HENSCHEN and ASSOCIATES, INC.

Ohio's leader in software development for Courts, Law Enforcement, Prosecutors, and Attorneys

* * * * * *

Over 15 years of service in Ohio

We offer case and event tracking, scheduling, accounting, time billing, form and report generation. Case information linked to word processing software for professional looking letters and forms. Leading technology including: document imaging, web-site development, e-payments, and e-filing via the Internet.

"One stop shop" for hardware, network, Internet "firewall", and software installations.

We **design and customize** our products to your specifications and provide **professional training** for your staff.

For information, please contact:

Bud L. Henschen, President
Henschen and Associates, Inc.
432 W. Gypsy Lane Road
Bowling Green, Ohio 43402
Telephone (419) 352-5454
Email: courts@henschen.com
www.henschen.com

PREFACE

The mission of our company is to provide the Ohio legal community with the most useful information available in a convenient format. To properly fulfill this mission we ask our readers for suggestions to help us continuously improve our publication. We listen carefully to each idea.

We are proud to present the *Ohio Legal Pages*®, our latest achievement towards meeting this mission. Our ultimate goal is to be the reference of choice for the communities of law and government in Ohio. We are proud to use our experience and expertise to provide you with the accurate, up-to-date source of information that you deserve.

There have been numerous changes since our 2005 edition went to press. Several courts in various counties have elected new judges. Also, due to recent legislation, several filing fees, especially those for county recorders, have been increased. Also, the post-judgment interest rate for the Ohio courts was changed by statute. We have followed these changes carefully, and have updated this edition to provide you with the latest information.

Our research staff has worked diligently to capture the movement of all members of the Ohio Bench and Bar. Almost 40,000 attorneys and law firms and over 800 judges are listed in this edition. Each one has been carefully verified through letters, phone calls and faxes.

Your comments and suggestions are welcome and appreciated. Please let us know how we can continue to improve your *Ohio Legal Pages*® and serve you better. You may reach us through any of a number of ways:

Mailing address:	P.O. Box 50, Newark, NJ 07101
Telephone:	(800) 444-4041
Fax:	(973) 642-4280
E-mail:	mail@lawdiary.com
Web site:	http://www.lawdiary.com

At our web site, you will find post-election information and many other useful materials, including information about obtaining our products on CD-ROM.

We wish you a successful and productive year.

The Legal Pages®

ISBN 1-57741-221-4

2005
OHIO EDITION

Includes:

- **Ohio Attorneys and Judges**
- **Ohio Courts**

- **Federal and State Departments and Agencies**
- **Professional Products and Services Directory**

The Reference of Choice for and about the Communities of Law and Government

TABLE OF CONTENTS

THE COURTS

DEPARTMENTS AND AGENCIES

LAW-RELATED INFORMATION

DIRECTORIES OF JUDGES AND ATTORNEYS

GOODS AND SERVICES FOR THE LEGAL PROFESSIONAL

UNITED STATES COURTS AND OFFICES

SUPREME COURT OF THE UNITED STATES

**U.S. Supreme Court Bldg., 1 First St. N.E.,
Washington, DC 20543
(202) 479-3000; Attorney Admissions: (202) 479-3387;
(202) 479-3018**

Chief Justice: William H. Rehnquist, Arizona

Justices:
John Paul Stevens, Illinois
Sandra Day O'Connor, Arizona
Antonin Scalia, Virginia
Anthony M. Kennedy, California
David H. Souter, New Hampshire
Clarence Thomas, Georgia
Ruth Bader Ginsburg, New York
Stephen G. Breyer, Massachusetts

Clerk: William K. Suter   (202) 479-3011

Reporter of Decisions: Frank D. Wagner   (202) 479-3390

Marshal: Pamela Talkin   (202) 479-3333

Librarian: Judith Gaskell   (202) 479-3175

Public Information Officer: Kathy Arberg
(202) 479-3211

Court Schedule: The Court holds one term annually, commencing on the first Mon. in October.

UNITED STATES COURT OF APPEALS
SIXTH CIRCUIT

(Kentucky, Michigan, Ohio, Tennessee)

Chief Judge:
Danny J. Boggs
220 Gene Snyder U.S. Courthouse, 601 W. Broadway,
Louisville, KY 40202
(502) 625-3900

Judges:
Alice M. Batchelder
143 W. Liberty St., Medina 44256   (330) 764-6026
Eric L. Clay
481 Theodore Levin U.S. Cthse.,
231 W. Lafayette Blvd., Detroit, MI 48226
(313) 234-5260
R. Guy Cole, Jr.
127 Joseph P. Kinneary U.S. Courthouse,
85 Marconi Blvd., Columbus 43215   (614) 719-3350
Deborah L. Cook
433 U.S. Courthouse & Fedl. Bldg., Two S. Main St.,
Akron 44308   (330) 375-5412
Martha Craig Daughtrey
304 U.S. Customs House, 701 Broadway,
Nashville, TN 37203   (615) 736-7678
Julia Smith Gibbons
1157 Clifford Davis Fedl. Bldg., 167 N. Main St.,
Memphis, TN 38103   (901) 495-1265
Ronald Lee Gilman
1176 Federal Bldg., 167 N. Main St.,
Memphis, TN 38103   (901) 495-1575
Boyce F. Martin, Jr.
209 Gene Snyder U.S. Courthouse, 601 W. Broadway,
Louisville, KY 40202   (502) 625-3800
Karen Nelson Moore
328 U.S. Courthouse, 201 Superior Ave.,
Cleveland 44114   (216) 522-7207
John M. Rogers
Community Trust Bldg., Suite 400, 100 E. Vine St.,
Lexington, KY 40507   (859) 233-2680
Jeffrey S. Sutton
10 W. Broad St., Suite 1150, Columbus 43215
(614) 849-0134

Senior Judges:
Ralph B. Guy, Jr.
P.O. Box 7910, Ann Arbor, MI 48107   (313) 741-2300
Damon J. Keith
240 Theodore Levin U.S. Cthse.,
231 W. Lafayette Blvd., Detroit, MI 48226
(313) 234-5245

Cornelia G. Kennedy
744 Theodore Levin U.S. Cthse.,
231 W. Lafayette Blvd., Detroit, MI 48226
(313) 234-5240
Gilbert S. Merritt
303 U.S. Customs House, 701 Broadway,
Nashville, TN 37203   (615) 736-5957
David A. Nelson
414 Potter Stewart U.S. Cthse., 5th & Walnut Streets,
Cincinnati 45202   (513) 564-7414
Alan E. Norris
328 Joseph P. Kinneary U.S. Courthouse,
85 Marconi Blvd., Columbus 43215   (614) 719-3330
James L. Ryan
611 Theodore Levin U.S. Cthse.,
231 W. Lafayette Blvd., Detroit, MI 48226
(313) 234-5250
Eugene E. Siler, Jr.
1380 W. Fifth St., London, KY 40741   (606) 878-6822
Richard F. Suhrheinrich
241 U.S. P.O. & Federal Bldg., 315 West Allegan St.,
Lansing, MI 48933   (517) 377-1513

Circuit Executive:
James A. Higgins
503 Potter Stewart U.S. Cthse., 100 E. Fifth St.,
Cincinnati 45202   (513) 564-7200

Clerk:
Leonard Green
532 Potter Stewart U.S. Cthse., 100 E. Fifth St.,
Cincinnati 45202-3988
(513) 564-7000; Fax: (513) 564-7096;
ABBS: (513) 564-7152

Librarian:
Kathy Welker
312 Potter Stewart U.S. Cthse., 100 E. Fifth St.,
Cincinnati 45202   (513) 564-7321

UNITED STATES DISTRICT COURT
Northern District of Ohio

**Carl B. Stokes U.S. Courthouse,
801 W. Superior Ave., Cleveland 44113-1830
PACER: (800) 676-6856
E-mail: www.ohnd.uscourts.gov**

U.S. Courthouse, Two S. Main St., Akron 44308-1813

**U.S. Courthouse, 1716 Spielbusch Ave.,
Toledo 43624-1363**

**Thomas D. Lambros Fedl. Bldg. & Courthouse,
125 Market St., Youngstown 44503-1780**

Jurisdiction—Counties of Allen, Ashland, Ashtabula, Auglaize, Carroll, Columbiana, Crawford, Cuyahoga, Defiance, Erie, Fulton, Geauga, Hancock, Hardin, Henry, Holmes, Huron, Lake, Lorain, Lucas, Mahoning, Marion, Medina, Mercer, Ottawa, Paulding, Portage, Putnam, Richland, Sandusky, Seneca, Stark, Summit, Trumbull, Tuscarawas, Van Wert, Williams, Wood, Wyandot; Eastern Division (Akron) consists of counties of Carroll, Holmes, Portage, Stark, Summitt, Tuscarawas and Wayne. Eastern Division (Cleveland) consists of counties of Ashland, Ashtabula, Crawford, Cuyahoga, Geauga, Lake, Lorain, Medina and Richland. Eastern Division (Youngstown) consists of Columbiana, Mahoning and Trumbull. Western Division (Toledo) consists of counties of Allen, Auglaize, Defiance, Erie, Fulton, Hancock, Hardin, Henry, Huron, Lucas, Marion, Mercer, Ottawa, Paulding, Putnam, Sandusky, Seneca, Van Wert, Williams, Wood and Wyandot.

Chief Judge: James G. Carr, Room 203, Toledo
(419) 259-6420; Fax: (419) 259-6427
E-mail: james_g_carr@ohnd.uscourts.gov

U.S. District Court, Northern Dist. of Ohio—Cont'd

Judges:

John R. Adams, Room 526, Akron
(330) 375-5900; Fax: (330) 375-5875
Christopher A. Boyko, Cleveland
(216) 357-7151; Fax: (216) 357-7156
Peter C. Economus, Room 313, Youngstown
(330) 746-7830; Fax: (330) 746-4195
Patricia A. Gaughan, Cleveland
(216) 357-7210; Fax: (216) 357-7215
James S. Gwin, Room 510, Akron
(330) 375-5934; Fax: (330) 375-5937
Donald C. Nugent, Cleveland
(216) 357-7160; Fax: (216) 357-7165
Kathleen M. O'Malley, Cleveland
(216) 357-7240; Fax: (216) 357-7246
Solomon Oliver, Jr., Cleveland
(216) 357-7171; Fax: (216) 357-7176
Dan A. Polster, Cleveland
(216) 357-7190; Fax: (216) 357-7195
E-mail: dan_polster@ohnd.uscourts.gov
Lesley Wells, Room 18-A, Cleveland
(216) 357-7120; Fax: (216) 357-7127

Senior Judges:

Ann Aldrich, Cleveland
(216) 357-7200; Fax: (216) 357-7205
David D. Dowd, Jr., Room 402, Akron
(330) 375-5836; Fax: (330) 375-5628
David A. Katz, Room 210, Toledo
(419) 259-7488; Fax: (419) 259-3744
John M. Manos, Cleveland
(216) 357-7265; Fax: (216) 357-7271
Paul R. Matia, Cleveland
(216) 357-7100; Fax: (216) 357-7110

U.S. Magistrate Judges:

Vernelis K. Armstrong, Room 318, Toledo
(419) 259-6217; Fax: (419) 259-3728
E-mail: vernelis_k_armstrong@ohnd.uscourts.gov
William H. Baughman, Jr., Room 10-A, Cleveland
(216) 357-7220; Fax: (216) 357-7224
James S. Gallas, Room 480, Akron
(330) 375-5466; Fax: (330) 375-5536
E-mail: james_s_gallas@ohnd.uscourts.gov
Patricia A. Hemann, Cleveland
(216) 357-7135; Fax: (216) 357-7139
George J. Limbert, Room 229, Youngstown
(330) 743-2987; Fax: (330) 746-8609
Kenneth S. McHargh, Cleveland
(216) 357-7230; Fax: (216) 357-7234
David S. Perelman (Retired, on recall)
Room 11-A, Cleveland
(216) 357-7140; Fax: (216) 357-7145
Nancy A. Vecchiarelli, Cleveland
(216) 357-7130; Fax: (216) 357-7134

Clerk: Geri M. Smith
Cleveland: (216) 357-7000;
Cleveland Fax: (216) 357-7040;
Toledo: (419) 259-6411, 12;
Youngstown: (330) 746-0019, 746-1906;
Akron: (330) 375-5407, 05

U.S. BANKRUPTCY COURT

Chief Judge: Randolph Baxter
3204 Key Tower, 127 Public Sq., Cleveland 44114-1309
(216) 522-4373, Ext. 3063

U.S. Bankruptcy Judges:

Arthur I. Harris
3101 Key Tower, 127 Public Sq., Cleveland 44114-1309
(216) 522-4373, Ext. 3022
Russ Kendig
Frank T. Bow Federal Bldg., 201 Cleveland Ave. S.W.,
Canton 44702 (330) 489-4430
Pat E. Morgenstern-Clarren
3201 Key Tower, 127 Public Sq., Cleveland 44114-1309
(216) 522-4373, Ext. 3059

Marilyn Shea-Stonum
240 U.S. Courthouse, 2 S. Main St., Akron 44308
(330) 375-5780
Richard L. Speer
113 U.S. Courthouse, 1716 Spielbusch Ave.,
Toledo 43624 (419) 259-7559
Mary Ann Whipple
111 U.S. Courthouse, 1716 Spielbusch Ave.,
Toledo 43624 (419) 259-6327
Kay Woods
Federal Bldg. & U.S. Courthouse, 10 E. Commerce St.,
Youngstown 44503-1621 (330) 746-7027, Ext. 4200

Clerk: Kenneth J. Hirz
3001 Key Tower, 127 Public Sq., Cleveland 44114-1309
(216) 522-7299, 522-4373; Fax: (216) 522-4082;
PACER: (330) 489-4779; (800) 579-5735;
VCIS: (330) 489-4731, 71
Internet: www.ohnb.uscourts.gov
455 U.S. Courthouse, Two S. Main St., Akron 44308
(330) 375-5840
411 U.S. Courthouse, 1716 Spielbusch Ave.,
Toledo 43624 (419) 259-6440
Frank T. Bow Federal Bldg., 201 Cleveland Ave., S.W.,
Canton 44702 (330) 489-4426
Federal Bldg. & U.S. Courthouse, 10 E. Commerce St.,
Youngstown 44503-1621 (330) 746-7027

U.S. ATTORNEY'S OFFICE

400 U.S. Cthse., 801 W. Superior Ave., Cleveland 44113
(216) 622-3600; Fax: (216) 522-3370
Four Seagate, 3rd Floor, Toledo 43604-2624
(419) 259-6376; Fax: (419) 259-6360
City Center One, Suite 325, 100 E. Federal Plz.,
Youngstown 44503
(330) 746-7974; Fax: (330) 746-0239
208 Federal Bldg., Two S. Main St., Akron 44308-1855
(330) 375-5716; Fax: (330) 375-5492

U.S. Atty.: Gregory A. White

U.S. MARSHALS SERVICE

12-100 Carl B. Stokes U.S. Courthouse,
801 W. Superior Ave., Cleveland 44113-1853
(216) 522-2150; Fax: (216) 522-7908

U.S. Marshal: Peter J. Elliott

U.S. PRETRIAL SERVICES OFFICE

Carl B. Stokes U.S. Courthouse, 3rd Floor,
801 W. Superior Ave., Cleveland 44113-1851
(216) 357-7375; Fax: (216) 357-7390

Chief: Jeffrey P. Johnson (216) 357-7383

U.S. PROBATION OFFICE

Carl B. Stokes U.S. Court House,
801 W. Superior Ave., Cleveland 44113-1850
(216) 357-7300; Fax: (216) 357-7350
Akron Office,
Courthouse and Federal Bldg., Suite B3-55,
Two S. Main St., Akron 44308-1810
(330) 375-5774; Fax: (330) 375-5897
215 N. Summit St., Suite A, Toledo 43604-2659
(419) 259-6432; Fax: (419) 259-7580
Youngstown Office,
210 Thomas D. Lambros Fedl. Bldg. & U.S. Cthse.,
125 Market St., Youngstown 44503-1478
(330) 743-0933; Fax: (330) 743-5829

Chief Probation Officer: Greg L. Johnson
E-mail: greg_johnson@ohnp.uscourts.gov

FEDERAL PUBLIC DEFENDER

Skylight Office Tower, Suite 750, 1660 W. Second St.,
Cleveland 44113
(216) 522-4856; Fax: (216) 522-4321
Akron Office,
U.S. Courthouse & Federal Bldg., Suite B3-56,
2 S. Main St., Akron 44308
(330) 375-5739; Fax: (330) 375-5738

Federal Public Defender: Michael G. Dane

UNITED STATES DISTRICT COURT
Southern District of Ohio
**Joseph P. Kinneary U.S. Courthouse,
85 Marconi Blvd., Columbus 43215
PACER: (614) 469-6990
Internet: www.ohsd.uscourts.gov
Potter Stewart U.S. Courthouse, 100 E. Fifth St.,
Cincinnati 45202
Federal Bldg., 200 W. Second St., Dayton 45402**

Jurisdiction—Counties of Adams, Athens, Belmont, Brown, Butler, Champaign, Clark, Clermont, Clinton, Coshocton, Darke, Delaware, Fairfield, Fayette, Franklin, Gallia, Greene, Guernsey, Hamilton, Harrison, Highland, Hocking, Jackson, Jefferson, Knox, Lawrence, Licking, Logan, Madison, Meigs, Miami, Monroe, Montgomery, Morgan, Morrow, Muskingum, Noble, Perry, Pickaway, Pike, Preble, Ross, Scioto, Shelby, Union, Warren; Eastern Division (Columbus) consists of counties of Athens, Belmont, Coshocton, Delaware, Fairfield, Fayette, Franklin, Gallia, Guernsey, Harrison, Hocking, Jackson, Jefferson, Knox, Licking, Logan, Madison, Meigs, Monroe, Morgan, Morrow, Muskingum, Noble, Perry, Pickaway, Pike, Ross, Union, Vinton and Washington counties. Western Division (Cincinnati) consists of counties of Adams, Brown, Butler, Clermont, Clinton, Hamilton, Highland, Lawrence, Scioto and Warren counties. Western Division (Dayton) consists of counties of Champaign, Clark, Darke, Greene, Miami, Montgomery, Preble and Shelby counties.

Chief Judge: Sandra S. Beckwith, Room 810, Cincinnati
(513) 564-7610
  Courtroom Deputy Clerk: Mary Brown (513) 564-7520

Judges:
Susan J. Dlott, Room 829, Cincinnati
(513) 564-7630; Fax: (513) 564-7638
  Courtroom Deputy Clerk: Stephen Snyder
  (513) 564-7633
Gregory L. Frost, Room 349, Columbus
(614) 719-3300; Fax: (614) 719-3305
E-mail: greg_frost@ohsd.uscourts.gov
  Courtroom Deputy Clerk: Scott E. Miller
  (614) 719-3014
Algenon L. Marbley, Room 319, Columbus
(614) 719-3260; Fax: (614) 719-3264
  Courtroom Deputy Clerk: Betty Clark
Thomas M. Rose, Room 910, Dayton
(937) 512-1600
E-mail: thomas_rose@ohsd.uscourts.gov
  Courtroom Deputy Clerk: Jeffrey S. Garey
  (937) 512-1603
Edmund A. Sargus, Jr., Room 301, Columbus
(614) 719-3240
  Courtroom Deputy Clerk: Andy Quisumbing
  (614) 719-3244
Michael H. Watson, Room 247, Columbus
(614) 719-3280
  Courtroom Deputy Clerk: Barbara Crum
  (513) 564-7692

Senior Judges:
James L. Graham, Room 169, Columbus
(614) 719-3200
  Courtroom Deputy Clerk: Beverly White
  (614) 719-3202
John D. Holschuh, Room 109, Columbus
(614) 719-3310
  Courtroom Deputy Clerk: Sherry Nichols
  (614) 719-3315
Walter H. Rice, Room 909, Dayton
(937) 512-1500
  Courtroom Deputy Clerk: Karla Evans-Clark
George C. Smith, Room 101, Columbus
(614) 719-3220
  Courtroom Deputy Clerk: Lisa Wright
  (614) 719-3222

S. Arthur Spiegel, Room 838, Cincinnati
(513) 564-7620
  Courtroom Deputy Clerk: Kevin Moser
  (513) 564-7623
Herman J. Weber, Room 801, Cincinnati
(513) 564-7603
  Admin. Asst.: Betsi Brockmeier

Chief U.S. Magistrate Judge: Michael R. Merz
Room 902, Dayton (937) 512-1550
E-mail: michael_merz@ohsd.uscourts.gov
  Courtroom Deputy Clerk: Gayle Hayes
  (937) 512-1553

U.S. Magistrate Judges:
Mark R. Abel, Room 208, Columbus
(614) 719-3370
E-mail: abel_chambers@ohsd.uscourts.gov
  Courtroom Deputy Clerk: Spencer Harris
  (614) 719-3027
Timothy S. Black, Room 716, Cincinnati
(513) 564-7640
  Courtroom Deputy Clerk: Jan Lahley
Timothy S. Hogan, Room 706, Cincinnati
(513) 564-7650
  Courtroom Deputy Clerk: Barbara Crum
  (513) 564-7652
Terence P. Kemp, Room 172, Columbus
(614) 719-3410
  Courtroom Deputy Clerk: Wanda Harrison
  (614) 719-3023
Norah McCann King, Room 235, Columbus
(614) 719-3390
  Courtroom Deputy Clerk: John Miller
  (614) 719-3026
Sharon L. Ovington, Room 810, Columbus
(937) 512-1570
  Courtroom Deputy Clerk: Lois Tipton
  (937) 512-1573

Clerk: James Bonini
Columbus: (614) 719-3000;
Columbus Fax: (614) 469-5953;
Cincinnati: (513) 564-7500; Dayton: (937) 512-1400

U.S. BANKRUPTCY COURT
Chief Judge: Thomas F. Waldron
120 W. Third St., Room 121, Dayton 45402-1819
(937) 225-2516, Ext. 338
  Judicial Asst.: Joni Behnken

U.S. Bankruptcy Judges:
J. Vincent Aug, Jr.
Atrium Two, 8th Floor, 221 E. 4th St., Cincinnati 45202
(513) 684-2572, Ext. 132
Charles M. Caldwell
170 N. High St., Columbus 43215-2403
(614) 469-6638, Ext. 260
Donald E. Calhoun, Jr.
170 N. High St., Columbus 43215-2403
(614) 469-6638, Ext. 240
William A. Clark
120 W. Third St., Dayton 45402
(937) 225-2516, Ext. 301
John E. Hoffman, Jr.
170 N. High St., Columbus 43215
(614) 469-6638, Ext. 282
Jeffery P. Hopkins
Atrium Two, Suite 800, 221 E. 4th St.,
Cincinnati 45202
(513) 684-2572, Ext. 146
Burton Perlman
Atrium Two, 8th Floor, 221 E. 4th St., Cincinnati 45202
(513) 684-2572, Ext. 131
Barbara J. Sellers
170 N. High St., Columbus 43215-2403
(614) 469-6638, Ext. 250
Lawrence S. Walter
120 W. Third St., Dayton 45402
(937) 225-2516, Ext. 307

U.S. Bankruptcy Court, South. Dist. of Ohio—Cont'd

Clerk: Michael D. Webb
120 W. Third St., Dayton 45402-1819
(937) 225-2516; Fax: (937) 225-2954;
PACER: (800) 793-7003;
VCIS: (800) 726-1004, (937) 225-2544
Atrium Two, Suite 800, 221 E. 4th St.,
Cincinnati 45202
(513) 684-2572; Fax: (513) 684-6727;
PACER: (800) 793-7003, (937) 225-7561;
VCIS: (800) 726-1004, (937) 225-2544
170 N. High St., Columbus 43215
(614) 469-6638; Fax: (617) 469-2478;
PACER: (800) 793-7003, (937) 225-7561;
VCIS: (800) 726-1006, (937) 225-2562

U.S. ATTORNEY'S OFFICE
303 Marconi Blvd., Suite 200, Columbus 43215
(614) 469-5715; Fax: (614) 469-2200
221 E. Fourth St., Suite 400, Cincinnati 45202
(513) 684-3711; Fax: (513) 684-6710
602 U.S. Courthouse, 200 W. Second St.,
Dayton 45402
(937) 225-2910; Fax: (937) 225-2564

U.S. Atty.: Gregory G. Lockhart

U.S. MARSHALS SERVICE
460 Joseph P. Kinneary U.S. Courthouse,
85 Marconi Blvd., Columbus 43215
(614) 469-5540; Fax: (614) 469-2298

U.S. Marshal: James M. Wahlrab

U.S. PRETRIAL SERVICES OFFICE
512 Joseph P. Kinneary U.S. Courthouse,
85 Marconi Blvd., Columbus 43215-2398
(614) 719-3070; Fax: (614) 469-2484
301 Potter Stewart U.S. Courthouse, 100 E. Fifth St.,
Cincinnati 45202
(513) 564-7590; Fax: (513) 564-7594
709 Federal Bldg. & Courthouse, 200 W. Second St.,
Dayton 45402-1411
(937) 512-1430; Fax: (937) 225-7204

Chief: Holly Renner High

U.S. PROBATION OFFICE
Joseph P. Kinneary U.S. Courthouse, Room 546,
85 Marconi Blvd., Columbus 43215
(513) 564-7573; Fax: (614) 469-2579
702 Federal Bldg. & Courthouse, 200 W. Second St.,
Dayton 45402-1411
(937) 512-1450; Fax: (937) 225-2755
110 Potter Stewart U.S. Courthouse, 100 E. Fifth St.,
Cincinnati 45202-3980
(513) 564-7575; Fax: (513) 564-7587

Chief U.S. Probation Officer: C. Patrick Crowley

FEDERAL PUBLIC DEFENDER
10 W. Broad St., Suite 1020, Columbus 43215-3469
(614) 469-2999; Fax: (614) 469-5999
36 E. Seventh St., Suite 2000, Cincinnati 45202
(513) 929-4834; Fax: (513) 929-4842
130 W. 2nd St., Suite 820, Dayton 45402-1819
(937) 225-7687; Fax: (937) 225-7688

Federal Public Defender: Steven R. Keller

OHIO STATE COURTS & OFFICES

SUPREME COURT OF OHIO

65 S. Front St., 9th Floor, Columbus 43215-3431
(614) 387-9000
Jurisdiction—State of OH

Chief Justice: Thomas J. Moyer, 9th Floor (614) 387-9010
    E-mail: moyert@sconet.state.oh.us

Justices:
  Judith A. Lanzinger
    (614) 387-9090; Fax: (614) 387-9099
  Maureen O'Connor, 9th Floor (614) 387-9060
  Terrence O'Donnell, 9th Floor (614) 387-9030
  Paul E. Pfeifer, 9th Floor (614) 387-9020
  Alice Robie Resnick, 9th Floor (614) 387-9040
    E-mail: resnicka@sconet.state.oh.us
  Evelyn Lundberg Stratton, 9th Floor
    (614) 387-9050; Fax: (617) 387-9059
    E-mail: strattonoe@sconet.state.oh.us

    Law Clerks:
     David Bartteson (614) 387-9053
     Connie Crim (614) 387-9054
     Kristina Hawk (614) 387-9052
Secretary: Sue A. Bowery (614) 387-9050
Clerk: Marcia J. Mengel, 8th Floor (614) 387-9530, 31

Administrative Director's Office
Supreme Court of Ohio
65 S. Front St., Columbus 43215-3431
(614) 387-9000, (800) 826-9010
Internet: www.sconet.state.oh.us

Admin. Dir.: Steven C. Hollon

Dir., Legal Resources Division: David Gormley
  8th Floor (614) 387-9560; Fax: (614) 387-9569

Dir., Policy & Programs/Attorney Svces. Div.:
  Richard A. Dove, 7th Floor (614) 387-9520

Dir., Building Operations Div.: Byron Wilson, 2nd Floor
  (614) 387-9296

Dir., Fiscal & Mgmt. Resources Division: Ronda Perri
  7th Floor (614) 387-9480

*Provides technical and logistical support, conducts court
statistical reporting, and makes judge assignments*

DISTRICT COURT OF APPEALS OF OHIO

FIRST APPELLATE DISTRICT
230 E. Ninth St., 12th Floor, Cincinnati 45202
(513) 946-3500; Fax: (513) 946-3412
Jurisdiction—County of Hamilton

Judges:
  Rupert A. Doan (513) 946-3441
  Robert H. Gorman (513) 946-3421
    E-mail: rgorman@cms.hamilton-co.org
  Sylvia Sieve Hendon (513) 946-3505; Fax: (513) 946-3411
  Lee H. Hildebrandt, Jr. (513) 946-3450
    E-mail: lhildebrandt@cms.hamilton-co.org
  Mark P. Painter (513) 946-3444; Fax: (513) 946-3411
    E-mail: mpainter@cms.hamilton-co.org
    Internet: www.judgepainter.org
  J. Howard Sundermann, Jr. (513) 946-3424

Court Administrator: Mark E. Combs
  (513) 946-3488; Fax: (513) 946-3412
  E-mail: mccombs@cms.hamilton-co.org

SECOND APPELLATE DISTRICT
41 N. Perry, P.O. Box 972, Dayton 45422
(937) 225-4464; Fax: (937) 496-7724

Clark County Courthouse, 101 N. Limestone St.,
Springfield 45502
(937) 328-2653; Fax: (937) 328-2652
Jurisdiction—Counties of Champaign, Clark, Darke,
Greene, Miami, Montgomery

Judges:
  James A. Brogan, Dayton; Fax: (937) 496-7724
    E-mail: broganj@mcohio.org
  Mary E. Donovan, 5th Floor, Dayton
  Mike Fain, Dayton; E-mail: fainm@mcohio.org
  Thomas J. Grady, Springfield
    E-mail: tjgrady@erinet.com
  William H. Wolff, Jr., Dayton; E-mail: wolffw@mcohio.org
    Law Clerks:
     Valerie Finn-DeLuca   Karen R. Lindsay
Secretary: Patty Edmondson

Court Administrator: Ronald E. Mount, Dayton

THIRD APPELLATE DISTRICT
204 N. Main St., Lima 45801
(419) 223-1861; Fax: (419) 224-3828
Internet: www.third.courts.state.oh.us
Jurisdiction—Counties of Allen, Auglaize, Crawford,
Defiance, Hancock, Hardin, Henry, Logan, Marion, Mercer,
Paulding, Putnam, Seneca, Shelby, Union, Van Wert,
Wyandot

Presiding Judge: Robert R. Cupp
  Law Clerks:
    Jennifer J. Mabry   Luke D. Mahoney

Judges:
  Stephen R. Shaw (Administrative Judge)
    Law Clerk: Terri Cannon
  Thomas F. Bryant
    E-mail: bryant@third.courts.state.oh.us
    Law Clerks:
     Tamara Bell   Anna Franceschelli
  Richard M. Rogers

Court Administrator: Gregory B. Miller
Administrative Counsel: Susan M. Prueter
Systems Administrator: Jeanne I. Shaw

FOURTH APPELLATE DISTRICT
121-A W. Franklin St., Circleville 43113
(740) 474-7841; Fax: (740) 474-6870
Jurisdiction—Counties of Adams, Athens, Gallia,
Highland, Hocking, Jackson, Lawrence, Meigs, Pickaway,
Pike, Ross, Scioto, Vinton, Washington

Judges:
  Peter B. Abele
    Athens Co. Cthse., 1 S. Court St., Athens 45701
    (740) 592-3247, 594-3250; Fax: (740) 594-3303
    E-mail: pbabele@eurekanet.com
    Law Clerks:
     Gary Garrison   Susan Satava
    Secretary: Teresa Yates
  William H. Harsha
    14 S. Paint St., Suite 38, Chillicothe 45601
    (740) 779-6662; Fax: (740) 779-6665
    Staff Atty.: Jim Jump
    Law Clerks:
     Sharon A. Maerten-Moore
     Lisa Ziegler
    Admin. Asst.: Nancy Argabright
    Secretary: Michelle Ratcliff
  Roger L. Kline
    (740) 474-7841; Fax: (740) 474-6870
    Staff Atty.: Susan Eyerman (740) 474-5237
    Law Clerks:
     Stacey Blasko   Sara Sampson
    Secretary: Barbara Large
  Matthew W. McFarland
    Scioto County Courthouse, 3rd Floor, 602 7th St.,
    Portsmouth 45662 (740) 355-9497; Fax: (740) 355-3934

Court Administrator: Aaron M. McHenry
  121-A W. Franklin St., Circleville 43113
  (740) 474-7841

FIFTH APPELLATE DISTRICT
110 Central Plaza S., Suite 320, Canton 44702-1411
(330) 451-7765; Fax: (330) 451-7249
Jurisdiction—Counties of Ashland, Coshocton, Delaware, Fairfield, Guernsey, Holmes, Knox, Licking, Morgan, Morrow, Muskingum, Perry, Richland, Stark, Tuscarawas
Judges:
John F. Boggins (330) 451-7245, 451-7839
Julie A. Edwards (330) 451-7766
  E-mail: info@fifthdist.org
    Staff Attys.:
      Melinda Cooper (330) 451-7240
      Debbie Roland (330) 451-7898
    Admin. Asst.: Margo Clore (330) 451-7766
Sheila G. Farmer (330) 451-7447
W. Scott Gwin (330) 451-7750
William B. Hoffman (330) 451-7448
John W. Wise (330) 451-7701
  E-mail: infor@fifthdist.org
Court Administrator: Trevor Buehler (330) 451-7768

SIXTH APPELLATE DISTRICT
One Constitution Ave., Toledo 43624
(419) 213-4755; Fax: (419) 213-4844
Jurisdiction—Counties of Erie, Fulton, Huron, Lucas, Ottawa, Sandusky, Williams, Wood
Judges:
Peter M. Handwork
  E-mail: handwork@co.lucas.oh.us
Dennis M. Parish
Mark L. Pietrykowski
  E-mail: pietry@co.lucas.oh.us
Arlene Singer; E-mail: singer@co.lucas.oh.us
William J. Skow; E-mail: 6thca@co.lucas.oh.us
Court Administrator: Donna Kiroff

SEVENTH APPELLATE DISTRICT
Mahoning County Cthse., 120 Market St.,
Youngstown 44503-1710
(330) 740-2180; Fax: (330) 740-2182
Jurisdiction—Counties of Belmont, Carroll, Columbiana, Harrison, Jefferson, Mahoning, Monroe, Noble
Presiding Judge: Cheryl L. Waite, 4th Floor
Judges:
Mary DeGenaro
  E-mail: mdegenaro@aol.com
    Law Clerks:
      Brad Catlin   Christina Rorick
    Secretary: Bobbie Knickerbocker
Gene Donofrio
Joseph J. Vukovich
Court Administrator: Robert Budinsky

EIGHTH APPELLATE DISTRICT
Cuyahoga County Courthouse, Suite 202, 1 Lakeside Ave., Cleveland 44113-1085
(216) 443-6350; Fax: (216) 443-2044
E-mail: anr@8thappeals.com
Jurisdiction—County of Cuyahoga
Judges:
Patricia Ann Blackmon (216) 443-6358
Anthony O. Calabrese, Jr. (216) 348-4837
  E-mail: cpaoc@www.cuyahoga.oh.us
Frank D. Celebrezze, Jr. (216) 443-6355
  Secretary: Suzanne M. Devera
  Clerks:
    Nick A. Nykulak (216) 443-6381
    Cara L. Santosuosso (216) 443-6373
Colleen Conway Cooney (216) 443-6357
  E-mail: ccc@8thappeals.com
Michael J. Corrigan
  (216) 443-6360; Fax: (216) 443-2044
  E-mail: mjc@8thappeals.com
Ann Dyke (216) 443-6356
Sean C. Gallagher (216) 348-4838

Diane Karpinski (216) 443-6354
Mary Eileen Kilbane (216) 443-6355
Christine T. McMonagle (216) 443-6377
Kenneth A. Rocco (216) 348-4810
James J. Sweeney (216) 348-4807
Court Administrator: Ute L. Vilfroy (216) 443-6396

NINTH APPELLATE DISTRICT
161 S. High St., Suite 504, Akron 44308-1602
(330) 643-2250; Fax: (330) 643-2091
Internet: www.ninth.courts.state.oh.us
Jurisdiction—Counties of Lorain, Medina, Summit, Wayne
Judges:
William G. Batchelder
  (330) 643-2259; Fax: (330) 643-2394
  E-mail: william@ninth.courts.state.oh.us
Donna J. Carr
  (330) 643-2259; Fax: (330) 643-2394
  E-mail: donna@ninth.courts.state.oh.us
Carla Moore
  (330) 643-2259; Fax: (330) 643-2394
Lynn C. Slaby
  (330) 643-2259; Fax: (330) 643-2394
  E-mail: lynn@ninth.courts.state.oh.us
Beth Whitmore
  (330) 643-2259; Fax: (330) 643-2394
  E-mail: beth@ninth.courts.state.oh.us
Court Administrator: C. Michael Walsh (330) 643-2254
  E-mail: cmwalsh@ninth.courts.state.oh.us

TENTH APPELLATE DISTRICT
373 S. High St., 24th Floor, Columbus 43215-4578
(614) 462-3580; Fax: (614) 462-7249
Internet: www.tenthdistrictcourt.org
Jurisdiction—County of Franklin
Presiding Judge: Susan Brown (614) 462-4022
  E-mail: sbrown@co.franklin.oh.us
Judges:
William A. Klatt (Administrative Judge) (614) 462-3610
Peggy Bryant (614) 462-3612
  E-mail: plbryant@co.franklin.oh.us
Judith L. French (614) 462-4032
Cynthia C. Lazarus (614) 462-3613
  E-mail: cclazarus@co.franklin.oh.us
Patrick M. McGrath (614) 462-7241
Charles R. Petree (614) 462-4049
  E-mail: crpetree@co.franklin.oh.us
Lisa L. Sadler (614) 462-4054
  E-mail: lisa_sadler@fccourts.org
Court Administrator: Jack Kullman, Jr. (614) 462-3580
  E-mail: jrkullman@co.franklin.oh.us

ELEVENTH APPELLATE DISTRICT
111 High St., N.E., Warren 44481
(330) 675-2650; Fax: (330) 675-2655
Jurisdiction—Counties of Ashtabula, Geauga, Lake, Portage, Trumbull
Judges:
Donald R. Ford
Diane V. Grendell
  Secretary: Sheryl A. Russell
  Law Clerks:
    William R. Knox   Mitchell J. Michaelec
William M. O'Neill
  E-mail: wmoneill-@11thappeal.co.trumbull.oh.us
Colleen M. O'Toole
Cynthia Westcott Rice
Chief Magistrate: Matthew O. Lamb
Deputy Admin.: Patricia A. Sontag (330) 675-2660

TWELFTH APPELLATE DISTRICT
1001 Reinartz Blvd., P.O. Box 1009,
Middletown 45042-1901
(513) 425-6609; Fax: (513) 425-8751
Jurisdiction—Counties of Brown, Butler, Clermont,
Clinton, Fayette, Madison, Preble, Warren
Judges:
  H. J. Bressler
    E-mail: bresslerhj@twelfth.courts.state.oh.us
  Stephen W. Powell
    E-mail: stephen@twelfth.courts.state.oh.us
  James E. Walsh
    E-mail: james@twelfth.courts.state.oh.us
  William W. Young
    E-mail: william@twelfth.courts.state.oh.us
Court Administrator: Bennett A. Manning
    E-mail: bennett@twelfth.courts.state.oh.us

COURT OF CLAIMS OF OHIO

65 S. Front St., 3rd Floor, Columbus 43215
(614) 387-9800; Toll Free: (800) 824-8263;
Panel Appeals: (614) 387-9862; Fax: (614) 387-9836
Internet: www.cco.state.oh.us
Judges:
  J. Warren Bettis
  Joseph T. Clark; E-mail: jsclark@cco.state.oh.us
  J. Craig Wright

Clerk: Miles C. Durfey
Deputy Clerks:
  Robert B. Belz
  Daniel R. Borchert

This court has exclusive, original jurisdiction of all civil actions against the State of Ohio permitted by the waiver of immunity contained in R.C. 2743.02, and exclusive jurisdiction of all parties in civil actions that are removed to this court. The court has appellate jurisdiction over claims for an award of reparations to victims of crime pursuant to R.C. 2743.51et seq. The court has full equity powers in all actions within its jurisdiction and may entertain and determine all counterclaims, cross-claims and third party claims.
Actions against the state of $2,500 or less are determined administratively by the clerk or a deputy clerk. Upon motion of a party, a judge of the court reviews the determination of the clerk and enters judgment accordingly. The judgment cannot be the subject of further appeal. Civil actions in excess of $2,500 are heard and determined by a judge of the court. Appeals from orders and judgments of the court lie to the same court under the same circumstances as appeals from the Court of Common Pleas of Franklin County. No claimant is entitled to have his civil action against the state determined by a trial by jury. Parties in removed cases retain their right to trial by jury in the court of any civil action not against the state.

COUNTY COURTS AND OFFICES

ADAMS COUNTY

ADAMS COUNTY COMMON PLEAS COURT
110 W. Main St., West Union 45693-1347
(937) 544-2921; Fax: (937) 544-8911
Judge: Brett M. Spencer

ADAMS COUNTY COURT
Courthouse, Room 25, 110 W. Main St., West Union 45693
(937) 544-2011; Fax: (937) 544-8911
Judge: Alan W. Foster
Clerk: Mary Ruth Mack
Court Schedule: Weekdays, 8:30 A.M.-4 P.M.

County Offices

ADAMS COUNTY BOARD OF COMMISSIONERS
110 W. Main St., West Union 45693-1395
(937) 544-3286; Fax: (937) 544-5992
Commissioners:
John Cluxton   Bill Seaman
Roger Rhonemus

ADAMS COUNTY CLERK OF COURTS
110 W. Main St., Room 207, West Union 45693-1391
(937) 544-2344; Fax: (937) 544-8971
Clerk of Courts: Gary K. Gardner

ADAMS COUNTY CORONER
223 N. Wilson Dr., West Union 45693
(937) 544-5698; Fax: (937) 544-2655
Coroner: Susan E. Dunkin-Blanton

ADAMS COUNTY ENGINEER
116 W. Mulberry St., West Union 45693
(937) 544-2943; Fax: (937) 544-7505
Engineer: David Hook

ADAMS COUNTY PROSECUTOR
110 W. Main St., West Union 45693
(937) 544-3600
Prosecutor: David Kelley

ADAMS COUNTY RECORDER
110 W. Main St., West Union 45693
(937) 544-5051
Recorder: Mark A. Tolle

ADAMS COUNTY AUDITOR
110 W. Main St., West Union 45693
(937) 544-1016; Fax: (937) 544-2316
Auditor: David Gifford

ADAMS COUNTY SHERIFF
110 W. Main St., West Union 45693
(937) 544-2314; Fax: (513) 544-2316
Sheriff: Kermit Howard

ADAMS COUNTY TREASURER
110 W. Main St., West Union 45693
(937) 544-2845
Treasurers:
Howard A. Harris
Resigning in September 2005
Lisa Newman
Effective September 2005

ALLEN COUNTY

ALLEN COUNTY COMMON PLEAS COURT
333 N. Main St., P.O. Box 1243, Lima 45802
(419) 228-3700; Fax: (419) 224-9269
Judges:
David R. Kinworthy (419) 223-8501; Fax: (419) 221-3432
Jeffrey L. Reed (419) 223-8525
Matt C. Staley (419) 223-8511; Fax: (419) 227-3162
Richard K. Warren (419) 223-8525

ALLEN COUNTY PROBATE COURT
301 N. Main St., P.O. Box 1243, Lima 45801
(419) 223-8501; Fax: (419) 221-3432
Internet: www.allencountyohio.com/
Judge: David R. Kinworthy
Magistrate/Court Administrator: Timothy C. Hamman
Hours: Weekdays, 8 A.M.-4:30 P.M.

ALLEN COUNTY JUVENILE COURT
1000 Wardhill Ave., P.O. Box 419, Lima 45802
(419) 227-5531; Fax: (419) 222-7403
E-mail: acjc@allencountyohio.com
Internet: www.co.allen.oh.us/cjuv.php
Judge: David R. Kinworthy
Chief Deputy Clerk: Debbie Cheney

ALLEN COUNTY DOMESTIC RELATIONS COURT
301 N. Main St., P.O. Box 1243, Lima 45802
(419) 223-8511; Fax: (419) 227-3162
Judge: Matt C. Staley

LIMA MUNICIPAL COURT
109 N. Union St., P.O. Box 1529, Lima 45802-1529
(419) 221-5275; Fax: (419) 998-5526
Judges:
William G. Lauber   Rickard A. Workman
Clerk: Robert V. Holmes

County Offices

ALLEN COUNTY BOARD OF COMMISSIONERS
301 N. Main St., Lima 45801
(419) 228-3700, Ext. 8725; Fax: (419) 224-0183
President: W. Dan Reiff
E-mail: dreiff@allencountyohio.com
Commissioners:
Sam B. Bassitt; E-mail: sbassitt@allencountyohio.com
Greg A. Sneary; E-mail: gsneary@allencountyohio.com
Clerk: Kelli A. Singhaus
E-mail: ksinghaus@allencountyohio.com
Administrator: Becky Saine
E-mail: bsaine@allencountyohio.com

ALLEN COUNTY CLERK OF COURTS
301 N. Main St., Lima 45801
(419) 223-8513; Fax: (419) 222-8427
Clerk of Courts: Gina C. Burley-Staley
Hours: Weekdays, 8 A.M.-4:30 P.M.

ALLEN COUNTY CORONER
2629 Shoreline Dr., Lima 45805 (419) 991-1096
Coroner: Gary Beasley

ALLEN COUNTY ENGINEER
301 N. Main St., Lima 45801
(419) 228-3196; Fax: (419) 227-2920
Engineer: Wayne Gerdeman
E-mail: coengr@allencountyohio.com

ALLEN COUNTY PROSECUTOR
301 N. Main St., Lima 45801
(419) 228-3700, Ext. 8876
Prosecutor: Juergen Waldick

ALLEN COUNTY RECORDER
301 N. Main St., Lima 45801
(419) 223-8517; Fax: (419) 222-8427
Recorder: Mona Losh

ALLEN COUNTY AUDITOR
301 N. Main St., Lima 45801
(419) 228-3700, Ext. 8520; Fax: (419) 222-8427
Auditor: Ben Diepenbrock
E-mail: bdiepenbrock@allencountyohio.com

Allen County—Cont'd

ALLEN COUNTY SHERIFF
301 N. Main St., Lima 45801
(419) 222-1844; Fax: (419) 227-3535
Sheriff: Daniel W. Beck
    E-mail: beck@acso-ohio.us

ALLEN COUNTY TREASURER
301 N. Main St., Lima 45801
(419) 228-3700, Ext. 8515
Treasurer: Rhonda Eddy
    E-mail: reddy@allencountyohio.com

ASHLAND COUNTY

ASHLAND COUNTY COMMON PLEAS COURT
Courthouse, 142 W. Second St., Ashland 44805-2101
Judge: Deborah E. Woodward
    (419) 282-4292; Fax: (419) 281-8315
Magistrate Judge: Jeffrey A. Linsker (419) 282-4290
Court Reporter: Carol Jung (419) 282-4285
Mediator: Walt Harrop (419) 282-4290

ASHLAND COUNTY PROBATE/JUVENILE COURT
Courthouse, 142 W. Second St., Ashland 44805-2190
(419) 282-4284; Fax: (419) 281-5699
Judge: Damian J. Vercillo
Court Administrator: Nancy J. Dyer

ASHLAND MUNICIPAL COURT
1209 E. Main St., P.O. Box 385, Ashland 44805-0385
(419) 289-8137
Judge: Jacob M. Fridline
Clerk: William E. Linson, Jr.

County Offices

ASHLAND COUNTY BOARD OF COMMISSIONERS
110 Cottage St., Ashland 44805-2114
(419) 289-0000; Fax: (419) 281-6939
President: Matt Miller
    E-mail: mattmiller@ashlandcounty.org
Commissioners:
    Marilyn Byers; E-mail: mbyers@ashlandcounty.org
    Michael E. Welch; E-mail: mwelch@ashlandcounty.org
Clerk: Gail Crossen

ASHLAND COUNTY CLERK OF COURTS
142 W. Second St., Ashland 44805
(419) 282-4242; Fax: (419) 282-4240
E-mail: clerkofcourts@ashlandcounty.org
Clerk of Courts: Annette Shaw

ASHLAND COUNTY CORONER
1207 E. Main St., Ashland 44805
(419) 289-6552
Coroner: William M. Emery

ASHLAND COUNTY ENGINEER
1511 Cleveland Ave., Ashland 44805
(419) 289-0000
Engineer: Ed Meixner

ASHLAND COUNTY PROSECUTOR
307 Orange St., Ashland 44805
(419) 289-0000
Prosecutor: Ramona Rogers

ASHLAND COUNTY RECORDER
142 W. Second St., Ashland 44805
(419) 289-0000
Recorder: Barbara J. Harding

ASHLAND COUNTY AUDITOR
142 W. Second St., Ashland 44805
(419) 289-0000
Auditor: Phillip H. Leboit

ASHLAND COUNTY SHERIFF
1205 E. Main St., Ashland 44805
(419) 289-6552
Sheriff: Wayne Risner

ASHLAND COUNTY TREASURER
142 W. Second St., Ashland 44805
(419) 289-0000
Treasurer: Cindy A. Funk

ASHTABULA COUNTY

ASHTABULA COUNTY COMMON PLEAS COURT
25 W. Jefferson St., Jefferson 44047-1092
(440) 576-3687; Fax: (440) 576-1426
Judges:
    Alfred W. Mackey (440) 576-3683
    Ronald W. Vettel (440) 576-3677
    Gary L. Yost (440) 576-3681

ASHTABULA COUNTY PROBATE COURT
25 W. Jefferson, Jefferson 44047
(440) 576-3451; Fax: (440) 576-3633
Judge: Charles G. Hague
    E-mail: cghague@co.ashtabula.oh.us

ASHTABULA COUNTY JUVENILE COURT
3816 Donahoe Dr., Ashtabula 44004
(440) 994-6000; Fax: (440) 994-6021
Judge: Charles G. Hague
    E-mail: cghague@co.ashtabula.oh.us

ASHTABULA COUNTY COURT EASTERN DISTRICT
Eastern District
25 W. Jefferson St., Jefferson 44047
(440) 576-3617; Fax: (440) 576-3441
Judge: Robert S. Wynn
Clerk: Rose Cole

ASHTABULA COUNTY COURT WESTERN DISTRICT
Western District
117 W. Main St., Geneva 44041
(440) 466-1184; Fax: (440) 466-7171
Judge: Richard L. Stevens
Clerk: Mickey L. Mihalick

ASHTABULA MUNICIPAL COURT
110 W. 44th St., Ashtabula 44004
(440) 992-7108; Fax: (440) 998-5786
Judge: Albert S. Camplese
Clerk: Janis Crowell

CONNEAUT MUNICIPAL COURT
290 Main St., Conneaut 44030
(440) 593-7410; Fax: (440) 593-6402
Judge: Thomas E. Harris
Clerk: Wendy M. Thomas

County Offices

ASHTABULA COUNTY BOARD OF COMMISSIONERS
25 W. Jefferson St., Jefferson 44047-1027
(440) 576-3750; Fax: (440) 576-2344
President: Robert J. Boggs (440) 576-3757
Commissioners:
    Joseph A. Moroski (440) 576-3760
    Deborah A. Newcomb (440) 576-3756
Clerk: Julie Chelciu (440) 576-3751

ASTABULA COUNTY CLERK OF COURTS
25 W. Jefferson St., Jefferson 44047
(440) 576-3639; Fax: (440) 576-2819
Clerk of Courts: Carol A. Mead

ASTABULA COUNTY CORONER
600 State Rd., Ashtabula 44004
(440) 998-4791; Fax: (440) 998-0642
Coroner: Robert A. Malinowski

Ashtabula County—Cont'd

ASTABULA COUNTY ENGINEER
25 W. Jefferson St., Jefferson 44047-1092
(440) 576-3707; Fax: (440) 576-5663
Engineer: Timothy T. Martin

ASTABULA COUNTY PROSECUTOR
25 W. Jefferson St., Jefferson 44047-1092
(440) 576-3694; Fax: (440) 576-3692
Prosecutor: Thomas Sartini

ASTABULA COUNTY RECORDER
25 W. Jefferson St., Jefferson 44047-1092
(440) 576-3762; Fax: (440) 576-3231
Recorder: Judith A. Barta

ASHTABULA COUNTY AUDITOR
25 W. Jefferson St., Jefferson 44047
(440) 576-3783; Fax: (440) 576-3797
Auditor: Sandra C. O'Brien

ASTABULA COUNTY SHERIFF
25 W. Jefferson St., Jefferson 44047-1092
(440) 576-3507; Fax: (440) 576-5915
Sheriff: William R. Johnson

ASTABULA COUNTY TREASURER
25 W. Jefferson St., Jefferson 44047-1092
(440) 576-3727; Fax: (440) 576-3221
Treasurer: Robert L. Harvey

ATHENS COUNTY

ATHENS COUNTY COMMON PLEAS COURT
Courthouse, 3rd Floor, One S. Court St., Athens 45701-2895
(740) 592-3238; Fax: (740) 592-3020
Judges:
  L. Alan Goldsberry (740) 592-3236
  E-mail: agoldsberry@athenscountygovernment.com
  Michael W. Ward (740) 593-3591
  E-mail: cpcward@athenscountygovernment.com

ATHENS COUNTY PROBATE/JUVENILE COURT
Courthouse, One S. Court St., Athens 45701-2897
(740) 593-9029; Fax: (740) 592-3268
Judge: Robert W. Stewart (740) 592-3256

ATHENS COUNTY MUNICIPAL COURT
City Hall, Eight E. Washington St., Athens 45701-2498
(740) 592-3328; Fax: (740) 592-3331
Judge: William A. Grim
Clerk: Pamela Walton

County Offices

ATHENS COUNTY BOARD OF COMMISSIONERS
15 S. Court St., Athens 45701
(740) 592-3219; Fax: (740) 594-8010
Commissioners:
  Lenny Eliason   William H (Bill) Theisen
  Mark Sullivan
Clerk: JoAnn Sikorski

ATHENS COUNTY CLERK OF COURTS
Courthouse, 4th Floor, One South Court, Athens 45701
(740) 592-3242; Fax: (740) 592-3282
Clerk of Courts: Ann Trout

ATHENS COUNTY CORONER
58 Eden Pl., Athens 45701 (740) 594-2490
Coroner: Scott Jenkinson

ATHENS COUNTY ENGINEER
555 E. State St., Athens 45701 (740) 593-5514
Engineer: Archie Stanley, Jr.

ATHENS COUNTY PROSECUTOR
Courthouse, 15 S. Court St., Athens 45701 (740) 592-3208
Prosecutor: C. David Warren

ATHENS COUNTY RECORDER
Courthouse, 2nd Floor, 15 S. Court St., Athens 45701
(740) 592-3225
Recorder: Julia Michael Scott

ATHENS COUNTY AUDITOR
Courthouse, Room 300, 15 S. Court St., Athens 45701-2896
(740) 592-3223
Auditor: Jill A. Thompson

ATHENS COUNTY SHERIFF
13 W. Washington Ave., Athens 45701 (740) 592-3264
Sheriff: Vern Castle

ATHENS COUNTY TREASURER
Courthouse, 3rd Floor, 15 S. Court St., Athens 45701
(740) 592-3231
Treasurer: Javon Kittle Cooper

AUGLAIZE COUNTY

AUGLAIZE COUNTY COMMON PLEAS COURT
201 Willipie St., Suite 217, Wapakoneta 45895-1994
(419) 739-6770; Fax: (419) 738-7953
Judge: Frederick D. Pepple; Fax: (419) 739-6771

AUGLAIZE COUNTY PROBATE/JUVENILE COURT
201 Willipie St., Suite 103, Wapakoneta 45895-1972
Juvenile: (419) 739-6776; Probate: (419) 739-6778;
Fax: (419) 739-7563
Judge: Mark E. Spees
Chief Deputy Clerks:
  Debra K. Bellman
  Sue Widney (Probate)

AUGLAIZE COUNTY DOMESTIC RELATIONS COURT
201 Willipie St., Suite 103, Wapakoneta 45895
(419) 739-9119; Fax: (419) 739-7563
Judge: Mark E. Spees
Clerk: Sue Ellen Kohler

AUGLAIZE COUNTY MUNICIPAL COURT
201 S. Willipie St., P.O. Box 11, Wapakoneta 45895
(419) 739-6780; Fax: (419) 738-7953
Judge: Gary W. Herman; E-mail: gwherman@bright.net
Clerk: Sue Ellen Kohler
  P.O. Box 409, Wapakoneta 45895

County Offices

AUGLAIZE COUNTY BOARD OF COMMISSIONERS
209 S. Blackhoof St., Room 201, Wapakoneta 45895-1972
(419) 739-6700; Fax: (419) 739-6711
President: Ivo Kramer
Commissioners:
  John N. Bergman   Hugh A. Core
Clerk: Connie Cordonnier

AUGLAIZE COUNTY CLERK OF COURTS
201 S. Willipie St., Suite 211, P.O. Box 409,
Wapakoneta 45895-0409
(419) 739-6765
Clerk of Courts: Sue Ellen Kohler

AUGLAIZE COUNTY CORONER
601 Warren Dr., Wapakoneta 45895
(419) 738-5151
Coroner: Thomas Robert Freytag

AUGLAIZE COUNTY ENGINEER
1014 S. Blackhoof St., P.O. Box 59, Wapakoneta 45895
(419) 739-6520
Engineer: Douglas P. Reinhart

AUGLAIZE COUNTY PROSECUTOR
Courthouse, P.O. Box 1992, Wapakoneta 45895
(419) 739-6785
Prosecutor: Edwin A. Pierce

Auglaize County—Cont'd

AUGLAIZE COUNTY RECORDER
209 S. Blackhoof St., Wapakoneta 45895 (419) 739-6735
Recorder: Ann A. Billings

AUGLAIZE COUNTY AUDITOR
P.O. Box 34, Wapakoneta 45895-4713 (419) 739-6705
Auditor: Karyn Schumann

AUGLAIZE COUNTY SHERIFF
1051 Dearbaugh Ave., P.O. Box 26, Wapakoneta 45895
(419) 738-2147
Sheriff: Larry R. Longsworth

AUGLAIZE COUNTY TREASURER
209 S. Blackhoof St., Wapakoneta 45895 (419) 739-6745
Treasurer: Genevie Pitchford

BELMONT COUNTY

BELMONT COUNTY COMMON PLEAS COURT
Courthouse, 101 W. Main St., Saint Clairsville 43950-1154
(740) 695-2121, 699-2137
Judges:
Jennifer L. Sargus (740) 699-2137
John M. Solovan II (740) 699-2138

BELMONT COUNTY PROBATE/JUVENILE COURT
101 W. Main St., Saint Clairsville 43950-1154
Juvenile: (740) 699-2141; Probate: (740) 699-2144;
Fax: (740) 699-2143
Judge: J. Mark Costine (740) 699-2141
E-mail: markcjmc@aol.com
Hours: Weekdays, 8:30 A.M.-4:30 P.M.

BELMONT COUNTY COURT EASTERN DISTRICT
400 W. 26th St., Suite 100, Bellaire 43906
(740) 676-4490; Fax: (740) 671-6100
Judge: D. William Davis
Clerk: D. Charlene Baker

BELMONT COUNTY COURT NORTHERN DISTRICT
302 Walnut St., P.O. Box 40, Martins Ferry 43935
(740) 633-3147; Fax: (740) 633-6631
Judge: Frank A. Fregiato
E-mail: fregiato@tfmhd-law.com
Clerk: Donna Cottage

BELMONT COUNTY COURT WESTERN DISTRICT
147 W. Main St., Saint Clairsville 43950
(740) 695-2875; Fax: (740) 695-7285
Judge: Harry W. White; E-mail: bankerwhite@1st.net
Clerk: Rosalee J. Ralston
E-mail: rosalee.western@comcast.net

County Offices

BELMONT COUNTY BOARD OF COMMISSIONERS
Courthouse, 101 W. Main St., Saint Clairsville 43950-1225
(740) 699-2155; Fax: (740) 699-2156
President: Mark Thomas
Commissioners:
Geordie W. Longshaw   Charles R. Probst, Jr.

BELMONT COUNTY CLERK OF COURTS
Courthouse, 101 W. Main St., Saint Clairsville 43950
(740) 699-2169
Clerk of Courts: Randy L. Marple

BELMONT COUNTY CORONER
187 W. Main St., Saint Clairsville 43950
(740) 699-1000
Cororner: Dr. Troy Balgo

BELMONT COUNTY ENGINEER
Courthouse, 101 W. Main St., Saint Clairsville 43950
(740) 699-2160
Engineer: Frederick F. Bennett

BELMONT COUNTY PROSECUTOR
147 W. Main St., Saint Clairsville 43950
(740) 695-4412
Prosecutor: Chris Berhalter

BELMONT COUNTY RECORDER
Courthouse, 101 W. Main St., Saint Clairsville 43950
(740) 699-2140
Recorder: Mary Catherine Nixon

BELMONT COUNTY AUDITOR
Courthouse, 101 W. Main St., Saint Clairsville 43950
(740) 699-2130; Fax: (740) 699-2156
Auditor: Joseph A. Pappano

BELMONT COUNTY SHERIFF
68137 Hammond Rd., Saint Clairsville 43950
(740) 695-7933
Sheriff: Fred Thompson

BELMONT COUNTY TREASURER
Courthouse, 101 W. Main St., Saint Clairsville 43950
(740) 699-2145
Treasurer: Joseph A. Gaudio

BROWN COUNTY

BROWN COUNTY COMMON PLEAS COURT
Courthouse, 101 S. Main St., Georgetown 45121
(937) 378-4101; Fax: (937) 378-4212
Judge: R. Alan Corbin

BROWN COUNTY PROBATE/JUVENILE COURT
510 E. State St., Suite 1, P.O. Box 379,
Georgetown 45121-0379
(937) 378-6549; Fax: (937) 378-4729
Judge: Margaret A. Clark
E-mail: mclark@browncountycourt.org

BROWN COUNTY MUNICIPAL COURT
770 Mt. Orab Pike, Georgetown 45121-1281
(937) 378-6358; Fax: (937) 378-2462
Judge: Thomas F. Zachman
E-mail: tzachman@browncountycourt.org
Clerk: Tina Meranda (937) 378-5062

County Offices

BROWN COUNTY BOARD OF COMMISSIONERS
County Administration Bldg., Suite 101,
800 Mt. Orab Pike, Georgetown 45121-1170
(937) 378-3956; Fax: (937) 378-6324
President: Dale Reynolds
Commissioners:
Kirby Cornett   Perry Ogden
Clerk: Beverly Gallimore

BROWN COUNTY CLERK OF COURTS
101 S. Main St., Georgetown 45121 (937) 378-3100
Clerk of Courts: Tina Meranda

BROWN COUNTY CORONER
111 Vandament Way, Mount Orab 45154 (937) 444-9186
Engineer: Tim McKinley

BROWN COUNTY ENGINEER
325 W. State St., Georgetown 45121 (937) 378-6456
Engineer: James G. Beasley

BROWN COUNTY PROSECUTOR
200 E. Cherry St., Georgetown 45121 (937) 378-4151
Prosecutor: Thomas F. Grennan

BROWN COUNTY RECORDER
800 Mt. Orab Pike, Suite 151, P.O. Box 149,
Georgetown 45121
(937) 378-6478; Fax: (937) 378-2848
Recorder: Gary Himes

Brown County—Cont'd

BROWN COUNTY AUDITOR
County Administration Bldg., Suite 181,
800 Mt. Orab Pike, Georgetown 45121
(937) 378-6398; Fax: (937) 378-6038
Auditor: Doug Green

BROWN COUNTY SHERIFF
750 Mt. Orab Pike, Georgetown 45121 (937) 378-4435
Sheriff: Dwayne Wenninger

BROWN COUNTY TREASURER
County Administration Bldg., Suite 171,
800 Mt. Orab Pike, Georgetown 45121
(937) 378-6705
Treasurer: Gail DeClaire

BUTLER COUNTY

BUTLER COUNTY COMMON PLEAS COURT
Government Services Ctr., 3rd Floor, 315 High St.,
Hamilton 45011 (513) 887-3950; Fax: (513) 785-5719
Judges:
　Matthew J. Crehan
　　(513) 887-3590; Fax: (513) 785-5667
　　E-mail: crehanm@butlercountyohio.org
　Daniel "Andy" Nastoff
　　(513) 887-3290; Fax: (513) 785-6582
　　E-mail: nastoffa@butlercountyohio.org
　Patricia Oney
　　(513) 887-3286; Fax: (513) 887-5646
　　E-mail: oneyps@butlercountyohio.org
　Charles L. Pater
　　(513) 785-5801; Fax: (513) 785-6582
　　E-mail: patercl@butlercountyohio.org
　Michael J. Sage
　　(513) 887-3283; Fax: (513) 887-3285
　　E-mail: sagem@butlercountyohio.org
　Keith Spaeth
　　(513) 887-3586; Fax: (513) 785-5757
　　E-mail: spaethkm@butlercountyohio.org
Administrator: Gary W. Yates
　County Courthouse, 3rd Floor, 101 High St.,
　Hamilton 45011 (513) 785-5851; Fax: (513) 785-5816

BUTLER COUNTY PROBATE COURT
Courthouse, 2nd Floor, 101 High St., Hamilton 45011
(513) 887-3294; Fax: (513) 887-3629
Judge: Randy T. Rogers
　E-mail: rogersr@butlercountyohio.org

BUTLER COUNTY JUVENILE COURT
280 N. Fair Ave., Hamilton 45011
(513) 887-3318; Fax: (513) 887-3698
Internet: www.butlercountyohio.org/juvenilejusticecenter
Judges:
　Ronald R. Craft　　　　David J. Niehaus
Director: Robert G. Clevenger, Jr.

BUTLER COUNTY DOMESTIC RELATIONS COURT
Government Services Ctr., 2nd Floor, 315 High St.,
Hamilton 45011
(513) 887-3351; Fax: (513) 887-5640, 785-5337
Judge: Sharon L. Kennedy (513) 887-3788
　E-mail: kennedysl@butlercountyohio.org

BUTLER COUNTY COURT NO. 1
118 W. High St., Oxford 45056
(513) 523-4748; Fax: (513) 523-4737
Judge: Robert Hagen Lyons
Court Administrator: Debbie Bolser

BUTLER COUNTY COURT NO. 2
101 High St., Hamilton 45011
(513) 887-3459; Fax: (513) 887-3568
Judge: John B. Connaughton
Court Clerk: Debbie Bolser

BUTLER COUNTY COURT NO. 3
9577 Beckett Rd., Suite 300, West Chester 45069
(513) 867-5070; Fax: (513) 777-0558
Judge: Robert A. Hendrickson
Court Administrator: Debbie Bolser

FAIRFIELD MUNICIPAL COURT
4951 Dixie Hwy., Fairfield 45014
(513) 867-6002; Fax: (513) 867-6001
Judge: Joyce Ann Campbell
　E-mail: jcampbell@fairfield-city.org
Clerk: Eddie Roberts (513) 867-6001

HAMILTON MUNICIPAL COURT
One Renaissance Center, 2nd. Floor, 345 High St.,
Hamilton 45011 (513) 785-7300; Fax: (513) 785-7315
Judge: John G. Rosmarin
Clerk: Paul R. Kidd

MIDDLETOWN MUNICIPAL COURT
I Donham Plaza, Middletown 45042
(513) 425-7802; Fax: (513) 425-7846
Jurisdiction—Counties of Butler, Warren
Judge: Mark W. Wall (513) 425-7822
　E-mail: markw@ci.middletown.oh.us
Clerk: Louis A. Rossi (513) 425-7811
　E-mail: budr@ci.middletown.oh.us

County Offices

BUTLER COUNTY BOARD OF COMMISSIONERS
315 High St., Hamilton 45011
(513) 887-3247; Fax: (513) 887-3505
President: Charles R. Furmon
Commissioners:
　Michael A. Fox　　　　　Greg V. Jolivette

BUTLER COUNTY CLERK OF COURTS
315 High St., 5th Floor, Hamilton 45011
(513) 887-3278; Fax: (513) 887-3966
E-mail: mail@butlercountyclerk.org
Internet: www.butlercountyclerk.org
Clerk of Courts: Cindy Carpenter

BUTLER COUNTY CORONER
315 High St., Hamilton 45011 (513) 785-5860
Coroner: Richard P. Burkhardt

BUTLER COUNTY ENGINEER
1921 Fairgrove Ave., Hamilton 45011
(513) 785-4107; Fax: (513) 785-4114
Engineer: Greg Wilkens

BUTLER COUNTY PROSECUTOR
315 High St., Hamilton 45012
(513) 887-3474; Fax: (513) 887-3489
Prosecutor: Robin Piper

BUTLER COUNTY RECORDER
130 High St., Hamilton 45011 (513) 887-3188
Recorder: Danny Crank

BUTLER COUNTY AUDITOR
130 High St., Hamilton 45011
(513) 887-3154; Fax: (513) 887-3149
Auditor: Kay Rogers

BUTLER COUNTY SHERIFF
705 Hanover St., Hamilton 45011 (513) 785-1000
Sheriff: Rick Jones

BUTLER COUNTY TREASURER
315 High St., Hamilton 45011 (513) 887-3181
Treasurer: Carole Mosketti

CARROLL COUNTY

CARROLL COUNTY COMMON PLEAS COURT
P.O. Box 367, Carrollton 44615
(330) 627-2450; Fax: (330) 627-0985
Judge: William J. Martin

CARROLL COUNTY PROBATE/JUVENILE COURT
Courthouse, Suite 202, 119 S. Lisbon St.,
Carrollton 44615-1497 (330) 627-2323; Fax: (330) 627-6004
Judge: John H. Weyand

CARROLL COUNTY COURT
119 S. Lisbon St., Suite 301, Carrollton 44615
(330) 627-5049; Fax: (330) 627-3662
Judge: Charles A. Johnston
    E-mail: judge@carrollcountycourt.org
Clerk: Vanita J. Leggett

County Offices

CARROLL COUNTY BOARD OF COMMISSIONERS
Courthouse, Suite 201, 119 S. Lisbon St., Carrollton 44615
(330) 627-4869; Fax: (330) 627-6656
President: Robert D. Herron
Commissioners:
  Terry L. Wagner   Thomas A. Wheaton

CARROLL COUNTY CLERK OF COURTS
119 S. Lisbon St., P.O. Box 367, Carrollton 44615
(330) 627-4886; Fax: (330) 627-6437
Clerk of Courts: William R. Wohlwend

CARROLL COUNTY CORONER
P.O. Box 338, Carrollton 44615
(330) 627-5527; Fax: (330) 627-8083
Coroner: Mandal B. Haas

CARROLL COUNTY ENGINEER
200 Kensington Rd., Carrollton 44615
(330) 627-4110; Fax: (330) 627-6656
Engineer: David A. Miskimen

CARROLL COUNTY PROSECUTOR
11 E. Main St., Carrollton 44615 (330) 627-4555
Prosecutor: Donald R. Burns, Jr.

CARROLL COUNTY RECORDER
119 S. Lisbon St., Carrollton 44615 (330) 627-4545
Recorder: Patricia J. Oyer

CARROLL COUNTY AUDITOR
119 S. Lisbon St., Suite 203, Carrollton 44615
(330) 627-2250; Fax: (330) 627-0426
Auditor: E. Leroy Van Horne

CARROLL COUNTY SHERIFF
43 2nd St. S.E., Carrollton 44615
(330) 627-2141; Fax: (330) 627-2143
Sheriff: Dale R. Williams

CARROLL COUNTY TREASURER
119 S. Lisbon St., Carrollton 44615 (330) 627-5649
Sheriff: Jeff Yeager

CHAMPAIGN COUNTY

CHAMPAIGN COUNTY COMMON PLEAS COURT
Courthouse, 200 N. Main St., Urbana 43078
(937) 484-1000; Fax: (937) 484-1025
Judge: Roger B. Wilson

CHAMPAIGN COUNTY PROBATE/JUVENILE COURT
200 N. Main St., Urbana 43078
Probate: (937) 484-1028; Juvenile: (937) 484-1027
Judge: John C. Newlin
Clerks:
  Suzy Aukerman (Probate)
  Jana Champ (Juvenile)

CHAMPAIGN COUNTY MUNICIPAL COURT
205 S. Main St., P.O. Box 85, Urbana 43078
(937) 653-7376; Fax: (937) 652-4333
Judge: Susan J. Fornof-Lippencott
Clerk: Judy Taylor

County Offices

CHAMPAIGN COUNTY BOARD OF COMMISSIONERS
1512 S. U.S. Hwy. 68, Suite A100, Urbana 43078-1677
(937) 484-1611; Fax: (937) 484-1609
President: Steven R. Hess
Commissioners:
  Max Coates   Bob E. Corbett
Clerk/Administrator: Andrea Millice
Clerk: Jami Hackworth

CHAMPAIGN COUNTY CLERK OF COURTS
200 N. Main St., Urbana 43078
(937) 484-1047; Fax: (937) 484-5325
Clerk of Courts: Edward L. Preston

CHAMPAIGN COUNTY CORONER
848 Scioto St., Urbana 43078 (937) 653-3825
Coroner: Joshua F. Richards

CHAMPAIGN COUNTY ENGINEER
428 Beech St., P.O. Box 38187, Urbana 43078 (937) 653-4848
Engineer: Fereidoun Shokouhi

CHAMPAIGN COUNTY PROSECUTOR
200 N. Main St., Urbana 43078 (937) 652-1555
Prosecutor: Nick A. Selvaggio

CHAMPAIGN COUNTY RECORDER
1512 S. U.S. Hwy. 68, Suite B200, Urbana 43078
(937) 484-1630
Recorder: Carolyn Jo Downing

CHAMPAIGN COUNTY AUDITOR
1512 S. U.S. Hwy. 68, Suite B300, Urbana 43078-1680
(937) 484-1600; Fax: (937) 484-1626
Auditor: Bonnie McGowen Warman

CHAMPAIGN COUNTY SHERIFF
214 N. Main St., Urbana 43078
(937) 652-1311; Fax: (937) 788-2468
Sheriff: David Deskins

CHAMPAIGN COUNTY TREASURER
1512 S. U.S. Hwy. 68, Suite B400, Urbana 43078
(937) 484-1640
Treasurer: Kermit D. Russell

CLARK COUNTY

CLARK COUNTY COMMON PLEAS COURT
Courthouse, 101 N. Limestone St., Springfield 45502-1120
(937) 328-2458; Fax: (937) 328-2436
Judges:
  Thomas J. Capper (937) 328-2464; Fax: (937) 328-2463
  Richard O'Neill (937) 328-2467; Fax: (937) 328-2674
  Douglas M. Rastatter (937) 328-2480; Fax: (937) 328-2674

CLARK COUNTY PROBATE COURT
50 E. Columbia St., Springfield 45502-1194
(937) 328-2435; Fax: (937) 328-2589
Judge: Richard P. Carey
    E-mail: rcarey@clarkcountyohio.gov

CLARK COUNTY JUVENILE COURT
101 E. Columbia St., Springfield 45502
(937) 328-2626; Fax: (937) 328-2639
Judge: Joseph N. Monnin; E-mail: ccjuvcourt@cs.com

CLARK COUNTY DOMESTIC RELATIONS COURT
101 N. Limestone St., Springfield 45502
(937) 328-4648; Fax: (937) 328-2463
Judge: Thomas J. Capper

Clark County—Cont'd

CLARK COUNTY MUNICIPAL COURT
50 E. Columbia St., Springfield 45502-1116
(937) 328-3700; Fax: (937) 328-3779;
Toll free: (800) 544-1694
Internet: www.clerkofcourts.municipal.co.clark.oh.us
Judges:
Denise L. Moody (937) 328-3773
Eugene S. Nevius (937) 328-3763
Thomas E. Trempe (937) 328-3768
Clerk: Guy A. Ferguson (937) 328-3711

County Offices

CLARK COUNTY BOARD OF COMMISSIONERS
50 E. Columbia St., P.O. Box 2639, Springfield 45501-2639
(937) 328-2405; Fax: (937) 328-4588
Commissioners:
John Detrick (President)
Roger D. Tackett (Vice President)
David Hartley

CLARK COUNTY CLERK OF COURTS
101 N. Limestone St., P.O. Box 1008, Springfield 45501
(937) 328-2458
Clerk of Courts: Ronald E. Vincent

CLARK COUNTY CORONER
135 E. Columbia St., Springfield 45502 (937) 328-2655
Coroner: Richard A. Marsh

CLARK COUNTY ENGINEER
4075 Laybourne Rd., Springfield 45505
(937) 328-2484; Fax: (937) 328-2473
Engineer: Bruce Smith

CLARK COUNTY PROSECUTOR
50 E. Columbia St., P.O. Box 1608, Springfield 45501
(937) 328-2574; Fax: (937) 328-4588
Prosecutor: Stephen A. Schumaker

CLARK COUNTY RECORDER
31 N. Limestone St., P.O. Box 1406, Springfield 45501-2639
(937) 328-2444
Recorder: Nancy Pence

CLARK COUNTY AUDITOR
P.O. Box 1325, Springfield 45501
(937) 328-2423; Fax: (937) 928-4579
Auditor: George Sodders

CLARK COUNTY SHERIFF
120 N. Fountain Ave., Springfield 45502 (937) 328-2523
Sheriff: Gene A. Kelly

CLARK COUNTY TREASURER
31 N. Limestone St., P.O. Box 1305, Springfield 45501-1305
(937) 328-2432
Treasurer: Stephen T. Metzger

CLERMONT COUNTY

CLERMONT COUNTY COMMON PLEAS COURT
270 Main St., Batavia 45103-3071
Civil: (513) 732-7560; Criminal: (513) 732-7130;
Fax: (513) 732-7050
Judges:
Jerry R. McBride (813) 732-7104
Robert P. Ringland
William Walker

CLERMONT COUNTY PROBATE COURT
76 S. Riverside Dr., Batavia 45103
(513) 732-7243; Fax: (513) 732-8183
Judge: Stephanie Wyler

CLERMONT COUNTY JUVENILE COURT
2340 Clermont Center Dr., Batavia 45103
(513) 732-7696; Fax: (513) 732-7695
Judge: Stephanie Wyler

CLERMONT COUNTY DOMESTIC RELATIONS COURT
2340 Clermont Center Dr., Suite 200, Batavia 45103
(513) 732-7327; Fax: (513) 732-7333
E-mail: domestic@fuse.net
Internet: www.domesticcourt.org
Judge: Michael J. Voris; E-mail: domestic@fuse.net
Clerk: Barbara Weidenbein

CLERMONT COUNTY MUNICIPAL COURT
4430 St. Rt. 222, Batavia 45103
(513) 732-7308; Fax: (513) 732-7831
Judges:
Victor M. Haddad (513) 732-7914
Thomas R. Herman (513) 732-7916
James A. Shriver (513) 732-7396
Clerk: Timothy R. Rudd (513) 732-7308

County Offices

CLERMONT COUNTY BOARD OF COMMISSIONERS
101 E. Main St., Batavia 45103-2960
(513) 732-7300; Fax: (513) 732-7826
Internet: www.co.clermont.oh.us
Commissioner:
R. Scott Croswell III (President)
Robert L. Proud
Mary C. Walker
Clerk: Judie Kocica

CLERMONT COUNTY CLERK OF COURTS
270 Main St., Batavia 45103
(513) 732-8119; Fax: (513) 732-7050
Internet: www.clermontclerk.org
Clerk of Courts: Barbara A. Weidenbien

CLERMONT COUNTY CORONER
333 E. Main St., Batavia 45103
(513) 732-8117; Fax: (513) 732-8118
Coroner: Brian Treon, M.D.

CLERMONT COUNTY ENGINEER
2381 Clermont Center Dr., Batavia 45103
(513) 732-8857; Fax: (513) 732-8875
Engineer: Pat Manger

CLERMONT COUNTY PROSECUTOR
123 N. Third St., Batavia 45103
(513) 732-7313; Fax: (513) 732-7592
Prosecutor: Donald W. White

CLERMONT COUNTY RECORDER
101 E. Main St., Batavia 45103
(513) 732-7236; Fax: (513) 732-7891
Internet: www.co.clermont.oh.us
Recorder: Carolyn Green

CLERMONT COUNTY AUDITOR
101 E. Main St., Batavia 45103
(513) 732-7150; Fax: (513) 732-7849
Internet: www.clermontauditor.org
Auditor: Linda Fraley

CLERMONT COUNTY SHERIFF
4470 State Rt. 222, Batavia 45103
(513) 732-7500; Fax: (513) 732-7515
Internet: www.clermontsheriff.org
Sheriff: Albert J. Rodenberg

CLERMONT COUNTY TREASURER
101 E. Main St., Batavia 45103
(513) 732-7254; Fax: (513) 732-7969
Internet: www.clermonttreasurer.org
Treasurer: J. Robert True

CLINTON COUNTY

CLINTON COUNTY COMMON PLEAS COURT
Courthouse, 46 S. South St., Wilmington 45177
(937) 382-3640; Fax: (937) 383-3455
Judge: John W. Rudduck
    E-mail: cpjg@erinet.com

CLINTON COUNTY PROBATE/JUVENILE COURT
Courthouse, 2nd Floor, 46 S. South St., Wilmington 45177
(937) 382-2391; Juvenile Fax: (937) 383-0823;
Probate Fax: (937) 383-1158
Judge: G. Allen Gano

CLINTON COUNTY MUNICIPAL COURT
69 N. South St., P.O. Box 71, Wilmington 45177
(937) 382-8985; Fax: (937) 383-0130
Judge: Chad Lee Carey; E-mail: ccmc@erinet.com
Clerk: Sarah J. Avey

County Offices

CLINTON COUNTY BOARD OF COMMISSIONERS
46 S. South St., Wilmington 45177-2245
(937) 382-2103; Fax: (937) 383-2884
Commissioners:
    Mike Curry (President)   Randy Riley
    Darleen M. Myers

CLINTON COUNTY CLERK OF COURTS
Courthouse, 3rd Floor, 46 S. South St.,
Wilmington 45177-2297
(937) 382-2316; Fax: (937) 383-3455
Clerk of Courts: Joann M. Chamberlin

CLINTON COUNTY CORONER
103 E. Main St., Wilmington 45177 (937) 383-1242
Coroner: Ronald G. Seaman

CLINTON COUNTY ENGINEER
1326 Fife Ave., Wilmington 45177
(937) 382-2078; Fax: (937) 382-7530
Engineer: William T. Temple

CLINTON COUNTY PROSECUTOR
103 E. Main St., Wilmington 45177
(937) 382-4559; Fax: (937) 382-6278
Prosecutor: William E. Peelle

CLINTON COUNTY RECORDER
46 S. South St., Wilmington 45177
(937) 382-1611; Fax: (937) 383-6653
Recorder: Sandra K. Wilt

CLINTON COUNTY AUDITOR
46 S. South St., Wilmington 45177
(937) 382-2250; Fax: (937) 382-7530
Auditor: Wanda E. Armstrong

CLINTON COUNTY SHERIFF
1645 Davids Dr., Wilmington 45177
(937) 382-1611; Fax: (937) 382-7530
Sheriff: Ralph D. Fizer, Jr.

CLINTON COUNTY TREASURER
46 S. South St., Wilmington 45177 (937) 382-2224
Treasurer: Joyce L. Atley

COLUMBIANA COUNTY

COLUMBIANA COUNTY COMMON PLEAS COURT
Courthouse, 105 S. Market St., Lisbon 44432
(330) 424-7777; Fax: (330) 424-3960
Judges:
    C. Ashley Pike; E-mail: apike@ccclerk.org
    David Tobin; E-mail: dtobin@epochi.com

COLUMBIANA COUNTY PROBATE COURT
Courthouse, 105 S. Market St., Lisbon 44432
(330) 424-9516; Fax: (330) 424-5067
Judge: Thomas M. Baronzzi

COLUMBIANA COUNTY JUVENILE COURT
260 W. Lincoln Way, Lisbon 44432
(330) 424-4071; Fax: (330) 424-6670
Judge: Thomas M. Baronzzi
    E-mail: tbaronzzi@raex.com

**COLUMBIANA COUNTY MUNICIPAL COURT
EASTERN DIVISION**
31 N. Market St., East Palestine 44413
(330) 426-3774; Fax: (330) 426-6328
Judges:
    Mark A. Frost (330) 426-3774
    Robert C. Roberts (330) 332-0297
Clerk: Anthony J. Dattilio
    (330) 424-7777; Fax: (330) 424-3960

**COLUMBIANA COUNTY MUNICIPAL COURT
NORTHWEST**
130 Penn Ave., Salem 44460-3125
(330) 332-0297; Fax: (330) 332-0904
Judge: Robert C. Roberts
Clerk: Anthony J. Dattilio
    (330) 424-7777; Fax: (330) 424-3960
Court Schedule: Mon. and Thurs.

**COLUMBIANA COUNTY MUNICIPAL COURT
SOUTHWEST**
41 N. Park Ave., Lisbon 44432
(330) 424-5326; Fax: (330) 424-6658
Judges:
    Mark A. Frost (330) 426-3774
    Robert C. Roberts (330) 332-0297
Clerk: Anthony J. Dattilio
    (330) 424-7777; Fax: (330) 424-3960

EAST LIVERPOOL MUNICIPAL COURT
126 W. Sixth St., East Liverpool 43920
(330) 385-5151; Fax: (330) 385-1566
Judge: Melissa Byers-Emmerling
Clerk: Candace Moore-Page

County Offices

COLUMBIANA COUNTY BOARD OF COMMISSIONERS
105 S. Market St., Lisbon 44432
(330) 424-9511; Fax: (330) 424-5067
President: Jim H. Hoppel, Ext. 621
Commissioners:
    Sean Logan, Ext. 620
    Gary Williams, Ext. 622
Clerk: Tracy Allen

COLUMBIANA COUNTY CLERK OF COURTS
Courthouse, 105 S. Market St., Lisbon 44432
(330) 424-7777; Fax: (330) 424-3960
Clerk of Courts: Anthony J. Dattilio
    E-mail: tdattilio@ccclerk.org

COLUMBIANA COUNTY CORONER
Basement, 873 Old County Home Rd., Lisbon 44432
(330) 424-5029
Coroner: William A. Graham

COLUMBIANA COUNTY ENGINEER
235 S. Market St., Lisbon 44432
(330) 424-1740; Fax: (330) 424-0259
Engineer: Bert Dawson

COLUMBIANA COUNTY PROSECUTOR
105 S. Market St., Lisbon 44432
(330) 420-0140; Fax: (330) 424-0944
Prosecutor: Robert L. Herron

COLUMBIANA COUNTY RECORDER
105 S. Market St., Lisbon 44432 (330) 424-9517
Recorder: Craig Brown

Columbiana County—Cont'd

COLUMBIANA COUNTY AUDITOR
105 S. Market St., Lisbon 44432
(330) 424-9511; Fax: (330) 424-9745
Auditor: Nancy Millken

COLUMBIANA COUNTY SHERIFF
105 S. Market St., Lisbon 44432 (330) 424-9519
Sheriff: David Smith

COLUMBIANA COUNTY TREASURER
105 S. Market St., Lisbon 44432 (330) 424-9514
Treasurer: Linda Bolon

COSHOCTON COUNTY

COSHOCTON COUNTY COMMON PLEAS COURT
Courthouse Sq., 318 Main St., Coshocton 43812-1595
(740) 622-1595; Fax: (740) 295-0021

Title Department, 706 S. Seventh St., Coshocton 43812
(740) 622-1459; Fax: (740) 622-1154
E-mail: irenemiller@coshoctoncounty.net
Judge: Richard I. Evans

COSHOCTON COUNTY PROBATE/JUVENILE COURT
426 Main St., Coshocton 43812-1593
(740) 622-1837; Fax: (740) 623-6514
Judge: C. Fenning Pierce

COSHOCTON MUNICIPAL COURT
760 Chestnut St., Coshocton 43812-1294
(740) 622-2871; Fax: (740) 623-5928
Internet: www.coshoctonmunicipalcourt.com
Judge: David L. Hostetler
　　E-mail: judge@coshoctonmunicipalcourt.com
Clerk: Marcia J. Turner

County Offices

COSHOCTON COUNTY BOARD OF COMMISSIONERS
349 1/2 Main St., Coshocton 43812-1586
(740) 622-1753; Fax: (740) 622-4917
President: Grant K. Daugherty
Commissioners:
　Dane R. Shryock　　　　Kathleen M. Thompson
Clerk: Mary Beck

COSHOCTON COUNTY CLERK OF COURTS
Courthouse Sq., 318 Main St., Coshocton 43812
(740) 622-1456; Fax: (740) 295-0020

Title Department, 706 S. Seventh St., Coshocton 43812
(740) 622-1459; Fax: (740) 622-1154
E-mail: irenemiller@coshoctoncounty.net
Clerk of Courts: Irene Crouso Miller

COSHOCTON COUNTY CORONER
28549 C.R. 12, Coshocton 43812 (740) 622-1266
Coroner: Robert B. Gwinn

COSHOCTON COUNTY ENGINEER
23194 C.R. 621, Coshocton 43812
(740) 622-2135; Fax: (740) 623-6512
Engineer: Frederick T. Wachtel

COSHOCTON COUNTY PROSECUTOR
324 Chestnut St., Coshocton 43812
(740) 622-3566; Fax: (740) 623-6520
Prosecutor: Robert J. Batchelor

COSHOCTON COUNTY RECORDER
349 Main St., P.O. Box 817, Coshocton 43812
(740) 622-2817; Fax: (740) 622-1090
Recorder: Sandra K. Corder

COSHOCTON COUNTY AUDITOR
349 Main St., Coshocton 43812
(740) 622-1243; Fax: (740) 622-4917
Auditor: Richard J. Tompkins

COSHOCTON COUNTY SHERIFF
328 Chestnut St., Coshocton 43812 (740) 622-2411
Sheriff: Timothy L. Rogers

COSHOCTON COUNTY TREASURER
349 Main St., Coshocton 43812 (740) 622-2731
Treasurer: Michelle Darner

CRAWFORD COUNTY

CRAWFORD COUNTY COMMON PLEAS COURT
112 E. Mansfield St., Suite 200, Bucyrus 44820
(419) 562-5771; Fax: (419) 562-8011
Judge: Russell B. Wiseman

CRAWFORD COUNTY PROBATE/JUVENILE COURT
112 E. Mansfield St., Bucyrus 44820-2386
(419) 562-1896; Fax: (419) 562-6538
Judge: Steven D. Eckstein

CRAWFORD MUNICIPAL COURT
112 E. Mansfield St., P.O. Box 550, Bucyrus 44820-0550
(419) 562-2731; Fax: (419) 562-7064
Judge: James L. Hoover; E-mail: hoov@bright.net
Clerk: David L. Christman

County Offices

CRAWFORD COUNTY BOARD OF COMMISSIONERS
112 E. Mansfield St., Suite 304, Bucyrus 44820-2349
(419) 562-5876; Fax: (419) 562-3491
Commissioners:
　Ron Hoeft (President)
　Carl W. Watt (Vice President)
　Mo Ressallat
Clerk: Barbara Leuthold

CRAWFORD COUNTY CLERK OF COURTS
112 E. Mansfield St., Suite 204, Bucyrus 44820
(419) 562-2766; Fax: (419) 562-8011
Clerk of Courts: Sue Seevers

CRAWFORD COUNTY CORONER
725 N. Sandusky Ave., Bucyrus 44820 (419) 562-7557
Coroner: Michael Johnson

CRAWFORD COUNTY ENGINEER
815 Whetstone St., Bucyrus 44820 (419) 562-7731
Engineer: Gerald W. Riedel

CRAWFORD COUNTY PROSECUTOR
112 E. Mansfield St., Suite 305, Bucyrus 44820
(419) 562-9782
Prosecutor: Stanley Flegm

CRAWFORD COUNTY RECORDER
112 E. Mansfield St., Suite 206, Bucyrus 44820
(419) 562-6961
Recorder: Karen Scott

CRAWFORD COUNTY AUDITOR
112 E. Mansfield St., Suite 105, Bucyrus 44820
(419) 562-7941; Fax: (419) 562-3171
Auditor: Robin Hildebrand

CRAWFORD COUNTY SHERIFF
3613 Stetezer Rd., Bucyrus 44820 (419) 562-7906
Sheriff: Ronny Shawber

CRAWFORD COUNTY TREASURER
Courthouse, Box 565, Bucyrus 44820-1565
(419) 562-7861; Fax: (419) 562-3171
Treasurer: Gary A. Cole

CUYAHOGA COUNTY

CUYAHOGA COUNTY COMMON PLEAS COURT
1200 Ontario St., Cleveland 44113-1678
(216) 443-8560; Fax: (216) 443-5424

Judges:
Richard J. McMonagle (Presiding)
(216) 443-8675; Fax: (216) 348-4038
Richard J. (Dick) Ambrose
(216) 443-8670; Fax: (216) 348-4036
Christopher A. Boyko
(216) 443-8726; Fax: (216) 348-4036
Mary J. Boyle
(216) 443-8738; Fax: (216) 348-4033
Janet R. Burnside
(216) 443-8671; Fax: (216) 348-4035
Kenneth R. Callahan
(216) 443-8748; Fax: (216) 348-4032
Brian J. Corrigan
(216) 443-8747; Fax: (216) 348-4032
William J. Coyne
(216) 443-8755; Fax: (216) 348-4092
Carolyn B. Friedland
(216) 443-8705; Fax: (216) 348-4034
Stuart A. Friedman
(216) 443-8708; Fax: (216) 348-4035
Nancy A. Fuerst
(216) 443-8687; Fax: (216) 348-4092
Eileen Gallagher
(216) 443-8686; Fax: (216) 348-4031
Daniel Gaul
(216) 443-8706; Fax: (216) 348-4035
Lillian J. Greene
(216) 443-8681; Fax: (216) 348-4038
Burt W. Griffin
(216) 443-8736; Fax: (216) 348-4033
Peggy Foley Jones
(216) 443-8725; Fax: (216) 348-4038
Judith Kilbane Koch
(216) 443-8685; Fax: (216) 348-4032
Ann T. Mannen
(216) 443-8698; Fax: (216) 348-4036
David T. Matia
(216) 443-8695; Fax: (216) 348-4037
Bridget M. McCafferty
(216) 443-8707; Fax: (216) 348-4033
Timothy P. McCormick
(216) 443-8745; Fax: (216) 348-4034
Nancy R. McDonnell
(216) 443-8756; Fax: (216) 348-4037
Timothy J. McGinty
(216) 443-8758; Fax: (216) 348-4033
John P. O'Donnell
(216) 443-8676; Fax: (216) 348-4037
Thomas J. Pokorny
(216) 443-8728; Fax: (216) 348-4038
Joseph D. Russo
(216) 443-8746; Fax: (216) 348-4032
Michael J. Russo
(216) 443-8757; Fax: (216) 348-4037
Nancy M. Russo
(216) 443-8688; Fax: (216) 348-4036
Shirley Strickland Saffold
(216) 443-8735; Fax: (216) 348-4036
Ronald Suster
(216) 443-8727; Fax: (216) 348-4034
John D. Sutula
(216) 443-8680; Fax: (216) 348-4031
Kathleen Ann Sutula
(216) 443-8697; Fax: (216) 348-4031
José A. Villanueva
(216) 443-8737; Fax: (216) 348-4034

Administrator: William L. Danko

CUYAHOGA COUNTY PROBATE COURT
One Lakeside Ave., Cleveland 44113
(216) 443-8764, 65; Fax: (216) 443-5446
Internet: www.cuyahoga.oh.us/probate
Presiding Judge: John J. Donnelly
Judge: John E. Corrigan
Administrator: John A. Polito

CUYAHOGA COUNTY JUVENILE COURT
2163 E. 22nd St., Cleveland 44115 (216) 443-8400
Judges:
Patrick F. Corrigan (216) 443-8417
Alison L. Floyd (216) 443-8406
John W. Gallagher (216) 443-8410
Joseph F. Russo (216) 443-8408
Peter M. Sikora (216) 443-5818
Kristin W. Sweeney (216) 443-8412
Court Administrator: Ken Lusnia (216) 443-8423

CUYAHOGA COUNTY DOMESTIC RELATIONS COURT
One W. Lakeside Ave., Cleveland 44113-1082
(216) 443-8800; Fax: (216) 443-4943
Judges:
James P. Celebrezze (216) 443-8806
Timothy M. Flanagan (216) 443-8812
Cheryl S. Karner (216) 443-8809
Kathleen O'Malley (216) 443-8815
Anthony J. Russo (216) 443-8849
Court Administrator: Frank J. Pokorny

BEDFORD MUNICIPAL COURT
165 Center Rd., Bedford 44146-2818
(440) 232-3420; Fax: (440) 232-2510
Judges:
Peter J. Junkin   Brian J. Melling
Clerk: Thomas E. Day, Jr.

BEREA MUNICIPAL COURT
11 Berea Commons, Berea 44017
(440) 826-5860; Fax: (440) 891-3387
Internet: www.bereamunicipalcourt.org
Judge: Mark A. Comstock
Clerk: Raymond J. Wohl

CLEVELAND MUNICIPAL COURT
1200 Ontario St., Cleveland 44113
Mailing Address: P.O. Box 94894, Cleveland 44101-4894
(216) 664-4700; Fax: (216) 664-4283
Judges:
Ronald B. Adrine (216) 664-4975
Emanuella D. Groves (216) 664-4984
Mabel M. Jasper (216) 664-4978
Larry A. Jones (Presiding & Administrative Judge)
(216) 664-4996
Kathleen A. Keough (216) 664-4990
Anita Laster Mays (216) 664-4982
Lauren C. Moore (216) 664-4972
Raymond L. Pianka (Cleveland Housing Court)
(216) 664-4989
Angela R. Stokes (216) 664-4986
Joan Synenberg (216) 664-4998
Pauline H. Tarver (216) 664-4994
Robert J. Triozzi (216) 664-4992
Joseph J. Zone (216) 664-4980
Court Administrator: Michael E. Flanagan, 11th Floor
(216) 664-4700;
Court Interpreters Unit: (216) 664-3952;
Fax: (216) 664-4283
Clerk: Earle B. Turner
(216) 664-4314; Civil Division: (216) 664-4870;
Criminal Traffic: (216) 664-4790;
Parking Violations: (216) 664-4744
Court Administrator, Housing Court: Kate M. Thomas
13th Floor
(216) 664-4295; Fax: (216) 664-6103

Cleveland Municipal Court—Cont'd

Dir., Central Scheduling: Mary Ann Koster
11th Floor
(216) 664-3915; Civil Division Fax: (216) 664-6917;
Criminal Division Fax: (216) 420-7929
Chief Magistrate: Gregory F Clifford, 12th Floor
(216) 664-4942; Fax: (216) 664-4949
Bailiff: Paul J. Mizerak, 10th Floor
(216) 664-3950; Fax: (216) 664-4146
Jury Commissioner: Barbra Washington, 4th Floor
(216) 664-3957; Fax: (216) 420-8014
Chief Court Reporter: Grace Evangelou, 10th Floor
(216) 664-4725; Fax: (216) 420-8040
Chief Probation Officer: Regina Daniel, 6th Floor
(216) 664-4930; Fax: (216) 664-4267;
Satellite Office East: (216) 664-6181;
Satellite Office East Fax: (216) 420-8762;
Satellite Office West: (216) 420-8830;
Satellite Office West Fax: (216) 420-8848

EAST CLEVELAND MUNICIPAL COURT
14340 Euclid Ave., E., Cleveland 44112
(216) 681-2220; Fax: (216) 681-2217
Judge: Una H.R. Keenon (216) 681-2220
Magistrate Judge: Warner Jackson (216) 681-2387
Clerk: Patricia M. Ivery (206) 451-5900
Court Administrator: Patricia M. Ivery (216) 451-5900

EUCLID MUNICIPAL COURT
555 E. 222nd St., Euclid 44123-2029
(216) 289-2888; Fax: (216) 289-8254
Judge: Deborah Ann LeBarron
E-mail: dlebarron@ci.euclid.oh.us
Clerk: Barbara M. Tercek

GARFIELD HEIGHTS MUNICIPAL COURT
5555 Turney Rd., Cleveland 44125-3778
(216) 475-1900; Fax: (216) 475-3087
Internet: www.ghmc.org
Judges:
Deborah J. Nicastro (216) 475-5045
E-mail: dnicastro@ghmc.org
Jennifer P. Weiler (216) 475-4927
E-mail: jweiler@ghmc.org
Clerk: Jeffrey W. Rose

LAKEWOOD MUNICIPAL COURT
12650 Detroit Ave., Lakewood 44107
(216) 529-6700; Fax: (216) 529-7687
Judge: Patrick Carroll
Clerk: Thomas J. Wagner

LYNDHURST MUNICIPAL COURT
5301 Mayfield Rd., Cleveland 44124
(440) 461-6500, Ext. 151; Fax: (440) 442-1910
Judge: Mary Kaye Bozza
Clerk: Kristina A. Furcsik; E-mail: tfurcsik@yahoo.com

PARMA MUNICIPAL COURT
5555 Powers Blvd., Parma 44129-5462
(440) 887-7400; Fax: (440) 887-7481
Judges:
Mary L. Dunning   Kenneth R. Spanagel
Timothy P. Gilligan
Clerk: Marty Vittardi

SHAKER HEIGHTS MUNICIPAL COURT
3355 Lee Rd., Cleveland 44120-3499
(216) 491-1300; Fax: (216) 491-1314
Judge: K.J. Montgomery
Clerk: Phillip P. Ertel

SOUTH EUCLID MUNICIPAL COURT
1349 S. Green Rd., South Euclid 44121
(216) 381-2880; Fax: (216) 381-1195
Judge: Patricia Ann Kleri
Clerk: Debra E. Roy

County Offices

CUYAHOGA COUNTY BOARD OF COMMISSIONERS
1219 Ontario St., 4th Floor, Cleveland 44113-1684
(216) 443-7178; Fax: (216) 443-7635
Internet: www.cuyahogacounty.us
President: Timothy F. Hagan (216) 443-7181
Commissioners:
Jimmy C. Dimori (216) 443-7180
Peter Lawson Jones (216) 443-7182
Meetings: Thurs., 10 A.M., unless otherwise advertised

CUYAHOGA COUNTY CLERK OF COURTS
Justice Ctr., Courts Tower, 1200 Ontario St.,
Cleveland 44113 (216) 443-7950; Fax: (216) 443-6868
Clerk of Courts: Gerald E. Fuerst

CUYAHOGA COUNTY CORONER
11001 Cedar Ave., Cleveland 44106
(216) 721-5610; Fax: (216) 721-2559
Coroner: Elizabeth K. Balraj, M.D.

CUYAHOGA COUNTY ENGINEER
2100 W. Superior Viaduct, Cleveland 44113
(216) 348-3800; Fax: (216) 348-3896
Engineer: Robert C. Klaiber, Jr.

CUYAHOGA COUNTY PROSECUTOR
1200 Ontario St., Cleveland 44113
(216) 443-7800; Fax: (216) 443-7601
Prosecutor: William D. Mason

CUYAHOGA COUNTY RECORDER
1219 Ontario St., Cleveland 44113
(216) 443-8194; Fax: (216) 443-8193
Recorder: Patrick J. O'Malley

CUYAHOGA COUNTY AUDITOR
1219 Ontario St., Cleveland 44113
(216) 443-7010; Fax: (216) 443-5090
Auditor: Frank Russo

CUYAHOGA COUNTY SHERIFF
1215 W. 3rd St., Cleveland 44113
(216) 443-6000; Fax: (216) 348-4353
Sheriff: Gerald T. McFaul

CUYAHOGA COUNTY TREASURER
1219 Ontario St., Room 135, Cleveland 44113
(216) 443-7400; Fax: (216) 443-7463
Treasurer: James Rokakis

DARKE COUNTY

DARKE COUNTY COMMON PLEAS COURT
Courthouse, 504 S. Broadway St., Greenville 45331
(937) 547-7325; Fax: (937) 547-7323
E-mail: commonpleas@co.darke.oh.us
Judge: Jonathan P. Hein

DARKE COUNTY PROBATE/JUVENILE COURT
300 Garst Ave., Greenville 45331
(937) 547-7350; Fax: (937) 547-1945
Judge: Michael D. McClurg

DARKE COUNTY MUNICIPAL COURT
Courthouse, 3rd Floor, 504 S. Broadway St.,
Greenville 45331-1990 (937) 547-7340; Fax: (937) 547-7378
Judge: Roger L. Hurley
Clerk: Karen K. Stubbs

Darke County—Cont'd

County Offices

DARKE COUNTY BOARD OF COMMISSIONERS
520 S. Broadway, Greenville 45331-1993
(937) 547-7370; Fax: (937) 547-7367
Commissioners:
  Robert L. Downing   Michael W. Rhoades
  Terry L. Haworth
Clerk: Margaret A. Hile

DARKE COUNTY CLERK OF COURTS
504 S. Broadway, Greenville 45331
(937) 547-7335; Fax: (937) 547-7305
Clerk of Courts: Cindy Pike
    E-mail: cpike@co.darke.oh.us

DARKE COUNTY CORONER
404 Wagner Ave., Greenville 45331-0451
(937) 548-8711; Fax: (937) 548-6724
Coroner: John Mobley

DARKE COUNTY ENGINEER
504 S. Broadway, Greenville 45331
(937) 547-7375; Fax: (937) 547-7364
Engineer: James P. Surber

DARKE COUNTY PROSECUTOR
504 S. Broadway, Greenville 45331
(937) 547-7380; Fax: (937) 547-9075
Prosecutor: Richard M. Howell

DARKE COUNTY RECORDER
504 S. Broadway, Greenville 45331
(937) 547-7390; Fax: (937) 547-7342
Recorder: Judy Sonner

DARKE COUNTY AUDITOR
504 S. Broadway, Greenville 45331
(937) 547-7310; Fax: (937) 547-7342
Auditor: Janice P. Anderson

DARKE COUNTY SHERIFF
5185 County Home Rd., Greenville 45331
(937) 548-3399; Fax: (937) 548-9235
Sheriff: Toby Spencer

DARKE COUNTY TREASURER
504 S. Broadway, Greenville 45331
(937) 547-7365; Fax: (937) 547-7342
Treasurer: Scott J. Zumbrink

DEFIANCE COUNTY

DEFIANCE COUNTY COMMON PLEAS COURT
221 Clinton St., P.O. Box 386, Defiance 43512-2182
(419) 782-5931; Fax: (419) 782-2437
Judge: Joseph N. Schmenk
Court Administrator: Cheryl Timbrook

DEFIANCE COUNTY PROBATE/JUVENILE COURT
221 Clinton St., Defiance 43512-2182
(419) 782-4181; Fax: (419) 782-2437
Judge: Stephen W. Ruyle
Clerk: Janet Davis-Dunbar

DEFIANCE MUNICIPAL COURT
324 Perry St., Defiance 43512-2194
(419) 782-5756; Civil: (419) 782-4092; Fax: (419) 782-2018
Judge: John T. Rohrs III
Clerk: Julie A. Fitzenrider
Hours: Weekdays, 7 A.M.-5 P.M.

County Offices

DEFIANCE COUNTY BOARD OF COMMISSIONERS
500 Court St., Suite A, Defiance 43512-2157
(419) 782-4761; Fax: (419) 782-8449
President: Richard Cromwell
Commissioners:
  Thomas L. Kime   Otto Nicely
Clerk: Alison Grimes

DEFIANCE COUNTY CLERK OF COURTS
221 Clinton St., P.O. Box 716, Defiance 43512
(419) 782-1936; Fax: (419) 782-2739
Clerk of Courts: Jean Ziegler

DEFIANCE COUNTY CORONER
1810 Tiffin Ct., Defiance 43512 (419) 782-9005
Coroner: James L. Preston

DEFIANCE COUNTY ENGINEER
500 Second St., Defiance 43512
(419) 782-4751; Fax: (419) 782-3031
Engineer: Warren Schlatler

DEFIANCE COUNTY PROSECUTOR
607 W. Third St., Defiance 43512
(419) 784-3700; Fax: (419) 782-0594
Prosecutor: Jeffrey Strausbaugh

DEFIANCE COUNTY RECORDER
221 Clinton St., Defiance 43512 (419) 782-4741
Recorder: Jane M. Tadsen

DEFIANCE COUNTY AUDITOR
221 Clinton St., Defiance 43512
(419) 782-1926; Fax: (419) 784-2761
Auditor: Marlene J. Goodwin

DEFIANCE COUNTY SHERIFF
113 Biede Ave., Defiance 43512
(419) 784-1155; Fax: (417) 784-1592
Sheriff: David J. Westrick

DEFIANCE COUNTY TREASURER
221 Clinton St., Defiance 43512
(419) 782-8741; Fax: (419) 782-4719
Treasurer: Karen A. Tubbs

DELAWARE COUNTY

DELAWARE COUNTY COMMON PLEAS COURT
91 N. Sandusky St., Delaware 43015-1795
Judges:
  Everett H. Krueger
    (740) 833-2550; Fax: (740) 833-2549
  W. Duncan Whitney
    (740) 833-2530; Fax: (740) 833-2529

DELAWARE COUNTY PROBATE/JUVENILE COURT
88 N. Sandusky St., Delaware 43015
(740) 833-2600; Fax: (740) 833-2599
Judge: Kenneth J. Spicer (740) 833-2596

DELAWARE MUNICIPAL COURT
Justice Ctr., 70 N. Union St., Delaware 43015
Criminal Division: (740) 368-1555;
Civil/Small Claims Division: (740) 368-1550;
Fax: (740) 368-1583
Internet: www.municipalcourt.org
Judge: David P. Sunderman
    (740) 368-1575; Fax: (740) 368-1583
    E-mail: dsunderman@municipalcourt.org
Clerk: Betty J. Porter (740) 368-1580

Delaware County—Cont'd

County Offices

DELAWARE COUNTY BOARD OF COMMISSIONERS
101 N. Sandusky St., Delaware 43015-1732
(740) 833-2000; Fax: (740) 833-2099
Internet: www.co.delaware.oh.us
Commissioners:
Glenn Evans   Kris Jordan
James D. Ward

DELAWARE COUNTY CLERK OF COURTS
91 N. Sandusky St., 1st Floor, Delaware 43015
(740) 833-2500
Clerk of Courts: Jan Antonoplos

DELAWARE COUNTY CORONER
149 N. Sandusky St., Delaware 43015
Coroner: Dr. David Rath

DELAWARE COUNTY ENGINEER
50 Channing St., Delaware 43015
(740) 833-2400; Fax: (740) 833-2399
Engineer: Christian Bauserman

DELAWARE COUNTY PROSECUTOR
140 N. Sandusky St., Delaware 43015
(740) 833-2690; Fax: (740) 833-2689
Prosecutor: David A. Yost

DELAWARE COUNTY RECORDER
91 N. Sandusky St., Delaware 43015
(740) 833-2460, 59
Recorder: Andrew Brenner

DELAWARE COUNTY AUDITOR
140 N. Sandusky St., Delaware 43015
(740) 833-2900; Fax: (740) 833-2899
Auditor: Todd Hanks

DELAWARE COUNTY SHERIFF
149 N. Sandusky St., Delaware 43015
(740) 833-2860; Fax: (740) 833-2859
Sheriff: Al Myers

DELAWARE COUNTY TREASURER
140 N. Sandusky St., Delaware 43015
(740) 833-2480; Fax: (740) 833-2479
Treasurer: Dale M. Wilgus

ERIE COUNTY

ERIE COUNTY COMMON PLEAS COURT
Courthouse, 323 Columbus Ave., Sandusky 44870-2602
(419) 627-7731; Fax: (419) 627-6602
Judges:
Roger E. Binette   Tygh M. Tone

ERIE COUNTY PROBATE COURT
323 Columbus Ave., Sandusky 44870-2691
(419) 627-7750; Fax: (419) 626-9120
Judges:
Roger E. Binette   Tygh M. Tone
Beverly K. McGookey

ERIE COUNTY DOMESTIC RELATIONS/JUVENILE COURT
323 Columbus Ave., 4th. Floor, Sandusky 44870-2697
(419) 627-7782; Fax: (419) 627-6600
Judge: Robert C. DeLamatre

ERIE COUNTY COURT
150 W. Mason Rd., Milan 44846
(419) 499-4689; Fax: (419) 499-3300
Judge: Paul G. Lux
Clerk: Janet S. Bartizal

HURON MUNICIPAL COURT
417 Main St., Huron 44839
(419) 433-5430; Fax: (419) 433-5120
Judge: Ralph C. Pisano, Jr.
Clerk: Julie Bollenbacher

SANDUSKY MUNICIPAL COURT
222 Meigs St., Sandusky 44870
(419) 627-5920; Fax: (419) 627-5950
Judge: Erich J. O'Brien (419) 627-5975
Clerk: Peggy A. Rice (419) 627-5926
Court Schedule: Weekdays, 8 A.M.-4 P.M.; Second & fourth
Wed., 8 A.M-1 P.M. and 5:30-7.30 P.M.

VERMILLION MUNICIPAL COURT
687 Decatur St., Vermilion 44089
(440) 967-6543; Fax: (440) 967-1467
Jurisdiction—Counties of Erie, Lorain
Judge: Elizabeth Wakefield
Clerk: Barbara L. Akers

County Offices

ERIE COUNTY BOARD OF COMMISSIONERS
2900 Columbus Ave., Sandusky 44870-5554
(419) 627-7682; Fax: (419) 627-7692
President: Nancy McKeen
Commissioners:
Thomas M. Ferrell   Sparky R. Weilnau
Clerk: Carolyn L. Hauenstein

ERIE COUNTY CLERK OF COURTS
Courthouse, 323 Columbus Ave., Sandusky 44870
(419) 627-7708; Fax: (419) 624-6873
Clerk of Courts: Barbara J. Johnson

ERIE COUNTY CORONER
2203 Eagles Nest Cir., Sandusky 44870 (419) 626-2367
Coroner: Dr. Brian A. Baxter
136 E. Perkins Ave., Sandusky 44870 (419) 625-0654

ERIE COUNTY ENGINEER
2700 Columbus Ave., Sandusky 44870
(419) 627-7710; Fax: (419) 625-9622
Engineer: John D. Farschman

ERIE COUNTY PROSECUTOR
247 Columbus Ave., Suite 319, Sandusky 44870
(419) 627-7697; Fax: (419) 627-7567
Prosecutor: Kevin J. Baxter

ERIE COUNTY RECORDER
247 Columbus Ave., Sandusky 44870
(419) 627-7684; Fax: (419) 627-6639
Recorder: Barbara A. Sessler

ERIE COUNTY AUDITOR
247 Columbus Ave., Suite 210, Sandusky 44870-2635
(419) 627-7746; Fax: (419) 627-7740
Auditor: Jude T. Hammond

ERIE COUNTY SHERIFF
2800 Columbus Ave., P.O. Box 2357, Sandusky 44870
(419) 627-7668
Sheriff: Terry M. Lyons

ERIE COUNTY TREASURER
247 Columbus Ave., 1st Floor, Sandusky 44870
(419) 627-7704; Fax: (419) 627-7733
Treasurer: JoDee Fantozz

FAIRFIELD COUNTY

FAIRFIELD COUNTY COMMON PLEAS COURT
Hall of Justice, 224 E. Main St., Lancaster 43130-3879
(740) 687-7030; Fax: (740) 687-0158
Judges:
  Richard E. Berens (740) 687-7040
  Chris A. Martin (740) 687-7059

FAIRFIELD COUNTY PROBATE/JUVENILE COURT
Hall of Justice, 224 E. Main St., Lancaster 43130-3863
Juvenile: (740) 681-7223; Probate: (740) 687-7090;
Fax: (740) 687-0942
Judge: Steven O. Williams
Court Director: Cheri J. Shaw

FAIRFIELD COUNTY DOMESTIC RELATIONS COURT
Hall of Justice, 4th Floor, 224 E. Main St.,
Lancaster 43130
(740) 687-7087; Fax: (740) 687-7169
Judge: S. Farrell Jackson
Clerk: Ron Balser

FAIRFIELD COUNTY MUNICIPAL COURT
104 E. Main St., P.O. Box 2390, Lancaster 43130
(740) 687-6621; Fax: (740) 681-5014
Internet: www.fairfieldcountymunicipalcourt.org
Judges:
  Patrick N. Harris (740) 687-6620, Ext. 35
  David A. Trimmer (740) 687-6620, Ext. 36
Clerk: Sherry L. Eckman

County Offices

FAIRFIELD COUNTY BOARD OF COMMISSIONERS
210 E. Main St., Lancaster 43130-3879
(740) 687-7190; Fax: (740) 687-6048
President: Judith K. Shupe
Commissioners:
  Mike Kiger   Jon Myers
Clerk: Jacqueline D. Long

FAIRFIELD COUNTY CLERK OF COURTS
224 E. Main St., Lancaster 43130
(740) 687-7030; Fax: (740) 687-0158
Clerk of Courts: Ron Balser

FAIRFIELD COUNTY CORONER
1587 Granville Pike, Lancaster 43130 (740) 687-6774
Coroner: Thomas R. Vajen

FAIRFIELD COUNTY ENGINEEER
3024 W. Fair Ave., Lancaster 43130
(740) 652-2300; Fax: (740) 687-7055
Engineer: Frank W. Anderson

FAIRFIELD COUNTY PROSECUTOR
201 S. Broad St., 4th Floor, Lancaster 43130
(740) 687-7168; Fax: (740) 653-4708
Prosecutor: David L. Landefeld

FAIRFIELD COUNTY RECORDER
210 E. Main St., P.O. Box 2420, Lancaster 43130
(740) 687-7100
Recorder: Gene Wood

FAIRFIELD COUNTY AUDITOR
210 E. Main St., Lancaster 43130
(740) 687-7021; Fax: (740) 687-6781
Auditor: Barbara Curtiss

FAIRFIELD COUNTY SHERIFF
221 E. Main St., Lancaster 43130
(740) 653-5223; Fax: (740) 687-6856
Sheriff: Dave Phalen

FAIRFIELD COUNTY TREASURER
210 E. Main St., Lancaster 43130 (740) 687-7140
Treasurer: Jon A. Slater

FAYETTE COUNTY

FAYETTE COUNTY COMMON PLEAS COURT
Courthouse, 110 E. Court St.,
Washington Court House 43160-1395
(740) 335-4750; Fax: (740) 333-3522
Judge: Steven P. Beathard

FAYETTE COUNTY PROBATE/JUVENILE COURT
110 E. Court St., Washington Court House 43160-1391
(740) 335-0640; Fax: (740) 333-3598
Judge: Nancy Drake Hammond

WASHINGTON COURT HOUSE MUNICIPAL COURT
119 N. Main St., Washington Court House 43160-1330
(740) 636-2350; Fax: (740) 636-2359
Judge: Gary C. Stout
Clerk: Kathy Robinson

County Offices

FAYETTE COUNTY BOARD OF COMMISSIONERS
133 S. Main St., Suite 401,
Washington Court House 43160-1395
(740) 335-0720; Fax: (740) 333-3530
Commissioners:
  Tony Anderson   Bob Peterson
  Jack DeWeese
Clerk: Judy Rambo

FAYETTE COUNTY CLERK OF COURTS
110 E. Court St., Washington Court House 43160
(740) 335-6371; Fax: (740) 333-3522
Clerk of Courts: Larry L. Long

FAYETTE COUNTY CORONER
5 Fayette Center, P.O. Box 457,
Washington Court House 43160 (740) 335-4201
Coroner: Albert G. Gay, M.D.

FAYETTE COUNTY ENGINEER
1600 Robinson Rd., Washington Court House 43160
(740) 335-1541; Fax: (740) 333-3573
Engineer: Steven G. Luebbe

FAYETTE COUNTY PROSECUTOR
110 E. Court St., Washington Court House 43160
(740) 335-0888; Fax: (740) 333-3539
Prosecutor: David Bender

FAYETTE COUNTY RECORDER
133 S. Main St., Suite 305,
Washington Court House 43160
(740) 335-1770; Fax: (740) 333-3521
Recorder: Cathy Templin

FAYETTE COUNTY AUDITOR
133 S. Main St., Suite 303,
Washington Court House 43160
(740) 335-6461; Fax: (740) 333-3530
Auditor: Penny S. Johnson

FAYETTE COUNTY SHERIFF
113 E. Market St., Washington Court House 43160
(740) 335-6170; Fax: (740) 333-3589
Sheriff: Vernon P. Stanford

FAYETTE COUNTY TREASURER
133 S. Main St., Suite 304,
Washington Court House 43160
(740) 335-4961; Fax: (740) 333-3560
Treasurer: Susan V. Dunn

FRANKLIN COUNTY

FRANKLIN COUNTY COMMON PLEAS COURT
369 S. High St., Columbus 43215-4554
(614) 462-3452; Fax: (614) 462-4480

Judges:
John F. Bender (614) 462-7200
John P. Bessey, Room 6A (614) 462-3550
Jennifer L. Brunner, Room 8B (614) 462-6281
David E. Cain, Room 7D (614) 462-3777
John A. Connor, Room 6D (614) 462-3660
Dale A. Crawford, Room 8D (614) 462-3811
David W. Fais, Room 6C (614) 462-3660
Richard Frye (614) 462-3550
Daniel T. Hogan, Room 9D (614) 462-3770
Beverly Y. Pfeiffer, Room 8C (614) 462-3811
Guy L. Reece II, Room 7A (614) 462-7200
Charles Schneider, Room 9B (614) 462-3664
Richard S. Sheward, Room 9C (614) 462-3770
Tommy Thompson, Room 9A (614) 462-3664
Alan C. Travis, Room 8A (614) 462-6281

Administrator: Atiba Jones, 4th Floor (614) 462-7492

FRANKLIN COUNTY PROBATE COURT
373 S. High St., 22nd Floor, Columbus 43215-6311
(614) 462-3894; Fax: (614) 462-7422

Judge: Lawrence A. Belskis
E-mail: ibelskis@co.franklin.oh.us

FRANKLIN COUNTY DOMESTIC RELATIONS/JUVENILE COURT
373 S. High St., 6th Floor, Columbus 43215
(614) 462-6320; Fax: (614) 719-2118

Judges:
Jim Mason (Administrative) (614) 462-4453
E-mail: james_mason@fccourts.org
Kim A. Browne (614) 462-4444
Kay Lias (614) 462-4445
E-mail: kalias @co.franklin.oh.us
Dana Suzanne Preisse (614) 462-5775
E-mail: dana_preisse@fccourts.org
Carole Squire (614) 462-5223
E-mail: carole_squire@fccourts.org

FRANKLIN COUNTY MUNICIPAL COURT
375 S. High St., Columbus 43215-4593
(614) 645-8214; Fax: (614) 645-8822

Judges:
Ted Barrows (614) 645-7655
Michael T. Brandt (614) 645-8296
E-mail: michael_brandt@fccourts.org
Julia L. Dorrian (614) 645-8205
Mark S. Froehlich (614) 645-8849
E-mail: mark_froehlich@fccourts.org
Carrie Glaeden (614) 645-8206
James E. Green (614) 645-8295
E-mail: james_green@fccourts.org
Janet A. Grubb (614) 645-8207
Harland H. Hale (Environmental), Ctrm. 15C
(614) 645-8740; Fax: (614) 645-8255
E-mail: haleh@femcclerk.com
Paul M. Herbert (614) 645-8287
Teresa L. Liston (614) 645-8280
E-mail: listont@fcmclerk.com
W. Dwayne Maynard (614) 645-8286
E-mail: dwayne_maynard@fccourts.org
H. William Pollitt, Jr. (614) 645-7745
E-mail: william_pollitt@fccourts.org
Amy Salerno (614) 645-8204
E-mail: amy_salerno@fccourts.org
Anne Taylor (614) 645-7643
E-mail: anne_taylor@fccourts.org
Scott D. VanDerKarr (614) 645-8288
E-mail: scott_vanderkarr@fccourts.org

Clerk: Mike Pirik (614) 645-7657
Court Administrator: Keith Bartlett (614) 645-8214

County Offices

FRANKLIN COUNTY BOARD OF COMMISSIONERS
373 S. High St., 26th Floor, Columbus 43215-6314
(614) 462-3322; Fax: (614) 462-5999

Commissioners:

Mary Jo Kilroy (President)	Paula Brookes
	Dewey R. Stokes

Clerk: Debra Willaman

FRANKLIN COUNTY CLERK OF COURTS
373 S. High St., 23rd Floor, Columbus 43215
(614) 462-3600; Fax: (614) 462-4325

Clerk of Courts: John O'Grady

FRANKLIN COUNTY CORONER
520 Kings Ave., Columbus 43201 (614) 462-5290

Coroner: Bradley J. Lewis, M.D.

FRANKLIN COUNTY ENGINEER
970 Dublin Rd., Columbus 43215 (614) 462-3030

Engineer: Dean C. Ringle

FRANKLIN COUNTY PROSECUTOR
373 S. High St., 14th. Floor, Columbus 43215
(614) 462-3555; Fax: (614) 462-6103

Prosecutor: Ron O'Brien

FRANKLIN COUNTY RECORDER
373 S. High St., 18th Floor, Columbus 43215
(614) 462-3930; Fax: (614) 462-4299

Recorder: Robert G. Montgomery

FRANKLIN COUNTY AUDITOR
373 S. High St., 21st Floor, Columbus 43215
(614) 462-3247; Fax: (614) 462-7384

Auditor: Joseph W. Testa

FRANKLIN COUNTY SHERIFF
369 S. High St., Columbus 43215 (614) 462-3360

Sheriff: James Karnes

FRANKLIN COUNTY TREASURER
373 S. High St., 17th Floor, Columbus 43215-6306
(614) 462-3438; Fax: (614) 221-8124

Treasurer: Richard Cordray

FULTON COUNTY

FULTON COUNTY COMMON PLEAS COURT
210 S. Fulton St., Wauseon 43567
(419) 337-9260; Fax: (419) 337-9293

Judge: James E. Barber
E-mail: jbarber@fultoncounty.oh.com

FULTON COUNTY PROBATE/JUVENILE COURT
210 S. Fulton St., Wauseon 43567
(419) 337-9242; Fax: (419) 337-9284

Judge: Michael J. Bumb

FULTON COUNTY COURT EASTERN DISTRICT
204 S. Main St., Swanton 43558-1091
(419) 826-5636; Fax: (419) 825-3324

Judge: Colin J. McQuade
E-mail: cjmcquade@fultoncountyoh.com

Clerk: Christine Mossing

FULTON COUNTY COURT WESTERN DISTRICT
224 S. Fulton St., Wauseon 43567-1352
(419) 337-9212; Fax: (419) 337-9286

Judge: Jeffrey L. Robinson
Clerk: Dianne Galbraith

Fulton County—Cont'd

County Offices

FULTON COUNTY BOARD OF COMMISSIONERS
152 S. Fulton St., Suite 270, Wauseon 43567-3309
(419) 337-9255; Fax: (419) 337-9285
Commissioners:
Paul Barnaby   Jack C. Graf
Dean Genter
Clerk: Rhonda Borton

FULTON COUNTY CLERK OF COURTS
210 S. Fulton St., Suite 102, Wauseon 43567
(419) 337-9230; Fax: (419) 337-9199
Clerk of Courts: Mary Gype

FULTON COUNTY CORONER
803 Eastwood Dr., Delta 43515 (419) 822-4664
Coroner: Harry Murtiff

FULTON COUNTY ENGINEER
9120 County Rd. 14, Wauseon 43567 (419) 335-3816
Engineer: Frank T. Onweller

FULTON COUNTY PROSECUTOR
123 Courthouse Plz., Wauseon 43567 (419) 337-9240
Prosecutor: Roger D. Nagel

FULTON COUNTY RECORDER
152 S. Fulton St., Suite 175, Wauseon 43567
(419) 337-9232
Recorder: Sandra K. Barber

FULTON COUNTY AUDITOR
152 S. Fulton St., Suite 165, Wauseon 43567
(419) 337-9200; Fax: (419) 337-9298
Auditor: Nancy Yackee

FULTON COUNTY SHERIFF
129 Courthouse Plz., Wauseon 43567 (419) 335-4010
Sheriff: Darrell E. Merillat

FULTON COUNTY TREASURER
152 S. Fulton St., Suite 155, Wauseon 43567
(419) 337-9252
Treasurer: Beverly Schlosser

GALLIA COUNTY

GALLIA COUNTY COMMON PLEAS COURT
Courthouse, Room 1200, 18 Locust St., Gallipolis 45631
(740) 446-4612
Judge: D. Dean Evans
   (740) 446-4702; Fax: (740) 441-2051

GALLIA COUNTY PROBATE/JUVENILE COURT
Courthouse, Room 1293, 18 Locust St.,
Gallipolis 45631-1244 (740) 446-3842; Fax: (740) 446-3144
Judges:
Thomas S. Malton   William S. Medley
Deputy Clerk: Mary Beth Coleman

GALLIPOLIS MUNICIPAL COURT
518 Second Ave., Gallipolis 45631-0988
(740) 446-9400; Fax: (740) 441-6025
Judge: Margaret Evans
Clerk: Lou Ellen Werry

County Offices

GALLIA COUNTY BOARD OF COMMISSIONERS
18 Locust St., Room 1292, Gallipolis 45631-1292
(740) 446-4612; Fax: (740) 446-4804
E-mail: gcboc@zoomnet.net
President: Harold G. Montgomery
Commissioners:
Fred Dell   David Smith
Administrator: Karen Sprague
Clerk: Barbara Unroe

GALLIA COUNTY CLERK OF COURTS
Courthouse, Room 1290, 18 Locust St., Gallipolis 45631
(740) 446-4612, Ext. 222; Fax: (740) 441-2932
499 Jackson Pike, Suite C, Gallipolis 45631
(740) 441-2186
Clerk of Courts: Noreen M. Saunders

GALLIA COUNTY CORONER
P.O. Box 344, Gallipolis 45631 (740) 446-5225
Coroner: Daniel H. Whitely

GALLIA COUNTY ENGINEER
1167 State Rte. 160, Gallipolis 45631
(740) 446-4009; Fax: (740) 446-2032
Engineer: Glenn A. Smith

GALLIA COUNTY PROSECUTOR
18 Locust St., Room 1267, Gallipolis 45631
(740) 446-0018; Fax: (740) 441-2050
Prosecutor: Brent A. Saunders

GALLIA COUNTY RECORDER
18 Locust St., Room 1265, Gallipolis 45631
(740) 446-4612
Recorder: Roger Walker

GALLIA COUNTY AUDITOR
18 Locust St., Room 1264, Gallipolis 45631
(740) 446-4612; Fax: (740) 446-9666
Auditor: Larry M. Betz

GALLIA COUNTY SHERIFF
18 Locust St., Room 1289, Gallipolis 45631
(740) 446-1221; Fax: (740) 441-4804
Sheriff: Dave Martin

GALLIA COUNTY TREASURER
Courthouse, Room 1291, 18 Locust St., Gallipolis 45631
(740) 446-4612; Fax: (740) 441-2092
Treasurer: Steven McGhee

GEAUGA COUNTY

GEAUGA COUNTY COMMON PLEAS COURT
Courthouse, 100 Short Court, Chardon 44024-1238
(440) 285-2222; Fax: (440) 286-2127
Judges:
Forrest W. Burt   David L. Fuhry
Court does not accept fax filings

GEAUGA COUNTY PROBATE/JUVENILE COURT
Courthouse Annex, Suite 200, 231 Main St., Chardon 44024
(440) 285-2222, Ext. 2000; Fax: (440) 285-5025
Judge: Charles E. Henry
Hours: Weekdays, 8 A.M.-4:30 P.M.

CHARDON MUNICIPAL COURT
111 Water St., Chardon 44024-1201
(440) 286-2670; Fax: (440) 286-2679
Judge: Mark J. Hassett
Clerk: Victoria Dailey
Hours: Weekdays, 8 A.M.-4 P.M.

County Offices

GEAUGA COUNTY BOARD OF COMMISSIONERS
Building 4, 470 Center St., Chardon 44024-1071
(440) 285-2222, Ext. 6150; Fax: (440) 286-9177
E-mail: commissioners@geaugabocc.org
Commissioners:
Craig S. Albert   William S. Young
Mary E. Samide
Clerk: Claudine Kozenko, Ext. 6180
Administrator: David Lair, Ext. 6800

GEAUGA COUNTY CLERK OF COURTS
100 Short Court St., Suite 2B, Chardon 44024
(440) 285-2222, Ext. 2380
Clerk of Courts: Denise M. Kaminski

Geauga County—Cont'd

GEAUGA COUNTY CORONER
13205 Aquilla Rd., Chardon 44024
(440) 285-2222; Fax: (440) 285-5390
Coroner: Albert S. Evans

GEAUGA COUNTY ENGINEER
470 Center St., Bldg. 5, Chardon 44024
(440) 285-2222; Fax: (440) 285-9864
Engineer: Robert L. Phillips

GEAUGA COUNTY PROSECUTOR
Courthouse Annex, 231 Main St., Chardon 44024
(440) 285-2222; Fax: (440) 286-4357
Prosecutor: David P. Joyce

GEAUGA COUNTY RECORDER
Courthouse Annex, Suite 1C, 231 Main St., Chardon 44024
(440) 285-2222
Recorder: Mary Margaret McBride

GEAUGA COUNTY AUDITOR
231 Main St., Suite 1A, Chardon 44024-1393
(440) 285-2222; Fax: (440) 286-4359
Auditor: Tracy Jemison

GEAUGA COUNTY SHERIFF
13281 Ravenna Rd., P.O. Box 224, Chardon 44024
(440) 285-2222
Sheriff: Daniel C. McClelland

GEAUGA COUNTY TREASURER
211 Main St., Chardon 44024-1249
(440) 285-2222; Fax: (440) 285-0940
Treasurer: Christopher P. Hitchcock

GREENE COUNTY

GREENE COUNTY COMMON PLEAS COURT
45 N. Detroit St., Xenia 45385-2998
(937) 562-5217; Fax: (937) 562-5142
Judges:
J. Timothy Campbell
Stephen A. Wolaver
(937) 562-5218; Fax: (937) 562-5137

GREENE COUNTY PROBATE COURT
45 N. Detroit St., Xenia 45385-2998
(937) 562-5280; Fax: (937) 562-5316
Judge: Robert A. Hagler
E-mail: rhagler@co.greene.oh.us
Chief Deputy Clerk: Marsha K. Linkhart

GREENE COUNTY JUVENILE COURT
2100 Greene Way Blvd., Xenia 45385
(937) 562-4000; Fax: (937) 562-4010
Judge: Robert W. Hutcheson
Administrator: Jan A. White

GREENE COUNTY DOMESTIC RELATIONS COURT
595 Ledbetter Rd., Xenia 45385-2998
(937) 562-6249; Fax: (937) 562-6233
Judge: Steven L. Hurley
Hours: Weekdays, 8 A.M.-4 P.M.

FAIRBORN MUNICIPAL COURT
1148 Kauffman Ave., Fairborn 45324
(937) 754-3040; Fax: (937) 879-4422
Judge: Catherine M. Barber
Clerk: William Litteral

XENIA MUNICIPAL COURT
101 N. Detroit St., Xenia 45385-2996
(937) 376-7294; Fax: (937) 376-7288
Judge: Susan L. Goldie
Clerk: C. Arch Grieve, Jr.
Court Schedule: Night Court: Mon. and Tues., 5.30 P.M.

County Offices

GREENE COUNTY BOARD OF COMMISSIONERS
35 Greene St., Xenia 45385-3101
(937) 562-5006; Fax: (937) 562-5331
Internet: www.co.greene.oh.us
Commissioners:
Ralph C. Harper   Marilyn J. Reid
Rick Perales
Clerk: Lisa Mock

GREENE COUNTY CLERK OF COURTS
45 N. Detroit St., Xenia 45385
(937) 562-5290; Fax: (937) 562-5309
Clerk of Courts: Terri A. Mazur

GREENE COUNTY CORONER
120 E. Main St., Xenia 45385 (937) 562-5050
Coroner: Kevin L. Sharett

GREENE COUNTY ENGINEER
615 Dayton-Xenia Rd., Xenia 45385 (937) 562-7500
Engineer: Robert N. Geyer

GREENE COUNTY PROSECUTOR
55 Greene St., Xenia 45385 (937) 562-5250
Prosecutor: William F. Schenck

GREENE COUNTY RECORDER
69 Greene St., Xenia 45385 (937) 562-5270
Recorder: Mary Morris

GREENE COUNTY AUDITOR
69 Greene St., Xenia 45385 (937) 562-5065
Auditor: Luwanna A. Delaney

GREENE COUNTY SHERIFF
120 E. Main St., Xenia 45385 (937) 562-4801
Sheriff: Eugene Fischer

GREENE COUNTY TREASURER
15 Greene St., Xenia 45385 (937) 562-5017
Treasurer: James W. Schmidt

GUERNSEY COUNTY

GUERNSEY COUNTY COMMON PLEAS COURT
801 Wheeling Ave., Room E, Cambridge 43725-2358
(740) 432-9252; Fax: (740) 432-7807
Judge: David A. Ellwood; E-mail: jdae33@yahoo.com

GUERNSEY COUNTY PROBATE COURT
Courthouse, Dept. D-203, 801 E. Wheeling Ave.,
Cambridge 43725 (740) 432-9262; Fax: (740) 439-5278
Judge: Robert S. Moorehead, Jr.

CAMBRIDGE MUNICIPAL COURT
134 Southgate Pkwy., Cambridge 43725
(740) 439-5585; Fax: (740) 439-5666
Judge: John Mark Nicholson
Clerk: Jane Patterson
E-mail: cambcrtclerk@cambridgemunicipalcourt.com

County Offices

GUERNSEY COUNTY BOARD OF COMMISSIONERS
627 Wheeling Ave., Suite 300, Cambridge 43725-2364
(740) 432-9200; Fax: (740) 432-9359
President: Steve Allen
Commissioners:
Thomas Laughman   Joe Secrest
Clerk: Cheryl Edwards

GUERNSEY COUNTY CLERK OF COURTS
627 Wheeling Ave., Cambridge 43725
(740) 432-9230; Fax: (740) 432-7807
Internet: www.guernseycountycpcourt.org
Clerk of Courts: Teresa A. Dankovic
E-mail: guernseycounty.clerkofcourts@verizon.net

Guernsey County—Cont'd

GUERNSEY COUNTY CORONER
6555 Mathews Rd., Cambridge 43725
(740) 432-2234; Fax: (740) 439-5484
Coroner: Janet M. Brockwell

GUERNSEY COUNTY ENGINEER
6782 Bennett Ave., Cambridge 43725
(740) 432-2234; Fax: (740) 432-7556
Engineer: Delmar E. George

GUERNSEY COUNTY PROSECUTOR
129 W. Eighth St., Cambridge 43725
(740) 439-2082; Fax: (740) 439-7161
Prosecutor: Dan Padden

GUERNSEY COUNTY RECORDER
627 Wheeling Ave., Cambridge 43725 (740) 432-9275
Recorder: Colleen Doutt Wheatley

GUERNSEY COUNTY AUDITOR
627 Wheeling Ave., Cambridge 43725
(740) 432-9243; Fax: (740) 432-9207
Auditor: Anthony Brown

GUERNSEY COUNTY SHERIFF
601 S. Gate Pkwy., Cambridge 43725 (740) 439-4455
Sheriff: Michael McCauley

GUERNSEY COUNTY TREASURER
627 Wheeling Ave., Cambridge 43725
(740) 432-7556; Fax: (740) 432-9251
Treasurer: James A. Caldwell

HAMILTON COUNTY

HAMILTON COUNTY COMMON PLEAS COURT
1000 Main St., Room 410, Cincinnati 45202
(513) 946-5800; Fax: (513) 946-5907
Judges:
　Kim Wilson Burke, Room 500 (513) 946-5770
　Ethna Marie Cooper, Room 485 (513) 946-5860
　Thomas H. Crush, Room 360 (513) 946-5750
　David P. Davis, Room 530 (513) 946-5890
　Patrick T. Dinkelacker, Room 310 (513) 946-5755
　Dennis S. Helmick, Room 510
　　(513) 946-5830; Fax: (513) 946-5833
　Charles Kubicki, Jr., Room 495 (513) 946-5760
　Melba D. Marsh, Room 330 (513) 946-5866
　Steven E. Martin, Room 340 (513) 946-5790
　Beth A. Myers, Room 370 (513) 946-5102
　Norbert A. Nadel, Room 560 (513) 946-5960
　Fred Nelson, Room 380 (513) 946-5840
　Richard A. Niehaus, Room 520 (513) 946-5835
　Robert P. Ruehlman, Room 300 (513) 946-5850
　Mark Schweikert, Room 320 (513) 946-5117
　John Andrew West, Room 595 (513) 946-5785
　Ralph E. (Ted) Winkler, Room 515 (513) 946-5175
Court Administrator: Michael Walton, Room 410
　(513) 946-5900; Fax: (513) 946-5808

HAMILTON COUNTY PROBATE COURT
230 E. Ninth St., 10th Floor, Cincinnati 45202-2145
(513) 946-3580; Fax: (513) 946-3581
Judge: James Cissell

HAMILTON COUNTY JUVENILE COURT
800 Broadway, Cincinnati 45202-1225
(513) 946-9400; Fax: (513) 946-9217; TDD: (513) 946-9340
Judges:
　Karla J. Grady (513) 946-9201
　　E-mail: kgrady@juvcourt.hamilton-co.org
　Thomas R. Lipps (513) 946-9211
　　E-mail: thomas.lipps@juvcourt.hamilton.co.org

Magistrates:
　Jack McManus (Chief) (513) 946-9460
　Brenda Anthony (513) 946-9380
　Katherine Boller-Koch (513) 946-9370
　Bernard Bouchard (513) 946-9476
　Paul DeMott (513) 946-9367
　Tina Ernst (513) 946-9468
　Karen Falter (513) 946-9372
　Thomas Flynn (513) 946-9461
　Rob Gray (513) 946-9467
　Carla Guenthner (513) 946-9371
　Denis Holtmeier (513) 946-9463
　Elizabeth Igoe (513) 946-9473
　Catherine Kelley (513) 946-9469
　Melinda Klenk (513) 946-9455
　William Melvin (513) 946-9475
　Charles Milazzo (513) 946-9477
　Allen Miller (513) 946-9459
　Connie Murdock (513) 946-9465
　Elisa Persley (513) 946-9326
　Kevin Reed (513) 946-9471
　Jacqueline Rellahan
　Sara Schoettmer
　Mary Schulcz (513) 946-9464
　Scheherazde Washington (513) 946-9369
　Donald Webb (513) 946-9470
Court Administrator: Mark Reed (513) 948-9221
Chief Deputy Clerk: John Cullum (513) 946-9431
Court Schedule: Weekdays, 8:30 A.M.-1 P.M. & 2-5 P.M.

HAMILTON COUNTY DOMESTIC RELATIONS COURT
800 Broadway, Room 225, Cincinnati 45202
(513) 946-9000
Judges:
　Penelope R. Cunningham
　　(513) 946-9030; Fax: (513) 946-9033
　Ronald A. Panioto
　　(513) 946-9020; Fax: (513) 946-9021
　Susan Laker Tolbert
　　(513) 852-8017; Fax: (513) 946-9019

HAMILTON COUNTY MUNICIPAL COURT
Courthouse, 1000 Main St., Cincinnati 45202
(513) 946-5200; Fax: (513) 946-5202
Judges:
　Lisa Allen (513) 946-5148
　Nadine L. Allen (513) 946-5154
　John H. Burlew (513) 946-5122
　Kendal M. Coes (513) 946-5127
　Cheryl D. Grant (513) 946-5165
　Guy C. Guckenberger (513) 946-5169
　William L. Mallory (513) 946-5112
　Elizabeth B. Mattingly (513) 946-5108
　Russell J. Mock (513) 946-5138
　Heather Russell (513) 946-5133
　Julia A. Stautberg (513) 946-5149
　David C. Stockdale (513) 946-5160
　Alex Triantafilou (513) 946-5175
　Robert C. Winkler (513) 946-5143
Clerk: Gregory Hartmann (513) 946-5127

County Offices

HAMILTON COUNTY BOARD OF COMMISSIONERS
138 E. Court St., Room 603, Cincinnati 45202
(513) 946-4400; Fax: (513) 946-4444
Commissioners:
　Pat DeWine (513) 946-4405
　Phil Heimlich (513) 946-4410
　Todd Portune (513) 946-4401
Clerk: Jacqueline Panioto (513) 946-4414

COUNTY COURTS AND OFFICES

Courts &
Officials

Hamilton County—Cont'd

HAMILTON COUNTY CLERK OF COURTS
Hamilton County Courthouse, Room 375, 1000 Main St.,
Cincinnati 45202 (513) 946-5666

Clerk of Courts: Gregory Hartmann

HAMILTON COUNTY CORONER
3159 Eden Ave., Cincinnati 45219 (513) 221-4524

Coroner: O'Dell Owens

HAMILTON COUNTY ENGINEER
County Administration Bldg., Room 700, 138 E. Court St.,
Cincinnati 45202 (513) 946-4250

Engineer: William W. Brayshaw

HAMILTON COUNTY PROSECUTOR
230 E. Ninth St., Cincinnati 45202
(513) 946-3000; Fax: (513) 946-3017

Prosecutor: Joseph T. Deters

HAMILTON COUNTY RECORDER
County Administration Bldg., Room 209, 138 E. Court St.,
Cincinnati 45202 (513) 946-4600

Recorder: Rebecca Prem Groppe

HAMILTON COUNTY AUDITOR
County Administration Bldg., Room 304, 138 E. Court St.,
Cincinnati 45202-1221 (513) 946-4000

Auditor: Dusty Rhodes

HAMILTON COUNTY SHERIFF
1000 Sycamore St., Room 110, Cincinnati 45202
(513) 946-6400

Sheriff: Simon L. Leis

HAMILTON COUNTY TREASURER
138 E. Court St., Room 402, Cincinnati 45202-1276
(513) 946-4800

Treasurer: Robert A. Goering

HANCOCK COUNTY

HANCOCK COUNTY COMMON PLEAS COURT
300 S. Main St., Findlay 45840-3345 (419) 424-7008

Judges:
Joseph H. Niemeyer
  (419) 424-7008; Fax: (419) 424-7437
Reginald J. Routson
  (419) 424-7009; Fax: (419) 424-7436

HANCOCK COUNTY PROBATE/JUVENILE COURT
308 Dorney Plz., Findlay 45840-3302
Juvenile: (419) 424-7066; Probate: (419) 424-7079;
Fax: (419) 424-7081

Judge: Allan H. Davis
  E-mail: ahdavis@co.hancock.oh.us

FINDLAY MUNICIPAL COURT
Municipal Bldg., Room 206, 318 Dorney Plaza, Findlay 45840
Administration: (419) 424-7144; Criminal: (419) 424-7141;
Civil: (419) 424-7143; Fax: (419) 424-7803

Judges:
Vernon L. Preston
  E-mail: vpreston@ci.findlay.oh.us
Vacancy at Press Time

Clerk: Patricia L. Walters (419) 424-7141

FOSTORIA MUNICIPAL COURT
213 S. Main St., P.O. Box 985, Fostoria 44830
(419) 435-8139; Fax: (419) 435-1150
Jurisdiction—Counties of Hancock, Seneca, Wood

Judge: John D. Hadacek; E-mail: fosmunct@bright.net
Clerk: Janice Russell

County Offices

HANCOCK COUNTY BOARD OF COMMISSIONERS
300 S. Main St., Findlay 45840-3345
(419) 424-7044; Fax: (419) 424-7828

Commissioners:
Edward D. Ingold   Emily A. Walton
David W. Spahr

Clerk: Cheryl Farlow

HANCOCK COUNTY CLERK OF COURTS
Court Records Division, Room 32, 300 S. Main St.,
Findlay 45840 (419) 424-7037
E-mail: clerkofcourts@co.hancock.oh.us
Internet: www.co.hancock.oh.us

Clerk of Courts: Cathy Wilcox

HANCOCK COUNTY CORONER
200 W. Pearl St., Findlay 45840 (419) 424-0380

Coroner: Leroy L. Schroeder

HANCOCK COUNTY ENGINEER
1900 Lima Ave., Findlay 45840
(419) 422-7433; Fax: (419) 424-5057

Engineer: Steven C. Wilson

HANCOCK COUNTY PROSECUTOR
202 Broadway, Room 104, Findlay 45840
(419) 424-7089; Fax: (419) 424-7889

Prosecutor: Robert A. Fry

HANCOCK COUNTY RECORDER
300 S. Main St., Findlay 45840 (419) 424-7091

Recorder: Anita M. Musgrave

HANCOCK COUNTY AUDITOR
300 S. Main St., Findlay 45840
(419) 424-7015; Fax: (417) 424-7825

Auditor: Charity A. Rauschenberg

HANCOCK COUNTY SHERIFF
200 W. Crawford St., Findlay 45840 (419) 424-7097

Sheriff: Michael Heldman

HANCOCK COUNTY TREASURER
300 S. Main St., Findlay 45840
(419) 424-7213; Fax: (419) 424-7003

Treasurer: Steve Welton

HARDIN COUNTY

HARDIN COUNTY COMMON PLEAS COURT
One Courthouse Sq., Suite 370, Kenton 43326-2301

Judge: William D. Hart
  (419) 674-2256; Fax: (419) 674-2264

HARDIN COUNTY PROBATE/JUVENILE COURT
One Courthouse Sq., Suite 210, Kenton 43326-2301
(419) 674-2230; Fax: (419) 674-2274
E-mail: probjuv@hardincourts.com

Judge: James S. Rapp

HARDIN COUNTY MUNICIPAL COURT
111 W. Franklin St., P.O. Box 250, Kenton 43326
(419) 674-4362; Fax: (419) 674-4096

Judge: Gregory A. Grimslid
Clerk: Elois A. Cramer

County Offices

HARDIN COUNTY BOARD OF COMMISSIONERS
One Courthouse Sq., Suite 100, Kenton 43326-1575
(419) 674-2205; Fax: (419) 674-2272

President: Gerald Potter
Commissioners:
Jerry E. Cross   Russell Ludwig
Clerk: Randy S. Paul

HARDIN COUNTY CLERK OF COURTS
One Courthouse Sq., Suite 310, Kenton 43326
(419) 674-2278; Fax: (419) 674-2273

Clerk of Courts: Lori Stevenson

Hardin County—Cont'd

HARDIN COUNTY CORONER
520 W. Lincoln Ave., Ada 45810 (419) 634-4085
Coroner: Lawrence Kuk, M.D.

HARDIN COUNTY ENGINEER
1040 W. Franklin, Kenton 43326-9401
(419) 674-2222; Fax: (419) 673-1232
Engineer: Michael L. Smith

HARDIN COUNTY PROSECUTOR
One Courthouse Sq., Suite 60, Kenton 43326
(419) 674-2284; Fax: (419) 674-4767
Prosecutor: Brad Bailey

HARDIN COUNTY RECORDER
One Courthouse Sq., Suite 220, Kenton 43326
(419) 674-2252
Recorder: Sharon A. Sams

HARDIN COUNTY AUDITOR
Suite 250, 2nd Floor, One Courthouse Sq., Kenton 43326
(419) 674-2239; Fax: (419) 674-4767
Auditor: Michael T. Bacon

HARDIN COUNTY SHERIFF
125 E. Carrol St., Kenton 43326 (419) 673-1268
Sheriff: Craig Leeth

HARDIN COUNTY TREASURER
One Courthouse Sq., Suite 230, Kenton 43326
(419) 674-2246; Fax: (419) 674-4023
Treasurer: Ruth Ann Cook

HARRISON COUNTY

HARRISON COUNTY COMMON PLEAS COURT
Courthouse, 100 W. Market St., Cadiz 43907-1132
(740) 942-8500; Juvenile: (740) 942-8862;
Probate: (740) 942-8868; Fax: (740) 942-3006
Judge: Michael K. Nunner

HARRISON COUNTY COURT
Courthouse, 100 W. Market St., Cadiz 43907-1132
(740) 942-8865; Fax: (740) 942-3541
Judge: Mark Beetham
Clerk: Michele R. Davis

County Offices

HARRISON COUNTY BOARD OF COMMISSIONERS
Courthouse, 100 W. Market St., Cadiz 43907
(740) 942-4623; Fax: (740) 942-4090
Commissioners:
William Host			Dennis Watson
Phillip Madzia
Clerk: Brandi Henry

HARRISON COUNTY CLERK OF COURTS
100 W. Market St., Cadiz 43907
(740) 942-8863; Fax: (740) 942-4963
Clerk of Courts: Barbara J. Yoho

HARRISON COUNTY CORONER
943 E. Market St., Cadiz 43907 (740) 942-2716
Coroner: Isam Tabbah (740) 942-2716

HARRISON COUNTY ENGINEER
100 W. Market St., Cadiz 43907
(740) 942-8867; Fax: (740) 942-3034
Engineer: Robert K. Sterling

HARRISON COUNTY PROSECUTOR
111 W. Warren St., P.O. Box 235, Cadiz 43907
(740) 942-2621
Prosecutor: Shawn Hervey

HARRISON COUNTY RECORDER
100 W. Market St., Cadiz 43907 (740) 942-8869
Recorder: Tracy L. Boyer

HARRISON COUNTY AUDITOR
100 W. Market St., Cadiz 43907
(740) 942-8861; Fax: (740) 942-3034
Auditor: Patrick J. Moore

HARRISON COUNTY SHERIFF
114 Court St., Cadiz 43907 (740) 942-2197
Sheriff: Mark J. Miller

HARRISON COUNTY TREASURER
100 W. Market St., Cadiz 43907 (740) 942-8864
Treasurer: George E. Campbell

HENRY COUNTY

HENRY COUNTY COMMON PLEAS COURT
660 N. Perry St., P.O. Box 70, Napoleon 43545-1747
(419) 592-5926; Fax: (419) 599-0803
E-mail: common.pleas@henrycountyohio.com
Judge: Keith P. Muehlfeld

NAPOLEON MUNICIPAL COURT
255 W. Riverview Ave., P.O. Box 502, Napoleon 43545-0502
(419) 592-2851; Fax: (419) 592-1805
Judge: John S. Collier; E-mail: lcollier@wcnet.org
Clerk: Betty Marihugh

County Offices

HENRY COUNTY BOARD OF COMMISSIONERS
1853 Oakwood Ave., Napoleon 43545
(419) 592-4876; Fax: (419) 592-4016
E-mail: commissioners@henrycountyohio.com
President: Rita M. Franz
Commissioners:
Steve A. Baden			Richard J. Bennett
Clerk: Vicki Glick

HENRY COUNTY CLERK OF COURT
660 N. Perry St., P.O. Box 71, Napoleon 43545
(419) 592-5886
Clerk of Courts: Judy Sonnenberg

HENRY COUNTY CORONER
11-600 S.R. 424, Napoleon 43545
(419) 592-8783; Fax: (419) 592-6042
Coroner: Marek Skoskiewicz

HENRY COUNTY ENGINEER
660 N. Perry St., Napoleon 43545
(419) 592-2976; Fax: (419) 592-5508
Engineer: Randolf L. Germann

HENRY COUNTY PROSECUTOR
P.O. Box 605, Napoleon 43545
(419) 599-1010; Fax: (419) 599-0770
Prosecutor: John H. Hanna

HENRY COUNTY RECORDER
660 N. Perry St., Napoleon 43545
(419) 592-1766; Fax: (419) 592-1652
Recorder: Sara Myles

HENRY COUNTY AUDITOR
660 N. Perry St., Napoleon 43545
(419) 592-1956; Fax: (419) 592-4024
Auditor: Ida L. Bostelman

HENRY COUNTY SHERIFF
123 E. Washington St., Napoleon 43545
(419) 592-8010; Fax: (419) 592-6915
Sheriff: John J. Nye

HENRY COUNTY TREASURER
P.O. Box 546, Napoleon 43545
(419) 592-1851; Fax: (419) 592-2004
Treasurer: Calvin G. Spiess

HIGHLAND COUNTY

HIGHLAND COUNTY COMMON PLEAS COURT
105 N. High St., Hillsboro 45133-1182
(937) 393-2422; Fax: (937) 393-6878
Judges:
 Jeffrey J. Hoskins (General Division) (937) 393-2161
 Kevin L. Greer (Probate & Juvenile) (937) 393-9981
 Cynthis Williams (Domestic Division), 2nd Floor
  (937) 393-3676

HIGHLAND COUNTY PROBATE/JUVENILE COURT
Courthouse, 105 N. High St., Hillsboro 45133-1182
(937) 393-9981; Fax: (937) 393-0926
Judge: Kevin L. Greer

HIGHLAND COUNTY COURT
300 Jefferson St., P.O. Box 378, Greenfield 45123
(937) 981-2139; Fax: (937) 981-2130
Judge: Robert J. Judkins
Clerk: Ronald W. Coffey

HILLSBORO MUNICIPAL COURT
130 Homestead Ave., Hillsboro 45133
(937) 393-3022; Fax: (937) 393-0517
Judge: David H. McKenna
Clerk: Dianna D. Workman

County Offices

HIGHLAND COUNTY BOARD OF COMMISSIONERS
114 Governor Foraker Pl., Hillsboro 45133
(937) 393-1911; Fax: (937) 393-5850
President: Michael E. Rector
Commissioners:
 Richard Graves Russell L. Newman
Clerk: Rosalind Newman

HIGHLAND COUNTY CLERK OF COURTS
105 N. High St., P.O. Box 821, Hillsboro 45133
(937) 393-9957; Fax: (937) 393-9878

Title Dept., 1575 N. High St., P.O. Box 821, Hillsboro 45133
Clerk of Courts: Paulette Donley
Hours: Legal Dept.: Weekdays, 8 A.M.-5 P.M.; Title Dept.:
Weekdays, 8 A.M.-4:30 P.M.; Sat., 8 A.M.-Noon

HIGHLAND COUNTY CORONER
6000 S.R. 247, P.O. Box 340, Hillsboro 45133
(937) 393-6512; Fax: (937) 393-6669
Coroner: Paul W. Terrell

HIGHLAND COUNTY ENGINEER
P.O. Box 297, Hillsboro 45133
(937) 393-3496; Fax: (937) 393-3498
Engineer: Dean Otworth

HIGHLAND COUNTY PROSECUTOR
112 Governor Foraker Pl., Hillsboro 45133
(937) 393-1851; Fax: (937) 393-6501
Prosecutor: James Grandey

HIGHLAND COUNTY RECORDER
114 Governor Fraker Pl., Hillsboro 45133
(937) 393-9954; Fax: (937) 393-5855
Recorder: Dwight O. Hodson

HIGHLAND COUNTY AUDITOR
P.O. Box 822, Hillsboro 45133
(937) 393-1915; Fax: (937) 393-3854
Auditor: Bill Fawley

HIGHLAND COUNTY SHERIFF
130 Homestead Dr., Hillsboro 45133
(937) 393-1421; Fax: (937) 840-6241
Sheriff: Ron Ward

HIGHLAND COUNTY TREASURER
114 Governor Fraker Pl., P.O. Box 824, Hillsboro 45133
(937) 393-9951
Treasurer: Ann Williams

HOCKING COUNTY

HOCKING COUNTY COMMON PLEAS COURT
1 E. Main St., 3rd Floor, Logan 43138-1207
(740) 385-4027; Fax: (740) 385-2614
E-mail: cpcourt@ohiohills.com
Judge: Thomas H. Gerken

HOCKING COUNTY PROBATE/JUVENILE COURT
1 E. Main St., Logan 43138-1288
(740) 385-3615; Fax: (740) 385-6892
Judge: Frederick E. Mong; E-mail: fmong@co.hocking.oh.us

HOCKING MUNICIPAL COURT
One E. Main St., P.O. Box 950, Logan 43138
(740) 385-2250; Fax: (740) 385-3826
Judge: Richard M. Wallar
 E-mail: rwallar@co.hocking.oh.us
Clerk: Michele L. Bell

County Offices

HOCKING COUNTY BOARD OF COMMISSIONERS
Courthouse, One E. Main St., Logan 43138-1276
(740) 385-5195; Fax: (740) 385-1105
President: Gary K. Starner
Commissioners:
 Greg Green John Walker
Clerk: Alison Redmond

HOCKING COUNTY CLERK OF COURTS
Courthouse, 1 E. Main St., P.O. Box 108, Logan 43138
(740) 385-2616; Fax: (740) 385-1822
Clerk of Courts: Narcie Stahr

HOCKING COUNTY CORONER
13468 S.R. 664, Logan 43138 (740) 385-5320
Coroner: David Cummin

HOCKING COUNTY ENGINEER
1286 California Ave., Logan 43138-8999 (740) 385-8543
Engineer: William R. Shaw

HOCKING COUNTY PROSECUTOR
88 S. Market St., Logan 43138-1221 (740) 385-5343
Prosecutor: Larry E. Beal

HOCKING COUNTY RECORDER
Courthouse, One E. Main St., Logan 43138 (740) 385-2031
Recorder: Sandra Leach-Hunt

HOCKING COUNTY AUDITOR
Courthouse, One E. Main St., Logan 43138
(740) 382-2127; Fax: (740) 385-9888
Auditor: Kenneth R. Wilson

HOCKING COUNTY SHERIFF
54 S. Market St., Logan 43138 (740) 385-2131
Sheriff: Larry North

HOCKING COUNTY TREASURER
P.O. Box 28, Logan 43138 (740) 385-3517
Treasurer: Kay Cook

HOLMES COUNTY

HOLMES COUNTY COMMON PLEAS COURT
Courthouse, Room 307, One E. Jackson St.,
Millersburg 44654-1249
(330) 674-5086; Fax: (330) 674-0289
E-mail: hccp@valkyrie.net
Judge: Thomas D. White

HOLMES COUNTY PROBATE/JUVENILE COURT
One E. Jackson St., Suite 201, Millersburg 44654
(330) 674-5881; Fax: (330) 674-5820
Judge: Thomas C. Lee
Court Administrator: Glennis R. Menuez
Hours: Weekdays, 8:30 A.M.-4:30 P.M.

Holmes County—Cont'd

HOLMES COUNTY DOMESTIC RELATIONS COURT
Courthouse, One E. Jackson St., Millersburg 44654
(330) 674-5086; Fax: (330) 674-0289

Magistrate: Jeffrey Ginsburg

Bailiff: Michael McElroy

HOLMES COUNTY COURT
One E. Jackson St., Suite 101, Millersburg 44654
(330) 674-4901; Fax: (330) 674-5514

Judge: Jane Irving

Clerk: Marcia J. Schie

County Offices

HOLMES COUNTY BOARD OF COMMISSIONERS
Two Court St., Suite 14, Millersburg 44654-2001
(330) 674-0286; Fax: (330) 674-0566
E-mail: hcc@valkyrie.net

Commissioners:
David L. Hall   Joe D. Miller
Ray L. Feikert

Clerk: Susan L. Haun

HOLMES COUNTY CLERK OF COURT
Courthouse, Suite 306, One E. Jackson St.,
Millersburg 44654
(330) 674-1876; Fax: (330) 674-0289

Clerk of Court: Dorcas L. Miller

HOLMES COUNTY CORONER
981 Wooster Rd., Millersburg 44654
(330) 674-1015, Ext. 785

Coroner: Robert J. Anthony

HOLMES COUNTY ENGINEER
10 S. Clay St., Suite 101, Millersburg 44654
(330) 674-5076

Engineer: Christopher R. Young, P.E.,P.S.

HOLMES COUNTY PROSECUTOR
91 S. Monroe St., Millersburg 44654 (330) 674-4841

Prosecutor: Steve Knowling

HOLMES COUNTY RECORDER
P.O. Box 213, Millersburg 44654 (330) 674-5916

Recorder: Sally E. Miller

HOLMES COUNTY AUDITOR
75 E. Clinton St., Millersburg 44654
(330) 674-1896; Fax: (330) 674-9428

Auditor: Jackie McKee

HOLMES COUNTY SHERIFF
8105 Township Rd. 574, Holmesville 44633 (330) 674-1936

Sheriff: Timothy W. Zimmerly

HOLMES COUNTY TREASURER
75 E. Clinton St., Suite 105, Millersburg 44654
(330) 674-5871; Fax: (330) 674-5860

Treasurer: Joyce L. Yoder

HURON COUNTY

HURON COUNTY COMMON PLEAS COURT
Two E. Main St., Norwalk 44857
(419) 668-6162; Fax: (419) 663-4048

Judge: Earl R. McGimpsey
E-mail: judge@huroncountyclerk.com

HURON COUNTY PROBATE/JUVENILE COURT
Two E. Main St., Norwalk 44857
(419) 668-1616, 668-4383; Fax: (419) 663-0944

Judge: Timothy L. Cardwell

BELLEVUE MUNICIPAL COURT
3000 Seneca Industrial Pkwy., Bellevue 44811
(419) 483-5880; Fax: (419) 484-8060
Jurisdiction—Counties of Huron, Sandusky; City of
Bellevue; Towns of Lyme, Sherman and York

Judge: Kenneth P. Fox

Clerk: Susan K. Meador

Court Schedule: Arraignments: Tues. mornings
Pre-trials: Mon. and Tues. morning
Civil and Small Claims: Thurs.

NORWALK MUNICIPAL COURT
45 N. Linwood Ave., Norwalk 44857
(419) 663-6750; Fax: (419) 663-6749
Jurisdiction—County of Huron; All of Huron Counties,
except Lyme & Sherman Townships

Judge: John S. Ridge (419) 663-6771
E-mail: jjsr@accnorwalk.com

Clerk: Pamela G. Boss

County Offices

HURON COUNTY BOARD OF COMMISSIONERS
180 Milan Ave., Norwalk 44857-1168
(419) 668-3092; Fax: (419) 663-3370

Commissioners:
Mike Adelman   Ralph A. Fegley
Gary W. Bauer

Clerk: Cheryl Nolan

HURON COUNTY CLERK OF COURTS
Courthouse, Two E. Main St., Norwalk 44857
(419) 668-5113; Fax: (419) 663-4048
Internet: www.huroncountyclerk.com

Clerk of Courts: Susan S. Hazel

HURON COUNTY CORONER
187 W. Main St., New London 44851 (419) 929-4357

Coroner: Jeffrey A. Harwood

HURON COUNTY ENGINEER
150 Jefferson St., Norwalk 44857
(419) 668-1997; Fax: (419) 668-8308

Engineer: Joseph Kovach

HURON COUNTY PROSECUTOR
12 E. Main St., Norwalk 44857
(419) 668-8215; Fax: (419) 663-3844

Prosecutor: Russell V. Leffler

HURON COUNTY RECORDER
12 E. Main St., Norwalk 44857
(419) 668-1916; Fax: (419) 663-4052

Recorder: Karen Fries

HURON COUNTY AUDITOR
12 E. Main St., Norwalk 44857
(419) 668-4304; Fax: (419) 663-6948

Auditor: John A. Elmlinger

HURON COUNTY SHERIFF
255 Shady Lane Dr., Norwalk 44857-2700
(419) 668-6912; Emergency: (419) 663-2828;
Fax: (419) 663-1380

Sheriff: Richard Sutherland

HURON COUNTY TREASURER
Courthouse, 16 E. Main St., Norwalk 44857
(419) 668-2090; Fax: (419) 668-4245

Treasurer: Roland Tkach

JACKSON COUNTY

JACKSON COUNTY COMMON PLEAS COURT
Courthouse, Suite 6, 226 E. Main St., Jackson 45640
(740) 286-3601; Fax: (740) 286-5203
Judge: Leonard F. Holzapfel

JACKSON COUNTY PROBATE/JUVENILE COURT
Courthouse, 226 E. Main St., Jackson 45640
(740) 286-6405; Fax: (740) 288-4836
Judge: Stephen D. Michael

JACKSON COUNTY MUNICIPAL COURT
350 Portsmouth St., Suite 101, Jackson 45640
(740) 286-2718; Fax: (740) 286-0679
Judge: Lorene Johnston
Clerk: Kimberly A. Riegel

County Offices

JACKSON COUNTY BOARD OF COMMISSIONERS
Annex Bldg., 275 Portsmouth St., Jackson 45640-1750
(740) 286-3301; Fax: (740) 286-4061
President: Rick McNelly
Commissioners:
Edward Armstrong   James P. Riepenhoff
Clerk: Martha Cosby
Admin. Asst.: Gloria J. Addington

JACKSON COUNTY CLERK OF COURTS
Courthouse, Suite 8, 226 E. Main St., Jackson 45640-1755
(740) 286-2006; Fax: (740) 286-5186
Clerk of Courts: Robert F. Walton

JACKSON COUNTY CORONER
200 E. Main St., Jackson 45640-1716 (740) 286-5094
Coroner: Gregory Hawker

JACKSON COUNTY ENGINEER
3062 Clary Rd., Jackson 45640
(740) 286-4139; Fax: (740) 286-4130
Engineer: Brian D. McPherson

JACKSON COUNTY PROSECUTOR
350 Portsmouth St., Suite 100, Jackson 45640-1755
(740) 286-5006; Fax: (740) 286-6556
Prosecutor: Jonathan Blanton

JACKSON COUNTY RECORDER
Courthouse, 3rd Floor, 226 E. Main St., Jackson 45640-1755
(740) 286-1919
Recorder: Linda L. Hoover

JACKSON COUNTY AUDITOR
226 E. Main St., Suite 5, Jackson 45640-1797
(740) 286-4231; Fax: (740) 286-6312
Auditor: Clyde Holdren

JACKSON COUNTY SHERIFF
350 Portsmouth St., Jackson 45640-1755
(740) 286-6464; Fax: (740) 286-5635
Sheriff: John Shasteen

JACKSON COUNTY TREASURER
Courthouse, Suite 4, 226 E. Main St., P.O. Box 980,
Jackson 45640-0980 (740) 286-2402; Fax: (740) 286-0922
Treasurer: Lee Hubbard

JEFFERSON COUNTY

JEFFERSON COUNTY COMMON PLEAS COURT
Courthouse, 301 Market St., Steubenville 43952-2149
(740) 283-8583; Fax: (740) 283-8686
Judges:
Joseph J. Bruzzese, Jr. (740) 283-8543
David E. Henderson (740) 283-8545

JEFFERSON COUNTY PROBATE/JUVENILE COURT
P.O. Box 549, Steubenville 43952-2184
(740) 283-8692; Juvenile Fax: (740) 283-8694;
Probate Fax: (740) 283-8653
Judge: Samuel W. Kerr

JEFFERSON COUNTY COURT NO. 1
1007 Franklin Ave., Toronto 43964
(740) 537-2020; Fax: (740) 537-1866
Judge: Joseph M. Corabi
Clerk: Elaine Zdinak

JEFFERSON COUNTY COURT NO. 2
P.O. Box 2207, Wintersville 43953
(740) 264-7644; Fax: (740) 264-3909
Judge: Michael C. Bednar
E-mail: mbednar@blakehersheybednar.com
Clerk: Emily Cola

JEFFERSON COUNTY COURT NO. 3
6 Liberty St., P.O. Box 495, Dillonvale 43917
(740) 769-2903; Fax: (740) 769-7640
Judge: David J. Scarpone
Court Schedule: Wed., 3 P.M.
Clerk: Barbara Donahue

STEUBENVILLE MUNICIPAL COURT
123 S. Third St., Steubenville 43952
(740) 283-6000; Fax: (740) 283-6167
Judge: G. Daniel Spahn, Ext. 2252
Clerk: Mary C. Murray, Ext. 2253

County Offices

JEFFERSON COUNTY BOARD OF COMMISSIONERS
Courthouse, 301 Market St., Steubenville 43952-2278
(740) 283-8500; Fax: (740) 283-8599
Commissioners:
Dr. Thomas E. Graham   Adam E. Scurti
Dave Maple
Clerk: Linda L. Porter
Commissioner: Richard Delatore

JEFFERSON COUNTY CLERK OF COURTS
P.O. Box 1326, Steubenville 43952 (740) 283-8583
Clerk of Courts: John Corrigan

JEFFERSON COUNTY CORONER
16001 St. Rt. 7, Steubenville 43952
(740) 283-2070; Fax: (740) 283-2002
Coroner: John W. Metcalf, Jr., M.D.

JEFFERSON COUNTY ENGINEER
598 State Rte. 43, Steubenville 43952 (740) 283-8574
Engineer: James F. Branagan

JEFFERSON COUNTY PROSECUTOR
Jefferson County Justice Ctr., 16001 State Rte. 7,
Steubenville 43952 (740) 283-1966; Fax: (740) 283-3409
Prosecutor: Thomas Straus

JEFFERSON COUNTY RECORDER
Courthouse, 301 Market St., Steubenville 43952
(740) 283-8566
Recorder: Paul R. McKeegan

JEFFERSON COUNTY AUDITOR
P.O. Box 159, Steubenville 43952
(740) 283-8511; Fax: (740) 283-8520
Auditor: Patrick J. Marshall

JEFFERSON COUNTY SHERIFF
Jefferson County Justice Ctr., 16001 State Rd. 7,
Steubenville 43952 (740) 283-8600
Sheriff: Fred J. Abdalla

JEFFERSON COUNTY TREASURER
Courthouse, P.O. Box 398, Steubenville 43952
(740) 283-8572; Fax: (740) 284-3343
Treasurer: Raymond A. Agresta

KNOX COUNTY

KNOX COUNTY COMMON PLEAS COURT
Courthouse, 111 E. High St., Mount Vernon 43050
(740) 393-6777; Fax: (740) 393-5096

Judge: Otho Eyster

KNOX COUNTY PROBATE/JUVENILE COURT
Courthouse, 111 E. High St., Mount Vernon 43050
(740) 393-6798; Fax: (740) 393-6832

Judge: James M. Ronk

MOUNT VERNON MUNICIPAL COURT
5 N. Gay St., Mount Vernon 43050
(740) 393-9510; Fax: (740) 393-5349
Internet: www.mountvernonmunicipalcourt.org

Judge: Paul E. Spurgeon

Clerk: Judy Smith

Court Schedule: Traffic-Criminal Arraignments: Tues-Fri., 9:30 A.M.

County Offices

KNOX COUNTY BOARD OF COMMISSIONERS
117 E. High St., Suite 161, Mount Vernon 43050-3493
(740) 393-6703; Fax: (740) 393-6705

President: Robert S. Wise

Commissioners:
Thomas C. McLarnan   Allen Stockberger

Clerk/Administrator: Rochelle Shackle

KNOX COUNTY CLERK OF COURTS
117 E. High St., Suite 201, Mount Vernon 43050
(740) 393-6788
E-mail: mjh@knoxcountyclerk.org

Clerk of Courts: Mary Jo Hawkins

Hours: Weekdays, 8 A.M.-4 P.M.

KNOX COUNTY CORONER
117 E. High St., Mount Vernon 43050 (740) 397-9339

Coroner: Jeffrey J. Bowers

KNOX COUNTY ENGINEER
422 Old Columbus Rd., Mount Vernon 43050
(740) 397-1590

Engineer: Jim Henry

KNOX COUNTY PROSECUTOR
117 E. High St., Suite 234, Mount Vernon 43050
(740) 393-6720

Prosecutor: John Thatcher

KNOX COUNTY AUDITOR
117 E. High St., Suite 120, Mount Vernon 43050
(740) 393-6750; Fax: (740) 393-6806

Auditor: Margaret Ann Ruhl

KNOX COUNTY RECORDER
117 E. High St., Suite 114, Mount Vernon 43050
(740) 393-6755

Recorder: John B. Lybarger

KNOX COUNTY SHERIFF
11540 Upper Gilchrist Rd., Mount Vernon 43050
(740) 397-3333

Sheriff: David B. Barber

KNOX COUNTY TREASURER
117 E. High St., Suite 103, Mount Vernon 43050
(740) 393-6740

Treasurer: Sandra L. Mizer

LAKE COUNTY

LAKE COUNTY COMMON PLEAS COURT
47 N. Park Pl., P.O. Box 490, Painesville 44077
(440) 350-2657

Judges:
Richard L. Collins (440) 350-2720
Vincent A. Culotta
Eugene A. Lucci (440) 350-2100
Paul H. Mitrovich (440) 350-2662
Court does not accept faxes

LAKE COUNTY PROBATE COURT
Courthouse, 25 N. Park Pl., Painesville 44077-3416
(440) 350-2626; Fax: (440) 350-2628

Judge: Ted R. Klammer

LAKE COUNTY JUVENILE COURT
Juvenile Justice Ctr., 53 E. Erie St.,
Painesville 44077-3907
(440) 350-3126; Fax: (440) 350-2724

Judge: William W. Weaver

Court Administrators:
Susan Y. Kish (440) 350-3137
Dennis J. Vidic (440) 350-3134

Hours: Weekdays, 7:45 A.M.-4:30 P.M.

LAKE COUNTY DOMESTIC RELATIONS COURT
47 N. Park Pl., P.O. Box 490, Painesville 44077
(440) 350-2709

Judge: Colleen A. Falkowski
(440) 350-2708; Fax: (440) 350-2717

MENTOR MUNICIPAL COURT
8500 Civic Center Blvd., Mentor 44060-2418
(440) 974-5744; Fax: (440) 974-5742
Jurisdiction—County of Lake; Cities of Mentor,
Mentor-on-the-Lake

Judge: John Trebets

Clerk: Nancy McClatchy

Court Schedule: Mon., Tues., Thurs. and Fri.,
8 A.M.-4 P.M.; Wed., 8 A.M.-6 P.M.

PAINESVILLE MUNICIPAL COURT
7 Richmond St., P.O. Box 601, Painesville 44077
(440) 392-5874; Fax: (440) 352-0028
Internet: www.pmcourt.com

Judge: Michael A. Cicconetti
(440) 392-5875; Fax: (440) 639-4927

Clerk: Debra G. Poe; E-mail: dpoe@pmcourt.com

WILLOUGHBY MUNICIPAL COURT
One Public Sq., Willoughby 44094-7888
(440) 953-4150; Fax: (440) 953-4149
Internet: www.willoughbycourt.com

Judge: Larry Allen; E-mail: judge@willoughbycourt.com

Clerk: Lisa B. Mastrangelo

Court Schedule: Mon., 7:30 A.M.-7:30 P.M.; Tues.-Fri.,
7:30 A.M.-4:30 P.M.

County Offices

LAKE COUNTY BOARD OF COMMISSIONERS
105 Main St., P.O. Box 490, Painesville 44077
(440) 350-2745; Fax: (440) 350-2672

President: Robert E. Aufuldish (440) 350-2754

Commissioners:
Raymond E. Sines (440) 350-2755
Daniel P. Troy (440) 350-2752

Clerk: Amy Elszasz (440) 350-2753

LAKE COUNTY CLERK OF COURTS
25 N. Park Pl., P.O. Box 490, Painesville 44077
(440) 350-2658

Clerk of Courts: Lynne L. Mazeika

LAKE COUNTY CORONER
104 E. Erie St., Painesville 44077 (440) 350-2789

Coroner: Salvatore Rizzo

Lake County—Cont'd

LAKE COUNTY ENGINEER
550 Blackbrook Rd., Painesville 44077
(440) 350-2770; Fax: (440) 352-8133
Engineer: James R. Gills

LAKE COUNTY PROSECUTOR
105 Main St., Painesville 44077
(440) 350-2683; Fax: (440) 350-2585
Prosecutor: Charles E. Coulson

LAKE COUNTY RECORDER
105 Main St., P.O. Box 490, Painesville 44077
(440) 350-2510; Fax: (440) 350-5940
Recorder: Frank A. Suponcic

LAKE COUNTY AUDITOR
105 Main St., P.O. Box 490, Painesville 44077-0490
(440) 350-2530; Fax: (440) 350-2667
Auditor: Edward H. Zupancic

LAKE COUNTY SHERIFF
104 E. Erie St., Painesville 44077
(440) 350-5569; Fax: (440) 350-5590
Sheriff: Daniel A. Dunlap

LAKE COUNTY TREASURER
105 E. Main St., Painesville 44077
(440) 350-2480; Fax: (440) 350-2623
Treasurer: John S. Crocker

LAWRENCE COUNTY

LAWRENCE COUNTY COMMON PLEAS COURT
Courthouse, One Veteran's Sq., Ironton 45638
(740) 533-4329; Fax: (740) 533-4377
Judges:
Frank J. McCown; E-mail: judgemac@hotmail.com
W. Richard Walton; E-mail: walton@zoomnet.net

LAWRENCE COUNTY PROBATE/JUVENILE COURT
Courthouse, One Veteran's Sq., Ironton 45638-1585
(740) 533-4372; Fax: (740) 533-4412
Judge: C. David Payne

IRONTON MUNICIPAL COURT
301 S. Third St., P.O. Box 237, Ironton 45638-0237
(740) 532-3062; Fax: (740) 533-6088
Judge: O. Clark Collins, Jr.
Clerk: Cheryl Ackinson

LAWRENCE MUNICIPAL COURT
10916 County Rd. 1, P.O. Box 126, Chesapeake 45619
(740) 867-3127; Fax: (740) 867-3547
Judge: Donald R. Capper
E-mail: dcapper@zoomnet.net
Clerk: Cynthia A. Lewis

County Offices

LAWRENCE COUNTY BOARD OF COMMISSIONERS
One Veteran's St., Ironton 45638
(740) 533-4300; Fax: (740) 533-4370
President: George R. Patterson
Commissioners:
Douglas Malone   Jason C. Stephens
Administrator: Kathleen R. Fraley

LAWRENCE COUNTY CLERK OF COURTS
P.O. Box 208, Ironton 45638 (740) 533-4355
Clerk of Courts: Les Boggs

LAWRENCE COUNTY CORONER
517 Park Ave., Ironton 45638 (740) 532-9454
Coroner: A. Burton Payne

LAWRENCE COUNTY ENGINEER
One Veteran's Sq., Ironton 45638 (740) 533-4317
Engineer: David R. Lynd

LAWRENCE COUNTY PROSECUTOR
One Veteran's Sq., Ironton 45638
(740) 533-4360; Fax: (740) 533-4387
Prosecutor: J.B. Collier

LAWRENCE COUNTY RECORDER
One Veteran's Sq., Ironton 45638 (740) 533-4312
Recorder: Sharon Gossett Nager

LAWRENCE COUNTY AUDITOR
One Veteran's Sq., Ironton 45638
(740) 533-4310; Fax: (740) 533-4370
Auditor: Ray T. Dutey

LAWRENCE COUNTY SHERIFF
115 S. Fifth St., Ironton 45638 (740) 533-3106
Sheriff: Tim Sexton

LAWRENCE COUNTY TREASURER
One Veteran's Sq., Ironton 45638
(740) 533-4304; Fax: (740) 533-3820
Treasurer: Stephen Burcham

LICKING COUNTY

LICKING COUNTY COMMON PLEAS COURT
Courthouse, Public Sq., Newark 43055
Judges:
Thomas M. Marcelain (740) 670-5781
E-mail: tmarcelain@msmisp.com
Jon R. Spahr (740) 670-5770
E-mail: jspahr@lcounty.com

LICKING COUNTY PROBATE/JUVENILE COURT
Courthouse, Public Sq., Newark 43055-5553
(740) 670-5624; Fax: (740) 670-5881
Judge: Robert H. Hoover

LICKING COUNTY DOMESTIC RELATIONS COURT
75 E. Main St., Newark 43055
(740) 349-6215; Fax: (740) 349-1485
Judge: Russell A. Steiner; E-mail: steiner@alltel.net
Clerk: Gary Walters (740) 349-1676

LICKING COUNTY MUNICIPAL COURT
40 W. Main St., Newark 43055
(740) 349-6627; Fax: (740) 345-4250
Judges:
W. David Branstool (740) 349-6640
Michael F. Higgins (740) 349-6652
E-mail: higginsmf@hotmail.com
Clerk: Larry R. Brown; E-mail: clerk@msmisp.com
Chief Deputy Clerk: Brad Feightner (740) 349-6636

County Offices

LICKING COUNTY BOARD OF COMMISSIONERS
County Administration Bldg., 4th Floor, 20 S. Second St.,
Newark 43055 (740) 349-6066; Fax: (740) 349-6114
Commissioners:
Tim Bubb   Marcia J. Phelps
Jay Baird
Clerk: Michael L. Smith

LICKING COUNTY CLERK OF COURTS
P.O. Box 4370, Newark 43058-4370 (740) 670-5797
Clerk of Courts: Gary Walters

LICKING COUNTY CORONER
2102 Cherry Valley Rd., Newark 43055 (740) 349-3633
Coroner: Robert P. Raker

LICKING COUNTY ENGINEER
County Administration Bldg., 20 S. Second St.,
Newark 43055 (740) 349-6055
Engineer: Timothy P. Lollo

LICKING COUNTY PROSECUTOR
County Administration Bldg., 4th Floor, 20 S. Second St.,
Newark 43055 (740) 349-6195
Prosecutor: Robert L. Becker

Licking County—Cont'd

LICKING COUNTY RECORDER
County Administration Bldg., P.O. Box 676,
Newark 43055-0676 (740) 349-6061
Prosecutor: Bryan Long

LICKING COUNTY AUDITOR
County Administration Bldg., 20 S. Second St.,
Newark 43055 (740) 349-6026
Auditor: J. Terry Evans

LICKING COUNTY SHERIFF
155 E. Main St., Newark 43055 (740) 349-6400
Sheriff: Gerry D. Billy

LICKING COUNTY TREASURER
County Administration Bldg., 20 S. Second St.,
Newark 43055 (740) 349-6046
Treasurer: William R. Kashner

LOGAN COUNTY

LOGAN COUNTY COMMON PLEAS COURT
101 S. Main St., Room 18, Bellefontaine 43311-3101
(937) 599-7260; Fax: (937) 593-3379
Judge: Mark S. O'Connor
E-mail: mo'connor@co.logan.oh.us

LOGAN COUNTY PROBATE/JUVENILE COURT
101 S. Main St., Room 6, Bellefontaine 43311
(937) 599-7249; Fax: (937) 599-7297
Judges:
Michael L. Brady
E-mail: mbrady@co.logan.oh.us
C. Douglas Chamberlain
E-mail: dchamberlain@co.logan.oh.us

BELLEFONTAINE MUNICIPAL COURT
226 W. Columbus Ave., Bellefontaine 43311
(937) 599-6127; Fax: (937) 599-2488
Judge: John L. Ross
Clerk: Marty Carmean

County Offices

LOGAN COUNTY BOARD OF COMMISSIONERS
117 E. Columbus Ave., Bellefontaine 43311-2074
(937) 599-7283; Fax: (937) 599-7268
President: David Knight
Commissioners:
John Bayliss   Jack Reser
Clerk: Kacy D. Sells

LOGAN COUNTY CLERK OF COURTS
101 S. Main St., Room 12, Bellefontaine 43311
(937) 599-7275
Clerk of Courts: Dottie Tuttle
E-mail: dtuttle@co.logan.oh.us

LOGAN COUNTY CORONER
990 Road 230, Bellefontaine 43311
Hospital: (937) 592-4015
Coroner: Michael E. Failor

LOGAN COUNTY ENGINEER
P.O. Box 427, Bellefontaine 43311
(937) 592-2791; Fax: (937) 599-2658
Engineer: Scott Coleman

LOGAN COUNTY PROSECUTOR
117 E. Columbus Ave., Suite 200, Bellefontaine 43311-2094
(937) 593-3755; Fax: (937) 599-7271
Prosecutor: Gerald L. Heaton

LOGAN COUNTY RECORDER
100 S. Madriver St., Suite A, Bellefontaine 43311
(937) 599-7202
Recorder: Linda L. Hanson

LOGAN COUNTY AUDITOR
100 S. Madriver St., Bellefontaine 43311
(937) 599-7209; Fax: (937) 599-7216
Auditor: Michael E. Yoder

LOGAN COUNTY SHERIFF
284 C.R. 32, S., P.O. Box 218, Bellefontaine 43311
(937) 599-3333; Fax: (937) 592-5731
Sheriff: Michael E. Henry

LOGAN COUNTY TREASURER
100 S. Madriver St., Room 104, Bellefontaine 43311
(937) 599-7227; Fax: (937) 599-7216
Treasurer: Dara Wren

LORAIN COUNTY

LORAIN COUNTY COMMON PLEAS COURT
Lorain County Justice Center, 225 Court St., Elyria 44035
(440) 329-5536; Fax: (440) 329-5404
Judges:
Mark A. Betleski
(440) 329-5722; Fax: (440) 329-5729
Thomas W. Janas
(440) 329-5518; Fax: (440) 284-3794
Lynett M. McGough
(440) 329-5416; Fax: (440) 284-3681
Christopher R. Rothgery
(440) 329-5570; Fax: (440) 284-3680
Edward M. Zaleski
(440) 329-5560; Fax: (440) 329-5562

LORAIN COUNTY PROBATE COURT
Lorain County Justice Center, 6th Floor, 225 Court St.,
Elyria 44035 (440) 329-5175; Fax: (440) 328-2157
Judge: Frank J. Horvath

LORAIN COUNTY DOMESTIC RELATIONS COURT
Justice Center, 4th Floor, 225 Court St., Elyria 44035-5629
(440) 329-5368; Fax: (440) 329-5438
Judges:
David A. Basinski
Lorain County Justice Center, 225 Court St.,
Elyria 44035 (440) 329-5365; Fax: (440) 328-2258
Debra L. Boros
348 Second St., Elyria 44035-5629
(440) 328-2201; Fax: (440) 328-2211
E-mail: jdboros@hotmail.com
Paulette J. Lilly
(440) 329-5357; Fax: (440) 329-5438
E-mail: judgelilly@centurytel.net
Court Administrator: Doug Messer (440) 329-5360

AVON LAKE MUNICIPAL COURT
32855 Walker Rd., Avon Lake 44012
(440) 930-4103; Fax: (440) 930-4128
Judge: John F. Mackin
Clerk: Melissa A. Dunham

ELYRIA MUNICIPAL COURT
328 Broad St., Elyria 44035-5577
(440) 323-1328; Fax: (440) 323-8095
Judges:
Lisa A. Locke-Graves (440) 323-6545; Fax: (440) 322-2206
John R. Musson (440) 323-4903; Fax: (440) 323-4012
Clerk: Donald J. Rothgery

LORAIN MUNICIPAL COURT
200 W. Erie Ave., Lorain 44052-1646
(440) 204-2140; Fax: (440) 204-2146
Judges:
Thomas Elwell (440) 204-2150
Mark Mihok
100 W. Erie Ave., 2nd Floor, Lorain 44052
(440) 204-2159; Fax: (440) 204-2162
Clerk: Stephen W. Bansek

Lorain County—Cont'd

OBERLIN MUNICIPAL COURT
85 S. Main St., P.O. Box 179, Oberlin 44074-0179
(440) 775-1751; Fax: (440) 775-0619
Internet: www.oberlinmunicipalcourt.org
Jurisdiction—County of Lorain; Serves cities of Amherst
and Oberlin; the villages of Wellington, South Amherst,
Kipton and Rochester; and the townships of Amherst,
Brighton, Camden, Henrietta, Huntington, New Russia,
Penfield, Pittsfield, Rochester and Wellington

Judge: Thomas Januzzi (440) 775-1751

Clerk: Sandra Kohart

VERMILLION MUNICIPAL COURT
687 Decatur St., Vermilion 44089
(440) 967-6543; Fax: (440) 967-1467
Jurisdiction—Counties of Erie, Lorain

Judge: Elizabeth Wakefield

Clerk: Barbara L. Akers

County Offices

LORAIN COUNTY BOARD OF COMMISSIONERS
226 Middle Ave., Elyria 44035-5641
(440) 329-5111; Fax: (440) 323-3357

Commissioners:
Elizabeth C. Blair   Lori Kokoski
Ted Kalo

Clerk: Theresa Upton (440) 329-5103

LORAIN COUNTY CLERK OF COURTS
Lorain County Justice Center, 1st. Floor, 225 Court St.,
P.O. Box 749, Elyria 44036
(440) 329-5536, 41; Fax: (440) 329-5404

Clerk of Courts: Ronald L. Nabakowski

LORAIN COUNTY CORONER
Five S. Main St., Suite 304, Oberlin 44074-1600
(440) 774-7300; Fax: (440) 774-7002

Coroner: Paul M. Matus

LORAIN COUNTY ENGINEER
247 Hadaway St., Elyria 44035
(440) 329-5586; Fax: (440) 329-5587

Engineer: Kenneth P. Carney

LORAIN COUNTY PROSECUTOR
255 Court St., 3rd Floor, Elyria 44035
(440) 329-5387; Fax: (440) 329-1015

Prosecutor: Dennis Will

LORAIN COUNTY RECORDER
226 Middle Ave., Elyria 44035 (440) 329-5148

Recorder: Judy Nedwick

LORAIN COUNTY AUDITOR
226 Middle Ave., Elyria 44035
(440) 329-5203; Fax: (440) 329-5199

Auditor: Mark R. Stewart

LORAIN COUNTY SHERIFF
9896 Murray Ridge, P.O. Box 389, Elyria 44036
(440) 329-3709

Sheriff: Phil Stammitti

LORAIN COUNTY TREASURER
County Administration Bldg., 226 Middle Ave.,
Elyria 44035 (440) 329-5252

Treasurer: Daniel J. Talarek

LUCAS COUNTY

LUCAS COUNTY COMMON PLEAS COURT
Courthouse, 700 Adams St., Toledo 43624-1678
(419) 213-4777; Fax: (419) 213-4184
Judges:
James D. Bates (419) 213-4578
Gary G. Cook (419) 213-4370
Denise Ann Dartt (419) 213-4575
Charles J. Doneghy (419) 213-4570
Ruth Ann Franks (416) 213-4572
James D. Jensen (419) 213-4538
Frederick H. McDonald (419) 213-4560
Thomas J. Osowik (419) 213-4565
Charles S. Wittenberg (419) 213-4580

LUCAS COUNTY PROBATE COURT
Courthouse, Suite 200, 700 Adams St., Toledo 43624-1676
(419) 213-4775; Fax: (419) 213-4764

Judge: Jack R. Puffenberger
E-mail: judgepuff@lucas-co-probate-ct.org

LUCAS COUNTY JUVENILE COURT
1801 Spielbusch Ave., Toledo 43624
(419) 213-6700; Fax: (413) 213-6898
Judges:
Denise N. Cubbon (419) 213-6778
James A. Ray (419) 213-6717

LUCAS COUNTY DOMESTIC RELATIONS COURT
429 N. Michigan St., Suite B, Toledo 43624-1689
(419) 213-6850
Judges:
David Lewandowski (419) 213-6824
E-mail: dlewan@co.lucas.oh.us
Norman G. Zemmelman (419) 213-6827

MAUMEE MUNICIPAL COURT
400 Conant St., Maumee 43537-3397
(419) 897-7136; Fax: (419) 897-7129
E-mail: court@maumee.org

Judge: Gary L. Byers (419) 897-7140

Clerk: Sharon A. Thomasson

OREGON MUNICIPAL COURT
5330 Seaman Rd., Oregon 43616
(419) 698-7173; Fax: (419) 698-7013

Judge: Donald Z. Petroff (419) 698-7009

Clerk: Stacy A. DeShetler (419) 698-7007

SYLVANIA MUNICIPAL COURT
6700 Monroe St., Sylvania 43560
Criminal/Traffic: (419) 885-8975;
Civil/Small Claims: (419) 885-8985; Fax: (419) 885-8987

Judge: M. Scott Ramey

Clerk: Bonnie Chromik

TOLEDO MUNICIPAL COURT
555 N. Erie St., Toledo 43624
(419) 245-1949; Fax: (419) 245-1802
Judges:
Amy J. Berling (419) 245-1941
E-mail: amy.berling@noris.org
Francis X. Gorman (419) 245-1944
E-mail: francis.gorman@noris.org
Timothy Kuhlman
E-mail: tim.kuhlman@noris.org
C. Allen McConnell (419) 245-1946
E-mail: callenmcc@noris.org
Mary Grace Trimboli (419) 245-1940
E-mail: mary.trimboli@noris.org
Gene Zmuda (419) 245-1942
E-mail: gene.zmuda@noris.org

Clerk: Vallie Bowman-English
(419) 245-1780; Fax: (419) 245-1801

Lucas County—Cont'd

County Offices

LUCAS COUNTY BOARD OF COMMISSIONERS
One Government Ctr., Suite 800, Toledo 43604-2259
(419) 213-4500; Fax: (419) 213-4532
Internet: www.lucascountyoh.gov
President: Pete Gerken (419) 213-4502
Commissioners:
  Tina Skeldon Wozniak (419) 213-4314
  Margaret B. Thurber (419) 213-4220
Clerk: Nancy Poskar (419) 213-4511

LUCAS COUNTY CLERK OF COURTS
700 Adams St., 3rd Floor, Toledo 43604 (419) 213-4484
Clerk of Court: Bernie Quilter

LUCAS COUNTY CORONER
2595 Arlington Ave., Toledo 43614 (419) 213-3900
Coroner: James R. Patrick

LUCAS COUNTY ENGINEER
One Government Ctr., Suite 870, Toledo 43604
(419) 213-4540; Fax: (419) 213-4598
Engineer: Keith Earley

LUCAS COUNTY PROSECUTOR
Adams & Erie St., Suite 250, Toledo 43624-1680
(419) 213-4700; Fax: (419) 213-4595
Prosecutor: Julia Bates

LUCAS COUNTY RECORDER
One Government Ctr., Suite 700, Toledo 43604-2256
(419) 213-4400
Recorder: Anita Lopez

LUCAS COUNTY AUDITOR
One Government Ctr., Suite 600, Toledo 43604-2255
(419) 213-4394; Fax: (419) 213-4399
Auditor: Larry A. Kaczala

LUCAS COUNTY SHERIFF
1622 Spielbusch Ave., Toledo 43624 (419) 213-4900
Sheriff: James A. Telb

LUCAS COUNTY TREASURER
One Government Ctr., Suite 670, Toledo 43604-2253
(419) 213-4301
Treasurer: Wade Kapsukiewicz

MADISON COUNTY

MADISON COUNTY COMMON PLEAS COURT
One N. Main St., P.O. Box 527, London 43140-0527
(740) 852-9568; Fax: (740) 852-7144
Judge: Robert D. Nichols

MADISON COUNTY PROBATE/JUVENILE COURT
Courthouse, Room 205, 1 N. Main St., London 43140
(740) 852-0756; Fax: (740) 852-7134
Judge: Glenn S. Hamilton

MADISON MUNICIPAL COURT
P.O. Box 646, London 43140
(740) 852-1669; Fax: (740) 852-0812
Judge: R. David Picken
Clerk: Linda L. Sollars

County Offices

MADISON COUNTY BOARD OF COMMISSIONERS
Courthouse, 1 N. Main St., P.O. Box 618,
London 43140-0618 (740) 852-2972; Fax: (740) 845-1660
Internet: www.co.madison.oh.us
Chair: David Dhume
Commissioners:
  Robert D. Hackett   Chris R. Snyder
Clerk: Regina Bogenrife

MADISON COUNTY CLERK OF COURTS
Courthouse, One N. Main St., P.O. Box 557, London 43140
(740) 852-9776
Clerk of Courts: Marie Parks

MADISON COUNTY CORONER
115 E. High St., London 43140 (740) 852-9660
Coroner: Martin Markus

MADISON COUNTY ENGINEER
825 U.S. 42 N.E., London 43140
(740) 852-9404; Fax: (740) 852-9530
Engineer: David Brand

MADISON COUNTY PROSECUTOR
23 W. High St., London 43140
(740) 852-2259; Fax: (740) 845-1750
Prosecutor: Stephen Pronal

MADISON COUNTY RECORDER
Courthouse, Room 40, One N. Main St., London 43140
(740) 852-1854
Recorder: Charles E. Reed

MADISON COUNTY AUDITOR
Courthouse, P.O. Box 47, London 43140
(740) 852-9717; Fax: (740) 852-5752
Auditor: Jim Williamson

MADISON COUNTY SHERIFF
12 N. Oak St., London 43140
(740) 852-1332; Fax: (740) 852-7142
Sheriff: Stephen V. Saltsman

MADISON COUNTY TREASURER
P.O. Box 675, London 43140-0675 (740) 852-1936
Treasurer: William M. Stidman

MAHONING COUNTY

MAHONING COUNTY COMMON PLEAS COURT
120 Market St., Youngstown 44503-1710
(330) 740-2100
Judges:
  Maureen A. Cronin
    (330) 740-2154; Fax: (330) 740-2529
    E-mail: mcronin@mahoningcountyoh.gov
  John M. Durkin
    (330) 740-2168; Fax: (330) 742-5898
    E-mail: jdurkin@mahoningcounty.oh.gov
  James C. Evans
    (330) 740-2152; Fax: (330) 742-5890
    E-mail: jevans@mahoningcounty.oh.gov
  R. Scott Krichbaum
    (330) 740-2156; Fax: (330) 742-5898
  Maureen A. Sweeney
    (330) 740-2150; Fax: (330) 742-5882
    E-mail: msweeney@mahoningcounty.oh.gov

MAHONING COUNTY PROBATE COURT
120 Market St., Youngstown 44503
(330) 740-2310; Fax: (330) 740-2325
E-mail: mcprobate@mahoningcountyoh.gov
Internet: www.mahoningcountyoh.gov/probate
Judge: Timothy P. Maloney
Chief Deputy Clerk/Court Administrator: Lucia Lovell

MAHONING COUNTY JUVENILE COURT
300 E. Scott St., Youngstown 44505
(330) 740-2278; Clerk's Fax: (330) 740-2286;
Administration Fax: (330) 740-2272
Judge: Theresa Dellick

MAHONING COUNTY DOMESTIC RELATIONS COURT
120 Market St., Youngstown 44503
(330) 740-2208; Fax: (330) 740-2503
Judge: Beth A. Smith

Mahoning County—Cont'd

MAHONING COUNTY COURT NO. 2
127 Boardman-Canfield Rd., Youngstown 44512
(330) 726-5546; Fax: (330) 740-2035
Judge: Joseph M. Houser; E-mail: jhouser@mbpu.com

MAHONING COUNTY COURT NO. 3
605 E. Ohio Ave., Sebring 44672
(330) 938-9873; Fax: (330) 938-6518
Judge: Diane Vettori
Clerk: Miriam Pagan
Court Schedule: Tues., 1.30 P.M.

MAHONING COUNTY COURT NO. 4
6000 Mahoning Ave., Youngstown 44515
(330) 740-2001; Fax: (330) 740-2036
Jurisdiction—County of Mahoning; Austintown,
Lake Milton, North Jackson
Judge: David A. D'Apolito

MAHONING COUNTY COURT NO. 5
72 N. Broad St., Canfield 44406
(330) 533-3643; Fax: (330) 740-2034
Judge: Scott D. Hunter

ALLIANCE MUNICIPAL COURT
470 E. Market, Room 16, Alliance 44601
(330) 823-6600; Fax: (330) 829-2231
Internet: www.alliancecourt.org; www.starkcjis.org
Jurisdiction—Counties of Mahoning, Stark
Judge: Robert G. Lavery
    (330) 823-6181; Fax: (330) 823-6183
Clerk: Kevin B. Ward

CAMPBELL MUNICIPAL COURT
351 Tenney Ave., Campbell 44405
(330) 755-2165; Fax: (330) 750-3058
Jurisdiction—County of Mahoning; City of Campbell;
Town of Coitsville
Judge: John P. Almasy
Clerk: Mary Helen Muntean
Court Schedule: Tues. and Fri., 9 A.M.

STRUTHERS MUNICIPAL COURT
6 Elm St., Struthers 44471-1904
(330) 755-1800; Fax: (330) 755-2790
Judge: James R. Lanzo
Clerk: Linda Aey

YOUNGSTOWN MUNICIPAL COURT
26 S. Phelps St., Youngstown 44501
(330) 742-8844; Fax: (330) 744-1768
Judges:
    Robert A. Douglas, Jr.
     (330) 742-8857; Fax: (330) 742-8725
     E-mail: rdoug31204@aol.com
    Elizabeth A. Kobly
     (330) 742-8853; Fax: (330) 742-8723
    Robert P. Milich
     (330) 742-8855; Fax: (330) 742-8716
     E-mail: bobmilich@aol.com
Clerk: Sarah Brown-Clark
     (330) 742-8858; Fax: (330) 742-8786
     E-mail: sbrownclark@cboss.com
Court Administrator: Laura M. McLaughlin
     (330) 742-8844
     E-mail: courtadmin@cityofyoungstownoh.com

County Offices

MAHONING COUNTY BOARD OF COMMISSIONERS
Administration Bldg., Suite 200, 21 W. Boardman St.,
Youngstown 44503 (330) 740-2130; Fax: (330) 740-2006
President: John A. McNally
Commissioners:
    David N. Ludt   Anthony T. Traficanti
Clerk: Nancy Laboy

MAHONING COUNTY CLERK OF COURTS
Courthouse, 120 Market St., Youngstown 44503
(330) 740-2100; Fax: (330) 740-2105
Clerk of Courts: Anthony Vivo

MAHONING COUNTY CORONER
Oakhill Renaissance Pl., Suite 320, 345 Oakhill Ave.,
Youngstown 44502 (330) 740-2175; Fax: (330) 742-5868
Coroner: David M. Kennedy, M.D.

MAHONING COUNTY ENGINEER
940 Bears Den Rd., Youngstown 44511
(330) 799-1581; Fax: (330) 799-4600
Engineer: Richard A. Marsico

MAHONING COUNTY PROSECUTOR
Administration Bldg., 21 W. Boardman St.,
Youngstown 44503 (330) 740-2330; Fax: (330) 740-2008
Prosecutor: Paul J. Gains

MAHONING COUNTY RECORDER
Courthouse, 120 Market St., Youngstown 44503
(330) 740-2345; Fax: (330) 740-2347
Recorder: Ronald Gerberry

MAHONING COUNTY SHERIFF
Justice Center, 110 Fifth Ave., Youngstown 44503
(330) 480-5020; Fax: (330) 480-5089
Sheriff: Randall A. Wellington

MAHONING COUNTY AUDITOR
Courthouse, 120 Market St., Youngstown 44503
(330) 740-2010; Fax: (330) 480-7571
Auditor: George J. Tablack

MAHONING COUNTY TREASURER
Courthouse, 120 Market St., Youngstown 44503
(330) 740-2460; Fax: (330) 740-2142
Treasurer: John B. Reardon

MARION COUNTY

MARION COUNTY COMMON PLEAS COURT
Courthouse Sq., 100 N. Main St., Marion 43302
(740) 223-4500
Judges:
    Robert S. Davidson
     (740) 223-4210; Fax: (740) 387-1321
    William Finnegan
     (740) 223-4220; Fax: (740) 387-7131
    Court does not accept fax filings.

MARION COUNTY PROBATE/JUVENILE COURT/DOMESTIC RELATIONS COURT
222 W. Center St., Marion 43302
(740) 223-4060; Fax: (740) 382-3798

Probate Division, 100 N. Main St., Marion 43302
(740) 223-4260
Judges:
    Deborah A. Alspach   Thomas K. Jenkins

MARION MUNICIPAL COURT
233 W. Center St., Marion 43302
Small Claims: (740) 383-6049;
Civil Division: (740) 383-5515;
Traffic/Criminal Division: (740) 387-0073;
Fax: (740) 382-5274
Judge: Teresa L. Ballinger (740) 387-0439
Clerk: Linda Bartley (740) 387-0439

Marion County—Cont'd

County Offices

MARION COUNTY BOARD OF COMMISSIONERS
222 W. Center St., Marion 43302
(740) 223-4001; Fax: (740) 383-1190
President: Ken Frayer
Commissioners:
  Andy Appelfeller   Dave Columber
County Administrator: Lenora Mayes
Administrative Clerk.: Sylvia Almendinger
  (740) 223-4001

MARION COUNTY CLERK OF COURTS
100 N. Main St., Marion 43302 (740) 223-4270
Clerk of Courts: Julie M. Kagel

MARION COUNTY CORONER
200 S. Elm St., Prospect 43342 (740) 494-2431
Coroner: Marc J. Comianos

MARION COUNTY ENGINEER
222 W. Center St., Marion 43302
(740) 223-4110; Fax: (740) 223-4119
Engineer: Brad Irons

MARION COUNTY PROSECUTOR
134 E. Center St., Marion 43302
(740) 223-4290; Fax: (740) 223-4299
Prosecutor: Jim Slagle

MARION COUNTY RECORDER
222 W. Center St., Marion 43302 (740) 223-4100
Recorder: Mary Jo Osmun

MARION COUNTY AUDITOR
225 W. Center St., Marion 43302 (740) 223-4020
Auditor: Joe Campbell

MARION COUNTY SHERIFF
899 Marion Williamsport Rd., Marion 43302
(740) 382-8244
Sheriff: Tim Bailey

MARION COUNTY TREASURER
222 W. Center St., Marion 43302 (740) 223-4030
Treasurer: Thomas J. Sheskey

MEDINA COUNTY

MEDINA COUNTY COMMON PLEAS COURT
93 Public Sq., Medina 44256-2205
(330) 725-9729
Judges:
  Christopher Collier (Courtroom 1)
    (330) 725-9729; Fax: (330) 764-8445
  James L. Kimbler (Courtroom 2)
    (330) 725-9736; Fax: (330) 764-8791
    E-mail: kimbler@apk.net

MEDINA COUNTY PROBATE/JUVENILE COURT
93 Public Sq., Medina 44256-2205
Juvenile: (330) 725-9709; Juvenile Fax: (330) 725-9173;
Probate: (330) 725-9703; Probate Fax: (330) 725-9119
Judge: John J. Lohn

MEDINA COUNTY DOMESTIC RELATIONS COURT
99 Public Sq., Medina 44256
(330) 725-9740; Fax: (330) 764-8794
Judge: Mary R. Kovack
  E-mail: mrkovack@medinaco.org

MEDINA MUNICIPAL COURT
135 N. Elmwood Ave., Medina 44256
(330) 723-3287; Fax: (330) 225-1108
Internet: www.medinamunicipalcourt.org
Judge: Dale H. Chase
Clerk: Lori A. Henry

WADSWORTH MUNICIPAL COURT
120 Maple St., Wadsworth 44281
(330) 335-1596; Fax: (330) 335-2723
Judge: Stephen B. McIlvaine
Clerk: Marjorie L. Laterza

County Offices

MEDINA COUNTY BOARD OF COMMISSIONERS
144 N. Broadway St., Medina 44256-1974
(330) 722-9208; Fax: (330) 722-9206
Internet: www.co.medina.oh.us
President: Patricia G. Geissman
Commissioners:
  Stephen D. Hambley   Sharon A. Ray
Clerk: Pamela J. Terrill

MEDINA COUNTY CLERK OF COURTS
93 Public Sq., Medina 44256-2292 (330) 725-9722
Clerk of Courts: Kathy Fortney

MEDINA COUNTY CORONER
6605 Center Rd., Valley City 44280 (330) 483-3135
Coroner: Neil F. Grabenstetter

MEDINA COUNTY ENGINEER
791 W. Smith Rd., P.O. Box 825, Medina 44258-0825
(330) 723-9561
Engineer: Mike Salay

MEDINA COUNTY PROSECUTOR
60 Public Sq., Medina 44256
(330) 723-9536; Fax: (330) 723-9532
Prosecutor: Dean Holman

MEDINA COUNTY RECORDER
144 N. Broadway St., Medina 44256 (330) 725-9782
Recorder: Nancy L. Abbott

MEDINA COUNTY AUDITOR
144 N. Broadway St., Medina 44256
(330) 725-9767; Fax: (330) 725-9136
Auditor: Michael E. Kovack

MEDINA COUNTY SHERIFF
555 Independence Dr., Medina 44256 (330) 725-9147
Sheriff: Neil F. Hassinger

MEDINA COUNTY TREASURER
144 N. Broadway St., Medina 44256
(330) 725-9748; Fax: (330) 725-9174
Treasurer: Burke A. John

MEIGS COUNTY

MEIGS COUNTY COMMON PLEAS COURT
100 E. Second St., Pomeroy 45769-1030
(740) 992-6439; Fax: (740) 992-3828
Judge: Frederick W. Crow III

MEIGS COUNTY PROBATE/JUVENILE COURT
100 E. Second St., 2nd. Floor, Pomeroy 45769-1030
Probate: (740) 992-3096; Juvenile: (740) 992-6205;
Fax: (740) 992-6727
Judge: L. Scott Powell

MEIGS COUNTY COURT
Courthouse, 100 E. Second St., Pomeroy 45769-1030
(740) 992-2279; Fax: (740) 992-4570
Judge: Steven L. Story

County Offices

MEIGS COUNTY BOARD OF COMMISSIONERS
Courthouse, 100 E. Second St., Pomeroy 45769
(740) 992-2895; Fax: (740) 992-2270
Commissioners:
  Mick Davenport   Jim Sheets
    (President)   Jeffrey L. Thornton
Clerk: Gloria Kloes

Meigs County—Cont'd

MEIGS COUNTY CLERK OF COURTS
Courthouse, 100 E. Second St., P.O. Box 151, Pomeroy 45769
(740) 992-5290; Fax: (740) 992-4429
Clerk of Courts: Marlene Harrison

MEIGS COUNTY CORONER
P.O. Box 458, Racine 45771 (740) 949-2683
Coroner: Douglas D. Hunter

MEIGS COUNTY ENGINEER
34110 Fair Grounds Rd., Pomeroy 45769 (740) 992-2911
Engineer: Eugene Triplett

MEIGS COUNTY PROSECUTOR
117 W. Second St., P.O. Box 685, Pomeroy 45769
(740) 992-6371
Prosecutor: Pat Story

MEIGS COUNTY RECORDER
Courthouse, 100 E. Second St., Pomeroy 45769
(740) 992-3806; Fax: (740) 992-2867
Recorder: Kay Hill

MEIGS COUNTY AUDITOR
P.O. Box 551, Pomeroy 45769
(740) 992-2698; Fax: (740) 992-5028
Auditor: Nancy J. Grueser

MEIGS COUNTY SHERIFF
104 E. Second St., Pomeroy 45769 (740) 992-3371
Sheriff: Robert Beegle

MEIGS COUNTY TREASURER
Courthouse, 100 E. Second St., Pomeroy 45769-0231
(740) 992-2004
Treasurer: Howard E. Frank

MERCER COUNTY

MERCER COUNTY COMMON PLEAS COURT
Courthouse, Room 301, 101 N. Main St., Celina 45822
Judge: Jeffrey R. Ingraham
   (419) 586-2122; Fax: (419) 586-4000
   E-mail: judge.ingraham@mercercountyohio.org

MERCER COUNTY PROBATE/JUVENILE COURT
101 N. Main St., Room 307, Celina 45822-1796
Juvenile: (419) 586-2418; Probate: (419) 586-8779;
Juvenile/Probate Fax: (419) 586-4506
Judge: Mary Pat Zitter (419) 586-1249

CELINA MUNICIPAL COURT
202 N. Main St., P.O. Box 362, Celina 45822-0362
(419) 586-6491; Fax: (419) 586-4735
E-mail: celmuncrtclk@bright.net
Judge: James J. Scheer
Clerk: Barbara A. Painter
Hours: Weekdays, 8 A.M.-5 P.M.

County Offices

MERCER COUNTY BOARD OF COMMISSIONERS
220 W. Livingston St., Room A201, Celina 45822-1671
(419) 586-3178; Fax: (419) 586-1699
President: Jim Zehringer
Commissioners:
   Jerry Laffin   Robert Nuding
Clerk: Kim Everman

MERCER COUNTY CLERK OF COURTS
101 N. Main St., Room 205, P.O. Box 28, Celina 45822
(419) 586-6461; Fax: (419) 586-5826
Clerk of Courts: James J. Highley
   E-mail: jim.highley@mercercountyohio.org

MERCER COUNTY CORONER
407 S. Oak St., Coldwater 45828-1697
(419) 678-2354; Fax: (419) 678-4716
Coroner: Timothy F. Heinrichs

MERCER COUNTY ENGINEER
321 Riley St., Celina 45822
(419) 586-7759; Fax: (419) 586-9887
Engineer: James Weichart
   E-mail: engineer@mercercountyohio.org

MERCER COUNTY PROSECUTOR
119 N. Walnut St., Celina 45822
(419) 586-8677; Fax: (419) 586-8747
Prosecutor: Andy Hinders
   E-mail: prosecutor@mercercountyohio.org

MERCER COUNTY RECORDER
101 N. Main St., Room 203, Celina 45822
(419) 586-4232; Fax: (419) 586-3541
Recorder: Tammy Barger
   E-mail: recorder@mercercountyohio.org

MERCER COUNTY AUDITOR
Courthouse, Room 105, 101 N. Main St., Celina 45822
(419) 586-6402; Fax: (419) 586-8089
Auditor: Mark R. Giesige
   E-mail: mark.giesige@mercercountyohio.org

MERCER COUNTY SHERIFF
125 W. Livingston St., Celina 45822
(419) 586-7724; Fax: (419) 586-2234
Sheriff: Jeff Grey
   E-mail: sheriff@mercercountyohio.org

MERCER COUNTY TREASURER
101 N. Main St., Room 201, Celina 45822-1789
(419) 586-2259; Fax: (419) 586-4319
Treasurer: Doris A. Rutschilling
   E-mail: treasurer@mercercountyohio.org

MIAMI COUNTY

MIAMI COUNTY COMMON PLEAS COURT
Safety Bldg., 3rd Floor, 201 W. Main St., Troy 45373-3239
(937) 440-6010; Fax: (937) 440-6011
Judges:
   Robert J. Lindeman (937) 440-6019
   Jeffrey M. Welbaum (937) 440-6021

MIAMI COUNTY PROBATE/JUVENILE COURT
Safety Bldg., 201 W. Main St., Troy 45373-2363
Juvenile: (937) 440-5970; Juvenile Fax: (937) 440-3531;
Probate: (937) 440-6050; Probate Fax: (937) 440-3529
Judge: Lynnita K.C. Wagner

MIAMI MUNICIPAL COURT
Courthouse, 201 W. Main St., Troy 45373
(937) 440-3910; Fax: (937) 440-3911
Internet: www.co.miami.oh.us/

110 S. Wayne St., Piqua 45356 (937) 773-0513
Judges:
   Elizabeth Gutmann (937) 440-3936
      E-mail: esg@woh.rr.com
   Mel Kemmer (937) 440-3933
      E-mail: mkemmer@co.miami.oh.us
Magistrate Judge: Gary E. Zuhl (937) 332-7084
Clerk: Thomas Elliott (937) 440-3918

County Offices

MIAMI COUNTY BOARD OF COMMISSIONERS
County Plz., 201 W. Main St., Troy 45373-2363
(937) 440-5910; Fax: (937) 440-5911
E-mail: commissioners@co.miami.oh.us
Internet: www.co.miami.oh.us
President: John F. Evans
Commissioners:
   D. Ann Baird   Ron Widener
Clerk: Tamara K. Shellhaas (937) 440-5906

MIAMI COUNTY CLERK OF COURTS
Safety Bldg., 3rd Floor, 201 W. Main St., Troy 45373
(937) 440-6010
Clerk of Courts: Jan A. Mottlinger

Miami County—Cont'd

MIAMI COUNTY CORONER
Safety Bldg., 201 W. Main St., Troy 45373 (937) 339-3838
Coroner: Judith Nickras

MIAMI COUNTY ENGINEER
2100 County Rd. 25-A, Troy 45373 (937) 440-5656
Engineer: Douglas L. Christian

MIAMI COUNTY PROSECUTOR
Safety Bldg., 201 W. Main St., Troy 45373
(937) 440-5960; Fax: (937) 440-5961
Prosecutor: Gary Nasal

MIAMI COUNTY RECORDER
P.O. Box 653, Troy 45373 (937) 440-6040
Recorder: John W. O'Brien

MIAMI COUNTY AUDITOR
Safety Bldg., 201 W. Main St., Troy 45373 (937) 440-5925
Auditor: Chris Peeples

MIAMI COUNTY SHERIFF
201 W. Main St., Troy 45373 (937) 440-6085
Sheriff: Charles A. Cox

MIAMI COUNTY TREASURER
Safety Bldg., 201 W. Main St ., Troy 45373 (937) 440-6045
Treasurer: Lydia Callison

MONROE COUNTY

MONROE COUNTY COMMON PLEAS COURT
Courthouse, 101 Main St., P.O. Box 563,
Woodsfield 43793-1099 (740) 472-0761
Judge: William D. Harris
    (740) 472-0841; Fax: (740) 472-2518
    E-mail: wmharris@1st.net

MONROE COUNTY PROBATE/JUVENILE COURT
101 N. Main St., Room 39, Woodsfield 43793-1099
(740) 472-5790; Fax: (740) 472-2520
Judge: Walter R. Starr

MONROE COUNTY COURT
101 N. Main St., Room 35, Woodsfield 43793
(740) 472-5181; Fax: (740) 472-2526
Judge: James W. Peters; E-mail: judgejpl@1st.net
Clerk: Brenda Roberts

County Offices

MONROE COUNTY BOARD OF COMMISSIONERS
Courthouse, Room 12, 101 N. Main St., Woodsfield 43793
(740) 472-1341; Fax: (740) 472-5156
Commissioners:
Gary L. Hudson   Francis Block
  (President)   Mark A. Forni
Clerk: Allyson Cox

MONROE COUNTY CLERK OF COURTS
Courthouse, Room 26, 101 N. Main St., Woodsfield 43793
(740) 472-0761; Fax: (740) 472-2549
Clerk of Courts: Beth Ann Rose

MONROE COUNTY CORONER
154 S. Main St., Woodsfield 43793 (740) 472-1330
Coroner: Jay Seidler

MONROE COUNTY ENGINEER
P.O. Box 555, Woodsfield 43793
(740) 472-2537; Fax: (740) 472-2530
Engineer: Lonnie E. Tustin

MONROE COUNTY PROSECUTOR
110 N. Main St., P.O. Box 430, Woodsfield 43793
(740) 472-1158
Prosecutor: Lynn Kent Riethmiller

MONROE COUNTY RECORDER
Courthouse, P.O. Box 152, Woodsfield 43793-0152
(740) 472-5264
Recorder: Martha Louise Reid

MONROE COUNTY AUDITOR
Courthouse, Room 22, 101 N. Main St., Woodsfield 43793
(740) 472-0873; Fax: (740) 472-2523
Auditor: Pandora J. Neuhart

MONROE COUNTY SHERIFF
P.O. Box 595, Woodsfield 43793
(740) 472-1612; Fax: (740) 472-5132
Sheriff: Tim Price

MONROE COUNTY TREASURER
Courthouse, Room 2, 101 N. Main St., Woodsfield 43793
(740) 472-1521
Treasurer: Judy A. Gramlich

MONTGOMERY COUNTY

MONTGOMERY COUNTY COMMON PLEAS COURT
41 N. Perry St., P.O. Box 972, Dayton 45422-2170
(937) 225-6000; Fax: (937) 225-5406
Judges:
  G. Jack Davis (937) 225-4368
  Jeffrey E. Froelich (937) 225-4440
    E-mail: froelicj@montcourt.org
  Barbara P. Gorman (937) 225-4392
    E-mail: gormanb@montcourt.org
  David A. Gowdown (937) 225-4416
    E-mail: gowdownd@montcourt.org
  Michael T. Hall (937) 496-7951
    E-mail: hallm@montcourt.org
  Mary Katherine Huffman (937) 496-7955
  John W. Kessler (937) 225-4384
    E-mail: kesslerj@montcourt.org
  Dennis J. Langer (937) 225-4055
    E-mail: langerd@montcourt.org
  Gregory F. Singer (937) 225-4376
    E-mail: singerg@montcourt.org
  Michael L. Tucker (937) 225-4448
    E-mail: tuckerm@montcourt.org
  A.J. Wagner (937) 225-4409
    E-mail: wagnera@montcourt.org
Court Administrator: James W. Drubert (937) 225-6000

MONTGOMERY COUNTY PROBATE COURT
41 N. Perry St., Dayton 45422-2155
(937) 225-4552; Fax: (937) 496-3181
Internet: www.mcohio.org/probate
Judge: Alice O. McCollum
    E-mail: mccolluma@mcohio.org

MONTGOMERY COUNTY JUVENILE COURT
303 W. Second St., Dayton 45422-4240
(937) 496-7908
Judges:
  Anthony Capizzi (937) 496-6600; Fax: (937) 496-6598
  Nick Kuntz (937) 225-4124; Fax: (937) 224-8603

MONTGOMERY COUNTY DOMESTIC RELATIONS COURT
301 W. Third St., 2nd. Floor, Dayton 45422-4248
(937) 225-4063; Fax: (937) 496-7835
Judges:
  Denise Martin Cross (937) 496-7538
    E-mail: crossd@mcohio.org
  Judith A. King (937) 496-7536
    E-mail: kingj@mcohio.org
Administrators:
  Michael Howley (Legal Director) (937) 225-4053
    E-mail: howleym@mcohio.org
  Robin Lehman (Operations Director) (937) 225-6060
    E-mail: lehmanr@mcohio.org

MONTGOMERY COUNTY COURT AREA ONE
195 S. Clayton Rd., New Lebanon 45345
(937) 687-9099; Fax: (937) 687-7119
Judges:
  James L. Manning; E-mail: manning@montcnty.oh.org
  Connie S. Price-Testerman; E-mail: pricejd@aol.com
  Adele Riley; E-mail: rileya@mcohio.org
Clerk: Dan Foley (937) 225-6118
Court Schedule: Mon., Noon-7 P.M.; Tues., Wed. and
Thurs., 8 A.M.-4 P.M.; Fri., 9 A.M.-4 P.M.

MONTGOMERY COUNTY COURT AREA TWO
6111 Taylorsville Rd., Huber Heights 45424
(937) 496-7231; Fax: (937) 496-7236
Internet: www.clerk.co.montgomery.oh.us
Judges:
  James A. Hensley, Jr.; E-mail: hensljrj@montcnty.org
  James D. Piergies; E-mail: piergiesj@montcnty.org

DAYTON MUNICIPAL COURT
301 W. Third St., Dayton 45402
(937) 333-4338; Fax: (937) 333-4468
Judges:
  James F. Cannon (937) 333-4367; Fax: (937) 333-5114
  Daniel G. Gehres (937) 333-4366; Fax: (937) 333-5114
  Carl S. Henderson (937) 333-4350; Fax: (937) 333-5079
  Bill C. Littlejohn (937) 333-4369; Fax: (937) 333-4496
  John S. Pickrel (937) 333-4364; Fax: (937) 333-5083
Clerk: Mark E. Owens

KETTERING MUNICIPAL COURT
3600 Shroyer Rd., Kettering 45429
(937) 296-2461; Fax: (937) 534-7017;
Judges' Fax: (937) 296-3284
Jurisdiction—County of Montgomery; Kettering,
Centerville, Washington Township and Moraine
Judges:
  Thomas M. Hanna (937) 296-3327
    E-mail: thomas.hanna@ketteringoh.org
  Robert L. Moore (937) 296-2542
    E-mail: moore136@yahoo.com
Clerk: Andrea J. White
    E-mail: andrea.white@ketteringoh.org

MIAMISBURG MUNICIPAL COURT
10 N. First St., Miamisburg 45342-2305
(937) 866-2203; Fax: (937) 866-0135
Internet: www.miamisburgcourts.com
Judge: Robert E. Messham, Jr.
Clerk: Cynthia A. Coffey

OAKWOOD MUNICIPAL COURT
30 Park Ave., Dayton 45419-3426
(937) 293-3058; Fax: (937) 297-2939
Judge: Robert L. Deddens
Clerk: V. Louise Ackerman

VANDALIA MUNICIPAL COURT
Justice Center, 2nd. Floor, 245 Bohanan Memorial Dr.,
P.O. Box 429, Vandalia 45377-2393
(937) 898-3996; Fax: (937) 898-6648
Judge: Richard J. Bannister
Clerk: Jerry M. Kaylor

County Offices

MONTGOMERY COUNTY BOARD OF COMMISSIONERS
421 W. Third St., P.O. Box 972, Dayton 45422
(937) 225-4690; Fax: (937) 496-7723
Commissioners:
  Vicki D. Pegg (President)
  Charles J. Curran
  Deborah A. Lieberman
Clerk: Juanita M. Hunn
    451 W. Third St., 11th Floor, Dayton 45422-1120
    (937) 225-4591; Fax: (937) 496-6560
    E-mail: hunnj@mcohio.org

MONTGOMERY COUNTY CLERK OF COURTS
41 N. Perry St., Room 106, Dayton 45422
(937) 496-7623; Fax: (937) 496-7627
Clerk of Courts: Dan Foley

MONTGOMERY COUNTY CORONER
361 W. Third St., Dayton 45402 (937) 225-4156
Coroner: James H. Davis

MONTGOMERY COUNTY ENGINEER
451 W. Third St., Dayton 45422
(937) 225-4889; Fax: (937) 225-4774
Engineer: Joseph Litvin

MONTGOMERY COUNTY PROSECUTOR
301 W. Third St., 5th Floor, Dayton 45402
(937) 225-5757; Fax: (937) 225-3470
Prosecutor: Mathias Heck

MONTGOMERY COUNTY RECORDER
451 W. Third St., P.O. Box 972, Dayton 45422
(937) 225-4275
Recorder: Judy Dodge

MONTGOMERY COUNTY AUDITOR
451 W. Third St., Dayton 45422
(937) 225-4333; Fax: (937) 225-5011
Auditor: Karl Keith

MONTGOMERY COUNTY SHERIFF
330 W. Second St., P.O. Box 972, Dayton 45422
(937) 225-4192; Fax: (937) 496-7986
Sheriff: Dave Vore

MONTGOMERY COUNTY TREASURER
451 W. Third St., Dayton 45422 (937) 225-4010
Treasurer: Hugh Quill

MORGAN COUNTY

MORGAN COUNTY COMMON PLEAS COURT
19 E. Main St., McConnelsville 43756-1197
(740) 962-4752
Judge: Dan W. Favreau
    (740) 962-3371; Fax: (740) 962-4589

MORGAN COUNTY COURT
37 E. Main St., McConnelsville 43756
(740) 962-4031; Fax: (740) 962-2895
E-mail: morgancountycourt@yahoo.com
Judge: Michael D. Lowe
Clerk: Alma J. Tennent

County Offices

MORGAN COUNTY BOARD OF COMMISSIONERS
155 E. Main St., Room 216, McConnelsville 43756-1172
(740) 962-3183; Fax: (740) 962-2014
President: Carl Dodrill, Jr.
Commissioners:
  Bruce J. Dozer   Ron Moore
Clerk: Sharon Travis

MORGAN COUNTY CLERK OF COURTS
19 E. Main St., McConnelsville 43756 (740) 962-4752
Clerk of Courts: Mary E. Gessel

MORGAN COUNTY CORONER
Prime Care of Southeastern Ohio, 1210 Ashland Ave.,
Zanesville 43701 (740) 454-8551
Coroner: David Parrett, M.D.

MORGAN COUNTY ENGINEER
155 E. Main St., Room 208, McConnelsville 43756
(740) 962-3171
Engineer: Richard L. Hardison

MORGAN COUNTY PROSECUTOR
109 E. Main St., McConnelsville 43756-1125
(740) 962-6478; Fax: (740) 962-6664
Prosecutor: Richard Welch

Morgan County—Cont'd

MORGAN COUNTY RECORDER
155 E. Main St., Room 160, McConnelsville 43756-1125
(740) 962-4051
Recorder: Rebecca Cooley

MORGAN COUNTY AUDITOR
155 E. Main St., Room 217, McConnelsville 43756
(740) 962-4475; Fax: (740) 962-2014
Auditor: Gary D. Woodward

MORGAN COUNTY SHERIFF
37 E. Main St., McConnelsville 43756 (740) 962-4044
Sheriff: Thomas C. Jenkins

MORGAN COUNTY TREASURER
155 E. Main St., Room 153, McConnelsville 43756
(740) 962-3561
Treasurer: Kaye S. Tatman

MORROW COUNTY
MORROW COUNTY COMMON PLEAS COURT
Courthouse, 48 E. High St., Mount Gilead 43338-1458
(419) 947-4515; Fax: (419) 947-6341;
Probate: (419) 947-5575; Juvenile: (419) 947-5545;
Juvenile Fax: (419) 946-1270;
Domestic Relations: (419) 947-4525
Judge: Howard E. Hall
Court Administrator: James D. Wallis (419) 947-5512
Assignment Commissioner: Daniel Rhodebeck
  (419) 947-4515
Fiscal Coordinator: Shirley Fissell (419) 947-4515

MORROW COUNTY MUNICIPAL COURT
48 E. High St., Mount Gilead 43338
(419) 947-5045; Fax: (419) 947-9161
Judge: Lee W. McClelland; E-mail: judgemac@rrohio.com
Clerk: Candy C. Dartt
Hours: Weekdays, 7:30 A.M.-5 P.M.

County Offices
MORROW COUNTY BOARD OF COMMISSIONERS
48 E. High St., Mount Gilead 43338-1490
(419) 947-4085; Fax: (419) 947-1860
Commissioners:
  Olen D. Jackson   Donald R. Staley
  Jean McClintock
Clerk: Charisse Gruber

MORROW COUNTY CLERK OF COURTS
Courthouse, 48 E. High St., Mount Gilead 43338
(419) 947-2085; Fax: (419) 947-5421
Clerk of Courts: Geraldine Park

MORROW COUNTY CORONER
117 E. Main St., Cardington 43315 (419) 864-2056
Coroner: Dr. William Lee

MORROW COUNTY ENGINEER
50 E. High St., Mount Gilead 43338
(419) 947-4530; Fax: (419) 947-1860
Engineer: L. Randy Bush

MORROW COUNTY PROSECUTOR
60 E. High St., Mount Gilead 43338
(419) 947-5515; Fax: (419) 947-5205
Prosecutor: Charles S. Howland

MORROW COUNTY RECORDER
48 E. High St., Mount Gilead 43338
(419) 947-3060; Fax: (419) 947-3709
Recorder: Dixie Shinaberry

MORROW COUNTY AUDITOR
48 E. High St., Mount Gilead 43338
(419) 946-4060; Fax: (419) 946-6713
Auditor: Mary M. Holtrey

MORROW COUNTY SHERIFF
101 Home Rd., P.O. Box 359, Mount Gilead 43338
(419) 946-4444; Fax: (419) 946-2406
Sheriff: Steve Brenneman

MORROW COUNTY TREASURER
48 E. High St., Mount Gilead 43338
(419) 947-6070; Fax: (419) 947-6231
Treasurer: Dan Green

MUSKINGUM COUNTY
MUSKINGUM COUNTY COMMON PLEAS COURT
401 Main St., Zanesville 43701
(740) 455-7142; Fax: (740) 455-7177
Judges:
  Mark C. Fleegle   Howard Zwelling

MUSKINGUM COUNTY PROBATE COURT
401 Main St., Zanesville 43701-3567
(740) 455-7113; Fax: (740) 455-7173
Judge: Joseph A. Gormley

MUSKINGUM COUNTY JUVENILE COURT
1860 E. Pike, Zanesville 43701
(740) 453-0351; Fax: (740) 453-1066
Judge: Joseph A. Gormley

MUSKINGUM COUNTY COURT
27 N. Fifth St., Zanesville 43701
(740) 455-7138; Fax: (740) 455-7157
Internet: www.muskingumcountycourt.org
Judges:
  Jay F. Vinsel   Vacancy at Press Time
Clerk: Jacqueline E. Garber

County Offices
MUSKINGUM COUNTY BOARD OF COMMISSIONERS
401 Main St., Zanesville 43701-3519
(740) 455-7100; Fax: (740) 455-3785
E-mail: commissioners@muskingumcounty.org
Commissioners:
  Brian Hill (President)   Dorothy M. Montgomery
  Don Madden
Clerk: Susan Culbertson

MUSKINGUM COUNTY CLERK OF COURTS
401 Main St., Zanesville 43701 (740) 455-7104
Clerk of Courts: Todd A. Bickle
Hours: Weekdays, 8:30 A.M.-4:30 P.M.

MUSKINGUM COUNTY CORONER
33 E. Main St., New Concord 43762 (740) 826-7626
Coroner: Howard J. Marsh

MUSKINGUM COUNTY ENGINEER
155 Rehl Rd., Zanesville 43701 (740) 454-0155
Engineer: Doug Davis

MUSKINGUM COUNTY PROSECUTOR
27 N. Fifth St., P.O. Box 1187, Zanesville 43702-1187
(740) 455-7123; Fax: (740) 455-7141
Prosecutor: Michael D. Haddox

MUSKINGUM COUNTY RECORDER
P.O. Box 2333, Zanesville 43702-2333
(740) 455-7107; Fax: (740) 455-7943
Recorder: Karen Bates Vincent

MUSKINGUM COUNTY AUDITOR
401 Main St., Zanesville 43701
(740) 455-7109; Fax: (740) 455-7182
Auditor: Anita J. Adams

MUSKINGUM COUNTY SHERIFF
28 N. Fourth St., Zanesville 43701
(740) 452-3637; Fax: (740) 455-7176
Sheriff: Bob Stephenson

MUSKINGUM COUNTY TREASURER
401 Main St., Zanesville 43701
(740) 455-7118; Fax: (740) 455-7908
Treasurer: Phillip Murphy

NOBLE COUNTY

NOBLE COUNTY COMMON PLEAS COURT
300 Courthouse, Caldwell 43724
(740) 732-4045; Fax: (740) 732-0100
Judge: John W. Nau

NOBLE COUNTY COURT
100 Courthouse, Caldwell 43724-1243
(740) 732-5795; Fax: (740) 732-1435
Judge: Lucien C. Young III
Clerk: Sandra Schott

County Offices

NOBLE COUNTY BOARD OF COMMISSIONERS
Courthouse Sq., Room 210, Caldwell 43724
(740) 732-2969; Fax: (740) 732-5702
Commissioners:
John H. Carter   Charles E. Cowgill
(President)   Danny Harmon
Clerk: Sue Shottis

NOBLE COUNTY CLERK OF COURTS
350 Courthouse, Caldwell 43724 (740) 732-4408
Clerk of Courts: Karen Starr

NOBLE COUNTY CORONER
304 Main St., Caldwell 43724 (740) 732-2339
Coroner: R. Alan Spencer

NOBLE COUNTY ENGINEER
Courthouse, Room 220, Caldwell 43724 (740) 732-4861
Engineer: John A. Foreman

NOBLE COUNTY PROSECUTOR
409 Popular St., Caldwell 43724 (740) 732-5685
Prosecutor: Robert Watson

NOBLE COUNTY RECORDER
260 Courthouse, Room 2E, Caldwell 43724 (740) 732-4319
Recorder: Phyllis Stritz

NOBLE COUNTY AUDITOR
Courthouse, Room 200, Caldwell 43724
(740) 732-2702; Fax: (740) 732-5702
Auditor: Alice L. Warner

NOBLE COUNTY SHERIFF
420 Olive St., Caldwell 43724 (740) 732-5631
Sheriff: Landon T. Smith

NOBLE COUNTY TREASURER
Courthouse Sq., Caldwell 43724 (740) 732-4895
Treasurer: Becky J. Hendershot

OTTAWA COUNTY

OTTAWA COUNTY COMMON PLEAS COURT
315 Madison St., Port Clinton 43452-1936
(419) 734-6755; Fax: (419) 734-6875
Internet: www.ottawacocpcourt.com
Judges:
Kathleen L. Giesler (Probate & General Div.), Room 306
(419) 734-6830
Paul C. Moon (General Div.), Room 301
(419) 734-6791
E-mail: amadeus43452@yahoo.com

OTTAWA COUNTY PROBATE/JUVENILE COURT
315 Madison St., Port Clinton 43452-1994
Probate: (419) 734-6830; Fax: (419) 732-8147;
Juvenile Court: (419) 734-6840; Fax: (419) 734-6851
Judge: Kathleen L. Giesler

OTTAWA MUNICIPAL COURT
1860 E. Perry St., Port Clinton 43452
(419) 734-4143; Fax: (419) 732-2862
Judge: Frederick C. Hany II
Clerk: Rebecca L. Szilagyi

County Offices

OTTAWA COUNTY BOARD OF COMMISSIONERS
315 Madison St., Room 103, Port Clinton 43452-1993
(419) 734-6710; Fax: (419) 734-6898
Commissioners:
John G. Papcun   Steven M. Arndt
(President)   Carl E. Koebel
Clerk/Asst. Admin.: Rhonda Slauterbeck

OTTAWA COUNTY CLERK OF COURTS
Courthouse, Room 304, 315 Madison St.,
Port Clinton 43452-1997 (419) 734-6756
E-mail: legal@co.ottawa.oh.us
Clerk of Courts: JoAn C. Monnett

OTTAWA COUNTY CORONER
1858 E. Perry St., Port Clinton 43452 (419) 732-7372
Coroner: Jerome McTague

OTTAWA COUNTY ENGINEER
315 Madison St., Room 106, Port Clinton 43452
(419) 734-6777; Fax: (419) 734-6768
Engineer: David Brunkhorst

OTTAWA COUNTY PROSECUTOR
315 Madison St., Port Clinton 43452
(419) 734-6845; Fax: (419) 734-3860
Prosecutor: Mark Mulligan

OTTAWA COUNTY RECORDER
315 Madison St., Port Clinton 43452
(419) 734-6730
Recorder: Virginia M. Park

OTTAWA COUNTY AUDITOR
315 Madison St., Room 202, Port Clinton 43452
(419) 734-6740; Fax: (419) 734-6592
Auditor: JoEllen Regal

OTTAWA COUNTY SHERIFF
315 Madison St., Room 110, Port Clinton 43452
(419) 734-4404; Fax: (419) 734-6876
Sheriff: Robert Bratton

OTTAWA COUNTY TREASURER
Courthouse, Room 201, Port Clinton 43452-1995
(419) 734-6750
Treasurer: Jacqueline Chapman

PAULDING COUNTY

PAULDING COUNTY COMMON PLEAS COURT
Courthouse, 2nd Floor, Suite 201, 115 N. Williams St.,
Paulding 45879-1298 (419) 399-8220; Fax: (419) 399-8224
Judge: J. David Webb

PAULDING COUNTY PROBATE/JUVENILE COURT
Courthouse, Room 202, 115 N. Williams St.,
Paulding 45879 (419) 399-8255; Fax: (419) 399-8261
Judge: John A. DeMuth

PAULDING COUNTY COURT
201 E. Caroline St., Suite 2, Paulding 45879-1204
(419) 399-2792; Fax: (419) 399-3421
Judge: Timothy R. Pieper
Clerk: Sandra C. Bowers

County Offices

PAULDING COUNTY BOARD OF COMMISSIONERS
Courthouse, Suite B1, 115 N. Williams St., Paulding 45879
(419) 399-8215; Fax: (419) 399-8299
President: Tony Burkley
Commissioners:
Martin Harmon   Ron Lane
Clerk: Joanne M. Goerlitz

Paulding County—Cont'd

PAULDING COUNTY CLERK OF COURTS
County Courthouse, Suite 104, 115 N. Williams St.,
Paulding 45879 (419) 399-8210; Fax: (419) 399-8248
Clerk of Courts: Elenor J. Edwards

PAULDING COUNTY CORONER
220 W. Perry St., Paulding 45879 (419) 399-3771
Coroner: Larry B. Fishbaugh

PAULDING COUNTY PROSECUTOR
1121/2 N. Water St., Paulding 45879
(419) 399-8270; Fax: (419) 399-2358
Prosecutor: Joseph R. Burkard

PAULDING COUNTY RECORDER
Courthouse, 115 N. Williams St., Paulding 45879
(419) 399-8275; Fax: (419) 399-2862
Recorder: Kathryn Sue Thrasher

PAULDING COUNTY AUDITOR
Courthouse, 115 N. Williams St., Paulding 45879
(419) 399-8205; Fax: (419) 399-5713
Auditor: Bill Bolenbaugh

PAULDING COUNTY SHERIFF
112 S. Williams St., Paulding 45879
(419) 399-3791; Fax: (419) 399-3216
Sheriff: David L. Harrow

PAULDING COUNTY TREASURER
115 N. Williams St., Paulding 45879
(419) 399-8281; Fax: (419) 399-8268
Treasurer: Greig Edwards

PERRY COUNTY

PERRY COUNTY COMMON PLEAS COURT
P.O. Box 7, New Lexington 43764
(740) 342-1204; Fax: (740) 342-5500
Judge: Linton D. Lewis, Jr.

PERRY COUNTY PROBATE/JUVENILE COURT
Courthouse, 105 Main St., P.O. Box 167,
New Lexington 43764
(740) 342-1118, 342-1493; Fax: (740) 342-5524
E-mail: pcjuv@perrycountycourt.com
Judge: Luann Cooperrider

PERRY COUNTY COURT
105 N. Main St., P.O. Box 207, New Lexington 43764-0207
(740) 342-3156; Fax: (740) 342-2188
Judge: Dean L. Wilson
Clerk: Lorinda Wollenberg

County Offices

PERRY COUNTY BOARD OF COMMISSIONERS
121 W. Brown St., P.O. Box 248, New Lexington 43764
(740) 342-2045; Fax: (740) 342-5505
Commissioners:
Thad Cooperrider   Lonnie Wood
Fred Shriner
Clerk: Gene Dibari

PERRY COUNTY CLERK OF COURTS
105 N. Main St., P.O. Box 67, New Lexington 43764
(740) 342-1022; Fax: (740) 342-5527
Clerk of Courts: Timothy Wollenberg

PERRY COUNTY CORONER
7756 State Rt. 37 E., New Lexington 43764
(740) 342-3540; Fax: (740) 342-3879
Coroner: Bradley C. Wilson

PERRY COUNTY ENGINEER
2645 Old Somerset Rd., P.O. Box 29, New Lexington 43764
(740) 342-2191; Fax: (740) 342-5502
Engineer: Kenton C. Cannon

PERRY COUNTY PROSECUTOR
111 N. High St., P.O. Box 569, New Lexington 43764
(740) 342-4582; Fax: (740) 342-3577
Prosecutor: Joseph A. Flautt

PERRY COUNTY RECORDER
105 N. Main St., P.O. Box 147, New Lexington 43764
(740) 342-2494; Fax: (740) 342-5539
Recorder: Barbara J. Fox

PERRY COUNTY AUDITOR
105 N. Main St., P.O. Box 127, New Lexington 43764
(740) 342-2074; Fax: (740) 342-1627
Auditor: Larry Householder

PERRY COUNTY SHERIFF
110 W. Brown St., P.O. Box 107, New Lexington 43764
(740) 342-4123; Fax: (740) 342-5521
Sheriff: William R. Barker

PERRY COUNTY TREASURER
105 N. Main St., P.O. Box 288, New Lexington 43764
(740) 342-1235; Fax: (740) 342-4710
Treasurer: David R. Wilson

PICKAWAY COUNTY

PICKAWAY COUNTY COMMON PLEAS COURT
Courthouse, 2nd Floor, 207 S. Court St., Circleville 43113
(740) 474-6026; Fax: (740) 477-6334
Judge: P. Randall Knece

PICKAWAY COUNTY PROBATE/JUVENILE COURT
Courthouse, 207 S. Court St., Circleville 43113
Probate: (740) 474-3950; Probate Fax: (740) 477-3852;
Juvenile: (740) 474-3117; Juvenile Fax: (740) 474-8451
Judge: Jan Michael Long; E-mail: jlong@pickaway.org
Chief Admin. Officers:
Dianne Hopkins   Andi Humphries

CIRCLEVILLE MUNICIPAL COURT
151 E. Franklin St., P.O. Box 128, Circleville 43113
(740) 474-3171; Fax: (740) 420-3041
Internet: www.circlevillecourt.com
Judge: John R. Adkins
(740) 474-3175; Fax: (740) 477-8291
E-mail: john@circlevillecourt.com
Clerk: Rob Reeser

County Offices

PICKAWAY COUNTY BOARD OF COMMISSIONERS
139 W. Franklin St., Circleville 43113
(740) 474-6093; Fax: (740) 474-8988
President: Ula Jean Metzler
Commissioners:
Glenn Reeser   John A. Stevenson
Clerk: Patricia A. Webb
Administrator: Daniel V. Bradhurst

PICKAWAY COUNTY CLERK OF COURTS
Courthouse, 207 S. Court St., Circleville 43113
(740) 474-5231; Fax: (740) 477-3976
Clerk of Courts: James W. Dean

PICKAWAY COUNTY CORONER
111 Island Rd., Circleville 43113
(740) 474-8818; Fax: (740) 477-6452
Coroner: Michael E. Geron

PICKAWAY COUNTY ENGINEER
Courthouse, 207 S. Court St., Circleville 43113
(740) 474-3360; Fax: (740) 477-1245
Engineer: Robert E. Parker

PICKAWAY COUNTY PROSECUTOR
118 E. Main St., P.O. Box 910, Circleville 43113
(740) 474-6066; Fax: (740) 477-7475
Prosecutor: P. Eugene Long

Pickaway County—Cont'd

PICKAWAY COUNTY RECORDER
Courthouse, 207 S. Court St., Circleville 43113
(740) 474-5826; Fax: (740) 477-6361
Recorder: Joyce R. Gilford

PICKAWAY COUNTY AUDITOR
Courthouse, 207 S. Court St., Circleville 43113
(740) 474-4765; Fax: (740) 474-4956
Auditor: Melissa A. Betz

PICKAWAY COUNTY SHERIFF
600 Island Rd., P.O. Box 710, Circleville 43113
(740) 477-6000; Fax: (740) 474-1798
Sheriff: Dwight E. Radcliff

PICKAWAY COUNTY TREASURER
Courthouse, 207 S. Court St., Circleville 43113
(740) 474-2370; Fax: (740) 477-2386
Treasurer: Ellery S. Elick

PIKE COUNTY

PIKE COUNTY COMMON PLEAS COURT
100 E. Second St., Waverly 45690-1302
(740) 947-2212; Fax: (740) 947-1729
Judge: Randy D. Deering; E-mail: judge@zoomnet.net

PIKE COUNTY PROBATE/JUVENILE COURT
230 Waverly Plaza, Suite 600, Waverly 45690-1385
Probate: (740) 947-2560; Juvenile: (740) 947-5914
Judge: William Wray Bevens
Court Administrator: Lori Caskey

PIKE COUNTY COURT
230 Waverly Plz., Suite 900, Waverly 45690
(740) 947-4003; Fax: (740) 947-7644
Judge: Cassandra Bolt-Meredith
Clerk: Theresa Parmeter

County Offices

PIKE COUNTY BOARD OF COMMISSIONERS
230 Waverly Plz., Suite 1000, Waverly 45690
(740) 947-4817; Fax: (740) 947-5065
Chairman: James A. Brushart
Commissioners:
John Harbert   Harry Rider
Clerk: Carolyn Remy

PIKE COUNTY CLERK OF COURTS
100 E. Second St., 2nd Floor, Waverly 45690
(740) 947-2715; Fax: (740) 947-1729
Clerk of Courts: John E. Williams
Hours: Weekdays, 8:30 A.M.-4 P.M.

PIKE COUNTY CORONER
100 Indian Ridge Dr., Piketon 45661 (740) 289-1548
Coroner: Thomas Valley

PIKE COUNTY ENGINEER
502 S. Pike St., Waverly 45690
(740) 947-4259; Fax: (740) 947-9339
Engineer: Denny Salisbury

PIKE COUNTY RECORDER
230 Waverly Plz., Suite 500, Waverly 45690
(740) 947-2622; Fax: (740) 947-7997
Recorder: Joyce Leeth

PIKE COUNTY AUDITOR
230 Waverly Plz., Suite 200, Waverly 45690
(740) 947-2713; Fax: (740) 947-5065
Auditor: Teddy L. Wheeler

PIKE COUNTY SHERIFF
116 Market St., Waverly 45690
(740) 947-2111; Fax: (740) 947-1049
Sheriff: Larry D. Travis

PIKE COUNTY TREASURER
230 Waverly Plz., Suite 300, Waverly 45690
(740) 947-2472; Fax: (740) 947-5065
Treasurer: Donald Ed Davis

PORTAGE COUNTY

PORTAGE COUNTY COMMON PLEAS COURT
Courthouse, 203 W. Main St., Ravenna 44266-2778
Civil, Criminal, Appeals: (330) 297-3644;
Fax: (330) 297-4554
Judges:
John A. Enlow (330) 297-3866; Fax: (330) 297-4589
Laurie J. Pittman (330) 297-3858; Fax: (330) 297-5370

PORTAGE COUNTY PROBATE COURT
203 W. Main St., 3rd Floor, P.O. Box 936, Ravenna 44266
(330) 297-3870; Fax: (330) 298-1100
Judge: Thomas J. Carnes

PORTAGE COUNTY JUVENILE COURT
8000 Infirmary Rd., Ravenna 44266
(330) 297-0881; Fax: (330) 297-2227
Judge: Thomas J. Carnes
Chief Magistrate: James J. Aylward
Magistrate: Joseph Szymanski
Chief Deputy Clerk: Sheila Cecora
Court Administrator: Denise Metropulos-Tharp

PORTAGE COUNTY DOMESTIC RELATIONS COURT
Courthouse, 203 W. Main St., Ravenna 44266-2788
(330) 297-3880; Fax: (330) 296-0190
Judge: Joseph Giulitto
Clerk: Linda K. Fankhauser (330) 297-3644

PORTAGE COUNTY MUNICIPAL COURT
Ravenna Division, 203 W. Main St., P.O. Box 958,
Ravenna 44266-0958
Criminal/Traffic: (330) 297-3639; Fax: (330) 297-5867;
Civil: (330) 297-3635; Fax: (330) 297-3526

Kent Division, 214 S. Water St., Kent 44240
Criminal/Traffic: (330) 678-9100;
Criminal/Traffic Fax: (330) 677-9944;
Civil: (330) 678-9170; Civil Fax: (330) 677-9944
Judges:
Barbara Roush Watson (Presiding)
(350) 297-4277; Fax: (350) 297-4283
William A. Nome
(330) 297-3629; Fax: (330) 298-3033
Court Administrator: Carolynne Sendry
(330) 297-3625; Fax: (330) 298-1112

County Offices

PORTAGE COUNTY BOARD OF COMMISSIONERS
County Administration Bldg., 449 S. Meridian St.,
Ravenna 44266-1217 (330) 297-3600; Fax: (330) 297-3610
Commissioners:
Christopher Smeiles (330) 297-3605
Maureen T. Frederick (330) 297-3604
Charles W. Keiper II (330) 297-3606
Clerk: Deborah Mazanec (330) 297-3895

PORTAGE COUNTY CLERK OF COURTS
203 W. Main St., P.O. Box 1035, Ravenna 44266
Domestic Relations: (330) 297-3475; Fax: (330) 297-4268;
Civil, Criminal, Appeals: (330) 297-3644;
Fax: (330) 297-4554
Clerk of Courts: Linda Fankhauser (330) 297-3644

PORTAGE COUNTY CORONER
449 S. Meridian St., Ravenna 44266
(330) 296-5015; Fax: (330) 298-2059
Coroner: Roger Marcial

Portage County—Cont'd

PORTAGE COUNTY ENGINEER
5000 Newton Falls Rd., Ravenna 44266
(330) 296-6411; Fax: (330) 296-2303
Engineer: Michael A. Marozzi

PORTAGE COUNTY PROSECUTOR
466 S. Chestnut St., Ravenna 44266
(330) 297-3850; Fax: (330) 297-3856
Prosecutor: Victor V. Vigluicci

PORTAGE COUNTY RECORDER
Administration Bldg., 449 S. Meridian St., Ravenna 44266
(330) 297-3553; Fax: (330) 297-7349
Recorder: Bonnie Howe

PORTAGE COUNTY AUDITOR
Administration Bldg., 449 S. Meridian St., Ravenna 44266
(330) 297-3561; Fax: (330) 297-4560
Auditor: Janet Esposito

PORTAGE COUNTY SHERIFF
8240 Infirmary Rd., Ravenna 44266
(330) 296-5100; Fax: (330) 297-3402
Sheriff: Duane W. Kaley

PORTAGE COUNTY TREASURER
Administration Bldg., 449 S. Meridian St., Ravenna 44266
(330) 297-3586; Fax: (330) 297-3393
Treasurer: Steve Shanafelt
    (330) 297-3566; Fax: (330) 297-3610

PREBLE COUNTY

PREBLE COUNTY COMMON PLEAS COURT
Courthouse, 101 E. Main St., Eaton 45320-1758
(937) 456-8165; Fax: (937) 456-9548
Judge: David N. Abruzzo

PREBLE COUNTY PROBATE/JUVENILE COURT
Courthouse, 2nd Floor, 101 E. Main St., Eaton 45320-1791
(937) 456-8136; Fax: (937) 456-5803
Judge: Wilfrid G. Dues

EATON MUNICIPAL COURT
1199 Preble Dr., P.O. Box 65, Eaton 45320
(937) 456-6204; Fax: (937) 456-4685
Internet: www.eatonmunicipalcourt.com
Judge: Paul D. Henry
Clerk: Bertha Miley-Kalil

County Offices

PREBLE COUNTY BOARD OF COMMISSIONERS
Courthouse, 101 E. Main St., Eaton 45320-1791
(937) 456-8143; Fax: (937) 456-8114
Commissioners:
Jane Marshall   David Wesler
  (President)   William B. Withrow
Clerk: Connie C. Crowell

PREBLE COUNTY CLERK OF COURTS
Courthouse, 3rd Floor, 101 E. Main St., Eaton 45320
(937) 456-8160; Fax: (937) 456-9548
Clerk of Court: Christopher B. Washington

PREBLE COUNTY CORONER
103 N. Barron, Eaton 45320 (937) 456-4618
Coroner: John A. Vosler

PREBLE COUNTY ENGINEER
1000 Preble Dr., Eaton 45320
(937) 456-4600; Fax: (937) 456-4606
Engineer: J. Stephen Simmons

PREBLE COUNTY PROSECUTOR
101 E. Main St., 1st Floor, Eaton 45320
(937) 456-8156; Fax: (937) 456-8199
Prosecutor: Martin P. Votel

PREBLE COUNTY RECORDER
101 E. Main St., Eaton 45320 (937) 456-8173
Recorder: William J. Spahr

PREBLE COUNTY AUDITOR
101 E. Main St., Eaton 45320
(937) 456-8148; Fax: (937) 456-8108
Auditor: Harold E. Yoder

PREBLE COUNTY SHERIFF
Courthouse, 101 E. Main St., Eaton 45320 (937) 456-6262
Sheriff: Michael Simpson

PREBLE COUNTY TREASURER
Courthouse, 2nd Floor, 101 E. Main St., Eaton 45320
(937) 456-8141
Treasurer: Brenda White

PUTNAM COUNTY

PUTNAM COUNTY COMMON PLEAS COURT
Courthouse, Suite 302, 245 E. Main St., Ottawa 45875
(419) 523-6200; Fax: (419) 523-5284
Judge: Randall L. Basinger
    E-mail: basinger@nwbright.net

PUTNAM COUNTY PROBATE/JUVENILE COURT
Courthouse, Suite 204, 245 E. Main St., Ottawa 45875-1963
(419) 523-3012; Fax: (419) 523-9291
Judge: Daniel R. Gerschutz
Deputy Clerk: Linda Schimmoeller

PUTNAM COUNTY COURT
Courthouse, 245 E. Main St., Ottawa 45875-1956
(419) 523-3110; Fax: (419) 523-5284
Judges:
    Chad Niese; E-mail: cniese@who.rr.com
    Michael E. O'Malley; E-mail: momalley@woh.rr.com
Clerk: Teresa Lammers

County Offices

PUTNAM COUNTY BOARD OF COMMISSIONERS
245 E. Main St., Suite 101, Ottawa 45875-1968
(419) 523-3656; Fax: (419) 523-9213
Commissioners:
Tom A. Price   Vincent T. Schroeder
Robert A. Riepenhoff
Clerk: Betty Schroeder

PUTNAM COUNTY CLERK OF COURTS
245 E. Main St., Suite 301, Ottawa 45875
(419) 523-3110; Fax: (419) 523-5284
Clerk of Courts: Teresa Lammers

PUTNAM COUNTY CORONER
5580 State Rt. 12, P.O. Box 299, Pandora 45877
(419) 384-3251
Coroner: Oliver N. Lugibihl

PUTNAM COUNTY ENGINEER
245 E. Main St., Suite 205, Ottawa 45875 (419) 523-6931
Engineer: Terrence R. Recker

PUTNAM COUNTY PROSECUTOR
125 W. Main St., Suite 303, Ottawa 45875 (419) 523-3600
Prosecutor: Gary Lammers

PUTNAM COUNTY RECORDER
245 E. Main St., Suite 202, Ottawa 45875
(419) 523-6490; Fax: (419) 523-4403
Recorder: Cathy Recker

PUTNAM COUNTY AUDITOR
245 E. Main St., P.O. Box 345, Ottawa 45875
(419) 523-6686; Fax: (419) 523-6390
Auditor: Marlene T. Lahey

PUTNAM COUNTY SHERIFF
1035 Heritage Trail, Ottawa 45875 (419) 523-3208
Sheriff: James Beutler

PUTNAM COUNTY TREASURER
245 E. Main St., Suite 203, Ottawa 45875 (419) 523-6588
Treasurer: Robert L. Benroth

RICHLAND COUNTY

RICHLAND COUNTY COMMON PLEAS COURT
50 Park Ave., E., Mansfield 44902-1888
Judges:
  James DeWeese
  (419) 774-5567; Fax: (419) 774-5516
  E-mail: judgedeweese@kosinet.com
  Jams D. Henson
  (419) 774-5570; Fax: (419) 774-5516
  E-mail: judgehenson@kosinet.com

RICHLAND COUNTY PROBATE COURT
50 Park Ave., E., Mansfield 44901-1896
(419) 774-5583; Fax: (419) 774-5865
Judge: Philip Alan B. Mayer

RICHLAND COUNTY JUVENILE COURT
411 S. Diamond St., Mansfield 44902
(419) 774-5578; Fax: (419) 774-5555
Judge: Ronald D. Spon

RICHLAND COUNTY DOMESTIC RELATIONS COURT
50 Park Ave., E., 3rd Floor, Mansfield 44902-1894
(419) 774-5573; Fax: (419) 774-5574
Judge: Robert L. Konstam
Clerk: Linda Frary (419) 774-5540

MANSFIELD MUNICIPAL COURT
30 N. Diamond St., Mansfield 44902
(419) 755-9633; Fax: (419) 755-9647
Judges:
  Jerry Ault (419) 755-9622
  Jeff Payton (419) 755-9616
Clerk: Gene E. Coffey

SHELBY MUNICIPAL COURT
18 W. Main St., Shelby 44875
(419) 342-2896; Fax: (419) 342-6404
Judge: Jon P. Schaefer
Clerk: Tina M. Griffitts

County Offices

RICHLAND COUNTY BOARD OF COMMISSIONERS
50 Park Ave., E., Mansfield 44902-1896
(419) 774-5550; Fax: (419) 774-5862
Commissioners:
  Edward W. Olson   Timothy A. Wert
  Gary Utt, Sr.
Clerk: Stacey L. Crall

RICHLAND COUNTY CLERK OF COURTS
50 Park Ave., E., Mansfield 44902
Mailing Address: P.O. Box 127, Mansfield 44901
Civil & Criminal: (419) 774-5690;
Domestic: (419) 774-5544;
Court of Appeals: (419) 774-5655; Fax: (419) 774-5547
Clerk of Court: Linda H. Frary

RICHLAND COUNTY CORONER
38 Park St., Suite 102, Mansfield 44902-1717
(419) 774-5868
Coroner: Stewart D. Ryckman

RICHLAND COUNTY ENGINEER
77 Mulberry St., N., Mansfield 44902-1289
(419) 774-5591; Fax: (419) 774-5539
Engineer: Thomas E. Beck

RICHLAND COUNTY PROSECUTOR
38 S. Park St., Mansfield 44902 (419) 774-5676
Prosecutor: James J. Mayer

RICHLAND COUNTY RECORDER
50 Park Ave., E., Mansfield 44902
(419) 774-5599; Fax: (419) 774-5603
Recorder: Sarah M. Davis

RICHLAND COUNTY AUDITOR
50 Park Ave., E., Mansfield 44902
(419) 774-5501; Fax: (419) 774-6309
Auditor: Patrick Dropsey

RICHLAND COUNTY SHERIFF
597 Park Ave. E., Mansfield 44905 (419) 522-6193
Sheriff: J. Steve Sheldon

RICHLAND COUNTY TREASURER
50 Park Ave., E., Mansfield 44902 (419) 774-5622
Treasurer: Daniel F. Smith

ROSS COUNTY

ROSS COUNTY COMMON PLEAS COURT
Courthouse, 2 N. Paint St., Chillicothe 45601-3109
(740) 702-3010; Fax: (740) 702-3018
Judges:
  William J. Corzine (740) 702-3036
  Nicholas H. Holmes, Jr. (740) 702-3038

ROSS COUNTY PROBATE/JUVENILE COURT
Two N. Paint St., Suite A, Chillicothe 45601-3181
Juvenile: (740) 774-1177; Juvenile Fax: (740) 774-3711;
Probate: (740) 774-1179; Probate Fax: (740) 774-3711
Judge: Richard G. Ward; E-mail: ctward@bright.net
Office Hours: Weekdays, 8 A.M.-4 P.M.

CHILLICOTHE MUNICIPAL COURT
26 S. Paint St., Chillicothe 45601-3202
(740) 773-3515; Fax: (740) 774-1101
Judges:
  Thomas E. Bunch; E-mail: tbunch@bright.net
  John B. Street (740) 774-4202
  E-mail: jbstreet@bright.net
Clerk: Roseanna J. Strong

County Offices

ROSS COUNTY BOARD OF COMMISSIONERS
2 N. Paint St., Suite H, Chillicothe 45601
(740) 702-3085; Fax: (740) 774-1602
President: James M. Caldwell
Commissioners:
  Frank X. Hirsch   Teresa Knott
Clerk: Leticia Dobbins (740) 702-3085

ROSS COUNTY CLERK OF COURTS
Courthouse, 2 N. Paint St., Chillicothe 45601
(740) 702-3010
Clerk of Courts: Ty D. Hinton

ROSS COUNTY CORONER
60 Capital Dr., Chillicothe 45601 (740) 775-7464
Coroner: John A. Gabis

ROSS COUNTY ENGINEER
755 Fairgrounds Rd., P.O. Box 458, Chillicothe 45601
(740) 702-3130
Engineer: Don E. Carnes

ROSS COUNTY PROSECUTOR
72 N. Paint St., Chillicothe 45601-2418
(740) 702-3115; Fax: (740) 702-3106
Prosecutor: Scott W. Nusbaum

ROSS COUNTY RECORDER
P.O. Box 6162, Chillicothe 45601 (740) 702-3000
Recorder: Kathy Dunn

ROSS COUNTY AUDITOR
2 N. Paint St., Suite G, Chillicothe 45601
(740) 702-3080; Fax: (740) 772-6748
Auditor: Stephen A. Neal

ROSS COUNTY SHERIFF
28 N. Paint St., Chillicothe 45601 (740) 773-1185
Sheriff: Ron Nichols

ROSS COUNTY TREASURER
Courthouse, Chillicothe 45601 (740) 702-3080
Treasurer: Jerald Byers

Courts &
Officials

SANDUSKY COUNTY

SANDUSKY COUNTY COMMON PLEAS COURT
Courthouse, 100 N. Park Ave., Fremont 43420-2454

Judges:
Harry A. Sargeant, Jr.
(419) 334-6169; Fax: (419) 334-6122
E-mail: judge2@co.sandusky.oh.us
James R. Sherck
(419) 334-6170; Fax: (419) 334-6171
E-mail: judge1@co.sandusky.oh.us

SANDUSKY COUNTY PROBATE/JUVENILE COURT
100 N. Park Ave., Fremont 43420-2476
(419) 334-6200; Fax: (419) 334-6210

Judge: Brad Culbert (419) 334-6417
E-mail: judgebc@co.sandusky.oh.us

SANDUSKY COUNTY COURT NO. 1
847 E. McPherson Hwy., P.O. Box 267, Clyde 43410-1998
(419) 547-0915; Fax: (419) 547-9198

Judge: John P. Dewey; E-mail: deweylaw@woh.rr..com
Deputy Clerk: Alice Adams

SANDUSKY COUNTY COURT NO. 2
215 W. Main St., P.O. Box 128, Woodville 43469
(419) 849-3961; Fax: (419) 849-3932

Judge: Herbert E. Adams
E-mail: woodvilljudge@co.sandusky.oh.us
Supervisor: Alice Adams
Hours: Weekdays, 8 A.M.-4:30 P.M.

BELLEVUE MUNICIPAL COURT
3000 Seneca Industrial Pkwy., Bellevue 44811
(419) 483-5880; Fax: (419) 484-8060
Jurisdiction—Counties of Huron, Sandusky; City of
Bellevue; Towns of Lyme, Sherman and York

Judge: Kenneth P. Fox
Clerk: Susan K. Meador

Court Schedule: Arraignments: Tues. mornings
Pre-trials: Mon. and Tues. morning
Civil and Small Claims: Thurs.

FREMONT MUNICIPAL COURT
323 S. Front St., P.O. Box 886, Fremont 43420-0071
(419) 332-1579; Fax: (419) 332-1570

Judge: Michael L. Burkett
Clerk: Raquel Molina

County Offices

SANDUSKY COUNTY BOARD OF COMMISSIONERS
622 Croghan St., Fremont 43420-2477
(419) 334-6100; Fax: (419) 334-6104

Commissioners:
Daniel Liskai (419) 333-6901
Brad Smith (419) 333-6903
Terry T. Thatcher (419) 333-6902
Clerk: Mary Ann Strausbaugh

SANDUSKY COUNTY CLERK OF COURTS
Courthouse, Suite 320, 100 N. Park Ave., Fremont 43420
(419) 334-6161; Fax: (419) 334-6164

Clerk of Courts: Warren Brown
Hours: Weekdays, 8 A.M.-4:30 P.M.

SANDUSKY COUNTY CORONER
2000 Countryside Dr., Fremont 43420 (419) 334-6517

Coroner: John J. Wukie

SANDUSKY COUNTY ENGINEER
2500 W. State St., Fremont 43420 (419) 334-9731

Engineer: James R. Moyer

SANDUSKY COUNTY PROSECUTOR
100 N. Park Ave., Suite 319, Fremont 43420
(419) 334-6222

Prosecutor: Thomas Stierwalt

SANDUSKY COUNTY RECORDER
100 N. Park Ave., Suite 217, Fremont 43420
(419) 334-6226

Recorder: Colleen Carmack

SANDUSKY COUNTY AUDITOR
100 N. Park Ave., Fremont 43420 (419) 334-6123

Auditor: William L. Farrell

SANDUSKY COUNTY SHERIFF
2323 Countryside Dr., Fremont 43420 (419) 332-2613

Sheriff: David G. Gangwer

SANDUSKY COUNTY TREASURER
100 N. Park Ave., Suite 227, Fremont 43420
(419) 334-6234

Treasurer: Irma Celestino

SCIOTO COUNTY

SCIOTO COUNTY COMMON PLEAS COURT
Courthouse, 602 Seventh St., Portsmouth 45662-3951

Judges:
Howard H. Harcha III
(740) 355-8207; Fax: (740) 355-8230
E-mail: hharcha@sciotocounty.net
William T. Marshall
(740) 355-8301; Fax: (740) 353-1209

SCIOTO COUNTY PROBATE/JUVENILE COURT
602 Seventh St., Portsmouth 45662-3998
Juvenile: (740) 355-8306; Probate: (740) 355-8351;
Fax: (740) 353-1095

Judge: James W. Kirsch
Magistrate Judge: Shane A. Tieman
Court Administrator: Dawn G. Keller
Chief Deputy Clerk: Pamela K. Hutchinson
Chief Probation Officer: Ronald C. Pendleton
Hours: Weekdays, 8:30 A.M.-4:30 P.M.

SCIOTO COUNTY DOMESTIC RELATIONS COURT
Courthouse, 602 Seventh St., Portsmouth 45662
(740) 355-8316; Fax: (740) 355-8205

Judge: David E. Spears

PORTSMOUTH MUNICIPAL COURT
728 Second St., Portsmouth 45662
(740) 354-3283; Fax: (740) 353-6645

Judges:
Russell D. Kegley   Richard T. Schisler
Clerk: Leroy Kegley

County Offices

SCIOTO COUNTY BOARD OF COMMISSIONERS
Courthouse, Room 1, 602 Seventh St., Portsmouth 45662
(740) 355-8313; Fax: (740) 353-7358

Commissioners:
Vern Riffe III (Chair)   Tom Reiser
Mike Crabtree
Clerk: Jane Kitts (740) 355-8202

SCIOTO COUNTY CLERK OF COURTS
Courthouse, Room 205, 602 Seventh St.,
Portsmouth 45662 (740) 355-8210

Clerk of Courts: Mildred E. Thompson

SCIOTO COUNTY CORONER
Courthouse, 602 Seventh St., Portsmouth 45662
(740) 355-0113

Coroner: Terry Johnson

SCIOTO COUNTY ENGINEER
Courthouse, Room 106, 602 Seventh St.,
Portsmouth 45662 (740) 355-8265

Engineer: Clyde S. Willis

Courts & Officials

Scioto County—Cont'd

SCIOTO COUNTY PROSECUTOR
Courthouse, 602 Seventh St., Portsmouth 45662
(740) 355-8215; Fax: (740) 355-5546
Prosecutor: Mark Kuhn

SCIOTO COUNTY RECORDER
Courthouse, 602 Seventh St., Portsmouth 45662
(740) 355-8303; Fax: (740) 355-8355
Recorder: Irene Ashley

SCIOTO COUNTY AUDITOR
Courthouse, Room 103, 602 Seventh St.,
Portsmouth 45662 (740) 355-8216
Auditor: David L. Green

SCIOTO COUNTY SHERIFF
Courthouse, Portsmouth 45662 (740) 355-8261
Sheriff: Marty V. Donini

SCIOTO COUNTY TREASURER
Courthouse, Room 102, 602 Seventh St.,
Portsmouth 45662 (740) 355-8272; Fax: (740) 355-8296
Treasurer: Margaret Gordley

SENECA COUNTY

SENECA COUNTY COMMON PLEAS COURT
Annex, Suite 4204, 117 E. Market St., Tiffin 44883
Judges:
 Michael P. Kelbley (419) 447-2982; Fax: (419) 448-7103
  E-mail: cpc1@acctiffin.com
 Steve C. Shuff (419) 448-1302; Fax: (419) 443-7927
  E-mail: scs-court@bright.net

SENECA COUNTY PROBATE/JUVENILE COURT
108 Jefferson St., Tiffin 44883-2898
Juvenile: (419) 447-4912; Probate: (419) 447-3121;
Fax: (419) 448-5060
Judge: Paul F. Kutscher, Jr.

FOSTORIA MUNICIPAL COURT
213 S. Main St., P.O. Box 985, Fostoria 44830
(419) 435-8139; Fax: (419) 435-1150
Jurisdiction—Counties of Hancock, Seneca, Wood
Judge: John D. Hadacek; E-mail: fosmunct@bright.net
Clerk: Janice Russell

TIFFIN MUNICIPAL COURT
51 E. Market St., P.O. Box 694, Tiffin 44883
(419) 448-5412; Fax: (419) 448-5419
Judge: Mark E. Repp
Clerk: Victoria Comer (419) 448-5411

County Offices

SENECA COUNTY BOARD OF COMMISSIONERS
81 Jefferson St., Suite 3202, Tiffin 44883-2354
(419) 447-4550; Fax: (419) 447-0556
Commissioners:
 Ben Nutter   Joseph E. Schock
 David Sauber
Clerk: Lucinda S. Keller (419) 443-7937

SENECA COUNTY CLERK OF COURTS
Annex-Legal Dept., Suite 4101, 117 E. Market St.,
Tiffin 44883 (419) 447-0671; Fax: (419) 443-7919
Internet: www.senecaco.org

Annex-Title Dept., Suite 4102, 117 E. Market St.,
Tiffin 44883 (419) 447-3433; Fax: (419) 443-7918
Clerk of Courts: Mary K. Ward

SENECA COUNTY CORONER
19 W. Market St., Tiffin 44883 (419) 447-8444
Coroner: Mark Akers

SENECA COUNTY ENGINEER
111 Madison St., Tiffin 44883 (419) 447-1011
Engineer: James R. Nimz

SENECA COUNTY PROSECUTOR
71 S. Washington St., Suite 1204, Tiffin 44883
(419) 448-4444; Fax: (419) 443-7911
Prosecutor: Kenneth H. Egbert, Jr.

SENECA COUNTY RECORDER
109 S. Washington St., Suite 2104, Tiffin 44883
(419) 447-4434
Recorder: Michael J. Dell

SENECA COUNTY AUDITOR
109 S. Washington St., Suite 2206, Tiffin 44883
(419) 447-0692; Fax: (419) 447-5055
Auditor: Larry Beidelschies

SENECA COUNTY SHERIFF
3040 S. State Rte. 100, Tiffin 44883
(419) 447-3456; Fax: (419) 448-5103
Sheriff: Thomas Steyer

SENECA COUNTY TREASURER
109 S. Washington St., Suite 2105, Tiffin 44883
(419) 447-1584
Treasurer: Marguerite O. Bernard

SHELBY COUNTY

SHELBY COUNTY COMMON PLEAS COURT
Courthouse, 100 E. Court St., P.O. Box 947,
Sidney 45365-0947 (937) 498-7230
Judge: John D. Schmitt
 (937) 498-7233; Fax: (937) 498-7824

SHELBY COUNTY PROBATE/JUVENILE COURT
Courthouse, 100 E. Court St., P.O. Box 4187,
Sidney 45365-4187
(937) 498-7255; Fax: (937) 498-7260;
Juvenile: (937) 498-7255; Probate: (937) 498-7263
E-mail: shelbycojuvenilecourt@earthlink.net
Judge: Norman P. Smith (937) 498-7255
Magistrate Judge: Melanie Ellis Guillozet

SIDNEY MUNICIPAL COURT
110 W. Court St., Sidney 45365
Mailing Address: 201 W. Poplar St., Sidney 45365
(937) 498-0011; Fax: (937) 498-8179
Judge: Donald G. Luce; E-mail: dluce@sidneyoh.com
Clerk: Karen S. Goffena

County Offices

SHELBY COUNTY BOARD OF COMMISSIONERS
County Annex, 129 E. Court St., Sidney 45365
(937) 498-7226; Fax: (937) 498-1293
Chairman: Dale DeLoye
Commissioners:
 Larry Kleinhans   Jack Toomey
Clerk: Pamela Steinke

SHELBY COUNTY CLERK OF COURTS
Courthouse, 100 E. Court St., P.O. Box 809, Sidney 45365
(937) 498-7221; Fax: (937) 498-4840
Clerk of Courts: Michele K. Mumford

SHELBY COUNTY CORONER
805 E. Pike St., Jackson Center 45334 (937) 596-0456
Coroner: Cheryl Mann, M.D.

SHELBY COUNTY ENGINEER
500 Gearhart Rd., Sidney 45365
(937) 498-7244; Fax: (937) 492-8411
Engineer: Robert B. Geuy

SHELBY COUNTY PROSECUTOR
126 N. Main Ave., P.O. Box 987, Sidney 45365
(937) 498-2101; Fax: (937) 492-2532
Prosecutor: James Stevenson

Shelby County—Cont'd

SHELBY COUNTY RECORDER
County Annex, 129 E. Court St., Sidney 45365
(937) 498-7270; Fax: (937) 498-7272
Recorder: Jodi Seigel

SHELBY COUNTY AUDITOR
County Annex, 129 E. Court St., Sidney 45365
(937) 498-7296; Fax: (937) 498-7292
Auditor: Joseph P. Deweese

SHELBY COUNTY SHERIFF
555 Gearhart Rd., Sidney 45365 (937) 498-1111
Sheriff: Kevin O'Leary

SHELBY COUNTY TREASURER
County Annex, 129 E. Court St., Sidney 45365
(513) 498-7298
Treasurer: Linda Meininger

STARK COUNTY

STARK COUNTY COMMON PLEAS COURT
115 Central Plz., N., Suite 400, Canton 44702-1490
(330) 451-7931; Fax: (330) 451-7740
Judges:
　Charles E. Brown (330) 451-7720
　John G. Haas (330) 451-7847
　Sara E. Lioi (330) 451-7708
　Richard D. Reinbold, Jr. (330) 451-7715
　V. Lee Sinclair (330) 451-7789

STARK COUNTY PROBATE COURT
501 Stark County Office Bldg., 110 Central Plz., S.,
Canton 44702-1413
(330) 451-7752; Fax: (330) 451-7040
Internet: www.probate.co.stark.oh.us
Judge: Dixie Park

STARK COUNTY FAMILY COURT
110 Central Plz., S., Suite 601, Canton 44702-1414
(330) 451-7415; Fax: (330) 451-7837
Judges:
　Michael L. Howard (330) 451-7922
　Jim D. James (330) 451-7307
　　E-mail: judgejames@co.stark.oh.us
　David E. Stucki (330) 451-7308
　　E-mail: judgestucki@co.stark.oh.us
Court Administrator: Richard DeHeer (330) 451-7413
　E-mail: rgdcheer@co.stark.oh.us

ALLIANCE MUNICIPAL COURT
470 E. Market, Room 16, Alliance 44601
(330) 823-6600; Fax: (330) 829-2231
Internet: www.alliancecourt.org; www.starkcjis.org
Jurisdiction—Counties of Mahoning, Stark
Judge: Robert G. Lavery
　(330) 823-6181; Fax: (330) 823-6183
Clerk: Kevin B. Ward

CANTON MUNICIPAL COURT
City Hall, 218 Cleveland Ave., S.W., Canton 44702
(330) 489-3078; Internet: www.cantoncourt.org
Judges:
　Stephen F. Belden (330) 489-3214; Fax: (330) 471-8869
　　E-mail: sfbelden@ci.canton.oh.us
　Mary A. Falvey (330) 489-3216; Fax: (330) 471-8860
　　E-mail: mafalvey@ci.canton.oh.us
　Richard J. Kubilus (330) 489-3210; Fax: (330) 471-8860
　　E-mail: rjkubilu@ci. canton.oh.us
　John A. Poulos (330) 489-3288; Fax: (330) 471-8860
Magistrate Judges:
　Lemuel Green (330) 489-3257; Fax: (330) 489-3296
　Taryn Heath (330) 489-3257; Fax: (330) 489-3296
Clerk: Tom Harmon (330) 489-3203; Fax: (330) 489-3075
Court Administrator: Michael Kochera
　(330) 430-7881; Fax: (330) 471-8860
　E-mail: mekochera@ci.canton.oh.us

MASSILLON MUNICIPAL COURT
2 James Duncan Plz., Massillon 44646
(330) 830-1730; Fax: (330) 830-1756
Judges:
　Edward J. Elum (330) 830-1727
　Richard T. Kettler (330) 830-1725
Court Administrator: Jeannie Shrider (330) 830-1729

County Offices

STARK COUNTY BOARD OF COMMISSIONERS
110 Central Plz., S., Suite 240, Canton 44702
(330) 451-7364; Fax: (330) 451-7906
Commissioners:
　Gayle A. Jackson　　　　　Jane Vignos
　Richard Regula
Clerk: Jeff Dutton

STARK COUNTY CLERK OF COURTS
115 Central Plz., N, Suite 101, P.O. Box 21160,
Canton 44701-1160 (330) 451-7795
Internet: www.starkclerk.org
Clerk of Courts: Phil G. Giavasis

STARK COUNTY CORONER
Doctor's Hospital, 400 Austin Ave., N.W., Massillon 44646
(330) 837-9299
Coroner: P.S. Murthy

STARK COUNTY ENGINEER
5165 Southway St., S.W., Canton 44706
(330) 477-6781; Fax: (330) 477-3926
Commissioner: Michael Rehfus

STARK COUNTY PROSECUTOR
110 Central Plz., S., Suite 510, Canton 44702
(330) 451-7897; Fax: (330) 451-7965
Prosecutor: John Ferrero

STARK COUNTY RECORDER
110 Central Plz., S., Suite 170, Canton 44702
(330) 451-7443; Fax: (330) 451-7394
Recorder: Rick Campbell

STARK COUNTY AUDITOR
110 Central Plz., S., Suite 240, Canton 44702
(330) 451-7357; Fax: (330) 438-0949
Auditor: Kim Perez

STARK COUNTY SHERIFF
4500 Atlantic Blvd., N.E., P.O. Box 9179, Canton 44711
(330) 430-3800
Sheriff: Timothy A. Swanson

STARK COUNTY TREASURER
110 Central Plz., S., Suite 250, Canton 44702
(330) 451-7814
Treasurer: Gary D. Zeigler

SUMMIT COUNTY

SUMMIT COUNTY COMMON PLEAS COURT
209 S. High St., Akron 44308-1610 (330) 643-2190
Judges:
　Jane Bond (330) 643-2238
　Patricia A. Cosgrove (330) 643-2228
　Judith Hunter (330) 643-2230
　James E. Murphy (330) 643-2239
　Marvin Shapiro (330) 643-2628
　Mary F. Spicer (330) 643-2247
　Brenda Burnham Unruh (330) 643-2233
　James R. Williams (330) 643-2241
Magistrate Judge: John H. Shoemaker
Court Administrator: Andrew J. Bauer

Summit County—Cont'd

SUMMIT COUNTY PROBATE COURT
209 S. High St., Akron 44308-1616
(330) 643-2330; Fax: (330) 643-2393

Judge: W. F. Spicer
E-mail: bspicer@summitohioprobate.com

SUMMIT COUNTY JUVENILE COURT
650 Dan St., Akron 44310
(330) 643-2900; Fax: (330) 643-2987

Judge: Linda Tucci Teodosio (330) 643-2995
E-mail: lteodosio@cpcourt.summitoh.net

SUMMIT COUNTY DOMESTIC RELATIONS COURT
209 S. High St., Akron 44308-1610
(330) 643-2365; Fax: (330) 643-2126

Judges:
Carol J. Dezso (330) 643-2357
John P. Quinn (330) 643-2080
Moving to new building, July 2005.

AKRON MUNICIPAL COURT
217 S. High St., Akron 44308-1611
(330) 375-2120

Judges:
Edna J. Boyle
(330) 375-2054; Fax: (330) 375-2238
E-mail: boyleed@ci.akron.oh.us
Lynne S. Callahan
(330) 375-2009; Fax: (330) 375-2123
E-mail: callaly@ci.akron.oh.us
Kathryn Culver
(330) 375-2053; Fax: (330) 375-2229
E-mail: culveka@ci.akron.oh.us
John E. Holcomb
(330) 375-2052; Fax: (330) 375-2474
E-mail: holcojo@ci.akron.oh.us
Alison McCarty
(330) 375-2611; Fax: (330) 375-2642
E-mail: mccaral@ci.akron.oh.us
Annalisa S. Williams
(330) 375-2007; Fax: (330) 375-2514
E-mail: willia@akron.oh.us

Court Administrator: Kenneth Kuckuck
(330) 375-2120; Fax: (330) 375-2303
E-mail: kuckuke@ci.akron.oh.us

BARBERTON MUNICIPAL COURT
Municipal Bldg., 576 W. Park Ave., Barberton 44203-2584
(330) 753-2261; Fax: (330) 848-6779
Internet: www.cityofbarberton.com/clerkofcourts
Jurisdiction—County of Summit; Cities of Barberton,
Green, Norton, Coventry, Franklin, Copley and Clinton

Judges:
Michael J. McNulty (330) 861-7215
Michael L. Weigand (330) 861-7217

Clerk: Andrea L. Norris (330) 861-7194
Court Schedule: Arraignments: Weekdays, 9 A.M or
1 P.M.; Sat., 9 A.M.
Hours: Weekdays, 8 A.M.-8 P.M.; Sat., 8-11 A.M.

CUYAHOGA FALLS MUNICIPAL COURT
2310 Second St., Cuyahoga Falls 44221
(330) 971-8280; Fax: (330) 928-7722

Judges:
Lisa Lynne Coates   Kim R. Hoover

Clerk: Eric M. Czetli
(330) 971-8110; Fax: (330) 971-8114

County Offices

SUMMIT COUNTY COUNCIL
175 S. Main St., 7th Floor, Akron 44308-1314
(330) 643-2725; Fax: (330) 643-2531
Members:
Nick Kostandaras (District 1)
Tom Teodosio (District 2)
Louise L. Heydorn (District 3)
Pete Crossland (District 4)
Cazzell M. Smith, Sr. (District 5)
Daniel Congrove (District 6)
Tim Crawford (District 7, V.P.)
Paula Prentice (District 8)
Paul Gallagher (At-Large)
Clair Dickinson (At-Large, President)
Michael T. Callahan (At-Large)
County Executive: James B. McCarthy
(330) 643-2510; Fax: (330) 643-2507
Clerk: David E. Hannan

SUMMIT COUNTY CLERK OF COURTS
53 University Ave., 2nd Floor, Akron 44308-1591
(330) 643-2217
Clerk of Courts: Diana Zaleski (330) 643-2211

SUMMIT COUNTY MEDICAL EXAMINER
85 N. Summit St., Akron 44308
(330) 643-2101; Fax: (330) 643-2100
Medical Examiner: Dr. Lisa Kohler

SUMMIT COUNTY ENGINEER
538 E. South St., Akron 44311
(330) 643-2850; Fax: (330) 762-7829
Engineer: Greg Bachman

SUMMIT COUNTY PROSECUTOR
53 University Ave., 6th Floor, Akron 44308-2137
(330) 643-2800; Fax: (330) 643-2137
Prosecutor: Sherri Bevan-Walsh

SUMMIT COUNTY SHERIFF
53 University Ave., 4th Floor, Akron 44308
(330) 643-2111; Fax: (330) 643-8117
Sheriff: Drew Alexander

SUMMIT COUNTY FISCAL OFFICER
175 S. Main St., 3rd Floor, Akron 44308
(330) 643-7934; Fax: (330) 643-2864
Fiscal Officer: John A. Donofrio

TRUMBULL COUNTY

TRUMBULL COUNTY COMMON PLEAS COURT
161 High St., N.W., Warren 44481-1006
Fax: (330) 675-2580
Judges:
Peter J. Kontos (330) 675-2569
Andrew D. Logan (330) 675-2564
W. Wyatt McKay (330) 675-2577
John M. Stuard (330) 675-2534

TRUMBULL COUNTY PROBATE COURT
161 High St., N.W., Warren 44481-1230
(330) 675-2521; Fax: (330) 675-3024
Internet: www.trumbullprobate.org
Judge: Thomas A. Swift
E-mail: swift@trumbullprobate.org

TRUMBULL COUNTY FAMILY COURT
220 S. Main St., Warren 44482
(330) 675-2600; Fax: (330) 675-2322
Judges:
Richard L. James (330) 675-2605
E-mail: drjames@co.trumbull.oh.us
Pamela A. Rintala (330) 675-2341
E-mail: drrintal@co.trumbull.oh.us
Clerk: Margaret O'Brien (330) 675-2302

Courts &
Officials

Trumball County—Cont'd

County Court

TRUMBULL COUNTY COURT CENTRAL DISTRICT
180 N. Mecca St., Cortland 44410
(330) 637-5023; Fax: (330) 637-5021
Jurisdiction—County of Trumbull; City of Cortland,
Bazetta Township, Johnston Township, Fowler Township,
Greene Township
Judge: Thomas A. Campbell
Clerk: Evelyn Shelton
Court Schedule: Mon., Wed. and Fri., 9 A.M.

TRUMBULL COUNTY COURT EASTERN DISTRICT
7130 Brookwood Dr., Brookfield 44403
Civil: (330) 448-4492; Traffic/Criminal: (330) 448-1726;
Probation: (330) 448-6210; Fax: (330) 448-6310
Judge: Ronald J. Rice; E-mail: rjcolpa@msn.com
Clerk: Rosemary Livingston
Court Schedule: Civil Court: Mon.; Traffic/Criminal Court:
Thurs.

GIRARD MUNICIPAL COURT
Girard Justice Center, Suite A, 100 N. Market St.,
Girard 44420 (330) 545-3177; Fax: (330) 545-7045
Jurisdiction—County of Trumbull; Cities of Girard and
Hubbard; Townships of Hubbard, Liberty and Vienna
Judge: Michael A. Bernard
Clerk: Karen A. Constantino

NEWTON FALLS MUNICIPAL COURT
19 N. Canal St., Newton Falls 44444
(330) 872-0302; Fax: (330) 872-3899
Judge: Thomas L. Old
Clerk: Betty A. Heber (330) 872-0232
Court Schedule: Arraignments: Mon.-Thurs., 9 A.M.; Civil:
Mon., 1 P.M; Contested Hearings: 1 P.M. Tues. and Thurs.

NILES MUNICIPAL COURT
15 E. State St., Niles 44446
(330) 652-5863; Fax: (330) 544-9025
Judge: Thomas W. Townley
Clerk: Paul D. Lawrence

WARREN MUNICIPAL COURT
141 South St., P.O. Box 1550, Warren 44482-1550
(330) 841-2525; Fax: (330) 841-2760
Judges:
  Thomas P. Gysegem; E-mail: tgysegem@warren.org
  Terry Ivanchak; E-mail: tyivan@warren.org
Clerk: Margaret M. Scott; E-mail: mscott@warren.org

County Offices

TRUMBULL COUNTY BOARD OF COMMISSIONERS
Administration Bldg., 160 High St., Warren 44481
(330) 675-2451; Fax: (330) 675-2462
President: Daniel E. Polivka
Commissioners:
Paul E. Heltzel   James G. Tsagaris

TRUMBULL COUNTY CLERK OF COURTS
Courthouse, 161 High St., Warren 44481 (330) 675-2557
Clerk of Courts: Karen Infante Allen

TRUMBULL COUNTY CORONER
1863 E. Market St., Warren 44483 (330) 675-2516
Coroner: Ted W. Soboslay

TRUMBULL COUNTY ENGINEER
650 N. River Rd., N.W., Warren 44483 (330) 675-2640
Engineer: John D. Latell

TRUMBULL COUNTY PROSECUTOR
160 High St., Warren 44481 (330) 675-2426
Prosecutor: Dennis Watkins

TRUMBULL COUNTY RECORDER
Administration Bldg., 160 High St., Warren 44481
(330) 675-2401; Fax: (330) 675-2404
Recorder: Diana J. Marchese

TRUMBULL COUNTY AUDITOR
Administration Bldg., 160 High St., Warren 44481
(330) 675-2420; Fax: (330) 675-2419
Auditor: David Hines

TRUMBULL COUNTY SHERIFF
150 High St., Warren 44481 (330) 675-2508
Sheriff: Thomas L. Altiere

TRUMBULL COUNTY TREASURER
160 High St., Warren 44481 (330) 675-2436
Treasurer: Christ Michelakis

TUSCARAWAS COUNTY

TUSCARAWAS COUNTY COMMON PLEAS COURT
Courthouse, 101 E. High Ave., New Philadelphia 44663-2599
(330) 365-3217
Judges:
  Edward E. O'Farrell (330) 365-3213
    E-mail: ofarrell@co.tuscarawas.oh.us
  Elizabeth Lehigh Thomakos (330) 365-3289
    E-mail: thomakos@co.tuscarawas.oh.us
Administrator: Elizabeth W. Stephenson (330) 365-3299

TUSCARAWAS COUNTY PROBATE/JUVENILE COURT
Courthouse, 101 E. High Ave.,
New Philadelphia 44663-2636
(330) 365-3266; Fax: (330) 364-3190
Judge: Linda A. Kate

TUSCARAWAS COUNTY COURT
220 E. Third St., Uhrichsville 44683
(740) 922-4795; Fax: (740) 922-7020
Judge: Brad L. Hillyer
Clerk: Carol A. Ross

NEW PHILADELPHIA MUNICIPAL COURT
166 E. High Ave., New Philadelphia 44663
(330) 343-6797; Fax: (330) 364-6885
Judge: Mary Wade Space
Clerk: Glorya J. Metzger

County Offices

TUSCARAWAS COUNTY BOARD OF COMMISSIONERS
Courthouse, 125 E. High Ave.,
New Philadelphia 44663-2573
(330) 364-8811, Ext. 3240; Fax: (330) 602-7483
President: Jim Seldenright
Commissioners:
Chris Aubihl   Kerry Metzger

TUSCARAWAS COUNTY CLERK OF COURTS
Courthouse, Room 230, 125 E. High Ave.,
New Philadelphia 44663-0628 (330) 365-3243
Internet: www.co.tuscarawas.oh.us
Clerk of Courts: Rockne W. Clarke
    E-mail: clerke@co.tuscarawas.oh.us

TUSCARAWAS COUNTY CORONER
Twin City Hospital, N. First & Fuhr St., Dennison 44621
(740) 922-2800
Coroner: James G. Hubert

TUSCARAWAS COUNTY ENGINEER
832 Front Ave., S.W., New Philadelphia 44663
(330) 339-6648
Engineer: Joe S. Bachman

TUSCARAWAS COUNTY PROSECUTOR
Courthouse, 125 E. High Ave., New Philadelphia 44663
(330) 364-8811, Ext. 3214
Prosecutor: Amanda Spies Bornhorst

Courts & Officials

Tuscarawas County—Cont'd

TUSCARAWAS COUNTY RECORDER
125 E. High Ave., New Philadelphia 44663
(330) 364-8811, Ext. 3284
Recorder: Lori Smith

TUSCARAWAS COUNTY AUDITOR
Courthouse, 125 E. High Ave., New Philadelphia 44663
(330) 364-8811, Ext. 3220
Auditor: J. Matthew Judy

TUSCARAWAS COUNTY SHERIFF
2295 Reiser Ave., S.E., New Philadelphia 44663
(330) 343-7731
Sheriff: Walt Wilson

TUSCARAWAS COUNTY TREASURER
Courthouse, 125 E. High Ave., P.O. Box 250,
New Philadelphia 44663 (330) 364-8811, Ext. 3254
Treasurer: Jeff Mamarella

UNION COUNTY

UNION COUNTY COMMON PLEAS COURT
Courthouse, 215 W. Fifth St., P.O. Box 723, Marysville 43040
(937) 645-3006
Internet: www.co.union.oh.us
Judge: Richard E. Parrott
(937) 645-3015; Fax: (937) 645-3149
E-mail: parrott@urec.net

UNION COUNTY PROBATE/JUVENILE COURT
Courthouse, 215 W. Fifth St., Marysville 43040
(937) 645-3029; Fax: (937) 645-3160
Judge: Charlotte Coleman Eufinger

MARYSVILLE MUNICIPAL COURT
125 E. Sixth St., P.O. Box 322, Marysville 43040
(937) 644-9102; Fax: (937) 644-1228
Judge: Michael J. Grigsby
Clerk: Charles E. Crowley
Hours: Weekdays, 8 A.M.-4 P.M.

County Offices

UNION COUNTY BOARD OF COMMISSIONERS
233 W. Sixth St., Marysville 43040-1526
(937) 645-3012; Fax: (937) 645-3002
E-mail: commissioners@co.union.oh.us
President: Thomas A. McCarthy
Commissioners:
Charles Hall   Gary Lee
Clerk: Rebecca Roush

UNION COUNTY CLERK OF COURTS
Courthouse, 215 W. Fifth St., Marysville 43040
(937) 645-3006; Fax: (937) 645-3162
Clerk of Courts: Paula P. Warner

UNION COUNTY CORONER
221 W. 5th St., Marysville 43040
(937) 645-4145; Fax: (937) 645-4170
Coroner: David T. Applegate II

UNION COUNTY ENGINEER
233 W. Sixth St., Marysville 43040
(937) 645-3018; Fax: (937) 645-3161
Engineer: Steve A. Stolte

UNION COUNTY PROSECUTOR
221 W. Fifth St., Marysville 43040
(937) 645-4190; Fax: (937) 645-4191
Prosecutor: Dave Phillips

UNION COUNTY RECORDER
233 W. Sixth St., Marysville 43040
(937) 645-3032; Fax: (937) 642-3397
Recorder: Teresa Markham

UNION COUNTY AUDITOR
233 W. Sixth St., P.O. Box 420, Marysville 43040
(937) 645-3003; Fax: (937) 645-3057
Auditor: Mary H. Snider

UNION COUNTY SHERIFF
221 W. Fifth St., Marysville 43040
(937) 645-4102; Fax: (934) 645-4170
Sheriff: Rocky Nelson

UNION COUNTY TREASURER
233 W. Sixth St., P.O. Box 420, Marysville 43040
(937) 645-3035; Fax: (937) 645-3094
Treasurer: Tamara K. Lowe

VAN WERT COUNTY

VAN WERT COUNTY COMMON PLEAS COURT
Courthouse, 121 E. Main St., Van Wert 45891-1729
(419) 238-6935; Fax: (419) 238-2874
Judge: Charles D. Steele
E-mail: steelecharles@yahoo.com

VAN WERT COUNTY PROBATE/JUVENILE COURT
108 E. Main St., Van Wert 45891-1786
Probate: (419) 238-0027; Juvenile: (419) 238-1118;
Fax: (419) 238-7315
Judge: Rex D. Fortney
E-mail: judge@vwprobjuvcourt.net

VAN WERT MUNICIPAL COURT
124 S. Market St., Van Wert 45891
(419) 238-5767; Fax: (419) 238-5865
Judge: Phil W. Campbell
Clerk: Debra Lichtensteiger

County Offices

VAN WERT COUNTY BOARD OF COMMISSIONERS
114 E. Main St., Suite 200, Van Wert 45891-1725
(419) 238-6159; Fax: (419) 238-4528
Commissioners:
Harold L. Merkle (Chair)
E-mail: vwcocomm.merkle@bright.net
Gary D. Adams
E-mail: vwcocomm.adams@bright.net
Mr. Clair Dudgeon
E-mail: vwcocomm.dudgeon@bright.net
Clerk: Larry E. Clouse
E-mail: vwcocomm.clouse@bright.net

VAN WERT COUNTY CLERK OF COURTS
Courthouse, 121 E. Main St., P.O. Box 366,
Van Wert 45891 (419) 238-1022; Fax: (419) 238-4760
Clerk of Courts: Carol A. Speelman

VAN WERT COUNTY CORONER
140 Fox Rd., Suite F, Van Wert 45891 (419) 238-7727
Coroner: Scott Jarvis; E-mail: swjmd@bright.net

VAN WERT COUNTY ENGINEER
220 S. Market St., Van Wert 45891
(419) 238-0210; Fax: (419) 238-6372
E-mail: kwvwce@earthlink.net
Engineer: Kyle Wendel; E-mail: kwvwce@earthlink.net

VAN WERT COUNTY PROSECUTOR
101 E. Main St., Van Wert 45891
(419) 238-0272; Fax: (419) 238-2743
E-mail: cfkiiico@bright.net
Prosecutor: Charles F. Kennedy III
E-mail: cfkiiico@bright.net

VAN WERT COUNTY RECORDER
Courthouse, Room 206, 121 E. Main St., Van Wert 45891
(419) 238-2558; Fax: (419) 238-5410
E-mail: vwrecorder@earthlink.net
Recorder: Nancy Harting

Van Wert County—Cont'd

VAN WERT COUNTY AUDITOR
Courthouse, 121 E. Main St., Van Wert 45891
(419) 238-0843; Fax: (419) 238-1111
E-mail: auditor@vanwertcounty.org
Auditor: Nancy Dixon

VAN WERT COUNTY SHERIFF
113 N. Market St., Van Wert 45891
(419) 238-3866; Fax: (419) 238-9531
E-mail: vwcsd@earthlink.net
Sheriff: Stan Owens

VAN WERT COUNTY TREASURER
Courthouse, 121 E. Main St., Van Wert 45891
(419) 237-5177
E-mail: treasurer@vanwertcounty.org
Treasurer: Beverly L. Fuerst

VINTON COUNTY

VINTON COUNTY COMMON PLEAS COURT
Courthouse, 100 E. Main St., McArthur 45651-1267
Judge: Jeffrey L. Simmons
(740) 596-4319; Fax: (740) 596-9611

VINTON COUNTY PROBATE/JUVENILE COURT
Courthouse, 100 E. Main St., McArthur 45651-1267
(740) 596-5480; Fax: (740) 596-3438
Judge: N. Robert Grillo

VINTON COUNTY COURT
Courthouse, 100 E. Main St., McArthur 45651
(740) 596-5000
Judge: James P. Salter
Clerk: Rita S. Ward

County Offices

VINTON COUNTY BOARD OF COMMISSIONERS
100 E. Main St., McArthur 45651
(740) 596-4571, Ext. 221; Fax: (740) 596-2462
President: Mike Bledsoe
Commissioners:
  James Harper   Matt Sowers
Clerk: Brande Minton

VINTON COUNTY CLERK OF COURTS
Courthouse, 100 E. Main St., McArthur 45651
(740) 596-3001; Fax: (740) 596-9611
E-mail: clerkofcourts@co.vinton.oh.us
Clerk of Courts: Lisa A. Gilliland

VINTON COUNTY ENGINEER
Courthouse, 100 E. Main St., McArthur 45651
(740) 596-5144, Ext. 241
Engineer: Ronald M. Sharrett

VINTON COUNTY PROSECUTOR
Courthouse, 100 E. Main St., McArthur 45651
(740) 596-5583; Fax: (740) 596-4702
Prosecutor: Timothy P. Gleeson

VINTON COUNTY RECORDER
100 E. Main St., McArthur 45651
(740) 596-4314, Ext. 225
Recorder: Lori Graman

VINTON COUNTY AUDITOR
Courthouse, 100 E. Main St., McArthur 45651-1267
(740) 596-5445, Ext. 231; Fax: (740) 596-2462
Auditor: Cindy Owings

VINTON COUNTY SHERIFF
106 S. Market St., McArthur 45651 (740) 596-5242
Sheriff: Dave Hickey

VINTON COUNTY TREASURER
Courthouse, 100 E. Main St., McArthur 45651-0301
(740) 596-4571, Ext. 227
Treasurer: Larry E. Clary

WARREN COUNTY

WARREN COUNTY COMMON PLEAS COURT
500 Justice Dr., Lebanon 45036
Judges:
  Neal B. Bronson (513) 695-1231; Fax: (513) 695-2920
  James L. Flannery (513) 695-1149; Fax: (513) 695-1303
  James J. Heath (513) 695-1159; Fax: (513) 695-1303

WARREN COUNTY PROBATE/JUVENILE COURT
570 Justice Dr., Lebanon 45036-2361
Juvenile: (513) 695-1161; Fax: (513) 695-2948;
Probate: (513) 695-1181; Fax: (513) 695-2945
Judge: Michael E. Powell
  E-mail: poweme@co.warren.oh.us

WARREN COUNTY DOMESTIC RELATIONS COURT
500 Justice Dr., Lebanon 45036-2398
(513) 695-1344; Fax: (513) 695-2929
Judge: Timothy A. Oliver (513) 695-1340
Court Administrator: Rhonda Denny (513) 695-2586

WARREN COUNTY COURT
550 Justice Dr., Lebanon 45036
(513) 695-1370; Fax: (513) 695-2990
Jurisdiction—County of Warren; Towns of Clearcreek,
Massie, Wayne, Washington, Hamilton, Salem and Union
Judges:
  Donald E. Oda II   Dallas P. Powers
Clerk: James L. Spaeth
  E-mail: spaejl@co.warren.oh.us

FRANKLIN MUNICIPAL COURT
1 Benjamin Franklin Way, P.O. Box 292, Franklin 45005
(513) 746-2858; Fax: (513) 743-7751
E-mail: smullins@franklinohio.org
Judge: James D. Ruppert
  E-mail: jruppert@franklinohio.org
Clerk: Sherry Mullins
Court Schedule: Tues., 4 P.M.; Fri., 1 P.M.

LEBANON MUNICIPAL COURT
City Bldg., 50 S. Broadway, Lebanon 45036
(513) 933-7210; Fax: (513) 933-7212
Judge: Mark R. Bogen
Clerk: Brenda Morgan

MASON MUNICIPAL COURT
5950 Mason Montgomery Rd., Mason 45040
(513) 398-7901; Fax: (513) 459-8085
Judge: George Parker
Clerk: William Scherpenberg

MIDDLETOWN MUNICIPAL COURT
I Donham Plaza, Middletown 45042
(513) 425-7802; Fax: (513) 425-7846
Jurisdiction—Counties of Butler, Warren
Judge: Mark W. Wall (513) 425-7822
  E-mail: markw@ci.middletown.oh.us
Clerk: Louis A. Rossi (513) 425-7811
  E-mail: budr@ci.middletown.oh.us

County Offices

WARREN COUNTY BOARD OF COMMISSIONERS
406 Justice Dr., Lebanon 45036
(513) 695-1250; Fax: (513) 695-2054
President: Patricia Arnold South
Commissioners:
  C. Michael Kilburn   David G. Young
Clerk: Tina Davis

WARREN COUNTY CLERK OF COURTS
500 Justice Dr., Lebanon 45036
(513) 695-1120; Fax: (513) 695-2965
Clerk of Courts: James L. Spaeth

Warren County—Cont'd

WARREN COUNTY CORONER
406 Justice Dr., Lebanon 45036 (513) 695-1137
Coroner: Warren C. Young

WARREN COUNTY ENGINEER
105 Markey Rd., Lebanon 45036
(513) 695-1364; Fax: (513) 695-1382
Engineer: Neil F. Tunison

WARREN COUNTY PROSECUTOR
500 Justice Dr., Lebanon 45036
(513) 695-1325; Fax: (513) 695-2962
Prosecutor: Rachel Hutzel

WARREN COUNTY RECORDER
406 Justice Dr., Lebanon 45036
(513) 695-1382; Fax: (513) 695-1382
Recorder: Beth Deckard

WARREN COUNTY AUDITOR
406 Justice Dr., Lebanon 45036
(513) 695-1239; Fax: (513) 695-2960
Auditor: Nick Nelson

WARREN COUNTY SHERIFF
550 Justice Dr., Lebanon 45036 (513) 695-1280
Sheriff: Tom Ariss

WARREN COUNTY TREASURER
406 Justice Dr., Lebanon 45036 (513) 695-1300
Treasurer: James R. Aumann

WASHINGTON COUNTY

WASHINGTON COUNTY COMMON PLEAS COURT
Courthouse, 205 Putnam St., Marietta 45750-2922
(740) 373-6623; Fax: (740) 373-5713
Judges:
  Susan E. Boyer   Norman E. Lane, Jr.

WASHINGTON COUNTY PROBATE/JUVENILE COURT
Courthouse, 205 Putnam St., Marietta 45750-2922
(740) 373-6623; Fax: (740) 376-7425
E-mail: juvenilecourt@washingtongov.org
Internet: www.washingtongov.org
Judge: Timothy A. Williams, Ext. 253
  E-mail: timw@frognet.net

MARIETTA MUNICIPAL COURT
301 Putnam St., P.O. Box 615, Marietta 45750-1615
(740) 373-4474; Fax: (740) 373-2547
E-mail: clerk@mariettacourt.com
Internet: www.mariettacourt.com
Judge: Milt Nuzum III
  E-mail: judge@mariettacourt.com
Clerk: Rosanne Buell

County Offices

WASHINGTON COUNTY BOARD OF COMMISSIONERS
223 Putnam St., Marietta 45750-3087
(740) 373-6623; Fax: (740) 374-7693
Commissioners:
  Samuel R. Cook   Larry Steinel
  John Grimes
Clerk: Teresa L. Smith

WASHINGTON COUNTY CLERK OF COURTS
Courthouse, 205 Putnam St., Marietta 45750
(740) 373-6623
Clerk of Courts: Judy R. Van Dyk, Ext. 280

WASHINGTON COUNTY CORONER
400 Matthews St., Suite 22, Marietta 45750
(740) 374-4273
Coroner: Kenneth J. Leopold

WASHINGTON COUNTY ENGINEER
204 Davis Ave., Marietta 45750
(740) 376-7430; Fax: (740) 376-7084
Engineer: Robert Badger

WASHINGTON COUNTY PROSECUTOR
205 Putnam St., Marietta 45750
(740) 373-7624
Prosecutor: James Schneider

WASHINGTON COUNTY RECORDER
Courthouse, 205 Putnam St., Marietta 45750
(740) 373-6623, Ext. 236; Fax: (740) 373-9643
Recorder: Tracey C. Wright

WASHINGTON COUNTY AUDITOR
Courthouse, 205 Putnam St., Marietta 45750
(740) 373-6623; Fax: (740) 373-2085
Auditor: William McFarland

WASHINGTON COUNTY SHERIFF
Courthouse, 205 Putnam St., Marietta 45750
(740) 376-7070
Sheriff: Larry Mincks

WASHINGTON COUNTY TREASURER
Courthouse, 205 Putnam St., Marietta 45750
(740) 373-6623
Treasurer: Dorothy K. Peppel

WAYNE COUNTY

WAYNE COUNTY COMMON PLEAS COURT
107 W. Liberty St., Wooster 44691 (330) 287-5591
Judges:
  Robert J. Brown (330) 287-5540; Fax: (330) 264-2560
  Mark K. Wiest (330) 287-5530; Fax: (330) 287-5416

WAYNE COUNTY PROBATE/JUVENILE COURT
107 W. Liberty St., Wooster 44691
Probate Court: (330) 287-5575;
Juvenile Court: (330) 287-5562; Fax: (330) 287-5427
Judge: Raymond E. Leisy

WAYNE MUNICIPAL COURT
215 N. Grant St., Wooster 44691-3499
(330) 287-5650; Fax: (330) 263-4043

207 N. Main St., Orrville 44667-1639
Judges:
  D. William Evans, Jr.   Stuart K. Miller
Clerk: Carol White Millhoan
Office Hours: Weekdays, 7:30 A.M.-4:30 P.M.

County Offices

WAYNE COUNTY BOARD OF COMMISSIONERS
428 W. Liberty St., Wooster 44691
(330) 287-5406; Fax: (330) 287-5407
President: Ann M. Obrecht
Commissioners:
  Cheryl A. Noah   Scott S. Wiggam
Clerk: Diane M. Austen

WAYNE COUNTY CLERK OF COURTS
107 W. Liberty St., P.O. Box 507, Wooster 44691
(330) 287-5591; Fax: (330) 287-5416
Clerk of Courts: Carol White Millhoan

WAYNE COUNTY CORONER
201 W. North St., Wooster 44691 (330) 287-5760
Coroner: Matthew D. Morris, M.D.

WAYNE COUNTY PROSECUTOR
115 W. Liberty St., Wooster 44691
(330) 262-3030; Fax: (330) 287-5412
Prosecutor: Martin Frantz

Wayne County—Cont'd

WAYNE COUNTY RECORDER
428 W. Liberty St., Wooster 44691
(330) 287-5460; Fax: (330) 287-5685
Recorder: Jane Carmicael

WAYNE COUNTY AUDITOR
428 W. Liberty St., Wooster 44691
(330) 287-5430; Fax: (330) 287-5436
Auditor: Jarra L. Underwood

WAYNE COUNTY SHERIFF
201 W. North St., Wooster 44691 (330) 287-5750
Sheriff: Thomas G. Maurer

WAYNE COUNTY TREASURER
428 W. Liberty St., Wooster 44691
(330) 287-5450; Fax: (330) 287-5454
Treasurer: Beverly A. Shaw

WILLIAMS COUNTY

WILLIAMS COUNTY COMMON PLEAS COURT
One Courthouse Sq., Bryan 43506
Judge: Anthony L. Gretick
    (419) 636-2644; Fax: (419) 636-9886
    E-mail: gretick@email.msn.com

WILLIAMS COUNTY PROBATE/JUVENILE COURT
One Courthouse Sq., 2nd. Floor, Bryan 43506
(419) 636-1548; Fax: (419) 636-5405
Internet: www.co.williams.oh.us
Judge: Steven R. Bird; E-mail: juvcourt@wmsco.org
Court Administrator: Holly A. Schlosser

BRYAN MUNICIPAL COURT
1399 E. High St., P.O. Box 546, Bryan 43506-1819
(419) 636-6939; Fax: (419) 636-3417
Judge: Kent L. North
Clerk: Trisha M. Russell

County Offices

WILLIAMS COUNTY BOARD OF COMMISSIONERS
One Courthouse Sq., Bryan 43506-1791
(419) 636-2059; Fax: (419) 636-0643
President: Thomas Stroup
Commissioners:
    Marvin Stuckey   Duane Votaw
Clerk: Nancy Kraemer

WILLIAMS COUNTY CLERK OF COURTS
One Courthouse Sq., 3rd Floor, Bryan 43506
(419) 636-1551; Fax: (419) 636-7877
Clerk of Courts: Kimberly Herman

WILLIAMS COUNTY CORONER
442 W. High St., Bryan 43506 (419) 636-4517
Coroner: Kevin Park

WILLIAMS COUNTY ENGINEER
12953 County Rd. G, Bryan 43506
(419) 636-2454; Fax: (419) 636-8687
Engineer: Dennis Bell

WILLIAMS COUNTY PROSECUTOR
1210 W. High St., Bryan 43506
(419) 636-4411; Fax: (419) 636-3919
Prosecutor: Craig Roth

WILLIAMS COUNTY RECORDER
One Courthouse Sq., Bryan 43506
(419) 636-3259; Fax: (419) 636-6940
Recorder: Patsy Mealer

WILLIAMS COUNTY AUDITOR
One Courthouse Sq., Bryan 43506
(419) 636-5639; Fax: (419) 636-8584
Auditor: Rob Rosswurm

WILLIAMS COUNTY SHERIFF
218 W. Bryan St., Bryan 43506
(419) 636-3151; Fax: (419) 636-2935
Sheriff: Kevin Beck

WILLIAMS COUNTY TREASURER
One Courthouse Sq., Bryan 43506 (419) 636-1850
Treasurer: Sharon Helbig

WOOD COUNTY

WOOD COUNTY COMMON PLEAS COURT NO. 1
One Courthouse Sq., Bowling Green 43402
Judge: Robert C. Pollex
    (419) 354-9210; Fax: (419) 354-7626
    E-mail: rpollex@co.wood.oh.us

WOOD COUNTY COMMON PLEAS COURT NO. 2
One Courthouse Sq., Bowling Green 43402
Judge: Reeve W. Kelsey
    (419) 354-9220; Fax: (419) 354-9223
    E-mail: rkelsey@co.wood.oh.us

WOOD COUNTY COMMON PLEAS COURT NO. 4
One Courthouse Sq., Bowling Green 43402
Judge: Alan Mayberry (419) 354-9600; Fax: (419) 354-9612

WOOD COUNTY PROBATE COURT
One Courthouse Sq., Bowling Green 43402
(419) 354-9230; Fax: (419) 354-9357
E-mail: probate-court@co.wood.oh.us
Judge: David E. Woessner

WOOD COUNTY JUVENILE COURT
11120 E. Gypsy Lane Rd., Bowling Green 43402
(419) 352-3554; Fax: (419) 352-6084
Judge: David E. Woessner

BOWLING GREEN MUNICIPAL COURT
711 S. Dunbridge Rd., P.O. Box 326,
Bowling Green 43402-0326
(419) 352-5263; Fax: (419) 352-9407
Judge: Mark B. Reddin; E-mail: bfmunict@wcnet.org
Clerk: Mary A. Cowell; E-mail: mary.cowell@bgohio.org
Court Schedule: Criminal Arraignments: Mon., 2:30 P.M.
and Wed. 10:30 A.M.; also first and third Wed., 5 P.M.
Traffic Arraignments: Mon., 1 P.M. and Wed. 8:30 A.M.;
also first and third Wed., 5 P.M.
Video Arraignments: Weekdays, 8:30 A.M.
Criminal/Traffic Contested Docket: Mon. and Fri.,
8:30 A.M. and Wed., 1 P.M.
Jury Trials: Tues., 8:30 A.M. and 1 P.M.
Civil Evictions: Thurs., 1:30 P.M.
Civil Pretrials: Fri., 1:30 P.M.
Civil Trials: Thurs., 9 A.M.
Debtor Exams: Thurs., 2 P.M.
Garnishment Hearings: Thurs., 2 P.M.
Nonsupport Contested Docket: Wed., 8:30 A.M.
Small Claims Mediations and Trials: Thurs., 9 A.M.
Weddings: Fri., 1:30 P.M.

FOSTORIA MUNICIPAL COURT
213 S. Main St., P.O. Box 985, Fostoria 44830
(419) 435-8139; Fax: (419) 435-1150
Jurisdiction—Counties of Hancock, Seneca, Wood
Judge: John D. Hadacek; E-mail: fosmunct@bright.net
Clerk: Janice Russell

PERRYSBURG MUNICIPAL COURT
300 Walnut St., Perrysburg 43551
(419) 872-7900; Fax: (419) 872-7905
Internet: www.perrysburgcourt.com
Judge: S. Dwight Osterud
    E-mail: sdosterud@ci.perrysburg.oh.us
Clerk: Janice I. Elkes
Court Schedule: Mon., Wed., Thur. and Fri.,
8 A.M.-4:30 P.M.; Tues., 8 A.M.-7 P.M.

Wood County—Cont'd

County Offices

WOOD COUNTY BOARD OF COMMISSIONERS
One Courthouse Sq., Bowling Green 43402-2431
(419) 354-9100; Fax: (419) 354-1522

President: James F. Carter

Commissioners:
Tim W. Brown   Alvin L. Perkins

Clerk: Kristy Muir

WOOD COUNTY CLERK OF COURTS
One Courthouse Sq., Bowling Green 43402
(419) 354-9280; Fax: (419) 354-9241

Clerk of Courts: Rebecca E. Bhaer

WOOD COUNTY CORONER
640 Wintergarden Rd., Bowling Green 43402
(419) 352-1452

Coroner: Douglas W. Hess

WOOD COUNTY ENGINEER
County Office Bldg., One Courthouse Sq.,
Bowling Green 43402
(419) 354-9060; Fax: (419) 354-1409

Engineer: Raymond A. Huber

WOOD COUNTY PROSECUTOR
One Courthouse Sq., Bowling Green 43402
(419) 354-9250; Fax: (419) 354-2904

Prosecutor: Raymond Fischer

WOOD COUNTY RECORDER
One Courthouse Sq., Bowling Green 43402-2473
(419) 354-9140

Recorder: Sue Kinder

WOOD COUNTY AUDITOR
One Courthouse Sq., Bowling Green 43402-0368
(419) 354-9150

Auditor: Michael Sibbersen

WOOD COUNTY SHERIFF
1960 E. Gypsy Lane Rd., Bowling Green 43402
(419) 354-9137; Fax: (419) 354-9086

Engineer: Mark Wasylyshyn

WOOD COUNTY TREASURER
County Office Bldg., One Courthouse Sq.,
Bowling Green 43402
(419) 354-9131; Fax: (419) 354-9619

Treasurer: Jill Engle

WYANDOT COUNTY

WYANDOT COUNTY COMMON PLEAS COURT
109 S. Sandusky Ave., Upper Sandusky 43351-1435
(419) 294-1727; Fax: (419) 209-0251

Judge: Kathleen A. Aubry

UPPER SANDUSKY MUNICIPAL COURT
119 N. Seventh St., Upper Sandusky 43351
(419) 294-3809; Fax: (419) 209-0474

Judge: Thomas E. Osborn

Clerk: Barbara Pagnard

County Offices

WYANDOT COUNTY BOARD OF COMMISSIONERS
Courthouse, 109 S. Sandusky Ave.,
Upper Sandusky 43351-1497
(419) 294-3836; Fax: (419) 294-6427

President: Joyce C. Morehart

Commissioners:
James J. Gilliland   Edward F. Kuenzli

WYANDOT COUNTY CLERK OF COURTS
Courthouse, Room 31, 109 S. Sandusky Ave.,
Upper Sandusky 43351-1493
(419) 294-1432; Fax: (419) 294-6414

Clerk of Courts: Ann K. Dunbar

WYANDOT COUNTY CORONER
Coroner: Vacancy at Press Time
Subject to election

WYANDOT COUNTY ENGINEER
350 N. Warpole St., Upper Sandusky 43351
(419) 294-2330; Fax: (419) 294-1627

Engineer: James A. Morris

WYANDOT COUNTY PROSECUTOR
137 S. Sandusky Ave., Upper Sandusky 43351
(419) 294-5878; Fax: (419) 294-6430

Prosecutor: E. Michael Pfeifer

WYANDOT COUNTY RECORDER
Courthouse, 109 S. Sandusky Ave., Upper Sandusky 43351
(419) 294-1442; Fax: (419) 294-6405

Recorder: Karen Kline

WYANDOT COUNTY AUDITOR
Courthouse, 109 S. Sandusky Ave., Upper Sandusky 43351
(419) 294-1531; Fax: (419) 294-6429

Auditor: Jeffrey A. McClain

WYANDOT COUNTY SHERIFF
125 E. Wyandot Ave., Upper Sandusky 43351
(419) 294-2362; Fax: (419) 294-1719

Sheriff: Michael R. Hetzel

WYANDOT COUNTY TREASURER
Courthouse, 109 S. Sandusky Ave., Upper Sandusky 43351
(419) 294-2131

Treasurer: Carolyn Frederick

Courts &
Officials

COSTS AND FEES IN OHIO

FEDERAL COURTS

UNITED STATES COURT OF APPEALS
SCHEDULE OF FEES

(Effective January 1, 2005)

Docket fee, Court of Appeals (a separate fee must be filed by each party filing a notice of appeal, but parties filing a joint notice of appeal are required to pay only one fee)	$250.00
Search of Court Records and certification of the results	26.00
Certifying any document or paper	9.00
Photographic (Xerox) copies (from documents or microfilm), per page	.50
Reproduction of magnetic tape recording, including materials..	26.00
For reproduction of the record in any appeal in which the requirement of an appendix is dispensed with by any court of appeals pursuant to Rule 30(f), F.R.A.P...	71.00
For each microfiche sheet of film or microfilm jacket copy of any court record, where available..	5.00
For retrieval of a record from a Federal Records Center, National Archives, or other storage location removed from the place of business of the court....	45.00
For a check paid into the court which is returned for lack of funds	45.00
To be paid by appellant or petitioner upon the filing of any separate or joint notice of appeal or application for appeal from the Bankruptcy Appellate Panel, or notice of the allowance of an appeal from the Bankruptcy Appellate Panel ...	5.00
Admission of attorney to practice (including certificate)..	150.00
Duplicate Certificate of Admission or Certificate of Good Standing................................	15.00

The clerk shall assess a charge for the handling of registry funds, to be assessed from interest earnings and in accordance with the detailed fee schedule issued by the Director of the Administrative Office of the United States Courts.

The court may charge and collect fees, commensurate with the cost of printing, for copies of the local rules of court. The court may also distribute copies of the local rules without charge.

The court may charge and collect a $200.00 per remote location for counsel's requested use of videoconferencing equipment in connection with each oral argument.

For usage of electronic access to court data, $.60 per minute of usage via dialup service, and $.08 per page ($2.40 maximum per document) for public users using a Federal judiciary Internet site [provided the court may, for good cause, exempt persons or classes of persons from the fees, in order to avoid unreasonable burdens and to promote public access to such information]. No fee is owed until an account holder accrues charges of more than $10.00 in a calendar year. All such fees collected shall be deposited to the Judiciary Information Technology Fund.

For printing copies of any record or document accessed electronically at a public terminal in the courthouse, $.10 per page. This fee shall apply to the United States.

For every search of court records conducted by the PACER Service Center, $20.00.

UNITED STATES DISTRICT COURT
SCHEDULE OF FEES AND DEPOSITS

Pursuant to 28 U.S.C. §1914 and the District Court Miscellaneous Fee Schedule
(effective February 7, 2005)

Commencing any civil proceeding other than habeas corpus	$250.00
Filing application for writ of habeas corpus	5.00
Filing notice or petition of appeal in any case—Civil or criminal (not including Court of Appeals docketing fees)	5.00
Filing notice of appeal to district judge from a judgment of conviction by a magistrate judge in a misdemeanor case	32.00
Search of District Court Records (each name or item)	26.00
Certifying any document or paper	9.00
Exemplifying any document or paper	18.00

Filing or indexing any paper not in a case or proceeding (i.e., petition to perpetuate testimony, Rule 27(a), Fed.R.Civ.P., the filing of papers by trustees under 28 U.S.C. §754, the filing of letters rogatory or letters of request, and registering of a judgment from another district pursuant to 28 U.S.C. § 1963)..	$ 39.00
Registration of foreign judgment	30.00
Admission of attorney to practice (including certificate)	
Northern Dist. of Ohio	190.00
Southern Dist. of Ohio	155.00
Motion for leave to appear (Pro hac vice)	50.00
Copies made by Clerk (does not include certification)	
Photographic (Xerox) copies (from documents or microfilm), per page	.50
Reproduction of magnetic tape recording, including materials...............................	26.00
For each microfiche sheet of film or microfilm jacket copy of any court record, where available..	5.00
For retrieval of a record from a Federal Records Center, National Archives, or other storage location removed from the place of business of the court....	45.00
For a check paid into the court which is returned for lack of funds	45.00
For filing an action brought under Title III of the Cuban Liberty and Democratic Solidarity (LIBERTAD) Act of 1996, P.L. 104-114, 110 Stat. § 785 (1996) (in addition to fee for commencing any civil proceeding other than habeas corpus)	5,431.00

The clerk shall assess a charge for the handling of registry funds, to be assessed from interest earnings and in accordance with the detailed fee schedule issued by the Director of the Administrative Office of the United States Courts.

The court may charge and collect fees, commensurate with the cost of printing, for copies of the local rules of court. The court may also distribute copies of the local rules without charge.

For usage of electronic access to court data, $.60 per minute of usage via dialup service, and $.08 per page ($2.40 maximum per document) for public users using a Federal judiciary Internet site [provided the court may, for good cause, exempt persons or classes of persons from the fees, in order to avoid unreasonable burdens and to promote public access to such information]. No fee is owed until an account holder accrues charges of more than $10.00 in a calendar year. All such fees collected shall be deposited to the Judiciary Information Technology Fund.

For printing copies of any record or document accessed electronically at a public terminal in the courthouse, $.10 per page. This fee shall apply to the United States.

For every search of court records conducted by the PACER Service Center, $20.00.

Checks and money orders may be made payable to the Clerk, United States District Court.

Federal Post Judgment Interest Rates

From Oct. 1, 1982 to Dec. 21, 2000, the interest rate on civil money judgments in federal district court was calculated from the date of entry of the judgment at a rate equal to the equivalent coupon issue yield (as determined by the Secretary of the Treasury) of 52-week U.S. Treasury Bills settled immediately prior to the date of the judgment. Effective Dec. 21, 2000, the interest rate is calcuated at a rate equal to the weekly average 1-year constant maturity Treasury yield, as published by the Board of Governors of the Federal Reserve System for the preceding calendar week. 28 U.S. §1961. For the latest yield rate releases, consult the Federal Reserve's website at www.federalreserve.gov/releases/h15.

Jan. 5, 1999	4.545%	May 25, 1999	4.879%
Feb. 2, 1999	4.584%	June 22, 1999	5.163%
Mar. 2, 1999	4.918%	July 20, 1999	4.966%
Mar. 30, 1999	4.732%	Aug. 17, 1999	5.224%
Apr. 27, 1999	4.727%	Sept. 14, 1999	5.285%

Federal Post-Judgment Interest Rates—Cont'd

Oct. 11, 1999...........5.411%	Feb. 8, 2002...............2.19%	June 13, 2003...........0.97%	May 14, 2004.............1.83%
Nov. 9, 1999............5.471%	Feb. 15, 2002 .... 2.24%	June 20, 2003...........0.95%	May 21, 2004.............1.83%
Dec. 7, 1999............5.670%	Feb. 22, 2002 .... 2.24%	June 27, 2003...........1.02%	May 28, 2004.............1.82%
Jan. 4, 2000............5.997%	Mar. 1, 2002 .... 2.28%	July 4, 2003............1.07%	June 4, 2004.............1.92%
Feb. 1, 2000............6.287%	Mar. 8, 2002 ....2.41%	July 11, 2003 ....1.08%	June 11, 2004 ....2.07%
Feb. 29, 2000...........6.197%	Mar. 15, 2002 ....2.58%	July 18, 2003............1.11%	June 18, 2004.............2.22%
May 31, 2000............6.375%	Mar. 22, 2002 ....2.66%	July 25, 2003............1.13%	June 25, 2004...........2.16%
Aug. 28, 2000 ....6.241%	Mar. 29, 2002 ....2.70%	Aug. 1, 2003.............1.22%	July 2, 2004.............2.14%
Nov. 28, 2000...........6.052%	Apr. 5, 2002 ....2.64%	Aug. 8, 2003.............1.26%	July 9, 2004.............2.04%
Dec. 22, 2001............5.44%	Apr. 12, 2002 ....2.53%	Aug. 8, 2003.............1.26%	July 16, 2004...........2.07%
Dec. 29, 2001............5.34%	Apr. 19, 2002 ....2.42%	Aug. 15, 2003 ....1.29%	July 23, 2004...........2.12%
Jan. 5, 2001.............4.89%	Apr. 26, 2002 ....2.36%	Aug. 22, 2003...........1.33%	July 30, 2004...........2.16%
Jan. 12, 2001............4.79%	May 3, 2002...............2.33%	Aug. 29, 2003...........1.35%	Aug. 6, 2004 ....2.07%
Jan. 19, 2001............4.85%	May 10, 2002.............2.23%	Sept. 5, 2003............1.33%	Aug. 13, 2004 ....1.99%
Jan. 26, 2001............4.83%	May 17, 2002.............2.40%	Sept. 12, 2003...........1.22%	Aug. 20, 2004 ....1.98%
Feb. 2, 2001.............4.66%	May 24, 2002.............2.38%	Sept. 19, 2003...........1.21%	Aug. 27, 2004 ....2.03%
Feb. 9, 2001.............4.72%	May 31, 2002.............2.35%	Sept. 26, 2003...........1.22%	Sept. 3, 2004............2.03%
Feb. 16, 2001............4.80%	June 7, 2002.............2.32%	Oct. 3, 2003 ....1.17%	Sept. 10, 2004..........2.10%
Feb. 23, 2001............4.69%	June 14, 2002.............2.24%	Oct. 10, 2003 ....1.20%	Sept. 17, 2004..........2.09%
Mar. 2, 2001 ....4.47%	June 21, 2002............2.13%	Oct. 17, 2003 ....1.29%	Sept. 24, 2004..........2.14%
Mar. 9, 2001 ....4.47%	June 28, 2002............2.10%	Oct. 24, 2003 ....1.30%	Oct. 1, 2004 ....2.20%
Mar. 16, 2001 ....4.31%	July 5, 2002..............2.06%	Oct. 30, 2003 ....1.30%	Oct. 8, 2004 ....2.24%
Mar. 23, 2001 ....4.17%	July 12, 2002.............2.00%	Nov. 7, 2003.............1.35%	Oct. 15, 2004 ....2.18%
Mar. 23, 2001 ....4.17%	July 19, 2002...........1.97%	Nov. 14, 2003............1.36%	Oct. 22, 2004 ....2.22%
Mar. 30, 2001 ....4.19%	July 26, 2002...........1.88%	Nov. 21, 2003............1.30%	Oct. 29, 2004 ....2.29%
Apr. 6, 2001 ....4.00%	Aug. 2, 2002.............1.82%	Nov. 28, 2003............1.35%	Nov. 5, 2004.............2.35%
Apr. 13, 2001............4.07%	Aug. 9, 2002.............1.67%	Dec. 5, 2003.............1.37%	Nov. 12, 2004...........2.49%
Apr. 20, 2001............4.04%	Aug. 16, 2002...........1.76%	Dec. 12, 2003............1.31%	Nov. 19, 2004...........2.53%
Apr. 27, 2001............3.82%	Aug. 23, 2002...........1.81%	Dec. 19, 2003............1.27%	Nov. 26, 2004...........2.60%
May 4, 2001.............3.90%	Aug. 30, 2002...........1.80%	Dec. 26, 2003............1.28%	Dec. 3, 2004.............2.62%
May 11, 2001............3.76%	Sept. 6, 2002............1.70%	Jan. 2, 2004.............1.29%	Dec. 10, 2004............2.60%
May 18, 2001............3.76%	Sept. 13, 2002...........1.78%	Jan. 9, 2004.............1.29%	Dec. 17, 2004............2.66%
May 25, 2001............3.78%	Sept. 20, 2002...........1.73%	Jan. 16, 2004............1.19%	Dec. 24, 2004............2.71%
June 1, 2001.............3.70%	Sept. 27, 2002...........1.68%	Jan. 23, 2004............1.20%	Dec. 31, 2004............2.77%
June 8, 2001.............3.64%	Oct. 4, 2002.............1.55%	Jan. 30, 2004............1.25%	Jan. 7, 2005 ....2.82%
June 15, 2001............3.59%	Oct. 11, 2002 ....1.59%	Feb. 6, 2004.............1.28%	Jan. 14, 2005............2.85%
June 22, 2001............3.46%	Oct. 18, 2002 ....1.77%	Feb. 13, 2004............1.24%	Jan. 21, 2005............2.87%
June 29, 2001............3.60%	Oct. 25, 2002 ....1.79%	Feb. 20, 2004............1.23%	Jan. 28, 2005............2.89%
July 6, 2001.............3.70%	Nov. 1, 2002..............1.46%	Feb. 27, 2004............1.22%	Feb. 4, 2005.............2.95%
July 13, 2001............3.62%	Nov. 8, 2002..............1.51%	Mar. 5, 2004 ....1.23%	Feb. 11, 2005............2.96%
July 20, 2001............3.60%	Nov. 15, 2002.............1.46%	Mar. 12, 2004 ....1.16%	Feb. 18, 2005............3.05%
July 27, 2001............3.59%	Nov. 22, 2002.............1.51%	Mar. 19, 2004 ....1.18%	Feb. 25, 2005............3.13%
Aug. 3, 2001 ....3.56%	Nov. 29, 2002.............1.55%	Mar. 26, 2004 ....1.17%	Mar. 4, 2005 ....3.20%
Aug. 10, 2001 ....3.50%	Dec. 6, 2002..............1.53%	Apr. 2, 2004 ....1.23%	Mar. 11, 2005............3.24%
Aug. 17, 2001 ....3.44%	Dec. 13, 2002.............1.47%	Apr. 9, 2004 ....1.32%	Mar. 18, 2005 ....3.31%
Aug. 24, 2001 ....3.45%	Dec. 20, 2002.............1.43%	Apr. 16, 2004 ....1.41%	Mar. 25, 2005............3.38%
Aug. 31, 2001 ....3.44%	Dec. 27, 2002.............1.41%	Apr. 23, 2004 ....1.50%	Apr. 1, 2005 ....3.38%
Sept. 7, 2001.............3.43%	Jan. 3, 2003..............1.38%	Apr. 30, 2004 ....1.55%	Apr. 8, 2005 ....3.33%
Sept. 14, 2001............3.02%	Jan. 10, 2003.............1.41%	May 7, 2004.............1.63%	Apr. 15, 2005 ....3.32%
Sept. 21, 2001............2.60%	Jan 17, 2003..............1.38%		
Sept. 28, 2001...........2.49%	Jan. 24, 2003.............1.32%		
Oct. 5, 2001 ....2.40%	Jan. 31, 2003.............1.32%		
Oct. 12, 2001 ....2.39%	Feb. 7, 2003..............1.32%		
Oct. 19, 2001 ....2.37%	Feb. 14, 2003.............1.30%		
Oct. 26, 2001 ....2.31%	Feb. 21, 2003.............1.30%		
Nov. 2, 2001..............2.11%	Feb. 28, 2003.............1.27%		
Nov. 9, 2001..............1.99%	Mar. 7, 2003..............1.22%		
Nov. 16, 2001............2.24%	Mar. 14, 2003 ....1.16%		
Nov. 23, 2001............2.35%	Mar. 21, 2003 ....1.32%		
Nov. 30, 2001............2.23%	Mar. 28, 2003 ....1.27%		
Dec. 7, 2001..............2.21%	Apr. 4, 2003 ....1.19%		
Dec. 14, 2001.............2.17%	Apr. 18, 2003 ....1.33%		
Dec. 21, 2001.............2.23%	Apr. 25, 2003 ....1.31%		
Dec. 28, 2001.............2.28%	May 2, 2003...............1.25%		
Jan. 4, 2002..............2.24%	May 9, 2003...............1.23%		
Jan. 11, 2002..............2.13%	May 16, 2003.............1.20%		
Jan. 18, 2002..............2.03%	May 23, 2003.............1.13%		
Jan. 25, 2002.............2.18%	May 30, 2003.............1.13%		
Feb. 1, 2002...............2.25%	June 6, 2003.............1.08%		

FEES OF U.S. BANKRUPTCY COURTS

Filing and Conversion Fees

To be collected by the clerk in Bankruptcy Code cases pursuant to 28 U.S.C. §1930 and the Bankruptcy Court Miscellaneous Fee Schedule (effective January 1, 2005)

For a case commenced under Chapter 7 of Title 11, (including $39.00 administrative fee and $15.00 trustee surcharge)................................	$209.00
For a case commenced under Chapter 13 of Title 11 (including $39.00 administrative fee)	194.00
For a case commenced under Chapter 9 of Title 11 (including $39.00 administrative fee)	839.00
For a case commenced under Chapter 12 of Title 11 (including $39.00 administrative fee)..	239.00
For a case commenced under Chapter 11 of Title 11 that does not concern a railroad, as defined in section 101 of Title 11 (including $39.00 administrative fee)	839.00

Fees of U.S. Bankruptcy Courts—Cont'd

For a case commenced under Chapter 11 of Title 11 concerning a railroad, as so defined (including $39.00 administrative fee)................................$ 1,039.00

For filing an Adversary proceeding................. 150.00

For a conversion from Chapter 7 or 13 of Title 11 to Chapter 11 on request of debtor

    Non-railroad... 645.00

    Railroad.. 845.00

For filing Notice of Appeal (including $250.00 docket fee)... 255.00

For filing a motion to convert a case to Chapter 7 of Title 11 or a notice of conversion pursuant to Section 1208(a) or Section 1307(a) of Title 11.... 15.00

For filing a petition ancillary to a foreign proceeding under 11 U.S.C.§304 (including $39.00 administrative fee)............................... 839.00

Note: Filing fees should also be collected when a case is reopened except in cases of administrative error or actions relating to the discharge (however, such fees are not subject to administrative fee or trustee surcharge.

Miscellaneous Fees
Promulgated under 28 U.S.C. §1930(b)
(including certain filing fees noted above)

For reproducing any record or paper, per page. $.50
This fee does not include certification. This fee shall apply to services rendered on behalf of the United States if the record or paper requested is available through electronic access.

For certifying any document or paper............. 9.00

For exemplifying any document or paper 18.00

For reproduction of magnetic tape audio recordings, either cassette or reel-to-reel, including the cost of materials, $26.00.

For amendments to debtor's schedules or lists of creditors, $26.00 for each amendment, provided the bankruptcy judge may, for good cause, waive the charge in any case.

For searches of court records, $26.00 per name or item searched. This fee shall apply to services rendered on behalf of the United States if the information requested is available through electronic access.

For filing a complaint, $150.00. If the United States, other than the United States Trustee acting as a trustee in a case under Title 11, or a debtor is the plaintiff, no fee is required. If a trustee or debtor in possession is the plaintiff, the fee shall be payable only from the estate and to the extent there is any estate realized. If a child support creditor or its representative is the plaintiff, and if such plaintiff files the form required by §304(g) of the Bankruptcy Reform Act of 1994, no fee is required.

For filing or indexing any paper not in a case or proceeding for which a filing fee has been paid, including registering a judgment from another district, $39.00.

In all cases filed under any chapter of Title 11, the clerk shall collect from the debtor a miscellaneous administrative fee of $39.00. This fee may be paid in installments in the same manner that the filing fee may be paid in installments, consistent with the procedure set forth in Federal Rule of Bankruptcy Procedure 1006.

Upon the filing of a petition under Chapter 7 of the Bankruptcy Code, the petitioner shall pay $15.00 to the clerk of the court for payment to trustees serving in cases as provided in 11 U.S.C §330(b)(2). An application to pay the fee in installments may be filed in the matter set forth in Federal Rule of Bankruptcy Procedure 1006(b).

Upon the filing of a motion to convert a case to Chapter 7 of the Bankruptcy Code, the movant shall pay $15.00 to the clerk of the court for payment to trustees serving in cases as provided in 11 U.S.C §330(b)(2). Upon the filing of a notice of conversion pursuant to Section 1208(a) or Section 1307(a) of the Code, $15.00 shall be paid to the clerk of the court for payment to trustees serving in cases as provided in 11 U.S.C §330(b)(2). If the trustee serving in the case before the conversion is the movant, the fee shall be payable only from the estate that exists prior to conversion.

For filing a motion to reopen a case, the same fee as for commencing a new case, unless the reopening is to correct an administrative error or for actions relating to the debtor's discharge. The court may waive the fee under appropriate circumstances or may defer payment of the fee from trustees pending discovery of additional assets.

For each microfiche sheet of film or microfilm jacket copy of any court record, where available, $5.00.

For retrieval of a record from a Federal Records Center, National Archives, or other storage location removed from the place of business of the court, $45.00.

For a check paid into the court which is returned for lack of funds, $45.00.

For docketing a proceeding on appeal or review from a final judgment of a bankruptcy judge pursuant to 28 U.S.C. §158(a) and (b), $250.00. A separate fee shall be paid by each party filing a notice of appeal in the bankruptcy court, but parties filing a joint notice of appeal in the bankruptcy court are required to pay only one fee. If a trustee or debtor in possession is the appellant, the fee shall be payable only from the estate and to the extent there is any estate realized.

The court may charge and collect fees, commensurate with the cost of printing, for copies of the local rules of court. The court may also distribute copies of the local rules without charge.

The clerk shall assess a charge for the handling of registry funds, to be assessed from interest earnings and in accordance with the detailed fee schedule issued by the Director of the Administrative Office of the United States Courts.

When a joint case filed under §302 of Title 11 is divided into two separate cases at the request of the debtor(s), a fee shall be charged equal to current filing fee for the chapter under which the joint case was commenced.

For filing a motion to terminate, annul, modify or condition the automatic stay provided under §362 of Title 11, a motion to compel abandonment of property of the estate pursuant to Rule 6007(b) of the Federal Rules of Bankruptcy Procedure, or a motion to withdraw the reference of a case or proceeding under 28 U.S.C. §157(d), $150.00. No fee is required for a motion for relief from the co-debtor stay or for a stipulation for court approval of an agreement for relief from a stay. If a child support creditor or its representative is the plaintiff, and if such plaintiff files the form required by §304(g) of the Bankruptcy Reform Act of 1994, no fee is required.

For docketing a cross appeal from a bankruptcy court determination, $250. If a trustee or debtor in possession is the appellant, the fee shall be payable only from the estate and to the extent there is any estate realized.

For usage of electronic access to court data, $.60 per minute of usage via dialup service, and $.08 per page ($2.40 maximum per document) for public users using a Federal judiciary Internet site [provided the court may, for good cause, exempt persons or classes of persons from the fees, in order to avoid unreasonable burdens and to promote public access to such information]. No fee is owed until an account holder accrues charges of more than $10.00 in a calendar year. All such fees collected shall be deposited to the Judiciary Information Technology Fund.

For printing copies of any record or document accessed electronically at a public terminal in the courthouse, $.10 per page. This fee shall apply to the United States.

For every search of court records conducted by the PACER Service Center, $20.00.

Note: None of the foregoing miscellaneous additional fees are to be charged for services rendered on behalf of the United States (except for those specifically enumerated), or to bankruptcy administrators appointed under P.L. 99-554, §302(d)(3)(I) as amended by P.L. 101-650, §317(a).

FEES OF STATE COURTS OF OHIO

SUPREME COURT

Docket Fee for Filing an Appeal	$ 40.00
Deposit for Original Actions	100.00

DISTRICT COURT OF APPEAL

Deposit Required for Filing, by District:

First Appellate District	$ 50.00
Additional deposit for subpoena in habeas corpus actions	10.00
Second Appellate District	75.00
Third Appellate District:	
Appeals	150.00
Original Actions (mandamus, prohibition, procedendo, or quo warranto, or, except where prohibited by law, habeas corpus).	150.00
Additional deposit for subpoena in habeas corpus actions	20.00
Fourth Appellate District	85.00
Fifth Appellate District:	
Appeals	90.00
Original Actions (mandamus, prohibition, procedendo, or quo warranto, or, except where prohibited by law, habeas corpus).	85.00
Additional deposit for subpoena in habeas corpus actions	10.00
Sixth Appellate District:	
Appeals	150.00
Original Actions (mandamus, prohibition, procedendo, or quo warranto, or, except where prohibited by law, habeas corpus).	100.00
Additional deposit for subpoena, per witness	10.00
Seventh Appellate District	50.00
Additional deposit for subpoena, per witness	20.00
Eighth Appellate District	125.00
Ninth Appellate District	85.00
Additional deposit for subpoena, per witness	20.00
Tenth Appellate District:	
Appeals	75.00
Original Actions (mandamus, prohibition, procedendo, or quo warranto, or, except where prohibited by law, habeas corpus).	100.00
Eleventh Appellate District	100.00
Additional deposit for subpoena, per witness	20.00
Twelfth Appellate District	125.00
Additional deposit for subpoena, per witness	20.00

FEES OF THE CLERK OF THE COURT OF COMMON PLEAS

Ohio Rev. Code, § 2303.20

Editor's Note: The clerk in each county requires that a deposit be submitted in each cause, against which fees are charged. The amount of deposit required varies by court. Also, pursuant to Rev. Code § 2303.201, the court in any county may impose an additional fee to pay for court computerization, or to support legal aid or other programs. Contact clerk before submitting payment.

For each cause of action, fee to include docketing in all dockets; filing necessary documents, noting the filing of the documents, except subpoena, on the dockets; issuing certificate of deposit in foreign writs; indexing pending suits and living judgments; noting on appearance docket all papers mailed; certificate for attorney's fee; certificate for stenographer's fee; preparing cost bill; entering on indictment any plea; and entering costs on docket and cash book	$ 25.00
Taking each undertaking, bond or recognizance	2.00
Issuing each writ, order or notice, except subpoena	2.00
Issuing subpoena, swearing witness, entering attendance and certifying fees, per name	2.00
Calling a jury in each cause	$ 25.00
Entering on journal, indexing, and posting on any docket, per page	2.00
Execution or transcript of judgment, including indexing, each	3.00
Making complete record, including indexing, each page	1.00
Certifying a plat recorded in the county recorder's office.	5.00
Issuing certificate to receiver or order of reference with oath	5.00
Entering satisfaction or partial satisfaction of each lien on record in the county recorder's office and the clerk of court's office	5.00
Certificate of fact under seal of the court (payable by the party demanding it)	1.00
Taking affidavit, including certificate and seal, each	1.00
Acknowledging instruments in writing	2.00
Certificate of judgment, making	5.00
Filing, docketing, and endorsing a certificate of judgment, including the indexing and noting the return of the certificate	10.00
Judgment by confession, including all docketing, indexing, and entries on the journal, for each cause of action	25.00
Recording commission of mayor or notary public.	5.00
Issuing a license except those pursuant to Rev. Code §§ 1533.101, 1533.11, 1533.13 and 1533.32	1.00
Docketing and indexing each aid in execution or petition to vacate, revive, or modify judgment, including the filing of all necessary documents.	15.00
Docketing and indexing each appeal, including the filing of all necessary documents	25.00
Commission for receiving and disbursing money, other than costs and fees, paid to or deposited with the clerk of courts in pursuance of a court order or on judgments, including moneys invested by order of the court and interest earned on them:	
First $10,000	2%
Money exceeding $10,000	1%
Numbering, docketing, indexing, and filing each authenticated or certified copy of the record, or any portion of an authenticated or certified copy of the record, of an extra county action or proceeding	5.00
Submitting certificate of divorce, annulment, or dissolution of marriage to the Bureau of Vital Statistics	2.00
Electronic transmission of a document (payable by the party requesting the document)	2.00
Plus additional charge, per page	1.00
Copies of pleadings, process, record or files, including certificate and seal, per page	1.00

INTEREST ON JUDGMENTS IN THE OHIO STATE COURTS

Prior to 2005, pursuant to Ohio Rev. Code § 1343.03, interest on judgments was at 10% per annum, except as otherwise provided.

Rev. Code § 1343.03 was amended in 2004 to provide that interest on judgments shall be determined according to a formula cited in Rev. Code § 5703.47, whereby the state tax commissioner shall determine, on Oct. 15 of each year, the "federal short-term rate", the rate of the average market rate of U.S. obligations with remaining terms to maturity of three years or less as per 26 U.S.C.A. 1274, for July of that year. That rate shall be rounded to the nearest whole number, and three percent shall be added to that number to determine the interest rate for the following calendar year.

The interest rate, as per Rev. Code § 5703.47, was determined for the year 2005 to be 5%.

The 2006 rate, when determined by the state tax commissioner, shall be posted on our website, www.lawdiary.com.

Costs & Fees

WITNESS FEES IN CIVIL CASES

Ohio Rev. Code § 2335.06

Full day's attendance	$ 12.00
Half day's attendance	6.00
Plus mileage to and from place of residence, per mile	.10

Full day's attendance means a day in which witness is requested or required before and after noon, regardless of whether the witness testifies. Half day's attendance means a day in which witness is requested or required either before or after noon, but not both, regardless of whether the witness testifies.

FEES OF THE PROBATE JUDGE

Ohio Rev. Code, § 2101.16

Editor's Note: Pursuant to Rev. Code § 2101.162, the court in any county may impose an additional fee to pay for court computerization, or for computerized legal research programs. Contact clerk before submitting payment.

The following fees shall be charged and collected, if possible, by the probate judge and shall be in full for all services rendered in the respective proceedings:

Account, in addition to advertising charges	$12.00
Waivers and proof of notice of hearing on account, per page, ($1.00 minimum)	1.00
Account of distribution, in addition to advertising charges	7.00
Adoption of child, petition for	50.00
Alter or cancel contract for sale or purchase of real estate, petition to	20.00
Application and order not otherwise provided for in this section or by rule	5.00
Appropriation suit, hearing in, per day	20.00
Birth, application for registration	7.00
Birth record, application to correct	5.00
Bond, application for new or additional	5.00
Bond, application for release of surety or reduction of	5.00
Bond, receipt for securities deposited in lieu of	5.00
Certified Copy of journal entry, record or proceeding, per page ($1.00 minimum)	1.00
Citation and issuing citation, application for	5.00
Change of name, petition	20.00
Claim, application of administrator or executor for allowance of administrator's or executor's own	10.00
Claim, application to compromise or settle	10.00
Claim, petition for authority to present	10.00
Commissioner, appointment of	5.00
Compensation for extraordinary services and attorney's fees for fiduciary, application for	5.00
Competency, application to procure adjudication of	20.00
Complete contract, application to	10.00
Concealment of assets, citation for	10.00
Construction of will, petition for	20.00
Continue decedent's business, application to	10.00
Monthly reports of operation	5.00
Declaratory judgment, petition for	20.00
Deposit of will	5.00
Designation of heir	20.00
Distribution in kind, application, assent and order for	5.00
Distribution under Rev. Code § 2109.36 (order of distribution of the assets of an estate or trust), application for an order of	7.00
Docketing and indexing proceedings, including the filing and noting of all necessary documents, maximum fee	15.00
Exceptions to any proceeding named in this section, contest of appointment or	10.00
Election of surviving partner to purchase assets of partnership, proceedings relating to	10.00

Election of surviving spouse under will	$ 5.00
Fiduciary, including an assignee or trustee of an insolvent debtor or any guardian or conservator accountable to the probate court, appointment of	35.00
Foreign will, application to record	10.00
Record of such will, additional, per page	1.00
Forms when supplied by the probate court, fee not to exceed	10.00
Heirship, petition to determine	20.00
Injunction proceedings	20.00
Improve real estate, petition to	20.00
Inventory with appraisement	10.00
Inventory without appraisement	7.00
Investment or expenditure of funds, application for	10.00
Invest in real estate, application to	10.00
Lease for oil, gas, coal, or other mineral, petition to	20.00
Lease or lease and improve real estate, petition to	20.00
Marriage license	10.00
Certified abstract of each marriage	2.00
Minor or mentally ill person, etc., disposal of estate under $10,000	10.00
Mortgage or mortgage and repair or improve real estate, petition to	20.00
Newly discovered assets, report of	7.00
Nonresident executor or administrator to bar creditors' claims, proceedings by	20.00
Power of attorney or revocation of power, bonding company	10.00
Presumption of death, petition to establish	20.00
Probating will	15.00
Proof of notice to beneficiaries	5.00
Purchase personal property, application of surviving spouse to	10.00
Purchase real estate at appraised value, petition of surviving spouse to	20.00
Receipts in addition to advertising charges, application and order to record	5.00
Record in excess of 1,500 words in any proceeding in the probate court, per page	1.00
Release of estate by mortgagee or other lienholder	5.00
Relieving an estate from administration under Rev. Code § 2113.03 or granting an order for a summary release from administration under Rev. Code § 2113.031	60.00
Removal of fiduciary, application for	10.00
Requalification of executor or administrator	10.00
Resignation of fiduciary	5.00
Sale bill, public sale of personal property	10.00
Sale of personal property and report, application for	10.00
Sale of real estate, petition for	25.00
Terminate guardianship, petition to	10.00
Transfer of real estate, application, entry, and certificate for	7.00
Unclaimed money, application to invest	7.00
Vacate approval of account or order of distribution, motion to	10.00
Writ of execution	5.00
Writ of possession	5.00
Wrongful death, application and settlement of claim for	20.00
Year's allowance, petition to review	7.00
Guardian's report, filing and review of	5.00

The probate court, by rule, may require an advance deposit for costs, not to exceed $125.00, at the time application is made for appointment as executor or administrator, or at the time a will is presented for probate.

The probate court may direct that an applicant or the estate pay any or all of the expenses of an investigation related to an application for the appointment of a guardian or the review of a report of a guardian under Rev. Code § 2111.49, pursuant to § 2111.041 or § 2111.49(A)(2). The court may waive the costs if the court finds an alleged incompetent or ward is indigent.

Fees of the Probate Judge—Cont'd

The probate court may direct that an applicant or the estate pay any or all of the expenses of an investigation related to the appointment or functioning of a guardian for a minor or the guardianship of a minor, pursuant to Rev. Code § 2111.042. The court may waive the costs if the court finds the guardian or applicant is indigent.

The probate court, by rule, shall establish a fee not to exceed $50.00 for the filing of a petition for the release of information regarding an adopted person's name by birth and the identity of the biological parents and siblings, pursuant to Rev. Code § 3107.41, all prceedings relative to the petition, entry of an order relative to the petition, and all services required to be performed in connection with the petition.

Fees of Probate Judge pursuant to Ohio Rev. Code § 1313.52 For services performed under Ohio Rev. Code §§ 1313.01 through 1313.59

Hearing and deciding each application	$ 2.00
Appointing or removing an assignee or trustee	1.00
Filing assignment, inventory, and schedule, each.	.10
Filing other papers, each	.05
Other services, the same compensation as for like services, in the settlement of the estate of deceased persons.	

FEES OF COUNTY RECORDERS

Ohio Rev. Code § 317.32; includes Housing Trust Fund fees

Recording and indexing when photocopy or other method is employed (8.5 by 14 inches or fraction of page, including caption page), first 2 pages	$ 28.00
Per additional page	8.00
Certifying photocopy from a record previously recorded employed (8.5 by 14 inches or fraction of page), per page	2.00
Certification where recorder's seal is required (except as to instuments issued by the U.S. Armed Forces)	1.00
Manual or typewritten recording of assignment or satisfaction of mortgage or lease or any other marginal entry	8.00
Entering any marginal reference by separate recorded instrument per marginal reference (in addition to fees set forth above)	4.00
Indexing in the real estate mortgage records, pursuant to Rev. Code § 1309.519, financing statements covering crops growing or to be grown, timber to be cut, minerals or the like, including oil or gas, accounts subject to Rev. Code § 1309.301, or fixture filings pursuant to Rev. Code § 1309.334, per name indexed	4.00
Recording manually any plat not exceeding six lines	4.00
Each additional line	.20
Filing zoning resolutions, including text and maps, as required under Rev. Code §§ 303.11 and 519.11, regardless of the size or length of the resolutions	100.00
Filing zoning amendments, including text and maps, as required under Rev. Code §§ 303.12 and 519.12, first page	20.00
Each additional page	8.00
Photocopying a document, other than at the time of recording and indexing (8.5 by 14 inches), per page or fraction of page	2.00
Local facsimile transmission of a document (8.5 by 14 inches), per page or fraction of page	2.00
Long distance transmission, per page	4.00
Recording a declaration executed under Rev. Code § 2133.02 (declaration regarding life-sustaining treatment) or durable power of attorney for health care pursuant to Rev. Code § 1337.12, or both, minimum fee $28.00, maximum fee not to exceed	40.00

In counties where photostatic or similar process used for recording maps, plats or prints, $.10 per square inch, minimum fee	$ 40.00
Certifying a copy from the record, $.04 per square inch, minimum fee	4.00
Records of Internal Revenue tax liens or other Federal liens (Rev. Code § 317.09):	
Filing, recording and indexing, or copying of lien	5.00
Filing, recording and indexing certificates of discharge or release of lien	3.00

FEES OF COUNTY SHERIFFS

Ohio Rev. Code, § 311.17

The sheriff shall charge the following fees, which the court or its clerk thereof shall tax in the bill of costs against the judgment debtor or those legally liable therefor for the judgment:

Service and Return of Writs and Orders

Execution:	
When money is paid without levy or when no property is found	$ 20.00
When levy is made on real property, first tract	25.00
Each additional tract	10.00
When levy is made on goods and chattels, including inventory	50.00
Writ of attachment of property, except for purpose of garnishment	40.00
Writ of attachment for purpose of garnishment	10.00
Writ of replevin	40.00
Warrant to arrest, per person named in the writ	10.00
Attachment for contempt, per person named in the writ	6.00
Writ of possession or restitution	60.00
Subpoena, per person named, civil or criminal case	6.00
Venire, per person named, civil or criminal case	6.00
Summoning each juror, other than on venire, civil or criminal case	6.00
Writ of partition	25.00
Order of sale on partition, first tract	50.00
Each additional tract	25.00
Other order of sale of real property, first tract	50.00
Each additional tract	25.00
Administering oath to appraisers, each	3.00
Furnishing copies for advertisements, per 100 words	1.00
Copy of indictment, each defendant	5.00
All summons, writ, orders or notices, first name	6.00
Each additional name	1.00

Additional fees

Mileage on each summons, writ, order or notice, first mile	$ 1.00
Each additional mile, going and returning	.50
Taking bail bond	3.00
Jail fees:	
Receiving a prisoner	5.00
Discharging or surrendering a prisoner	5.00
Taking a prisoner before a judge or court, per day	5.00
Calling action	1.00
Calling jury	3.00
Calling each witness	3.00
Bringing prisoner before court on habeas corpus	6.00
Poundage on all moneys actually made and paid to the sheriff on execution, decree, or sale of real estate	1½%
Making and executing a deed of land sold on execution, decree, or order of the court (to be paid by purchaser)	50.00

OHIO FEDERAL DEPARTMENTS AND AGENCIES

LEGISLATIVE BRANCH

THE SENATE
Washington, DC 20510
(202) 224-3121
Internet: www.senate.gov/

Secretary: Emily Reynolds

All legislative power of the United States is vested in the Congress, made of two houses. The Senate has 100 members. The Senate approves all presidential appointments to the Cabinet, the Supreme Court, Ambassadorial positions, tries impeachments, and approves treaties. The Vice President sits as president of the Senate. *U.S. Const. Art. I sec. 1*

THE HOUSE OF REPRESENTATIVES
Office of the Clerk, H-154, The Capitol,
Washington, DC 20515
(202) 225-7000
Internet: clerkweb.house.gov

Clerk: Jeff Trandahl
(202) 225-7000; Fax: (202) 225-1776

All legislative power of the United States is vested in Congress, made of two houses. The House of Representatives has 435 members. The House originates all legislative provisions raising revenue, and makes all impeachments. *U.S. Const. Art. I sec. 1*

GOVERMENT ACCOUNTABILITY OFFICE
441 G St. N.W., Washington, DC 20548
(202) 512-3000; Public Affairs: (202) 512-4800
Internet: www.gao.gov

Comptroller General of the United States:
David M. Walker (202) 512-5500

Investigates all matters relating to the receipt and disbursement of public funds including research into the effects of proposed legislative action. Acts as an independent arm of Congress to carry out its public audit duties. *31 U.S.C. 702*
Formerly General Accounting Office

Dayton Office
AMC Branch, P.O. Box 33626,
Wright Patterson Afb, OH 45433

GOVERNMENT PRINTING OFFICE
732 N. Capitol St. N.W., Washington, DC 20401
(202) 512-0000; Public Affairs: (202) 512-1957
Internet: www.access.gpo.gov

Public Printer: Bruce R. James
(202) 512-1000; Fax: (202) 512-1347

General Counsel: Anthony J. Zagami
(202) 512-0033; Fax: (202) 512-0076

Dir., Office of Congressional Relations:
Andrew M. Sherman
(202) 512-1991; Fax: (202) 512-1293

Prints, binds, and distributes the publications and printed materials of the Congress and the executive departments of the Federal government. *44 U.S.C. 301 et seq.*

LIBRARY OF CONGRESS
101 Independence Ave. S.E., Washington, DC 20540
(202) 707-8000; General Information: (202) 707-5000
Internet: www.loc.gov

Librarian of Congress: James H. Billington
(202) 707-5205; Fax: (202) 707-1714

Contains the national library of the United States containing nearly 128 million items and provides such books as may be necessary for the operation and duties of the Congress. Operates the system of copyrights. Operates the largest law library in the world with 2.4 million items. (foreign & domestic) *2 U.S.C. 131.*

EXECUTIVE BRANCH

EXECUTIVE OFFICE OF THE PRESIDENT
The White House, 1600 Pennsylvania Ave. N.W.,
Washington, DC 20500
White House Operator: (202) 456-1414;
Comment Line: (202) 456-1111; Fax: (202) 456-2461
Internet: www.whitehouse.gov

President: George W. Bush
Chief of Staff: Andrew H. Card, Jr.
Sr. White House Advisor: Karl Rove
Counsel to the President: Harriet Miers
Ciounselor to the President: Dan Bartlett
Asst. to the President for Natl. Security Affairs:
Stephen Hadley
Press Secretary: Scott McClellan

Office of Management and Budget
New Executive Office Bldg., 725 17th St. N.W.,
Washington, DC 20503
(202) 395-3080; Fax: (202) 395-3888
Internet: www.whitehouse.gov/OMB

Director: Joshua Bolten
(202) 395-4840; Fax: (202) 395-3888

Deputy Dir.: Joel Kaplan
(202) 395-4742; Fax: (202) 456-5938

Deputy Dir. for Management: Clay Johnson III
(202) 456-7070; Fax: (202) 456-5938

Exec. Assoc. Dir.: Austin Smythe (202) 395-4844

Evaluates, formulates, and coordinates management procedures and program objectives within and among the Federal departments and agencies. Controls the administration of the budget and makes recommendations to the President regarding budget proposals and legislation. *5 U.S.C. app. Reorganization Plan No. 1*

Council of Economic Advisers
1800 G St., N.W., 8th Floor, Washington, DC 20502
(202) 395-5084

Chair: Dr. Harvey S. Rosen
(202) 395-5042; Fax: (202) 395-6958

Analyzes and appraises the national economy to provide policy recommendations to the President. *15 U.S.C. 1023*

National Security Council
Eisenhower Executive Office Bldg., Washington, DC 20504
(202) 456-1414
Internet: www.whitehouse.gov/nsc/

Asst. to the President for Natl. Security Affairs:
Stephen J. Hadley

Advises and assists the President in the formation of an integrated national security policy for the United States in conjunction with the National Economic Council. *50 U.S.C. 402*

Office of the United States Trade Representative
600 17th St. N.W., Washington, DC 20508
(202) 395-USTR: (202) 395-8787; (888) 473-8787;
Public Information Fax: (202) 395-3911
E-mail: contactustr@ustr.gov
Internet: www.ustr.gov

U.S. Trade Representative: Robert B. Zoellick
(202) 395-6890

General Counsel: John Veroneau (202) 395-3150

Formulates all trade policy and directs all trade negotiations for the United States. *19 U.S.C. 1921*

Council on Environmental Quality
722 Jackson Pl. N.W., Washington, DC 20503
(202) 395-5750; Fax: (202) 456-6546

Chair: James L. Connaughton

General Counsel: Dinah Bear (202) 395-7421

Deputy General Counsel: Edward Boling (202) 395-3449

Researches, develops, analyzes, and recommends environmental policy to the President for the preservation and improvement of the quality of the environment. Also oversees federal agencies' implementation of the National Environmental Policy Act. *42 U.S.C. 4341, 42 U.S.C. 4321 et seq., Exec. Order 11991*

Executive Office of the President—Cont'd

Office of Science and Technology Policy
1600 Pennsylvania Ave., N.W., Washington, DC 20502
(202) 395-7347;
Science Div.: (202) 456-6130; Fax: (202) 456-6027;
Technology Div.: (202) 456-6046; Fax: (202) 456-6021
E-mail: ostpinfo@ostp.eop.gov
Internet: www.ostp.gov

Asst. to the President and Dir.: John H. Marburger III
(202) 456-7116; Fax: (202) 456-6021
Acts as a source of information and policy recommendations for the President in the fields of science, engineering, and technology. *42 U.S.C. 6611*

Office of National Drug Control Policy
750 17th St. N.W., Washington, DC 20503
(202) 395-6700; Fax: (202) 395-6680
E-mail: ondcp@ncjrs.org
Internet: www.whitehousedrugpolicy.gov

Director: John P. Walters
Coordinates and plans national, state, and local efforts to control illegal drug trafficking and drug abuse. *21 U.S.C. 1501*

Office of Administration
725 17th St. N.W., EEOB, Room 145,
Washington, DC 20503
(202) 456-2861; Fax: (202) 456-1655
Internet: www.whitehouse.gov/WH/EOP/html/OA.html

Director: Timothy A. Campen
(202) 456-2861; Fax: (202) 456-6512
General Counsel: Vacancy at Press Time
Provides administrative support services to all units within the Executive Office of the President. *5 U.S.C. app. Reorganization Plan No. 1*

Office of the Vice President of the United States
Eisenhower Executive Office Bldg.,
1650 Pennsylvania Ave. N.W., Washington, DC 20501
(202) 456-7549; Fax: (202) 456-7044
E-mail: vice.president@whitehouse.gov
Internet: www.whitehouse.gov/vicepresident

Vice President: Richard B. Cheney
Participates in the Cabinet meetings, acts as member of the National Security Council, sits on the Board of Regents of the Smithsonian Institution, and is President of the Senate. *U.S. Const. Art. II sec. 1*

DEPARTMENT OF AGRICULTURE
Whitten Bldg., 1400 Independence Ave. S.W., Washington, DC 20250
(202) 720-4623; Employee Locator: (202) 720-8732; Fax: (202) 720-5023
Internet: www.usda.gov

Secretary of Agriculture: Michael O. Johanns
Room 200-A (202) 720-3631

General Counsel: Nancy S. Bryson, Room 107-W
(202) 720-3351
Works to improve and develop agricultural production, income and markets; to stop hunger through food programs; to protect the environment, soil, water and forests; and inspects and grades food products for sale. *7 U.S.C. 2201*

Animal and Plant Health Inspection Services (APHIS), Plant Protection and Quarantine Programs
Eastern Regional Office
920 Main Campus Dr., Suite 200, Raleigh, NC 27606-5213
(919) 855-7300; Fax: (919) 855-7393

Regional Dir.: Jerry L. Fowler

Animal and Plant Health Inspection Services (APHIS), Animal Care
Eastern Regional Office
920 Main Campus Dr., Unit 30-40, Suite 200,
Raleigh, NC 27606
(919) 855-7100; Fax: (919) 855-7123

Regional Dir.: Dr. Elizabeth Goldentyer

Animal and Plant Health Inspection Service, Investigative and Enforcement Services
Eastern Regional Office
920 Main Campus Dr., Suite 200, Raleigh, NC 27606
(919) 716-5618; Fax: (919) 716-5626
Regional Dir.: John S. Kinsella
Asst. Regional Dirs.:
William T. Groce
Herbert Jordan
Allison Khroustalev

Animal and Plant Health Inspection Services (APHIS), Veterinary Services
Eastern Regional Office
920 Main Campus Dr., Suite 200, Raleigh, NC 27606
(919) 855-7250; Fax: (919) 855-7295
Regional Dir.: Jere Dick

Food and Nutrition Service Regional Office
200 N. High St., Room 750, Columbus, OH 43215-2476
(614) 469-6864; Fax: (614) 469-6849
Officer in Charge: Sheila M. Jacobs

Food and Nutrition Service—Cincinnati Satellite Office
Federal Bldg., Room 10405, 550 Main St.,
Cincinnati, OH 45202-3276
(513) 684-3568; Fax: (513) 684-6043

Food and Nutrition Service—Cleveland Satellite Office
Anthony J. Celebrezze Federal Bldg., Room 1661,
1240 E. Ninth St., Cleveland, OH 44199
(216) 522-4990; Fax: (216) 522-4994

Office of the Inspector General
111 N. Canal St., Suite 1130, Chicago, IL 60606-7295
Audits: (312) 353-1352; Audits Fax: (312) 353-3017;
Investigations: (312) 353-1358;
Investigations Fax: (312) 353-8963
Regional, Inspector General: Edward R. Krivus (Audits)
Special Agent in Charge: Vacancy at Press Time
(Investigations)

Rural Development
Washington Office
1400 Independence Ave. S.W., Mailstop 0705,
Washington, DC 20250
Public Affairs: (202) 720-4323; Fax: (202) 690-4083
Internet: www.rurdev.usda.gov
Under Secretary: Gilbert G. Gonzalez (Acting)
Mailstop 0107 (202) 720-4581; Fax: (202) 720-2080
Develops sustainable communities by improving the economy and quality of life in rural areas; offers financial programs, technical assistance and educational materials; helps rural Americans build, buy or rent housing; helps rural communities build or expand vital community facilities; offers financial and technical assistance to rural businesses and cooperatives; and ensures that rural communities are served by modern utilities.
Formerly known as Farmer's Home Admin. and Rural Economic & Community Development

Ohio State Office
Federal Bldg., Rm. 507, 200 N. High St., Columbus, OH 43215
(614) 255-2400
State Dir.: Randall C. Hunt
(614) 255-2390; Fax: (614) 255-2559
E-mail: Randall.Hunt@oh.usda.gov
Dir., Administrative Programs: Beth Huhn
(614) 255-2515; Fax: (614) 255-2558
E-mail: Beth.Huhn@oh.usda.gov
Public Information Coordinator: Michael Jones
(614) 255-2394; Fax: (614) 255-2559
E-mail: Michael.Jones@oh.usda.gov
Dir., Housing Programs: Gerald Arnott
(614) 255-2401; Fax: (614) 255-2561
E-mail: Gerald.Arnott@oh.usda.gov
Dir., Business Programs: James Cogan
(614) 255-2420; Fax: (614) 255-2562
E-mail: Jim.Cogan@oh.usda.gov
Dir., Community Programs: David Douglas
(614) 255-2391; Fax: (614) 255-2562
E-mail: David.Douglas@oh.usda.gov

Dept. of Agriculture, Rural Development—Cont'd

Area Dir., Findlay Area Office: Christopher Spellmire
7868 C.R. 140, Suite D, Findlay, OH 45840
(419) 422-0242; Fax: (419) 422-5423
E-mail: chris.spellmire@oh.usda.gov

Area Dir., Hillsborough Area Office: Lynn Stevens
514 Harry Sauner Rd., Suite 3, Hillsboro, OH 45133
(937) 393-1921; Fax: (937) 393-1656
E-mail: lynn.stevens@oh.usda.gov

Area Dir., Massillon Area Office: John Miller
2650 Richville Dr. S.E., Suite 102, Massillon, OH 44646
(330) 830-7700; Fax: (330) 830-7701
E-mail: john.miller@oh.usda.gov

Area Dir., Marietta Area Office: Carol Costanzo
21330 State Rt. 676, Suite A, Marietta, OH 45750
(740) 373-7113; Fax: (740) 373-4838
E-mail: carol.costanzo@oh.usda.gov

Milk Market Administration

1325 Industrial Pkwy. N., P.O. Box 5102, Brunswick, OH 44212
(330) 225-4758; Fax: (330) 220-6675
Internet: www.fmmaclev.com

Market Administrator: David Z. Walker
E-mail: dwalker@fmmaclev.com

Marketing Specialist: Gino M. Tosi
USDA-AMS Dairy Programs,
South Building, Room 2971, P.O. Box 96456,
Washington, DC 20090-6456
(202) 720-7183; Fax: (202) 690-0552

Food Safety Inspection Services—Program Enforcement Evaluation & Review (PEER)

1919 S. Highland Ave., Suite 120C, Lombard, IL 60148
(630) 916-6226, Ext. 264; Fax: (630) 620-7876

Regional Mgr.: Michael Bird
Administrator: Karen Higgs

United States Forest Service

Eastern Regional Office
626 E. Wisconsin Ave., Suite 800, Milwaukee, WI 53202
(414) 297-3600; Fax: (414) 944-3963; TTY: (414) 297-3507

Regional Forester: Randy Moore
(414) 297-3765; Fax: (414) 944-3973
Special Asst. to RF: Kathy Gorman (414) 297-3765
Deputy Regional Foresters:
Skip Starkey (Operations) (414) 297-3765
Jim Sanders (Resources—Acting) (414) 297-3765

Eastern Regional Office of the General Counsel
626 E. Wisconsin Ave., Milwaukee, WI 53202-4616
Fax: (414) 944-3967

Assoc. Regional Atty.: Mike Danaher (414) 297-1891
Dep. Assoc. Regional Atty.: Vacancy at Press Time
(414) 297-3776

DEPARTMENT OF COMMERCE
Office of the Secretary, Herbert C. Hoover Bldg., 1401 Constitution Ave. N.W., Washington, DC 20230
**(202) 482-2000; Fax: (202) 482-2741;
Legislative and Intergovernmental Affairs:
(202) 482-3663; Public Affairs: (202) 482-4883;
Business Liaison: (202) 482-1360;
Small & Disadvantaged Business Utilization:
(202) 482-1472; OSDBU Fax: (202) 482-0501
Internet: www.doc.gov**

Secretary of Commerce: Carlos Gutierrez, Room 5516
(202) 482-2112; E-mail: cgutierrez@doc.gov
Deputy Secretary: Theodore W. Kassinger, Room 5838
(202) 482-8376 E-mail: tkassinger@doc.gov
General Counsel: Jane T. Dana (Acting), Room 5870
(202) 482-4772; Fax: (202) 482-0042
E-mail: ogcexecutiveoffice@doc.gov

Promotes job creation, economic growth, sustainable development and improved living standards for all Americans, by working in partnership with businesses, universities, communities, and workers to: build for the future and promote U.S. competitiveness in the global marketplace, by strengthening and safeguarding the nation's economic infrastructure; keeps America competitive with cutting-edge science and technology; provides effective management and stewardship of our nation's resources and assets.

Bureau of the Census

4700 Silver Hill Rd., Bldg. 3, Washington, DC 20233-0001
Administration: (301) 763-2917;
Public Information Office: (301) 763-3030
Internet: www.census.gov

Director: Charles Louis Kincannon, Room 2049
(301) 763-2135
Collects and compiles statistical information on the population and economy of the United States. *13 U.S.C. 1*

Regional Office
1395 Brewery Park Blvd., Detroit, MI 48207
(313) 656-0100; Fax: (313) 259-5045
E-mail: detroit.regional.office@census.gov

Regional Dir.: Dwight P. Dean

Bureau of Economic Analysis

1441 L St. N.W., Room M-100, Washington, DC 20230
(202) 606-9900; Administrative Office: (202) 606-5556;
Fax: (202) 606-5310
E-mail: webmaster@bea.doc.gov
Internet: www.bea.gov

Director: J. Steven Landefeld (202) 606-9600
Produces and disseminates economic accounts statistics that provide government, businesses and individuals with a comprehensive, up-to-date picture of economic activity; presents basic information on such key issues as U.S. economic growth, regional economic development, and the Nation's position in the world economy. *Organization Order No. 35-1A*

Economic Development Administration

Herbert C. Hoover Bldg., 1401 Constitution Ave. N.W., Washington, DC 20230
(202) 482-2309
Internet: www.eda.gov

Asst. Secretary: David A. Sampson, Room 7804
(202) 482-5081; Fax: (202) 273-4781

Chief Counsel: Benjamin Erulkar, Room 7005
(202) 482-4687; Fax: (202) 501-5671
Works to aid in the creation of new jobs; helps protect existing jobs; and stimulates industrial and commercial growth in distressed areas with low income, high unemployment or in a state of economic dislocation. *42 U.S.C. 3121, et seq.*

Regional Office
111 N. Canal St., Suite 855, Chicago, IL 60606-7208
(312) 353-7706; Fax: (312) 353-8575

Regional Dir.: C. Robert Sawyer
E-mail: rsawyer@eda.doc.gov

Economics and Statistics Administration

Herbert C. Hoover Bldg., Room 4885,
14th St. & Constitution Ave. N.W., Washington, DC 20230
(202) 482-3727; Fax: (202) 482-0432;
(800) STAT-USA: (800) 782-8872; (202) 482-2198
E-mail: stat-usa@doc.gov
Internet: www.esa.doc.gov

Under Secretary of Commerce for Economic Affairs:
Kathleen B. Cooper
Advises the Secretary and other governmental officials on the economy and economic policy and oversees the Census Bureau, Bureau of Economic Analysis, and STAT-USA.

Bureau of Industry and Security

Herbert C. Hoover Bldg., Room 2093,
14th St. & Constitution Ave. N.W., Washington, DC 20230
(202) 482-3825; Fax: (202) 482-0751
Internet: www.bis.doc.gov

Under Secretary: Peter Lichtenbaum
(202) 482-1455; Fax: (202) 482-2387

Chief Counsel: Roman Sloniewsky (Acting)
(202) 482-5301; Fax: (202) 482-0085
Supervises the administration of export promotion and export control including licensing, studies for export restriction decontrol, and enforcement of export restrictions. *50 U.S.C. app. 2401*
Formerly called Bureau of Export Administration

Department of Commerce—Cont'd

International Trade Administration
Herbert C. Hoover Bldg., 14th & Constitution Ave. N.W.,
Washington, DC 20230
1-800-USA-TRADE: (800) 872-8723;
Public Affairs: (202) 482-3809
Internet: www.ita.doc.gov
Under Secretary: Grant D. Aldonis, Room 3850
  (202) 482-2867; Fax: (202) 484-4821
Deputy Under Secretary for Intl. Trade:
  Timothy J. Hauser, Room 3842
  (202) 482-3917; Fax: (202) 482-2925
Chief Counsel: John D. McInerney, Room 3622
  (202) 482-5589; Fax: (202) 482-4912
Works to promote world trade and strengthen the
international trade and investment position of the United
States through the following departments: Market Access
and Compliance, Import Administration, Trade
Development, and U.S. and Foreign Commercial Service.

U.S. Commercial Service
3802 Herbert C. Hoover Bldg.,
14th & Constitution Ave. N.W., Washington, DC 20230
(202) 482-0725, (800) 872-8723; Fax: (202) 482-5013
Internet: www.buyusa.gov
  Asst. Secy. & Director General (Acting): Carlos Poza
Operates 107 U.S. Export Assistance Centers throughout
the country, and more than 150 offices overseas, to assist
U.S. Companies, particularly small and medium-sized
businesses, make sales in international markets; also seeks
to protect U.S. business interests abroad.

  U.S. Export Assistance Center
  Northern Ohio Office
  600 Superior Ave., Suite 700, Cleveland, OH 44114
  (216) 522-4750; Fax: (216) 522-2235
    E-mail: office.cleveland@mail.doc.gov
    Office Dir.: Susan Whitney
  Akron Office
  One Cascade Plz., 8th Floor, Akron, OH 44308
  (330) 237-1264
    Contact: Ricardo Pelaez
    E-mail: rpelaez@mail.doc.gov
  Cincinnati Office
  36 E. 7th St., Suite 2650, Cincinnati, OH 45202
  (513) 684-2944; Fax: (513) 684-3227
    E-mail: office.cincinnati@mail.doc.gov
    Director: Dao Le (513) 684-3829
  Columbus Office
  280 N. High St., Suite 1400, Columbus, OH 43215
  (614) 365-9510; Fax: (614) 365-9598
    Contact: Roberta Ford
    E-mail: roberta.ford@mail.doc.gov
  Toledo Office
  300 Madison Ave., Suite 270, Toledo, OH 43604
  (419) 241-0683; Fax: (419) 241-0684
    E-mail: office.toledo@mail.doc.gov
    Intl. Trade Specialist: Robert Abrahams

Minority Business Development Agency
1401 Constitution Ave. N.W., Room 5053,
Washington, DC 20230
(202) 482-5061, (888) 324-1551
Internet: www.mbda.gov
National Dir.: Ronald N. Langson
Develops and coordinates a national program for minority
business enterprise investment, participation, and
management through technical assistance and granting
market opportunities. *Executive Order 11625*

Chicago National Enterprise Center
55 E. Monroe St., Suite 1406, Chicago, IL 60603
(312) 353-0182; Fax: (312) 353-0191
E-mail: cro-info@mbda.gov
  Regional Dir.: Eric Dobyne
  Ohio Office
  7162 Reading Rd., Suite 630,
  Cincinnati, OH 45237-4757
  (513) 631-7666; Fax: (513) 631-7613
    E-mail: omartin@ohiostatewidembdc.org

National Oceanic and Atmospheric Administration
Herbert C. Hoover Bldg., 14th & Constitution Ave. N.W.,
Washington, DC 20230
(202) 482-6090; Fax: (202) 482-3154
Internet: www.noaa.gov
Under Secretary of Commerce for Oceans and Atmosphere:
  Vice Adm. Conrad C. Lautenbacher, Jr., Room 5128
  (202) 482-3436; Fax: (202) 408-9674
Deputy Administrator: James R. Mahoney, Ph.D., Room 5804
  (202) 482-3567; Fax: (202) 482-6318
General Counsel: James R. Walpole
  (202) 482-4080; Fax: (202) 482-4893
Responsible for all U.S. weather and climate forecasting,
monitoring and archiving of ocean and atmospheric data,
management of marine fisheries and mammals, mapping
and charting of all U.S. waters, coastal zone management,
and research and development in all of these areas. NOAA is
the largest agency in the Department of Commerce and
manages the U.S. operational weather and environmental
satellites, a fleet of ships and aircraft for oceanographic,
surveying, fisheries, coastal, and atmospheric studies,
twelve environmental research laboratories, and several
large supercomputers.

Patent and Trademark Office
2900 Crystal Dr., Suite 906, Arlington, VA 22202
Mailing Address: P.O. Box 1450, Alexandria, VA 22313-1450
(800) 786-9199, (703) 308-4357; Fax: (703) 305-7786
Internet: www.uspto.gov
Under Secretary of Commerce for Intellectual Property
and Deputy Dir.: Jon W. Dudas
  (571) 272-8600; Fax: (571) 273-0464
Commissioner for Patents: Nicholas P. Godici
  (571) 880-0800; Fax: (571) 273-0125
Commissioner for Trademarks: Anne H. Chasser
  (571) 272-8900; Fax: (571) 273-8900
General Counsel: James A. Toupin
  (571) 272-7000; Fax: (571) 273-0099
Dir., Public Affairs: Richard G. Maulsby, Suite 0100
  (571) 272-8400; Fax: (571) 273-0340
Examines, researches, and issues design, plant, and utility
patents for the protection of innovation, research and
invention. Issues, researches, and protects trademarks of
symbols, words, devices or any combination thereof.
Maintains records of attorneys qualified to practice before
the office and patent agents. *35 U.S.C. 1*

Technology Administration
Herbert C. Hoover Bldg., 1401 Constitution Ave. N.W.,
Washington, DC 20230 (202) 482-1575; Fax: (202) 482-5687
Internet: www.technology.gov
Under Secretary for Technology: Phillip J. Bond, Room 4824
  (202) 482-1091; Fax: (202) 501-2595
Asst. Secretary for Technology Policy: Benjamin H. Wu
  Room 4822 (202) 482-1575; Fax: (202) 501-2595
Chief Counsel for Technology: Craig S. Burkhardt
  (202) 482-1065
Aids in the advancement of U.S. business in innovation,
technological development, and productivity.

National Institute of Standards and Technology
100 Bureau Dr., Mail-Stop 1070,
Gaithersburg, MD 20899-1070
(301) 975-2000; General Inquiries: (301) 975-6478;
Fax: (301) 926-1630
E-mail: inquiries@nist.gov; Internet: www.nist.gov
125 Broadway, Boulder, CO 80303-3328
(303) 497-3000; Public Inquiries: (303) 497-3246
  Director: Dr. Hratch G. Semerjian (Acting) (301) 975-2300
  Dir. of Media Relations: Michael E. Newman (301) 975-3025
  Counsel for NIST: Michael R. Rubin
  (301) 975-2803; Fax: (301) 926-6241
  Freedom of Information Act Officer: Sharon Bisco
  (301) 975-4074; Fax: (301) 926-8091
Promotes U.S. economic growth by working with industry to
develop and apply technology, measurements and
standards. Oversees the Measurement and Standards
Laboratories, Advanced Technology Program, the
Manufacturing Extension Partnership and the Malcolm
Baldrige National Quality Award.

Dept. of Commerce, Technology Admin.—Cont'd

National Technical Information Service
5285 Port Royal Rd., Springfield, VA 22161
(703) 605-6000; Fax: (703) 605-6900
E-mail: info@ntis.gov; Internet: www.ntis.gov
   Director: Ron Lawson
     (703) 605-6400; Fax: (703) 605-6715
Serves as the nation's clearinghouse for research and development results and other information produced by and for the U.S. Government.

National Telecommunications and Information Administration

Herbert C. Hoover Bldg., Room 4898,
1401 Constitution Ave. N.W., Washington, DC 20230
(202) 482-7002; Internet: www.ntia.doc.gov
Asst. Secretary, for Communication & Information:
   Michael D. Gallagher (202) 482-1840
Chief Counsel: Kathy Smith (202) 482-1816
Advises the President on telecommunications and information policy, develops and presents plans at international conferences, manages Federal use of the radio frequency spectrum and serves as the principal Federal communications research lab. *47 U.S.C. 901*

United States Travel and Tourism Administration

All functions now assumed by the International Trade Administration, supra.

DEPARTMENT OF DEFENSE
Office of the Secretary, 1000 Defense Pentagon, Washington, DC 20301-1000
Public Affairs: (703) 428-0711
Internet: www.defenselink.mil

Secretary of Defense: Donald H. Rumsfeld
Deputy Secretary: Dr. Paul Wolfowitz
   1010 Defense Pentagon, Washington, DC 20301-1010
General Counsel: William J. Haynes II
   The Pentagon, Room 3E980, Washington, DC 20301
   (703) 695-3341
Asst. Secretary for Public Affairs: Lawrence DiRita (Acting)
   Room 2E556 (703) 697-9312; Fax: (703) 695-4299
Provides the military forces necessary to deter war and protect the security of the United States through the maintenance of the Army, Navy, Air Force, and Marine Corps consisting of 1.7 million active duty personnel (247,000 overseas) and 67,000 ships at sea. *5 U.S.C. 101*

Department of the Air Force

The Pentagon, Washington, DC 20330-1670
(703) 545-6700; Internet: www.af.mil
Secretary of the Air Force: Peter B. Teets (Acting), Room 1670
   (703) 697-7376
General Counsel: Mary L. Walker, Room 4E856
   (703) 697-0941; Fax: (703) 693-9355
Preserves the peace of the United States through the effective control of air and space activities.

Defense Contract Management Agency

General Counsel's Office
6350 Walker Lane, Suite 300, Alexandria, VA 22310-3241
Internet: www.dcma.mil
Director: Maj. Gen. Darryl A. Scott (Air Force)
   (703) 428-1700; Fax: (703) 428-1942
General Counsel: Nicholas Retson (703) 428-1824

Department of the Army

101 Army Pentagon, Washington, DC 20310-0101
(703) 695-3211; Fax: (703) 697-8036
Internet: www.army.mil
Secretary of the Army: Francis J. Harvey
General Counsel: Avon N. Williams II
   104 Army Pentagon, Washington, DC 20310-0104
   (703) 697-9235; Fax: (703) 693-9254
Organizes, trains, and equips more than one million men and women on active duty and reserve forces for the preservation of peace, security, and the defense of the nation. Carries out programs for the protection of the environment, improving waterways, flood and erosion control, beach erosion control, and water resource development. *50 U.S.C. 401*

United States Army Corps of Engineers

441 G St. N.W., Washington, DC 20314
(202) 761-0008
Internet: www.usace.army.mil
Commander: Lt. Gen Carl A. Strock (202) 761-1024
Chief Counsel: Earl Stockdale, Room 3A29
   (202) 761-0018; Fax: (202) 761-4932

Department of the Navy

1000 Navy Pentagon, Washington, DC 20350-1000
(703) 695-3131; Information: (703) 545-6700
Internet: www.navy.mil
Secretary of the Navy: Gordon R. England
General Counsel: Alberto J. Mora, Room 4E516
   (202) 685-7000; Fax: (202) 685-6580
Protects the United States by the effective prosecution of war at sea including, with the Marine Corps component, the seizure or defense of advance naval bases, supports all military departments of the United States. Maintains the freedom of the seas. *10 U.S.C. 5011*

DEPARTMENT OF EDUCATION
400 Maryland Ave. S.W., Washington, DC 20202
Information Resource Ctr.: (202) 401-2000;
(800) 872-5327; Fax: (202) 401-0689
Internet: www.ed.gov

Secretary of Education: Margaret Spellings, Room 7W301
   (202) 401-3000; Fax: (202) 401-0596
General Counsel: Kent Talbert (Acting), Room 6E313
   (202) 401-6000
Establishes policy for, administers, and coordinates federal assistance to educational efforts and programs. *20 U.S.C. 3411*

Regional Office

111 N. Canal St., Chicago, IL 60606-7204
(312) 353-8192; Fax: (312) 353-5147
Secretary's Regional Representative: Kristine Cohn

Regional Office of Inspector General
111 N. Canal St., Suite 940, Chicago, IL 60606-7204
   Regional Inspector General: Richard Dowd (Audits)
   (312) 886-6503
   Special Agent in Charge: Christopher Fox (312) 353-7891

Office for Civil Rights, Cleveland Office
Bank One Center, Suite 750, 600 E. Superior Ave.,
Cleveland, OH 44114-2611
(216) 522-4970; Fax: (216) 522-2573; TDD: (216) 522-4944
E-mail: OCR_Cleveland@ed.gov

Office for Civil Rights, Chicago
111 N. Canal, Suite 1053, Chicago, IL 60606-7204
(312) 886-8434
   Regional Dir.: Linda McGovern

DEPARTMENT OF ENERGY
Forrestal Bldg., 1000 Independence Ave. S.W., Washington, DC 20585
(800) 342-5363; Information Officer: (202) 586-5575;
Fax: (202) 586-4403
Internet: www.energy.gov

Secretary of Energy: Dr. Samuel W. Bodman, Room 7A-257
   (202) 586-6210; Fax: (202) 586-4403
General Counsel: Lee Liberman Otis, Room 6A-245
   (202) 586-5281; Fax: (202) 586-1499
   E-mail: lee.otis@hq.doe.gov
Provides the framework for a coordinated national energy plan. Conducts long-term and high-risk energy research, markets federal power, works for the conservation of energy, oversees the nuclear weapons program, energy regulatory programs, and a central energy data collection and analysis program. *42 U.S.C. 7131*

Regional Office

9800 S. Cass Ave., Lemont, IL 60439
(630) 252-2110
   Manager: Marvin E. Gunn, Jr.

Ohio Field Office
175 Tri-County Pkwy., Springdale, OH 45246-3222
(513) 246-0074
   Manager: Robert F. Warther

DEPARTMENT OF HEALTH AND HUMAN SERVICES
200 Independence Ave. S.W., Washington, DC 20201
(202) 619-0257, (877) 696-6775
E-mail: hhsmail@os.dhhs.gov
Internet: www.dhhs.gov
Secretary of Health and Human Services:
Michael O. Leavitt, Room 615F
(202) 690-7000; Fax: (202) 690-7203
General Counsel: Alex M. Azar II, Room 713-F
(202) 690-7741; Fax: (202) 690-7998
E-mail: alex.azar@hhs.gov
Internet: www.dhhs.gov/ogc

Acts as the personal and living services department of government providing assistance and aid in all aspects of life from medical and health care services and aid to addiction and mental health services. *20 U.S.C. 3508*

Region V Office
233 N. Michigan Ave., Suite 700, Chicago, IL 60601
(312) 353-1921
Secretary's Regional Representative: Suzanne Krohn (Acting)
(312) 353-5160
Regional Chief Counsel: Donna Morros Weinstein
(312) 886-1709

Administration on Aging
1 Massachusetts Ave. N.W., Washington, DC 20201
(202) 619-0724; Eldercare Locator: (800) 677-1116;
Public Inquiries: (202) 619-0724; Fax: (202) 357-3523
E-mail: aoainfo@aoa.hhs.gov
Internet: www.aoa.gov
Asst. Secretary for Aging: Josefina G. Carbonell
(202) 401-4541
Established by the Older Americans Act of 1965, this office acts as the leading advocate within the Federal Government for older Americans. Disburses funds for various programs including group and home-delivered meals, in-home assistance for the frail elderly, transportation services, legal assistance, nursing home ombudsman services, employment help and senior center programs. Also funds research, demonstration and training programs.

Administration for Children and Families
370 L'Enfant Promenade S.W., Room Aerospace 6th F,
Washington, DC 20447
(202) 401-2337; Fax: (202) 401-4678
E-mail: wade.horn@acf.hhs.gov
Internet: www.acf.hhs.gov
Asst. Secretary: Wade F. Horn, Ph.D.
Coordinates the efforts and programs for the advancement and preservation of the welfare and conditions of children and families.

Regional Office
233 N. Michigan Ave., Suite 400, Chicago, IL 60601-5519
(312) 353-4237; Fax: (312) 353-2204
E-mail: chicago@acf.hhs.gov
Regional Administrator: Joyce A. Thomas

Center for Disease Control and Prevention
1600 Clifton Rd. N.E., Atlanta, GA 30333
(404) 639-3311; Public Inquiries: (404) 498-1530;
(800) 311-3435
Internet: www.cdc.gov
Director: Julie L. Gerberding, M.D., M.P.H.

Education Information Div.
Robert A. Taft Laboratory, 4676 Columbia Pkwy.,
Cincinnati, OH 45226
(513) 533-8302; Publications: (513) 533-8120;
Fax: (513) 533-8588
Director: Paul Schulte, Ph.D.

National Institute for Occupational Safety and Health (NIOSH)
Alice Hamilton Laboratory
5555 Ridge Ave., Cincinnati, OH 45213
(513) 841-4428; Fax: (513) 841-4483
Dir., Div. of Surveillance, Hazard Evaluation & Field Studies: Theresa Schnoor
Assoc. Dir. for Surveillance: John P. Sestito, J.D., MS Room R12 (513) 841-4428; Fax: (404) 929-2666

Food and Drug Administration
Parklawn Bldg., 5600 Fishers Lane,
Rockville, MD 20857-0001
(301) 827-2410, (888) 463-6332
Internet: www.fda.gov
Commissioner: Lester M. Crawford, Jr., D.V.M., Ph.D. (Acting)
Mail Stop HF-1, Room 1471,
(301) 827-2410; Fax: (301) 443-3100
E-mail: d.commissioner@fda.hhs.gov
General Counsel: Gerald F. Masoudi (Acting), Room 605
(301) 827-1137; Fax: (301) 827-3054

Office of the Administrative Law Judge
5600 Fishers Ln. (HF-3), Room 9-57, Rockville, MD 20857
(301) 827-7120; Fax: (301) 594-6800
Admin. Law Judge: Daniel J. Davidson

Regional Office (Central Region)
900 U.S. Customhouse, 200 Chestnut St.,
Philadelphia, PA 19106
(215) 597-4390; Fax: (215) 597-5798
Internet: www.fda.gov
1600 Watermark Dr., Suite 105, Columbus, OH 43215
(614) 487-1273
Regional Director: Susan M. Setterberg (215) 597-4390
E-mail: ssetterb@ora.fda.gov

Regional Office (Central Region)
20 N. Michigan Ave., Suite 510, Chicago, IL 60602
(312) 596-6520; Fax: (312) 886-1682
Deputy Regional Dir.: Andy Bonnano

Cincinnati District Office
6751 Steger Dr., Cincinnati, OH 45237-3097
(513) 679-2700; Fax: (513) 679-2771
District Dir.: Carol Heppe

Centers for Medicare and Medicaid Services
7500 Security Blvd., Baltimore, MD 21244-1850
(410) 786-3000, (877) 267-2323
Internet: www.cms.hhs.gov
Administrator: Mark B. McClellan, M.D., Ph.D.
(410) 786-3151; E-mail: mmcclellan@cms.hhs.gov
Acts mainly as the purchaser of health care services for Medicare and Medicaid beneficiaries; assures proper administration by its contractors and state agencies; establishes policies for the reimbursement of health care providers; conducts research on the effectiveness of various methods of health care management, treatment and financing; and assesses the quality of health care facilities and services. *56 CFR 123474*
Formerly called Health Care Financing Administration

Regional Office
233 N. Michigan Ave., Suite 600, Chicago, IL 60601-5519
(312) 886-6432; Fax: (312) 353-0252
Regional Dir.: Jackie Garner

Office of Public Health and Science
Hubert H. Humphrey Bldg., Suite 716G,
200 Independence Ave. S.W., Washington, DC 20201
(202) 690-7694; Fax: (202) 690-7425
Internet: www.osophs.dhhs.gov/ophs
Asst. Secretary for Health: Cristina V. Beato, M.D. (Acting)
Deputy Asst. Secretary for Health: Howard Zucker, M.D. (Designee)
Chief Counsel, Public Health Service: David Benor
Parklawn Bldg., Room 4A-53, 5600 Fishers Lane,
Rockville, MD 20857 (301) 443-2644; Fax: (301) 443-2639
Coordinates with the states and administers the public health efforts; coordinates and upholds international health-related agreements; conducts medical and biomedical research; develops programs for planning public and private institutional medical programs; and enforces laws for the protection of foods, drugs, and medical apparatus and supplies. *42 U.S.C. 201*
Formerly known as The Office of the Asst. Secy. for Health

Region V Office
233 N. Michigan Ave., Suite 1300, Chicago, IL 60601
(312) 353-1385; Fax: (312) 353-0718
Regional Health Administrator:
Steven R. Potsic, M.D., M.P.H.
E-mail: spotsic@osophs.dhhs.gov

Dept. of Health and Human Services—Cont'd

Substance Abuse and Mental Health Services Administration
1 Choke Cherry Rd., 8th Floor, Rockville, MD 20857
(240) 276-2000, 276-2130; Fax: (240) 276-2010, 276-2135
Internet: www.samhsa.gov
Administrator: Charles G. Curie, M.D., M.A., A.C.S.W.
  (240) 276-2000; Fax: (240) 276-2010
Deputy Admin.: Vacancy at Press Time
Provides prevention, diagnosis, and treatment services for people at risk for or experiencing substance abuse or mental illnesses. Works in partnership with States, communities and private organizations to address the needs of individuals with substance abuse and mental illnesses, and to identify and respond to the community risk factors that contribute to these illnesses. *P.L. 102-321 and P.L. 106-310. If using private courier service use zip code 20850*

Office of the Surgeon General
5600 Fishers Ln., Room 1866, Rockville, MD 20857
(301) 443-4000; Fax: (301) 443-3574
Surgeon General:
  Richard H. Carmona, M.D., M.P.H., F.A.C.S.

DEPARTMENT OF HOMELAND SECURITY
Nebraska Ave. Complex, Washington, DC 20528
Mailing Address: U.S. Dept. of Homeland Security, Washington, DC 20528
(202) 282-8000
Internet: www.dhs.gov/dhspublic
Secretary: Michael Chertoff
Deputy Secretary: Admiral James Loy
General Counsel: Philip J. Perry (pending confirmation)
Dir. of FOIA, Privacy Act and Disclosure:
  (202) 772-9848; Fax: (202) 772-5036
  E-mail: FOIA@dhs.gov
All correspondence must be sent to mailing address—do not use "Nebraska Ave. Complex" in address.

Border and Transportation Security
(202) 282-8355; Fax: (202) 282-8407
Under Secretary for Border and Transportation Security:
  Vacancy at Press Time
Responsible for maintaining the security of our nation's borders and transportation systems.

Bureau of Customs and Border Protection
1300 Pennsylvania Ave. N.W., Washington, DC 20229
(202) 344-2001; Public Affairs: (202) 344-1780;
Commissioner's Fax: (202) 344-1380
Internet: www.cbp.gov
  Commissioner: Robert C. Bonner
  Deputy Commissioner: Deborah Spero (202) 344-1010
  Asst. Commissioner, Office of Regulations & Rulings:
    Michael Schmitz (202) 572-8700
  Chief Counsel: Alfonso Robles, Room 4.4B
    (202) 344-2990; Fax: (202) 344-2950
Collects duties from imports and enforces customs, immigration and related laws, including the seizure of contraband and narcotics. *19 U.S.C. 2071*
Formerly components of the U.S. Customs Service, Department of the Treasury, Department of Agriculture and Immigration and Naturalization Service, Department of Justice

  Mid America Custom Management Center
  610 S. Canal St., Room 900, Chicago, IL 60607
  (312) 983-9100; Fax: (312) 886-4921
    Director: Anne Lombardi

Bureau of Immigration and Customs Enforcement
425 I St. N.W., Washington, DC 20536
(202) 514-2648; Fax: (202) 307-1918
Internet: www.ice.gov
  Asst. Secretary: Michael J. Garcia
  Asst. Dir., Internal Communication: Cathy Bridwell (Acting)
  Dir., Office of Public Affairs: Russ Knocke
  Deputy Asst. Dir., Media: Manny Van Pelt

The primary investigative arm of the Department of Homeland Security, this agency is a law enforcement agency and does not facilitate or provide assistance with immigration issues. Enforces immigration and customs laws and prevents violations by terrorists and other criminals who threaten national security. Combines the investigative, detention & removal, and intelligence functions of the former Immigration and Naturalization Service with the investigative, intelligence, and air & marine functions of the former Customs Service.

Emergency Preparedness and Response
(202) 282-8000

Under Secretary for Emergency Preparedness and Response: Michael D. Brown
  FEMA, 500 C St. S.W., Washington, DC 20472
Responsible for ensuring the nation's preparation for, and ability to recover from, terrorist attacks and natural disasters.

Federal Emergency Management Agency
500 C St. S.W., Washington, DC 20472
Public Affairs: (202) 646-4600;
Contracts and Procurements: (202) 646-3742;
Personnel Locator: (202) 566-1600
Internet: www.fema.gov
  Under Secretary: Michael D. Brown (202) 646-3900
    E-mail: michael.brown@fema.gov
  General Counsel: David A. Trissell (202) 646-4105
  Dir., Response Div.: Ed Buikema (Acting) (202) 646-3692
  Dir., Recovery Div.: Daniel A. Craig (202) 646-3642
  Administrator, Fed. Insurance & Mitigation Directorate:
    David Maurstad (Acting) (202) 646-2781
  Asst. Dir., Admin. & Resource Planning Directorate:
    Vacancy at Press Time
  Dir., Regional Operations Directorate: Vallee Bunting
    (202) 646-4289
  Chief Info. Officer: Barry West
    (202) 646-3336; Fax: (202) 646-4655
  Division Dir., Public Affairs, Office of External Affairs:
    Vacancy at Press Time (202) 646-4600
  Administrator, U.S. Fire Administration:
    R. David Paulison (301) 646-4223; Fax: (301) 646-4301
Acts as the Federal focal point of emergency planning, preparedness, mitigation, response, and recovery. Funds emergency programs, provides technical guidance and training, and ensures a broad based program to protect public safety and property. *5 U.S.C. app. Reorganization Plan No. 3 of 1978*
Formerly an independent agency

  Regional Office
  536 S. Clark St., Chicago, IL 60605
  (312) 408-5500

    Regional Dir.: Edward G. Buikema (312) 408-5504
    Deputy Regional Dir.: Janet M. Odeshoo (312) 408-5504

Information Analysis and Infrastructure Protection
(202) 282-8000

Under Secretary for Information Analysis and Infrastructure Protection: Frank Libutti
Responsible for identifing and assessing intelligence information concerning threats to the homeland, issuing warnings, and taking appropriate preventive and protective action.

Science and Technology Directorate
(202) 282-8000

Under Secretary for Science and Technology:
  Dr. Charles E. McQeary
Coordinates the Department's efforts in research and development, including preparing for and responding to terrorist threats involving weapons of mass destruction.

Management Directorate
(202) 205-4613

Under Secretary for Management: Janet Hale
Responsible for budget, management and personnel issues.

Dept. of Homeland Security—Cont'd

United States Coast Guard
2100 2nd St. S.W., Rm. 3310, Washington, DC 20593-0001
Public Affairs: (202) 267-1587; Internet: www.uscg.mil
Commandant: Admiral Thomas H. Collins (202) 267-2390
Judge Advocate General: RADM John Crowley (202) 267-1617
Chief Judge, Admin. Law: Joseph N. Ingolia (202) 267-2940
Acts as the Federal Maritime law enforcement agency except when called into service of the United States Navy during times of war or when the President orders. *14 U.S.C. 1*
Formerly a component of the Department of Transportation

Legal Office
Mlclant Legal Division, 300 E. Main St., Suite 400,
Norfolk, VA 23510-9100
(757) 628-4192; Fax: (757) 628-4217
Internet: www.uscg.mil/mlclant/ldiv/ldiv.htm
  Chief of Legal Division: Jeneen Howard-Williams

United States Secret Service
950 H St. N.W., Suite 8400, Washington, DC 20001
Public Affairs: (202) 406-5708
Internet: www.secretservice.gov
245 Murray Dr., Bldg. 410, Washington, DC 20223
Director: W. Ralph Basham (202) 406-5700
Chief Counsel: John J. Kelleher
    (202) 406-5771; Fax: (202) 406-6544
Protects the President, Vice President, former Presidents, their immediate families, the White House Complex, major Presidential candidates, and foreign dignitaries. Enforces laws regarding counterfeiting, financial institution fraud, telecommunications and computer fraud, false identification, access device fraud, advance fee fraud, electronic funds transfers and money laundering. *Title 3 & 18 U.S.C.*
Formerly a component of the Department of the Treasury

Akron Resident Office
Grant-Washington Professional Bldg. 2,
441 Wolf Ledges Pkwy., Akron, OH 44311
(330) 761-0544; Fax: (330) 761-0540
  Resident Agent-in-Charge: David Lee

Cincinnati Field Office
Cincinnati, OH 45202
(513) 684-3585; Fax: (513) 684-3436

Cleveland Field Office
6450 Rockside Woods Blvd. S., Suite 200,
Independence, OH 44131-2230
(216) 706-4365; Fax: (216) 706-4445

Columbus Resident Office
500 S. Front St., Columbus, OH 43215
(614) 469-7370; Fax: (614) 469-2049
  Resident Agent-in-Charge: Kurt Douglass

Dayton Resident Office
200 W. Second St., Dayton, OH 45402
(937) 222-2013; Fax: (937) 225-2724
  Resident Agent-in-Charge: Todd Bagby

Toledo Resident Office
Four Seagate, Toledo, OH 43604
(419) 259-6434; Fax: (419) 259-6437
  Resident Agent-in-Charge: Vacancy at Press Time

Bureau of Citizenship and Immigration Services
425 Eye St. N.W., Room 7100, Washington, DC 20536
(202) 514-1900; Fax: (202) 307-9911
Internet: www.uscis.gov
Director: Eduardo Aguirre, Jr.
Chief, Office of Citizenship: Alfonso Aguilar
Facilitates the entry of persons legally admissable as visitors or as immigrants to the United States; grants benefits under the Immigration and Nationality Act, as amended, including providing assistance to those seeking permanent resident status or naturalization; prevents unlawful entry, employment or receipt of benefits by those who are not entitled to them; and apprehends or removes those aliens who enter or remain illegally in the United States and/or whose stay is not in the public interest. *(8 U.S.C. 1551 note) (8 U.S.C. 1101 note)*
Formerly Immigration and Nationalization Service, Department of Justice

Cleveland District Office
A.J.C. Federal Bldg., Room 501, 1240 E. Ninth St.,
Cleveland, OH 44199
Legal: (216) 535-0530; Detention: (216) 535-0510;
Duty Officer: (216) 535-0515;
Freedom of Information Act: (216) 535-0355;
Press Information Officer: (216) 535-0500
  District Dir.: Mark B. Hanson

  Cincinnati Sub Office
  J.W. Peck Federal Bldg., Room 4001, 550 Main St.,
  Cincinnati, OH 45202
  (513) 684-2934; Duty Officer: (513) 684-2930;
  Press Information Office: (216) 535-0500
    Officer-in-Charge: Helaine Tasch

  Columbus Satellite Office
  Leveque Tower, Suite 306, 50 W. Broad St.,
  Columbus, OH 43215
  Detention: (614) 469-2904;
  Press Information Office: (216) 535-0500
    Officer-in-Charge: Cheryl Gallegos

Office of Inspector General
(202) 254-4100; Hotline: (800) 323-8603
Inspector General: Richard L. Skinner (Acting)
General Counsel to the Inspector General:
  Richard N. Reback

Federal Law Enforcement Training Center
Glynco, GA 31524 (912) 267-2100; Fax: (912) 554-4608
Internet: www.fletc.gov
Director: Connie L. Patrick
Chief Counsel: Willis C. Hunter
    (912) 267-2441; Fax: (912) 267-2847
Deputy Chief Counsel: David H. Brunjes (912) 267-2441
Atty. Advisors:
    Trisha Besselman (912) 267-2441
    Diane Buchli (912) 267-2441
    W. Kent Davis (912) 267-2441
Formerly a component of the Department of the Treasury

DEPARTMENT OF HOUSING AND URBAN DEVELOPMENT
451 7th St. S.W., Washington, DC 20410
(202) 708-1112; Personnel Locator: (202) 708-1422;
TTY: (202) 708-1455
Internet: www.hud.gov

Secretary of Housing and Urban Development:
  Alphonso Jackson, Room 10000
  (202) 708-0417; Fax: (202) 619-8365
General Counsel: Vacancy at Press Time (202) 708-2244
Creates and administers programs for the meeting of the nation's housing needs, fair housing opportunity, and improvement and development of the nation's communities. *42 U.S.C. 3532*

Office of Administrative Law Judges
409 Third St. S.W., Suite 320, Washington, DC 20024
(202) 708-5004; Fax: (202) 708-5014
Chief Admin. Law Judge: Arthur A. Liberty
Admin. Law Judges:
    Robert A. Andretta
    Thomas C. Heinz
    Constance T. O'Bryant

Chicago Regional Office
Ralph H. Metcalfe Federal Bldg., Room 2608,
77 W. Jackson Blvd., Chicago, IL 60604-3507
(312) 353-5680; Fax: (312) 886-2729
Regional Dir.: Joseph P. Galvan

Columbus Field Office
200 N. High St., Columbus, OH 43215-2463
(614) 469-5737; Fax: (614) 469-2432
  Director: Thomas H. Leach, Ext. 8110

Cincinnati Field Office
15 E. Seventh St., Cincinnati, OH 45202-2401
(513) 684-3451; Fax: (513) 684-6224
  Director: James A. Cunningham

Cleveland Field Office
1350 Euclid Ave., Suite 500, Cleveland, OH 44115-1815
(216) 522-4058; Fax: (216) 522-4067
  Director: Douglas W. Shelby

Departments & Agencies

Dept. of Housing & Urban Development—Cont'd

Federal Housing Administration
451 7th St. S.W., Room 9100, Washington, DC 20410-8000
(202) 708-3600; Fax: (202) 708-2580
Internet: www.hud.gov/fha
Federal Housing Commissioner: John C. Weicher
   (202) 708-2601
Administers and underwrites housing loans and programs
for the elderly, physically challenged, chronically ill, and low
income persons. Develops and aids in the development of
multi-family housing projects.

Office of Community Planning and Development
451 7th St. S.W., Suite 7100, Washington, DC 20410
(202) 708-2690; Fax: (202) 708-3336
Internet: www.hud.gov/cpd
Asst. Secretary: Vacancy at Press Time
Advises the Secretary on the development and planning of
community programs and projects to meet the department's
goals.

Policy Development and Research
451 7th St. S.W., Room 8100, Washington, DC 20410-6000
(202) 708-1600; Fax: (202) 619-8000
Asst. Secy. for Policy Development and Research:
  Dennis C. Shea
Evaluates and advises on existing and proposed projects
and programs.

Office of Fair Housing and Equal Opportunity
451 7th St. S.W., Room 5100, Washington, DC 20410
(202) 708-4252; Fax: (202) 708-4483
Internet: www.hud.gov/fhe/fheo.html
Asst. Secretary: Carolyn Y. Peoples
General Deputy Asst. Secy.: Floyd O. May
Administers laws that prohibit discrimination in housing
based on race, color, religion, sex, national origin, familial
status and handicap

Government National Mortgage Association
550 12th St. S.W., Room B-133, Washington, DC 20024
Mailing Address: 451 7th St. S.W., Room B-133,
Washington, DC 20410
(202) 708-1535, (888) 446-6434; Fax: (202) 708-0490
Internet: www.ginniemae.gov
President: Vacancy at Press Time (202) 708-0926
Exec. V.P.: Michael J. Frenz
Supports the government's housing efforts through
financing and guarantees for home financing.

DEPARTMENT OF THE INTERIOR
1849 C St. N.W., Washington, DC 20240
Personnel Locator/Information: (202) 208-3100
Internet: www.doi.gov
Secretary of the Interior: Gale Norton, Room 6150
  (202) 208-7351; Fax: (202) 208-6956
Solicitor: Sue Ellen Wooldridge, Room 6352
  (202) 208-4423; Fax: (202) 208-5584

Encourages and provides for the management, preservation
and operation of the Nation's public lands and natural
resources; develops and uses resources in an
environmentally sound manner; carries out related
scientific research and trust responsibilities of the U.S.
government with respect to American and Alaskan natives.
The Department also manages more than 441 million acres
of Federal lands. *43 U.S.C. 1451*

United States Fish and Wildlife Service

Regional Office
BHW Federal Bldg., 1 Federal Dr.,
Fort Snelling, MN 55111-4056
(612) 713-5301; Fax: (612) 713-5284
Regional Dir.: Robyn Thorson

Delaware Law Enforcement Office
359 Main Rd., Delaware, OH 43015
(740) 368-0137; TTY: (800) 877-8339; Fax: (740) 368-0135
E-mail: Delaware@fws.gov

Sandusky Law Enforcement Office
6100 Columbus Ave., Sandusky, OH 44870
(419) 625-9713; TTY: (800) 877-8339; Fax: (419) 625-0250
E-mail: Sandusky@fws.gov

Reynoldsburg Ecological Services Office
6950-H Americana Pkwy., Reynoldsburg, OH 43068-4127
(614) 469-6923; Fax: (614) 469-6919
E-mail: Reynoldsburg@fws.gov
  Field Supervisor: Mary Knapp

Pennsylvania Avenue National Historic Site
National Capital Parks Central, 900 Ohio Dr. S.W.,
Washington, DC 20242
(202) 485-9880; Fax: (202) 426-1835
Superintendent: Vikki Keys (Acting)
Sidewalks, parks and memorials along Pennsylvania
Avenue from 3rd St. to 15th St., including John Marshall
Park, Navy Memorial, Freedom Plaza, Pershing Park,
Hancock Memorial, GAR Memorial, Mellon Fountain and
Temperance Fountain. *40 U.S.C. 871*
*Formerly known as Pennsylvania Avenue Development
Corporation*

DEPARTMENT OF JUSTICE
950 Pennsylvania Ave. N.W.,
Washington, DC 20530-0001
(202) 514-2000; Fax: (202) 514-4371
E-mail: web@usdoj.gov
Internet: www.usdoj.gov
Attorney General of the United States:
  Alberto R. Gonzales (202) 353-1555; Fax: (202) 307-6777
Represents the interests of the nation and its citizens in the
prosecution of all Federal criminal and civil actions taken to
the Supreme Court. Ensures healthy competition in
business, protects the nation from illegal immigration and
drug trade, and renders legal advice to the President and
the heads of the executive departments. *28 U.S.C. 501*

Bureau of Alcohol, Tobacco, Firearms and Explosives
650 Massachusetts Ave. N.W., Washington, DC 20226
Public Information: (202) 927-8500;
Public Information Fax: (202) 927-8112
Director: Carl J. Truscott
Chief Counsel: Stephen R. Rubenstein
  (202) 927-7772; Fax: (202) 927-6117, 927-8673
Enforces and administers the Federal laws relating to
firearms and explosives and the Anti-Arson Act of 1982.
Administers the U.S. Criminal Code provisions concerning
alcohol and tobacco smuggling and diversion. *18 U.S.C. 2341*
Formerly a component of the Department of Treasury

Columbus Field Division
37 W. Broad St., Suite 200, Columbus, OH 43215-4167
(614) 827-8400; Fax: (614) 827-8401
  Division Dir./Special Agent in Charge:
    Christopher P. Sadowski
  Division Counsel: Joyce T. Rybak

Office of the Solicitor General
950 Pennsylvania Ave., N.W., Washington, DC 20530-0001
(202) 514-2203; Case Mgmt.: (202) 514-2217
Internet: www.usdoj.gov/osg
Solicitor General: Paul D. Clement (Acting)
Supervises and conducts government litigation in the
United States Supreme Court. *28 U.S.C. 505.*

Drug Enforcement Administration
2401 Jefferson Davis Hwy., Mailstop AXS,
Alexandria, VA 22301
(202) 307-1000; Public Affairs: (202) 307-7977;
Fax: (202) 307-7965
Internet: www.usdoj.gov/dea/
Administrator: Karen P. Tandy (202) 307-8000
Chief Counsel: Wendy H. Goggin
  (202) 307-7322; Fax: (202) 307-4364

Office of Administrative Law Judges
E-2123, Washington, DC 20537
(202) 307-8188; Fax: (202) 307-8198

600 Army-Navy Dr., Arlington, VA 22202
  Chief Admin. Law Judge: Mary Ellen Bittner
  Admin. Law Judge: Gail A. Randall

Detroit Field Division
431 Howard St., Detroit, MI 48226 (313) 234-4000
  Special Agent in Charge: John P. Gilbride; Fax: (313) 234-4141

Dept. of Justice, Drug Enforcement Admin.—Cont'd

Cincinnati Resident Office
Federal Office Bldg., Suite 1900, 36 E. 7th St.,
Cincinnati, OH 45202
(513) 684-3671; Fax: (513) 684-3672
  Resident Agent-in-Charge: James Shroba

Cleveland Resident Office
310 Lakeside St., Suite 395, Cleveland, OH 44113
(216) 522-3705; Fax: (216) 522-3704
  Resident Agent-in-Charge: Reginald Cheney

Dayton Resident Office
1 Prestige Pl., Suite 450, Miamisburg, OH 45342
(937) 291-1988; Fax: (937) 291-0535
  Resident Agent-in-Charge: Russell E. Neville

Toledo Resident Office
433 N. Summit St., Suite 700, Toledo, OH 43604
(419) 259-6490
  Resident Agent-in-Charge: Vernon Dunn

Youngstown Resident Office
100 Federal Plz. E., Suite 422, Youngstown, OH 44503
(330) 740-7000; Fax: (330) 740-6969
  Resident Agent-in-Charge: Doug Lamplugh

Federal Bureau of Investigation
J. Edgar Hoover Bldg., 935 Pennsylvania Ave. N.W.,
Washington, DC 20535-0001
(202) 324-3000; Internet: www.fbi.gov/
Director: Robert S. Mueller III
General Counsel: Valerie E. Caproni

Field Division (Cleveland)
1501 Lakeside Ave., Cleveland, OH 44114
(216) 522-1400; Fax: (216) 622-6717
E-mail: cleveland@fbi.gov
  Special Agent in Charge: Theodore R. Wasky
  Asst. Special Agent in Charge: John G. Kavanagh
    Gary D. Klein

Field Division Office (Cincinnati)
John Weld Peck Federal Bldg., Suite 9000, 550 Main St.,
Cincinnati, OH 45202
(513) 421-4310; Fax: (513) 562-5650
E-mail: cincinnati@fbi.gov
  Special Agent in Charge: Stanley J. Borgia
  Asst. Special Agent in Charge: James H. Robertson

Community Relations Service
600 E St. N.W., Suite 6000, Washington, DC 20530
(202) 305-2935; Fax: (202) 305-3005
Internet: www.usdoj.gov/crs/crs.htm
Director: Sharee M. Freeman
Atty. Advisor: George E. Henderson
  (202) 305-2964; Fax: (202) 305-3005
Provides mediation, conciliation and prevention services for
community disputes, disagreements and misunderstandings
based on race, color and national origin.

Regional Office
55 W. Monroe St., Suite 420, Chicago, IL 60603
(312) 353-4391; Fax: (312) 353-4390
  Administrator: Sister Patricia Campbell Glenn

Executive Office for U.S. Trustees
20 Massachusetts Ave. N.W., Suite 8000, Washington, DC 20530
(202) 307-1391; Fax: (202) 307-0672
Internet: www.usdoj.gov/ust
Director: Lawrence A. Friedman
Ensures compliance with the United States Bankruptcy
Code. 11 U.S.C. 101

Executive Office of the U.S. Trustee
Regional Office (Cleveland)
200 Public Sq., Suite 20-3300, Cleveland, OH 44114
(216) 522-7800; Fax: (216) 522-7193
  U.S. Trustee: Saul Eisen
  Asst. U.S. Trustee: Daniel M. McDermott

  Cincinnati Office
  36 E. Seventh St., Suite 2030, Cincinnati, OH 45202
  (513) 684-6988; Fax: (513) 684-6994
    Asst. U.S. Trustee: Neil J. Weill

Columbus Office
170 N. High St., Suite 200, Columbus, OH 43215-2403
(614) 469-7411; Fax: (614) 469-7448
  Asst. U.S. Trustee: Alexander G. Barkan

Bureau of Prisons
320 First St. N.W., Washington, DC 20534
Public Information Office: (202) 307-3198;
Fax: (202) 514-6620
Internet: www.bop.gov
Director: Harley G. Lappin
  (202) 307-3250; Fax: (202) 514-6878
General Counsel: Kathleen Kenney
  (202) 307-3062; Fax: (202) 307-2995

Northeast Regional Office
U.S. Customs House, 7th Floor, 2nd and Chestnut Streets,
Philadelphia, PA 19106
(215) 521-7300
  Regional Dir.: D. Scott Dodrill; Fax: (215) 597-1893
  Community Corrections Regional Administrator:
    Edward Hughes
    (215) 521-7460; Fax: (215) 521-7476

  Community Corrections Mgmt. Office
  36 E. Seventh St., Suite 2107-A, Cincinnati, OH 45202
  (513) 684-2603; Fax: (513) 684-2590

National Institute of Corrections
320 First St. N. W., Washington, DC 20534
Toll Free: (800) 995-6423; (202) 307-3106;
Fax: (202) 307-3361
Internet: www.nicic.org

1960 Industrial Circle, Longmont, CO 80501
Toll Free: (800) 995-6429; Fax: (303) 682-0469;
Information Center: (303) 682-0213
  Director: Morris L. Thigpen, Sr.
  Academy Chief: Robert M. Brown, Jr.
    (303) 682-0382, Ext. 111
    E-mail: rbrown@bop.gov
  Prisons Division Chief: Susan M. Hunter
  Jails Division Chief: Virginia A. Hutchinson
    E-mail: ghutchinson@bop.gov
  Community Corrections Chief: George Keiser
    E-mail: gkeiser@bop.gov
Provides leadership and assistance to the field of
corrections. Responds directly to the needs identified by
those working in state and local corrections agencies. Public
Law 93-415 (1974)

Parole Commission
5550 Friendship Blvd., Suite 420, Chevy Chase, MD 20815
(301) 492-5990; Legal Fax: (301) 492-6694
Internet: www.usdoj.gov/uspc
Chairman: Edward F. Reilly, Jr. (301) 492-5933
Commissioners:
    Patricia Cushwa
    Isaac Fulwood
    Cranston J. Mitchell (301) 492-5954
    Deborah A. Spagnoli
General Counsel: Rockne Chickinell (301) 492-5959
Exec. Officer: Judy I. Carter (301) 492-5974
Chief of Staff: Tom Hutchison (301) 492-5953
Case Operation Administrator: Stephen Husk
    (301) 492-5952
Administrator, Case Services: Sheley Witenstein
    (301) 492-5821
Has sole authority to grant, modify or revoke parole of
eligible Federal and District of Columbia prisoners serving
sentences of more than one year. Responsible for supervision
of parolees and prisoners released upon expiration of their
sentences with allowances for statutory good time, and
determination of supervisory conditions and terms.

Antitrust Division
950 Pennsylvania Ave. N.W., Washington, DC 20530
(202) 514-2401; Fax: (202) 616-2645
E-mail: antitrust@usdoj.gov
Internet: www.usdoj.gov/atr/index.html
Asst. Atty. General: R. Hewitt Pate

Dept. of Justice, Antitrust Division—Cont'd

Cleveland Field Office
Plaza 9 Bldg., Suite 700, 55 Erieview Plz.,
Cleveland, OH 44114
(216) 522-4070; Fax: (216) 522-8332
E-mail: Cleveland.ATR@usdoj.gov
  Chief: Scott M. Watson
  Asst. Chief: Michael F. Wood

Civil Division
950 Pennsylvania Ave. N.W., Room 3141,
Washington, DC 20530 (202) 514-3301
Internet: www.usdoj.gov/civil
Asst. Atty. General: Peter D. Keisler; Fax: (202) 514-8071
Represents the United States, its departments and
agencies, members of Congress, cabinet officers, and other
Federal employees.

Civil Rights Division
950 Pennsylvania Ave. N.W., Room 3623,
Washington, DC 20530
(202) 514-4609
Internet: www.usdoj.gov/crt/crt-home.html
Asst. Atty. General: R. Alexander Acosta
  (202) 514-2151; Fax: (202) 514-0293
Secures effective enforcement of Federal civil rights.

Office of Special Counsel for Immigration Related Unfair
Employment Practices
950 Pennsylvania Ave., N.W., Washington, DC 20030
(202) 616-5594, (800) 255-7688; Fax: (202) 616-5509;
TDD: (202) 616-5525, (800) 237-2515;
Employer Hotline: (800) 255-8155;
Employer Hotline TDD: (800) 362-2735
E-mail: osc.crt@usdoj.gov
Internet: www.usdoj.gov/crt/osc
  Special Counsel: William J. Sanchez
  Deputy Special Counsel: Katherine A. Baldwin
Enforces the antidiscrimination provisions of the
Immigration and Nationality Act, and ensures that
proceeded individuals and aliens authorized to work in the
United States are not discriminated against with respect to
hiring and firing based on their citizenship status or
national origin. 8 U.S.C. 1324b

Criminal Division
950 Pennsylvania Ave. N.W., Room 2107,
Washington, DC 20530-0001
(202) 514-2601; Fax: (202) 514-9412
Internet: www.usdoj.gov/criminal/criminal-home.html
Asst. Atty. General in Charge: Christopher A. Wray
Formulates criminal law enforcement policy and prosecutes
criminal law violations not assigned to other departments.

Environment and Natural Resources Division
950 Pennsylvania Ave. N.W., Room 2143,
Washington, DC 20530
(202) 514-2701; Fax: (202) 514-0557
Internet: www.usdoj.gov/enrd
Asst. Atty. General: Thomas L. Sansonetti
Litigates all aspects of environmental law for the
government.

Tax Division
950 Pennsylvania Ave. N.W., Room 4141,
Washington, DC 20530
(202) 514-2901; Fax: (202) 514-5479
Internet: www.usdoj.gov/tax/
Asst. Atty. General: Eileen J. O'Connor
Investigates and prosecutes all civil and criminal matters
arising under the internal revenue laws other than those in
the Tax Court of the United States.

Executive Office for Immigration Review
5107 Leesburg Pike, Falls Church, VA 22041
(703) 305-0289; Clerk's Office: (703) 605-1007;
Case Information: (800) 898-7180; TDD: (800) 828-1120;
Fax: (703) 605-0365
Director: Kevin D. Rooney (703) 305-0169
Deputy Dir.: Kevin Ohlson (703) 305-0169
General Counsel: Mary Beth Keller (703) 305-0470
Chair, Board of Immigration Appeals: Lori L. Scialabba
  (703) 305-1194

Vice Chair, Board of Immigration Appeals:
  David B. Holmes (Acting) (703) 305-1194
Chief Immigration Judge: Michael J. Creppy (703) 305-1247
Deputy Chief Immigration Judges:
  Brian M. O'Leary (703) 305-1247
  Thomas L. Pullen (703) 305-1247
Chief Admin. Hearing Officer: Vacancy at Press Time
  (703) 305-0864
Deputy Chief Admin. Hearing Officer: Louis J. Ruffino
  (703) 305-0864
Adjudicates immigration cases, including cases involving
detained aliens, criminal aliens, and aliens seeking asylum
as a form of relief from removal, while ensuring the
standards of due process and fair treatment.

DEPARTMENT OF LABOR
200 Constitution Ave. N.W., Washington, DC 20210
(202) 693-5000, (866) 487-2365
Internet: www.dol.gov/
Secretary of Labor: Elaine L. Chao, Room S-2018
  (202) 693-6000; Fax: (202) 693-6111
Office of the Solicitor: Howard M. Radzely, Suite S-2002
  (202) 693-5260; Fax: (202) 693-5278
Fosters, develops, and promotes the welfare of workers,
improves the working conditions of workers, enhances
employment opportunities, guarantees worker's rights to
safe working conditions, a minimum wage, freedom from
discrimination, unemployment compensation,
nondiscrimination policies, free collective bargaining, and
job training and retraining. 29 U.S.C. 551

Office of Administrative Law Judges
800 K St. N.W., Suite 400 North,
Washington, DC 20001-8002
(202) 693-7300; Fax: (202) 693-7365
Chief Judge: John M. Vittone (202) 693-7542
Associate Chief Judge for Black Lung and Traditional:
  Thomas M. Burke (202) 693-7542
Associate Chief Judge for Longshore: A.A. Simpson, Jr.
  (202) 693-7542
Judges:
  Linda Chapman (202) 693-7500
  Alice M. Craft (202) 693-7500
  Stuart Levin (202) 693-7500
  Edward Terhune Miller (202) 693-7500
  Stephen L. Purcell (202) 693-7500
  Daniel Solomon (202) 693-7500
  Richard T. Stansell-Gamm (202) 693-7500
  Jeffrey Tureck (202) 693-7500
  Pamela Lakes Wood (202) 693-7500
Dir., Office of Program Operations: P.J. Soto
  (202) 693-7542
Chief Docket Clerk: Beverly Queen
  (202) 693-7300; Fax: (202) 693-7365
Chief, Information Resources Division: Victor V. Soto
  (202) 693-7400
FOIA Disclosure Officer: Andrea Thomas (202) 693-7348
Chief, Budget and Administration: Alice Greer (202) 693-7440

Office of the Solicitor of Labor
200 Constitution Ave. N.W., Room S-2002,
Washington, DC 20210
(202) 693-5260
E-mail: contact.sol@dol.gov
Solicitor: Howard M. Radzely; Fax: (202) 693-5278
Deputy Solicitor: Gregory F. Jacob
Provides the Secretary and the departmental officials with
legal services as required to accomplish the mission of the
department.

Regional Office
230 S. Dearborn St., Room 844, Chicago, IL 60604
(312) 886-5260; Fax: (312) 353-5698
  Regional Solicitor: Joan A. Gestrin
  Deputy Regional Solicitor: Janet E. Gestin

    Cleveland Office
    Federal Office Bldg., Room 881, 1240 E. Ninth St.,
    Cleveland, OH 44199
    (216) 522-3870; Fax: (216) 522-7172
      Associate Regional Solicitor: Benjamin J. Chinni

Dept. of Labor—Cont'd

Employment and Training Administration

200 Constitution Ave. N.W., Room S-2307,
Washington, DC 20210
(202) 693-2700, (877) 872-5627; Fax: (202) 693-2725
Internet: www.doleta.gov/
Asst. Secretary: Emily Stover DeRocco
Fulfills duties assigned to the Department of Labor relating to job training and retraining, unemployment compensation, and employment services.

Regional Office
230 S. Dearborn St., 6th Floor, Chicago, IL 60604
(312) 596-5400; Fax: (312) 596-5401;
Alien Certification Unit (ACU): (312) 353-2595;
ACU Automated Search: (312) 353-1059;
ACU Fax: (312) 596-5410;
Job Corps/Youth: (312) 596-5470;
Office of Job Corps Fax: (312) 596-5471; ATELS: (312) 596-5500;
Bureau of Apprenticeship & Training Fax: (312) 596-5501
  Regional Administrator: Byron Zuidema

Employee Benefits Security Administration

200 Constitution Ave. N.W., Suite S-2524,
Washington, DC 20210
(202) 693-8300; Fax: (202) 219-5526
Internet: www.dol.gov/dol/ebsa/
Asst. Secretary: Ann L. Combs
Deputy Asst. Secretary for Policy: Bradford P. Campbell
  Suite S-2524 (202) 693-8300; Fax: (202) 219-5526
Deputy Asst. Secretary for Program Operations:
  Alan D. Lebowitz, Suite N-5677
  (202) 693-8315; Fax: (202) 219-6531
Protects the economic future and retirement security of working Americans through regulation of private pension and retirement benefits and is guardian of the national workers retirement and welfare system; enforces and provides advice regarding Title I of the Employee Retirement Income Security Act (ERISA) *29 U.S.C. 1001 Formerly Pension and Welfare Benefits Administration*

Cincinnati Regional Office
1885 Dixie Hwy., Suite 210, Ft. Wright, KY 41011-2664
(859) 578-4680; Fax: (859) 578-4688
  Director: Joseph Menez

Employment Standards Administration

200 Constitution Ave. N.W., Room C-3201,
Washington, DC 20210
(202) 693-0001; Fax: (202) 693-1451
Internet: www.dol.gov/dol/esa/
Asst. Secretary: Victoria Lipnic (202) 693-0200
Enforces standards that affect labor practices of Federal workers. *29 U.S.C. 401; 5 U.S.C. 8101; 33 U.S.C. 901; 30 U.S.C. 901; 49 U.S.C. 53; 29 U.S.C. 201; 40 U.S.C. 276(a); 41 U.S.C. 351; 41 U.S.C. 35; 18 U.S.C. 874 and 40 U.S.C. 276(c); 40 U.S.C. 327; 29 U.S.C. 1801; 29 U.S.C. 2601; 29 U.S.C. 2001; 15 U.S.C. 1671; 8 U.S.C. 1101; 20 U.S.C. 954(c) and 20 U.S.C. 956(g); 29 U.S.C. 706; 29 U.S.C. 793; 38 U.S.C. 4211; 38 U.S.C.. 4212*

Office of Labor Management Standards
Regional Office
1000 Liberty Ave., Room 801, Pittsburgh, PA 15222
(412) 395-6925; Fax: (412) 395-5409
  Regional Director: John Pegula

  Cincinnati District Office
  36 E. Seventh St., Suite 2550, Cincinnati, OH 45202
  (513) 684-6840; Fax: (513) 684-6845
    District Dir.: Lesta Chandler

  Cleveland District Office
  1240 E. Ninth St., Rm. 831, Cleveland, OH 44199-2053
  (216) 357-5455
    District Dir.: James Gearhart

Wage and Hour Division
200 Constitution Ave. N.W., Room S-3502,
Washington, DC 20210
(202) 693-0051; Fax: (202) 693-1406
Internet: www.dol.gov/dol/esa/public/whd_org.htm
  Administrator: Alfred B. Robinson, Jr. (Acting)

Administers and enforces labor standards statutes that are national in scope. Enforces Federal minimum wage, overtime pay, record keeping, and child labor requirements of the Fair Labor Standards Act. Enforces the Family and Medical Leave Act (FMLA), the Employee Polygraph Protection Act, the Migrant and Seasonal Agricultural Worker Protection Act (MSPA), field sanitation and housing standards in the Occupational Safety and Health Act, and a number of employment standards and worker protections provided in the immigration law. Administers and enforces the prevailing wage requirements of the Davis-Bacon Act and the McNamara O'Hara Service Contract Act and other statutes applicable to Federal contracts for construction and for the provision of goods and services.

  Cleveland District Office
  Federal Office Bldg., Room 817, 1240 E. Ninth St.,
  Cleveland, OH 44199-2054
  (216) 357-5400; Fax: (216) 357-5422
    District Dir.: Barry Haber

  Columbus District Office
  200 N. High St., Room 646, Columbus, OH 43215-2475
  (614) 469-5677; Fax: (614) 469-5428
    District Dir.: George Victory

  Cincinnati Area Office
  550 Main St., Room 10-409,
  Cincinnati, OH 45202-5208
  (513) 684-2908; Fax: (513) 684-2906
    Asst. District Dir.: Donald W. Harrison

Office of Workers' Compensation Programs (OWCP)

200 Constitution Ave. N.W., Room S-3524,
Washington, DC 20210
(202) 693-0031
Internet: www.dol.gov/esa/owcp_org.htm
Director: Shelby Hallmark
  (202) 693-0031; Fax: (202) 693-1378
Dir. of Federal Employee Compensation:
  Douglas C. Fitzgerald (202) 693-1035
Administers the Federal Employees Compensation Act, the Longshore and Harbor Workers' Compensation Act, the Black Lung Benefits Act, and the Energy Employees Occupational Illness Compensation Program Act.

Midwest Regional Office
230 S. Dearborn St., 8th Floor, Chicago, IL 60604
(312) 596-7131
  Regional Dir.: Nancy Jenson

  Cleveland District Office
  1240 E. Ninth St., Room 851, Cleveland, OH 44199
  (216) 357-5390; Fax: (216) 357-5378
    District Dir.: Robert Sullivan

Occupational Safety and Health Administration

200 Constitution Ave. N.W., Room 3718,
Washington, DC 20210
Standards: (202) 693-1950, (800) 321-6742;
Public Affairs: (202) 693-1999; TTY: (877) 889-5627
Internet: www.osha.gov
Asst. Secretary: Jonathan L. Snare (Acting), Room S2315
  (202) 693-2000; Fax: (202) 693-2106
Assoc. Solicitor: Joseph M. Woodward (202) 693-5445
Develops and promulgates occupational safety and health standards, develops and issues regulations, and conducts investigations and inspections to enforce compliance. *29 U.S.C. 615*

Regional Office
230 S. Dearborn St., Room 3244, Chicago, IL 60604
(312) 353-2220; Fax: (312) 353-7774
  Information Specialist & Resource Contact:
  Susan Thompson

  Cincinnati Area Office
  36 Triangle Park Dr., Cincinnati, OH 45246
  (513) 841-4132; Fax: (513) 841-4114
    Area Dir.: Richard Gilgrist

  Cleveland Area Office
  Federal Office Bldg., Room 899, 1240 E. Ninth St.,
  Cleveland, OH 44199
  (216) 522-3818; Fax: (216) 771-6148
    Area Dir.: Rob Madlock

Departments &
Agencies

Dept. of Labor, Occupational Safety and Health Administration—Cont'd

Columbus Area Office
Federal Office Bldg., Room 620, 200 N. High St.,
Columbus, OH 43215
(614) 469-5582; Fax: (614) 469-6791
  Area Dir.: Deborah Zubaty

Toledo Area Office
420 Madison Ave., Suite 600, Toledo, OH 43604
(419) 259-7542; Fax: (419) 259-6355
  Area Dir.: Jule Jones

Mine Safety and Health Administration

1100 Wilson Blvd., Arlington, VA 22209-3939
(703) 235-1452; Fax: (703) 235-4323
Internet: www.msha.gov
Asst. Secretary: David G. Dye (Acting), Room 622
  (202) 693-9414; Fax: (202) 693-9401
  E-mail: asmsha@msha.gov
Mgr., Office of Program Education and Outreach Services:
  Layne Lathram (202) 693-9400; Fax: (202) 693-9421
  E-mail: lathram.layne@dol.gov
Assoc. Solicitor: Edward P. Clair (202) 693-9333
Asst. Secretary: David D. Lauriski, Room 622
  (202) 693-9414; Fax: (202) 693-9401
Protects miner safety and health through enforcement, education and technical assistance. *30 U.S.C. 801*

Bureau of Labor Statistics

Commissioner's Office
2 Massachusetts Ave. N.E., Room 4040,
Washington, DC 20212
(202) 691-5200; Fax: (202) 691-5899;
Fax-on-demand: (202) 691-6325
Internet: www.bls.gov
Commissioner: Kathleen P. Utgoff
  (202) 691-7802; Fax: (202) 691-7797
Collects, processes, and analyzes labor information and statistics.

Regional Office
J.C. Kluczynski Federal Office Bldg., Room 960,
230 S. Dearborn St., Chicago, IL 60604
(312) 353-1880; Fax: (312) 353-1886
E-mail: BLSinfoChicago@bls.gov

Veterans' Employment and Training Service

200 Constitution Ave. N.W., Room S-1325,
Washington, DC 20210
(202) 693-4700; Fax: (202) 693-4754
Internet: www.dol.gov/vets
Asst. Secretary: Frederico Juarbe, Jr.
Administers veterans' training and employment programs. Work with and provides technical assistance to State Employment Security Agencies and Job Training Partnership Act grant recipients to ensure mandated priority services for veterans. Assists federal contractors in compliance with and reporting of veterans affirmative action requirements. Investigates complaints from veterans, reservists and National Guard members regarding their employment and reemployment rights under Uniformed Services Employment and Reemployment Rights Act. *U.S.C. Title 38, Chap. 43*

Women's Bureau

Frances Perkins Bldg., Room S-3002,
200 Constitution Ave. N.W., Washington, DC 20210
(202) 693-6710, (800) 827-5335; Fax: (202) 693-6725
Internet: www.dol.gov/wb
Director: Shinae Chun
The Women's Bureau is responsible for formulating standards and policies that promote the welfare of wage-earning women, improve their working conditions, increase their efficiency, and advance their opportunities for profitable employment.

Regional Office
230 S. Dearborn St., Room 1022, Chicago, IL 60604
(312) 353-6985, (800) 827-5335; Fax: (312) 353-6986
  Regional Administrator: Nancy S. Chen
    E-mail: chen-nancy@dol.gov

DEPARTMENT OF STATE
2201 C St. N.W., Washington, DC 20520
(202) 647-4000; Fax: (202) 261-8577;
TTY: (800) 877-8339
E-mail: secretary@state.gov
Internet: www.state.gov

Secretary of State: Condoleezza Rice
  (202) 647-5291; Fax: (202) 261-8577
Legal Advisor: William H. Taft IV, Room 6423
  (202) 647-9598; Fax: (202) 647-1037, 647-7096
Advises the President in the formulation and execution of foreign policy and carries out established foreign policy on behalf of the nation. *1 Stat. 68*

Chicago Passport Agency

Kluczynski Fedl. Bldg., 18th Floor, 230 S. Dearborn St.,
Chicago, IL 60604-1564
(312) 341-6020, (877) 487-2778

National Passport Center

31 Rochester Ave., Portsmouth, NH 03801-2900
Processing center for applications

Special Issuance Agency

1111 19th St. N.W., Room 200,
Washington, DC 20522-1705
(202) 955-0198; Dept. of Defense Inquiries: (703) 696-1463;
Fax: (202) 955-0347
Director: Barbara M. Chesman
Asst. Dir.: Randall J. Bevins
Applications for Diplomatic, Official and No Fee passports; also Fee passports accompanied by Congressional referrals

United States Information Agency

Internet: www.usia.gov
Effective October 1, 1999, the agency was consolidated into the Department of State as per P.L. 105-277 acts of 1999. For further information on the Voice of America or other related entities, call (202) 619-4700.

DEPARTMENT OF TRANSPORTATION
400 7th St. S.W., Washington, DC 20590
(202) 366-2332; Personnel Locator: (202) 366-4000;
Fax: (202) 366-9634
Internet: www.dot.gov

Secretary of Transportation: Norman Y. Mineta
  (202) 366-1111; Fax: (202) 366-7202
General Counsel: Jeffrey A. Rosen
  (202) 366-4702; Fax: (520) 236-6338
Establishes the nation's overall transportation policy, administers highway development, restoration, maintenance, mass transit, rail, aviation, and waterway programs. *49 U.S.C. app. 1651 note*

Office of Hearings

Mailcode M-20, Room 5411, 400 Seventh St. S.W.,
Washington, DC 20590
(202) 366-2142; Fax: (202) 366-7536
E-mail: ronnie.yoder@ost.dot.gov
Internet: www.dot.gov/ost/hearings
Chief Admin. Law Judge: Ronnie A. Yoder
    E-mail: ronnie.yoder@ost.dot.gov
Admin. Law Judges:
    Richard C. Goodwin
    Burton S. Kolko
Responsible for conduct and initial disposition of formal proceedings falling within the purview of the A.P.A. and instituted under legislation vesting executive authority and responsibility in the Secretary of Transportation, except as prescribed by statue or otherwise ordered by the Secretary.

Federal Aviation Administration

800 Independence Ave. S.W., Washington, DC 20591
(202) 267-3883; Employee Locator: (202) 366-4000
Internet: www.faa.gov/
Administrator: Marion C. Blakey, Room 1010
  (202) 267-3111; Fax: (202) 267-5047
General Counsel: Andrew B. Steinberg, Room 900E
  (202) 267-3222; Fax: (202) 267-3227
Regulates air commerce; controls the use of navigable airspace for both civil and military use; promotes the development of civil aeronautics; conducts research; installs and operates air navigation facilities; and promotes the limitation of environmental effects of aviation. *49 U.S.C. 706*

Dept. of Transportation, Fed. Aviation Admin.—Cont'd

Great Lakes Regional Office
2300 E. Devon Ave., Des Plaines, IL 60018
(847) 294-7294; 24-Hour Phone: (847) 294-7410;
Fax: (847) 294-7498

Regional Administrator: Christopher Blum

Regional Counsel: Perry Kupietz (847) 294-9109

Federal Highway Administration
400 7th St. S.W., Washington, DC 20590
(202) 366-0537
Internet: www.fhwa.dot.gov/

Administrator: Mary E. Peters, Room 4218
(202) 366-0650; Fax: (202) 366-3244

Chief Counsel: D.J. Gribbin, Room 4213
(202) 366-0740; Fax: (202) 366-7499
Coordinates and administers Federal funding for all aspects of highway transportation, construction, maintenance, management, and Federal regulation. *49 U.S.C. app. 1651 note*

Midwestern Resource Center
19900 Governors Dr., Suite 301,
Olympia Fields, IL 60461-1021
(708) 283-3500; Fax: (708) 283-3501
Internet: www.fhwa.dotgov/resourcecenter

Manager: Ronald Moses

Maritime Administration
400 7th St. S.W., Washington, DC 20590
(800) 996-2723
Internet: www.marad.dot.gov

Administrator: Capt. William G. Schubert

Assoc. Administrator: Eileen Roberson
(202) 366-5802; E-mail: eileen.roberson@marad.dot.gov

Deputy Admin.: John Jamian

Chief Counsel: Robert B. Ostrom (202) 366-5711
E-mail: robert.ostrom@marad.dot.gov
Promotes the development and maintenance of the merchant marine, to carry domestic waterborne commerce and a substantial portion of the nation's waterborne commerce, and to serve as a naval and military auxiliary during wartime or national emergency. Also seeks to ensure adequate shipbuilding and repair service, efficient ports, effective intermodal water and land transportation systems, and reserve shipping capacity in time of national emergency.

Great Lakes Regional Office
1701 E. Woodfield Rd., Suite 203, Schaumburg, IL 60173
(847) 995-0122; Fax: (847) 995-0133

Regional Dir.: Doris J. Bautch
E-mail: Doris.Bautch@marad.dot.gov

Federal Railroad Administration
1120 Vermont Ave. N.W., Washington, DC 20590
(202) 493-6000; Office of Chief Counsel: (202) 493-6052;
Fax: (202) 493-6068;
Office of Public Affairs: (202) 493-6024
Internet: www.fra.dot.gov

Administrator: Robert D. Jamison (Acting)
Mail Stop 5 (202) 493-6014; Fax: (202) 493-6009

Chief Counsel: S. Mark Lindsey, Mail Stop 10
(202) 493-6052; Fax: (202) 493-6068
Promulgates and enforces rail safety regulations, rail assistance programs, research and development in support of improved rail facilities. *49 U.S.C. app. 1652*

Regional Office
2 International Plz., Suite 550, Philadelphia, PA 19113
(610) 521-8200; Fax: (610) 521-8225;
Hot Line: (800) 724-5992

Regional Administrator: David Myers
E-mail: David.Myers@fra.dot.gov

Deputy Regional Administrators:
Daniel C. Buckley; E-mail: Daniel.Buckley@fra.dot.gov
Brian Hontz; E-mail: Brian.Hontz@fra.dot.gov

National Highway Traffic Safety Administration
400 7th St. S.W., Washington, DC 20590
Auto Safety Hotline: (202) 366-0123, (888) 327-4236
Internet: www.nhtsa.dot.gov
Administrator: Jeffrey W. Runge, M.D. (202) 366-1836
Chief Counsel: Jacqueline Glassman
(202) 366-9511; Fax: (202) 366-3820
Carries out programs related to driver safety, motor vehicle and related equipment performance. *23 U.S.C. chapter 4; 49 U.S.C. chapter 301.*

Regional Office
19900 Governors Dr., Suite 201, Olympia Fields, IL 60461-1021
(708) 503-8822; Fax: (708) 503-8991
E-mail: region5@nhtsa.dot.gov

Federal Transit Administration
400 7th St. S.W., Room 9328, Washington, DC 20590
(202) 366-4042; Public Affairs: (202) 366-4043;
Fax: (202) 366-3472; Internet: www.fta.dot.gov/
Administrator: Jennifer L. Dorn (202) 366-4040
Chief Counsel: Judith Kaleta (Acting), Room 9316
(202) 366-4063; Fax: (202) 366-3809
Assists in the development of mass transit facilities; encourages the planning and establishment of urban mass transit systems; and aids state governments in the development and operation of mass transit systems.
5 U.S.C. app. Reorganization Plan No. 2 of 1968

Office of Hazardous Materials Safety, Research and Special Programs Administration
400 7th St. S.W., Room 8321, Washington, DC 20590
(202) 366-0656
Internet: http://hazmat.dot.gov
Assoc. Administrator: Robert A. McGuire
(202) 366-0656; Fax: (202) 366-5713
Chief Counsel: Elaine E. Joost
(202) 366-4400; Fax: (202) 366-7041
Asst. Chief Counsel for Hazardous Materials Safety and Emergency Transportation Law: Joseph Solomey
(202) 366-4400; Fax: (202) 366-7041
Develops and issues regulations for the transportation of hazardous materials, provides training and enforces those regulations. Issues preemption determinations. Provides emergency response support.

Office of Airline Information
400 7th St. S.W., Room 4125, Washington, DC 20590
(202) 366-9059; Fax: (202) 366-3383
Internet: www.bts.gov/oai
Assistant Director: Donald W. Bright (202) 366-4373
E-mail: donald.bright@bts.gov

Surface Transportation Board
1925 K St. N.W., Washington, DC 20423-0001
(202) 565-1500; Fax: (202) 565-9016
Internet: www.stb.dot.gov
Chairperson: Roger Nober
(202) 565-1510; Fax: (202) 565-9013
Vice Chair: W. Douglas Buttrey
(202) 565-1505; Fax: (202) 565-9015
Commissioner: Francis P. Mulvey
(202) 565-1505; Fax: (202) 565-9018
General Counsel: Ellen D. Hanson
(202) 565-1558; Fax: (202) 565-9001
Secretary: Vernon A. Williams
(202) 565-1718; Fax: (202) 565-9019
Dir., Office of Congressional and Public Services:
Dan G. King (202) 565-1594; Fax: (202) 565-9016
Dir., Ofc. of Economics, Environmental Analysis and Admin.: Leland L. Gardner
(202) 565-1532; Fax: (202) 565-9000
Dir., Office of Proceedings: David M. Konschnik
(202) 565-1600; Fax: (202) 565-9002
Dir., Office of Compliance and Enforcement:
Melvin F. Clemens, Jr. (202) 565-1573; Fax: (202) 565-9011
Adjudicates disputes and regulates interstate surface transportation through various laws pertaining to the different modes of surface transportation. *49 U.S.C. 10101*
Formerly known as Interstate Commerce Commission

Departments & Agencies

Dept. of Transportation—Cont'd

Bureau of Transportation Statistics

400 7th St. S.W., Room 3103, Washington, DC 20590
Main Office: (202) 366-9510;
BTS Products: (202) 366-DATA;
Statistical Questions: (800) 853-1351; Fax: (202) 366-3640
E-mail: info@bts.gov; Internet: www.bts.gov
Director: Rick Kowalewski (Acting) (202) 366-6268
Atty. Advisor: Bob Monniere (202) 366-5498
Compiles, analyzes, and publishes transportation related statistics. *49 U.S.C. 111*

Volpe National Transportation Systems Center

55 Broadway, Kendall Sq., Cambridge, MA 02142-1093
(617) 494-2000
Internet: www.volpe.dot.gov
Director: Curtis J. Tompkins
    (617) 494-2222; Fax: (617) 494-3731
Chief Counsel: David S. Glater (617) 494-2727

DEPARTMENT OF THE TREASURY
1500 Pennsylvania Ave. N.W., Washington, DC 20220
(202) 622-2000; Fax: (202) 622-6415
Internet: www.ustreas.gov

Secretary of the Treasury: John W. Snow
General Counsel: Arnold I. Havens, Room 4330
    (202) 622-0283; Fax: (202) 622-2882

Formulates and recommends economic, financial, tax, and fiscal policies; serves as financial agent for the U.S. government; enforces the law; and manufactures coin and currency. *31 U.S.C. 1001*

Office of the Comptroller of the Currency

250 E St. S.W., Washington, DC 20219
(202) 874-5000
Internet: www.occ.treas.gov
Comptroller: Julie L. Williams (Acting) (202) 874-4900
Chief Counsel: Daniel P. Stipano (Acting) (202) 874-5200
Promulgates rules and regulations for the operation of the national banks and examines the banks for compliance with banking regulations. *12 Stat. 665*

Central District Office
One Financial Place, Suite 2700, 440 S. LaSalle St., Chicago, IL 60605
(312) 360-8800; TDD: (312) 360-8827;
General Fax: (312) 435-0951;
Executive/Legal Fax: (312) 435-9632;
Human Resources Fax: (312) 435-1370
  Deputy Comptroller: Bert A. Otto (312) 360-8802
  District Counsel: Coreen S. Arnold
    (312) 360-8805; Fax: (312) 435-0951
    Cincinnati Field Office
    West Lake Center, Suite 610, 455 Lake Forest Dr., Blue Ash, OH 45242
    (513) 769-6601; Fax: (513) 769-6723
     Asst. Deputy Comptroller: Larry L. Hattix
    Cleveland Field Office
    Summit Office Park, Suite 530, 3 Summit Park Dr., Independence, OH 44131
    (216) 447-8866; Fax: (216) 447-9335
     Asst. Deputy Comptroller: Lance J. Ciroli
    Columbus Field Office
    325 Cramer Creek Ct., Suite 101, Dublin, OH 43017
    (614) 766-6296; Fax: (614) 766-6545
     Asst. Deputy Comptroller: Larry L. Hattix

Bureau of Engraving and Printing

14th & C Sts. S.W., Washington, DC 20228
External Relations: (202) 874-3019;
External Relations Fax: (202) 874-3177
Internet: www.moneyfactory.gov
9000 Blue Mound Rd., Fort Worth, TX 76131
(817) 847-3800
Director: Thomas A. Ferguson
    (202) 874-2002; Fax: (202) 874-3879
Chief Counsel: Michael J. Davidson
    (202) 874-5363; Fax: (202) 874-5710
Pursuant to *31 U.S.C. 5114* the Bureau produces United States obligations and securities.

Financial Management Service

401 14th St. S.W., Washington, DC 20227
(202) 874-6950; Fax: (202) 874-7016
Internet: www.fms.treas.gov/
Commissioner: Richard L. Gregg
    (202) 874-7000; Fax: (202) 874-6743
Dir., Office of Legislative & Public Affairs:
  Alvina A. McHale (202) 874-6740
Chief Counsel: Margaret Marquette (Acting)
    (202) 874-6680; Fax: (202) 874-6627
The Financial Management Services disburses Federal payments like Social Security, veterans' benefits and income tax refunds, collects Federal revenues, oversees a daily cash flow, provides centralized debt collection services to most Federal agencies and provides government-wide accounting and reporting.

Internal Revenue Service

1111 Constitution Ave. N.W., Washington, DC 20224
(202) 622-5000;
Federal Tax Forms (800) 829-FORM: (800) 829-3676;
Tax Assistance, Information and Problem Resolution:
(800) 829-1040
Internet: www.irs.gov
Commissioner: Mark W. Everson, Room 3000
    (202) 622-9511
Chief Counsel: Donald L. Korb
    (202) 622-3300; Fax: (202) 622-4277
Administers and enforces all internal revenue laws except those relating to alcohol, tobacco, firearms, and explosives. *26 U.S.C. 7802*

Local Offices
2 S. Main St., Akron, OH 44308 (330) 253-7013

201 Cleveland Ave. S.W., Canton, OH 44702 (330) 588-4717

550 Main St., Cincinnati, OH 45202 (513) 263-3333

200 N. High St., Room 425, Columbus, OH 43215
(614) 280-8691

1240 E. Ninth St., Cleveland, OH 44199 (216) 522-4048

200 W. Second St., Dayton, OH 45402 (937) 610-2182

401 W. North St., Lima, OH 45801 (419) 223-5873

180 N. Diamond St., Mansfield, OH 44902
(419) 522-9204

Four Seagate, 433 N. Summit St., Toledo, OH 43604
(419) 213-5165

9075 Centre Pointe Dr., West Chester, OH 45069
(513) 263-3333

10 E. Commerce St., Youngstown, OH 44503 (330) 746-0006

Bureau of the Public Debt

799 9th St. N.W., Washington, DC 20239
(202) 504-3502
Internet: www.publicdebt.treas.gov
200 Third St., P.O. Box 1328, Parkersburg, WV 26106
Commissioner: Van Zeck
Chief Counsel: Brian Ferrell (202) 504-3520
Finances and accounts for the nation's public debt; handles all Treasury Debt finance and accounting operations; administers the regulations governing the Government Securities Market.

Office of Thrift Supervision

1700 G St. N.W., Washington, DC 20552
(202) 906-6000; Internet: www.ots.treas.gov
Director: James E. Gilleran, 5th Floor
    (202) 906-6590; Fax: (202) 898-0230
Ombudsman: Randy W. Thomas
    (202) 906-7945; Fax: (202) 906-6260
Chief Counsel: John E. Bowman, 5th Floor
    (202) 906-6372; Fax: (202) 906-7606
    E-mail: john.bowman@ots.treas.gov
Regulates and supervises the nation's thrift industry; ensures the safety and soundness of thrift institutions and supports their role as home and mortgage lenders and providers of other community credit and financial services. Regulation of savings associations. *12 U.S.C. 1461* et seq.

OHIO FEDERAL DEPARTMENTS AND AGENCIES 83

Dept. of the Treasury, Office of Thrift Supervision—Cont'd

Office of Regional Counsel—Northeast
Harborside Financial Center Plaza Five, Suite 1600,
Jersey City, NJ 07311
(201) 413-1000; Fax: (201) 413-7543
Internet: www.ots.treas.gov
    Regional Enforcement Counsel, Enforcement and
    Litigation Matters: Steven A. Rosenberg
        (201) 413-7381
    Regional Counsel, Corporate Matters and Regulatory
    Advice: James Porreca (201) 413-7304

Northeast Regional Office
Harborside Financial Center Plaza Five, Suite 1600,
Jersey City, NJ 07311
(201) 413-1000
    Regional Dir.: Robert C. Albanese

United States Mint
801 9th St. N.W., Washington, DC 20220
(202) 354-7200; Fax: (202) 874-6282
Internet: www.usmint.gov
Director: Henrietta Holsman Fore, 8th Floor
    (202) 354-7200; Fax: (202) 756-6160
Chief Counsel: Daniel Shaver, 8th Floor
    (202) 354-7280; Fax: (202) 756-6110
Produces and distributes coins; maintains and protects government's gold and silver reserves.

DEPARTMENT OF VETERANS AFFAIRS
810 Vermont Ave. N.W., Washington, DC 20420
Internet: www.va.gov
Secretary of Veterans Affairs: James Nicholson
(Pending Confirmation)
General Counsel: Tim S. McClain, Mailcode 02
(202) 273-6660; Fax: (202) 273-6671

Operates programs for the benefit of veterans and their survivors, including disability compensation, pensions, education, rehabilitation, home loan guarantee, medical and hospital program, and death and burial benefits. *38 U.S.C. 201 note*

Independent Establishments and Government Corporations

AFRICAN DEVELOPMENT FOUNDATION
1400 Eye St. N.W., 10th Floor,
Washington, DC 20005-2248
(202) 673-3916; Fax: (202) 673-3810
E-mail: info@adf.gov
Internet: www.adf.gov
President: Nathaniel Fields
General Counsel: Doris Mason Martin
Supports the self-help projects and programs of the poor in Africa. Provides economic assistance to African grassroots organizations engaged in development activities. *22 U.S.C. 290*

CENTRAL INTELLIGENCE AGENCY
Washington, DC 20505
(703) 482-0623;
Public Communications Branch: (703) 482-0623, 24;
Fax (Public Communications): (703) 482-1739
Internet: www.cia.gov
Director: Porter J. Goss
Deputy Dir.: Vacancy at Press Time
Exec. Dir.: Vacancy at Press Time
General Counsel: Scott W. Muller
Collects, evaluates, and disseminates valuable information on political, military, economic, scientific, and other developments abroad needed to safeguard national security. *50 U.S.C. 401*

COMMISSION ON CIVIL RIGHTS
624 9th St. N.W., Room 700, Washington, DC 20425
(202) 376-7700; Fax: (202) 376-7672
Internet: www.usccr.gov
Chairman: Gerald A. Reynolds
General Counsel: Vacancy at Press Time
Deputy General Counsel: Debra A. Carr, Room 620
(202) 376-8351; Fax: (202) 376-1163

Collects, studies, and evaluates information on discrimination or denials of equal protection of the laws under the Constitution because of race, color, religion, sex, age, disability, or national origin. *42 U.S.C. 1975*

Midwestern Regional Office
55 W. Monroe St., Suite 410, Chicago, IL 60603
(312) 353-8311; Fax: (312) 353-8324
Director: Constance M. Davis

COMMODITY FUTURES TRADING COMMISSION
Three Lafayette Centre, 1155 21st St. N.W.,
Washington, DC 20581
(202) 418-5000; Fax: (202) 418-5521
Internet: www.cftc.gov
Chair: Sharon Brown-Hruska, Room 9060
    (202) 418-5050; Fax: (202) 418-5533
General Counsel: Patrick J. McCarty, Room 8062
    (202) 418-5120; Fax: (202) 418-5524
Promotes healthy economic growth; protects the rights of customers; and ensures fairness and integrity through the efficient regulation of the trading of futures in commodities. *7 U.S.C. 4a*

Office of Proceedings
Three Lafayette Centre, 4th Floor, 1155 21st St., N.W.,
Washington, DC 20581
(202) 418-5000; Fax: (202) 418-5532
Admin. Law Judges:
    Bruce C. Levine (202) 418-5503; E-mail: blevine@cftc.gov
    George H. Painter (202) 418-5504
        E-mail: gpainter@cftc.gov
Hears and decides enforcement and reparations cases arising under the Commodities and Exchange Act as amended. *7 U.S.C. 1-25*

CONSUMER PRODUCT SAFETY COMMISSION
East West Towers, 4330 East West Highway,
Bethesda, MD 20814-4408
Mailing Address: , Washington, DC 20207
(301) 504-6816; Public Affairs: (301) 504-7908;
CPSC Consumer Hotline: (800) 638-2772;
Fax: (301) 504-0025, 504-0124
E-mail: info@cpcs.gov
Internet: www.cpsc.gov
Chairperson: Hal Stratton
General Counsel: John G. Mullan, Suite 700
    (301) 504-7626; Fax: (301) 504-0403
    E-mail: jmullen@cpsc.gov
Protects the public against unreasonable risk of injury from consumer products, develops uniform safety standards for consumer products, negotiates recalls of defective products, and promotes research and investigation into the causes and prevention of product-related illness, death, and injury. *15 U.S.C. 2051*

Central Office
230 S. Dearborn St., Room 2944, Chicago, IL 60604-8260
(312) 353-8260; Fax: (312) 353-5013
Regional Dir.: Eric Ault; E-mail: eault@cpsc.gov

CORPORATION FOR NATIONAL
AND COMMUNITY SERVICE
1201 New York Ave. N.W., Washington, DC 20525
(202) 606-5000; Fax: (202) 565-2796
Internet: www.cns.gov
C.E.O.: David Eisner
General Counsel: Frank R. Trinity
Mobilizes Americans for voluntary service throughout the United States through programs that help meet the basic human needs and support self-help efforts of low-income individuals and communities. *42 U.S.C. 4951 and 42 U.S.C. 12501*
Formerly called ACTION

Ohio Office
51 N. High St., Suite 800, Columbus, OH 43215
(614) 469-7441; Fax: (614) 469-2125
E-mail: OH@cns.gov
Regional Dir.: Paul Schrader (Area Manager)

DEFENSE NUCLEAR FACILITIES SAFETY BOARD
625 Indiana Ave. N.W., Suite 700,
Washington, DC 20004
(202) 694-7000, (800) 788-4016; Fax: (202) 208-6518
Internet: www.dnfsb.gov

Chairman: John T. Conway

General Counsel: Richard A. Azzaro

Reviews and evaluates the content and implementation of the safety standards relating to the design, construction, operation, and decommissioning of defense nuclear facilities of the Department of Energy. *42 U.S.C. 2286*

ENVIRONMENTAL PROTECTION AGENCY
Ariel Rios Bldg., 1200 Pennsylvania Ave., N.W.,
Washington, DC 20460
(202) 272-0167
Internet: www.epa.gov

Commissioner: Stephen L. Johnson (pending confirmation) Mailbox 1101A   (202) 564-4700

Protects and enhances the environment through rigorous enforcement of all environmental legislation, including pesticide, radiation, and toxic substances regulation. Cooperates and coordinates with state and local enforcement efforts. *5 U.S.C. app. Reorganization Plan No. 3 of 1970*

Regional Office
77 W. Jackson Blvd., Chicago, IL 60604
(312) 353-2000, (800) 621-8431
E-mail: reshkin.karen@epa.gov

Regional Administrator: Bharat Mathur (Acting)
     (312) 886-3000; E-mail: mathur.bharat@epa.gov

Deputy Regional Administrator: Norman Niedergang (Acting)
     (312) 886-3000

Office of Administrative Law Judges
1099 14th St. N.W., Suite 350, Washington, DC 20005
Mailing Address:
1200 Pennsylvania Ave. N.W., Mailcode 1900L,
Washington, DC 20460
(202) 564-6255; Fax: (202) 565-0044
Internet: www.epa.gov

Chief Admin. Law Judge: Susan L. Biro

Admin. Law Judges:
     Carl C. Charneski
     Barbara Gunning
     William B. Moran
     Spencer T. Nissen

Docket Clerk: Knolyn Jones   (703) 603-0061

Conduct hearings and render decisions under the Clean Air Act (CAA); the Clean Water Act (CWA); the Comprehensive Environmental Response, Compensation and Liability Act (CERCLA); the Emergency Planning and Community Right-To-Know Act (EPCRA); the Federal Insecticide, Fungicide and Rodenticide Act (FIFRA); the Marine Protection, Research and Sanctuaries Act (MPRSA); the Safe Drinking Water Act (SDWA); the Solid Waste Disposal Act, as amended by the Resource Conservation and Recovery Act (RCRA); the Toxic Substances Control Act (TSCA); and the Asbestos Hazard Emergency Response Act (AHERA). Also serve as mediators in Superfund (CERCLA) cases.

Office for Administration and Resources Management (OARM)
1200 Pennsylvania Ave. N.W., Mailcode 3101A,
Washington, DC 20460
(202) 564-4600; Fax: (202) 564-0233

Asst. Administrator: David J. O'Connor (Acting)

Office of Air and Radiation (OAR)
1200 Pennsylvania Ave. N.W., Mailcode 6101A,
Washington, DC 20460
(202) 564-7400; Fax: (202) 501-0986

Asst. Administrator: Jeffrey R. Holmstead
     E-mail: holmstead.jeff@epa.gov

Office of Enforcement and Compliance Assurance (OECA)
1200 Pennsylvania Ave. N.W., Mailcode 2201A,
Washington, DC 20460
(202) 564-2440; Fax: (202) 501-3842

Asst. Administrator: Thomas V. Skinner (Acting)

Office of Inspector General (OIG)
1301 Connecticut Ave. N.W., Room 3216, Mailcode 2410T,
Washington, DC 20004
(202) 566-2391; Hotline: (888) 546-8740;
Fax: (202) 566-2549
Internet: www.epa.gov/oigearth

Inspector General: Nikki L. Tinsley   (202) 566-0847

Counsel: Mark Bialek   (202) 566-0863
     E-mail: bialek.mark@epa.gov

Office of International Affairs (OIA)
1200 Pennsylvania Ave. N.W., Mailcode 2610R,
Washington, DC 20460
(202) 564-6613; Fax: (202) 565-2411

Asst. Administrator: Judith E. Ayres

Office of Policy, Economics & Innovation (OPEI)
1200 Pennsylvania Ave. N.W., Mailcode 1803A,
Washington, DC 20004
(202) 564-4332; Fax: (202) 501-1688

Associate Administrator: Stephanie N. Daigle (Acting)

Office of Prevention, Pesticides and Toxic Substances (OPPTS)
1200 Pennsylvania Ave. N.W., Mailcode 7101M,
Washington, DC 20460
(202) 564-2910; Fax: (202) 564-0512
Internet: www.epa.gov/oppts

Asst. Administrator: Vacancy at Press Time

Principal Dep. Asst. Administrator: Susan B. Hazen
Implementation of Federal Insecticide, Fungicide & Rodenticide Act; Food Quality Protection Act; Toxic Substances Control Act; Emergency Planning and Community Right to Know Act.

Office of Research and Development (ORD)
1200 Pennsylvania Ave. N.W., Mailcode 8101-R,
Washington, DC 20460
(202) 564-6620; Fax: (202) 565-2431

Assoc. Asst. Administrator: Michael Brown   (202) 564-6766

Office of Solid Waste and Emergency Response (OSWER)
1301 Constitution Ave. N.W., Room 3146,
Washington, DC 20004
Mailing Address:
1200 Pennsylvania Ave. N.W., Mailcode 5101T,
Washington, DC 20460
(202) 566-0200; Fax: (202) 566-0207

Office of Water (OW)
1200 Pennsylvania Ave. N.W., Mailcode 4101M,
Washington, DC 20460
(202) 564-5700; Fax: (202) 564-0488

Asst. Administrator: Benjamin Grumbles

EQUAL EMPLOYMENT OPPORTUNITY COMMISSION
1801 L St. N.W., Washington, DC 20507
Personnel Locator: (202) 663-4900;
TTY: (202) 663-4494;
Outside of Washington, DC: (800) 669-4000;
TTY (Outside of Washington, DC): (800) 669-6820
Internet: www.eeoc.gov

Chairman: Cari M. Dominquez, Room 10006
     (202) 663-4001

Chief Operating Officer: Leonora L. Guarraia, Room 10010
     (202) 663-4007

General Counsel: Eric Dreiband, (202) 663-4705

Inspector General: Aletha L. Brown, Room 3003
     (202) 663-4379

Dir., Office of Communication & Legislative Affairs:
     Karen Pedrick   (202) 663-4900

Eliminates discrimination in employment hiring, promotion, training, apprenticeship, testing, training, and wages. Conducts investigations, files lawsuits, attempts mediation, and assists employers in voluntary program implementation. *42 U.S.C. 2000e; Title VII; Americans with Disabilities Act; Age Discrimination In Employment or Equal Pay Act*

Equal Employment Opportunity Commission—Cont'd

Cleveland District Office
Tower City—Skylight Office Tower, Suite 850,
1660 W. Second St., Cleveland, OH 44113-1412
(216) 522-2003; TTY: (216) 522-8441; Fax: (216) 522-7395

Director: Michael C. Fetzer

Regional Atty.: C. Larry Watson

Cincinnati Area Office
John W. Peck Federal Office Bldg., 10th Floor,
550 Main St., Cincinnati, OH 45202
(513) 684-2851, (800) 669-4000;
TTY: (513) 684-2074, (800) 669-6820; Fax: (513) 684-2361

Director: Wilma L. Javey

Regional Atty.: C. Larry Watson (Cleveland)

EXPORT IMPORT BANK OF THE UNITED STATES
811 Vermont Ave. N.W., Washington, DC 20571
(202) 565-3946, (800) 565-3946; Fax: (202) 565-3380
Internet: www.exim.gov

President and Chairman: Philip Merrill, Room 1215
(202) 565-3500

Vice Chair and V.P.: April Foley, Room 1229
(202) 565-3540

General Counsel and C.O.O.: Peter Saba, Room 947
(202) 565-3430

Facilitates financing of exports of U.S. goods and services through loans, loan guarantees, and export credit insurance where private sector financing otherwise would not be available. *12 U.S.C. 635*

Midwest Regional Office
200 W. Adams, Suite 2450, Chicago, IL 60606
(312) 353-8081; Fax: (312) 353-8098
Internet: www.exim.gov

Director: Michael Howard

Officer (Ohio, Nebraska, Iowa and Northern Illinois):
Barry Bint (312) 353-8071

FARM CREDIT ADMINISTRATION
1501 Farm Credit Dr., McLean, VA 22102-5090
(703) 883-4000; Fax: (703) 734-5784
E-mail: info.line@fca.gov
Internet: www.fca.gov

Chairperson: Nancy C. Pellett (703) 883-4008

General Counsel: Charles R. Rawls (703) 883-4020

Ensures safe and sound operation of the banks, associations, affiliated service organizations, and other entities that comprise the Farm Credit System. *12 U.S.C. 2241*

CoBank
5500 S. Quebec St., Greenwood Village, CO 80111
Mailing Address: P.O. Box 5110, Denver, CO 80217
(800) 542-8072
Internet: www.cobank.com

C.E.O.: Douglas D. Sims (303) 740-4062
E-mail: dsims@cobank.com

President/C.O.O.: Robert B. Engel (303) 740-6498
E-mail: bengel@cobank.com

Exec. V.P. & C.F.O.: Brian P. Jackson (303) 694-5869
E-mail: bjackson@cobank.com

General Counsel: Allan S. Kantrowitz (303) 740-4142
E-mail: akantrowitz@cobank.com

Board Chairman: J. Roy Orton
E-mail: rorton@cobank.com

First Vice Chair: D. Sheldon Brown
E-mail: sbrown@cobank.com
Cooperative bank serving agricultural and rural needs. Part of the Farm Credit System, a privately owned Federally chartered organization regulated by the Farm Credit Administration.

FEDERAL COMMUNICATIONS COMMISSION
445 12th St. S.W., Washington, DC 20554
Consumer Information:
(202) 418-0260, (888) 225-5322;
Library: (202) 418-0450;
Media Bureau: (202) 418-7200;
Public Affairs: (202) 418-0503;
TDD: (202) 418-2555, (888) 835-5322;
Procurement Branch: (202) 418-0930;
Personnel: (202) 418-0130;
Personnel Locator: (202) 418-0126;
Fax: (866) 418-0232
E-mail: fccinfo@fcc.gov
Internet: www.fcc.gov

Chairman: Michael K. Powell, (202) 418-1000
E-mail: michael.powell@fcc.gov

General Counsel: Austin C. Schlick (Acting) (202) 418-1774
E-mail: austin.schlick@fcc.gov

Regulates interstate and foreign communication by radio, television, wire, satellite, and cable. Oversees the orderly development and operation of broadcast services, telephone and telegraph services at reasonable rates. *15 U.S.C.; 21 U.S.C.; 47 U.S.C. 35, 151*

District Office
Park Ridge Office Center, Room 306,
1550 Northwest Hwy., Park Ridge, IL 60068-1460
(888) 225-5322

District Dir.: G. Michael Moffitt
(847) 813-4660; Fax: (847) 298-5403

Office of Administrative Law Judges
445 12th St. S.W., Washington, DC 20554

Chief Admin. Law Judge: Richard L. Sippel, Room 1-C768
(202) 418-2280

Admin. Law Judge: Arthur I. Steinberg, Room 1-C861
(202) 418-2255

Media Bureau
445 12th St. S.W., Room 3-C734, Washington, DC 20554
(202) 418-7200, 418-1198; Fax: (202) 418-2376
Internet: www.fcc.gov/mb

Chief: Deborah E. Klein (Acting)
Administers the regulatory program for AM, FM, low power FM, low power TV, Television; Cable television and post-licensing satellite matters.

Wireline Competition Bureau
445 12th St. S.W., 5th Floor, Washington, DC 20554
(202) 418-1500; TTY: (202) 418-0484

Chief: Jeffrey Carlisle; Fax: (202) 418-2825
Responsible for FCC policies concerning telephone companies that provide interstate telecommunications services to the public through the use of wire-based transmission facilities. These companies, called common carriers, provide voice, data and other transmission services.
Formerly called Common Carrier Bureau

Wireless Telecommunications Bureau
445 12th St. S.W., Washington, DC 20554
(202) 418-0600; Fax: (202) 418-0787

Chief: John B. Muletta, Room 3-C252
Develops, recommends and administers the Commission's policies, programs and rules governing domestic wireless telecommunications except satellite communications.
Formerly called Private Radio Communications

Office of Engineering and Technology
445 12th St. S.W., Suite 7C155, Washington, DC 20554
(202) 418-2470; Fax: (202) 418-1944
Internet: www.fcc.gov/oet

Chief: Edmond J. Thomas
Administers the table of frequency allocations, the Experimental Radio Service, and Equipment Authorization Program.

Consumer and Governmental Affairs Bureau
445 12th St. S.W., Room CYB514, Washington, DC 20554
(888) 225-5322; Fax: (866) 418-0232; TTY: (888) 835-5322

Chief: Jay Keithley (Acting), Room 5C758
(202) 418-1400; Fax: (202) 418-2983

Departments & Agencies

FEDERAL DEPOSIT INSURANCE CORPORATION
550 17th St. N.W., Washington, DC 20429-9990
(202) 736-0000
E-mail: publicinfo@fdic.gov
Internet: www.fdic.gov

Chairman: Donald E. Powell (202) 898-6974
General Counsel: William F. Kroener III (202) 898-3680
Dir., Division of Supervision & Consumer Protection: Michael J. Zamorski (202) 898-8946
Dir., Division of Finance: Frederick S. Selby (202) 416-6965
Dir., Division of Resolutions and Receiverships:
  Mitchell L. Glassman (202) 898-6525
Dir., Division of Information Resources Management: Michael E. Bartell (703) 516-5781
Dir., Division of Insurance and Research:
  Arthur J. Murton (202) 898-3938

Promotes and preserves public confidence in the banking system and protects the money supply by providing insurance for bank deposits and periodic examinations of state chartered banks that are not members of the Federal Reserve System. *12 U.S.C. 1811*

Regional Office
500 W. Monroe St., Suite 3300, Chicago, IL 60661-3697
(312) 382-7500, (800) 944-5343; Fax: (312) 382-6901

Regional Dir.: Sylvia Plunkett (Acting)
Regional Counsel: Timothy E. Divis

FEDERAL ELECTION COMMISSION
999 E St. N.W., Washington, DC 20463
(202) 694-1100, (800) 424-9530; TTY: (202) 219-3336
Internet: www.fec.gov

Chair: Scott E. Thomas (202) 694-1000
General Counsel: Lawrence Norton
  (202) 694-1650; Fax: (202) 219-3923

Exercises exclusive jurisdiction over the administration and civil enforcement of federal laws pertaining to acquisition and expenditure of funds to influence elections to federal office. *2 U.S.C. 431-455 and 26 U.S.C. 9001-9042*

FEDERAL HOUSING FINANCE BOARD
1777 F St. N.W., Washington, DC 20006-5210
(202) 408-2500
Internet: www.fhfb.gov

Chairman: Alicia R. Castaneda (202) 408-2542
General Counsel: Mark J. Tenhundfeld
  (202) 408-2536; Fax: (202) 408-2580
Deputy General Counsel: Neil R. Crowley (202) 408-2990
Administers and enforces the Federal Home Loan Bank Act.
12 U.S.C. 1421

Federal Home Loan Bank of Cincinnati
1000 Atrium Two, 221 E. 4th St., Cincinnati, OH 45202
Mailing Address: P.O. Box 598, Cincinnati, OH 45201
(513) 852-7500, (888) 852-6500; Fax: (513) 852-7655
Internet: www.fhlbcin.com

FEDERAL LABOR RELATIONS AUTHORITY
1400 K St. N.W., Washington, DC 20424-0001
(202) 218-7770; Fax: (202) 482-6659
Internet: www.flra.gov

Chairman: Dale Cabaniss (202) 218-7900
Exec. Dir.: Vacancy at Press Time (202) 218-7960
General Counsel: Vacancy at Press Time
  (202) 218-7910; Fax: (202) 482-6608

Oversees the Federal Service Labor-Management Relations Program in the protection of the rights of federal employees to bargain collectively. *5 U.S.C. Chapter 71*

Regional Office
55 W. Monroe St., Suite 1150, Chicago, IL 60603-9729
(312) 886-3465; Fax: (312) 886-5977

Regional Dir.: Peter Sutton (Acting), Ext. 4022
  E-mail: psutton@flra.gov
Regional Atty.: Ayo Glanton, Ext. 4017

Office of Administrative Law Judges
1400 K St. N.W., Washington, DC 20424
(202) 218-7950; Fax: (202) 482-6629
Chief Admin. Law Judge: Eli Nash
Admin. Law Judges:
  Susan Jelen   Richard Pearson
  Paul Lang

FEDERAL MARITIME COMMISSION
800 North Capitol St. N.W.,
Washington, DC 20573-0001
(202) 523-5707
Internet: www.fmc.gov

Chairman: Steven R. Blust
  (202) 523-5911; Fax: (202) 523-4224
  E-mail: chairman@fmc.gov
Secretary: Bryant L. VanBrakle
  (202) 523-5725; Fax: (202) 523-0014
  E-mail: secretary@fmc.gov
General Counsel: Amy W. Larson
  (202) 523-5740; Fax: (202) 523-5738

Regulates the waterborne foreign commerce of the United States including licensing ocean transportation intermediaries reviewing agreements among carriers and enforcement of the shipping statutes as related to foreign commerce. *5 U.S.C. app. Reorganization Plan No. 7 of 1961*

Office of Administrative Law Judges
800 N. Capitol St., N.W., Room 1088,
Washington, DC 20573
(202) 523-5750; Fax: (202) 566-0042
Internet: www.fmc.gov

Chief Admin. Law Judge: Norman D. Kline

Admin. Law Judges:
  Irwin Schroeder
  Miriam A. Trudelle
The judges act as trial judges presiding over and issuing decisions in formal proceedings involving alleged violation of Federal shipping regulatory law.

FEDERAL MEDIATION AND CONCILIATION SERVICE
2100 K St. N.W., Washington, DC 20427
(202) 606-8100;
Communication Services: (202) 606-8100;
Arbitration Division: (202) 606-5111;
Fax: (202) 606-4251
Internet: www.fmcs.gov

Director: Scot L. Beckenbaugh (Acting)
Chief of Staff: John J. Toner
General Counsel: Arthur B. Pearlstein (202) 606-5444

Prevents work stoppages, advocates collective bargaining, and promotes sound labor-management relations through effective mediation and voluntary arbitration programs. *29 U.S.C. 172.*

Eastern Regional Office
6161 Oak Tree Blvd., Suite 120, Independence, OH 44131
(216) 520-4800; Fax: (216) 520-4815

Regional Dir.: Jack Buettner

D.M.S.: Louis Manchise
  (Field Station Responsibility—Cleveland, Columbus, Dayton, Toledo)
  (513) 684-2951; E-mail: lmanchise@fmcs.gov

FEDERAL MINE SAFETY AND HEALTH REVIEW COMMISSION
601 New Jersey Ave. N.W., Suite 9500,
Washington, DC 20001-2021
(202) 434-9900; Fax: (202) 434-9944
E-mail: info@fmshrc.gov
Internet: www.fmshrc.gov
1244 Speer Blvd., Room 280, Denver, CO 80204
(303) 844-5267; Fax: (303) 844-5268

Chairperson: Michael F. Duffy
  (202) 434-9924; Fax: (202) 434-9944
General Counsel: Thomas A. Stock
  (202) 434-9935; Fax: (202) 434-9944

Adjudicates disputes regarding compliance with occupational safety and health standards in the Nation's surface and underground metal, coal, and non-metal mines. *30 U.S.C. 801*

FEDERAL RESERVE SYSTEM
Board of Governors of the Federal Reserve System
**20th St. & Constitution Ave. N.W.,
Washington, DC 20551
(202) 452-3000; Publications: (202) 452-3245;
Fax: (202) 452-3819
Internet: www.federalreserve.gov**

Chairman: Alan Greenspan
General Counsel: Scott G. Alvarez, Room B-1046
(202) 452-3430; Fax: (202) 452-3101
Leads the Nation's monetary and credit affairs as the central bank of the United States. Supervises and regulates the banking system to ensure a sound and capable system that can respond to the needs of the Nation. *12 U.S.C. 221*

FEDERAL RETIREMENT THRIFT INVESTMENT BOARD
**1250 H St. N.W., Suite 200, Washington, DC 20005
(202) 942-1600; Fax: (202) 942-1676
Internet: www.tsp.gov; www.frtib.gov**

Exec. Dir.: Gary A. Amelio
General Counsel: Elizabeth S. Woodruff (202) 942-1660
Administers the Thrift Savings Plan which provides federal employees the same type of savings and tax benefits that many private corporations offer their employees under so-called 401 (k) plans. *5 U.S.C.8351 and 8401-8479.*

FEDERAL TRADE COMMISSION
**600 Pennsylvania Ave. N.W., Washington, DC 20580
General Information: (202) 326-2222;
Antitrust: (202) 326-3300;
Consumer Protection: (877) 382-4357;
Inspector General: (202) 326-2800;
Procurement: (202) 326-2258;
Personnel (Employee Development & Relations):
(202) 326-2021; Press Office: (202) 326-2180;
Phone Mail System: (202) 326-2000
Internet: www.ftc.gov**

Chair: Deborah Platt Majoras, Room 440
(202) 326-2100; Fax: (202) 326-2396
General Counsel: William E. Kovacic (202) 326-2424
Maintains the competitive nature of the United States by working to prevent monopolies, unfair trade practices, and restraints to trade, keeping competition free and fair. *15 U.S.C. 41*

Office of Administrative Law Judges
600 Pennsylvania Ave. N.W., Washington, DC 20580
Chief Admin. Law Judge: Stephen J. McGuire, Room 113
(202) 326-3637; Fax: (202) 326-2427
Admin. Law Judge: D. Michael Chappell, Room 113
(202) 326-3637; Fax: (202) 326-2427

East Central Regional Office
1111 Superior Ave., Suite 200, Cleveland, OH 44114-2507
(216) 263-3418
Internet: www.ftc.gov
Director: John M. Mendenhall

GENERAL SERVICES ADMINISTRATION
**1800 F St. N.W., Washington, DC 20405
(202) 501-0800
Internet: www.gsa.gov**

Administrator: Stephen A. Perry
(202) 501-0800; Fax: (202) 219-1243
E-mail: stephen.perry@gsa.gov
General Counsel: George N. Barclay (Acting)
(202) 501-2200; Fax: (202) 501-2509
E-mail: george.barclay@gsa.gov
Establishes policy for and administers management of real estate and other property of the U.S. government including construction and operation of buildings; procurement and distribution of supplies, furnishings, and equipment; utilization and disposal of property; and procurement and management of transportation, technology, telecommunications, and other administrative services. *40 U.S.C. 471*

Regional Office
230 S. Dearborn St., Room 3700, Chicago, IL 60604
(312) 353-5395; Fax: (312) 886-5595
Regional Administrator: James C. Handley

Federal Citizen Information Center
Pueblo, CO 81009
(800) 333-4636
Internet: www.firstgov.gov; www.pueblo.gsa.gov
A clearinghouse for information about the Federal Government. Persons with questions about a Government Program or Agency, and who are unsure of which office can help, may call or write the Center. A specialist will either answer the question or locate an expert who can.

Chief Information Office
General Services Bldg., 1800 F St. N.W.,
Washington, DC 20405
(202) 501-1000; Fax: (202) 501-0022
Chief Information Officer: Michael W. Carleton
E-mail: michael.carleton@gsa.gov
Manages the operation and procurement of government wide automatic data processing equipment, resources, and procedures.

Federal Supply Service
1901 S. Bell St., Arlington, VA 22202-4502
Mailing Address: Washington, DC 20406
(703) 605-5400
Internet: www.fss.gsa.gov
Commissioner: Donna D. Bennett
E-mail: donna.bennett@gsa.gov
Contracts for and distributes personal property and services for the Federal agencies.

Public Buildings Service
General Services Administration, Room 6340,
1800 F St. N.W., Washington, DC 20405
(202) 501-1100; Fax: (202) 219-2310
Commissioner: F. Joseph Moravac
E-mail: joseph.moravec@gsa.gov
Oversees and manages the design, construction, lease, purchase, repair, appraisal, maintenance, and protection of many public buildings comprising 250 million square feet of space.

Office of Real Property Disposal
General Services Bldg., Room 4244, 1800 F St. N.W.,
Washington, DC 20405
(202) 501-0084; Fax: (202) 208-1714
Internet: www.gsa.gov/pbs/pr/prhome.htm
Asst. Commissioner: Brian K. Polly
E-mail: brian.polly@gsa.gov
Deputy Asst. Commissioner: Gordon S. Creed
E-mail: gordon.creed@gsa.gov
Manages the utilization and disposal of federal real and related personal property.
Formerly known as Federal Property Resources Service

Human Resources Division
Office of Chief People Officer
1800 F St. N.W., Room 6242, Washington, DC 20405
(202) 501-0398; Fax: (202) 219-0982
Chief People Officer: Gail T. Lovelace

OFFICE OF GOVERNMENT ETHICS
**1201 New York Ave. N.W., Suite 500,
Washington, DC 20005-3917
(202) 482-9300; Fax: (202) 482-9237
Internet: www.usoge.gov**

Director: Marilyn L. Glynn (Acting)
General Counsel: Stuart D. Rick (Acting)
(202) 482-9292; Fax: (202) 482-9237
Provides overall direction to the Executive branch in the prevention and management of conflicts of interest. This is the lead agency in the administration and interpretation of the Ethics in Government Act for the Executive branch. *5 U.S.C. app. 401*

INTER-AMERICAN FOUNDATION
**901 Stuart St., 10th Floor, Arlington, VA 22203
(703) 306-4301; Fax: (703) 306-4365
Internet: www.iaf.gov**

Chairperson: Roger W. Wallace
President: David Valenzuela (703) 306-4359
General Counsel: Jocelyn Nieva (Acting) (703) 306-4314
Supports economic and social development in Latin America and the Caribbean. *22 U.S.C. 290f*

Departments & Agencies

MERIT SYSTEMS PROTECTION BOARD
1615 M St. N.W., Washington, DC 20036
(202) 653-7200; Fax: (202) 653-7130
E-mail: mspb@mspb.gov
Internet: www.mspb.gov

Chair: Neil A.G. McPhie

General Counsel: Martha Schneider (202) 653-7171

Protects the integrity of the Federal Merit principles and the rights of the workers in the system. Adjudicates Federal employee appeals of removals and other significant employment actions. Conducts studies of the Civil Service and other Federal Merit systems; reviews regulations of the Office of Personnel Management. *5 U.S.C. 1201*

Central Regional Office
230 S. Dearborn St., Room 3100, Chicago, IL 60604-1669
(312) 353-2923; Fax: (312) 886-4231

Regional Dir.: Martin Baumgaertner

U.S. Office of Special Counsel
1730 M St. N.W., Suite 300, Washington, DC 20036-4505
(202) 254-3600; Fax: (202) 653-5161
Internet: www.osc.gov

Special Counsel: Scott J. Bloch
   (202) 254-3610; Fax: (202) 653-5161

The U.S. Office of Special Counsel (OSC) is an independent investigative and prosecutorial agency and operates as a secure channel for disclosures of whistleblower complaints and abuse of authority. Its primary mission is to safeguard the merit system in Federal employment by protecting Federal employees and applicants from prohibited personnel practices, especially retaliation for whistleblowing. OSC also has jurisdiction over the Hatch Act and the Uniformed Services Employment and Reemployment Rights Act. For more information please visit our web site at www.osc.gov or call 1-800-872-9855.

NATIONAL AERONAUTICS
AND SPACE ADMINISTRATION
300 E St. S.W., Washington, DC 20024-3210
Mailing Address: NASA Headquarters,
Washington, DC 20496-0001
(202) 358-0000; Internet: www.nasa.gov

Administrator: Dr. Michael Griffin (202) 358-1010

General Counsel: Michael Wholley
   (202) 358-2450; Fax: (202) 358-2741

Conducts research for the solution of problems of flights within and outside the Earth's atmosphere and develops, tests, constructs, and operates aeronautical and space vehicles, explores space with manned and unmanned projects, and utilizes the resources of the United States and other nations engaged in space activities for peaceful purposes. *42 U.S.C. 2451*

NATIONAL ARCHIVES
AND RECORDS ADMINISTRATION
8601 Adelphi Rd., College Park, MD 20740-6001
(866) 272-6272;
Public Reference/Customer Service: (301) 713-6779;
Public Affairs Information: (301) 713-6000;
Records Mgmt. Programs: (301) 713-7110
Internet: www.archives.gov

Archivist of the United States: Allen Weinstein
   Room 4200 (301) 837-1600; Fax: (301) 837-3218

General Counsel: Gary M. Stern, Room 3110
   (301) 837-1750; Fax: (301) 837-0293
   E-mail: garym.stern@nara.gov

Ensures ready access to essential evidence that documents the rights of American citizens, the actions of Federal officials, and the national experience; establishes policies and procedures for managing U.S. Government records assists Federal agencies in documenting their activities, administering records management programs, scheduling records, and retiring noncurrent records; NARA accessions, arranges, describes, preserves, and provides access to the essential documentation of the three branches of Government; manages the Presidential Libraries system; and publishes the laws, regulations, and Presidential and other public documents; assists the Information Security oversight Office, which manages Federal classification and declassification policies, and the National Historical Publications and Records Commission. *44 U.S.C. 2101*

Great Lakes Regional Office
7358 S. Pulaski Rd., Chicago, IL 60629-5898
(773) 948-9000; Fax: (312) 948-9059

Regional Administrator: David Kuehl

Asst. Regional Administrator: Denis Paskauskas

Office of Regional Records Services
National Archives at College Park, 8601 Adelphi Rd., College Park, MD 20740
(301) 837-2950; Fax: (301) 837-1617

Director: Tom Mills

Office of Records Services
National Archives at College Park, 8601 Adelphi Rd., College Park, MD 20740
(301) 837-3110

Asst. Archivist: Michael J. Kurtz, Room 3400
   E-mail: mike.kurtz@arch2.nara.gov
Formerly known as Office of Records Management

National Archives—Museum Programs
700 Pennsylvania Ave. N.W., G9, Washington, DC 20408
(202) 501-5210; Fax: (202) 501-5239
E-mail: museumprograms@nara.gov
Internet: www.archives.gov
   Director: Marvin Pinkert

Brings the rich and varied resources of the National Archives to the public through its educational workshops and materials, exhibitions, film programs, publications, lectures, genealogy programs, tours, museum shop and other outreach activities.

Office of Special and Regional Archives
All functions now handled by the Office of Regional Records Services, supra

Office of the Federal Register
National Archives and Records Administration,
800 North Capitol St. N.W., Suite 700, Washington, DC 20408
(202) 741-6000; Fax: (202) 741-6012
E-mail: fedreg.info@nara.gov
Internet: www.archives.gov/federal_register;
www.gpoaccess.gov/nara

Director: Raymond A. Mosley
   E-mail: ray.mosley@nara.gov

Dir., Legal Affairs and Policy: Michael L. White
   (202) 741-6030

Provides ready access to the official text of the Public Laws, Presidential documents, Federal administrative regulations and notices, and descriptions of Federal organizations, programs and actitivies. Publishes the daily *Federal Register* and the *Code of Federal Regulations* (CFR) in print and online formats. Administers the constitutional amendment process and coordinates the functions of the Electoral College. *44 U.S.C. Chap. 15.*

Office of Records Administration
All functions now handled by the Office of Records Services, supra

Office of Presidential Libraries
National Archives at College Park, 8601 Adelphi Rd., College Park, MD 20740-6001
(301) 837-3250; Fax: (301) 837-3199

Asst. Archivist for Presidential Libraries:
   Richard Claypoole (301) 837-3250

NATIONAL CAPITAL PLANNING COMMISSION
401 9th St., N.W., North Lobby, Suite 500,
Washington, DC 20576
(202) 482-7200; Fax: (202) 482-7272
Internet: www.ncpc.gov

Chairman: John V. Cogbill III

Exec. Dir.: Patricia E. Gallagher

General Counsel: Wayne Costa

The National Capital Planning Commission is the federal government's central planning agency charged with protecting the federal interest in the National Capital Region. NCPC's jurisdiction covers 2,500 square miles, and includes the District of Columbia and surrounding counties in Maryland and Virginia. The Commission reviews development plans and projects, reviews Federal Capital Improvement Programs, and conducts comprehensive and long-range planning. *40 U.S.C. 71*

NATIONAL CONSUMER COOPERATIVE BANK
d.b.a. National Cooperative Bank
1725 Eye St. N.W., Suite 600, Washington, DC 20006
(202) 336-7700, (800) 955-9622; Fax: (202) 336-7800
Internet: www.ncb.com
President and Chief Executive Officer:
   Charles E. Snyder (202) 336-7610
   E-mail: csnyder@ncb.com
Counsel: Shea & Gardner (202) 828-2080

A unique financial services company that provides financial products and services to U.S. commercial and real estate ventures governed by certain cooperative principles. Primary lines of business include: real estate lending, commercial lending, small business lending, capital markets capabilities, community development expertise and retail banking through its subsidiary, NCB Savings Bank FSB.

NATIONAL CREDIT UNION ADMINISTRATION
1775 Duke St., Alexandria, VA 22314-3428
(703) 518-6300; Fax: (703) 518-6319, 518-6660
E-mail: boardmail@ncua.gov
Internet: www.ncua.gov
Chair: JoAnn Johnson
General Counsel: Robert M. Fenner
   (703) 518-6540; Fax: (703) 518-6569, 518-6667
   E-mail: ogcmail@ncua.gov

Charters, insures, supervises, and examines Federal Credit Unions and administers the National Credit Union Share Insurance Fund. Manages the Central Liquidity Facility which provides emergency loans to member credit unions. *12 U.S.C. 1752*

Region III
7000 Central Pkwy., Suite 1600, Atlanta, GA 30328
(678) 443-3000; Fax: (678) 443-3020
Regional Dir.: Alonzo A. Swann III

NATIONAL ENDOWMENT FOR THE ARTS
1100 Pennsylvania Ave. N.W., Washington, DC 20506
(202) 682-5400; Fax: (202) 682-5572
E-mail: webmgr@arts.endow.gov
Internet: www.nea.gov
Chairperson: Dana Gioia (202) 682-5414
General Counsel: Claudia Nadig (202) 682-5595

Fosters the excellence, diversity and vitality of the arts in the United States; and broadens public access to the arts. *20 U.S.C. 951*

NATIONAL ENDOWMENT FOR THE HUMANITIES
1100 Pennsylvania Ave. N.W., Washington, DC 20506
Public Information Office: (202) 606-8400;
Fax: (202) 606-8240;
TDD: (866) 372-2930, (202) 606-8282
E-mail: info@neh.gov
Internet: www.neh.gov
Chairman: Dr. Bruce Cole, Room 503
   (202) 606-8310; E-mail: bcole@neh.gov
General Counsel: Daniel Schneider, Room 530
   (202) 606-8322; E-mail: dschneider@neh.gov

Supports research, education, and public programs in the humanities through a grant-making program. *20 U.S.C. 951*

NATIONAL LABOR RELATIONS BOARD
1099 14th St. N.W., Washington, DC 20570-0001
(202) 273-1000; Public Information: (202) 273-1991;
TDD: (202) 273-4300
Internet: www.nlrb.gov
Chairman: Robert J. Battista (202) 273-1770
General Counsel: Arthur F. Rosenfeld (202) 273-3700
Assoc. Dir., Div. of Information: Patricia Gilbert
   (202) 273-1991
Dir., Division of Administration: Gloria J. Joseph
   (202) 273-3890
Dir., Division of Equal Employment Opportunity:
   Robert J. Poindexter (202) 273-3891

Administers the National Labor Relations Act as the principal labor law of the United States governing relations between unions and employers in the private sector. Prevents and remedies unfair labor practices; determines, through secret-ballot elections, the free democratic choice by employees to be represented by a union and if so, which union. *29 U.S.C. 167*

Division of Judges
1099 14th St. N.W., Suite 5400E,
Washington, DC 20570-0001
(202) 501-8800; Fax: (202) 501-8686
Chief Admin. Law Judge: Robert A. Giannasi
Deputy Chief Admin. Law Judge: Richard A. Scully
Admin. Law Judges:

George Aleman	Martin Linsky
Arthur Amchan	C. Richard Miserendino
Paul A. Bogas	Wallace A. Nations
Karl Buschmann	Michael Rosas
Paul Buxbaum	Bruce D. Rosenstein
John Clark	Mark Rubin
David L. Evans	Ira Sandron
Eric Fine	Benjamin Schlesinger
Joseph Gontram	Earl Shamwell, Jr.
Margaret Kern	Jane VanDeventer
William Kocol	

Cleveland Regional Office
Anthony J. Celebrezze Federal Bldg., Room 1695,
1240 E. Ninth St., Cleveland, OH 44199-2086
(216) 522-3716; Fax: (216) 522-2418
Regional Dir.: Frederick Calatrello

Cincinnati Regional Office
Federal Office Bldg., Room 3003, 550 Main St.,
Cincinnati, OH 45202-3271
(513) 684-3686; Fax: (513) 684-3946
Regional Dir.: Gary W. Muffley (513) 684-3621

NATIONAL MEDIATION BOARD
1301 K St. N.W., Suite 250 East,
Washington, DC 20005
(202) 692-5000
Internet: www.nmb.gov
Chair: Harry R. Hoglander
   (202) 692-5022; Fax: (202) 692-5082
Members:
   Edward J. Fitzmaurice, Jr.
      (202) 692-5016; Fax: (202) 692-5082
   Read Van de Water (202) 692-5019; Fax: (202) 692-5082
Dir., Mediation Services: Larry Gibbons
   (202) 692-5030; Fax: (202) 692-5083
Dir., ADR Services: Daniel Rainey
   (202) 692-5030; Fax: (202) 692-5083
General Counsel: Mary Johnson
   (202) 692-5040; Fax: (202) 692-5085
Arbitration Services Dir.: Roland Watkins
   (202) 692-5055; Fax: (202) 692-5086
Finance & Admin. Dir.: June D.W. King
   (202) 692-5010; Fax: (202) 692-5081

Resolves disputes in rail and airline management-labor relations in accordance with the Railway Labor Act and provides administrative and financial support in adjusting minor grievances in the railroad industry. *45 U.S.C. 151*

NATIONAL RAILROAD PASSENGER CORPORATION (AMTRAK)
60 Massachusetts Ave. N.E., Washington, DC 20002
(202) 906-3000; Fax: (202) 906-3865
Internet: www.amtrak.com
President & C.E.O.: David L. Gunn
   (202) 906-3960; Fax: (202) 906-2850
General Counsel & Corporate Secretary:
   Alicia Serfaty (202) 906-2198; Fax: (202) 906-2821

Develops, operates, and improves a modern inter-city rail transportation system for the nation's transportation needs. *Now a Private Corporation operating passenger rail service.*

NATIONAL SCIENCE FOUNDATION
4201 Wilson Blvd., Arlington, VA 22230
(703) 292-5111; TDD: (703) 292-5090
Internet: www.nsf.gov
Director: Arden Bement (703) 292-8000
General Counsel: Lawrence Rudolph
   (703) 292-8060; Fax: (703) 292-9041

Promotes the progress of science and engineering through the support of research and education programs. *42 U.S.C. 1861*

Departments & Agencies

NATIONAL TRANSPORTATION SAFETY BOARD
490 L'Enfant Plaza S.W., Washington, DC 20594
(202) 314-6000; Fax: (202) 314-6293
E-mail: pubinq@ntsb.gov
Internet: www.ntsb.gov

Chair: Ellen Engelman-Connors
Vice Chair: Mark Rosenker
Managing Dir.: Daniel Campbell (202) 314-6060
General Counsel: Ron Battocchi (202) 314-6080

Ensures that all types of transportation are conducted safely by investigating accidents, conducting studies, and making recommendations to government agencies and industry.

Office of Administrative Law Judges
490 L'Enfant Plaza East, S.W., Washington, DC 20594
(202) 314-6150; Fax: (202) 314-6158
4760 Oakland St., Denver, CO 80239
624 Six Flags Dr., Suite 150, Arlington, TX 76011
Chief Admin. Law Judge: William E. Fowler, Jr.
    (Washington, D.C.); Fax: (202) 314-6158
        E-mail: fowlerw@ntsb.gov
        Circuit I (Generally the Northeastern States)
Admin. Law Judges:
    William A. Pope (Washington, D.C.); Fax: (202) 314-6158
        E-mail: popew@ntsb.gov
        Circuit II (Generally the Southeastern States)
    Patrick G. Geraghty (Denver, Col.)
        (303) 373-3511; Fax: (303) 373-3507
        E-mail: geraghp@ntsb.gov
        Circuit III (Generally the Western States)
    William R. Mullins (Arlington, Tex.)
        (817) 652-7860; Fax: (817) 652-7868
        E-mail: mullinsw@ftwntsb.gov
        Circuit IV (Generally the Central States)

Aviation, Highway, Northeast Regional Office
2001 Rt. 46, Suite 504, Parsippany, NJ 07054
Highway: (973) 334-6615; Aviation: (973) 334-6420;
Fax: (973) 334-6759

Regional Dir., Aviation: Robert Pearce

Engineer, Highway Div.: Vacancy at Press Time

NUCLEAR REGULATORY COMMISSION
One White Flint North, 11555 Rockville Pike,
Rockville, MD 20852-2738
Mailing Address: , Washington, DC 20555
(301) 415-8200, (800) 368-5642
Internet: www.nrc.gov

Chair: Nils J. Diaz
    (301) 415-1759; Fax: (301) 415-1672
General Counsel: Karen D. Cyr (301) 415-1743

Licenses and regulates civilian use of nuclear reactors and materials to protect the safety of the public and the environment. *42 U.S.C. 5801*

Regional Office
2443 Warrenville Rd., Suite 210, Lisle, IL 60532-4351
(630) 829-9500; TDD: (301) 415-5575; Fax: (630) 515-1078
Regional Administrator: James L. Caldwell
Regional Counsel: Bruce A. Berson

OCCUPATIONAL SAFETY AND HEALTH REVIEW COMMISSION
One Lafayette Ctr., 9th Floor, 1120 20th St. N.W.,
Washington, DC 20036-3419
(202) 606-5398; Fax: (202) 606-5050
Internet: www.oshrc.gov

Exec. Dir.: Patricia A. Randle (202) 606-5380
Chairperson: W. Scott Railton
    (202) 606-2082; Fax: (202) 418-3487
General Counsel: Vacancy at Press Time
    (202) 606-5410
Public Information Officer: Linda A. Gravely
    (202) 606-5398; E-mail: lgravely@oshrc.gov

Issues decisions in disputes between O.S.H.A. and private employers over whether job safety standards were violated. *29 U.S.C. 651-678*

PEACE CORPS
1111 20th St. N.W., Washington, DC 20526
(800) 424-8580; Fax: (202) 692-2151
Internet: www.peacecorps.gov

Director: Gaddi H. Vasquez (202) 692-2100
General Counsel: Tyler S. Posey (202) 692-2150

Promotes world peace and friendship, helps other countries meet their needs for trained individuals, and helps promote understanding between the people of the United States and the people of the rest of the world. *22 U.S.C. 2501*

PENSION BENEFIT GUARANTY CORPORATION
1200 K St. N.W., Washington, DC 20005
(202) 326-4000
E-mail: www.pbgc.gov

Exec. Dir.: Bradley D. Belt
    (202) 326-4010; Fax: (202) 326-4016
General Counsel: James J. Keightley (202) 326-4020

Protects the retirement incomes of more than 44 million American workers in about 32,500 defined benefit pension plans. *29 U.S.C. 1301*

OFFICE OF PERSONNEL MANAGEMENT
1900 E St. N.W., Room 5A09,
Washington, DC 20415-1000
(202) 606-1800; Fax: (202) 606-2573
Internet: www.opm.gov

Director: Dan G. Blair (Acting)
    (202) 606-1000; Fax: (202) 606-2183
General Counsel: Mark A. Robbins, Room 7355
    (202) 606-1700; Fax: (202) 606-2609

Administers a merit system for federal employment that includes the examination, recruiting, training, and promotion of persons on the basis of their knowledge and skills regardless of their race, color, religion, political influence or other non-merit factors. *5 U.S.C. app Reorganization Plan No. 2 of 1978*

POSTAL RATE COMMISSION
1333 H St. N.W., Suite 300,
Washington, DC 20268-0001
(202) 789-6800; T.T.Y.: (202) 789-6881;
Fax: (202) 789-6886
Internet: www.prc.gov

Chair: George A. Omas (202) 789-6801
Chief Admin. Officer: Steven W. Williams (202) 789-6840
General Counsel: Stephen L. Sharfman
    (202) 789-6820; Fax: (202) 789-6861
Dir., Office of the Consumer Advocate:
    Shelley Dreifuss (202) 789-6830

Submits recommended decisions to the United States Postal Governors on postage rates, fees, and mail classifications. *39 U.S.C. 3601*

RAILROAD RETIREMENT BOARD
844 N. Rush St., Chicago, IL 60611-2092
(312) 751-4500; Fax: (312) 751-7154
E-mail: ola@rrb.gov
Internet: www.rrb.gov
Office of Legislative Affairs,
1310 G St. N.W., Suite 500,
Washington, DC 20005-3004
(202) 272-7742; Fax: (202) 272-7728
E-mail: ola@rrb.gov

Chair: Michael S. Schwartz
    (312) 751-4900; Fax: (312) 751-7193
Labor Member: V.M. Speakman, Jr.
    (312) 751-4905; Fax: (312) 751-7194
Management Member: Jerome F. Kever
    (312) 751-4910; Fax: (312) 751-7189
General Counsel: Steven A. Bartholow
    (202) 272-7742; Fax: (202) 272-7728

Administers retirement, survivor, unemployment and sickness benefits for railroad workers under the Railroad Retirement Act of 1974 and the Railroad Unemployment Insurance Act. *45 U.S.C. 231-231u, 45 U.S.C. 351-369*

District Office
U.R.S. Bldg., Suite 201, 36 E. Seventh St., Cincinnati, OH 45202
(513) 684-3188; Fax: (513) 684-3182
E-mail: cincinnati@rrb.gov

Railroad Retirement Board—Cont'd

District Office
AJC Federal Bldg., Room 907, 1240 E. Ninth St.,
Cleveland, OH 44199-2093
(216) 522-4053; Fax: (216) 522-2320;
Toledo area calls: (419) 259-7442; E-mail: cleveland@rrb.gov
District Mgr.: Richard Friedauer

SECURITIES AND EXCHANGE COMMISSION
450 5th St. N.W., Washington, DC 20549-0601
(202) 942-8088;
Office of Filings and Info. (Paper Filings): (202) 942-8050;
Office of Filings and Info. (Electronic Filing):
(202) 942-8900;
Office of Filings and Info. (Electronic Filing Fees):
(202) 942-8989;
Administrative and Personnel Management:
(202) 942-4000;
Investor Assistance and Complaints: (800) 732-0330;
Public Reference Room: (202) 942-8090;
Small Business Activities: (202) 942-2950
Chair: William H. Donaldson, Room 6000
(202) 942-0100; Fax: (202) 942-9646
General Counsel: Giovanni P. Prezioso, Room 6134
(202) 942-0900; Fax: (202) 942-9625
Administers the federal securities laws that seek to provide protection for investors, ensure that markets are fair and honest, and where necessary enforce securities laws with sanctions. *15 U.S.C. 78a-78jj*

Office of Administrative Law Judges
Mail Stop 1106, 450 Fifth St., N.W., Washington, DC 20549-1106
(202) 942-0399; Fax: (202) 942-9655
Chief Admin. Law Judge: Brenda P. Murray

Admin. Law Judges:
Carol Fox Foelak
James T. Kelly
Robert G. Mahony
Lillian A. McEwen

Midwest Regional Office
175 W. Jackson Blvd., Suite 900, Chicago, IL 60604
(312) 353-7390; Fax: (312) 353-7398
E-mail: chicago@sec.gov
Senior Counsel: Emlee Hilliard-Smith

SELECTIVE SERVICE SYSTEM
1515 Wilson Blvd., Arlington, VA 22209-2425
(703) 605-4100; Fax: (703) 605-4106
E-mail: info@sss.gov
Internet: www.sss.gov
Director: William A. Chatfield (703) 605-4005
General Counsel: Rudy Sanchez (703) 605-4066
Prepares to conduct a military draft in a national emergency. Registers virtually all young men and informs them about opportunities to serve America in peace time. *50 App. U.S.C. 451 et seq.*

SMALL BUSINESS ADMINISTRATION
409 3rd St. S.W., Washington, DC 20416
General Information/Personnel Locator:
(202) 205-6600;
Answer Desk (800) U-ASK-SBA: (800) 827-5722;
Inspector General: (202) 205-6586;
Office of Financial Assistance: (202) 205-6490;
Office of Disaster Assistance: (202) 205-6734;
Investment Division: (202) 205-6510;
Office of Surety Guarantee: (202) 205-6540;
Office of Procurement Assistance: (202) 205-6460;
Office of Business Initiatives, Education & Training:
(202) 205-6665;
Office of Minority Enterprise Development:
(202) 205-6412; Office of Advocacy: (202) 205-6533;
Office of Women's Business Ownership: (202) 205-6673;
Office of Veterans Affairs: (202) 205-6773;
Office of Technology: (202) 205-6450;
Office of International Trade: (202) 205-6720;
Office of Small Business Development Centers:
(202) 205-6766
Internet: www.sba.gov
Administrator: Hector V. Barreto, Suite 7000
(202) 205-6605; Fax: (202) 481-4600
General Counsel: David A. Javdan, Suite 7200
(202) 205-6642; Fax: (202) 481-0434

Aids, counsels, and protects the interests of small business, ensures that small business concerns receive a fair share of government business, makes loans to small businesses, and licenses, regulates, and makes loans to small business investment companies. *15 U.S.C. 631*

Office of Hearings and Appeals
409 Third St., S.W., Suite 5900, Washington, DC 20416
(202) 401-8200; Fax: (202) 205-7059
Admin. Law Judge: Richard S. Arkow
Admin. Judge: Christopher Holleman
Asst. Administrator for Hearings and Appeals:
Delorice P. Ford

Regional Office
Citicorp Center, Suite 1240, 500 W. Madison St.,
Chicago, IL 60661-2511
(312) 353-0357; Fax: (312) 353-3426
Regional Administrator: Patrick E. Rea

Columbus District Office
Two Nationwide Plaza, Suite 1400,
Columbus, OH 43215-2542
(614) 469-6860; Fax: (614) 469-2391
District Dir.: Thomas K. Mueller, Ext. 287

Small Business Administration Cleveland District Office
1350 Euclid Ave., Suite 211, Cleveland, OH 44115
(216) 522-4182; Fax: (216) 522-2038
District Dir.: Gilbert B. Goldberg

Cincinnati District Office
550 Main St., Room 2-522, Cincinnati, OH 45202
(513) 684-2814, Ext. 205; Fax: (513) 684-3251
Cincinnati Branch Mgr.: Ronald A. Carlson

SOCIAL SECURITY ADMINISTRATION
Windsor Park Bldg., 6401 Security Blvd.,
Baltimore, MD 21235
(410) 965-8882, (800) 772-1213;
Employer Hotline: (800) 772-6270; TTY: (800) 325-0778
Internet: www.ssa.gov
Commissioner: JoAnne B. Barnhart
General Counsel: Lisa de Soto
(410) 965-0600; Fax: (410) 966-3146
Press Officer: Mark Lassiter
449 Altmeyer Bldg., 6401 Security Blvd.,
Baltimore, MD 21235
(410) 965-8904; Fax: (410) 966-9973
E-mail: press.office@ssa.gov
Administers a national plan of contributory social insurance for retired or disabled persons and their survivors and dependents. *42 U.S.C. 1305, Public Law 103-296, (August 15, 1994)*

Regional Office
P.O. Box 8280, Chicago, IL 60680-8280
(800) 772-1213
Regional Commissioner: James F. Martin

Akron Office
2 S. Main St., 2nd Floor, Akron, OH 44308
(330) 375-5790
Manager: Michael Cooley

Akron West Office
Walter Mitchell Bldg., 2nd Floor, 1655 W. Market St.,
Akron, OH 44313
(330) 375-5830
Manager: Stephen Geary

Ashtabula Office
4314 Main Ave., Ashtabula, OH 44004
(440) 992-4198
Manager: Mary Jo Trent

Athens Office
Athens Mall, 743A E. State St., Athens, OH 45701
(740) 592-4448; TTY: (740) 594-1032
Manager: Elizabeth Crump

Batavia Office
1050 Hospital Dr., Batavia, OH 45103
(513) 732-2405
Manager: Virginia Pryce

Social Security Administration—Cont'd

Bowling Green Office
440 E. Poe Rd., Room 202, Bowling Green, OH 43402
(419) 352-8481
  Manager: Lois F. Dimaria

Cambridge Office
1225 Woodlawn Ave., Cambridge, OH 43725
(740) 439-4422
  Manager: Jim Thomas

Canton Office
1370 Market Ave. N., Canton, OH 44714
(330) 489-4457; TTY: (330) 489-4492
  Manager: Quinzella E. Hobbs

Chillicothe Office
606 Central Center Mall, Chillicothe, OH 45601
(740) 775-0206; TTY: (740) 773-4608
  Manager: Conception L. Doolen

Cincinnati Downtown Office
Federal Bldg., Room 2000, 550 Main St.,
Cincinnati, OH 45202
(513) 357-5505
  Manager: Robert M. Mendenhall

Cincinnati North Office
15 E. Sunnybrook Dr., Cincinnati, OH 45237
(513) 821-9424
  Manager: Ned Morrell

Cleveland Downtown Office
A.J.C. Federal Bldg., Room 793, 1240 E. Ninth St.,
Cleveland, OH 44199
(800) 772-1213
  Manager: Richard E. Warsinskey

Cleveland East Office
Beachwood Corporate Park, Suite 211,
3355 Richmond Rd., Cleveland, OH 44122
(216) 464-5951
  Manager: Roman Frayman

Cleveland Northeast Office
14930 St. Clair Ave., Cleveland, OH 44110
(216) 268-5164
  Manager: Bobby Reynolds

Cleveland Northwest Office
Seymour Bldg., 1st Floor, 2519 Detroit Ave.,
Cleveland, OH 44113
(216) 621-7363
  Manager: Lisa Allen

Cleveland Southeast Office
18711 Miles Rd., Warrensville Hts, OH 44128
(216) 518-0360
  Manager: Bobby Reynolds

Cleveland University Circle Office
1950 E. 117th St., Cleveland, OH 44106
(216) 791-3682
  Manager: Sue Mastrodonato

Columbus Downtown Office
225 Federal Bldg., 200 N. High St., Columbus, OH 43215
(614) 469-6855; TTY: (614) 228-0226
  Manager: Michael Link

Columbus East Office
4177 E. Broad St., Columbus, OH 43213
(614) 235-3710; TTY: (614) 228-0226
  Manager: Dennis C. Warstler

Columbus West Office
1060 Georgesville Rd., Columbus, OH 43228
(614) 274-9628
  Manager: Lyn Garfinkle

Dayton Office
Federal Bldg., Room 209, 200 W. Second St.,
Dayton, OH 45402
(937) 225-2542
  Manager: Henry D. Johnson

West Dayton Office
4375 Hoover Ave., Dayton, OH 45417
(937) 263-0450
  Manager: Jim Bitzer

Defiance Office
205 E. Second St., Defiance, OH 43512
(419) 782-3950; TTY: (419) 782-0368
  Manager: Donna M. Polce

East Liverpool Office
212 E. Fifth St., East Liverpool, OH 43920
(330) 385-9224
  Manager: Greg Hartman

Euclid Office
22802 Lake Shore Blvd., Euclid, OH 44123
(216) 289-8706
  Manager: Larry Soliday

Findlay Office
1665 Tiffin Ave., Findlay, OH 45840
(419) 423-9373; TTY: (419) 423-3130
  Manager: Teri Snook

Fremont Office
225 E. State St., Fremont, OH 43420
(419) 334-9771
  Manager: Robert Wood

Gallipolis Office
2455 S.R. 160, Gallipolis, OH 45631
(740) 446-7660; TTY: (740) 446-7905
  Manager: Dan Dearth

Hamilton Office
6553 Winford Ave., Hamilton, OH 45011
(513) 867-1530
  Manager: Virginia Pryce

Ironton Office
405 S. Third St., Ironton, OH 45638
(740) 533-1200; TTY: (740) 533-1068
  Manager: Bette L. Backus

Lakewood Office
Lakewood Center West, Suite 200, 14650 Detroit Ave.,
Lakewood, OH 44107
(800) 772-1213
  Manager: Kathleen Pepera

Lancaster Office
River Valley Mall, Suite 5046, 1635 River Valley Cir.,
Lancaster, OH 43130
(740) 689-2936
  Manager: Peter Gerds

Lima Office
Federal Bldg., 401 W. North St., Lima, OH 45801
(419) 228-7401; TTY: (419) 227-8262
  Manager: Roy N. Baldridge

Lorain Office
City Center Bldg., Room 306, 300 Broadway,
Lorain, OH 44052
(440) 245-3208
  Manager: Darrin K. Morgan

Mansfield Office
1287 S. Trimble Rd., Mansfield, OH 44902
(419) 522-8425
  Manager: Larry G. Moore

Marietta Office
1301 Greene St., Marietta, OH 45750
(740) 373-5007; TTY: (740) 373-5703
  Manager: Patricia Escalante

Marion Office
1363 Wellness Dr., Marion, OH 43302
(740) 389-3140
  Manager: Sarah Markofski

Medina Office
805 E. Washington St., Suite 130, Medina, OH 44256
(330) 725-0095
  Manager: Craig Enoch

Social Security Administration—Cont'd

Middleburg Heights Office
Commerce Place Bldg., Suite 200, 7123 Pearl Rd.,
Middleburg Heights, OH 44130 (440) 845-9863
Manager: William Norris

Middletown Office
3860 Towne Blvd., Franklin, OH 45005 (513) 423-4915
Manager: Carolyn Reeves

Newark Office
1671 W. Main St., Newark, OH 43055
(740) 788-9448; TTY: (740) 349-7892
Manager: Christine Vess

New Philadelphia Office
2419 E. High Ave. N.E., New Philadelphia, OH 44663
(330) 339-8910
Manager: Robert Eikenburg

Painesville Office
55 W. Jackson St., Painesville, OH 44077 (880) 772-1213
Manager: Hector Lamourt

Piqua Office
215 Looney Rd., Piqua, OH 45356
(937) 773-8098; TTY: (937) 773-3410
Manager: Jim Blair

Portsmouth Office
945 Fourth St., Portsmouth, OH 45662
(740) 354-3163; TTY: (740) 354-6282
Manager: Donald W. Davis

Ravenna Office
Key Bank Bldg., Suite 201, 145 N. Chestnut St.,
Ravenna, OH 44266 (330) 296-7427
Manager: Wanda I. Colón-Mollfulleda

Sandusky Office
200 Hancock St., Sandusky, OH 44870 (419) 625-6052
Manager: Al Kares

Springfield Office
2026 W. Main St., Springfield, OH 45501 (937) 325-0674
Manager: George M. Schild

Steubenville Office
2nd Natl. Bank Bldg., 4th Floor, 500 Market St.,
Steubenville, OH 43952 (740) 282-6265; TTY: (740) 282-6450
Manager: Michael Reynolds

Toledo Office
Four Seagate, Suite 1000, Toledo, OH 43604
(419) 259-6250; TTY: (419) 259-3870
Manager: Phil Walton

West Toledo Office
5151 Monroe St., Suite 112 W, Toledo, OH 43623
(419) 843-7751; TTY: (419) 259-3870
Manager: Rebecca Contreras

Warren Office
1353 E. Market St., 2nd Floor, Warren, OH 44483
(330) 399-7518; TTY: (330) 399-2380
Manager: Barry Linville

Wooster Office
1985 Eagle Pass, Wooster, OH 44691 (330) 264-0771
Manager: Tom Fortune

Worthington Office
AAA Bldg., Suite 160, 90 E. Wilson Bridge Rd.,
Worthington, OH 43085
(614) 888-5339; TTY: (614) 288-0226
Manager: Sharon Johnson

Xenia Office
Greene Park Plaza, 469 Dayton Ave., Xenia, OH 45385
(937) 372-9813; TTY: (800) 325-0778
Manager: Rick Meyer

Youngstown Office
101 Federal Plaza E., Suite 206, Youngstown, OH 44503
(330) 747-1496; TTY: (330) 747-3557
Manager: Carolyn Nixon

Zanesville Office
3089 Maple Ave., Zanesville, OH 43701
(740) 452-7539; TTY: (740) 452-3049
Manager: Terry Washington

TENNESSEE VALLEY AUTHORITY
400 West Summit Hill Dr., Knoxville, TN 37902-1499
(865) 632-2101
E-mail: tvainfo@tva.gov
Internet: www.tva.gov
One Massachusetts Ave, N.W., Suite 300,
Washington, DC 20444-0001
(202) 898-2999
Chairman: Glenn L. McCullough, Jr., Room ET12A
(865) 632-2600; Fax: (865) 632-2601
General Counsel: Maureen H. Dunn, Room ET11A
(865) 632-4131; Fax: (865) 632-3307
Conducts a unified program of resource development for the
advancement of economic growth in the Tennessee Valley
region. *16 U.S.C. 831*

U.S. TRADE AND DEVELOPMENT AGENCY
1000 Wilson Blvd., Suite 1600, Arlington, VA 22209
(703) 875-4357; Fax: (703) 875-4009
E-mail: info@ustda.gov
Internet: www.ustda.gov
Director: Thelma J. Askey
General Counsel: Leocadia I. Zak
Promotes economic development and market penetration in
developing and middle-income countries. *22 U.S.C. 2421*

UNITED STATES AGENCY
FOR INTERNATIONAL DEVELOPMENT
1300 Pennsylvania Ave., N.W.,
Washington, DC 20523-1000
(202) 712-0000; Fax: (202) 216-3524
E-mail: pinquries@usaid.gov
Internet: www.usaid.gov
Administrator: Andrew S. Natsios, Room 6.9
(202) 712-4040; Fax: (202) 216-3455
E-mail: anatsios@usaid.gov
Plans, coordinates, and formulates policy on international
issues affecting developing countries. *5 U.S.C. app.
Reorganization Plan No. 2 of 1979*
*Formerly known as the Agency for International
Development*

Overseas Private Investment Corporation
1100 New York Ave. N.W., Washington, DC 20527
(202) 336-8400; Fax: (202) 408-9859
Internet: www.opic.gov
President and Chief Executive Officer: Dr. Peter S. Watson
V.P./General Counsel: Mark Garfinkel
(202) 336-8410; Fax: (202) 218-0256

UNITED STATES INTERNATIONAL TRADE
COMMISSION
500 E St. S.W., Washington, DC 20436
(202) 205-2000; Fax: (202) 205-2104
Internet: www.usitc.gov
Chairman: Stephen Koplan (202) 708-2880
General Counsel: James M. Lyons (Acting) (202) 205-3061
Furnishes studies, reports, and recommendations involving
international trade and tariffs to the president, the
Congress, and other governmental agencies. *19 U.S.C. 2231*

UNITED STATES POSTAL SERVICE
475 L'Enfant Plaza S.W., Washington, DC 20260-1100
(202) 268-2960
Internet: www.usps.gov
Postmaster General: John E. Potter
Sr. V.P. and General Counsel: Mary Anne Gibbons
Room 6004 (202) 268-2950; Fax: (202) 268-6981
Provides mail processing and delivery services to businesses
and individuals in the United States. *39 U.S.C. 101*

United States Postal Inspection Service
1001 California Ave., Pittsburgh, PA 15290-9000
(412) 359-7900; Fax: (412) 359-7682
Inspector-in-Charge: Robin Dalgleish

Quasi-Official Agencies

LEGAL SERVICES CORPORATION
3333 K St., N.W., 3rd Floor,
Washington, DC 20007-3522
(202) 295-1500; Fax: (202) 337-6797
Internet: www.lsc.gov
President: Helaine M. Barnett
  E-mail: hbarnett@lsc.gov
General Counsel: Victor M. Fortuno
  E-mail: fortunov@lsc.gov
Provides funding for the provision of civil legal assistance to those unable to afford it, and oversees the national legal services program. *42 U.S.C. 2996*

SMITHSONIAN INSTITUTION
1000 Jefferson Dr. S.W., P.O. Box 37012,
Washington, DC 20013-7012
(202) 357-1300; T.T.Y.: (202) 357-1729
E-mail: info@si.edu
Internet: http://www.si.edu
Secretary: Lawrence M. Small, Room 205
  (202) 357-1846
General Counsel: John Huerta, Room 302
  (202) 357-1997, 357-2583; Fax: (202) 357-4310
Operates as an independent trust instrumentality of the United States that fosters the increase and diffusion of knowledge. *20 U.S.C. 41*

STATE JUSTICE INSTITUTE
1650 King St., Suite 600, Alexandria, VA 22314
(703) 684-6100; Fax: (703) 684-7618
Internet: www.statejustice.org
Chair: Hon. Robert A. Miller
(Chief Justice, S.D. Supreme Court, retired)
Exec. Dir.: Kevin Linskey, Ext. 214
Deputy Dir.: Kathy Schwartz, Ext. 215
Awards grants to further the development and adoption of improved judicial administration in the state courts of the United States. *42 U.S.C. 10701*

UNITED STATES INSTITUTE OF PEACE
1200 17th St. N.W., Suite 200,
Washington, DC 20036-3011
(202) 457-1700; Fax: (202) 429-6063;
TDD: (202) 457-1719; Job Line: (202) 775-4111
E-mail: publicaffairs@usip.org
Internet: www.usip.org
President: Richard H. Solomon
  (202) 429-3835
Dir., Rule of Law Program: Neil Kritz
  (202) 429-3833; Fax: (202) 429-6063
An independent, nonpartisan Federal institution created by Congress to promote research, policy analysis, education, and training on international peace and conflict resolution.

CONGRESSIONAL DELEGATION

U.S. SENATORS

SENATOR, Mike DeWine
Republican; next election November 2006
140 Russell Senate Bldg., Washington, DC 20510
(202) 224-2315; TDD: (202) 224-9921; Fax: (202) 224-6519
Internet: www.dewine.senate.gov

District Offices:

Xenia Office
100 W. Main St., 2nd Floor, Xenia 45385
(937) 376-3080; Fax: (937) 376-3387
State Dir.: Barbara Schenck

Cleveland Office
600 E. Superior Ave., Room 2450, Cleveland 44114
(216) 522-7272; Fax: (216) 522-2239
State Dir.: Barbara Schenck

Cincinnati Office
312 Walnut St., Suite 2030, Cincinnati 45202
(513) 763-8260; Fax: (513) 763-8268
State Dir.: Barbara Schenck
Regional Dir.: Scott Noyes

Columbus Office
37 W. Broad St., Suite 300, Columbus 43215
(614) 469-5186; Fax: (614) 469-2982
State Dir.: Barbara Schenck

Marietta Office
121 Putnam St., Suite 102, Marietta 45750
(740) 373-2317; Fax: (740) 373-8689
State Dir.: Barbara Schenck

Toledo Office
420 Madison Ave., Room 1225, Toledo 43604
(419) 259-7536; Fax: (419) 259-7575
State Dir.: Barbara Schenck

SENATOR, George V. Voinovich
Republican; next election November 2006
524 Hart Senate Office Bldg., Washington, DC 20510
(202) 224-3353; TDD: (202) 224-6997; Fax: (202) 228-1382
Internet: www.voinovich.senate.gov

District Offices:

Cleveland Office
1240 E. 9th St., Room 2955, Cleveland 44199
(216) 522-7095; Fax: (216) 522-7097
E-mail: cleveland_voinovich@voinovich.senate.gov

Cincinnati Office
36 E. 7th St., Room 2615, Cincinnati 45202
(513) 684-3265; Fax: (513) 684-3269
E-mail: cincinnati_voinovich@voinovich.senate.gov

Columbus Office
37 W. Broad St., Room 310, Columbus 43215
(614) 469-6697; Fax: (614) 469-7733
E-mail: columbus_ voinovich@voinovich.senate.gov

Toledo Office
420 Madison Ave., Room 1210, Toledo 43604
(419) 259-3895; Fax: (419) 259-3899
E-mail: toledo_voinovich@voinovich.senate.gov

U.S. REPRESENTATIVES

REPRESENTATIVE, John A. Boehner
8th District, Republican
1011 Longworth House Office Bldg.,
Washington, DC 20515
(202) 225-6205; Ohio Residents: (800) 582-1001;
Fax: (202) 225-0704
Internet: www.johnboehner.house.gov

District Offices:

Butler County Office
7969 Cincinnati-Dayton Rd., Suite B,
West Chester 45069
(513) 779-5400; Fax: (513) 779-5315
District Chief of Staff: Mick Krieger

Miami County Office
12 S. Plum St., Troy 45373
(937) 339-1524; Fax: (937) 339-1878
Field Representative: Ryan Day

REPRESENTATIVE, Sherrod Brown
13th District, Democrat
2332 Rayburn House Office Bldg., Washington, DC 20515
(202) 225-3401; Fax: (202) 225-2266
E-mail: sherrod@mail.house.gov
Internet: www.house.gov/sherrodbrown

District Offices:

Lorain County Office
205 W. 20th St., Suite M230, Lorain 44052
(440) 245-5350, 365-5877;
District Residents: (800) 234-6413; Fax: (440) 245-5355
District Dir.: Beth Thames

Summit County Office
1655 W. Market St., Suite E, Akron 44313
(330) 865-8450; Fax: (330) 865-8470
Community Liaison: Laura Pechaitis

REPRESENTATIVE, Steve Chabot
1st District, Republican
129 Cannon House Office Bldg., Washington, DC 20515
(202) 225-2216; Fax: (202) 225-3012
Internet: www.house.gov/chabot

District Office:

Cincinnati Office
3003 Carew Tower, 441 Vine St., Cincinnati 45202
(513) 684-2723; Fax: (513) 421-8722
District Dir.: Mike Cantwell

REPRESENTATIVE, Paul E. Gillmor
5th District, Republican
1203 Longworth House Office Bldg., Washington, DC 20515
(202) 225-6405; Ohio Residents: (800) 541-6446;
Ohio Residents Fax: (800) 278-8203; Fax: (202) 225-1985
Internet: http://gillmor.house.gov

District Offices:

Defiance Office
613 W. Third St., Defiance 43512
(419) 782-1996; Fax: (419) 784-9808
Office Mgr.: Kathy Shaver

Norwalk Office
130 Shady Lane Dr., Norwalk 44857
(419) 668-0206
District Representative: Chris Strumsky
Temporary Office; Tues. only

Tiffin Office
96 S. Washington St., Suite 400, Tiffin 44883
(419) 448-9016; Fax: (419) 448-9201
District Representatives:
   Chris Strumsky
   Everett Woodel
District Dir.: Barbara Barker

REPRESENTATIVE, David L. Hobson
7th District, Republican
2346 Rayburn House Office Bldg., Washington, DC 20515
(202) 225-4324; Fax: (202) 225-1984
Internet: www.house.gov/hobson

District Offices:

Lancaster Office
212 S. Broad St., Room 55, Lancaster 43130
(740) 654-5149; Fax: (740) 654-7825
District Representative: Bob Clark

Springfield Office
5 W. North St., Suite 200, P.O. Box 269,
Springfield 45501
(937) 325-0474; Fax: (937) 325-9188
District Dir.: Eileen Austria

Departments & Agencies

REPRESENTATIVE, Stephanie Tubbs Jones
11th District, Democrat
1009 Longworth House Office Bldg.,
Washington, DC 20515
(202) 225-7032; Fax: (202) 225-1339
Internet: www.house.gov/tubbsjones

District Office:

Shaker Heights Office
3645 Warrensville Center Rd., Suite 204,
Shaker Heights 44122
(216) 522-4900; Fax: (216) 522-4908
District Dir.: Betty K. Pinkney

REPRESENTATIVE, Marcy Kaptur
9th District, Democrat
2366 Rayburn House Office Bldg., Washington, DC 20515
(202) 225-4146; Fax: (202) 225-7711
Internet: www.house.gov/kaptur

District Office:

Northwest Ohio Office
One Maritime Plz., 6th Floor, Toledo 43604-1853
(419) 259-7500, (800) 964-4699; Fax: (419) 255-9623
Admin. Asst.: Steve Katich

REPRESENTATIVE, Dennis J. Kucinich
10th District, Democrat
1730 Longworth House Office Bldg., Washington, DC 20515
(202) 225-5871; Fax: (202) 225-5745
Internet: www.house.gov/kucinich

District Offices:

Lakewood Office
14400 Detroit Ave., Lakewood 44107
(216) 228-8850; Fax: (216) 228-6465
District Dir.: Pat Vecchio

Parma Office
5983 W. 54th St., Parma 44129
(440) 845-2707; Fax: (440) 845-2743
District Dir.: Pat Vecchio
  14400 Detroit Ave., Lakewood 44107

REPRESENTATIVE, Steven C. LaTourette
14th District, Republican
2453 Rayburn House Office Bldg., Washington, DC 20515
(202) 225-5731; Fax: (202) 225-3307
Internet: www.house.gov/latourette

District Office:

Painesville Office
1 Victoria Pl., Room 320, Painesville 44077
(440) 352-3939, (800) 447-0529;
District Residents Fax: (440) 352-3622
District Dir.: Dino Disanto

REPRESENTATIVE, Robert W. Ney
18th District, Republican
2438 Rayburn House Office Bldg., Washington, DC 20515
(202) 225-6265; Fax: (202) 225-3394
E-mail: bobney@mail.house.gov
Internet: www.ney.house.gov

District Offices:

Chillicothe Office
126 E. 2nd St., Suite D, Chillicothe 45601-2593
(740) 779-1634; Fax: (740) 779-1641
District Dir.: John Poe

Jackson Office
200 Broadway, Jackson 45640-1702
(740) 288-1430; Fax: (740) 286-7630
District Dir.: John Poe

New Philadelphia Office
152 Second St. N.E., Suite 200,
New Philadelphia 44663-2854
(330) 364-6380; Fax: (330) 364-7675
District Dir.: John Poe

St. Clairsville Office
146A W. Main St., Saint Clairsville 43950-1225
(740) 699-2704; Fax: (740) 699-2769
District Dir.: John Poe

Zanesville Office
38 N. 4th St., Room 502, Zanesville 43701
(740) 452-7023; Fax: (740) 452-7191
District Dir.: John Poe

REPRESENTATIVE, Michael G. Oxley
4th District, Republican
2308 Rayburn House Office Bldg., Washington, DC 20515
(202) 225-2676; Ohio Residents: (800) 472-4154;
Fax: (202) 226-0577
Internet: www.oxley.house.gov

District Offices:

Findlay District Office
100 E. Main Cross St., Findlay 45840
(419) 423-3210; Fax: (419) 422-2838
District Dir.: Bonnie Dunbar

Lima District Office
3121 W. Elm Plz., Lima 45805
(419) 999-6455; Fax: (419) 999-4238
District Dir.: Kelly Kirk

Mansfield Office
24 W. Third St., Room 314, Mansfield 44902
(419) 522-5757; Fax: (419) 525-2805
District Dir.: Phil Holloway

REPRESENTATIVE, Rob Portman
2nd District, Republican
238 Cannon House Office Bldg., Washington, DC 20515
(202) 225-3164; Fax: (202) 225-1992
Internet: www.house.gov/portman

District Offices:

Cincinnati Office
8044 Montgomery Rd., Room 540, Cincinnati 45236
(513) 791-0381; Ohio Residents: (800) 784-6366;
Fax: (513) 791-1696
District Dir.: Nan Cahall

Portsmouth Office
601 Chillicothe St., Portsmouth 45662
(740) 354-1440; Fax: (740) 354-1144
District Representative: Mary Glasgow

Batavia Office
175 E. Main St., Batavia 45103
(513) 732-2948; Fax: (513) 791-1696
District Dir.: Nan Cahall

REPRESENTATIVE, Deborah Pryce
15th District, Republican
204 Cannon House Office Bldg., Washington, DC 20515
(202) 225-2015; Fax: (202) 225-3529
E-mail: pryce.oh15@mail.house.gov
Internet: www.house.gov/pryce

District Office:

Columbus Office
500 S. Front St., Suite 1130, Columbus 43215
(614) 469-5614; Fax: (614) 469-7469
District Dir.: Marcy McCreary

REPRESENTATIVE, Ralph Regula
16th District, Republican
2306 Rayburn House Office Bldg., Washington, DC 20515
(202) 225-3876; Fax: (202) 225-3059
Internet: wwwc.house.gov/regula

District Offices:

Canton Office
4150 Belden Village St. N.W., Suite 408,
Canton 44718-2553
(330) 489-4414; Ohio Residents: (800) 826-9015;
Fax: (330) 489-4448
District Staff Dir.: Robert Mullen

Medina Office
124 W. Washington St., Suite 1A, Medina 44256
(330) 722-3793; Fax: (330) 723-1319
District Staff Dir.: Robert Mullen

REPRESENTATIVE, Timothy J. Ryan
17th District, Democrat
222 Cannon House Office Bldg., Washington, DC 20515
(202) 225-5261, (800) 856-4152; Fax: (202) 225-3719
Internet: http://timryan.house.gov

District Offices:

Akron Office
1030 Tallmadge Ave., Akron 44310
(330) 630-7311; Fax: (330) 630-7314
Constituent Liaison: Sean Buchanan

Warren Office
197 W. Market St., Warren 44481
(330) 373-0074; Fax: (330) 373-0098
District Dir.: Rick Leonard

Youngstown Office
241 Federal Plz. W., Youngstown 44503
(330) 740-0193; Fax: (330) 740-0182
District Dir.: Rick Leonard

REPRESENTATIVE, Ted Strickland
6th District, Democrat
336 Cannon House Office Bldg., Washington, DC 20515
(202) 225-5705; Ohio Residents: (888) 706-1833;
Fax: (202) 225-5907
Internet: www.house.gov/strickland

District Offices:

Boardman Office
374 Boardman-Poland Rd., Boardman 44512
(330) 965-4220; Fax: (330) 965-4224
District Dir.: Patrick Lorelli

Marietta Office
254 Front St., Marietta 45750
(740) 376-0868; Fax: (740) 376-0886
District Dir.: Jess Goode
Scheduler: Carolyn Jones (740) 376-0868

Martins Ferry Office
35 S. 5th St., Martins Ferry 43935
(740) 633-2275; Fax: (740) 633-2280
District Dir.: Anthony Trevena

Wheelersburg Office
11692 Gallia Pike, Suite A, Wheelersburg 45694
(740) 574-2676; Fax: (740) 574-5337
District Dir.: Jess Goode

REPRESENTATIVE, Patrick J. Tiberi
12th District, Republican
113 Cannon House Office Bldg., Washington, DC 20515
(202) 225-5355; Fax: (202) 226-4523
Internet: www.house.gov/tiberi

District Office:

Columbus Office
2700 E. Dublin-Granville Rd., Suite 525,
Columbus 43231
(614) 523-2555; Fax: (614) 818-0887
District Dir.: Sally Testa

REPRESENTATIVE, Michael R. Turner
3rd District, Republican
1740 Longworth House Office Bldg.,
Washington, DC 20515
(202) 225-6465; Fax: (202) 225-6754
Internet: www.house.gov/miketurner

District Offices:

Dayton Office
120 W. Third St., Suite 305, Dayton 45402
(937) 225-2843; Fax: (937) 225-2752
District Dir.: Michael Gaynor

Wilmington Office
15 E. Main St., Wilmington 45177
(937) 383-8931; Fax: (937) 383-8910
Field Representative: Jennifer Taylor

Departments & Agencies

OHIO STATE DEPARTMENTS AND AGENCIES

EXECUTIVE OFFICE OF THE GOVERNOR
Vern Riffe Center, 77 S. High St.,
Columbus 43215-6117
(614) 466-3555, 644-4357; Fax: (614) 752-4858
Internet: www.governor.ohio.gov

Governor: Bob Taft
Lt. Governor: Bruce Johnson (614) 466-3379
Chief of Staff: John Allison (614) 644-0986
Chief Legal Counsel: Elizabeth Luper Schuster (Acting) (614) 644-0872
Dir. of Communications: Orest Holubec (614) 644-0957
Press Secretary: Mark L. Rickel (614) 644-0957

ACCOUNTANCY BOARD OF OHIO
77 S. High St., 18th Floor, Columbus 43215-6128
(614) 466-4135; Fax: (614) 466-2628
Internet: www.acc.ohio.gov

Exec. Dir.: Ronald Rotaru
Asst. Dir.: Robert Joseph, Ph.D., C.P.A. (614) 466-1660
Investigators:
Jesse Dixon (614) 728-3004
Faith Ottavi (614) 752-2468
Chair: Theodore W. Long, Jr.
Vice Chair: Ray G. Stephens
Board Secretary: Albert J. Cannon

Regulates the practice of public accounting in Ohio; determines the requirements for the CPA examination, CPA certification, CPA licensing, and public accounting firm registration; and conducts disciplinary hearings against CPAs and public accounting firms for violations of the accountancy law.

ADJUTANT GENERAL'S DEPARTMENT
2825 W. Dublin Granville Rd., Columbus 43235
(614) 336-6000; Records Library: (614) 336-7038

Adjutant General: Maj. Gen. Gregory L. Wayt

DEPARTMENT OF ADMINISTRATIVE SERVICES
Rhodes Tower, 40th Floor, 30 E. Broad St.,
Columbus 43215-3414
(614) 466-6511; Fax: (614) 644-8151
Internet: www.das.ohio.gov

Director: Scott Johnson
Asst. Dir.: Nikki Guilford
Chief Information Officer: Mary F. Carroll (Acting) (614) 644-6446
Legislative Liaison: Rick Frank (614) 644-6056
Chief Legal Counsel: Deborah Archie (614) 644-1773; Fax: (614) 752-6557
Human Resources Administrator: Allison Shaeffer (614) 466-2136; Fax: (614) 466-7949
Finance Administrator: Peter Coccia (614) 644-7340; Fax: (614) 728-2541
State EEO Coordinator/Deputy Dir., Equal Opportunity Div.: Wiley Clodfelder (614) 466-8308; Fax: (614) 728-5628
Deputy Dir., General Services: Richard Hickman (614) 466-4459; Fax: (614) 466-1040
Deputy Dir., Communications: Gretchen Hull (614) 752-9521; Fax: (614) 728-0490
MIS Administrator: J. Scott Seilhamer (614) 387-1602; Fax: (614) 644-9910
Quality Coordinator: Barcy McNeal
Deputy Dir., Collective Bargaining: Steven Loeffler (614) 466-0570; Fax: (614) 644-0121
Deputy Dir., Human Resources: Clare Long (614) 466-3455; Fax: (614) 728-2785
Deputy Dir., Investment and Governance Div.: Mary Carroll (614) 466-6930; Fax: (614) 644-1428
Deputy Dir., IT Service Delivery: Walter Callahan (614) 752-7320; Fax: (614) 644-2133
Executive Asst.: Julie Trackler

Provides centralized services and specialized support to state agencies, boards and commissions and local governments and state universities.

COMMISSION ON AFRICAN-AMERICAN MALES
35 E. Chestnut, 5th Floor, Columbus 43215
(614) 644-5143, (800) 370-4566; Fax: (614) 387-0136
E-mail: caam@caam.state.oh.us
Internet: www.caam.ohio.gov

Exec. Dir.: Marv West
Chair: Leonard Huebert
Senior Project Dir.: Gregory Lewis, Jr.
Project Coordinator: Michael Gregory

Serves African-American males who are experiencing problems and/or difficulties within the health care, unemployment, education and criminal justice areas; conducts community education and public awareness programs, as well as holding public hearings.

DEPARTMENT OF AGING
LeVeque Tower, 9th Floor, 50 W. Broad St.,
Columbus 43215-3363
(614) 466-5500; Fax: (614) 466-5741
Internet: www.goldenbuckeye.com

Director: Joan W. Lawrence

Oversees programs and services for residents age 60 and over.

DEPARTMENT OF AGRICULTURE
8995 E. Main St., Reynoldsburg 43068
(614) 728-6201, (800) 282-1955; Fax: (614) 466-4346
E-mail: communications@mail.agri.state.oh.us
Internet: www.ohioagriculture.gov

Director: Fred L. Dailey
Asst. Dir.: Howard Wise (Acting)

Provides regulatory protection to producers, agribusinesses and the consuming public; promotes Ohio agricultural products in domestic and international markets; educates the public about the agricultural business.

Division of Animal Industry
8995 E. Main St., Reynoldsburg 43068
(614) 728-6220; Fax: (614) 728-6310
Responsibilities include testing and inspecting livestock and poultry, licensing, controlling animal diseases and providing veterinary diagnostic laboratory services; supervises the exhibition livestock testing; and cooperates with the Food and Drug Administration to investigate drug residue violation cases.

Consumer Analytical Laboratory
8995 E. Main St., Reynoldsburg 43068
(614) 728-6230; Fax: (614) 728-6322
Serves as the state's primary food safety laboratory and works with other ODA divisions to help assure food safety.

Division of Dairy
8995 E. Main St., Reynoldsburg 43068
(614) 466-5550; Fax: (614) 728-2652
Inspects, licenses, and maintains records on milk producers, milk haulers, milk processors, milk transfer stations, and milk receiving stations.

Division of Enforcement
8995 E. Main St., Reynoldsburg 43068
(614) 728-6240; Fax: (614) 728-6328
Provides investigative support, both criminal and administrative, for all of the Department of Agriculture's regulatory divisions; The Auctioneer Program regulates auctions in Ohio under *Rev. Code, Chap. 4707* which is responsible for investigation of complaints, testing and licensing auctioneer's and apprentice auctioneers in the state. The Ohio Auctioneers Commission oversees the auction education fund and serves in an advisory capacity to the Department.

Office of Fairs
8995 E. Main St., Reynoldsburg 43068
(614) 728-6218; Fax: (614) 752-2282

Office of Farmland Preservation
8995 E. Main St., Reynoldsburg 43068
(614) 728-2732; Fax: (614) 752-2282
Educates the public about preserving farmland and helps local officials with farmland protection efforts; administers the agricultural easement donation and purchase programs.

Dept. of Agriculture—Cont'd

Division of Food Safety
8995 E. Main St., Reynoldsburg 43068
(614) 728-6250; Fax: (614) 644-0720
Secures compliance with the laws and rules that pertain to food safety. The regulations cover good manufacturing practices and sanitation, adulteration, false advertising, misbranding and illegal labeling, and fraud incidental to the preparation, processing, handling, packaging, storage, transportation, refrigeration, and other hazards connected with the merchandising of foods including dairy products, beverages, dietary supplements, and over-the-counter drugs.

Ohio Grape Industries Program
8995 E. Main St., Reynoldsburg 43068
(614) 728-4216; Fax: (614) 644-5017
Oversees and implements how promotional funds for the grape and wine industries are spent.

Human Resources
8995 E. Main St., Reynoldsburg 43068
(614) 466-4595; Fax: (614) 728-2622
Recruits employees, administers labor relations policy, promotes professional development, and oversees Equal Employment Opportunity compliance.

Livestock Environmental Permitting Program
8995 E. Main St., Reynoldsburg 43068
(614) 387-0470; Fax: (614) 728-6335
Regulates livestock and poultry farms to ensure that they are operating in an environmentally safe manner.

Division of Markets
8995 E. Main St., Reynoldsburg 43068
(614) 752-9814; Fax: (614) 644-5017
Responsible for the domestic and international marketing of agricultural products to provide employment opportunities; works cooperatively with commodity organizations to conduct their marketing programs; responsible for public information and communication regarding agricultural issues.

Division of Meat Inspection
8995 E. Main St., Reynoldsburg 43068
(614) 728-6260; Fax: (614) 728-6434
Responsible for administering the Ohio Meat Law in such a manner as to conform to the provisions of the Wholesome Meat Act passed by Congress in 1967; assures that meat and poultry products are wholesome, unadulterated, and properly labeled.

Division of Plant Industry
8995 E. Main St., Reynoldsburg 43068
(614) 728-6270; Fax: (614) 728-4235
Performs feed mill inspections to monitor animal protein to prevent BSE; verifies label statements of feed and fertilizers; inspects nursery stock; works to prevent the spread of invasive pests (i.e., Gypsy Moth and Emerald Ash Borer); performs phytosanitary certificates for products being shipped intrastate and internationally; monitors the financial stability of grain elevators; and oversees indemnity fund. The Pesticide Section registers pesticides, licenses applicators and responds to consumer complaints of pesticide misuse.

Ohio Rural Development Partnership
A.B. Graham Bldg., 8995 E. Main St., Reynoldsburg 43068
(614) 728-4937; Fax: (614) 728-2652

Exec. Dir.: William N. Morgan (Acting)
Brings together citizens, community-based organizations, representatives of the private sector, federal, state, and local officials to address the needs of rural Ohio communities.

Ohio Tobacco Program
8995 E. Main St., Reynoldsburg 43068
(614) 728-2303; Toll-free: (800) 282-1955;
Fax: (614) 995-6453
E-mail: tobacco@mail.agri.state.oh.us
Administers the annual National Tobacco Growers Trust program, helping the state's tobacco growers and quota owners get financial assistance as demand for Burley tobacco decreases.

Division of Weights & Measures
8995 E. Main St., Reynoldsburg 43068
(614) 728-6290; Fax: (614) 728-6424
Helps to ensure equity in the marketplace by administering and enforcing all laws pertaining to true and uniform weights and measures standards; and works with county and city weights and measures programs to test devices ranging from fuel meters and retail store scanners to vehicle and livestock scales for consistent measuring standards.

AIR QUALITY DEVELOPMENT AUTHORITY
50 W. Broad St., Suite 1718, Columbus 43215-5910
(614) 224-3383; Fax: (614) 752-9188
Internet: www.ohioairquality.org

Exec. Dir.: Mark R. Shanahan
General Counsel: Darrell A. Fields

DEPARTMENT OF ALCOHOL & DRUG ADDICTION SERVICES
280 N. High St., 12th Floor, Columbus 43215-2550
(614) 466-3445; Fax: (614) 752-8645;
TDD/TTY: (614) 644-9140
Internet: www.odadas.state.oh.us

Director: Gary Q. Tester; E-mail: tester@ada.state.oh.us
Asst. Dir.: Carolyn Givens; E-mail: givens@ada.state.oh.us
Chief Counsel: Jodi Elsass-Locker
E-mail: locker@ada.state.oh.us
Chief of Comunication and Training:
Stacey Frohnapfel-Hasson
E-mail: frohnapfel@ada.state.oh.us
Legislative Liaison: Merissa McKinstry
E-mail: mckinstry@ada.state.oh.us

Provides statewide supervision for alcohol and other drug addiction prevention and treatment services for the health, safety and productivity of all Ohioans.

ARTS COUNCIL
727 E. Main St., Columbus 43205-1796
(614) 466-2613; Fax: (614) 466-4494
Internet: www.oac.state.oh.us

Exec. Dir.: Wayne P. Lawson
E-mail: wayne.lawson@oac.state.oh.us
Deputy Dir.: Julie Henahan
E-mail: julie.henahan@oac.state.oh.us
Dir., Grants Office: Kevin Cary
E-mail: kevin.cary@oac.state.oh.us
Fiscal Dir.: Carolyn McClaskey
E-mail: carolyn.mcclaskey@oac.state.oh.us
Dir., Public Information: Gregg Dodd
E-mail: gregg.dodd@oac.state.oh.us
Dir., Riffe Gallery: Mary Gray
E-mail: mary.gray@oac.state.oh.us
Chair: Susan R. Sofia

OFFICE OF THE ATTORNEY GENERAL
30 E. Broad St., 17th Floor, Columbus 43215-3428
(614) 466-4320; Fax: (614) 644-6135
Internet: www.ag.state.oh.us

Cincinnati Regional Office, 1700 Carew Tower,
441 Vine Street, Cincinnati 45202-2809
(513) 852-3497; Fax: (513) 852-3484

Cleveland Regional Office,
615 W. Superior Ave., 11th Floor,
Cleveland 44113-1899
(216) 787-3030; Fax: (216) 787-3480

Toledo Regional Office, One SeaGate, Suite 2150,
Toledo 43604-1551
(419) 245-2550; Fax: (419) 245-2520

Atty. General: Jim Petro (614) 728-8194
First Asst. Atty. General: D. Michael Grodhaus
(614) 466-1339
Chief Deputy Atty. General, Criminal Justice:
James V. Canepa (614) 466-4638
Chief Deputy Atty. General, Public Protection:
Melissa J. Iannotta (416) 466-9511
Chief of Staff: Lana T. Ruebel (614) 466-0846
Chief of Communications: Kim Norris (614) 466-3840
Chief Counsel: Elizabeth T. Smith (614) 728-6069
State Solicitor: Douglas R. Cole (614) 466-8980
Internal Auditor: Joe Bell (614) 644-6669

Office of the Attorney General—Cont'd

Sr. Deputy Atty. General, Antitrust: Jennifer L. Pratt (614) 466-4328

Sr. Deputy Atty. General, Appeals: Stephen P. Carney (614) 466-8980

Sr. Deputy Atty. General, Business Counsel: O'Neal Saunders (614) 644-6342

Sr. Deputy Atty. General, Capital Crimes: Timothy D. Prichard (614) 728-7055

Sr. Deputy Atty. General, Charitable Law: Brian Cook (614) 466-3180

Sr. Deputy Atty. General, Child & Elder Protection: Jeffrey W. Clark (740) 845-2447

Sr. Deputy Atty. General, Civil Rights: Stephanie R. Bostos-Demers (614) 466-7900

Sr. Deputy Atty. General, Collections Enforcement: Sue Pohler (614) 466-4510

Constituent Services: Mark Gribben (614) 644-8529; Fax: (614) 644-6135

Sr. Deputy Atty. General, Constitutional Offices: Arthur J. Marziale (614) 466-2872

Sr. Deputy Atty. General, Consumer Protection: Michael Gonidakis (614) 466-1305; Fax: (614) 466-8898

Sr. Deputy Atty. General, Corrections Litigation: Stephanie Watson (614) 644-7233

Sr. Deputy Atty. General, Court of Claims: Paula Paoletti (614) 466-7447

Sr. Deputy Atty. General, Crime Victims Services: Jonathan Bowman (614) 466-7447

Sr. Deputy Atty. General, Education: Roger F. Carroll (614) 644-7250

Sr. Deputy Atty. General, Employment Law: Eric Harrell (614) 644-7257

Sr. Deputy Atty. General, Environmental: Dale T. Vitale (614) 466-2766

Sr. Deputy Atty. General, Executive Agencies: Peter M. Thomas (614) 466-2980

Fiduciary and Public Integrity Counsel: (614) 644-1234

Sr. Deputy Atty. General, Health & Human Services: Sheryl L. Maxfield (614) 466-8600

Sr. Deputy Atty. General, Health Care Fraud: John A. Guthrie (614) 466-0722

Sr. Deputy Atty. General, Opinions: Kevin M. McIver (614) 752-6417

Policy & Legislative Affairs: Andrea Hill (614) 644-1234

Sr. Deputy Atty. General, Public Utilities: Duane W. Luckey (614) 466-4395

Sr. Deputy Atty. General, Special Counsel: Kari B. Hertel (614) 466-8240

Sr. Deputy Atty. General, Taxation: Richard C. Farrin (614) 466-3142

Sr. Deputy Atty. General, Transportation: Stephanie B. McCloud (614) 466-4656

Sr. Deputy Atty. General, Workers Compensation: James A. Barnes (614) 466-6696

Bureau of Criminal Identification & Investigation
1560 SR 56, S.W., P.O. Box 365, London 43140
(740) 845-2000

Superintendent: John Monce, Jr.

AUDITOR OF STATE
88 E. Broad St., P.O. Box 1140, Columbus 43216-1140
(614) 466-4514, (800) 282-0370; Fax: (614) 466-4490
Internet: www.auditor.state.oh.us

Athens Mall, 743B E. State St., Athens 45701-2246
(740) 594-3300, (800) 441-1389; Fax: (740) 594-2110

One Government Center, Room 1420,
Toledo 43604-2246
(419) 245-2811, (800) 443-9276; Fax: (419) 245-2484

Voinovich Government Center, Suite 302,
242 Federal Plz. W., Youngstown 44503
(330) 797-9900, (800) 443-9271; Fax: (330) 797-9949

2146 Southgate Pkwy., Cambridge 43725
(740) 432-6371; Fax: (740) 432-6212

410 N. Dixie Hwy., Wapakoneta 45895
(419) 739-7600; Fax: (419) 739-7604

4320 Old Scioto Rd., Portsmouth 45662
(740) 353-2150; Fax: (740) 353-3831

Lausche Bldg., 12th Floor, 615 Superior Ave. N.W.,
Cleveland 44113
(216) 787-3665, (800) 626-2297; Fax: (216) 787-3361

11117 Kenwood Rd., Blue Ash 45242
(513) 361-8550, (800) 368-7419; Fax: (513) 361-8577

700 BankOne Tower, 101 Central Plaza S.,
Canton 44702
(330) 438-0617, (800) 443-9272; Fax: (330) 471-0001

One First National Plaza, Suite 2040,
130 W. Second St., Dayton 45402
(937) 285-6677, (800) 443-9274; Fax: (937) 285-6688

State Auditor: Betty Montgomery
Chief Deputy Auditor: David Varda
Chief of Staff: Deb Shanahan Hackathorn
Chief Legal Counsel: Craig Mayton
Dir., Public Affairs: Vacancy at Press Time

BARBER BOARD
77 S. High St., 16th Floor, Columbus 43215-6108
(614) 466-5003; Fax: (614) 387-1694
Internet: www.barber.ohio.gov

Exec. Dir.: Howard L. Warner
Chair: Edwin C. Jeffers

OFFICE OF BUDGET AND MANAGEMENT
30 E. Broad St., 34th Floor, Columbus 43215-3457
(614) 466-4034; Fax: (614) 466-3813
E-mail: obm@obm.state.oh.us
Internet: www.obm.ohio.gov

Exec. Dir.: Thomas W. Johnson
Asst. Dir.: Timothy S. Keen
Chief Legal Counsel: Beth Scott
(614) 466-4034; Fax: (614) 466-3813

Provides fiscal accounting and budgeting services to state government. Services include the coordination, development, and monitoring of agency operating and capital budgets and the review, processing, and reporting of financial transactions made by state agencies by providing policy and management support relative to the state's fiscal activities.

Controlling Board
30 E. Broad St., 34th Floor, Columbus 43215-3457
(614) 466-5721; Fax: (614) 466-3813
Internet: www.obm.ohio.gov/cb

President: Lisa H. Dodge (614) 752-6392
Executive Secretary: Francene Johnson

Provides legislative oversight over certain capital and operating expenditures by state agencies; has approval authority over various state fiscal activities including the waivers of competitive selection to agencies when an agency's purchases or leases from a specific vendor exceed the amounts specified in law; releases appropriation for capital construction projects, loans and grants made through the Department of Development, loans and subsidies made through the Department of Education to local school districts, and transfer of appropriation authority between line items within a fund in an agency and increases in appropriation authority in some funds.

OHIO BUILDING AUTHORITY
30 E. Broad St., Suite 4020, Columbus 43215
(614) 466-5959; Fax: (614) 644-6478
Internet: www.oba.ohio.gov

Exec. Dir.: Paul E. Goggin
Asst. Exec. Dir., Facilities Mgmt.: Mark A. Haberman
Asst. Exec. Dir., Financial Affairs: Kevin T. Fenlon

CAPITOL SQUARE REVIEW AND ADVISORY BOARD
Statehouse, Columbus 43215-4210
(614) 752-9777; Fax: (614) 752-5209
Internet: www.statehouse.state.oh.us

Exec. Dir.: Ronald T. Keller
Deputy Dir., Administration: Mark Hedges
Deputy Dir., Buildings and Grounds: Dennis Trimble
Deputy Dir., Communications: Pat Groseck

Oversees the preservation, maintenance, and security of the Historic Ohio Statehouse; *Ohio Rev. Code, Chap. 105.4*

BOARD OF CAREER COLLEGES AND SCHOOLS
35 E. Gay St., Suite 403, Columbus 43215-3138
(614) 466-2752, (877) 275-4219; Fax: (614) 466-2219
E-mail: bpsr@scr.state.oh.us
Internet: www.scr.ohio.gov

Exec. Dir.: John P. Ware
Chair: Linda Hanaway
Vice Chair: Dr. Leonard D. Kingsley
Board Secretary: Neil Collins
Investigator: Kimberly Stein

Provides regulatory structure for programs, operations, and consumer protection mechanisms, which promote quality proprietary education.

CHEMICAL DEPENDENCY PROFESSIONALS BOARD
Huntington Plaza, Suite 785, 37 W. Broad St.,
Columbus 43215
(614) 387-1110; Fax: (614) 387-1109
Internet: www.ocdp.ohio.gov

Exec. Dir.: Robert Field
Deputy Dir.: Amanda Ferguson
Ohio Rev. Code, §4758

STATE CHIROPRACTIC BOARD
77 S. High St., 16th Floor, Columbus 43215
(614) 644-7032, (888) 772-1384; Fax: (614) 752-2539
E-mail: chirobd@mail.peps.state.oh.us
Internet: www.chirobd.ohio.gov

Exec. Dir.: Kelly A. Caudill
Licensing Coordinator: Laurie Allison
Investigators:
Thomas J. Hollis   Rex J. Waldenmeyer
Lawrence E. Phillips
Ohio Rev. Code, Chap. 4734

CIVIL RIGHTS COMMISSION
1111 E. Broad St., 3rd Floor, Columbus 43205
(614) 466-2785, (888) 278-7101
Internet: www.state.oh.us/crc

Exec. Dir.: G. Michael Payton
Chair: Aaron Wheeler, Sr.
Commissioners:
Jeanine P. Donaldson   Nirmal Sinha
Attagracia Ramos   Charles Winburn

Investigates charges of discrimination and determines whether or not the law has been broken; governed under *Ohio Rev. Code, Chap. 4112*

Akron Regional Office
Akron Government Bldg., Suite 205, 161 S. High St.,
Akron 44308
(330) 643-3100; Fax: (330) 643-3120

Regional Dir.: Diane Citrino
Carroll, Columbiana, Coshocton, Harrison, Holmes, Jefferson, Knox, Mahoning, Portage, Stark, Summit, Trumbull, Tuscarawas, Wayne

Cincinnati Regional Office
Corporate Tower, Suite 1001, 7162 Reading Rd.,
Cincinnati 45237
(513) 852-3344; Fax: (513) 852-3357

Regional Dir.: H. Jean Marshall-McEntire
Adams, Brown, Butler, Clermont, Clinton, Fayette, Gallia, Hamilton, Highland, Jackson, Lawrence, Meigs, Pike, Scioto, Vinton, Warren

Cleveland Regional Office
615 W. Superior Ave., Room 885, Cleveland 44113
(216) 787-3150; TTY: (216) 787-3150; Fax: (216) 787-4121

Regional Dir.: Iris Choi
Ashland, Ashtabula, Cuyahoga, Erie, Geauga, Huron, Lake, Lorain, Medina, Richland

Columbus Regional Office
1111 E. Broad St., Suite 301, Columbus 43205
(614) 466-5928; TTY: (614) 752-2391; Fax: (614) 466-6250

Regional Dir.: Beleta Ebron
Athens, Belmont, Delaware, Fairfield, Franklin, Guernsey, Hocking, Licking, Madison, Marion, Monroe, Morgan, Morrow, Noble, Perry, Pickaway, Ross, Union, Washington

Dayton Regional Office
Miami Valley Tower, Suite 1900, 40 W. 4th St.,
Dayton 45402
(937) 285-6500; Fax: (937) 285-6606

Regional Dir.: Marguerite Walker
Allen, Auglaize, Champaign, Clark, Darke, Greene, Hardin, Logan, Mercer, Miai, Montgomery, Preble, Shelby, Van Wert

Toledo Regional Office
One Government Center, Suite 936, Jackson and Erie Sts.,
Toledo 43604
(419) 245-2900; Fax: (419) 245-2668

Regional Dir.: Darlene Sweeney-Newbern
Crawford, Defiance, Fulton, Hancock, Henry, Lucas, Ottawa, Paulding, Putnam, Sandusky, Seneca, Williams, Wood, Wyandot

DEPARTMENT OF COMMERCE
Vern Riffe Ctr., 23rd Floor, 77 S. High St.,
Columbus 43266-0544
(614) 466-3636; Receptionist: (614) 644-7381;
Enforcement: (614) 466-6140;
Registration: (614) 466-3440;
Licensing: (614) 466-3466; Records: (614) 466-3001
Internet: www.securities.state.oh.us

Director: Doug White
Commissioner: Dale Jewell

Oversees the securities marketplace; responsible for providing investor protection and enhancing capital formation by administering and enforcing the Ohio Securities Act; *Ohio Rev. Code, Chap. 1707.*

Division of Financial Institutions
77 S. High St., 21st Floor, Columbus 43215-6120
(614) 728-8400; Fax: (614) 644-1631
Internet: www.com.state.oh.us/dfi

Superintendent: F. Scott O'Donnell

Deputy Superintendent, Banks: Michael O. Roark

Deputy Superintendent, Credit Unions:
Kenneth A. Roberts (Acting)

Deputy Superintendent, Savings and Loans/Savings Banks:
Neil G. Danzinger

Deputy Superintendent, Consumer Finance:
Robert M. Grieser
Regulates various state-chartered or licensed institutions, including banks, savings and loans, and credit unions.

Division of Real Estate and Professional Licensing
77 S. High St., 20th Floor, Columbus 43215-6133
(614) 466-4100; Fax: (614) 644-0584
615 W. Superior Ave., Cleveland 44113-1801
(216) 787-3100; Fax: (216) 787-4449

Superintendent: Anne M. Petit
Responsible for licensing real estate brokers and salespeople, real estate appraisers, foreign real estate dealers and salespeople, the registration of cemeteries located in Ohio and the registration of real estate developments located in other states but marketed in Ohio; also responsible for the licensing of private investigators and security guards. Real estate appraisers & cemetery registration handled in Cleveland office.

Division of Unclaimed Funds
77 S. High St., 20th Floor, Columbus 43215-6108
(614) 644-6094; Fax: (614) 752-5078
E-mail: webunfd.claims@com.state.oh.us
Internet: www.com.state.oh.us/unfd

Superintendent: David L. Moore
Collects unclaimed property (including bank accounts, security deposits, undelivered stock dividends, and safe deposit box contents) and manages the property and returns it to the rightful owners.

State Fire Marshal
8895 E. Main St., Reynoldsburg 43068
(614) 752-8200; Fax: (614) 752-7213

Fire Marshal: Stephen K. Woltz

COUNSELOR, SOCIAL WORKER AND MARRIAGE & FAMILY THERAPIST BOARD
77 S. High St., 16th Floor, Columbus 43215-6108
(614) 466-0912; Fax: (614) 728-7790
Internet: www.cswmft.ohio.gov

Exec. Dir.: Vacancy at Press Time

Ohio Rev. Code, Chap. 4757; Ohio Admin. Code, Chap. 4757

OFFICE OF CRIMINAL JUSTICE SERVICES
140 E. Town St., Suite 1400, Columbus 43215
(614) 466-7782, (888) 448-4842; Fax: (614) 466-0308
E-mail: webmaster@ocjs.oh.gov
Internet: www.ocjs.state.oh.us

Director: Karen J. Huey

Chief Counsel: Karhlton F. Moore (614) 466-4792

Ohio Rev. Code, § 181.52

CULTURAL FACILITIES COMMISSION
20 E. Broad St., Suite 200, Columbus 43215-3416
(614) 752-2770; Fax: (614) 752-2775
Internet: www.culture.ohio.gov

Exec. Dir.: Kathleen M. Fox, FASLA
E-mail: kfox@culture.ohio.gov

Dir., Information Systems: Jim Armstrong
(614) 728-3328; E-mail: jarmstrong@culture.ohio.gov

Project Mgrs.:
Todd O'Donnell (614) 752-2774
E-mail: todonnell@culture.ohio.gov
Bob Talbott (614) 728-8925
E-mail: btalbott@culture.ohio.gov
Jayne A. Williams, AIA (614) 728-6924
E-mail: jwilliams@culture.ohio.gov

Dir., Community Relations: Jerry Emig (614) 995-7552
E-mail: jemig@culture.ohio.gov

Executive Asst.: Annie Fullerton
E-mail: afullerton@culture.ohio.gov

Admin. Asst.: Myra LaCava
E-mail: mlacava@culture.ohio.gov

Establishes and implements operational policies and oversight mechanisms to ensure that the state resources appropriated by the General Assembly and Governor for planning, construction, renovation and expansion projects at theatres, museums, historical sites and publicly-owned professional sports venues are spent properly; *Ohio Rev. Code, Chap. 3383*
Formerly known as Arts & Sports Facilities Commission

DENTAL BOARD
77 S. High St., Columbus 43215-6135
(614) 466-2580; Fax: (614) 752-8995
E-mail: ohdental@mail.peps.state.oh.us
Internet: www.dental.ohio.gov

Exec. Dir.: Lili C. Reitz

Responsible for examining and licensing dentists, dental hygienists, and dental assistant radiographers for practice; adopts rules establishing standards for the safe practice of dentistry and dental hygiene; acts on complaints through investigations, inquiries and inspections; holds administrative hearings pursuant to Ohio Revised Code *Chapter 119*; monitors continuing education compliance of its licensees; keeps a register of all licensees and all disciplinary action taken against licensees; *Ohio Rev. Code, Chap. 4715 & Ohio Admin. Code, Chap. 4715.*

DEPARTMENT OF DEVELOPMENT
77 S. High St., 29th Floor, Columbus 43215
(614) 466-2480, (800) 848-1300; Fax: (614) 644-5167;
Administration: (614) 466-3379;
Legal Office: (614) 466-7611
Internet: www.odod.state.oh.us

Director: Lt. Governor Bruce Johnson

Promotes economic opportunities to foster industry growth; provides financial, informative and technical assistance. Programs include business attraction and retention, small business growth, technology commercialization, export promotion, travel promotion, energy efficiency, affordable housing, community infrastructure, downtown revitalization and brownfield clean-up.

COMMISSION ON DISPUTE RESOLUTION & CONFLICT MANAGEMENT
Riffe Ctr., 24th Floor, 77 S. High St.,
Columbus 43215-6108
(614) 752-9595; Fax: (614) 752-9682
Internet: www.disputeresolution.ohio.gov

Exec. Dir.: Maria Mone

Associate Dir.: Maggie Lewis

Dir. of Court & Community Programs: Ed Krauss

Dir. of Education Programs: Jennifer Batton

Program Asst.: Portia Gray

Promotes the use of alternative dispute resolution through training and education, initiation of pilot projects, and casework and referrals for government agencies seeking assistance in conflict resolution.

DEPARTMENT OF EDUCATION
25 S. Front St., Columbus 43215-4183
(877) 644-6338
Internet: www.ode.state.oh.us

Superintendent of Public Instruction:
Susan Tave Zelman (614) 466-7578

Deputy Superintendent: Bob Bowers (614) 466-3175

Special Asst. to Superintendent: Joe Johnson
(614) 387-2195

Chief of Staff: Jeanette Oxender (614) 466-3125

C.O.O.: Steven Burgiana (614) 995-1129

Assoc. Superintendent, Center for Curriculum & Assessment: Stan Heffner (614) 995-4839

Assoc. Superintendent, Center for the Teaching Profession: Marilyn Troyer (614) 728-5865

Assoc. Superintendent, Center for Students, Families and Communities: Jane Wiechel
(614) 995-4695

Assoc. Superintendent, Center for School Reform & Options: Pamela Young (614) 466-5834

Asst. Superintendent, Internal Operations & Risk Mgmt.: Steven Puckett (614) 466-2517

Chief Information Officer, Information Technology Office: Robert Luikart (614) 752-6840

Asst. Superintendent, Policy Development: Mitch Chester (614) 466-3175

Budget Dir.: Susan Tavakolian (614) 466-7578

Administrator, Internal Audit: Donna Hairston
(614) 644-7812

State Board of Education
25 S. Front St., 7th Floor, Columbus 43215-4183
(614) 466-4838

President: Sue Westendorf (419) 352-2908

V.P.: Jennifer H. Stewart (740) 452-4558

Secretary: Susan Tave Zelman (Superintendent of Public Instruction) (614) 466-7578

EMPLOYMENT RELATIONS BOARD
65 E. State St., 12th Floor, Columbus 43215-4213
(614) 644-8573; Fax: (614) 466-3074
Internet: www.serb.state.oh.us

Exec. Dir.: Patricia E. Snyder, J.D. (614) 466-3013

General Counsel: J. Russell Keith (614) 466-3014

Board Chair: Carol Nolan Drake (614) 466-3206

Vice Chair: Karen L. Gillmor, Ph.D. (614) 466-3206

Board Member: Michael G. Verich (614) 466-3206

Jurisdiction is over public sector collective bargaining, including schools, police and fire, township, city, county and staff employees. *Ohio Rev. Code, Chap. 4117*

ENVIRONMENTAL PROTECTION AGENCY
122 S. Front St., Columbus 43215
Mailing Address: P.O. Box 1049,
Columbus 43216-1049
(614) 644-3020; Fax: (614) 644-3184
Internet: www.epa.state.oh.us

Director: Joseph Koncelik (614) 644-2782
Chief Legal Counsel: Bill Fischbein
  (614) 644-2782; Fax: (614) 728-2782
Deputy Dir., Policy: Laura Powell (614) 644-2782
Deputy Dir., Communications: Pat Madigan
  (614) 644-2782
Chief, Strategic Mgmt.: Al Franks (614) 644-3347
Hearing Officer: W. Samuel Wilson
  (614) 644-3037; Fax: (614) 728-1803

Implements laws and regulations regarding air and water quality standards; solid, hazardous and infectious waste disposal standards; water quality planning, supervision of sewage treatment and public drinking water supplies; and cleanup of unregulated hazardous waste sites; cooperates with government and private agencies, manages some federally funded pollution control projects, obtains technical and laboratory services, establishes advisory boards, investigates environmental problems, and disseminates information on environmental programs; also authorizes enforcement actions against violators of pollution laws and regulations.

Division of Air Pollution Control
122 S. Front St., Columbus 43215
Mailing Address: P.O. Box 1049, Columbus 43216-1049
(614) 644-2270; Fax: (614) 644-3681

Chief: Robert Hodonbosi

Asst. Chief: Cindy DeWulf

Division of Drinking and Ground Waters
Lazarus Government Center, 122 S. Front St.,
Columbus 43215
Mailing Address: P.O. Box 1049, Columbus 43216-1049
(614) 644-2752; Fax: (614) 644-2909

Chief: Michael Baker

Asst. Chiefs:
  Tom Allen (Ground Water)
  Kirk Leifheit (Drinking Water)

Division of Emergency and Remedial Response
Lazarus Government Center, 122 S. Front St.,
Columbus 43215
Mailing Address: Lazarus Government Center,
P.O. Box 1049, Columbus 43216-1049
(614) 644-2924; Fax: (614) 644-3146

Chief: Cindy Hafner

Asst. Chief: Peter Whitehouse

Division of Environmental and Financial Assistance
122 S. Front St., Columbus 43215
Mailing Address: P.O. Box 1049, Columbus 43216-1049
(614) 644-2798; Fax: (614) 644-3687

Chief: Greg Smith

Asst. Chief: Sanat Barua

Division of Environmental Services
1571 Perry St., Columbus 43201
(614) 644-4247; Fax: (614) 644-4272

Chief: Linda Friedman
Provides chemical and biological data and technical assistance to other EPA divisions and state and local agencies in order to help monitor and protect human health and the environment.

Division of Solid and Infectious Waste Management
122 S. Front St., Columbus 43215
Mailing Address: P.O. Box 1049, Columbus 43216-1049
(614) 644-2621; Fax: (614) 728-5315

Chief: Dan Harris

Asst. Chief: Vacancy at Press Time

Division of Surface Water
Lazarus Government Center, 122 S. Front St.,
Columbus 43215
Mailing Address: P.O. Box 1049, Columbus 43216-1049
(614) 644-2001; Fax: (614) 644-2745
Internet: www.epa.state.oh.us/dsw

Chief: George Elmaraghy (Acting) (614) 644-2041

Permits and Compliance Section: Paul Novak
  (614) 644-2035

Central District Office Surface Water Mgr.: Bill McCarthy
  3232 Alum Creek Dr., Columbus 43207-3417
  (614) 728-3839; Fax: (614) 728-3898

Northeast District Office Surface Water Mgr.:
  John Januska, 2110 E. Aurora Rd., Twinsburg 44087
  (330) 963-1100; Fax: (216) 487-0769

Northwest District Office Surface Water Mgr.: Allen Rupp
  347 N. Dunbridge Rd., Bowling Green 43402
  (419) 373-3000; Fax: (419) 352-8468

Southeast District Office Surface Water Mgr.:
  Dave Schuetz, 2195 Front St., Logan 43138
  (740) 380-5212; Fax: (740) 385-6490

Southwest District Office Surface Water: Jim Simpson
  401 E. Fifth St., Dayton 54502-2911
  (937) 285-6357; Fax: (937) 285-6249

Division of Hazardous Waste Management
122 S. Front St., Columbus 43215
Mailing Address: P.O. Box 1049, Columbus 43216-1049
(614) 644-2917; Fax: (614) 728-1245

Chief: Mike Savage

Asst. Chief: Dave Sholtis

ETHICS COMMISSION
8 E. Long St., 10th Floor, Columbus 43215
(614) 466-7090; TTY/TDD: (800) 750-0750;
Fax: (614) 466-8368
Internet: www.ethics.ohio.gov

Exec. Dir.: David Freel (614) 466-7093
  E-mail: david.freel@ethics.ohio.gov
Commissioners:
  Merom Brachman (Chair)
  Sarah M. Brown (Vice Chair)
  Josiah Blackmore
  Dean Robert Browning
  Ann Marie Tracey
Chief Investigative Atty.: Paul Nick
  E-mail: paul.nick@ethics.ohio.gov
Chief Advisory Atty.: Jennifer A. Hardin
  E-mail: jennifer.hardin@ethics.ohio.gov
Financial Disclosure Coordinator: Sue McVey
Education Coordinator: Lynn Honeck
  E-mail: lynn.honeck@ethics.ohio.gov
Office Mgr.: Susan J. Loe
  E-mail: susan.loe@ethics.ohio.gov
IT Administrator: Angela Atwell
  E-mail: angela.atwell@ethics.ohio.gov

Administers the Ohio Ethics Law and related statues for all public officials and employees at the state and local levels of government, except for state legislators and their employees, and judges and their employees.

BOARD OF EXAMINERS OF ARCHITECTS
77 S. High St., 16th Floor, Columbus 43215-6108
(614) 466-2316; Fax: (614) 644-9048

Exec. Dir.: Amy Kobe
Investigator: Chad B. Holland
Executive Secretary: Cheryl L. Thaxton
Admin. Asst.: Danielle Karvois

Establishes standards for architectural registration, practice and professional conduct; enforces the laws and rules governing the practice of architecture; communicates with and educates the public and profession.

OHIO EXPO CENTER AND STATE FAIR
Ohio Expo Ctr., 717 E. 17th Ave., Columbus 43211
(614) 644-4000, (888) 686-3976; Fax: (614) 644-4031

Departments & Agencies

FAMILY AND CHILDREN FIRST
30 E. Broad St., 34th Floor, Columbus 43215
(614) 752-4044; Fax: (614) 728-3813
Internet: www.ohiofcf.org
Chief of Staff: Jessica Cannon
Regional Coordinators:
Joyce Calland (Southwest District)
1512 So. U.S. Highway 68, Suite B100, Urbana 43078
(937) 484-1526; Fax: (937) 484-1540
Janice Houchins (Northeast District)
1680 Madison Ave., Wooster 44691
(330) 263-3831; Fax: (330) 263-3667
Cindy Lafollett (East District)
16714 S.R. 215, Caldwell 43724
(740) 732-2381; Fax: (740) 732-5992
Teresa Reed McGlashan (Northwest District)
1219 W. Main Cross St., Suite 202, Findlay 45840
(419) 422-6106; Fax: (419) 422-7595
Sherry Ward (South District)
P.O. Box 958, Jackson 45640
(750) 286-2177; Fax: (750) 286-1578

GOVERNOR'S OFFICE OF VETERANS AFFAIRS
77 S. High St., 30th Floor, Columbus 43215
(614) 644-0898; Fax: (614) 728-9498
Internet: www.veteransaffairs.ohio.gov
Director: Col. Robert J. Labadie
Deputy Dir.: Anthony (Jim) Forster (614) 752-8942
Records Mgr.: Carla Brown (614) 752-8942
Oversees the operations of the 88 county veterans service offices, the Ohio Veterans Hall of Fame and the Ohio Veterans Plaza; responsible for the training, certification and accreditation of more than 600 county veterans service officers, commissioners and staff; monitors federal funding and federal agency programs that provide services and benefits to veterans; serves as the custodian of records for Ohio veterans who served in the military during World War II, Korea and Vietnam; serves as the legislative agent for the office of the Governor regarding any legislation relating to Ohio veterans and their needs; *Ohio Rev. Code, § 5902.02*

DEPARTMENT OF HEALTH
246 N. High St., Columbus 43216-0118
(614) 466-3543
Internet: www.odh.state.oh.us
Director: J. Nick Baird, M.D. (614) 466-2253
Asst. Dir.: Anne Harnish (614) 466-0041
Asst. Dir.,: Jim Pearsol
(Center for Public Health Data & Statistics)
(614) 466-9838
General Counsel: Jodi A. Govern (614) 466-4882
Dir., Governmental Affairs: D. Mike Carroll
(614) 466-8251
Dir., Public Affairs: Jay Carey (614) 644-8562
Chief, Div. of Family & Community Health Svces.:
David P. Schor, M.D. (614) 466-3263
Chief, Div. of Quality Assurance: Rebecca Maust
(614) 466-7857
Chief, Div. of Prevention: Deborah L. Arms, R.N., Ph.D.
(614) 466-0302

HISPANIC/LATINO AFFAIRS COMMISSION
77 S. High St., 18th Floor, Columbus 43215
(614) 466-8333; Fax: (614) 995-0896
Internet: www.ochla.ohio.gov
Exec. Dir.: Ezra C. Escudero
Chair: Michael Florez
119 E. Court St., Suite 501, Cincinnati 45202
(513) 977-4777; Fax: (513) 621-7086
E-mail: mgflorez@cinci.rr.com
Vice Chair: Maritza Perez
14800 Lenox Dr., Strongsville 44136
(216) 687-9283; Fax: (216) 687-5442
E-mail: m.l.perez@csuohio.edu
Secretary: V. Anthony Simms-Howell
5402 Kingway West, Cincinnati 45215
(513) 761-5696; Fax: (513) 761-5552
E-mail: jsimms@cincin.rr.com

Commissioners:
Donna M. Alvarado
P.O. Box 266, Granville 43023
(740) 587-3549; Fax: (740) 587-4519
E-mail: DMAlva@aol.com
Phillip R. Barbosa
902 Broadway Ave., Toledo 43609
(419) 215-7941; Fax: (419) 825-1164
E-mail: phil@philbarbosa.com
Humberto Gonzalez
41 S. High St., Suite 2410, Columbus 43215
(614) 224-6077; Fax: (614) 224-3865
E-mail: Hgonzlez@LLMUS.LeggMason.com
Simon Rodriguez
4530 Stengel Ave., Toledo 43614
(419) 380-0550; Fax: (419) 380-0590
E-mail: sgiltd@buckeye-express.com
Richard Romero
1405 W. Erie Ave., Lorain 44052
(440) 282-6015; Fax: (440) 282-3704
E-mail: lkeerie@centurytel.net
Mary Santiago
4146 Elyria Ave., Lorain 44055
Fax: (440) 233-4323
E-mail: JRSProductions@centurytel.net
Serves as a liason between government and the Hispanic/ Latino community and advocates the development and the implementation of policies and programs to address needs in education, employment, economic development, health and housing, and other issues.

OHIO HISTORICAL SOCIETY
1982 Velma Ave., Columbus 43211
(614) 297-2300; Fax: (614) 297-2352
Internet: www.ohiohistory.org
Exec. Dir.: Dr. William K. Laidlaw, Jr.
Private nonprofit organization; preserves and interprets Ohio's history and offers educational programs and services.

INDUSTRIAL COMMISSION OF OHIO
30 W. Spring St., Columbus 43215-2233
(614) 466-6136, (800) 521-2691; TDD: (800) 686-1589;
Fax: (614) 728-7004
E-mail: asklc@ic.state.oh.us
Internet: www.ohioic.com
Chair: William E. Thompson (614) 466-3711
Commissioners:
Patrick J. Gannon (614) 466-5733
Donna Owens (614) 466-3010
Conducts hearings on disputed worker's compensation claims; adjudicates claims involving an employer's violation of specific safety requirements; determines eligibility for Permanent Total Disability benefits.

Akron Hearing Administrator Office
161 S. High St., Suite 301, Akron 44308-1602
(330) 643-3554; Fax: (330) 643-3153
Hearing Administrator: Ann Lischner

Cincinnati Hearing Administrator Office
125 E. Court St., Suite 600, Cincinnati 45202-1211
(513) 357-9764; Fax: (513) 721-7503
Hearing Administrator: Steven Kirchner

Cleveland Hearing Administrator Office
615 Superior Ave., N.W., 7th Floor, Cleveland 44113-1898
(216) 787-3633; Fax: (216) 787-5289
Hearing Administrator: James Augusta

Columbus Hearing Administrator Office
30 W. Spring St., 7th Floor, Columbus 43215-2233
(614) 644-8351; Fax: (614) 466-7043
Hearing Administrator: Cynthia Day Slocum

Toledo Hearing Administrator Office
One Government Center, Suite 1500, Toledo 43604
(419) 245-2747; Fax: (419) 245-2673
Hearing Administrator: Lloyd Grant

OFFICE OF INFORMATION TECHNOLOGY
30 E. Broad St., 40th Floor, Columbus 43215-3414
(614) 644-6446; Fax: (614) 644-9152
E-mail: contact@oit.ohio.gov
Internet: www.oit.ohio.gov

Chief Information Officer: Mary F. Carroll (Acting)
Deputy C.I.O., Investment & Governance Div.:
Cynthia Doughtery (Acting)
(614) 466-6930; Fax: (614) 644-9152
Deputy C.I.O., Service Delivery Div.: Walter Callahan
(614) 752-7320; Fax: (614) 644-2133
Administrator, Administration: Katrina Flory
(614) 995-5466
Administrator, Digital Government: Mark Smith
(614) 466-2701
Technical Advisor: Rico Singleton (614) 728-4618

INSPECTOR GENERAL
30 E. Broad St., 18th Floor, Columbus 43215
(614) 644-9110, (800) 686-1525
Internet: www.watchdog.ohio.gov

Inspector General: Thomas P. Charles
Chief Legal Counsel: Richard A. Whitehouse
First Deputy Inspector General: Gregg B. Thornton
Deputy Inspectors General:
Jane M. Lengel   Arnie Schropp
Joseph R. Montgomery
Executive Secretary: Vicki L. Davies
Case Mgr.: Judy Celnicken

Investigates fraud, waste, abuse, and corruption within the executive branch of state government. The jurisdiction of this office extends to the Governor, his staff, state agencies, departments, boards, commissions, and any other entities appointed, employed, controlled, directed, or subject to the authority of the Governor.

DEPARTMENT OF INSURANCE
2100 Stella Ct., Columbus 43215-1067
(614) 644-2658; Fax: (614) 644-3743
Internet: www.ohioinsurance.gov

Director: Ann Womer Benjamin (614) 644-2651
Deputy Dir.: Holly S. Saelens (614) 719-1518
E-mail: holly.saelens@ins.state.oh.us
Asst. Dir., General Counsel: John Pouliot
(614) 644-3345; E-mail: john.pouliot@ins.state.oh.us
Asst Dir., Communications: Michael Fulwider
(614) 644-3481; E-mail: michael.fulwider@ins.state.oh.us
Asst. Dir., Policy & Legislation: Brent Walls
(614) 719-1511; E-mail: brent.walls@ins.state.oh.us
Asst. Dir., General Services: Anne Thomson
(614) 644-3490; E-mail: anne.thomson@ins.state.oh.us
Asst. Dir., Financial Regulation: Bill Rossbach
(614) 644-2648; E-mail: bill.rossbach@ins.state.oh.us
Asst. Dir., Property & Casualty Svces.: Peg Ising
(614) 644-3355; E-mail: peg.ising@ins.state.oh.us
Asst. Dir., Consumer Services: Nancy Colley
(614) 644-3378; E-mail: nancy.colley@ins.state.oh.us
Asst. Dir., Investigative & Licensing Svces.: Sue Stead
(614) 644-2438; E-mail: sue.stead@ins.state.oh.us

DEPARTMENT OF JOB & FAMILY SERVICES
30 E. Broad St., 32nd Floor, Columbus 43215
(614) 466-6282; TDD/TTY: (614) 752-3951;
Child Support Payment Central: (888) 965-2676;
Fax: (614) 466-2815
Internet: www.jfs.ohio.gov

Director: Barbara Riley
Chief Inspector: Wm. Eric Minameyer
(614) 466-3015; Fax: (614) 466-0207
Deputy Dir., Child Support: Joseph J. Pilat, 30th Floor
(614) 752-6561; Fax: (614) 752-9760
Deputy Dir., Local Operations: John Trott
4300 E. Fifth Ave., Suite 4318, Columbus 43219
(614) 466-4951; Fax: (614) 466-5025
Deputy Dir., Office of Management Information Services: Kimberly Liston
4200 E. 5th Ave., Columbus 43219
(614) 466-2303; Fax: (614) 752-6815
Deputy Dir., Communications: Jon Allen
(614) 466-6650; Fax: (614) 466-0292

Deputy Dir., Fiscal Services: Quentin Potter, 38th Floor
(614) 466-2924; Fax: (614) 995-5004
Deputy Dir., Employee and Business Services:
Katherine Nowack, 32nd Floor
(614) 466-4503; Fax: (614) 644-1208
Deputy Dir., Unemployment Compensation: Pat Paver
4300 Kimberly Pkwy., 4th Floor, Columbus 43232
(614) 995-7066; Fax: (614) 466-6873

Develops and oversees programs that provide health care, employment and economic assistance, child support and services to families and children.

Office of Legal Services
30 E. Broad St., 31st Floor, Columbus 43215
(614) 466-4605; Fax: (614) 752-8298;
TTY/TDD: (614) 728-2985

Chief Legal Counsel: Bob Mullinax

Deputy Legal Counsel: Marcia Slotnick
Oversees hearings in appealed cases to seek fairness, objectivity, promptness, efficiency, and timely decisions.

Ohio Health Plans
30 E. Broad St., 31st Floor, Columbus 43215
(614) 644-0140; Fax: (614) 752-3986;
Consumer Hotline: (800) 324-8680;
TTY/TDD: (800) 292-3572
Internet: www.jfs.ohio.gov/ohp

Deputy Dir.: Barbara Coulter Edwards

Bureau Chief, Consumer & Program Support: Brenda Lucas
33rd Floor (614) 728-8476; Fax: (614) 728-9201

Bureau Chief, Long Term Care Facilities: Harry Saxe
(614) 466-9243

Bureau Chief, Managed Health Care: Jon Barley
(614) 466-4693; Fax: (614) 728-4516

Bureau Chief, Health Plan Policy: Robin Colby
(614) 466-6420

Bureau Chief, Plan Operations: Sheila Fujii
(614) 466-2365

Bureau Chief, Home & Community Svces.: Sara Abbott
(614) 466-6742

Bureau Chief, Community Access: Tim Ferguson
(614) 466-6742

Office for Children and Families
255 E. Main St., 3rd Floor, Columbus 43215-3414
(614) 466-1213; Fax: (614) 466-6185

Deputy Dir.: Rick Smith

Bureau Chief, Family Svces.: Fran Rembert
(614) 466-9274; Fax: (614) 726-6426

Bureau Chief, Child Care and Development: Terrie Hare
(614) 466-1043; Fax: (614) 728-6803

Exec. Dir., Children's Trust Fund: Sally Pedon
(614) 466-1822; Fax: (614) 466-9682
Responsible for state level administration and oversight of programs that prevents and protects abused/neglected children and their families; licenses foster and child care homes and residential facilities; and guides county agencies by providing technical assistance and developing policies and procedures for program implementation.

Office of Unemployment Compensation
4300 Kimberly Pkwy., 4th Floor, Columbus 43232
(614) 995-7066; Claims: (877) 644-6562;
Fax: (614) 466-6873

Deputy Dir.: Patrick J. Power

Asst. Deputy Dir., Benefits: Joe Duda (614) 752-4699

Asst. Deputy Dir., Tax: William Lind (614) 752-7995

Asst. Deputy Dir.: Douglas Holmes (614) 644-9178
Pays unemployment benefits to eligible unemployed workers; administers the tax and wage records provisions of the Ohio Unemployment Compensation Law; responsible for several specialized unemployment program functions, including labor dispute determinations, representation of the Director before the Unemployment Compensation Review Commission, internal security and administration of the profiling program; and helps support the Unemployment Compensation Advisory Council

LAKE ERIE COMMISSION
One Maritime Plaza, 4th Floor, Toledo 43604
(419) 245-2514; Fax: (419) 245-2519
Internet: www.epa.state.oh.us/oleo

Exec. Dir.: Edwin J. Hammett
Chair: Dr. Samuel Speck (Dir., Dept. of Natural Resources)
(614) 265-6879
Secretary: Cash Misel (Asst. Dir., Dept. of Transportation)
(614) 644-8241

Coordinates policies and programs of state government pertaining to water quality, toxins and coastal resource management; seeks to protect and improve environmental quality of the Lake Erie Basin through coordination with the development of tourism, recreation, the fishing industry and the maintenance of the Lake Erie ports.

OHIO LEGAL RIGHTS SERVICE
8 E. Long St., Suite 500, Columbus 43215-2999
(614) 466-7264, (800) 282-9181; T.T.Y.: (614) 728-2553;
Fax: (614) 644-1888
Internet: www.olrs.ohio.gov

Exec. Dir.: Carolyn S. Knight
Chair: William Crum

Protects and advocates the human, civil, and legal rights of people with disabilities; enables people with disabilities to realize self-determination, equality of opportunity, and full participation.

LEGISLATIVE SERVICE COMMISSION
Vern Riffe Center, 9th Floor, 77 S. High St.,
Columbus 43215-6136
(614) 466-3615
Internet: www.lsc.state.oh.us

Director: James W. Burley
Assoc. Dir.: Richard E. Masek (614) 466-5709
Asst. Dir.: Tom Manuel
Legal Review & Technical Services: Randy Anderson
(614) 466-0339
Register of Ohio & Administrative Rules Unit:
Julie Hartzell (614) 387-6117
Librarian: Debbie Tavenner (614) 466-2241
Chair: Bill Harris
Vice Chair: Jon Husted

Researches and drafts legislation, including amendments, requested by any member of the General Assembly; maintains the laws of Ohio in an orderly and uniform system; reviews all bills introduced in the General Assembly to insure that each bill is drafted in conformity with required technical standards; monitors all legislation moving through the General Assembly and attempts to minimize the possibility of technical conflict that could occur if two bills amending the same section of law are enacted during the same session of the General Assembly.

STATE LIBRARY
Main Library, 274 E. First Ave., Ste. 100, Columbus 43201
(614) 644-7061, (800) 686-1532; Fax: (614) 466-3584
Internet: www.winslo.state.oh.us
Southeastern Ohio Library Center,
40780 State Route 821, Caldwell 43724

State Librarian: Joanne Budler
Deputy State Librarian: Cynthia McLaughlin (614) 644-6847
Public Information Officer: Jane Byrnes (614) 644-6875

Provides access to information for Ohio's state government; leads and partners in the development of library services throughout Ohio; enables resource sharing among libraries and library networks; provides specialized services to Ohio's citizens.

OHIO LOTTERY
615 W. Superior Ave., Cleveland 44113
(216) 787-3990; Customer Service: (216) 787-3200;
Fax: (216) 787-3313
Internet: www.ohiolottery.com

Exec. Dir.: Thomas J. Hayes
Asst. Dir.: Constance Miller
Deputy Dir., Finance: Dennis R. Berg
Deputy Dir., Administration: Duane Miller

Protects the integrity of the Ohio Lottery with its employees, sales retailers and its players; maintains the annual commitment to the Lottery Profits for Education Fund; promotes the accessibility of lottery games; evaluates retailers on the basis of revenues generated, but with consideration to their location and the population they serve; seeks to evaluate and improve operational efficiency.

MEDICAL BOARD
77 S. High St., 17th Floor, Columbus 43215-6127
(614) 466-3934; Complaint Line: (800) 554-7717;
Fax: (614) 728-5946

Exec. Dir.: Thomas A. Dilling
Senior Staff Atty.: Lauren Lubow
Board President: Patricia J. Davidson

Regulates medical doctors, doctors of osteopathic medicine, doctors of podiatric medicine, physician assistants, massage therapists, cosmetic therapists, anesthesiology assistants and acupuncturists.

DEPARTMENT OF MENTAL HEALTH
30 E. Broad St., 8th Floor, Columbus 43215-3430
(614) 466-2596; Fax: (614) 752-9453
Internet: www.mh.state.oh.us

Director: Michael F. Hogan
Deputy Dir.: Debra M. Belinky, J.D. (614) 466-8288

Cabinet-level agency; funds and oversees the administration of public mental health in partnership with 50 independent, county-level Community Mental Health (CMH) & Alcohol and Drug Addiction and Mental Health Services (ADAMHS) boards; licenses and certifies mental health providers, including provider agencies, private psychiatric hospitals, and select residential programs; operates five behaviorial healthcare organizations that provide outpatient and inpatient hospital services at nine sites throughout the state. *Ohio Rev. Code, Chapters 340 and 5119*

DEPARTMENT OF MENTAL RETARDATION AND DEVELOPMENTAL DISABILITIES
1810 Sullivant Ave., Columbus 43223-1239
(614) 466-5214, (877) 464-6733; Fax: (614) 466-3141
Internet: www.odmrdd.state.oh.us

Director: Kenneth W. Ritchey (614) 466-0129
E-mail: kenneth.ritchey@dmr.state.oh.us
Asst. Dir.: Constance Ament (614) 644-7596
E-mail: connie.ament@dmr.state.oh.us
Deputy Dir., Community Services: Dana Charlton
(614) 752-8878, 995-7078
E-mail: dana.charlton@dmr.state.oh.us
Deputy Dir., Constituent Services: Jeff Davis
(614) 644-6300; E-mail: jeff.davis@dmr.state.oh.us
Deputy Dir., Legal Services: Christine Oliver
(614) 466-5216; E-mail: christine.oliver@dmr.state.oh.us
Deputy Dir., Medicaid Policy: Linda Lewis-Day
(614) 728-2736; E-mail: linda.lewis-day@dmr.state.oh.us

COMMISSION ON MINORITY HEALTH
77 S. High St., 7th Floor, Columbus 43215
(614) 466-4000; Fax: (614) 752-9049
E-mail: minhealth@ocmh.state.oh.us
Internet: www.mih.ohio.gov

Exec. Dir.: Cheryl A. Boyce, M.S.
Program Mgr.: Bounthanh Phommasathit (Acting)
Legal Counsel: Shakeba DuBose (614) 466-8600
Assoc. Dir.: Lisa B. Stafford, B.S.
Chair: Ray Miller (614) 466-5131
Vice Chair: Gregory L. Hall, M.D. (216) 881-5055
Secretary: Gina Austin Lewis, M.S.A., F.A.C.H.E.
(937) 429-3901
Commissioners:
J. Nick Baird, Jr., M.D. (614) 466-2253
Walter T. Bowers II, M.D. (513) 381-6161
Edna Brown (614) 466-1401
Kenneth G. Cowens, M.D. (330) 747-3390
Mary I. Gregory, R.N., M.Ed. (419) 535-9561
Thomas J. Hayes (614) 466-6283
Michael F. Hogan, Ph.D. (614) 466-2337
Maria Julia, Ph.D. (614) 292-3521
Cora Munoz, Ph.D., R.N. (614) 236-6382
Kenneth Ritchey (614) 644-0378
Kirk Schuring (614) 466-0626
Olivia M. Thomas, M.D. (614) 722-4950
May L. Wykle, Ph.D. (216) 368-2545
Susan Tave Zelman (614) 466-7578

Funds projects toward reduction of the incidence and severity of conditions which are responsible for excess morbidity and mortality in minority populations.

BOARD OF MOTOR VEHICLE COLLISION REPAIR REGISTRATION
37 W. Broad St., Suite 880, Columbus 43215
(614) 995-0714; Fax: (614) 995-0717
Internet: www.collisionboard.com
Exec. Dir.: Robert L. Cassidy (614) 995-0715
Deputy Dir.: Diane Hoenig

DEPARTMENT OF NATURAL RESOURCES
2045 Morse Rd., Bldg. D-3, Columbus 43229-6693
(614) 265-6879; Fax: (614) 261-9601
E-mail: dnrmail@dnr.state.oh.us
Internet: www.ohiodnr.com
Director: Dr. Samuel Speck
Chief Counsel: Joan Weiser (614) 265-6819

Division of Parks and Recreation
2045 Morse Rd., Bldg. C-3, Columbus 43229-6693
(614) 265-6561
Internet: www.ohiodnr.com/parks
Chief: Daniel West

BOARD OF NURSING
17 S. High St., Suite 400, Columbus 43215-3413
(614) 466-3947; Fax: (614) 466-0388
Internet: www.nursing.ohio.gov
Exec. Dir.: John M. Brion
President: Yvonne Smith, M.S.N., R.N., C.N.S.

OCCUPATIONAL THERAPY, PHYSICAL THERAPY AND ATHLETIC TRAINERS BOARD
77 S. High St., 16th Floor, Columbus 43215-6108
(614) 466-3774; Fax: (614) 995-0816
Internet: www.otptat.ohio.gov
Exec. Dir.: Jeffrey M. Rosa

Regulates and licenses occupational therapists, occupational therapy assistants, physical therapists, physical therapist assistants, and athletic trainers. *Ohio Rev. Code Chap. 4755, Ohio Admin. Code 4755-1 to 4755-48.*

OPTICAL DISPENSERS BOARD
77 S. High St., 16th Floor, Columbus 43215-6108
(614) 466-9709; Fax: (614) 995-5392
Internet: www.optical.ohio.gov
Exec. Dir.: Linda E. Hoshor

BOARD OF OPTOMETRY
77 S. High St., 16th Floor, Columbus 43215-6108
(614) 466-5115, (888) 565-3044; Fax: (614) 644-3937
E-mail: optometry.board@exchange.state.oh.us
Internet: www.optometry.ohio.gov
Exec. Dir.: Michael R. Everhart
Investigator: Jeff A. May
President: Lawrence J. Barger, O.D.
  Valley Vision Center, 1480 N. Portage Path, Akron 44313
  (330) 867-2020; Fax: (330) 867-4666
Secretary: Dennis O. Roark, O.D.
  1674 N. Limestone St., Springfield 45503
  (937) 399-4101; Fax: (937) 399-2346

BOARD OF ORTHOTICS, PROSTHETICS & PEDORTHICS
77 S. High St., 18th Floor, Columbus 43215
(614) 466-1157; Fax: (614) 387-7347
E-mail: bopp@exchange.state.oh.us
Internet: www.opp.ohio.gov
Director: Mark B. Levy
President: Manuel R. Garcia

Protects the public by assuring that orthotists, prosthetists and pedorthists have appropriate minimum qualifications by virtue of recognized or demonstrated background, education, experience and training; reviews license applications, issues licenses, promulgates rules, investigates complaints, addresses issues of unlicensed practice and conducts disciplinary process; *Ohio Rev. Code, Chap. 4779 and Ohio Admin. Code, Chap. 4779*

PERSONNEL BOARD OF REVIEW
65 E. State St., 12th Floor, Columbus 43215-4213
(614) 466-7046; Fax: (614) 466-6539
Internet: www.pbr.ohio.gov
Exec. Dir.: James R. Sprague
Admin. Law Judges:
  Jeannette E. Gunn   Christopher R. Young
  Marcie M. Scholl
Contract Admin. Law Judge: Howard D. Silver
Staff Atty.: Elaine K. Stevenson
Docket Clerk: Barbara J. Dorsey
Chair: Roger W. Tracy
Vice Chair: J. Richard Lumpe
Member: Paul M. Booth

Provides a forum for administrative appeal by classified employees of state agencies, county agencies and general health districts; also answers inquiries from the general public, as well as civil service commissions and attorneys, regarding civil service law and procedures.

BOARD OF PHARMACY
77 S. High St., Room 1702, Columbus 43215-6126
(614) 466-4143; Fax: (614) 752-4836
Internet: www.pharmacy.ohio.gov
Exec. Dir.: William T. Winsley, M.S., R.Ph.
Board Counsel: Sally Ann Steuk (614) 466-8600

POWER SITING BOARD
180 E. Broad St., Columbus 43215
(866) 270-6772; Fax: (614) 752-8352
Internet: www.opsb.ohio.gov
Exec. Dir.: Kim Wissman (614) 466-6692
Chair: Alan R. Schriber

Supports energy policies that provide for the installation of energy capacity and transmission infrastructure.

BOARD OF PSYCHOLOGY
Vern Riffe Center, Suite 1830, 77 S. High St., Columbus 43215-6108
(614) 466-8808; Fax: (614) 728-7081
Internet: www.psychology.ohio.gov
Exec. Dir.: Ronald R. Ross, Ph.D., CPM (614) 466-1085
  E-mail: psy.dir@exchange.state.oh.us
Admin. Assts.:
  Chiquana Campbell; E-mail: psy.ce@exchange.state.oh.us
  Carla Daniels; E-mail: psy.sup@exchange.state.oh.us
Investigators:
  Kelli Coleman Delguzzo (614) 644-9176
  E-mail: psy.enforce@exchange.state.oh.us
  Carolyn Knauss (614) 644-9177
  E-mail: psy.enforce2@exchange.state.oh.us

Ensures that appropriately trained professionals are providing psychological services; stops illegal practice of psychology/school psychology; provides safeguards to consumers needs; establishes rules to guide professionals.

OFFICE OF THE PUBLIC DEFENDER
8 E. Long St., 11th Floor, Columbus 43215
(614) 466-5394, (800) 686-1573; Fax: (614) 644-9972
Internet: www.opd.ohio.gov
Athens County Branch Office, 80 N. Court St., Athens 45701
(740) 593-6400; Fax: (740) 594-2074
Ross County Branch Office, 14 S. Paint St., Suite 54, Chillicothe 45601
(740) 772-4772; Fax: (740) 772-4825
Washington County Branch Office, 200 Putnam St., Suite 200, Marietta 45750
(740) 373-1441; Fax: (740) 373-2133
Trumbull County Branch Office, 328 Mahoning Ave., Warren 44483
(330) 393-7727; Fax: (330) 393-7076
Public Defender: David H. Bodiker
Of Counsel: Gregory W. Meyers
Chief, Legal Div.: John A. Bay
Dir., Administrative Div.: John D. Alge
Chief Counsel, Death Penalty Div.: Joseph E. Wilhelm
Provides, supervises and coordinates legal representation at state expense for indigents and other persons, *Ohio Rev. Code 120.01*

Departments & Agencies

DEPARTMENT OF PUBLIC SAFETY
1970 W. Broad St., P.O. Box 182081, Columbus 43218-2081
(614) 466-2550; Fax: (614) 466-0433
Internet: www.ohiopublicsafety.com

Director: Kenneth L. Morckel
E-mail: director@dps.state.oh.us

Emergency Management Agency
2855 W. Dublin-Granville Rd., Columbus 43235-2206
(614) 889-7150; Fax: (614) 889-7183
Internet: www.ema.ohio.gov

Exec. Dir.: Nancy Dragani
Serves as the central point of coordination within the state for response and recovery to disasters; ensures that the state is prepared to respond to an emergency or disaster and to lead mitigation efforts against the effects of future disasters; *Ohio Rev. Code, Chap. 5502.*

Emergency Medical Services Division
1970 W. Broad St., P.O. Box 182073, Columbus 43218-2073
(614) 466-9447, (800) 233-0785; Fax: (614) 466-9461
Internet: www.ems.ohio.gov

Exec. Dir.: Richard Rucker
    E-mail: rnrucker@dps.state.oh.us
Asst. Administrator: Mike Glenn
    E-mail: mglenn@dps.state.oh.us
Certifies emergency medical technicians, firefighters and fire safety inspectors; issues accreditation and approval of EMS training sites for certification and continuing education programs; develops statewide EMS disaster response planning.

Homeland Security
1970 W. Broad St., Columbus 43223
(614) 387-6171; Fax: (614) 752-2419

Exec. Dir.: John Overly
Oversees the licensing and regulation of private investigators and security guards; and addresses new threats and challenges of terrorism.

Investigative Unit
1970 W. Broad St., P.O. Box 182081, Columbus 43218-2081
(614) 644-2415; Fax: (614) 644-2463

Deputy Dir.: Ed Duvall, Jr.
Comprised of agents who are fully-certified undercover, plain-clothed peace officers who investigate violations of liquor and tobacco laws, as well as food stamp fraud. Agents have criminal jurisdiction and serve as the sole law enforcement agency in the state with the power to administratively cite a liquor permit premise before the Liquor Control Commission; Also educates the community on underage drinking and smoking.

Bureau of Motor Vehicles
1970 W. Broad St., P.O. Box 16520, Columbus 43216-6520
(614) 752-7500; T.D.D.: (614) 752-4559
Internet: www.ohiobmv.com

Registrar: Franklin Caltrider

State Highway Patrol
1970 W. Broad St., Columbus 43223
(614) 466-2660; Fax: (614) 752-6409
Internet: www.statepatrol.ohio.gov

Superintendent: Col. Paul McClellan (614) 466-2990
Asst. Superintendents:
    Lt. Col. Michael W. Finamore (Administration)
    Lt. Col. Arthur A. Reitz (Operations)
Provides statewide traffic, emergency response and support services to the public and the criminal justice community; investigates criminal activities on state-owned and leased property throughout Ohio; provides security for the Governor and other dignitaries.

Ashland Patrol Post
805 U.S. 250, Ashland 44805 (419) 289-0911
Ashtabula Patrol Post
4860 N. Ridge West, Ashtabula 44004 (440) 969-1155
Athens Patrol Post
13600 Della Dr., Athens 45701 (740) 593-6611
Batavia Patrol Post
1000 Hospital Dr., Batavia 45103 (513) 732-1510
Berea Patrol Post
682 Prospect St., Berea 44017 (440) 234-2096

Bucyrus Patrol Post
3665 State Route 4, Bucyrus 44820 (419) 562-8040
Cambridge Patrol Post
7051 Glenn Highway Rd., Cambridge 43725
(740) 439-1388
Canfield Patrol Post
500 S. Broad St., Canfield 44406 (330) 533-6866
Canton Patrol Post
4710 Shuffel Rd., North Canton 44720 (330) 433-6200
Chardon Patrol Post
530 Center St., Chardon 44024 (440) 286-6612
Chillicothe Patrol Post
201 Hospital Rd., Chillicothe 45601 (740) 775-7770
Circleville Patrol Post
16395 U.S. Route 23, Ashville 43103 (740) 983-2538
Cleveland Operations
12323 Broadway Ave., Garfield Heights 44125
(216) 587-4305
Columbus District Headquarters
2855 W. Dublin-Granville Rd., Columbus 43235
(614) 799-9241
Dayton Patrol Post
400 Smith Dr., Englewood 45322 (937) 832-4794
Defiance Patrol Post
2350 Baltimore Rd., Defiance 43512 (419) 784-1025
Delaware Patrol Post
1500 Columbus Pike, Delaware 43015 (740) 548-6011
Elyria Patrol Post
38000 Cletus Dr., Elyria 44035 (440) 365-5045
Findlay Patrol Post
3201 N. Main St., Findlay 45840 (419) 423-1414
Fremont Patrol Post
2226 Commerce Dr., Fremont 43420 (419) 332-8246
Gallipolis Patrol Post
396 Jackson Pike, Gallipolis 45631 (740) 446-2433
Georgetown Patrol Post
9240 U.S. 68, Georgetown 45121 (937) 378-6191
Granville Patrol Post
3855 Outville Rd. S.W., Granville 43023 (740) 927-0065
Hamilton Patrol Post
4751 Hamilton-Middletown Rd., Hamilton 45011
(513) 863-4606
Hiram Patrol Post
P.O. Box 149, Ravenna 44266 (330) 527-2168
Ironton Patrol Post
1336 County Rd. 60, South Point 45680 (740) 377-4311
Jackson Patrol Post
10179 Chillicothe Pike, Jackson 45640 (740) 286-4141
Lancaster Patrol Post
1125 Ety Rd., Lancaster 43130 (740) 654-1523
Lebanon Patrol Post
184 Nelson Rd., Lebanon 45036 (513) 932-4444
Lima Patrol Post
2005 E. Fourth St., Lima 45804 (419) 228-2421
Lisbon Patrol Post
9423 State Route 45, Lisbon 44432-9505 (330) 424-7783
Mansfield Patrol Post
2255 S. Main St., Mansfield 44907 (419) 756-2222
Marietta Patrol Post
27761 State Route 7, Marietta 45750 (740) 374-6616
Marion Patrol Post
2284 Marion-Upper Sandusky Rd., Marion 43302
(740) 383-2181
Marysville Patrol Post
22600 Northwest Pkwy., Marysville 43040 (937) 644-8811
Medina Patrol Post
3149 Frantz Rd., Medina 44256 (330) 725-4921
Milan Patrol Post
Ohio Tpke., Exit 118, Toll Plaza 7, P.O. Box 524, Milan 44846
(419) 499-4808
Mt. Gilead Patrol Post
3980 County Rd. 172, Mount Gilead 43338 (419) 768-3955
New Philadelphia Patrol Post
2454 E. High Ave., New Philadelphia 44663 (330) 339-1103

State Highway Patrol—Cont'd

Norwalk Patrol Post
300 S. Norwalk Rd., Norwalk 44857 (419) 668-3711

Piqua Patrol Post
401 W. U.S. Route 36, Piqua 45356 (937) 773-1131

Portsmouth Patrol Post
U.S. Route 23, Lucasville 45648 (740) 354-2888

Ravenna Patrol Post
6259 State Route 14, Ravenna 44266 (330) 297-1441

St. Clairsville Patrol Post
51400 National Rd., St. Clairsville 43950 (740) 695-0915

Sandusky Patrol Post
511 Fremont Ave., Sandusky 44870 (419) 625-6565

Springfield Patrol Post
4201 Gateway Blvd., Springfield 45502 (937) 323-9781

Steubenville Patrol Post
1377 Cadiz Rd., Wintersville 43953 (740) 264-1641

Swanton Patrol Post
8891 County Rd. 1, Swanton 43558 (419) 826-5871

Toledo Patrol Post
10391 Airport Highway, Swanton 43558 (419) 865-5544

Van Wert Patrol Post
1230 E. Ridge Rd., Van Wert 45891 (419) 238-3055

Walbridge Patrol Post
29256 Lemoyne Rd., Millbury 43447 (419) 666-1323

Wapakoneta Patrol Post
15472 Wapak-Fisher Rd., Rt. 5, Wapakoneta 45895
(419) 738-8010

Warren Patrol Post
3424 State Route 422, Southington 44470 (330) 898-2311

West Jefferson Patrol Post
1485 W. Main St., West Jefferson 43162 (614) 879-7626

Wilmington Patrol Post
950 Rombach Ave., Wilmington 45177 (937) 382-2551

Wooster Patrol Post
1786 Dover Rd., Wooster 44691 (330) 264-0575

Xenia Patrol Post
517 Union Rd., Xenia 45385 (937) 372-7671

Zanesville Patrol Post
3760 East Pike, Zanesville 43701 (740) 453-0541

PUBLIC UTILITIES COMMISSION
180 E. Broad St., Columbus 43215-3793
(614) 466-3292; Fax: (614) 752-8351;
Consumer Hotline Toll Free: (800) 686-7826
E-mail: webmaster@puc.state.oh.us
Internet: www.puco.ohio.gov

Chair: Alan R. Schriber (614) 466-3016

PUBLIC WORKS COMMISSION
65 E. State St., Suite 312, Columbus 43215
(614) 466-0880; Fax: (614) 466-4664
E-mail: pwc_is@pwc.state.oh.us
Internet: www.pwc.state.oh.us

Director: W. Laurence Bicking
E-mail: laurence.bicking@pwc.state.oh.us

Assists in financing local public infrastructure improvements under the State Capital improvements Program (SCIP) and the Local Transportation Improvements Program (LTIP); provides grants, loans, and financing for local debt support and credit enhancement. Eligible projects include improvements to roads, bridges, culverts, water supply systems, wastewater systems, storm water collection systems, and solid waste disposal facilities.

STATE RACING COMMISSION
77 S. High St., 18th Floor, Columbus 43215-6108
(614) 466-2757; Fax: (614) 466-1900
Internet: www.racing.ohio.gov

Exec. Dir.: Sam Zonak
Chief Legal Counsel: Tom Michael
E-mail: tml@osrc.state.oh.us
Public Information: Martin Evans
E-mail: mje@osrc.state.oh.us

BOARD OF REGENTS
30 E. Broad St., 36th Floor, Columbus 43215-3414
(614) 466-6000; Fax: (614) 466-5866
E-mail: regents@regents.state.oh.us
Internet: www.regents.state.oh.us

Chancellor: Roderick G.W. Chu
Chair: Thomas W. Noe
Vice Chair: Edmund J. Adams

Advocates for and recommends spending of the state's higher education budget; works with the state Board of Educaton to coordinate primary, secondary and higher educaton systems; authorizes and approves degree programs; manages state-funded financial aid programs for students; develops and supports higher education policy.

DEPARTMENT OF REHABILITATION & CORRECTION
1050 Freeway Dr., N., Columbus 43229
(614) 752-1150; Fax: (614) 752-1171
Internet: www.drc.state.oh.us

Director: Reginald A. Wilkinson (614) 752-1164
Deputy Dir.: Michael Randle (614) 752-1271
Chief Counsel: Greg Trout (614) 752-1765
Chief Inspector: Cheryl Jorgenson-Martinez
Chief of Policy: Maureen Black (614) 752-0627

Protects and supports by ensuring that adult felony offenders are effectively supervised in environments that are safe, humane and appropriately secure; promotes citizen safety and victim reparation through rehabilitative and restorative programming.

RESPIRATORY CARE BOARD
77 S. High St., 16th Floor, Columbus 43215
(614) 752-9218; Fax: (614) 728-8691
E-mail: rcb.logsdon@rcb.state.oh.us
Internet: www.respiratorycare.ohio.gov

Exec. Dir.: Christopher H. Logsdon

Responsible for the regulation of the practice of respiratory care; licenses properly qualified providers and issues limited permits to respiratory care program students, graduates, and experienced-based providers; maintains the active status of the board's licensees; acts on complaints filed with the agency through investigation, inquiry and on site inspection of facilities; establishes educational standards for respiratory care educational programs; and monitors compliance of mandatory continuing education for respiratory care providers; recommends improvements to the practice of respiratory care to the Governor and Ohio General Assembly; also regulates and licenses home medical equipment services; *Ohio Rev. Code, Chaps. 4752 and 4761.*

BOARD OF SANITARIAN REGISTRATION
77 S. High St., 16th Floor, Columbus 43215-6108
(614) 466-1772; Fax: (614) 644-8112
Internet: www.sanitarian.ohio.gov

Exec. Secretary: Lynn Jones

SCHOOL FACILITIES COMMISSION
10 W. Broad St., Suite 1400, Columbus 43215
(614) 466-6290; Fax: (614) 466-7749, 995-9908
Internet: www.osfc.state.oh.us

Exec. Dir.: Mary Lynn Readey
Chair: Thomas Johnson (Office of Budget & Management) (614) 466-4034

Provides funding, management oversight and technical assistance to Ohio school districts for the construction and renovation of school facilities in order to create and appropriate learning environment.

SECRETARY OF STATE
180 E. Broad St., 16th Floor, Columbus 43215
(614) 466-2655, (877) 767-6446; Fax: (614) 644-0649;
Business Services: (877) 767-3453;
Business Services Fax: (614) 995-2238;
Elections: (614) 466-2585;
Elections Fax: (614) 752-4360
E-mail (Business Services): busserv@sos.state.oh.us;
E-mail (Elections): election@sos.state.oh.us
Internet: www.sos.state.oh.us
Client Service Center, 30 E. Broad St., Lower Level, Columbus 43215

Departments & Agencies

Secretary of State—Cont'd

Secretary of State: J. Kenneth Blackwell
E-mail: blackwell@sos.state.oh.us
General Counsel: Cassandra Hicks (614) 644-1373
E-mail: cihicks@sos.state.oh.us
Dir., Public Affairs: Carol Taylor (614) 466-7691

BOARD OF SPEECH-LANGUAGE PATHOLOGY AND AUDIOLOGY
77 S. High St., 16th Floor, Columbus 43215
(614) 466-3145; Fax: (614) 995-2286
Exec. Dir.: Michael J. Setty
Legal Counsel: Dominick Chieffo
30 E. Broad St., 26th Floor, Columbus 43266
(614) 466-8600

Licenses and regulates the practice of speech-language pathology and audiology. *Chapter 4753 of the Ohio Revised Code and Ohio Administrative Code.*

BOARD OF TAX APPEALS
Rhodes Office Tower, 24th Floor, 30 E. Broad St., Columbus 43215-3414
(614) 466-6700; Fax: (614) 644-5196
Internet: www.bta.ohio.gov
Secretary/Exec. Dir.: Julia M. Snow
Chief Attorney Examiner: Bradford P. Arnold
Chair: Louise A. Jackson
Vice Chair: Pamela L. Margulies
Commission Member: Robert L. Eberhart

Resolves appeals from decisions and orders of the Tax Commissioner; has jurisdiction of appeals from county boards of revision regarding real property valuation and appeals from county budget commissions.

DEPARTMENT OF TAXATION
30 E. Broad St., 22nd Floor, Columbus 43215
(614) 466-2166; Fax: (614) 466-6401
Internet: www.tax.ohio.gov
Commissioner: William W. Wilkins
Deputy Commissioner, Chief Counsel: Fred Nicely
Deputy Commissioner, Tax Operations: Boris Slogar
Deputy Commissioner, Tax Policy: Frederick G. Church
(614) 466-3960
Deputy Commissioner, Tax Service: Rick Anthony

Audit Division
30 E. Broad St., 20th Floor, Columbus 43215
(614) 644-1701; Fax: (614) 466-1082
Exec. Administrator: Ron Potorff (614) 466-2425
Administrators:
Vaughn Lombardo (614) 995-0726
John Trippier (614) 995-0724

Bankruptcy Division
30 E. Broad St., 23rd Floor, Columbus 43215
Fax: (614) 995-0164
Administrator: Rebecca Daum (614) 752-6864

Budget and Accounts Payable Division
30 E. Broad St., 22nd Floor, Columbus 43215
(614) 466-7150; Fax: (614) 466-8393
C.F.O.: Kevin McNeil
Fiscal Officer: Teri Knox

Chief Counsel
30 E. Broad St., 23rd Floor, Columbus 43215
(614) 466-6750; Fax: (614) 466-7979
Appeals Mgmt.: Marge Brewer
Tax Appeals: Charles Rhilinger, Jr.

Communications Office
30 E. Broad St., 22nd Floor, Columbus 43215
(614) 644-6903; Fax: (614) 466-8922
Director: Gary Gudmundson

Compliance Division
830 Freeway Dr. N., Columbus 43229
(614) 387-1701; Fax: (614) 387-1847
Administrator: Deborah Eckert
Asst. Administrator: Mary Tillman

Corporate Franchise Tax
1030 Freeway Dr. N., Columbus 43229
(614) 433-7615; Fax: (614) 846-9504
Administrator: Tom Duncan

Employee Development and Training Division
30 E. Broad St., 23rd Floor, Columbus 43215
(614) 466-7560; Fax: (614) 728-8466
Administrator: Arthur L. Flesch

Estate Tax Division
800 Freeway Dr. N., Columbus 43229
(800) 977-7711; Fax: (614) 387-1984
Administrator: Michael R. Dundon
Asst. Administrator: John Lynch
Legal Counsel: Marc Friedman

Excise and Motor Fuel Tax Division
30 E. Broad St., 19th Floor, Columbus 43215
Excise & Assessments: (614) 466-3410;
IFTA/Fuel Use/Compliance & Assessments:
(614) 466-6410;
IFTA/Fuel Use Trucking Permits: (614) 466-3921;
Motor Fuel Compliance & Refunds: (614) 466-3503;
Motor Fuel Refunds: (614) 466-3503; Fax: (614) 752-8644
Administrator: Dale Bischoff (614) 466-3794
Asst. Administrator: Richard Carter (614) 466-3794

Facilities Management Division
1030 Freeway Dr. N., Columbus 43229
(614) 433-7791; Fax: (614) 433-7691
Administrator: Greg Stratton

Forecasting & Special Projects
30 E. Broad St., 22nd Floor, Columbus 43215
(614) 466-3960; Fax: (614) 752-0700
Administrator: Mike Sobul

Forms Purchasing Division
990 Freeway Dr. N., Columbus 43229
(614) 433-7632; Fax: (614) 438-5300
Administrator: Julie Carpenter

Human Resources Division
30 E. Broad St., 22nd Floor, Columbus 43215
(614) 466-3020; Fax: (614) 466-9867
Executive Administrator: Francie Adams
Asst. Administrators:
Leslie Cassady					Elissa Nagy

Income & School District Tax
1030 Freeway Dr. N., Columbus 43229
(614) 433-7606; Fax: (614) 846-9504
Administrator: James Baumann

Information Services Computer Division
1320 Arthur E. Adams Dr., Columbus 43221
(614) 752-1967; Fax (2nd Fl.): (614) 752-1990;
Fax (3rd Fl.): (614) 752-0738, 995-5270
Administrator: James McAndrew

Investigation and Enforcement Division
830 Freeway Dr. N., Columbus 43229
(614) 466-6939; Fax: (614) 752-1929
1150 W. 8th St., Suite 253, Cincinnati 45203
(513) 852-3313; Fax: (513) 852-3221
615 W. Superior Ave., Room 510, Cleveland 44113
(216) 787-3123; Fax: (216) 787-5256
One Government Center, Suite 1450, Toledo 43604
(419) 245-3005; Fax: (419) 245-3006
Administrator: Robert Bray

Legislation Division
30 E. Broad St., 22nd Floor, Columbus 43215
(614) 644-6896; Fax: (614) 466-8922
Administrator: Kimberly Wisecup
Legal Counsel: Leslie Akers

Problem Resolution Office
30 E. Broad St., Columbus 43215
Fax: (614) 466-6401
Officer: Einon Plummer (614) 466-0832
Supervisor: Dale Carter (614) 466-3359

Department of Taxation—Cont'd

Revenue Accounting Division
30 E. Broad St., 19th Floor, Columbus 43215
(614) 466-7150; Fax: (614) 995-0988
Administrator: Michael J. O'Leary

Sales and Use Tax Division
30 E. Broad St., 20th Floor, Columbus 43215
(614) 466-7351; Fax: (614) 466-4977
Administrator: Bryan Hairston
Legal Counsel: William Riesenberger

Tangible Personal Property Tax
30 E. Broad St., 21st Floor, Columbus 43215
(614) 466-8123; Fax: (614) 466-8654
Exec. Administrator: Shelley Wilson
Property Administrator: William T. Peters
Asst. Administrator: John Nolfi

Tax Analysis & Research Division
30 E. Broad St., 22nd Floor, Columbus 43215
(614) 466-3960; Fax: (614) 752-0700
Administrator: Chris Hall

Tax Equalization Division
30 E. Broad St., 21st Floor, Columbus 43215
(614) 466-5744; Fax: (614) 752-9822
Executive Administrator: Shelley Wilson
Administrator: Chris Kantzer
Asst. Administrator: Robert Everhart
Legal Counsel: Edward Samsel

Taxpayer Service Center Administration
800 Freeway Dr. N., Columbus 43229
(614) 995-0729; Fax: (614) 387-1851
Administrator: Keith Farrell

Taxpayer Services Division
800 Freeway Dr. N., Columbus 43229
Taxpayer Services: (614) 387-1801;
Taxpayer Services Fax: (614) 387-1851
Exec. Administrator: Mark Walker
Administrators:
    Deborah Eckert (Compliance)
    Cal Skaates (Compliance Support)
Asst. Administrators:
    Joseph Hammond (Taxpayer Services)
    Del Harlan (Taxpayer Services)
    Mary Tillman (Compliance)

DEPARTMENT OF TRANSPORTATION
1980 W. Broad St., Columbus 43223
(614) 466-7170; Fax: (614) 644-8662
Internet: www.dot.state.oh.us
Director: Gordon Proctor (614) 466-2336
Chief of Staff: Andrew Gall (614) 466-8991
Chief Legal Counsel: Lisa Conomy (614) 466-3664
Asst. Dir., Planning & Production: Cash Misel
    (614) 466-8991
Deputy Dir., Div. of Planning: Howard Wood
    (614) 466-8969
Deputy Dir., Div. of Local Programs: Carla L. Cefaratti
    (614) 466-8969
Deputy Dir., Div. of Production Mgmt.: Tim McDonald
    (614) 728-9544
Asst. Dir. of Highway Mgmt.: Rich Martinko (614) 466-2336
Deputy Dir., Div. of Contract Admin.: Mark Kelsey
    (614) 466-3778
Deputy Dir., Div. of Highway Operations: Tony Vogal
    (614) 752-5396
Plans, builds and maintains the state transportation infrastructure; responsible for the state roads system.

District 1 Office
1885 North McCullough St., Lima 45801
(419) 222-9055; TDD: (419) 222-5652; Fax: (419) 222-0438
District Deputy Dir.: Norman R. Redick

District 2 Office
317 East Poe Rd., Bowling Green 43402-1330
(419) 353-8131; Fax: (419) 353-1468
District Deputy Dir.: Todd Audet

District 3 Office
906 N. Clark St., Ashland 44805
(800) 276-4188; Fax: (419) 281-0874
District Deputy Dir.: Thomas O'Leary

District 4 Office
2088 S. Arlington Rd., Akron 44306
(330) 786-3100, (800) 603-1054; TDD: (330) 297-0369;
Fax: (330) 786-2232
District Deputy Dir.: Mohamed Darwish

District 5 Office
9600 Jacksontown Rd. S.E., Jacksontown 43030
(740) 323-4400; TDD: (740) 323-4746; Fax: (740) 323-3715
District Deputy Dir.: Christopher T. Engle

District 6 Office
400 E. William St., Delaware 43015
(740) 363-1251, (800) 372-7714; Fax: (740) 369-7437
District Deputy Dir.: Jack Marchbanks

District 7 Office
1001 St. Marys Ave., P.O. Box 969, Sidney 45365
(937) 492-1141; Fax: (937) 497-9734
District Deputy Dir.: William L. Harrison

District 8 Office
505 S. St. Rt. 741, Lebanon 45036
(513) 932-3030, (800) 831-2142; Fax: (513) 932-7651
District Deputy Dir.: Michael C. Flynn

District 9 Office
650 Eastern Ave., Chillicothe 45601-0467
(740) 773-2691, (888) 819-8501; Fax: (740) 775-4889
District Deputy Dir.: Harry Fry

District 10 Office
338 Muskingum Dr., Marietta 45750
(740) 373-0212; Fax: (740) 373-7317
District Deputy Dir.: George M. Collins

District 11 Office
2201 Reiser Ave. S.E., New Philadelphia 44663
(330) 339-6633; Fax: (330) 308-3942
District Deputy Dir.: Myron Pakush

District 12 Office
5500 Transportation Blvd., Cleveland 44125
(866) 737-8112, (216) 581-2100; Fax: (216) 587-1730
District Deputy Dir.: David J. Coyle

Rail Development Commission
50 W. Broad St., Suite 1510, Columbus 43215
(614) 644-0306; Fax: (614) 728-4520
Exec. Dir.: James E. Seney (614) 728-9497
Associate Asst. Atty. General: Alan H. Klodell
    (614) 466-7020; Fax: (614) 466-1756
Coordinates freight and passenger rail systems in Ohio as an integral part of a seamless intermodal transportation network.

TREASURER OF STATE
30 E. Broad St., 9th Floor, Columbus 43215
(614) 466-2160; TTY: (800) 228-1102;
Fax: (614) 644-7313
Internet: www.treasurer.state.oh.us
State Treasurer: Jennette B. Bradley (614) 466-3639
Deputy Treasurer: Pat McDonald (614) 466-2191
Dir., Operations: Kevin Talty (614) 466-8358
Dir., Accounting: Tom McFarland (614) 752-8491
Dir., Center for Public Investment Mgmt.:
    Victoria Gatien (614) 728-4198
Dir., Communications: John Meyer (614) 644-0169
Deputy Press Secretary: Merle Madrid (614) 752-1973
Dir., Community Education Programs: Tom Kelly
    (614) 752-2748
Dir., Human Resources and Fiscal Services Dept.:
    Jacqueline Leisenheimer (614) 466-5486
Dir., Information Systems and Services: James Davis
    (614) 466-0777
Dir., Internal Audit: Toni L. Powell (614) 752-2163
Dir., Investments: James Hartley (614) 466-3511
Dir., Legislative Affairs: Matthew Ottiger (614) 466-5341
Dir., Revenue Management: Jennifer E. Day
    (614) 752-8496
Dir, Trust Department: Cindy Beck (614) 466-8046

Departments & Agencies

Treasurer of State—Cont'd

Responsible for assuring the absolute safety of all public funds collected, managed, disbursed, and invested by the Treasury; emphasis on providing necessary liquidity and, within the context of safety and liquidity, maximum yield.

Central Regional Office
30 E. Broad St., 9th Floor, Columbus 43215
(614) 644-1287
Representative: Scott Brown
Serves Coshocton, Delaware, Fairfield, Franklin, Guernsey, Hocking, Knox, Licking, Madison, Marion, Morgan, Morrow, Muskingum, Pickaway, Perry and Union Counties.

Eastern Regional Office
242 Federal Plaza W., 3rd Floor, Youngstown 44503-1206
(330) 793-5492
Representative: Mike Wellendorf
Serves Ashtabula, Belmont, Carroll, Columbiana, Harrison, Jefferson, Mahoning, Monroe, Noble, Portage, Trumbull and Tuscarawas Counties.

Northeast Regional Office
Lausche Building, 12th Floor, 615 Superior Ave. N.W., Cleveland 44113
(216) 787-3305
Representative: Bill White
Serves Cuyahoga, Geauga, Lake and Lorrain Counties.

Northeast Regional Office
615 W. Superior Ave., Suite 1210, Cleveland 44113
(216) 787-5050; Fax: (216) 787-3924
Representative: Jim Richison
Serves Ashland, Holmes, Medina, Stark, Summit and Wayne Counties.

Northeast Regional Office
615 Superior Ave., Cleveland 44113
(216) 787-3737
Representative: Matt Moennich
Serves Crawford, Erie, Huron and Richland Counties

Northwest Regional Office
One Government Center, 12th Floor, Toledo 43604
(419) 241-2951
Representative: Mike Goetz
Serves Counties of Allen, Defiance, Fulton, Hancock, Hardin, Henry, Lucas, Ottawa, Paulding, Putnam, Sandusky, Seneca, Van Wert, Williams, Wood and Wyandot Counties.

Southern Regional Office
8790 Governor's Hill, Suite 201, Cincinnati 45249
(513) 677-7901
Representative: Brandon Hopkins
Serves Adams, Athens, Brown, Clermont, Gallia, Highland, Jackson, Lawrence, Meigs, Pike, Ross, Scioto, Washington and Vinton Counties.

Southwest Regional Office
8790 Governor's Hill, Suite 201, Cincinnati 45249
(513) 659-1333; Fax: (513) 677-7905
Representative: Matt Davis
Serves Champaign, Clark, Clinton, Fayette, Greene, Hamilton, Logan and Warren Counties.

Western Regional Office
1478-A Miamisburg-Centerville Rd., Centerville 45459
(937) 433-9223
Representative: Michael McNamara
Serves Auglaize, Butler, Darke, Mercer, Miami, Montgomery, Preble and Sandusky Counties.

OHIO TRUST TUITION AUTHORITY
580 S. High St., Suite 208, Columbus 43215
(614) 752-9400; Customer Service: (800) 233-6734;
Fax: (614) 644-5009
E-mail: info@otta.state.oh.us
Internet: www.collegeadvantage.com
Exec. Dir.: Jacqueline Williams

Offers a safe and affordable way to help Ohio families save for a college education, offers additional market-based college savings options along with the guaranteed option to form the College Advantage 529 Savings Plan.

TURNPIKE COMMISSION
682 Prospect St., Berea 44017
(440) 234-2081; Fax: (440) 234-4618
Internet: www.ohioturnpike.org
Exec. Dir.: Gary C. Suhadolnik
E-mail: gsuhadolnik@ohioturnpike.org
Deputy Exec. Dir.: Gerald L. Pursley
C.F.O./Comptroller: James T. Steiner
Chief Engineer: Daniel Castrigano
Chair: Thomas Noe
General Counsel: Noelle Tsevdos

A 241-mile toll road which crosses the northern part of the state from Indiana to Pennsylvania; autonomous and financially independent instrumentality of the state; *Ohio Rev. Code, Chap. 5537*

UNEMPLOYMENT COMPENSATION REVIEW COMMISSION
145 S. Front St., 5th Floor, Columbus 43215
Mailing Address: P.O. Box 182292,
Columbus 43218-2292
(866) 833-8272; Fax: (614) 752-8862
Internet: www.web.ucrc.state.oh.us
Chair: E.J. Thomas
Vice Chair: John D. Jacob
Commissioner: Kenny E. Delaney
Secretary to Commission: Helen L. Detrick
Chief Admin. Hearing Officer: David F. Kubli

Hears, on appeal, Ohio Department of Job & Family Services unemployment compensation decisions and provides parties an opportunity for a hearing before an independent tribunal.

VETERANS HOME
3416 Columbus Ave., Sandusky 44870
(419) 625-2454; Administration Fax: (419) 625-3207;
Admissions Office: (800) 572-7934
Internet: www.ovh.state.oh.us
2003 Veterans Blvd., Georgetown 45121
(937) 378-2900
Network Superintendent: Col. Christine M. Cook
Ext. 1200
Deputy Superintendents:
Steve Matune (Sandusky), Ext. 1202
Stan Weigman (Georgetown) (937) 378-2900, Ext. 2701
Dir., Operations: Debbie DeRose, Ext. 1236
E-mail: dsderose@ovh.state.oh.us
Chief Legal Counsel: Greg Kowalski, Ext. 1253
Public Relations Officer: Gary Chetwood, Ext. 1219

Provides a home environment for eligible Ohio veterans under the authority of *Ohio Rev. Code, Chap. 5907*

VETERINARY MEDICAL LICENSING BOARD
77 S. High St., 16th Floor, Columbus 43215-6108
(614) 644-5281; Fax: (614) 644-9038
E-mail: info@ovmlb.state.oh.us
Internet: www.state.oh.us/ovmlb
Exec. Dir.: Heather Hissom

Issues veterinary licenses; provides examinations for license; approves continuing education courses required for the license; investigates complaints involving licensed veterinarians or violations of the practice act; provides compliance inspections of veterinary facilities and establishing liaison with all federal, state and local regulatory agencies relating to veterinary medicine; *Ohio Rev. Code, Chapter 4741.*

WATER DEVELOPMENT AUTHORITY
480 S. High St., Columbus 43215-3516
(614) 466-5822, (877) 693-1123; Fax: (614) 644-9964
Internet: www.owda.org
Exec. Dir.: Steve Grossman
C.O.O.: Scott Campbell
Chief Engineer: Ken Heigel

Provides financing to local governments for drinking water, wastewater and solid waste facilities; also issues private activity bonds for sewage facilities, solid waste facilities, facilities that furnish potable water, and facilities for the disposal of hazardous waste.

BUREAU OF WORKERS' COMPENSATION
30 W. Spring St., Columbus 43215-2256
(800) 644-6292; Fax: (877) 520-6446
Internet: www.ohiobwc.com

Administrator/C.E.O.: James Conrad

Administrator/C.O.O.: Tina Kielmeyer

Chief Legal Officer: John Annarino

Chief Information Officer: Chuck Quinlan

C.F.O.: Tracy Valentino (Acting)

Chief of Human Resources: Barbara Young

Chief, Employer Management Services: John Romig

Chief, Injury Management Services: Joel Donchess

Chief, Field Operations: Jeff Redman

Dir., Communications: Victoria Pannell

Provides medical and compensation benefits for work-related injuries, diseases, and deaths; *Ohio Rev. Code, Chap. 4121 & 4123*.

DEPARTMENT OF YOUTH SERVICES
51 N. High St., Columbus 43215
(614) 466-4314; Victims Services: (800) 872-3132;
Fax: (614) 752-9078

Director: Thomas Stickrath (Acting) (614) 466-8783
Chief of Staff: Kevin Miller (614) 728-9319
Deputy Dir., Human Resources: Tina Kruger
(614) 644-7569
Deputy Dir., Legal Services: Sara Vollmer
(614) 728-3576
Deputy Dir., Corrections: Gary Mohr (614) 466-9318
Deputy Dir., Parole and Community Services:
David Schroot (614) 466-4906
Deputy Dir., Finance and Planning: Harry Kamdar
(614) 466-4841
Deputy Dir., Treatment and Rehabilitation Services:
Monique Marrow (614) 728-9319
Chief Inspector: Rufus Thomas (614) 728-2118
Public Information Officer: Andrea Kruse
(614) 466-9854

Juvenile corrections system for the state; statutorily mandated to confine felony offenders; adjudicated and committed by Ohio's 88 county juvenile courts; operates eight correctional and rehabilitation facilities and provides parole services from seven regional sites.

Departments &
Agencies

OHIO CORRECTIONAL INSTITUTIONS

Allen Correctional Institution (ACI)
2338 N. West St., P.O. Box 4501, Lima 45801
(419) 224-8000; Fax: (419) 224-5828
Warden: Jesse Williams
Medium Security

Belmont Correctional Institution (BECI)
68518 Bannock Rd., St. Rt. 331, P.O. Box 540,
Saint Clairsville 43950-0540
(740) 695-5169; Fax: (740) 695-8272
Warden: Michelle Eberlin
Minimum / Medium Security

Camp Reams (Boot Camp)
Southeastern Correctional Institution, 5900 B.I.S. Rd.,
Lancaster 43130
(740) 653-4324, Ext. 2900
Warden: Mark Saunders

Chillicothe Correctional Institution (CCI)
15802 St. Rt. 104 N., P.O. Box 5500, Chillicothe 45601
(740) 774-7080; Fax: (740) 773-8296
Warden: Tim Brunsman
Minimum / Medium Security

Correctional Reception Center (CRC)
11271 State Route 762, P.O. Box 300, Orient 43146
(614) 877-2441; Fax: (614) 877-3853
Warden: Ginny Lamneck
Close Security

Corrections Medical Center (CMC)
1990 Harmon Ave., P.O. Box 23658, Columbus 43223
(614) 445-5960; Fax: (614) 445-7040
Warden: Kay Northrup
Close Security

Dayton Correctional Institution (DCI)
4104 Germantown St., P.O. Box 17249, Dayton 45417
(937) 263-0058; Fax: (937) 263-9285
Warden: Lawrence Mack
Medium Security

Franklin Pre-Release Center (FPRC)
1800 Harmon Ave., P.O. Box 23651, Columbus 43223
(614) 445-8600; Fax: (614) 444-8267
Warden: Tracy Tyson-Parker
Minimum Security; Women

Grafton Correctional Institution (GCI)
2500 S. Avon Beldon Rd., Grafton 44044
(440) 748-1161; Fax: (216) 748-2521
Warden: Carl Anderson
Medium Security

Hocking Correctional Facility (HCF)
16759 Snake Hollow Rd., P.O. Box 59, Nelsonville 45764
(740) 753-1917; Fax: (740) 753-4277
Warden: Sam Tambi
Medium Security

Lake Erie Correctional Institution (LaeCI)
501 Thompson Rd., P.O. Box 8000, Conneaut 44030
(440) 599-5000; Fax: (440) 593-4536
Warden: Rich Gransheimer
Minimum / Medium Security; Privately Operated

Lebanon Correctional Institution (LeCI)
State Route 63, P.O. Box 56, Lebanon 45036
(513) 932-1211; Fax: (513) 932-1320
Warden: Ernie Moore
Minimum / Close Security

Lima Correctional Institution (LCI)
2235 N.W. St., P.O. Box 4571, Lima 45802
*Institution closed June 2004; for more information contact
The Department of Rehabilitation & Correction, Public
Information Office at (614) 752-1150*

London Correctional Institution (LoCI)
1580 State Route 56, P.O. Box 69, London 43140-0069
(740) 852-2454; Fax: (740) 852-4854
Warden: Deb Timmerman-Cooper
Minimum / Medium Security

Lorain Correctional Institution (LorCI)
2075 S. Avon Belden Rd., Grafton 44044
(440) 748-1049; Fax: (440) 748-2191
Warden: Bennie Kelly
Close Security

Madison Correctional Institution (MaCI)
1851 State Route 56, P.O. Box 740, London 43140-0740
(740) 852-9777; Fax: (740) 852-3666
Warden: Alan Lazaroff
Medium / Close Security

Mansfield Correctional Institution (ManCI)
P.O. Box 788, Mansfield 44901
(419) 525-4455; Fax: (419) 524-8022
Warden: Margaret Bradshaw
Close Security

Marion Correctional Institution (MCI)
940 Marion-Williamsport Rd., P.O. Box 57, Marion 43302
(740) 382-5781; Fax: (740) 387-8736
Warden: Christine M. Money
Minimum / Medium Security

Montgomery Ed. and Pre-Release Center (MEPRC)
P.O. Box 17399, Dayton 45418
(937) 262-9853; Fax: (937) 268-7960
Warden: Bobby Bogan, Jr.
Minimum Security

Noble Correctional Institution (NCI)
15708 State Route 78, P.O. Box 278, Caldwell 43724
(740) 732-5188; Fax: (740) 732-2651
Warden: Jeffrey A. Wolfe
Medium Security

North Central Correctional Institution (NCCI)
670 Marion Williamsport Rd. E., P.O. Box 1812,
Marion 43302
(740) 387-7040; Fax: (740) 387-5575
Warden: Rob Jeffreys
Minimum Security; Privately Operated

**North Coast Correctional Treatment Facility
(NCCTF)**
2000 S. Avon Belden Rd., Grafton 44044
(440) 748-5000; Fax: (440) 748-5010
Warden: Jacqueline Thomas
Minimum Security; Privately Operated

Northeast Pre-Release Center (NEPRC)
2675 E. 30th St., P.O. Box 93943, Cleveland 44115
(216) 771-6460; Fax: (216) 787-3540
Warden: Frank Shewalter
Minimum Security; Women

Oakwood Correctional Facility (OCE)
3200 N. West Rd., Lima 45801
(419) 225-8052; Fax: (419) 225-8000
Warden: Christopher Yanai
Close Security; Men and Women

Ohio Reformatory for Women (ORW)
1479 Collins Ave., Marysville 43040
(937) 642-1065; Fax: (937) 642-7678
Warden: Patricia Andrews
All Security Levels

Ohio State Penitentiary (OSP)
878 Coitsville-Hubbard Rd., Youngstown 44505
(330) 743-0700; Fax: (330) 743-0841
Warden: Marc Houk
Administrative Maximum Security

Pickaway Correctional Institution (PCI)
11781 St. Rt. 762, P.O. Box 209, Orient 43146
(614) 877-4362; Fax: (614) 877-1660
Warden: Jim Erwin
Minimum Security

Richland Correctional Institution (RiCI)
1001 Olivesburg Rd., P.O. Box 8107, Mansfield 44901
(419) 526-2100; Fax: (419) 521-2810
Warden: Julius Wilson
Minimum, Medium and Close Security

Ross Correctional Institution (RCI)
16149 State Route 104, P.O. Box 7010, Chillicothe 45601
(740) 774-7050; Fax: (740) 774-7055
Warden: Pat Hurley
Minimum / Medium Security

Southeastern Correctional Institution (SCI)
5900 B.I.S. Rd., P.O. Box 200, Lancaster 43130
(740) 653-4324; Fax: (740) 653-6155
Warden: Mark Saunders
Medium Security

Southern Ohio Correctional Facility (SOCF)
1724 St. Rt. 728, P.O. Box 45699, Lucasville 45699
(740) 259-5544; Fax: (740) 259-2882
Warden: James Haviland
Maximum Security

Toledo Correctional Institution (ToCI)
2001 E. Central Ave., Toledo 43608
(419) 726-7977; Fax: (419) 726-7157
Warden: Khelleh Konteh
Minimum / Close Security

Trumbull Correctional Institution (TCI)
5701 Burnett Rd., P.O. Box 901, Leavittsburg 44430
(330) 898-0820; Fax: (330) 898-0848
Warden: David Bobby
Close Security

Warren Correctional Institution (WCI)
State Route 63, P.O. Box 120, Lebanon 45036
(513) 932-3388; Fax: (513) 933-0150
Warden: Wanza Jackson
Close Security

OHIO JUVENILE FACILITIES

Circleville Juvenile Correctional Facility
640 Island Rd., Circleville 43113
(740) 477-2500
Superintendent: Damita Perry
State Operated

Cuyahoga Hills Juvenile Correctional Facility
4321 Green Rd., Highland Hills 44128
(216) 464-8200
Superintendent: Ben Bower
State Operated

Freedom Center
8101 Dublin Rd., Delaware 43015
(740) 881-3337
Superintendent: Marci Sutherland
State Operated; Drug and alcohol treatment center

Indian River Juvenile Correctional Facility
1775 Indian River Rd., Massillon 44647
(330) 837-4211
Superintendent: Vacancy at Press Time
State Operated

Marion Juvenile Correctional Facility
332 Marion Williamsport Rd., Marion 43302
(740) 223-2400
Superintendent: Norm Hills
State Operated

Mohican Juvenile Correctional Facility
P.O. Box 150, Loudonville 44842
(419) 994-4127
Superintendent: Martha Spown
State Operated

Ohio River Valley Juvenile Correctional Facility
4696 Gallica Pike, P.O. Box 1000, Franklin Furnace 45629
(740) 354-7000
Superintendent: Aldine Gaspers
State Operated

Paint Creek Youth Center
P.O. Box 455, Bainbridge 45612
(614) 634-3094
Director: John Kelly
State Operated; Private, nonprofit

Scioto Juvenile Correctional Facility
5993 Home Rd., Delaware 43015
(740) 881-3250
Superintendent: Robert Pritchett
State Operated

Allen County Juvenile Justice Center
1000 Wardhill Ave., Lima 45805
(419) 998-5240; Fax: (419) 222-7403
Director: Larry Webb

Ashland County Juvenile Detention Center
1260 S. Center St., Ashland 44805
(419) 289-3988; Fax: (419) 281-8710
Director: Duane Botdorf

Ashtabula County Youth Detention Center
3816 Donohoe Dr., Ashtabula 44004
(440) 992-3390; Fax: (440) 992-7835
Director: Dan Sheldon

Butler County Juvenile Detention Center
280 N. Fair Ave., Hamilton 45011
(513) 887-3865; Fax: (513) 328-2639
Superintendent: Thomas Barnes

Central Ohio Youth Center
18100 State Route #4, Marysville 43040
(937) 642-1015; Fax: (937) 642-5900
Superintendent: Victoria Jordan

Clark County Juvenile Detention Center
101 E. Columbia St., Springfield 45502
(937) 328-2632; Fax: (937) 328-2639
Director: Fred Thomas

Clermont County Juvenile Detention Center
2339 Clermont Center Dr., Batavia 45103
(513) 732-7154; Fax: (513) 732-7695
Superintendent: Tom Del Grande

Cuyahoga County Juvenile Detention Center
2209 Central Ave., Cleveland 44115
(216) 443-3300; Fax: (216) 443-5019
Superintendent: Leonard Munks

Edward J. Ruzzo Juvenile Justice Center
1440 Mt. Vernon Ave., Marion 43302
(740) 389-5476; Fax: (740) 389-2060
Director: Gloria Craig

Erie County Juvenile Detention Center
1319 Tiffin Ave., Sandusky 44870-2038
(419) 627-7611; Fax: (419) 627-6672
Administrator: Lee Millhouse

Franklin County Juvenile Detention Center
399 S. Front St., Columbus 43215
(614) 462-4490; Fax: (614) 462-4838
Superintendent: Andrea Morbitzer

Greene County Juvenile Detention Center
2100 Greeneway Blvd., Xenia 45385
(937) 562-4100; Fax: (937) 562-4118
Director: Gary Neidenthal

Hamilton County Juvenile Detention Center
2020 Auburn Ave., Cincinnati 45219
(513) 946-2644; Fax: (513) 946-2675
Director: Harvey Reed

Jefferson County Juvenile Detention Center
16001 State Route 7, P.O. Box 549, Steubenville 43952
(740) 283-8563; Fax: (740) 283-8653
Director: William M. Ward

Lake County Youth Detention Center
53 E. Erie St., P.O. Box 490, Painesville 44077
(440) 350-3159; Fax: (440) 350-2724
Superintendent: Rich Sivula

Linda Martin Juvenile Attention Center
6807 Non-Pariel Rd., Route 4, Wooster 44691
(330) 264-9050; Fax: (330) 262-9058
Administrator: Leon Horton
Formerly Wayne-Holmes Attention Center

Logan County Juvenile Detention Center
104 S. Madriver St., Bellefontaine 43311
(937) 593-9513; Fax: (937) 292-4069
Administrator: Lt. Andrew J. Smith

Lorain County Juvenile Detention Home
9967 S. Murray Ridge Rd., Elyria 44035
(440) 326-4040; Female Detention Center: (440) 329-3764;
Fax: (440) 329-0811
Director: Lorie Simon

Louis Tobin Attention Center
8363 County Home Rd., Lisbon 44432
(330) 424-9809; Fax: (330) 424-0429
Administrator: Denna Bryant

Lucas County Child Study Institute
1801 Spielbusch Ave., Toledo 43624
(419) 213-6704; Fax: (419) 213-6898
Director: Tony Garrett

Martin P. Joyce Detention Center
300 E. Scott St., Youngstown 44505
(330) 740-2261; Fax: (330) 742-5877
Director: Kevin Douglas

Medina County Juvenile Detention Center
655 Independence Dr., Medina 44256
(330) 764-8408; Fax: (330) 764-8412
Superintendent: Nancy Peteya

Montgomery County Detention Center
303 W. Second St., Dayton 45422
(937) 225-5901; Fax: (937) 946-7270
Director: Jimmie Carter

Muskingum County Detention Center
1860 East Pike, Zanesville 43701
(740) 588-4335; Fax: (740) 588-4354
Superintendent: Daniel B. Kieffer

Northwest Ohio Juvenile Detention Center
3389 County Rd. 24.25, Stryker 43557
(419) 428-2322; Fax: (419) 428-6303
Superintendent: April Cook

Portage-Geauga Detention Center
8000 Infirmary Rd., Ravenna 44266
(330) 297-5233; Fax: (330) 297-1533
Director: Thomas Rehnert

Richland County Attention Center
411 S. Diamond St., Mansfield 44902
(419) 774-6388; Fax: (419) 774-6391
Director: Cindy Hoover

Sandusky County Juvenile Detention Center
2100 Castalia Rd., Fremont 43420
(419) 334-6498; Fax: (419) 334-6505
Director: Dale Mitchell

Sargus Juvenile Detention Center
210 Fox Shannon Rd., Saint Clairsville 43950
(740) 695-9750; Fax: (740) 695-6001
Administrator: Beth Oprisch

Scioto County Juvenile Detention Center
526 5th St., Portsmouth 45662
(740) 351-0931; Fax: (740) 353-0860
Superintendent: Dean Novinger

Seneca County Youth Center
3484 S. Township Rd. 151, Tiffin 44883
(419) 447-7852; Fax: (419) 448-5061
Director: Kurt Baumgartner (Acting)

South Central Ohio Regional Juvenile Detention Center
182 Cattail Rd., Chillicothe 45601
(740) 773-4169; Fax: (740) 773-3714
Superintendent: Michael T. Oyer

Stark Attention Center
815 Faircrest St. S.W., Canton 44706
(330) 484-6471; Fax: (330) 484-8112
Director: Rod Schneider

Summit County Juvenile Detention Services
650 Dan St., Akron 44310
(330) 643-2960, 62; Fax: (330) 643-2987
Superintendent: Dave Bailey

Trumbull County Juvenile Detention Center
220 Main Ave., S.W., Box 1209, Warren 44482
(330) 675-2612; Fax: (330) 675-2619
Director: John Cickelli

Tuscarawas Attention Center
241 University Dr., N.E., New Philadelphia 44663
(330) 339-7775; Fax: (330) 339-1311
Director: Pam Watkins

Warren County Juvenile Justice Center
570 Justice Dr., Lebanon 45036
(513) 695-1617; Fax: (513) 695-1394
Director: Desiree Batsche

West Central Juvenile Detention Center
2044 N. County Rd. 25-A, Troy 45373
(937) 440-5651; Fax: (937) 335-3843
Director: Gregory Simmons

Wood County Juvenile Detention Center
11120 Gypsy Lane Rd., Bowling Green 43402
(419) 352-3554; Fax: (419) 352-6503
Director: Richard Schmidbauer

OHIO PUBLIC DEFENDERS

Counties without agencies listed use court-appointed private counsel only

STATEWIDE

Office of the Public Defender
8 E. Long St., 11th Floor, Columbus 43215
(614) 466-5394, (800) 686-1573
Director: David H. Bodiker; Fax: (614) 644-9972

ADAMS COUNTY

Office of the Public Defender
  Athens County Branch Office
See Athens County

ASHTABULA COUNTY

Ashtabula County Public Defender
4817 State Rd., Suite 202, Ashtabula 44004
(440) 998-2628; Fax: (440) 998-2972
Public Defender: Marie Lane
Non-profit corporation providing public defender services

ATHENS COUNTY

Office of the Public Defender
Athens County Branch Office
80 N. Court St., Athens 45701
(740) 593-6400; Fax: (740) 594-2074;
Toll Free: (800) 383-0533
Public Defender: Mike Westfall
Also serves counties of Adams, Brown, Fayette, Jackson,
Meigs, Pickaway, Pike, Ross

AUGLAIZE COUNTY

Auglaize County Public Defender
119 W. Auglaize St., P.O. Box 180, Wapakoneta 45895
(419) 738-7111; Fax: (419) 739-9389
Public Defender: S. Mark Weller

BELMONT COUNTY

Belmont County Public Defender
100 West Main St., Saint Clairsville 43950
(740) 695-5263; Fax: (740) 695-5639
E-mail: bcpubdef@1st.net
Public Defender: James L. Nichelson

BROWN COUNTY

Office of the Public Defender
  Athens County Branch Office
See Athens County

CARROLL COUNTY

Carroll County Public Defender
See Tuscarawas County

CLARK COUNTY

Clark County Public Defender
50 E. Columbia St., 4th Floor, Springfield 45502
(937) 328-2640; Fax: (937) 328-2715
Public Defender: William N. Merrell

CLERMONT COUNTY

Clermont County Public Defender
10 S. Third St., Batavia 45103
(513) 732-7223; Fax: (513) 732-5382
Director: R. Daniel Hannon

CLINTON COUNTY

Clinton County Public Defender
32 E. Sugartree St., 2nd Floor, Wilmington 45177
(937) 382-1316; Fax: (937) 382-8670
Dir. & Public Defender: Joseph H. Dennis
Asst. Public Defenders:
  Sharon Kornman   Steven N. Szelagiewicz

COLUMBIANA COUNTY

Columbiana County Criminal Defense Co.
248 E. State St., P.O. Box 61, Salem 44460
(330) 337-9578; Fax: (330) 337-1223
Managing Atty.: Frederic E. Naragon
Non-profit corporation providing public defender services

COSHOCTON COUNTY

Coshocton County Public Defender
239 N. 4th St., Coshocton 43812
(740) 623-0800; Fax: (740) 623-0296
Public Defender: Jeffrey A. Mullen

CUYAHOGA COUNTY

Cuyahoga County Public Defender
1200 W. Third St., Cleveland 44113
(216) 443-7223; Fax: (216) 443-3632
Public Defender: Robert L. Tobik

ERIE COUNTY

Erie County Public Defender
220 Columbus Ave., Sandusky 44870
(419) 627-6620; Fax: (419) 627-6633
Public Defender: Jeffrey J. Whitacre

FAYETTE COUNTY

Office of the Public Defender
  Athens County Branch Office
See Athens County

FRANKLIN COUNTY

Franklin County Public Defender
373 S. High St., 12th Floor, Columbus 43215-6302
(614) 462-3194; Fax: (614) 461-6470
Public Defender: Yeura R. Venters

GEAUGA COUNTY

Geauga County Public Defender
211 Main St., Chardon 44024
(440) 285-2222, Ext. 5130; Fax: (440) 286-4136
Public Defender: R. Robert Umholtz

GREENE COUNTY

Greene County Public Defender
90 E. Main St., Xenia 45385
(937) 562-5041; Fax: (937) 562-5671
Public Defender: Arthur L. Sidell III

HAMILTON COUNTY

Hamilton County Public Defender
230 E. Ninth St., 2nd Floor, Cincinnati 45202
(513) 946-3700; Fax: (513) 946-3707
Internet: www.hamilton-co.org/pub_def
Public Defender: Louis F. Strigari

HANCOCK COUNTY

Hancock County Public Defender
316 Dorney Plaza, Findlay 45840
(419) 424-7276; Fax: (419) 424-7274
Chief Public Defender: Michael Galose
Asst. Public Defenders:
  Paul V. Maekask   Kenneth J. Sass
  Aaron J. Ried

HARRISON COUNTY

Harrison County Public Defender
112 N. Main St., P.O. Box 427, Cadiz 43907-0427
(740) 942-2010
Public Defender: C. Adrian Pincola

HURON COUNTY

Huron County Public Defender
16 E. Main St., 2nd Floor, Norwalk 44857
(419) 668-3702; Fax: (419) 668-3703
E-mail: hcpdef@accnorwalk.com
Public Defender: George C. Ford
Please call first, before faxing any documents.

JACKSON COUNTY

Office of the Public Defender
  Athens County Branch Office
See Athens County

KNOX COUNTY

Knox County Public Defender
One Public Sq., Mount Vernon 43050
(740) 393-6734; Fax: (740) 397-6611
Public Defender: Fred E. Mayhew

LAKE COUNTY

Lake County Public Defender
125 E. Erie St., Suite 50, Painesville 44077
(440) 350-3200; Fax: (440) 350-5715, 918-5715
Public Defender: R. Paul LaPlante

LUCAS COUNTY

Toledo Legal Aid Society
Defender Division
55 N. Erie St., Suite 248, Toledo 43624
(419) 244-8351; Fax: (419) 244-4833
Atty.: Henry B. Herschel
Non-profit corporation providing public defender services

MEIGS COUNTY

Office of the Public Defender
  Athens County Branch Office
See Athens County

MIAMI COUNTY

Miami County Public Defender
Courthouse, 215 W. Main St., Troy 45373
(937) 440-3950; Fax: (937) 440-3951
Public Defender: John E. Hemm (Director)

MONROE COUNTY

Monroe County Public Defender
117 N. Main St., Woodsfield 43793
(740) 472-0703; Fax: (740) 472-9190
Public Defender: C. Mark Morrison

MONTGOMERY COUNTY

Montgomery County Public Defender
117 S. Main St., Suite 400, P.O. Box 972, Dayton 45422
(937) 225-4652; Fax: (937) 225-3449
Public Defender: Glen Dewar

PICKAWAY COUNTY

Office of the Public Defender
  Athens County Branch Office
See Athens County

PIKE COUNTY

Office of the Public Defender
  Athens County Branch Office
See Athens County

PORTAGE COUNTY

Portage County Public Defender
209 S. Chestnut St., Suite 400, Ravenna 44266
(330) 297-3665; Fax: (330) 298-2064
E-mail: pcpubdef@portageco.com
Public Defender: Dennis D. Lager

ROSS COUNTY

Office of the Public Defender
Ross County Branch Office
14 S. Paint St., Suite 54, Chillicothe 45601
(740) 772-4772; Fax: (740) 772-4825
Public Defender: Daniel L. Silcott
Asst. Public Defenders:
  Gary D. McCleese   Lori J. Rankin
  Ben A. Rainsberger   John M. Scherff

SHELBY COUNTY

Shelby County Public Defender
108 E. Poplar St., Sidney 45365
(937) 498-1714; Fax: (937) 492-6957
Public Defender: William R. Zimmerman

STARK COUNTY

Stark County Public Defender
200 W. Tuscarawas St., Suite 200, Canton 44702
(330) 451-7200; Fax: (330) 451-7227
Public Defender: Tammi R. Johnson

SUMMIT COUNTY

Legal Defender of Summit County, Ohio Inc.
One Cascade Plaza, Suite 1940, Akron 44308
(330) 434-3461; Fax: (330) 434-3371
Director: Joseph S. Kodish
Non-profit corporation providing public defender services

TRUMBULL COUNTY

Office of the Public Defender
Trumbull County Branch Office
328 Mahoning Ave., Warren 44483
(330) 393-7727; Fax: (330) 393-7076
Director: Jim Lewis

TUSCARAWAS COUNTY

Tuscarawas County Public Defender Office
153 N. Broadway, New Philadelphia 44663
(330) 364-3523; Fax: (330) 364-7616
Public Defender: Gerald A. Latanich

UNION COUNTY

Union County Criminal Defense Lawyers
111 W. Sixth St., Marysville 43040
(937) 644-3144
Director: Perry Parsons
Non-profit corporation providing public defender services

VAN WERT COUNTY

Van Wert County Public Defender Office
124 E. Main St., Van Wert 45891
(419) 238-6621; Fax: (419) 238-4705
Public Defender: Steven L. Diller
Contract service

WASHINGTON COUNTY

Office of the Public Defender
Washington County Branch Office
200 Putnam St., Suite 200, Marietta 45750
(740) 373-1441, (800) 618-6549; Fax: (740) 373-2133
Public Defender: Janet McKim

WAYNE COUNTY

Wayne County Public Defender
113 W. Liberty St., Wooster 44691
(330) 287-5490; Fax: (330) 287-5479
Public Defender: Beverly J. Wire

WOOD COUNTY

Wood County Public Defender
123 N. Summit St., Bowling Green 43402
(419) 354-9244; Fax: (419) 353-9865
Public Defender: Kathleen M. Hamm
  E-mail: wcdefender@co.wood.oh.us

OHIO LAW SCHOOLS

CAPITAL UNIVERSITY LAW SCHOOL
303 E. Broad St., Columbus 43215-3200
(614) 236-6500; Fax: (614) 236-6972
Internet: www.law.capital.edu
Dean: Jack A. Guttenberg (614) 236-6383
Assoc. Dean for Academic Affairs: Athornia Steele
(614) 236-6441
Asst. Dean for Admission and Financial Aid:
Linda Mihely (614) 236-6310
Dir. of Career Services: Mary Ann Willis (614) 236-6887
Dir. of Development and Alumni Relations:
John Strick (614) 236-6603
Dir. of Business Operations: Linda Gorsuch
(614) 236-6426
Dir. of Student and Minority Affairs: Torian L. Lee
(614) 236-6392
Dir. of Graduate & Certificate Programs:
James Hatch (614) 236-6402
Dir. of Law Library: Donald A. Hughes, Jr.
(614) 236-6476

**CASE WESTERN RESERVE UNIVERSITY
SCHOOL OF LAW**
Gund Bldg., 11075 East Blvd., Cleveland 44106-7148
(800) 756-0036; Fax: (216) 368-1042;
Registrar: (216) 368-3280; Registrar Fax: (216) 368-6144;
Admissions: (216) 368-3600
Internet: www.law.case.edu
Dean: Gerald Korngold (216) 368-3283
Assoc. Dean for Student Services: Barbara Andelman
(216) 368-3600
Assoc. Dean for Academic Affairs: Hiram E. Chodosh
(216) 368-1796
Assoc. Dean for Development & Public Affairs:
Sonia Winner (216) 368-4495
Asst. Dean for Career Services: Elizabeth Klusas
(216) 366-6353
Dir. of Student Finances: Tonya Phillips (216) 368-3602
Dir. of Law Library: Kathleen M. Carrick (216) 368-6357

**CLAUDE W. PETTIT COLLEGE OF LAW/
OHIO NORTHERN UNIVERSITY**
525 S. Main St., Ada 45810
(419) 772-2211
Internet: www.law.onu.edu
Dean: David C. Crago (419) 772-2205
E-mail: d-crago@onu.edu
Assoc. Dean for Academic Affairs: John Paul Christoff
(419) 772-2206
Asst. Dean for Administration & Student Services:
Mindi Wells (419) 772-2230
Asst. Dean for Admissions: Linda English
(419) 772-2211
Dir. of Financial Aid: Wendall Schick (419) 772-2272
Dir. of Law, Alumni & Career Services:
Cheryl A. Kitchen (419) 772-2220
Dir., Law Library: Nancy A. Armstrong (419) 772-2692
E-mail: librarian@eugene.onu.edu

**CLEVELAND-MARSHALL COLLEGE OF
LAW/CLEVELAND STATE UNIVERSITY**
2121 Euclid Ave., LB 138, Cleveland 44115-2214
Reception: (216) 687-2344; Fax: (216) 687-6881
Internet: www.law.csuohio.edu;
www.law.csuohio.edu/lawlibrary
Dean: Steven H. Steinglass (216) 687-2300
Assoc. Deans:
Linda Ammons (216) 687-2300
Lloyd Snyder (216) 687-3889
Asst. Dean: Jean B. Lifter (216) 687-4557
Asst. Dean, Student Affairs: Gary Williams
(216) 687-2297
Asst. Dean, Admissions: Melody Stewart (216) 687-2344

Asst. Dean, External Affairs: Louise Dempsey
(216) 687-2300
Exec. Dir., Law Alumni Assn.: Mary McKenna
(216) 687-2368
Dir., Career Planning: Jayne Geneva (216) 687-2540
Assoc. Dean & Dir. of Law Library: Michael J. Slinger
(216) 687-2250; Fax: (216) 687-5098

**MORITZ COLLEGE OF LAW/
OHIO STATE UNIVERSITY**
55 W. 12th Ave., Columbus 43210-1391
(614) 292-2631; Law Library: (614) 292-3987;
Fax: (614) 292-1383
E-mail: moritzlaw@osu.edu
Internet: www.moritzlaw.osu.edu
Dean: Nancy Hardin Rogers
Assoc. Dean for Academic & Student Affairs:
Kathy Northern (614) 292-7750
Assoc. Dean for Information Svces.: Bruce Johnson
(614) 292-2964
Asst. Dean for Admissions & Financial Aid:
Robert Solomon II (614) 292-5354
Asst. Dean for Alumni Affairs: Pamela H. Lombardi
(614) 292-8809
Asst. Dean for Professional Development:
Amee McKim (614) 292-8814
Dir. of Communications: Liz Cutler Gates
(614) 292-0283

UNIVERSITY OF AKRON SCHOOL OF LAW
150 University Ave., Akron 44325-2901
(330) 972-7331; Fax: (330) 258-2343
Internet: www.uakron.edu/law
Dean: Richard Aynes; E-mail: raynes@uakron.edu
Assoc. Dean: Elizabeth Reilly; E-mail: reilly@ukron.edu
Asst. Dean for Student Affairs: Lauri File (Acting)
E-mail: lfile@uakron.edu
Asst. Dean, Finance & Administration:
Rosemary Cannon (330) 972-6366
E-mail: rcannon@uakron.edu
Asst. Dean, Law Admissions & Financial Aid:
Lauri File; E-mail: lfile@uakron.edu
Asst. Dean, External Law Program: William Rickett
E-mail: wrickett@uakron.edu
Dir., Career Planning & Placement: Jay Levine
E-mail: jay10@uakron.edu
Dir., Law Library: Paul Richert (330) 972-7330
E-mail: richert@uakron.edu

UNIVERSITY OF CINCINNATI COLLEGE OF LAW
Clifton Ave. & Calhoun St., P.O. Box 210040,
Cincinnati 45221-0040
(513) 556-6805; Fax: (513) 556-2391
Internet: www.law.uc.edu
Dean: Donna M. Nagy (Acting) (513) 556-0113
E-mail: donna.nagy@uc.edu
Assoc. Dean, Curriculum & Student Affairs:
Barb Watts (513) 556-0065; E-mail: barb.watts@uc.edu
Asst. Dean, Admissions & Financial Aid: Al Watson
(513) 556-0077; E-mail: alfred.watson@uc.edu
**Asst. Dean & Dir. of the Center for Professional
Development:** Mina Jones Jefferson (513) 556-6810
E-mail: mina.jefferson@uc.edu
Dir., Development: Michael Volan (513) 556-0066
E-mail: mike.volan@uc.edu
Asst. Dir., Alumni & Development: Lauren Scharf
(513) 556-0071; E-mail: lauren.scharf@uc.edu
Dir., Law Library & Information Technology:
Virginia C. Thomas (513) 556-0159
E-mail: virginia.thomas@uc.edu

UNIVERSITY OF DAYTON SCHOOL OF LAW
300 College Park, Dayton 45469-2760
(937) 229-3211; Fax: (937) 229-4194
Internet: www.law.udayton.edu

Dean: Lisa Kloppenberg (937) 229-3795

Assoc. Dean, Academic Affairs: Kelvin H. Dickinson
(937) 229-3794

Assoc. Dean, Student Affairs: Lori Shaw (937) 229-3794

Asst. Dean, Admissions & Financial Aid: Janet Hein
(937) 229-3555

Asst. Dean, External Affairs: Timothy Stonecash
(937) 229-3793

Dir., Career Services: Timothy Swensen (937) 229-3215

Dir., Law Library: Thomas Hanley (937) 229-2444

UNIVERSITY OF TOLEDO COLLEGE OF LAW
2801 W. Bancroft St., Toledo 43606-3390
(419) 530-4131
Internet: www.utlaw.edu
Dean: Phillip J. Closius
(419) 530-2379; Fax: (419) 530-4526
E-mail: phillip.closius@utoledo.edu
Assoc. Dean for Academic Affairs: Beth A. Eisler
(419) 530-2937; Fax: (419) 530-4526
E-mail: beisler@utnet.utoledo.edu
Asst. Dean for Law Admissions: Carol E. Frendt
(419) 530-4131; Fax: (419) 530-4345
Dir., Alumni & Communication: Linda Packo
(419) 530-2712
Asst. Dean, Law Career Services: Heather Karns
(419) 530-2851
Asst. Dir., Financial Aid: Beth Solo (419) 530-7929
Dir., Law Library: Donald A. Arndt, Jr. (Acting)
(419) 530-2945

OHIO HOSPITALS

Note: Pursuant to Revised Code § 3701.741, the maximum fees for copies of hospital records are:
•Search fee of no more than $15.00 per patient per request; plus
•$1.00 per page for the first ten pages; $.50 per page exceeding Page 10; $.20 per page exceeding Page 51; plus
•Actual mailing costs.
•Many of the hospitals listed below charge the maximum statutory fee, as listed here.

AKRON   **Summit County**

Akron Children's Hospital
One Perkins Sq., Akron 44308
(330) 543-1000; Fax: (330) 543-3008
Internet: www.akronchildrens.org
C.E.O.: William Considine
General Counsel: Shawn Lyden
Records Administrator: Nancy Gloyd
Fee for Copy of Records: See statutory fee, *supra*
Formerly Children's Hospital Medical Center of Akron

Akron City Hospital
Summa Health System
525 E. Market St., P.O. Box 2090, Akron 44304
(330) 375-3000; Medical Records: (330) 375-3930
C.E.O.: Thomas J. Strauss
President/C.O.O.: Robert Harrigan
V.P./General Counsel: William A. Powel III
Records Administrator: Diane Kramanak
     (330) 375-4997
Fee for Copy of Records: See statutory fee, *supra*

Akron General Medical Center
400 Wabash Ave., Akron 44307
(330) 344-6000; Medical Records: (330) 344-6320
Medical Records E-mail: medrec@agmc.org
Internet: www.agmc.org
President/C.E.O.: Alan J. Bleyer
Senior V.P., Legal Affairs: Daniel P. Cunningham
Fee for Copy of Records: See statutory fee, *supra*
Affiliate of Akron General Health System

Edwin Shaw Hospital for Rehabilitation
1621 Flickinger Rd., Akron 44312
(330) 784-1271; Fax: (330) 784-1968
Internet: www.edwinshaw.com
President/C.E.O.: Sue Gill (Acting), Ext. 5201

St. Thomas Hospital
Summa Health System
444 N. Main St., P.O. Box 2090, Akron 44310
(330) 375-3000; Medical Records: (330) 379-5171
C.E.O.: Thomas J. Strauss (Summa Health System)
President/C.O.O.: Robert Harrigan
V.P., Legal Services: William A. Powel III
Records Administrator: Diane Kramanak
Fee for Copy of Records: See statutory fee, *supra*

Select Specialty Hospital of Akron
400 Wabash Ave., Akron 44307
(330) 344-6910
C.E.O.: Patricia Mahovich
Records Administrator: Ila Snyder
Fee for Copy of Records: See statutory fee, *supra*
Located within Riverside Methodist Hospital

Sempercare Hospital of Akron
525 E. Market St., Akron 44309
(330) 375-6500; Fax: (330) 375-4218
C.E.O.: Vacancy at Press Time
Fee for Copy of Records: Contact Medical Records Coordinator
Affiliate of Summa Health System

ALLIANCE   **Stark County**

Alliance Community Hospital
264 E. Rice St., Alliance 44601
(330) 829-4000; Medical Records: (330) 829-4153
Internet: www.achosp.org
C.E.O.: Stanley W. Jonas
Fee for Copy of Records: See statutory fee, *supra*

AMHERST   **Lorain County**

The Hospital for Orthopaedic and Specialty Services
254 Cleveland Ave., Amherst 44001
(440) 988-6000; Medical Records: (440) 988-6157
Internet: www.emh-healthcare.org
President/C.E.O.: Kevin Martin
     (EMH Regional Healthcare System)
Fee for Copy of Records: See statutory fee, *supra*
Affiliate of EMH Regional Healthcare System; Formerly Amherst Hospital

ARCHBOLD   **Fulton County**

Archbold Hospital & Medical Center
Community Hospitals of Williams County
121 Westfield Dr., Archbold 43502
(419) 445-4415; Chart Analysis: (419) 636-1131, Ext. 1155
Internet: www.chwchospital.com
President/C.E.O.: Rusty O. Brunicardi
Records Administrator: Teresa Monroe
     433 W. High St., Bryan 43506-1679
Supervisor, Chart Analysis: Natasha Eicher
Fee for Copy of Records: See statutory fee, *supra*

ASHLAND   **Ashland County**

Samaritan Hospital
1025 Center St., Ashland 44805
(419) 289-0491, (800) 257-9917;
Health Information Mgmt.: (419) 289-0491
Internet: www.samaritanhospital.org
President/C.E.O.: Danny L. Boggs
Dir., Health Information Mgmt.: Emma Shoemaker
Fee for Copy of Records: See statutory fee, *supra*

ASHTABULA   **Ashtabula County**

Ashtabula County Medical Center
2420 Lake Ave., Ashtabula 44004
(440) 997-2262; Fax: (440) 997-6644
E-mail: info@acmchealth.org
Internet: www.acmchealth.org
President/C.E.O.: Kevin Miller
Fee for Copy of Records: See statutory fee, *supra*
Affiliate of Cleveland Clinic Health System

ATHENS   **Athens County**

O'Bleness Memorial Hospital
55 Hospital Dr., Athens 45701
(740) 593-5551; Administration: (740) 592-9292;
Medical Records: (740) 592-9388
Internet: www.obleness.org
President: Richard F. Castrop
Records Administrator: Tammy Johnson
Fee for Copy of Records: See statutory fee, *supra*

BARBERTON   Summit County

Barberton Citizens Hospital
155 Fifth St., N.E., Barberton 44203
(330) 745-1611; Fax: (330) 848-7820;
Health Information Svces.: (330) 848-7760;
Health Information Svces. Fax: (330) 745-8533
Internet: www.barbertonhospital.com
C.E.O.: Willard Roderick
Dir., Health Information Svces.: Elizabeth Gash
Fee for Copy of Records: See statutory fee, *supra*
Affiliate of Triad Corporation

BARNESVILLE   Belmont County

Barnesville Hospital Assoc., Inc.
639 W. Main St., Barnesville 43713
(740) 425-3941; Administration: (740) 425-5101
Internet: www.barnesvillehospital.com
C.E.O.: Richard Doan
Records Administrator: Tiffany Gramby
Fee for Copy of Records: See statutory fee, *supra*

BATAVIA   Clermont County

Mercy Hospital Clermont
3000 Hospital Dr., Batavia 45103
(513) 732-8200
Internet: www.e-mercy.com
C.E.O.: Mark Shugarman
Mgr., Public Relations: Debbie Copeland-Bloom
   (513) 981-6312; Fax: (513) 981-6102
Affiliate of Catholic Healthcare Partners and Mercy Health Partners

BEACHWOOD   Cuyahoga County

Glenbeigh Outpatient Center of Beachwood
3789 B S. Green Rd., Beachwood 44122
(216) 464-5800; Fax: (216) 464-1840
E-mail: beachwood@gleinbeigh.com
Exec. Dir.: Patricia Weston-Hall
Fee for Copy of Records: $.50 per page
A chemical dependency treatment center

BEDFORD   Cuyahoga County

UHHS—Bedford Medical Center
44 Blaine Ave., Bedford 44146
(440) 735-3900; Medical Records: (440) 735-3572
Internet: www.uhhs.com
President: Sean McKibben
Fee for Copy of Records: See statutory fee, *supra*
Affiliate of University Hospitals Health System

BELLAIRE   Belmont County

Belmont Community Hospital
4697 Harrison St., Bellaire 43906
(740) 671-1200; Medical Records: (740) 671-1243
C.E.O.: Gary R. Gould
Fee for Copy of Records: See statutory fee, *supra*
Affiliate of Wheeling Hospital

BELLEFONTAINE   Logan County

Mary Rutan Hospital
205 Palmer Ave., Bellefontaine 43311
(937) 592-4015; Medical Records: Ext. 4231
Internet: www.maryrutan.org
President/C.E.O.: Mandy Goble
Dir., Public Relations: Tammy Allison
   (937) 599-7003
      E-mail: tallison@maryrutan.org
Fee for Copy of Records: Contact Medical Records Dept. for fees

BELLEVUE   Huron County

Bellevue Hospital
811 Northwest St., Bellevue 44811
(419) 483-4040; T.D.D.: (419) 483-0400;
Fax: (419) 483-9718
Internet: www.bellevuehospital.com
C.E.O.: Mike Winthrop, Ext. 4200
Mgr., Health Information Svces.: Marianne Schoen
   Ext. 4264
Fee for Copy of Records: See statutory fee, *supra*

BLUFFTON   Allen County

Blanchard Valley Regional Health Center
Bluffton Campus
139 Garau St., Bluffton 45817
(419) 358-9010
Internet: www.bvha.org
C.E.O.: Scott Malaney (419) 423-5201
Risk Mgr.: Lori Curry (419) 423-5454
Fee for Copy of Records: Contact Medical Records Dept.

BOWLING GREEN   Wood County

Wood County Hospital
950 W. Wooster St., Bowling Green 43402
(419) 354-8900; Fax: (419) 354-8957;
Administration: (419) 354-8930;
Health Information Mgmt. (Medical Records):
(419) 354-8934
E-mail: woodhosp@wch.net
President/C.E.O.: Stanley Korducki
Records Administrator: Lin Cox
Fee for Copy of Records: See statutory fee, *supra*

BRYAN   Williams County

Community Hospital & Wellness Centers—Bryan
433 W. High St., Bryan 43506
(419) 636-1131; Chart Analysis (Medical Records): Ext. 1155
Internet: www.chwchospital.com
President: Rusty O. Brunicardi
Mgr., Medical Records: Teresa Monroe
Supervisor, Chart Analysis: Natasha Eicher
   (Medical Records)
Fee for Copy of Records: See statutory fee, *supra*

BUCYRUS   Crawford County

Bucyrus Community Hospital
629 N. Sandusky Ave., Bucyrus 44820 (419) 562-4677
Internet: www.bchonline.org
President/C.E.O.: Gerard Klein
Mgr., Health Information Svces.: Joanne Beasley
   (419) 563-9347
Fee for Copy of Records: See statutory fee, *supra*

CADIZ   Harrison County

Harrison Community Hospital
951 E. Market St., Cadiz 43907
(740) 942-4631; Fax: (740) 942-2749; Administration: Ext. 206
E-mail: hchosp@1st.net
Internet: www.harrisoncommunity.com
C.E.O.: Terry M. Carson
Fee for Copy of Records: See statutory fee, *supra*

CAMBRIDGE   Guernsey County

Southeastern Ohio Regional Medical Center
1341 Clark St., Cambridge 43725
(740) 439-8000; Fax: (740) 439-8658;
Administration: (740) 439-8112
Internet: www.seormc.org
President/C.E.O.: James W. Keller, M.D. (740) 439-8111
Records Administrator: Dan Cohen (740) 439-8655
Fee for Copy of Records: Contact ChartOne representative in the Medical Records Dept.

CANTON   Stark County

Aultman Hospital and Health Foundation
2600 Sixth St., S.W., Canton 44710
(330) 452-9911; Fax: (330) 438-6356
Internet: www.aultman.com
President/C.E.O.: Edward J. Roth III
V.P., Legal Affairs: Mark N. Rose, M.D., J.D.
    (330) 363-7463; Fax: (330) 580-5549
Fee for Copy of Records: See statutory fee, *supra*

Mercy Medical Center
1320 Mercy Dr., N.W., Canton 44708
(330) 489-1000;
Health Information Mgmt. (Medical Records):
(330) 489-1230;
Health Information Mgmt. Fax: (330) 489-1241
Internet: www.thequalityhospital.com
C.E.O.: Thomas E. Cecconi
Legal Officer: Ronald Bennington
Fee for Copy of Records: See statutory fee, *supra*
*Partnered with University Hospitals and the Sisters of
Charity of St. Augustine Health Systems*

CHAGRIN FALLS   Cuyahoga County

Windsor Hospital
115 E. Summit St., Chagrin Falls 44022
(440) 247-5300; Fax: (440) 247-6648
Internet: www.ardenthealth.com
C.E.O.: Richard W. Warden
Affiliate of Ardent Health Services

CHARDON   Geauga County

UHHS—Geauga Regional Hospital
13207 Ravenna Rd., Chardon 44024
(440) 285-6000; Fax: (440) 286-7219;
Health Information Svces.: (440) 285-6373
E-mail: info@uhhsgrh.com
Internet: www.uhhsgrh.com
President: Richard J. Frenchie
Dir., Health Information Svces.: Julie Novak
Fee for Copy of Records: See statutory fee, *supra*
Affiliate of University Hospitals Health System

UHHS—Heather Hill Hospital and Health Partnership
12340 Bass Lake Rd., Chardon 44024
(440) 285-4040;
Health Information Mgmt. Fax: (440) 279-2501
E-mail: info@heatherhill.org
Internet: www.heatherhill.org
President/C.E.O.: Richard J. Frenchie
Dir., Health Information Mgmt.: Laura Corbo
Fee for Copy of Records: See statutory fee, *supra*
Affiliate of University Hospitals Health System

CHILLICOTHE   Ross County

Adena Regional Medical Center
272 Hospital Rd., Chillicothe 45601
(740) 779-7500, (877) 779-7585
Internet: www.adena.org
President/C.E.O.: Allen V. Rupiper (740) 779-7778
Fee for Copy of Records: See statutory fee, *supra*
Member of Adena Health System

CINCINNATI   Hamilton County

Bethesda North Hospital
10500 Montgomery Rd., Cincinnati 45242-9508
(513) 745-1111; Fax: (513) 745-1136;
Medical Records: (513) 745-1101
Internet: www.trihealth.com
President/C.E.O., TriHealth: John Prout (513) 569-6509
V.P./C.O.O.: Sher McClanahan
Fee for Copy of Records: See statutory fee, *supra*
Affiliate of TriHealth

Christ Hospital
2139 Auburn Ave., Cincinnati 45219
(513) 585-2000; Fax: (513) 585-3200;
Administration: (513) 585-1139;
Medical Records: (513) 585-2514
Internet: www.christhospitalcincinnati.com
Senior V.P.: Susan Croushore
Fee for Copy of Records: See statutory fee, *supra*
Affiliate of Health Alliance of Greater Cincinnati

Cincinnati Children's Hospital Medical Center
3333 Burnet Ave., Cincinnati 45229-3039
(513) 636-4200, (800) 344-2462; Fax: (513) 636-7194;
Medical Records Fax: (513) 636-1086
Internet: www.cincinnatichildrens.org
President/C.E.O.: James M. Anderson (513) 636-4000
Fee for Copy of Records: Contact SourceCorp HealthSERVE
representative in the Health Information Mgmt. Dept.;
microfilm/microfiche/CD copies, $1.50 per page

Deaconess Hospital
311 Straight St., Cincinnati 45219
(513) 559-2100; Fax: (513) 475-5251;
Medical Records: (513) 559-2208
President/C.E.O.: Bryan Burklow
General Counsel: Thomas Anthony (513) 559-2190
Records Administrator: Nancy Wilson (513) 559-2265
Fee for Copy of Records: Contact Smart Corporation
representative in the Medical Records Dept.

Drake Center, Inc.
151 W. Galbraith Rd., Cincinnati 45216-1096
(513) 948-2500; Fax: (513) 948-2501
Internet: www.drakecenter.com
President/C.E.O.: Roberta J. Bradford
Fee for Copy of Records: See statutory fee, *supra*
Long-term Care Facility

Good Samaritan Hospital
375 Dixmyth Ave., Cincinnati 45220-2489
(513) 872-1400; Fax: (513) 872-1190;
Medical Records: (513) 872-2628
President/C.E.O., TriHealth: John Prout (513) 569-6141
V.P./C.O.O.: David Dornheggen (513) 872-2601
Fee for Copy of Records: Contact Smart Corporation
representative in the Medical Records Dept.
Affiliate of TriHealth

Jewish Hospital
4777 E. Galbraith Rd., Cincinnati 45236-2891
(513) 686-3000; Fax: (513) 686-3003;
Medical Records: (513) 686-3190
Internet: www.health-alliance.com/Jewish.html
Senior V.P.: M. Aurora Lambert
Fee for Copy of Records: See statutory fee, *supra*
Affiliate of HealthAlliance of Greater Cincinnati

Mercy Franciscan Hospital Western Hills
3131 Queen City Ave., Cincinnati 45238
(513) 389-5000; Medical Records: (513) 389-5130
Internet: www.e-mercy.com
President/C.E.O.: James C. Patrick
Mgr., Public Relations: Aaron Bley
    (513) 389-5745; Fax: (513) 389-9141
    E-mail: aabley@health-partners.org
Fee for Copy of Records: Contact SourceCorp HealthSERVE
representative in the Medical Records Dept.
*Affiliate of Catholic Healthcare Partners and Mercy Health
Partners*

Cincinnati—Cont'd

Mercy Hospital Anderson
7500 State Rd., Cincinnati 45255
(513) 624-4500; Medical Records: (513) 624-4073
Internet: www.e-mercy.com
President: Patricia Schroer (513) 624-4501
Mgr., Public Relations: Debbie Copeland-Bloom
   (513) 981-6312; Fax: (513) 981-6102
   E-mail: ddcopeland-bloom@health-partners.org
Fee for Copy of Records: See statutory fee, *supra*
Affiliate of Catholic Healthcare Partners and Mercy Health Partners

Mercy Hospital Mt. Airy
2446 Kipling Ave., Cincinnati 45239
(513) 853-5000
Internet: www.e-mercy.com
President: Rodney Reider (513) 853-5774
Mgr., Public Relations: Brandie Whitmer
   (513) 853-5803; Fax: (513) 853-5910
   E-mail: bswhitmer@health-partners.org
Fee for Copy of Records: Contact SourceCorp HealthSERVE representative in the Medical Records Dept.
Affiliate of Catholic Healthcare Partners and Mercy Health Partners

Select Specialty Hospital—Cincinnati
375 Dixmyth Ave., Cincinnati 45220
(513) 487-4100; Fax: (513) 872-3435
Administrator/C.E.O.: John Baird, M.B.A.
Fee for Copy of Records: Contact Medical Records Dept.
Long-term Acute Care Facility; affiliate of Select Medical Corp.

Shriners Hospitals for Children
3229 Burnet Ave., Cincinnati 45229-3095 (513) 636-4200
Internet: www.shrinershq.org/shc/cincinnati
Administrator: Ronald R. Hitzler
Records Administrator: Linda Miller (513) 872-6035
Fee for Copy of Records: See statutory fee, *supra*

The University Hospital
234 Goodman St., Cincinnati 45219
(513) 584-1000; Administration: (513) 584-3000;
Fax: (513) 584-3755; Medical Records: (513) 584-0141
Internet: www.healthalliance.com/University.html
Exec. Dir.: James Kingsbury
Fee for Copy of Records: See statutory fee, *supra*
Affiliate of Health Alliance

CIRCLEVILLE   Pickaway County

Berger Hospital
600 N. Pickaway St., Circleville 43113
(740) 474-2126; Administration: (740) 420-8231;
Medical Records: (740) 420-8237
Internet: www.bergerhealth.com
C.E.O.: Larry W. Thornhill
Records Administrator: Lori Martin
Fee for Copy of Records: Contact Medical Records Dept.

CLEVELAND   Cuyahoga County

Cleveland Clinic Children's Hospital for Rehabilitation
2801 Martin Luther King Jr. Dr., Cleveland 44104
(216) 721-5400; Fax: (216) 791-1012
President: Vacancy at Press Time
Records Administrator: Gayla Sirmons, R.H.I.T.,C.M.C.
Fee for Copy of Records: See statutory fee, *supra*
Affiliate of the Cleveland Clinic Health System

Cleveland Clinic Foundation
9500 Euclid Ave., Cleveland 44195
(216) 444-2200; Toll-free: (800) 223-2273
Internet: www.clevelandclinic.org
C.E.O.: Delos M. Cosgrove, M.D.
C.O.O.: Frank L. Lordeman
Dir., Health Data Svces.: Erica Foster (Medical Records)
Fee for Copy of Records: See statutory fee, *supra*
Affiliate of the Cleveland Clinic Health System

Deaconess Hospital
4229 Pearl Rd., Cleveland 44109
*Hospital closed November 28, 2003,
please contact (216) 459-6300 for more information.*

Euclid Hospital
18901 Lake Shore Blvd., Cleveland 44119
(216) 531-9000;
Health Information Svces. (Medical Records): (216) 692-8670
Internet: www.euclidhospital.org
C.A.O.: Lauren Rock
Dir., Health Information Svces.: Donna Misch
Fee for Copy of Records: See statutory fee, *supra*
Member of the Cleveland Clinic Health System

Fairview Hospital
18101 Lorain Ave., Cleveland 44111
(216) 476-7000; Fax: (216) 227-2621
Internet: www.fairviewhospital.org
C.E.O.: Fred M. DeGrandis
C.A.O.: Jeffrey A. Leimgruber
Fee for Copy of Records: See statutory fee, *supra*
Member of Cleveland Clinic Health System

Grace Hospital
2307 W. 14th St., Cleveland 44113
(216) 687-1500; Administration Fax: (216) 687-4090;
Medical Records: (216) 476-2802
C.E.O.: Robert Range
Records Administrator: Heather Pesarchick
Fee for Copy of Records: See statutory fee, *supra*;
microfilm, additional $1.50 per page
Affiliate of Cleveland Clinic Health System

Huron Hospital
13951 Terrace Rd., Cleveland 44112
(216) 761-3300; Health Information Svces.: (216) 761-7992
Internet: www.huronhospital.org
C.A.O.: Michael Trainer (Acting)
Dir., Health Information Svces.: Donna Misch
Fee for Copy of Records: See statutory fee, *supra*
Member of Cleveland Clinic Health System

Kindred Hospital—Cleveland
2351 E. 22nd St., 7th Floor, Cleveland 44115
(216) 592-2830; Fax: (216) 592-2831
Internet: www.kindredcleveland.com
C.E.O.: Rick Pletz (216) 592-2834
Fee for Copy of Records: See statutory fee, *supra*
Affiliate of Kindred Health System; located within St. Vincent Charity Hospital

Lutheran Hospital
1730 W. 25th St., Cleveland 44113
(216) 696-4300; Medical Records: (216) 363-2195
Internet: www.lutheranhospital.org
C.E.O.: Fred DeGrandis
   (Cleveland Clinic Health System—Western Region)
C.A.O.: Steven Ruwoldt
Fee for Copy of Records: See statutory fee, *supra*
Affiliate of Cleveland Clinic Health System

Marymount Hospital
12300 McCracken Rd., Cleveland 44125
(216) 581-0500; Medical Records: (216) 587-8222
Internet: www.marymount.org
President/C.E.O.: David J. Kilarski
Fee for Copy of Records: See statutory fee, *supra*
Affiliate of the Cleveland Clinic Health System

MetroHealth Medical Center
2500 Metrohealth Dr., Cleveland 44109
(216) 778-7800; Health Information Mgmt.: (216) 778-4252
Internet: www.metrohealth.org
C.E.O.: John F. Sideras
Dir., Health Information Mgmt.: Susan Pemberton
Fee for Copy of Records: See statutory fee, *supra*
Affiliate of MetroHealth System

Cleveland—Cont'd

St. Vincent Charity Hospital
2351 E. 22nd St., Cleveland 44115
(216) 861-6200; Fax: (216) 363-2796
Internet: www.svch.net
President: Jeffrey S. Janey
Records Administrator: Erin Lamb
Fee for Copy of Records: See statutory fee, *supra*
Affiliate of University Hospitals Health System and CSA Health System

Southwest General Health Center
18697 Bagley Rd., Cleveland 44130 (440) 816-8000
Internet: www.swgeneral.com
President/C.E.O.: L. Jon Schurmeier
V.P./Chief Legal Officer: Susan O. Scheutzow
Assoc. Dir., Health Information Svces.: Kathy Koch
Fee for Copy of Records: See statutory fee, *supra*
Affiliate of University Hospitals Health System

UHHS—St. Michael Hospital
5163 Broadway Ave., Cleveland 44127
Fee for Copy of Records: See statutory fee, *supra*
Hospital closed December 19, 2003. Please contact University Hospitals Health System at (216) 844-3825

University Hospitals of Cleveland
11100 Euclid Ave., Cleveland 44106
(216) 844-1000;
Health Information Mgmt. (Medical Records): (216) 844-3554
Internet: www.uhhs.com
President/C.E.O.: Fred C. Rothstein, M.D.
Fee for Copy of Records: See statutory fee, *supra*
Partnered with University Hospitals Health System

COLDWATER   Mercer County

Mercer County Community Hospital
800 W. Main St., Coldwater 45828
(419) 678-2341; T.D.D.: (419) 678-5677;
Administration: (419) 678-5104;
Administration Fax: (419) 678-3271
E-mail: info@mercerhospital.com
Internet: www.mercerhospital.com
C.E.O.: Terrance J. Padden
Records Administrator: Deb Grieshop (419) 678-5114
Fee for Copy of Records: See statutory fee, *supra*

COLUMBUS   Franklin County

Arthur G. James Cancer Hospital & Richard L. Solve Research Institute
300 W. 10th Ave., Columbus 43210
(614) 293-5066; Administration: (614) 293-4878
Internet: www.jamesline.com
C.E.O.: Dr. David Shuller
Dir., Medical Information Svces.: Elizabeth Curtis
Fee for Copy of Records: See statutory fee, *supra*
Affiliate of the Ohio State University Medical Center

Children's Hospital Inc.
700 Children's Dr., Columbus 43205
(614) 722-2000; Health Information Mgmt.: (614) 722-3658
Internet: www.childrenscolumbus.org
C.E.O.: Thomas N. Hansen, M.D.
Dir., Health Information Mgmt.: Jill Choi
Fee for Copy of Records: See statutory fee, *supra*

Doctors Hospital
5100 W. Broad St., Columbus 43228
(614) 297-4000; Health Information Mgmt.: (614) 544-5779
Internet: www.doctorshospital.org
President: Kreg Gruber (614) 429-6030
Dir., Health Information Mgmt.: Sandy Shelton
Fee for Copy of Records: See statutory fee, *supra*
Affiliate of OhioHealth

Grant Medical Center
111 S. Grant Ave., Columbus 43215
(614) 566-9000; Health Information Mgmt.: (614) 566-5444
Internet: www.ohiohealth.com
President: Robert Falcone, M.D. (614) 566-9978
Fee for Copy of Records: See statutory fee, *supra*
Affiliate of OhioHealth

Mount Carmel East
6001 E. Broad St., Columbus 43213
(614) 234-6000; Health Information Mgmt.: (614) 898-4075
Internet: www.mountcarmelhealth.com
President/C.E.O.: Joseph Calvaruso
Fee for Copy of Records: Contact ChartOne representative in the Medical Records Dept.
Member of Trinity Health

Mount Carmel West
793 W. State St., Columbus 43222 (614) 234-5000
Internet: www.mountcarmelhealth.com
President/C.E.O.: Joseph Calvaruso
Fee for Copy of Records: See statutory fee, *supra*
Affiliate of Trinity Health

Ohio State University Hospital—East
1492 E. Broad St., Columbus 43205
(614) 257-3700; Administration: (614) 257-3100;
Administration Fax: (614) 257-3439;
Medical Information Mgmt.: (614) 257-2544;
Medical Information Fax: (614) 257-2545
Internet: www.medicalcenter.osu.edu
C.E.O.: Peter E. Geier (Acting)
Exec. Dir.: Karen Mlawsky
Administrative Dir., Talbot Hall & Legal Svces.: Dennis Ehrie
Dir., Medical Information Mgmt.: Elizabeth Curtis
Fee for Copy of Records: See statutory fee, *supra*

Ohio State University Hospital
410 W. 10th Ave., Columbus 43210
(614) 293-8000; Medical Information Mgmt.: (614) 293-8657
Internet: www.medicalcenter.osu.edu
C.E.O.: Peter E. Geier (Acting)
C.O.O.: Kamilla Sigafoos
Dir., Medical Information Mgmt.: Elizabeth Curtis
Fee for Copy of Records: See statutory fee, *supra*

Riverside Methodist Hospital
3535 Olentangy River Rd., Columbus 43214
(614) 566-5000; Medical Records: (614) 566-5444
Internet: www.ohiohealth.com
President/C.E.O.: David Blom (OhioHealth) (614) 544-5430
President: Bruce Hagen (614) 566-3602
Dir., Medical Records Svces.: Diane Setty
Fee for Copy of Records: Contact ChartOne representative in the Medical Records Dept.
Affiliate of OhioHealth

Select Specialty Hospital—Columbus
1492 E. Broad St., Tower 8, Columbus 43205
(614) 252-4440; Medical Records: Ext. 158
C.E.O.: Albert Wright
Fee for Copy of Records: See statutory fee, *supra*
Located within University Hospital—East

Select Specialty Hospital at Ohio State University (OSU)
Doan Hall, 11th Floor, 410 W. 10th Ave., Columbus 43210
(614) 293-6960;
Health Information Svces. (Medical Records): (614) 293-6942
Fee for Copy of Records: Contact Health Information Mgmt. for fee information

Select Specialty Hospital at Riverside
3535 Olentangy River Rd., Columbus 43214
(614) 566-5451
C.E.O.: Terry Mayberry
Fee for Copy of Records: See statutory fee, *supra*

CONNEAUT   Ashtabula County

UHHS—Brown Memorial Hospital
158 W. Main Rd., Conneaut 44030
(440) 593-1131; Administration: (440) 593-0272
President/C.E.O.: Thomas F. Zenty III
   (University Hospitals Health System)
President: William P. Lawrence
Coordinator, Health Information Mgmt.:
   Patricia Kenney (Medical Records) (440) 593-0250
Fee for Copy of Records: See statutory fee, *supra*
Affiliate of University Hospitals Health System

COSHOCTON   Coshocton County

Coshocton County Memorial Hospital
1460 Orange St., Coshocton 43812
(740) 622-6411; Medical Records: (740) 623-4121;
Medical Records Fax: (740) 623-4146
Internet: www.ccmh.com
C.E.O./Administrator: Gregory Nowak
Records Administrator: Karen Erman
Fee for Copy of Records: See statutory fee, *supra*

CUYAHOGA FALLS   Summit County

Cuyahoga Falls General Hospital
1900 23rd St., Cuyahoga Falls 44223 (330) 971-7000
Internet: www.summahealth.org
President/C.O.O.: Kathleen A. Rice
Records Administrator: Diane Burns (330) 971-7414
Fee for Copy of Records: See statutory fee, *supra*
Affiliate of Summa Health System

DAYTON   Montgomery County

Children's Medical Center
One Children's Plaza, Dayton 45404-1815
(937) 641-3000, (800) 228-4055;
Health Information Mgmt.: (937) 641-3395
Internet: www.childrensdayton.org
President: David Kinsaul
Dir., Health Information Mgmt.: Dan Gross, R.H.I.A.
   (937) 641-3395

Dayton Heart Hospital
707 S. Edwin C. Moses Blvd., Dayton 45408
(937) 221-8000, (800) 975-9996
Internet: www.daytonhearthospital.com
President/C.E.O.: Chad Carpenter
Team Leader, Health Information Svces.:
   Donna Edmondson (Medical Records)
   (937) 221-8421; Fax: (937) 221-8426
Fee for Copy of Records: See statutory fee, *supra*
Affiliate of MedCath, Inc.

Good Samaritan Hospital
2222 Philadelphia Dr., Dayton 45406-1891
Automated Attendant: (937) 278-6251;
Receptionist: (937) 278-2612
Internet: www.goodsamdayton.com
President/C.E.O.: James R. Pancoast
Corporate Counsel: Geoff P. Walker
   (937) 276-8258; Fax: (937) 276-8277
Mgr., Health Information Svces.: Bonnie Vaughn
   (Medical Records) (937) 278-6251, Ext. 2581
Fee for Copy of Records: See statutory fee, *supra*
Affiliate of Premier Health Partners

Grandview Hospital & Medical Center
405 Grand Ave., Dayton 45405 (937) 226-3200
President: Roy Chew (937) 226-3410
Dir., Health Information Mgmt.: Debbie Schrubb
   (937) 439-6299
Fee for Copy of Records: See statutory fee, *supra*
Affiliate of Kettering Medical Center Network

Kettering Hospital Youth Services
5350 Lamme Rd., Dayton 45439 (937) 534-4600
Internet: www.kmcnetwork.org/kys
Administrative Dir.: David Drawbaugh, Ph.D.
   (937) 534-4633
*Affiliate of the Kettering Medical Center Network; A
behavioral health hospital specializing in child and
adolescent health.*

Miami Valley Hospital
One Wyoming St., Dayton 45409-2793 (937) 208-8000
Internet: www.mvh.org
President/C.E.O.: Willam M. Thornton
General Counsel: Dale Creech, Jr. (937) 208-2205
Fee for Copy of Records: See statutory fee, *supra*
In partnership with Premier Health Partners

Southview Hospital and Family Health Center
1997 Miamisburg-Centerville Rd., Dayton 45459
(937) 439-6000
C.E.O.: Francisco J. Perez
   (Kettering Medical Center Network)
President: Dr. Roy Chew
Dir., Health Information Mgmt.: Debbie Schrubb
   (937) 439-6299
Fee for Copy of Records: See statutory fee, *supra*
Affiliate of Kettering Medical Center Network

DEFIANCE   Defiance County

Defiance Regional Medical Center
1200 Ralston Ave., Defiance 43512 (419) 783-6955
C.E.O.: John E. Horns
Fee for Copy of Records: See statutory fee, *supra*
Affiliate of ProMedica Health System

DENNISON   Tuscarawas County

Twin City Hospital
819 N. First St., Dennison 44621
(740) 922-2800; Fax: (740) 922-6945
Internet: www.twincityhospital.org
President/C.E.O.: Frederick J. Makowski
Fee for Copy of Records: See statutory fee, *supra*

DOVER   Tuscarawas County

Union Hospital Association
659 Boulevard St., Dover 44622
(330) 343-3311; Fax: (330) 364-0951;
Administration: (330) 364-0803;
Health Information Mgmt.: Ext. 2421
E-mail: information@unionhospital.org
Internet: www.unionhospital.org
President/C.E.O.: William W. Harding
Dir., Health Information Mgmt.: Cheryl A. Hicks
Fee for Copy of Records: See statutory fee, *supra*

EAST LIVERPOOL   Columbiana County

East Liverpool City Hospital
425 W. Fifth St., East Liverpool 43920
(330) 385-7200; Medical Information Svces.: (330) 386-2081
Internet: www.elch.org
C.E.O.: Melvin Creeley
Dir., Medical Information Svces.: Patricia Ruppersberg
Fee for Copy of Records: See statutory fee, *supra*

ELYRIA   Lorain County

EMH Regional Medical Center
630 E. River St., Elyria 44035
(440) 329-7500;
Health Information Mgmt. (Medical Records): (440) 329-7570
Internet: www.emh-healthcare.org
President/C.E.O.: Kevin Martin
Fee for Copy of Records: See statutory fee, *supra*
Affiliate of EMH Regional Healthcare System

ERIE   **Erie County**

Glenbeigh Outpatient Center of Erie
4906 Richmond Rd., Erie, PA 16509
(814) 864-4226; Fax: (814) 864-4238
E-mail: erie@glenbeigh.com
Exec. Dir.: Patricia Weston-Hall
Fee for Copy of Records: $.50 per page
A chemical dependency treatment center

FAIRFIELD   **Butler County**

Mercy Hospital Fairfield
3000 Mack Rd., Fairfield 45014
(513) 870-7000; Medical Records: (513) 870-7104;
Medical Records Fax: (513) 870-7187
Internet: www.e-mercy.com
C.E.O.: Mark Hood
Mgr., Public Relations: Greg Ossmann (513) 603-8850
Records Administrator: Cherie Puthoff
Fee for Copy of Records: See statutory fee, *supra*
*Affiliate of Catholic Healthcare Partners and Mercy Health
Partners of Southwest Ohio*

FINDLAY   **Hancock County**

Blanchard Valley Regional Health Center
145 W. Wallace St., Findlay 45840
(419) 423-4500; Fax: (419) 423-5358;
Health Information Svces.: (419) 423-5330
Internet: www.bvha.org
C.E.O.: Scott Malaney (419) 423-5201
Risk Mgr.: Lori Curry (419) 423-5454
Fee for Copy of Records: See statutory fee, *supra*

FOSTORIA   **Seneca County**

Fostoria Community Hospital
501 Van Buren St., Fostoria 44830
(419) 435-7734, (800) 815-0575; Fax: (419) 436-6602;
Health Information Svces.: (419) 436-6658;
Health Information Svces. Fax: (419) 436-6628
Internet: www.fchosp.org
President: Timothy J. Jakacki; Fax: (419) 436-6603
Dir., Health Information Svces.: Mary Higgins
Fee for Copy of Records: See statutory fee, *supra*
Affiliate of ProMedica Health System

FREMONT   **Sandusky County**

Memorial Hospital
715 S. Taft Ave., Fremont 43420
(419) 332-7321;
Health Information (Medical Records): (419) 334-6640;
Health Information Fax: (419) 332-7332
E-mail: webmaster@fremontmemorial.org
Internet: www.fremontmemorial.org
C.E.O.: John Gorman (419) 334-6617
Fee for Copy of Records: See statutory fee, *supra*

GAHANNA   **Franklin County**

The Woods at Parkside
349 Olde Ridenour Rd., Gahanna 43230
(614) 471-2552, (800) 282-5512
Administrator: Susan Carmichael
Fee for Copy of Records: $1.00 per page
Formerly Parkside Behavioral Health Care

GALION   **Crawford County**

Galion Community Hospital
Portland Way South, Galion 44833
(419) 468-4841; Fax: (419) 468-2381;
Medical Records: (419) 468-0538
Internet: www.galionhospital.org
President/C.E.O.: LaMar Wyse
Affiliate of OhioHealth

GALLIPOLIS   **Gallia County**

Holzer Medical Center
100 Jackson Pike, Gallipolis 45631 (740) 446-5000
Internet: www.holzer.org
President/C.E.O.: Thomas E. Tope (Acting) (740) 446-5050
Fee for Copy of Records: Contact Medical Records Dept.

GENEVA   **Ashtabula County**

UHHS—Memorial Hospital of Geneva
870 W. Main St., Geneva 44041
(440) 466-1141; Health Information Mgmt.: (440) 415-0203
President/C.E.O.: Laurie S. Lewis
Dir., Health Information Mgmt.: Stephanie Annick
Fee for Copy of Records: See statutory fee, *supra*
Affiliate of University Hospitals Health System

GEORGETOWN   **Brown County**

Brown County General Hospital
425 Home St., Georgetown 45121
(937) 378-7500, (800) 866-0657;
Administration: (937) 378-7800;
Health Information Svces.: (937) 378-7760;
Health Information Svces. Fax: (937) 378-7766
Internet: www.browncountygeneralhospital.org
President: David T. Wallace
Dir., Health Information Svces.: Sandra Schumann
Fee for Copy of Records: See statutory fee, *supra*

GREEN SPRINGS   **Seneca County**

St. Francis Health Care Centre
401 N. Broadway, Green Springs 44836
(419) 639-2626; Medical Records Fax: (419) 639-6239
Internet: www.sfhcc.org
Exec. Dir.: Dan Schwanke
Records Administrator: Cheryl Desjardins
Fee for Copy of Records: See statutory fee, *supra*
Long-term care facility

GREENFIELD   **Highland County**

Greenfield Area Medical Center
550 Mirabeau St., Greenfield 45123 (937) 981-9400
Internet: www.adena.org
Administrator: Jeff Graham
Fee for Copy of Records: See statutory fee, *supra*
Affiliate of Adena Health System

GREENVILLE   **Darke County**

Wayne Hospital
835 Sweitzer St., Greenville 45331
(937) 548-1141; Administration: (937) 547-5723;
Medical Records: (937) 547-5732;
Medical Records Fax: (937) 547-5738
Internet: www.waynehospital.com
President/C.E.O.: Raymond E. Laughlin, Jr.
   Fax: (937) 547-5712
Records Administrator: Julie Hewitt
Fee for Copy of Records: See statutory fee, *supra*

GROVEPORT   **Franklin County**

Barix Clinics of Ohio
3964 Hamilton Square Blvd., Groveport 43125
(614) 834-6800; Fax: (614) 834-6875;
Corporate Office: (800) 282-0066
Internet: www.barixclinics.com
*Specializes in Gastric Bypass Surgery; formerly Bariatric
Care Center of Ohio*

HAMILTON   Butler County

Fort Hamilton Hospital
630 Eaton Ave., Hamilton 45013
(513) 867-2000; Administration: (513) 867-2124
President/C.E.O.: Rick Hinds (Acting)
Fee for Copy of Records: See statutory fee, *supra*
Affiliate of Health Alliance

HICKSVILLE   Defiance County

Community Memorial Hospital
208 N. Columbus St., Hicksville 43526
(419) 542-6692; Medical Records: (419) 542-5664;
Medical Records Fax: (419) 542-6440
Internet: www.cmhosp.com
C.E.O.: Melvin H. Fahs; E-mail: csw@cmhosp.com
Records Administrator: Teresa Hildebrandt
    E-mail: thildebrandt@cmhosp.com
Fee for Copy of Records: See statutory fee, *supra*
Affiliate of the Lutheran Health Network

HILLSBORO   Highland County

Highland District Hospital
1275 N. High St., Hillsboro 45133-8273
(937) 393-6100, (866) 393-6100; Fax: (937) 393-6278;
Medical Records: (937) 393-6292
Internet: www.hdh.org
President/C.E.O.: Paula Detterman
Fee for Copy of Records: $.50 per page

JACKSON   Jackson County

Holzer Medical Center—Jackson
500 Burlington Rd., Jackson 45640 (740) 288-4625
Internet: www.holzer.org
President/C.E.O.: Ross Matlack
Fee for Copy of Records: Contact Medical Records Dept. for
fees

KENTON   Hardin County

Hardin Memorial Hospital
921 E. Franklin St., Kenton 43326
(419) 673-0761, 675-8140; Fax: (419) 673-1097;
Health Information Mgmt. Fax: (419) 673-9366
Internet: www.hardinmemorial.org
President/C.E.O.: Mark Seckinger
Dir., Health Information Mgmt.: Shelly Dodds
Fee for Copy of Records: See statutory fee, *supra*
Affiliates of OhioHealth

KETTERING   Montgomery County

Charles F. Kettering Memorial Hospital
3535 Southern Blvd., Kettering 45429
(937) 298-4331; Fax: (937) 395-8142;
Corporate Office: (937) 395-8167;
Medical Records Fax: (937) 395-8857
C.E.O.: Francisco J. Perez
    (Kettering Medical Center Network)
President: Fred Manchur
Records Administrator: Debbie Schrubb
Fee for Copy of Records: See statutory fee, *supra*
Member of the Kettering Medical Center Network

LAKEWOOD   Cuyahoga County

Lakewood Hospital
14519 Detroit Ave., Lakewood 44107
(216) 521-4200; Administration: Ext. 7602;
Health Information Svces. (Medical Records): (216) 529-7138
Internet: www.lakewoodhospital.org
C.E.O.: Fred M. DeGrandis
C.A.O.: Richard A. Stelzer
Fee for Copy of Records: See statutory fee, *supra*
Affiliates of Cleveland Clinic Health System

LANCASTER   Fairfield County

Fairfield Medical Center
401 N. Ewing St., Lancaster 43130
(740) 687-8000, (800) 548-2627;
Administration: (740) 687-8001;
Medical Information Svces. (Medical Records): (740) 687-8053
Internet: www.fmchealth.org
President/C.E.O.: Mina Ubbing
Fee for Copy of Records: See statutory fee, *supra*

LIMA   Allen County

Lima Memorial Health System
1001 Bellefontaine Ave., Lima 45804 (419) 228-3335
Internet: www.limamemorial.org
President/C.E.O.: Michael D. Swick; Fax: (419) 226-5017
Records Administrator: Anita Good
Fee for Copy of Records: See statutory fee, *supra*

St. Rita's Medical Center
730 W. Market St., Lima 45801
(419) 227-3361, (800) 232-7762;
Medical Records: (419) 226-9018
Internet: www.stritas.org
President/C.E.O.: James P. Reber (419) 226-9020
Fee for Copy of Records: See statutory fee, *supra*
Affiliate of the Catholic Healthcare Partners

SCCI Hospital—Lima
730 W. Market St., 6th Floor, Lima 45801 (419) 224-1888
Internet: www.sccihospitals.com
C.E.O.: Sheila Wheeler
    E-mail: sheila.wheeler@sccihospitals.com
Fee for Copy of Records: Contact Smart Corporation
representative in the Medical Records Dept.
Located within St. Rita's Medical Center

LODI   Medina County

Lodi Community Hospital
225 Elyria St., Lodi 44254
(330) 948-1222, (888) 520-6000;
Medical Records: Ext. 39225
Internet: www.lodihospital.com
President: Thomas Whelan
Fee for Copy of Records: See statutory fee, *supra*
Affiliate of Akron General Health System

LOGAN   Hocking County

Hocking Valley Community Hospital
601 State Route 664 N., Logan 43138
(740) 380-8000, (800) 479-2351
Internet: www.hvch.org
President: Clifford Harmon
Fee for Copy of Records: See statutory fee, *supra*

LONDON   Madison County

Madison County Hospital
210 N. Main St., London 43140
(740) 845-7000, 852-1372;
Medical Records: (740) 845-7102;
Medical Records Fax: (740) 845-7104
Internet: www.madisoncountyhospital.org
President/C.E.O.: Fred L. Kolb
Records Administrator: Dana Harms
Fee for Copy of Records: Search fee: If record is less than six
months old, no search fee; if record is six months to one year
old, $5.00; if record is 1-3 years old, $7.50; if record is older
than 3 years, $15.00. Copy fee: See statutory fee, *supra*
Affiliate of OSU/Mount Carmel Health Alliance

LORAIN   Lorain County

Community Health Partners Hospital and Surgical Center
3700 Kolbe Rd., Lorain 44053 (440) 960-4000
Internet: www.ehealthconnection.com
President/C.E.O.: Brian C. Lockwood
Fee for Copy of Records: See statutory fee, *supra*
Affiliate of Mercy Health Partners and Catholic Healthcare Partners

Specialty Hospital of Lorain
205 W. 20th St., Suite 200, Lorain 44052
(440) 204-3500; Fax: (440) 245-2197
Internet: www.specialtyhospitaloflorain.com
President/C.E.O.: Susan M. Gregg
Fee for Copy of Records: Contact Medical Records Dept. for fees
Long-term Acute Care Facility

MANSFIELD   Richland County

MedCentral Health System—Mansfield
335 Glessner Ave., Mansfield 44903
(419) 526-8000
E-mail: medcentral@medcentral.org
Internet: www.medcentral.org
President: James E. Meyer
Records Administrator: James Freimark (419) 526-8525
Fee for Copy of Records: See statutory fee, *supra*

SCCI Hospital—Mansfield
335 Glessner Ave., 5th Floor, Mansfield 44903
(419) 526-0777; Fax: (419) 526-0929
Internet: www.sccihospitals.com
C.E.O.: Karen Caywood
    E-mail: karen.caywood@sccihospitals.com
Mgr., Health Information Mgmt.: Gail Wright
Fee for Copy of Records: See statutory fee, *supra*
Located within MedCentral Health System—Mansfield

MARIETTA   Washington County

Marietta Memorial Hospital
401 Matthew St., Marietta 45750
(740) 374-1400; Fax: (740) 374-1787
Internet: www.mmhospital.org
President: Larry J. Unroe
Fee for Copy of Records: See statutory fee, *supra*

Selby General Hospital
1106 Colgate Dr., Marietta 45750 (740) 568-2000
E-mail: information@selbygeneralhospital.com
C.E.O.: Kevin P. Calhoun
Fee for Copy of Records: See statutory fee, *supra*; one copy provided free for patient filing for benefits from Social Security Admin., Workers' Comp., Industrial Commission, or Dept. of Job and Family Services
An osteopathic teaching hospital

MARION   Marion County

Marion Area Health Center
1050 Delaware Ave., Marion 43302
(740) 383-8000; Medical Records: (740) 383-7751
Internet: www.marionareahealth.com
Out-patient surgery facility

Marion General Hospital
1000 McKinley Park Dr., Marion 43302
(740) 383-8400; Administration: (740) 383-8700;
Medical Records: (740) 383-8714;
Medical Records Correspondence: (740) 383-8592
Internet: www.mariongeneral.com
President/C.E.O.: Ron Bachman
Records Administrator: Cheryl Born, RHIA
Fee for Copy of Records: See statutory fee, *supra*;
microfilm/microfiche, additional $1.50 per page
Affiliate of OhioHealth

MARTINS FERRY   Belmont County

East Ohio Regional Hospital
90 North 4th St., Martins Ferry 43935
(740) 633-1100; Medical Records Fax: (740) 633-4399
Internet: www.eastohioregionalhospital.com
C.E.O.: Brian Felici
Records Administrator: Mary McClure
Fee for Copy of Records: See statutory fee, *supra*

MARYSVILLE   Union County

Memorial Hospital of Union County
500 London Ave., Marysville 43040
(937) 644-6115;
Health Information Mgmt.: (937) 578-2365;
Health Information Mgmt. Fax: (937) 578-2844
Internet: www.memorialhosp.org
C.E.O.: Olas A. Hubbs III
V.P., Legal Svces.: Sue Dill Calloway
Dir., Health Information Mgmt.: Carla Worthington (Medical Records) (937) 578-2298
Fee for Copy of Records: See statutory fee, *supra*

MASSILLON   Stark County

Doctors Hospital of Stark County
400 Austin Ave., N.W., Massillon 44646
(330) 837-7200; Medical Records: (330) 837-7224
Internet: www.drshospital.com
C.E.O.: Janie Sinacore-Jaberg
Records Administrator: Shelley Morgan
Fee for Copy of Records: See statutory fee, *supra*

Massillon Community Hospital
875 8th St., N.E., Massillon 44646
(330) 832-8761; Medical Records: (330) 837-6885;
Medical Records Fax: (330) 837-6802
Internet: www.mchosp.org
President: Michael Reichfield
Fee for Copy of Records: See statutory fee, *supra*
Member of Akron General Health System

MAUMEE   Lucas County

Focus Healthcare of Ohio—Arrowhead Park
1725 Timberline Rd., Maumee 43537 (419) 891-9333
Internet: www.focushealthcare.com
C.E.O.: Carey W. Plummer
Fee for Copy of Records: See statutory fee, *supra*
An adult chemical dependency rehabilitation center

St. Luke's Hospital
5901 Monclova Rd., Maumee 43537-1899 (419) 893-5911
Internet: www.stlukeshospital.com
President/C.E.O.: Frank J. Bartell III
V.P./General Counsel: Kathleen Zouhary (419) 893-5908
Dir., Health Information Mgmt.: Betsy Woodring
Fee for Copy of Records: See statutory fee, *supra*

MAYFIELD HEIGHTS   Cuyahoga County

Hillcrest Hospital
6780 Mayfield Rd., Mayfield Heights 44124 (440) 449-4500
Internet: www.hillcresthospital.org
C.O.O.: Catherine Leary
Dir., Health Information Svces.: Donna Misch
Fee for Copy of Records: See statutory fee, *supra*
Member of Cleveland Clinic Health System

MEDINA   **Medina County**

Medina General Hospital
1000 E. Washington St., Medina 44256
(330) 725-1000; Administration: (330) 721-5098;
Administration Fax: (330) 721-4906;
Medical Records: (330) 721-5790;
Medical Records Fax: (330) 721-4903
E-mail: administration@medinahospital.org
Internet: www.medinahospital.org
President/C.E.O.: Gary D. Hallman
V.P., Legal Affairs: Debra Zanath
Records Administrator: Darla Parcher
Fee for Copy of Records: See statutory fee, *supra*

MIAMISBURG   **Montgomery County**

Lifecare Hospitals of Dayton
2150 Leiter Rd., 3rd Floor, Miamisburg 45342
(937) 384-8300; Medical Records: (937) 384-8313
C.E.O.: Ken D. D'Amico
Fee for Copy of Records: See statutory fee, *supra*
Long-term acute care facility; located within Sycamore Hospital

Sycamore Hospital
2150 Leiter Rd., Miamisburg 45342 (937) 866-0551
President/C.E.O.: Francisco J. Perez
   (Kettering Medical Center Network)
Senior Exec. Dir.: Richard Haas
Dir., Health Information Mgmt.: Debbie Schrubb
   (937) 298-3399
Fee for Copy of Records: See statutory fee, *supra*
Affiliate of Kettering Medical Center Network

MIDDLETOWN   **Butler County**

Middletown Regional Hospital
105 McKnight Dr., Middletown 45044
(513) 424-2111, (800) 338-4057;
Medical Records: (513) 420-5200
Internet: www.middletownhospital.org
President/C.E.O.: Douglas W. McNeil
Records Administrator: Tammy Valentine
Fee for Copy of Records: See statutory fee, *supra*

MILLERSBURG   **Holmes County**

Pomerene Hospital
981 Wooster Rd., Millersburg 44654
(330) 674-1015; Administration: Ext. 1252;
Health Information Mgmt.: (330) 674-1015, Ext. 4147
Internet: www.pomerenehospital.org
Administrator/C.E.O.: P.W. Smith, Jr.
Fee for Copy of Records: See statutory fee, *supra*

MONTPELIER   **Williams County**

Community Hospitals & Wellness Centers—Montpelier
909 E. Snyder Ave., Montpelier 43543
(419) 485-3154; Chart Analysis: (419) 636-1131, Ext. 1155
Internet: www.chwchospital.com
C.E.O.: Rusty O. Brunicardi (419) 636-1131, Ext. 1141
Mgr., Medical Records: Teresa Monroe
   433 W. High St., Bryan 43506
Supervisor, Chart Analysis: Natasha Eicher
Fee for Copy of Records: See statutory fee, *supra*

MOUNT GILEAD   **Morrow County**

Morrow County Hospital
651 W. Marion Rd., Mount Gilead 43338
(419) 946-5015;
Health Information Mgmt. Fax: (419) 949-3122
Internet: www.morrowcountyhospital.com
President/C.E.O.: Diana D. Fisher
Dir., Health Information Mgmt.: Kay Beveridge
Fee for Copy of Records: See statutory fee, *supra*
Affiliate of OhioHealth

MOUNT VERNON   **Knox County**

Knox Community Hospital
1330 Coshocton Rd., Mount Vernon 43050
(740) 393-9000; Fax: (740) 393-3487
Internet: www.knoxcommhosp.org
President/C.E.O.: Kevin Rogols (740) 393-9601
Fee for Copy of Records: See statutory fee, *supra*

NAPOLEON   **Henry County**

Henry County Hospital
11-600 State Route 424, Napoleon 43545
(419) 592-4015; Fax: (419) 592-8964;
Administration: (419) 591-3844;
Medical Records: (419) 591-3809
Internet: www.henrycountyhospital.org
C.E.O.: Kim Bordenkircher
Fee for Copy of Records: Contact Medical Records Dept. for fee information

NELSONVILLE   **Athens County**

Doctors Hospital Nelsonville
1950 Mount St. Marys Dr., Nelsonville 45764
(740) 753-1931
Internet: www.ohiohealth.com
C.E.O.: Steven Swart (740) 753-1931
Records Administrator: Ellen Robertson
Fee for Copy of Records: See statutory fee, *supra*
Affiliate of OhioHealth

NEWARK   **Licking County**

Licking Memorial Behavioral Health at Shepherd Hill
200 Messimer Dr., Newark 43055
(740) 348-4870;
Medical Records (In-Patient): (740) 348-4894;
Medical Records (Out-Patient): (740) 348-4891
Director: Anna Rehl
Fee for Copy of Records: Contact Medical Records Dept. for fee information

Licking Memorial Hospital
1320 W. Main St., Newark 43055 (740) 348-4000
E-mail: info@lmhealth.org
Internet: www.lmhealth.org
President: William J. Andrews
Fee for Copy of Records: See statutory fee, *supra*

NILES   **Trumbull County**

Glenbeigh Outpatient Center of Niles
29 North Rd. S.E., Niles 44446
(330) 652-6770; Fax: (330) 652-2069
E-mail: Niles@glenbeigh.com
Exec. Dir.: Patricia Weston-Hall
Fee for Copy of Records: $.50 per page
A chemical dependency treatment center

NORWALK   **Huron County**

Fisher-Titus Medical Center
272 Benedict Ave., Norwalk 44857
(419) 668-8101, (800) 589-3862
Internet: www.fisher-titus.com
President/C.E.O.: Patrick J. Martin
Fee for Copy of Records: See statutory fee, *supra*

OBERLIN   **Lorain County**

Allen Medical Center
200 W. Lorain St., Oberlin 44074
(440) 775-1211; Fax: (440) 775-9118
Internet: www.ehealthconnection.com
President/C.E.O.: Edwin Oley
Risk Mgr.: Kathleen Neptune
Records Administrator: Michael Majoras
Fee for Copy of Records: Contact Medical Records Dept.
Member of Community Health Partners

OREGON   **Lucas County**

St. Charles Mercy Hospital
2600 Navarre Ave., Oregon 43616 (419) 696-7200
Internet: www.mercyweb.org
C.E.O.: David J. Ameen
Dir., Health Information Svces.: Amy Szymkowiak
Fee for Copy of Records: See statutory fee, *supra*;
microfiche, additional $1.00 per page
Affiliate of Mercy Health Partners

ORRVILLE   **Wayne County**

Dunlap Memorial Hospital
832 S. Main St., Orrville 44667
(330) 682-3010; Fax: (330) 683-2130;
Medical Records: (330) 684-4720
Internet: www.dunlaphospital.org
C.E.O.: Lynn V. Horner
Records Administrator: Linda Heffner
Fee for Copy of Records: Contact Medical Records Dept. for
fees

OXFORD   **Butler County**

McCullough-Hyde Memorial Hospital
110 N. Poplar St., Oxford 45056
(513) 523-2111; Fax: (513) 524-5647
Internet: www.mhmh.org
C.E.O.: Richard A. Daniels (513) 524-5501
General Counsel: James Michael
Records Administrator: Kim Belec
Fee for Copy of Records: See statutory fee, *supra*

PAINESVILLE   **Lake County**

LakeEast Hospital
10 E. Washington St., Painesville 44077
(440) 354-2400;
Health Information Mgmt. Fax: (440) 354-1966
E-mail: info@lhs.net
Internet: www.lhs.net
President/C.E.O.: Cynthia Moore-Hardy
Dir., Health Information Mgmt.: Susan Meyer
    (440) 354-1998
Fee for Copy of Records: See statutory fee, *supra*
Member of Lake Health System

PARMA   **Cuyahoga County**

Parma Community General Hospital
7007 Powers Blvd., Parma 44129
(440) 743-3000; Health Information Mgmt.: (440) 743-4242
Internet: www.parmahospital.org
President/C.E.O.: Patricia A. Ruflin
    E-mail: pruflin@parmahospital.org
Dir., Health Information Mgmt.: Terry Byrne
Fee for Copy of Records: See statutory fee, *supra*

PAULDING   **Paulding County**

Paulding County Hospital
1035 W. Wayne St., Paulding 45879
(419) 399-4080; Fax: (419) 399-5560;
Medical Records: (419) 399-1172;
Medical Records Fax: (419) 399-1167
Internet: www.pauldingcountyhospital.com
C.E.O.: Gary W. Adkins
Records Administrator: Rebecca Ringler
    E-mail: bringler@saa.net
Fee for Copy of Records: See statutory fee, *supra*

PORT CLINTON   **Ottawa County**

Magruder Memorial Hospital
615 Fulton St., Port Clinton 43452 (419) 734-3131
Internet: www.magruderhospital.com
President/C.E.O.: David R. Norwine
Fee for Copy of Records: See statutory fee, *supra*

PORTSMOUTH   **Scioto County**

Southern Ohio Medical Center
1805 27th St., Portsmouth 45662
(740) 356-5000; Health Information Mgmt.: (740) 356-8286
Internet: www.somc.org
President/C.E.O.: Randal M. Arnett
Dir., Health Information Mgmt.: Juanita Gammon
Fee for Copy of Records: See statutory fee, *supra*
Affiliate of OhioHealth

RAVENNA   **Portage County**

Robinson Memorial Hospital
6847 N. Chestnut St., Ravenna 44266-1204
(330) 297-0811; Administration: (330) 297-2300;
Medical Records: (330) 297-2560;
Medical Records Fax: (330) 297-2309
Internet: www.robinsonmemorial.org
President/C.E.O.: Stephen Colecchi
General Counsel: Ted Zawadski
Records Administrator: Thelma Hajes
Fee for Copy of Records: See statutory fee, *supra*

RICHMOND HEIGHTS   **Cuyahoga County**

UHHS—Richmond Heights Hospital
27100 Chardon Rd., Richmond Heights 44143
(440) 585-6500; Administration: (440) 585-6136;
Health Information Svces.: (440) 585-6413
Internet: www.uhhsrh.org
C.E.O.: William Lawrence
Dir., Health Information Svces.: Clo Kempt-Mitchell
Fee for Copy of Records: Contact Smart Corporation
representative in the Health Information Svces. Dept.
Affiliate of University Hospitals Health System

ROCK CREEK   **Ashtabula County**

Glenbeigh Hospital & Outpatient Ctrs.
2863 St. Rt. 45, Rock Creek 44084-0298
(440) 563-3400, (800) 234-1001
Internet: www.glenbeigh.com
Exec. Dir.: Patricia Weston-Hall
Fee for Copy of Records: $.50 per page
A chemical dependency treatment center

ROCKY RIVER   **Cuyahoga County**

Glenbeigh Outpatient Center of Rocky River
20800 Center Ridge Rd., Suite 410, Rocky River 44116
(440) 356-7620; Fax: (440) 356-7623
E-mail: rockyriver@glenbeigh.com
C.E.O.: Patricia Weston-Hall
Fee for Copy of Records: $.50 per page
A chemical dependency treatment center

SAINT CLAIRSVILLE   **Belmont County**

BHC—Fox Run Hospital
67670 Traco Dr., Saint Clairsville 43950
(740) 695-2131; Fax: (740) 695-7158
C.E.O.: Karen Maxwell
Records Administrator: Wanda Baker
Fee for Copy of Records: Retrieval fee, $10.00; $.25 per page
Affiliate of Ardent Health Services; a behavioral health facility

SAINT MARYS   **Auglaize County**

Joint Township District Memorial Hospital
200 St. Clair St., Saint Marys 45885
(419) 394-3335, (877) 564-6897
Internet: www.jtdmh.org
C.E.O.: James R. Chick
Records Administrator: Vacancy at Press Time
Fee for Copy of Records: See statutory fee, *supra*

SALEM   **Columbiana County**

Salem Community Hospital
1995 E. State St., Salem 44460
(330) 332-1551; Medical Records: (330) 332-7346
Internet: www.salemhosp.com
C.E.O.: Howard Rohleder
Records Administrator: Sam Failla
Fee for Copy of Records: See statutory fee, *supra*

SANDUSKY   **Erie County**

Firelands Regional Medical Center—Main Campus
1101 Decatur St., Sandusky 44870
(419) 626-7400; Medical Records: (419) 626-7435
Internet: www.firelands.com
President/C.E.O.: Charles A. Stark, F.A.C.H.E.
Fee for Copy of Records: See statutory fee, *supra*

Firelands Regional Medical Center—South Campus
1912 Hayes Ave., Sandusky 44870
(419) 621-7000; Medical Records: (419) 626-7435
President/C.E.O.: Charles A. Stark, F.A.C.H.E.
Fee for Copy of Records: See statutory fee, *supra*

SHELBY   **Richland County**

MedCentral Health System—Shelby Hospital
20 Morris Rd., Shelby 44875
(419) 342-5015; Medical Records: (419) 342-1715
E-mail: medcentral@medcentral.org
Internet: www.medcentral.org
President: James E. Meyer
    MedCentral Health System, 335 Glessner Ave.,
    Mansfield 44905-2263 (419) 526-8000
Records Administrator: James Freimark
    335 Glessner Ave., Mansfield 44903 (419) 526-8525
Fee for Copy of Records: See statutory fee, *supra*

SIDNEY   **Shelby County**

Wilson Memorial Hospital
915 W. Michigan St., Sidney 45365
(937) 498-2311, (800) 589-9641; Fax: (937) 497-8251
Internet: www.wilsonhospital.com
C.E.O.: Thomas J. Boecker
Fee for Copy of Records: See statutory fee, *supra*

SPRINGFIELD   **Clark County**

Community Hospital
2615 E. High St., Springfield 45505 (937) 325-0531
Internet: www.CommunityHospital.com
President: Andrew R. McCulloch
Fee for Copy of Records: See statutory fee, *supra*

Mercy Medical Center
1343 N. Fountain Blvd., Springfield 45504
(937) 390-5000; Fax: (937) 390-5507
Internet: www.mercy-health.org
President/C.E.O.: Andrew R. McCulloch (937) 328-8027
Fee for Copy of Records: See statutory fee, *supra*
*Affiliate of Catholic Healthcare Partners and Mercy Health
Partners*

STEUBENVILLE   **Jefferson County**

Trinity Medical Center East
380 Summit Ave., Steubenville 43952
(740) 283-7000; Administration: (740) 283-7212;
Medical Records: (740) 264-8107
Internet: www.trinityhealth.com
President/C.E.O.: Fred Brower
Records Administrator: Kim Dudich
Fee for Copy of Records: Contact ChartOne representative
in the Medical Records Dept.
Affiliate of Trinity Health System

Trinity Medical Center West
4000 Johnson Rd., Steubenville 43952
(740) 264-8000; Medical Records: (740) 264-8107
Internet: www.trinityhealth.com
President/C.E.O.: Fred Brower
Records Administrator: Kim Dudich
Fee for Copy of Records: Contact ChartOne representative
in the Medical Records Dept.
Affiliate of Trinity Health System

SYLVANIA   **Lucas County**

Flower Hospital
5200 Harroun Rd., Sylvania 43560
(419) 824-1444; Health Information Mgmt.: (419) 824-1956;
Health Information Mgmt. Fax: (419) 824-1768
President: Kevin Webb
Dir., Health Information Mgmt.: Nicole Stenberg
Fee for Copy of Records: See statutory fee, *supra*
Affiliate of ProMedica Health System

TIFFIN   **Seneca County**

Mercy Hospital of Tiffin
485 W. Market St., Tiffin 44883 (419) 447-3130
President/C.E.O.: Dale E. Thornton
Fee for Copy of Records: See statutory fee, *supra*
*Affiliate of Catholic Healthcare Partners and Mercy Health
Partners*

TOLEDO   **Lucas County**

Medical College of Ohio
3000 Arlington Ave., Toledo 43614
(419) 383-4000, (800) 321-8383
Internet: www.mco.edu
President: Dr. Lloyd A. Jacobs
Fee for Copy of Records: See statutory fee, *supra*

St. Anne Mercy Hospital
3404 W. Sylvania Ave., Toledo 43623 (419) 407-2663
Internet: www.mercyweb.org
President/C.E.O.: Karen Connors
Fee for Copy of Records: See statutory fee, *supra*
Affiliate of Catholic Health Partners

St. Vincent Mercy Medical Center
2213 Cherry St., Toledo 43608 (419) 251-3232
Internet: www.mercyweb.org
C.E.O.: Steven L. Mickus
Fee for Copy of Records: See statutory fee, *supra*
Affiliate of Mercy Health Partners

The Toledo Hospital & Toledo Children's Hospital
2142 N. Cove Blvd., Toledo 43606
(419) 291-4000; Toledo Children's Hospital: (419) 291-5437
Internet: www.promedica.org
Presidents:
    Barbara Steele (The Toledo Hospital) (419) 291-4245
    Kathy Carlson, M.D. (Toledo Children's Hospital)
        (419) 291-4210
General Counsel: Jeffrey Kuhn (419) 291-2034
Fee for Copy of Records: See statutory fee, *supra*
Affiliate of ProMedica Health System

TROY   **Miami County**

Upper Valley Medical Center
3130 N. Dixie Hwy., Troy 45373 (937) 440-4000
E-mail: info@uvmc.com
Internet: www.uvmc.com
President/C.E.O.: David Meckstroth (937) 440-7921
Fee for Copy of Records: See statutory fee, *supra*
*Affiliate of Upper Valley Medical Center Health Care
System*

UPPER SANDUSKY   Wyandot County

Wyandot Memorial Hospital
885 N. Sandusky Ave., Upper Sandusky 43351
(419) 294-4991; Fax: (419) 294-2233
C.E.O.: Joseph D'Ettorre
Records Administrator: Darlene Clabaugh, Ext. 2211
Fee for Copy of Records: First page, $2.50; $.50 per page,
pages 2-50; $.20 each additional page

URBANA   Champaign County

Mercy Memorial Hospital
904 Scioto St., Urbana 43078
(937) 653-5231; Health Information Svces.: Ext. 6161
Administrator: Karl Zalar
Dir., Health Information Svces.: Lisa Anderson
    (937) 390-5348
Fee for Copy of Records: Contact ChartOne representative
in the Health Information Svces. Dept.
Affiliate of Mercy Health Partners

VAN WERT   Van Wert County

Van Wert County Hospital
1250 S. Washington St., Van Wert 45891
(419) 238-2390; Medical Records: Ext. 245;
Medical Records Fax: (419) 238-4668
Internet: www.vanwerthospital.com
President/C.E.O.: Mark J. Minick
Dir., Patient Financial Services: Debbie Lewis
    (419) 238-8639
Fee for Copy of Records: See statutory fee, *supra*

WADSWORTH   Medina County

Wadsworth—Rittman Hospital
195 Wadsworth Rd., Wadsworth 44281
(330) 334-1504, (800) 828-1789;
Administration: (330) 334-2703
E-mail: wrh@wrhospital.com
Internet: www.wrhospital.com
President/C.E.O.: James W. Brumlow, Jr.
Fee for Copy of Records: See statutory fee, *supra*

WARREN   Trumbull County

Forum Health Hillside Rehabilitation Hospital
8747 Squires Lane, N.E., Warren 44484
(330) 841-3700; Fax: (330) 841-3633
Internet: www.forumhealth.org
C.O.O.: Rodney Jones
Partnered with Forum Health

St. Joseph Health Center
667 Eastland Ave., S.E., Warren 44484
(330) 841-4000; Medical Records: (330) 841-4043
C.E.O.: Robert Shroder
Fee for Copy of Records: See statutory fee, *supra*
Affiliate of Humility of Mary Health Partners

Trumbull Memorial Hospital—Forum Health
1350 E. Market St., Warren 44482
(330) 841-9011; Medical Records: (330) 841-9151
Internet: www.forumhealth.org
President/C.E.O.: N. Kristopher Hoce, C.H.E.
    (Forum Health) (330) 841-9820
Affiliate of Forum Health Services

WARRENSVILLE HEIGHTS   Cuyahoga County

South Pointe Hospital
4110 Warrensville Center Rd., Warrensville Heights 44122
(216) 491-6000; Administration: (216) 491-7100;
Health Information Svces.: (216) 491-7285;
Health Information Svces. Fax: (216) 491-7276
Internet: www.southpointehospital.org
C.A.O.: Beverly Lozar
Dir., Health Information Svces.: Donna Misch
Member of Cleveland Clinic Health System

WASHINGTON COURT HOUSE   Fayette County

Fayette County Memorial Hospital
1430 Columbus Ave., Washington Court House 43160
(740) 335-1210; Fax: (740) 333-2998
Internet: www.fcmh.org
C.E.O.: Francis G. Albarano (740) 333-2705
Records Administrator: Bonnie Hall (740) 333-2828

WAUSEON   Fulton County

Fulton County Health Center
725 S. Shoop Ave., Wauseon 43567
(419) 335-2015; Health Information Mgmt.: (419) 330-2662
Internet: www.fultoncountyhealthcenter.org
Administrator: E. Dean Beck
Fee for Copy of Records: See statutory fee, *supra*

WEST UNION   Adams County

Adams County Hospital
210 N. Wilson Dr., West Union 45693
(937) 544-5571; Fax: (937) 544-5693
C.E.O.: Linda Niles
Records Administrator: Penny Prater
Fee for Copy of Records: $.50 per page

WESTERVILLE   Franklin County

Mount Carmel St. Ann's
500 S. Cleveland Ave., Westerville 43081
(614) 898-4000; Health Information Mgmt.: (614) 898-4075;
Health Information Mgmt. Fax: (614) 898-8609
Internet: www.mountcarmelhealth.com
President/C.E.O.: Joseph Calvaruso
Dir., Health Information Mgmt.: Marcia Newkirk
Fee for Copy of Records: See statutory fee, *supra*;
Electronic Chart, $1.00 per page
Member of Trinity Health

WESTLAKE   Cuyahoga County

St. John West Shore Hospital
29000 Center Ridge Rd., Westlake 44145
(440) 835-8000; Fax: (440) 827-5015;
Medical Records: (440) 827-5030
Internet: www.sjws.net
President: Keith Poisson
    E-mail: keith.poisson@csauh.com
Records Administrator: Erin Lamb
Fee for Copy of Records: See statutory fee, *supra*
*Affiliate of the University Hospitals Health System and the
CSA Health System*

WILLARD   Huron County

Mercy Hospital of Willard
110 E. Howard St., Willard 44890 (419) 964-5000
Internet: www.ehealthconnection.com
President/C.E.O.: Robert E. Gospodarek
Fee for Copy of Records: See statutory fee, *supra*
*Member of Catholic Healthcare Partners and Mercy Health
Partners*

WILLOUGHBY   Lake County

LakeWest Hospital
36000 Euclid Ave., Willoughby 44094-4662
(440) 953-9600;
Health Information Mgmt. Fax: (440) 953-6092
E-mail: info@lhs.net
Internet: www.lhs.net
President/C.E.O.: Cynthia Moore-Hardy
Dir., Health Information Mgmt.: Susan Meyer
    (440) 354-1998
Fee for Copy of Records: See statutory fee, *supra*
Member of Lake Health System

Willoughby—Cont'd

Laurelwood Hospital & Counseling Centers
35900 Euclid Ave., Willoughby 44094
(440) 953-3000, (800) 438-4673; Fax: (440) 953-3344;
Medical Records: Ext. 3150
E-mail: access@laurelwoodhospital.com
Internet: www.laurelwoodhospital.com
President: Farshid Afsarifard, Ph.D., C.H.E.
(440) 953-3310
Fee for Copy of Records: See statutory fee, *supra*
Affiliate of University Hospitals Health System; full service psychiatric hospital

WILMINGTON   Clinton County

Clinton Memorial Hospital
610 W. Main St., P.O. Box 600, Wilmington 45177
(937) 382-6611; Fax: (937) 382-6633;
Medical Records: (937) 382-9220;
Medical Records Fax: (937) 382-9557
Internet: www.cmhregional.com
President/C.E.O.: Timothy J. Crowley (937) 382-9201
Records Administrator: Suzanne Sammaghandi
(937) 382-9216
Fee for Copy of Records: See statutory fee, *supra*

WOOSTER   Wayne County

Wooster Community Hospital
1761 Beall Ave., Wooster 44691 (330) 263-8100
Internet: www.woosterhospital.org
C.E.O.: Bill Sheron
Fee for Copy of Records: See statutory fee, *supra*

XENIA   Greene County

Greene Memorial Hospital, Inc.
1141 N. Monroe Dr., Xenia 45385
(937) 372-8011; Health Information Mgmt.: Ext. 5497
Internet: www.greene-memorial.org
President: Michael R. Stephens
Dir., Health Information Mgmt.: Sheila Harris
Fee for Copy of Records: See statutory fee, *supra*

YOUNGSTOWN   Mahoning County

Belmont Pines Hospital
615 Churchill-Hubbard Rd., Youngstown 44505
(330) 759-2700; Fax: (330) 759-2776
Internet: www.bhcbelmontpines.com
C.E.O.: Dr. George H. Perry
Fee for Copy of Records: See statutory fee, *supra*
Member of Ardent Health Services; a behavioral health hospital

Mahoning Valley Hospital
345 Oak Hill Ave., Suite 210, Youngstown 44502
(330) 480-1250
President/C.E.O.: Michael Senchak
Fee for Copy of Records: See statutory fee, *supra*
Formerly Specialty Hospital of Mahoning Valley

Neil Kennedy Recovery Clinic
2151 Rush Blvd., Youngstown 44507
(330) 744-1181; Fax: (330) 740-2849
Internet: www.nkrc.org

160 Clifton Dr. N.E., Warren 44484
(330) 609-5441; Fax: (330) 609-5448

25 N. Canfield Niles Rd., Suite 14, Austintown 44515
(330) 792-4724; Fax: (330) 792-1848
Exec. Dir.: Gerald Carter
Drug and alcohol dependency treatment center

Northside Medical Center & Tod Children's Hospital
500 Gypsy Lane, Youngstown 44501
Northside Medical Center: (330) 884-1000;
Tod Children's Hospital: (330) 884-3000;
Medical Records: (330) 884-1126
Internet: www.forumhealth.org
President/C.E.O.: N. Kristopher Hoce
(Forum Health Services)
Fee for Copy of Records: Contact Medical Records Dept. for fee information
Affiliate of Forum Health Services

St. Elizabeth Health Center
1044 Belmont Ave., Youngstown 44501
(330) 746-7211; Administration: (330) 480-3570;
Administration Fax: (330) 480-7974
Internet: www.hmpartners.org
President/C.E.O.: Robert W. Shroder
Fee for Copy of Records: Contact Medical Records Dept.
Affiliate of Humility of Mary Health Partners

Select Specialty Hospital—Youngstown, Inc.
1044 Belmont Ave., Youngstown 44501 (330) 480-2349
C.E.O.: Marijo Shuntich
Fee for Copy of Records: No fee

ZANESVILLE   Muskingum County

Bethesda Hospital
Genesis Maple Ave. Campus
2951 Maple Ave., Zanesville 43701
(740) 454-4000; Health Information Mgmt.: (740) 454-5905
C.E.O.: Thomas L. Sieber
Mgr., Health Information Mgmt.: Misty Dickinson
(740) 455-7768
Fee for Copy of Records: See statutory fee, *supra*
Member of Genesis Health Care System

Good Samaritan Hospital
800 Forest Ave., Zanesville 43701
(740) 454-5000; Health Information Mgmt.: (740) 454-5905
C.E.O.: Thomas L. Sieber
Mgr., Health Information Mgmt.: Misty Dickinson
(740) 455-7768
Fee for Copy of Records: See statutory fee, *supra*
Affiliates of Genesis Healthcare System

OHIO BAR ASSOCIATIONS

American Bar Association
750 N. Lake Shore Dr., Chicago, IL 60611
(312) 988-5000; Fax: (312) 988-5151
Internet: www.abanet.org

740 15th St. N.W., Washington, DC 20005
(202) 662-1000
Exec. Dir.: Robert A. Stein   (312) 988-5225
   E-mail: robertstein@staff.abanet.org
Annual Meeting: August
Mid-year Meeting: February

Ohio State Bar Association
1700 Lake Shore Dr., Columbus 43204
(614) 487-2050, (800) 282-6556; Fax: (614) 487-1008
E-mail: osba@ohiobar.org
Internet: http://www.ohiobar.org
Exec. Dir.: Denny Ramey
   E-mail: dramey@ohiobar.org
President: Heather G. Sowald
   Sowald Sowald & Clouse, 400 S. 5th St., Suite 101,
   Columbus 43215
   (614) 464-1877; Fax: (614) 464-2035
President-Elect: E. Jane Taylor
   Guy Lambert & Towne, 106 S. Main St., Suite 2210,
   Akron 44308
   (330) 535-2151; Fax: (330) 535-9048

Adams County Bar Association
President: Douglas E. McIlwain
   217 W. Main St., West Union 45693
   (937) 544-7900
Secretary-Treasurer: Kenneth L. Armstrong, Jr.
   107 E. Main St., P.O. Box 236, West Union 45693
   (937) 544-3331; Fax: (937) 544-5107

Akron Bar Association
7 W. Bowery St., Suite 1100, Akron 44308
(330) 253-5007; Fax: (330) 253-2140
Internet: www.akronbar.org
Exec. Dir.: Susan D. Lengal
President: Peter T. Cahoon
   50 S. Main St., P.O. Box 1500, Akron 44309
   (330) 376-5300; Fax: (330) 252-5539
President-Elect: L. Terence Ufholz
   304 N. Cleveland-Massillon Rd., Akron 44333
   (330) 670-0770; Fax: (330) 670-0297
Secretary: Michael L. Robinson
   750 Spring Water Dr., Akron 44333
   (330) 762-9300; Fax: (330) 665-1117
Treasurer: Karen A. Bozzelli
   P.O. Box 2130, Akron 44309-2130
   (330) 375-8471; Fax: (330) 375-8434
Elections: June

Allen County Bar Association
204 N. Main St., Lima 45801
(419) 223-1426
President: Deborah Drexler
   Allen County Common Pleas Court, 333 N. Main St.,
   P.O. Box 1243, Lima 45802-1243
   (419) 223-8511; Fax: (419) 227-3162
V.P.: Hon. Jeffrey L. Reed
   Allen County Common Pleas Court, 333 N. Main St.,
   P.O. Box 1243, Lima 45802-1243
   (419) 223-8525; Fax: (419) 224-9269
Secretary: Richard W. Miller III
   1728 Allentown Rd., Lima 45801
   (419) 227-9595; Fax: (419) 227-3177
Treasurer: Andrew B. King
   212 N. Elizabeth St., Lima 45801
   (419) 224-1353; Fax: (419) 224-5305

Ashland County Bar Association
President: Erin Poplar
   930 Claremont Ave., Ashland 44805
   (419) 281-3561
V.P.: Timothy E. Potts
   Harpster,Vanosvalo & Findley, 60 W. Second St.,
   Ashland 44805
   (419) 289-6888; Fax: (419) 281-2461
Secretary/Treasurer: Thomas R. Gilman
   Kick & Gilman, L.L.C., 133 S. Market St.,
   Loudonville 44842
   (419) 994-4892; Fax: (419) 994-4886

Ashtabula County Bar Association
P.O. Box 1675, Ashtabula 44005-1675
Internet: www.ashtabulacountybar.com
President: Lori B. Lamer
Secretary: Thomas D. Anderson
   First Merit Bank, 4200 Park Age., Ashtabula 44004
   (440) 994-8418; Fax: (440) 992-0674
Treasurer: Alfred W. Mackey
   Ashtabula County Common Pleas Court,
   25 W. Jefferson St., Jefferson 44047
   (440) 576-3683; Fax: (440) 576-6394

Asian American Bar Association
Organizers:
   James Chin
   745 Leader Bldg., 526 Superior Ave. E., Cleveland 44114
   (216) 241-0646; Fax: (216) 241-4246
   Sanjiv K. Kapur
   Jones, Day, 901 Lakeside Ave., Cleveland 44114
   (216) 586-7114; Fax: (216) 579-0212
   Sonja C. Rice
   Hahn, Loeser & Parks, L.L.P., 3300 BP Tower,
   200 Public Sq., Cleveland 44114
   (216) 274-2479; Fax: (216) 241-2824
   Monica Verma
   Baker & Hostetler, L.L.P., 3200 National Center,
   1900 E. 9th. St., Cleveland 44114
   (216) 861-7370; Fax: (216) 696-0740
   Margaret W. Wong
   Margaret W. Wong & Assoc., MWW Center,
   3150 Chester Ave., Cleveland 44114
   (216) 566-9908; Fax: (216) 566-1125

Auglaize County Bar Association
P.O. Box 180, Wapakoneta 45895
President: John Brunner (419) 738-2552
V.P.: Mike Burton (419) 738-8165
Secretary/Treasurer: S. Mark Weller
   (419) 738-7025; Fax: (419) 739-9389
Meeting: Last Thurs., monthly
Election: December

Belmont County Bar Association
President: Jack Kigerel
   P.O. Box 248, Saint Clairsville 43950
   (740) 695-5866; Fax: (740) 695-3947
Secretary: Grace L. Hoffman
   Hoffman Law Office, 160 E. Main St., P.O. Box 310,
   Barnesville 43713-0310
   (740) 425-2372; Fax: (740) 425-4021
Elections: May
Meetings: First Tues., Jan., May & Sept.

Black Lawyers Association of Cincinnati
P.O. Box 3181, Cincinnati 45202
Internet: www.cincinnatiblac.org
President: Bryant L. Brewer
   Baker & Hosletter, 312 Walnut St., Suite 3200,
   Cincinnati 45202
   (513) 852-2605; Fax: (513) 929-0303
V.P.: Tawanda J. Edwards
   105 E. Fourth St., 4th Floor, Cincinnati 45202
   (513) 721-5151; Fax: (513) 621-9285

Black Lawyers Assn. of Cincinnati—Cont'd

Secretary: Barbara Barber
  Ohio Atty. General's Office, Taxation Section,
  30 E. Broad St., 16th Floor, Columbus 43215
  (614) 466-5967; Fax: (614) 466-8226
Treasurer: Brian C. Thomas
  Graydon, Head & Richey, L.L.P., 1900 Fifth Third Center,
  511 Walnut St., Cincinnati 45202
  (513) 629-2859; Fax: (513) 651-3836
Meetings: First Thurs., monthly

Butler County Bar Association
118 S. 2nd St., Hamilton 45011
(513) 896-6671; Fax: (513) 868-7022
E-mail: bcbarassn@aol.com
Internet: www.butlercountybar.org
Exec. Dir.: Mary Lou Kusel
President: Stephen C. Lane
  Fiehrer, Lane & Copeland, 10 Journal Sq., Suite 400,
  Hamilton 45011 (513) 887-7300
V.P.: Elizabeth A. Yauch
  240 E. State St., Trenton 45067 (513) 988-6169
Treasurer: Casandra Kiesey
  Butler County Prosecutor's Office,
  315 High St., 11th Floor, P.O. Box 515, Hamilton 45012
  (513) 887-3474

Carroll County Bar Association
President: John S. Campbell
  130 Public Sq., P.O. Box 25, Carrollton 44615-0025
  (330) 627-5577
V.P.: Donald Burns
  11 E. Main St., Carrollton 44615 (330) 627-4555
Secretary-Treasurer: Kathleen Allmon Stoneman
  63 Second St., S.W., P.O. Box 235, Carrollton 44615
  (330) 627-6642

Champaign County Bar Association
President: Kevin S. Talebi
  Paulig, Singer & Talebi, 40 Monument Sq., Suite 300,
  Urbana 43078 (937) 653-5257; Fax: (937) 653-3027
Treasurer: Joe Valore
  120 N. Main St., Suite B, Urbana 43078 (937) 653-1729

Cincinnati Bar Association
225 E. Sixth St., 2nd Floor, Cincinnati 45202-3209
(513) 381-8213; Fax: (513) 381-0528
Internet: www.cincybar.org
Exec. Dir.: John C. Norwine
President: John W. McNally, Jr.
  Jacobs, Kleinman, Seibel & McNally Co., L.P.A.,
  2300 Kroger Building, 1014 Vine St., Cincinnati 45202
  (513) 381-6600; Fax: (513) 381-4150
President-Elect: Hon. Beth A. Myers
  Hamilton County Common Pleas Court,
  1000 Main St., Room 370, Cincinnati 45202
  (513) 946-5102
Elections: April

Clark County Bar Association
President: Jerome M. Strozdas
  20 S. Limestone St., Suite 330, Springfield 45502
  (937) 323-1010; Fax: (937) 323-1953

Clermont County Bar Association
Clermont County Law Library, 270 Main St.,
Batavia 45103
(513) 732-7109; Fax: (513) 732-0974
President: Kathleen Rodenberg
  Rodenberg & Kennedy, 247 E. Main St., Batavia 45103
  (513) 732-2040

Cleveland Bar Association
1301 E. Ninth St., 2nd Level, Cleveland 44114
(216) 696-3525; Fax: (216) 696-2413
Internet: www.clevelandbar.org
Exec. Dir./Secretary: D. Larkin Chenault
President: David A. Kutik
  Jones Day, North Point, 901 Lakeside Ave.,
  Cleveland 44114-1190 (216) 586-7186
President-Elect: P. Kelly Tompkins
  RPM International Inc., 2628 Pearl Rd., P.O. Box 777,
  Medina 44258 (330) 273-8883
Treasurer: Thomas M. Turner
  Turner & Associates,
  Executive Commons East, Suite 206,
  29525 Chagrin Blvd., Beachwood 44122-4601
  (216) 595-1700

Clinton County Bar Association
Clinton County Law Library, 46 S. South St.,
Wilmington 45177
(937) 382-2428; Fax: (937) 382-7632
President: Richard Federle, Jr.
  Law Offices of Rose & Dobyns, 97 N. South St.,
  Wilmington 45177 (937) 382-2838

Columbiana County Bar Association
Secretary-Treasurer: C. Brooke Zellers
  166 N. Union Ave., Salem 44460
  (330) 337-4820; Fax: (330) 332-2907
Elections: April
Meetings: Second Mon. in Jan., April and Sept., except
holidays

Columbus Bar Association
175 S. Third St., Suite 1100, Columbus 43215
(614) 221-4112; Fax: (614) 221-4850
Internet: www.cbalaw.org
Exec. Dir.: Alex Lagusch
** E-mail: alex@cbalaw.org**
President: Sally W. Bloomfield
  Bricker & Eckler, L.L.P., 100 S. Third St.,
  Columbus 43215-4291
  (614) 227-2300; Fax: (614) 227-2390
  E-mail: sbloomfield@bricker.com
President-Elect: Belinda S. Barnes
  Lane, Alton & Horst, L.L.C., 175 S. Third St., Suite 700,
  Columbus 43215-5100
  (614) 233-4709; Fax: (614) 228-0146
  E-mail: bbarnes@lah4law.com
Annual Elections: May

Coshocton County Bar Association
President: Robert E. Weir
  305 Main St., Coshocton 43812
  (740) 622-6464; Fax: (740) 622-8107
Secretary-Treasurer: Paul R. Scherbel
  240 S. 4th St., P.O. Box 880, Coshocton 43812-0880
  (740) 622-0166; Fax: (740) 622-0174

Crawford County Bar Association
President: David R. Cory
  Cory & Cory, P.L.L., 221 S. Poplar St., P.O. Box 510,
  Bucyrus 44820-0510
  (419) 562-7762; Fax: (419) 562-6514
V.P.: Debra A. Garverick
  112 W. Church St., Galion 44833
  (419) 468-4933; Fax: (419) 468-8428
Secretary-Treasurer: Edward L. Kurek
  112 E. Mansfield St., Bucyrus 44820
  (419) 562-1896; Fax: (419) 562-6538
Meetings: First Wed., Monthly

Cuyahoga County Bar Association
Leader Bldg., Suite 1240, 526 Superior Ave.,
Cleveland 44114
(216) 621-5112; Fax: (216) 523-2259
Internet: www.cuybar.org
Exec. Dir.: Barbara C. Greenberg
President: Justin J. Madden
    Landskroner, Greico & Madden,
    1360 W. 9th St., Suite 200, Cleveland 44113
    (216) 522-9000; Fax: (216) 522-9001
President-Elect: Diana M. Thimmig
    One Cleveland Center, 10th Floor, 1375 E. 9th St.,
    Cleveland 44114
    (216) 623-0150; Fax: (216) 623-0134
Secretary: Howard R. Besser
    U.S. E.E.O. Commission, 1660 W. 2nd St., Suite 850,
    Cleveland 44113-1454
    (216) 522-7675; Fax: (216) 381-0250
Treasurer: David Webster
    Webster, Webster & Kvale, 1260 W. 6th St., Suite 600,
    Cleveland 44113
    (216) 566-1144; Fax: (216) 566-1221

Darke County Bar Association
President: Phil Hoover
    Darke County Ohio Prosecutor's Office,
    Darke County Courthouse, 3rd Floor, Greenville 45331
    (937) 547-7380; Fax: (937) 457-9075
V.P.: John F. Marchal, Jr.
    Marchal & Brown, 116-118 W. Fourth St., Greenville 45331
    (937) 548-1125; Fax: (937) 548-6409
Secretary-Treasurer: Gail M. Dues
    Hanes, Schipfer, Cooper, Graber, Guillozet & Detling, Ltd.,
    507 S. Broadway, Greenville 45331
    (937) 548-1157; Fax: (937) 548-2734

Annual Elections: December
Meetings: First Thurs., monthly

Dayton Bar Association
600 Performance Pl., 109 N. Main St., Dayton 45402
(937) 222-7902; Fax: (937) 222-1308
Internet: www.daybar.org
Exec. Dir.: William B. Wheeler
President: Susan Blasik-Miller
    Freund, Freeze & Arnold, One S. Main St., Suite 1800,
    Dayton 45402
    (937) 222-2424; Fax: (937) 222-5369
First V.P.: Jeffrey A. Swillinger
    Crew & Buchanan, 2850 Kettering Tower,
    40 N. Main St., Dayton 45423
    (937) 223-6211
Second V.P.: Hon. Alice O. McCollum
    Montgomery County Probate Court, 41 N. Perry St.,
    Dayton 45422
    (937) 225-4552; Fax: (937) 496-3181
    E-mail: mccolluma@mcohio.org
Secretary: Karen D. Bradley
    Skelton, McQuiston, Gounaris & Henry Attorneys &
    Counselors-at-Law, 130 W. Second St., Suite 1818,
    Dayton 45402 (937) 226-1224
    E-mail: bradlw@main-net.com
Treasurer: Paul B. Roderer, Jr.
    4 E. Schantz Ave., P.O. Box 897, Dayton 45409
    (937) 293-9189; Fax: (937) 293-9372
    E-mail: rodererlaw@aol.com

Defiance County Bar Association
President: Maurice J. Murray
    500 Court St., Defiance 43512
    (419) 784-2123; Fax: (419) 782-7680
V.P.: Barbara Rath
    Common Pleas Court, 221 Clinton St., P.O. Box 386,
    Defiance 43512 (419) 782-5931
Secretary: Jeff Strausbaugh
    414 3rd St., Defiance 43512 (419) 784-3700
Treasurer: Denis Trimboli
    U.A.W.G.M.Legal Services, 1500 Baltimore Road,
    Defiance 43512 (419) 782-2253; Fax: (419) 784-2756

Delaware County Bar Association
President: G. Scott Miller
    103 N. Union St., Delaware 43015
    (740) 363-1324; Fax: (740) 548-5443

Erie County Bar Association
P.O. Box 905, Sandusky 44871-0905
Internet: www.erie-county-ohio.net
President: Gary A. Lickfelt
    Erie County Services Center,
    2900 Columbus Ave., Room 204, Sandusky 44870
    (419) 627-7696
V.P.: Victor Kademenos
    502 W. Washington St., Sandusky 44870
    (419) 625-7770
Secretary: E. Ann S. Giesler
    8 Harbour Pkwy., Sandusky 44870-4141
    (419) 624-1501
Treasurer: Pamela A. Gross
    3710 Mathhes Ave., Sandusky 44870
    (419) 621-0577

Meetings: First Fri., monthly
Election: January

Fairfield County Bar Association
Internet: www.fairfieldcountybar.org
President: David Shaver
    P.O. Box 320, Pickerington 43147
    (614) 837-8433; Fax: (614) 837-8634
V.P.: Jason Price
    126 E. Chestnut, Lancaster 43130
    (740) 689-3000; Fax: (740) 689-3506
Secretary: Peggy Smith
    136 Mulberry St., Lancaster 43130
    (740) 681-9499; Fax: (740) 653-4118
Treasurer: Scott Wood
    144 E. Main St., Lancaster 43130
    (740) 653-6464; Fax: (740) 653-8522
Elections: May
Meetings: Third Thurs., Sept.-April

Fayette County Bar Association
President: Landis Terhune-Olaker
    P.O. Box 895, Washington Court House 43160
    (740) 636-1830
Secretary-Treasurer: Melissa Simmons-Upthegrove
    129 N. Hinde St., Washington Court House 43160
    (740) 335-2087

Federal Bar Association, Northern Dist. of Ohio
P.O. Box 16562, Columbus 43216-6562
E-mail: admin@fba-ndohio.org
President: Keven Drummond Eiber
    Brouse, McDowell, L.P.A.,
    1001 Lakeside Ave., Suite 1600, Cleveland 44114
    (216) 830-6830; Fax: (216) 830-6807
President-Elect: Lori White Laisure
    U.S. Attorney's Office, 1800 Bank One Center,
    600 Superior Ave. E., Cleveland 44114-2600
    (216) 622-3600; Fax: (216) 522-3370
V.P.: Arthur M. Kaufman
    Hahn, Loeser & Parks, L.L.P., 3300 BP Tower,
    200 Public Sq., Cleveland 44114-2301
    (216) 621-0150; Fax: (216) 241-2824
Secretary: Hugh E. McKay
    Porter, Wright, Morris & Arthur L.L.P.,
    925 Euclid Ave., Suite 1700, Cleveland 44115-1483
    (216) 443-9000; Fax: (216) 443-9011
Treasurer: Diane P. Chapman
    Baker & Hostetler, 3200 National City Center,
    1900 E. Ninth St., Cleveland 44114-3485
    (216) 861-7343; Fax: (215) 696-0740
    E-mail: dchapman@bakerlaw.com

Findlay-Hancock County Bar Association
President: J. Michael Wilder
  Marathon Ashland Petroleum L.L.C., 539 S. Main St.,
  Findlay 45840-3295
  (419) 421-2470; Fax: (419) 421-3124
President-Elect: Robert A. Fry
  222 W. Broadway, Findlay 45840 (419) 424-7089
Secretary-Treasurer: Douglas Melin
  Marathon Ashland Petroleum L.L.C., 539 S. Main St.,
  Findlay 45840-3295 (419) 422-2121

Franklin County Trial Lawyers Association
37 W. Broad St., Suite 480, Columbus 43215-4132
(614) 228-1017; Fax: (614) 241-2215
Exec. Dir.: Thomas J. King
President: Michael Miller
  Volkema, Thomas, Miller, Burkett, Scott & Merry,
  140 E. Town St., Suite 1100, Columbus 43215
  (614) 221-4400
Meetings: Monthly
Elections: May

Fulton County Bar Association
President: Jeffrey L. Robinson
  Barber, Kaper, Stamm & Robinson, 124 N. Fulton St.,
  P.O. Box 531, Wauseon 43567
  (419) 337-5065; Fax: (419) 337-1136
V.P.: Mark L. Powers
  142 N. Fulton St., Wauseon 43567
  (419) 337-2531; Fax: (419) 335-5040
Secretary-Treasurer: Timothy W. Hallett
  Hallett, Hallett & Nagel, 132 S. Fulton St.,
  Wauseon 43567-1388
  (419) 335-5011; Fax: (419) 335-3187
Meetings: Second Tues., Sept.-May

Gallia County Bar Association
President: Douglas Cowles
  Douglas M Cowles Co LPA, 435 2nd. Ave., P.O. Box 969,
  Gallipolis 45631-0449
  (740) 446-0644; Fax: (740) 446-8433

Geauga County Bar Association
P.O. Box 750, Chardon 44024
(440) 286-7160
E-mail: gcll@nls.net
President: Ann D'Amico
  5001 Mayfield Rd., Lyndhurst 44124
  (440) 286-7160; Fax: (440) 285-3603
V.P.: Stephen G. Macek
  First Merit Bank, N.A., 111 Cascade Plaza, CAS 81,
  Akron 44308
  (330) 849-8753; Fax: (330) 384-7133
Secretary: Bruce Smacheek
  114 E. Park St., Chardon 44024
  (440) 286-6177; Fax: (440) 286-6158
Treasurer: Lisa J. Carey
  Svete McGee & Carrabine Co., L.P.A., 100 Parker Ct.,
  Chardon 44024
  (440) 286-9571; Fax: (440) 286-7504
Meetings: Fourth Wed.

Greene County Bar Association
Greene County Law Library,
45 N. Detroit St., 3rd Floor, Xenia 45385
(937) 562-5115; Fax: (937) 562-5116
President: Ronald C. Lewis
  101 N. Detroit Ave., Xenia 45385 (937) 376-7303
First V.P.: Kristen Kelly
  Greene County Domestic Relations Court,
  45 N. Detroit Ave., Xenia 45385-2255
  (937) 562-5249
Second V.P.: J. Andrew Root
  Gibney, Stephan, Barrett & Root,
  1354 N. Monroe Dr., Suite B, Xenia 45385
  (937) 372-4404; Fax: (937) 372-5435
Secretary-Treasurer: Charles M. Rowland, II
  2190 Gateway Dr., Fairborn 45324
  (937) 879-9542

Guernsey County Bar Association
President: Stephanie L. Mitchell
  139 W. 8th St., Cambridge 43725
  (740) 432-6322; Fax: (740) 439-1795
V.P.: Matthew T. Smith
  Advantage Bank, 814 Wheeling Ave., Cambridge 43725
  (740) 432-6363; Fax: (740) 439-1765
Secretary/Treasurer: Mary B. Keith
  58885 Grisak Rd., P.O. Box 82, Byesville 43723
  (740) 685-7611
Elections: May
Meetings: First Fri., monthly

Henry County Bar Association
P.O. Box 201, Napoleon 43545
President: Melissa Pepper-Firestone
  555 Monroe St., Napoleon 43545
  (419) 592-3816
Secretary-Treasurer: David Busick
  S671 Road 9, Liberty Center 43532
  (419) 533-4516

Hocking County Bar Association
President: James Lewis
  Citizens Bank, 188 W. Main St., Logan 43138-0388
  (740) 385-8561
V.P.: Sandra L. Brandon
  38 1/2 N. Market St., P.O. Box 943, Logan 43138-0943
  (740) 380-2941; Fax: (740) 380-2787
Secretary/Treasurer: Stephen E. Proctor
  G. Drew Roston, 61 N. Market St. Rear,
  Logan 43138-1291
  (740) 385-5604; Fax: (740) 385-0145

Holmes County Bar Association
President: Jeffrey G. Kellogg
  5 S. Washington St., Millersburg 44654
  (330) 674-0442; Fax: (330) 674-0443
V.P.: Sean M. Warner
  138 E. Jackson St., Millersburg 44654
  (330) 674-3055; Fax: (330) 674-4469
Secretary/Treasurer: Ellis Miller
  P.O. Box 250, Berlin 44610
  (330) 893-2600

Huron County Bar Association
President: James Martin
  111B Walton Ave., Willard 44890
  (419) 964-0423; Fax: (419) 964-0433
V.P.: Reese Wineman
  6 W. Main St., Norwalk 44857
  (419) 668-6840; Fax: (419) 668-7720
Secretary: Stuart O'Hara
  Asst. Norwalk City Law Director,
  38 Whittlesey Ave., Norwalk 44857
  (419) 663-6785
Treasurer: Davia S. Kaspar
  12 E. Main St., 4th Floor, Norwalk 44857
  (419) 668-8215

Jackson County Bar Association
President: William C. Martin III
  141 Portsmouth St., P.O. Box 926, Jackson 45640
  (740) 286-8054
V.P.: Aaron Michael
  233 Main St., Jackson 45640-1715
  (740) 286-4649
Secretary: Dana E. Glliland
  23 E. Broadway St., P.O. Box 284, Wellston 45692
  (740) 384-5440
Treasurer: Shannon Weber
  16 E. Broadway, Wellston 45692
  (740) 384-2111
Elections: January
Meetings: Third Thurs., monthly

Jefferson County Bar Association
Jefferson County Courthouse, 301 Market St.,
Steubenville 43952
(740) 283-8553; Fax: (740) 283-8629
E-mail: law_library@jeffcch.com
President: S. Gary Repellla
  212 City Annex Bldg., 308 Market St.,
  Steubenville 43952 (740) 282-7929
First V.P.: Emanuela Agresta
  300 Sinclair Bldg., P.O. Box 1506, Steubenville 43952
  (740) 282-5323
Second V.P.: Samuel A. Pate
  708 Sinclair Bldg., Steubenville 43952 (740) 282-2000
Secretary: John J. Mascio
  329 N. Fourth St., Steubenville 43952 (740) 282-1544
Elections: October

John Mercer Langston Bar Association
President: Cynthia N. Callender
  Ohio State Auditors Office, 88 E. Broad St.,
  P.O. Box 1140, Columbus 43216-1140 (614) 728-8537
V.P.: James Barnes
  Ohio Atty. General's Office, 150 E. Gay St.,
  Columbus 43215 (614) 466-6696
Secretary: Janine Jones
  Baker & Hostetler, L.L.P., 65 E. State St., Suite 2100,
  Columbus 43215 (614) 462-2668; Fax: (614) 462-7616
Elections: April
2004-05 Officers

Knox County Bar Association
President: Heidi Mallory
  5 N. Gay St., Suite 222, Mount Vernon 43050
  (740) 393-5085
V.P.: Wendi M. Fowler
  121 E. High St., Mount Vernon 43050 (740) 397-5262
Secretary: P. Robert Broeren
  110 E. Gambier St., Mount Vernon 43050
  (740) 397-7474; Fax: (740) 397-5466
Treasurer: Robert D. Lee
  136 S. Main St., Mount Vernon 43050
  (740) 392-8838; Fax: (740) 392-8838
Meetings: Third Wed., monthly

Lake County Bar Association
25 N. Park Pl., P.O. Box 490, Painesville 44077
(440) 352-6044; Fax: (440) 350-2298
E-mail: lcba@lcba-ohio.org
Internet: www.lcba-ohio.org
Exec. Dir.: Diane R. Cochrane
President: David S. Sternberg
  Sternberg & Zeid, 7547 Mentor Ave., Suite 301,
  Mentor 44060 (440) 942-6267; Fax: (440) 942-6504
V.P.: Geoffrey W. Weaver
  Centre Plaza South, Suite 530, 35350 Curtis Blvd.,
  Eastlake 44094 (440) 942-6262; Fax: (440) 942-7211
Secretary: Walter J. McNamara
  McNamara, Hanrahan, Callender & Loxterman,
  8440 Station St., Mentor 44060
  (440) 255-9100; Fax: (440) 974-1585
Treasurer: Robert A. Gambol
  Lake County Prosecutor's Office, 125 Main St.,
  Painesville 44077 (440) 350-2683; Fax: (440) 350-2585
Annual Election: June
Hours: Second Wed., monthly

Lawrence County Bar Association
Lawrence County Law Library,
1 Veterans Sq., 4th Annex Floor, Ironton 45638
(740) 533-0582
President: Patricia Sanders
  (740) 533-4340; Fax: (740) 533-4377

Licking County Bar Association
President: Richard M. Van Winkle
  8 Arcade Pl., Suite 200, Newark 43055
  (740) 345-3488; Fax: (740) 349-7526
V.P.: James Hostetter
  40 W. Main St., Newark 43055
  (740) 349-6663; Fax: (740) 349-6638
Secretary: Robert Handelman
  29 S. Park Pl., Newark 43055
  (740) 349-8581; Fax: (740) 345-4101
Treasurer: Joseph A. Robison
  Jones Norpell List Miller & Howarth, 2 N. 1st St.,
  P.O. Box 4010, Newark 43058-4010
  (740) 345-9801; Fax: (740) 345-6031

Logan County Bar Association
President: Dane M. Hanna
  Thompson, Dunlap & Heydinger, 1111 Rush Ave.,
  P.O. Box 68, Bellefontaine 43311
  (937) 593-6065; Fax: (937) 593-9978
V.P.: Amy Billiar
  Logan County Common Pleas Court, Room 18,
  101 S. Main St., Bellefontaine 43311
  (937) 599-7260
Secretary: Kathryn Dougherty
  125 W. Sandusky Ave., Bellefontaine 43311
  (937) 592-3785
Treasurer: Bridget Hawkins
  Beck, Beck & Hawkins, 709 N. Main St.,
  Bellefontaine 43311 (937) 599-6242

Lorain County Bar Association
205 Robinson Bldg., 401 Broad St., Elyria 44035
(440) 323-8416; Fax: (440) 323-1922
President: Richard R. Mellott, Jr.
  Triglio & Stephenson, P.L.L.,
  5750 Cooper Foster Park Rd., Suite 102, Lorain 44053
  (440) 988-9500; Fax: (440) 988-9511
V.P.: Kim R. Meyers
  McCray, Muzilla, Smith & Meyers Co. L.P.A.,
  260 Burns Rd., Suite 150, Elyria 44035
  (440) 366-9930; Fax: (440) 366-1910
Secretary-Treasurer: James N. Taylor
  James N. Taylor Co., L.P.A., 409 East Ave., Suite B,
  Elyria 44035 (440) 323-5700

Lucas County Bar Association
President: John R. Wanick
  Anspach Meeks Ellenberger, L.L.P.,
  300 Madison Ave., Suite 1600, Toledo 43604-2633
  (419) 246-5757; Fax: (419) 321-6979
First V.P.: Patricia Hayden Kurt
  Spengler Nathanson P.L.L.,
  608 Madison Ave., Suite 1000, P.O. Box 2027,
  Toledo 43603-2027
  (419) 241-2201; Fax: (419) 241-8599
Treasurer: Steven K. Lauer
  Internal Revenue Service, 4 SeaGate, Room 226,
  Toledo 43604-2638
  (419) 213-5131; Fax: (419) 213-5120
Elections: December
Meetings: Jan.-June & Sept.-Dec.: Mon., Noon

Madison County Bar Association
Madison County Law Library,
1 N. Main St., Room 205, London 43140
(740) 852-9515
President: Rachel M. Price
  Prosecutors Office, 23 W. High St., London 43140
  (740) 852-2259; Fax: (740) 845-1694
V.P.: Eric M. Schooley
  Wildman and Schooley, 26 E. Fourth St., London 43140
  (740) 852-8383; Fax: (740) 852-1699
Secretary: Zahid H. Siddiqi
  58 E. High St., Suite B, London 43140
  (740) 845-0195
Treasurer: Shannon M. Treynor
  58 E. High St., Suite C, London 43140
  (740) 845-0195

Mahoning County Bar Association
114 E. Front St., Youngstown 44503
(330) 746-2933
President: Clair M. Carlin
  62 S. Main St., P.O. Box 5369, Poland 44514
  (330) 707-0377; E-mail: info@carlin-law.com
President-Elect: Larry D. Wilkes
  300 Commerce Bldg., 201 E. Commerce St.,
  Youngstown 44503
  (330) 743-1717; E-mail: lwilkes@dyyoungstown.com
Secretary-Treasurer: Joseph D. DeSanto
  807 Southwestern Run, Poland 44514-3688
  (330) 758-3878
Elections: June
Meetings: Third Thurs., monthly

Marion County Bar Association
President: Malcolm Goodman
  131 S. Prospect St., Suite 102, Marion 43302
  (740) 302-4445
V.P.: Hon. William Finnegan
  Marion County Common Pleas Court, 100 N. Main St.,
  Marion 43302 (740) 223-4220; Fax: (740) 387-7131
Secretary-Treasurer: Robert D. Fragale
  Nemo & Fragale, L.P.A., 495 S. State St.,
  Marion 43302-5033 (740) 387-7438; Fax: (740) 387-6367

Meigs County Bar Association
President: Bernard V. Fultz
  111 1/2 W. Second St., P.O. Box 723, Pomeroy 45769-0723
  (740) 992-7101; Fax: (740) 992-5457
Secretary-Treasurer: Jennifer L. Sheets
  Little Sheets & Warner, 211-213 E. 2nd St.,
  P.O. Box 686, Pomeroy 45769-0686
  (740) 992-2151; Fax: (740) 922-5168
V.P.: Frederick W. Crow
  Meigs County Common Pleas Court, 100 E. 2nd St.,
  Pomeroy 45769-1030
  (740) 992-6439; Fax: (740) 992-3828

Mercer County Bar Association
President: Kathryn W. Speelman
  201 E. Vine St., Coldwater 45828
  (419) 678-2378; Fax: (419) 678-8653
Secretary: Ross J. Finke
  110½ W. Market St., Celina 45822
  (419) 586-1334; Fax: (419) 586-0120
Treasurer: Angela R.M. Nickell
  Koester Law Office, 201 E. Vine St., Coldwater 45828
  (419) 678-2378

Miami County Bar Association
President: Samuel Huffman
  80 S. Plum St., Troy 45373 (937) 335-0550
V.P.: Frank J. Patrizio
  123 Market St., P.O. Box 910, Piqua 45356
  (937) 773-3212; Fax: (937) 773-9672

Monroe County Bar Association
President: Julie R. Selmon
  107 W. Court St., Woodsfield 43793
  (740) 472-5768; Fax: (740) 472-1718
V.P.: Robert Coury
  Smith & Coury, 316 S. Main St., P.O. Box 599,
  Woodsfield 43793
  (740) 472-1647; Fax: (740) 472-5288
Secretary-Treasurer: Richard A. Yoss
  122 N. Main St., P.O. Box 271, Woodsfield 43793
  (740) 472-0707; Fax: (740) 472-0770

Morgan County Bar Association
President: Robert J. Christie
  400 Ralston Dr., P.O. Box 419, McConnelsville 43756
  (740) 962-2262; Fax: (740) 962-4992
Secretary-Treasurer: Michael D. Lowe
  59 N. 7th St., McConnelsville 43756-1101
  (740) 962-3862

Morrow County Bar Association
President: Robert C. Hickson, Jr.
  22 S. Main St., P.O. Box 166, Mount Gilead 43338-0166
  (419) 946-6055; Fax: (419) 946-5904
Treasurer: Amy Steiger
  48 E. High St., Mount Gilead 43338 (419) 947-5515

Muskingum County Bar Association
President: Crystal I. Zellar
  720 Market St., P.O. Box 2172, Zanesville 43701
  (740) 452-8439; Fax: (740) 450-8499
  E-mail: czellar@zellarlaw.com
Secretary: Susan E. Small
  825 Adair Ave., Zanesville 43701 (740) 455-3350
Treasurer: David J. Tarbert
  Kincaid Taylor & Geyer, 50 N. Fourth St., P.O. Box 1030,
  Zanesville 43702-1030
  (740) 454-2591; Fax: (740) 455-6975

Noble County Bar Association
President: John W. Nau
  Common Pleas Court, Courthouse, Room 300,
  Caldwell 43724 (740) 732-4045; Fax: (740) 732-0100
V.P.: Lucien C. Young, Jr.
  508 North St., Caldwell 43724-1224 (740) 732-8441
Secretary: Sharon L. Tanner
  421 West St., Caldwell 43724
  (740) 732-7667; Fax: (740) 732-2986

Norman S. Minor Bar Association
President: Russell W. Tye
  75 Public Sq., Cleveland 44113-2001 (216) 324-7893

Ohio Association of Civil Trial Attorneys
17 S. High St., Suite 200, Columbus 43215
(614) 221-1900; Fax: (614) 221-1989
President: James R. Gallagher
  Gallagher Gams Pryor Tallan & Littrel, L.L.P.,
  471 E. Broad St., 19th Floor, Columbus 43215-3872
  (614) 228-5151; Fax: (614) 228-0032
  E-mail: jgallagher@ggptl.com
V.P.: Steven V. Freeze
  Freund, Freeze and Arnold,
  One Dayton Centre, Suite 1800, One S. Main St.,
  Dayton 45402-2017 (937) 222-2424; Fax: (937) 222-5369
  E-mail: sfreeze@ffalaw.com
Secretary: Scott A. Gilliam
  The Cincinnati Insurance Companies,
  6200 S. Gilmore Rd., Fairfield 45014
  (513) 870-2811; Fax: (513) 870-2985
  E-mail: scott_gilliam@cinfin.com
Treasurer: Gregory E. O'Brien
  Weston, Hurd, Fallon, Paisley & Howley, L.L.P.,
  2500 Terminal Tower, 50 Public Sq., Cleveland 44113
  (216) 241-6602; Fax: (216) 621-8369
  E-mail: gobrien@westonhurd.com
Meetings: Summer Conference, June 16-18;
Winter Conference, Dec. 1-2

Ohio Association of Criminal Defense Lawyers
2720 Airport Dr., Suite 100, Columbus 43219
(614) 418-1824, (800) 443-2626; Fax: (614) 418-1825
Internet: www.oacdl.org
President: Paul Skendelas
  Franklin Cty. Public Defender,
  373 S. High St., 12th. Floor, Columbus 43215
  (614) 462-3194; Fax: (614) 461-6470
President-Elect: R. Daniel Hannon
  10 S. Third St., Batavia 45103-3042
  (513) 732-2214; Fax: (513) 732-9400
Secretary: Donald Schumacher
  755 S. High St., Columbus 43206-1908
  (614) 444-3900; Fax: (614) 444-9086
Treasurer: James Phillips
  Vorys, Sater, Seymour & Pease, 52 E. Gay St.,
  P.O. Box 1008, Columbus 43216-1008
  (614) 464-5610; Fax: (614) 464-6350

Ohio Municipal Attorneys Association

President: Barbara E. Herring
  City of Toledo, Law Dept.,
  One Government Center, Suite 2250, Toledo 43604
  (419) 245-1020; Fax: (419) 245-1090
First V.P.: Bruce E. Bailey
  33 E. Schrock Rd., Westerville 43081
  (614) 882-2327; Fax: (614) 882-5150
Second V.P.: Richard Pfeiffer, Jr.
  Columbus City Atty., 90 W. Broad St., Columbus 43215
  (614) 645-7385
Secretary/General Counsel: John E. Gotherman
  The Ohio Municipal League, 175 S. 3rd St., Suite 510,
  Columbus 43215-7100
  (614) 221-4349; Fax: (614) 221-4390

Ohio Women's Bar Association
9705 State Rd., North Royalton 44133
(440) 582-2769; Fax: (440) 582-2856
Internet: www.owba.org
Exec. Dir.: I. Violet Imre
Preisdent: Halle M. Hebert
  Oldham & Dowling, 195 S. Main St., Suite 300,
  Akron 44308 (330) 762-7377; Fax: (330) 762-7390
  E-mail: hherbert@oldham-dowling.com
President-Elect: Monique Bradley Lampke
  Porter, Wright, Morris & Arthur, L.L.P., 41 S. High St.,
  Columbus 43215 (614) 227-2058; Fax: (614) 227-2100
  E-mail: mlampke@porterwright.com
V.P.: Pamela D. Houston
  Andrews & Pontius, L.L.C., 4817 State Rd., Suite 100,
  P.O. Box 10, Ashtabula 44005
  (440) 998-6835; Fax: (440) 992-6336
  E-mail: phouston@andrewpointius.com
Secretary: Susan E. Petersen
  Spangenberg, Shibley & Liber,
  2400 National City Center, 1900 E. Ninth St.,
  Cleveland 44114 (216) 696-3232; Fax: (216) 696-3924
  E-mail: sep@spanglaw.com
Treasurer: Clare K. Smith
  Marshall & Melhorn, L.L.C., Four SeaGate, 8th Floor,
  Toledo 43604 (419) 249-7100; Fax: (419) 249-7151
  E-mail: smith@marshall-melhorn.com

Ottawa County Bar Association

President: Sarah Nation
  318 Madison St., Port Clinton 43452
  (419) 734-2412; Fax: (419) 734-2123
  E-mail: polarrays@yahoo.com
V.P.: Catherine E. Heigel
  Kocher & Gillum, 101½ Madison St., Port Clinton 43452
  (419) 732-3135; Fax: (419) 734-5644
  E-mail: catherine@kochbergillum.com
Secretary/Treasurer: Roger Stark
  UAW-GM Legal Service Plan, 3116 Bardshar Rd.,
  Sandusky 44870 (419) 625-0536
  E-mail: rogerst@uawlsp.com
Meetings: 1st Mon., monthly

Parma Bar Association

President: Richard P. Dell'Aquilla
  5800 Lombardo Ctr., Suite 255, Seven Hills 44131
  (216) 642-5357
Secretary: David R. Boldt
  Kirner & Boldt Co., L.P.A., 8025 Corporate Cir.,
  North Royalton 44133
  (440) 884-4300; Fax: (440) 884-4302
Treasurer: David L. Nobili
  Leary Shifko Novili & Lang, 5700 Pearl Rd., Suite 306,
  Cleveland 44129-2537
  (216) 886-3000; Fax: (440) 886-3171
2004-05 Officers

Perry County Bar Association

President: Maureen E. Dodd
  106 N. Main St., New Lexington 43764 (740) 342-7324
V.P.: Nancy Ridenour
  P.O. Box 827, New Lexington 43764 (740) 342-1109
Secretary: Cindy O'Neil
  113 N. Main St., P.O. Box 508,
  New Lexington 43764-0508 (740) 342-3582
Treasurer: Riley Crandell
  P.O. Box 610, Thornville 43076 (740) 246-5624

Pike County Bar Association

President: William W. Bevens
  230 Waverly Plaza, Suite 600, Waverly 45690
  (740) 947-2560; Fax: (740) 947-5065
Treasurer: Dave Self

Putnam County Bar Association

President: Todd C. Schroeder
  315 E. Main St., P.O. Box 110, Ottawa 45875
  (419) 523-5658; Fax: (419) 523-6500
V.P.: Matthew Cunningham
  749 N. Perry St., Ottawa 45875 (419) 523-3396
Secretary/Treasurer: Gary Lammers
  125 W. Main St., Ottawa 45875 (419) 523-5400

Richland County Bar Association, Inc.
Richland County Law Library,
50 Park Ave. E., 2nd Floor, Mansfield 44902
(419) 774-5595
President: Donald E. Hoover
  Weldon, Huston & Keyser, L.L.P.,
  28 Park Ave. West, 9th Floor, Mansfield 44902
  (419) 524-9811; Fax: (419) 522-5758
V.P.: Loré Whitney
  Inscore, Rinehardt, Whitney & Enderle Co. L.P.A.,
  13 Park Ave. W., Mansfield 44902
  (419) 522-2733; Fax: (419) 522-5165
Secretary: David Haring
  Brown, Bemiller, Murray, McIntyre, Vetter & Heck, L.L.P.,
  70 Park Ave. W., P.O. Box 728, Mansfield 44901-0728
  (419) 525-1811; Fax: (419) 525-3810
Treasurer: C. Richard Thompson
  Thompson & Cockley, L.P.A., 13 Park Ave. W., Suite 300,
  Mansfield 44902 (419) 522-5297; Fax: (419) 524-8017

Ross County Bar Association

President: Hon. Thomas E. Bunch
  Chillicothe Municipal Court, 26 Paint St.,
  Chillicothe 45601-3202
  (740) 773-3515; Fax: (740) 774-1101

Sandusky County Bar Association

President: Lisa Snyder
  714 Court St., Fremont 43420
  (419) 333-9918; Fax: (419) 333-9054
Secretary/Treasurer: Beth Bales
  107 N. Main St., Clyde 43410 (419) 547-9471

Seneca County Bar Association

President: Dawn Root
  5219 N. State Rt. 53, Tiffin 44883
  (419) 447-8332; Fax: (419) 447-8332
V.P.: Lisa Miller
  120½ S. Washington St., Suite 216, Tiffin 44883
  (419) 443-8985; Fax: (419) 443-9476
Secretary: Barbara L. Marley
  100 N. Poplar St., P.O. Box 866, Fostoria 44830-0866
  (419) 435-7786; Fax: (419) 435-6062
Treasurer: Derek W. DeVine
  Lange & DeVine Law Offices, 174 S. Washington St.,
  Tiffin 44883 (419) 448-9250

Shelby County Bar Association

President: William Zimmerman
Shelby County Public Defender Office, 101 E. Poplar St.,
Sidney 45365 (937) 492-1969
V.P.: Thomas W. Kerrigan II
Kerrigan, Boller, Stevenson & Goettemoeller Co., L.P.A.,
126 N. Main St., P.O. Box 987, Sidney 45365
(937) 492-6125; Fax: (937) 492-2532
Secretary/Treasurer: Michael Staudt
Faulkner, Garmhausen, Keister & Shenk, L.P.A.,
100 S. Main St., Suite 300, Sidney 45365
(937) 492-1271; Fax: (937) 498-1306

Stark County Bar Association

Exec. Dir.: Tina McCort
116 Cleveland Ave. N.W., Suite 400, Canton 44702-0685
(330) 453-0685; Fax: (330) 453-0180
President: Pericles G. Stergios
2859 Aaronwood Ave., N.E., Suite 101, Massillon 44646
(330) 832-9878
First V.P.: Hon. Jim D. James
Stark County Family Court,
Stark County Office Bldg., Suite 601, 110 Central Plz. S.,
Canton 44702 (330) 451-7307

Thurgood Marshall Law Society

President: Mia Wortham Spells
P.O. Box 60792, Dayton 45406 (937) 224-4600
Secretary: Hazel Rountree
Office of Affirmative Action Programs Wrights State
University, 436 Millett Hall, 3640 Colonel Glenn Hwy.,
Dayton 45435-0001 (937) 775-3207; Fax: (937) 775-3027

Toledo Bar Association

311 N. Superior St., Toledo 43604
(419) 242-9363; Fax: (419) 242-3614
E-mail: tba@toledobar.org
Internet: www.toledobar.org
Exec. Dir.: Trish Branam
President: Steven R. Smith
Connelly Jackson & Collier, L.L.P.,
405 Madison Ave., Suite 1600, Toledo 43604
(419) 243-2100; Fax: (419) 243-7119
First V.P.: Stuart F. Cubbon
Cubbon & Associates, Co., L.P.A., 405 N. Huron, Suite 500,
P.O. Box 387, Toledo 43697-0387 (419) 243-7243
Second V.P.: Louise A. Jackson
Spengler Nathason P.L.L., 608 Madison Ave., Suite 1000,
P.O. Box 2027, Toledo 43603-2027
(419) 241-2201; Fax: (419) 241-8599
Third V.P.: James H. Irmen
Marshall & Melhorn, LLC, Four SeaGate, 8th Floor,
Toledo 43604 (419) 249-7123
Secretary: Catherine Garcia-Feehan
U.S. District Court, 1716 Spielbusch Ave., Suite 210,
Toledo 43624 (419) 259-7488
Treasurer: Laurie J. Pangle
Spengler Nathanson, P.L.L.,
608 Madison Ave., Suite 1000, Toledo 43604
(419) 252-6251; Fax: (419) 241-8599
Elections: May

Toledo Women's Bar Association

President: Yolanda D. Gwynn
U.S. District Court, 1716 Spielbusch Ave., Room 318,
Toledo 43624 (419) 259-6217; Fax: (419) 259-3728
President-Elect: Bridgett Root
Marshall & Melhorn, 4 Seagate, 8th Floor,
Toledo 43604-1599 (419) 249-7100; Fax: (419) 249-7151

Trumbull County Bar Association

Executive Secretary: Dolores Bloom
120 High St., P.O. Box 4222, Warren 44482-0422
(330) 675-2415; Fax: (330) 675-2412
President: Daniel G. Keating
170 Monroe N.W., Warren 44483
(330) 393-4611; Fax: (330) 394-0101
Annual Meeting: September
Elections: May/June

Tuscarawas County Bar Association

President: Ryan Styer
111 W. Main St., Newcomerstown 43832
(740) 498-7252
V.P.: Judith Dzigiel
New Philadelphia Municipal Court, 166 E. High Ave.,
New Philadelphia 44663
(330) 343-6797; Fax: (330) 364-6885
Secretary: Harry Tolhurst
Miller & Kyler, L.P.A., 405 Chauncey Ave.,
New Philadelphia 44663 (330) 343-5585
Treasurer: Traci Berry
154 Second St. N.E., New Philadelphia 44663
(330) 343-0099

Union County Bar Association

President: Tim Aslaner
110 S. Court St., Marysville 43040 (937) 644-8151
Secretary: Steve Dunbar
110 S. Court St., Marysville 43040 (937) 644-8151
Treasurer: Monica Overly
Law Library, 215 W. 6th St., Marysville 43040
(937) 645-3000; Fax: (937) 645-3149
Meetings: Second Thurs., monthly

Van Wert County Bar Association

President: Scott R. Gordon
116 W. Main St., Van Wert 45891
(419) 238-0114; Fax: (419) 238-0195
Secretary-Treasurer: Shaun A. Putnam
111 E. Main St., Suite 105, Van Wert 45891
(419) 238-2200; Fax: (419) 238-1694
Elections: Every two years
Meetings: First Wed., alternate months

Vinton County Bar Association

President: Jeffrey L. Simmons
100 E. Main St., McArthur 45651
(740) 596-4319; Fax: (740) 596-9611
V.P.: N. Robert Grillo
100 E. Main St., McArthur 45651-0466
(740) 596-5480; Fax: (740) 596-3438

Washington County Bar Association

President: John Halliday
Bertram & Halliday, L.L.C., 412 Third St.,
Marietta 45750
(740) 373-1155; Fax: (740) 373-3140
V.P.: Abraham Sellers
Thiesen Brock, L.P.A., 424 2nd. St., P.O. Box 739,
Marietta 45750-2101
(740) 373-5455; Fax: (740) 373-4409
Secretary: Ethan Vessels
Theisen Brock, L.P.A., 424 2nd St., P.O. Box 739,
Marietta 45750-2101
(740) 373-5455; Fax: (743) 373-4409
Treasurer: Robin A. Bozian
S.E.Ohio Legal Svces., 427 2nd. St., Marietta 45750
(740) 374-2629
Annual Meeting: February
2004 Officers

Wayne County Bar Association

President: John E. Johnson, Sr.
Johnson & Helmuth, 343 S. Crownhill Rd., P.O. Box 149,
Orrville 44667 (330) 683-0015; Fax: (330) 682-4925
President-Elect: John C. Johnston III
Critchfield Law Firm, 225 N. Market St., Wooster 44691
(330) 264-4444; Fax: (330) 263-9278
Secretary-Treasurer: James J. Lanham
Taggart Law Firm, 142 W. Liberty St., P.O. Box 218,
Wooster 44691-0218
(330) 264-5141; Fax: (330) 262-1046
Annual Meeting: January

Williams County Bar Association
President: Ryan Breininger
  Newcomer, Shaffer, Spangler & Breininger,
  117 W. Maple St., Bryan 43506 (419) 636-3196
V.P.: Rhonda Fisher
  1399 E. High St., Bryan 43506 (419) 636-2596
Secretary: Ryan Thompson
  Bish, Butler & Thompson, Ltd., 1210 W. High St.,
  Bryan 43506 (419) 636-5666; Fax: (419) 636-3919
Treasurer: Bruce O'Donnell
  Edon State Bank, 101 North Michigan Ave., Edon 43518
  (419) 272-2521

Women Lawyers of Franklin County
President: Angela G. Phelps-White (Magistrate)
  Franklin County Court of Common Pleas,
  375 S. High St., Columbus 43215-4520 (614) 462-4242

Wood County Bar Association
P.O. Box 780, Bowling Green 43402
Internet: www.woodcobarassociation.org
President: Bruce Stevens
  Middleton, Roebke & Nelson, 521 N. Main St.,
  Bowling Green 43402
  (419) 352-7522; Fax: (419) 353-4899

V.P.: Robert D. Strauss
  Koder & Strauss, LLC,
  3361 Executive Parking, Suite 101, Toledo 43606
  (419) 472-9041; Fax: (419) 472-9071

Secretary-Treasurer: Mimi S. Yoon
  Spitler, Huffman, Yoon & Newlove, 131 E. Court St.,
  Bowling Green 43402
  (419) 352-2535; Fax: (419) 353-8728
Meetings: First Mon, monthly

Wyandot County Bar Association

President: Mary E. Fox
  Osburn & Fox, 116 E. Wyandot Ave.,
  Upper Sandusky 43351
  (419) 294-2336; Fax: (419) 294-5669

V.P.: Douglas D. Rowland
  Pfeifer & Pfeifer, 114 W. Wyandot Ave., P.O. Box 240,
  Upper Sandusky 43351 (419) 294-1200

Secretary: Stephanie Weaver
  Wyandot County CSEA, 120 E. Johnson St.,
  Upper Sandusky 43351-1420 (419) 294-4977

OHIO MUNICIPALITIES WITH THEIR COUNTIES, AREA CODES AND ZIP CODES

(Note: An X indicates that the municipality has more than one Zip Code)

Aberdeen (Brown)(937) ... 45101
Ada (Hardin)(419, 567) ... 45810
Adams Mills (Muskingum)(740) ... 43821
Adamsville (Muskingum)(740) ... 43802
Addyston (Hamilton)(513) ... 45001
Adelphi (Ross)(740) ... 43101
Adena (Jefferson)(740) ... 43901
Adrian (Seneca)(419, 567) ... 44801
Akron (Summit)(330, 234) ... 443XX
Albany (Athens)(740) ... 45710
Alexandria (Licking)(740) ... 43001
Alger (Hardin)(419, 567) ... 45812
Alledonia (Belmont)(740) ... 43902
Allensville (Vinton)(740) ... 45651
Alliance (Stark)(330, 234) ... 44601
Alpha (Greene)(937) ... 45301
Alvada (Seneca)(419, 567) ... 44802
Alvordton (Williams)(419, 567) ... 43501
Amanda (Fairfield)(740) ... 43102
Amelia (Clermont)(513) ... 45102
Amesville (Athens)(740) ... 45711
Amherst (Lorain)(440) ... 44001
Amlin (Franklin)(614) ... 43002
Amsden (Seneca)(419, 567) ... 44803
Amsterdam (Jefferson)(740) ... 43903
Anderson (Hamilton)(513) ... 452XX
Andover (Ashtabula)(440) ... 44003
Anna (Shelby)(937) ... 45302
Ansonia (Darke)(937) ... 45303
Antioch (Monroe)(740) ... 43793
Antwerp (Paulding)(419, 567) ... 45813
Apple Creek (Wayne)(330) ... 44606
Arcadia (Hancock)(419, 567) ... 44804
Arcanum (Darke)(937) ... 45304
Archbold (Fulton)(419, 567) ... 43502
Arlington (Hancock)(419, 567) ... 45814
Armstrong Mills (Belmont)(740) ... 43933
Ashland (Ashland)(419,567) ... 44805
Ashley (Delaware)(740) ... 43003
Ashtabula (Ashtabula)(440) ... 4400X
Ashville (Pickaway)(740) ... 43103
Athens (Athens)(740) ... 45701
Attica (Seneca)(419, 567) ... 44807
Atwater (Portage)(330, 234) ... 44201
Augusta (Carroll)(330, 234) ... 44607
Aurora (Portage)(330, 234) ... 44202
Austinburg (Ashtabula)(440) ... 44010
Austintown (Mahoning)(330, 234) ... 44515
Ava (Noble)(740) ... 43711
Avon (Lorain)(440) ... 44011
Avon Lake (Lorain)(440) ... 44012
Bainbridge (Ross)(740) ... 45612
Bakersville (Coshocton)(740) ... 43803
Baltic (Tuscarawas)(330, 234) ... 43804
Baltimore (Fairfield)(740) ... 43105
Bannock (Belmont)(740) ... 43972
Barberton (Summit)(330, 234) ... 44203
Barlow (Washington)(740) ... 45712
Barnesville (Belmont)(740) ... 43713
Bartlett (Washington)(740) ... 45713
Barton (Belmont)(740) ... 43905
Bascom (Seneca)(419, 567) ... 44809
Batavia (Clermont)(513) ... 45103
Bath (Summit)(330, 234) ... 44210
Bay Village (Cuyahoga)(440) ... 44140
Beach City (Stark)(330, 234) ... 44608
Beachwood (Cuyahoga)(216) ... 44122
Beallsville (Monroe)(740) ... 43716
Beaver (Pike)(740) ... 45613
Beavercreek (Montgomery)(937) ... 454XX
Beaverdam (Allen)(419,567) ... 45808
Bedford (Cuyahoga)(440) ... 44146
Bellaire (Belmont)(740) ... 43906
Bellbrook (Greene)(937) ... 45305
Belle Center (Logan)(937) ... 43310
Bellefontain (Logan)(937) ... 43311
Belle Valley (Noble)(740) ... 43717
Bellevue (Huron)(419, 567) ... 44811
Bellville (Richland)(419, 567) ... 44813
Belmont (Belmont)(740) ... 43718
Belmore (Putnam)(419, 567) ... 45815
Beloit (Mahoning)(330, 234) ... 44609
Belpre (Washington)(740) ... 45714
Bentleyville (Cuyahoga)(440) ... 4402X
Benton Ridge (Hancock)(419, 567) ... 45816
Bentonville (Adams)(937) ... 45105
Berea (Cuyahoga)(440) ... 44017
Bergholz (Jefferson)(740) ... 43908
Berkey (Lucas)(419, 567) ... 43504
Berlin (Holmes)(330, 234) ... 44610
Berlin Center (Mahoning)(330, 234) ... 44401
Berlin Heights (Erie)(419, 567) ... 44814
Bethel (Clermont)(513) ... 45106
Bethesda (Belmont)(740) ... 43719
Bettsville (Seneca)(419, 567) ... 44815
Beverly (Washington)(740) ... 45715
Bexley (Franklin)(614) ... 43XXX
Bidwell (Gallia)(740) ... 45614
Big Prairie (Holmes)(330, 234) ... 44611
Birmingham (Erie)(419, 567) ... 44816
Blacklick (Franklin)(614) ... 43004
Bladensburg (Knox)(740) ... 43005
Blaine (Belmont)(740) ... 43909
Blakeslee (Williams)(419, 567) ... 43505
Blanchester (Clinton)(937) ... 45107
Blissfield (Coshocton)(740) ... 43805
Bloomdale (Wood)(419, 567) ... 44817
Bloomingburg (Fayette)(740) ... 43106
Bloomingdale (Jefferson)(740) ... 43910
Bloomville (Seneca)(419, 567) ... 44818
Blue Creek (Adams)(937) ... 45616
Blue Rock (Muskingum)(740) ... 43720
Bluffton (Allen)(419,567) ... 45817
Boardman (Mahoning)(330, 234) ... 445XX
Bolivar (Tuscarawas)(330, 234) ... 44612
Botkins (Shelby)(937) ... 45306
Bourneville (Ross)(740) ... 45617
Bowerston (Harrison)(740) ... 44695
Bowersville (Greene)(937) ... 45307
Bowling Green (Wood)(419, 567) ... 43402
Bradford (Miami)(937) ... 45308
Bradner (Wood)(419, 567) ... 43406
Brady Lake (Portage)(330, 234) ... 44211
Bratenahl (Cuyahoga)(216) ... 441XX
Brecksville (Cuyahoga)(440) ... 44141
Bremen (Fairfield)(740) ... 43107
Brewster (Stark)(330, 234) ... 44613
Brice (Franklin)(614) ... 43109
Bridgeport (Belmont)(740) ... 43912
Brilliant (Jefferson)(740) ... 43913
Brinkhaven (Knox)(740) ... 43006
Bristolville (Trumbull)(330, 234) ... 44402
Broadview Heights (Cuyahoga)(440) ... 44147
Broadway (Union)(937) ... 43007
Brook Park (Cuyahoga)(216) ... 44142
Brookfield (Trumbull)(330, 234) ... 44403
Brooklyn (Cuyahoga)(216) ... 441XX
Brookville (Montgomery)(937) ... 45309
Brownsville (Licking)(740) ... 43721
Brunswick (Medina)(330) ... 44212
Bryan (Williams)(419, 567) ... 43506
Buchtel (Athens)(740) ... 45716
Buckeye Lake (Licking)(740) ... 43008
Buckland (Auglaize)(419, 567) ... 45819
Bucyrus (Crawford)(419, 567) ... 44820
Buffalo (Guernsey)(740) ... 43722
Buford (Highland)(937) ... 45110
Burbank (Wayne)(330) ... 44214
Burghill (Trumbull)(330, 234) ... 44404
Burgoon (Sandusky)(419, 569) ... 43407
Burkettesville (Mercer)(419, 567) ... 45310
Burton (Geauga)(440) ... 44021
Butler (Richland)(419, 567) ... 44822
Byesville (Guernsey)(740) ... 43723
Cable (Champaign)(937) ... 43009
Cadiz (Harrison)(740) ... 43907
Cairo (Allen)(419,567) ... 45820
Calcutta (Columbiana)(330, 234) ... 43920
Caldwell (Noble)(740) ... 43724
Caledonia (Marion)(740) ... 43314
Cambridge (Guernsey)(740) ... 43725
Camden (Preble)(937) ... 45311
Cameron (Monroe)(740) ... 43914
Campbell (Mahoning)(330, 234) ... 44405
Camp Dennison (Hamilton)(513) ... 45111
Canal Fulton (Stark)(330, 234) ... 44614
Canal Winchester (Franklin)(614) ... 43110
Canfield (Mahoning)(330, 234) ... 44406
Canton (Stark)(330, 234) ... 447XX
Carbondale (Athens)(740) ... 45717
Carbon Hill (Hocking)(740) ... 43111
Cardington (Morrow)(419, 567) ... 43315
Carey (Wyandot)(419, 567) ... 43316
Carlisle (Warren)(330, 234) ... 45005
Carroll (Fairfield)(740) ... 43112
Carrollton (Carroll)(330, 234) ... 44615
Carrothers (Seneca)(419, 567) ... 44807
Carthagena (Mercer)(419, 567) ... 45822
Casstown (Miami)(937) ... 45312
Castalia (Erie)(419, 567) ... 44824
Castine (Darke)(937) ... 45304
Catawba (Clark)(937) ... 43010
Cecil (Paulding)(419, 567) ... 45821
Cedarville (Greene)(937) ... 45314
Celina (Mercer)(419, 567) ... 45822
Cedarville (Greene)(937) ... 45314
Celina (Mercer)(419, 567) ... 45822
Centerburg (Knox)(740) ... 43011
Centerville (Montgomery)(937) ... 454XX
Chagrin Falls (Cuyahoga)(440) ... 440XX
Chandlersville (Muskingum)(740) ... 43727
Chardon (Geauga)(440) ... 44024
Charm (Holmes)(330, 234) ... 44617
Chatfield (Crawford)(419, 567) ... 44825
Chauncey (Athens)(740) ... 45719
Cherry Fork (Adams)(937) ... 45618
Chesapeake (Lawrence)(740) ... 45619
Cheshire (Gallia)(740) ... 45620
Chester (Meigs)(740) ... 45720
Chesterhill (Morgan)(740) ... 43728
Chesterland (Geauga)(440) ... 44026
Chesterville (Morrow)(419, 567) ... 43317
Chickasaw (Mercer)(419, 567) ... 45826
Chillicothe (Ross)(740) ... 45601
Chilo (Clermont)(513) ... 45112
Chippewa Lake (Medina)(330) ... 44215
Christiansburg (Champaign)(937) ... 45389
Cincinnati (Hamilton)(513) ... 452XX
Circleville (Pickaway)(740) ... 43113
Clarington (Monroe)(740) ... 43915
Clarksburg (Ross)(740) ... 43115
Clarksville (Clinton)(937) ... 45113
Clay Center (Ottawa)(419, 567) ... 43408
Claysville (Guernsey)(740) ... 43725
Clayton (Montgomery)(937) ... 45315
Cleveland (Cuyahoga)(216) ... 441XX
Cleveland Heights (Cuyahoga)(216) ... 441XX
Cleves (Hamilton)(513) ... 45002
Clifton (Greene)(937) ... 45316
Clinton (Summit)(330, 234) ... 44216
Cloverdale (Putnam)(419, 567) ... 45827
Clyde (Sandusky)(419, 569) ... 43410
Coal Run (Washington)(740) ... 45721
Coalton (Jackson)(740) ... 45621
Coldwater (Mercer)(419, 567) ... 45828
Colerain (Belmont)(740) ... 43916
College Corner (Butler)(513) ... 45003
College Hill Station (Hamilton)(513) ... 452XX
Collins (Huron)(419, 567) ... 44826
Collinsville (Butler)(513) ... 45004
Colton (Henry)(419, 567) ... 43510
Columbiana (Columbiana)(330, 234) ... 44408
Columbia Station (Lorain)(440) ... 44028
Columbus (Franklin)(614) ... 432XX
Columbus Grove (Putnam)(419, 567) ... 45830
Commercial Point (Pickaway)(740) ... 43116
Conesville (Coshocton)(740) ... 43811
Conneaut (Ashtabula)(440) ... 44030
Conover (Miami)(937) ... 45317
Continental (Putnam)(419, 567) ... 45831

Municipality	Zip
Convoy (Van Wert)(419, 567)	45832
Coolville (Athens)(740)	45723
Copley (Summit)(330, 234)	443XX
Corning (Perry)(740)	43730
Cortland (Trumbull)(330, 234)	44410
Coshocton (Coshocton)(740)	43812
Covington (Miami)(937)	45318
Creola (Vinton)(740)	45622
Crestline (Crawford)(419, 567)	44827
Creston (Wayne)(330)	44217
Cridersville (Allen)(419,567)	4580X
Crooksville (Perry)(740)	43731
Croton (Licking)(740)	43013
Crown City (Gallia)(740)	45623
Cuba (Clinton)(937)	45114
Cumberland (Guernsey)(740)	43732
Curtice (Ottawa)(419, 567)	43412
Custar (Wood)(419, 567)	43511
Cutler (Washington)(740)	45724
Cuyahoga Falls (Summit)(330, 234)	4422X
Cuyahoga Heights (Cuyahoga)(216)	441XX
Cygnet (Wood)(419, 567)	43413
Cynthiana (Pike)(740)	45624
Dalton (Wayne)(330)	44618
Damascus (Mahoning)(330, 234)	44619
Danville (Knox)(740)	43014
Day Heights (Clermont)(513)	45150
Dayton (Montgomery)(937)	454XX
Decatur (Brown)(937)	45115
Deerfield (Portage)(330, 234)	44411
Deersville (Harrison)(740)	44693
Defiance (Defiance)(419, 567)	43512
De Graff (Logan)(937)	43318
Delaware (Delaware)(740)	43015
Dellroy (Carroll)(330, 234)	44620
Delphos (Allen)(419,567)	45833
Delta (Fulton)(419, 567)	43515
Dennison (Tuscarawas)(330, 234)	44621
Derby (Pickaway)(740)	43117
Derwent (Guernsey)(740)	43733
Deshler (Henry)(419, 567)	43516
Dexter (Meigs)(740)	45741
Dexter City (Noble)(740)	45727
Diamond (Portage)(330, 234)	44412
Dillonvale (Jefferson)(740)	43917
Dola (Hardin)(419, 567)	45835
Donnelsville (Clark)(937)	45319
Dorset (Ashtabula)(440)	44032
Dover (Tuscarawas)(330, 234)	44622
Doylestown (Wayne)(330)	44230
Dresden (Muskingum)(740)	43821
Dublin (Warren)(330, 234)	45005
Dunbridge (Wood)(419, 567)	43414
Duncan Falls (Muskingum)(740)	43734
Dundee (Tuscarawas)(330, 234)	44624
Dunkirk (Hardin)(419, 567)	45836
Dupont (Putnam)(419, 567)	45837
East Canton (Stark)(330, 234)	447XX
East Claridon (Geauga)(440)	44033
East Cleveland (Cuyahoga)(216)	441XX
East Fultonham (Muskingum)(740)	43735
Eastlake (Lake)(440)	4409X
East Liberty (Logan)(937)	43319
East Liverpool (Columbiana)(330, 234)	43920
East Orwell (Ashtabula)(440)	44076
East Palestine (Columbiana)(330, 234)	44413
East Rochester (Columbiana)(330, 234)	44625
East Sparta (Stark)(330, 234)	44626
East Springfield (Jefferson)(740)	43925
Eaton (Preble)(937)	45320
Edgerton (Williams)(419, 567)	43517
Edgewater (Cuyahoga)(216)	44107
Edison (Morrow)(419, 567)	43320
Edon (Williams)(419, 567)	43518
Eldorado (Preble)(937)	45321
Elgin (Van Wert)(419, 567)	45838
Elida (Allen)(419,567)	4580X
Elkton (Columbiana)(330, 234)	44415
Elliston (Ottawa)(419, 567)	43432
Ellsworth (Mahoning)(330, 234)	44416
Elmore (Ottawa)(419, 567)	43416
Elyria (Lorain)(440)	4403X
Empire (Jefferson)(740)	43926
Englewood (Montgomery)(937)	45322
Enon (Clark)(937)	45323
Etna (Licking)(740)	43018
Euclid (Cuyahoga)(216)	441XX
Evansport (Defiance)(419, 567)	43519
Fairborn (Greene)(937)	45324
Fairfield (Butler)(513)	4501X
Fairlawn (Summit)(330, 234)	44334
Fairpoint (Belmont)(740)	43927
Fairport Harbor (Lake)(440)	44077
Fairview (Guernsey)(740)	43736
Fairview Park (Cuyahoga)(440)	441XX
Farmdale (Trumbull)(330, 234)	44417
Farmer (Defiance)(419, 567)	43520
Farmersville (Montgomery)(937)	45325
Fayette (Fulton)(419, 567)	43521
Fayetteville (Brown)(937)	45119
Felicity (Clermont)(513)	45120
Findlay (Hancock)(419, 567)	458XX
Flat Rock (Seneca)(419, 567)	44828
Fleming (Washington)(740)	45729
Fletcher (Miami)(937)	45326
Flushing (Belmont)(740)	43977
Fly (Washington)(740)	45767
Forest (Hardin)(419, 567)	45843
Fort Jennings (Putnam)(419, 567)	45844
Fort Loramie (Shelby)(937)	45845
Fort Recovery (Mercer)(419, 567)	45846
Fort Seneca (Seneca)(419, 567)	44883
Fostoria (Seneca)(419, 567)	44830
Fowler (Trumbull)(330, 234)	44418
Frankfort (Ross)(740)	45628
Franklin (Warren)(937)	45005
Franklin Furnace (Scioto)(740)	45629
Frazeysburg (Muskingum)(740)	43822
Fredericksburg (Wayne)(330)	44627
Fredericktown (Knox)(740)	43019
Freeport (Harrison)(740)	43973
Fremont (Sandusky)(419, 569)	43420
Fresno (Coshocton)(740)	43824
Friendship (Scioto)(740)	45630
Fulton (Morrow)(419, 567)	43321
Fultonham (Muskingum)(740)	43738
Gahanna (Franklin)(614)	432XX
Galena (Delaware)(740)	43021
Galion (Crawford)(419, 567)	44833
Gallipolis (Gallia)(740)	45631
Galloway (Franklin)(614)	43119
Gambier (Knox)(740)	43022
Garfield Heights (Cuyahoga)(216)	441XX
Garrettsville (Portage)(330, 234)	44231
Gates Mills (Cuyahoga)(440)	44040
Geneva (Ashtabula)(440)	44041
Genoa (Ottawa)(419, 567)	43430
Georgetown (Brown)(937)	45121
Germantown (Montgomery)(937)	45327
Gettysburg (Darke)(937)	45328
Gibsonburg (Sandusky)(419, 569)	43431
Gilboa (Putnam)(419, 567)	45875
Girard (Trumbull)(330, 234)	44420
Glandorf (Putnam)(419, 567)	45848
Glencoe (Belmont)(740)	43928
Glenford (Perry)(740)	43739
Glenmont (Holmes)(330, 234)	44628
Glouster (Athens)(740)	45732
Gnadenhutten (Tuscarawas)(330, 234)	44629
Gomer (Allen)(419,567)	45809
Goshen (Clermont)(513)	45122
Grafton (Lorain)(440)	44044
Grand Rapids (Wood)(419, 567)	43522
Grand River (Lake)(440)	44045
Granville (Licking)(740)	43740
Gratis (Preble)(937)	45330
Graysville (Monroe)(740)	45734
Graytown (Ottawa)(419, 567)	43432
Green (Summit)(330, 234)	44232
Green Camp (Marion)(740)	43322
Greenfield (Highland)(937)	45123
Greenford (Mahoning)(330, 234)	44422
Green Springs (Seneca)(419, 567)	44836
Greentown (Stark)(330, 234)	44630
Greenville (Darke)(937)	45331
Greenwich (Huron)(419, 567)	44837
Grelton (Henry)(419, 567)	43523
Groesbeck (Hamilton)(513)	452XX
Grove City (Franklin)(614)	43123
Groveport (Franklin)(614)	43125
Grover Hill (Paulding)(419, 567)	45849
Guernsey (Guernsey)(740)	43749
Guysville (Athens)(740)	45735
Gypsum (Ottawa)(419, 567)	43433
Hallsville (Ross)(740)	45633
Hamden (Vinton)(740)	45634
Hamersville (Brown)(937)	45130
Hamilton (Butler)(513)	4501X
Hamler (Henry)(419, 567)	43524
Hammondsville (Jefferson)(740)	43930
Hannibal (Monroe)(740)	43931
Hanoverton (Columbiana)(330, 234)	44423
Harbor View (Lucas)(419, 567)	43434
Harlem Springs (Carroll)(330, 234)	44631
Harpster (Wyandot)(419, 567)	43323
Harrisburg (Franklin)(614)	43126
Harrison (Hamilton)(513)	45030
Harrisville (Harrison)(740)	43974
Harrod (Allen)(419,567)	45850
Hartford (Trumbull)(330, 234)	44424
Hartville (Stark)(330, 234)	44632
Harveysburg (Warren)(937)	45032
Haskins (Wood)(419, 567)	43525
Haverhill (Scioto)(740)	45636
Haviland (Paulding)(419, 567)	45851
Haydenville (Hocking)(740)	43127
Hayesville (Ashland)(419,567)	44838
Heath (Licking)(740)	43025
Hebron (Licking)(740)	43025
Helena (Sandusky)(419, 569)	43435
Hemlock (Perry)(740)	43730
Hicksville (Defiance)(419, 567)	43526
Higginsport (Brown)(937)	45131
Highland (Highland)(937)	45132
Highland Heights (Cuyahoga)(440)	441XX
Highland Hills (Cuyahoga)(216)	44122
Hilliard (Franklin)(614)	43026
Hillsboro (Highland)(937)	45133
Hinckley (Medina)(330)	44233
Hiram (Portage)(330, 234)	44234
Hockingport (Athens)(740)	45739
Holgate (Henry)(419, 567)	43527
Holland (Lucas)(419, 567)	43528
Hollansburg (Darke)(937)	45332
Holloway (Belmont)(740)	43985
Holmesville (Holmes)(330, 234)	44633
Homer (Licking)(740)	43027
Homerville (Medina)(330)	44235
Homeworth (Columbiana)(330, 234)	44634
Hooven (Hamilton)(513)	45033
Hopedale (Harrison)(740)	43976
Hopewell (Muskingum)(740)	43746
Houston (Shelby)(937)	45333
Howard (Knox)(740)	43028
Hoytville (Wood)(419, 567)	43529
Hubbard (Trumbull)(330, 234)	44425
Huber Heights (Montgomery)(937)	454XX
Hudson (Summit)(330, 234)	44236
Huntsburg (Geauga)(440)	44046
Huntsville (Logan)(937)	43324
Huron (Erie)(419, 567)	44839
Iberia (Morrow)(419, 567)	43325
Idaho (Pike)(740)	45661
Independence (Cuyahoga)(216)	44131
Irondale (Jefferson)(740)	43932
Ironton (Lawrence)(740)	45638
Irwin (Union)(937)	43029
Isle Saint George (Ottawa)(419, 567)	43436
Ithaca (Darke)(937)	45304
Jackson (Jackson)(740)	45135
Jackson Belden (Stark)(330,234)	44735
Jackson Center (Shelby)(937)	45334
Jacksontown (Licking)(740)	43030
Jacksonville (Athens)(740)	45740
Jacobsburg (Belmont)(740)	43933
Jamestown (Greene)(937)	45335
Jasper (Pike)(937)	45642
Jefferson (Ashtabula)(440)	44047
Jeffersonville (Fayette)(740)	43128
Jenera (Hancock)(419, 567)	45841
Jeromesville (Ashland)(419,567)	44840
Jerry City (Wood)(419, 567)	43437
Jerusalem (Monroe)(740)	43747
Jewell (Defiance)(419, 567)	43530
Jewett (Harrison)(740)	43986
Johnstown (Licking)(740)	43031
Junction City (Perry)(740)	43748
Kalida (Putnam)(419, 567)	45853

Kansas (Seneca)(419, 567) 44841
Keene (Coshocton)(740) 43828
Kelleys Island (Erie)(419, 567) 43438
Kensington (Columbiana)(330, 234) 44427
Kent (Portage)(330, 234) 4424X
Kenton (Hardin)(419, 567) 43326
Kerr (Gallia)(740) 45643
Kettering (Montgomery)(937) 454XX
Kettlersville (Shelby)(937) 45336
Kidron (Wayne)(330) 44636
Kilbourne (Delaware)(740) 43032
Killbuck (Holmes)(330, 234) 44637
Kimbolton (Guernsey)(740) 43749
Kings Mills (Warren)(330, 234) 45034
Kingston (Ross)(740) 45644
Kingsville (Ashtabula)(440) 44048
Kinsman (Trumbull)(330, 234) 44428
Kipling (Guernsey)(740) 43750
Kipton (Lorain)(440) 44049
Kirby (Wyandot)(419, 567) 43330
Kirkersville (Licking)(740) 43033
Kirtland (Lake)(440) 4409X
Kitts Hill (Lawrence)(740) 45645
Kunkle (Williams)(419, 567) 43531
Lacarne (Ottawa)(419, 567) 43439
Lafayette (Allen)(419,567) 45854
Lafferty (Belmont)(740) 43951
Lagrange (Lorain)(440) 44050
Laings (Monroe)(740) 43752
Lakeline (Lake)(440) 4409X
Lake Milton (Mahoning)(330, 234) 44429
Lakemore (Summit)(330, 234) 44250
Lakeside (Ottawa)(419, 567) 43440
Lakeside Marblehead (Ottawa)(419, 567) 43440
Lakeview (Logan)(937) 43331
Lakeville (Holmes)(330, 234) 44638
Lakewood (Cuyahoga)(216) 44107
Lancaster (Fairfield)(740) 43130
Langsville (Meigs)(740) 45741
Lansing (Belmont)(740) 43934
La Rue (Marion)(740) 43332
Latham (Pike)(740) 45646
Latty (Paulding)(419, 567) 45855
Laura (Miami)(937) 45337
Laurelville (Hocking)(740) 43135
Leavittsburg (Trumbull)(330, 234) 44430
Lebanon (Warren)(330, 234) 45036
Leesburg (Highland)(937) 45135
Lees Creek (Clinton)(937) 45138
Leesville (Carroll)(330, 234) 44639
Leetonia (Columbiana)(330, 234) 44431
Leipsic (Putnam)(419, 567) 45856
Lemoyne (Wood)(419, 567) 43441
Lewisburg (Preble)(937) 45338
Lewis Center (Delaware)(740) 43035
Lewistown (Logan)(937) 43333
Lewisville (Monroe)(740) 43754
Lexington (Richland)(419, 567) 4490X
Liberty Center (Henry)(419, 567) 43532
Lima (Allen)(419,567) 4580X
Limaville (Stark)(330, 234) 44640
Lincoln Village Fin Unit (Franklin)(614) 43XXX
Lindenwald (Butler)(513) 4501X
Lindsey (Sandusky)(419, 569) 43442
Lisbon (Columbiana)(330, 234) 44432
Litchfield (Medina)(330) 44253
Lithopolis (Fairfield)(740) 43136
Little Hocking (Washington)(740) 45742
Lockbourne (Pickaway)(740) 43137
Lockland (Hamilton)(513) 452XX
Lodi (Medina)(330) 44254
Logan (Hocking)(740) 43138
London (Madison)(740) 43140
Londonderry (Ross)(740) 45647
Long Bottom (Meigs)(740) 45743
Lorain (Lorain)(440) 4405X
Lore City (Guernsey)(740) 43755
Loudonville (Ashland)(419,567) 44842
Louisville (Stark)(330, 234) 44641
Loveland (Clermont)(513) 45140
Lowell (Washington)(740) 45744
Lowellville (Mahoning)(330, 234) 44436
Lower Salem (Washington)(740) 45745
Lucas (Richland)(419, 567) 44843
Lucasville (Scioto)(740) 45648
Luckey (Wood)(419, 567) 43443
Ludlow Falls (Miami)(937) 45339
Lynchburg (Highland)(937) 45142
Lyndhurst (Cuyahoga)(440) 441XX
Lynx (Adams)(937) 45650
Lyons (Fulton)(419, 567) 43533
Macedonia (Summit)(330, 234) 44056
Macksburg (Washington)(740) 45746
Madeira (Hamilton)(513) 452XX
Madison (Lake)(440) 44057
Magnetic Springs (Union)(937) 43036
Magnolia (Stark)(330, 234) 44643
Maineville (Warren)(330, 234) 45039
Malaga (Monroe)(740) 43757
Malinta (Henry)(419, 567) 43535
Malta (Morgan)(740) 43758
Malvern (Carroll)(330, 234) 44644
Manchester (Adams)(937) 45144
Mansfield (Richland)(419, 567) 4490X
Mantua (Portage)(330, 234) 44255
Maple Heights (Cuyahoga)(216) 44137
Maplewood (Shelby)(937) 45340
Marathon (Clermont)(513) 45145
Marblehead (Lake)(440) 43440
Marengo (Morrow)(419, 567) 43334
Maria Stein (Mercer)(419, 567) 45860
Marietta (Washington)(740) 45750
Marion (Marion)(740) 4330X
Mark Center (Defiance)(419, 567) 43536
Marshallville (Wayne)(330) 44645
Martel (Marion)(740) 43335
Martin (Ottawa)(419, 567) 43445
Martinsburg (Knox)(740) 43037
Martins Ferry (Belmont)(740) 43935
Martinsville (Clinton)(937) 45146
Marysville (Union)(937) 43040
Mason (Warren)(330, 234) 45040
Massillon (Stark)(330, 234) 4464X
Masury (Trumbull)(330, 234) 44438
Maumee (Lucas)(419, 567) 43537
Maximo (Stark)(330, 234) 44650
Mayfield (Cuyahoga)(440) 441XX
Mayfield Heights (Cuyahoga)(440) 441XX
Maynard (Belmont)(740) 43937
McArthur (Vinton)(740) 45651
McClure (Henry)(419, 567) 43534
McComb (Hancock)(419, 567) 45858
McConnelsville (Morgan)(740) 43756
McCutchenville (Wyandot)(419, 567) 44844
McDermott (Scioto)(740) 45652
McDonald (Trumbull)(330, 234) 44437
McGuffey (Hardin)(419, 567) 45859
Mechanicsburg (Champaign)(937) 43044
Mechanicstown (Carroll)(330, 234) 44651
Medina (Medina)(330) 4425X
Medway (Clark)(937) 45341
Melmore (Seneca)(419, 567) 44845
Melrose (Paulding)(419, 567) 45861
Mendon (Mercer)(419, 567) 45862
Mentor (Lake)(440) 4406X
Mentor On The Lake (Lake)(440) 44060
Mesopotamia (Trumbull)(330, 234) 44439
Metamora (Fulton)(419, 567) 43540
Miamisburg (Montgomery)(937) 4534X
Miamitown (Hamilton)(513) 45041
Miamiville (Clermont)(513) 45147
Middletown (Butler)(513) 4504X
Midland (Clinton)(937) 45148
Midvale (Tuscarawas)(330, 234) 44653
Milan (Erie)(419, 567) 44846
Milford (Clermont)(513) 45150
Milford Center (Union)(937) 43045
Millbury (Wood)(419, 567) 43447
Milledgeville (Fayette)(740) 43142
Miller City (Putnam)(419, 567) 45864
Millersburg (Holmes)(330, 234) 44654
Millersport (Fairfield)(740) 43046
Millersville (Sandusky)(419, 569) 43435
Millfield (Athens)(740) 45761
Milton Center (Wood)(419, 567) 43541
Mineral City (Tuscarawas)(330, 234) 44656
Mineral Ridge (Trumbull)(330, 234) 44440
Minerva (Stark)(330, 234) 44657
Minford (Scioto)(740) 45653
Mingo (Champaign)(937) 43047
Mingo Junction (Jefferson)(740) 43938
Minster (Auglaize)(419, 567) 45865
Mogadore (Portage)(330, 234) 44260
Monclova (Lucas)(419, 567) 43542
Monroe (Butler)(513) 45050
Monroeville (Huron)(419, 567) 44847
Montezuma (Mercer)(419, 567) 45866
Montpelier (Williams)(419, 567) 43543
Montville (Geauga)(440) 44064
Moorefield (Harrison)(740) 43907
Moreland Hills (Cuyahoga)(440) 4402X
Morral (Marion)(740) 43337
Morristown (Belmont)(740) 43759
Morrow (Warren)(330, 234) 45152
Moscow (Clermont)(513) 45153
Mount Blanchard (Hancock)(419, 567) 45867
Mount Cory (Hancock)(419, 567) 45868
Mount Eaton (Wayne)(330) 44659
Mount Gilead (Morrow)(419, 567) 43338
Mount Healthy (Hamilton)(513) 452XX
Mount Hope (Holmes)(330, 234) 44660
Mount Liberty (Knox)(740) 43048
Mount Orab (Brown)(937) 45154
Mount Perry (Perry)(740) 43760
Mount Pleasant (Jefferson)(740) 43939
Mount Saint Joseph (Hamilton)(513) 45051
Mount Sterling (Madison)(740) 43143
Mount Vernon (Knox)(740) 43050
Mount Victory (Hardin)(419, 567) 43340
Mowrystown (Highland)(937) 45155
Moxahala (Perry)(740) 43761
Munroe Falls (Summit)(330, 234) 44262
Murray City (Hocking)(740) 43144
Nankin (Ashland)(419,567) 44848
Napoleon (Henry)(419, 567) 43545
Nashport (Muskingum)(740) 43830
Nashville (Holmes)(330, 234) 44661
Navarre (Stark)(330, 234) 44662
Neapolis (Lucas)(419, 567) 43547
Neffs (Belmont)(740) 43940
Negley (Columbiana)(330, 234) 44441
Nelsonville (Athens)(740) 45764
Nevada (Wyandot)(419, 567) 44849
Neville (Clermont)(513) 45156
New Albany (Franklin)(614) 43054
Newark (Licking)(740) 43055
New Athens (Harrison)(740) 43981
New Bavaria (Henry)(419, 567) 43548
New Bloomington (Marion)(740) 43341
New Bremen (Auglaize)(419, 567) 45869
Newburgh Heights (Cuyahoga)(216) 441XX
Newbury (Geauga)(440) 44065
New Carlisle (Clark)(937) 45344
Newcomerstown (Tuscarawas)(330, 234) 43832
New Concord Muskungum 43762
New Hampshire (Auglaize)(419, 567) 45870
New Haven (Huron)(419, 567) 44850
New Holland (Pickaway)(740) 43145
New Knoxville (Auglaize)(419, 567) 45871
New Lebanon (Montgomery)(937) 45345
New Lexington (Perry)(740) 43764
New London (Huron)(419, 567) 44581
New Madison (Darke)(937) 45346
New Marshfield (Athens)(740) 45766
New Matamoras (Washington)(740) 45767
New Middletown (Mahoning)(330, 234) 44442
New Paris (Preble)(937) 45347
New Philadelphia (Tuscarawas)(330, 234) 44663
New Plymouth (Vinton)(740) 45654
Newport (Washington)(740) 45768
New Richmond (Clermont)(513) 45757
New Riegel (Seneca)(419, 567) 44853
New Rumley (Harrison)(740) 43984
New Springfield (Mahoning)(330, 234) 44443
New Straitsville (Perry)(740) 43766
Newton Falls (Trumbull)(330, 234) 44444
Newtonsville (Clermont)(513) 45158
Newtown (Hamilton)(513) 452XX
New Vienna (Clinton)(937) 45159
New Washington (Crawford)(419, 567) 44854
New Waterford (Columbiana)(330, 234) 44445
New Weston (Darke)(937) 45348
Ney (Defiance)(419, 567) 43549
Niles (Trumbull)(330, 234) 44446
North Baltimore (Wood)(419, 567) 45872
North Bend (Hamilton)(513) 45052
North Benton (Mahoning)(330, 234) 44449
North Bloomfield (Trumbull)(330, 234) 44450

Municipality	ZIP
North Canton (Stark)(330, 234)	447XX
Northfield (Summit)(330, 234)	44067
North Georgetown (Columbiana)(330, 234)	44665
North Hampton (Clark)(937)	45349
North Industry (Stark)(330, 234)	44707
North Jackson (Mahoning)(330, 234)	44451
North Kingsville (Ashtabula)(440)	44068
North Lawrence (Stark)(330, 234)	44666
North Lewisburg (Champaign)(937)	43060
North Lima (Mahoning)(330, 234)	44452
North Olmsted (Cuyahoga)(440)	44070
North Ridgefield (Lorain)(440)	44039
North Ridgeville (Lorain)(440)	4403X
North Robinson (Crawford)(419, 567)	44856
North Royalton (Cuyahoga)(440)	44133
North Star (Darke)(937)	45350
Northwood (Wood)(419, 567)	43619
Northwood (Lucas)(419, 567)	436XX
Norton (Summit)(330, 234)	44203
Norwalk (Huron)(419, 567)	44857
Norwich (Muskingum)(740)	43767
Norwood (Hamilton)(513)	452XX
Nova (Ashland)(419,567)	44859
Novelty (Geauga)(440)	44072
Oak Harbor (Ottawa)(419, 567)	43449
Oak Hill (Jackson)(740)	45656
Oakwood Village (Cuyahoga)(440)	44146
Oberlin (Lorain)(440)	44074
Oceola (Crawford)(419, 567)	44860
Ohio City (Van Wert)(419, 567)	45874
Okeana (Butler)(513)	45053
Okolona (Henry)(419, 567)	43550
Old Fort (Seneca)(419, 567)	44861
Old Washington (Guernsey)(740)	43768
Olmsted Falls (Cuyahoga)(440)	44138
Ontario (Richland)(419, 567)	44862
Orangeville (Trumbull)(330, 234)	44453
Oregon (Lucas)(419, 567)	436XX
Oregonia (Warren)(330, 234)	45054
Orient (Pickaway)(740)	43146
Orrville (Wayne)(330)	44667
Orwell (Ashtabula)(440)	44076
Osgood (Darke)(937)	45351
Ostrander (Delaware)(740)	43061
Ottawa (Putnam)(419, 567)	45875
Otterbien Home (Warren)(330, 234)	45036
Ottoville (Putnam)(419, 567)	45876
Otway (Scioto)(740)	45657
Overpeck (Butler)(513)	45055
Owensville (Clermont)(513)	45160
Oxford (Butler)(513)	45056
Painesville (Lake)(440)	44077
Palestine (Darke)(937)	45352
Pandora (Putnam)(419, 567)	45877
Paris (Stark)(330, 234)	44669
Parkdale (Hamilton)(513)	452XX
Parkman (Geauga)(440)	44080
Parma (Cuyahoga)(440)	441XX
Parma Heights (Cuyahoga)(440)	441XX
Pataskala (Licking)(740)	43062
Patriot (Gallia)(740)	45658
Patterson (Hardin)(419, 567)	45843
Paulding (Paulding)(419, 567)	45879
Payne (Paulding)(419, 567)	45880
Pedro (Lawrence)(740)	45659
Peebles (Adams)(937)	45660
Pemberton (Shelby)(937)	45353
Pemberville (Wood)(419, 567)	43450
Peninsula (Summit)(330, 234)	44264
Pennsville (Morgan)(740)	43787
Pepper Pike (Cuyahoga)(216)	441XX
Perry (Lake)(440)	44081
Perrysburg (Wood)(419, 567)	4355X
Perrysville (Ashland)(419,567)	44864
Petersburg (Mahoning)(330, 234)	44454
Pettisville (Fulton)(419, 567)	43553
Phillipsburg (Montgomery)(937)	45354
Philo (Muskingum)(740)	43771
Phoneton (Miami)(937)	45371
Pickerington (Fairfield)(740)	43147
Piedmont (Belmont)(740)	43983
Pierpont (Ashtabula)(440)	44082
Piketon (Pike)(740)	45661
Piney Fork (Jefferson)(740)	43941
Pioneer William	43554
Piqua (Miami)(937)	45356
Pitsburg (Darke)(937)	45358
Plain City (Madison)(740)	43064
Plainfield (Coshocton)(740)	43836
Pleasant City (Guernsey)(740)	43772
Pleasant Hill (Miami)(937)	45359
Pleasant Plain (Warren)(330, 234)	45162
Pleasantville (Fairfield)(740)	43148
Plymouth (Huron)(419, 567)	44865
Poland (Mahoning)(330, 234)	445XX
Polk (Ashland)(419,567)	44866
Pomeroy (Meigs)(740)	45769
Portage (Wood)(419, 567)	43451
Port Clinton (Ottawa)(419, 567)	43452
Port Jefferson (Shelby)(937)	45360
Portland (Meigs)(740)	45770
Portsmouth (Scioto)(740)	45662
Port Washington Tuscarawas	43837
Port William (Clinton)(937)	45164
Potsdam (Miami)(937)	45361
Powell (Delaware)(740)	43065
Powhatan Point (Belmont)(740)	43942
Proctorville (Lawrence)(740)	45669
Prospect (Marion)(740)	43342
Put In Bay (Ottawa)(419, 567)	43456
Quaker City (Guernsey)(740)	43773
Queen City (Hamilton)(513)	452XX
Quincy (Logan)(937)	43343
Racine (Meigs)(740)	45771
Radcliff (Vinton)(740)	45695
Radnor (Delaware)(740)	43066
Randolph (Portage)(330, 234)	44265
Rarden (Scioto)(740)	45671
Ravenna (Portage)(330, 234)	44266
Rawson (Hancock)(419, 567)	45881
Ray (Vinton)(740)	45672
Rayland (Jefferson)(740)	43943
Raymond (Union)(937)	43067
Reading (Hamilton)(513)	452XX
Reedsville (Meigs)(740)	45772
Reesville (Clinton)(937)	45166
Reminderville (Portage)(330, 234)	44202
Reno (Washington)(740)	45773
Republic (Seneca)(419, 567)	44867
Reynoldsburg (Franklin)(614)	43068
Richfield (Summit)(330, 234)	44286
Richmond (Jefferson)(740)	43944
Richmond Dale (Ross)(740)	45673
Richmond Heights (Cuyahoga)(216)	441XX
Richwood (Union)(937)	43344
Ridgeville Corners (Henry)(419, 567)	43555
Ridgeway (Hardin)(419, 567)	43345
Rinard Mills (Monroe)(740)	45734
Rio Grande (Gallia)(740)	45674
Ripley (Brown)(937)	45167
Risingsun (Wood)(419, 567)	43457
Rittman (Wayne)(330)	44270
Robertsville (Stark)(330, 234)	44670
Rochester (Lorain)(440)	44090
Rockbridge (Hocking)(740)	43149
Rock Camp (Lawrence)(740)	45675
Rock Creek (Ashtabula)(440)	44084
Rockford (Mercer)(419, 567)	45882
Rocky Ridge (Ottawa)(419, 567)	43458
Rocky River (Cuyahoga)(440)	44116
Rogers (Columbiana)(330, 234)	44455
Rome (Ashtabula)(440)	44085
Rootstown (Portage)(330, 234)	44272
Roselawn Finance (Hamilton)(513)	452XX
Roseville (Muskingum)(740)	43777
Rosewood (Champaign)(937)	43070
Ross (Butler)(513)	45061
Rossburg (Darke)(937)	45362
Rossford (Wood)(419, 567)	43460
Rossville (Butler)(513)	4501X
Roundhead (Hardin)(419, 567)	43346
Rudolph (Wood)(419, 567)	43462
Rushsylvania (Logan)(937)	43347
Rushville (Fairfield)(740)	43150
Russells Point (Logan)(937)	43348
Russellville (Brown)(937)	45168
Russia (Shelby)(937)	45363
Rutland (Meigs)(740)	45775
Sabina (Clinton)(937)	45169
Saint Bernard (Hamilton)(513)	452XX
Saint Clairsville (Belmont)(740)	43950
Saint Henry (Mercer)(419, 567)	45883
Saint Johns (Auglaize)(419, 567)	45884
Saint Louisville (Licking)(740)	43071
Saint Marys (Auglaize)(419, 567)	45885
Saint Paris (Champaign)(937)	43072
Salem (Columbiana)(330, 234)	44460
Salesville (Guernsey)(740)	43778
Salineville (Columbiana)(330, 234)	43945
Sandusky (Erie)(419, 567)	4487X
Sandyville (Tuscarawas)(330, 234)	44671
Sarahsville (Noble)(740)	43779
Sardinia (Brown)(937)	45171
Sardis (Monroe)(740)	43946
Savannah (Ashland)(419,567)	44874
Sayler Park Finance (Hamilton)(513)	452XX
Scio (Harrison)(740)	43988
Scioto Furnace (Scioto)(740)	45677
Sciotoville (Scioto)(740)	45662
Scott (Van Wert)(419, 567)	45886
Scottown (Lawrence)(740)	45678
Seaman (Adams)(937)	45679
Sebring (Mahoning)(330, 234)	44672
Sedalia (Madison)(740)	43151
Selma (Clark)(937)	45368
Senecaville (Guernsey)(740)	43780
Seven Hills (Cuyahoga)(216)	44131
Seven Mile (Butler)(513)	45062
Seville (Medina)(330)	44273
Shade (Meigs)(740)	45776
Shadyside (Belmont)(740)	43947
Shaker Heights (Cuyahoga)(216)	44112
Shandon (Butler)(513)	45063
Sharon Center (Medina)(330)	44274
Sharonville (Hamilton)(513)	452XX
Sharpsburg (Athens)(740)	45777
Shauck (Morrow)(419, 567)	43349
Shawnee (Perry)(740)	43782
Sheffield Lake (Lorain)(440)	44054
Shelby (Richland)(419, 567)	44875
Sherrodsville (Carroll)(330, 234)	44675
Sherwood (Defiance)(419, 567)	43556
Shiloh (Richland)(419, 567)	44878
Shinrock (Erie)(419, 567)	44839
Short Creek (Harrison)(740)	43989
Shreve (Wayne)(330)	44676
Sidney (Shelby)(937)	45365
Silver Lake (Summit)(330, 234)	44224
Sinking Spring (Highland)(937)	45172
Smithfield (Jefferson)(740)	43948
Smithville (Wayne)(330)	44677
Solon (Cuyahoga)(440)	44139
Somerdale (Tuscarawas)(330, 234)	44678
Somerset (Perry)(740)	43783
Somerton (Belmont)(740)	43713
Somerville (Butler)(513)	45064
Sonora (Muskingum)(740)	4370X
South Amherst (Lorain)(440)	44001
South Bloomingville (Hocking)(740)	43152
South Charlestown (Clark)(937)	45368
South Euclid (Cuyahoga)(216)	441XX
Southington (Trumbull)(330, 234)	44470
South Lebanon (Warren)(330, 234)	45065
South Point (Lawrence)(740)	45680
South Salem (Ross)(740)	45681
South Solon (Madison)(740)	43153
South Vienna (Clark)(937)	45369
South Webster (Scioto)(740)	45682
Sparta (Morrow)(419, 567)	43350
Spencer (Medina)(330)	44275
Spencerville (Allen)(419,567)	45887
Springboro (Warren)(330, 234)	45066
Springfield (Clark)(937)	4550X
Spring Valley (Greene)(937)	45370
Stafford (Monroe)(740)	43786
Sterling (Wayne)(330)	44276
Steubenville (Jefferson)(740)	4395X
Stewart (Athens)(740)	45778
Stillwater (Tuscarawas)(330, 234)	44679
Stockdale (Pike)(740)	45683
Stockport (Morgan)(740)	43787
Stone Creek (Tuscarawas)(330, 234)	43840
Stony Ridge (Wood)(419, 567)	43463
Stout (Scioto)(740)	45684
Stoutsville (Fairfield)(740)	43154
Stow (Summit)(330, 234)	44224
Strasburg (Tuscarawas)(330, 234)	44680
Stratton (Jefferson)(740)	43961

Streetsboro (Portage)(330, 234) 44241	Valley View (Cuyahoga)(216) 441XX	West Mitlon (Miami)(937) 45383
Strongsville (Cuyahoga)(440) 441XX	Van Buren (Hancock)(419, 567) 45889	Weston (Wood)(419, 567) 43569
Struthers (Mahoning)(330, 234) 44471	Vandalia (Montgomery)(937) 45377	West Point (Columbiana)(330, 234) 44492
Stryker (Williams)(419, 567) 43557	Vanlue (Hancock)(419, 567) 45890	West Portsmouth (Scioto)(740) 45663
Sugarcreek (Tuscarawas)(330, 234) 44681	VanWert (Van Wert)(419, 567) 45891	West Rushville (Fairfield)(740) 43163
Sugar Grove (Fairfield)(740) 43155	Vaughnsville (Putnam)(419, 567) 45893	West Salem (Wayne)(330) 44287
Sullivan (Ashland)(419,567) 44880	Venedocia (Van Wert)(419, 567) 45894	West Union (Adams)(937) 45693
Sulphur Springs (Crawford)(419, 567) 44881	Vermillion (Erie)(419, 567) 44089	West Unity (Williams)(419, 567) 43570
Summerfield (Noble)(740) 43788	Verona (Preble)(937) 45378	Westville (Champaign)(937) 43083
Summit Station (Licking)(740) 43073	Versailles (Darke)(937) 45380	Westwood (Hamilton)(513) 452XX
Summitville (Columbiana)(330, 234) 43962	Vickery (Sandusky)(419, 569) 43464	Wharton (Wyandot)(419, 567) 43359
Sunbury (Delaware)(740) 43074	Vienna (Trumbull)(330, 234) 44473	Wheelersburg (Scioto)(740) 45694
Swanton (Fulton)(419, 567) 43558	Vincent (Washington)(740) 45784	Whipple (Washington)(740) 45788
Sycamore (Wyandot)(419, 567) 44882	Vinton (Gallia)(740) 45686	White Cottage (Muskingum)(740) 43791
Sycamore Valley (Monroe)(740) 43789	Wadsworth (Medina)(330) 4428X	Whitehall (Franklin)(614) 432XX
Sylvania (Lucas)(419, 567) 43560	Waite Hill (Lake)(440) 44094	Whitehouse (Lucas)(419, 567) 43571
Symmes (Hamilton)(513) 452XX	Wakefield (Pike)(740) 45687	Wickliffe (Lake)(440) 44092
Syracuse (Meigs)(740) 45779	Wakeman (Huron)(419, 567) 44889	Wilberforce (Greene)(937) 45384
Taft (Hamilton)(513) 452XX	Walbridge (Wood)(419, 567) 43465	Wilkesville (Vinton)(740) 45695
Tallmadge (Summit)(330, 234) 44278	Waldo (Marion)(740) 43356	Willard (Huron)(419, 567) 44890
Tarlton (Pickaway)(740) 43156	Walhonding (Coshocton)(740) 43843	Williamsburg (Clermont)(513) 45176
Terrace Park (Hamilton)(513) 45174	Walnut Creek (Holmes)(330, 234) 44687	Williamsfield (Ashtabula)(440) 44093
The Plains (Athens)(740) 45780	Wapakoneta (Auglaize)(419, 567) 45895	Williamsport (Pickaway)(740) 43164
Thompson (Geauga)(440) 44086	Warner (Washington)(740) 45745	Williamstown (Hancock)(419, 567) 45897
Thornville (Perry)(740) 43076	Warnock (Belmont)(740) 43967	Williston (Ottawa)(419, 567) 43468
Thurman (Gallia)(740) 45685	Warren (Trumbull)(330, 234) 4428X	Willoughby (Lake)(440) 4409X
Thurston (Fairfield)(740) 43157	Warrensville Heights (Cuyahoga)(216) 44122	Willowick (Lake)(440) 4409X
Tiffin (Seneca)(419, 567) 44883	Warsaw (Coshocton)(740) 43844	Willow Wood (Lawrence)(740) 45696
Tiltonsville (Jefferson)(740) 43963	Washington Court House (Fayette)(740) 43160	Willshire (Van Wert)(419, 567) 45898
Tipp City (Miami)(937) 45371	Washington Township (Montgomery)(937) . . . 454XX	Wilmington (Clinton)(937) 45177
Tippecanoe (Harrison)(740) 44699	Washingtonvill (Columbiana)(330, 234) 44490	Wilmot (Stark)(330, 234) 44689
Tiro (Crawford)(419, 567) 44887	Waterford (Washington)(740) 45786	Winchester (Adams)(937) 45697
Toledo (Lucas)(419, 567) 436XX	Waterloo (Lawrence)(740) 45688	Windham (Portage)(330, 234) 44288
Tontogany (Wood)(419, 567) 43565	Watertown (Washington)(740) 45787	Windsor (Ashtabula)(440) 44099
Torch (Athens)(740) 45781	Waterville (Lucas)(419, 567) 43566	Winesburg (Holmes)(330, 234) 44690
Toronto (Jefferson)(740) 43964	Wauseon (Fulton)(419, 567) 43567	Wingett Run (Washington)(740) 45789
Tremont City (Clark)(937) 45372	Waverly (Pike)(740) 45690	Winona (Columbiana)(330, 234) 44493
Trenton (Butler)(513) 45067	Wayland (Portage)(330, 234) 44285	Wintersville (Jefferson)(740) 4395X
Trimble (Athens)(740) 45782	Wayne (Wood)(419, 567) 44366	Wolf Run (Jefferson)(740) 43970
Trinway (Muskingum)(740) 43842	Waynesburg (Stark)(330, 234) 44688	Woodsfield (Monroe)(740) 43793
Trotwood (Montgomery)(937) 454XX	Waynesfield (Auglaize)(419, 567) 45896	Woodstock (Champaign)(937) 43084
Troy (Miami)(937) 45373	Waynesville (Warren)(330, 234) 45068	Woodville (Sandusky)(419, 569) 43469
Tuppers Plains (Meigs)(740) 45783	Wellington (Lorain)(440) 44090	Wooster (Wayne)(330) 44691
Tuscarawas (Tuscarawas)(330, 234) 44682	Wellston (Jackson)(740) 45692	Worthington (Franklin)(614) 43XXX
Twinsburg (Summit)(330, 234) 44087	Wellsville (Columbiana)(330, 234) 43968	Wren (Van Wert)(419, 567) 45899
Uhrichsville (Tuscarawas)(330, 234) 44683	West Alexandria (Preble)(937) 45381	Wright Patterson (Montgomery)(937) 454XX
Union (Montgomery)(937) 45322	West Carrollton (Montgomery)(937) 454XX	Xenia (Greene)(937) 45385
Union City (Darke)(937) 45390	West Chester (Butler)(513) 450XX	Yellow Springs (Greene)(937) 45387
Union Furnace (Hocking)(740) 43158	West Elkton (Preble)(937) 45070	Yorkshire (Darke)(937) 45388
Unionport (Jefferson)(740) 43966	Western Hills (Hamilton)(513) 452XX	Yorkville (Jefferson)(740) 43971
Uniontown (Stark)(330, 234) 44685	Westerville (Franklin)(614) 4308X	Youngstown (Mahoning)(330, 234) 445XX
Unionville (Ashtabula)(440) 44088	West Farmington (Trumbull)(330, 234) 44491	Zaleski (Vinton)(740) 45698
Unionville Center (Union)(937) 43077	Westfield Center (Medina)(330) 44251	Zanesfield (Logan)(937) 43360
Uniopolis (Auglaize)(419, 567) 45888	West Jefferson (Madison)(740) 43162	Zanesville (Muskingum)(740) 4370X
University Heights (Cuyahoga)(216) 44122	West Lafayette (Coshocton)(740) 43845	Zoar (Tuscarawas)(330, 234) 44697
Upper Arlington (Franklin)(614) 43XXX	Westlake (Cuyahoga)(440) 44145	Zoarville (Tuscarawas)(330, 234) 44656
Upper Sandusky (Wyandot)(419, 567) 43351	West Liberty (Logan)(937) 43357	
Urbana (Champaign)(937) 43078	West Manchester (Preble)(937) 45382	
Utica (Licking)(740) 43080	West Mansfield (Logan)(937) 43358	
Valley City (Medina)(330) 44280	West Millgrove (Wood)(419, 567) 43467	

NATIONAL DIRECTORY OF STATES

ALABAMA
Capital: Montgomery

4,447,100 (2000 Census)
State Information: (334) 242-8000
State Web Site: www.alabama.gov

Administrative Office of the Courts
Administrative Office of the Courts
300 Dexter Ave., Montgomery, AL 36104
(334) 242-0300; Fax: (334) 242-2099
Internet: www.alacourt.org
Admin. Dir. of the Courts: Randy Helms

Attorney Discipline
Alabama State Bar Center for Professional Responsibility
415 Dexter Ave., Montgomery, AL 36104
(334) 269-1515; Fax: (334) 261-6311
E-mail: tmclain@alabar.org; Internet: www.alabar.org
General Counsel: J. Anthony McLain

Attorney General
Office of the Attorney General
State House, 3rd Floor, 11 S. Union St.,
Montgomery, AL 36130-0152
(334) 242-7300; Fax: (334) 242-7458
Internet: www.ago.state.al.us
Atty. General: Troy King
Appointed to fill a vacancy; next election Nov. 2006

Banking Department
State Banking Department
401 Adams Ave., Suite 680, Montgomery, AL 36104
(334) 242-3452; Fax: (334) 242-3500
Internet: www.bank.state.al.us
Superintendent: Anthony Humphries

Bar Admissions
Alabama State Bar
Admissions Office
415 Dexter Ave., Montgomery, AL 36104
Mailing Address: P.O. Box 671, Montgomery, AL 36101
(334) 269-1515; Fax: (334) 261-6310
E-mail: admit@alabar.org
Internet: www.alabar.org/admissions/admis.html
12 hours CLE required per year.
Admission on motion only for law professors teaching in an Alabama ABA-accredited law school.

Bar Association
Alabama State Bar
415 Dexter Ave., Montgomery, AL 36104
Mailing Address: P.O. Box 671, Montgomery, AL 36101
(334) 269-1515; Fax: (334) 261-6310
Internet: www.alabar.org
Exec. Dir.: Keith B. Norman
President: J. Douglas McElvy
Integrated Bar
Annual Meeting—July, 2006

Client Protection Fund
Client Security Fund
Alabama State Bar
415 Dexter Ave., P.O. Box 671, Montgomery, AL 36101
(334) 269-1515; Fax: (334) 261-6310, 11
Internet: www.alabar.org
Administrator: Laurie Blazer

Commerce Department
See Economic Development Administration

Corporations Officers
Corporations Division
State House, Room 207, 11 S. Union St.,
Montgomery, AL 36130
(334) 242-7200; Corporations Section: (334) 242-5324;
Name Availabilities: (334) 242-5324;
Annual Reports: (334) 353-7923; Fax: (334) 240-3138;
Limited Partnerships: (334) 242-5324;
UCC: (334) 242-5231; Trademarks: (334) 242-5325;
Notaries: (334) 242-7205
E-mail: alabiz@sos.al.gov

Supervisor, Corporations Division: Sharon Viox
Information Systems Division
State House, Suite 205, 11 S. Union St.,
Montgomery, AL 36130
(334) 242-7222
Director: Mickey Moore; E-mail: moore@sos.al.gov
Office of the Secretary of State
State Capitol, Room E-201, P.O. Box 5616,
Montgomery, AL 36103
(334) 242-7202; E-mail: alabiz@alalinc.net
General Counsel: Trey Granger; E-mail: tgranger@sos.al.gov
Dir., Information Svces. Div.: Mickey Moore
    (334) 242-7222; E-mail: mmoore@alalinc.net
Office of the Secretary of State
UCC Division
11 S. Union St., P.O. Box 5616,
Montgomery, AL 36103-5616
(334) 242-5231
Supervisor: Karl Frost; E-mail: kfrost@sos.al.gov
Office of the Secretary of State
Lands and Trademarks Division
P.O. Box 5616, Montgomery, AL 36103-5616
(334) 242-7200
Supervisor: Eliza Marshall; E-mail: emarshall@sos.al.gov

Criminal History Board
Criminal Justice Information Center
770 Washington Ave., Suite 350, Montgomery, AL 36130
(334) 242-4900; Fax: (334) 242-0577

Economic Development Administration
Development Office
401 Adams St., Suite 670, Montgomery, AL 36130-4160
(334) 242-0400, (800) 248-0033; Fax: (334) 242-5669
E-mail: idinfo@ado.state.al.us
Internet: www.ado.state.al.us
Director: Neal Wade

Governor's Office
Office of the Governor
State Capitol, N104, 600 Dexter Ave.,
Montgomery, AL 36130
(334) 242-7100; Fax: (334) 242-0937
Internet: www.governor.state.al.us
Governor: Bob Riley (Republican)
Next election Nov. 2006

Highest State Court
Supreme Court
300 Dexter Ave., Montgomery, AL 36104-3701
(334) 242-4609; Clerk's Office Fax: (334) 242-0588;
Court Fax: (334) 242-4483
Chief Justice: Gorman Houston (Acting)
Clerk of the Supreme Court: Robert G. Esdale, Sr.

Insurance Department
Department of Insurance
201 Monroe St., Suite 1700, Montgomery, AL 36104
Mailing Address: P.O. Box 303351, Montgomery, AL 36130-3351
(334) 269-3550; Fax: (334) 241-4192; Legal: (334) 241-4117;
Fax (Legal Division): (334) 240-7581
E-mail: insdept@insurance.alabama.gov
Internet: www.aldoi.org
Commissioner: Walter Bell
Chief Examiner: Richard Ford

Motor Vehicle Office
Alabama Department of Public Safety
301 S. Ripley St., Montgomery, AL 36104
Mailing Address:
For Driver Abstracts: Driver License Division,
P.O. Box 1471, Montgomery, AL 36102-1471
(334) 242-4400
Internet: www.dps.state.al.us
Driver's Licenses
Fee for obtaining abstract: $5.75; Accident Reports $15.00; cash or money order only (include self-addressed stamped envelope)

National Directory of States

Motor Vehicle Office—Cont'd

Alabama Department of Revenue
Motor Vehicle Division, Gordon Persons Bldg., Room 1202,
50 N. Ripley St., Montgomery, AL 36130
Mailing Address: P.O. Box 327630,
Montgomery, AL 36132-7630
(334) 242-9000; Fax: (334) 353-8038
E-mail: bcoone@revenue.state.al.us
Internet: www.ador.state.al.us/
Vehicle Registration, Intl. Registration & Title Certification
$15.00 for a complete title history; $3.00 per year for
certified copy of registration

Police

Alabama Department of Public Safety
301 S. Ripley St., Montgomery, AL 36104
Mailing Address: P.O. Box 1511,
Montgomery, AL 36102-1511
(334) 242-4371; Driver's Licenses: (334) 242-4400;
Fax: (334) 242-0934, 242-0512
E-mail: info@dps.state.al.us
Internet: www.dps.state.al.us/

Accident Records Unit, P.O. Box 1471,
Montgomery, AL 36102-1471 (334) 242-4241
Director: Col. W. M. Coppage
Fee for obtaining accident report: $15.00

Probate, Recording and Notary Certificate Offices

Estate & Wills: County Probate Judge's Office
Deeds and Mortgages: County Probate Judge's Office
Notary Certificates: Cty. Judge of Probate and Circuit
Clerk each of Alabama's Counties (fee varies); certified by
Secretary of State for Apostille Certification ($5.00)

Senators, U.S.

Jeff Sessions (Republican)
335 Russell Senate Office Bldg., Washington, DC 20510
(202) 224-4124; Fax: (202) 224-3149
Internet: http://sessions.senate.gov
Richard C. Shelby (Republican)
110 Hart Senate Office Bldg., Washington, DC 20510
(202) 224-5744; Fax: (202) 224-3416
E-mail: senator@shelby.senate.gov
Internet: http://shelby.senate.gov

Secretary of State

Office of the Secretary of State
600 Dexter Ave., Room S-105, Montgomery, AL 36104
Mailing Address: P.O. Box 5616,
Montgomery, AL 36103-5616
(334) 242-7205; Executive Fax: (334) 242-4993
E-mail: sos@sos.al.gov; Internet: www.sos.state.al.us
Secretary of State: Nancy L. Worley (Democrat)
Elected; next election Nov. 2006

Tax Department

Department of Revenue
Gordon Persons Bldg., Room 4112, 50 N. Ripley St.,
P.O. Box 327001, Montgomery, AL 36132-7001
Commissioner's Office: (334) 242-1175;
Fax: (334) 242-0550; Administrative Law: (334) 242-1075;
Fax: (334) 242-2060; Collection Services: (334) 242-1220;
Fax: (334) 242-8342;
Individual & Corporate: (334) 242-1000; Fax: (334) 242-0064;
Legal: (334) 242-9690; Fax: (334) 242-9782;
Sales, Use & Business Tax: (334) 242-1490;
Fax: (334) 353-7666
Internet: www.ador.state.al.us
Commissioner: G. Thomas Surtees

Victim Compensation Program

Alabama Crime Victims Compensation Commission
RSA Union Bldg., Suite 778, 100 N. Union St.,
Montgomery, AL 36102
Mailing Address: P.O. Box 1548,
Montgomery, AL 36102-1548
(334) 242-4007; Fax: (334) 353-1401
Internet: www.acvcc.state.al.us/
Amended by Act 98-492, Effective May 1, 1998

Vital Statistics

Center for Health Statistics
201 Monroe St., Suite 1150, Montgomery, AL 36104
Mailing Address: P.O. Box 5625,
Montgomery, AL 36103-5625
(334) 206-5418; Administration: (334) 206-5426;
Fax: (334) 206-2659, 262-9563
Internet: www.adph.org
*Births—1908, Deaths—1908, Marriages—1936,
Divorces—1950. Birth and death records are restricted to
authorized individuals.*
$12.00 first copy, $4.00 each additional copy ordered at
same time. Exemplified copies—$20.00 each. Payable by
money order, certified or personal check to State Board of
Health. Expedited service—$10.00 in addition to copy fee.
Overnight service by telephone using credit card—$39.50
total fee.

ALASKA *Capital: Juneau*

626,932 (2000 Census)
State Information: (907) 465-3500
State Web Site: www.state.ak.us

Administrative Office of the Courts

Administrative Director of the Courts
303 K St., Anchorage, AK 99501
(907) 264-0547; Fax: (907) 264-0881
Internet: www.state.ak.us/courts
Administrative Dir. of the Courts: Stephanie J. Cole
 E-mail: scole@courts.state.ak.us

Attorney Discipline

Alaska Bar Association Discipline Section
550 W. 7th Ave., Suite 1900, Anchorage, AK 99501
Mailing Address: P.O. Box 100279,
Anchorage, AK 99510-0279
(907) 272-7469; Fax: (907) 272-2932
E-mail: info@alaskabar.org
Internet: www.alaskabar.org
Bar Counsel: Stephen J. Van Goor

Attorney General

Office of the Attorney General
Dimond Courthouse, 6th Floor, 123 Fourth St.,
Juneau, AK 99801
Mailing Address: P.O. Box 110300, Juneau, AK 99811-0300
(907) 465-3600; Fax: (907) 465-2075
Internet: www.law.state.ak.us/ag.html

Anchorage Office, 1031 W. 4th Ave., Suite 200,
Anchorage, AK 99501-1994
(907) 269-5100; Fax: (907) 276-3697
E-Mail: usprobation of c@vtnet.com

Fairbanks Office, 100 Cushman St., Suite 400,
Fairbanks, AK 99701-4679
(907) 451-2811; Fax: (907) 451-2846
Atty. General: Gregg D. Renkes (Republican)
Appointed

Banking Department

Division of Banking, Securities & Corporations
150 Third St., Suite 217, Juneau, AK 99801
Mailing Address: P.O. Box 110807, Juneau, AK 99811-0807
(907) 465-2521; Fax: (907) 465-2549
Internet: www.commerce.state.ak.us/bsc
Director: Mark R. Davis

Bar Admissions

Board of Governors
550 W. 7th Ave., Suite 1900, Anchorage, AK 99501
Mailing Address: P.O. Box 100279,
Anchorage, AK 99510-0279
(907) 272-7469; Fax: (907) 272-2932
Internet: www.alaskabar.org
No CLE required. Reduced bar dues and other incentives
granted for participation in voluntary CLE. Admission on
motion with five of the last seven years in practice in a
Reciprocal Jurisdiction which requires a written bar exam,
and mandatory Ethics course.

Bar Association

Alaska Bar Association
550 W. 7th Ave., Suite 1900, P.O. Box 100279,
Anchorage, AK 99510
(907) 272-7469; Fax: (907) 272-2932
E-mail: alaskabar@alaskabar.org
Internet: www.alaskabar.org

Exec. Dir.: Deborah O'Regan

President: Keith Levy
Integrated Bar
Annual Meeting—May, 2005

Chief Medical Examiner

Office of Chief Medical Examiner
4500 S. Boniface Pkwy., Anchorage, AK 99507-1264
(907) 334-2200; Fax: (907) 334-2216
Internet: www.hss.state.ak.us/dph/sme

Chief Medical Examiner: Dr. Franc G. Fallico
    (907) 334-2214; E-mail: franc_fallico@health.state.ak.us

Client Protection Fund

Lawyers' Fund for Client Protection
Alaska Bar Association
550 W. 7th Ave., Suite 1900, Anchorage, AK 99510
Mailing Address: P.O. Box 100279,
Anchorage, AK 99510-0279
(907) 272-7469; Fax: (907) 272-2932
E-mail: info@alaskabar.org
Internet: www.alaskabar.org

Exec. Dir.: Deborah O'Regan

Commerce Department

See Economic Development Administration

Corporations Officers

Department of Community & Economic Development
Division of Banking, Securities & Econ. Dev.
150 3rd St., Suite 217, P.O. Box 110807,
Juneau, AK 99811-0807
(907) 465-2521; Fax: (907) 465-2549;
Corporation, Limited Partnership and Limited Liability
Company Information: (907) 465-2530
Internet: www.dced.state.ak.us/bsc/bsc.htm

Director: Mark Davis
    (907) 465-2521; Fax: (907) 465-2549

Department of Community & Economic Development
Division of Banking, Securities & Corps.
150 3rd St., Suite 217, P.O. Box 110808,
Juneau, AK 99811-0808
(907) 465-2297; Fax: (907) 465-3257

Records & Licensing Supervisor: Alyce Houston
    E-mail: alyce_houston@dced.state.ak.us

Office of the State Recorder
Department of Natural Resources
550 W. 7th Ave., Suite 1210, Anchorage, AK 99501-3564
Internet: www.dnr.state.ak.us/ucc

State Recorder: Sharon Young
    (907) 269-8882; Fax: (907) 269-8912
    E-mail: sharon_young@dnr.state.ak.us

Recorder Mgr.: Paula Kelsey
    (907) 269-8881; Fax: (907) 269-8912
    E-mail: paula_kelsey@dnr.state.ak.us

Criminal History Board

Department of Public Safety
Records & Identification Section
450 Whittier Ave., Room 103, Juneau, AK 99801
(907) 465-4343; Fax: (907) 465-5327

Economic Development Administration

Department of Community & Economic Development
State Office Bldg., 9th Floor, 333 Willoughby Ave.,
Juneau, AK 99811-0800
Mailing Address: P.O. Box 110800, Juneau, AK 99811-0800
(907) 465-2500; Fax: (907) 465-5442
E-mail: questions@dced.state.ak.us
Internet: www.dced.state.ak.us

Commissioner: Edgar Blatchford

Governor's Office

Office of the Governor
240 Main St., Suite 300, Juneau, AK 99801
Mailing Address: State Capitol, P.O. Box 110001,
Juneau, AK 99811-0001
(907) 465-3500; Fax: (907) 465-3532
Internet: http://www.gov.state.ak.us

550 W. 7th Ave., Suite 1700, Anchorage, AK 99501
(907) 269-7450; Fax: (907) 269-7461

675 7th Ave., Station H5, Fairbanks, AK 99701-4526
(907) 451-2920; Fax: (907) 451-2858

444 N. Capitol St. N.W., Suite 336,
Washington, DC 20001-1512
(202) 624-5858; Fax: (202) 624-5857

Governor: Frank H. Murkowski (Republican)
Next election Nov. 2006

Highest State Court

Supreme Court
Appellate Courts, 303 K St., 4th Floor,
Anchorage, AK 99501-2083
(907) 264-0612; Fax: (907) 264-0878
Internet: www.state.ak.us/courts/

Chief Justice: Alexander O. Bryner

Clerk of the Supreme Court: Marilyn May

Insurance Department

Division of Insurance
333 Willoughby Ave., 9th Floor, Juneau, AK 99801
Mailing Address: P.O. Box 110805, Juneau, AK 99811-0805
(907) 465-2515; TDD: (907) 465-5437; Fax: (907) 465-3422
E-mail: insurance@commerce.state.ak.us
Internet: www.dced.state.ak.us/insurance

550 W. 7th Ave., Suite 1560, Anchorage, AK 99501-3567
(907) 269-7900; TDD: (907) 465-5437; Fax: (907) 269-7910

Director: Linda S. Hall

Chief Financial Examiner: Gloria Glover

Motor Vehicle Office

Alaska Division of Motor Vehicles
Department of Administration, 3300-B Fairbanks St.,
Anchorage, AK 99503
(907) 269-5559; Fax: (907) 269-6084
Internet: www.state.ak.us/dmv

For Abstracts write: DMV, Attn.: Research, Suite 200,
1300 W. Benson Blvd., Anchorage, AK 99503
(907) 269-5551; Fax: (907) 561-3108
Fee for obtaining abstract: $5.00

Police

Alaska State Troopers
5700 E. Tudor Rd., Anchorage, AK 99507-1225
(907) 269-5511; Fax: (907) 337-2059
Internet: http://www.dps.state.ak.us/ast

Deputy Dir.: Maj. Howard Starbard

Director: Col. Julio Grimes
    (907) 269-5641

Deputy Dir.: Maj. Joseph Masters
Fee for obtaining accident report: $1.00 for first page; $.25
each additional page; must contact individual troop where
accident occurred.

Probate, Recording and Notary Certificate Offices

Estate & Wills: Superior Court each Judicial District
Deeds and Mortgages: District Recorders Offices
Notary Certificates: Office of Lieutenant Governor, Notary
Division

Senators, U.S.

Lisa Murkowski (Republican)
322 Hart Senate Office Bldg., Washington, DC 20510
(202) 224-6665; Fax: (202) 224-5301
Internet: http://murkowski.senate.gov

Ted Stevens (Republican)
522 Hart Senate Office Bldg., Washington, DC 20510
(202) 224-3004; Fax: (202) 224-2354
Internet: http://stevens.senate.gov

National Directory of States

Secretary of State

Office of the Lieutenant Governor
State Capitol, Suite 300, 120 Fourth St.,
Juneau, AK 99801
Mailing Address: P.O. Box 110015, Juneau, AK 99811-0015
(907) 465-3520; Fax: (907) 465-5400
Internet: www.ltgov.state.ak.us
Lieutenant Governor: Loren Leman
Elected; next election Nov. 2006

Tax Department

Department of Revenue
Tax Division
State Office Bldg., 11th Floor, P.O. Box 110420,
Juneau, AK 99811-0420
(907) 465-2320; Fax: (907) 465-2375
Internet: www.revenue.state.ak.us

550 W. 7th Ave., Suite 500, Anchorage, AK 99501-3556
(907) 269-6620; Fax: (907) 269-6644
Director: Dan Dickinson (Anchorage Office)
    E-mail: dan_dickinson@revenue.state.ak.us
Deputy Director: Larry Meyers (Anchorage Office)

Victim Compensation Program

Violent Crimes Compensation Board
450 Whittier, Suite 101, P.O. Box 110230,
Juneau, AK 99811-0230
Mailing Address: P.O. Box 111200, Juneau, AK 99811-1200
(907) 465-3040, (800) 764-3040; Fax: (907) 465-2379
Internet: www.state.ak.us/admin/vccb/
Alaska Stat. tit. 18 §§18.67.01 to 18.67.180

Vital Statistics

Bureau of Vital Statistics
Department of Health and Social Services,
5441 Commercial Blvd., Juneau, AK 99801
Recording: (907) 465-3391;
Director's Office: (907) 465-3392; Fax: (907) 465-3618
Internet: www.hss.state.ak.us/dph/bvs
Births, Deaths, Marriages, Divorces.
At press time a fee increase was pending.
Certified copies—$20.00. Search fees—$20.00 for first
three years; $1.00 for each additional year. Additional
copies—$20.00. Service using a credit card (Visa,
Mastercard, Discover or American Express), may be
obtained for an additional charge of $11.00.

ARIZONA   *Capital: Phoenix*

5,130,632 (2000 Census)
State Information: (602) 542-4900
State Web Site: www.state.az.us

Administrative Office of the Courts

Administrative Office of the Courts
Arizona State Courts Bldg., 1501 W. Washington,
Phoenix, AZ 85007-3327
(602) 542-9301; Fax: (602) 542-9484
Administrative Dir. of the Courts: David K. Byers

Attorney Discipline

State Bar of Arizona Office of Lawyer Regulation
111 W. Monroe, Suite 1800, Phoenix, AZ 85003-1742
(602) 252-4804; Fax: (602) 271-4930
Chief Bar Counsel: Robert B. Van Wyck

Attorney General

Office of the Attorney General
1275 W. Washington St., Phoenix, AZ 85007
(602) 542-4266; Fax: (602) 542-4085
Atty. General: Terry Goddard (Democrat)
Elected; next election Nov. 2006

Banking Department

Department of Banking
2910 N. 44th St., Suite 310, Phoenix, AZ 85018
(602) 255-4421; Fax: (602) 381-1225
E-mail: mailbox@azbanking.com
Internet: www.azbanking.com
Superintendent: Richard C. Houseworth

Bar Admissions

Committee on Character & Fitness
Arizona Supreme Court
1501 W. Washington, Suite 104, Phoenix, AZ 85007-3231
(602) 364-0371
Internet: www.supreme.state.az.us/admis
15 hours CLE required per year.
No admission without exam.

Bar Association

State Bar of Arizona
111 W. Monroe St., Suite 1800, Phoenix, AZ 85003-1742
(602) 252-4804; Fax: (602) 271-4930
Internet: www.azbar.org

Southern Regional Office, 320 S. Convent St.,
Tucson, AZ 85701-2215
(520) 623-9944; Fax: (520) 623-9974
Exec. Dir.: Teresa Schmid
President: Charles W. Wirken
    E-mail: charles.wirken@azbar.org
Integrated Bar
Annual Meeting: June, 2005

Client Protection Fund

Client Protection Fund
State Bar of Arizona
111 W. Monroe, Suite 1800, Phoenix, AZ 85003
(602) 340-7286; Fax: (602) 271-4930
Internet: www.azbar.org/Discipline/cpf_form.pdf
Client Protection Fund Administrator: Ann Hetzler
    E-mail: ann.hetzler@staff.azbar.org

Commerce Department

Department of Commerce
Executive Tower, Suite 600, 1700 W. Washington,
Phoenix, AZ 85007
(602) 771-1100; Fax: (602) 771-1200
Internet: www.commerce.state.az.us/

Corporations Officers

Arizona Corporation Commission
Corporations Division
1300 W. Washington, Phoenix, AZ 85007
(602) 542-3521; General Information: (602) 542-3026;
Corporate Filing Section: (602) 542-3135;
Name Reservation: (602) 542-3230;
Annual Reports: (602) 542-3285;
Corporations Fax: (602) 542-0900
Internet: www.cc.state.az.us
Director: Joanne C. MacDonnell
    E-mail: jmacdonnell@cc.state.az.us
Deputy Dir.: Steve McCance
    (602) 542-0776; E-mail: smccance@cc.state.az.us
Chief Information Officer: Clark Lathram
    1200 W. Washington, Phoenix, AZ 85007
    (602) 542-0671; E-mail: clathram@cc.state.az.us
Office of the Secretary of State
1700 W. Washington, 7th Floor, Phoenix, AZ 85007-2888
General Information: (602) 542-4285;
Limited Partnerships: (602) 542-6187;
UCC: (602) 542-6187; Notaries: (602) 542-4758;
Fax: (602) 542-7386
Internet: www.sos.state.az.us
Chief Information Officer: Bill Maaske
    (602) 542-6170; E-mail: bmaaske@sos.state.az.us
Dir. of Business Services: Gene Palma
    (602) 542-3060; E-mail: gpalma@sos.state.az.us
UCC, Trade Names and Limited Partnerships Office

Criminal History Board

Department of Public Safety
Criminal History Records Section
Mail Drop 1120, 2102 W. Encanto Blvd.,
Phoenix, AZ 85009
Mailing Address: P.O. Box 18450, Phoenix, AZ 85005-8450
(602) 223-2222; Fax: (602) 223-2983

Economic Development Administration

See Commerce Department

Governor's Office

Office of the Governor
1700 W. Washington St., Phoenix, AZ 85007
(602) 542-4331; Fax: (602) 542-1381
E-mail: azgov@az.gov
Internet: http://www.governor.state.az.us
Governor: Janet Napolitano (Democrat)
Next election Nov. 2006

Highest State Court

Arizona Supreme Court
State Courts Bldg., 1501 W. Washington St.,
Phoenix, AZ 85007-3231
(602) 542-9300
Internet: http://www.supreme.state.az.us
Chief Justice: Charles E. Jones
    (602) 542-4531
Clerk of the Supreme Court: Noel K. Dessaint
    Room 402

Insurance Department

Department of Insurance
2910 N. 44th St, 2nd Floor, Phoenix, AZ 85018-7256
(602) 912-8400; Statewide: (800) 325-2548;
Fax: (602) 912-8452
E-mail: info@id.state.az.us
Internet: www.state.az.us/id

Tucson Office, 400 W. Congress, Suite 152,
Tucson, AZ 85701
(520) 628-6370, 71; Fax: (520) 628-6633
Director: Christina Urias
Asst. Dir. of Financial Examination Div.:
    Steve Ferguson

Motor Vehicle Office

Arizona Motor Vehicle Division
Department of Transportation
1801 W. Jefferson Ave., Mail Drop 500M,
Phoenix, AZ 85007
(602) 255-0072; Director's Office: (602) 712-8152;
Fax: (602) 712-6539
E-mail: mvdinfo@dot.state.az.us
Internet: www.azdot.gov

For Abstracts write:, Motor Vehicle Division,
1801 W. Jefferson Ave., Mail Drop 539M, P.O. Box 2100,
Phoenix, AZ 85007-1200
Fee for obtaining abstract: $3.00 for 39 months; $5.00 for
five years, certified; notarized request required.

Police

Arizona Department of Public Safety
2102 W. Encanto Blvd., Phoenix, AZ 85009
Mailing Address: P.O. Box 6638, Phoenix, AZ 85005-6638
(602) 223-2000; Accident Reports: (602) 223-2230, 36;
Accident Reports Fax: (602) 223-2915
Internet: www.dps.state.az.us
Director: Dennis A. Garrett
    (602) 223-2359
Fee for obtaining accident report: $9.00,
Attn: Department Records Section, Mail Drop 1110

Probate, Recording and Notary Certificate Offices

Estate & Wills: Superior Court, each County
Deeds and Mortgages: County Recorders Offices
Notary Certificates: Secretary of State, Business Services
& Notary Division ($3.00)

Senators, U.S.

Jon L. Kyl (Republican)
730 Hart Senate Office Bldg., Washington, DC 20510
(202) 224-4521; Fax: (202) 228-1239
Internet: http://kyl.senate.gov

John McCain (Republican)
241 Russell Senate Office Bldg., Washington, DC 20510
(202) 224-2235; Fax: (202) 228-2862
Internet: http://mccain.senate.gov

Secretary of State

1700 W. Washington, 7th Floor, Phoenix, AZ 85007-2888
(602) 542-4285; Administrative Fax: (602) 542-1575;
Publication Fax: (602) 542-4366
Internet: www.azsos.gov
Secretary of State: Janice K. Brewer (Republican)
Elected; next election Nov. 2006

Tax Department

Department of Revenue
1600 W. Monroe, Phoenix, AZ 85007
(602) 716-6090; Fax: (602) 542-4772
Internet: www.azdor.gov
Director: J. Elliott Hibbs

Victim Compensation Program

Arizona Criminal Justice Commission
1110 W. Washington, Suite 230, Phoenix, AZ 85007
(602) 364-1146; Fax: (602) 364-1175
Internet: www.acjc.state.az.us
*Separate Boards in each county; contact County Attorney's
office*

Vital Statistics

Office of Vital Records
Arizona Dept. of Health Services, 1818 W. Adams St.,
Phoenix, AZ 85007
Mailing Address: P.O. Box 3887, Phoenix, AZ 85030-3887
(602) 364-1300; Credit Card Purchases: (602) 364-1253;
Fax: (602) 249-3040
Internet: www.hs.state.az.us/vitalrcd
*Births, Deaths. Marriage and Divorce records from Clerk of
Superior Court of county where event occurred.*
Certified photocopy of birth records, prior to 1990—$15.00;
after 1990—$10.00; death records—$10.00.

ARKANSAS   *Capital: Little Rock*

2,673,400 (2000 Census)
State Information: (501) 682-3000
State Web Site: www.state.ar.us

Administrative Office of the Courts

Administrative Office of the Courts
1100 Justice Bldg., 625 Marshall St.,
Little Rock, AR 72201
(501) 682-9400; TDD: (501) 682-9412; Fax: (501) 682-9410
E-mail: aoc@arkansas.gov
Internet: www.courts.state.ar.us
Dir. of Court Administration: James D. Gingerich

Attorney Discipline

Arkansas Supreme Court Office on Professional Conduct
Justice Bldg., Rm. 110, 625 Marshall St., Little Rock, AR 72201
(501) 376-0313; Fax: (501) 376-3438
Internet: www.courts.state.ar.us
Exec. Dir.: Stark Ligon

Attorney General

Office of the Attorney General
323 Center St., Suite 200, Little Rock, AR 72201-2610
(501) 682-2007; In-State: (800) 482-8982; Fax: (501) 682-8084
Internet: www.ag.state.ar.us/
Atty. General: Michael D. Beebe (Democrat)
Elected; next election Nov. 2006

Banking Department

State Bank Department
400 Hardin Rd., Suite 100, Little Rock, AR 72211
(501) 324-9019; Fax: (501) 324-9028
Internet: www.accessarkansas.org/bank
Commissioner: Robert H. Adcock, Jr.

Bar Admissions

Supreme Court of Arkansas
State Board of Law Examiners
120 Justice Bldg., 625 Marshall St., Little Rock, AR 72201
(501) 374-1855; Fax: (501) 374-1853
Internet: http://courts.state.ar.us
12 hours CLE required per year.
Admission on motion available
MPRE is prerequisite for admission.

Bar Association

Arkansas Bar Association
400 W. Markham, Little Rock, AR 72201-1408
(501) 375-4606; Instate: (800) 609-5668;
Fax: (501) 375-4901
E-mail: arkbar1@swbell.net
Internet: www.arkbar.com

Exec. Dir.: Don Hollingsworth
    E-mail: dhollingsworth@arkbar.com
President: Glenn Vasser
Non-Integrated Bar
Annual Meeting—June, 2006

Chief Medical Examiner

Office of Chief Medical Examiner
Arkansas State Crime Lab, 3 Natural Resources Dr.,
P.O. Box 8500, Little Rock, AR 72215
(501) 227-5936; Fax: (501) 221-1653
Chief Medical Examiner: William Q. Sturner, M.D.

Client Protection Fund

Client Security Fund
Arkansas Supreme Court
Supreme Ct. Clerk's Office, Justice Bldg.,
625 Marshall St., Little Rock, AR 72201
(501) 682-6849
Clerk: Leslie William Steen

Commerce Department

See Economic Development Administration

Corporations Officers

Office of the Secretary of State
Business & Special Services Division
State Capitol, Room 058, Little Rock, AR 72201
General Information: (501) 682-3409;
Name Availability: (501) 682-3409;
Franchise Tax/Annual Reports: (501) 682-3409;
Limited Partnerships: (501) 682-3409;
Notaries: (501) 682-3409;
Trademarks, Boards & Commissions: (501) 682-3409;
Corporations Fax: (501) 682-3437;
UCC Searches & Inquiries: (501) 682-5078;
UCC Fax: (501) 682-3500
Internet: www.sosweb.state.ar.us

Business Services Mgr.: Charolett B. Martin
    (501) 682-3404; Fax: (501) 682-3437
    E-mail: cbmartin@sosmail.state.ar.us

Criminal History Board

Crime Information Center
One Capitol Mall, 4D200, Little Rock, AR 72201
(501) 682-2222; Fax: (501) 682-7444

Economic Development Administration

Department of Economic Development
One Capitol Mall, Little Rock, AR 72201
(501) 682-1121, (800) 275-2672; Fax: (501) 682-7394
E-mail: info@1800arkansas.com
Internet: www.1800arkansas.com/home.cfm
Director: Larry Walther

Governor's Office

Office of the Governor
State Capitol, Little Rock, AR 72201
(501) 682-2345; Fax: (501) 682-3597
Internet: http://www.state.ar.us/governor/governor.html
Governor: Mike D. Huckabee (Republican)
Next election Nov. 2006

Highest State Court

Supreme Court of Arkansas
Justice Bldg., 625 Marshall St., Little Rock, AR 72201
(501) 682-6849; Fax: (501) 682-6877
Internet: http://www.state.ar.us/supremecourt/arksct.htm
Chief Justice: Betty C. Dickey
Clerk of the Supreme Court: Leslie W. Steen

Insurance Department

Arkansas Insurance Department
1200 W. 3rd St., Little Rock, AR 72201-1904
(501) 371-2600, (800) 282-9134; Fax: (501) 371-2618
E-mail: seleta.yearian@arkansas.gov
Internet: www.arkansas.gov/insurance

Commissioner: Julie Benafield Bowman

**Deputy Commissioner, Financial Regulation &
Audit:** Lenita Blasingame
Chief Examiner: William Woodall, Jr.

Motor Vehicle Office

Arkansas Office of Driver Services
Div. of Revenue
Department of Finance and Administration, Room 1130,
P.O. Box 1272, Little Rock, AR 72203
(501) 682-7060; Administration Fax: (501) 682-7688
Internet: www.arkansas.gov/dfa

For Abstracts write: DFA Driving Records,
1900 W. 7th St., Room 1130, Little Rock, AR 72201

Mailing Address: DFA Driving Records, Room 1130,
P.O. Box 1272, Little Rock, AR 72203
(501) 682-7207
Fee for obtaining abstract: commercial (employment)
$10.00; insurance $7.00, three-years.

Police

Arkansas State Police
1 State Police Plaza Dr., Little Rock, AR 72209
(501) 618-8000; Emergency: (501) 618-8100;
Fax: (501) 618-8222; Accident Records: (501) 618-8130
Internet: www.asp.state.ar.us

Director: Col. Steve Dozier
    (501) 618-8200
Fee for obtaining accident report: $10.00

Probate, Recording and Notary Certificate Offices

Estate & Wills: County Probate Clerks Offices
Deeds and Mortgages: Circuit Clerks, each County
Notary Certificates: Secretary of State, Notary Division
($5.00, Apostille Certification $10.00)

Senators, U.S.

Blanche L. Lincoln (Democrat)
355 Dirksen Senate Office Bldg., Washington, DC 20510
(202) 224-4843; Fax: (202) 228-1371
Internet: http://lincoln.senate.gov

Mark Pryor (Democrat)
217 Russell Senate Office Bldg., Washington, DC 20510
(202) 224-2353
Internet: http://pryor.senate.gov

Secretary of State

Office of the Secretary of State
256 State Capitol, Little Rock, AR 72201
(501) 682-1010; Fax: (501) 682-3510
E-mail: sos@sosmail.state.ar.us
Internet: www.sosweb.state.ar.us

Secretary of State: Charlie Daniels (Democrat)
Elected; next election Nov. 2006

Tax Department

Department of Finance & Administration
Revenue Division
1800 W. 7th St., Little Rock, AR 72201
Mailing Address: P.O. Box 3278, Little Rock, AR 72203
Exec. Offices: (501) 682-2242;
Exec. Offices Fax: (501) 682-1029; Forms: (501) 682-1100;
Form Fax: (501) 682-7692;
Excise Tax Admin. Ofc.: (501) 682-7200
Internet: www.arkansas.gov/dfa/

Commissioner/Deputy Dir.: Timothy J. Leathers
    E-mail: tim.leathers@dfa.state.ar.us
Dir., Dept. of Finance & Admin.: Richard A. Weiss
    E-mail: richard.weiss@dfa.state.ar.us

Victim Compensation Program

Crime Victims Reparations Board
323 Center St., Suite 1100, Little Rock, AR 72201
(501) 682-1020; Arkansas only: (800) 448-3014;
Fax: (501) 682-5313
E-mail: oag@arkansasag.gov
Internet: www.arkansasag.gov
Ark. Code Ann. §§16-90-701 to 16-90-719

Vital Statistics

Division of Vital Records
Department of Health
4815 W. Markham St., Slot 44, Little Rock, AR 72205-3867
(501) 661-2174; Fax: (501) 661-2869
Internet: www.healthyarkansas.com
Births, Deaths, Marriages, Divorces.
Certified copies of births—$12.00 (extra copies $10.00 each if ordered at same time); certified copy of deaths, marriages and divorces—$10.00 (extra copies of death certificates $8.00 each if ordered at same time); Vital Chek (866) 209-9482; U.S. Certs. (866) 300-8534; Internet: www.vitalchek.com.

CALIFORNIA   *Capital: Sacramento*

33,871,648 (2000 Census)
State Information: (916) 322-9900
State Web Site: www.ca.gov

Administrative Office of the Courts

Administrative Office of the Courts
455 Golden Gate Ave., San Francisco, CA 94102-3688
(415) 865-4200; Fax: (415) 865-4228
Internet: http://www.courtinfo.ca.gov/aoc/

Administrative Dir. of the Courts: William C. Vickrey

Attorney Discipline

State Bar of California Attorney Discipline
180 Howard Street, San Francisco, CA 94015
(415) 538-2000;
Attorney Discipline Complaint Hotline in CA:
(800) 843-9053; Outside of CA: (213) 765-1200;
Fax: (213) 765-1168
Internet: www.calbar.ca.gov

1149 S. Hill St., Los Angeles, CA 90015-2299
(213) 765-1000

Court & Certification, 180 Howard St.,
San Francisco, CA 94105-1639
(415) 538-2000

Chief Trial Counsel: Mike Nisperos

Attorney General

Office of the Attorney General
1300 I St., Sacramento, CA 95814
Mailing Address: Public Inquiry Unit, P.O. Box 944255,
Sacramento, CA 94244-2550
(916) 445-9555; Fax: (916) 323-5341
E-mail: piu@doj.ca.gov
Internet: www.ag.ca.gov

Atty. General: Bill Lockyer (Democrat)
Elected; next election Nov. 2006

Banking Department

Department of Financial Institutions
111 Pine St., Suite 1100, San Francisco, CA 94111-5613
(415) 263-8500; Fax: (415) 989-5310
Internet: www.dfi.ca.gov/

300 S. Spring St., Suite 15513,
Los Angeles, CA 90013-1204
(213) 897-2085; Fax: (213) 897-8860

1810 13th St., Sacramento, CA 95814
(916) 322-5966; Examination Policy Fax: (916) 322-5976

7575 Metropolitan Dr., Suite 108, San Diego, CA 92108
(619) 682-7227; Fax: (619) 682-7217

Commissioner: Howard Gould

Bar Admissions

Committee of Bar Examiners/Office of Admissions
The State Bar of California
180 Howard St., San Francisco, CA 94105-1639
(415) 538-2303; CLE Office: (415) 538-2130
Internet: www.cdlbar.ca.gov

1149 S. Hill St., 4th Floor, Los Angeles, CA 90015-2212
(213) 765-1500
25 hours CLE required per three years, including 4 hours of Ethics, 1 hour of Substance Abuse and 1 hour of Elimination of Bias.
No admission without exam.

Bar Association

State Bar of California
180 Howard St., San Francisco, CA 94105-1639
(415) 538-2000; Fax: (415) 538-2305
Internet: www.calbar.ca.gov, Internet (Member Records): www.calsb.org
Exec. Dir.: Judy Johnson
President: Anthony P. Capozzi
Integrated Bar
Annual Meeting—October, 2005

Client Protection Fund

Client Security Fund
State Bar of California, 1149 S. Hill St.,
Los Angeles, CA 90015-2299
(213) 765-1140; Fax: (213) 765-1158
Director: Martha J. Gonzales

Commerce Department

Commerce & Economic Deveopment Program
980 9th St., Suite 2450, Sacramento, CA 95831
(916) 323-5400; Fax: (916) 323-7166
Internet: www.commerce.ca.gov/state/ttca/ttca_homepage.jsp
Deputy Secretary: Patricia Garamendi (Commerce)
(916) 327-7222

Corporations Officers

Business Programs Division
1500 11th St., 3rd Floor, Sacramento, CA 95814
Business Programs: (916) 657-5448
Chief: Cathy Mitchell
(916) 653-0721; Fax: (916) 653-1315
E-mail: cmitchel@ss.ca.gov
Sr. Staff Counsel Supervisor: Betsy Bogart
(916) 653-6244; Fax: (916) 653-0138
E-mail: bbogart@ss.ca.gov
Managers, Business Entities:
Stacy Hirakana (916) 653-6364; Fax: (916) 653-1315
E-mail: shirakana@ss.ca.gov
Susan Hiuga (916) 654-4155; Fax: (916) 654-1315
E-mail: shiuga@ss.ca.gov
Department of State
Information Technology
1500 11th St., 4th Floor, Sacramento, CA 95814
(916) 653-7735; Fax: (916) 653-2151
Database Administrator: Lynnette Wong
(916) 653-2652; Fax: (916) 653-2151
E-mail: lwong@ss.ca.gov
UCC Section
1500 11th St., 2nd Floor, Sacramento, CA 95814
General Information, UCC: (916) 653-8153;
Annual Reports: (916) 653-4834
Manager: Kathleen Vasquez
(916) 653-8153; Fax: (916) 653-4834
E-mail: kvasquez@ss.ca.gov

Criminal History Board

Department of Justice
Bureau of Criminal Identification & Information
Records Review Unit, P.O. Box 903417,
Sacramento, CA 94203-4170
General Information: (916) 227-3832;
Sealing and Dismissal: (916) 227-2405;
Visa Clearances: (916) 227-3832;
Criminal Record Purge Inquiries: (916) 227-2405

Economic Development Administration

Commerce & Economic Development Program
980 9th St., Suite 2450, Sacramento, CA 95831
(916) 322-5400; Fax: (916) 323-2887
Internet: http://commerce.ca.gov

Deputy Secretary, Commerce: Patricia Garamendi
   (916) 327-7222; Fax: (916) 327-7166
See Commerce & Economic Development Program

Governor's Office

Office of the Governor
State Capitol Bldg., Sacramento, CA 95814
(916) 445-2841; Fax: (916) 445-4633
E-mail: governor@governor.ca.gov
Internet: http://www.governor.ca.gov

444 N. Capitol St. N.W., Washington, DC 20001
(202) 624-5270; Fax: (202) 624-5280

Governor: Arnold Schwarzenegger (Republican)
   E-mail: governor@governor.ca.gov
Next election Nov. 2006

Highest State Court

Supreme Court
350 McAllister St., San Francisco, CA 94102
(415) 865-7000; Fax: (415) 865-7183
Internet: www.courtinfo.ca.gov/courts/supreme

300 S. Spring St., Los Angeles, CA 90013
(213) 830-7570

Library & Courts Bldg., Room 100, Sacramento, CA 95814
(916) 322-5957

Chief Justice: Ronald M. George
Clerk/Administrator of the Supreme Court:
   Frederick K. Ohlrich

Insurance Department

Office of the Insurance Commissioner
300 Capital Mall, Suite 1700, Sacramento, CA 95814
(916) 492-3500; Fax: (916) 445-5280
Internet: www.insurance.ca.gov

300 S. Spring St., South Tower, Los Angeles, CA 90013
(213) 346-6400; Fax: (213) 897-6771

45 Fremont St., San Francisco, CA 94105
(415) 538-4010; Fax: (415) 904-5889
Commissioner: John Garamendi

Motor Vehicle Office

California Department of Motor Vehicles
2415 1st Ave., E-128, P.O. Box 932382,
Sacramento, CA 95818
(916) 657-6469; Director's Office: (916) 657-6940;
Fax: (916) 657-6243; Director's Fax: (916) 657-7393;
Abstracts: (916) 957-8298
Internet: www.dmv.ca.gov

For Abstracts write:, P.O. Box 944247,
Sacramento, CA 94244-2470
Fee for obtaining abstract: $5.00

Police

California Highway Patrol
2555 First Ave., Sacramento, CA 95818
Mailing Address: P.O. Box 942898, Sacramento, CA 94298-0001
(916) 957-7261, 657-7152;
Accident Reports, Valley Division: (916) 464-2090;
Fax: (916) 657-7324
Internet: http://www.chp.ca.gov/

Commissioner: D. O. Helmick, Jr.
Fee for obtaining accident report: $6.00 up to 12 pages;
$12.00 up to 24 pages; Accident reports are available from
the CHP Area office that handled the accident
investigation.

Probate, Recording and Notary Certificate Offices

Estate & Wills: County Clerks Offices
Deeds and Mortgages: County Recorders Offices
Notary Certificates: County Clerk/Recorder in County of
Notary's Commission (fee varies); Secretary of State,
Notary Public Section for Apostille Certification ($20.00)

Senators, U.S.

Barbara Boxer (Democrat)
112 Hart Senate Office Bldg., Washington, DC 20510
(202) 224-3553; Fax: (202) 956-6701
Internet: http://boxer.senate.gov

Dianne Feinstein (Democrat)
331 Hart Senate Office Bldg., Washington, DC 20510
(202) 224-3841; Fax: (202) 228-3954
Internet: http://feinstein.senate.gov

Secretary of State

Office of the Secretary of State
1500 11th St., Sacramento, CA 95814
(916) 653-7244; Fax: (916) 653-4620
E-mail: webmaster@ss.ca.gov
Internet: www.ss.ca.gov

Secretary of State: Kevin Shelley (Democrat)
Elected; next election Nov. 2006

Tax Department

Franchise Tax Board
9646 Butterfield Way, Sacramento, CA 95827
Mailing Address: P.O. Box 942840,
Sacramento, CA 94240-0040
(800) 852-5711, (916) 845-6500;
Forms: (800) 338-0505, (916) 845-6600;
TDD: (800) 822-6268; Calif. Relay Service: (800) 735-2922
Internet: www.ftb.ca.gov

Exec. Officer: Gerald H. Goldberg; Fax: (916) 845-6614
Chief Counsel: John Davies

Victim Compensation Program

Victim Compensation and Government Claims Board
630 K St., Sacramento, CA 95814
Mailing Address: P.O. Box 3036, Sacramento, CA 95812-3036
(800) 777-9229, (916) 322-4426; Fax: (916) 323-2695
Internet: www.boc.ca.gov
Calif. Govt. Code Ann. §§13950 et seq.

Vital Statistics

Office of Vital Records
M.S. 5103, P.O. Box 997410, Sacramento, CA 95899-7410
(916) 445-1719, 445-2684
Internet: www.dhs.ca.gov

Physical Address (for overnight couriers only),
M.S. 5103, Suite 71.1110, 1501 Capitol Ave.,
Sacramento, CA 95814
*Births, Deaths—July 1905. Marriage—1949-1986 and
1998-1999; Marriages 1905-1948, 1987-1997, and
2000-present located at the county recorder where marriage
occurred; Indexes of Divorce from January 1962 through
June 1984; other marriage and divorce records in county
clerk's office in county where event occurred.*
Certified copies: births—$15.00; deaths, marriages,
divorces—$13.00. If exact date is unknown, fee includes
record search of up to 10 years. Notarized statement
required for certified copy of birth or death record: consult
website for details.

COLORADO   *Capital: Denver*

4,301,261 (2000 Census)
State Information: (303) 866-5000
State Web Site: www.state.co.us

Administrative Office of the Courts

Office of the State Court Administrator
1301 Pennsylvania, Suite 300, Denver, CO 80203
(303) 861-1111; Fax: (303) 837-2340
Internet: www.courts.state.co.us/exec/scaoindex.htm
State Court Administrator: Gerald A. Marroney

Attorney Discipline

Colorado Supreme Court
Office of Attorney Regulation Counsel
Dominion Plaza Bldg., Suite 200 South, 600 17th St.,
Denver, CO 80202-5435
(303) 893-8121; Toll Free: (877) 888-1370
Internet: www.coloradosupremecourt.com
Regulation Counsel: John S. Gleason

Attorney General

Office of the Attorney General
1525 Sherman St., 7th Floor, Denver, CO 80203
(303) 866-4500; Fax: (303) 866-4745
Internet: www.ago.state.co.us

Atty. General: John W. Suthers
Elected; next election Nov. 2006

Banking Department

Division of Banking
1560 Broadway, Suite 1175, Denver, CO 80202
(303) 894-7575; Fax: (303) 894-7570
Internet: www.dora.state.co.us/banking

Commissioner: Richard Fulkerson

Bar Admissions

Board of Law Examiners
Colorado Supreme Court
Dominion Plaza Bldg., Suite 520-S, 600 17th St.,
Denver, CO 80202-5451
(303) 893-8096
E-mail: information@lawexaminers.courts.state.co.us
Internet: www.courts.state.co.us
45 hours CLE required per three years; seven hours must
be in ethics.
Admission on motion with five of the last seven years law
practice in a Reciprocal Jurisdiction.

Bar Association

Colorado Bar Assn.
1900 Grant St., Suite 900, Denver, CO 80203
(303) 860-1115; Fax: (303) 894-0821
E-mail: comments@cobar.org
Internet: www.cobar.org

Exec. Dir.: Charles C. Turner
E-mail: cturner@cobar.org

President: Steve C. Briggs
Non-Integrated Bar

Chief Medical Examiner

Office of Chief Medical Examiner
660 Bannock St., Denver, CO 80204-4507
(303) 436-7711; Fax: (303) 436-7709
Internet: www.denvergov.org/dephome.asp?depid=50

Chief Medical Examiner: Dr. Thomas E. Henry
E-mail: tom.henry@ci.denver.co.us

Commerce Department

See Economic Development Administration

Corporations Officers

Department of State
Division of Commercial Recordings
1560 Broadway, Suite 200, Denver, CO 80202-5169
Business Division, Annual Reports (press option 2):
(303) 894-2200;
Licensing/Notaries (press option 4): (303) 894-2200;
UCC (press option 2): (303) 894-2200;
Business Entities, Tradenames & Trademarks (press
option 2): (303) 894-2200;
Elections (press option 3): (303) 894-2200;
Forms Fax on Demand: (303) 860-6975;
Administration (press option 5): (303) 894-2200
Internet: www.sos.state.co.us

Director: Keith Whitelaw
(303) 849-2200, Ext. 6201
E-mail: keith.whitelaw@sos.state.co.us

Records Administrator: Alberta Bennett
(303) 894-2200, Ext. 6203
E-mail: alberta.bennett@sos.state.co.us

Criminal History Board

Bureau of Investigation (CBI)
Program Support Unit
690 Kipling St., Room 3000, Denver, CO 80215-5844
(303) 239-4222, 239-4300; Fax: (303) 239-4661
Internet: www.cbi.state.co.us

Economic Development Administration

Office of Economic Development & Intl. Trade
1625 Broadway, Suite 1700, Denver, CO 80202
(303) 892-3840; Fax: (303) 892-3848
Internet: www.advancecolorado.com

Director: Brian Vogt

Governor's Office

Office of the Governor
136 State Capitol, Denver, CO 80203-1792
(303) 866-2471; Fax: (303) 866-2003
Internet: http://www.state.co.us/governor_office.html

Governor: Bill Owens (Republican)
E-mail: governorowens@state.co.us
Next election Nov. 2006

Highest State Court

Supreme Court
Judicial Bldg., Room 400, 2 E. 14th Ave., Denver, CO 80203
(303) 837-3790
Internet: http://www.courts.state.co.us

Chief Justice: Mary J. Mullarkey

Clerk of the Supreme Court: Susan J. Festag

Insurance Department

Division of Insurance
1560 Broadway, Suite 850, Denver, CO 80202
(303) 894-7499; Fax: (303) 894-7455
Internet: www.dora.state.co.us/insurance

Commissioner: Doug Dean

Motor Vehicle Office

Colorado Motor Vehicle Division
1881 Pierce St., Lakewood, CO 80214
Mailing Address:
For Driver Records write: Driver Control Section,
Denver, CO 80261-0016
(303) 205-5613; Fax: (303) 205-5990
Internet: www.mv.state.co.us/mv.html

Titles & Registrations: Motor Vehicle Division,
Dept. of Revenue Registration Section,
Denver, CO 80261-0016
Fee for obtaining abstract: $2.20; $2.70 certified, available
in person only; checks payable to Department of Revenue

Police

Colorado State Patrol
700 Kipling St., Lakewood, CO 80215
(303) 239-4500; Fax: (303) 239-4481
Internet (State Police): http://csp.state.co.us, Internet
(Motor Vehicles/Accident Reports): www.mv.state.co.us

For Accident Reports (Regular & Priority Mail) write: ,
Motor Vehicle Div., Driver Services,
Denver, CO 80261-0016

For Accident Reports (Deliveries only, i.e., FedEx): ,
Motor Vehicle Div., Driver Services, 1881 Pierce St.,
Lakewood, CO 80214
(303) 205-5613; Fax: (303) 205-5990

Chief: Col. Mark V. Trostel
(303) 239-4403
Fee for obtaining accident report: $2.20; $2.70 certified

Probate, Recording and Notary Certificate Offices

Estate & Wills: District Court Probate Division
Deeds and Mortgages: County Clerks and Recorders
Offices
Notary Certificates: Secretary of State, Notary Division
($2.00, same day service $17.00)

Senators, U.S.

Wayne Allard (Republican)
525 Dirksen Senate Office Bldg., Washington, DC 20510
(202) 224-5941; Fax: (202) 224-6471
Internet: http://allard.senate.gov

Ken Salazar (Democrat)
B-40A Dirksen Senate Office Bldg., Washington, DC 20510
(202) 224-5852; Fax: (202) 228-5036
Internet: http://salazar.senate.gov

Secretary of State
Office of the Secretary of State
1560 Broadway, Suite 200, Denver, CO 80202
(303) 894-2200; Fax: (303) 869-4860
E-mail: sos.administration@sos.state.co.us
Internet: www.sos.state.co.us
Secretary of State: Donetta Davidson (Republican)
Elected; next election Nov. 2006

Tax Department
Department of Revenue
1375 Sherman St., Room 409, Denver, CO 80261
Forms & Telefile: (303) 238-3278;
Income, Sales and Witholding Tax Info: (303) 238-7378;
Tax Auditing Compliance: (303) 866-3711;
Fuel Tax: (303) 205-5602
Internet: www.revenue.state.co.us
Exec. Dir.: M. Michael Cooke
(303) 866-3091
E-mail: edo@spike.dor.state.co.us

Victim Compensation Program
Office for Victims Program
Division of Criminal Justice
700 Kipling, Suite 1000, Denver, CO 80215
(303) 239-4442, 239-5719; Fax: (303) 239-5743
Internet: www.cdpsweb.state.co.us/ovp
*Victims Compensation Boards in each of the state's 22
judicial districts. See Colorado Revised Statutes 1981
(amended 1995). §§24-4.1-100*

Vital Statistics
Department of Public Health & Environment
Vital Records Section,
4300 Cherry Creek Dr. S., Suite A145,
Denver, CO 80246-1530
(303) 692-2200, 756-4464; Fax outside US: (303) 691-9307;
Fax within US: (800) 423-1108
Internet: www.cdphe.state.co.us/hs/certs.asp
*Births—1910-present, Deaths—1900-present,
Marriages—1900-1939 and 1975-present,
Divorces—1900-1939 and 1968-present.*
Certified copies: births and deaths—$15.00; Additional
copies: $6.00 if ordered at the same time. Convenience
charge for the use of a credit card—$6.00
Marriage & Divorce Records: Considered open records and
available for review on website except marriages
1900-1939. www.cdphe.state.co.us/hs/certs.asp.
Department can verify for $15.00 fee for index information
or people can contact county in which event occurred for
the actual record.

CONNECTICUT   *Capital: Hartford*
3,405,565 (2000 Census)
State Information: (860) 566-2211
State Web Site: www.state.ct.us

Administrative Office of the Courts
Office of the Chief Court Administrator
Supreme Court Bldg., 231 Capitol Ave.,
Hartford, CT 06106
(860) 757-2100; Fax: (860) 757-2130
Chief Court Administrator: Judge Joseph H. Pellegrino

Attorney Discipline
Statewide Grievance Committee
287 Main St., Suite Two, East Hartford, CT 06118-1885
(860) 568-5157
Statewide Bar Counsel: Daniel B. Horwitch

Attorney General
Office of the Attorney General
55 Elm St., Hartford, CT 06106
(860) 808-5318; Fax: (860) 808-5387
E-mail: attorney.general@po.state.ct.us
Internet: www.cslib.org/attygenl/
Atty. General: Richard Blumenthal (Democrat)
Elected; next election Nov. 2006

Banking Department
Department of Banking
260 Constitution Plaza, Hartford, CT 06103-1800
(860) 240-8299; Fax: (860) 240-8178
Internet: www.state.ct.us/dob/
Commissioner: John P. Burke

Bar Admissions
Connecticut Bar Examining Committee
100 Washington St., Hartford, CT 06106-4411
Internet: www.jud.state.ct.us/cbec
No CLE required.
Admission on motion with five of the last seven years in
practice in Reciprocal Jurisdiction.

Bar Association
Connecticut Bar Assn.
30 Bank Street, New Britain, CT 06050-0350
(860) 223-4400; Fax: (860) 223-4488
E-mail: ctbar@ctbar.org; Internet: www.ctbar.org
Exec. Dir.: Tim Hazen
President: Louis R. Pepe
Non-Integrated Bar
Annual Meeting—June, 2006

Chief Medical Examiner
Office of Chief Medical Examiner
11 Shuttle Rd., Farmington, CT 06032-1939
(860) 679-3980; Fax: (860) 679-1257
Chief Medical Examiner: H. Wayne Carver II, M.D.

Client Protection Fund
Clients' Security Fund
287 Main St., Suite 1, 2nd Floor,
East Hartford, CT 06118-1885
(860) 568-3450; Fax: (860) 568-4953
E-mail: security.fund@jud.state.ct.us
Internet: www.jud.state.ct.us
Chairperson: Joette Katz
Staff Atty.: Christopher Blanchard

Commerce Department
See Economic Development Administration

Corporations Officers
Office of the Secretary of State
Commercial Recording Division
30 Trinity St., Hartford, CT 06106
Mailing Address: P.O. Box 150470,
Hartford, CT 06115-0470
(860) 509-6001; Business Information: (860) 509-6002;
Document Review: (860) 509-6003;
Form Orders: (860) 509-6079;
Form Orders by Fax: (860) 509-6080;
Research and Response Unit (UCC copies, certificates):
(860) 509-6004
Internet: www.sots.state.ct.us
Dep. Secy. of State and General Counsel:
Maria Marena Greenslade
(860) 509-6212; Fax: (860) 509-6131
E-mail: maria.greenslade@po.state.ct.us
Mgr., Commercial Recording Div.: Diane Steir
(860) 509-6006; Fax: (860) 509-6068
E-mail: diane.steir@po.state.ct.us
Information Technology: Terrance Babcock
(860) 509-6212; Fax: (860) 509-6131
E-mail: terry.babcock@po.state.ct.us

Criminal History Board
State Police Bureau of Identification (SPBI)
1111 Country Club Rd., P.O. Box 2794,
Middletown, CT 06457-9294
(860) 685-8480; Fax: (860) 685-8361
Internet: www.state.ct.us/dps/spbi.htm

Economic Development Administration
Department of Economic & Community Development
505 Hudson St., Hartford, CT 06105-7106
(860) 270-8000; Fax: (860) 270-8008
Internet: www.ct.gov/ecd
Commissioner: James F. Abromaitis

Governor's Office

Office of the Governor
State Capitol, Room 200, 210 Capitol Ave.,
Hartford, CT 06106
(860) 566-4840; Fax: (860) 524-7395, 96
Internet: http://www.state.ct.us/governor

444 N. Capitol St. N.W., Suite 317, Washington, DC 20001
(202) 347-4535; Fax: (202) 347-7151
Governor: M. Jodi Rell (Republican)
Next election Nov. 2006

Highest State Court

Supreme Court
Supreme Court Bldg., 231 Capitol Ave.,
Hartford, CT 06106
(860) 757-2200; Fax: (860) 757-2217
E-mail: chief.clerk@connapp.state.ct.us
Internet: www.jud.state.ct.us
Chief Justice: William J. Sullivan (860) 757-2116
Clerk of the Supreme Court: Michele T. Angers

Insurance Department

Insurance Department
153 Market St., Hartford, CT 06103
Mailing Address: P.O. Box 816, Hartford, CT 06142-0816
(860) 297-3800; Fax: (860) 566-7410
Internet: www.ct.gov/cid
Commissioner: Susan F. Cogswell
Chief Examiner: Kathryn Belfi

Motor Vehicle Office

Connecticut Department of Motor Vehicles
60 State St., Wethersfield, CT 06161-0503
(860) 263-5700
E-mail: mail@dmvct.org
Internet: http://dmvct.org/
Abstracts not available by Fax
Fee for obtaining abstract: $20.00

Police

Connecticut State Police
1111 Country Club Rd., Middletown, CT 06457-9294
Commissioner's Office: (860) 685-8000;
Fax: (860) 685-8354
Internet: www.state.ct.us/dps

Reports & Records, P.O. Box 2794, Middletown, CT 06457
(860) 685-8250; Fax: (860) 685-8361
Commissioner: Arthur L. Spada
Deputy Commissioner: Col. Timothy F. Barry
Fee for obtaining accident report: $8.00; $9.00 certified
copies

Probate, Recording and Notary Certificate Offices

Estate & Wills: District Probate Courts
Deeds and Mortgages: Town Clerks Offices—Land Records
Notary Certificates: Secretary of State, Authentication
Unit ($20.00; if used in an adoption—$5.00; expedited
service is an additional $25.00 per document)

Senators, U.S.

Christopher J. Dodd (Democrat)
448 Russell Senate Office Bldg., Washington, DC 20510
(202) 224-2823; Fax: (202) 224-1083
Internet: http://dodd.senate.gov
Joseph I. Lieberman (Democrat)
706 Hart Senate Office Bldg., Washington, DC 20510
(202) 224-4041; Fax: (202) 224-9750
Internet: http://lieberman.senate.gov

Secretary of State

Office of Secretary of the State
210 Capitol Ave., Room 104, Hartford, CT 06106
(860) 509-6200; Capitol Office Fax: (860) 509-6209
Internet: www.sots.state.ct.us

30 Trinity St., P.O. Box 150470, Hartford, CT 06106
(860) 509-6212; Fax: (860) 509-6131
Secretary of State: Susan Bysiewicz (Democrat)
Elected; next election Nov. 2006

Tax Department

Department of Revenue Services
Taxpayer Services Div.
25 Sigourney St., Hartford, CT 06106-5032
(860) 297-5962; In-State: (800) 382-9463;
Forms Fax: (860) 297-5698;
Administration Div.: (860) 297-5660;
Audit Div.: (860) 541-7500;
Collections & Enforcement Div.: (860) 297-5909;
Legal Division: (860) 297-5776;
Operations Division: (860) 297-4700;
Appellate Division: (860) 297-4775
E-mail: drs@po.state.ct.us
Internet: www.ct.gov/drs
Commissioner: Pam Law

Victim Compensation Program

Office of Victim Services
31 Cooke St., Plainville, CT 06062
(860) 747-6070; Fax: (860) 747-6428
Internet: www.jud.state.ct.us
Conn. Gen. Stat. Ann. §§54-201 to 54-233

Vital Statistics

Department of Public Health
Vital Records Section, 410 Capital Ave., 1st Floor,
Hartford, CT 06134
Mailing Address: MS11VRS, P.O. Box 340308,
Hartford, CT 06134-0308
(860) 509-7897; Fax: (860) 509-7964
*Births, Deaths, Marriages. Divorce records at clerk of
Superior Court where decree was granted.
Temporarily closed effective March 1996, until further
notice; until service resumes, contact Town Clerk where
event occurred.*
Certified copies—Births: $5.00; Marriages and Deaths:
$5.00.

DELAWARE   *Capital: Dover*

783,600 (2000 Census)
State Information: (302) 739-4000
State Web Site: www.state.de.us

Administrative Office of the Courts

Administrative Office of the Courts
New Castle County Courthouse, Suite 11600,
500 N. King St., Wilmington, DE 19801-3734
(302) 255-0088; Fax: (302) 255-2218
Internet: www.courts.state.de.us
Court Administrator: Patricia Walther Griffin
    E-mail: patricia.griffin@state.de.us

Attorney Discipline

Office of Disciplinary Counsel
Supreme Court of the State of Delaware
Carvel State Office Bldg., 11th Floor, 820 N. French St.,
Wilmington, DE 19801
(302) 577-7042; Fax: (302) 577-7048
Internet: http://courts.state.de.us/odc
Chief Counsel: Andrea L. Rocanelli
Deputy Counsel:
    Michael S. McGinniss
    Mary Susan Much
    Patricia Bartley Schwartz
Administrator: Margot R. Millar
At press time, an address change was anticipated.

Attorney General

Office of the Attorney General
Carvel State Office Bldg., 6th Floor, 820 N. French St.,
Wilmington, DE 19801
Administration: (302) 577-8400; Criminal: (302) 577-8500;
Fax: (302) 577-6630; TTY: (302) 577-5783
Internet: www.state.de.us/attgen/index.htm

102 W. Water St., Dover, DE 19904 (302) 739-4211

114 E. Market St., Georgetown, DE 19947 (302) 856-5353
Atty. General: M. Jane Brady (Republican)
Elected; next election Nov. 2006

National Directory of States

Banking Department

Office of the State Bank Commissioner
555 E. Loockerman St., Suite 210, Dover, DE 19901
(302) 739-4235; Fax: (302) 739-3609
Internet: www.state.de.us/bank

Commissioner: Robert A. Glen

Bar Admissions

Board of Bar Examiners of the Delaware Supreme Court
Carvel State Bldg., 11th Floor, 820 N. French St.,
Wilmington, DE 19801
(302) 577-7038; Fax: (302) 577-7037;
CLE Office: (302) 577-7040
E-mail: sarah.arnold@state.de.us
Internet: http://courts.state.de.us/bbe/
24 credits CLE required per two years; 4 hours must be in enhanced ethics.
No admission without exam.

Bar Association

Delaware State Bar Assn.
301 N. Market St., Wilmington, DE 19801
(302) 658-5279; Fax: (302) 658-5212
Internet: www.dsba.org

Exec. Dir.: Rina Marks, Ext. 218
   E-mail: rmarks@dsba.org

President: Robert B. Young
Non-Integrated Bar
Annual Meeting—June, 2005

Chief Medical Examiner

Office of Chief Medical Examiner
200 S. Adam St., Wilmington, DE 19801
(302) 577-3420; Fax: (302) 577-3416

Chief Medical Examiner: Richard T. Callery, M.D.

Client Protection Fund

Lawyers' Fund for Client Protection of the Bar of Delaware
820 N. French St., 11th Floor, Wilmington, DE 19801
(302) 577-7034; Fax: (302) 577-7037
E-mail: maureen.mcgovern@state.de.us
Internet: http://courts.state.de.us/lfcp

Executive Secretary: Maureen F. McGovern

Commerce Department

See Economic Development Administration

Corporations Officers

Division of Corporations
John G. Townsend Bldg., 401 Federal St., P.O. Box 898,
Dover, DE 19903
(302) 739-3077;
Corporate General Information: (302) 739-3073;
Name Reservation: (900) 420-8042;
Franchise Tax Information: (302) 739-3073;
UCC: (302) 739-3073;
Expedited Services, Limited Partnerships: (302) 739-3073;
Corporate Status (900) 555-CORP: (900) 555-2677;
Fax: (302) 739-3812, 13
Internet: www.state.de.us/corp

Asst. Secretary of State: Richard J. Geisenberger
   Suite 3   (302) 739-4111; Fax: (302) 739-3811
   E-mail: richard.geisenberger@state.de.us

Corporations Administrator: Robert Mathers, Suite 4
   (302) 739-3077; Fax: (302) 739-2238
   E-mail: robert.mathers@state.de.us

Technical Support Admin.: Sandra M. Miller, Suite 4
   (302) 739-3077, Ext. 1320; Fax: (302) 739-2859
   E-mail: sandra.miller@state.de.us

Franchise Tax Admin.: Eileen H. Simpson, Suite 4
   (302) 739-3077, Ext. 1600; Fax: (302) 739-2565
   E-mail: eileen.simpson@state.de.us

Criminal History Board

State Bureau of Identification
Criminal History
1407 N. Dupont Hwy., P.O. Box 430, Dover, DE 19903
(302) 739-5882; Fax: (302) 739-5888

Economic Development Administration

Delaware Economic Development Office
99 Kings Hwy., Dover, DE 19901-7305
(302) 739-4271; Fax: (302) 739-5749
Internet: www.state.de.us/dedo

820 N. French St., Wilmington, DE 19801
(302) 577-8477; Fax: (302) 577-8499

Director: Judy McKinney-Cherry

Governor's Office

Office of the Governor
Tatnall Bldg., 2nd Floor, 150 William Penn St.,
Dover, DE 19901
(302) 744-4101; Fax: (302) 739-2775
Internet: https://delaware/gov/

444 N. Capitol St. N.W., Suite 230, Washington, DC 20001
(202) 624-7724; Fax: (202) 624-5495

Governor: Ruth Ann Minner (Democrat)
Next election Nov. 2008

Highest State Court

Supreme Court
55 The Green, Supreme Court Bldg., Dover, DE 19901
Mailing Address: P.O. Box 476, Dover, DE 19903
(302) 739-4155; Clerk's Fax: (302) 739-3751
Internet: http://courts.state.de.us

Court of Chancery Cthse., 34 The Circle, P.O. Box 369,
Georgetown, DE 19947

820 N. French St., 11th Floor, Wilmington, DE 19801

Chief Justice: Myron T. Steele

Clerk of the Supreme Court: Cathy L. Howard

Insurance Department

Department of Insurance
The Rodney Bldg., 841 Silver Lake Blvd., Dover, DE 19904
(302) 739-4251; Fax: (302) 739-5280
Internet: www.state.de.us/inscom/index.html

Carvel State Bldg., 5th Floor, 820 French St.,
Wilmington, DE 19801

Commissioner: Donna Lee H. Williams

Chief Financial Examiner: Darryl Reese

Motor Vehicle Office

Delaware Division of Motor Vehicles
Dept. of Transportation, 303 Transportation Circle,
Dover, DE 19901
Mailing Address: P.O. Box 698, Dover, DE 19903
General Information: (302) 744-2500;
Director's Office: (302) 744-2510; Fax: (302) 739-3152;
Motor Vehicles Records: (302) 744-2511
Internet: www.dmv.de.gov

Georgetown Lane, Rt. 113 and S. Bedford St. Ext.,
P.O. Box 399, Georgetown, DE 19947
(302) 853-1000; Fax: (302) 856-5886

Greater Wilmington DMV, 2230 Hessler Blvd.,
New Castle, DE 19720
(302) 434-3203; Fax: (302) 577-5658

New Castle Lane, 161 Airport Road,
New Castle, DE 19720
(302) 326-5000; Fax: (302) 326-6168
Fee for obtaining abstract: $15.00; $20.00 certified

Police

Delaware State Police
1441 N. Dupont Hwy., P.O. Box 430, Dover, DE 19903-0430
Mailing Address: Traffic Records, P.O. Box 430,
Dover, DE 19903-0430
(302) 739-5911; Headquarters Fax: (302) 739-5966;
Traffic Records: (302) 739-5931;
Traffic Fax: (302) 739-5982
Internet: www.state.de.us/dsp/

Superintendent: Col. L. Aaron Chaffinch
   (302) 739-5901
Fee for obtaining accident report: $25.00 for regular
accident report; $60.00 for fatal accident

Probate, Recording and Notary Certificate Offices

Estate & Wills: County Registers of Wills
Deeds and Mortgages: County Recorders of Deeds Offices
Notary Certificates: Office of the S.O.S., Div. of Corporations, 401 Federal St., Suite 4, Dover, DE 19901
(302) 739-3073
($20.00; $30.00 total for 2 or more documents)

Senators, U.S.

Joseph R. Biden, Jr. (Democrat)
201 Russell Senate Office Bldg., Washington, DC 20510
(202) 224-5042; Fax: (202) 224-0139
E-mail: senator@biden.senate.gov
Internet: http://biden.senate.gov
Thomas R. Carper (Democrat)
513 Hart Senate Office Bldg., Washington, DC 20501
(202) 224-2441
Internet: http://carper.senate.gov

Secretary of State

Office of the Secretary of State
Townsend Bldg., Suite 3, 401 Federal St., Dover, DE 19901
(302) 739-4111; Fax: (302) 739-3811
Internet: www.state.de.us/sos/sos.shtml

Carvel State Office Bldg., 4th Floor, 820 N. French St., Wilmington, DE 19801
(302) 577-8767; Fax: (302) 577-2694
Internet: www.state.de.us/sos/sos.shtml
Secretary of State: Dr. Harriet Smith Windsor
Appointed

Tax Department

Division of Revenue
Carvel State Office Bldg., 8th Floor, 820 N. French St., Wilmington, DE 19801
Public Service: (302) 577-8200;
Billing/Collections: (302) 577-8208;
Public Relations: (302) 577-8667;
Legal Matters: (302) 577-8643; Fax: (302) 577-8656
Internet: www.state.de.us/revenue

Thomas Collins Bldg., Suite 2, 540 S. Dupont Hwy., Dover, DE 19901
(302) 744-1085; Fax: (302) 744-1095

422 N. Dupont Hwy., Suite 2, Georgetown, DE 19947
(302) 856-5358; Fax: (302) 856-5697
Director: Patrick T. Carter

Victim Compensation Program

Violent Crimes Compensation Board
240 N. James St., Suite 203, Newport, DE 19804
(302) 995-8383; Fax: (302) 995-8387
Internet: http://Courts.state.de.us/vccb/
Exec. Dir.: Gertrude Burke
    E-mail: gburke@state.de.us
Del. Code Ann. tit. 11 §§9001 to 9020 (amended July 2000)

Vital Statistics

Office of Vital Statistics
Division of Public Health,
Jesse S. Cooper Bldg., Room 144, 417 Federal St., Dover, DE 19901
Mailing Address: P.O. Box 637, Dover, DE 19903
(302) 744-4549; Fax: (302) 736-1862
Internet: www.vitalchek.com,
www.state.de.us/dhss/dph/vs.htm
Births-from 1933; Deaths, Marriages-from 1965.
Certified copy—Search fee (includes certified copy if record found)—$10.00

Delaware Public Archives
121 Duke of York St., Dover, DE 19901
(302) 744-5000; Fax: (302) 739-6710
Birth records older than 72 years; Death and Marriage records older than 40 years.
$5.00 for up to four copies.

DISTRICT OF COLUMBIA

572,059 (2000 Census)
State Information: (202) 727-1000
State Web Site: www.dc.gov

Administrative Office of the Courts

Executive Office of the D.C. Courts
500 Indiana Ave. N.W., Room 1500, Washington, DC 20001
(202) 879-1700; Fax: (202) 879-4829
Internet: www.dccourts.gov
Executive Officer of the District of Columbia Courts:
   Anne B. Wicks

Attorney Discipline

District of Columbia Office of Bar Counsel
515 5th St. N.W., Bldg. A, Room 127,
Washington, DC 20001-2797
(202) 638-1501; Fax: (202) 638-0862
Bar Counsel: Joyce E. Peters

Banking Department

Department of Banking and Financial Institutions
1400 L St. N.W., Suite 400, Washington, DC 20005
(202) 727-1563; Fax: (202) 727-1290
E-mail: dbfi@dc.gov
Internet: www.dbfi.dc.gov
Commissioner: Albert L. Elder III (Acting)

Bar Admissions

Committee on Admissions
District of Columbia Court of Appeals
500 Indiana Ave. N.W., Room 4200, Washington, DC 20001
(202) 879-2710
E-mail: coa@dcca.state.dc.us
Internet: www.dccourts.gov
No CLE required; one day Professional Conduct and D.C. Practice course
required of new admittees.
Admission on motion with five years bar membership in good standing or passing bar exam of another Jurisdiction with MBE scaled score of 133, MPRE scaled score of 75, JD from ABA-approved law school, and admission in other jurisdiction.

Bar Association

Bar Assn. of the District of Columbia
1225 19th St. N.W., Suite 800, Washington, DC 20036
(202) 223-6600; Fax: (202) 293-3388
Internet: www.badc.org
Exec. Dir./Exec. V.P.: Mary Eva Candon
President: Nicholas S. McConnell
Annual Meeting—June, 2005
The District of Columbia Bar
1250 H St. N.W., Sixth Floor, Washington, DC 20005-5937
(202) 737-4700; Fax: (202) 626-3471
Internet: www.dcbar.org
Exec. Dir.: Katherine A. Mazzaferri
   Ext. 221
President: John C. Keeney, Jr.
Integrated Bar
Annual Meeting—June, 2005

Chief Medical Examiner

Office of Chief Medical Examiner
1910 Massachusetts Ave. S.E., Bldg. 27,
Washington, DC 20003
(202) 698-9000; Fax: (202) 698-9100
Chief Medical Examiner: Marie Pierre-Louis, M.D.

Client Protection Fund

Clients' Security Fund of the District of Columbia Bar
1250 H St. N.W., 6th Floor, Washington, DC 20005-5937
(202) 737-4700, Ext. 237; Fax: (202) 626-3471
Internet: www.dcbar.org
Programs Coordinator: Suhana A. Rai
Director: Carla J. Freudenberg

National Directory of States

Corporations Officers

Department of Consumer & Regulatory Affairs
941 N. Capitol St. N.E., 9th Floor, Washington, DC 20002
(202) 442-4432; Fax: (202) 442-4523

Director: David Clark
   (202) 442-8947

Superintendent of Corporations: Patricia Grays
   (202) 442-4312; E-mail: patricia.grays@dc.gov

Recorder of Deeds
515 D St. N.W., Washington, DC 20001
(202) 727-0419

Director: Larry J. Todd; E-mail: larry.todd@dc.gov

Deputy Recorder of Deeds: John Mowery
   (202) 727-0420; E-mail: john.mowery@dc.gov

Criminal History Board

Metropolitan Police Department
Criminal History
300 Indiana Ave. N.W., Washington, DC 20001
(202) 727-4245; Fax: (202) 727-4889

Governor's Office

Office of the Mayor
John A. Wilson Bldg., Suite 600,
1350 Pennsylvania Ave. N.W., Washington, DC 20004
(202) 727-6263; Fax: (202) 727-0505

Mayor: Anthony A. Williams; E-mail: mayor@dc.gov
   Internet: www.dc.gov
Next election Nov. 2006

Highest State Court

District of Columbia Court of Appeals
500 Indiana Ave. N.W., Room 6000,
Washington, DC 20001-2131
(202) 879-2700; Fax: (202) 626-8840
Internet: www.dccourts.gov

Chief Judge: Annice M. Wagner

Clerk of the Court of Appeals: Garland Pinkston, Jr.

Insurance Department

Dept. of Insurance, Securities & Banking
810 First St., N.E., Suite 701, Washington, DC 20002
(202) 727-8000; Fax: (202) 535-1196
E-mail: disb@dc.gov
Internet: www.disb.dc.gov

Commissioner: Lawrence H. Mirel

Asst. Dir. of Financial Examination Div.:
   Phillip Barlow

Motor Vehicle Office

District of Columbia, Dept. of Motor Vehicles
Municipal Bldg., 301 C Street N.W.,
Washington, DC 20001
(202) 727-5000; Fax: (202) 727-0463;
Director's Office: (202) 724-2034;
Director's Fax: (202) 727-5017
E-mail: dmv@dc.gov
Internet: www.dmv.washingtondc.gov

For Abstracts write: Attn.: Driver's Records, 65 K St. N.E.,
Washington, DC 20001
Fee for obtaining abstract: Three and five-year history,
$7.00; ten-year history, $13.00

Police

Metropolitan Police Department
300 Indiana Ave. N.W., Room 3061, Washington, DC 20001
(202) 727-4218; Fax: (202) 727-9524;
Accident Report: (202) 727-4357
Internet: http://mpdc.dc.gov/main.shtm

Chief: Charles H. Ramsey, Room 5080
Fee for obtaining accident report: $3.00; money orders
preferred

Probate, Recording and Notary Certificate Offices

Estate & Wills: Superior Court, Register of Wills
Deeds and Mortgages: Recorder of Deeds Office
Notary Certificates: Office of the Secretary of the District
of Columbia, Notary Public Section ($10.00)

Tax Department

Office of Tax and Revenue
941 N. Capitol St., N.E., 1st Floor, Washington, DC 20002
Customer Service Help Line (202) 727-4Tax:
(202) 442-6200; Forms Center: (202) 442-6546;
Compliance Administration: (202) 442-6852;
Chief Counsel: (202) 442-6500;
Office of Tax Appeals: (202) 442-6945
E-mail: otr@dc.gov; Internet: www.cfo.washingtondc.gov

Chief Financial Officer: Natwar M. Gandhi
   1350 Pennsylvania Ave. S.W., Suite 203,
   Washington, DC 20004
   (202) 727-2476; Fax: (202) 727-1643; E-mail: ocfo@dc.gov

Deputy Chief Finance Officer: Herbert J. Huff

Victim Compensation Program

Crime Victims Compensation Program
District of Columbia Superior Court, Bldg. A,
515 5th St. N.W., Rm. 104, Washington, DC 20001
(202) 879-4216; Fax: (202) 879-4230
D.C. Official Code §§4-501 to 4-518 (2001 Edition)

Vital Statistics

Marriage Bureau
500 Indiana Ave. N.W., Room 4485, Washington, DC 20001
(202) 879-4840; Fax: (202) 879-1280;
Marriage Bureau Info. Line: (202) 879-4840
Marriages, 1811 to present.
Fee varies

Vital Records Division
825 N. Capitol St. N.E., 1st Floor, Washington, DC 20002
Information: (202) 442-9009;
Vital Chek Network, Inc.: (800) 255-2414; Fax: (800) 843-0485
Internet: www.dchealth.dc.gov
*Births, Deaths, from 1874 to present; Record available only
to immediate nuclear family.*
Computer copy (short form)—$18.00; Archival copy (long
form)—$23.00. Death copy—$18.00; Searches—$18.00 (3
consecutive years). Make checks payable to D.C. Treasurer.

FLORIDA   *Capital: Tallahassee*

15,982,378 (2000 Census)
State Information: (850) 488-1234
State Web Site: www.myflorida.com

Administrative Office of the Courts

Office of the State Courts Administrator
Supreme Court Bldg., 500 S. Duval St.,
Tallahassee, FL 32399-1900
(850) 922-5081; Fax: (850) 488-0156
E-mail: osca@flcourts.org; Internet: www.flcourts.org

Court Administrator: Elisabeth Goodner

Attorney Discipline

Department of Lawyer Regulation
The Florida Bar
651 E. Jefferson St., Tallahassee, FL 32399-2300
(850) 561-5839; Fax: (850) 561-5665;
(800) 342-8060, Ext. 5839
Internet: www.flabar.org

Cypress Financial Center, Suite 900,
5900 N. Andrews Ave., Fort Lauderdale, FL 33309
(954) 772-2245; Fax: (954) 772-0660

444 Brickell Ave., Suite M100, Miami, FL 33131
(305) 377-4445; Fax: (305) 377-4519

1200 Edgewater Dr., Orlando, FL 32804-6314
(407) 425-5424; Fax: (407) 841-5403

Dir. of Lawyer Regulation: Kenneth Marvin

Attorney General

Office of the Attorney General
The Capitol, PL-01, Tallahassee, FL 32399-1050
Switchboard: (850) 414-3300;
Citizen Services: (850) 414-3990;
Fraud Hotline (toll free within FL): (866) 966-7226
Internet: www.myfloridalegal.com

Atty. General: Charles J. Crist, Jr. (Republican)
Elected; next election Nov. 2006

Banking Department

Department of Financial Services
200 E. Gaines St., Tallahassee, FL 32399-0300
(850) 413-3100; Internet: www.fldfs.com
C.F.O.: Tom Gallagher; E-mail: cfo@dfs.state.fl.us

Bar Admissions

Florida Board of Bar Examiners
Tippin-Moore Bldg., 1891 Eider Ct., Tallahassee, FL 32399-1750
(850) 487-1292; Fax: (850) 414-6822
Internet: www.floridabarexam.org
30 hours CLE required per three years.
No admission without exam. Legal Ethics and
Professionalism course required for admittance.

Bar Association

The Florida Bar
651 E. Jefferson St., Tallahassee, FL 32399-2300
(850) 561-5600; Fax: (850) 561-5826
Internet: www.flabar.org
Exec. Dir.: John F. Harkness, Jr.
President: Alan B. Bookman
Integrated Bar
Annual Meeting—June, 2005

Client Protection Fund

Clients' Security Fund, The Florida Bar
651 E. Jefferson St., Tallahassee, FL 32399-2300
(850) 561-5812; Fax: (850) 561-5818
Internet: www.flabar.org
Coordinator: Suzanne Dunn; E-mail: sdunn@flabar.org

Commerce Department

Enterprise Florida, Inc.
390 N. Orange Ave., Suite 1300, Orlando, FL 32801
(407) 316-4600; Fax: (407) 316-4599
E-mail: information@enterprise.state.fl.us
Internet: http://www.eflorida.com

Tallahassee Regional Office, 325 John Knox Rd., Suite 201, Tallahassee, FL 32303
(850) 488-6300; Fax: (850) 922-9595

Miami Regional Office, 2801 Ponce de Leon Blvd., Suite 700, Coral Gables, FL 33134
(305) 569-2650; Fax: (305) 569-2686

Corporations Officers

Bureau of Commercial Applications
409 E. Gaines St., Tallahassee, FL 32399
Mailing Address: P.O. Box 6327, Tallahassee, FL 32314
(850) 245-6812
Chief: Don Roberts; E-mail: droberts@mail.dos.state.fl.us
Bureau of Commercial Information Services
409 E. Gaines St., Tallahassee, FL 32399
Mailing Address: P.O. Box 6327, Tallahassee, FL 32314
(850) 245-6862
Chief: Joan Jones; E-mail: jjones@mail.dos.state.fl.us
Bureau of Commercial Recordings
409 E. Gaines St., Tallahassee, FL 32399
Mailing Address: P.O. Box 6327, Tallahassee, FL 32314
(850) 245-6900; Fax: (850) 245-6013
Chief: Karon Beyer; E-mail: kbeyer@mail.dos.state.fl.us
Division of Corporations
Department of State
409 E. Gaines St., Tallahassee, FL 32399
Mailing Address: P.O. Box 6327, Tallahassee, FL 32314
(850) 245-6000; Fictitious Names: (850) 245-6058;
General Corporate Information: (850) 488-9000;
Domestic, Non-Profit & Profit: (850) 245-6052;
Trademarks, LLC's, Limited Partnerships: (850) 245-6051;
Amendments, Dissolutions, Mergers: (850) 245-6050;
Foreign Qualifications: (850) 245-6051;
Certification: (850) 245-6053;
Reinstatements: (850) 245-6059;
Annual Reports: (850) 245-6056;
Bureau of Commercial Recordings' Fax: (850) 245-6013
Director: Jay Kassees
　(850) 245-6000; Fax: (850) 245-6014
　E-mail: jkassees@mail.dos.state.fl.us

Judgment Liens
P.O. Box 6250, Tallahassee, FL 32314
(850) 656-7463; Internet: www.sunbiz.org
Florida UCC, Inc.
P.O. Box 5588, Tallahassee, FL 32314
(850) 222-8526; Internet: www.floridaucc.com

Criminal History Board

Department of Law Enforcement
CJIS User Services
Public Records, 2331 Phillips Rd., Tallahassee, FL 32308
Mailing Address: P.O. Box 1489, Tallahassee, FL 32302
(850) 410-8109; Internet: www.fdle.state.fl.us

Economic Development Administration

See Commerce Department

Governor's Office

Office of the Governor
PL-05 The Capitol, 400 S. Monroe St., Tallahassee, FL 32399
(850) 488-7146; Fax: (850) 487-0801
Internet: www.myflorida.com

444 N. Capitol St. N.W., Suite 349, Washington, DC 20001
(202) 624-5885; Fax: (202) 624-5886
Governor: John Ellis (Jeb) Bush (Republican)
Next election Nov. 2006

Highest State Court

Supreme Court
Supreme Court Bldg., 500 S. Duval St.,
Tallahassee, FL 32399-1927 (850) 488-0125
Internet: www.floridasupremecourt.org
Chief Justice: Barbara J. Pariente
Clerk of the Supreme Court: Thomas D. Hall

Insurance Department

Department of Financial Services
200 E. Gaines St., Tallahassee, FL 32399-0300
C.F.O.'s: (850) 413-2850; Fax: (850) 488-6581
Chief Financial Officer: Tom Gallagher
Deputy: Karen Chandler

Motor Vehicle Office

Florida Division of Driver Licenses
Neil Kirkman Bldg., 2900 Apalachee Pkwy.,
Tallahassee, FL 32399-0500
(850) 922-9000; TTY: (850) 488-4461; Fax: (850) 922-5015
Internet: www.hsmv.state.fl.us

For Abstracts write: Bureau of Records,
2900 Apalachee Pkwy., MS 90, Tallahassee, FL 32399-0575
Driver's Licenses
Fee for obtaining abstract: $2.10 for 3 years; $3.10 for 3-year certified or 7-year certified or complete certified abstract
Florida Dept. of Highway Safety and Motor Vehicles
Neil Kirkman Bldg., 2900 Apalachee Pkwy.,
Tallahassee, FL 32399-0600
(850) 922-9000; TTY: (850) 488-4461; Fax: (850) 922-4456;
Registration Renewal: (866) 467-3639
E-mail: hsmv-info@hsmv.state.fl.us
Internet: http://express.hsmv.state.fl.us, Internet
(Registration Renewal): www.hsmv.state.fl.us
Vehicle Registrations & Titles; Also contact local county tax collector's office for expedited service—$7.00 plus standard title fees
Fee for obtaining abstract: 3 years, $2.10; 7 years, $3.10 (complete history)

Police

Florida Highway Patrol
Neil Kirkman Bldg., 2900 Apalachee Pkwy.,
Tallahassee, FL 32399-0500
(850) 488-4885; Fax: (850) 922-0148
Internet: www.fhp.state.fl.us

Accident Reports: Crash Records Dept.,
Neil Kirkman Bldg., Room A325, 2900 Apalachee Pkwy.,
Tallahassee, FL 32399-5017
(850) 488-5017; Fax: (850) 922-0488
Director: Christopher A. Knight
Fee for obtaining accident report: $2.00

National Directory of States

Probate, Recording and Notary Certificate Offices

Estate & Wills: Clerk of Court's Offices, each county
Deeds and Mortgages: Clerk of Court's Offices, each county
Notary Certificates: Certification Section (850) 245-6975 ($10.00)

Senators, U.S.

Mel Martinez Senator: (Republican)
C-2 Russell Senate Office Bldg., Washington, DC 20510
(202) 224-3041; Fax: (202) 228-5171
Internet: http://martinez.senate.gov
Bill Nelson (Democrat)
716 Hart Senate Office Bldg., Washington, DC 20510
(202) 224-5274
Internet: http://billnelson.senate.gov

Secretary of State

Office of the Secretary of State
R.A. Gray Bldg., 500 S. Bronough St., Tallahassee, FL 32399
(850) 245-6500
Internet: www.dos.state.fl.us
Secretary of State: Glenda E. Hood (Republican)
Appointed

Tax Department

Department of Revenue
5050 W. Tennessee St., Tallahassee, FL 32399-0100
Mailing Address: Tax Information Svces.,
1379 Blountstown Hwy., Tallahassee, FL 32304-2716
(850) 488-6800, (800) 352-3671;
TDD: (800) 367-8331, (850) 922-1115;
Forms Fax: (850) 922-3676
Internet: http://sun6.dms.state.fl.us/dor/
Exec. Dir.: Jim Zingale
   (850) 488-5050; Fax: (850) 488-0024
General Counsel: Bruce Hoffman
   Mailing Address: P.O. Box 6668, Tallahassee, FL 32399-6668
   (850) 488-0712; Fax: (850) 488-7112

Victim Compensation Program

Bureau of Victim's Compensation
Office of the Attorney General
The Capitol, PL-01, Tallahassee, FL 32399-1050
(800) 226-6667, (850) 414-3300; Fax: (850) 487-1595
Internet: http://myfloridalegal.com
Fla. Stat. Ann. §§960.01 to 960.297 (1996 Supp.)

Vital Statistics

Office of Vital Statistics
Department of Health, 1217 Pearl St.,
Jacksonville, FL 32202
Mailing Address: P.O. Box 210,
Jacksonville, FL 32231-0042
(904) 359-6900, Ext. 9000; Fax: (904) 359-6633
Internet & E-mail: www.doh.state.fl.us
Internet & E-mail: www.doh.state.fl.us
Limited Births from 1865, Deaths from 1877, Birth & Death, Marriages and Divorces from 1927.
Non-refundable fee for search—births: $9.00 for first year searched; deaths, marriages and divorces: $5.00 for first year searched; $2.00 for each additional year up to $55.00 maximum. Fee includes one certification of record (if not found-certified statement to that effect). Additional copies—$4.00 each. Rush orders by credit card—VISA, MasterCard, Discover or American Express $15.00 processing charge, in addition to search fee stated above.

GEORGIA   *Capital: Atlanta*

8,186,453 (2000 Census)
State Information: (404) 656-2000
State Web Site: www.state.ga.us

Administrative Office of the Courts

Administrative Office of the Courts
244 Washington Street S.W., Suite 300,
Atlanta, GA 30334-5900
(404) 656-5171; Fax: (404) 651-6449
Internet: www.georgiacourts.org
Administrative Dir. of the Courts: David L. Ratley

Attorney Discipline

Office of General Counsel
State Bar of Georgia
104 Marietta St. N.W., Suite 100, Atlanta, GA 30303
(404) 527-8720; Fax: (404) 527-8744
Internet: www.gabar.org
General Counsel: William P. Smith III

Attorney General

Office of the Attorney General
40 Capitol Sq. S.W., Atlanta, GA 30334-1300
(404) 656-3300; Fax: (404) 657-8733
Internet: www.ganet.org/ago
Atty. General: Thurbert E. Baker (Democrat)
Elected; next election Nov. 2006

Banking Department

Department of Banking and Finance
2990 Brandywine Rd., Suite 200, Atlanta, GA 30341-5565
(770) 986-1633; Fax: (770) 986-1654, 55
Internet: http://www.state.ga.us/dbf/
Commissioner: David G. Sorrell

Bar Admissions

Office of Bar Admissions
Supreme Court of Georgia, 244 Washington St., Suite 440, Atlanta, GA 30334
Mailing Address: P.O. Box 38466, Atlanta, GA 30334-0466
(404) 656-3490; Fax: (404) 657-9108
Internet: http://www.gabaradmissions.org
12 hours CLE (including one hour of professionalism) required per year.
Admission on motion for attorneys in Reciprocal Jurisdiction.

Bar Association

State Bar of Georgia
104 Marietta St. N.W., Suite 100, Atlanta, GA 30303
(404) 527-8700; Fax: (404) 527-8717
Internet: www.gabar.org
Exec. Dir.: Cliff Brashier (404) 527-8755
   E-mail: cliff@gabar.org
President: George R. Reinhardt, Jr.
Integrated Bar
Annual Meeting—June, 2005

Client Protection Fund

Clients' Security Fund of the State Bar of Georgia
104 Marietta St. N.E., Suite 100, Atlanta, GA 30303
(404) 527-8720; Fax: (404) 527-8744
Internet: www.gabar.org
Deputy General Counsel: Robert E. McCormack

Commerce Department

See Economic Development Administration

Corporations Officers

Corporations Division
West Tower, Suite 315, 2 Martin Luther King, Jr. Dr., Atlanta, GA 30334-1530
(404) 656-2817
Internet: www.georgiacorporations.org
Director: Warren Rary
   (404) 657-8371
   E-mail: wrary@sos.state.ga.us
Asst. Dir.: Enrico M. Robinson
   (404) 657-4988
   E-mail: erobinson@sos.state.ga.us
Corp. Services Mgr.: Susan Golden
   (404) 657-1374
   E-mail: sgolden@sos.state.ga.us
Georgia Superior Court Clerks' Cooperative Authority (UCC Filing)
1875 Century Blvd., Suite 100, Atlanta, GA 30345
(404) 327-9058; Fax: (404) 327-7877
Internet: www.gsccca.org
Communications Dir.: Mike Smith
   E-mail: mike.smith@gsccca.org

Criminal History Board

Bureau of Investigation
Crime Information Center
3121 Panthersville Rd., Decatur, GA 30034
(404) 244-2601; Fax: (404) 270-8637
Internet: www.state.ga.us/gbi/

Economic Development Administration

Georgia Dept. of Industry, Trade & Tourism
Marquis II Tower, Suite 1100, 285 Peachtree Center Ave.,
Atlanta, GA 30303
(404) 656-3545; Fax: (404) 651-6505
Internet: www.georgia.org
Deputy Commissioner: Charlie Gatlin
  (404) 656-3573
    E-mail: cgatlin@georgia.org

Governor's Office

Office of the Governor
203 State Capitol, Atlanta, GA 30334
(404) 656-1776; Fax: (404) 657-7332
Internet: www.gov.state.ga.us
Governor: Sonny Perdue (Republican)
Next election Nov. 2006

Highest State Court

Supreme Court of Georgia
244 Washington St. S.W., Room 572, Atlanta, GA 30334
(404) 656-3470; Fax: (404) 656-2253
E-mail: scinfo@gasupreme.us
Internet: www.gasupreme.us
Chief Justice: Norman S. Fletcher
Clerk of the Supreme Court: Sherie M. Welch

Insurance Department

Office of the Commissioner of Insurance and Fire Safety
2 Martin L. King, Jr. Dr., West Tower, Suite 704,
Atlanta, GA 30334
(404) 656-2070, (800) 656-2298; Fax: (404) 656-8532
Internet: www.gainsurance.org
Commissioner: John W. Oxendine

Motor Vehicle Office

Georgia Department of Motor Vehicle Safety
Driver Services Division
2206 E. View Pkwy., Conyers, GA 30013
Mailing Address:
For Driver's Abstracts write: GA Dept. of Motor Vehicle So
ciety, Unit MVR, P.O. Box 80447, Conyers, GA 30013
(678) 413-8650; Driver Licensing: (678) 413-8400;
Commissioner Office: (678) 413-8660;
Commissioner Fax: (678) 413-8661;
Motor Vehicle Records: (678) 413-8441;
Motor Vehicle Records Fax: (678) 413-8460;
Fax: (678) 418-8489
Internet: www.dmvs.ga.gov
Fee for Obtaining Abstract: M.V.R. Abstract: $5.00 for 3
year record; $7.00 for 7 year record (no personal checks).
Fee for Obtaining Accident Report: $5.00

Police

Georgia State Patrol
959 E. Confederate Ave., Atlanta, GA 30316
Mailing Address: P.O. Box 1456, Atlanta, GA 30371-1456
(404) 624-7710; Fax: (404) 624-6706
Internet: http://www.ganet.org
Commissioner: Col. George Ellis
Fee for obtaining accident report: $5.00

Probate, Recording and Notary Certificate Offices

Estate & Wills: Judge of Probate Court, each county
Deeds and Mortgages: Clerk of Superior Court, each
county
Notary Certificates: Superior Court Clerk's Cooperative
Authority
1875 Century Blvd., Atlanta, GA 30345
Internet: www.gsccca.org; (404) 327-6023
(Apostille Certification, $3.00)

Senators, U.S.

Saxby Chambliss (Republican)
416 Russell Senate Office Bldg., Washington, DC 20510
(202) 224-3521
Internet: http://chambliss.senate.gov
Johnny Isakson (Republican)
Washington, DC 20510
(202) 224-3643; Fax: (202) 228-0724

Secretary of State

Office of the Secretary of State
214 State Capitol, Atlanta, GA 30334
(404) 656-2881; Fax: (404) 656-0513
E-mail: sosweb@sos.state.ga.us
Internet: www.sos.state.ga.us
Secretary of State: Cathy Cox (Democrat)
Elected; next election Nov. 2006

Tax Department

Department of Revenue
1800 Century Center Blvd., Suite 2225,
Atlanta, GA 30345-3205
(404) 417-2111; Sales & Use Tax Div.: (404) 417-6601;
Fax: (404) 417-6650;
Compliance Dir.'s Office: (404) 417-6458;
Local Government Services Dir.'s Office: (404) 968-0707;
Taxpayer Services Dir.'s Office: (404) 417-2309;
Taxpayer Acctg. Dir.'s Office: (404) 417-4201;
Alcohol & Tobacco Dir.'s Office: (404) 417-4902
Internet: www.gatax.org

4245 International Pkwy., Hapeville, GA 30354-3904
(404) 968-0707
Commissioner: Bart L. Graham (404) 417-2100

Victim Compensation Program

Georgia Crime Victims Compensation Board
Office of Criminal Justice Coordinating Council
503 Oak Pl., Suite 540, Atlanta, GA 30349
(404) 559-4949; Fax: (404) 559-4960
Internet: www.ganet.org/cjcc/victimscomp.html
Ga. Code Ann. §§17-15-1 to 17-15-13 (amended 1994; 2002)

Vital Statistics

Department of Human Resources
Vital Records Service, 2600 Skyland Dr. N.E.,
Atlanta, GA 30319-3640
General Info.: (404) 679-4701; Fax: (404) 679-4730
Internet: www.ph.dhr.state.ga.us/programs/vitalrecords/
Births and Deaths from 1919. Marriages from June, 1952.
However, Vital Records Service can only issue copies of
marriage records June 1952-December 1996. Other
marriage records must be obtained from Probate Court in
county where the marriage occurred. Central registration of
Divorces from June 1952. Divorce records on file with the
Clerk of the Superior Court in the county in which the
divorce was obtained.
Non-refundable search fee—$10.00 includes copy if found.
Additional copies paid for at same time—$5.00 each.
Copies of marriage certificates—$10.00. For charge card
service, contact VitalChek at (877) 572-6343

HAWAII   *Capital: Honolulu*

1,211,537 (2000 Census)
State Information: (808) 586-2211
State Web Site: www.hawaii.gov

Administrative Office of the Courts

Administrative Director of the Courts
Aliiolani Hale, Room 206A, 417 S. King St.,
Honolulu, HI 96813
(808) 539-4900; Fax: (808) 539-4855
E-mail: admindir@courts.state.hi.us
Internet: www.courts.state.hi.us
Administrative Dir. of the Courts: Thomas R. Keller

Attorney Discipline

Disciplinary Board of the Hawaii Supreme Court
1132 Bishop St., Suite 300, Honolulu, HI 96813
(808) 521-4591
Chief Disciplinary Counsel: Carole R. Richelieu

Attorney General

Department of the Attorney General
425 Queen St., Honolulu, HI 96813
(808) 586-1500; Fax: (808) 586-1239
E-mail: hawaiiag@hawaii.gov
Internet: www.state.hi.us/ag/index.html

Atty. General: Mark J. Bennett
Appointed

Banking Department

Division of Financial Institutions
335 Merchant St., Room 221, Honolulu, HI 96813
Mailing Address: P.O. Box 2054, Honolulu, HI 96805
(808) 586-2820; Fax: (808) 586-2818
E-mail: dfi@lscca.hawaii.gov
Internet: www.hawaii.gov/dcca/dfi

Commissioner: D. B. Griffin III

Bar Admissions

Board of Examiners
Supreme Court of Hawaii
417 S. King St., Honolulu, HI 96813-2911
(808) 539-4977; Fax: (808) 539-4978
Internet: www.state.hi.us/jud
No CLE required.
No admission without exam. Legal Professionalism course
required for admittance.

Bar Association

Hawaii State Bar Assn.
1132 Bishop St., Suite 906, Honolulu, HI 96813
(808) 537-1868; Fax: (808) 521-7936
Internet: www.hsba.org

Exec. Dir.: Lyn Flanigan Anzai

President: Wayne D. Parsons
Integrated Bar
Annual Meeting: October, 2005

Chief Medical Examiner

Office of Chief Medical Examiner
835 Iwilei Rd., Honolulu, HI 96817
(808) 527-6777; Fax: (808) 524-8797

Chief Medical Examiner: Dr. Kanthi Von Guenthner

Client Protection Fund

Lawyers' Fund for Client Protection
1132 Bishop St., Suite 300, Honolulu, HI 96813
(808) 599-2483

Fund Administrator: Carole R. Richelieu

Commerce Department

Department of Commerce and Consumer Affairs
335 Merchant St., Honolulu, HI 96813
Mailing Address: P.O. Box 541, Honolulu, HI 96809
Director's Office: (808) 586-2850; Fax: (808) 586-2856;
Consumer Dial: (808) 587-1234
Internet: www.state.hi.us/dcca

Corporations Officers

Bureau of Conveyances (UCC Filings)
Department of Land and Natural Resources
1151 Punchbowl St., Honolulu, HI 96813
Mailing Address: P.O. Box 2867, Honolulu, HI 96803
(808) 587-0120; UCC Information: (808) 587-0154;
Fax: (808) 587-0136

Registrar of Conveyances: Carl T. Watanabe
    E-mail: watact@pixi.com

Department of Commerce & Consumer Affairs
Business Registration Division
335 Marchant St., Room 204, Honolulu, HI 96813
Mailing Address: P.O. Box 40, Honolulu, HI 96810
General Information, Corporations Section, Name
Availabilities, Annual Reports & Limited Partnerships:
(808) 586-2727; Securities Salespersons: (808) 586-2730;
Broker/Dealers, Securities Offering, Franchise:
(808) 586-2722; Fax: (808) 586-2733

Commissioner of Securities: Ryan S. Ushijima
    (808) 586-2744; E-mail: ryan.s.ushijima@dcca.state.hi.us

Documents Registration Supervisor: Amy Iha
    E-mail: amy.iha@dcca.state.hi.us

Criminal History Board

Criminal Justice Data Center
465 S. King St., Room 101, Honolulu, HI 96813
(808) 587-3100
Internet: www.state.hi.us/hcjdc

Economic Development Administration

Dept. of Business, Economic Development & Tourism
No. 1 Capitol District Bldg., 250 S. Hotel St.,
Honolulu, HI 96813
Mailing Address: P.O. Box 2359, Honolulu, HI 96804
(808) 586-2423; Fax: (808) 587-2790
Internet: www.hawaii.gov/dbedt

Director: Theodore E. Liu

Governor's Office

Office of the Governor
State Capitol, 5th Floor, 415 S. Beretania St.,
Honolulu, HI 96813
(808) 586-0034; Fax: (808) 586-0006
E-mail: governor.lingle@hawaii.gov
Internet: www.hawaii.gov/gov

Governor: Linda Lingle (Republican)
Next election Nov. 2006

Highest State Court

Supreme Court
Office of the Chief Clerk, Room 103, 417 S. King St.,
Honolulu, HI 96813-2911
(808) 539-4919; Fax: (808) 539-4928
Internet: http://www.state.hi.us/jud/SC.HTM

Chief Justice: Ronald T.Y. Moon

Clerk of the Supreme Court: Darrell N. Phillips

Insurance Department

Insurance Division
Dept. of Commerce & Consumer Affairs
335 Merchant St., Room 213, Honolulu, HI 96813
Mailing Address: P.O. Box 3614, Honolulu, HI 96811-3614
(808) 586-2790; Fax: (808) 586-2806
Internet: www.hawaii.gov/dcca/ins

Commissioner: J.P. Schmidt

Chief Examiner: William Koppenheffer

Motor Vehicle Office

City and County of Honolulu
Drivers License Section,
1199 Dillingham Blvd., Room A101, Honolulu, HI 96817
Mailing Address: P.O. Box 30340,
Honolulu, HI 96820-0340
(808) 532-7730

For Abstracts write: Traffic Violations Bureau,
District Court of the 1st Circuit, 2nd Floor,
1111 Alakea St., Honolulu, HI 96813
(808) 538-5500
Fee for obtaining abstract: $7.00

County of Hawaii Police Department
Driver's License Section, 349 Kapiolani St., Hilo, HI 96720
(808) 961-2222; Fax: (808) 961-8861

For Abstracts write: Traffic Violations, District Court of th
e 3rd Circuit, Hilo State Office Bldg., Room 205,
75 Aupuni St., Hilo, HI 96720
Fee for obtaining abstract: $10.00

Department of Public Safety
Division of Motor Vehicles and Licensing
P.O. Box 30320, Honolulu, HI 96820-0320
Ewa/Pearl City Court: (808) 454-5488;
Honolulu: (808) 538-5500; Kaneohe: (808) 234-0800;
Wahiawa-Waialua: (808) 621-5097, 621-8045;
Waianae: (808) 668-1509
E-mail: info@dmv.express.com
Internet: www.dmv-department-of-motor-vehicles.com

For Abstracts write: District Court of the 2nd Circuit,
2145 Main St., Suite 137, Wailuku, HI 96793
(808) 244-2800
Fee for obtaining abstract: $21.00

Police

Department of Public Safety Sheriff Division
1111 Alakea St., Honolulu, HI 96813
(808) 538-5656; Fax: (808) 538-5684

Records and Identification Div., Honolulu Police Dept.,
801 S. Beritania St., Honolulu, HI 96813 (808) 529-3271
Internet: www.honolulupd.org

First Deputy Commissioner: F. Cappy Caminos
  (808) 538-5686
*Statewide law enforcement agency for judicial security;
Hawaii does not have a State Police or Highway Patrol*
Fee for obtaining accident report: From Dept. of Public
Safety: No fee; from Honolulu Police Dept.: $1.00 first
page, $.25 each additional page

Probate, Recording and Notary Certificate Offices

Estate & Wills: State Circuit Courts
Deeds and Mortgages: State Bureau of Conveyances
Notary Certificates: Department of the Attorney General
(Chapter 456, Hawaii Revised Statutes)

Senators, U.S.

Daniel K. Akaka (Democrat)
141 Hart Senate Office Bldg., Washington, DC 20510
(202) 224-6361; Fax: (202) 224-2126
Internet: www.akaka.senate.gov

Daniel K. Inouye (Democrat)
722 Hart Senate Office Bldg., Washington, DC 20510
(202) 224-3934; Fax: (202) 224-6747
Internet: http://inouye.senate.gov

Secretary of State

Office of the Lieutenant Governor
P.O. Box 3226, Honolulu, HI 96801-3226
(808) 586-0255; Fax: (808) 586-0231
E-mail: ltgov@hawaii.gov
Internet: www.hawaii.gov/ltgov

Lieutenant Governor: James (Duke) R. Aiona, Jr.
  (Republican)
Elected; next election Nov. 2006

Tax Department

Department of Taxation
Oahu District Office, Princess Ruth Keelikolani Bldg.,
830 Punchbowl St., Honolulu, HI 96813-5094
Mailing Address: P.O. Box 259, Honolulu, HI 96809-0259
Taxpayer Services Branch: (808) 587-4242, (800) 222-3229;
Taxpayer Services Branch (Jan.-Apr. 20): (808) 587-6515;
Taxpayer Services Branch Fax: (808) 587-1488;
Office Audit Branch: (808) 587-1660;
Office Audit Fax: (808) 587-1633;
Collection Branch: (808) 587-1600;
Collection Branch Fax: (808) 587-1720;
Tax Services and Processing (Hearing Impaired):
(808) 587-1418;
Tax Services and Processing (Hearing Impaired Toll-Free):
(808) 887-8974;
Compliance Division (Hearing Impaired): (808) 587-1419;
Administrative Services Ofc. (Hearing Impaired):
(808) 587-1501
E-mail: director_office@tax.state.hi.us
Internet: www.state.hi.us/tax/tax.html

Hawaii District Office, State Office Bldg., Room 101,
75 Aupuni St., Hilo, HI 96720-4245
Mailing Address: P.O. Box 833, Hilo, HI 96721-0833
(808) 974-6321; Fax: (808) 974-6300
E-mail: hilo_office@tax.state.hi.us

Kauai District Office, State Office Bldg., Room 105,
3060 Eiwa St., Lihue, HI 96766-1889
(808) 274-3456; Fax: (808) 274-3461
E-mail: kauai_office@tax.state.hi.us

Maui District Office, State Office Bldg., Room 208,
54 S. High St., Wailuku, HI 96793-2198
Mailing Address: P.O. Box 1169, Wailuku, HI 96793-6169
(808) 984-8500; Fax: (808) 984-8522
E-mail: maui_office@tax.state.hi.us

Director: Kurt Kawafuchi

Victim Compensation Program

Criminal Victim Compensation Commission
1136 Union Mall, Suite 600, Honolulu, HI 96813
(808) 587-1143; Fax: (808) 587-1146
Internet: www.ehawaiigov.org/cvcc
*Haw. Rev. Stat. tit. 20 §§351-1 to 351-70 (1993 Supp.;
amended 1995, 1996, 1997, 1998, 1999, 2000, 2001, 2002)*

Vital Statistics

Office of Health Status Monitoring
1250 Punchbowl St., Room 103, Honolulu, HI 96801
Mailing Address: Issuance/Vital Statistics Section,
P.O. Box 3378, Honolulu, HI 96801-9984
(808) 586-4533; Fax: (808) 586-4606
Internet: http://www.hawaii.gov/doh
Births, Deaths, Marriages, Divorces.
Certified copy—$10.00. Search fee of $10.00 charged if no
record found. Person actually named in birth or marriage
record may order record via Internet for $1.50 surcharge.

IDAHO   *Capital: Boise*

1,293,953 (2000 Census)
State Information: (208) 334-2411
State Web Site: www.state.id.us

Administrative Office of the Courts

Administrative Office of the Courts
Idaho Supreme Court, 451 W. State St., Boise, ID 83702
Mailing Address: P.O. Box 83720, Boise, ID 83720-0101
(208) 334-2246; Fax: (208) 334-2146
Internet: www.isc.idaho.gov

Administrative Dir. of the Courts: Patti Tobias
Financial Officer of the Courts: Roland Gammill

Attorney Discipline

Office of Bar Counsel
525 W. Jefferson, Boise, ID 83702
Mailing Address: P.O. Box 895, Boise, ID 83701-0895
(208) 334-4500; Fax: (208) 334-2764
Internet: www.state.id.us/isb

Bar Counsel: Bradley G. Andrews

Attorney General

Office of the Attorney General
State House, Room 210, 700 W. Jefferson St.,
P.O. Box 83720, Boise, ID 83720-0010
(208) 334-2400; Fax: (208) 334-2530
Internet: www.state.id.us/ag

Atty. General: Lawrence G. Wasden (Republican)
Elected; next election Nov. 2006

Banking Department

Department of Finance
700 W. State St., 2nd Floor, Boise, ID 83702
Mailing Address: P.O. Box 83720, Boise, ID 83720-0031
(208) 332-8000; Director: (208) 332-8010;
Director's Fax: (208) 332-8097
E-mail: finance@fin.state.id.us; Internet: http://finance.idaho.gov

Director: Gavin M. Gee

Bar Admissions

Idaho State Bar
525 W. Jefferson St., Boise, ID 83702
Mailing Address: P.O. Box 895, Boise, ID 83701
(208) 334-4500; Fax: (208) 334-2764
Internet: www.idaho.gov/isb
30 hours CLE required per three years.
Reciprocity with Oregon and Washington, Utah &
Wyoming only. Required bar exam for all other states.

Bar Association

Idaho State Bar
525 W. Jefferson St., Boise, ID 83702
Mailing Address: P.O. Box 895, Boise, ID 83701
(208) 334-4500; Fax: (208) 334-4515
Internet: www.idaho.gov/isb

Exec. Dir.: Diane K. Minnich
President: Hon. Rice Carnaroli
Integrated Bar
Annual Meeting—July, 2006

National Directory
of States

Client Protection Fund

Idaho State Bar
525 W. Jefferson, Boise, ID 83702
Mailing Address: P.O. Box 895, Boise, ID 83701
(208) 334-4500; Fax: (208) 334-4515
Internet: www.idaho.gov/isb

Exec. Dir.: Diane K. Minnich

Contact for Client Assistance Fund: Robin Marker
    Fax: (208) 334-2764

Commerce Department

Department of Commerce
700 West State St., P.O. Box 83720, Boise, ID 83720-0093
(208) 334-2470; Fax: (208) 334-2631
Internet: www.cl.idaho.gov

Corporations Officers

Department of State, Commercial Division
State Capitol, 700 W. Jefferson, Boise, ID 83702
Mailing Address: P.O. Box 83720, Boise, ID 83720-0080
General Information: (208) 334-2300;
Corporations, LLC's, Limited Partnerships, Name
Availabilities & Annual Reports: (208) 334-2301;
UCC: (208) 334-3191;
Trademarks and Notaries: (208) 334-2300;
Information Services: (208) 334-5354; Fax: (208) 334-2847

Dep. Secy. of State, Commercial Div.:
    Chuck Goodenough (208) 332-2862

Dir., Information Technology Div.: Garry Snyder
    (208) 332-2824; E-mail: gsnyder@idsos.state.id.us

Criminal History Board

Bureau of Criminal Identification
700 S. Stratford Dr., Meridian, ID 83642
Mailing Address: P.O. Box 700, Meridian, ID 83680-0700
(208) 884-7130; Fax: (208) 884-7193
Internet: www.isp.state.id.us

Economic Development Administration

Economic Development Division
Idaho Department of Commerce and Labor
700 West State St., P.O. Box 83720, Boise, ID 83720-0093
(208) 334-2650; Fax: (208) 334-2631
Internet: www.idahoworks.com

Administrator: Jay Engstrom

Governor's Office

Office of the Governor
700 W. Jefferson, 2nd Floor, Boise, ID 83720
(208) 334-2100; Fax: (208) 334-2175
Internet: www.state.id.us/gov

Governor: Dirk Kempthorne (Republican)
Next election Nov. 2006

Highest State Court

Idaho Supreme Court
451 W. State St., Boise, ID 83702
Mailing Address: P.O. Box 83720, Boise, ID 83720-0101
(208) 334-2210; Fax: (208) 334-2616
Internet: www.isc.idaho.gov

Chief Justice: Gerald Schroeder

Clerk of the Supreme Court: Stephen W. Kenyon

Insurance Department

Office of the Insurance Director
700 W. State St., 3rd Floor, P.O. Box 83720, Boise, ID 83720-0043
(208) 334-4250; Fax: (208) 334-4398
Internet: www.doi.idaho.gov

Director: Gary L. Smith

Chief Examiner: Georgia Hill

Motor Vehicle Office

Idaho Transportation Department
Division of Motor Vehicles, 3311 W. State St.,
P.O. Box 7129, Boise, ID 83707-1129
Driver's Licenses: (208) 334-8736; Fax: (208) 334-8739;
Registration and Records: (208) 334-8649;
Fax: (208) 334-8542; Titles: (208) 334-8663;
Fax: (208) 334-8658
Internet: www.dmv.idaho.gov

For Driver's Records write: Driver's Services, P.O. Box 34,
Boise, ID 83731

For Motor Vehicle Records write:, P.O. Box 34,
Boise, ID 83707-1129
Fee for obtaining abstract: $4.00

Police

Idaho State Police
700 S. Stratford Dr., Meridian, ID 83642
Mailing Address: P.O. Box 700, Meridian, ID 83680-0700
(208) 884-7200; Fax: (208) 884-7290
Internet: http://www.isp.state.id.us

Region 1—Patrol, 602 W. Prairie Ave.,
Coeur d'Alene, ID 83815
(208) 772-6055; Fax: (208) 772-0924

Region 2—Patrol, 2700 North & South Hwy. N.,
Lewiston, ID 83501-1732
(208) 799-5151; Fax: (208) 799-5146

Region 3—Patrol, 3056 Elder St., Boise, ID 83705
(208) 334-3731; Fax: (208) 334-2691

Region 4—Patrol, 18 W. 200th S., Jerome, ID 83338-5904
(208) 324-6000; Fax: (208) 324-7897

Region 5—Patrol, 5205 S. 5th, Pocatello, ID 83204-2299
(208) 236-6466; Fax: (208) 236-6068

Region 6—Patrol, 1540 Foote Dr.,
Idaho Falls, ID 83402-1899
(208) 525-7377; Fax: (208) 525-7294

Director: Col. R. Dan Charboneau
    (208) 884-7000, 03; Fax: (208) 884-7090
For accident reports, contact Region Patrol office.
Fee for obtaining accident report: No fee; send SASE with
written request

Probate, Recording and Notary Certificate Offices

Estate & Wills: County District Courts
Deeds and Mortgages: County Clerks Offices
Notary Certificates: Secretary of State, Attn.: Notary Dept.
($10.00; use suite 203 for over-night delivery services)

Senators, U.S.

Larry E. Craig (Republican)
520 Hart Senate Office Bldg., Washington, DC 20510
(202) 224-2752; Fax: (202) 228-1067
Internet: http://craig.senate.gov

Mike Crapo (Republican)
239 Dirksen Senate Office Bldg., Washington, DC 20510
(202) 224-6142; Fax: (202) 224-5893
Internet: http://crapo.senate.gov

Secretary of State

Office of the Secretary of State
700 W. Jefferson St., P.O. Box 83720, Boise, ID 83720-0080
(208) 334-2300; Fax: (208) 334-2282
Internet: www.idsos.state.id.us

Secretary of State: Ben Ysursa
Elected; next election Nov. 2006

Tax Department

State Tax Commission
Plaza IV, 800 Park Blvd., P.O. Box 36, Boise, ID 83722
Comissioners: (208) 334-7500;
Taxpayer Services: (208) 334-7660; Fax: (208) 334-7844;
Audit & Collection Div.: (208) 334-7615;
Legal and Tax Policy: (208) 334-7530

Tax Commissioners:
    Coleen Grant   Sam Haws
    DuWayne D. Hammond, Jr.   Larry Watson

Counsel: Theodore V. Spangler, Jr.

Victim Compensation Program

Idaho Crime Victims Comp. Program
317 Main St., P.O. Box 83720, Boise, ID 83720-0041
(208) 334-6080; Fax: (208) 332-7559
Internet: www2.state.id.us/iic/crimevictims.htm
Idaho Code §72-1001, et seq.

Vital Statistics

Bureau of Health Policy and Vital Statistics
450 W. State St., 1st Floor, P.O. Box 83720,
Boise, ID 83720-0036
(208) 334-5980; Fax: (208) 334-0685;
Recording: (208) 334-5988; Order by Fax: (208) 389-9096
Internet: www.state.id.us/dhw/health/index.htm
Births and Deaths from 1911. Marriages and Divorces from 1947.
Certified copies of all certificates—$13.00; Faxed
orders—$10.50 surcharge.

ILLINOIS
Capital: Springfield

12,419,293 (2000 Census)
State Information: (217) 782-2000
State Web Site: www.state.il.us

Administrative Office of the Courts

Administrative Office of the Illinois Courts
222 N. LaSalle St., 13th Floor, Chicago, IL 60601
(312) 793-3250; Fax: (312) 793-1335
Internet: www.state.il.us/court

3101 Old Jacksonville Rd., Springfield, IL 62704-6488
(217) 558-4490; Fax: (217) 785-3905
Administrative Dir. of the Courts: Cynthia Y. Cobbs

Attorney Discipline

Illinois Attorney Registration and Disciplinary
Commission
One Prudential Plaza, Suite 1500, 130 E. Randolph Dr.,
Chicago, IL 60601
(312) 565-2600; Fax: (312) 565-1409

One Old Capitol Plaza N., Springfield, IL 62701
(217) 522-6838; Fax: (217) 522-2417
Administrator: Mary Robinson

Attorney General

Office of the Attorney General
100 W. Randolph St., 12th Floor, Chicago, IL 60601
(312) 814-3000; TTY: (312) 814-3374;
Fax: (312) 814-2549, 814-3806
Internet: www.ag.state.il.us

Springfield Office, 500 S. Second St., Springfield, IL 62706
(217) 782-1090; TTY: (217) 785-2771; Fax: (217) 785-2551

1001 E. Main St., Carbondale, IL 62901
(618) 529-6400; TTY: (618) 529-6403
Atty. General: Lisa Madigan (Democrat)
Elected; next election Nov. 2006

Banking Department

Illinois Department of Financial & Professional Regulation
500 E. Monroe St., Springfield, IL 62701-1509
(217) 782-3000; Fax: (217) 524-5941
Internet: www.idfpr.com

310 S. Michigan Ave., Suite 2130, Chicago, IL 60604-4278
(312) 793-3000; Fax: (312) 793-7097
Director: D. Lorenzo Padron

Department of Financial Institutions
James R. Thompson Center, Suite 15-700,
100 W. Randolph St., Chicago, IL 60601
(312) 814-2000; TDD: (312) 814-7138; Fax: (312) 814-5168
Internet: www.state.il.us/dfi/

500 Iles Park Pl., Suite 510, Springfield, IL 62718
(217) 782-2831, 32; TDD: (217) 785-3022;
Fax: (217) 785-6999
Director: Michele V. Latz

Bar Admissions

Illinois Board of Admissions to the Bar
625 S. College St., Springfield, IL 62704
(217) 522-5917; Fax: (217) 522-3728
Internet: www.ibaby.org
No CLE required.
Admission on motion with five of the last seven years
practice in a Reciprocal Jurisdiction.

Bar Association

Illinois State Bar Assn.
Illinois Bar Center, 424 S. Second St., Springfield, IL 62701-1779
(217) 525-1760; Fax: (217) 525-0712
E-mail: info@isba.org; Internet: www.isba.org

20 S. Clark St., 9th Floor, Chicago, IL 60603-1802
(312) 726-8775; Fax: (312) 726-9071
Exec. Dir.: Robert E. Craghead
President: Ole B. Pace III
Non-Integrated Bar
Annual Meeting—June, 2005

Chief Medical Examiner

Office of the Medical Examiner
2121 W. Harrison St., Chicago, IL 60612-3705
(312) 997-4500; Fax: (312) 997-4516
Chief Medical Examiner: Edmund R. Donoghue, M.D.
(Cook County)

Client Protection Fund

Client Protection Program
Attorney Registration & Disciplinary Commission of the
Illinois Supreme Court
One Prudential Plaza, Suite 1500, 130 E. Randolph Dr.,
Chicago, IL 60601-6219
(312) 565-2600; Fax: (312) 565-2320
Internet: www.iardc.org
Counsel: Eileen Donahue

Commerce Department

Department of Commerce and Economic Opportunity
620 E. Adams St., Springfield, IL 62701
(217) 782-7500; TDD: (800) 785-6055; Fax: (217) 785-6454
Internet: www.commerce.state.il.us

100 W. Randolph, Suite 3-400, Chicago, IL 60601
(312) 814-7179; TDD: (800) 419-0667; Fax: (312) 814-2370

Corporations Officers

Department of Business Services
Howlett Bldg., Springfield, IL 62756
General Information: (217) 782-7880;
Corporations Section: (217) 782-6961;
Name Availabilities: (217) 782-9521;
Annual Reports: (217) 782-7808;
Trademarks: (217) 524-0400; UCC: (217) 782-7518;
Limited Liability Companies: (217) 524-8008;
Limited Partnerships: (217) 785-8960; Fax: (217) 524-8281
Director: Kenneth V. Buzbee, Room 350 (217) 524-1159
Corporations Div. Administrator: Robert Durchholz
Room 330 (217) 782-4909
Liability Limitation Div. Administrator: Mike Vincent
Room 351 (217) 782-4875
Uniform Commercial Code Administrator:
Pete Campo, Room 350 (217) 785-3356
Limited Partnership Section Supervisor: Don White
Room 357 (214) 782-4868
Annual Report Section Supervisor: Wanda Corn
Room 330 (217) 782-9587

Criminal History Board

Bureau of Identification
260 N. Chicago St., Joliet, IL 60432-4075
(815) 740-5160; Fax: (815) 740-5174

Governor's Office

Office of the Governor
State Capitol, Room 207, Springfield, IL 62706
(217) 782-6830; Fax: (217) 782-3560
E-mail: governor@state.il.us
Internet: www.state.il.us/gov/

100 W. Randolph St., 16th Floor, Chicago, IL 60601
(312) 814-2121; Fax: (312) 814-5512

444 N. Capitol St. N.W., Suite 240, Washington, DC 20001
(202) 624-7760; Fax: (202) 724-0689
Governor: Rod Blagojevich (Democrat)
Next election Nov. 2006

Highest State Court

Supreme Court
Supreme Court Bldg., 200 E. Capitol Ave.,
Springfield, IL 62701-1721
(Clerk's Office): (217) 782-2035
Internet: www.state.il.us/court

160 N. LaSalle St., 20th Floor, Chicago, IL 60601
(312) 793-5490
Chief Justice: Mary Ann G. McMorrow
Clerk of the Supreme Court: Juleann Hornyak

Insurance Department

Department of Insurance
320 W. Washington St., 4th Floor,
Springfield, IL 62767-0001
(217) 782-4515; TDD: (217) 524-4872; Fax: (217) 782-5020
Internet: www.ins.state.il.us

100 W. Randolph St., Suite 15-100, Chicago, IL 60601
(312) 814-2427; TDD: (312) 814-2603; Fax: (312) 814-5435
Director: Deirdre K. Manna

Motor Vehicle Office

Drivers Services Department
Office of the Secretary of State, 2701 S. Dirksen Pkwy.,
Springfield, IL 62723
(217) 782-5356; Fax: (217) 558-4942;
Abstracts: (217) 785-3003
Internet: www.sos.state.il.us
Driver's Licenses
Fee for obtaining abstract: $12.00

Illinois Vehicle Services Department
Office of the Secretary of State, Record Inquiry Section,
501 S. Second, Room 408, Springfield, IL 62756-7000
(217) 782-6992; Fax: (217) 524-0122
Vehicle Registration and Titles
Fee for obtaining abstract: Title and Registration Search,
$5.00; Certified Title and Registration, $10.00.

Police

Illinois State Police
125 E. Monroe St., Room 103, Springfield, IL 62706
Mailing Address: P.O. Box 19461,
Springfield, IL 62794-9461
(217) 782-7263; Fax: (217) 785-2821
Internet: www.isp.state.il.us

Illinois State Police—Traffic Crash Report Unit (official na
me), 500 Iles Park Pl., Suite 200,
Springfield, IL 62703-2982
(217) 785-0614; Fax: (217) 785-2325
Director: Larry G. Trent
Fee for obtaining accident report: $5.00

Probate, Recording and Notary Certificate Offices

Estate & Wills: Circuit Court Clerks Offices, each county
Deeds and Mortgages: County Clerks or Recorders Offices
Notary Certificates: Secretary of State, Attn: Index Dept.

Senators, U.S.

Richard J. Durbin (Democrat)
332 Dirksen Senate Office Bldg., Washington, DC 20510
(202) 224-2152; Fax: (202) 228-0400
Internet: http://durbin.senate.gov

Barack Obama (Democrat)
B-40 Dirksen Senate Office Bldg., Washington, DC 20510
(202) 224-2854; Fax: (202) 228-5417
Internet: http://obama.senate.gov

Secretary of State

Office of the Secretary of State
213 Capitol Bldg., Springfield, IL 62706
(217) 782-2201, (800) 252-8980; Fax: (217) 785-0358
Internet: www.cyberdrilleillinois.com
Secretary of State: Jesse White (Democrat)
Elected; next election Nov. 2006

Tax Department

Department of Revenue
Willard Ice Bldg., 101 W. Jefferson St.,
Springfield, IL 62702
(800) 732-8866; TDD: (800) 544-5304; (217) 782-3336;
Business Hot Line: (217) 524-4772; Forms: (800) 356-6302;
Forms by Fax: (217) 785-3400; Audit: (217) 782-9800;
Collections: (217) 782-2988;
Administrative Svcs. Bur.: (217) 782-2220;
Bd. of Appeals: (312) 814-3004;
Legal Svces.: (217) 782-7054;
Sales Tax (Specific account inquiries only): (212) 782-7897
Internet: www.revenue.state.il.us/

James R. Thompson Center, 100 W. Randolph St.,
Chicago, IL 60601-3274
(312) 814-5232
Director: Brian Hamer
General Counsel: Lynne Raimondo

Victim Compensation Program

Crime Victim Services Division
Attorney General's Office
Crime Victims' Compensation Bureau,
100 W. Randolph, 13th Floor, Chicago, IL 60601
(312) 814-2581; In-State: (800) 228-3368;
Fax: (312) 814-7105
E-mail: jkuhn@atg.state.il.us, evitell@atg.state.il.us
Internet: www.illinoisattorneygeneral.gov
740 ILCS 45 / 1, et seq. (1993) (2002)

Vital Statistics

Division of Vital Records
Department of Public Health, 605 W. Jefferson St.,
Springfield, IL 62702-5097
(217) 782-6553; TTY: (800) 547-0466;
Credit Card Orders Fax: (217) 523-2648;
Main Office Fax: (217) 785-3209
Internet: http://www.idph.state.il.us/410ilcs535/1-27
*Births, Deaths, 1916 to present. State office has central
index to Marriages, Divorces and annulments from
January 1, 1962. Only county clerks issue certified copies of
Marriages. Only circuit clerks issue certified copies of
Divorce decrees.*
Certified copies of births —$15.00; short-form
copy—$17.00; deaths—$17.00; additional copies issued at
the same time—$2.00 each. Marriage and Divorce fee for
index search and verification—$5.00.

INDIANA   *Capital: Indianapolis*

6,080,485 (2000 Census)
State Information: (317) 232-3140
State Web Site: www.state.in.us

Administrative Office of the Courts

Administrative Office of the Courts
115 W. Washington St., Suite 1080, Indianapolis, IN 46204
(317) 232-2542; Fax: (317) 233-6586
Exec. Dir. of State Court Administration:
Lilia G. Judson

Attorney Discipline

Indiana Supreme Court Disciplinary Commission
115 W. Washington St., Suite 1165,
Indianapolis, IN 46204-3417
(317) 232-1807; Fax: (317) 233-0261
Internet: www.state.in.us/judiciary/agencies/dis.html
Executive Secretary: Donald R. Lundberg

Attorney General

Office of the Attorney General
Ind. Govt. Center South, Room C553,
302 W. Washington St., Indianapolis, IN 46204
(317) 232-6201; Fax: (317) 232-7979
Internet: http://www.in.gov/attorneygeneral
Atty. General: Stephen Carter (Republican)
Elected; next election Nov. 2008

Banking Department

Department of Financial Instituitions
30 S. Meridian St., Suite 300, Indianapolis, IN 46204
(317) 232-3955; Fax: (317) 232-7655
Internet: www.dfi.state.in.us

Director: Vacancy at Press Time
Supervisor of Administration: Gina Williams

Bar Admissions

Supreme Court of Indiana
State Board of Law Examiners
South Tower, Suite 1370, 115 W. Washington St.,
Indianapolis, IN 46204-3417
(317) 232-2552; Fax: (317) 233-3960
Internet: www.in.gov./judiciary/ble
36 hours CLE, including 3 hours of Ethics, required per
three years, minimum six hours per year.
Admission on motion with five of the last seven years in
practice; attorney must intend to practice predominantly
in Indiana.
Business counsel license available to corporate counsel,
single employer not in business of practicing law.

Bar Association

Indiana State Bar Assn.
One Indiana Sq., Suite 530, Indianapolis, IN 46204
(317) 639-5465; Fax: (317) 266-2588
E-mail: isbaadmin@inbar.org
Internet: www.inbar.org

Exec. Dir.: Thomas A. Pyrz; E-mail: tpyrz@inbar.org
President: James W. Riley, Jr.
Non-Integrated Bar
Annual Meeting—October, 2005

Chief Medical Examiner

Office of Chief Medical Examiner
521 W. McCarty St., Indianapolis, IN 46225
(317) 327-4744; Fax: (317) 327-4563

Chief Medical Examiner: John P. McGoff, M.D.
  (Marion County)
Contact Medical Examiner in specific county

Client Protection Fund

Clients Financial Assistance Fund
Indiana State Bar Association
One Indiana Sq., Suite 530, Indianapolis, IN 46204
(317) 639-5465; Fax: (317) 266-2588
Internet: www.inbar.org

Exec. Dir.: Thomas A. Pyrz

Commerce Department

Department of Commerce
One N. Capitol Ave., Suite 700,
Indianapolis, IN 46204-2288
(317) 232-8800; Fax: (317) 233-4146
Internet: www.indianacommerce.com

Corporations Officers

Department of State
Corporations Division
302 W. Washington St., Indianapolis, IN 46204
Corporations Information: (317) 232-6576;
UCC: (317) 233-3984; Notaries: (317) 232-6542;
Fax: (317) 233-3387
Internet: www.sos.in.gov

Deputy Secy./Chief of Staff: Heather Willis
  201 State House (317) 232-6584
  E-mail: hwillisl@sos.state.in.us

Dir. of Business Services: Liz Keele, Room E018
  (317) 232-6583
  E-mail: lkeele@sos.state.in.us

Deputy Dir.: Beth Swindle, Room E-018
  (317) 234-1553
  E-mail: bswindle@sos.state.in.us

Criminal History Board

Criminal Justice Institute
One N. Capitol, Suite 1000, Indianapolis, IN 46204-2038
(317) 232-1233; Fax: (317) 232-4979

Economic Development Administration

Division of Economic Development
Dept. of Commerce
One N. Capitol, Suite 700, Indianapolis, IN 46204
(317) 232-8847, (800) 463-8081; Fax: (317) 232-4146
Internet: www.indianacommerce.com

Director: Vacancy at Press Time

Governor's Office

Office of the Governor
206 State House, Indianapolis, IN 46204
(317) 232-4567; Fax: (317) 232-3443
Internet: http://www.ai.org/gov/index.html

444 N. Capitol Ave., Suite 428, Washington, DC 20001
(202) 624-1474; Fax: (202) 624-1475

Governor: Mitchell E. Daniels, Jr. (Republican)
Next election Nov. 2008

Highest State Court

Indiana Supreme Court
315 State House, 200 W. Washington St.,
Indianapolis, IN 46204
(317) 232-2504; Fax: (317) 232-8372
Internet: www.in.gov/judiciary/supreme

402 W. Washington St., Room W062,
Indianapolis, IN 46204
(317) 232-7225

Chief Justice: Randall T. Shepard
**Clerk of the Indiana Supreme Court, Appellate &
Tax Courts:** David C. Lewis, Room 217
  (317) 232-1930; Fax: (317) 232-8365

Insurance Department

Department of Insurance
311 W. Washington St., Suite 300,
Indianapolis, IN 46204-2787
(317) 232-2385; Fax: (317) 232-5251
E-mail: doi@state.in.us
Internet: www.in.gov/idoi

Commissioner: Jim Atterholt (Acting)
Chief Examiner: Mark Pufahl

Motor Vehicle Office

Indiana Bureau of Motor Vehicles
Legal Department
N440 Indiana Govt. Center-North, 100 North Senate Ave.,
Indianapolis, IN 46204
(317) 232-7043; Fax: (317) 233-3135
Internet: www.bmvexpress.org

For Abstracts write: Drivers Record Section,
100 N. Senate Ave., Room N405, Indianapolis, IN 46204
(317) 233-6000

Chief Legal Counsel: David Cesto
Fee for obtaining abstract: Driving Record only, $4.00;
Complete Record, History & Documents, $8.00; $12.00
certified; checks payable to Bureau of Motor Vehicles

Police

Indiana State Police Department
Indiana Government Center North, 3rd Floor,
100 N. Senate Ave., Indianapolis, IN 46204-2259
Operations: (317) 232-8248;
Public Information Officer: (317) 232-8200;
Fax: (317) 232-0652, 232-5682

Vehicle Crash Records Section,
Indiana State Police, 3rd Floor,
Indiana Government Center N., 100 N. Senate Ave.,
Indianapolis, IN 46204-2259
(317) 232-8286

Superintendent: Paul Whitesell, Ph.D.
Fee for obtaining accident report: $3.00

Probate, Recording and Notary Certificate Offices

Estate & Wills: Circuit or Probate Court Clerks, each county
Deeds and Mortgages: County Recorders Offices
Notary Certificates: Secretary of State, Attn.:
Authentications (No Fee)

Senators, U.S.

Evan Bayh (Democrat)
463 Russell Senate Office Bldg., Washington, DC 20510
(202) 224-5623; Fax: (202) 228-3924
Internet: http://bayh.senate.gov

Richard G. Lugar (Republican)
306 Hart Senate Office Bldg., Washington, DC 20510
(202) 224-4814; Fax: (202) 228-0360
E-mail: senator_lugar@lugar.senate.gov
Internet: http://lugar.senate.gov

Secretary of State

Office of the Secretary of State
The State House, Room 201, Indianapolis, IN 46204
(317) 232-6531; Fax: (317) 233-3283
E-mail: aa@sos.state.in.us; Internet: www.sos.in.gov
Secretary of State: Todd Rokita
Elected; next election Nov. 2006

Tax Department

Department of Revenue
100 N. Senate Ave., Indianapolis, IN 46204
Taxpayer Service: (317) 232-2240; Fax: (317) 233-3201;
Forms: (317) 615-2581;
Forms Fax: (317) 232-2329, 615-2692;
Collection Div.: (317) 232-2165; Audit Div.: (317) 233-5015
Internet: www.in.gov/dor/
Commissioner: T.F. Obsitnik (Acting)

Victim Compensation Program

Victim Services Div., Indiana Criminal Justice Inst.
One N. Capital, Suite 1000, Indianapolis, IN 46204
(317) 232-1233; Fax: (317) 233-3912
Internet: www.state.in.us/cji
*Ind. Stat. Ann. §§5-2-6.1-1 through 48 and 5-2-6.3-1
through 7*

Vital Statistics

Division of Vital Records
Dept. of Health, 6 W. Washington St., Indianapolis, IN 46204
(317) 233-2700; Fax: (317) 233-7210
E-mail: bstultz@isdh.state.in.us
Internet: http://www.state.in.us/isdh/bdcertifs/bdcert.html
*Births—1907; Deaths—1900 (Marriages and Divorces are filed
with County Clerks; Indiana State Library, Geneology Dept.
prepares annual index of marriages beginning with 1958).*
Search fee $10.00 for birth record; $8.00 for death record.
Fee includes one certified copy if record is found.
Additional copies $4.00. Amendment additional $8.00.
Certificates sent by FedEx are $28.45 additional (credit
card orders only).

IOWA　　　　　　　*Capital: Des Moines*

2,926,324 (2000 Census)
State Information: (515) 281-5011
State Web Site: www.state.ia.us

Administrative Office of the Courts

Administrative Office of the Courts
Judicial Branch Bldg., 1111 E. Court Ave.,
Des Moines, IA 50319
(515) 281-5241; Fax: (515) 242-0014
Internet: www.judicial.state.ia.us
Court Administrator: David K. Boyd

Attorney Discipline

The Iowa Supreme Court Board of Professional Ethics and
Conduct
Iowa Judicial Branch Bldg., 1111 E. Court Ave.,
Des Moines, IA 50319
(515) 725-8017; Fax: (515) 725-8013
Ethics Administrator: Charles L. Harrington

Attorney General

Office of the Attorney General
1305 E. Walnut St., Des Moines, IA 50319
(515) 281-5164; Fax: (515) 281-4209
Internet: www.iowaattorneygeneral.org
Atty. General: Thomas J. Miller (Democrat)
Elected; next election Nov. 2006

Banking Department

Division of Banking
East Grand Office Park, Suite 300, 200 E. Grand Ave.,
Des Moines, IA 50309-1827
(515) 281-4014; Fax: (515) 281-4862
Internet: www.idob.state.ia.us
Superintendent: Thomas B. Gronstal

Bar Admissions

Supreme Court of Iowa
Judicial Branch Bldg., 1111 E. Court Ave.,
Des Moines, IA 50319
(515) 281-5911; Fax: (515) 242-6164
Internet: www.judicial.state.ia.us
15 hours CLE required per year; must include two hours of
ethic courses every other year.
Admission on motion with five of the last seven years in
practice.

Bar Association

Iowa State Bar Assn.
521 E. Locust St., 3rd Floor, Des Moines, IA 50309-1939
(515) 243-3179; Fax: (515) 243-2511
Internet: www.iowabar.org
Exec. Dir.: Dwight Dinkla
President: J. C. Salvo
Non-Integrated Bar
Annual Meeting—June, 2005

Client Protection Fund

Client Security & Attorney Disciplinary Commission
Judicial Branch Bldg., 1111 E. Court Ave.,
Des Moines, IA 50319
(515) 725-8029; Fax: (515) 725-8032
E-mail: client.security@jb.state.ia.us
Internet: www.judicial.state.ia.us/regs/csc.asp
Asst. Court Administrator: Paul H. Wieck II

Commerce Department

Department of Commerce
200 E. Grand Ave., Suite 300, Des Moines, IA 50309-1827
Commerce Director's Office/Banking Div.: (515) 281-4014;
Banking Div. Fax: (515) 281-4862;
Credit Unions: (515) 281-6514
Internet: www.state.ia.us/government/com/

350 Maple St., Des Moines, IA 50319-0065
Insurance Div.: (515) 281-5705; Toll-Free: (877) 955-1212;
Fax: (515) 281-3059; Utilities Div.: (515) 281-5979

1918 S.E. Hulsizer Rd., Ankeny, IA 50021
Alcoholic Beverages: (515) 281-7400;
Professional Licensing: (515) 281-7393;
Professional Licensing Fax: (515) 281-7411

Corporations Officers

Department of State
Business Services Division
Lucas Bldg., 1st Floor, Des Moines, IA 50319
General Information and Name Availabilies:
(515) 281-5204; Corporations Section: (515) 281-5204;
Notaries: (515) 281-8363;
Limited Partnerships: (515) 281-5204;
Annual Reports: (515) 281-7796; UCC: (515) 281-5204;
Fax: (515) 242-5953
Deputy Secretary of State: Steve Mandernach
　　(515) 281-5865; E-mail: smandernach@sos.state.ia.us
Dir., Admin. Services: Harry Davis (515) 281-6560
　　E-mail: harry@sos.state.ia.us

Criminal History Board

Division of Criminal Investigation
Wallace State Office Bldg., 502 E. 9th St.,
Des Moines, IA 50319
(515) 281-4776; Fax: (515) 242-6876

Economic Development Administration

Dept. of Economic Development
200 E. Grand Ave., Des Moines, IA 50309
(515) 242-4700; Fax: (515) 242-4809
Internet: www.iowalifechanging.com
Director: Michael T. Blouin

Governor's Office

State Capitol, Des Moines, IA 50319
(515) 281-5211; Fax: (515) 281-6611
Internet: www.state.ia.us/governor/

444 N. Capitol St. N.W., Suite 359, Washington, DC 20001
(202) 624-5442; Fax: (202) 624-8189
Governor: Tom Vilsack (Democrat)
Next election Nov. 2006

Highest State Court

Supreme Court
State Capitol, 1111 E. Court Ave., Des Moines, IA 50319
(515) 281-3952, 53; Fax: (515) 242-6164
Internet: www.judicial.state.ia.us
Chief Justice: Louis A. Lavorato
Clerk of the Supreme Court: R.K. Richardson

Insurance Department

Division of Insurance
330 Maple St., Des Moines, IA 50319-0065
(515) 281-5705; Fax: (515) 281-3059;
Toll Free: (877) 955-1212
Internet: www.iid.state.ia.us/
Commissioner: Susan E. Voss

Motor Vehicle Office

Iowa Motor Vehicle Division
Park Fair Mall, 100 Euclid Ave., P.O. Box 9204,
Des Moines, IA 50306-9204
(515) 244-9124; Director's Office: (515) 237-3121;
Information Center: (515) 244-8725, (800) 532-1121;
Fax: (515) 237-3087, 239-1837

For Abstracts write: Driver Services, 100 Euclid Ave.,
P.O. Box 9204, Des Moines, IA 50306-9204
Fee for obtaining abstract: $5.50

Police

Iowa State Patrol
Wallace State Office Bldg., 3rd Floor,
Des Moines, IA 50319-0044
(515) 281-5824; Fax: (515) 242-6305
Internet: www.state.ia.us/government/dps/isp/

Accident Reports: Office of Driver's Services,
100 Euclid Ave., P.O. Box 9204,
Des Moines, IA 50306-9204
(515) 244-9124; In-state: (800) 532-1121
Chief: Col. Robert Garrison
Attorneys should not use automated system; wait on line for attendant
Fee for obtaining accident report: $4.00

Probate, Recording and Notary Certificate Offices

Estate & Wills: Clerk of Court, each county
Deeds and Mortgages: County Recorders Offices
Notary Certificates: Secretary of State, Notary Dept. (5.00)

Senators, U.S.

Charles E. Grassley (Republican)
135 Hart Senate Office Bldg., Washington, DC 20510
(202) 224-3744; Fax: (202) 224-6020
Internet: http://grassley.senate.gov

Tom Harkin (Democrat)
731 Hart Senate Office Bldg., Washington, DC 20510
(202) 224-3254; Fax: (202) 224-9369
Internet: http://harkin.senate.gov

Secretary of State

Office of the Secretary of State
Lucas State Office Bldg., 1st Floor, Des Moines, IA 50319
(515) 281-5204; Fax: (515) 242-5953
Internet: www.sos.state.ia.us
Secretary of State: Chester J. Culver (Democrat)
Elected; next election Nov. 2006

Tax Department

Department of Revenue & Finance
Hoover State Office Bldg., 4th Floor, 1305 E. Walnut,
Des Moines, IA 50319
Mailing Address: P.O. Box 10460, Des Moines, IA 50306

(515) 281-3114; In-State: (800) 367-3388;
Fax: (515) 242-6040; Forms (Mail): (515) 281-7239;
Forms (Fax): (800) 572-3943;
Compliance Dir.: (515) 281-3254;
Operations Dir.: (515) 281-7654;
Property Tax Dir.: (515) 281-4040
Internet: www.state.ia.us/tax/, Internet (Forms):
www.state.ia.us/government/drf/index.html
Director: Michael D. Ralston
(515) 281-3204
E-mail: michael.ralston@idrf.state.ia.us

Victim Compensation Program

Crime Victim Assistance Division
Iowa Attorney General
Lucas Bldg., Ground Fl., 321 E. 12th St.,
Des Moines, IA 50319
(515) 281-5044; Fax: (515) 281-8199
Internet: www.state.ia.us/government/ag/cva.html
Iowa Code Ch. 915, Amended 2000

Vital Statistics

Bureau of Vital Records
Iowa Department of Public Health,
Lucas State Office Bldg., 321 E. 12th St.,
Des Moines, IA 50319-0075
(515) 281-4944; Credit Card Orders: (515) 281-4944;
Fax: (515) 281-0479
Internet: www.idph.state.ia.us/pa/vr.htm
Births, Deaths, Marriages since 1880. Divorces—not available through this office. Original dissolution records are available in the county only.
Non-Refundable fee for searching or certified
copy—$15.00. May be ordered by phone (using a credit card) for a $5.50 additional charge.

KANSAS *Capital: Topeka*

2,688,418 (2000 Census)
State Information: (913) 296-0111
State Web Site: www.state.ks.us

Administrative Office of the Courts

Administrative Office of the Courts
Judicial Center, Room 337, 301 S.W. Tenth Ave.,
Topeka, KS 66612-1507
(785) 296-4873; Fax: (785) 296-7076
Internet: www.kscourts.org
Judicial Administrator: Howard Schwartz

Attorney Discipline

Office of the Disciplinary Administrator
701 Jackson St., 1st Floor, Topeka, KS 66603
(785) 296-2486; Fax: (785) 296-6049
Internet: www.kscourts.org/attydisc/
Disciplinary Administrator: Stanton A. Hazlett
E-mail: shazlett.@kscourts.org
Deputy Disciplinary Admins.:
Janith A. Davis
Frank D. Diehl; E-mail: fdiehl@kscourts.org
Alexander M. Walczak; E-mail: awalczak@kscourts.org
Admissions Atty.: Gayle B. Larkin

Attorney General

Office of the Attorney General
Memorial Hall, 2nd Floor, 120 S.W. 10th Ave.,
Topeka, KS 66612-1597
(785) 296-2215; Fax: (785) 296-6296
Internet: www.ksag.org
Atty. General: Phill Kline (Republican)
Elected; next election Nov. 2006

Banking Department

Office of the State Bank Commissioner
700 Jackson St., Suite 300, Topeka, KS 66603
(785) 296-2266; Fax: (785) 296-0168
Internet: www.osbckansas.org
Commissioner: Clarence W. Norris

Bar Admissions

Supreme Court of Kansas
Judicial Center, Room 374, 301 S.W. Tenth Ave.,
Topeka, KS 66612-1507
(785) 296-8410; Fax: (785) 296-1028
E-mail: admissions@kscourts.org
Internet: www.kscourts.org
12 hours CLE required per year, including two hours of
professional responsibility.
Admission without examination approved, effective July 1,
2005.

Bar Association

Kansas Bar Assn.
1200 S.W. Harrison St., Topeka, KS 66612
(785) 234-5696; Fax: (785) 234-3813
Internet: www.ksbar.org
Exec. Dir.: Jeffrey Alderman
President: richard F. Hayse
Non-Integrated Bar
Annual Meeting—June, 2005

Client Protection Fund

Client Protection Fund Commission
Judicial Center, Room 374, 301 S.W. Tenth Ave.,
Topeka, KS 66612-1507
(785) 296-3229; Fax: (785) 296-1028
Internet: www.kscourts.org/programs/cpf.htm
Clerk of the Supreme Court: Carol Gilliam Green

Commerce Department

Department of Commerce and Housing Legal
100 S.W. Jackson St., Suite 100, Topeka, KS 66612-3481
(785) 296-1913; TTY: (785) 296-3487; Fax: (785) 296-6809
Internet: www.kansascommerce.com

Corporations Officers

Department of State
Business Services Division
Memorial Hall, 1st Floor, 120 S.W. 10th Ave.,
Topeka, KS 66612-1594
General Information, Corporations Section & Name
Availabilities: (785) 296-4564;
Annual Reports: (785) 296-4564;
Corporations Fax: (785) 296-4570;
UCC Fax: (785) 296-3659
Deputy Asst. Secretary/Legal Counsel:
  Melissa Wangemann
    (785) 296-4801; Fax: (785) 368-8032
    E-mail: melissaw@kssos.org
Deputy Asst. Secretary, Corporations:
  Fariba Pouraryan, Room 100
    (785) 296-7456; Fax: (785) 296-4570
    E-mail: faribap@kssos.org
Deputy Asst. Secy. of State, E-Government Svces.:
  Kathy M. Sachs (785) 296-3828; Fax: (785) 296-3659
    E-mail: kathys@kssos.org

Criminal History Board

Bureau of Investigation
1620 S.W. Tyler St., Topeka, KS 66612-1837
(785) 296-8200; Fax: (785) 296-6781

Economic Development Administration

Business Development Division
Dept. of Commerce and Housing
1000 S.W. Jackson, Suite 100, Topeka, KS 66612-1354
(785) 296-5298; Fax: (785) 296-3490
Internet: www.kansascommerce.com
Director: Steve R. Kelly; Fax: (785) 296-3490
    E-mail: skelly@kansascommerce.com

Governor's Office

Office of the Governor
State Capitol, Room 212-S, 300 SW 10th St.,
Topeka, KS 66612-1590
(785) 296-3232; Fax: (785) 296-7973
E-mail: governor@state.ks.us
Internet: www.ksgovernor.org
Governor: Kathleen Sebelius (Democrat)
Next election Nov. 2006

Highest State Court

Supreme Court
Judicial Center, 301 S.W. Tenth Ave.,
Topeka, KS 66612-1507
(785) 296-3229; Fax: (785) 296-1028
Internet: www.kscourts.org
Chief Justice: Kay McFarland
Clerk of the Supreme Court: Carol G. Green

Insurance Department

Insurance Department
420 S.W. 9th St., Topeka, KS 66612-1678
(785) 296-3071; Fax: (785) 296-2283
Internet: www.ksinsurance.org
Commissioner: Sandy Praeger
Chief Examiner: Don Gaskill

Motor Vehicle Office

Kansas Division of Motor Vehicles
Department of Revenue
Docking State Office Bldg., 915 S.W. Harrison St.,
Topeka, KS 66626-0001
Records Dept.: (785) 296-3671;
Fax: (785) 291-3755, 296-6851;
Title & Registration: (785) 296-3621; Fax: (785) 296-3852;
Driver Licensing: (785) 296-3963; Fax: (785) 296-0691;
Motor Carriers: (785) 291-3384; Fax: (785) 296-7872;
Medical Review: (785) 296-3601
E-mail: dc@kdor.state.ks.us
Internet: www.ink.org/public/kdor/dmv

For Abstracts write: Driver Control Bureau,
P.O. Box 12021, Topeka, KS 66612-2021
(785) 296-3671; Fax: (785) 296-6851
Fee for obtaining abstract: $6.00; multiple
documents/folders $10.00

Police

Kansas Highway Patrol
122 S.W. 7th St., Topeka, KS 66603-3847
(785) 296-6800; Fax: (785) 296-3049
Internet: www.kansashighwaypatrol.org
Superintendent: Col. William R. Seck
Fee for obtaining accident report: $2.00

Probate, Recording and Notary Certificate Offices

Estate & Wills: Probate Division of District Court
Deeds and Mortgages: County Register of Deeds Offices
Notary Certificates: Secretary of State, Attn.: Notary
Division ($10.00)

Senators, U.S.

Sam Brownback (Republican)
303 Hart Senate Office Bldg., Washington, DC 20510
(202) 224-6521; Fax: (202) 228-1265
Internet: http://brownback.senate.gov

Pat Roberts (Republican)
109 Hart Senate Office Bldg., Washington, DC 20510
(202) 224-4774; Fax: (202) 224-3514
Internet: http://roberts.senate.gov

Secretary of State

Office of the Secretary of State
120 S.W. 10th Ave., 1st Floor, Topeka, KS 66612-1594
(785) 296-4564; Fax: (785) 296-4570
Internet: www.kssos.org
Secretary of State: Ron Thornburgh (Republican)
    E-mail: ron_thornburgh@kssos.org
Elected; next election Nov. 2006

Tax Department

Department of Revenue
Office of Policy & Research
915 S.W. Harrison St., Topeka, KS 66612-1588
(785) 296-3081; Forms: (785) 296-4937;
Fax: (785) 296-7928; Audit Svces.: (785) 296-7719;
Legal Svcs. Bur.: (785) 296-2381
Internet: www.ksrevenue.org
Secretary: Joan Wagnon

Victim Compensation Program

Crime Victims Compensation Board
120 S.W. 10th Ave., 2nd Floor, Topeka, KS 66612-1597
(785) 296-2359; Fax: (785) 296-0652
*Kan. Stat. Ann. §§74-7301 to 74-7321 (1978) Amended
1995, 2004*

Vital Statistics

Kansas Department of Health and Environment
Office of Vital Statistics, 1000 S.W. Jackson St., Suite 120,
Topeka, KS 66612-2221
(785) 296-1400; Fax: (785) 296-8075;
Order by Fax: (785) 357-4332
Internet: www.kdhe.state.ks.us/vital/
Births, Deaths—1911; Marriages—1913; Divorces—1951.
Certified copies—for the first copy: $12.00 for birth,
marriage, and divorce and each additional copy of the same
record ordered at the same time: $7.00; $13.00 for death
records and each additional copy of the same record ordered
at the same time $8.00. Expedited requests may be ordered
by telephone (785) 296-3253, for a $9.00 additional priority
shipping & handling fee (order by credit card).

KENTUCKY
Capital: Frankfort

4,041,769 (2000 Census)
State Information: (502) 564-3130
State Web Site: www.state.ky.us

Administrative Office of the Courts

Administrative Office of the Courts
100 Millcreek Park, Frankfort, KY 40601
(502) 573-2350; Fax: (502) 695-1759
Dir., Administrative Office of the Courts:
  Cicely Jaracz Lambert

Attorney Discipline

Office of Bar Counsel
Kentucky Bar Association
Kentucky Bar Center, 514 W. Main St.,
Frankfort, KY 40601-1883
(502) 564-3795; Fax: (502) 564-3225
Internet: www.kybar.org
Chief Bar Counsel: Linda A. Gosnell, Ext. 271

Attorney General

Office of the Attorney General
700 Capitol Ave., Suite 118, Frankfort, KY 40601
(502) 696-5300; Fax: (502) 564-8310
Internet: www.ag.ky.gov
Atty. General: Gregory Stumbo (Democrat)
Elected; next election Nov. 2007

Banking Department

Office of Financial Institutions
1025 Capitol Center Dr., Suite 200, Frankfort, KY 40601
(502) 573-3390, (800) 223-2579; Fax: (502) 573-8787
Internet: www.dfi.state.ky.us
Exec. Dir.: Vacancy at Press Time
Deputy Executive Dir.: Keith A. Talley

Bar Admissions

Kentucky Office of Bar Admissions
1510 Newtown Pike, Suite 156, Lexington, KY 40511
(859) 246-2381; Fax: (859) 246-2385
Internet: www.kyoba.org
12.5 hours CLE required per year, including two hours
ethics or professional responsibility.
Admission on motion with five of the last seven years
practice in a Reciprocal Jurisdiction. Must have graduated
from an ABA-approved law school and passed the MPRE.

Bar Association

Kentucky Bar Assn.
514 W. Main St., Frankfort, KY 40601-1883
(502) 564-3795; Fax: (502) 564-3225
Internet: www.kybar.org
Exec. Dir.: Bruce K. Davis, Ext. 248; E-mail: bdavis@kybar.org
President: R. Kent Westberry
Integrated Bar
Annual Meeting—June, 2005

Client Protection Fund

Clients' Security Fund
Kentucky Bar Association, 514 W. Main St.,
Frankfort, KY 40601-1883
(502) 564-3795; Fax: (502) 564-3225
Internet: www.kybar.org
Chief Bar Counsel: Linda A. Gosnell

Commerce Department

See Economic Development Administration

Corporations Officers

Office of the Secretary of State
152 State Capitol Bldg., 700 Capital Ave.,
Frankfort, KY 40601
Annual Reports, Name Availibilities, Filing Information:
(502) 564-2848; Records Section: (502) 564-7330;
UCC Branch: (502) 573-0265;
Administration: (502) 564-3490; Fax: (502) 564-4075;
Fax Assistance: (502) 564-7330
Internet: www.kysos.com
Dir. of Corporations: Tracy Goff Herman
  (502) 564-3490
  E-mail: therman@kysos.com
UCC Branch Mgr.: Ann Clay Hanly
  Mare Manor, 363-C Versailles Rd.,
  Frankfort, KY 40601
  (502) 573-0265
  E-mail: ahanly@mail.sos.state.ky.us
Business Filing Branch Mgr.: M. Gail Hance
  (502) 564-2848
  E-mail: ghance@mail.sos.state.ky.us
Dir., Information Technology: Lisa Rowe
  (502) 564-3490
  E-mail: lrowe@kysos.com

Criminal History Board

Criminal ID & Record Section
Kentucky State Police
1250 Louisville Rd., Frankfort, KY 40601
(502) 227-8700; Fax: (502) 226-7422
Internet: www.kentuckystatepolice.org

Economic Development Administration

Cabinet for Economic Development
2400 Capital Plaza Tower, 500 Mero St.,
Frankfort, KY 40601
(502) 564-7670, (800) 626-2930; Fax: (502) 564-1535
Internet: www.thinkkentucky.com
Secretary: Marvin E. Strong, Jr.

Governor's Office

Office of the Governor
700 Capitol Ave., Frankfort, KY 40601
(502) 564-2611; Fax: (502) 564-0437
Internet: http://governor.ky.gov
Governor: Ernie Fletcher (Republican)
Next election Nov. 2007

Highest State Court

Supreme Court of Kentucky
State Capitol, Room 235, 700 Capitol Ave.,
Frankfort, KY 40601
(502) 564-5444; Fax: (502) 564-2665
Internet: www.kycourts.net
Chief Justice: Joseph E. Lambert
Clerk of the Supreme Court: Susan Stokley Clary

Insurance Department

Office of Insurance
215 W. Main St., Frankfort, KY 40601
Mailing Address: P.O. Box 517, Frankfort, KY 40602
(502) 564-3630; Fax: (502) 564-1453;
Legal Fax: (502) 564-1456
Internet: http://doi.ppr.ky.gov/kentucky/
Commisioner: Martin J. Koetters (Exec. Dir.)
Chief Financial Examiner: David Hurt

Motor Vehicle Office

Kentucky Department of Vehicle Regulation
State Office Bldg., Room 308, 200 Mero St.,
Frankfort, KY 40622
(502) 564-7000; Fax: (502) 564-6403;
Driver Licensing: (502) 564-6800
Internet: www.transportation.ky.gov/drlic/,
www.transportation.ky.gov/mvl/
Fee for obtaining abstract: $3.00

Police

Kentucky State Police
919 Versailles Rd., Frankfort, KY 40601
(502) 695-6300; Records Custodian: (502) 695-6300;
Fax: (502) 573-1479
Internet: www.kentuckystatepolice.org
Commissioner: Mark L. Miller
Fee for obtaining accident report: $.10 per page

Probate, Recording and Notary Certificate Offices

Estate & Wills: District Courts (estates) and County
Clerks (wills)
Deeds and Mortgages: County Clerks Offices
Notary Certificates: County Clerk where affidavit
originated (fee varies); Secretary of State for Apostille
certification ($5.00)

Senators, U.S.

Jim Bunning (Republican)
316 Hart Senate Office Bldg., Washington, DC 20510
(202) 224-4343; Fax: (202) 228-1373
Internet: http://bunning.senate.gov

Mitch McConnell (Republican)
361-A Russell Senate Office Bldg., Washington, DC 20510
(202) 224-2541; Fax: (202) 224-2499
Internet: http://mcconnell.senate.gov

Secretary of State

Office of the Secretary of State
State Capitol, Suite 152, 700 Capitol Ave.,
Frankfort, KY 40601-3493
(502) 564-3490; Fax: (502) 564-5687
Internet: www.kysos.com
Secretary of State: Trey Grayson
Elected; next election Nov. 2007

Tax Department

Revenue Cabinet
200 Fair Oaks Lane, Frankfort, KY 40620
(502) 564-4581; TYY: (502) 564-3058;
Property Valuation Dept.: (502) 564-8358;
Tax Administration Dept.: (502) 564-3111;
Law Dept.: (502) 564-6866
Internet: http://revenue.ky.gov/revhome.htm
Secretary: Dana Bynum Mayton
(502) 564-3226; Fax: (502) 564-3875

Victim Compensation Program

Crime Victims Compensation Board
130 Brighton Park Blvd., Frankfort, KY 40601-3714
(502) 573-2290; Fax: (502) 573-4817
E-mail: cvcb@ky.gov
*Ky. Rev. Stat. Ann. §§346.010 to 346.190 (Bobbs-Merrill
Co., 1990)*

Vital Statistics

Office of Vital Records
275 E. Main St., Suite 1E-A, Frankfort, KY 40621-0001
(502) 564-4212; Order by Credit Card: (877) 817-3632;
Order by Credit Card Fax: (877) 435-5584
Internet: http://chfs.ky.gov/dph/vital
*Births, Deaths Jan. 1911 to present, Marriages, Divorces
Marriages & Divorce Records from June 1958 to present.
Marriage records before June 1, 1958 are in County Court
Clerk's Office. Divorces prior to same date are in the Circuit
Court Clerk's Office.*
Certified Copies—birth certificates: $10.00; all other
certificates: $6.00.

LOUISIANA   *Capital: Baton Rouge*

4,468,976 (2000 Census)
State Information: (504) 342-6600
State Web Site: www.state.la.us

Administrative Office of the Courts

Office of the Judicial Administrator
400 Royal St., New Orleans, LA 70112
(504) 568-5747; Fax: (504) 568-5687
Internet: www.lasc.org
**Judicial Administrator of the Judicial Council of
the Supreme Court:** Hugh M. Collins, Ph.D.

Attorney Discipline

Attorney Disciplinary Board
Office of the Disciplinary Counsel
4000 S. Sherwood Forest Blvd., Suite 607,
Baton Rouge, LA 70816
(225) 293-3900, (800) 326-8022; Fax: (225) 293-3300
E-mail: ladb@ladb.org
Internet: www.ladb.org

Administrator's Office, 2800 Veterans Blvd., Suite 310,
Metairie, LA 70002
(504) 834-1488, (800) 489-8411; Fax: (504) 834-1449
Chief Disciplinary Counsel: Charles B. Plattsmier
Board Administrator: Donna L. Roberts

Attorney General

Office of the Attorney General
1885 N. 3rd St., 7th Floor, P.O. Box 94005,
Baton Rouge, LA 70804-9005
(225) 326-6705; Fax: (225) 326-6797
Internet: www.ag.state.la.us/
Atty. General: Charles C. Foti, Jr. (Democrat)
Elected; next election Nov. 2007

Banking Department

Office of Financial Institutions
8660 United Plaza Blvd., 2nd Floor,
Baton Rouge, LA 70809-7024
Mailing Address: P.O. Box 94095,
Baton Rouge, LA 70804-9095
(225) 925-4660; Depository & Admin. Fax: (225) 925-4548;
Legal, Non-Depository & Securities Fax: (225) 925-4524
Internet: www.ofi.state.la.us
Commissioner: John P. Ducrest
Deputy Commissioner: Doris B. Gunn

Bar Admissions

Committee on Bar Admissions
Supreme Court of Louisiana
2800 Veterans Memorial Blvd., Suite 310,
Metairie, LA 70002
(504) 836-2420; Fax: (504) 834-1449
E-mail: denisel@lascba.org
Internet: www.lascba.org
12.5 hours CLE required per year, including one hour of
ethics and one hour of professionalism.
No admission without exam.

Bar Association

Louisiana State Bar Assn.
601 St. Charles Ave., New Orleans, LA 70130-3411
(504) 566-1600; Fax: (504) 566-0930
Internet: www.lsba.org
Exec. Dir.: Loretta L. Topey
President: Michael W. McKay
Integrated Bar
Annual Meeting—June, 2005

Client Protection Fund

Client Protection Fund
Louisiana State Bar, 601 St. Charles Ave.,
New Orleans, LA 70130
(504) 566-1600; Fax: (504) 598-6753
Internet: www.lsba.org
Practice Assistance Counsel: Cheri Cotogno Grodsky
(504) 619-0107, (800) 421-5722, Ext. 107
E-mail: cgrodsky@lsba.org

Commerce Department
See Economic Development Administration

Corporations Officers
Department of State
Commercial Division
8549 United Plz., Baton Rouge, LA 70809
Mailing Address: P.O. Box 94125,
Baton Rouge, LA 70804-9125
General Information, Corporations Section, Annual
Reports, Name Availabilities, Limited Partnerships &
Trademarks: (225) 925-4704; UCC: (225) 342-5542;
Fax: (225) 925-4726; UCC Fax: (225) 342-7011
E-mail (Commercial Div.): commercial@sec.state.la.us,
E-mail (UCC Div.): ucc@sec.state.la.us
Internet: www.sec.state.la.us

Administrator: Helen J. Cumbo (225) 925-4716
E-mail: hcumbo.@sec.state.la.us

Commercial Mgrs., Corporations:
Jan Cobb (225) 925-4702
Debra O'Banion (225) 922-0434

UCC Commercial Mgr.: Janice Newton (225) 342-0500
E-mail: jnewton@sec.state.la.us

I.T. Applications Mgr.: Cathy Matherne Hansen
(225) 925-1392; E-mail: chansen@sec.state.la.us

Criminal History Board
Bureau of Criminal Identification and Information
7919 Independence, Baton Rouge, LA 70806
(225) 925-6095; Fax: (225) 925-7005

Economic Development Administration
Department of Economic Development
Capitol Annex, Room 229, 1051 N. Third St.,
Baton Rouge, LA 70802
Mailing Address: P.O. Box 94185, Baton Rouge, LA 70804-9185
(225) 342-3000; Fax: (225) 342-5389
Internet: www.lded.state.la.us
Secretary: Don J. Hutchinson

Governor's Office
Office of the Governor
900 N. Third St., Baton Rouge, LA 70802
Mailing Address: P.O. Box 94004, Baton Rouge, LA 70804
(225) 342-7015; Fax: (225) 342-7099
Internet: http://www.gov.state.la.us/
Governor: Kathleen Babineaux Blanco (Democrat)
Next election Nov. 2007

Highest State Court
Supreme Court
Supreme Court Bldg., 400 Royal St.,
New Orleans, LA 70130-8102
(504) 310-2300; Internet: www.lasc.org
Chief Justice: Pascal F. Calogero, Jr. (504) 568-5727
Clerk of the Supreme Court: John Tarlton Olivier

Insurance Department
Office of the Insurance Commissioner
1702 N. Third St., Baton Rouge, LA 70802
Mailing Address: P.O. Box 94214, Baton Rouge, LA 70804
(225) 342-5900; Fax: (225) 342-8622
E-mail: public@ldi.state.la.us
Internet: www.ldi.state.la.us
Commissioner: J. Robert Wooley

Motor Vehicle Office
Louisiana Office of Motor Vehicles
7979 Independence Blvd., P.O. Box 64886,
Baton Rouge, LA 70896-4886
(225) 922-2821, (877) 368-5463;
Driver's Licenses: (225) 922-1175;
Vehicle Registration: (225) 925-6146; (877) 368-5463;
Fax: (225) 925-3979; Internet: www.expresslane.org

For Abstracts write: Driver Records,
Office of Motor Vehicles, P.O. Box 64886,
Baton Rouge, LA 70896 (225) 925-6388
Fee for obtaining abstract: $15.00 (on-line service—add
$2.00 for electronic commerce as per La Rev. Stat. 49: 316.1)

Police
Louisiana State Police
7919 Independence Blvd., Baton Rouge, LA 70806
Mailing Address: P.O. Box 66614, Baton Rouge, LA 70896
(225) 925-6157; Internet: www.lsp.org/index.html

Accident Reports: Traffic Records Unit,
Office of State Police, P.O. Box 66614, Baton Rouge, LA 70896
(225) 925-6157
Superintendent: Henry Whitehorn (225) 925-6118
Fee for obtaining accident report: $7.50

Probate, Recording and Notary Certificate Offices
Estate & Wills: Clerk of Courts Office, each parish
Deeds and Mortgages: Clerk of Courts Office, each parish;
Recorder of Mortgages in Orleans Parish
Notary Certificates: Secretary of State, Commissions
Division ($20.00; except Adoptions are $10.00 per document)
E-mail: notaries@sec.state.la.us

Senators, U.S.
Mary L. Landrieu (Democrat)
724 Hart Senate Office Bldg., Washington, DC 20510
(202) 224-5824; Fax: (202) 224-9735
Internet: http://landrieu.senate.gov
David Vitter (Republican)
825-A Hart Senate Office Bldg., Washington, DC 20510
(202) 224-4623; Fax: (202) 228-5061
Internet: http://vitter.senate.gov

Secretary of State
Office of the Secretary of State
333 State Capitol Dr., P.O. Box 94125,
Baton Rouge, LA 70804-9125
(225) 922-1000; Apostille/Authentications: (225) 922-0330;
Fax: (225) 342-5577; Internet: www.sec.state.la.us
Secretary of State: W. Fox McKeithen
Elected; next election Nov. 2007

Tax Department
Department of Revenue
617 N. Third St., Baton Rouge, LA 70802
Mailing Address: P.O. Box 201,
Baton Rouge, LA 70821-0201
Personal Income Tax Ofc: (225) 219-0102;
Sales Tax Ofc.: (225) 219-7356;
Severence Tax Ofc.: (225) 219-2500; Forms: (225) 219-2113;
Tax Administration Group 1: (225) 219-2152;
Tax Administration Group II: (225) 219-2150;
Excise Tax Ofc.: (225) 219-7656;
Corp. Income & Franchise Tax: (225) 219-0067;
Legal Division: (225) 219-2080;
Tax Administration Group III: (225) 219-2157;
Inheritance & Gift Taxes: (225) 219-0067;
Withholding Tax: (225) 219-0102;
Alcohol & Tobacco Control: (225) 925-4041
Internet: www.revenue.louisiana.gov
Secretary: Cynthia Bridges
P.O. Box 66258, Baton Rouge, LA 70896
(225) 219-2700

Victim Compensation Program
Crime Victims Reparations Bd.
Commission on Law Enforcement
1885 Wooddale Blvd., Room 1230, Baton Rouge, LA 70806
(225) 925-4437; Fax: (225) 925-6649;
Victim/Claimants (In-State only): (888) 684-2846
Internet: www.cole.state.la.us/cvr.htm
La. Rev. Stat. §§46:1801-1823, 46:1831-1839 (1950)

Vital Statistics
Vital Records Registry
Dept. of Health and Hospitals, Office of Public Health,
325 Loyola Ave., New Orleans, LA 70112
Mailing Address: P.O. Box 60630, New Orleans, LA 70160-0630
(504) 568-5152; Information lines: (800) 454-9570
Internet: www.oph.dhh.state.la.us/recordsstatistics/vital
*Birth records dating back 100 years. Death records dating
back 50 years. Orleans Parish Marriage records dating
back 50 years.*

MAINE   *Capital: Augusta*

1,274,923 (2000 Census)
State Information: (207) 582-9500
State Web Site: www.state.me.us

Administrative Office of the Courts

Administrative Office of the Courts
62 Elm St., P.O. Box 4820, Portland, ME 04112
(207) 822-0792; Fax: (207) 822-0781
Internet: www.courts.state.me.us

State Court Administrator: James T. (Ted) Glessner

Attorney Discipline

Maine Board of Overseers of the Bar
97 Winthrop St., Augusta, ME 04330
Mailing Address: P.O. Box 527, Augusta, ME 04332-0527
(207) 623-1121; Fax: (207) 623-4175
Internet: www.mebaroverseers.org

Bar Counsel: J. Scott Davis
    E-mail: jscottdavis@mebaroverseers.org

Attorney General

Office of Attorney General
Burton M. Cross Office Bldg., 111 Sewell St.,
Augusta, ME 04330-6830
(207) 626-8800; Fax: (207) 287-3145
Internet: www.maine.gov/us

6 State House Station, Augusta, ME 04333-0006
Atty. General: G. Steven Rowe (Democrat)
Elected; next election Dec. 2006

Banking Department

Bureau of Financial Institutions
122 Northern Ave., Gardiner, ME 04345
Mailing Address: 36 State House Station,
Augusta, ME 04333-0036
(207) 624-8570, (800) 965-5235; Fax: (207) 624-8590
Internet: www.mainebankingreg.org

Superintendent: Colette L. Mooney (Acting)

Bar Admissions

Board of Bar Examiners
59 Court St., Augusta, ME 04330
Mailing Address: P.O. Box 140, Augusta, ME 04332-0140
(207) 623-2464; Fax: (207) 622-0059
E-mail: execdir@mainebarexaminers.org
Internet: www.mainebarexaminers.org
CLE required
Reciprocity for attorneys admitted in NH or VT who meet
eligibility requirements. (See H.B.A.R. 11A)

Bar Association

Maine State Bar Assn.
124 State St., P.O. Box 788, Augusta, ME 04332-0788
(207) 622-7523; Fax: (207) 623-0083
E-mail: info@mainebar.org
Internet: www.mainebar.org

Exec. Dir.: Julie G. Rowe
    E-mail: jrowe@mainebar.org

President: Meris J. Bickford
Non-Integrated Bar
Annual Meeting—Jan., 2005; June, 2005

Chief Medical Examiner

Office of Chief Medical Examiner
34A Hospital St., Augusta, ME 04330
Mailing Address: 37 State House Station,
Augusta, ME 04333
(207) 624-7180; Fax: (207) 624-7178

Chief Medical Examiner: Margaret Greenwald, M.D.
Administrator: James Ferland

Commerce Department

Department of Professional & Financial Regulation
122 Northern Ave., Gardiner, ME 04345
Mailing Address: 35 State House Station,
Augusta, ME 04333
(207) 624-8500; TTY: (207) 624-8563; Fax: (207) 624-8690
Internet: www.state.me.us/pfr

Corporations Officers

Department of State, Division of Corporations & UCC
Burton M. Cross State Office Bldg., 4th Floor,
109 Seawell St., Augusta, ME 04333-0101
Mailing Address: 101 State House Station,
Augusta, ME 04333-0101
General Information: (207) 624-7736;
Annual Reports: (207) 624-7752;
New Filings: (207) 624-7740; Notaries: (207) 624-7650;
UCC: (207) 624-7760; Fax: (207) 287-5874
Internet: www.state.me.us/sos/cec/cec.htm

Dir. of Corporations & UCC: Timothy R. Poulin
    (207) 624-7734; Fax: (207) 287-5428
    E-mail: tim.poulin@maine.gov
Asst. Dir. of Corporations & UCC: Carol Hanks
    (207) 624-7734; Fax: (207) 287-5428
    E-mail: carol.hanks@maine.gov
Corporate Reporting & Information Supervisor:
    Cathy Beaudoin (207) 624-7752; Fax: (207) 287-5874
    E-mail: cathy.beaudoin@state.me.us
UCC Supervisor: Claudia Veilleux
    (207) 624-7760; Fax: (207) 287-5874

Department of State
Corporate Examining Section
101 State House Station, Augusta, ME 04333-0101
(207) 627-7740; Fax: (207) 287-5874

Supervisor: Nancy Wright
    E-mail: nancy.wright@maine.gov

Department of State
Bureau of Corporations, Elections and Commissions
101 State House Station, Augusta, ME 04333-0101
(207) 624-7734; Fax: (207) 287-5428

Dep. Secy. of State: Julie L. Flynn
    E-mail: julie.flynn@maine.gov

Criminal History Board

State Bureau of Identification
State House Station 42, 36 Hospital St.,
Augusta, ME 04333
(207) 624-7009; Fax: (207) 624-7088
E-mail: jackie.theriault@maine.gov

Economic Development Administration

Economic and Community Development
111 Sewall St., 3rd Floor, Augusta, ME 04333-0059
(207) 624-9800; Fax: (207) 287-8461
Internet: www.econdevmaine.com

Commissioner: Jack Cashman

Governor's Office

Office of the Governor
1 State House Station, Augusta, ME 04333-0001
(207) 287-3531; Fax: (207) 287-1034
Internet: http://www.maine.gov

Governor: John E. Baldacci (Democrat)
Next election Nov. 2006

Highest State Court

Supreme Judicial Court
205 Newbury St., Room 139, Portland, ME 04101
Mailing Address: P.O. Box 368, Portland, ME 04112-0368
(207) 822-4146, 822-4270
Internet: www.courts.state.me.us

Judicial Center, 65 Stone St., Augusta, ME 04330
Chief Justice: Leigh Ingalls Saufley
located at Portland Address

Clerk of the Supreme Judicial Court: James Chute
located at Portland Address

Insurance Department

Bureau of Insurance
Dept. of Professional & Financial Regulation
124 Northern Ave., Gardiner, ME 04345
Mailing Address: 34 State House Station,
Augusta, ME 04333
(207) 624-8475; Fax: (207) 624-8599

Superintendent: Alessandro Iuppa
Director of Examiners: James Williams

Motor Vehicle Office

Maine Bureau of Motor Vehicles
Driver License Services Div.
29 State House Station, 101 Hospital St.,
Augusta, ME 04333-0029
Driver Records: (207) 624-9000, Ext. 52116;
TTY: (207) 624-9105; Fax: (207) 624-9090;
Registration: (207) 624-9000, Ext. 52149;
Fax: (207) 624-9204, 624-9312
Internet: www.maine.gov/sos,
http://www.maine.gov/portal/contactus.html
Fee for obtaining abstract: $5.00 (mailed in request); $1.00
for certification; $2.00 for fax (per 10 pages); 3 yr driving
record on line service. www.informe.org/bmv/drc

Police

Maine State Police
Station 42, Suite 1, 45 Commerce Dr.,
Augusta, ME 04333-0042
(207) 624-7200; Fax: (207) 287-3042
Internet: www.maine.gov/mcrs/

For Accident Reports write: Maine State Police,
State House Station 20, 36 Hospital St.,
Augusta, ME 04333-0020
Automated: (207) 624-8939; Voice: (207) 624-8944
Chief of State Police: Col. Craig A. Poulin
     E-mail: craig.a.poulin@maine.gov
Fee for obtaining accident report: $5.00

Probate, Recording and Notary Certificate Offices

Estate & Wills: County Registers of Probate
Deeds and Mortgages: County Registers of Deeds
Notary Certificates: Div. of Elections & Commissions, 101
State House Station, Augusta, ME 04333-0101 (207)
624-7650; Fax: (207) 287-6545 ($10.00)

Senators, U.S.

Susan M. Collins (Republican)
172 Russell Senate Office Bldg., Washington, DC 20510
(202) 224-2523; Fax: (202) 224-2693
Internet: http://collins.senate.gov

Olympia J. Snowe (Republican)
154 Russell Senate Office Bldg., Washington, DC 20510
(202) 224-5344; Fax: (202) 224-1946
E-mail: olympia@snowe.senate.gov
Internet: http://snowe.senate.gov

Secretary of State

Office of the Secretary of State
148 State House Station, Augusta, ME 04333-0148
(207) 626-8400; Fax: (207) 287-8598
Internet: www.state.me.us/sos/
Secretary of State: Dan A. Gwadosky
Elected; next election Dec. 2008

Tax Department

Maine Revenue Services Income/Estate Tax Division
24 State House Station, 26 Edison Dr.,
Augusta, ME 04333-0024
(207) 287-2076, 626-8475; Forms: (207) 624-7894;
Fax: (207) 624-9694;
Collections & Enforcement: (207) 624-9595;
Collections & Enforcement Fax: (207) 287-6627;
Corporate Tax: (207) 624-9670;
Corporate Tax Fax: (207) 287-6627;
Estate Tax: (207) 626-8480; Excise Tax: (207) 287-3851;
Fiduciary Income Tax: (207) 626-8484;
Partnerships/Corporations: (207) 626-8475;
Property Tax: (207) 287-2011;
Property Tax Fax: (207) 287-6396;
Sales Tax: (207) 624-9693;
Sales, Fuel & Special Tax Div.: (207) 624-9745;
TTY: (207) 287-4477
E-mail: income.tax@maine.gov
Internet: www.maine.gov/revenue
Exec. Dir.: Jerome D. Gerard (Acting)

Victim Compensation Program

Victims Compensation Program
Attorney General's Office
State Office Bldg., Station 6, Augusta, ME 04333-0006
(207) 624-7882; Within State Victims only: (800) 903-7882;
Fax: (207) 624-7730
5 M.R.S.A. §3360-3360-M (2001 Supp.; amended 2002)

Vital Statistics

Department of Human Services
Office of Vital Records, State House, Station 11,
Augusta, ME 04333-0011
(207) 287-3181; Fax: (207) 287-1093;
Fax (Ordering) Toll free: (877) 523-2659
*Birth, Death, Marriage Records before 1892 must contact
Clerk in town where event occurred; 1892-1922 records
located at Maine State Archives. Also Divorce Records
before 1892 contact Maine State Archives (207) 287-5795*
Certified copy—Divorce since 1892: $15.00; $10.00 plain copy;
Birth, Death & Marriage since 1923: $15.00; $10.00 plain
copy; Expedited service—VitalChek, $12.95 plus $10.00 for
search and copy; Birth, Death & Marriage certified copies
from 1892-1922 (located at Maine State Archives (207)
287-5795): $10.00; $6.00 plain copy; or regular mail $27.95
requests are sent by Fed Ex; cost $26.95.

MARYLAND   *Capital: Annapolis*

5,296,486 (2000 Census)
State Web Site: www.mec.state.md.us

Administrative Office of the Courts

Administrative Office of the Courts
Maryland Judicial Center, 580 Taylor Ave.,
Annapolis, MD 21401
(410) 260-1295; Fax: (410) 974-2066
Internet: www.courts.state.md.us
Court Administrator: Frank Broccolina

Attorney Discipline

Attorney Grievance Commission of Maryland
100 Community Pl., Suite 3301,
Crownsville, MD 21032-2027
(410) 514-7051; (within MD): (800) 492-1660; Fax: (410) 987-4690
E-mail: agcmd@courts.state.md.us
Internet: www.courts.state.md.us/attygrievance/index.html
Bar Counsel: Melvin Hirshman

Attorney General

Office of the Attorney General
200 St. Paul Pl., Baltimore, MD 21202
(410) 576-6300; Fax: (410) 576-7003
Internet: www.oag.state.md.us
Atty. General: J. Joseph Curran, Jr. (Democrat)
Elected; next election Nov. 2006

Banking Department

Financial Regulation
500 N. Calvert St., Suite 402, Baltimore, MD 21202
(410) 230-6100; Fax: (410) 333-0475
Internet: www.dllr.state.md.us
Commissioner: Charles W. Turnbaugh

Bar Admissions

State Board of Law Examiners
Robert F. Sweeney District Court Bldg., Room 307,
251 Rowe Blvd., Annapolis, MD 21401
(410) 260-1975; E-mail: sble@courts.state.md.us
Internet: www.courts.state.md.us
Legal professionalism course required for admittance.
No admission without exam.

Bar Association

Maryland State Bar Assn., Inc.
520 W. Fayette St., Baltimore, MD 21201
(410) 685-7878; Fax: (410) 837-0518
E-mail: msba@msba.org; Internet: www.msba.org
Exec. Dir.: Paul V. Carlin
President: J. Michael Conroy
Non-Integrated Bar
Annual Meeting—June, 2005

Chief Medical Examiner

Office of Chief Medical Examiner
111 Penn St., Baltimore, MD 21201
(410) 333-3250; Fax: (410) 333-3063

Chief Medical Examiner: David R. Fowler

Client Protection Fund

Client Protection Fund
Robert F. Sweeney District Ct. Bldg., Suite 341,
251 Rowe Blvd., Annapolis, MD 21401
(410) 260-1950; Fax: (410) 260-1954
Internet: www.courts.state.md.us/cpf

Administrator: Janet C. Moss

Commerce Department

See Economic Development Administration

Corporations Officers

State Department of Assessments & Taxation
301 W. Preston St., Room 808, Baltimore, MD 21201
General Information: (410) 767-1340;
Corporations Section & Limited Partnerships:
(410) 767-1340;
Name Availabilities & Resident Agent Information:
(410) 767-1330; Forms: (410) 767-1180;
Annual Reports: (410) 767-1170; UCC: (410) 767-1459;
Fax: (410) 333-7097

Assoc. Dir.: Robert E. Young
(410) 767-1191
E-mail: ryoung@dat.state.md.us

Programs Mgr., UCC & Charter: Phyllis Levi
(410) 767-5759

DP Functional Analyst: Nancy Grueninger
(410) 767-1838
E-mail: ngreuninger@dat.state.md.us

Criminal History Board

Information Technology & Communications Division
6776 Reisterstown Rd., Suite 209, Baltimore, MD 21215
Mailing Address: P.O. Box 5743, Pikeville, MD 21282-5743
(410) 585-3100; Fax: (410) 318-6004
Internet: www.dpscs.state.md.us

Economic Development Administration

Department of Business & Economic Development
217 E. Redwood St., Baltimore, MD 21202
(410) 767-6300; Fax: (410) 333-8628
Internet: www.choosemaryland.org

Secretary: Aris Melissaratos

Governor's Office

Office of the Governor
State House, 100 State Circle, Annapolis, MD 21401-1991
(410) 974-3901; Fax: (410) 974-3275
E-mail: governor@gov.state.md.us
Internet: http://www.gov.state.md.us

444 N. Capitol St. N.W., Suite 311, Washington, DC 20001
(202) 624-1430; Fax: (202) 783-3061

Governor: Robert L. Ehrlich, Jr. (Republican)
Next election Nov. 2006

Highest State Court

Court of Appeals of Maryland
Robert C. Murphy Courts of Appeal Bldg., 361 Rowe Blvd.,
Annapolis, MD 21401
(410) 260-1500

Chief Judge: Robert M. Bell
Clerk of the Court of Appeals: Alexander L. Cummings

Insurance Department

Insurance Administration
525 St. Paul Pl., Baltimore, MD 21202-2272
(800) 492-6116; Examination & Audit Fax: (410) 468-2101;
Insurance Fraud Fax: (410) 347-5350;
Life & Health Fax: (410) 468-2204;
Property & Casualty Fax: (410) 468-2306;
Compliance & Enforcement Fax: (410) 468-2289
Internet: www.mdinsurance.state.md.us

Commissioner: Alfred W. Redmer, Jr.
Chief Examiner: P. Sean O'Donnell

Motor Vehicle Office

Maryland Motor Vehicle Administration
6601 Ritchie Hwy. N.E., Glen Burnie, MD 21062
Media Relations: (410) 768-7386;
Driver Records: (410) 768-7034, 35;
Driver Records Fax.: (410) 424-3678;
Vehicle Records: (410) 424-3647;
Vehicle Records Fax: (410) 768-7653
Internet: www.marylandmva.com
Fee for obtaining abstract:$7.00, non-certified; $10.00,
certified

Police

Maryland State Police
1201 Reisterstown Rd., Pikesville, MD 21208-3899
(410) 486-3101; TDD: (410) 486-0677; (800) 525-5555;
Fax: (410) 653-4269
Internet: www.mdsp.org

Central Records Division,
Motor Vehicle Accident Report Unit, 1711 Belmont Ave.,
Baltimore, MD 21244
(410) 298-3390

Secretary: Col. Thomas E. Hutchins
Fee for obtaining accident report: $4.00; non-refundable
document search fee.

Probate, Recording and Notary Certificate Offices

Estate & Wills: Register of Wills, each county and
Baltimore City
Deeds and Mortgages: Circuit Court Clerk, each county
and Baltimore City
Notary Certificates: Clerk of Circuit Court in notary's
place of authority (fee varies);   Clerk's identity certified by
Secretary of State, Certification Desk ($5.00)

Senators, U.S.

Barbara A. Mikulski (Democrat)
709 Hart Senate Office Bldg., Washington, DC 20510
(202) 224-4654; Fax: (202) 224-8858
Internet: htp://mikulski.senate.gov

Paul S. Sarbanes (Democrat)
309 Hart Senate Office Bldg., Washington, DC 20510
(202) 224-4524; Fax: (202) 224-1651
Internet: http://sarbanes.senate.gov

Secretary of State

Office of the Secretary of State
State House, Annapolis, MD 21401
(410) 974-5521; Main Office (In-State): (888) 874-0013;
Fax: (410) 974-5190;
Charities Div. (In-State): (800) 825-4510;
Charities Div. Fax: (410) 974-5527
Internet: www.sos.state.md.us

Secretary of State: R. Karl Aumann (Republican)
Appointed

Tax Department

Comptroller of Maryland
Revenue Administration Division,
Revenue Administration Center, 110 Carroll St.,
Annapolis, MD 21411-0001
(410) 260-7980; Fax (Taxpayer Service): (410) 974-5808
E-mail: taxhelp@comp.state.md.us
Internet: www.marylandtaxes.com

Business Taxpayer Service, 301 W. Preston St., Room 206,
Baltimore, MD 21201
(410) 767-1995

Compliance Division, 301 W. Preston St., Room 203,
Baltimore, MD 21201
(410) 767-1555; Fax: (410) 767-1310

Comptroller: William Donald Schaefer
Comptroller of Maryland, 80 Calvert St.,
Annapolis, MD 21401
(413) 260-7300
E-mail: wdschaefer@comp.state.md.us

Victim Compensation Program

Criminal Injuries Compensation Board
6776 Reistertown Rd., Suite 312,
Baltimore, MD 21215-2341
(410) 585-3010; Fax: (410) 764-3815
Internet: www.dpscs.state.md.us/cicb

Chair: Benjamin R. Wolman
*Md. Ann. Code art. 27 §§ 815 to 832; Criminal Procedure
11-809*

Vital Statistics

State Department of Health and Mental Hygiene
Division of Vital Records, 6550 Reisterstown Rd.,
Baltimore, MD 21215
(410) 764-3038; Fax: (410) 358-0738
*Births from 1898 (Baltimore City from 1875), Deaths from
1973 (Baltimore City from 1950), Marriages from June,
1951, Divorces (verification only) from July, 1961.
Marriages prior to 1951 and Certified Divorce records at
County Circuit Courts.*
$6.00 per copy; expedited orders (using overnight delivery
service) fee set by delivery service; credit card orders
(using VitalChek) $7.00.

MASSACHUSETTS   *Capital: Boston*

6,349,097 (2000 Census)
State Information: (617) 727-2121
State Web Site: www.state.ma.us

Administrative Office of the Courts

Administrative Office of the Trial Court
Two Center Plaza, Suite 540, Boston, MA 02108-1905
(617) 742-8575; Fax: (617) 742-0968

Chief Justice for Admin. and Mgmt.:
Robert A. Mulligan

Attorney Discipline

Massachusetts Board of Bar Overseers
99 High St., 5th Floor, Boston, MA 02110
(617) 728-8700
Internet: www.state.ma.us/obcbbo/

Administrator: Laurie G. Aaron

Attorney General

Office of the Attorney General
One Ashburton Pl., 20th Floor, Boston, MA 02108-1518
(617) 727-2200; TTY: (617) 727-4765; Fax: (617) 727-3251
Internet: www.ago.state.ma.us

Atty. General: Thomas F. Reilly (Democrat)
Elected; next election Nov. 2006

Banking Department

Division of Banks
One South Station, 3rd Floor, Boston, MA 02110
(617) 956-1500, Ext. 510; Fax: (617) 956-1599
Internet: www.mass.gov/dob

Commissioner: Steven L. Antonakes

Bar Admissions

Board of Bar Examiners
3 Pemberton Sq., 7th Floor, Boston, MA 02108
(617) 482-4466
Internet: www.mass.gov/bbe
No CLE required.
Admission on motions for attorneys of another state,
district or territory of the United States for five or more
years who meet the criteria in Supreme Judicial Court
Rule 3:01 Section 6. Details are on the Board's Website.

Bar Association

Massachusetts Bar Assn.
20 West St., Boston, MA 02111-1218
(617) 338-0500; Fax: (617) 338-0650
Internet: www.massbar.org

Exec. Dir.: Vacancy at Press Time
President: Kathleen M. O'Donnell
Non-Integrated Bar
Annual Meeting—January, 2005

Chief Medical Examiner

Office of Chief Medical Examiner
720 Albany St., Boston, MA 02118
(617) 267-6767; 24-hour Hotline: (800) 962-7877;
Fax: (617) 266-6763

Chief Medical Examiner: Richard J. Evans, M.D.
General Counsel: Jacqueline Faherty

Client Protection Fund

Clients' Security Board
99 High St., Boston, MA 02110
(617) 728-8700; Fax: (617) 482-8000

Board Counsel: Michael Fredrickson
Asst. Board Counsel: Adam Lutynski
Karen D. O'Toole

Commerce Department

See Economic Development Administration

Corporations Officers

Secretary of the Commonwealth
Corporations Office
One Ashburton Pl., Room 1710, Boston, MA 02108
Corporations Section, Name Availabilities & Annual
Reports: (617) 727-9640; UCC: (617) 727-2860;
Limited Partnerships: (617) 727-2859;
Trademarks: (617) 727-8329;
Dissolutions & Service of Process: (617) 727-2853;
Non-Profit: (617) 727-4176;
Business Trusts: (617) 727-2859; Forms: (617) 727-9440

Chief Legal Counsel/Director: Laurie Flynn
(617) 727-4919; Fax: (617) 727-4528
E-mail: laurie.flynn@sec.state.ma.us
Compliance Officer: Daniel Wandell
(617) 878-3010; Fax: (617) 742-4538
E-mail: daniel.wandell@sec.state.ma.us

Criminal History Board

Criminal History Systems Board
200 Arlington St., Suite 2200, Chelsea, MA 02150
(617) 660-4600; Fax: (617) 660-4613

Economic Development Administration

Department of Business and Technology
One Ashburton Place, Room 2101, Boston, MA 02108
(617) 727-8380; Fax: (617) 727-4426
Internet: www.mass.gov/econ

Director: Barbara B. Berke
Formerly Department of Economic Development

Governor's Office

Office of the Governor
State House, Room 360, Boston, MA 02133
(617) 725-4005; TTY: (617) 717-3666; Fax: (617) 727-9725
E-mail: goffice@state.ma.us
Internet: www.state.ma.us/gov

Springfield Office, 436 Dwight St., Room 300,
Springfield, MA 01103
(413) 784-1200; Fax: (413) 784-1202

444 N. Capitol St. N.W., Suite 208, Washington, DC 20001
(202) 624-7713; Fax: (202) 624-7714

Governor: Mitt Romney (Republican)
Next election Nov. 2006

Highest State Court

Supreme Judicial Court
One Beacon St., 3rd Floor, Boston, MA 02108
Judges's Lobby: (617) 557-1000

Chief Justice: Margaret H. Marshall
**Clerk of the Supreme Judicial Court for the
Commonwealth:** Susan Mellen
**Clerk of the Supreme Judicial Court for Suffolk
County:** Maura S. Doyle, 4th Floor
Case Information: (617) 557-1100;
Bar Information: (617) 557-1050; Fax: (617) 523-1540
Internet: sjccountyclerk.com

Insurance Department

Division of Insurance
One South Station, Boston, MA 02110-2208
(617) 521-7794; Legal Division Fax: (617) 521-7475
Internet: www.state.ma.us/doi

Commissioner: Julie Bowler

Director of Finance: Robert Dynan

General Counsel: Elisabeth Ditomassi

Motor Vehicle Office

Massachusetts Registry of Motor Vehicles
630 Washington St., Boston, MA 02108
Mailing Address: P.O. Box 199100, Boston, MA 02119-9100
(617) 351-4500; Records: (617) 351-7200;
Fax: (617) 351-9524
Internet: www.mass.gov/rmv

For Abstracts write: Attn.: Mail Listings Driver Control Unit,
Registry of Motor Vehicles, P.O. Box 199150,
Roxbury, MA 02119-9100
Fee for obtaining abstract: Driver's Record, $15.00,
Accident Reports, $10.00

Police

Massachusetts State Police
470 Worcester Rd., Framingham, MA 01702
(508) 820-2300; Fax: (508) 820-9630

Superintendent: Thomas G. Robbins
Accident Reports: Contact Motor Vehicles Registry

Probate, Recording and Notary Certificate Offices

Estate & Wills: Register of Probate, each county
Deeds and Mortgages: County or District Registry of Deeds
Notary Certificates: Secretary of State, Commission
Section; One Ashburton Pl., Room 1719, Boston, MA.
02108 ($3.00)

Senators, U.S.

Edward M. Kennedy (Democrat)
317 Russell Senate Office Bldg., Washington, DC 20510
(202) 224-4543; Fax: (202) 224-2417
Internet: http://kennedy.senate.gov

John F. Kerry (Democrat)
304 Russell Senate Office Bldg., Washington, DC 20510
(202) 224-2742; Fax: (202) 224-8525
Internet: http://kerry.senate.gov

Secretary of State

Office of the Secretary of the Commonwealth
State House, Room 337, Boston, MA 02133
(617) 727-9180; Fax: (617) 742-4722
E-mail: cis@sec.state.ma.us
Internet: www.state.ma.us/sec/

Secretary of the Commonwealth: William F. Galvin
(Democrat)
Elected; next election Nov. 2006

Tax Department

Department of Revenue
100 Cambridge St., Boston, MA 02114
(617) 887-MDOR: (617) 887-6367;
Toll Free (In-State): (800) 392-6089;
Forms: (617) 626-2201; Fax: (617) 626-2299;
General Counsel: (617) 626-3200;
Appeal & Review Bureau: (617) 626-3300
Internet: www.massdor.com

Commissioner: Alan LeBovidge
(617) 626-2201

Victim Compensation Program

Department of the Attorney General
Victim Comp. & Assistance Div.
100 Cambridge St., 12th Floor, Boston, MA 02108
(617) 727-2200; Fax: (617) 722-3066
Internet: www.ago.state.ma.us
Mass. Gen. Laws Ann. ch. 258C
Temporary location; At press time, relocation was pending.

Vital Statistics

Registry of Vital Records & Statistics
Department of Public Health,
150 Mt. Vernon St., 1st Floor, Dorchester, MA 02125
General Public: (617) 740-2600;
Credit Card Orders: (617) 740-2606;
Fax Orders: (617) 825-7755
Internet: www.state.ma.us/dph/bhsre/rvr/rvr.htm
*Births, Deaths, Marriages from 1911-present; Divorce
records in Probate & Family courts, each county.*
Regular mail: Search fee—$28.00 (includes one certified
copy); Credit Card orders—ordered by phone with delivery
via regular mail $44.00; ordered by phone with overnight
delivery $61.50; additional copies ordered by phone $37.00
each. Expedited mail service (2 weeks)—$37.00 for each
certified certificate requested. Walk-in service: Search
fee—$18.00 (includes certified copy).

MICHIGAN   *Capital: Lansing*

9,938,444 (2000 Census)
State Information: (517) 373-1837
State Web Site: www.michigan.gov

Administrative Office of the Courts

State Court Administrative Office
Michigan Hall of Justice, 925 W. Ottawa,
Lansing, MI 48915
Mailing Address: P.O. Box 30048, Lansing, MI 48909
(517) 373-0130; Fax: (517) 373-2112
Internet: courts.michigan.gov/scao

State Court Administrator: John D. Ferry, Jr.
E-mail: ferryj@jud.state.mi.us

Attorney Discipline

Michigan Attorney Grievance Commission
Marquette Bldg., Suite 256, 243 W. Congress St.,
Detroit, MI 48226
(313) 961-6585; Fax: (313) 961-5819
Internet: www.agcmi.com

Grievance Administrator: Robert L. Agacinski

Attorney General

G. Mennen Williams Bldg., 525 W. Ottawa,
P.O. Box 30212, Lansing, MI 48909
(517) 373-1110; Fax: (517) 373-3042
Internet: www.michigan.gov/ag

Atty. General: Mike Cox (Republican)
Elected; next election Nov. 2006

Banking Department

Office of Financial and Insurance Services
Office of Financial Evaluation
Bank and Trust Division, 611 W. Ottawa, 3rd Floor,
Lansing, MI 48933
Mailing Address: P.O. Box 30220, Lansing, MI 48909
(517) 373-6950; Fax: (517) 373-9475;
Commissioner's Fax: (517) 373-4870
Internet: www.michigan.gov/ofis

Commissioner: Linda A. Watters

Bar Admissions

Board of Bar Examiners
Hall of Justice, 4th. Floor, 925 W. Ottawa St., Lansing, MI 48915
Mailing Address: P.O. Box 30104, Lansing, MI 48909
(517) 373-4453; Fax: (517) 373-5038
No CLE required.
Admission on motion with three of the last five years in practice.
Must have graduated from an ABA-approved law school, and
intend in good faith to maintain a law office in the state.

Bar Association

State Bar of Michigan
306 Townsend St., Lansing, MI 48933-2083
(517) 346-6300; Fax: (517) 482-6248
Internet: www.michbar.org

Exec. Dir.: John T. Berry (517) 346-6331
E-mail: jberry@mail.michbar.org

President: Nancy J. Diehl
Integrated Bar
Annual Meeting—September, 2005

Client Protection Fund

Client Protection Fund
State Bar of Michigan
306 Townsend St., Lansing, MI 48933-2083
(517) 346-6379; Fax: (517) 482-6248
Administrator: Robin Lawnichak

Commerce Department

Department of Labor & Economic Growth
611 W. Ottawa St., Lansing, MI 48933
Mailing Address: P.O. Box 30004, Lansing, MI 48909
(517) 373-1820; Fax: (517) 373-2129
Internet: www.michigan.gov

Corporations Officers

Department of Consumer & Industry Services
Corporations Division
7150 Harris Dr., Lansing, MI 48909
Mailing Address: P.O. Box 30054, Lansing, MI 48909
(517) 241-6470;
Trademark/Service Mark Forms: (517) 241-6450
Internet: www.michigan.gov/corporations
Director: G. Ann Baker (517) 241-3838
    E-mail: abaker@michigan.gov
UCC Section
Department of State
7064 Crowner Dr., Dimondale, MI 48821
Mailing Address: P.O. Box 30197, Lansing, MI 48909-7697
(517) 322-1144; Fax: (517) 322-5434
Supervisor: Jeff Nickerson (517) 322-1495
    E-mail: nickersonj@michigan.gov

Criminal History Board

Department of State Police
Criminal Justice Information
7150 Harris Dr., A Wing, Lansing, MI 48913
(517) 322-1957; Fax: (517) 322-0635
Internet: www.michigan.gov/msp

Economic Development Administration

See Department of Commerce

Governor's Office

Office of the Governor
111 S. Capitol Ave., P.O. Box 30013, Lansing, MI 48909
(517) 373-3400; Fax: (517) 335-6863
Internet: www.michigan.gov

444 N. Capitol St. N.W., Suite 411, Washington, DC 20001
(202) 624-5840; Fax: (202) 624-5841
Governor: Jennifer M. Granholm (Democrat)
Next election Nov. 2006

Highest State Court

Supreme Court
Hall of Justice, 4th Fl., 925 W. Ottawa St., Lansing, MI 48915
Mailing Address: P.O. Box 30052, Lansing, MI 48909-7552
(517) 373-0120
Internet: www.courts.michigan.gov/supremecourt/
Chief Justice: Clifford W. Taylor
Clerk of the Supreme Court: Corbin Davis

Insurance Department

Dept. of Labor & Economic Growth
Office of Financial & Insurance Svces.
611 W. Ottawa St., 2nd. Floor N., Lansing, MI 48933
Mailing Address: P.O. Box 30220, Lansing, MI 48909-7720
(517) 373-9273; Fax: (517) 335-4978
Commissioner: Linda A. Watters
Chief Field Examiner: Robert Lamberjack

Motor Vehicle Office

Michigan Department of State
Department of State Information Center,
Secondary Complex, 7064 Crowner Dr., Lansing, MI 48918
(517) 322-1460; Fax: (517) 322-1968
Internet: www.michigan.gov/sos

For Abstracts write: Commercial Lookup Unit,
Michigan Department of State, 7064 Crowner Dr.,
Lansing, MI 48918 (517) 322-1624; Fax: (517) 322-1181
Fee for obtaining abstract: $7.00; $8.00 for certified copies.

Police

Michigan State Police
714 S. Harrison Rd., East Lansing, MI 48823
(517) 332-2521; Fax: (517) 336-6551
Internet: www.michigan.gov/msp

Accident Reports: Criminal Justice Information Center,
7150 Harris Dr., Suite 1A, Lansing, MI 48913
(517) 322-5531; Fax: (517) 322-6326
Director: Col. Tadarial Sturdivant (517) 336-6157
*Form RI 101 (Request for Public Records/FOI) required;
available on website*
Fee for obtaining accident report: No fee for standard reports.

Probate, Recording and Notary Certificate Offices

Estate & Wills: County Probate Courts
Deeds and Mortgages: County Register of Deeds
Notary Certificates: Dept. of State, Office of the Great Seal

Senators, U.S.

Carl Levin (Democrat)
269 Russell Senate Office Bldg., Washington, DC 20510
(202) 224-6221; Fax: (202) 224-1388
Internet: http://levin.senate.gov
Debbie Stabenow (Democrat)
702 Hart Senate Office Bldg., Washington, DC 20510
(202) 224-4822
Internet: http://stabenow.senate.gov

Secretary of State

Office of the Secretary of State
Department of State, Treasury Bldg., 4th Floor,
430 W. Allegan St., Lansing, MI 48918
(517) 373-2510; Fax: (517) 373-0727
Internet: www.michigan.gov/sos
Secretary of State: Terri Lynn Land (Republican)
Elected; next election Nov. 2006

Tax Department

Michigan Department of Treasury
Bureau of Revenue
Treasury Bldg., 430 W. Allegan St., Lansing, MI 48933
(517) 373-3196; Fax: (517) 373-4023;
Audit Div.: (517) 636-4171; Collection Div.: (517) 241-4900;
Technical Services: (517) 636-4230;
Audit Region I-Discovery: (517) 636-4121;
Customer Contact: (517) 636-4001;
Return Processing: (517) 636-4282;
Tax Processing Center: (517) 636-4282
E-mail: taxquestions@michigan.gov
Internet: www.michigan.gov/treasury
Dir., Bureau of Tax Policy: Vacancy at Press Time
State Treasurer: Jay B. Rising

Victim Compensation Program

Crime Victims' Services Commission
320 S. Walnut, Lansing, MI 48913
(517) 373-7373; Fax: (517) 334-9462
Internet: www.mdch.state.mi.us/cv/index.htm
Mich. Comp. Laws Ann. §§18.351-18.368 (1978 Supp.)

Vital Statistics

Michigan Department of Community Health
Div. for Vital Records & Health Statistics,
3423 N. Martin Luther King Jr. Blvd., P.O. Box 30721,
Lansing, MI 48909 (517) 335-8666;
Changes unit customer service: (517) 335-8660;
Request Applications: (517) 335-8656
E-mail: sopocyc@michigan.gov
Internet: www.michigan.gov/mdch
Births, Deaths, & Marriages from 1867. Divorces from 1897.
Search fee—-$26.00, (non refundable) including certified
copy if record found. Additional copies are $12.00 each,
and a search of more than three years is $12.00 for each
additional year beyond three years. Expedited copy
through website using credit card (birth orders restricted
to person named on record or parent named on record).
Person age 65 plus requesting own birth record $7.00.
Expedited service also available by mail for an addl.
$10.00 fee. No phone or fax orders.

MINNESOTA

Capital: Saint Paul

4,919,479 (2000 Census)
State Information: (612) 296-6013
State Web Site: www.state.mn.us

Administrative Office of the Courts

State Court Administrator's Office
25 Rev. Dr. Martin Luther King Jr. Blvd.,
St. Paul, MN 55155
(651) 296-2474; Fax: (651) 215-6004
State Court Administrator: Sue K. Dosal

Attorney Discipline

Minnesota Office of Lawyers Professional Responsibility
1500 Landmark Towers, 345 St. Peter St.,
Saint Paul, MN 55102-1218
(800) 657-3601, (651) 296-3952; TTY: (800) 627-3529;
Fax: (651) 297-5801
Internet: www.courts.state.mn.us/lprb
Director: Kenneth L. Jorgensen

Attorney General

Office of the Attorney General
102 State Capitol, St. Paul, MN 55155
(651) 296-6196; TTY: (651) 297-7206; Fax: (651) 297-4193
E-mail: attorney.general@state.mn.us
Internet: www.ag.state.mn.us

525 Park St., Suite 200, Saint Paul, MN 55103-2106

1400 NCL Tower, 445 Minnesota St.,
Saint Paul, MN 55101-2130
Atty. General: Mike Hatch (Democrat)
Elected; next election Nov. 2006

Banking Department

Division of Financial Examinations
Department of Commerce
85 Seventh Place East, Suite 500, St. Paul, MN 55101
(651) 296-2715; Fax: (651) 296-8591
E-mail: financial.comerce@state.mn.us
Internet: www.commerce.state.mn.us
Deputy Commissioner: Kevin M. Murphy
   E-mail: kmurphy@commerce.state.mn.us

Bar Admissions

Board of Law Examiners
Galtier Plaza, Suite 201, 380 Jackson St.,
Saint Paul, MN 55101
(651) 297-1800; Fax: (651) 297-1196
E-mail: ble.cle.blc@mbcle.state.mn.us
Internet: www.ble.state.mn.us
45 hours CLE required per three years.
Admission on motion with five of the last seven years in
practice, or 145 scaled score on MBE taken within two
years of application.

Bar Association

Minnesota State Bar Assn.
600 Nicollet Mall, No. 380, Minneapolis, MN 55402
(612) 333-1183; Fax: (612) 333-4927
Internet: www.mnbar.org
Exec. Dir.: Tim Groshens
President: Susan M. Holden
Non-Integrated Bar
Annual Meeting—June, 2006

Client Protection Fund

Client Security Board
1500 Landmark Towers, 345 St. Peter St.,
Saint Paul, MN 55102-1218
(651) 296-3952, (800) 657-3601; TTY: (800) 627-3529;
Fax: (651) 297-5801
Internet: www.courts.state.mn.us/csb/csb.html
Director: Kenneth L. Jorgensen

Commerce Department

Department of Commerce
85 7th Pl. E., Suite 500, St. Paul, MN 55101
(651) 296-4026; Fax: (651) 297-1959
Internet: www.commerce.state.mn.us/

Corporations Officers

Department of State, Business Services Division
180 State Office Bldg., 100 Constitution Ave.,
St. Paul, MN 55155
General Information: (651) 296-2803;
Toll-Free: (877) 551-6767;
Fax-Back Forms Library: (651) 296-2803;
Corporations Fax: (651) 297-5844
Business & Legal Analyst: Bert Black (651) 215-1441
Business Services Dir.: Peggy Steineck (651) 284-4057
Department of State, Uniform Commercial Code Division
60 Empire Dr., Room 100, Saint Paul, MN 55103
(651) 296-9232; UCC Filing Information: (651) 296-2803;
Fax, UCC: (651) 215-1009
Internet: www.sos.state.mn.us
UCC Dir.: Bonita Harvieux
   E-mail: bonita.b.harvieux@state.mn.us

Criminal History Board

Criminal Justice Information Systems
Bureau of Criminal Apprehension
Dept. of Public Safety, 1430 Maryland Ave. E.,
Saint Paul, MN 55106-2802
(651) 793-2400; Fax: (651) 793-2401
Internet: www.bca.state.mn.us

Economic Development Administration

Department of Employment & Economic Development
500 Metro Square Bldg., 121 7th Pl. E., St. Paul, MN 55101
(651) 297-1291, (800) 657-3858; Fax: (651) 296-1290
Internet: www.dted.state.mn.us
Commissioner: Matt Kramer; Fax: (651) 296-4772

Governor's Office

Office of the Governor
130 State Capitol, 75 Rev. Dr. Martin Luther King Jr. Blvd.,
Saint Paul, MN 55155
(651) 296-3391; In-State: (800) 657-3717;
Fax: (651) 296-0674, 296-2089
Internet: http://www.governor.state.mn.us/

400 N. Capitol St. N.W., Suite 365, Washington, DC 20001
(202) 624-5308; Fax: (202) 624-5425
Governor: Timothy Pawlenty (Democrat)
   E-mail: tim.pawlenty@state.mn.us
Next election Nov. 2006

Highest State Court

Supreme Court
25 Rev. Dr. Martin Luther King Blvd., St. Paul, MN 55155
(651) 296-2581; Fax: (651) 282-5115
Internet: www.courts.state.mn.us/
Chief Justice: Kathleen A. Blatz
Clerk of the Appellate Courts: Frederick K. Grittner

Insurance Department

Insurance Division
Dept. of Commerce
85 E. 7th Pl., Suite 500, St. Paul, MN 55101
(651) 296-6848; Fax: (651) 282-2568
Internet: www.commerce.state.mn.us
Commissioner: Glenn Wilson

Motor Vehicle Office

Dept. of Public Safety Driver & Vehicle Services Division
Administrative Office, Town Square Bldg., Suite 195,
445 Minnesota St., St. Paul, MN 55101-5195
(651) 296-2001; Customer Service: (651) 296-6911;
Fax: (651) 296-3141
E-mail: motor.vehicles@state.mn.us
Internet: www.mndriveinfo.org

For Abstracts write: License & Records Administration,
Driver's License, Town Square Bldg., Suite 180,
445 Minnesota St., Saint Paul, MN 55101-5180
(651) 296-2277
Fee for obtaining abstract: $4.00. For a copy of Motor
Vehicle Ownership record-contact Records Unit; $4.50 if
requestor is not the subject of the data. For Certified
records, add $1.00 to the above fees.

Police

Minnesota State Patrol
444 Cedar St., Suite 130, Saint Paul, MN 55101-5130
(651) 282-6870; Fax: (651) 296-5937
Internet: www.dps.state.mn.us/patrol/

Accident Records,
Minnesota Dept. of Public Safety, Suite 181,
445 Minnesota St., Saint Paul, MN 55101-5181
(651) 296-2060; Fax: (651) 282-2360
Chief: Col. Steven J. Mengelkoch
    (651) 282-6870
Fee for obtaining accident report: $4.00

Probate, Recording and Notary Certificate Offices

Estate & Wills: County or District Probate Courts
Deeds and Mortgages: County Recorders Offices
Notary Certificates: Secretary of State ($5.00)

Senators, U.S.

Norman Coleman (Republican)
320 Hart Senate Office Bldg., Washington, DC 20510
(202) 224-5641
Internet: http://coleman.senate.gov
Mark Dayton (Democrat)
346 Russell Senate Office Bldg., Washington, DC 20510
(202) 224-3244
Internet: http://dayton.senate.gov

Secretary of State

Office of the Secretary of State
180 State Office Bldg.,
100 Rev. Dr. Martin Luther King Jr. Blvd.,
St. Paul, MN 55155-1299
(651) 296-2803; Fax: (651) 297-7067
Internet: www.sos.state.mn.us/
Secretary of State: Mary Kiffmeyer (Republican)
Elected; next election Nov. 2006

Tax Department

Department of Revenue
Mail Station 7100, 600 N. Robert,
Saint Paul, MN 55146-7100
Forms: (651) 296-4444;
Internal Audit Div.: (651) 556-6017;
Sales and Use Tax: (651) 296-6181;
Individual Income Tax: (651) 296-3781;
Corporate Tax: (651) 297-7000; Estate Tax: (651) 556-6747;
Nonprofit Organization Franchise Tax: (651) 297-7000;
Partnership Tax: (651) 556-6765
E-mail: DORWeb.com@state.mn.us
Internet: www.taxes.state.mn.us
Commissioner: Daniel A. Salomone

Victim Compensation Program

Crime Victims Reparations Board
445 Minnesota St., Suite 2300, Saint Paul, MN 55101
(651) 282-6256; Fax: (651) 296-5787
Internet:
www.ojp.state.mn.us/mccvs/FinancialHelp/index.htm
Minn. Stat. Ann. §§611A.51-.67; §611A.70-71 (West) (1990 Supp.)

Vital Statistics

Office of the State Registrar
Department of Health, 717 Delaware St. S.E.,
Minneapolis, MN 55414-9441
Mailing Address: P.O. Box 9941,
Minneapolis, MN 55440-9441
(612) 676-5120; Fax: (612) 331-5776
Internet: www.health.state.mn.us
Births since 1900. Deaths since 1908. Marriages and Divorces—filed with the County Registrar.
County Registrar locations available on website; No walk in service
Certified copy—Birth record: $13.00, additional copy: $7.00; Death record: $10.00, additional copy: $4.00.

MISSISSIPPI   *Capital: Jackson*

2,844,658 (2000 Census)
State Information: (601) 359-1000
State Web Site: www.state.ms.us

Administrative Office of the Courts

Administrative Office of Courts
656 N. State, Jackson, MS 39201
Mailing Address: P.O. Box 117, Jackson, MS 39205
(601) 354-7406; Fax: (601) 354-7459
Internet: www.mssc.state.ms.us
Administrative Dir. of the Courts: Kevin Lackey
    E-mail: lackeyjk@mssc.state.ms.us

Attorney Discipline

The Mississippi Bar, Office of Professional Responsibility
643 N. State St., Jackson, MS 39202
Mailing Address: P.O. Box 2168, Jackson, MS 39225-2168
(601) 948-4471; Fax: (601) 355-8635
Exec. Dir.: Larry Houchins
General Counsel: Michael B. Martz

Attorney General

Office of the Attorney General
Carroll Gartin Justice Bldg., 450 High St., P.O. Box 220,
Jackson, MS 39201
Mailing Address: P.O. Box 220, Jackson, MS 39205
(601) 359-3680; Fax: (601) 359-3441
Internet: www.ago.state.ms.us
Atty. General: Jim Hood (Republican)
Elected; next election Nov. 2007

Banking Department

Department of Banking and Consumer Finance
901 Woolfolk Bldg., Suite A, 501 N. West St., Jackson, MS 39201
Mailing Address: P.O. Drawer 23729,
Jackson, MS 39225-3729
(601) 359-1031; Fax: (601) 359-3557
Internet: www.dbcf.state.ms.us
Commissioner: John S. Allison
Deputy Commissioner: Theresa L. Brady

Bar Admissions

Mississippi Board of Bar Admissions
Courts of Appeals Bldg., 1st Floor, 656 N. State St.,
Jackson, MS 39202
Mailing Address: P.O. Box 1449, Jackson, MS 39215-1449
(601) 354-6055; Fax: (601) 354-6054
Internet: http://www.mssc.state.ms.us/baradmissions
12 hours CLE required per year.
Admission by special "attorneys' examination" with five years practice in a Reciprocal Jurisdiction. Also, must establish within 30 days of admission, a permanent office for the active practice of Law in Mississippi.

Bar Association

The Mississippi Bar
643 N. State St., Jackson, MS 39202
Mailing Address: P.O. Box 2168, Jackson, MS 39225-2168
(601) 948-4471; Fax: (601) 355-8635
E-mail: info@msbar.org
Internet: www.msbar.org
Exec. Dir.: Larry Houchins
    E-mail: houchins@msbar.org
President: Jam Lambert Phillips
Integrated Bar
Annual Meeting—July, 2006

Chief Medical Examiner

Office of State Medical Examiner
1700 E. Woodrow Wilson, Jackson, MS 39216
(601) 987-1440; Fax: (601) 987-1445
Administrator: Sam Howell; E-mail: showell@mcl.state.ms.us

Client Protection Fund

Client Security Fund
643 N. State St., Jackson, MS 39202
Mailing Address: P.O. Box 2168, Jackson, MS 39225-2168
(601) 948-0568; Fax: (601) 355-8635
Internet: www.msbar.org
Asst. General Counsel: Adam Kilgore

National Directory of States

Commerce Department

See Economic Development Administration

Corporations Officers

Department of State, Business Services Division
700 North St., Jackson, MS 39202
Mailing Address: P.O. Box 136, Jackson, MS 39205-0136
(601) 359-1626; Corporations Toll-Free: (800) 256-3494;
Fax: (601) 359-1607

Bureau Dir., Filing Service/Customer Service:
Rita Bingham (601) 359-1633
E-mail: rbingham@sos.state.ms.us

Asst. Secretarys:
James Anderson (UCC and Corporations)
(601) 359-1633; E-mail: janderson@sos.state.ms.us
Bill Thompson (Business Services) (601) 359-1633
E-mail: bthompson@sos.state.ms.us

Criminal History Board

Criminal Information Center
3891 Hwy. 468 W., Pearl, MS 39208
Mailing Address: P.O. Box 958, Jackson, MS 39205
(601) 933-2600; Fax: (601) 933-2676

Economic Development Administration

Development Authority
501 North West St., Jackson, MS 39201
Mailing Address: P.O. Box 849, Jackson, MS 39205
(601) 359-3449; Fax: (601) 359-2832
Internet: www.mississippi.org

Exec. Dir.: Leland R. Speed

Governor's Office

Office of the Governor
Woolfolk Bldg., 15th Fl., 501 N. West St., Jackson, MS 39201
Mailing Address: P.O. Box 139, Jackson, MS 39205-0139
(601) 359-3100, 50; Fax: (601) 359-3741
Internet: http://www.governor.state.ms.us

Governor: Haley Barbour (Republican)
Next election Nov. 2007

Highest State Court

Supreme Court
Gartin Justice Bldg., 450 High St., P.O. Box 245,
Jackson, MS 39201
Clerk's Office: (601) 359-3694; Clerk's Fax: (601) 359-2407
Internet: www.mssc.state.ms.us

Chief Justice: James W. Smith, Jr.

Court Administrator of the Supreme Court:
Stephen Kirchmayr

Clerk of the Supreme Court: Betty Sephton

Insurance Department

Department of Insurance
1001 Woolfolk Bldg., 10th Fl., 501 N.West St., Jackson, MS 39201
Mailing Address: P.O. Box 79, Jackson, MS 39205
(601) 359-3569; Legal Division Fax: (601) 359-2474
Internet: www.doi.state.ms.us/

Commissioner: George Dale
E-mail: commissioner@mid.state.ms.us

Deputy Commissioner: Lee Harrell

Chief Financial Examiner: Debra Vernon

Special Asst. Atty General/Chief Counsel: Mark Haire
E-mail: mark.haire@mid.state.ms.us

Motor Vehicle Office

Mississippi State Tax Commission
1577 Springridge Rd., Raymond, MS 39154
Internet: www.mstc.state.ms.us

Motor Vehicle Licensing, P.O. Box 1140,
Jackson, MS 39215-1140
(601) 923-7100; Fax: (601) 923-7133, 34
E-mail: pholeman@mstc.state.ms.us

Title, P.O. Box 1383, Jackson, MS 39215-1383
(601) 923-7200; Fax: (601) 923-7224

Highway Patrol (Abstracts), P.O. Box 958, Jackson, MS 39205
(601) 987-1271, 74, 75
Fee for obtaining abstract: $7.00

Mississippi Department of Public Safety
Driver Services Bureau
1900 E. Woodrow Wilson, Jackson, MS 39216
Mailing Address: P.O. Box 958, Jackson, MS 39205
(601) 987-1200; Fax: (601) 987-1280;
Abstracts: (601) 987-1271
Internet: www.dps.state.ms.us
*Driver's Licenses; Notarized request or subpoena required
for obtaining abstract*
Fee for obtaining abstract: $7.00

Police

Mississippi Highway Safety Patrol
P.O. Box 958, Jackson, MS 39205
(601) 987-1212; Fax: (601) 987-1419
Internet: www.dps.state.ms.us/dps/dps.nsf/main?OpenForm

Accident Reports: Safety Responsibility Bureau,
P.O. Box 958, Jackson, MS 39205
(601) 987-1255

Commissioner: Rusty Fortenberry
Fee for obtaining accident report: $10.00

Probate, Recording and Notary Certificate Offices

Estate & Wills: Chancery Court Clerks Office, each county
Deeds and Mortgages: Chancery Court Clerks Office, each
county
Notary Certificates: Secretary of State, Notary Dept.
($2.00)

Senators, U.S.

Thad Cochran (Republican)
113 Dirksen Senate Office Bldg., Washington, DC 20510
(202) 224-5054; Fax: (202) 224-9450
Internet: http://cochran.senate.gov

Trent Lott (Republican)
487 Russell Senate Office Bldg., Washington, DC 20510
(202) 224-6253; Fax: (202) 224-2262
E-mail: senatorlott@lott.senate.gov
Internet: http://lott.senate.gov

Secretary of State

Office of the Secretary of State
401 Mississippi St., Jackson, MS 39201
Mailing Address: P.O. Box 136, Jackson, MS 39205-0136
(601) 359-1350; Fax: (601) 359-1499, 359-1607, 359-6700
E-mail: administrator@sos.state.ms.us
Internet: www.sos.state.ms.us

700 North St., Jackson, MS 39201
Business Services: (601) 359-1633
E-mail: customerservice@sos.state.ms.us

Hatten Bldg., Suite 107, 1400 24th Ave., P.O. Box 97,
Gulfport, MS 39501
(228) 864-0254

Secretary of State: Eric Clark
Elected; next election Nov. 2007

Tax Department

State Tax Commission
1577 Springridge Rd., Raymond, MS 39154-9602
Mailing Address: P.O. Box 22828, Jackson, MS 39225
(601) 923-7000;
Ofc. of Audit & Compliance: (601) 923-7305;
Legal Bur.: (601) 923-7412
Internet: www.mstc.state.ms.us

Chairman & Revenue Commissioner: Joseph L. Blount

Victim Compensation Program

Mississippi Crime Victim Compensation Program
1301 Woolfolk Bldg., Suite D, 501 N. West St.,
Jackson, MS 39201
Mailing Address: P.O. Box 267, Jackson, MS 39205
(800) 829-6766, (601) 359-6766; Fax: (601) 359-3262
E-mail: crimevictimcomp@dfa.state.ms.us
Internet: www.dfa.state.ms.us/cvcompx.html

Director: Sandra Morrison
MCA §99-41-1; et seq. (enacted 1990; amended 2002)

Vital Statistics
Vital Records Unit
Public Health Statistics, 571 Stadium Dr., Jackson, MS 39216
Mailing Address: P.O. Box 1700, Jackson, MS 39215-1700
(601) 576-7981, 60; Fax: (601) 576-7505
Internet: www.msdh.state.ms.us
*Births, Deaths, Marriages. Divorce certificates secured from
Chancery Clerk of County in which decree was granted.*
Birth Records: Short Form Birth Certificate—$7.00; Long
Form Birth Certificate—$12.00; Duplicate Copies—$3.00.
Death and Marriage Certificates—$10.00; Duplicate
Copies—$2.00 each. Multi-year search of records—$20.00
per hour.

MISSOURI   *Capital: Jefferson City*
5,595,211 (2000 Census)
State Information: (573) 751-2000
State Web Site: www.state.mo.us

Administrative Office of the Courts
Office of State Courts Administrator
2112 Industrial Dr., P.O. Box 104480,
Jefferson City, MO 65110-4480
(573) 751-4377; Fax: (573) 751-5540
Internet: www.osca.state.mo.us
State Court Administrator: Mike Buenger

Attorney Discipline
Office of Chief Disciplinary Counsel
3335 American Ave., Jefferson City, MO 65109
(573) 635-7400; Fax: (573) 635-2240
Internet: www.mochiefcounsel.org
Chief Disciplinary Counsel: Maridee F. Edwards

Attorney General
Office of the Attorney General
Supreme Court Bldg., 207 W. High St., P.O. Box 899,
Jefferson City, MO 65102
(573) 751-3321; Fax: (573) 751-0774
E-mail: ag@ago.mo.gov; Internet: www.ago.mo.gov

Penntower Office Bldg., Suite 609, 3100 Broadway,
Kansas City, MO 64111
(816) 889-5000; Fax: (816) 889-5006

Springfield State Office Bldg., Suite 1017,
149 Park Central Sq., Springfield, MO 65806
(417) 895-6567; Fax: (417) 895-6382

Wainwright State Office Bldg., 111 N. 7th St., Suite 934,
Saint Louis, MO 63101
Atty. General: Jeremiah W. (Jay) Nixon (Democrat)
Elected; next election Nov. 2008

Banking Department
Division of Finance
Truman State Office Bldg., North Wing, Room 630,
301 W. High St., Jefferson City, MO 65101
Mailing Address: P.O. Box 716, Jefferson City, MO 65102
(573) 751-2545; Fax: (573) 751-9192
E-mail: finance@ded.mo.gov
Internet: www.missouri-finance.org
Commissioner: D. Eric McClure

Bar Admissions
Missouri Board of Law Examiners
407 Jefferson St., Jefferson City, MO 65101
(573) 751-9814; Fax: (573) 751-5335
E-mail: mble@osca.state.mo.us; Internet: www.mble.org
Admission on motion with five of the last ten years in
practice in Reciprocal Jurisdiction or employment as an
In-House Counsel

Bar Association
The Missouri Bar
326 Monroe St., P.O. Box 119, Jefferson City, MO 65102
(573) 635-4128; Fax: (573) 635-2811
E-mail: mobar@mobar.org; Internet: www.mobar.org
Exec. Dir.: Keith A. Birkes
President: Douglas A. Copeland
Integrated Bar
Annual Meeting—Sept. 2006

Client Protection Fund
Client Security Fund
Missouri Bar
326 Monroe, P.O. Box 119, Jefferson City, MO 65102
(573) 635-4128; Fax: (573) 635-2811
Dir. of Programs: Christopher Janku

Commerce Department
See Economic Development Administration

Corporations Officers
Corporations Division
Business Services
600 W. Main St., Jefferson City, MO 65101
Mailing Address: P.O. Box 778, Jefferson City, MO 65102
(573) 751-4153
Internet: http://sos.state.mo.us
Deputy Secretary: Trish Vincent (573) 751-1812
   E-mail: vincent@sosmail.state.ma.us
Corporations Dir.: Katherine Barondeau (573) 751-3200
   E-mail: baronk@sosmail.state.ma.us

Criminal History Board
State Highway Patrol
Criminal Records & Identification Division
1510 E. Elm St., Jefferson City, MO 65101
Mailing Address: P.O. Box 9500,
Jefferson City, MO 65102-9500
(573) 526-6153; Fax: (573) 751-9382
E-mail: mshpcrid@mshp.dps.mo.gov
Internet: www.mshp.dps.mo.gov

Economic Development Administration
Department of Economic Development
Harry S. Truman Bldg., Room 680, 301 W. High St.,
Jefferson City, MO 65109
Mailing Address: P.O. Box 1157, Jefferson City, MO 65102
(573) 751-4962; Fax: (573) 526-7700
E-mail: ecodev@ded.state.mo.us
Internet: www.ded.state.mo.us
Director: Kelvin L. Simmons

Governor's Office
Office of the Governor
State Capitol, Room 216, Jefferson City, MO 65101
(573) 751-3222; Fax: (573) 751-1495
Internet: www.mo.gov
Governor: Matt Blunt (Republican)
Next election Nov. 2008

Highest State Court
Supreme Court
Supreme Court Bldg., 207 W. High St., P.O. Box 150,
Jefferson City, MO 65102
(573) 751-4144; Fax: (573) 751-7514
Internet: www.courts.mo.gov
Chief Justice: Michael A. Wolff
Clerk of the Supreme Court: Thomas F. Simon

Insurance Department
Department of Insurance
301 W. High St., Suite 530, Jefferson City, MO 65102-0690
Mailing Address: P.O. Box 690,
Jefferson City, MO 65102-0690
(573) 751-4126
Internet: www.insurance.mo.gov
Director: W. Dale Finke
Chief Financial Examiner: Kirk Schmidt
Chief Market Conduct Examiner: Mike Woolbright

Motor Vehicle Office
Missouri Dept. of Revenue
Division of Motor Vehicle and Drivers Licensing,
Harry S. Truman State Office Bldg., 301 W. High St.,
P.O. Box 200, Jefferson City, MO 65105-0200
General information: (573) 751-4600;
Record Sales: (573) 751-4300; Fax: (573) 526-7367
E-mail: dlbmail@mail.dor.state.mo.us
Internet: www.dor.state.mo.us/mvdl/drivers/
Fee for obtaining abstract: $1.25 non-certified; $4.00
certified

Police

Missouri State Highway Patrol
P.O. Box 568, Jefferson City, MO 65102
(573) 751-3313; Fax: (573) 751-9921
Internet: www.mshp.dps.mo.gov

Accident Reports: Traffic Division,
Missouri State Highway Patrol, 1510 E. Elm St.,
P.O. Box 568, Jefferson City, MO 65102
(573) 526-6113

Superintendent: Col. Roger D. Stottlemyre
(573) 526-6120
Fee for obtaining accident report: $4.00; send case with
letter of request and self-addressed stamped envelope. Add
$2.00 for certified copy. Must call for fee on Reconstructed
Accident Reports.

Probate, Recording and Notary Certificate Offices

Estate & Wills: Circuit Ct., Probate Div., each county & St.
Louis City
Deeds and Mortgages: Recorders of Deeds each county &
St. Louis City
Notary Certificates: Secretary of State, Commission
Division ($10.00)

Senators, U.S.

Christopher S. (Kit) Bond (Republican)
274 Russell Senate Office Bldg., Washington, DC 20510
(202) 224-5721; Fax: (202) 224-8149
Internet: http://bond.senate.gov

James M. Talent (Republican)
493 Russell Senate Office Bldg., Washington, DC 20510
(202) 224-6154
Internet: http://talent.senate.gov

Secretary of State

Office of the Secretary of State
600 W. Main St., P.O. Box 1767,
Jefferson City, MO 65102-0078
(573) 751-4936; Fax: (573) 526-4903
E-mail: sosmain@sos.mo.gov
Internet: www.sos.mo.gov

513 Kansas City State Office Bldg., 5th Floor,
615 E. 13th St., Kansas City, MO 64106
(816) 889-2925

Wainwright State Office Bldg., Room 234,
111 N. Seventh St., Saint Louis, MO 63101
(314) 340-7490

Springfield State Office Bldg., Room 624,
149 Park Central Sq., Springfield, MO 65806
(417) 895-6330

Secretary of State: Robin Carnahan (Democrat)
Elected; next election Nov. 2008

Tax Department

Department of Revenue
301 W. High St., P.O. Box 311,
Jefferson City, MO 65105-0311
(573) 751-4450; Fax: (573) 751-7150;
Forms: (573) 751-5337, (800) 877-6881;
Field Audit: (573) 751-3736;
Taxation & Collection Div.: (573) 751-3470;
General Counsel's Office: (573) 751-2633
Internet: www.dor.mo.gov

Director: Trish Vincent

Victim Compensation Program

Crime Victims Compensation Program
Div. of Workers Compensation
1700 S. Jefferson, Jefferson City, MO 65102
Mailing Address: P.O. Box 3001,
Jefferson City, MO 65102-3001
(573) 526-6006; Fax: (573) 526-4940
Internet: www.dolir.mo.gov/wc/cv_help.htm
Mo. Rev. Stat. Ch. 595 (1998 Supp.)

Vital Statistics

Bureau of Vital Records
Missouri Department of Health and Senior Services,
930 Wildwood, Jefferson City, MO 65109
Mailing Address: P.O. Box 570,
Jefferson City, MO 65102-0570
(573) 751-6387; Births and Deaths: (573) 751-6387;
Fax: (573) 526-3846
Internet: www.dhss.mo.gov
*Births, Deaths. Marriages filed with the County Recorders,
Divorces with Clerks of the Circuit Courts.*
Births—$15.00 for each five year search; Deaths—$13.00
for each five year search; Additional copies—$10.00.
Expedited service available through VitalChek, for a $9.95
additional surcharge, by calling (877) 817-7363.

MONTANA   *Capital: Helena*

902,195 (2000 Census)
State Information: (406) 444-2511
State Web Site: www.mt.gov

Administrative Office of the Courts

Administrative Office of the Courts
Justice Bldg., Room 315, 215 N. Sanders, Helena, MT 59620
Mailing Address: P.O. Box 203002, Helena, MT 59620-3002
(406) 444-2621; Fax: (406) 444-0834

Court Administrator: Jim Oppedahl

Attorney Discipline

Commission on Practice of the Supreme Court of Montana
Justice Bldg., Room 315, 215 N. Sanders, P.O. Box 203002,
Helena, MT 59620-3002
(406) 444-2608; Fax: (406) 444-0834

Staff: Shauna Ryan

Office of Disciplinary Counsel
301 S. Park, Suite 334, P.O. Box 203007,
Helena, MT 59620-3007
(406) 841-2980; Fax: (406) 841-2984

Disciplinary Counsel: Timothy B. Strauch
E-mail: strauch@state.mt.us

Attorney General

Justice Bldg., 215 N. Sanders Ave., P.O. Box 201401,
Helena, MT 59620-1401
(406) 444-2026; Fax: (406) 444-3549
Internet: www.doj.state.mt.us

Atty. General: Michael McGrath (Democrat)
Elected; next election Nov. 2008

Banking Department

Division of Banking and Financial Institutions
Department of Administration
301 S. Park, Suite 316, P.O. Box 200546,
Helena, MT 59620-0546
(406) 841-2920; Fax: (406) 841-2930
Internet: www.discoveringmontana.com/doa/banking

Commissioner: Annie M. Goodwin
E-mail: agoodwin@state.mt.us

Bar Admissions

Bar Admissions Administrator
7 W. 6th Ave., Suite 2B, P.O. Box 577, Helena, MT 59624
(406) 442-7660; Fax: (406) 442-7763
Internet: www.montanabar.org
15 hours CLE required per year.
Require JD degree from ABA accredited law school. No
admission without exam.

Bar Association

State Bar of Montana
7 W. 6th Ave., Suite 2-B, Helena, MT 59624
Mailing Address: P.O. Box 577, Helena, MT 59624-0577
(406) 442-7660; Fax: (406) 442-7763
E-mail: mailbox@montanabar.org
Internet: www.montanabar.org

Exec. Dir.: Chris Manos
E-mail: cmanos@montanabar.org

President: Keith A. Maristuen
Integrated Bar
Annual Meeting—September, 2005

Chief Medical Examiner

Department of Justice
Division of Forensic Science
2679 Palmer, Missoula, MT 59808
(406) 728-4970; Fax: (406) 549-1067
Chief Medical Examiner: Gary Dale, M.D.

Client Protection Fund

Lawyers' Fund for Client Protection
State Bar of Montana
7 W. Sixth Ave., Suite 2-B, Helena, MT 59624
Mailing Address: P.O. Box 577, Helena, MT 59624-0577
(406) 447-2204; Fax: (406) 442-7763
Internet: www.montanabar.org
Exec. Dir.: Christopher L. Manos

Commerce Department

Montana Department of Commerce
301 S. Park Ave., Helena, MT 59601
Mailing Address: P.O. Box 200501,
Helena, MT 59620-0501
(406) 841-2700; Fax: (406) 841-2701
Internet: www.commerce.state.mt.us

Corporations Officers

Business Services Bureau
State Capitol, Room 260, 1236 E. Sixth Ave.,
Helena, MT 59620
Mailing Address: P.O. Box 202801,
Helena, MT 59620-2801
General Information: (406) 444-2034;
Corporations Section, Name Availabilities, Annual Reports
& Limited Partnerships: (406) 444-3665;
Notaries: (406) 444-5379; UCC: (406) 444-1212;
Fax: (406) 444-3976
Internet: www.sos.state.mt.us
Chief Legal Counsel: Janice Frankino Doggett
    (406) 444-2034
    E-mail: jdoggett@state.mt.us
Deputy: Pat Haffey
    (406) 444-2034
    E-mail: phaffey@state.mt.us
UCC Administrator: Tana Gormely
    (406) 444-2896
    E-mail: tgormely@state.mt.us

Criminal History Board

Department of Justice
Criminal Justice Information Services Bureau
Criminal Records & Identification Services Section,
303 N. Roberts, P.O. Box 201403, Helena, MT 59620-1403
(406) 444-3625; Fax: (406) 444-0689

Economic Development Administration

Business Resources Division
Department of Commerce
301 S. Park Ave., Helena, MT 59601
Mailing Address: P.O. Box 200505,
Helena, MT 59620-0501
(406) 841-2700; Fax: (406) 841-2701
Internet: www.commerce.state.mt.us
Administrator: Andy Poole

Governor's Office

Office of the Governor
State Capitol, 1301 E. 6th Ave., Helena, MT 59620-0801
(406) 444-3111; Fax: (406) 444-5529
Internet: www.state.mt.us/governor
Governor: Brian Schweitzer (Democrat)
Next election Nov. 2008

Highest State Court

Supreme Court
Justice Bldg., Room 323, 215 N. Sanders,
Helena, MT 59620-3003
Mailing Address: P.O. Box 203003,
Helena, MT 59620-3003
(406) 444-3858; Fax: (406) 444-5705
Chief Justice: Karla M. Gray
Clerk of the Supreme Court: Ed Smith

Insurance Department

Department of Insurance
840 Helena Ave., Helena, MT 59601
(406) 444-2040; TDD: (406) 444-3246; Fax: (406) 444-3497
Internet: www.state.mt.us/sao
Commissioner/State Auditor: John Morrison
Chief Examiner: Steve Matthews
Legal Counsel: Patrick Driscoll

Motor Vehicle Office

Montana Motor Vehicles Division
Scott-Hart Bldg., 303 N. Roberts St., Helena, MT 59620
Mailing Address: P.O. Box 201430,
Helena, MT 59620-1430
(406) 444-4536; Fax: (406) 444-1631
E-mail (for Registrations only): mvdtitleinfo@state.mt.us
Internet: www.onlinedmv.com/MT

Title & Registration Bureau, 1032 Buckskin Dr.,
Deer Lodge, MT 59722
(406) 846-6000; Fax: (406) 846-6039
E-mail: mvdtitleinfo@state.mt.us
Fee for obtaining driver license history abstract: $6.50 for
lifetime.; $10.00 for certified record. These are obtained
from the Discovering Montana website at
www.doj.state.mt.us/driving/default.asp

Police

Montana Highway Patrol
2550 Prospect Ave., P.O. Box 201419,
Helena, MT 59620-1419
(406) 444-3780; Accident Reports: (406) 444-3278;
Fax: (406) 444-4169
E-mail: contactdoj@state.mt.us
Internet: www.doj.state.mt.us
Chief: Col. Randy Yaeger
Fee for obtaining accident report: $2.00. At press time a
fee change was anticipated.

Probate, Recording and Notary Certificate Offices

Estate & Wills: County District Courts
Deeds and Mortgages: County Clerks and Recorders
Notary Certificates: Secretary of State,
Notary/Certification Dept., P.O. Box 202801, Helena, MT
59620-2801; for priority courier service use: 1236 Sixth
Ave., Helena, MT 59620 ($10.00)

Senators, U.S.

Max Baucus (Democrat)
511 Hart Senate Office Bldg., Washington, DC 20510
(202) 224-2651
Internet: http://baucus.senate.gov

Conrad Burns (Republican)
187 Dirksen Senate Office Bldg., Washington, DC 20510
(202) 224-2644; Fax: (202) 224-8594
Internet: http://burns.senate.gov

Secretary of State

Office of the Secretary of State
State Capitol, Room 260, Helena, MT 59620-2801
Mailing Address: P.O. Box 202801,
Helena, MT 59620-2801
(406) 444-2034; Fax: (406) 444-3976
Internet: http://sos.state.mt.us
Secretary of State: Brad Johnson (Republican)
Elected; next election Nov. 2008

Tax Department

Department of Revenue
Sam W. Mitchell Bldg., 3rd Floor, 125 N. Roberts St.,
Helena, MT 59601
Mailing Address: P.O. Box 5805, Helena, MT 59604-5805
(406) 444-6900; TDD: (406) 444-2830;
Director's Office Fax: (406) 444-3696;
Business & Misc. Taxes Fax: (406) 444-0629;
Income Taxes Fax: (406) 444-1505
Internet: www.state.mt.us/revenue/
Director: Don Hoffman (Acting)

National Directory
of States

Victim Compensation Program

Crime Victims Compensation Program
Dept. of Justice
1712 Ninth Ave., P.O. Box 201410, Helena, MT 59620-1410
(406) 444-3653; Fax: (406) 444-4303
Mont. Code Ann. §§53-9-101 to 53-9-133

Vital Statistics

Office of Vital Statistics
Dept. of Public Health and Human Services
111 N. Sanders, P.O. Box 4210, Helena, MT 59604-4210
(406) 444-2685; Fax: (406) 444-1803
Internet: www.dphhs.mt.gov
*Births, Deaths from late 1907. Marriages and Divorces
July 1943.*
Certified copies—$12.00. Search fee—$10.00 per five-year
search, $1.00 for each additional year. Express mail
service may be obtained by fax or via Internet at
www.vitalchek.com if charged through American Express,
Discover, VISA or MasterCard, for a $6.00 handling fee
plus Federal Express charges. No requests by telephone;
must have written request.

NEBRASKA   *Capital: Lincoln*

1,711,263 (2000 Census)
State Information: (402) 471-2311
State Web Site: www.state.ne.us

Administrative Office of the Courts

Administrative Office of the Courts
1220 State Capitol, P.O. Box 98910, Lincoln, NE 68509
(402) 471-3730; Fax: (402) 471-2197
Court Administrator: Frank E. Goodroe

Attorney Discipline

Counsel for Discipline of the Nebraska Supreme Court
3808 Normal Blvd., Lincoln, NE 68506
(402) 471-1040; Fax: (402) 471-1014
Counsel for Discipline: Dennis G. Carlson
    E-mail: dcarlson@nsc.state.ne.us

Attorney General

Office of the Attorney General
2115 State Capitol, P.O. Box 98920,
Lincoln, NE 68509-8920
(402) 471-2682; Fax: (402) 471-3297
Internet: www.ago.state.ne.us/
Atty. General: Jon Bruning (Republican)
Elected; next election Nov. 2006

Banking Department

Department of Banking & Finance
1230 O St., Suite 400, Lincoln, NE 68508
Mailing Address: P.O. Box 95006, Lincoln, NE 68509-5006
(402) 471-2171; Fax: (402) 471-3062
Internet: www.ndbf.org
Director: John Munn

Bar Admissions

Nebraska State Bar Commission
635 S. 14th St., Suite 200, Lincoln, NE 68508
Mailing Address: P.O. Box 81809, Lincoln, NE 68501-1809
(402) 475-7091; Fax: (402) 475-7098
E-mail: ns21448@alltel.net
Internet: www.nebar.com/memberinfo/nsbc/index.htm
No CLE required.
Admission on motion permitted.

Bar Association

Nebraska State Bar Assn.
635 S. 14th St., 2nd Floor, Lincoln, NE 68508
Mailing Address: P.O. Box 81809, Lincoln, NE 68501
(402) 475-7091; Fax: (402) 475-7098
Internet: www.nebar.com
Exec. Dir.: Jane L. Schoenike
    E-mail: jschoenike@nebar.com
President: John O. Sennett
Integrated Bar
Annual Meeting—October, 2005

Client Protection Fund

Client Assistance Fund
Nebraska State Bar Association
635 S. 14th St., 2nd Floor, P.O. Box 81809,
Lincoln, NE 68501-1809
(402) 475-7091; Fax: (402) 475-7098
Internet: www.nebar.com
Exec. Dir.: Jane L. Schoenike

Commerce Department

See Economic Development Administration

Corporations Officers

Business Services Division
1305 State Capitol, P.O. Box 95104, Lincoln, NE 68509
General Information: (402) 471-4070;
Corporations Section: (402) 471-4079;
Notaries: (402) 471-2558; UCC: (402) 471-4080;
Fax (Corporations): (402) 471-3666;
Fax (UCC & Notary): (402) 471-4429
Dir., Business Services Div.: Debbie Pester
    (402) 471-4080; E-mail: sos07@nol.org

Criminal History Board

Criminal Justice Information Systems
Criminal Records & Identification Division
1600 Nebraska Hwy. 2, Lincoln, NE 68502
Mailing Address: P.O. Box 94907, Lincoln, NE 68509-4907
(402) 479-4099; Fax: (402) 479-4054

Economic Development Administration

Department of Economic Development
301 Centennial Mall S., P.O. Box 94666,
Lincoln, NE 68509-4666
(402) 471-3111, (800) 426-6505; Fax: (402) 471-3778
Internet: www.neded.org
Director: Richard Baier

Governor's Office

Office of the Governor
State Capitol, Room 2316, 2nd Floor, Lincoln, NE 68509
Mailing Address: P.O. Box 94848, Lincoln, NE 68509-4848
(402) 471-2244; Fax: (402) 471-6031
Internet: http://gov.nol.org
Governor: David Heineman (Republican)
    Appointed to fill vacancy; Next election Nov. 2006

Highest State Court

Supreme Court
2413 State Capitol, 1445 K St., P.O. Box 98910,
Lincoln, NE 68509-8910
(402) 471-3731; Fax: (402) 471-3480
Internet: www.nebraskacourt.com
Chief Justice: John V. Hendry
Clerk of the Supreme Court: Lanet S. Asmussen

Insurance Department

Department of Insurance
Office of the Insurance Director
Terminal Bldg., Suite 400, 941 O St., Lincoln, NE 68508
(402) 471-2201; TDD: (800) 833-7352; Fax: (402) 471-4610
Internet: www.nol.org/home/NDOI/
Director: L. Tim Wagner
Chief Examiner: David L. Krumm

Motor Vehicle Office

Nebraska Department of Motor Vehicles
Driver and Vehicle Records Division
301 Centennial Mall South, P.O. Box 94789,
Lincoln, NE 68509-4789
(402) 471-3918; Fax: (402) 471-8694
E-mail: dvrweb@dmv.state.ne.us
Internet: www.dmv.state.ne.us/dvr/drvrec/drivrecreq.html

For Abstracts write: Driver Records,
Nebraska Department of Motor Vehicles, P.O. Box 94789,
Lincoln, NE 68509-4789
Fee for obtaining abstract: $3.00; include SASE. Must use
DMV prescribed "Application for Copy of Driving Record"
form when requesting an abstract. Call 402-471-3918 to
request an application form, or download at:
www.dmv.state.ne.us/dvr/drvrec/drivrecreq.html

Police

Nebraska State Patrol
1600 Nebraska Highway 2, Lincoln, NE 68502
Mailing Address: P.O. Box 94907, Lincoln, NE 68509
(402) 471-4545; Fax: (402) 479-4002
Internet: www.nsp.state.ne.us

Highway Safety (Accident Reports), Department of Roads,
1500 Nebraska Hwy. 2, P.O. Box 94669, Lincoln, NE 68509
(402) 479-4645
Superintendent: Col. Tom Nesbitt (402) 479-4931
Fee for obtaining accident report: $6.00

Probate, Recording and Notary Certificate Offices

Estate & Wills: County Court Clerks
Deeds and Mortgages: County Register of Deeds Offices
Notary Certificates: Secretary of State, Notary Division
(Authentication or Apostille $10.00)

Senators, U.S.

Charles (Chuck) Hagel (Republican)
248 Russell Senate Office Bldg., Washington, DC 20510
(202) 224-4224; Fax: (202) 224-5213
Internet: http://hagel.senate.gov
E. Benjamin Nelson (Democrat)
720 Hart Senate Office Bldg., Washington, DC 20510
(202) 224-6551
Internet: http://bennelson.senate.gov

Secretary of State

Office of the Secretary of State
2300 State Capitol, Suite 2300, 1445 K St.,
P.O. Box 94608, Lincoln, NE 68509-4608
(402) 471-2554; Fax: (402) 471-3237
E-mail: sos04@nol.org, katie.clark@sos.ne.gov
Internet: www.sos.state.ne.us, www.sos.state.ne.us
Secretary of State: John A. Gale (Republican)
  John A. Gale (Republican)
Elected; next election Nov. 2006

Tax Department

Department of Revenue
301 Centennial Mall S., Lincoln, NE 68509-4818
Mailing Address: P.O. Box 94818, Lincoln, NE 68509-4818
(402) 471-2971; Taxpayer Assistance: (402) 471-5729;
Toll Free in Nebraska & Iowa: (800) 742-7474;
Forms: (402) 471-5601; Federal Forms: (800) 626-7899;
Finance & Management Services: (402) 471-5890;
Audit Services: (402) 471-5751;
Legal Services: (402) 471-5915;
Operations & Taxpayer Services: (402) 471-5805;
Motor Fuels: (402) 471-5678;
Taxpayer Assistance—Motor Fuels: (800) 554-3835
Internet: www.revenue.state.ne.us
Tax Commissioner: Mary Jane Egr Edson

Victim Compensation Program

Crime Victims Reparations Committee
301 Centennial Mall South, P.O. Box 94946,
Lincoln, NE 68509-4946
(402) 471-2828; Fax: (402) 471-2837
Neb. Rev. Stat. §§81-1801 to 81-1850 (1992)

Vital Statistics

Vital Statistics Section
Health and Human Services System
State Office Bldg., 3rd Floor, 301 Centennial Mall S.,
Lincoln, NE 68509-5007
Mailing Address: P.O. Box 95065, Lincoln, NE 68509-5065
(402) 471-2871; Fax: (402) 471-8238
E-mail: vitalrecords@hhss.ne.gov
Internet: www.hhs.state.ne.us
Births and Deaths from 1904. Marriages and Divorces from 1909.
File search—Birth—$8.00; Death, Marriage and
Divorce—$7.00 (includes copy if found). Credit card
service available for next day Federal Express service in
emergency situations; Birth—$31.00 for first copy; Death,
Marriage and Divorce—$30.00 for first copy. If ordered by
3:00 P.M. Central Time, certificate is mailed the same day.

NEVADA   *Capital: Carson City*

1,998,257 (2000 Census)
State Information: (702) 687-5000
State Web Site: www.state.nv.us

Administrative Office of the Courts

Administrative Office of the Courts
Supreme Court Bldg., Capitol Complex, Suite 250,
201 S. Carson St., Carson City, NV 89701-4702
(775) 684-1700; Fax: (775) 684-1723
Internet: www.nvsupremecourt.us
Director: Ronald R. Titus

Attorney Discipline

State Bar of Nevada Ethics Department
600 E. Charleston Blvd., Las Vegas, NV 89104
(702) 382-2200; Fax: (702) 382-8747
Internet: www.nvbar.org
Bar Counsel: Rob W. Bare

Attorney General

Office of the Attorney General
100 N. Carson St., Carson City, NV 89701-4717
(775) 684-1100; Fax: (775) 684-1108
Internet: www.ag.state.nv.us

Las Vegas Office, 555 E. Washington Ave., Suite 3900,
Las Vegas, NV 89101
(702) 486-3420

Reno Office, 5420 Kietzke Lane, Suite 202,
Reno, NV 89511
(775) 688-1818
Atty. General: Brian Sandoval (Republican)
Elected; next election Nov. 2006

Banking Department

Financial Institutions Division
406 E. Second St., Suite 3, Carson City, NV 89701-4758
(775) 684-1830; Fax: (775) 684-1845
Internet: www.fid.state.nv.us

2501 E. Sahara Ave., Suite 300, Las Vegas, NV 89104
(702) 486-4120
Commissioner: Carol J. Tidd (Las Vegas Office)

Bar Association

State Bar of Nevada
600 E. Charleston Blvd., Las Vegas, NV 89104
(702) 382-2200; Fax: (702) 385-2878
Internet: www.nvbar.org
Exec. Dir.: Allen Kimbrough
President: Ann Price McCarthy
Integrated Bar
Annual Meeting—June, 2005

Client Protection Fund

Clients' Security Fund
State Bar of Nevada
600 E. Charleston Blvd., Las Vegas, NV 89104
(800) 254-2797, (702) 382-2200;
Fax: (702) 385-2878, (888) 660-6767
E-mail: georgiat@nvbar.org
Internet: www.nvbar.org
Exec. Dir.: Allen Kimbrough
Coordinator, Fee Dispute & Clients' Security Fund:
  Georgia Taylor

Commerce Department

See Economic Development Administration

Corporations Officers

Department of State
Corporations Division
202 N. Carson St., Carson City, NV 89701-4201
(775) 684-5708; Fax: (775) 684-5725;
Fax Corporate Copies & Certification: (775) 684-5645
Internet: www.sos.state.nv.us
Deputy Secretary for Commercial Recordings:
  Scott W. Anderson
    E-mail: scotta@sosmail.state.nv.us

Criminal History Board

Records Division
555 Wright Way, Carson City, NV 89711
(775) 684-4590; Fax: (775) 684-4899
Internet: www.dmvnv.com

Economic Development Administration

Commission on Economic Development
108 E. Proctor St., Carson City, NV 89701-4240
(775) 687-4325, (800) 336-1600; Fax: (775) 687-4450
Internet: www.expand2Nevada.com

555 E. Washington, Suite 5400, Las Vegas, NV 89101
(702) 486-2700; Fax: (702) 486-2701
Chair: Lorraine T. Hunt (Lt. Governor)

Governor's Office

Office of the Governor
Capitol Complex, 101 N. Carson St.,
Carson City, NV 89701
(775) 684-5670; Fax: (775) 684-5683
Internet: http://gov.state.nv.us

444 N. Capitol St. N.W., Suite 209, Washington, DC 20001
(202) 624-5405; Fax: (202) 624-8181

555 E. Washington St., Suite 5100, Las Vegas, NV 89101
(702) 486-2500; Fax: (702) 486-2505
Governor: Kenny C. Guinn (Republican)
Next election Nov. 2006

Highest State Court

Supreme Court of Nevada
Supreme Court Bldg., 201 S. Carson St.,
Carson City, NV 89701-4702
(775) 684-1600
Internet: www.nvsupremecourt.us
Chief Justice: Nancy A. Becker
Clerk of the Supreme Court: Janette Bloom

Insurance Department

Division of Insurance
788 Fairview Dr., No. 300, Carson City, NV 89701-5491
(775) 687-4270; Fax: (775) 687-3937
Internet: http://doi.state.nv.us

2501 E. Sahara Ave., Suite 302, Las Vegas, NV 89104
(702) 486-4009; Fax: (702) 486-4007
Commissioner: Alice A. Molasky-Arman

Motor Vehicle Office

Nevada Department of Motor Vehicles
Records Section, 555 Wright Way,
Carson City, NV 89711-0250
From Rural Nevada/Out-of-State: (877) 368-7828;
Fax: (775) 684-4899; Director: (775) 684-4549;
Records Dept.: (775) 684-4590;
From Las Vegas Area: (702) 486-4368;
From Reno/Sparks/Carson City: (775) 684-4590
E-mail: info@dmv.state.nv.us
Internet: www.dmvnv.com
Fee for obtaining abstract: $7.00

Police

Nevada Highway Patrol
555 Wright Way, Carson City, NV 89711-0525
(775) 687-5300; Fax: (775) 684-4879
Internet: www.ps.state.nv.us/nhp/

Accident Reports, 2601 E. Sahara Ave.,
Las Vegas, NV 89158
(702) 486-4100; Fax: (702) 486-4297

Accident Reports, 357 Hammill Lane, Reno, NV 89511
(775) 688-2500; Fax: (775) 688-2772

Accident Reports, 3920 E. Idaho St., Elko, NV 89801
(775) 753-1111; Fax: (775) 753-7790
Chief: David S. Hosmer
    E-mail: lgillespie@dps.state.nv.us
Fee for obtaining accident report: $3.50 first 10 pages. Any record over 3 yrs. must be obtained from Carson City Office.

Probate, Recording and Notary Certificate Offices

Estate & Wills: County Clerks Offices or Carson City Clerk
Deeds and Mortgages: County Recorders Office or Carson City Recorder
Notary Certificates: Secretary of State, Notary Division;
204 N. Carson St., Carson City, NV 89701-4299 ($20.00)

Senators, U.S.

John Ensign (Republican)
364 Russell Senate Office Bldg., Washington, DC 20510
(202) 224-6244; Internet: http://ensign.senate.gov
Harry M. Reid (Democrat)
528 Hart Senate Office Bldg., Washington, DC 20510
(202) 224-3542; Fax: (202) 224-7327
Internet: http://reid.senate.gov

Secretary of State

Office of the Secretary of State
Capitol Bldg., Suite 3, 101 N. Carson St.,
Carson City, NV 89701-3714
(775) 684-5708; Fax: (775) 684-5725
E-mail: sosmail@govmail.state.nv.us
Internet: www.sos.state.nv.us

555 E. Washington Ave., 4th Floor, Las Vegas, NV 89101
(702) 486-2880; Fax: (702) 486-2888
Secretary of State: Dean Heller (Republican)
Elected; next election Nov. 2006

Tax Department

Department of Taxation
1550 E. College Pkwy., Suite 115, Carson City, NV 89706
(775) 684-2000; Fax: (775) 684-2020
Internet: http://tax.state.nv.us

555 E.Wasington St., Suite 1300, Las Vegas, NV 89101
(702) 486-2300; Fax: (702) 486-2373

Bldg. L, Suite 235, 4600 Kietzke Lane, Reno, NV 89502
(775) 688-1295; Fax: (775) 688-1303
Exec. Dir.: Charles E. Chinnock

Victim Compensation Program

Victims of Crime Program
2200 N. Rancho Dr., Suite 130, Las Vegas, NV 89102-4413
(702) 486-2740; Fax: (702) 486-2825
E-mail: tbedford@hearings.state.nv.us

4600 Kietzke L., Bldg. I, Room 205, Reno, NV 89502
(775) 688-2900; Fax: (775) 688-2912
Nev. Rev. Stat. §§217.010 to 217.480 (enacted 1969, amended 1981, 1983, 1985, 1987, 1989 & 1995)

Vital Statistics

Department of Human Resources
Division of Health
Office of Vital Records, 505 E. King St., Room 102,
Carson City, NV 89701-4749
(775) 684-4242; Fax: (775) 684-4156
Internet: www.vitalrec.com/nv.html
Births & Death records available from July 1, 1911-present. Marriages and Divorces—filed in each county; Index of Marriages, Divorces and Annulments—June 1, 1968-present.
Certified copies—Birth—$13.00; Death—$10.00. For marriage and divorce verification of records or search of index—$8.00. Certified birth card (short form birth certificate)—$13.00.

NEW HAMPSHIRE   *Capital: Concord*

1,235,786 (2000 Census)
State Information: (603) 271-1110
State Web Site: www.state.nh.us

Administrative Office of the Courts

Administrative Office of the Courts
Two Noble Dr., Concord, NH 03301
(603) 271-2521; Fax: (603) 271-3977
E-mail: aoc@courts.state.nh.us
Internet: www.courts.state.nh.us
Director: Donald D. Goodnow

Attorney Discipline

New Hampshire Supreme Court
Attorney Discipline Office
4 Park St., Suite 304, Concord, NH 03301
(603) 224-5828; Fax: (603) 228-9511
General Counsel: James L. DeHart
Deputy General Counsel: Thomas V. Trevethick
Asst. General Counsel: Janet F. DeVito
Disciplinary Counsel: Landya B. McCafferty

Attorney General

Office of the Attorney General
33 Capitol St., Concord, NH 03301-6397
(603) 271-3658; Fax: (603) 271-2110
Internet: www.doj.nh.gov
Atty. General: Kelly Ayotte (Republican)
Appointed

Banking Department

Banking Department
64B Old Suncook Rd., Concord, NH 03301
(603) 271-3561; Fax: (603) 271-1090
Internet: www.state.nh.us/banking
Commissioner: Peter C. Hildreth

Bar Admissions

Supreme Court of New Hampshire
Frank R. Kenison Bldg., 1 Noble Dr., Concord, NH 03301
(603) 271-2646; Fax: (603) 271-6630
Internet: www.courts.nh.us.
12 hours CLE required per year. Reciprocal admission
after 5 years of practice in Reciprocal Jurisdiction. Special
rule applicable to Vermont and Maine lawyers after 3
years of practice.

Bar Association

New Hampshire Bar Assn.
112 Pleasant St., Concord, NH 03301
(603) 224-6942; Fax: (603) 224-2910
Internet: www.nhbar.org
Exec. Dir.: Jeannine L. McCoy
President: Richard Y. Uchida
Integrated Bar
Annual meeting—June, 2006

Chief Medical Examiner

Office of Chief Medical Examiner
246 Pleasant St., Suite 218, Concord, NH 03301
(603) 271-1235; Fax: (603) 271-6308
Chief Medical Examiner: Dr. Thomas A. Andrew
  E-mail: tandrew@doj.state.nh.us

Client Protection Fund

Public Protection Fund
New Hampshire Bar Association
112 Pleasant St., Concord, NH 03301-2947
(603) 224-6942; Fax: (603) 224-2910
Internet: www.nhbar.org
Exec. Dir.: Jeannine L. McCoy
Staff Liaison: Tom Manter
  E-mail: tmanter@nhbar.org

Commerce Department

See Economic Development Administration

Corporations Officers

Department of State
State House, Room 204, 107 N. Main St.,
Concord, NH 03301-4989
Corporations Section: (603) 271-3244;
Corporate Information & Name Availabilities:
(603) 271-3246; UCC: (603) 271-3276; Fax: (603) 271-6316
Deputy Secretary: David Scanlan (603) 271-3242
  E-mail: dscanlan@sos.state.nh.us
Supvr., Corporate Div.: Jane Northcott (603) 271-3278
  E-mail: jnorthcott@sos.state.nh.us
Supvr., UCC Div.: Joan Stewartson (603) 271-3276
  E-mail: jstewartson@sos.state.nh.us
Business Analyst: Debra A. Ulmanis (603) 271-3234
  E-mail: dulmanis@sos.state.nh.us

Criminal History Board

State Police
Criminal Records Unit, James H. Hayes Safety Bldg.,
33 Hazen Dr., Concord, NH 03305
(603) 271-2538; Fax: (603) 271-2339

Economic Development Administration

Department of Resources & Economic Development
Division of Economic Development
172 Pembroke Rd., P.O. Box 1856,
Concord, NH 03302-1856
(603) 271-2341; Fax: (603) 271-6784
Internet: www.nheconomy.com
Director: Stuart Arnett

Governor's Office

Office of the Governor
State House, 107 N. Main St., Concord, NH 03301-4990
(603) 271-2121; Fax: (603) 271-8788
Internet: http://www.state.nh.us/governor/
Governor: John Lynch (Democrat)
Next election Nov. 2006

Highest State Court

Supreme Court
Frank R. Kenison Bldg., 1 Noble Dr.,
Concord, NH 03301-6160
(603) 271-2646; Fax: (603) 271-6630
Internet: www.courts.state.nh.us
Chief Justice: John T. Broderick, Jr.
Clerk of the Supreme Court: Eileen Fox

Insurance Department

Department of Insurance
21 S. Fruit St., Suite 14, Concord, NH 03301
(603) 271-2261; Fax: (603) 271-1406
E-mail: requests@ins.nh.gov
Internet: www.nh.gov/insurance
Commissioner: Roger A. Sevigny, SCLA
Deputy Commissioner: Alexander K. Feldvebel
Director, Examination Div.pd: Thomas S. Burke, CPA
Director of Operations:
  Barbara D. Richardson, MBA, JD
Legal Counsel: James Zemp, JD, MBA, CPCU

Motor Vehicle Office

New Hampshire Division of Motor Vehicles
Department of Safety, 33 Hazen Dr.,
Concord, NH 03305-0002
Mailing Address:
Driver's Records write: D.OS., D.M.V., FR Driving Records,
23 Haven Dr., Concord, NH 03305
(603) 271-2484; Abstracts: (603) 271-2514;
Driver Records: (603) 271-2322;
Registration: (603) 271-2251; Repro: (603) 271-2128;
Title: (603) 271-3111; Fax: (603) 271-1061
Internet: http://www.state.nh.us/dmv/
Fee for obtaining abstract: $10.00 certified copy, driver
record; $8.00 non-certified driver record; $8.00 for
insurance copy of motor vehicle record.

Police

New Hampshire State Police
33 Hazen Dr., Concord, NH 03305
(603) 271-3636; Fax: (603) 271-2527

Department of Motor Vehicles Accident Section,
23 Hazen Dr., Concord, NH 03305
Director: Col. Frederick H. Booth
  (603) 271-2450
Fee for obtaining accident report: $1.00 per page

Probate, Recording and Notary Certificate Offices

Estate & Wills: County Register of Probate
Deeds and Mortgages: County Register of Deeds
Notary Certificates: Secretary of State ($10.00)

National Directory
of States

Senators, U.S.

Judd Gregg (Republican)
393 Russell Senate Office Bldg., Washington, DC 20510
(202) 224-3324; Fax: (202) 224-4952
E-mail: mailbox@gregg.senate.gov
Internet: http://gregg.senate.gov

John E. Sununu (Republican)
111 Russell Senate Office Bldg., Washington, DC 20510
(202) 224-2841
Internet: http://sununu.senate.gov

Secretary of State

State House, Rm. 204, 107 N. Main St., Concord, NH 03301-4989
Elections: (603) 271-3242; Elections Fax: (603) 271-6316;
Corporations: (603) 271-3244;
Corp. Records: (603) 271-3246; Securities: (603) 271-1463
E-mail: elections@sos.state.nh.us,
E-mail (for business questions): corporate@sos.state.nh.us
Internet: www.sos.nh.gov

Secretary of State: William M. Gardner
Elected by Legislature; next election Dec. 2006

Tax Department

Department of Revenue Administration
45 Chenell Dr., Concord, NH 03301
Taxpayer Assistance: (603) 271-2191;
Audit Division: (603) 271-3400; Fax: (603) 271-6146;
Collection: (603) 271-3701; Appeals: (603) 271-1304;
Taxpayer Advocate: (603) 271-8481
Internet: www.revenue.nh.gov

Administrative Hearings, 57 Regional Dr., Concord, NH 03301
(603) 271-1304

Commissioner: G. Philip Blatsos

Victim Compensation Program

Victims' Assistance Commission
Department of Justice
33 Capitol St., Concord, NH 03301-6397
(603) 271-1284; In-State only: (800) 300-4500;
TDD: (800) 735-2964
Internet: www.doj.nh.gov/victim/compensation.html

Victim's Compensation Coordinator:
  Bette Jane Riordan
RSA 21-M:8-g to 21-M:8-j

Vital Statistics

Department of Health and Human Services
Division of Vital Records Administration
Registration/Certification, 29 Hazen Dr.,
Concord, NH 03301-6527
(603) 271-4650, (800) 852-3345, Ext. 4651;
TDD: (800) 735-2964; Fax: (603) 271-3447
Internet: www.dhhs.state.nh.us
Births, Deaths, Marriages, Divorces from 1640.
Search fee—$12.00, which includes certified copy if record
is on file. Additional copies issued at the same
time—$8.00. Payment by credit card is an additional
$6.00. Expedited service is an additional $25.00.

NEW JERSEY   *Capital: Trenton*

8,414,350 (2000 Census)
State Information: (609) 292-2121
State Web Site: www.state.nj.us

Administrative Office of the Courts

Administrative Office of the Courts
Richard J. Hughes Justice Complex, 7th Floor,
25 W. Market St., P.O. Box 037, Trenton, NJ 08625
(609) 984-0275; Fax: (609) 292-3320
Internet: www.njcourtsonline.com

Administrative Dir. of the Courts:
  Philip S. Carchman, J.A.D. (Acting)

Attorney Discipline

Supreme Court of New Jersey Office of Attorney Ethics
Mountainview Office Park, 840 Bear Tavern Rd.,
West Trenton, NJ 08628
Mailing Address: P.O. Box 963, Trenton, NJ 08625
(609) 530-4008, (800) 406-8594
Internet: www.judiciary.state.nj.us/oae/index.htm
Director: David E. Johnson, Jr.

Attorney General

Office of the Attorney General
Hughes Justice Complex, 25 Market St., P.O. Box 080,
Trenton, NJ 08625-0080
(609) 292-4925; Fax: (609) 292-3508
Internet: www.state.nj.us/lps/

Atty. General: Peter Harvey
Appointed

Banking Department

Department of Banking and Insurance
20 W. State St., Trenton, NJ 08625
Mailing Address: P.O. Box 325, Trenton, NJ 08625-0325
(609) 292-5360; Fax: (609) 984-5273
Internet: www.njdobi.org

Commissioner: Donald Bryan (Acting)
Dir., Division of Banking: H. Robert Tillman

Bar Admissions

New Jersey Board of Bar Examiners
Hughes Justice Complex, 8th Floor, North Wing,
25 W. Market St., Trenton, NJ 08625
Mailing Address: P.O. Box 973, Trenton, NJ 08625-0973
(609) 984-2111; Fax: (609) 984-6859
Internet: www.njbarexams.org
CLE skills courses required during first three years of
admission; 30 hours during first six months, 8 hours each
during second and third years.
No admission without exam.

Bar Association

New Jersey State Bar Assn.
N.J. Law Center, One Constitution Sq.,
New Brunswick, NJ 08901-1520
(732) 249-5000; Fax: (732) 249-2815
Internet: www.njsba.com

Exec. Dir.: Harold L. Rubenstein
President: Stuart A. Hoberman
Non-Integrated Bar
Annual Meeting—May, 2005

Chief Medical Examiner

Office of the State Medical Examiner
3131 Princeton Pike, Lawrenceville, NJ 08648
Mailing Address: P.O. Box 094, Trenton, NJ 08625-0094
(609) 896-8900; Fax: (609) 896-8697

State Medical Examiner: John Krolikowski, M.D.
  (Acting)

Client Protection Fund

N.J. Lawyers' Fund for Client Protection
Hughes Justice Complex, 25 W. Market St., P.O. Box 961,
Trenton, NJ 08625-0961
Claims: (609) 984-7179; Fax: (609) 394-3637
Internet: www.judiciary.state.nj.us/cpf/index.htm
Dir. and Counsel: Kenneth J. Bossong

Commerce Department

N.J. Commerce and Economic Growth Commission
20 W. State St., P.O. Box 820, Trenton, NJ 08625-0839
(609) 777-0885; Fax: (609) 777-4097
Internet: www.newjerseycommerce.org

Corporations Officers

Department of Treasury
Business Services Branch
225 West State St., 3rd Floor, P.O. Box 308,
Trenton, NJ 08625-0308
(609) 292-9292
Internet: www.state.nj.us/njbgs

Chief, Div. of Revenue: Andrew Pantelides
  (609) 633-8294; Fax: (609) 984-6832
  E-mail: apanteli@sos.state.us

Asst. Dir.: James Fruscione
  (609) 984-8467; Fax: (609) 777-3535
  E-mail: info@revenue.state.nj.us

Criminal History Board

Identification and Information Technology Section
State Police, River Rd., West Trenton, NJ 08628-0068
(609) 882-2000, Ext. 2368; Fax: (609) 530-4856

Economic Development Administration

Economic Development Authority
36 W. State St., P.O. Box 990, Trenton, NJ 08625-0990
(609) 292-1800; Fax: (609) 984-4301
E-mail: njeda@njeda.com
Internet: www.njeda.com
C.E.O.: Caren S. Franzini

Governor's Office

Office of the Governor
State House, 125 W. State St., P.O. Box 001,
Trenton, NJ 08625-0001
(609) 292-6000; Fax: (609) 292-3454
Internet: http://www.state.nj.us/governor/

444 N. Capitol St. N.W., Suite 201, Washington, DC 20001
(202) 638-0631; Fax: (202) 638-2296

State Office Bldg., 101 Hadden Ave., Camden, NJ 08102
(856) 614-3200; Fax: (856) 614-3210

153 Halsey St., Newark, NJ 07102
(973) 648-2640; Fax: (973) 648-3939
Governor: Richard J. Codey (Acting)
Next election Nov. 2005

Highest State Court

Supreme Court
Richard J. Hughes Justice Complex, 25 W. Market St.,
Trenton, NJ 08625
Mailing Address: Hughes Justice Complex, P.O. Box 970,
Trenton, NJ 08625-0970
(609) 292-4837
Chief Justice: Deborah T. Poritz
Clerk of the Supreme Court: Stephen W. Townsend

Insurance Department

Department of Banking & Insurance
20 W. State St., P.O. Box 325, Trenton, NJ 08625-0325
(609) 292-5360, 341-2511;
Commissioner's Fax: (609) 984-5273
Internet: www.njdobi.org
Asst. Commissioner, Office of Solvency Regulation:
Raymond K. Conover
Commissioner: Holly Bakke

Motor Vehicle Office

New Jersey Motor Vehicles Commission
225 E. State St., P.O. Box 160, Trenton, NJ 08666
Suspension Unit: (609) 292-7500;
General Information: (609) 292-6500
Internet: www.state.nj.us/mvc

Abstract Unit, 225 E. State St., P.O. Box 142, Trenton, NJ 08666
(609) 292-6100
Fee for obtaining abstract: $10.00

Police

New Jersey Division of State Police
River Rd., West Trenton, NJ 08628
Mailing Address: P.O. Box 7068,
West Trenton, NJ 08628-0068
(609) 882-2000
Internet: www.njsp.org

Criminal Justice Records Bureau, Bldg. 15, River Rd.,
P.O. Box 7068, West Trenton, NJ 08628
Superintendent: Joseph R. (Rick) Fuentes
Fee for obtaining certified accident report: $10.00 (1-3
pages); each additional page $2.00; over 6 pages no
additional cost

Probate, Recording and Notary Certificate Offices

Estate & Wills: County Surrogate's Offices & Superior
Court
Deeds and Mortgages: County Clerks or Registers Office
Notary Certificates: Dept. of Treasury, Div. of Revenue,
Notary Unit, P.O. Box 452, Trenton, NJ 08625; via priority
courier service use: 225 W. State St., 3rd Fl., Trenton, NJ
08608-1001 ($25.00*) (609) 292-9292
*except for adoption purposes—then fee for certification or
Apostille is $5*

Senators, U.S.

Jon S. Corzine (Democrat)
502 Hart Senate Office Bldg., Washington, DC 20510
(202) 224-4744
Internet: http://corzine.senate.gov
Frank R. Lautenberg (Democrat)
324 Hart Senate Office Bldg., Washington, DC 20510
(202) 224-3224; Fax: (202) 228-4054
Internet: http://lautenberg.senate.gov

Secretary of State

Office of the Secretary of State
Department of State, State House, 125 W. State St.,
Trenton, NJ 08625
Mailing Address: P.O. Box 300, Trenton, NJ 08625-0300
(609) 777-2581; Fax: (609) 777-1764
Internet: www.state.nj.us/state/
Secretary of State: Regena L. Thomas (Democrat)
(609) 777-2581
Appointed

Tax Department

Division of Taxation
50 Barrack St., P.O. Box 269, Trenton, NJ 08695-0269
(800) 323-4400, (609) 826-4400;
Taxpayer Hotline: (609) 292-6400
E-mail: taxation@tax.state.nj.us
Internet: www.state.nj.us/treasury/taxation
Director: Robert K. Thompson

Victim Compensation Program

Victims of Crime Compensation Board
50 Park Pl., 6th Floor, Newark, NJ 07102
(973) 648-2107; Fax: (973) 648-3937, 648-7031
Internet: www.njvictims.org

140 E. Front St., 3rd Floor, Trenton, NJ 08625
(609) 292-8446
N.J. Stat. Ann. §52:4B-1 et seq. (West) (1983 Supp.)

Vital Statistics

Superior Court Records Center
Bldg. 2, 1st Floor, Jersey & Tremont Sts., P.O. Box 967,
Trenton, NJ 08625-0967
(609) 777-0092; Fax: (609) 777-0094
*Divorces—1900-1995—Depending upon the county where
divorce took place. Fax requests are only processed for
attorneys or companies that have an account with Superior
Court.*
Certified copy—$10.00.

Vital Statistics
Office of the State Registrar
State Dept. of Health and Senior Services,
John Fitch Plaza, Room 504, Health & Agricultural Bldg.,
P.O. Box 370, Trenton, NJ 08625-0370
(609) 292-4087; Fax: (609) 777-1337
Internet: www.state.nj.us/health/vital/vital.htm
*Births, Deaths, Marriages. Same day service for walk-ins.
Expedited service available through a company called Vital
Chek, for a $10.95 additional surcharge, plus $15.75 for
express delivery if desired (billing through Visa,
MasterCard or Discover). Order by phone, (877) 622-7549,
or via the Internet at www.vitalchek.com.*
When year of event is supplied search fee is $4.00 for one
name. Search fee includes certified copy if found.
Additional copies ordered at same time $2.00 per copy.

NEW MEXICO   *Capital: Santa Fe*

1,819,046 (2000 Census)
State Information: (505) 827-4011
State Web Site: www.sos.state.nm.us

Administrative Office of the Courts

Administrative Office of the Courts
Supreme Court Bldg., Room 25, 237 Don Gaspar St.,
Santa Fe, NM 87504-2178
(505) 827-4800; Fax: (505) 827-4824
Internet: www.nmcourts.com
Administrator: Gina M. Maestas

Attorney Discipline

Disciplinary Board of the Supreme Court of New Mexico
400 Gold Ave. S.W., Suite 800, P.O. Box 1809,
Albuquerque, NM 87103-1809
(505) 842-5781; Fax: (505) 766-6833
Internet: www.nmdisboard.org

Chief Disciplinary Counsel: Virginia L. Ferrara

Attorney General

Office of the Attorney General
260 Bataan Memorial Bldg., 407 Galisteo St.,
Santa Fe, NM 87501
Mailing Address: P.O. Drawer 1508,
Santa Fe, NM 87504-1508
(505) 827-6000; Fax: (505) 827-5826
Internet: www.ago.state.nm.us

111 Lomas Blvd. N.W., Suite 300, Albuquerque, NM 87102
(505) 222-9000; Fax: (505) 222-9006

Atty. General: Patricia A. Madrid (Democrat)
Elected; next election Nov. 2006

Banking Department

Financial Institutions Division
2550 Cerrillos Rd., Santa Fe, NM 87505
Mailing Address: P.O. Box 25101, Santa Fe, NM 87504
(505) 476-4885; Fax: (505) 476-4670
Internet: www.rld.state.nm.us

Director: William J. Verant

Bar Admissions

Board of Bar Examiners
Supreme Court of New Mexico
9420 Indian School Rd. N.E., Albuquerque, NM 87112
(505) 271-9706; Fax: (505) 271-9768;
CLE Office: (505) 797-6020
Internet: www.nmexam.org
15 hours CLE required per year including one hour of
ethics and 2 hours of professionalism.
No admission without exam.

Bar Association

State Bar of New Mexico
5121 Masthead N.E., Albuquerque, NM 87109
Mailing Address: P.O. Box 92860,
Albuquerque, NM 87125-2860
(505) 797-6000; Fax: (505) 828-3765
E-mail: sbnm@nmbar.org
Internet: www.nmbar.org

Exec. Dir.: Joe Conte
    (505) 797-6099
    E-mail: jconte@nmbar.org

President: Charles J. Vigil
Integrated Bar
Annual Meeting: November

Chief Medical Examiner

Office of the Medical Investigator
MSC 11 6030
1 University of New Mexico, Albuquerque, NM 87131-0001
(505) 272-3053; Fax: (505) 272-0727
Internet: http://omi.unm.edu

Chief Medical Investigator: Ross E. Zumwalt, M.D.

Client Protection Fund

Client Protection Fund
State Bar of New Mexico
5121 Masthead N.E., Albuquerque, NM 87109
Mailing Address: P.O. Box 92860,
Albuquerque, NM 87199-2860
(505) 797-6000; Fax: (505) 828-3765
E-mail: sbnm@nmbar.org
Internet: www.nmbar.org

Exec. Dir.: Joe Conte
    (505) 797-6099
    E-mail: jconte@nmbar.org

Commerce Department

See Economic Development Administration

Corporations Officers

Department of State
Public Regulation Commission
413 P.E.R.A. Bldg., 1120 Paseo de Peralta, P.O. Box 1269,
Santa Fe, NM 87504-1269
General Information:
(505) 827-4508, (800) 947-4722, Ext. 2;
Corporations Section: (505) 827-4502;
Name Availabilities: (505) 827-4504;
Annual Reports & Good Standing Certificates:
(505) 827-4510; Certified Copies: (505) 827-4513;
Fax: (505) 827-4387

Bureau Chief: Ann Echols (505) 827-4508
    E-mail: ann.echols@state.nm.us

Administrator of Corporations: Tillie M. Martinez
    (505) 827-4508; E-mail: tillie.martinez@state.nm.us
UCC, Partnerships, Notaries, Agricultural Liens, Service
of Process,
Trademarks/Service Mark, International Wills Divisions
300 State Capitol Bldg., 325 Don Gaspar,
Santa Fe, NM 87503
(505) 827-3600, (800) 477-3632; Fax: (505) 827-3611

Operations Dir.: Patricia Herrera
    E-mail: patricia.herrera@state.nm.org

Criminal History Board

Department of Public Safety
Law Enforcement Records Bureau
4491 Cerrillos Rd., Santa Fe, NM 87507
Mailing Address: P.O. Box 1628, Santa Fe, NM 87504-1628
(505) 827-9181; Fax: (505) 827-9189
Internet: www.dps.nm.org

Economic Development Administration

Economic Development Department
1100 St. Francis Dr., Santa Fe, NM 87505-4147
Mailing Address: P.O. Box 20003,
Santa Fe, NM 87504-5003
(505) 827-0300, (800) 374-3061; Fax: (505) 827-0328
Internet: www.newmexicodevelopment.com

Secretary: Rick Homans

Governor's Office

Office of the Governor
State Capitol, Room 400, 1120 Paseo de Peralta,
Santa Fe, NM 87501
(505) 476-2200; Fax: (505) 476-2226
Internet: www.governor.state.nm.us

Governor: William Richardson (Democrat)
Next election Nov. 2006

Highest State Court

Supreme Court of New Mexico
Supreme Court Bldg., Room 104, 237 Don Gaspar Ave.,
Santa Fe, NM 87501
Mailing Address: P.O. Box 848, Santa Fe, NM 87504-0848
(505) 827-4860; Fax: (505) 827-4837
Internet: www.supremecourt.nm.org

Chief Justice: Richard C. Bosson
Clerk of the Supreme Court: Kathleen Jo Gibson

Insurance Department

Insurance Department
1120 Paseo de Peralta, Santa Fe, NM 87501
Mailing Address: P.O. Box 1269, Santa Fe, NM 87504-1269
(505) 827-4601; Fax: (505) 476-0326

Superintendent: Eric P. Serna
    (505) 827-4299

Motor Vehicle Office

New Mexico Motor Vehicle Division
Joseph Montoya Bldg., 1100 S. St. Francis Dr.,
Santa Fe, NM 87505
Mailing Address: P.O. Box 1028, Santa Fe, NM 87504-1028
Records: (505) 827-2234; Driver's Licenses: (505) 827-2241;
Fax: (505) 827-2267;
Toll Free (888) MVD-INFO: (888) 683-4636
Internet: www.state.nm.us/tax
Fee for obtaining abstract: No fee; must be a written
request

Police

New Mexico Department of Public Safety
State Police Division
4491 Cerrillos Rd., P.O. Box 1628,
Santa Fe, NM 87504-1628
(505) 827-9002; Fax: (505) 827-3395
Internet: www.dps.nm.org

Accident Reports: Law Enforcement Records Bureau,
4491 Cerrillos Rd., P.O. Box 1628,
Santa Fe, NM 87504-1628
(505) 827-9181; Fax: (505) 827-3388

Cabinet Secretary: John Denko
  (505) 827-3370; Fax: (505) 827-3434
Fee for obtaining accident report: $1.00 per page

Probate, Recording and Notary Certificate Offices

Estate & Wills: Probate Court Clerks Offices, each County
Deeds and Mortgages: County Clerks Offices
Notary Certificates: Secretary of State, Attn: Notary
Division ($3.00)

Senators, U.S.

Jeff Bingaman (Democrat)
703 Hart Senate Office Bldg., Washington, DC 20510
(202) 224-5521; Fax: (202) 224-2852
Internet: http://bingaman.senate.gov

Pete V. Domenici (Republican)
328 Hart Senate Office Bldg., Washington, DC 20510
(202) 224-6621; Fax: (202) 224-7371
Internet: http://domenici.senate.gov

Secretary of State

Office of the Secretary of State
325 Don Gaspar, Suite 300, Santa Fe, NM 87503
(505) 827-3600; Fax: (505) 827-8081
Internet: www.sos.state.nm.us

Secretary of State: Rebecca D. Vigil-Giron (Democrat)
Elected; next election Nov. 2006

Tax Department

Taxation & Revenue Department
Joseph Montoya Bldg., 1100 St. Francis Dr.,
Santa Fe, NM 87509
Mailing Address: P.O. Box 630, Santa Fe, NM 87504-0630
(505) 827-0700; Fax: (505) 827-0331;
D.W.I. Legal: (505) 827-9807;
Inspector General: (505) 827-0570;
Legal Svces.: (505) 827-0730;
Tax Info. and Policy: (505) 827-0908
Internet: www.state.nm.us/tax

Secretary: Jan Goodwin

Victim Compensation Program

Crime Victims Reparation Commission
8100 Mountain Road, N.E., Suite 106,
Albuquerque, NM 87110
(505) 841-9432; Fax: (505) 841-9437
E-mail: cvrc@state.nm.us
Internet: www.state.nm.us/cvrc
N.M. Stat. 1978 §§31-22-1 to 31-22-21

Vital Statistics

New Mexico Vital Records and Health Statistics
1105 St. Francis Dr., P.O. Box 26110, Santa Fe, NM 87502
(505) 827-2338; Credit Card Orders: (877) 284-0963;
Fax: (505) 827-1751
Internet:
www.dohewbs2.health.state.nm.us/vitalrec/default
Births & Deaths since 1920.
Birth records—$10.00. Additional $39.75 handling fee for
Credit Card Orders. Death records—$5.00

NEW YORK   *Capital: Albany*

18,976,457 (2000 Census)
State Information: (518) 474-2121
State Web Site: www.state.ny.us

Administrative Office of the Courts

Office of Court Administration
25 Beaver St., New York, NY 10004
(212) 428-2100; Fax: (212) 428-2188
Internet: www.nycourts.gov
Chief Administrative Judge: Jonathan Lippman

Attorney Discipline

New York Departmental Disciplinary Committee: First Dept.
(Manhattan and Bronx)
61 Broadway, 2nd Floor, New York, NY 10006
(212) 401-0800; Fax: (212) 401-0810
Chief Counsel: Thomas J. Cahill

New York Grievance Committee: Second Dept.,
Second and Eleventh Dists.
(Brooklyn, Queens and Staten Island)
335 Adams St., 24th Floor, Brooklyn, NY 11201
(718) 923-6300

Chief Counsel: Diana Maxfield Kearse

New York Grievance Committee:
Appellate Div., Second Dept., Tenth Dist. (Long Island)
150 Motor Pkwy., Suite 102, Hauppauge, NY 11788
(631) 231-3775

Chief Counsel: Faith Lorenzo

New York State Committee on Professional Standards
Third Judicial Department
40 Steuben St., Suite 502, Albany, NY 12270
(518) 474-8816; Fax: (518) 474-0389
Internet: www.courts.state.ny.us/ad3

Chief Counsel: Mark S. Ochs

Attorney Grievance Committee: Fourth Dept., Fifth Dist.
224 Harrison St., Suite 408, Syracuse, NY 13202-3066
(315) 471-1835; Fax: (315) 479-0123
Internet: www.courts.state.ny.us/ad4

Chief Counsel: David L. Edmunds, Jr.
Principal Counsel: Anthony J. Gigliotti

New York Departmental Disciplinary Committee:
Fourth Dept., Eighth Dist.
295 Main St., Suite 1036, Buffalo, NY 14203-2560
(716) 858-1190; Fax: (716) 856-2701
Internet: www.courts.state.ny.us/ad4

Chief Counsel: David L. Edmunds, Jr.

New York Departmental Disciplinary Committee:
Fourth Dept., Seventh Dist.
50 East Ave., Suite 404, Rochester, NY 14604-2206
(585) 530-3180; Fax: (585) 530-3191
Internet: www.courts.state.ny.us/ad4

Chief Counsel: David L. Edmunds, Jr.

State of New York Grievance Committee Second Dept.,
Ninth Dist.
399 Knollwood Rd., Suite 200, White Plains, NY 10603
(914) 949-4540; Fax: (914) 949-0997

Chief Counsel: Gary L. Casella

Attorney General

Office of the Attorney General
The Capitol, Albany, NY 12224-0341
(518) 474-7330; Fax: (518) 402-2472
Internet: www.oag.state.ny.us/

NYC Office, 120 Broadway, New York, NY 10271-0332
(212) 416-8000; Fax: (212) 416-8942
Atty. General: Eliot Spitzer (Democrat)
Elected; next election Nov. 2006

Banking Department

Department of Banking
One State St., New York, NY 10004-1417
(212) 709-5470; Fax: (212) 709-3520
Internet: www.banking.state.ny.us/

5 Empire State Plaza, Suite 2310, Albany, NY 12223-1555
(518) 473-6160

National Directory of States

Banking Department—Cont'd

333 E. Washington St., Suite 521, Syracuse, NY 13202
(315) 428-4049
Superintendent: Diana L. Taylor

Bar Admissions

New York State Board of Law Examiners
Corporate Plaza, Bldg. 3, 254 Washington Ave. Ext.,
Albany, NY 12203
(518) 452-8700; Fax: (518) 452-5729
Internet: www.nybarexam.org
The Board holds examinations twice each year in each
Judicial Department under Rules of the Court of Appeals
for admission of attorneys and counselors-at-law.
Admission on motion with five of the last seven years
practice in a Reciprocal Jurisdiction.

Bar Association

New York State Bar Assn.
One Elk St., Albany, NY 12207
(518) 463-3200; Fax: (518) 487-5564
Internet: www.nysba.org
Exec. Dir.: Patricia K. Bucklin
President: A. Vincent Buzard
Non-Integrated Bar
Annual Meeting—January 23-28, 2006

Client Protection Fund

Lawyers Fund for Client Protection
119 Washington Ave., 3rd Floor, Albany, NY 12210
(518) 434-1935, (800) 442-3863; Fax: (518) 434-5641
Internet: www.nylawfund.org
Exec. Dir. and Counsel: Timothy O'Sullivan

Commerce Department

See Economic Development Administration

Corporations Officers

Department of State
Division of Corporations, State Records and Uniform
Commercial Code
41 State St., Albany, NY 12231
General Information: (518) 473-2492;
Corporate Records Section (900) TEL-CORP:
(900) 835-2677; UCC: (518) 474-4763;
Corporate Fax: (518) 474-5173; UCC Fax: (518) 474-4478
Director: Daniel E. Shapiro (518) 473-2281
    E-mail: dshapiro@dos.state.ny.us
Asst. Dir.: Howard J. Carr (518) 486-6111
    E-mail: hcarr@dos.state.ny.us
Supervisor, Corporate & Business Filings:
    Denise A. Lauer (518) 473-4103
    E-mail: dlauer@dos.state.ny.us
Supervisor, Corporate & Business Information:
    Joseph E. Terry
    (518) 473-2492 E-mail: jterry@dos.state.ny.us
Supervisor, UCC Operations: Paul LaPointe
    (518) 474-5418
    E-mail: plapoint@dos.state.ny.us
Supervisor, Biennial Statement Unit:
    Mary (Sue) Zouky (518) 473-6385
    E-mail: szouky@dos.state.ny.us

Criminal History Board

Office of Justice Information Services
Division of Criminal Justice Services
4 Tower Pl., Albany, NY 12203-3764
(518) 485-2995

Economic Development Administration

Empire State Development
30 S. Pearl St., Albany, NY 12245
(518) 292-5100, (800) 782-8369; Fax: (518) 292-5888
E-mail: esd@empire.state.ny.us
Internet: www.empire.state.ny.us/

633 Third Ave., New York, NY 10017
(212) 803-3100; Fax: (212) 803-3175
Chair/Commissioner: Charles A. Gargano

Governor's Office

Office of the Governor
State Capitol, Executive Chamber, Albany, NY 12224
(518) 474-8390
Internet: www.state.ny.us/governor

633 Third Ave., 39th Floor, New York, NY 10017
(212) 681-4580

444 N. Capitol St. N.W., Suite 301, Washington, DC 20001
(202) 434-7100
Governor: George E. Pataki (Republican)
Next election Nov. 2006

Highest State Court

Court of Appeals
Court of Appeals Hall, 20 Eagle St., Albany, NY 12207-1095
(518) 455-7700
Internet: www.courts.state.ny.us/ctapps
Chief Judge: Judith S. Kaye
Clerk of the Court of Appeals: Stuart M. Cohen

Insurance Department

Department of Insurance
25 Beaver St., New York, NY 10004 (212) 480-4701
Internet: www.ins.state.ny.us

One Commerce Plaza, Albany, NY 12257
(518) 474-4550; Fax: (518) 473-4600
Superintendent: Howard Mills (Acting)

Motor Vehicle Office

New York Department of Motor Vehicles
Swan Street Bldg., Room 136, Empire State Plaza,
Albany, NY 12228-0001
(800) 225-5368; From all other area codes: (518) 473-5595
Internet: www.nysdmv.com
*Use Toll Free number from area codes (315, 518, 585, 607
or 716) only*
Fee for obtaining driver abstract: $6.00 per search in a
personal check or money order made payable to
"Commissioner of Motor Vehicles," (there is a $5.00 fee to
process orders by phone. The total for telephone orders is
$11.00—payable by credit card)

Police

New York State Police
1220 Washington Ave., Bldg. 22, Albany, NY 12226-2252
(518) 457-6811
Internet: www.troopers.state.ny.us
Superintendent: Wayne E. Bennett
Fee for obtaining accident report: $15.00; Certified copy:
$30.00; All requests must be made in writing to the
appropriate Troop Headquarters.

Probate, Recording and Notary Certificate Offices

Estate & Wills: County Surrogates Offices
Deeds and Mortgages: County Clerks Offices & N.Y.C.
Registers Offices
Notary Certificates: Clerk of County of Commission (fee
varies); Secretary of State, Miscellaneous Records
Division ($10.00)

Senators, U.S.

Hillary Rodham Clinton (Democrat)
476 Russell Senate Office Bldg., Washington, DC 20510
(202) 224-4451; Fax: (202) 228-0282
Internet: http://clinton.senate.gov
Charles E. Schumer (Democrat)
313 Hart Senate Office Bldg., Washington, DC 20510
(202) 224-6542; Fax: (202) 224-5871
Internet: http://schumer.senate.gov

Secretary of State

Office of the Secretary of State
Department of State, 41 State St., Albany, NY 12231-0001
(518) 474-4750; Fax: (518) 474-4765
E-mail: info@dos.state.ny.us
Internet: www.dos.state.ny.us
Secretary of State: Randy A. Daniels (Republican)
Appointed

Tax Department

Department of Taxation & Finance
W.A. Harriman Campus, Albany, NY 12227
General Tax Information: (800) 225-5829;
Tax Forms & Publications: (800) 462-8100
Internet: http://www.tax.state.ny.us/

Service of Legal Papers, write: Office of Counsel,
W.A. Harriman Campus, Bldg. 9, Albany, NY 12227
Commissioner: Andrew S. Eristoff
Counsel: Barbara Billet

Victim Compensation Program

Crime Victims Board
845 Central Ave., South 3, Suite 107,
Albany, NY 12206-1588
(518) 457-8727, (800) 247-8035; TTY: (888) 289-9747;
Fax: (518) 457-8658
E-mail: cvbinfo@cvb.state.ny.us
Internet: www.cvb.state.ny.us

65 Court St., Room 308, Buffalo, NY 14202-3406
(716) 847-7992, (800) 247-8035; Fax: (716) 847-7995

55 Hanson Place, Room 1000, Brooklyn, NY 11217-1523
(718) 923-4325, (800) 247-8035; Fax: (718) 923-4352
N.Y. Exec. Law Ann. §§620 to 635 (McKinney)

Vital Statistics

State Department of Health
Vital Records Office, 733 Broadway,
Albany, NY 12237-0023
Mailing Address: Certification Unit, Vital Records Section,
P.O. Box 2602, Albany, NY 12220-2602
Application Forms: (518) 474-3077;
Credit Card Orders: (877) 854-4481;
(Fax) Credit Card Processing: (877) 854-4607
E-mail: vr@health.state.ny.us
Internet: www.health.state.ny.us, www.vitalcheck.com
*Births—since 1881; Deaths—since 1880; Marriages—since
1881; (except New York City; Also no records for Albany,
Buffalo or Yonkers for 1881-1914; Contact city clerk where
event occurred for those records); Divorces—since 1963;
Before 1963, contact county clerk where divorce is filed.*
Certified copies: $30.00; $15.00 surcharge for priority
handling; Searches of more than three years—$5.00 per
ten years searched.
Geneology fee: $22.00 for a 1-3 year search for birth, death
and marriages; $42.00 per 10 yrs, $20.00 for each
additional 10 yrs.
Credit card orders—$45.00 per copy, plus $11.95
transaction fee (regardless of number of copies ordered) for
record or no-record statement. Birth records only.
Applicant must call himself/herself. Fee is non-refundable.
N.Y.C. Department of Health
Office of Vital Records, 125 Worth St., Room 133,
New York, NY 10013
Mailing Address: , CN 4, New York, NY 10013
(212) 788-4520; Fax: (212) 442-0946;
Order by Phone: (212) 788-4520;
Order by Fax: (212) 962-6105
Internet: www.nyc.gov/html/doh/html/vr/vr.html
*Five Boroughs of New York City: Births—1910.
Deaths—1949.*
Births and Deaths—Search fee: $15.00. Includes one
certified copy of record, if found. If not found, a certified
certificate stating that the record was not found is issued.
Additional copies ordered at same time: $15.00. Phone
orders additional $5.50 mailing and service charge payable
by credit card; $11.00 additional shipping and handling fee
for expedited delivery on credit card phone orders. There is
no credit card service for death certificates. Attorneys
must indicate purpose for requiring birth certificate and
written consent of client.

City Clerk
Municipal Bldg., Room 252 South, 1 Centre St.,
New York, NY 10007
(212) 669-8090; Fax: (212) 669-3300; (212) 669-2400
Internet: http://nycmarriagebureau.com
*Marriage licenses and/or ceremonies within the five
boroughs of New York City.*

Fees for certified copies of marriage records is $15.
Payable to City Clerk by money order or certified check
only; additional copies—$10.00
Municipal Archives
Department of Records and Information Services,
31 Chambers St., New York, NY 10007
(212) 639-9675; Fax: (212) 788-8583
Internet: www.nyc.gov/records
*New York City: Births before 1910. Deaths before 1949.
Marriages before 1938.*
Copies—$15.00, including search.

NORTH CAROLINA   *Capital: Raleigh*

8,049,313 (2000 Census)
State Information: (919) 733-1110
State Web Site: www.state.nc.us

Administrative Office of the Courts

Administrative Office of the Courts
Justice Bldg., 2 E. Morgan St., Raleigh, NC 27601
Mailing Address: P.O. Box 2448, Raleigh, NC 27602-2448
(919) 733-7107; Fax: (919) 715-5779
Internet: www.nccourts.org
Director: John Kennedy

Attorney Discipline

Office of the Counsel
North Carolina State Bar
208 Fayetteville St. Mall, Raleigh, NC 27601
Mailing Address: P.O. Box 25908, Raleigh, NC 27611
(919) 828-4620; Fax: (919) 834-8156
Internet: www.ncbar.com
Counsel: Carolin D. Bakewell

Attorney General

Office of the Attorney General
114 W. Edenton St., Raleigh, NC 27603
Mailing Address: 9001 Mail Service Center,
Raleigh, NC 27699-9001
(919) 716-6400; Fax: (919) 716-6750
E-mail: ncago@ncdoj.com
Internet: www.ncdoj.com
Atty. General: Roy Cooper (Democrat)
Elected; next election Nov. 2008

Banking Department

Office of the Commissioner of Banks
316 W. Edenton St., Raleigh, NC 27603
Mailing Address: 4309 Mail Service Center,
Raleigh, NC 27699-4309
(919) 733-3016; Fax: (919) 733-6918
Internet: www.nccob.org
Commissioner: Joseph A. Smith, Jr.

Bar Admissions

Board of Law Examiners of the State of North Carolina
One Exchange Plaza, Suite 700, Raleigh, NC 27601
Mailing Address: P.O. Box 2946, Raleigh, NC 27602
(919) 828-4886; Fax: (919) 828-2251
Internet: www.ncble.org
12 hours CLE (including seven hours over a three-year
period which must be in professionalism, one hour of
which must be on substance-abuse instruction or
debilitating mental conditions) required per year.
Admission on motion with four of the last six years in full
time practice in a Reciprocal Jurisdiction.

Bar Association

The North Carolina State Bar
208 Fayetteville St. Mall, Raleigh, NC 27611
Mailing Address: P.O. Box 25908, Raleigh, NC 27601-5908
(919) 828-4620; Fax: (919) 821-9168
Internet: www.ncstatebar.org
Exec. Dir.: L. Thomas Lunsford II
       E-mail: tlunsford@ncbar.com
President: Robert (Bud) F. Siler
Integrated Bar
Annual Meeting—October, 2005

National Directory
of States

Bar Associations—Cont'd

North Carolina Bar Assn.
8000 Weston Pkwy., Cary, NC 27513
Mailing Address: P.O. Box 3688, Cary, NC 27519-3688
(919) 677-0561; Fax: (919) 677-0761
Internet: www.ncbar.org
Exec. Dir.: Allan B. Head
President: G. Gray Wilson
Non-Integrated Bar
Annual Meeting—June, 2005

Chief Medical Examiner

Office of Chief Medical Examiner
Brinkhous-Bullitt Bldg., 10th Floor,
Chapel Hill, NC 27599-7580
(919) 966-2253; Fax: (919) 962-6263
Internet: www.ocme.unc.edu
Chief Medical Examiner: John D. Butts, M.D.

Client Protection Fund

Client Security Fund
North Carolina State Bar
208 Fayetteville St. Mall, Raleigh, NC 27601
Mailing Address: P.O. Box 25908, Raleigh, NC 27611-5908
(919) 828-4620; Fax: (919) 834-8156
Internet: www.ncbar.com
Counsel to the Board: A. Root Edmonson, Ext. 229
    E-mail: redmonson@ncbar.com

Commerce Department

Department of Commerce
301 N. Wilmington St., Raleigh, NC 27601-2825
Mailing Address: 4301 Mail Service Center,
Raleigh, NC 27699-4301
(919) 733-4151; Fax: (919) 733-9265
Internet: www.nccommerce.com

Corporations Officers

Department of State
Corporations Division
Old Revenue Bldg., 2 S. Salisbury St., P.O. Box 29622,
Raleigh, NC 27626-0622
General Information: (919) 807-2000;
Corporations Section, Name Availabilities & Limited
Partnerships: (919) 807-2225; Notaries: (919) 807-2131;
Trademarks: (919) 807-2162; UCC: (919) 807-2111;
Corporations Fax: (919) 807-2039;
Notaries Fax: (919) 807-2130; UCC Fax: (919) 807-2120
Director: Charlene P. Dawkins (919) 807-2050
    E-mail: cdawkins@sosnc.com
Dir., Certification & Filing: Gayle P. Holder
    One Exchange Plz., P.O. Box 29626,
    Raleigh, NC 27626-0626
    (919) 807-2288; E-mail: gholder@sosnc.com
Dir., UCC Division: Vacancy at Press Time
    One Exchange Plz., P.O. Box 29626,
    Raleigh, NC 27626-0626
    (919) 807-2100

Criminal History Board

State Bureau of Investigation
3320 Garner Rd., Raleigh, NC 27610
Mailing Address: P.O. Box 29500, Raleigh, NC 27626
(919) 662-4500; Fax: (919) 662-4523

Economic Development Administration

Economic Development Board
Department of Commerce
4301 Mail Service Center, Raleigh, NC 27699-4301
(919) 733-3309; Fax: (919) 733-8356
Internet: www.nccommerce.com/econbrd
Chair: Robert Stolz

Governor's Office

Office of the Governor
116 W. Jones St., Raleigh, NC 27603
Mailing Address: 20301 Mail Service Center,
Raleigh, NC 27699-0301
(919) 733-5811; Fax: (919) 715-3175
Internet: www.governor.state.nc.us

444 N. Capitol St., Suite 332, Washington, DC 20001
(202) 624-5830; Fax: (202) 624-5836
Governor: Michael F. Easley (Democrat)
Next election Nov. 2008

Highest State Court

Supreme Court
Justice Bldg., 2 E. Morgan St., Raleigh, NC 27601-1445
Mailing Address: P.O. Box 2170, Raleigh, NC 27602
(919) 733-3723; Fax: (919) 733-0105
Internet: www.nccourts.org
Chief Justice: I. Beverly Lake, Jr.
Clerk of the Supreme Court: Christie Speir Cameron

Insurance Department

Department of Insurance
Dobbs Bldg., 430 N. Salisbury St., Raleigh, NC 27603
Mailing Address: 1201 Mail Service Center,
Raleigh, NC 27611
(919) 733-7343; Commissioner's Fax: (919) 733-6495
Internet: www.ncdoi.com

New Bern Regional Office, 233 Middle St., P.O. Box 1691,
New Bern, NC 28563
(252) 514-4813

Asheville Regional Office, 537 College St.,
Asheville, NC 28801
(704) 251-6483
Commissioner: James E. Long
Chief Examiner: Ray Martinez

Motor Vehicle Office

North Carolina Division of Motor Vehicles
1100 New Bern Ave., Raleigh, NC 27697
Commissioner's Office: (919) 861-3015;
Commissioner's Office Fax: (919) 733-0126
Internet: www.dmv.dot.state.nc.us

For Driver's Abstracts write: Driver's License Section,
1100 New Bern Ave., Raleigh, NC 27697-0001
(919) 715-7000

Vehicle Registration, 1100 New Bern Ave., Room 132,
Raleigh, NC 27697
(919) 861-3332; Fax: (919) 733-6948

For Traffic Records write:, 1100 New Bern Ave., Suite 407,
Raleigh, NC 27697
(919) 861-3062; Fax: (919) 715-9099

License and Theft Bureau, 1100 New Bern Ave.,
Raleigh, NC 27697
(919) 861-3185; Fax: (919) 715-0169
Fee for obtaining abstract: $5.00; $7.00 certified

Police

North Carolina State Highway Patrol
512 N. Salisbury St., Raleigh, NC 27699
Mailing Address: 4702 Mail Service Center,
Raleigh, NC 27699-4702
(919) 733-7952; Fax: (919) 733-1189

Collision Reports, Division of Motor Vehicles,
1100 New Bern Ave., Raleigh, NC 27697
(919) 733-7250
Commander: Col. R. W. Holden
Fee for obtaining accident report: Certified copy, $4.00

Probate, Recording and Notary Certificate Offices

Estate & Wills: Clerk of Superior Court, each county
Deeds and Mortgages: County Register of Deeds
Notary Certificates: County Register of Deeds

Senators, U.S.

Richard Burr (Republican)
40-C Dirksen Senate Office Bldg., Washington, DC 20510
(202) 224-3154

Elizabeth H. Dole (Republican)
120 Russell Senate Office Bldg., Washington, DC 20510
(202) 224-6342
Internet: http://dole.senate.gov

Secretary of State

Department of the Secretary of State
2 South Salisbury Street, Raleigh, NC 27601
Mailing Address: P.O. Box 29622, Raleigh, NC 27626-0622
(919) 807-2000; Fax: (919) 807-2010
Internet: www.sosnc.com
Secretary of State: Elaine F. Marshall (Democrat)
Elected; next election Nov. 2008

Tax Department

Department of Revenue
501 N. Wilmington St., Raleigh, NC 27604-8001
Mailing Address: P.O. Box 25000, Raleigh, NC 27640-0640
(919) 733-7211; Forms: (919) 715-0397; Fax: (919) 733-0023
Internet: http://www.dor.state.nc.us/
Secretary: E. Norris Tolson

Victim Compensation Program

Crime Victims Compensation Commission
Victims Compensation Services
4703 Mail Svc. Center, Raleigh, NC 27699-4703
(919) 733-7974; Fax: (919) 715-4209
Internet: www.nccrimecontrol.org/vjs
N.C. Gen. Stat §§15B-1, et seq.

Vital Statistics

North Carolina Vital Records Unit
Cooper Bldg., 225 N. McDowell St., Raleigh, NC 27603
Mailing Address: North Carolina Vital Records,
1903 Mail Service Center, Raleigh, NC 27699-1903
(919) 733-3526; Fax: (919) 715-5044, 733-1511
Internet: http://vitalrecords.dhhs.state.nc.us/schs
Births—1913-present. Deaths—1930-present.
Divorces—1958-present. Divorces prior to this date filed
with Clerk of Court in county of divorce.
Marriages—1962-present. Marriages prior to this date
filed with Register of Deeds in county of marriage.
Search fee—$15.00. Includes copy of record if found.
Additional copies—$5.00 each. Expedited service available
by telephone for an additional surcharge (billing by credit
card) through VitalChek at (800) 669-8310.

NORTH DAKOTA   *Capital: Bismarck*

642,200 (2000 Census)
State Information: (701) 328-2000
State Web Site: www.state.nd.us

Administrative Office of the Courts

Office of State Court Administrator
State Capitol, Judicial Wing,
600 E. Boulevard Ave., Dept. 180,
Bismarck, ND 58505-0530
(701) 328-4216; Fax: (701) 328-2092
Internet: www.ndcourts.com
State Court Administrator: Ted Gladden
    E-mail: tgladden@ndcourts.com

Attorney Discipline

Disciplinary Board of the Supreme Court of North Dakota
515 1/2 Broadway, Bismarck, ND 58501
Mailing Address: P.O. Box 2297,
Bismarck, ND 58502-2297
(701) 328-3925; Fax: (701) 328-3964
Contact: Paul W. Jacobson

Attorney General

Office of the Attorney General
State Capitol, 600 E. Boulevard Ave., Dept. 125,
Bismarck, ND 58505-0040
(701) 328-2210; Fax: (701) 328-2226
Internet: http://www.state.nd.us/ndag/
Atty. General: Wayne Stenehjem (Republican)
Elected; next election Nov. 2008

Banking Department

Department of Financial Institutions
2000 Schafer St., Suite G, Bismarck, ND 58501-1204
(701) 328-9933; Fax: (701) 328-9955
Internet: www.state.nd.us/dfi
Commissioner: Timothy J. Karsky

Bar Admissions

State Board of Law Examiners
Judicial Wing, 1st Floor, 600 E. Boulevard Ave., Dept. 180,
Bismarck, ND 58505-0530
(701) 328-4201; Fax: (701) 328-4480
Internet: www.ndcourts.com
45 hours CLE required per three years including three
hours of ethics or professional responsibility.
Admission on motion with five years' membership of the
bar of another jurisdiction and four of the last five years in
practice; or admission on motion based on a scaled score of
150 or higher on MBE taken within two years of
application and admission in jurisdiction of examination;
or admission by bar exam.

Bar Association

State Bar Assn. of North Dakota
504 N. Washington St., P.O. Box 2136, Bismarck, ND 58502-2136
(701) 255-1404; Fax: (701) 224-1621
E-mail: info@sband.org; Internet: www.sband.org
President: Michael J. Williams
Integrated Bar
Annual Meeting—June, 2006

Chief Medical Examiner

State Forensics Medical Examiner
North Dakota Dept. of Health
2635 E. Main St., Bismarck, ND 58504
Mailing Address: P.O. Box 937, Bismarck, ND 58502-0937
(701) 328-6138; Fax: (701) 328-6145
Chief Medical Examiner: George R. Mizell, M.D.

Commerce Department

See Economic Development Administration

Corporations Officers

Department of State
600 E. Boulevard Ave., Dept. 108, Bismarck, ND 58505-0500
(701) 328-4284; Fax: (701) 328-2992
Dir., Business Division: Clara M. Jenkins
    (701) 328-4284; Fax: (701) 328-2992
    E-mail: cjenkins@state.nd.us
Central Indexing Dir.: Llona Sailing
    (701) 328-3663; Fax: (701) 328-4214
    E-mail: lsailing@state.nd.us

Criminal History Board

Bureau of Criminal Investigation
Information Services Section
P.O. Box 1054, Bismarck, ND 58502
(701) 328-5500; Fax: (701) 328-5510

Economic Development Administration

Economic Development & Finance Division
Dept. of Commerce
1600 E. Century Ave., Suite 2, P.O. Box 2057,
Bismarck, ND 58501
(701) 328-5300; TTY: (800) 366-6888; Fax: (701) 328-5320
Internet: www.growingnd.com
Commissioner: Lee Peterson
Dir., Economic Dev. & Finance Div.: Linda Butts

Governor's Office

Office of the Governor
State Capitol, Dept. 101, 600 E. Boulevard Ave.,
Bismarck, ND 58505-0001
(701) 328-2200; TTY (Relay ND): Ext. 711; Fax: (701) 328-2205
E-mail: governor@state.nd.us
Internet: www.governor.state.nd.us
Governor: John Hoeven
Next election Nov. 2008

Highest State Court

Supreme Court
600 E. Boulevard Ave., Dept. 180,
Bismarck, ND 58505-0530
(701) 328-2221; Fax: (701) 328-4480
Internet: www.ndcourts.com
Chief Justice: Gerald W. VandeWalle
Clerk of the Supreme Court: Penny Miller
    E-mail: pmiller@ndcourts.com

Insurance Department

Department of Insurance
Dept. 401, 600 East Boulevard Ave.,
Bismarck, ND 58505-0320
(701) 328-2440, (800) 247-0560; Fax: (701) 328-4880
Internet: www.state.nd.us/ndins/
Commissioner: Jim Poolman
Chief Examiner: Carole Kessel

Motor Vehicle Office

North Dakota Drivers License & Traffic Safety Division
Dept. of Transportation, 608 E. Blvd. Ave.,
Bismarck, ND 58505-0700
(701) 328-2600; Fax: (701) 328-2435
Internet: www.state.nd.us/dot/
Driver's Licenses
Fee for obtaining abstract: $3.00
North Dakota Motor Vehicle Division
Dept. of Transportation, 608 E. Boulevard Ave.,
Bismarck, ND 58505-0780
(701) 328-2725; Vehicle Registration Fax: (701) 328-1487
E-mail: kkiser@state.nd.us
Internet: www.state.nd.us/dot/
Vehicle Registration
Fee for obtaining abstract: $3.00

Police

North Dakota State Highway Patrol
State Capitol, 600 E. Boulevard Ave., Dept. 504,
Bismarck, ND 58505-0240
(701) 328-2455; Fax: (701) 328-1717
E-mail: ndhpinfo@state.nd.us
Internet: www.state.nd.us/ndhp

Accident Reports: Driver License and Traffic Safety Div.,
North Dakota Dept. of Transportation,
608 E. Boulevard Ave., Bismarck, ND 58505-0700
(701) 328-2601; Fax: (701) 328-4545
E-mail: dl@state.nd.us
Internet: www.state.nd.us/dot/dl&ts.html
Superintendent: Col. Bryan Klipfel
Fee for obtaining accident report: $7.00

Probate, Recording and Notary Certificate Offices

Estate & Wills: District Courts
Deeds and Mortgages: County Recorder
Notary Certificates: Secretary of State ($10.00)

Senators, U.S.

Kent Conrad (Democrat)
530 Hart Senate Office Bldg., Washington, DC 20510
(202) 224-2043; Fax: (202) 224-7776
Internet: http://conrad.senate.gov
Byron L. Dorgan (Democrat)
713 Hart Senate Office Bldg., Washington, DC 20510
(202) 224-2551; Fax: (202) 224-1193
Internet: http://dorgan.senate.gov

Secretary of State

Office of the Secretary of State
Dept. 108, 600 E. Boulevard Ave.,
Bismarck, ND 58505-0500
(701) 328-2900; Fax: (701) 328-2992
E-mail: sos@state.nd.us
Internet: www.state.nd.us/sec/
Secretary of State: Alvin A. Jaeger (Republican)
Elected; next election Nov. 2006

Tax Department

Office of State Tax Commissioner
Dept. 127, 600 E. Boulevard Ave.,
Bismarck, ND 58505-0599
(701) 328-2770; Forms Mail Room: (701) 328-3017;
Fax: (701) 328-3700; Legal Div.: (701) 328-2775
E-mail: taxinfo@state.nd.us
Internet: www.ndtaxdepartment.com
Commissioner: Rick Clayburgh

Victim Compensation Program

Crime Victims Compensation
Div. of Parole and Probation
3100 Railroad Ave., P.O. Box 5521,
Bismarck, ND 58506-5521
(701) 328-6195; In-state: (800) 445-2322;
Fax: (701) 328-6186
E-mail: pcoughli@state.nd.us
N.D. Cent. Code Chap. 54-23.4, §§1-18

Vital Statistics

Division of Vital Records
North Dakota Department of Health
600 E. Boulevard Ave., Bismarck, ND 58505-0200
(701) 328-2360; Fax: (701) 328-1850
Internet: www.vitalnd.com
Births—1870; Deaths—1881; Marriages—1925.
Divorces—Clerks of District Court. Prior to 1925, requests
for copies of marriage licenses and certificates should be
addressed to the Local Recorder of the county where the
license was obtained.
Certified copies—Births: $7.00, additional copies $4.00;
Deaths: $5.00, additional copies $2.00.

OHIO   *Capital: Columbus*
11,353,140 (2000 Census)
State Information: (614) 466-2000
State Web Site: www.ohio.gov

Administrative Office of the Courts

Administrative Director's Office
Supreme Court of Ohio, 65 S. Front St.,
Columbus, OH 43215-3431
(614) 387-9000; Fax: (614) 387-9509
Internet: www.sconet.state.oh.us
Administrative Dir.: Steven C. Hollon

Attorney Discipline

Office of the Disciplinary Counsel of the Supreme Court of Ohio
250 Civic Center Dr., Suite 325,
Columbus, OH 43215-7411
(614) 461-0256; Fax: (614) 461-7205
Internet: www.sconet.state.oh.us/boc/odc/
Disciplinary Counsel: Jonathan E. Coughlan

Attorney General

Office of the Attorney General
30 East Broad Street, 17th Floor,
Columbus, OH 43215-3428
(614) 466-4320; Fax: (614) 644-6135
Internet: www.ag.state.oh.us
Atty. General: Jim Petro (Republican)
Elected; next election Nov. 2006

Banking Department

Division of Financial Institutions
77 S. High St., 21st Floor, Columbus, OH 43215
(614) 728-8400; Fax: (614) 644-1631
Internet: www.com.state.oh.us/dfi
Supt. of Div. of Financial Institutions:
   F. Scott O'Donnell
Deputy Superintendent of Banks: Michael Roark

Bar Admissions

Bar Admissions Office
Supreme Court of Ohio
65 S. Front St., 5th Floor, Columbus, OH 43215-3431
(614) 387-9340; Fax: (614) 387-9349
E-mail: admissions@sconet.state.oh.us
Internet: www.sconet.state.oh.us
24 hours CLE required per two years.
Admission on motion at least five full years of practice out
of the last ten years.

Bar Association

Ohio State Bar Assn.
1700 Lake Shore Dr., Columbus, OH 43204
Mailing Address: P.O. Box 16562,
Columbus, OH 43216-6562
In-State: (800) 282-6556; (614) 487-2050; Fax: (614) 487-1008
E-mail: osba@ohiobar.org
Internet: www.ohiobar.org

Exec. Dir.: Denny L. Ramey, CAE

President: Heather Sowald
Non-Integrated Bar
Annual Meeting—May, 2005

Client Protection Fund

Clients' Security Fund
Supreme Court of Ohio
Ohio Judicial Center, 65 S. Front St.,
Columbus, OH 43215-3431
(614) 387-9390; Fax: (614) 387-9399

Administrator: Janet Green Marbley

Commerce Department

Department of Commerce
77 S. High St., 20-23rd Floor, Columbus, OH 43215
(614) 466-3636; Fax: (614) 644-8292
Internet: www.com.state.oh.us

Corporations Officers

Corporations Office
180 E. Broad St., 16th Floor, Columbus, OH 43215
(614) 466-3910, (877) 767-3453; Fax: (614) 466-2892
E-mail: busserv@sos.state.oh.us
Internet: www.state.oh.us/sos/

Chief of Staff: Sherri A. Dembinski (614) 995-1527
   E-mail: sdembins@sos.state.oh.us

General Counsel: Cassandra L. Hicks (614) 644-1373
   E-mail: clhicks@sos.state.oh.us

Asst. Secy. of State: Monty Lobb, 15th Floor
   (614) 752-2450; E-mail: mlobb@sos.state.oh.us

Asst. Dir., Business Filings Services: Vincent L. Mason
   (614) 995-3361; E-mail: vmason@sos.state.oh.us

Dir. of Business Services: Timothy L. Sturkie
   (614) 728-6855; E-mail: tsturkie@sos.state.oh.us

Criminal History Board

Bureau of Criminal Identification & Investigation
Identification Division
1560 State Route 56 S.W., P.O. Box 365,
London, OH 43140
(740) 845-2000; Fax: (740) 845-2020

Economic Development Administration

Department of Development
77 S. High St., 29th Floor, Columbus, OH 43215-6130
(614) 466-3379, (800) 848-1300; Fax: (614) 644-5167
Internet: www.odod.state.oh.us

Director: Bruce E. Johnson (Lt. Governor)

Governor's Office

Office of the Governor
77 S. High St., 30th Floor, Columbus, OH 43215-6117
(614) 466-3555; Fax: (614) 752-4858
Internet: http://governor.ohio.gov

444 N. Capitol St. N.W., Suite 546, Washington, DC 20001
(202) 624-5844; Fax: (202) 624-5847

Governor: Bob Taft (Republican)
Next election Nov. 2006

Highest State Court

Supreme Court of Ohio
65 S. Front St., Columbus, OH 43215-3431
Clerk: (614) 387-9530; Fax (Clerk): (614) 387-9539;
Fax (Administration): (614) 387-9500
Internet: www.sconet.state.oh.us

Chief Justice: Thomas J. Moyer

Clerk of the Supreme Court: Marcia J. Mengel, 8th Fl.
   (614) 387-9530, 31

Insurance Department

Department of Insurance
2100 Stella Ct., Columbus, OH 43215-1067
(614) 644-2658; Legal Division Fax: (614) 644-3742
Internet: www.ohioinsurance.gov

Director: Ann Womer Benjamin

Chief of Financial Regulations: Bill Rossbach

Motor Vehicle Office

Ohio Bureau of Motor Vehicles
Legal Counsel Office
1970 W. Broad St., Columbus, OH 43223-1101
(614) 752-7500; Driver's Licenses: (614) 752-7600;
Registration: (614) 752-7800; TDD: (614) 752-4559
Internet: www.ohiobmv.com/

P.O. Box 16520, Columbus, OH 43266-0020
(614) 466-7014; Fax: (614) 752-6063
Fee for obtaining abstract: $2.00

Police

Ohio State Highway Patrol
1970 W. Broad St., Columbus, OH 43223
Mailing Address: P.O. Box 182074, Columbus, OH 43218
(614) 466-2660; Accident Reports: (614) 466-3536;
Fax: (614) 644-9749
Internet: www.ohio.gov/ohiostatepatrol/

Superintendent: Paul D. McClellan
Fee for obtaining accident report: $4.00

Probate, Recording and Notary Certificate Offices

Estate & Wills: Probate Court, each county
Deeds and Mortgages: Clerk of Court of Common Pleas,
each county
Notary Certificates: Commissioned by the Secretary of
State upon recommendation of a judge; Certified by
Secretary of State ($15.00)

Senators, U.S.

Mike DeWine (Republican)
140 Russell Senate Office Bldg., Washington, DC 20510
(202) 224-2315; Fax: (202) 224-6519
Internet: http://dewine.senate.gov

George V. Voinovich (Republican)
524 Hart Senate Office Bldg., Washington, DC 20510
(202) 224-3353; Fax: (202) 228-1382
Internet: http://voinovich.senate.gov

Secretary of State

Office of the Secretary of State
180 E. Broad St., 16th Floor, Columbus, OH 43215
(614) 466-2655; Fax: (614) 644-0649
E-mail: blackwell@sos.state.oh.us
Internet: www.sos.state.oh.us

Walk-in Client Service Center,
30 E. Broad St., Lower Level, Columbus, OH 43215

Secretary of State: J. Kenneth Blackwell (Republican)
Elected; next election Nov. 2006

Tax Department

Department of Taxation
30 E. Broad St., 22nd Floor, P.O. Box 530,
Columbus, OH 43216-0530
Income Tax: (800) 282-1780; Fax: (614) 387-1851;
Sales Tax: (614) 466-4810; Estate Tax: (614) 387-1976;
Excise Tax: (614) 466-3794;
Personal Property Tax: (614) 466-3280;
Public Utility Tax: (614) 466-7371;
Tax Equalization: (614) 466-5744
Internet: www.tax.ohio.gov

Tax Commissioner: William Wilkins

Victim Compensation Program

Victims of Crime Division
150 E. Gay St., 25th Floor, Columbus, OH 43215
(614) 466-5610, 11; Victim Hotline: (800) 582-2877;
Fax: (614) 752-2732, 995-5412
Internet: www.ag.state.oh.us
Ohio Rev. Code §§2743.51 to 2743.72

Vital Statistics

Vital Statistics
Ohio Department of Health, 35 E. Chestnut St.,
P.O. Box 15098, Columbus, OH 43215-0098
(614) 466-2531; Fax: (614) 728-9181
E-mail: vitalstat@odh.ohio.gov
Internet: www.odh.state.oh.us, Credit Card Orders via
Internet: www.vitalcheck.com
*Births from Dec. 20, 1908-present. Births and deaths prior
to Dec. 20, 1908, contact the local county probate court.
Deaths from Jan. 1, 1955-present. Marriage and Divorce
indexes from 1955-present. Certified copies of marriage
records may be obtained from probate court that issued
marriage license. Certified copies of divorce decrees may be
obtained from Common Pleas Court where divorce was
decreed.*
Certified copy—$15.00.

OKLAHOMA   *Capital: Oklahoma City*

3,450,654 (2000 Census)
State Information: (405) 521-2011
State Web Site: www.state.ok.us

Administrative Office of the Courts

Administrative Office of the Courts
1915 N. Stiles, Suite 305, Oklahoma City, OK 73105
(405) 521-2450; Fax: (405) 521-6815
Internet: www.oscn.net
Administrative Dir. of the Courts: Howard W. Conyers

Attorney Discipline

Oklahoma Bar Association Office of the General Counsel
1901 N. Lincoln Blvd., Oklahoma City, OK 73105
Mailing Address: P.O. Box 53036,
Oklahoma City, OK 73152
(405) 416-7007; Fax: (405) 416-7003
General Counsel: Dan Murdock

Attorney General

Office of the Attorney General
112 State Capitol, 2300 N. Lincoln Blvd.,
Oklahoma City, OK 73105
(405) 521-3921; Fax: (405) 521-6246
Internet: www.oag.state.ok.us/
Atty. General: W.A. Drew Edmondson (Democrat)
Elected; next election Nov. 2006

Banking Department

State Banking Department
4545 N. Lincoln Blvd., Suite 164,
Oklahoma City, OK 73105
(405) 521-2782; Fax: (405) 522-2993
Internet: www.osbd.state.ok.us
Commissioner: Mick Thompson

Bar Admissions

Board of Bar Examiners
1901 N. Lincoln Blvd., Oklahoma City, OK 73105
Mailing Address: P.O. Box 53036,
Oklahoma City, OK 73152-3036
(405) 416-7075; Fax: (405) 528-4103
Internet: www.okbbe.com
12 hours CLE required per year.
Admission on motion with five of the last seven years
practice in a Reciprocal Jurisdiction.

Bar Association

Oklahoma Bar Assn.
1901 N. Lincoln Blvd., Oklahoma City, OK 73105
Mailing Address: P.O. Box 53036,
Oklahoma City, OK 73152-3036
(405) 416-7000; Fax: (405) 416-7001
Internet: www.okbar.org
Exec. Dir.: John Morris Williams
President: Michael D. Evans
Integrated Bar
Annual Meeting—November, 2005

Chief Medical Examiner

Office of Chief Medical Examiner
901 N. Stonewall St., Oklahoma City, OK 73117
(405) 239-7141; Fax: (405) 239-2430
Chief Medical Examiner: Dr. Fred Jordan

Client Protection Fund

Client Security Fund, Oklahoma Bar Association
1901 N. Lincoln, Oklahoma City, OK 73105
Mailing Address: P.O. Box 53036,
Oklahoma City, OK 73152
(405) 416-7000; Fax: (405) 416-7003
Internet: www.okbar.org
Exec. Dir.: John Morris Williams

Commerce Department

Department of Commerce
900 N. Stiles, Oklahoma City, OK 73104-3234
Mailing Address: P.O. Box 26980,
Oklahoma City, OK 73126-0980
(405) 815-6552, (800) 879-6552; Fax: (405) 815-5199
E-mail: info@odoc.state.ok.us
Internet: www.okcommerce.gov

Corporations Officers

Department of State
Corporations Department
2300 N. Lincoln, Room 101,
Oklahoma City, OK 73105-4897
(405) 521-3911; Certification Dept.: (405) 521-4211;
Fax: (405) 521-3771
Internet: www.sos.state.ok.us
Business Division Dir.: Vickie Mitchell (405) 521-3912
   E-mail: vickie.mitchell@sos.state.ok.us
UCC Dir.: Gary Brownlee
   Oklahoma County Clerk's Office, Suite 107,
   320 Robert S. Kerr Ave., Oklahoma City, OK 73102
   (405) 713-1522
   E-mail: uccoffice@oklahomacounty.org
   Internet: www.oklahomacounty.org

Criminal History Board

State Bureau of Investigation
Criminal History Reporting Unit
6600 N. Harvey Pl., Bldg. 6, Oklahoma City, OK 73116
(405) 848-6724; Fax: (405) 843-3804
Internet: www.osbi.state.ok.us

Economic Development Administration

See Commerce Department

Governor's Office

Office of the Governor
State Capitol Bldg., Room 212, 2300 N. Lincoln Blvd.,
Oklahoma City, OK 73105
(405) 521-2342; Fax: (405) 523-3353
Internet: www.governor.state.ok.us

440 S. Houston St., Suite 304, Tulsa, OK 74127
(918) 581-2801; Fax: (918) 581-2835
Governor: Brad Henry (Democrat)
Next election Nov. 2006

Highest State Court

Supreme Court
State Capitol, Room 245, Oklahoma City, OK 73105
(405) 521-2163
Internet: www.oscn.net
Chief Justice: Joseph M. Watt
Clerk of the Supreme Court: Michael S. Richie
   State Capitol, Room B-2, Oklahoma City, OK 73105

Insurance Department

Office of the Insurance Commissioner
2401 N.W. 23rd St., Suite 28, Oklahoma City, OK 73107
Mailing Address: P.O. Box 53408,
Oklahoma City, OK 73152-3408
(405) 521-2828; In-State: (800) 522-0071;
Fax: (405) 521-6635; Legal: (405) 521-2746;
Legal and Financial Fax: (405) 522-0125
E-mail: okinsdept@insurance.state.ok.us
Internet: www.oid.state.ok.us

Insurance Department—Cont'd

3105 E. Skelly Dr., Suite 305, Tulsa, OK 74105
(918) 747-7700, (800) 728-2906
Commissioner: Carroll Fisher
Chief Examiner: John Beers

Motor Vehicle Office

Oklahoma Department of Public Safety
For Driver History write: Attn.: Driving Records,
3600 N. Martin Luther King Blvd., P.O. Box 11415,
Oklahoma City, OK 73136 (405) 425-2262
Internet: www.dps.state.ok.us

For Collision Reports write: Attn.: Records Mgmt. Div.,
P.O. Box 11415, Oklahoma City, OK 73136
(405) 425-2192
Driver's Records
Fee for obtaining abstract: $10.00
Fee for obtaining Collision Reports: $10.00—certified
copies; $7.00—uncertified copies

Oklahoma Motor Vehicle Division
Oklahoma Tax Commission
409 N.E. 28th, Oklahoma City, OK 73194
Mailing Address: 2501 Lincoln Blvd.,
Oklahoma City, OK 73194
(405) 521-3221; Fax: (405) 522-0991
Internet: www.oktax.state.ok.us
Vehicle Registration and Title Information
Fee for obtaining abstract: $7.50 per copy; $10.00 for
certified copy

Police

Oklahoma Highway Patrol
3600 N. Martin Luther King Blvd.,
Oklahoma City, OK 73111
Mailing Address: P.O. Box 11415,
Oklahoma City, OK 73136
(405) 425-2424; Fax: (405) 425-7039
Internet: www.dps.state.ok.us/

Records Management Division, P.O. Box 11415,
Oklahoma City, OK 73136
(405) 425-2192; Fax: (405) 425-2046

Chief: Col. Gary Adams (405) 425-2003
Fee for obtaining accident report: Certified copy, $10.00
per report; Uncertified $7.00 per report include SASE

Probate, Recording and Notary Certificate Offices

Estate & Wills: District Court Clerks
Deeds and Mortgages: County Clerks
Notary Certificates: Certified by Secretary of State
(including Apostille Certification, $25, Apostille Adoption
$10; Authentication $20)

Senators, U.S.

Tom Coburn (Republican)
B-400 Dirksen Senate Office Bldg., Washington, DC 20510
(202) 224-5754; Fax: (202) 224-6008

James M. Inhofe (Republican)
453 Russell Senate Office Bldg., Washington, DC 20510
(202) 224-4721; Fax: (202) 228-0380
Internet: http://inhofe.senate.gov

Secretary of State

Office of the Secretary of State
101 State Capitol, 2300 N. Lincoln Blvd.,
Oklahoma City, OK 73105-4897
(405) 521-3912; Fax: (405) 521-3771
Internet: www.sos.state.ok.us

Secretary of State: M. Susan Savage
Appointed

Tax Department

Oklahoma Tax Commission
Connors Bldg., Capitol Complex, 2501 N. Lincoln Blvd.,
Oklahoma City, OK 73194
Mailing Address: P.O. Box 26800, Oklahoma City, OK 73126-0800

Taxpayer Assistance: (405) 521-3160;
Tax Policy & Research: (405) 521-3133;
Audit Div.: (405) 521-3251;
Collections Div.: (405) 521-3281;
Legal Div.: (405) 521-3141;
Administration Fax: (405) 521-2035;
Legal Fax: (405) 521-2036
Internet: http://www.oktax.state.ok.us
Chairman: Thomas E. Kemp, Jr. (405) 521-3637

Victim Compensation Program

Crime Victims Compensation Board
421 N.W. 13th St., Suite 290, Oklahoma City, OK 73103
(405) 264-5006; Fax: (405) 264-5097; Toll-Free: (800) 745-6098
Internet: www.dac.state.ok.us
Okla. Stat. Title 21, §§142.1-et seq.

Vital Statistics

Vital Records Division
State Health Department, 1000 N.E. 10th St., Room 111,
Oklahoma City, OK 73117
Mailing Address: P.O. Box 53551,
Oklahoma City, OK 73152-3551
(405) 271-4040
Births, Deaths—1908-present. Marriages and
Divorces—filed in each county.
Fee for search of birth records—$10.00. Fee for search of
death records—$10.00. If a certificate is on record the
searching fee pays for a certified copy. If record of birth
certificate is not located in file the search fee is credited
toward the filing of a delayed certificate of birth and an
additional $5.00 is charged for the issuance of the first
certified copy.

OREGON   *Capital: Salem*

3,421,399 (2000 Census)
State Web Site: www.state.or.us

Administrative Office of the Courts

Office of the State Court Administrator
Justice Bldg., Room 510, 1162 Court St.,
Salem, OR 97301-4096
Mailing Address: Supreme Court Bldg., 1163 State St.,
Salem, OR 97301
(503) 986-5500; Fax: (503) 986-5503
Internet: www.ojd.state.or.us
State Court Administrator: Kingsley W. Click

Attorney Discipline

Oregon State Bar Disciplinary Counsel's Office
5200 S.W. Meadows Rd., P.O. Box 1689,
Lake Oswego, OR 97035-0889
(503) 620-0222; Fax: (503) 968-4457
Disciplinary Counsel: Jeffrey D. Sapiro

Attorney General

Office of the Attorney General
1162 Court St. N.E., Salem, OR 97301-4096
(503) 378-4400; Fax: (503) 378-4017
Internet: www.doj.state.or.us/
Atty. General: Hardy Myers (Democrat)
Elected; next election Nov. 2008

Banking Department

Division of Finance and Corporate Securities
350 Winter St. N.E., Room 410, Salem, OR 97301-3881
Mailing Address: P.O. Box 14480, Salem, OR 97309-0405
(503) 378-4140; Fax: (503) 947-7862
Internet: www.oregondfcs.org
Administrator: Floyd G. Lanter

Bar Admissions

State Board of Bar Examiners
5200 S.W. Meadows Rd., P.O. Box 1689,
Lake Oswego, OR 97035-0889
(503) 620-0222, Exts. 310, 311, 316, 410; Fax: (503) 598-6990
E-mail: mgholston@osbar.org
Internet: www.osbar.org
45 hrs. CLE required per three years (includes six hrs. ethics).
No admission without exam, except for Reciprocity
between Idaho, Utah and Washington.

Bar Association

Oregon State Bar
5200 S.W. Meadows Rd., P.O. Box 1689,
Lake Oswego, OR 97035
(503) 620-0222; Oregon In-State: (800) 452-8260;
Fax: (503) 684-1366
E-mail: info@osbar.org
Internet: www.osbar.org

Exec. Dir.: Karen L. Garst; E-mail: kgarst@osbar.org

President: Nena Cook
Integrated Bar
Annual Meeting—September, 2005

Chief Medical Examiner

Office of Chief Medical Examiner
13309 S.E. 84th Ave., Suite 100, Clackamas, OR 97015
(503) 451-2200; Fax: (503) 657-6831
Internet: www.osp.state.or.us

Chief Medical Examiner: Karen Gunson, M.D.

Client Protection Fund

Client Security Fund
Oregon State Bar
5200 S.W. Meadows Rd., P.O. Box 1689,
Lake Oswego, OR 97035
(503) 620-0222; Fax: (503) 624-8326
Internet: www.osbar.org

Exec. Dir.: Karen L. Garst

Commerce Department

See Economic Development Administration

Corporations Officers

Department of State
Corporation Division
151 Public Service Bldg., 255 Capitol St. N.E.,
Salem, OR 97310-1327
General Information: (503) 986-2200;
Copies/Certificates: (503) 986-2317; Fax: (503) 986-6355;
Fax Notaries: (503) 986-2300; Fax UCC: (503) 373-1166;
Fax Corporations: (503) 378-4381

Director: Peter Threlkel (503) 986-2205
    E-mail: peter.threlkel@state.or.us

Manager, Business Registry/Business Info. Center:
    Twila Coakley (503) 986-2219
    E-mail: twila.k.coakley@state.or.us

Manager, UCC/Notary Public: Gary L. Johnson
    (503) 986-2207
    E-mail: gary.l.johnson@state.or.us

Division Policy Analyst: Tom Wrosch (503) 986-1522
    E-mail: thomas.e.wrosch@state.or.us

Research Analyst: Carolyn Thrasher (503) 986-2227
    E-mail: carolyn.m.thrasher@state.or.us

Criminal History Board

State Police
Identification Services Section
3772 Portland Rd. N.E., Bldg. C, Salem, OR 97303
(503) 378-3070; Fax: (503) 378-2121

Economic Development Administration

Economic and Community Development Department
775 Summer St. NE, Suite 200, Salem, OR 97301
(503) 986-0123; In-State: (800) 233-3306;
Fax: (503) 581-5115
Internet: www.econ.state.or.us/

International Trade, One World Trade Center, Suite 205,
121 S.W. Salmon, Portland, OR 97204
(503) 229-6051; TTY: (800) 735-2900; Fax: (503) 222-5050
Director: Martin Brantley

Governor's Office

Office of the Governor
State Capitol, Room 160, 900 Court St., N.E.,
Salem, OR 97310-4047
(503) 378-3111; Fax: (503) 378-6827
E-mail: governor@state.wy.us
Internet: www.governor.oregon.gov

Governor: Theodore R. Kulongoski (Democrat)
Next election Nov. 2006

Highest State Court

Supreme Court
Supreme Court Bldg., 1163 State St.,
Salem, OR 97301-2563
(503) 986-5555; Fax: (503) 986-5730
Internet: www.ojd.state.or.us/courts/supreme

Chief Justice: Wallace P. Carson, Jr.

State Court Administrator: Kingsley W. Click
    (503) 986-5500; Fax: (503) 986-5730

Insurance Department

Dept. of Consumer & Business Services
Insurance Division
350 Winter St. N.E., Room 440, Salem, OR 97301-3883
(503) 947-7980; Fax: (503) 378-4351
E-mail: dcbs.insmail@state.or.us
Internet: www.insurance.oregon.gov

Director: Cory Streisinger
Administrator: Joel Ario
Deputy Administrator: Carl Lundberg

Motor Vehicle Office

Oregon Department of Transportation
Driver and Motor Vehicle Services, 1905 Lana Ave. N.E.,
Salem, OR 97314
Salem Area: (503) 945-5000;
Portland Area: (503) 299-9999; Fax: (503) 945-0893
Internet: www.odot.state.or.us/dmv, www.oregondmv.com
See website for fees.

Police

Oregon State Police
400 Public Service Bldg., 255 Capitol St. N.E.,
Salem, OR 97310
(503) 378-3720, 25; Fax: (503) 378-8282
Internet: www.osp.state.or.us

Accident Reports Unit, Department of Motor Vehicles,
1905 Lana Ave. N.E., Salem, OR 97314
(503) 945-5098; Fax: (503) 945-5267
Superintendent: Ronald C. Ruecker
Fee for obtaining accident report: $8.50

Probate, Recording and Notary Certificate Offices

Estate & Wills: Circuit Court Clerk, Probate Section, each county
Deeds and Mortgages: County Clerks
Notary Certificates: Secretary of State, Attn.: Corporation Division, 255 Capitol St. N.E., Suite 151, Salem OR 97310
(Certificate or Apostille $10.00)

Senators, U.S.

Gordon Smith (Republican)
404 Russell Senate Office Bldg., Washington, DC 20510
(202) 224-3753; Fax: (202) 228-3997
Internet: http://gsmith.senate.gov

Ron Wyden (Democrat)
516 Hart Senate Office Bldg., Washington, DC 20510
(202) 224-5244; Fax: (202) 228-2717
Internet: http://wyden.senate.gov

Secretary of State

Office of the Secretary of State
136 State Capitol, Salem, OR 97310-0722
(503) 986-1500; Fax: (503) 986-1616
Internet: www.sos.state.or.us

Secretary of State: Bill Bradbury (Democrat)
    (503) 986-1523
    E-mail: oregon.sos@state.or.us
Elected; next election Nov. 2008

Tax Department

Department of Revenue
955 Center St. N.E., Salem, OR 97301-2555
(503) 378-4988
Internet: www.dor.state.or.us

Director: Elizabeth Harchenko
    (503) 945-8214; Fax: (503) 945-8290

Victim Compensation Program

Crime Victims Assistance Section
Department of Justice
1162 Court St. N.E., Salem, OR 97301-4096
(503) 378-5348; TDD: (503) 378-5938; Fax: (503) 378-5738
E-mail: cvas.email@doj.state.or.us
Internet: www.doj.state.or.us/CrimeV/welcome1.htm
Or. Rev. Stat. §§147.005 to 147.365.471 (enacted 1977; amended Jan. 2004)

Vital Statistics

Department of Human Services/Vital Records
Portland State Office Bldg., Suite 225,
800 N.E. Oregon St., Portland, OR 97232-2162
Mailing Address: Oregon Vital Records, P.O. Box 14050,
Portland, OR 97293-0050
Recorded Information: (503) 731-4095;
Order by Phone: (503) 731-4108; Order by Fax: (503) 234-8417;
General Fax: (503) 731-4084, 731-3076
Internet: www.healthoregon.org
Births from July 1903. Deaths from July 1903. Marriages from 1906. Divorces 1925.
Fee for search—$20.00, includes one certified copy.
Additional copies—$15.00 each. Credit Card
Orders—$32.50 each. These may be ordered by phone, Fax or the Internet.

PENNSYLVANIA   *Capital: Harrisburg*

12,281,054 (2000 Census)
State Information: (717) 787-2121
State Web Site: www.state.pa.us

Administrative Office of the Courts

Administrative Office of Pennsylvania Courts
1515 Market St., Suite 1414, Philadelphia, PA 19102
(215) 560-6300; Fax: (215) 560-6315
Internet: www.courts.state.pa.us
State Court Administrator: Zygmont A. Pines

Attorney Discipline

The Disciplinary Board of the Supreme Court of Pennsylvania
2 Lemoyne Dr., 1st Floor, Lemoyne, PA 17043
(717) 731-7073
Chief Disciplinary Counsel: Paul J. Killion

Attorney General

Office of the Attorney General
Strawberry Sq., 16th Floor, Harrisburg, PA 17120
(717) 787-3391; Fax: (717) 783-1107
Internet: www.attorneygeneral.gov/
Atty. General: Thomas W. Corbett, Jr. (Republican)
Elected; next election Nov. 2008

Banking Department

Department of Banking
333 Market St., 16th Floor, Harrisburg, PA 17101-2290
(717) 787-6991; Fax: (717) 787-8773
Internet: www.banking.state.pa.us
Secretary: A. William Schenck III
E-mail is available by accessing our website.

Bar Admissions

Pennsylvania Board of Law Examiners
5070A Ritter Rd., Suite 300, Mechanicsburg, PA 17055
(717) 795-7270; Fax: (717) 795-8194
Internet: www.pabarexam.org
Admission on motion with five of the last seven years practice in a Reciprocal Jurisdiction or currently admitted in good standing in any Jurisdiction and graduate (JD) of an ABA accredited law school (Rule 204).

Bar Association

Pennsylvania Bar Assn.
100 South St., P.O. Box 186, Harrisburg, PA 17108
(717) 238-6715; Fax: (717) 238-1204
Internet: www.pabar.org
Exec. Dir.: Barry M. Simpson
President: Michael H. Reed
Integrated Bar
Annual Meeting—May, 2005

Client Protection Fund

Pennsylvania Lawyers Fund for Client Security
4909 Louise Dr., Suite 101, Mechanicsburg, PA 17055
(717) 691-7503, (800) 962-4618; Fax: (717) 691-9005
E-mail: admin@palawfund.com
Internet: www.palawfund.com
Exec. Dir.: Kathryn J. Peifer

Commerce Department

See Economic Development Administration

Corporations Officers

Corporations Bureau
206 North Office Bldg., Harrisburg, PA 17120
Mailing Address: P.O. Box 8722,
Harrisburg, PA 17105-8722
(717) 787-1057; Fax: (717) 783-2244
Internet: www.dos.state.pa.us/corps/
Director: Richard K. House (717) 783-9210
E-mail: rihouse@state.pa.us
Admin. Asst.: Travis Blouch (717) 783-9210
E-mail: tblouch@state.pa.us
Chief, UCC Division: Patricia A. Hegedus
P.O. Box 8721, Harrisburg, PA 17105-8721
(717) 772-2149; E-mail: phegedus@state.pa.us
Division Chief, Customer Service: Lyndelle Butler
(717) 783-3584; E-mail: lybutler@state.pa.us
Legal Asst. Supervisor: Joy Drake (717) 772-2147
E-mail: jdrake@state.pa.us
Operations Mgr.: Charles W. Bowser, Jr. (717) 772-1093
E-mail: charlbowse@state.pa.us

Criminal History Board

Bureau of Records & Identification
1800 Elmerton Ave., Harrisburg, PA 17110
(717) 783-5588; Fax: (717) 783-5589

Economic Development Administration

Department of Community and Economic Development
Keystone Bldg., 4th Floor, 400 North St.,
Harrisburg, PA 17120-0225
Customer Service: (800) 379-7448;
Chief Counsel: (717) 783-8452; Fax: (717) 772-3103
Internet: www.inventpa.com
Secretary: Dennis Yablonsky (717) 787-3003

Governor's Office

225 Main Capitol Bldg., Harrisburg, PA 17120
(717) 787-2500; Fax: (717) 772-8284
Internet: www.state.pa.us/
Governor: Edward G. Rendell (Democrat)
Next election Nov. 2006

Highest State Court

Supreme Court
Supreme Court, 468 City Hall, Philadelphia, PA 19107
(215) 560-6370
Internet: www.aopc.org

434 Main Capitol Building, Harrisburg, PA 17120
(717) 787-6181

801 City-County Bldg., Pittsburgh, PA 15219 (412) 565-2816
Chief Justice: Ralph J. Cappy
Clerk of the Supreme Court: Charles W. Johns

Insurance Department

Insurance Department
1326 Strawberry Sq., Harrisburg, PA 17120
(717) 783-0442; Fax: (717) 772-1969
Internet:
www.state.pa.us/PA_Exec/Insurance/overview.html

State Office Bldg., Room 1701, 1400 Spring Garden St.,
Philadelphia, PA 19130 (215) 560-2630; Fax: (215) 560-2648

State Office Bldg., Room 304, 300 Liberty Ave.,
Pittsburgh, PA 15222 (412) 565-2020; Fax: (412) 565-7648
Commissioner: M. Diane Koken
Chief Counsel: Steven Davis
Dir., Bureau of Licensing and Financial Analysis:
Willard A. Smith

Motor Vehicle Office

Pennsylvania Bureau of Motor Vehicles
Dept. of Transportation, Riverfront Office Center,
1101 S. Front St., Harrisburg, PA 17104
In-State Toll Free: (800) 932-4600; (717) 391-6190
Internet: www.dmv.state.pa.us

For Abstracts write: Dept. of Transportation,
Bur. of Driver Licensing, P.O. Box 68695,
Harrisburg, PA 17106-8695
Fee for obtaining abstract: $5.00; $10.00 certified

Police

Pennsylvania State Police
1800 Elmerton Ave., Harrisburg, PA 17110
(717) 783-5599; Fax: (717) 787-2948;
Traffic Accident Records Unit: (717) 783-5516
Commissioner: Jeffrey B. Miller (717) 772-6924
Fee for obtaining accident report: $8.00, checks payable to
Commonwealth of Pennsylvania

Probate, Recording and Notary Certificate Offices

Estate & Wills: County Registers of Wills
Deeds and Mortgages: County Recorder of Deeds or
Philadelphia Commissioner of Records
Notary Certificates: Department of State, Bureau of
Commisions Elections and Legislation ($15.00 Apostille Fee)

Senators, U.S.

Rick Santorum (Republican)
511 Dirksen Senate Office Bldg., Washington, DC 20510
(202) 224-6324; Fax: (202) 228-0604
Internet: http://santorum.senate.gov

Arlen Specter (Republican)
711 Hart Senate Office Bldg., Washington, DC 20510
(202) 224-4254; Fax: (202) 228-1229
Internet: http://specter.senate.gov

Secretary of State

Office of the Secretary of the Commonwealth
Department of State, 302 N. Office Bldg.,
Commonwealth Ave. & North St., Harrisburg, PA 17120
(717) 787-6458; Fax: (717) 787-1734
Internet: www.dos.state.pa.us
Secretary of the Commonwealth: Pedro A. Cortes
Appointed

Tax Department

Department of Revenue
1133 Strawberry Sq., Harrisburg, PA 17128-1100
(717) 772-9739; Forms: (888) 728-2937;
Bureau of Administration: (717) 787-8293;
Administrative Svcs. Bur.: (717) 986-4603;
Audit Bur.: (717) 783-1731
Internet: www.revenue.state.pa.us/

Tax Forms Service Unit, 711 Gibson Blvd.,
Harrisburg, PA 17104-3200
Tax Information: (717) 985-3207;
Forms: (717) 985-3236, 37, 38, 39, 41; Fax: (717) 985-3243
Secretary: Gregory C. Fajt
Chief Counsel: Christopher Zettlemoyer

Victim Compensation Program

Victims' Compensation Assistance Program
Pennsylvania Commission on Crime and Delinquency
3101 N. Front St., P.O. Box 1167, Harrisburg, PA 17108-1167
(717) 783-5153; Fax: (717) 787-4306
Internet: www.pccd.state.pa.us
Pa. Stat. Ann. titl. 18 §§11.704 (enacted 1976)

Vital Statistics

Division of Vital Records
101 S. Mercer St., Room 401, New Castle, PA 16103-1528
Mailing Address: P.O. Box 1528, New Castle, PA 16101
(724) 656-3100; Credit Card Orders by Fax: (724) 652-8951
Internet: www.health.state.pa.us/vitalrecords
*Births, Deaths—1906-present. Marriage—Marriage
License Clerk of county where license issued.
Divorces—Prothonotary of county where divorce decreed.*
Certified copy—Births—$10.00. Deaths—$9.00. Expedited
service ordered by fax with a credit card—$7.00, in
addition to certified copy fee.

RHODE ISLAND   *Capital: Providence*

1,048,319 (2000 Census)
State Information: (401) 277-2000
State Web Site: www.state.ri.us

Administrative Office of the Courts

Administrative Office of the Courts
250 Benefit St., Room 705, Providence, RI 02903
(401) 222-3266; Fax: (401) 222-5131
Internet: www.courts.state.ri.gov
Court Administrator: J. Joseph Baxter

Attorney Discipline

Supreme Court Disciplinary Board
John E. Fogarty Judicial Annex, 2nd Floor,
24 Weybosset St., Providence, RI 02903
(401) 222-3270; Fax: (401) 222-1191
Chief Disciplinary Counsel: David D. Curtin

Attorney General

Office of the Attorney General
150 S. Main St., Providence, RI 02903
(401) 274-4400; Fax: (401) 222-1331
Internet: http://www.riag.state.ri.us
Atty. General: Patrick C. Lynch (Democrat)
Elected; next election Nov. 2006

Banking Department

Department of Business Regulation
Division of Banking
233 Richmond St., Suite 231, Providence, RI 02903-4231
(401) 222-2405; Fax: (401) 222-5628
Superintendent: Dennis F. Ziroli

Bar Admissions

Supreme Court of Rhode Island
Board of Bar Examiners
250 Benefit St., Providence, RI 02903
(401) 222-3272; Fax: (401) 222-3599
Internet: www.courts.state.ri.us
Ten hours CLE required per year; at least two hours must
be ethics courses.
No admission without exam.

Bar Association

Rhode Island Bar Assn.
115 Cedar St., Providence, RI 02903
(401) 421-5740; Fax: (401) 421-2703
Internet: www.ribar.com
Exec. Dir.: Helen Desmond McDonald, Ext. 107
    E-mail: hmcdonald@ribar.com
President: Philip M. Weinstein
Integrated Bar
Annual Meeting—June, 2005

Chief Medical Examiner

Office of Chief Medical Examiner
Dept. of Health, 48 Orms St., Providence, RI 02904
(401) 222-5500; Fax: (401) 222-5517
Chief Medical Examiner: Elizabeth A. Laposata, M.D.

Client Protection Fund

Lawyers Fund for Client Reimbursement
Rhode Island Bar Association
115 Cedar St., Providence, RI 02903
(401) 421-5740; Fax: (401) 421-2703
Exec. Dir.: Helen Desmond McDonald

Commerce Department

Department of Business Regulation
233 Richmond St., Providence, RI 02903
(401) 222-2246; Fax: (401) 222-6098
E-mail: dstg@dbr.state.ri.us
Internet: www.dbr.state.ri.us

Corporations Officers

Corporations Office
100 N. Main St., Providence, RI 02903-1335
Corporations/UCC: (401) 222-3040;
Notaries & Trademark Division: (401) 222-1487;
Fax, Corporations: (401) 222-1309;
Fax, UCC, Notaries, Trademarks: (401) 222-3879
Internet: www.sec.state.ri.us

Director: Sandra M. Williams
  (401) 222-3040
  E-mail: swilliams@sec.state.ri.us

Notary Supervisor: Justine Santoro Almeida
  (401) 222-1487
  E-mail: jalmeida@sec.state.ri.us

UCC Supervisor: Terrance Jackson
  (401) 222-3040
  E-mail: tjackson@sec.state.ri.us

Criminal History Board

Office of the Attorney General
Bureau of Criminal Identification
150 S. Main St., Providence, RI 02903
(401) 421-5268; Fax: (401) 222-1331

Economic Development Administration

Economic Development Corporation
One W. Exchange St., 5th Floor, Providence, RI 02903
(401) 222-2601; Fax: (401) 222-2102
E-mail: riedc@riedc.com
Internet: www.riedc.com

Exec. Dir./C.E.O.: Michael McMahon

Governor's Office

Office of the Governor
115 State House, Providence, RI 02903
(401) 222-2080; Fax: (401) 222-8096
E-mail: rigov@gov.state.ri.us
Internet: www.governor.state.ri.us

444 N. Capitol St. N.W., Suite 619, Washington, DC 20001
(202) 624-3605; Fax: (202) 624-3607

Governor: Donald Carcieri (Republican)
Next election Nov. 2006

Highest State Court

Supreme Court
250 Benefit St., Providence, RI 02903
(401) 222-3272; Fax: (401) 222-3599
Internet: www.courts.state.ri.us

Chief Justice: Frank J. Williams
Clerk of the Supreme Court: Pamela Woodcock Pfeiffer

Insurance Department

Insurance Division
233 Richmond St., Suite 233, Providence, RI 02903-4233
(401) 222-2223; Fax: (401) 222-5475
Internet: www.dbr.state.ri.us

Commissioner: Marilyn Shannon McConaghy
Assoc. Dir./Supt.: Joseph Torti
Chief Insurance Examiner: Sharon K. Gordon

Motor Vehicle Office

Rhode Island Division of Motor Vehicles
Operator Control for Abstracts Section, 286 Main Street, Pawtucket, RI 02860
(401) 588-3020; Abstracts: (401) 721-2650;
TTY: (401) 721-2618; Titles: (401) 588-3018
Internet: www.dmv.state.ri.us
Fee for obtaining abstract: $16.00

Police

Rhode Island State Police
311 Danielson Pike, North Scituate, RI 02857
(401) 444-1000; Fax: (401) 444-1105
Internet: www.risp.state.ri.us

Superintendent: Col. Steven M. Pare
Fee for obtaining accident report: $10.00

Probate, Recording and Notary Certificate Offices

Estate & Wills: Probate Court Clerks Office, each town or city
Deeds and Mortgages: Recorder or Land Records Office, each city or town
Notary Certificates: Secretary of State, Notary Division (Certificate or Apostille $5.00)

Senators, U.S.

Lincoln D. Chafee (Republican)
141A Russell Senate Office Bldg., Washington, DC 20510
(202) 224-2921
Internet: http://chafee.senate.gov

John Reed (Democrat)
728 Hart Senate Office Bldg., Washington, DC 20510
(202) 224-4642
Internet: http://reed.senate.gov

Secretary of State

Office of the Secretary of State
State House, Room 217, 82 Smith St.,
Providence, RI 02903
(401) 222-2357; Fax: (401) 222-1356
Internet: www.state.ri.us

Secretary of State: Matthew A. Brown (Democrat)
Elected; next election Nov. 2006

Tax Department

Division of Taxation
One Capitol Hill, Providence, RI 02908-5800
(401) 222-2905; Fax: (401) 222-6006;
Sales & Excise Tax Unit: (401) 222-2950
Internet: www.tax.state.ri.us

Tax Administrator: R. Gary Clark (401) 222-3050
Asst. Tax Administrator: Robert M. Gerusso
  (401) 222-3050
Chief Legal Counsel: Marcia McGair Ippolito
  (401) 222-2337

Victim Compensation Program

Crime Victim Compensation Program
Office of the General Treasurer, 40 Fountain St.,
Providence, RI 02903
(401) 222-8590; Fax: (401) 222-4577
Internet: www.treasury.state.ri.us
R.I. Gen. Laws §§12-25-18 (b) (1991 Supp.) 1999 as Amended.

Vital Statistics

Department of Health
Division of Vital Records, 3 Capitol Hill, Room 101,
Providence, RI 02908-5097
(401) 222-2811, 12
Internet: www.health.ri.gov
Births—1904; Deaths—1954. Marriages—1904.
Certified copy—$15.00 (includes two-year search).
Additional copies—$10.00 each. $ .50 per additional year searched. Priority handling—$5.00 surcharge (indicate "Rush" on letter and envelope). Make checks payable to Rhode Island General Treasurer.

SOUTH CAROLINA   *Capital: Columbia*

4,012,012 (2000 Census)
State Information: (803) 734-1000
State Web Site: www.state.sc.us

Administrative Office of the Courts

Court Administration
1015 Sumter St., Suite 200, Columbia, SC 29201
(803) 734-1800; Fax: (803) 734-1355
Internet: www.sccourts.org

Director: Rosalyn W. Frierson

Attorney Discipline

Office of Disciplinary Counsel
1015 Sumter St., Room G.08, Columbia, SC 29201
Mailing Address: P.O. Box 12159, Columbia, SC 29211
(803) 734-2038

Disciplinary Counsel: Henry B. Richardson, Jr.

Attorney General

Rembert C. Dennis Office Bldg., Room 519,
1000 Assembly St., P.O. Box 11549,
Columbia, SC 29211-1549
(803) 734-3970; Fax: (803) 253-6283
Internet: www.scattorneygeneral.org/
Atty. General: Henry McMaster (Republican)
Elected; next election Nov. 2006

Banking Department

Department of Banking
State Board of Financial Institutions
Examination Division, Calhoun Office Bldg., Room 309,
1015 Sumter St., Columbia, SC 29201
Mailing Address: P.O. Box 12549, Columbia, SC 29211
(803) 734-2001; Fax: (803) 734-2013
Commissioner: Louie A. Jacobs

Bar Admissions

Supreme Court of South Carolina
1231 Gervais St., Columbia, SC 29201
Mailing Address: P.O. Box 11330, Columbia, SC 29211
(803) 734-1080; Fax: (803) 734-0394
Internet: www.sccourts.org
14 hrs. CLE required per year including two hrs. of ethics.
No admission without exam.

Bar Association

South Carolina Bar
950 Taylor St., P.O. Box 608, Columbia, SC 29202-0608
(803) 799-6653; Fax: (803) 799-4118
Internet: www.scbar.org
Exec. Dir.: Robert S. Wells
President: Daniel B. White
Integrated Bar
Convention: January, 2006

Client Protection Fund

Lawyers' Fund for Client Protection, South Carolina Bar
950 Taylor St., P.O. Box 608, Columbia, SC 29202
(803) 799-6653; Fax: (803) 799-4118
E-mail: sarah.steen@scbar.org
Contact: Sarah K. Steen; E-mail: sarah.steen@scbar.org

Commerce Department

Department of Commerce
South Trust Bldg., Suite 1600, 1201 Main Street,
Columbia, SC 29201
(803) 737-0400; Fax: (803) 737-0418
Internet: www.sccommerce.com

Corporations Officers

Department of State
Corporation UCC/Department
1205 Pendleton St., Columbia, SC 29201
Mailing Address: P.O. Box 11350, Columbia, SC 29211
General Information: (803) 734-2170;
Fax: (803) 734-1614, 734-2164
Mgr., Business Filings Div.: Amy Ziegler (803) 734-1116

Criminal History Board

State Law Enforcement Division, Criminal Records
4400 Broad River Rd., Columbia, SC 29212
Mailing Address: P.O. Box 21398,
Columbia, SC 29221-1398
(803) 896-7043; Fax: (803) 896-7022
Internet: www.sled.state.sc.us

Economic Development Administration

See Commerce Department

Governor's Office

State House, 1st Fl., 1100 Gervais St., Columbia, SC 29201
Mailing Address: P.O. Box 12267, Columbia, SC 29211
(803) 734-2100; Fax: (803) 734-0396, 734-5167
E-mail: governor@govoepp.state.sc.us
Internet: www.scgovernor.com

444 N. Capitol St. N.W., Suite 203, Washington, DC 20001
(202) 624-7793; Fax: (202) 624-7800
Governor: Mark Sanford (Republican)
Next election Nov. 2006

Highest State Court

Supreme Court
1231 Gervais St., Columbia, SC 29201
Mailing Address: P.O. Box 11330, Columbia, SC 29211
(803) 734-1080; Fax: (803) 734-1499
Chief Justice: Jean H. Toal
Clerk of the Supreme Court: Daniel E. Shearouse

Insurance Department

Department of Insurance
300 Arbor Lake Dr., Suite 1200, Columbia, SC 29223
Mailing Address: P.O. Box 100105, Columbia, SC 29202
(803) 737-6160; Director's Fax: (803) 737-6229
Internet: www.doi.state.sc.us
Director: Eleanor Kitzman
Chief Examiner: Linda G. Haralson

Motor Vehicle Office

South Carolina Department of Motor Vehicles
Driver's Records Division
10311 Wilson Blvd., Columbia, SC 29201
Mailing Address: P.O. Box 1498, Blythewood, SC 29016
(803) 896-5000; Fax: (803) 896-5018
Internet: www.scdmvonline.com
Driver's Licenses
Fee for obtaining abstract: $6.00
South Carolina Department of Motor Vehicles
10311 Wilson Blvd., Blythewood, SC 29016
Mailing Address: P.O. Box 1498, Blythewood, SC 29016
(803) 896-5000
Internet: www.scdmvonline.com
Vehicle Registration and Title
Fee for obtaining abstract: $6.00

Police

South Carolina State Highway Patrol
10311 Wilson Blvd., P.O. Box 1993, Blythewood, SC 29016
(803) 896-7920; Fax: (803) 896-7922
Internet: www.schp.org

Financial Responsibility, Dept. of Motor Vehicles,
P.O. Box 1498, Blythewood, SC 29016
(803) 737-4000
Deputy Dir.: Col. Russell F. Roark III
Fee for obtaining accident report: $6.00

Probate, Recording and Notary Certificate Offices

Estate & Wills: County Probate Judges Office
Deeds and Mortgages: County Clerks of Cts. or Register of
Deeds, where office exists
Notary Certificates: Secretary of State, Notary Div. ($2.00)

Senators, U.S.

Jim DeMint (Republican)
825 Hart Senate Office Bldg., Washington, DC 20510
(202) 224-6121; Fax: (202) 228-5143
Internet: http://demint.senate.gov
Lindsey O. Graham (Republican)
290 Russell Senate Office Bldg., Washington, DC 20510
(202) 224-5972
Internet: http://lgraham.senate.gov

Secretary of State

Office of the Secretary of State
Edgar Brown Bldg., Suite 525, 1205 Pendleton St.,
Columbia, SC 29201
Mailing Address: P.O. Box 11350, Columbia, SC 29211
(803) 734-0629, 734-2170; Fax: (803) 734-1661
Internet: www.scsos.com
Secretary of State: Mark Hammond (Republican)
Elected; next election Nov. 2006

Tax Department

Department of Revenue
301 Gervais St., Columbia, SC 29201
Mailing Address: P.O. Box 125, Columbia, SC 29214-0402
(803) 898-5000; Fax: (803) 898-5446;
Fax (Forms): (800) 768-3676
Internet: www.sctax.org
Director: Burnet R. Maybank III (803) 898-5040

Victim Compensation Program

State Office of Victim Assistance
Edgar A. Brown Bldg., 1205 Pendleton St., Room 401,
Columbia, SC 29201
(803) 734-1900; Fax: (803) 734-1708;
Victims Only: (800) 220-5370
S.C. Code of Laws, 1976 §§16-3-1110 to 16-3-1420 (As amended)

Vital Statistics

Office of Public Health Statistics & Information Services
Division of Vital Records
Department of Health and Environmental Control,
2600 Bull St., Columbia, SC 29201
(803) 898-3630; Fax: (803) 898-3761
Internet: www.scdhec.net/vr
*Births, Deaths—1915. Marriages—July, 1950.
Divorces—July, 1962.*
Search fee—$12.00 fee for records includes certified copy of record, if located. Additional copies: $3.00 each. Additional expedite fee: $5.00

SOUTH DAKOTA   *Capital: Pierre*

754,844 (2000 Census)
State Information: (605) 773-3011
State Web Site: www.state.sd.us

Administrative Office of the Courts

Administrative Office of the Courts
State Capitol, 500 E. Capital, Pierre, SD 57501-5070
(605) 773-3474; Fax: (605) 773-5627
State Court Administrator: D. J. Hanson
E-mail: dj.hanson@ujs.state.sd.us

Attorney Discipline

Disciplinary Board, State Bar of South Dakota
222 E. Capitol Ave., Pierre, SD 57501-2596
(605) 224-7554; Fax: (605) 224-0282
Executive Director/Treasurer: Tom Barnett

Attorney General

500 E. Capitol, Pierre, SD 57501-5070
(605) 773-3215; Fax: (605) 773-4106
E-mail: atghelp@state.sd.us
Internet: www.state.sd.us/atg
Atty. General: Larry Long (Republican)
Elected; next election Nov. 2006

Banking Department

Division of Banking
217 1/2 W. Missouri Ave., Pierre, SD 57501
(605) 773-3421; Fax: (605) 773-5367
Internet: www.state.sd.us/banking
Commissioner: Roger Novotny

Bar Admissions

South Dakota Board of Bar Examiners
500 E. Capitol Ave., Pierre, SD 57501-5070
(605) 773-4898; Fax: (605) 773-6128
Internet: www.sdjudicial.com
No CLE required.
Admission on motion with last five years in practice in another jurisdiction.

Bar Association

State Bar of South Dakota
222 E. Capitol Ave., Pierre, SD 57501-2596
(605) 224-7554; Fax: (605) 224-0282
Internet: www.sdbar.org
Exec. Dir.: Thomas C. Barnett, Jr.
President: Robert C. Riter, Jr.
Integrated Bar
Annual Meeting—June, 2006

Client Protection Fund

Client Security Fund
State Bar of South Dakota
222 E. Capitol Ave., Pierre, SD 57501-2596
(605) 224-7554; Fax: (605) 224-0282
Exec. Dir.: Thomas C. Barnett, Jr.

Commerce Department

Department of Public Safety
118 W. Capitol Ave., Pierre, SD 57501-2000
(605) 773-3178; Fax: (605) 773-3018
Internet: www.state.sd.us/dps/

Corporations Officers

Department of State
Corporations & UCC Central Filings
500 E. Capitol Ave., Pierre, SD 57501-5077
General Information: (605) 773-3537;
Corporations Section, Name Availabilities, Annual Reports & Limited Partnerships: (605) 773-4845;
Notaries: (605) 773-3539; UCC: (605) 733-4422;
Fax: (605) 773-4550
Internet: www.state.sd.us/sos/sos/htm
Supervisor: Beverly Wilson (605) 773-4845
E-mail: bev.wilson@state.sd.us
UCC Dir./Dakota Fast File Supvr.: Shelley Pitlick
(605) 773-5006; E-mail: shelley.pitlick@state.sd.us

Criminal History Board

Office of the Attorney General
Division of Criminal Investigation
500 E. Capitol Ave., Pierre, SD 57501-5070
(605) 773-3331; Fax: (605) 773-7163

Economic Development Administration

Governors Office of Economic Development
711 E. Wells Ave., Pierre, SD 57501-3369
(605) 773-5032, (800) 872-6190; Fax: (605) 773-3256
Internet: www.sdgreatprofits.com
Commissioner: Jim Hagen

Governor's Office

500 E. Capitol Ave., Pierre, SD 57501-5070
(605) 773-3212; Fax: (605) 773-4711
E-mail: governor@state.sd.us
Internet: www.state.sd.us/governor/
Governor: M. Michael Rounds (Republican)
Next election Nov. 2006

Highest State Court

Supreme Court of South Dakota
500 E. Capitol Ave., Pierre, SD 57501-5070
Clerk: (605) 773-3511; Chief Justice: (605) 773-6254;
Fax: (605) 773-6128
Internet: www.state.sd.us/state/judicial/
Chief Justice: David Gilbertson
Clerk of the Supreme Court: Shirley A. Jameson-Fergel

Insurance Department

Division of Insurance
445 E. Capitol, Pierre, SD 57501-3185
(605) 773-3563; Fax: (605) 773-5369
Internet: www.state.sd.us/drr
Director: Gary Steuck

Motor Vehicle Office

South Dakota Division of Motor Vehicles
445 E. Capitol Ave., Pierre, SD 57501-3185
(605) 773-3541; Fax: (605) 773-2549
E-mail: motorv@rev.state.sd.us
Internet: www.state.sd.us/drr/revenue.html

For Abstracts write: Dept. of Public Safety, Driver's License, 118 W. Capitol Ave., Pierre, SD 57501
(605) 773-6883
Fee for obtaining abstract: $4.00 plus state and city tax—no sales tax for out of state requests. MV abstracts: Division of Motor Vehicles (must complete DPPA form and meet criteria for obtaining information) record search $2.00 & title history $5.00

Police

South Dakota Highway Patrol
118 W. Capitol Ave., Pierre, SD 57501-5070
(605) 773-3105; Fax: (605) 773-6046
Internet: http://hp.state.sd.us

State Police—Cont'd

Accident Reports: Office of Accident Records,
118 W. Capitol Ave., Pierre, SD 57501
(605) 773-3868; Fax: (605) 773-6893

Superintendent: Daniel C. Mosteller
Fee for obtaining accident report: $4.00

Probate, Recording and Notary Certificate Offices

Estate & Wills: County Clerk of Courts
Deeds and Mortgages: County Register of Deeds
Notary Certificates: Secretary of State, Notary Division
($5.00)

Senators, U.S.

Tim Johnson (Democrat)
136 Hart Senate Office Bldg., Washington, DC 20510
(202) 224-5842; Fax: (202) 228-0368
Internet: http://johnson.senate.gov

John Thune Senator: (Republican)
, Washington, DC 20510
(202) 224-2321

Secretary of State

Office of the Secretary of State
500 E. Capitol Ave., Suite 204, Pierre, SD 57501-5070
(605) 773-3537; Fax: (605) 773-6580
Internet: www.sdsos.gov

Secretary of State: Chris Nelson (Republican)
Elected; next election Nov. 2006

Tax Department

Department of Revenue and Regulation
445 E. Capitol Ave., Pierre, SD 57501-3185
(605) 773-3311; Fax: (605) 773-5129
Internet: www.state.sd.us/drr

Secretary: Gary R. Viken

Victim Compensation Program

Crime Victims' Compensation Program
Department of Social Services, Office of Adult Services and
Aging
700 Governors Dr., Pierre, SD 57501-2291
(605) 773-6317; In-State Only: (800) 696-9476;
Fax: (605) 773-6834
Internet: www.sdvictims.com
S.D. Codified Laws, 1991 §§ 23A-28B-1 to 23A-28B-44

Vital Statistics

Office of Vital Records
State Department of Health, 600 E. Capitol,
Pierre, SD 57501-2536
(605) 773-4961; Fax: (605) 773-5683
Internet: www.state.sd.us/doh/vitalrec/vital.htm
Births, Deaths, Marriages, Divorces.
Certified copy—marriage and divorce records—$7.00.
Birth and death records—$10.00. Fee subject to change at
press time.

TENNESSEE   *Capital: Nashville*
5,689,283 (2000 Census)
State Information: (615) 741-3011
State Web Site: www.state.tn.us

Administrative Office of the Courts

Administrative Office of the Courts
511 Union St., Suite 600, Nashville, TN 37219
(615) 741-2687; Fax: (615) 741-6285
Internet: www.tsc.state.tn.us

Director: Cornelia A. Clark

Attorney Discipline

Board of Professional Responsibility of the Supreme Court
of Tennessee
1101 Kermit Dr., Suite 730, Nashville, TN 37217-5111
(615) 361-7500; Fax: (615) 367-2480

Chief Disciplinary Counsel: Lance B. Bracy

Attorney General

Office of the Attorney General
425 5th Ave. N., Nashville, TN 37243
Mailing Address: P.O. Box 20207, Nashville, TN 37202
(615) 741-3491; Fax: (615) 741-2009

Atty. General: Paul G. Summers
Appointed

Banking Department

Department of Financial Institutions
Nashville City Center, Suite 400, 511 Union St.,
Nashville, TN 37219
(615) 741-2236; Fax: (615) 253-6306
Internet: www.tennessee.gov/financialinst

Commissioner: Kevin P. Lavender

Bar Admissions

State Board of Law Examiners
706 Church St., Suite 100, Nashville, TN 37243-0740
(615) 741-3234; Fax: (615) 741-5867
Internet: www.state.tn.us/lawexaminers
15 hours CLE required per year.
Admission on motion with five out of last seven years in
practice immediately preceding application, ABA law
school, successful bar exam and intent to practice in state.

Bar Association

Tennessee Bar Assn.
221 Fourth Ave. N., Suite 400, Nashville, TN 37219-2198
(615) 383-7421; Fax: (615) 297-8058
E-mail: email@tnbar.org
Internet: www.tba.org

Exec. Dir.: Allan F. Ramsaur
    E-mail: aramsaur@tnbar.org

President: Bill Haltom
Non-Integrated Bar
Annual Meeting—June, 2005

Chief Medical Examiner

Office of Chief Medical Examiner
Department of Health
Center for Forensic Medicine, 850 R.S. Gass Blvd.,
Nashville, TN 37216
(615) 743-1800; Fax: (615) 743-1890
Internet: www.forensicmed.com

Chief Medical Examiner: Bruce P. Levy, M.D.

Client Protection Fund

Tennessee Lawyers' Fund for Client Protection
221 4th Ave. N., Suite 300, Nashville, TN 37219
(615) 741-3097; Fax: (615) 532-2477

Exec. Dir.: David N. Shearon

Commerce Department

Department of Commerce & Insurance
500 James Robertson Pkwy., 5th Floor,
Nashville, TN 37243
(615) 741-1900; Fax: (615) 532-6934
Internet: http://www.state.tn.us/commerce/

Corporations Officers

Department of State
Corporate Section
Wm. R. Snodgrass Tower, 6th Floor, 312 Eighth Ave. N.,
Nashville, TN 37243
Apostilles/Authentications: (615) 741-3699;
Corporate Information: (615) 741-2286;
Motor Vehicle Temporary Liens: (615) 741-0529;
UCC: (615) 741-3276; Notaries: (615) 741-3699;
Trademarks: (615) 741-0531;
Certifications/Copies: (615) 741-6488;
Service of Process: (615) 741-1799;
Administration Fax: (615) 741-7310;
Corporation Fax: (615) 741-7310; UCC Fax: (615) 532-2892

Dir. of Business Services: Bob Grunow
    (615) 741-0584
    E-mail: bob.grunow@state.tn.us

Asst. Dir.: Reba Barker
    (615) 741-0584
    E-mail: reba.barker@state.tn.us

Criminal History Board

Bureau of Investigation
Professional Standards Unit
901 R.S. Gass Blvd., Nashville, TN 37216-2639
(615) 744-4032; Fax: (615) 744-4656

Economic Development Administration

Department of Economic & Community Development
Wm. R. Snodgrass Tennessee Tower, 11th Floor,
312 Eighth Ave. N., Nashville, TN 37243-0405
(615) 741-1888; Fax: (615) 741-7306
Internet: www.state.tn.us/ecd/
Commissioner: Matt Kisber

Governor's Office

Office of the Governor
State Capitol, 1st Floor, 600 Charlotte Ave.,
Nashville, TN 37243-0001
(615) 741-2001; Fax: (615) 532-9711
Internet: www.state.tn.us/governor/
Governor: Phil Bredesen (Democrat)
    E-mail: phil.bredesen@state.tn.us
Next election Nov. 2006

Highest State Court

Supreme Court
Middle Division, 401 Seventh Ave. N.,
Nashville, TN 37219-1407
(615) 253-1470; Fax: (615) 532-8757
Internet: www.tsc.state.tn.us

Supreme Court Bldg., P.O. Box 909, Jackson, TN 38302
(731) 423-5840; Fax: (731) 423-6453

Supreme Court Bldg., P.O. Box 444, Knoxville, TN 37901
(865) 594-6700; Fax: (865) 594-6497

Chief Justice: Frank F. Drowota III
    Fax: (615) 741-5809

Clerk of the Supreme Court: Michael W. Catalano

Insurance Department

Dept. of Commerce and Insurance
Davy Crockett Tower, 5th Floor,
500 James Robertson Pkwy., Nashville, TN 37243-0565
(615) 741-6007; Commissioner's Fax: (615) 532-6934
Internet: www.state.tn.us/commerce
Commissioner: Paula A. Flowers
Chief Examiner: Donnie Spann

Motor Vehicle Office

Tennessee Department of Safety
Driver Records Unit, Financial Responsibility Section,
1150 Foster Ave., Nashville, TN 37210
Mailing Address: P.O. Box 945, Nashville, TN 37202-0945
(615) 741-3954; Fax: (615) 253-2093
E-mail: finresp.safety@state.tn.us
Internet: www.tennessee.gov/safety
Driver's Abstracts
Fee for obtaining abstract: $5.00

Tennessee Safety Title & Registration Division
44 Vantage Way, Suite 160, Nashville, TN 37243-8050
(615) 741-3101; Fax: (615) 253-4259
Internet: www.state.tn.us/safety/
Vehicle Registration
Fee for obtaining abstract: $5.00 must complete a form for
request; make checks or money orders payable to State of
Tennessee.

Police

Tennessee Department of Safety
1150 Foster Ave., Nashville, TN 37249-1000
(615) 251-5166; Fax: (615) 253-2091
E-mail: safety@mail.state.tn.us
Internet: www.tennessee.gov/safety

Accident Reports, Financial Responsibility Div.,
1150 Foster Ave., Nashville, TN 37249-1000
(615) 741-3954
Commissioner: Fred Phillips
For Fed. Ex. packages, use zip code 37210
Fee for obtaining accident report: $5.00

Probate, Recording and Notary Certificate Offices

Estate & Wills: Circuit Court Clerk, each county
Deeds and Mortgages: County Register of Deeds
Notary Certificates: County Ct. Clerk of County of
Notary's Commission (fee varies); Secy. of State, Notary
Section, for Notaries-at-large before 7/1/93 ($2.00)

Senators, U.S.

Lamar Alexander (Republican)
302 Hart Senate Office Bldg., Washington, DC 20510
(202) 224-4944
Internet: http://alexander.senate.gov/index.html
William Frist (Republican)
461 Dirksen Senate Office Bldg., Washington, DC 20510
(202) 224-3344; Fax: (202) 228-1264
Internet: http://frist.senate.gov

Secretary of State

Office of the Secretary of State
Wm. R. Snodgrass Tower, 6th Floor, 312 Eighth Ave. N.,
Nashville, TN 37243
Mailing Address: State Capitol, 1st Floor,
Nashville, TN 37243
Corporations Information: (615) 741-2286;
Executive Office: (615) 741-2819;
Executive Office Fax: (615) 741-5962
Internet: www.state.tn.us/sos/sos.htm
Secretary of State: Riley C. Darnell
    E-mail: riley.darnell@state.tn.us
Appointed

Tax Department

Department of Revenue
500 Deaderick St., 3rd Floor, Nashville, TN 37242
(615) 253-0600; Tax Practitioner Hotline: (615) 253-0700;
Tax Practitioner Hotline Statewide Toll Free:
(800) 397-8395; Tax Practitioner Fax: (615) 253-3580;
Tax Fraud Hot Line: (800) 372-8389;
Franchise and Excise Tax Reinstatements and
Dissolutions: (615) 253-4142, 532-6036;
Inheritance, Estate and Gift Taxes: (615) 532-6438;
Audit Division: (615) 741-3680;
Legal Office: (615) 741-2348; Bankruptcy: (615) 532-6322
E-mail: tn.revenue@state.tn.us
Internet: www.tennessee.gov/revenue
Commissioner: Loren L. Chumley
    (615) 741-2461
**Asst. Commissioner for Operations and Support
Services:** Sam Chessor
    (615) 741-5884
Asst. Commissioner for Tax Administration:
Reagan Farr
    (615) 741-5884
Chief Financial Officer: Ed Eldridge
    (615) 741-5884

Victim Compensation Program

Criminal Injuries Compensation Program
Division of Claims Administration
Andrew Jackson Office Bldg., 500 Deaderick St., 9th Floor,
Nashville, TN 37243-0243
(615) 741-2734; Fax: (615) 532-4979
Internet: www.treasury.state.tn.us/injury
Tenn. Code Ann. §29-13-101 (et seq.)

Vital Statistics

Vital Records
Tennessee Department of Health,
Central Services Bldg., 1st Floor, 421 5th Ave. N.,
Nashville, TN 37247
(615) 741-1763; Fax: (615) 741-9860
Internet: https://health.state.tn.us/vrocs/vr.aspx
Births, Deaths, Marriages, Divorces.
Search and certified copy deaths—$7.00; Birth long
form—$12.00; Birth short form (1949-present
only)—$7.00; Marriage and divorce—$12.00; Additional
copies of birth, marriage, or divorce record—$4.00.

NATIONAL DIRECTORY OF STATES

TEXAS
Capital: Austin

20,851,820 (2000 Census)
State Information: (512) 463-4630
State Web Site: www.texas.gov

Administrative Office of the Courts
Office of Court Administration
205 W. 14th St., 6th Floor, Austin, TX 78701
Mailing Address: P.O. Box 12066, Austin, TX 78711-2066
(512) 463-1625; Fax: (512) 463-1648
Internet: www.courts.state.tx.us
Administrative Dir.: Carrice Marcovich (Acting)

Attorney Discipline
State Bar of Texas Attorney Discipline
La Costa Centre, Suite 300, 6300 La Calma,
Austin, TX 78752
Mailing Address: P.O. Box 12487, Austin, TX 78711
(512) 453-5535, (877) 953-5535; Fax: (512) 453-6667
Internet: www.texasbar.com
Chief Disciplinary Counsel: Dawn Miller

Attorney General
Office of the Attorney General
209 W. 14th St., 8th Floor, Austin, TX 78701
Mailing Address: P.O. Box 12548, Austin, TX 78711-2548
(512) 463-2191; Fax: (512) 463-2063
Internet: www.oag.state.tx.us/
Atty. General: Greg Abbott (Republican)
Elected; next election Nov. 2006

Banking Department
Department of Banking
2601 North Lamar Blvd., Austin, TX 78705
(512) 475-1300; Fax: (512) 475-1313
Internet: http://www.banking.state.tx.us/
Commissioner: Randall S. James

Bar Admissions
Board of Law Examiners
Tom C. Clark Bldg., Suite 500, 205 W. 14th St., Austin, TX 78701
Mailing Address: P.O. Box 13486, Austin, TX 78711-3486
(512) 463-1621; Fax: (512) 463-5300
E-mail: ble@mail.capnet.state.tx.us
Internet: www.ble.state.tx.us
15 hours CLE required per year; three hours must be
ethics (administered by the State Bar of Texas, Dept. of
Continuing Legal Education). Admission on motion for
persons who meet the requirements set out in Rule XIII (a)
(i) of the Rules Governing Admission to the Bar of Texas.

Bar Association
State Bar of Texas
1414 Colorado St., P.O. Box 12487, Austin, TX 78711-2487
(512) 463-1463, (800) 204-2222; Fax: (512) 463-1475
Internet: www.texasbar.com
Exec. Dir.: Antonio Alvarado
President: Kelly Frels
Integrated Bar
Annual Meeting—June, 2005

Client Protection Fund
Client Security Fund
State Bar of Texas
6300 LaCalma, Suite 300, Austin, TX 78701
Mailing Address: P.O. Box 12487, Austin, TX 78711-2487
(512) 453-5535, (877) 953-5535; Fax: (512) 453-6667
Staff Liaison: Maureen Ray

Commerce Department
See Economic Development Administration

Corporations Officers
Department of State, Business & Public Filings Division
1019 Brazos, Austin, TX 78701
Mailing Address: P.O. Box 13697, Austin, TX 78711-3697
General Information, Name Availabilities, Trademarks,
Limited Partnerships & Assumed Names: (512) 463-5555;
Certifying: (512) 463-5578; Legal Staff: (512) 463-5586;
Forms ($1.00 per minute): (900) 263-0060;
Fax: (512) 463-5709
Internet (Forms): www.sos.state.tx.us/corp/forms.shtml

Director: Lorna Wassdorf (512) 463-5591
E-mail: lwassdorf@sos.state.tx.us
Mgr. of Legal Compliance: Robert Sumners
(512) 463-5590; E-mail: rsumners@sos.state.tx.us
Mgr. of Public Information: Tina Passell (512) 463-9856
Department of State
Uniform Commercial Code Section
Business & Public Filings Division, 1019 Brazos,
Austin, TX 78701
Mailing Address: P.O. Box 13193, Austin, TX 78711-3193
UCC: (512) 475-2700; UCC Searches: (512) 475-2705;
Financing Statements & Amendments: (512) 475-2703
Internet: www.sos.state.tx.us
Director: Randy Moes (512) 475-2709; Fax: (512) 463-5904
E-mail: rmoes@sos.state.tx.us
Office Mgr. & Asst. to the Dir.: Mary Jackson
(512) 475-2710; Fax: (512) 463-5904
Business & Public Filings Division

Criminal History Board
Department of Public Safety, Crime Records Service
5805 North Lamar Blvd., Bldg. G, Austin, TX 78752
Mailing Address: P.O. Box 4143, Austin, TX 78765-4143
(512) 424-2079; Fax: (512) 424-2961

Economic Development Administration
Department of Economic Development
1700 N. Congress Ave., Austin, TX 78701
Mailing Address: P.O. Box 12728, Austin, TX 78711-2728
(512) 936-0100; Fax: (512) 936-0440
Internet: www.tded.state.tx.us
Exec. Dir.: Jeff Moseley
Formerly Department of Commerce

Governor's Office
Office of the Governor
State Insurance Bldg., 1100 San Jacinto, Austin, TX 78701
Mailing Address: P.O. Box 12428, Austin, TX 78711-2428
(512) 463-2000; Fax: (512) 463-1849
Internet: www.governor.state.tx.us/

122 C St. N.W., Suite 200, Washington, DC 20001
(202) 638-3927; Fax: (202) 628-1943
Governor: Rick Perry (Republican)
Next election Nov. 2006

Highest State Court
Supreme Court of Texas
201 W. 14th St., Room 104, Austin, TX 78701
Mailing Address: P.O. Box 12248, Austin, TX 78711
(512) 463-1312; Fax: (512) 463-1365
Internet: www.courts.state.tx.us
Chief Justice: Wallace B. Jefferson
Clerk of the Supreme Court: Andrew Weber
*Use 14th St. address for Express/Courier only; P.O. Box
address for regular mail (Fax Filings not accepted)*

Insurance Department
Department of Insurance
333 Guadalupe St., Austin, TX 78701
Mailing Address: P.O. Box 149104, Austin, TX 78714-9104
(512) 463-6169; Fax: (512) 475-2005
E-mail: pio@tdi.state.tx.us; Internet: www.tdi.state.tx.us/
Commissioner: José Montemayor
Chief Financial Examiner: Danny Saenz
General Counsel/Chief Clerk: Gene Jarmon (Acting)
(512) 305-7351; Fax: (512) 475-2025

Motor Vehicle Office
Texas Department of Public Safety
Driver Records Bureau, P.O. Box 149246,
Austin, TX 78714-9246
(512) 424-2600; Fax: (512) 424-2948
Internet: www.txdps.state.tx.us

Accident Records Bureau, P.O. Box 4087,
Austin, TX 78773-0350   (512) 424-2600
*Driver's Records: Use mailing address if sending money to
dept.*
Fee for obtaining abstract: Driver's record, certified abstract,
$20.00; accident reports, $6.00; certified copy, $8.00

Motor Vehicle Office—Cont'd

Texas Department of Transportation
Vehicle Titles and Registration Division
125 E. 11th St., Austin, TX 78701-2483
(512) 465-7611; Fax: (512) 302-2162
Internet: www.dot.state.tx.us
Vehicle Registration

Police

Texas Department of Public Safety
5805 N. Lamar Blvd., Austin, TX 78752-4422
(512) 424-2000; Fax: (512) 424-2603
Internet: www.txdps.state.tx.us

Accident Records Bureau, P.O. Box 15999,
Austin, TX 78761-5999
(512) 424-7121; Fax: (512) 424-2741
Director: Col. Thomas A. Davis, Jr.
Fee for obtaining accident report $6.00; certified copy, $8.00

Probate, Recording and Notary Certificate Offices

Estate & Wills: County Clerks Office, Probate Section
Deeds and Mortgages: County Clerks Offices
Notary Certificates: Secretary of State, Notary Public
Section ($10.00)

Senators, U.S.

John Cornyn (Republican)
517 Hart Senate Office Bldg., Washington, DC 20510
(202) 224-2934
Internet: http://cornyn.senate.gov
Kay Bailey Hutchison (Republican)
284 Russell Senate Office Bldg., Washington, DC 20510
(202) 224-5922; Fax: (202) 224-0776
Internet: http://hutchison.senate.gov

Secretary of State

Office of the Secretary of State
1019 Brazos, Austin, TX 78701
Mailing Address: P.O. Box 12887, Austin, TX 78711-2887
(512) 463-5701; Fax: (512) 475-2761
Internet: www.sos.state.tx.us
Secretary of State: J. Roger Williams
Appointed

Tax Department

State Comptroller's Office
Lyndon B. Johnson State Office Bldg., 111 E. 17th St.,
Austin, TX 78774 (512) 463-4600; Fax: (512) 305-9711;
Audit Div.: (512) 463-3900, 463-4007
Internet: www.window.state.tx.us

Texas Comptroller of Public Accounts, Capitol Station,
P.O. Box 13528, Austin, TX 78711-3528
Comptroller: Carole Keeton Strayhorn (512) 463-4444
General Counsel: Jesse Ancira (512) 463-4384

Victim Compensation Program

Office of the Attorney General
Crime Victim Services Division
300 W. 15th St., 15th Fl., P.O. Box 12198, Austin, TX 78711-2198
(512) 936-1200; Fax: (512) 476-7526
Internet: www.oag.state.tx.us
Tex. Code Crim. Proc. Art. 56B (West 1994)

Vital Statistics

Bureau of Vital Statistics
Dept. of Health, 1100 W. 49th St., Austin, TX 78756-3191
(512) 458-7111; Fax: (512) 458-7506;
Order by Fax: (512) 458-7711
Internet: www.tdh.state.tx.us/bvs
*Births and deaths from 1903 to Present. Applications for
Marriage license since January 1, 1966, Reports of Divorce
or Annulment of Marriage since January 1, 1968. For
certified copy of marriage license, contact county clerk of the
county where issued. For certified copy of divorce decree,
contact the district clerk of the county where divorce granted.*
Copies—birth record: $11.00: death record: $9.00; Additional
copies of the same death record, ordered at the same
time—$3.00. Fax or overnight service—surcharge $5.00 fax or
overnight service (Call (512) 458-7111 for instructions or see
the website) Verification of a divorce or annulment of
marriage or application for marriage license—$13.00.

UTAH   *Capital: Salt Lake City*

2,233,169 (2000 Census)
State Information: (801) 538-3000
State Web Site: www.state.ut.us

Administrative Office of the Courts

Administrative Office of the Courts
450 S. State St., 3rd Floor, Salt Lake City, UT 84111
Mailing Address: P.O. Box 140241,
Salt Lake City, UT 84114-0241
(801) 578-3800; Fax: (801) 578-3843
Internet: www.utcourts.gov
State Court Administrator: Daniel J. Becker

Attorney Discipline

Utah State Bar Office of Professional Conduct
645 S. 200 E., Salt Lake City, UT 84111
(801) 531-9110; Fax: (801) 531-9912
Internet: www.utahbar.org
Senior Counsel: Billy L. Walker

Attorney General

Office of the Attorney General
Utah State Capitol Complex, 320 East Office Bldg.,
Salt Lake City, UT 84114
Mailing Address: P.O. Box 142320, Salt Lake City, UT 84114-2320
(801) 538-9600; Fax: (801) 538-1121
Internet: http://attorneygeneral.utah.gov

160 E. 300 South, Suite 600, Salt Lake City, UT 84114
Atty. General: Mark L. Shurtleff (Republican)
Elected; next election Nov. 2008

Banking Department

Department of Financial Institutions
324 S. State St., Suite 201, Salt Lake City, UT 84111
Mailing Address: P.O. Box 146800, Salt Lake City, UT 84114-6800
(801) 538-8830; Fax: (801) 538-8894
E-mail: slong@utah.gov
Internet: www.dfi.utah.gov
Commissioner: G. Edward Leary

Bar Admissions

Utah State Bar
645 S. 200 E., Salt Lake City, UT 84111-3834
(801) 531-9077; Fax: (801) 531-0660
Internet: www.utahbar.org
24 hours CLE required per two years.
Admission on motion for attorneys admitted in a
Reciprocal Jurisdiction, on the same terms as those in the
reciprocal jurisdiction.

Bar Association

Utah State Bar
645 S. 200 E., Suite 310, Salt Lake City, UT 84111-3834
(801) 531-9077; Fax: (801) 531-0660
Internet: www.utahbar.org
Exec. Dir.: John C. Baldwin; E-mail: jbaldwin@utahbar.org
President: David R. Bird
Integrated Bar
Annual Meeting—July, 2006

Chief Medical Examiner

Office of Medical Examiner
48 N. Medical Dr., Salt Lake City, UT 84113
(801) 584-8410; Fax: (801) 584-8435
Chief Medical Examiner: Dr. Todd Grey

Client Protection Fund

Fund for Client Protection
Utah State Bar
645 South 200 E., Salt Lake City, UT 84111-3834
(801) 531-9077; Fax: (801) 531-0660
Internet: www.utahbar.org
Bar Program Coordinator: Christine Critchley

Commerce Department

Department of Commerce
160 E. 300 S., P.O. Box 146701,
Salt Lake City, UT 84114-6701
(801) 530-6701; Fax: (801) 530-6446; TDD: (801) 530-6917
E-mail: commerce@utah.gov; Internet: www.commerce.utah.gov

Corporations Officers
Utah Division of Corporations and Commercial Code
160 E. 300 South, 2nd Floor, P.O. Box 146705,
Salt Lake City, UT 84114-6705
(877) 526-3994; Corporations Section: (801) 530-4849;
UCC: (801) 530-6143; Fax: (801) 530-6438
Internet: www.commerce.utah.gov

Director: Kathy Berg (801) 530-6024
　　E-mail: kberg@utah.gov
Deputy Dir.: Vacancy at Press Time (801) 530-6005
Office Mgr. & Asst. to the Dir.: Mary Ester Allers
　　(801) 530-6024; E-mail: mallers@utah.gov
UCC Mgr.: Sean Reed
　　(801) 530-6143; Fax: (801) 530-6438

Criminal History Board
Department of Public Safety
Bureau of Criminal Identification
3888 W. 5400 S., Salt Lake City, UT 84118
Mailing Address: P.O. Box 148280,
Salt Lake City, UT 84114-8280
(801) 965-4445; Fax: (801) 965-4944
Internet: www.bci.utah.gov

Economic Development Administration
Governor's Office of Economic Development
324 S. State St., Suite 500, Salt Lake City, UT 84111
(801) 538-8700, (877) 488-3233; Fax: (801) 538-8888
Internet: www.dced.utah.gov
Dir.: Martin Frey

Governor's Office
East Office Bldg., Suite E220,
Utah State Capitol Complex, P.O. Box 142220,
Salt Lake City, UT 84114-2220
(801) 538-1000; Fax: (801) 538-1528
Internet: www.utah.gov/governor

444 N. Capitol St. N.W., Suite 388, Washington, DC 20001
(202) 624-7704; Fax: (202) 624-7707
Governor: Jon M. Huntsman, Jr. (Republican)
Next election Nov. 2008

Highest State Court
Supreme Court
450 S. State, P.O. Box 140210,
Salt Lake City, UT 84114-0210
Appellate Clerks Office: (801) 578-3900;
Supreme Court: (801) 238-7967; Fax: (801) 238-7980
Internet: www.utcourts.gov
Chief Justice: Christine M. Durham
Clerk of the Supreme Court: Patricia H. Bartholomew

Insurance Department
Department of Insurance
3110 State Office Bldg., Salt Lake City, UT 84114-6901
(801) 538-3800, 05; TDD: (801) 538-3826;
Fax: (801) 538-3829
Internet: www.insurance.utah.gov
Commissioner: D. Kent Michie
Chief Examiner: Steven Fry (801) 538-3811

Motor Vehicle Office
Department of Public Safety
Driver License Division
4501 S. 2700 W., West Valley City, UT 84119
Mailing Address: P.O. Box 30560,
Salt Lake City, UT 84130-0560
(801) 965-4437; Fax: (801) 965-4496
Internet: www.driverlicense.utah.gov
Driver's Licenses
Fee for obtaining M.V.R. abstract: $4.25
Utah State Tax Commission
Motor Vehicle Division
210 N. 1950 W., Salt Lake City, UT 84134
(801) 297-7780; Administrative Offices: (801) 297-7500;
In-State: (800) 368-8824; Fax: (801) 297-3570
Internet: www.tax.ex.state.ut.us, www.dmv.utah.gov
Vehicle Registration

Police
Utah Dept. of Public Safety
Calvin Rampton Complex, 4501 S. 2700 W.,
Salt Lake City, UT 84114
Mailing Address: Box 141775,
Salt Lake City, UT 84114-1775
Commissioner's Office: (801) 965-4461;
Commissioner's Office Fax: (801) 965-4608;
Utah Highway Patrol: (801) 965-4518;
Utah Highway Patrol Fax: (801) 965-4716
Internet: www.publicsafety.utah.gov

Accident Reports: Driver License Section, P.O. Box 30560,
Salt Lake City, UT 84130-0560
(801) 965-4428; Fax: (801) 964-4536
Commissioner: Robert L. Flowers
Fee for obtaining accident report: $5.00

Probate, Recording and Notary Certificate Offices
Estate & Wills: District Court Offices, Probate Division
Deeds and Mortgages: County Recorders Offices
Notary Certificates: Authentications/Notarizations Office
(801) 538-1040 ($10.00; Apostille Certification $5.00)

Senators, U.S.
Robert F. Bennett (Republican)
431 Dirksen Senate Office Bldg., Washington, DC 20510
(202) 224-5444
Internet: http://bennett.senate.gov
Orrin G. Hatch (Republican)
104 Hart Senate Office Bldg., Washington, DC 20510
(202) 224-5251; Fax: (202) 224-6331
Internet: http://hatch.senate.gov

Secretary of State
Office of the Lieutenant Governor
220E State Capitol, Salt Lake City, UT 84114
(801) 538-1000; Fax: (801) 538-1557
Internet: www.utah.gov/ltgovernor
Lieutenant Governor: Gary R. Herbert (Republican)
Elected; next election Nov. 2008

Tax Department
Utah State Tax Commission
210 N. 1950 W., Salt Lake City, UT 84134
(801) 297-2200, (800) 662-4335; Fax: (801) 297-7699;
Taxpayer Services: (801) 297-2200; TDD: (801) 297-2020
E-mail (Tax & Filing Questions): taxmaster@utah.gov
Internet: www.tax.utah.gov
Chairman: Pam Hendrickson
Exec. Dir.: Rodney G. Marrelli

Victim Compensation Program
Crime Victim Reparations Office
350 East 500 South, Suite 200, Salt Lake City, UT 84111
(801) 238-2360, (800) 621-7444; Fax: (801) 533-4127
E-mail: ddavis@utah.gov
Internet: www.crimevictim.utah.gov
Utah Code Ann. §63-25a-401 (enacted 1986, amended 1996)

Vital Statistics
Office of Vital Records and Statistics
Cannon Health Bldg., 288 North 1460 W.,
P.O. Box 141012, Salt Lake City, UT 84114-1012
(801) 538-6105; Vital Records: (801) 538-6380;
Vital Statistics: (801) 538-6843
E-mail: vrequest@utah.gov
Internet: http://health.utah.gov/vitalrecords,
www.vitalchek.com
Births and Deaths since 1905. Marriage transcript and Divorce records are filed in state office of Vital Statistics. Certified copies for marriages or divorces occuring prior to 1978 must be obtained from County Clerk.
Births—$15.00 per five years searched; Death—$13.00;
Marriage and Divorce—$9.00. $50.00 for search of entire file for any record; includes one certified copy if record found. $8.00 for additional copies obtained at the same time. Same day service using a credit card for an additional service charge of $15.50. Special handling fees are charged for credit card orders and priority mail service.

VERMONT
Capital: Montpelier

608,827 (2000 Census)
State Information: (802) 828-1110
State Web Site: www.state.vt.us

Administrative Office of the Courts
Office of the Court Administrator
111 State St., Montpelier, VT 05609-0701
Mailing Address: 109 State St., Montpelier, VT 05609-0701
(802) 828-3278; Fax: (802) 828-3457
Internet: www.vermontjudiciary.org
Court Administrator: Lee Suskin

Attorney Discipline
Professional Responsibility Program
Vermont Supreme Court Bldg., 109 State Street,
Montpelier, VT 05609-0703
(802) 828-3204; Fax: (802) 828-3457
Internet: www.vermontjudiciary.org

Office of Disciplinary Counsel, 32 Cherry St., Suite 213,
Burlington, VT 05401
Bar Counsel: Wendy S. Collins
Disciplinary Counsel: Michael Kennedy
Deputy Disciplinary Counsel: Beth DeBernardi
Program Administrator: Deb Laferriere

Attorney General
Office of the Attorney General
109 State St., 2nd Floor, Montpelier, VT 05609-1001
(802) 828-3171; Fax: (802) 828-2154
E-mail: aginfo@atg.state.vt.us
Internet: www.atg.state.vt.us
Atty. General: William H. Sorrell (Democrat)
Elected; next election Nov. 2006

Banking Department
Banking Division
Department of Banking, Insurance, Securities &
HealthCare Administration
89 Main St., Drawer 20, Montpelier, VT 05620-3101
(802) 828-3301; Fax: (802) 828-3306
Internet: www.bishca.state.vt.us
Commissioner: John P. Crowley
Deputy Commissioner: Thomas J. Candon

Bar Admissions
Vermont Board of Bar Examiners
2412B Airport Rd., Suite 2, Barre, VT 05641
Mailing Address: 109 State St., Montpelier, VT 05609-0702
(802) 828-3281; Fax: (802) 828-1695
E-mail: licensing@mail.crt.state.vt.us
Internet: www.vermontjudiciary.org
20 hrs. CLE required per two years with at least 2 hrs. in ethics.
Admission on motion with five of the last ten years in
practice; fewer years in practice for a Reciprocal Jurisdiction.

Bar Association
Vermont Bar Assn.
35-37 Court St., P.O. Box 100, Montpelier, VT 05601-0100
(802) 223-2020; Fax: (802) 223-1573
Internet: www.vtbar.org
Exec. Dir.: Robert M. Paolini; E-mail: bpaolini@vtbar.org
President: Thomas A. Zonay
Non-Integrated Bar
Annual Meeting—September, 2005

Chief Medical Examiner
Office of Chief Medical Examiner
Baird 1, 111 Colchester Ave., Burlington, VT 05401
(802) 863-7320
Chief Medical Examiner: Vacancy at Press Time

Client Protection Fund
Client Security Fund
Vermont Bar Association
35-37 Court St., Montpelier, VT 05602
Mailing Address: P.O. Box 100, Montpelier, VT 05601-0100
(802) 223-2020; Fax: (802) 223-1573
Internet: www.vtbar.org
Exec. Dir.: Robert M. Paolini

Commerce Department
Agency of Commerce and Community Development
National Life Bldg., North, Drawer 20,
Montpelier, VT 05620-0501
(802) 828-3211; Fax: (802) 828-3383
Internet: www.dca.state.vt.us
Secretary: Kevin Dorn
General Counsel: John Kessler

Corporations Officers
Corporations/UCC Office
Business Registry Division
81 River St., Drawer 09, Montpelier, VT 05609-1104
(802) 828-2386; Fax: (802) 828-2853
Corporations Dir.: Betty Poulin
E-mail: bpoulin@sec.state.vt.us

Criminal History Board
Department of Public Safety
Criminal Information Center
103 S. Main St., Waterbury, VT 05671-2101
(802) 244-8781; Fax: (802) 241-5552

Economic Development Administration
Department of Economic Development
National Life Bldg., Drawer 20,
Montpelier, VT 05620-0501
(802) 828-3080; Fax: (802) 828-3258
E-mail: info@thinkvermont.com
Internet: www.thinkvermont.com
Commissioner: Mike Quinn
(802) 828-5239

Governor's Office
Office of the Governor
Pavilion Office Bldg., 109 State St.,
Montpelier, VT 05609-0101
(802) 828-3333; Fax: (802) 828-3339
Internet: www.vermont.gov/governor
Governor: James H. Douglas (Republican)
Next election Nov. 2008

Highest State Court
Supreme Court of Vermont
111 State St., Montpelier, VT 05602
Mailing Address: 109 State St., Montpelier, VT 05609-0801
(802) 828-3278; Fax: (802) 828-3457
Internet: www.vermontjudiciary.org
Chief Justice: Jeffrey L. Amestoy
Clerk of the Supreme Court: Lee Suskin

Insurance Department
Division of Insurance
Dept. of Banking, Insurance, Securities and Health Care
Administration
89 Main St., Drawer 20, Montpelier, VT 05620-3101
(802) 828-3301; Fax: (802) 828-3306
Internet: www.bishca.state.vt.us
Commissioner: John P. Crowley
Deputy Commissioner of Insurance:
J. Peter Yankowski
Deputy Commissioner of Banking: Thomas J. Candon
Chief Examiner: Ken McGuckin
Deputy Commissioner of Securities:
Phillips B. Keller III
**Deputy Commissioner of Health Care
Administration:** Paulette Thabault
Deputy Commissioner of Captives: Leonard Crouse

Motor Vehicle Office
Vermont Department of Motor Vehicles
120 State St., Montpelier, VT 05603-0001
(802) 828-2000; Fax: (802) 828-2098
Internet: www.dmv.state.vt.us
Fee for obtaining abstract: $8.00 for 3 year record; $16.00
for Complete record

Police

Vermont Department of Public Safety
103 S. Main St., Waterbury State Complex,
Waterbury, VT 05671-2101
(802) 244-8718; Fax: (802) 241-5551
Internet: www.state.vt.us/dps

Accident Reports: Department of Motor Vehicles,
120 State St., Montpelier, VT 05602
(802) 828-2000

Commissioner: Kerry L. Sleeper
Fee for obtaining motor vehicle accident report: $12.00;
Fee for obtaining all other investigative reports from Dept.
of Public Safety is $15.00 per report.

Probate, Recording and Notary Certificate Offices

Estate & Wills: District Probate Courts
Deeds and Mortgages: Town or City Clerks Offices
Notary Certificates: Secretary of State ($2.00)

Senators, U.S.

James M. Jeffords (Independent)
413 Dirksen Senate Office Bldg., Washington, DC 20510
(202) 224-5141
Internet: http://jeffords.senate.gov
Patrick J. Leahy (Democrat)
433 Russell Senate Office Bldg., Washington, DC 20510
(202) 224-4242; Fax: (202) 224-3595
Internet: http://leahy.senate.gov

Secretary of State

Office of the Secretary of State
26 Terrace St., Drawer 09, Montpelier, VT 05609-1101
(802) 828-2363; Fax: (802) 828-2496
Internet: www.sec.state.vt.us

Secretary of State: Deborah L. Markowitz (Democrat)
Elected; next election Nov. 2008

Tax Department

Department of Taxes
109 State St., Montpelier, VT 05609-1401
Mailing Address: P.O. Box 429, Montpelier, VT 05601-0429
Income Taxes: (802) 828-2865;
Income Taxes Fax: (802) 828-2728;
Income Taxes Toll Free: (866) 828-2865;
Business Taxes: (802) 828-2551;
Business Taxes Fax: (802) 828-5787;
Corporations: (802) 828-5723;
Corporations Fax: (802) 828-5787
Internet: www.state.vt.us/tax

Commissioner: Tom Pelham

Victim Compensation Program

Vermont Center for Crime Victims' Services
58 S. Main St., Suite 1, Waterbury, VT 05676-1599
(802) 241-1250; Fax: (802) 241-1253; TTY: (802) 241-1258
E-mail: info@ccvs.state.vt.us
Internet: www.ccvs.state.vt.us
Vt. Stat. Ann. Title 13, Chap. 167 §§5363 to 5359 & 5361 (2003 Supp.)

Vital Statistics

General Services Center, Public Records Division
Reference/Research Section, U.S. Route 2—Middlesex,
Drawer 33, Montpelier, VT 05633-7601
(802) 828-3286; Fax: (802) 828-3710;
Voice Mail: (802) 828-3701, 828-3286
Births, Deaths, Marriages—1760-1998;
Divorces—1861-1998.
Certified copy—$9.50; Fax service available for some
records—$2.50 up to 5 pages, $.50 each page thereafter per
Fax. Accepts AmEx, Mastercard, Discover and Visa—$6.00
service charge for credit card transactions.
Vital Records
Department of Health, 108 Cherry St., P.O. Box 70,
Burlington, VT 05402-9962
(802) 863-7275; Fax: (802) 651-1787
Internet: http://www.healthyvermonters.info/
Births, Deaths, Marriages. Divorces—1999-Present.
Certified copy—$7.00.

VIRGINIA   *Capital: Richmond*

7,078,515 (2000 Census)
State Information: (804) 786-0000
State Web Site: www.state.va.us

Administrative Office of the Courts

Administrative Office of the Courts
Supreme Court of Virginia, 3rd Floor, 100 N. 9th St.,
Richmond, VA 23219
(804) 786-6455; Fax: (804) 786-4542

Executive Secretary: Vacancy at Press Time

Attorney Discipline

Virginia State Bar Attorney Discipline
Eighth & Main Bldg., Suite 1500, 707 E. Main St.,
Richmond, VA 23219-2800
(804) 775-0500; Fax: (804) 775-0597
Internet: www.vsb.org

100 N. Pitt St., Suite 310, Alexandria, VA 22314-3133
(703) 518-8045; Fax: (703) 518-8052

Clerk of Disciplinary System: Barbara S. Lanier
Bar Counsel: Barbara Ann Williams
Deputy Bar Counsel: Harry M. Hirsch
Sr. Asst. Bar Counsel: Noel D. Sengel

Attorney General

Office of the Attorney General
900 E. Main St., Richmond, VA 23219
(804) 786-2071; Fax: (804) 786-1991
Internet: www.vaag.com

Atty. General: Judith Williams Jagdmann
Elected; next election Nov. 2005

Banking Department

Bureau of Financial Institutions
Tyler Bldg., Suite 800, 1300 E. Main St., P.O. Box 640,
Richmond, VA 23218-0640
(804) 371-9657; Fax: (804) 371-9416
Internet: www.state.va.us/scc

Commissioner: E. Joseph Face, Jr.

Bar Admissions

Virginia Board of Bar Examiners
Shockoe Centre, Suite 225, 11 S. 12th St.,
Richmond, VA 23219
(804) 786-7490; Fax: (804) 786-0816
Internet: www.vbbe.state.va.us
12 hours CLE required per year, two hours must be in
ethics (Contact Virginia State Bar).
Admission on motion by Supreme Court with five years
practice in a Reciprocal Jurisdiction.

Bar Association

Virginia State Bar
Eighth & Main Bldg., Suite 1500, 707 E. Main St.,
Richmond, VA 23219-2800
(804) 775-0500; Fax: (804) 775-0501
Internet: www.vsb.org

Exec. Dir.: Thomas A. Edmonds
President: Phillip V. Anderson
Integrated Bar
Annual Meeting—June, 2005
The Virginia Bar Assn.
701 E. Franklin St., Suite 1120, Richmond, VA 23219
(804) 644-0041; Fax: (804) 644-0052
E-mail: thevba@vba.org
Internet: www.vba.org

Exec. V.P.: C. B. Arrington, Jr.
President: William R. Van Buren III
Non-Integrated Bar
Annual Meeting—January, 2006

Chief Medical Examiner

Office of Chief Medical Examiner
400 E. Jackson St., Richmond, VA 23219
(804) 786-3174; Fax: (804) 371-8595
Internet: www.vdh.virginia.gov

Chief Medical Examiner: Marcella F. Fierro, M.D.

Client Protection Fund

Clients' Protection Fund
Virginia State Bar
Eighth and Main Bldg., Suite 1500, 707 E. Main St.,
Richmond, VA 23219-2800
(804) 775-0524; Fax: (804) 775-0501
Internet: www.vsb.org
Exec. Dir.: Thomas A. Edmonds

Commerce Department

See Economic Development Administration

Corporations Officers

State Corporation Commission
Tyler Bldg., 1300 E. Main St., Richmond, VA 23219
Mailing Address: P.O. Box 1197, Richmond, VA 23218
(804) 371-9733; Fax: (804) 371-9654
Clerk: Joel H. Peck (804) 371-9834
Deputy Clerk: Charlotte E. Daniel (804) 371-9364
Asst. Deputy Clerk: Robert Lindsey (804) 371-9424
    E-mail: rlindsey@scc.state.va.us
Business Entity Mgr.: Carolyn Thon (804) 371-9639
    E-mail: cthon@sec.state.va.us
UCC Mgr.: Richard Whitt (804) 371-9271
Principal Charter Examiner: Charles L. Rogers
    (804) 371-9803; E-mail: crogers@scc.state.va.us

Criminal History Board

Virginia State Police
Central Criminal Records Exchange
7700 Midlothian Turnpike, Richmond, VA 23235
(804) 323-2001; Fax: (804) 323-0862
E-mail: vgunn@vsp.state.va.us, tturner@vsp.state.va.us
Internet: www.vsp.state.va.us

Economic Development Administration

Economic Development Partnership
901 East Byrd St., West Tower, 19th Fl., Richmond, VA 23219
Mailing Address: P.O. Box 798, Richmond, VA 23218-0798
(804) 371-8100; Business: (804) 371-8202; Fax: (804) 371-8112
Internet: www.yesvirginia.org
Exec. Director: Mark R. Kilduff

Governor's Office

Office of the Governor
State Capitol, Richmond, VA 23219
(804) 786-2211; Fax: (804) 371-6351
Internet: www.governor.virginia.gov/

444 N. Capitol St. N.W., Suite 214, Washington, DC 20001
(202) 783-1769; Fax: (202) 783-7687
Governor: Mark R. Warner (Democrat)
Next election Nov. 2005

Highest State Court

Supreme Court
Supreme Court Bldg., 5th Floor, 100 N. 9th St.,
Richmond, VA 23219
(804) 786-2251; Fax: (804) 786-6249
Internet: www.courts.state.va.us
Chief Justice: Leroy Rountree Hassell, Sr.
Clerk of the Supreme Court: Patricia L. Harrington
    E-mail: scvclerk@courts.state.va.us

Insurance Department

Bureau of Insurance
Tyler Bldg., 1300 E. Main St., Richmond, VA 23219
Mailing Address: P.O. Box 1157, Richmond, VA 23218
(804) 371-9741; Fax: (804) 371-9873
Internet: www.scc.virginia.gov/division/boi/
Commissioner: Alfred W. Gross
Chief Examiner: David H. Smith

Motor Vehicle Office

Virginia Department of Motor Vehicles
2300 W. Broad St., Richmond, VA 23220
Mailing Address: P.O. Box 27412, Richmond, VA 23269-0001
(804) 367-6602, (866) 368-5463; TDD: (800) 272-9268;
Fax: (804) 367-6631
Internet: www.dmv.state.va.us
Fee for obtaining abstract: $8.00; certified copies $13.00

Police

Virginia Department of State Police
7700 Midlothian Turnpike, Richmond, VA 23235
Mailing Address: P.O. Box 27472, Richmond, VA 23261-7472
(804) 674-2000; Fax: (804) 323-0862
Internet: www.vsp.state.va.us
Superintendent: Col. Steven Flaherty   (804) 674-2087
Fee for obtaining accident report: $6.00

Probate, Recording and Notary Certificate Offices

Estate & Wills: Chancery or Circuit Court Clerks, each
county/city
Deeds and Mortgages: Circuit Court Clerks, each county/city
Notary Certificates: Secretary of Commonwealth, Notary
Public Division ($10.00)

Senators, U.S.

George Allen (Republican)
204 Russell Senate Office Bldg., Washington, DC 20510
(202) 224-4024; Internet: http://allen.senate.gov

John W. Warner (Republican)
225 Russell Senate Office Bldg., Washington, DC 20510
(202) 224-2023; Fax: (202) 224-6295
Internet: http://warner.senate.gov

Secretary of State

Office of the Secretary of the Commonwealth
1200 E. Broad St., 4th Floor, Richmond, VA 23219
Mailing Address: P.O. Box 2454, Richmond, VA 23218-2454
(804) 786-2441; Fax: (804) 371-0017
Internet: www.commonwealth.virginia.gov
Secretary of the Commonwealth: Anita A. Rimler
Appointed

Tax Department

Virginia Department of Taxation
3600 Centre, 3610 W. Broad St.,
P.O. Box 1115 (23218-1115), Richmond, VA 23230
Mailing Address: P.O. Box 1880, Richmond, VA 23218-1880
Customer Services Individual: (804) 367-8031;
Customer Services Corporation: (804) 367-8037;
Fax (Cust. Svces.—Indiv. & Bus.): (804) 786-2643;
Fax (Tax Forms): (804) 236-2779; Fax (Compliance):
E-mail: tax-indivrtn@state.va.us
Internet: www.tax.virginia.gov

Forms Request, P.O. Box 1317, Richmond, VA 23218-1317
(804) 236-2760, 61, 62; Fax: (804) 236-2779
Tax Commissioner: Kenneth W. Thorson

Victim Compensation Program

Criminal Injuries Compensation Fund
Workers' Compensation Commission
11513 Allecingie Pkwy., Richmond, VA 23235
(804) 378-3434; Fax: (804) 378-4390
Internet: www.cicf.state.va.us
Director: Mary Vail Ware
*Va. Code §§19.2-368.1 to 368.18 (enacted 1977; 1979 Supp.;
amended 2002)*

Vital Statistics

Office of Vital Records Health Statistics
Department of Health, 1601 Willow Lawn Dr., Suite 275,
Richmond, VA 23230
Mailing Address: P.O. Box 1000, Richmond, VA 23218-1000
(804) 662-6200
Internet: www.vdh.virginia.gov
*Births, Deaths—1853-1896 and 1912-Present;
Marriages—1853; Divorces—1918.*
Certified copy—$12.00; expedited service via
VitalCheck—$46.00. Note: see website for I.D.
requirements.

National Directory
of States

WASHINGTON
Capital: Olympia

5,894,121 (2000 Census)
State Information: (360) 753-5000
State Web Site: www.wa.gov/wahome.html

Administrative Office of the Courts
Office of the Administrator for the Courts
Temple of Justice, 415 12th Ave., S.W., P.O. Box 41174,
Olympia, WA 98504-1174
(360) 357-2121; Fax: (360) 357-2127
Internet: www.courts.wa.gov
Court Administrator: Janet L. McLane

Attorney Discipline
Washington State Bar Association—Office of Disciplinary
Counsel
2101 Fourth Ave., Suite 400, Seattle, WA 98121-2330
(206) 727-8207; Fax: (206) 727-8325
Internet: www.wsba.org
Office of Disciplinary Counsel: Joy McLean

Attorney General
Office of the Attorney General
1121 Washington St. S.E., P.O. Box 40100,
Olympia, WA 98504-0100
(360) 753-6200; Fax: (360) 664-0228
E-mail: emailago@atg.wa.gov
Internet: http://access.wa.gov
Atty. General: Rob McKenna (Republican)
Elected; next election Nov. 2008

Banking Department
Department of Financial Institution
150 Israel Rd. S.W., Tumwater, WA 98501
Mailing Address: P.O. Box 41200,
Olympia, WA 98504-1200
(360) 902-8704; Fax: (360) 753-6070
Internet: dfi.wa.gov/banks
Dir., Division of Banks: David G. Kroeger

Bar Admissions
Washington State Bar Association
2101 Fourth Ave., Suite 400, Seattle, WA 98121-2330
(206) 443-9722, (800) 945-9722; Fax: (206) 727-8320
Internet: www.wsba.org
45 hours CLE required per three years (6 hours in ethics),
new admits exempt for two years. Admission on motion by
attorney from Reciprocal Jurisdiction.

Bar Association
Washington State Bar Assn.
2101 Fourth Ave., Suite 400, Seattle, WA 98121-2330
(206) 443-9722; Fax: (206) 727-8319; (800) 945-9722
E-mail: questions@wsba.org
Internet: www.wsba.org
Exec. Dir.: M. Janice Michels
President: Ronald R. Ward
Integrated Bar

Client Protection Fund
Lawyers' Fund for Client Protection
Washington State Bar Association
2101 Fourth Ave., Suite 400, Seattle, WA 98121-2330
(206) 727-8252; Fax: (206) 727-8319
E-mail: questions@wsha.org
Internet: www.wsba.org
General Counsel: Robert D. Welden

Commerce Department
See Economic Development Administration

Corporations Officers
Department of Licensing
Uniform Commercial Code, Business and Professions
Division
405 Black Lake Blvd., Olympia, WA 98502
Mailing Address: P.O. Box 9660, Olympia, WA 98507-9660
(360) 664-1530; Fax: (360) 586-4414
Internet: www.dol.wa.gov/unfc/uccfront.htm
Administrator: Jon Donnellan (360) 664-1528
    E-mail: jdonnellan@dol.wa.gov

Department of State Corporations Division
James M. Dollver Bldg., 801 Capitol Way S.,
P.O. Box 40234, Olympia, WA 98504-0234
(360) 753-7115; Fax: (360) 664-8781
Internet: www.secstate.wa.gov/corps
Director: Mike Ricchio (360) 753-2896
    E-mail: mricchio@secstate.wa.gov

Criminal History Board
Washington State Patrol
Criminal Records Division
P.O. Box 42619, Olympia, WA 98504-2619
(360) 570-5252; Fax: (360) 570-5274

Economic Development Administration
Community, Trade & Economic Development
128 10th Ave. S.W., Olympia, WA 98504-2525
Mailing Address: P.O. Box 42525, Olympia, WA 98504
(360) 725-4000; Fax: (360) 586-8440
Internet: www.cted.wa.gov
Director: Juli Wilkerson

Governor's Office
Office of the Governor
Legislative Bldg., Olympia, WA 98504
Mailing Address: P.O. Box 40002,
Olympia, WA 98504-0002
(360) 753-6780, 902-4111; Fax: (360) 753-4110
Internet: www.governor.wa.gov
Governor: Christine O. Gregoire (Democrat)
Next election Nov. 2008

Highest State Court
Supreme Court
Temple of Justice, Capitol Campus, 415 12th St. W.,
P.O. Box 40929, Olympia, WA 98504-0929
(360) 357-2077; Fax: (360) 357-2102
E-mail: supreme@courts.wa.gov
Internet: www.courts.wa.gov
Chief Justice: Gerry L. Alexander
Clerk of the Supreme Court: C.J. Merritt

Insurance Department
Office of the Insurance Commissioner
5000 Capitol Blvd., Tumwater, WA 98501
Mailing Address: P.O. Box 40255,
Olympia, WA 98504-0255
(360) 725-7000; Legal Affairs: (360) 725-7047;
Legal Affairs Fax: (360) 586-3109
E-mail: cad@oic.wa.gov
Internet: www.insurance.wa.gov/
Commissioner: Mike Kreidler
Deputy Commissioner, Legal Affairs: Carol Sureau

Motor Vehicle Office
Washington Department of Licensing
Driver Services, 1125 Washington St. S.E.,
Olympia, WA 98504
Mailing Address: P.O. Box 9030, Olympia, WA 98507
(360) 902-3900; TDD: (360) 664-0116; Fax: (360) 586-9044
Internet: www.dol.wa.gov
Fee for obtaining abstract: $5.00

Police
Washington State Patrol
General Administration Bldg., Olympia, WA 98504
Mailing Address: P.O. Box 42600,
Olympia, WA 98504-2600
(360) 753-6540; Fax: (360) 753-2492
Internet: www.wa.gov/wsp/wsphome.htm

Collision Records Section, P.O. Box 47382,
Olympia, WA 98504-7382 (360) 570-5200
Chief: John R. Batiste
Fee for obtaining accident report: $5.00

Probate, Recording and Notary Certificate Offices
Estate & Wills: Superior Court Clerks Offices, each county
Deeds and Mortgages: County Auditors Offices
Notary Certificates: Secretary of State ($15.00)

Senators, U.S.
Maria Cantwell (Democrat)
717 Hart Senate Office Bldg., Washington, DC 20510
(202) 224-3441; Fax: (202) 228-0514
Internet: http://cantwell.senate.gov
Patty Murray (Democrat)
173 Russell Senate Office Bldg., Washington, DC 20510
(202) 224-2621; Fax: (202) 224-0238
Internet: http://murray.senate.gov

Secretary of State
Office of the Secretary of State
Legislative Bldg., Room 250, 416 14th Ave.,
P.O. Box 40220, Olympia, WA 98504-0220
(360) 902-4151; Fax: (360) 586-5629
Internet: www.secstate.wa.gov
Corporations Division, 801 Capitol Way S., P.O. Box 40234,
Olympia, WA 98504-0234 (360) 753-7115
Secretary of State: Sam Reed
Elected; next election Nov. 2008

Tax Department
Department of Revenue
6500 Linderson Way, Suite 102, Tumwater, WA 98501
Mailing Address: P.O. Box 47478, Olympia, WA 98504-7478
(800) 647-7706; Fax: (360) 705-6655
Internet: www.dor.wa.gov
Director: William N. Rice

Victim Compensation Program
Crime Victims Compensation Program
Dept. of Labor and Industries
7273 Linderson Way S.W., Tumwater, WA 98501
Mailing Address: P.O. Box 44520, Olympia, WA 98504-4520
(360) 902-5355, (800) 762-3716; Fax: (360) 902-5333
Internet: www.lni.wa.gov/claimsinsurance/crimevictims
Wash. Rev. Code Ann. §§7.68.010 to 7.68.915 (1982 Supp., Amended 1992)

Vital Statistics
Department of Health
Center for Health Statistics, 101 Israel Rd. S.E.,
P.O. Box 7814, Olympia, WA 95804-7814
(360) 236-4300; Credit Card Orders by Phone: (360) 236-4313;
Credit Card Orders by Fax: (360) 352-2586
Internet: www.doh.wa.gov

Street address for private couriers only,
101 Israel Rd. S.E., Tumwater, WA 98501
Births and Deaths from July 1, 1907. Marriages from Jan. 1, 1968; older records filed with County Auditors. Divorces from Jan. 1, 1968; older records filed with County Clerks.
Certified Copies—$17.00. Expedited service available, using credit card. Fees for expedited service start at $28.00.

WEST VIRGINIA   *Capital: Charleston*
1,808,344 (2000 Census)
State Information: (304) 558-3456
State Web Site: wvweb.com

Administrative Office of the Courts
Administrative Office of the Courts
Supreme Court of Appeals of W.Va., E-100 State Capitol,
Charleston, WV 25305
(304) 558-0145; Fax: (304) 558-1212
Internet: www.state.wv.us/wvsca
Administrative Dir. of the Courts:
  Linda Richmond Artimez, J.D.

Attorney Discipline
West Virginia Office of Disciplinary Counsel
2008 Kanawha Blvd. East, Charleston, WV 25311
(304) 558-7999; Fax: (304) 558-4015
Chief Disciplinary Counsel: Lawrence J. Lewis

Attorney General
Office of the Attorney General
State Capitol, Room E-26, 1900 Kanawha Blvd. E.,
Charleston, WV 25305-0220
(304) 558-2021; Fax: (304) 558-0140
Internet: www.wvs.state.wv.us\wvag
Atty. General: Darrell V. McGraw, Jr. (Democrat)
Elected; next election Nov. 2008

Banking Department
Division of Banking
State Office Bldg. 3, Suite 311, Charleston, WV 25305-0240
(304) 558-2294; Fax: (304) 558-0442
Internet: www.wvdob.org
Commissioner: Larry A. Stark

Bar Admissions
Board of Law Examiners
Supreme Court of West Virginia
910 Quarrier St., Suite 212, Charleston, WV 25301-2613
(304) 558-7815; Fax: (304) 558-0831
E-mail: suerubenstein@courtswv.org
Internet: www.state.wv.us/wvsca
24 hours CLE required per two years, including at least three ethics, office management, substance abuse or elimination of bias in the legal profession, credits.
Admission on motion with five years practice within the last seven years in a Reciprocal Jurisdiction.

Bar Association
The West Virginia State Bar
2006 Kanawha Blvd. E., Charleston, WV 25311-2204
(304) 558-2456; Fax: (304) 558-2467
Internet: www.wvbar.org
Exec. Dir.: Thomas R. Tinder
President: Charles M. Love III
Integrated Bar
Annual Meeting— May, 2005
The West Virginia Bar Assn.
1111 6th Ave., Huntington, WV 25701
Mailing Address: P.O. Box 2162, Huntington, WV 25722
(304) 522-2652; Fax: (304) 522-2795
E-mail: director@wvbarassociation.org
Internet: www.wvbarassociation.org
Exec. Dir.: Pryce M. Haynes II
President: Charles M. Love III
President-Elect: Richard A. Pill
Non-Integrated Bar
Annual Meeting—Sept. 2006

Chief Medical Examiner
Office of Chief Medical Examiner
619 Virginia St. West, Charleston, WV 25302
(304) 558-3920; Fax: (304) 558-7886
Chief Medical Examiner: James A. Kaplan, M.D.

Client Protection Fund
Client Protection Fund
West Virginia State Bar
2006 Kanawha Blvd. E., Charleston, WV 25311
(304) 558-2456; Fax: (304) 558-2467
Internet: www.wvbar.org
Contact: Thomas R. Tinder

Commerce Department
Bureau of Commerce
90 MacCorkle Ave. S.W., South Charleston, WV 25303
(304) 558-2200; Fax: (304) 558-2956
Internet: www.boc.state.wv.us

Corporations Officers
Department of State
Corporations/UCC Division
Bldg. 1, Room W-139, 1900 Kanawha Blvd. E.,
Charleston, WV 25305-0776
General Information & UCC: (304) 558-6000;
Corporations Section, Name Availabilities, Limited Partnerships & Limited Liability Companies:
(304) 558-8000; Notaries: (304) 558-6000;
Fax: (304) 558-0900; Corporations & UCC Fax: (304) 558-5758
Supervisor, Corporations: Penney Barker
  (304) 558-8000, Ext. 236; E-mail: pbarker@wvsos.com
Supervisor, UCC: Vicki Haught, Room W-131
  (304) 558-6000, Ext. 233; E-mail: vhaught@wvsos.com

Criminal History Board
West Virginia State Police, Criminal Records
725 Jefferson Rd., South Charleston, WV 25309
(304) 746-2177; Fax: (304) 746-2402

Economic Development Administration

West Virginia Development Office
Capitol Complex, Bldg. 6, Room 553,
1900 Kanawha Blvd. E., Charleston, WV 25305-0311
(304) 558-2234, (800) 982-3386; Fax: (304) 558-0449

Exec. Dir.: David Satterfield

Governor's Office

Capitol, 1900 Kanawha Blvd. E., Charleston, WV 25305-0370
(304) 558-2000; Fax: (304) 342-7025
Internet: www.state.wv.us/governor/

Governor: Joseph Manchin III (Democrat)
Next election Nov. 2008

Highest State Court

Supreme Court of Appeals of West Virginia
1900 Kanawha Blvd. E., Rm. E-317, Charleston, WV 25305
(304) 558-2601; Fax: (304) 558-3815
Internet: www.state.wv.us/wvsca

Chief Justice: Joseph P. Albright
Clerk of the Supreme Court: Rory L. Perry II
Deputy Clerk: Edythe A. Nash

Insurance Department

Office of the Insurance Commissioner
1124 Smith St., Charleston, WV 25301
Mailing Address: P.O. Box 50540,
Charleston, WV 25305-0540
(304) 558-3394; Fax: (304) 558-0412
Internet: www.wvinsurance.gov

Commissioner: Jane L. Cline
Chief Insurance Examiner: Leah Cooper

Motor Vehicle Office

West Virginia Division of Motor Vehicles
Dept. of Transportation,
State Capitol Complex, Bldg. 3, Room 124,
1800 Kanawha Blvd. E., Charleston, WV 25317
(304) 558-0238; Vehicle Services Fax: (304) 558-2013
E-mail: www.state.wv.us/dmv
Driver Licenses
Fee for obtaining abstract: $5.00 with driver's license
number; additional $1.00 with Social Security number.
(request must be notorized or a must present a copy of the
requestor's I.D.)
West Virginia Division of Motor Vehicles
Vehicle Records Section, 1606 Washington St. E.,
Charleston, WV 25311 (304) 558-0282; Fax: (304) 558-1012
Internet: www.wvdot.com
Vehicle Records
Vehicle Registration Records: $1.00; Title Copy $5.00; Title
History: $15.00

Police

West Virginia State Police
725 Jefferson Rd., South Charleston, WV 25309-1698
(304) 746-2111; Fax: (304) 746-2246;
Traffic Records Section: (304) 746-2121;
Accident Records Clerk: (304) 746-2128;
Fax: (304) 746-2206
Internet: www.wvstatepolice.com

Superintendent: D. L. Lemmon
Fee for obtaining accident report: $20.00, mailed; $25.00, faxed

Probate, Recording and Notary Certificate Offices

Estate & Wills: Clerk of the County Commission
Deeds and Mortgages: Clerk of the County Commission
Notary Certificates: Secretary of State, Authentication
Division ($10.00)

Senators, U.S.

Robert C. Byrd (Democrat)
311 Hart Senate Office Bldg., Washington, DC 20510
(202) 224-3954; Fax: (202) 228-0002
Internet: http://byrd.senate.gov

John D. (Jay) Rockefeller IV (Democrat)
531 Hart Senate Office Bldg., Washington, DC 20510
(202) 224-6472; Fax: (202) 224-4656
Internet: http://rockefeller.senate.gov

Secretary of State

Office of the Secretary of State
State Capitol, Bldg. 1, Suite 157K,
1900 Kanawha Blvd. E., Charleston, WV 25305-0770
(304) 558-6000; Fax: (304) 558-0900
E-mail: wvsos@wvsos.com
Internet: www.wvsos.com

Secretary of State: Betty Ireland (Republican)
Elected; next election Nov. 2008

Tax Department

Department of Tax & Revenue
Taxpayer Services Division, P.O. Box 3784,
Charleston, WV 25337-3784
(304) 558-3333; Fax: (304) 558-3269;
Auditing Div.: (304) 558-8500; Legal Div.: (304) 558-5330
Internet: www.state.wv.us/taxdiv/

1206 Quarrier St., Charleston, WV 25301

1001 Lee St., Charleston, WV 25301
Secretary: John C. Musgrave (Acting)

Victim Compensation Program

Court of Claims
Crime Victims Compensation Fund
Bldg. 1, Room W-334, 1900 Kanawha Blvd. E.,
Charleston, WV 25305-0610
(304) 347-4850; Fax: (304) 347-4915
W. Va. Code §§14-2A-1 to 14-2A-29

Vital Statistics

Vital Registration Office
350 Capitol St., Room 165, Charleston, WV 25301-3701
(304) 558-2931; Fax: (304) 558-1051
E-mail: vitalreg@wvdhhr.org
Internet: www.wvdhhr.org
*1917-present—Birth, Death. Certified copies of
Marriage—1964-present. Central index of
Marriages—1921 to present. Central index of
Divorces—1967 to present. Certified copies, Marriage prior
to 1964 and Divorce, from county of event.
Mailing and physical address for ordering certificates only;
Mailing address for court orders: adoptions, legal name
change, court ordered determination of paternity, etc. write:
Attn.: Corrections Unit Vital Registration Office, P.O. Box
11012, Charleston WV 25339-1012*
Search or certified copy—$5.00. Expedited service
available through VitalChek, via Internet at
www.vitalchek.com.

WISCONSIN

Capital: Madison

5,363,675 (2000 Census)
State Information: (608) 266-2211
State Web Site: www.state.wi.us

Administrative Office of the Courts

Director of State Courts Office
16 E. State Capitol, Madison, WI 53702
Mailing Address: Supreme Court, P.O. Box 1688,
Madison, WI 53701-1688
(608) 266-6828; Fax: (608) 267-0980
Internet: www.wicourts.gov

Dir. of State Courts: A. John Voelker

Attorney Discipline

Wisconsin Office of Lawyer Regulation
315 Tenney Bldg., 110 E. Main St.,
Madison, WI 53703-3383
(608) 267-7274; Toll Free: (877) 315-6941;
Fax: (608) 267-1959
Internet: www.wicourts.gov/olr

Director: Keith L. Sellen

Attorney General

Office of the Attorney General
114 E. State Capitol, Madison, WI 53702
(608) 266-1221; Fax: (608) 267-2779
Internet: www.doj.state.wi.us

Atty. General: Peggy A. Lautenschlager (Democrat)
Elected; next election Nov. 2006

Banking Department

Department of Financial Institutions
Banking Division
345 W. Washington Ave., 4th Floor, Madison, WI 53703
Mailing Address: P.O. Box 7876, Madison, WI 53707-7876
(608) 261-7578; Fax: (608) 267-6889
Internet: www.wdfi.org

Administrator: Michael J. Mach

Bar Admissions

Board of Bar Examiners
Supreme Court of Wisconsin
715 Tenney Bldg., 110 E. Main St.,
Madison, WI 53703-3328
(608) 266-9760; Fax: (608) 266-1196
E-mail: bbe@wicourts.gov; Internet: www.wicourts.gov
30 hours CLE required per two years including three
hours of ethics.
Admission on motion with discretionary years practice in a
Reciprocal Jurisdiction.

Bar Association

State Bar of Wisconsin
5302 Eastpark Blvd., Madison, WI 53718
Mailing Address: P.O. Box 7158, Madison, WI 53707-7158
(608) 257-3838; Fax: (608) 257-5502
Internet: www.wisbar.org, www.legalexplorer.com

Exec. Dir.: George C. Brown

President: Michelle A. Behnke
Integrated Bar
Annual Meeting—May, 2005

Client Protection Fund

Clients' Security Fund
State Bar of Wisconsin
5302 Eastpark Blvd., Madison, WI 53718
Mailing Address: P.O. Box 7158, Madison, WI 53707-7158
(608) 257-3838; Fax: (608) 257-5502
Internet: www.legalexplorer.com

Client Protection Fund Administrator: Kris E. Wenzel
    E-mail: kwenzel@wisbar.org

Commerce Department

Department of Commerce
201 W. Washington Ave., Madison, WI 53717-7970
Mailing Address: P.O. Box 7970, Madison, WI 53707
(608) 266-1018; Main Fax: (608) 266-3447
Internet: www.commerce.state.wi.us

Corporations Officers

Department of Financial Institutions
Division of Corporate and Consumer Services
P.O. Box 7846, Madison, WI 53707-7846
General Information: (608) 261-9555;
Corporations Section: (608) 261-7577;
Domestic Annual Reports: (608) 264-7810;
Foreign Annual Reports: (608) 267-3218;
Limited Partnerships & Foreign Corporations:
(608) 267-6808;
Name Reservation by Phone: (608) 261-7577;
UCC: (608) 261-9548; Fax: (608) 267-6813;
UCC Fax: (608) 264-7965

Deputy Administrator: Ray Allen
    (608) 264-7950; Fax: (608) 267-6813
    E-mail: ray.allen@dfi.state.wi.us

UCC Dir.: Dave Duecker
    (608) 261-9566; Fax: (608) 264-7965
    E-mail: david.duecker@dfi.state.wi.us

Criminal History Board

Crime Information Bureau
Record Check Unit
17 W. Main St., Suite 461, Madison, WI 53701
Mailing Address: P.O. Box 2688, Madison, WI 53701-2688
(608) 266-5764; Fax: (608) 267-4558

Economic Development Administration

See Commerce Department

Governor's Office

Office of the Governor
115 E. State Capitol, Madison, WI 53702
(608) 266-1212; TTY: (608) 261-6790; Fax: (608) 267-8983
Internet: www.wisgov.state.wi.us

444 N. Capitol St. N.W., Suite 613, Washington, DC 20001
(202) 624-5870; Fax: (202) 624-5871

Governor: Jim Doyle (Democrat)
Next election Nov. 2006

Highest State Court

Supreme Court
110 E. Main St., Room 215, Madison, WI 53703
Mailing Address: P.O. Box 1688, Madison, WI 53701-1688
(608) 266-1880; Clerk's Fax: (608) 267-0640;
Chief Justice's Fax: (608) 261-8299
Internet: www.wicourts.gov

Chief Justice: Shirley S. Abrahamson

Clerk of the Supreme Court: Cornelia G. Clark

Insurance Department

Office of the Commissioner of Insurance
125 S. Webster St., Madison, WI 53702
Mailing Address: P.O. Box 7873, Madison, WI 53707-7873
(608) 266-3586; Fax: (608) 266-9935
E-mail: information@oci.state.wi.us
Internet: http://oci.wi.gov

Commissioner: Jorge Gomez

Chief Examiner: Roger Peterson

Motor Vehicle Office

Wisconsin Division of Motor Vehicles
Department of Transportation, 4802 Sheboygan Ave.,
P.O. Box 7995, Madison, WI 53707-7911
(608) 266-2353
E-mail: driverrecords.dmv@dot.state.wi.us
Internet: www.dot.state.wi.us

For Abstracts write: Driver Records,
Dept. of Transportation, 4802 Sheboygan Ave.,
P.O. Box 7995, Madison, WI 53707-7995
(608) 266-2353; Fax: (608) 261-8201
Fee for obtaining abstract: $5.00 alone; $10.00 abstract
with search

Police

Wisconsin State Patrol
P.O. Box 7912, Madison, WI 53707-7912
Fax: (608) 267-4495

Superintendent: David L. Collins (608) 267-7102
Fee for obtaining accident report: $1.75, plus $.35 per
additional side of page; for accidents of three or four cars,
$3.15, plus $.35 per additional side of page

Probate, Recording and Notary Certificate Offices

Estate & Wills: County Register in Probate
Deeds and Mortgages: County Clerks Offices
Notary Certificates: Secy. of State, Notary Records ($10.00)

Senators, U.S.

Russell D. Feingold (Democrat)
506 Hart Senate Office Bldg., Washington, DC 20510
(202) 224-5323; Fax: (202) 224-2725
Internet: http://feingold.senate.gov

Herbert H. Kohl (Democrat)
330 Hart Senate Office Bldg., Washington, DC 20510
(202) 224-5653; Fax: (202) 224-9787
Internet: http://kohl.senate.gov

Secretary of State

Office of the Secretary of State
30 W. Mifflin St., 10th Floor, P.O. Box 7848,
Madison, WI 53707-7848
(608) 266-8888; Fax: (608) 266-3159
Internet: http://www.state.wi.us/agencies/sos/

Secretary of State: Douglas La Follette (Democrat)
Elected; next election Nov. 2006

Tax Department

Department of Revenue
2135 Rimrock Rd., Madison, WI 53713
Mailing Address: Room 624A, P.O. Box 8933,
Madison, WI 53708-8933
Audit: (608) 266-2486; Forms Fax: (608) 261-6229;
General Fax: (608) 266-5718;
Enterprise Svcs. Div.: (608) 264-8175;
Income, Sales & Excise Tax Div.: (608) 266-3360;
Audit Bur.: (608) 266-2772
Internet: http://www.dor.state.wi.us/
Secretary: Michael L. Morgan

Victim Compensation Program

Office of Crime Victim Services, Department of Justice
17 W. Main St., Rm. 843, P.O. Box 7951, Madison, WI 53707-7951
(608) 264-9497; Fax: (608) 264-6368
Wis. Stat. Ann. §§949.01 to 949.18 (West) (rev. 1986)

Vital Statistics

Dept. of Health & Family Services
Vital Records Section, Room 158, 1 W. Wilson St.,
P.O. Box 309, Madison, WI 53701-0309
General Information Records: (608) 266-1371;
Customer Service: (608) 266-1373;
Credit Card Orders by Fax: (608) 255-2035
E-mail: vitalrecords@dhfs.state.wi.us
Internet: www.dhfs.wisconsin.gov
*Births, Deaths, Marriages, Divorces—1907-present; Also
Divorces—1987-present from Clerk of Court in county
where divorce occurred.*
Search fee including certified copy—$12.00 for birth
records; by fax add $16.00 per record; $7.00 for other
records. Additional copies, $3.00.

WYOMING   *Capital: Cheyenne*

493,782 (2000 Census)
State Information: (307) 777-7220
State Web Site: www.state.wy.us

Administrative Office of the Courts

Administrative Office of the Courts
233 Supreme Court Bldg., 2301 Capitol Ave.,
Cheyenne, WY 82002
(307) 777-7583, 777-7678; Fax: (307) 777-3447
Internet: http://courts.state.wy.us/
Court Administrator: Holly A. Hansen

Attorney Discipline

Wyoming State Bar Board of Professional Responsibility
500 Randall Ave., Cheyenne, WY 82001
Mailing Address: P.O. Box 109, Cheyenne, WY 82003-0109
(307) 632-9061; Fax: (307) 632-3737
E-mail: beckyalewis@aol.com; Internet: www.wyomingbar.org
Bar Counsel: Rebecca A. Lewis

Attorney General

123 State Capitol, Cheyenne, WY 82002
(307) 777-7841; Fax: (307) 777-6869
Atty. General: Patrick J. Crank
Appointed

Banking Department

Division of Banking, Department of Audit
Herschler Bldg., 3rd Floor East, Cheyenne, WY 82002
(307) 777-7797; Fax: (307) 777-3555
Internet: http://audit.state.wy.us/banking
Commissioner: Jeffrey C. Vogel

Bar Admissions

Wyoming State Bar
500 Randall Ave., Cheyenne, WY 82001
Mailing Address: P.O. Box 109, Cheyenne, WY 82003-0109
(307) 632-9061; Fax: (307) 632-3737
Internet: www.wyomingbar.org
15 hrs. CLE required per year including one hour of ethics.
Admission on motion with five of the last seven years in
practice in a Reciprocal Jurisdiction. Requests for
applications should be made to Wyoming State Bar, P.O.
Box 109, Cheyenne, WY 82003 (307) 632-9061 or at
www.wyomingbar.org.

Bar Association

Wyoming State Bar
500 Randall Ave., Cheyenne, WY 82001
(307) 632-9061; Fax: (307) 632-3737
Internet: www.wyomingbar.org
Exec. Dir.: Mary B. Guthrie
President: Mark W. Harris
Integrated Bar
Annual Meeting—September, 2005

Client Protection Fund

Client Security Fund
Wyoming State Bar
P.O. Box 109, Cheyenne, WY 82003-0109
(307) 632-9061; Fax: (307) 632-3737
Internet: www.wyomingbar.org
Executive Dir.: Mary B. Guthrie

Commerce Department

Wyoming Business Council
214 W. 15th St., Cheyenne, WY 82002
(307) 777-2800; Toll-Free: (800) 262-3425;
Fax: (307) 777-2838
Internet: www.wyomingbusiness.org

Corporations Officers

Department of State
Corporation and UCC Department
110 Capitol Bldg., Cheyenne, WY 82002-0020
General Information, Corporations Section, Annual
Reports & Name Availabilities: (307) 777-7311;
UCC: (307) 777-5372; Notaries: (307) 777-5407;
Fax: (307) 777-5339
Internet: http://soswy.state.wy.us
Director: Jeanne Sawyer (307) 777-5334
    E-mail: jsawye@state.wy.us

Criminal History Board

Division of Criminal Investigation
316 W. 22nd St., Cheyenne, WY 82002
(307) 777-7523; Fax: (307) 777-7252

Economic Development Administration

See Commerce Department

Governor's Office

Office of the Governor
State Capitol, Room 124, 200 W. 24th St.,
Cheyenne, WY 82002-0010
(307) 777-7434; Fax: (307) 632-3909
Internet: www.wyoming.gov/governor/governor_home.asp
Governor: Dave Freudenthal (Democrat)
Next election Nov. 2006

Highest State Court

Supreme Court
Supreme Court Bldg., 2301 Capitol Ave.,
Cheyenne, WY 82002
(307) 777-7316; Fax: (307) 777-6129
Internet: www.courts.state.wy.us
Chief Justice: William U. Hill
Clerk of the Supreme Court: Judy Pacheco

Insurance Department

Department of Insurance
Herschler Bldg., 122 W. 25th St., 3rd Fl. E.,
Cheyenne, WY 82002-0440
(307) 777-7401; Fax: (307) 777-5895
E-mail: wyinsdep@state.wy.us
Internet: http://insurance.state.wy.us
Commissioner: Kenneth G. Vines
Chief Examiner: Linda Johnson

Motor Vehicle Office

Wyoming Department of Transportation
For Abstracts write: Attn.: Driver Services,
5300 Bishop Blvd., Cheyenne, WY 82009-3340
Customer Service/Abstracts: (307) 777-4800;
Abstracts Fax: (307) 777-4773
Internet: http://wydotweb.state.wy.us
Fee for obtaining abstract: $5.00

Police

Wyoming Highway Patrol
5300 Bishop Blvd., Cheyenne, WY 82009-3340
(307) 777-4301; Fax: (307) 777-3897
Internet: www.whp.state.wy.us

Accident Reports: Wyoming Department of Transportation,
5300 Bishop Blvd., Cheyenne, WY 82009-3310
(307) 777-4450; Fax: (307) 777-4250

Administrator: Col. John F. Cox
Fee for obtaining accident report: $3.00

Probate, Recording and Notary Certificate Offices

Estate & Wills: County District Court Clerks Offices
Deeds and Mortgages: County Clerks Offices
Notary Certificates: Secretary of State, Notary Division
(Apostille and Certification $3.00)

Senators, U.S.

Michael B. Enzi (Republican)
379-A Russell Senate Office Bldg., Washington, DC 20510
(202) 224-3424
Internet: http://enzi.senate.gov

Craig Thomas (Republican)
307 Dirksen Senate Office Bldg., Washington, DC 20510
(202) 224-6441; Fax: (202) 224-1724
Internet: http://thomas.senate.gov

Secretary of State

Office of the Secretary of State
106 State Capitol Bldg., 200 W. 24th St.,
Cheyenne, WY 82002-0020
(307) 777-7378; Fax: (307) 777-6217
E-mail: secofstate@state.wy.us
Internet: http://soswy.state.wy.us

Secretary of State: Joseph B. Meyer (Republican)
Elected; next election Nov. 2006

Tax Department

Department of Revenue
Herschler Bldg., 2nd W. Floor, 122 W. 25th St.,
Cheyenne, WY 82002-0110
Excise Tax Div.: (307) 777-5220;
Mineral Tax Div.: (307) 777-5327;
Administrative Svces.: (307) 777-3724;
Ad Valorem/Property Tax (Local): (307) 777-5325;
Ad Valorem/Property Tax (State): (307) 777-5232;
Estate Tax: (307) 777-5200;
Director's Office: (307) 777-7961;
Director's Office Fax: (307) 777-7722
E-mail: DirectorOfRevenue@wy.gov
Internet: http://revenue.state.wy.us

Director: Edmund J. Schmidt

Victim Compensation Program

Victim Services Division
Office of the Attorney General
Herschler Bldg., 1st Floor West, 122 W. 25th St.,
Cheyenne, WY 82002
(307) 777-7200; Fax: (307) 777-6683
Internet: http://vssi.state.wy.us
*Wyo. Stat. §§1-40-101 to 1-40-119 and 1-40-201 to 1-40-210
(1985 Cum. Supp., Amended 1987, 1989, 1991, 1993,1997)*

Vital Statistics

Vital Records Services
Hathaway Bldg., Cheyenne, WY 82002
(307) 777-7591; Fax: (307) 635-4103
Internet: http://wdh.state.wy.us/vital_records
Births, Deaths since July 1909; Marriages, Divorces since May, 1941.
Search fee including certified copy—Deaths: $9.00 if exact year of death is known; otherwise $12.00 per five years searched. All other records: $12.00
Expedited Service: Available via Fax for $30.25 (including overnight delivery). Details can be obtained by calling (307) 777-7591, or on Internet.

PUERTO RICO   *Capital: San Juan*

3,808,610 (2000 Census)
State Web Site: www.gobierno.pr

Administrative Office of the Courts

Office of Courts Administration
General Court of Justice
César González St. and Jésus T. Piñero Ave.,
Hato Rey, PR 00919
Mailing Address: P.O. Box 190917,
San Juan, PR 00919-0917
(787) 641-6600, 24; Fax: (787) 250-7448
Internet: www.tribunalpr.org

Administrative Dir.: Sonia Ivette Vëlez Colón

Attorney Discipline

Comision de Etica Professional
Avenida Ponce de Leon 808,
Colegio de Abogados de Puerto Rico, San Juan, PR 00907
Mailing Address: P.O. Box 9021900,
San Juan, PR 00902-1900
(787) 721-3358; Fax: (787) 725-0330
Internet: www.capr.org

President: Julio Fontanet

Attorney General

Edificio Principal del Depto. de Justicia, Piso 11,
Calle Olimpo, Esquina Axtmayer, Parada 11, Num. 6,
Miramar, PR 00907
Mailing Address: G.P.O. Box, San Juan, PR 00902-0192
(787) 721-2900; Fax: (787) 724-4770
Internet: www.justicia.gobierno.pr

Secretary of Justice: Anabelle Rodriguez (787) 721-7700, 71
Appointed

Bar Association

The Bar Assn. of Puerto Rico
Colegio de Abogados de Puerto Rico
808 Ave. Ponce de Leon 80, Miramar, PR 00908
Mailing Address: P.O. Box 9021900,
San Juan, PR 00902-1900
(787) 721-3358; Fax: (787) 725-0330
E-mail: dircapr@capr.org
Internet: www.capr.org

Exec. Dir.: José M. Montalvo Trias
President: Julio E. Fontanet Maldonado
Integrated Bar
Annual Meeting—September, 2005 and 2006

Corporations Officers

Department of State
Corporation & Trademark Division
San Francisco St., Old San Juan Station, P.O. Box 3271,
San Juan, PR 00902-3271
General Information: (787) 722-2121;
Corporations Section & Annual Reports: (787) 722-2121;
Notaries: (787) 722-2121, Ext. 3336;
Filing Division: (787) 722-2121, Ext. 6255

Dir., Corporate Div.: Marcos Vélez Green (Acting)
Dir., Trademark Div.: Raquel Mercado

Governor's Office

Office of the Governor
La Fortaleza, 52 Fortaleza St., P.O. Box 9020082,
San Juan, PR 00901
Mailing Address: P.O. Box 9020082, San Juan, PR 00902-0082
(787) 721-7000; Fax: (787) 725-7763
Internet: www.fortaleza.gobierno.pr

Governor: Aníbal Acevedo Vílá
Next election Nov. 2008

Highest State Court

Supreme Court of Puerto Rico
Muñoz Rivera Ave., Stop 8, Puerta de Tierra,
San Juan, PR 00902
Mailing Address: P.O. Box 9022392, San Juan, PR 00902-2392
(787) 723-6033; Fax: (787) 722-9177
Internet: www.tribunalpr.org

Chief Justice: Miriam Naviera Merly
Clerk of the Court: Patricia Oton

Probate, Recording and Notary Certificate Offices
Estate & Wills: Clerk, General Ct. of Justice, Supreme Ct.
Deeds and Mortgages: Property Registry, each district
Notary Certificates: Dept. of State, Division of
Certification and Regulations ($3.00)

Secretary of State
Office of the Secretary of State
Department of State, Real Intendencia Bldg., San Jose St.,
San Juan, PR 00902
Mailing Address: P.O. Box 9023271,
San Juan, PR 00902-3271
(787) 722-2121; Fax: (787) 725-7303; Internet:
www.estado.gobierno.pr
Secretary of State: Hon. Marisara Pont Marchese
Appointed

Victim Compensation Program
Oficina de Compensación a Víctimas de Delito
(Office of Crime Victim Compensation)
Ave. Juan Ponce de León 804, Suite 101, Miramar,
G.P.O. Box 9020192, San Juan, PR 00902-0192
(787) 641-7480, 76, 85, 647-7478, 79; Fax: (787) 641-7477
Internet: www.justicia.gobierno.pr
Directora: Lidice A. Cardelario

Vital Statistics
Demographic Registry
Dept. of Health, 171 Quisqueya St., Hato Rey, PR 00917
Mailing Address: P.O. Box 11854, San Juan, PR 00910
(787) 767-9120; Fax: (787) 751-5003
Internet: www.salud.gov.pr
Births, Deaths, Marriages, Divorces—1931 (local registry records 1885-1931).
Certified copies: $5.00 money order for first copy payable to Secretary of the Treasury. Additional copies ordered at the same time are $4.00 each for the same person. No checks accepted.

VIRGIN ISLANDS
Capital: Charlotte Amalie, St. Thomas
108,612 (2000 Census)
State Web Site: www.usvi.org

Bar Association
Virgin Islands Bar Association
27 & 28 King Cross St., Phoenix Court,
Christiansted, St. Croix, VI 00822
Mailing Address: P.O. Box 4108,
Christiansted, St. Croix, VI 00820
(340) 778-7497; Fax: (340) 773-5060
E-mail: vibar@viaccess.net
Internet: www.vibar.org
Exec. Dir.: Hinda Richards
President: Maxwell P. McIntosh
President-Elect: Joycelyn Hewlett
Integrated Bar
Annual Meeting—December, 2005

Corporations Officers
Division of Corporations and Trademarks
Office of the Lieutenant Governor
Kogens Gade No. 18,
Charlotte Amalie, Saint Thomas, VI 00802
(340) 776-8515; Fax: (340) 776-4612
Chief: Lorna Webster

Governor's Office
Office of the Governor
Government House, 21-22 Kongens Gade,
St. Thomas, VI 00802
(340) 774-0001; Fax: (340) 776-4912
E-mail: rcanton@govhse.gov.vi

Government House 3009,
Christiansted, St. Croix, VI 00820
(340) 773-1404; Fax: (340) 713-9806
Governor: Charles W. Turnbull, Ph.D.
Next election Nov. 2006

Highest State Court
Territorial Court of the Virgin Islands
5400 Veteran's Dr., Saint Thomas, VI 00802
Mailing Address: P.O. Box 70, Saint Thomas, VI 00804
(340) 774-6680; Fax: (340) 776-8690
Presiding Judge: Maria M. Cabret
Clerk of the Court: Denise D. Abramsen

Probate, Recording and Notary Certificate Offices
Estate & Wills: Territorial Court of the Virgin Islands
Deeds and Mortgages: Recorder of Deeds in each district
Notary Certificates: Office of the Lieutenant Governor ($25.00)

Victim Compensation Program
V.I. Criminal Victims Compensation Commission
Dept. of Human Services
Knud Hansen Complex—Bldg. A,
1303 Hospital Ground, Charlotte Amalie,
St. Thomas, VI 00802
(340) 774-0930, Ext. 4104, 774-1166; Fax: (340) 774-3466
Administrator: Alrick Brooks
V.I. Code Ann. tit. 34 chap. 7, §§151 to 179

Vital Statistics
Clerk of the District Court
3013 Estate Golden Rock, Lot 13,
Christiansted, St. Croix, VI 00820-4355
(340) 773-1130; Fax: (340) 773-1563
Internet: www.vid.uscourts.gov

5500 Veteran's Dr., Room 310,
Saint Thomas, VI 00802-6424
(340) 774-0640; Fax: (340) 774-1293
Divorces before 1977. For Divorces after 1977, contact the Territorial Court in the appropriate area.
Certified copy—$10.00 and $25.00, separate money order and/or certified check required.

Clerk of the District Court
5500 Veteran's Dr., Suite 310,
Charlotte Amalie, St. Thomas, VI 00802-6424
(340) 774-0640; Fax: (340) 774-1293
Internet: www.vid.uscourts.gov
Divorces before 1977. For divorces after 1977, contact the Territorial Court in the appropriate area.
Certified copy—$10.00, plus $25.00 for a Registry Stamp; two checks or Money Orders must be drafted.

Clerk of the Territorial Court
Alexander Farrelly Justice Complex, Veterans Dr.,
Saint Thomas, VI 00802
Mailing Address: P.O. Box 70, Saint Thomas, VI 00801
(340) 774-6680; Fax: (340) 776-8690
Internet: www.vitalrec.com/vi.html
St. Thomas and St. John: Marriages.
Certified copy—Marriages: $2.00; Divorces: $5.00

Clerk of the Territorial Court
Chief Deputy Clerk, Family Div.
R.F.D. 2, Kingshill, Kingshill, St. Croix, VI 00850
Mailing Address: P.O. Box 929, Christiansted, VI 00820
(340) 778-9750; Fax: (340) 778-4044
St. Croix: Marriages.
Certified copy—Marriages: $2.00; Divorces: $5.00

Vital Statistics
Department of Health, 3500 Richmond,
Christiansted, St. Croix, VI 00820-4370
(340) 773-4050, 773-1311, Ext. 3086
St. Croix: Births, Deaths.
Certified copy—$15.00

Vital Statistics
Department of Health,
Knud Hansen Complex, Hospital Ground,
Saint Thomas, VI 00802
(340) 774-9000, Ext. 4621, Ext. 4623
Internet: www.vitalrec.com/vi.html
St. Thomas and St. John: Births, Deaths since July 1906.
Births, Deaths: $10.00; Marriage: $2.00; Divorce: $5.00

AFFIDAVIT OF NON-MILITARY SERVICE SOURCES

Whenever an affidavit of non-military service is required, certificates in accordance with Section 601 of the (Soldiers and Sailors) Civil Relief Act may be obtained from the various military services as follows:

Requests for such certificates should contain the defendant's full name, service number, rank or grade, social security account number, date and place of birth, last known address, former organizations to which assigned, or other information to properly identify the individual in question. The reason for requiring such a certificate must be stated. Each request must be accompanied by a postal money order, certified, cashier or personal check made payable to the Treasurer of the United States (unless otherwise indicated) in the amount of $5.20 (cash or stamps will not be accepted) payable as indicated.

Air Force Worldwide Locator
HQ AFPC/MSIDL
550 C St. W., Suite 50, Randolph AFB, TX 78150-4752
(210) 565-2660
Make check payable to DAO-DE RAFB. Enclose a self-addressed stamped envelope.

Bureau of Naval Personnel
Department of the Navy
Navy Personnel Command,
5751 Honor Dr. Bldg. 769, PERS-312,
Millington, TN 38055-3120
Mailing Address: Navy Personnel Command,
5720 Integrity Drive, PERS-312,
Millington, TN 38055-3120
(901) 874-3350
Internet: www.bupers.navy.mil/pers312/index.htm
Make check payable to Treasurer of the United States, $5.20 per name.

Commandant of the Marine Corps (MMSB10)
Headquarters U.S. Marine Corps,
Personnel Mgmt. Support BR MMSB 10, 2008 Elliot Rd.,
Quantico, VA 22134-5030
(703) 784-3940
Please mark on bottom of envelope "OFFICIAL BUSINESS"

Defense Manpower Data Center
1600 Wilson Blvd., Suite 400, Arlington, VA 22209-2593
(703) 696-6762, 67; Fax: (703) 696-4156

Verifies non-military status for defense branches of armed services. No fee for verification, but must be requested on form provided by Manpower Data Center. Contact Center for copy of appropriate form. Provide self-addressed, stamped envelope for reply. If toll-free Fax number is available for party making request, Center will reply by Fax.

U.S. Army Enlisted Records and Evaluation Center
Commander
Attn: PCRE-RP, 8899 E. 56th St.,
Indianapolis, IN 46249-5301
(317) 510-3644
Make check payable to Finance Officer

U.S. Coast Guard
Commander
U.S. Dept. of Transportation/U.S.C.G.,
2100 Second St. S.W., Washington, DC 20593-0001
(202) 267-1613
Enclose a self-addressed stamped envelope. Mark bottom of envelope,"ADM-3" and "DO NOT OPEN IN MAIL ROOM". Make check payable to U.S. Coast Guard.

WEATHER RECORDS

American Meteorological Society
45 Beacon St., Boston, MA 02108-3693
(617) 227-2425; Fax: (617) 742-8718
E-mail: amsinfo@ametsoc.org
Internet: www.ametsoc.org/ams

Publishes and distributes a free directory of private consulting meteorologists for testimony (available on website).

National Climatic Data Center (NCDC)
Federal Bldg., Room 120, 151 Patton Ave.,
Asheville, NC 28801-5001
(828) 271-4800; Fax: (828) 271-4876
E-mail: ncdc.orders@noaa.gov
Internet: www.ncdc.noaa.gov

The collection, publication and archiving of official weather records are the responsibility of the National Oceanic and Atmospheric Administration (NOAA) of the Department of Commerce. Supplies certified records of daily high and low temperatures and precipitation for thousands of U.S. cities, and data recorded on an hourly basis of temperature, precipitation, wind, humidity, type of weather, pressure, visibility and clouds at most National Weather Service offices, for legal cases not involving the Federal Government. Costs of reproduction charged for data and services. For an additional charge, written translations of specific information in plain language can be obtained. With consent of NOAA counsel, the NCDC can supply data for federal cases. Most uncertified data can be obtained from the Internet site.

National Weather Service
Attn: W/OS523, Forensic Services,
1325 East-West Highway, Room 14400,
Silver Spring, MD 20910
(301) 713-0090, Ext. 147; Fax: (301) 713-1598
A component of the National Oceanic and Atmospheric Administration (NOAA) of the Department of Commerce. Provides certified copies of weather warnings and forecasts.

OVERSEAS BIRTH AND DEATH RECORDS

National Personnel Records Center
Military Personnel Records
9700 Page Ave., Saint Louis, MO 63132-5100
Army: (314) 538-4261; Air Force: (314) 538-4243;
Navy/Marines/Coast Guard: (314) 538-4141;
Fax: (314) 538-4175
E-mail: center@stlouis.nara.gov
Internet: www.nara.gov/regional/mpr.html

The National Personnel Records Center, Military Personnel Records is the repository of millions of military personnel, health, and medical records of discharged and deceased veterans of all services during the 20th century. No fee for death record (Report of Casualty: D.D. Form 1300) but consent of next of kin is required. Information from the records is made available upon written request.

U.S. Department of State
Passport Correspondence Office, 1111 19th
St. N.W., Suite 510, Washington, DC 20524
(202) 955-0307; automated: (202) 647-0518
Internet: http://travel.state.gov/consular_records.html

Record of Births (Form FS-240), Cetification of Births (Form DS 1350) and deaths (Form OF 180) occurring to U.S. citizens while abroad (except deaths of Armed Forces personnel). Also certificates of witness to marriage for American citizens.

Certified copies—$40.00 for one copy; $20.00 for first copy, $10.00 for each additional copy

MARRIAGE LAWS

Revised by Gary N. Skoloff of the New Jersey Bar, lecturer on Matrimonial Law for the Institute for Continuing Legal Education, and author, New Jersey Family Law Practice

State or other jurisdiction	Age at which marriage can be contracted with parental consent		Age below which parental consent is required		Common-law marriage recognized	Physical examination and blood test for male and female		Waiting period	
	Male	Female	Male	Female		Maximum period between examination and issuance of license	Scope of medical examination	Before issuance of license	After issuance of license (Expiration)
Alabama	16(33)	16(33)	18	18	*(33)			(33)	30 da.
Alaska	14(14)	14(14)	18	18	recognized before 1917			3 da.(25)	90 da.
Arizona	16(14)(33)	16(14)(33)	18	18	(30)				12 mo.
Arkansas	17(6)(33)	16(6)(33)	18	18	(30)			(24)	
California	(2)(27)	(2)(27)	18	18	(30)	(31)			90 da.
Colorado (22)	16(29)	16(29)	18	18	*(30)				30 da.
Connecticut	16(14)(44)	16(14)(44)	18	18	(30)		(4)(25)	4 da.(25)	65 da.
Delaware	18(6)(29)(46)	16(6)(29)(45)(46)	18	18	(30)			24 hrs.(9)	30 da.
Florida	16(1)(6)(29)(49)	16(1)(6)(29)(49)	18	18	recognized before 1/1/1968			3 da.(25)(50)	60 da.
Georgia	16(6)(33)	16(6)(33)	16	16	recognized before 1/1/1997(30)		(41)	3 da.	30 da.
Hawaii	15(14)	15(14)	18	18	(30)			3 da.	30 da.
Idaho	16(14)	16(14)	18	18	recognized before 1/1/1996(30)		(34)(11)	3 da.(24)(25)	90 da.
Illinois	16(43)	16(43)	18	18	recognized before 6/30/1905		(51)	1 da.	60 da.
Indiana	17(6)(14)	17(6)(14)(29)	18	18	recognized before 1/1/1958		(35)		60 da.
Iowa	16(14)	16(14)	18	18	*(30)			3 da.(25)	20 da.
Kansas	14(14)	12(14)	18	18	*			3 da.(25)	180 da.
Kentucky	16(6)(14)(44)	16(6)(14)(44)	18	18	(30)		(19)		30 da.
Louisiana	16(14)(52)	16(14)(52)	18	18			(3)	2 da.	30 da.
Maine	16(14)	16(14)	18	18		10 da.		3 da.(24)(25)	90 da.
Maryland	16(6)(10)	16(6)(10)	18	18				48 hrs.(25)	180 da.
Massachusetts	14(14)	12(14)	18	18	(30)	3-60 da.	(16)	3 da.(24)	60 da.
Michigan	16(29)	16(29)	18	18	recognized before 1/1/1957(30)			3 da.(25)	33 da.
Minnesota	16(29)	16(29)	18	18	recognized before 4/26/1941(30)			5 da.(25)	180 da.
Mississippi	17(2)(29)(53)	15(2)(29)(53)	17	15	recognized before 4/5/1956(30)	30 da.	(3)	3 da.(25)	
Missouri	15(8)	15(8)	18	18	recognized before 3/31/1921(30)			3 da.(25)	30 da.
Montana (23)	16(29)(33)	16(29)(33)	18	18	*(30)		(57)		180 da.
Nebraska (23)	17(29)	17(29)	19	19	recognized before 1/1/1923(30)		(35)		1 yr.
Nevada	16(1)(29)(44)	16(1)(29)(44)	18	18	recognized before 3/12/1943(55)				1 yr.
New Hampshire	14(15)	13(15)	18	18	*(30)			3 da.(26)	90 da.
New Jersey	16(6)(29)	16(6)(29)	18	18	recognized before 12/1/1939(30)			72 hrs.(25)	30 da.
New Mexico (37)	16(6)(8)	16(6)(8)	18	18	(30)	30 da.	(3)		
New York (38)	16(15)(29)	16(15)(29)	18	18	recognized before 4/29/1933(30)		(19)	24 hrs.(12)	60 da.
North Carolina	16(6)(29)	16(6)(29)	18	18	(30)(55)				
North Dakota	16	16	18	18	recognized before 10/10/1991(30)				60 da.
Ohio	18(6)(29)	16(6)(29)	18	18	*(30)(55)		(3)	(17)	60 da.
Oklahoma	16(6)(29)	16(6)(29)	18	18	*(30)(55)	30 da.(25)		(20)	30 da.
Oregon	17(21)	17(21)	18	18	(30)			3 da.(25)	60 da.
Pennsylvania	16(8)(29)	16(8)(29)	18	18	*			3 da.(25)	60 da.
Puerto Rico (22)(39)	18(6)(8)(29)	16(6)(8)(29)	21(6)	21(6)			(3)(33)		60 da.
Rhode Island (58)	18(8)(29)	18(8)(29)	18	18	*(13)				90 da.
South Carolina	16(6)(29)	14(6)(29)	18	18	*			1 da.	
South Dakota	16(6)(29)	16(6)(29)	18	18	recognized before 7/1/1959(13)				20 da.
Tennessee	16(8)(29)	16(8)(29)	18	18			(41)	3 da.(7)(25)	30 da.
Texas (22)(23)	14(14)(15)	14(14)(15)	18	18	*(30)		(41)	72 hrs.(25)(33)	30 da.
Utah	15(1)(14)(33)	15(1)(14)(33)	18(27)(1)	18(27)(1)	(40)		(41)		30 da.
Vermont	16(29)	16(29)	18	18		(30)(25)	(3)	1 da.(25)	30 da.

MARRIAGE LAWS

Revised by Gary N. Skoloff of the New Jersey Bar, lecturer on Matrimonial Law for the Institute for Continuing Legal Education, and author, New Jersey Family Law Practice

State or other jurisdiction	Age at which marriage can be contracted with parental consent		Age below which parental consent is required		Common-law marriage recognized	Physical examination and blood test for male and female — Scope of medical examination	Maximum period between examination and issuance of license	Waiting period — Before issuance of license	Waiting period — After issuance of license (Expiration)
	Male	Female	Male	Female					
Virginia	16(1)(6)	16(1)(6)	18(1)	18(1)	(30)	(41)			60 da.
Washington	17(8)(29)	17(8)(29)	18	18	(30)	(5)		3 da.	60 da.
West Virginia	18(6)	18(6)	18	18	(30)			3 da.(25)	
Wisconsin	16(29)	16(29)	18	18		(32)		5 da.(25)	30 da.
Dist. of Columbia (48)	16(8)(29)(33)	16(8)(29)(33)	16	16	(30)	(3)(47)	30 da.	3 da.(26)	
Virgin Islands	16(1)	14(1)	18	18	(30)			8 da.(25)	

* Indicates common-law marriage recognized.

(1) Parental consent not required if minor was previously married.
(2) No age limits.
(3) Venereal diseases. In West Virginia and Oklahoma, Circuit Court judge may waive requirement. In Mississippi, Oklahoma, Pennsylvania and West Virginia, applicant must be free of syphilis. In Puerto Rico, applicant must be free from mental illness or idiocy.
(4) Venereal diseases and Rubella (for female). In some states Rubella test requirements may be waived. In Connecticut, rubella only.
(5) No exam required, but parties must file affidavit of non-affliction of contagious sexually-transmitted disease.
(6) Younger parties may obtain licence in case of pregnancy or birth of child.
(7) Unless parties are over 18 years of age.
(8) Statute establishes procedure whereby younger parties may obtain license in special circumstances.
(9) Residents before expiration of the 24-hr. waiting period; non-residents before expiration of the 96-hr. waiting period.
(10) If parties are at least 16 years of age, proof of age and the consent of parents in person required. If a parent is ill, an affidavit by the incapacitated parent and a physician's affidavit to that effect required.
(11) Applicants must receive AIDS information pamphlet and certify having read it.
(12) License effective 1 day after issuance, unless court orders otherwise, valid for 60 days only.
(13) No case law or statutes as to recognition of out-of-state common law marriages.
(14) Parental consent and permission of judge required.
(15) Judge can grant marriage to anyone under 18, no younger than 14 year old male and 13 year old female. In New York, female must be at least 14.
(16) Doctor's certificate must be filed 30 days prior to notice of intention.
(17) Applicants under age 18 must state that they have had marriage counseling.
(18) Venereal diseases; test for sickle cell anemia given at request of examining physician.
(19) Test for sickle cell anemia may be requested for certain applicants.
(20) If one or both parties are below the age for marriage without parental consent (3 day waiting period).
(21) If a party has no parent residing within state, and one party has residence within state for six months, no permission required.
(22) Marriages by proxy are valid.
(23) Statute authorizes proxy marriage under certain conditions.
(24) Parties must file notice of intention to marry with local clerk.
(25) Statute establishes procedure whereby waiting period may be avoided.
(26) Time may be shortened. In West Virginia, requirement may be waived by a Circuit Court judge.
(27) Counties may require premarital counseling for persons under 19 or previously divorced.
(28) Not generally valid except for limited purpose of recovery in Workers Compensation cases.
(29) Younger parties may marry with parental consent and/or permission of judge. In Connecticut, judicial approval.
(30) Common law marriage, if valid where contracted, recognized. In New York, including post-1933 good faith relationships started in New York if sojourn in common-law jurisdiction.
(31) When unmarried man and unmarried woman, not minors, have been living together as man and wife, they may, without health certificate, be married upon issuance of appropriate authorization.
(32) Application shall contain such information as directed by Dept. of Health & Social Services.
(33) Other statutory requirements apply.
(34) Rubella for female, but there are certain exceptions, and district judge may waive medical examination on proof that emergency exists.

(35) Any unsterilized female under 50 must submit with application for license a medical report stating whether she has immunological response to rubella, or written record that rubella vaccine was administered on or after her first birthday. Judge may by order dispense with these requirements.
(36) Parties must sign affidavit affirming that they have received and discussed brochure prepared by Division of Public Health Services, Department of Health and Human Services.
(37) No statutory authorization for proxy marriage, but May 11, 1943 opinion of Attorney General that such marriage is valid, but new ceremony when possible recommended.
(38) Proxy marriages are not explicitly authorized by statute but are not contrary to public policy if valid in state where contracted.
(39) Proxy marriage between a person present in Puerto Rico and one absent is permitted.
(40) Unsolemnized marriage arising out of contract is valid if court or administrative order finds two parties: (i) capable of consent; (ii) legally capable of solemnized marriage; (iii) have cohabitated; (iv) mutually assume marital rights, duties and obligations; and (v) contend and are believed to be husband and wife. Determination must be made during or within 1 year of termination of relationship.
(41) Must be provided with information on AIDS and tests available.
(42) Medical exam requirement repealed; applicant must show certificate of HIV counseling, transmission/prevention of venerial diseases.
(43) Judicial consent may be given when parents refuse to consent.
(44) If under age party is under care of guardian or conservator, written consent signed in presence of witness and notarized must be filed with the registrar.
(45) Physician's certificate stating the underage female is pregnant is required.
(46) Consent forms shall be signed in the presence of two reputable witnesses unless signed by a judge.
(47) If individual cannot afford services of physician or other authorized for tests or required statement, a medical officer of the Dept. of Human Services may conduct tests and provide statement at no cost. Medical exam may be waived at discretion of Superior Court Judge in case of public policy or emergency.
(48) Two unmarried individuals may register themselves as a "Domestic Partnership" and obtain certain benefits.
(49) No consent required if both parents are deceased.
(50) Both parties must file a statement specifying completion of a premarital preparatory course and both parties have read or accessed information from the Family Law Handbook. Failure to do so will delay effective date of marriage.
(51) All parties shall be provided a brochure concerning sexually transmitted diseases and inherited metabolic diseases. A judge in county where license is to be issued may waive medical exam for religious reasons.
(52) In certain circumstances, marriage between two minors is not void or voidable merely because it was contracted without parental consent.
(53) If either party is not of legal age to marry, parental consent as well as written waiver of minimum age requirements is necessary.
(54) No pre-trial serological tests required. However, test will be required on the woman; however, tests will be required on the woman or on the umbilical cord upon birth of the child.
(55) Marriages according to Native American customs are recognized.
(56) Certificate of genetic counseling from physician must be filed with notice of marriage intention between a man and a daughter of his father's brother or sister, or corresponding marriage by a woman.
(57) Each female applicant for license, unless exempted for medical reasons, must present pre-marital certification of physician on official form stating she has had standard seriological tests.
(58) Marriages between Jews within degrees of consanguinity permitted by their religion are valid. **Note: All states prohibit marriage between persons of varying degrees of consanguinity.**

DIVORCE LAWS

There are presently pending, in most states, proposed divorce reform laws. The data set forth herein is correct as of July 2004. It is suggested that the attorney utilizing this chart consult amendments to local statutes.

State or other jurisdiction	Residence required before filing suit of divorce	Grounds for absolute divorce						
		Adultery	Mental and/or physical cruelty	Abandonment	Alcoholism	Impotency	Non-support	Insanity
Alabama	6 mos. (82)	*	*	1 yr.	*		2 yrs.	5 yrs.(4)(66)
Alaska	(1)	*	*	1 yr.	1 yr.	*		18 mos.(66)
Arizona	90 da.					*		
Arkansas	60 da. (83)	*†	*		1 yr.	*	*	3 yrs.
California	6 mos. (13)							*(66)
Colorado	90 da.							
Connecticut	(16)	*	*	1 yr.(14)	*		*	5 yrs.
Delaware	6 mos.		*			(29)		*
Florida	6 mos.							3 yrs.
Georgia	6 mos.	*	*	1 yr.	*	*		2 yrs.(66)
Hawaii	6 mos.				*			
Idaho	6 wks.	*	*		*			3 yrs.(66)
Illinois	90 da.	*	*	1 yr.	*	*		
Indiana	6 mos. (13)				2 yrs.	*		2 yrs.(66)
Iowa	1 yr. (28)					(29)		(4)
Kansas	60 da.							
Kentucky	180 da.					(29)		2 yrs.
Louisiana	6 mos. (84)	*†						
Maine	6 mos.(31)	*	*	3 yrs.	*	*	*(100)	7 yrs. (4)
Maryland	(38)	*	*	1 yr. †	*	*	*(100)	3 yrs.(66)
Massachusetts	1 yr. (41)	*	*	1 yr. †	*	*	†	(4)
Michigan	180 da. (42)(43)							
Minnesota	180 da.							
Mississippi	6 mos.	*	*	1 yr.	*	(4)	†	3 yrs.(4)(46)(66)
Missouri	90 da.	†		†				
Montana	90 da.					(29)		

DIVORCE LAWS

There are presently pending, in most states, proposed divorce reform laws. The data set forth herein is correct as of July 2004. It is suggested that the attorney utilizing this chart consult amendments to local statutes.

Grounds for absolute divorce

State or other jurisdiction	Residence required before filing suit of divorce	Adultery	Mental and/or physical cruelty	Abandonment	Alcoholism	Impotency	Non-support	Insanity
Nebraska	1 yr. (50)					(29)		(4)
Nevada	6 wks.			90 da.†				2 yrs.†
New Hampshire	1 yr. (51)	*†	*†	2 yrs.†	2 yrs.†	*†	*2 yrs.†	
New Jersey	1 yr. (57)	*†	*†	1 yr.†	†	(29)		2 yrs.†
New Mexico	6 mos.	*	*	*				
New York	1 yr. (59)	*†	*1 yr.†	*1 yr.†			†	(4)
North Carolina	6 mos.	(3)	(3)	(3)	(3)	(29)		3 yrs.(66)
North Dakota	6 mos.	*	*	*	*			5 yrs.(66)
Ohio	6 mos.	*†	*†	1 yr.†	*†		*	
Oklahoma	6 mos. (87)	*†	*†	1 yr.†	*	*†	*	5 yrs.(66)†
Oregon	6 mos. (41)							
Pennsylvania	6 mos.	*	*	1 yr.				*18 mos.
Rhode Island	1 yr.	*†	*	5 yrs.(71)	*	*†	1 yr.	
South Carolina	1 yr. (11)	*	*	1 yr.	*			
South Dakota	(68)	*†	*†	†	1 yr.†		1 yr.†	
Tennessee	6 mos.(41)	*†	*†	1 yr.†	*†	*†	*†	
Texas	6 mos.(13)	*	*	1 yr.		(29)		3 yrs.
Utah	3 mos.(13)	*	*	1 yr.†	*	(29)	*	*(66)
Vermont	6 mos.(73)(74)	*†	*†	7 yrs.†			*†	5 yrs.†(66)
Virginia	6 mos.	*	*†	1 yr.†		(29)		(4)
Washington	bona fide resid. (79)							
West Virginia	1 yr. (41)(86)	*†	*†	*6 mo.†	*†	(29)		*3 yrs.(66)
Wisconsin	6 mos.(87)					(29)		
Wyoming	2 mos.(76)							2 yrs.†(66)
District of Columbia	6 mos.	(3)	(3)					(4)
Virgin Islands	6 wks.							(4)
Puerto Rico	1 yr.(41)	*	*	1 yr.	*	*		7 yrs.(66)

DIVORCE LAWS

There are presently pending, in most states, proposed divorce reform laws. The data set forth herein is correct as of July 2004. It is suggested that the attorney utilizing this chart consult amendments to local statutes.

State or other jurisdiction	Grounds for absolute divorce							Grounds for "no-fault" divorce			Other Grounds	Period before parties may remarry after final decree	
	Bigamy	Felony Conviction or imprisonment	Drug Addiction	Fraud, force or duress	Prior decree of limited divorce	Irreconcilable Differences or Irretrievable Breakdown	Incompatibility	Living Separate and Apart	Judicial Separation or Maintenance	Mutual Consent	Other	Plaintiff	Defendant
Alabama	(4)	(9)	*	(4)	(12)	*	*	2yrs.	2yrs.(25)		(7)(17)(23)(89)(103)	60da.	60da.
Alaska		*	*	(4)			*(98)				(90)	(90)	
Arizona						*				(3)	(23)	
Arkansas		*†		(4)				18mos.	2yrs.†	*	(5)(7)(15)(23)(90)(94)	
California	(4)			(4)		*				†	(5)(7)(23)	
Colorado	(4)			(4)	(12)	*†				(7)(23)(90)	(70)	(70)	
Connecticut	(4)	(15)		(4)	(12)	*		18mos.			(23)(30)(91)	
Delaware	(4)			(4)		(2)(18)	*	*			(7)(23)(29)	
Florida						*	*	*			(7)(23)	
Georgia	(4)	(21)	*	*		*	*				(5)(7)(20)(23)(44)	
Hawaii	(4)			(4)	(12)	*		*(35)	2yrs.(25)		(7)(23)(88)	
Idaho	(4)	*	2yrs.	(4)		*		5yrs.			(5)(7)(20)(23)(30)(100)	
Illinois	*	*		(4)		(64)		(64)†			(7)(23)(27)(90)	
Indiana	(4)	*		(4)		*†				(64)	(5)(7)(23)(102)	
Iowa	(4)					*†					(7)(23)	
Kansas	(4)			(4)			*†				(5)(23)(30)	
Kentucky	(4)			(4)		*†					(5)(7)(23)(90)	
Louisiana	(4)	*(32)†		(4)				*(33)†			(6)(23)	
Maine	(4)		*	(4)		*		†(8)		†	(5)(23)	
Maryland	(4)	*(36)		(4)				†(35)		(37)	(23)	
Massachusetts	(4)	(39)	*	(4)		*		†			(23)	
Michigan				(4)		*†					(5)(7)(23)	
Minnesota						*		180da.			(5)(7)(23)	
Mississippi	(4)	*	*	(4)		(47)				(65)	(5)(7)(17)(23)(44)(99)	(85)	(85)
Missouri	(4)		*	(4)	*	*		24mo.†		†	(7)(23)	
Montana	(4)			(4)		*		180da.			(5)(7)(23)(90)	

DIVORCE LAWS

There are presently pending, in most states, proposed divorce reform laws. The data set forth herein is correct as of July 2004. It is suggested that the attorney utilizing this chart consult amendments to local statutes.

State or other jurisdiction	Grounds for absolute divorce					Grounds for "no-fault" divorce					Other Grounds	Period before parties may remarry after final decree	
	Bigamy	Felony Conviction or imprisonment	Drug Addiction	Fraud, force or duress	Prior decree of limited divorce	Irreconcilable Differences or Irretrievable Breakdown	Incompatibility	Living Separate and Apart	Judicial Separation or Maintenance	Mutual Consent	Other	Plaintiff	Defendant
Nebraska	(4)			(4)		*					(5)(23)		
Nevada	(4)			(4)			*†	1yr.†			(7)(23)		
New Hampshire	(4)	(52)*†		(4)		*†		2yrs.†			(23)(49)(54)(55)(56)		
New Jersey	(4)	18mos.†	†	(4)				18mos.†		*	(5)(7)(23)(58)		
New Mexico							*	†		*	(7)(23)		
New York	(4)	*3yrs.†		(4)	1yr.			1yr.	1yr.	(65)	(5)(7)(23)		
North Carolina	(4)		(3)	(4)				1yr.			(5)(7)(23)		
North Dakota	(4)			(4)		*					(5)(7)(23)(100)	(62)	(62)
Ohio	*	*†		*(4)(91)			*†	1yr.†(40)		(65)	(5)(7)(23)(63)(90)(100)	(62)	(62)
Oklahoma	(4)	*		(91)†			*				(7)(23)(44)(63)(100)	6mos.(67)	6 mos. (67)
Oregon	(4)			*		*†		*1yr.†		*	(5)(7)(23)		
Pennsylvania	*	*2yr.				*(69)		2yr.		(69)	(5)(7)(23)(94)		
Rhode Island	*†	*	*			*†		3yrs.†			(7)(23)(100)(104)		
South Carolina	*	*	*			*		1yr.			(7)(22)(23)		
South Dakota	(4)	*		(4)		*(34)			†		(5)(7)(23)(100)		
Tennessee	*†	*†	*†	(4)	2yrs.	*(60)†		2yrs.†			(5)(15)(22)(23)(26)(44)(61)(93)(100)	30da.(71)	30da.(71)
Texas	*	1yr.		(4)		*		3yrs.			(7)(23)		
Utah	(4)	*			*	*		3yrs.†	3yrs.		(7)(23)(27)(75)(100)	(70)	(70)
Vermont	(4)	3yrs.†		(4)				6mos.†			(5)(7)(23)(78)(90)(100)	(70)	(70)
Virginia	(4)	1yr.†				*†		1yr.(77)			(5)(7)(23)(44)(96)	(70)	(70)
Washington	(4)			(4)		*†		*		*	(7)(23)	(70)	(70)
West Virginia	(4)	*†	*†			*†		1yr.			(5)(7)(15)(19)(23)(27)(44)(95)(101)		
Wisconsin	(4)			(4)		*†		1yr.			(5)(7)(23)(90)	6mos.	6mos.
Wyoming	(4)			(4)		*†			†		(5)(7)(20)(23)		
Dist. of Columbia	(4)			(4)	(92)			6mos.(10)†			(7)(20)(23)		
Virgin Islands	(4)			(4)†		*					(5)(7)(23)		
Puerto Rico	(4)	*	*			*		2yrs.		*	(5)(23)(27)(80)(81)		

Footnotes

* Indicates ground for absolute divorce.

†Indicates ground for limited divorce or legal separation.

(1) No residency requirement where plaintiff a resident and marriage solemnized in state. If marriage not solemnized in state, suit may be filed regardless of residency.

(2) Irreconcilable differences or irretrievable breakdown must be accompanied by one of the "traditional" grounds.

(3) Ground for separation from bed and board.

(4) Ground for annulment. In Hawaii, lack of mental capacity.

(5) Personal indignities, unsound mind, mental incapacity at time of marriage.

(6) Effective July 15, 1997, statute provides for an optional, voluntary form of marriage that is more difficult to dissolve through divorce. The covenant marriage requires pre-marriage counseling and limits grounds for divorce to such issues as spousal or child abuse, imprisonment, adultery or abandonment of the matrimonial domicile for one year.

(7) Lacked capacity to consent to marriage at time of marriage.

(8) Where one party has deserted the other or is living apart from the other for justifiable cause for at least 60 days.

(9) Imprisonment for 2 years of a 7 year (or longer) sentence.

(10) 6 months by voluntary separation, one year living separate and apart.

(11) Three months (plaintiff) if both parties reside in state.

(12) Legal separation that may be enlarged into an absolute divorce; Colorado, 6 months after decree of separation; Hawaii, after decree for separation from bed and board (issued by any court of competent jurisdiction) has expired or 2 years after decree of separate maintenance.

(13) 3 months in county.

(14) Also seven years absence.

(15) Infamous crime; in Connecticut, life imprisonment or crime involving violation of conjugal duty punishable by imprisonment of excess of one year.

(16) For certain circumstances a lesser period of time may be required; one party may be domiciled in state at time of marriage and returned to state before filing of complaint with intention of permanently residing in state, or cause of dissolution arose after either party moved into the state.

(17) Pregnancy at time of marriage.

(18) A marriage is irretrievably broken down when it is characterized by (i) voluntary separation or (ii) separation caused by respondent's misconduct or (iii) separation caused by respondent's mental illness or (iv) separation caused by incompatibility where reconciliation is impossible.

(19) Ground for annulment if, before marriage, husband was a notorious, licentious person without the wife's knowledge.

(20) Mental incompetence.

(21) Conviction of offense involving moral turpitude and under which party is sentenced to two year term.

(22) Abandonment by one party for five years without the abandonee knowing where the abandoner is living creates a presumption of abandoner's death, and remarriage is possible. In South Carolina, seven years.

(23) Intermarriage by persons within the prohibited degrees of consanguinity or affinity. Ground for divorce or annulment. In Georgia, such marriages may be voidable, not void.

(24) If there are minor children, or if claim of irretrievable breakdown is denied, court may order counseling, continue the proceeding for up to three months to enable the parties to effect a reconciliation, or take such other actions as may be in the best interest of the parties and minor children of the marriage.

(25) In addition to living separate and apart for two years after decree of separation or execution of a properly filed and executed separation agreement, or where terms of court ordered separation has expired.

(26) Attempted murder of other spouse by poison or other means showing malice.

(27) Infected the other spouse with venereal disease and/or AIDS. Ground for divorce or annulment.

(28) None if both parties are residents.

(29) Annulment due to impotency at time of marriage.

(30) Failure to perform marital duty or obligations.

(31) 3 months for member of Armed Forces stationed in Maine, or spouse.

(32) Felony conviction plus sentence to death or imprisonment at hard labor.

(33) 6 months for living separate and apart; also, divorce shall be granted upon rule to show cause filed by spouse when either spouse has filed petition for divorce and upon proof that 180 days have elapsed from service of petition and that spouses have lived separate and apart continously since filing of petition.

(34) "Irreconcilable differences" is defined as "those grounds which are determined to be substantial reasons for not continuing the marriage, and which make it appear that the marriage should be dissolved." Both parties are required to consent to the no-fault divorce unless one party has not made a general appearance.

(35) Living apart voluntarily twelve months or uninterrupted separation for two years.

(36) At least 12 months of 3 year sentence have been served prior to filing complaint.

(37) Without cohabitation, for 12 consecutive months, prior to filing with no reasonable expectation of reconciliation.

(38) No specific period required, except one year if cause occurred out of state and two years if on ground of insanity.

(39) Confinement for life or five years or more in a state or federal institution. A later pardon does not restore conjugal rights.

(40) Joint Bill—parties must execute separation agreement and reaffirm agreement in court.

(41) None if libellant domiciled in state and cause accrued within state.

(42) One year residency where cause of action occurred out of state.

(43) Ten days in the county, unless the defendant was born in or is a citizen in another country and the parties have a child who is at risk of being taken out of the U.S. and retained in another country by the defendant.

(44) Pregnancy of wife, at time of marriage, by another than husband, is ground for divorce; in Tennessee, without husband's knowledge.

(45) Cause of divorce must have occurred or existed within five years before commencement of suit.

(46) Or at time of the marriage.

(47) Mutual consent divorce for irreconcilable differences upon joint bill or where defendant personally served and no contest or denial.

(48) If contested, petitioner must show adultery, incompatibility, six month's abandonment, living apart by mutual consent for one year, or two year's living separate and apart.

(49) Serious injury to health or endangerment to reason.

(50) No requirement if marriage solemnized in state and continued residency in state until filing of petition.

(51) None except where defendant is non-resident; then one year continued residency or defendant personally served with process within state. Cause must have arisen in state.

(52) One year sentence or longer and actual imprisonment under such sentence.

(53) 90-day waiting period between date of service and hearing, unless court waives this requirement on grounds of emergency or necessity.

(54) Either party joins a religious sect or society which professes to believe the relation of husband and wife is unlawful and has refused cohabitation for six months or more.

(55) Where wife residing outside of state for two years without his consent and without returning to claim marital rights.

(56) Where wife is alien or citizen of another state who resides in New Hampshire for two years, left the U.S. with intention of becoming citizen of another country and not having come into the state to claim marital rights nor provide suitable support.

(57) Except adultery if cause of action arose in state.

(58) Deviant sexual conduct.

(59) No residence requirement when cause occurred in state and both parties are residents at time of commencement. One year residence requirement in all other cases except when neither the marriage nor the cause of action occurred within the state, then two years.

(60) 60-day waiting period if there are minor children; 90-day period if no minor children.

(61) Refusing to live in same state with the spouse.

(62) In court's discretion.

(63) Defendant obtained divorce from plaintiff in another state.

(64) Irretrievable breakdown and two years living separate and apart required; if both parties consent the period becomes 6 months.

(65) Mutual consent divorce—Mississippi, irreconcilable differences upon joint bill or where defendant personally served and no contest or denial; Ohio, petition by both spouses, and execution of separation agreement; New York, legal separation is implied consent to a divorce one year later.

(66) If incurable.

(67) Longer if appeal taken.

(68) Plaintiff must be resident when action begun and maintain residency during pendency of the action.

(69) Mutual consent divorce for irretrievable breakdown if both parties have filed affidavits of consent and 90 days have elapsed.

(70) Remarriage of either party (except to each other) is prohibited during period allowed for appeal or pending appeal.

(71) Or lesser time in court's discretion.

(72) Condonation is defense only if there is finding of reasonable expectation of reconciliation.

(73) No divorce is granted unless the plaintiff has resided in state for one year next preceding the date of the final hearing.

(74) No divorce is granted where the grounds for divorce are insanity, unless the plaintiff has resided in the state for two years.

(75) Decree becomes absolute on date signed by court and entered by clerk if both parties who have a child or children have completed attendance at mandatory course for divorcing parents, unless court waives that requirement, or at expiration of court-designated time period.

(76) Unless marriage solemnized in state and plaintiff resided in state from time of marriage to filing of petition.

(77) Separate and apart for one year is sufficient, six months if there is a separation agreement and there are no children.

(78) Decree issued is a divorce nisi in first instance; becomes absolute in three months; court has discretion to fix earlier date.

(79) Petitioner must be state resident or married to a resident. 90-day cooling-off period after filing required.

(80) Attempt of husband or wife to corrupt their sons or to prostitute their daughters and connivance in their corruption or prostitution.

(81) Proposal of husband to prostitute his wife.

(82) None if plaintiff is domiciled in state and defendant submits to jurisdiction. If nonsupport, two years of separation.

(83) Residence in state also for at least 3 months next preceding final judgment of divorce.

(84) 6 months, creates rebuttable presumption of domicile in state and parish of such residence.

(85) Judge may remove prohibition after 1 year upon petition and evidence of reformation.

(86) Where cause is adultery, one of the parties must be a bona fide resident of West Virginia.

(87) Action may be brought in county in which plaintiff has resided for 30 days immediately preceding filing, or in county in which plaintiff resides.

(88) One party suffered from leprosy or loathsome disease, and this fact was concealed from or unknown by party seeking annulment.

(89) Crime against nature before or after marriage is ground for divorce.

(90) Failure to consummate at time of marriage and continuing at commencement of action is ground for divorce.

(91) Fraudulent contract is ground for divorce.

(92) Decree of legal separation may be enlarged to absolute divorce if court finds that no reconciliation has taken place or is probable and separation has continued voluntarily and without interruption for 6 month period or without interruption for 1 year.

(93) Grounds for divorce from bed and board: (i) abandonment; (ii) maliciously turning other out of doors, (iii) cruel and barbarous treatment endangering life; (iv) indignities to person, rendering life burdensome and conditions intolerable; (v) rendering life unbearable by excessive use of alcohol or drugs (except in Tennessee); (vi) adultery (except in Tennessee).

(94) Indignities rendering condition intolerable and life burdensome is ground for divorce.

(95) Abuse, neglect of child is ground for divorce.

(96) Annulment for prostitution of a party before marriage without knowledge of other party.

(97) If parties were married in state, and at least one of parties is a resident at the time action is commenced, no length of residency is required.

(98) Husband and wife may together petition court if they have agreed on custody, support and property rights. Either spouse may petition court if other spouse's whereabouts are unknown and spouse cannot be served personally within or without the state.

(99) Failure to procure a valid license; grounds for annulment.

(100) Gross neglect of duty.

(101) Homosexuality.

(102) Marriages entered into after Sept. 1, 1977 between first cousins 65 or older not void.

(103) Fraudulent intent not to perform marriage vows is grounds for annulment.

(104) Gross misbehavior and wickedness, in either of parties, repugnant to and in violation of marriage covenant.

DEGREES OF KINDRED

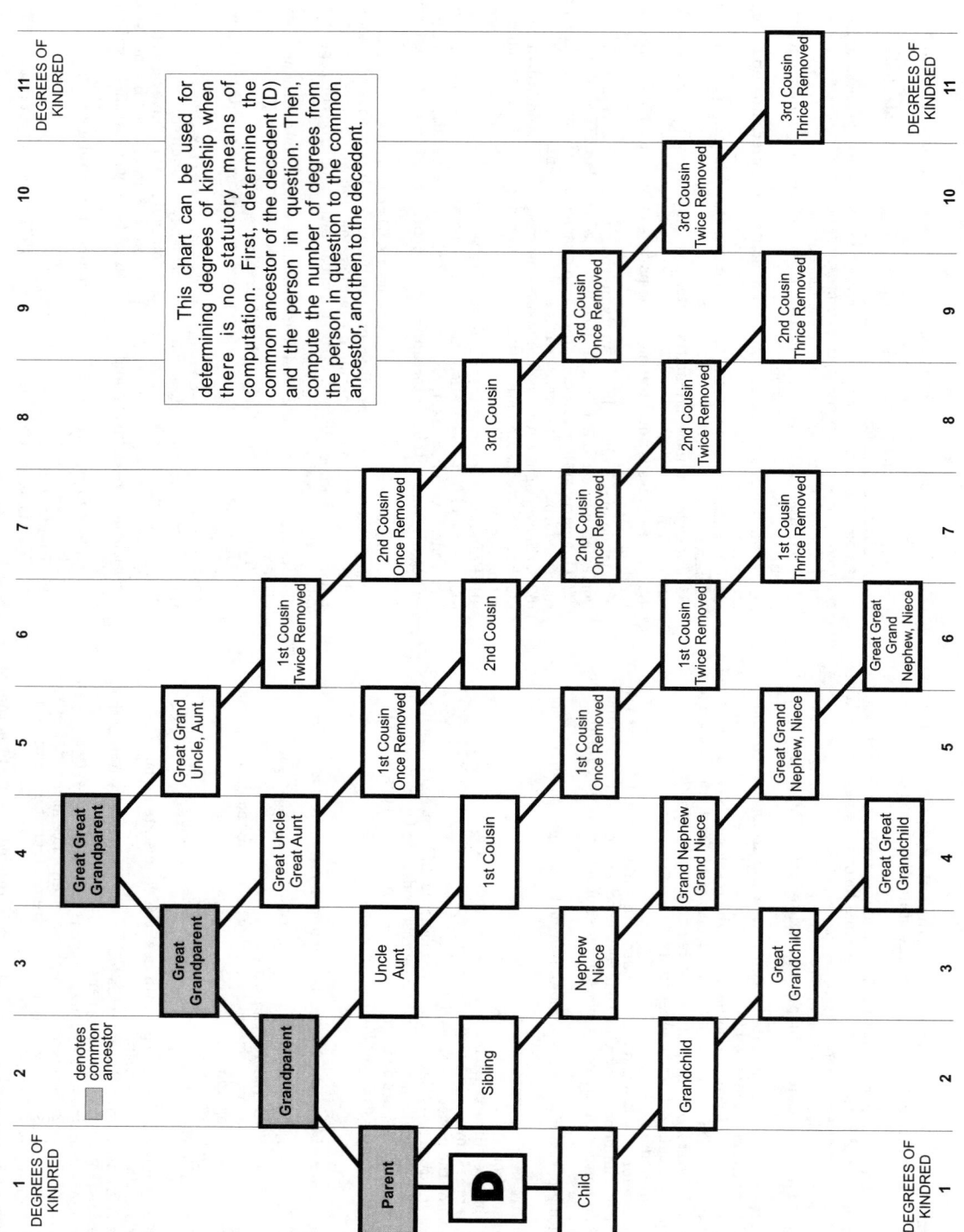

This chart can be used for determining degrees of kinship when there is no statutory means of computation. First, determine the common ancestor of the decedent (D) and the person in question. Then, compute the number of degrees from the person in question to the common ancestor, and then to the decedent.

2005 HOLIDAYS—FEDERAL AND ALL STATES AND TERRITORIES†

Editor's Note: Federal legislation has changed Veterans' Day back to the traditional November 11 but has not changed Memorial Day from the last Monday in May, Washington's Birthday from the 3rd Monday in February or Columbus Day from the 2nd Monday in October. Most States have followed these Federal dates. Local statutes as well as executive orders or proclamations should be checked for possible change during the year after our press time. We have verified the dates listed below but can not be responsible for changes that are pending.

Also, in most States, where a holiday falls on a Sunday it is observed on the following Monday and in some States where a holiday falls on a Saturday it is observed on the preceding Friday. Consult local statutes and case law for specific applications.

2005 Federal Public Holidays observed as Holidays in most States:

*January 1—(New Year's Day).
3rd Monday in January—January 17 (Dr. Martin Luther King, Jr.'s Birthday; called Human Rights Day or Civil Rights Day in some states). Now observed in most States.
3rd Monday in February—February 21 (called Washington's Birthday or Presidents Day in most States).
Last Monday in May—May 30 (Memorial Day). Vermont always celebrates Memorial Day on May 30. Each State celebration is listed below.
July 4—(Independence Day).
1st Monday in September—September 5 (Labor Day).
2nd Monday in October—October 10 (Columbus Day) celebrated by most States.
November 11—(Veterans' Day) celebrated by most States.
4th Thursday in November—November 24. (Thanksgiving Day). Many States close courts and public offices on the day after Thanksgiving.
*December 25—(Christmas Day). Many States close courts and public offices on the day before and after Christmas Day.

2005 State and Territorial Holidays in addition to Federal Public Holidays above.

Alabama—3rd Mon. in Jan.–Jan. 17 (Robert E. Lee's and Dr. Martin Luther King's Birthday); Feb. 8 (Mardi Gras, Mobile & Baldwin Counties); 3rd Mon. in Feb.–Feb. 21 (Thomas Jefferson's Birthday); 4th Mon. in April–April 25 (Confederate Memorial Day); last Mon. in May–May 30 (Memorial Day); 1st Mon. in June–June 6 (Jefferson Davis' Birthday).

Alaska—Last Mon. in March–March 28 (Seward's Day); last Mon. in May—May 30 (Memorial Day); Oct. 18 (Alaska Day).

Arizona—last Mon. in May–May 30 (Memorial Day).

Arkansas—3rd Mon. in Jan.–Jan. 17 (Dr. Martin Luther King's and Robert E. Lee's Birthday); 3rd Mon. in Feb.—Feb. 21 (Washington's Birthday and Daisy Bates Day); last Mon. in May–May 30 (Memorial Day); *Dec. 24 (Christmas Eve Day).

California—*Feb. 12 (Lincoln Day); March 31 (Cesar Chavez Day); March 25 (Good Friday); last Mon. in May–May 30 (Memorial Day); Sept. 9 (Admission Day).

Colorado—last Mon. in May–May 30 (Memorial Day).

Connecticut—*Feb. 12 (Lincoln's Birthday); last Mon. in May–May 30 (Memorial Day).

Delaware—March 25 (Good Friday); last Mon. in May–May 30 (Memorial Day); Thurs. following Election Day–Nov. 9 (Return Day—noon, Sussex County); last Fri. in Nov.–Nov. 24 (Day after Thanksgiving); (General Election Day, when applicable).

District of Columbia—Jan. 20 (Presidential Inauguration Day, when Applicable); last Mon. in May–May 30 (Memorial Day).

Florida—Jan. 19 (Robert E. Lee's Birthday); *Feb. 12 (Lincoln's Birthday); Feb. 8 (Shrove Tuesday); Feb. 15 (Susan B. Anthony's Birthday); March 25 (Good Friday); *April 2 (Pascua Florida Day); April 26 (Confederate Memorial Day); last Mon. in May–May 30 (Memorial Day); June 3 (Jefferson Davis' Birthday); June 14 (Flag Day); (General Election Day, when applicable).

Georgia—Jan. 19 (Robert E. Lee's Birthday); April 26 (Confederate Memorial Day); last Mon. in May–May 30 (Memorial Day); June 3 (Jefferson Davis' Birthday). Certain holidays require Gubernatorial Proclamation. Statutes must be consulted for particular applications.

Guam—1st Mon. in March–March 7 (Guam Discovery Day); March 25 (Good Friday); last Mon. in May—May 30 (Memorial Day); July 21 (Liberation Day); Nov. 2 (All Soul's Day); Dec. 8 (Lady of Camarin Day); (General Election Day, when applicable).

Hawaii—March 25 (Good Friday); *March 26 (Kuhio Day); last Mon. in May–May 30 (Memorial Day); *June 11 (Kamehameha Day); 3rd Fri. in Aug.–Aug. 19 (Admission Day); (General Election Day, when applicable).

Idaho—last Mon. in May–May 30 (Memorial Day).

Illinois—*Feb. 12 (Lincoln's Birthday); 1st Mon. in March–March 7 (Casimir Pulaski Day); last Mon. in May—May 30 (Memorial Day); General Election Day, when applicable.

Indiana—*Feb. 12 (Lincoln's Birthday); March 25 (Good Friday); last Mon. in May–May 30 (Memorial Day); (Primary and General Election Days, when applicable).

Iowa—*Feb. 12 (Lincoln's Birthday); last Mon. in May–May 30 (Memorial Day).

Kansas—*Feb. 12 (Lincoln's Birthday); last Mon. in May–May 30 (Memorial Day).

Kentucky—Jan. 19 (Robert E. Lee Day); *Jan. 30 (Franklin D. Roosevelt Day); *Feb. 12 (Lincoln's Birthday); last Mon. in May–May 30 (Memorial Day); June 3 (Confederate Memorial Day and Jefferson Davis Day); (General Election Day, when applicable).

Louisiana—*Jan. 8 (Battle of New Orleans Day); Jan. 19 (Robert E. Lee Day); Feb. 8 (Mardi Gras); March 25 (Good Friday); last Mon. in May–May 30 (Memorial Day); June 3 (Confederate Memorial Day); Aug. 30 (Huey P. Long Day); Nov. 1 (All Saints Day); (General Election Day, when applicable); last Fri. in Nov.–Nov. 25 (Acadian Day); Certain holidays require Gubernatorial Proclamation. Statutes must be consulted for particular applications.

Maine—3rd Mon. in April–April 18 (Patriots' Day) last Mon. in May–May 30 (Memorial Day).

Maryland—*Feb. 12 (Lincoln's Birthday); March 25 (Maryland Day); March 25 (Good Friday); last Mon. in May–May 30 (Memorial Day); Sept. 12 (Defender's Day); (General Election Day, when applicable).

Massachusetts—March 17 (Evacuation Day, Suffolk Co.); 3rd Mon. in April–April 18 (Patriots' Day); last Mon. in May–May 30 (Memorial Day); June 17 (Bunker Hill Day, Suffolk Co.).

Michigan—*Feb. 12 (Lincoln's Birthday); last Mon. in May–May 30 (Memorial Day).

Minnesota—last Mon. in May–May 30 (Memorial Day).

Mississippi—3rd Mon. in Jan.–Jan. 17 (Robert E. Lee's and Dr. Martin Luther King, Jr.'s Birthday); Feb. 8 (Mardi Gras, Coastal counties only); last Mon. in April–April 25 (Confederate Memorial Day); last Mon. in May–May 30 (Memorial Day and Jefferson Davis' Birthday); last Fri. in November–Nov. 26 (Day after Thanksgiving).

Missouri—*Feb. 12 (Lincoln's Birthday); *May 8 (Truman's Birthday); last Mon. in May–May 30 (Memorial Day).

†**For the legal consequences of these holidays consult local statutes and case law.**
*Denotes holidays falling on a Saturday or Sunday.

Montana—last Mon. in May–May 30 (Memorial Day); (General Election Day, when applicable).

Nebraska—Last Fri. in April–April 29 (Arbor Day); last Mon. in May–May 30 (Memorial Day).

Nevada—last Mon. in May–May 30 (Memorial Day); last Fri. in Oct.—Oct. 28 (Nevada Day); last Fri. in Nov.–Nov. 25 (Family Day).

New Hampshire—last Mon. in May–May 30 (Memorial Day); (General Election Day, when applicable).

New Jersey—*Feb. 12 (Lincoln's Birthday); March 25 (Good Friday); last Mon. in May–May 30 (Memorial Day); (General Election Day, when applicable).

New Mexico—last Mon. in May–May 30 (Memorial Day).

New York—*Feb. 12 (Lincoln's Birthday); last Mon. in May–May 30 (Memorial Day); *2nd Sun. in June–June 12 (Flag Day); (General Election Day, when applicable).

North Carolina—Jan. 19 (Robert E. Lee's Birthday); March 25 (Greek Independence Day); March 25 (Good Friday); April 12 (Halifax Resolves Anniversary); May 10 (Confederate Memorial Day); May 20 (Mechlenberg Declaration of Independence Anniversary); last Mon. in May–May 30 (Memorial Day); Oct. 13 (Yom Kippur); (General Election Day, when applicable).

North Dakota—March 25 (Good Friday); last Mon. in May–May 30 (Memorial Day).

Ohio—last Mon. in May—May 30 (Memorial Day); (General Election Day, when applicable).

Oklahoma—last Mon. in May–May 30 (Memorial Day).

Oregon—last Mon. in May–May 30 (Memorial Day).

Pennsylvania—March 25 (Good Friday); last Mon. in May–May 30 (Memorial Day); June 14 (Flag Day); (General Election Day, when applicable).

Puerto Rico—Jan. 6 (Three Kings Day); second Mon. in Jan.–Jan. 10 (De Hostos' Birthday); March 22 (Emancipation Day); March 25 (Good Friday); third Mon. in April–April 18 (de Diego's Birthday and Spanish Only Day); last Mon. in May–May 30 (Memorial Day); third Mon. in July–July 18 (Muñoz Rivera's Birthday); July 25 (E.L.A. Constitution Day); July 27 (Barbosa's Birthday); *Nov. 19 (Discovery of Puerto Rico).

Rhode Island—last Mon. in May–May 30 (Memorial Day); 2nd Mon. in Aug.–Aug. 8 (Victory Day); (General Election Day, when applicable).

South Carolina—May 10 (Confederate Memorial Day); last Mon. in May–May 30 (Memorial Day); last Fri. in Nov.–Nov. 25 (Day after Thanksgiving); Dec. 26 (Day after Christmas).

South Dakota—last Mon. in May–May 30 (Memorial Day); 2nd Mon. in Oct.–Oct. 10 (Native Americans' Day).

Tennessee—March 25 (Good Friday); last Mon. in May–May 30 (Memorial Day).

Texas—Jan. 19 (Confederate Heroes Day); March 2 (Texas Independence Day); April 21 (San Jacinto Day); last Mon. in May–May 30 (Memorial Day); *June 19 (Emancipation Day); *Aug. 27 (Lyndon B. Johnson's Birthday); (General Election Day, when applicable).

Utah—last Mon. in May–May 30 (Memorial Day); *July 24 (Pioneer Day).

Vermont—*Feb. 12 (Lincoln's Birthday); 1st Tues. in March–March 1 (Town Meeting Day); May 30 (Memorial Day); Aug. 16 (Bennington Battle Day).

Virginia—Fri. preceding 3rd Mon. in Jan–Jan. 14 (Lee-Jackson Day); last Mon. in May–May 30 (Memorial Day); last Fri. in Nov.–Nov. 25 (Day after Thanksgiving).

Virgin Islands—Jan. 6 (Three Kings Day); March 24 (Holy Thursday); March 25 (Good Friday); March 28 (Easter Monday); March 31 (Transfer Day); last Mon. in May–May 30 (Memorial Day); 3rd Mon. in June–June 20 (Organic Act Day); *July 3 (Virgin Islands Emancipation Day); 4th Mon. in July–July 25 (Supplication Day); 2nd Mon. in Oct–Oct. 10 (Puerto Rico–Virgin Islands Friendship Day); 3rd Mon. in Oct.–Oct. 17 (Local Thanksgiving Day); Nov. 1 (D. Hamilton Jackson Day); Dec. 26 (Christmas, second day/Boxing Day); (Primary and General Election Days, when applicable).

Washington—last Mon. in May–May 30 (Memorial Day); last Fri. in Nov.–Nov. 25 (Day after Thanksgiving).

West Virginia—*Feb. 12 (Lincoln's Birthday); last Mon. in May–May 30 (Memorial Day); June 20 (West Virginia Day); (Primary and General Election Days, when applicable).

Wisconsin—March 25 (Good Friday); last Mon. in May–May 30 (Memorial Day); (Primary and General Election Days, when applicable).

Wyoming—last Mon. in May–May 30 (Memorial Day).

---

*Denotes holidays falling on a Saturday or Sunday.

OHIO HOLIDAYS 2005

January 1—New Year's Day
January 17—Dr. Martin Luther King, Jr. Day
February 21—Washington's Birthday
May 30—Memorial Day
July 4—Independence Day
September 5—Labor Day
October 10—Columbus Day
November 8—Election Day
November 11—Veterans' Day
November 24—Thanksgiving Day
December 25—Christmas Day
December 26—Christmas Day observed

2005 Tax Deadlines to Remember

January 17—Final Payment on Estimated Federal Income Tax Due Unless Return in Lieu of Final Declaration is Filed by January 31

January 17—Ohio State Estimated Personal Income and Unincorporated Business Tax Installment Due for Calendar Year Taxpayers

Janurary 31—Quarterly Form 941 Return Due

January 31—Federal Unemployment Form 940 Due for 2004

January 31—Deadline to Furnish Employees Withholding Statements (Forms W-2) and Statements to Recipients of Dividends and Interest Payments (Forms 1099) for the preceding year.

March 15—Federal Corporation Income Tax Returns on Calendar Year Basis Due

April 15—Federal Individual Income Tax Returns on Calendar Year Basis Due

April 15—Ohio State Personal Income Tax Returns Due for Calendar Year Basis Taxpayers

April 15—Quarterly Estimated Federal Income Tax Payment Due

April 15—Ohio Quarterly Estimated Personal Income Payment Due for Calendar Year Taxpayers

May 2—Quarterly Form 941 Return Due

May 2—Federal Unemployment Tax Deposit Due

May 2—Final Date to File Ohio Personal Property Tax Return

June 15—Quarterly Estimated Federal Income Tax Payment Due

June 15—Ohio State Estimated Personal Tax Payment Due for Calendar Year Taxpayers

August 1—Quarterly Form 941 Return Due

August 1—Federal Unemployment Tax Deposit Due

September 15—Quarterly Estimated Federal Income Tax Payment Due

September 15—Ohio State Estimated Personal Income Tax Payment Due for Calendar Year Taxpayers

October 31—Quarterly Form 941 Return Due

October 31—Federal Unemployment Tax Deposit Due

If any date falls on a Saturday, Sunday or holiday (national or state-wide) a required act will be timely if performed the following business day. U.S. Postmark controls timely filing. I.R.C. § 7503.

OHIO FEDERAL, STATE AND COUNTY COURT JUDGES
Federal Court

(614) 719-3370   **Abel, Mark R.** (US Magis J South Dist) Joseph P. Kinneary U.S. Cthse., Rm. 208, 85 Marconi Blvd., Columbus 43215; **E-mail:** abel_chambers@ohsd.uscourts.gov

(330) 375-5900   **Adams, John R.** (J US Dist Ct North Dist) U.S. Cthse., Rm. 526, Two S. Main St., Akron 44308-1813; **Fax:** (330) 375-5875

(216) 357-7200   **Aldrich, Ann** (Sr J US Dist Ct North Dist) Carl B. Stokes U.S. Cthse., 801 W. Superior Ave., Cleveland 44113-1830; **Fax:** (216) 357-7205

(419) 259-6217   **Armstrong, Vernelis K.** (US Magis J North Dist) U.S. Cthse., Rm. 318, 1716 Spielbusch Ave., Toledo 43624-1363; **Fax:** (419) 259-3728; **E-mail:** vernelis_k_armstrong@ohnd.uscourts.gov

(513) 684-2572 Ext. 132   **Aug, J. Vincent, Jr.** (J US Bank Ct South Dist) Atrium Two, 8th Fl., 221 E. 4th St., Cincinnati 45202

(330) 764-6026   **Batchelder, Alice M.** (J US Ct of App 6th Circ) 143 W. Liberty St., Medina 44256

(216) 357-7220   **Baughman, William H., Jr.** (US Magis J North Dist) Carl B. Stokes U.S. Cthse., Rm. 10-A, 801 W. Superior Ave., Cleveland 44113-1830; **Fax:** (216) 357-7224

(216) 522-4373 Ext. 3063   **Baxter, Randolph** (Chief J US Bank Ct North Dist) 3204 Key Tower, 127 Public Sq., Cleveland 44114-1309

(513) 564-7610   **Beckwith, Sandra S.** (Chief J US Dist Ct South Dist) Potter Stewart U.S. Cthse., Rm. 810, 100 E. Fifth St., Cincinnati 45202

(513) 564-7640   **Black, Timothy S.** (US Magis J South Dist) Potter Stewart U.S. Cthse., Rm. 716, 100 E. Fifth St., Cincinatti 45202

(502) 625-3900   **Boggs, Danny J.** (Chief J US Ct of App 6th Circ) 220 Gene Snyder U.S. Cthse., 601 W. Broadway, Louisville, KY 40202

(216) 357-7151   **Boyko, Christopher A.** (J US Dist Ct North Dist) Carl B. Stokes U.S. Cthse., 801 W. Superior Ave., Cleveland 44113-1830; **Fax:** (216) 357-7156

(614) 469-6638 Ext. 260   **Caldwell, Charles M.** (J US Bank Ct South Dist) 170 N. High St., Columbus 43215-2403

(614) 469-6638 Ext. 240   **Calhoun, Donald E., Jr.** (J US Bank Ct South Dist) 170 N. High St., Columbus 43215-2403

(419) 259-6420   **Carr, James G.** (Chief J US Dist Ct North Dist) U.S. Cthse., Rm. 203, 1716 Spielbusch Ave., Toledo 43624-1363; **Fax:** (419) 259-6427; **E-mail:** james_g_carr@ohnd.uscourts.gov

(937) 225-2516 Ext. 301   **Clark, William A.** (J US Bank Ct South Dist) 120 W. Third St., Dayton 45402

(313) 234-5260   **Clay, Eric L.** (J US Ct of App 6th Circ) 481 Theodore Levin U.S. Cthse., 231 W. Lafayette Blvd., Detroit, MI 48226

(614) 719-3350   **Cole, R. Guy, Jr.** (J US Ct of App 6th Circ) 127 Joseph Kinneary U.S. Cthse., 85 Marconi Blvd., Columbus 43215

(330) 375-5412   **Cook, Deborah L.** (J US Ct of App 6th Circ) 433 U.S. Cthse. & Fedl. Bldg., Two S. Main St., Akron 44308

(615) 736-7678   **Daughtrey, Martha Craig** (J US Ct of App 6th Circ) 304 U.S. Customs House, 701 Broadway, Nashville, TN 37203

(513) 564-7630   **Dlott, Susan J.** (J US Dist Ct South Dist) Potter Stewart U.S. Cthse., Rm. 829, 100 E. Fifth St., Cincinatti 45202; **Fax:** (513) 564-7638

(330) 375-5836   **Dowd, David D., Jr.** (Sr J US Dist Ct North Dist) U.S. Cthse., Rm. 402, Two S. Main St., Akron 44308-1813; **Fax:** (330) 375-5628

(330) 746-7830   **Economus, Peter C.** (J US Dist Ct North Dist) Thomas D. Lambros Fedl. Bldg. & Cthse., Rm. 313, 125 Market St., Youngstown 44503-1780; **Fax:** (330) 746-4195

(614) 719-3300   **Frost, Gregory L.** (J US Dist Ct South Dist) Joseph P. Kinneary U.S. Cthse., Rm. 349, 85 Marconi Blvd., Columbus 43215; **Fax:** (614) 719-3305; **E-mail:** greg_frost@ohsd.uscourts.gov

(330) 375-5466   **Gallas, James S.** (US Magis J North Dist) U.S. Cthse., Rm. 480, Two S. Main St., Akron 44308-1813; **Fax:** (330) 375-5536; **E-mail:** james_s_gallas@ohnd.uscourts.gov

(216) 357-7210   **Gaughan, Patricia A.** (J US Dist Ct North Dist) Carl B. Stokes U.S. Cthse., 801 W. Superior Ave., Cleveland 44113-1830; **Fax:** (216) 357-7215

(901) 495-1265   **Gibbons, Julia Smith** (J US Ct of App 6th Circ) 1157 Clifford Davis Fedl. Bldg., 167 N. Main St., Memphis, TN 38103

(901) 495-1575   **Gilman, Ronald Lee** (J US Ct of App 6th Circ) 1176 Federal Bldg., 167 N. Main St., Memphis, TN 38103

(614) 719-3200   **Graham, James L.** (Sr J US Dist Ct South Dist) Joseph P. Kinneary U.S. Cthse., Rm. 169, 85 Marconi Blvd., Columbus 43215

(313) 741-2300   **Guy, Ralph B., Jr.** (Sr J US Ct of App 6th Circ) P.O. Box 7910, Ann Arbor, MI 48107

(330) 375-5934   **Gwin, James S.** (J US Dist Ct North Dist) U.S. Cthse., Rm. 510, Two S. Main St., Akron 44308-1813; **Fax:** (330) 375-5937

(216) 522-4373 Ext. 3022   **Harris, Arthur I.** (J US Bank Ct North Dist) 3101 Key Tower, 127 Public Sq., Cleveland 44114-1309

(216) 357-7135   **Hemann, Patricia A.** (US Magis J North Dist) Carl B. Stokes U.S. Cthse., 801 W. Superior Ave., Cleveland 44113-1830; **Fax:** (216) 357-7139

(614) 469-6638 Ext. 282   **Hoffman, John E., Jr.** (J US Bank Ct South Dist) 170 N. High St., Columbus 43215

(513) 564-7650   **Hogan, Timothy S.** (US Magis J South Dist) Potter Stewart U.S. Cthse., Rm. 706, 100 E. Fifth St., Cincinnati 45202

(614) 719-3310   **Holschuh, John D.** (Sr J US Dist Ct South Dist) Joseph P. Kinneary U.S. Cthse., Rm. 109, 85 Marconi Blvd., Columbus 43215

(513) 684-2572 Ext. 146   **Hopkins, Jeffery P.** (J US Bank Ct South Dist) Atrium Two, Suite 800, 221 E. 4th St., Cincinnati 45202

(419) 259-7488   **Katz, David A.** (Sr J US Dist Ct North Dist) U.S. Cthse., Rm. 210, 1716 Spielbusch Ave., Toledo 43624-1363; **Fax:** (419) 259-3744

(313) 234-5245   **Keith, Damon J.** (Sr J US Ct of App 6th Circ) 240 Theodore Levin U.S. Cthse., 231 W. Lafayette Blvd., Detroit, MI 48226

(614) 719-3410   **Kemp, Terence P.** (US Magis J South Dist) Joseph P. Kinneary U.S. Cthse., Rm. 172, 85 Marconi Blvd., Columbus 43215

(330) 489-4430   **Kendig, Russ** (J US Bank Ct North Dist) Frank T. Bow Fedl. Bldg., 201 Cleveland Ave. S.W., Canton 44702

(313) 234-5240   **Kennedy, Cornelia G.** (Sr J US Ct of App 6th Circ) 744 Theodore Levin U.S. Cthse., 231 W. Lafayette Blvd., Detroit, MI 48226

(614) 719-3390   **King, Norah McCann** (US Magis J South Dist) Joseph P. Kinneary U.S. Cthse., Rm. 235, 85 Marconi Blvd., Columbus 43215

(330) 743-2987   **Limbert, George J.** (US Magis J North Dist) Thomas D. Lambros Fedl. Bldg. & Cthse., Rm. 229, 125 Market St., Youngstown 44503-1780; **Fax:** (330) 746-8609

(216) 357-7265   **Manos, John M.** (Sr J US Dist Ct North Dist) Carl B. Stokes U.S. Cthse., 801 W. Superior Ave., Cleveland 44113-1830; **Fax:** (216) 357-7271

(614) 719-3260   **Marbley, Algenon L.** (J US Dist Ct South Dist) Joseph P. Kinneary U.S. Cthse., Rm. 319, 85 Marconi Blvd., Columbus 43215; **Fax:** (614) 719-3264

(502) 625-3800   **Martin, Boyce F., Jr.** (J US Ct of App 6th Circ) 209 Gene Snyder U.S. Cthse., 601 W. Broadway, Louisville, KY 40202

(216) 357-7100   **Matia, Paul R.** (Sr J US Dist Ct North Dist) Carl B. Stokes U.S. Cthse., 801 W. Superior Ave., Cleveland 44113-1830; **Fax:** (216) 357-7110

(216) 357-7230   **McHargh, Kenneth S.** (US Magis J North Dist) Carl B. Stokes U.S. Cthse., 801 W. Superior Ave., Cleveland 44113-1830; **Fax:** (216) 357-7234

(615) 736-5957   **Merritt, Gilbert S.** (Sr J US Ct of App 6th Circ) 303 U.S. Customs House, 701 Broadway, Nashville, TN 37203

(937) 512-1550   **Merz, Michael R.** (Chief US Magis J South Dist) Fedl. Bldg., Rm. 902, 200 W. Second St., Dayton 45402; **E-mail:** michael_merz@ohsd.uscourts.gov

(216) 522-7207   **Moore, Karen Nelson** (J US Ct of App 6th Circ) 328 U.S. Cthse., 201 Superior Ave., Cleveland 44114

(216) 522-4373 Ext. 3059   **Morgenstern-Clarren, Pat E.** (J US Bank Ct North Dist) 3201 Key Tower, 127 Public Sq., Cleveland 44114-1309

(513) 564-7414   **Nelson, David A.** (Sr J US Ct of App 6th Circ) 414 Potter Stewart U.S. Cthse., 5th & Walnut Streets, Cincinnati 45202

(614) 719-3330   **Norris, Alan E.** (Sr J US Ct of App 6th Circ) 328 Joseph P. Kinneary U.S. Cthse., 85 Marconi Blvd., Columbus 43215

(216) 357-7160   **Nugent, Donald C.** (J US Dist Ct North Dist) Carl B. Stokes U.S. Cthse., 801 W. Superior Ave., Cleveland 44113-1830; **Fax:** (216) 357-7165

(216) 357-7240   **O'Malley, Kathleen M.** (J US Dist Ct North Dist) Carl B. Stokes U.S. Cthse., 801 W. Superior Ave., Cleveland 44113-1830; **Fax:** (216) 357-7246

(216) 357-7171   **Oliver, Solomon, Jr.** (J US Dist Ct North Dist) Carl B. Stokes U.S. Cthse., 801 W. Superior Ave., Cleveland 44113-1830; **Fax:** (216) 357-7176

(937) 512-1570   **Ovington, Sharon L.** (US Magis J South Dist) Joseph P. Kinneary U.S. Cthse., Rm. 810, 85 Marconi Blvd., Columbus 43215

(216) 357-7140   **Perelman, David S.** (US Magis J North Dist) Carl B. Stokes U.S. Cthse., Rm. 11-A, 801 W. Superior Ave., Cleveland 44113-1830; **Fax:** (216) 357-7145

(513) 684-2572 Ext. 131   **Perlman, Burton** (J US Bank Ct South Dist) Atrium Two, 8th Fl., 221 E. 4th St., Cincinnati 45202

(216) 357-7190   **Polster, Dan A.** (J US Dist Ct North Dist) Carl B. Stokes U.S. Cthse., 801 W. Superior Ave., Cleveland 44113-1830; **Fax:** (216) 357-7195; **E-mail:** dan_polster@ohnd.uscourts.gov

(937) 512-1500   **Rice, Walter H.** (Sr J US Dist Ct South Dist) Fedl. Bldg., Rm. 909, 200 W. Second St., Dayton 45402

(859) 233-2680   **Rogers, John M.** (J US Ct of App 6th Circ) Community Trust Bldg., Suite 400, 100 E. Vine St., Lexington, KY 40507

(937) 512-1600   **Rose, Thomas M.** (J US Dist Ct South Dist) Federal Bldg., Rm. 910, 200 W. Second St., Dayton 45402; **E-mail:** thomas_rose@ohsd.uscourts.gov

(313) 234-5250   **Ryan, James L.** (Sr J US Ct of App 6th Circ) 611 Theodore Levin U.S. Cthse., 231 W. Lafayette Blvd., Detroit, MI 48226

(614) 719-3240   **Sargus, Edmund A., Jr.** (J US Dist Ct South Dist) Joseph P. Kinneary U.S. Cthse., Rm. 301, 85 Marconi Blvd., Columbus 43215

(614) 469-6638 Ext. 250   **Sellers, Barbara J.** (J US Bank Ct South Dist) 170 N. High St., Columbus 43215-2403

(330) 375-5780   **Shea-Stonum, Marilyn** (J US Bank Ct North Dist) 240 U.S. Cthse., 2 S. Main St., Akron 44308

(606) 878-6822   **Siler, Eugene E., Jr.** (Sr J US Ct of App 6th Circ) 1380 W. Fifth St., London, KY 40741

(614) 719-3220   **Smith, George C.** (Sr J US Dist Ct South Dist) Joseph P. Kinneary U.S. Cthse., Rm. 101, 85 Marconi Blvd., Columbus 43215

(419) 259-7559   **Speer, Richard L.** (J US Bank Ct North Dist) 113 U.S. Cthse., 1716 Spielbusch Ave., Toledo 43624

(513) 564-7620   **Spiegel, S. Arthur** (Sr J US Dist Ct South Dist) Potter Stewart U.S. Cthse., Rm. 838, 100 E. Fifth St., Cincinnati 45202

(517) 377-1513   **Suhrheinrich, Richard F.** (Sr J US Ct of App 6th Circ) 241 U.S. P.O. & Federal Bldg., 315 West Allegan St., Lansing, MI 48933

(614) 849-0134   **Sutton, Jeffrey S.** (J US Ct of App 6th Circ) 10 W. Broad St., Suite 1150, Columbus 43215

(216) 357-7130   **Vecchiarelli, Nancy A.** (US Magis J North Dist) Carl B. Stokes U.S. Cthse., 801 W. Superior Ave., Cleveland 44113-1830; **Fax:** (216) 357-7134

(937) 225-2516 Ext. 338   **Waldron, Thomas F.** (Chief J US Bank Ct South Dist) 120 W. Third St., Rm. 121, Dayton 45402-1819

(937) 225-2516 Ext. 307   **Walter, Lawrence S.** (J US Bank Ct South Dist) 120 W. Third St., Dayton 45402

(614) 719-3280   **Watson, Michael H.** (J US Dist Ct South Dist) Joseph P. Kinneary U.S. Cthse., Rm. 247, 85 Marconi Blvd., Columbus 43215

Judges Directory

(513) 564-7603   **Weber, Herman J.** (Sr J US Dist Ct South Dist) Potter Stewart U.S. Cthse., Rm. 801, 100 E. Fifth St., Cincinnati 45202

(216) 357-7120   **Wells, Lesley** (J US Dist Ct North Dist) Carl B. Stokes U.S. Cthse., Rm. 18-A, 801 W. Superior Ave., Cleveland 44113-1830; **Fax:** (216) 357-7127

(419) 259-6327   **Whipple, Mary Ann** (J US Bank Ct North Dist) 111 U.S. Cthse., 1716 Spielbusch Ave., Toledo 43624

(330) 746-7027   **Woods, Kay** (J US Bank Ct North Dist) Fedl. Bldg. & U.S. Cthse., 10 E. Commerce St.,
Ext. 4200   Youngstown 44503-1621

State Judges

(740) 592-3247   **Abele, Peter B.** (J Dist Ct of App 4th App Dist) Athens Co. Cthse., 1 S. Court St., Athens 45701; **Fax:** (740) 594-3303; **E-mail:** pbabele@eurekanet.com

(937) 456-8165   **Abruzzo, David N.** (J Preble Cty Common Pleas Ct) Cthse., 101 E. Main St., Eaton 45320-1758; **Fax:** (937) 456-9548

(419) 849-3961   **Adams, Herbert E.** (J Sandusky Cty Ct No 2) 215 W. Main St., P.O. Box 128, Woodville 43469; **Fax:** (419) 849-3932; **E-mail:** woodvilljudge@co.sandusky.oh.us

(740) 474-3175   **Adkins, John R.** (J Circleville Munic Ct) 151 E. Franklin St., P.O. Box 128, Circleville 43113; **Fax:** (740) 477-8291; **E-mail:** john@circlevillecourt.com

(216) 664-4975   **Adrine, Ronald B.** (J Cleveland Munic Ct) 1200 Ontario St., Cleveland 44113
Mailing Address: P.O. Box 94894, Cleveland 44101-4894; **Fax:** (216) 664-4283

(440) 953-4150   **Allen, Larry** (J Willoughby Munic Ct) One Public Sq., Willoughby 44094-7888; **Fax:** (440) 953-4149; **E-mail:** judge@willoughbycourt.com

(513) 946-5148   **Allen, Lisa** (J Hamilton Cty Munic Ct) Cthse., 1000 Main St., Cincinnati 45202; **Fax:** (513) 946-5202

(513) 946-5154   **Allen, Nadine L.** (J Hamilton Cty Munic Ct) Cthse., 1000 Main St., Cincinnati 45202; **Fax:** (513) 946-5202

(330) 755-2165   **Almasy, John P.** (J Campbell Munic Ct) 351 Tenney Ave., Campbell 44405; **Fax:** (330) 750-3058

(740) 223-4060   **Alspach, Deborah A.** (J Marion Cty Probate/Juv/Dom Rel Ct) 222 W. Center St., Marion 43302; **Fax:** (740) 382-3798

(216) 443-8670   **Ambrose, Richard J. (Dick)** (J Cuyahoga Cty Common Pleas Ct) 1200 Ontario St., Cleveland 44113-1678; **Fax:** (216) 348-4036

(419) 294-1727   **Aubry, Kathleen A.** (J Wyandot Cty Common Pleas Ct) 109 S. Sandusky Ave., Upper Sandusky 43351-1435; **Fax:** (419) 209-0251

(419) 755-9622   **Ault, Jerry** (J Mansfield Munic Ct) 30 N. Diamond St., Mansfield 44902; **Fax:** (419) 755-9647

(740) 387-0439   **Ballinger, Teresa L.** (J Marion Munic Ct) 233 W. Center St., Marion 43302; **Fax:** (740) 382-5274

(937) 898-3996   **Bannister, Richard J.** (J Vandalia Munic Ct) Justice Center, 2nd. Fl., 245 Bohanan Mem. Dr., P.O. Box 429, Vandalia 45377-2393; **Fax:** (937) 898-6648

(937) 754-3040   **Barber, Catherine M.** (J Fairborn Munic Ct) 1148 Kauffman Ave., Fairborn 45324; **Fax:** (937) 879-4422

(419) 337-9260   **Barber, James E.** (J Fulton Cty Common Pleas Ct) 210 S. Fulton St., Wauseon 43567; **Fax:** (419) 337-9293; **E-mail:** jbarber@fultoncounty.oh.com

(330) 424-4071   **Baronzzi, Thomas M.** (J Columbiana Cty Juv Ct) 260 W. Lincoln Way, Lisbon 44432; **Fax:** (330) 424-6670; **E-mail:** tbaronzzi@raex.com

(330) 424-9516   (J Columbiana Cty Probate Ct) Cthse., 105 S. Market St., Lisbon 44432; **Fax:** (330) 424-5067

(614) 645-7655   **Barrows, Ted** (J Franklin Cty Munic Ct) 375 S. High St., Columbus 43215-4520; **Fax:** (614) 645-8822

(419) 523-6200   **Basinger, Randall L.** (J Putnam Cty Common Pleas Ct) Cthse., Suite 302, 245 E. Main St., Ottawa 45875; **Fax:** (419) 523-5284; **E-mail:** basinger@nwbright.net

(440) 329-5365   **Basinski, David A.** (J Lorain Cty Dom Rel Ct) Lorain Cty. Justice Center, 225 Court St., Elyria 44035; **Fax:** (440) 328-2258

(330) 643-2259   **Batchelder, William G.** (J Dist Ct of App 9th App Dist) 161 S. High St., Suite 504, Akron 44308-1602; **Fax:** (330) 643-2394; **E-mail:** william@ninth.courts.state.oh.us

(419) 213-4578   **Bates, James D.** (J Lucas Cty Common Pleas Ct) Cthse., 700 Adams St., Toledo 43624-1678; **Fax:** (419) 213-4184

(740) 335-4750   **Beathard, Steven P.** (J Fayette Cty Common Pleas Ct) Cthse., 110 E. Court St., Washington Court House 43160-1395; **Fax:** (740) 333-3522

(740) 264-7644   **Bednar, Michael C.** (J Jefferson Cty Ct No 2) P.O. Box 2207, Wintersville 43953; **Fax:** (740) 264-3909; **E-mail:** mbednar@blakehersheybednar.com

(740) 942-8865   **Beetham, Mark** (J Harrison Cty Ct) Cthse., 100 W. Market St., Cadiz 43907-1132; **Fax:** (740) 942-3541

(330) 489-3214   **Belden, Stephen F.** (J Canton Munic Ct) City Hall, 218 Cleveland Ave., S.W., Canton 44702; **Fax:** (330) 471-8869; **E-mail:** sfbelden@ci.canton.oh.us

(614) 462-3894   **Belskis, Lawrence A.** (J Franklin Cty Probate Ct) 373 S. High St., 22nd Fl., Columbus 43215-6311; **Fax:** (614) 462-7422; **E-mail:** lbelskis@co.franklin.oh.us

(614) 462-7200   **Bender, John F.** (J Franklin Cty Common Pleas Ct) 369 S. High St., Columbus 43215-4554; **Fax:** (614) 462-4480

(740) 687-7040   **Berens, Richard E.** (J Fairfield Cty Common Pleas Ct) Hall of Justice, 224 E. Main St., Lancaster 43130-3879; **Fax:** (740) 687-0158

(419) 245-1941   **Berling, Amy J.** (J Toledo Munic Ct) 555 N. Erie St., Toledo 43624; **Fax:** (419) 245-1802; **E-mail:** amy.berling@noris.org

(330) 545-3177   **Bernard, Michael A.** (J Girard Munic Ct) Girard Justice Ctr., Suite A, 100 N. Market St., Girard 44420; **Fax:** (330) 545-7045

(614) 462-3550   **Bessey, John P.** (J Franklin Cty Common Pleas Ct) 369 S. High St., Rm. 6A, Columbus 43215-4554; **Fax:** (614) 462-4480; **E-mail:** john_bessey@fccourts.org

(440) 329-5722   **Betleski, Mark A.** (J Lorain Cty Common Pleas Ct) Lorain Cty. Justice Center, 225 Court St., Elyria 44035; **Fax:** (440) 329-5729

(614) 387-9800   **Bettis, J. Warren** (J Ct of Claims) 65 S. Front St., 3rd Fl., Columbus 43215; **Fax:** (614) 387-9836

(740) 947-2560   **Bevens, William Wray** (J Pike Cty Probate/Juv Ct) 230 Waverly Plaza, Suite 600, Waverly 45690-1385

(419) 627-7731   **Binette, Roger E.** (J Erie Cty Common Pleas Ct) Cthse., 323 Columbus Ave., Sandusky 44870-2602; **Fax:** (419) 627-6602

(419) 627-7750   (J Erie Cty Probate Ct) 323 Columbus Ave., Sandusky 44870-2691; **Fax:** (419) 626-9120

(419) 636-1548   **Bird, Steven R.** (J Williams Cty Probate/Juv Ct) One Courthouse Sq., 2nd. Fl., Bryan 43506; **Fax:** (419) 636-5405; **E-mail:** juvcourt@wmsco.org

(216) 443-6358   **Blackmon, Patricia Ann** (J Dist Ct of App 8th App Dist) Cuyahoga Cty. Cthse., Suite 202, 1 Lakeside Ave., Cleveland 44113-1085; **Fax:** (216) 443-2044

(513) 933-7210   **Bogen, Mark R.** (J Lebanon Munic Ct) City Bldg., 50 S. Broadway, Lebanon 45036; **Fax:** (513) 933-7212

(330) 451-7245   **Boggins, John F.** (J Dist Ct of App 5th App Dist) 110 Central Plaza S., Suite 320, Canton 44702-1411; **Fax:** (330) 451-7249

(740) 947-4003   **Bolt-Meredith, Cassandra** (J Pike Cty Ct) 230 Waverly Plz., Suite 900, Waverly 45690; **Fax:** (740) 947-7644

(330) 643-2238   **Bond, Jane** (J Summit Cty Common Pleas Ct) 209 S. High St., Akron 44308-1610

(440) 328-2201   **Boros, Debra L.** (J Lorain Cty Dom Rel Ct) 348 Second St., Elyria 44035-5629; **Fax:** (440) 328-2211; **E-mail:** jdboros@hotmail.com

(740) 373-6623   **Boyer, Susan E.** (J Washington Cty Common Pleas Ct) Cthse., 205 Putnam St., Marietta 45750-2922; **Fax:** (740) 373-5713

(216) 443-8726   **Boyko, Christopher A.** (J Cuyahoga Cty Common Pleas Ct) 1200 Ontario St., Cleveland 44113-1678; **Fax:** (216) 348-4036

(330) 375-2054   **Boyle, Edna J.** (J Akron Munic Ct) 217 S. High St., Akron 44308-1611; **Fax:** (330) 375-2238; **E-mail:** boyleed@ci.akron.oh.us

(216) 443-8738   **Boyle, Mary J.** (J Cuyahoga Cty Common Pleas Ct) 1200 Ontario St., Cleveland 44113-1678; **Fax:** (216) 348-4033

(440) 461-6500 Ext. 151   **Bozza, Mary Kaye** (J Lyndhurst Munic Ct) 5301 Mayfield Rd., Cleveland 44124; **Fax:** (440) 442-1910

(937) 599-7249   **Brady, Michael L.** (J Logan Cty Probate/Juv Ct) 101 S. Main St., Rm. 6, Bellefontaine 43311; **Fax:** (937) 599-7297; **E-mail:** mbrady@co.logan.oh.us

(614) 645-8296   **Brandt, Michael T.** (J Franklin Cty Munic Ct) 375 S. High St., Columbus 43215-4520; **Fax:** (614) 645-8822

(740) 349-6640   **Branstool, W. David** (J Licking Cty Munic Ct) 40 W. Main St., Newark 43055; **Fax:** (740) 345-4250

(513) 425-6609   **Bressler, H. J.** (J Dist Ct of App 12th App Dist) 1001 Reinartz Blvd., P.O. Box 1009, Middletown 45042-1901; **Fax:** (513) 425-8751; **E-mail:** bresslerhj@twelfth.courts.state.oh.us

(937) 496-7724   **Brogan, James A.** (J Dist Ct of App 2nd App Dist) 41 N. Perry, P.O. Box 972, Dayton 45422; **Fax:** (937) 496-7724; **E-mail:** broganj@mcohio.org

(513) 695-1231   **Bronson, Neal B.** (J Warren Cty Common Pleas Ct) 500 Justice Dr., Lebanon 45036; **Fax:** (513) 695-2920

(330) 451-7720   **Brown, Charles E.** (J Stark Cty Common Pleas Ct) 115 Central Plz., N., Suite 400, Canton 44702-1490; **Fax:** (330) 451-7740

(330) 287-5540   **Brown, Robert J.** (J Wayne Cty Common Pleas Ct) 107 W. Liberty St., Wooster 44691; **Fax:** (330) 264-2560

(614) 462-4022   **Brown, Susan** (Pres J Dist Ct of App 10th App Dist) 373 S. High St., 24th Fl., Columbus 43215-4578; **Fax:** (614) 462-7249; **E-mail:** sbrown@co.franklin.oh.us

(614) 462-4444   **Browne, Kim A.** (J Franklin Cty Dom Rel/Juv Ct) 373 S. High St., 6th Fl., Columbus 43215; **Fax:** (614) 719-2118

(614) 462-6281   **Brunner, Jennifer L.** (J Franklin Cty Common Pleas Ct) 369 S. High St., Rm. 8B, Columbus 43215-4554; **Fax:** (614) 462-4480; **E-mail:** jennifer_brunner@fccourts.org

(740) 283-8543   **Bruzzese, Joseph J., Jr.** (J Jefferson Cty Common Pleas Ct) Cthse., 301 Market St., Steubenville 43952-2149; **Fax:** (740) 283-8686

(614) 462-3612   **Bryant, Peggy** (J Dist Ct of App 10th App Dist) 373 S. High St., 24th Fl., Columbus 43215-4578; **Fax:** (614) 462-7249; **E-mail:** plbryant@co.franklin.oh.us

(419) 223-1861   **Bryant, Thomas F.** (J Dist Ct of App 3rd App Dist) 204 N. Main St., Lima 45801; **Fax:** (419) 224-3828; **E-mail:** bryant@third.courts.state.oh.us

(216) 291-4901   **Buchanan, A. Deane** (J Cleveland Heights Munic Ct) 40 Severance Cir., Cleveland 44118; **Fax:** (216) 291-2459

(419) 337-9242   **Bumb, Michael J.** (J Fulton Cty Probate/Juv Ct) 210 S. Fulton St., Wauseon 43567; **Fax:** (419) 337-9284

(740) 773-3515   **Bunch, Thomas E.** (J Chillicothe Munic Ct) 26 S. Paint St., Chillicothe 45601-3202; **Fax:** (740) 774-1101; **E-mail:** tbunch@bright.net

(513) 946-5770   **Burke, Kim Wilson** (J Hamilton Cty Common Pleas Ct) 1000 Main St., Rm. 500, Cincinnati 45202; **Fax:** (513) 946-5907

(419) 332-1579   **Burkett, Michael L.** (J Fremont Munic Ct) 323 S. Front St., P.O. Box 886, Fremont 43420-0071; **Fax:** (419) 332-1570

(513) 946-5122   **Burlew, John H.** (J Hamilton Cty Munic Ct) Cthse., 1000 Main St., Cincinnati 45202; **Fax:** (513) 946-5202

(216) 443-8671   **Burnside, Janet R.** (J Cuyahoga Cty Common Pleas Ct) 1200 Ontario St., Cleveland 44113-1678; **Fax:** (216) 348-4035

(440) 285-2222   **Burt, Forrest W.** (J Geauga Cty Common Pleas Ct) Cthse., 100 Short Court, Chardon 44024-1238; **Fax:** (440) 286-2127

(419) 897-7140   **Byers, Gary L.** (J Maumee Munic Ct) 400 Conant St., Maumee 43537-3397; **Fax:** (419) 897-7129

(330) 385-5151   **Byers-Emmerling, Melissa** (J East Liverpool Munic Ct) 126 W. Sixth St., East Liverpool 43920; **Fax:** (330) 385-1566

(614) 462-3777   **Cain, David E.** (J Franklin Cty Common Pleas Ct) 369 S. High St., Rm. 7D, Columbus 43215-4554; **Fax:** (614) 462-4480; **E-mail:** david_cain@fccourts.org

(216) 348-4837   **Calabrese, Anthony O., Jr.** (J Dist Ct of App 8th App Dist) Cuyahoga Cty. Cthse., Suite 202, 1 Lakeside Ave., Cleveland 44113-1085; **Fax:** (216) 443-2044; **E-mail:** cpaoc@www.cuyahoga.oh.us

(216) 443-8748   **Callahan, Kenneth R.** (J Cuyahoga Cty Common Pleas Ct) 1200 Ontario St., Cleveland 44113-1678; **Fax:** (216) 348-4032

(330) 375-2009   **Callahan, Lynne S.** (J Akron Munic Ct) 217 S. High St., Akron 44308-1611; **Fax:** (330) 375-2123; **E-mail:** callaly@ci.akron.oh.us

(513) 867-6002 **Campbell, Joyce Ann** (J Fairfield Munic Ct) 4951 Dixie Hwy., Fairfield 45014; **Fax:** (513) 867-6001; **E-mail:** jcampbell@fairfield-city.org

(419) 238-5767 **Campbell, Phil W.** (J Van Wert Munic Ct) 124 S. Market St., Van Wert 45891; **Fax:** (419) 238-5865

(330) 637-5023 **Campbell, Thomas A.** (J Trumbull Cty Ct Central Dist) 180 N. Mecca St., Cortland 44410; **Fax:** (330) 637-5021

(440) 992-7108 **Camplese, Albert S.** (J Ashtabula Munic Ct) 110 W. 44th St., Ashtabula 44004; **Fax:** (440) 998-5786

(937) 333-4367 **Cannon, James F.** (J Dayton Munic Ct) 301 W. Third St., Dayton 45402; **Fax:** (937) 333-5085

(937) 496-6600 **Capizzi, Anthony** (J Montgomery Cty Juv Ct) 303 W. Second St., Dayton 45422-4240; **Fax:** (937) 496-6598

(740) 867-3127 **Capper, Donald R.** (J Lawrence Munic Ct) 10916 County Rd. 1, P.O. Box 126, Chesapeake 45619; **Fax:** (740) 867-3547; **E-mail:** dcapper@zoomnet.net

(937) 328-2464 **Capper, Thomas J.** (J Clark Cty Common Pleas Ct) Cthse., 101 N. Limestone St., Springfield 45502-1120; **Fax:** (937) 328-2463

(937) 328-4648 (J Clark Cty Dom Rel Ct) 101 N. Limestone St., Springfield 45502; **Fax:** (937) 328-2463

(419) 668-4383 **Cardwell, Timothy L.** (J Huron Cty Probate/Juv Ct) Two E. Main St., Norwalk 44857; **Fax:** (419) 663-0944

(937) 382-8985 **Carey, Chad Lee** (J Clinton Cty Munic Ct) 69 N. South St., P.O. Box 71, Wilmington 45177; **Fax:** (937) 383-0130; **E-mail:** ccmc@erinet.com

(937) 328-2435 **Carey, Richard P.** (J Clark Cty Probate Ct) 50 E. Columbia St., Springfield 45502-1194; **Fax:** (937) 328-2589; **E-mail:** rcarey@clarkcountyohio.gov

(330) 297-0881 **Carnes, Thomas J.** (J Portage Cty Juv Ct) 8000 Infirmary Rd., Ravenna 44266; **Fax:** (330) 297-2227

(330) 297-3870 (J Portage Cty Probate Ct) 203 W. Main St., 3rd Fl., P.O. Box 936, Ravenna 44266; **Fax:** (330) 298-1100

(330) 643-2259 **Carr, Donna J.** (J Dist Ct of App 9th App Dist) 161 S. High St., Suite 504, Akron 44308-1602; **Fax:** (330) 643-2394; **E-mail:** donna@ninth.courts.state.oh.us

(216) 529-6700 **Carroll, Patrick** (J Lakewood Munic Ct) 12650 Detroit Ave., Lakewood 44107; **Fax:** (216) 529-7687

(216) 443-6355 **Celebrezze, Frank D., Jr.** (J Dist Ct of App 8th App Dist) Cuyahoga Cty. Cthse., Suite 202, 1 Lakeside Ave., Cleveland 44113-1085; **Fax:** (216) 443-2044

(216) 443-8806 **Celebrezze, James P.** (J Cuyahoga Cty Dom Rel Ct) One W. Lakeside Ave., Cleveland 44113-1082; **Fax:** (216) 443-4943

(937) 599-7249 **Chamberlain, C. Douglas** (J Logan Cty Probate/Juv Ct) 101 S. Main St., Rm. 6, Bellefontaine 43311; **Fax:** (937) 599-7297; **E-mail:** dchamberlain@co.logan.oh.us

(330) 723-3287 **Chase, Dale H.** (J Medina Munic Ct) 135 N. Elmwood Ave., Medina 44256; **Fax:** (330) 225-1108

(440) 392-5875 **Cicconetti, Michael A.** (J Painesville Munic Ct) 7 Richmond St., P.O. Box 601, Painesville 44077; **Fax:** (440) 639-4927

(513) 946-3580 **Cissell, James** (J Hamilton Cty Probate Ct) 230 E. Ninth St., 10th Fl., Cincinnati 45202-2145; **Fax:** (513) 946-3581

(614) 387-9800 **Clark, Joseph T.** (J Ct of Claims) 65 S. Front St., 3rd Fl., Columbus 43215; **Fax:** (614) 387-9836; **E-mail:** jsclark@cco.state.oh.us

(937) 378-6549 **Clark, Margaret A.** (J Brown Cty Probate/Juv Ct) 510 E. State St., Suite 1, P.O. Box 379, Georgetown 45121-0379; **Fax:** (937) 378-4729; **E-mail:** mclark@browncountycourt.org

(513) 946-5127 **Coes, Kendal M.** (J Hamilton Cty Munic Ct) Cthse., 1000 Main St., Cincinnati 45202; **Fax:** (513) 946-5202

(937) 645-3029 **Coleman Eufinger, Charlotte** (J Union Cty Probate/Juv Ct) Cthse., 215 W. Fifth St., Marysville 43040; **Fax:** (937) 645-3160

(330) 725-9729 **Collier, Christopher** (J Medina Cty Common Pleas Ct) 93 Public Sq., Medina 44256-2205; **Fax:** (330) 764-8445

(419) 592-2851 **Collier, John S.** (J Napoleon Munic Ct) 255 W. Riverview Ave., P.O. Box 502, Napoleon 43545-0502; **Fax:** (419) 592-1805; **E-mail:** lcollier@wcnet.org

(740) 532-3062 **Collins, O. Clark, Jr.** (J Ironton Munic Ct) 301 S. Third St., P.O. Box 237, Ironton 45638-0237; **Fax:** (740) 533-6088

(440) 350-2720 **Collins, Richard L.** (J Lake Cty Common Pleas Ct) 47 N. Park Pl., P.O. Box 490, Painesville 44077

(440) 826-5860 **Comstock, Mark A.** (J Berea Munic Ct) 11 Berea Commons, Berea 44017; **Fax:** (440) 891-3387

(513) 887-3459 **Connaughton, John B.** (J Butler Cty Ct) 101 High St., Hamilton 45011; **Fax:** (513) 887-3568

(614) 462-3660 **Connor, John A.** (J Franklin Cty Common Pleas Ct) 369 S. High St., Rm. 6D, Columbus 43215-4554; **Fax:** (614) 462-4480; **E-mail:** john_connor@fcccourts.org

(419) 213-4370 **Cook, Gary G.** (J Lucas Cty Common Pleas Ct) Cthse., 700 Adams St., Toledo 43624-1678; **Fax:** (419) 213-4184

(216) 443-6357 **Cooney, Colleen Conway** (J Dist Ct of App 8th App Dist) Cuyahoga Cty. Cthse., Suite 202, 1 Lakeside Ave., Cleveland 44113-1085; **Fax:** (216) 443-2044; **E-mail:** ccc@8thappeals.com

(513) 946-5860 **Cooper, Ethna Marie** (J Hamilton Cty Common Pleas Ct) 1000 Main St., Rm. 485, Cincinnati 45202; **Fax:** (513) 946-5907

(740) 342-1118 **Cooperrider, Luann** (J Perry Cty Probate/Juv Ct) Cthse., 105 Main St., P.O. Box 167, New Lexington 43764; **Fax:** (740) 342-5524

(740) 537-2020 **Corabi, Joseph M.** (J Jefferson Cty Ct No 1) 1007 Franklin Ave., Toronto 43964; **Fax:** (740) 537-1866

(937) 378-4101 **Corbin, R. Alan** (J Brown Cty Common Pleas Ct) Cthse., 101 S. Main St., Georgetown 45121; **Fax:** (937) 378-4212

(216) 443-8747 **Corrigan, Brian J.** (J Cuyahoga Cty Common Pleas Ct) 1200 Ontario St., Cleveland 44113-1678; **Fax:** (216) 348-4032

(216) 443-8764 **Corrigan, John E.** (J Cuyahoga Cty Probate Ct) One Lakeside Ave., Cleveland 44113; **Fax:** (216) 443-5446

(216) 443-6360 **Corrigan, Michael J.** (J Dist Ct of App 8th App Dist) Cuyahoga Cty. Cthse., Suite 202, 1 Lakeside Ave., Cleveland 44113-1085; **Fax:** (216) 443-2044; **E-mail:** mjc@8thappeals.com

(216) 443-8417 **Corrigan, Patrick F.** (J Cuyahoga Cty Juv Ct) 2163 E. 22nd St., Cleveland 44115

(740) 702-3036 **Corzine, William J.** (J Ross Cty Common Pleas Ct) Cthse., 2 N. Paint St., Chillicothe 45601-3109; **Fax:** (740) 702-3018

(330) 643-2228 **Cosgrove, Patricia A.** (J Summit Cty Common Pleas Ct) 209 S. High St., Akron 44308-1610

(740) 699-2141 **Costine, J. Mark** (J Belmont Cty Probate/Juv Ct) Cthse., 101 W. Main St., St. Clairsville 43950-1154; **Fax:** (740) 699-2143; **E-mail:** markcjmc@aol.com

(216) 443-8755 **Coyne, William J.** (J Cuyahoga Cty Common Pleas Ct) 1200 Ontario St., Cleveland 44113-1678; **Fax:** (216) 348-4092

(614) 462-3811 **Crawford, Dale A.** (J Franklin Cty Common Pleas Ct) 369 S. High St., Rm. 8D, Columbus 43215-4554; **Fax:** (614) 462-4480; **E-mail:** dale_crawford@fccourts.org

(513) 887-3590 **Crehan, Matthew J.** (J Butler Cty Common Pleas Ct) Govt. Svces. Ctr., 3rd Fl., 315 High St., Hamilton 45011; **Fax:** (513) 785-5667; **E-mail:** crehanm@butlercountyohio.org

(330) 740-2154 **Cronin, Maureen A.** (J Mahoning Cty Common Pleas Ct) 120 Market St., Youngstown 44503-1710; **Fax:** (330) 740-2529; **E-mail:** mcronin@mahoningcountyoh.gov

(937) 496-7538 **Cross, Denise Martin** (J Montgomery Cty Dom Rel Ct) 301 W. Third St., 2nd. Fl., Dayton 45422-4248; **Fax:** (937) 496-7835; **E-mail:** crossd@mcohio.org

(740) 992-6439 **Crow, Frederick W., III** (J Meigs Cty Common Pleas Ct) 100 E. Second St., Pomeroy 45769-1030; **Fax:** (740) 992-3828

(513) 946-5750 **Crush, Thomas H.** (J Hamilton Cty Common Pleas Ct) 1000 Main St., Rm. 360, Cincinnati 45202; **Fax:** (513) 946-5907

(419) 213-6778 **Cubbon, Denise N.** (J Lucas Cty Juv Ct) 1801 Spielbusch Ave., Toledo 43624; **Fax:** (413) 213-6898

(419) 334-6417 **Culbert, Brad** (J Sandusky Cty Probate/Juv Ct) 100 N. Park Ave., Fremont 43420-2476; **Fax:** (419) 334-6210; **E-mail:** judgebc@co.sandusky.oh.us

(440) 350-2657 **Culotta, Vincent A.** (J Lake Cty Common Pleas Ct) 47 N. Park Pl., P.O. Box 490, Painesville 44077

(330) 375-2053 **Culver, Kathryn** (J Akron Munic Ct) 217 S. High St., Akron 44308-1611; **Fax:** (330) 375-2229; **E-mail:** culveka@ci.akron.oh.us

(513) 946-9030 **Cunningham, Penelope R.** (J Hamilton Cty Dom Rel Ct) 800 Broadway, Rm. 225, Cincinnati 45202; **Fax:** (513) 946-9033

(419) 223-1861 **Cupp, Robert R.** (Pres J Dist Ct of App 3rd App Dist) 204 N. Main St., Lima 45801; **Fax:** (419) 224-3828

(330) 740-2001 **D'Apolito, David A.** (J Mahoning Cty Ct No 4) 6000 Mahoning Ave., Youngstown 44515; **Fax:** (330) 740-2036

(419) 213-4575 **Dartt, Denise Ann** (J Lucas Cty Common Pleas Ct) Cthse., 700 Adams St., Toledo 43624-1678; **Fax:** (419) 213-4184

(740) 223-4210 **Davidson, Robert S.** (J Marion Cty Common Pleas Ct) Courthouse Sq., 100 N. Main St., Marion 43302; **Fax:** (740) 387-1321

(419) 424-7081 **Davis, Allan H.** (J Hancock Cty Probate/Juv Ct) 308 Dorney Plz., Findlay 45840-3302; **Fax:** (419) 424-7081; **E-mail:** ahdavis@co.hancock.oh.us

(740) 676-4490 **Davis, D. William** (J Belmont Cty Ct, Eastern Dist) 400 W. 26th St., Suite 100, Bellaire 43906; **Fax:** (740) 671-6100

(513) 946-5890 **Davis, David P.** (J Hamilton Cty Common Pleas Ct) 1000 Main St., Rm. 530, Cincinnati 45202; **Fax:** (513) 946-5907

(937) 225-4368 **Davis, G. Jack** (J Montgomery Cty Common Pleas Ct) 41 N. Perry St., P.O. Box 972, Dayton 45422-2170; **Fax:** (937) 225-5406

(937) 293-3058 **Deddens, Robert L.** (J Oakwood Munic Ct) 30 Park Ave., Dayton 45419-3426; **Fax:** (937) 297-2939

(740) 947-2212 **Deering, Randy D.** (J Pike Cty Common Pleas Ct) 100 E. Second St., Waverly 45690-1302; **Fax:** (740) 947-1729; **E-mail:** judge@zoomnet.net

(330) 740-2180 **DeGenaro, Mary** (J Dist Ct of App 7th App Dist) Mahoning Cty. Cthse., 120 Market St., Youngstown 44503-1710; **Fax:** (330) 740-2182; **E-mail:** mdegenaro@aol.com

(419) 627-7782 **DeLamatre, Robert C.** (J Erie Cty Dom Rel/Juv Ct) 323 Columbus Ave., 4th. Fl., Sandusky 44870-2697; **Fax:** (419) 627-6600

(330) 740-2278 **Dellick, Theresa** (J Mahoning Cty Juv Ct) 300 E. Scott St., Youngstown 44505; **Fax:** (330) 740-2286

(419) 774-5567 **DeWeese, James** (J Richland Cty Common Pleas Ct) 50 Park Ave., E., Mansfield 44902-1888; **Fax:** (419) 774-5516; **E-mail:** judgedeweese@kosinet.com

(419) 547-0915 **Dewey, John P.** (J Sandusky Cty Ct No 1) 847 E. McPherson Hwy., P.O. Box 267, Clyde 43410-1998; **Fax:** (419) 547-9198; **E-mail:** deweylaw@woh.rr..com

(330) 643-2357 **Dezso, Carol J.** (J Summit Cty Dom Rel Ct) 209 S. High St., Akron 44308-1610; **Fax:** (330) 643-2126

(513) 946-5755 **Dinkelacker, Patrick T.** (J Hamilton Cty Common Pleas Ct) 1000 Main St., Rm. 310, Cincinnati 45202; **Fax:** (513) 946-5907

(513) 946-3441 **Doan, Rupert A.** (J Dist Ct of App 1st App Dist) 230 E. Ninth St., 12th Fl., Cincinnati 45202; **Fax:** (513) 946-3412

(419) 213-4570 **Doneghy, Charles J.** (J Lucas Cty Common Pleas Ct) Cthse., 700 Adams St., Toledo 43624-1678; **Fax:** (419) 213-4184

(216) 443-8764 **Donnelly, John J.** (Pres J Cuyahoga Cty Probate Ct) One Lakeside Ave., Cleveland 44113; **Fax:** (216) 443-5446

(330) 740-2180 **Donofrio, Gene** (J Dist Ct of App 7th App Dist) Mahoning Cty. Cthse., 120 Market St., Youngstown 44503-1710; **Fax:** (330) 740-2182

(937) 225-4464 **Donovan, Mary E.** (J Dist Ct of App 2nd App Dist) 41 N. Perry, 5th Fl., P.O. Box 972, Dayton 45422; **Fax:** (937) 496-7724

(614) 645-8205 **Dorrian, Julia L.** (J Franklin Cty Munic Ct) 375 S. High St., Columbus 43215-4520; **Fax:** (614) 645-8822

(330) 742-8857 **Douglas, Robert A., Jr.** (J Youngstown Munic Ct) 26 S. Phelps St., Youngstown 44501; **Fax:** (330) 742-8725; **E-mail:** rdoug31204@aol.com

(937) 456-8136 **Dues, Wilfrid G.** (J Preble Cty Probate/Juv Ct) Cthse., 2nd Fl., 101 E. Main St., Eaton 45320-1791; **Fax:** (937) 456-5803

(440) 887-7400 **Dunning, Mary L.** (J Parma Munic Ct) 5555 Powers Blvd., Parma 44129-5462; **Fax:** (440) 887-7481

(330) 740-2168   **Durkin, John M.** (J Mahoning Cty Common Pleas Ct) 120 Market St., Youngstown 44503-1710; **Fax:** (330) 742-5898; **E-mail:** jdurkin@mahoningcounty.oh.gov

(216) 443-6356   **Dyke, Ann** (J Dist Ct of App 8th App Dist) Cuyahoga Cty. Cthse., Suite 202, 1 Lakeside Ave., Cleveland 44113-1085; **Fax:** (216) 443-2044

(419) 562-1896   **Eckstein, Steven D.** (J Crawford Cty Probate/Juv Ct) 112 E. Mansfield St., Bucyrus 44820-2386; **Fax:** (419) 562-6538

(330) 451-7766   **Edwards, Julie A.** (J Dist Ct of App 5th App Dist) 110 Central Plaza S., Suite 320, Canton 44702-1411; **Fax:** (330) 451-7249; **E-mail:** info@fifthdist.org

(740) 432-9252   **Ellwood, David A.** (J Guernsey Cty Common Pleas Ct) 801 Wheeling Ave., Rm. E, Cambridge 43725-2358; **Fax:** (740) 432-7807; **E-mail:** jdae33@yahoo.com

(330) 830-1727   **Elum, Edward J.** (J Massillon Munic Ct) 2 James Duncan Plz., Massillon 44646; **Fax:** (330) 830-1756

(440) 204-2150   **Elwell, Thomas** (J Lorain Munic Ct) 200 W. Erie Ave., Lorain 44052-1646; **Fax:** (440) 204-2146

(330) 297-3866   **Enlow, John A.** (J Portage Cty Common Pleas Ct) Cthse., 203 W. Main St., Ravenna 44266-2778; **Fax:** (330) 297-4589

(740) 446-4702   **Evans, D. Dean** (J Gallia Cty Common Pleas Ct) Cthse., Rm. 1200, 18 Locust St., Gallipolis 45631; **Fax:** (740) 441-2051

(330) 287-5650   **Evans, D. William, Jr.** (J Wayne Munic Ct) 215 N. Grant St., Wooster 44691-3499; **Fax:** (330) 263-4043

(330) 740-2152   **Evans, James C.** (J Mahoning Cty Common Pleas Ct) 120 Market St., Youngstown 44503-1710; **Fax:** (330) 742-5890; **E-mail:** jevans@mahoningcounty.oh.gov

(740) 446-9400   **Evans, Margaret** (J Gallipolis Munic Ct) 518 Second Ave., Gallipolis 45631-0988; **Fax:** (740) 441-6025

(740) 622-1595   **Evans, Richard I.** (J Coshocton Cty Common Pleas Ct) Courthouse Sq., 318 Main St., Coshocton 43812-1595; **Fax:** (740) 295-0021

(740) 393-6777   **Eyster, Otho** (J Knox Cty Common Pleas Ct) Cthse., 111 E. High St., Mount Vernon 43050; **Fax:** (740) 393-5096

(937) 225-4464   **Fain, Mike** (J Dist Ct of App 2nd App Dist) 41 N. Perry, P.O. Box 972, Dayton 45422; **Fax:** (937) 496-7724; **E-mail:** fainm@mcohio.org

(614) 462-3660   **Fais, David W.** (J Franklin Cty Common Pleas Ct) 369 S. High St., Rm. 6C, Columbus 43215-4554; **Fax:** (614) 462-4480

(440) 350-2708   **Falkowski, Colleen A.** (J Lake Cty Dom Rel Ct) 47 N. Park Pl., P.O. Box 490, Painesville 44077; **Fax:** (440) 350-2717

(330) 489-3216   **Falvey, Mary A.** (J Canton Munic Ct) City Hall, 218 Cleveland Ave., S.W., Canton 44702; **Fax:** (330) 471-8860; **E-mail:** mafalvey@ci.canton.oh.us

(330) 451-7447   **Farmer, Sheila G.** (J Dist Ct of App 5th App Dist) 110 Central Plaza S., Suite 320, Canton 44702-1411; **Fax:** (330) 451-7249

(740) 962-3371   **Favreau, Dan W.** (J Morgan Cty Common Pleas Ct) 19 E. Main St., McConnelsville 43756-1197; **Fax:** (740) 962-4589

(740) 223-4220   **Finnegan, William** (J Marion Cty Common Pleas Ct) Courthouse Sq., 100 N. Main St., Marion 43302; **Fax:** (740) 387-7131

(440) 333-0066   **Fitzsimmons, Donna Congeni** (J Rocky River Munic Ct) 21012 Hilliard Blvd., Rocky River 44116; **Fax:** (440) 356-5613

(216) 443-8812   **Flanagan, Timothy M.** (J Cuyahoga Cty Dom Rel Ct) One W. Lakeside Ave., Cleveland 44113-1082; **Fax:** (216) 443-4943

(513) 695-1149   **Flannery, James L.** (J Warren Cty Common Pleas Ct) 500 Justice Dr., Lebanon 45036; **Fax:** (513) 695-1303

(740) 455-7142   **Fleegle, Mark C.** (J Muskingum Cty Common Pleas Ct) 401 Main St., Zanesville 43701; **Fax:** (740) 455-7177

(216) 443-8406   **Floyd, Alison L.** (J Cuyahoga Cty Juv Ct) 2163 E. 22nd St., Cleveland 44115

(330) 675-2650   **Ford, Donald R.** (J Dist Ct of App 11th App Dist) 111 High St., N.E., Warren 44481; **Fax:** (330) 675-2655

(937) 653-7376   **Fornof-Lippencott, Susan J.** (J Champaign Cty Munic Ct) 205 S. Main St., P.O. Box 85, Urbana 43078; **Fax:** (937) 652-4333

(419) 238-7315   **Fortney, Rex D.** (J Van Wert Cty Probate/Juv Ct) 108 E. Main St., Van Wert 45891-1786; **Fax:** (419) 238-7315; **E-mail:** judge@vwprobjuvcourt.net

(937) 544-2011   **Foster, Alan W.** (J Adams Cty Ct) Cthse., Rm. 25, 110 W. Main St., West Union 45693; **Fax:** (937) 544-8911

(419) 483-5880   **Fox, Kenneth P.** (J Bellevue Munic Ct) 3000 Seneca Industrial Pkwy., Bellevue 44811; **Fax:** (419) 484-8060

(416) 213-4572   **Franks, Ruth Ann** (J Lucas Cty Common Pleas Ct) Cthse., 700 Adams St., Toledo 43624-1678; **Fax:** (419) 213-4184

(740) 633-3147   **Fregiato, Frank A.** (J Belmont Cty Ct, Northern Dist) 302 Walnut St., P.O. Box 40, Martins Ferry 43935; **Fax:** (740) 633-6631; **E-mail:** fregiato@tfmhd-law.com

(614) 462-4032   **French, Judith L.** (J Dist Ct of App 10th App Dist) 373 S. High St., 24th Fl., Columbus 43215-4578; **Fax:** (614) 462-7249

(419) 289-8137   **Fridline, Jacob M.** (J Ashland Munic Ct) 1209 E. Main St., P.O. Box 385, Ashland 44805-0385

(216) 443-8705   **Friedland, Carolyn B.** (J Cuyahoga Cty Common Pleas Ct) 1200 Ontario St., Cleveland 44113-1678; **Fax:** (216) 348-4034

(216) 443-8708   **Friedman, Stuart A.** (J Cuyahoga Cty Common Pleas Ct) 1200 Ontario St., Cleveland 44113-1678; **Fax:** (216) 348-4035

(614) 645-8849   **Froehlich, Mark S.** (J Franklin Cty Munic Ct) 375 S. High St., Columbus 43215-4520; **Fax:** (614) 645-8822

(937) 225-4440   **Froelich, Jeffrey E.** (J Montgomery Cty Common Pleas Ct) 41 N. Perry St., P.O. Box 972, Dayton 45422-2170; **Fax:** (937) 225-5406; **E-mail:** froelicj@montcourt.org

(330) 426-3774   **Frost, Mark A.** (J Columbiana Cty Munic Ct Southwest) 41 N. Park Ave., Lisbon 44432; **Fax:** (330) 424-6658

(330) 426-3774   (J Columbiana Cty Munic Ct Eastern Div) 31 N. Market St., East Palestine 44413; **Fax:** (330) 426-6328

(614) 462-3550   **Frye, Richard** (J Franklin Cty Common Pleas Ct) 369 S. High St., Columbus 43215-4554; **Fax:** (614) 462-4480

(216) 443-8687   **Fuerst, Nancy A.** (J Cuyahoga Cty Common Pleas Ct) 1200 Ontario St., Cleveland 44113-1678; **Fax:** (216) 348-4092

(440) 285-2222   **Fuhry, David L.** (J Geauga Cty Common Pleas Ct) Cthse., 100 Short Court, Chardon 44024-1238; **Fax:** (440) 286-2127

(216) 443-8686 **Gallagher, Eileen** (J Cuyahoga Cty Common Pleas Ct) 1200 Ontario St., Cleveland 44113-1678; **Fax:** (216) 348-4031

(216) 443-8410 **Gallagher, John W.** (J Cuyahoga Cty Juv Ct) 2163 E. 22nd St., Cleveland 44115

(216) 348-4838 **Gallagher, Sean C.** (J Dist Ct of App 8th App Dist) Cuyahoga Cty. Cthse., Suite 202, 1 Lakeside Ave., Cleveland 44113-1085; **Fax:** (216) 443-2044

(937) 382-2391 **Gano, G. Allen** (J Clinton Cty Probate/Juv Ct) Cthse., 2nd Fl., 46 S. South St., Wilmington 45177; **Fax:** (937) 383-0823

(216) 443-8706 **Gaul, Daniel** (J Cuyahoga Cty Common Pleas Ct) 1200 Ontario St., Cleveland 44113-1678; **Fax:** (216) 348-4035

(937) 333-4366 **Gehres, Daniel G.** (J Dayton Munic Ct) 301 W. Third St., Dayton 45402; **Fax:** (937) 333-5114

(740) 385-4027 **Gerken, Thomas H.** (J Hocking Cty Common Pleas Ct) 1 E. Main St., 3rd Fl., Logan 43138-1207; **Fax:** (740) 385-2614

(419) 523-3012 **Gerschutz, Daniel R.** (J Putnam Cty Probate/Juv Ct) Cthse., Suite 204, 245 E. Main St., Ottawa 45875-1963; **Fax:** (419) 523-9291

(419) 734-6830 **Giesler, Kathleen L.** (J Ottawa Cty Common Pleas Ct Probate & General Div) 315 Madison St., Rm. 306, Port Clinton 43452-1936; **Fax:** (419) 734-6875

(419) 734-6851 (J Ottawa Cty Probate/Juv Ct) 315 Madison St., Port Clinton 43452-1994; **Fax:** (419) 734-6851

(440) 887-7400 **Gilligan, Timothy P.** (J Parma Munic Ct) 5555 Powers Blvd., Parma 44129-5462; **Fax:** (440) 887-7481

(330) 297-3880 **Giulitto, Joseph** (J Portage Cty Dom Rel Ct) Cthse., 203 W. Main St., Ravenna 44266-2788; **Fax:** (330) 296-0190

(614) 645-8206 **Glaeden, Carrie** (J Franklin Cty Munic Ct) 375 S. High St., Columbus 43215-4520; **Fax:** (614) 645-8822

(937) 376-7294 **Goldie, Susan L.** (J Xenia Munic Ct) 101 N. Detroit St., Xenia 45385-2996; **Fax:** (937) 376-7288

(740) 592-3236 **Goldsberry, L. Alan** (J Athens Cty Common Pleas Ct) Cthse., 3rd Fl., One S. Court St., Athens 45701-2895; **Fax:** (740) 592-3020; **E-mail:** agoldsberry@athenscountygovernment.com

(937) 225-4392 **Gorman, Barbara P.** (J Montgomery Cty Common Pleas Ct) 41 N. Perry St., P.O. Box 972, Dayton 45422-2170; **Fax:** (937) 225-5406; **E-mail:** gormanb@montcourt.org

(419) 245-1944 **Gorman, Francis X.** (J Toledo Munic Ct) 555 N. Erie St., Toledo 43624; **Fax:** (419) 245-1802; **E-mail:** francis.gorman@noris.org

(513) 946-3421 **Gorman, Robert H.** (J Dist Ct of App 1st App Dist) 230 E. Ninth St., 12th Fl., Cincinnati 45202; **Fax:** (513) 946-3412; **E-mail:** rgorman@cms.hamilton-co.org

(740) 453-0351 **Gormley, Joseph A.** (J Muskingum Cty Juv Ct) 1860 E. Pike, Zanesville 43701; **Fax:** (740) 453-1066

(740) 455-7113 (J Muskingum Cty Probate Ct) 401 Main St., Zanesville 43701-3567; **Fax:** (740) 455-7173

(937) 225-4416 **Gowdown, David A.** (J Montgomery Cty Common Pleas Ct) 41 N. Perry St., P.O. Box 972, Dayton 45422-2170; **Fax:** (937) 225-5406; **E-mail:** gowdownd@montcourt.org

(513) 946-9201 **Grady, Karla J.** (J Hamilton Cty Juv Ct) 800 Broadway, Cincinnati 45202-1225; **Fax:** (513) 946-9217; **E-mail:** kgrady@juvcourt.hamilton-co.org

(937) 328-2653 **Grady, Thomas J.** (J Dist Ct of App 2nd App Dist) Clark Cty. Cthse., 101 N. Limestone St., Springfield 45502; **Fax:** (937) 328-2652; **E-mail:** tjgrady@erinet.com

(513) 946-5165 **Grant, Cheryl D.** (J Hamilton Cty Munic Ct) Cthse., 1000 Main St., Cincinnati 45202; **Fax:** (513) 946-5202; **E-mail:** cgrant@cms.hamilton-co.org

(440) 333-0066 **Gravens, Maureen Adler** (J Rocky River Munic Ct) 21012 Hilliard Blvd., Rocky River 44116; **Fax:** (440) 356-5613

(614) 645-8295 **Green, James E.** (J Franklin Cty Munic Ct) 375 S. High St., Columbus 43215-4520; **Fax:** (614) 645-8822

(216) 443-8681 **Greene, Lillian J.** (J Cuyahoga Cty Common Pleas Ct) 1200 Ontario St., Cleveland 44113-1678; **Fax:** (216) 348-4038

(937) 393-9981 **Greer, Kevin L.** (J Highland Cty Probate/Juv Ct) Cthse., 105 N. High St., Hillsboro 45133-1182; **Fax:** (937) 393-0926

(937) 393-9981 (J Highland Cty Common Pleas Ct Probate & Juv Div) 105 N. High St., Hillsboro 45133-1182; **Fax:** (937) 393-6878

(330) 675-2650 **Grendell, Diane V.** (J Dist Ct of App 11th App Dist) 111 High St., N.E., Warren 44481; **Fax:** (330) 675-2655

(419) 636-2644 **Gretick, Anthony L.** (J Williams Cty Common Pleas Ct) One Courthouse Sq., Bryan 43506; **Fax:** (419) 636-9886; **E-mail:** gretick@email.msn.com

(216) 443-8736 **Griffin, Burt W.** (J Cuyahoga Cty Common Pleas Ct) 1200 Ontario St., Cleveland 44113-1678; **Fax:** (216) 348-4033

(937) 644-9102 **Grigsby, Michael J.** (J Marysville Munic Ct) 125 E. Sixth St., P.O. Box 322, Marysville 43040; **Fax:** (937) 644-1228

(740) 596-5480 **Grillo, N. Robert** (J Vinton Cty Probate/Juv Ct) Cthse., 100 E. Main St., McArthur 45651-1267; **Fax:** (740) 596-3438

(740) 592-3328 **Grim, William A.** (J Athens Cty Munic Ct) City Hall, Eight E. Washington St., Athens 45701-2498; **Fax:** (740) 592-3331

(419) 674-4362 **Grimslid, Gregory A.** (J Hardin Cty Munic Ct) 111 W. Franklin St., P.O. Box 250, Kenton 43326; **Fax:** (419) 674-4096

(216) 664-4984 **Groves, Emanuella D.** (J Cleveland Munic Ct) 1200 Ontario St., Cleveland 44113 Mailing Address: P.O. Box 94894, Cleveland 44101-4894; **Fax:** (216) 664-4283

(614) 645-8207 **Grubb, Janet A.** (J Franklin Cty Munic Ct) 375 S. High St., Columbus 43215-4520; **Fax:** (614) 645-8822

(513) 946-5169 **Guckenberger, Guy C.** (J Hamilton Cty Munic Ct) Cthse., 1000 Main St., Cincinnati 45202; **Fax:** (513) 946-5202

(937) 440-3936 **Gutmann, Elizabeth** (J Miami Munic Ct) Cthse., 201 W. Main St., Troy 45373; **Fax:** (937) 440-3911; **E-mail:** esg@woh.rr.com

(330) 451-7750 **Gwin, W. Scott** (J Dist Ct of App 5th App Dist) 110 Central Plaza S., Suite 320, Canton 44702-1411; **Fax:** (330) 451-7249

(330) 841-2525 **Gysegem, Thomas P.** (J Warren Munic Ct) 141 South St., P.O. Box 1550, Warren 44482-1550; **Fax:** (330) 841-2760; **E-mail:** tgysegem@warren.org

Judges Directory

(330) 451-7847 **Haas, John G.** (J Stark Cty Common Pleas Ct) 115 Central Plz., N., Suite 400, Canton 44702-1490; **Fax:** (330) 451-7740

(419) 435-8139 **Hadacek, John D.** (J Fostoria Munic Ct) 213 S. Main St., P.O. Box 985, Fostoria 44830; **Fax:** (419) 435-1150; **E-mail:** fosmunct@bright.net

(513) 732-7914 **Haddad, Victor M.** (J Clermont Cty Munic Ct) 4430 St. Rt. 222, Batavia 45103; **Fax:** (513) 732-7831

(937) 562-5280 **Hagler, Robert A.** (J Greene Cty Probate Ct) 45 N. Detroit St., Xenia 45385-2998; **Fax:** (937) 562-5316; **E-mail:** rhagler@co.greene.oh.us

(440) 576-3451 **Hague, Charles G.** (J Ashtabula Cty Probate Ct) 25 W. Jefferson, Jefferson 44047; **Fax:** (440) 576-3633

(440) 994-6000 (J Ashtabula Cty Juv Ct) 3816 Donahoe Dr., Ashtabula 44004; **Fax:** (440) 994-6021; **E-mail:** cghague@co.ashtabula.oh.us

(614) 645-8740 **Hale, Harland H.** (J Franklin Cty Munic Ct) 375 S. High St., Ctrm. 15C, Columbus 43215-4520; **Fax:** (614) 645-8255; **E-mail:** haleh@femcclerk.com

(419) 947-4515 **Hall, Howard E.** (J Morrow Cty Common Pleas Ct) Cthse., 48 E. High St., Mount Gilead 43338-1458; **Fax:** (419) 947-6341

(937) 496-7951 **Hall, Michael T.** (J Montgomery Cty Common Pleas Ct) 41 N. Perry St., P.O. Box 972, Dayton 45422-2170; **Fax:** (937) 225-5406; **E-mail:** hallm@montcourt.org

(740) 852-0756 **Hamilton, Glenn S.** (J Madison Cty Probate/Juv Ct) Cthse., Rm. 205, 1 N. Main St., London 43140; **Fax:** (740) 852-7134

(740) 335-0640 **Hammond, Nancy Drake** (J Fayette Cty Probate/Juv Ct) 110 E. Court St., Washington Court House 43160-1391; **Fax:** (740) 333-3598

(419) 213-4755 **Handwork, Peter M.** (J Dist Ct of App 6th App Dist) One Constitution Ave., Toledo 43624; **Fax:** (419) 213-4844; **E-mail:** handwork@co.lucas.oh.us

(937) 296-3327 **Hanna, Thomas M.** (J Kettering Munic Ct) 3600 Shroyer Rd., Kettering 45429; **Fax:** (937) 534-7017; **E-mail:** thomas.hanna@ketteringoh.org

(419) 734-4143 **Hany, Frederick C., II** (J Ottawa Munic Ct) 1860 E. Perry St., Port Clinton 43452; **Fax:** (419) 732-2862

(740) 355-8207 **Harcha, Howard H., III** (J Scioto Cty Common Pleas Ct) Cthse., 602 Seventh St., Portsmouth 45662-3951; **Fax:** (740) 355-8230; **E-mail:** hharcha@sciotocounty.net

(740) 687-6620 Ext. 35 **Harris, Patrick N.** (J Fairfield Cty Munic Ct) 104 E. Main St., P.O. Box 2390, Lancaster 43130; Fax: (740) 681-5014

(440) 593-7410 **Harris, Thomas E.** (J Conneaut Munic Ct) 290 Main St., Conneaut 44030; **Fax:** (440) 593-6402

(740) 472-0841 **Harris, William D.** (J Monroe Cty Common Pleas Ct) Cthse., 101 Main St., P.O. Box 563, Woodsfield 43793-1099; **Fax:** (740) 472-2518; **E-mail:** wmharris@1st.net

(740) 779-6662 **Harsha, William H.** (J Dist Ct of App 4th App Dist) 14 S. Paint St., Suite 38, Chillicothe 45601; **Fax:** (740) 779-6665

(419) 674-2256 **Hart, William D.** (J Hardin Cty Common Pleas Ct) One Courthouse Sq., Suite 370, Kenton 43326-2301; **Fax:** (419) 674-2264

(440) 286-2670 **Hassett, Mark J.** (J Chardon Munic Ct) 111 Water St., Chardon 44024-1201; **Fax:** (440) 286-2679

(513) 695-1159 **Heath, James J.** (J Warren Cty Common Pleas Ct) 500 Justice Dr., Lebanon 45036; **Fax:** (513) 695-1303

(937) 547-7325 **Hein, Jonathan P.** (J Darke Cty Common Pleas Ct) Cthse., 504 S. Broadway St., Greenville 45331; **Fax:** (937) 547-7323

(513) 946-5830 **Helmick, Dennis S.** (J Hamilton Cty Common Pleas Ct) 1000 Main St., Rm. 510, Cincinnati 45202; **Fax:** (513) 946-5833

(937) 333-4350 **Henderson, Carl S.** (J Dayton Munic Ct) 301 W. Third St., Dayton 45402; **Fax:** (937) 333-5077

(740) 283-8545 **Henderson, David E.** (J Jefferson Cty Common Pleas Ct) Cthse., 301 Market St., Steubenville 43952-2149; **Fax:** (740) 283-8686

(513) 946-3505 **Hendon, Sylvia Sieve** (J Dist Ct of App 1st App Dist) 230 E. Ninth St., 12th Fl., Cincinnati 45202; **Fax:** (513) 946-3411

(513) 867-5070 **Hendrickson, Robert A.** (J Butler Cty Ct) 9577 Beckett Rd., Suite 300, West Chester 45069; **Fax:** (513) 777-0558

(440) 285-2222 Ext. 2000 **Henry, Charles E.** (J Geauga Cty Probate/Juv Ct) Cthse. Annex, Suite 200, 231 Main St., Chardon 44024; **Fax:** (440) 285-5025

(937) 456-6204 **Henry, Paul D.** (J Eaton Munic Ct) 1199 Preble Dr., P.O. Box 65, Eaton 45320; **Fax:** (937) 456-4685

(937) 496-7231 **Hensley, James A., Jr.** (J Montgomery Cty Ct Area Two) 6111 Taylorsville Rd., Huber Heights 45424; **Fax:** (937) 496-7236; **E-mail:** hensljrj@montcnty.org

(419) 774-5570 **Henson, Jams D.** (J Richland Cty Common Pleas Ct) 50 Park Ave., E., Mansfield 44902-1888; **Fax:** (419) 774-5516; **E-mail:** judgehenson@kosinet.com

(614) 645-8287 **Herbert, Paul M.** (J Franklin Cty Munic Ct) 375 S. High St., Columbus 43215-4520; **Fax:** (614) 645-8822

(419) 739-6780 **Herman, Gary W.** (J Auglaize Cty Munic Ct) 201 S. Willipie St., P.O. Box 11, Wapakoneta 45895; **Fax:** (419) 738-7953; **E-mail:** gwherman@bright.net

(513) 732-7916 **Herman, Thomas R.** (J Clermont Cty Munic Ct) 4430 St. Rt. 222, Batavia 45103; **Fax:** (513) 732-7831

(740) 349-6652 **Higgins, Michael F.** (J Licking Cty Munic Ct) 40 W. Main St., Newark 43055; **Fax:** (740) 345-4250; **E-mail:** higginsmf@hotmail.com

(513) 946-3450 **Hildebrandt, Lee H., Jr.** (J Dist Ct of App 1st App Dist) 230 E. Ninth St., 12th Fl., Cincinnati 45202; **Fax:** (513) 946-3412; **E-mail:** lhildebrandt@cms.hamilton-co.org

(740) 922-4795 **Hillyer, Brad L.** (J Tuscarawas Cty Ct) 220 E. Third St., Uhrichsville 44683; **Fax:** (740) 922-7020

(330) 451-7448 **Hoffman, William B.** (J Dist Ct of App 5th App Dist) 110 Central Plaza S., Suite 320, Canton 44702-1411; **Fax:** (330) 451-7249

(614) 462-3770 **Hogan, Daniel T.** (J Franklin Cty Common Pleas Ct) 369 S. High St., Rm. 9D, Columbus 43215-4554; **Fax:** (614) 462-4480; **E-mail:** daniel_hogan@fccourts.org

(330) 375-2052 **Holcomb, John E.** (J Akron Munic Ct) 217 S. High St., Akron 44308-1611; **Fax:** (330) 375-2474; **E-mail:** holcojo@ci.akron.oh.us

(740) 702-3038 **Holmes, Nicholas H., Jr.** (J Ross Cty Common Pleas Ct) Cthse., 2 N. Paint St., Chillicothe 45601-3109; **Fax:** (740) 702-3018

(740) 286-3601   **Holzapfel, Leonard F.** (J Jackson Cty Common Pleas Ct) Cthse., Suite 6, 226 E. Main St., Jackson 45640; **Fax:** (740) 286-5203

(740) 455-7190   **Hooper, Jeffrey A.** (J Muskingum Cty Dom Rel Ct) 22 N. Fifth St., Zanesville 43701

(419) 562-2731   **Hoover, James L.** (J Crawford Munic Ct) 112 E. Mansfield St., P.O. Box 550, Bucyrus 44820-0550; **Fax:** (419) 562-7064; **E-mail:** hoov@bright.net

(330) 971-8280   **Hoover, Kim R.** (J Cuyahoga Falls Munic Ct) 2310 Second St., Cuyahoga Falls 44221; **Fax:** (330) 928-7722

(440) 329-5175   **Horvath, Frank J.** (J Lorain Cty Probate Ct) Lorain Cty. Justice Center, 6th Fl., 225 Court St., Elyria 44035; **Fax:** (440) 328-2157

(937) 393-2161   **Hoskins, Jeffrey J.** (J Highland Cty Common Pleas Ct General Div) 105 N. High St., Hillsboro 45133-1182; **Fax:** (937) 393-6878

(740) 622-2871   **Hostetler, David L.** (J Coshocton Munic Ct) 760 Chestnut St., Coshocton 43812-1294; **Fax:** (740) 623-5928; **E-mail:** judge@coshoctonmunicipalcourt.com

(330) 726-5546   **Houser, Joseph M.** (J Mahoning Cty Ct No 2) 127 Boardman-Canfield Rd., Youngstown 44512; **Fax:** (330) 740-2035; **E-mail:** jhouser@mbpu.com

(330) 451-7922   **Howard, Michael L.** (J Stark Cty Family Ct) 110 Central Plz., S., Suite 601, Canton 44702-1414; **Fax:** (330) 451-7837

(937) 496-7955   **Huffman, Mary Katherine** (J Montgomery Cty Common Pleas Ct) 41 N. Perry St., P.O. Box 972, Dayton 45422-2170; **Fax:** (937) 225-5406

(330) 643-2230   **Hunter, Judith** (J Summit Cty Common Pleas Ct) 209 S. High St., Akron 44308-1610

(330) 533-3643   **Hunter, Scott D.** (J Mahoning Cty Ct No 5) 72 N. Broad St., Canfield 44406; **Fax:** (330) 740-2034

(937) 547-7340   **Hurley, Roger L.** (J Darke Cty Munic Ct) Cthse., 3rd Fl., 504 S. Broadway St., Greenville 45331-1990; **Fax:** (937) 547-7378

(937) 562-6249   **Hurley, Steven L.** (J Greene Cty Dom Rel Ct) 595 Ledbetter Rd., Xenia 45385-2998; **Fax:** (937) 562-6233

(937) 562-4000   **Hutcheson, Robert W.** (J Greene Cty Juv Ct) 2100 Greene Way Blvd., Xenia 45385; **Fax:** (937) 562-4010

(419) 586-2122   **Ingraham, Jeffrey R.** (J Mercer Cty Common Pleas Ct) Cthse., Rm. 301, 101 N. Main St., Celina 45822; **Fax:** (419) 586-4000; **E-mail:** judge.ingraham@mercercountyohio.org

(330) 674-4901   **Irving, Jane** (J Holmes Cty Ct) One E. Jackson St., Suite 101, Millersburg 44654; **Fax:** (330) 674-5514

(330) 841-2525   **Ivanchak, Terry** (J Warren Munic Ct) 141 South St., P.O. Box 1550, Warren 44482-1550; **Fax:** (330) 841-2760; **E-mail:** tyivan@warren.org

(740) 687-7087   **Jackson, S. Farrell** (J Fairfield Cty Dom Rel Ct) Hall of Justice, 4th Fl., 224 E. Main St., Lancaster 43130; **Fax:** (740) 687-7169

(216) 681-2387   **Jackson, Warner** (Magis J East Cleveland Munic Ct) 14340 Euclid Ave., E., Cleveland 44112; **Fax:** (216) 681-2217

(330) 451-7307   **James, Jim D.** (J Stark Cty Family Ct) 110 Central Plz., S., Suite 601, Canton 44702-1414; **Fax:** (330) 451-7837; **E-mail:** judgejames@co.stark.oh.us

(330) 675-2605   **James, Richard L.** (J Trumbull Cty Family Ct) 220 S. Main St., Warren 44482; **Fax:** (330) 675-2322; **E-mail:** drjames@co.trumbull.oh.us

(440) 329-5518   **Janas, Thomas W.** (J Lorain Cty Common Pleas Ct) Lorain Cty. Justice Center, 225 Court St., Elyria 44035; **Fax:** (440) 284-3794

(440) 775-1751   **Januzzi, Thomas** (J Oberlin Munic Ct) 85 S. Main St., P.O. Box 179, Oberlin 44074-0179; **Fax:** (440) 775-0619

(216) 664-4978   **Jasper, Mabel M.** (J Cleveland Munic Ct) 1200 Ontario St., Cleveland 44113 Mailing Address: P.O. Box 94894, Cleveland 44101-4894; **Fax:** (216) 664-4283

(740) 223-4060   **Jenkins, Thomas K.** (J Marion Cty Probate/Juv/Dom Rel Ct) 222 W. Center St., Marion 43302; **Fax:** (740) 382-3798

(419) 213-4538   **Jensen, James D.** (J Lucas Cty Common Pleas Ct) Cthse., 700 Adams St., Toledo 43624-1678; **Fax:** (419) 213-4184

(330) 627-5049   **Johnston, Charles A.** (J Carroll Cty Ct) 119 S. Lisbon St., Suite 301, Carrollton 44615; **Fax:** (330) 627-3662; **E-mail:** judge@carrollcountycourt.org

(740) 286-2718   **Johnston, Lorene** (J Jackson Cty Munic Ct) 350 Portsmouth St., Suite 101, Jackson 45640; **Fax:** (740) 286-0679

(216) 664-4996   **Jones, Larry A.** (Pres & Admin J Cleveland Munic Ct) 1200 Ontario St., Cleveland 44113 Mailing Address: P.O. Box 94894, Cleveland 44101-4894; **Fax:** (216) 664-4283

(216) 443-8725   **Jones, Peggy Foley** (J Cuyahoga Cty Common Pleas Ct) 1200 Ontario St., Cleveland 44113-1678; **Fax:** (216) 348-4038

(740) 454-3269   **Joseph, William D.** (J Zanesville Munic Ct) 322 South St., P.O. Box 566, Zanesville 43702; **Fax:** (740) 455-0739; **E-mail:** wdjoseph@prodigy.net

(937) 981-2139   **Judkins, Robert J.** (J Highland Cty Ct) 300 Jefferson St., P.O. Box 378, Greenfield 45123; **Fax:** (937) 981-2130

(440) 232-3420   **Junkin, Peter J.** (J Bedford Munic Ct) 165 Center Rd., Bedford 44146-2818; **Fax:** (440) 232-2510

(216) 443-8809   **Karner, Cheryl S.** (J Cuyahoga Cty Dom Rel Ct) One W. Lakeside Ave., Cleveland 44113-1082; **Fax:** (216) 443-4943

(216) 443-6354   **Karpinski, Diane** (J Dist Ct of App 8th App Dist) Cuyahoga Cty. Cthse., Suite 202, 1 Lakeside Ave., Cleveland 44113-1085; **Fax:** (216) 443-2044

(330) 365-3266   **Kate, Linda A.** (J Tuscarawas Cty Probate/Juv Ct) Cthse., 101 E. High Ave., New Philadelphia 44663-2636; **Fax:** (330) 364-3190

(216) 681-2220   **Keenon, Una H.R.** (J East Cleveland Munic Ct) 14340 Euclid Ave., E., Cleveland 44112; **Fax:** (216) 681-2217

(740) 354-3283   **Kegley, Russell D.** (J Portsmouth Munic Ct) 728 Second St., Portsmouth 45662; **Fax:** (740) 353-6645

(419) 447-2982   **Kelbley, Michael P.** (J Seneca Cty Common Pleas Ct) Annex, Suite 4303, 117 E. Market St., Tiffin 44883; **Fax:** (419) 448-7103; **E-mail:** cpc1@acctiffin.com

(419) 354-9220   **Kelsey, Reeve W.** (J Wood Cty Common Pleas Ct No 2) One Courthouse Sq., Bowling Green 43402; **Fax:** (419) 354-9223; **E-mail:** rkelsey@co.wood.oh.us

(937) 440-3933   **Kemmer, Mel** (J Miami Munic Ct) Cthse., 201 W. Main St., Troy 45373; **Fax:** (937) 440-3911; **E-mail:** mkemmer@co.miami.oh.us

(513) 887-3788   **Kennedy, Sharon L.** (J Butler Cty Dom Rel Ct) Govt. Svces. Ctr., 2nd Fl., 315 High St., Hamilton 45011; **Fax:** (513) 785-5337; **E-mail:** kennedysl@butlercountyohio.org

Judges Directory

(216) 664-4990   **Keough, Kathleen A.** (J Cleveland Munic Ct) 1200 Ontario St., Cleveland 44113
Mailing Address: P.O. Box 94894, Cleveland 44101-4894; **Fax:** (216) 664-4283

(740) 283-8692   **Kerr, Samuel W.** (J Jefferson Cty Probate/Juv Ct) P.O. Box 549, Steubenville 43952-2184; **Fax:** (740) 283-8694

(937) 225-4384   **Kessler, John W.** (J Montgomery Cty Common Pleas Ct) 41 N. Perry St., P.O. Box 972,
Dayton 45422-2170; **Fax:** (937) 225-5406; **E-mail:** kesslerj@montcourt.org

(330) 830-1725   **Kettler, Richard T.** (J Massillon Munic Ct) 2 James Duncan Plz., Massillon 44646; **Fax:** (330) 830-1756

(216) 443-6355   **Kilbane, Mary Eileen** (J Dist Ct of App 8th App Dist) Cuyahoga Cty. Cthse., Suite 202,
1 Lakeside Ave., Cleveland 44113-1085; **Fax:** (216) 443-2044

(330) 725-9736   **Kimbler, James L.** (J Medina Cty Common Pleas Ct) 93 Public Sq., Medina 44256-2205;
Fax: (330) 764-8791; **E-mail:** kimbler@apk.net

(937) 496-7536   **King, Judith A.** (J Montgomery Cty Dom Rel Ct) 301 W. Third St., 2nd. Fl., Dayton 45422-4248;
Fax: (937) 496-7835; **E-mail:** kingj@mcohio.org

(419) 223-8501   **Kinworthy, David R.** (J Allen Cty Common Pleas Ct & Probate Ct) 301 N. Main St., P.O. Box 1243,
Lima 45801; **Fax:** (419) 221-3432

(419) 227-5531   (J Allen Cty Juv Ct) 1000 Wardhill Ave., P.O. Box 419, Lima 45802; **Fax:** (419) 222-7403

(740) 353-1095   **Kirsch, James W.** (J Scioto Cty Probate/Juv Ct) 602 Seventh St., Portsmouth 45662-3998; **Fax:** (740) 353-1095

(440) 350-2626   **Klammer, Ted R.** (J Lake Cty Probate Ct) Cthse., 25 N. Park Pl., Painesville 44077-3416; **Fax:** (440) 350-2628

(614) 462-3610   **Klatt, William A.** (Admin J Dist Ct of App 10th App Dist) 373 S. High St., 24th Fl.,
Columbus 43215-4578; **Fax:** (614) 462-7249

(216) 381-2880   **Kleri, Patricia Ann** (J South Euclid Munic Ct) 1349 S. Green Rd., South Euclid 44121; **Fax:** (216) 381-1195

(740) 474-7841   **Kline, Roger L.** (J Dist Ct of App 4th App Dist) 121-A W. Franklin St., Circleville 43113; **Fax:** (740) 474-6870

(740) 474-6026   **Knece, P. Randall** (J Pickaway Cty Common Pleas Ct) Cthse., 2nd Fl., 207 S. Court St.,
Circleville 43113; **Fax:** (740) 477-6334

(330) 742-8853   **Kobly, Elizabeth A.** (J Youngstown Munic Ct) 26 S. Phelps St., Youngstown 44501; **Fax:** (330) 742-8723

(216) 443-8685   **Koch, Judith Kilbane** (J Cuyahoga Cty Common Pleas Ct) 1200 Ontario St., Cleveland 44113-1678;
Fax: (216) 348-4032

(419) 774-5573   **Konstam, Robert L.** (J Richland Cty Dom Rel Ct) 50 Park Ave., E., 3rd Fl., Mansfield 44902-1894;
Fax: (419) 774-5574

(330) 675-2569   **Kontos, Peter J.** (J Trumbull Cty Common Pleas Ct) 161 High St., N.W., Warren 44481-1006;
Fax: (330) 675-2580

(330) 725-9740   **Kovack, Mary R.** (J Medina Cty Dom Rel Ct) 99 Public Sq., Medina 44256; **Fax:** (330) 764-8794;
E-mail: mrkovack@medinaco.org

(330) 740-2156   **Krichbaum, R. Scott** (J Mahoning Cty Common Pleas Ct) 120 Market St., Youngstown 44503-1710;
Fax: (330) 742-5898

(740) 833-2550   **Krueger, Everett H.** (J Delaware Cty Common Pleas Ct) 91 N. Sandusky St., Delaware 43015-1795;
Fax: (740) 833-2549

(513) 946-5760   **Kubicki, Charles, Jr.** (J Hamilton Cty Common Pleas Ct) 1000 Main St., Rm. 495, Cincinnati 45202;
Fax: (513) 946-5907

(330) 489-3210   **Kubilus, Richard J.** (J Canton Munic Ct) City Hall, 218 Cleveland Ave., S.W., Canton 44702;
Fax: (330) 471-8860; **E-mail:** rjkubilu@ci. canton.oh.us

(419) 245-1950   **Kuhlman, Timothy** (J Toledo Munic Ct) 555 N. Erie St., Toledo 43624; **Fax:** (419) 245-1802;
E-mail: tim.kuhlman@noris.org

(937) 225-4124   **Kuntz, Nick** (J Montgomery Cty Juv Ct) 303 W. Second St., Dayton 45422-4240; **Fax:** (937) 224-8603

(419) 448-5060   **Kutscher, Paul F., Jr.** (J Seneca Cty Probate/Juv Ct) 108 Jefferson St., Tiffin 44883-2898; **Fax:** (419) 448-5060

(740) 373-6623   **Lane, Norman E., Jr.** (J Washington Cty Common Pleas Ct) Cthse., 205 Putnam St.,
Marietta 45750-2922; **Fax:** (740) 373-5713

(937) 225-4055   **Langer, Dennis J.** (J Montgomery Cty Common Pleas Ct) 41 N. Perry St., P.O. Box 972,
Dayton 45422-2170; **Fax:** (937) 225-5406; **E-mail:** langerd@montcourt.org

(614) 387-9090   **Lanzinger, Judith A.** (Justice Supreme Ct) 65 S. Front St., 9th Fl., Columbus 43215-3431; **Fax:** (614) 387-9099

(330) 755-1800   **Lanzo, James R.** (J Struthers Munic Ct) 6 Elm St., Struthers 44471-1904; **Fax:** (330) 755-2790

(419) 221-5275   **Lauber, William G.** (J Lima Munic Ct) 109 N. Union St., P.O. Box 1529, Lima 45802-1529;
Fax: (419) 998-5526

(330) 823-6181   **Lavery, Robert G.** (J Alliance Munic Ct) 470 E. Market, Rm. 16, Alliance 44601; **Fax:** (330) 823-6183

(614) 462-3613   **Lazarus, Cynthia C.** (J Dist Ct of App 10th App Dist) 373 S. High St., 24th Fl., Columbus 43215-4578;
Fax: (614) 462-7249; **E-mail:** cclazarus@co.franklin.oh.us

(216) 289-2888   **LeBarron, Deborah Ann** (J Euclid Munic Ct) 555 E. 222nd St., Euclid 44123-2029;
Fax: (216) 289-8254; **E-mail:** dlebarron@ci.euclid.oh.us

(330) 674-5881   **Lee, Thomas C.** (J Holmes Cty Probate/Juv Ct) One E. Jackson St., Suite 201, Millersburg 44654;
Fax: (330) 674-5820

(330) 287-5427   **Leisy, Raymond E.** (J Wayne Cty Probate/Juv Ct) 107 W. Liberty St., Wooster 44691; **Fax:** (330) 287-5427

(419) 213-6824   **Lewandowski, David** (J Lucas Cty Dom Rel Ct) 429 N. Michigan St., Suite B, Toledo 43624-1689;
E-mail: dlewan@co.lucas.oh.us

(740) 342-1204   **Lewis, Linton D., Jr.** (J Perry Cty Common Pleas Ct) P.O. Box 7, New Lexington 43764; **Fax:** (740) 342-5500

(614) 462-4445   **Lias, Kay** (J Franklin Cty Dom Rel/Juv Ct) 373 S. High St., 6th Fl., Columbus 43215;
Fax: (614) 719-2118; **E-mail:** kalias @co.franklin.oh.us

(440) 329-5357   **Lilly, Paulette J.** (J Lorain Cty Dom Rel Ct) Justice Center, 4th Fl., 225 Court St., Elyria 44035-5629;
Fax: (440) 329-5438; **E-mail:** judgelilly@centurytel.net

(937) 440-6019   **Lindeman, Robert J.** (J Miami Cty Common Pleas Ct) Safety Bldg., 3rd Fl., 201 W. Main St.,
Troy 45373-3239; **Fax:** (937) 440-6011

(330) 451-7708   **Lioi, Sara E.** (J Stark Cty Common Pleas Ct) 115 Central Plz., N., Suite 400, Canton 44702-1490;
Fax: (330) 451-7740

(513) 946-9211   **Lipps, Thomas R.** (J Hamilton Cty Juv Ct) 800 Broadway, Cincinnati 45202-1225; **Fax:** (513) 946-9217;
E-mail: thomas.lipps@juvcourt.hamilton.co.org

(614) 645-8280   **Liston, Teresa L.** (J Franklin Cty Munic Ct) 375 S. High St., Columbus 43215-4520; **Fax:** (614) 645-8822

(937) 333-4369   **Littlejohn, Bill C.** (J Dayton Munic Ct) 301 W. Third St., Dayton 45402; **Fax:** (937) 333-4496

(440) 323-6545   **Locke-Graves, Lisa A.** (J Elyria Munic Ct) 328 Broad St., Elyria 44035-5577; **Fax:** (440) 322-2206

(330) 675-2564   **Logan, Andrew D.** (J Trumbull Cty Common Pleas Ct) 161 High St., N.W., Warren 44481-1006; **Fax:** (330) 675-2580

(330) 725-9119   **Lohn, John J.** (J Medina Cty Probate/Juv Ct) 93 Public Sq., Medina 44256-2205; **Fax:** (330) 725-9173

(740) 474-8451   **Long, Jan Michael** (J Pickaway Cty Probate/Juv Ct) Cthse., 207 S. Court St., Circleville 43113; **Fax:** (740) 477-3852; **E-mail:** jlong@pickaway.org

(740) 962-4031   **Lowe, Michael D.** (J Morgan Cty Ct) 37 E. Main St., McConnelsville 43756; **Fax:** (740) 962-2895

(440) 350-2100   **Lucci, Eugene A.** (J Lake Cty Common Pleas Ct) 47 N. Park Pl., P.O. Box 490, Painesville 44077

(937) 498-0011   **Luce, Donald G.** (J Sidney Munic Ct) 110 W. Court St., Sidney 45365
     Mailing Address: 201 W. Poplar St., Sidney 45365; **Fax:** (937) 498-8179; **E-mail:** dluce@sidneyoh.com

(419) 499-4689   **Lux, Paul G.** (J Erie Cty Ct) 150 W. Mason Rd., Milan 44846; **Fax:** (419) 499-3300

(513) 523-4748   **Lyons, Robert Hagen** (J Butler Cty Ct) 118 W. High St., Oxford 45056; **Fax:** (513) 523-4737

(440) 576-3683   **Mackey, Alfred W.** (J Ashtabula Cty Common Pleas Ct) 25 W. Jefferson St., Jefferson 44047-1092; **Fax:** (440) 576-1426

(440) 930-4103   **Mackin, John F.** (J Avon Lake Munic Ct) 32855 Walker Rd., Avon Lake 44012; **Fax:** (440) 930-4128

(513) 946-5112   **Mallory, William L.** (J Hamilton Cty Munic Ct) Cthse., 1000 Main St., Cincinnati 45202; **Fax:** (513) 946-5202

(330) 740-2310   **Maloney, Timothy P.** (J Mahoning Cty Probate Ct) 120 Market St., Youngstown 44503; **Fax:** (330) 740-2325

(740) 446-3842   **Malton, Thomas S.** (J Gallia Cty Probate/Juv Ct) Cthse., Rm. 1293, 18 Locust St., Gallipolis 45631-1244; **Fax:** (740) 446-3144

(216) 443-8698   **Mannen, Ann T.** (J Cuyahoga Cty Common Pleas Ct) 1200 Ontario St., Cleveland 44113-1678; **Fax:** (216) 348-4036

(937) 687-9099   **Manning, James L.** (J Montgomery Cty Ct Area One) 195 S. Clayton Rd., New Lebanon 45345; **Fax:** (937) 687-7119; **E-mail:** manning@montcnty.oh.org

(740) 670-5781   **Marcelain, Thomas M.** (J Licking Cty Common Pleas Ct) Cthse., Public Sq., Newark 43055; **E-mail:** tmarcelain@msmisp.com

(513) 946-5866   **Marsh, Melba D.** (J Hamilton Cty Common Pleas Ct) 1000 Main St., Rm. 330, Cincinnati 45202; **Fax:** (513) 946-5907

(740) 355-8301   **Marshall, William T.** (J Scioto Cty Common Pleas Ct) Cthse., 602 Seventh St., Portsmouth 45662-3951; **Fax:** (740) 353-1209

(740) 687-7059   **Martin, Chris A.** (J Fairfield Cty Common Pleas Ct) Hall of Justice, 224 E. Main St., Lancaster 43130-3879; **Fax:** (740) 687-0158

(513) 946-5790   **Martin, Steven E.** (J Hamilton Cty Common Pleas Ct) 1000 Main St., Rm. 340, Cincinnati 45202; **Fax:** (513) 946-5907

(330) 627-2450   **Martin, William J.** (J Carroll Cty Common Pleas Ct) P.O. Box 367, Carrollton 44615; **Fax:** (330) 627-0985

(614) 462-4453   **Mason, Jim** (Admin J Franklin Cty Dom Rel/Juv Ct) 373 S. High St., 6th Fl., Columbus 43215; **Fax:** (614) 719-2118; **E-mail:** james_mason@fccourts.org

(216) 443-8695   **Matia, David T.** (J Cuyahoga Cty Common Pleas Ct) 1200 Ontario St., Cleveland 44113-1678; **Fax:** (216) 348-4037

(513) 946-5108   **Mattingly, Elizabeth B.** (J Hamilton Cty Munic Ct) Cthse., 1000 Main St., Cincinnati 45202; **Fax:** (513) 946-5202; **E-mail:** ematting@hamilton-co.org

(419) 354-9600   **Mayberry, Alan** (J Wood Cty Common Pleas Ct No 4) One Courthouse Sq., Bowling Green 43402; **Fax:** (419) 354-9612

(614) 645-8286   **Maynard, W. Dwayne** (J Franklin Cty Munic Ct) 375 S. High St., Columbus 43215-4520; **Fax:** (614) 645-8822

(216) 664-4982   **Mays, Anita Laster** (J Cleveland Munic Ct) 1200 Ontario St., Cleveland 44113
     Mailing Address: P.O. Box 94894, Cleveland 44101-4894; **Fax:** (216) 664-4283

(813) 732-7104   **McBride, Jerry R.** (J Clermont Cty Common Pleas Ct) 270 Main St., Batavia 45103-3071; **Fax:** (513) 732-7050

(216) 443-8707   **McCafferty, Bridget M.** (J Cuyahoga Cty Common Pleas Ct) 1200 Ontario St., Cleveland 44113-1678; **Fax:** (216) 348-4033

(330) 375-2611   **McCarty, Alison** (J Akron Munic Ct) 217 S. High St., Akron 44308-1611; **Fax:** (330) 375-2642; **E-mail:** mccaral@ci.akron.oh.us

(419) 947-5045   **McClelland, Lee W.** (J Morrow Cty Munic Ct) 48 E. High St., Mount Gilead 43338; **Fax:** (419) 947-9161; **E-mail:** judgemac@rrohio.com

(937) 547-7350   **McClurg, Michael D.** (J Darke Cty Probate/Juv Ct) 300 Garst Ave., Greenville 45331; **Fax:** (937) 547-1945

(419) 599-5951   **McColley, Denise Herman** (J Henry Cty Dom Rel Ct) 660 N. Perry St., Suite 401, Napoleon 43545

(937) 225-4552   **McCollum, Alice O.** (J Montgomery Cty Probate Ct) 41 N. Perry St., Dayton 45422-2155; **Fax:** (937) 496-3181; **E-mail:** mccolluma@mcohio.org

(419) 245-1946   **McConnell, C. Allen** (J Toledo Munic Ct) 555 N. Erie St., Toledo 43624; **Fax:** (419) 245-1802; **E-mail:** callenmcc@noris.org

(216) 443-8745   **McCormick, Timothy P.** (J Cuyahoga Cty Common Pleas Ct) 1200 Ontario St., Cleveland 44113-1678; **Fax:** (216) 348-4034

(740) 533-4329   **McCown, Frank J.** (J Lawrence Cty Common Pleas Ct) Cthse., One Veteran's Sq., Ironton 45638; **Fax:** (740) 533-4377; **E-mail:** judgemac@hotmail.com

(419) 213-4560   **McDonald, Frederick H.** (J Lucas Cty Common Pleas Ct) Cthse., 700 Adams St., Toledo 43624-1678; **Fax:** (419) 213-4184

(216) 443-8756   **McDonnell, Nancy R.** (J Cuyahoga Cty Common Pleas Ct) 1200 Ontario St., Cleveland 44113-1678; **Fax:** (216) 348-4037

(740) 355-9497   **McFarland, Matthew W.** (J Dist Ct of App 4th App Dist) Scioto Cty. Cthse., 3rd Fl., 602 7th St., Portsmouth 45662; **Fax:** (740) 355-3934

(419) 668-6162   **McGimpsey, Earl R.** (J Huron Cty Common Pleas Ct) Two E. Main St., Norwalk 44857;
    Fax: (419) 663-4048; **E-mail:** judge@huroncountyclerk.com

(216) 443-8758   **McGinty, Timothy J.** (J Cuyahoga Cty Common Pleas Ct) 1200 Ontario St., Cleveland 44113-1678;
    Fax: (216) 348-4033

(419) 627-7750   **McGookey, Beverly K.** (J Erie Cty Probate Ct) 323 Columbus Ave., Sandusky 44870-2691; **Fax:** (419) 626-9120

(440) 329-5416   **McGough, Lynett M.** (J Lorain Cty Common Pleas Ct) Lorain Cty. Justice Center, 225 Court St.,
    Elyria 44035; **Fax:** (440) 284-3681

(614) 462-7241   **McGrath, Patrick M.** (J Dist Ct of App 10th App Dist) 373 S. High St., 24th Fl., Columbus 43215-4578;
    Fax: (614) 462-7249; **E-mail:** patrick_mcgrath@fccourts.org

(330) 335-1596   **McIlvaine, Stephen B.** (J Wadsworth Munic Ct) 120 Maple St., Wadsworth 44281; **Fax:** (330) 335-2723

(330) 675-2577   **McKay, W. Wyatt** (J Trumbull Cty Common Pleas Ct) 161 High St., N.W., Warren 44481-1006;
    Fax: (330) 675-2580

(937) 393-3022   **McKenna, David H.** (J Hillsboro Munic Ct) 130 Homestead Ave., Hillsboro 45133; **Fax:** (937) 393-0517

(216) 443-6377   **McMonagle, Christine T.** (J Dist Ct of App 8th App Dist) Cuyahoga Cty. Cthse., Suite 202,
    1 Lakeside Ave., Cleveland 44113-1085; **Fax:** (216) 443-2044

(216) 443-8675   **McMonagle, Richard J.** (Pres J Cuyahoga Cty Common Pleas Ct) 1200 Ontario St.,
    Cleveland 44113-1678; **Fax:** (216) 348-4038

(330) 861-7215   **McNulty, Michael J.** (J Barberton Munic Ct) Munic. Bldg., 576 W. Park Ave., Barberton 44203-2584;
    Fax: (330) 848-6779

(419) 826-5636   **McQuade, Colin J.** (J Fulton Cty Ct, Eastern Dist) 204 S. Main St., Swanton 43558-1091;
    Fax: (419) 825-3324; **E-mail:** cjmcquade@fultoncountyoh.com

(740) 446-3842   **Medley, William S.** (J Gallia Cty Probate/Juv Ct) Cthse., Rm. 1293, 18 Locust St., Gallipolis 45631-1244;
    Fax: (740) 446-3144; **E-mail:** juvjudge@gallianet.net

(440) 232-3420   **Melling, Brian J.** (J Bedford Munic Ct) 165 Center Rd., Bedford 44146-2818; **Fax:** (440) 232-2510

(937) 866-2203   **Messham, Robert E., Jr.** (J Miamisburg Munic Ct) 10 N. First St., Miamisburg 45342-2305;
    Fax: (937) 866-0135

(740) 286-6405   **Michael, Stephen D.** (J Jackson Cty Probate/Juv Ct) Cthse., 226 E. Main St., Jackson 45640;
    Fax: (740) 288-4836

(440) 204-2159   **Mihok, Mark** (J Lorain Munic Ct) 100 W. Erie Ave., 2nd Fl., Lorain 44052; **Fax:** (440) 204-2162

(330) 742-8855   **Milich, Robert P.** (J Youngstown Munic Ct) 26 S. Phelps St., Youngstown 44501; **Fax:** (330) 742-8716;
    E-mail: bobmilich@aol.com

(330) 287-5650   **Miller, Stuart K.** (J Wayne Munic Ct) 215 N. Grant St., Wooster 44691-3499; **Fax:** (330) 263-4043

(440) 350-2662   **Mitrovich, Paul H.** (J Lake Cty Common Pleas Ct) 47 N. Park Pl., P.O. Box 490, Painesville 44077

(513) 946-5138   **Mock, Russell J.** (J Hamilton Cty Munic Ct) Cthse., 1000 Main St., Cincinnati 45202; **Fax:** (513) 946-5202

(740) 385-3615   **Mong, Frederick E.** (J Hocking Cty Probate/Juv Ct) 1 E. Main St., Logan 43138-1288;
    Fax: (740) 385-6892; **E-mail:** fmong@co.hocking.oh.us

(937) 328-2626   **Monnin, Joseph N.** (J Clark Cty Juv Ct) 101 E. Columbia St., Springfield 45502; **Fax:** (937) 328-2639;
    E-mail: ccjuvcourt@cs.com

(216) 491-1300   **Montgomery, K.J.** (J Shaker Heights Munic Ct) 3355 Lee Rd., Cleveland 44120-3499; **Fax:** (216) 491-1314

(937) 328-3773   **Moody, Denise L.** (J Clark Cty Munic Ct) 50 E. Columbia St., Springfield 45502-1116;
    Fax: (937) 328-3779

(419) 734-6791   **Moon, Paul C.** (J Ottawa Cty Common Pleas Ct General Div) 315 Madison St., Rm. 301,
    Port Clinton 43452-1936; **Fax:** (419) 734-6875; **E-mail:** amadeus43452@yahoo.com

(330) 643-2259   **Moore, Carla** (J Dist Ct of App 9th App Dist) 161 S. High St., Suite 504, Akron 44308-1602; **Fax:** (330) 643-2394

(216) 664-4972   **Moore, Lauren C.** (J Cleveland Munic Ct) 1200 Ontario St., Cleveland 44113
    Mailing Address: P.O. Box 94894, Cleveland 44101-4894; **Fax:** (216) 664-4283

(937) 296-2542   **Moore, Robert L.** (J Kettering Munic Ct) 3600 Shroyer Rd., Kettering 45429; **Fax:** (937) 534-7017;
    E-mail: moore136@yahoo.com

(740) 432-9262   **Moorehead, Robert S., Jr.** (J Guernsey Cty Probate Ct) Cthse., Dept. D-203, 801 E. Wheeling Ave.,
    Cambridge 43725; **Fax:** (740) 439-5278

(614) 387-9010   **Moyer, Thomas J.** (Chief Justice Supreme Ct) 65 S. Front St., 9th Fl., Columbus 43215-3431;
    E-mail: moyert@sconet.state.oh.us

(419) 592-5926   **Muehlfeld, Keith P.** (J Henry Cty Common Pleas Ct) 660 N. Perry St., P.O. Box 70,
    Napoleon 43545-1747; **Fax:** (419) 599-0803

(330) 643-2239   **Murphy, James E.** (J Summit Cty Common Pleas Ct) 209 S. High St., Akron 44308-1610

(440) 323-4903   **Musson, John R.** (J Elyria Munic Ct) 328 Broad St., Elyria 44035-5577; **Fax:** (440) 323-4012

(513) 946-5102   **Myers, Beth A.** (J Hamilton Cty Common Pleas Ct) 1000 Main St., Rm. 370, Cincinnati 45202;
    Fax: (513) 946-5907

(513) 946-5960   **Nadel, Norbert A.** (J Hamilton Cty Common Pleas Ct) 1000 Main St., Rm. 560, Cincinnati 45202;
    Fax: (513) 946-5907

(513) 887-3290   **Nastoff, Daniel (Andy)** (J Butler Cty Common Pleas Ct) Govt. Svces. Ctr., 3rd Fl., 315 High St.,
    Hamilton 45011; **Fax:** (513) 785-6582; **E-mail:** nastoffa@butlercountyohio.org

(740) 732-4045   **Nau, John W.** (J Noble Cty Common Pleas Ct) 300 Cthse., Caldwell 43724; **Fax:** (740) 732-0100

(513) 946-5840   **Nelson, Fred** (J Hamilton Cty Common Pleas Ct) 1000 Main St., Rm. 380, Cincinnati 45202;
    Fax: (513) 946-5907

(937) 328-3763   **Nevius, Eugene S.** (J Clark Cty Munic Ct) 50 E. Columbia St., Springfield 45502-1116;
    Fax: (937) 328-3779

(937) 484-1027   **Newlin, John C.** (J Champaign Cty Probate/Juv Ct) 200 N. Main St., Urbana 43078

(216) 475-5045   **Nicastro, Deborah J.** (J Garfield Heights Munic Ct) 5555 Turney Rd., Cleveland 44125-3778;
    Fax: (216) 475-3087; **E-mail:** dnicastro@ghmc.org

(740) 852-9568   **Nichols, Robert D.** (J Madison Cty Common Pleas Ct) One N. Main St., P.O. Box 527,
    London 43140-0527; **Fax:** (740) 852-7144

(740) 439-5585   **Nicholson, John Mark** (J Cambridge Munic Ct) 134 Southgate Pkwy., Cambridge 43725; **Fax:** (740) 439-5666

(513) 887-3318   **Niehaus, David J.** (J Butler Cty Juv Ct) 280 N. Fair Ave., Hamilton 45011; **Fax:** (513) 887-3698

(513) 946-5835   **Niehaus, Richard A.** (J Hamilton Cty Common Pleas Ct) 1000 Main St., Rm. 520, Cincinnati 45202; **Fax:** (513) 946-5907

(419) 424-7008   **Niemeyer, Joseph H.** (J Hancock Cty Common Pleas Ct) 300 S. Main St., Findlay 45840-3345; **Fax:** (419) 424-7437

(419) 523-3110   **Niese, Chad** (J Putnam Cty Ct) Cthse., 245 E. Main St., Ottawa 45875-1956; **Fax:** (419) 523-5284; **E-mail:** cniese@who.rr.com

(330) 297-3629   **Nome, William A.** (J Portage Cty Munic Ct) Ravenna Div., 203 W. Main St., P.O. Box 958, Ravenna 44266-0958; **Fax:** (330) 298-3033

(419) 636-6939   **North, Kent L.** (J Bryan Munic Ct) 1399 E. High St., P.O. Box 546, Bryan 43506-1819; **Fax:** (419) 636-3417

(740) 942-8500   **Nunner, Michael K.** (J Harrison Cty Common Pleas Ct) Cthse., 100 W. Market St., Cadiz 43907-1132; **Fax:** (740) 942-3006

(740) 373-4474   **Nuzum, Milt, III** (J Marietta Munic Ct) 301 Putnam St., P.O. Box 615, Marietta 45750-1615; **Fax:** (740) 373-2547; **E-mail:** judge@mariettacourt.com

(419) 627-5975   **O'Brien, Erich J.** (J Sandusky Munic Ct) 222 Meigs St., Sandusky 44870; **Fax:** (419) 627-5950

(937) 599-7260   **O'Connor, Mark S.** (J Logan Cty Common Pleas Ct) 101 S. Main St., Rm. 18, Bellefontaine 43311-3101; **Fax:** (937) 593-3379; **E-mail:** mo'connor@co.logan.oh.us

(614) 387-9060   **O'Connor, Maureen** (Justice Supreme Ct) 65 S. Front St., 9th Fl., Columbus 43215-3431

(614) 387-9030   **O'Donnell, Terrence** (Justice Supreme Ct) 65 S. Front St., 9th Fl., Columbus 43215-3431

(330) 365-3213   **O'Farrell, Edward E.** (J Tuscarawas Cty Common Pleas Ct) Cthse., 101 E. High Ave., New Philadelphia 44663-2599; **E-mail:** ofarrell@co.tuscarawas.oh.us

(216) 443-8815   **O'Malley, Kathleen** (J Cuyahoga Cty Dom Rel Ct) One W. Lakeside Ave., Cleveland 44113-1082; **Fax:** (216) 443-4943

(419) 523-3110   **O'Malley, Michael E.** (J Putnam Cty Ct) Cthse., 245 E. Main St., Ottawa 45875-1956; **Fax:** (419) 523-5284; **E-mail:** momalley@woh.rr.com

(937) 328-2467   **O'Neill, Richard** (J Clark Cty Common Pleas Ct) Cthse., 101 N. Limestone St., Springfield 45502-1120; **Fax:** (937) 328-2674

(330) 675-2650   **O'Neill, William M.** (J Dist Ct of App 11th App Dist) 111 High St., N.E., Warren 44481; **Fax:** (330) 675-2655; **E-mail:** wmoneill-@11thappeal.co.trumbull.oh.us

(330) 675-2650   **O'Toole, Colleen M.** (J Dist Ct of App 11th App Dist) 111 High St., N.E., Warren 44481; **Fax:** (330) 675-2655

(513) 695-1370   **Oda, Donald E., II** (J Warren Cty Ct) 550 Justice Dr., Lebanon 45036; **Fax:** (513) 695-2990

(513) 695-1340   **Oliver, Timothy A.** (J Warren Cty Dom Rel Ct) 500 Justice Dr., Lebanon 45036-2398; **Fax:** (513) 695-2929

(513) 887-3286   **Oney, Patricia** (J Butler Cty Common Pleas Ct) Govt. Svces. Ctr., 3rd Fl., 315 High St., Hamilton 45011; **Fax:** (513) 887-5646; **E-mail:** oneyps@butlercountyohio.org

(419) 294-3809   **Osborn, Thomas E.** (J Upper Sandusky Munic Ct) 119 N. Seventh St., Upper Sandusky 43351; **Fax:** (419) 209-0474

(419) 213-4565   **Osowik, Thomas J.** (J Lucas Cty Common Pleas Ct) Cthse., 700 Adams St., Toledo 43624-1678; **Fax:** (419) 213-4184

(419) 872-7900   **Osterud, S. Dwight** (J Perrysburg Munic Ct) 300 Walnut St., Perrysburg 43551; **Fax:** (419) 872-7905; **E-mail:** sdosterud@ci.perrysburg.oh.us

(513) 946-3444   **Painter, Mark P.** (J Dist Ct of App 1st App Dist) 230 E. Ninth St., 12th Fl., Cincinnati 45202; **Fax:** (513) 946-3411; **E-mail:** mpainter@cms.hamilton-co.org

(513) 946-9020   **Panioto, Ronald A.** (J Hamilton Cty Dom Rel Ct) 800 Broadway, Rm. 225, Cincinnati 45202; **Fax:** (513) 946-9021

(419) 213-4755   **Parish, Dennis M.** (J Dist Ct of App 6th App Dist) One Constitution Ave., Toledo 43624; **Fax:** (419) 213-4844

(513) 398-7901   **Parker, George** (J Mason Munic Ct) 5950 Mason Montgomery Rd., Mason 45040; **Fax:** (513) 459-8085

(937) 645-3015   **Parrott, Richard E.** (J Union Cty Common Pleas Ct) Cthse., 215 W. Fifth St., P.O. Box 723, Marysville 43040; **Fax:** (937) 645-3149; **E-mail:** parrott@urec.net

(513) 785-5801   **Pater, Charles L.** (J Butler Cty Common Pleas Ct) Govt. Svces. Ctr., 3rd Fl., 315 High St., Hamilton 45011; **Fax:** (513) 785-6582; **E-mail:** patercl@butlercountyohio.org

(740) 533-4372   **Payne, C. David** (J Lawrence Cty Probate/Juv Ct) Cthse., One Veteran's Sq., Ironton 45638-1585; **Fax:** (740) 533-4412

(419) 755-9616   **Payton, Jeff** (J Mansfield Munic Ct) 30 N. Diamond St., Mansfield 44902; **Fax:** (419) 755-9647

(419) 739-6771   **Pepple, Frederick D.** (J Auglaize Cty Common Pleas Ct) 201 Willipie St., Suite 217, Wapakoneta 45895-1994; **Fax:** (419) 739-6771

(740) 472-5181   **Peters, James W.** (J Monroe Cty Ct) 101 N. Main St., Rm. 35, Woodsfield 43793; **Fax:** (740) 472-2526; **E-mail:** judgejpl@1st.net

(614) 462-4049   **Petree, Charles R.** (J Dist Ct of App 10th App Dist) 373 S. High St., 24th Fl., Columbus 43215-6313; **Fax:** (614) 462-7249; **E-mail:** crpetree@co.franklin.oh.us

(419) 698-7009   **Petroff, Donald Z.** (J Oregon Munic Ct) 5330 Seaman Rd., Oregon 43616; **Fax:** (419) 698-7013

(614) 387-9020   **Pfeifer, Paul E.** (Justice Supreme Ct) 65 S. Front St., 9th Fl., Columbus 43215-3431

(614) 462-3811   **Pfeiffer, Beverly Y.** (J Franklin Cty Common Pleas Ct) 369 S. High St., Rm. 8C, Columbus 43215-4554; **Fax:** (614) 462-4480; **E-mail:** beverly_pfeiffer@fccourts.org

(216) 664-4989   **Pianka, Raymond L.** (J Cleveland Munic Ct Housing Ct Div) 1200 Ontario St., Cleveland 44113 Mailing Address: P.O. Box 94894, Cleveland 44101-4894; **Fax:** (216) 664-4283

(740) 852-1669   **Picken, R. David** (J Madison Munic Ct) P.O. Box 646, London 43140; **Fax:** (740) 852-0812

(937) 333-4375   **Pickrel, John S.** (J Dayton Munic Ct) 301 W. Third St., Dayton 45402; **Fax:** (937) 333-5079

(419) 399-2792   **Pieper, Timothy R.** (J Paulding Cty Ct) 201 E. Caroline St., Suite 2, Paulding 45879-1204; **Fax:** (419) 399-3421

(740) 622-1837   **Pierce, C. Fenning** (J Coshocton Cty Probate/Juv Ct) 426 Main St., Coshocton 43812-1593; **Fax:** (740) 623-6514

(937) 496-7231   **Piergies, James D.** (J Montgomery Cty Ct Area Two) 6111 Taylorsville Rd., Huber Heights 45424; **Fax:** (937) 496-7236; **E-mail:** piergiesj@montcnty.org

Judges Directory

(419) 213-4755   **Pietrykowski, Mark L.** (J Dist Ct of App 6th App Dist) One Constitution Ave., Toledo 43624; **Fax:** (419) 213-4844; **E-mail:** pietry@co.lucas.oh.us

(330) 424-7777   **Pike, C. Ashley** (J Columbiana Cty Common Pleas Ct) Cthse., 105 S. Market St., Lisbon 44432; **Fax:** (330) 424-3960; **E-mail:** apike@ccclerk.org

(419) 433-5430   **Pisano, Ralph C., Jr.** (J Huron Munic Ct) 417 Main St., Huron 44839; **Fax:** (419) 433-5120

(330) 297-3858   **Pittman, Laurie J.** (J Portage Cty Common Pleas Ct) Cthse., 203 W. Main St., Ravenna 44266-2778; **Fax:** (330) 297-5370

(216) 443-8728   **Pokorny, Thomas J.** (J Cuyahoga Cty Common Pleas Ct) 1200 Ontario St., Cleveland 44113-1678; **Fax:** (216) 348-4038

(419) 354-9210   **Pollex, Robert C.** (J Wood Cty Common Pleas Ct No 1) One Courthouse Sq., Bowling Green 43402; **Fax:** (419) 354-7626; **E-mail:** rpollex@co.wood.oh.us

(614) 645-7745   **Pollitt, H. William, Jr.** (J Franklin Cty Munic Ct) 375 S. High St., Columbus 43215-4520; **Fax:** (614) 645-8822

(330) 489-3288   **Poulos, John A.** (J Canton Munic Ct) City Hall, 218 Cleveland Ave., S.W., Canton 44702; **Fax:** (330) 471-8860

(513) 695-2948   **Powell, Michael E.** (J Warren Cty Probate/Juv Ct) 570 Justice Dr., Lebanon 45036-2361; **Fax:** (513) 695-2948; **E-mail:** poweme@co.warren.oh.us

(513) 425-6609   **Powell, Stephen W.** (J Dist Ct of App 12th App Dist) 1001 Reinartz Blvd., P.O. Box 1009, Middletown 45042-1901; **Fax:** (513) 425-8751; **E-mail:** stephen@twelfth.courts.state.oh.us

(513) 695-1370   **Powers, Dallas P.** (J Warren Cty Ct) 550 Justice Dr., Lebanon 45036; **Fax:** (513) 695-2990; **E-mail:** poweda@co.warren.oh.us

(614) 462-5775   **Preisse, Dana Suzanne** (J Franklin Cty Dom Rel/Juv Ct) 373 S. High St., 6th Fl., Columbus 43215; **Fax:** (614) 719-2118; **E-mail:** dana_preisse@fccourts.org

(419) 424-7803   **Preston, Vernon L.** (J Findlay Munic Ct) Munic. Bldg., Rm. 206, 318 Dorney Plaza, Findlay 45840; **Fax:** (419) 424-7803; **E-mail:** vpreston@ci.findlay.oh.us

(937) 687-9099   **Price-Testerman, Connie S.** (J Montgomery Cty Ct Area One) 195 S. Clayton Rd., New Lebanon 45345; **Fax:** (937) 687-7119; **E-mail:** pricejd@aol.com

(419) 213-4775   **Puffenberger, Jack R.** (J Lucas Cty Probate Ct) Cthse., Suite 200, 700 Adams St., Toledo 43624-1676; **Fax:** (419) 213-4764; **E-mail:** judgepuff@lucas-co-probate-ct.org

(330) 643-2080   **Quinn, John P.** (J Summit Cty Dom Rel Ct) 209 S. High St., Akron 44308-1610; **Fax:** (330) 643-2126

(419) 885-8987   **Ramey, M. Scott** (J Sylvania Munic Ct) 6700 Monroe St., Sylvania 43560; **Fax:** (419) 885-8987

(419) 674-2230   **Rapp, James S.** (J Hardin Cty Probate/Juv Ct) One Courthouse Sq., Suite 210, Kenton 43326-2301; **Fax:** (419) 674-2274

(937) 328-2480   **Rastatter, Douglas M.** (J Clark Cty Common Pleas Ct) Cthse., 101 N. Limestone St., Springfield 45502-1120; **Fax:** (937) 328-2674

(419) 213-6717   **Ray, James A.** (J Lucas Cty Juv Ct) 1801 Spielbusch Ave., Toledo 43624; **Fax:** (413) 213-6898

(419) 352-5263   **Reddin, Mark B.** (J Bowling Green Munic Ct) 711 S. Dunbridge Rd., P.O. Box 326, Bowling Green 43402-0326; **Fax:** (419) 352-9407; **E-mail:** bfmunict@wcnet.org

(614) 462-7200   **Reece, Guy L., II** (J Franklin Cty Common Pleas Ct) 369 S. High St., Rm. 7A, Columbus 43215-4554; **Fax:** (614) 462-4480

(419) 223-8525   **Reed, Jeffrey L.** (J Allen Cty Common Pleas Ct) 333 N. Main St., P.O. Box 1243, Lima 45802; **Fax:** (419) 224-9269

(330) 451-7715   **Reinbold, Richard D., Jr.** (J Stark Cty Common Pleas Ct) 115 Central Plz., N., Suite 400, Canton 44702-1490; **Fax:** (330) 451-7740

(419) 448-5412   **Repp, Mark E.** (J Tiffin Munic Ct) 51 E. Market St., P.O. Box 694, Tiffin 44883; **Fax:** (419) 448-5419

(614) 387-9040   **Resnick, Alice Robie** (Justice Supreme Ct) 65 S. Front St., 9th Fl., Columbus 43215-3431; **E-mail:** resnicka@sconet.state.oh.us

(330) 675-2650   **Rice, Cynthia Westcott** (J Dist Ct of App 11th App Dist) 111 High St., N.E., Warren 44481; **Fax:** (330) 675-2655

(330) 448-6310   **Rice, Ronald J.** (J Trumbull Cty Ct Eastern Dist) 7130 Brookwood Dr., Brookfield 44403; **Fax:** (330) 448-6310; **E-mail:** rjcolpa@msn.com

(419) 663-6771   **Ridge, John S.** (J Norwalk Munic Ct) 45 N. Linwood Ave., Norwalk 44857; **Fax:** (419) 663-6749; **E-mail:** jjsr@accnorwalk.com

(937) 687-9099   **Riley, Adele** (J Montgomery Cty Ct Area One) 195 S. Clayton Rd., New Lebanon 45345; **Fax:** (937) 687-7119; **E-mail:** rileya@mcohio.org

(513) 732-7050   **Ringland, Robert P.** (J Clermont Cty Common Pleas Ct) 270 Main St., Batavia 45103-3071; **Fax:** (513) 732-7050

(330) 675-2341   **Rintala, Pamela A.** (J Trumbull Cty Family Ct) 220 S. Main St., Warren 44482; **Fax:** (330) 675-2322; **E-mail:** drrintal@co.trumbull.oh.us

(330) 332-0297   **Roberts, Robert C.** (J Columbiana Cty Munic Ct Eastern Div) 31 N. Market St., East Palestine 44413; **Fax:** (330) 426-6328

(330) 332-0297   (J Columbiana Cty Munic Ct Northwest) 130 Penn Ave., Salem 44460-3125; **Fax:** (330) 332-0904

(330) 332-0297   (J Columbiana Cty Munic Ct Southwest) 41 N. Park Ave., Lisbon 44432; **Fax:** (330) 424-6658

(419) 337-9212   **Robinson, Jeffrey L.** (J Fulton Cty Ct, Western Dist) 224 S. Fulton St., Wauseon 43567-1352; **Fax:** (419) 337-9286

(216) 348-4810   **Rocco, Kenneth A.** (J Dist Ct of App 8th App Dist) Cuyahoga Cty. Cthse., Suite 202, 1 Lakeside Ave., Cleveland 44113-1085; **Fax:** (216) 443-2044

(513) 887-3294   **Rogers, Randy T.** (J Butler Cty Probate Ct) Cthse., 2nd Fl., 101 High St., Hamilton 45011; **Fax:** (513) 887-3629; **E-mail:** rogersr@butlercountyohio.org

(419) 223-1861   **Rogers, Richard M.** (J Dist Ct of App 3rd App Dist) 204 N. Main St., Lima 45801; **Fax:** (419) 224-3828

(419) 782-5756   **Rohrs, John T., III** (J Defiance Munic Ct) 324 Perry St., Defiance 43512-2194; **Fax:** (419) 782-2018

(513) 785-7300   **Rosmarin, John G.** (J Hamilton Munic Ct) One Renaissance Center, 2nd. Fl., 345 High St., Hamilton 45011; **Fax:** (513) 785-7315

(937) 599-6127   **Ross, John L.** (J Bellefontaine Munic Ct) 226 W. Columbus Ave., Bellefontaine 43311; **Fax:** (937) 599-2488

(440) 329-5570   **Rothgery, Christopher R.** (J Lorain Cty Common Pleas Ct) Lorain Cty. Justice Center, 225 Court St., Elyria 44035; **Fax:** (440) 284-3680

(419) 424-7009   **Routson, Reginald J.** (J Hancock Cty Common Pleas Ct) 300 S. Main St., Findlay 45840-3345; **Fax:** (419) 424-7436

(937) 382-3640   **Rudduck, John W.** (J Clinton Cty Common Pleas Ct) Cthse., 46 S. South St., Wilmington 45177; **Fax:** (937) 383-3455; **E-mail:** cpjg@erinet.com

(513) 946-5850   **Ruehlman, Robert P.** (J Hamilton Cty Common Pleas Ct) 1000 Main St., Rm. 300, Cincinnati 45202; **Fax:** (513) 946-5907

(513) 746-2858   **Ruppert, James D.** (J Franklin Munic Ct) 1 Benjamin Franklin Way, P.O. Box 292, Franklin 45005; **Fax:** (513) 743-7751; **E-mail:** jruppert@franklinohio.org

(513) 946-5133   **Russell, Heather** (J Hamilton Cty Munic Ct) Cthse., 1000 Main St., Cincinnati 45202; **Fax:** (513) 946-5202

(216) 443-8849   **Russo, Anthony J.** (J Cuyahoga Cty Dom Rel Ct) One W. Lakeside Ave., Cleveland 44113-1082; **Fax:** (216) 443-4943

(216) 443-8746   **Russo, Joseph D.** (J Cuyahoga Cty Common Pleas Ct) 1200 Ontario St., Cleveland 44113-1678; **Fax:** (216) 348-4032

(216) 443-8408   **Russo, Joseph F.** (J Cuyahoga Cty Juv Ct) 2163 E. 22nd St., Cleveland 44115

(216) 443-8757   **Russo, Michael J.** (J Cuyahoga Cty Common Pleas Ct) 1200 Ontario St., Cleveland 44113-1678; **Fax:** (216) 348-4037

(216) 443-8688   **Russo, Nancy M.** (J Cuyahoga Cty Common Pleas Ct) 1200 Ontario St., Cleveland 44113-1678; **Fax:** (216) 348-4036

(419) 782-4181   **Ruyle, Stephen W.** (J Defiance Cty Probate/Juv Ct) 221 Clinton St., Defiance 43512-2182; **Fax:** (419) 782-2437

(614) 462-4054   **Sadler, Lisa L.** (J Dist Ct of App 10th App Dist) 373 S. High St., 24th Fl., Columbus 43215-4578; **Fax:** (614) 462-7249; **E-mail:** lisa_sadler@fccourts.org

(216) 443-8735   **Saffold, Shirley Strickland** (J Cuyahoga Cty Common Pleas Ct) 1200 Ontario St., Cleveland 44113-1678; **Fax:** (216) 348-4036

(513) 887-3283   **Sage, Michael J.** (J Butler Cty Common Pleas Ct) Govt. Svces. Ctr., 3rd Fl., 315 High St., Hamilton 45011; **Fax:** (513) 887-3285; **E-mail:** sagem@butlercountyohio.org

(614) 645-8204   **Salerno, Amy** (J Franklin Cty Munic Ct) 375 S. High St., Columbus 43215-4520; **Fax:** (614) 645-8822; **E-mail:** amy_salerno@fccourts.org

(740) 596-5000   **Salter, James P.** (J Vinton Cty Ct) Cthse., 100 E. Main St., McArthur 45651

(419) 334-6169   **Sargeant, Harry A., Jr.** (J Sandusky Cty Common Pleas Ct) Cthse., 100 N. Park Ave., Fremont 43420-2454; **Fax:** (419) 334-6122; **E-mail:** judge2@co.sandusky.oh.us

(740) 699-2137   **Sargus, Jennifer L.** (J Belmont Cty Common Pleas Ct) Cthse., 101 W. Main St., St. Clairsville 43950-1154

(740) 769-2903   **Scarpone, David J.** (J Jefferson Cty Ct No 3) 6 Liberty St., P.O. Box 495, Dillonvale 43917; **Fax:** (740) 769-7640

(419) 342-2896   **Schaefer, Jon P.** (J Shelby Munic Ct) 18 W. Main St., Shelby 44875; **Fax:** (419) 342-6404

(419) 586-6491   **Scheer, James J.** (J Celina Munic Ct) 202 N. Main St., P.O. Box 362, Celina 45822-0362; **Fax:** (419) 586-4735

(740) 354-3283   **Schisler, Richard T.** (J Portsmouth Munic Ct) 728 Second St., Portsmouth 45662; **Fax:** (740) 353-6645

(419) 782-5931   **Schmenk, Joseph N.** (J Defiance Cty Common Pleas Ct) 221 Clinton St., P.O. Box 386, Defiance 43512-2182; **Fax:** (419) 782-2437

(937) 498-7233   **Schmitt, John D.** (J Shelby Cty Common Pleas Ct) Cthse., 100 E. Court St., P.O. Box 947, Sidney 45365-0947; **Fax:** (937) 498-7824

(614) 462-3664   **Schneider, Charles** (J Franklin Cty Common Pleas Ct) 369 S. High St., Rm. 9B, Columbus 43215-4554; **Fax:** (614) 462-4480

(513) 946-5117   **Schweikert, Mark** (J Hamilton Cty Common Pleas Ct) 1000 Main St., Rm. 320, Cincinnati 45202; **Fax:** (513) 946-5907

(330) 643-2628   **Shapiro, Marvin** (J Summit Cty Common Pleas Ct) 209 S. High St., Akron 44308-1610

(419) 223-1861   **Shaw, Stephen R.** (Admin J Dist Ct of App 3rd App Dist) 204 N. Main St., Lima 45801; **Fax:** (419) 224-3828

(419) 334-6170   **Sherck, James R.** (J Sandusky Cty Common Pleas Ct) Cthse., 100 N. Park Ave., Fremont 43420-2454; **Fax:** (419) 334-6171; **E-mail:** judge1@co.sandusky.oh.us

(614) 462-3770   **Sheward, Richard S.** (J Franklin Cty Common Pleas Ct) 369 S. High St., Rm. 9C, Columbus 43215-4554; **Fax:** (614) 462-4480; **E-mail:** richard_sheward@fccourts.org

(513) 732-7396   **Shriver, James A.** (J Clermont Cty Munic Ct) 4430 St. Rt. 222, Batavia 45103; **Fax:** (513) 732-7831

(419) 448-1302   **Shuff, Steve C.** (J Seneca Cty Common Pleas Ct) Annex, Suite 4204, 117 E. Market St., Tiffin 44883; **Fax:** (419) 443-7927; **E-mail:** scs-court@bright.net

(216) 443-5818   **Sikora, Peter M.** (J Cuyahoga Cty Juv Ct) 2163 E. 22nd St., Cleveland 44115

(740) 596-4319   **Simmons, Jeffrey L.** (J Vinton Cty Common Pleas Ct) Cthse., 100 E. Main St., McArthur 45651-1267; **Fax:** (740) 596-9611

(330) 451-7789   **Sinclair, V. Lee** (J Stark Cty Common Pleas Ct) 115 Central Plz., N., Suite 400, Canton 44702-1490; **Fax:** (330) 451-7740

(419) 213-4755   **Singer, Arlene** (J Dist Ct of App 6th App Dist) One Constitution Ave., Toledo 43624; **Fax:** (419) 213-4844; **E-mail:** singer@co.lucas.oh.us

(937) 225-4376   **Singer, Gregory F.** (J Montgomery Cty Common Pleas Ct) 41 N. Perry St., P.O. Box 972, Dayton 45422-2170; **Fax:** (937) 225-5406; **E-mail:** singerg@montcourt.org

(419) 213-4755   **Skow, William J.** (J Dist Ct of App 6th App Dist) One Constitution Ave., Toledo 43624; **Fax:** (419) 213-4844; **E-mail:** 6thca@co.lucas.oh.us

(330) 643-2259   **Slaby, Lynn C.** (J Dist Ct of App 9th App Dist) 161 S. High St., Suite 504, Akron 44308-1602; **Fax:** (330) 643-2394; **E-mail:** lynn@ninth.courts.state.oh.us

(330) 740-2208   **Smith, Beth A.** (J Mahoning Cty Dom Rel Ct) 120 Market St., Youngstown 44503; **Fax:** (330) 740-2503

(937) 498-7255   **Smith, Norman P.** (J Shelby Cty Probate/Juv Ct) Cthse., 100 E. Court St., P.O. Box 4187, Sidney 45365-4187; **Fax:** (937) 498-7260

(740) 699-2138   **Solovan, John M., II** (J Belmont Cty Common Pleas Ct) Cthse., 101 W. Main St., St. Clairsville 43950-1154

(330) 343-6797   **Space, Mary Wade** (J New Philadelphia Munic Ct) 166 E. High Ave., New Philadelphia 44663; **Fax:** (330) 364-6885

(513) 887-3586   **Spaeth, Keith** (J Butler Cty Common Pleas Ct) Govt. Svces. Ctr., 3rd Fl., 315 High St., Hamilton 45011; **Fax:** (513) 785-5757; **E-mail:** spaethkm@butlercountyohio.org

(740) 283-6000 Ext. 2252   **Spahn, G. Daniel** (J Steubenville Munic Ct) 123 S. Third St., Steubenville 43952; **Fax:** (740) 283-6167

(740) 670-5770   **Spahr, Jon R.** (J Licking Cty Common Pleas Ct) Cthse., Public Sq., Newark 43055;
     E-mail: jspahr@lcounty.com

(440) 887-7400   **Spanagel, Kenneth R.** (J Parma Munic Ct) 5555 Powers Blvd., Parma 44129-5462;
     Fax: (440) 887-7481

(740) 355-8316   **Spears, David E.** (J Scioto Cty Dom Rel Ct) Cthse., 602 Seventh St., Portsmouth 45662;
     Fax: (740) 355-8205

(419) 739-9119   **Spees, Mark E.** (J Auglaize Cty Dom Rel Ct) 201 Willipie St., Suite 103, Wapakoneta 45895;
     Fax: (419) 739-7563

(419) 739-7563   (J Auglaize Cty Probate/Juv Ct) 201 Willipie St., Suite 103, Wapakoneta 45895-1972; **Fax:** (419) 739-7563

(937) 544-2921   **Spencer, Brett M.** (J Adams Cty Common Pleas Ct) 110 W. Main St., West Union 45693-1347;
     Fax: (937) 544-8911

(740) 833-2596   **Spicer, Kenneth J.** (J Delaware Cty Probate/Juv Ct) 88 N. Sandusky St., Delaware 43015;
     Fax: (740) 833-2599

(330) 643-2247   **Spicer, Mary F.** (J Summit Cty Common Pleas Ct) 209 S. High St., Akron 44308-1610

(330) 643-2330   **Spicer, W. F.** (J Summit Cty Probate Ct) 209 S. High St., Akron 44308-1616; **Fax:** (330) 643-2393;
     E-mail: bspicer@summitohioprobate.com

(419) 774-5578   **Spon, Ronald D.** (J Richland Cty Juv Ct) 411 S. Diamond St., Mansfield 44902; **Fax:** (419) 774-5555

(740) 393-9510   **Spurgeon, Paul E.** (J Mount Vernon Munic Ct) 5 N. Gay St., Mount Vernon 43050;
     Fax: (740) 393-5349

(614) 462-5223   **Squire, Carole** (J Franklin Cty Dom Rel/Juv Ct) 373 S. High St., 6th Fl., Columbus 43215;
     Fax: (614) 719-2118; **E-mail:** carole_squire@fccourts.org

(419) 223-8511   **Staley, Matt C.** (J Allen Cty Common Pleas Ct) 301 N. Main St., P.O. Box 1243, Lima 45802; **Fax:** (419) 227-3162

(419) 223-8511   (J Allen Cty Dom Rel Ct) 333 N. Main St., P.O. Box 1243, Lima 45802; **Fax:** (419) 227-3162

(740) 472-5790   **Starr, Walter R.** (J Monroe Cty Probate/Juv Ct) 101 N. Main St., Rm. 39, Woodsfield 43793-1099;
     Fax: (740) 472-2520

(513) 946-5149   **Stautberg, Julia A.** (J Hamilton Cty Munic Ct) Cthse., 1000 Main St., Cincinnati 45202;
     Fax: (513) 946-5202

(419) 238-6935   **Steele, Charles D.** (J Van Wert Cty Common Pleas Ct) Cthse., 121 E. Main St., Van Wert 45891-1729;
     Fax: (419) 238-2874; **E-mail:** steelecharles@yahoo.com

(740) 349-6215   **Steiner, Russell A.** (J Licking Cty Dom Rel Ct) 75 E. Main St., Newark 43055; **Fax:** (740) 349-1485;
     E-mail: steiner@alltel.net

(440) 466-1184   **Stevens, Richard L.** (J Ashtabula Cty Ct Western Dist) 117 W. Main St., Geneva 44041; **Fax:** (440) 466-7171

(740) 592-3256   **Stewart, Robert W.** (J Athens Cty Probate/Juv Ct) Cthse., One S. Court St., Athens 45701-2897;
     Fax: (740) 592-3268

(513) 946-5160   **Stockdale, David C.** (J Hamilton Cty Munic Ct) Cthse., 1000 Main St., Cincinnati 45202;
     Fax: (513) 946-5202; **E-mail:** dstockda@cms.hamilton-co.org

(216) 664-4986   **Stokes, Angela R.** (J Cleveland Munic Ct) 1200 Ontario St., Cleveland 44113
     Mailing Address: P.O. Box 94894, Cleveland 44101-4894; **Fax:** (216) 664-4283

(740) 992-2279   **Story, Steven L.** (J Meigs Cty Ct) Cthse., 100 E. Second St., Pomeroy 45769-1030; **Fax:** (740) 992-4570

(740) 636-2350   **Stout, Gary C.** (J Washington Court House Munic Ct) 119 N. Main St.,
     Washington Court House 43160-1330; **Fax:** (740) 636-2359

(614) 387-9050   **Stratton, Evelyn Lundberg** (Justice Supreme Ct) 65 S. Front St., 9th Fl., Columbus 43215-3431;
     Fax: (617) 387-9059; **E-mail:** strattonoe@sconet.state.oh.us

(740) 774-4202   **Street, John B.** (J Chillicothe Munic Ct) 26 S. Paint St., Chillicothe 45601-3202; **Fax:** (740) 774-1101;
     E-mail: jbstreet@bright.net

(330) 675-2534   **Stuard, John M.** (J Trumbull Cty Common Pleas Ct) 161 High St., N.W., Warren 44481-1006;
     Fax: (330) 675-2580

(330) 451-7308   **Stucki, David E.** (J Stark Cty Family Ct) 110 Central Plz., S., Suite 601, Canton 44702-1414;
     Fax: (330) 451-7837; **E-mail:** judgestucki@co.stark.oh.us

(740) 368-1575   **Sunderman, David P.** (J Delaware Munic Ct) Justice Ctr., 70 N. Union St., Delaware 43015;
     Fax: (740) 368-1583; **E-mail:** dsunderman@municipalcourt.org

(513) 946-3424   **Sundermann, J. Howard, Jr.** (J Dist Ct of App 1st App Dist) 230 E. Ninth St., 12th Fl.,
     Cincinnati 45202; **Fax:** (513) 946-3412

(216) 443-8727   **Suster, Ronald** (J Cuyahoga Cty Common Pleas Ct) 1200 Ontario St., Cleveland 44113-1678; **Fax:** (216) 348-4034

(216) 443-8680   **Sutula, John D.** (J Cuyahoga Cty Common Pleas Ct) 1200 Ontario St., Cleveland 44113-1678;
     Fax: (216) 348-4031

(216) 443-8697   **Sutula, Kathleen Ann** (J Cuyahoga Cty Common Pleas Ct) 1200 Ontario St., Cleveland 44113-1678;
     Fax: (216) 348-4031

(216) 348-4807   **Sweeney, James J.** (J Dist Ct of App 8th App Dist) Cuyahoga Cty. Cthse., Suite 202, 1 Lakeside Ave.,
     Cleveland 44113-1085; **Fax:** (216) 443-2044

(216) 443-8412   **Sweeney, Kristin W.** (J Cuyahoga Cty Juv Ct) 2163 E. 22nd St., Cleveland 44115

(330) 740-2150   **Sweeney, Maureen A.** (J Mahoning Cty Common Pleas Ct) 120 Market St., Youngstown 44503-1710;
     Fax: (330) 742-5882; **E-mail:** msweeney@mahoningcounty.oh.gov

(330) 675-2521   **Swift, Thomas A.** (J Trumbull Cty Probate Ct) 161 High St., N.W., Warren 44481-1230;
     Fax: (330) 675-3024; **E-mail:** swift@trumbullprobate.org

(216) 664-4998   **Synenberg, Joan** (J Cleveland Munic Ct) 1200 Ontario St., Cleveland 44113
     Mailing Address: P.O. Box 94894, Cleveland 44101-4894; **Fax:** (216) 664-4283

(614) 645-7643   **Taylor, Anne** (J Franklin Cty Munic Ct) 375 S. High St., Columbus 43215-4520; **Fax:** (614) 645-8822

(330) 643-2995   **Teodosio, Linda Tucci** (J Summit Cty Juv Ct) 650 Dan St., Akron 44310; **Fax:** (330) 643-2987;
     E-mail: lteodosio@cpcourt.summitoh.com

(330) 365-3289   **Thomakos, Elizabeth Lehigh** (J Tuscarawas Cty Common Pleas Ct) Cthse., 101 E. High Ave.,
     New Philadelphia 44663-2599; **E-mail:** thomakos@co.tuscarawas.oh.us

(614) 462-3664   **Thompson, Tommy** (J Franklin Cty Common Pleas Ct) 369 S. High St., Rm. 9A, Columbus 43215-4554;
     Fax: (614) 462-4480

(330) 424-7777   **Tobin, David** (J Columbiana Cty Common Pleas Ct) Cthse., 105 S. Market St., Lisbon 44432; **Fax:** (330) 424-3960; **E-mail:** dtobin@epochi.com

(513) 852-8017   **Tolbert, Susan Laker** (J Hamilton Cty Dom Rel Ct) 800 Broadway, Rm. 225, Cincinnati 45202; **Fax:** (513) 946-9019

(419) 627-7731   **Tone, Tygh M.** (J Erie Cty Common Pleas Ct) Cthse., 323 Columbus Ave., Sandusky 44870-2602; **Fax:** (419) 627-6602

(419) 627-7750   (J Erie Cty Probate Ct) 323 Columbus Ave., Sandusky 44870-2691; **Fax:** (419) 626-9120

(330) 652-5863   **Townley, Thomas W.** (J Niles Munic Ct) 15 E. State St., Niles 44446; **Fax:** (330) 544-9025

(614) 462-6281   **Travis, Alan C.** (J Franklin Cty Common Pleas Ct) 369 S. High St., Rm. 8A, Columbus 43215-4554; **Fax:** (614) 462-4480; **E-mail:** alan_travis@fccourts.org

(440) 974-5744   **Trebets, John** (J Mentor Munic Ct) 8500 Civic Center Blvd., Mentor 44060-2418; **Fax:** (440) 974-5742

(937) 328-3768   **Trempe, Thomas E.** (J Clark Cty Munic Ct) 50 E. Columbia St., Springfield 45502-1116; **Fax:** (937) 328-3779

(513) 946-5175   **Triantafilou, Alex** (J Hamilton Cty Munic Ct) Cthse., 1000 Main St., Cincinnati 45202; **Fax:** (513) 946-5202

(419) 245-1940   **Trimboli, Mary Grace** (J Toledo Munic Ct) 555 N. Erie St., Toledo 43624; **Fax:** (419) 245-1802; **E-mail:** mary.trimboli@noris.org

(740) 687-6620 Ext. 36   **Trimmer, David A.** (J Fairfield Cty Munic Ct) 104 E. Main St., P.O. Box 2390, Lancaster 43130; **Fax:** (740) 681-5014

(216) 664-4992   **Triozzi, Robert J.** (J Cleveland Munic Ct) 1200 Ontario St., Cleveland 44113 Mailing Address: P.O. Box 94894, Cleveland 44101-4894; **Fax:** (216) 664-4283

(937) 225-4448   **Tucker, Michael L.** (J Montgomery Cty Common Pleas Ct) 41 N. Perry St., P.O. Box 972, Dayton 45422-2170; **Fax:** (937) 225-5406; **E-mail:** tuckerm@montcourt.org

(330) 643-2233   **Unruh, Brenda Burnham** (J Summit Cty Common Pleas Ct) 209 S. High St., Akron 44308-1610

(614) 645-8288   **VanDerKarr, Scott D.** (J Franklin Cty Munic Ct) 375 S. High St., Columbus 43215-4520; **Fax:** (614) 645-8822

(419) 282-4284   **Vercillo, Damian J.** (J Ashland Cty Probate/Juv Ct) Cthse., 142 W. Second St., Ashland 44805-2190; **Fax:** (419) 281-5699

(440) 576-3677   **Vettel, Ronald W.** (J Ashtabula Cty Common Pleas Ct) 25 W. Jefferson St., Jefferson 44047-1092; **Fax:** (440) 576-1426

(330) 938-9873   **Vettori, Diane** (J Mahoning Cty Ct No 3) 605 E. Ohio Ave., Sebring 44672; **Fax:** (330) 938-6518

(216) 443-8737   **Villanueva, José A.** (J Cuyahoga Cty Common Pleas Ct) 1200 Ontario St., Cleveland 44113-1678; **Fax:** (216) 348-4034

(740) 455-7138   **Vinsel, Jay F.** (J Muskingum Cty Ct) 27 N. Fifth St., Zanesville 43701; **Fax:** (740) 455-7157

(513) 732-7327   **Voris, Michael J.** (J Clermont Cty Dom Rel Ct) 2340 Clermont Center Dr., Suite 200, Batavia 45103; **Fax:** (513) 732-7333; **E-mail:** domestic@fuse.net

(330) 740-2180   **Vukovich, Joseph J.** (J Dist Ct of App 7th App Dist) Mahoning Cty. Cthse., 120 Market St., Youngstown 44503-1710; **Fax:** (330) 740-2182

(937) 225-4409   **Wagner, A.J.** (J Montgomery Cty Common Pleas Ct) 41 N. Perry St., P.O. Box 972, Dayton 45422-2170; **Fax:** (937) 225-5406; **E-mail:** wagnera@montcourt.org

(937) 440-3529   **Wagner, Lynnita K.C.** (J Miami Cty Probate/Juv Ct) Safety Bldg., 201 W. Main St., Troy 45373-2363; **Fax:** (937) 440-3531

(330) 740-2180   **Waite, Cheryl L.** (Pres J Dist Ct of App 7th App Dist) Mahoning Cty. Cthse., 4th Fl., 120 Market St., Youngstown 44503-1710; **Fax:** (330) 740-2182

(440) 967-6543   **Wakefield, Elizabeth** (J Vermillion Munic Ct) 687 Decatur St., Vermilion 44089; **Fax:** (440) 967-1467

(513) 732-7050   **Walker, William** (J Clermont Cty Common Pleas Ct) 270 Main St., Batavia 45103-3071; **Fax:** (513) 732-7050

(513) 425-7822   **Wall, Mark W.** (J Middletown Munic Ct) I Donham Plaza, Middletown 45042; **Fax:** (513) 425-7846; **E-mail:** markw@ci.middletown.oh.us

(740) 385-2250   **Wallar, Richard M.** (J Hocking Munic Ct) One E. Main St., P.O. Box 950, Logan 43138; **Fax:** (740) 385-3826; **E-mail:** rwallar@co.hocking.oh.us

(513) 425-6609   **Walsh, James E.** (J Dist Ct of App 12th App Dist) 1001 Reinartz Blvd., P.O. Box 1009, Middletown 45042-1901; **Fax:** (513) 425-8751; **E-mail:** james@twelfth.courts.state.oh.us

(740) 533-4329   **Walton, W. Richard** (J Lawrence Cty Common Pleas Ct) Cthse., One Veteran's Sq., Ironton 45638; **Fax:** (740) 533-4377; **E-mail:** walton@zoomnet.net

(740) 593-3591   **Ward, Michael W.** (J Athens Cty Common Pleas Ct) Cthse., 3rd Fl., One S. Court St., Athens 45701-2895; **Fax:** (740) 592-3020; **E-mail:** cpcward@athenscountygovernment.com

(740) 774-3711   **Ward, Richard G.** (J Ross Cty Probate/Juv Ct) Two N. Paint St., Suite A, Chillicothe 45601-3181; **Fax:** (740) 774-3711; **E-mail:** ctward@bright.net

(419) 223-8525   **Warren, Richard K.** (J Allen Cty Common Pleas Ct) 333 N. Main St., P.O. Box 1243, Lima 45802; **Fax:** (419) 224-9269

(350) 297-4277   **Watson, Barbara Roush** (Pres J Portage Cty Munic Ct) Ravenna Div., 203 W. Main St., P.O. Box 958, Ravenna 44266-0958; **Fax:** (350) 297-4283

(440) 350-3126   **Weaver, William W.** (J Lake Cty Juv Ct) Juvenile Justice Ctr., 53 E. Erie St., Painesville 44077-3907; **Fax:** (440) 350-2724

(419) 399-8220   **Webb, J. David** (J Paulding Cty Common Pleas Ct) Cthse., 2nd Floor, Suite 201, 115 N. Williams St., Paulding 45879-1298; **Fax:** (419) 399-8224

(330) 861-7217   **Weigand, Michael L.** (J Barberton Munic Ct) Munic. Bldg., 576 W. Park Ave., Barberton 44203-2584; **Fax:** (330) 848-6779

(216) 475-4927   **Weiler, Jennifer P.** (J Garfield Heights Munic Ct) 5555 Turney Rd., Cleveland 44125-3778; **Fax:** (216) 475-3087; **E-mail:** jweiler@ghmc.org

(937) 440-6021   **Welbaum, Jeffrey M.** (J Miami Cty Common Pleas Ct) Safety Bldg., 3rd Fl., 201 W. Main St., Troy 45373-3239; **Fax:** (937) 440-6011

(513) 946-5785   **West, John Andrew** (J Hamilton Cty Common Pleas Ct) 1000 Main St., Rm. 595, Cincinnati 45202; **Fax:** (513) 946-5907

Judges Directory

(330) 627-2323   **Weyand, John H.** (J Carroll Cty Probate/Juv Ct) Cthse., Suite 202, 119 S. Lisbon St., Carrollton 44615-1497; **Fax:** (330) 627-6004

(740) 695-2875   **White, Harry W.** (J Belmont Cty Ct, Western Dist) 147 W. Main St., St. Clairsville 43950; **Fax:** (740) 695-7285; **E-mail:** bankerwhite@1st.net

(330) 674-5086   **White, Thomas D.** (J Holmes Cty Common Pleas Ct) Cthse., Rm. 307, One E. Jackson St., Millersburg 44654-1249; **Fax:** (330) 674-0289

(330) 643-2259   **Whitmore, Beth** (J Dist Ct of App 9th App Dist) 161 S. High St., Suite 504, Akron 44308-1602; **Fax:** (330) 643-2394; **E-mail:** beth@ninth.courts.state.oh.us

(740) 833-2530   **Whitney, W. Duncan** (J Delaware Cty Common Pleas Ct) 91 N. Sandusky St., Delaware 43015-1795; **Fax:** (740) 833-2529

(330) 287-5530   **Wiest, Mark K.** (J Wayne Cty Common Pleas Ct) 107 W. Liberty St., Wooster 44691; **Fax:** (330) 287-5416

(330) 375-2007   **Williams, Annalisa S.** (J Akron Munic Ct) 217 S. High St., Akron 44308-1611; **Fax:** (330) 375-2514; **E-mail:** willia@akron.oh.us

(937) 393-3676   **Williams, Cynthis** (J Highland Cty Common Pleas Ct Dom Div) 105 N. High St., 2nd Fl., Hillsboro 45133-1182; **Fax:** (937) 393-6878

(330) 643-2241   **Williams, James R.** (J Summit Cty Common Pleas Ct) 209 S. High St., Akron 44308-1610

(740) 687-0942   **Williams, Steven O.** (J Fairfield Cty Probate/Juv Ct) Hall of Justice, 224 E. Main St., Lancaster 43130-3863; **Fax:** (740) 687-0942

(740) 373-6623   **Williams, Timothy A.** (J Washington Cty Probate/Juv Ct) Cthse., 205 Putnam St.,
Ext. 253   Marietta 45750-2922; **Fax:** (740) 376-7425; **E-mail:** timw@frognet.net

(740) 342-3156   **Wilson, Dean L.** (J Perry Cty Ct) 105 N. Main St., P.O. Box 207, New Lexington 43764-0207; **Fax:** (740) 342-2188

(937) 484-1000   **Wilson, Roger B.** (J Champaign Cty Common Pleas Ct) Cthse., 200 N. Main St., Urbana 43078; **Fax:** (937) 484-1025

(513) 946-5175   **Winkler, Ralph E. (Ted)** (J Hamilton Cty Common Pleas Ct) 1000 Main St., Rm. 410, Cincinnati 45202; **Fax:** (513) 946-5907

(513) 946-5143   **Winkler, Robert C.** (J Hamilton Cty Munic Ct) Cthse., 1000 Main St., Cincinnati 45202; **Fax:** (513) 946-5202

(330) 451-7701   **Wise, John W.** (J Dist Ct of App 5th App Dist) 110 Central Plaza S., Suite 320, Canton 44702-1411; **Fax:** (330) 451-7249; **E-mail:** infor@fifthdist.org

(419) 562-5771   **Wiseman, Russell B.** (J Crawford Cty Common Pleas Ct) 112 E. Mansfield St., Suite 200, Bucyrus 44820; **Fax:** (419) 562-8011

(419) 213-4580   **Wittenberg, Charles S.** (J Lucas Cty Common Pleas Ct) Cthse., 700 Adams St., Toledo 43624-1678; **Fax:** (419) 213-4184

(419) 354-9230   **Woessner, David E.** (J Wood Cty Probate Ct) One Courthouse Sq., Bowling Green 43402; **Fax:** (419) 354-9357
(419) 352-3554   (J Wood Cty Juv Ct) 11120 E. Gypsy Lane Rd., Bowling Green 43402; **Fax:** (419) 352-6084

(937) 225-4464   **Wolff, William H., Jr.** (J Dist Ct of App 2nd App Dist) 41 N. Perry, P.O. Box 972, Dayton 45422; **Fax:** (937) 496-7724; **E-mail:** wolffw@mcohio.org

(419) 282-4292   **Woodward, Deborah E.** (J Ashland Cty Common Pleas Ct) Cthse., 142 W. Second St., Ashland 44805-2101; **Fax:** (419) 281-8315

(419) 221-5275   **Workman, Rickard A.** (J Lima Munic Ct) 109 N. Union St., P.O. Box 1529, Lima 45802-1529; **Fax:** (419) 998-5526

(614) 387-9800   **Wright, J. Craig** (J Ct of Claims) 65 S. Front St., 3rd Fl., Columbus 43215; **Fax:** (614) 387-9836

(513) 732-7243   **Wyler, Stephanie** (J Clermont Cty Probate Ct) 76 S. Riverside Dr., Batavia 45103; **Fax:** (513) 732-8183
(513) 732-7696   (J Clermont Cty Juv Ct) 2340 Clermont Center Dr., Batavia 45103; **Fax:** (513) 732-7695

(440) 576-3617   **Wynn, Robert S.** (J Ashtabula Cty Ct Eastern Dist) 25 W. Jefferson St., Jefferson 44047; **Fax:** (440) 576-3441

(440) 576-3681   **Yost, Gary L.** (J Ashtabula Cty Common Pleas Ct) 25 W. Jefferson St., Jefferson 44047-1092; **Fax:** (440) 576-1426

(740) 732-5795   **Young, Lucien C., III** (J Noble Cty Ct) 100 Cthse., Caldwell 43724-1243; **Fax:** (740) 732-1435

(513) 425-6609   **Young, William W.** (J Dist Ct of App 12th App Dist) 1001 Reinartz Blvd., P.O. Box 1009, Middletown 45042-1901; **Fax:** (513) 425-8751; **E-mail:** william@twelfth.courts.state.oh.us

(937) 378-6358   **Zachman, Thomas F.** (J Brown Cty Munic Ct) 770 Mt. Orab Pike, Georgetown 45121-1281; **Fax:** (937) 378-2462; **E-mail:** tzachman@browncountycourt.org

(440) 329-5560   **Zaleski, Edward M.** (J Lorain Cty Common Pleas Ct) Lorain Cty. Justice Center, 225 Court St., Elyria 44035; **Fax:** (440) 329-5562

(419) 213-6827   **Zemmelman, Norman G.** (J Lucas Cty Dom Rel Ct) 429 N. Michigan St., Suite B, Toledo 43624-1689

(419) 586-1249   **Zitter, Mary Pat** (J Mercer Cty Probate/Juv Ct) 101 N. Main St., Rm. 307, Celina 45822-1796; **Fax:** (419) 586-4506

(419) 245-1942   **Zmuda, Gene** (J Toledo Munic Ct) 555 N. Erie St., Toledo 43624; **Fax:** (419) 245-1802; **E-mail:** gene.zmuda@noris.org

(216) 664-4980   **Zone, Joseph J.** (J Cleveland Munic Ct) 1200 Ontario St., Cleveland 44113
                 Mailing Address: P.O. Box 94894, Cleveland 44101-4894; **Fax:** (216) 664-4283

(740) 455-7142   **Zwelling, Howard** (J Muskingum Cty Common Pleas Ct) 401 Main St., Zanesville 43701; **Fax:** (740) 455-7177

Explanatory Note: The date immediately following individual names denotes the year of admission to the Ohio Bar. The "%" indicates that the attorney is an associate/employee of the law firm, company or agency. Parentheses around a firm, company or agency name indicates a partner/shareholder/owner/officer/principal/member/responsible party of the law firm, company or agency.

Facsimile telephone numbers have been included in the listings when available.

Every effort has been made to obtain accuracy in the listings but the publishers do not guarantee its accuracy. Difficulty is sometimes experienced in securing information as to changes of addresses. In instances where communications requesting address and firm data have elicited no response, the old addresses have been retained without comment.

(740) 353-7548 .. **Aalyson**, Mark E '80 -711 Findlay -Portsmouth 45662
-Fx:353-1984

(859) 525-9800 .. **Aaron**, Donald W '98 -9758 Windsor Way -Florence, KY 41042

(216) 522-1555 .. **Abakumov**, Georg '77 -1701 E 12th -Ste 3G -Cleveland 44114
-Fx:522-1558

(513) 852-5600 .. **Abaray**, Janet G '82 (Lopez HRM&S) -312 Walnut -Ste 2090
-Cincinnati 45202 Fx:852-5611

(513) 723-4000 .. **Abare**, Terri Reyering '83 (Vorys SS&P LLP) -221 E 4th
-Ste 2000 Atrium Two -Bx0236 -Cincinnati 45201 Fx:723-4056

(216) 687-1311 .. **Abbarno**, Kenneth P '92 (Reminger & R) -101 Prospect Av W
-1400 Mdlnd Bldg -Cleveland 44115 Fx:687-1841

(216) 583-1160 .. **Abbass**, Rolla Z '99 Ernst & Young LLP -925 Euclid Av -Ste 1300
-Cleveland 44115

(513) 243-2245 .. **Abbott**, David L '84 GE -1 Neumann Way -MD S24
-Cincinnati 45215

(937) 252-2592 .. **Abbott**, John M '72 Primerica -4140 Linden Av -Ste 110
-Dayton 45432

(937) 226-1212 .. **Abboud**, Antony A '04 %Skelton MG&H -130 W 2nd -Ste 450
-Dayton 45402

(216) 292-8500 .. **Abbuhl**, David W '81 (D Abbuhl Co,LPA) -23230 Chagrin Blvd
-Ste 605 -Beachwood 44122

(937) 643-3770 .. **Abdallah**, Bahjat M '04 (Santiago & A,LLC) -2310 Far Hills Av
-Ste 3 -Dayton 45419 Fx:643-3704

Abdoulkarim, Abdoul R '74 -333 S Main -408 The Evans Bldg
-Akron 44308

(716) 849-1700 .. **Abdulla**, Karim A '99 %Stenger & F -70 Niagara -3rd Fl
-Buffalo, NY 14202 Fx:849-1717

(513) 621-1045 .. **Abel**, Frederick Bruce '64 -885 Greenvll Av -Cincinnati 45246

(317) 236-2217 .. **Abel**, George H II '00 OfCnsl Ice Miller -One Amer Sq -Ste 82001
-Indianapolis, IN 46282 Fx:592-4850

(216) 621-6138 .. **Abel**, Jack W '74 (Abel & Z,LPA) -815 Superior Av
-The Superior Bldg Ste 1915 -Cleveland 44114 Fx:241-5620

Abel, Michael A '95 -4096 Holiday NW -Canton 44718

(215) 597-3442 .. **Abele**, Joseph M '64 IRS-Ofc Chief Counsel -701 Market
-Philadelphia, PA 19106

(216) 443-8602 .. **Abens**, Matthew B '02 Cuyahoga Cnty Ct Cmmn Pleas
-1200 Ontario -Justice Ctr 11th Fl -Cleveland 44113

(419) 241-6000 .. **Abercrombie**, Gene R '96 %Eastman & S Ltd -1 Seagate -24th Fl
-Bx10032 -Toledo 43699 Fx:247-1777

(513) 621-2120 .. **Abernethy**, William S Jr. '67 Strauss & T,LPA -150 E 4th -4th Fl
-Cincinnati 45202 Fx:241-8259

(330) 865-7722 .. **Aberth**, Joel R '71 (Aberth & C Co LPA) -3296 W Market
-Akron 44333 Fx:865-9742

(513) 977-8200 .. **Abes**, Alan H '93 (Dinsmore & S LLP) -255 E 5th -Ste 1900
-Cincinnati 45202 Fx:977-8141

(419) 421-2815 .. **Abke**, Hope B '99 Marathon Ashland Petroleum LLC -539 S Main
-Rm 4130 -Findlay 45840 Fx:421-8415

Abood, Charles D '70 -2 Ginger Hill Ln -Toledo 43623

(330) 273-3208 .. **Abood**, Mark S '98 -2787 Francena Ct -Brunswick 44212

(419) 474-1218 .. **Abou-Arraj**, Rochelle A '96 -3126 W Sylvania Av -Toledo 43613

(916) 497-0331 .. **Abouhassan**, Evelyn M '99 Prtctn & Advccy Inc -555 Cptl Mall
-Ste 747 -Sacramento, CA 95814

Abraham, Alfred '03 -(Address Unavailable)

(614) 228-6453 .. **Abraham**, Daniel N '83 (Colley S&A Co,LPA) -536 S High
-Columbus 43215 Fx:228-7122

(614) 221-5474 .. **Abraham**, Joseph R '97 Abraham Law Ofcs -24 N High
-Columbus 43215

(614) 221-5474 .. **Abraham**, Rick J '87 -24 N High -Columbus 43215

Abraham, Steven G '02 -9071 E Mississippi Av -#32F
-Denver, CO 80247

(202) 686-0600 .. **Abrahams**, Adam L '96 %A Konopka -4530 Wscnsn Av NW
-Ste 200 -Washington, DC 20016 Fx:686-0896

(202) 624-3970 .. **Abrahams**, Jessica C '90 (Powell GF&M LLP) -1001 Penn Av NW
-6th Fl -Washington, DC 20004 Fx:624-7222

(614) 225-8528 .. **Abrahamsen**, Erik E '86 Motorists Mutual Ins Co -471 E Broad
-Columbus 43215

(216) 691-2405 .. **Abramoff**, Howard B '77 -1500 S Green Rd -Ste 200
-Cleveland 44121

(517) 371-8100 .. **Abramowitz**, Jerrold '82 Foster SC&S,PC -313 S Wshngtn Sq
-Lansing, MI 48933

(740) 283-3330 .. **Abrams**, Amanda Jo '02 -Bank One Bldg -Ste 1210 -Bx608
-Steubenville 43952

(614) 221-4000 .. **Abrams**, James D '03 %Chester W&S LLP -65 E State -10th Fl
-Columbus 43215 Fx:221-4012

(740) 283-3330 .. **Abrams**, James T '73 -Bank One Bldg -Ste 1210 -Bx608
-Steubenville 43952

(330) 742-4255 .. **Abrams**, Karen H '81 Natl City Bank NE -20 Fed Plz -Bx450
-Youngstown 44501 Fx:742-4290

(614) 466-1943 .. **Abrams**, Kevin R '82 Workers Comp -30 W Spring -Level 26
-Columbus 43215

(513) 721-4876 .. **Abrams**, Laura A '91 (Sirkin P&S LLP) -105 W 4th
-920 4th & Race Twr -Cincinnati 45202 Fx:721-0876

(330) 743-5101 .. **Abrams**, Richard A '80 Green H&S,Co LPA -16 Wick Av -Ste 400
-Youngstown 44503 Fx:743-3451

(740) 369-2423 .. **Abrams**, Robert A '93 Cnsl Celina Ins Grp -163 N Sandusky
-Ste 205 -Delaware 43015 Fx:362-5553

(513) 983-7854 .. **Abrams**, Sharon E '85 Procter & Gamble Co-Legal
-1 Procter & Gamble Plz -Cincinnati 45202

(614) 461-6066 .. **Abramson**, Lawrence D '78 (Abramson & O,LLC) -695 Bryden Rd
-Columbus 43205 Fx:461-4524

(419) 724-2600 .. **Abramson**, Mark C '81 (Udell & A Ltd) -5738 Main
-Sylvania 43560

(330) 668-1324 .. **Abramson**, Susan H '84 -660 N Medina Line Rd -Medina 44256

(513) 977-8200 .. **Abreu**, Steven A '04 %Dinsmore & S LLP -255 E 5th -Ste 1900
-Cincinnati 45202 Fx:977-8141

(614) 221-8448 .. **Abromowitz**, David M '91 (Buckingham D&B,LLP)
-191 W Nationwide Blvd -Ste 300 -Bx151120 -Columbus 43215
Fx:221-8590

(614) 443-7000 .. **Abroms**, Hillard M '72 -753 S Front -Columbus 43206

(937) 225-5779 .. **Abshire**, Steven M '01 Montgomery Cnty Pros -3304 N Main
-Children Srvcs -Dayton 45405

(419) 213-4700 .. **Accettola**, Judith K '81 %Lucas Cnty Pros -Adams & Erie
-Lucas Cnty Cthse -Toledo 43624

(419) 241-1150 .. **Accettola**, Paul E '75 (Herschel ABM&M) -615 Adams
-Toledo 43604 Fx:241-7825

(513) 241-7111 .. **Acciani**, Henry D '79 (O'Connor A&L Co,LPA) -1014 Vine -22nd Fl
-Cincinnati 45202 Fx:241-7197

(513) 651-6800 .. **Acheson**, Edwin R Jr. '89 (Frost BT LLC) -201 E 5th
-2200 PNC Ctr -Cincinnati 45202 Fx:651-6981

(614) 220-8877 .. **Acker**, Alan S '90 -145 E Rich -4th Fl -Columbus 43215
Fx:220-8876

(412) 656-1333 .. **Acker**, Thomas S '56 -500 1st Fed Plz -New Castle, PA 16101
Fx:658-6010

Ackerman, Glen H '00 -Bx3176 -Clearwater Beach, FL 33767

(937) 445-2966 .. **Ackermann**, John R Jr. '91 NCR Corp -1611 S Main -SDC-2
-Dayton 45409

(614) 433-9612 .. **Acklin**, Kristina L '96 Kagay AD&G -6877 N High -Ste 300
-Worthington 43085

(440) 232-6288 .. **Acosta**, Lori A '89 (Acosta & L) -318 Solon Rd -Bedford 44146

(412) 434-0201 .. **Acton**, Mary Ann C '93 Bashline & Hutton -210 6th Av -Ste 3500
-Pittsburgh, PA 15222

(216) 575-0777 .. **Acton**, Shawn M '00 %Kelley & F,LLP -1300 E 9th -Ste 1901
-Cleveland 44114 Fx:575-0799

(614) 462-3960 .. **Adair**, Allen V '72 Franklin Cnty Pub Def -373 S High -12th Fl
-Columbus 43215

(330) 867-0363 .. **Adair**, Delilah A '84 -1939 Burlngtn Rd -Akron 44313

(216) 751-8183 .. **Adair**, James G '75 -21625 Chagrin Blvd -#250
-Beachwood 44122 Fx:751-9911

(614) 451-6050 .. **Adair**, James W III '74 -1170 Old Henderson Rd -Ste 109
-Columbus 43220

(440) 888-6660 .. **Adamczyk**, Beverly A '90 (B Adamczyk Co,LPA) -6929 W 130th
-Rm 660 -Cleveland 44130 Fx:888-6100

(216) 586-3939 .. **Adamo**, Kenneth R '84 (Jones D) -901 Lakeside Av
-Cleveland 44114 Fx:579-0212

(216) 621-0200 .. **Adams**, Albert T '77 (Baker & H LLP) -1900 E 9th -Ste 3200
-Cleveland 44114 Fx:696-0740

(614) 464-2392 .. **Adams**, Andrew S '75 (Earl WA&D,LPA) -136 W Mound
-Columbus 43215 Fx:464-0754

(937) 224-5300 .. **Adams**, Audrey S '01 %Cooper & G Co,LPA -118 W 1st -Ste 850
-Dayton 45402

(216) 664-6900 .. **Adams**, Beth M '02 %Brzytwa Q&M LLC -1660 W 2nd
-900 Skylight Ofc Twr -Cleveland 44113 Fx:664-6901

(216) 443-8589 .. **Adams**, Beverly A '02 Cuyahoga Cnty Ct Cmmn Pleas
-1200 Ontario -Justice Ctr 11th Fl -Cleveland 44113

(614) 221-8448 .. **Adams**, Bret A '84 -191 W Nationwide Blvd -Ste 300 -Bx151120
-Columbus 43215 Fx:221-8590

(704) 374-6247 .. **Adams**, Carmen R '92 Wachovia Corp -301 S Cllg -TW30
-Charlotte, NC 28288

(513) 732-2214 .. **Adams**, Catherine '83 Clermont Cnty Pub Def -10 S 3rd
-Batavia 45103 Fx:732-9400

(440) 967-5195 .. **Adams**, Charles F '70 -667 Sunnyside Rd -Vermilion 44089

(216) 991-0731 .. **Adams**, Craig A '85 -3068 Warrington Rd -Shaker Heights 44120

(440) 326-1464 .. **Adams**, Cynthia M '92 City Law Dir Ofc -131 Court -Ste 120
-Elyria 44035

(513) 651-6800 .. **Adams**, Deborah S '82 (Frost BT LLC) -201 E 5th -2200 PNC Ctr
-Cincinnati 45202 Fx:651-6981

(513) 868-7100 .. **Adams**, Dennis L '97 Davidson A&C Co,LPA -127 N 2nd
-Hamilton 45011 Fx:868-9579

(513) 381-9200 .. **Adams**, Donald C '82 (Rendigs FK&D,LLP) -One W 4th -Ste 900
-Cincinnati 45202 Fx:381-9206

(513) 651-6800 .. **Adams**, Edmund J '63 Cnsl Frost BT LLC -201 E 5th
-2200 PNC Ctr -Cincinnati 45202 Fx:651-6981

(440) 746-1500 .. **Adams**, Gary S '83 Grtr Cleveland Auto Dealers Assn
-10100 Brecksvll Rd -Brecksville 44141

(216) 502-0600 .. **Adams**, Gregory J '98 %Eschweiler & Assoc,LLC -629 Euclid Av
-Ste 1210 -Cleveland 44114

(513) 241-5670 .. **Adams**, Gregory L '77 Croswell & A Co,LPA -1208 Sycamore
-Cincinnati 45210

(513) 977-8200 .. **Adams,** Gregory P '91 (Dinsmore & S LLP) -255 E 5th -Ste 1900 -Cincinnati 45202 **Fx:**977-8141

(419) 355-1372 .. **Adams,** Herbert E '72 -714 Court -Fremont 43420 **Fx:**332-1566

(513) 651-6800 .. **Adams,** James R '63 Cnsl Frost BT LLC -201 E 5th -2200 PNC Ctr -Cincinnati 45202 **Fx:**651-6981

(330) 869-9849 .. **Adams,** Jason T '89 -1830 Stabler Rd -Akron 44313

(937) 294-2778 .. **Adams,** Jay A '00 -424 Patterson Rd -Dayton 45419

(513) 542-7111 .. **Adams,** Jeffrey L '92 -1538 Cedar Av -Cincinnati 45224

(216) 931-6000 .. **Adams,** Jennifer Lawry '96 (Ulmer & B LLP) -1300 E 9th -Ste 900 Penton Media Bldg -Cleveland 44114 **Fx:**931-6001

(312) 558-5600 .. **Adams,** Jennifer P '95 Winston & S -35 W Wacker Dr -Chicago, IL 60601

(216) 443-7223 .. **Adams,** John F '76 Cuyahoga Cnty Pub Def -1200 W 3rd NW -100 Lakeside Pl -Cleveland 44113

Adams, John M '54 -2535 Canterbury Rd -Columbus 43221

(504) 576-2095 .. **Adams,** John M Jr. '83 Entergy Srvcs,Inc -639 Loyola Av -Bx61000 -New Orleans, LA 70161

(937) 449-2800 .. **Adams,** Karen R '91 (Chernesky H&K PLL) -10 Cthse Plz SW -Ste 1100 -Dayton 45402 **Fx:**449-2821

(859) 431-3313 .. **Adams,** Kimberely J '89 Childrens Law Ctr -104 E 7th -2nd Fl -Covington, KY 41011

(216) 787-3407 .. **Adams,** Margaret E '92 Dept Job & Family Srvcs -615 W Superior Av -Cleveland 44113 **Fx:**787-3299

(614) 475-9511 .. **Adams,** Mark A '78 (Blumenstiel HA&E,LLC) -261 W Johnstown Rd -Columbus 43230 **Fx:**475-0348

Adams, Mark W '90 -3912 LaGrange -Ste B -Toledo 43612

(304) 723-2674 .. **Adams,** Michael A '01 (Schrader B&C,PLLC) -2112 Penn Av -Bx2785 -Weirton, WV 26062 **Fx:**723-2876

Adams, Michael W '01 -1190 Yllwstn Rd -Cleveland 44121

(703) 720-7800 .. **Adams,** Nathaniel W '01 %Squire S&D LLP -8000 Towers Crescent Dr -14th Fl -Tysons Corner, VA 22182 **Fx:**720-7801

(513) 946-3000 .. **Adams,** Paula E '98 Hamilton Cnty Pros -230 E 9th -Cincinnati 45202 **Fx:**946-3017

(202) 339-8400 .. **Adams,** Rachel A '94 Orrick H&S LLP -3050 K NW -Washington, DC 20007

(740) 587-2889 .. **Adams,** Russell J '76 -11 N Prospect -Granville 43023

(513) 929-9333 .. **Adams,** Steven R '91 -215 E 9th -Ste 102 -Cincinnati 45202 **Fx:**651-2570

(330) 761-2333 .. **Adams,** Tanzie D '85 FirstEnergy Corp -76 S Main -Rm GO-12 -Akron 44308

(614) 415-7078 .. **Adams,** Theodore L '91 Limited Brands,Inc -3 Limited Pkwy -Columbus 43230 **Fx:**415-7080

(216) 621-1113 .. **Adams,** Thomas W '92 (Renner OB&S,LLP) -1621 Euclid Av -19th Fl -Cleveland 44115 **Fx:**621-6165

(614) 221-3155 .. **Adams,** William A '85 (Bailey C LLC) -10 W Broad -Columbus 43215 **Fx:**221-0479

(740) 373-1335 .. **Adams,** William J '85 -200 Putnam -Ste 426 -Marietta 45750

(740) 965-5119 .. **Adams,** William Mark '87 -241 Greenbrier Rd -Sunbury 43074

(216) 696-3332 .. **Adamson,** Charles Z '78 -815 Superior Av E -Ste 1915 -Cleveland 44114

(330) 253-7171 .. **Adamson,** Paul F '82 Burdon & M -137 S Main -Ste 201 -Akron 44308 **Fx:**253-7174

(614) 221-0944 .. **Addesa,** Thomas J '85 %Artz & D,LLP -560 E Town -Columbus 43215 **Fx:**221-2340

(513) 626-1602 .. **Addington,** Eric T '03 Procter & Gamble Co -11450 Grooms Rd -Cincinnati 45242

(505) 873-7276 .. **Addis,** Richard B '56 -Bx25923 -Albuquerque, NM 87125

(614) 464-6400 .. **Addison,** Colborn M '60 OfCnsl Vorys SS&P LLP -52 E Gay -Bx1008 -Columbus 43216 **Fx:**464-6350

(740) 373-6688 .. **Addison,** James R Jr. '53 (Addison & F) -202 WesBanco Bldg -Marietta 45750

(513) 554-1110 .. **Addy,** Robert Mark '87 Phillips Edison & Co -11690 Grooms Rd -Cincinnati 45242

(440) 843-9944 .. **Ade,** Mark A '98 -10007 Concord Ct -Parma 44130

(513) 771-4800 .. **Adee,** Jonathan D '98 OH Vlly Goodwill Ind -10600 Sprngfld Pike -Cincinnati 45215

(614) 462-3194 .. **Adel,** Mitchell J '01 Franklin Cnty Pub Def -373 S High -12th Fl -Columbus 43215

(216) 932-5556 .. **Adelman,** Eugene M '56 -2620 Warrensvll Ctr Rd -#205 -University Heights 44118

(216) 983-1053 .. **Adelman,** Harlin G '90 Univ Hosp -10524 Euclid Av -Ste 1100 -Cleveland 44106

(440) 247-0003 .. **Adelman,** Kelly G '96 %Turner & G LLC -100 N Main -Ste 350 -Chagrin Falls 44022 **Fx:**247-8903

Adelman, Robert E '98 -1391 Vandermar -Cleveland Heights 44121

(513) 785-5880 .. **Adelmann,** Laura A '99 Butler Cnty CSEA -315 High -7th Fl -Hamilton 45011

(216) 781-0755 .. **Adelstein,** Carol B '88 -2043 Random Rd -Cleveland 44106

(216) 883-0509 .. **Adelstein,** Louis S '86 -4108 Cullen Dr -Cleveland 44105

(713) 653-3404 .. **Adewale-Mendes,** Rose E '76 EEOC -1919 Smith -Ste 735 -Houston, TX 77002

(330) 535-8771 .. **Adgate,** Thomas L '87 (Adgate & K) -159 S Main -Ste 830 -Akron 44308 **Fx:**253-8578

(614) 478-9472 .. **Adjoua,** Hakim B '99 -670 Frances Ct -Gahanna 43230

(740) 446-0644 .. **Adkins,** Charles Jeffrey '86 -435 2nd Av -Gallipolis 45631

(937) 223-1201 .. **Adkins,** Dennis J '86 (Altick & C Co,LPA) -1 S Main -1700 One Dayton Ctr -Dayton 45402 **Fx:**223-5100

(513) 684-6023 .. **Adkins,** Douglas D '03 US Dept of Labor -36 E 7th -Ste 2525 -Cincinnati 45202

(216) 277-0702 .. **Adkins,** Ilah M '03 Charter One Bk -1215 Superior Av -SU 530 -Cleveland 44115 **Fx:**566-0405

(614) 464-3563 .. **Adkins,** Jonathan E '04 %Loveland & B -50 W Broad -Ste 3300 -Columbus 43215

(216) 623-0150 .. **Adkins,** Lewis W Jr. '93 (Roetzel & A,LPA) -1375 E 9th -One Cleve Ctr 9th Fl -Cleveland 44114 **Fx:**623-0134

(949) 255-3534 .. **Adkins,** Mitchell D '93 IBM -15440 Laguna Canyon Rd -Irvine, CA 92618

Adkins, Stuart A '92 -12048 Purity Rd -Saint Louisville 43071

(330) 643-7786 .. **Adkins,** Yamini K '93 Summit Cnty Sheriffs Ofc -175 S Main -2nd Fl -Akron 44308

(614) 469-1882 .. **Adkinson,** Christopher D '01 %Kephart & F LLP -207 N 4th -Columbus 43215

(937) 431-9660 .. **Adkinson,** Patrick K '80 P Adkinson,LLC -4244 Indn Ripple Rd -Ste 150 -Dayton 45440 **Fx:**431-9670

Adler, Allen P '71 -948 Riva Ridge Blvd -Gahanna 43230

(216) 696-4200 .. **Adler,** Charles F III '83 (Schneider SR&L PLL) -1111 Superior Av -Ste 1000 -Cleveland 44114 **Fx:**696-7303

(216) 586-3939 .. **Adler,** David F '87 (Jones D) -901 Lakeside Av -Cleveland 44114 **Fx:**579-0212

(937) 223-1201 .. **Adler,** Deborah J '82 (Altick & C Co,LPA) -1 S Main -1700 One Dayton Ctr -Dayton 45402 **Fx:**223-5100

(330) 758-3878 .. **Adler,** Jeffrey D '90 -807 Southwestern Run -Poland 44514

(216) 332-0400 .. **Adler,** Steven M '97 -5706 Turney Rd -Ste 308 -Garfield Heights 44125

(330) 456-8376 .. **Adlon,** James P '81 -101 Central Plz S -Ste 401 -Canton 44702

(216) 566-5086 .. **Adorno,** Juan E '79 Cleveland Regional Transit -1240 W 6th -Cleveland 44113

(440) 356-0373 .. **Adrain-Piccorelli,** Suzanne H '86 -255 Falmouth Dr -Rocky River 44116

(419) 241-2000 .. **Adray,** James S '76 (Adray & G) -709 Mad Av -Ste 209 -Toledo 43624

(216) 241-0286 .. **Adrine,** Ethel M '93 Progressive House Cnsl -55 Pub Sq -Ste 1331 -Cleveland 44113

(216) 664-4974 .. **Adrine,** Ronald B '73 Mun Ct Judge -1200 Ontario -Bx94894 -Cleveland 44101

(740) 282-6233 .. **Adulewicz,** Casimir T '63 -409 Sinclair Bldg -Bx1388 -Steubenville 43952

(757) 262-0128 .. **Aduma,** Kenyetta T '94 MC African American Mennonite Assn -2311 Twr Pl -Hampton, VA 23666

(313) 792-6432 .. **Adusei-Poku,** Kwadjo S '97 Masco Corp -21001 Van Born Rd -Taylor, MI 48180

(419) 252-8152 .. **Adusei-Poku,** Marilyn S '97 Columbia Gas of Ohio,Inc -333 S Erie -Toledo 43602

(419) 947-4515 .. **Aebi,** Ana Luz '00 Morrow Cnty Dom Rltns Ct -48 E High -Mount Gilead 43338

(740) 393-0771 .. **Aebi,** John W '79 -13600 Old Mansfld Rd -Mount Vernon 43050

(614) 764-6895 .. **Aebker,** Jill E '97 Wendys Intl -4288 W Dublin-Granvll Rd -Bx256 -Dublin 43017

Aeschliman, Reed J '91 US Agency for Intl Development-USAID -US State Dept -New Delhi India -Washington, DC 20521

(330) 723-9797 .. **Afarin,** Lisa M '87 -3540 Autumn Tree Dr -Medina 44256

(614) 464-3332 .. **Affeldt,** Kelly I '93 -60 E Broad -Ste 400 -Columbus 43215

(614) 469-5715 .. **Affeldt,** Kenneth F '91 US Atty -303 Marconi Blvd -Ste 200 -Columbus 43215

(513) 241-5670 .. **Agar,** Elizabeth E '80 Croswell & A Co,LPA -1208 Sycamore -Cincinnati 45210

(412) 566-6183 .. **Agarwal,** Brij K '97 %Eckert SC&M,LLC -600 Grant -44th Fl -Pittsburgh, PA 15219

(937) 865-6800 .. **Agarwal,** Neil P '96 Lexis/Nexis -Bx933 -Dayton 45401

(216) 479-8500 .. **Agati,** Andrew '95 (Squire S&D LLP) -127 Pub Sq -4900 Key Twr -Cleveland 44114 **Fx:**479-8780

(202) 220-1200 .. **Agbapuruonwu,** Fidelis I '02 %Pepper H LLP -600 14th NW -Ste 600 -Washington, DC 20005 **Fx:**220-1665

(614) 221-3318 .. **Agee Clymer Mitchell & Laret** -89 E Nationwide Blvd -Ste 200 -Columbus 43215

(216) 765-8520 .. **Aggers,** David F '83 (Aggers J&C Co,LPA) -29565 Chagrin Blvd -Ste 306 Exec Cmmns E -Pepper Pike 44122 **Fx:**765-8817

(216) 765-8520 .. **Aggers Joseph & Cheverine Co, LPA** -29565 Chagrin Blvd -Ste 306 Exec Cmmns E -Pepper Pike 44122 **Fx:**765-8817

(440) 460-1415 .. **Agin,** Bernard I '75 (Agin & A Co,LPA) -5910 Landerbrook Dr -Ste 200 -Mayfield Heights 44124

(614) 476-5540 .. **Agin,** Frank J '88 -150 W Johnstown Rd -Bx30724 -Gahanna 43230

(740) 474-2000 .. **Agin,** Kevin T '91 -143 W Franklin -Circleville 43113 **Fx:**474-2007

(440) 460-1415 .. **Agin,** Sandra K '78 (Agin & A Co,LPA) -5910 Landerbrook Dr -Ste 200 -Mayfield Heights 44124

(216) 291-1300 .. **Agins,** Kerry M '00 %N Siegel Co,LPA -4070 Mayfld Rd -Cleveland 44121

(216) 321-5068 .. **Agle,** Katherine S '98 -2593 Hmpshr Rd -19 -Cleveland Heights 44106

(614) 466-3191 .. **Agler,** Alfred P '74 PUCO -180 E Broad -Columbus 43266

(440) 268-4355 .. **Agnello Russo,** Christine L '89 -11005 Pearl Rd -Ste 4 -Strongsville 44136 **Fx:**268-7670

(216) 696-1550 .. **Agopian,** Richard V '75 -1419 W 9th -2nd Fl -Cleveland 44113

(216) 586-3939 .. **Agozzino,** Leozino '85 Cnsl Jones D -901 Lakeside Av -Cleveland 44114 **Fx:**579-0212

(614) 466-0108 .. **Agranoff,** Jay S '88 PUCO -180 E Broad -Columbus 43266

(740) 282-5323 .. **Agresta,** Emanuela '90 (Bruzzese & C) -300 Sinclair Bldg -Bx1506 -Steubenville 43952 **Fx:**282-5328

(937) 276-6580 .. **Ahearn,** Todd M '98 Montgomery Cnty Pros -301 W 3rd -Bx972 -Dayton 45422 **Fx:**225-3470

(216) 575-1002 .. **Ahern,** Ann-Marie R '98 Simon Law Firm,LLC -1300 E 9th -Ste 1717 -Cleveland 44114

(419) 243-6148 .. **Ahern,** Stephen F '76 Manahan PB&D -414 N Erie -Bx2328 -Toledo 43603

Ahern, William R '72 -30185 Hickory Hill Dr -Perrysburg 43551

(513) 681-8616 .. **Ahlers,** Donald B '53 -6045 Budmar Av -Cincinnati 45224

(513) 621-1652 .. **Ahlers,** Edward C '82 (Crowley A&R Co,LPA) -414 Walnut -Ste 707 -Cincinnati 45202 **Fx:**621-8430

(513) 533-8347 .. **Ahlers,** Heinz W '76 Natl Inst for Occ Safety & Health -4676 Columbia Pkwy -Mail Drop C-31 -Cincinnati 45226

(513) 751-4420 .. **Ahlers,** Laurie K '95 -2345 Ashland Av -Cincinnati 45206 **Fx:**751-3095

(407) 425-2786 .. **Ahlers,** Mark F '82 (Fishback DBSAA&B,LLP) -170 E Wshngtn -Orlando, FL 32801 **Fx:**425-2863

(513) 251-1247 .. **Ahlrichs & Ahlrichs** -4037 Glenway Av -Cincinnati 45205

(513) 251-1247 .. **Ahlrichs,** James W '56 %Ahlrichs & A -4037 Glenway Av -Cincinnati 45205

(513) 251-1247 .. **Ahlrichs,** Susan M '85 (Ahlrichs & A) -4037 Glenway Av -Cincinnati 45205

(312) 353-5868 .. **Ahmed,** Mona B '96 Social Security Admin -200 W Adams -30th Fl -Chicago, IL 60606

(330) 860-6762 .. **Ahonen,** Robert M '87 Babcock & Wilcox Co -20 S Van Buren Av -Barberton 44203

(219) 455-3717 ..**Ahrendt,** David L '87 Delaware Investments -915 S Clinton
-Bx2248 -Fort Wayne, IN 46801

(513) 579-1100 ..**Ahrens,** Gerard J '77 Talbots -441 Vine -Carew Twr
-Cincinnati 45202

(513) 241-2324 ..**Ahrens,** Gregory F '87 (Wood H&E LLP) -441 Vine -Ste 2700
-Cincinnati 45202 **Fx:**421-7269

(513) 583-4200 ..**Ahrens,** Megan Cochran '03 %Schroeder MB&P
-11935 Mason Rd -Ste 110 -Cincinnati 45249

(419) 337-9240 ..**Ahroni,** Orly '94 Fulton Cnty Pros -123 Cthse Plz -Wauseon 43567

(212) 334-1222 ..**Aieta,** Mario '84 (Garvey S&B) -599 Bway -8th Fl
-New York, NY 10012 **Fx:**334-1278

(419) 483-2141 ..**Aigler & Paul** -202½ W Main -Bellevue 44811

(419) 483-2141 ..**Aigler,** Thomas L '83 (Aigler & P) -202½ W Main -Bellevue 44811

(419) 483-2141 ..**Aigler,** William F '43 OfCnsl Aigler & P -202½ W Main
-Bellevue 44811

(301) 588-8066 ..**Aikman,** Susan F '99 D Goren -8600 2nd Av
-Silver Spring, MD 20910

(520) 547-1412 ..**Aikman-Scalese,** Ann E '78 Lisa Frank,Inc -6760 S Lisa Frank Av
-Tucson, AZ 85706

(740) 845-0300 ..**Ailes,** Aleita J '72 (A Ailes,LLC) -Bx588 -London 43140
Fx:845-0500

(740) 654-2325 ..**Aiman,** Scott A '69 -1465 Redwood Dr NE -Bx2571
-Lancaster 43130

Ainley, Gary L '86 -Bx99185 -Cleveland 44199

(614) 464-6400 ..**Airey,** Wilfred Jonathan '73 (Vorys SS&P LLP) -52 E Gay -Bx1008
-Columbus 43216 **Fx:**464-6350

(216) 241-5310 ..**Aitken,** Janice P '96 % Gallagher SF&N -1501 Euclid Av -6th Fl
-Cleveland 44115 **Fx:**241-1608

(614) 443-4063 ..**Akamine,** Nathan Sei '95 (McCord & A,LLP) -844 S Front
-Columbus 43206

(330) 456-8376 ..**Ake,** David S '72 (D Ake Co,LPA) -401 Bank One Twr
-Canton 44702

(419) 289-2183 ..**Akers,** Eric J '73 -Bx483 -Ashland 44805 **Fx:**289-2802

(614) 365-2700 ..**Akers,** Laing P '00 %Squire S&D LLP -41 S High
-1300 Huntngtn Ctr -Columbus 43215 **Fx:**365-2499

(614) 644-6896 ..**Akers,** Leslie A '86 OH Dept Taxation -30 E Broad -22nd Fl
-Columbus 43215 **Fx:**466-8922

(216) 623-9999 ..**Akers-Parry,** Deborah '76 (Wolf & A,LPA) -1717 E 9th -Ste 1515
-Cleveland 44114 **Fx:**623-0629

(937) 865-6800 ..**Akerson,** Valerie L '95 Lexis/Nexis -Bx933 -Dayton 45401

(740) 587-4150 ..**Akin,** Dain C '78 Paramount Finl Grp -4009 Columbus Rd SW
-Granville 43023

(513) 381-2838 ..**Akin,** Edward P '01 %Taft S&H LLP -425 Walnut -Ste 1800
-Cincinnati 45202 **Fx:**381-0205

(614) 898-9900 ..**Akin Guthrie LLC** -100 Drchstr Sq Ln -Ste 202 -Westerville 43081
Fx:898-9685

(614) 898-9900 ..**Akin,** Sherrille D '92 (Akin G LLC) -100 Drchstr Sq Ln -Ste 202
-Westerville 43081 **Fx:**898-9685

(330) 740-2073 ..**Akins,** Kim T '90 Mahoning Cnty CSEA -112 W Commerce -Bx119
-Youngstown 44503

(412) 777-2340 ..**Akorli,** Godfried '79 Bayer Corp -100 Bayer Rd
-Pittsburgh, PA 15205

(216) 931-6000 ..**Al-Shidhani,** Lynnette L '03 %Ulmer & B LLP -1300 E 9th
-Ste 900 Penton Media Bldg -Cleveland 44114 **Fx:**931-6001

Alabasi, Kim K '04 -(Address Unavailable)

(803) 502-9767 ..**Alan,** Matthew W '87 Westinghouse Sfty Mgmt Solutions
-1993 S Centennial Av SE -Bx5388 -Aiken, SC 29804
Fx:502-9999

(614) 466-6696 ..**Alatis,** Andrew J '89 Atty Gen -150 E Gay -Columbus 43215
Fx:752-2538

(314) 340-4830 ..**Alatorre,** Salvador L '83 MO Dept Labor & Indstrl Rltns
-505 Wshngtn Av -St. Louis, MO 63101

(216) 586-3939 ..**Alavi,** Atossa M '03 %Jones D -901 Lakeside Av -Cleveland 44114
Fx:579-0212

(513) 651-6800 ..**Albainy-Jenei,** Stephen R '95 (Frost BT LLC) -201 E 5th
-2200 PNC Ctr -Cincinnati 45202 **Fx:**651-6981

(614) 340-4044 ..**Alban,** David R '55 (Alban & C LLP) -7100 N High -Ste 102
-Worthington 43085

(614) 340-4044 ..**Alban,** Glenn F '92 (Alban & C LLP) -7100 N High -Ste 102
-Worthington 43085

(440) 354-8859 ..**Alban,** Robert J '73 -411 Valley Vw Dr -Painesville 44077

(513) 946-6611 ..**Albanese,** Francis D '65 Hamilton Cnty Sheriffs Dept
-1000 Sycamore -Director of Safety -Cincinnati 45202

(440) 826-0125 ..**Albanese,** Michael A '97 Global Ground Srvcs,Inc -Bx811150
-Cleveland 44181 **Fx:**826-0328

(513) 576-0111 ..**Albenze-Smith,** Nadine A '94 Record Express LLC
-400 Technecenter Dr -Ste 101 -Milford 45150 **Fx:**576-1148

(216) 368-6353 ..**Alber,** Alyson S '98 CWRU Law Schl -11075 East Blvd
-Cleveland 44106

(614) 464-4414 ..**Albers,** James B '50 Albers & A -88 N 5th -Columbus 43215
Fx:464-0604

(614) 464-4414 ..**Albers,** James S '77 Albers & A -88 N 5th -Columbus 43215
Fx:464-0604

(614) 464-4414 ..**Albers,** John B II '82 Albers & A -88 N 5th -Columbus 43215
Fx:464-0604

(216) 479-6100 ..**Albers,** Matthew E '02 %Vorys SS&P LLP -1375 E 9th
-Ste 2100 One Cleve Ctr -Cleveland 44114 **Fx:**479-6060

(614) 466-8600 ..**Albers,** Rebecca Jo '92 Atty Gen -30 E Broad -Columbus 43215
Fx:466-6090

(937) 275-7170 ..**Albert,** Jeffrey P '71 (Albert & K) -4403 N Main -Dayton 45405

(513) 946-3000 ..**Albert,** John E '78 Hamilton Cnty Pros -230 E 9th
-Cincinnati 45202 **Fx:**946-3017

(440) 395-0251 ..**Albert,** Peter J '88 Progressive Ins Co -300 N Cmmns Blvd
-OHF 11 -Mayfield Village 44143

(614) 433-9612 ..**Albert,** Robert H '60 (Kagay AD&G) -6877 N High -Ste 100
-Worthington 43085

(216) 931-6000 ..**Albert,** Steven W '71 (Ulmer & B LLP) -1300 E 9th
-Ste 900 Penton Media Bldg -Cleveland 44114 **Fx:**931-6001

(330) 666-3833 ..**Alberti,** John Curtis '79 (JC Alberti Co,LPA)
-525 N Cleveland-Massillon Rd -Akron 44333

(513) 732-5950 ..**Albi,** Joy M '95 -7374 Riverpoint Dr -Cincinnati 45255

(216) 241-8172 ..**Albin,** Jason T '04 %J Chapman & Assoc,LLC -700 W St Clair Av
-Ste 300 -Cleveland 44113 **Fx:**241-8175

(800) 736-3973 ..**Albl,** Suzanne Scheiner '01 ABX Air Inc -145 Hunter Dr
-Wilmington 45177

Albores, Oscar E '02 -(Address Unavailable)

(614) 221-1216 ..**Albrecht,** Benjamin S '00 Downes H&F -400 S 5th -Ste 200
-Columbus 43215 **Fx:**221-8769

(614) 752-6889 ..**Albrecht,** Cynthia L '92 Industrial Commssn of OH -30 W Spring
-9th Fl -Columbus 43215 **Fx:**752-8785

(513) 737-5100 ..**Albrecht,** David S '98 -304 N 2nd -Hamilton 45011

(614) 445-8811 ..**Albrecht,** Geoffrey E '75 (G Albrecht Co,LPA) -673 Mohawk
-Ste 203 -Columbus 43206

(800) 783-9655 ..**Albrecht,** Mark A '92 -1791 Franklin Park S -Columbus 43205

(859) 655-4200 ..**Albrecht,** Ryan J '03 %Greenebaum D&M PLLC
-50 E RiverCenter Blvd -Ste 1800 -Covington, KY 41011
Fx:655-4239

(330) 375-2285 ..**Albrecht,** Sophie E '78 Akron Municipal Ct -217 S High
-Akron 44308

(419) 841-8584 ..**Albrechta & Coble** -3230 Cntrl Pk W Dr -Ste 200 -Toledo 43617

(419) 332-9999 ..**Albrechta,** Joseph F '84 (Albrechta & C) -2255 Christy Rd
-Fremont 43420

(419) 471-1489 ..**Albright,** Alfred Jr. '79 UAW Legal Srvcs -3360 W Laskey Rd
-Toledo 43606 **Fx:**471-0498

(740) 345-3431 ..**Albright,** Mary M '97 (Reese PD&M,PLL) -36 N 2nd -Bx919
-Newark 43058 **Fx:**349-5116

(508) 646-3189 ..**Albright,** Michael S '92 Lightolier -631 Airport Rd
-Fall River, MA 02720

(216) 587-6500 ..**Albright,** Mylayna S '00 City of Warrensville Hts
-4301 Warrensvll Ctr Rd -Cleveland 44128

(614) 228-5711 ..**Albright,** Robert E '50 (Lucas PAG&N) -600 S High
-Columbus 43215 **Fx:**228-0982

(513) 475-8027 ..**Albrinck,** Daniel E '96 Univ of Cincinnati Medical Assoc
-222 Piedmont Av -Ste 1200 -Cincinnati 45219 **Fx:**475-8020

(513) 612-3095 ..**Albrinck,** John Jeffrey '87 (JJ Albrinck Co,LPA)
-11275 Sprngfld Pike -Cincinnati 45246

(252) 753-3433 ..**Albritton,** Lesley Wiseman '01 %SB Fulford Rhodes,PA
-3396 N Walnut -Bx253 -Farmville, NC 27828

(614) 469-5577 ..**Albu,** George M '93 Fed Mediation & Conciliation Srvcs
-1682 Schrock Rd -Columbus 43229

(216) 398-0591 ..**Albu,** John F '92 -2009 Mayview Av -Cleveland 44109

(330) 456-0050 ..**Albu,** Thomas P '75 -2223 Fulton Rd NW -Ste 206 -Canton 44709

(312) 332-0777 ..**Alcala,** Brian V '97 %Matkov SM&G -55 E Monroe -Ste 2900
-Chicago, IL 60603 **Fx:**332-6130

(216) 575-1560 ..**Alcox,** Patrick J '76 -75 Pub Sq -Ste 650 -Cleveland 44113

(216) 586-3939 ..**Alden,** David B '83 (Jones D) -901 Lakeside Av -Cleveland 44114
Fx:579-0212

(614) 410-6726 ..**Alden,** Erick R '72 (E Alden Co,LLC) -470 Olde Worthngtn Rd
-Ste 200 -Columbus 43082

(614) 221-1306 ..**Alden,** John L '72 -1 E Lvngstn Av -Columbus 43215 **Fx:**221-3551

(614) 410-6726 ..**Alden,** Matthew L '95 %E Alden Co,LLC -470 Olde Worthngtn Rd
-Ste 200 -Columbus 43082

(740) 397-5262 ..**Alden,** Noel B '96 Zelkowitz B&C -121 E High
-Mount Vernon 43050

(216) 252-7300 ..**Alden,** Phyllis C '89 Amer Greetings Corp -1 Amer Rd
-Cleveland 44144

(901) 544-3895 ..**Alden,** Randolph W '93 Federal Defender Ofc -200 Jffrsn Av
-Ste 200 -Memphis, TN 38103

(740) 852-3065 ..**Alderman,** Elizabeth C '02 Madison Cnty Health Dept -13 N Oak
-London 43140

(440) 930-4001 ..**Alderman,** Larry D '75 (Baumgartner & O)
-5455 Detroit Rd (Rte 254) -Sheffield Village 44054 **Fx:**934-7205

(248) 952-5444 ..**Aldrich,** James G Jr. '92 Romanzi N&C,PLLC -4555 Investment Dr
-Ste 200 -Troy, MI 48098 **Fx:**952-5466

(937) 443-6600 ..**Aldrich,** Jeff Jr. '02 %Thompson H LLP -2000 Cthse Plz NE
-Bx8801 -Dayton 45401 **Fx:**443-6635

(614) 846-2000 ..**Aldrich,** Misty H '85 Campbell HC&V,LLC -7650 Rvrs Edge Dr
-Columbus 43235 **Fx:**846-2003

(216) 566-5749 ..**Aldrich,** Thomas A '82 (Thompson H LLP) -127 Pub Sq
-3900 Key Ctr -Cleveland 44114 **Fx:**566-5800

(513) 887-3474 ..**Aldridge,** Averil A '98 Butler Cnty Pros -315 High -11th Fl -Bx515
-Hamilton 45012

(330) 928-7976 ..**Aldridge,** James D '73 -2731 Oak Park Blvd
-Cuyahoga Falls 44221

(330) 253-1555 ..**Alejars,** Stacey L '03 %D Booher & Assoc Co,LPA
-3180 W Market -Fairlawn 44333

(606) 431-8100 ..**Alerding,** Dennis C '95 -303 Greenup -Ste 300
-Covington, KY 41011

(419) 755-9455 ..**Alesch-Scholl,** Carol M '85 Mansfield Mun Ct -30 W Diamond
-Mansfield 44902

(614) 799-2800 ..**Alex,** Spero M '82 (Zaino & H LPA) -5775 Perimeter Dr -Ste 275
-Dublin 43017 **Fx:**799-1500

(216) 430-1200 ..**Alexander,** Andrew C '89 Boykin Lodging Co -45 W Prospect Av
-Guildhall Bldg Ste 1500 -Cleveland 44115

(330) 384-5793 ..**Alexander,** Anthony J '76 FirstEnergy Corp -76 S Main
-Akron 44308

(614) 559-2501 ..**Alexander,** Arlene K '87 White Castle Mgmt Co -555 W Goodale
-Columbus 43215

(513) 587-2884 ..**Alexander,** Christopher M '01 C Alexander Co,LPA -114 E 8th
-Cincinnati 45202 **Fx:**621-2525

(614) 365-2700 ..**Alexander,** David W '82 (Squire S&D LLP) -41 S High
-1300 Huntngtn Ctr -Columbus 43215 **Fx:**365-2499

(202) 887-4064 ..**Alexander,** Donald C '54 (Akin GSH&F,LLP) -1333 NH Av NW
-Ste 400 -Washington, DC 20036 **Fx:**887-4288

(412) 391-3228 ..**Alexander,** Efstathia G '86 (Reich A&R) -1350 Koppers Bldg
-436 7th Av -Pittsburgh, PA 15219 **Fx:**391-5323

(419) 241-9000 ..**Alexander,** Gregory G '54 OfCnsl Shumaker L&K,LLP
-1000 Jackson -Toledo 43624 **Fx:**241-6894

(404) 572-6600 ..**Alexander,** Halle R '01 %Powell GF&M LLP -191 Pchtree NE
-16th Fl -Atlanta, GA 30303 **Fx:**572-6999

(513) 621-6464 ..**Alexander,** Henry G '75 (Graydon H&R LLP) -511 Walnut
-1900 Fifth Third Ctr -Cincinnati 45202 **Fx:**651-3836

(216) 382-8586 ..**Alexander,** James Jr. '71 -2940 Noble Rd -Ste 202
-Cleveland Heights 44121 **Fx:**382-8580

(419) 213-4590 ..**Alexander,** John P '85 Lucas Cnty Chief of Staff -One Govt Ctr
-Ste 800 -Toledo 43604

(330) 785-3337 .. **Alexander,** John P '01 D Looney Co LPA -1735 S Main
-Akron 44301 Fx:785-3337

(216) 928-1010 .. **Alexander,** Joseph P '81 (Rotatori BGS&A Co LPA)
-526 Superior Av E -800 Leader Bldg -Cleveland 44114
Fx:928-1007

Alexander, Kadra D '01 -5200 Mdwcrk Dr -#1011
-Dallas, TX 75248

(614) 466-4605 .. **Alexander,** Linette M '94 OH Dept Job & Fam Srvcs -30 E Broad
-32nd Fl -Columbus 43266

(216) 621-1530 .. **Alexander,** Louis P Jr. '03 %Shapiro & F,LLP -1500 W 3rd
-Ste 400 -Cleveland 44113 **Fx:**621-1551

Alexander, Michael T '76 -1005 W 70th -Kansas City, MO 64113

(614) 823-6243 .. **Alexander,** Nicholas Z '64 Century Insurance Grp
-465 Cleveland Av -Westerville 43082

(513) 622-1268 .. **Alexander,** Richard L '02 Procter&Gamble Co
-Health Care Rsrch Ctr -Mason 45040

(330) 688-8820 .. **Alexander,** Ronald E '71 -44 Munroe Fls Av -Munroe Falls 44262

(614) 221-5627 .. **Alexander,** Suzanne K '03 Cnty Commssnrs Assn -37 W Broad
-Ste 650 -Columbus 43215

(513) 241-3100 .. **Alexander,** Tony M '00 %Lerner S&R -120 E 4th -8th Fl
-Cincinnati 45202

(585) 546-5530 .. **Alexander,** Yasmin E '01 West Grp -50 E Broad
-Rochester, NY 14694

(216) 241-5310 .. **Alexandersen,** Kevin C '86 (Gallagher SF&N) -1501 Euclid Av
-6th Fl -Cleveland 44115 **Fx:**241-1608

(248) 645-0800 .. **Alexopoulos,** Alex L '00 (Hardy L&P,PC)
-401 S Old Woodward Av -Ste 400 -Birmingham, MI 48009
Fx:645-2602

(614) 248-7973 .. **Alexsy,** Steven F '89 Bank One Corp -100 E Broad
-18th Fl -OH1-0158 -Columbus 43271

(330) 745-5061 .. **Alfera,** Vincent J '75 -480 W Tuscarawas Av -Ste 10 -Bx751
-Barberton 44203

(419) 422-8906 .. **Alge,** William S Jr. '73 (Snyder A&W,LPA) -233 S Main
-Findlay 45840

(513) 533-2996 .. **Algenio,** Rebecca N '01 %Finney SS&K Co,LPA -2623 Erie Av
-Bx8804 -Cincinnati 45208

(513) 723-2212 .. **Algie,** Glenn E '89 (Weltman W&R Co,LPA) -525 Vine -Ste 800
-Cincinnati 45202 **Fx:**723-2239

(614) 227-2000 .. **Ali,** Karim A '03 %Porter WM&A LLP -41 S High -Columbus 43215
Fx:227-2100

(216) 443-6350 .. **Aliberti,** Louis S '99 8th Dist Ct of Appls -1 Lakeside Av -#202
-Cleveland 44113 **Fx:**443-2044

(703) 607-6096 .. **Alich,** Keith R '83 US Air Force/Def Info Sys Agncy
-701 S Ct Hse Rd -Arlington, VA 22204

(513) 241-3685 .. **Alig,** Wesly A '02 %White G&M Co,LPA -1 W 4th -Ste 1700
-Cincinnati 45202 **Fx:**241-2399

(440) 572-1450 .. **Alikhan,** Cheryl A '89 -Bx360382 -Strongsville 44136

(216) 348-5400 .. **Alikhan,** Mariam '04 %McDonald H Co,LPA -600 Superior Av E
-Ste 2100 -Cleveland 44114 **Fx:**348-5474

(513) 352-6743 .. **Alkire,** Erin M '01 %Thompson H LLP -312 Walnut -14th Fl
-Cincinnati 45202 **Fx:**241-4771

Alkire, Laura '04 -319 N Buckeye -Bellevue 44811

(216) 674-0550 .. **Alkire,** Richard C '80 (RC Alkire Co,LPA)
-6060 Rockside Wds Blvd -Ste 250 -Independence 44131
Fx:674-0104

(513) 352-6658 .. **Allaer,** Paul A '86 (Thompson H LLP) -312 Walnut -14th Fl
-Cincinnati 45202 **Fx:**241-4771

(202) 781-2986 .. **Allahut,** Louis '72 %Ofc of Cnsl/NAVSEA-00L52
-1333 Isaac Hull Av SE -MS 1160 Rm 197/4W3035
-Washington, DC 20376 **Fx:**781-4628

(330) 376-5300 .. **Allan,** Ronald C '66 (Buckingham D&B,LLP) -50 S Main -Bx1500
-Akron 44309 **Fx:**781-4628

(216) 377-0598 .. **Allan,** Sean P '89 (Allan & G,LLP) -614 W Superior Av -Ste 1300
-Cleveland 44113

(937) 228-5912 .. **Allbery,** Charles F III '78 (Allbery C&F) -137 N Main -Ste 500
-Dayton 45402

(937) 228-5912 .. **Allbery Cross & Fogarty** -137 N Main -Ste 500 -Dayton 45402

(216) 523-5000 .. **Allbery,** Scott E '87 Eaton Corp -1111 Superior Av
-Cleveland 44114

(614) 645-8500 .. **Allbritain,** Michael C '02 Franklin Cnty Mun Ct -375 S High
-16th Fl -Columbus 43215

(309) 793-5884 .. **Allegro,** Donald B '90 US Atty -1830 2nd Av -Ste 320
-Rock Island, IL 61201

(614) 436-6690 .. **Alleman,** Brenda B '81 -4819 Sharon Av -Columbus 43214

(614) 868-0009 .. **Allen,** Anthony J '89 (Hallowes A&H) -6445 E Lvngstn Av
-Reynoldsburg 43068 **Fx:**868-0029

(216) 691-8472 .. **Allen,** Bruce C '80 (Allen & H) -1481 Warrensvll Ctr Rd
-South Euclid 44121

(440) 953-4183 .. **Allen,** Bruce L '72 Mun Ct Judge -1 Pub Sq -Willoughby 44094

(216) 433-2317 .. **Allen,** Carolyn W '72 Chief Cnsl Ofc -21000 Brookpark Rd
-Cleveland 44135

(513) 621-2120 .. **Allen,** Claudia G '88 (Strauss & T,LPA) -150 E 4th -4th Fl
-Cincinnati 45202 **Fx:**241-8259

(740) 533-1700 .. **Allen,** Craig A '66 -311 S 3rd -Bx1 -Ironton 45638

(740) 537-4687 .. **Allen,** Craig J '90 -1117 Fed -Toronto 43964

(614) 228-1174 .. **Allen,** Daniel D '89 -338 S High -Columbus 43215 **Fx:**228-7121

(937) 642-4070 .. **Allen,** David F '61 (Allen Y&M) -233 W 5th -Bx391
-Marysville 43040

(216) 241-2838 .. **Allen,** David V '87 (Taft S&H LLP) -200 Pub Sq -3500 BP Twr
-Cleveland 44114 **Fx:**241-3707

(419) 738-7180 .. **Allen,** Eric J '01 %Poppe Law Ofc -1100 W Auglaize
-Wapakoneta 45895

(513) 241-7111 .. **Allen,** Eric P '89 (O'Connor A&L Co,LPA) -1014 Vine -22nd Fl
-Cincinnati 45202 **Fx:**241-7197

(216) 691-8472 .. **Allen & Hodgman** -1481 Warrensvll Ctr Rd -South Euclid 44121

(419) 259-2791 .. **Allen,** James B '98 Hylant Group -1505 Jffrsn Av -Bx1687
-Toledo 43603

(703) 720-7800 .. **Allen,** James F '78 Cnsl Squire S&D LLP
-8000 Towers Crescent Dr -14th Fl -Tysons Corner, VA 22182
Fx:720-7801

(248) 901-4001 .. **Allen,** James L '04 (Plunkett & C,PC) -38505 Woodward -Ste 2000
-Bloomfield Hills, MI 48304

(513) 844-1300 .. **Allen,** James M '68 (JM Allen & Assoc) -240A Park Av
-Hamilton 45013 **Fx:**868-9876

(614) 462-3555 .. **Allen,** Jeffrey R '72 Franklin Cnty Pros -373 S High
-Columbus 43215

(614) 227-8834 .. **Allen,** Jerry O '84 (Bricker & E LLP) -100 S 3rd -Columbus 43215
Fx:227-2390

(740) 450-9301 .. **Allen,** John R '68 (Allen & B) -Bx1909 -South Zanesville 43701

(614) 224-4114 .. **Allen,** John R '73 (Mitchell AC&B Co,LPA) -580 S High -Ste 200
-Columbus 43215 **Fx:**224-3804

(419) 524-7788 .. **Allen,** John W '74 (Allen & Assoc) -24 W 3rd -Ste 200
-Mansfield 44902 **Fx:**524-7789

(513) 425-2602 .. **Allen,** Jonathan P '92 AK Steel Corp -703 Curtis
-Mlddletown 45043

(740) 342-1534 .. **Allen,** Joseph M '62 (Allen & A) -107 S Main -Bx61
-New Lexington 43764

(614) 221-8500 .. **Allen Kuehnle & Stovall LLP** -21 W Broad -Ste 400
-Columbus 43215

(513) 946-5203 .. **Allen,** Lisa C '84 Hamilton Cnty Ct -1000 Main -Rm 205
-Cincinnati 45202

(614) 466-2980 .. **Allen,** Michael D '80 Atty Gen -30 E Broad -Columbus 43215
Fx:728-9470

(513) 946-3210 .. **Allen,** Michael K '84 Hamilton Cnty Pros -230 E 9th
-Cincinnati 45202 **Fx:**946-3017

(513) 933-9011 .. **Allen,** Mitchell W '91 M Allen,LPA -52 E Mulberry -Bx435
-Lebanon 45036

(513) 946-5154 .. **Allen,** Nadine L '77 Mun Ct Judge -1000 Main -#205
-Cincinnati 45202

(937) 225-4464 .. **Allen,** Pamela K '96 2nd Dist Ct of Appls -41 N Perry -Rm 515
-Bx972 -Dayton 45422

(513) 424-2401 .. **Allen,** Patrick W '65 Casper & C -1 N Main -Bx510
-Middletown 45042 **Fx:**424-0622

(614) 222-0521 .. **Allen,** Philip Lon '86 -600 S High -Ste 201 -Columbus 43215

(440) 826-4100 .. **Allen Ramsey Maynard & Associates** -7530 Lucerne Dr
-Ste 200 -Middleburg Heights 44130

(407) 425-9044 .. **Allen,** Richard L Jr. '80 (Mateer & H,PA) -225 E Robnsn -Ste 600
-Bx2854 -Orlando, FL 32802 **Fx:**423-2016

(513) 621-2120 .. **Allen,** Samuel M '57 OfCnsl Strauss & T,LPA -150 E 4th -4th Fl
-Cincinnati 45202 **Fx:**241-8259

(513) 422-2001 .. **Allen,** Thomas B '94 (Frost BT LLC) -300 N Main -Ste 200
-Middletown 45042 **Fx:**422-3010

(440) 356-1345 .. **Allen,** Thomas E '54 -3591 Wooster Rd -Rocky River 44116

(216) 771-4000 .. **Allen,** Thomas F '68 -1801 E 9th -Ste 1300 -Cleveland 44114

(614) 221-8500 .. **Allen,** Thomas R '81 (Allen K&S LLP) -21 W Broad -Ste 400
-Columbus 43215

(216) 689-5775 .. **Allen,** Thomas S '79 Key Bank,NA -127 Pub Sq -17th Fl
-Cleveland 44114

(330) 841-0985 .. **Allen,** Thomas W '70 2nd Natl Bank -105 High NE -Bx1311
-Warren 44482

(614) 462-3555 .. **Allen,** Thomas W '98 Franklin Cnty Pros -373 S High
-Columbus 43215

(859) 264-0216 .. **Allen,** Timothy W '96 -501 Darby Crk Rd -Ste 58 -Lexington,
KY 40509

(513) 424-2401 .. **Allen,** William P '94 (Casper & C) -1 N Main -Bx510
-Middletown 45042 **Fx:**424-0622

(513) 241-2324 .. **Allen,** William R '00 %Wood H&E LLP -441 Vine -Ste 2700
-Cincinnati 45202 **Fx:**421-7269

(937) 642-4070 .. **Allen Yurasek & Merklin** -233 W 5th -Bx391 -Marysville 43040

(801) 777-2940 .. **Allen-McCoy,** Michelle D '98 US Air Force JAG -6026 Cedar Ln
-Hill AFB, UT 84056

(614) 462-7312 .. **Allendorf,** Thea L '99 %Hon WA Klatt -373 S High -24th Fl
-Columbus 43215

(614) 444-5700 .. **Allerding,** Michael P '75 -895 S High -Columbus 43206

(304) 340-3800 .. **Allevato,** John F '79 (Spilman T&B,PLLC) -300 Kanawha Blvd E
-Bx273 -Charleston, WV 25301

(859) 282-8800 .. **Alley,** Paul '03 %Graydon H&R,LLP -2500 Chmbr Ctr Dr -Ste 300
-Ft Mitchell, KY 41017

(419) 381-9368 .. **Alley,** Timothy R '02 %Cook K & Assoc,PLLC
-1918 Heatherdale Dr -Toledo 43609

(513) 729-3198 .. **Allf,** Rebecca J '86 Scholles & S -8970 Winton Rd
-Cincinnati 45231

(216) 755-5500 .. **Allgood,** Joan U '77 Developers Diversified Rlty Corp
-3300 Enterprise Pkwy -Beachwood 44122

(440) 356-1100 .. **Allington,** Frances Fitzgerald '97 -21300 Lorain Rd
-Fairview Park 44126 **Fx:**895-1233

(614) 466-5638 .. **Allison,** Adrian E '98 OH Dept of Edu -25 S Front -7th Fl
-Columbus 43215

(330) 426-9076 .. **Allison,** David M '02 -50345 SR 14 -East Palestine 44413

(330) 426-9491 .. **Allison,** James B '90 Allison & B -139 N Market
-East Palestine 44413

(614) 848-6500 .. **Allison,** James H '68 (Hill A&D) -7737 Olentangy Rvr Rd
-Columbus 43235 **Fx:**848-6516

(614) 221-8668 .. **Allison,** John J II '80 -165 E Lvngstn Av -Columbus 43215

(614) 644-0986 .. **Allison,** Jonathan A '94 Governors Ofc -77 S High -30th Fl
-Columbus 43215

(513) 977-8200 .. **Allison,** Jonathan B '01 %Dinsmore & S LLP -255 E 5th -Ste 1900
-Cincinnati 45202 **Fx:**977-8141

Allison, Kreg T '03 -(Address Unavailable)

(614) 462-7450 .. **Allison,** Linda K '00 CASA Franklin Cnty -373 S High -6th Fl
-Columbus 43215 **Fx:**462-5070

(614) 337-5140 .. **Allison,** Michael R '82 Victorias Secret Direct -3425 Morse Xing
-Columbus 43219

(330) 761-4306 .. **Allison,** Paul W '79 FirstEnergy Corp -76 S Main -Akron 44308

(216) 297-7000 .. **Allison,** Thomas H '87 The Cleveland Clinic Foundation
-1950 Richmond Rd -TR38 -Cleveland 44124

(513) 352-6712 .. **Allman,** Bruce W '74 (Thompson H LLP) -312 Walnut -14th Fl
-Cincinnati 45202 **Fx:**241-4771

(973) 426-3200 .. **Allman,** Thomas Y '65 BASF Corp -3000 Continental Dr N
-Budd Lake, NJ 07828 **Fx:**426-3213

(419) 535-0075 .. **Allotta Farley & Widman Co, LPA** -2222 Centennial Rd
-Toledo 43617 **Fx:**535-1935

(419) 874-7188 .. **Allotta Farley & Widman Co, LPA** -27457 Holiday Ln -Ste W
-Perrysburg 43551 **Fx:**874-7189

(216) 621-0200 .. **Allotta,** John J '01 %Baker & H LLP -1900 E 9th -Ste 3200
-Cleveland 44114 **Fx:**696-0740

(419) 535-0075 .. **Allotta,** Joseph J '72 (Allotta F&W Co,LPA) -2222 Centennial Rd
-Toledo 43617 **Fx:**535-1935

Alloy, Mark W '81 -627 Georgia Av -Palo Alto, CA 94306

(216) 765-5013 .. **Allport**, William W '69 Penske Logistics -3000 Auburn Dr
-2 Chagrin Highlands -Beachwood 44122

(419) 668-8211 .. **Allton**, John D '72 (Hiltz WA&K Co,LPA) -401 Ctzns Natl Bk Bldg
-Bx640 -Norwalk 44857 **Fx:**668-2813

Alluis, Louise J '82 -657 Beautyvw Ct -Columbus 43214

Ally, Bassil S '99 -219 W Boardmen -Youngstown 44503

(513) 684-8000 .. **Almaguer**, Alejandro E '98 US Postal Inspctn Srvc -895 Central Av
-3 Centennial Plz Ste 400 -Cincinnati 45202

(216) 443-7800 .. **Almaro**, Isadora A '00 Cuyahoga Cnty Pros -1200 Ontario -8th Fl
-Cleveland 44113 **Fx:**698-2270

(330) 742-8791 .. **Almasy**, Dionne M '92 Law Dept -26 S Phelps -Youngstown 44503

(330) 755-2165 .. **Almasy**, John P '55 Mun Ct Judge -351 Tenney Av
-Campbell 44405 **Fx:**750-3058

Almeida, Joseph A '03 -(Address Unavailable)

(614) 224-2428 .. **Alo**, Mohammed N '04 %Shihab & Assoc -65 E State -Ste 1550
-Columbus 43215 **Fx:**224-5080

(216) 464-7015 .. **Alperin**, Mitchell L '77 -3690 Orange Pl -Ste 575 -Cleveland 44122

(330) 394-1501 .. **Alpern**, Jack N '71 (J Alpern Co,LPA) -103 W Market -Ste 202
-Bx727 -Warren 44482

(502) 587-5400 .. **Alphin**, Elizabeth B '03 %Mapother & M,PSC -801 W Jffrsn
-Louisville, KY 40202

(513) 271-8242 .. **Alsfelder**, Deborah T '91 %R Alsfelder Jr -3700 Ctr
-Cincinnati 45227

(513) 271-8242 .. **Alsfelder**, Robert F Jr. '81 -3700 Ctr -Cincinnati 45227

(859) 341-1881 .. **Alsip**, Reneé L '97 %Deters B&L,PSC -2701 Turkeyfoot Rd
-207 Thomas More Pkwy -Crestview Hills, KY 41017 **Fx:**341-1469

Alston, Richard N '79 -3963 Tennyson Ln -North Olmsted 44070

Alt, Damon D '04 -118 W Center -1 -Fostoria 44830

(216) 696-7600 .. **Alten**, Heidi L '97 %Duvin C&H -1301 E 9th -20th Fl Erievw Twr
-Cleveland 44114 **Fx:**696-2038

(216) 931-6000 .. **Alten**, John M '99 %Ulmer & B LLP -1300 E 9th
-Ste 900 Penton Media Bldg -Cleveland 44114 **Fx:**931-6001

(513) 629-1702 .. **Altenau**, Michael J '88 Western & Southern Life Ins Co -400 Bway
-Cincinnati 45202

(703) 588-6720 .. **Altenburg**, John D Jr. '73 US Army JAG -Dept of the Army
-Washington, DC 20310

(937) 332-7016 .. **Altenburger**, Scott R '85 Miami Cnty Crt Cmmn Pls -Safety Bldg
-Troy 45373

(614) 224-8160 .. **Alter**, Mitchell J '81 (Vickery R&A) -500 S Front -Ste 200
-Columbus 43215 **Fx:**224-4943

(954) 769-5560 .. **Alter**, Robert T '00 Hon Gonzalez -299 E Broward Blvd -205D
-Fort Lauderdale, FL 33301

(856) 667-7338 .. **Alterman**, Stuart J '86 (Alterman & Assoc) -800 Kings Hwy N
-Ste 301 -Cherry Hill, NJ 08034 **Fx:**667-0550

(614) 475-3178 .. **Althauser**, Martha G '80 Physicians Ins Co of Ohio -One
Easton Oval -Ste 530 -Columbus 43219

(202) 508-9100 .. **Altherr**, Robert F Jr. '80 (Banner & W,Ltd.) -1001 G NW -Ste 1100
-Washington, DC 20001 **Fx:**508-9299

(216) 696-6776 .. **Althouse**, Philip D '91 -2012 W 25th -Ste 715 -Cleveland 44113
Fx:696-9824

(937) 223-1201 .. **Altick & Corwin Co,LPA** -1 S Main -1700 One Dayton Ctr
-Dayton 45402 **Fx:**223-5100

(440) 964-2700 .. **Altier**, Christopher T '89 -3503 Carpenter Rd -Ashtabula 44004
Fx:964-7710

(937) 332-6848 .. **Altier**, Mark W '73 Miami Cnty Pros -201 W Main -Troy 45373
Fx:440-5961

(330) 836-2636 .. **Altier**, Mary W '79 -534 Garnette Rd -Akron 44313

(440) 964-3311 .. **Altier**, Samuel L Jr. '82 -1027 Lk Av -Ashtabula 44004

(419) 269-2156 .. **Altiere**, James N III '90 Professional Corp Mgmt Co
-5967 Telegraph Rd -Ste C -Toledo 43612

(216) 383-2708 .. **Altieri**, Bruce E '85 Lincoln Elctrc Co -22801 St Clair Av
-Cleveland 44117

(440) 930-8072 .. **Altieri**, Mark P '80 Wickens HPC&B -35765 Chester Rd
-Avon 44011 **Fx:**937-4466

(513) 621-6699 .. **Altimari**, Rita M '88 SW Fincl Srvcs -537 E Pete Rose Way
-Ste 300 -Cincinnati 45202

(740) 345-9611 .. **Altmaier**, Martin D '67 (Morrow G&B,Ltd) -33 W Main -Bx4190
-Newark 43058

(215) 599-1500 .. **Altman**, David '83 %Weltman W&R Co,LPA -325 Chestnut
-Ste 1120 -Philadelphia, PA 19106 **Fx:**599-1505

(513) 721-2180 .. **Altman**, Dennis D '74 (DD Altman Co,LPA) -15 E 8th -Ste 200W
-Cincinnati 45202

(614) 462-3194 .. **Altman**, Marylou G '91 Franklin Cnty Pub Def -373 S High -12th Fl
-Columbus 43215

(419) 592-5105 .. **Altman**, Richard L '83 Henry-Defiance-Fulton Med Srvc -Bx70
-Napoleon 43545

(317) 848-8710 .. **Altman**, Robert L '93 HH Gregg,Inc -4151 E 96th
-Indianapolis, IN 46240

(304) 232-6810 .. **Altmeyer**, Henry Brann '86 (Phillips GK&A) -61 14th
-Wheeling, WV 26003 **Fx:**232-4918

(216) 861-5070 .. **Altmeyer**, Susan M '91 Cleveland Law Library -1 Lakeside Av
-Cleveland 44113

(814) 824-9626 .. **Altomare**, Joseph E '03 -22 E Central Av -Bx373 -Titusville, PA
16354

(614) 221-6751 .. **Alton**, John M '77 JM Alton Co LPA -175 S 3rd -Ste 360
-Columbus 43215

(330) 867-6600 .. **Altwies**, David J '76 Glinsek & H -88 S Portage Path -Ste 301
-Akron 44303 **Fx:**867-9720

(513) 381-9200 .. **Aluotto**, Christopher J '92 %Rendigs FK&D,LLP -One W 4th
-Ste 900 -Cincinnati 45202 **Fx:**381-9206

(216) 687-1311 .. **Alusheff**, Charles P '85 (Reminger & R) -101 Prospect Av W
-1400 Mdlnd Bldg -Cleveland 44115 **Fx:**687-1841

(305) 523-5750 .. **Alvarez**, Tatiana '02 US Dist Ct SDFL -301 N Miami Av
-Miami, FL 33128

(513) 287-2649 .. **Alvaro**, Jay R '95 Cnsl Cinergy Corp -139 E 4th -25 Atrium II
-Bx960 -Cincinnati 45201

(216) 274-0800 .. **Amaddio**, Mark D '89 MD Amaddio Co,LPA -1801 E 9th
-1710 Ohio Svngs Plz -Cleveland 44114

(330) 456-8389 .. **Aman**, Gary J '54 -1101 Bk One Twr -Canton 44702

Aman, Mara C '03 -(Address Unavailable)

(859) 491-5118 .. **Amann**, Thomas W '75 -27 E 4th -Covington, KY 41011

(937) 276-6560 .. **Amarante**, John J '87 Montgomery Cnty Pros -301 W 3rd -Bx972
-Dayton 45422 **Fx:**276-1875

(717) 630-3324 .. **Amata**, Mario A '84 ESAB Group -801 Wilson Av
-Hanover, PA 17331

(216) 443-7295 .. **Amata**, Salvatore '81 Cuyahoga Cnty Pub Def -1849 Prospect Av
-Ste 222 -Cleveland 44115

(216) 651-5000 .. **Amata**, Theodore A '95 -1831 W 54th -Cleveland 44102

Amato, Anthony J '92 -6325 York Rd -Ste 305 -Cleveland 44130

(330) 532-4658 .. **Amato**, Charles C '90 -991 Main -Wellsville 43968

(216) 431-8405 .. **Amato**, Darlene D '91 Cuyahoga Cnty Juv Ct -2163 E 22nd
-Cleveland 44115

(216) 696-1400 .. **Amato**, Marion B '62 (M Amato Co,LPA) -700 W St Clair Av
-Ste 210 -Cleveland 44113 **Fx:**696-4919

(330) 532-4658 .. **Amato**, Nicholas T '89 -991 Main -Wellsville 43968

(216) 573-6000 .. **Amato**, Thomas S '92 %Licata & Assoc Co,LPA
-6480 Rockside Wds Blvd S -Ste 390 -Independence 44131
Fx:573-6333

(216) 621-0200 .. **Ambriola-Anastos**, Lori M '97 %Baker & H LLP -1900 E 9th
-Ste 3200 -Cleveland 44114 **Fx:**696-0740

(614) 461-4444 .. **Ambro**, George R '76 -264 S Wshngtn Av -Columbus 43215

(937) 229-9999 .. **Ambrose**, James T '75 (Ambrose & D) -130 W 2nd -Ste 999
-Dayton 45402 **Fx:**229-7898

(330) 375-2030 .. **Ambrose**, Patricia C '77 Law Dept -161 S High -Ste 202
-Akron 44308

(614) 221-6755 .. **Ambrosio**, Lawrence J '76 -975 S High -Columbus 43206
Fx:445-6494

(330) 393-6400 .. **Ambrosy**, Curtis J '77 (Ambrosy & F) -144 N Park Av -Ste 200
-Warren 44481 **Fx:**392-5685

Amendola, Mark A '89 -33478 Vineyard Park -Avon 44011

(330) 629-9030 .. **Amendolara**, Samuel G '79 -1032 Boardman Canfld Rd
-Youngstown 44512 **Fx:**629-9036

(330) 762-2411 .. **Amer Cunningham Co,LPA** -159 S Main -6th Fl -Akron 44308
Fx:762-9918

(216) 586-3939 .. **Amer**, Kathleen M '04 %Jones D -901 Lakeside Av
-Cleveland 44114 **Fx:**579-0212

(216) 581-8200 .. **Amer**, Margaret E '94 %Robey & R -14402 Granger Rd
-Cleveland 44137

(216) 644-2640 .. **Amerine**, Amy C '81 Dept Ins -2100 Stella Ct -Columbus 43215

(614) 792-3409 .. **Amerine**, Hal D '86 -6360 Fiesta Dr -Columbus 43235

(614) 464-6400 .. **Amerine**, Marjorie Frazier '04 %Vorys SS&P LLP -52 E Gay
-Bx1008 -Columbus 43216 **Fx:**464-6350

(804) 672-1599 .. **Amernick**, Terri G '89 CL Amernick CPA,PC -2505 Waco
-Richmond, VA 23294

(440) 255-4600 .. **Amery**, Eric J '83 AA Importing Inc -6760 Hopkins Rd
-Mentor 44060

(937) 461-4646 .. **Ames**, Arthur A '69 (Ames & A) -131 N Ludlow
-Ste 1311 Talbott Twr -Dayton 45402 **Fx:**461-4747

(330) 792-6611 .. **Ames**, Clarence D '92 Heller MM&M Co LPA -54 Wstchstr Dr
-Bx4144 -Youngstown 44515

(614) 421-5605 .. **Ames**, Kristen M '00 Franklin Cnty Children Srvcs -855 W Mound
-Columbus 43223 **Fx:**275-2589

(614) 577-9970 .. **Ames**, Stephen P '85 (S Ames & Assoc) -6100 Channingway Blvd
-Ste 301 -Columbus 43232

(937) 548-1920 .. **Amick & Breaden** -414 Walnut -Greenville 45331

(937) 548-1920 .. **Amick**, Jeffrey L '77 (Amick & B) -414 Walnut -Greenville 45331

(614) 583-5020 .. **Amid**, Jeanine A '85 %City Atty -3600 Tremont Rd
-Columbus 43221

(330) 492-8717 .. **Amiet**, Ralph D '67 (Buckingham D&B,LLP) -4518 Fulton Dr NW
-Bx35548 -Canton 44735 **Fx:**492-9625

(216) 589-0640 .. **Amigoni**, Albert R '75 -1280 W 3rd -Cleveland 44113

(216) 696-8730 .. **Amin**, Himanshu S '95 (Amin & T LLP) -1900 E 9th
-24th Fl Natl City Ctr -Cleveland 44114 **Fx:**696-8731

(216) 696-8730 .. **Amin & Turocy LLP** -1900 E 9th -24th Fl Natl City Ctr
-Cleveland 44114 **Fx:**696-8731

(216) 932-5100 .. **Amini**, Saeid Baradaran '99 -13916 Cedar Rd -Cleveland 44118

(937) 456-8420 .. **Amiott**, Laura M '95 Cnsl Henny Penny Corp -1219 US Rte 35 W
-Bx60 -Eaton 45320 **Fx:**456-8424

(216) 514-4981 .. **Amirault**, Donald P '01 %CW Relman Co,LPA
-23875 Commerce Pk -Ste 105 -Beachwood 44122

(614) 462-3555 .. **Amlin**, Renee L '99 Franklin Cnty Pros -373 S High
-Columbus 43215

(502) 582-2424 .. **Amlung**, Jonathon N '98 -616 S 5th -Louisville, KY 40202
Fx:589-3004

(513) 533-2996 .. **Amlung**, Pamela K '91 Finney SS&K Co,LPA -2623 Erie Av
-Bx8804 -Cincinnati 45208

(513) 241-4722 .. **Ammer**, Timothy C '98 %Montgomery R&J,LPA -36 E 7th
-Ste 2100 -Cincinnati 45202 **Fx:**241-8775

(513) 634-1873 .. **Ammons**, Bridget D '01 Procter & Gamble Co,Inc -6110 Ctr Hill Av
-Winton Hill Tech Ctr FC2S65 -Cincinnati 45224

(216) 687-2300 .. **Ammons**, Linda L '87 CSU-Marshall Cllg of Law -2121 Euclid Av
-LB138 -Cleveland 44115 **Fx:**687-6881

(216) 781-1212 .. **Ammons**, Randal G '92 %Walter & H LLP -1301 E 9th -Ste 3500
-Cleveland 44114 **Fx:**575-0911

(330) 725-8816 .. **Amodio**, James A '78 %Brown & A,LPA -109 W Lbrty -Bx1117
-Medina 44258

(937) 224-8806 .. **Amos**, John C '00 Montgomery Cnty Pros -301 W 3rd -Bx972
-Dayton 45422 **Fx:**225-3470

(216) 928-2200 .. **Amos**, Marc D '04 %Sutter OM&F -1301 E 9th -3600 Erievw Twr
-Cleveland 44114 **Fx:**928-4400

(330) 535-6650 .. **Amourgis**, Julius P '98 -611 W Market -Ste 1 -Akron 44303

(216) 664-4407 .. **Amponsah**, Kim D '85 City Div of Taxation -1701 Lakeside Av
-Cleveland 44114

(330) 471-4044 .. **Amrhein**, Christine D '87 Timken Corp -1835 Dueber Av SW
-GNW-11 -Canton 44706

(513) 651-6800 .. **Amrine**, Kimberly S '00 %Frost BT LLC -201 E 5th -2200 PNC Ctr
-Cincinnati 45202 **Fx:**651-6981

(330) 702-9700 .. **Ams**, John A '02 %Pfau P&M -6715 Tippecanoe Rd -Bx9070
-Youngstown 44513

(330) 821-1430 .. **Amsden-Michel**, Alissa A '01 Geiger TS&H -1844 W State -Ste A
-Alliance 44601 **Fx:**821-2217

(216) 575-3283 .. **Amstadt**, Nancy Rae '99 Natl City Corp -1900 E 9th
-Loc 2101 17th Fl -Cleveland 44114

(330) 744-4137 .. **Amstutz**, Clarence John Jr. '60 OfCnsl Friedman & R Co,LPA
-100 Fed Plz E -Ste 300 City Centre One -Youngstown 44503
Fx:744-9962

(330) 375-8349 .. **Amundsen**, Richard S '74 Natl City Bank -Bx2130 -Akron 44309

(419) 242-7985 .. **Anagnos**, Joyce '04 %Roetzel & A,LPA -One SeaGate -9th Fl
-Toledo 43604 **Fx:**242-0316

(216) 741-8552 .. **Anastos**, James M '97 Capstone Rlty Advisors,LLC
-1120 Chester Av -Ste 300 -Cleveland 44114

(216) 664-2737 .. **Anastos**, Thomas Leo '89 Dept of Law -601 Lakeside Av
-Rm 106 City Hall -Cleveland 44114 **Fx:**664-2663

(513) 731-8080 .. **Anaya**, George Antonio '97 -6215 Cortelyou Av -Cincinnati 45213
    Anaya, Rebecca K '96 -293 Millstead Ct -Lawrenceville, GA 30043

(513) 721-1997 .. **Ancona**, Perry L '72 P Ancona Co,LPA -917 Main -2nd Fl
-Cincinnati 45202

(216) 368-3600 .. **Andelman**, Barbara F '86 CWRU Law Schl -11075 East Blvd
-Cleveland 44106

(216) 443-9000 .. **Anderle**, Robert D '95 (Porter WM&A LLP) -925 Euclid Av
-Ste 1700 -Cleveland 44115 **Fx:**443-9011

(937) 667-4481 .. **Andersen**, Nicholas I '04 %Dysinger S&D -249 S Garber Dr
-Tipp City 45371 **Fx:**667-5393

(202) 966-8287 .. **Andersen**, Robert M '76 SrCnsl LeBoeuf LG&M
-1875 Conn Av NW -Ste 1200 -Washington, DC 20009
Fx:986-8102

(216) 861-2388 .. **Andersen**, Todd J '87 (TJ Andersen Co,LPA) -526 Superior Av
-Ste 455 -Cleveland 44114
    Andersen, Wendy L '98 -9546 Benchmark Ln -Cincinnati 45242

(937) 372-4436 .. **Anderson**, Alan G '73 (Wead AP&A) -53 W Main -BxH
-Xenia 45385

(440) 988-7918 .. **Anderson**, Alan W '72 -238 Church -Amherst 44001 **Fx:**988-9521

(216) 781-1111 .. **Anderson**, Benjamin H '97 Weisman G&W Co,LPA
-101 Prospect Av -1600 Mdlnd Bldg -Cleveland 44115
Fx:781-6747

(937) 227-3700 .. **Anderson**, Bradley D '93 %Faruki I&C PLL -10 N Ludlow
-500 Cthse Plz SW -Dayton 45402 **Fx:**227-3717

(740) 532-7779 .. **Anderson**, Brigham M '04 %Anderson & A -408 Park Av -Bx712
-Ironton 45638
    Anderson, Candace C '92 -(Address Unavailable)

(717) 787-1471 .. **Anderson**, Carl E II '81 PA Dept of Banking -333 Market -16th Fl
-Harrisburg, PA 17101 **Fx:**783-8427

(800) 224-7914 .. **Anderson**, Carl W '90 (LAWO) -125 W Water -Sandusky 44870
Fx:(419) 609-9173

(419) 289-6500 .. **Anderson**, Charles D '59 (Wilson & A) -46 W Main -Bx650
-Ashland 44805 **Fx:**281-8492

(419) 245-2740 .. **Anderson**, Charles R II '78 Industrial Commssn of OH
-One Govt Ctr -Ste 1500 -Toledo 43604

(937) 865-6800 .. **Anderson**, Christopher J '95 Lexis/Nexis -Bx933 -Dayton 45401

(912) 644-5772 .. **Anderson**, Corinne E '00 %Bouhan W&L,LLP -447 Bull -Bx2139
-Savannah, GA 31402

(740) 532-4554 .. **Anderson**, Curtis B '97 (Edwards KA&S Co LPA) -211 Center
-Ironton 45638

(419) 798-5857 .. **Anderson**, Daniel D '87 -234 Golf Club Dr -Key West, FL 33040

(614) 462-5013 .. **Anderson**, Daniel M '96 (Schottenstein Z&D) -250 West
-Bx165020 -Columbus 43216 **Fx:**462-5135

(518) 426-4600 .. **Anderson**, David G '97 %Couch W,LLP -540 Bway -7th Fl
-Bx22222 -Albany, NY 12201 **Fx:**426-0376

(419) 358-2464 .. **Anderson**, David L '79 -334 S Jackson -Bluffton 45817

(614) 719-1579 .. **Anderson**, Douglas L '91 Dept Ins -2100 Stella Ct -Columbus
43215

(614) 529-7099 .. **Anderson**, Douglas R '93 -4440 Dublin Rd -Columbus 43221

(330) 535-4000 .. **Anderson**, Dreama '90 (Anderson M&L) -120 E Mill -Ste 315
-Akron 44308

(419) 447-0507 .. **Anderson**, Eleanor J '01 %JT Barga -120 Jffrsn -Bx200
-Tiffin 44883 **Fx:**447-4447

(740) 349-8581 .. **Anderson**, Eric L '97 OfCnsl Calig & H,LPA -29 S Park Pl
-Newark 43055 **Fx:**345-4101

(440) 639-0300 .. **Anderson**, George F '81 -1610 Mentor Av -Ste 2
-Painesville 44077
    Anderson, Gerald L '77 -Bx555 -Saint Paris 43072

(614) 539-2533 .. **Anderson**, Harold J III '92 SWACO -6220 Young Rd
-Grove City 43123

(614) 433-7941 .. **Anderson**, Hugh Russell III '72 -399 Highgate Av
-Worthington 43085

(513) 965-8302 .. **Anderson**, Isaac L III '88 -1157 St Rt 131 -Ste A -Milford 45150
Fx:248-2829

(419) 252-6268 .. **Anderson**, James C '79 (Spengler N PLL) -608 Mad Av -Ste 1000
-Toledo 43604 **Fx:**241-8599

(419) 213-4700 .. **Anderson**, James Christopher '80 %Lucas Cnty Pros -Adams &
Erie -Lucas Cnty Cthse -Toledo 43624

(513) 636-4000 .. **Anderson**, James M '67 Childrens Hosp & Med Ctr
-3333 Burnet Av -Cincinnati 45229

(614) 875-4895 .. **Anderson**, Jeffrey S '89 -3083 Columbus -Grove City 43123

(740) 362-8341 .. **Anderson**, John R '87 -187 W Lincoln Av -Delaware 43015

(614) 227-2000 .. **Anderson**, Jon M '61 (Porter WM&A LLP) -41 S High
-Columbus 43215 **Fx:**227-2100

(219) 425-4657 .. **Anderson**, Kathleen M '01 (Barnes & T) -600 1 Summit Sq
-Fort Wayne, IN 46802

(318) 456-2561 .. **Anderson**, Keith S '04 US Air Force SJAG -334 Davis Av -Ste 100
-Barksdale AFB, LA 71110

(513) 695-1325 .. **Anderson**, Keith W '83 Warren Cnty Pros -500 Justice Dr
-Lebanon 45036 **Fx:**695-2962

(859) 669-8000 .. **Anderson**, Kevin T '93 Shire US Inc -1 Rvrfrnt Pl -Ste 900
-Newport, KY 41071 **Fx:**669-8414

(614) 644-7342 .. **Anderson**, Kimberly C '93 Dept Mntl Rtrdtn -1810 Sullivant Av
-Columbus 43266 **Fx:**752-8551

(440) 934-3700 .. **Anderson**, Kurt D '90 (Fauver K-W&D) -5333 Meadow Ln Ct
-Elyria 44035 **Fx:**934-3708

(614) 692-3284 .. **Anderson**, Kyle B '03 Defense Supply Cntr Columbus
-3990 E Broad -Columbus 43216

(216) 586-3939 .. **Anderson**, Laura R '97 %Jones D -901 Lakeside Av
-Cleveland 44114 **Fx:**579-0212

(601) 206-9450 .. **Anderson**, Lula M '78 -Bx31147 -Jackson, MS 39286
Fx:206-9451

(614) 466-3132 .. **Anderson**, Mark S '70 OH Liquor Control Comm -77 S High
-18th Fl -Columbus 43215 **Fx:**466-4564

(614) 464-1877 .. **Anderson**, Marty '77 (Sowald S&C) -400 S 5th -Ste 101
-Columbus 43215

    Anderson, Mary K '96 -6716 Wooden Shoe Ct
-Liberty Township 45044

(937) 865-6800 .. **Anderson**, Maureen H '96 Lexis/Nexis -Bx933 -Dayton 45401

(614) 644-1414 .. **Anderson**, McDonald E '82 Workers Comp -30 W Spring
-Level 26 -Columbus 43215

(614) 462-3194 .. **Anderson**, Melani C '87 Franklin Cnty Pub Def -373 S High
-12th Fl -Columbus 43215

(419) 228-6365 .. **Anderson**, Michael P '87 (Cory MWR&C,LPA) -101 N Elizabeth
-Ste 607 -Bx1217 -Lima 45802 **Fx:**228-5319

(330) 535-4000 .. **Anderson Miller & Lowry** '82 -120 E Mill -Ste 315 -Akron 44308

(614) 462-3194 .. **Anderson**, Norman Q '77 Franklin Cnty Pub Def -373 S High
-12th Fl -Columbus 43215

(614) 464-6400 .. **Anderson**, Raymond D '79 (Vorys SS&P LLP) -52 E Gay -Bx1008
-Columbus 43216 **Fx:**464-6350

(740) 532-7779 .. **Anderson**, Robert C '78 (Anderson & A) -408 Park Av -Bx712
-Ironton 45638
    Anderson, Robert N '94 -1070 Rainbow Trl -Milford 45150

(614) 460-4645 .. **Anderson**, Rodney W '85 Columbia Gas of OH Inc
-200 Civic Ctr Dr -Bx117 -Columbus 43216

(614) 464-6400 .. **Anderson**, Sandra Jo '76 (Vorys SS&P LLP) -52 E Gay -Bx1008
-Columbus 43216 **Fx:**464-6350

(614) 387-9305 .. **Anderson**, Scott A '91 OH Criminal Sentencing Commssn
-65 S Front -2nd Fl -Columbus 43215
    Anderson, Scott A '93 -6989 Rochelle Ln -Blacklick 43004

(614) 221-2121 .. **Anderson**, Scyld D '95 %Isaac BL&T,LLP -250 E Broad
-Ste 900 Mdlnd Bldg -Columbus 43215 **Fx:**365-9516
    Anderson, Shirley L '04 -1 Maplevw Ct -Cincinnati 45236

(330) 364-1614 .. **Anderson**, Steven A '96 Fitzpatrick Z&R Co LPA -140 Fair Av NW
-Bx1014 -New Philadelphia 44663 **Fx:**343-3077

(937) 328-2574 .. **Anderson**, Susan H '82 Cnty Mun Ct Judge -50 E Columbia
-Ste 317 -Springfield 45502

(937) 225-7687 .. **Anderson**, Thomas W Jr. '00 Fed Pub Def -130 W 2nd
-Dayton 45402

(617) 720-0438 .. **Anderson**, Thurman E '71 SSA-OHA -One Bowdoin Sq -10th Fl
-Boston, MA 02114

(216) 696-7600 .. **Anderson**, Timothy S '99 %Duvin C&H -1301 E 9th -20th
Fl Erievw Twr -Cleveland 44114 **Fx:**696-2038

(614) 644-2840 .. **Anderson**, Todd A '91 EPA -122 S Front -Bx1049
-Columbus 43216

(740) 382-3221 .. **Anderson**, Todd A '96 -198 E Center -Marion 43302

(340) 774-5666 .. **Anderson**, Wayne G '94 Dept Justice -488-50C
Kronprindsens Gade -2nd Fl -St Thomas, VI 00801

(419) 524-8200 .. **Anderson Will O'Donnell & Kitzler LLP** -3 N Main -Ste 703
-Mansfield 44902

(513) 735-9100 .. **Anderson**, William H '69 Sportsmans Market,Inc
-Clermont Cnty Airport -Batavia 45103

(513) 263-4687 .. **Anderson**, William H II '94 IRS -550 Main -Rm 5120
-Cincinnati 45202 **Fx:**263-4624

(513) 946-3000 .. **Anderson**, William H Jr. '87 Hamilton Cnty Pros -230 E 9th
-Cincinnati 45202 **Fx:**946-3017

(740) 532-7779 .. **Anderson**, William M '77 (Anderson & A) -408 Park Av -Bx712
-Ironton 45638

(440) 328-2206 .. **Anderson-White**, Charlita '88 Lorain Cnty Juvenile Ct -225 Court
-2nd Fl -Elyria 44035

(216) 592-5000 .. **Anderton**, A Michael '93 (Tucker E&W LLP) -925 Euclid Av
-1150 Huntngtn Bldg -Cleveland 44115 **Fx:**592-5009

(419) 422-2121 .. **Andes**, Ronald L '88 Marathon Ashland Petro LLC -539 S Main
-Findlay 45840 **Fx:**421-8402

(513) 243-5955 .. **Andes**, William S '92 GE -1 Neumann Way -H-17, Rm E-125
-Cincinnati 45215

(440) 327-1925 .. **Andolsen**, Robert R '94 -36100 Maple Dr -North Ridgeville 44039
Fx:327-5629

(216) 621-0200 .. **Andorka**, Frank H '75 (Baker & H LLP) -1900 E 9th -Ste 3200
-Cleveland 44114 **Fx:**696-0740

(614) 224-1222 .. **Andorka**, Gary P '86 %Maguire & S,LLP -250 Civic Ctr Dr
-Ste 200 -Columbus 43215 **Fx:**224-1236

(422) 281-3330 .. **Andracki**, Richard F '97 Andracki Law Offices -1801 Lawyers Bldg
-Pittsburgh, PA 15219

(937) 226-9354 .. **Andrade**, David '00 %Macey & C -40 W 4th -Ste 2160
-Dayton 45402 **Fx:**226-9359

(216) 621-0200 .. **Andrassy**, Dana R '94 (Baker & H LLP) -1900 E 9th -Ste 3200
-Cleveland 44114 **Fx:**696-0740
    Andreas, Frederick W '91 -70 E 208th -Euclid 44123

(330) 253-5060 .. **Andreeff**, Nickolas P '60 Brennan M&D,LLC -75 E Market -Akron
44308 **Fx:**253-1977

(216) 586-3939 .. **Andreini**, Mark J '94 %Jones D -901 Lakeside Av -Cleveland
44114 **Fx:**579-0212

(937) 323-9783 .. **Andreoff**, Alexander '62 (A Andreoff & Assoc) -31 E High -2nd Fl
-Springfield 45502 **Fx:**525-1573

(419) 241-3213 .. **Andres**, Van P '89 Ritter RM&J -405 Mad Av -Ste 1850
-Toledo 43604 **Fx:**241-4925

(614) 464-1999 .. **Andrew**, Craig D '80 -454 E Main -Ste 200 -Columbus 43215

(216) 520-0088 .. **Andrew**, Donna M '96 Pepple & W Ltd -5005 Rockside Rd
-Ste 260 -Cleveland 44131 **Fx:**520-0044

(513) 381-2838 .. **Andrew**, Marcia V '88 (Taft S&H LLP) -425 Walnut -Ste 1800
-Cincinnati 45202 **Fx:**381-0205

(614) 228-8400 .. **Andrews**, Alexander M '81 (Ulmer & B LLP) -88 E Broad
-Ste 1600 -Columbus 43215 **Fx:**228-8561

(330) 830-1718 .. **Andrews**, Amy Sue '98 Massillon Law Dept -2 James Duncan Plz
-Massillon 44646 **Fx:**833-7144

(216) 621-0200 .. **Andrews**, Barry W '95 (Baker & H LLP) -1900 E 9th -Ste 3200
-Cleveland 44114 **Fx:**696-0740
    Andrews, Carol E '04 -(Address Unavailable)

(216) 621-0150 .. **Andrews**, Catherine V '00 %Hahn L&P LLP
-3300 BP Twr/200 Pub Sq -Ste 3300 -Cleveland 44114
Fx:241-2824

(614) 248-6035 .. **Andrews**, Charles F '74 Banc One Mgt Corp -100 E Broad
-OH1-0158 -Columbus 43271

(937) 225-4652 .. **Andrews**, Charles G '80 Montgomery Cnty Pub Def -117 S Main
-Ste 400 -Dayton 45422 **Fx:**225-4669

(440) 942-7757 .. **Andrews**, Charles M '78 -35110 Euclid Av -Willoughby 44094

(216) 447-1551 .. **Andrews**, David T '93 (Ross B&S Co LPA)
-6000 Freedom Square Dr -Ste 540 -Cleveland 44131
Fx:447-1554

(614) 224-1222 .. **Andrews**, Donald S '98 %Maguire & S,LLP -250 Civic Ctr Dr
-Ste 200 -Columbus 43215 **Fx:**224-1236

(216) 771-1430 .. **Andrews**, Douglas A '84 (Masters & Assoc,LPA) -1111 Superior
Av -Cleveland 44114 **Fx:**771-2070

(212) 737-1592 .. **Andrews**, Eleanor S '90 -80 E End Av -New York, NY 10028

(330) 757-2454 .. **Andrews**, James H '82 James H. Andrews -Bx5250
-Poland 44514

(440) 942-7757 .. **Andrews**, Junior Melvin '50 -35110 Euclid Av -Willoughby 44094

(440) 998-6835 .. **Andrews**, Mark W '76 (Andrews & P LLC) -4817 State Rd
-Ste 100 -Bx10 -Ashtabula 44005

(216) 621-0200 .. **Andrews**, Oakley V '65 (Baker & H LLP) -1900 E 9th -Ste 3200
-Cleveland 44114 **Fx:**696-0740

(440) 998-6835 .. **Andrews & Pontius LLC** -4817 State Rd -Ste 100 -Bx10
-Ashtabula 44005

(440) 357-4601 .. **Andrews**, Richard C '69 Isk Americas Inc -7474 Auburn Rd
-Bx8011 -Concord 44077

(330) 740-2330 .. **Andrews**, Robert J '89 Mahoning Cnty Pros -21 W Boardman
-6th Fl -Youngstown 44503 **Fx:**740-2008

(614) 228-5931 .. **Andrews**, Scott R '02 %Mazanec R&R Co,LPA -250 Civic Ctr Dr
-Ste 400 -Columbus 43215 **Fx:**228-5934

(330) 499-0900 .. **Andrews**, Timothy G '73 -4808 Munson NW -Canton 44718

(216) 299-7508 .. **Andrews**, William H III '02 Andrews Fin & Est Planning
-24803 Detroit Rd -Ste A -Westlake 44145

Andrews-Singh, April L '01 -5188 NW 47th Av
-Coconut Creek, FL 33073

(801) 364-0123 .. **Andrewsen**, Brent A '00 %T Bowen,PC -175 SW Temple
-Bx11637 -Salt Lake City, UT 84147 **Fx:**595-0976

(614) 221-2700 .. **Andrioff**, James J '85 (J Andrioff Co, LPA) -42 E Gay -Ste 1500
-Columbus 43215

(614) 228-5931 .. **Anelli**, Dianna M '94 Mazanec R&R Co,LPA -250 Civic Ctr Dr
-Ste 400 -Columbus 43215 **Fx:**228-5934

(216) 687-1311 .. **Anenson**, T Leigh '94 %Reminger & R -101 Prospect Av W
-1400 Mdlnd Bldg -Cleveland 44115 **Fx:**687-1841

(330) 262-8871 .. **Anfang**, William F III '83 -434 N Market -Wooster 44691

(614) 462-4283 .. **Angel**, Michael W '78 Franklin Cnty Cmn Pleas Ct -375 S High
-Columbus 43215 **Fx:**462-6292

(440) 244-4839 .. **Angel**, Stephen B '72 -750 Bway -#205 -Lorain 44052

(740) 282-2676 .. **Angel-Shaffer**, Arlene B '81 (Shaffer & S) -316 N 4th
-Steubenville 43952

(614) 466-2766 .. **Angell**, Lauren C '89 Atty Gen -30 E Broad -Columbus 43215
Fx:644-1926

(614) 471-5881 .. **Angell**, Robert C '93 RC Angell,LLC -346 Halsbury Cir -Bx30788
-Gahanna 43230 **Fx:**471-5881

(330) 545-6912 .. **Angelo**, Barbara J '85 -103 Crumlin Av -Girard 44420

(216) 789-5536 .. **Angelo**, Michael J '84 -920 Trmnl Twr -50 Pub Sq
-Cleveland 44113 **Fx:**(480) 785-8592

(937) 223-5200 .. **Angelo**, Thomas III '83 Flanagan LH&S -318 W 4th -Dayton 45402
Fx:223-3335

(216) 443-5710 .. **Angelotta**, John L '52 -1250 Ontario -Cnty Justice Ctr
-Cleveland 44113

(937) 322-0891 .. **Angle**, Tammi J '94 (Cole AH&D) -333 N Limestone -Bx1687
-Springfield 45501 **Fx:**322-9931

(440) 284-5100 .. **Anglewicz**, Gregory A '04 Cnsl LandAmerica Financial Grp
-424 Middle Av -Elyria 44035 **Fx:**284-5161

(216) 443-8579 .. **Angley**, Sonia R '98 Ct of Common Pleas -1200 Ontario -11th Fl
-Cleveland 44113

(216) 363-4500 .. **Angney**, Jessica L '01 %Benesch FC&A LLP -200 Pub Sq
-Ste 2300 -Cleveland 44114 **Fx:**363-4588

(703) 248-0333 .. **Angres**, Mark B '03 %Davidson BK&J,LLP -4501 N Fairfax Dr
-Ste 920 -Arlington, VA 22203 **Fx:**248-9558

(614) 466-6750 .. **Angus**, George P '78 OH Dept Taxation -30 E Broad -22nd Fl
-Columbus 43215

(216) 931-2346 .. **Anhold**, Gordon A '71 Northern Trust Bank -127 Pub Sq -Ste 5150
-Cleveland 44114

(330) 650-0088 .. **Ania**, Anthony J '91 Bevan & Assoc LPA,Inc -10360 Nrthfld Rd
-Northfield 44067 **Fx:**467-4493

(614) 466-1158 .. **Aninao**, Joseph G '84 Legis Srvc Commssn -77 S High
-Columbus 43215

(614) 297-4483 .. **Anker**, Ruth L '02 Pathology Srvcs Inc -1087 Dennison Av
-Columbus 43201

(248) 645-1483 .. **Ankers**, Gary C '97 %Howard & H -39400 Woodward Av -Ste 101
-Bloomfield Hills, MI 48304

(216) 241-8333 .. **Ankuda**, Christopher J '01 Ritzler C&S,Ltd -1001 Lakeside Av
-1550 North Pnt Twr -Cleveland 44114 **Fx:**241-5890

(440) 331-0599 .. **Annandale**, Melinda J '91 -20033 Detroit Road
-Rocky River 44116

(614) 466-1938 .. **Annarino**, John A '85 Workers Comp -30 W Spring -Level 26
-Columbus 43215

(513) 421-1313 .. **Anness**, Harold L '78 (Griffin-F,LLP) -3500 Redbank Rd
-Cincinnati 45227 **Fx:**421-1118

(216) 360-7200 .. **Annos**, George J '92 %Carlisle MRK&U Co,LPA
-24755 Chagrin Blvd -Ste 200 -Cleveland 44122 **Fx:**360-7210

(330) 675-2426 .. **Annos**, LuWayne '91 Trumbull Cnty Pros -160 High NW
-Warren 44481

(216) 621-0150 .. **Ansberry**, Sean M '99 %Hahn L&P LLP -3300 BP Twr/200 Pub Sq
-Ste 3300 -Cleveland 44114 **Fx:**241-2824

(216) 485-1040 .. **Anselmo**, Christopher A '89 (Anselmo & Co,LLC) -4161 Ridge Rd
-Cleveland 44144

(216) 621-0200 .. **Anselmo**, Michelle B '04 %Baker & H LLP -1900 E 9th -Ste 3200
-Cleveland 44114 **Fx:**696-0740

(216) 566-0064 .. **Anselmo**, Victor V '88 %Armstrong MD&Z -101 Prospect Av W
-1725 The Mdlnd Bldg -Cleveland 44115 **Fx:**566-0224

(937) 223-8177 .. **Anspach**, Douglas C Jr. '01 %Coolidge WW&L -33 W 1st -Ste 600
-Dayton 45402 **Fx:**223-6705

(419) 246-5757 .. **Anspach Meeks & Nunn,LLP** -300 Mad Av -Ste 1600
-Toledo 43604 **Fx:**321-6979

(419) 246-5757 .. **Anspach**, Robert M '73 (Anspach M&N,LLP) -300 Mad Av
-Ste 1600 -Toledo 43604 **Fx:**321-6979

(614) 221-2121 .. **Anspaugh**, Donald Lee '80 Isaac BL&T,LLP -250 E Broad
-Ste 900 Mdlnd Bldg -Columbus 43215 **Fx:**365-9516

(614) 628-8000 .. **Anstaett**, Elizabeth L '91 Dreher L&T LLP -41 S High
-2250 Huntngtn Ctr -Columbus 43215 **Fx:**628-1600

(513) 621-2100 .. **Anstaett**, Jennifer G '01 %Beckman W&S LLC -120 E 4th
-1200 Mercantile Ctr -Cincinnati 45202 **Fx:**621-0106

(419) 334-7436 .. **Ansted**, Barbara J '78 -201 N Park Av -Fremont 43420

(513) 721-1311 .. **Antaki**, Vincent P '00 %Reminger & R -7 W 7th -Ste 1990
-Cincinnati 45202 **Fx:**721-2553

(419) 695-7050 .. **Antalis**, Gregory M '78 -125 E 3rd -Bx17 -Delphos 45833

(513) 248-0088 .. **Antell**, Barbara J '77 -228 Mill -Ste 205 -Milford 45150

(513) 241-6748 .. **Anten**, Brian J '79 A Levine -324 Reading Rd -Cincinnati 45202

(609) 750-3805 .. **Anthony**, Anil V '95 ITXC Corp -750 Cllg Rd E
-Princeton, NJ 08540

(513) 946-9200 .. **Anthony**, Brenda A '99 Hamilton Cnty Juv Ct -800 Bway
-Cincinnati 45202 **Fx:**946-9217

(614) 827-7300 .. **Anthony**, Carl A '91 (Freund F&A) -65 E State -Ste 800
-Columbus 43215 **Fx:**827-7303

(440) 230-1700 .. **Anthony**, David S '01 %Sindyla A&S -7425 Royalton Rd
-North Royalton 44133 **Fx:**230-1699

(901) 544-0102 .. **Anthony**, Draga G '89 EEOC -1407 Union Av -Memphis,
TN 38104

(216) 241-3400 .. **Anthony**, Hilary J '00 Cuyahoga Cnty Mental Health Bd
-1400 W 25th -3rd Fl -Cleveland 44113

(330) 492-5151 .. **Anthony**, John F II '77 -4450 Belden Vllg NW -Ste 800
-Canton 44718

(614) 227-2366 .. **Anthony**, Laura G '95 (Bricker & E LLP) -100 S 3rd
-Columbus 43215 **Fx:**227-2390

(513) 852-3497 .. **Anthony**, Lori A '97 Atty Gen -441 Vine -1600 Carew Twr
-Cincinnati 45202 **Fx:**852-3484

(614) 771-1010 .. **Anthony**, Marcell R '72 -3688 Buchmill Falls Dr -Columbus 43221

(614) 340-0011 .. **Anthony**, Michael J '96 Anthony Law Ofc,LLC -555 S Front
-Ste 320 -Columbus 43215

(513) 651-6800 .. **Anthony**, Thomas D '77 (Frost BT LLC) -201 E 5th -2200 PNC Ctr
-Cincinnati 45202 **Fx:**651-6981

(412) 366-3333 .. **Antinone**, Ruth A '84 (Willman & A,LLP) -705 McKnight Park Dr
-Pittsburgh, PA 15237

(312) 861-2000 .. **Antinossi**, Matthew J '03 %Kirkland & E -200 E Randolph Dr
-Chicago, IL 60601

(614) 621-1500 .. **Antipova**, Yelena Y '03 Calfee H&G LLP -21 E State
-1100 Fifth Third Ctr -Columbus 43215 **Fx:**621-0010

(330) 673-3444 .. **Antognoli**, Benito C '79 %Williams W&K -11 S River -Bx396
-Kent 44240

(614) 442-3355 .. **Antolino**, Ralph Jr. '80 Antolino & Assoc,Inc -3240
W Henderson Rd -Ste A -Columbus 43220

(216) 861-2222 .. **Antonelli**, Dominic M '87 (Rieth & A) -200 Pub Sq -Ste 2940
-Cleveland 44114

Antonelli, Mariellen M '02 -2548 Charney Rd -Cleveland 44118

(419) 885-7442 .. **Antonini**, Jennifer J '90 -6034 Needle Rock Ct -Sylvania 43560

(419) 242-2131 .. **Antonini**, Michael J '83 -520 Mad Av -Ste 902 -Toledo 43604

(419) 249-7900 .. **Antonini**, Thomas J '88 (Robison C&O) -Four SeaGate -9th Fl
-Toledo 43604 **Fx:**249-7911

(330) 535-1555 .. **Antoniotti**, Erica L '99 -1 Cascade Plz -Ste 1000 -Akron 44308

(330) 399-6450 .. **Antonucci**, Anthony L '80 -175 Franklin SE -Warren 44481
Fx:399-6457

Antonuk, Theodore E '86 -2434 W Market -Akron 44313

(513) 860-7803 .. **Antony**, John P '89 -1 Katherine Ct -Highland Heights, KY 41076

(614) 221-8448 .. **Antrim**, Donald A '74 (Buckingham D&B,LLP)
-191 W Nationwide Blvd -Ste 300 -Bx151120 -Columbus 43215
Fx:221-8590

(216) 479-8279 .. **Anway**, Stephen P '02 %Squire S&D LLP -127 Pub Sq
-4900 Key Twr -Cleveland 44114 **Fx:**479-8780

(330) 792-6033 .. **Anzellotti Sperling Pazol & Small Co, LPA** -21 N Wickliffe Cir
-Youngstown 44515 **Fx:**793-3384

(614) 645-7483 .. **Anzelmo**, James A '97 City Pros -375 S High -7th Fl
-Columbus 43215

(740) 353-2146 .. **Apel**, John P '97 (Apel & M) -617 5th -Portsmouth 45662
Fx:354-3148

(740) 353-2146 .. **Apel-Miller**, Margaret B '89 (Apel & M) -617 5th
-Portsmouth 45662 **Fx:**354-3148

(216) 771-6597 .. **Apelt**, Ronald A '90 -1422 Euclid Av -Ste 717 -Cleveland 44115

(216) 696-3550 .. **Apicella**, Felix M '54 (Apicella & T) -1300 E 9th
-1200 Penton Media Bldg -Cleveland 44114 **Fx:**696-3830

(419) 782-3010 .. **Aplin**, Robert D '00 Weaner ZBY&H,Ltd -401 Wayne Av
-Defiance 43512 **Fx:**782-8426

(513) 791-8600 .. **Apocotos**, Thomas G '92 Spherion -5151 Pfeiffer Rd -Ste 120
-Cincinnati 45242

(614) 728-7055 .. **Appel**, Henry G '97 Atty Gen -30 E Broad -Columbus 43215
Fx:728-8600

(614) 848-9600 .. **Appel**, Jeffrey L '99 %H Minton & Assoc -6641 N High
-Worthington 43085

(513) 651-6800 .. **Appel**, John H '74 (Frost BT LLC) -201 E 5th -2200 PNC Ctr
-Cincinnati 45202 **Fx:**651-6981

(216) 566-5548 .. **Appelbaum**, Jeffrey R '77 (Thompson H LLP) -127 Pub Sq
-3900 Key Ctr -Cleveland 44114 **Fx:**566-5800

(513) 425-5000 .. **Appenzeller**, Rebecca H '89 AK Steel,Inc -703 Curtis
-Middletown 45043

(330) 337-6624 .. **Apple**, Kenneth B '87 (Williams & A Co LPA) -1376 E State
-Salem 44460 **Fx:**337-0424

(216) 514-4125 .. **Apple**, Sheldon A '63 -25550 Chagrin Blvd -Ste 101
-Cleveland 44122

(513) 651-6800 .. **Applegarth**, Barbara C '79 Cnsl Frost BT LLC -201 E 5th
-2200 PNC Ctr -Cincinnati 45202 **Fx:**651-6981

(614) 239-4822 .. **Applegate**, Amanda M '98 Executive Jet -4111 Brdgway Av
-Columbus 43219

(812) 855-8684 .. **Applegate**, Amy G '88 Indiana Univ Schl of Law -211 S Indna Av
-Child Advcy Clinic -Bloomington, IN 47405

(513) 528-1414 .. **Applegate**, James E '54 (Masters & Co,LPA)
-4760 Sandra Lee Ln -Cincinnati 45244 **Fx:**528-0213

(513) 929-3400 .. **Appleton**, William J '78 (Baker & H LLP) -312 Walnut -Ste 3200
-Cincinnati 45202 **Fx:**929-0303

(216) 621-4636 .. **Arabian**, Anjanette C '01 %Gallup B & Assoc -815 Superior Av E
-Ste 1810 The Superior Bldg -Cleveland 44114

(440) 356-0838 .. **Aragones**, Neil F '95 Lexis Nexis -22242 Rvr Walk Rd
-Rocky River 44116

(740) 654-4141 .. **Aranda**, James C '73 (Stebelton A&S,LPA) -109 N Broad -Bx130
-Lancaster 43130 **Fx:**654-2521

(614) 644-7467 .. **Arata**, Jane S '87 OH Dept Commerce -77 S High
-Columbus 43266

(513) 732-7683 ..**Arbaugh,** Anne M '91 Clermont Cnty CSEA -2400 Clermont Ctr Dr -Ste 106C -Batavia 45103

(216) 622-3600 ..**Arbeznik,** Gary D '76 US Atty -801 W Superior -Ste 400 -Cleveland 44113 **Fx:**622-3370

(330) 399-5518 ..**Arbie,** Phillip S '73 -155 S Park -Ste 100 -Warren 44481

(216) 443-3674 ..**Arbie-McClelland,** Valerie R '93 Cuyahoga Cnty Pub Def -1200 W 3rd NW -100 Lakeside Pl -Cleveland 44113

(502) 587-8974 ..**Arbogast,** Janet R '93 Cnsl Bush Law Ofc -713 E Market -Ste 200 -Louisville, KY 40202 **Fx:**587-8975

(614) 866-9999 ..**Arbuckle,** Charles H '90 Dynalab,Inc -555 Lncstr Av -Reynoldsburg 43068

(216) 787-3638 ..**Arcangelini,** F. M '93 Industrial Commssn of OH -615 Superior Av NW -Cleveland 44113 **Fx:**787-3483

(440) 720-8500 ..**Arcara,** Kristina A '01 Pioneer Stndrd Elec -6065 Parkland Blvd -Mayfield Heights 44124

(419) 249-7100 ..**Arce,** Roman '92 (Marshall & M,LLC) -Four Seagate -8th Fl -Toledo 43604 **Fx:**249-7151

  Arceci, Richard M '81 -7599 Brinmore Rd -Sagamore Hills 44067

(330) 455-0173 ..**Archer,** John P '01 %Day KRW&R,Ltd -200 Market Av N -Ste 300 -Bx24213 -Canton 44701 **Fx:**455-2633

(740) 376-2400 ..**Archer,** Michael D '00 Cnsl Pioneer Pipe,Inc -2021 Hanna Rd -Marietta 45750 **Fx:**373-8964

(419) 784-5622 ..**Archer,** Stephen R '78 -106 Clinton -Defiance 43512 **Fx:**784-5909

(740) 477-8887 ..**Archer,** William L Jr. '88 -Bx482 -Circleville 43113

(304) 345-5200 ..**Archibald,** Ellen R '02 Kesner K&B -112 Cptl -Bx2587 -Charleston, WV 25329

(216) 621-9870 ..**Archibald,** Robert D '56 OfCnsl McNeal SA&B Co,LPA -123 W Prospect Av -Ste 250 Van Sweringen Arcade -Cleveland 44115 **Fx:**522-1112

(614) 466-6511 ..**Archie,** Deborah '85 Dept Admin Srvcs -30 E Broad -Columbus 43215

  Archinal, David D '92 -5726 Heritage Av -Madison 44057

  Arciaga, Arthur A '81 -Bx42104 -Cleveland 44142

(419) 756-7711 ..**Ardis,** Frank Jr. '74 (Bayer J&A) -362 Lex Av -Mansfield 44907 **Fx:**756-9566

(216) 931-6000 ..**Arendt,** Michelle R '98 %Ulmer & B LLP -1300 E 9th -Ste 900 Penton Media Bldg -Cleveland 44114 **Fx:**931-6001

(317) 387-3800 ..**Arens,** David J '96 %Locke R,LLP -201 N Illinois -Ste 1000 -Bx44961 -Indianapolis, IN 46244 **Fx:**387-3900

(614) 799-2800 ..**Arenstein,** Gilbert G '94 (Zaino & H LPA) -5775 Perimeter Dr -Ste 275 -Dublin 43017 **Fx:**799-1500

(513) 651-5666 ..**Arenstein,** Hal R '79 (Arenstein & G) -114 E 8th -Cincinnati 45202

(216) 623-0150 ..**Arfons,** Walter Chad II '97 %Roetzel & A,LPA -1375 E 9th -One Cleve Ctr 9th Fl -Cleveland 44114 **Fx:**623-0134

(412) 355-8668 ..**Argentieri,** Kenneth M '97 (Kirkpatrick & LNG LLP) -535 Smithfld -Henry W Oliver Bldg -Pittsburgh, PA 15222 **Fx:**355-6501

(440) 449-3333 ..**Argie D'Amico & Vitantonio** -6449 Wilson Mills Rd -Mayfield Village 44143

(440) 449-3333 ..**Argie,** George J '82 Argie D&V -6449 Wilson Mills Rd -Mayfield Village 44143

(513) 579-6980 ..**Argo,** Susan M '96 Fifth Third Bank -38 Fountain Sq Plz -Cincinnati 45263

(901) 544-3153 ..**Arguello,** Pedro M '00 NLRB -1407 Union Av -Ste 800 -Memphis, TN 38104

(216) 443-7295 ..**Arinze,** Francis M '98 Cuyahoga Cnty Pub Def -1849 Prospect Av -Ste 222 -Cleveland 44115

(216) 515-1660 ..**Arison,** Barbara J '75 (Frantz W LLP) -127 Pub Sq -2500 Key Center -Cleveland 44114 **Fx:**515-1650

(937) 278-4214 ..**Arkenberg,** Kenneth J '53 -4133 N Dixie Dr -Dayton 45414

(614) 466-6928 ..**Arkenberg,** Tina M '96 Workers Comp -30 W Spring -Level 26 -Columbus 43215

(330) 437-0025 ..**Arkow,** Seth W '98 -101 Central Plz S -300 Bank One Twr -Canton 44702

(859) 331-2000 ..**Arlinghaus,** Christopher J '97 %O'Hara RTS&S -25 Crestvw Hills Mall Rd -Ste 201 -Bx17411 -Covington, KY 41017

(419) 213-3000 ..**Armacost,** James S '76 Lucas Cnty CSEA -701 Adams -Toledo 43624

(937) 225-5751 ..**Armanini,** Debra B '82 Montgomery Cnty Pros -301 W 3rd -Bx972 -Dayton 45422 **Fx:**225-3470

(937) 296-4902 ..**Armanini,** Joseph S '82 LM Berry & Co -3170 Kettering Blvd -Dayton 45439

(216) 676-4600 ..**Armanini,** Todd T '87 -5231 Engle Rd -Brook Park 44142

(330) 491-5216 ..**Armatas,** Steven A '84 (Buckingham D&B,LLP) -4518 Fulton Dr NW -Bx35548 -Canton 44735 **Fx:**492-9625

(419) 327-4303 ..**Armbruster,** Clare C '86 Wise & D,Ltd -151 N Mich -Ste 333 -Toledo 43624 **Fx:**327-4302

(330) 434-2113 ..**Armbruster Kelley Kot Honeck & Baker** -159 S Main -Ste 720 -Akron 44308

(330) 434-2113 ..**Armbruster,** Robert '78 Armbruster KKH&B -159 S Main -Ste 720 -Akron 44308

(740) 387-1613 ..**Armengau,** Javier H '98 -208 S Main -Marion 43302

(937) 393-3397 ..**Armintrout,** George W '84 (Armintrout Law Ofc) -120 Governor Trimble Pl -Hillsboro 45133

(305) 375-0111 ..**Armour,** Pamela Ann '94 %Ferraro & Assoc,PA -4000 Pnc de Leon Blvd -Ste 700 -Miami, FL 33146 **Fx:**379-6222

(937) 382-1494 ..**Armour,** Scott A '85 R&L Carriers -600 Gillam Rd -Wilmington 45177

(937) 225-4892 ..**Armstead,** Thaddeus J '82 Montgomery Cnty Pros/CSEA -14 W 4th -Ste 510 -Dayton 45402

(216) 363-1400 ..**Armstrong,** Barbara L '87 (Buckley K,LPA) -600 E Superior Av -Ste 1400 -Cleveland 44114 **Fx:**579-1020

(330) 505-1811 ..**Armstrong,** Charles R '73 Untd Steel Wrkrs Intl Union -950 Youngstown Warren Rd -Niles 44446

(614) 237-6718 ..**Armstrong,** Daniel G '01 Capital Univ -303 E Broad -Columbus 43215

(440) 243-5010 ..**Armstrong,** Erin A '97 %D Briller Co,LPA -7379 Pearl Rd -Middleburg Heights 44130 **Fx:**243-0105

  Armstrong, Heidi A '93 The V Co -2136 Noble Rd -Cleveland 44112

(937) 461-4648 ..**Armstrong,** James S '78 (Ames & A) -131 N Ludlow -Ste 1311 Talbott Twr -Dayton 45402 **Fx:**461-4747

(330) 643-2900 ..**Armstrong,** James W '91 Summit Cnty Juv Ct -650 Dan -Akron 44310

(513) 977-8200 ..**Armstrong,** Jody H '92 %Dinsmore & S LLP -255 E 5th -Ste 1900 -Cincinnati 45202 **Fx:**977-8141

(330) 499-8648 ..**Armstrong,** John A '98 PatentHlth,LLC -5080 Aultman Av NW -Canton 44720

(513) 458-2320 ..**Armstrong,** John B '73 Chester Lab,Inc -2900 Section Rd -Cincinnati 45237

(513) 665-3500 ..**Armstrong,** Kelly A '03 %Freund F&A -105 E 4th -Ste 1400 -Cincinnati 45202 **Fx:**665-3503

(941) 366-9692 ..**Armstrong,** Kenneth E '73 Venvest Inc -2 N Tamiami Trl -Ste 506 -Sarasota, FL 34236 **Fx:**366-9592

(937) 544-3331 ..**Armstrong,** Kenneth L Jr. '77 -107 E Main -Bx236 -West Union 45693

(419) 259-7488 ..**Armstrong,** Kristopher J '04 US Dist Ct-Nrthn Dist -1716 Spielbusch Av -Rm #210 -Toledo 43624

(614) 326-0919 ..**Armstrong,** Leslie '89 Leslie Armstrong -2244 Woodstock Rd -Columbus 43221

(216) 696-3311 ..**Armstrong,** Lester W '86 (Kahn K) -1301 E 9th -2600 Erievw Twr -Cleveland 44114 **Fx:**623-4912

(614) 227-8821 ..**Armstrong,** Maria J '87 %Bricker & E LLP -100 S 3rd -Columbus 43215 **Fx:**227-2390

(937) 327-1700 ..**Armstrong,** Melinda M '04 Clark Co CSEA -1346 Lagonda Av -Springfield 45503

(216) 566-0064 ..**Armstrong Mitchell Damiani & Zaccagnini** -101 Prospect Av W -1725 The Mdlnd Bldg -Cleveland 44115 **Fx:**566-0224

(216) 566-0064 ..**Armstrong,** Timothy J '72 (Armstrong MD&Z) -101 Prospect Av W -1725 The Mdlnd Bldg -Cleveland 44115 **Fx:**566-0224

  Armstrong, Wendy R '97 -2515 Legends Way -Crestview Hills, KY 41017

(216) 348-0041 ..**Armstrong,** William E '67 (Deacon H&A,Ltd) -127 Pub Sq -Ste 4110 -Cleveland 44114 **Fx:**348-0040

(216) 664-3584 ..**Armstrong,** William H Jr. '92 Dept of Law -601 Lakeside Av -Rm 106 City Hall -Cleveland 44114 **Fx:**664-2663

(706) 791-7812 ..**Arn,** Denise J '78 OSJA -US Army Signal Ctr -Fort Gordon, GA 30905

(404) 562-4213 ..**Arnao,** Kimberly L '97 AFLSA -60 Forsyth SW -Ste 8M80 -Atlanta, GA 30303

(330) 675-2426 ..**Arnaut,** Gina B '02 -624 Angeline Dr -Boardman 44512

(614) 462-2235 ..**Arndt,** Randall S '81 (Schottenstein Z&D) -250 West -Bx165020 -Columbus 43216 **Fx:**462-5135

(614) 481-8416 ..**Arnebeck,** Clifford O Jr. '70 -1351 King Av -1st Fl -Columbus 43212 **Fx:**481-8387

(513) 287-3024 ..**Arnett,** Bradley C '95 SrCnsl Cinergy Corp -139 E 4th -25 Atrium II -Bx960 -Cincinnati 45201

(765) 584-2057 ..**Arnett,** Dale W '87 -817 E Wshngtn -Bx488 -Winchester, IN 47394

(614) 224-7771 ..**Arnett,** Henry A '76 (Livorno & A Co,LPA) -280 N High -Ste 1410 -Columbus 43215 **Fx:**224-7775

(912) 767-2955 ..**Arnett,** Laura J '98 GA Sthrn Univ -Dept Political Science -Bx8101 -Statesboro, GA 30460

(216) 360-3737 ..**Arnoff,** Fred J '75 (Persky S&A Co,LPA) -25101 Chagrin Blvd -Ste 350 Signature Sq II -Beachwood 44122 **Fx:**593-0921

(330) 764-9823 ..**Arnold,** Alanna S '01 -226 Bway -Upstairs -Medina 44256 **Fx:**764-9890

(800) 998-9454 ..**Arnold,** Alanna S '01 Cmmnty Lgl Aid Srvcs,Inc -265 S Main -3rd Fl -Akron 44308 **Fx:**(330) 535-0728

(614) 466-6700 ..**Arnold,** Bradford P '88 Tax Appeals -30 E Broad -Columbus 43215 **Fx:**644-5196

(440) 247-4420 ..**Arnold,** Carol '79 -34 S Main -Chagrin Falls 44022

(419) 241-2200 ..**Arnold & Caruso,Ltd** -1822 Cherry -Toledo 43608 **Fx:**255-7623

(614) 752-7204 ..**Arnold,** Daren G '00 OH Dept of Admin Srvcs -30 E Broad -39th Fl -Columbus 43215

(216) 241-6602 ..**Arnold,** David G '66 (Weston HFP&H LLP) -50 Pub Sq -2500 Trmnl Twr -Cleveland 44113 **Fx:**621-8369

(603) 646-2444 ..**Arnold,** Ellen L '79 %Dartmouth Cllg -14 S Main -Ste 2C -Hanover, NH 03755 **Fx:**646-2447

(614) 485-1800 ..**Arnold,** Gayle E '80 (Arnold T&W) -2075 Marble Cliff Ofc Park -Columbus 43215 **Fx:**485-1944

(614) 487-1335 ..**Arnold,** George J '70 HR Gray & Assoc,Inc -1335 Dublin Rd -Ste 100B -Columbus 43215 **Fx:**487-1335

(937) 222-2424 ..**Arnold,** Gordon D '75 (Freund F&A) -1 S Main -Ste 1800 -Dayton 45402 **Fx:**222-5369

(419) 241-4441 ..**Arnold,** Gregory L '80 -608 Mad Av -Ste 1400 -Toledo 43604

(216) 664-2693 ..**Arnold,** Jack M '78 Dept of Law -601 Lakeside Av -Rm 106 City Hall -Cleveland 44114 **Fx:**664-2663

(614) 469-1400 ..**Arnold,** James E '87 Clark PR&S Co,LPA -471 E Broad -Ste 1400 -Columbus 43215 **Fx:**469-0900

(513) 984-8313 ..**Arnold,** James S '93 (J Arnold & Assoc) -9737 Loveland-Madeira Rd -Loveland 45140 **Fx:**984-8040

(513) 351-1174 ..**Arnold,** Jason D '96 -2325 Wshngtn Av -Cincinnati 45212

(330) 456-7702 ..**Arnold,** Jennifer L '99 %R Tscholl -220 Market Av S -Ste 1120 -Canton 44702

(513) 946-3044 ..**Arnold,** John J '78 Hamilton Cnty Pros -230 E 9th -Cincinnati 45202 **Fx:**946-3017

(216) 642-7878 ..**Arnold,** Kemper D '80 (Vantage Fin Grp,Inc) -6200 Rockside Rd -Ste 100 -Bx318082 -Cleveland 44131

(219) 769-2323 ..**Arnold,** Matthew U '96 %Spangler J&D -8396 Mississippi -Merrillville, IN 46410

(419) 947-9111 ..**Arnold,** Michael F '03 Cnty Job & Family Srvcs -619 W Marion Rd -Mount Gilead 43338

(330) 455-0173 ..**Arnold,** Richard W '94 (Day KRW&R,Ltd) -200 Market Av N -Ste 300 -Bx24213 -Canton 44701 **Fx:**455-2633

(614) 462-3555 ..**Arnold,** Stephen W '03 Franklin Cnty Pros -373 S High -Columbus 43215

(330) 375-8648 ..**Arnold,** Suzanne E '98 Natl City Bank -1 Cascade Plz -5th Fl -Akron 44308

(614) 485-1800 ..**Arnold Todaro & Welch** -2075 Marble Cliff Ofc Park -Columbus 43215 **Fx:**485-1944

(937) 222-3322 ..**Arnold Todaro & Welch** -130 W 2nd -Ste 940 -Dayton 45402

(216) 761-7601 ..**Arnold,** Wanda R '80 -1098 E 98th -Cleveland 44108

(419) 241-2200 ..**Arnold,** William D '87 (Arnold & C,Ltd) -1822 Cherry -Toledo 43608 **Fx:**255-7623

(614) 436-0093 ..**Arnold,** William H '77 -6848 Alloway W -Worthington 43085

(216) 621-0200 ..**Arnold,** William L '77 OfCnsl Baker & H LLP -1900 E 9th -Ste 3200 -Cleveland 44114 **Fx:**696-0740

(330) 425-4201 ..Arnovitz, Michael S '86 (Reimer L&A Co,LPA) -2450 Edison Blvd
-Bx968 -Twinsburg 44087 Fx:487-0923
(419) 843-3955 ..Arnsby, Jeanette F '89 -6613 Elmer Dr -Toledo 43615
(419) 897-7085 ..Arnsby, John B '90 City of Maumee -400 Conant -Maumee 43537
(440) 498-4353 ..Arnson, Gerald I '65 (G Arnson Co,LPA) -37177 Cherrybank Dr
-Solon 44139 Fx:498-4357
(859) 344-1919 ..Arnsperger-Hammerle, Amy J '97 KY Land Title Agncy,Inc -2362
Grandvw Dr -Ft Mitchell, KY 41017
(937) 224-0036 ..Arntz, Matthew R '82 -411 E 5th -Bx4235 -Dayton 45401
(513) 556-0072 ..Arnzen, Melissa L '02 Univ of Cinn -Bx210040 -Cincinnati 45221
(216) 363-4500 ..Aronoff, George N '58 (Benesch FC&A LLP) -200 Pub Sq
-Ste 2300 -Cleveland 44114 Fx:363-4588
(216) 566-5504 ..Aronoff, James B '84 (Thompson H LLP) -127 Pub Sq
-3900 Key Ctr -Cleveland 44114 Fx:566-5800
(513) 241-0400 ..Aronoff Rosen & Hunt Co,LPA -425 Walnut -Ste 2400
-Cincinnati 45202 Fx:241-2877
(513) 241-0400 ..Aronoff, Stanley J '58 (Aronoff R&H Co,LPA) -425 Walnut
-Ste 2400 -Cincinnati 45202 Fx:241-2877
(216) 787-3030 ..Aronoff, Steven K '86 Atty Gen -615 W Superior Av -11th Fl
-Cleveland 44113 Fx:787-3480
Arons, Murray H '95 -2611 Ashurst Rd -University Heights 44118
(330) 643-2788 ..Aronson, Beth E '99 Summit Cnty Pros-Crim -53 Univ Av -7th Fl
-Akron 44308 Fx:643-8277
(330) 385-3900 ..Aronson Fineman & Davis Co, LPA -124 E 5th
-East Liverpool 43920
(330) 836-5506 ..Aronson, Stanley P '72 Aronson & Assoc -3085 W Market
-Ste 130 -Akron 44333
Arostegui, Julie L '99 -4173 Stonecreek Way -Cincinnati 45241
(419) 729-3752 ..Arquette, James A '90 -4825 298th -Toledo 43611
(937) 208-2525 ..Arquilla, Thomas J '84 Miami Valley Hosp -1 Wyoming
-Dayton 45409
(440) 328-2205 ..Arredondo, Michele S '81 Lorain Cnty Dom Rltns Ct -225 Court
-Elyria 44035
(216) 621-0040 ..Arrighi, Amy L '98 %Strachan MO&R Co LPA -925 Euclid Av
-Ste 1940 -Cleveland 44115
(216) 932-9302 ..Arrington, Curtis R '76 BP America Inc -19341 Fairmount Blvd
-Shaker Heights 44118
(216) 443-8868 ..Arrington, Joan K '93 Cuyahoga Cnty Pros -1 Lakeside Av
-Rm 49 -Cleveland 44115 Fx:443-3777
(330) 971-8190 ..Arrington, Virgil E Jr. '82 Cuyahoga Falls Pros -2310 2nd
-Cuyahoga Falls 44221
(740) 779-7593 ..Arrowsmith, Monica S '94 Adena Regional Med Ctr -272 Hsptl Rd
-Chillicothe 45601
(440) 960-2520 ..Arroyo, Angel L '77 HUD -4223 Edgewood Dr -Lorain 44053
(614) 462-3555 ..Arsenault, Laurie A '00 Franklin Cnty Pros -373 S High
-Columbus 43215
(202) 514-2895 ..Arsenault, Moira A '01 DHS Ofc Prncpl Lgl Adv -425 I NW
-Rm 6100 -Washington, DC 20536
(614) 221-4000 ..Art, Andrew J '90 (Chester W&S LLP) -65 E State -10th Fl
-Columbus 43215 Fx:221-4012
(440) 942-9980 ..Arthur, Douglas W '93 D Arthur Co,LPA -8039 Broadmoor Rd
-Ste 23 -Mentor 44060
(330) 673-1535 ..Arthur, Francis L '74 (Arthur & N) -1325 S Water -Kent 44240
(614) 228-0326 ..Arthur, Geoffrey W '91 -37 W Broad -Ste 1100 -Columbus 43215
(216) 360-2124 ..Arthur, Harry L '82 (Moriarty & J,PLL) -30000 Chagrin Blvd
-Ste 200 -Pepper Pike 44124
Arthur, James E '82 -3281 Brdgt Dr -Columbus 43221
(419) 782-9881 ..Arthur O'Neil Mertz & Michel Co,LPA -901 Ralston Av -Bx781
-Defiance 43512
(937) 254-3738 ..Arthur, Richard P '86 -1634 S Smithvll Rd -Dayton 45410
(419) 782-9881 ..Arthur, Rodney M '69 (Arthur OM&M Co,LPA) -901 Ralston Av
-Bx781 -Defiance 43512
(614) 227-2000 ..Arthur, William E '53 OfCnsl Porter WM&A LLP -41 S High
-Columbus 43215 Fx:227-2100
(216) 692-6369 ..Artuso, John D '86 Marine Mechanical Corp -23555 Euclid Av
-Euclid 44117
(614) 221-0944 ..Artz, Brian S '80 (Artz & D,LLP) -560 E Town -Columbus 43215
Fx:221-2340
(614) 221-0944 ..Artz & Dewhirst,LLP -560 E Town -Columbus 43215
Fx:221-2340
(614) 462-2700 ..Arville, Alan J '03 %Schottenstein Z&D -250 West -Bx165020
-Columbus 43216 Fx:462-5135
(216) 523-1500 ..Arvin, Ashley M '04 %Mansour GG&M Co,LPA -55 Pub Sq
-Ste 2150 -Cleveland 44113 Fx:523-1705
(614) 459-3868 ..Ary, Richard E '87 (Ary & Roepke) -1500 Lk Shr Dr -Ste 350
-Columbus 43204
(270) 766-5160 ..Ary, William R '95 Dept of Public Advocate -916 N Mulberry Av
-Ste 160 -Bx628 -Elizabethtown, KY 42702
(216) 443-7800 ..Asad, Faris Y '98 Cuyahoga Cnty Pros -1200 Ontario -8th Fl
-Cleveland 44113 Fx:698-2270
(216) 696-5580 ..Asale, Shirley M '94 -815 Superior Bldg -Ste 1725
-Cleveland 44114
(216) 586-3939 ..Asam, Michael R '01 %Jones D -901 Lakeside Av
-Cleveland 44114 Fx:579-0212
(513) 569-1500 ..Asante, Lori S '95 Cincinnati Tech Cmmnty Cllg -3520 Cntrl Pkwy
-Cincinnati 45223
(614) 275-5935 ..Asbury, Damon A '93 SrCnsl Cntrl OH Transit Auth
-1600 McKinley Av -Columbus 43222
(419) 891-1510 ..Asbury, Karen E '88 -Bx950 -Maumee 43537
(513) 241-9400 ..Asbury, Mary '80 Legal Aid -215 E 9th -Ste 200 -Cincinnati 45202
(517) 467-2736 ..Aschemeier, Charles R '75 -540 N Kilkenny Dr -Onsted, MI 49265
(614) 365-2700 ..Aschenbrand, Tara A '02 %Squire S&D LLP -41 S High
-1300 Huntngtn Ctr -Columbus 43215 Fx:365-2499
(908) 276-4000 ..Ascher, David M '78 Newark Grp,Inc -20 Jackson Dr
-Cranford, NJ 07016 Fx:276-2888
(614) 228-1541 ..Asensio, Manuel J III '85 (Baker & H LLP) -65 E State -Ste 2100
-Columbus 43215 Fx:462-2616
(740) 369-8229 ..Ash, Charles W '93 -Bx1401 -Delaware 43015
(513) 785-7030 ..Ash, Kenya D '03 City of Hamilton -345 High -1st Fl
-Hamilton 45011
(513) 977-8200 ..Ash, Linda A '91 (Dinsmore & S LLP) -255 E 5th -Ste 1900
-Cincinnati 45202 Fx:977-8141
(513) 762-4423 ..Ash, Patricia T '79 Kroger Co -1014 Vine -Cincinnati 45202

(513) 762-6200 ..Ash, Reuel D '91 (Ulmer & B LLP) -600 Vine -Ste 2800
-Cincinnati 45202 Fx:762-6245
(614) 466-6935 ..Ashanin, Janine S '00 %OH Admin Srvcs -100 E Broad -15th Fl
-Columbus 43215
(440) 930-8052 ..Ashar, Linda C '85 Wickens HPC&B -35765 Chester Rd
-Avon 44011 Fx:937-4466
(440) 967-2680 ..Ashar, Michael K '85 (M Ashar & Assoc) -13010 W Darrow Rd
-Vermilion 44089
(937) 496-7428 ..Ashbery, Lynda K '97 -14 W 4th -Dayton 45402
(330) 966-9990 ..Ashbrook, Julie D '88 Allison, Ashbrook & Co
-7555 Freedom Av NW -North Canton 44720
(614) 645-7385 ..Ashbrook, Susan E '87 City Atty -90 W Broad -Columbus 43215
(740) 354-2334 ..Ashburn, Randy D '89 Ohio Industrial Commission -1005 Fourth
-Portsmouth 45662
(513) 936-8062 ..Ashby, Todd P '96 Advanced Land Title Agncy
-10979 Reed Hartman Hwy -Cincinnati 45242
Ashcraft, Amy R '01 -(Address Unavailable)
(513) 621-2120 ..Ashdown, Charles C '86 (Strauss & T,LPA) -150 E 4th -4th Fl
-Cincinnati 45202 Fx:241-8259
(513) 621-2120 ..Ashdown, Philomena S '86 OfCnsl Strauss & T,LPA -150 E 4th
-4th Fl -Cincinnati 45202 Fx:241-8259
(937) 775-5857 ..Ashelman, Scott A '01 Wright State/Stdnt Lgl Srvcs
-3640 Colonel Glenn Hwy -W015 Student Union -Dayton 45435
Fx:775-5858
(440) 349-9000 ..Asher, Anthony J '63 Guardian Title -29300 Aurora Rd -Solon
44139
(216) 522-5560 ..Asher, Kenneth D '91 Defense Finance&AccountingSrvc
-1240 E 9th -Cleveland 44199
(248) 746-2728 ..Asher, Michael J '00 (Sullivan WBT&A,PC) -25800 Nrthwstrn Hwy
-1000 Maccabees Ctr -Bx222 -Southfield, MI 48037 Fx:746-2760
(216) 522-3870 ..Ashley, Elizabeth R '90 US Dept of Labor/Solicitor Ofc -1240 E 9th
-881 -Cleveland 44199
(330) 867-2808 ..Ashley, Richard W '74 (R Ashley Co,LPA) -88 N Miller Rd
-Akron 44333
(419) 242-8900 ..Ashley, William L '98 -416 N Erie -Ste 200 -Toledo 43624
Ashman, Eric J '04 -(Address Unavailable)
(216) 515-1660 ..Ashmus, Keith A '74 (Frantz W LLP) -127 Pub Sq
-2500 Key Center -Cleveland 44114 Fx:515-1650
Ashshaheed, Zakiyyah N '03 -(Address Unavailable)
(513) 381-2838 ..Ashton, Amy C '00 %Taft S&H LLP -425 Walnut -Ste 1800
-Cincinnati 45202 Fx:381-0205
(614) 478-6000 ..Ashton, Rick L '04 %Karr & S Co,LPA -1 Easton Oval -Ste 550
-Columbus 43219
Ashton, Robert E '84 -190 S Cassingham Rd -Bexley 43209
(216) 443-6350 ..Ashwill, Ellen L '86 8th Dist Ct of Appls -1 Lakeside Av -#202
-Cleveland 44113 Fx:443-2044
(304) 485-4516 ..Ashworth, Colleen C '93 Goldenberg G&S,PLLC -200 Star Av
-Ste 222 -Parkersburg, WV 26101
(330) 836-9300 ..Askin, William P '98 %Smythe Cramer Co -3070 W Market
-Akron 44333
(937) 644-8151 ..Aslaner, Tim M '98 (Coleman E&A) -110 S Court -Bx266
-Marysville 43040
(937) 548-1920 ..Aslinger, Jason R '96 %Amick & B -414 Walnut -Greenville 45331
(419) 244-8384 ..Aslinger, Julie A '03 Pub Def -520 Madison -Ste 740
-Toledo 43604
(330) 627-4555 ..Asper, Edward S '95 Pros -49 Pub Sq -Carrollton 44615
(513) 985-0515 ..Asquith, Susan S '98 Jewish Vocational Srvc -4300 Ross Plain Rd
-Cincinnati 45236
(216) 664-2716 ..Assad, Awatef '95 Dept of Law -601 Lakeside Av
-Rm 106 City Hall -Cleveland 44114 Fx:664-2663
(330) 864-5916 ..Assaf, Timothy P '83 -230 White Pond Dr -Ste A -Akron 44313
(216) 447-3061 ..Asseff, Carl F '84 -6638 Kings Cote Park -Independence 44131
(216) 443-8600 ..Asseff, Michael C '97 Cuyahoga Co Common Pleas Ct
-1200 Ontario -Justice Ctr -Cleveland 44113
(313) 442-6407 ..Astolfi, Paul J '01 %Foley & L -150 W Jffrsn -Ste 1000
-Detroit, MI 48226
(216) 781-7455 ..Astrab, Michael K '97 -2000 E 9th -Ste 710 -Cleveland 44115
(614) 227-2000 ..Atchison, Julie L '98 %Porter WM&A LLP -41 S High
-Columbus 43215 Fx:227-2100
(740) 775-1700 ..Ater, Jennifer L '95 (Blair & A LLP) -6 W Main -Chillicothe 45601
(740) 702-3100 ..Ater, Michael M '94 (Nusbaum A&W) -72 N Paint
-Chillicothe 45601
(202) 463-0662 ..Atienza, Alberto M '92 (Atienza C&C) -1717 K NW -Ste 600
-Washington, DC 20036
(419) 213-4749 ..Atkin, Jean E '79 Lucas Co Common Pleas Ct -700 Adams
-Cnty Cthse 3rd Fl -Toledo 43624
(513) 621-2120 ..Atkins, Charles G '62 Strauss & T,LPA -150 E 4th -4th Fl
-Cincinnati 45202 Fx:241-8259
(513) 422-3658 ..Atkins, Christopher G '84 -1081 N Univ Blvd -Ste B
-Middletown 45042
(859) 344-1188 ..Atkins, E Jason '99 %Hemmer SPD PLLC -250 Grandvw Dr
-Ste 200 -Fort Mitchell, KY 41017 Fx:578-3869
(513) 977-8200 ..Atkins, Katrina R '03 %Dinsmore & S LLP -255 E 5th -Ste 1900
-Cincinnati 45202 Fx:977-8141
(614) 854-8672 ..Atkins, Lisa Ann '96 Cnsl Nationwide Ins Co -1 Nationwide Plz
-Columbus 43215
(419) 213-4700 ..Atkins, Maureen O '94 Lucas Cnty Pros -Adams & Erie
-Lucas Cnty Cthse -Toledo 43624
(609) 720-2901 ..Atkins, Thomas H '72 Washington Grp Intl -510 Carnegie Ctr
-Princeton, NJ 08540 Fx:720-2690
(419) 354-9278 ..Atkins, Timothy C '93 %Wood Cnty Pros -One Cthse Sq
-Bowling Green 43402 Fx:353-2904
Atkins, William M '94 -300 Keever -Lebanon 45036
(740) 373-4633 ..Atkinson & Burton -312 Putnam -Bxl -Marietta 45750
(419) 866-8900 ..Atkinson, James R '80 -6904 Sprng Vlly Dr -Ste 303
-Holland 43528
(216) 687-1311 ..Atkinson, Kathleen A '02 %Reminger & R -101 Prospect Av W
-1400 Mdlnd Bldg -Cleveland 44115 Fx:687-1841
(740) 373-4633 ..Atkinson, Thomas R '69 (Atkinson & B) -312 Putnam -Bxl
-Marietta 45750
Atleson, Jessica Bryce '04 -(Address Unavailable)
(614) 365-2700 ..Atriano, Vincent '88 (Squire S&D LLP) -41 S High
-1300 Huntngtn Ctr -Columbus 43215 Fx:365-2499
(216) 623-1901 ..Attali, Michael D '02 -629 Euclid Av -Ste 519 -Cleveland 44114

(513) 784-0600 .. **Attenborough**, Bruce W '84 -617 Vine -Enquirer Bldg Ste 1311 -Cincinnati 45202

(513) 772-8588 .. **Attix**, Harold B '71 -230 Northland Blvd -Ste 221 -Cincinnati 45246

(937) 866-9933 .. **Attkisson**, Kevin W '97 -101 N 1st -Miamisburg 45342

(330) 743-6300 .. **Atway & Cochran,LLC** -19 E Front -Ste 1 -Youngstown 44503

(330) 743-6300 .. **Atway**, Neal G '92 (Atway & C,LLC) -19 E Front -Ste 1 -Youngstown 44503

(614) 203-2729 .. **Atway**, Saed W '01 -545 Chardonnay Ln -Lewis Center 43035

(330) 375-1311 .. **Atwell**, D Cheryl '80 (Reminger & R) -80 S Summit -200 Courtyard Sq -Akron 44308 **Fx:**375-9075

(513) 870-5000 .. **Atwell**, Kevin H '85 Automanage,Inc -5726 Dixie Hwy -Fairfield 45014

(513) 522-5800 .. **Atwood**, Daniel C '89 -7722 Hmltn Av -Cincinnati 45231

(216) 443-7223 .. **Atzberger**, Jennifer N '00 Cuyahoga Cnty Pub Def -1200 W 3rd NW -100 Lakeside Pl -Cleveland 44113

(614) 436-3555 .. **Atzberger**, Thomas W '76 Money Fndtn -100 W Old Wilson Bridge Rd -Ste 101 -Worthington 43085

(513) 421-7500 .. **Aubin**, Arthur N '83 (Faulkner & T,LLP) -5 W 4th -2200 4th & Vine Twr -Cincinnati 45202

(614) 224-8178 .. **Aubrey**, Joanne E '81 -519 S 4th -Columbus 43206

(419) 242-1400 .. **Aubry**, Jude T '66 -608 Mad Av -Ste 1400 -Toledo 43604

(419) 241-9000 .. **Aubry**, M Scott '95 (Shumaker L&K,LLP) -1000 Jackson -Toledo 43624 **Fx:**241-6894

(419) 874-3569 .. **Aubry**, P M '82 -110 W 2nd -Perrysburg 43551

(216) 241-5310 .. **Auciello**, Ernest W Jr. '85 (Gallagher SF&N) -1501 Euclid Av -6th Fl -Cleveland 44115 **Fx:**241-1608

(614) 464-4100 .. **AuCoin DuPont Hetterscheidt & Younkin LLC** -495 S High -Ste 250 -Columbus 43215

(614) 464-4100 .. **AuCoin**, Paul M '76 (AuCoin DH&Y LLC) -495 S High -Ste 250 -Columbus 43215

(216) 443-6350 .. **Audey**, Susan M '94 8th Dist Ct of Appls -1 Lakeside Av -#202 -Cleveland 44113 **Fx:**443-2044

(216) 698-6410 .. **Audi**, Frederick R '88 Pros -2210 Cedar Av -3rd Fl-Juvenile Ct -Cleveland 44115

(937) 865-6800 .. **Audi**, Joseph F '97 Lexis/Nexis -Bx933 -Dayton 45401 **Audi-DeGidio**, Annette R '92 -28007 W Oviatt Rd -Bay Village 44140

(513) 579-7881 .. **Auerbach**, Boris '54 -332 Ardon Ln -Cincinnati 45215 **Aufdenkampe**, Mark A '87 -733 Sorrento Inlet -Nokomis, FL 34275

(505) 678-1263 .. **Aug**, Thomas R '93 US Army -Ofc of SJAoct -Bldg 1460 -White Sands Missile Range, NM 88002

(614) 464-6400 .. **Auge**, Craig R '97 (Vorys SS&P LLP) -52 E Gay -Bx1008 -Columbus 43216 **Fx:**464-6350

(614) 995-4868 .. **Augsburger**, Mary Amos '02 OH Senate -Ohio Statehse -Columbus 43215

(419) 738-9688 .. **Augsburger**, Robert A '95 Auglaize Cnty Pros -201 Willipie -Ste G4 -Bx1992 -Wapakoneta 45895

(937) 865-6800 .. **August**, James E '97 Lexis/Nexis -Bx933 -Dayton 45401

(216) 292-4666 .. **August**, Steven L '92 S August Co,LPA -2101 Richmond Rd -Ste 39 -Beachwood 44122

(216) 787-3633 .. **Augusta**, James M '96 Industrial Commssn of OH -615 Superior Av NW -Cleveland 44113 **Fx:**787-3483

(216) 787-3649 .. **Augusta**, Lori A '89 Industrial Commssn of OH -615 Superior Av NW -Cleveland 44113 **Fx:**787-3483

(216) 429-5251 .. **Augustine**, Katherine A '95 3rd Fed Savings & Loan -7007 Bway Av -Compliance Dept -Cleveland 44105

(216) 662-8631 .. **Augustine**, Susan M '89 Outdoors,Inc -17388 Bway Av -#2 -Maple Heights 44137

(216) 443-8505 .. **Augustyn**, Kevin C '92 Cuyahoga Cmmn Pleas Ct -1200 Ontario -Cleveland 44113

(614) 559-1188 .. **Auker**, Jeffrey A '83 Chicago Title Ins Co -100 S 4th -Ste 100 -Columbus 43215

(765) 492-3350 .. **Aukerman**, Malcolm H '52 -350 Poplar -Bx69 -Newport, IN 47966 **Aukerman**, Russell R '89 -330 Yrktwn Pl -Unit A-1 -Vermilion 44089

(614) 336-7022 .. **Aukland**, Duncan D '82 Adjutant Generals Dept-OH AGOH-JA -2825 W Dublin Granvll Rd -Columbus 43235 **Fx:**336-7488

(419) 755-9622 .. **Ault**, Jerry E '78 Mun Ct Judge -30 N Diamond -Mansfield 44902 **Fx:**755-9650

(216) 443-7800 .. **Ault**, Micah R '04 Cuyahoga Cnty Pros -1200 Ontario -8th Fl -Cleveland 44113 **Fx:**698-2270

(419) 843-1333 .. **Ault**, Tim A '86 (Malone A&F) -7654 W Bancroft -Toledo 43617 **Fx:**843-3888

(614) 436-2750 .. **Aultman**, Mark H '68 -150 E Wilson Bridge Rd -Ste 200 -Worthington 43085

(937) 223-6003 .. **Auman**, Gary W '76 (Dunlevey M&F) -110 N Main -Ste 1000 -Dayton 45402 **Fx:**223-8550

(330) 534-1901 .. **Aurilio**, Beth A '01 -48 W Lbrty -Hubbard 44425

(216) 382-7114 .. **Aurslanian**, Richard N '68 -5001 Mayfld Rd -Ste 301 -Bx24005 -Cleveland 44124

(330) 726-1654 .. **Ausnehmer**, John E '80 -120 Marwood Cir -Bx3965 -Youngstown 44513 **Fx:**726-5608

(216) 736-4540 .. **Ausprunk**, Karen S '85 Comm Fund Mgmt Fndtn -1275 Lakeside Av E -Cleveland 44114

(216) 830-6830 .. **Aussem**, James S '75 (Brouse M) -1001 Lakeside Av -Ste 1600 -Cleveland 44114 **Fx:**830-6807

(419) 531-9559 .. **Austin**, Douglas V '78 Austin Fncl Srvcs Inc -3450 W Central Av -Ste 260 -Toledo 43606

(216) 771-4445 .. **Austin**, Gregg A '81 -614 Superior Av -Ste 650 -Cleveland 44113

(216) 566-5927 .. **Austin**, Heather A '93 %Thompson H LLP -127 Pub Sq -3900 Key Ctr -Cleveland 44114 **Fx:**566-5800

(216) 241-4100 .. **Austin**, Jeffrey L '98 %Keis/G LLP -55 Pub Sq -Ste 800 -Cleveland 44113 **Fx:**771-3111

(614) 421-5609 .. **Austin**, Linda M '00 Franklin Cnty Children Srvcs -855 W Mound -Columbus 43223 **Fx:**275-2589

(937) 449-5767 .. **Austin**, Matthew D '03 %Coolidge WW&L -33 W 1st -Ste 600 -Dayton 45402 **Fx:**223-6705

(216) 381-3400 .. **Austin**, Nicholas A '98 (Petronzio S Co,LPA) -5001 Mayfld Rd -Ste 201 -Cleveland 44124

(440) 232-6399 .. **Austin**, Pamela J '01 -26170 Forbes Rd -Oakwood Village 44146 **Fx:**232-6399

(340) 773-2626 .. **Austin**, Richard '69 Legal Srvcs of VI -3017 Orange Grv -St Croix, VI 00820

(302) 774-8553 .. **Austin**, Ross E '66 El Du Pont de Nemours & Co -1007 Market -Leg Dept -Wilmington, DE 19893

(614) 424-5400 .. **Austin**, Russell P '86 D O'Bryan -505 King Av -Columbus 43201

(216) 621-1000 .. **Austria**, Robert L '98 %Moscarino & T,LLP -1422 Euclid Av -Hanna Bldg Ste 630 -Cleveland 44115 **Fx:**622-1556

(614) 221-7711 .. **Auten**, Anthony R '72 %Grossman Law Ofcs -32 W Hoster -Ste 100 -Columbus 43215 **Fx:**221-7145 **Autero**, Brian K '04 -1218 Oxford Rd -Cleveland 44121

(513) 721-4532 .. **Auttonberry**, Sheri E '99 %Katz TB&H -255 E 5th -Ste 2400 -Cincinnati 45202

(216) 363-4500 .. **Auvil**, Steven M '94 (Benesch FC&A LLP) -200 Pub Sq -Ste 2300 -Cleveland 44114 **Fx:**363-4588

(614) 237-8050 .. **Avellano**, Andrew P '94 (A Avellano,LLC) -4181 E Main -Columbus 43213

(312) 341-1070 .. **Avellone**, Frank G '82 Lgl Asst Fndtn of Chicago -111 W Jackson -3rd Fl -Chicago, IL 60604

(440) 357-5537 .. **Aveni**, Anthony J '66 (Cannon SA&L Co,LPA) -41 E Erie -Painesville 44077 **Fx:**357-9234

(440) 357-5537 .. **Aveni**, Benjamin L '03 %Cannon SA&L Co,LPA -41 E Erie -Painesville 44077 **Fx:**357-9234

(614) 227-2000 .. **Aveni**, Carl A II '99 %Porter WM&A LLP -41 S High -Columbus 43215 **Fx:**227-2100

(440) 684-1600 .. **Aveni**, James V '93 (Ranallo & A LLC) -6685 Beta Dr -Cleveland 44143 **Fx:**684-1601 **Averbach**, Mark D '72 -Bx1377 -Chautauqua, NY 14722

(513) 684-3211 .. **Averbeck**, Linda R '98 IRS Dist Cnsl -312 Elm -Ste 2300 -Cincinnati 45202

(330) 673-9118 .. **Averill**, Sue N '95 AAUP-KSU -1100 E Summit -#9 -Kent 44240

(614) 841-1994 .. **Avery**, Barbara J '75 -488 Greenglade Av -Worthington 43085

(419) 254-1311 .. **Avery**, Laura J '98 (Reminger & R) -405 Mad Av -Ste 2300 -Toledo 43604 **Fx:**243-7830

(312) 269-4103 .. **Avery**, Robert D '71 (Jones DR&P) -77 W Wacker Dr -35th Fl -Chicago, IL 60601 **Fx:**782-8585

(718) 643-6555 .. **Averyhart**, Lisa Chrishon '99 %Marcus Attys -13 Greene Av -Brooklyn, NY 11238 **Fx:**643-9111

(202) 879-5401 .. **Avil**, Richard D Jr. '78 (Jones DR&P) -51 Louisiana Av NW -Washington, DC 20001 **Fx:**626-1700

(419) 243-2100 .. **Avila**, Janine T '91 (Connelly J&C LLP) -405 Mad Av -Ste 1600 -Toledo 43604 **Fx:**243-7119

(216) 363-4500 .. **Avsec**, Mark E '95 %Benesch FC&A LLP -200 Pub Sq -Ste 2300 -Cleveland 44114 **Fx:**363-4588 **Awadallah**, Mahmoud S '03 -1285 W 115th -Cleveland 44102

(216) 443-7800 .. **Awadallah**, Saleh S '94 Cuyahoga Cnty Pros -1200 Ontario -8th Fl -Cleveland 44113 **Fx:**698-2270

(216) 689-4959 .. **Axel**, Michael A '83 KeyBank NA -127 Pub Sq -2nd Fl -Cleveland 44114

(614) 464-6400 .. **Axelrod**, David F '78 (Vorys SS&P LLP) -52 E Gay -Bx1008 -Columbus 43216 **Fx:**464-6350

(330) 762-8111 .. **Axner**, Edward A '62 -80 S Summit -#400 -Akron 44308

(216) 781-1710 .. **Axner**, Gary R '71 -614 W Superior Av -Ste 1440 -Cleveland 44113

(614) 644-6530 .. **Axtell**, Amanda M '99 OH Dept Commerce -77 S High -Columbus 43266

(937) 443-6877 .. **Axtell**, Stephen J '88 (Thompson H LLP) -2000 Cthse Plz NE -Bx8801 -Dayton 45401 **Fx:**443-6635

(419) 861-7800 .. **Ayers**, Andrew J '79 Bahret & Assoc Co,LPA -7050 Spring Meadow W Dr -Holland 43528 **Ayers**, April C '89 -8450 Dellinger Rd -Galloway 43119

(330) 492-2323 .. **Ayers**, Charles Stephen '87 -4884 Dressier Rd NW -Ste 704 -Canton 44718

(614) 791-4121 .. **Ayers**, Elizabeth A '95 Peterson & Assoc -5060 Bradenton Av -Ste D -Dublin 43017

(513) 651-6800 .. **Ayers**, G Randall '88 (Frost BT LLC) -201 E 5th -2200 PNC Ctr -Cincinnati 45202 **Fx:**651-6981

(212) 813-5900 .. **Ayers**, Irene S '99 %Fross ZL&Z,PC -866 UN Plz -6th Fl -New York, NY 10017 **Fx:**813-5901

(614) 221-0770 .. **Ayers**, James C '97 %Casey Law Ofc -165 N High -Columbus 43215

(614) 249-1002 .. **Ayers**, Stephen F '04 Nationwide Financial -One Nationwide Plz -1-10-05 -Columbus 43215

(330) 297-0881 .. **Aylward**, James J '81 Portage Cnty Juv Ct -8000 Infirmary Rd -Ravenna 44266

(330) 451-7884 .. **Aylward**, Kristen B '85 Stark Cnty Pros -110 Central Plz -Ste 510 -Canton 44702

(770) 955-3555 .. **Aymond**, Amanda Joy '00 %Hartman SS&W -6400 Powers Ferry Rd -Ste 400 -Atlanta, GA 30339 **Fx:**303-1171

(330) 643-2250 .. **Aynes**, Kathleen S '77 9th Dist Ct of Appls -161 S High -Ste 504 -Akron 44308

(330) 972-7331 .. **Aynes**, Richard Lee '75 Univ of Akron Law Schl -302 Buchtel Mall -136K C Blake McDowell Law Ctr -Akron 44325 **Fx:**972-7337

(410) 293-1921 .. **Ayres**, Julia G '98 Navy JAG -USNA -Annapolis, MD 21412

(804) 284-2512 .. **Ayres**, Paul S '90 Capital One -15000 Cptl One Way -Richmond, VA 23238

(937) 224-5300 .. **Azallion**, Melissa G '95 Cooper & G Co,LPA -118 W 1st -Ste 850 -Dayton 45403

(216) 621-0200 .. **Azoff**, Elliot S '73 (Baker & H LLP) -1900 E 9th -Ste 3200 -Cleveland 44114 **Fx:**696-0740

(937) 324-4566 .. **Baader**, William F '75 -451 Upper Valley Pike -Springfield 45504

(513) 521-2929 .. **Baas**, Patricia A '83 -3091 W Galbraith Rd -Ste 310 -Cincinnati 45239

(330) 493-1570 .. **Baasten**, Cornelius J '73 (Macala BM&G,LLC) -4150 Belden Vllg NW -Ste 604 -Canton 44718 **Fx:**493-7042

(614) 734-0991 .. **Baba**, Martin N '91 -3010 Hayden Rd -Columbus 43235

(513) 579-6400 .. **Babb**, Brian M '86 (Keating M&K PLL) -1 E 4th -1400 Provident Twr -Cincinnati 45202 **Fx:**579-6457

(216) 622-8306 .. **Babbit**, Harold W '67 (Calfee H&G LLP) -800 Superior Av -Ste 1400 -Cleveland 44114 **Fx:**241-0816

(330) 344-6005 .. **Babbitt**, Craig M '97 Akron Gen Hlth Syst-Legal -400 Wabash Av -Akron 44307

(937) 255-6111 .. **Babbitt**, Edwin R III '81 AFCLC/JABB -2240 B -Rm C1 -Wright Patterson AFB 45433

(614) 228-4200 .. **Babbitt**, Gerald J '79 (Babbitt & W LLP) -503 S Front -Ste 200 -Columbus 43215 **Fx:**228-4224

(216) 363-4500 ..**Babbitt**, Lindsay C '04 %Benesch FC&A LLP -200 Pub Sq
-Ste 2300 -Cleveland 44114 **Fx**:363-4588

(216) 328-8700 ..**Babbitt**, Michael R '75 ICX Corp -2 Summit Park Dr -Ste 300
-Cleveland 44131

(216) 621-0150 ..**Babbitt**, Ross M '00 %Hahn L&P LLP -3300 BP Twr/200 Pub Sq
-Ste 3300 -Cleveland 44114 **Fx**:241-2824

(614) 228-4200 ..**Babbitt & Wellbaum LLP** -503 S Front -Ste 200
-Columbus 43215 **Fx**:228-4224

(216) 367-7744 ..**Babcock**, Clifford G '90 (Babcock & W Co,LPA) -55 Pub Sq
-Ste 700 -Cleveland 44113
Babcock, Douglas W '03 -(Address Unavailable)

(513) 229-7996 ..**Babcock**, Kelly E '94 %Kircher,LLC -4824 Socialville-Foster Rd
-Ste 110 -Mason 45040

(216) 367-7744 ..**Babcock & Wasserman Co,LPA** -55 Pub Sq -Ste 700
-Cleveland 44113

(740) 773-0012 ..**Babcox**, Josephine M '04 %SE OH Lgl Srvcs -11 E 2nd
-Chillicothe 45601

(937) 415-3300 ..**Babel**, Thomas S '98 Evanflo-Legal -770 Crssrd Ct
-Vandalia 45377

(740) 223-4290 ..**Babich**, Lawrence H '75 Marion Cnty Pros -134 E Center
-Marion 43302 **Fx**:223-4299

(740) 387-5900 ..**Babich**, Ted B '80 -117 E Center -Marion 43302
Babin, Mara L '75 (Squire S&D LLP) -60 Cannon
-London EC4N 6NP England

(513) 579-6400 ..**Babinec**, Gehl P '67 OfCnsl Keating M&K PLL -1 E 4th
-1400 Provident Twr -Cincinnati 45202 **Fx**:579-6457
Babington, Margaret M '84 -6988 N Renwood Rd
-Cleveland 44131

(216) 443-6373 ..**Babinski**, Michael T '98 OH 8th Dist Ct of Appeals -1 Lakeside Av
-Cleveland 44113
Babner, David W '93 -7566 Heatherwood Ln -Dublin 43017

(330) 458-2411 ..**Baca**, Rodney A '99 -101 Central Plz S -Ste 1000 -Canton 44702

(216) 443-7800 ..**Bacchus**, Renee A '94 Cuyahoga Cnty Pros -1200 Ontario -8th Fl
-Cleveland 44113 **Fx**:698-2270

(702) 433-3150 ..**Baccus**, Charles W '81 Dept Justice -3373 Pepper Ln
-Las Vegas, NV 89120

(216) 830-8800 ..**Bacevice**, John P '84 -1468 W 9th -Ste 240 -Cleveland 44113

(513) 721-8831 ..**Bacevich**, Michael P '96 Virgin Ventures Inc -1 W 4th -Ste 415
-Cincinnati 45202

(480) 554-4413 ..**Bach**, Bryan M '93 Intel Corp -5000 W Chandler Blvd
-Mailstop:ADC -Chandler, AZ 85226

(330) 434-3000 ..**Bach**, Lawrence R '84 (Roderick & L) -One Cascade Plz -Ste 1500
-Akron 44308 **Fx**:434-9220

(513) 489-7522 ..**Bach**, Michael B '87 (DeHaan & B) -11256 Cornell Park Dr
-Ste 500 -Bx429321 -Cincinnati 45242

(937) 223-8177 ..**Bach**, Michelle D '95 %Coolidge WW&L -33 W 1st -Ste 600
-Dayton 45402 **Fx**:223-6705

(614) 716-1615 ..**Bacha**, James R '79 Amer Elec Pwr Co -1 Riverside Plz
-Columbus 43215

(419) 353-5615 ..**Bachman**, Evelyn J '62 -242 S Main -Bowling Green 43402

(513) 946-3700 ..**Bachman**, Laura A '99 Hamilton Cnty Pub Def -230 E 9th -3rd Fl
-Cincinnati 45202 **Fx**:946-3707

(513) 946-3000 ..**Bachman**, Michael L '84 Hamilton Cnty Pros -230 E 9th -Cincinnati
45202 **Fx**:946-3017

(614) 249-9092 ..**Bachmann**, Gregg H '87 Cnsl Nationwide Ins Co
-1 Nationwide Plz -Columbus 43215

(419) 474-1190 ..**Bacho**, Teresa M '94 -3126 W Sylvania Av -Toledo 43613
Fx:472-2088

(330) 725-4209 ..**Bachtell**, David J '92 -148 Koons Av -Medina 44256

(513) 731-9571 ..**Back**, David A '96 -3735 Grovedale Pl -Cincinnati 45208

(513) 797-0802 ..**Backscheider**, Clifford R '79 Blue Horse Custom Homes
-2018 Plumb Ln -Batavia 45103 **Fx**:797-0803

(513) 421-0045 ..**Backsman**, Mary Goeke '58 (Goeke & G) -630 Vine
-1000 Provident Bk Bldg -Cincinnati 45202

(216) 696-9100 ..**Backus**, Russell P '95 KPMG, LLP -1375 E 9th -One Cleve Ctr
-Cleveland 44114

(305) 373-2190 ..**Bacon**, Belinda A '03 Falke Florida,Inc -44 W Flagler -Ste 1600
-Miami, FL 33130 **Fx**:373-2377

(216) 515-1660 ..**Bacon**, Brett K '72 (Frantz W LLP) -127 Pub Sq -2500 Key Center
-Cleveland 44114 **Fx**:515-1650

(614) 249-7452 ..**Bacon**, Brian M '84 Nationwide Ins Co -1 Nationwide Plz
-Columbus 43215

(419) 294-2232 ..**Bacon**, David F '77 (Roth BY) -50 Court -Upper Sandusky 43351
Fx:294-2488

(419) 294-2232 ..**Bacon**, Forrest H '51 (Roth BY) -50 Court -Upper Sandusky 43351
Fx:294-2488

(419) 626-3712 ..**Bacon**, John O '75 Mack Iron Works Co -124 Warren
-Sandusky 44870

(614) 799-3207 ..**Bacon**, Kevin R '98 Farmers Ins -2545 Farmers Dr -Ste 380
-Columbus 43235 **Fx**:764-1018

(937) 865-6800 ..**Bacon**, Leanna E '92 Lexis/Nexis -Bx933 -Dayton 45401

(937) 224-0963 ..**Bacon**, Steven E '92 %Breidenbach O&B -131 N Ludlow
-Ste 1060 -Dayton 45402

(513) 772-6508 ..**Bacon**, Todd D '92 -308 Albion Av -Cincinnati 45246

(216) 381-9878 ..**Baczewski**, Barbara A '89 -5247 Wilson Mills Rd -Ste 264
-Cleveland 44143

(757) 873-8000 ..**Baddar**, Lauren Cunningham '03 %Jones BW&K,PC
-701 Town Ctr Dr -Ste 800 -Newport News, VA 23606

(216) 621-0200 ..**Baddeley**, Jeffrey A '83 (Baker & H LLP) -1900 E 9th -Ste 3200
-Cleveland 44114 **Fx**:696-0740

(917) 206-8000 ..**Baden**, Alan P '73 (Vinson & E LLP) -666 5th Av -26th Fl
-New York, NY 10103 **Fx**:206-8100

(440) 892-3000 ..**Baden**, Steven L '84 Scott Fetzer Co -28800 Clemens Rd
-Westlake 44145

(419) 245-1503 ..**Bader**, Carol J '01 Law Dept -One Govt Ctr -Ste 2250
-Toledo 43604 **Fx**:245-1090

(419) 242-1555 ..**Bader**, David A '91 (Spitler & W-Y Co,LPA) -1000 Adams -Ste 200
-Toledo 43624

(216) 351-0100 ..**Bader**, Thomas J '56 United Security Mgt Srvc,Inc -1440 Snow Rd
-Parma 44134

(216) 357-7098 ..**Badertscher**, Sharon J '92 US Dist Ct-NDOH -801 W Superior Av
-Cleveland 44113

(330) 297-5531 ..**Badger**, Richard J '73 -4922 Industry Rd -Ravenna 44266

(330) 455-0173 ..**Badger**, William B '61 (Day KRW&R,Ltd) -200 Market Av N
-Ste 300 -Bx24213 -Canton 44701 **Fx**:455-2633

(419) 525-0800 ..**Badnell**, David C '94 -3 N Main -Ste 803 -Mansfield 44902

(419) 524-6682 ..**Badnell**, Kelly L '94 (Baran PTF&T Co,LPA) -3 N Main -Ste 500
-Mansfield 44902 **Fx**:525-4511

(937) 512-2376 ..**Badonsky**, Deborah K '73 Sinclair Cmmnty Coll -444 W 3rd
-Dayton 45402

(440) 285-2401 ..**Badovick**, George L '83 -11850 Mayfld Rd -Ste 2 -Chardon 44024

(614) 387-2243 ..**Badurina**, Elizabeth M '86 OH Dept of Educ -25 S Front
-Columbus 43205

(513) 948-5061 ..**Baechle**, Lisa G '98 Givaudan -1199 Edison Dr -Cincinnati 45216

(216) 523-4101 ..**Baechle**, Thomas J '72 Eaton Corp -1111 Superior Av
-Cleveland 44114

(513) 621-6464 ..**Baechtold**, William J '72 (Graydon H&R LLP) -511 Walnut
-1900 Fifth Third Ctr -Cincinnati 45202 **Fx**:651-3836

(419) 247-1032 ..**Baehren**, James W '78 Owens-Illinois,Inc -One SeaGate
-Toledo 43666

(216) 566-5500 ..**Baek**, Annie Jinyun '04 %Thompson H LLP -127 Pub Sq
-3900 Key Ctr -Cleveland 44114 **Fx**:566-5800
Baenen, Steven A '93 -(Address Unavailable)

(440) 350-2299 ..**Baeppler**, Michelle M '95 Lake Cnty Pros -105 Main -Bx490
-Painesville 44077 **Fx**:350-2585

(614) 866-6593 ..**Baer**, Christopher J '82 -777 Waggoner Rd -Reynoldsburg 43068

(740) 594-8093 ..**Baer**, David G '80 Cntr Stdnt Advccy -Bx755 -Athens 45701

(419) 254-4300 ..**Baer**, Elizabeth E '95 %Marshall & M,LLC -420 Mad Av -Ste 1100
-Toledo 43604

(937) 339-0511 ..**Baer**, Michael A '74 (Dungan & L Co,LPA) -210 W Main
-Troy 45373 **Fx**:335-5802

(740) 773-5941 ..**Baerkircher**, Alfred E '73 -68 N Walnut -Chillicothe 45601

(740) 283-1966 ..**Baes**, Maresa R '03 Jefferson Cnty Pros -16001 State Route 7
-Steubenville 43952

(440) 639-4890 ..**Baetzel**, Robert C '96 City of Painesville -7 Richmond
-Painesville 44077

(330) 535-5711 ..**Bagga**, Rajesh '97 %Brouse M -106 S Main -500 First Natl Twr
-Akron 44308 **Fx**:253-8601

(440) 326-4011 ..**Baggett**, Jessica Ann '94 Lorain Cnty Juv Ct
-9967 S Murray Ridge Rd -Elyria 44035 **Fx**:323-0188

(937) 223-1201 ..**Baggott**, Thomas M '71 OfCnsl Altick & C Co,LPA -1 S Main
-1700 One Dayton Ctr -Dayton 45402 **Fx**:223-5100

(440) 247-0775 ..**Bagley**, Donald B III '93 OfCnsl Weiss & F LLP -35 River
-Chagrin Falls 44022 **Fx**:893-9138

(513) 241-7111 ..**Bagliore**, Jayma C '80 %O'Connor A&L Co,LPA -1014 Vine
-22nd Fl -Cincinnati 45202 **Fx**:241-7197

(216) 443-8505 ..**Bagnato**, Elizabeth R '82 Cuyahoga Cnty Cmmn Pleas Ct
-1200 Ontario -10th Fl -Cleveland 44113
Bagnola, William E '01 -6804 Killdeer Dr -Canfield 44406

(718) 515-6400 ..**Bahamonde**, Pedro L '94 MSM Academy -4300 Murdock Av
-Bronx, NY 10466

(614) 221-4911 ..**Bahgat**, Abe '87 -338 S High -Columbus 43215

(732) 625-3368 ..**Bahleda**, Michael D '96 Prudential Ins Co -23 Main
-Holmdel, NJ 07733

(614) 424-7360 ..**Bahlmann**, Jerome R '67 Battelle Memorial Inst -505 King Av
-Columbus 43201

(614) 583-0088 ..**Bahnsen**, Deborah Nay '84 (Jewel & B,LLC) -230 E Town -1st Fl
-Columbus 43215

(248) 851-9500 ..**Bahorski**, Timothy A '95 %Secrest WLHT&M
-30903 Nrthwstrn Hwy -Bx3040 -Farmington Hills, MI 48333
Fx:851-2158

(813) 962-0817 ..**Bahr**, Donald R '65 -2608 Meridia Ln -Tampa, FL 33618

(419) 861-7800 ..**Bahret**, Robert J '80 (Bahret & Assoc Co,LPA)
-7050 Spring Meadow W Dr -Holland 43528

(602) 382-2816 ..**Baich**, Dale A '83 %Fed Public Def -850 W Adams -#201
-Phoenix, AZ 85007

(937) 227-6473 ..**Bailes**, Michael S '93 Fifth Third Bk -110 N Main -MD 332952
-Dayton 45402 **Fx**:229-8202

(919) 545-0257 ..**Bailes**, Richard H '82 Pennsylvania Life Ins Co
-360 Meadow Vw Dr -Moncure, NC 27559

(513) 983-4154 ..**Bailey**, Ann K '76 Procter & Gamble -1 Procter & Gamble Plz
-Cincinnati 45202
Bailey, Barbara E '92 -2310 2nd -Cuyahoga Falls 44221

(419) 673-8188 ..**Bailey**, Bradford W '79 Bailey Law Ofc -28 N Main -Kenton 43326

(614) 882-2327 ..**Bailey**, Bruce E '78 (Metz & B) -33 E Schrock Rd
-Westerville 43081

(614) 221-3155 ..**Bailey Cavalieri LLC** -10 W Broad -Columbus 43215
Fx:221-0479

(937) 223-4701 ..**Bailey Cavalieri LLC** -40 N Main -Ste 2310 -Dayton 45423
Fx:223-0170

(614) 221-3155 ..**Bailey**, Daniel A '78 (Bailey C LLC) -10 W Broad
-Columbus 43215 **Fx**:221-0479

(937) 225-4652 ..**Bailey**, Dennis L '82 Montgomery Cnty Pub Def -117 S Main
-Ste 400 -Dayton 45422 **Fx**:225-3449

(513) 745-0400 ..**Bailey**, Donyetta D '00 %Furnier T,LLP -1 Fncl Way -Ste 312
-Cincinnati 45242 **Fx**:792-6724

(606) 833-0260 ..**Bailey**, Dwight O '92 -2412 Argillite Rd -Bx862
-Flatwoods, KY 41139

(630) 377-1554 ..**Bailey**, Earl P '71 Wessels & P PC -2035 Foxfld Dr
-Saint Charles, IL 60174

(330) 425-4201 ..**Bailey**, Edward A '97 %Reimer L&A Co,LPA -2450 Edison Blvd
-Bx968 -Twinsburg 44087 **Fx**:487-0923

(937) 323-6475 ..**Bailey**, Edward G '70 Bailey & B -4 W Main -Ste 428
-Springfield 45502

(216) 928-0600 ..**Bailey**, Erika D '02 %Levin & Assoc -1301 E 9th -Ste 1100
-Cleveland 44114

(816) 753-9390 ..**Bailey**, Jennifer A '94 Laver Agency -4534 Worwalll
-Kansas City, MO 64111

(304) 232-6675 ..**Bailey**, John Preston '78 (Bailey RB&H,LC) -900 Riley Bldg
-53 14th -Bx631 -Wheeling, WV 26003 **Fx**:232-9897
Bailey, Jonathan A '97 -3273 Clarendon Rd
-Cleveland Heights 44118

(281) 363-0456 ..**Bailey**, Karen D '92 %Hewitt Assoc LLC -2601 Rsrch Forest Dr
-The Woodlands, TX 77381

(513) 946-3000 ..**Bailey**, Kathleen H '92 Hamilton Cnty Pros -230 E 9th
-Cincinnati 45202 **Fx**:946-3017

(937) 228-8080 .. **Bailey,** Kenneth L '60 K Bailey Co,LPA -226 Talbott Twr -Dayton 45402

(330) 675-2426 .. **Bailey,** Kenneth N '71 %Trumbull Cnty Pros -160 High NW -Warren 44481

(419) 625-6740 .. **Bailey,** Kenneth R '83 (KR Bailey & Assoc Co,LPA) -220 W Market -Bx830 -Sandusky 44871

(330) 287-5575 .. **Bailey,** Kenneth W '78 Cnty Probate/Juvenile Ct -107 W Lbrty -Wooster 44691

(304) 525-9115 .. **Bailey,** Larry A '92 (Greene KB&T) -419 11th -Bx2389 -Huntington, WV 25724

(859) 292-7011 .. **Bailey,** Mark W '73 Sencorp -1 Rvrfrnt Pl -Newport, KY 41071

(513) 852-5600 .. **Bailey,** Melanie S '03 %Lopez HRM&S -312 Walnut -Ste 2090 -Cincinnati 45202 **Fx:**852-5611

(513) 631-0022 .. **Bailey,** Michael S '91 (Bailey & G Co,LPA) -5257 Mntgmry Rd -Cincinnati 45212

(614) 885-8272 .. **Bailey,** Richard W '57 (Bailey & S) -6877 N High -Ste 303 -Columbus 43085

(614) 885-8272 .. **Bailey & Slavin** -6877 N High -Ste 303 -Columbus 43085

(513) 333-0990 .. **Bailey,** Stephen A '71 (Martin & B) -120 E 4th -Ste 420 -Cincinnati 45202 **Fx:**333-0066

(330) 725-0030 .. **Bailey,** Steve C '89 (Marco M&B) -52 Pub Sq -Medina 44256 **Fx:**722-4888

(513) 455-7600 .. **Bailey,** Todd H '76 (Greenebaum D&M PLLC) -255 E 5th -2800 Chemed Ctr -Cincinnati 45202 **Fx:**455-8500

(216) 222-2974 .. **Bailey,** William J Jr. '94 Natl City Corp -1900 E 9th -# 01-2174 -Cleveland 44114

(513) 977-5690 .. **Bailey-Newell,** Susan M '94 Cincinnati Metro Housing Auth -16 W Cntrl Pkwy -Cincinnati 45202

(216) 371-1154 .. **Bain,** Jeffrey M '77 -2562 Coventry Rd -Shaker Heights 44120

(216) 363-1400 .. **Bain,** Richard M '79 (Buckley K,LPA) -600 E Superior Av -Ste 1400 -Cleveland 44114 **Fx:**579-1020

(614) 224-9223 .. **Bainbridge,** Andrew J '96 Ward KBM&M -199 S 5th -Columbus 43215

(419) 247-2523 .. **Bainbridge,** David R '83 (Fuller & H,Ltd) -One SeaGate -Ste 1700 -Bx2088 -Toledo 43603 **Fx:**247-2665

(419) 213-4700 .. **Bainbridge,** Jennifer T '83 %Lucas Cnty Pros -Adams & Erie -Lucas Cnty Cthse -Toledo 43624

(614) 224-9223 .. **Bainbridge,** Thomas H Jr. '67 (Ward KBM&M) -199 S 5th -Columbus 43215

(614) 224-4114 .. **Bainter,** David T '69 (St Clair & B,LLP) -580 S High -Ste 200 -Columbus 43215 **Fx:**224-3804

(419) 865-1251 .. **Bair,** C William '83 (Wagoner & S,Ltd) -7445 Airport Hwy -Holland 43528 **Fx:**866-8798

(937) 227-3700 .. **Bair,** Erin A '04 %Faruki I&C PLL -10 N Ludlow -500 Cthse Plz SW -Dayton 45402 **Fx:**227-3717

(614) 466-3016 .. **Bair,** Jodi J '94 PUCO -180 E Broad -Columbus 43266

(419) 668-2311 .. **Baird,** John D '75 -85 Benedict Av -Norwalk 44857 **Fx:**668-2311

(513) 831-2492 .. **Baird,** Sharon C '82 -1 Crestvw Dr -Milford 45150

(614) 227-2300 .. **Baird-Veley,** Catherine J '04 %Bricker & E LLP -100 S 3rd -Columbus 43215 **Fx:**227-2390

(614) 895-3007 .. **Baisden,** Larry J '76 -6000 Cleveland Av -Bx29189 -Columbus 43229

(216) 622-8200 .. **Baisden,** W Eric '91 %Calfee H&G LLP -800 Superior Av -Ste 1400 -Cleveland 44114 **Fx:**241-0816

(419) 249-7900 .. **Baither,** C Philip III '80 (Robison C&O) -Four SeaGate -9th Fl -Toledo 43604 **Fx:**249-7911

(216) 524-5717 .. **Bajorek,** Christine C '89 %Independent Advsrs -3 Summit Park Dr -#610 -Independence 44131

(216) 222-9139 .. **Bajus,** Susan M '90 Natl City Bank -1900 E 9th -# 01-2174 -Cleveland 44114

(513) 347-7800 .. **Bajwa,** Loveleen K '02 -5948 Glenway Av -Cincinnati 45238

(216) 622-3600 .. **Bakeman,** Ronald B '73 US Atty -801 W Superior -Ste 400 -Cleveland 44113 **Fx:**622-3370

(740) 592-9043 .. **Baker,** Adam J '92 -8 N Court -Ste 212 -Athens 45701

(216) 771-3966 .. **Baker,** Adam S '98 Baker B&B -55 Pub Sq -Ste 1330 -Cleveland 44113

(440) 946-9646 .. **Baker,** Benjamin B '99 All Craft Wellman Prdcts,Inc -4839 E 345th -Willoughby 44094

(614) 221-2253 .. **Baker,** Blaise G '83 -600 S High -Ste 201 -Columbus 43215

(614) 227-2000 .. **Baker,** Bradley K '91 %Porter WM&A LLP -41 S High -Columbus 43215 **Fx:**227-2100

(330) 747-4404 .. **Baker,** Brent E '00 %Newman O&K,LPA -11 Fed Plz Central -Ste 1200 -Youngstown 44503 **Fx:**747-6056

(419) 893-3360 .. **Baker,** Chad R '99 %Weber & S,LLC -1721 Indn Wd Cir -Ste 1 -Maumee 43537 **Fx:**893-7146

(859) 431-5881 .. **Baker,** Clell D '87 -30 19th -Newport, KY 41071

(404) 705-9067 .. **Baker,** David A '75 ARAG Ins Co -5291 Lk Forrest Dr -Atlanta, GA 30342

(614) 227-2364 .. **Baker,** David G '72 (Bricker & E LLP) -100 S 3rd -Columbus 43215 **Fx:**227-2390

(740) 753-1111 .. **Baker,** David S '93 Fndtn for Appalachian OH -36 Pub Sq -Bx456 -Nelsonville 45764

(330) 562-4623 .. **Baker,** Douglas R '79 -840 Nautilus Trl -Aurora 44202

(330) 499-6000 .. **Baker Dublikar Beck Wiley & Mathews** -400 S Main -Canton 44720 **Fx:**449-6423

(440) 324-7577 .. **Baker,** Edward J '89 Apex Investment Mgt,LLC -347 Midway Blvd -Elyria 44035

(614) 444-2200 .. **Baker,** Elizabeth J '85 -897 S Front -Columbus 43206

(216) 566-8200 .. **Baker,** Eric D '98 %Seeley S&E Co LPA -600 Superior Av E -800 Bank One Ctr -Cleveland 44114 **Fx:**566-0213

(614) 227-2487 .. **Baker,** Frederick L '82 Columbus State Comm Cllg -550 E Spring -CL 295 -Columbus 43215

(216) 664-6079 .. **Baker,** Gail D '95 Dept of Law -601 Lakeside Av -Rm 106 City Hall -Cleveland 44114 **Fx:**664-2663

(614) 224-3504 .. **Baker,** Geoffrey L '95 -640 Brust -Columbus 43206

(330) 492-1001 .. **Baker,** Gerald L '68 -3311 Whipple Av NW -Canton 44718

(614) 462-2344 .. **Baker,** Gregory S '98 %Schottenstein Z&D -250 West -Bx165020 -Columbus 43216 **Fx:**462-5135

(440) 354-4364 .. **Baker & Hackenberg Co,LPA** -77 N St Clair -Painesville 44077 **Fx:**639-8901

(419) 354-9250 .. **Baker,** Heather M '04 Wood Cnty Pros -One Cthse Sq -Bowling Green 43402 **Fx:**353-2904

(740) 452-8426 .. **Baker,** Herbert W Jr. '76 -301 Main -Bx400 -Zanesville 43702

(216) 621-0200 .. **Baker & Hostetler LLP** -1900 E 9th -Ste 3200 -Cleveland 44114 **Fx:**696-0740

(513) 929-3400 .. **Baker & Hostetler LLP** -312 Walnut -Ste 3200 -Cincinnati 45202 **Fx:**929-0303

(614) 228-1541 .. **Baker & Hostetler LLP** -65 E State -Ste 2100 -Columbus 43215 **Fx:**462-2616

(330) 499-6000 .. **Baker,** Jack R '69 (Baker DBW&M) -400 S Main -Canton 44720 **Fx:**449-6423

(216) 896-2138 .. **Baker,** James A '70 Parker Hannifin Corp -6035 Parkland Blvd -Cleveland 44124

(216) 771-3966 .. **Baker,** Jason T '99 Baker B&B -55 Pub Sq -Ste 1330 -Cleveland 44113

(419) 774-5676 .. **Baker,** John W '81 Richland Cnty Pros -38 S Park -2nd Fl -Mansfield 44902 **Fx:**774-5589

(513) 241-7600 .. **Baker,** Joseph R '96 %Scacchetti & S -601 Main -3rd Fl -Cincinnati 45202

(216) 623-0000 .. **Baker,** Kenneth D '76 (Javitch B&R) -1300 E 9th -14th Fl -Cleveland 44114 **Fx:**623-0190

(419) 241-6000 .. **Baker,** Kenneth C '77 (Eastman & S Ltd) -1 Seagate -24th Fl -Bx10032 -Toledo 43699 **Fx:**247-1777

(419) 241-6000 .. **Baker,** Kimberly Sue '00 %Eastman & S Ltd -1 Seagate -24th Fl -Bx10032 -Toledo 43699 **Fx:**247-1777

(614) 645-7483 .. **Baker,** Lara N '94 City Pros -375 S High -7th Fl -Columbus 43215

(216) 696-1158 .. **Baker,** Lawrence M '61 -629 Euclid Av -Ste 727 -Cleveland 44114 **Fx:**696-5159

(216) 443-2054 .. **Baker,** Linda Lou '88 Cuyahoga Cnty Cmmn Pleas Ct -1 Lakeside -Rm 26 -Cleveland 44113

(216) 771-3966 .. **Baker,** Martin '71 Baker B&B -55 Pub Sq -Ste 1330 -Cleveland 44113

(614) 791-3245 .. **Baker,** Matthew B '02 Cnsl OH Patrolmens Benevolent Assn -555 Metro Pl N -Ste 100 -Dublin 43017 **Fx:**791-3246

(330) 650-0328 .. **Baker,** Michael D '61 -233 Aurora -Hudson 44236

(216) 241-0673 .. **Baker,** Michael D '94 -925 Euclid Av -Ste 2010 -Cleveland 44115

(859) 426-1300 .. **Baker,** Michael L '82 Ziegler & S,PSC -541 Buttermilk Pike -Ste 500 -Bx175710 -Covington, KY 41017

(216) 875-3167 .. **Baker,** Michael R '88 PricewaterhouseCoopers LLP -200 Pub Sq -27th Fl -Cleveland 44114

(513) 977-8200 .. **Baker,** Neal D '84 (Dinsmore & S LLP) -255 E 5th -Ste 1900 -Cincinnati 45202 **Fx:**977-8141

(937) 372-8055 .. **Baker,** R J '92 Miller FM&B -20 King Av -Bx610 -Xenia 45385

(740) 432-6397 .. **Baker,** Richard A '67 (DeSelm & B) -819 Steubenvll Av -Cambridge 43725

(614) 752-1200 .. **Baker,** Richard L '93 Parole Brd -1050 Fwy Dr N -Columbus 43229

(419) 536-3260 .. **Baker,** Richard S '57 -2819 Falmouth Rd -Toledo 43615

(330) 434-2113 .. **Baker,** Robert C '77 Armbruster KKH&B -159 S Main -Ste 720 -Akron 44308

(614) 236-8036 .. **Baker,** Samuel M '72 -3319 E Lvngstn Av -Columbus 43227

(513) 753-4303 .. **Baker,** Scott W '93 -1197 Birch Bark Ct -Amelia 45102

(614) 466-7919 .. **Baker,** Shelagh F '79 Legis Srvc Commssn -77 S High -Columbus 43215

(216) 687-1311 .. **Baker,** Stacie L '99 %Reminger & R -101 Prospect Av W -1400 Mdlnd Bldg -Cleveland 44115 **Fx:**687-1841

(216) 928-2200 .. **Baker,** Stuart D '04 %Sutter OM&F -1301 E 9th -3600 Erievw Twr -Cleveland 44114 **Fx:**928-2201

(330) 264-4444 .. **Baker,** Susan E '92 (Critchfield C&J Ltd) -225 N Market -Bx599 -Wooster 44691 **Fx:**263-9278

(937) 226-1990 .. **Baker,** Theresa A '92 W Kinney III Co,LPA -120 W 2nd -1700 Lbrty Twr -Dayton 45402

(614) 488-2202 .. **Baker,** Thomas S Jr. '68 (T Baker Jr LLC) -1371 W 3rd Av -Columbus 43212

(216) 592-5000 .. **Baker,** Thomas W '99 Cnsl Tucker E&W LLP -925 Euclid Av -1150 Huntngtn Bldg -Cleveland 44115 **Fx:**592-5009

(502) 564-5576 .. **Baker,** Virginia M '98 Natl Rsrcs & EPA -Cptl Plz Twr -5th Fl -Frankfort, KY 40601

.. **Baker,** Wendy J '95 -(Address Unavailable)

(937) 882-9305 .. **Baker,** Wilburn L '03 (Baker & N,LLC) -926 Bischoff Rd -New Carlisle 45344

(216) 781-7777 .. **Baker,** William Joseph '00 %Wuliger F&B -1340 Sumner Ct -Brownell Bldg -Cleveland 44115 **Fx:**781-0621

(419) 213-3000 .. **Baker-Johnson,** Elaine '89 Lucas Cnty CSEA -701 Adams -Toledo 43624

(419) 352-4621 .. **Bakies,** Gregory E '85 (Maurer N&B) -224 E Wooster -Bowling Green 43402

(216) 371-5220 .. **Bakst,** Gary N '82 -2000 Lee Rd -Ste 23 -Cleveland Heights 44118

(513) 381-2221 .. **Bakst,** Jeffrey S '83 (J Bakst & Assoc) -2406 Auburn Av -Cincinnati 45219

(216) 447-9500 .. **Bakula,** Charles A '92 OfCnsl O'Rourke & Assoc Co,LPA -2 Summit Park Dr -Ste 650 -Independence 44131 **Fx:**447-9501

(614) 716-0500 .. **Balaloski,** Daniel K '97 Onda L&R Co,LPA -266 N 4th -Ste 100 -Columbus 43215 **Fx:**716-0511

(216) 696-1422 .. **Balantzow,** Robert S '65 (McCarthy LC&L Co,LPA) -101 Prospect Av W -1800 Mdlnd Bldg -Cleveland 44115 **Fx:**696-1210

(513) 421-4225 .. **Balash,** Paul E '76 (Burke FB&B,LLP) -817 Main -Ste 800 -Cincinnati 45202

(216) 566-9700 .. **Balazs,** James A '99 %Rankin HP&C,LLP -925 Euclid Av -Ste 700 -Cleveland 44115 **Fx:**566-9711

(216) 241-2838 .. **Balazs,** Mary G '80 (Taft S&H LLP) -200 Pub Sq -3500 BP Twr -Cleveland 44114 **Fx:**241-3707

(202) 408-4613 .. **Balbach,** Amy E '94 %Cohen MH&T -1100 NY Av NW -Ste 500 -Washington, DC 20005

(216) 241-4482 .. **Balbier,** Ronald C '73 -400 Trmnl Twr -Cleveland 44113

(614) 538-1840 .. **Balcerzak,** Thomas J '89 -4656 Exec Dr -Columbus 43220

(614) 224-2329 .. **Balch,** Jacintha M '79 Balch Law Firm -1335 Dublin Rd -Ste 200A -Columbus 43215

(614) 224-2329 .. **Balch,** John R '84 OfCnsl Balch Law Firm -1335 Dublin Rd -Ste 200A -Columbus 43215

(304) 340-3837 .. **Balderson,** Lisa L '90 %Spilman T&B,PLLC -300 Kanawha Blvd E -Bx273 -Charleston, WV 25321 **Fx:**340-3801

(614) 228-9550 .. **Baldree,** Cheri M '04 %Javitch B&R -33 N 3rd -Ste 300 -Columbus 43215 **Fx:**228-2818

(859) 431-6100 .. **Baldridge,** E Douglas '02 %Arnzen WML&S,PSC -600 Greenup -Covington, KY 41011 **Fx:**431-3778

(937) 225-5887 .. **Baldwin**, Bradley S '98 Montgomery Cnty Pros -301 W 3rd -Bx972 -Dayton 45422 Fx:225-3470

(317) 916-1300 .. **Baldwin**, Charles B '83 (Ogletree DNS&S,PC) -1 Indna Square -Ste 2300 -Indianapolis, IN 46204 Fx:916-9076

(740) 349-6575 .. **Baldwin**, Craig R '92 Licking Cnty CSEA -65 E Main -Bx338 -Newark 43058

(330) 352-1439 .. **Baldwin**, David C '95 -Bx66 -Doylestown 44230

(513) 651-6800 .. **Baldwin**, Gerald L '69 (Frost BT LLC) -201 E 5th -2200 PNC Ctr -Cincinnati 45202 Fx:651-6981

(614) 273-0171 .. **Baldwin**, Melissa W '96 -4656 Burbank Dr -Columbus 43220

(614) 794-0386 .. **Baldwin**, Richard T '70 Land America -921 Eastwind Dr -Ste 129 -Westerville 43081

(614) 466-8944 .. **Baldwin**, Shannon Freed '02 State Med Brd -77 S High -17th Fl -Columbus 43215

(740) 454-2545 .. **Baldwin**, Steven R '83 (Micheli BN Co,LPA) -3808 James Ct -Ste 2 -Bx788 -Zanesville 43702

(513) 872-5162 .. **Baldwin**, Thomas A '75 -2345 Kemper Ln -Bx6129 -Cincinnati 45206

(513) 723-4000 .. **Baldwin**, William D '97 (Vorys SS&P LLP) -221 E 4th -Ste 2000 Atrium Two -Bx0236 -Cincinnati 45201 Fx:723-4056

(614) 895-5600 .. **Bale**, David G '78 (Bale B & Assoc,Ltd) -140 Commerce Park Dr -Westerville 43082

(419) 420-3055 .. **Balega**, Joseph R '86 Golden Key Title Agncy,Inc -239 S Main -Findlay 45840

(440) 365-2000 .. **Balena**, William J '78 -633 W Broad -#200 -Elyria 44035

(419) 547-9471 .. **Bales**, Beth A '04 %Dewey & D -107 N Main -Bx28 -Clyde 43410 Fx:547-0139

(216) 781-5470 .. **Bales**, Stephen M '83 (Ziegler M&M LLP) -925 Euclid Av -2020 Huntngtn Bldg -Cleveland 44115 Fx:781-0714

(440) 257-5000 .. **Balin**, Paulette F '78 -7372 Lk Shr Blvd -Mentor 44060

(419) 865-8021 .. **Balk Hess & Miller** -5744 Southwyck Blvd -Toledo 43614 Fx:865-9105

(330) 262-3030 .. **Ball**, Brian A '04 Wayne Cnty Pros -115 W Lbrty -Wooster 44691 Fx:287-5412

(614) 228-1357 .. **Ball**, Claire M Jr. '67 -503 S 3rd -Columbus 43215

(937) 485-1708 .. **Ball**, David E '92 Reynolds & Reynolds Co -One Reynolds Way -Dayton 45430 Fx:485-0973

(513) 732-5900 .. **Ball**, Douglas A '90 -233 E Main -Ste 3 -Batavia 45103 Fx:732-5904

(216) 451-1133 .. **Ball**, Fred J '45 -804 Bratenahl Pl -Cleveland 44108 Fx:541-6431

(614) 464-6400 .. **Ball**, James M '74 (Vorys SS&P LLP) -52 E Gay -Bx1008 -Columbus 43216 Fx:464-6350

(419) 627-0414 .. **Ball**, John R '88 Buckingham LM&Z Co,LPA -414 Wayne -Bx929 -Sandusky 44870 Fx:627-0009

(202) 835-6867 .. **Ball**, Julian C '84 Riggs & Co -808 17th NW -Washington, DC 20006

(614) 488-6166 .. **Ball**, Karen L '87 Flex Mgmt Inc -Bx2813 -Columbus 43216

(614) 624-5017 .. **Ball**, Michael D '94 Ross Product-Div of Abbott Labs -300 Stelzer Rd -Columbus 43219

(614) 447-8550 .. **Ball**, Steven L '74 (Ball & T) -700 Ackerman -Ste 450 -Columbus 43202 Fx:447-1673

(614) 523-1798 .. **Ball**, Theodore C '54 -8331 Cleveland Av NW -Westerville 43081

(614) 224-8374 .. **Ballam**, William F '80 %Legal Aid -40 W Gay -Columbus 43215

(216) 622-8269 .. **Ballard**, Brent D '85 (Calfee H&G LLP) -800 Superior Av -Ste 1400 -Cleveland 44114 Fx:241-0816

(614) 227-8806 .. **Ballard**, Catherine M '85 (Bricker & E LLP) -100 S 3rd -Columbus 43215 Fx:227-2390

(330) 643-2943 .. **Ballard**, Charmine T '02 Summit Cnty Pros-Juv -650 Dan -Akron 44310 Fx:379-3647

(317) 544-4040 .. **Ballard**, Duard D II '76 Rapid Logistics,Inc -5770 Dividend Dr -Indianapolis, IN 46241

(216) 621-5300 .. **Ballard**, John F Jr. '78 (Buckingham D&B,LLP) -1375 E 9th -Ste 1700 -Cleveland 44114 Fx:621-5440

(216) 328-8700 .. **Ballard**, Lynn A '91 SrCnsl ICX Corp -2 Summit Park Dr -Ste 300 -Cleveland 44131 Fx:328-8710

(937) 225-4168 .. **Ballard**, Nadine L '80 Montgomery Cnty Common Pleas Ct -41 N Perry -Bx972 -Dayton 45422

(614) 466-3636 .. **Ballard**, Steven '83 OH Dept Commerce -77 S High -Columbus 43266

(937) 225-6104 .. **Ballard**, Tracey L '98 Montgomery Cnty Pros -301 W 3rd -Bx972 -Dayton 45422 Fx:225-3470

Ballard-Dunlap, Alisa R '99 -(Address Unavailable)

(216) 696-1275 .. **Ballard-Eisman**, Mary B '78 Chicago Title Ins -1360 E 9th -Ste 500 -Cleveland 44114

(513) 723-9222 .. **Ballard-Salyer**, Susan M '96 Educational Lending Group -6 E 4th -Ste 300 -Cincinnati 45202

(937) 534-0500 .. **Ballato**, Lynnette P '95 (Subashi W&B) -2305 Far Hills Av -Oakwood Bldg -Dayton 45419 Fx:534-0505

(937) 228-2306 .. **Ballato**, Thomas A '94 %Brannon & Assoc -130 W 2nd -Ste 900 -Dayton 45402

(419) 698-1040 .. **Ballenger**, Brian J '85 Ballenger & M Co,LPA -3401 Woodvll Rd -Northwood 43619

(614) 888-3185 .. **Ballenger**, Kathleen A '79 (Kessler & B Co,LPA) -7650 Rvrs Edge Dr -Ste 101 -Columbus 43235

(614) 466-4100 .. **Ballenger**, Mark J '89 OH Dept Commerce -77 S High -Columbus 43266

(216) 479-8500 .. **Ballin**, Stacy D '83 (Squire S&D LLP) -127 Pub Sq -4900 Key Twr -Cleveland 44114 Fx:479-8780

(740) 383-3377 .. **Ballinger**, Teresa L '94 -383 S Main -Marion 43302

(216) 469-9337 .. **Ballou**, Emily A '92 Case Western Reserve Univ -10900 Euclid Av -Rsrch Marketing -Cleveland 44106

(740) 459-0116 .. **Ballou**, Marie E '90 -2887 Pebble Dr -Lewis Center 43035

(216) 776-9000 .. **Ballou**, Scott H '80 -1370 Ontario -Ste 1130 -Cleveland 44113

(614) 644-2489 .. **Bally**, James P '61 Dept Cmmrce/Liquor Cntrl -6606 Tussing Rd -Bx4005 -Reynoldsburg 43068 Fx:644-3740

(937) 293-2141 .. **Balmer**, Joseph E III '89 %Holzfaster CM&M -1105 Wilmngtn Av -Dayton 45420 Fx:293-0914

(330) 208-1000 .. **Balmert**, F Daniel '76 (Vorys SS&P LLP) -106 S Main -First Natl Twr -Akron 44308

(216) 479-6100 .. **Balmert**, F Daniel '76 (Vorys SS&P LLP) -1375 E 9th -Ste 2100 One Cleve Ctr -Cleveland 44114 Fx:479-6060

(859) 292-5500 .. **Balnes**, Sean C '02 Corporex Cos,Inc -100 E River Ctr Blvd -Ste 1100 -Covington, KY 41011

(216) 447-0070 .. **Balog**, Joseph A '76 Dalad Grp -6200 Rockside Wds Blvd -#105 -Independence 44131

(216) 351-3935 .. **Baloga**, David M '94 -7001 Plainfld Av -Cleveland 44144

(216) 348-7741 .. **Balogh**, Virginia E '92 Travelers Ins -1660 W 2nd -5th Fl -Cleveland 44113

(440) 934-0044 .. **Balser**, Brian K '87 (BK Balser Co,LPA) -5311 Meadow Ln -Ste 1 -Elyria 44035

(614) 469-3226 .. **Balthaser**, James H '78 (Thompson H LLP) -10 W Broad -Ste 700 -Columbus 43215 Fx:469-3361

Balunek, Adelbert A '66 -2227 Grdn Dr -Avon 44011

(419) 227-9595 .. **Balyeat**, Clay W '85 Daley B&L LLC -1728 Allentown Rd -Lima 45805 Fx:227-3177

(419) 321-6444 .. **Balyeat**, Thomas M '76 (Cline C&W Co,LPA) -300 Mad Av -Ste 1100 -Toledo 43604 Fx:321-6430

(419) 227-9595 .. **Balyeat**, William B '57 Daley B&L LLC -1728 Allentown Rd -Lima 45805 Fx:227-3177

(513) 603-5346 .. **Balzano**, David J '93 The Cincinnati Ins Co -6200 S Gilmore -Fairfield 45014

(440) 526-6722 .. **Balzano**, Laura A '80 (Wadsworth & B) -8927 Brecksvll Rd -Brecksville 44141

(513) 983-1100 .. **Bamber**, Jeffrey V '84 Procter & Gamble Co-Legal -1 Procter & Gamble Plz -Cincinnati 45202

(614) 445-8287 .. **Bamberger**, Kathryn A '91 -825 S Front -Columbus 43206

(216) 621-0200 .. **Bamberger**, Richard H '72 (Baker & H LLP) -1900 E 9th -Ste 3200 -Cleveland 44114 Fx:696-0740

(216) 622-3881 .. **Bamberger**, Roger S '72 US Atty -801 W Superior -Ste 400 -Cleveland 44113 Fx:622-3370

(419) 352-8100 .. **Bamburowski**, Thomas J '75 -133 N Prospect -Bowling Green 43402 Fx:354-8485

(614) 236-2483 .. **Bametzrieder**, Lori A '03 Nesbit Law Firm -447 E Main -Columbus 43215

(440) 930-3825 .. **Ban**, Woodrow W '81 Poly One Corp -33587 Walker -Avon Lake 44012

(330) 492-8717 .. **Banas**, Gary A '57 OfCnsl Buckingham D&B,LLP -4518 Fulton Dr NW -Bx35548 -Canton 44735 Fx:492-9625

(330) 706-1831 .. **Banas**, James E '83 -3067 Wadsworth Rd -Norton 44203

(330) 643-2788 .. **Banbury**, Michelle L '98 Summit Cnty Pros-Crim -53 Univ Av -7th Fl -Akron 44308 Fx:643-8277

(614) 462-2274 .. **Banchefsky**, Mitchell H '83 (Schottenstein Z&D) -250 West -Bx165020 -Columbus 43216 Fx:462-5135

(216) 566-7666 .. **Banchek**, Melvin H '73 -55 Pub Sq -Ste 918 -Cleveland 44113

(216) 443-7223 .. **Bancroft**, Michael R '83 Cuyahoga Cnty Pub Def -1200 W 3rd NW -100 Lakeside Pl -Cleveland 44113

(216) 781-0111 .. **Bancsi**, Joseph '72 -323 W Lakeside Av -Ste 450 -Cleveland 44113

(614) 848-5975 .. **Bandman**, Marc B '87 Bandman Consulting Co -1429 Royal Gold Dr -Columbus 43240

(419) 399-2351 .. **Bandy**, Erwin J '77 Paulding Cnty Ct -108 E Jackson -Bx174 -Paulding 45879

(330) 537-3739 .. **Bandy**, Kenneth L '74 -28787 Salem-Alliance Rd -Bx157 -Damascus 44619

(216) 861-5582 .. **Bandy**, Mark E '91 (Fay SFM&M LLP) -1100 Superior Av -7th Fl -Cleveland 44114 Fx:241-1666

(908) 595-3890 .. **Banerjee**, Krishna G '97 Clariant Corp -70 Meister Av -Somerville, NJ 08876

(740) 779-6662 .. **Banfield**, Amanda L '04 Hon W Harsha 4th Dist Ct of Appls -14 S Paint -Ste 18 -Chillicothe 45601

(304) 691-8412 .. **Banford**, Craig R '94 %Huddleston BBP&C -611 Third Av -Bx2185 -Huntington, WV 25722 Fx:522-4312

(216) 522-4870 .. **Bang**, Jun S '01 NLRB -1240 E 9th -Rm 1695 -Cleveland 44199 Fx:522-2418

(614) 236-6245 .. **Bank**, Danny W '90 %Capital Univ Lw Schl -303 E Broad -Columbus 43215 Fx:236-6970

(614) 227-8836 .. **Bank**, H Randy '84 (Bricker & E LLP) -100 S 3rd -Columbus 43215 Fx:227-2390

(216) 566-5555 .. **Bank**, Malvin E '57 (Thompson H LLP) -127 Pub Sq -3900 Key Ctr -Cleveland 44114 Fx:566-5800

(216) 471-6900 .. **Banker**, Amanda M '04 Office Max,Inc -3605 Warensvll Ctr Rd -Shaker Heights 44122

(740) 676-2111 .. **Banker**, Floyd A '57 (Banker & W) -3201 Belmont -Bellaire 43906

(513) 946-3435 .. **Banker**, Marcia A '84 1st Dist Ct of Appeals -230 E 9th -12th Fl Wm Howard Taft Law Ctr -Cincinnati 45202

(740) 676-2111 .. **Banker**, Megan '94 (Banker & W) -3201 Belmont -Bellaire 43906

(614) 469-3939 .. **Bankovich**, Candace A '02 %Jones D -325 John H McConnell Blvd -Ste 600 -Bx165017 -Columbus 43216 Fx:461-4198

(419) 222-9933 .. **Banks**, Farley K '95 -Bx363 -Lima 45802

Banks, Gerald T '75 -3509 Fleming Rd -Middletown 45042

(419) 255-7044 .. **Banks**, Gerald W '73 -709 Mad Av -314 Bell Bldg -Toledo 43624

(614) 866-0666 .. **Banks**, James H '80 SrCnsl J Banks -Bx40 -Dublin 43017 Fx:766-1203

(216) 566-5100 .. **Banks**, Kenneth E '73 Grtr Clvlnd Reg Trans Auth -1240 W 6th -Cleveland 44113

(216) 443-8580 .. **Banks**, Marie C '01 Cuyahoga Cnty Ct Cmmn Pleas -1200 Ontario -Justice Ctr 11th Fl -Cleveland 44113

(513) 221-5510 .. **Banner**, John G '80 Cinncinati Ofc of Admin Hearing -805 Central Av -Ste 110 -Cincinnati 45202 Fx:221-5540

(614) 294-5040 .. **Bannerman**, Robert C '97 %M Cohen LLC -1299 Olentangy Rvr Rd -2nd Fl Ste C -Columbus 43212

(937) 898-3996 .. **Bannister**, Richard J '61 Mun Ct Judge -245 James E Bohanan Mem'l Dr -Bx429 -Vandalia 45377

Bannon, Charles J '58 -968 Ottawa Dr -Youngstown 44511

(740) 353-1157 .. **Bannon Howland & Dever** -325 Masonic Bldg -Bx1384 -Portsmouth 45662

(330) 758-6731 .. **Bannon**, Robert W '84 -421 Glenwoods Ct -Youngstown 44512

(216) 566-0770 .. **Banta**, Michael E '73 -75 Pub Sq -Ste 525 -Cleveland 44113

(614) 365-9900 .. **Banvard**, Kris '03 %Zeiger TL&L,LLP -41 S High -Ste 3500 Huntngtn Ctr -Columbus 43215 Fx:365-7900

(517) 279-9745 .. **Bappert**, Charles R '03 %Biringer HL&B -100 W Chicago -Coldwater, MI 49036

(419) 524-6682 .. **Baran**, Edward C Jr. '67 OfCnsl Baran PTF&T Co,LPA -3 N Main -Ste 500 -Mansfield 44902 Fx:525-4571

(419) 524-6682 .. **Baran**, Gregory G '70 (Baran PTF&T Co,LPA) -3 N Main -Ste 500 -Mansfield 44902 Fx:525-4571

(937) 435-7500 ..**Baran**, Heidi L '98 %Botros B&S,LLC -5785 Far Hills Av
-Dayton 45429 **Fx:**435-7511

(440) 442-6677 ..**Baran**, Mark R '01 Elk & E Co,LPA -6100 Parkland Blvd
-Mayfield Heights 44124 **Fx:**442-7944

(440) 442-6677 ..**Baran**, Mindy E '98 Elk & E Co,LPA -6100 Parkland Blvd
-Mayfield Heights 44124 **Fx:**442-7944

(419) 524-6682 ..**Baran Piper Tarkowsky Fitzgerald & Theis Co,LPA** -3 N Main
-Ste 500 -Mansfield 44902 **Fx:**525-4571

(419) 227-5858 ..**Baran Piper Tarkowsky Fitzgerald & Theis Co,LPA**
-121 W High -Ste 905 -Bx568 -Lima 45802 **Fx:**227-4569

(419) 241-2900 ..**Baran Piper Tarkowsky Fitzgerald & Theis Co,LPA**
-608 Mad Av -Ste 1620 -Toledo 43604 **Fx:**241-3002

(440) 746-1177 ..**Baran Piper Tarkowsky Fitzgerald & Theis CO,LPA**
-8748 Brecksvll Rd -Ste 200 -Cleveland 44141 **Fx:**746-9637

(614) 436-0539 ..**Baran Piper Tarkowsky Fitzgerald & Theis Co,LPA**
-6877 N High -Ste 105 -Columbus 43085 **Fx:**436-1713

(614) 227-2000 ..**Baranowski**, Edwin M '82 (Porter WM&A LLP) -41 S High
-Columbus 43215 **Fx:**227-2100

(216) 348-5400 ..**Baraona**, Robert C '98 %McDonald H Co,LPA -600 Superior Av E
-Ste 2100 -Cleveland 44114 **Fx:**348-5474

(614) 462-2311 ..**Barath**, William J '89 (Schottenstein Z&D) -250 West -Bx165020
-Columbus 43216 **Fx:**462-5135

(513) 241-0400 ..**Barbanel**, Roberta J '02 Aronoff R&H Co,LPA -425 Walnut
-Ste 2400 -Cincinnati 45202 **Fx:**241-2877

(937) 223-9133 ..**Barbato**, Matthew J '03 %Rion R&R Co,LPA -130 W 2nd
-Ste 2150 -Bx1262 -Dayton 45402

(513) 721-2157 ..**Barbeau**, Jeannine C '93 -8 W 9th -Cincinnati 45202

(330) 744-5211 ..**Barbee**, David S '86 Roth BRS&L,LPA -100 Fed Plz E -Ste 600
-Youngstown 44503 **Fx:**744-3184

(614) 466-5967 ..**Barber**, Barbara L '97 Atty Gen -30 E Broad -Columbus 43215
Fx:466-8226

(937) 754-3040 ..**Barber**, Catherine Mae '79 Mun Ct Judge -44 W Hebble Av
-Fairborn 45324

(937) 865-6800 ..**Barber**, Darin S '94 Lexis/Nexis -Bx933 -Dayton 45401

(330) 675-2426 ..**Barber**, Diane L '98 %Trumbull Cnty Pros -160 High NW
-Warren 44481

(419) 337-5065 ..**Barber Kaper Stamm & Robinson** -124 N Fulton
-Wauseon 43567 **Fx:**337-1136

(419) 822-3211 ..**Barber Kaper Stamm & Robinson** -206 Main -Delta 43515
Fx:822-4593

(301) 415-1572 ..**Barber**, Kathryn M '00 US NRC -MS 0-15 D21
-Washington, DC 20555

(330) 334-2468 ..**Barber**, Mark H '87 Medina Cnty CSEA -Bx1389 -Medina 44258

(419) 241-6612 ..**Barber**, Matthew J '04 -316 N Mich -Ste 418 -Toledo 43624

(973) 360-6200 ..**Barber**, Peter K '82 %Heim & M -12 Vreeland Rd
-Florham Park, NJ 07932 **Fx:**360-6262

(513) 922-5200 ..**Barber**, Raymond P '73 -5115 Delhi Av -Cincinnati 45238

                    Barbera, Richard '94 -Bx1117 -Medina 44258

(513) 583-4200 ..**Barbiere**, Lawrence J '77 (Schroeder MB&P) -11935 Mason Rd
-Ste 110 -Cincinnati 45249

(561) 997-5700 ..**Barbieri**, Frank A Jr. '80 (Barbieri SW&R,PLLC) -3200 N
Military Trl -Ste 200 -Boca Raton, FL 33431 **Fx:**997-4737

(717) 533-3280 ..**Barbin**, Andrew W '85 James SD&C LLP -Bx650 -Hershey, PA
17033

(330) 424-3211 ..**Barborak**, Nicholas M '00 -120 S Market -Lisbon 44432

(330) 424-3211 ..**Barborak**, Virginia M '97 -120 S Market -Lisbon 44432

(614) 995-4934 ..**Barbosky**, Pamella A '92 Ohio Bd of Nursing -17 S High -Ste 400
-Columbus 43215

(216) 771-4050 ..**Barbour**, James E '88 (Jeffries KF&M Co,LPA) -101 W Prospect Av
-1650 Mdlnd Bldg -Cleveland 44115 **Fx:**771-0732

(614) 231-0003 ..**Barch**, Bryan C '03 %Goldstein & Assoc -4517 E Main -Columbus
43213

                    Barciz, Rosemarie A '83 -707 E Carisbrook Dr -Maumee 43537

(740) 452-8439 ..**Barclay**, Adam T '03 Zellar & Z -720 Market -Zanesville 43701

(614) 221-6969 ..**Barclay**, Craig D '73 Wolske & B,LPA -580 S High -Ste 300
-Columbus 43215

(740) 454-8585 ..**Barclay**, Katherine M '04 Graham M&R Co,LPA -11 N 4th -Bx340
-Zanesville 43702

(513) 421-3940 ..**Bardach**, Richard B '95 %Whitman Law Ofcs -3536 Edwards Rd
-Ste 100 -Cincinnati 45208

(513) 621-2666 ..**Bardach**, Robert A '89 (Statman HS&E LLC) -255 E 5th
-Ste 2900 Chemed Ctr -Cincinnati 45202 **Fx:**587-4477

(614) 310-0200 ..**Bardash**, James T '97 Stump-Bardash -730 Mt Airyshire Blvd
-Ste B -Columbus 43235 **Fx:**310-0205

(513) 946-3865 ..**Barden**, Barbara K '74 Pub Def Ofc - Guardian Ad Litem
-230 E 9th -3rd Fl -Cincinnati 45202 **Fx:**946-3808

(614) 445-6757 ..**Bardwell**, Robert E Jr. '88 -995 S High -Columbus 43206

(330) 376-2700 ..**Bare**, Betsy L '04 %Roetzel & A,LPA -222 S Main -Akron 44308
Fx:376-4577

(614) 227-2000 ..**Bares**, Bryce A '04 %Porter WM&A LLP -41 S High
-Columbus 43215 **Fx:**227-2100

                    Barette, Tammy S '02 -214 Melrose Av -Front
-Clarks Summit, PA 18411

(419) 447-0507 ..**Barga**, John T '76 -120 Jffrsn -Bx200 -Tiffin 44883 **Fx:**447-4447

(419) 885-3000 ..**Barger**, Brian P '84 (Brady C&S LLP) -4052 Holland-Sylvania Rd
-Toledo 43623 **Fx:**885-1120

                    Bargmeyer, Brian A '01 -2624 S Taylor Rd
-Cleveland Heights 44118

(312) 263-1070 ..**Barhorst**, Stacie E '00 %Statman HS&E,LLC -333 W Wacker Dr
-Ste 1710 -Chicago, IL 60606 **Fx:**263-1201

(440) 329-5357 ..**Barilla**, James V '92 Lorain Co Common Pleas Ct -226 Middle Av
-Elyria 44035

(440) 326-4835 ..**Barilla**, Jody L '92 Lorain Co Domestic Relations Ct
-226 Middle Av -Elyria 44035

(216) 586-3939 ..**Baringer**, Jennifer H '02 Jones D -901 Lakeside Av
-Cleveland 44114 **Fx:**579-0212

(216) 586-3939 ..**Baringer**, Randal S '90 (Jones D) -901 Lakeside Av
-Cleveland 44114 **Fx:**579-0212

(614) 469-7417 ..**Barkan**, Alexander G '71 US DOJ -170 N High -Ste 200
-Columbus 43215

(614) 461-1551 ..**Barkan**, Irving '57 (Barkan & B Co LPA) -81 S 4th -Ste 300
-Columbus 43215

(614) 461-1551 ..**Barkan**, Neal J '78 (Barkan & B Co LPA) -81 S 4th -Ste 300
-Columbus 43215

(614) 221-4221 ..**Barkan + Neff** -360 S Grant Av -Bx1989 -Columbus 43216
Fx:221-5423

(419) 897-6500 ..**Barkan & Robon Ltd** -1701 Woodlnds Dr -Maumee 43537
Fx:897-6200

(419) 897-6500 ..**Barkan**, William Ira '55 (Barkan & R Ltd) -1701 Woodlnds Dr
-Maumee 43537 **Fx:**897-6200

(602) 744-3210 ..**Barkel**, Edwin A '88 Sun Amer Sec,Inc -2800 N Central Av
-Ste 2100 -Phoenix, AZ 85004

(440) 353-9462 ..**Barker**, James E '85 -33278 Mills Rd -Avon 44011

(614) 888-9611 ..**Barker**, Larry D '74 (Innis & B Co,LPA) -8415 Pulsar Pl -Ste 380
-Columbus 43240 **Fx:**888-8499

(216) 348-1700 ..**Barker**, Pamela A '82 OfCnsl Davis & Y -101 Prospect Av W
-Ste 1700 -Cleveland 44115 **Fx:**621-0602

(513) 381-0656 ..**Barker**, Peggy M '95 (Kohnen & P LLP) -201 E 5th -Ste 800
-Cincinnati 45202 **Fx:**381-5823

(859) 232-3668 ..**Barker**, Scott N '98 Lexmark Intl,Inc -740 W New Circle Rd
-Lexington, KY 40550

(440) 277-1259 ..**Barkus**, Michael M '79 -Bx1236 -Lorain 44055

(614) 644-6905 ..**Barley**, Christopher E '93 OH Dept of Human Srvcs -30 E Broad
-32nd Fl -Columbus 43266

(614) 228-6885 ..**Barley-McBride**, Mary '86 (Lane A&H LLC) -175 S 3rd -Ste 700
-Columbus 43215 **Fx:**228-6340

(513) 621-2120 ..**Barlow**, Anthony M '90 (Strauss & T,LPA) -150 E 4th -4th Fl
-Cincinnati 45202 **Fx:**241-8259

(216) 623-0150 ..**Barlow**, J C Jeffrey '02 %Roetzel & A,LPA -1375 E 9th
-One Cleve Ctr 9th Fl -Cleveland 44114 **Fx:**623-0134

(703) 707-9110 ..**Barlow**, James E '90 (Posz & B,PLC) -12040 S Lakes Dr -Ste 101
-Reston, VA 20191 **Fx:**707-9112

(216) 687-1311 ..**Barmen**, Bradley J '03 %Reminger & R -101 Prospect Av W
-1400 Mdlnd Bldg -Cleveland 44115 **Fx:**687-1841

(440) 786-1910 ..**Barnabee**, Randi A '04 (Smith B & Co,LPA) -934 Archer Rd
-Bedford 44146

(216) 341-2022 ..**Barnak**, Andrew M '73 Heat Sealing Equipment Mfg Co
-4580 E 71st -Cleveland 44125

(330) 264-9456 ..**Barnard**, Bryan K '03 -322 W Lbrty -Ste B -Wooster 44691
Fx:262-4895

(216) 321-1234 ..**Barnard**, Geoffrey W '93 Cleveland Hts Police Dept
-40 Severance Cir Dr -Cleveland Heights 44118

(330) 264-9456 ..**Barnard**, George K '71 -248 N Walnut -Bx1041 -Wooster 44691

(440) 525-7352 ..**Barnard**, Laura '83 Lakeland Cmmnty Cllg -7700 Clocktower Dr
-Kirtland 44094 **Fx:**525-7653

(216) 931-6000 ..**Barnard**, Thomas H Jr. '64 (Ulmer & B LLP) -1300 E 9th
-Ste 900 Penton Media Bldg -Cleveland 44114 **Fx:**931-6001

(440) 350-2683 ..**Barner**, Donald R '86 Lake Cnty Pros -105 Main -Bx490
-Painesville 44077 **Fx:**350-2585

(216) 687-1902 ..**Barnes**, Austin B III '91 %S Haygood & Assoc -1422 Euclid Av
-Ste 1510 -Cleveland 44115 **Fx:**687-1906

(614) 228-6885 ..**Barnes**, Belinda S '87 (Lane A&H LLC) -175 S 3rd -Ste 700
-Columbus 43215 **Fx:**228-0146

(513) 684-3711 ..**Barnes**, Christopher K '75 US Atty -221 E 4th -Ste 400
-Cincinnati 45202 **Fx:**684-6385

(202) 283-7953 ..**Barnes**, David K '90 IRS -1111 Const Av NW -Ste 216
-Washington, DC 20224

(740) 695-2929 ..**Barnes**, David L '58 -Masonic Temple Bldg -Bx22
-Saint Clairsville 43950

(216) 479-8500 ..**Barnes**, Geoffrey K '73 (Squire S&D LLP) -127 Pub Sq
-4900 Key Twr -Cleveland 44114 **Fx:**479-8780

(330) 535-5711 ..**Barnes**, Heather M '99 %Brouse M -106 S Main
-500 First Natl Twr -Akron 44308 **Fx:**253-8601

(614) 466-6696 ..**Barnes**, James E '85 Atty Gen -150 E Gay -Columbus 43215
Fx:752-2538

(614) 716-1925 ..**Barnes**, Jenny C '94 Amer Elec Pwr Co -1 Riverside Plz
-Columbus 43215

(513) 977-8200 ..**Barnes**, John E '83 (Dinsmore & S LLP) -255 E 5th -Ste 1900
-Cincinnati 45202 **Fx:**977-8141

(202) 861-1633 ..**Barnes**, Johnine P '95 %Baker & H LLP -1050 Conn Av NW
-Ste 1100 -Washington, DC 20036

(740) 653-3281 ..**Barnes**, Kenneth M '57 -420 E Main -Lancaster 43130

(216) 696-3311 ..**Barnes**, Kevin D '79 (Kahn K) -1301 E 9th -2600 Erievw Twr
-Cleveland 44114 **Fx:**623-4912

(937) 496-7740 ..**Barnes**, Kevin R '94 Montgomery Cnty Juv Ct -303 W 2nd
-Rm 1146 -Dayton 45422

(419) 244-6788 ..**Barnes**, Mark S '95 Bugbee & C -405 Mad Av -Ste 1300 -Toledo
43604 **Fx:**244-7145

(513) 636-3100 ..**Barnes**, Michael D '96 Johnson Trust Co -3777 W Fork Rd
-Cincinnati 45247 **Fx:**661-3160

(216) 566-5578 ..**Barnes**, Nancy M '02 (Thompson H LLP) -127 Pub Sq
-3900 Key Ctr -Cleveland 44114 **Fx:**566-5800

(614) 249-8169 ..**Barnes**, Thomas E '78 Nationwide Ins Co -1 Nationwide Plz
-Columbus 43215

(312) 876-7700 ..**Barnes**, Timothy A '96 %Latham & W LLC -233 S Wacker Dr
-Ste 5800 Sears Twr -Chicago, IL 60606 **Fx:**993-9767

(614) 728-1922 ..**Barnes**, Yolanda L '87 OH Dept Rehab & Correction
-1050 Fwy Dr N -Columbus 43229

(937) 322-0891 ..**Barnett**, Cynthia S '94 (Cole AH&D) -333 N Limestone -Bx1687
-Springfield 45501 **Fx:**322-9931

(614) 228-1541 ..**Barnett**, Eric R '04 %Baker & H LLP -65 E State -Ste 2100
-Columbus 43215 **Fx:**462-2616

(937) 324-5541 ..**Barnett**, Hugh D '62 (Martin BH&H) -1 S Limestone -Ste 800
-Bx1488 -Springfield 45501 **Fx:**325-5432

(614) 757-4514 ..**Barnett**, James E '99 Cnsl Cardinal Health,Inc -7000 Cardinal Pl
-Dublin 43017 **Fx:**757-2243

(216) 443-7800 ..**Barnett**, Kelley J '99 Cuyahoga Cnty Pros -1200 Ontario -8th Fl
-Cleveland 44113 **Fx:**698-2270

(216) 698-3204 ..**Barnett**, Kimberly G '01 Cuyahoga Cnty Pub Def -1200 W 3rd NW
-100 Lakeside Pl -Cleveland 44113

(513) 629-1473 ..**Barnett**, Michael N '90 Wstrn & Sthrn Life Ins -400 Bway
-Cincinnati 45202

(419) 241-6000 ..**Barnett**, Michael R '02 %Eastman & S Ltd -1 Seagate -24th Fl
-Bx10032 -Toledo 43699 **Fx:**247-1777

(216) 524-0710 ..**Barnett**, Michelle L '04 Allegro Realty Advsrs Ltd
-8111 Rockside Rd -Ste 250 -Cleveland 44125

(513) 965-2962 ..**Barnett**, Richard S '92 Cnsl Intl Paper Co -6285 Tri-Ridge Blvd
-Loveland 45140

(330) 627-5577 ..**Barnett**, Steven D '04 (Campbell & B) -130 Pub Sq -Bx25
-Carrollton 44615

(330) 385-3900 ..**Barnett**, Troy D '00 Aronson F&D Co, LPA -124 E 5th
-East Liverpool 43920

(614) 462-2315 ..**Barnett**, Valerie T '04 %Schottenstein Z&D -250 West -Bx165020
-Columbus 43216 **Fx:**462-5135

(216) 861-7114 ..**Barnett**, William A '81 State Industrial Products Corp
-3100 Hmltn Av -Cleveland 44114

(908) 231-4551 ..**Barney**, Charlotte L '96 Aventis Pharmaceuticals,Inc
-Route 202-206 -Bx6800 -Bridgewater, NJ 08807

(419) 732-3135 ..**Barney**, James C '94 Kocher & G -101½ Madison
-Port Clinton 43452 **Fx:**734-5644

(937) 223-6003 ..**Barney**, William H III '77 (Dunlevey M&F) -110 N Main -Ste 1000
-Dayton 45402 **Fx:**223-8550

(614) 224-3838 ..**Barnhart**, David B '81 F Fulton & Assoc -89 E Nationwide Blvd
-Ste 300 -Columbus 43215 **Fx:**224-3933

(330) 456-8341 ..**Barnhart**, Gene '53 OfCnsl Black MS&A,LPA -220 Market Av S
-Ste 1000 -Canton 44702 **Fx:**456-5756

(614) 462-2246 ..**Barnhart**, Richard A '79 (Schottenstein Z&D) -250 West
-Bx165020 -Columbus 43216 **Fx:**462-5135

(513) 455-2301 ..**Barnhart**, Thomas M II '90 Information Leasing Corp -995 Dalton
-Cincinnati 45203

(216) 687-2315 ..**Barnhizer**, David R '73 CSU-Marshall Cllg of Law -2121 Euclid Av
-LB138 -Cleveland 44115 **Fx:**687-6881

(216) 443-3662 ..**Barnhizer**, Joshua R '01 Pub Def -1849 Prospect -#222
-Cleveland 44115

(330) 364-5538 ..**Barnhouse**, James R '51 (Sani & B Co) -120 N Bway
-New Philadelphia 44663

(602) 256-3018 ..**Barnhouse**, James W '67 Renaud C&D -40 N Central Av
-Ste 1600 -Phoenix, AZ 85004

(440) 446-1100 ..**Barni**, Thomas A '95 (Dinn H&P,LLC) -5910 Landerbrook Dr
-Ste 200 -Cleveland 44124 **Fx:**446-1240

(614) 883-7680 ..**Barnitz**, David W '90 Amer Elec Pwr -700 Morrison Dr
-Gahanna 43230

(614) 228-6885 ..**Barno**, John C '94 Lane A&H LLC -175 S 3rd -Ste 700
-Columbus 43215 **Fx:**228-0146

(330) 877-8850 ..**Barnoff**, Michelle S '88 -Bx816 -Uniontown 44685

(740) 321-7162 ..**Barns**, Stephen W '95 Owen Corning -2790 Columbus Rd
-Route 16 -Granville 43023

Barnum, Carol L '77 -1608 Sandy Side Dr -Columbus 43235

(313) 964-5026 ..**Barnwell**, Wendy '87 -1150 Griswold Av -Ste 3100
-Detroit, MI 48226

(419) 243-0020 ..**Baron**, Joanna E '02 -1900 Monroe -Ste 113 -Toledo 43624

(513) 946-3003 ..**Baron**, Lawrence C '84 Hamilton Cnty Pros -230 E 9th -Cincinnati
45202 **Fx:**946-3017

Baron, Michael S '03 -(Address Unavailable)

(216) 443-7800 ..**Baron**, Nicole '00 Cuyahoga Cnty Pros -1200 Ontario -8th Fl
-Cleveland 44113 **Fx:**698-2270

(216) 781-3858 ..**Baron**, Russell Z '55 (Ticktin B Co,LPA) -1621 Euclid Av -Ste 1700
-Cleveland 44115

(419) 242-0280 ..**Baronas**, Ann M '93 -413 N Mich Av -Toledo 43624

(330) 489-5065 ..**Barone**, Anthony N '91 Nationwide Ins -1000 Market Av N
-Canton 44702 **Fx:**489-5181

(330) 297-3850 ..**Barone**, Christina M '00 Portage Cnty Pros -466 S Chestnut
-Ravenna 44266

(419) 248-1432 ..**Barone**, Gaetano '73 (Barone & D) -320 N Mich -4th Fl
-Toledo 43624 **Fx:**244-0765

(513) 765-6331 ..**Barone**, James J '95 EyeMed Vision Care -4000 Luxottica Pl
-Mason 45040

(614) 901-5700 ..**Barone**, Joseph J '75 (Magnuson & B) -570 Polaris Pkwy -Ste 140
-Westerville 43082 **Fx:**901-5800

(614) 466-8600 ..**Barone**, Juliane E '01 Atty Gen -30 E Broad -Columbus 43215
Fx:466-6090

(419) 354-9244 ..**Barone**, Mary S '88 Wood Cnty Pub Def -123 N Summit
-Bowling Green 43402

(330) 744-1111 ..**Baronzzi**, Christopher J '04 %Harrington H&M,Ltd -26 Market
-Ste 1200 -Youngstown 44503 **Fx:**744-2029

(216) 651-3400 ..**Barr**, Anthony S '02 Langenau Mfg Co -7306 Mad Av
-Cleveland 44102

(330) 451-7897 ..**Barr**, Dennis E '84 Stark Cnty Pros -110 Central Plz -Ste 510
-Canton 44702

(216) 363-1400 ..**Barr**, Douglas N '72 (Buckley K,LPA) -600 E Superior Av -Ste 1400
-Cleveland 44114 **Fx:**579-1020

(513) 422-1997 ..**Barr**, Eric J '81 -1523 1st Av -Middletown 45044

(740) 695-9202 ..**Barr**, Jason '04 %Harper & H -185 W Main -Saint Clairsville 43950
Fx:695-9211

(216) 931-6000 ..**Barr**, Lewis T '67 (Ulmer & B LLP) -1300 E 9th
-Ste 900 Penton Media Bldg -Cleveland 44114 **Fx:**931-6001

Barr, Lisa J '97 -5240 Brunnerdale Av NW -Canton 44718

(740) 335-2037 ..**Barr**, Michael L '75 -318 E Court -Washington Court House 43160
Fx:335-5996

(859) 231-3000 ..**Barr**, Philip D '83 (Stoll K&P,LLP) -300 W Vine -Ste 2100
-Lexington, KY 40507

(216) 696-6000 ..**Barr**, Robert D '96 (Dettelbach S&B,LPA) -1801 E 9th
-1100 Ohio Svngs Plz -Cleveland 44114 **Fx:**696-3338

(214) 665-2143 ..**Barra**, Michael C '81 US EPA -1445 Ross Av -Dallas, TX 75202

(216) 586-3939 ..**Barragate**, Brett P '96 %Jones D -901 Lakeside Av
-Cleveland 44114 **Fx:**579-0212

(216) 263-3402 ..**Barragate**, Dana C '95 FTC -1111 Superior Av E -Ste 200
-Cleveland 44114

(216) 621-1530 ..**Barragate**, Phillip C '94 %Shapiro & F,LLP -1500 W 3rd -Ste 400
-Cleveland 44113 **Fx:**621-1551

(440) 349-0044 ..**Barrat**, Elliott S '86 -33840 Aurora Rd -Ste 200 -Solon 44139

(614) 776-1000 ..**Barren & Merry Co,LPA** -110 Polaris Pkwy -Ste 302
-Westerville 43082 **Fx:**865-3396

(614) 776-1000 ..**Barren**, Michael J '83 (Barren & M Co,LPA) -110 Polaris Pkwy
-Ste 302 -Westerville 43082 **Fx:**865-3396

(937) 225-5757 ..**Barrentine**, Ward C '01 Montgomery Cnty Pros -301 W 3rd
-Bx972 -Dayton 45422 **Fx:**225-3470

(513) 361-1200 ..**Barresi**, James J '91 (Squire S&D LLP) -312 Walnut -Ste 3500
-Cincinnati 45202 **Fx:**361-1201

(513) 737-8000 ..**Barrett**, Amanda R '02 %Gattermeyer & M LLC -2 S 3rd -Ste 570
-Hamilton 45011

(440) 233-1100 ..**Barrett**, Benjamin F '66 (Miraldi & B Co,LPA) -6061 S Bway
-Lorain 44053

(440) 233-1100 ..**Barrett**, Benjamin F Jr. '87 (Miraldi & B Co,LPA) -6061 S Bway
-Lorain 44053

(513) 721-2120 ..**Barrett**, Charles F '71 (Barrett & W) -105 E 4th -Ste 500
-Cincinnati 45202

(614) 210-1840 ..**Barrett**, David C Jr. '81 (Barrett EC&E LLP) -7269 Sawmill Rd
-Dublin 43016 **Fx:**210-1841

(330) 762-6281 ..**Barrett & Davis** -159 S Main -416 Key Bldg -Akron 44308

(614) 210-1840 ..**Barrett Easterday Cunningham & Eselgroth LLP**
-7269 Sawmill Rd -Dublin 43016 **Fx:**210-1841

(330) 687-9605 ..**Barrett**, Gene C '04 -1461 W Exchange -Akron 44313

(330) 762-2323 ..**Barrett**, Gerald Van '85 Barrett & Assoc,Inc -1772 State Rd
-Cuyahoga Falls 44223

(216) 696-1545 ..**Barrett**, Joyce E '71 -1370 Ontario -800 Standard Bldg
-Cleveland 44113 **Fx:**696-2104

(216) 514-9500 ..**Barrett**, Lisa M '92 %Norchi & Assoc,LLC -23240 Chagrin Blvd
-Ste 600 -Beachwood 44122

(614) 462-3310 ..**Barrett**, Mark J '82 Cnty Sheriffs Ofc -370 S Front
-Columbus 43215

(440) 356-4604 ..**Barrett**, Mary C '90 -19300 Detroit Av -Ste 202 -Rocky River
44116 **Fx:**356-2873

(440) 233-1100 ..**Barrett**, Matthew H '96 Miraldi & B Co,LPA -6061 S Bway
-Lorain 44053

(574) 631-8121 ..**Barrett**, Matthew J '85 Notre Dame Law Sch -312 Law Schl -BxR
-Notre Dame, IN 46556 **Fx:**631-4197

(513) 721-2120 ..**Barrett**, Michael R '77 Barrett & W -105 E 4th -Ste 500
-Cincinnati 45202

(937) 372-4404 ..**Barrett**, Paul W '80 (Gibney SB&R) -1354 N Monroe Dr -Ste B
-Xenia 45385 **Fx:**372-5435

(614) 227-2000 ..**Barrett**, Phillip H '68 (Porter WM&A LLP) -41 S High
-Columbus 43215 **Fx:**227-2100

(419) 674-4031 ..**Barrett**, Scott N '76 (Roof & B) -218 W Columbus -Kenton 43326

Barrett, Sharon M '97 -10109 Bennington Dr -Tampa, FL 33626

(740) 349-2299 ..**Barrett**, Thomas H II '86 -51 N 3rd -Ste 605 -Bx920
-Newark 43058

(513) 618-8700 ..**Barrett**, Tina Jo '04 The Wolfe Practice -5151 Pfeiffer Rd -Ste 105
-Cincinnati 45242

(513) 721-2120 ..**Barrett & Weber** -105 E 4th -Ste 500 -Cincinnati 45202

(317) 888-1121 ..**Barrett**, William W '89 Williams H&R LLP -600 N Emerson Av
-Bx405 -Greenwood, IN 46142

(202) 514-6249 ..**Barrick**, Andrew J '67 US DOJ -10th & Penn Av NW
-Rm 5632 PHB -Washington, DC 20035

(614) 227-2000 ..**Barrick**, Penny L '01 %Porter WM&A LLP -41 S High
-Columbus 43215 **Fx:**227-2100

(740) 772-5000 ..**Barrington**, Deborah Douglas '77 -134 S Paint -Chillicothe 45601

(740) 774-2121 ..**Barrington**, James E '74 -41 E 4th -Chillicothe 45601

(330) 264-8679 ..**Barrington**, John C '68 -322 W Lbrty -Bx624 -Wooster 44691
Fx:262-4895

(330) 764-8752 ..**Barrington**, Teresa '96 Medina County Juvenile Ct -93 Pub Sq
-Medina 44256

(513) 721-1975 ..**Barron**, Carrie A '95 Freking & B -215 E 9th -5th Fl
-Cincinnati 45202 **Fx:**651-2570

(513) 651-6800 ..**Barron**, Dennis J '56 Cnsl Frost BT LLC -201 E 5th -2200 PNC Ctr
-Cincinnati 45202 **Fx:**651-6981

(513) 871-2369 ..**Barron**, Dennis P '85 -Bx8190 -Cincinnati 45208

(419) 241-9000 ..**Barron**, John C '78 (Shumaker L&K,LLP) -1000 Jackson
-Toledo 43624 **Fx:**241-6894

(614) 644-0876 ..**Barron**, John W '01 Governors Ofc -77 S High -30th Fl
-Columbus 43215

(513) 721-1350 ..**Barron**, Michael S '93 (Barron PB&S) -3074 Madison Rd
-Cincinnati 45209

(513) 721-1350 ..**Barron**, Norman J '60 (Barron PB&S) -3074 Madison Rd
-Cincinnati 45209

(513) 721-1350 ..**Barron Peck Bennie & Schlemmer** -3074 Madison Rd
-Cincinnati 45209

(330) 364-2881 ..**Barrow**, James J '87 Camco Title Ins Agncy,Inc -1320 4th NW
-Ste D -New Philadelphia 44663

(202) 404-1551 ..**Barrow**, Jane M '87 Dept of the Navy-Naval Res Lab
-855 Overlook Av -IP-Code 1008.2 -Washington, DC 20375

(216) 566-1600 ..**Barrows**, Melissa E '03 %Schwarzwald & M -1300 E 9th -Ste 616
-Cleveland 44114 **Fx:**566-1814

(216) 479-8500 ..**Barry**, George R '64 Cnsl Squire S&D LLP -127 Pub Sq
-4900 Key Twr -Cleveland 44114 **Fx:**479-8780

(419) 241-6285 ..**Barry**, Gordon R '76 (Barry & F) -520 Mad Av -Ste 930
-Toledo 43604

(330) 337-8761 ..**Barry**, Timothy A '87 Fitch KCR&B -600 E State -Bx590
-Salem 44460 **Fx:**337-9453

(440) 542-1324 ..**Barsham**, Kelly J '00 ERICO Intl Corp -30575 Bainbrdg Rd
-Solon 44139

(513) 621-4006 ..**Barsman**, Marvin J '50 -830 Main -607 Second Natl Bldg
-Cincinnati 45202

(614) 462-5458 ..**Barsotti**, Stephen C '02 %Kegler BH&R -65 E State -Ste 1800
-Columbus 43215 **Fx:**464-2634

(216) 687-1311 ..**Barsoum**, Marianne K '99 %Reminger & R -101 Prospect Av W
-1400 Mdlnd Bldg -Cleveland 44115 **Fx:**687-1841

(614) 338-1800 ..**Barstow**, Todd W '91 -4185 E Main -Columbus 43213

(937) 438-1001 ..**Bart**, David R '71 (D Bart Co,LPA) -6776 Loop Rd -Dayton 45459

(614) 693-6842 ..**Barta**, Mark B '91 -DFAS-CO-D6 -Bx182317 -Columbus 43218

(330) 784-8580 ..**Bartek**, Dennis J '71 -2300 E Market -Ste E -Akron 44312

(216) 861-6000 ..**Bartel**, Willard E '74 (Miller S&B) -2000 E 9th -Ste 1100
-Cleveland 44115

(216) 771-1900 ..**Bartell**, Jonathan A '00 %M Peterson & Assoc -700 W St Clair Av
-Ste 100 -Cleveland 44113

(216) 621-1180 ..**Bartell**, Laurence A '72 Sustin Bartell & Waldman,Ltd
-920 Ohio Svngs Plz -Cleveland 44114

(330) 746-8491 ..**Bartell**, Charles B '96 %Henkin T&H -6 Fed Plz Central -Ste 905
-Youngstown 44503

(419) 222-5045 ..**Bartels**, N Shannon '94 %Siferd & M LPA -212 N Elizabeth
-Ste 504 -Lima 45801

(440) 323-8240 ..**Bartels**, Victoria T '88 Legal Aid -538 W Broad -Elyria 44035

(614) 227-2379 ..**Bartemes,** Amy S '93 Bricker & E LLP -100 S 3rd
-Columbus 43215 **Fx:**227-2390

(614) 777-1750 ..**Barth,** David A '88 -5105B Cemetery Rd -Hilliard 43026

(513) 852-8228 ..**Barth,** David L '78 Cors & B LLC -537 E Pete Rose Way -Ste 400
-Cincinnati 45202

(412) 566-6173 ..**Barth,** Douglas K '77 (Eckert SC&M,LLC) -600 Grant -44th Fl
-Pittsburgh, PA 15219

(419) 294-2924 ..**Bartholomew,** Charles L '72 Wyandot Cnty Pros -Bx26
-Upper Sandusky 43351

(614) 228-1541 ..**Bartholomew,** Kirsten L '04 %Baker & H LLP -65 E State
-Ste 2100 -Columbus 43215 **Fx:**462-2616

(330) 535-2151 ..**Bartilson,** Thomas R '04 %Guy L&T -106 S Main -Ste 2210
-Akron 44308 **Fx:**535-9048

(216) 771-1760 ..**Bartimole,** Todd W '93 Smith & C LLP -1801 E Ninth
-Ste 900 Ohio Svngs Plz -Cleveland 44114 **Fx:**771-3387

(616) 752-2522 ..**Bartish,** Anne M '01 %Warner N&J LLP -111 Lyon NW
-900 Fifth Third Ctr -Grand Rapids, MI 49503 **Fx:**222-2522

(616) 458-1477 ..**Bartish,** Michael R '98 %Smith HR&R PC -250 Monroe Av
-200 Calder Plz -Grand Rapids, MI 49503 **Fx:**774-2461

(330) 643-3550 ..**Bartko,** James J '92 Industrial Commssn of OH -161 S High
-Ste 301 -Akron 44308

(419) 624-3000 ..**Bartle,** William H '75 %Murray & M Co,LPA -111 E Shoreline Dr
-Bx19 -Sandusky 44871

(330) 425-4696 ..**Bartlebaugh,** Thomas E '85 -1790 Enterprise Pkwy
-Twinsburg 44087

(614) 466-2926 ..**Bartleson,** David T '92 %Hon EL Stratton -30 E Broad -3rd Fl
-Columbus 43215

(513) 977-4212 ..**Bartlett,** Charles H Jr. '79 -917 Main -Ste 300 -Cincinnati 45202

(734) 242-3434 ..**Bartlett,** James P '98 Czeryba & G -19 E Front -Bx 587
-Monroe, MI 48161

(614) 466-1551 ..**Bartlett,** Keith T '81 Supreme Ct of OH -30 E Broad -3rd Fl
-Columbus 43266

(937) 845-8989 ..**Bartlett,** Kelli A '04 -1115 Langdale Av -New Carlisle 45344

(614) 249-2300 ..**Bartlett,** Philip B '85 KPMG LLP -191 W Nationwide Blvd
-Columbus 43215

(937) 227-3700 ..**Bartlett,** Robert P '64 OfCnsl Faruki I&C PLL -10 N Ludlow
-500 Cthse Plz SW -Dayton 45402 **Fx:**227-3717

(513) 241-3992 ..**Bartlett & Weigle Co,LPA** -432 Walnut -Ste 1100
-Cincinnati 45202 **Fx:**241-1816

(513) 241-3992 ..**Bartlett,** William T '74 (Bartlett & W Co,LPA) -432 Walnut
-Ste 1100 -Cincinnati 45202 **Fx:**241-1816

(614) 466-2766 ..**Bartley,** John P '87 Atty Gen -30 E Broad -Columbus 43215
Fx:644-1926

Bartman, Christi S '94 -12945 Watervll Swanton Rd
-Whitehouse 43571

(216) 696-3311 ..**Bartman,** Douglas V '00 (Kahn K) -1301 E 9th -2600 Erievw Twr
-Cleveland 44114 **Fx:**623-4912

(216) 928-2200 ..**Barto,** Victoria D '99 %Sutter OM&F -1301 E 9th -3600 Erievw Twr
-Cleveland 44114 **Fx:**928-4400

(419) 421-4203 ..**Barto,** Vincent A '85 Marathon Ashland Petroleum LLC
-539 S Main -Findlay 45840

(440) 350-2684 ..**Bartolotta,** Mark J '92 Lake Cnty Pros -105 Main -Bx490
-Painesville 44077 **Fx:**350-2585

(410) 916-1994 ..**Barton,** Ellen L '78 -19 Overshot Ct -Phoenix, MD 21131
Fx:667-8429

(513) 871-2720 ..**Barton,** James R '61 -3412 Sawgrss Ln -Cincinnati 45209

(513) 533-1885 ..**Barton,** Jery E '72 Barton & B LLC -3412 Sawgrss Ln -Cincinnati
45209

(614) 480-5423 ..**Barton,** L Scott '97 Huntington Bancshares Inc -41 S High
-Columbus 43215

(412) 560-3375 ..**Barton,** Lisa H '01 %Morgan L&B LLP -One Oxford Centre
-32nd Fl -Pittsburgh, PA 15219 **Fx:**560-7001

Barton, Rebecca S '93 -3030 Fairmont Av -Dayton 45429

(216) 228-1166 ..**Bartos,** David S '99 -13363 Mad Av -Lakewood 44107

(240) 243-8000 ..**Bartosh,** Concetta E '91 Panacea Pharmaceuticals Inc
-207 Perry Pkwy -Ste 2 -Gaithersburg, MD 20877

(740) 387-6000 ..**Bartram,** John C '73 (Bartram & B) -146 E Center -Bx3
-Marion 43301

(304) 523-5400 ..**Bartram,** Steven R '80 Lamp OBL&T -Bx2488
-Huntington, WV 25725

(440) 247-7083 ..**Bartunek,** Clarence J '67 -270 Hickory Hill Rd -Chagrin Falls
44022

(513) 381-2838 ..**Barty,** Lawrence J '73 (Taft S&H LLP) -425 Walnut -Ste 1800
-Cincinnati 45202 **Fx:**381-0205

(714) 513-3145 ..**Bartyczak,** Michael A '86 Geologistics Americas Inc
-1251 E Dyer Rd -Santa Ana, CA 92705

(419) 627-7697 ..**Barylski,** Mary A '87 Erie Cnty Pros -247 Columbus Av -Ste 319
-Sandusky 44870 **Fx:**627-7567

(216) 351-6300 ..**Barz,** Patricia '85 Cleveland Metroparks -4101 Fulton Pkwy
-Cleveland 44144

(216) 664-4397 ..**Bascone,** Joan M '00 Prosecutor -1200 Ontario Av
-8th Fl Justice Ctr -Cleveland 44113 **Fx:**664-4399

(330) 674-4300 ..**Baserman,** Mark W Sr. '78 -45 S Monroe -Millersburg 44654
Fx:674-4818

(216) 621-0200 ..**Bash,** Brian A '75 (Baker & H LLP) -1900 E 9th -Ste 3200
-Cleveland 44114 **Fx:**696-0740

(330) 643-3330 ..**Bash,** Gary M '81 Industrial Commssn of OH -161 S High -Ste 301
-Akron 44308

(216) 771-3239 ..**Bashein & Bashein Co, LPA** -50 Pub Sq -Ste 3500 Trmnl Twr
-Cleveland 44113 **Fx:**781-5876

(216) 771-3239 ..**Bashein,** Richard W '89 (Bashein & B Co,LPA) -50 Pub Sq
-Ste 3500 Trmnl Twr -Cleveland 44113 **Fx:**781-5876

(216) 771-3239 ..**Bashein,** William Craig '86 (Bashein & B Co,LPA) -50 Pub Sq
-Ste 3500 Trmnl Twr -Cleveland 44113 **Fx:**781-5876

(866) 794-7282 ..**Bashore,** Sandra K '84 LAWO -545 W Market -Ste 301
-Lima 45801 **Fx:**(419) 224-9947

(216) 321-7150 ..**Basie,** Ramon '62 -15381 Brwstr Rd -East Cleveland 44112

(216) 443-7295 ..**Basil,** Autumn '95 Cuyahoga Cnty Pub Def -1849 Prospect Av
-Ste 222 -Cleveland 44115

(513) 381-9605 ..**Basil,** Beth L '91 Intrieve,Inc -312 Plum -Bx5412 -Cincinnati 45201

(614) 469-0400 ..**Basil,** Brian A '95 (Murray MM&B LLP) -326 S High -Ste 400
-Columbus 43215 **Fx:**469-0402

(216) 689-0512 ..**Basil,** David A '80 KeyBank NA -127 Pub Sq -OH-01-27-0200
-Cleveland 44114

(440) 349-9000 ..**Basil,** Deborah B '80 Cnsl Weston Inc -29300 Aurora Rd -2nd Fl
-Solon 44139 **Fx:**349-9001

(513) 793-6650 ..**Basil,** Mark A '83 -9000 Plainfld Rd -Cincinnati 45236

(330) 395-9555 ..**Basile,** Andrew R '86 NE OH Title Agncy,Inc -1129
Niles Crtland Rd SE -Warren 44484

(216) 685-9500 ..**Basinger,** Matthew R '03 %JM Smaili,LLC -1468 W 9th -Ste 330
-Cleveland 44113 **Fx:**685-9685

(330) 471-7362 ..**Basinski,** David A Jr. '89 Timken Co -1835 Dueber Av SW
-GNE-03 -Bx6928 -Canton 44706

(513) 651-6800 ..**Baskett,** William D III '64 OfCnsl Frost BT LLC -201 E 5th
-2200 PNC Ctr -Cincinnati 45202 **Fx:**651-6981

(216) 621-3346 ..**Baskin,** Sheldon E '62 %Kendis & Assoc Co,LPA
-614 Superior Av W -15th Fl Rckfllr Bldg -Cleveland 44113
Fx:621-3672

(440) 779-6636 ..**Basladynsky,** Myroslava A '94 %J Duffy & Assoc
-23823 Lorain Rd -Ste 270 -North Olmsted 44070

(513) 451-1443 ..**Basler,** Susan M '93 -Bx58228 -Cincinnati 45258

(614) 462-3194 ..**Basnett,** Jeffrey M '91 Franklin Cnty Pub Def -373 S High -12th Fl
-Columbus 43215

(216) 464-4340 ..**Bass,** Debra D '79 -30799 Pinetree Rd -Ste 123 -Cleveland 44124

(513) 579-1414 ..**Bass,** Herbert J '49 OfCnsl Schwartz M&R -441 Vine -Ste 2900
-Cincinnati 45202 **Fx:**579-1418

(614) 431-2277 ..**Bass,** Leon D '98 -122 E Main -3rd Fl -Columbus 43215

(216) 443-7725 ..**Bassett,** Benton '64 Cuyahoga Cnty Pros -1200 Ontario -8th Fl
-Cleveland 44113 **Fx:**698-2270

(513) 852-8200 ..**Bassett,** Kenneth B '56 OfCnsl Cors & B LLC
-537 E Pete Rose Way -Ste 400 -Cincinnati 45202

(216) 765-0550 ..**Bassett,** Stephen J '65 -23230 Chagrin Blvd -Ste 900
-Beachwood 44122

(513) 684-3201 ..**Bassin,** Jeffrey L '85 IRS Chief Cnsl -312 Elm -Ste 2350
-Cincinnati 45202

(208) 331-7385 ..**Bassler,** Thomas B '76 Blue Cross of ID -3000 E Pine Av
-Meridian, ID 83642

(614) 224-9207 ..**Basta,** Angie W '93 Title First Agncy,Inc -555 S Front -Ste 400
-Columbus 43213

(216) 357-5900 ..**Basta,** Samuel W '95 -2189 Professor Av -Ste 100
-Cleveland 44113

(513) 651-6800 ..**Bastian,** Eliot G '99 %Frost BT LLC -201 E 5th -2200 PNC Ctr
-Cincinnati 45202 **Fx:**651-6981

(513) 732-2800 ..**Bastin,** Dexter K '77 -285 Main -Prof Bldg -Batavia 45103

(440) 331-8850 ..**Batal,** Susan E '84 (Shalala & B) -2600 Wooster Rd
-Rocky River 44116

(330) 887-0101 ..**Batchelder,** John T '82 Westfield Grp -1 Park Cir -Bx5001
-Westfield Center 44251 **Fx:**887-2588

(330) 725-6666 ..**Batchelder,** William G '39 SrCnsl Williams & B,LLP -105 W Lbrty
-Bx394 -Medina 44258

(208) 395-4781 ..**Batcheler,** Colleen R '98 Albertsons Inc -250 Park Ctr Dr
-Boise, ID 83726

(740) 622-3566 ..**Batchelor,** Robert J '92 Cnty Prosecutor -318 Chestnut
-Coshocton 43812

(330) 740-2180 ..**Bateman,** Melissa F '01 %Hon JJ Vukovich -120 Market
-Youngstown 44503

(614) 891-2410 ..**Bates,** Anna L '84 (Bates & H LLP) -168 S State
-Westerville 43081

(330) 972-7869 ..**Bates,** Christine R '02 Univ of Akron-Ofc of Gen Cnsl
-302 Buchtel Cmmn -Akron 44325

(330) 650-0088 ..**Bates,** David S '92 %Bevan & Assoc LPA,Inc -10360 Nrthfld Rd
-Northfield 44067 **Fx:**467-4493

(419) 782-9500 ..**Bates,** E C '86 -922 E 2nd -Defiance 43512

Bates, George Del '51 -1056 Kirtland Av -Lakewood 44107

(440) 546-0483 ..**Bates,** James C '97 DP Seink Co,Ltd -8180 Brecksvll Rd
-Brecksville 44141 **Fx:**526-4548

(614) 221-3630 ..**Bates,** John H '93 -495 S High -Ste 400 -Columbus 43215
Fx:358-6633

(330) 364-6441 ..**Bates,** John R '93 -123 W High Av -New Philadelphia 44663
Fx:602-3255

(419) 213-4700 ..**Bates,** Julia R '77 (Lucas Cnty Pros) -Adams & Erie
-Lucas Cnty Cthse -Toledo 43624

(614) 224-0531 ..**Bates,** Lorri J '97 %Williams & P Co,LLC -338 S High -2nd Fl
-Columbus 43215 **Fx:**224-0553

(440) 734-6162 ..**Bates,** Mickey C '89 -4596 Porter Rd -North Olmsted 44070

(419) 241-2100 ..**Bates,** William F '69 (Watkins B&C) -405 Mad Av -Ste 1900
-Toledo 43604 **Fx:**241-1960

(330) 699-6102 ..**Bates Bostian,** Geneva R '80 -13330 Cleveland Av NW -Bx374
-Uniontown 44685

(614) 221-8448 ..**Bathija,** Priya J '04 %Buckingham D&B,LLP
-191 W Nationwide Blvd -Ste 300 -Bx151120 -Columbus 43215
Fx:221-8590

(216) 479-6100 ..**Batista,** Bruce P '94 %Vorys SS&P LLP -1375 E 9th
-Ste 2100 One Cleve Ctr -Cleveland 44114 **Fx:**479-6060

(440) 930-8066 ..**Batista,** Daniel P '59 Wickens HPC&B -35765 Chester Rd
-Avon 44011 **Fx:**937-4466

(330) 499-0900 ..**Batista,** Roy H '65 -4808 Munson NW -Canton 44718

(614) 221-3155 ..**Batke,** Gary S '85 (Bailey C LLC) -10 W Broad -Columbus 43215
Fx:221-0479

(513) 423-1100 ..**Batliner,** Jennifer J '82 -1440 S Breiel Blvd -Middletown 45044
Fx:423-4889

(847) 402-7755 ..**Batman,** Cynthia P '86 Cnsl Allstate Ins Co -2775 Sanders Rd
-Ste A6 -Northbrook, IL 60062

(216) 621-0200 ..**Bator,** Chris '87 OfCnsl Baker & H LLP -1900 E 9th -Ste 3200
-Cleveland 44114 **Fx:**696-0740

(614) 262-9600 ..**Batross,** Martin E '77 -200 Canyon Dr -Columbus 43214

(513) 398-8901 ..**Batsche,** David A '96 %Batsche & B -300 W Main -Bx75
-Mason 45040

(513) 398-8901 ..**Batsche,** David K '66 (Batsche & B) -300 W Main -Bx75
-Mason 45040

(216) 622-8225 ..**Batt,** John P '78 OfCnsl Calfee H&G LLP -800 Superior Av
-Ste 1400 -Cleveland 44114 **Fx:**241-0816

(216) 274-4536 ..**Battaglia,** Lisa R '90 McKinsey & Co Inc -200 Pub Sq -Ste 3900
-Cleveland 44114

Battaglia, Timothy J '72 -122 Trinity Oaks Cir -Spring, TX 77381

(330) 535-5711 ..**Battagline,** Richard F '70 (Brouse M) -106 S Main
-500 First Natl Twr -Akron 44308 **Fx:**253-8601

(419) 885-0805 .. **Battani**, Joseph A Jr. '87 Lenavitt Law Ofc
-4032 N Holland-Sylvania Rd -Toledo 43623

(248) 865-0866 .. **Battersby**, Michael L '01 -31100 Nrthwstrn Hwy
-Farmington Hills, MI 48334

(419) 832-0626 .. **Battin**, Robert C '88 -12520 Patton Rd -Grand Rapids 43522

(330) 868-4248 .. **Battista**, Clark E '83 (Battista & B Co,LPA) -211 N Market
-Minerva 44657

(614) 444-3003 .. **Battisti**, Eugene F Jr. '87 -987 S High -Columbus 43206

(614) 469-7411 .. **Battisti**, Linda M '79 US DOJ -170 N High -Ste 200
-Columbus 43215

(440) 895-9700 .. **Battle**, Colleen P '86 (Battle & M PLL) -1340 Depot -Ste 201
-Rocky River 44116

(440) 895-9700 .. **Battle & Miller PLL** -1340 Depot -Ste 201 -Rocky River 44116

(419) 213-3639 .. **Battles**, Cynthia L '87 Lucas Cnty Chldrn Srvcs Brd -705 Adams
-Toledo 43624

Battles, John M '90 -(Address Unavailable)

(216) 502-0350 .. **Baucco**, Anthony A '03 %Repicky & K -526 Superior Av
-530 Leader Bldg -Cleveland 44114

(312) 368-4000 .. **Bauders**, Heidi L '94 %Piper R LLP -203 N LaSalle -Ste 1800
-Chicago, IL 60601 Fx:236-7516

(330) 287-5545 .. **Bauders**, Jerry A '74 Wayne County Dom Rltns Ct -107 W Lbrty
-Pub Square -Wooster 44691

(216) 241-1010 .. **Bauders**, Robert S '70 -1370 Ontario -Ste 1700 -Cleveland 44113
Fx:241-0269

(419) 241-6000 .. **Bauer**, Albin II '93 (Eastman & S Ltd) -1 Seagate -24th Fl
-Bx10032 -Toledo 43699 Fx:247-1777

(419) 423-2673 .. **Bauer**, Bernard K '72 (BK Bauer Co,LPA) -410 W Sandusky
-Bx932 -Findlay 45839 Fx:423-2127

(614) 791-1600 .. **Bauer**, Christy L '89 Foresight Corp -4950 Blazer Pkwy -Dublin
43017

(419) 259-6376 .. **Bauer**, David O '76 US Atty -4 Seagate -Ste 308 -Toledo 43604
Fx:259-6360

(330) 364-6553 .. **Bauer**, Erick L '91 (Black MHD&B) -130 W 3rd -Bx2330
-Dover 44622 Fx:364-2739

(216) 426-4753 .. **Bauer**, Fred D '90 Applied Indstrl Tech Inc -1 Applied Plz
-Cleveland 44115

(440) 746-2117 .. **Bauer**, George J '75 Dept of Vets Affrs -10000 Brecksvll Rd
-5th Fl Bldg1 -Cleveland 44141

(216) 586-3939 .. **Bauer**, Gregory A '97 %Jones D -901 Lakeside Av -Cleveland
44114 Fx:579-0212

(216) 621-7227 .. **Bauer**, James P '93 %Nicola G&C,LLC -25 W Prospect Av
-Republic Bldg Ste 1400 -Cleveland 44115 Fx:621-3999

(513) 922-7505 .. **Bauer**, John C '72 -5319 Delhi Pike -Cincinnati 45238

(440) 347-5668 .. **Bauer**, Joseph W '81 Lubrizol Corp -29400 Lakelnd Blvd
-Wickliffe 44092

(301) 981-5357 .. **Bauer**, Ralph A '82 %Lt Col RA Bauer -1535 Command Av
-Ste AA210 -Andrews AFB, MD 20762

(937) 497-7222 .. **Bauer**, Ralph A '88 (R Bauer Co,LPA) -108 E Poplar -Bx4713
-Sidney 45365

(513) 683-3221 .. **Bauer**, Robert C '78 -501 W Loveland Av -Loveland 45140

(330) 393-3818 .. **Bauer**, Roger R '73 -244 Seneca Av -Warren 44481

(330) 849-6500 .. **Bauer**, Roland H '80 Cypress Co Inc -670 W Market -Akron 44303

(330) 375-5716 .. **Bauer**, Thomas M '72 US Atty -2 S Main -Ste 208 -Akron 44308

(330) 253-7171 .. **Bauer**, Thomas M Jr. '01 %Burdon & M -137 S Main -Ste 201
-Akron 44308 Fx:253-7174

(412) 355-2605 .. **Bauerle**, James F '00 (Doepken K&W) -600 Grant -58th Fl
-Pittsburgh, PA 15219

(216) 566-8500 .. **Bauernschmidt**, Charles J '74 KH Bauernschmidt Co,LPA
-700 W St Clair Av -Ste 214 -Cleveland 44113 Fx:566-0942

(216) 566-8500 .. **Bauernschmidt**, Karen H '76 (KH Bauernschmidt Co,LPA)
-700 W St Clair Av -Ste 214 -Cleveland 44113 Fx:566-0942

(919) 765-7599 .. **Bauers**, Joseph J '95 BC/BS of NC -Bx2291 -Durham, NC 27702

Baughman, Amy C '04 -(Address Unavailable)

(740) 450-9301 .. **Baughman**, Janice M '97 (Allen & B) -Bx1909
-South Zanesville 43701

Baughman, Kenneth D '03 -(Address Unavailable)

(216) 687-1244 .. **Baughman**, R Patrick '63 (Baughman & J LLC) -2500 Brook
Park Rd -Ste E -Cleveland 44141

(614) 227-2000 .. **Baughman**, Scott E '92 (Porter WM&A LLP) -41 S High
-Columbus 43215 Fx:227-2100

(419) 213-4700 .. **Baum**, Eric A Jr. '91 %Lucas Cnty Pros -Adams & Erie
-Lucas Cnty Cthse -Toledo 43624

Baum, James L '89 -102 Woodmont Blvd -Ste 235 -Nashville, TN
37205

(248) 362-3707 .. **Bauman**, Kenneth A '75 %Ogne A&S,PC -1869 E Maple Rd
-Ste 100 -Troy, MI 48083 Fx:362-0422

(614) 466-2966 .. **Baumann**, M Elizabeth '99 Legis Srvc Commssn -77 S High
-Columbus 43215 Fx:995-9987

Baumbick, John J '98 -19096 Coffinberry Blvd
-Fairview Park 44126

(419) 999-1256 .. **Baumeister**, Michelle L '96 -3495 Woodhvn Ln -Lima 45806
Fx:999-5495

(216) 781-5245 .. **Baumgarten**, Lorraine R '80 (Berkman GM&D) -55 Pub Sq
-2121 The Illuminating Bldg -Cleveland 44113 Fx:781-8207

(216) 696-6000 .. **Baumgart**, Richard A '78 (Dettelbach S&B,LPA) -1801 E 9th
-1100 Ohio Svngs Plz -Cleveland 44114 Fx:696-3338

(740) 373-2420 .. **Baumgartel**, Rolf E '89 -100 Putman -Marietta 45750

(614) 466-8288 .. **Baumgarten**, Marc T '86 Mntl Hlth -30 E Broad -8th Fl
-Columbus 43215

(216) 621-0200 .. **Baumgartner**, Bruce O '67 (Baker & H LLP) -1900 E 9th
-Ste 3200 -Cleveland 44114 Fx:696-0740

(440) 930-4001 .. **Baumgartner**, Charles E '73 (Baumgartner & O)
-5455 Detroit Rd (Rte 254) -Sheffield Village 44054 Fx:934-7205

Baumgartner, Garry L '78 -6184 Willow Hill Ct
-Florence, KY 41042

(330) 220-8383 .. **Baumgartner**, Matthew J '95 Foundation Software Inc
-150 Pearl Rd -Brunswick 44212

(440) 930-4001 .. **Baumgartner & O'Toole** -5455 Detroit Rd (Rte 254)
-Sheffield Village 44054 Fx:934-7205

(440) 647-4219 .. **Baumgartner & O'Toole** -110 Herrick Av W -Wellington 44090
Fx:647-4715

(440) 930-4001 .. **Baumgartner**, Todd C '02 %Baumgartner & O
-5455 Detroit Rd (Rte 254) -Sheffield Village 44054 Fx:934-7205

(419) 427-2406 .. **Baumgartner-Novak**, Patti '91 -615 S Main -104 Heck Bldg
-Findlay 45840

(330) 451-7897 .. **Baumoel**, Jonathan S '92 Stark Cnty Pros -110 Central Plz
-Ste 510 -Canton 44702

(330) 456-8361 .. **Baumoel**, Lynn R '90 Cmmnty Lgl Aid Srvcs,Inc -306 Market Av N
-Ste 730 -Canton 44702

(614) 221-6088 .. **Baumwell**, Howard E '85 -211 E Lvngstn Av -Columbus 43215

Bautista, Minerva F '04 -(Address Unavailable)

(216) 696-3311 .. **Bautista**, Philip R '01 %Kahn K -1301 E 9th -2600 Erievw Twr
-Cleveland 44114 Fx:623-4912

(513) 621-6621 .. **Bavely**, Ernest Hanlin '64 -432 Walnut -850 Tri State Bldg
-Cincinnati 45202

(937) 225-2516 .. **Baxley**, Jessica Y '00 US Bankrptcy Ct -120 W 3rd -Dayton 45402

Baxter, Howard H '56 -18107 Clifton Rd -Lakewood 44107

(419) 627-7697 .. **Baxter**, Kevin J '82 Erie Cnty Pros -247 Columbus Av -Ste 319
-Sandusky 44870 Fx:627-7567

(614) 227-2314 .. **Baxter**, Martha P '82 (Bricker & E LLP) -100 S 3rd
-Columbus 43215 Fx:227-2390

(440) 775-1411 .. **Baxter**, Norman T Jr. '69 Green Circle Growers,Inc
-15650 State Route 511 -Oberlin 44074

(740) 622-3171 .. **Baxter**, Terrence J '91 -239 N 4th -Coshocton 43812

(614) 431-8110 .. **Baxter**, Thomas E '74 (TE Baxter & Assoc Co,LPA)
-150 W Wilson Bridge Rd -Ste 101 -Worthington 43085
Fx:431-8120

(614) 466-5394 .. **Bay**, John A '80 Pub Def -8 E Long -Columbus 43215

(330) 376-2700 .. **Bayer**, Cynthia P '04 %Roetzel & A,LPA -222 S Main
-Akron 44308 Fx:376-4577

(419) 756-7711 .. **Bayer Jerger & Ardis** -362 Lex Av -Mansfield 44907 Fx:756-9566

(440) 998-2628 .. **Bayer**, Leigh A '02 Ashtabula Cnty Pub Def -4817 State Rd
-Ste 202 -Ashtabula 44004 Fx:998-2972

(419) 891-8884 .. **Bayer Papay & Steiner Co,LPA** -1925 Indn Wd Cir
-Maumee 43537 Fx:891-8889

(440) 734-7600 .. **Bayer**, Paul A '88 %Crombie Law Firm -4615 Great Nrthrn Blvd
-North Olmsted 44070 Fx:734-1054

(202) 761-7525 .. **Bayert**, William K '86 US Army Corps of Engrs -441 G NW
-Washington, DC 20314

(419) 472-0077 .. **Bayford**, Anthony '74 -3126 W Sylvania Av -Toledo 43613

(304) 242-2300 .. **Bayhan**, Holly S '95 (Herndon MH&Y) -83 Edgington Ln
-Wheeling, WV 26003

(513) 352-4705 .. **Baylen**, Kenneth B '74 Law Dept -801 Plum -Rm 214
-Cincinnati 45202 Fx:352-1515

(216) 561-8999 .. **Baylog**, Richard L '54 -19201 Van Aken Blvd -Ste 510
-Shaker Heights 44122

(740) 869-2393 .. **Baynes**, Gerald T '64 -16 N Market -Bx147 -Mount Sterling 43143

(216) 875-6122 .. **Bays**, James C '74 Ferro Corp -1000 Lakeside Av
-Cleveland 44114

(304) 485-8500 .. **Bays**, Robert L '77 Bowles RMG&L -501 Avry -5th Fl -Bx49
-Parkersburg, WV 26102

(410) 691-9028 .. **Baysinger**, Christina M '91 US Army Corps of Engrs
-1099 Winterson Rd -Ste 160 -Linthicum Heights, MD 21090

(440) 884-5015 .. **Bazarko**, Volodymyr O '70 -5566 Pearl Rd -Parma 44129

(937) 222-2424 .. **Bazelak**, Leonard J '94 (Freund F&A) -1 S Main -Ste 1800
-Dayton 45402 Fx:222-5993

(717) 892-3000 .. **Bazeley**, Alison '97 Roda & N,PC -801 Estelle Dr -Lancaster,
PA 17601

(937) 328-2653 .. **Bazeley**, Christopher C '04 2nd Dist Ct of Appeals -41 N Perry
-Bx972 -Dayton 45422

(513) 369-0200 .. **Bazeley & LaDue** -13 E Court -#400 -Cincinnati 45202

(513) 369-0200 .. **Bazeley**, Terrence D '80 (Bazeley & L) -13 E Court -#400
-Cincinnati 45202

(937) 335-6495 .. **Bazler**, Frank E '53 -1156 Premwood Dr -Troy 45373

(440) 225-1747 .. **Beach**, Michael T '00 Tax Harbor -7955 Fieldstone Ct -Mentor
44060

(513) 287-2215 .. **Beach**, Richard G '99 Cnsl Cinergy Corp -139 E 4th -25 Atrium II
-Bx960 -Cincinnati 45201

Beach, Victoria M '78 -9830 Barr Rd -Brecksville 44141

(419) 249-7900 .. **Beach**, William V '88 (Robison C&O) -Four SeaGate -9th Fl
-Toledo 43604 Fx:249-7911

(614) 466-6192 .. **Beachler**, Jayne S '76 Industrial Commssn of OH -30 W Spring
-9th Fl -Columbus 43215 Fx:752-8785

(614) 252-5116 .. **Beachler**, Jinx S '79 (Bidwell & B Co,LPA) -865 Bryden Rd
-Bx6810 -Columbus 43205

(513) 533-1551 .. **Beacock**, Kathy A '79 -2444 Madison Rd -102 The Regency
-Cincinnati 45208

(614) 444-2020 .. **Beagle**, Peter F '78 -412 S Yearling Rd -Whitehall 43213

(216) 771-1760 .. **Beal**, David A '82 Smith & C LLP -1801 E Ninth -Ste
900 Ohio Svngs Plz -Cleveland 44114 Fx:771-3387

(740) 385-5343 .. **Beal**, Larry E '78 Hocking Cnty -88 S Market -Bx873 -Logan 43138

(614) 444-3900 .. **Beal**, Thomas D '75 -755 S High -Columbus 43206

(614) 227-2000 .. **Beale**, Jennifer E '01 %Porter WM&A LLP -41 S High
-Columbus 43215 Fx:227-2100

(614) 387-1935 .. **Beale**, Victoria F '04 OH DOT -1980 W Broad -Columbus 43223

(614) 224-8187 .. **Beals**, David A '87 (Lamkin VTB&D) -500 S Front -Ste 200
-Columbus 43215 Fx:224-4943

(937) 325-8822 .. **Beals**, Scott B '91 (Spencer & B) -30 Warder -Ste 250
-Springfield 45504

(303) 783-8884 .. **Beam**, Jack M '00 Beam & R Assoc -2770 Arapahoe Rd
-Ste 132, PMB 135 -Lafayette, CO 80026

(740) 452-7555 .. **Beam**, James R '60 (Gottlieb JB&D,PLL) -320 Main -Bx190
-Zanesville 43702 Fx:452-2257

(740) 452-7555 .. **Beam**, Jeff R '82 (Gottlieb JB&D,PLL) -320 Main -Bx190
-Zanesville 43702 Fx:452-2257

(248) 477-6300 .. **Beamer**, Dirk A '93 Wright Penning -27655 Middlebelt Rd -Ste 170
-Farmington Hills, MI 48334

(740) 695-0532 .. **Bean**, Charles H '72 (Thornburg B&G) -113 W Main -Bx96
-Saint Clairsville 43950

(330) 384-7305 .. **Bean**, Gregory R '77 First Natl Bnk -121 S Main -Akron 44308

(614) 802-0150 .. **Bean**, Mark W '79 (Bean & N) -85 E Wilson Bridge Rd
-Worthington 43085

(216) 491-8446 .. **Bean**, Marva J '87 -3645 Warrensvll Ctr Rd -Ste 136
-Shaker Heights 44122

(330) 656-1272 .. **Bean**, Thomas F '72 -7941 Ravenna Rd -Hudson 44236

(330) 452-6567 .. **Beane**, Frank L '73 -1134 3rd SE -Massillon 44646

(513) 867-8000 .. **Beane,** Gregory S '80 -350 N 2nd -Hamilton 45011 Fx:867-0979
Bear, Matthew T '04 -(Address Unavailable)

(614) 464-6400 .. **Beard,** Douglas M '01 %Vorys SS&P LLP -52 E Gay -Bx1008 -Columbus 43216 Fx:464-6350

(202) 622-4173 .. **Beard,** Gene W '93 IRS-Ofc Asst Chief Cnsl -1111 Const Av NW -Washington, DC 20224

(803) 458-6319 .. **Beard,** Gerald A '89 Michelin Tire Corp -Bx19001 -Greenville, SC 29602

(330) 451-7765 .. **Beard,** Kristine W '89 5th Dist Ct of Appeals -110 Central Plz S -Rm 320 -Canton 44702

(937) 372-4411 .. **Beard,** Phillip L '73 Brandabur FJW&B -260 N Detroit -Xenia 45385 Fx:372-4415

(330) 744-1111 .. **Beard,** Ralph A '75 (Harrington H&M,Ltd) -26 Market -Ste 1200 -Youngstown 44503 Fx:744-2029

(937) 454-0039 .. **Beasley,** Jesse B Jr. '88 -303 Hacker Rd -Dayton 45415 Fx:454-1961

(937) 495-3092 .. **Beasley,** John H '93 Mead Corp -Cthse Plz NE -Dayton 45463

(216) 664-2680 .. **Beasley,** Teresa M '93 %Dept of Law -601 Lakeside Av -Rm 106 City Hall -Cleveland 44114 Fx:664-2663

(740) 852-9706 .. **Beathard,** Maurice E '50 (Beathard & B) -63 N Main -London 43140

(740) 852-9706 .. **Beathard,** Steven P '78 (Beathard & B) -63 N Main -London 43140

(614) 294-7067 .. **Beatley,** Jack K '79 -70 W Northwood -Ste 1E -Columbus 43201

(614) 464-6400 .. **Beatley,** James R Jr. '65 (Vorys SS&P LLP) -52 E Gay -Bx1008 -Columbus 43216 Fx:464-6350

(513) 695-1325 .. **Beaton,** James D Jr. '73 Warren Cnty Pros -500 Justice Dr -Lebanon 45036 Fx:695-2962

(330) 743-1171 .. **Beatrice,** Mark A '81 (Manchester BP&U) -201 E Commerce -Atrium Level 2 Commerce Bldg -Youngstown 44503 Fx:743-1190

(614) 263-7000 .. **Beattey,** Robert A Jr. '03 %D McTigue -3886 N High -Columbus 43214 Fx:263-7078

(513) 977-8200 .. **Beatty,** John W '65 OfCnsl Dinsmore & S LLP -255 E 5th -Ste 1900 -Cincinnati 45202 Fx:977-8141

(614) 221-2400 .. **Beatty,** Laurel A '99 %O Beatty Jr Co,LPA -233 S High -Ste 300 -Columbus 43215

(614) 228-1541 .. **Beatty,** Otto III '94 (Baker & H LLP) -65 E State -Ste 2100 -Columbus 43215 Fx:462-2616

(614) 221-2400 .. **Beatty,** Otto Jr. '66 (O Beatty Jr Co,LPA) -233 S High -Ste 300 -Columbus 43215

(614) 466-4605 .. **Beatty,** Patrick W '92 OH Dept Job & Fam Srvcs -30 E Broad -32nd Fl -Columbus 43266

(614) 224-0919 .. **Beauchamp,** Sarah H '86 (Beauchamp & F) -118 E Main -Columbus 43215

(216) 241-5310 .. **Beaudry,** Stephen M '03 %Gallagher SF&N -1501 Euclid Av -6th Fl -Cleveland 44115 Fx:241-1608

(330) 925-9080 .. **Beaumont,** Lynn A '72 -43 W Ohio Av -Rittman 44270

(614) 224-8166 .. **Beausay,** Thomas J '87 Twyford & D -495 S High -Ste 100 -Columbus 43215

(614) 222-4734 .. **Beaver,** Michael P '04 %Spater Law Ofc -565 E Town -Columbus 43215 Fx:222-4738

(614) 227-2361 .. **Beavers,** John P '72 (Bricker & E LLP) -100 S 3rd -Columbus 43215 Fx:227-2390
Beavers, Timothy C '99 -363 N Main -Waynesville 45068

(740) 387-9704 .. **Bebout,** Bradley C '80 Marion Cmmnty Fndtn -504 S State -Marion 43302

(513) 352-6790 .. **Bechhold,** Christopher M '80 (Thompson H LLP) -312 Walnut -14th Fl -Cincinnati 45202 Fx:241-4771

(513) 753-9114 .. **Bechmann,** Anita M '92 -Bx512 -Batavia 45103

(309) 765-5574 .. **Becht,** James H '79 Deere & Co -One John Deere Pl -Moline, IL 61265

(317) 575-1814 .. **Becht,** Stephen M '86 Becht Co,Inc -3155 Jason -Carmel, IN 46033

(419) 257-3121 .. **Bechtel,** Allen H '51 (Bechtel & T) -119 E Bway -North Baltimore 45872

(419) 624-3000 .. **Bechtel,** Steven C '83 Murray & M Co,LPA -111 E Shoreline Dr -Bx19 -Sandusky 44871

(419) 485-3284 .. **Bechtol,** Denver G '77 -205 W Main -Bx313 -Montpelier 43543
Bechtol, Lew A II '89 %OH Atty Gen -Bx968 -Grove City 43123

(614) 464-6400 .. **Bechtold,** Timothy J '78 Vorys SS&P LLP -52 E Gay -Bx1008 -Columbus 43216 Fx:464-6350

(614) 221-7201 .. **Beck,** Amanda M '00 Cnsl OSLSA -555 Buttles Av -Columbus 43215

(937) 599-6242 .. **Beck,** Ann E '86 (Beck B&H) -709 N Main -Bx549 -Bellefontaine 43311

(614) 340-2329 .. **Beck,** Bethany A '77 Battelle Pulmonary Therapeutics Inc -1801 Watermark Dr -Columbus 43215

(901) 255-9311 .. **Beck,** Bradley D '88 Butler SOS&C -Bx171443 -Memphis, TN 38187

(419) 294-5781 .. **Beck,** Bruce J '81 Commerical Savings Bk -118 S Sandusky -Bx90 -Upper Sandusky 43351

(603) 695-7562 .. **Beck,** Carter A '88 %Anthem BCBS -3000 Goffs Falls Rd -Manchester, NH 03111 Fx:695-7912

(412) 394-2437 .. **Beck,** Christopher A '99 %Thorp R&A,LLP -301 Grant -One Oxford Ctr 14th Fl -Pittsburgh, PA 15219 Fx:394-2555

(614) 469-3939 .. **Beck,** David A '00 %Jones D -325 John H McConnell Blvd -Ste 600 -Bx165017 -Columbus 43216 Fx:461-4198

(740) 354-3214 .. **Beck,** David B '97 %Kimble & C -622 6th -Portsmouth 45662
Beck, David F '72 -1896 W 1st Av -Columbus 43212

(614) 273-3300 .. **Beck,** Donald P '01 %AW Sheppard -1900 Crown Park Ct -Columbus 43235

(330) 499-6000 .. **Beck,** Gregory A '81 (Baker DBW&M) -400 S Main -Canton 44720 Fx:449-6423

(513) 367-5401 .. **Beck,** Gregory G '82 %Kreiner & P Co,LPA -Bx1209 -Dublin 43017

(330) 533-2601 .. **Beck,** James H '59 -7 Court -Olde Cthse Bldg -Canfield 44406

(440) 546-1404 .. **Beck,** Janet R '77 -7650 Chippewa Rd -Ste 308 -Brecksville 44141
Beck, Jennifer Boyle '03 -(Address Unavailable)

(614) 464-6400 .. **Beck,** Jonathan P '81 Vorys SS&P LLP -52 E Gay -Bx1008 -Columbus 43216 Fx:464-6350
Beck, Jonathon L '03 -(Address Unavailable)

(419) 637-2168 .. **Beck,** Ladd W '80 (Kuhlman & B) -4590 State Route 600 -Bx63 -Gibsonburg 43431

(419) 396-6190 .. **Beck,** Linden J '73 (Burson & B) -102 E Findlay -Carey 43316

(419) 247-2500 .. **Beck,** Margaret G '92 (Fuller & H,Ltd) -One SeaGate -Ste 1700 -Bx2088 -Toledo 43603 Fx:247-2665

(330) 747-2661 .. **Beck,** Mark J '91 Cafaro Co -2445 Belmont Av -Bx2186 -Youngstown 44504

(614) 871-9555 .. **Beck,** Mary J '82 -3971 Hoover Rd -Bx179 -Grove City 43123
Beck, Nancy F '86 -33070 Woodleigh Rd -Cleveland 44124

(513) 336-2503 .. **Beck,** Patrick E '92 Anthem BCBS -4361 Irwin Simpson Rd -Mason 45040

(614) 462-3194 .. **Beck,** Robert J Jr. '98 Franklin Cnty Pub Def -373 S High -12th Fl -Columbus 43215

(740) 345-2400 .. **Beck,** Roland S '63 -50 N 4th -Newark 43055

(614) 228-2531 .. **Beck,** Stacey L '00 -600 S High -Ste 203 -Columbus 43215 Fx:228-2571

(513) 315-5541 .. **Beck,** Suzanne H '00 -9983 Walnutrdg Ct -Cincinnati 45242
Beck, William T '04 -(Address Unavailable)

(216) 464-8181 .. **Becker,** Amy A '84 Adler Norman & Assoc Co -24700 Chagrin Blvd -Beachwood 44122

(304) 233-3100 .. **Becker,** Carol E '95 %Bailey & W,PLLC -1219 Chapline -Wheeling, WV 26003

(330) 675-2426 .. **Becker,** Christopher D '90 Trumbull Cnty Pros -160 High NW -Warren 44481

(513) 721-7522 .. **Becker,** Dennis A '77 -22 W 9th -Cincinnati 45202

(513) 977-8200 .. **Becker,** Gary E '84 (Dinsmore & S LLP) -255 E 5th -Ste 1900 -Cincinnati 45202 Fx:977-8141

(440) 423-6532 .. **Becker,** Gordon P '78 Alcan Aluminum Corp -6060 Parkland Blvd -Mayfield Heights 44124

(614) 457-7863 .. **Becker,** James C '80 -4380 Braunton Rd -Columbus 43220

(614) 464-6400 .. **Becker,** Jeffrey R '02 %Vorys SS&P LLP -52 E Gay -Bx1008 -Columbus 43216 Fx:464-6350

(330) 376-2700 .. **Becker,** John W '95 (Roetzel & A,LPA) -222 S Main -Akron 44308 Fx:376-4577

(614) 387-2635 .. **Becker,** Julie E '94 Pub Emplyees Retirement Sys -277 E Town -Columbus 43215

(440) 323-7070 .. **Becker,** Michael F '76 (Becker & M Co,LPA) -134 Middle Av -Elyria 44035 Fx:323-1879

(614) 469-4778 .. **Becker,** Michael R '76 (Becker & L LLC) -100 E Broad -Ste 2320 -Columbus 43215 Fx:469-4779

(216) 241-2600 .. **Becker & Mishkind Co,LPA** -1660 W 2nd -Ste 660 -Cleveland 44113 Fx:241-5757

(440) 323-7070 .. **Becker & Mishkind Co,LPA** -134 Middle Av -Elyria 44035 Fx:323-1879

(513) 424-2429 .. **Becker,** Paul A '78 -1701 S Breiel Blvd -Middletown 45044

(513) 241-6748 .. **Becker,** Raymond '89 A Levine -324 Reading Rd -Cincinnati 45202

(330) 375-5716 .. **Becker,** Robert J '82 US Atty -2 S Main -Ste 208 -Akron 44308

(740) 349-6195 .. **Becker,** Robert L '74 Licking Cnty Pros -20 S 2nd -4th Fl -Newark 43055

(419) 227-3423 .. **Becker,** Stephen L '75 (Huffman KB&B LLC) -127-129 N Pierce -Bx546 -Lima 45802 Fx:228-1937

(216) 687-2323 .. **Becker,** Susan J '84 CSU-Marshall Cllg of Law -2121 Euclid Av -LB138 -Cleveland 44115 Fx:687-6881

(216) 226-9463 .. **Becker,** Thea G '84 -1239 Donald Av -Lakewood 44107

(614) 466-7447 .. **Becker,** William C Jr. '81 Atty Gen -150 E Gay -Columbus 43215

(614) 227-2000 .. **Beckett,** Donald L '57 OfCnsl Porter WM&A LLP -41 S High -Columbus 43215 Fx:227-2100

(937) 255-6111 .. **Beckett,** Janice C '85 USAF AFMCLO/JAN -1864 4th -Bldg 15 -Wright Patterson AFB 45433
Beckler, Mark M '02 -2600 Eastwood Dr -Wooster 44691

(614) 470-2063 .. **Beckley,** John G '91 -Bx1242 -Worthington 43085

(614) 415-7468 .. **Beckman,** Michelle F '96 The Limited,Inc -3 Limited Pkwy -Columbus 43230

(614) 461-0256 .. **Beckman,** Stacy S '94 Ofc Dscplnry Cnsl -250 Civic Ctr Dr -#325 -Columbus 43215 Fx:461-7205

(419) 782-9492 .. **Beckman,** Tiffany R '99 (Borland & B) -110 Clinton -Defiance 43512 Fx:782-5482

(513) 621-2100 .. **Beckman Weil & Shepardson LLC** -120 E 4th -1200 Mercantile Ctr -Cincinnati 45202 Fx:621-0106

(937) 449-6400 .. **Beckmann,** Richard J '74 (Dinsmore & S LLP) -1 S Main -Ste 1300 One Dayton Centre -Dayton 45402 Fx:449-6405

(216) 344-1040 .. **Beckor,** Colin '03 -50 Pub Sq #4000 -Trmnl Twr -Cleveland 44113 Fx:344-1330

(216) 622-8501 .. **Beckstrom,** Sean C '95 %Calfee H&G LLP -800 Superior Av -Ste 1400 -Cleveland 44114 Fx:241-0816

(714) 639-5114 .. **Beckwith,** Richard E '50 -10971 Glen Robin Ln -Bx2194 -Orange, CA 92859

(513) 345-4160 .. **Bedall,** Thomas G '78 Pro Seniors,Inc -7162 Redding Rd -Ste 1150 -Cincinnati 45237

(419) 522-6242 .. **Beddow,** Kenneth R '81 (Sauter H&B) -24 W 3rd -Ste 306 -Mansfield 44902

(513) 621-8770 .. **Bedell,** Christopher J '95 David J Joseph Co -300 Pike -Cincinnati 45202
Bedell, Melissa H '96 -(Address Unavailable)

(440) 746-2118 .. **Bedell,** Michael L '73 Dept of Veterans Affairs -10000 Brecksvll Rd -Bldg 1 - 5th Fl -Brecksville 44141

(216) 586-3939 .. **Bedell,** Richard J Jr. '87 (Jones D) -901 Lakeside Av -Cleveland 44114 Fx:579-0212

(513) 732-7385 .. **Bedinghaus,** Kate E '00 Hon R Ringland -270 Main -Batavia 45103

(440) 943-7600 .. **Bednar,** Gerald J '74 -28700 Euclid Av -Wickliffe 44092

(216) 664-6924 .. **Bednar,** Michael A '83 Cleveland Municipal Ct -1200 Ontario -12th Fl -Cleveland 44113

(740) 264-1651 .. **Bednar,** Michael C '84 (Blake H&B) -4110 Sunset Blvd -Steubenville 43952

(513) 932-3263 .. **Bednarczuk,** Robert '62 -2283 Bone Rd -Lebanon 45036

(330) 865-9635 .. **Bednarski,** Holly '03 (Bednarski R&L) -159 S Main -Ste 300 -Akron 44308

(513) 723-4000 .. **Bedree,** Melvin A '84 (Vorys SS&P LLP) -221 E 4th -Ste 2000 Atrium Two -Bx0236 -Cincinnati 45201 Fx:723-4056

(513) 381-2838 .. **Bee,** Gregory W '02 %Taft S&H LLP -425 Walnut -Ste 1800 -Cincinnati 45202 Fx:381-0205
Beebe, David K '75 -2520 Canterbury Rd -Columbus 43221

(440) 331-0200 .. **Beebe,** Linda G '82 -19111 Detroit Rd #205 -Rocky River 44116 Fx:331-0203

(419) 244-8500 ..**Beebe**, Raymond L '81 -1107 Adams -Toledo 43624
(216) 579-4214 ..**Beebe**, Richard A '73 -1370 Ontario -Ste 2000 -Cleveland 44113
(513) 939-3300 ..**Beeber**, Kerry A '95 -1244 Nilles Rd -Ste 9 -Fairfield 45014
(330) 532-5955 ..**Beech**, Andrew A '85 Columbiana Cnty -611 Main -Bx352
    -Wellsville 43968
(260) 668-8778 ..**Beech**, Beth E '88 -830 W South Boundary -3 -Perrysburg 43551
(513) 381-0656 ..**Beech**, Joseph III '73 (Kohnen & P LLP) -201 E 5th -Ste 800
    -Cincinnati 45202 Fx:381-5823
(614) 365-4100 ..**Beekhuizen**, Michael N '95 OfCnsl Carpenter & L LLP -280 N High
    -Ste 1300 280 Plz -Columbus 43215 Fx:365-9145
(404) 705-7950 ..**Beelen**, Gary D '98 %Neel & R,LLC -100 N Pnt Ctr E -Ste 510
    -Alpharetta, GA 30022
(614) 227-2000 ..**Beeler**, John C '76 (Porter WM&A LLP) -41 S High
    -Columbus 43215 Fx:227-2100
(419) 396-6662 ..**Beeler**, Robert L '83 (Cassel & B) -3727 Cnty Rd 96 -Carey 43316
(614) 466-4396 ..**Beeler**, Steven Logan '04 Atty Gen -30 E Broad -Columbus 43215
    Fx:644-8764
(614) 466-5394 ..**Beeler-Andrews**, Jill E '98 Pub Def -8 E Long -Columbus 43215
(513) 419-3249 ..**Beerck**, Daniel R '94 1st Grp America -705 Central Av
    -Cincinnati 45202
(937) 332-6993 ..**Beers**, Gretchen K '84 Miami Cnty Probate/Juv Ct -201 W Main
    -Troy 45373
(513) 618-8700 ..**Beers**, Janet E '04 The Wolfe Practice -5151 Pfeiffer Rd -Ste 105
    -Cincinnati 45242
(740) 687-6513 ..**Beery**, Edward T '70 -371 Baldwin Dr -Lancaster 43130
(614) 228-8575 ..**Beery**, Eric W '96 (Beery & S Co,LPA) -275 E State -Columbus
    43215 Fx:228-1408
(937) 393-1906 ..**Beery**, Forrest F '50 Beery Law Ofc -125 N High -Hillsboro 45133
(937) 393-1907 ..**Beery**, Fred J '82 Beery Law Ofc -125 N High -Hillsboro 45133
(859) 594-4529 ..**Beetem**, Angela P '95 -258 Main -Florence, KY 41042
(740) 942-8282 ..**Beetham**, Rupert N '72 -110 S Main -Bx262 -Cadiz 43907
(740) 942-2356 ..**Beetham**, Thomas Mark '75 -146 S Main -Bx128 -Cadiz 43907
(216) 622-8639 ..**Beg**, Murad A '01 (Calfee H&G LLP) -800 Superior Av -Ste 1400
    -Cleveland 44114 Fx:241-0816
(703) 547-2001 ..**Begeman**, Gary D '83 XO Comm,Inc -11111 Sunset Hills Rd
    -Reston, VA 20190
(216) 687-3948 ..**Beggs**, Gordon J '74 CSU-Marshall Cllg of Law -2121 Euclid Av
    -LB138 -Cleveland 44115 Fx:687-6881
(614) 538-1277 ..**Beggs**, Robert J '82 -1675 Old Henderson Rd -Columbus 43220
(614) 895-5600 ..**Begin**, James S '73 (Bale B & Assoc,Ltd) -140 Commerce Park Dr
    -Westerville 43082
(216) 281-3838 ..**Begin**, Robert T '77 Catholic Diocese Of Cleveland
    -7800 Detroit Av -Cleveland 44102
(614) 464-2025 ..**Behal**, Robert J '77 (Connor B LLP) -501 S High -Columbus 43215
    Fx:224-8708
(513) 684-3711 ..**Behlen**, Robert A Jr. '80 US Atty -221 E 4th -Ste 400
    -Cincinnati 45202 Fx:684-6385
(614) 466-2766 ..**Behlen**, Thomas P '89 Atty Gen -30 E Broad -Columbus 43215
    Fx:644-1926
(330) 264-6464 ..**Behlke**, William M '97 Newell Rubbermaid,Inc -3320 W Market
    -Fairlawn 44333
(614) 466-6696 ..**Behm**, Dennis H '94 Atty Gen -150 E Gay -Columbus 43215
    Fx:752-2538
(419) 448-4575 ..**Behm & Henry** -187 S Wshngtn -Tiffin 44883 Fx:448-0543
(419) 448-4575 ..**Behm**, Karen S '89 (Behm & H) -187 S Wshngtn -Tiffin 44883
    Fx:448-0543
(440) 942-7935 ..**Behnke**, Mark L '81 -Bx1172 -Willoughby 44096
(937) 435-7500 ..**Behnke**, Stephen D '00 (Botros B&S,LLC) -5785 Far Hills Av
    -Dayton 45429 Fx:435-7511
(419) 424-1365 ..**Behrendt**, Elizabeth A '94 -Bx1218 -Findlay 45839
(419) 893-7300 ..**Behrendt**, Harry M Jr. '67 Interactive Rtrmnt Plans,Inc
    -2321 Rvr Rd -Ste 2 -Maumee 43537
(937) 644-9111 ..**Behrens**, Daniel E '68 Marysville Newspapers,Inc -207 N Main
    -Bx226 -Marysville 43040
(216) 771-1144 ..**Behrens Gioffre & Schroeder Co, LPA** -1360 W 9th -Ste 400
    -Cleveland 44113 Fx:736-7136
(216) 771-1144 ..**Behrens**, James E '78 (Behrens G&S Co,LPA) -1360 W 9th
    -Ste 400 -Cleveland 44113 Fx:736-7136
(614) 668-4517 ..**Behrens**, Shanda M '02 -Bx329130 -Columbus 43232
    Fx:856-3579
(614) 876-2689 ..**Behringer**, Douglas J '96 %S Craig -5251 Norwich -Hilliard 43026
    Fx:876-0279
(513) 946-6464 ..**Beiderbeck**, Janice H '02 %Hamilton Cnty Mun Ct -1000 Main
    -Cincinnati 45202
(330) 434-3000 ..**Beidler**, Craig W '86 %Roderick & L -One Cascade Plz -Ste 1500
    -Akron 44308 Fx:434-9220
(419) 666-3417 ..**Beier**, Gayle K '00 %SA Skiver -30025 E River Rd
    -Perrysburg 43551
(412) 937-2851 ..**Beiersdorfer**, Amy M '02 US Dept of the Interior -3 Pkwy Ctr
    -Pittsburgh, PA 15220
(937) 492-6125 ..**Beigel**, Jeffrey J '86 (Kerrigan BSG&B) -126 N Main Av -Bx987
    -Sidney 45365
(419) 867-1800 ..**Beightol**, Sharon S '80 -4917 Alexis Rd -Sylvania 43560
(330) 399-3601 ..**Beil**, Patricia S '93 ADS Machinery Corp -1201 Vine NE -Bx1027
    -Warren 44482
(419) 522-2706 ..**Beilstein**, Kathryn A '84 Kathryn A. Beilstein -1530 Maxwell Dr
    -Mansfield 44906
(513) 651-4130 ..**Beirne**, Patrick J '96 %Lawrence Firm -8044 Mntgmry Rd -Ste 700
    -Cincinnati 45236
(859) 578-1030 ..**Beirne**, Patrick J '96 %Lawrence Firm -606 Phila -Covington, KY
    41011 Fx:578-1032
(513) 221-1745 ..**Beirne & Wirthlin Co,LPA** -1745 Madison Rd -Bx6111
    -Cincinnati 45206 Fx:221-6666
(330) 376-5300 ..**Beistel**, Peggy Sue '99 %Buckingham D&B,LLP -50 S Main
    -Bx1500 -Akron 44309 Fx:258-6559
(937) 291-2209 ..**Beitel**, Stephanie A '82 -Bx41336 -Dayton 45441
(330) 384-5795 ..**Beiting**, Michael R '85 FirstEnergy Corp -76 S Main -Akron 44308
(937) 440-9220 ..**Beitzel**, David E '76 -22 N Shourt -Troy 45373
(216) 592-5000 ..**Bekeny**, Karl A '02 %Tucker E&W LLP -925 Euclid Av
    -1150 Huntngtn Bldg -Cleveland 44115 Fx:592-5009
(614) 855-0383 ..**Belan**, Laurie A '87 -1222 Pond Hllw Ln -New Albany 43054
(440) 934-2199 ..**Belardo**, Lee E '95 LE Belardo,LLC -36368-A Detroit Rd -Bx419
    -Avon 44011 Fx:934-2289

(216) 586-3939 ..**Belasic**, Mark A '86 (Jones D) -901 Lakeside Av -Cleveland 44114
    Fx:579-0212
(419) 241-2200 ..**Belazis**, Paul T '79 (Arnold & C,Ltd) -1822 Cherry -Toledo 43608
    Fx:255-7623
(440) 329-5389 ..**Belcher**, Billie J '00 Lorain Cnty Pros -225 Court -3rd Fl
    -Elyria 44035
(216) 664-4959 ..**Belcher**, Gayle A '81 Cleveland Mun Ct -1200 Ontario -Bx94894
    -Cleveland 44101
(216) 696-5887 ..**Belcher**, Michael L '77 -75 Pub Sq -Ste 910 -Cleveland 44113
(216) 431-4500 ..**Belcher**, Robin Donnell '02 %Cuyahoga Cnty Pros
    -3955 Euclid Av -Jane Edna Hunter Bldg -Cleveland 44115
    Fx:431-4113
(330) 489-3214 ..**Belden**, Stephen F '79 Mun Ct Judge -218 Cleveland Av SW
    -Bx24218 -Canton 44701 Fx:471-8869
(216) 621-7860 ..**Belden**, Thomas G '71 (Cavitch FD&F) -1717 E 9th -14th Fl
    -Cleveland 44114 Fx:621-3415
(614) 249-7111 ..**Beldy**, Michael D '97 Cnsl Nationwide Ins Co -1 Nationwide Plz
    -Columbus 43215
(216) 583-3156 ..**Belenkaya**, Tatiana '02 Ernst & Young LLP -925 Euclid Av
    -Ste 1300 -Cleveland 44115
(614) 466-4882 ..**Belenker**, Rachel L '81 OH Dept Hlth -246 N High -Bx118
    -Columbus 43215
(330) 535-0505 ..**Belfance**, Eve V '90 %K Belfance & Assoc -One Cascade Plz
    -Ste 2100 -Akron 44308
(330) 535-0505 ..**Belfance**, Kathryn A '77 (K Belfance & Assoc) -One Cascade Plz
    -Ste 2100 -Akron 44308
(330) 796-9731 ..**Belfiglio**, Ralph A Jr. '84 Lockheed Martin Def Syst
    -1210 Massillon Rd -Akron 44315
(202) 208-3000 ..**Belin**, Jeremy S '99 NLRB -1099 14th NW
    -Washington, DC 20570
(216) 520-1464 ..**Belinger**, Robert J '75 Cleveland Title Srvc Agency,Ltd
    -4200 Rockside Rd -101 -Independence 44131
(614) 464-0400 ..**Belinky**, David A '77 -326 S High -Ste 300 -Columbus 43215
(614) 466-8288 ..**Belinky**, Debra M '78 Mntl Hlth -30 E Broad -8th Fl
    -Columbus 43215
(330) 744-3523 ..**Belinky**, Mark A '77 -600 Metro Twr -Youngstown 44503
(216) 696-7600 ..**Belkin**, Jeffrey A '65 OfCnsl Duvin C&H -1301 E 9th
    -20th Fl Erievw Twr -Cleveland 44114 Fx:696-2038
(216) 283-8970 ..**Belkin**, Keith E '76 (Luria & B) -20600 Chagrin Blvd -#1111
    -Beachwood 44122
(440) 247-2722 ..**Belkin-Laureno**, Lisa '88 -44 N Main -Chagrin Falls 44022
(614) 278-6762 ..**Bell**, Albert J '85 Big Lots Inc -300 Phillipi Rd -Columbus 43228
(614) 899-1447 ..**Bell**, Albert L '59 -1103 Bryan Dr -Westerville 43081 Fx:899-6174
(216) 622-8200 ..**Bell**, Alyssa J '02 %Calfee H&G LLP -800 Superior Av -Ste 1400
    -Cleveland 44114 Fx:241-0816
(614) 464-6400 ..**Bell**, Anker M '82 (Vorys SS&P LLP) -52 E Gay -Bx1008
    -Columbus 43216 Fx:464-6350
(330) 796-1818 ..**Bell**, Bertram '76 Goodyear Tire & Rubber Co -1144 E Market
    -Akron 44316
(330) 430-6109 ..**Bell**, Catherine M '99 -610 Market Av N -Canton 44702
(330) 535-5711 ..**Bell**, Daniel L '90 (Brouse M) -106 S Main -500 First Natl Twr
    -Akron 44308 Fx:253-8601
(630) 821-2273 ..**Bell**, David L '77 SrCnsl BP America Inc -4101 Winfld Rd -4 W
    -Warrenville, IL 60555
(440) 247-7800 ..**Bell**, Denise D '86 (McSherry & Co) -178 E Wshngtn -Chagrin Falls
    44022 Fx:247-7801
(216) 861-1148 ..**Bell**, Edward J '83 Gries Finl LLC -1801 E 9th -Ste 1600
    -Cleveland 44114
(216) 831-6100 ..**Bell**, Eric E '92 Goldberg Co,Inc -25101 Chagrin Blvd -Ste 300
    -Beachwood 44122
(216) 295-8491 ..**Bell**, Everett A '76 -20475 Farnsleigh Rd -Ste 205
    -Cleveland 44122
(717) 237-4040 ..**Bell**, George T '72 OfCnsl Morgan L&B LLP -417 Walnut
    -Harrisburg, PA 17101 Fx:237-4004
(440) 292-6445 ..**Bell**, Helen M '89 -31870 Hiram Trl -Moreland Hills 44022
(614) 777-9917 ..**Bell**, Irene D '89 -4143 Main -Hilliard 43026
(440) 449-4560 ..**Bell**, Irving '59 -1392 Som Ctr Rd -Lyndhurst 44124
(513) 271-6554 ..**Bell**, James R '84 -6700 Chestnut -215 Mariemont Exec Bldg
    -Cincinnati 45227
(513) 721-2120 ..**Bell**, Janet L '84 (Barrett & W) -105 E 4th -Ste 500 -Cincinnati
    45202
(440) 285-2222 ..**Bell**, Janette A '90 Geauga Cnty Pros -231 Main -Cthse Annx
    -Chardon 44024 Fx:286-4357
(614) 586-1310 ..**Bell**, Jessica Rodriguez '02 %Nesbit Law Firm -447 E Main
    -Ste 200 -Columbus 43215
(614) 266-2961 ..**Bell**, John A '84 -2700 E Main -Ste 102 -Bx091022 -Bexley 43209
    Fx:239-0543
(740) 597-1819 ..**Bell**, Kelli L '99 Ohio Univ -210 McGuffey Hall -Athens 45701
(440) 998-2628 ..**Bell**, Kimberly E '02 Ashtabula Cnty Pub Def -4817 State Rd
    -Ste 202 -Ashtabula 44004 Fx:998-2972
(614) 228-0704 ..**Bell**, Langdon D '63 (Bell R&S Co,LPA) -33 S Grant Av
    -Columbus 43215
(216) 363-4500 ..**Bell**, Lawrence M '61 (Benesch FC&A LLP) -200 Pub Sq -Ste 2300
    -Cleveland 44114 Fx:363-4588
(330) 492-8717 ..**Bell**, Lee J '73 (Buckingham D&B,LLP) -4518 Fulton Dr NW
    -Bx35548 -Canton 44735 Fx:492-9625
(330) 384-3864 ..**Bell**, Mary E '97 FirstEnergy Corp -76 S Main -Akron 44308
(404) 523-5398 ..**Bell**, Meredith E '00 ACLU Fndtn -233 Pchtree NE
    -2725 Harris Twr -Atlanta, GA 30303
(419) 842-8200 ..**Bell**, Michael D '99 %GW Osborne -7150 Granite Cir Dr
    -Toledo 43617
(513) 946-3700 ..**Bell**, Nathan C '03 Hamilton Cnty Pub Def -230 E 9th -3rd Fl
    -Cincinnati 45202 Fx:946-3707
(419) 241-9000 ..**Bell**, Neema M '87 (Shumaker L&K,LLP) -1000 Jackson
    -Toledo 43624 Fx:241-6894
(216) 443-7800 ..**Bell**, Richard A '89 Cuyahoga Cnty Pros -1200 Ontario -8th Fl
    -Cleveland 44113 Fx:698-2270
(614) 464-6400 ..**Bell**, Robert A '00 %Vorys SS&P LLP -52 E Gay -Bx1008
    -Columbus 43216 Fx:464-6350
(330) 644-5404 ..**Bell**, Robin L '84 Clemans Nelson & Assoc -2351 S Arlngtn Rd
    -Ste A -Akron 44319
(513) 361-1200 ..**Bell**, Ronald A '94 (Squire S&D LLP) -312 Walnut -Ste 3500
    -Cincinnati 45202 Fx:361-1201
(614) 228-0704 ..**Bell Royer & Sanders Co,LPA** -33 S Grant Av -Columbus 43215

(614) 865-4700 ..Bell, Sandra F '86 OCSEA-AFSCME Local 11 -390 Worthngtn Rd -Ste A -Westerville 43082

(216) 575-1002 ..Bell, Steven D '79 Simon Law Firm,LLC -1300 E 9th -Ste 1717 -Cleveland 44114

(513) 852-8200 ..Bell, Susan R '98 %Cors & B LLC -537 E Pete Rose Way -Ste 400 -Cincinnati 45202

(614) 239-5032 ..Bell, Suzanne P '97 Regional Airport Auth -4600 Intl Gtwy -Columbus 43219 Fx:238-7834

(419) 223-1861 ..Bell, Tamara M '96 %Hon TF Bryant -204 N Main -Lima 45801

(614) 645-8906 ..Bell, Tannisha D '03 City Pros -375 S High -7th Fl -Columbus 43215

(513) 241-2355 ..Bell, William D '77 (WD Bell & Assoc) -830 Main -Ste 604 -Cincinnati 45202

(419) 244-9500 ..Bella, Johna M '86 (Goranson P&B) -405 Mad Av -Ste 2200 -Toledo 43604 Fx:(414) 244-9510

(513) 241-7111 ..Bella, Ronald T '79 %O'Connor A&L Co,LPA -1014 Vine -22nd Fl -Cincinnati 45202 Fx:241-7197

(513) 455-7600 ..Bellamy, Glenn D '99 OfCnsl Greenebaum D&M PLLC -255 E 5th -2800 Chemed Ctr -Cincinnati 45202 Fx:455-8500

(212) 657-0585 ..Belle, Lisa M '95 Salomon Smith Barney -77 Water -19th Fl -New York, NY 10005

(614) 621-1500 ..Belleville, Mark L '95 %Calfee H&G LLP -21 E State -1100 Fifth Third Ctr -Columbus 43215 Fx:621-0010

(614) 444-6556 ..Belli, Dennis C '79 -844 S Front -Columbus 43206

(614) 761-0402 ..Bellinger, Scott P '92 (Bellinger & D) -6065 Frantz Rd -Ste 106 -Dublin 43017

(740) 973-4326 ..Bellman, Daniel A '80 -320 N Pearl -Granville 43023

(513) 621-2260 ..Bellman, Gregory W Sr. '97 Weber D&B -813 Bway -1st Fl -Cincinnati 45202

(412) 231-3000 ..Bello, Sean H '91 Advantage Equity Srvc -1501 Reedsdale -Ste 1001 -Pittsburgh, PA 15233

(713) 356-4680 ..Belman, Bruce J '78 Pricewaterhouse Coopers -1201 Louisisana -Ste 2900 -Houston, TX 77002

(216) 566-5547 ..Belman, Susan L '77 %Thompson H LLP -127 Pub Sq -3900 Key Ctr -Cleveland 44114 Fx:566-5800

(614) 227-8885 ..Belo, Vladimir P '99 %Bricker & E LLP -100 S 3rd -Columbus 43215 Fx:227-2390

(440) 238-4622 ..Belock, Wayne J '82 Belock & Co LPA -14761 Pearl Rd -Ste 125 -Cleveland 44136

(440) 884-8018 ..Belovich, Barbara A '86 -5638 Ridge Rd -Parma 44129

(440) 884-8018 ..Belovich, Robert F '52 -5638 Ridge Rd -Parma 44129 Fx:884-8021

(440) 884-8018 ..Belovich, Robert S '77 -5638 Ridge Rd -Parma 44129

(419) 241-9000 ..Belt, Jenifer A '95 (Shumaker L&K,LLP) -1000 Jackson -Toledo 43624 Fx:241-6894

(614) 457-2034 ..Belton, John T '77 -2066 W Henderson Rd -Columbus 43220

(614) 716-1647 ..Belville, Barbara A '80 Amer Elec Pwr Co -1 Riverside Plz -Columbus 43215

(614) 644-7250 ..Belville, Dan E '88 Atty Gen -30 E Broad -Columbus 43215 Fx:644-7634

(614) 466-7190 ..Belz, Robert B '74 Ct of Claims -65 E State -Ste 1100 -Columbus 43215

(440) 248-7906 ..Belzer, Geoffrey A '00 %Mazanec R&R Co,LPA -34305 Solon Rd -Ste 100 -Cleveland 44139 Fx:248-8861

(314) 232-0248 ..Beman, Thomas J '76 Boeing Co -Bx516 -Saint Louis, MO 63166

(216) 579-1700 ..Bembenick, Brian G '98 (Pearne & G LLP) -1801 E 9th -Ste 1200 -Cleveland 44114 Fx:579-6073

(216) 566-8200 ..Bemer, Andrew D Jr. '73 (Seeley S&E Co LPA) -600 Superior Av E -800 Bank One Ctr -Cleveland 44114 Fx:566-0213

(419) 525-1611 ..Bemiller, F Loyal '58 OfCnsl Brown BM&M -70 Park Av W -Mansfield 44902 Fx:525-3810

(513) 984-1160 ..Benadum, Frederick L '58 -9737 Loveland Madeira Rd -Loveland 45140

(419) 252-5997 ..Benavides, John J '87 Manor Care Inc -333 N Summit -Bx10086 -Toledo 43699

(419) 228-0189 ..Benavidez, Joseph A '89 (Dugan & B) -138 W High -Lima 45801

(740) 453-6475 ..Benbow, Brian W '99 -45 N 4th -Zanesville 43701 Fx:453-6475

(513) 651-6800 ..Bence, David S '90 (Frost BT LLC) -201 E 5th -2200 PNC Ctr -Cincinnati 45202 Fx:651-6981

(740) 635-6259 ..Bench, Kevin W '01 Industrial Commission -56104 Natl Rd -Bridgeport 43912 Fx:635-6260

(740) 695-1444 ..Bench, Rebecca L '02 %Hanlon DE&M Co,LPA -46457 Natl Rd W -Saint Clairsville 43950 Fx:695-1563

(440) 946-7739 ..Bencin, Patricia D '81 -5800 Andrews Rd -Mentor 44060
Bencivengo, Mary L '80 -34208 Aurora Rd PMB 288 -Solon 44139

(216) 241-0715 ..Bencivenni, Michael R '88 -425 W Lakeside Av -Ste 100 -Cleveland 44113

(216) 464-6666 ..Bendau, James M '72 -23200 Chagrin Blvd -Bldg 2-Ste 200 -Beachwood 44122

(859) 431-7886 ..Bendel, David E '82 -1336 Old State Rd -Park Hills, KY 41011

(419) 243-4788 ..Bender, Anthony J '83 -7456 Annin -Holland 43528

(740) 335-3826 ..Bender, David B '86 -251 E Court -Washington Court House 43160

(513) 852-6002 ..Bender, Edward D '95 %Wood & L LLP -600 Vine -Ste 2500 -Cincinnati 45202 Fx:852-6087

(513) 891-5630 ..Bender, Eric D '91 (ED Bender Co,LPA) -9764 Kenwood Rd -Blue Ash 45242

(513) 946-3000 ..Bender, Gwendolyn M '91 Hamilton Cnty Pros -230 E 9th -Cincinnati 45202 Fx:946-3017

(859) 291-0202 ..Bender, James D '99 -100 E RiverCenter Blvd -Ste 250 -Covington, KY 41011

(740) 687-7155 ..Bender, Jeffrey F '86 Fairfield Cnty CSEA -239 W Main -Lancaster 43130

(216) 928-1010 ..Bender, John Timothy '78 (Rotatori BGS&A Co LPA) -526 Superior Av E -800 Leader Bldg -Cleveland 44114 Fx:928-1007

(216) 579-9782 ..Bender, Kyle R '98 Major Legal Srvcs -1111 Chester Av -Cleveland 44114

(440) 285-4332 ..Bender, Mary K '81 (MK Bender Co,LPA) -401 South -#4A -Chardon 44024 Fx:285-9562

(419) 229-2931 ..Bender, Michael J Jr. '66 -316 E Main -Elida 45807

(740) 353-4191 ..Bender, Stanley C '76 -707 6th -Portsmouth 45662

Bendetta, Gina M '00 -610 N Main -North Canton 44720

(614) 878-7251 ..Bendig, Charles H III '78 (Wilcox S&B Co LPA) -4937 W Broad -Columbus 43228

(419) 448-8755 ..Bendure, Randall S '73 -Bx834 -Tiffin 44883

(614) 274-0033 ..Bendycki, Mary L '84 %Goldstein & Assoc -3649 W Broad -Columbus 43228
Bendycki, Richard T '81 -3838 Faversham Rd -University Heights 44118

(216) 778-4991 ..Benedict, James J Jr. '96 Metro Health Systm -2500 Metro Health Dr -K151 -Cleveland 44109
Benedict, Louis M '93 -(Address Unavailable)

(330) 753-6416 ..Benedict, Robert L '77 -480 W Tuscarawas Av -Ste 101 -Barberton 44203

(513) 794-6316 ..Benedict, Ronald L '68 Ohio Natl Life Ins Co -One Fncl Way -Cincinnati 45242

(614) 228-7775 ..Benedict, Spencer R '76 -400 S 5th -Ste 102 -Columbus 43215

(216) 363-4500 ..Benesch Friedlander Coplan & Aronoff LLP -200 Pub Sq -Ste 2300 -Cleveland 44114 Fx:363-4588

(614) 223-9300 ..Benesch Friedlander Coplan & Aronoff LLP -88 E Broad -Ste 900 -Columbus 43215 Fx:223-9330

(216) 781-4522 ..Benford, Sheryl King '80 Cnsl Grtr Cleveland Reg Transit Auth -1240 W 6th -Cleveland 44113 Fx:781-4152
Benge, Klarysa J '04 -(Address Unavailable)

(419) 347-4900 ..Benham, Frank L III '79 (F Benham Co,LPA) -150 Mansfld Av -Shelby 44875

(216) 481-0020 ..Beni, Franklin '79 -20050 Lakeshr Blvd -Euclid 44123

(513) 977-8200 ..Benintendi, Christopher A '90 (Dinsmore & S LLP) -255 E 5th -Ste 1900 -Cincinnati 45202 Fx:977-8141

(513) 870-2000 ..Benintendi, John K '94 Cincinnati Ins Co -6200 S Gilmore Rd -Leg Dept -Bx145496 -Cincinnati 45250 Fx:870-2900

(513) 336-2701 ..Benintendi, Laurie H '91 Anthem BCBS -4361 Irwin Simpson Rd -Mason 45040
Benintendi, Robert F '92 -4801 Beechwd Farms Dr -Mount Carmel 45244

(513) 241-2324 ..Benintendi, Steven W '03 %Wood H&E LLP -441 Vine -Ste 2700 -Cincinnati 45202 Fx:421-7269

(614) 463-1551 ..Benis, Stuart A '71 -326 S High -Ste 300 -Columbus 43215

(614) 719-1589 ..Benjamin, Ann Womer '78 Dept Ins -2100 Stella Ct -Columbus 43215 Fx:644-3743

(330) 562-6800 ..Benjamin, David M '77 -199 S Chillicothe Rd -Bx511 -Aurora 44202

(513) 721-5672 ..Benjamin, Jack A '40 (Benjamin Y&H LLC) -312 Elm -Ste 1850 -Cincinnati 45202 Fx:562-4388

(216) 831-8234 ..Benjamin, Lawrence S '74 -23230 Chagrin Blvd -Ste 900 -Cleveland 44122 Fx:831-8254

(513) 352-1565 ..Benjamin, Marva K '96 Law Dept -801 Plum -Rm 214 -Cincinnati 45202 Fx:352-1515

(216) 622-8200 ..Benjamin, Virginia D '76 (Calfee H&G LLP) -800 Superior Av -Ste 1400 -Cleveland 44114 Fx:241-0816

(513) 721-5672 ..Benjamin Yocum & Heather LLC -312 Elm -Ste 1850 -Cincinnati 45202 Fx:562-4388

(317) 582-2471 ..Benkert, Ronald J '78 Estridge Group,Inc -1041 W Main -Carmel, IN 46032

(216) 861-1365 ..Benko, Kerilyn '98 Hawkins & Co,LPA -1267 W 9th -Ste 500 -Cleveland 44113 Fx:861-0714

(614) 464-3900 ..Bennett, Adam J '04 %Browning & C -243 N 5th -3rd Fl -Columbus 43215

(614) 488-1161 ..Bennett, Bradley E '03 %Kennedy & K -3040 Riverside Dr -Ste 103 -Columbus 43221

(330) 394-1539 ..Bennett, Bruce W '86 W Urban Co LPA -434 High NE -Warren 44481
Bennett, Chad M '03 -610 Geron Dr -Springfield 45505

(937) 686-4625 ..Bennett, Charles A '81 -6986 Cnty Rd 39 -Huntsville 43324

(513) 932-7699 ..Bennett, Charles K '73 -801 Wildwood Ct -Lebanon 45036

(216) 241-7000 ..Bennett, Charles W '99 %Landskroner & Assoc -55 Pub Sq -Ste 1040 -Cleveland 44113

(937) 225-7687 ..Bennett, Cheryl A '94 Fed Pub Def -130 W 2nd -Ste 820 -Dayton 45402

(513) 977-8200 ..Bennett, Clyde II '92 (Dinsmore & S LLP) -255 E 5th -Ste 1900 -Cincinnati 45202 Fx:977-8141

(937) 593-3655 ..Bennett, Daniel L '00 -111 S Madriver -Bellefontaine 43311

(740) 439-2719 ..Bennett, David B '85 (Knowlton & B) -126 N 9th -Cambridge 43725

(216) 522-4914 ..Bennett, Donald E '76 SSA/OHA -1350 Euclid Av -7th Fl -Cleveland 44115

(419) 435-5566 ..Bennett, Donald S '89 (D Bennett & Assoc) -125 S Main -Ste 301 -Fostoria 44830

(740) 592-3328 ..Bennett, Douglas J '75 Cnty Mun Ct Judge -8 E Wshngtn Av -Athens 45701

(419) 253-6091 ..Bennett, Earl W '75 -20 W Walnut -Marengo 43334
Bennett, Erin Davies '03 -(Address Unavailable)

(419) 547-9585 ..Bennett, Frank H '56 -107 W Buckeye -Clyde 43410

(330) 744-4351 ..Bennett, Franklin S Jr. '80 Butler Wick & Co,Inc -700 City Ctr One -Youngstown 44503

(440) 323-1808 ..Bennett, Gary C '77 St Marie Law Firm Co,LPA -409 East Av -Ste A -Elyria 44035 Fx:323-6135

(614) 761-8323 ..Bennett, George H Jr. '78 (GH Bennett Jr,LLC) -7669 Serenity Dr -Dublin 43017

(937) 456-4100 ..Bennett, Gray W '91 -200 W Main -Eaton 45320

(937) 440-5960 ..Bennett, James D '85 Miami Cnty Pros -201 W Main -Troy 45373 Fx:440-5961

(330) 723-9536 ..Bennett, James R II '99 Medina Cnty Pros -72 Pub Sq -Medina 44256

(716) 852-3540 ..Bennett, James W '71 (Watson BCJ&S) -600 Fleet Bk Bldg -Buffalo, NY 14202 Fx:852-3546

(513) 523-4104 ..Bennett, Jay C '74 -5995 Fairfld Rd -Ste 5 -Oxford 45056

(614) 757-5132 ..Bennett, Jeffrey R '98 Cardinal Health -7000 Cardinal Pl -Dublin 43017

(216) 447-1551 ..Bennett, Jennifer A '94 %Ross B&S Co LPA -6000 Freedom Square Dr -Ste 540 -Cleveland 44131 Fx:447-1554

(937) 449-6810 ..Bennett, John Francis '02 %Porter WM&A LLP -1 S Main -Ste 1600 -Dayton 45402 Fx:449-6820

(614) 462-4450 ..**Bennett**, John Ira '73 Franklin Cnty Domestic Relations Ct -373 S High -5th Fl -Columbus 43215

(513) 793-4400 ..**Bennett**, Lawrence T '79 (Katzman LH&B) -9000 Plainfld Rd -Cincinnati 45236 **Fx:**793-4691

(330) 643-2985 ..**Bennett**, Linda M '00 Summit Cnty Juv Ct -650 Dan -Akron 44310

(216) 241-6602 ..**Bennett**, Mark S '98 %Weston HFP&H LLP -50 Pub Sq -2500 Trmnl Twr -Cleveland 44113 **Fx:**621-8369

(419) 249-7100 ..**Bennett**, Marshall A Jr. '80 (Marshall & M,LLC) -Four Seagate -8th Fl -Toledo 43604 **Fx:**249-7151

Bennett, Michael J '88 -Bx16305 -Rocky River 44116

(216) 221-2984 ..**Bennett**, Paul E '73 -1455 W Clifton Blvd -Lakewood 44107

(216) 515-1660 ..**Bennett**, Rebecca J '98 %Frantz W LLP -127 Pub Sq -2500 Key Center -Cleveland 44114 **Fx:**515-1650

(740) 355-8215 ..**Bennett**, Rebecca L '92 Scioto Cnty Pros -602 7th -Rm 310 -Portsmouth 45662 **Fx:**354-5546

(330) 865-9369 ..**Bennett**, Richard J '84 -773 Cliffside Dr -Akron 44313

(740) 927-8386 ..**Bennett**, Richard T '75 -275 Forward Pass Rd SW -Pataskala 43062 **Fx:**927-2211

Bennett, Robert P Jr. '85 -(Address Unavailable)

(440) 333-4848 ..**Bennett**, Robert T '67 -4800 Valley Pkwy -Fairview Park 44126

(216) 514-1566 ..**Bennett**, Stanley '60 -2652 Edgewood Rd -Beachwood 44122

(419) 929-8352 ..**Bennett**, Stephen K '75 -136 W Main -New London 44851

Bennett, Steven A '95 -2313 Lockhill Selma Rd -Ste 291 -San Antonio, TX 78230

(614) 645-8988 ..**Bennett**, Sue A '83 Franklin Cnty Pub Def -373 S High -12th Fl -Columbus 43215

(216) 787-3030 ..**Bennett**, Thomas D '03 Atty Gen -615 W Superior Av -11th Fl -Cleveland 44113 **Fx:**787-3480

(330) 535-5711 ..**Bennett**, Timothy D '02 (Brouse M) -106 S Main -500 First Natl Twr -Akron 44308 **Fx:**253-8601

(740) 439-2719 ..**Bennett**, William M '77 (Knowlton & B) -126 N 9th -Cambridge 43725

(419) 254-3106 ..**Bennett**, Yvonne D '92 (Bunda S&D,PLL) -One SeaGate -Ste 650 -Toledo 43604 **Fx:**241-4697

(513) 721-1350 ..**Bennie**, Daniel M '73 (Barron PB&S) -3074 Madison Rd -Cincinnati 45209

(937) 224-9291 ..**Bennington**, C Christopher '04 %Young & A Co,LPA -130 W 2nd -Ste 2000 -Dayton 45402 **Fx:**224-9679

(937) 233-8492 ..**Bennington**, Christopher '76 Bennington P&S -7229 Taylorsvll Rd -Huber Heights 45424

(740) 368-1673 ..**Bennington**, Daniel B '73 City of Delaware -1 S Sandusky -Delaware 43015 **Fx:**368-1525

(614) 645-7483 ..**Bennington**, Jeffrey R '00 City Pros -375 S High -7th Fl -Columbus 43215

(740) 474-7561 ..**Bennington**, Kevin G '99 (Bennington & B) -149 W Franklin -Bx682 -Circleville 43113

(740) 474-7561 ..**Bennington**, Roger E '64 (Bennington & B) -149 W Franklin -Bx682 -Circleville 43113

(330) 489-1001 ..**Bennington**, Ronald K '61 Mercy Med Ctr -1320 Mercy Dr NW -Canton 44708

(410) 865-5405 ..**Benoit**, Michael A '93 (Hudson C LLP) -971 Corp Blvd -Ste 301 -Linthicum, MD 21090

(419) 843-2689 ..**Benore**, Charles J '85 -2440 Cannons Park Rd -Toledo 43617

(216) 535-0446 ..**Benos**, Wayne F '80 Dept Homeland Security -1240 E 9th -Ste 519 -Cleveland 44199

(419) 245-4907 ..**Bensen**, Eileen W '94 Lucas Cnty Sheriffs Ofc -1622 Spielbusch Av -Toledo 43624

(216) 241-6650 ..**Bensing**, Russell S '75 -1148 Euclid Av -Ste 300 -Cleveland 44115

(216) 583-1234 ..**Bensinger**, Valerie J '99 Cap Gemini Ernst & Young LLC -1660 W 2nd -Ste 1200 -Cleveland 44113

(937) 492-1271 ..**Bensman**, Daniel A '94 (Faulkner GK&S,LPA) -100 S Main Av -Ste 300 -Sidney 45365 **Fx:**498-1306

(216) 241-2510 ..**Benson**, David M '93 DM Benson LLC -1422 Euclid Av -Rm 1672 -Bx1672 -Cleveland 44115 **Fx:**241-2510

(330) 499-1016 ..**Benson**, Don M '65 (Herbert & B) -4571 Stephen Cir NW -Canton 44718 **Fx:**499-0790

(740) 773-3600 ..**Benson**, James J '82 (Benson Law Ofc) -36 S Paint -Chillicothe 45601 **Fx:**773-3610

(419) 427-3679 ..**Benson**, Jeffrey L '76 Marathon Ashland Petro LLC -539 S Main -Findlay 45840 **Fx:**421-3720

(513) 241-3992 ..**Benson**, Matthew L '03 %Bartlett & W Co,LPA -432 Walnut -Ste 1100 -Cincinnati 45202 **Fx:**241-1816

(614) 418-4740 ..**Benson**, Michael E '97 -109 Town -Gahanna 43230 **Fx:**418-5045

(419) 422-2121 ..**Benson**, Molly R '98 Marathon Ashland Petro LLC -539 S Main -Findlay 45840 **Fx:**421-8402

(614) 827-1625 ..**Benson**, Pamela C '90 Def Ofc of Hearings & Appls -2780 Airport Dr -Columbus 43219

(330) 627-5314 ..**Benson**, Paul F '50 -219 Timberline Ln SW -Carrollton 44615

(330) 263-5248 ..**Benson**, Richard R Jr. '82 Law Dept -538 N Market -Wooster 44691

(330) 762-4757 ..**Benson**, Walter J '94 -159 S Main -Ste 800 -Akron 44308

(614) 221-5216 ..**Benson**, William B '90 (Wiles BB&B Co,LPA) -300 Spruce -1st Fl -Columbus 43215 **Fx:**221-5692

(859) 331-0111 ..**Benson-Blasch**, Barbara A '94 Abstractors Plus Inc -2508 Champions Way -Crestview HIlls, KY 41017

(614) 221-4000 ..**Bentine**, John W '75 (Chester W&S LLP) -65 E State -10th Fl -Columbus 43215 **Fx:**221-4012

(216) 524-9438 ..**Bentkowski**, David A '97 NE OH Concrete Promotion Cncl -Bx31007 -Independence 44131

Bentley, Michael L '02 -123 E William -Maumee 43537

(740) 532-7000 ..**Bentley**, Richard F '78 (Wolfe & B) -425 Center -Ironton 45638 **Fx:**532-7722

(216) 861-1234 ..**Bentoff & Duber Co,LPA** -55 Pub Sq -Ste 1200 -Cleveland 44113

(216) 363-1323 ..**Bentoff**, Freddie J '61 -1140 Leader Bldg -Cleveland 44113

(216) 861-9899 ..**Bentoff**, Jerome L '54 Bentoff & S Co,LPA -526 Superior Av E -440 Leader Bldg -Cleveland 44114

(614) 445-3962 ..**Benton**, Frederick D Jr. '80 -786 S Front -Ste 204 -Columbus 43206

(513) 765-6902 ..**Benton**, James S '80 Lens Crafters -4000 Luxoticca Pl -Mason 45040

(614) 258-6000 ..**Benton**, Shannon K '00 %Brenner BG&M Co,LPA -2109 Stella Ct -Columbus 43215 **Fx:**258-6006

(252) 937-2200 ..**Bentz**, Curtis L '76 Battle WS&W,PA -2343 Prof Dr -Bx7100 -Rocky Mount, NC 27804

(330) 879-2105 ..**Bentzel**, Todd H '83 -105 N Main -Bx34 -Navarre 44662

(614) 752-6417 ..**Benyo**, Steven J '89 Atty Gen -30 E Broad -Columbus 43215 **Fx:**466-0013

(330) 384-5802 ..**Benz**, Gary D '84 FirstEnergy Corp -76 S Main -Akron 44308

(216) 241-0520 ..**Benza**, Michael J '93 -526 Superior Av -1540 Leader Bldg -Cleveland 44114

(419) 249-7900 ..**Benziger**, Julia E '02 %Robison C&O -Four SeaGate -9th Fl -Toledo 43604 **Fx:**249-7911

(330) 244-1174 ..**Beoglos**, Laura L '92 Sand & S -4940 Munson NW -Ste 1100 -Canton 44718

(513) 412-4925 ..**Beraha**, Stephen C '97 Great American Ins Co -580 Walnut -10th Fl -Cincinnati 45202

(614) 469-7404 ..**Beran**, Barbara L '82 SSA-OHA, Columbus -280 N High -3rd Fl -Columbus 43215

(828) 369-1163 ..**Beran**, Milo R '68 -595 Bailey Rd -Franklin, NC 28734

(440) 871-4022 ..**Beranek**, Stephen '96 (Corsaro & Assoc Co,LPA) -2001 Crocker Rd -Ste 400 -Westlake 44145

(703) 588-6603 ..**Berardinelli**, Nancy L '02 US Army Legal Srvcs Agency -901 N Stuart -Ste 740 -Arlington, VA 22203

(513) 621-2666 ..**Berberich**, Gregory J '89 %Statman HS&E LLC -255 E 5th -Ste 2900 Chemed Ctr -Cincinnati 45202 **Fx:**587-4477

(440) 414-6050 ..**Bercik**, Joseph E '02 St John West Shore Hospt -29000 Ctr Ridge -Attn:Physical Therapy -Westlake 44145

(513) 946-3000 ..**Berding**, Anita P '96 Hamilton Cnty Pros -230 E 9th -Cincinnati 45202 **Fx:**946-3017

(419) 255-6500 ..**Berebitsky**, Michael J '73 -500 Mad Av -Ste 400 -Toledo 43604

(216) 479-8500 ..**Beredo**, Cipriano S III '99 %Squire S&D LLP -127 Pub Sq -4900 Key Twr -Cleveland 44114 **Fx:**479-8780

(216) 621-0200 ..**Beredo**, Gina A '99 %Baker & H LLP -1900 E 9th -Ste 3200 -Cleveland 44114 **Fx:**696-0740

(216) 621-0200 ..**Beredo**, Mathew B '98 %Baker & H LLP -1900 E 9th -Ste 3200 -Cleveland 44114 **Fx:**696-0740

(614) 227-8870 ..**Berendsen**, James R '71 Bricker & E LLP -100 S 3rd -Columbus 43215 **Fx:**227-2390

(216) 937-4000 ..**Berenger**, Lori A '93 Watson Wyatt & Co -1001 Lakeside Av E -Ste 1900 -Cleveland 44114

(216) 514-9879 ..**Berenholz**, Jeffrey S '98 (JS Berenholz LLC) -23240 Chagrin Blvd -Ste 180 -Beachwood 44122

(740) 687-5555 ..**Berens**, Randall S '78 (Berens & B) -126 E Main -Lancaster 43130

(740) 687-5555 ..**Berens**, Richard E '85 (Berens & B) -126 E Main -Lancaster 43130

(330) 650-2090 ..**Beres**, Steven A '79 UAW Legal Srvcs Plan -8536 Crow Dr -Ste 110 -Macedonia 44056

(216) 787-3030 ..**Beres**, Susan Ann '81 Atty Gen -615 W Superior Av -11th Fl -Cleveland 44113 **Fx:**787-3480

(216) 586-3939 ..**Beresh-Taylor**, Laura '00 %Jones D -901 Lakeside Av -Cleveland 44114 **Fx:**579-0212

(440) 352-3391 ..**Berezin**, Alec '74 (Dworken & B Co,LPA) -60 S Park Pl -Painesville 44077 **Fx:**352-3469

(216) 696-6500 ..**Berg**, Aaron P '01 %Caravona & C,PLL -50 Pub Sq -Ste 1900 Trmnl Twr -Cleveland 44113 **Fx:**696-1411

(513) 793-8282 ..**Berg**, John L '76 -9000 Plainfld Rd -Cincinnati 45236

(614) 445-2348 ..**Berg**, John R '92 Grange Ins -650 S Front -Bx1218 -Columbus 43216

(313) 226-7999 ..**Berg**, Leslie K '80 US DOJ -211 W Fort -Ste 700 -Detroit, MI 48226

(216) 781-5470 ..**Berg**, Megan S '00 %Ziegler M&M LLP -925 Euclid Av -2020 Huntgtn Bldg -Cleveland 44115 **Fx:**781-0714

(330) 745-1000 ..**Berg**, Sharon '76 -754 Kenmore Blvd -Akron 44314

(440) 954-3111 ..**Bergen**, Ann S '92 -38040 Euclid Av -Willoughby 44094

(330) 298-0065 ..**Bergener**, Karin C '91 -8034 Limerdg Rd -Ravenna 44266

(740) 474-6900 ..**Berger**, Allan '59 -Bx123 -Circleville 43113

(513) 721-4532 ..**Berger**, Andrew R '78 (Katz TB&H) -255 E 5th -Ste 2400 -Cincinnati 45202

(440) 338-4150 ..**Berger**, Christopher J '86 ITC Corp -312 Whitetail Dr -South Russell 44022

(216) 443-7800 ..**Berger**, Gayl M '00 Cuyahoga Cnty Pros -1200 Ontario -8th Fl -Cleveland 44113 **Fx:**698-2270

(330) 253-2195 ..**Berger**, Gerald W '75 -106 S Main -Ste 2500 -Akron 44308 **Fx:**996-8175

(216) 830-9000 ..**Berger**, Isreal Joseph '50 (Berger & Z Co,LPA) -614 W Superior Av -Ste 1425 Rckfllr Bldg -Cleveland 44113 **Fx:**830-4200

(419) 683-2214 ..**Berger**, J Sebastian '03 %Garner & B -211 N Seltzer -Bx29 -Crestline 44827

(419) 683-2214 ..**Berger**, John W '66 (Garner & B) -211 N Seltzer -Bx29 -Crestline 44827

(330) 376-5300 ..**Berger**, Joshua S '97 %Buckingham D&B,LLP -50 S Main -Bx1500 -Akron 44309 **Fx:**258-6559

Berger, Lisa J '98 -2464 Dale Av -Bexley 43209

(614) 461-0256 ..**Berger**, Robert R '95 Ofc Dscplnry Cnsl -250 Civic Ctr Dr -#325 -Columbus 43215 **Fx:**461-7205

(330) 296-3884 ..**Berger**, Robert W '78 (Giulitto & B) -222 W Main -Bx350 -Ravenna 44266

Berger, Sanford J '52 -1032 Som Ctr Rd -Cleveland 44143

(216) 691-4692 ..**Berger**, Steven B '93 Berger Law Inc -23968 Glenhill Dr -Beachwood 44122

(216) 830-9000 ..**Berger & Zavesky Co, LPA** -614 W Superior Av -Ste 1425 Rckfllr Bldg -Cleveland 44113 **Fx:**830-4200

(513) 361-1200 ..**Bergeron**, Pierre H '99 %Squire S&D LLP -312 Walnut -Ste 3500 -Cincinnati 45202 **Fx:**361-1201

(330) 456-1112 ..**Bergert**, Jennifer L '01 P Schandel Co,LPA -116 Cleveland Av NW -Ste 709 -Canton 44702

(330) 454-1967 ..**Bergert**, Todd A '90 -400 3rd SE -Ste 150 -Canton 44702

(513) 946-3000 ..**Berghausen**, Andrew A '93 Hamilton Cnty Pros -230 E 9th -Cincinnati 45202 **Fx:**946-3017

(614) 227-2000 ..**Bergman**, Andrew S '91 OfCnsl Porter WM&A LLP -41 S High -Columbus 43215 **Fx:**227-2100

(419) 244-8138 ..**Bergman**, Charles S '97 -316 N Mich -Ste 600 -Toledo 43624

(419) 244-8138 ..**Bergman**, Melissa A '97 -316 N Mich -Ste 600 -Toledo 43624

(614) 279-7058 ..**Bergman**, Robert D '70 (Bergman & Y) -3099 Sullivant Av -Columbus 43204

(513) 621-2666 ..**Bergman,** Thomas H '78 (Statman HS&E LLC) -255 E 5th
-Ste 2900 Chemed Ctr -Cincinnati 45202 **Fx:**587-4477

(614) 466-9559 ..**Bergmann,** David C '76 OH Consumers' Cnsl -10 W Broad
-Ste 1800 -Columbus 43215 **Fx:**466-9475

(513) 385-5574 ..**Bergmann,** Michael J '82 (MJ Bergmann,LLC) -6020 Cheviot Rd
-Cincinnati 45247

(216) 831-6580 ..**Bergrin,** Irving S '76 %Hartman & K Co,LPA -27600 Chagrin Blvd
-Ste 340 -Woodmere 44122

           Bergsmark, Jean M '00 -3160 Stone Wall Rd -Maumee 43537

(740) 633-5551 ..**Berhalter,** Christopher M '96 (Sommer L&B Co,LPA) -409 Walnut
-Bx279 -Martins Ferry 43935 **Fx:**633-5660

(216) 479-8500 ..**Berick,** Daniel G '92 (Squire S&D LLP) -127 Pub Sq
-4900 Key Twr -Cleveland 44114 **Fx:**479-8780

(513) 352-3618 ..**Beridon,** Thomas O '99 Law Dept -801 Plum -Rm 214
-Cincinnati 45202 **Fx:**352-1515

(614) 233-5603 ..**Bering,** Adam D '97 Ernst & Young -41 S High -Ste 1100
-Columbus 43215

(216) 771-8121 ..**Berk,** Gerald A '70 (Steuer EB&B Co,LPA) -55 Pub Sq -Ste 1828
-Cleveland 44113 **Fx:**771-8120

(330) 668-7777 ..**Berk,** Robert C '84 Creative Tech -137 Heritage Woods Dr
-Akron 44321

(216) 241-3880 ..**Berk,** Robert J '69 R Berk Co LPA -75 Pub Sq -Ste 1425
-Cleveland 44113 **Fx:**241-5366

(330) 208-1000 ..**Berke,** Aaron S '00 %Vorys SS&P LLP -106 S Main -First Natl Twr
-Akron 44308

(216) 932-6045 ..**Berkeley,** Jerome S '60 -3229 Fairmount Blvd
-Cleveland Heights 44118

(614) 274-6700 ..**Berkemer,** Frederick L '77 -79 N Wilson Rd -Columbus 43204

(614) 716-1648 ..**Berkemeyer,** Thomas G '86 Amer Elec Pwr Co -1 Riverside Plz
-Columbus 43215

(412) 394-4460 ..**Berkey,** Todd '99 %Edgar S & Assoc -707 Grant -16th Fl
-Pittsburgh, PA 15219

(440) 323-0687 ..**Berki,** Jenifer C '04 (Berki & N,LLC) -124 Middle Av -Ste 800
-Elyria 44035 **Fx:**323-2332

(216) 781-5245 ..**Berkman Gordon Murray & DeVan** -55 Pub Sq
-2121 The Illuminating Bldg -Cleveland 44113 **Fx:**781-8207

(330) 762-0755 ..**Berkowitz,** Richard E '96 -113 Portage Trl -Bx67128
-Cuyahoga Falls 44222

(515) 223-1036 ..**Berkson,** Edward J '67 -3420 Briar Ridge Rd
-West Des Moines, IA 50265

(216) 781-5515 ..**Berkson,** Hugh D '94 %Hermann C&S,LLP -1301 E 9th -Ste 500
-Cleveland 44114 **Fx:**781-1030

(614) 791-9413 ..**Berky,** Robert R '88 -5900 Sawmill Rd -Ste 220 -Dublin 43017

(513) 621-2120 ..**Berliant,** Mark H '57 Strauss & T,LPA -150 E 4th -4th Fl
-Cincinnati 45202 **Fx:**241-8259

(216) 479-0400 ..**Berlin,** Jennifer W '97 Berlin Financial Ltd -1325 Carnegie Av
-3rd Fl -Cleveland 44115

(614) 751-8611 ..**Berlin,** Lawrence A '70 -6422 E Main -Reynoldsburg 43068

(614) 469-3268 ..**Berliner,** Alan F '76 (Thompson H LLP) -10 W Broad -Ste 700
-Columbus 43215 **Fx:**469-3361

(216) 696-3311 ..**Berliner,** Irving H '79 (Kahn K) -1301 E 9th -2600 Erievw Twr
-Cleveland 44114 **Fx:**623-4912

(216) 622-8200 ..**Berliner,** Stacy '03 %Calfee H&G LLP -800 Superior Av -Ste 1400
-Cleveland 44114 **Fx:**241-0816

(419) 245-1941 ..**Berling,** Amy J '87 Mun Ct Judge -555 N Erie -Toledo 43624

(419) 255-5058 ..**Berling,** Mark D '83 -520 Madison -670 Spitzer Bldg
-Toledo 43604

(513) 821-5536 ..**Berlon,** Henry G Jr. '65 -540 Larchmont Dr -Cincinnati 45215

(440) 248-7005 ..**Berman,** David L '88 -5135 Leighton Ct -Solon 44139

(313) 761-3780 ..**Berman,** Harvey W '77 (Bodman L&D LLP) -110 Miller -Ste 300
-Ann Arbor, MI 48104

(513) 674-1111 ..**Berman,** Ira M '75 (Lieberman L&B) -415 Glensprings Dr -Ste 102
-Cincinnati 45246

(216) 621-5980 ..**Berman,** Keevin J '77 Legal Aid -1223 W 6th -Cleveland 44113

           Berman, Paul B '80 -24105 Duffld Rd -Shaker Heights 44122

(330) 492-2900 ..**Bernabei,** Thomas M '75 -441 Lakecrest NW -Canton 44709

(937) 229-4211 ..**Bernal-Olson,** Patricia '98 Univ of Dayton Schl of Law
-300 Cllg Park -Dayton 45469

(330) 759-3758 ..**Bernard,** Anthony M '46 SrCnsl Mun Ct -966 Villa Pl -Girard 44420

(330) 376-2700 ..**Bernard,** Aretta K '87 (Roetzel & A,LPA) -222 S Main
-Akron 44308 **Fx:**376-4577

(614) 923-6534 ..**Bernard,** Bruce D '85 Rea & Assoc,Inc -5775 Perimeter Dr
-Ste 200 -Dublin 43017

(513) 769-9396 ..**Bernard,** Christopher J '91 -2 W Benson -Reading 45215

(440) 546-7500 ..**Bernard,** Dale A '84 (Bernard Law Firm) -5005 Rockside Rd
-Ste 600 Crown Centre Bldg -Independence 44131 **Fx:**546-7501

(330) 744-5284 ..**Bernard,** Elizabeth A '88 (Harshman B&R) -105 E Boardman
-Youngstown 44503

(216) 291-3600 ..**Bernard & Haffey Co,LPA** -5001 Mayfld Rd -Ste 301
-Cleveland 44124 **Fx:**291-0159

(513) 651-1111 ..**Bernard,** Kathryn S '79 CBS Personnel Srvcs -435 Elm -Ste 300
-Cincinnati 45202

(301) 698-4605 ..**Bernard,** Louis A '84 Farmers Mechanics Natl Bk
-110 Thomas Johnson Dr -Bx460 -Frederick, MD 21705

(859) 655-3700 ..**Bernard,** Lucian J '90 (Pearson & B,PSC) -1224 Hwy Av
-Covington, KY 41011

(614) 462-3194 ..**Bernard,** Robert M '79 Franklin Cnty Pub Def -373 S High -12th Fl
-Columbus 43215

(330) 799-7711 ..**Bernard,** Roberta M '00 UAW Legal Srvcs
-1570 S Canfld-Niles Rd -Ste 101 -Youngstown 44515

(513) 946-5820 ..**Bernat,** Richard A '75 Hamilton Cnty Cmmn Pleas Ct -1000 Main
-Rm 240 -Cincinnati 45202

(513) 421-4646 ..**Bernat,** Stephen M '98 McCaslin I&M,LPA -632 Vine -Ste 900
-Cincinnati 45202 **Fx:**421-7929

(614) 225-4382 ..**Berndt,** Ellen G '84 Borden Inc -180 E Broad -Columbus 43215

(614) 280-9300 ..**Berndt,** Jeffrey A '83 -575 S High -Columbus 43215

(513) 636-4070 ..**Berner,** Melissa A '90 Chldrns Hosp Med Ctr -3333 Burnet Av
-Cincinnati 45229

(614) 464-6400 ..**Berner,** Michael G '03 %Vorys SS&P LLP -52 E Gay -Bx1008
-Columbus 43216 **Fx:**464-6350

(513) 753-2800 ..**Berner,** Milton T '74 -7682 Clough Pike -Cincinnati 45244
Fx:753-2808

(937) 223-4701 ..**Berner,** Robert B '84 (Bailey C LLC) -40 N Main -Ste 2310
-Dayton 45423 **Fx:**223-0170

(614) 228-1541 ..**Bernert,** Edward J '77 (Baker & H LLP) -65 E State -Ste 2100
-Columbus 43215 **Fx:**462-2616

(440) 808-4242 ..**Berney,** Sean F '92 Douglass & Assoc Co,LPA -551 Dover Ctr Rd
-Bx40480 -Cleveland 44140 **Fx:**808-4215

(513) 946-3000 ..**Bernhard,** Dale H '77 Hamilton Cnty Pros -230 E 9th
-Cincinnati 45202 **Fx:**946-3017

(419) 628-3232 ..**Bernhold,** James A '72 -12 Eagle Dr -Ste B -Bx26 -Minster 45865

(513) 852-3497 ..**Berning,** Randal C '78 Atty Gen -441 Vine -1600 Carew Twr
-Cincinnati 45202 **Fx:**852-3484

(513) 852-6088 ..**Berninger,** Paul R '71 (Wood & L LLP) -600 Vine -Ste 2500
-Cincinnati 45202 **Fx:**852-6087

(713) 831-6133 ..**Bernlohr,** Kurt W '87 Amer Gen Entrprse Srvcs,Inc -2929
Allen Pkwy -L4-01 -Houston, TX 77019

(330) 434-1000 ..**Bernlohr,** Mark W '87 (Bernlohr W,LLP) -23 S Main -3rd Fl -Akron
44308 **Fx:**434-1001

(330) 434-1000 ..**Bernlohr Wertz, LLP** -23 S Main -3rd Fl -Akron 44308
Fx:434-1001

(412) 338-7512 ..**Bernot,** Joseph E '86 (Deloitte & Touche LLP) -2500 One PPG Pl
-Pittsburgh, PA 15222

(216) 831-8838 ..**Berns,** Jordan B '90 (Berns O&G,LLC) -3733 Park East Dr
-Ste 200 -Beachwood 44122 **Fx:**464-4489

(216) 831-8838 ..**Berns Ockner & Greenberger, LLC** -3733 Park East Dr -Ste 200
-Beachwood 44122 **Fx:**464-4489

(216) 831-8838 ..**Berns,** Sheldon I '60 (Berns O&G,LLC) -3733 Park East Dr
-Ste 200 -Beachwood 44122 **Fx:**464-4489

(937) 277-0505 ..**Bernsen,** Kenneth J '99 Multi-Hlth Srvcs,Inc -5020 Phila
-Dayton 45415

(440) 349-4889 ..**Bernstein,** David J '83 -33111 Seneca Dr -Solon 44139

(937) 496-3686 ..**Bernstein,** Elaine S '89 -130 W 2nd -Ste 1818 -Dayton 45402
Fx:226-1224

(440) 255-5550 ..**Bernstein,** Harry S '88 Heritage Beverage Co -7333 Corp Blvd
-Mentor 44060

(937) 775-3488 ..**Bernstein,** J Michael '71 Wright State Univ Dept Mgt & Law
-3640 Colonial Glenn Hwy -Rm 212K Rike Hall -Dayton 45435

(248) 737-8400 ..**Bernstein,** Samuel I '97 -31100 Nrthwstrn Hwy
-Farmington Hills, MI 48334

(216) 328-8080 ..**Bernstein,** Stephen C '01 Fedeli Group -5005 Rockside Rd
-Ste 500 Crown Centre -Independence 44131

(850) 438-3111 ..**Beroset,** Barry W '71 (Beroset & K) -417 E Zaragoza
-Pensacola, FL 32501 **Fx:**432-1919

(614) 249-0878 ..**Berridge,** Thomas E '72 Nationwide Ins Co -1 Nationwide Plz
-Columbus 43215

(614) 728-7055 ..**Berrien,** Tara L '01 Atty Gen -30 E Broad -Columbus 43215
Fx:728-8600

(216) 781-1111 ..**Berris,** Richard J '80 Weisman G&W Co,LPA -101 Prospect Av
-1600 Mdlnd Bldg -Cleveland 44115 **Fx:**781-6747

(937) 652-1606 ..**Berry,** B Bradley '03 Champaign Cnty CSEA -1512 S US Hwy 68
-Ste F100 -Urbana 43078

(843) 686-5432 ..**Berry,** David H '77 -Bx6717 -Hilton Head Island, SC 29938

(937) 322-6611 ..**Berry,** James A '53 -10 W Columbia -Bx1885 -Springfield 45501
Fx:322-4497

(330) 376-0000 ..**Berry,** James F '78 Cnsl Lwyrs Title Ins Co -195 S Main -Ste 202
-Akron 44308 **Fx:**873-9529

(740) 353-4191 ..**Berry,** John F '76 -707 6th -Portsmouth 45662

(216) 520-5546 ..**Berry,** Melissa D '93 West Grp -6111 Oak Tree Blvd -Bx318063
-Cleveland 44131

(419) 228-7640 ..**Berry,** Melvin D '72 -212 N Elizabeth -Lima 45801

(216) 348-5400 ..**Berry,** Patrick J '89 (McDonald H Co,LPA) -600 Superior Av E
-Ste 2100 -Cleveland 44114 **Fx:**348-5474

(440) 816-0600 ..**Berry,** Ralph A Jr. '73 Largent BP&J Co,LPA -1 Berea Cmmns
-Ste 216 -Berea 44017 **Fx:**816-0604

(419) 248-7769 ..**Berry,** Richard L Jr. '83 Owens Corning -1 Owens Corning Pkwy
-Leg Dept -Toledo 43659

(330) 723-6404 ..**Berry,** Robert C '91 (Critchfield C&J Ltd) -3985 Medina Rd
-Ste 100 -Medina 44256

(614) 221-1215 ..**Berry,** Robert L '76 (R Berry Co LPA) -503 S High -Ste 200
-Columbus 43215 **Fx:**221-4161

(513) 671-1744 ..**Berry,** Theodore N '89 -225 Pictoria Dr -Ste 220 -Cincinnati 45246

(937) 778-0022 ..**Berry,** Thomas D '81 (Berry & V) -4612 Salem Av -Dayton 45440

(330) 365-3502 ..**Berry,** Traci A '94 Tuscarawas Cnty CSEA -154 2nd -Bx1016
-New Philadelphia 44663

(740) 349-6227 ..**Berryhill,** John C '70 Licking Cnty Domestic Relations Ct
-75 E Main -Newark 43055

(734) 769-6190 ..**Berryman,** Patrick D '96 Comshare,Inc -555 Briarwood Cir
-Ann Arbor, MI 48108

(216) 736-7219 ..**Bersticker,** Steven C '86 (Kohrman J&K PLL) -1375 E 9th
-One Cleve Ctr 20th Fl -Cleveland 44114 **Fx:**621-6536

(440) 244-3177 ..**Berta,** David J '94 -4606 Timbervw Dr -Lorain 44053

(216) 378-4136 ..**Bertea,** Craig J '85 Sky Trust -30050 Chagrin Blvd -Ste 150
-Pepper Pike 44124

           Bertoch, Carl A '57 -Bx880848 -Port Saint Lucie, FL 34988

(330) 953-7588 ..**Bertolo,** Peter F '86 FirstEnergy Corp -76 S Main -Akron 44308

(216) 664-3312 ..**Bertovich,** Richard '92 Dept of Law -601 Lakeside Av
-Rm 106 City Hall -Cleveland 44114 **Fx:**664-2663

(740) 373-1155 ..**Bertram & Halliday,LLC** -412 3rd -Marietta 45750

(614) 221-0725 ..**Bertram,** Pamela J '82 -8425 Pulsar Pl -Ste 240 -Columbus 43240

(740) 373-1155 ..**Bertram,** Paul G III '89 (Bertram & H,LLC) -412 3rd
-Marietta 45750

(740) 373-1155 ..**Bertram,** Paul G Jr. '62 Bertram & H,LLC -412 3rd -Marietta 45750

(216) 265-2658 ..**Bertram,** Ricky L '84 Park Corp -6200 Riverside Dr
-Cleveland 44135

(614) 436-8100 ..**Bertram,** William C '82 Aon Consulting -445 Hutchnsn Av -Ste 900
-Columbus 43235

(330) 296-2811 ..**Bertrand,** Louis R '68 -409 S Prospect -Bx268 -Ravenna 44266

(330) 376-5300 ..**Bertsch,** David P '78 (Buckingham D&B,LLP) -50 S Main -Bx1500
-Akron 44309 **Fx:**258-6559

(330) 643-2946 ..**Bertsch,** Eva K '85 Summit Cnty Juv Ct -650 Dan -Akron 44310

(216) 621-1000 ..**Bertsch,** Michael J '82 Moscarino & T,LLP -1422 Euclid Av
-Hanna Bldg Ste 630 -Cleveland 44115 **Fx:**622-1556

(330) 395-6444 ..**Berzonski,** Laura Odenweller '04 %JP Morgan,Ltd -173 W Market
-Warren 44481 **Fx:**394-6548

(614) 268-8410 ..**Beshears,** Ruth E '91 -560 E Royal Forest Blvd -Columbus 43214

(440) 349-5757 ..Besman, Douglas B '90 Nestle USA -30003 Bainbrdg Rd
-Solon 44139
(847) 949-7753 ..Besore, Thomas G '97 -27554 S Turf Hill Dr -Mundelein, IL 60060
(912) 267-2693 ..Besselman, John P '95 Fed Law EnvirTraining Ctr -Bldg 69
-Glynco, GA 31524
(912) 261-4551 ..Besselman, Trisha T '91 Fed Law Enfrcmnt Training Cntr
-Townhse 400 D -Ofc of Leg Cnsl -Glynco, GA 31524
(216) 382-2500 ..Besser, Barbara Kaye '73 (Elfvin & B) -4070 Mayfld Rd
-Cleveland 44121 Fx:381-0250
(216) 522-7675 ..Besser, Howard R '66 US EEOC -1660 W 2nd -Ste 850
-Cleveland 44113
Besser, Jason A '03 -1225 Warren Dr -Wilmington 45177
(614) 206-4945 ..Besser, Kenneth R '97 -2616 Brookwood Rd -Columbus 43209
(814) 464-9646 ..Besser, Matthew E '04 US Ct of Appeals-3rd Cir -17 S Park Row
-Ste 230B -Erie, PA 16507
(216) 664-2806 ..Best, Christel '92 Dept of Law -601 Lakeside Av -Rm 106 City Hall
-Cleveland 44114 Fx:664-2663
(248) 362-6139 ..Best, Daniel E '91 (Weltman W&R Co,LPA) -755 W Big Beaver Rd
-Ste 1820 -Troy, MI 48084 Fx:273-2444
(330) 665-1855 ..Best, David M '75 (D Best Co,LPA) -4900 W Bath Rd
-Akron 44333 Fx:666-5755
(419) 321-1326 ..Best, Eileen M '93 Shumaker L&K,LLP -1000 Jackson
-Toledo 43624 Fx:241-6894
Best, Eryn M '99 Global Signal Services LLC -301 N Cattlemen Rd
-Ste 300 -Sarasota, FL 34232
(419) 241-1200 ..Best, Libbey W '97 Cooper & W,LPA -900 Adams -Toledo 43624
Fx:242-5675
(419) 241-5522 ..Best, Louis M '87 Amer 1st Title Agncy -241 N Superior -Toledo
43604
(513) 241-6848 ..Best, Scott A '02 -324 Reading Rd -Cincinnati 45202
(419) 344-7355 ..Best, Steven K '99 -5575 Eagle Ter -Sylvania 43560
(202) 898-3812 ..Best, Valerie J '78 FDIC -550 17th NW -Rm F-4080
-Washington, DC 20429
(513) 563-1400 ..Betagole, Marty '94 Mike Albert Leasing,Inc -10340 Evendale Dr
-Cincinnati 45241
(770) 564-6188 ..Betchkal, Gregory J '89 Primerica Financial Srvcs
-3120 Breckingrdg Blvd -Duluth, GA 30099
(304) 529-1173 ..Beter, George D '59 -522 10th -Huntington, WV 25701
(614) 464-2200 ..Bethel, Blythe M '84 -400 S 5th -Ste 102 -Columbus 43215
Fx:464-2226
(812) 855-3892 ..Bethel, Terry A '71 Indiana Univ Schl of Law -211 S Indna Av
-Ofc 333 -Bloomington, IN 47405
(330) 746-8484 ..Betras, David J '85 (Betras M&K LLC) -6630 Sevll Dr -Bx129
-Canfield 44406 Fx:702-8280
(330) 746-8484 ..Betras Maruca & Kopp LLC -6630 Sevll Dr -Bx129
-Canfield 44406 Fx:702-8280
(440) 232-9303 ..Bettasso, Katharine Lang '79 -466 Nrthfld Rd -1st Fl
-Bedford 44146 Fx:232-9301
(216) 822-4723 ..Bettendorf, Edward L '81 Ameritech -45 Erievw Plz -Ste 1443
-Cleveland 44114
(614) 463-4201 ..Bettendorf, Margaret C '97 %Littler M,PC -21 E State -Ste 1600
-Columbus 43215 Fx:221-3301
(508) 520-2200 ..Bettigole, Bruce J '64 Gilmore R&C PC -1000 Franklin Village Dr
-Franklin, MA 02038
(513) 556-0958 ..Bettman, Marianna B '77 Univ of Cincinnati Law Schl -Bx210040
-Cincinnati 45221
Betts, Carolyn A '84 -6929 Lynfld Ct -Apt 104 -Cincinnati 45243
(740) 833-2690 ..Betts, Christopher D '97 %Delaware Cnty Pros -140 N Sandusky
-3rd Fl -Delaware 43015
(216) 781-1212 ..Betts, James E '76 OfCnsl Walter & H LLP -1301 E 9th -Ste 3500
-Cleveland 44114 Fx:575-0911
(419) 422-5565 ..Betts Miller & Russo -101 W Sandusky -Findlay 45840
Fx:423-1868
(419) 422-5565 ..Betts, Stephen C '73 (Betts M&R) -101 W Sandusky
-Findlay 45840 Fx:423-1868
(216) 241-5310 ..Betz, Thomas E '68 OfCnsl Gallagher SF&N -1501 Euclid Av
-6th Fl -Cleveland 44115 Fx:241-1608
(216) 622-3600 ..Betzer, Linda M '76 %US Atty -801 W Superior -Ste 400
-Cleveland 44113 Fx:622-3370
(216) 622-8200 ..Beus, Karl S '92 (Calfee H&G LLP) -800 Superior Av -Ste 1400
-Cleveland 44114 Fx:241-0816
(419) 422-4014 ..Beutler, Robert A Jr. '71 (Hackenberg B&R) -314 W Crawford
-Bx1544 -Findlay 45839
(312) 558-5600 ..Beutler, Todd M '97 %Winston & S -35 W Wacker Dr
-Chicago, IL 60601
(440) 357-5537 ..Bevack, Gina M '03 %Cannon SA&L Co,LPA -41 E Erie
-Painesville 44077 Fx:357-9234
(330) 650-0088 ..Bevan, Keith D '72 (Bevan & Assoc LPA,Inc) -10360 Nrthfld Rd
-Northfield 44067 Fx:467-4493
(513) 487-5985 ..Bevan, Patricia M '90 Milacron Inc -2090 Florence Av
-Cincinnati 45206
(330) 650-0088 ..Bevan, Thomas W '91 Bevan & Assoc LPA,Inc -10360 Nrthfld Rd
-Northfield 44067 Fx:467-4493
(419) 352-8095 ..Bevelhymer, Darlene P '87 -914 N Prospect
-Bowling Green 43402
Bevens, Tonya R '95 -245 Stillpass Way -Monroe 45050
(513) 618-7800 ..Bever, Mark S '84 (Graf S&M,LPA) -425 Walnut -Ste 2400
-Cincinnati 45202 Fx:618-7801
(713) 507-6823 ..Beverick, Timothy A '89 Dynegy Power Corp -1000 Louisiana
-Ste 5800 -Houston, TX 77002
(513) 943-7100 ..Bevington, Maria D '98 Midland Co -7000 Mdlnd Blvd
-Amelia 45102
(740) 226-4191 ..Bevins, Walter A '91 -112 N Market -Waverly 45690
(313) 961-0200 ..Beyer, Daniel G '98 (Kerr R&W,PLC) -500 Woodward Av
-Ste 2500 -Detroit, MI 48226 Fx:961-0138
(937) 449-6400 ..Beyer, James E '95 (Dinsmore & S LLP) -1 S Main
-Ste 1300 One Dayton Centre -Dayton 45402 Fx:449-6405
(937) 222-2500 ..Beyer, Martin A '92 (Sebaly S&D) -1900 Kettering Twr
-Dayton 45423 Fx:222-6554
(216) 781-7777 ..Beyer, William D '69 (Wuliger F&B) -1340 Sumner Ct
-Brownell Bldg -Cleveland 44115 Fx:781-0621
Beyke, Joseph L '04 -(Address Unavailable)
(937) 224-1427 ..Beyoglides, Harry G Jr. '78 -130 W 2nd -Ste 1900 -Dayton 45402

Bhaerman, David A '04 -(Address Unavailable)
(513) 745-0400 ..Bhakta, Suraj J '03 %Furnier T,LLP -1 Fncl Way -Ste 312
-Cincinnati 45242 Fx:792-6724
(330) 668-9479 ..Bhakuni, Pravin S '04 -474 S Medina Line Rd -Akron 44321
(937) 223-8177 ..Bhat, Aniruddha D '01 %Coolidge WW&L -33 W 1st -Ste 600
-Dayton 45402 Fx:223-6705
(440) 285-4040 ..Bhatia, Megan H '94 UHHS-Hosp & Hlth Partnership
-12340 Bass Lk Rd -Chardon 44024
(614) 222-4900 ..Bhatt, Sanjay K '94 -155 W Main -Ste 100 -Columbus 43215
(419) 724-0030 ..Bhatti, Kaser S '93 LAWO -520 Mad Av -Ste 640 -Toledo 43604
Fx:321-1582
(770) 850-0370 ..Bialczak, Jeanette E '73 DuCharme M & Assoc
-1000 Parkwood Cir SE -Ste 320 -Atlanta, GA 30339
(614) 466-3280 ..Bialczak, Stanley T '84 OH Dept Taxation -30 E Broad -22nd Fl
-Columbus 43215
(419) 865-1251 ..Bialecki, Korleen M '89 Wagoner & S,Ltd -7445 Airport Hwy
-Holland 43528 Fx:866-8798
(216) 574-9128 ..Bialer, Bruce A '75 -833 Leader Bldg -Cleveland 44114
(440) 266-1700 ..Biales, Robert C '93 (RC Biales & Co) -6966A Heisley Rd
-Mentor 44060
(614) 866-9143 ..Biancamano, John J '76 OSU-Ofc of Leg Affrs -33 W 11th Av
-Columbus 43201
(440) 843-6670 ..Bianchi, Robert C '84 -6325 York Rd -Ste 305
-Parma Heights 44130
(740) 282-6271 ..Bianco, Dominic J '42 -120 Shirley Cir -Steubenville 43952
(614) 241-2154 ..Bibbo, Jeffrey R '91 (DeLibera L&B) -336 S High
-Columbus 43215
(330) 451-7200 ..Bible, April R '92 Stark Cnty Pub Def -200 W Tuscarawas -Ste 200
-Canton 44702
(813) 289-3400 ..Bible, Robert W Jr. '84 (Lopez & K,PA) -4600 W Cypress Av
-Ste 500 -Tampa, FL 33607 Fx:287-5775
(740) 653-6464 ..Bibler, Robert M '81 (Dagger JMO&H) -144 E Main -Bx667
-Lancaster 43130 Fx:653-8522
(513) 662-0300 ..Bibus, Thomas W '76 -2962 Harrison Av -Cincinnati 45211
(602) 255-0330 ..Bickart, Allen B '56 -111 W Monroe -Ste #1212
-Phoenix, AZ 85003
Bickel, Leif P '03 -23483 Smith Hulse Rd -Circleville 43113
(216) 664-2070 ..Bickerstaff, Linda L '91 City Div of Taxation -1701 Lakeside Av
-Cleveland 44114
(216) 443-7800 ..Bickerstaff, Valerie D '95 %Cuyahoga Cnty Pros -1200 Ontario
-8th Fl -Cleveland 44113 Fx:698-2270
(330) 375-5716 ..Bickett, James L '74 US Atty -2 S Main -Ste 208 -Akron 44308
(330) 643-2765 ..Bickett, William W II '72 Summit Cnty Pros-CSEA -171 S Main
-Akron 44308 Fx:643-2822
(614) 939-9409 ..Bicking, Carol D '94 Velocity Title Rrsch -664 Bugle Ct
-Gahanna 43230 Fx:939-0785
Bickis, Michael S '02 -1010 18th NW -Canton 44703
(216) 621-7860 ..Bidar, Mohammed J '84 (Cavitch FD&F) -1717 E 9th -14th Fl
-Cleveland 44114 Fx:621-3415
(440) 892-8846 ..Bidari, Jayashree Y '92 -31025 Ctr Ridge Rd -Ste 6
-Westlake 44145
(440) 350-3200 ..Biddell, Nancy L '02 Lake Cnty Pub Def -125 E Erie
-Painesville 44077
(614) 236-6496 ..Biddle, James H '75 Capital Univ -2199 E Main -Columbus 43209
(740) 592-6399 ..Biddlestone, William R Jr. '84 (Biddlestone & W Co,LPA)
-8 N Court -Ste 308 -Athens 45701 Fx:573-6341
(614) 252-5116 ..Bidwell, David M '80 (Bidwell & B Co,LPA) -865 Bryden Rd
-Bx6810 -Columbus 43205
(513) 241-8313 ..Bieber, Alan E '86 (Barnes Dennig & Co,Ltd) -441 Vine
-Ste 200 Carew Twr -Cincinnati 45202
(440) 577-1738 ..Bieganski, Walter R '85 High Grwth Ventures LLC
-39056 Lochmoor Dr -Solon 44139
(937) 291-8646 ..Biegel, Alan A '67 A Biegel Co,LPA -5975 Kentshire Dr
-Kettering 45440
(740) 432-6322 ..Biegler, Kent D '82 Tribbie SP&P -139 Ct Hse Sq -Bx640
-Cambridge 43725 Fx:439-1795
(614) 221-3155 ..Biehl, Adam J '95 %Bailey C LLC -10 W Broad -Columbus 43215
Fx:221-0479
(606) 357-7227 ..Biehl, John C '71 Valvoline Co -Bx14000 -Lexington, KY 40512
(219) 461-4138 ..Biehl, Thomas R Jr. '97 Essex Grp,Inc -1601 Wall
-Fort Wayne, IN 46802
(312) 984-7788 ..Biek, John A '87 (McDermott W&E) -227 W Monroe
-Chicago, IL 60606 Fx:984-7700
(614) 463-6661 ..Bielby, Jeanine L '87 Natl City Bank -Leg Dept -155 E Broad
-Columbus 43251
(513) 651-3505 ..Bieler, Cole A '78 -432 Walnut -Ste 601 -Cincinnati 45202
(216) 781-1609 ..Bielinis, Arunas P '76 -8000 Plz Blvd -#311 -Mentor 44060
Bierce, James M '65 -4119 E Mooresdock Rd -Port Clinton 43452
(937) 223-3277 ..Bierman, Mary-Karen '02 %Bieser G&L LLP -6 N Main
-400 Natl City Ctr -Dayton 45402 Fx:223-6339
(216) 595-0071 ..Bierman, Victor J III '99 (Roth B LLP) -5196 Richmond Rd
-Bedford Heights 44146 Fx:595-0073
(216) 586-3939 ..Biernacki, John V '01 %Jones D -901 Lakeside Av
-Cleveland 44114 Fx:579-0212
(937) 223-3277 ..Bieser Greer & Landis LLP -6 N Main -400 Natl City Ctr -Dayton
45402 Fx:223-6339
(937) 223-3277 ..Bieser, Irvin G Jr. '66 (Bieser G&L LLP) -6 N Main -400 Natl
City Ctr -Dayton 45402 Fx:223-6339
(419) 243-6678 ..Biesiada, Shawn T '00 -500 Mad Av -Ste 555 -Toledo 43604
(440) 835-5396 ..Biesterfeldt, John P '99 -30305 Lk Rd -Bay Village 44140
(419) 843-2001 ..Biggert, Wayne W '04 %Gallon & T Co,LPA -3516 Granite Cir
-Bx352018 -Toledo 43635 Fx:843-6665
(440) 333-9270 ..Biggins, Brian P '96 (B Biggins & Assoc Co,LPA)
-19071 Old Detroit Rd -Ste 200 -Rocky River 44116 Fx:333-9271
(310) 899-3808 ..Biggins, Douglas C '99 (Biggins & Assoc) -233 Wilshire Blvd
-Ste 400 -Santa Monica, CA 90401 Fx:899-3804
(216) 586-3939 ..Bigler, Laura A '01 %Jones D -901 Lakeside Av -Cleveland 44114
Fx:579-0212
(513) 929-3400 ..Bigler, Michael F '84 (Baker & H LLP) -312 Walnut -Ste 3200
-Cincinnati 45202 Fx:929-0303
(330) 643-2788 ..Biglow, Michael K '02 Summit Cnty Pros-Crim -53 Univ Av -7th Fl
-Akron 44308 Fx:643-8277
(419) 691-6844 ..Bihn, Jane F '83 -860 Ansonia -Ste 11 -Oregon 43616

(440) 323-1650 .. **Bilancini**, Darrel A '78 (Savoy & B) -595 W Broad -Elyria 44035

(202) 783-7220 .. **Bilas**, Kurt W '89 Reliant Resources Inc -801 Penn Av NW -Ste 620 -Washington, DC 20004

(419) 355-5349 .. **Bilby**, Cynthia A '95 Dept of Human Srvcs -2511 Cntryside Dr -Fremont 43420

(216) 363-4500 .. **Bilchik**, Gary B '71 (Benesch FC&A LLP) -200 Pub Sq -Ste 2300 -Cleveland 44114 **Fx**:363-4588

(614) 716-2759 .. **Bilenko**, David '03 American Electric Power -1 Riverside Plz -Intl Tax & Planning -Columbus 43215

(216) 696-5297 .. **Bilfield**, Murray D '74 Bilfield & S Co,LPA -1301 E 9th -Ste 1000 Erievw Twr -Cleveland 44114 **Fx**:696-2316

(216) 696-5297 .. **Bilfield & Sandel Co, LPA** -1301 E 9th -Ste 1000 Erievw Twr -Cleveland 44114 **Fx**:696-2316

(330) 740-0200 .. **Billak**, Damian A '95 -103 E Boardman -Youngstown 44503 **Fx**:740-0201

Billec, Brett R '02 -649 Chapel Ln -Campbell 44405

(202) 533-3078 .. **Billett**, Brian A '93 KPMG -2001 M NW -Washington, DC 20036

(937) 599-7260 .. **Billiar**, Amy J '93 Logan Cnty Cmmn Pleas Ct -101 S Main -Cthse -Bellefontaine 43311

(216) 696-7600 .. **Billick**, John T '73 (Duvin C&H) -1301 E 9th -20th Fl Erievw Twr -Cleveland 44114 **Fx**:696-2038

(330) 342-8203 .. **Billick**, Timothy R '77 J Clunk Co LPA -5061 Hudson Dr -Ste 400 -Hudson 44236 **Fx**:342-8205

(513) 858-2400 .. **Billig**, Gary A '75 -447 Nilles Rd -#9 -Fairfield 45014

(937) 361-1835 .. **Billingham**, Katherine L '84 -10803 Portside Ct -Indianapolis, IN 46236

(614) 236-8000 .. **Billings**, James R '93 Zacks Law Grp LLC -33 S James Rd -3rd Fl -Columbus 43213

(606) 357-7419 .. **Billings**, John F '98 Ashland Inc -3475 Blazer Pkwy -Lexington, KY 40509

(859) 572-5340 .. **Billings**, Roger D Jr. '69 Chase Coll of Law/NKU -Nunn Dr -Rm514 -Highland Heights, KY 41099

(216) 592-5000 .. **Billingsley**, Henry E II '78 (Tucker E&W LLP) -925 Euclid Av -1150 Huntngtn Bldg -Cleveland 44115 **Fx**:592-5009

(216) 431-4500 .. **Billingsley**, Yvonne C '84 Cuyahoga Cnty Pros -3955 Euclid Av -Jane Edna Hunter Bldg -Cleveland 44115 **Fx**:431-4113

(216) 371-5551 .. **Billington**, Glenn E '70 (GE Billington Co,LPA) -1991 Lee Rd -#102 -Cleveland Heights 44118

(330) 972-7302 .. **Billow**, Patricia M '81 Univ of Akron -302 Buchtel Hall -Coll of Business Admin -Akron 44325

(614) 228-6885 .. **Bills**, Joshua R '99 Lane A&H LLC -175 S 3rd -Ste 700 -Columbus 43215 **Fx**:228-0146

(937) 333-4413 .. **Bilott**, Raymond L '83 Law Dept -101 W 3rd -Bx22 -Dayton 45402

(513) 381-2838 .. **Bilott**, Robert A '90 (Taft S&H LLP) -425 Walnut -Ste 1800 -Cincinnati 45202 **Fx**:381-0205

(216) 831-8900 .. **Bilsky**, Jeremy L '01 Cnsl Advance Payroll Funding,Ltd -3401 Enterprise Pkwy -Ste 520 -Beachwood 44122 **Fx**:831-8819

(614) 464-2572 .. **Binau**, Dan J '76 (Harris MB&C,PLL) -37 W Broad -9th Fl -Columbus 43215 **Fx**:464-2245

(614) 228-6888 .. **Binder**, Maura E '04 %Havens W LLC -141 E Town -Ste 200 -Columbus 43215 **Fx**:228-6878

(216) 522-4083 .. **Binder**, Paul L '72 US DOJ -55 Erievw Pl -Ste 70 -Cleveland 44114

(740) 323-4888 .. **Bindley**, Richard S '78 (Morrison & B) -987 Prof Pkwy -Unit B -Heath 43056

(216) 363-4500 .. **Binford**, Gregory G '73 (Benesch FC&A LLP) -200 Pub Sq -Ste 2300 -Cleveland 44114 **Fx**:363-4588

(330) 492-8865 .. **Bing**, Jason N '00 Stark Cnty Common Pleas Ct -Cnty Ofc Bldg -Market Av -Canton 44702

(330) 452-1343 .. **Bing**, Richard George '56 -116 Cleveland Av NW -Ste 804 -Canton 44702 **Fx**:453-0180

(419) 243-9876 .. **Bingle**, William J '71 -520 Mad Av -Ste 524 -Toledo 43604

(614) 752-5081 .. **Binkovitz**, David J '78 Industrial Commssn of OH -30 W Spring -9th Fl -Columbus 43215 **Fx**:752-8785

(614) 224-1979 .. **Binning**, John B '76 -592 S 3rd -Columbus 43215

(614) 224-1982 .. **Binning**, Peter J T '04 -592 S 3rd -Columbus 43215

(301) 215-6723 .. **Binns**, Carl D '01 NASD Mrkt Regulation -5500 Friendship Blvd -#2305N -Chevy Chase, MD 20815

(216) 344-8398 .. **Binns**, Cynthia A '95 Glidden Co -925 Euclid Av -9th Fl -Cleveland 44115

(513) 988-9357 .. **Binns**, Patrick A '76 -102 E State -Trenton 45067

(330) 744-0291 .. **Bins-Castronovo**, Matthew N '99 %Boyd RC&C Co LPA -400 Sky Bk Bldg -Bx6565 -Youngstown 44501

(301) 495-5623 .. **Binzel**, William P '81 Natl Fndtn for Credit Cnslng -801 Roeder Rd -Ste 900 -Silver Spring, MD 20910

(216) 566-7995 .. **Binzley**, Richard C '66 (Thompson H LLP) -127 Pub Sq -3900 Key Ctr -Cleveland 44114 **Fx**:566-5800

(614) 227-2325 .. **Birath**, John F Jr. '71 (Bricker & E LLP) -100 S 3rd -Columbus 43215 **Fx**:227-2390

(740) 363-2223 .. **Birch**, David H '85 -2 W Winter -Ste 31 -Delaware 43015

(614) 764-1444 .. **Birch**, Elizabeth J '89 Mowery & Y -425 Metro Pl N -Ste 420 -Dublin 43017 **Fx**:760-8654

(216) 443-8780 .. **Birch**, Wanda J '91 Cuyahoga Cnty Probate Ct -1 Lakeside Av -Cleveland 44113

(513) 732-7313 .. **Birck**, Mary L '94 Clermont Cnty Pros -123 N 3rd -Batavia 45103

(937) 255-6111 .. **Bird**, Karl C '88 USAF AFMCLO/JAB -1864 4th -Bldg 15 -Wright Patterson AFB 45433

Bird, Pooja Alag '04 -(Address Unavailable)

(843) 815-3900 .. **Bird**, Stephen S '81 (S Bird,LLC) -15 Clarks Summit Dr -Bluffton, SC 29910

Bird, Thomas E '04 -(Address Unavailable)

(330) 297-3850 .. **Bird**, Tiffany D '97 %Portage Cnty Pros -466 S Chestnut -Ravenna 44266

(419) 531-9559 .. **Bires**, Steven A '99 Austin Fncl Srvcs Inc -3450 W Central Av -Ste 260 -Toledo 43606

(330) 656-0495 .. **Birmingham**, Fletcher A '88 Summit Bus Cons Inc -679 Norbury Dr -Hudson 44236

(419) 255-6810 .. **Birmingham**, John D '90 -1107 Adams -Toledo 43624

(517) 323-1506 .. **Birn**, Stuart R '73 Auto Owners Ins Co -6101 Anacapri -Lansing, MI 48917

(734) 930-5600 .. **Birnbaum**, Renee '79 Garan LM,PC -101 N Main -Ste 460 -Ann Arbor, MI 48104

(614) 878-4281 .. **Birnbrich**, Gilbert J '99 -7680 Feder Rd -Galloway 43119

(216) 292-4900 .. **Birne**, Kenneth A '81 (Peltz & B) -23230 Chagrin Blvd -Ste 715 -Beachwood 44122 **Fx**:292-4942

(330) 395-3419 .. **Birrell**, Bruce '53 -106 E Market -712 Bank One Bldg -Warren 44481

(614) 461-1100 .. **Birrer**, Scott B '94 %Swedlow BLL&D Co,LPA -10 W Broad -Ste 2400 -Columbus 43215 **Fx**:461-8178

(937) 222-1148 .. **Birt**, James E '63 -111 W 1st -Ste 1000 -Dayton 45402

(614) 223-9300 .. **Bisesi**, Phillip P '98 %Benesch FC&A LLP -88 E Broad -Ste 900 -Columbus 43215 **Fx**:223-9330

(419) 636-5666 .. **Bish Butler & Thompson,Ltd** -1210 W High -Bryan 43506 **Fx**:636-3919

(419) 636-5666 .. **Bish**, William A '69 (Bish B&T,Ltd) -1210 W High -Bryan 43506 **Fx**:636-3919

(419) 865-1251 .. **Bish Wagoner**, Helen '80 Wagoner & S,Ltd -7445 Airport Hwy -Holland 43528 **Fx**:866-8798

(330) 744-5211 .. **Bishara**, Joseph C '96 Roth BRS&L,LPA -100 Fed Plz E -Ste 600 -Youngstown 44503 **Fx**:744-3184

(513) 241-2025 .. **Bishop**, Alvertis W Jr. '84 -917 Main -2nd Fl -Cincinnati 45202 **Fx**:241-0154

(859) 426-9000 .. **Bishop**, Bryan N '04 CE Massey -2643 Erlanger Crescent Springs Rd -Erlanger, KY 41017 **Fx**:426-9001

Bishop, Cary B '04 -(Address Unavailable)

(330) 753-6874 .. **Bishop**, Christy B '03 Thompson Law Ofcs -2719 Mnchstr Rd -Akron 44319

(419) 242-1400 .. **Bishop**, Daniel A '78 -608 Mad Av -Ste 1400 -Toledo 43604 **Fx**:246-5764

(419) 354-9250 .. **Bishop**, Gary D '87 %Wood Cnty Pros -One Cthse Sq -Bowling Green 43402 **Fx**:353-2904

(330) 638-1529 .. **Bishop**, Jami L '03 -143 W Main -Cortland 44410

(513) 352-4708 .. **Bishop**, Jennifer I '84 Law Dept -801 Plum -Rm 214 -Cincinnati 45202 **Fx**:352-1515

(513) 721-4532 .. **Bishop**, Jerome C '02 %Katz TB&H -255 E 5th -Ste 2400 -Cincinnati 45202

(419) 536-2066 .. **Bishop**, Jerry J II '79 (Chase G&B) -2650 N Reynolds Rd -Ste 3 -Toledo 43615 **Fx**:536-2239

(317) 881-6751 .. **Bishop**, Kurt D '96 OMS Intl,Inc -941 Fry Rd -Greenwood, IN 46142

(216) 445-6653 .. **Bishop**, Sherri L '91 Cleveland Clinic Fndtn -9500 Euclid Av -Cleveland 44195

(440) 423-0606 .. **Bissell**, Robert K '52 (Bissell & B) -1540 Chagrin Rvr Rd -Bx310 -Gates Mills 44040

(513) 723-4084 .. **Bissinger**, Charles C Jr. '79 (Vorys SS&P LLP) -221 E 4th -Ste 2000 Atrium Two -Bx0236 -Cincinnati 45201 **Fx**:723-4056

(513) 352-3346 .. **Bissinger**, Julie F '84 Law Dept -801 Plum -Rm 214 -Cincinnati 45202 **Fx**:352-1515

(513) 977-8200 .. **Bissinger**, Mark C '83 (Dinsmore & S LLP) -255 E 5th -Ste 1900 -Cincinnati 45202 **Fx**:977-8141

(937) 228-2666 .. **Bissonnette**, Brett R '03 %Hochman R&P Co,LPA -118 W 1st -Ste 650 -Dayton 45402 **Fx**:228-0508

(614) 657-6944 .. **Biswas**, Naren '59 -131 Wnthrp Rd -Columbus 43214

(440) 871-0516 .. **Bittel**, Patricia T '83 -30628 Detroit Rd PMB 254 -Westlake 44145

(330) 762-2600 .. **Bittel**, Timothy M '71 (Joondeph & B,LLP) -50 S Main -Ste 700 -Akron 44308 **Fx**:762-2604

(440) 449-9690 .. **Bittenbender**, Charles A '80 Nacco Industries,Inc -5875 Landerbrook Dr -Mayfield Heights 44124

(216) 621-0200 .. **Bittence**, Mary M '82 (Baker & H LLP) -1900 E 9th -Ste 3200 -Cleveland 44114 **Fx**:696-0740

(216) 586-3939 .. **Bittence**, Stephen L '04 %Jones D -901 Lakeside Av -Cleveland 44114 **Fx**:579-0212

(513) 721-5672 .. **Bitter**, Lisa M '91 (Benjamin Y&H LLC) -312 Elm -Ste 1850 -Cincinnati 45202 **Fx**:562-4388

(216) 739-5125 .. **Bitterman**, Eileen M '97 %Weltman W&R Co,LPA -323 W Lakeside Av -Ste 200 -Cleveland 44113 **Fx**:363-4121

(419) 255-5058 .. **Bittner**, Diana L '98 -520 Mad Av -Ste 670 -Toledo 43604

(614) 462-2228 .. **Bittner**, Paul L '93 (Schottenstein Z&D) -250 West -Bx165020 -Columbus 43216 **Fx**:462-5135

(937) 444-0403 .. **Bitzer**, Frank J '88 Phoenix Rsrch Inc -Bx859 -Mount Orab 45154

(614) 716-3068 .. **Bivens**, Gina S '99 Cnsl Amer Elec Pwr Co -1 Riverside Plz -Columbus 43215

(614) 253-4744 .. **Bivens**, Michael T '03 -2255 Kimberley Pkwy E -Columbus 43232

(330) 392-5000 .. **Biviano**, William R '74 -108 Main Av SW -7th Fl -Warren 44481

(216) 931-6000 .. **Bixenstine**, Barton A '81 (Ulmer & B LLP) -1300 E 9th -Ste 900 Penton Media Bldg -Cleveland 44114 **Fx**:931-6001

(216) 983-1911 .. **Bixenstine**, Kim F '82 Univ Hosp Health Sys -10524 Euclid Av -Cleveland 44106

(419) 252-5770 .. **Bixler**, Robert J '72 Manor Care,Inc -333 N Summit -Toledo 43604

(440) 526-1202 .. **Bjelovuk**, Gordana L '92 G Bjelovuk & Assoc -8181 Avry Rd -Cleveland 44147

(614) 228-1541 .. **Bjerke**, Jack A '70 (Baker & H LLP) -65 E State -Ste 2100 -Columbus 43215 **Fx**:462-2616

(513) 352-6536 .. **Blachman**, Gary D '95 %Thompson H LLP -312 Walnut -14th Fl -Cincinnati 45202 **Fx**:241-4771

Blachman, Marci L '95 -420 Madison -Ste 1100 -Toledo 43604

(216) 586-3939 .. **Black**, Carl E '98 %Jones D -901 Lakeside Av -Cleveland 44114 **Fx**:579-0212

(614) 761-8113 .. **Black**, Christopher G '97 %Maguire & S,LLP -250 Civic Ctr Dr -Ste 200 -Columbus 43215 **Fx**:224-1236

(513) 977-8200 .. **Black**, David G '94 (Dinsmore & S LLP) -255 E 5th -Ste 1900 -Cincinnati 45202 **Fx**:977-8141

(614) 241-2174 .. **Black**, David P '01 Kelly Law Ofcs -118 E Main -Columbus 43215

(727) 771-7727 .. **Black**, James A Jr. '67 Zurich NA -334 Eastlake Rd -PMB 136 -Palm Harbor, FL 34685

(440) 350-1616 .. **Black**, Jeffrey H '92 (Black & Assoc Co,LPA) -1501 Mad Av -Painesville 44077 **Fx**:350-1691

(513) 474-6532 .. **Black**, Kevin M '97 -8085 Ashgrove Dr -Cincinnati 45244

(216) 334-2904 .. **Black**, Lisa G '92 Catholic Charities-Hlth & Human Srvcs -7911 Detroit Av -Cleveland 44102

(614) 224-6257 .. **Black**, Lori A '90 Rector & Assoc,Inc -172 E State -Ste 305 -Columbus 43215

(330) 364-6553 .. **Black McCuskey Hanhart Deeds & Bauer** -130 W 3rd -Bx2330 -Dover 44622 **Fx**:364-2739

(330) 456-8341 .. **Black McCuskey Souers & Arbaugh, LPA** -220 Market Av S -Ste 1000 -Canton 44702 **Fx**:456-5756

(614) 752-4219 ..**Black**, Rachael T '92 Industrial Commssn of OH -30 W Spring -9th Fl -Columbus 43215 Fx:752-8785

Black, Sharon L '02 -2777 Carrington NW -Canton 44720

(330) 455-0173 ..**Black**, Sheila Markley '72 (Day KRW&R,Ltd) -200 Market Av N -Ste 300 -Bx24213 -Canton 44701 Fx:455-2633

Black, Sher A '98 -2988 S Brdg -Chillicothe 45601

(513) 621-6464 ..**Black**, Stephen L '74 (Graydon H&R LLP) -511 Walnut -1900 Fifth Third Ctr -Cincinnati 45202 Fx:651-3836

(513) 946-5138 ..**Black**, Timothy S '83 Cnty Mun Ct Judge -1000 Main -Cincinnati 45202

(813) 223-6773 ..**Blackburn**, Catherine E '82 (Fiol G&B,PA) -400 N Tampa -Ste 2630 -Tampa, FL 33602 Fx:223-7702

(440) 617-1900 ..**Blackburn**, Douglas C '75 (Direnfeld G&B Co,LPA) -24441 Detroit Rd -Ste 200 -Westlake 44145 Fx:871-2661

(561) 746-9800 ..**Blackburn**, James M '61 -1001 N Hwy A1A Alt -#109 -Jupiter, FL 33477

(614) 225-0760 ..**Blackburn**, John D '74 -220 Wnthrp Rd -Columbus 43214

(513) 621-3550 ..**Blackburn**, Katherine B '89 Cincinnati Bengals -1 Paul Brown Stadium -Cincinnati 45202

(513) 983-7676 ..**Blackburn**, Kenneth L '03 Cnsl Procter & Gamble Co -1 Procter & Gamble Plz -Cincinnati 45202 Fx:983-4274

(937) 645-3082 ..**Blackburn**, Marcia V '85 Union Cnty Common Pleas Ct -215 W 5th -Marysville 43040

(937) 223-8177 ..**Blackburn**, R Scott '79 (Coolidge WW&L) -33 W 1st -Ste 600 -Dayton 45402 Fx:223-6705

(614) 461-5600 ..**Blackburn**, Thomas I '79 (Buckley K,LPA) -10 W Broad -Ste 1300 -Columbus 43215

(513) 621-3550 ..**Blackburn**, Troy A '92 Cincinnati Bengals -1 Paul Brown Stadium -Cincinnati 45202

(216) 241-6602 ..**Blackford**, Jason C '64 OfCnsl Weston HFP&H LLP -50 Pub Sq -2500 Trmnl Twr -Cleveland 44113 Fx:621-8369

(614) 466-3957 ..**Blackford**, Megan Davis '04 OH DOT-Claims -1980 W Broad -Div of Construction Mgmt -Columbus 43223 Fx:752-6534

(216) 623-0150 ..**Blackham**, Robert E '87 (Roetzel & A,LPA) -1375 E 9th -One Cleve Ctr 9th Fl -Cleveland 44114 Fx:623-0134

(216) 291-7359 ..**Blackhurst**, Scott D '90 Northrop Grumman -1900 Richmond Rd -Cleveland 44124

(440) 838-8800 ..**Blackie**, William E III '79 OfCnsl Millisor & N Co,LPA -9150 S Hills Blvd -Ste 300 -Cleveland 44147 Fx:838-8805

(614) 272-6951 ..**Blackman**, Gordon A '75 %Am Commerce Ins Co -3590 Twin Crks Dr -Columbus 43204

(614) 464-0082 ..**Blackmer**, Mark R '82 Johrendt C&E -471 E Broad -Ste 800 -Columbus 43215

(412) 366-3333 ..**Blackmer**, Steven G '00 %Willman & A,LLP -700 McKnight Park Dr -Ste 705-708 -Pittsburgh, PA 15237 Fx:366-3462

(614) 939-1510 ..**Blackmore**, Josiah H II '62 Capital Univ Law Schl -7639 Clark State Rd -Blacklick 43004

(614) 221-1341 ..**Blackmore**, Margaret L '81 (Tyack B&L Co,PA) -536 S High -Columbus 43215 Fx:228-0253

(330) 744-0440 ..**Blackstone**, Jay C '83 -130 Overhill Rd -Youngstown 44512

(330) 339-2806 ..**Blackwell**, David L '94 -3405 Curtis Rd SE -New Philadelphia 44663

(303) 673-3988 ..**Blackwell**, Karen J '76 SrCnsl Storage Tech -1 Storagetek Dr -MS 4309 -Louisville, CO 80028

(419) 423-2200 ..**Blackwell**, Robert B '89 (Blackwell Law Firm) -519 S Blanchard -Findlay 45840

(513) 651-6800 ..**Blade**, Bryan S '95 (Frost BT LLC) -201 E 5th -2200 PNC Ctr -Cincinnati 45202 Fx:651-6981

(440) 729-7996 ..**Blageff**, Lillian V '91 Business Laws,Inc -11630 Chillicothe Rd -Bx185 -Chesterland 44026

(440) 333-3386 ..**Blaha**, Keith E '86 -20220 Ctr Ridge Rd -Ste 304 -Rocky River 44116

(614) 891-5378 ..**Blaine**, Craig J '82 -1195 Hoovervw Dr -Westerville 43082

(614) 466-0722 ..**Blair**, Adrianne M '90 Atty Gen -150 E Gay -Columbus 43215 Fx:644-9973

(937) 223-8171 ..**Blair**, Amy R '01 %Rogers & G -2160 Kettering Twr -Dayton 45423 Fx:223-1649

(740) 775-1700 ..**Blair & Ater LLP** -6 W Main -Chillicothe 45601

(216) 687-2538 ..**Blair**, Beverly J '85 CSU-Marshall Cllg of Law -2121 Euclid Av -LB138 -Cleveland 44115 Fx:687-6881

(330) 702-2830 ..**Blair**, Harry G '95 Progressive Ins Co -3660 Stutz Dr -Ste 100 -Canfield 44406

(419) 224-1353 ..**Blair**, James F '74 (King & B) -212 N Elizabeth -Lima 45801 Fx:224-5305

(740) 775-1700 ..**Blair**, John G '59 (Blair & A LLP) -6 W Main -Chillicothe 45601

Blair, Julie A '04 -(Address Unavailable)

(513) 469-6908 ..**Blair**, Linda A '86 -10726 Escondido Dr -Cincinnati 45249

(330) 544-4002 ..**Blair**, Matthew J Jr. '84 (Blair & L Co,LPA) -724 Youngstown Rd -Niles 44446

(216) 622-8361 ..**Blair**, Mitchell G '82 (Calfee H&G LLP) -800 Superior Av -Ste 1400 -Cleveland 44114 Fx:241-0816

(216) 781-5245 ..**Blair**, Nancy P '03 -55 Pub Sq -2121 The Illuminating Bldg -Cleveland 44113 Fx:781-8207

(216) 574-9474 ..**Blair**, Rebecca S '86 -815 Superior Av -Ste 1915 -Cleveland 44114

(330) 744-5211 ..**Blair**, Richard B '70 (Roth BRS&L,LPA) -100 Fed Plz E -Ste 600 -Youngstown 44503 Fx:744-3184

(614) 442-1331 ..**Blair**, Roger S '68 1st Community Bk -4300 E Broad -Whitehall 43213

(330) 499-1016 ..**Blair**, William P III '71 -4571 Stephen Cir NW -Canton 44718 Fx:499-0790

(202) 879-3604 ..**Blais**, Travis L '00 %Jones D -51 Louisiana Av NW -Washington, DC 20001 Fx:626-1700

(740) 653-4259 ..**Blaisdell**, Julie S '92 Fairfield Cnty Pros -201 S Broad -4th Fl -Lancaster 43130

(330) 451-7200 ..**Blake**, Allyson J '99 Stark Cnty Pub Def -200 W Tuscarawas -Ste 200 -Canton 44702

(216) 621-0150 ..**Blake**, Christopher S '99 %Hahn L&P LLP -3300 BP Twr/200 Pub Sq -Ste 3300 -Cleveland 44114 Fx:241-2824

(614) 481-4480 ..**Blake**, Curtis R '89 Koffel & J -2130 Arlngtn Av -Columbus 43221

(740) 264-1651 ..**Blake Hershey & Bednar** -4110 Sunset Blvd -Steubenville 43952

(330) 455-0173 ..**Blake**, James R '73 (Day KRW&R,Ltd) -200 Market Av N -Ste 300 -Bx24213 -Canton 44701 Fx:455-2633

(614) 462-3555 ..**Blake**, Jeffrey A '88 Franklin Cnty Pros -373 S High -Columbus 43215

(937) 382-4030 ..**Blake**, John F '70 -799 Ward Rd -Wilmington 45177

(937) 296-2384 ..**Blake**, Jonathan I '01 LM Beery & Co -3170 Kettering Blvd -Dayton 45439

Blake, Joseph G II '02 -5803 Scenic Edge Blvd -Dublin 43017

(937) 497-1000 ..**Blake**, Kara M '04 %Blake Law Co -124 W Poplar -Sidney 45365 Fx:497-8117

(216) 464-7600 ..**Blake**, Martin C '57 -23200 Chagrin Blvd -Cleveland 44122

(423) 229-1793 ..**Blake**, Michael J '91 Eastman Chem Co -Bx511 -Kingsport, TN 37662

(614) 752-4153 ..**Blake**, Richard E '85 Workers Comp -30 W Spring -Level 26 -Columbus 43215

(937) 497-1000 ..**Blake**, Rodney R Jr. '66 (Blake Law Co) -124 W Poplar -Sidney 45365 Fx:497-8117

(419) 255-5900 ..**Blake**, Scott A '95 %MacMillan S&T,LLC -720 Water -4th Fl -Toledo 43604 Fx:255-9639

(740) 264-1651 ..**Blake**, Shawn M '99 Blake H&B -4110 Sunset Blvd -Steubenville 43952

(440) 245-3111 ..**Blake**, Stephen K '00 -215 W 8th -Lorain 44052

(740) 264-1651 ..**Blake**, William F Jr. '74 (Blake H&B) -4110 Sunset Blvd -Steubenville 43952

(216) 689-4129 ..**Blake**, William J '81 KeyBank NA -127 Pub Sq -2nd Fl -Cleveland 44114

(216) 514-4981 ..**Blakely**, Jonathan P '89 -23875 Commerce Park Rd -Ste 105 -Beachwood 44122

(330) 297-3850 ..**Blakemore**, Allison B '89 Portage Cnty Pros -466 S Chestnut -Ravenna 44266

(216) 928-2200 ..**Blakemore**, Edward H '00 %Sutter OM&F -1301 E 9th -3600 Erievw Twr -Cleveland 44114 Fx:928-4400

(330) 253-3337 ..**Blakemore Meeker & Bowler Co,LPA** -19 N High -Akron 44308 Fx:253-4131

(850) 245-2242 ..**Blakemore**, Trina Lynn '96 DEP -3900 Cmmnwlth Blvd -MS 35 -Tallahassee, FL 32399 Fx:245-2303

(513) 551-1988 ..**Blaker**, Joseph A '01 Unemploymnt Comp Commssn -225 Pictoria Dr -Pictoria Twr 5th Fl -Cincinnati 45246

(740) 732-7559 ..**Blakeslee**, Jack A '76 (JA Blakeslee Co,LPA) -421 West -Bx284 -Caldwell 43724

(419) 873-8401 ..**Blakly**, Kim G '88 (KG Blakley,LPA) -117 Louisiana Av -Ste #200 -Perrysburg 43551

(740) 622-0130 ..**Blanchard**, Van II '86 -402 Main -Coshocton 43812

(330) 742-8941 ..**Blanchard**, William J '96 Youngstown Police Dept -116 W Boardman -Youngstown 44503

(305) 381-6073 ..**Blanco**, Chrisana C '01 %ME Trenzada -150 W Flagler -1650 Museum Twr -Miami, FL 33130

(614) 424-7352 ..**Blanda**, John J '70 Battelle Memorial Inst -505 King Av -Columbus 43201

(513) 381-0656 ..**Blandford**, Colleen M '83 (Kohnen & P LLP) -201 E 5th -Ste 800 -Cincinnati 45202 Fx:381-5823

(419) 249-7900 ..**Blandin**, Bradley L '04 %Robison C&O -Four SeaGate -9th Fl -Toledo 43604 Fx:249-7011

(561) 624-0291 ..**Blaney**, Jerri M '81 -11380 Prosperity Farms Rd -Ste 203 -Palm Beach Gardens, FL 33410

(330) 384-5431 ..**Blank**, David M '78 FirstEnergy Corp -76 S Main -Akron 44308

(859) 655-3000 ..**Blank**, David M '91 -36 W 5th -Covington, KY 41011 Fx:655-3004

(202) 202-3908 ..**Blank**, Harvey P '79 US Dept of the Interior -18th & C NW -SOL/DMR -Washington, DC 20240

(330) 451-7456 ..**Blank**, Norma H '84 Stark Cnty Fam Ct -110 Central Plz S -Ste 601 -Canton 44702 Fx:451-7837

(513) 362-8700 ..**Blank Rome** -201 E 5th -Ste 1700 -Cincinnati 45202 Fx:362-8787

(419) 241-9000 ..**Blank**, Thomas C '81 (Shumaker L&K,LLP) -1000 Jackson -Toledo 43624 Fx:241-6894

(419) 523-5658 ..**Blankemeyer**, Anna M '81 (Schroeder B&S) -315 E Main -Bx110 -Ottawa 45875 Fx:523-6500

(614) 249-0295 ..**Blankenship**, Alice K '83 Nationwide Ins Co -One Nationwide Plz -Columbus 43215

(614) 572-0046 ..**Blankenship**, Arnold D II '93 -336 S High -Columbus 43215

(614) 274-2889 ..**Blankenship**, Jeffrey A '83 -3303 Sullivant Av -Columbus 43204

(440) 576-3662 ..**Blankenship**, Jodi Misinec '01 Ashtabula Cnty Pros -25 W Jffrsn -Jefferson 44047

(859) 283-1140 ..**Blankenship**, Norman J '85 (Monohan & B) -7711 Ewing Blvd -Ste 100 -Florence, KY 41042

(513) 721-3330 ..**Blankenship**, Randy J '86 (Robbins KP&T) -7 W 7th -Ste 1400 -Cincinnati 45202

(606) 877-7930 ..**Blankley**, Kristen M '04 Hon E Siler -310 S Main -US Circuit Ct -London, KY 40741

(740) 286-5006 ..**Blanton**, Jonathan D '98 Jackson Cnty -350 Portsmouth -Ste 100 -Jackson 45640

(937) 544-5095 ..**Blanton**, Kristofer D '01 %Young & C -225 N Cross -West Union 45693

(937) 252-1414 ..**Blaschak**, Thomas R '92 -1692 Woodman Dr -Dayton 45432 Fx:252-6124

(330) 426-9491 ..**Blasdell**, Daniel A '73 (Allison & B) -139 N Market -East Palestine 44413

(614) 224-5205 ..**Blaser**, Jennifer R '99 %Peck S&W,LLP -175 S 3rd -Ste 600 -Columbus 43215 Fx:224-0069

(937) 222-2424 ..**Blasik-Miller**, Susan '84 (Freund F&A) -1 S Main -Ste 1800 -Dayton 45402 Fx:222-5369

(513) 852-6003 ..**Blaske**, Nathan H '03 %Wood & L LLP -600 Vine -Ste 2500 -Cincinnati 45202 Fx:852-6087

(734) 747-7055 ..**Blaske**, Thomas H '03 (Blaske & B) -320 N Main -Ste 303 -Ann Arbor, MI 48104

(614) 324-5969 ..**Blasko**, Joseph C '97 Scotts Co -50 W Broad -Ste 2400 -Columbus 43215

(740) 474-7231 ..**Blasko**, Stacey L '96 4th Dist Ct of Appls -121-A W Franklin -Circleville 43113 Fx:474-6870

(304) 242-8410 ..**Blass**, Scott S '93 Bordas & B,PLLC -1358 Natl Rd -Wheeling, WV 26003

(440) 366-5440 ..**Blaszak**, James L '70 -258 N Abbe Rd -Elyria 44035

(513) 745-9019 ..**Blatt**, Henry J '97 John Henry Homes,Inc -10925 Reed Hartman Hwy -Ste 312 -Cincinnati 45242

Blatt, Nancy M '91 -(Address Unavailable)

(513) 241-2324 .. **Blatt,** Paul A '98 %Wood H&E LLP -441 Vine -Ste 2700
-Cincinnati 45202 **Fx:**421-7269

(937) 222-2424 .. **Blatt,** Shawn M '91 (Freund F&A) -1 S Main -Ste 1800
-Dayton 45402 **Fx:**222-5369

(937) 485-4388 .. **Blattner,** Elizabeth H '89 Reynolds & Reynolds Co -115 S Ludlow
-Bx2608 -Dayton 45401

(937) 443-6539 .. **Blattner,** James Wray '80 (Thompson H LLP) -2000 Cthse Plz NE
-Bx8801 -Dayton 45401 **Fx:**443-6635

(440) 247-5995 .. **Blattner,** Robert A '59 -30799 Pinetree Rd -Ste 415
-Cleveland 44124 **Fx:**247-2655

(419) 255-7250 .. **Blaufuss,** John A '91 -709 Mad Av -Rm 218 -Toledo 43624
Fx:242-7085

(614) 764-0681 .. **Blaugrund,** David S '77 (Blaugrund H&M,Inc) -5455 Rings Rd
-Ste 500 -Dublin 43017 **Fx:**764-0774

(614) 764-0681 .. **Blaugrund Herbert & Martin,Inc** -5455 Rings Rd -Ste 500
-Dublin 43017 **Fx:**764-0774

(513) 892-8251 .. **Blauvelt,** Scott N '97 %Holcomb & H LLP -6 S 2nd
-311 Key Bk Bldg -Hamilton 45011 **Fx:**737-6854

(419) 529-8764 .. **Blazef,** Jaceda '00 -13 Park Av -Barrington One Bldg
-Mansfield 44902

(614) 841-2635 .. **Blazek,** James N '93 -33 E North -Worthington 43085

(440) 238-7887 .. **Blech,** Kenneth A '79 (KA Blech Co,LPA) -10850 Pearl Rd -D-3
-Strongsville 44136 **Fx:**238-9532

(614) 728-5100 .. **Bledsoe,** Tony W Jr. '99 Legis Insp Gen -50 W Broad -Ste 1308
-Columbus 43215

(513) 564-0088 .. **Bleile,** Adam B '99 (Bleile & S) -114 E 8th -Cincinnati 45202

(216) 642-2273 .. **Bleisch,** N D '98 LTV Steel Co,Inc -5860 Lombardo Ctr
-Seven Hills 44131

(440) 248-8787 .. **Bleiweiss,** Gary L '81 Saltz Shamis & Goldfarb,Inc
-32125 Solon Rd -Ste 200 -Solon 44139

                 Bleser, Donald L '82 -6220 Cedarbluff Ct -Cincinnati 45233

(513) 621-9191 .. **Blessing,** David S '04 W Blessing -119 E Court -Ste 500
-Cincinnati 45202

(513) 385-1234 .. **Blessing,** Louis W Jr. '76 OfCnsl Lyons & F Co,LPA
-3672 Sprngdl Rd -Cincinnati 45251

(513) 621-9191 .. **Blessing,** William H '76 -119 E Court -Ste 500 -Cincinnati 45202

(440) 366-9930 .. **Blevins,** Anne-Marie N '98 -222 Columbus -Elyria 44035

(614) 873-3421 .. **Blevins,** Melissa D '04 -128 W Main -Plain City 43064

(440) 366-9930 .. **Blevins,** Paul E '93 %McCray MS&M Co,LPA -260 Burns Rd
-Ste 150 -Elyria 44035 **Fx:**366-1910

                 Bley, Kellie S '97 -(Address Unavailable)

(513) 651-6800 .. **Blickensderfer,** Matthew C '00 (Frost BT LLC) -201 E 5th
-2200 PNC Ctr -Cincinnati 45202 **Fx:**651-6981

(937) 692-5278 .. **Blinn,** Caroline R '01 Garbig & B,LLC -2840 Alt State Rt 49 N
-Ste A -Bx100 -Arcanum 45304 **Fx:**692-6544

(609) 252-4814 .. **Blischak,** Matthew P '90 Bristol-Myers Squibb Co -Bx4000
-Princeton, NJ 08543

(440) 356-2600 .. **Bliss,** Thomas P '76 (Bliss & H-B) -20899 Lorain Rd
-Fairview Park 44126

(202) 273-1722 .. **Blitz,** Daniel A '98 NLRB -1099 14th NW -Ste 11500
-Washington, DC 20570

(614) 629-5357 .. **Bloch,** Daniel D '02 PricewaterhouseCoopers,LLP -100 E Broad
-Ste 2100 -Columbus 43215

(216) 696-7600 .. **Bloch,** Marc J '69 (Duvin C&H) -1301 E 9th -20th Fl Erievw Twr
-Cleveland 44114 **Fx:**696-2038

(513) 751-4420 .. **Bloch,** Randal S '73 (Wagner & B) -2345 Ashland Av
-Cincinnati 45206 **Fx:**751-4555

(614) 236-6560 .. **Blocher,** Janet G '90 %Capital Univ Law Sch -303 E Broad
-Columbus 43215

(513) 621-3394 .. **Blocher,** Mark D '79 (Peck S&W,LLP) -201 E 5th -Ste 900
-Cincinnati 45202 **Fx:**621-3813

(937) 443-6964 .. **Block,** Barry M '75 (Thompson H LLP) -2000 Cthse Plz NE
-Bx8801 -Dayton 45401 **Fx:**443-6635

(216) 623-0000 .. **Block,** Brian C '03 %Javitch B&R -1300 E 9th -14th Fl
-Cleveland 44114 **Fx:**623-0190

(216) 623-0000 .. **Block,** Bruce A '76 (Javitch B&R) -1300 E 9th -14th Fl
-Cleveland 44114 **Fx:**623-0190

                 Block, Drew L '03 -(Address Unavailable)

(513) 241-3100 .. **Block,** Patricia K '98 Lerner S&R -120 E 4th -8th Fl
-Cincinnati 45202

(513) 721-1504 .. **Block,** Robert G '75 Droder & M Co,LPA -125 W Cntrl Pkwy
-Cincinnati 45202 **Fx:**721-0310

(216) 696-1422 .. **Blocker,** David S '02 %McCarthy LC&L Co,LPA
-101 Prospect Av W -1800 Mdlnd Bldg -Cleveland 44115
Fx:696-1210

(859) 491-4444 .. **Bloemer,** Donna M '95 Wolnitzek & R,PSC -502 Greenup -Bx352
-Covington, KY 41012 **Fx:**491-1001

(513) 651-6800 .. **Blomeke,** Stacy C '00 %Frost BT LLC -201 E 5th -2200 PNC Ctr
-Cincinnati 45202 **Fx:**651-6981

(513) 947-9490 .. **Blomer,** Philip J '04 -1166 W Ohio Pike -Amelia 45102

(216) 771-6500 .. **Blomgren,** Gilbert E '95 %K Weiner & Assoc Co,LPA -75 Pub Sq
-4th Fl -Cleveland 44113 **Fx:**771-6540

(330) 744-1111 .. **Blomstrom,** James L '74 Harrington H&M,Ltd -26 Market
-Ste 1200 -Youngstown 44503 **Fx:**744-2029

(513) 946-3582 .. **Bloniarz,** Mindy M '03 Hamilton Cnty Probate Ct -230 E 9th
-10th Fl -Cincinnati 45202 **Fx:**946-3581

(419) 241-1150 .. **Bloom,** Charles E '72 (Herschel ABM&M) -615 Adams
-Toledo 43604 **Fx:**241-7825

(216) 781-4110 .. **Bloom,** Douglas E '01 %C Kampinski Co,LPA -1370 Ontario
-1530 Standard Bldg -Cleveland 44113 **Fx:**781-4178

(216) 522-3380 .. **Bloom,** Richard S '77 IRS -1375 E 9th -1200 -Cleveland 44114

(440) 729-7336 .. **Bloom,** Robert M '73 Bloom Brothers Supply -7941 Mayfld Rd
-Chesterland 44026

(216) 575-9100 .. **Bloom,** Stephen E '85 -526 Superior Av -Ste 833
-Cleveland 44114

(614) 236-8020 .. **Bloom,** Theodore S '80 Baker Rental Co -3319 E Lvngstn Av
-Columbus 43227

(202) 694-1605 .. **Bloom,** Tracy L '93 Fed Election Comm -999 E NW -6th Fl
-Washington, DC 20463 **Fx:**219-3923

(614) 224-9221 .. **Bloomfield,** David S '69 (Bloomfield & K) -199 S 5th
-Columbus 43215

(614) 227-2000 .. **Bloomfield,** David S Jr. '97 %Porter WM&A LLP -41 S High
-Columbus 43215 **Fx:**227-2100

(614) 224-9221 .. **Bloomfield & Kempf** -199 S 5th -Columbus 43215

(937) 438-5310 .. **Bloomfield,** Roger E '74 -Bx9218 -Dayton 45409 **Fx:**439-0022

(614) 227-2368 .. **Bloomfield,** Sally W '69 (Bricker & E LLP) -100 S 3rd -Columbus
43215 **Fx:**227-2390

(513) 742-6163 .. **Bloomhuff,** Amy B '91 ACGIH Worldwide
-1330 Kemper Meadow Dr -Cincinnati 45240

(614) 224-3080 .. **Blosser,** Jeffery M '98 %K O'Brien & Assoc Co,LPA -995 S High
-Columbus 43206

(614) 466-6696 .. **Blosser,** Keith D '90 Atty Gen -150 E Gay -Columbus 43215
Fx:752-2538

(314) 774-2929 .. **Blosser,** Timothy J '76 -Bx525 -Waynesville, MO 65583

                 Blough, Donna M '04 -(Address Unavailable)

                 Blower, George H '02 -38415 Forest -Columbus 43206

(704) 377-9200 .. **Blowers,** Erik B '89 FBI -400 S Tryon -Ste 900
-Charlotte, NC 28285

(614) 223-9300 .. **Blubaugh,** Marc S '97 (Benesch FC&A LLP) -88 E Broad -Ste 900
-Columbus 43215 **Fx:**223-9330

(740) 549-2202 .. **Blue,** Allan M '67 -5542 Columbus Pike -Ste D -Lewis Center
43035

(937) 298-1054 .. **Blue,** Charles M '01 %Murr CC&M -401 E Stroop Rd
-Kettering 45429 **Fx:**293-1766

(614) 224-6969 .. **Blue,** Douglas J '92 (Blue W+B LLC) -471 E Broad
-Columbus 43206 **Fx:**224-6999

(614) 224-6969 .. **Blue,** Jason A '64 (Blue W+B LLC) -471 E Broad
-Columbus 43215 **Fx:**224-6999

(614) 224-6969 .. **Blue Wilson + Blue LLC** -471 E Broad -Columbus 43215
Fx:224-6999

(330) 399-4554 .. **Bluedorn,** Samuel F '92 (Bluedorn & O Co,LPA) -144 N Park Av
-Ste 310 -Warren 44481 **Fx:**399-5112

(303) 443-1484 .. **Bluestein,** Philip M '93 -864 W S Boulder Rd -Ste 100
-Louisville, CO 80027

(614) 939-0985 .. **Bluestone,** Charles L '93 -6530 W Campus Oval -Ste 300
-New Albany 43054

(419) 241-6000 .. **Bluhm,** Graham A '95 (Eastman & S Ltd) -1 Seagate -24th Fl
-Bx10032 -Toledo 43699 **Fx:**247-1777

(614) 445-8416 .. **Blum,** Charles J '66 -52 W Whittier -Columbus 43206

(614) 445-8416 .. **Blum,** Jason C '00 -52 W Whittier -Columbus 43206

(216) 292-1144 .. **Blum,** Kevin R '93 -29325 Chagrin Blvd -Ste 200 -Cleveland 44122

(740) 574-2521 .. **Blume,** Thurl K '81 (Mowery & B) -9050 Ohio Rvr Rd
-Wheelersburg 45694

(215) 963-5000 .. **Blumenfeld,** Jeremy P '97 %Morgan,L&B LLP -1701 Market
-Philadelphia, PA 19103 **Fx:**963-5001

(614) 475-9511 .. **Blumenstiel,** Braden A '04 %Blumenstiel HA&E,LLC
-261 W Johnstown Rd -Columbus 43230 **Fx:**475-0348

(614) 475-9511 .. **Blumenstiel Huhn Adams & Evans,LLC** -261 W Johnstown Rd
-Columbus 43230 **Fx:**475-0348

(614) 475-9511 .. **Blumenstiel,** James B '67 (Blumenstiel HA&E,LLC)
-261 W Johnstown Rd -Columbus 43230 **Fx:**475-0348

(614) 475-9511 .. **Blumenstiel,** Laura C '97 Blumenstiel HA&E,LLC
-261 W Johnstown Rd -Columbus 43230 **Fx:**475-0348

(937) 224-7200 .. **Blumenthal,** Gary M '74 (Horenstein N&B) -124 E 3rd -5th Fl
-Dayton 45402 **Fx:**224-3353

(614) 220-9200 .. **Blumenthal,** Kenneth S '83 (Rourke & B,LLP) -495 S High
-Ste 450 -Columbus 43215 **Fx:**220-7900

(216) 514-9400 .. **Blumenthal,** Michael R '89 (Waxman B LLC) -29225 Chagrin Blvd
-Ste 350 -Cleveland 44122

(202) 994-6503 .. **Blumer,** Dennis H '67 GWU -2100 Penn Av NW -Rm 690
-Washington, DC 20052

(419) 522-6168 .. **Blunt,** James L II '94 -105 Sturges Av -Mansfield 44903

(216) 830-6823 .. **Bluso,** Linda L '82 (Brouse M) -1001 Lakeside Av -Ste 1600
-Cleveland 44114 **Fx:**830-6807

(513) 732-9191 .. **Blust,** Thomas L '73 -237 E Main -Batavia 45103

(614) 236-6124 .. **Bluth,** William H '70 Capital Univ Law Sch -303 E Broad
-Columbus 43215

(937) 223-1130 .. **Bly,** Loren M '89 Pickrel S&E -40 N Main -2700 Kettering Twr
-Dayton 45423 **Fx:**223-0339

(216) 360-7200 .. **Blythe-Glaze,** Amy M '99 %Carlisle MRK&U Co,LPA
-24755 Chagrin Blvd -Ste 200 -Cleveland 44122 **Fx:**360-7210

(330) 746-7575 .. **Boano,** Michael L '80 -412 Boardman-Canfld Rd -Boardman
44512 **Fx:**259-0603

(614) 221-2121 .. **Boatright,** Douglas C '89 Isaac BL&T,LLP -250 E Broad
-Ste 900 Mdlnd Bldg -Columbus 43215 **Fx:**365-9516

(440) 838-7600 .. **Boatwright,** Joseph W IV '04 %Janik & D,LLP -9200 S Hills Blvd
-Ste 300 -Cleveland 44147 **Fx:**838-7601

(330) 376-1242 .. **Bobak,** Donald J '73 Renner KGBT&W,LPA -106 S Main
-4th Fl First Natl Twr -Akron 44308 **Fx:**376-9646

(614) 462-3194 .. **Bobbitt,** Geoffrey C '82 Franklin Cnty Pub Def -373 S High
-12th Fl -Columbus 43215

(614) 889-2531 .. **Bobbitt,** Lawrence C '93 (Sanborn BD&B Co,LPA)
-2515 W Granvll Rd -Columbus 43235

(440) 234-1314 .. **Bobinsky,** Sylvester F '49 -31 E Brdg -203 -Bx367 -Berea 44017

(216) 771-6500 .. **Bobka,** Todd A '99 %K Weiner & Assoc Co,LPA -75 Pub Sq
-4th Fl -Cleveland 44113 **Fx:**771-6540

(937) 323-8777 .. **Boblitt,** Ronald R '86 -1 S Limestone -Ste 777 -Springfield 45502

(513) 421-3514 .. **BoBo,** Kevin T '96 -601 Main -3rd Fl -Cincinnati 45202

(330) 792-3313 .. **Bobovnyik,** David A '86 Industrial Commssn of OH
-242 Fed Plz W -Ste 303 -Youngstown 44503

(419) 241-6000 .. **Bobowick,** Morton '66 (Eastman & S Ltd) -1 Seagate -24th Fl
-Bx10032 -Toledo 43699 **Fx:**247-1777

(216) 696-3311 .. **Bobrow,** Howard J '96 (Kahn K) -1301 E 9th -2600 Erievw Twr
-Cleveland 44114 **Fx:**623-4912

(440) 998-4214 .. **Bobulsky,** William P '72 SrCnsl W Bobulsky Co,LPA
-1612 E Prospect Rd -Ashtabula 44004 **Fx:**992-7392

(216) 241-6045 .. **Boccardi,** Maria '94 1st Amer/Midland Title -1111 Superior Av
-Ste 700 -Cleveland 44114

(216) 587-1245 .. **Bocci,** Lawrence M '98 -20676 Southgate Park Blvd -103 -Maple
Heights 44137

(740) 587-4150 .. **Bocciardi,** John G '96 Paramount Finl Grp
-4009 Columbus Rd SW -Granville 43023

(216) 642-0323 .. **Bocciarelli,** Kathryn I '03 %Britton SP&K Co,LPA
-4700 Rockside Rd -Ste 540 Summit One -Cleveland 44131
Fx:642-0747

(216) 928-2200 .. **Bocciarelli**, Marco G '03 %Sutter OM&F -1301 E 9th
-3600 Erievw Twr -Cleveland 44114 Fx:928-4400

(419) 882-4570 .. **Bocik**, Edward J '74 Honeywell -7857 Saltwood Ct
-Sylvania 43560

(859) 341-1881 .. **Bock**, Angela '03 %Deters B&L -207 Thomas More Pkwy
-Crestview Hills, KY 41017

(330) 342-9778 .. **Bockanic**, William N '73 John Carroll Univ -7536 Warren Pnt Ln
-Hudson 44236

(614) 466-8600 .. **Bockbrader**, Katherine J '96 Atty Gen -30 E Broad
-Columbus 43215 Fx:466-6090

(614) 224-4114 .. **Boda**, Daniel K '75 (Mitchell AC&B Co,LPA) -580 S High -Ste 200
-Columbus 43215 Fx:224-3804

(920) 491-7001 .. **Bodager**, Brian R '80 Associated Banc-Corp -1200 Hansen Rd
-Green Bay, WI 54304

(937) 271-2727 .. **Boddie**, Kelvin L '85 -120 W 2nd -Ste 701 -Bx423 -Dayton 45402
Fx:837-3359

(216) 222-2991 .. **Boddy**, Carla D '96 Natl City Bank -1900 E 9th
-17th Fl Loc 01-2174 -Cleveland 44114

(216) 687-1311 .. **Bode**, Hugh J '78 (Reminger & R) -101 Prospect Av W
-1400 Mdlnd Bldg -Cleveland 44115 Fx:687-1841

(216) 579-1700 .. **Bodi**, Robert F '00 %Pearne & G LLP -1801 E 9th -Ste 1200
-Cleveland 44114 Fx:579-6073

(419) 254-4300 .. **Bodie**, John F Jr. '91 Marshall & M,LLC -420 Mad Av -Ste 1100
-Toledo 43604

(614) 466-5394 .. **Bodiker**, David H '63 Pub Def -8 E Long -Columbus 43215

(937) 223-3277 .. **Bodin**, John D '03 %Bieser G&L LLP -6 N Main -400 Natl City Ctr
-Dayton 45402 Fx:223-6339

(614) 644-7233 .. **Bodine**, John J Jr. '89 Atty Gen -150 E Gay -Columbus 43215
Fx:728-9327

(513) 677-1645 .. **Bodley**, James C '78 -957 Ashire Ct -Loveland 45140

(216) 692-1222 .. **Bodnar**, Brenda T '84 A Sirvaitis & Assoc -880 E 185th
-Cleveland 44119 Fx:531-8687

(216) 579-9100 .. **Bodnar**, Carol G '92 (Bodnar & B) -14805 Detroit Av -Ste 230
-Lakewood 44107

(513) 421-7300 .. **Bodnar**, Julie M '84 (Howard & B Co,LPA) -120 E 4th
-960 Mercantile Ctr -Cincinnati 45202

(216) 579-9100 .. **Bodnar**, Mark S '91 (Bodnar & B) -14805 Detroit Av -Ste 230
-Lakewood 44107

(440) 460-3600 .. **Bodnar**, Rebecca J '99 Marconi Comm Inc -5900 Landerbrook Dr
-Ste 300 -Cleveland 44124

(937) 898-1465 .. **Bodoh**, Emily D '00 %Scheuer M&B LLC -8565 N Dixie Dr
-Dayton 45414 Fx:898-1478

(614) 464-1211 .. **Bodoh**, William T '64 (Frost BT LLC) -10 W Broad -Ste 1000
-Columbus 43215 Fx:464-1737

(330) 393-4060 .. **Bodor**, Csaba A '72 (C Bodor Co,LPA) -280 N Park -Ste 108
-Warren 44481

(330) 399-2233 .. **Bodor**, Frank R '56 -157 Porter NE -Warren 44483 Fx:399-5165

(614) 777-4600 .. **Bodycombe**, Paul A '80 -3535 Fishinger Blvd -Ste 220
-Hilliard 43026

(330) 792-1063 .. **Bodzenta**, Dwayne J '88 Industrial Commssn of OH
-242 Fed Plz W -Ste 303 -Youngstown 44503

(330) 864-0500 .. **Boecker**, Gary J '83 OfCnsl Boecker & P,LPA -55 S Miller Rd
-Ste 200 -Fairlawn 44333 Fx:864-0520

(614) 228-1541 .. **Boeckman**, Joseph P '87 (Baker & H LLP) -65 E State -Ste 2100
-Columbus 43215 Fx:462-2616

(740) 522-8567 .. **Boeckman**, Ronald P '87 -619 Indstrl Pkwy -Bx2312 -Heath 43056

(419) 626-3800 .. **Boehk**, Robert P '85 (Reno B&F Co,LPA) -725 Sycamore Line
-Sandusky 44870 Fx:626-3638

(216) 621-1113 .. **Boehlefeld**, Heidi A '90 (Renner OB&S,LLP) -1621 Euclid Av
-19th Fl -Cleveland 44115 Fx:621-6165

(513) 421-2255 .. **Boehm**, David F '72 (Boehm K&L) -36 E 7th -2110 Society Bk Ctr
-Cincinnati 45202

(216) 623-0900 .. **Boehm**, David H '00 %McLaughlin & M,LLP -1111 Superior Av E
-Ste 1350 Eaton Ctr -Cleveland 44114 Fx:623-0935

(440) 734-8087 .. **Boehm**, Keith D '81 -25105 Linda Dr -North Olmsted 44070

(513) 421-2255 .. **Boehm**, Kurt J '03 %Boehm K&L -36 E 7th -2110 Society Bk Ctr
-Cincinnati 45202

(513) 421-2255 .. **Boehm Kurtz & Lowry** -36 E 7th -2110 Society Bk Ctr
-Cincinnati 45202

.. **Boesch**, James D '75 -5091 Lord Alfred Ct -Cincinnati 45241

(330) 744-1111 .. **Boetcher**, Martin J '87 Harrington H&M,Ltd -26 Market -Ste 1200
-Youngstown 44503 Fx:744-2029

(937) 767-2741 .. **Boettcher**, Barbara E '03 -105 W North Cllg
-Yellow Springs 45387

(248) 901-4035 .. **Boettcher**, Matthew J '02 %Plunkett & C,PC
-38505 Woodward Av -Ste 3000 -Bloomfield Hills, MI 48304

(330) 455-0173 .. **Boettler**, Louis A '55 Day KRW&R,Ltd -200 Market Av N -Ste 300
-Bx24213 -Canton 44701 Fx:455-2633

(304) 797-0602 .. **Bogarad**, Sharon N '85 -3412 West -Weirton, WV 26062

(614) 415-7100 .. **Bogart**, Amy '95 The Limited,Inc -3 Limited Pkwy
-Columbus 43230

(216) 443-4698 .. **Bogart**, Bruce P '75 -614 Superior Av W -Ste 836
-Cleveland 44113

(330) 497-0700 .. **Bogdan**, Michael J '04 %Krugliak WG&D Co,LPA
-4775 Munson NW -Bx36963 -Canton 44735 Fx:497-4020

(330) 643-2791 .. **Bogdanoff**, Philip D '81 Summit Cnty Pros-Crim -53 Univ Av
-7th Fl -Akron 44308 Fx:643-8277

(216) 583-1038 .. **Bogdanski**, Tammy L '99 Ernst & Young LLP -925 Euclid Av
-Cleveland 44115

(419) 626-3800 .. **Bogden**, Kenneth E '78 (Reno B&F Co,LPA) -725 Sycamore Line
-Sandusky 44870 Fx:626-3638

(330) 652-4529 .. **Bogen**, Curt P '89 -42 S Main -Ste 1000 -Niles 44446

(513) 503-7251 .. **Bogen**, James F '02 -119 E Court -Bx632 -Cincinnati 45202

(513) 932-4284 .. **Bogen**, Mark R '73 -41 N Bway -Lebanon 45036

(937) 766-4861 .. **Bogenschutz**, Stephen A '73 -61 N Main -Bx273
-Cedarville 45314

(740) 363-9412 .. **Boger**, Keith A '81 -61 N Sandusky -Delaware 43015

(330) 452-3003 .. **Boggins**, John V '86 -1428 Market Av N -Canton 44714

(419) 325-2458 .. **Boggioni**, Nicholas A '95 -2302 Gibley Park Rd -Toledo 43617

(513) 751-0115 .. **Boggs**, Duane A '84 -3936 Rose Hill Av -Cincinnati 45229

(202) 942-0572 .. **Boggs**, Elaine M '91 SEC -450 5th NW -Washington, DC 20549

(419) 241-6000 .. **Boggs**, John H '72 (Eastman & S Ltd) -1 Seagate -24th Fl
-Bx10032 -Toledo 43699 Fx:247-1777

(614) 464-6400 .. **Boggs**, Kelly A '98 %Vorys SS&P LLP -52 E Gay -Bx1008
-Columbus 43216 Fx:464-6350

(614) 451-9646 .. **Boggs**, Kenneth R '80 -1170 Old Henderson Rd -Ste 109
-Columbus 43220

(614) 228-4546 .. **Boggs**, Patrick H '85 Shuler P&B,LPA -145 E Rich -Ste 400
-Columbus 43215

(859) 647-9100 .. **Boggs**, Paul R III '84 (Boggs & C) -73 Cavalier Blvd -Ste 316
-Florence, KY 41042

(614) 464-6400 .. **Boggs**, Theodore A '86 OfCnsl Vorys SS&P LLP -52 E Gay
-Bx1008 -Columbus 43216 Fx:464-6350

(937) 226-1200 .. **Bogin Patterson & Bohman** -131 N Ludlow -1200 Talbot Twr
-Dayton 45402

(513) 241-3447 .. **Bogner**, Eugene P '88 -906 Main -405 Schwart Bldg
-Cincinnati 45202

(330) 497-0700 .. **Bogniard**, John J '72 (Krugliak WG&D Co,LPA)
-4775 Munson NW -Bx36963 -Canton 44735 Fx:497-4020

(216) 861-8888 .. **Bohac**, Edward T '97 %L Weiser Co,LPA -1419 W 9th
-Cleveland 44113

(614) 891-6920 .. **Bohan**, Gerald F '77 -1001 Eastwind Dr -Ste 203
-Westerville 43081

(614) 861-1350 .. **Bohan**, Michelle L '00 Oasis Corp -265 N Hmltn Rd
-Columbus 43213

(419) 476-7525 .. **Bohl**, Steven C '80 -534 Laskey Rd -Toledo 43612

(815) 939-1133 .. **Bohlen**, Christopher W '73 Barmann K&B -200 E Court -Ste 502
-Bx1787 -Kankakee, IL 60901

(513) 621-6556 .. **Bohlen**, Monica R '74 -36 E 7th -1520 CBLD Ctr -Cincinnati 45202

.. **Bohm**, Anneliese A '99 -88 Olentangy Pnt -Columbus 43202

(216) 464-2400 .. **Bohm**, Lori B '85 Austin Powder Co -25800 Science Park Dr
-Beachwood 44122

(216) 831-0284 .. **Bohm**, Marvin R '77 -24800 Chagrin Blvd -Beachwood 44122

(937) 226-1200 .. **Bohman**, Jerome B '59 (Bogin P&B) -131 N Ludlow -1200
Talbot Twr -Dayton 45402

(419) 213-4755 .. **Bohmer**, Julie E '96 %Hon ML Pietrykowski -800 Jackson
-Toledo 43624

(419) 241-2100 .. **Bohmer**, Robert W '94 Watkins B&C -405 Mad Av -Ste 1900
-Toledo 43604 Fx:241-1960

(414) 297-3395 .. **Bohn**, James F '84 US Dept of Justice -1000 N Water -Ste 1010
-Milwaukee, WI 53202

.. **Bohner**, Michael D '04 -1012 S Byrne Rd -Ste 34 -Toledo 43609

(330) 425-4201 .. **Bohnert**, Edward G '80 -2450 Edison Blvd -Bx968
-Twinsburg 44087

(419) 876-3600 .. **Bohrer**, Bruce B '83 -11413 Road G -Ottawa 45875

(330) 343-8848 .. **Bohse**, Frederick H '68 Woodard & B -121 W 3rd -Dover 44622
Fx:343-3496

(614) 466-8911 .. **Boiarsky**, Megan H '04 Atty Gen -30 E Broad -Columbus 43215
Fx:728-7582

(216) 459-1405 .. **Boigner**, David P '77 -7520 Wefel Av -Brooklyn 44144

(888) 901-4647 .. **Boikova**, Nataliya A '03 Mortg Info Srvc -4877 Galaxy Pkwy
-Cleveland 44128

(216) 566-5785 .. **Boise**, April V '00 (Thompson H LLP) -127 Pub Sq -3900 Key Ctr
-Cleveland 44114 Fx:566-5800

(216) 368-8849 .. **Boise**, Craig M '00 %CWRU Law Schl -11075 East Blvd
-Cleveland 44106

(216) 621-1113 .. **Boisselle**, Armand P Sr. '65 (Renner OB&S,LLP) -1621 Euclid Av
-19th Fl -Cleveland 44115 Fx:621-6165

(419) 843-2001 .. **Boissoneault**, Kevin J '88 (Gallon & T Co,LPA) -3516 Granite Cir
-Bx352018 -Toledo 43635 Fx:843-6665

(614) 252-8066 .. **Boiston**, Bernard G '69 -1620 E Broad -Ste 107 -Columbus 43203

.. **Bojanowski**, Timothy J '83 -Bx16261 -Phoenix, AZ 85011

(614) 227-2000 .. **Bojko**, Andrew M '98 %Porter WM&A LLP -41 S High
-Columbus 43215 Fx:227-2100

(614) 466-7967 .. **Bojko**, Kimberly W '98 OH Consumers' Cnsl -10 W Broad
-Ste 1800 -Columbus 43215 Fx:466-9475

(419) 636-3166 .. **Bok**, Kelli S '03 %Gallagher S&Y,Ltd -216 S Lynn -Bryan 43506
Fx:636-5743

(614) 462-3555 .. **Bokelman**, Christopher '99 Franklin Cnty Pros -373 S High
-Columbus 43215

(330) 544-4002 .. **Boker**, David E '75 -724 Youngstown Rd -Niles 44446
Fx:544-4110

(216) 749-0808 .. **Bokor**, David B '93 %L Kravitz -4508 State Rd -Cleveland 44109

(513) 627-7533 .. **Bolam**, Brian M '93 Procter & Gamble Co -5299 Spring Grove Av
-Ivorydale Tech Ctr -Cincinnati 45217

(937) 848-6711 .. **Boland**, Amy S '81 -45 W Franklin -Bellbrook 45305

(216) 635-0636 .. **Boland**, Dean M '95 -3723 Pearl Rd -Cleveland 44109

(614) 734-1270 .. **Boland**, James A Jr. '02 %Farlow & Assoc LLC -270 Bradenton Av
-Dublin 43017 Fx:923-1031

(419) 726-3450 .. **Boldt**, Daniel J '86 -4912 N Summit -Toledo 43611

(419) 734-6845 .. **Boldt**, David R '85 Ottawa Cnty Pros -315 Madison -2nd Fl
-Port Clinton 43452 Fx:734-3862

(440) 884-4300 .. **Boldt**, David R '86 (Kirner & B Co,LPA) -8025 Corp Cir
-North Royalton 44133 Fx:884-4302

(513) 946-6611 .. **Boldt**, Edwin H Jr. '68 Hamilton Cnty Sheriffs Ofc -1000 Sycamore
-Rm 110 -Cincinnati 45202

(216) 623-1123 .. **Bolek**, Cathleen M '92 (Sindell YG&S,PLL) -55 Pub Sq -Ste 1020
-Cleveland 44113 Fx:623-1124

(216) 831-0004 .. **Bolek**, Joseph F Jr. '67 -3659 Green Rd -Ste 200
-Cleveland 44122 Fx:831-5051

(614) 430-9258 .. **Bolen**, Alan L '83 -1000 High -Ste G -Worthington 43085

(304) 529-6181 .. **Bolen**, Richard J '98 (Huddleston BBP&C,LLP) -611 3rd Av
-Bx2185 -Huntington, WV 25722 Fx:522-4310

(440) 205-3600 .. **Boles**, Edgar H II '73 Driggs LB&H Co,LPA -8522 East Av
-Mentor 44060 Fx:205-3601

(419) 586-1072 .. **Boley**, Leisa R '94 -4590 Miller Rd -Celina 45822

(330) 753-7777 .. **Boley**, Thomas R '74 City of Barberton -682 W Tuscarawas Av
-Barberton 44203

(513) 523-6369 .. **Bolin**, Larry R '97 -29 N Beech -Oxford 45056

(513) 421-2500 .. **Bolin**, Linda S '85 McKinney & N Co,LPA -15 E 8th -Cincinnati
45202 Fx:632-5898

.. **Boling**, Ellis D '82 -6106 Catawba Dr -Grove City 43123

(513) 422-4861 .. **Bolinger**, Bradley D '88 -16 N Main -Middletown 45042

(216) 621-2234 .. **Bolinger**, Brian W '02 %Tarolli SC&T -526 Superior Av
-1111 Leader Bldg -Cleveland 44114 Fx:621-4072

(336) 293-9000 ..**Bolinger,** Maureen Connolly '97 %Blanco TC&M,PA
-110 S Stratford Rd -5th Fl -Drwr25008
-Winston Salem, NC 27114

(513) 241-3100 ..**Boll,** Edward J III '00 %Lerner S&R -120 E 4th -8th Fl
-Cincinnati 45202

(814) 833-2222 ..**Bolla,** Lawrence C '97 %Quinn BLT&K -2222 W Grandvw Blvd
-Erie, PA 16506

(614) 466-3339 ..**Boller,** Jack A '81 Industrial Commssn of OH -30 W Spring -9th Fl
-Columbus 43215 **Fx:**752-8785

(937) 492-6125 ..**Boller,** Michael F '64 (Kerrigan BSG&B) -126 N Main Av -Bx987
-Sidney 45365

(513) 946-9000 ..**Boller-Koch,** Kathryn M '89 Hamilton Cnty Juv Ct -800 Bway
-Cincinnati 45202 **Fx:**946-9217

(513) 421-4248 ..**Bollhauer,** Raymond G '90 Amer Lgl Pub Corp -432 Walnut
-Ste 1200 -Cincinnati 45202 **Fx:**763-3562

(216) 566-5786 ..**Bollin,** Kip T '95 (Thompson H LLP) -127 Pub Sq -3900 Key Ctr
-Cleveland 44114 **Fx:**566-5800

(419) 222-1040 ..**Bollinger,** Christine M '02 -400 W North -Lima 45801

(419) 690-7100 ..**Bollinger,** Ernest E '92 -Bx167796 -Oregon 43616

(419) 690-7100 ..**Bollinger,** Mary M '84 -Bx167796 -Oregon 43616

(216) 781-7990 ..**Bolmeyer,** Franklin G Jr. '81 (Sammon & B Co,LPA)
-614 Superior Av NW -1160 Rckfllr Bldg -Cleveland 44113

(614) 338-8485 ..**Bolon,** David D '92 Foundation Title Agency -2831 E Main
-Columbus 43209

Bolon, Gordon K '53 -Bx493 -Granville 43023

(614) 236-2222 ..**Bolon,** Thomas M Jr. '91 Bolon Co -2513A E Main -Bexley 43209

(614) 693-6841 ..**Bolon,** William T '88 DFAS -3990 E Broad -Bldg 21 -Bx182317
-Columbus 43218

(216) 861-4357 ..**Bolotin,** Fredric N '90 Krainess Law Firm -13882 Cedar Rd
-Rm 1 Lwr Level -Cleveland 44118

(513) 721-1200 ..**Bolotin,** Jay A '96 %Young R&M Co,LPA -1014 Vine -Ste 2400
-Cincinnati 45202 **Fx:**721-7116

(419) 472-1900 ..**Bolotin,** Samuel G '75 -4349 Talmadge Rd -Toledo 43623

(419) 866-6060 ..**Bolotin,** Sandra C '79 -5241 Southwyck Blvd -Ste 107
-Toledo 43614

(513) 621-7878 ..**Bolsinger,** Gregg D '86 (Bolsinger & B) -830 Main
-Cincinnati 45202 **Fx:**621-7880

(305) 232-9035 ..**Bolton,** Donald E '67 Plumbers Parts Inc -8789 SW 129 Ter
-Miami, FL 33176

(614) 891-6530 ..**Bolton,** James G '82 -14 Huber Vllg Blvd -Westerville 43081

(216) 443-7800 ..**Bolton,** Pamela A '99 Cuyahoga Cnty Pros -1200 Ontario -8th Fl
-Cleveland 44113 **Fx:**698-2270

(330) 743-1171 ..**Bolton,** Stephen T '72 (Manchester BP&U) -201 E Commerce
-Atrium Level 2 Commerce Bldg -Youngstown 44503
Fx:743-1190

(740) 653-1902 ..**Boltz,** G Brian '59 -109 E Main -Ste 205 Fairfld Fed Bldg
-Lancaster 43130 **Fx:**653-1951

(614) 365-2700 ..**Bolyard,** Beth C '01 %Squire S&D LLP -41 S High
-1300 Huntngtn Ctr -Columbus 43215 **Fx:**365-2499

(734) 261-4700 ..**Bolz,** Ronald J '91 Consumer Leg Srvcs -30928 Ford Rd
-Garden City, MI 48135

(330) 373-7298 ..**Bombeck,** Scott C '84 -269 Seneca Av NE -Warren 44481

(216) 479-8500 ..**Bomberger,** Jeffrey A '86 Cnsl Squire S&D LLP -127 Pub Sq
-4900 Key Twr -Cleveland 44114 **Fx:**479-8780

(216) 443-7800 ..**Bombik,** Richard J '78 Cuyahoga Cnty Pros -1200 Ontario -8th Fl
-Cleveland 44113 **Fx:**698-2270

(989) 799-3033 ..**Bommarito,** Alexander D '99 %Collison & C,PC
-5811 Colony Dr N -Bx6010 -Saginaw, MI 48608

(216) 621-2034 ..**Bompiedi,** Michelle T '04 %Margolius M & Assoc,LPA -55 Pub Sq
-Ste 1100 -Cleveland 44113 **Fx:**621-1908

(248) 948-1010 ..**Bon,** William A Jr. '83 BMWE -20300 Civic Ctr Dr -Ste 320
-Southfield, MI 48076 **Fx:**948-7150

(216) 664-4844 ..**Bonacci,** Louis M '73 Prosecutor -1200 Ontario Av
-8th Fl Justice Ctr -Cleveland 44113 **Fx:**664-4399

(216) 896-1410 ..**Bonaguro,** Mark N '90 Tyco Suppession Sys -200 Auburn Dr
-Ste 400 -Beachwood 44122

(814) 452-6232 ..**Bonanti,** John M '96 (Bernard S&B) -234 W 6th -Erie, PA 16507

(859) 431-3333 ..**Bonar,** Barbara D '90 -3611 Decoursey Av -Covington, KY 41015

(866) 837-8847 ..**Bonar,** Byron K '79 LAWO -20 S Limestone -Ste 220
-Springfield 45502 **Fx:**(937) 323-0291

(859) 431-6100 ..**Bonar,** John A '83 Arnzen & W,PSC -600 Greenup
-Covington, KY 41011 **Fx:**431-3778

(614) 461-1100 ..**Bonasera,** Michael D '03 %Swedlow BLL&D Co,LPA -10 W Broad
-Ste 2400 -Columbus 43215 **Fx:**461-8178

(614) 469-3259 ..**Bonasera,** Thomas J '75 (Thompson H LLP) -10 W Broad
-Ste 700 -Columbus 43215 **Fx:**469-3361

(614) 466-2766 ..**Bonaventura,** Mark G '79 Atty Gen -30 E Broad -Columbus 43215
Fx:644-1926

(216) 321-0388 ..**Boncella,** Elizabeth W '77 -2297 Lamberton Rd
-Cleveland Heights 44118

(216) 328-0436 ..**Boncella,** Gary A '78 Local 436 Pension Fund -6051 Carey Dr
-Valley View 44125

(330) 384-7306 ..**Bonchack,** Robert M '75 FirstMerit Trust -121 S Main -#200
-Akron 44308

(614) 462-5200 ..**Bond,** Anthony R '93 Franklin Cnty CSEA -80 E Fulton
-Columbus 43215

(440) 285-3123 ..**Bond,** Daniel E '75 (Bond & S,LPA) -109 Main -Chardon 44024

(513) 852-3497 ..**Bond,** Dianna K '90 Atty Gen -441 Vine -1600 Carew Twr
-Cincinnati 45202 **Fx:**852-3484

(330) 492-4717 ..**Bond,** Douglas C '89 -1428 Market Av N -Canton 44714

(513) 651-6800 ..**Bond,** Kasey L '04 %Frost BT LLC -201 E 5th -2200 PNC Ctr
-Cincinnati 45202 **Fx:**651-6981

(614) 462-3555 ..**Bond,** Kimberly MacVicar '03 Franklin Cnty Pros -373 S High
-Columbus 43215

(440) 930-4001 ..**Bond,** Stephen P '76 (Baumgartner & O)
-5455 Detroit Rd (Rte 254) -Sheffield Village 44054 **Fx:**934-7205

(330) 225-1288 ..**Bonda,** Thomas J '92 RocCorp Inc -1113 Indstrl Pkwy N
-Brunswick 44212

(216) 595-4903 ..**Bonder,** Daniel L '84 Cleveland Finl Grp -28601 Chagrin Blvd
-Ste 300 -Cleveland 44122

(216) 381-8470 ..**Bondra,** Anthony J '86 -1414 S Green Rd -Ste 310
-Cleveland 44121

(440) 933-4469 ..**Bonds,** William T '64 Helical Line Products -659 Miller Rd -Bx217
-Avon Lake 44012

(614) 222-8686 ..**Bondy,** Melissa Martinez '96 %Scott S&W LLP -50 W Broad
-2500 LeVeque Twr -Columbus 43215 **Fx:**222-8688

(614) 865-8515 ..**Bondy,** Michael S '01 Exel -570 Polaris Pkwy -Westerville 43082

(859) 491-2300 ..**Bonecutter-Tulley,** Brenda L '98 -530 York -Barrister Bldg
-Newport, KY 41071

(330) 376-9691 ..**Bonetti,** Albert E Jr. '87 -441 Wolf Ledges Pkwy -Ste 302
-Akron 44311

(419) 241-1200 ..**Boney,** Jacqueline M '76 %Cooper & W,LPA -900 Adams
-Toledo 43624 **Fx:**242-5675

(216) 875-2767 ..**Bonezzi Switzer Murphy & Polito Co LPA** -526 Superior Av
-Ste 1400 -Cleveland 44114 **Fx:**875-1570

(216) 875-2767 ..**Bonezzi,** William D '73 (Bonezzi SM&P Co LPA) -526 Superior Av
-Ste 1400 -Cleveland 44114 **Fx:**875-1570

(614) 258-6063 ..**Bonfield,** Lauren B '03 -206 N Drexel Av -Bexley 43209

(937) 333-4100 ..**Bonfield,** Patrick J '73 Law Dept -101 W 3rd -Bx22 -Dayton 45402

(419) 243-2100 ..**Bonfiglio,** Michael A '85 (Connelly J&C LLP) -405 Mad Av
-Ste 1600 -Toledo 43604 **Fx:**243-7119

(419) 241-9770 ..**Bonfiglio,** Paul R '89 (Vassar DD&B,LLC) -420 Mad Av -Ste 1102
-Toledo 43604 **Fx:**241-9771

(740) 676-3473 ..**Bonfini,** Emilio M '50 -57661 48th -Bellaire 43906

(859) 357-7342 ..**Bongard,** Charles M '85 Ashland Inc -Bx14000
-Lexington, KY 40512

(216) 522-3530 ..**Bongiovanni,** Franklin V '84 US DVA -1240 E 9th
-Cleveland 44199

(440) 366-4792 ..**Bonham,** Brian W '03 OSU Ext -1005 Abbe Rd N -SP 220
-Elyria 44035

(513) 695-1569 ..**Bonham,** Mitchell W '76 Warren Cnty CSEA -500 Justice Dr
-Lebanon 45036

(614) 478-8020 ..**Bonham,** William T '88 -107 W Johnstown Rd -Gahanna 43230

(513) 861-9978 ..**Bonhaus,** Laurence A '76 -948 Dana Av -Cincinnati 45229

(419) 241-9000 ..**Bonini,** Aleta M '79 (Shumaker L&K,LLP) -1000 Jackson
-Toledo 43624 **Fx:**241-6894

(216) 621-8484 ..**Bonk,** Colleen M '96 %Climaco LPW&G Co,LPA -1228 Euclid Av
-Ste 900 Halle Bldg -Cleveland 44115 **Fx:**771-1632

(216) 622-8200 ..**Bonko,** Robert J '93 Calfee H&G LLP -800 Superior Av -Ste 1400
-Cleveland 44114 **Fx:**241-0816

(312) 641-2100 ..**Bonneau,** Steven M '94 %Handler T&D,LLC -191 N Wacker Dr
-23rd Fl -Chicago, IL 60606 **Fx:**641-6866

(216) 622-8200 ..**Bonner,** Chet J '02 %Calfee H&G LLP -800 Superior Av -Ste 1400
-Cleveland 44114 **Fx:**241-0816

(216) 514-1100 ..**Bonsall,** Eric J '03 %Rolf & G Co,LPA -30100 Chagrin Blvd
-Ste 350 Corp Cir -Cleveland 44124 **Fx:**514-0030

(330) 666-3591 ..**Bonsky,** Jack A '64 -4234 Idlebrook Dr -Akron 44333

(330) 456-8361 ..**Bonta,** Darlene B '94 Cmmnty Lgl Aid Srvcs,Inc -306 Market Av N
-Ste 730 -Canton 44702

(216) 687-1900 ..**Bonthius,** Robert H Jr. '76 Legal Aid -1223 W 6th
-Cleveland 44113 **Fx:**687-0779

(330) 253-1555 ..**Booher,** Debra E '97 (D Booher & Assoc Co,LPA) -3180 W Market
-Fairlawn 44333

Booher, Mark S '90 -1120 E Rookwood Dr -Cincinnati 45208

(937) 775-5857 ..**Booher,** Michael R '81 Cnsl Wright State/Stdnt Lgl Srvcs
-3640 Colonel Glenn Hwy -W015 Student Union -Dayton 45435
Fx:775-5858

(740) 355-0073 ..**Book,** Thomas T '94 -800 Gallia -Ste 800 -Bx548
-Portsmouth 45662

(216) 787-5224 ..**Booker,** Lisa '92 State of OH -615 Superior Av -Cleveland 44113

(513) 946-3000 ..**Books,** Diane E '82 Hamilton Cnty Pros -230 E 9th
-Cincinnati 45202 **Fx:**946-3017

(937) 866-2485 ..**Bookwalter,** Thomas E '70 (Baver & B Co,LPA) -202 E Central Av
-Miamisburg 45342

(740) 654-5704 ..**Boone,** Mary A '92 -260 Scott Dr -Lancaster 43130

(614) 228-0200 ..**Boone,** Timothy J '76 (TJ Boone Co,LPA) -1349 E Broad -2nd Fl
-Columbus 43205 **Fx:**358-9814

(216) 241-5310 ..**Boop,** Gregory K '97 %Gallagher SF&N -1501 Euclid Av -6th Fl
-Cleveland 44115 **Fx:**241-1608

(513) 651-6800 ..**Boord,** L Roger '03 Cnsl Frost BT LLC -201 E 5th -2200 PNC Ctr
-Cincinnati 45202 **Fx:**651-6981

(614) 785-0054 ..**Boord,** Lawrence F '75 (Boord & Assoc) -951B High
-Worthington 43085

(614) 895-1070 ..**Bootes,** Wendi S '98 Countrytyme Inc -4218 Hoover Rd
-Grove City 43123

(614) 692-3284 ..**Booth,** Gail L '90 US Dfnse Lgstcs Agncy -Bx3990
-Columbus 43218

(937) 222-2500 ..**Booth,** Michael A '95 (Sebaly S&D) -1900 Kettering Twr
-Dayton 45423 **Fx:**222-6554

(740) 432-3281 ..**Booth,** Russell H Jr. '57 -745 Steubenvll Av -Cambridge 43725

(614) 784-9451 ..**Booth,** Sandra E '79 -3620 N High -Ste 310 -Columbus 43214

(740) 654-1892 ..**Booth,** Victoria M '79 -1826 Plsnt Vw Dr NE -Lancaster 43130

(304) 485-8500 ..**Boothby,** Richard S '03 %Bowles RMG&L -501 Avry -5th Fl
-Parkersburg, WV 26101

(740) 769-7219 ..**Boothe,** Lawrence I '79 Boothe Law Ofc -Main & Lbrty -Bx684
-Dillonvale 43917

(734) 764-2178 ..**Boothman,** Richard C '97 Univ of Michigan -300 N Ingalls Bldg
-Rm 3804 -Ann Arbor, MI 48109

(740) 454-2545 ..**Bopeley,** Thomas R '58 OfCnsl Micheli BN Co,LPA
-3808 James Ct -Ste 2 -Bx788 -Zanesville 43702

(216) 687-1311 ..**Borchelt,** Joseph W '02 %Reminger & R -101 Prospect Av W
-1400 Mdlnd Bldg -Cleveland 44115 **Fx:**687-1841

(614) 466-8838 ..**Borchert,** Daniel R '78 OH Ct of Claims -65 S Front -1st Fl
-Columbus 43215

(216) 344-9220 ..**Borchert,** Kimberly L '02 %McGinty GH&S Co,LPA
-614 W Superior Av -Ste 1300 -Cleveland 44113

(330) 499-2396 ..**Borcoman,** Tom A '74 -5438 Isl Dr NW -Canton 44718

(304) 242-8410 ..**Bordas,** James G III '01 (Bordas & B,PLLC) -1358 Natl Rd
-Wheeling, WV 26003 **Fx:**242-3936

(304) 242-8410 ..**Bordas,** Linda M '85 (Bordas & B,PLLC) -1358 Natl Rd
-Wheeling, WV 26003

(614) 239-4014 ..**Borden,** Rod C '81 Regional Airport Auth -4600 Intl Gtwy
-Columbus 43219 **Fx:**238-7834

(330) 796-6738 ..**Bordenkircher,** Steven C '98 Goodyear Tire & Rubber Co
-1144 E Market -Akron 44316

(216) 263-6200 ..**Borders,** Keith L '00 Rauser & Assoc,LPA -614 W Superior Av
-Ste 950 -Cleveland 44113 **Fx:**263-6202

Bordner, Kellie D '93 -6892 Slippery Rock Dr -Canfield 44406
(419) 213-2001 ..**Borell**, John A '81 %Lucas Cnty Pros -Adams & Erie
   -Lucas Cnty Cthse -Toledo 43624
(419) 249-7100 ..**Borell**, John A Jr. '97 Marshall & M,LLC -Four Seagate -8th Fl
   -Toledo 43604 **Fx:**249-7151
(202) 434-1300 ..**Borer**, David A '83 Cnsl Assn Flght Attndnts CWA AFL-CIO
   -501 3rd NW -Washington, DC 20001 **Fx:**434-0690
(419) 523-3322 ..**Borer**, Michael A '86 -125 W Main -Bx327 -Ottawa 45875
   Fx:523-6285
(513) 556-6361 ..**Borger**, Patricia A '93 Univ of Cincinnati Fndtn -Bx19970
   -Cincinnati 45219
(419) 841-9623 ..**Borgess**, Pamela A '00 Zoll & K -6620 W Central Av -Ste 200
   -Toledo 43617
(513) 744-9600 ..**Borgmann**, Barbara A '00 %Javitch B&R -602 Main -Ste 500
   -Cincinnati 45202 **Fx:**744-9602
(419) 842-1166 ..**Borgstahl**, Gene T '84 (Borgstahl & Z) -6591 W Central Av
   -Ste 201 -Toledo 43617
(419) 842-1166 ..**Borgstahl & Zychowicz** -6591 W Central Av -Ste 201
   -Toledo 43617
   Boring, Deron M '04 -(Address Unavailable)
(317) 861-4497 ..**Boring**, Gary L '95 (Boring & C PC) -11782 N Main -Bx100
   -Fountaintown, IN 46130
(216) 566-5527 ..**Bork**, Derek D '96 (Thompson H LLP) -127 Pub Sq -3900 Key Ctr
   -Cleveland 44114 **Fx:**566-5800
(202) 418-0626 ..**Borkowski**, John J '76 FCC-Wireless Telecomm Bur
   -445 12th SW -Rm 6604 -Washington, DC 20554
(330) 670-7300 ..**Borla**, Robert B '04 %Hanna C&P,LLP -3737 Embssy Pkwy
   -Bx5521 -Akron 44334 **Fx:**670-0977
(513) 721-5151 ..**Borland**, Cheryl L '95 %Katz G&N,LLP -105 E 4th -4th Fl
   -Cincinnati 45202 **Fx:**621-9285
(419) 782-9492 ..**Borland**, James S '69 (Borland & B) -110 Clinton -Defiance 43512
   Fx:782-5482
(937) 323-0966 ..**Borley**, Robert L '75 -4 W Main -Ste 720 -Springfield 45502
(216) 522-4914 ..**Borling**, David C '74 SSA/OHA -1350 Euclid Av -7th Fl
   -Cleveland 44115
(419) 247-1716 ..**Borman**, Amy J '90 (Eastman & S Ltd) -1 Seagate -24th Fl
   -Bx10032 -Toledo 43699 **Fx:**247-1777
(614) 463-9441 ..**Born**, Michael E '88 (Shumaker L&K,LLP) -41 S High -Ste 2210
   -Columbus 43215 **Fx:**463-1108
(513) 768-4626 ..**Borne**, Troy A '95 PricewaterhouseCoopers -720 E
   Pete Rose Way -Ste 400 -Cincinnati 45202
(330) 365-3214 ..**Bornhorst**, Amanda S '89 Tuscarawas Cnty Pros -101 E High Av
   -Ste 103 -New Philadelphia 44663 **Fx:**364-4135
(860) 522-5175 ..**Bornhorst**, Kathleen F '84 (Pepe & H LLP) -225 Asylum
   -Goodwin Sq -Hartford, CT 06103 **Fx:**522-2796
(216) 222-9038 ..**Bornhorst**, Nicole K '95 Natl City Bk -1900 E 9th
   -Cleveland 44114
(740) 687-5645 ..**Bornstein**, Meredith L '00 K Burkett -118 W Chestnut
   -Lancaster 43130
   Bornstein, Michael D '89 -67 E Kossuth -Columbus 43206
(216) 689-3918 ..**Boron**, Martin C '82 KeyBank NA -127 Pub Sq -Cleveland 44114
(440) 843-8089 ..**Borosh**, Lawrence P '70 -6691 Big Crk Pkwy -Cleveland 44130
(614) 431-8110 ..**Borowicz**, Louis M '04 %TE Baxter & Assoc Co,LPA
   -150 W Wilson Bridge Rd -Ste 101 -Worthington 43085
   Fx:431-8120
(614) 227-2000 ..**Borowicz**, Stacey A '03 %Porter WM&A LLP -41 S High
   -Columbus 43215 **Fx:**227-2100
(740) 455-7123 ..**Borowitz**, Paul J '65 Muskingum Cnty Pros -27 N 5th
   -Zanesville 43701
(419) 291-5826 ..**Borrillo**, Donato J '97 ProMedica Hlth Syst -2150 W Central Av
   -Toledo 43606
(619) 557-5081 ..**Borsh**, Judith A '76 Ofc of Hearings & Appls -750 B -Ste 1100
   -San Diego, CA 92101
(513) 785-7327 ..**Borst**, Samuel D '89 Hamilton Law Dept -345 High -2nd Fl
   -Hamilton 45011
(216) 696-8730 ..**Bortnick**, Daniel B '00 %Amin & T LLP -1900 E 9th
   -24th Fl Natl City Ctr -Cleveland 44114 **Fx:**696-8731
(513) 381-8696 ..**Bortz**, Christopher N '03 Towne Properties -1055 St Paul Pl
   -Cincinnati 45202
(513) 772-7844 ..**Bortz**, Lee '50 -9941 Hunters Pl -Cincinnati 45249
(419) 727-5442 ..**Borysiak**, David E '83 Faurecia -543 Matzinger Rd -Bx64010
   -Toledo 43612
   Bosak, Jodi L '04 -(Address Unavailable)
(303) 336-4568 ..**Bosch**, Anthony R '90 Berger, LLC -210 Univ Av -Ste 900
   -Denver, CO 80206
(440) 944-4443 ..**Bosco**, John W '72 (J Bosco Co,LPA) -31805 Vine -Willowick
   44095
(404) 897-4425 ..**Boshinski**, Thomas A '81 Mead Corp -4850D N Church Ln
   -Smyrna, GA 30080
(412) 263-2000 ..**Bosick**, Joseph J '91 (Pietragallo B&G) -One Oxford Ctr
   -Pittsburgh, PA 15219 **Fx:**261-5295
(231) 946-6428 ..**Bosio**, Christopher J '97 Cintas Corp -10753 E. Cherry Bend Dr
   -Traverse City, MI 49684
(330) 455-6400 ..**Boske**, Michael A '95 -122 Market Av N -Canton 44702
(614) 840-3697 ..**Bosko**, Marybeth '93 Worthington Ind,Inc -1205 Dearborn Dr
   -Columbus 43085
(614) 469-5715 ..**Bosley**, David J '78 US Atty -303 Marconi Blvd -Ste 200
   -Columbus 43215
(419) 893-5555 ..**Boss**, Charles M '81 (Boss & V Co,LPA) -111 W Dudley
   -Maumee 43537 **Fx:**893-2797
(419) 241-6000 ..**Boss**, Mark H '97 %Eastman & S Ltd -1 Seagate -24th Fl
   -Bx10032 -Toledo 43699 **Fx:**247-1777
(419) 893-5555 ..**Boss & Vitou Co,LPA** -111 W Dudley -Maumee 43537
   Fx:893-2797
(614) 464-2572 ..**Bossart**, Emily J '04 %Harris MB&C,PLL -37 W Broad -9th Fl
   -Columbus 43215 **Fx:**464-2245
(513) 397-7730 ..**Bosse**, Thomas W '95 Broadwing Inc -201 E 4th -Ste 102-620
   -Cincinnati 45202
(614) 659-1644 ..**Bosserman**, Eric L '97 WA Butler Co -5600 Blazer Pkwy
   -Dublin 43017
(440) 646-1881 ..**Bossin**, Kenneth A '71 -1392 SOM Center Rd
   -Mayfield Heights 44124
(513) 421-4420 ..**Bossin**, Phyllis G '77 (P Bossin Co,LPA) -36 E 4th -Ste 1210
   -Cincinnati 45202

(419) 247-2500 ..**Bostelman**, Lisa L '01 %Fuller & H,Ltd -One SeaGate -Ste 1700
   -Bx2088 -Toledo 43603 **Fx:**247-2665
(513) 762-6200 ..**Boster**, B Scott '85 (Ulmer & B LLP) -600 Vine -Ste 2800
   -Cincinnati 45202 **Fx:**762-6245
(614) 529-8600 ..**Bostic**, Amy L '88 OfCnsl Nobile N&T,LLC -4511 Cemetery Rd
   -Ste B -Hilliard 43026 **Fx:**529-8656
(330) 281-3936 ..**Bostick**, Robin G '97 -Bx1040 -Ravenna 44266
(419) 724-7000 ..**Bostleman**, William Lee '91 Bostleman Corp -Bx1390
   -Maumee 43537
(614) 890-2111 ..**Boston**, Shannon C '97 Porter Drywall -297 Old Cnty Line Rd
   -Bx550 -Westerville 43086 **Fx:**890-0375
(440) 333-8960 ..**Bostwick**, John M Jr. '86 %Kenneally & Assoc Co
   -20525 Ctr Ridge Rd -Ste 505 -Rocky River 44116 **Fx:**333-8170
(216) 664-2689 ..**Bosu**, Linda M '99 Dept of Law -601 Lakeside Av -Rm
   106 City Hall -Cleveland 44114 **Fx:**664-2663
(740) 283-2535 ..**Boswell**, Jerry L '75 -139 N 3rd -Steubenville 43952
(614) 481-6999 ..**Bosworth**, Angela L '91 Open Online -1650 Lk Shr Dr -Ste 350
   -Columbus 43204
   Botek, Frederick G '96 -2932 Sherbrook Valley Ct
   -Willoughby 44094
(937) 299-7482 ..**Bothmann**, Randall N '70 -2550 S Patterson Blvd -Dayton 45409
   Botnick, Robert B '04 -(Address Unavailable)
(937) 435-7500 ..**Botros Behnke & Schulte,LLC** -5785 Far Hills Av -Dayton 45429
   Fx:435-7511
(937) 435-7500 ..**Botros**, Michael R '96 (Botros B&S,LLC) -5785 Far Hills Av
   -Dayton 45429 **Fx:**435-7511
   Botschner, Andrew T '88 -5676 Eaglesrdg Ln -Cincinnati 45230
(614) 221-4000 ..**Bott**, April R '96 SrCnsl Chester W&S LLP -65 E State -10th Fl
   -Columbus 43215 **Fx:**221-4012
(734) 622-4476 ..**Bott**, Cynthia M '99 Pfizer Inc -2800 Plymouth Rd -Bldg 16/4th Fl
   -Ann Arbor, MI 48105
(412) 394-2435 ..**Botta**, Frank C '98 Thorp R&A -301 Grant -14th Fl
   -Pittsburgh, PA 15219
(614) 227-2000 ..**Botti**, James P '82 (Porter WM&A LLP) -41 S High
   -Columbus 43215 **Fx:**227-2100
(513) 326-5555 ..**Bottoms**, James M '01 Young & A Co,LPA -110 Boggs Ln
   -Ste 350 -Cincinnati 45246
(513) 946-9200 ..**Bouchard**, Bernard A '95 Hamilton Cnty Juv Ct -800 Bway
   -Cincinnati 45202 **Fx:**946-9217
   Bouchard, Roger P '02 -2723 Cyclorama Dr -Cincinnati 45211
(937) 223-0122 ..**Boucher**, Richard A '86 (Boucher & B Co,LPA)
   -12 W Monument Av -Ste 200 -Dayton 45402
(912) 261-3617 ..**Bouchillon**, Lynn H '96 US DOJ-Fed Bur of Prisons -Bldg 21
   -Fed Law Enfrcmnt Training Ctr -Glynco, GA 31524
(317) 276-0755 ..**Boudreaux**, William R '93 Eli Lilly & Co -Lilly Corp Ctr-DC 1152
   -Indianapolis, IN 46285
(513) 579-6400 ..**Bouffard**, Alison J '04 %Keating M&K PLL -1 E 4th
   -1400 Provident Twr -Cincinnati 45202 **Fx:**579-6457
(330) 726-5518 ..**Bouffard**, Robert S '79 -721 Boardman-Poland Rd -Ste 201
   -Youngstown 44512 **Fx:**726-7538
(330) 723-4599 ..**Bougher**, Frederick C '82 -326 North Ct -Medina 44256
(330) 643-2765 ..**Boughton**, Lisa A '98 Summit Cnty Pros-CSEA -171 S Main
   -Akron 44308 **Fx:**643-2822
(216) 621-1424 ..**Boukalik**, William T '68 US Title Agncy Inc -1111 Chester Av
   -Ste 400 -Cleveland 44114
(216) 696-1076 ..**Boukis**, Christ '65 Hohmann B&C Co,LPA -1370 Ontario
   -Ste 520 Standard Bldg -Cleveland 44113 **Fx:**696-2317
(216) 696-1076 ..**Boukis**, Kenneth '66 Hohmann B&C Co,LPA -1370 Ontario
   -Ste 520 Standard Bldg -Cleveland 44113 **Fx:**696-2317
(216) 524-9007 ..**Boulas**, James E '98 (J Boulas Co,LPA) -6221 Cabrini Ln
   -Seven Hills 44131
(859) 491-2206 ..**Bouldin**, Michael W '95 -120 W 5th -Covington, KY 41011
(740) 775-5312 ..**Boulger**, James T '79 -2 W 4th -Chillicothe 45601
(740) 773-1666 ..**Boulger**, William C '51 -45 W 4th -Bx204 -Chillicothe 45601
(419) 524-6011 ..**Bourdeau**, Julia M '99 %Calhoun KH&C Co,LPA -6 W 3rd
   -Ste 200 -Bx268 -Mansfield 44901 **Fx:**526-1431
(330) 609-5515 ..**Bourne**, Nicholas A '95 Title Works Agncy -8228 E Market -Ste A
   -Warren 44484
(216) 221-2930 ..**Boutall**, Thomas B '91 -2013 Riverside Dr -Lakewood 44107
(216) 228-8850 ..**Bouvier**, Jaime M '99 %Hon DJ Kucinich -14400 Detroit Av
   -Lakewood 44107
(419) 483-7119 ..**Bova**, Barry W '88 -817 Kilbourne -Bellevue 44811
(419) 526-1176 ..**Bove**, Ralph R '78 -16 W 2nd -Mansfield 44902 **Fx:**522-8731
(419) 243-1770 ..**Bovee**, Megan E '88 (Bovee C Co,LPA) -421 N Mich -Ste E
   -Toledo 43624
(614) 466-4320 ..**Bowe**, Carolyn S '02 Atty Gen -150 E Gay -Columbus 43215
(330) 945-6931 ..**Bowen**, Kathleen K '98 -311 Hillbrook Dr -Cuyahoga Falls 44223
(404) 236-2600 ..**Bowen**, Sean A '85 Internet Security Sys -6303 Barfld Rd
   -Atlanta, GA 30328
(513) 424-2050 ..**Bowen**, William L '78 -1 N Main -Middletown 45042 **Fx:**424-2983
(614) 629-3000 ..**Bower**, Amelia J '84 %Plunkett & C,PC -300 E Broad -Ste 590
   -Columbus 43215 **Fx:**629-3019
(330) 674-0499 ..**Bower**, Blair A '89 -111 S Wshngtn -Ste B -Millersburg 44654
(614) 621-4060 ..**Bower**, Eileen R '95 Schneider Downs & Co,Inc -10 W Broad
   -Ste 1500 -Columbus 43215
(330) 927-5100 ..**Bower**, George K '76 -19 N Main -Ste B -Rittman 44270
(937) 223-8177 ..**Bower**, Glenn J '77 (Coolidge WW&L) -33 W 1st -Ste 600 -Dayton
   45402 **Fx:**223-6705
(419) 475-7422 ..**Bower**, Karen L '83 -Bx2696 -Toledo 43606
(419) 627-7774 ..**Bower**, Mary M '86 Erie Cnty Fam Ct -323 Columbus Av
   -Sandusky 44870
(330) 376-5756 ..**Bower**, Terry L '71 Emershaw M&S -120 E Mill -#437
   -Akron 44308 **Fx:**762-5980
(614) 728-7244 ..**Bowers**, Andrew D '99 State Auditors Ofc -88 E Broad -5th Fl
   -Columbus 43215
(614) 464-6400 ..**Bowers**, Brenda K '90 Vorys SS&P LLP -52 E Gay -Bx1008
   -Columbus 43215 **Fx:**464-6350
(216) 241-2838 ..**Bowers**, Charles A '94 (Taft S&H LLP) -200 Pub Sq -3500 BP Twr
   -Cleveland 44114 **Fx:**241-3707
(216) 431-4500 ..**Bowers**, Cynthia '81 Cleveland Mun Ct -Bx94894
   -Cleveland 44101
(419) 228-3700 ..**Bowers**, David '70 Allen Cnty Pros -204 N Main -#302
   -Lima 45801

Bowers, Edmond F '86 -6440 Ryan Rd -Medina 44256
(937) 461-9297 .. **Bowers,** Gwendolyn R '78 (G Bowers Co,LPA) -1712 W 3rd
-Dayton 45407
(330) 335-2304 .. **Bowers,** Harold F Jr. '78 -102 Main -Ste 201 -Wadsworth 44281
(330) 343-1614 .. **Bowers,** Henry T '49 (Bowers & M) -108½ E High Av
-New Philadelphia 44663
(740) 477-1361 .. **Bowers,** John E '79 -233 N Court -Circleville 43113
(614) 443-6548 .. **Bowers,** John S '58 -720 S High -Columbus 43206 **Fx:**443-6540
(317) 808-6163 .. **Bowers,** Kellye J '98 Duke Realty Corp -600 E 96th -Ste 100
-Indianapolis, IN 46240
(207) 990-5855 .. **Bowers,** Nanon L '94 WR Foote -157 Park -Bangor, ME 04401
(713) 296-3904 .. **Bowers,** Ricky C '95 Marathon Oil Co -5555 San Filipe Rd
-Tax Dept -Houston, TX 77056
Bowersock, William L '85 -334 E Lake Rd
-Palm Harbor, FL 34685
(216) 689-5089 .. **Bowes,** Robert C '78 KeyBank NA -127 Pub Sq -Cleveland 44114
(513) 632-4506 .. **Bowie,** Karen L '95 Firstar Bank -425 Walnut -Location 7128
-Cincinnati 45202
(419) 855-7718 .. **Bowland,** Denise M '85 (Bowland Law Ofc) -629 Main -Bx127
-Genoa 43430
(585) 724-2577 .. **Bowler,** John R '91 Eastman Kodak Co-Legal Dept -343 State
-Rochester, NY 14650
(330) 253-3337 .. **Bowler,** Michael B '73 (Blakemore M&B Co,LPA) -19 N High
-Akron 44308 **Fx:**253-4131
(502) 589-4200 .. **Bowles,** Claude R Jr. '87 Greenebaum D&M PLLC -101 S 5th
-Ste 3300 -Louisville, KY 40202
(216) 479-8500 .. **Bowling,** Chandra S '93 %Squire S&D LLP -127 Pub Sq
-4900 Key Twr -Cleveland 44114 **Fx:**479-8780
(740) 532-4333 .. **Bowling,** Daniel S '97 (Lambert M&B) -215 S 4th -Bx725
-Ironton 45638
(513) 892-3400 .. **Bowling,** Jeffrey W '98 (Brandabur & B Co,LPA) -306 S 3rd
-Hamilton 45011
(937) 383-1422 .. **Bowling,** Larry R '88 Bowling Law Office -1366 State Route 134 N
-Wilmington 45177
Bowling, Leigh Anne '93 -1924 Sandee Cres
-Virginia Beach, VA 23454
(419) 332-8260 .. **Bowlus,** Thomas M '94 (Bowlus & B Ltd) -207 N Park Av
-Fremont 43420
(419) 332-8260 .. **Bowlus,** William R '62 (Bowlus & B Ltd) -207 N Park Av
-Fremont 43420
(614) 221-1166 .. **Bowman,** John S '98 %Plymale & Assoc -495 S High -Ste 400
-Columbus 43215 **Fx:**221-6633
(614) 466-3180 .. **Bowman,** Jonathan M '94 Atty Gen -150 E Gay -Columbus 43215
Fx:466-9788
(614) 221-3155 .. **Bowman,** Katharine B '83 (Bailey C LLC) -10 W Broad
-Columbus 43215 **Fx:**221-0479
(937) 222-2500 .. **Bowman,** Kevin A '97 %Sebaly S&D -1900 Kettering Twr
-Dayton 45423 **Fx:**222-6554
(330) 337-9173 .. **Bowman,** Scott M '92 -Bx558 -Salem 44460
(513) 721-2120 .. **Bowman,** Stephanie K '00 %Barrett & W -105 E 4th -Ste 500
-Cincinnati 45202
(419) 843-2001 .. **Bowman,** Theodore A '79 (Gallon & T Co,LPA) -3516 Granite Cir
-Bx352018 -Toledo 43635 **Fx:**843-6665
(330) 643-8301 .. **Bown,** Thomas D '04 Hon Shapiro Ct -209 S High -Akron 44308
(614) 221-0922 .. **Bownas,** James H '71 Gamble HJ Co,LPA -1 E Lvngstn Av
-Columbus 43215 **Fx:**365-9741
(216) 586-3939 .. **Bownas,** Pearson N '97 %Jones D -901 Lakeside Av
-Cleveland 44114 **Fx:**579-0212
(614) 466-3998 .. **Bowshier,** Denis J '90 Unemploymnt Comp Commssn
-145 S Front -Bx182299 -Columbus 43218
(614) 875-1777 .. **Bowshier,** Stephen J '81 -4030 Bway -Ste 100 -Grove City 43123
(330) 376-2700 .. **Box,** Susan S '85 (Roetzel & A,LPA) -222 S Main -Akron 44308
Fx:376-4577
(419) 243-6281 .. **Boxell,** Charles K '74 (Shindler NH&S,LLP) -300 Mad Av
-Ste 1200 -Toledo 43604 **Fx:**243-0129
(216) 931-6000 .. **Boxer,** Yelena B '99 %Ulmer & B LLP -1300 E 9th
-Ste 900 Penton Media Bldg -Cleveland 44114 **Fx:**931-6001
(216) 586-3939 .. **Boyce,** Jennifer Hanley '96 %Jones D -901 Lakeside Av
-Cleveland 44114 **Fx:**579-0212
(216) 586-3939 .. **Boyce,** Kevin D '96 %Jones D -901 Lakeside Av -Cleveland 44114
Fx:579-0212
(330) 829-0150 .. **Boyce,** Richard M '85 -1617 W State -Alliance 44601
(703) 696-9055 .. **Boyce,** William B '90 USAF AFLSA/JAC -1501 Wilson Blvd -8th Fl
-Arlington, VA 22209
(513) 946-3158 .. **Boychan,** Thomas J Jr. '88 Hamilton Cnty Pros -230 E 9th
-Cincinnati 45202 **Fx:**946-3017
Boychuk, Andrew M '88 -(Address Unavailable)
(614) 280-8718 .. **Boyd,** Alan B '74 IRS -200 N High -#425 -Columbus 43215
(614) 466-3615 .. **Boyd,** Bethany R '90 Legis Srvc Commssn -77 S High
-Columbus 43215
(513) 241-2382 .. **Boyd,** David J '64 -7 W 7th -Rm 1800 -Cincinnati 45202
(614) 224-8374 .. **Boyd,** Eric R '86 Legal Aid -40 W Gay -Columbus 43215
(508) 855-4013 .. **Boyd,** George M '77 %Allmerica Fncl -440 Lincoln
-Ofc of Gen Cnsl -Worcester, MA 01653 **Fx:**856-9526
(614) 891-6584 .. **Boyd,** James W Sr. '73 -6090 Ashtree Pl -Columbus 43229
(419) 734-6790 .. **Boyd,** Jason E '02 Ottawa Cnty Ct of Common Pleas
-315 Madison -Rm 301 -Port Clinton 43452
(614) 885-4980 .. **Boyd,** Jeffrey D '82 -5655 N High -Ste 202 -Worthington 43085
(330) 744-0291 .. **Boyd,** John C '66 (Boyd RC&C Co LPA) -400 Sky Bk Bldg -Bx6565
-Youngstown 44501
(216) 222-3330 .. **Boyd,** John W '85 Natl City Bank -1900 E 9th -17th Fl Loc 01-2174
-Cleveland 44114
(419) 241-8171 .. **Boyd,** Kenneth E '80 Moran & M -626 Mad Av -Ste 300
-Toledo 43604
(615) 251-5583 .. **Boyd,** Martha L '99 %Frost BT LLC -424 Church -Ste 1600
-Nashville, TN 37219
(419) 626-3241 .. **Boyd,** Melanie S '87 -158 E Market -Ste 202 -Sandusky 44870
(419) 246-5757 .. **Boyd,** Nathan R '04 %Anspach M&N,LLP -300 Mad Av -Ste 1600
-Toledo 43604 **Fx:**321-6979
(216) 696-0800 .. **Boyd,** Robert A '80 %Gibson BZ&M -55 Pub Sq -Ste 2075
-Cleveland 44113 **Fx:**696-0702
Boyd, Robert C II '94 -7380 Hawksbeard Dr -Westerville 43082

(614) 229-3888 .. **Boyd,** Robert E '97 Cheek & Z,LLP -471 E Broad -18th Fl
-Bx15069 -Columbus 43215 **Fx:**241-5865
(614) 716-0500 .. **Boyd,** Robert E III '79 %Onda L&R Co,LPA -266 N 4th -Ste 100
-Columbus 43215 **Fx:**716-0511
Boyd, Robert E Jr. '52 -2511 Barcelona Dr
-Fort Lauderdale, FL 33301
(614) 451-5000 .. **Boyd,** Roy F '76 Ayliss Mortgage Co -1335 Dublin Rd -Ste 200A
-Columbus 43215
(330) 744-0291 .. **Boyd Rummell Carach & Curry Co LPA** -400 Sky Bk Bldg
-Bx6565 -Youngstown 44501
(614) 462-4492 .. **Boyd,** Sally W '81 Franklin Cnty Dom Ct -373 S High
-Columbus 43215
(614) 462-3555 .. **Boyd,** Tracie M '98 Franklin Cnty Pros -373 S High
-Columbus 43215
(216) 622-8270 .. **Boyd,** William A '74 -800 Superior Av -Ste 1400 -Cleveland 44114
(513) 455-7600 .. **Boydston,** Richard M Jr. '77 (Greenebaum D&M PLLC) -255 E 5th
-2800 Chemed Ctr -Cincinnati 45202 **Fx:**455-8500
(212) 656-2633 .. **Boyer,** Allen D '82 %NYSE -14 Wall -Enforcement Division
-New York, NY 10005 **Fx:**656-2309
(614) 645-6763 .. **Boyer,** Betsy A '03 City Atty Ofc -375 S High -17th Fl
-Columbus 43215
(614) 464-6400 .. **Boyer,** John N '00 %Vorys SS&P LLP -52 E Gay -Bx1008
-Columbus 43216 **Fx:**464-6350
(614) 224-8446 .. **Boyer,** Kelly S '03 Ohio Capital Corp for Housing -88 E Broad
-Ste 1800 -Columbus 43215 **Fx:**241-5938
Boyer, Patricia A '01 -5292 Riverside Dr -Columbus 43220
(419) 241-2300 .. **Boyer,** Peter G '92 -316 N Mich -Ste 800 -Toledo 43624
(740) 342-5520 .. **Boyer,** Tina M '94 Perry Cnty Cmmn Pleas Ct -105 N Main -Bx167
-New Lexington 43764 **Fx:**342-5524
Boyer, Todd F '99 -6202 Spring Lk Dr -Hamilton 45011
(419) 241-1395 .. **Boyk,** Charles E '83 -520 Mad Av -Ste 655 -Toledo 43604
(419) 327-6160 .. **Boyk,** Fredric M '94 -520 Mad Av -655 Spitzer Bldg -Toledo 43604
(216) 987-5037 .. **Boyko,** Michael E '84 Cuyahoga Comm College -11000 W
Plsnt Vlly Rd -Cleveland 44130
(440) 886-3800 .. **Boyko,** Timothy A '89 (Boyko & D) -6741 Ridge Rd -Parma 44129
(513) 421-4020 .. **Boylan,** Michael J '76 (Cohen TK&S,LLC) -250 E 5th -Ste 1200
-Cincinnati 45202 **Fx:**241-4490
(513) 361-0250 .. **Boylan,** Peter J '82 SSA-OHA -312 Elm -Ste 2100
-Cincinnati 45202
(614) 461-6973 .. **Boylan,** Richard L '68 RLB Grp,Inc -21 E State -Ste 220
-Columbus 43215
(330) 451-8892 .. **Boyle,** Alicia L '99 Stark Cnty CSEA -116 Cleveland Av -Bx21337
-Canton 44701 **Fx:**481-8871
(216) 623-1123 .. **Boyle,** James P '91 (Sindell YG&S,PLL) -55 Pub Sq -Ste 1020
-Cleveland 44113 **Fx:**623-1124
(419) 213-4061 .. **Boyle,** Joseph P III '89 %Lucas Cnty Pros-Foreclosure
-One Govt Ctr -Ste 500 -Toledo 43604
(614) 221-5216 .. **Boyle,** Kerry T '00 %Wiles BB&B Co,LPA -300 Spruce -1st Fl
-Columbus 43215 **Fx:**221-5692
(859) 292-7015 .. **Boyle,** Marie M '85 SENCORP -1 Rvrfrnt Pl -10th Fl -Newport,
KY 41071
(513) 629-2443 .. **Boyle,** Mark S '84 Eagle-Picher Ind,Inc -250 E 5th -Ste 500 -Bx779
-Cincinnati 45201
(614) 457-7219 .. **Boyle,** Sean O '88 -490 S High -Columbus 43215
(513) 352-6700 .. **Boyle,** Tanya L '03 %Thompson H LLP -312 Walnut -14th Fl
-Cincinnati 45202 **Fx:**241-4771
(614) 221-5216 .. **Boyle,** Thomas E '72 (Wiles BB&B Co,LPA) -300 Spruce -1st Fl
-Columbus 43215 **Fx:**221-5692
(330) 878-5501 .. **Boynton,** John R '69 AJ Weigand,Inc -Bx130 -Dover 44622
(440) 323-5813 .. **Boyson,** Frank A Jr. '74 -105 Court -Ste 300 -Elyria 44035
(614) 443-8731 .. **Boyuk,** Walter C '68 -34 W Whittier -Columbus 43206
Fx:445-8810
(330) 375-2030 .. **Bozeka,** George A '81 Law Dept -161 S High -Ste 202
-Akron 44308
Bozell, Catherine L '02 -10600 Clifton Blvd -#10 -Cleveland 44102
(740) 374-2629 .. **Bozian,** Robin A '77 SE OH Lgl Srvcs -427 2nd -Marietta 45750
(650) 833-7735 .. **Bozicevic,** Karl '87 Bozicevic F&F LLP -200 Middlefld Rd -Ste 200
-Menlo Park, CA 94025
(330) 375-8471 .. **Bozzelli,** Karen A '87 Natl City Bank -1 Cascade Plz
-Private Client Group -Bx2130 -Akron 44309
(513) 723-1600 .. **Brabenec-Page,** Susan '02 %Mezibov & J -1726 Young
-Cincinnati 45202
(614) 442-1953 .. **Bracco,** Robert A '82 (R Bracco & Assoc)
-1170 Old Henderson Rd -Ste 109 -Columbus 43220
(502) 588-4016 .. **Brackett,** Alexander P '95 %Greenebaum D&M -101 S 5th
-3300 Nat'l City Twr -Louisville, KY 40202
Bracy, Michele L '02 -47255 Middle Range Rd -Amherst 44001
(216) 689-0346 .. **Bradbury,** Petra J '88 KeyBank NA -127 Pub Sq
-Mail Code OH-01-27-0200 -Cleveland 44114
(859) 331-8883 .. **Braden,** Roger N '90 (Sutton HLG&B PLC) -130 Dudley Rd
-Ste 250 -Edgewood, KY 41017 **Fx:**341-2777
(440) 892-6800 .. **Bradford,** Dale A '83 Carnegie Mgmt -27500 Detroit Rd -Ste 300
-Westlake 44145
(513) 732-1141 .. **Bradford,** Douglas J '74 (Burreson B&H) -40 S 3rd -Batavia 45103
(419) 238-1010 .. **Bradford,** Kent M '73 Cntrl Mutual Ins Co -800 S Wshngtn
-Van Wert 45891
(216) 566-5500 .. **Bradford,** Matthew '01 %Thompson H LLP -127 Pub Sq
-3900 Key Ctr -Cleveland 44114 **Fx:**566-5800
(740) 593-5828 .. **Bradford,** Melinda K '97 %Shostak Law Ofc -18 W State
-Athens 45701 **Fx:**594-6446
(937) 333-4100 .. **Bradford,** Tracy L '92 %Law Dept -101 W 3rd -Bx22
-Dayton 45402
(614) 416-5120 .. **Bradigan,** Brian J '81 (BJ Bradigan,Inc) -3948 Townfair Way
-Ste 230 -Columbus 43219
(256) 772-0723 .. **Bradley,** Aldean S '64 AL Reading Systms -Bx6032 -Huntsville, AL
35824
Bradley, David P '89 -735 Manatee Bay Dr
-Boynton Beach, FL 33435
(614) 716-2934 .. **Bradley,** Elizabeth M '03 American Electric Power -1 Riverside Pl
-29th Fl -Columbus 43215
(859) 257-4784 .. **Bradley,** Geoffrey J '94 Univ of KY Residence Life
-537 Patterson Ofc Twr -Lexington, KY 40506
(440) 244-1811 .. **Bradley,** Jack W '77 -520 Bway -3rd Fl -Lorain 44052

(937) 226-1212 ..**Bradley**, Karen D '96 (Skelton MG&H) -130 W 2nd -Ste 450
    -Dayton 45402

(330) 535-5711 ..**Bradley**, Kate M '01 %Brouse M -106 S Main -500 First Natl Twr
    -Akron 44308 **Fx:**253-8601

(216) 522-7546 ..**Bradley**, Mary L '00 US Dept of Labor -1240 E 9th -Rm 881
    -Cleveland 44199 **Fx:**522-7172

(614) 239-1389 ..**Bradley**, Philip Raymond '50 -2599 E Main #125
    -Columbus 43209

(440) 989-4100 ..**Bradley**, Sam R '87 (S Bradley,LPA) -1958 Kresge Dr
    -Amherst 44001 **Fx:**989-4104

(216) 781-0722 ..**Bradley**, Steven L '90 (Marein & B) -526 Superior Av E -Ste 222
    -Cleveland 44114

(847) 604-0187 ..**Bradner**, James H Jr. '67 -Bx415 -Highwood, IL 60040

(330) 434-3000 ..**Bradshaw**, Duard D '73 (Roderick & L) -One Cascade Plz
    -Ste 1500 -Akron 44308 **Fx:**434-9220

Bradstreet, Tanya R '03 -(Address Unavailable)

(330) 486-4007 ..**Brady**, Brooke M '00 Cole Vision Corp -1925 Enterprise Pkwy
    -Twinsburg 44087 **Fx:**486-3981

(419) 885-3000 ..**Brady Coyle & Schmidt LLP** -4052 Holland-Sylvania Rd
    -Toledo 43623 **Fx:**885-1120

(419) 621-9214 ..**Brady**, Daniel J '74 -516 W Wshngtn -Sandusky 44870

(440) 808-4242 ..**Brady**, David T '00 Douglass & Assoc Co,LPA -551 Dover Ctr Rd
    -Bx40480 -Cleveland 44140 **Fx:**808-4215

(419) 885-3000 ..**Brady**, Jack J '84 (Brady C&S LLP) -4052 Holland-Sylvania Rd
    -Toledo 43623 **Fx:**885-1120

(440) 286-7460 ..**Brady**, Joanne C '82 -12665 Gwendolyn Farms Rd
    -Chardon 44024

(614) 227-2000 ..**Brady**, John E '70 (Porter WM&A LLP) -41 S High
    -Columbus 43215 **Fx:**227-2100

(216) 523-5000 ..**Brady**, Matthew T '85 Eaton Corp -1111 Superior Av
    -Cleveland 44114

(210) 671-2007 ..**Brady**, Robert J '97 USAF JAG -1701 Kenly Av -Ste 117
    -Lackland AFB, TX 78236

Brady, Robert M Jr. '74 -36 Andvr Rd -Cincinnati 45218

(419) 535-0075 ..**Brady**, William D II '04 %Allotta F&W Co,LPA -2222 Centennial Rd
    -Toledo 43617 **Fx:**535-1935

(970) 243-1921 ..**Braffett**, Fielding G '66 Dalby Wendland & Co PC -Bx430
    -Grand Junction, CO 81502

(216) 861-3810 ..**Bragg**, Caprice H '89 The Cleveland Foundation -1422 Euclid Av
    -Ste 1300 -Cleveland 44115 **Fx:**861-6754

(216) 696-4659 ..**Bragg**, Charles H '84 -1370 Ontario -Ste 1520 -Cleveland 44113

(937) 910-4173 ..**Bragg**, Holly J '83 Natl City Corp -3232 Newmark Dr
    -Miamisburg 45342

(419) 252-6271 ..**Bragg**, Michael W '85 (Spengler N PLL) -608 Mad Av -Ste 1000
    -Toledo 43604 **Fx:**241-8599

(419) 252-6216 ..**Bragg**, Ralph E '59 (Spengler N PLL) -608 Mad Av -Ste 1000
    -Toledo 43604 **Fx:**241-8599

(312) 648-2244 ..**Bragga**, Terri Barton '98 %Zulkie Prtnrs LLC -222 S Riverside Plz
    -Ste 2300 -Chicago, IL 60606 **Fx:**648-9848

(330) 335-2748 ..**Brague**, Norman E '71 Wadsworth Law Dept -120 Maple
    -Wadsworth 44281 **Fx:**335-2711

(614) 228-4546 ..**Brahm**, Richard C '70 (Shuler P&B,LPA) -145 E Rich -Ste 400
    -Columbus 43215

(937) 593-8510 ..**Braig**, Kevin P '93 %Smith S&M -112 N Main -Bellefontaine 43311

(440) 461-6000 ..**Brainard**, Patrick J '93 NESCO,Inc -6140 Parkland Blvd
    -Mayfield Heights 44124

(330) 847-8383 ..**Brainard**, Todd L '91 -925 State Rd NW -Warren 44481

Braithwaite, Melanie J '81 -5022 Hibbs Dr -Columbus 43220

(937) 382-1494 ..**Brake**, Daniel J '93 %R&L Carriers -600 Gillam Rd -Bx271
    -Wilmington 45177

(510) 437-3330 ..**Bralliar**, Rachael B '98 US Coast Guard -Bldg #54-C
    -Coast Guard Isl -Alameda, CA 94501

(440) 942-8544 ..**Bralliar**, Thomas B Jr. '95 -691 Robin Dr -Eastlake 44095

(304) 345-5200 ..**Bramble**, Mark A '97 (Kesner K&B) -112 Cptl -Bx2587
    -Charleston, WV 25329

(330) 725-6666 ..**Bramley**, Jeffrey L '81 (Williams & B,LLP) -105 W Lbrty -Bx394
    -Medina 44258

(740) 965-8452 ..**Brammer**, Celeste E '90 -13290 Centerbury Rd -Sunbury 43074

(612) 348-1774 ..**Brammer**, Florence I '81 NLRB -330 2nd Av S -Ste 790
    -Minneapolis, MN 55401

(513) 762-6200 ..**Brammer**, Matthew V '93 %Ulmer & B LLP -600 Vine -Ste 2800
    -Cincinnati 45202 **Fx:**762-6245

(216) 751-6214 ..**Branagan**, James J '68 -19801 Van Aken Blvd -Ste 203
    -Shaker Heights 44122

(440) 946-6958 ..**Brancatelli**, Frank R '73 -Bx790 -Willoughby 44096

(270) 926-4545 ..**Brancato**, Frank A '80 OfCnsl Bamberger & A,PLC -111 W 2nd
    -Bx1676 -Owensboro, KY 42302 **Fx:**684-0064

(440) 933-2029 ..**Branch**, David A '96 -524 Rockwood Ct -Avon Lake 44012

(513) 621-9100 ..**Branch**, Jennifer L '87 %Laufman & G -617 Vine
    -1409 Enquirer Bldg -Cincinnati 45202

(937) 548-2211 ..**Brand**, Eric H '78 (Goubeaux & G) -100 Wshngtn Av -Bx158
    -Greenville 45331

(513) 531-3428 ..**Brand**, Jack I '86 -6530 Hudson Pkwy -Cincinnati 45213

(937) 372-4411 ..**Brandabur Finlay Johnson Weckstein & Beard** -260 N Detroit
    -Xenia 45385 **Fx:**372-4415

(937) 372-4411 ..**Brandabur**, James F '59 OfCnsl Brandabur FJW&B -260 N Detroit
    -Xenia 45385 **Fx:**372-4415

(513) 892-3400 ..**Brandabur**, Michael J '96 (Brandabur & B Co,LPA) -306 S 3rd
    -Hamilton 45011

(330) 722-6611 ..**Brandel**, Lawrence S '75 -122 Pub Sq -Medina 44256

(937) 748-1004 ..**Brandenburg**, Cynthia L '86 %Kirby & T LPA -4 Sycamore Crk Dr
    -Springboro 45066 **Fx:**748-2390

(513) 752-5350 ..**Brandenburg**, George P '78 (Smith B&N) -905 Ohio Pike
    -Cincinnati 45245

(216) 443-8290 ..**Brandenburg**, Valerie '85 Domestic Relations Ct -1 Lakeside
    -Cleveland 44113

(513) 785-7006 ..**Brandenburger**, Mark '74 City of Hamilton -345 High -7th Fl
    -Hamilton 45011

(304) 368-2700 ..**Brandfass**, Robert L '86 WV United Health Sys -1000 Tech Dr
    -Ste 2320 -Fairmont, WV 26554

(740) 380-2941 ..**Brandon**, Sandra L '88 -38½ N Market -Bx943 -Logan 43138

(614) 464-6400 ..**Brandt**, Adam K '96 (Vorys SS&P LLP) -52 E Gay -Bx1008
    -Columbus 43216 **Fx:**464-6350

(937) 224-3741 ..**Brandt**, Daniel J '97 Montgomery Cnty Pros -301 W 3rd -Bx972
    -Dayton 45422 **Fx:**225-3470

(216) 621-1610 ..**Brandt**, Jean M '89 -1028 Kenilworth Av -Cleveland 44113

(513) 381-8033 ..**Brandt**, Jeffrey M '95 -11331 Grooms Rd -Ste 3000
    -Cincinnati 45242

(212) 344-5680 ..**Brandt**, Katherine D '89 (Thompson H LLP) -1 Chase Manh Plz
    -58th Fl -New York, NY 10005 **Fx:**809-6890

(937) 225-5543 ..**Brandt**, Kirsten A '98 Montgomery Cnty Pros -301 W 3rd -Bx972
    -Dayton 45422 **Fx:**225-3470

(614) 645-8296 ..**Brandt**, Michael T '68 Cnty Mun Ct Judge -375 S High
    -Columbus 43215

(440) 808-9743 ..**Brandt**, Natasha E '90 Park Pl/Level Propane Co
    -830 Canterbury Rd -Westlake 44145

(937) 465-2002 ..**Brandt**, Philip A '82 (Brandt & M) -109 S Detroit -Bx910
    -West Liberty 43357

(937) 222-9687 ..**Brandt**, Stephen D '76 -22 Brown -Bx3340 -Dayton 45401
    Fx:222-3551

(216) 586-3939 ..**Brandt**, Tamara S '00 %Jones D -901 Lakeside Av
    -Cleveland 44114 **Fx:**579-0212

(831) 372-3266 ..**Brandwein**, William A '69 (W Brandwein,PLC) -215 W Franklin
    -BxLAW -Monterey, CA 93942

(740) 474-6026 ..**Branham**, Elisa M '93 Pickaway Cnty Cmmn Pleas Ct
    -207 S Court -Circleville 43113

Branham, Jacquelyn J '97 -Bx200615 -Anchorage, AK 99520

(313) 871-3000 ..**Branigan**, Thomas P '99 (Bowman and B LLP) -50 W Big Beaver
    Rd -Ste 600 -Troy, MI 48084

(215) 977-2742 ..**Branigin**, Roger D III '91 %Wolf BS&S-C,LLP -1650 Arch -22nd Fl
    -Philadelphia, PA 19103

(614) 431-1500 ..**Brankamp**, Joshua W '04 %Perez & M LLC -8000 Ravines
    Edge Ct -Ste 300 -Columbus 43235 **Fx:**431-3885

(404) 888-4000 ..**Brannan**, Arthur D '93 (Hunton & W) -600 Pchtree NE -Ste 4100
    -Atlanta, GA 30308 **Fx:**888-4190

(330) 455-0173 ..**Brannen**, John H '75 (Day KRW&R,Ltd) -200 Market Av N
    -Ste 300 -Bx24213 -Canton 44701 **Fx:**455-2633

(330) 533-1700 ..**Brannigan**, Mary E '90 -3870 Starr Centre Dr -Canfield 44406

(614) 326-5544 ..**Brannock**, Keith W '57 (K Brannock Co,LPA)
    -1550 Old W Henderson Rd -Ste N-130 -Columbus 43220

(937) 228-2306 ..**Brannon**, Douglas D '03 %Brannon & Assoc -130 W 2nd -Ste 900
    -Dayton 45402

(937) 228-2306 ..**Brannon**, Dwight D '74 (Brannon & Assoc) -130 W 2nd -Ste 900
    -Dayton 45402

(330) 239-1230 ..**Brannon**, Ellis B '51 (E Brannon Co,LPA) -6294 Ridge Rd -Bx189
    -Sharon Center 44274

(312) 236-5907 ..**Bransfield**, Thomas D '99 (JF Bransfield Prtnrshp)
    -One N La Salle -Ste 2046 -Chicago, IL 60602

(202) 463-8400 ..**Bransford**, William L '75 (Shaw BV&R) -1100 Conn Av NW
    -Ste 900 -Washington, DC 20036

(513) 946-3000 ..**Branson**, Dorothy K '98 Hamilton Cnty Pros -230 E 9th
    -Cincinnati 45202 **Fx:**946-3017

(937) 226-9354 ..**Branson**, Paul M '01 %Macey & C -40 W 4th -Ste 2160
    -Dayton 45402 **Fx:**226-9359

(740) 345-5535 ..**Branstool**, William D '94 -35 S Park Pl -Ste 201 -Newark 43055

(614) 221-2121 ..**Brant**, Charles E '59 (Isaac BL&T,LLP) -250 E Broad
    -Ste 900 Mdlnd Bldg -Columbus 43215 **Fx:**365-9516

(513) 721-4532 ..**Brant**, Joel S '97 %Katz TB&H -255 E 5th -Ste 2400
    -Cincinnati 45202

Brant, John F '04 -(Address Unavailable)

(614) 644-2613 ..**Brant**, John W '77 Dept of Commerce -Bx4009
    -Reynoldsburg 43068

(513) 721-4532 ..**Brant**, Joseph A '61 OfCnsl Katz TB&H -255 E 5th -Ste 2400
    -Cincinnati 45202

(503) 846-8855 ..**Brant**, Judith A '96 DA -150 N 1st Av -Rm 300
    -Hillsboro, OR 97124

(614) 460-4658 ..**Brant**, Marjorie H '83 Columbia Gas of OH,Inc -200 Civic Ctr Dr
    -Bx117 -Columbus 43216

(513) 721-4532 ..**Brant**, Robert E '74 (Katz TB&H) -255 E 5th -Ste 2400
    -Cincinnati 45202

Brant, Travis W '90 -2180 Marlow Rd -Toledo 43613

(216) 222-3331 ..**Brantley**, Sandra J '80 Natl City Bank-Leg Dept -1900 E 9th
    -Cleveland 44114

(216) 522-1400 ..**Brantley**, William S Jr. '80 FBI -1501 Lakeside Av
    -Cleveland 44114

(614) 459-5200 ..**Brantner**, Jeffrey W '74 (Rance PBK&E Co,LPA)
    -1720 Zollinger Rd -Ste 200 -Columbus 43221 **Fx:**459-1151

(614) 757-5913 ..**Brasel**, Christine E '99 Cardinal Health Inc -7000 Cardinal Pl
    -Dublin 43017

(440) 234-1100 ..**Brasfield**, Lynne S '97 -13801 Byron Blvd
    -Middleburg Heights 44130

(937) 222-3000 ..**Brasier**, Susan M '88 Falke & D LLC -30 Wyoming -Dayton 45409
    Fx:222-1414

(330) 342-6000 ..**Brasselle**, Susan Curry '03 %Pauley CS&V -Bx2786
    -Charleston, WV 25330

(937) 834-5000 ..**Bratka**, Dan W '87 Tri-County Rgnl Jail -4099 SR 559
    -Mechanicsburg 43044

(304) 422-7193 ..**Bratke**, Steven R '98 %McNeer HM&V,LC -404 Market -Ste 204
    -Bx1507 -Parkersburg, WV 26102

(800) 325-4916 ..**Brattain**, James A '79 Army Rsrve JAG -1 Reserve Way
    -ATTN:ARPC-OPB -Saint Louis, MO 63132

(606) 572-5447 ..**Bratton**, Robert M Jr. '64 Chase Law Schl -528 Nunn Hall
    -Highland Heights, KY 41076

(216) 566-9908 ..**Bratton**, Scott E '97 M Wong & Assoc Co,LPA -3150 Chester Av
    -Ste 200 -Cleveland 44114 **Fx:**566-1125

(216) 621-0150 ..**Brauer**, Jeffrey A '98 (Hahn L&P LLP) -3300 BP Twr/200 Pub Sq
    -Ste 3300 -Cleveland 44114 **Fx:**241-2824

(614) 644-3037 ..**Brault**, Eva M '98 EPA -122 S Front -Bx1049 -Columbus 43216

(937) 396-0089 ..**Braum**, Scott L '99 (SL Braum & Assoc) -3131 S Dixie Dr -Ste 400
    -Dayton 45439 **Fx:**396-1046

(330) 491-5222 ..**Braun**, Dianne Blocker '76 (Buckingham D&B,LLP)
    -4518 Fulton Dr NW -Bx35548 -Canton 44735 **Fx:**492-9625

Braun, Fredrick H '57 -650 Windings Ln -Clifton 45220

(330) 716-0855 ..**Braun**, Gary L '83 -333 Fuller Dr NE -Warren 44484

(614) 463-9770 ..**Braun**, Jeffrey S '02 %Roetzel & A,LPA -155 E Broad
    -Natl City Ctr 12th Fl -Columbus 43215 **Fx:**463-9792

(614) 410-6500 ..**Braun,** JoAnna Christie '92 -445 Hutchnsn Av -Ste 800
-Columbus 43235

(513) 621-2120 ..**Braun,** Joseph J '98 %Strauss & T,LPA -150 E 4th -4th Fl
-Cincinnati 45202 **Fx:**241-8259

(216) 621-6684 ..**Braun,** Katherine M '93 %Kordic & Assoc -1422 Euclid Av
-The Hanna Bldg Ste 350 -Cleveland 44115

(513) 863-6600 ..**Braun,** Michael P '81 -616 Dayton -Bx1166 -Hamilton 45012

(419) 213-4700 ..**Braun,** Timothy F '87 %Lucas Cnty Pros -Adams & Erie
-Lucas Cnty Cthse -Toledo 43624

(614) 469-3939 ..**Braun,** Tonya Blosser '02 %Jones D -325 John H McConnell Blvd
-Ste 600 -Bx165017 -Columbus 43216 **Fx:**461-4198

(314) 512-3079 ..**Braunstein,** Brian S '84 Enterprise Rent-A-Car -600 Corp Park Dr
-Clayton, MO 63105

(614) 292-2342 ..**Braunstein,** Michael '93 OSU Moritz Cllg of Law -55 W 12th Av
-Columbus 43210 **Fx:**292-1383

(216) 781-1212 ..**Braverman,** Herbert L '72 (Walter & H LLP) -1301 E 9th -Ste 3500
-Cleveland 44114 **Fx:**575-0911

(216) 689-5369 ..**Braverman,** Jeffrey L '92 KeyBank NA -127 Pub Sq -16th Fl
-Cleveland 44114

(614) 365-5673 ..**Braverman,** Loren L '77 %Columbus Pub Sch -270 E State
-Columbus 43215

(216) 621-3346 ..**Braverman,** Sheldon L '65 %Kendis & Assoc Co,LPA
-614 Superior Av W -15th Fl Rckfllr Bldg -Cleveland 44113
Fx:621-3672

(513) 521-8499 ..**Braverman,** Tobie A '79 -Bx53022 -Cincinnati 45253

(614) 463-9770 ..**Bravo,** Eric S '90 %Roetzel & A,LPA -155 E Broad
-Natl City Ctr 12th Fl -Columbus 43215 **Fx:**463-9792

(216) 931-6000 ..**Bravo,** Kenneth A '67 (Ulmer & B LLP) -1300 E 9th
-Ste 900 Penton Media Bldg -Cleveland 44114 **Fx:**931-6001

(513) 381-2838 ..**Braxton,** Patricia D '90 %Taft S&H LLP -425 Walnut -Ste 1800
-Cincinnati 45202 **Fx:**381-0205

Bray, Angela D '02 -48098 Century Dr -Macomb, MI 48044

(216) 464-2153 ..**Bray,** Christopher P '01 Sterling Bk -3550 Lander Rd
-Pepper Pike 44124

(419) 249-7900 ..**Brazeau,** James E '78 (Robison C&O) -Four SeaGate -9th Fl
-Toledo 43604 **Fx:**249-7911

(216) 271-5665 ..**Brdar,** Robert A '84 -Bx32177 -Euclid 44132

(937) 548-1920 ..**Breaden,** Randall E '79 (Amick & B) -414 Walnut
-Greenville 45331

(330) 670-8400 ..**Breaux,** Alison M '01 H Tipping -525 N Cleveland Massillon Rd
#207 -Akron 44333

(419) 255-5111 ..**Brebberman,** James A '82 -520 Mad Av -Ste 1030 -Toledo 43604
Fx:255-3231

(330) 364-1112 ..**Brechbill,** John M '96 %ND Von Allman Co LPA -134 2nd NW
-New Philadelphia 44663

(614) 875-3227 ..**Breckenridge,** Donald O '85 -3009 Columbus -Ste 103
-Grove City 43123

(937) 484-7303 ..**Brecount,** Steven T '95 -108 Miami -Bx795 -Urbana 43078

(513) 852-6076 ..**Breed,** Thomas J '74 (Wood & L LLP) -600 Vine -Ste 2500
-Cincinnati 45202 **Fx:**852-6087

(702) 384-5800 ..**Breeden,** Adam '03 %Hafen & P -525 S 9th -Las Vegas, NV
89108 **Fx:**384-6580

(614) 486-7716 ..**Breen,** John E '82 Breen Law Ofc -650 Harrison Dr
-Columbus 43204

(330) 374-9444 ..**Breen,** Kevin J '86 Breen & Co -39 E Market -Ste 101 -Akron
44308 **Fx:**762-2936

(513) 784-5701 ..**Breen,** Timothy P '86 Convergys Info Mgt Group Inc -600 Vine
-Bx1638 -Cincinnati 45201

(419) 536-8600 ..**Breese,** Charles E '55 -3361 Exec Pkwy -Ste 100 -Toledo 43606

(740) 363-1213 ..**Brehm,** David J '93 (Firestone BHNW&Y,LLP) -15 W Winter
-Delaware 43015 **Fx:**369-0875

(513) 583-8888 ..**Brehm,** John E Jr. '82 %Heath & Assoc -8977 Columbia Rd -Ste A
-Bx4770 -Maineville 45039

(513) 556-6530 ..**Brehm,** Marianne Jones '02 Univ of Cincinnati/Coll of Edu
-301 Teachers Cllg -Cincinnati 45221

(614) 351-8570 ..**Brehmer,** Marcia L '76 -2047 Charmingfare -Columbus 43228

(419) 422-2121 ..**Breidenbach,** David C '77 Marathon Ashland Petro LLC
-539 S Main -Findlay 45840 **Fx:**421-8402

(937) 224-0963 ..**Breidenbach,** Heidi S '95 %Breidenbach O&B -131 N Ludlow
-Ste 1060 -Dayton 45402

(937) 224-0963 ..**Breidenbach,** John E '68 (Breidenbach O&B) -131 N Ludlow
-Ste 1060 -Dayton 45402

(216) 991-4236 ..**Breidenbach,** Paul C '49 -3310 Drchstr Rd -Shaker Heights 44120

(513) 721-2120 ..**Breidenstein,** Thomas W '94 %Barrett & W -105 E 4th -Ste 500
-Cincinnati 45202

(330) 434-2300 ..**Breiding,** Leonard J II '90 -572 W Market -Ste 11 -Akron 44303

(419) 690-8022 ..**Breier,** Gary A '78 (Breier & W,Ltd) -2741 Navarre Av -Ste 402
-Oregon 43616

(419) 885-4149 ..**Breier,** Gregory J '81 -4149 Holland-Sylvania Rd -Ste 2
-Toledo 43623

(419) 636-3196 ..**Breininger,** Ryan S '99 %Newcomer S&S -117 W Maple
-Bryan 43506 **Fx:**636-0867

(513) 779-4961 ..**Breissinger,** Kirc J '96 -7343 Cinnamon Woods Dr
-West Chester 45069

(513) 621-6464 ..**Breitenbach,** Thomas A '90 (Graydon H&R LLP) -511 Walnut
-1900 Fifth Third Ctr -Cincinnati 45202 **Fx:**651-3836

(614) 464-4201 ..**Breitfeller,** Ralph E '78 (McGrath & B LLP) -140 E Town
-Ste 1070 -Columbus 43215

(513) 984-0074 ..**Breitholle,** Howard F '50 -9789 Cooper Woods Ct
-Cincinnati 45241 **Fx:**984-0074

(513) 381-2838 ..**Breitkreutz,** Brenda M '98 %Taft S&H LLP -425 Walnut -Ste 1800
-Cincinnati 45202 **Fx:**381-0205

(614) 249-4572 ..**Breitstadt,** Charles P '74 Nationwide Ins Co -1 Nationwide Plz
-27 T -Columbus 43215

(800) 243-0210 ..**Brej,** Christopher J '04 Westfield Grp -1 Park Cir -Bx5001
-Westfield Center 44251 **Fx:**(330) 887-2588

(216) 696-0800 ..**Brelo,** Clayton E '67 (Gibson BZ&M) -55 Pub Sq -Ste 2075
-Cleveland 44113 **Fx:**696-0702

(513) 247-0077 ..**Brendamour,**
Douglas P '82 Brendamour Warehsng Distrbtn & Srvc Inc
-11400 Grooms Rd -Cincinnati 45242

(513) 241-3685 ..**Brendamour,** Reeta H '96 OfCnsl White G&M Co,LPA -1 W 4th
-Ste 1700 -Cincinnati 45202 **Fx:**241-2399

(614) 846-5005 ..**Brengartner,** Beth A '99 Kenric Fine Homes -2728 Jewett Rd
-Powell 43065

(216) 621-0200 ..**Brennan,** Bridget M '00 %Baker & H LLP -1900 E 9th -Ste 3200
-Cleveland 44114 **Fx:**696-0740

(330) 253-5060 ..**Brennan,** David L '57 Brennan M&D,LLC -75 E Market
-Akron 44308 **Fx:**253-1977

(330) 743-4116 ..**Brennan Frederick Vouros & Yarwood,Ltd** -29 E Front -2nd Fl
-Youngstown 44503

(937) 224-9291 ..**Brennan,** James M '57 Young & A Co,LPA -130 W 2nd -Ste 2000
-Dayton 45402 **Fx:**224-9769

(440) 951-8889 ..**Brennan,** Jane L '96 Brewster & Brewster,Inc -7575 Tyler Blvd
-A-4 -Mentor 44060

(513) 556-6814 ..**Brennan,** Kellie L '04 Univ of Cincinnati -Ofc of Judcl Affairs
-Ste 745 -Cincinnati 45219

(614) 751-1000 ..**Brennan,** Kevin J '89 Medical Assurance Inc -630 Morrison Rd
-Columbus 43230

Brennan, Kevin J '02 -7141 W Cross Crk Trl -Brecksville 44141

(216) 696-1422 ..**Brennan,** Kimberly A '93 %McCarthy LC&L Co,LPA
-101 Prospect Av W -1800 Mdlnd Bldg -Cleveland 44115
Fx:696-1210

(330) 253-5060 ..**Brennan Manna & Diamond, LLC** -75 E Market -Akron 44308
Fx:253-1977

(216) 621-0200 ..**Brennan,** Maureen A '89 (Baker & H LLP) -1900 E 9th -Ste 3200
-Cleveland 44114 **Fx:**696-0740

(216) 781-5515 ..**Brennan,** Michael D '96 Hermann C&S,LLP -1301 E 9th -Ste 500
-Cleveland 44114 **Fx:**781-1030

(216) 621-0200 ..**Brennan,** Terry M '95 (Baker & H LLP) -1900 E 9th -Ste 3200
-Cleveland 44114 **Fx:**696-0740

(513) 621-6464 ..**Brennan,** Thomas A '66 (Graydon H&R LLP) -511 Walnut
-1900 Fifth Third Ctr -Cincinnati 45202 **Fx:**651-3836

(419) 241-3601 ..**Brennan,** William J '80 Assoc Gen Contractors -1845 Collingwood
-Toledo 43624

(513) 352-6638 ..**Brenneman,** Deborah S '93 (Thompson H LLP) -312 Walnut
-14th Fl -Cincinnati 45202 **Fx:**241-4771

(216) 991-5391 ..**Brenneman,** Kathryn R '84 -14325 Drexmore Rd -Shaker Heights
44120

(614) 258-6000 ..**Brenner Brown Golian & McCaffrey Co,LPA** -2109 Stella Ct
-Columbus 43215 **Fx:**258-6006

(937) 586-3100 ..**Brenner,** Joan B '81 (ES Gallon & Assoc) -40 W 4th -22nd Fl
-Dayton 45402 **Fx:**586-3100

(216) 689-8064 ..**Brenner,** Paul M '86 KeyBank NA -127 Pub Sq -17th Fl
-Cleveland 44114

(937) 427-9450 ..**Brenner,** Robert A '97 -Bx341021 -Beavercreek 45434

(440) 247-5555 ..**Brenner,** Robert C '79 (Brenner K LLP) -50 E Wshngtn
-Chagrin Falls 44022 **Fx:**247-5551

(614) 258-6000 ..**Brenner,** Todd A '91 (Brenner BG&M Co,LPA) -2109 Stella Ct
-Columbus 43215 **Fx:**258-6006

(419) 682-6661 ..**Brenner,** William J '77 -112 N Defiance -Stryker 43557
Fx:682-7152

(614) 462-5472 ..**Brenning,** Mary F '96 %Kegler BH&R -65 E State -Ste 1800
-Columbus 43215 **Fx:**464-2634

(614) 716-2147 ..**Breseman,** Ross E '93 American Electric Power
-155 W Nationwide Blvd -Ste 500 -Columbus 43215

(330) 702-0780 ..**Bresko,** Andrew G '75 (Luckhart MZ&R) -3810 Starrs Centre Dr
-Canfield 44406

(330) 656-2702 ..**Breslin,** Jordan K '84 (Scheuer M&B LLC) -110 W Streetsboro Rd
-Ste 2A -Hudson 44236 **Fx:**656-2755

(614) 466-3576 ..**Bressler,** Marla K '92 OH DYS -51 N High -Columbus 43215

(614) 538-1116 ..**Bressman,** David A '90 -3011 Bethel Rd -Ste 103
-Columbus 43220

(440) 933-6718 ..**Bretnall,** Dorothy H '81 -317 Long Pnte Dr -Avon Lake 44012

(216) 621-4268 ..**Brett,** Maureen '98 Ofc of Chptr 13 Trustees -200 Pub Sq
-Ste 3860 BP Twr -Cleveland 44114

(513) 530-9595 ..**Bretz,** Charles G Jr. '71 -4725 Cornell Rd -Cincinnati 45241

(419) 241-1200 ..**Bretzloff,** Margaret E '85 Cooper & W,LPA -900 Adams
-Toledo 43624 **Fx:**242-5675

(440) 323-5700 ..**Breunig,** Erik A '04 %Taylor B&R Co,LPA -409 East Av -Ste B
-Elyria 44035

(440) 323-5700 ..**Breunig,** Kurt A '79 (Taylor B&R Co,LPA) -409 East Av -Ste B
-Elyria 44035

(330) 643-2943 ..**Brevetta,** Nicholas A '02 Summit Cnty Pros-Juv -650 Dan
-Akron 44310 **Fx:**379-3647

(216) 642-8234 ..**Brewer,** Blake O '84 -4807 Rockside Rd -Ste 400
-Cleveland 44131

(513) 929-3400 ..**Brewer,** Bryant L '00 %Baker & H LLP -312 Walnut -Ste 3200
-Cincinnati 45202 **Fx:**929-0303

(412) 394-2452 ..**Brewer,** Christopher B '96 (Thorp R&A LLP) -301 Grant -Ste 1400
-Pittsburgh, PA 15219 **Fx:**394-2555

(513) 868-3663 ..**Brewer,** David B '98 -723 Dayton -Hamilton 45011

(513) 721-5151 ..**Brewer,** Kevin R '97 %Katz G&N,LLP -105 E 4th -4th Fl
-Cincinnati 45202 **Fx:**621-9285

(614) 890-5632 ..**Brewer,** Lee M '89 (Brewer McGraw & Assoc) -1001 Eastwind Dr
-Ste 203 -Westerville 43081

(614) 466-6750 ..**Brewer,** Margaret A '85 OH Dept Taxation -30 E Broad -22nd Fl
-Columbus 43215 **Fx:**466-7979

(330) 336-7377 ..**Brewer,** Scott E '88 (SE Brewer Co,LPA) -676 High
-Wadsworth 44281 **Fx:**336-3200

(513) 412-5400 ..**Brewer,** Stephen J '77 (Buckley K,LPA) -201 E 5th -Ste 1420
-Cincinnati 45202 **Fx:**412-5401

(937) 222-2424 ..**Brewer,** Steven L '98 %Freund F&A -1 S Main -Ste 1800
-Dayton 45402 **Fx:**222-5369

(614) 466-8980 ..**Brey,** Diane R '88 Atty Gen -30 E Broad -Columbus 43215
Fx:466-5087

(614) 221-4000 ..**Brey,** Donald C '81 (Chester W&S LLP) -65 E State -10th Fl
-Columbus 43215 **Fx:**221-4012

(513) 732-7313 ..**Breyer,** Daniel J '77 Clermont Cnty Pros -123 N 3rd
-Batavia 45103

Breyer, William E '74 -(Address Unavailable)

(330) 837-9735 ..**Breyfogle,** Edwin H '76 -11 Lincoln Way W -Ste 2B
-Massillon 44647

(937) 879-2261 ..**Brezine & Bowers** -188 W Hebble Av -Fairborn 45324

(937) 879-2261 ..**Brezine,** Donald F '84 (Brezine & B) -188 W Hebble Av
-Fairborn 45324

(440) 646-3375 ..**Brezovec,** Brian P '97 Rockwell Automation Allen-Bradley Co
-1 Allen-Bradley Dr -Mayfield Heights 44124

(330) 758-0080 ..**Briach,** George G '82 (White & B) -755 Boardman-Canfld Rd
-Bx9304 -Youngstown 44513 **Fx:**758-9533

(330) 494-2121 ..**Brian,** Richard F '82 -5770 Dressler Rd NW -Ste 101
-Canton 44720

(330) 494-2121 ..**Brian,** Steven J '88 -5770 Dressler Rd NW -Ste 101
-Canton 44720

(440) 286-9549 ..**Brice,** Edward T '74 (Newman & B) -214 E Park -Chardon 44024

(937) 845-3878 ..**Brichacek,** John I '75 (Brichacek & G) -101 S Main
-New Carlisle 45344

(513) 684-3711 ..**Brichler,** Robert C '74 US Atty -221 E 4th -Ste 400
-Cincinnati 45202 **Fx:**684-6385

(216) 241-5310 ..**Brick,** Timothy T '88 (Gallagher SF&N) -1501 Euclid Av -6th Fl
-Cleveland 44115 **Fx:**241-1608

(614) 227-2312 ..**Bricker,** Christine A '95 (Bricker & E LLP) -100 S 3rd
-Columbus 43215 **Fx:**227-2390

(330) 965-5195 ..**Bricker,** Dale E '61 -100 DeBartolo Pl -Bx3232
-Youngstown 44513 **Fx:**726-7993

(614) 488-1161 ..**Bricker,** Derek F '01 Kennedy & K -3040 Riverside Dr -Ste 103
-Columbus 43221

(614) 269-4900 ..**Bricker,** Douglas M '69 (Bricker & M,LLC) -4100 Regent -Ste T
-Columbus 43219 **Fx:**269-4901

(614) 227-2300 ..**Bricker & Eckler LLP** -100 S 3rd -Columbus 43215 **Fx:**227-2390

(216) 523-5405 ..**Bricker & Eckler LLP** -1375 E 9th -Ste 1500 -Cleveland 44114
Fx:523-7071

(330) 392-1541 ..**Bricker,** Gina DeGenova '00 %Harrington H&M,Ltd
-108 Main Av SW -Ste 500 -Bx1510 -Warren 44482 **Fx:**394-6890

(614) 269-4900 ..**Bricker & Maxfield,LLC** -4100 Regent -Ste T -Columbus 43219
Fx:269-4901

(330) 259-0612 ..**Bricker,** Thomas R '00 -4531 Belmont Av -Ste C
-Youngstown 44505

(614) 365-4100 ..**Bricker,** Timothy R '93 (Carpenter & L LLP) -280 N High
-Ste 1300 280 Plz -Columbus 43215 **Fx:**365-9145

(201) 592-1300 ..**Brickman,** James T '72 PricewaterhouseCoopers LLP
-2100 N Central Rd -Bx1400 -Fort Lee, NJ 07024

(513) 421-4248 ..**Brickner,** Lisa M '92 Amer Lgl Pub Corp -432 Walnut -Ste 1200
-Cincinnati 45202 **Fx:**763-3562

(216) 522-7690 ..**Brickner,** Paul '66 SSA -1350 Euclid Av -7th Fl -Cleveland 44115

(513) 455-7600 ..**Bride,** Nancy J '97 Greenebaum D&M PLLC -255 E 5th
-2800 Chemed Ctr -Cincinnati 45202 **Fx:**455-8500

(330) 451-7897 ..**Bridenstine,** David M '80 Stark Cnty Pros -110 Central Plz
-Ste 510 -Canton 44702

(419) 255-0814 ..**Bridges,** Angelita C '00 ABLE -520 Mad Av -740 Spitzer Bldg
-Toledo 43604 **Fx:**259-2880

(614) 228-1541 ..**Bridges,** Michael D '93 (Baker & H LLP) -65 E State -Ste 2100
-Columbus 43215 **Fx:**462-2616

(937) 644-9125 ..**Bridges,** Robert L '79 (Cannizzaro FB&J) -302 S Main
-Marysville 43040 **Fx:**644-0754

(614) 464-6400 ..**Bridgman,** G Ross Jr. '73 (Vorys SS&P LLP) -52 E Gay -Bx1008
-Columbus 43216 **Fx:**464-6350

(202) 626-6600 ..**Briggs,** Alan L '67 (Squire S&D LLP) -1201 Penn Av NW -Bx407
-Washington, DC 20044 **Fx:**626-6780

Briggs, Beverly M '72 -10629 Elmwood Av
-Garfield Heights 44125

(216) 781-7990 ..**Briggs,** David A '81 Sammon & Co,LPA -614 Superior Av NW
-1160 Rckfllr Bldg -Cleveland 44113

(330) 643-2519 ..**Briggs,** Kasie L '98 Summit Cnty Exec Ofc -175 S Main -8th Fl
-Akron 44308

(513) 579-6400 ..**Briggs,** Laurie A '89 (Keating M&K PLL) -1 E 4th
-1400 Provident Twr -Cincinnati 45202 **Fx:**579-6457

(330) 644-7922 ..**Briggs,** Randy D '83 -4367 State Rd -Akron 44319

(330) 376-5300 ..**Briggs,** Robert W '66 (Buckingham D&B,LLP) -50 S Main -Bx1500
-Akron 44309 **Fx:**258-6559

(216) 586-3939 ..**Briggs,** Thomas A '94 (Jones D) -901 Lakeside Av
-Cleveland 44114 **Fx:**579-0212

Brigham, Anne T '99 -12659 Girdled Rd -Concord 44077

(513) 621-2244 ..**Brigham,** Charles A III '85 Brigham & B -4931 Delhi Pike
-Cincinnati 45238

(216) 696-4700 ..**Bright,** James R '76 (Spieth BM&N Co,LPA) -925 Euclid Av
-2000 Huntngtn Bldg -Cleveland 44115 **Fx:**696-2706

(216) 983-1058 ..**Bright,** Mary C '76 Univ Hospitals Hlth System -10524 Euclid Av
-Cleveland 44106

Bright, Robert P '04 -290 Apache Trl -Loveland 45140

(330) 374-0300 ..**Brightbill,** James E '87 -One Cascade Plz -Ste 710 -Akron 44308
Fx:374-0433

(216) 443-6381 ..**Brighton,** Anthony R '98 %OH Crt Appls -1 Lakeside Av
-Cleveland 44113

(614) 221-7777 ..**Brightwell,** Julie M '93 %Ohio Ins Co -155 E Broad -13th Fl
-Columbus 43215

(614) 221-0240 ..**Brigner,** Julie E '96 %Hahn L&P LLP -65 E State -Ste 1400
-Columbus 43215 **Fx:**221-5909

(614) 462-5015 ..**Brigner,** Nancy A '92 OfCnsl Schottenstein Z&D -250 West
-Bx165020 -Columbus 43216 **Fx:**462-5135

(937) 512-2950 ..**Brigner,** Victor M '77 Sinclair Cmmnty Coll -414 W 3rd
-Dayton 45402

(419) 898-0000 ..**Brikmanis,** John A '89 -139 E Water -Oak Harbor 43449

(419) 241-9000 ..**Briley,** Michael M '69 (Shumaker L&K,LLP) -1000 Jackson
-Toledo 43624 **Fx:**241-6894

(440) 324-5353 ..**Brill,** Douglas M '78 %Spike & M,LLP -1551 W River Rd N
-Elyria 44035 **Fx:**324-6529

(614) 221-5216 ..**Brill,** Lauren S '03 %Wiles BB&B Co,LPA -300 Spruce -1st Fl
-Columbus 43215 **Fx:**221-5692

(614) 466-3269 ..**Brill,** William L '80 Industrial Commssn of OH -30 W Spring -9th Fl
-Columbus 43215 **Fx:**752-8785

(440) 243-5010 ..**Briller,** David D '77 (D Briller Co,LPA) -7379 Pearl Rd
-Middleburg Heights 44130 **Fx:**243-0105

Brillian, John H Jr. '02 -8372 Stationhouse Ct -Lorton, VA 22079

(419) 422-8000 ..**Brimley,** J Bruce '78 -337 S Main -Ste 300 -Findlay 45840
Fx:422-0399

(216) 752-9930 ..**Brindza,** Robert A II '89 (RA Brindza Co.,LPA)
-3645 Warrensvll Ctr Rd -Ste 219 -Shaker Heights 44122

Briner, Merlin G '66 -Bx9217 -Canton 44711

Bring, Dale V '74 -667 Clotts Rd -Gahanna 43230

(614) 221-5216 ..**Bringardner,** Daniel E '78 (Wiles BB&B Co,LPA) -300 Spruce
-1st Fl -Columbus 43215 **Fx:**221-5692

(614) 221-5216 ..**Bringardner,** Richard D '78 (Wiles BB&B Co,LPA) -300 Spruce
-1st Fl -Columbus 43215 **Fx:**221-5692

(740) 694-3015 ..**Bringman,** William P '70 -13 E Cllg -Fredericktown 43019

(614) 481-4480 ..**Brininger,** Tod A '98 %Koffel & J -2130 Arlngtn Av
-Columbus 43221

(216) 830-6830 ..**Brink,** Michael C '03 %Brouse M -1001 Lakeside Av -Ste 1600
-Cleveland 44114 **Fx:**830-6807

(513) 665-4888 ..**Brinker,** John R '87 -414 Walnut -Ste 1220 -Cincinnati 45202

(513) 922-3200 ..**Brinker,** Stephen G '77 (Haverkamp BR&R Co,LPA)
-5856 Glenway Av -Cincinnati 45238 **Fx:**922-8096

(614) 438-3001 ..**Brinkman,** Dale T '77 Worthington Industries Inc
-1205 Dearborn Dr -Columbus 43085

(937) 226-1996 ..**Brinkman,** Daniel E '82 -120 W 2nd -2000 LIberty Twr
-Dayton 45402

(513) 241-2324 ..**Brinkman,** David H '94 (Wood H&E LLP) -441 Vine -Ste 2700
-Cincinnati 45202 **Fx:**421-7269

(937) 223-8177 ..**Brinkman,** Justin D '03 %Coolidge WW&L -33 W 1st -Ste 600
-Dayton 45402 **Fx:**223-6705

(513) 632-5310 ..**Brinkman,** Karen R '84 (Brinkman & Assoc) -119 E Court
-Cincinnati 45202

Brinkman, Kathleen M '75 -address not available
-Cincinnati 45202

(513) 241-3100 ..**Brinkman,** Michael R '88 %Lerner S&R -120 E 4th -8th Fl
-Cincinnati 45202

(513) 621-2120 ..**Brinn,** Stuart C '76 Strauss & T,LPA -150 E 4th -4th Fl
-Cincinnati 45202 **Fx:**241-8259

(419) 882-7100 ..**Brinning,** Leslie B '02 %Lydy & M,Ltd -4930 Holland Sylvania Rd
-Sylvania 43560 **Fx:**882-1120

(937) 223-6003 ..**Brinsfield,** Gary T '68 (Dunlevey M&F) -110 N Main -Ste 1000
-Dayton 45402 **Fx:**223-8550

(617) 523-2700 ..**Bris-Bois,** Marie A '98 %Holland & K -10 St James Av
-Boston, MA 02116

(614) 224-4149 ..**Briscoe,** Colleen H '77 -500 S Front -Ste 125 -Columbus 43215
Fx:224-0738

(614) 466-3998 ..**Briscoe,** Emily K '96 Unemploymnt Comp Commssn -145 S Front
-Bx182299 -Columbus 43218

(614) 445-8461 ..**Brisk,** Marlene B '89 Schottenstein Mgt Co -1798 Frebis Av
-Columbus 43206

(440) 838-8800 ..**Briskin,** Seth P '95 %Millisor & N Co,LPA -9150 S Hills Blvd
-Ste 300 -Cleveland 44147 **Fx:**838-8805

(937) 222-3000 ..**Brissie,** William J '02 %Falke & D LLC -30 Wyoming
-Dayton 45409 **Fx:**222-1414

(419) 332-7161 ..**Bristley,** C Wesley '51 -323 S High -Fremont 43420 **Fx:**332-7354

(216) 781-7956 ..**Bristol,** Jason R '00 (Cohen R&K LLP) -1468 W 9th -Ste 705
-Cleveland 44113 **Fx:**781-8061

(614) 228-4526 ..**Bristol,** Rachelle E '98 OH Educ Assn -Leg Srvcs -225 E Broad
-Columbus 43215

(513) 564-9222 ..**Bristol,** William M '01 -120 E 4th -Ste 1040 -Cincinnati 45202

(859) 441-7800 ..**Bristow,** William S '91 Jeff Wyler Dealer Grp -100 Alexandria Pike
-Fort Thomas, KY 41075

(813) 655-6363 ..**Britt,** Anthony '87 -1381 Oakfld Dr -Oakfld Business Ctr
-Brandon, FL 33511

(614) 224-8339 ..**Britt Campbell Nagel & Sproat** -490 City Park Av
-Columbus 43215 **Fx:**224-2001

(513) 794-4020 ..**Britt,** Curtis D '99 Guarantee Title & Trust Co -8230 Mntgmry Rd
-Ste 210 -Cincinnati 45236 **Fx:**794-4027

(614) 224-8339 ..**Britt,** James C Jr. '73 (Britt CN&S) -490 City Park Av
-Columbus 43215 **Fx:**224-2001

(513) 723-4000 ..**Britt,** Kent A '97 %Vorys SS&P LLP -221 E 4th
-Ste 2000 Atrium Two -Bx0236 -Cincinnati 45201 **Fx:**723-4056

(216) 485-7970 ..**Britt,** Stephen T '89 %McCauley & Assoc Co,LPA -5454 State Rd
-Parma 44134 **Fx:**485-7979

(216) 447-1551 ..**Brittain,** Brian K '81 (Ross B&S Co LPA) -6000 Freedom
Square Dr -Ste 540 -Cleveland 44131 **Fx:**447-1554

(216) 622-8200 ..**Brittain,** Michael P '79 (Calfee H&G LLP) -800 Superior Av
-Ste 1400 -Cleveland 44114 **Fx:**241-0816

(513) 977-8200 ..**Brittingham,** J David '93 (Dinsmore & S LLP) -255 E 5th
-Ste 1900 -Cincinnati 45202 **Fx:**977-8141

(202) 408-4158 ..**Brittingham,** Smith R IV '87 (Finnegan HFG&D,LLP) -1300 I NW
-Ste 700 -Washington, DC 20005 **Fx:**408-4400

(419) 321-1348 ..**Britton,** Eric D '92 (Shumaker L&K,LLP) -1000 Jackson
-Toledo 43624 **Fx:**241-6894

(614) 251-4000 ..**Britton,** John B '98 %Columbus Fndtn -1234 E Broad
-Columbus 43205

(216) 642-0323 ..**Britton,** John E '81 (Britton SP&K Co,LPA) -4700 Rockside Rd
-Ste 540 Summit One -Cleveland 44131 **Fx:**642-0747

(216) 642-0323 ..**Britton Smith Peters & Kalail Co, LPA** -4700 Rockside Rd
-Ste 540 Summit One -Cleveland 44131 **Fx:**642-0747

(419) 242-7415 ..**Britz,** Harland M '56 (Britz & Z) -416 N Erie -Ste 100 -Toledo
43624 **Fx:**241-7818

(513) 943-7100 ..**Brizzolara,** Paul T '82 Midland Co -7000 Mdlnd Blvd
-Amelia 45102

(901) 866-5323 ..**Broadhurst,** Jerome A '73 (Armstrong A,PLLC) -80 Monroe Av
-Ste 700 Brinkley Plz -Memphis, TN 38103 **Fx:**524-4936

(216) 896-2584 ..**Brobst,** Claudia Mae '81 Parker Hannifin Corp
-6035 Parkland Blvd -Cleveland 44124

(330) 722-1152 ..**Brobst,** Lorie K '94 -209 W Lbrty -Medina 44256

(513) 732-7313 ..**Brock,** Anthony W '93 Clermont Cnty Pros -123 N 3rd
-Batavia 45103

(740) 373-5455 ..**Brock,** Jerry A '63 (Theisen B,LPA) -424 2nd -Bx739
-Marietta 45750 **Fx:**373-4409

(513) 977-8200 ..**Brock,** Louise S '96 (Dinsmore & S LLP) -255 E 5th -Ste 1900
-Cincinnati 45202 **Fx:**977-8141

(419) 227-3423 ..**Brock,** Terry B '93 (Huffman KB&B LLC) -127-129 N Pierce
-Bx546 -Lima 45802 **Fx:**228-1937

(614) 620-2196 ..**Brock,** Thomas J '96 -5 E Long -Ste 902 -Columbus 43215

(513) 946-3032 ..**Brocker,** Nanci H '98 Hamilton Cnty Pros -230 E 9th
-Cincinnati 45202 **Fx:**946-3017

(213) 443-3236 ..**Brockett,** Daniel L '92 (Quinn EUO&H LLP) -865 S Figueroa
-10th Fl -Los Angeles, CA 90017 **Fx:**624-0643

(216) 246-9033 .. **Brockler**, Aaron J '04 -2683 Hmpshr Rd #2
-Cleveland Heights 44106

(614) 879-4143 .. **Brockman**, Blaine P '01 Brockman Leg Srvcs -765 Lakevw Dr
-West Jefferson 43162

(513) 243-2264 .. **Brockman**, Cynthia K '82 GE -1 Neumann Way -S24
-Cincinnati 45215

(513) 421-6630 .. **Brockman**, James F '81 Lindhorst & D Co,LPA -312 Walnut
-Ste 2300 -Cincinnati 45202

(800) 243-0210 .. **Brockman**, Phoebe M '83 Westfield Grp -1 Park Cir -Bx5001
-Westfield Center 44251 **Fx:**(330) 887-2588

(614) 225-7020 .. **Brockman**, Vincent C '88 Borden Foods Corp -180 E Broad
-20th Fl -Columbus 43215

Brockmeyer, Jennifer L '04 -(Address Unavailable)

(740) 439-1499 .. **Brockwell**, Jeremy W '84 -67816 Read Rd -Cambridge 43725

(740) 374-2629 .. **Brockwell**, Joseph H '81 SE OH Lgl Srvcs -427 2nd
-Marietta 45750

(330) 297-3850 .. **Brode**, David M '90 Portage Cnty Pros -466 S Chestnut
-Ravenna 44266

(513) 579-7560 .. **Broderick**, Dennis J '76 Federated Dept Stores,Inc -7 W 7th
-Cincinnati 45202

(216) 696-3232 .. **Brodhead**, Peter J '79 (Spangenberg S&L,LLP) -1900 E 9th
-2400 Natl City Ctr -Cleveland 44114 **Fx:**696-3924

(216) 443-7800 .. **Brodnik**, Louis J '83 Cuyahoga Cnty Pros -1200 Ontario -8th Fl
-Cleveland 44113 **Fx:**698-2270

(614) 228-8400 .. **Brodnik**, Martyn T '80 OfCnsl Ulmer & B LLP -88 E Broad
-Ste 1600 -Columbus 43215 **Fx:**228-8561

(330) 995-7702 .. **Brodsky**, Jerry '87 Aurora City Schools -102 E Garfld Rd
-Aurora 44202

(216) 781-5550 .. **Brodsky**, Philip R '52 -614 W Superior Av -Ste 814
-Cleveland 44113 **Fx:**781-5550

(614) 462-5456 .. **Brody**, John P '79 (Kegler BH&R) -65 E State -Ste 1800
-Columbus 43215 **Fx:**464-2634

(330) 264-9897 .. **Broehl**, Margo E '77 -105 W Pine -Wooster 44691

(740) 393-6720 .. **Broeren**, P Robert Jr. '98 Knox Cnty Pros -117 E High -Ste 234
-Mount Vernon 43050

(216) 875-9843 .. **Broering-Jacobs**, Carolyn '94 CSU-Marshall Cllg of Law
-2121 Euclid Av -LB138 -Cleveland 44115 **Fx:**687-6881

(419) 893-4880 .. **Brogan**, Allan J '58 Marsh M Ltd -204 W Wayne -Maumee 43537

(216) 621-1511 .. **Brogley**, Joycelyn '91 -457 Leader Bldg -Cleveland 44114

(513) 272-1200 .. **Brokamp**, Larry J '97 (Doan K&B,LLC) -5710 Wooster Pike
-Ste 212 -Cincinnati 45227

(216) 524-2212 .. **Brokaw**, Glenn J '82 -4890 Hickory Nut Ln -Independence 44131

(216) 896-5600 .. **Brokaw**, Kevin M '00 %Levy & D -25200 Chagrin Blvd -Ste 310
-Beachwood 44122 **Fx:**896-5601

(513) 977-8200 .. **Bromberg**, Barbara S '73 (Dinsmore & S LLP) -255 E 5th
-Ste 1900 -Cincinnati 45202 **Fx:**977-8141

(513) 651-0100 .. **Bromberg**, Robert S '72 -1144 Rookwood Dr -Cincinnati 45208

(216) 522-2763 .. **Brommer**, Carolyn T '85 Fed Med & Conc Srvc
-6161 Oak Tree Blvd -Ste 100 -Independence 44131

(216) 363-5220 .. **Brondou**, Derek M '00 (Lindner WC&B,LLP) -55 Pub Sq -Ste 1600
-Cleveland 44113

(937) 746-2832 .. **Bronson**, Barbara J '73 (Ruppert B&R Co,LPA) -1063 E 2nd
-Bx369 -Franklin 45005 **Fx:**746-2855

(513) 723-4000 .. **Bronson**, Michael J '01 %Vorys SS&P LLP -221 E 4th
-Ste 2000 Atrium Two -Bx0236 -Cincinnati 45201 **Fx:**723-4056

(513) 241-9400 .. **Bronson**, Mya E '99 Legal Aid -215 E 9th -Ste 200
-Cincinnati 45202

(937) 449-2800 .. **Broock**, Richard A '72 (Chernesky H&K PLL) -10 Cthse Plz SW
-Ste 1100 -Dayton 45402 **Fx:**449-2821

(330) 455-0173 .. **Brooker**, James K '62 (Day KRW&R,Ltd) -200 Market Av N
-Ste 300 -Bx24213 -Canton 44701 **Fx:**455-2633

(303) 675-4421 .. **Brooker**, Joseph M '89 Medicine Bow Energy Corp -1225 17th
-Ste 1900 -Denver, CO 80202

Brooker, Shoshanna M '04 -(Address Unavailable)

(330) 638-7347 .. **Brooker**, William H '81 -197C W Main -Cortland 44410

(614) 848-4300 .. **Brookes**, Mark C '83 (Maney & B) -92 Northwoods Blvd -Ste B
-Columbus 43235

(330) 386-5964 .. **Brookes**, Timothy R '79 -517 Bway -Bx15 -East Liverpool 43920

(859) 282-3900 .. **Brooking**, John R '60 (Brooking B&K PLLC) -1717 Dixie Hwy
-Ste 920 -Fort Wright, KY 41011

(859) 581-5898 .. **Brooking**, John S '91 (Brooking R&H PLLC) -1717 Dixie Hwy
-Ste 920 -Ft Wright, KY 41011

(937) 228-9790 .. **Brooks**, Adrienne D '04 %LP Mulligan & Assoc LPA,Co
-28 N Wilkinson -2nd Fl -Bx10838 -Dayton 45402

(216) 241-6045 .. **Brooks**, Christopher F '94 Cnsl Midland Title Sec,Inc
-1111 Superior Av E -Ste 700 -Cleveland 44114

(216) 932-1069 .. **Brooks**, Ellen M '87 -14444 E Carroll Blvd
-University Heights 44118

(216) 591-1610 .. **Brooks**, Jeffrey M '69 -23215 Commerce Park Rd -#316
-Beachwood 44122

Brooks, Jennifer M '04 -(Address Unavailable)

(614) 224-9900 .. **Brooks**, Keith H '75 -172 E State -Ste 550 -Columbus 43215

(440) 285-3511 .. **Brooks**, Keith K '69 OfCnsl Petersen & I -401 South
-Chardon 44024 **Fx:**285-3363

(513) 721-1350 .. **Brooks**, Kyle C '88 (Barron PB&S) -3074 Madison Rd
-Cincinnati 45209

(740) 869-4400 .. **Brooks**, L Steven '87 (L Brooks Law Ofc LLC) -23 E Columbus
-Bx201 -Mount Sterling 43143 **Fx:**869-3364

(614) 457-1010 .. **Brooks & Logan Co,LPA** -4921 Dierker Rd -Columbus 43220

Brooks, Lori A '04 -(Address Unavailable)

(216) 479-8500 .. **Brooks**, Patrick J '98 %Squire S&D LLP -127 Pub Sq
-4900 Key Twr -Cleveland 44114 **Fx:**479-8780

(614) 457-1010 .. **Brooks**, Paula L '83 (Brooks & L Co,LPA) -4921 Dierker Rd
-Columbus 43220

(216) 621-2929 .. **Brooks**, Phyllis E '81 -75 Pub Sq -Ste 600 -Cleveland 44113

(937) 225-4609 .. **Brooks**, Richard C '68 Montgomery Cnty Probate Ct -41 N Perry
-Bx972 -Dayton 45422

(937) 222-2424 .. **Brooks**, Richard C Jr. '00 %Freund F&A -1 S Main -Ste 1800
-Dayton 45402 **Fx:**222-5369

(614) 221-3155 .. **Brooks**, Richard D Jr. '72 (Bailey C LLC) -10 W Broad
-Columbus 43215 **Fx:**221-0479

(330) 628-1446 .. **Brooks**, Richard R '87 -3808 Mogadore Rd -Mogadore 44260

(216) 522-1920 .. **Brooks**, Robert C II '88 -600 Superior Av -Ste 1300
-Cleveland 44114

(614) 462-3996 .. **Brooks**, Stephanie L '86 10th Dist Ct of Appls -373 S High -24th Fl
-Columbus 43215

(216) 741-2365 .. **Brooks**, Sylvester Jr. '75 UAW Legal Srvcs -707 Brookpark Rd
-Brooklyn Heights 44109

(216) 694-4307 .. **Brooks**, William M '79 Hyatt Legal Plans,Inc -1111 Superior Av
-Cleveland 44114

(937) 339-0511 .. **Brookshire**, James D '91 %Dungan & L Co,LPA -210 W Main
-Troy 45373 **Fx:**335-5802

(216) 928-1010 .. **Broome**, Jeffrey Scott '89 %Rotatori BGS&A Co LPA
-526 Superior Av E -800 Leader Bldg -Cleveland 44114
Fx:928-1007

(614) 771-6933 .. **Broschak**, Thomas J '80 -5785 Middlebay Dr -PMB 112 -Hilliard
43026

Brose, James J '91 -(Address Unavailable)

Brosh, Lenee M '02 -(Address Unavailable)

(614) 464-3563 .. **Brosius**, Donald F '80 (Loveland & B) -50 W Broad -Ste 3300
-Columbus 43215

(216) 526-2068 .. **Broski**, Gerald F '68 Maple Hts Bd of Ed -15785 Bway
-Maple Heights 44137

(216) 737-5000 .. **Broski**, Todd A '00 Chernett WY&P -1301 E 9th -Ste 3300
-Cleveland 44114 **Fx:**737-0011

(440) 282-9109 .. **Brosky**, Michael E '92 -4463 Oberlin Av -Lorain 44053

(440) 282-6188 .. **Brosky**, Robert E '69 1st Fed Savings of Lorain -3721 Oberlin Av
-Lorain 44053

(330) 865-9980 .. **Brosnan**, Margaret A '73 -906 Sturbrdg Dr -Akron 44313

(513) 381-0656 .. **Bross**, David J '04 %Kohnen & P LLP -201 E 5th -Ste 800
-Cincinnati 45202 **Fx:**381-5823

(304) 347-3350 .. **Brossart**, Joseph A '99 Fed Pub Def -300 VA E -Ste 3400
-Charleston, WV 25301

(216) 831-0042 .. **Brosse**, Peter D '84 Meyers RF&L LPA -28601 Chagrin Blvd
-Ste 500 -Cleveland 44122 **Fx:**831-0542

(419) 243-4006 .. **Brossia**, Anne M '01 %Kitch DWD&V,PC -405 Mad Av -Ste 1500
-Toledo 43604 **Fx:**243-7333

(616) 651-2445 .. **Brothers**, Robert P '86 Bird SBS&P -227 W Chicago Rd
-Sturgis, MI 49091

(330) 533-8323 .. **Brott**, Gary N '83 -6600 Summit Dr -Canfield 44406 **Fx:**533-8324

(216) 861-4533 .. **Brouhard**, Julia R '89 (Ray RC&D PLL) -1717 E 9th
-Cleveland 44114 **Fx:**861-4568

(216) 765-8004 .. **Brouman**, Alvin '55 OfCnsl SE Stein & Assoc,LPA
-3509 Kersdale Rd -Pepper Pike 44124 **Fx:**765-0119

(330) 928-7878 .. **Brouse**, Karen H '02 -1013 Portage Trl -Ste 7 -Bx3792
-Cuyahoga Falls 44223 **Fx:**920-1832

(330) 535-5711 .. **Brouse McDowell** -106 S Main -500 First Natl Twr -Akron 44308
Fx:253-8601

(216) 830-6830 .. **Brouse McDowell** -1001 Lakeside Av -Ste 1600 -Cleveland
44114 **Fx:**830-6807

(216) 464-7988 .. **Brover**, David R '85 Brover & Assoc -29425 Chagrin Blvd -#310
-Pepper Pike 44122

(216) 363-6036 .. **Browarek**, Matthew F '88 -1370 Ontario -Ste 2000
-Cleveland 44113

(419) 534-2200 .. **Browarsky**, Phillip D '78 (P Browarsky & Co,LLC)
-3425 Exec Pkwy -Ste 206 -Toledo 43606

(614) 491-1080 .. **Browell**, Douglas K '78 Obetz Village Admin -4175 Alum Crk Dr
-Columbus 43207

(937) 643-9329 .. **Brown**, Alan I '79 Brown Tax Cnsltng,Inc -3131 S Dixie Dr -#421
-Dayton 45439

(513) 621-2825 .. **Brown**, Albert T Jr. '66 (Brown & W) -1014 Vine -2550 Kroger Bldg
-Cincinnati 45202

(614) 227-2344 .. **Brown**, Alexander M '99 %Bricker & E LLP -100 S 3rd
-Columbus 43215 **Fx:**227-2390

(614) 337-8366 .. **Brown**, Amanda B '02 %Pencheff & F -2176A CityGate Dr
-Columbus 43219

(330) 725-8816 .. **Brown & Amodio, LPA** -109 W Lbrty -Bx1117 -Medina 44258

(614) 221-6800 .. **Brown**, Angela F '88 -536 S High -Columbus 43215

Brown, Anne M '00 -325 Groveland Club Dr -Cleveland 44110

(330) 499-6000 .. **Brown**, Anthony E '98 %Baker DBW&M -400 S Main
-Canton 44720 **Fx:**449-6423

(617) 495-0959 .. **Brown**, Ashley Corson '77 -79 JFK B317 -Cambridge, MA 02138

(513) 851-4646 .. **Brown**, Barbara M '80 -868 Waycross Rd -Cincinnati 45240

(419) 525-1611 .. **Brown Bemiller Murray & McIntyre** -70 Park Av W
-Mansfield 44902 **Fx:**525-3810

(614) 466-3998 .. **Brown**, Blaine W '95 Unemploymnt Comp Commssn -145 S Front
-Bx182299 -Columbus 43218

(937) 228-8088 .. **Brown**, Branford D '89 LAWO -333 W 1st -Ste 500A
-Dayton 45402 **Fx:**449-8131

(419) 732-3145 .. **Brown**, Bree Noblitt '01 (Noblitt & B LPA) -318 Madison
-Port Clinton 43452 **Fx:**734-2123

(513) 475-0200 .. **Brown**, Caleb Jr. '74 -527 Linton -Cincinnati 45219

(216) 830-2312 .. **Brown**, Catherine M '96 Charter 1 Bank FSB -1215 Superior Av
-2nd Fl -Cleveland 44114

(740) 983-4074 .. **Brown**, Charles D '90 Teays Valley Middle Schl -383 Circlevll Av
-Ashville 43103

(419) 243-6281 .. **Brown**, Charles E '49 OfCnsl Shindler NH&S,LLP -300 Mad Av
-Ste 1200 -Toledo 43604 **Fx:**243-0129

(513) 977-8200 .. **Brown**, Charles H III '87 (Dinsmore & S LLP) -255 E 5th -Ste 1900
-Cincinnati 45202 **Fx:**977-8141

(419) 524-4711 .. **Brown**, Charles M '72 (Cole B&F) -28 Park Av -Mansfield 44902
Fx:522-8905

(216) 443-8970 .. **Brown**, Charles T '85 Cuyahoga Cnty Probate Ct -1 Lakeside Av
-Rm 254 -Cleveland 44113

(419) 225-8987 .. **Brown**, Christi L '94 -850 Bellefontaine Av -Ste B -Lima 45801

(312) 673-0360 .. **Brown**, Christina L '91 (Baniak P&G) -150 N Wacker Dr -Ste 1200
-Chicago, IL 60606 **Fx:**673-0361

(740) 852-2445 .. **Brown**, Christopher J '97 C Brown LPA -58 E High -Ste A
-London 43140

(937) 449-2800 .. **Brown**, Christopher M '03 %Chernesky H&K PLL
-10 Cthse Plz SW -Ste 1100 -Dayton 45402 **Fx:**449-2821

(216) 696-7600 .. **Brown**, Craig W '79 (Duvin C&H) -1301 E 9th -20th Fl Erievw Twr
-Cleveland 44114 **Fx:**696-2038

(614) 469-5715 .. **Brown**, Daniel A '73 US Atty -303 Marconi Blvd -Ste 200
-Columbus 43215

(513) 422-2001 .. **Brown**, Daniel A '88 Cnsl Frost BT LLC -300 N Main -Ste 200
-Middletown 45042 **Fx:**422-3010

(513) 861-9830 ..Brown, Darrell '79 -Bx17134 -Cincinnati 45217
(937) 257-6142 ..Brown, Darryl D '93 US Air Force 88th ABW/JAG
-5135 Pearson Rd -Ste 2 -Wright Patterson AFB 45433
(704) 344-6222 ..Brown, David A '79 US Atty Ofc -227 W Trade
-Charlotte, NC 28202
(614) 481-6000 ..Brown, David A '92 Cooper & E LLC -2175 Riverside Dr
-Columbus 43221 Fx:481-6001
(440) 838-7600 ..Brown, David H '02 %Janik & D,LLP -9200 S Hills Blvd -Ste 300
-Cleveland 44147 Fx:838-7601
(330) 725-8816 ..Brown, David N '72 %Brown & A,LPA -109 W Lbrty -Bx1117
-Medina 44258
(937) 461-5310 ..Brown, Diana S '96 %Doll J&F -111 W 1st -Ste 1100
-Dayton 45402 Fx:461-7219
(440) 247-9100 ..Brown, Don P '61 -10 Center -Chagrin Falls 44022
(614) 464-6400 ..Brown, Donald A '77 %Vorys SS&P LLP -52 E Gay -Bx1008
-Columbus 43216 Fx:464-6350
(740) 432-5638 ..Brown, Donald D '76 -803 Steubenvll Av -Cambridge 43725
(513) 542-8811 ..Brown, Donté P '03 -1963 Crest Rd -Cincinnati 45240
(440) 564-7987 ..Brown, Douglas B '85 (D Brown,LLC) -13715 Clover Lk Dr
-Ste 100 -Chardon 44024 Fx:564-7989
(740) 773-3952 ..Brown, Edward J '74 -97 W Main -Chillicothe 45601
(614) 466-9546 ..Brown, Emily M '99 OH Brd of Nursing -17 S High -Ste 400
-Columbus 43215
(614) 258-9595 ..Brown, Eric L '91 -225 S Drexel Av -Bx09770 -Columbus 43209
(614) 462-6288 ..Brown, Eric S '79 Franklin Cnty Cmn Pleas Ct -375 S High
-Columbus 43215 Fx:462-6292
Brown, Erin C '03 -(Address Unavailable)
(419) 423-0242 ..Brown, Garth W '93 (Drake PK&C) -301 S Main -Ste 3
-Findlay 45840 Fx:423-0186
(614) 488-3159 ..Brown, Gary E '73 Grandview Heights Law Dept
-1016 Grandvw Av -Columbus 43212 Fx:481-6224
(937) 548-1125 ..Brown, Gary L '72 (Marchal & B) -116 W 4th -Greenville 45331
(304) 242-8410 ..Brown, Geoffrey C '00 Bordas & B,PLLC -1358 Natl Rd
-Wheeling, WV 26003
(216) 363-4500 ..Brown, Harry M '72 (Benesch FC&A LLP) -200 Pub Sq -Ste 2300
-Cleveland 44114 Fx:363-4588
(216) 831-3175 ..Brown, Harvey A '65 -29525 Chargin Blvd -Ste 312
-Pepper Pike 44102
(614) 221-4225 ..Brown, Herbert R '56 -145 N High -11th Fl -Columbus 43215
Brown, Hugh D '79 -1801 E 12th -Ste 601 -Cleveland 44114
(740) 355-9000 ..Brown, J Rick '76 -625 7th -Portsmouth 45662
(513) 248-0560 ..Brown, Jack G '72 -621 Wooster Pike -Bx33 -Terrace Park 45174
(937) 227-3700 ..Brown, Jacqueline V '04 %Faruki I&C PLL -10 N Ludlow
-500 Cthse Plz SW -Dayton 45402 Fx:227-3717
(614) 445-2647 ..Brown, James D '91 Grange Ins Co -650 S Front
-Columbus 43206
(330) 762-0700 ..Brown, James E '83 %Slater Z&G -One Cascade Plz -Ste 2210
-Akron 44308 Fx:762-3923
(740) 453-0888 ..Brown, James P '84 (Cultice & B) -121 N 4th -Bx490
-Zanesville 43702
(614) 734-3337 ..Brown, James R '94 -5500 Frantz Rd -Ste 157 -Dublin 43017
(614) 224-4114 ..Brown, James W '82 -490 S High -Columbus 43215
(216) 622-8200 ..Brown, Jaron R '02 %Calfee H&G LLP -800 Superior Av -Ste 1400
-Cleveland 44114 Fx:241-0816
Brown, Jeffery S '01 -24078 Frank -North Olmsted 44070
(614) 224-4114 ..Brown, Jeffrey A '78 -490 S High -Columbus 43215
(614) 221-4255 ..Brown, Jeffrey L '79 (Smith & H) -37 W Broad -Columbus 43215
(740) 282-1911 ..Brown, Jeffrey Orr '79 (Fisher B&P) -2017 Sunset Blvd
-Steubenville 43952
(312) 286-8893 ..Brown, Jeffrey T '82 Cincinnati Stock Exchange -440 S LaSalle
-Chicago, IL 60605
(740) 474-6900 ..Brown, Jennifer Lyn '89 -Bx123 -Circleville 43113
(419) 782-9881 ..Brown, Jennifer N '01 Arthur OM&M Co,LPA -901 Ralston Av
-Bx781 -Defiance 43512
(216) 851-3304 ..Brown, Joanne '77 -2136 Noble Dr -Cleveland 44112
(216) 241-2838 ..Brown, John D '69 (Taft S&H LLP) -200 Pub Sq -3500 BP Twr
-Cleveland 44114 Fx:241-3707
(419) 525-1611 ..Brown, John T '58 (Brown BM&M) -70 Park Av W
-Mansfield 44902 Fx:525-3810
(740) 702-3115 ..Brown, Judith H '89 Ross Cnty Pros -72 N Paint -Chillicothe 45601
(270) 781-6500 ..Brown, Kelli E '97 %English LP&O -1101 Cllg -Bx770
-Bowling Green, KY 42102 Fx:782-7782
(614) 487-4426 ..Brown, Kenneth A '84 OH State Bar Assn -1700 Lk Shr Dr
-Columbus 43204
(614) 331-9554 ..Brown, Kerry T '93 Huntington Natl Bank -7 Easton Oval -EA4E83
-Columbus 43219
(330) 425-9282 ..Brown, Kevin E '80 -8737 Darrow -Twinsburg 44087
(614) 237-2595 ..Brown, Kevin W '82 -3140 E Broad -Bx09765 -Columbus 43209
(614) 227-8894 ..Brown, Kimberly J '95 (Bricker & E LLP) -100 S 3rd
-Columbus 43215 Fx:227-2390
(614) 365-2700 ..Brown, Kristen J '90 %Squire S&D LLP -41 S High
-1300 Huntngtn Ctr -Columbus 43215 Fx:365-2499
(216) 378-0804 ..Brown, Kristin M '91 -3044 Bremerton Rd -Pepper Pike 44124
(330) 455-0173 ..Brown, Larry R '60 OfCnsl Day KRW&R,Ltd -200 Market Av N
-Ste 300 -Bx24219 -Canton 44701 Fx:455-2633
(513) 763-5514 ..Brown, Leon F '96 Clear Channel WKRC-TV -1906 Highland Av
-Cincinnati 45219
(216) 481-8100 ..Brown, Leslie S '96 Lincoln Electric Co -22801 St Clair Av
-Cleveland 44117
(513) 241-1950 ..Brown Lippett Heile & Evans -7 W 7th -Ste 1950
-Cincinnati 45202 Fx:241-4095
(330) 287-5490 ..Brown, Lisa A '95 Wayne Cnty Pub Def -113 W Lbrty
-Wooster 44691 Fx:287-5479
(440) 350-2781 ..Brown, Lora L '97 Lake Cnty Cmmn Pleas Ct -25 N Park Pl
-W Annx -Painesville 44077
Brown, Lori A '04 -(Address Unavailable)
(216) 241-5310 ..Brown, Lori E '99 %Gallagher SF&N -1501 Euclid Av -6th Fl
-Cleveland 44115 Fx:241-1608
(614) 461-0256 ..Brown, Lori J '88 Ofc Dscplnry Cnsl -250 Civic Ctr Dr -#325
-Columbus 43215 Fx:461-7205
(614) 223-9300 ..Brown, Lyle B '98 %Benesch FC&A LLP -88 E Broad -Ste 900
-Columbus 43215 Fx:223-9330

(419) 873-0009 ..Brown, Matthew S '04 Westfield Grp -740 Commerce Dr -Ste A
-Perrysburg 43551
(513) 221-2510 ..Brown, Michael A '97 -1523 Madison Rd -Ste C-2
-Cincinnati 45206
(216) 464-6700 ..Brown, Michael C '88 -23230 Chagrin Blvd -#940
-Cleveland 44122
(513) 455-7600 ..Brown, Michael H '82 (Greenebaum D&M PLLC) -255 E 5th
-2800 Chemed Ctr -Cincinnati 45202 Fx:455-8500
(314) 872-5138 ..Brown, Michael K '89 USPS -Bx66640 -Saint Louis, MO 63166
(614) 225-4358 ..Brown, Nancy D '74 Borden Foods Corp -180 E Broad
-Columbus 43215
(216) 363-1031 ..Brown, Neil A '81 H & I Advisors Inc -1422 Euclid Av -Ste 1030
-Cleveland 44115
(614) 252-2026 ..Brown, Paul R '75 Culbreath & Assoc -90 N Nelson Rd
-Columbus 43219
(614) 464-2000 ..Brown, Paula M '97 Kravitz & K -145 E Rich -Columbus 43215
Fx:464-2002
(614) 464-6400 ..Brown, Philip A '74 (Vorys SS&P LLP) -52 E Gay -Bx1008
-Columbus 43216 Fx:464-6350
(513) 258-6000 ..Brown, Philip F '85 (Brenner BG&M Co,LPA) -2109 Stella Rd
-Columbus 43215 Fx:258-6006
(513) 241-6466 ..Brown, Phyllis E '86 (P Brown,LLC) -119 E Court -Ste 510
-Cincinnati 45202
Brown, Rafael '03 -(Address Unavailable)
(614) 451-2555 ..Brown, Ray G '61 -4581 Helston Ct -Columbus 43220
(614) 461-5600 ..Brown, Richard D '81 (Buckley K,LPA) -10 W Broad -Ste 1300
-Columbus 43215
(440) 247-9100 ..Brown, Richard H '68 R Brown & Assoc -10 Center
-Chagrin Falls 44022
(419) 294-1333 ..Brown, Richard R '68 -114 E Wyandot Av -Bx403
-Upper Sandusky 43351
(937) 879-9542 ..Brown, Richard T '82 -2190 Gtwy Dr -Fairborn 45324
(513) 381-9200 ..Brown, Robert F '88 (Rendigs FK&D,LLP) -One W 4th -Ste 900
-Cincinnati 45202 Fx:381-9206
(330) 376-3000 ..Brown, Robert H '65 -120 E Mill -Ste 407 -Akron 44308
(937) 443-6557 ..Brown, Robert J '68 (Thompson H LLP) -2000 Cthse Plz NE
-Bx8801 -Dayton 45401 Fx:443-6635
(216) 861-4414 ..Brown, Robert L '92 (Brown M LLC) -1468 W 9th -Ste 210
-Cleveland 44113
(513) 381-2121 ..Brown, Robert S '67 (Brown Firm Inc,LPA) -2199 Victory Pkwy
-Cincinnati 45206
(330) 722-4686 ..Brown, Robert W '82 Goodyear -3414 Huffman Rd -Medina 44256
(864) 862-2528 ..Brown, Rodney M '83 Younts, Alford, Brown & Goodson
-210 S Main -Bx566 -Fountain Inn, SC 29644
(440) 473-1634 ..Brown, Ronald B '68 Lancer Ins -6563 Wilson Mills Rd -Ste 101
-Mayfield Village 44143
(513) 487-5584 ..Brown, Ronald D '78 Milacron Inc -2090 Florence Av
-Cincinnati 45206
(419) 884-0655 ..Brown, Russell J '84 -32 Lutz Av -Lexington 44904 Fx:884-3416
(216) 664-3765 ..Brown, Russell R '91 Cleveland Municipal Ct -1200 Ontario
-11th Fl -Bx94894 -Cleveland 44101
(304) 243-5440 ..Brown, Scott C '97 %F Jackson -1031 Natl Rd
-Wheeling, WV 26003
(412) 777-8306 ..Brown, Scott G '80 Bayer Corp -100 Bayer Rd
-Pittsburgh, PA 15205
(513) 651-6800 ..Brown, Scott R '95 (Frost BT LLC) -201 E 5th -2200 PNC Ctr
-Cincinnati 45202 Fx:651-6981
Brown, Seymour R '53 -1344 Continental Av
-Melbourne, FL 32940
(330) 725-7045 ..Brown, Stephen J '70 (SJ Brown Co,LPA) -326 N Court
-Medina 44256 Fx:722-5909
(614) 488-1169 ..Brown, Stephen W '75 Crown NorthCorp,Inc -1251 Dublin Rd
-Columbus 43215
(614) 241-5550 ..Brown, Steven M '84 OfCnsl Brunner Law Firm Co,LPA
-545 E Town -Columbus 43215 Fx:241-5551
(740) 593-5046 ..Brown, Susan A
'93 Delaware County Child Support Enforcement Agy -140 N
Sandusky -Delaware 43015
(614) 464-6400 ..Brown, Susan E '71 (Vorys SS&P LLP) -52 E Gay -Bx1008
-Columbus 43216 Fx:464-6350
Brown, Susan R '87 Lexis-Nexis Inc -5639 Huron
-Vermilion 44089
(216) 228-7200 ..Brown & Szaller -14222 Mad Av -Cleveland 44107
(216) 443-7791 ..Brown, Thomas C '74 Cuyahoga Cnty Pros -1200 Ontario -8th Fl
-Cleveland 44113 Fx:698-2270
(614) 460-4203 ..Brown, Thomas J Jr. '75 Columbia Gas of OH,Inc
-200 Civic Ctr Dr -Bx117 -Columbus 43216
(216) 781-1212 ..Brown, Timothy Christopher '97 %Walter & H LLP -1301 E 9th
-Ste 3500 -Cleveland 44114 Fx:575-0911
(419) 872-5337 ..Brown, Timothy J '84 -10960 Sprngbrook Ct -Whitehouse 43571
(513) 352-6800 ..Brown, Timothy R '87 (Thompson H LLP) -312 Walnut -14th Fl
-Cincinnati 45202 Fx:241-4771
(216) 443-8812 ..Brown, Timothy R '88 Cuyahoga Cnty Domestic Relatns Ct
-1 Lakeside Av -Cleveland 44113
(614) 462-5064 ..Brown, Tonia R '03 Franklin Cnty Children Srvcs -855 W Mound
-Columbus 43223 Fx:275-2589
(216) 292-5807 ..Brown, Troy R '72 (Singerman MD&K) -3401 Enterprise Pkwy -Ste
200 -Beachwood 44122 Fx:292-5867
(740) 681-9290 ..Brown, Tyler E '04 %Linehan & Assoc,LPA -120½ E Main
-Lancaster 43130
(216) 851-3304 ..Brown, Virgil A '74 -2136 Noble Rd -Cleveland 44112
(614) 445-8287 ..Brown, Wayne A '73 -825 S Front -Columbus 43206
(216) 771-8121 ..Brown, William D '91 (Steuer EB&B Co,LPA) -55 Pub Sq
-Ste 1828 -Cleveland 44113 Fx:771-8120
Brown, William F Jr. '73 -12406 Butterfld Dr NW
-Pickerington 43147
(614) 890-9099 ..Brown, William W '60 -2999 E Dublin Granvll Rd -Ste 217
-Columbus 43231
(614) 722-4044 ..Brown, Yvette M '85 Ctr for Child & Fam Advcy -700 Childrens Dr
-Columbus 43205 Fx:722-4044
(216) 932-0762 ..Brown-Daniels, Barbara C '91 -1620 Eddington Rd
-Cleveland Heights 44118
(614) 488-6005 ..Brown-Schwart, Mary A '92 Schwart,LLC -1620 W 1st Av
-Columbus 43212

(330) 365-3289 ..**Brown-Tolloti**, Lisa M '96 Tuscarawas Cnty Cmn Pleas Ct
-101 E High Av -Ste 205 -New Philadelphia 44663 **Fx**:602-8811

(216) 696-0808 ..**Brown-Williams**, Tabitha L '99 %Wilkerson & Assoc Co,LPA
-1422 Euclid Av -Ste 248 -Cleveland 44115 **Fx**:696-4970

(419) 294-5781 ..**Browne**, David J '88 Commerical Savings Bk -118 S Sandusky Av
-Bx90 -Upper Sandusky 43351

(330) 761-9960 ..**Browne**, Susan E '88 State & Fed Communications Inc
-80 S Summit -Ste 100 -Akron 44308

(312) 922-8833 ..**Browne**, Vincent B '03 %Harrington TA&H -310 S Mich Av
-Ste 2000 -Chicago, IL 60604

(216) 774-0000 ..**Browner**, Jeremy T '03 (Browner & H,LLC) -526 Superior Av E
-Ste 545 -Cleveland 44114 **Fx**:774-0493

(614) 464-2201 ..**Brownfield**, C William '71 -2551 Charing Rd -#1 -Columbus 43221

(513) 361-0300 ..**Brownfield**, Matthew '84 (M Brownfield Co,LPA) -414 Walnut
-Ste 707 -Cincinnati 45202

(614) 464-3900 ..**Browning & Cook** -243 N 5th -3rd Fl -Columbus 43215

(212) 872-9800 ..**Browning**, Jackson B Jr. '73 (Squire S&D LLP) -350 Park Av
-15th Fl -New York, NY 10022 **Fx**:872-9815

(623) 587-2213 ..**Browning**, Jennifer S '99 Petsmart,Inc -19601 N 27th Av
-Leg Dept -Phoenix, AZ 85027

(614) 464-3900 ..**Browning**, Jon M '86 (Browning & C) -243 N 5th -3rd Fl
-Columbus 43215

(216) 586-3939 ..**Browning**, Marc D '98 %Jones D -901 Lakeside Av
-Cleveland 44114 **Fx**:579-0212

(419) 213-4755 ..**Browning**, Melvin L '88 %Hon JR Sherck -800 Jackson
-Toledo 43624

(614) 471-0085 ..**Browning & Meyer Co,LPA** -8101 N High -Ste 370
-Columbus 43235 **Fx**:471-8132

(614) 462-3117 ..**Browning**, Pamela B '83 Franklin Cnty Cmn Pleas Ct -375 S High
-Columbus 43215 **Fx**:462-6292

(614) 464-6400 ..**Browning**, Stephen D '93 (Vorys SS&P LLP) -52 E Gay -Bx1008
-Columbus 43216 **Fx**:464-6350

Browning, Susan C '03 -(Address Unavailable)

(614) 471-0085 ..**Browning**, William J '83 Browning & M Co,LPA -8101 N High
-Ste 370 -Columbus 43235 **Fx**:471-8132

(248) 540-9636 ..**Browning-Smith**, Tammy L '00 %Foley & M -24255 W 13 Mile Rd
-Ste 200 -Franklin, MI 48025

(614) 227-2301 ..**Brownlee**, Thomas R Jr. '89 (Bricker & E LLP) -100 S 3rd
-Columbus 43215 **Fx**:227-2390

(440) 647-4219 ..**Brownsberger**, Alecia J '93 %Baumgartner & O
-110 Herrick Av W -Wellington 44090 **Fx**:647-4715

Broxterman, Eric L '02 -(Address Unavailable)

(202) 326-2805 ..**Broyles**, Phillip L '80 FTC -601 NJ Av NW -Washington, DC 20580
Fx:326-3383

(614) 464-6400 ..**Broz**, Alycia N '98 %Vorys SS&P LLP -52 E Gay -Bx1008
-Columbus 43216 **Fx**:464-6350

(440) 237-1100 ..**Broz**, Glenn A '74 -6060 Royalton Rd -North Royalton 44133

(216) 523-5405 ..**Brozovic**, Maura L '00 %Bricker & E LLP -1375 E 9th -Ste 1500
-Cleveland 44114 **Fx**:523-7071

(440) 205-3600 ..**Brubaker**, Carl Richard '60 (Driggs LB&H Co,LPA) -8522 East Av
-Mentor 44060 **Fx**:205-3601

(937) 904-2156 ..**Brubaker**, James D '77 88 ABW/JA -5135 Pearson Rd -Rm 122
-Wright Patterson AFB 45433

(419) 241-6000 ..**Brubaker**, Marcus J '81 (Eastman & S Ltd) -1 Seagate -24th Fl
-Bx10032 -Toledo 43699 **Fx**:247-1777

(614) 227-2000 ..**Brubaker**, Robert L '72 (Porter WM&A LLP) -41 S High
-Columbus 43215 **Fx**:227-2100

(304) 645-4182 ..**Bruce**, Barry L '77 B Bruce & Assoc -101 W Randolph -Bx388
-Lewisburg, WV 24901

(216) 464-6700 ..**Bruce**, Gordon S '76 Master Credit Cnslts -23230 Chagrin Blvd
-#640 -Beachwood 44122

(419) 245-1829 ..**Bruce**, Kerry D '77 City of Toledo -420 Mad Av -Ste 100
-Toledo 43604

(937) 225-4652 ..**Bruce**, Kimberly L '04 Montgomery Cnty Pub Def -117 S Main
-Ste 400 -Dayton 45422 **Fx**:225-3449

(734) 944-2269 ..**Bruce**, Ronald T Jr. '00 Lahn M&B,PLC -208 E Mich Av
-Saline, MI 48176

(513) 977-8200 ..**Bruch**, Charles A '03 %Dinsmore & S LLP -255 E 5th -Ste 1900
-Cincinnati 45202 **Fx**:977-8141

(805) 815-4645 ..**Bruckelmeyer**, Lynn Y '00 -169 W Alta Green
-Port Hueneme, CA 93041

(937) 323-1171 ..**Brucker**, Joseph C '52 -14 N Fountain Av -Springfield 45502

(949) 855-1246 ..**Brucker**, William J '90 (Stetina BG&B,PC) -75 Enterprise -Ste 250
-Aliso Viejo, CA 92656 **Fx**:855-6371

(937) 223-8888 ..**Bruder**, Matthew D '98 Dyer GM&S -131 N Ludlow -Ste 1400
-Dayton 45402 **Fx**:223-0127

(614) 292-0795 ..**Brudney**, James J '95 OSU Moritz Cllg of Law -55 W 12th Av
-Columbus 43210 **Fx**:292-1383

(614) 461-1311 ..**Brudny**, James J Jr. '83 (Reminger & R) -65 E State
-4th Fl Cptl Sq Ofc Bldg -Columbus 43215 **Fx**:232-2410

(419) 334-8884 ..**Brudzinski**, Daniel L '91 -501 W State -Fremont 43420
Fx:334-8840

(513) 268-8887 ..**Brueggeman**, Edward P '72 -10507 Butterworth Rd
-Loveland 45140 **Fx**:683-7526

Bruenderman, Katherine R '88 -(Address Unavailable)

(513) 361-0200 ..**Bruestle**, Eric G '77 (Roetzel & A,LPA) -250 E 5th
-310 Chiquita Ctr -Cincinnati 45202 **Fx**:361-0335

(513) 892-8329 ..**Bruewer**, Henry J '49 -521 Vinnedge Ct -Fairfield 45014

(513) 887-3313 ..**Bruewer**, John T '88 Butler Cnty Juv Ct -280 N Fair Av
-Hamilton 45011

(330) 376-2700 ..**Bruggeman**, Amie L '82 (Roetzel & A,LPA) -222 S Main
-Akron 44308 **Fx**:376-4577

(419) 213-4061 ..**Bruggeman**, Carol L '84 %Lucas Cnty Pros-Foreclosure
-One Govt Ctr -Ste 500 -Toledo 43604

Bruhl, David C '04 -(Address Unavailable)

(216) 363-4500 ..**Brule**, Thomas R '93 (Benesch FC&A LLP) -200 Pub Sq -Ste 2300
-Cleveland 44114 **Fx**:363-4588

(740) 373-4633 ..**Brum**, Nancy E '82 Atkinson & B -312 Putnam -Bxl
-Marietta 45750

(937) 547-7360 ..**Brumbaugh**, Anne J '78 Darke Cnty Cmmn Pleas Ct -Ct Hse
-Greenville 45331

(937) 332-0138 ..**Brumbaugh**, Jeffrey S '01 Brumbaugh Law Firm -121 W Franklin
-Bx950 -Troy 45373

(440) 333-5991 ..**Brumbaugh**, Marian C '83 -20525 Ctr Ridge Rd -Ste 136
-Rocky River 44116

(937) 547-0218 ..**Brumbaugh**, Michael L '91 %S Rudnick,Ltd -121 W 3rd
-Greenville 45331

Brumbaugh, Suzanne P '04 -(Address Unavailable)

(937) 225-5757 ..**Brumby**, Jennifer D '03 %Montgomery Cnty Pros -301 W 3rd
-Bx972 -Dayton 45422 **Fx**:225-3470

(513) 579-6400 ..**Brun**, James H '76 (Keating M&K PLL) -1 E 4th
-1400 Provident Twr -Cincinnati 45202 **Fx**:579-6457

(502) 627-3945 ..**Bruner**, Cheryl E '97 LG&E Energy LLC -220 W Main -Louisville,
KY 40202

(216) 566-9477 ..**Bruner**, Harvey B '74 (Bruner & J Co LPA) -55 Pub Sq -Ste 1600
-Cleveland 44113

(216) 566-9477 ..**Bruner & Jordan Co LPA** -55 Pub Sq -Ste 1600 -Cleveland
44113

(614) 464-6400 ..**Brunetto**, Joseph A '80 (Vorys SS&P LLP) -52 E Gay -Bx1008
-Columbus 43216 **Fx**:464-6350

(412) 281-8000 ..**Bruni**, John W '90 %Zimmer K,PLLC -600 Grant
-Pittsburgh, PA 15219

(330) 497-3681 ..**Brunk**, Richard C '59 -4809 Munson NW -Canton 44718

(216) 623-7300 ..**Brunn**, Thomas L Sr. '67 (Brunn Law Firm Co,LPA)
-700 W St Clair Av -Ste 208 Hoyt Block -Cleveland 44113
Fx:623-7330

(216) 623-7300 ..**Brunn**, Thomas L Jr. '89 (Brunn Law Firm Co,LPA)
-700 W St Clair Av -Ste 208 Hoyt Block -Cleveland 44113
Fx:623-7330

(419) 739-6510 ..**Brunner**, John D '93 Cnsl Auglaize Cnty CSEA -12 N Wood
-Bx2003 -Wapakoneta 45895 **Fx**:739-6511

(216) 621-0200 ..**Brunner**, Kimberly C '02 %Baker & H LLP -1900 E 9th -Ste 3200
-Cleveland 44114 **Fx**:696-0740

(937) 228-5600 ..**Brunner**, Lowell K '73 -36 W 3rd -Dayton 45402

(614) 241-5550 ..**Brunner**, Rick L '80 (Brunner Law Firm Co,LPA) -545 E Town
-Columbus 43215 **Fx**:241-5551

(419) 246-5700 ..**Bruno**, Dominic M '64 -608 Madison -Ste 1400 -Bx1336
-Toledo 43603

(330) 965-2323 ..**Bruno**, Lynn S '83 -412 Boardman-Canfld Rd -Youngstown 44512

(419) 241-1395 ..**Bruno**, Michael A '83 C Boyk,LLC -520 Mad Av -Ste 655
-Toledo 43604

(419) 678-4317 ..**Bruns**, David W '75 -123 W Main -Coldwater 45828

(513) 381-2838 ..**Bruns**, Jeanne M '99 %Taft S&H LLP -425 Walnut -Ste 1800
-Cincinnati 45202 **Fx**:381-0205

(937) 512-1680 ..**Bruns**, Julie A '96 Montgomery Cnty Pros -301 W 3rd -Bx972
-Dayton 45422 **Fx**:225-3470

(513) 651-6800 ..**Bruns**, Julie M '99 %Frost BT LLC -201 E 5th -2200 PNC Ctr
-Cincinnati 45202 **Fx**:651-6981

(513) 621-3394 ..**Bruns**, Robert T '75 (Peck S&W,LLP) -201 E 5th -Ste 900
-Cincinnati 45202 **Fx**:621-3813

(937) 456-1776 ..**Bruns**, Stephen R '83 -123 W Main -Eaton 45320 **Fx**:456-7182

(513) 665-3500 ..**Bruns**, Thomas B '90 (Freund F&A) -105 E 4th -Ste 1400
-Cincinnati 45202 **Fx**:665-3503

(513) 674-5259 ..**Brunsman**, Theresa M '84 Union Cntrl Life Ins Co
-1876 Waycross Rd -Cincinnati 45240

(216) 265-1630 ..**Brunst**, Christa D '85 Dept Homeland Security
-20445 Emerald Pkwy -1 Intl Pl -Cleveland 44135

(614) 461-1311 ..**Brunton**, Gregory D '93 (Reminger & R) -65 E State
-4th Fl Cptl Sq Ofc Bldg -Columbus 43215 **Fx**:232-2410

(954) 689-3147 ..**Bruscino**, David A '88 AOL Latin America -6600 N Andrews Av
-Ste 400 -Fort Lauderdale, FL 33309

(740) 927-2219 ..**Brush**, C Bernard '75 -5530 Columbia Rd SW -Pataskala 43062
Fx:927-7799

(513) 421-1108 ..**Brush**, Thomas B '64 Natl Resrc Ctr on Prisons & Communities
-617 Vine -Ste 1301 -Cincinnati 45202 **Fx**:562-3200

(614) 863-0018 ..**Brusk**, Norman '92 (Brusk & B) -7100 E Lvngstn Av
-Reynoldsburg 43068

(614) 863-0018 ..**Brusk**, Susan P '92 (Brusk & B) -7100 E Lvngstn Av
-Reynoldsburg 43068

(440) 930-2600 ..**Brusnahan**, Kreig J '81 (K Brusnahan & Assoc) -158-A Lear Rd
-Avon Lake 44012 **Fx**:930-2602

(419) 247-2500 ..**Bruss**, Howard G Jr. '67 OfCnsl Fuller & H,Ltd -One SeaGate
-Ste 1700 -Bx2088 -Toledo 43603 **Fx**:247-2665

(330) 609-5045 ..**Brutz**, James M '84 (Brutz & K,Ltd) -405 Niles Courtland Rd SE
-Ste 203 -Warren 44484

(937) 449-2800 ..**Bruzzese**, Anthony E '03 %Chernesky H&K PLL -10 Cthse Plz SW
-Ste 1100 -Dayton 45402 **Fx**:449-2821

(740) 282-5323 ..**Bruzzese & Calabria** -300 Sinclair Bldg -Bx1506
-Steubenville 43952 **Fx**:282-5328

(740) 282-5323 ..**Bruzzese**, Frank J '74 (Bruzzese & C) -300 Sinclair Bldg -Bx1506
-Steubenville 43952 **Fx**:282-5328

(740) 282-5323 ..**Bruzzese**, Jeffrey J '04 %Bruzzese & C -300 Sinclair Bldg -Bx1506
-Steubenville 43952 **Fx**:282-5328

(440) 686-9000 ..**Bryan**, Bradric T '90 (Goodwin & B LLP) -22050 Mastick Rd
-Fairview Park 44126 **Fx**:686-9001

(419) 243-1239 ..**Bryan**, David A '76 (Wasserman BL&H,LLP) -405 N Huron
-Ste 300 -Toledo 43604

(216) 522-4856 ..**Bryan**, Edward G '91 Fed Pub Def -1660 W 2nd -Ste 750
-Cleveland 44113

(859) 655-7004 ..**Bryan**, Jennifer W '02 %Nielson & S,PSC -639 Wshngtn Av
-Newport, KY 41071

(330) 744-1148 ..**Bryan**, Jerome M '91 (Henderson CMN&T Co,LPA) -34 Fed Plz W
-Ste 600 Wick Bldg -Youngstown 44503 **Fx**:744-3807

(614) 228-6131 ..**Bryan**, Jonathan M '95 McNamara & M,LLP -88 E Broad
-Ste 1250 -Columbus 43215 **Fx**:228-6126

(740) 452-8484 ..**Bryan**, Michael T '01 %Stubbins W&E Co LPA -59 N 4th -Bx488
-Zanesville 43702

(513) 564-7656 ..**Bryan-Caron**, Mary C '92 US District Ct SDOH -706 US
Cthse Bldg -Cincinnati 45202

(937) 382-7777 ..**Bryant**, Jerry D '74 -21 N South -Wilmington 45177

(513) 423-9291 ..**Bryant**, Jerry M '72 (Bryant & S) -1600 1st Av -Middletown 45044

(216) 382-3559 ..**Bryant**, Juanita '86 -3675 Runnymede Blvd -Cleveland 44121

Bryant, Kevin L '01 -150 S Westmoor Av -Columbus 43204

(614) 228-1541 ..**Bryant**, Letitia S '04 %Baker & H LLP -65 E State -Ste 2100
-Columbus 43215 **Fx**:462-2616

(248) 338-8980 ..**Bryant**, Michael D '97 (Ward AP&B) -300 Enterprise Ct -Ste 100
-Bloomfield Hills, MI 48302

(937) 449-2800 .. **Bryant**, Todd E '00 %Chernesky H&K PLL -10 Cthse Plz SW -Ste 1100 -Dayton 45402 **Fx:**449-2821
(216) 522-2084 .. **Bryce**, Rita M '90 US DOJ-Antitrust Div -55 Erievw Plz -Bldg 9-Ste 700 -Cleveland 44114
(419) 691-2435 .. **Bryce**, Robert W '81 (Schlageter & B Co,LPA) -715 S Coy Rd -Oregon 43616
(216) 621-0200 .. **Bryenton**, Gary L '65 (Baker & H LLP) -1900 E 9th -Ste 3200 -Cleveland 44114 **Fx:**696-0740
(440) 327-5487 .. **Bryer**, Terry A '85 -37 Cadet Dr -North Ridgeville 44039
(513) 651-6800 .. **Bryson**, Craig M '03 %Frost BT LLC -201 E 5th -2200 PNC Ctr -Cincinnati 45202 **Fx:**651-6981
(513) 595-2341 .. **Bryson**, Gary A '78 Union Cntrl Life Ins Co -1876 Waycross Rd -Bx40888 -Cincinnati 45240
(412) 372-5138 .. **Brzuszek**, Joseph L '67 -106 Monticello Dr -Monroeville, PA 15146
(216) 664-6900 .. **Brzytwa**, Edward John Jr. '68 (Brzytwa Q&M LLC) -1660 W 2nd -900 Skylight Ofc Twr -Cleveland 44113 **Fx:**664-6901
(216) 664-6900 .. **Brzytwa Quick & McCrystal LLC** -1660 W 2nd -900 Skylight Ofc Twr -Cleveland 44113 **Fx:**664-6901
(440) 845-9050 .. **Bubna**, Walter P '80 -5700 Pearl Rd -Ste 304 -Parma 44129
(937) 544-2581 .. **Bubp**, Danny R '84 -307 N Market -West Union 45693 **Fx:**544-1802
(614) 466-4605 .. **Bubutiev**, Jim K '94 OH Dept Job & Fam Srvcs -30 E Broad -32nd Fl -Columbus 43266
(216) 621-8700 .. **Bucalo**, John C '94 %Wincek & D Co,LPA -1370 Ontario -1500 Standard Bldg -Cleveland 44113
Bucci, Christin M '96 -21693 Fall Rvr Dr -Boca Raton, FL 33428
(937) 652-2224 .. **Bucci**, Christopher M '01 Feinstein E Co,LPA -1052 S Main -Urbana 43078
(614) 575-3530 .. **Bucci**, Tammie S '01 Franklin Cnty Children Srvcs -855 W Mound -Columbus 43223 **Fx:**275-2589
(513) 891-5580 .. **Bucciere**, Robert L '97 (Bucciere Firm,Inc) -8044 Mntgmry Rd -Ste 410 -Cincinnati 45236
(216) 443-8505 .. **Bucha**, Stephen M III '95 Cuyahoga Cnty Cmmn Pleas Ct -1200 Ontario -10th Fl -Cleveland 44113
(216) 291-3184 .. **Buchanan**, Alan Deane '73 Mun Ct Judge -40 Severance Cir -Cleveland Heights 44118
(513) 651-6800 .. **Buchanan**, Beth A '97 %Frost BT LLC -201 E 5th -2200 PNC Ctr -Cincinnati 45202 **Fx:**651-6981
(216) 363-0982 .. **Buchanan Ingersoll PC** -600 Superior Av E -Ste 1300 -Cleveland 44114
(937) 223-6211 .. **Buchanan**, Joseph P '56 (Crew & B) -2580 Kettering Twr -Dayton 45423
Buchanan, Leslie S '80 -2257 N Fountain Blvd -Springfield 45504
(757) 563-1600 .. **Buchanan**, Richard L '75 Al-Anon Fam Grp Hdqurtrs -1600 Corp Lndng Pkwy -Virginia Beach, VA 23454
(740) 773-0012 .. **Buchanan**, Robert J Jr. '85 SE OH Lgl Srvcs -11 E 2nd -Chillicothe 45601
(330) 296-7152 .. **Buchanan**, Thomas R '87 -206 S Meridian -Ste B -Ravenna 44266
(614) 464-6400 .. **Buchenroth**, Stephen R '74 (Vorys SS&P LLP) -52 E Gay -Bx1008 -Columbus 43216 **Fx:**464-6350
(843) 552-4066 .. **Bucher**, Stephen P '80 (Bucher Firm,PC) -3782 Ashley Phosphate Rd -North Charleston, SC 29418 **Fx:**552-8894
(513) 946-3800 .. **Buchert**, Christopher B '98 Hamilton Cnty Pub Def -230 E 9th -3rd Fl -Cincinnati 45202 **Fx:**946-3808
(614) 480-3110 .. **Buchholz**, Thomas M '90 Huntington Natl Bank -41 S High -HCO548 -Columbus 43287
(614) 462-3555 .. **Buchman**, David M '77 Franklin Cnty Pros -373 S High -Columbus 43215
(727) 363-3026 .. **Buchmann**, Alan P '60 -3910 Belle Vista E -Saint Petersburg, FL 33706 **Fx:**363-3045
(937) 332-9300 .. **Bucio**, Christopher R '03 (Bucio & E,LLP) -10 N Market -Troy 45373 **Fx:**339-6549
(937) 332-9300 .. **Bucio & Ehinger,LLP** -10 N Market -Troy 45373 **Fx:**339-6549
Buck, Christian L '01 -1034 Yorkshire Dr -Marion 43302
(614) 538-2901 .. **Buck**, Elaine S '81 -1560 Fishinger Rd -Upper Arlington 43221
(216) 696-7600 .. **Buck**, Frank W '80 (Duvin C&H) -1301 E 9th -20th Fl Erievw Twr -Cleveland 44114 **Fx:**696-2038
(704) 344-7571 .. **Buck**, James T '03 Pricewaterhouse Coopers -214 N Tryon -Ste 3600 -Charlotte, NC 28202
(216) 622-3712 .. **Buck**, Lynne H '84 US Atty -801 W Superior -Ste 400 -Cleveland 44113 **Fx:**622-3370
(330) 746-5643 .. **Buck**, Marshall D '81 (Comstock S&W Co,LPA) -100 Fed Plz E -Ste 926 -Youngstown 44503 **Fx:**746-4925
(513) 579-6400 .. **Buck**, Matthew K '96 %Keating M&K PLL -1 E 4th -1400 Provident Twr -Cincinnati 45202 **Fx:**579-6457
(216) 363-4500 .. **Buck**, Maynard A III '83 (Benesch FC&A LLP) -200 Pub Sq -Ste 2300 -Cleveland 44114 **Fx:**363-4588
(740) 453-0351 .. **Buck**, Steven E '75 Muskingum Cnty Juv Ct -1860 E Pike -Zanesville 43701
(248) 569-4646 .. **Buckfire**, Lawrence J '03 %Buckfire & B -17117 W 9 Mile Rd -Ste 535 -Southfield, MI 48075
(678) 375-3761 .. **Buckham**, William C '70 Checkfree Corp -4411 E Jones Brdg Rd -Norcross, GA 30092
(330) 376-5300 .. **Buckingham Doolittle & Burroughs, LLP** -50 S Main -Bx1500 -Akron 44309 **Fx:**258-6559
(614) 221-8448 .. **Buckingham Doolittle & Burroughs, LLP** -191 W Nationwide Blvd -Ste 300 -Bx151120 -Columbus 43215 **Fx:**221-8590
(330) 492-8717 .. **Buckingham Doolittle & Burroughs, LLP** -4518 Fulton Dr NW -Bx35548 -Canton 44735 **Fx:**492-9625
(216) 621-5300 .. **Buckingham Doolittle & Burroughs, LLP** -1375 E 9th -Ste 1700 -Cleveland 44114 **Fx:**621-5440
(216) 522-4820 .. **Buckingham**, George W Jr. '92 Fed Med & Conc Srvc -6161 Oak Tree Blvd -Ste 100 -Independence 44131
(419) 627-0414 .. **Buckingham Lucal McGookey & Zeiher Co, LPA** -414 Wayne -Bx929 -Sandusky 44870 **Fx:**627-0009
(440) 967-6136 .. **Buckingham Lucal McGookey & Zeiher Co, LPA** -1513 State Route 60 -Vermilion 44089
(740) 353-6604 .. **Buckler**, Barry A '02 Buckler Law Ofc -531 6th -Portsmouth 45662
(740) 353-6604 .. **Buckler**, Jerry L '96 -531 6th -Portsmouth 45662
(740) 353-6604 .. **Buckler**, Ruth A '02 Buckler Law Ofc -531 6th -Portsmouth 45662
(216) 252-8436 .. **Buckles**, Howard E '76 White Consolidated Industries Inc -11770 Berea Rd -Cleveland 44111
(330) 643-2250 .. **Buckles**, Tammy R '01 9th Dist Ct of Appls -161 S High -Ste 504 -Akron 44308
(330) 896-7821 .. **Bucklew**, Roger D '91 Motorists Mutual Ins Co -3532 Maassillon Rd -Uniontown 44685
(216) 363-1400 .. **Buckley**, Brent M '82 (Buckley K,LPA) -600 E Superior Av -Ste 1400 -Cleveland 44114 **Fx:**579-1020
(937) 865-6800 .. **Buckley**, Brian P '01 Lexis/Nexis -Bx933 -Dayton 45401
(513) 723-4000 .. **Buckley**, Daniel J '74 (Vorys SS&P LLP) -221 E 4th -Ste 2000 Atrium Two -Bx0236 -Cincinnati 45201 **Fx:**723-4056
(859) 750-2667 .. **Buckley**, Dennis J '73 -638 Pnt Benton Ln -Covington, KY 41014
(937) 382-4454 .. **Buckley**, Frederick J '50 -209 Leyland Park Dr -Wilmington 45177
(330) 652-8000 .. **Buckley & George Co, LPA** -5704 Youngstown-Warren Rd -Niles 44446
(713) 951-9400 .. **Buckley**, Jennifer A '02 %Littler M,PC -1301 McKinney -Ste 1900 -Houston, TX 77010 **Fx:**951-9212
(216) 443-7223 .. **Buckley**, Joseph D '89 Cuyahoga Cnty Pub Def -1200 W 3rd NW -100 Lakeside Pl -Cleveland 44113
(937) 382-0946 .. **Buckley**, Karen '86 (Buckley M&W) -145 N South -Wilmington 45177
(419) 213-4772 .. **Buckley**, Kevin P '82 Lucas Cnty Probate Ct -700 Adams -Toledo 43624
(216) 363-1400 .. **Buckley King,LPA** -600 E Superior Av -Ste 1400 -Cleveland 44114 **Fx:**579-1020
(614) 461-5600 .. **Buckley King,LPA** -10 W Broad -Ste 1300 -Columbus 43215
(513) 412-5400 .. **Buckley King,LPA** -201 E 5th -Ste 1420 -Cincinnati 45202 **Fx:**412-5401
(614) 798-1600 .. **Buckley**, Michael E '98 %Eichenberger & Assoc -6099 Frantz Rd -Dublin 43017
(937) 382-0946 .. **Buckley Miller & Wright** -145 N South -Wilmington 45177
(330) 652-8000 .. **Buckley**, Robert J '80 (Buckley & G Co,LPA) -5704 Youngstown-Warren Rd -Niles 44446
(614) 460-4664 .. **Buckley**, Shalu T '96 NiSource Corp Srvcs -200 Civic Ctr Dr -Columbus 43215
(770) 261-6120 .. **Buckley**, Thomas C '98 YKK Corp of Amer -1850 Pkwy Pl -Ste 300 -Marietta, GA 30067
(330) 343-6080 .. **Buckley-Mirhaidari**, Sharon '84 -707 N Wooster Av -Dover 44622
(216) 241-6602 .. **Buckman**, Herbert Jr. '40 OfCnsl Weston HFP&H LLP -50 Pub Sq -2500 Trmnl Twr -Cleveland 44113 **Fx:**621-8369
(216) 875-2767 .. **Buckner**, Andrew P '67 %Bonezzi SM&P Co LPA -526 Superior Av -Ste 1400 -Cleveland 44114 **Fx:**875-1570
(937) 372-6000 .. **Buckwalter**, Michael A '84 -Bx580 -Xenia 45385
(859) 669-8000 .. **Buda**, Aaron P '93 Shire US Inc -1 Rvrfrnt Pl -Newport, KY 41071 **Fx:**669-8414
(614) 221-3456 .. **Buda**, David M '74 -35 E Lvngstn Av -Columbus 43215
Budd, Andrea E '04 -(Address Unavailable)
(419) 289-2220 .. **Budd**, Thomas J II '78 -128 Church -Ashland 44805
(513) 684-3211 .. **Budde**, John E '88 IRS Dist Cnsl -312 Elm -Ste 2300 -Cincinnati 45202
(614) 286-9670 .. **Budde**, Joseph E '83 -6306 Mem'l Dr -Dublin 43017
(614) 761-9775 .. **Budde**, Oscar A '99 -5650 Blazer Pkwy -Dublin 43017
(513) 421-9222 .. **Budinger**, Carrie L '88 Cnsl Allstate Ins Co -1014 Vine -Ste 2322 -Cincinnati 45202 **Fx:**421-9555
(330) 740-2180 .. **Budinsky**, Robert '78 7th Dist Court of Appls -120 Market -4th Fl -Youngstown 44503 **Fx:**740-2182
(216) 765-0123 .. **Budish**, Armond D '79 (Budish & S Ltd) -23240 Chagrin Blvd -Ste 450 Commerce Park 4 -Beachwood 44122 **Fx:**595-2787
(216) 765-0123 .. **Budish & Solomon Ltd** -23240 Chagrin Blvd -Ste 450 Commerce Park 4 -Beachwood 44122 **Fx:**595-2787
(440) 989-5700 .. **Budway**, R J '93 -1958 Kresge Dr -Amherst 44001
(216) 696-5222 .. **Budzik**, James A '85 %Johnson & C,LLC -1001 Lakeside Av -Ste 1700 N Pnt Twr -Cleveland 44114 **Fx:**696-5288
(513) 684-3093 .. **Budzynski**, Kristin E '92 US Army Corps of Engineers -Great Lks & Ohio Rvr Div -Bx1159 -Cincinnati 45201
(859) 578-6600 .. **Buechel**, Edward J '77 (Buechel & C) -25 Crestvw Hills Mall Rd -Ste 104 -Crestview Hills, KY 41017
(513) 579-1500 .. **Buechner Haffer O'Connell Meyers & Healey Co,LPA** -105 E 4th -Ste 300 -Cincinnati 45202 **Fx:**977-4361
(513) 579-1500 .. **Buechner**, Robert W '74 (Buechner HOM&H Co,LPA) -105 E 4th -Ste 300 -Cincinnati 45202 **Fx:**977-4361
(937) 778-8000 .. **Buecker**, Thomas J '69 (T Buecker Co,LPA) -306 W High -Bx1215 -Piqua 45356 **Fx:**778-1111
(641) 787-6464 .. **Bueckman**, Lynn A '00 Maytag Corp -Bx39 -Newton, IA 50208
(330) 451-7768 .. **Buehler**, Trevor K '73 Ohio 5th Dist Ct of Appeals -110 Central Plz S -Ste 320 -Canton 44702 **Fx:**451-7249
(419) 822-3211 .. **Buehrer**, Stephen P '97 %Barber KS&R -206 Main -Delta 43515 **Fx:**822-4593
(330) 376-5300 .. **Buehrle**, Edward V '93 (Buckingham D&B,LLP) -50 S Main -Bx1500 -Akron 44309 **Fx:**258-6559
(740) 373-3219 .. **Buell**, Michael D '78 (Buell & S Co,LPA) -322 3rd -Marietta 45750 **Fx:**373-2892
(216) 664-4823 .. **Buelow**, Edward T '82 Prosecutor -1200 Ontario Av -8th Fl Justice Ctr -Cleveland 44113 **Fx:**664-4399
(330) 872-0918 .. **Buente**, Victor O Jr. '80 Cadle Co -100 N Center -Newton Falls 44444
(614) 298-8150 .. **Buergenthal**, Alan E '96 American Kidney Stone Mgmt -100 W 3rd Av -Ste 350 -Columbus 43201
(513) 621-2666 .. **Buerger**, Kathryn E '97 %Statman HS&E LLC -255 E 5th -Ste 2900 Chemed Ctr -Cincinnati 45202 **Fx:**587-4477
(937) 372-8888 .. **Buerger**, Robert E '00 -Bx103 -Alpha 45301 **Fx:**372-5135
(216) 566-5657 .. **Buescher**, Stephen L '69 (Thompson H LLP) -127 Pub Sq -3900 Key Ctr -Cleveland 44114 **Fx:**566-5800
(330) 877-9479 .. **Buetel**, Veronica K '00 Lake Township -12360 Market Av N -Hartville 44632
(419) 891-2024 .. **Bueter**, Christopher R '02 Dana Corp -1480 Ford -Maumee 43537
(216) 621-6101 .. **Bufe**, Eric T '96 %Kahn & Assoc,LLC -55 Pub Sq -Ste 650 -Cleveland 44113 **Fx:**621-6006
(513) 684-2572 .. **Buffington**, Carolyn B '85 US Bankrptcy Ct -221 E 4th -Ste 800 -Cincinnati 45202
(513) 977-8200 .. **Buford**, Calvin D '85 (Dinsmore & S LLP) -255 E 5th -Ste 1900 -Cincinnati 45202 **Fx:**977-8141
(216) 241-3222 .. **Buford**, Thomas C '77 -75 Pub Sq -Ste 650 -Cleveland 44113
(216) 348-5056 .. **Bugaj**, Dale S '89 Cuyahoga Metro Housing Auth -1441 W 25th -Cleveland 44113

(216) 579-3108 ..**Bugaj**, Rebecca '99 Federal Reserve Bk -E 6th & Superior -Cleveland 44101

(419) 244-6788 ..**Bugbee & Conkle** -405 Mad Av -Ste 1300 -Toledo 43604 **Fx:**244-7145

(740) 775-3300 ..**Bugg**, Clifford N '92 %Phillips & S -37 N Paint -Chillicothe 45601

(614) 645-4980 ..**Bui**, Hoang Diem '04 -90 W Broad -Rm 200 -Columbus 43215

(330) 928-7840 ..**Buie**, Mark J '86 -Bx1701 -Stow 44224

(419) 241-9000 ..**Bula**, Megan A '00 %Shumaker L&K,LLP -1000 Jackson -Toledo 43624 **Fx:**241-6894

(330) 455-0173 ..**Bules**, Raymond T '81 (Day KRW&R,Ltd) -200 Market Av N -Ste 300 -Bx24213 -Canton 44701 **Fx:**455-2633

(330) 375-5716 ..**Bulford**, Robert E Jr. '76 US Atty -2 S Main -Ste 208 -Akron 44308

(614) 466-0118 ..**Bulgrin**, Richard M '87 PUCO -180 E Broad -Columbus 43266

(614) 487-1106 ..**Bull**, John A '84 -Bx12633 -Columbus 43212

(614) 688-5699 ..**Bull**, Joseph O '86 OSU -2400 Olentangy Rvr Rd -Columbus 43210

(614) 466-8950 ..**Bull**, Julianna F '84 Envrnmntl Review Appl Comm -309 S 4th -Ste 222 -Columbus 43215

(614) 249-6276 ..**Bull**, Mary M '95 SrCnsl Nationwide Ins Co -1 Nationwide Plz -Columbus 43215

(248) 362-3707 ..**Bullard**, Jeffrey '92 (Ogne A&S,PC) -1869 E Maple Rd -Ste 100 -Troy, MI 48083 **Fx:**362-0422

                    Bullard, Kathleen I '04 -(Address Unavailable)

                    Bullard, Marc D '04 -(Address Unavailable)

(440) 892-8456 ..**Bullard**, Marcia J '84 -24441 Detroit Rd -Ste 300 -Westlake 44145

(216) 479-8500 ..**Buller**, Carolyn J '81 (Squire S&D LLP) -127 Pub Sq -4900 Key Twr -Cleveland 44114 **Fx:**479-8780

(216) 621-1000 ..**Bulloch**, John T '91 %Moscarino & T,LLP -1422 Euclid Av -Hanna Bldg Ste 630 -Cleveland 44115 **Fx:**622-1556

(216) 689-5109 ..**Bulloch**, Steven N '74 KeyBank NA -127 Pub Sq -2nd Fl -Cleveland 44114

(614) 677-8224 ..**Bulloch**, Elizabeth S '80 Cnsl Nationwide Ins Co -1 Nationwide Plz -Columbus 43215

(215) 965-1200 ..**Bullock**, Kristyne A '98 %Akin GSH&F,LLP -2005 Market -Ste 2200 -Philadelphia, PA 19103

(502) 226-6500 ..**Bullock**, Robert V '66 (Bullock & C LLP) -101 St Clair -Frankfort, KY 40601

(513) 634-1948 ..**Bullock**, Roddy M '97 Procter & Gamble -6110 Ctr Hill Av -Rm 1500 -Cincinnati 45224

(216) 696-3030 ..**Bulloff**, Aaron H '81 %Kadish H&W,LPA -1717 E 9th -Ste 2112 -Cleveland 44114 **Fx:**696-3492

(216) 932-1930 ..**Bulloff**, Frances W '78 -2684 Claythorne Rd -Shaker Heights 44122

(724) 779-6698 ..**Bulman**, Cornelius Jr. '79 Amer Eagle Outfitters,Inc -150 Thorn Hill Dr -Warrendale, PA 15086

(216) 621-1113 ..**Bulson**, Don W '76 (Renner OB&S,LLP) -1621 Euclid Av -19th Fl -Cleveland 44115 **Fx:**621-6165

(614) 387-9571 ..**Bumbico**, James F '99 OH Sup Ct -65 S Front -Columbus 43215

(614) 294-1900 ..**Bumgarner**, Christopher D '04 -929 Harrison Av -Ste 302 -Columbus 43215

(941) 778-1132 ..**Bumgarner**, Ray Q '75 -1007 Gulf Dr N -#210/211 -Bradenton Beach, FL 34217

(614) 486-0297 ..**Bumgarner**, Robert B '95 %S Jurus -1375 Dublin Rd -Columbus 43215 **Fx:**486-8580

(330) 471-3949 ..**Bump**, Mark W '83 Timken Co -1835 Dueber Av SW -GNE-03 -Canton 44706

(216) 515-1660 ..**Bumpass**, Thomas Merritt Jr. '72 (Frantz W LLP) -127 Pub Sq -2500 Key Center -Cleveland 44114 **Fx:**515-1650

(330) 373-1035 ..**Bumstead**, Mark E '80 Letson GWL&R -155 S Park Av -Ste 250 -Bx151 -Warren 44482 **Fx:**392-5419

(740) 992-5730 ..**Bunce**, Denise L '89 -105 2nd -Bx711 -Pomeroy 45769

(937) 704-0220 ..**Bunce**, Jack P '73 -56 Westline Dr -Franklin 45005

(513) 241-3685 ..**Bunch**, Nicholas E '80 (White G&M Co,LPA) -1 W 4th -Ste 1700 -Cincinnati 45202 **Fx:**241-2399

(740) 774-4710 ..**Bunch**, Thomas E '80 Mun Ct Judge -26 S Paint -Chillicothe 45601

(419) 241-2777 ..**Bunda**, Robert A '79 (Bunda S&D,PLL) -One SeaGate -Ste 650 -Toledo 43604 **Fx:**241-4697

(419) 241-2777 ..**Bunda Stutz & DeWitt,PLL** -One SeaGate -Ste 650 -Toledo 43604 **Fx:**241-4697

(216) 787-3030 ..**Bundy**, Charlett A '91 Atty Gen -615 W Superior Av -11th Fl -Cleveland 44113 **Fx:**787-3480

(850) 882-4611 ..**Bundy**, Randall G '79 US Air Force -501 Van Matre Av -AAC/JA -Eglin AFB, FL 32542

(216) 781-1720 ..**Bundy**, Roger M Jr. '02 -75 Pub Sq -Ste 1414 -Cleveland 44113 **Fx:**622-2714

(330) 456-8341 ..**Bundy**, Todd S '80 (Black MS&A,LPA) -220 Market Av S -Ste 1000 -Canton 44702 **Fx:**456-5756

(216) 664-3584 ..**Bungard**, Susan M '92 Dept of Law -601 Lakeside Av -Rm 106 City Hall -Cleveland 44114 **Fx:**664-2663

(216) 263-3403 ..**Bungo**, Larissa L '96 FTC -1111 Superior Av E -Ste 200 -Cleveland 44114

(813) 948-2442 ..**Bunin**, Myra J '93 -422 Pine Bluff Dr -Lutz, FL 33549

(740) 323-1545 ..**Bunning**, Karen J '77 -275 Upson Downs Rd -Newark 43055

(314) 694-5201 ..**Bunning-Stevens**, Barbara A '88 Monsanto Co -800 N Lindbergh Blvd -Law Dept -Saint Louis, MO 63167

(740) 775-5600 ..**Bunstine**, Edward R '81 -32 S Paint -Chillicothe 45601

(734) 779-1509 ..**Buntele**, Richard A '85 Aramark,Inc -20255 Victor Pkwy -Ste 375 -Livonia, MI 48152

                    Bunyan, George W Jr. '52 -5842 Robison Rd -Apt 1 -Cincinnati 45213

(330) 562-6538 ..**Buonpane**, Susan K '85 -480 Wheatfld Dr -Aurora 44202

(440) 603-2376 ..**Burba**, Christopher M '78 Progressive Casualty Ins Co -6055 Parkland Blvd -Mayfield Heights 44124

                    Burchell, Traci L '04 -(Address Unavailable)

(859) 344-9171 ..**Burchett**, Milton E '63 -1843 Mt Vernon Dr -Fort Wright, KY 41011

(614) 252-1131 ..**Burchfield**, James R '78 -1313 E Broad -Columbus 43205 **Fx:**252-1132

(419) 238-6553 ..**Burchfield**, Martin D '86 -124 N Wshngtn -Van Wert 45891

(614) 228-5800 ..**Burchinal**, Christopher J '99 Graff & Assoc -604 E Rich -Columbus 43215 **Fx:**228-8811

(216) 479-8500 ..**Burchmore**, David W '86 (Squire S&D LLP) -127 Pub Sq -4900 Key Twr -Cleveland 44114 **Fx:**479-8780

(513) 793-9950 ..**Burd**, Jeffrey A '96 -10999 Reed Hartman Hwy -Ste 229 -Cincinnati 45242

(216) 221-8825 ..**Burda**, Joan M '82 -2035 Elmwood Av -Lakewood 44107

(614) 789-9600 ..**Burda**, Robert T '81 -6114 Quin Abbey Ct -Dublin 43017 **Fx:**789-5888

(216) 621-2424 ..**Burdell-Ware**, Andrea L '03 -75 Pub Sq #714 -Cleveland 44113 **Fx:**621-5633

(614) 224-2590 ..**Burden**, Eric J '81 -35 E Lvngstn Av -Columbus 43215

(330) 729-9124 ..**Burdette**, Kevin S '92 -8255 South Av -Ste A -Boardman 44512

                    Burdge, Matthew D '02 -88 W Mound -Columbus 43215

(937) 224-1981 ..**Burdge**, Michael J '78 Young PL&J -130 W 2nd -Ste 800 -Dayton 45402

(937) 432-9500 ..**Burdge**, Ronald L '78 -2299 Miamisburg-Centervll Rd -Dayton 45459 **Fx:**432-9503

(740) 345-4429 ..**Burdick**, Nancy N '88 -2437 Swans Rd NE -Newark 43055

(813) 632-4500 ..**Burditt**, Gerald T '92 Washington Mutual Fin -8900 Grand Oak Cir -Tampa, FL 33637

(330) 253-7171 ..**Burdon**, James L '67 (Burdon & M) -137 S Main -Ste 201 -Akron 44113

(330) 253-7171 ..**Burdon & Merlitti** -137 S Main -Ste 201 -Akron 44308 **Fx:**253-7174

(740) 695-4821 ..**Burech**, Stanley G '69 (Burech & C) -121 Newell Av -Saint Clairsville 43950

(216) 443-8610 ..**Burg**, Matthew G '00 Ct of Common Pleas -1200 Ontario -Cleveland 44113

(216) 621-0200 ..**Burgan**, Kelly S '01 %Baker & H LLP -1900 E 9th -Ste 3200 -Cleveland 44114 **Fx:**696-0740

                    Burgazli, Cenk R '04 -(Address Unavailable)

(216) 921-8900 ..**Burge**, David A '71 -2901 S Park Blvd -Cleveland 44120

(440) 244-1808 ..**Burge**, James M '75 (J Burge Co,LPA) -600 Bway -Lorain 44052

(440) 244-1808 ..**Burge**, Susan C '97 %J Burge Co,LPA -600 Bway -Lorain 44052

(513) 671-3201 ..**Burger**, John J '99 Harmon,Inc -12021 Centron Pl -Cincinnati 45246

(419) 435-4809 ..**Burger**, Robert M '54 -131 W North -Bx468 -Fostoria 44830

(216) 566-5790 ..**Burger**, Robert W '97 %Thompson H LLP -127 Pub Sq -3900 Key Ctr -Cleveland 44114 **Fx:**566-5800

(513) 241-2324 ..**Burger**, Thomas J '86 (Wood H&E LLP) -441 Vine -Ste 2700 -Cincinnati 45202 **Fx:**421-7269

(216) 696-8700 ..**Burger**, Todd M '02 %Kohrman J&K PLL -1375 E 9th -One Cleve Ctr 20th Fl -Cleveland 44114 **Fx:**621-6536

(412) 471-1180 ..**Burgess**, John A '94 %Dell ML&L -525 Wm Penn Pl -Ste 3700 -Pittsburgh, PA 15219

(216) 222-2963 ..**Burgess**, Julia E '80 Natl City Bank -1900 E 9th -Cleveland 44114

(216) 348-5400 ..**Burgess**, M John '02 %McDonald H Co,LPA -600 Superior Av E -Ste 2100 -Cleveland 44114 **Fx:**348-5474

(216) 566-5500 ..**Burgess**, Patricia A '02 %Thompson H LLP -127 Pub Sq -3900 Key Ctr -Cleveland 44114 **Fx:**566-5800

(859) 231-3000 ..**Burgess**, Patricia K '94 (Stoll K&P,LLP) -300 W Vine -Ste 2100 -Lexington, KY 40507

(330) 743-9383 ..**Burgess**, Richard L '84 7th Dist Ct of Appls -120 Market -4th Fl -Youngstown 44503

(513) 724-2252 ..**Burgess**, Terry David '71 -110 N 3rd -Williamsburg 45176

(513) 384-5225 ..**Burgess**, Thomas C '86 FirstEnergy Corp -76 S Main -Akron 44308

                    Burgett, Clifford W '94 -30951 Walden Dr -Westlake 44145

(740) 223-4290 ..**Burggraf**, Rhonda G '92 Marion Cnty Pros -134 E Center -Marion 43302 **Fx:**223-4299

(513) 891-3270 ..**Burgin**, Lester J '82 (Harris & B) -9545 Kenwood Rd -Ste 301 -Cincinnati 45242

(614) 481-0332 ..**Burgoon**, Jerry J Jr. '59 -2621 Dorset Rd -Columbus 43221

(330) 456-3200 ..**Burick**, Elizabeth A '84 (E Burick Co,LPA) -1428 Market Av N -Canton 44714

(937) 443-6625 ..**Burick**, Lawrence T '68 (Thompson H LLP) -2000 Cthse Plz NE -Bx8801 -Dayton 45401 **Fx:**443-6635

(937) 847-6477 ..**Burk**, Christine L '90 City of Miamisburg -10 N 1st -Miamisburg 45342

(330) 384-5861 ..**Burk**, James W '91 FirstEnergy Corp -76 S Main -Akron 44308

(740) 363-2600 ..**Burkam Fuller & Herzog** -43 E Central Av -Delaware 43015

(740) 363-2600 ..**Burkam**, Jeffrey A '79 (Burkam F&H) -43 E Central Av -Delaware 43015

(419) 399-2181 ..**Burkard**, Joseph R '92 (Cook T&B,Ltd) -112 N Water -Paulding 45879

(219) 455-1847 ..**Burke**, Brian M '85 Lincoln Natl Life Ins Co -1300 S Clinton -Fort Wayne, IN 46802

(330) 394-1501 ..**Burke**, Charlene E '89 %J Alpern Co,LPA -103 W Market -Ste 202 -Bx727 -Warren 44482

(212) 326-3939 ..**Burke**, Christopher M '00 %Jones D -222 E 41st -4th Fl -New York, NY 10017 **Fx:**755-7306

(513) 621-6464 ..**Burke**, Daniel E '88 (Graydon H&R LLP) -511 Walnut -1900 Fifth Third Ctr -Cincinnati 45202 **Fx:**651-3836

(513) 708-1096 ..**Burke**, Daniel F Jr. '77 -866 Genenbill Dr -Cincinnati 45238 **Fx:**946-4577

(216) 241-2838 ..**Burke**, David E '64 OfCnsl Taft S&H LLP -200 Pub Sq -3500 BP Twr -Cleveland 44114 **Fx:**241-3707

(216) 381-8747 ..**Burke**, Delia A '81 -3562 Radcliffe Rd -Cleveland Heights 44121

(614) 436-0600 ..**Burke**, Diane E '98 %Mueller & S,LPA -7700 Rvrs Edge Dr -Columbus 43235

(513) 421-4225 ..**Burke Fitzgerald Burns & Balash,LLP** -817 Main -Ste 800 -Cincinnati 45202

(419) 243-2283 ..**Burke**, Hal D '98 Scheer G&B Co,LPA -520 Mad Av -Bx1335 -Toledo 43603

(513) 579-6400 ..**Burke**, James E '78 (Keating M&K PLL) -1 E 4th -1400 Provident Twr -Cincinnati 45202 **Fx:**579-6457

(440) 746-0707 ..**Burke**, James F '77 (Burke & H) -3505 E Royalton Rd -#218 -Broadview Heights 44147

(216) 586-3939 ..**Burke**, James P '01 %Jones D -901 Lakeside Av -Cleveland 44114 **Fx:**579-0212

(440) 777-6500 ..**Burke**, James W Jr. '70 Burke V&G -22649 Lorain Rd -Fairview Park 44126 **Fx:**777-0507

(614) 464-6400 ..**Burke**, Jennifer M '01 %Vorys SS&P LLP -52 E Gay -Bx1008 -Columbus 43216 **Fx:**464-6350

(216) 267-0445 ..**Burke**, Jerome L '71 -4544 Rocky Rvr Dr -Cleveland 44135

(216) 523-1500 ..**Burke,** John F III '92 Mansour GG&M Co,LPA -55 Pub Sq
-Ste 2150 -Cleveland 44113 **Fx:**523-1705

(216) 328-2590 ..**Burke,** John T '69 Realty 1 -6000 Rockside Wds Blvd -Ste 328
-Independence 44131

(614) 249-6716 ..**Burke,** Joseph E '03 %Nationwide Ins Co -1 Nationwide Plz
-Columbus 43215

(440) 835-8200 ..**Burke,** Joseph T '91 -24500 Ctr Ridge Rd -Ste 175
-Westlake 44145

(216) 586-3939 ..**Burke,** Kathleen B '73 (Jones D) -901 Lakeside Av
-Cleveland 44114 **Fx:**579-0212

(216) 696-6525 ..**Burke,** Kevin T '96 Catholic Diocese of Cleveland -1404 E 9th
-8th Fl -Cleveland 44114 **Fx:**696-8084

(513) 381-2838 ..**Burke,** Kim K '81 (Taft S&H LLP) -425 Walnut -Ste 1800
-Cincinnati 45202 **Fx:**381-0205

(216) 622-8200 ..**Burke,** Matthew E '95 %Calfee H&G LLP -800 Superior Av
-Ste 1400 -Cleveland 44114 **Fx:**241-0816

(419) 243-9650 ..**Burke,** Megan E '97 M Burke LLC -1709 Spielbusch Av -Ste 100
-Toledo 43624 **Fx:**243-9680

(419) 243-2283 ..**Burke,** Michael J '73 (Scheer G&B Co,LPA) -520 Mad Av -Bx1335
-Toledo 43603

(937) 225-5798 ..**Burke,** Nicole C '97 Montgomery Cnty Pros -301 W 3rd -Bx972
-Dayton 45422 **Fx:**225-3470

(216) 479-8500 ..**Burke,** Patrick J '03 %Squire S&D LLP -127 Pub Sq
-4900 Key Twr -Cleveland 44114 **Fx:**479-8780

(513) 381-4700 ..**Burke,** Rachel '96 %Porter WM&A LLP -250 E 5th -Ste 2200
-Cincinnati 45202 **Fx:**421-0991

(330) 253-5060 ..**Burke,** Richard W '83 (Brennan M&D,LLC) -75 E Market
-Akron 44308 **Fx:**253-1977

(859) 341-1881 ..**Burke,** Riley Stephen '91 (Deters B&L,PSC) -2701 Turkeyfoot Rd
-207 Thomas More Pkwy -Crestview Hills, KY 41017 **Fx:**341-1469

(937) 223-8888 ..**Burke,** Robert A '79 Dyer GM&S -131 N Ludlow -Ste 1400
-Dayton 45402 **Fx:**223-0127

(419) 882-7100 ..**Burke,** Steven M '82 (Lydy & M,Ltd) -4930 Holland Sylvania Rd
-Sylvania 43560 **Fx:**882-7100

(513) 723-4000 ..**Burke,** Tara K '00 %Vorys SS&P LLP -221 E 4th
-Ste 2000 Atrium Two -Bx0236 -Cincinnati 45201 **Fx:**723-4056

(513) 721-5525 ..**Burke,** Timothy M '73 (Manley B) -225 W Court -Cincinnati 45202
Fx:721-4268

(440) 777-6500 ..**Burke Vannucci & Gallagher** -22649 Lorain Rd
-Fairview Park 44126 **Fx:**777-0507

(614) 221-4400 ..**Burkett,** Elizabeth S '86 Volkema TMBS&M,LPA -140 E Town
-Ste 1100 -Columbus 43215 **Fx:**221-6010

(740) 345-0417 ..**Burkett,** Julia Kristin '90 -21 W Church -Ste 201 -Newark 43055

(330) 393-3200 ..**Burkey Burkey & Scher Co, LPA** -200 Chestnut Av NE
-Warren 44483 **Fx:**393-6436

(330) 393-3200 ..**Burkey,** Elise M '88 Burkey B&S Co,LPA -200 Chestnut Av NE
-Warren 44483 **Fx:**393-6436

(330) 393-3200 ..**Burkey,** Robert F '66 Burkey B&S Co,LPA -200 Chestnut Av NE
-Warren 44483 **Fx:**393-6436

(803) 777-8178 ..**Burkhard,** James R '68 USC-Law School -Main & Greene
-Columbia, SC 29208

(216) 642-3342 ..**Burkhardt,** Amy M '95 %Wegman H&V,LPA
-6055 Rockside Wds Blvd -Ste 200 -Cleveland 44131
Fx:642-8826

(419) 245-1020 ..**Burkhardt,** James G '76 %Law Dept -One Govt Ctr -Ste 2250
-Toledo 43604 **Fx:**245-1090

(216) 787-3145 ..**Burkhart,** Elizabeth L '84 Industrial Commssn of OH
-615 Superior Av NW -Cleveland 44113 **Fx:**787-3483

(614) 221-3155 ..**Burkhart,** Matthew J '97 %Bailey C LLC -10 W Broad
-Columbus 43215 **Fx:**221-0479

(216) 520-1345 ..**Burkhart,** Robert C '98 NY Life Ins -6000 Lombardo Ctr -Ste 300
-Seven Hills 44131

(772) 341-5038 ..**Burkhart,** Sandra Edwards '01 -1225 Taft SW
-Sherrodsville 44675

(937) 324-7353 ..**Burkholder,** Andrew J '77 Law Directors Ofc -76 E High
-Springfield 45502

(614) 221-5216 ..**Burkholder,** Bruce H '80 (Wiles BB&B Co,LPA) -300 Spruce
-1st Fl -Columbus 43215 **Fx:**221-5692

(419) 536-6038 ..**Burkholder,** Fred J '83 -4303 Talmadge Rd -Ste 201
-Toledo 43623

(513) 621-4496 ..**Burks,** Margaret A '85 Ofc of Chapter 13 Trustee -36 E 4th
-Ste 700 -Cincinnati 45202

Burland, Bradley D '80 -23300 Chagrin Blvd -Ste 203
-Beachwood 44122

(614) 464-1877 ..**Burleigh,** Barbra A '03 %Sowald S&C -400 S 5th -Ste 101
-Columbus 43215

(513) 241-4110 ..**Burleigh,** David W '95 (Deters B&L,PSC) -441 Vine
-Ste 3500 Carew Twr -Cincinnati 45202 **Fx:**241-4551

(330) 526-0104 ..**Burleson,** David G '92 (Zollinger & B Ltd) -Bx2368 -Canton 44720
Fx:(866) 311-9964

(513) 946-5122 ..**Burlew,** John H '75 Cnty Mun Ct Judge -1000 Main
-Cincinnati 45202

(614) 466-3615 ..**Burley,** James W '80 Legis Srvc Commssn -77 S High
-Columbus 43215

(614) 857-3102 ..**Burley,** John D '84 Red Capital Grp -2 Miranova Pl -12th Fl
-Columbus 43215

(216) 479-8500 ..**Burlingame,** Alexander G '98 %Squire S&D LLP -127 Pub Sq
-4900 Key Twr -Cleveland 44114 **Fx:**479-8780

(614) 221-8900 ..**Burman,** Robert N '73 (Burman & R) -601 S High
-Columbus 43215 **Fx:**221-8912

(614) 221-8900 ..**Burman & Robinson** -601 S High -Columbus 43215 **Fx:**221-8912

(419) 535-0075 ..**Burnard,** Justin D '02 %Allotta F&W Co,LPA -2222 Centennial Rd
-Toledo 43617 **Fx:**535-1935

(937) 865-6800 ..**Burneka,** Joseph W III '96 Lexis/Nexis -Bx933 -Dayton 45401

(614) 469-3939 ..**Burnell,** Brigette A '02 %Jones D -325 John H McConnell Blvd
-Ste 600 -Bx165017 -Columbus 43216 **Fx:**461-4198

(614) 227-8804 ..**Burnes,** James P '78 (Bricker & E LLP) -100 S 3rd
-Columbus 43215 **Fx:**227-2390

(330) 643-2242 ..**Burnett,** Crystal D '03 Hon J Williams -209 S High
-Ct of Cmmn Pleas -Akron 44308

(440) 323-7070 ..**Burnett,** John W '87 %Becker & M Co,LPA -134 Middle Av
-Elyria 44035 **Fx:**323-1879

(330) 675-2426 ..**Burnett,** Michael A '01 %Trumbull Cnty Pros -160 High NW
-Warren 44481

(216) 443-7223 ..**Burnett,** Rochelle A '81 Cuyahoga Cnty Pub Def -1200 W 3rd NW
-100 Lakeside Pl -Cleveland 44113

(630) 724-6729 ..**Burney,** Jon R '68 -3113 Woodcreek Dr -Downers Grove, IL 60515

(216) 615-7600 ..**Burney,** Stephanie B '00 Acxiom Corp -1616 Oak Tree Blvd
-Ste 400 -Independence 44131

(440) 777-5354 ..**Burnham,** Francis N '68 -26720 Caton Pl -North Olmsted 44070
Fx:777-5354

(513) 241-4722 ..**Burnham,** Ralph E '97 %Montgomery R&J,LPA -36 E 7th
-Ste 2100 -Cincinnati 45202 **Fx:**241-8775

(330) 821-6411 ..**Burnquist,** John A '84 -1844 W State -Ste C -Alliance 44601

(513) 891-3270 ..**Burns,** Andrea L '97 %Harris & B -9545 Kenwood Rd -Ste 301
-Cincinnati 45242

(610) 280-3950 ..**Burns,** Anne F '94 Bazil & Assoc -102 Pickering Way -#402
-Exton, PA 19341

(937) 443-5426 ..**Burns,** Belinda A '79 Deloitte & Touche LLP -1700 Cthse Plz NE
-Dayton 45402

(419) 661-0800 ..**Burns,** Brian P '94 Impact Cutoff Srvc -129 Dixie Hwy
-Rossford 43460

(419) 898-6210 ..**Burns,** Charles R '91 Benton-Carroll-Salem Schools
-11685 W State Route 163 -Oak Harbor 43449

(419) 249-7100 ..**Burns,** Craig P '90 %Marshall & M,LLC -Four Seagate -8th Fl
-Toledo 43604 **Fx:**249-7151

(614) 438-1217 ..**Burns,** Darla J '85 OH Rehab Srvc Comm
-400 E Campus Vw Blvd -Columbus 43266

(740) 622-2011 ..**Burns,** David W '68 (Pomerene B&S) -309 Main
-Coshocton 43812

(330) 627-4555 ..**Burns,** Donald R Jr. '88 Carroll Cnty Pros -49 Pub Sq
-Carrollton 44615

(216) 621-1200 ..**Burns,** James L '90 -526 Superior Av -Ste 1130 -Cleveland 44114

(212) 306-1822 ..**Burns,** Jeffrey P '88 Amer Stock Exch -86 Trinity Pl
-New York, NY 10006

(614) 444-1190 ..**Burns,** John A '73 Cnsl Jochim Co,LPA -673 S Mohawk
-Columbus 43206 **Fx:**445-5850

(740) 593-2626 ..**Burns,** John F '69 %Ohio Univ -10 E Union -Pilcher Hse
-Athens 45701

(216) 292-5807 ..**Burns,** John J '98 %Singerman MD&K -3401 Enterprise Pkwy
-Ste 200 -Beachwood 44122 **Fx:**292-5867

(219) 460-1630 ..**Burns,** John R III '74 (Baker & D) -111 E Wayne -Ste 800
-Fort Wayne, IN 46802

(937) 865-6800 ..**Burns,** Jonathan P '01 Lexis/Nexis -Bx933 -Dayton 45401

(513) 852-8200 ..**Burns,** Joseph S '02 %Cors & B LLC -537 E Pete Rose Way
-Ste 400 -Cincinnati 45202

(937) 746-2832 ..**Burns,** Joshua G '01 %Ruppert B&R Co,LPA -1063 E 2nd -Bx369
-Franklin 45005 **Fx:**746-2855

(615) 791-1031 ..**Burns,** Joy D '96 (Sutter OM&F) -217 2nd Av S
-Franklin, TN 37064 **Fx:**790-7468

(216) 621-4636 ..**Burns,** Kenneth B '62 (Gallup B & Assoc) -815 Superior Av E
-Ste 1810 The Superior Bldg -Cleveland 44114

(419) 248-3585 ..**Burns,** Mary A '83 Cnty Brd of Mntl Rtrdtn -2001 Collingwood Blvd
-Toledo 43620

(330) 867-9717 ..**Burns,** Mary Lou '99 -304 N Cleveland-Massillon Rd -Akron 44333

(859) 394-6200 ..**Burns,** Mary Pyle '02 %Adams SW&D -40 W Pike -Bx861
-Covington, KY 41012 **Fx:**291-7902

(614) 469-5715 ..**Burns,** Michael J '79 US Atty -303 Marconi Blvd -Ste 200
-Columbus 43215

(513) 618-7800 ..**Burns,** Nancy J '95 %Graf S&M,LPA -425 Walnut -Ste 2400
-Cincinnati 45202 **Fx:**618-7801

(202) 942-4425 ..**Burns,** Robert E '76 SEC -450 5th NW -Washington, DC 20549

(614) 292-9307 ..**Burns,** Robert E '78 Natl Regulatory Rsrch Inst -1080 Carmack Rd
-Ste 406 -Columbus 43210

(216) 689-4970 ..**Burns,** Robert J '80 KeyBank Natl Assoc -127 Pub Sq -2nd Fl
-Cleveland 44114

(440) 349-9000 ..**Burns,** Robert S '85 Weston Design Build Inc -29300 Aurora Rd
-Solon 44139

(513) 421-4225 ..**Burns,** Robert W '74 (Burke FB&B,LLP) -817 Main -Ste 800
-Cincinnati 45202

Burns, Stacey L '04 -(Address Unavailable)

(330) 743-2987 ..**Burns,** Susan A '97 %Hon GJ Limbert -125 Market
-Youngstown 44503

(330) 478-4333 ..**Burns,** Susan H '94 -3704 Lincoln Way E -Massillon 44646

(330) 454-2136 ..**Burns,** Thomas A '75 -116 Cleveland Av NW -Ste 717
-Canton 44702

(614) 466-7853 ..**Burns,** William M '76 Legis Srvc Commssn -77 S High
-Columbus 43215

(859) 491-5200 ..**Burns-Gerakos,** Tonya S '01 -27 E 4th -Covington, KY 41011

(937) 333-4400 ..**Burns-Smith,** Andrea J '99 Dayton Pros -335 W 3rd -Ste 372
-Dayton 45402

Burnside, Jeremy M '04 -(Address Unavailable)

(440) 576-3662 ..**Burnside,** Teri L '96 Ashtabula Cnty Pros -25 W Jffrsn
-Jefferson 44047

(614) 428-6969 ..**Burnside-Kelly,** Susan B '91 (Burnside-Kelly Law Ofc)
-348 Granvll -Gahanna 43230

(740) 374-2241 ..**Burnworth,** Randall G '76 -429 2nd -Marietta 45750

(614) 387-9024 ..**Burpee,** Robert L '96 %Hon PE Pfeifer -65 Front
-Columbus 43215

(440) 473-1634 ..**Burr,** Andrew M '93 Lancer Ins Co -6563 Wilson Mills Blvd
-Ste 801 -Mayfield Village 44143

(513) 412-0068 ..**Burr,** Heather M '01 Great Amer Fncl Rsrcs,Inc -250 E 5th
-Cincinnati 45202

(513) 721-1350 ..**Burr,** Peter A '88 %Barron PB&S -3074 Madison Rd
-Cincinnati 45209

(513) 852-6000 ..**Burrell,** Peter M '90 Wood & L LLP -600 Vine -Ste 2500
-Cincinnati 45202 **Fx:**852-6087

(513) 732-1141 ..**Burreson Bradford & Hill** -40 S 3rd -Batavia 45103

(513) 887-3474 ..**Burress,** Brad A '00 Butler Cnty Pros -315 High -11th Fl -Bx515
-Hamilton 45012

(216) 583-2539 ..**Burridge-Olah,** Christee S '84 Ernst & Young LLP -925 Euclid Av
-Ste 1300 -Cleveland 44115

(614) 224-8824 ..**Burrier,** Brian C '92 (Gerrity & B Ltd) -400 S 5th -Ste 302
-Columbus 43215 **Fx:**224-3810

(740) 353-1540 ..**Burris,** Diane '87 -1625 Offnere -Bx1222 -Portsmouth 45662

(954) 262-6176 ..**Burris,** Johnny C '79 NSU-Shepard Broad Law Ctr -3305 Cllg Av
-Fort Lauderdale, FL 33314

(513) 946-3000 ..**Burroughs,** Katie M '97 Hamilton Cnty Pros -230 E 9th
 -Cincinnati 45202 **Fx:**946-3017

Burroughs, Nancy H '82 -7496 Chagrin Rd -Chagrin Falls 44023

(614) 466-7424 ..**Burrow,** Marcie P '98 State Med Bd of OH -77 S High -17th Fl
 -Columbus 43215

(317) 326-3131 ..**Burrow,** Michael R '01 Hancock Telecom -2331 E 600 N -Bx108
 -Maxwell, IN 46154

(937) 223-8000 ..**Bursey,** Charles E II '01 -333 W 1st -Ste 445 -Dayton 45402

(419) 241-9000 ..**Burson,** John H '68 (Shumaker L&K,LLP) -1000 Jackson
 -Toledo 43624 **Fx:**241-6894

(419) 396-6190 ..**Burson,** Paul A '49 (Burson & B) -102 E Findlay -Carey 43316

(740) 382-1121 ..**Burt,** Jasper N '66 -284 S State -Marion 43302 **Fx:**383-3094

(614) 876-3862 ..**Burt,** LoAnn Q '96 OH Dept of Admin Srvcs -30 E Broad -28th Fl
 -Columbus 43215

(614) 466-4882 ..**Burtch,** James M III '75 OH Dept Hlth -246 N High -Bx118
 -Columbus 43216

(614) 228-1541 ..**Burtch,** John H '74 (Baker & H LLP) -65 E State -Ste 2100
 -Columbus 43215 **Fx:**462-2616

(513) 352-4719 ..**Burtch,** Karla J '83 Law Dept -801 Plum -Rm 214
 -Cincinnati 45202 **Fx:**352-1515

(419) 447-6181 ..**Burtis,** Paul F '90 Dell B&A,LLP -60 Sycamore -Tiffin 44883
 Fx:477-6332

(216) 787-3297 ..**Burton,** Andre L '95 OH Lottery Cmmssn -615 W Superior Av
 -Cleveland 44113

(937) 227-3700 ..**Burton,** Chad E '04 %Faruki I&C PLL -10 N Ludlow
 -500 Cthse Plz SW -Dayton 45402 **Fx:**227-3717

(419) 738-8165 ..**Burton,** Courtney W '95 %RC Wiesenmayer -15 Willipie -Ste 300
 -Bx299 -Wapakoneta 45895

(330) 451-7770 ..**Burton,** Diane C '91 5th Dist Ct of Appls -110 Central Plz S
 -Ste 320 -Canton 44702 **Fx:**451-7249

(937) 227-3700 ..**Burton,** Donald E '88 %Faruki I&C PLL -10 N Ludlow
 -500 Cthse Plz SW -Dayton 45402 **Fx:**227-3717

(301) 897-6951 ..**Burton,** Frederick H Jr. '90 Lockheed Martin Cop
 -6801 Rockldg Dr -Bethesda, MD 20817

(732) 274-0600 ..**Burton,** John F Jr. '60 Rutgers Univ/Sch of Mngmnt
 -56 Primrose Cir -Princeton, NJ 08540 **Fx:**274-0678

(419) 522-2889 ..**Burton,** Jon K '74 (Renwick W&B) -9 N Mulberry -Mansfield 44902

(419) 352-1581 ..**Burton,** Julie A '95 %Mitchell S&H -112 E Oak
 -Bowling Green 43402

(614) 888-6067 ..**Burton,** Martin D '95 -1933 E Dublin Granvll Rd -Ste 278
 -Columbus 43229

(937) 227-3700 ..**Burton,** Melinda K '95 %Faruki I&C PLL -10 N Ludlow
 -500 Cthse Plz SW -Dayton 45402 **Fx:**227-3717

(419) 738-8165 ..**Burton,** Michael A '95 %RC Wiesenmayer -15 Willipie -Ste 300
 -Bx299 -Wapakoneta 45895

(614) 798-0971 ..**Burton,** Robert E Jr. '87 Natl Realty Srvcs,Inc -5131 Post Rd
 -Ste 350 -Dublin 43017

(513) 977-8200 ..**Burton,** Shawn P '04 %Dinsmore & S LLP -255 E 5th -Ste 1900
 -Cincinnati 45202 **Fx:**977-8141

(740) 373-4633 ..**Burton,** William L '76 (Atkinson & B) -312 Putnam -Bxl
 -Marietta 45750

(216) 574-7184 ..**Burtzlaff,** Kevin J '88 Bd of Ed -1380 E 6th -3rd Fl
 -Cleveland 44114

(614) 387-2065 ..**Burwell,** David W '76 OH Dept Taxation -800 Fwy Dr N
 -Columbus 43229

(304) 529-5531 ..**Burwell,** Karen E '79 SSA-OHA -1108 3rd Av -Ste 400
 -Huntington, WV 25701

(202) 267-3515 ..**Bury,** Mark W '84 FAA -800 Indpndnc Av -Washington, DC 20591

(513) 352-6700 ..**Busacker,** Bret F '00 %Thompson H LLP -312 Walnut -14th Fl
 -Cincinnati 45202 **Fx:**241-4771

(859) 371-3600 ..**Busald,** E André '89 (Busald FZ) -226 Main -Bx6910
 -Florence, KY 41022 **Fx:**525-1040

(614) 258-1983 ..**Busam,** David R '91 (DR Busam Co,LPA) -923 E Broad
 -Columbus 43205

(937) 324-8482 ..**Busam,** Thomas C '98 %D Harkins & Assoc -333 N Limestone
 -Bx1125 -Springfield 45501

(216) 830-2106 ..**Busby,** Mary S '88 Gallagher Pipino,Inc -1500 W 3rd -Ste 450
 -Cleveland 44113

(216) 431-9900 ..**Busby,** William C '99 Athersys,Inc -3201 Carnegie Av
 -Cleveland 44115

(614) 421-1980 ..**Buscemi,** Anthony W '93 West Grp -365 W Hubbard Av
 -Columbus 43215

(216) 766-5712 ..**Busch,** Lawrence J '79 -3401 Enterprise Pkwy #340
 -Beachwood 44122 **Fx:**371-5583

(513) 965-9002 ..**Buschbacher,** Michael S '73 -1019 Main -Milford 45150

(513) 983-1479 ..**Buse,** Jennifer D '92 Procter & Gamble-Tax Div -Bx599
 -Cincinnati 45201

(513) 421-4499 ..**Busemeyer,** William A '65 (WA Busemeyer Co,LPA)
 -3805 Edwards Rd -Ste 105 -Cincinnati 45209

(330) 659-3142 ..**Buser,** Daniel C '88 Crain Langner & Co -3728 Waitley Dr
 -Richfield 44286

(419) 422-2919 ..**Busey,** Nicole M '02 %Marathon Ashland Petro LLC -539 S Main
 -Findlay 45840 **Fx:**421-8402

(330) 424-7781 ..**Bush,** Florence '84 Child Support -110 N Nelson Av -Lisbon 44432

(330) 799-5940 ..**Bush,** Joseph J III '87 (Schiavoni S&B Co,LPA) -87 Wstchstr Dr
 -Youngstown 44515

(614) 280-1100 ..**Bush,** Kevin R '85 (Keener DC&P,LPA) -88 E Broad -Ste 1750
 -Columbus 43215

(440) 954-4170 ..**Bush,** Mary E '90 -9373 Kings Hllw Ct -Mentor 44060

(330) 743-5101 ..**Bush,** Richard T '83 (Green H&S,Co LPA) -16 Wick Av -Ste 400
 -Youngstown 44503 **Fx:**743-3451

(330) 742-8921 ..**Bush,** Robert E Jr. '92 City of Youngstown Police Dept
 -116 W Boardman -Youngstown 44503

(614) 466-3998 ..**Bush,** Robert S '90 Unemploymnt Comp Commssn -145 S Front
 -Bx182299 -Columbus 43218

(216) 621-9800 ..**Bush,** Theodore J '94 Lawyers Title Ins -1300 E 9th -Ste 1201
 -Cleveland 44114

Bushey, Jason D '03 -228 S Main -North Baltimore 45872

(330) 743-1171 ..**Bushey,** Martha L '89 (Manchester BP&U) -201 E Commerce
 -Atrium Level 2 Commerce Bldg -Youngstown 44503
 Fx:743-1190

(740) 695-1327 ..**Busic,** Amy L '99 Tri-Cnty Mediator -100 W Main -Cthse
 -Saint Clairsville 43950

(419) 533-6472 ..**Busick,** David M '93 -S671 Rd 9 -Liberty Center 43532

(800) 327-0117 ..**Buskey,** Joanne '93 -2345 Crystal Dr -Exec Ofcs -Arlington, VA
 22227

(614) 875-7220 ..**Buskirk,** Jeffrey E '84 -4178 Bway -Grove City 43123

(419) 522-7776 ..**Busler,** David E '77 -3 N Main -Ste 812 -Mansfield 44902

(440) 876-6338 ..**Buss,** Dennis A '74 Van Dorn Demag Corp -11792 Alameda Dr
 -Strongsville 44149

(440) 946-2322 ..**Buss,** Ralph C '66 -111 E Wshngtn -Ste 1 -Bx705
 -Painesville 44077

(216) 397-1270 ..**Buss,** William D II '70 -2214 Delamere Dr
 -Cleveland Heights 44106

(513) 932-8000 ..**Busse,** Robert L '84 Fujitec Amer Inc -401 Fujitec Dr
 -Lebanon 45036

(216) 241-6220 ..**Bustamante,** Michael T '88 Project Grp -1400 W 6th -4th Fl
 -Cleveland 44113

(614) 445-6265 ..**Butauski,** Joseph A '87 (Caborn & B Co,LPA) -765 S High
 -Columbus 43206

(216) 363-4500 ..**Butch,** Mariann E '96 OfCnsl Benesch FC&A LLP -200 Pub Sq
 -Ste 2300 -Cleveland 44114 **Fx:**363-4588

(216) 781-2258 ..**Butcher,** Samuel V '84 (Stewart & D Co,LPA) -1370 Ontario
 -Ste 1440 Standard Bldg -Cleveland 44113 **Fx:**781-8210

(216) 523-4625 ..**Butensky Brehm,** Ilene '86 Eaton Corp -1111 Superior Av
 -Cleveland 44114

(330) 438-0976 ..**Butera,** Constance D '82 Stark Cnty Fam Crt -100 Central Plz S
 -Canton 44702

(404) 870-2237 ..**Butera,** Deborah S '94 %Shapiro F -1360 Pchtree -Ste 1200
 -Atlanta, GA 30309 **Fx:**870-2222

(330) 491-5217 ..**Butera,** Karen D '99 %Buckingham D&B,LLP -4518 Fulton Dr NW
 -Bx35548 -Canton 44735 **Fx:**492-9625

(574) 631-6368 ..**Butkovich,** John E '68 Univ Notre Dame Ofc of Planned Giving
 -1100 Grace Hall -Notre Dame, IN 46556 **Fx:**631-6957

(513) 621-1414 ..**Butkovich,** Joseph A '93 Butkovich SS&G Co,LPA -36 E 7th
 -Ste 2600 -Cincinnati 45202 **Fx:**977-5580

(513) 621-1414 ..**Butkovich Schimpf Schimpf & Ginocchio Co,LPA** -36 E 7th
 -Ste 2600 -Cincinnati 45202 **Fx:**977-5580

(419) 213-4751 ..**Butler,** Amy L '02 Lucas Cnty Cthse -700 Adams -Toledo 43624

(216) 622-3718 ..**Butler,** Annette G '73 US Atty -801 W Superior -Ste 400
 -Cleveland 44113 **Fx:**622-3370

(440) 933-5442 ..**Butler,** Barbara A '00 %J Marcie,PC -32730 Walker Rd -Ste I-6
 -Avon Lake 44012

(330) 670-7300 ..**Butler,** Brian J '01 Hanna C&P,LLP -3737 Embssy Pkwy -Bx5521
 -Akron 44334 **Fx:**670-0977

(419) 636-5666 ..**Butler,** Charles C '92 (Bish B&T,Ltd) -1210 W High -Bryan 43506
 Fx:636-3919

(216) 691-9404 ..**Butler,** Charles S '67 -35 Severance Circle Dr -Ste 809 -Cleveland
 44118

(614) 221-3151 ..**Butler Cincione & DiCuccio** -50 W Broad -Ste 700
 -Columbus 43215

(303) 676-7514 ..**Butler,** Clark W Jr. '82 Defense Finance & Accounting Srvc
 -6760 E Irvngtn Pl -Denver, CO 80279

(614) 221-4000 ..**Butler,** David J '97 (Chester W&S LLP) -65 E State -10th Fl
 -Columbus 43215 **Fx:**221-4012

(216) 621-3870 ..**Butler,** Dennis F '70 -2401 Superior Viaduct -Cleveland 44113

(216) 621-7260 ..**Butler,** Donald '82 (D Butler & Assoc) -75 Pub Sq -Ste 600
 -Cleveland 44113

(614) 221-3882 ..**Butler,** Eugene R '86 -326 S High -Ste 400 -Columbus 43215

(317) 233-4133 ..**Butler,** Eugene W Jr. '75 IN Public Employees Ret Fund
 -143 W Market -Indianapolis, IN 46204

(216) 621-0200 ..**Butler,** Geraldine J '00 Baker & H LLP -1900 E 9th -Ste 3200
 -Cleveland 44114 **Fx:**696-0740

(440) 323-5443 ..**Butler,** Harry F '52 -475 Middle Av -Elyria 44035

Butler, Heather '03 -(Address Unavailable)

(513) 946-3000 ..**Butler,** James E '75 Hamilton Cnty Pros -230 E 9th
 -Cincinnati 45202 **Fx:**946-3017

(740) 335-4381 ..**Butler,** James L '74 (Butler & M) -200 E Market
 -Washington Court House 43160

(614) 461-1100 ..**Butler,** John C '72 (Swedlow BLL&D Co,LPA) -10 W Broad
 -Ste 2400 -Columbus 43215 **Fx:**461-8178

(317) 265-2120 ..**Butler,** Jolynn Barry '76 SBC Indiana -240 N Meridian -Rm 1801
 -Indianapolis, IN 46204 **Fx:**265-4354

(216) 241-9990 ..**Butler,** Kevin M '01 %J Jerome & Assoc -55 Pub Sq -Ste 2020
 -Cleveland 44113 **Fx:**241-2920

(440) 329-5416 ..**Butler,** Linda M '88 Lorain Cnty Common Pleas Ct -308 2nd
 -Cthse -Elyria 44035

(937) 297-1150 ..**Butler,** Mariah D '03 %Hochwalt & S,LLP -500 Lincoln Park Blvd
 -Ste 216 -Dayton 45429

(513) 621-2120 ..**Butler,** Martin C '77 (Strauss & T,LPA) -150 E 4th -4th Fl
 -Cincinnati 45202 **Fx:**241-8259

(216) 241-7255 ..**Butler,** Michael P '83 -2401 Superior Viaduct -Cleveland 44113

(513) 891-7087 ..**Butler,** Robert T '90 (Donnellon D&M) -9079 Mntgmry Rd
 -Cincinnati 45242

(513) 352-6587 ..**Butler,** Stephen J '77 (Thompson H LLP) -312 Walnut -14th Fl
 -Cincinnati 45202 **Fx:**241-4771

(440) 329-5408 ..**Butler,** Terrence R '84 Lorain Cnty Dom Rltns Ct -226 Middle Av
 -Elyria 44035

(937) 445-7438 ..**Butler,** Timothy R '83 NCR Corp -1700 S Patterson Blvd
 -WHQ-4W -Dayton 45479

(513) 946-3000 ..**Butler,** Yvette S '97 Hamilton Cnty Pros -230 E 9th
 -Cincinnati 45202 **Fx:**946-3017

(502) 581-6526 ..**Butrum,** Gregory W '90 -513 S 5th -Ste 7A -Louisville, KY 40202

(216) 928-7540 ..**Butscher,** Alisa C '96 (Vanik & B,LLP) -1406 W 6th -3rd Fl
 -Cleveland 44113 **Fx:**928-7548

(330) 830-0083 ..**Buttacavoli,** Glen F '84 -30 1st SE -Massillon 44646

(330) 253-5060 ..**Butterworth,** Jason A '00 %Brennan M&D,LLC -75 E Market
 -Akron 44308 **Fx:**253-1977

(216) 642-3342 ..**Button,** David R '92 %Wegman H&V,LPA
 -6055 Rockside Wds Blvd -Ste 200 -Cleveland 44131
 Fx:642-8826

(513) 621-6464 ..**Buttress,** Christine A '79 (Graydon H&R LLP) -511 Walnut
 -1900 Fifth Third Ctr -Cincinnati 45202 **Fx:**651-3836

(614) 854-9968 ..**Butts,** Diana F '89 Gallagher Benefit Admin,Inc
 -130 E Wilson Bridge Rd -#310 -Worthington 43085

(330) 723-2200 ..**Butts,** Michael T '90 %G Piszczek Co, LPA -412 N Court
 -Medina 44256

(330) 497-0700 ..**Butz**, David E '87 (Krugliak WG&D Co,LPA) -4775 Munson NW
-Bx36963 -Canton 44735 **Fx:**497-4020

(260) 422-0800 ..**Butz**, James A '86 (Beckman L LLP) -800 Standard Fed Plz
-Bx800 -Fort Wayne, IN 46801 **Fx:**420-1013

(937) 322-0891 ..**Butz**, John R '69 Cole AH&D -333 N Limestone -Bx1687
-Springfield 45501 **Fx:**322-9931

(614) 486-3585 ..**Butzer**, Dane C '00 -681 Woodduck Ct -Columbus 43215

(312) 353-1110 ..**Buvinger**, David D '71 US Atty Ofc -219 S Dearborn -#5080
-Chicago, IL 60604

(330) 725-6666 ..**Bux**, Robert J '78 (Williams & B,LLP) -105 W Lbrty -Bx394
-Medina 44258

(216) 575-2284 ..**Buxton**, Mark W '93 Natl City Bank -Bx5756 -Cleveland 44101

(330) 262-7555 ..**Buytendyk**, Michael G '86 (Kennedy CK&B) -558 N Market
-Wooster 44691

(614) 764-6057 ..**Buzash**, George E '90 OCLC,Inc -6565 Frantz Rd -Dublin 43017

(614) 227-2000 ..**Buzby**, Brian L '74 (Porter WM&A LLP) -41 S High
-Columbus 43215 **Fx:**227-2100

(216) 861-0360 ..**Buzney**, Sandra J '99 %Hickman & L Co,LPA -1370 Ontario
-Ste 1620 -Cleveland 44113 **Fx:**861-3113

(330) 392-8551 ..**Buzulencia**, Michael D '84 -150 E Market -Ste 300 -Warren 44481
Fx:392-7030

(330) 385-8590 ..**Buzzard**, John D '69 -517 Bway -East Liverpool 43920

(330) 376-8019 ..**Buzzelli**, Laurence F '73 Allstate Ins Co -50 So Main -Ste 620
-Akron 44308 **Fx:**376-5713

(330) 725-9709 ..**Buzzelli**, Russell A '87 Medina Cmmn Pleas Ct -93 Pub Sq
-Medina 44256

(330) 376-5297 ..**Buzzi**, Paul F '68 -631 W Exchange -Akron 44302 **Fx:**376-7611

(614) 442-5626 ..**Byard**, Robert R '89 (Hunter CS&B) -3360 Tremont Rd -2nd Fl
-Columbus 43221 **Fx:**442-5625

(614) 462-3580 ..**Byers**, Brad A '89 Franklin County Ct Appeals -37 S High -24th Fl
-Columbus 43215

(972) 618-0481 ..**Byers**, David W '66 Emplymnt Law Cnsltng Grp,LLC
-3425 Swanson Dr -Ste 101 -Plano, TX 75025 **Fx:**618-1731

(419) 241-8013 ..**Byers**, Frederick '84 -520 Mad Av -824 Spitzer Bldg -Toledo 43604

(419) 897-7140 ..**Byers**, Gary L '81 Mun Ct Judge -400 Conant -Maumee 43537

(614) 228-6283 ..**Byers**, Kevin P '88 KP Byers Co,LPA -21 E State -Ste 220
-Columbus 43215 **Fx:**228-6425

(614) 221-2838 ..**Byers**, Michael A '78 (Taft S&H LLP) -21 E State -12th Fl
-Columbus 43215 **Fx:**221-2007

(614) 752-7811 ..**Byers**, Renee L '99 OH Dept of Pub Safety -1970 W Broad
-Columbus 43223

(614) 527-6740 ..**Byers**, William L IV '03 OH State Medical Assn -3401 Mill Run Dr
-Govt Relations Ofc -Hilliard 43026

(330) 385-5151 ..**Byers-Emmerling**, Melissa '82 Mun Ct Judge -126 W 6th
-East Liverpool 43920

(212) 736-4500 ..**Byler**, Philip A '76 OfCnsl Nesenoff & M,LLP -363 7th Av -5th Fl
-New York, NY 10001 **Fx:**736-2260

(937) 865-6800 ..**Byrd**, James E '84 Lexis/Nexis -Bx933 -Dayton 45401

(216) 479-8500 ..**Byrd**, Nailah K '02 %Squire S&D LLP -127 Pub Sq -4900 Key Twr
-Cleveland 44114 **Fx:**479-8780

(254) 690-6745 ..**Byrd**, Wilbert '76 Byrd & Assoc -806 Woodlawn Dr
-Harker Heights, TX 76548

(216) 491-1381 ..**Byrne**, Cornelia A '75 Shaker Hts Mun Crt -3355 Lee Rd
-Shaker Heights 44120

(216) 621-1312 ..**Byrne**, James A '90 %McMahon DH&L LLP -812 Huron Rd
-Ste 650 The Caxton Bldg -Cleveland 44115 **Fx:**621-0577

(513) 612-2300 ..**Byrne**, Kenneth L '71 Cincom Systms,Inc -55 Merchant
-Cincinnati 45246

(614) 761-1000 ..**Byrne**, Laura D '84 (Byrne & B,LLP) -5695 Avry Rd -Ste C
-Dublin 43016 **Fx:**495-9001

(513) 381-6600 ..**Byrne**, Mark J '83 (Jacobs KS&M) -1014 Vine -Ste 2300
-Cincinnati 45202

(614) 466-4510 ..**Byrne**, Robert J '88 Atty Gen -150 E Gay -Columbus 43215
Fx:995-0501

(614) 469-3939 ..**Byrne**, Sean P '04 %Jones D -325 John H McConnell Blvd
-Ste 600 -Bx165017 -Columbus 43216 **Fx:**461-4198

(614) 761-1000 ..**Byrne**, Thomas J '88 (Byrne & B,LLP) -5695 Avry Rd -Ste C
-Dublin 43016 **Fx:**495-9001

(419) 213-6850 ..**Byrne**, William A '81 Lucas Cnty Cmmn Pleas Ct -429 Mich Av
-Ste A -Toledo 43624

(937) 445-6327 ..**Byrnes**, John J '82 NCR Corp -1700 S Patterson Blvd -WHQ 3E
-Dayton 45479

(614) 466-3615 ..**Byrnett**, Megan E '04 Legis Srvc Commssn -77 S High
-Columbus 43215

(216) 771-6650 ..**Byroads**, Shaun D '04 Kreiner & P Co,LPA -Bx6599
-Cleveland 44101

(614) 224-8374 ..**Byrom**, Robert G '77 Legal Aid -40 W Gay -Columbus 43215

(440) 951-2303 ..**Byron**, Barry M '56 (Byron & B Co,LPA) -4230 SR 306 -#240
-Willoughby 44094

(614) 645-8815 ..**Byron**, Linda '98 City Pros -375 S High -7th Fl -Columbus 43215

(440) 951-2303 ..**Byron**, Stephen L '91 Byron & B Co,LPA -4230 SR 306 -#240
-Willoughby 44094

(419) 247-2611 ..**Cabanski**, Robert W '79 (Fuller & H,Ltd) -One SeaGate -Ste 1700
-Bx2088 -Toledo 43603 **Fx:**247-2665

(614) 462-3555 ..**Cable**, Daniel J '92 Franklin Cnty Pros -373 S High
-Columbus 43215

(419) 448-4444 ..**Cable**, Jonathan H '02 Seneca Cnty Pros -71 S Wshngtn -Ste E
-Bx667 -Tiffin 44883 **Fx:**448-7911

(330) 643-2365 ..**Cable**, Ronald L Jr. '01 Summit Cnty Dom Rltns Ct -209 S High
-Akron 44308

(440) 779-5920 ..**Cables**, Thomas A '61 -25746 Yeoman Dr -Westlake 44145

(614) 445-6265 ..**Caborn**, David A '86 (Caborn & D,LPA) -765 S High
-Columbus 43206

Caborn, Leslie Thorpe '89 -2100 Cheltenham Rd
-Columbus 43220

(614) 461-8103 ..**Cabot**, Jeffery A '87 -60 E Broad -Ste 300 -Columbus 43215

(419) 734-6699 ..**Cabral**, Allen M '75 -419 E 2nd -Port Clinton 43452 **Fx:**734-6699

(216) 241-5310 ..**Cabral**, Thomas J '86 (Gallagher SF&N) -1501 Euclid Av -6th Fl
-Cleveland 44115 **Fx:**241-1608

(440) 323-6098 ..**Cabrera**, Robert '94 -300 4th -Elyria 44035

(330) 759-9350 ..**Caccarozzo**, Joey L '03 Assn in Anesthesiology Inc
-3622 Belmont Av -Ste 1 -Youngstown 44505 **Fx:**759-9387

(440) 871-8900 ..**Cada**, Dennis C '96 Radiometer Amer Inc -810 Sharon Dr
-Westlake 44145

(216) 241-0715 ..**Cada**, Gregory A '78 -425 W Lakeside Av -Ste 100
-Cleveland 44113

(513) 887-3364 ..**Cade**, Daniel S '82 Butler Cnty CSE -315 High -8th Fl
-Hamilton 45011

(513) 721-7522 ..**Cade**, Howard D III '88 -22 W 9th -Cincinnati 45202

(216) 479-8500 ..**Cadle**, Amy L '02 %Squire S&D LLP -127 Pub Sq -4900 Key Twr
-Cleveland 44114 **Fx:**479-8780

(614) 464-1211 ..**Cadwallader**, John I '78 (Frost BT LLC) -10 W Broad -Ste 1000
-Columbus 43215 **Fx:**464-1737

(888) 224-3993 ..**Cadwallader**, John R '83 Nationwide Ins -5900 Parkwood Dr
-Dublin 43016

(513) 887-3586 ..**Cady**, Heather L '03 Butler Cnty Common Pleas Ct -315 High
-3rd Fl -Hamilton 45011

Caffarel, Christopher J '04 -(Address Unavailable)

(216) 363-6014 ..**Cafferkey**, Kevin M '85 -1370 Ontario -Ste 2000 -Cleveland 44113

(216) 522-3872 ..**Cafferkey**, Maureen M '85 US Dept of Labor -1240 E 9th -Rm 881
-Cleveland 44199

(860) 527-9699 ..**Caffrey**, Robert J '84 %Berman & S -100 Pearl
-Hartford, CT 06103

(419) 281-3561 ..**Cahill**, Erin N '99 %Lutz & O Co,LPA -930 Claremont Av -Bx0220
-Ashland 44805 **Fx:**281-6999

(614) 249-9001 ..**Cahill**, John C '83 %Nationwide Ins Co -2 Nationwide Plz -Ste 810
-Columbus 43215

(440) 352-8977 ..**Cahill**, Kenneth J '91 J Ulrich Co,LPA -1959 Mentor Av
-Painesville 44077

(216) 664-6900 ..**Cahill**, Robert E '00 %Brzytwa Q&M LLC -1660 W 2nd
-900 Skylight Ofc Twr -Cleveland 44113 **Fx:**664-6901

Cahill, Ronald R '99 -878 S Court -Medina 44256

(216) 443-7800 ..**Cahill**, Thomas M '94 Cuyahoga Cnty Pros -1200 Ontario -8th Fl
-Cleveland 44113 **Fx:**698-2270

(216) 781-5515 ..**Cahn**, James S '73 (Hermann C&S,LLP) -1301 E 9th -Ste 500
-Cleveland 44114 **Fx:**781-1030

(216) 696-7600 ..**Cahn**, Stephen J '61 (Duvin C&H) -1301 E 9th -20th Fl Erievw Twr
-Cleveland 44114 **Fx:**696-2038

(330) 376-5300 ..**Cahoon**, Peter T '77 (Buckingham D&B,LLP) -50 S Main -Bx1500
-Akron 44309 **Fx:**258-6559

(440) 338-4650 ..**Caimi**, Paul A '86 (P Caimi Co,LPA) -46 Chagrin Plz -#106
-Chagrin Falls 44022

(513) 985-0550 ..**Cain**, Charles C '80 Insured Land Title -8044 Mntgmry Rd -#505
-Cincinnati 45236

(419) 244-8989 ..**Cain**, Dwight L '81 %Cosme D&S -202 N Erie -Toledo 43624

(216) 281-6122 ..**Cain**, Elizabeth A '82 -1268 W Blvd -Cleveland 44102

(216) 622-3600 ..**Cain**, James M '72 US Atty -801 W Superior -Ste 400
-Cleveland 44113 **Fx:**622-3370

(440) 846-2434 ..**Cain**, Julia A '89 Barristers Title Agncy -16600 Sprague Rd
-Ste 390 -Middleburg Heights 44130

(614) 644-8381 ..**Cain**, Kenneth R Jr. '96 Workers Comp -30 W Spring -Level 26
-Columbus 43215

(614) 222-8686 ..**Cain**, Lacey L '00 %Scott S&W LLP -50 W Broad
-2500 LeVeque Twr -Columbus 43215 **Fx:**222-8688

(440) 248-2482 ..**Caine**, Steven R '92 -6775 Ridgecliff Dr -Cleveland 44139

(216) 443-7808 ..**Caine**, William R '79 Cuyahoga Cnty Pros -1200 Ontario -8th Fl
-Cleveland 44113 **Fx:**698-2270

(419) 213-6744 ..**Cairl**, Susan M '87 Lucas Cnty Cmmn Pleas Ct -1801 Speilbusch
-Family Court Ctr -Toledo 43624

Cairns, Danielle D '04 -(Address Unavailable)

(216) 696-4700 ..**Cairns**, J Donald '58 (Spieth BM&N Co,LPA) -925 Euclid Av
-2000 Huntngtn Bldg -Cleveland 44115 **Fx:**696-2706

(614) 464-2000 ..**Cairns**, Jacob A '03 %Kravitz & K -145 E Rich -Columbus 43215
Fx:464-2002

(937) 865-6800 ..**CaJacob**, Jennifer G '00 Lexis/Nexis -Bx933 -Dayton 45401

(440) 243-8330 ..**Calabase**, Mark '86 -Two Berea Cmmns -Ste #1 -Berea 44017

(216) 479-6100 ..**Calabrese**, Anthony O III '97 (Vorys SS&P LLP) -1375 E 9th
-Ste 2100 One Cleve Ctr -Cleveland 44114 **Fx:**479-6060

(216) 479-8500 ..**Calabrese**, J Philip '00 %Squire S&D LLP -127 Pub Sq
-4900 Key Twr -Cleveland 44114 **Fx:**479-8780

(330) 499-8387 ..**Calabretta**, Joseph W '71 -4571 Stephens Cir NW -Canton 44718

(740) 282-5323 ..**Calabria**, Michael J '77 (Bruzzese & C) -300 Sinclair Bldg -Bx1506
-Steubenville 43952 **Fx:**282-5328

(513) 946-3000 ..**Calambas**, Linda '02 Hamilton Cnty Pros -230 E 9th
-Cincinnati 45202 **Fx:**946-3017

(419) 242-7985 ..**Calamunci**, Anthony J '94 (Roetzel & A,LPA) -One SeaGate
-9th Fl -Toledo 43604 **Fx:**242-0316

(440) 746-1177 ..**Calandra**, John P '64 (Baran PTF&T Co,LPA) -8748 Brecksvll Rd
-Ste 200 -Cleveland 44141 **Fx:**746-9637

(513) 598-5000 ..**Calardo**, Stephen P '81 Calardo Mediation Srvc -5608 Harrison Av
-Cincinnati 45248 **Fx:**598-5000

(937) 225-4652 ..**Calaway**, Scott M '97 Montgomery Cnty Pub Def -117 S Main
-Ste 400 -Dayton 45422 **Fx:**225-3449

(937) 225-4652 ..**Calaway**, Todd E '99 Montgomery Cnty Pub Def -117 S Main
-Ste 400 -Dayton 45422 **Fx:**225-3449

(513) 351-9400 ..**Calaway**, Wendy R '98 (WR Calaway Co,LPA) -2089 Sherman Av
-Ste 20 -Cincinnati 45212 **Fx:**351-4345

(419) 885-4149 ..**Calcamuggio**, Larry G '77 -4149 Holland-Sylvania Rd -Ste 2
-Toledo 43623

(614) 469-3200 ..**Calcaterra**, Craig A '98 %Thompson H LLP -10 W Broad -Ste 700
-Columbus 43215 **Fx:**469-3361

(703) 834-4273 ..**Calciu**, Andrei D '99 NEC America, Inc. -14040 Park Ctr Rd
-Mail Stop VA 4480 -Herndon, VA 20171

(513) 977-8200 ..**Calder**, Thomas S '57 OfCnsl Dinsmore & S LLP -255 E 5th
-Ste 1900 -Cincinnati 45202 **Fx:**977-8141

(216) 621-0150 ..**Calderas**, Erica L '94 (Hahn L&P LLP) -3300 BP Twr/200 Pub Sq
-Ste 3300 -Cleveland 44114 **Fx:**241-2824

(513) 576-1060 ..**Calderhead**, David C '87 -200 TechneCenter Dr -Ste 100
-Milford 45150 **Fx:**576-8792

(419) 354-4632 ..**Calderon**, Reina A '92 Calderon Energy Co -500 Lehman Av
-Bx126 -Bowling Green 43402

(330) 434-6685 ..**Calderone**, Andrew J '73 -511 N Main -Akron 44310

(330) 670-7300 ..**Calderone**, Kenneth A '90 (Hanna C&P,LLP) -3737 Embssy Pkwy
-Bx5521 -Akron 44334 **Fx:**670-0977

(216) 479-6100 .. **Caldwell,** Carrie M '02 %Vorys SS&P LLP -1375 E 9th
-Ste 2100 One Cleve Ctr -Cleveland 44114 **Fx:**479-6060

(937) 332-6936 .. **Caldwell,** David J '93 Municipal Ct Pros -Old Ct Hse -Troy 45373

(330) 971-7067 .. **Caldwell,** Deborah A '98 Summa Health System -1900 23rd
-Cuyahoga Falls 44223

(330) 497-0700 .. **Caldwell,** Jacqueline B '85 (Krugliak WG&D Co,LPA)
-4775 Munson NW -Bx36963 -Canton 44735 **Fx:**497-4020

(937) 544-5095 .. **Caldwell,** John B '73 (Young & C) -225 N Cross
-West Union 45693

Caldwell, Raberta A '03 -(Address Unavailable)

(330) 451-7897 .. **Caldwell,** Ronald M '85 Stark Cnty Pros -110 Central Plz -Ste 510
-Canton 44702

(513) 721-2506 .. **Caldwell,** Sean M '91 Lexis Nexis -842 Dayton -Cincinnati 45214

(740) 345-6454 .. **Calesaric,** Robert E '94 -35 S Park Pl -Ste 201 -Newark 43055
Fx:349-0869

(419) 496-3680 .. **Caley,** Beverly A '92 -Bx946 -Ashland 44805

(216) 622-8200 .. **Calfee Halter & Griswold LLP** -800 Superior Av -Ste 1400
-Cleveland 44114 **Fx:**241-0816

(614) 621-1500 .. **Calfee Halter & Griswold LLP** -21 E State -1100 Fifth Third Ctr
-Columbus 43215 **Fx:**621-0010

(859) 252-6721 .. **Calhoun,** Dustin J '00 Boehl S&G LLP -444 W 2nd
-Lexington, KY 40507

(330) 253-1111 .. **Calhoun,** Howard L '51 Calhoun W&H -159 S Main -Ste 707
-Akron 44308

(614) 644-9632 .. **Calhoun,** Jason H '82 OH Bureau of Workers Comp -30 W Spring
-28th Fl -Columbus 43215

(419) 524-6011 .. **Calhoun Kademenos Heichel & Childress Co,LPA** -6 W 3rd
-Ste 200 -Bx268 -Mansfield 44901 **Fx:**526-1431

(419) 625-7770 .. **Calhoun Kademenos Heichel & Childress Co,LPA**
-502 W Wshngtn -Sandusky 44870 **Fx:**625-8552

(330) 424-7937 .. **Calhoun,** Melody M '84 -37½ N Park Av -Bx365 -Lisbon 44432

(740) 446-7890 .. **Calhoun,** Ronald R '58 -444 2nd Av -Bx787 -Gallipolis 45631

(330) 253-1111 .. **Calhoun Waddell & Hunt** -159 S Main -Ste 707 -Akron 44308

(513) 621-2120 .. **Calico,** Paul B '80 Strauss & T,LPA -150 E 4th -4th Fl
-Cincinnati 45202 **Fx:**241-8259

(614) 252-2300 .. **Calig & Handelman,LPA** -854 E Broad -Columbus 43205

(740) 349-8581 .. **Calig & Handelman,LPA** -29 S Park Pl -Newark 43055
Fx:345-4101

(740) 653-4400 .. **Calig & Handelman,LPA** -204 N Columbus -Lancaster 43130

(614) 252-2300 .. **Calig,** Samuel L '74 (Calig & H,LPA) -854 E Broad
-Columbus 43205

(614) 461-0256 .. **Caligiuri,** Joseph M '02 Ofc Dscplnry Cnsl -250 Civic Ctr Dr -#325
-Columbus 43215 **Fx:**461-7205

(216) 696-4700 .. **Calkins,** Benjamin '83 (Spieth BM&N Co,LPA) -925 Euclid Av
-2000 Huntngtn Bldg -Cleveland 44115 **Fx:**696-2706

(216) 397-9749 .. **Calkins,** Hugh '51 -3345 N Park Blvd -Cleveland 44118

(414) 299-6860 .. **Call,** Laurel K '80 Fortis Hlth -501 W Mich Av
-Milwaukee, WI 53203

(216) 464-5255 .. **Callaghan,** Gregory J '69 -30000 Chagrin Blvd -Cleveland 44124

(216) 781-4868 .. **Callaghan,** Thomas M '53 -2628 Detroit Av -Cleveland 44113

(202) 326-4020 .. **Callaghan,** Tim M '78 Ofc of the Genl Cnsl -1200 K NW -Ste 340
-Washington, DC 20005

(440) 205-9303 .. **Callahan,** Dennis M '70 -8000 Plz Blvd -PMB #203 -Mentor 44060

(330) 376-9260 .. **Callahan Green Rilley & Sinn LLC** -7 W Bowery -Ste 907
-Akron 44308 **Fx:**376-9807

(419) 885-3597 .. **Callahan,** John J '52 -5580 Monroe -Sylvania 43560

(937) 866-9933 .. **Callahan,** Karl P '90 -101 N 1st -Miamisburg 45342

(216) 443-7900 .. **Callahan,** Michael F '85 Cuyahoga Cnty Cmmn Pleas Crt
-1200 Ontario Av -Cleveland 44113

(330) 376-9260 .. **Callahan,** Michael T '82 (Callahan GR&S LLC) -7 W Bowery
-Ste 907 -Akron 44308 **Fx:**376-9807

(216) 291-1718 .. **Callahan,** Michael W '91 -5001 Mayfld Rd -Ste 301
-Cleveland 44124

(614) 461-4455 .. **Callahan,** Rory P '00 %Cloppert LS&W -225 E Broad
-Columbus 43215 **Fx:**461-0072

(740) 549-1320 .. **Callahan,** Thomas C '79 -1233 Westwood Dr -Lewis Center 43035

(216) 566-5612 .. **Callahan,** Thomas J '85 (Thompson H LLP) -127 Pub Sq
-3900 Key Ctr -Cleveland 44114 **Fx:**566-5800

(419) 421-3343 .. **Callahan-Brown,** Linda J '93 Marathon Ashland Petro LLC
-539 S Main -Findlay 45840 **Fx:**421-3578

(614) 466-5394 .. **Callais,** Melissa J '94 Pub Def -8 E Long -Columbus 43215

(513) 977-8200 .. **Callan,** Sean P '93 (Dinsmore & S LLP) -255 E 5th -Ste 1900
-Cincinnati 45202 **Fx:**977-8141

(614) 899-6611 .. **Callander,** Robert D '67 -576 Charring Cross Dr -Ste G
-Westerville 43081

(330) 456-8341 .. **Callas,** Gust '78 (Black MS&A,LPA) -220 Market Av S -Ste 1000
-Canton 44702 **Fx:**456-5756

(419) 354-1244 .. **Callejas,** Esteban R '89 -1180 N Main -Ste 4
-Bowling Green 43402 **Fx:**353-2733

(330) 744-3198 .. **Callen,** James B '76 NE OH Legal Srvcs -11 Fed Plz Central
-Ste 800 -Youngstown 44503

(419) 874-1633 .. **Callender,** Calvin D '67 -130 Cedar Ct -Perrysburg 43551

(614) 527-6199 .. **Callender,** Carma L '03 Gates McDonald & Co -3455 Mill Run Dr
-Hilliard 43026

(614) 728-8537 .. **Callender,** Cynthia N '96 State Auditor Ofc -88 E Broad -5th Fl
-Bx1140 -Columbus 43216

(614) 224-5700 .. **Callender,** Gwen E '91 %FOP/OH Labor Cncl -222 E Town
-Columbus 43215

(440) 255-9100 .. **Callender,** James S Jr. '92 (McNamara HC&L) -8440 Station
-Mentor 44060

(202) 661-2200 .. **Callender,** Ryan K '99 %Ballard SA&I,LLP -601 13th NW
-Ste 1000 S -Washington, DC 20005 **Fx:**661-2299

(216) 621-0200 .. **Callesen,** Phillip M '87 (Baker & H LLP) -1900 E 9th -Ste 3200
-Cleveland 44114 **Fx:**696-0740

(614) 210-1840 .. **Callicoat,** Troy A '03 %Barrett EC&E LLP -7269 Sawmill Rd
-Dublin 43016 **Fx:**210-1841

Callinan, Maureen A '04 -(Address Unavailable)

(513) 852-6012 .. **Callow,** Amy G '94 %Wood & L LLP -600 Vine -Ste 2500
-Cincinnati 45202 **Fx:**852-6087

(513) 579-6400 .. **Callow,** Joseph M Jr. '93 (Keating M&K PLL) -1 E 4th
-1400 Provident Twr -Cincinnati 45202 **Fx:**579-6457

(330) 334-6446 .. **Callow,** Michael J '95 -1 Park Centre Dr -Ste 100
-Wadsworth 44281

(614) 645-7385 .. **Calloway,** George H '83 City Atty -90 W Broad -Columbus 43215

(937) 578-4202 .. **Calloway,** Sue Dill '83 Memorial Hospital -500 London Av
-Leg Dept -Marysville 43040

(847) 646-7046 .. **Calloway,** Valerie Lyn '99 Kraft Foods -Three Lks Dr -NF 346
-Northfield, IL 60093

(513) 721-1975 .. **Calloway-Campbell,** Marsha G '85 Freking & B -215 E 9th -5th Fl
-Cincinnati 45202 **Fx:**651-2570

(216) 696-2286 .. **Calo,** Julie A '93 Cnsl Tucker E&W LLP -925 Euclid Av
-1150 Huntngtn Bldg -Cleveland 44115 **Fx:**592-5009

(973) 439-3430 .. **Calore,** William J '82 Atlas Copco NA,Inc -34 Maple Av
-Pinebrook, NJ 07058

(440) 442-6800 .. **Calta,** Diane A '99 %JW Diemert Jr & Assoc Co,LPA -1360
SOM Center Rd -Mayfield Heights 44124 **Fx:**442-0825

(937) 913-2539 .. **Calvert,** Christopher J '97 Brady Ware Capital,Inc -1 S Main
-Ste 600 -Dayton 45402

(859) 331-1560 .. **Calvert,** Robert J '74 Toebben Co -541 Buttermilk Pike -Ste 104
-Crescent Springs, KY 41017

(304) 232-0361 .. **Camastro,** Diane A '94 WV Business Cllg -1052 Main
-Wheeling, WV 26003

(312) 880-3000 .. **Cambria,** David G '95 Huron Consulting Grp -550 W Van Buren
-Ste 900 -Chicago, IL 60607

(513) 946-3800 .. **Cambron,** Robyn W '00 Hamilton Cnty Pub Def -230 E 9th -3rd Fl
-Cincinnati 45202 **Fx:**946-3808

(513) 977-8200 .. **Camden,** Bonnie G '89 (Dinsmore & S LLP) -255 E 5th -Ste 1900
-Cincinnati 45202 **Fx:**977-8141

(440) 245-4000 .. **Camera,** Michael J '80 -520 Bway -Ste 200 -Lorain 44052

(440) 526-8888 .. **Cameratta,** Karen Jo '93 (KJ Cameratta Co,LPA)
-500 E Royalton Rd -180 Security Fed Plz -Broadview Heights
44147

(614) 487-3202 .. **Cameron,** Bruce L '69 -1161 Bethel Rd -Ste 101 -Columbus 43220

(440) 247-2477 .. **Cameron,** David K '78 -3951 Ellendale Rd -Moreland Hills 44022

(216) 443-7800 .. **Cameron,** Denise R '79 Cuyahoga Cnty Pros -1200 Ontario -8th Fl
-Cleveland 44113 **Fx:**698-2270

(419) 255-0571 .. **Cameron,** Donald H '80 (Konop & C) -413 N Mich -Toledo 43624
Fx:255-6227

(614) 221-3318 .. **Cameron,** Eric B '04 %Agee CM&L -89 E Nationwide Blvd
-Ste 200 -Columbus 43215

(330) 722-8989 .. **Cameron,** John B '91 (J Cameron & Assoc) -247 E Smith Rd
-Medina 44256

(614) 387-0605 .. **Cameron,** Julie A '03 Lgsltv Srvc Comm -77 S High -Riffe Ctr
-Columbus 43215

(513) 946-3700 .. **Cameron,** Kendra M '02 %Hamilton Cnty Pub Def -230 E 9th
-3rd Fl -Cincinnati 45202 **Fx:**946-3707

(614) 846-2946 .. **Cameron,** Phillip D '69 -8382 Kirkaldy Ct -Dublin 43017

(513) 241-8844 .. **Cameron,** Phillip F '71 -441 Vine -4400 Carew Twr
-Cincinnati 45202

(216) 292-3300 .. **Cameron,** Sondra R '76 (Conway MWK&K Co,LPA)
-30195 Chagrin Blvd -Ste 300 -Cleveland 44124

(216) 622-8200 .. **Cameron,** Stacy '03 %Calfee H&G LLP -800 Superior Av
-Ste 1400 -Cleveland 44114 **Fx:**241-0816

(419) 843-4499 .. **Camick,** Daniel G '87 (Camick & K Ltd) -3230 Cntrl Pk W -Ste 106
-Toledo 43617

(614) 469-3939 .. **Camillus,** John C '04 %Jones D -325 John H McConnell Blvd
-Ste 600 -Bx165017 -Columbus 43216 **Fx:**461-4198

(216) 241-1907 .. **Camino,** Carmine '80 -1370 Ontario -Ste 330 -Cleveland 44113

(216) 685-1360 .. **Camino,** Paula E '91 (Karp & C,Ltd) -2000 E 9th -Ste 710
-Cleveland 44115 **Fx:**781-3130

(216) 443-8355 .. **Camino,** Walter '79 Cuyahoga Cnty Pub Def -1200 W 3rd NW
-100 Lakeside Pl -Cleveland 44113

(513) 626-3371 .. **Camp,** Jason J '98 Cnsl Procter & Gamble Co -11520 Reed
Hartman Hwy -Cincinnati 45241

(440) 260-6612 .. **Camp,** Margaret A '95 Compli Source/CCH -7055 Engle Rd
-Bldg 4;Ste 403 -Middleburg Heights 44130 **Fx:**239-8533

(330) 434-3461 .. **Camp,** Miles A '94 Legal Defenders -One Cascade Plz
-Akron 44308

Camp, Patricia T '93 -Bx922 -Graham, NC 27253

(216) 241-5310 .. **Campagna,** Maria A '93 %Gallagher SF&N -1501 Euclid Av -6th Fl
-Cleveland 44115 **Fx:**241-1608

(216) 566-5500 .. **Campana,** Jeremy M '02 %Thompson H LLP -127 Pub Sq
-3900 Key Ctr -Cleveland 44114 **Fx:**566-5800

Campanella, Phillip J '66 -7059 Gates Rd -Gates Mills 44040

(216) 621-0200 .. **Campanella,** Thomas S '77 OfCnsl Baker & H LLP -1900 E 9th
-Ste 3200 -Cleveland 44114 **Fx:**696-0740

Campbell, Barbara '04 -(Address Unavailable)

(614) 340-2053 .. **Campbell,** Bruce A '65 Columbus Bar Assn -175 S 3rd -Ste 11
-Columbus 43215

(419) 352-3554 .. **Campbell,** Craig W '90 Wood Cnty Probate Ct
-11120 E Gypsy Lane Rd -Bowling Green 43402

(216) 479-6100 .. **Campbell,** David A III '96 (Vorys SS&P LLP) -1375 E 9th
-Ste 2100 One Cleve Ctr -Cleveland 44114 **Fx:**479-6060

(330) 922-2123 .. **Campbell,** David A Jr. '74 -3773 State Rd -Bx2010 -Akron 44309

(937) 257-5958 .. **Campbell,** Douglas L '76 US Air Force -AFMC LO/JANA
-AFMC Law Ofc -Wright Patterson AFB 45433

(513) 576-2801 .. **Campbell,** Douglas W '88 SDRC -2000 Eastman Dr
-Milford 45150

(419) 425-8594 .. **Campbell,** Dow L '97 St Francis Senior Ministries
-182 St Francis Av -Tiffin 44883

(614) 227-2319 .. **Campbell,** Drew H '90 (Bricker & E LLP) -100 S 3rd
-Columbus 43215 **Fx:**227-2390

(216) 651-2061 .. **Campbell,** Edward J '79 -11515 Lk Av -Cleveland 44102

(216) 621-9338 .. **Campbell,** Eloise A '94 Christian Legal Srvcs -1468 W 25th
-Cleveland 44113

(614) 846-2000 .. **Campbell,** Fred M '54 (Campbell HC&V,LLC) -7650 Rvrs Edge Dr
-Columbus 43235 **Fx:**846-2003

(614) 846-2000 .. **Campbell Hornbeck Chilcoat & Veatch,LLC**
-7650 Rvrs Edge Dr -Columbus 43235 **Fx:**846-2003

(513) 762-5126 .. **Campbell,** Hugh K '84 -2011 Madison Rd -Cincinnati 45208

(330) 645-0431 .. **Campbell,** James M '84 -500 Portage Lks Dr -Akron 44319

(513) 421-4020 .. **Campbell,** Janet B '79 %Cohen TK&S,LLC -250 E 5th -Ste 1200
-Cincinnati 45202 **Fx:**241-4490

(216) 621-1113 .. **Campbell,** Jay R '89 (Renner OB&S,LLP) -1621 Euclid Av -19th Fl
-Cleveland 44115 **Fx:**621-6165

(614) 224-8339 .. **Campbell,** Joel R '72 (Britt CN&S) -490 City Park Av
-Columbus 43215 **Fx:**224-2001

(513) 381-0656 .. **Campbell**, John L '77 (Kohnen & P LLP) -201 E 5th -Ste 800
  -Cincinnati 45202 **Fx:**381-5823

(330) 627-5577 .. **Campbell**, John S '77 (Campbell & B) -130 Pub Sq -Bx25
  -Carrollton 44615

(216) 651-2061 .. **Campbell**, Joseph P '83 -11515 Lk Av -Cleveland 44102

(216) 443-8589 .. **Campbell**, Kathrin D '97 Ct of Common Pleas -1200 Ontario
  -Cleveland 44113

(330) 721-7819 .. **Campbell**, Kevin R '82 %Campbell Assoc -4065 Fairway Dr
  -Medina 44256

(330) 305-6400 .. **Campbell**, Kristen E '96 %Pelini & F,Ltd -8040 Cleveland Av NW
  -Ste 400 -North Canton 44720 **Fx:**305-0042

(440) 350-3200 .. **Campbell**, Margaret S '95 Lake Cnty Pub Def -125 E Erie
  -Painesville 44077

(513) 621-2666 .. **Campbell**, Maura Moran '96 %Statman HS&E LLC -255 E 5th
  -Ste 2900 Chemed Ctr -Cincinnati 45202 **Fx:**587-4477

(937) 382-2838 .. **Campbell**, Michael T '98 %Rose & D Co,LPA -97 N South
  -Wilmington 45177

(937) 445-6662 .. **Campbell**, Noelle D '94 NCR - Law Dept -1700 S Patterson Blvd
  -WHQ-3 -Dayton 45409 **Fx:**445-7531

(510) 444-3770 .. **Campbell**, Patrick C '78 -1970 Bway -Ste 1200 -Oakland, CA 94612
  Fx:451-4115

(570) 893-2114 .. **Campbell**, Peter A '95 Lock Haven Univ -142 E Bald Eagle
  -Lock Haven, PA 17745

(419) 238-5767 .. **Campbell**, Phil W '76 Mun Ct Judge -124 S Market
  -Van Wert 45891

(513) 241-9400 .. **Campbell**, Regina R '96 Legal Aid -215 E 9th -Ste 200
  -Cincinnati 45202

(740) 354-5659 .. **Campbell**, Richard W '83 -1024 Kinney's Ln -Bx1324
  -Portsmouth 45662 **Fx:**354-5650

(330) 725-0030 .. **Campbell**, Robert B '92 Marco M&B -52 Pub Sq -Medina 44256
  Fx:722-4888

(330) 253-6121 .. **Campbell**, Robert P '80 Title One Agncy -2800 W Market
  -Akron 44333

(937) 865-6800 .. **Campbell**, Samuel A '02 LexisNexis -Bx933 -Dayton 45401

(614) 469-3311 .. **Campbell**, Scott A '95 (Thompson H LLP) -10 W Broad -Ste 700
  -Columbus 43215 **Fx:**469-3361

(614) 644-7233 .. **Campbell**, Scott M '99 Atty Gen -150 E Gay -Columbus 43215
  Fx:728-9327

(740) 349-8505 .. **Campbell**, Thomas K '74 (Schaller C&U) -32 N Park Pl
  -Newark 43055

(330) 670-7300 .. **Campbell**, Timothy C '82 (Hanna C&P,LLP) -3737 Embssy Pkwy
  -Bx5521 -Akron 44334 **Fx:**670-0977

(216) 621-7743 .. **Campbell**, William P '93 %Schiff & D,LLC -1370 Ontario
  -Standard Bldg 6th Fl -Cleveland 44113

(713) 939-9444 .. **Campigotto**, Frank J '94 %Streets & S -13831 Northwest Fwy
  -Ste 355 -Houston, TX 77040 **Fx:**939-9508

(440) 992-7196 .. **Camplese**, Albert S '85 Mun Ct Judge -110 W 44th
  -Ashtabula 44004

(330) 673-3444 .. **Can**, Errol A '92 %Williams W&K -11 S River -Bx396 -Kent 44240

(440) 974-1273 .. **Canala**, John S '89 -9240 Kathleen Dr -Mentor 44060

(216) 586-3939 .. **Canala**, Robert L '86 (Jones D) -901 Lakeside Av
  -Cleveland 44114 **Fx:**579-0212

(614) 449-0926 .. **Canale**, David M '85 -1141 S High -Columbus 43206

(614) 644-1583 .. **Canan**, Crystal A '86 OH Schl Facilities Comm -10 W Broad
  -Ste 1400 -Columbus 43215

(216) 241-0033 .. **Canaris**, James E '56 -614 Superior Av NW -820 Rckfllr Bldg
  -Cleveland 44113

(561) 833-5900 .. **Canary**, Nancy H '68 -125 Worth Av -Ste 117
  -Palm Beach, FL 33480 **Fx:**833-5951

(502) 587-5400 .. **Canary**, Thomas L Jr. '87 Mapother & M -801 W Jffrsn
  -Louisville, KY 40202

(216) 696-6500 .. **Canda**, Ronald J '86 %Caravona & C,PLL -50 Pub Sq
  -Ste 1900 Trmnl Twr -Cleveland 44113 **Fx:**696-1411

(419) 841-0792 .. **Candiello**, Vedo R '73 -4859 W Sylvania Av -Ste A -Toledo 43623

(513) 891-5666 .. **Candito**, Joseph '86 -9403 Kenwood Rd -Ste A-106
  -Blue Ash 45242

(419) 424-7066 .. **Candler**, Elizabeth P '80 Hancock Cnty Juvenile Ct -308 Dorney
  Plz -Findlay 45840

(614) 462-3555 .. **Canepa**, Angela R '91 Franklin Cnty Pros -373 S High
  -Columbus 43215

(614) 466-4638 .. **Canepa**, James V '89 Atty Gen -30 E Broad -Columbus 43215
  Fx:466-5087

(513) 241-8600 .. **Caneris**, Adonis A '93 Legg Mason -425 Walnut -Ste 1100
  -Cincinnati 45201

(513) 425-2617 .. **Caneris**, Thomas A '87 AK Steel Corp -703 Curtis
  -Middletown 45043

(614) 221-3318 .. **Canestraro**, Carl R '93 Agee CM&L -89 E Nationwide Blvd
  -Ste 200 -Columbus 43215

(216) 663-4552 .. **Canestraro**, Donald C '66 -15950 Libby Rd -Maple Heights 44137
  Fx:663-4556

(419) 321-6444 .. **Canestraro**, Eugene F '85 (Cline C&W Co,LPA) -300 Mad Av
  -Ste 1100 -Toledo 43604 **Fx:**321-6430

(216) 443-6350 .. **Canfil**, Ellen J '83 8th Dist Ct of Appls -1 Lakeside Av -#202
  -Cleveland 44113 **Fx:**443-2044

(216) 363-6033 .. **Canfil**, Steve W '77 -1370 Ontario -Ste 2000 -Cleveland 44113

Cannata, Sam P '04 -(Address Unavailable)

(937) 644-9125 .. **Cannizzaro Fraser Bridges & Jillisky** -302 S Main
  -Marysville 43040 **Fx:**644-0754

(937) 644-9125 .. **Cannizzaro**, John F '80 (Cannizzaro FB&J) -302 S Main
  -Marysville 43040 **Fx:**644-0754

(937) 443-4367 .. **Cannon**, James F '78 Mun Ct Judge -301 W 3rd -Dayton 45402
  Cannon, James H '03 -(Address Unavailable)

(419) 755-9659 .. **Cannon**, Karen L '92 Law Dir Ofc -30 N Diamond
  -Mansfield 44902

(419) 245-1020 .. **Cannon**, Marci L '97 %Law Dept -One Govt Ctr -Ste 2250 -Toledo
  43604 **Fx:**245-1090

(216) 241-2838 .. **Cannon**, Margaret A '73 (Taft S&H LLP) -200 Pub Sq
  -3500 BP Twr -Cleveland 44113

(440) 357-5537 .. **Cannon Stern Aveni & Loiancono Co,LPA** -41 E Erie
  -Painesville 44077 **Fx:**357-9234

(440) 357-5537 .. **Cannon**, Timothy P '80 (Cannon SA&L Co,LPA) -41 E Erie
  -Painesville 44077 **Fx:**357-9234

(440) 247-4765 .. **Canonico**, Jesse W '03 %SG Thomas,LPA -35 River -Level B
  -Chagrin Falls 44022

(614) 722-3940 .. **Canowitz**, Robin L '92 Childrens Hospital -700 Childrens Dr
  -Columbus 43205

(440) 964-5125 .. **Cantagallo**, Anthony J Jr. '64 -2910 Saybula Dr -Ashtabula 44004

(330) 373-1717 .. **Cantalamessa**, Enzo C '03 %Davis & Y -108 Main SW -10th Fl
  -Warren 44481 **Fx:**395-0610

(614) 464-6400 .. **Canter**, Michael J '72 (Vorys SS&P LLP) -52 E Gay -Bx1008
  -Columbus 43216 **Fx:**464-6350

(513) 762-7700 .. **Cantleberry**, Jill C '84 AXA Advisors,LLC -1055 St Paul Pl
  -Cincinnati 45202

(513) 381-2838 .. **Canton**, Doreen '88 (Taft S&H LLP) -425 Walnut -Ste 1800
  -Cincinnati 45202 **Fx:**381-0205

(440) 942-7750 .. **Cantor**, Abraham '73 -9930 Johnnycake Ridge Rd -Ste 4F
  -Concord 44060

(440) 953-9355 .. **Cantrell**, Doreen M '88 -37121 Euclid Av -Willoughby 44094

(513) 777-2222 .. **Caparella**, Courtney N '03 Lyons & L Co,LPA
  -8310 Prnctn-Glendale Rd -Ste B -West Chester 45069

(614) 873-2219 .. **Capehart**, Curtis R A '03 -6418 Wynwright Dr -Dublin 43016

(304) 529-6181 .. **Capehart**, Marvin II '97 %Huddleston BBP&C,LLP -611 3rd Av
  -Bx2185 -Huntington, WV 25722

(216) 881-5411 .. **Capers**, Jean M '45 -4614 Prospect Av -Ste 222 -Cleveland 44103

(330) 643-2943 .. **Capes**, Robert C '02 Summit Cnty Pros-Juv -650 Dan
  -Akron 44310 **Fx:**379-3647

(937) 461-8800 .. **Capizzi**, Anthony '79 (Harker C&H) -130 W 2nd -Ste 2103
  -Dayton 45402 **Fx:**461-8818

(216) 431-7700 .. **Capka**, Paul V '96 Rysar Properties Inc -4317 Chester Av
  -Cleveland 44103

(216) 514-5997 .. **Caplan**, Leah M '86 %Margulies & L -30100 Chagrin Blvd -Ste 250
  -Pepper Pike 44124 **Fx:**514-5996

(614) 252-2026 .. **Caplan**, Robert L '94 -90 N Nelson Rd -Columbus 43219

(330) 376-5300 .. **Caplan**, William L '80 (Buckingham D&B,LLP) -50 S Main -Bx1500
  -Akron 44309 **Fx:**258-6559

(330) 455-4555 .. **Caplea**, Don E '72 (D Caplea Co,LPA) -116 Cleveland Av NW
  -500 Courtyard Ctr Bldg -Canton 44702

(513) 946-9064 .. **Caplinger**, Candace C '82 Domestic Relations Ct -800 Bway
  -Rm 3-15 -Cincinnati 45202
  Caplinger, James L '62 -3157 Meadow Wood Dr
  -Springfield 45505

(330) 535-5711 .. **Capotosto**, Nicholas P '03 %Brouse M -106 S Main -500
  First Natl Twr -Akron 44308 **Fx:**253-8601

(216) 621-9870 .. **Cappara**, Janeane R '00 %McNeal SA&B Co,LPA
  -123 W Prospect Av -Ste 250 Van Sweringen Arcade
  -Cleveland 44115 **Fx:**522-1112

(216) 241-6602 .. **Cappel**, Carolyn M '77 (Weston HFP&H LLP) -50 Pub Sq
  -2500 Trmnl Twr -Cleveland 44113 **Fx:**621-8369

(513) 621-6464 .. **Cappel**, Harry W '96 (Graydon H&R LLP) -511 Walnut
  -1900 Fifth Third Ctr -Cincinnati 45202 **Fx:**651-3836

(216) 586-3939 .. **Cappellazzo**, Ronald L '89 Jones D -901 Lakeside Av
  -Cleveland 44114 **Fx:**579-0212

(330) 376-7500 .. **Capriolo**, Ralph A '74 Mentzer & M,Ltd -1 Cascade Plz -20th Fl
  -Akron 44308 **Fx:**376-8018

(440) 331-2478 .. **Caputo**, Diane J '80 -20525 Ctr Ridge Rd -Ste 350
  -Rocky River 44116

(520) 284-4085 .. **Carabell**, Robert S '67 -50 Skyline Cir -Sedona, AZ 86351

(330) 744-0291 .. **Carach**, Herman J Jr. '77 (Boyd RC&Co LPA) -400 Sky Bk Bldg
  -Bx6565 -Youngstown 44501

(330) 762-2411 .. **Carano**, Sergio A '89 %Amer C Co,LPA -159 S Main -6th Fl
  -Akron 44308 **Fx:**762-9918

(937) 223-2200 .. **Caras**, Sam G '80 -130 W 2nd -Ste 310 -Dayton 45402
  Fx:223-8989

(216) 696-6500 .. **Caravona & Czack, PLL** -50 Pub Sq -Ste 1900 Trmnl Twr
  -Cleveland 44113 **Fx:**696-1411

(216) 696-6500 .. **Caravona**, Donald E '73 (Caravona & C,PLL) -50 Pub Sq
  -Ste 1900 Trmnl Twr -Cleveland 44113 **Fx:**696-1411

(330) 497-9700 .. **Carbenia**, Brian P '03 %Machan & Assoc Co,LPA
  -6647 Frank Av NW -Ste 110 -North Canton 44720

(216) 861-3000 .. **Carbone**, Joseph A Jr. '75 -1370 Ontario -Ste 800
  -Cleveland 44113

(440) 473-1025 .. **Carbone**, Rocco J '72 (Carbone & M Co,LPA) -6690 Beta Dr
  -Ste 106 -Mayfield 44143

(216) 433-1300 .. **Cardaman**, Victoria L '95 Brook Park Law Dept -6161 Engle Rd
  -Brook Park 44142

(248) 244-1100 .. **Cardelli**, Thomas G '04 (Cardelli H&L,PC) -322 W Lincoln
  -Royal Oak, MI 48067

(216) 623-0150 .. **Cardenas**, Ricardo J '96 %Roetzel & A,LPA -1375 E 9th
  -One Cleve Ctr 9th Fl -Cleveland 44114 **Fx:**623-0134

(419) 213-6951 .. **Carder**, Kevin J '86 Lucas Cnty Pros-Juv Div -1801 Spielbusch Av
  -Toledo 43624

(330) 938-2161 .. **Cardinal**, Kenneth J '74 -758 N 15th -Bx207 -Sebring 44672

(812) 537-0100 .. **Cardis**, Francis J '99 Cardis & Assoc -318 Walnut -Lawrenceburg,
  IN 47025

(740) 354-7563 .. **Cardosi**, Mark J '88 SE OH Lgl Srvcs -800 Gallia -Ste 700
  -Portsmouth 45662

(614) 785-4676 .. **Carducci**, Daniel G '81 Wendys Intl,Inc -1105 Schrock Rd
  -Ste 401 -Columbus 43229

(614) 224-5205 .. **Cardwell**, Richard D '91 Peck S&W,LLP -175 S 3rd -Ste 600
  -Columbus 43215 **Fx:**224-0069

(614) 410-6740 .. **Carelli**, Gail E '02 Contract Counsel -470 Olde Worthngtn Rd
  -Ste 200 -Westerville 43082

(216) 443-9000 .. **Caresani**, Ann M '94 %Porter WM&A LLP -925 Euclid Av
  -Ste 1700 -Cleveland 44115 **Fx:**443-9011

(216) 357-7160 .. **Carey**, Amy H '00 Hon D Nugent -801 W Superior Av
  -Cleveland 44113

(330) 725-0531 .. **Carey**, Chris D '94 %Laribee H&K -325 N Bway -Bx445
  -Medina 44258

(937) 325-4077 .. **Carey**, Daniel D '91 -4 W Main -Ste 404 -Springfield 45502

(781) 356-9689 .. **Carey**, Harry M Jr. '79 Cnsl Haemonetics Corp -400 Wood Rd
  -Braintree, MA 02184 **Fx:**356-3558

(419) 241-2100 .. **Carey**, John M '78 (Watkins B&C) -405 Mad Av -Ste 1900
  -Toledo 43604 **Fx:**241-1960

(440) 925-2802 .. **Carey**, John T '83 -1991 Crocker Rd -Ste 600 -Westlake 44145

(614) 227-4891 .. **Carey**, Kimball H '79 OfCnsl Bricker & E LLP -100 S 3rd
  -Columbus 43215 **Fx:**227-2390

(614) 228-9707 .. **Carey**, Laura M '98 Mallory & T Co,LPA -88 E Broad -Ste 1560
  -Columbus 43215

(440) 286-9571 .. **Carey,** Lisa J '93 %Svete M&C Co,LPA -100 Parker Ct
-Chardon 44024

(937) 328-2435 .. **Carey,** Richard P '83 Cnty Mun Ct Judge -50 E Columbia
-Springfield 45502

(614) 278-6800 .. **Carey,** Rick V '03 Cnsl Big Lots Stores -300 Phillipi Rd
-Columbus 43228

(513) 231-0262 .. **Carey,** Robert P '80 (RP Carey LLC) -7189 Grantham Way
-Cincinnati 45230

(937) 382-0955 .. **Carey,** Ronald C '64 (R Carey,LPA) -283 N South
-Wilmington 45177 **Fx:**382-0956

(330) 392-1541 .. **Carey,** Thomas G Jr. '78 Harrington H&M,Ltd -108 Main Av SW
-Ste 500 -Bx1510 -Warren 44482 **Fx:**394-6890

(210) 351-5115 .. **Carey,** Timothy M '89 SBC Comm,Inc -175 E Houston -Ste 212
-San Antonio, TX 78205

(216) 622-8200 .. **Carfagna,** Peter A '79 SrCnsl Calfee H&G LLP -800 Superior Av
-Ste 1400 -Cleveland 44114 **Fx:**241-0816

(330) 788-2480 .. **Carfolo,** Mark A '91 -4800 Market -Ste C -Youngstown 44512

(937) 339-0511 .. **Cargill,** Michael L '79 (Dungan & L Co,LPA) -210 W Main
-Troy 45373 **Fx:**335-5802

(216) 443-6350 .. **Cargill,** Newton S '01 8th Dist Ct of Appls -1 Lakeside Av -#202
-Cleveland 44113 **Fx:**443-2044

(330) 375-1311 .. **Cargle,** Amy Elizabeth '98 %Reminger & R -80 S Summit
-200 Courtyard Sq -Akron 44308 **Fx:**375-9075

(513) 579-7573 .. **Cariappa,** Padma T '82 Federated Dept Stores,Inc -7 W 7th
-Cincinnati 45202

(216) 696-9310 .. **Cariglio,** Terrence Lee '81 (Cariglio & Assoc Co,LPA) -75 Pub Sq
-Ste 920 -Cleveland 44113 **Fx:**696-0075

(740) 284-8008 .. **Carinci,** Francesca T '94 -100 N 4th -Ste 904-911
-Steubenville 43952

(216) 266-2545 .. **Carino,** Philip J '90 Cnsl GE -1975 Noble Rd -Nela Park MD 310B
-Cleveland 44112

(216) 522-3718 .. **Carissimi,** Mark M '76 NLRB -1240 E 9th -1695 Celebrezze Bldg
-Cleveland 44199 **Fx:**522-2418

(216) 586-3939 .. **Carkhuff,** Denise A '95 (Jones D) -901 Lakeside Av
-Cleveland 44114 **Fx:**579-0212

(216) 426-9708 .. **Carl,** Terrence P '99 -1445 E 52nd -Cleveland 44103

(216) 861-4533 .. **Carle,** William D III '55 SrCnsl Ray RC&D PLL -1717 E 9th
-Cleveland 44114 **Fx:**861-4568

(614) 276-4000 .. **Carleton,** Betsy A '94 Roxane Lab Inc -Bx16532 -Columbus 43216

(602) 667-3957 .. **Carleton,** Katherine L '90 Medicis Pharmctcl Corp
-8125 N Hayden Rd -Scottsdale, AZ 85258

(513) 732-7243 .. **Carlier,** Lawrence W '59 Clermont Cnty Probate Ct
-76 S Riverside Dr -Batavia 45103

(937) 443-6520 .. **Carlile,** Richard F '69 (Thompson H LLP) -2000 Cthse Plz NE
-Bx8801 -Dayton 45401 **Fx:**443-6635

(216) 241-6602 .. **Carlin,** Angela G '55 (Weston HFP&H LLP) -50 Pub Sq
-2500 Trmnl Twr -Cleveland 44113 **Fx:**621-8369

(330) 707-0377 .. **Carlin,** Clair M '73 (C Carlin,LLC) -62 S Main -Bx5369
-Poland 44514

(440) 686-9000 .. **Carlin,** Hugh A '83 (H Carlin Co,LPA) -22050 Mastick Rd
-Fairview Park 44126

(440) 256-3323 .. **Carlin,** Joan L '86 -486 Sandhurst Dr -Highland Heights 44143

(216) 622-0700 .. **Carlin,** John H '73 -55 Pub Sq -Ste 2219 -Cleveland 44113

(216) 831-4935 .. **Carlin,** William A '78 (Carlin & C) -29425 Chagrin Blvd -Ste 305
-Pepper Pike 44122

(216) 781-4680 .. **Carlini,** Lawrence J '73 OfCnsl Van Aken W&W -629 Euclid Av
-1000 Natl City Bk Bldg -Cleveland 44114 **Fx:**241-1421

(614) 280-1100 .. **Carlino,** Steven G '01 %Keener DC&P,LPA -88 E Broad -Ste 1750
-Columbus 43215

(404) 652-4000 .. **Carlisle,** Calvin E '76 Georgia-Pacific Corp -133 Pchtree NE
-Atlanta, GA 30303

(216) 360-7200 .. **Carlisle,** Gerald K '60 (Carlisle MRK&U Co,LPA)
-24755 Chagrin Blvd -Ste 200 -Cleveland 44122 **Fx:**360-7210

(419) 535-1301 .. **Carlisle,** James E '98 -110 Harmony Ln -Toledo 43615

(937) 865-1711 .. **Carlisle,** Lynn A '85 Lexis/Nexis -Bx933 -Dayton 45401

(740) 373-5455 .. **Carlisle,** Matthew C '98 %Theisen B,LPA -424 2nd -Bx739
-Marietta 45750 **Fx:**373-4409

(216) 360-7200 .. **Carlisle McNellie Rini Kramer & Ulrich Co,LPA**
-24755 Chagrin Blvd -Ste 200 -Cleveland 44122 **Fx:**360-7210

(614) 837-6504 .. **Carlisle,** Robert P '85 -13175 Pickerington Rd N -Ste 104
-Pickerington 43147

(216) 622-8200 .. **Carlisle,** Zoe K '04 %Calfee H&G LLP -800 Superior Av -Ste 1400
-Cleveland 44114 **Fx:**241-0816

(440) 842-3500 .. **Carlisle-Kesling,** Kathryn J '99 (Carlisle-Kesling & Assoc LLC)
-7083 Pearl Rd -Middleburg Heights 44130

(330) 376-4444 .. **Carlozzi,** Joyce E '87 Edminister & Assoc -159 S Main -Akron
44308

(216) 241-6277 .. **Carlozzi,** Louis J '94 (Carlozzi & Assoc Co,LPA) -1382 W 9th
-Ste 215 -Cleveland 44113 **Fx:**241-6343

(612) 336-3000 .. **Carlson,** Beth E '96 %Faegre & B,LLP -90 S 7th
-Minneapolis, MN 55402 **Fx:**336-3026

(925) 838-2044 .. **Carlson,** Bruce A '83 Image Advertising -383 Diablo Rd -Ste 100
-Danville, CA 94526

(614) 728-5693 .. **Carlson,** Christopher T '91 OH Dept of Job & Fam Srvcs
-30 E Broad -32nd Fl -Columbus 43266

(614) 227-2000 .. **Carlson,** Craig R '91 (Porter WM&A LLP) -41 S High
-Columbus 43215 **Fx:**227-2100

(216) 621-0150 .. **Carlson,** Douglas C '75 (Hahn L&P LLP)
-3300 BP Twr/200 Pub Sq -Ste 3300 -Cleveland 44114
Fx:241-2824

(440) 930-4001 .. **Carlson,** Frank S '74 Baumgartner & O -5455 Detroit Rd (Rte 254)
-Sheffield Village 44054 **Fx:**934-7205

(216) 566-5556 .. **Carlson,** James R '75 (Thompson H LLP) -127 Pub Sq
-3900 Key Ctr -Cleveland 44114 **Fx:**566-5800

(612) 973-2845 .. **Carlson,** Jennie P '85 US Bancorp -800 Nicollet Mall
-BC-MN-H17A -Minneapolis, MN 55402

(937) 276-6577 .. **Carlson,** John P '03 Montgomery Cnty -3304 N Main
-Dayton 45405

(614) 231-8900 .. **Carlson,** Leonard A '78 -2700 E Main -Ste 111 -Columbus 43209

(614) 462-3888 .. **Carlson,** Melinda S '88 Franklin Cnty CSEA -80 E Fulton
-Columbus 43215

(612) 342-0370 .. **Carlson,** Nels E '96 %Parsinen KR&G,PA -100 S 5th -Ste 1100
-Minneapolis, MN 55402

(513) 868-3200 .. **Carlson,** Timothy W '86 -301 High -Ste 220 -Hamilton 45011

(614) 340-4044 .. **Carlson,** Valerie H '90 (Alban & C LLP) -7100 N High -Ste 102
-Worthington 43085

Carlton, Jamie M '04 -(Address Unavailable)

(330) 666-5545 .. **Carlyon,** Candice J '94 Summit County Engineer -171 Court Dr
-#301 -Fairlawn 44333

(614) 464-6400 .. **Carman,** Corrine S '92 %Vorys SS&P LLP -52 E Gay -Bx1008
-Columbus 43216 **Fx:**464-6350

(513) 352-1575 .. **Carman,** Dorothy N '80 Law Dept -801 Plum -Rm 214
-Cincinnati 45202 **Fx:**352-1515

(419) 609-0143 .. **Carman,** Heather L '03 -Bx2033 -Sandusky 44871 **Fx:**609-0495

(614) 501-1460 .. **Carmany,** Margaret R '89 Methodist Eldercare
-2225 State Route 256 -Reynoldsburg 43068 **Fx:**501-1461

(513) 868-7474 .. **Carmella,** Bradley R '86 -6 S 2nd -Ste 821 -Hamilton 45011

(216) 831-1400 .. **Carmen,** Fred N '81 -27800 Cedar Rd -Beachwood 44122

(317) 569-4837 .. **Carmichael,** Daniel P '68 Cnsl Baker & D -600 E 96th -Ste 600
-Indianapolis, IN 46240

(216) 222-2894 .. **Carnahan,** Anne S '79 Natl City Bank -#2020 -Bx5756
-Cleveland 44101

(216) 520-5540 .. **Carnahan,** James R Jr. '87 West Grp -6111 Oak Tree Blvd
-Bx318063 -Cleveland 44131

(216) 581-2600 .. **Carnahan,** John A '55 XLO Grp -4495 Cranwood Pkwy
-Cleveland 44128

(614) 445-6499 .. **Carnahan,** John A '55 -767 S 5th -Columbus 43206 **Fx:**449-8442

(614) 442-5626 .. **Carnahan,** Russell E '84 (Hunter CS&B) -3360 Tremont Rd
-2nd Fl -Columbus 43221 **Fx:**442-5625

(216) 621-7227 .. **Carnahan,** Timothy D '79 (Nicola G&C,LLC) -25 W Prospect Av
-Republic Bldg Ste 1400 -Cleveland 44115 **Fx:**621-3999

(740) 345-9611 .. **Carnes,** Carolyn J '96 %Morrow G&B,Ltd -33 W Main -Bx4190
-Newark 43058

Carnes, Conrad D '66 -205 Warrior Dr -169
-Murfreesboro, TN 37128

(419) 246-5757 .. **Carnes,** James R '98 %Anspach M&N,LLP -300 Mad Av -Ste 1600
-Toledo 43604 **Fx:**321-6979

(216) 830-6830 .. **Carney,** Christopher J '86 (Brouse M) -1001 Lakeside Av
-Ste 1600 -Cleveland 44114 **Fx:**830-6807

(216) 861-0111 .. **Carney,** Christopher J '93 (Klein & C Co,LPA) -55 Pub Sq
-Ste 1200 -Cleveland 44113 **Fx:**861-8203

(216) 368-3301 .. **Carney,** David J '89 CWRU Law Schl -11075 East Blvd
-Cleveland 44106

(440) 892-4900 .. **Carney,** James A '73 (Carney & C) -2001 Crocker Rd -Ste 420
-Cleveland 44145

(440) 892-4900 .. **Carney,** John J '69 (Carney & C) -2001 Crocker Rd -Ste 420
-Cleveland 44145

(614) 227-2000 .. **Carney,** John P '01 %Porter WM&A LLP -41 S High
-Columbus 43215 **Fx:**227-2100

(440) 899-1551 .. **Carney,** Joseph D '77 (JD Carney & Assoc,LLC) -2001 Crocker Rd
-440 Gemini Twr II -Westlake 44145

(513) 352-4703 .. **Carney,** Julia B '04 Law Dept -801 Plum -Rm 214
-Cincinnati 45202 **Fx:**352-1515

(937) 859-1323 .. **Carney,** Patrick G '66 (Carney & Assoc) -534 Dixie Dr
-West Carrollton 45449

(614) 466-8980 .. **Carney,** Stephen P '94 Atty Gen -30 E Broad -Columbus 43215
Fx:466-5087

(740) 369-7567 .. **Carney-DeBord,** Jack W '91 -305 S Sandusky -Delaware 43015

Carnie, William T '79 -2346 Selma Av -Youngstown 44504

Carolin, Thomas M '77 -7183 Rustic Oval -Seven Hills 44131

(330) 740-2073 .. **Caroline,** John C '95 Mahoning Cnty CSEA -112 W Commerce
-Bx119 -Youngstown 44503

(440) 734-7600 .. **Caron,** Brian L '95 Crombie Law Firm -4615 Great Nrthrn Blvd
-North Olmsted 44070 **Fx:**734-1054

(330) 626-2926 .. **Carothers,** Deborah A '00 -8474 State Route 43
-Streetsboro 44241

(412) 394-2325 .. **Carothers,** Patrick '03 %Thorp R&A -301 Grant -14th Fl
-Pittsburgh, PA 15219

(770) 932-3552 .. **Carothers,** Richard A '79 (Carothers & M,LLC) -4350 S Lee
-Ste 200 -Buford, GA 30518 **Fx:**932-6348

(302) 282-8431 .. **Carpenter,** David W '83 1st USA Bank,NA -201 N Walnut
-3 Christina Ctr -Wilmington, DE 19801

(330) 392-6171 .. **Carpenter,** Dennis L '77 %Rieger SC&D -410 Mahoning Av
-Bx1429 -Warren 44482 **Fx:**394-5507

(614) 228-6885 .. **Carpenter,** James C '75 OfCnsl Lane A&H LLC -175 S 3rd
-Ste 700 -Columbus 43215 **Fx:**228-0146

(513) 528-5788 .. **Carpenter,** James W '66 -1143 Telluride Dr #405
-Cincinnati 45202 **Fx:**528-3190

(614) 444-6467 .. **Carpenter,** Kendra L '01 (Carpenter Law Ofc,LLC) -987 S High
-Columbus 43206 **Fx:**444-3320

(614) 365-4100 .. **Carpenter & Lipps LLP** -280 N High -Ste 1300 280 Plz
-Columbus 43215 **Fx:**365-9145

(614) 365-4100 .. **Carpenter,** Michael H '77 (Carpenter & L LLP) -280 N High
-Ste 1300 280 Plz -Columbus 43215 **Fx:**365-9145

(330) 995-0971 .. **Carpenter,** Paul E '82 -165 Eldrdg Rd -Aurora 44202

(513) 977-8200 .. **Carpenter,** Robert A '95 (Dinsmore & S LLP) -255 E 5th -Ste 1900
-Cincinnati 45202 **Fx:**977-8141

(402) 471-2505 .. **Carpenter,** Stanley H '76 NE State Cllgs System -Bx94605
-Lincoln, NE 68509

(937) 225-5782 .. **Carper,** Margaret M '91 Montgomery Cnty Pros -301 W 3rd -Bx972
-Dayton 45422 **Fx:**225-3470

(614) 718-4416 .. **Carper,** Tina L '91 Amer Cancer Society -5555 Frantz Av
-Dublin 43017

(330) 659-5842 .. **Carpinelli,** Ralph R '66 -4800 Townsend Rd -Richfield 44286

(480) 816-3482 .. **Carpinelli,** Rick R '93 -15248 E Mustang Dr
-Fountain Hills, AZ 85268

(740) 859-5209 .. **Carpino,** Joseph S '64 (Carpino & C) -Bx874 -Steubenville 43952

(330) 405-5061 .. **Carr,** Adam E '93 (Williams S&S Co,LPA) -2241 Pinnacle Pkwy
-Twinsburg 44087 **Fx:**405-5586

Carr, Cathleen '85 -2549 Sloop Lndng -Wilmington, NC 28409

(216) 736-7223 .. **Carr,** Connie S '94 %Kohrman J&K PLL -1375 E 9th
-One Cleve Ctr 20th Fl -Cleveland 44114 **Fx:**621-6536

(716) 856-5012 .. **Carr,** Daria A '98 %Anspach M&N,LLP -2400 Main Pl Twr
-Buffalo, NY 14202 **Fx:**852-2485

Carr, David M '04 -(Address Unavailable)

(440) 255-1080 .. **Carr,** Douglas L '94 Tridelta Ind -Bx780 -Mentor 44061

(216) 241-5310 ..**Carr,** George H '98 %Gallagher SF&N -1501 Euclid Av -6th Fl -Cleveland 44115 **Fx:**241-1608

(770) 591-0085 ..**Carr,** J David '55 Carr Consultants Intl -3009 Ironhill Way -Woodstock, GA 30189 **Fx:**591-0086

(614) 466-8911 ..**Carr,** James A '80 Atty Gen -30 E Broad -Columbus 43215 **Fx:**728-7582

(330) 373-1221 ..**Carr,** James C '73 First Place Bank -185 E Market -Bx551 -Warren 44482 **Fx:**373-9906

(513) 651-5651 ..**Carr,** Joseph G '69 (Carr & S) -817 Main -Ste 200 -Cincinnati 45202 **Fx:**651-5402

(440) 473-2277 ..**Carr,** Leonard B '96 LB Carr Co,LPA -1392 SOM Center Rd -Mayfield Heights 44124

(440) 473-2277 ..**Carr,** Leonard F '74 (LF Carr Co,LPA) -1392 SOM Center Rd -Mayfield Heights 44124

(734) 241-8892 ..**Carr,** Leslie M '93 -25 S Monroe -Ste 202 -Monroe, MI 48161

(216) 621-0200 ..**Carr,** Lidia V '01 Baker & H LLP -1900 E 9th -Ste 3200 -Cleveland 44114 **Fx:**696-0740

(216) 515-1660 ..**Carr,** Lindsey A '01 %Frantz W LLP -127 Pub Sq -2500 Key Center -Cleveland 44114 **Fx:**515-1650

(330) 715-3573 ..**Carr,** Melissa B '04 (Schafer & C Co,LPA) -1745 W Market -Akron 44313 **Fx:**864-7157

(513) 295-3067 ..**Carr,** Michael G '01 M Carr & Assoc -5582 Penway Ct -Cincinnati 45239

(216) 443-7800 ..**Carr,** Pinkey S '93 Cuyahoga Cnty Pros -1200 Ontario -8th Fl -Cleveland 44113 **Fx:**698-2270

(419) 865-8021 ..**Carr,** Richard H '83 (Balk H&M) -5744 Southwyck Blvd -Toledo 43614 **Fx:**865-9105

(937) 223-6003 ..**Carr,** Richard L Jr. '84 (Dunlevey M&F) -110 N Main -Ste 1000 -Dayton 45402 **Fx:**223-8550

(513) 651-5651 ..**Carr & Shiverdecker** -817 Main -Ste 200 -Cincinnati 45202 **Fx:**651-5402

(614) 846-7160 ..**Carr,** Steven C '80 -51 N High -Ste 401 -Columbus 43215

(419) 246-5757 ..**Carr,** Steven E '99 %Anspach M&N,LLP -300 Mad Av -Ste 1600 -Toledo 43604 **Fx:**321-6979

(419) 351-4005 ..**Carr,** Tonya L '04 -413 N Mich -Toledo 43624 **Fx:**255-6227

(440) 286-9571 ..**Carrabine,** James P '84 (Svete M&C Co,LPA) -100 Parker Ct -Chardon 44024

(859) 291-9900 ..**Carran,** Robert W '69 Taliaferro MSC&K,PLLC -1005 Mad Av -Bx468 -Covington, KY 41012

(937) 372-4431 ..**Carrera,** Nicholas A '62 -1465 Foust Rd -Xenia 45385

(614) 921-8976 ..**Carrier,** Frank L Jr. '00 Nationwide Ins -5525 Park Ctr Cir -Dublin 43017

　　　　　　　　　Carrigan, Martin D '85 -3700 Forest Trl Dr -Findlay 45840

(937) 222-2424 ..**Carrigg,** Christopher W '85 (Freund F&A) -1 S Main -Ste 1800 -Dayton 45402 **Fx:**222-5369

(800) 243-0210 ..**Carrino,** Frank A '87 Westfield Grp -1 Park Cir -Bx5001 -Westfield Center 44251 **Fx:**(330) 887-2588

(330) 972-7751 ..**Carro,** J D '78 %Univ of Akron/Sch of Law -150 Univ Av -Leg Clinic -Akron 44325

(614) 547-0350 ..**Carroll,** David W '76 (Carroll U&H,LLC) -7100 N High -Ste 301 -Columbus 43085 **Fx:**547-0354

(614) 221-3155 ..**Carroll,** Donald D '90 (Bailey C LLC) -10 W Broad -Columbus 43215 **Fx:**221-0479

(412) 762-4285 ..**Carroll,** Donald F '79 PNC Fin Srvcs Grp -620 Lbrty Av -10th Fl -Pittsburgh, PA 15222 **Fx:**705-0161

(937) 544-8655 ..**Carroll,** Gregory A '88 -503 E Main -West Union 45693 **Fx:**544-9774

　　　　　　　　　Carroll, Heidi R '02 -2024 Marks Rd -Valley City 44280

(330) 376-1112 ..**Carroll,** Helen S '92 %Whalen & C,LPA -565 Wolf Ledges Pkwy -Bx2020 -Akron 44309 **Fx:**376-3200

(513) 852-8205 ..**Carroll,** James J '78 OfCnsl Cors & B LLC -537 E Pete Rose Way -Ste 400 -Cincinnati 45202

(513) 852-3489 ..**Carroll,** James M '76 Atty Gen -441 Vine -1600 Carew Twr -Cincinnati 45202 **Fx:**852-3484

(513) 381-0656 ..**Carroll,** Karen A '87 (Kohnen & P LLP) -201 E 5th -Ste 800 -Cincinnati 45202 **Fx:**381-5823

(330) 643-2788 ..**Carroll,** Michael E '72 Summit Cnty Pros-Crim -53 Univ Av -7th Fl -Akron 44308 **Fx:**643-8277

(513) 241-6748 ..**Carroll,** Patrick F '84 A Levine -324 Reading Rd -Cincinnati 45202

(216) 529-6700 ..**Carroll,** Patrick J '77 Mun Ct Judge -12650 Detroit Av -Lakewood 44107

(513) 732-8100 ..**Carroll,** Rebecca R '90 Clermont Cnty Municipal Ct -289 E Main -Batavia 45103

(614) 644-7250 ..**Carroll,** Roger F '79 Atty Gen -30 E Broad -Columbus 43215 **Fx:**644-7634

(513) 723-4000 ..**Carroll,** Scott A '93 (Vorys SS&P LLP) -221 E 4th -Ste 2000 Atrium Two -Bx0236 -Cincinnati 45201 **Fx:**723-4056

(614) 547-0350 ..**Carroll Ucker & Hemmer,LLC** -7100 N High -Ste 301 -Columbus 43085 **Fx:**547-0354

　　　　　　　　　Carrothers, Jack Dayton L '01 -10275 St Augustine Rd -#808 -Jacksonville, FL 32257

(330) 339-6444 ..**Carrothers,** James M '73 (Stephenson S&C) -206 W High Av -New Philadelphia 44663 **Fx:**339-6228

(614) 481-9655 ..**Carruthers,** David F '79 -1500 W 3rd Av -Ste 400 -Columbus 43212

(440) 285-7065 ..**Carse,** William O '73 -12860 Mayfld Rd -Lot 99 -Chardon 44024

(513) 368-5221 ..**Carson,** Cheryl L '90 -2576 Eastern Av -Cincinnati 45202

(614) 716-3849 ..**Carson,** Cynthia Butler '96 Amer Elec Pwr Co -1 Riverside Plz -Columbus 43215

　　　　　　　　　Carson, Dennis A '04 -7699 E Visao Dr -Scottsdale, AZ 85262

(937) 890-8883 ..**Carson,** Douglas T '86 -7825 N Dixie Dr -Ste B -Dayton 45414

(216) 696-3366 ..**Carson,** Drew A '86 (Goodman WM LLP) -100 Erievw Plz -27th Fl -Cleveland 44114 **Fx:**363-5835

(330) 545-3424 ..**Carson,** Edward L '81 -285 E Howard -Girard 44420

(440) 526-9440 ..**Carson,** Gayle J '76 -7023 Mill Rd -Brecksville 44141

(740) 594-8388 ..**Carson,** Herman A '80 (Sowash C&F) -39 N Cllg -Bx2629 -Athens 45701

(216) 515-1660 ..**Carson,** Jay R '97 %Frantz W LLP -127 Pub Sq -2500 Key Center -Cleveland 44114 **Fx:**515-1650

(216) 771-3303 ..**Carson,** John H Jr. '64 -614 Superior Av NW -Rckfllr Bldg Ste 800 -Cleveland 44113

(330) 887-1036 ..**Carson,** Kandie L '93 -Bx887 -Westfield Center 44251

(937) 898-7070 ..**Carson,** Lloyd T '49 -7825 N Dixie Dr -Ste B -Dayton 45414

(419) 424-7818 ..**Carson,** Loretta A '82 Hancock Cnty Cmmn Pleas Ct -300 S Main -Domestic Relations Div -Findlay 45840

　　　　　　　　　Carson, Peter '03 -(Address Unavailable)

(440) 439-5959 ..**Carson,** Robert Otto '73 -653 Bway -Ste 200 -Bedford 44146 **Fx:**439-5984

(216) 479-8500 ..**Carson,** Van '66 (Squire S&D LLP) -127 Pub Sq -4900 Key Twr -Cleveland 44114 **Fx:**479-8780

(301) 680-6319 ..**Carson,** Walter E '68 -12501 Old Columbia Pk -Silver Spring, MA 20904

(614) 223-9300 ..**Carsonie,** Frank W '92 (Benesch FC&A LLP) -88 E Broad -Ste 900 -Columbus 43215 **Fx:**223-9330

(419) 836-8246 ..**Carstensen,** William J '94 -22631 Toledo -Bx261 -Curtice 43412

(330) 643-7955 ..**Carter,** Allen G Sr. '86 Summit Cnty Dom Rltns Ct -209 S High -Akron 44308

(513) 785-5805 ..**Carter,** Barbara S '91 Butler Cnty Domestic Relatns Ct -315 High -3rd Fl -Hamilton 45011

(513) 829-4579 ..**Carter,** Bruce '92 -5458 Yosemite Dr -Fairfield 45014

(330) 761-9960 ..**Carter,** Cornell P '94 State & Federal Communication Inc -80 S Summit -Ste 100 -Akron 44308

(404) 521-3939 ..**Carter,** Dan T '78 (Jones DR&P) -303 Pchtree NE -Atlanta, GA 30308

(216) 363-1400 ..**Carter,** Daniel P '02 (Buckley K,LPA) -600 E Superior Av -Ste 1400 -Cleveland 44114 **Fx:**579-1020

(614) 221-2121 ..**Carter,** Danielle M '99 Isaac BL&T,LLP -250 E Broad -Ste 900 Mdlnd Bldg -Columbus 43215 **Fx:**365-9516

(937) 328-2575 ..**Carter,** Darnell E '79 Clark Cnty Pros -50 E Columbia -Bx1608 -Springfield 45501

(513) 732-1420 ..**Carter,** David E '91 %Nichols S&N -237 Main -Batavia 45103

(419) 259-7778 ..**Carter,** David W '98 Natl City Bank -405 Mad Av -Toledo 43604

(937) 498-7230 ..**Carter,** Gary J '83 Shelby Cnty Cmmn Pleas Ct -Cthse -Bx947 -Sidney 45365

(740) 345-9722 ..**Carter,** Gregory E '87 -21 W Church -Ste 208 -Newark 43055

(937) 335-7366 ..**Carter,** Jack L '83 -Bx881 -Troy 45373

(513) 651-6800 ..**Carter,** Janda' M '02 %Frost BT LLC -201 E 5th -2200 PNC Ctr -Cincinnati 45202 **Fx:**651-6981

(937) 222-1366 ..**Carter,** Jay B '89 -111 W 1st -Ste 519 -Dayton 45402 **Fx:**222-1399

(513) 671-1744 ..**Carter,** Karen E '94 Ohio Casualty Grp -225 Pictoria Dr -Ste 220 -Cincinnati 45246

　　　　　　　　　Carter, Kathleen Yates '02 -221 Hosea Av -#2 -Cincinnati 45220

(614) 645-5817 ..**Carter,** Melinda D '89 Columbus EBOCO -109 N Front -4th Fl -Columbus 43215

(330) 471-9522 ..**Carter,** Ross A '90 -819 9th NW -Canton 44703

(843) 785-2171 ..**Carter,** Stephen E '80 (Bethea J&G,PA) -23-B Shelter Cove Ln -#400 -Drwr3 -Hilton Head Island, SC 29938 **Fx:**686-5991

(614) 645-8300 ..**Carter,** Theresa L '85 Columbus Civil Srvc Comm -50 W Gay -Columbus 43215

(330) 376-5756 ..**Carter,** Trina M '98 Emershaw M&S -120 E Mill -#437 -Akron 44308 **Fx:**762-5980

(216) 831-8331 ..**Carter,** Van D '80 -3401 Enterprise Pkwy -Ste 410 -Beachwood 44122

(614) 459-4140 ..**Carter,** Wanda L '82 (Moots C&H) -3600 Olentangy Rvr Rd -Ste 501 -Columbus 43214 **Fx:**459-4503

(419) 524-9811 ..**Carto,** David D '81 (Weldon H&K,LLP) -28 Park Av W -Bank One Bldg -Mansfield 44902 **Fx:**522-5758

　　　　　　　　　Carton, Thomas W Jr. '73 -5745 Newbank Cir -Ste 102 -Dublin 43017

(440) 243-1198 ..**Cartwright,** Mark J '98 Codonics -17991 Englewood Dr -Middleburg Heights 44130

(440) 442-6800 ..**Cartwright-Jones,** Rhys B '04 %JW Diemert Jr & Assoc Co,LPA -1360 SOM Center Rd -Mayfield Heights 44124 **Fx:**442-0825

(614) 645-7483 ..**Carty,** Bridget E '00 City Pros -375 S High -7th Fl -Columbus 43215

(440) 442-6677 ..**Carty,** Matthew J '02 Elk & E Co,LPA -6100 Parkland Blvd -Mayfield Heights 44124 **Fx:**442-7944

(216) 623-0150 ..**Carulas,** Anna Moore '86 (Roetzel & A,LPA) -1375 E 9th -One Cleve Ctr 9th Fl -Cleveland 44114 **Fx:**623-0134

(513) 381-0656 ..**Caruso,** Anthony J '88 (Kohnen & P LLP) -201 E 5th -Ste 800 -Cincinnati 45202 **Fx:**381-5823

　　　　　　　　　Caruso, Daniel R '95 -273 Colonial Av -Worthington 43085

(419) 241-2200 ..**Caruso,** James D '78 (Arnold & C,Ltd) -1822 Cherry -Toledo 43608 **Fx:**255-7623

(330) 451-7900 ..**Carver,** Aletha M '92 5th Dist Ct of Appls -110 Central Plz S -Ste 320 -Canton 44702 **Fx:**451-7249

　　　　　　　　　Carver, Stephanie N '04 -(Address Unavailable)

(937) 445-2088 ..**Carver,** Todd B '91 NCR Corp -1700 S Patterson Blvd -Dayton 45479

(513) 381-9200 ..**Carville,** Christopher R '97 %Rendigs FK&D,LLP -One W 4th -Ste 900 -Cincinnati 45202 **Fx:**381-9206

(937) 223-8177 ..**Cary,** Dina M '97 %Coolidge WW&L -33 W 1st -Ste 600 -Dayton 45402 **Fx:**223-6705

(216) 522-4914 ..**Cary,** Judith D '96 SSA/OHA -1350 Euclid Av -7th Fl -Cleveland 44115

(614) 464-6400 ..**Cary,** Nelson D '01 %Vorys SS&P LLP -52 E Gay -Bx1008 -Columbus 43216 **Fx:**464-6350

(216) 592-5000 ..**Caryl,** Christopher J '98 %Tucker E&W LLP -925 Euclid Av -1150 Huntngtn Bldg -Cleveland 44115 **Fx:**592-5009

(330) 793-4419 ..**Casale,** Carl L '84 -5917 Yrktwn Ln -Youngstown 44515

(330) 821-0701 ..**Casale,** Joseph A '59 Casale & C -1021 W State -Alliance 44601 **Fx:**821-0702

(330) 821-0701 ..**Casale,** Ned J '84 (Casale & C) -1021 W State -Alliance 44601 **Fx:**821-0702

(330) 867-8422 ..**Casalinova,** Gregory Jerry '54 -41 Merz Blvd -Akron 44333

(330) 376-1350 ..**Casalinuovo,** John A '84 (Colopy & C Co) -159 S Main -Ste 420 -Akron 44308

(724) 983-3477 ..**Casalnova,** Charles C '02 FNB Corp -1 FNB Blvd -Hermitage, PA 16148

(616) 456-2002 ..**Casamatta,** Daniel J '82 DOJ-Ofc of the US Trustee -330 Ionia Av NW -Ste 202 -Grand Rapids, MI 49503 **Fx:**456-2550

(614) 224-1222 ..**Casanova,** Janice E '02 Maguire & S,LLP -250 Civic Ctr Dr -Ste 200 -Columbus 43215 **Fx:**224-1236

(216) 623-0150 ..**Casarona,** Robert B '86 (Roetzel & A,LPA) -1375 E 9th -One Cleve Ctr 9th Fl -Cleveland 44114 **Fx:**623-0134

(216) 781-1212 .. **Cascarilla,** Ralph E '76 (Walter & H LLP) -1301 E 9th -Ste 3500
-Cleveland 44114 Fx:575-0911
Case, Douglas M '91 -501 Bay Dr -Vero Beach, FL 32963
(937) 255-6111 .. **Case,** John A '83 USAF -AFMC LO/Jaf -Bx33574
-Wright Patterson AFB 45433
(614) 480-4891 .. **Case,** Larry D '82 Huntington Natl Bank -41 S High
-Columbus 43287
(614) 469-3208 .. **Case,** William R '73 (Thompson H LLP) -10 W Broad -Ste 700
-Columbus 43215 Fx:469-3361
(314) 244-2826 .. **Casey,** Brian P '04 US Ct of Appeals-8th Ct -111 S 10th
-Ste 23365 -Saint Louis, MO 63102
(513) 946-3000 .. **Casey,** Deborah A '94 Hamilton Cnty Pros -230 E 9th
-Cincinnati 45202 Fx:946-3017
(330) 535-0177 .. **Casey,** James D '88 -686 W Market -Akron 44303
(304) 675-3999 .. **Casey,** James M '80 -611 Viand -Bx427 -Point Pleasant,
WV 25550
(408) 474-7001 .. **Casey,** James N '86 Cnsl Philips Semiconductors -1109 McKay Dr
-MS 545J -San Jose, CA 95131 Fx:474-7100
(440) 442-6677 .. **Casey,** James S '93 Elk & E Co,LPA -6100 Parkland Blvd
-Mayfield Heights 44124 Fx:442-7944
(614) 564-2666 .. **Casey,** John F '65 (J Casey,LPA) -600 S High -Columbus 43215
(419) 255-3153 .. **Casey,** Julia K '74 (Casey & S) -520 Mad Av -727 Spitzer Bldg
-Toledo 43604
(614) 462-7492 .. **Casey,** Karen S '91 Franklin Cnty Common Pleas Ct -369 S High
-Columbus 43215
(419) 241-6000 .. **Casey,** Peter R III '74 (Eastman & S Ltd) -1 Seagate -24th Fl
-Bx10032 -Toledo 43697 Fx:247-1777
(614) 227-2300 .. **Casey,** Peter R IV '01 %Bricker & E LLP -100 S 3rd
-Columbus 43215 Fx:227-2390
(614) 222-0800 .. **Casey,** Sean M '99 -Bx710 -New Albany 43054
(513) 621-2602 .. **Cash,** Albert D Jr. '59 (Cash & C) -432 Walnut -1001 Tri-State Bldg
-Cincinnati 45202
(513) 243-2000 .. **Cash,** Joshua N '97 Cnsl GE Aircraft Engines -1 Neumann Way
-MD J104 -Cincinnati 45215
(513) 621-2602 .. **Cash,** Robert B '64 (Cash & C) -432 Walnut -1001 Tri-State Bldg
-Cincinnati 45202
(330) 255-0037 .. **Casolari,** Samuel Guy Jr. '86 Marshall DWC&G -120 E Mill
-Ste 240 -Akron 44308 Fx:255-0040
(614) 939-1235 .. **Cason-Adams,** Sharon '97 %Demers & C -3 N High -Bx430
-New Albany 43054
(937) 449-2800 .. **Caspar,** Frederick J '85 (Chernesky H&K PLL) -10 Cthse Plz SW
-Ste 1100 -Dayton 45402 Fx:449-2821
(937) 236-6444 .. **Caspar,** Robert L Jr. '88 -7460 Brandt Pike -Huber Heights 45424
(513) 424-2401 .. **Casper,** Arthur B '67 (Casper & C) -1 N Main -Bx510
-Middletown 45042 Fx:424-0622
(513) 424-2401 .. **Casper & Casper** -1 N Main -Bx510 -Middletown 45042
Fx:424-0622
(513) 424-2401 .. **Casper,** Douglas W '75 (Casper & C) -1 N Main -Bx510
-Middletown 45042 Fx:424-0622
(513) 424-2401 .. **Casper,** E Jeffrey '72 (Casper & C) -1 N Main -Bx510
-Middletown 45042 Fx:424-0622
(440) 461-0928 .. **Casper,** Michael J '75 -459 Locklie Dr -Highland Heights 44143
(513) 651-6800 .. **Casper,** Paul W Jr. '81 (Frost BT LLC) -201 E 5th -2200 PNC Ctr
-Cincinnati 45202 Fx:651-6981
(513) 424-2401 .. **Casper,** Sanford I '81 (Casper & C) -1 N Main -Bx510
-Middletown 45042 Fx:424-0622
(513) 942-8855 .. **Casper,** Sheldon Robert '72 -8469 Eagle Rdg Dr
-West Chester 45069
(216) 241-5310 .. **Cass,** Edward J '62 OfCnsl Gallagher SF&N -1501 Euclid Av
-6th Fl -Cleveland 44115 Fx:241-1608
(937) 222-1232 .. **Cass,** William O Jr. '86 (Schneble C & Assoc Co,LPA)
-111 W Monument Av -Ste 402 -Dayton 45402
(513) 621-2100 .. **Cassady,** Peter L '83 (Beckman W&S LLC) -120 E 4th
-1200 Mercantile Ctr -Cincinnati 45202 Fx:621-0106
(216) 696-4442 .. **Cassaro,** Bessie J '67 Cassaro & C Co,LPA -1370 Ontario
-Ste 330 Standard Bldg -Cleveland 44113
(216) 696-4442 .. **Cassaro,** Charles T '70 Cassaro & C Co,LPA -1370 Ontario
-Ste 330 Standard Bldg -Cleveland 44113
(330) 864-6611 .. **Cassetty,** Michael T '93 %McCarty & P -1655 W Market -Ste 400
-Akron 44313
(216) 443-7800 .. **Cassidy,** Marilyn B '83 Cuyahoga Cnty Pros -1200 Ontario -8th Fl
-Cleveland 44113 Fx:698-2270
(859) 331-2000 .. **Cassidy,** Mary S '93 %O'Hara RTS&S -25 Crestvw Hills Mall Rd
-Ste 201 -Bx17411 -Covington, KY 41017
(216) 520-5980 .. **Cassidy,** Michael P '83 (Cassidy & Assoc LPA)
-4700 Rockside Rd -Ste 603 -Independence 44131 Fx:520-5984
(513) 248-9332 .. **Cassidy,** Michael W '84 -19 Water -Milford 45150
(304) 232-8100 .. **Cassidy,** Patrick S '74 (Cassidy MCV&T,LC) -1413 Eoff
-The 1st State Cptl -Wheeling, WV 26003 Fx:232-8200
(216) 520-5980 .. **Cassidy,** Paul W '47 OfCnsl Cassidy & Assoc LPA
-4700 Rockside Rd -Ste 603 -Independence 44131 Fx:520-5984
(404) 331-4463 .. **Cassidy,** William A '81 US DOJ/INS -77 Forsyth
-Atlanta, GA 30303
(513) 721-1311 .. **Cassinelli,** Tracy A '95 (Reminger & R) -7 W 7th -Ste 1990
-Cincinnati 45202 Fx:721-2553
(937) 444-2626 .. **Cassity,** Michael E '72 -107 E Main -Bx478 -Mount Orab 45154
(614) 228-6888 .. **Cassone,** Michael J '04 %Havens W LLC -141 E Town -Ste 200
-Columbus 43215 Fx:228-6878
(202) 739-5101 .. **Castaldi,** Terra E '97 %Morgan L&B LLP -1111 Penn Av NW
-Washington, DC 20004 Fx:739-3001
(513) 852-6058 .. **Castaneda,** Janet Y '96 %Wood & L LLP -600 Vine -Ste 2500
-Cincinnati 45202 Fx:852-6087
(937) 866-9933 .. **Casteel,** Douglas '75 -101 N 1st -Miamisburg 45342
(216) 241-7255 .. **Castele,** John T '92 -2401 Superior Viaduct -Cleveland 44113
(440) 720-3283 .. **Castell,** Rebecca J '03 B Guyuron MD,Inc -29001 Mayfld Rd
-Ste 325 -Lyndhurst 44124 Fx:461-3285
(513) 621-2345 .. **Castelli,** Anthony D '81 -11085 Mntgmry Rd -Ste 200
-Cincinnati 45249
(513) 871-1083 .. **Castellini,** Richard A '64 -3525 Springvw Dr -Cincinnati 45208
(216) 583-3373 .. **Castelluccio,** Tracy W '94 Ernst & Young LLP -925 Euclid Av
-Ste 1300 -Cleveland 44115
(440) 886-7460 .. **Caster,** Cynthia M '90 State Farm Ins -7088 W 130th
-Middleburg Heights 44130

(513) 621-9100 .. **Caster,** Donald R '04 %Laufman & G -617 Vine
-1409 Enquirer Bldg -Cincinnati 45202
(330) 425-8520 .. **Casterline,** Christopher S '01 Lerner S&R -8972 Darrow Rd
-Ste A304 -Twinsburg 44087
(614) 692-9704 .. **Castillo,** Maria B '84 DSIO -3990 E Broad -DSIO-MSCB
-Whitehall 43216
(212) 644-8600 .. **Castle,** David A '92 -150 E 58th -37th Fl -New York, NY 10155
(614) 645-7385 .. **Castle,** Kelly M '86 City Atty -90 W Broad -Columbus 43215
(202) 331-8800 .. **Castleton,** Todd B '04 %Thompson H,LLP -1920 N NW -Ste 800
-Washington, DC 20036 Fx:331-8330
(740) 345-5171 .. **Castner,** Joseph F '80 (J Castner Co,LPA) -1 S Park Pl
-Newark 43055 Fx:349-9327
(614) 228-5331 .. **Casto,** Don M III '72 (Don M Casto Org) -191 W Nationwide Blvd
-Ste 200 -Columbus 43215
(614) 249-8782 .. **Casto,** Jamie R '96 Nationwide Ins Co -1 Nationwide Plz -1-09-V3
-Columbus 43215
(330) 376-2700 .. **Casto,** Jeffrey J '81 (Roetzel & A,LPA) -222 S Main -Akron 44308
Fx:376-4577
(304) 347-8355 .. **Casto,** Matthew S '99 %Robinson & M PLLC -500 VA E
-600 United Ctr -Bx1791 -Charleston, WV 25326 Fx:344-9566
(419) 774-5676 .. **Castor,** Robert D '76 Richland Cnty Pros -38 S Park -2nd Fl
-Mansfield 44902 Fx:774-5589
(440) 717-9595 .. **Castro,** Michael M '80 (MM Castro & Assoc) -9286 Province Ln
-Brecksville 44141
(216) 664-4855 .. **Castro,** Pablo A '02 Prosecutor -1200 Ontario Av
-8th Fl Justice Ctr -Cleveland 44113 Fx:664-4399
(614) 761-9273 .. **Castrodale,** Gloria P '88 -5170 Reddington Dr -Dublin 43017
(216) 931-6000 .. **Castrodale,** Joseph A '83 (Ulmer & B LLP) -1300 E 9th
-Ste 900 Penton Media Bldg -Cleveland 44114 Fx:931-6001
(312) 372-5520 .. **Castrogiovanni,** Tanya Lenko '01 %Littler M -200 N LaSalle
-Ste 2900 -Chicago, IL 60601 Fx:372-7880
Castrovinci, Juliet P '04 -(Address Unavailable)
(404) 965-4928 .. **Cataland,** Andrea K '92 OfCnsl Carter & A -1180 W Pchtree NE
-Ste 2300 -Atlanta, GA 30309 Fx:658-9726
(440) 442-8800 .. **Catalano,** Cynthia A '73 Wilson Mill Foods,Inc -5612 Wilson Mills
-Highland Heights 44143
(614) 224-4114 .. **Catalano,** William A Jr. '74 (Mitchell AC&B Co,LPA) -580 S High
-Ste 200 -Columbus 43215 Fx:224-3804
Catanzarite, Jeffrey A '79 -88 S Portage Path -Akron 44303
(216) 522-3530 .. **Catanzarite,** Marc T '99 US DVA -1240 E 9th -Cleveland 44199
(866) 837-8847 .. **Catanzariti,** Frank P '85 LAWO -20 S Limestone -Ste 220
-Springfield 45502 Fx:(937) 323-0291
(740) 947-2176 .. **Catanzaro,** Jerome D '77 (Catanzaro & R) -112 W 3rd -Bx26
-Waverly 45690
(937) 325-2459 .. **Catanzaro,** Michael A '77 (Pavlatos C&L Co,LPA) -700 E High
-Springfield 45505
(740) 947-2176 .. **Catanzaro & Rosenberger** -112 W 3rd -Bx26 -Waverly 45690
Cater, Lyndsey R '04 -(Address Unavailable)
(216) 676-8131 .. **Caterini,** Joseph W '62 -16097 Ramona Dr
-Middleburg Heights 44130
(216) 751-1490 .. **Caterino,** Bartholomew M '61 (B Caterino & Assoc)
-3550 Warrensvll Ctr Rd -Ste 102N -Shaker Heights 44122
Fx:751-1492
(216) 523-1500 .. **Cathcart,** David B '75 Mansour GG&M Co,LPA -55 Pub Sq
-Ste 2150 -Cleveland 44113 Fx:523-1705
(440) 248-7906 .. **Cathcart,** Robert F IV '99 %Mazanec R&R Co,LPA
-34305 Solon Rd -Ste 100 -Cleveland 44139 Fx:248-8861
(860) 251-5000 .. **Cathcart,** Robert J '62 (Shipman & G LLP) -One Const Plz
-Hartford, CT 06103 Fx:251-5099
(513) 762-6200 .. **Cathey,** Christopher D '99 %Ulmer & B LLP -600 Vine -Ste 2800
-Cincinnati 45202 Fx:762-6245
(216) 291-2400 .. **Caticchio,** Michael J '82 (Zimmerman CE&M) -5001 Mayfld Rd
-Ste 105 -Cleveland 44124
(216) 297-0910 .. **Caticchio,** Pasquale '64 -5001 Mayfld Rd -Ste 209
-Cleveland 44124
(419) 329-6500 .. **Catignani,** Dean A '89 -4005 W Central Av -The Vllg Grn
-Toledo 43606 Fx:329-7832
Catipay, Christina T '03 -8654 Squirrel Hill Dr NE -Warren 44484
Catlett, Charlotte W '88 -1623 Clarke Sprngs Dr -Allen, TX 75002
(312) 782-3939 .. **Catlett,** Steven T '86 (Jones DR&P) -77 W Wacker Dr -Ste 3500
-Chicago, IL 60601
(614) 761-3200 .. **Catri,** Jeffrey A '84 Cnsl J Catri Co, LLC -220 W Brdg -Ste 220
-Dublin 43017 Fx:761-3222
Catron, Gregory W '95 -Bx871 -Burlington, KY 41005
(330) 638-1200 .. **Catuogno,** J V '95 -1165 Wilson-Sharpsvll Rd -Cortland 44410
(606) 692-2238 .. **Caudill,** April K '80 Natl Underwriter Co -5081 Olympic Blvd
-Erlanger, KY 41018
(614) 481-4480 .. **Caudill,** Christal L '97 %Koffel & J -2130 Arlngtn Av
-Columbus 43221
(937) 382-1497 .. **Caudill,** David R Jr. '91 %Peelle Law Ofcs Co,LPA
-1929 Rombach Av -Bx950 -Wilmington 45177
(937) 461-0306 .. **Caudill,** Mary B '83 -306 S Patterson Blvd -Dayton 45402
(513) 634-1368 .. **Caudill,** Rhonda L '94 Procter & Gamble Co -6090 Ctr Hill Av
-Bx 119 -Cincinnati 45224
(330) 392-2505 .. **Cauffield,** William G '70 (Meermans Z&C) -8799 E Market
-Warren 44484
(614) 854-8673 .. **Caughey,** Stacey L '95 Nationwide -5900 Parkwood Dr PW-01-08
-Dublin 43016
(419) 872-1688 .. **Caughey,** William C '75 -900 W Boundary S -Ste 8-A
-Perrysburg 43551
(859) 655-3007 .. **Cauhorn,** Jay P '91 -36 W 5th -Covington, KY 41011
(912) 752-3415 .. **Caulfield,** James M '71 SSA-OHA -640 D N Av -Macon, GA 31211
(740) 373-7624 .. **Cauthorn-Kreiss,** Alison L '89 Washington Cnty Pros
-205 Putnam -Marietta 45750
(614) 221-4255 .. **Cavalaris,** Nicholas C '93 Smith & H -37 W Broad
-Columbus 43215
(614) 221-3155 .. **Cavalieri,** Nick V '73 (Bailey C LLC) -10 W Broad
-Columbus 43215 Fx:221-0479
(216) 443-7295 .. **Cavallo,** Francis J '01 Cuyahoga Cnty Pub Def -1849 Prospect Av
-Ste 222 -Cleveland 44115
(330) 864-7155 .. **Cavanagh,** Mark C '75 (Cavanagh & C) -1745 W Market
-Akron 44313 Fx:864-7157
(216) 433-0542 .. **Cavanaugh,** Mary A '93 Kemper Co -15583 Brookpark Rd
-CLeveland 44142 Fx:433-0562

(517) 482-5800 .. **Cavanaugh,** Michael E '69 Fraser TD&D,PC -1000 Mich Natl Twr -Lansing, MI 48933

(513) 381-2838 .. **Cavanaugh,** Natasha M '02 %Taft S&H LLP -425 Walnut -Ste 1800 -Cincinnati 45202 **Fx:**381-0205

(330) 434-1000 .. **Cavanaugh,** Sarah B '04 %Bernlohr W,LLP -23 S Main -3rd Fl -Akron 44308 **Fx:**434-1001

(937) 257-4124 .. **Cavanaugh,** William D Jr. '86 HQ AFMC/JAG -4225 Logistics Av -Wright Patterson AFB 45433

(216) 687-1311 .. **Cavasinni,** Joseph E '95 (Reminger & R) -101 Prospect Av W -1400 Mdlnd Bldg -Cleveland 44115 **Fx:**687-1841

Cave, Christopher R '04 -Address Unavailable

Cave, Gilbert T '60 -7834 Brakeman Rd -Painesville 44077

(703) 549-6075 .. **Cave,** Philip D '79 -107 N Payne -Alexandria, VA 22314

(614) 224-5205 .. **Cavezza,** Edward '82 (Peck S&W,LLP) -175 S 3rd -Ste 600 -Columbus 43215 **Fx:**224-0069

(216) 621-7860 .. **Cavitch Familo Durkin & Frutkin** -1717 E 9th -14th Fl -Cleveland 44114 **Fx:**621-3415

(419) 354-9238 .. **Cavitt,** Valencia G '96 Wood Cnty Cmn Pleas Ct -1 Cthse Sq -Bowling Green 43402 **Fx:**354-9357

(216) 696-7600 .. **Cawley,** Michael Terence '90 %Duvin C&H -1301 E 9th -20th Fl Erievw Twr -Cleveland 44114 **Fx:**696-2038

(216) 621-7860 .. **Cawley,** Thomas M '82 (Cavitch FD&F) -1717 E 9th -14th Fl -Cleveland 44114 **Fx:**621-3415

(513) 665-3500 .. **Cawood,** James M '04 %Freund F&A -105 E 4th -Ste 1400 -Cincinnati 45202 **Fx:**665-3503

(614) 466-2766 .. **Cayton,** John F '00 Atty Gen -30 E Broad -Columbus 43215 **Fx:**644-1926

(330) 922-4830 .. **Cazin,** Tyler K '98 -1944 13th -Cuyahoga Falls 44223

(614) 529-8000 .. **Cecil,** Andrew W '86 (Plymale & Assoc) -495 S High -Ste 400 -Columbus 43215 **Fx:**221-6633

(419) 241-6000 .. **Cecil,** Daniel O '04 %Eastman & S Ltd -1 Seagate -24th Fl -Bx10032 -Toledo 43699 **Fx:**247-1769

(330) 337-8761 .. **Cecil,** Larry G '72 Fitch KCR&B -600 E State -Bx590 -Salem 44460 **Fx:**337-9453

(239) 593-2900 .. **Cecil,** W Jeffrey '79 (Porter WM&A,LLP) -5801 Pelican Bay Blvd -Ste 300 -Naples, FL 34108 **Fx:**593-2990

(330) 253-5678 .. **Cek,** Derek '00 -137 S Main -Ste 202 -Akron 44308 **Fx:**762-5063

(216) 664-4942 .. **Celebrezze,** Leslie A '99 Cleveland Mun Ct -Justice Ctr -12th Fl -Bx94894 -Cleveland 44101

Celebrezze, Nicholas J '04

(419) 872-5695 .. **Celley & Sanderson,LLP** -27457 Holiday Ln -#E -Perrysburg 43551 **Fx:**872-4476

(419) 872-5695 .. **Celley,** Walter J '87 (Celley & S,LLP) -27457 Holiday Ln -#E -Perrysburg 43551 **Fx:**872-4476

(614) 882-6334 .. **Cellura,** Frank A '78 -5450 Hoover Rd -Grove City 43123

(614) 221-0888 .. **Cennamo,** Louis W '77 -5 E Long -Ste 605 -Columbus 43215

(216) 692-0020 .. **Centa,** Emil J '54 -763 E 185th -Cleveland 44119

(216) 692-0020 .. **Centa,** Ernest R '55 -763 E 185th -Cleveland 44119

(440) 392-7643 .. **Centanni,** Michael A '84 Steris Corp -5960 Heisley Rd -Mentor 44060

Center, April H '86 -353½ S Drexel Av -Bexley 43209

Centifanti, Dina L '89 -(Address Unavailable)

(614) 793-7600 .. **Centolella,** Paul A '81 %SAIC,Inc -4900 Blazer Pkwy -Dublin 43017

(330) 830-2682 .. **Centrone,** Cataldo R '80 Massillon Mun Ct -2 James Duncan Plz -Massillon 44646

(330) 456-8341 .. **Centrone,** Francis G '68 (Black MS&A,LPA) -220 Market Av S -Ste 1000 -Canton 44702 **Fx:**456-5756

(216) 696-0250 .. **Cerio,** Arthur R '55 -4545 Hinckley Pkwy -Cleveland 44109

(248) 816-3982 .. **Cermak,** Bryan '86 IWKA Holding Corp -2855 Coolidge Hwy -Ste 107 -Troy, MI 48084

(216) 586-3939 .. **Cernansky,** Justin M '04 %Jones D -901 Lakeside Av -Cleveland 44114 **Fx:**579-0212

(216) 622-8200 .. **Cernelich,** John R '86 (Calfee H&G LLP) -800 Superior Av -Ste 1400 -Cleveland 44114 **Fx:**241-0816

(937) 223-1201 .. **Certo,** Peter R Jr. '79 (Altick & C Co,LPA) -1 S Main -1700 One Dayton Ctr -Dayton 45402 **Fx:**223-5100

(202) 326-3576 .. **Cerullo,** Michele M '02 FTC -601 NJ Av NW -Drop 5222 -Washington, DC 20001

(937) 228-2666 .. **Cervay,** John A '68 %Hochman R&P Co,LPA -118 W 1st -Ste 650 -Dayton 45402 **Fx:**228-0508

(330) 545-5506 .. **Cervello,** Mark C '91 -52 Townsend Av -Girard 44420

(202) 514-6429 .. **Cervoni,** Rena J '95 US DOJ -950 Penn Av NW -Rm 7254 -Washington, DC 20530

Cesarik, Joseph M '81 -6414 Canterbury Dr -Hudson 44236

(419) 673-1292 .. **Cesner,** Robert E Jr. '68 Cnsl Tudor Law,LLC -22 N Main -Kenton 43326 **Fx:**675-2145

(330) 456-4590 .. **Cespedes,** Anthony J '78 -437 Market Av N -Canton 44702

(859) 331-4900 .. **Cetrulo,** Susanne M '85 (Cetrulo & M) -130 Dudley Pike -Ste 200 -Crescent Springs, KY 41017

(513) 731-3188 .. **Cettel,** Robert W '74 -7265 Kenwood Rd -Ste 175 -Cincinnati 45236 **Fx:**731-7245

(419) 841-3311 .. **Chabler,** Allan J '61 -6800 W Central Av -Ste G-2 -Toledo 43617

(937) 437-3567 .. **Chachula,** Bernard M '01 -2261 Hunters Ridge Blvd -Beavercreek 45434

(330) 868-4210 .. **Chaddock,** Susan C '97 (Clark C&C) -201 N Market -Minerva 44657

(440) 988-0340 .. **Chadwick,** Geneva C '83 -199 N Leavitt Rd -#201 -Amherst 44001

(216) 586-3939 .. **Chaffee,** Eric C '02 %Jones D -901 Lakeside Av -Cleveland 44114 **Fx:**579-0212

(740) 387-5297 .. **Chaffin,** Steven E '81 -1671 Weiss Av -Marion 43302

(614) 466-6700 .. **Chafin,** Matthew H '93 Tax Appeals -30 E Broad -Columbus 43215 **Fx:**644-5196

(818) 995-4540 .. **Chahine,** Linda M '91 Price Law Grp -15760 Ventura Blvd -Ste 1100 -Encino, CA 91436

(513) 352-6550 .. **Chaiken,** Frank D '94 (Thompson H LLP) -312 Walnut -14th Fl -Cincinnati 45202 **Fx:**241-4771

(513) 684-7376 .. **Chain,** Donald J '80 SSA-OHA -312 Elm -Ste 2100 -Cincinnati 45202

(614) 849-0134 .. **Chaiten,** Louis A '00 Hon J Sutton US Ct Appeals 6th Circ -85 Marconi Blvd -Columbus 43215

(614) 457-7989 .. **Chakeres,** David J '77 -3307 Kirkham Rd -Columbus 43221

(740) 282-9784 .. **Chalfant,** Robert P '65 -Bx39 -Steubenville 43952

(513) 381-8616 .. **Chalfie,** James J '66 (J Chalfie Co,LPA) -36 E 7th -Ste 1600 -Cincinnati 45202

(937) 436-1893 .. **Chalker,** Brad A '81 (B Chalker,LLC) -7953 Wshngtn Woods Dr -Dayton 45459

(216) 486-1777 .. **Chalko,** Paul P '52 -880 E 185th -Cleveland 44119

(440) 729-7996 .. **Chaloupka,** Robert S '01 Business Laws,Inc -11630 Chillicothe Rd -Bx185 -Chesterland 44026

(937) 593-3655 .. **Chamberlain,** Charles D '69 -111 S Madriver -Bellefontaine 43311

(419) 224-7133 .. **Chamberlain,** Frank S '88 -Bx1314 -Lima 45802

(216) 781-1111 .. **Chamberlain,** Henry W '90 Weisman G&W Co,LPA -101 Prospect Av -1600 Mdlnd Bldg -Cleveland 44115 **Fx:**781-6747

(937) 593-3655 .. **Chamberlain,** Matthew R '03 -412 E Columbus -Bellefontaine 43311

(419) 891-8884 .. **Chamberlain,** Richard M '99 Bayer P&S Co,LPA -1925 Indn Wd Cir -Maumee 43537 **Fx:**891-8889

(440) 785-8319 .. **Chambers,** Gregory J '76 (GJ Chambers & Assoc,Inc) -13629 Heath Rd -Novelty 44072 **Fx:**338-4241

(513) 241-2324 .. **Chambers,** J R '74 (Wood H&E LLP) -441 Vine -Ste 2700 -Cincinnati 45202 **Fx:**421-7269

(937) 223-8177 .. **Chambers,** John C '85 (Coolidge WW&L) -33 W 1st -Ste 600 -Dayton 45402 **Fx:**223-8197

(740) 369-2423 .. **Chambers,** Lester A '90 %Celina Grp -163 N Sandusky -Ste 205 -Delaware 43015

(614) 459-7109 .. **Chambers,** Yvonne F '82 Nationwide Ins Co -1 Nationwide Plz -01-24-16 -Columbus 43215

(614) 228-6135 .. **Champ,** Stephanie D '02 %Carlile P&M,LLP -366 E Broad -Columbus 43215 **Fx:**221-0216

(248) 767-4930 .. **Champion,** David C '84 -20390 Woodcreek Blvd -Northville, MI 48167

(330) 865-7722 .. **Champion,** Timothy H '88 (Aberth & C Co LPA) -3296 W Market -Akron 44333 **Fx:**865-9742

(817) 498-1248 .. **Chan,** David C '89 -7500 Acts Ct -Fort Worth, TX 76180

(330) 759-2044 .. **Chan,** Grace Y '93 -4503 Logan Way -Ste A -Hubbard 44425

(937) 445-4956 .. **Chan,** Michael '88 NCR Corp -1700 S Patterson Blvd -Law Dept WHQ-5E -Dayton 45479

(614) 462-7237 .. **Chance,** Sharlene I '99 10th Dist Ct of Appls -373 S High -24th Fl -Columbus 43215 **Fx:**462-7249

(202) 482-6690 .. **Chandler,** Adam A '98 US Fed Labor Relations Auth -607 14th NW -Ste 701 -Washington, DC 20424

(515) 226-6662 .. **Chandler,** Darlene K '84 Farm Bureau Finl Srvcs -5400 Univ Av -West Des Moines, IA 50266

(740) 226-2113 .. **Chandler,** James A '82 -2993 Dutch Run Rd -Beaver 45613

(216) 443-3436 .. **Chandler,** Johnny Mac '82 Cuyahoga Cnty Juv Ct -2163 E 22nd -Cleveland 44115

(330) 723-9536 .. **Chandler,** Maryann C '04 %Medina Cnty Pros -72 Pub Sq -Medina 44256

(713) 308-9520 .. **Chandler,** Richard E Jr. '81 M-I LLC -Bx42842 -Houston, TX 77242

(216) 221-7044 .. **Chandra,** Ashvin '93 -1584 Orchrd Grove Av -Lakewood 44107

(415) 556-9363 .. **Chandra,** Kalyani A '02 Ct of Appeals 9th Circ -95 7th -San Francisco, CA 94103

(216) 522-2677 .. **Chandra,** Meenakshi M '93 US Dept of Ed-Civil Rights Ofc -600 Superior Av E -Ste 750 -Cleveland 44114

(216) 443-8868 .. **Chaney,** Cathleen J '93 Cuyahoga Cnty Pros -1 Lakeside Av -Rm 49 -Cleveland 44115 **Fx:**443-3777

(330) 395-9500 .. **Chaney,** John H III '91 -106 E Market -Warren 44481

(202) 879-3939 .. **Chaney,** John L '00 %Jones DR&P -51 Louisiana Av NW -Washington, DC 20001

(740) 425-1211 .. **Chaney,** William E '53 (Chaney & C) -111 E Main -Bx365 -Barnesville 43713

(330) 451-8970 .. **Chaney-Hopwood,** Kimberly R '90 Stark Cnty CSEA -116 Cleveland Av -Bx21337 -Canton 44701

(614) 527-0779 .. **Chanfrau,** Graciela M '98 (Chanfrau & Assoc,LPA) -3742 Plsntbrook Dr -Hilliard 43026

Chanfrau, Jose M IV '00 -Bx403102 -Miami Beach, FL 33140

(513) 232-1800 .. **Chang,** Nadya '88 ME Clancey -7200 Paddison Rd -Cincinnati 45230

(513) 509-9961 .. **Chang,** Nancy Schadler '96 Torogordo Ventures LLC -Bx48 -Miamiville 45147

(330) 830-2689 .. **Chapanar,** Lawrence E '84 %City of Navarre -27 W Canal -Navarre 44662

(419) 584-1004 .. **Chapel,** Matthew W '95 -110 W Market -Bx613 -Celina 45822

(614) 799-0602 .. **Chapin,** Don H '89 -5960 Wilcox Pl -Ste B -Dublin 43016 **Fx:**799-8910

(614) 221-9100 .. **Chapin,** Lance A '98 (Stein C & Assoc LLC) -32 W Hoster -Ste 200 -Columbus 43215 **Fx:**221-9272

(330) 833-6315 .. **Chapis,** Richard M '75 -611 Andrew Av NE -Bx179 -Massillon 44648

(216) 861-0660 .. **Chaplin,** Daniel S '83 -1148 Euclid Av -Ste 300 -Cleveland 44115

(330) 644-4508 .. **Chaplin,** Mardis R '97 -1999 Killian Rd -Akron 44312

(419) 627-8075 .. **Chapman,** Benjamin M '79 -602 Jackson -Sandusky 44870

(513) 723-2202 .. **Chapman,** Brian E '88 %Weltman W&R Co,LPA -525 Vine -Ste 800 -Cincinnati 45202 **Fx:**723-2239

(310) 979-4700 .. **Chapman,** Christopher P '93 All Student Loan Grp -6701 Ctr Dr W -Ste 500 -Los Angeles, CA 90045

(330) 652-8000 .. **Chapman,** Dawn L '04 %Buckley & G Co,LPA -5704 Youngstown-Warren Rd -Niles 44446

(216) 621-0200 .. **Chapman,** Diane P '78 (Baker & H LLP) -1900 E 9th -Ste 3200 -Cleveland 44114 **Fx:**696-0740

(419) 537-2926 .. **Chapman,** Douglas K '74 Univ of Toledo Law Schl -2801 W Bancroft -Toledo 43606

(615) 284-2340 .. **Chapman,** Erie D III '69 Baptist Healing Hosp Trust -1919 Charlotte Av -Ste 320 -Nashville, TN 37203 **Fx:**284-2683

(216) 696-1133 .. **Chapman,** Frank H II '96 (Chapman Law Firm Co,LPA) -123 W Prospect Av -Ste 150 -Cleveland 44115

(330) 405-3391 .. **Chapman,** George B III '83 Chapman & C, Inc -2307 E Aurora Rd -Ste #B-13 -Twinsburg 44087

(513) 732-7313 .. **Chapman,** Gregory A '78 Clermont Cnty Pros -123 N 3rd -Batavia 45103

(440) 439-3400 .. **Chapman,** Howard S '71 TransCon Builders Inc -25250 Rockside Rd -Bedford Heights 44146 **Fx:**439-6710

(330) 945-8110 .. **Chapman,** James B '66 -1407 Sackett Hills Dr -Akron 44313

(440) 946-9469 .. **Chapman**, James E '03 %CP Kasunic Co,LPA -38033 Euclid Av -#1 -Willoughby 44094
Chapman, John E '02 -1270 Hunters Lk Dr W -Cuyahoga Falls 44221
(216) 241-8172 .. **Chapman**, John S '84 (J Chapman & Assoc,LLC) -700 W St Clair Av -Ste 300 -Cleveland 44113 **Fx:**241-8175
(614) 466-6594 .. **Chapman**, Joseph "Ted" '00 Atty Gen -150 E Gay -Columbus 43215 **Fx:**752-9070
(804) 675-3471 .. **Chapman**, Lynn M '87 Nationwide Mutual Ins Co -7545 Midlothian Tpk -Richmond, VA 23225 **Fx:**675-3595
(330) 868-6400 .. **Chapman**, Martin A '85 -215 N Market -Minerva 44657
(513) 744-9600 .. **Chapman**, Michael J '03 %Javitch B&R -602 Main -Ste 500 -Cincinnati 45202 **Fx:**744-9602
(614) 466-4656 .. **Chapman**, Shirley E '93 Atty Gen -150 E Gay -Columbus 43215 **Fx:**466-1756
(941) 366-8100 .. **Chapnick**, Bruce P '74 (Icard MCTF&G,PA) -2033 Main -Ste 600 -Bx4195 -Sarasota, FL 34230 **Fx:**366-6384
(614) 228-4422 .. **Chappano**, Perry M '86 (Chappano W PLL) -8 E Long -9th Fl -Columbus 43215 **Fx:**228-4423
(614) 228-4422 .. **Chappano Wood PLL** -8 E Long -9th Fl -Columbus 43215 **Fx:**228-4423
(937) 374-0077 .. **Chappars**, Timothy S '78 -Bx280 -Xenia 45385
(614) 221-0240 .. **Chappelear**, Stephen E '77 (Hahn L&P LLP) -65 E State -Ste 1400 -Columbus 43215 **Fx:**221-5909
(419) 867-8900 .. **Chappell**, Erik Grant '96 (Lyden L&C,Ltd) -5565 Airport Hwy -Ste 101 -Toledo 43615 **Fx:**867-8909
(216) 931-6000 .. **Chappell**, Inajo D '88 (Ulmer & B LLP) -1300 E 9th -Ste 900 Penton Media Bldg -Cleveland 44114 **Fx:**931-6001
(216) 426-0890 .. **Character**, Dea L '89 (Character C & Assoc) -3055 Ludlow Rd -Shaker Heights 44120
(216) 426-0890 .. **Character-Johnson**, Darla M '95 (Character C & Assoc) -3055 Ludlow Rd -Shaker Heights 44120
(419) 861-7800 .. **Charles**, Jeffrey B '95 Bahret & Assoc Co,LPA -7050 Spring Meadow W Dr -Holland 43528
(513) 627-4229 .. **Charles**, Mark A '04 Procter & Gamble Co -5299 Spring Grove Av -Cincinnati 45217
(614) 462-3194 .. **Charlesworth**, Thomas F '89 Franklin Cnty Pub Def -373 S High -12th Fl -Columbus 43215
(513) 367-1332 .. **Charls**, Jerome J '82 -10150 Harrison Av -Harrison 45030
(513) 661-1332 .. **Charls**, Joseph E '71 -3165 Harrison Av -Cincinnati 45211
(216) 689-5258 .. **Charlton**, Melody K '97 Key Corp -127 Pub Sq -Cleveland 44114
(216) 781-4900 .. **Charms**, Stephen J '81 (S Charms Co,LPA) -323 Lakeside Pl W -Ste 450 -Cleveland 44113
(202) 857-1757 .. **Charnas**, Douglas W '78 (McGuire W LLP) -1050 Conn Av NW -Ste 1200 -Washington, DC 20036
(614) 752-6890 .. **Charney**, Deborah J '92 Industrial Commssn of OH -30 W Spring -9th Fl -Columbus 43215 **Fx:**752-8785
(740) 592-3332 .. **Charriez**, Gilberto J '04 %Athens Pros -8 E Wshngtn -Ste 301 -Athens 45701
(614) 644-7342 .. **Charvat**, Marie '78 Dept Mntl Rtrdtn -1810 Sullivant Av -Columbus 43266 **Fx:**752-8551
(513) 621-2120 .. **Chasar**, Matthew R '02 Strauss & T,LPA -150 E 4th -4th Fl -Cincinnati 45202 **Fx:**241-8259
(937) 865-6800 .. **Chase**, Barry E '01 Lexis/Nexis -Bx933 -Dayton 45401
(508) 335-0798 .. **Chase**, Beth Anne '95 -22 June Ter -Dennis Port, MA 02639
(650) 404-4285 .. **Chase**, Bradley D '03 Bearing Point Inc -500 E Middlefld Rd -Mountain View, CA 94043
(330) 723-3287 .. **Chase**, Dale H '75 Mun Ct Judge -135 N Elmwood Av -Medina 44256
(419) 536-2066 .. **Chase Goff & Bishop** -2650 N Reynolds Rd -Ste 3 -Toledo 43615 **Fx:**536-2239
(937) 645-4190 .. **Chase**, Melissa A '89 Union Cnty Pros -221 W 5th -Ste 333 -Marysville 43040 **Fx:**645-4191
(216) 901-9111 .. **Chase**, Michael G '98 Cnsl ChromaScape Inc -2055 Enterprise Pkwy -Twinsburg 44087 **Fx:**901-9115
(419) 536-2066 .. **Chase**, Richard A '67 (Chase G&B) -2650 N Reynolds Rd -Ste 3 -Toledo 43615 **Fx:**536-2239
Chase, Timothy S '00 -310 St Clair -#106 -Frankfort, KY 40601
(614) 777-7610 .. **Chasser**, Timothy G '76 Chasser Law Ofc -4615 Leap Ct -Hilliard 43026
Chasteen, Kathleen C '02 -Bx152 -Reynoldsburg 43068
(216) 522-5020 .. **Chatfield**, Hedy S '92 Dept of Defense -Bx998002 -Cleveland 44199
(513) 621-5428 .. **Chatfield & Marshall** -7 W 7th -Ste 1800 -Cincinnati 45202
(513) 621-5428 .. **Chatfield**, Melanchthon W '85 (Chatfield & M) -7 W 7th -Ste 1800 -Cincinnati 45202
(513) 621-5428 .. **Chatfield**, William H '72 (Chatfield & M) -7 W 7th -Ste 1800 -Cincinnati 45202
(614) 249-5276 .. **Chatterton**, Lisa A '94 Nationwide Ins Co -One Nationwide Plz -1-09-V3 -Columbus 43215
(216) 621-5300 .. **Chattman**, Gerald B '67 (Buckingham D&B,LLP) -1375 E 9th -Ste 1700 -Cleveland 44114 **Fx:**621-5440
(513) 534-4847 .. **Chattoraj**, Tarun K '00 Cnsl Fifth Third Bank -38 Fountain Sq Plz -MD 10AT76 -Cincinnati 45263
Chavanne, Michelle L '01 -1209 Westwood Av -Columbus 43212
(216) 698-2698 .. **Chavers**, Dana C '82 Cuyahoga Cnty Juv Ct -3343 Comm Cllg Av -Cleveland 44115
(614) 462-3194 .. **Chavers**, Dane C '81 Franklin Cnty Pub Def -373 S High -12th Fl -Columbus 43215
(614) 469-5576 .. **Chavers**, Darlene E '87 Fed Mediation & Conciliation Svc -1682 Schrock Rd -Columbus 43229
(937) 328-2640 .. **Chavez**, Bjorn J '98 Clark Cnty Pub Def -50 E Columbia -4th Fl -Springfield 45502 **Fx:**328-2715
(614) 224-3827 .. **Chavez**, Margaret L '00 Parking Co of Amer -250 S Civic Ctr -Ste 410 -Columbus 43215
(440) 934-3700 .. **Chavez**, Stephen P '95 Fauver K-W&D -5333 Meadow Ln Ct -Elyria 44035 **Fx:**934-3708
(330) 451-7897 .. **Chawla**, Kathi W '98 Stark Cnty Pros -110 Central Plz -Ste 510 -Canton 44702
(614) 262-2539 .. **Cheadle**, Michele M '74 %Anadem Pblshng -3620 N High -#201 -Columbus 43214
(614) 480-4647 .. **Cheap**, Richard A '80 Huntington Natl Bank -41 S High -Columbus 43287

(440) 350-2146 .. **Cheatham**, Amy E '97 Lake Cnty Pros -105 Main -Bx490 -Painesville 44077 **Fx:**350-2585
(216) 588-5945 .. **Cheatham**, Stephen V '77 OH Savings Bank -1801 E 9th -Ste 200 -Cleveland 44114
(614) 229-3888 .. **Cheek**, Emerson III '70 (Cheek & Z,LLP) -471 E Broad -18th Fl -Bx15069 -Columbus 43215 **Fx:**241-5865
(330) 725-4935 .. **Cheek**, Todd E '03 %JB Palmquist III Co,LPA -5 Pub Sq -Medina 44256
(614) 229-3888 .. **Cheek & Zeehandelar,LLP** -471 E Broad -18th Fl -Bx15069 -Columbus 43215 **Fx:**241-5865
(419) 352-4659 .. **Cheetwood**, John S '69 -300 N Main -Bowling Green 43402 **Fx:**354-4550
(202) 662-1050 .. **Chellis**, Michael R '84 Labat-Anderson Inc -529 14th NW -#452 -Washington, DC 20045
(937) 225-2910 .. **Chema**, J David '81 US Atty -200 W 2nd -602 Fed Bldg -Dayton 45402
(937) 445-9787 .. **Chema**, Susan R '82 NCR Corp -Leg Dept -1700 S Patterson Blvd -Dayton 45479
(216) 592-5000 .. **Chema**, Thomas V '71 OfCnsl Tucker E&W LLP -925 Euclid Av -1150 Huntngtn Bldg -Cleveland 44115 **Fx:**592-5009
(440) 639-3000 .. **Chemnitz**, Gregory R '84 Avery Dennison Materials -7590 Auburn Rd -Painesville 44077
(937) 365-6800 .. **Chen**, Huiling K '93 Lexis/Nexis -Bx933 -Dayton 45401
(216) 621-8742 .. **Chenette**, Frank A '76 -55 Pub Sq -Ste 2121 -Cleveland 44113
(419) 228-6365 .. **Cheney**, David A '74 (Cory MWR&C,LPA) -101 N Elizabeth -Ste 607 -Bx1217 -Lima 45802 **Fx:**228-5319
(513) 632-4085 .. **Cheng**, Lan-Lan J '00 US Bancorp -425 Walnut -ML: CN-WN-09 AD -Cincinnati 45202
(216) 222-2979 .. **Chenin**, Avery M '89 Natl City Corp -1900 E 9th -17th Fl -Cleveland 44114
(330) 376-5300 .. **Chenoweth**, Richard A '48 OfCnsl Buckingham D&B,LLP -50 S Main -Bx1500 -Akron 44309 **Fx:**258-6559
(216) 588-5193 .. **Cherchiglia**, Dean K '84 OH Savings Bnk -1801 E 9th -Ste 200 -Cleveland 44114
(330) 255-5016 .. **Cherkala**, Brian L '78 KeyBank Natl Assoc -222 S Main -Ste 200 -Akron 44308 **Fx:**255-5029
(330) 629-8882 .. **Chermely**, Diane L '89 -945 Windham Ct -Ste 3 -Boardman 44512 **Fx:**726-5926
(330) 425-4201 .. **Chernek**, Ronald J '89 Reimer L&A Co,LPA -2450 Edison Blvd -Bx968 -Twinsburg 44087 **Fx:**487-0923
(937) 449-2800 .. **Chernesky Heyman & Kress PLL** -10 Cthse Plz SW -Ste 1100 -Dayton 45402 **Fx:**449-2821
(937) 449-2800 .. **Chernesky**, Richard J '66 (Chernesky H&K PLL) -10 Cthse Plz SW -Ste 1100 -Dayton 45402 **Fx:**449-2821
(216) 737-5000 .. **Chernett**, Robert I '73 (Chernett WY&P) -1301 E 9th -Ste 3300 -Cleveland 44114 **Fx:**737-0011
(216) 737-5000 .. **Chernett Wasserman Yarger & Pasternak** -1301 E 9th -Ste 3300 -Cleveland 44114 **Fx:**737-0011
(937) 449-2800 .. **Cherney**, Andrew K '73 (Chernesky H&K PLL) -10 Cthse Plz SW -Ste 1100 -Dayton 45402 **Fx:**449-2821
(216) 621-6101 .. **Chernosky**, David J '90 %Kahn & Assoc,LLC -55 Pub Sq -Ste 650 -Cleveland 44113 **Fx:**621-6006
(719) 575-9260 .. **Chernushin**, Gregory '77 -1530 S Tejon -Colorado Springs, CO 80906
(440) 446-5769 .. **Cherosky**, Michael R '00 Progressice Ins Co -Bx43258 -Richmond Heights 44143
(330) 645-4907 .. **Cherpas**, Christopher T '52 Cnsl Quality Mold,Inc -2200 Massilon Rd -Akron 44312 **Fx:**645-4827
(740) 446-2922 .. **Cherrington Moulton & Evans** -Bx409 -Gallipolis 45631 **Fx:**446-1738
(312) 655-1500 .. **Cherry**, Daniel R '76 (Welsh & K,Ltd) -120 S Riverside Plz -22nd Fl -Chicago, IL 60606 **Fx:**655-1501
(419) 242-4969 .. **Cherry**, Jonathan B '75 Toledo Bar Assoc -311 N Superior -Toledo 43604
(216) 928-3082 .. **Cheselka**, Michael J Jr. '03 (Cheselka & P,LLC) -1940 E 6th -8th Fl Baker Bldg -Cleveland 44114 **Fx:**619-7420
(212) 770-7976 .. **Cheshire**, Sandra K '82 Intl Cos. -70 Pine -54th Fl -New York, NY 10270 **Fx:**(732) 671-0402
(440) 967-1513 .. **Chesky**, Stuart B '03 -13703 W Lake Rd -Vermilion 44089
Chesler, Lisa M '91 -8061 Chagrin Mills Rd -Chagrin Falls 44022
Chesler, Steven B '84 -3443 Green Rd -Apt 3B -Cleveland 44122
(312) 782-3939 .. **Chesley**, Richard A '85 (Jones DR&P) -77 W Wacker Dr -Ste 3500 -Chicago, IL 60601
(513) 621-0267 .. **Chesley**, Stanley M '60 (Waite SB&C) -1 W 4th -1513 4th & Vine Twr -Cincinnati 45202
(614) 644-5470 .. **Chesley-Lahm**, Diane M '77 Supreme Ct of OH -30 E Broad -35th Fl -Columbus 43266
(216) 515-1660 .. **Chesney**, Michael N '92 (Frantz W LLP) -127 Pub Sq -2500 Key Center -Cleveland 44114 **Fx:**515-1650
(740) 349-6640 .. **Chesrown**, Jennifer L '95 Cnty Mun Ct Judge -40 W Main -Newark City Bldg -Newark 43055
(740) 455-7123 .. **Chess**, Walter K Jr. '75 Muskingum Cnty Pros -27 N 5th -Zanesville 43701
(330) 489-3251 .. **Chessler**, Craig E '83 Law Dept -218 Cleveland Av SW -Bx24218 -Canton 44702
(216) 696-5580 .. **Chestang-Fossett**, Renee S '85 -815 Superior Bldg -Ste 1725 -Cleveland 44114
(614) 447-3812 .. **Chester**, Casey E '92 Chemical Abstrcts Srvcs -2540 Olentangy Rvr Rd -Columbus 43202
(330) 253-5678 .. **Chester**, David M '95 Patent Cpyrt & Trdmrk Law Grp,LLC -137 S Main -Ste 202 -Akron 44308 **Fx:**762-5063
(614) 221-4000 .. **Chester**, James J '87 (Chester W&S LLP) -65 E State -10th Fl -Columbus 43215 **Fx:**221-4012
(614) 221-4000 .. **Chester**, John J '48 (Chester W&S LLP) -65 E State -10th Fl -Columbus 43215 **Fx:**221-4012
(614) 221-4000 .. **Chester**, John J Jr. '89 (Chester W&S LLP) -65 E State -10th Fl -Columbus 43215 **Fx:**221-4012
(513) 287-7019 .. **Chester**, Victoria L '92 Cincinnati Museum Ctr -1301 Wstrn Av -Cincinnati 45203
(614) 221-4000 .. **Chester Willcox & Saxbe LLP** -65 E State -10th Fl -Columbus 43215 **Fx:**221-4012
(614) 466-2766 .. **Cheugh**, Robert W II '79 Atty Gen -30 E Broad -Columbus 43215 **Fx:**644-1926

(216) 241-5310 ..**Cheung**, Jeremy G '04 %Gallagher SF&N -1501 Euclid Av -6th Fl
-Cleveland 44115 **Fx:**241-1608

(216) 689-0509 ..**Cheverine**, Carolyn E '96 KeyBank NA -127 Pub Sq
-Law Group, 2nd Fl -Cleveland 44114

(216) 765-8520 ..**Cheverine**, Vincent L '95 (Aggers J&C Co,LPA)
-29565 Chagrin Blvd -Ste 306 Exec Cmmns E
-Pepper Pike 44122 **Fx:**765-8817

(513) 381-9200 ..**Chiaro**, Cynthia M '96 %Rendigs FK&D,LLP -One W 4th -Ste 900
-Cincinnati 45202 **Fx:**381-9206

(440) 349-2712 ..**Chiarucci**, Regina L '90 -35520 Spicebush Ln -Solon 44139

(937) 743-1500 ..**Chicarelli**, David A '75 (D Chicarelli Co,LPA) -614 E 2nd
-Franklin 45005

(330) 376-8336 ..**Chicatelli**, Joy L '00 %Goldman & R,Ltd -11 S Forge
-Akron 44304 **Fx:**376-2522

(614) 293-7802 ..**Chicoine**, Julie E '03 OH State Univ Med Ctr -410 W 10th Av
-Columbus 43210

(614) 466-8600 ..**Chieffo**, Dominic J '66 Atty Gen -30 E Broad -Columbus 43215
Fx:466-6090

(614) 846-2000 ..**Chilcoat**, David L '84 (Campbell HC&V,LLC) -7650 Rvrs Edge Dr
-Columbus 43235 **Fx:**846-2003

(614) 846-2000 ..**Chilcoat**, Jeffrey R '98 (Campbell HC&V,LLC) -7650 Rvrs Edge Dr
-Columbus 43235 **Fx:**846-2003

(216) 795-4117 ..**Chilcote**, Lee A '72 (Chilcote Law Firm) -12434 Cedar Rd -Ste 1
-Cleveland Heights 44106 **Fx:**795-4245

(216) 831-5904 ..**Chilcote**, Nancy A '83 -30900 Edgewood Rd -Pepper Pike 44124

(330) 627-4770 ..**Childers**, John C '78 (Childers & S) -70 Pub Sq -Bx252
-Carrollton 44615

(740) 887-4987 ..**Childers**, Pamela C '98 -Bx327 -Londonderry 45647

(330) 375-6696 ..**Childers**, William E '88 Summa Hlth Syst -525 E Market -1st Fl
-Bx2090 -Akron 44309

(419) 524-6011 ..**Childress**, James L '85 (Calhoun KH&C Co,LPA) -6 W 3rd
-Ste 200 -Bx268 -Mansfield 44901 **Fx:**526-1431

(330) 643-8003 ..**Childress**, Marilyn R '90 %Summit Cnty Cmmn Pleas Ct
-209 S High -Akron 44308

(440) 526-1021 ..**Childs**, Carol A '91 -6636 Westvw Dr -Brecksville 44141

(513) 352-6700 ..**Childs**, Erin Cunniff '02 %Thompson H LLP -312 Walnut -14th Fl
-Cincinnati 45202 **Fx:**241-4771

Childs, Ishmael C '56 -3105 Keswick Rd -Shaker Heights 44120

(330) 253-5060 ..**Childs**, John N '74 (Brennan M&D,LLC) -75 E Market
-Akron 44308 **Fx:**253-1977

(937) 865-1419 ..**Chillinsky**, Michael J '88 Lexis/Nexis -Bx933 -Dayton 45401

(937) 224-9291 ..**Chilson**, Mark R '81 Young & A,LPA -130 W 2nd -Ste 2000
-Dayton 45402 **Fx:**224-9679

(614) 462-3194 ..**Chimbidis**, Peter E '96 Franklin Cnty Pub Def -373 S High -12th Fl
-Columbus 43215

(216) 443-8427 ..**Chimo**, Elaine J '62 Cuyahoga Cnty Juv Ct -1910 Carnegie Av
-Cleveland 44115

(216) 362-1880 ..**Chimples**, Constantine G '73 AMAC Enterprises Inc
-5909 W 130th -Parma 44130

(216) 479-8500 ..**Chin**, Elleanor H '99 %Squire S&D LLP -127 Pub Sq -4900 Key
Twr -Cleveland 44114 **Fx:**479-8780

(216) 241-0646 ..**Chin**, James W '76 (Chin & Assoc) -526 Superior Av -Ste 745
-Cleveland 44114

(330) 376-9260 ..**Chin**, Maria E '02 -7 W Bowery -Ste 907 -Akron 44308

(513) 946-3000 ..**Chin**, Nee F '87 Hamilton Cnty Pros -230 E 9th -Cincinnati 45202
Fx:946-3017

(937) 226-9354 ..**Chinault**, Elizabeth M '03 %Macey & C -40 W 4th -Ste 2160
-Dayton 45402 **Fx:**226-9359

(937) 223-8888 ..**Chinault**, Jeffrey G '03 %Dyer GM&S -131 N Ludlow -Ste 1400
-Dayton 45402 **Fx:**223-0127

(216) 522-3881 ..**Chinni**, Benjamin T '70 Dept of Labor -1240 E 9th -Rm 881
-Cleveland 44199

(412) 928-4206 ..**Chiodo**, Julie E '93 Honeywell,Inc -1005 S Bee -Pittsburgh,
PA 15220

(716) 856-5012 ..**Chiriboga**, J Christine '93 %Anspach M&N,LLP -2400 Main Pl Twr
-Buffalo, NY 14202 **Fx:**852-2485

(212) 455-2000 ..**Chisling**, Brian E '94 %Simpson T&B LLP -425 Lex Av
-New York, NY 10017 **Fx:**455-2502

(440) 349-9966 ..**Chisling**, Stephanie A '97 -6732 Winston Ln -Solon 44139

(419) 529-4560 ..**Chisnell**, Brian J '80 UAW Legal Srvcs Plan -1075 Natl Pkwy
-Bx2668 -Mansfield 44906 **Fx:**529-5350

(216) 368-2655 ..**Chisolm**, Laura B '81 CWRU Law Schl -11075 East Blvd
-Cleveland 44106

(614) 322-9500 ..**Chiu**, Alicia M '04 -7906 Blacklick Vw Dr -Blacklick 43004

(614) 462-3555 ..**Chiu**, Vincent S '04 Franklin Cnty Pros -373 S High -Columbus
43215

(440) 842-6800 ..**Chizmar**, Gregory A '77 -5851 Pearl Rd -Ste 203
-Parma Heights 44130 **Fx:**663-1201

(216) 696-8700 ..**Chlarson**, Kevin L '03 %Kohrman J&K PLL -1375 E 9th
-One Cleve Ctr 20th Fl -Cleveland 44114 **Fx:**621-6536

(330) 670-7300 ..**Chlysta**, John R '92 %Hanna C&P,LLP -3737 Embssy Pkwy
-Bx5521 -Akron 44334 **Fx:**670-0977

(304) 367-3295 ..**Chmiel**, Arthur J '86 Allegheny Power -1310 Fairmont Av
-Fairmont, WV 26554

(216) 621-8484 ..**Chmielewski**, Dawn M '04 %Climaco LPW&G Co,LPA
-1228 Euclid Av -Ste 900 Halle Bldg -Cleveland 44115
Fx:771-1632

(614) 338-0700 ..**Chodosh**, Louis J '77 (Chodosh & C) -2392 E Main
-Columbus 43209

(614) 338-0700 ..**Chodosh**, Sheila R '86 (Chodosh & C) -2392 E Main
-Columbus 43209

(216) 522-3715 ..**Choe**, Iva Y '95 NLRB -1240 E 9th -1695 Celebrezze Bldg
-Cleveland 44199 **Fx:**522-2418

(614) 247-5853 ..**Choe**, Susan A '96 OSU Student Housing Lgl Clinic -1739 N High
-Rm 345 Ohio Union -Columbus 43210

(703) 720-7800 ..**Choi**, Alicia M '99 %Squire S&D LLP -8000 Towers Crescent Dr
-14th Fl -Tysons Corner, VA 22182 **Fx:**720-7801

(440) 395-0274 ..**Choi**, Catherine K '98 Progressive Ins Co -300 N Cmmns Blvd
-OHF 11 -Mayfield Village 44143

(614) 789-0240 ..**Choi**, Monica H '98 -4243 Hertford Ln -Dublin 43017

(419) 252-6208 ..**Choka**, Byron S '80 (Spengler N PLL) -608 Mad Av -Ste 1000
-Toledo 43604 **Fx:**241-8599

(330) 865-4949 ..**Choken**, Charles Vincent '99 -3020 W Market -Akron 44333
Fx:865-3777

(614) 466-4314 ..**Cholar**, Richard T Jr. '92 OH DYS -51 N High -Columbus 43215

(440) 257-1658 ..**Chopra**, Mira B '92 -7372 Lakeshr Blvd #4 -Mentor 44060
Fx:(866) 566-9444

(602) 264-3289 ..**Chornenky**, O J '70 (O Chornenky,PC) -301 E Bethany Home Rd
-Bldg A/ste 209 -Phoenix, AZ 85012

(614) 469-1301 ..**Chorpenning**, Brian E '83 (Chorpenning G&P Co,LPA)
-585 S Front -Ste 250 -Columbus 43215

(614) 469-1301 ..**Chorpenning Good & Pandora Co,LPA** -585 S Front -Ste 250
-Columbus 43215

(312) 230-3503 ..**Chorzempa**, David J '02 SrCnsl AT&T -222 W Monroe
-Chicago, IL 60606

(216) 621-0200 ..**Chotlos**, Elaine A '83 (Baker & H LLP) -1900 E 9th -Ste 3200
-Cleveland 44114 **Fx:**696-0740

(614) 229-5124 ..**Chou**, Chun-Yi K '02 Ernst & Young LLP -41 S High -Ste 1100
-Columbus 43215 **Fx:**229-5127

(216) 522-3715 ..**Choudhury**, Rudra '99 NLRB -1240 E 9th -1695 Celebrezze Bldg
-Cleveland 44199 **Fx:**522-2418

(614) 464-1211 ..**Chouinard**, Erika J '04 %Frost BT LLC -10 W Broad -Ste 1000
-Columbus 43215 **Fx:**464-1737

(614) 227-5835 ..**Chretien**, Alfred M '92 Intellinetics,Inc -2190 Dividend Dr
-Columbus 43228

(330) 434-3000 ..**Chris**, William G '85 (Roderick & L) -One Cascade Plz -Ste 1500
-Akron 44308 **Fx:**434-9220

(614) 249-7875 ..**Chrisley**, Gail D '99 Nationwide Life -1 Nationwide Plz -1-07-10
-Columbus 43215 **Fx:**249-9075

(937) 492-4250 ..**Chrisman**, James J '79 -223½ N Main Av -Bx442 -Sidney 45365

(716) 664-1558 ..**Chrispell**, David J '02 -815 Busti-Sugargrove -Jamestown, NY
14701

(216) 291-7380 ..**Christ**, Paula B '91 Northrop Grumman -1900 Richmond Rd
-Cleveland 44124

(330) 489-5243 ..**Christ**, Roger A '87 Nationwide Ins Co -1000 Market Av N -Bx8379
-Canton 44711

(419) 843-2001 ..**Christen**, Dawn T '01 %Gallon & T Co,LPA -3516 Granite Cir
-Bx352018 -Toledo 43635 **Fx:**843-6665

(419) 249-7100 ..**Christensen**, Allen T '77 Marshall & M,LLC -Four Seagate -8th Fl
-Toledo 43604 **Fx:**249-7151

(330) 375-2030 ..**Christensen**, Bruce H Jr. '86 Law Dept -161 S High -Ste 202
-Akron 44308

(614) 221-1830 ..**Christensen Christensen & DeVillers** -401 N Front -Ste 350
-Columbus 43215

(614) 221-1830 ..**Christensen**, Jon A '81 (Christensen C&D) -401 N Front -Ste 350
-Columbus 43215

(614) 275-3444 ..**Christensen**, Lisa M '04 MD Christensen,LLC -3184 W Broad
-Ste D -Columbus 43204

(614) 221-1830 ..**Christensen**, Mary W '83 (Christensen C&D) -401 N Front
-Ste 350 -Columbus 43215

(614) 275-3444 ..**Christensen**, Michael D '99 -3184 W Broad -Ste D
-Columbus 43204

(440) 473-1634 ..**Christensen**, Romie M '03 Lancer Ins Co -6563 Wilson Mills Rd
-Ste 101 -Mayfield Village 44143

Christensen, Susan M '00 -7852 Saddle Run -Powell 43065

(614) 443-4606 ..**Christensen**, William J '68 -765 S High -Columbus 43206

(216) 222-3668 ..**Christhilf**, George H '96 Natl City Bank -Bx94651
-Cleveland 44101

Christian, Kristin L '02 -1396 St Louis Av -Bay Shore, NY 11706

(330) 744-2125 ..**Christian**, Robert J '77 -26 Market -Ste 904 -Youngstown 44503

(513) 381-2838 ..**Christian**, Ronald C '87 (Taft S&H LLP) -425 Walnut -Ste 1800
-Cincinnati 45202 **Fx:**381-0205

(330) 744-1111 ..**Christian**, Shirley J '86 Harrington H&M,Ltd -26 Market -Ste 1200
-Youngstown 44503 **Fx:**744-2029

(740) 653-3281 ..**Christian**, Thomas M '72 -420 E Main -Lancaster 43130

(216) 535-0520 ..**Christian**, Victoria A '80 US DHS,ICE -1240 E 9th -Rm 519
-Cleveland 44199

Christians, Elizabeth A '93 -(Address Unavailable)

(740) 349-7414 ..**Christiansen**, Vicky M '79 (Christiansen & W) -172 Hudson Av
-Newark 43055

(515) 280-2535 ..**Christianson**, Carol A '91 EMC Ins Co -717 Mulberry
-Des Moines, IA 50309

(614) 645-6323 ..**Christie**, Chester C '83 City Deptof Human Resources
-90 W Broad -Ste 311 -Columbus 43215

(216) 382-8422 ..**Christie**, Edward C '70 -4320 Elmwood Rd -Ste 2
-South Euclid 44121

(216) 579-1602 ..**Christie**, John R '97 Rawlins G&F Co,LPA -55 Pub Sq -Ste 850
-Cleveland 44113

(330) 376-7334 ..**Christie**, Michael G '88 -631 W Exchange -Akron 44302

(419) 898-2671 ..**Christie**, Michelle L '93 (Graves K&C) -142 W Water
-Oak Harbor 43449

(740) 962-2262 ..**Christie**, Robert J '74 (Christie & W) -36 W Main -Bx419
-McConnelsville 43756

(603) 373-2046 ..**Christie**, Sheila K '93 (Pierce Atwood) -One NH Av -Ste 350
-Portsmouth, NH 03801

(330) 394-1539 ..**Christine**, Anthony P '84 W Urban Co LPA -434 High NE
-Warren 44481

(330) 562-3156 ..**Christley Herington & Pierce** -215 W Garfld -Ste 230
-Aurora 44202 **Fx:**562-9540

(330) 562-3156 ..**Christley**, Norman L '68 (Christley H&P) -215 W Garfld -Ste 230
-Aurora 44202 **Fx:**562-9540

(330) 643-2921 ..**Christman**, Bradford J '86 Summit Cnty Juv Ct -650 Dan
-Akron 44310

(440) 942-6675 ..**Christman**, Katie E '03 %MJ Clair -4132 Erie -Ste 202
-Willoughby 44094

(412) 572-7159 ..**Christman**, Kenneth W '74 Columbia Gas of PA -650 Wshngtn Rd
-Pittsburgh, PA 15228

(216) 241-5019 ..**Christman**, Leif B '98 -1370 Ontario -Ste 2000 -Cleveland 44113

(412) 392-5240 ..**Christof**, Joseph S II '01 %Dickie M&C,PC -Two PPG Pl -Ste 400
-Pittsburgh, PA 15222

(419) 772-2205 ..**Christoff**, John P '77 ONU-Pettit Clg of Law -525 S Main
-Ada 45810 **Fx:**772-2404

(614) 644-9326 ..**Christoff**, Susan B '88 OH Supreme Ct -30 E Broad -2nd Fl
-Columbus 43215

(330) 832-5999 ..**Christoff**, William Z '76 -26 S Erie -Massillon 44646

(937) 461-0796 ..**Christon**, Jimmie '87 -15 E 4th -Ste 625 -Dayton 45402

(614) 466-6227 ..**Christopher**, Jack L '98 State Auditor Ofc -88 E Broad -Bx1140
-Columbus 43216

(513) 977-8200 ..**Christopher**, John E Jr. '95 (Dinsmore & S LLP) -255 E 5th
-Ste 1900 -Cincinnati 45202 Fx:977-8141

(614) 221-4747 ..**Christopher**, Judith E '75 -326 S High -3rd Fl -Columbus 43215

(216) 622-8200 ..**Christopher**, S Paige '96 %Calfee H&G LLP -800 Superior Av
-Ste 1400 -Cleveland 44114 Fx:241-0816

(419) 422-7176 ..**Christopher**, Steven D '84 -330 S Main -Findlay 45840

(216) 514-6400 ..**Christy**, Chastity L '03 %Zipkin W Co LPA -3637 S Green Rd
-Zipkin Whiting Bldg -Cleveland 44122 Fx:514-6406

(513) 651-6800 ..**Christy**, Diana R '01 %Frost BT LLC -201 E 5th -2200 PNC Ctr
-Cincinnati 45202 Fx:651-6981

(703) 810-1072 ..**Christy**, James T '73 NW Financial Srvcs -200 Spring -Ste 120
-Herndon, VA 20170 Fx:810-1079

(419) 248-7957 ..**Christy**, John W '97 Owens Corning -1 Owens Corning Pkwy
-Leg Dept -Toledo 43659

(216) 443-7800 ..**Christyson**, Robert J Jr. '85 Cuyahoga Cnty Pros -1200 Ontario
-8th Fl -Cleveland 44113 Fx:698-2270

(216) 621-7227 ..**Chriszt**, James R '87 OfCnsl Nicola G&C,LLC -25 W Prospect Av
-Republic Bldg Ste 1400 -Cleveland 44115 Fx:621-3999

(305) 529-1500 ..**Chrystal**, Neil R '73 (Dunwody W&L,PA) -550 Biltmore Way
-Ste 810 -Coral Gables, FL 33134 Fx:529-8855

(216) 586-3939 ..**Chu**, Howard W '04 %Jones D -901 Lakeside Av -Cleveland 44114
Fx:579-0212

(937) 342-1896 ..**Chu**, Jeannette A '04 -6320 Plateau Dr -Springfield 45502
Fx:342-1897

(440) 729-7551 ..**Chubb**, Kathryn A '91 -11165 Chillicothe Rd -Chesterland 44026

(770) 951-6589 ..**Chubb**, Robert A '95 (Hartman SS&W LLP)
-6400 Powers Ferry Rd NW -Ste 400 -Atlanta, GA 30339
Fx:303-1131

(216) 931-6000 ..**Chudakoff**, Robert E '87 (Ulmer & B LLP) -1300 E 9th
-Ste 900 Penton Media Bldg -Cleveland 44114 Fx:931-6001

(216) 671-3364 ..**Chudner**, Richard '98 -3715 W 139th -Cleveland 44111

(216) 523-1900 ..**Chudyk**, Peter J '80 Hausser & Taylor,LLP -1001 Lakeside Av
-Ste 1400 -Cleveland 44114

(419) 232-8810 ..**Chudzinski**, Anthony A '76 -621 Croghan -Fremont 43420

(513) 627-5145 ..**Chuey**, Steven R '94 Cnsl Procter & Gamble
-5299 Spring Grove Av -Cincinnati 45217

(614) 873-8566 ..**Chuha**, Edward F '68 -10856 Tioga Sprngs Cir -Plain City 43064

(317) 263-2441 ..**Chumlea**, Kevin L '92 Simon Prop Grp -115 W Wshngtn
-Indianapolis, IN 46204

(513) 579-6400 ..**Chumley**, Mark J '96 (Keating M&K PLL) -1 E 4th -1400
Provident Twr -Cincinnati 45202 Fx:579-6457

Chunat, Thomas R '04 -(Address Unavailable)

(614) 466-2166 ..**Chung**, Eun Sook '02 OH Dept Taxation -30 E Broad -22nd Fl
-Columbus 43215

(216) 586-3939 ..**Chunyo**, Jennifer J '96 Jones D -901 Lakeside Av
-Cleveland 44114 Fx:579-0212

(419) 243-6148 ..**Chuparkoff**, David F '88 Manahan PB&D -414 N Erie -Bx2328
-Toledo 43603

(614) 464-2392 ..**Chuparkoff**, Mark A '00 %Earl WA&D,LPA -136 W Mound
-Columbus 43215 Fx:464-0754

(330) 835-0500 ..**Chuparkoff**, Michael A '96 %Chuparkoff & C -1655 W Market
-Ste 430 -Akron 44313 Fx:835-0500

Chuparkoff, Stephen J '87 -406 W 5th -Mc Donald 44437

(330) 835-0500 ..**Chuparkoff**, Theodore '62 SrCnsl Chuparkoff & C -1655 W Market
-Ste 430 -Akron 44313 Fx:835-0500

(440) 248-5010 ..**Church**, Joseph Jeffrey '79 -32915 Aurora Rd -#180 -Solon 44139
Fx:248-9036

(812) 945-3561 ..**Church**, Larry R '91 Wyatt T&C -101 W Spring -5th Fl
-New Albany, IN 47150

(513) 661-1888 ..**Church**, William B III '73 Hamilton Cnty Pub Def -230 E 9th -3rd Fl
-Cincinnati 45202 Fx:946-3707

(614) 462-3194 ..**Churchill**, Philip T '80 Franklin Cnty Pub Def -373 S High -12th Fl
-Columbus 43215

(440) 439-7700 ..**Churchmack**, Allan G '89 Arhaus Furniture -7700 Nrthfld Rd
-Walton Hills 44146 Fx:439-7075

(216) 781-5515 ..**Chylla**, Heidi P '99 %Hermann C&S,LLP -1301 E 9th -Ste 500
-Cleveland 44114 Fx:781-1030

(216) 896-5600 ..**Chyun**, Edward H '03 %Levy & D -25200 Chagrin Blvd -Ste 310
-Beachwood 44122 Fx:896-5601

(330) 729-9240 ..**Ciambotti**, Anna M '87 -755 Boardman-Canfld Rd -Ste P-4
-Boardman 44512

(937) 443-6568 ..**Ciambrone**, Richard A '80 Thompson H LLP -2000 Cthse Plz NE
-Bx8801 -Dayton 45401 Fx:443-6635

(614) 487-4439 ..**Cianca**, Stephen P '93 OH State Bar Assoc -1700 Lakeshr Dr
-Columbus 43204

(216) 687-1311 ..**Ciano**, Mario C '68 (Reminger & R) -101 Prospect Av W
-1400 Mdlnd Bldg -Cleveland 44115 Fx:687-1841

(216) 658-9900 ..**Ciano**, Phillip A '96 (Ciano & G,LLP) -1500 W 3rd -Ste 460
-Cleveland 44113

(216) 328-0002 ..**Ciaravino**, Michael G '91 -5005 Rockside Rd
-Crown Centre-Ste 600 -Independence 44131

(330) 255-6348 ..**Ciavarella**, Nick E '97 Gojo Ind -Bx991 -Akron 44309

(216) 344-9220 ..**Cibella**, Mary L '84 OfCnsl McGinty GH&S Co,LPA -614 W
Superior Av -Ste 1300 -Cleveland 44113

(216) 622-8200 ..**Cicarella**, Thomas A '74 (Calfee H&G LLP) -800 Superior Av
-Ste 1400 -Cleveland 44114 Fx:241-0816

(614) 466-4605 ..**Cicatiello**, Judith L '92 OH Dept Job & Fam Srvcs -30 E Broad
-32nd Fl -Columbus 43266

(330) 382-7455 ..**Ciccarelli**, Mark A '99 Kent State Univ -400 E 4th -East Liverpool
43920 Fx:382-7561

(330) 753-1051 ..**Ciccolini**, Eliodoro '53 Germano R&C Co,LPA -2715 Mnchstr Rd
-Akron 44319

(330) 722-5000 ..**Ciccolini**, James F '92 -209 S Bway -Medina 44256

(330) 753-1051 ..**Ciccolini**, Michael E '84 Germano R&C Co,LPA -2715 Mnchstr Rd
-Akron 44319

(330) 753-1051 ..**Ciccolini**, Thomas A '73 Germano R&C Co,LPA
-2715 Mnchstr Rd -Akron 44319

(330) 796-4565 ..**Ciccolini**, Vincent N '91 Goodyear Tire & Rubber Co
-1144 E Market -Akron 44316

(330) 262-7555 ..**Cicconetti**, Francis E '69 (Kennedy CK&B) -558 N Market
-Wooster 44691

(937) 424-5390 ..**Cicero**, Anthony R '95 (Cicero & K,PLL) -500 E 5th -Ste 100
-Dayton 45402 Fx:424-5393

(614) 228-2600 ..**Cicero**, Christopher T '88 -1308 W Mound -Columbus 43223

(216) 621-7227 ..**Cicero**, Michael E '92 %Nicola G&C,LLC -25 W Prospect Av
-Republic Bldg Ste 1400 -Cleveland 44115 Fx:621-3999

(561) 630-5055 ..**Cich**, Brian C '95 Rendina Cos -3801 PGA Blvd -Ste 600
-Palm Beach Gardens, FL 33410

Cich, Frank A '74 -3307 Cherrywood -Barberton 44203

(216) 749-2203 ..**Cichocki**, Bruce M '75 -2525 Brookpark -Parma 44134

(216) 642-3777 ..**Cichocki**, Charles F '77 -6911 Delmur Dr -Independence 44131

(513) 579-7371 ..**Ciclet**, Donna R '93 Federated Dept Stores,Inc -7 W 7th
-Cincinnati 45202

(614) 387-9040 ..**Ciecka**, Emily H '04 Hon A Resnick Supreme Ct -65 S Front -9th Fl
-Columbus 43215

(212) 446-4800 ..**Cieri**, Richard M '81 (Kirkland & E LLP) -153 E 53rd -39th Fl
-New York, NY 10022 Fx:446-4900

(216) 987-2310 ..**Cieslak**, James L '78 Cuyahoga CC -4250 Richmond Rd
-Highland Hills 44122

(216) 581-7400 ..**Cifelli**, Leo L '59 -5250 Transportation Blvd -Ste 100
-Garfield Heights 44125

(202) 307-3278 ..**Cihon**, Jennifer L '97 US DOJ -325 7th NW -Ste 500
-Washington, DC 20530

(440) 329-5456 ..**Cillo**, Anthony D '93 Lorain Cnty Pros -225 Court -3rd Fl
-Elyria 44035

(305) 381-6073 ..**Cimballa**, George L III '01 GEICO Ins -150 W Flagler -Ste 1650
-Miami, FL 33130

(419) 242-8214 ..**Cimerman**, Adrian P '79 (Zaner & C) -520 Mad Av -Ste 545
-Toledo 43604 Fx:242-8658

(412) 394-6966 ..**Cimini**, Sally G '97 %Babst CC&Z,PC -Two Gtwy Ctr -8th Fl
-Pittsburgh, PA 15222

(330) 297-5788 ..**Cimino**, Frank J '72 -250 S Chestnut -Ste 18 -Ravenna 44266

(440) 992-6067 ..**Cimorell**, Bret J '85 -Bx2259 -Ashtabula 44005

(614) 267-7966 ..**Cimperman**, Anthony J '89 -3130 N High -Ste 214
-Columbus 43202

(440) 449-2662 ..**Cimperman**, Marilyn L '96 Annashae Corp -673 Alpha Dr -Ste C
-Cleveland 44143

(614) 221-3151 ..**Cincione**, Alphonse P '61 (Butler C&D) -50 W Broad -Ste 700
-Columbus 43215

(614) 464-6400 ..**Cincione**, Karen A '89 Vorys SS&P LLP -52 E Gay -Bx1008
-Columbus 43216 Fx:464-6350

(614) 221-3151 ..**Cincione**, Matthew P '85 %Butler C&D -50 W Broad -Ste 700
-Columbus 43215

(330) 562-4862 ..**Cindric**, Michael J '97 -Bx357 -Aurora 44202

(440) 333-5700 ..**Ciocco**, Mary B '94 (M Ciocco & Assoc,LLC) -22255 Ctr Ridge Rd
-Ste 106 -Rocky River 44116

Ciocia, James A '71 -5277 Graham Dr -Lyndhurst 44124

(513) 362-8700 ..**Cioffi**, Michael A '03 %Blank R -201 E 5th -Ste 1700
-Cincinnati 45202 Fx:362-8787

(513) 362-8700 ..**Cioffi**, Michael L '79 (Blank R) -201 E 5th -Ste 1700
-Cincinnati 45202 Fx:362-8787

(330) 864-7285 ..**Ciotola**, Janet M '89 -612 Deering Dr -Akron 44313

(330) 533-8885 ..**Ciotola**, Robert A '77 (R Ciotola Co,LPA)
-4590 Boardman Canfld Rd -Canfield 44406

(216) 222-8441 ..**Cipiti**, Anthony Jr. '01 Natl City Corp -1300 E 9th
-Cleveland 44114

(216) 622-8200 ..**Cipolla**, John S '89 (Calfee H&G LLP) -800 Superior Av -Ste 1400
-Cleveland 44114 Fx:241-0816

(440) 974-0505 ..**Cipollo**, Todd D '98 (TD Cipollo Co,LPA) -6990 Lindsay Dr -Ste 7
-Mentor 44060

(202) 879-1689 ..**Cipullo**, Daniel W '84 DC-Superior Ct -500 Indna Av -Rm 4016
-Washington, DC 20001

(614) 464-6400 ..**Ciriaco**, Anthony C '83 (Vorys SS&P LLP) -52 E Gay -Bx1008
-Columbus 43216 Fx:464-6350

Cirigliano, Joseph E '52 -140 Windbrook Dr -Elyria 44035

(440) 942-1034 ..**Cisan**, Heidi M '89 (Thrasher D&D,LPA) -100 7th Av -Ste 150
-Chardon 44024 Fx:285-9423

(513) 946-3580 ..**Cissell**, James C '66 Hamilton Cnty Probate Ct -230 E 9th -10th Fl
-Cincinnati 45202 Fx:946-3581

(440) 835-6603 ..**Ciszczon**, William J '83 United Cnsmr Finl Srvcs -865 Bassett Rd
-Westlake 44145

(216) 931-6000 ..**Citeroni**, Maria A '01 %Ulmer & B LLP -1300 E 9th
-Ste 900 Penton Media Bldg -Cleveland 44114 Fx:931-6001

(330) 643-3100 ..**Citrino**, Diane E '94 OH Civil Rghts Cmmssn -161 S High -Ste 205
-Akron 44308

(440) 884-2036 ..**Ciulla**, Joseph F '65 -6364 Pearl Rd -Cleveland 44130

Ciupak, Scott P '03 -382 Arbor Ct -Medina 44256

(216) 363-4500 ..**Clady**, Susan E '96 %Benesch FC&A LLP -200 Pub Sq -Ste 2300
-Cleveland 44114 Fx:363-4588

(440) 483-2373 ..**Clair**, Eugene E III '94 Philips Medical Sys,Inc -595 Miner Rd
-Cleveland 44143

(419) 842-0313 ..**Clair**, Mark D '97 -7135 W Sylvania Av -Ste 2B -Sylvania 43560
Fx:842-1539

(440) 942-6675 ..**Clair**, Mary J '77 -4132 Erie -Ste 202 -Willoughby 44094

Claire, Grace '02 -Bx1711 -Dayton 45401

(513) 232-1800 ..**Clancey**, Michael E '88 -7200 Paddison Rd -Cincinnati 45230

(614) 526-1013 ..**Clancey**, Michael T '96 HBD Ind,Inc -5200 Uppr Metro Pl -Ste 110
-Dublin 43017

(216) 368-6280 ..**Clancy**, Daniel T '62 Case Wstrn Reserve Univ -10900 Euclid Av
-D54425D -Cleveland 44106

(216) 443-7800 ..**Clancy**, Maureen E '91 Cuyahoga Cnty Pros -1200 Ontario -8th Fl
-Cleveland 44113 Fx:698-2270

(440) 354-2600 ..**Clancy**, Timothy G '88 Steris Corp -5960 Heisley Rd
-Mentor 44060

(614) 837-1029 ..**Clapham**, Edward Geoffrey '63 -8575 Wnchstr Rd NW
-Carroll 43112

(216) 861-1400 ..**Clapp**, Jane E '91 %RJ Clapp & Assoc Co,LPA -1375 E 9th
-One Cleve Ctr #2420 -Cleveland 44114 Fx:861-1401

(216) 861-1400 ..**Clapp**, Robert Jack '90 (RJ Clapp & Assoc Co,LPA) -1375 E 9th
-One Cleve Ctr #2420 -Cleveland 44114 Fx:861-1401

(440) 350-3200 ..**Clapp**, Vanessa R '92 Lake Cnty Pub Def -125 E Erie
-Painesville 44077

(614) 469-2999 ..**Clark**, Alison M '99 Fed Pub Def -10 W Broad -Ste 1020
-Columbus 43215

(614) 224-3838 ..**Clark**, Allison A '04 P Fulton & Assoc -89 E Nationwide Blvd
-Ste 300 -Columbus 43215 Fx:224-3933

(330) 220-9170 ..**Clark**, Amy L '92 -51 Clearwtr Dr -Brunswick 44212

(937) 335-5658 ..**Clark,** Christopher D '95 %Lopez S&P Co,LPA -18 E Water
-Troy 45373 **Fx:**339-6446
Clark, Christopher J '04 -(Address Unavailable)

(419) 524-6011 ..**Clark,** Christopher S '91 %Calhoun KH&C Co,LPA -6 W 3rd
-Ste 200 -Bx268 -Mansfield 44901 **Fx:**526-1431

(330) 868-4210 ..**Clark Clark & Chaddock** -201 N Market -Minerva 44657

(513) 381-2011 ..**Clark,** Craig S '63 %Hammond Law Grp,LLC -441 Vine
-3311 Carew Twr -Cincinnati 45202 **Fx:**381-2227

(614) 365-2700 ..**Clark,** D Lewis Jr. '90 (Squire S&D LLP) -41 S High
-1300 Huntngtn Ctr -Columbus 43215 **Fx:**365-2499

(440) 995-5100 ..**Clark,** Daniel J '85 Evergreen/UNI -6140 Parkland Blvd
-Mayfield Heights 44124

(614) 464-6400 ..**Clark,** Daniel J '02 %Vorys SS&P LLP -52 E Gay -Bx1008
-Columbus 43216 **Fx:**464-6350

(419) 241-1200 ..**Clark,** E Sharon '01 Cooper & W,LPA -900 Adams -Toledo 43624
Fx:242-5675

(419) 691-5745 ..**Clark,** Edward V '67 -617 Miami -Toledo 43605

(513) 352-6700 ..**Clark,** Eric S '99 %Thompson H LLP -312 Walnut -14th Fl
-Cincinnati 45202 **Fx:**241-4771

(330) 668-2464 ..**Clark,** George A '66 (G Clark & Assoc)
-875 N Cleveland-Massillon Rd -Akron 44333

(513) 574-9713 ..**Clark,** George W '71 -4343 Marcrest Dr -Cincinnati 45211

(513) 425-6609 ..**Clark,** Gregory M '86 12th Dist Ct of Appls -1001 Reinartz Blvd
-Middletown 45042 **Fx:**425-8751

(314) 877-7106 ..**Clark,** J S '89 SrCnsl Ralcorp Hldngs,Inc -Bx618 -St. Louis,
MO 63188

(937) 225-9947 ..**Clark,** Jan A '75 Dayton Fndtn -2300 Kettering Twr -Dayton 45423

(216) 689-4118 ..**Clark,** Janet C '94 Key Corp Mgmt Co -127 Pub Sq -2nd Fl
-Cleveland 44114

(614) 644-0729 ..**Clark,** Jeffery W '81 Atty Gen -30 E Broad -Columbus 43215
Fx:728-7582
Clark, Jill G '79 -3119 Courtland Blvd -Shaker Heights 44122

(330) 497-0700 ..**Clark,** John D '97 (Krugliak WG&D Co,LPA) -4775 Munson NW
-Bx36963 -Canton 44735 **Fx:**497-4020

(740) 384-5641 ..**Clark,** John K Jr. '90 -213 E Bway -Wellston 45692

(330) 971-8273 ..**Clark,** John W '90 Cuyahoga Falls Mun Ct -2310 2nd
-Cuyahoga Falls 44221

(740) 653-6464 ..**Clark,** Jonathan C '02 %Dagger JMO&H -144 E Main -Bx667
-Lancaster 43130 **Fx:**653-8522

(440) 930-4001 ..**Clark,** Jonathan D '93 Baumgartner & O
-5455 Detroit Rd (Rte 254) -Sheffield Village 44054 **Fx:**934-7205

(440) 967-0759 ..**Clark,** Jonathan F '84 -5551 Lbrty Av -Bx433 -Vermilion 44089

(740) 687-7044 ..**Clark,** Joseph T '66 Fairfield Cnty Common Pleas Ct -224 E Main
-Lancaster 43130

(513) 622-3949 ..**Clark,** Karen F '87 Procter & Gamble -8700 Mason-Mntgmry Rd
-Cincinnati 45040 **Fx:**622-3300

(937) 456-9999 ..**Clark,** Karen M '90 -101 N Barron -Ste 204 -Eaton 45320

(216) 566-9700 ..**Clark,** Kenneth A '86 (Rankin HP&C,LLP) -925 Euclid Av -Ste 700
-Cleveland 44115 **Fx:**566-9711

(419) 422-2121 ..**Clark,** Kristi L '96 Marathon Ashland Petroleum LLC -539 S Main
-Findlay 45840

(513) 721-3236 ..**Clark,** Lisa M '97 %Weisser & W -1014 Vine -Ste 1650
-Cincinnati 45202

(740) 477-2173 ..**Clark,** Lori D '94 %Hill Law Ofc -408 E Main -Circleville 43113

(330) 868-4210 ..**Clark,** Luther J Jr. '56 (Clark C&C) -201 N Market -Minerva 44657

(330) 376-6191 ..**Clark,** Lynn M '90 Fair Housing Contact Srvc -333 S Main -Ste 300
-Akron 44308

(330) 925-9010 ..**Clark,** Mark C '74 (Flynn & C) -99 E Ohio Av -Bx116
-Rittman 44270

(614) 757-5000 ..**Clark,** Marla D '96 %Cardinal Hlth -7000 Cardinal Pl -Dublin 43017
Clark, Marshall L '61 -6121 N Golden Eagle Dr -Tucson, AZ 85750

(419) 872-1290 ..**Clark,** Mary C '93 -444 E Front -Perrysburg 43551

(513) 721-1975 ..**Clark,** Megan E '95 Freking & B -215 E 9th -5th Fl
-Cincinnati 45202 **Fx:**651-2570

(419) 242-3900 ..**Clark,** Michael Leo '89 Cincinnati Ins Co -300 Mad Av -Ste 1406
-Toledo 43604

(419) 692-9055 ..**Clark,** Nicholas J '89 (Shenk CW&C,LLC) -214 W 2nd -Bx304
-Delphos 45833

(419) 213-3328 ..**Clark,** Patricia J '82 Cnty Chldrns Srvcs Brd -705 Adams
-Toledo 43624

(614) 469-1400 ..**Clark Perdue Roberts & Scott Co,LPA** -471 E Broad -Ste 1400
-Columbus 43215 **Fx:**469-0900

(216) 522-0183 ..**Clark,** Pinkie L '92 %DS Nance,LPA -11811 Shaker Blvd -Ste 420
-Cleveland 44120

(614) 466-5988 ..**Clark,** Ralph D '89 Legis Srvc Commssn -77 S High
-Columbus 43215

(513) 587-2887 ..**Clark,** Ravert J '89 -114 E 8th -Ste 400 -Cincinnati 45202

(614) 538-5381 ..**Clark,** Richard M '92 (Clark & H) -2000 Bethel Rd -Columbus
43220

(330) 868-4210 ..**Clark,** Robert A '91 (Clark C&C) -201 N Market -Minerva 44657

(330) 864-5550 ..**Clark,** Robert J '96 %Hahn L&P LLP -One GOJO Plz -Ste 300
-Akron 44311 **Fx:**864-7986

(937) 294-6551 ..**Clark,** Robert L '01 -3033 S Kettering Blvd -Ste 110 -Dayton 45439

(419) 213-4700 ..**Clark,** Robert L Jr. '80 %Lucas Cnty Pros -Adams & Erie
-Lucas Cnty Cthse -Toledo 43624

(740) 354-3214 ..**Clark,** Roger L '68 (Kimble & C) -622 6th -Portsmouth 45662

(419) 841-4672 ..**Clark,** Roger N '67 -2451 Cherry Hill Rd -Toledo 43615

(614) 340-3895 ..**Clark,** Sheila A '80 (Clark & L,LLC) -1500 W 3rd Av -Ste 310
-Bx12310 -Columbus 43212

(614) 221-2838 ..**Clark,** Shelli T '00 %Taft S&H LLP -21 E State -12th Fl
-Columbus 43215 **Fx:**221-2007

(740) 349-6181 ..**Clark,** Stephanie A '96 Licking Cnty Cmmn Pleas Ct -Cnty Ct Hse
-2nd Fl -Newark 43055

(213) 624-2500 ..**Clark,** Terence J '69 (Squire S&D) -801 S Figueroa -14th Fl
-Los Angeles, CA 90017

(740) 363-9412 ..**Clark,** Thomas C '60 -61 N Sandusky -Delaware 43015

(740) 363-9412 ..**Clark,** Thomas C II '91 -61 N Sandusky -Delaware 43015

(513) 241-6998 ..**Clark,** Thomas H '49 -537 E Pete Rose Way -Ste 450
-Cincinnati 45202

(614) 875-4895 ..**Clark,** Thomas R '75 -3083 Columbus -Grove City 43123

(513) 762-6200 ..**Clark,** Tiffany Reece '02 %Ulmer & B LLP -600 Vine -Ste 2800
-Cincinnati 45202 **Fx:**762-6245

(614) 224-2125 ..**Clark,** Toki M '89 -233 S High -3rd Fl -Columbus 43215

(614) 228-1144 ..**Clark,** Trevor M '02 %P Collins & Assoc -21 E State -Ste 1130
-Columbus 43215
Clark, Victoria R '03 -(Address Unavailable)

(216) 622-8200 ..**Clark,** Wade D '80 Calfee H&G LLP -800 Superior Av -Ste 1400
-Cleveland 44114 **Fx:**241-0816

(614) 221-3911 ..**Clark,** William A '81 -600 S High -Ste 202 -Columbus 43215

(419) 423-0242 ..**Clark,** William E '68 (Drake PK&C) -301 S Main -Ste 3
-Findlay 45840 **Fx:**423-0186

(614) 766-8475 ..**Clark,** William J '77 (Clark Legal Assoc Co,LPA) -78 E Scioto Dr
-Powell 43065 **Fx:**766-8465

(614) 459-1012 ..**Clark,** William L '60 -1167 Millcreek Ln -Columbus 43220
Clarke, Arthur F '74 -1504 Westford Cir -Westlake 44145

(216) 479-8500 ..**Clarke,** Charles F '46 (Squire S&D LLP) -127 Pub Sq
-4900 Key Twr -Cleveland 44114 **Fx:**479-8780

(513) 651-6800 ..**Clarke,** Deanne E '00 %Frost BT LLC -201 E 5th -2200 PNC Ctr
-Cincinnati 45202 **Fx:**651-6981

(513) 352-6534 ..**Clarke,** Jeffrey M '99 %Thompson H LLP -312 Walnut -14th Fl
-Cincinnati 45202 **Fx:**241-4771

(513) 684-3650 ..**Clarke,** Naima R '95 NLRB -550 W Main -Rm 3003
-Cincinnati 45202
Clarke, Timothy P '93 -1504 Westford Cir -#211 -Westlake 44145
Clarke, Tricia L '04 -(Address Unavailable)

(419) 213-4755 ..**Clarkson,** Karin L '04 6th Dist Ct of Appeals -1 Const Av
-Toledo 43624

(513) 474-1508 ..**Clary,** Daniel K '84 -1446 Sigma Cir -Cincinnati 45255

(614) 236-6685 ..**Clary,** Lori A '96 Capital Univ Law Schl -303 E Broad
-Academic Support -Columbus 43215

(614) 227-2000 ..**Clary,** Mary Beth M '83 (Porter WM&A LLP) -41 S High
-Columbus 43215 **Fx:**227-2100

(614) 463-4201 ..**Clary,** Wendy K '04 %Littler M,PC -21 E State -Ste 1600
-Columbus 43215 **Fx:**221-3301

(419) 627-0414 ..**Claus,** David J '99 Buckingham LM&Z Co,LPA -414 Wayne
-Bx929 -Sandusky 44870 **Fx:**627-0009

(513) 723-2208 ..**Clausen,** Cynthia R '02 %Weltman W&R Co,LPA -525 Vine
-Ste 800 -Cincinnati 45202 **Fx:**723-2239

(216) 443-7800 ..**Claussen,** Scott D '01 Cuyahoga Cnty Pros -1200 Ontario -8th Fl
-Cleveland 44113 **Fx:**698-2270

(937) 222-2500 ..**Clawson,** Carissa E '03 %Sebaly S&D -1900 Kettering Twr
-Dayton 45423 **Fx:**222-6554
Clawson, Sandra A '86 -11000 Plsnt Vlly Rd -Cleveland 44130

(513) 626-0575 ..**Clay,** Cynthia L '02 Procter & Gamble Co
-11511 Reed Hartman Hwy -HB3N14 -Cincinnati 45241

(216) 781-1212 ..**Clay,** Darrell A '97 %Walter & H LLP -1301 E 9th -Ste 3500
-Cleveland 44114 **Fx:**575-0911

(216) 443-5809 ..**Clay,** Pamela S '96 Cuyahoga Cnty Pros -1910 Carnegie Av
-Whitlatch Bldg -Cleveland 44115 **Fx:**443-5815

(202) 327-5760 ..**Claybon,** Marc A '97 Ernst & Young -1225 Conn Av NW
-Washington, DC 20036

(513) 771-8500 ..**Claybon,** Stanley L '71 -11499 Lippelman Rd -Cincinnati 45246

(216) 642-0323 ..**Clayborne,** Sherrie D '96 %Britton SP&K Co,LPA
-4700 Rockside Rd -Ste 540 Summit One -Cleveland 44131
Fx:642-0747

(513) 381-3525 ..**Claycomb,** Gregory J '89 Kircher R&W -1014 Vine -Ste 2520
-Cincinnati 45202

(419) 447-5255 ..**Claydon,** Julianne '00 -107 E Perry -Bx946 -Tiffin 44883

(513) 421-5999 ..**Claymon,** Allan W '64 -914 Main -Ste 500 -Cincinnati 45202

(937) 224-1427 ..**Claypool,** Charles A '73 -130 W 2nd -Ste 400 -Dayton 45402

(440) 871-1122 ..**Claypool,** Oliver H Jr. '74 -2500 Bradley Rd -Westlake 44145

(937) 224-3740 ..**Claypoole,** Erin L '97 Montgomery Cnty Pros -301 W 3rd -Bx972
-Dayton 45422 **Fx:**225-3470

(703) 547-2480 ..**Clayton,** Denise C '89 XO Comm,Inc -11111 Sunset Hills Rd
-Reston, VA 20190

(614) 898-8903 ..**Clayton,** Kelly L '91 Mt Camel Hlth -500 S Cleveland Av
-Ste 208 W -Westerville 43081

(937) 904-2176 ..**Clayton,** Robert B '71 JAG -5135 Pearson Rd
-Wright Patterson AFB 45433

(386) 267-1665 ..**Clayton,** Thomas M '81 Oceans Resorts -600 N Atl Av
-Daytona Beach, FL 32118

(513) 684-8042 ..**Claytor,** William G '76 US Postal Srvc -895 Central Av -Ste 400
-Cincinnati 45202

(614) 475-4598 ..**Cleamons,** Geneva G '78 -3067 Oak Sprngs -Columbus 43219
Clear, Rory T '78 -7265 Kenwood Rd -Cincinnati 45236

(216) 522-4856 ..**Cleary,** Amy B '97 Fed Pub Def -1660 W 2nd -Ste 750
-Cleveland 44113

(216) 443-7800 ..**Cleary,** Daniel A '02 Cuyahoga Cnty Pros -1200 Ontario -8th Fl
-Cleveland 44113 **Fx:**698-2270

(440) 331-8844 ..**Cleary,** Edward P '77 -20800 Ctr Ridge Rd -Ste 211
-Rocky River 44116 **Fx:**331-8322

(614) 487-8210 ..**Cleary,** Lora H '91 -1500 W 3rd Av -Ste 127 -Columbus 43212

(216) 642-7878 ..**Cleary,** Michael F '84 Vantage Fincl Grp -6200 Rockside Rd
-Ste 100 -Cleveland 44131

(614) 237-7440 ..**Cleary,** Michael P '77 -2740 E Main -Bexley 43209

(216) 573-1776 ..**Cleary,** Timothy R '75 (Cleary & Assoc Co,LPA)
-6000 Lombardo Ctr Dr -Ste 635 -Independence 44131

(216) 222-9963 ..**Cleary,** Vicki M '86 Natl City Bank -1900 E 9th -Cleveland 44114

(330) 499-8899 ..**Cleaver,** Sandra W '88 (Simmons & C) -4690 Munson NW
-Canton 44718

(330) 673-8600 ..**Clegg,** C Bailey '76 B Clegg & Assoc -131 Columbus -Kent 44240
Fx:678-1984

(216) 447-6412 ..**Clegg,** Christopher R '88 Noveon, Inc -9911 Brecksvll Rd
-Brecksville 44141

(304) 455-1751 ..**Clegg,** Whitney G '95 Jackson & K -256 Russell Av -Drwr68
-New Martinsville, WV 26155

(330) 678-6030 ..**Clem,** Christopher '87 -Bx1366 -Stow 44224

(419) 782-6055 ..**Clemens Korhn Liming & Warncke, Ltd** -419 5th -Ste 2000
-Bx787 -Defiance 43512

(440) 365-1310 ..**Clemens,** Timothy J '98 Nationwide Ins Co -994 N Abbe Rd
-Elyria 44035

(248) 593-3019 ..**Clemens,** William J '74 Butzel L,PC -100 Blmfld Hills Pkwy
-Ste 200 -Bloomfield Hills, MI 48304 **Fx:**258-1439

(850) 644-9214 ..**Clement,** Annie '85 Florida State Univ -110 Tully Gymnasium
-Tallahassee, FL 32306

(419) 726-2645 .. **Clement,** John K Jr. '87 Bock Engineered Prdcts Inc
-3600 Summit -Bx5127 -Toledo 43611

(330) 755-1437 .. **Clemente,** Michael C '53 (Clements & W Co,LPA) -700 5th
-Struthers 44471

(216) 621-7227 .. **Clements,** Arthur L III '87 OfCnsl Nicola G&C,LLC -25 W Prospect
Av -Republic Bldg Ste 1400 -Cleveland 44115 **Fx:**621-3999

(513) 721-6500 .. **Clements Mahin & Cohen** -35 E 7th -Ste 710 -Cincinnati 45202
Fx:763-6415

(513) 721-6500 .. **Clements,** William E '79 (Clements M&C) -35 E 7th -Ste 710
-Cincinnati 45202 **Fx:**763-6415

(513) 829-6700 .. **Clemmons,** John H '76 (Millikin & F) -530 Wessel Dr -Ste 2A
-Fairfield 45014 **Fx:**829-0258

(513) 421-6630 .. **Clemons,** Michelle L '97 %Lindhorst & D Co,LPA -312 Walnut
-Ste 2300 -Cincinnati 45202

(605) 371-0998 .. **Clendenon,** Donn A '79 -2709 S Sandstone Cir
-Sioux Falls, SD 57103

(216) 443-7875 .. **Cleveland,** Phyllis E '89 Cuyahoga Cnty Pros -1200 Ontario -8th Fl
-Cleveland 44113 **Fx:**698-2270

(614) 466-4605 .. **Clevenger,** Bonnie L '81 OH Dept Job & Fam Srvcs -30 E Broad
-32nd Fl -Columbus 43266

(216) 228-7250 .. **Clevenger,** Daniel E II '98 %J Saurman -14650 Detroit Av
-Ste 450 -Lakewood 44107

(440) 322-4548 .. **Clevenger,** Sherman G '70 %DC George -105 Court -Rm 715
-Elyria 44035

Clevenger, Tehra Newman '04 -(Address Unavailable)

(513) 531-1777 .. **Cleves,** Cynthia M '85 Interlube Corp -4646 Baker Av
-Cincinnati 45212

(859) 341-1881 .. **Cleves,** Joseph A Jr. '78 (Deters B&L,PSC) -2701 Turkeyfoot Rd
-207 Thomas More Pkwy -Crestview Hills, KY 41017 **Fx:**341-1469

(513) 333-4054 .. **Cliffe,** David W '92 %Weltman W&R Co,LPA -525 Vine -Ste 800
-Cincinnati 45202 **Fx:**723-2239

(614) 222-3152 .. **Cliffel,** Albert P III '90 Ernst & Young LLP -41 S High -Ste 100
-Columbus 43215 **Fx:**229-5127

(513) 723-8400 .. **Cliffel,** Susan K '90 %Coley & Assoc -9334 Union Centre Blvd
-Ste 200 -West Chester 45069

(614) 224-0933 .. **Clifford,** Damion M '04 %Frost & M Co,LPA -400 S 5th -Ste 301
-Columbus 43215

(216) 664-4955 .. **Clifford,** Gregory F '81 Cleveland Mun Ct -1200 Ontario -Bx94894
-Cleveland 44101 **Fx:**664-4949

(937) 443-6829 .. **Clifford,** Joanne E '01 %Thompson H LLP -2000 Cthse Plz NE
-Bx8801 -Dayton 45401 **Fx:**443-6635

(216) 241-0022 .. **Clifford,** Lisa A '01 Hyatt Leg Plans,Inc -1111 Superior Av
-Cleveland 44114

(614) 644-7250 .. **Clifford,** Mary-Kathleen '99 Atty Gen -30 E Broad -Columbus
43215 **Fx:**644-7634

(419) 660-8167 .. **Clifford,** Timothy D '01 -Bx228 -Norwalk 44857

(216) 621-8484 .. **Climaco,** John R '67 (Climaco LPW&G Co,LPA) -1228 Euclid Av
-Ste 900 Halle Bldg -Cleveland 44115 **Fx:**771-1632

(216) 621-8484 .. **Climaco Lefkowitz Peca Wilcox & Garofoli Co, LPA** -1228
Euclid Av -Ste 900 Halle Bldg -Cleveland 44115 **Fx:**771-1632

(440) 893-9588 .. **Climaco,** Michael L '73 -100 Stonewood Dr -Moreland Hills 44022

(440) 248-7906 .. **Climer,** James A '80 (Mazanec R&R Co,LPA) -34305 Solon Rd
-Ste 100 -Cleveland 44139 **Fx:**248-8861

(937) 498-4981 .. **Clinard,** Nathan '94 Shelby Cnty CSEA -227 S Ohio Av
-Sidney 45365

(330) 656-3633 .. **Cline,** Carl L '94 Vestax Sec Corp -1931 Georgtwn Rd
-Hudson 44236

(614) 764-0681 .. **Cline,** Christopher T '75 Blaugrund H&M,Inc -5455 Rings Rd
-Ste 300 -Dublin 43017 **Fx:**764-0774

(513) 723-3463 .. **Cline,** Claudia L '87 Convergys Corp -201 E 4th -Cincinnati 45202

(419) 321-6444 .. **Cline Cook & Weisenburger Co,LPA** -300 Mad Av -Ste 1100
-Toledo 43604 **Fx:**321-6430

(216) 481-8100 .. **Cline,** Guy G Jr. '78 Lincoln Electric Co -22801 St Clair Av
-Cleveland 44117

(937) 222-5552 .. **Cline,** James T Jr. '70 (Cline & C) -32 N Main -934 -Dayton 45402
Fx:222-5554

(216) 447-1551 .. **Cline,** Jerry P '02 %Ross B&S Co LPA -6000 Freedom Square Dr
-Ste 540 -Cleveland 44131 **Fx:**447-1554

(614) 752-4650 .. **Cline,** Jo E '94 OH Supreme Ct -30 E Broad -Columbus 43215

(614) 464-6400 .. **Cline,** Michael A '79 (Vorys SS&P LLP) -52 E Gay -Bx1008
-Columbus 43216 **Fx:**464-6350

(614) 224-4114 .. **Cline,** Richard A '81 OfCnsl Mitchell AC&B Co,LPA -580 S High
-Ste 200 -Columbus 43215 **Fx:**224-3804

(216) 348-5400 .. **Cline,** Richard W '97 %McDonald H Co,LPA -600 Superior Av E
-Ste 2100 -Cleveland 44114 **Fx:**348-5474

(330) 455-0173 .. **Cline,** William S '78 (Day KRW&R,Ltd) -200 Market Av N -Ste 300
-Bx24213 -Canton 44701 **Fx:**455-2633

(740) 363-1925 .. **Clinger,** Terrie L '86 -103 N Union -Ste D -Delaware 43015

(614) 878-0287 .. **Clinkscale,** Debra L '87 -5832 Wellbird Dr -Galloway 43119
Fx:878-0287

(614) 752-9271 .. **Clodfelder,** Wiley H '83 Dept Admin Srvcs -30 E Broad
-Columbus 43215

(513) 621-5252 .. **Clodfelter,** David C '92 (Clodfelter & G) -36 E 4th -Ste 1208
-Cincinnati 45202

(513) 621-5252 .. **Clodfelter & Gutzwiller** -36 E 4th -Ste 1208 -Cincinnati 45202

(330) 742-7031 .. **Cloonan,** Terrence F '81 Sky Trust,NA -Trust Dept -Bx479
-Youngstown 44501

(216) 689-4117 .. **Cloonan,** William P '92 KeyBank NA -127 Pub Sq
-Cleveland 44114

(614) 461-4455 .. **Cloppert,** Frederick G Jr. '72 (Cloppert LS&W) -225 E Broad
-Columbus 43215 **Fx:**461-0072

(614) 461-4455 .. **Cloppert Latanick Sauter & Washburn** -225 E Broad
-Columbus 43215 **Fx:**461-0072

(513) 984-2640 .. **Clore,** W Edward '96 Cnsl UAW-Ford Legal Srvcs
-4010 Exec Park Dr -Ste 225 -Cincinnati 45241 **Fx:**984-1665

(330) 788-3971 .. **Close,** Arthur L Jr. '58 -4859 Oak Knoll Dr -Youngstown 44514

(614) 221-5216 .. **Close,** Michael L '75 (Wiles BB&B Co,LPA) -300 Spruce -1st Fl
-Columbus 43215 **Fx:**221-5692

(614) 529-2900 .. **Close,** Stephen P '79 Coinmach Corp -3021 Intl -Columbus 43228

(212) 326-3939 .. **Clossey,** David F III '68 (Jones DR&P) -222 E 41st
-New York, NY 10017 **Fx:**326-3428

Cloud, Claire A '03 -(Address Unavailable)

(614) 436-3211 .. **Cloud,** Clifford R '61 (Cloud & O) -5354 N High -Ste 3D
-Columbus 43214

(937) 426-3230 .. **Cloud,** Darrel G '88 -3973 Dayton-Xenia Rd -Beavercreek 45432

Cloud, Joel B '03 -(Address Unavailable)

(937) 223-8171 .. **Cloud,** John M '76 (Rogers & G) -2160 Kettering Twr
-Dayton 45423 **Fx:**223-1649

(614) 436-3211 .. **Cloud & Owen** -5354 N High -Ste 3D -Columbus 43214

(513) 831-8700 .. **Cloud,** Robert L '76 -2646 Blackhoof Trl -Milford 45150

(216) 443-7800 .. **Clough,** John A III '77 Cuyahoga Cnty Pros -1200 Ontario -8th Fl
-Cleveland 44113 **Fx:**698-2270

(937) 223-1130 .. **Clough,** John E '94 Pickrel S&E -40 N Main -2700 Kettering Twr
-Dayton 45423 **Fx:**223-0339

Clough-Brewerton, Carroll '03 -521 2nd -Traverse City, MI 49684

Clous, Aimee A '99 -(Address Unavailable)

(614) 464-1877 .. **Clouse,** Gerard J '84 (Sowald S&C) -400 S 5th -Ste 101
-Columbus 43215

(614) 485-1800 .. **Clouse,** Karen L '86 %Arnold T&W -2075 Marble Cliff Ofc Park
-Columbus 43215 **Fx:**485-1944

(614) 292-7745 .. **Clovis,** Albert Lee '62 OSU Moritz Cllg of Law -55 W 12th Av
-Columbus 43210 **Fx:**292-1383

(614) 466-5394 .. **Clovis,** Charles B '00 Pub Def -8 E Long -Columbus 43215

(740) 345-3431 .. **Clovis,** Siobhan R '98 %Reese PD&M,PLL -36 N 2nd -Bx919
-Newark 43058 **Fx:**349-5116

(202) 879-5173 .. **Clubok,** Andrew B '94 (Kirkland & E) -655 15th NW -Ste 1200
-Washington, DC 20005 **Fx:**879-5200

Clucas, Amber L '03 -(Address Unavailable)

(330) 374-0207 .. **Clum,** Ronald '03 -137 S Main -Ste 206 -Akron 44308

(330) 823-9142 .. **Clunk,** Dennis R '82 -2040 S Union Av -Alliance 44601

(330) 342-8203 .. **Clunk,** John D '82 J Clunk Co LPA -5061 Hudson Dr -Ste 400
-Hudson 44236 **Fx:**342-8205

(330) 887-6930 .. **Cluse,** Mark E '95 Westfield Grp -1 Park Cir -Bx5001
-Westfield Center 44251 **Fx:**887-2588

Clutter, Mary E '04 -(Address Unavailable)

(614) 752-8919 .. **Clyde,** Robert M Jr. '72 OH Leg Assistance Fdtn -42 E Gay
-Ste 900 -Columbus 43215

(614) 221-3318 .. **Clymer,** James G '74 (Agee CM&L) -89 E Nationwide Blvd
-Ste 200 -Columbus 43215

(614) 374-4997 .. **Clymer,** Tony A '91 -1420 Matthias Dr -Columbus 43224

(614) 253-8723 .. **Coady,** Michael F '82 Coady Construction Inc -1455 E 5th Av
-Columbus 43219

(614) 227-2000 .. **Coady,** Thomas C '64 (Porter WM&A LLP) -41 S High
-Columbus 43215 **Fx:**227-2100

(520) 228-4705 .. **Coakley,** Brett L '85 H Q IZ AF\JA -2915 S 12th Air Force Dr
-Ste 157 -Davis Monthan AFB, AZ 85707

(216) 687-1311 .. **Coakley,** George S '75 (Reminger & R) -101 Prospect Av W
-1400 Mdlnd Bldg -Cleveland 44115 **Fx:**687-1841

(216) 444-2200 .. **Coate,** Brian R '95 Cleveland Clinic Fndtn -9500 Euclid Av
-Cleveland 44195

(412) 374-4124 .. **Coates,** Frank R '71 Westinghouse Elec Co,LLC -Bx355
-Pittsburgh, PA 15230

(937) 586-4654 .. **Coates,** Joseph A '88 Cashland -36 W 3rd -Dayton 45402

(614) 228-6888 .. **Coates,** Kristen C '04 %Havens W LLC -141 E Town -Ste 200
-Columbus 43215 **Fx:**228-6878

(330) 971-8256 .. **Coates,** Lisa L '94 Mun Ct Judge -2310 2nd
-Cuyahoga Falls 44221

(330) 652-0190 .. **Coates,** Michael J Jr. '86 M Coates Cnstrctn Co Inc
-800 Summit Av -Niles 44446

(614) 221-2993 .. **Coatney,** Jennifer A '02 %DL Day,LPA -400 S 5th -Ste 300
-Columbus 43215

(937) 865-6800 .. **Coats,** Wanda P '80 Lexis/Nexis -Bx933 -Dayton 45401

(216) 621-5300 .. **Coaxum,** Edward C Jr. '71 (Buckingham D&B,LLP) -1375 E 9th
-Ste 1700 -Cleveland 44114 **Fx:**621-5440

(216) 621-0150 .. **Cobb,** Arthur L '77 (Hahn L&P LLP) -3300 BP Twr/200 Pub Sq
-Ste 3300 -Cleveland 44114 **Fx:**241-2824

(301) 585-9025 .. **Cobb,** Carolyn C '89 Cobb & Assoc -612 McNeill Rd -Silver
Spring, MD 20910

(614) 438-2648 .. **Cobb,** Craig S '82 -100 E Compus Vw Blvd -Ste 250
-Columbus 43235 **Fx:**438-2650

(313) 961-3433 .. **Cobb,** James C Jr. '79 (JC Cobb Jr,PC) -615 Griswold -Ste 1415
-Detroit, MI 48226

(614) 464-6400 .. **Cobb,** Tiffany Strelow '97 %Vorys SS&P LLP -52 E Gay -Bx1008
-Columbus 43216 **Fx:**464-6350

(513) 421-4020 .. **Cobey,** John G '69 (Cohen TK&S,LLC) -250 E 5th -Ste 1200
-Cincinnati 45202 **Fx:**241-4490

(419) 841-8584 .. **Coble,** John A '84 Albrechta & C -3230 Cntrl Pk W Dr -Ste 200
-Toledo 43617

(419) 841-8584 .. **Coble,** Richard A '69 (Albrechta & C) -3230 Cntrl Pk W Dr -Ste 200
-Toledo 43617

(216) 689-5436 .. **Coburn,** Howard E '84 KeyBank NA -127 Pub Sq -2nd Fl
-Cleveland 44114

Cocca, Caterina M '04 -(Address Unavailable)

(202) 349-0220 .. **Cocci,** Melissa '94 Stewart Title Grp -11 Dupont Cir NW -Ste 750
-Washington, DC 20036 **Fx:**349-0224

(330) 867-8422 .. **Cochran,** Charles C Jr. '90 -41 Merz Blvd -Fairlawn 44333

(317) 882-9543 .. **Cochran,** Charles W '85 -7548 Tarragon Pl
-Indianapolis, IN 46237

(216) 586-3939 .. **Cochran,** David B '96 OfCnsl Jones D -901 Lakeside Av
-Cleveland 44114 **Fx:**579-0212

(216) 751-5546 .. **Cochran,** Edward W '76 -20030 Marchmont Rd -Shaker Heights
44122

(330) 626-5600 .. **Cochran,** George W Jr. '79 (Cochran & C) -9170 State Route 43
-Streetsboro 44241

(216) 443-7800 .. **Cochran,** James C '78 Cuyahoga Cnty Pros -1200 Ontario -8th Fl
-Cleveland 44113 **Fx:**698-2270

(740) 254-9429 .. **Cochran,** Michael A '75 -116 N Cherry -Bx790
-Gnadenhutten 44629

(614) 863-0045 .. **Cochran,** Michael H '71 -5969 Ar Lvngstn Av -Columbus 43232

(941) 366-7550 .. **Cochran,** Michael W '02 %Nelson H -2070 Ringling Blvd
-Sarasota, FL 34230 **Fx:**955-3708

(781) 237-4400 .. **Cochran,** Molly '85 %Seegel Lipshutz & W,PC -60 William
-Ste 200 -Wellesley, MA 02481 **Fx:**235-2333

(614) 469-3292 .. **Cochran,** Philip B '81 Thompson H LLP -10 W Broad -Ste 700
-Columbus 43215 **Fx:**469-3361

(937) 229-2332 .. **Cochran**, Rebecca A '92 Univ of Dayton Schl of Law
-300 Cllg Park -Dayton 45469
(614) 462-2248 .. **Cochran**, Robert J '91 OfCnsl Schottenstein Z&D -250 West
-Bx165020 -Columbus 43216 **Fx**:462-5135
(330) 743-6300 .. **Cochran**, Scott R '95 (Atway & C,LLC) -19 E Front -Ste 1
-Youngstown 44503
(614) 863-4775 .. **Cochran**, Shirley A '79 -2897 Lbrty Bell Ln -Reynoldsburg 43068
(937) 667-6684 .. **Cochran**, Thomas R '88 (T Cochran Co LPA) -17 W Main
-Tipp City 45371 **Fx**:667-4629
(330) 477-2539 .. **Cochrane**, William Jr. '50 -237 Grandvw Av NW -Canton 44708
(216) 381-8800 .. **Cocirteu**, Cosmin '03 (Cocirteu H&S,LLC) -4040 Mayfld Rd
-Cleveland 44121
Cockerill, Curtis A '93 -Bx2738 -Columbus 43216
(419) 522-8844 .. **Cockley**, Mark W '92 M Cockley Co,LPA -16 W 2nd
-Mansfield 44902
(419) 522-2001 .. **Cockley**, Stephen '76 -13 Park Av W -609 Barrington One
-Mansfield 44902
(614) 221-7025 .. **Cockrum**, William G '75 -400 S 5th -Ste 202 -Columbus 43215
(330) 821-3293 .. **Coco**, Anthony J '56 -114 E Bway -Alliance 44601
(614) 464-2572 .. **Coco**, Mark S '77 (Harris MB&C,PLL) -37 W Broad -9th Fl
-Columbus 43215 **Fx**:464-2245
(419) 241-5506 .. **Cocoves**, Spiros P '85 -610 Adams -2nd Fl -Toledo 43604
(614) 221-8448 .. **Cocroft**, Kimberly '00 %Buckingham D&B,LLP
-191 W Nationwide Blvd -Ste 300 -Bx151120 -Columbus 43215
Fx:221-8590
(216) 687-9318 .. **Codinach**, Maria J '76 Cleveland State Univ -2121 Euclid Av
-KB 1401 -Cleveland 44115 **Fx**:687-9274
(330) 535-4191 .. **Codrea**, John Eli '75 Cmmnty Lgl Aid Srvcs,Inc -265 S Main -3rd Fl
-Akron 44308 **Fx**:535-0728
(330) 376-6766 .. **Cody**, Daniel S '90 M Djordjevic Co,LPA -17 S Main -Ste 201
-Akron 44308 **Fx**:376-7344
(419) 352-4621 .. **Cody**, David A '81 Maurer N&B -224 E Wooster -Bowling
Green 43402
(330) 796-7095 .. **Cody**, Nancy C '81 Goodyear -1144 E Market -Akron 44316
(614) 466-8669 .. **Cody**, Robert M '82 OH Sup Crt -30 E Broad -35th Fl
-Columbus 43266
(907) 276-6173 .. **Coe**, Charles W '76 -805 W 3nd Av -#100 -Anchorage, AK 99501
(419) 893-4836 .. **Coe**, Helen M '73 -302 Conant -Maumee 43537
Coe, Stefanie L '04 -(Address Unavailable)
(440) 892-1580 .. **Coen**, Beverly J '77 Nordson Corp -28601 Clemens Rd -Westlake
44145 **Fx**:414-5611
(740) 653-7825 .. **Coen Wexler & Wentz** -323 E Main -Bx1028 -Lancaster 43130
Fx:653-3719
(937) 293-2200 .. **Coen**, William R '53 WR Coen Co, LPA -2323 W Schantz Av
-Kettering 45409 **Fx**:293-2224
(248) 596-3500 .. **Coerdt**, Thomas R '85 Waste Mngmnt,Inc -48797 Alpha Dr
-Ste 100 -Wixom, MI 48393
(513) 852-8084 .. **Coes**, Kendal M '94 Hamilton Cnty Dom Rltns Ct -800 Bway
-Rm 315 -Cincinnati 45202
(330) 492-8717 .. **Coey**, G Brenda '03 %Buckingham D&B,LLP -4518 Fulton Dr NW
-Bx35548 -Canton 44735 **Fx**:492-9625
(440) 930-4001 .. **Coey**, Laurent E '73 OfCnsl Baumgartner & O
-5455 Detroit Rd (Rte 254) -Sheffield Village 44054 **Fx**:934-7205
(513) 741-9800 .. **Coffaro**, Joseph M '69 -3537 Epley Ln -Cincinnati 45247
(513) 569-6331 .. **Coffaro**, Katrina L '95 TriHealth,Inc -619 Oak -Cincinnati 45206
(513) 579-6400 .. **Coffaro**, Steve C '95 (Keating M&K PLL) -1 E 4th
-1400 Provident Twr -Cincinnati 45202 **Fx**:579-6457
(330) 253-8877 .. **Coffee**, Thomas P '87 -50 S Main -Ste 502 -Akron 44308
(440) 395-0234 .. **Coffey**, David M '86 Progressive Ins Co -300 N Cmmns Blvd
-OHF 11 -Mayfield Village 44143
(440) 639-9000 .. **Coffey**, David D '60 -9853 Johnnycake Ridge Rd -Ste 207
-Concord 44060
(216) 368-2282 .. **Coffey**, Ronald J '61 CWRU Law Schl -11075 East Blvd
-Cleveland 44106
(513) 621-8333 .. **Coffey**, Shirley A '92 %Shea & Assoc -250 E 5th -Ste 444
-Cincinnati 45202
(216) 592-5000 .. **Coffey**, Thomas W '90 Cnsl Tucker E&W LLP -925 Euclid Av
-1150 Huntngtn Bldg -Cleveland 44115 **Fx**:592-5009
(415) 553-7400 .. **Coffin**, Steven C '93 FBI -450 Golden Gate Av -13th Fl
-San Francisco, CA 94102
(330) 325-1624 .. **Coffman**, Brian L '98 Coffman & Co,LPA -4124 Hattrick Rd
-Rootstown 44272
(202) 942-4574 .. **Coffman**, James T '79 US SEC -450 5th NW -Washington, DC
20549
(614) 848-7882 .. **Coffman**, Joseph G '75 -150 W Wilson Bridge Rd
-Worthington 43085
(740) 454-1010 .. **Coffman**, Ward D III '78 -604 Main -Bx159 -Zanesville 43702
(614) 224-1884 .. **Cogan**, Anthony M '94 -336 S High -Columbus 43215
(614) 469-3939 .. **Cogan**, J Kevin '78 (Jones D) -325 John H McConnell Blvd
-Ste 600 -Bx165017 -Columbus 43216 **Fx**:461-4198
(304) 232-8100 .. **Cogan**, Timothy F '80 (Cassidy MCV&T,LC) -1413 Eoff
-The 1st State Cptl -Wheeling, WV 26003 **Fx**:232-8200
(716) 646-6192 .. **Cogar**, Rae N '90 RCS Consulting -5874 Shmrck Ct
-Hamburg, NY 14075
(513) 460-3365 .. **Cogen**, Richard M '98 OH River Fndtn -4480 Classic Dr
-Cincinnati 45241
(419) 352-2614 .. **Coggin**, Betty F '86 -406 Donbar Dr -Bx441 -Bowling Green 43402
(216) 451-2323 .. **Coghill**, George J '75 -10211 Lakeshr Blvd -Bratenahl 44108
(216) 991-6200 .. **Coghlan**, Owen Scott '92 -20133 Farnsleigh Rd
-Shaker Heights 44122
(614) 466-2872 .. **Coglianese**, Richard N '96 Atty Gen -30 E Broad
-Columbus 43215 **Fx**:728-7592
Cogswell, Laura Gregory '04 -(Address Unavailable)
(216) 621-7860 .. **Cohan**, Michael C '77 (Cavitch FD&F) -1717 E 9th -14th Fl
-Cleveland 44114 **Fx**:621-3415
(614) 523-1927 .. **Cohan**, Sanford J '74 -2500 Corp Exchange -Ste 151
-Columbus 43231
(208) 734-1155 .. **Cohara**, Christine A '03 Twin Falls Cnty Pub Def Ofc -231 4th Av N
-Twin Falls, ID 83303
(513) 421-4020 .. **Cohen**, Alfred M '53 OfCnsl Cohen TK&S,LLC -250 E 5th
-Ste 1200 -Cincinnati 45202 **Fx**:241-4490
(216) 621-0200 .. **Cohen**, Avery S '61 (Baker & H LLP) -1900 E 9th -Ste 3200
-Cleveland 44114 **Fx**:696-0740

(202) 296-2960 .. **Cohen**, Barry '76 Cnsl Miller BO,PC -1140 19th NW -Ste 700
-Washington, DC 20036 **Fx**:296-0166
(614) 224-8176 .. **Cohen**, Bernard '52 -50 W Broad -Ste 1800 -Columbus 43215
(614) 583-7606 .. **Cohen**, David M '72 Amer Elec Pwr Co -1 Riverside Plz
-Columbus 43215
(513) 721-6500 .. **Cohen**, Edward '82 (Clements M&C) -35 E 7th -Ste 710
-Cincinnati 45202 **Fx**:763-6415
(561) 776-0017 .. **Cohen**, Elissa D '91 -18 St Geo Pl
-Palm Beach Gardens, FL 33418
(513) 621-9016 .. **Cohen**, Gregory A '93 -114 E 8th -The Citadel -Cincinnati 45202
(440) 639-4494 .. **Cohen**, Gretchen Y '93 US Endoscopy Grp,Inc -5976 Heisley Rd
-Mentor 44060
(412) 281-3000 .. **Cohen**, Harry S '80 (H Cohen & Assoc) -2 Chatham Ctr -Ste 985
-Pittsburgh, PA 15219
(513) 977-8200 .. **Cohen**, Harvey Jay '87 (Dinsmore & S LLP) -255 E 5th -Ste 1900
-Cincinnati 45202 **Fx**:977-8141
(216) 442-9295 .. **Cohen**, Hyman '69 -Bx22360 -Cleveland 44122
(513) 896-4547 .. **Cohen**, Jack E '75 D Cohen Ent,Inc -1000 Maple Av
-Hamilton 45011
(513) 579-6400 .. **Cohen**, Jason M '03 %Keating M&K PLL -1 E 4th
-1400 Provident Twr -Cincinnati 45202 **Fx**:579-6457
(937) 865-6800 .. **Cohen**, Jonathan D '99 Lexis/Nexis -Bx933 -Dayton 45401
(513) 781-7956 .. **Cohen**, Joshua R '84 (Cohen R&K LLP) -1468 W 9th -Ste 705
-Cleveland 44113 **Fx**:781-8061
Cohen, Kenneth S '69 -6573 Marissa Loop -PH 3
-Naples, FL 34108
(513) 721-6500 .. **Cohen**, Lane N '88 %Clements M&C -35 E 7th -Ste 710
-Cincinnati 45202 **Fx**:763-6415
(614) 939-1235 .. **Cohen**, Lawrence H '97 (Demers & C) -3 N High -Bx430
-New Albany 43054
(740) 393-6780 .. **Cohen**, Linda M '90 Knox Cnty Cmmn Pleas Ct -111 E High
-Mount Vernon 43050
(614) 444-4211 .. **Cohen**, Lloyd D '79 -824 S High -Columbus 43206
(614) 294-5040 .. **Cohen**, Marshall D '90 (M Cohen LLC) -1299 Olentangy Rvr Rd
-2nd Fl Ste C -Columbus 43212
(440) 238-3331 .. **Cohen**, Martin '85 Natl Engineering & Cntrctng -12608 Alameda Dr
-Strongsville 44149
Cohen, Michael A '02 -80 Riva Ridge Dr
-Cranberry Twp, PA 16066
Cohen, Mitchell I '94 -5319 Sebastian Ct -Cleveland 44143
(614) 289-5410 .. **Cohen**, Richard '80 Garden City Grp -6525 W Campus Oval
-Ste 175 -New Albany 43054
(419) 255-8260 .. **Cohen**, Richard A '70 (Sharfman & C) -626 Madison -Ste 711
-Toledo 43604 **Fx**:255-4240
(614) 428-8540 .. **Cohen**, Robert D '76 -658 Laurel Rdg Dr -Gahanna 43230
(614) 462-5400 .. **Cohen**, Robert G '89 (Kegler BH&R) -65 E State -Ste 1800
-Columbus 43215 **Fx**:464-2634
(614) 227-2000 .. **Cohen**, Robert H '76 (Porter WM&A LLP) -41 S High
-Columbus 43215 **Fx**:227-2100
(216) 781-7956 .. **Cohen Rosenthal & Kramer LLP** -1468 W 9th -Ste 705
-Cleveland 44113 **Fx**:781-8061
(216) 696-4009 .. **Cohen**, Ryan W '04 %Kraig & K -614 Superior Av W -Ste 900
-Cleveland 44113 **Fx**:696-1835
(513) 931-1890 .. **Cohen**, Stephen '60 -7860 Gapstow Brdg -Cincinnati 45231
Fx:931-1556
(614) 464-6400 .. **Cohen**, Susan A '87 (Vorys SS&P LLP) -52 E Gay -Bx1008
-Columbus 43216 **Fx**:464-6350
(513) 421-4020 .. **Cohen Todd Kite & Stanford,LLC** -250 E 5th -Ste 1200
-Cincinnati 45202 **Fx**:241-4490
(703) 605-8480 .. **Cohen**, Zoe A '88 SpclCnsl SSA -5107 Leesburg Pk
-Falls Church, VA 22041
(216) 752-0955 .. **Cohn**, Howard M '92 -21625 Chagrin Blvd -Ste 220
-Cleveland 44122
(216) 696-1422 .. **Cohn**, Mark B '74 (McCarthy LC&L Co,LPA) -101 Prospect Av W
-1800 Mdlnd Bldg -Cleveland 44115 **Fx**:696-1210
(614) 223-1000 .. **Cohn**, Robert G '91 Amer Elec Pwr Co -1 Riverside Plz
-Columbus 43215
(440) 717-1517 .. **Cohn**, Wendy J '88 M Termini Assoc,Inc -8934 Brecksvll Rd -#417
-Brecksville 44141
(513) 754-0564 .. **Coll**, Nicole T '96 -6589 Chrstn Park Dr -Mason 45040
(304) 353-8000 .. **Cokeley**, Bryan R '00 (Steptoe & J) -Bank One Ctr -7th Fl -Bx1588
-Charleston, WV 25326
Colabianchi, James Jr. '99 -407 Front -Berea 44017
(216) 883-5451 .. **Colabianchi**, Nicholas A '86 -5325 Bway -Cleveland 44127
(216) 586-3939 .. **Colacarro**, Robert J '02 %Jones D -901 Lakeside Av
-Cleveland 44114 **Fx**:579-0212
(216) 696-5222 .. **Colaluca**, Thomas L '78 (Johnson & C,LLC) -1001 Lakeside Av
-Ste 1700 N Pnt Twr -Cleveland 44114 **Fx**:696-5288
(614) 224-1222 .. **Colantonio**, Lawrence J '04 %Maguire & S,LLP -250 Civic Ctr Dr
-Ste 200 -Columbus 43215 **Fx**:224-1236
(304) 723-4400 .. **Colantonio**, Mark A '95 Frankovitch AC&S -337 Penco Rd
-Weirton, WV 26062
(614) 451-7711 .. **Colasurd**, Christopher P '86 (Colasurd & C) -941 Chatham Ln
-Ste 326 -Columbus 43221
(614) 221-8401 .. **Colasurd**, Michael D '84 (Kennedy & C,LPA) -30 Spruce -3rd Fl
-Columbus 43215 **Fx**:222-4799
(614) 888-0040 .. **Colasurdo**, Kelly M '97 DLZ Corp -6121 Huntley Rd
-Columbus 43229
(330) 920-1210 .. **Colavecchio**, Diana M '89 -612 Graham Rd
-Cuyahoga Falls 44221
(330) 467-5030 .. **Colavecchio**, Paul V '81 UAW Legal Srvcs Plan -8536 Crow Rd
-Ste 110 -Macedonia 44056
(513) 621-6464 .. **Colbert**, John P '96 %Graydon H&R LLP -511 Walnut
-1900 Fifth Third Ctr -Cincinnati 45202 **Fx**:651-3836
(614) 466-7502 .. **Colbert**, Paul A '92 Cinergy -155 E Broad -21st Fl
-Columbus 43215
(937) 225-3991 .. **Colbert**, Valerie L '01 J Greene,III & Assoc -120 W 2nd -Dayton
45402
(419) 865-3923 .. **Colburn**, Anthony J '95 -Bx67 -Monclova 43542
(614) 430-8175 .. **Colburn**, Joseph L Jr. '78 -1765 Ivyhill Loop N -Columbus 43229
(614) 461-1516 .. **Colby**, Richard D '74 -169 E Livington Av -Columbus 43215
(513) 474-1712 .. **Coldiron**, James F '75 -8312 Richland Dr -Cincinnati 45255
(740) 363-1324 .. **Coldren**, Robert H '59 GS Miller -103 N Union -Ste A
-Delaware 43015 **Fx**:548-5443

(937) 322-0891 .. **Cole** Acton Harmon & Dunn -333 N Limestone -Bx1687
  -Springfield 45501 **Fx:**322-9931

(216) 566-2000 .. **Cole,** Allison E '00 Sherwin-Williams Co -101 Prospect Av NW
  -Cleveland 44115 **Fx:**566-1708

(740) 363-1443 .. **Cole,** April B '98 -41 N Sandusky -Ste 314 -Bx1040
  -Delaware 43015

(419) 524-4711 .. **Cole** Brown & Fesmier -28 Park Av -Mansfield 44902
  Fx:522-8905

(419) 327-4303 .. **Cole,** Christy L '01 Wise & D,Ltd -151 N Mich -Ste 333 -Toledo
  43624 **Fx:**327-4302

(330) 972-7960 .. **Cole,** Dana K '86 Univ of Akron Law Schl -150 Univ Av
  -Akron 44325

(419) 244-8336 .. **Cole,** David A '86 (Gressley K&P) -608 Mad Av -Ste 930
  -Toledo 43604 **Fx:**244-1914

(216) 765-8080 .. **Cole,** David G '93 -3659 S Green Rd -Ste 315 -Beachwood 44122

(740) 779-7500 .. **Cole,** Denise Lanier '04 Adena Regl Med Ctr -272 Hsptl Rd
  -Chillicothe 45601

(614) 466-8980 .. **Cole,** Douglas R '99 Atty Gen -30 E Broad -Columbus 43215
  Fx:466-5087

(419) 244-1742 .. **Cole,** Eddie M '51 (E Cole Co,LPA) -1117 Mackow Dr
  -Toledo 43607

(614) 221-1827 .. **Cole,** Eric R '02 %Manring & F -167 N High -Bx15037
  -Columbus 43215

(330) 376-6339 .. **Cole,** Gary M '91 -1024 Dan -Akron 44310

(937) 225-4255 .. **Cole,** James D '80 Montgomery Cnty Pros -303 W 2nd -Rm 113
  -Dayton 45402

(330) 761-4074 .. **Cole,** James L '94 FirstEnergy Corp -76 S Main -Akron 44308

(330) 643-2788 .. **Cole,** Jay A '92 Summit Cnty Pros-Crim -53 Univ Av -7th Fl
  -Akron 44308 **Fx:**643-8277

(216) 623-5012 .. **Cole,** John M '00 Cleveland Police -1300 Ontario -Rm 929
  -Cleveland 44113

(313) 792-6314 .. **Cole,** Kenneth G '93 Masco Corp -21001 Van Born Rd
  -Taylor, MI 48180

(216) 579-2848 .. **Cole,** Kevin P '80 Federal Reserve Bk -Bx6387 -Cleveland 44101

(614) 466-1385 .. **Cole,** Kimber L '93 OH Dept Commerce -77 S High
  -Columbus 43266

(330) 666-5550 .. **Cole,** Leland D '69 (Cole Co,LPA) -863 N Cleveland-Massillon Rd
  -Akron 44333

(330) 923-5315 .. **Cole,** Leza A '02 %MH Kreiner -2020 Front -Ste 200
  -Cuyahoga Falls 44221

(614) 442-6601 .. **Cole,** Linda J '93 %OH Ins Guaranty Assoc -1840 Mackenzie Dr
  -Columbus 43220

(216) 566-7100 .. **Cole,** Michael L '00 %SS Keller -1422 Euclid Av
  -330 The Hanna Bldg -Cleveland 44115 **Fx:**566-5430

(484) 865-5000 .. **Cole,** Mitzi G '87 Wyeth-Ayerst Labs -Bx6000
  -Collegeville, PA 19426

(614) 224-8500 .. **Cole,** Philip E '82 OACAA -50 W Broad -Ste 1616
  -Columbus 43215

(216) 586-3939 .. **Cole,** Randall A '73 Cnsl Jones D -901 Lakeside Av
  -Cleveland 44114 **Fx:**579-0212

(614) 644-7233 .. **Cole,** Stuart A '77 Atty Gen -150 E Gay -Columbus 43215
  Fx:728-9327

(419) 524-4711 .. **Cole,** Thomas L '61 (Cole B&F) -28 Park Av -Mansfield 44902
  Fx:522-8905

(614) 466-2980 .. **Cole,** William J '97 Atty Gen -30 E Broad -Columbus 43215
  Fx:728-9470

(740) 286-5460 .. **Cole,** William S '77 -227 E Main -Bx427 -Jackson 45640
  Fx:288-2161

(330) 297-2310 .. **Colecchi,** Stephen '79 Robinson Meml Hsptl -6847 N Chestnut
  -Ravenna 44266

(724) 837-2320 .. **Colecchia,** David A '93 Law Care -542 Hamel Av
  -Greensburg, PA 15601 **Fx:**834-5773

(440) 988-9000 .. **Colella,** Richard '60 (Colella & W,PLL) -6055 Park Square Dr
  -Oak Pnt Prof Park -Lorain 44053 **Fx:**988-9002

(440) 988-9000 .. **Colella,** Richard J '93 (Colella & W,PLL) -6055 Park Square Dr
  -Oak Pnt Prof Park -Lorain 44053 **Fx:**988-9002

(440) 988-9000 .. **Colella** & Weir, PLL -6055 Park Square Dr -Oak Pnt Prof Park
  -Lorain 44053 **Fx:**988-9002

(614) 252-7853 .. **Coleman,** Alicia R '94 -1123 Seymour Av -Bx7938
  -Columbus 43207 **Fx:**252-7848

(614) 462-3655 .. **Coleman,** Cindy A '89 Franklin Cnty CSEA -80 E Fulton
  -Columbus 43215

(937) 222-2500 .. **Coleman,** Danyelle S '00 %Sebaly S&D -1900 Kettering Twr
  -Dayton 45423 **Fx:**222-6554

(914) 766-1220 .. **Coleman,** David W '80 IBM -Route 100 -Somers, NY 10589

(216) 621-0150 .. **Coleman,** Deborah A '76 (Hahn L&P LLP)
  -3300 BP Twr/200 Pub Sq -Ste 3300 -Cleveland 44114
  Fx:241-2824

 Coleman, Debra P '92 -4 Stonebrook Farm Way
  -Greenville, SC 29615

(937) 644-8151 .. **Coleman** Eufinger & Aslaner -110 S Court -Bx266
  -Marysville 43040

(330) 451-8796 .. **Coleman,** Jerry A '99 Stark Cnty Job/Fam Srvcs
  -220 E Tuscarawas -Canton 44702

(513) 946-3700 .. **Coleman,** John K '99 Hamilton Cnty Pub Def -230 E 9th -3rd Fl
  -Cincinnati 45202 **Fx:**946-3707

(412) 261-1600 .. **Coleman,** Kimberly A '96 %Leech TF&L,LLC -525 William Penn Pl
  -30th Fl Ctzns Bk Ctr -Pittsburgh, PA 15219 **Fx:**227-5551

(216) 771-8121 .. **Coleman,** L Christopher '02 %Steuer EB&B Co,LPA -55 Pub Sq
  -Ste 1828 -Cleveland 44113 **Fx:**771-8120

(614) 445-2649 .. **Coleman,** LaVawn D '89 Grange Mutual Cslty Co -650 S Front
  -Bx1218 -Columbus 43216

(210) 977-2291 .. **Coleman,** Lori T '86 USAF -67IOW/JA -Lackland AFB
  -San Antonio, TX 78243

(614) 464-2572 .. **Coleman,** Michael A '86 (Harris MB&C,PLL) -37 W Broad -9th Fl
  -Columbus 43215 **Fx:**464-2245

(419) 241-1200 .. **Coleman,** Pariss M II '96 %Cooper & W,LPA -900 Adams
  -Toledo 43624 **Fx:**242-5675

(614) 235-3653 .. **Coleman,** Paul H '68 -1299 Hddn Rd -Columbus 43209

(502) 326-9795 .. **Coleman,** Stephen G '77 -6808 Fallen Leaf Cir
  -Louisville, KY 40241

(614) 766-7910 .. **Coles,** Carl E '91 -6735 Ballantrae Pl -Dublin 43016

(937) 228-8104 .. **Coles,** Gwendolyn D '93 ABLE -333 W 1st -Ste 500B
  -Dayton 45402 **Fx:**449-8131

(330) 740-2158 .. **Coles-Jones,** Jacquelyn '01 Hon C Waite 7th Dist Ct Appls
  -120 Market -Mahoning Cnty Cths -Youngstown 44503

(216) 622-2727 .. **Coletta,** Dominic J '04 %R Synenberg,LLC -55 Pub Sq -Ste 1200
  -Cleveland 44113 **Fx:**622-2707

(513) 579-6400 .. **Coletti,** Robert E '82 (Keating M&K PLL) -1 E 4th
  -1400 Provident Twr -Cincinnati 45202 **Fx:**579-6457

(513) 723-8400 .. **Coley,** William P II '86 (Coley & Assoc) -9334 Union Centre Blvd
  -Ste 200 -West Chester 45069

(440) 576-3662 .. **Colgan,** Catherine R '01 %Ashtabula Cnty Pros -25 W Jffrsn
  -Jefferson 44047

(216) 271-8049 .. **Colgrove,** John K '69 BP Amer,Inc -4850 E 49th -MBC3-157
  -Cuyahoga Heights 44125

(513) 603-5032 .. **Collett,** Keith W '98 Cincinnati Insurance -6200 S Gilmore Rd
  -Fairfield 45014

(440) 930-8083 .. **Collett,** Marsha L '80 Wickens HPC&B -35765 Chester Rd
  -Avon 44011 **Fx:**937-4466

(513) 621-5959 .. **Collett,** Thomas E '75 Investment of Cincinnati Inc -312 Plum
  -#1200 -Cincinnati 45202

(419) 424-7286 .. **Collette,** Daniel M '71 Hancock Cnty Pros -222 Bway -#104
  -Findlay 45840 **Fx:**424-7889

(248) 822-6461 .. **Collette,** David R '96 Collette & Assoc,PC -5445 Corp Dr -Ste 360
  -Troy, MI 48098

(614) 487-8887 .. **Colley,** David A '78 -1820 Northwest Blvd -Ste 100
  -Columbus 43212

(614) 228-6453 .. **Colley,** Michael F '61 (Colley S&A Co,LPA) -536 S High
  -Columbus 43215 **Fx:**228-7122

(614) 228-6453 .. **Colley** Shroyer & Abraham Co,LPA -536 S High -Columbus
  43215 **Fx:**228-7122

(216) 765-1199 .. **Collier,** Brandon S '02 %Collier S & Assoc Inc
  -30195 Chagrin Blvd -Ste 100 -Cleveland 44124

(937) 324-5541 .. **Collier,** Glenn W '68 (Martin BH&H) -1 S Limestone -Ste 800
  -Bx1488 -Springfield 45501 **Fx:**325-5432

(740) 532-8034 .. **Collier,** James B Jr. '70 (Collier & C) -411 Center -Ironton 45638

(419) 278-7015 .. **Collier,** John S '79 Gribbell S&C -114 E Main -Bx54 -Deshler
  43516

(513) 361-8390 .. **Collier,** Julia A '87 Workers Comp -125 E Court -Cincinnati 45202
  Fx:361-8322

(763) 514-3279 .. **Collier,** Kenneth J '94 Medtronic,Inc -710 Medtronic Pkwy NE
  -MS 301 -Minneapolis, MN 55432

(614) 223-9300 .. **Collier,** Orla E III '75 (Benesch FC&A LLP) -88 E Broad -Ste 900
  -Columbus 43215 **Fx:**223-9330

(216) 765-1199 .. **Collier,** Richard A '70 (Collier S & Assoc Inc) -30195 Chagrin Blvd
  -Ste 100 -Cleveland 44124

(216) 765-1199 .. **Collier** Sarner & Assoc Inc -30195 Chagrin Blvd -Ste 100
  -Cleveland 44124

(419) 243-2100 .. **Collier,** Steven P '81 (Connelly J&C LLP) -405 Mad Av -Ste 1600
  -Toledo 43604 **Fx:**243-7119

(216) 621-0200 .. **Collier,** Wan C '02 %Baker & H LLP -1900 E 9th -Ste 3200
  -Cleveland 44114 **Fx:**696-0740

(216) 621-9190 .. **Collier-Williams,** Cassandra '91 -2103 St Clair -2nd Fl -Bx94062
  -Cleveland 44114 **Fx:**621-9020

(216) 902-6062 .. **Collin,** James M '95 US DOT -1240 E 9th -9th CG Dist
  -Cleveland 44199

(216) 566-5509 .. **Collin,** Thomas J '75 (Thompson H LLP) -127 Pub Sq
  -3900 Key Ctr -Cleveland 44114 **Fx:**566-5800

 Collins, Alan E '94 -1380 Darien Ln -Springfield 45505

 Collins, Amy B '92 -899 E Broad -Columbus 43205

(216) 671-6542 .. **Collins,** Daisy G '70 -Bx110051 -Cleveland 44111

(937) 865-6800 .. **Collins,** David A '89 Lexis/Nexis -Bx933 -Dayton 45401

(412) 765-2500 .. **Collins,** Dean E '96 %Rabner Law Ofc,PC -429 4th Av -Ste 800
  -Pittsburgh, PA 15219

(614) 466-2765 .. **Collins,** Donald M '87 Industrial Commssn of OH -30 W Spring
  -9th Fl -Columbus 43215 **Fx:**752-8785

(513) 721-1504 .. **Collins,** Edward J '77 Droder M & Co,LPA -125 W Cntrl Pkwy
  -Cincinnati 45202 **Fx:**721-0310

(440) 526-0610 .. **Collins,** Forrest L '73 (Collins & Assoc) -Bx41040
  -Brecksville 44141

(419) 255-3544 .. **Collins,** Francis C '87 -1122 Adams -Toledo 43624

(330) 376-1717 .. **Collins,** Gregory H '88 (Davis & Y) -One Cascade Plz -Ste 800
  -Akron 44308

(513) 579-1177 .. **Collins,** James M III '69 -128 E 6th -900 Schmidt Bldg
  -Cincinnati 45202

(330) 374-6906 .. **Collins,** John C '82 Collins & G -333 S Main -Ste 304
  -Akron 44308

(419) 294-3132 .. **Collins,** Kathryn M '98 (Mason M&E) -110 S Sundusky Av -Bx8
  -Upper Sandusky 43351

(740) 233-1470 .. **Collins,** Kevin P '85 (Collins & L) -125 S Main -Marion 43302
  Fx:223-1467

(440) 255-4244 .. **Collins,** Leo R '62 (L Collins Co,LPA) -7333 Ctr -Mentor 44060
  Fx:255-5570

(937) 445-3690 .. **Collins,** Lori J '87 NCR Corp -1700 S Patterson Blvd -WHQ-SE
  -Dayton 45479

(740) 233-1470 .. **Collins** & Lowther -125 S Main -Marion 43302 **Fx:**223-1467

(513) 794-6230 .. **Collins,** Marcus L '97 OH Natl Fin Srvcs -1 Fncl Way
  -Cincinnati 45242

(740) 532-9772 .. **Collins,** Mark A '82 M Collins Co,LPA -119 N 5th -Ironton 45638

(614) 443-3100 .. **Collins,** Mark C '93 -673 Mohawk -Ste 202 -Columbus 43206
  Fx:443-3102

(614) 443-4866 .. **Collins,** Michael J '94 %J Nemeth & Assoc -21 E Frankfort
  -Columbus 43206 **Fx:**443-4860

(419) 241-6000 .. **Collins,** Myron C '95 (Eastman & S Ltd) -1 Seagate -24th Fl
  -Bx10032 -Toledo 43699 **Fx:**247-1777

(216) 696-5400 .. **Collins,** Patrick S '84 Crosby O & Assoc Co,LPA -55 Pub Sq
  -Ste 1475 -Cleveland 44113 **Fx:**696-2610

(614) 228-1144 .. **Collins,** Philip M '73 (P Collins & Assoc) -21 E State -Ste 1130
  -Columbus 43215

(513) 946-3000 .. **Collins,** Rebecca L '01 Hamilton Cnty Pros -230 E 9th
  -Cincinnati 45202 **Fx:**946-3017

(513) 632-5342 .. **Collins,** Regina A '97 R Collins LPA -119 E Court
  -Cincinnati 45202 **Fx:**721-5824

(330) 602-7767 .. **Collins,** Ronald L '73 -135 2nd SE -New Philadelphia 44663

(216) 696-0022 .. **Collins** & Scanlon LLP -50 Pub Sq -3300 Trmnl Twr
  -Cleveland 44113 **Fx:**696-1166

(330) 643-2083 ..**Collins**, Stephan B '98 Summit Cnty Cmmn Pleas Ct -209 S High
-Akron 44308

(937) 328-2574 ..**Collins**, Stephen C '90 Clark Cnty Pros -50 E Columbia -Bx1608
-Springfield 45501

(330) 372-2010 ..**Collins**, Susan P '88 Trumbull Cnty Chldrn Srvcs
-2282 Reeves Rd NE -Warren 44483

(502) 564-8006 ..**Collins**, Thomas D '97 Dept of Pub Advoc -100 Fair Oaks Ln
-Ste 302 -Frankfort, KY 40601

(216) 696-0022 ..**Collins**, Tim L '86 (Collins & S LLP) -50 Pub Sq -3300 Trmnl Twr
-Cleveland 44113 Fx:696-1166

(330) 788-3666 ..**Collins**, William M '58 -4319 Market -Youngstown 44512

(330) 762-8638 ..**Collins-Berger**, Susan M '87 -159 S Main -Ste 912 -Akron 44308
Fx:762-6301

(606) 441-7841 ..**Collinsworth**, Holly B '88 -31 Crow Hill -Fort Thomas, KY 41075

(614) 486-3909 ..**Collis**, Elizabeth Y '93 (Collis S&C,LLC) -1650 Lk Shr Dr -Ste 225
-Columbus 43204 Fx:486-2129

(614) 486-3909 ..**Collis**, Todd W '91 (Collis S&C,LLC) -1650 Lk Shr Dr -Ste 225
-Columbus 43204 Fx:486-2129

(513) 744-9600 ..**Collister**, Scott E '99 %Javitch B&R -602 Main -Ste 500
-Cincinnati 45202 Fx:744-9602

(513) 860-2560 ..**Colloton**, Margaret C '82 LandAmerica -8892 Beckett Rd
-West Chester 45069

(330) 499-1016 ..**Collum**, James J '99 OfCnsl Herbert B & -4571 Stephen Cir NW
-Canton 44718 Fx:499-0790

(216) 787-3030 ..**Collyer**, Michael L '93 Atty Gen -615 W Superior Av -11th Fl
-Cleveland 44113 Fx:787-3480

(614) 228-6040 ..**Colner**, James D '79 (Smith & C) -261 S Front -Columbus 43215

(614) 462-2232 ..**Colombo**, J Corey '00 %Schottenstein Z&D -250 West -Bx165020
-Columbus 43216 Fx:462-5135

(216) 621-0200 ..**Colombo**, Louis A '73 (Baker & H LLP) -1900 E 9th -Ste 3200
-Cleveland 44114 Fx:696-0740

(330) 376-1350 ..**Colopy**, Daniel M '81 (Colopy & C Co) -159 S Main -Ste 420
-Akron 44308

(405) 739-2695 ..**Colopy**, Michael L '81 USAF -7460 Arnold -OC-ALC/JA
-Tinker AFB, OK 73145

(216) 621-5500 ..**Colovas**, Dean A '86 -1350 Illuminating Bldg -Cleveland 44113

(440) 333-7330 ..**Coltman**, Thomas J '64 Valore & C Co,LPA -23550 Ctr Ridge Rd
-Westlake 44145

(419) 245-1020 ..**Colturi**, Jeffrey S '80 Law Dept -One Govt Ctr -Ste 2250
-Toledo 43604 Fx:245-1090

(440) 979-0233 ..**Columbro**, James R '78 -24726 Meadow Ln -Westlake 44145

Columbus, Michael T '03 -(Address Unavailable)

(317) 574-3505 ..**Colussi**, Ann L '87 Duke Realty Corp -600 E 96th -Ste 100
-Indianapolis, IN 46240

(513) 721-4532 ..**Colvin**, Adam D '03 %Katz TB&H -255 E 5th -Ste 2400
-Cincinnati 45202

(859) 283-7532 ..**Colvin**, Charles R '01 (Boggs & C) -73 Cavaller Blvd -Ste 316
-Florence, KY 41042

(513) 977-8200 ..**Colvin**, Sterling W '98 (Dinsmore & S LLP) -255 E 5th -Ste 1900
-Cincinnati 45202 Fx:977-8141

(614) 466-7900 ..**Colvin**, Terra L '99 Atty Gen -30 E Broad -Columbus 43215
Fx:466-2437

(843) 577-9440 ..**Colwell**, Angelica M '99 SpclCnsl Nexsen P LLC -205 King
-Ste 400 -Bx486 -Charleston, SC 29402 Fx:720-1777

(513) 732-8121 ..**Colyer**, Jason M '04 Clermont Cnty Pub Def -10 S 3rd
-Batavia 45103

(330) 643-1028 ..**Comanor**, Lawrence B '73 Industrial Commssn of OH -161 S High
-Ste 301 -Akron 44308

(513) 381-0656 ..**Combs**, Ann R '77 (Kohnen & P LLP) -201 E 5th -Ste 800
-Cincinnati 45202 Fx:381-5823

(513) 424-1660 ..**Combs**, Charles E Jr. '73 (Combs & S) -1081 N Univ Blvd -Ste B
-Middletown 45042

(513) 981-6342 ..**Combs**, Claire G '88 Mercy Hlth Prtnrs of SW Ohio
-4600 McAuley Pl -6th Fl -Cincinnati 45242

(513) 381-2838 ..**Combs**, Eric K '96 (Taft S&H LLP) -425 Walnut -Ste 1800
-Cincinnati 45202 Fx:381-0205

(937) 223-4800 ..**Combs**, Gardner J '90 -1091 Watkins Rd -Jamestown 45335

(513) 946-3500 ..**Combs**, Mark E '77 1st Dist Ct of Appls -230 E 9th -12th Fl
-Cincinnati 45202 Fx:946-3412

(513) 424-1660 ..**Combs & Schaefer** -1081 N Univ Blvd -Ste B -Middletown 45042

(513) 844-1300 ..**Combs-Valerio**, Traci M '04 %JM Allen & Assoc -240A Park Av
-Hamilton 45013 Fx:868-9876

(614) 213-1828 ..**Comeaux**, James F '97 Bank One -1111 Polaris Pkwy -Ste 1K
-Columbus 43215

(216) 932-5659 ..**Comella**, Ignatius A '51 -2624 Courtland Oval -Cleveland 44118

(330) 343-5542 ..**Comella**, John J '82 -211 W 4th -Dover 44622

(216) 664-3559 ..**Comer**, Michele R '93 Dept of Law -601 Lakeside Av
-Rm 106 City Hall -Cleveland 44114 Fx:664-2663

(937) 324-5541 ..**Comer**, Randall M '00 %Martin BH&H -1 S Limestone -Ste 800
-Bx1488 -Springfield 45501 Fx:325-5432

(614) 457-6662 ..**Comeras**, Leonard A '75 Easton Shoes,Inc -2052 Crown Plz Dr
-Columbus 43235

(330) 650-7697 ..**Comery**, Franklin B Jr. '75 Alltel Comm -50 Exec Pkwy
-Hudson 44236

(419) 724-0030 ..**Comes**, Robert J '82 LAWO -520 Mad Av -Ste 640 -Toledo 43604
Fx:321-1582

(216) 464-1610 ..**Comet-Epstein**, Sharon J '92 -2421 Allen Blvd
-Beachwood 44122

(513) 232-4449 ..**Comey**, Margaret W '77 -1095 Nimitzvw Dr -Ste 103
-Cincinnati 45230

(614) 228-3372 ..**Comisford**, Tracy S '91 (Comisford & P LLC) -1243 S High
-Columbus 43206 Fx:228-3584

(419) 535-4500 ..**Commons**, Donald W '82 Dana Corp -4500 Dorr -Bx1000
-Toledo 43697

(513) 977-8200 ..**Comodeca**, James A '87 (Dinsmore & S LLP) -255 E 5th
-Ste 1900 -Cincinnati 45202 Fx:977-8141

(216) 622-8830 ..**Comodeca**, Peter J '91 (Calfee H&G LLP) -800 Superior Av
-Ste 1400 -Cleveland 44114 Fx:241-0816

(304) 233-3390 ..**Companion**, James F '89 Schrader B&C,PLLC -32-20th
-Maxwell Centre,Ste 500 -Wheeling, WV 26003

(216) 481-6700 ..**Compoli**, Joseph R Jr. '82 -652 E 185th -Cleveland 44119

(614) 752-8805 ..**Compson**, Christopher C '80 OH Dept Hlth -246 N High -Bx118
-Columbus 43216

(937) 298-1054 ..**Compton**, Brooks A '79 (Murr CC&M) -401 E Stroop Rd
-Kettering 45429 Fx:293-1766

(330) 376-1112 ..**Compton**, George F Jr. '73 Whalen & C,LPA
-565 Wolf Ledges Pkwy -Bx2020 -Akron 44309 Fx:376-3200

(502) 589-4440 ..**Compton**, Gregory A '03 (Goldberg & S,PSC) -3000 Natl City Twr
-101 S 5th -Louisville, KY 40202 Fx:581-1344

(614) 875-7233 ..**Compton**, Jeffrey P '89 -4178 Bway -Grove City 43123
Fx:875-0480

(614) 888-3177 ..**Compton**, John S '77 -6463 Proprietors Rd -Worthington 43085

Compton, Lori '82 -65 Stonewood Dr -Moreland Hills 44022

(330) 451-8796 ..**Compton**, Quay D '99 Stark Cnty Job/Fam Srvcs
-220 E Tuscarawas -Canton 44702

Compton, Robert H '63 -Bx391 -Ashland, KY 41114

(330) 746-5643 ..**Comstock**, David C '59 (Comstock S&W Co,LPA) -100 Fed Plz E
-Ste 926 -Youngstown 44503 Fx:746-4925

(330) 746-5643 ..**Comstock**, David C Jr. '88 (Comstock S&W Co,LPA) -100
Fed Plz E -Ste 926 -Youngstown 44503 Fx:746-4925

(330) 746-5643 ..**Comstock Springer & Wilson Co,LPA** -100 Fed Plz E -Ste 926
-Youngstown 44503 Fx:746-4925

(937) 227-3310 ..**Comunale**, Anthony F '93 -130 W 2nd -Ste 2050 -Dayton 45402

(937) 225-4652 ..**Comunale**, Kristine E '93 Montgomery Cnty Pub Def -117 S Main
-Ste 400 -Dayton 45422 Fx:225-3449

(937) 223-8177 ..**Conard**, Christopher R '88 %Coolidge WW&L -33 W 1st -Ste 600
-Dayton 45402 Fx:223-6705

(614) 227-2351 ..**Conard**, William T '83 (Bricker & E LLP) -100 S 3rd
-Columbus 43215 Fx:227-2390

(937) 237-9485 ..**Conboy**, Patrick J '98 P Conboy,PC -5613 Brandt Pike
-Dayton 45424 Fx:237-1978

(513) 421-4646 ..**Concannon**, John P '76 McCaslin I&M,LPA -632 Vine -Ste 900
-Cincinnati 45202 Fx:421-7929

(216) 623-0150 ..**Conde**, Stephenie L '94 %Roetzel & A,LPA -1375 E 9th
-One Cleve Ctr 9th Fl -Cleveland 44114 Fx:623-0134

(216) 771-1760 ..**Condeni**, Joseph A '82 (Smith & C LLP) -1801 E Ninth
-Ste 900 Ohio Svngs Plz -Cleveland 44114 Fx:771-3387

(513) 985-9333 ..**Condit**, James J '62 -9403 Kenwood Rd
-Ste D205 Kenwood Prof Bldg -Cincinnati 45242

(513) 965-9260 ..**Condit**, Thomas W '89 -Bx275 -Milford 45150

(440) 248-6728 ..**Condon**, Amanda A '00 -Bx39663 -Solon 44139

(440) 350-2683 ..**Condon**, Eric A '88 Lake Cnty Pros -105 Main -Bx490
-Painesville 44077 Fx:350-2585

(440) 248-6728 ..**Condon**, Frederick J '70 -Bx39663 -Solon 44139

(216) 222-2542 ..**Condon**, Maurice J Jr. '83 Natl City Bank -1900 E 9th
-Loc 01-2030 -Cleveland 44114

(440) 350-2683 ..**Condon**, Patrick J '99 Lake Cnty Pros -105 Main -Bx490
-Painesville 44077 Fx:350-2585

(216) 443-7223 ..**Condosta**, Thomas J '86 Cuyahoga Cnty Pub Def
-1200 W 3rd NW -100 Lakeside Pl -Cleveland 44113

(216) 752-4286 ..**Cone**, Sanford A '61 -3028 Woodbury Rd -Shaker Heights 44120

(410) 832-2000 ..**Cones**, Maureen E '96 %Whiteford T&P LLP -210 W Penn Av
-Towson, MD 21204 Fx:832-2015

(513) 737-7044 ..**Conese**, Mark A '83 -21 Ludlow -Hamilton 45011

(330) 253-3337 ..**Congeni**, Christopher B '04 %Blakemore M&B Co,LPA -19 N High
-Akron 44308 Fx:253-4131

(440) 244-7350 ..**Conger**, Neal A '69 Lorain Natl Bank -457 Bway -Lorain 44052
Fx:245-4511

(614) 275-2783 ..**Congrove**, Kathryn P '94 Franklin Cnty Children Srvcs
-855 W Mound -Columbus 43223 Fx:275-2589

(216) 861-4533 ..**Coniam**, Robert T '86 (Ray RC&D PLL) -1717 E 9th
-Cleveland 44114 Fx:861-4568

(330) 533-8980 ..**Coniglio**, Shirley J '89 -Olde Cthse Bldg -7 Court -Canfield 44406

(513) 651-3456 ..**Conkin**, Elizabeth '95 (Gonzalez S&H LLP) -441 Vine -Ste 3615
-Cincinnati 45202 Fx:651-3446

(419) 244-6788 ..**Conkle**, Allan J '48 OfCnsl Bugbee & C -405 Mad Av -Ste 1300
-Toledo 43604 Fx:244-7145

(614) 677-5932 ..**Conkle**, Thomas J '89 Nationwide Mutual Ins Co -2 Nationwide Plz
-Ste 810 -Columbus 43215

(419) 244-8336 ..**Conklin**, George J '78 %Gressley K&P -608 Mad Av -Ste 930
-Toledo 43604 Fx:244-1914

(937) 228-1111 ..**Conley**, Andrew P '03 %Hall & M,LPA -51 Irongate Park Dr
-Dayton 45459 Fx:912-8920

(937) 912-9810 ..**Conley**, Andrew P '03 %Hall & M,LPA -3040 Prsdntl Dr -Ste 222
-Fairborn 45324 Fx:912-6920

(606) 329-1974 ..**Conley**, Christopher A '86 (Campbell WBE&M) -1608 Carter Av
-Bx1862 -Ashland, KY 41105

(216) 586-3939 ..**Conley**, Colleen A '01 %Jones D -901 Lakeside Av
-Cleveland 44114 Fx:579-0212

(330) 453-1900 ..**Conley**, Craig T '83 -220 Market Av S -604 United Bk Bldg
-Canton 44702

(330) 830-2688 ..**Conley**, James M '77 Massillon Mun Ct -2 James Duncan Plz
-Bx 1040 -Massillon 44646

(859) 578-6604 ..**Conley**, Joseph E Jr. '77 (Buechel & C) -25 Crestvw Hills Mall Rd
-Ste 104 -Crestview Hills, KY 41017 Fx:578-6609

(614) 464-8241 ..**Conley**, Robert W '04 %Vorys SS&P LLP -52 E Gay -Bx1008
-Columbus 43216 Fx:464-6350

(740) 446-0603 ..**Conley**, William D '72 -537 2nd Av -Gallipolis 45631 Fx:446-3411

(513) 860-5355 ..**Conliff**, Charles M '92 -6660 Dixie Hwy -Ste 302 -Fairfield 45014

(440) 526-9301 ..**Conlon**, James E '86 Stein Inc -1929 E Royalton Rd
-Broadview Heights 44147 Fx:526-9230

(419) 255-7600 ..**Conn**, Charles L '75 -608 Mad Av -Ste 1523 -Toledo 43604

(330) 337-6586 ..**Conn**, Harry R '73 Harrington H&M,Ltd -2235 E Pershing
-Salem 44460 Fx:337-6662

(330) 746-6301 ..**Conn**, Paul C '92 -219 W Boardman -Youngstown 44503

(216) 664-4972 ..**Connally**, Cecelia E '71 Mun Ct Judge -Bx94894
-Cleveland 44101

(513) 868-7500 ..**Connaughton**, John B '64 -2332 Morman Rd -Hamilton 45013

(859) 231-3000 ..**Connell**, Anetria K '04 %Stoll K&P,LLP -300 W Vine -Ste 2100
-Lexington, KY 40507 Fx:253-1093

(216) 696-7600 ..**Connell**, Daniel M '04 %Duvin C&H -1301 E 9th -20th Fl Erievw
Twr -Cleveland 44114 Fx:696-2038

(937) 225-5762 ..**Connell**, James M '69 Montgomery Cnty Pros -301 W 3rd -Bx972
-Dayton 45422 Fx:225-3470

(937) 222-2424 ..**Connell**, Kevin C '94 (Freund F&A) -1 S Main -Ste 1800
-Dayton 45402 Fx:222-5369

(216) 479-8500 ..**Connell**, Michele L Ondako '03 %Squire S&D LLP -127 Pub Sq -4900 Key Twr -Cleveland 44114 **Fx:**479-8780

(330) 643-2247 ..**Connell**, Todd M '02 Summit Cnty Ct of Common Pleas -209 S High -Akron 44308

(330) 832-5211 ..**Connelly**, Alan M '57 A Connelly Co,LPA -2830 Conn Av SW -#30 -Massillon 44646

(614) 464-6400 ..**Connelly**, Christopher L '04 %Vorys SS&P LLP -52 E Gay -Bx1008 -Columbus 43216 **Fx:**464-6350

(419) 243-2100 ..**Connelly Jackson & Collier LLP** -405 Mad Av -Ste 1600 -Toledo 43604 **Fx:**243-7119

(330) 264-9454 ..**Connelly**, James J '79 Cmmnty Lgl Aid Srvcs,Inc -121 W North -Ste 100 -Wooster 44691

(513) 290-5646 ..**Connelly**, John C '96 J Connelly Co LLC -700 Walnut -Ste 413 -Cincinnati 45202

(614) 438-1214 ..**Connelly**, John M II '80 OH Rehab Srvcs Comm -400 E Campus Vw Blvd -Columbus 43235

(419) 213-4700 ..**Connelly**, Kathleen M '88 %Lucas Cnty Pros -Adams & Erie -Lucas Cnty Cthse -Toledo 43624

(419) 254-4300 ..**Connelly**, Kristen A '98 %Marshall & M,LLC -420 Mad Av -Ste 1100 -Toledo 43604

(419) 243-2100 ..**Connelly**, William M '64 (Connelly J&C LLP) -405 Mad Av -Ste 1600 -Toledo 43604 **Fx:**243-7119

(419) 255-5990 ..**Connelly**, William L Jr. '00 %Kerger & K -33 S Mich -Ste 201 -Toledo 43602 **Fx:**255-5997

(330) 923-2451 ..**Conner**, James W '67 -1615 Akron Pennisula Rd -#102 -Akron 44313

(216) 515-1660 ..**Conner**, Larry W II '97 %Frantz W LLP -127 Pub Sq -2500 Key Center -Cleveland 44114 **Fx:**515-1650

(330) 673-9511 ..**Conner**, Marjorie L '94 Davey Tree Expert Co -1500 N Mantua -Kent 44240

(513) 381-5700 ..**Conner**, Mia L '04 %Ritter & R,LLC -105 E 4th -Ste 1200 -Cincinnati 45202 **Fx:**381-0014

(216) 479-8500 ..**Conner**, William H '67 (Squire S&D LLP) -127 Pub Sq -4900 Key Twr -Cleveland 44114 **Fx:**479-8780

(614) 464-6400 ..**Conners**, Kevin R '89 OfCnsl Vorys SS&P LLP -52 E Gay -Bx1008 -Columbus 43216 **Fx:**464-6350

(513) 751-7056 ..**Conners**, Thomas J '50 -125 Calhoun -Cincinnati 45219

(740) 694-6315 ..**Connett**, Kimberly M '96 Kokosing Cnstrctn Co -Bx246 -Fredericktown 43019

(216) 367-1150 ..**Connick**, Michael J '90 (Connick & Assoc Co LPA) -1301 E 9th -Ste 1420 -Cleveland 44114

(216) 348-1700 ..**Connick**, Thomas J '99 %Davis & Y -101 Prospect Av W -Ste 1700 -Cleveland 44115 **Fx:**621-0602

(740) 922-4161 ..**Connolly Hillyer & Welch** -201 N Main -Bx272 -Uhrichsville 44683

(304) 723-4442 ..**Connolly**, James G '92 (J Connolly,LLC) -3071 Penn Av -Ste B -Weirton, WV 26062

(202) 514-1244 ..**Connolly**, Kevin P '77 DOJ-Crim Div -1400 NY Av -Washington, DC 20530

(330) 971-8191 ..**Connolly**, Lisa A '89 Cuyahoga Falls Pros -2310 2nd -Cuyahoga Falls 44221

(419) 478-2889 ..**Connolly**, Thomas M '77 (Papps & C) -1026 W Sylvania -Toledo 43612

(614) 464-2025 ..**Connor Behal LLP** -501 S High -Columbus 43215 **Fx:**224-8708

(614) 464-2025 ..**Connor**, Daniel D '68 (Connor B LLP) -501 S High -Columbus 43215 **Fx:**224-8708

(614) 461-8000 ..**Connor**, David A '82 Connor Land Title Agncy,Ltd -35 N 4th -Ste 301 -Columbus 43215

(614) 751-0444 ..**Connor**, Kevin H '86 Retail Pharmacy Assets -630 Morrison Rd -Ste 150 -Gahanna 43230

Connor, Kevin T '89 Squire S&D LLP -Andrássy út 64 -1062 Budapest Hungary

(202) 564-5114 ..**Connor**, Paul N '84 EPA -1200 Penn Av NW -Washington, DC 20460

(614) 341-1900 ..**Connor**, Roger L Jr. '76 %Old Rpblc Natl Title Ins -141 E Town -Columbus 43215

(614) 466-8189 ..**Connor**, Thomas S '91 Industrial Commssn of OH -30 W Spring -9th Fl -Columbus 43215 **Fx:**752-8785

(614) 221-6868 ..**Connors**, James P '86 -221 S High -Columbus 43215

Connors, Maureen '01 -5566 Pearl Rd -Parma 44129

(330) 456-8341 ..**Connors**, Thomas W '78 (Black MS&A,LPA) -220 Market Av S -Ste 1000 -Canton 44702 **Fx:**456-5756

(216) 622-8200 ..**Connors**, Timothy J '89 (Calfee H&G LLP) -800 Superior Av -Ste 1400 -Cleveland 44114 **Fx:**241-0816

(440) 248-7906 ..**Conomy**, Christopher P '00 %Mazanec R&R Co,LPA -34305 Solon Rd -Ste 100 -Cleveland 44139 **Fx:**248-8861

(614) 466-3664 ..**Conomy**, Lisa J '91 OH DOT -1980 W Broad -Columbus 43223

(216) 771-3336 ..**Cononico**, Vincent E '94 Allstate Ins Co -113 St Clair Av -Ste 525 -Cleveland 44114

(740) 653-6464 ..**Conrad**, Aaron R '02 %Dagger JMO&H -144 E Main -Bx667 -Lancaster 43130 **Fx:**653-8522

(330) 253-7171 ..**Conrad**, Bruce R '79 %Burdon & M -137 S Main -Ste 201 -Akron 44308 **Fx:**253-7174

(614) 227-2304 ..**Conrad**, David K '80 (Bricker & E LLP) -100 S 3rd -Columbus 43215 **Fx:**227-2390

(216) 621-0200 ..**Conrad**, Deanna M '04 %Baker & H LLP -1900 E 9th -Ste 3200 -Cleveland 44114 **Fx:**696-0740

Conrad, Earl W Jr. '83 -22 Westervll Sq N -#222 -Westerville 43081

(216) 781-5515 ..**Conrad**, Jane K '00 %Hermann C&S,LLP -1301 E 9th -Ste 500 -Cleveland 44114 **Fx:**781-1030

Conrad, Kelly R '02 -1608 Dartmth Ln -Brunswick 44212

(419) 891-7775 ..**Conrad**, Mark A '83 Eaton Corp -1660 Indn Wd Ctr -Maumee 43537

(216) 485-7970 ..**Conrad**, Michelle L '03 %McCauley & Assoc Co,LPA -5454 State Rd -Parma 44134 **Fx:**485-7979

(513) 579-1414 ..**Conrad**, Ralph J '87 %Schwartz M&R -441 Vine -Ste 2900 -Cincinnati 45202 **Fx:**579-1418

(740) 593-2631 ..**Conrad**, Robert F '93 Ohio Univ Fdn -209 McGuffey Hall -Athens 45701

(216) 781-1212 ..**Conroy**, James P '74 (Walter & H LLP) -1301 E 9th -Ste 3500 -Cleveland 44114 **Fx:**575-0911

(614) 326-3353 ..**Conroy**, John T '62 -3363 Tremont Rd -Ste 104C -Columbus 43221

Conroy, Michelle A '04 -(Address Unavailable)

(216) 622-8200 ..**Conroy**, Suzanne M '95 %Calfee H&G LLP -800 Superior Av -Ste 1400 -Cleveland 44114 **Fx:**241-0816

(440) 988-4537 ..**Conry**, Martin J '74 -141 Park Av -Amherst 44001

(513) 369-5747 ..**Consalvi**, Genina '80 Great American Ins Co -580 Walnut -Ste 1050 -Cincinnati 45202

(216) 566-7744 ..**Consiglio**, Charles J '61 -850 Euclid Av -801 City Club Bldg -Cleveland 44114

(330) 393-7727 ..**Consoldane**, Anthony V '72 OH Pub Def Comm -328 Mahoning Av -Warren 44483

(216) 696-5400 ..**Consolo**, Frank '89 Crosby O & Assoc Co,LPA -55 Pub Sq -Ste 1475 -Cleveland 44113 **Fx:**696-2610

(216) 348-5400 ..**Consolo**, Jeffrey P '79 (McDonald H Co,LPA) -600 Superior Av E -Ste 2100 -Cleveland 44114 **Fx:**348-5474

(937) 229-3211 ..**Conte**, Francis J '88 Univ of Dayton Schl of Law -300 Cllg Park -Dayton 45469

(513) 762-6200 ..**Conte**, Jason P '99 %Ulmer & B LLP -600 Vine -Ste 2800 -Cincinnati 45202 **Fx:**762-6245

(513) 362-8700 ..**Conte**, Jonathan A '93 %Blank R -201 E 5th -Ste 1700 -Cincinnati 45202 **Fx:**362-8787

Conte, Richard M '83 -31200 Gates Mills Blvd -Pepper Pike 44124

Conte, Vincent A III '04 -(Address Unavailable)

(216) 696-7600 ..**Conti**, Patricia S '95 %Duvin C&H -1301 E 9th -20th Fl Erievw Twr -Cleveland 44114 **Fx:**696-2038

(330) 497-0700 ..**Contini**, James F II '92 (Krugliak WG&D Co,LPA) -4775 Munson NW -Bx36963 -Canton 44735 **Fx:**497-4020

(740) 587-4066 ..**Contini**, Stephen A '83 -210 Sunrise -Granville 43023

(419) 841-4400 ..**Contrada**, Carol A '79 %Contrada & Assoc -6641 Sylvania Av -Ste 8 -Sylvania 43560

(419) 841-4400 ..**Contrada**, Charles L '79 (Contrada & Assoc) -6641 Sylvania Av -Ste 8 -Sylvania 43560

(614) 227-2000 ..**Conway**, Daniel R '80 (Porter WM&A LLP) -41 S High -Columbus 43215 **Fx:**227-2100

(419) 668-1616 ..**Conway**, Danita G '91 Huron Cnty Probate/Juv Ct -2 E Main -Norwalk 44857

(216) 292-3300 ..**Conway**, James J '55 (Conway MWK&K Co,LPA) -30195 Chagrin Blvd -Ste 300 -Cleveland 44124

(216) 368-5845 ..**Conway**, James P '61 Case Wstrn Reserve Univ -10900 Euclid Av -Ste 124,Adelbert Hall -Cleveland 44106

(419) 663-6785 ..**Conway**, James W '88 City Law Dept -38 Whittlesey Av -Norwalk 44857

(248) 362-3707 ..**Conway**, John M '95 (Ogne A&S,PC) -1869 E Maple Rd -Troy, MI 48083 **Fx:**362-0422

(216) 861-1365 ..**Conway**, Kara A '02 %Hawkins & Co,LPA -1267 W 9th -Ste 500 -Cleveland 44113 **Fx:**861-0714

(937) 443-6840 ..**Conway**, Mark A '91 (Thompson H LLP) -2000 Cthse Plz NE -Bx8801 -Dayton 45401 **Fx:**443-6635

(216) 292-3300 ..**Conway Marken Wyner Kurant & Kern Co,LPA** -30195 Chagrin Blvd -Ste 300 -Cleveland 44124

(330) 220-7660 ..**Conway**, Michael T '92 -180 Aster Pl -Brunswick 44212

(858) 558-1550 ..**Conway**, Michelle K '98 Global Renewable Enrgy Prtnrs,Inc -4225 Exec Sq -Ste 1650 -La Jolla, CA 92037

(440) 942-6957 ..**Conway**, Neil J III '83 Conway Land Title Co -162 Main -Bx728 -Painesville 44077

(513) 621-2044 ..**Conway**, Patrick J '82 (Macey & C) -1014 Vine -2500 Kroger Bldg -Cincinnati 45202

(215) 979-1000 ..**Conway**, Robert M '76 (Duane M LLP) -1 Lbrty Pl -Ste 4200 -Philadelphia, PA 19103

(216) 210-0470 ..**Conway**, Thomas E '84 -13363 Mad Av -Lakewood 44107

(330) 745-2175 ..**Conway**, Thomas P '91 Lombardi HHC&E -2745 Nesbitt Av -Akron 44319

(937) 294-8807 ..**Conway**, William M '77 -500 Lincoln Park Blvd -Ste 208 -Dayton 45429

(216) 574-9550 ..**Conwell**, Jocelyn '89 -1370 Ontario -Ste 330 -Cleveland 44113 **Fx:**574-9556

(513) 381-6810 ..**Conyers**, Sallie A '02 %Reisenfeld & Assoc -2355 Auburn Av -Cincinnati 45219 **Fx:**381-0255

(330) 678-4677 ..**Coogan**, Alan H '77 Coogan & Assoc,Inc -Bx3052 -Kent 44240

(513) 621-8210 ..**Coogan**, James H '61 (Drew & W Co,LPA) -1 W 4th -Ste 2400 -Cincinnati 45202 **Fx:**621-5444

(937) 645-2787 ..**Coogle**, Andrew B '96 Scotts Co -14111 Scottslawn Rd -Marysville 43041

(614) 462-3555 ..**Cook**, Aldous B '03 Franklin Cnty Pros -373 S High -Columbus 43215

(513) 977-4213 ..**Cook**, Barbara J '77 -917 Main -Ste 300 -Cincinnati 45202

(440) 892-0400 ..**Cook**, Brian A '92 (Hunt & C,LLC) -2001 Crocker Rd -Ste 530 -Westlake 44145 **Fx:**892-1966

(614) 466-3180 ..**Cook**, Brian C '87 Atty Gen -150 E Gay -Columbus 43215 **Fx:**466-9788

(401) 275-3000 ..**Cook**, Brian C '88 Factory Mutual Ins Co -1301 Atwood Av -Bx7500 -Johnston, RI 02919

(216) 687-3613 ..**Cook**, Brian S '85 Cleveland State Univ -1983 E 24th -Cleveland 44115

Cook, Bryn A '94 -4458 Wetmore Rd E -Columbus 43224

(513) 241-4029 ..**Cook**, Cathy R '82 -114 E 8th -Cincinnati 45202

(937) 382-1497 ..**Cook**, Charles T '00 %Peelle Law Ofcs Co,LPA -1929 Rombach Av -Bx950 -Wilmington 45177

(513) 627-0032 ..**Cook**, Christopher B '93 Procter & Gamble Co -Miami Valley Labs -Bx538707 -Cincinnati 45253

(740) 373-5455 ..**Cook**, Colleen E '83 (Theisen B,LPA) -424 2nd -Bx739 -Marietta 45750 **Fx:**373-4409

(216) 252-0372 ..**Cook**, Craig D '91 Precision Prdctn Inc -15215 Chatfld Av -Cleveland 44111

(440) 246-2665 ..**Cook**, D Christopher '93 -209 W 6th -Ste 10 -Lorain 44052

(614) 221-5216 ..**Cook**, Dale D '82 %Wiles BB&B Co,LPA -300 Spruce -1st Fl -Columbus 43215 **Fx:**221-5692

(440) 930-8045 ..**Cook**, David A '68 Wickens HPC&B -35765 Chester Rd -Avon 44011 **Fx:**937-4466

(440) 333-0031 ..**Cook**, David J '58 -2989 Macbeth Dr -Rocky River 44116 **Fx:**333-0059

(513) 721-7500 ..**Cook**, David M '78 (D Cook LLC) -22 W 9th -Cincinnati 45202

(216) 221-0560 ..**Cook**, David R '76 KKSG & Assoc -14600 Detroit Av -#1230 -Lakewood 44107

(614) 464-6400 .. **Cook**, David W '88 (Vorys SS&P LLP) -52 E Gay -Bx1008 -Columbus 43216 **Fx**:464-6350
(216) 831-1434 .. **Cook**, Denise M '00 %A Rickel & Assoc -3690 Orange Pl -Ste 440 -Beachwood 44122 **Fx**:831-6376
(330) 535-5711 .. **Cook**, Deron A '00 %Brouse M -106 S Main -500 First Natl Twr -Akron 44308 **Fx**:253-8601
(216) 241-5900 .. **Cook**, Francis X '79 (Payne P&C) -6100 Oak Tree Blvd -200 Park Ctr I -Independence 44131
(614) 645-7385 .. **Cook**, Frank H '96 City Atty -90 W Broad -Columbus 43215
(216) 261-8839 .. **Cook**, Gary '76 -27801 Euclid Av -Ste 640 -Euclid 44132
(614) 854-3280 .. **Cook**, Gwendolyn A '83 Nationwide Ins Co -1 Nationwide Plz -Grp Contracts -Columbus 43215
Cook, Jared D '02 -(Address Unavailable)
(202) 624-7790 .. **Cook**, Jennifer R '94 Natl Assn of Ins Comm -444 N Cptl NW -Ste 701 -Washington, DC 20001
(216) 348-5400 .. **Cook**, Jerome W '86 (McDonald H Co,LPA) -600 Superior Av E -Ste 2100 -Cleveland 44114 **Fx**:348-5474
(614) 757-5957 .. **Cook**, John K '96 Cardinal Hlth -7000 Cardinal Pl -Dublin 43017
(614) 464-0082 .. **Cook**, John W '77 (Johrendt C&E) -471 E Broad -Ste 800 -Columbus 43215
(614) 227-2383 .. **Cook**, John W III '78 (Bricker & E LLP) -100 S 3rd -Columbus 43215 **Fx**:227-2390
(614) 248-5703 .. **Cook**, Joseph R '71 Banc 1 Mgmt Corp -1111 Polaris Pkwy -OH1-0152 -Columbus 43271
(330) 867-5105 .. **Cook**, Katarina V '90 -Bx13674 -Akron 44334
(202) 752-7000 .. **Cook**, Kathleen B '76 Fannie Mae -3900 Wscnsn Av NW -Washington, DC 20016
(614) 228-6061 .. **Cook**, Laura F '99 Hammond & S -556 E Town -Columbus 43215
(330) 836-3385 .. **Cook**, Lawrence J '77 -563 HmptnRidge Dr -Akron 44313
(740) 773-0012 .. **Cook**, Linda I '87 SE OH Lgl Srvcs -11 E 2nd -Chillicothe 45601
(419) 882-6285 .. **Cook**, Linda S '93 -5646 Roan Rd -Sylvania 43560
(330) 972-5787 .. **Cook**, Maria C '87 Univ Of Akron/Gen Cnsl -302 Buchtel Hall -Ste 63 -Akron 44325
(513) 381-2221 .. **Cook**, Michael A '92 %J Bakst & Assoc -2406 Auburn Av -Cincinnati 45219
(419) 399-2181 .. **Cook**, Norman E '68 (Cook T&B,Ltd) -112 N Water -Paulding 45879
(740) 775-1700 .. **Cook**, Rebecca E '02 Blair & A LLP -6 W Main -Chillicothe 45601
(614) 227-2000 .. **Cook**, S Ronald Jr. '70 (Porter WM&A LLP) -41 S High -Columbus 43215 **Fx**:227-2100
Cook, Schuyler M '88 -801 E 232nd -Euclid 44123
(313) 322-2358 .. **Cook**, Shannon J '96 Ford Motor Co -3 Parklane Blvd -1500 Parklane Twrs W -Dearborn, MI 48126
(614) 228-5151 **Cook**, Sonya L '04 %Gallagher GPT&L LLP -471 E Broad -19th Fl -Columbus 43215 **Fx**:228-0032
(419) 243-1818 .. **Cook**, Stacy H '94 -413 N Mich -Toledo 43624
(330) 972-2358 .. **Cook**, Stephen R '96 Univ of Akron Schl of Law -West Hall 127 -Akron 44325
(614) 629-3000 .. **Cook**, Todd A '91 %Plunkett & C,PC -300 E Broad -Ste 590 -Columbus 43215 **Fx**:629-3019
(513) 281-2000 .. **Cook**, Tracy B '90 Prokids Inc -2320 Kemper Ln -Cincinnati 45206
(419) 399-2181 .. **Cook Troth & Burkard,Ltd** -112 N Water -Paulding 45879
(937) 863-7593 .. **Cook**, William R '98 Cnsl Speedway SuperAmerica LLC -500 Speedway Dr -Enon 45323
(513) 870-4980 .. **Cook-Reich**, Melynda W '96 (Schad & C) -8240 Beckett Park Dr -Ste A -Indian Springs 45011
(440) 365-8388 .. **Cooke**, Amanda M '03 %RA Piazza -10247 Dewhurst Dr -Elyria 44035 **Fx**:366-5265
(614) 464-3900 .. **Cooke**, Andrew P '88 (Browning & C) -243 N 5th -3rd Fl -Columbus 43215
(516) 742-4343 .. **Cooke**, Dermott J '89 %Scully SM&P -400 Grdn City Plz -Garden City, NY 11530 **Fx**:742-4366
(614) 688-3069 .. **Cooke**, Elizabeth I '94 OSU Moritz Cllg of Law -55 W 12th Av -Columbus 43210 **Fx**:292-1383
(614) 222-0531 .. **Cooke**, Reginald A '84 -338 S High -Columbus 43215
(630) 378-8800 .. **Cooke**, Thomas F II '87 Tellabs Oprtns,Inc -1415 W Diehl Rd -Naperville, IL 60563
(614) 248-5700 .. **Cookson**, Eloise G '76 Bank One Corp -1111 Polaris Pkwy -Ste 4P -Columbus 43271
(614) 462-5400 .. **Cookson**, Kenneth Ray '77 (Kegler BH&R) -65 E State -Ste 1800 -Columbus 43215 **Fx**:464-2634
(216) 586-3939 .. **Coolbaugh**, Stephen P '01 %Jones D -901 Lakeside Av -Cleveland 44114 **Fx**:579-0212
(937) 865-6800 .. **Cooley**, Brian H '00 Lexis/Nexis -Bx933 -Dayton 45401
(216) 696-6570 .. **Cooley**, Sheila P '76 -1370 Ontario -Ste 330 -Cleveland 44113
(937) 223-8177 .. **Coolidge Wall Womsley & Lombard** -33 W 1st -Ste 600 -Dayton 45402 **Fx**:223-6705
(513) 684-3711 .. **Coombe**, James M '84 US Atty -221 E 4th -Ste 400 -Cincinnati 45202 **Fx**:684-6385
(330) 744-1111 .. **Coombs**, Frederick S III '75 Harrington H&M,Ltd -26 Market -Ste 1200 -Youngstown 44503 **Fx**:744-2029
(330) 644-5208 .. **Coombs**, William D '66 -1226 Marycano Av -Akron 44319
(419) 354-4442 .. **Coon**, Scott T '84 (Rayle M&C) -100 S Main -Bowling Green 43402
(513) 977-8200 .. **Cooney**, J Michael '75 (Dinsmore & S LLP) -255 E 5th -Ste 1900 -Cincinnati 45202 **Fx**:977-8141
(513) 868-3663 .. **Cooney**, James E '75 -723 Dayton -Hamilton 45011
(216) 443-6350 .. **Cooney**, John G '79 8th Dist Ct of Appls -1 Lakeside Av -#202 -Cleveland 44113 **Fx**:443-2044
(513) 651-6800 .. **Cooney**, Kevin L '98 (Frost BT LLC) -201 E 5th -2200 PNC Ctr -Cincinnati 45202 **Fx**:651-6981
(216) 771-9750 .. **Cooney**, Patrick J III '91 -1370 Ontario -Ste 800 -Cleveland 44113
(330) 376-5600 .. **Cooper**, Angela T '79 HM Life Opportunity Srvcs -321 W Exchange -Akron 44302
Cooper, Brant B '04 -(Address Unavailable)
(419) 213-4700 .. **Cooper**, Candace C '74 %Lucas Cnty Pros -Adams & Erie -Lucas Cnty Cthse -Toledo 43624
(419) 241-1200 .. **Cooper**, Cary R '69 Cooper & W,LPA -900 Adams -Toledo 43624 **Fx**:242-5675
(937) 443-6909 .. **Cooper**, Charles D II '01 %Thompson H LLP -2000 Cthse Plz NE -Bx8801 -Dayton 45401 **Fx**:443-6635
(614) 481-6000 .. **Cooper**, Charles H Jr. '86 (Cooper & E LLC) -2175 Riverside Dr -Columbus 43221 **Fx**:481-6001
(614) 252-2352 .. **Cooper**, Christopher M '84 -1724 E Lvngstn Av -Columbus 43205
(614) 223-2417 .. **Cooper**, Curt D '86 Amer Elec Power Co -1 Riverside Plz -Employee Benefits -Columbus 43215
(419) 241-6000 .. **Cooper**, David F '74 (Eastman & S Ltd) -1 Seagate -24th Fl -Bx10032 -Toledo 43699 **Fx**:247-1777
(419) 241-1200 .. **Cooper**, David R '95 Cooper & W,LPA -900 Adams -Toledo 43624 **Fx**:242-5675
(248) 553-5362 .. **Cooper**, Douglas K '74 GDX Automotive -34975 W 12 Mile Rd -Bx9067 -Farmington Hills, MI 48333
(614) 481-6000 .. **Cooper & Elliott LLC** -2175 Riverside Dr -Columbus 43221 **Fx**:481-6001
(419) 535-4569 .. **Cooper**, Emily K '96 Dana Corp -4500 Dorr -Bx1000 -Toledo 43697
(330) 666-3777 .. **Cooper**, Gary G '78 (Cooper & P) -525 N Cleveland-Massillon Rd -Akron 44333
(937) 224-5300 .. **Cooper & Gentile Co,LPA** -118 W 1st -Ste 850 -Dayton 45402
(216) 696-3844 .. **Cooper**, Gerald F '57 (Cooper S&W Co,LPA) -801 Trmnl Twr -50 Pub Sq -Cleveland 44113 **Fx**:696-6364
(440) 275-1333 .. **Cooper**, Hal D '63 -3561 Clay -Austinburg 44010
(330) 455-0173 .. **Cooper**, Jack B '98 (Day KRW&R,Ltd) -200 Market Av N -Ste 300 -Bx24213 -Canton 44701 **Fx**:455-2633
(330) 761-4208 .. **Cooper**, Jacqueline Sue '97 FirstEnergy -76 S Main -Akron 44308
(740) 345-9611 .. **Cooper**, James R '72 (Morrow G&B,Ltd) -33 W Main -Bx4190 -Newark 43058
(513) 227-9398 .. **Cooper**, James T '94 -Bx265 -Hamilton 45012
(937) 224-5300 .. **Cooper**, Janet K '78 Cooper & G Co,LPA -118 W 1st -Ste 850 -Dayton 45402
(513) 412-1001 .. **Cooper**, Jeffrey R '87 Great Amer Fncl Resrc, Inc -250 E 5th -10th Fl -Cincinnati 45202
(216) 592-5000 .. **Cooper**, Jonathan R '86 Cnsl Tucker E&W LLP -925 Euclid Av -1150 Huntngtn Bldg -Cleveland 44115 **Fx**:592-5009
(440) 356-7255 .. **Cooper**, Julianne B '98 %Grady & Assoc -20950 Ctr Ridge Rd -Ste 100 -Rocky River 44116 **Fx**:356-7255
(419) 242-1555 .. **Cooper**, Kevin J '01 %Spitler & W-Y Co,LPA -1000 Adams -Ste 200 -Toledo 43624
(614) 228-9723 .. **Cooper**, Kitt C Sr. '87 Cooper Law Ofc -35 E Lvngstn Av -Columbus 43215
Cooper, Kymberly R '01 -3117 Lk Park Dr -Columbus 43232
(440) 357-6211 .. **Cooper**, Linda D '78 (Cooper & F) -166 Main -Painesville 44077 **Fx**:357-1634
(216) 586-3939 .. **Cooper**, Lorri W '02 %Jones D -901 Lakeside Av -Cleveland 44114 **Fx**:579-0212
(216) 621-6101 .. **Cooper**, Margaret E '00 %Kahn & Assoc,LLC -55 Pub Sq -Ste 650 -Cleveland 44113 **Fx**:621-6006
(614) 644-3037 .. **Cooper**, Martha J '83 EPA -122 S Front -Bx1049 -Columbus 43216
(513) 425-6609 .. **Cooper**, Matthew S '01 12th Dist Ct of Appls -1001 Reinartz Blvd -Middletown 45042 **Fx**:425-8751
Cooper, Melinda S '79 -(Address Unavailable)
(330) 451-7240 .. **Cooper**, Melinda S '93 5th Dist Ct of Appls -110 Central Plz S -Ste 320 -Canton 44702 **Fx**:451-7249
(716) 854-2020 .. **Cooper**, Michael J '02 (Cellino & B) -17 Ct -7th Fl -Buffalo, NY 14202
(440) 285-7536 .. **Cooper**, Patricia A '96 -12154 Fowlers Mill Rd -Chardon 44024
(216) 621-7227 .. **Cooper**, Richard A '77 (Nicola G&C,LLC) -25 W Prospect Av -Republic Bldg Ste 1400 -Cleveland 44115 **Fx**:621-3999
(216) 348-5400 .. **Cooper**, Richard S '81 (McDonald H Co,LPA) -600 Superior Av E -Ste 2100 -Cleveland 44114 **Fx**:348-5474
(216) 696-3844 .. **Cooper Spector & Weil Co, LPA** -801 Trmnl Twr -50 Pub Sq -Cleveland 44113 **Fx**:696-6364
(740) 625-5215 .. **Cooper**, Thom L '83 (T Cooper Co,LPA) -36 W Main -Bx747 -Centerburg 43011
(740) 345-9611 .. **Cooper**, Timothy M '98 Morrow G&B,Ltd -33 W Main -Bx4190 -Newark 43058
(513) 621-3394 .. **Cooper**, Todd L '81 (Peck S&W,LLP) -201 E 5th -Ste 900 -Cincinnati 45202 **Fx**:621-3813
(419) 241-1200 .. **Cooper & Walinski,LPA** -900 Adams -Toledo 43624 **Fx**:242-5675
(740) 532-4366 .. **Cooper**, William C '73 -407 Center -Ironton 45638
(937) 548-1157 .. **Cooper**, William H '77 (Hanes SCGG&D,Ltd) -507 S Bway -Greenville 45331
(216) 502-0600 .. **Cooper**, William J '98 %Eschweiler & Assoc,LLC -629 Euclid Av -Ste 1210 -Cleveland 44114
(304) 345-0200 .. **Cooper**, William J '78 (Flaherty S&B,PLLC) -200 Cptl -Bx3843 -Charleston, WV 25338 **Fx**:345-0260
(330) 668-4080 .. **Cooperman**, Jonathan M '94 Rehab & Hlth Ctr -3975 Embssy Pkwy -#103 -Akron 44333
(419) 247-1500 .. **Cooperman**, Ronald M '73 (Stockwell & C,LPA) -One Seagate -Ste 1610 -Toledo 43604 **Fx**:247-1575
(614) 459-4300 .. **Cope**, Jon M '68 Jon M Cope,LLC -3600 Olentangy Rvr Rd -Ste 501 -Columbus 43214
(614) 459-4300 .. **Cope**, Jonathan M '97 -3600 Olentangy Rvr Rd -Ste 501 -Columbus 43214 **Fx**:459-4503
(330) 966-2869 .. **Cope**, Leland H '53 -5247 Beverly Av NE -Canton 44714
(614) 857-4320 .. **Cope**, Monette W '97 %Weltman W&R Co,LPA -175 S 3rd -Ste 900 -Columbus 43215 **Fx**:222-2193
(513) 887-7300 .. **Copeland**, K Brent '90 (Fiehrer L&C) -10 Jrnl Sq -Ste 400 -Hamilton 45011
(216) 696-9077 .. **Copeland**, Terence E '74 Cncl for Econ Opportunities -1228 Euclid Av -Halle Bldg, Ste 700 -Cleveland 44115
(513) 574-5598 .. **Copeland**, William M '78 (WM Copeland,LLC) -5324 Timberhollow Ln -Cincinnati 45247 **Fx**:574-0040
(714) 476-2002 .. **Copenbarger**, Lloyd G '76 (L Copenbager & Assoc) -4675 MacArthur Ct -Ste 700 -Newport Beach, CA 92660
(304) 599-4229 .. **Copenhaver**, Brent P '89 %Colombo & S, PLLC -1054 Maple Dr -Morgantown, WV 26505
(513) 684-6022 .. **Copenhaver**, David T '00 US Dept of Labor -36 E 7th -Ste 2525 -Cincinnati 45202
(513) 352-6696 .. **Copetas**, Theodore C '97 %Thompson H LLP -312 Walnut -14th Fl -Cincinnati 45202 **Fx**:241-4771
(937) 436-0699 .. **Copley**, Charles Douglas '96 -854 E Franklin -Centerville 45459
(614) 221-8448 .. **Copley**, Michael F '86 (Buckingham D&B,LLP) -191 W Nationwide Blvd -Ste 300 -Bx151120 -Columbus 43215 **Fx**:221-8590
(419) 755-9659 .. **Copp**, Dianna B '85 Law Dir Ofc -30 N Diamond -Mansfield 44902

(614) 276-8959 ..**Copp,** Matthew R '94 OfCnsl Nein Law Ofcs -2291 Scioto Harper Dr -Columbus 43204 **Fx:**276-8959

(419) 734-3174 ..**Coppeler,** John A '75 (Flynn P&K,LPA) -115 W Perry -Port Clinton 43452 **Fx:**734-3175

(703) 602-6799 ..**Coppins,** Cray J Jr. '71 US Navy -1000 Navy Pentagon -Washington, DC 20350

(216) 586-3939 ..**Coquillette,** William H '75 (Jones D) -901 Lakeside Av -Cleveland 44114 **Fx:**579-0212

(740) 283-3388 ..**Corabi,** Joseph M '77 (Corabi & C) -424 Market -Steubenville 43952

(740) 283-3388 ..**Corabi-Flenniken,** Mary F '88 Corabi & C -424 Market -Steubenville 43952

(614) 759-7100 ..**Corban,** William V '71 -7596 Slate Ridge Blvd -Reynoldsburg 43068

(440) 354-4445 ..**Corbett,** James J '78 Ranpak Corp -7990 Auburn Rd -Concord 44077

(212) 422-0202 ..**Corbin,** Camille A '96 SpclCnsl Sedgewick DM&A -125 Broad -39th Fl -New York, NY 10004

Corbin, Gregory J '85 -(Address Unavailable)

(419) 394-7274 ..**Corbin,** Sara T '00 %Jones DR&P -500 Grant -31st Fl -Pittsburgh, PA 15219

(740) 687-1450 ..**Corbin,** Thomas J '78 -842 N Columbus -Lancaster 43130

(614) 464-6400 ..**Corbin,** Trisha M '01 %Vorys SS&P LLP -52 E Gay -Bx1008 -Columbus 43216 **Fx:**464-6350

(216) 781-8543 ..**Corchado,** Carlos Jr. '98 -1370 Ontario -Ste 2000 -Cleveland 44113

(440) 247-6960 ..**Corcoran,** Daniel R '52 -5 S Franklin -Ste 10 -Chagrin Falls 44022

(216) 397-0777 ..**Corcoran,** James J '66 -2915 Fairfax Rd -Cleveland 44118

(440) 327-9495 ..**Corcoran,** Kevin '98 Bob Schmitt Homes Inc -8501 Woodbrigde Ctr -North Ridgeville 44039

(614) 469-3939 ..**Corcoran,** Matthew C '04 %Jones D -325 John H McConnell Blvd -Ste 600 -Bx165017 -Columbus 43216 **Fx:**461-4198

(216) 621-0200 ..**Corcoran,** Melanie S '91 Baker & H LLP -1900 E 9th -Ste 3200 -Cleveland 44114 **Fx:**696-0740

(651) 730-1978 ..**Corcoran,** Peter '90 -7579 Teal Rd -Woodbury, MN 55125

(513) 625-1111 ..**Corcoran,** T J '94 -6177 State Route 132 -Goshen 45122

(216) 299-2451 ..**Cord,** Daniel A '04 -22299 Calverton Rd -Shaker Heights 44122

(479) 246-9933 ..**Cordas,** Kimberly A '02 -2200 S 18th Pl -Rogers, AR 72758

(440) 997-6175 ..**Cordell,** Stuart W '81 (Warren & Y,PLL) -134 W 46th -Bx2300 -Ashtabula 44005 **Fx:**992-9114

(216) 357-5900 ..**Corder,** Bradley S '90 -2189 Professor Av -Ste 100 -Cleveland 44113

(614) 466-4656 ..**Cordero,** Leandro Martin '95 Atty Gen -150 E Gay -Columbus 43215 **Fx:**466-1756

(412) 471-8500 ..**Cordes,** Samuel J '88 (Ogg CM&I) -245 Ft Pitt Blvd -Pittsburgh, PA 15222

(513) 352-6666 ..**Cordes,** William H '73 (Thompson H LLP) -312 Walnut -14th Fl -Cincinnati 45202 **Fx:**241-4771

(330) 451-7897 ..**Cordova,** Michelle L '96 Stark Cnty Pros -110 Central Plz -Ste 510 -Canton 44702

(440) 998-6835 ..**Cordova,** Philip E '01 %Andrews & P LLC -4817 State Rd -Ste 100 -Bx10 -Ashtabula 44005

(614) 539-1661 ..**Cordray,** Richard A '87 -4900 Grv Cty Rd -Grove City 43123

(513) 227-5765 ..**Cordrey,** Aimee N '99 Lexis-Nexis -Bx58352 -Cincinnati 45258

(740) 382-2611 ..**Cordrick,** Robert C '01 -117 E Center -Marion 43302

(937) 468-9921 ..**Core,** Anthony E '90 -3339 Cnty Road 20 -Rushsylvania 43347

(440) 884-2675 ..**Corea,** Charles '87 -6202 Thoreau Dr -Parma 44129 **Fx:**(216) 736-2756

(216) 861-3086 ..**Coreno,** Terese M '99 %Reid M&W -55 Pub Sq -Ste 2010 -Cleveland 44113 **Fx:**861-4409

(614) 464-6400 ..**Corey,** George H '73 (Vorys SS&P LLP) -52 E Gay -Bx1008 -Columbus 43216 **Fx:**464-6350

(330) 753-6874 ..**Corgan,** Jacquenette G '00 Thompson Law Ofcs -2719 Mnchstr Rd -Akron 44319

(330) 376-5756 ..**Corgan,** William H III '01 Emershaw M&S -120 E Mill -#437 -Akron 44308 **Fx:**762-5980

(614) 854-4840 ..**Coridan,** Mary F '81 Nationwide Ins Co -5525 Parkcenter Cir -Claims Dept -Dublin 43017

(614) 857-4393 ..**Coriell,** Angela K '03 %Weltman W&R Co,LPA -175 S 3rd -Ste 900 -Columbus 43215 **Fx:**222-2193

(614) 462-3555 ..**Coriell,** Jennifer L '00 Franklin Cnty Pros -373 S High -Columbus 43215

Coriston, Kerri '04 -(Address Unavailable)

(513) 984-2040 ..**Corker,** Robert S '82 (Scheuer M&B LLC) -11025 Reed Hartman Hwy -Cincinnati 45242 **Fx:**984-6590

(804) 832-2749 ..**Corkran,** Thomas D '74 Cnsl Framatome Technologies -3315 Old Forest Rd -Lynchburg, VA 24501 **Fx:**832-2325

(614) 466-2434 ..**Corletzi,** Carl J '77 OH Dept Hlth -246 N High -1st Fl -Columbus 43266

(419) 524-1361 ..**Corley,** Byron D '04 -3 N Main -Ste 714 -Mansfield 44902

(614) 644-2640 ..**Corley,** Edward C '83 Dept Ins -2100 Stella Ct -Columbus 43215

(216) 241-5210 ..**Corman,** Lawrence W '69 -55 Pub Sq -Ste 2240 -Cleveland 44113

(440) 248-7906 ..**Cormany,** Carl E '80 %Mazanec R&R Co,LPA -34305 Solon Rd -Ste 100 -Cleveland 44139 **Fx:**248-8861

(216) 348-1700 ..**Cormier,** Shawn A '98 %Davis & Y -101 Prospect Av W -Ste 1700 -Cleveland 44115 **Fx:**621-0602

(614) 466-7447 ..**Corn,** Peggy W '89 Atty Gen -150 E Gay -Columbus 43215

(614) 480-3869 ..**Corn,** Ronald J '74 Huntington Trust Co -41 S High -Columbus 43215

(614) 764-0681 ..**Corna,** Maryellen '92 Blaugrund H&M,Inc -5455 Rings Rd -Ste 500 -Dublin 43017 **Fx:**764-0774

(440) 350-2683 ..**Cornachio,** Marisa L '04 Lake Cnty Pros -105 Main -Bx490 -Painesville 44077 **Fx:**350-2683

(614) 466-5610 ..**Cornelius,** Melanie '85 Atty Gen -150 E Gay -Columbus 43215 **Fx:**752-2732

(614) 365-2700 ..**Cornelius,** Patrick D '97 %Squire S&D LLP -41 S High -1300 Huntgtn Ctr -Columbus 43215 **Fx:**365-2499

(256) 876-7153 ..**Cornelius,** Roger W '75 US Army -Leg Ofc AMSAM-L -Redstone Arsenal, AL 35898

(212) 326-3939 ..**Cornell,** John R '82 (Jones D) -222 E 41st -4th Fl -New York, NY 10017 **Fx:**755-7306

(740) 653-4000 ..**Cornell,** Raina D '94 -329 E Main -Lancaster 43130

(216) 861-5582 ..**Cornely,** John P '95 (Fay SFM&M LLP) -1100 Superior Av -7th Fl -Cleveland 44114 **Fx:**241-1666

(614) 228-5711 ..**Cornely,** John R '00 %Lucas PAG&N -600 S High -Columbus 43215 **Fx:**228-0982

(216) 664-2775 ..**Cornely,** Mary Z '96 Dept of Law -601 Lakeside Av -Rm 106 City Hall -Cleveland 44114 **Fx:**664-2663

(614) 466-7264 ..**Corner,** Barbara S '95 OH Legal Rghts Srvc -8 E Long -5th Fl -Columbus 43215

(614) 294-0313 ..**Corner,** Beverly J '89 -2572 Cleveland Av -Bx11502 -Columbus 43211

(513) 771-2444 ..**Cornetet,** John B '87 (Lutz CM&F Co,LPA) -130 Tri-Cnty Pkwy -Ste 208 -Cincinnati 45246 **Fx:**771-2447

(216) 241-2838 ..**Cornett,** Adam D '04 %Taft S&H LLP -200 Pub Sq -3500 BP Twr -Cleveland 44114 **Fx:**241-3707

(513) 852-8226 ..**Cornett,** Curtis L '93 Cors & B LLC -537 E Pete Rose Way -Ste 400 -Cincinnati 45202

(216) 592-5000 ..**Cornett,** Harry D Jr. '71 (Tucker E&W LLP) -925 Euclid Av -1150 Huntngtn Bldg -Cleveland 44115 **Fx:**592-5009

(513) 863-5333 ..**Cornett,** Jackie L '78 -1400 Eaton Av -Hamilton 45013

(330) 675-2542 ..**Cornicelli,** Anthony M '79 Trumbull Cnty Cmmn Pleas Ct -160 High -Warren 44481 **Fx:**675-2580

(941) 483-4246 ..**Cornish,** David R '76 -355 W Venice Av -Venice, FL 34285

(740) 594-2788 ..**Cornn,** Thomas L '73 -8 N Court -Ste 407 -Athens 45701

(216) 514-9999 ..**Cornrich,** Neil M '83 (Cornrich & C Co,LPA) -2000 Auburn Dr -Ste 315 -Cleveland 44122 **Fx:**514-8500

(216) 514-9999 ..**Cornrich,** Sidney M '51 (Cornrich & C Co,LPA) -2000 Auburn Dr -Ste 315 -Cleveland 44122 **Fx:**514-8500

(330) 434-3000 ..**Corns,** Frederick J '67 OfCnsl Roderick & L -One Cascade Plz -Ste 1500 -Akron 44308 **Fx:**434-9220

(419) 222-1155 ..**Cornwell,** Ted E '76 (Scherner H&C,LLC) -714 W North -Lima 45801 **Fx:**227-3131

(614) 225-9316 ..**Cornwell,** Virginia C '99 -155 W Main -Ste 101 -Columbus 43215

(937) 748-9447 ..**Cornyn,** Christopher J '79 (C Cornyn Co,LPA) -10 Fairway Dr -Springboro 45066

(419) 797-2377 ..**Corogin,** Thomas L '53 -5314 E Marina Av -Port Clinton 43452

(419) 244-3053 ..**Corpening,** Sarah A '00 Fam & Chld Abuse Prvntn Ctr -1 Stranahan Sq -Ste 532 -Toledo 43604 **Fx:**244-1100

(216) 622-8200 ..**Corpora,** Corine R '92 Calfee H&G LLP -800 Superior Av -Ste 1400 -Cleveland 44114 **Fx:**241-0816

(216) 642-3342 ..**Corpus,** Christopher A '00 %Wegman H&V,LPA -6055 Rockside Wds Blvd -Ste 200 -Cleveland 44131 **Fx:**642-8826

(216) 696-8730 ..**Corpus,** Deborah Liu '00 %Amin & T LLP -1900 E 9th -24th Fl Natl Cty Ctr -Cleveland 44114 **Fx:**696-8731

(513) 561-7755 ..**Corr,** Elizabeth D '81 -7243 Wooster Pike -Cincinnati 45227

(513) 229-1000 ..**Corrado,** Barry V '81 Thomson Learning -5191 Natorp Blvd -Mason 45040

(216) 696-0222 ..**Corrado,** David A '91 -1660 W 2nd -Ste 410 Skylight Ofc Twr -Cleveland 44113 **Fx:**696-0226

(216) 781-2895 ..**Corrado,** Paul J '86 -2000 E 9th -Ste 300 -Cleveland 44115

(216) 928-2200 ..**Corrigall,** Amy K '01 %Sutter OM&F -1301 E 9th -3600 Erievw Twr -Cleveland 44114 **Fx:**928-4400

(216) 348-5400 ..**Corrigan,** Anne T '92 (McDonald H Co,LPA) -600 Superior Av E -Ste 2100 -Cleveland 44114 **Fx:**348-5474

(216) 696-0606 ..**Corrigan,** Brian T '94 RE Sweeney Co,LPA -55 Pub Sq -Ste 1500 -Cleveland 44113 **Fx:**696-0679

(216) 696-7445 ..**Corrigan,** Christopher M '99 Glowacki & Assoc -526 Superior Av E -510 Leader Bldg -Cleveland 44114 **Fx:**696-0318

(216) 443-7223 ..**Corrigan,** Daniel P '87 Cuyahoga Cnty Pub Def -1200 W 3rd NW -100 Lakeside Pl -Cleveland 44113

(216) 443-7800 ..**Corrigan,** Edward J '89 Cuyahoga Cnty Pros -1200 Ontario -8th Fl -Cleveland 44113 **Fx:**698-2270

(216) 622-8200 ..**Corrigan,** Heather C '01 %Calfee H&G LLP -800 Superior Av -Ste 1400 -Cleveland 44114 **Fx:**241-0816

(614) 752-6888 ..**Corrigan,** Hugh A Jr. '95 Industrial Commssn of OH -30 W Spring -9th Fl -Columbus 43215 **Fx:**752-8785

(216) 861-1177 ..**Corrigan,** James E '81 -1370 Ontario -Ste 1130 -Cleveland 44113

(216) 621-8484 ..**Corrigan,** John F '86 %Climaco LPW&G Co,LPA -1228 Euclid Av -Ste 900 Halle Bldg -Cleveland 44115 **Fx:**771-1632

(216) 586-3939 ..**Corrigan,** Karen J '93 Jones D -901 Lakeside Av -Cleveland 44114 **Fx:**579-0212

(330) 725-3456 ..**Corrigan,** Mary B '89 Bowers & C -6440 Ryan Rd -Medina 44256

(330) 443-5772 ..**Corrigan,** Michael J '96 -137 S Main -Ste 202 -Akron 44308

(216) 696-6454 ..**Corrigan,** Patrick S '90 Cincinnati Ins Co -930 The 55 Bldg -55 Pub Sq -Cleveland 44113

(216) 443-7800 ..**Corrigan,** Peter J '96 Cuyahoga Cnty Pros -1200 Ontario -8th Fl -Cleveland 44113 **Fx:**698-2270

(440) 350-2663 ..**Corrigan,** Victoria M '99 Lake Cnty Ct of Common Pleas -47 N Park Pl -Bx490 -Painesville 44077

(216) 771-0875 ..**Corrigan,** William H '52 -3008 Clinton Av -Cleveland 44113

(330) 455-6112 ..**Corroto,** Gary A '91 (Tzangas PM&R) -220 Market Av S -8th Fl -Canton 44702 **Fx:**455-2108

(740) 368-1545 ..**Corroto,** Mark T '87 City Pros -70 N Union -Delaware 43015

(330) 743-4116 ..**Corroto,** Thomas L Jr. '48 Brennan FV&Y,Ltd -29 E Front -2nd Fl -Youngstown 44503

(513) 852-8200 ..**Cors & Bassett LLC** -537 E Pete Rose Way -Ste 400 -Cincinnati 45202

(513) 852-8200 ..**Cors,** L B '61 (Cors & B LLC) -537 E Pete Rose Way -Ste 400 -Cincinnati 45202

(440) 871-4022 ..**Corsaro,** Joseph G '82 Corsaro & Assoc Co,LPA -2001 Crocker Rd -Ste 400 -Westlake 44145

(330) 747-2661 ..**Corsell,** Joseph D '96 Cnsl Cafaro Co -2445 Belmont Av -Bx2186 -Youngstown 44504

(330) 364-4414 ..**Corsi,** Mario D '51 -117 E 3rd -Dover 44622

(216) 241-7660 ..**Corsi,** Mary J '93 %Stanard & C Co,LPA -1370 Ontario -Ste 748 -Cleveland 44113 **Fx:**241-7661

(216) 241-7660 ..**Corsi,** Megan J '97 (Stanard & C Co,LPA) -1370 Ontario -Ste 748 -Cleveland 44113 **Fx:**241-7661

(216) 241-2200 ..**Corso,** Heather L '99 %Zoller & S -812 Huron Rd -Caxton Bldg, Ste 490 -Cleveland 44115

(216) 642-3342 ..**Corso,** Jennifer A '94 %Wegman H&V,LPA -6055 Rockside Wds Blvd -Ste 200 -Cleveland 44131 **Fx:**642-8826

(440) 356-6380 ..**Corso**, Joseph J '61 -19111 Detroit Rd -Ste 302
-Rocky River 44116 **Fx:**356-6397

(216) 579-1700 ..**Corso**, Joseph J '69 (Pearne & G LLP) -1801 E 9th -Ste 1200
-Cleveland 44114 **Fx:**579-6073

(513) 626-4756 ..**Corstanje**, Brahm J '89 Procter & Gamble Co
-11511 Reed Hartman Hwy -Cincinnati 45241

(216) 622-3600 ..**Corts**, Robert F '89 US Atty -801 W Superior -Ste 400
-Cleveland 44113 **Fx:**622-3370

(614) 719-3390 ..**Corwin**, Jonathan P '02 Hon N King -85 Marconi Blvd
-Columbus 43215

(513) 621-0267 ..**Corwin**, Melanie S '90 Waite SB&C -1 W 4th -1513 4th & Vine Twr
-Cincinnati 45202

(440) 395-0281 ..**Corwin**, Patricia M '87 Progressive Ins Co -300 N Cmmns Blvd
-Mayfield Village 44143

(419) 562-7762 ..**Cory**, David R '82 (Cory & C) -221 S Poplar -Bx510
-Bucyrus 44820

(419) 228-6365 ..**Cory**, Frank B '55 (Cory MWR&C,LPA) -101 N Elizabeth -Ste 607
-Bx1217 -Lima 45802 **Fx:**228-5319

(419) 228-6365 ..**Cory Meredith Witter Rumer & Cheney,LPA** -101 N Elizabeth
-Ste 607 -Bx1217 -Lima 45802 **Fx:**228-5319

(419) 562-7762 ..**Cory**, Richard L '51 (Cory & C) -221 S Poplar -Bx510
-Bucyrus 44820

(330) 670-0770 ..**Corzin**, Christine K '00 %Corzin SU&F
-304 N Cleveland-Massillon Rd -Akron 44333

(330) 670-0770 ..**Corzin**, Harold A '75 (Corzin SU&F)
-304 N Cleveland-Massillon Rd -Akron 44333

(330) 670-0770 ..**Corzin Sanislo Ufholz & Freedman**
-304 N Cleveland-Massillon Rd -Akron 44333

(216) 566-5769 ..**Coscarelli**, Dianne S '78 (Thompson H LLP) -127 Pub Sq
-3900 Key Ctr -Cleveland 44114 **Fx:**566-5800

(216) 348-5400 ..**Cosentino**, Leonard M '87 (McDonald H Co,LPA)
-600 Superior Av E -Ste 2100 -Cleveland 44114 **Fx:**348-5474

(304) 485-0990 ..**Cosenza**, George J '78 (Cosenza M&W,PLLC) -515 Market -Bx4
-Parkersburg, WV 26102 **Fx:**485-1090

(617) 374-9001 ..**Cosgrove**, Anita D '91 Worldcare Inc -One Cmbrdg Ctr
-Cambridge, MA 02142

Cosgrove, Genylynn M '04 -(Address Unavailable)

(513) 946-3055 ..**Cosgrove**, Jonathan B '01 Hamilton Cnty Pros -230 E 9th
-Cincinnati 45202 **Fx:**946-3017

(216) 664-3574 ..**Cosgrove**, Michael F '00 Dept of Law -601 Lakeside Av
-Rm 106 City Hall -Cleveland 44114 **Fx:**664-2663

(513) 762-6200 ..**Cosgrove**, Paul J '01 %Ulmer & B LLP -600 Vine -Ste 2800
-Cincinnati 45202 **Fx:**762-6245

(513) 352-4701 ..**Cosgrove**, Terrence R '76 Law Dept -801 Plum -Rm 214
-Cincinnati 45202 **Fx:**352-1515

(216) 479-8500 ..**Cosgrove**, Timothy J '87 (Squire S&D LLP) -127 Pub Sq
-4900 Key Twr -Cleveland 44114 **Fx:**479-8780

(216) 443-8933 ..**Cosiano**, Ralph V '59 Cuyahoga Cnty Probate Ct -1 Lakeside Av
-Rm 107 -Cleveland 44113

(214) 346-7255 ..**Cosman**, Shawn D '97 Landamerica Finl Grp,Inc
-101 Gtwy Ctr Pkwy -Richmond, VA 23235

(419) 244-8989 ..**Cosme**, Keila D '94 (Cosme D&S) -202 N Erie -Toledo 43624

(937) 393-1850 ..**Coss**, Rocky A '76 -149 E Main -Hillsboro 45133

(216) 479-8500 ..**Cossler**, Christine T '02 %Squire S&D LLP -127 Pub Sq
-4900 Key Twr -Cleveland 44114 **Fx:**479-8780

(614) 461-0256 ..**Costa**, Carol A '90 Ofc Dscplnry Cnsl -250 Civic Ctr Dr -#325
-Columbus 43215 **Fx:**461-7205

(440) 871-5020 ..**Costa**, Gregory J '93 DK Fifner Co,LPA -24441 Detroit Rd -Ste 300
-Westlake 44145

(440) 243-2800 ..**Costabile**, Gregory S '93 (Phillips M&C Co,LPA) -7530 Lucerne Dr
-Ste 200 -Middleburg Heights 44130 **Fx:**243-2852

(202) 305-0375 ..**Costantini**, Christopher J '86 US DOJ -601 D NW -Rm 2012
-Washington, DC 20004

(440) 835-6304 ..**Costanza**, James F '67 Westlake City Schls Superintendent
-27200 Hilliard Blvd -Westlake 44145

(330) 392-9329 ..**Costanzo**, Maridee L '92 -244 Seneca Av -Warren 44481
Fx:393-9943

(216) 226-8241 ..**Costanzo**, Raymond J '78 (Costanzo & L) -13317 Mad Av
-Lakewood 44107

(972) 652-3026 ..**Costas**, Stephen J '77 Assoc Commercial Corp -300
E Carpenter Fwy -18th Fl -Irving, TX 75062

(330) 644-0076 ..**Costello**, Anthony J '82 -2666 S Arlngtn Rd -Akron 44319

Costello, Catherine C '81 -158 Oaklnd Park Av -Columbus 43214

(614) 227-2000 ..**Costello**, Daniel W '80 (Porter WM&A LLP) -41 S High
-Columbus 43215 **Fx:**227-2100

(740) 852-2259 ..**Costello**, Eamon P '93 Madison Cnty Pros -23 W High
-London 43140 **Fx:**845-1649

Costello, Fred P III '03 -7730 Ravenna Rd -#4 -Hudson 44236

(203) 968-3813 ..**Costello**, Mark '82 Xerox Corp -800 Long Ridge Rd
-Stamford, CT 06902

(404) 521-3939 ..**Costello**, Sean P '97 %Jones D -303 Pchtree NE
-Atlanta, GA 30308

(937) 223-8177 ..**Costello**, Shannon L '98 %Coolidge WW&L -33 W 1st -Ste 600
-Dayton 45402 **Fx:**223-6705

(216) 378-6220 ..**Costello**, William L '88 (WL Costello Co,LPA)
-3401 Enterprise Pkwy -Ste #406 -Beachwood 44122

(859) 341-9411 ..**Costin**, James W '86 -15 W Crittenden Av -Fort Wright, KY 41011

(740) 695-0371 ..**Costine**, Eric N '85 (Costine Law Firm) -136 W Main
-Saint Clairsville 43950

(740) 695-0371 ..**Costine**, John O '51 (Costine Law Firm) -136 W Main
-Saint Clairsville 43950

(216) 861-6622 ..**Coticchia**, Joseph L '75 -1370 Ontario -Ste 1640
-Cleveland 44113

(216) 687-1311 ..**Coticchia**, Lori A '88 %Reminger & R -101 Prospect Av W
-1400 Mdlnd Bldg -Cleveland 44115 **Fx:**687-1841

(216) 426-4511 ..**Coticchia**, Michael L '88 Applied Industrial Tech -1 Applied Plz
-Cleveland 44115

(937) 335-0570 ..**Cotner**, John M '70 -22 N Short -Troy 45373

(216) 621-0200 ..**Cotronakis**, Emanuel J '98 %Baker & H LLP -1900 E 9th
-Ste 3200 -Cleveland 44114 **Fx:**696-0740

(202) 326-6059 ..**Cotter**, Paula T '79 Natl Assn of Atty Genls -750 1st -Ste 1100
-Washington, DC 20002

(419) 241-9000 ..**Cotter**, Thomas A '88 (Shumaker L&K,LLP) -1000 Jackson
-Toledo 43624 **Fx:**241-6894

(419) 242-8214 ..**Cottier**, Geoffrey A '76 -520 Mad Av -Ste 545 -Toledo 43604

(419) 243-1770 ..**Cottle**, Christopher C '00 (Bovee C Co,LPA) -421 N Mich -Ste E
-Toledo 43624

(216) 781-2787 ..**Cottle**, Cullen J '00 %Lavelle & L Co,LPA -526 Superior Av E
-Ste 522 -Cleveland 44114

(216) 755-5660 ..**Cotton**, Eric C '89 Developers Diversified Rlty Corp
-3300 Enterprise Pkwy -Beachwood 44122

(614) 523-3575 ..**Cottone**, Carl N '03 -2864 Heatherleaf Way -Columbus 43231
Fx:794-7220

(740) 283-1966 ..**Cottrell**, Cerryn R '01 Jefferson Cnty Pros -16001 State Route 7
-Steubenville 43952

(419) 855-9955 ..**Cottrell**, Ernest E Jr. '85 -21980 State Route 51 -Genoa 43430

(419) 855-7731 ..**Cottrell**, Stephen E '73 -634 Main -Bx36 -Genoa 43430

(419) 774-5676 ..**Couch**, Bambi S '82 Richland Cnty Pros -38 S Park -2nd Fl
-Mansfield 44902 **Fx:**774-5589

(614) 213-4505 ..**Couch**, James E '83 Bank One Mgt Corp -1111 Polaris Pkwy
-OH1-1085 -Columbus 43240

(440) 324-5353 ..**Couch**, James R '75 %Spike & M,LLP -1551 W River Rd N
-Elyria 44035 **Fx:**324-6529

(740) 453-1130 ..**Couch**, Ronald C '83 -Bx2771 -Zanesville 43702

(330) 384-7146 ..**Couchman**, David M '88 FirstMerit Corp -106 S Main -Ste 900
-Akron 44308

Coughanour, William L '01 -(Address Unavailable)

(614) 461-0256 ..**Coughlan**, Jonathan E '78 Ofc Dscplnry Cnsl -250 Civic Ctr Dr
-#325 -Columbus 43215 **Fx:**461-7205

(859) 431-6340 ..**Coughlan**, Peter B '91 -509 E 10th -Newport, KY 41071

(937) 224-1981 ..**Coughlin**, Robert B '80 (Young PL&J) -130 W 2nd -Ste 800
-Dayton 45402

(216) 241-8333 ..**Coughlin**, Thomas M Jr. '91 Ritzler C&S,Ltd -1001 Lakeside Av
-1550 North Pnt Twr -Cleveland 44114 **Fx:**241-5890

(216) 566-5523 ..**Coughlin**, Timothy J '84 (Thompson H LLP) -127 Pub Sq
-3900 Key Ctr -Cleveland 44114 **Fx:**566-5800

(216) 622-8334 ..**Coughlin**, William E '83 (Calfee H&G LLP) -800 Superior Av
-Ste 1400 -Cleveland 44114 **Fx:**241-0816

(216) 586-3939 ..**Couhig**, Stephanie S '02 %Jones D -901 Lakeside Av
-Cleveland 44114 **Fx:**579-0212

Couhig, Thomas N '02 -6623 Ocean Pt -Mentor 44060

(440) 350-2684 ..**Coulson**, Charles E '74 (Lake Cnty Pros) -105 Main -Bx490
-Painesville 44077 **Fx:**350-2585

(614) 224-0531 ..**Coulter**, Lisa Weekley '88 OfCnsl Williams & P Co,LLC
-338 S High -2nd Fl -Columbus 43215 **Fx:**224-0553

(740) 223-3322 ..**Coulter**, Ted I '81 -391 S Main -Marion 43302

(513) 651-3505 ..**Counts**, Paul W '77 -432 Walnut -Ste 601 -Cincinnati 45202

(614) 227-7867 ..**Counts**, Thomas S '85 Tchrs Retirement Syst of OH -275 E Broad
-Columbus 43215

(216) 485-7970 ..**Courey**, Bruce M '89 -5454 State Rd -Parma 44134

(614) 462-3194 ..**Courtney**, Amy Sue '00 Franklin Cnty Pub Def -373 S High
-12th Fl -Columbus 43215

(513) 933-5527 ..**Courtney**, Darren L '96 Fujitec Amer Inc -401 Fujitec Dr
-Lebanon 45036

(330) 725-8474 ..**Courtney**, Lawrence J '73 -203 N Bway -Bx277 -Medina 44258
Fx:725-8518

(216) 520-7060 ..**Courtney**, Mary L '78 IRS-OH Div -5990 W Crk Rd
-Independence 44131

(614) 462-3664 ..**Courtney**, Michael J '01 %Hon DP O'Neill -369 S High
-Courtroom 9A -Columbus 43215

(216) 696-0600 ..**Courtney**, Michael M '75 (Rapoport SF&C) -55 Pub Sq -Ste 1750
-Cleveland 44113 **Fx:**696-2929

(937) 898-3980 ..**Courtney**, Paul M '82 -575 S Dixie Dr -Vandalia 45377

(248) 209-8435 ..**Courtney**, Ronald S '87 SrCnsl Valeo Inc -4100 N Atl Blvd
-Auburn Hills, MI 48326

(216) 696-4441 ..**Courtright**, Joy Zeiler '00 Zashin & R Co,LPA -55 Pub Sq
-Ste 1490 -Cleveland 44113 **Fx:**696-1618

(614) 461-1311 ..**Courtwright**, Angela M '04 %Reminger & R -65 E State
-4th Fl Cptl Sq Ofc Bldg -Columbus 43215 **Fx:**232-2410

(216) 443-7800 ..**Coury**, Donna M '00 Cuyahoga Cnty Pros -1200 Ontario -8th Fl
-Cleveland 44113 **Fx:**698-2270

(440) 835-0660 ..**Coury**, Elias J '87 Coury & C LPA -24340 Sperry Dr
-Westlake 44145

(440) 243-5668 ..**Coury**, John M '90 Generations Healthcare Mgt
-Two Berea Cmmns -Ste 1 -Berea 44017

(330) 454-2136 ..**Coury**, John S '77 J Coury & Assoc -116 Cleveland Av NW
-Ste 717 -Canton 44702

(216) 443-7800 ..**Coury**, Robert F '86 Cuyahoga Cnty Pros -1200 Ontario -8th Fl
-Cleveland 44113 **Fx:**698-2270

(740) 472-1647 ..**Coury**, Robert G '67 (Smith & C) -316 S Main -Bx599
-Woodsfield 43793

(937) 224-1611 ..**Cousineau**, Richard L '59 -120 W 2nd -Ste 733 -Dayton 45402

(216) 241-3366 ..**Couture**, Bernard P '91 -815 Superior Av E -Ste 1810
-Cleveland 44114

(614) 464-6400 ..**Coval**, Paul J '79 (Vorys SS&P LLP) -52 E Gay -Bx1008
-Columbus 43216 **Fx:**464-6350

(513) 621-8210 ..**Covatta**, Anthony G Jr. '79 (Drew & W Co,LPA) -1 W 4th
-Ste 2400 -Cincinnati 45202 **Fx:**621-5444

(216) 621-2234 ..**Covell**, Calvin G '68 (Tarolli SC&T) -526 Superior Av
-1111 Leader Bldg -Cleveland 44114 **Fx:**621-4072

(330) 796-3079 ..**Coven**, Christine L '74 Lockheed Martin Tactical Dfnse Sys
-1210 Massillon Rd -Akron 44315

(440) 352-3391 ..**Coven**, Steven H '03 %Dworken & B Co,LPA -60 S Park Pl
-Painesville 44077 **Fx:**352-3469

(513) 381-2838 ..**Cover**, Melissa Kurzhals '00 %Taft S&H LLP -425 Walnut
-Ste 1800 -Cincinnati 45202 **Fx:**381-0205

(614) 462-4553 ..**Coverdale**, Tracie A '91 Franklin Cnty CSEA -80 E Fulton
-Columbus 43215

(216) 696-7600 ..**Covey**, Christine C '80 (Duvin C&H) -1301 E 9th
-20th Fl Erievw Twr -Cleveland 44114 **Fx:**696-2038

(419) 535-1840 ..**Covrett**, Clinton C '75 (CC Covrett) -2727 N Holland-Sylvania Rd
-Ste E -Toledo 43615

(937) 222-2030 ..**Cowan**, Christopher F '81 (Cowan & H) -12 W Monument Av
-Dayton 45402

(216) 524-7979 ..**Cowan**, Dale H '81 -6100 W Crk Rd -#15 -Independence 44131

(440) 895-1811 ..**Cowan**, Elmer G Jr. '52 -2639 Wooster Rd -Rocky River 44116
Fx:356-2873

(440) 442-6677 .. **Cowan,** Gary '88 Elk & E Co,LPA -6100 Parkland Blvd
-Mayfield Heights 44124 **Fx:**442-7944

(513) 651-6800 .. **Cowan,** Grant S '85 (Frost BT LLC) -201 E 5th -2200 PNC Ctr
-Cincinnati 45202 **Fx:**651-6981

(614) 222-8686 .. **Cowans,** Timothy E '88 (Scott S&W LLP) -50 W Broad
-2500 LeVeque Twr -Columbus 43215 **Fx:**222-8688

(216) 241-2880 .. **Cowden,** Gerald W '75 (Cowden HN&L) -50 Pub Sq -Ste 1414
-Cleveland 44113 **Fx:**241-2881

(216) 241-2880 .. **Cowden Humphrey Nagorney & Lovett** -50 Pub Sq -Ste 1414
-Cleveland 44113 **Fx:**241-2881

(937) 222-1090 .. **Cowdrey,** Robert F '75 OfCnsl Statman HS&E LLC -110 N Main
-Ste 1520 -Dayton 45402 **Fx:**222-1046

(419) 774-4100 .. **Cowell,** Sheryl M '94 Children Services Board of Richland County
-731 Scholl Rd -Mansfield 44907

                Cowen, William B '79 -5712 10th Rd N -7 -Arlington, VA 22205

(570) 474-7579 .. **Cowger,** Alfred R Jr. '85 New Dana Perfumes Corp
-470 Oakhill Rd -Mountain Top, PA 18707

(913) 315-9164 .. **Cowin,** Joseph P '78 Sprint -6450 Sprint Pkwy
-Overland Park, KS 66251

(740) 446-0644 .. **Cowles,** Douglas M '76 (D Cowles Co,LPA) -435 2nd Av -Bx969
-Gallipolis 45631

(216) 566-5747 .. **Cox,** Andrew H '99 %Thompson H LLP -127 Pub Sq -3900 Key Ctr
-Cleveland 44114 **Fx:**566-5800

(713) 888-5026 .. **Cox,** Angela B '87 Minute Maid Co -2000 St James Pl
-Houston, TX 77056

(330) 656-1266 .. **Cox,** Anthony A Jr. '65 -118 W Streetsboro -#95 -Hudson 44236

(937) 228-1975 .. **Cox,** Bobby Joe '73 -130 W 2nd -Ste 810 -Dayton 45402

(513) 887-3474 .. **Cox,** Brenda S '94 Butler Cnty Pros -315 High -11th Fl -Bx515
-Hamilton 45012

(513) 381-6810 .. **Cox,** Daniel A '03 %Reisenfeld & Assoc -2355 Auburn Av
-Cincinnati 45219 **Fx:**381-0255

(248) 720-0290 .. **Cox,** Darcy E '03 %Simon G&F,PLC -363 W Big Beaver Rd
-Ste 300 -Troy, MI 48084 **Fx:**720-0291

(614) 228-6885 .. **Cox,** David G '89 Lane A&H LLC -175 S 3rd -Ste 700
-Columbus 43215 **Fx:**228-0146

(937) 372-6921 .. **Cox,** David W '76 (Cox K&R) -85 W Main -Xenia 45385

(216) 228-0415 .. **Cox,** Diane E '98 -1233 Arlngtn Rd -Lakewood 44107

(740) 286-6408 .. **Cox,** Donald A '79 (D Cox & Assoc) -239 Main -Jackson 45640

(703) 547-2677 .. **Cox,** Douglas B '89 XO Comm,Inc -11111 Sunset Hills Rd
-Reston, VA 20190

(216) 621-6684 .. **Cox,** Duane E '79 -1422 Euclid Av -Ste 350 The Hanna Bldg
-Cleveland 44115

(216) 522-4300 .. **Cox,** Earl G '70 US HUD -1350 Euclid Av -Ste 500
-Cleveland 44115

(614) 224-4357 .. **Cox,** Edward J Jr. '72 Cox S&P Co,LPA -115 W Main -Ste 400
-Columbus 43215 **Fx:**228-0701

(937) 644-3849 .. **Cox,** Faye D '01 (Schulze H&C) -110 S Main -Bx562
-Marysville 43040 **Fx:**644-1426

(614) 464-2572 .. **Cox,** Garth G '81 (Harris MB&C,PLL) -37 W Broad -9th Fl
-Columbus 43215 **Fx:**464-2245

(937) 328-2640 .. **Cox,** Gregory D '91 Clark Cnty Pub Def -50 E Columbia -4th Fl
-Springfield 45502 **Fx:**328-2715

(513) 333-0990 .. **Cox,** James S '91 (Martin & B) -120 E 4th -Ste 420
-Cincinnati 45202 **Fx:**333-0066

(937) 227-3700 .. **Cox,** Jeffrey T '91 (Faruki I&C PLL) -10 N Ludlow -500 Cthse
Plz SW -Dayton 45402 **Fx:**227-3717

                Cox, John M Jr. '78 -8150 Shaw Dr -Reynoldsburg 43068

(614) 645-7385 .. **Cox,** Joshua T '85 City Atty -90 W Broad -Columbus 43215

(937) 372-6921 .. **Cox Keller & Rowland** -85 W Main -Xenia 45385

(330) 244-8000 .. **Cox,** Kevin C '01 %RE Soles Jr -1401 S Main -Ste 202
-North Canton 44720 **Fx:**244-8002

(513) 528-6000 .. **Cox,** Lance S '70 (LS Cox Co,LPA) -480 Ohio Pike
-Cincinnati 45255

(216) 752-9341 .. **Cox,** Marion N '89 -3715 Warrensvll Ctr Rd -Ste 419
-Shaker Heights 44122

(614) 267-2871 .. **Cox,** Michael A '02 (Hall G&C) -3763 N High -Ste C
-Columbus 43214 **Fx:**267-2873

(513) 877-2900 .. **Cox,** Michael G '81 -8872 Debold-Koebel Rd
-Pleasant Plain 45162

(614) 645-7483 .. **Cox,** Michelle L '03 City Pros -375 S High -7th Fl -Columbus 43215

(614) 621-2313 .. **Cox,** Paul L III '75 -222 E Town -Columbus 43215

(606) 784-6418 .. **Cox,** Paul W Jr. '89 KY Dept of Pblc Advcy -Bx1038
-Morehead, KY 40351

(937) 434-7114 .. **Cox,** Ray A '68 (Cox & G) -267 Regency Ridge Dr -Dayton 45459

(202) 622-2880 .. **Cox,** Richard H Jr. '64 IRS -1111 Const Av NW
-Washington, DC 20024

(937) 548-4699 .. **Cox,** Robert J '51 -8903 State Route 571 -Arcanum 45304
Fx:548-4699

(937) 225-4652 .. **Cox,** Steven M '75 Montgomery Cnty Pub Def -117 S Main
-Ste 400 -Dayton 45422 **Fx:**225-3449

(330) 376-2700 .. **Cox,** Steven S '94 (Roetzel & A,LPA) -222 S Main -Akron 44308
Fx:376-4577

(330) 296-7447 .. **Cox,** Thomas A '75 -213 S Chestnut -Ravenna 44266

(937) 496-3210 .. **Cox,** William C '89 Montgomery Cnty Juv Ct -303 W 2nd -Rm 1144
-Dayton 45422

(614) 221-3155 .. **Cox,** Yvette A '79 (Bailey C LLC) -10 W Broad -Columbus 43215
Fx:221-0479

(419) 536-8600 .. **Cox-Doty,** Beverly J '91 %Dixon & H,Ltd -3361 Exec Pkwy
-Ste 100 -Toledo 43606

(440) 593-6211 .. **Coxon,** Gary L '71 (Kauffman & C) -180 Wshngtn -Bx97
-Conneaut 44030

(440) 997-6175 .. **Coxon,** Jeffrey L '92 (Warren & Y,PLL) -134 W 46th -Bx2300
-Ashtabula 44005 **Fx:**992-9114

(216) 426-4000 .. **Coy,** Betsy H '00 Applied Indstrl Technologies,Inc -One Applied Plz
-E 36th & Euclid -Cleveland 44115

(419) 249-7900 .. **Coy,** Edwin A '74 (Robison C&O) -Four SeaGate -9th Fl
-Toledo 43604 **Fx:**249-7911

(419) 243-8251 .. **Coy,** Mary F '85 Toledo-Lucas Cnty Port Auth -One Maritime Plz
-Toledo 43604

(513) 412-1463 .. **Coy,** Rhonda S '85 Great Amer Fncl Resrcs Inc -Bx5420
-Cincinnati 45202

(419) 241-9000 .. **Coyle,** David J '87 (Shumaker L&K,LLP) -1000 Jackson
-Toledo 43624 **Fx:**241-6894

(419) 248-2600 .. **Coyle,** Lori A '98 OfCnsl Rohrbachers LC&T Co,LPA -405 Mad Av
-8th Fl -Toledo 43604 **Fx:**248-2614

(513) 361-1200 .. **Coyle,** Timothy L '87 OfCnsl Squire S&D LLP -312 Walnut
-Ste 3500 -Cincinnati 45202 **Fx:**361-1201

(216) 523-1500 .. **Coyne,** Anthony J '88 %Mansour GG&M Co,LPA -55 Pub Sq
-Ste 2150 -Cleveland 44113 **Fx:**523-1705

(216) 781-9162 .. **Coyne,** Dennis M '85 -1428 Hmltn Av -Cleveland 44114

(216) 687-1311 .. **Coyne,** John C '01 (Reminger & R) -101 Prospect Av W
-1400 Mdlnd Bldg -Cleveland 44115 **Fx:**687-1841

(330) 376-2700 .. **Coyne,** John M III '95 (Roetzel & A,LPA) -222 S Main -Akron
44308 **Fx:**376-4577

(216) 781-1980 .. **Coyne,** John P '56 -1459 Hmltn Av -Cleveland 44114

(513) 922-3200 .. **Coyne,** Kenneth P '98 %Haverkamp BR&R Co,LPA
-5856 Glenway Av -Cincinnati 45238 **Fx:**922-8096

(440) 891-8388 .. **Coyne,** Loretta A '70 -7055 Engle Rd -Ste 6-606 -Cleveland 44130
Fx:891-8399

(216) 664-4850 .. **Coyne,** Lorraine '96 Prosecutor -1200 Ontario Av
-8th Fl Justice Ctr -Cleveland 44113 **Fx:**664-4399

                Coyne, Michael F '90 -127 Pub Sq -Cleveland 44114

(440) 835-0600 .. **Coyne,** Michael P '79 (Waldheger C,LPA) -1991 Crocker Rd
-Ste 550 -Westlake 44145 **Fx:**835-1511

(216) 642-3342 .. **Coyne,** Richard T '89 (Wegman H&V,LPA)
-6055 Rockside Wds Blvd -Ste 200 -Cleveland 44131
Fx:642-8826

(216) 566-5781 .. **Coyne,** Thomas J '85 (Thompson H LLP) -127 Pub Sq
-3900 Key Ctr -Cleveland 44114 **Fx:**566-5800

(513) 244-6648 .. **Coz,** Thomas A '79 -Bx5039 -Cincinnati 45205

(216) 348-9878 .. **Cozart,** Stacy E '99 %Sharon & K LLC -55 Pub Sq -Ste 750
-Cleveland 44113 **Fx:**348-9879

                Cozine, John C '98 -5024 Revere Ct -Mason 45040

(740) 284-1682 .. **Cozza,** Piero P '00 %Dickie M&C,PC -500 Market -Ste 10
-Steubenville 43952 **Fx:**284-1692

(614) 227-2000 .. **Crabtree,** Mark S '01 %Porter WM&A LLP -41 S High
-Columbus 43215 **Fx:**227-2100

                Crabtree, Valleri J '83 -930 Spring Loop -Celebration, FL 34747

(513) 870-2399 .. **Cracas,** Teresa C '98 Cincinnati Ins Co -6200 S Gilmore Rd
-Fairfield 45014

                Craemer-Smith, Melissa E '04 -(Address Unavailable)

(330) 643-2765 .. **Craft,** James D '90 Summit Cnty Pros-CSEA -171 S Main
-Akron 44308 **Fx:**643-2822

(606) 473-7303 .. **Craft,** Paul '04 %McBrayer ML&K -Bx280 -Greenup, KY 41144

(800) 890-5001 .. **Crafton,** Constance J '95 Becker Gallagher
-8790 Governors Hill Dr -Ste 102 -Cincinnati 45249

(502) 815-5000 .. **Crafton,** Thomas E '03 (Alber C,PSC) -9300 Shelbyvll Rd
-Ste 1300 Hurstbourne Pl -Louisville, KY 40222 **Fx:**815-5005

(419) 772-2205 .. **Crago,** David C '77 ONU-Pettit Clg of Law -525 S Main
-Ada 45810

(440) 603-2377 .. **Craig,** Andre A '84 Progressive Co -NY Div -6055 Parkland Dr
-Mayfield Heights 44124

                Craig, Barton J '75 -359 Amity Rd -Bethany, CT 06524

(419) 866-8900 .. **Craig,** Brian D '80 -6904 Sprng Vlly Dr -Ste 303 -Holland 43528

(937) 865-6800 .. **Craig,** Christopher J '99 Lexis/Nexis -Bx933 -Dayton 45401

(216) 443-7800 .. **Craig,** Kathleen S '84 Cuyahoga Cnty Pros -1200 Ontario -8th Fl
-Cleveland 44113 **Fx:**698-2270

                Craig, Kristen L '02 -155 Brookvalley Dr -Elyria 44035

(513) 381-2838 .. **Craig,** L Clifford '64 (Taft S&H LLP) -425 Walnut -Ste 1800
-Cincinnati 45202 **Fx:**381-0205

(216) 615-7302 .. **Craig,** Mark F '02 %Buckingham D&B,LLP -1375 E 9th -Ste 1700
-Cleveland 44114 **Fx:**621-5440

(859) 331-2838 .. **Craig,** Robert B '81 (Taft S&H LLP) -1717 Dixie Hwy -Ste 340
-Covington, KY 41011 **Fx:**(513) 381-6613

(614) 249-7683 .. **Craig,** Roger A '89 Nationwide Ins Co -1 Nationwide Plz
-Columbus 43215

(614) 876-2689 .. **Craig,** Steve A '76 -5251 Norwich -Hilliard 43026 **Fx:**876-0279

(330) 456-0061 .. **Craig,** Steven L '84 Heichel C&P Co,LPA -437 Market Av N
-Canton 44702

(513) 422-2001 .. **Crain,** Donald L '73 (Frost BT LLC) -300 N Main -Ste 200
-Middletown 45042 **Fx:**422-3010

(614) 224-7193 .. **Craine,** Kevin A '82 (Kincaid R&C) -2201 Riverside Dr
-Columbus 43221 **Fx:**586-4051

(419) 449-7800 .. **Crall,** Matthew E '02 %Leuthold & L -92 S Wshngtn -Tiffin 44883

(419) 535-0111 .. **Cramer,** Bruce A '68 -3170 W Central Av -Toledo 43606
Fx:531-9862

(937) 293-2016 .. **Cramer,** Carl A '73 C Cramer Co,LPA -2323 W Schantz Av
-Ste 216 -Kettering 45409

(513) 241-9400 .. **Cramer,** David C '73 Legal Aid -215 E 9th -Ste 200
-Cincinnati 45202

(304) 845-2580 .. **Cramer,** Jeffrey D '99 Berry KC&T -514 7th
-Moundsville, WV 26041

(216) 622-3600 .. **Cramer,** Marily A '77 US Atty -801 W Superior -Ste 400
-Cleveland 44113 **Fx:**622-3370

(513) 529-4848 .. **Cramer,** Philip W '71 Miami Univ -Dept of DS & MIS
-310 Upham Hall -Oxford 45056

(740) 387-9093 .. **Cramer,** Ronald D '75 Michel D&C -116 S Main -Marion 43302

(513) 703-5127 .. **Cramerding,** Jeffrey M '01 -1050 Academy Av -Cincinnati 45205

(216) 622-8200 .. **Crandall,** David J '91 (Calfee H&G LLP) -800 Superior Av
-Ste 1400 -Cleveland 44114 **Fx:**241-0816

(704) 383-4604 .. **Crandall,** Erika J '96 Wachovia Bank,NA -201 S Tryon
-Charlotte, NC 28202

(440) 442-6677 .. **Crandall,** Stephen S '94 Elk & E Co,LPA -6100 Parkland Blvd
-Mayfield Heights 44124 **Fx:**442-7944

(216) 622-8200 .. **Crandall,** Tracy D '97 %Calfee H&G LLP -800 Superior Av
-Ste 1400 -Cleveland 44114 **Fx:**241-0816

(740) 246-5624 .. **Crandell,** Riley C '01 -14578 Twp Rd -#1061 -Bx610
-Thornville 43076 **Fx:**246-5718

                Crane, Andrew B '04 -(Address Unavailable)

(937) 223-1201 .. **Crane,** Brent A '95 %Altick & C Co,LPA -1 S Main
-1700 One Dayton Ctr -Dayton 45402 **Fx:**223-5100

(513) 603-2213 .. **Crane,** Debra K '96 Ohio Casualty Ins Co -9450 Seward Rd
-Fairfield 45014

(216) 931-6000 .. **Crane**, James M '04 %Ulmer & B LLP -1300 E 9th -Ste 900 Penton Media Bldg -Cleveland 44114 **Fx:**931-6001

(216) 443-2791 .. **Crane**, Jonathan O '81 McDonald & Co -800 Superior Av -Ste 2100 -Cleveland 44114

(216) 861-1400 .. **Crane**, Kyle L '95 RJ Clapp & Assoc Co,LPA -1375 E 9th -One Cleve Ctr #2420 -Cleveland 44114 **Fx:**861-1401

(216) 621-0200 .. **Crane**, Matthew B '02 %Baker & H LLP -1900 E 9th -Ste 3200 -Cleveland 44114 **Fx:**696-0740

(330) 655-5800 .. **Crane**, Robert L Jr. '73 -2777 Blue Heron Dr -Hudson 44236

(216) 363-5220 .. **Crane**, Robert P '94 (Lindner WC&B,LLP) -55 Pub Sq -Ste 1600 -Cleveland 44113

(330) 796-9435 .. **Crane**, Robyn L '77 Goodyear Tire & Rubber Co -1144 E Market -Akron 44316

(440) 446-3078 .. **Crane**, Roderick J '83 Progressive Ins -Bx43258 -Richmond Heights 44143

Cranley, John J IV '00 -2426 Marylnd Av -Cincinnati 45204

(937) 225-4250 .. **Cranmer**, David J '87 Montgomery Cnty Juv Ct -303 W 2nd -Dayton 45422

(330) 454-5612 .. **Cranston**, Thomas K '76 -1369 Market Av N -Canton 44714

(513) 977-8200 .. **Crase**, Charles S '04 %Dinsmore & S LLP -255 E 5th -Ste 1900 -Cincinnati 45202 **Fx:**977-8141

(419) 673-1128 .. **Crates**, James L '65 (McKinley & C) -936 E Franklin -Bx207 -Kenton 43326

(740) 594-3558 .. **Crates**, Katrina O '04 SE OH Lgl Srvcs -1005 E State -Athens 45701 **Fx:**594-3791

(419) 673-5212 .. **Crates**, Randy L '86 -618 W Kohler -Kenton 43326

(617) 345-3000 .. **Craver**, James B '80 (Burns & L LLP) -125 Summer -8th Fl -Boston, MA 02110 **Fx:**345-3299

(330) 743-4116 .. **Crawford**, Anne F '91 Brennan FV&Y,Ltd -29 E Front -2nd Fl -Youngstown 44503

(314) 259-5810 .. **Crawford**, David E Jr. '93 (Sonnenschein N&R) -1 Metro Sq -Ste 3000 -Saint Louis, MO 63102

(614) 466-8911 .. **Crawford**, Franklin E '03 Atty Gen -30 E Broad -Columbus 43215 **Fx:**728-7582

(330) 452-6773 .. **Crawford**, George Ian '84 -101 Central Plz S -Ste 303 -Canton 44702

(440) 248-5151 .. **Crawford**, James D '74 (Glazer & C Co,LPA) -28815 Aurora Rd -Solon 44139

(740) 345-3431 .. **Crawford**, John A '81 (Reese PD&M,PLL) -36 N 2nd -Bx919 -Newark 43058 **Fx:**349-5116

(330) 836-0409 .. **Crawford**, Joseph A '87 -1849 Brookside Rd -Akron 44313

(419) 229-0224 .. **Crawford**, Leslie L '00 Investor Life Srvcs,Inc -825 S Cable Rd -Lima 45805

(614) 466-1154 .. **Crawford**, Linda S '84 Legis Srvc Commssn -77 S High -Columbus 43215

Crawford, Lisa K '91 -895 Central Av -Ste 840 -Cincinnati 45202

(216) 692-7197 .. **Crawford**, Matthew V '94 Park OH Industries Inc -23000 Euclid Av -Cleveland 44117

(216) 522-2918 .. **Crawford**, Richard D '90 IRS -1240 E 9th -Rm 409 -Cleveland 44199

(513) 412-2311 .. **Crawford**, Shawn J '94 Annuity Investors Life Ins Co -525 Vine -11th Fl -Cincinnati 45202

(216) 479-8500 .. **Crawford**, Stephen J '97 %Squire S&D LLP -127 Pub Sq -4900 Key Twr -Cleveland 44114 **Fx:**479-8780

(614) 249-3398 .. **Crawford**, Timothy D '97 Nationwide Life Ins Co -1 Nationwide Plz -01-09-V2 -Columbus 43215

(740) 455-7123 .. **Crawmer**, Shawn E '95 Muskingum Cnty Pros -27 N 5th -Zanesville 43701

(513) 361-1200 .. **Craycraft**, Kenneth R Jr. '01 %Squire S&D LLP -312 Walnut -Ste 3500 -Cincinnati 45202 **Fx:**361-1201

(513) 868-7100 .. **Creach**, Larry H Jr. '99 Davidson A&C Co,LPA -127 N 2nd -Hamilton 45011 **Fx:**868-9579

(216) 348-1700 .. **Creagan**, John M '85 OfCnsl Davis & Y -101 Prospect Av W -Ste 1700 -Cleveland 44115 **Fx:**621-0602

(440) 838-5104 .. **Creager**, Michael J '78 -6622 Morningside Dr -Brecksville 44141

(419) 241-9000 .. **Creamer**, Jeffrey S '79 (Shumaker L&K,LLP) -1000 Jackson -Toledo 43624 **Fx:**241-6894

(740) 852-7130 .. **Creamer**, Michael E Jr. '99 Madison Cnty Common Pleas Ct -Bx527 -London 43140 **Fx:**852-7144

(919) 929-8270 .. **Creatore**, Ronald M '92 -509 Weaver Mine Trl -Chapel Hill, NC 27517

(937) 208-2205 .. **Creech**, Dale E Jr. '78 Premier Hlth Prtnrs -1 Wyoming -Dayton 45409

(937) 434-6227 .. **Creech**, Herbert Jr. '73 -200 Jamestwn Cir -F -Dayton 45458

(440) 349-3813 .. **Creech**, Nancy N '92 -31860 Burlwood Dr -Solon 44139

(216) 443-8591 .. **Creed**, Laura W '93 Cuyahoga Cnty Ct Cmmn Pleas -1200 Ontario -Justice Ctr 11th Fl -Cleveland 44113

(614) 471-5150 .. **Creed**, Lawrence C '97 Evans Mechwart Hambleton & Tilton -170 Mill -Gahanna 43230

(614) 462-3555 .. **Creedon**, William R '95 Franklin Cnty Pros -373 S High -Columbus 43215

(216) 252-7300 .. **Creger**, Michelle B '81 Amer Greetings Corp -1 Amer Rd -Cleveland 44144

(513) 381-9200 .. **Crehan**, Kenneth J '02 %Rendigs FK&D,LLP -One W 4th -Ste 900 -Cincinnati 45202 **Fx:**381-9206

(216) 931-6000 .. **Crehore**, Charles A '76 OfCnsl Ulmer & B LLP -1300 E 9th -Ste 900 Penton Media Bldg -Cleveland 44114 **Fx:**931-6001

(513) 579-6400 .. **Creighton**, Richard L Jr. '73 (Keating M&K PLL) -1 E 4th -1400 Provident Twr -Cincinnati 45202 **Fx:**579-6457

(330) 750-9636 .. **Creighton**, William S '91 -295 Sexton -Struthers 44471

(614) 244-5700 .. **Cremeans**, Kay E '88 FOP-OH Labor Cncl -222 E Town -Columbus 43215

(216) 522-4914 .. **Crespy**, Gregory P '87 SSA/OHA -1350 Euclid Av -7th Fl -Cleveland 44115

Cretella, Michael A '04 -(Address Unavailable)

(330) 865-4434 .. **Creveling**, Michael A '94 (Creveling & C) -88 S Portage Path -Ste 306 -Akron 44303

(330) 865-4434 .. **Creveling**, Wendy S '95 (Creveling & C) -88 S Portage Path -Ste 306 -Akron 44303

(937) 223-6211 .. **Crew & Buchanan** -2580 Kettering Twr -Dayton 45423

(937) 223-6211 .. **Crew**, Robert B '36 (Crew & B) -2580 Kettering Twr -Dayton 45423

(937) 434-6040 .. **Crews**, Virginia L '04 -7501 Paragon Rd -Dayton 45459

(202) 761-7565 .. **Cribbin**, Robert D '84 US Army Corps of Engnrs -20 Mass Av NW -Washington, DC 20314

(216) 523-7240 .. **Cribbs**, Nancy J '72 CSU Univ Devlpmnt -2121 Euclid Av -MM103 -Cleveland 44115

(765) 742-4394 .. **Criblez**, Jennifer M '04 E McCoy -424 Columbia -Lafayette, IN 47901

(614) 464-1626 .. **Crider**, Benjamin W '01 %L Smith & Assoc -929 Harrison Av -Ste 300 -Columbus 43215

(419) 772-1870 .. **Crider**, Cecily A '93 ONU-Pettit Clg of Law -525 S Main -Ada 45810

(859) 586-9950 .. **Crigler**, Larry J '71 -6024 Rogers Ln -Bx169 -Burlington, KY 41005

(513) 793-9170 .. **Crilley**, Patrick R '77 Crilley Homes,Inc -Bx42222 -Cincinnati 45242

(330) 336-6666 .. **Crilly**, John R '97 -126 King -Wadsworth 44281

(614) 752-8984 .. **Crim**, Connie A '89 OH Supreme Ct -30 E Broad -3rd Fl -Columbus 43215

(937) 276-5770 .. **Crim**, Gary W '73 -943 Manh Av -Dayton 45406

(216) 663-1650 .. **Crimaldi**, Lisa M '98 -5706 Turney Rd -Ste 103 -Cleveland 44125

(309) 874-5890 .. **Cring**, Faith D '99 -809 Valley Vw Cir -Bloomington, IL 61704

(216) 574-2550 .. **Crisafi**, David A '92 -1370 Ontario -Ste 600 -Cleveland 44113

(216) 592-5000 .. **Crisafi**, Marilyn M '92 %Tucker E&W LLP -925 Euclid Av -1150 Huntngtn Bldg -Cleveland 44115 **Fx:**592-5009

(330) 394-9692 .. **Crisan**, James J '95 %M White Co,LPA -156 Park Av NE -Bx1150 -Warren 44482 **Fx:**394-8589

(216) 931-6000 .. **Crisci**, George S '83 (Ulmer & B LLP) -1300 E 9th -Ste 900 Penton Media Bldg -Cleveland 44114 **Fx:**931-6001

(513) 977-8200 .. **Crisler**, Scott A '01 %Dinsmore & S LLP -255 E 5th -Ste 1900 -Cincinnati 45202 **Fx:**977-8141

(330) 730-4317 .. **Crislip**, Kenneth M '04 -3793 S Hametown Rd -Norton 44203 **Fx:**825-5913

(419) 738-7180 .. **Crisp**, Jamie L '02 %Poppe Law Ofc -1100 W Auglaize -Wapakoneta 45895

(614) 644-7233 .. **Criss**, Michael Scott '97 Atty Gen -150 E Gay -Columbus 43215 **Fx:**728-9327

Crissman, Charlotte M '00 -400 Crestvw Blvd -Columbus 43202

(607) 248-1918 .. **Crist**, Karen M '88 Corning,Inc -1 Rvrfrnt Plz -SP-TI-03 13E09W -Corning, NY 14831

(415) 875-5722 .. **Crist**, Paul G '74 (Jones Day) -555 Calif -26th FL -San Francisco, CA 94104 **Fx:**875-5700

(513) 932-2115 .. **Crist**, Renee L '01 Rittgers & R -12 E Warren -Lebanon 45036

(216) 363-4500 .. **Crist**, Thomas O '95 (Benesch FC&A LLP) -200 Pub Sq -Ste 2300 -Cleveland 44114 **Fx:**363-4588

(614) 462-2243 .. **Crist**, Tyson A '99 %Schottenstein Z&D -250 West -Bx165020 -Columbus 43216 **Fx:**462-5135

(440) 248-7906 .. **Cristallo**, Paul J '93 %Mazanec R&R Co,LPA -34305 Solon Rd -Ste 100 -Cleveland 44139 **Fx:**248-8861

(614) 221-1166 .. **Critchett**, Eugene R '01 %Plymale & Assoc -495 S High -Ste 400 -Columbus 43215 **Fx:**221-6633

(330) 264-4444 .. **Critchfield Critchfield & Johnston Ltd** -225 N Market -Bx599 -Wooster 44691 **Fx:**263-9278

(740) 397-4040 .. **Critchfield Critchfield & Johnston Ltd** -10 S Gay -Mount Vernon 43050 **Fx:**397-6775

(330) 723-6404 .. **Critchfield Critchfield & Johnston Ltd** -3985 Medina Rd -Ste 100 -Medina 44256

(330) 674-3055 .. **Critchfield Critchfield & Johnston Ltd** -138 E Jackson -Ste A -Millersburg 44654

(330) 497-5131 .. **Critchfield**, Maureen C '98 East OH Gas -7015 Freedom Av -North Canton 44720

(216) 363-6056 .. **Crites**, Andrew J '89 -1370 Ontario -Ste 2000 -Cleveland 44113

(614) 228-5822 .. **Crites**, Don Michael '78 (Rich C&D,LLC) -300 E Broad -Ste 300 -Columbus 43215 **Fx:**228-2725

(513) 381-4700 .. **Croall**, David T '81 (Porter WM&A LLP) -250 E 5th -Ste 2200 -Cincinnati 45202 **Fx:**421-0991

(440) 323-8174 .. **Crobaugh**, Christopher J '99 -300 4th -Ste C -Elyria 44035

(330) 643-2112 .. **Croce**, Christine L '94 Summit Cnty Sheriffs Ofc -53 Univ Av -Akron 44308

(419) 882-0877 .. **Crocker**, Douglas J '04 -4149 Holland Sylvania Rd -Ste 7 -Toledo 43623

(330) 643-2902 .. **Crocker**, Robin G '96 Summit Cnty Juv Ct -650 Dan -Akron 44310 **Fx:**643-8682

Croghan, Harold H '67 -1217 Robert Dickey Pkwy -Dayton 45409

(614) 462-2281 .. **Crognale**, Corey V '80 (Schottenstein Z&D) -250 West -Bx165020 -Columbus 43216 **Fx:**462-5135

(843) 971-8801 .. **Crombie**, John R '76 Custom Devlpmnt Solutions -1470 Ben Sawyer Blvd -Mount Pleasant, SC 29464

Cromer, Carol A '82 -205 McWilliams Rd -Eubank, KY 42567

(614) 466-8457 .. **Cromley**, Charles T Jr. '97 -631 W Greene -Piqua 45356

Cromley, Robert E Jr. '82 Industrial Commssn of OH -30 W Spring -9th Fl -Columbus 43215 **Fx:**752-8785

(505) 986-1334 .. **Cron**, Daniel R '91 (D Cron Law Firm, PC) -125 Lincoln Av -Bx40 -Santa Fe, NM 87504

(419) 248-2600 .. **Cron**, Nicholas J '74 (Rohrbachers LC&T Co,LPA) -405 Mad Av -8th Fl -Toledo 43604 **Fx:**248-2614

(614) 466-7264 .. **Cronheim**, George K '98 OH Legal Rghts Srvc -8 E Long -5th Fl -Columbus 43215

(708) 354-2097 .. **Cronin**, Christopher J '98 Air Liquide -5230 E Av -La Grange, IL 60525

(330) 887-8365 .. **Cronin**, Michael C '04 Westfield Grp -1 Park Cir -Bx5001 -Westfield Center 44251 **Fx:**887-2588

(704) 331-3536 .. **Cronin**, Michael T '96 %Moore & V PLLC -100 N Tryon -Ste 4700 -Charlotte, NC 28202 **Fx:**339-5836

(513) 721-8210 .. **Cronin**, Patrick J '77 OfCnsl Spraul V&D -830 Main -Ste 200 -Cincinnati 45202

(419) 259-6376 .. **Croniser**, Gretchen E '96 US Atty -4 Seagate -Ste 308 -Toledo 43604 **Fx:**259-6360

(513) 241-6166 .. **Croog**, Charles F '94 Financial Stocks,Inc -441 Vine -Ste 507 -Cincinnati 45202

(330) 208-1000 .. **Crookes**, Thomas R '87 OfCnsl Vorys SS&P LLP -106 S Main -First Natl Twr -Akron 44308

(330) 864-5550 .. **Crooks**, Walter E '02 %Hahn L&P LLP -One GOJO Plz -Ste 300 -Akron 44311 **Fx:**864-7986

(513) 287-2209 .. **Cropper**, Leanne Rauh '92 Cinergy Corp -139 E 4th -Rm 260 -Cincinnati 45202

(800) 323-1331 .. **Crosbie**, Thomas B '69 Modern Mgmt,Inc -253 Commerce Dr -Ste 105 -Grayslake, IL 60030

Crosby, D Lee '03 -(Address Unavailable)
(216) 696-5400 .. **Crosby,** Elizabeth A '89 (Crosby O & Assoc Co,LPA) -55 Pub Sq
-Ste 1475 -Cleveland 44113 **Fx:**696-2610
(216) 696-5959 .. **Crosby,** Fred C '88 (Pomerantz & C Co,LPA)
-20676 Southgate Park Blvd -Ste 103 -Cleveland 44137
(216) 696-5400 .. **Crosby O'Brien & Associates Co, LPA** -55 Pub Sq -Ste 1475
-Cleveland 44113 **Fx:**696-2610
(216) 771-4648 .. **Crosby,** William M '82 (Crosby Law Ofc,LLC) -55 Pub Square
-Ste 1475 -Cleveland 44113
(419) 868-8788 .. **Crosgrove,** Darrell M '93 -5660 Southwyck -100-H -Toledo 43614
(513) 701-5529 .. **Croskery,** Robert F '95 -6860 Tylersvll Rd -Ste 1 -Mason 45040
Fx:701-5528
(740) 223-4290 .. **Croskey,** Jennifer S '00 Marion Cnty Pros -134 E Center
-Marion 43302 **Fx:**223-4299
(937) 866-2922 .. **Croskey,** Thomas P '80 Croskey Law Ofc -126 S 7th
-Miamisburg 45342 **Fx:**866-2922
(419) 399-8270 .. **Crosley,** Casey R '02 Paulding Cnty Pros Ofc -112 ½ N Water
-Paulding 45879
(513) 397-1463 .. **Cross,** Anita S '91 Cincinnati Bell Telephone Co -201 E 4th
-Atrium I -Cincinnati 45202
(937) 225-2516 .. **Cross,** Colleen R '96 US Bankrptcy Ct -120 W 3rd -Dayton 45402
(614) 716-1580 .. **Cross,** Jeffrey D '82 Amer Elec Pwr Co -1 Riverside Plz
-Columbus 43215
(216) 363-4500 .. **Cross,** Robert C '87 OfCnsl Benesch FC&A LLP -200 Pub Sq
-Ste 2300 -Cleveland 44114 **Fx:**363-4588
(330) 477-8535 .. **Cross & Rose Co,LPA** -2884 Whipple Av NW -Canton 44708
Fx:477-2611
(513) 861-7100 .. **Cross,** Wende C '93 (Cross S & Assoc Co,LPA)
-3460 Reading Rd -Cincinnati 45229 **Fx:**861-7101
(419) 666-6188 .. **Crosser,** Joan M '93 -Bx60436 -Rossford 43460
(614) 677-2406 .. **Crossett,** Kevin S '02 Nationwide Ins Co -One Nationwide Plz
-1-35-10 -Columbus 43215
(513) 933-9011 .. **Crossley,** Paige A '92 -52 E Mulberry -Bx435 -Lebanon 45036
(216) 861-3086 .. **Crossman,** Darryl H '93 Reid M&W -55 Pub Sq -Ste 2010
-Cleveland 44113 **Fx:**861-4409
(937) 294-6000 .. **Crossman,** Frances A '89 (Winwood C & Assoc)
-3077 Kettering Blvd -Ste 210 -Dayton 45439
(216) 363-4500 .. **Crossman,** Jeffrey A '01 %Benesch FC&A LLP -200 Pub Sq
-Ste 2300 -Cleveland 44114 **Fx:**363-4588
(419) 297-3771 .. **Crossmock,** Steven L '89 -520 Mad Av -1037 Spitzer Bldg
-Bx1507 -Toledo 43603
(513) 621-1414 .. **Crosthwaite,** Daryl A '89 Butkovich SS&G Co,LPA -36 E 7th
-Ste 2600 -Cincinnati 45202 **Fx:**977-5580
(513) 241-5670 .. **Croswell & Adams Co,LPA** -1208 Sycamore -Cincinnati 45210
(513) 241-5670 .. **Croswell,** Robert S III '74 Croswell A & Co,LPA -1208 Sycamore
-Cincinnati 45210
(419) 627-7782 .. **Croteau,** Bruce R '87 Erie Cnty Family Ct -323 Columbus Av
-Sandusky 44870
(440) 209-0609 .. **Crotser,** Michele L '85 -Bx1091 -Willoughby 44096
(614) 224-8374 .. **Crotte,** Alberto D '94 Legal Aid -40 W Gay -Columbus 43215
(419) 244-4605 .. **Crouch,** Victor R '78 Port Lwrnce Title -616 Mad Av -Toledo 43604
(513) 721-4876 .. **Crouse,** Candace C '00 %Sirkin P&S LLP -105 W 4th -920 4th &
Race Twr -Cincinnati 45202 **Fx:**721-0876
(513) 225-6666 .. **Croushore,** Paul G '91 -Bx75170 -Cincinnati 45275
(513) 721-7002 .. **Crout,** Daniel W '76 -632 Vine -Ste 800 -Cincinnati 45202
(740) 695-4821 .. **Crow,** Donna L '90 (Burech & C) -121 Newell Av
-Saint Clairsville 43950
(740) 992-5132 .. **Crow,** Irving C '75 (Crow & C) -110 W 2nd -Bx668
-Pomeroy 45769
(419) 425-2769 .. **Crow,** Robroy L '86 -124 W Front -Ste 201 -Findlay 45840
Fx:427-4673
(614) 463-9770 .. **Crow,** Scot C '97 %Roetzel & A,LPA -155 E Broad
-Natl City Ctr 12th Fl -Columbus 43215 **Fx:**463-9792
(800) 837-2508 .. **Crowder,** Marjorie B '75 SE OH Lgl Srvcs -800 Gallia -Ste 700
-Portsmouth 45662
(740) 387-0800 .. **Crowder,** Mary K '92 -334 E Center -Bx544 -Marion 43301
(740) 474-2179 .. **Crowder-Dorsey,** Kathy Jo '89 Huffer & H Co,LPA
-130 W Franklin -Bx464 -Circleville 43113
(216) 241-8111 .. **Crowe,** Frances N '04 %Sullivan & S Ltd -815 Superior Av E
-Ste 2016 -Cleveland 44114
(513) 352-6641 .. **Crowe,** James J '66 Cnsl Thompson H LLP -312 Walnut -14th Fl
-Cincinnati 45202 **Fx:**241-4771
(614) 466-3947 .. **Crowe,** Jodi F '93 OH Brd of Nursing -17 S High -Ste 400
-Columbus 43215
(513) 831-8511 .. **Crowe,** Stephen C '76 (Crowe & W) -1019 Main -Bx296
-Milford 45150
(614) 462-3555 .. **Crowell,** Adam E '02 %Franklin Cnty Pros -373 S High
-Columbus 43215
(704) 387-1359 .. **Crowell,** James D '75 Bank of America -101 S Tryon
-Charlotte, NC 28255
(937) 836-1013 .. **Crowell,** Larry G '75 (LG Crowell Co,LPA) -207 S Main -Bx339
-Englewood 45322 **Fx:**836-7363
(937) 225-6258 .. **Crowl,** Thomas L Jr. '78 Montgomery Cnty Juv Ct -303 W 2nd
-Dayton 45422
(513) 621-1652 .. **Crowley Ahlers & Roth Co,LPA** -414 Walnut -Ste 707
-Cincinnati 45202 **Fx:**621-8430
(614) 846-3870 .. **Crowley,** Charles E '63 -4967 Lyle Rd -Bx16562 -Columbus 43216
(513) 621-1652 .. **Crowley,** James C IV '76 (Crowley A&R Co,LPA) -414 Walnut
-Ste 707 -Cincinnati 45202 **Fx:**621-8430
(614) 876-7511 .. **Crowley,** James W '85 -4149 Maystar Way -Hilliard 43026
(614) 848-7883 .. **Crowley,** Timothy G '75 -150 W Wilson Bridge Rd -Ste 101
-Worthington 43085
(216) 761-4203 .. **Crowther,** Denise C '96 Huron Hospital -13951 Terrace Rd
-Cleveland 44112
(216) 642-3342 .. **Crowther,** Lawrence A '84 (Wegman H&V,LPA)
-6055 Rockside Wds Blvd -Ste 200 -Cleveland 44131
Fx:642-8826
(419) 874-5610 .. **Croy & Hendel,LLP** -801 W South Boundary -Ste C
-Perrysburg 43551
(419) 734-6845 .. **Croy,** Lorrain R '95 Ottawa Cnty Pros -315 Madison -2nd Fl
-Port Clinton 43452 **Fx:**734-3862
(419) 874-5610 .. **Croy,** Paul E '89 (Croy & H,LLP) -801 W South Boundary -Ste C
-Perrysburg 43551

(800) 243-0210 .. **Croyle,** Sherry A '87 Westfield Ins -1 Park Cir -Bx501 -Westfield
Center 44251
(412) 429-1250 .. **Crozier,** Ryan E '03 Cindrich & Co -525 Wshngtn Av
-Carnegie, PA 15106
(440) 352-4484 .. **Cruikshank,** David E '73 -8 N State -Ste 376 -Painesville 44077
(760) 597-4635 .. **Crumbaker,** Brian R '99 Unitrin Direct Ins -2790 Business Park Dr
-Vista, CA 92081
(937) 910-2851 .. **Crumbley,** Aimee L '02 Natl City Mortgage -3232 Newmark Dr
-Bldg 9 -Miamisburg 45342
(937) 223-8177 .. **Crump,** Edith E '91 %Coolidge WW&L -33 W 1st -Ste 600
-Dayton 45402 **Fx:**223-6705
(937) 264-5116 .. **Crump,** James R '89 Industrial Commssn of OH -3401 Park Ctr Dr
-Ste 300 -Dayton 45414
(216) 781-1212 .. **Crump,** Robert J '68 (Walter & H LLP) -1301 E 9th -Ste 3500
-Cleveland 44114 **Fx:**575-0911
(440) 333-7330 .. **Cruse,** Brian C '89 (Valore & C Co,LPA) -23550 Ctr Ridge Rd
-Westlake 44145
(513) 751-2148 .. **Crutcher,** John T '75 Cembex Physician Prtnrs,Inc
-2522 Highland Av -Cincinnati 45219
(202) 653-6772 .. **Cruz,** Ivelisse '96 US Merit Syst Protectn Brd -1615 M NW
-Washington, DC 20419
(513) 574-9600 .. **Cruze,** John J '70 -6470 Glenway Av -Ste 270 -Cincinnati 45211
(216) 696-1422 .. **Crystal,** Larry '65 (McCarthy LC&L Co,LPA) -101 Prospect Av W
-1800 Mdlnd Bldg -Cleveland 44115 **Fx:**696-1210
(440) 572-5083 .. **Csank,** James F '66 -11610 Rvr Moss Rd -Strongsville 44136
(216) 592-5000 .. **Csikos,** Debra '94 %Tucker E&W LLP -925 Euclid Av
-1150 Huntngtn Bldg -Cleveland 44115 **Fx:**592-5009
(440) 884-1309 .. **Csiszar-Highman,** Debbie A '97 -1962 Hope Haven Dr
-Parma 44134
(440) 329-5193 .. **Csokmay,** Jeffrey R '93 Lorain Cnty Dom Rltns Ct -226 Middle Av
-Cnty Admin Bldg -Elyria 44035
(216) 621-0200 .. **Csomos,** Andrea L '01 %Baker & H LLP -1900 E 9th -Ste 3200
-Cleveland 44114 **Fx:**696-0740
(419) 872-6600 .. **Csomos,** Laura A '00 %Handwork & K -900 W South Boundary
-Bldg 8-B -Perrysburg 43551
(864) 422-4644 .. **Csontos,** Alan A '75 Michelin NA Inc -515 Michelin Rd -IP/MARC
-Greenville, SC 29602
(216) 621-9870 .. **Cubar,** John C '78 (McNeal SA&B Co,LPA) -123 W Prospect Av
-Ste 250 Van Sweringen Arcade -Cleveland 44115 **Fx:**522-1112
(419) 243-7243 .. **Cubbon,** Frank W Jr. '53 (Cubbon & Assoc Co,LPA) -405 N Huron
-Ste 500 -Toledo 43604
(419) 243-7243 .. **Cubbon,** Kyle A '84 Cubbon & Assoc Co,LPA -405 N Huron
-Ste 500 -Toledo 43604
(419) 243-7243 .. **Cubbon,** Stuart F '81 Cubbon & Assoc Co,LPA -405 N Huron
-Ste 500 -Toledo 43604
(614) 466-3703 .. **Cuckler,** Steven R '02 OH House Rep Caucus -77 S High -14th Fl
-Columbus 43215
(216) 523-4077 .. **Cudak,** Gail L '77 Eaton Corp -1111 Superior Av -Cleveland 44114
Cudnik, Jonathan L '04 -(Address Unavailable)
(440) 995-3008 .. **Cuellar,** Michael M '92 Danaher Corp -6095 Parkland Blvd
-Ste 310 -Cleveland 44124
(216) 771-6500 .. **Cuilli,** Leonard A '97 %K Weiner & Assoc Co,LPA -75 Pub Sq
-4th Fl -Cleveland 44113 **Fx:**771-6540
(419) 332-5587 .. **Culbert,** Roger A '73 (Culbert & C) -200 S Arch -Fremont 43420
Fx:332-1422
(419) 242-1555 .. **Culbert,** William M '64 OfCnsl Spitler & W-Y Co,LPA -1000 Adams
-Ste 200 -Toledo 43624
(330) 753-1151 .. **Culbertson,** David E '65 -2447 Mnchstr Rd -Akron 44314
Fx:848-0372
(216) 931-6000 .. **Culbertson,** Mary M '95 %Ulmer & B LLP -1300 E 9th
-Ste 900 Penton Media Bldg -Cleveland 44114 **Fx:**931-6001
(216) 621-0200 .. **Culbertson,** William J '95 %Baker & H LLP -1900 E 9th -Ste 3200
-Cleveland 44114 **Fx:**696-0740
(614) 252-2026 .. **Culbreath,** Stanlee E '75 (Culbreath & Assoc) -90 N Nelson Rd
-Columbus 43219
Cull, William J '72 -561 Coy Ln -Chagrin Falls 44022
(513) 619-1549 .. **Cullen,** Blake W '02 Prasco,LLC -7155 K Kemper Rd
-Cincinnati 45249
(216) 268-6511 .. **Cullen,** Craig E '76 Soft Winds -11801 Clifton Blvd
-Lakewood 44107
(312) 861-8000 .. **Cullen,** Daniel F '98 %Baker & M -130 E Randolph Dr
-Ste 3500 One Pru Plz -Chicago, IL 60601 **Fx:**861-2899
(440) 356-0062 .. **Cullen,** James P '85 (Rego C&H Co,LPA) -21270 Lorain Rd
-Fairview Park 44126
(216) 292-5807 .. **Cullen,** Jean M '91 %Singerman MD&K -3401 Enterprise Pkwy
-Ste 200 -Beachwood 44122 **Fx:**292-5867
(216) 621-2090 .. **Cullen,** John L '93 (Gibbons & C LLP) -815 Superior Av -Ste 1210
-Cleveland 44114 **Fx:**621-2062
(808) 655-8329 .. **Cullen,** Steven P '97 US ARMY JAG -OSJA 2510/USAHI Hawaii
-Attn: APVG-JA -Schofield Barracks, HI 96857
(216) 621-0150 .. **Culler,** M Patricia '85 OfCnsl Hahn L&P LLP
-3300 BP Twr/200 Pub Sq -Ste 3300 -Cleveland 44114
Fx:241-2824
(740) 397-5262 .. **Cullers,** James J '59 OfCnsl Zelkowitz B&C -121 E High
-Mount Vernon 43050
(216) 479-8500 .. **Cullers,** Michael A '95 %Squire S&D LLP -127 Pub Sq
-4900 Key Twr -Cleveland 44114 **Fx:**479-8780
(216) 875-7500 .. **Cullers,** Romney B '91 (Krembs & C Co,LPA) -55 Pub Sq
-Ste 1700 -Cleveland 44113 **Fx:**875-7501
(614) 292-0582 .. **Culley,** Christopher M '82 %OSU -190 N Oval Mall
-103 Bricker Hall -Columbus 43210
Cullis, David H '80 -1809 Sherck Blvd -Wooster 44691
(614) 287-2592 .. **Cullison,** Daryl L '82 Columbus State Cmmnty Cllg -550 E Spring
-Columbus 43215
(859) 431-8200 .. **Cullison,** Richard A '77 Legal Aid -302 Greenup
-Covington, KY 41011
(740) 593-5046 .. **Culp,** Barbara V '84 Athens Cnty CSEA -Bx37 -The Plains 45780
(540) 434-5502 .. **Culp,** Trisha A '02 %Wharton A&W,PC -100 S Mason -Bx20028
-Harrisonburg, VA 22801 **Fx:**434-0316
(614) 466-5394 .. **Culshaw,** Kelly L '96 Pub Def -8 E Long -Columbus 43215
(740) 453-0888 .. **Cultice & Brown** -121 N 4th -Bx490 -Zanesville 43702
(740) 453-0888 .. **Cultice,** Peter N '83 (Cultice & B) -121 N 4th -Bx490
-Zanesville 43702

(740) 453-0888 ..**Cultice Brown**, Susan C '83 (Cultice & B) -121 N 4th -Bx490
-Zanesville 43702

(330) 394-6711 ..**Culver**, Fred A '60 -239 Marylnd NE -Warren 44483

(419) 517-7000 ..**Culver**, Jeffery A '02 %Kenney & N,Ltd -5470 Main -Ste 300
-Sylvania 43560 **Fx:**517-7001

(330) 762-9933 ..**Culver**, Kathryn F '82 Ferguson & H -120 E Mill -Ste 415
-Akron 44308

(937) 436-0033 ..**Cumbo**, Jennifer S '01 %Ruffolo SD&L -7501 Paragon Rd
-Dayton 45459

(937) 496-7797 ..**Cumming**, John A '73 Montgomery Cnty Pros -301 W 3rd -Bx972
-Dayton 45422 **Fx:**225-3470

(937) 865-6800 ..**Cummings**, Brian K '95 Lexis/Nexis -Bx933 -Dayton 45401

(937) 865-7925 ..**Cummings**, Carrie W '93 Lexis/Nexis -Bx933 -Dayton 45401

(614) 693-8134 ..**Cummings**, Cynthia C '78 Ofc of General Cnsl -DFAS-GA/CO
-Bx182317 -Columbus 43218

Cummings, Dana E '82 -117 Swoxford Pl
-Lees Summit, MO 64063

(440) 331-9599 ..**Cummings**, David A '94 -20800 Ctr Ridge Rd -Ste 200
-Rocky River 44116

Cummings, Joel P '03 US Army JAG Corp -1st Armored Div
-Unit 23746B37 -APO, AE 09034

(513) 762-7620 ..**Cummings**, John C '94 (Cummings & Co,LPA) -312 Walnut
-Ste 1600 -Cincinnati 45202

(510) 505-0722 ..**Cummings**, John P '73 (Cummings & Assoc -37161 Niles Blvd
-Ste B -Fremont, CA 94536 **Fx:**791-3306

Cummings, Lisa M '95 -5837 Karric Sq Dr -362 -Dublin 43016

(513) 946-3000 ..**Cummings**, Philip R '89 Hamilton Cnty Pros -230 E 9th
-Cincinnati 45202 **Fx:**946-3017

(513) 634-1906 ..**Cummings**, Theodore P '03 Procter & Gamble
-One Procter & Gamble Plz -Cincinnati 45202

(513) 868-9985 ..**Cummins**, Bill W '96 -105 Court -Ste 204 -Hamilton 45011

(513) 621-0267 ..**Cummins**, James R '67 Waite SB&C -1 W 4th
-1513 4th & Vine Twr -Cincinnati 45202

(513) 683-9000 ..**Cummins**, John R '86 (Slovin & C) -9435 Waterstone Blvd
-Ste 270 -Cincinnati 45249

(216) 566-2381 ..**Cummins**, Michael T '83 Sherwin Williams Co -101 Prosepect Av
-Cleveland 44115

(502) 589-5400 ..**Cummins**, Peter M '01 %Frost BT,LLC -400 W Market -Ste 3200
-Louisville, KY 40202

(937) 281-6273 ..**Cummiskey**, John P '87 Quantrum LLC -714 E Monument -#104
-Dayton 45402

(614) 228-5125 ..**Cummiskey**, Thomas M '97 Park Natl Bank -140 E Town
-Ste 1010 -Columbus 43215

(419) 609-1311 ..**Cuneo**, Richard P '98 (Reminger & R) -237 W Wshngtn Row
-2nd Fl -Sandusky 44870 **Fx:**626-4805

(513) 771-6768 ..**Cuni Ferguson & LeVay Co,LPA** -10655 Sprngfld Pike
-Cincinnati 45215

(513) 771-6768 ..**Cuni**, Thomas L Jr. '75 (Cuni F&L Co,LPA) -10655 Sprngfld Pike
-Cincinnati 45215

Cunliffe, Erika B '01 -2223 S Overlook Rd -Cleveland 44106

(330) 864-5550 ..**Cunniff**, John J '99 %Hahn L&P LLP -One GOJO Plz -Ste 300
-Akron 44311 **Fx:**864-7986

(609) 896-3600 ..**Cunniff**, Thomas A '95 %Fox R LLP -997 Lenox Dr -Bldg 3
-Lawrenceville, NJ 08648 **Fx:**896-1469

(330) 743-5101 ..**Cunning**, Patrick P '84 (Green H&S,Co LPA) -16 Wick Av -Ste 400
-Youngstown 44503 **Fx:**743-3451

(330) 364-9070 ..**Cunningham**, Arthur B '63 OfCnsl Hardin & S,LPA -132
Fair Av NW -New Philadelphia 44663 **Fx:**364-9073

(614) 228-4546 ..**Cunningham**, Catherine A '83 %Shuler P&B,LPA -145 E Rich
-Ste 400 -Columbus 43215

(330) 375-2030 ..**Cunningham**, Cheri B '82 Law Dept -161 S High -Ste 202
-Akron 44308

(330) 344-7626 ..**Cunningham**, Daniel P '78 Akron Gen Hlth Syst-Legal
-400 Wabash Av -Akron 44307

(614) 424-4566 ..**Cunningham**, Guy H '98 Battelle Memorial Inst -505 King Av
-Columbus 43201

(513) 871-0447 ..**Cunningham**, James J '73 Triannic LLC -3171 Portsmouth Av
-Cincinnati 45208

(513) 863-6600 ..**Cunningham**, Lyn A '89 L Cunningham Co,LPA -616 Dayton
-Bx1166 -Hamilton 45012

(908) 730-4113 ..**Cunningham**, Marc S '92 %Foster Wheeler Inc
-Perryvll Corp Park -Law Dept - Litigation -Clinton, NJ 08809

(419) 523-3396 ..**Cunningham**, Margaret A '68 (Cunningham & C) -749 N Perry
-Bx7 -Ottawa 45875 **Fx:**523-6428

(419) 222-1155 ..**Cunningham**, Mariah M '03 %Scherner H&C,LLC -714 W North
-Lima 45801 **Fx:**227-3131

(740) 797-7909 ..**Cunningham**, Matthew A '98 Ohio Dept of Jobs & Family Services
-Bx2630 -Athens 45701

(419) 523-3396 ..**Cunningham**, Matthew A '99 Cunningham & C -749 N Perry -Bx7
-Ottawa 45875 **Fx:**523-6428

(937) 865-6800 ..**Cunningham**, Melissa A '95 Lexis/Nexis -Bx933 -Dayton 45401

(513) 241-4110 ..**Cunningham**, Pierce E '60 OfCnsl Deters B&L,PSC -441 Vine
-Ste 3500 Carew Twr -Cincinnati 45202 **Fx:**241-4551

(330) 767-3143 ..**Cunningham**, Priscilla J '95 -404 3rd Av SW -Beach City 44608

(330) 535-5711 ..**Cunningham**, Richard T '53 OfCnsl Brouse M -106 S Main
-500 First Natl Twr -Akron 44308 **Fx:**253-8601

(614) 210-1840 ..**Cunningham**, Russell N '89 (Barrett EC&E LLP) -7269 Sawmill Rd
-Dublin 43016 **Fx:**210-1841

(859) 371-7300 ..**Cunningham**, Teresa L '88 -71 Cavalier Blvd -Ste 111
-Florence, KY 41042 **Fx:**371-7326

(304) 232-8100 ..**Cunningham**, Thomas M '95 (Cassidy MCV&T,LC) -1413 Eoff
-The 1st State Cptl -Wheeling, WV 26003 **Fx:**232-8200

(513) 793-4400 ..**Cunningham**, William D '75 Katzman LH&B -9000 Plainfld Rd
-Cincinnati 45236 **Fx:**793-4691

(304) 737-3737 ..**Cuomo**, Jason A '02 -1511 Commerce -Wellsburg, WV 26070

(216) 348-5400 ..**Cupar**, David B '99 %McDonald H Co,LPA -600 Superior Av E
-Ste 2100 -Cleveland 44114 **Fx:**348-5474

(216) 621-8484 ..**Cuppage**, David M '90 (Climaco LPW&G Co,LPA) -1228 Euclid Av
-Ste 900 Halle Bldg -Cleveland 44115 **Fx:**771-1632

(614) 464-6400 ..**Cupps**, David S '72 (Vorys SS&P LLP) -52 E Gay -Bx1008
-Columbus 43216 **Fx:**464-6350

(330) 493-4443 ..**Curati**, Jennifer E '00 EMP -4535 Dressler Rd NW -Canton 44718

(440) 808-0011 ..**Curatolo**, Joseph G '77 (Renner KGBT&W,LPA) -24500 Ctr
Ridge Rd -Ste 280 -Westlake 44145 **Fx:**808-0657

(440) 282-7539 ..**Curci**, Nicholas R '65 -1700 Cooper Foster Park Rd -Lorain 44053

(614) 280-1100 ..**Curley**, William C '78 (Keener DC&P,LPA) -88 E Broad -Ste 1750
-Columbus 43215

(219) 235-9544 ..**Curliss**, Laura A '94 St Joseph Cnty Pros -227 W Jffrsn Blvd
-10th Fl -South Bend, IN 46601

(614) 221-2838 ..**Curp**, John P '95 (Taft S&H LLP) -21 E State -12th Fl
-Columbus 43215 **Fx:**221-2007

(937) 255-6111 ..**Curp**, Sharon A '89 AFMC LO/JAB B -2240 B -Bldg11, Rm C1
-Wright Patterson AFB 45433

(614) 227-2000 ..**Curphey**, James D '83 (Porter WM&A LLP) -41 S High
-Columbus 43215 **Fx:**227-2100

(727) 726-8624 ..**Curphey**, William E III '73 (W Curphey & Assoc)
-2605 Enterprise Rd E -Ste 155 -Clearwater, FL 33759
Fx:726-8654

(330) 253-5060 ..**Curran**, Colleen C '97 %Brennan M&D,LLC -75 E Market
-Akron 44308 **Fx:**253-1977

(216) 521-7151 ..**Curran**, John J '57 -13363 Mad Av -Lakewood 44107

(216) 687-1900 ..**Curran**, Mallory C '02 Legal Aid -1223 W 6th -Cleveland 44113
Fx:687-0779

(513) 352-6647 ..**Curran**, Matthew C '03 %Thompson H LLP -312 Walnut -14th Fl
-Cincinnati 45202 **Fx:**241-4771

(772) 288-0048 ..**Curran**, Maura S '00 %Kramer S&L,PA
-853 SE Monterey Cmmns Blvd -Stuart, FL 34996 **Fx:**288-0049

(937) 981-7318 ..**Curren**, Conrad A '59 -330 Jffrsn -Bx149 -Greenfield 45123

(614) 227-2000 ..**Currence**, Kysha L '02 %Porter WM&A LLP -41 S High
-Columbus 43215 **Fx:**227-2100

(216) 589-8399 ..**Currie**, Douglas F '88 %Surety Title Agncy -1010 Leader Bldg
-Cleveland 44114

(614) 469-3241 ..**Currie**, Michael W '83 (Thompson H LLP) -10 W Broad -Ste 700
-Columbus 43215 **Fx:**469-3361

(614) 227-2000 ..**Currin**, Joseph H '99 %Porter WM&A LLP -41 S High
-Columbus 43215 **Fx:**227-2100

(216) 586-3939 ..**Currivan**, John D '78 (Jones D) -901 Lakeside Av
-Cleveland 44114 **Fx:**579-0212

(614) 430-8885 ..**Curry**, Bruce A '91 (Curry RS&M Co,LLC) -8000 Ravines Edge Ct
-Ste 103 -Columbus 43235 **Fx:**430-8890

(804) 290-2946 ..**Curry**, Edith L '97 Capital One Srvcs -4870 Sadler Rd
-12015-0350 -Glen Allen, VA 23060

(816) 426-5446 ..**Curry**, John C '67 FAA -901 Locust -Rm 506, DOT Bldg
-Kansas City, MO 64106

(216) 771-6500 ..**Curry**, Matthew P '04 %K Weiner & Assoc Co,LPA -75 Pub Sq
-4th Fl -Cleveland 44113 **Fx:**771-6540

(330) 744-0291 ..**Curry**, Robert J '95 (Boyd RC&C Co LPA) -400 Sky Bk Bldg
-Bx6565 -Youngstown 44501

(937) 443-6511 ..**Curry**, Robert M '78 (Thompson H LLP) -2000 Cthse Plz NE
-Bx8801 -Dayton 45401 **Fx:**443-6635

(614) 430-8885 ..**Curry Roby Schoenling & Mulvey Co,LLC**
-8000 Ravines Edge Ct -Ste 103 -Columbus 43235 **Fx:**430-8890

(330) 376-7245 ..**Curtin**, Cynthia K '89 %Curtin & Assoc -159 S Main -920 Key Bldg
-Akron 44305 **Fx:**376-8128

(330) 376-7245 ..**Curtin**, G Michael '83 (Curtin & Assoc) -159 S Main -920 Key Bldg
-Akron 44305 **Fx:**376-8128

(614) 221-2702 ..**Curtin**, James B '85 (Jackson & C Co,LPA) -171 E Lvngstn Av
-Columbus 43215

(216) 586-3939 ..**Curtin**, John D '03 (Jones D) -901 Lakeside Av -Cleveland 44114
Fx:579-0212

(419) 443-0689 ..**Curtin**, John V '88 -2578 W Twp Rd 18 -Ste 100 -Tiffin 44883

(614) 523-2251 ..**Curtin**, Richard A '76 Amer Alliance of Creditor Atty Inc
-2550 Corp Exchange Dr -Ste 204 -Columbus 43231

(859) 572-8930 ..**Curtis**, Beth A '88 Genl Cable Corp -4 Tesseneer Dr
-Highland Heights, KY 41076

(614) 442-9300 ..**Curtis**, Douglas E '87 (D Curtis & Co LLP) -Bx21075
-Columbus 43221

(216) 696-1076 ..**Curtis**, Jack S '85 Hohmann B&C Co,LPA -1370 Ontario
-Ste 520 Standard Bldg -Cleveland 44113 **Fx:**696-2317

(301) 738-2081 ..**Curtis**, Lawrence T '75 Ringler Assoc -15502 Avry Rd
-Rockville, MD 20855

(513) 765-6000 ..**Curtis**, Mildred A '81 LensCrafters,Inc -4000 Luxottica Pl
-Mason 45040

(216) 681-2393 ..**Curtis**, Ronda G '92 East Cleveland Law Dept -14340 Euclid Av
-East Cleveland 44112

(216) 642-9969 ..**Curtis**, Scott D '93 -4141 Rockside Rd -Ste 230
-Seven Hills 44131

(937) 865-6800 ..**Curtis-Austin**, Kelli C '00 Lexis/Nexis -Bx933 -Dayton 45401

(216) 443-7800 ..**Curtis-Patrick**, Saundra J '80 Cuyahoga Cnty Pros -1200 Ontario
-8th Fl -Cleveland 44113 **Fx:**698-2270

(817) 521-8609 ..**Curzan**, James N '84 Lexis Nexis -2814 Hedgeway Dr
-Arlington, TX 76016

(937) 878-8030 ..**Cusack**, David J '94 (Mayer & C LLC) -510 W Main
-Fairborn 45324 **Fx:**878-8031

(614) 880-0888 ..**Cusack**, Mary Jo '59 -5655 N High -Ste 200 -Worthington 43085
Fx:880-0085

(614) 469-5737 ..**Cusack**, William W '85 US HUD -200 N High -7th Fl
-Columbus 43215

(216) 371-2438 ..**Cushing**, Mary T '81 -2171 N St James Pkwy
-Cleveland Heights 44106 **Fx:**932-3983

(513) 831-8511 ..**Cushman**, Christopher S '97 %Crowe & W -1019 Main -Bx296
-Milford 45150

(937) 325-3022 ..**Cushman**, Linda J '89 -2 W Columbia -Ste 200 -Springfield 45502

(216) 622-8200 ..**Cushwa**, Mara E '90 (Calfee H&G LLP) -800 Superior Av
-Ste 1400 -Cleveland 44114 **Fx:**241-0816

(330) 746-7027 ..**Cusick**, Kelly R '03 Fed Bankruptcy Ct -10 E Commerce
-Youngstown 44503

(216) 479-8500 ..**Cusick**, Mark A '75 (Squire S&D LLP) -127 Pub Sq -4900 Key Twr
-Cleveland 44114 **Fx:**479-8780

(330) 945-8070 ..**Cusimano**, Christopher D '93 -2428 23rd -Cuyahoga Falls 44223

(216) 771-1760 ..**Cusimano**, Jennifer B '93 Smith & C LLP -1801 E Ninth -Ste
900 Ohio Svngs Plz -Cleveland 44114 **Fx:**771-3387

(216) 696-0650 ..**Cusimano**, Joseph J III '92 (Kaman & C) -50 Pub Sq
-Ste 600 Trmnl Twr -Cleveland 44113

(330) 456-7922 ..**Cusma**, Patrick L '96 -315 W Tuscarawas
-Ste 301 Natl City Bk Bldg -Canton 44702

(513) 421-4646 ..**Cussen**, Michael P '95 McCaslin I&M,LPA -632 Vine -Ste 900
-Cincinnati 45202 **Fx:**421-7929

(513) 421-6630 ..**Cussen,** William M '69 Lindhorst & D Co,LPA -312 Walnut
-Ste 2300 -Cincinnati 45202

(740) 992-2117 ..**Custer,** John S '87 Meigs Cnty Dept of Human Srvcs -175 Race
-Bx191 -Middleport 45760

(513) 684-7376 ..**Custis,** Douglass L '67 SSA-OHA -312 Elm -Ste 2100
-Cincinnati 45202

(513) 381-1234 ..**Cutcher,** Timothy R '74 -1019 Main -Cincinnati 45202

(216) 443-8590 ..**Cuthbert,** Amy R '02 Cuyahoga Cnty Ct Cmmn Pleas
-1200 Ontario -Justice Ctr 11th Fl -Cleveland 44113

(216) 515-1635 ..**Cuthbertson,** Jennifer L '04 %Frantz W LLP -127 Pub Sq
-2500 Key Center -Cleveland 44114 **Fx:**515-1650

(216) 621-1000 ..**Cuthbertson,** Patricia R '90 %Moscarino & T,LLP -1422 Euclid Av
-Hanna Bldg Ste 630 -Cleveland 44115 **Fx:**622-1556

(330) 493-9611 ..**Cutler,** Jay L '83 -4618 Dressler Rd NW -Canton 44718

(614) 791-9112 ..**Cutler,** Kimberly M '02 %Wright Law Co,LPA -4266 Tuller Rd
-Ste 101 -Dublin 43017 **Fx:**791-9116

(513) 946-3820 ..**Cutler,** Nancy J '93 Hamilton Cnty Pub Def -230 E 9th -3rd Fl
-Cincinnati 45202 **Fx:**946-3707

(937) 378-6165 ..**Cutrell,** Jay D '76 (McConn & C) -118 S Main -Georgetown 45121
Fx:378-6567

(740) 772-5595 ..**Cutright,** James K '84 (Cutright & C) -76 W 2nd -Chillicothe 45601

(740) 772-5595 ..**Cutright,** James M '50 (Cutright & C) -76 W 2nd -Chillicothe 45601

(614) 221-1400 ..**Cutter,** James M '77 -85 E Gay -Ste 500 -Columbus 43215

(614) 221-3155 ..**Cvetanovich,** Danny L '77 Bailey C LLC -10 W Broad
-Columbus 43215 **Fx:**221-0479

(216) 696-4200 ..**Cvetkovic,** Adrienne N '04 %Schneider SR&L PLL
-1111 Superior Av -Ste 1000 -Cleveland 44114 **Fx:**696-7303

(440) 277-8265 ..**Cwalina,** Daniel R '94 LorMet Cmmnty Fed Credit Union
-1825 E 28th -Lorain 44055
Cwalinski, Stanley C '04 -(Address Unavailable)

(888) 397-9499 ..**Cweiber,** Bruce E '94 Precision Title Agncy,Inc -13967 Cedar Rd
-Ste 205 -South Euclid 44118 **Fx:**(216) 397-9455

(216) 781-2600 ..**Cybulski,** Donald F '75 OfCnsl Lowe EW&M Co,LPA -1660 W 2nd
-610 Skylight Ofc Twr -Cleveland 44113 **Fx:**781-2610

(602) 792-7164 ..**Cybulsky,** Joseph '71 Bank One -Bx13779 -Tucson, AZ 85732
Cydrus, Michael S '04 -(Address Unavailable)

(216) 595-9225 ..**Cydulka,** Michele L '85 -33 Lyman Cir -Shaker Heights 44122

(937) 836-3648 ..**Cyester,** Tod A '89 -310 S Union Blvd -Englewood 45322

(216) 755-5500 ..**Cyncynatus,** Jerry M '83 Developers Diversified Rlty Corp
-3300 Enterprise Pkwy -Beachwood 44122

(330) 471-3530 ..**Cyperski,** Nancy L '84 Timken Co -1835 Dueber Av SW -Bx6927
-Canton 44706

(330) 492-6659 ..**Cyperski,** Robert H '84 -1201 30th NW -Ste 04-B -Canton 44709

(216) 781-1212 ..**Cyphert,** Michael A '73 (Walter & H LLP) -1301 E 9th -Ste 3500
-Cleveland 44114 **Fx:**575-0911

(216) 696-6500 ..**Czack,** Michael W '84 (Caravona & C,PLL) -50 Pub Sq
-Ste 1900 Trmnl Twr -Cleveland 44113 **Fx:**696-1411

(937) 227-3700 ..**Czanik,** Kara A '02 %Faruki I&C PLL -10 N Ludlow
-500 Cthse Plz SW -Dayton 45402 **Fx:**227-3717

(419) 241-1200 ..**Czarnecki,** John '72 Cooper & W,LPA -900 Adams -Toledo 43624
Fx:242-5675

(937) 748-2522 ..**Czechowski,** Donna K '89 %J Smith Co,LPA -130 N Main
-Springboro 45066 **Fx:**748-2712

(937) 449-2800 ..**Czechowski,** Thomas L '74 (Chernesky H&K PLL)
-10 Cthse Plz SW -Ste 1100 -Dayton 45402 **Fx:**449-2821

(419) 382-6888 ..**Czerniakowski,** Joseph L '54 -3626 S Detroit Av -Toledo 43614

(614) 464-6400 ..**Czerwonka,** Kevin M '90 (Vorys SS&P LLP) -52 E Gay -Bx1008
-Columbus 43216 **Fx:**464-6350

(313) 242-3434 ..**Czeryba,** Dennis J '77 (Czeryba and G,PC) -19 E Front
-Monroe, MI 48161

(330) 726-2441 ..**Czopur,** Edward C '73 -945 Windham -Ste 3 -Boardman 44512

(330) 740-2180 ..**Czopur-Gaffney,** Melanie A '01 %Hon G Donofrio -120 Market
-Youngstown 44503 **Fx:**740-2182
Czupik, Nancy M '84 -Bx81531 -Cleveland 44181

(330) 494-6666 ..**Daane,** Robert B '75 -4429 Fulton Dr NW -Canton 44718

(216) 621-0200 ..**Dabb,** Wayne C Jr. '71 (Baker & H LLP) -1900 E 9th -Ste 3200
-Cleveland 44114 **Fx:**696-0740

(770) 955-5070 ..**Dabbiere,** David K '84 Manhattan Assoc Inc
-2300 Windy Ridge Pkwy -7th Flr -Atlanta, GA 30339

(440) 526-5875 ..**Dacek,** James S '76 -6696 Farview Rd -Brecksville 44141

(614) 236-1950 ..**Dachner,** David A '72 -2369 E Main -Columbus 43209

(800) 646-0400 ..**Dacoros,** Carol L '97 First Energy -76 S Main -Akron 44308

(513) 579-6400 ..**D'Addesa,** Danielle M '03 %Keating M&K PLL -1 E 4th
-1400 Provident Twr -Cincinnati 45202 **Fx:**579-6457

(216) 574-2600 ..**Daddona,** David S '83 Lasko & L Co,LPA -1406 W 6th -Ste 200
-Cleveland 44113

(919) 483-6983 ..**Dadswell,** Charles E Jr. '93 Glaxo SmithKline -5 Moore Dr
-Bx13358 -Research Triangle Park, NC 27709

(513) 381-4888 ..**Dady,** James P '94 Mapother & M,PSC -1014 Vine
-Ste 2320 Kroger Bldg -Cincinnati 45202 **Fx:**381-3117

(440) 871-5899 ..**Daffner-Gulla,** Laura A '91 -27025 Knckrbckr Rd -Ste 10
-Bay Village 44140

(937) 223-1788 ..**Daganhardt,** Robert Casey '82 (Hess & D Co,LPA)
-3946 Kettering Blvd -Kettering 45439 **Fx:**223-1789

(740) 653-6464 ..**Dagger Johnston Miller Ogilvie & Hampson** -144 E Main
-Bx667 -Lancaster 43130 **Fx:**653-8522

(513) 232-1700 ..**Daggett,** John K '82 (Moore M&M) -7416 Jager Ct
-Cincinnati 45230
D'Agostino, Paul A '04 -(Address Unavailable)

(216) 443-7800 ..**Daher,** Paul A '01 %Cuyahoga Cnty Pros -1200 Ontario -8th Fl
-Cleveland 44113 **Fx:**698-2270

(202) 267-0094 ..**Dahill,** Charles D '83 Ofc of the Chief Cnsl -2100 2nd SW
-Rm 3400 -Washington, DC 20593

(513) 629-1853 ..**Dahl,** Elisabeth A '95 Wstrn & Sthrn Life Ins Co -400 Bway
-Cincinnati 45202

(330) 451-7716 ..**Dahl,** Milton Dean '96 Stark Cnty Cmn Pleas Ct -115 Central Plz N
-Canton 44702

(216) 348-5400 ..**Dahl,** Sherri L '01 %McDonald H Co,LPA -600 Superior Av E
-Ste 2100 -Cleveland 44114 **Fx:**348-5474

(614) 228-4200 ..**Dahlberg,** Carl G '01 %Babbitt & W LLP -503 S Front -Ste 200
-Columbus 43215 **Fx:**228-4224

(330) 451-7241 ..**Dahler,** Fred W '92 5th Dist Ct of Appls -110 Central Plz S
-Ste 320 -Canton 44702 **Fx:**451-7249

(614) 857-4330 ..**Dahmer,** Douglas M '93 %Weltman W&R Co,LPA -175 S 3rd
-Ste 900 -Columbus 43215 **Fx:**222-2193

(937) 224-1514 ..**Dahms,** Kenneth C '73 Montgomery Cnty Hlth Dist -117 S Main
-Dayton 45402

(937) 225-5766 ..**Daidone,** Leon J '81 Montgomery Cnty Pros -301 W 3rd -Bx972
-Dayton 45422 **Fx:**225-3470

(216) 592-5000 ..**Daiker,** Matthew M '04 %Tucker E&W LLP -925 Euclid Av
-1150 Huntngtn Bldg -Cleveland 44115 **Fx:**592-5009

(216) 696-0900 ..**Daiker,** Paul B '93 (Zukerman D&L,LPA) -2000 E 9th -Ste 700
-Cleveland 44115 **Fx:**696-8800

(513) 868-3911 ..**Daiker,** Victoria A '77 -301 High -Fifth Third Bk Bldg
-Hamilton 45011

(216) 687-6878 ..**Daiker-Middaugh,** Pamela A '89 CSU-Marshall Cllg of Law
-2121 Euclid Av -LB138 -Cleveland 44115 **Fx:**687-6881
Dailey, Bruce R '03 -400 E 5th Av -Lancaster 43130

(330) 424-7777 ..**Dailey,** Coleen H '81 Columbiana Cnty Cmmn Pleas Ct
-105 S Market -Lisbon 44432

(614) 677-2989 ..**Dailey,** Gerald E '82 Cnsl Nationwide Ins Co -1 Nationwide Plz
-Columbus 43215

(513) 977-8200 ..**Dailey,** Michael G '99 %Dinsmore & S LLP -255 E 5th -Ste 1900
-Cincinnati 45202 **Fx:**977-8141

(859) 669-8000 ..**Dailey,** Patricia J '96 Shire US Inc -1 Rvrfrnt Pl
-Newport, KY 41071 **Fx:**669-8414

(330) 674-0457 ..**Dailey,** Stephen P '80 -225 E Jackson -Millersburg 44654

(330) 762-9191 ..**Daily & Haskins** -7 W Bowery -Ste 604 -Akron 44308
Fx:762-4244

(330) 762-9191 ..**Daily,** John A '63 (Daily & H) -7 W Bowery -Ste 604 -Akron 44308
Fx:762-4244

(614) 277-9001 ..**Daily,** Ruth A '99 -2500 Gantz Rd -Grove City 43123 **Fx:**539-7290

(216) 479-8500 ..**Dakin,** Carol F '69 (Squire S&D LLP) -127 Pub Sq -4900 Key Twr
-Cleveland 44114 **Fx:**479-8780

(513) 381-2011 ..**Dalal,** Amy N '04 %Hammond Law Grp,LLC -441 Vine
-3311 Carew Twr -Cincinnati 45202 **Fx:**381-2227

(330) 315-1060 ..**Dalayanis,** Antoni '97 -12 E Exchange -Akron 44308

(419) 774-5569 ..**Dalbey,** Garry D '79 Richland Cnty Cmmn Pleas Ct -50 Park Av E
-Mansfield 44902

(301) 986-6708 ..**Dale-Bartow,** Dawn '87 Bank of America -5550 Friendship Blvd
-Chevy Chase, MD 20815

(419) 354-9244 ..**Daler,** Justin E '01 Wood Cnty Pub Def -123 N Summit
-Bowling Green 43402

(614) 469-5715 ..**D'Alessandro,** Mark T '79 US Atty -303 Marconi Blvd -Ste 200
-Columbus 43215

(419) 227-9595 ..**Daley Balyeat & Leahy LLC** -1728 Allentown Rd -Lima 45805
Fx:227-3177

(419) 227-9595 ..**Daley,** Charles W '49 Daley B&L LLC -1728 Allentown Rd
-Lima 45805 **Fx:**227-3177

(419) 227-9595 ..**Daley,** Douglas A '80 Daley B&L LLC -1728 Allentown Rd
-Lima 45805 **Fx:**227-3177

(216) 443-7800 ..**Daley,** Paul D '83 Cuyahoga Cnty Pros -1200 Ontario -8th Fl
-Cleveland 44113 **Fx:**698-2270

(614) 280-4000 ..**Daley,** Richard C Jr. '78 Pizzuti Dvlpmnt Inc -2 Miranova Pl
-Ste 800 -Columbus 43215

(440) 357-5654 ..**Dalheim,** Theodore J '70 -10255 Cherry Hill Dr -Painesville 44077

(440) 357-6372 ..**Dalheim,** Theodore J Jr. '90 -10401 Stuart Dr -Concord 44077

(330) 545-1550 ..**Daliman,** John P '86 Windsor House,Inc -101 W Lbrty
-Girard 44420

(513) 762-6946 ..**Dallob,** Naomi C '79 Chemed Corp -255 E 5th -Cincinnati 45202

(216) 566-5818 ..**Daloia,** Andrea B '01 %Thompson H LLP -127 Pub Sq
-3900 Key Ctr -Cleveland 44114 **Fx:**566-5800

(740) 452-7555 ..**Dal Ponte,** Don A '73 (Gottlieb JB&D,PLL) -320 Main -Bx190
-Zanesville 43702 **Fx:**452-2257
Dalrymple, Daniel W '04 -(Address Unavailable)

(713) 403-8092 ..**Dalton,** John T '80 Intl Bus Cnsl -4400 Post Oak Pkwy -Ste 1000
-Houston, TX 77027

(330) 255-5910 ..**Daly,** Brendan J '00 Ernst & Young, LLP -222 S Main -Ste 300
-Akron 44308

(937) 291-7025 ..**Daly,** Denis G '69 Amcast Indstrl Corp -7887 Wshngtn Vllg Dr
-Dayton 45459

(513) 241-9400 ..**Daly,** Gerald R '72 Legal Aid -10 Jrnl Sq -Hamilton 45011

(513) 241-9400 ..**Daly,** Hugh F '87 Legal Aid -215 E 9th -Ste 200 -Cincinnati 45202

(330) 825-9858 ..**Daly,** James E '71 -146 25th NW -Barberton 44203

(419) 372-2030 ..**Daly,** Lawrence J '87 Bowling Green State Univ -16 Williams Hall
-Bowling Green 43403

(937) 222-0500 ..**Daly,** William T '98 -120 W 2nd -Ste 1717 -Dayton 45402

(614) 466-2980 ..**Damaser,** Hilary R '92 Atty Gen -30 E Broad -Columbus 43215
Fx:728-9470

(937) 525-5549 ..**D'Ambrosi,** Bernard Jr. '93 Konecranes,Inc -4401 Gtwy Blvd
-Springfield 45502

(440) 942-6262 ..**Dame,** Stacy E '02 (Wiles & R) -35350 Curtis Blvd -Ste 530
-Eastlake 44095 **Fx:**942-7211

(216) 464-6776 ..**Damelio,** Anthony A Jr. '78 -23240 Chagrin Blvd -Ste 100
-Beachwood 44122

(216) 623-1155 ..**Damelio,** Marilyn F '78 Nationwide Ins -323 Lakeside Av W
-Ste 410 Lakeside Pl -Cleveland 44113

(513) 587-2882 ..**Dameron,** Jonathan P '91 (JP Dameron Co,LPA) -2662
Madison Rd -Cincinnati 45208

(513) 241-6650 ..**Dameron,** Nancy J '93 %M Godbey & Assoc -914 Main -Ste 200
-Cincinnati 45202 **Fx:**241-6649

(216) 566-0064 ..**Damiani,** Louis C '79 (Armstrong MD&Z) -101 Prospect Av W
-1725 The Mdlnd Bldg -Cleveland 44115 **Fx:**566-0224

(216) 291-2400 ..**D'Amico,** Ann M '88 %Zimmerman CE&M -5001 Mayfld Rd
-Ste 105 -Cleveland 44124

(216) 622-8200 ..**D'Amico,** Cheryl A '96 (Calfee H&G LLP) -800 Superior Av
-Ste 1400 -Cleveland 44114 **Fx:**241-0816

(412) 995-3000 ..**Damico,** David A '91 (Burns W&H) -106 Isabella
-Four Northshore Ctr -Pittsburgh, PA 15212 **Fx:**995-3300

(614) 864-8210 ..**D'Amico,** Jodelle M '83 -7110 E Lvngstn Av -Reynoldsburg 43068

(440) 449-3333 ..**D'Amico,** Louis A '88 (Argie D&V) -6449 Wilson Mills Rd
-Mayfield Village 44143

(937) 748-1004 ..**D'Amico,** Michael J '92 %Kirby & T LPA -4 Sycamore Crk Dr
-Springboro 45066 **Fx:**748-2390

(440) 205-0188 ..**D'Amico,** Mitchell '96 (D'Amico & Assoc Co,LPA) -7333 Ctr
-Mentor 44060

(937) 434-3197 .. **D'Amico,** Rudolph A '51 -5173 Sugar Maple Dr -Dayton 45440
(330) 721-0131 .. **D'Amico,** Tanya '01 -5192 Hanover Dr -Medina 44256
(419) 897-6500 .. **Damicone,** Jason S '03 %Barkan & R Ltd -1701 Woodlnds Dr -Maumee 43537 **Fx:**897-6200
(330) 688-3355 .. **Damicone,** Mary T '92 -100 Ridge Side Ct -Munroe Falls 44262 **Fx:**688-3352
Damon, Geoffrey P '84 -441 Vine -Ste 2900 -Cincinnati 45202
(419) 407-4355 .. **Damrauer,** Carol L '82 -1018 Adams -Toledo 43624 **Fx:**241-7267
(614) 995-1629 .. **Damschroder,** William R '88 OH Dept Commerce -77 S High -Columbus 43266
(614) 222-6465 .. **Damsel,** William R II '86 OH PERS -277 E Town -Columbus 43215 **Fx:**857-1061
(614) 253-1010 .. **Dana & Pariser Co,LPA** -800 E Broad -Columbus 43205 **Fx:**253-3310
(440) 352-8500 .. **Dana,** Richard L Jr. '95 %LJ Talikka -2603 Riverside Dr -Ste 100 -Painesville 44077
(614) 221-6424 .. **Danchak,** Michael G '78 (Frost & D LLP) -50 W Broad -Ste 1602 -Columbus 43215 **Fx:**221-7122
(937) 461-8656 .. **Dancing,** Tara C '04 Folkerth & F PLL -1812 Kettering Twr -Dayton 45423
(330) 376-5050 .. **D'Andrea,** Patrick J '81 (D'Andrea & Assoc) -697 W Market -Ste 200 -Akron 44303
(330) 928-1576 .. **Dandrea,** Victor A '71 -2845 Landon Dr -Cuyahoga Falls 44224
(216) 522-4856 .. **Dane,** Michael G '71 Fed Pub Def -1660 W 2nd -Ste 750 -Cleveland 44113
(614) 365-2700 .. **Dane,** Philomena M '90 (Squire S&D LLP) -41 S High -1300 Huntngtn Ctr -Columbus 43215 **Fx:**365-2499
(419) 873-1814 .. **Dane,** Stephen M '81 %Relman & Assoc -312 Louisiana Av -Perrysburg 43551
(513) 232-4165 .. **Danehy,** James S '85 -760 Roundtree Ct -Cincinnati 45230
(614) 337-0960 .. **Daneman,** Sara J '79 -62 Mill -Gahanna 43230
(740) 373-9324 .. **Danford,** Barbara N '91 Washington Cnty Child Spprt Enf -205 Putnam -4th Fl -Marietta 45750
(614) 387-9370 .. **Dangel,** Ruth B '87 Bd Comm on Grievances & Discipline -65 S Front -5th Fl -Columbus 43215 **Fx:**387-9379
(419) 244-8989 .. **D'Angelo,** Joseph M '94 (Cosme D&S) -202 N Erie -Toledo 43624
(440) 336-0720 .. **Dangelo,** Kathleen B '90 -8450 Whsprng Pines Dr -Russell 44072
(440) 942-5232 .. **D'Angelo,** Nicholas A '87 (Cannon SA&L Co,LPA) -41 E Erie -Painesville 44077 **Fx:**357-9234
(216) 623-7311 .. **D'Angelo,** Patrick A '77 (P D'Angelo,LLC) -1370 Ontario -Ste 2000 -Cleveland 44113
(859) 426-8090 .. **Daniel,** Amy M '00 -2643 Erlanger-Crescent Springs -Erlanger, KY 41017
(216) 696-5400 .. **Daniel,** Eric S '04 %Crosby O & Assoc Co,LPA -55 Pub Sq -Ste 1475 -Cleveland 44113 **Fx:**696-2610
(614) 837-5992 .. **Daniel,** F Toby T '75 (FT Daniel & Assoc) -49 Hill Rd N -Pickerington 43147
(937) 845-9485 .. **Daniel,** Theodore D '73 -133 S Main -New Carlisle 45344
(614) 486-5392 .. **Daniell,** Ric '78 (Mattis DV&V) -1350 W 5th Av -Columbus 43212
(216) 622-8200 .. **Daniels,** Anthea R '89 (Calfee H&G LLP) -800 Superior Av -Ste 1400 -Cleveland 44114 **Fx:**241-0816
(216) 861-5582 .. **Daniels,** Edward Kent Jr. '71 OfCnsl Fay SFM&M LLP -1100 Superior Av -7th Fl -Cleveland 44114 **Fx:**241-1666
(614) 365-2700 .. **Daniels,** Gregory R '01 %Squire S&D LLP -41 S High -1300 Huntngtn Ctr -Columbus 43215 **Fx:**365-2499
(330) 972-5965 .. **Daniels,** Isiah III '76 Univ of Akron -302 E Buchtel Av -Lincoln Bldg Rm 308 -Akron 44325
(614) 221-7201 .. **Daniels,** James M '78 OSLSA -555 Buttles Av -Columbus 43215
(937) 225-4652 .. **Daniels,** Ramona E '98 Montgomery Cnty Pub Def -117 S Main -Ste 400 -Dayton 45422 **Fx:**225-3449
(216) 621-1312 .. **Daniels,** Stephen H '78 (McMahon DH&L LLP) -812 Huron Rd -Ste 650 The Caxton Bldg -Cleveland 44115 **Fx:**621-0577
(937) 393-9285 .. **Daniels,** Susan M '99 -Bx589 -Hillsboro 45133
(216) 586-3939 .. **Daniels,** Thomas C '86 (Jones D) -901 Lakeside Av -Cleveland 44114 **Fx:**579-0212
(330) 609-9999 .. **Daniluk,** Daniel P '79 -1129 Niles-Crtland Rd SE -Warren 44484
(937) 333-4100 .. **Danish,** John J '90 Law Dept -101 W 3rd -Bx22 -Dayton 45402
(614) 798-1800 .. **Danison,** Nancy L '77 (NL Danison,LPA) -4757 Aberdeen Av -Dublin 43016
(216) 443-8560 .. **Danko,** William L '73 %Cuyahoga Cnty Cmmn Pleas Ct -1200 Ontario -11th Fl -Cleveland 44113
(937) 643-9999 .. **Dankof,** Steven K '76 (Weisbrod & D) -580 Lincoln Park Blvd -Ste 222 -Dayton 45429 **Fx:**643-0777
(614) 249-3281 .. **Dankovic,** Rae Ann '98 Cnsl Nationwide Ins Co -1 Nationwide Plz -Columbus 43215
(330) 759-4155 .. **Dann,** Marc E '87 (Dann & F,LLC) -4531 Belmont Av -Ste C Churchill Sq Plz -Youngstown 44505 **Fx:**759-9012
(937) 228-8104 .. **Dannemann,** Stephanie L '04 ABLE -333 W First -Ste 500B -Dayton 45402
(513) 745-0400 .. **Dannenfelser,** Jeanette N '98 %Furnier T,LLP -1 Fncl Way -Ste 312 -Cincinnati 45242 **Fx:**792-6724
Danner, John H Jr. '97 -2339 Timbervw -Portsmouth 45662
(740) 282-6705 .. **D'Anniballe,** Robert J Jr. '81 -100 N 4th -Steubenville 43952
Danolfo, Richard R '03 -(Address Unavailable)
(614) 227-2000 .. **Dansa,** Jaime A '02 %Porter WM&A LLP -41 S High -Columbus 43215 **Fx:**227-2100
(419) 843-2001 .. **Dansack,** Michael P Jr. '85 (Gallon & T Co,LPA) -3516 Granite Cir -Bx352018 -Toledo 43635 **Fx:**843-6665
(216) 566-2482 .. **Danzig,** Allen J '91 Sherwin-Williams Co -101 Prospect Av NW -Cleveland 44115
(216) 479-6807 .. **Danzinger,** Robert K '92 (Schottenstein Z&D) -1350 Euclid Av -Ste 1400 -Cleveland 44115 **Fx:**621-6502
(330) 783-9222 .. **D'Apolito,** Anthony M '94 D'Apolito & D -4800 Market -Youngstown 44512
(330) 783-9222 .. **D'Apolito,** David A '89 D'Apolito & D -4800 Market -Youngstown 44512
(330) 783-9222 .. **D'Apolito,** Loumano A '73 D'Apolito & D -4800 Market -Youngstown 44512
(843) 577-4000 .. **DaPore,** Joseph E '76 (Young CR&T,LLP) -28 Broad -Bx993 -Charleston, SC 29402 **Fx:**724-6600
(216) 525-4283 .. **Daprile,** Joseph R '86 Premier Farnell Corp -7061 E Plsnt Vlly Rd -Independence 44131
(440) 835-8200 .. **Daray,** Stephen E '97 (Sciangula & D) -24500 Ctr Ridge Rd -Ste 175 -Westlake 44145
(217) 787-2080 .. **Darby,** Karen S '80 IL Inst for CLE -2395 W Jffrsn -Springfield, IL 62702 **Fx:**787-5986
(419) 473-1346 .. **D'Arcangelo,** Bradley M '97 %Kroncke DS&F -2255 W Laskey Rd -Toledo 43613 **Fx:**473-0218
(419) 473-1346 .. **D'Arcangelo,** Joseph M '84 Kroncke DS&F -2255 W Laskey Rd -Toledo 43613 **Fx:**473-0218
(419) 473-1346 .. **D'Arcangelo,** Michael J '63 (Kroncke DS&F) -2255 W Laskey Rd -Toledo 43613 **Fx:**473-0218
(216) 781-2227 .. **D'Arcy,** Charles J '78 Bank One OH Trust Co -Bx91308 -Cleveland 44101
(614) 225-8749 .. **Dardinger,** Debora C '96 PricewaterhouseCoopers -100 E Broad -Columbus 43215
(330) 345-8100 .. **Dark,** Edward A '89 Wayne Mutual Ins Co -3873 Cleveland Rd -Wooster 44691
(440) 871-2985 .. **Darling,** Brian J '04 -31011 Kilgour Dr -Westlake 44145 **Fx:**871-6327
(614) 236-6517 .. **Darling,** Stanton G II '84 Capital Univ Schl of Law -303 E Broad -Columbus 43215
(513) 933-0032 .. **Darling,** Suzanne J '02 -9 ½ N Bway -Lebanon 45036
(216) 781-5470 .. **Darlington,** Stephen M '67 (Ziegler M&M LLP) -925 Euclid Av -2020 Huntngtn Bldg -Cleveland 44115 **Fx:**781-0714
(312) 214-4836 .. **Darnell,** Marc E '02 %Barnes & T LLP -One N Wacker Dr -Ste 4400 -Chicago, IL 60606 **Fx:**759-5646
(440) 605-6660 .. **Daroff,** Charles II '88 (Hurtuk & D Co,LPA) -6120 Parkland Blvd -Ste 100 -Cleveland 44124 **Fx:**605-6666
(859) 372-5250 .. **Darpel,** Matthew L '96 -71 Cavalier Blvd -Ste 210 -Florence, KY 41042
(859) 578-6606 .. **Darpel,** Paul J '95 -25 Crestvw Hills Mall Rd -Ste 104 -Crestview Hills, KY 41017
(614) 462-2237 .. **Darr,** Elaine M '01 %Schottenstein Z&D -250 West -Bx165020 -Columbus 43216 **Fx:**462-5135
(740) 833-2690 .. **Darr,** Frank P '82 Delaware Cnty Pros -140 N Sandusky -3rd Fl -Delaware 43015
(513) 977-8200 .. **Darrow,** Helana A '98 %Dinsmore & S LLP -255 E 5th -Ste 1900 -Cincinnati 45202 **Fx:**977-8141
(614) 221-1111 .. **Darvishi,** Michelle R '99 %Shayne & G -221 S High -Columbus 43215 **Fx:**221-4070
(330) 744-4137 .. **Dascenzo,** Daniel P '98 %Friedman & R Co,LPA -100 Fed Plz E -Ste 300 City Centre One -Youngstown 44503 **Fx:**744-9962
(614) 224-6969 .. **D'Ascenzo,** Rocco O '04 %Blue W+B LLC -471 E Broad -Columbus 43215 **Fx:**224-6999
(216) 861-7572 .. **DasVarma,** Jay R '96 Baker & H LLP -1900 E 9th -Ste 3200 -Cleveland 44114 **Fx:**696-0740
(617) 330-6669 .. **Datillo,** Katherine K '87 Investors Bank & Trust Co -200 Clarendon -Boston, MA 02116
(330) 497-2886 .. **D'Atri,** Edward L '63 (Zollinger DGT & Co) -6370 Mt Plsnt NW -Bx2985 -Canton 44720
Dattilo, Anthony P '81 USAF AIMCLO/JAB -2240 B St -Bldg 11 -Wright Patterson AFB 45433
(440) 988-9500 .. **Dattilo,** Brian G '01 Trigilio & S -5750 Cooper Foster Park Rd -Ste 102 -Lorain 44053
(513) 887-3474 .. **Dattilo,** Christina R '02 %Butler Cnty Pros -315 High -11th Fl -Bx515 -Hamilton 45012
(216) 830-6830 .. **Dattilo,** Joseph T '73 (Brouse M) -1001 Lakeside Av -Ste 1600 -Cleveland 44114 **Fx:**830-6807
(937) 228-1525 .. **Dauber,** Eric L '94 Nationwide Mutl Ins-Trail Div -130 W 2nd -Ste 410 -Dayton 45402
(312) 861-3261 .. **Dauchot,** Luke L '88 %Kirkland & E,LLP -200 E Randolph -Chicago, IL 60601
Daugherty, David D Jr. '73 -4110 Route 743 -Moscow 45153
(330) 392-6171 .. **Daugherty,** David D '80 %Rieger SC&D -410 Mahoning Av -Bx1429 -Warren 44482 **Fx:**394-5507
(614) 227-2000 .. **Daugherty,** Greg M '04 %Porter WM&A LLP -41 S High -Columbus 43215 **Fx:**227-2100
(513) 528-6444 .. **Daugherty,** Kendra L '82 -4529 Aicholtz Rd -Cincinnati 45245
(937) 382-0045 .. **Daugherty,** Michael T '94 (Peterson & D) -111 E Sugartree -Wilmington 45177
(440) 205-3600 .. **Daugherty,** Patrick J '93 %Driggs LB&H Co,LPA -8522 East Av -Mentor 44060 **Fx:**205-3601
(614) 210-0222 .. **Daugherty,** Scott P '89 -9071 Moors Pl N -Dublin 43017
(330) 534-1901 .. **Daugherty,** Teresa R '78 -48 W Lbrty -Hubbard 44425
(614) 224-1884 .. **Daulton,** Stephen W '74 (S Daulton & Assoc Co,LPA) -336 S High -Columbus 43215
(614) 752-6864 .. **Daum,** Rebecca L '90 OH Dept Taxation -30 E Broad -22nd Fl -Columbus 43215
(831) 649-1125 .. **Daunt,** Robert T '77 OfCnsl Terra Law LLP -215 W Franklin -Rm 407 -Monterey, CA 93940
(330) 535-8116 .. **D'Aurelio,** Gina M '99 Oriana House,Inc -Bx1501 -Akron 44309
(440) 729-7450 .. **D'Aurelio,** Michael J '96 %D'Aurelio & M -96 Church -Chagrin Falls 44022
(614) 221-7663 .. **D'Aurora,** Jack '91 OfCnsl Luper N&L,LPA -50 W Broad -1200 LeVeque Twr -Columbus 43215 **Fx:**464-2425
(440) 285-8190 .. **Dauscher,** Raymond G '58 -492 South -Chardon 44024
(419) 435-9273 .. **Dauterman,** Kurt A '03 -307 N Main -Fostoria 44830
(513) 579-5678 .. **Dauterman,** Steven L '78 Fifth 3rd Bank-Trust Div -38 Fountain Sq Plz -Cincinnati 45263
(419) 435-9273 .. **Dauterman,** William D '59 -307 N Main -Fostoria 44830 **Fx:**435-9274
(330) 451-7855 .. **Dave,** Jennifer L '94 Stark Cnty Pros -110 Central Plz -Ste 510 -Canton 44702
(937) 603-5326 .. **Davenport,** Andrew T '01 -1927 Waterstone Blvd -Ste 208 -Miamisburg 45342
(419) 422-8713 .. **Davenport,** Julie A '79 Oxley MHO&W,PLL -301 E Main Cross -Bx1086 -Findlay 45840 **Fx:**422-6495
(937) 777-1903 .. **Davenport,** Michael S '97 Quality Home Imprvmnts -10601 Milton-Carlisle Rd -New Carlisle 45344
(216) 621-0200 .. **Davet,** Anne M '04 %Baker & H LLP -1900 E 9th -Ste 3200 -Cleveland 44114 **Fx:**696-0740
(216) 696-5959 .. **Davey,** James A '04 %Pomerantz & C Co,LPA -20676 Southgate Park Blvd -Ste 103 -Cleveland 44137
(216) 241-6602 .. **Davey,** Karen A '80 (Weston HFP&H LLP) -50 Pub Sq -2500 Trmnl Twr -Cleveland 44113 **Fx:**621-8369

David, Audrey D '79 -3076 Fairmount Blvd
-Cleveland Heights 44118
(412) 232-3555 .. **David,** Wendy S '02 Pittsburgh Family Practice -120 Marion
-Pittsburgh, PA 15219
(937) 223-6211 .. **Davidek,** Robert J '81 Crew & B -2580 Kettering Twr
-Dayton 45423
(612) 313-8761 .. **Davido,** Scott J '87 NRG Energy,Inc -901 Marquette Av -Ste 2300
-Minneapolis, MN 55402
(216) 696-5510 .. **Davidoff,** Jason A '99 -925 Euclid Av -Ste 1025 -Cleveland 44115
(513) 868-7100 .. **Davidson Adams & Creach Co,LPA** -127 N 2nd
-Hamilton 45011 **Fx:**868-9579
(614) 463-8989 .. **Davidson,** Alan J '81 Natl City Bank -155 E Broad
-Columbus 43251
(513) 352-3333 .. **Davidson,** Allison A '99 Law Dept -801 Plum -Rm 214
-Cincinnati 45202 **Fx:**352-1515
(952) 351-3070 .. **Davidson,** Ann D '79 Alliant Techsystems,Inc -5050 Lincoln Dr
-Edina, MN 55436
(513) 893-6122 .. **Davidson,** Brian J '00 %Morgenstern & M -300 High -Ste 604
-Hamilton 45011
(859) 261-5777 .. **Davidson,** David E '81 (Oldfield DR, PLLC) -213 E 4th -Bx1078
-Covington, KY 41012
(513) 868-7100 .. **Davidson,** David T '86 Davidson A&C Co,LPA -127 N 2nd
-Hamilton 45011 **Fx:**868-9579
(330) 375-2030 .. **Davidson,** Elaine B '78 Law Dept -161 S High -Ste 202
-Akron 44308
(513) 887-3474 .. **Davidson,** Elizabeth A '87 Butler Cnty Pros -315 High -11th Fl
-Bx515 -Hamilton 45012
(216) 771-5300 .. **Davidson,** Gerry '72 OfCnsl P Yates Co,LPA -1370 Ontario
-800 Standard Bldg -Cleveland 44113 **Fx:**621-0575
(937) 653-7174 .. **Davidson,** Harley A '77 (Wagner MD&G) -117 W Court
-Urbana 43078
(740) 373-7572 .. **Davidson Heckler Riggs & Fouss** -311 4th -Bx567
-Marietta 45750 **Fx:**373-7081
(614) 462-2286 .. **Davidson,** James E '80 (Schottenstein Z&D) -250 West
-Bx165020 -Columbus 43216 **Fx:**462-5135
(513) 891-2100 .. **Davidson,** James P '86 (Davidson & G LLP) -10250 Alliance Rd
-Ste 120 -Cincinnati 45242
(513) 241-2324 .. **Davidson,** Kristi L '97 %Wood H&E LLP -441 Vine -Ste 2700
-Cincinnati 45202 **Fx:**421-7269
(216) 676-9840 .. **Davidson,** Lauren E '03 Cnsl Toolbold Corp
-5330 Commerce Pkwy W -Parma 44130 **Fx:**676-9870
(513) 793-5297 .. **Davidson,** Laurence J '93 Monnie & O Co,LPA
-8035 Hosbrook Rd -Ste 200 -Cincinnati 45236
(419) 529-1367 .. **Davidson,** Lisa L '95 Industrial Commssn of OH -240 Tappen Dr N
-Bx8051 -Mansfield 44906 **Fx:**529-3084
(330) 382-0371 .. **Davidson,** Marian D '96 -420 Market -East Liverpool 43920
(513) 362-8700 .. **Davidson,** Patricia A '85 %Blank R -201 E 5th -Ste 1700
-Cincinnati 45202 **Fx:**362-8787
(330) 376-9691 .. **Davidson,** Roger K '77 -441 Wolf Ledges Pkwy -Ste 302
-Akron 44311
(740) 635-0162 .. **Davies,** Albert E III '93 (Thomas FMH&D) -320 Howard
-Bridgeport 43912 **Fx:**635-1601
(216) 861-4533 .. **Davies,** David G '62 OfCnsl Ray RC&D PLL -1717 E 9th
-Cleveland 44114 **Fx:**861-4568
(440) 953-2000 .. **Davies,** David H '73 -Bx1264 -Willoughby 44096
(614) 221-3155 .. **Davies,** Donald A '62 (Bailey C LLC) -10 W Broad
-Columbus 43215 **Fx:**221-0479
Davies, Elizabeth A '03 -(Address Unavailable)
Davies, Erin E '04 -(Address Unavailable)
(419) 698-6626 .. **Davies,** James L '99 %7 Sun Co Inc -1819 Woodvll Rd -Oregon 43616
(330) 867-9998 .. **Davies,** Richard '80 %Kastner W&W,LLC -3480 W Market
-Ste 300 -Akron 44333 **Fx:**867-3786
(419) 287-3233 .. **Davies,** Richard N '76 (Davies & R) -427 W Cllg Av -Bx412
-Pemberville 43450 **Fx:**287-3215
(937) 222-2500 .. **Davies,** Scott S '03 %Sebaly S&D -1900 Kettering Twr
-Dayton 45423 **Fx:**222-6554
Davies, Steven W '02 -6081 Isl Dr NW -Canton 44718
(289-7600 .. **Davies,** William B '83 W Davies Co,LPA -21801 Lakeshr Blvd
-Euclid 44123
(614) 462-3555 .. **Davies,** William J '99 %Franklin Cnty Pros -373 S High
-Columbus 43215
(513) 579-6400 .. **D'Avignon,** David A '73 OfCnsl Keating M&K PLL -1 E 4th
-1400 Provident Twr -Cincinnati 45202 **Fx:**579-6457
(614) 249-2019 .. **Davin,** Elizabeth A '89 Nationwide Ins Co -1 Nationwide Plz
-Columbus 43215
(330) 643-2800 .. **Davis,** Anita L '83 Summit Cnty Pros-Civil -53 Univ Av -6th Fl
-Akron 44308 **Fx:**643-2137
(740) 353-9805 .. **Davis,** Anna Eva '00 Ruggiero & H -800 Gallia -Ste 600 -Bx150
-Portsmouth 45662
(216) 348-5056 .. **Davis,** Audrey H '77 Cuyahoga Metro Housing Auth -1441 W 25th
-Cleveland 44113
(419) 448-8000 .. **Davis,** B Mark '80 -100 E Perry -Tiffin 44883 **Fx:**448-1584
(419) 524-1213 .. **Davis,** Bernard R '72 -3 N Main -Ste 706 -Mansfield 44902
(513) 398-8885 .. **Davis,** Betty J '87 -3948 Hanover Dr -Mason 45040
Davis, Bruce T '04 -(Address Unavailable)
(419) 242-8214 .. **Davis,** Carla B '84 Zaner & C -520 Mad Av -Ste 545 -Toledo 43604
Fx:242-8658
(937) 981-3326 .. **Davis,** Carol A '86 -9185 State Route 41N -Greenfield 45123
(614) 757-7775 .. **Davis,** Carolyn L '04 Cardinal Hlth -7000 Cardinal Pl -Dublin 43017
Davis, Carrie L '03 -(Address Unavailable)
(216) 241-5310 .. **Davis,** Catherine A '98 %Gallagher SF&N -1501 Euclid Av -6th Fl
-Cleveland 44115 **Fx:**241-1608
(513) 721-4500 .. **Davis,** Charles J '77 %Patsfall Y&P LLC -1 W 4th -Ste 1800
-Cincinnati 45202 **Fx:**639-7554
(219) 391-2117 .. **Davis,** Christopher S '74 LTV Steel -3001 Dickey Rd
-East Chicago, IL 46312
(419) 472-2123 .. **Davis,** Christopher W '93 -5749 Park Ctr Ct -Toledo 43615
(614) 793-1799 .. **Davis,** Claudia L '02 -6099 Riverside Dr -Ste 102 -Dublin 43017
Davis, Clifford L '62 -2218 Canterbury Cir -Akron 44319
(614) 728-0276 .. **Davis,** Cynthia D '91 Workers Comp -30 W Spring -Level 26
-Columbus 43215
(937) 773-3212 .. **Davis,** Dale G '76 (McCulloch FF&G Co,LPA) -123 Market -Bx910
-Piqua 45356 **Fx:**773-9672

(330) 455-0173 .. **Davis,** David D L '03 %Day KRW&R,Ltd -200 Market Av N
-Ste 300 -Bx24213 -Canton 44701 **Fx:**455-2633
(740) 635-1217 .. **Davis,** David W '73 -407A Howard -Bridgeport 43912
(614) 466-7788 .. **Davis,** Delores L '97 OH Ct of Claims -65 E State -Ste 1100
-Columbus 43215
(419) 241-9000 .. **Davis,** Diane V '83 (Shumaker L&K,LLP) -1000 Jackson
-Toledo 43624 **Fx:**241-6894
(330) 762-0700 .. **Davis,** Donald W Jr. '85 (Slater Z&G) -One Cascade Plz -Ste 2210
-Akron 44308 **Fx:**762-3923
(304) 558-8986 .. **Davis,** Douglas L '89 Atty Genl Ofc -812 Quarrier -4th Fl
-Charleston, WV 25301
(330) 376-2700 .. **Davis,** Elizabeth N '84 (Roetzel & A,LPA) -222 S Main
-Akron 44308 **Fx:**376-4577
(513) 721-7295 .. **Davis,** Francis G '42 (Davis & H) -830 Main -Ste 200
-Cincinnati 45202
(419) 530-4236 .. **Davis,** Gabrielle '91 Univ of Toledo Law Schl -2801 W Bancroft
-Toledo 43606
(614) 464-6400 .. **Davis,** Gary E '76 (Vorys SS&P LLP) -52 E Gay -Bx1008
-Columbus 43216 **Fx:**464-6350
(513) 852-6085 .. **Davis,** Gary Jon '79 (Wood & L LLP) -600 Vine -Ste 2500
-Cincinnati 45202 **Fx:**852-6087
(419) 245-1020 .. **Davis,** Geoffrey H '73 %Law Dept -One Govt Ctr -Ste 2250
-Toledo 43604 **Fx:**245-1090
(740) 353-4661 .. **Davis,** George L III '80 -602 Chillicothe -Portsmouth 45662
(717) 761-1880 .. **Davis,** Glenn R '04 (Latsha DY&M,PC) -4720 Old Gettysburg Rd
-Ste 101 -Mechanicsburg, PA 17055 **Fx:**761-2286
(419) 756-3687 .. **Davis,** Harold H '68 -1436 Beechdale Dr -Mansfield 44907
(330) 533-4373 .. **Davis,** Henry W '55 (Davis & D) -6715 Tippecanoe Rd -Bldg A-103
-Canfield 44406 **Fx:**533-9954
(740) 532-8744 .. **Davis,** J B '99 McCown & D,LPA -311 Park Av -Ironton 45638
(336) 777-8901 .. **Davis,** James A '85 -150 Stratford Rd -Ste 322
-Winston Salem, NC 27104
(440) 564-1480 .. **Davis,** James B '59 -10808 Kinsman Rd -Bx296 -Newbury 44065
(330) 434-3000 .. **Davis,** James E '61 OfCnsl Roderick & L -One Cascade Plz
-Ste 1500 -Akron 44308 **Fx:**434-9220
(513) 632-8701 .. **Davis,** James F '75 Hamilton Cnty Pub Def -230 E 9th -3rd Fl
-Cincinnati 45202 **Fx:**946-3707
(330) 533-4373 .. **Davis,** James H '79 (Davis & D) -6715 Tippecanoe Rd -Bldg A-103
-Canfield 44406 **Fx:**533-9954
(330) 494-5504 .. **Davis,** Jane M '96 Suarez Corp -7800 Whipple Av NW
-Canton 44720 **Fx:**490-2861
(262) 373-0880 .. **Davis,** Janet E Fasse '93 -19015 Glacier Pkwy
-Brookfield, WI 53045
(614) 462-3555 .. **Davis,** Jeffrey R '94 Franklin Cnty Pros -373 S High
-Columbus 43215
(614) 485-1800 .. **Davis,** Jeffrey T '92 %Arnold T&W -2075 Marble Cliff Ofc Park
-Columbus 43215 **Fx:**485-1944
(614) 242-4242 .. **Davis,** Jennifer M '01 Decker VSL&V Co LPA -620 E Broad
-Columbus 43215 **Fx:**242-4243
(614) 463-9770 .. **Davis,** Jessica L '02 %Roetzel & A,LPA -155 E Broad
-Natl City Ctr 12th Fl -Columbus 43215 **Fx:**463-9792
(216) 241-1430 .. **Davis,** Jillian S '96 %Friedman & G -1370 Ontario
-1700 Standard Bldg -Cleveland 44113
(740) 363-1213 .. **Davis,** Joanna R '03 %Firestone BHNW&Y,LLP -15 W Winter
-Delaware 43015 **Fx:**369-0875
(907) 452-5181 .. **Davis,** Jody L '93 Alaska Legal Srvcs Corp -1648 Cushman
-Ste 300 -Fairbanks, AK 99701
(513) 241-2324 .. **Davis,** John P '01 %Wood H&E LLP -441 Vine -Ste 2700
-Cincinnati 45202 **Fx:**421-7269
(614) 229-5025 .. **Davis,** John R '86 Ernst & Young LLP -41 S High -Ste 1100
-Columbus 43215 **Fx:**229-5127
(614) 723-4197 .. **Davis,** Jon T '96 WorldCom,Inc -5000 Britton Rd -Hilliard 43026
(614) 478-3424 .. **Davis,** Julia A '85 Value City Dept Stores -3241 Westervll Rd
-Columbus 43224
(614) 222-8686 .. **Davis,** Kathleen Vivian '03 %Scott S&W LLP -50 W Broad
-2500 LeVeque Twr -Columbus 43215 **Fx:**222-8685
Davis, Kenneth R III '78 -317 Mill Crk Trl -Cleveland, TN 37323
(330) 434-6600 .. **Davis,** Kevin G '79 (K Davis & Assoc Co,LPA) -12 Exchange
-8th Fl -Akron 44308
(216) 363-6000 .. **Davis,** Leonard '66 -1370 Ontario -Ste 1020 -Cleveland 44113
(216) 523-1300 .. **Davis,** Marilyn T '82 Medimetrix Grp -25 W Prospect Av -Ste 1100
-Cleveland 44115
(419) 297-5088 .. **Davis,** Mark A '99 -500 Mad Av -Ste 525 -Toledo 43604
Davis, Mark E '99 -400 W North -Lima 45801
(216) 621-0995 .. **Davis,** Mark R '82 -1735 E 23rd -Cleveland 44114
(216) 297-7000 .. **Davis,** Marleina Thomas '00 Cleveland Clinic Fndtn
-1950 Richmond Rd TR 38 -Ofc Gen Cnsl -Cleveland 44124
(614) 462-3987 .. **Davis,** Martin L '92 10th Dist Ct Of Appls -373 S High
-Columbus 43215
(216) 566-8200 .. **Davis,** Mary '88 (Seeley S&E Co LPA) -600 Superior Av E
-800 Bank One Ctr -Cleveland 44114 **Fx:**566-0213
(614) 461-1922 .. **Davis,** McKenzie K '02 OH Acdmy of Nursing -2 Miranova Pl
-Ste 210 -Columbus 43215
(727) 726-1900 .. **Davis,** Michael G '74 -Bx906 -Safety Harbor, FL 34695
(513) 398-9500 .. **Davis,** Michael J '90 -3611 Sociaville-Foster Rd -Ste 103
-Mason 45040
(513) 621-3366 .. **Davis,** Michael W '73 -8549 Mntgmry Rd -Cincinnati 45236
(614) 237-3525 .. **Davis,** Murray A '91 Clean Title Inc -2715 E Main
-Columbus 43209
(513) 241-9773 .. **Davis,** Myron Y Jr. '69 -700 Walnut -Ste 310 -Cincinnati 45202
(614) 410-4643 .. **Davis,** Natasha N '01 City of Dublin -5800 Shier-Rings Rd
-Dublin 43016
(937) 223-8177 .. **Davis,** Nicholas E Jr. '90 (Coolidge WW&L) -33 W 1st -Ste 600
-Dayton 45402 **Fx:**223-6705
(513) 751-8495 .. **Davis,** Norma H '82 -415 Clinton Sprngs Av -Cincinnati 45217
(419) 874-2535 .. **Davis,** Paul A '81 Dold Co -26610 Eckel Rd -Perrysburg 43551
(513) 241-1991 .. **Davis,** Perry Jr. '87 (Harmon D & Assoc Co,LPA) -1200 Cypress
-Cincinnati 45206
(614) 752-1200 .. **Davis,** Peter '75 Parole Brd -1050 Fwy Dr N -Columbus 43229
(937) 445-2914 .. **Davis,** Peter W '91 NCR Corp -101 W Schantz Av -Law Dept
ECD-3 -Dayton 45409
(419) 242-7447 .. **Davis,** Philip C '77 -626 Mad Av -Ste 700 -Toledo 43604

(216) 566-5782 .. **Davis**, Renee L '03 %Thompson H LLP -127 Pub Sq
-3900 Key Ctr -Cleveland 44114 Fx:566-5800
(330) 762-9700 .. **Davis**, Rhonda G '94 %AW Zavarello Co,LPA -313 S High
-Akron 44308 Fx:762-1680
(330) 497-0700 .. **Davis**, Richard E II '76 (Krugliak WG&D Co,LPA)
-4775 Munson NW -Bx36963 -Canton 44735 Fx:497-4020
(937) 667-2466 .. **Davis**, Richard S '74 (R Davis Co LPA) -108 E Main
-Tipp City 45371
(330) 747-2661 .. **Davis**, Richard T '76 Cafaro Co -2445 Belmont Av -Bx2186
-Youngstown 44504
(216) 696-0606 .. **Davis**, Robert E '77 RE Sweeney Co,LPA -55 Pub Sq -Ste 1500
-Cleveland 44114 Fx:696-0679
(419) 897-6500 .. **Davis**, Robert E '01 Barkan & R Ltd -1701 WoodInds Dr
-Maumee 43537 Fx:897-6200
(513) 553-3421 .. **Davis**, Robert H '67 -Bx45 -New Richmond 45157
(513) 241-3500 .. **Davis**, Robert L '58 -3600 Carew Twr -441 Vine -Cincinnati 45202
Fx:241-5869
(440) 356-7456 .. **Davis**, Robert S '83 -1189 Woodside Dr -Rocky River 44116
(614) 228-2945 .. **Davis**, Ronald E '62 (Folkerth H&D) -250 Civic Ctr Dr -Ste 460
-Columbus 43215
(740) 654-4141 .. **Davis**, Sandra W '91 (Stebelton A&S,LPA) -109 N Broad -Bx130
-Lancaster 43130 Fx:654-2521
(216) 664-2677 .. **Davis**, Scott J '02 Dept of Law -601 Lakeside Av -Rm 106 City Hall
-Cleveland 44114 Fx:664-2663
(614) 227-2300 .. **Davis**, Scott W '04 %Bricker & E LLP -100 S 3rd -Columbus 43215
Fx:227-2390
(740) 353-1157 .. **Davis**, Sherry D '97 %Bannon H&D -325 Masonic Bldg -Bx1384
-Portsmouth 45662
(513) 761-4415 .. **Davis**, Sherry L '85 -307 Wyoming Av -Cincinnati 45215
(513) 721-1350 .. **Davis**, Steven C '96 (Barron PB&S) -3074 Madison Rd
-Cincinnati 45209
(937) 443-6533 .. **Davis**, Steven J '87 Thompson H LLP -2000 Cthse Plz NE
-Bx8801 -Dayton 45401 Fx:443-6635
(216) 781-3311 .. **Davis**, Steven S '75 -1370 Ontario -Ste 450 Standard Bldg
-Cleveland 44113 Fx:781-3312
(937) 393-4000 .. **Davis**, Susan L '80 (Davis Law Ofc) -107 Governor Foraker Pl
-Hillsboro 45133
(419) 241-9000 .. **Davis**, Terrance K '89 (Shumaker L&K,LLP) -1000 Jackson
-Toledo 43624 Fx:241-6894
(330) 762-6281 .. **Davis**, Thomas E '80 (Barrett & D) -159 S Main -416 Key Bldg
-Akron 44308
(614) 444-0566 .. **Davis**, Thomas E '94 -65 Parsons Av -Ste 202 -Columbus 43215
(614) 464-2392 .. **Davis**, Thomas L '82 (Earl WA&D,LPA) -136 W Mound
-Columbus 43215 Fx:464-0754
(614) 883-1072 .. **Davis**, Thomas R '73 Continental Real Estate Co -150 E Broad
-Ste 800 -Columbus 43215
(304) 232-8888 .. **Davis**, Tiffany E '04 %Jividen Law Ofc -729 N Main
-Wheeling, WV 26003
(216) 464-4105 .. **Davis**, Todd S '89 -25825 Science Park Dr -Ste 265
-Cleveland 44122
Davis, Wesley R '03 -233 Main -Zanesville 43701
(614) 221-3151 .. **Davis**, William A '74 Butler C&D -50 W Broad -Ste 700
-Columbus 43215
(513) 731-5980 .. **Davis**, William B '95 -1776 Mentor Av -Cincinnati 45212
Fx:731-5982
(330) 385-3900 .. **Davis**, William J '73 Aronson F&D Co, LPA -124 E 5th
-East Liverpool 43920
(216) 464-6744 .. **Davis**, William T '86 Galt Enterprises Inc -28601 Chagrin Blvd
-Ste 400 -Woodmere 44122
(216) 348-1700 .. **Davis & Young** -101 Prospect Av W -Ste 1700 -Cleveland 44115
Fx:621-0602
(330) 373-1717 .. **Davis & Young** -108 Main SW -10th Fl -Warren 44481
Fx:395-0610
(330) 376-1717 .. **Davis & Young** -One Cascade Plz -Ste 800 -Akron 44308
(330) 743-1717 .. **Davis & Young** -201 E Commerce -Ste 100 -Youngstown 44503
Fx:743-6347
(614) 866-5455 .. **Davis**, Yvette Carmon '85 -1266 Idlewild Dr -Columbus 43232
Fx:367-0546
(216) 987-8834 .. **Davis-Momon**, Andrea Y '95 Chubb Grp -600 Superior Av -11th Fl
-Cleveland 44114
(515) 235-1443 .. **Davison**, Darrel R '96 Principal Fncl Grp -711 High
-Des Moines, IA 50392 Fx:248-0483
(330) 867-0215 .. **Davison**, Edward Larry '77 (Davison & G) -59 Shiawassee Av
-Akron 44333 Fx:867-0216
(216) 241-2838 .. **Davison**, Lawrence C '91 %Taft S&H LLP -200 Pub Sq -3500
BP Twr -Cleveland 44114 Fx:241-3707
(614) 462-5400 .. **Davisson**, E Rod '02 %Kegler BH&R -65 E State -Ste 1800
-Columbus 43215 Fx:464-2634
(740) 623-0800 .. **Davitt**, Norman S '77 Pub Def Ofc -239 N 4th -Coshocton 43812
(765) 664-0669 .. **Dawalt**, Phillip R Jr. '79 -Bx1389 -Marion, IN 46952
(937) 865-6800 .. **Dawe**, Timothy J '90 Lexis/Nexis -Bx933 -Dayton 45401
(614) 854-0615 .. **Dawicke**, Jason E '01 Granger Co,LPA -132 Northwoods Blvd
-Columbus 43235
(614) 462-2290 .. **Dawley**, Kris M '85 (Schottenstein Z&D) -250 West -Bx165020
-Columbus 43216 Fx:462-5135
(614) 404-2691 .. **Dawsey**, David J '02 (Gallagher & D) -1487 W 5th Av -Bx 226
-Columbus 43212
(330) 379-1840 .. **Dawson**, Chester C Jr. '70 Summit Cnty Chldrn Srvcs
-264 S Arlngtn -Akron 44306 Fx:379-1897
(614) 488-9668 .. **Dawson**, Clyde W Jr. '64 -1350 W 5th Av -Ste 328
-Columbus 43212
(440) 323-7066 .. **Dawson**, Corinne K '78 -Bx1106 -Elyria 44036
(614) 246-1000 .. **Dawson**, Cynthia J '98 %R Kelm -37 W Broad -Ste 860
-Columbus 43215 Fx:246-8110
(216) 687-1900 .. **Dawson**, David B '73 Legal Aid -1223 W 6th -Cleveland 44113
Fx:687-0779
(330) 438-0865 .. **Dawson**, Deborah A '81 Stark Cnty Pros -110 Central Plz -Ste 510
-Canton 44702
(216) 382-9109 .. **Dawson**, James G '79 -4881 Foxlair Trl -Richmond Heights 44143
(419) 249-7100 .. **Dawson**, Jennifer J '84 %Marshall & M,LLC -Four Seagate -8th Fl
-Toledo 43604 Fx:249-7151
(419) 241-9770 .. **Dawson**, Joseph P '81 (Vassar DD&B,LLC) -420 Mad Av
-Ste 1102 -Toledo 43604 Fx:241-9771

(937) 644-1010 .. **Dawson**, Kerry B '89 Union Cnty CSEA -Bx389 -Marysville 43040
(740) 474-7841 .. **Dawson**, Laura W '97 4th Dist Ct of Appls -121-A W Franklin
-Circleville 43113 Fx:474-6870
(216) 622-8200 .. **Dawson**, Philip M '72 (Calfee H&G LLP) -800 Superior Av
-Ste 1400 -Cleveland 44114 Fx:241-0816
(513) 929-3312 .. **Dawson**, Phyllis I '94 Deloitte & Touche LLP -250 E 5th -Ste 1900
-Cincinnati 45202 Fx:929-3301
(614) 269-4900 .. **Dawson**, Shane M '96 Bricker & M,LLC -4100 Regent -Ste T
-Columbus 43219 Fx:269-4901
(330) 740-2055 .. **Dawson**, Thomas D '88 Mahoning Cnty Dom Rltns Ct -120 Market
-4th Fl -Youngstown 44503
(216) 621-0200 .. **Dawson**, Todd A '98 %Baker & H LLP -1900 E 9th -Ste 3200
-Cleveland 44114 Fx:696-0740
(937) 449-6400 .. **Dawson**, Wayne H '67 (Dinsmore & S LLP) -1 S Main
-Ste 1300 One Dayton Centre -Dayton 45402 Fx:449-6405
(216) 766-5777 .. **Dawson**, William L '00 -3401 Enterprise Pkwy -Ste 340
-Cleveland 44122
(614) 734-1270 .. **Day**, Barbara A '00 %Farlow & Assoc LLC -270 Bradenton Av
-Dublin 43017 Fx:923-1031
(440) 285-3511 .. **Day**, Carol L '93 (Petersen & I) -401 South -Chardon 44024
Fx:285-3363
(614) 221-2993 .. **Day**, David L '67 (DL Day,LPA) -400 S 5th -Ste 300
-Columbus 43215
(614) 224-7291 .. **Day**, Dennis G '82 -330 S High -Columbus 43215 Fx:224-7268
(614) 752-8496 .. **Day**, Jennifer E '91 Treasury Dept-Revenue Mgmt -30 E Broad
-9th Fl -Columbus 43266 Fx:752-8592
(513) 723-2206 .. **Day**, John L Jr. '81 %Weltman W&R Co,LPA -525 Vine -Ste 800
-Cincinnati 45202 Fx:723-2239
(330) 467-1065 .. **Day**, John R '89 -9735 Valley Vw Rd -The Pavillion Bx One
-Macedonia 44056
(615) 791-1031 .. **Day**, Joy B '96 Sutter OM&F -217 2nd Av S -Franklin, TN 37064
(330) 455-0173 .. **Day Ketterer Raley Wright & Rybolt, Ltd** -200 Market Av N
-Ste 300 -Bx42213 -Canton 44701 Fx:455-2633
(330) 489-3395 .. **Day**, Melissa '99 %Pros -218 Cleveland Av SW -Bx24218
-Canton 44702
(415) 278-4369 .. **Day**, Michael F '95 SrCnsl Providian Finl Corp -201 Mission
-San Francisco, CA 94105
(513) 621-5631 .. **Day**, Stephanie M '00 %Goodson & M,Ltd -110 E 8th -Ste 200
-Cincinnati 45202
(614) 462-3555 .. **Day**, Susan E '78 Franklin Cnty Pros -373 S High
-Columbus 43215
(440) 943-1200 .. **Day**, Suzanne F '93 Cnsl Lubrizol Corp -29400 Lakelnd Blvd
-Wickliffe 44092
(216) 241-9999 .. **Day**, William J '79 -8748 Brecksvll Rd -#216 -Brecksville 44141
(419) 476-8000 .. **Day**, Willis F IV '80 Willis Day Prop,Inc -Bx676 -Toledo 43697
(330) 456-8341 .. **Dayton**, Joel K '77 (Black MS&A,LPA) -220 Market Av S -Ste 1000
-Canton 44702 Fx:456-5756
(614) 882-3213 .. **Ddumba**, James '03 Cnsl J Ddumba & Assoc,LLC
-2151 E Dublin Granvll Rd -Ste 218 -Columbus 43229
Fx:882-4347
(513) 361-1200 .. **Deabler**, Christopher A '04 %Squire S&D LLP -312 Walnut
-Ste 3500 -Cincinnati 45202 Fx:361-1201
(216) 348-0041 .. **Deacon**, Robert F '79 (Deacon H&A,Ltd) -127 Pub Sq -Ste 4110
-Cleveland 44114 Fx:348-0040
(740) 622-6464 .. **Deadman**, William G '77 OfCnsl Frase WB&M Co,LPA -305 Main
-4th Fl -Coshocton 43812 Fx:622-8107
Deal, Christopher A '04 -(Address Unavailable)
(614) 340-9823 .. **Deal**, John C '74 OfCnsl Robol & W,LLC -555 City Park Av
-Columbus 43215 Fx:559-3846
(614) 291-6096 .. **Deal**, Roger F '88 -97 E Oaklnd Av -Columbus 43201
(239) 542-7512 .. **Deal**, Sharon E '84 -1616-102 W Cape Coral Pkwy -PMB 271
-Cape Coral, FL 33914
(703) 883-4036 .. **Dean**, Elizabeth M '81 Farm Credit Admin -1501 Farm Credit Dr
-McLean, VA 22102
(216) 443-0450 .. **Dean**, Jeffrey L '80 (Malek D & Assoc,LLC) -323 W Lakeside
-Ste 350 -Cleveland 44113
(513) 732-3200 .. **Dean**, John R '79 -285 Main -Batavia 45103
(440) 354-5636 .. **Dean**, John T '59 (Blakely & D) -56 Lbrty -Ste 304
-Painesville 44077
(614) 837-5030 .. **Dean**, Melissa C '99 -234 Portage Trl -Cuyahoga Falls 44221
Dean, Melissa K '99 -7125 Navarre Rd SW -Massillon 44646
(614) 464-2235 .. **Dean**, Nannette B '95 J McInturff -50 W Broad -Ste 2250
-Columbus 43215
(419) 586-5181 .. **Dean**, Rebecca L '98 Celina Ins -1 Insurance Sq -Celina 45822
(216) 592-5000 .. **Dean**, Richard A '73 (Tucker E&W LLP) -925 Euclid Av
-1150 Huntngtn Bldg -Cleveland 44115 Fx:592-5009
(216) 579-4114 .. **Dean**, Scott J '98 %McIntyre K&K Co LPA -1301 E 9th -Ste 1200
-Cleveland 44114
(513) 522-2100 .. **Dean**, Sheila C '83 -8624 Winton Rd -Cincinnati 45231
(937) 224-9291 .. **Dean**, Steven O '83 Young & A Co,LPA -130 W 2nd -Ste 2000
-Dayton 45402 Fx:224-9679
Dean, Warren T '91 -16301 Edwards Av -Southfield, MI 48076
Deane, T Mitchell '03 -(Address Unavailable)
(330) 726-0484 .. **DeAngelo**, Edward S '85 -1040 S Cmmns Pl -Ste 200
-Youngstown 44514
(614) 621-1500 .. **DeAngelo**, Peter M '69 (Calfee H&G LLP) -21 E State -1100 Fifth
Third Ctr -Columbus 43215 Fx:621-0010
(419) 478-0474 .. **Dear**, Harry J '87 -4817 Walker Av -Toledo 43612
(937) 435-2530 .. **Dearbaugh**, William C '84 Nationwide Ins Co
-6525 Centervll Business Pkwy -Centerville 45459
(513) 946-3700 .. **Deardorff**, Julie A '87 Hamilton Cnty Pub Def -230 E 9th -3rd Fl
-Cincinnati 45202 Fx:946-3707
(513) 872-7900 .. **Deardorff**, Timothy J '79 -2645 Erie Av -Ste 41 -Cincinnati 45208
(513) 559-1300 .. **Deardurff**, Dayle D '79 Public Allies -2905 Burnet Av
-Cincinnati 45219 Fx:559-1333
(513) 421-4428 .. **Dearfield**, George T '88 -602 Main -Ste 1010 -Cincinnati 45202
(513) 932-2115 .. **Dearie**, James A '00 %Rittgers & R -12 E Warren -Lebanon 45036
(919) 468-5979 .. **Dearth**, Miles B '95 Lord Corp -111 Lord Dr -Cary, NC 27511
(614) 220-5611 .. **Deas**, Brian T '93 (Manley D&K,LLC) -495 S High -Ste 300
-Columbus 43215 Fx:220-5613
(937) 449-6810 .. **Deas**, William G III '72 (Porter WM&A LLP) -1 S Main -Ste 1600
-Dayton 45402 Fx:449-6820

(770) 392-5326 ..**Deaton**, Michael F '87 Ashland Inc -900 Ashwood Pkwy -Ste #700 -Atlanta, GA 30338

(606) 789-1200 ..**Deaton**, Paul D '69 (P Deaton,PSC) -805 Bway -Paintsville, KY 41240

(614) 221-2121 ..**Deavers**, Maribeth M '91 Isaac BL&T,LLP -250 E Broad -Ste 900 Mdlnd Bldg -Columbus 43215 **Fx:**365-9516

(419) 734-1528 ..**DeBacco**, Thomas J '79 (T DeBacco & Assoc) -537 W Lakeshr Dr -Ste 800 -Port Clinton 43452

(614) 444-3900 ..**DeBacco**, Thomas J '79 (T DeBacco & Assoc) -755 S High -Columbus 43206

DeBacker, Gretchen S '04 -(Address Unavailable)

(216) 696-6373 ..**DeBaggis**, Henry F II '81 -55 Pub Sq -Ste 2240 -Cleveland 44113

(216) 621-2034 ..**De Baltzo**, Michelle L '97 %Margolius M & Assoc,LPA -55 Pub Sq -Ste 1100 -Cleveland 44113 **Fx:**621-1908

(216) 522-3879 ..**DeBaltzo**, Michelle M '97 US Dept of Labor -1240 E 9th -Rm 881 -Cleveland 44199 **Fx:**522-7172

(216) 696-5222 ..**DeBaltzo**, Nicholas J Jr. '99 %Johnson & C,LLC -1001 Lakeside Av -Ste 1700 N Pnt Twr -Cleveland 44114 **Fx:**696-5288

(850) 882-4611 ..**De Balzo**, Sandra M '96 US Air Force -501 Van Matre Av -AAC/JA -Eglin AFB, FL 32542

(513) 621-6464 ..**Debbeler**, J Michael '80 (Graydon H&R LLP) -511 Walnut -1900 Fifth Third Ctr -Cincinnati 45202 **Fx:**651-3836

(937) 324-7350 ..**DeBell**, Robin B '78 City Law Dir Ofc -76 E High -Springfield 45502

(614) 457-1911 ..**DeBeneditto**, Umberto A '94 -1170 Old Henderson Rd -Ste 109 -Columbus 43220

Debernardi, Linda M '96 -Bx23644 -Chagrin Falls 44023

(216) 696-3232 ..**Debevec**, Rhonda Baker '97 %Spangenberg S&L,LLP -1900 E 9th -2400 Natl City Ctr -Cleveland 44114 **Fx:**696-3924

(216) 621-0150 ..**Debitetto**, Rocco I '01 %Hahn L&P LLP -3300 BP Twr/200 Pub Sq -Ste 3300 -Cleveland 44114 **Fx:**241-2824

(513) 241-3100 ..**DeBlasis**, Rick D '80 Lerner S&R -120 E 4th -8th Fl -Cincinnati 45202

(614) 847-1660 ..**DeBoard**, James C '77 (JC Deboard & Co,LPA) -5878 N High -Worthington 43085

(614) 466-2766 ..**DeBoe**, Todd K '00 Atty Gen -30 E Broad -Columbus 43215 **Fx:**644-1926

(740) 498-7860 ..**De Boer**, Dirk P '00 PL Tarr Co,LPA -223 N Brdg -Newcomerstown 43832

(614) 466-3145 ..**Debolt**, Sallie J '87 Bd of Speech-Language Patholog & Audiology -77 S High -16th Fl -Columbus 43266

(330) 744-5211 ..**DeBonis**, Scott R '95 %Roth BRS&L,LPA -100 Fed Plz E -Ste 600 -Youngstown 44503 **Fx:**744-3184

(216) 586-3939 ..**DeBord**, David L '03 %Jones D -901 Lakeside Av -Cleveland 44114 **Fx:**579-0212

(216) 363-1400 ..**Debose**, Lorraine '03 %Buckley K,LPA -600 E Superior Av -Ste 1400 -Cleveland 44114 **Fx:**579-1020

(310) 443-6176 ..**de Brier**, Donald P '88 Occidental Petroleum Corp -10889 Wilshire Blvd -Ste 1500 -Los Angeles, CA 90024

(937) 443-6664 ..**DeBrosse**, Thomas E '80 (Thompson H LLP) -2000 Cthse Plz NE -Bx8801 -Dayton 45401 **Fx:**443-6635

(216) 447-1551 ..**Debski**, Christopher R '97 %Ross B&S Co LPA -6000 Freedom Square Dr -Ste 540 -Cleveland 44131 **Fx:**447-1554

(330) 494-2121 ..**Debski**, Dana M '96 %Brian Law Ofc -5770 Dressler Rd NW -Ste 101 -Canton 44720

DeCamp, Andrea R '03 -(Address Unavailable)

(330) 867-9242 ..**DeCamp**, Clifford Lee '85 (DeCamp R&D) -3250 W Market -Ste 203 -Akron 44333 **Fx:**867-9282

(330) 867-9242 ..**DeCamp Roth & Devany** -3250 W Market -Ste 203 -Akron 44333 **Fx:**867-9282

(216) 721-7700 ..**de Caris**, Gian M '89 -11510 Buckeye Rd -Cleveland 44104

(216) 937-2000 ..**de Caris**, Mario D '83 Farmers Insurance Exchaneg -815 Superior Av -Ste 1605 -Cleveland 44114

(330) 434-3000 ..**DeCarlo**, Michael '86 (Roderick & L) -One Cascade Plz -Ste 1500 -Akron 44308 **Fx:**434-9220

(216) 621-7860 ..**DeCaro**, Sara E '00 %Cavitch FD&F -1717 E 9th -14th Fl -Cleveland 44114 **Fx:**621-3415

(513) 732-0442 ..**Decatur**, Caitlin L '87 (Decatur & L Co,LPA) -350 E Main -Ste 4 -Bx605 -Batavia 45103

(419) 530-5508 ..**Decatur**, William R '83 Univ of Toledo Law Schl -2801 W Bancroft -Toledo 43606

(216) 687-7190 ..**Decensi**, Patricia B '87 Med Mutual of OH -2060 E 9th -CC 1900 -Cleveland 44115

(513) 721-4450 ..**DeCenso**, William A '79 (Santen & H) -312 Walnut -Ste 3100 -Cincinnati 45202

(419) 241-5506 ..**Dech**, Merle N Jr. '91 -610 Adams -Toledo 43604

(216) 781-2258 ..**DeChant**, Thomas H '58 Stewart & D Co,LPA -1370 Ontario -Ste 1440 Standard Bldg -Cleveland 44113 **Fx:**781-8210

(513) 931-1837 ..**Decile**, Jeffrey M '77 -7226 Greenfarms Dr -Cincinnati 45224

(614) 644-7257 ..**Decker**, Jack W '78 Atty Gen -150 E Gay -Columbus 43215 **Fx:**752-4677

(419) 249-7100 ..**Decker**, Lori W '78 Marshall & M,LLC -Four Seagate -8th Fl -Toledo 43604 **Fx:**249-7151

(614) 242-4242 ..**Decker**, Mark '73 (Decker VSL&V Co LPA) -620 E Broad -Columbus 43215 **Fx:**242-4243

(419) 255-5465 ..**Decker**, Michael E '82 Hileman Assoc -124 N Summit -Ste 140 -Toledo 43604

(859) 331-2000 ..**Decker**, Raymond H Jr. '98 %O'Hara RTS&S -25 Crestvw Hills Mall Rd -Ste 201 -Bx17411 -Covington, KY 41017

(614) 242-4242 ..**Decker Vonau Seguin Lackey & Viets Co LPA** -620 E Broad -Columbus 43215 **Fx:**242-4243

(937) 228-8088 ..**Decker-Hall**, Sarah J '00 LAWO -333 W 1st -Ste 500A -Dayton 45402 **Fx:**449-8131

(216) 443-7800 ..**Deckert**, Brian S '99 Cuyahoga Cnty Pros -1200 Ontario -8th Fl -Cleveland 44113 **Fx:**698-2270

Deckman, Adrienne L '78 -26613 Annesley Rd -Beachwood 44122

(419) 241-2122 ..**DeClark**, Peter O '95 %Williams JLG&S Co,LPA -416 N Erie -Ste 500 -Toledo 43624 **Fx:**245-3849

(216) 771-2300 ..**DeCosky**, Richard L '81 -812 Huron Rd E -Ste 315 -Cleveland 44115 **Fx:**803-3377

(513) 829-7519 ..**DeCresce**, Michele A '91 -5458 Yosemite Dr -Fairfield 45014

(937) 293-3058 ..**Deddens**, Robert L '67 Mun Ct Judge -30 Park Av -Dayton 45419 **Fx:**297-2939

(614) 876-7361 ..**DeDent**, Pamela A '91 City of Hilliard Law Dept -3800 Mncpl Way -Hilliard 43026

(513) 412-4324 ..**Dedischew**, Carol L '84 Great Amer Ins Co -49 E 4th -Ste 700 -Cincinnati 45202 **Fx:**412-4370

(216) 622-8466 ..**Dedmon**, Shelly Gail '88 (Calfee H&G LLP) -800 Superior Av -Ste 1400 -Cleveland 44114 **Fx:**241-0816

(440) 953-9064 ..**Deeb**, Charles G '76 -4230 SR 306 -Ste 240 -Willoughby 44094 **Fx:**953-1427

(440) 953-9064 ..**Deeb**, Timothy S '98 -4230 SR 306 -Ste 240 -Willoughby 44094

(330) 364-6888 ..**Deedrick**, Robert S '92 -300B E High Av -New Philadelphia 44663

(330) 364-6553 ..**Deeds**, Charles J '89 (Black MHD&B) -130 W 3rd -Bx2330 -Dover 44622 **Fx:**364-2739

(614) 231-9478 ..**Deeds**, Gary W '77 -3901 E Lvngstn Av -Ste 207 -Columbus 43227

(614) 466-2766 ..**Deeds**, Holly N '03 %Atty Gen -30 E Broad -Columbus 43215 **Fx:**644-1926

(937) 492-1271 ..**Deeds**, John M '03 %Faulkner GK&S,LPA -100 S Main Av -Ste 300 -Sidney 45365 **Fx:**498-1306

Deedy, Judith G '96 -6516 Overbrook Rd -Mission Hills, KS 66208

(216) 566-0500 ..**Deegan**, F Timothy '73 (Deegan & M) -1468 W 9th -Ste 240 -Cleveland 44113

(216) 443-6388 ..**Deegan**, Hallie M '02 %8th Dist Ct of Appls -1 Lakeside Av -#202 -Cleveland 44113 **Fx:**443-2044

(216) 328-2590 ..**Deegan**, Jon F '86 Realty 1 -6000 Rockside Wds Blvd -Ste 328 -Independence 44131

(412) 804-7602 ..**Deegan**, Joseph E '95 Ernst & Young,LLP -2100 One PPG Pl -Pittsburgh, PA 15222

(412) 434-5200 ..**Deemer**, Elizabeth E '87 %Brown & L -600 Gulf Twr -Pittsburgh, PA 15219

(614) 466-0637 ..**Deemer**, Michael W '02 OH Senate Minority Legal Cnsl -State Hse -Columbus 43215

(513) 981-6282 ..**Deen**, Jana B '91 Mercy Hlth Prtnrs -4600 McAuley Pl -Cincinnati 45242

(614) 469-3939 ..**Deep**, Colleen A '93 (Jones D) -325 John H McConnell Blvd -Ste 600 -Bx165017 -Columbus 43216 **Fx:**461-4198

(859) 291-9000 ..**Deering**, Dana E '97 OfCnsl Parry DF&S -411 Garrard -Covington, KY 41012 **Fx:**291-9300

(513) 946-3000 ..**Deering**, Jennifer K '96 Hamilton Cnty Pros -230 E 9th -Cincinnati 45202 **Fx:**946-3017

(440) 329-5389 ..**Deery**, Amanda R '04 %Lorain Cnty Pros -225 Court -3rd Fl -Elyria 44035

(440) 323-9500 ..**Deery**, James A '77 -300 4th -Elyria 44035

(419) 524-3337 ..**Dees**, Jodie D '87 -3 N Main -Richland Trust Bldg #405 -Mansfield 44902

(440) 356-5056 ..**Deese**, James L '80 -20325 Ctr Ridge Rd -Ste 512 -Rocky River 44116

(614) 224-2319 ..**Deeter**, Leann R '83 GP Price,LLC -555 City Park Av -Columbus 43215

(330) 782-3000 ..**DeFabio**, Louis M '92 -4822 Market -#220 -Youngstown 44512

(330) 533-0916 ..**DeFazio**, John T '73 Nationwide Ins -6715 Tippecanoe Rd -Ste 201 -Canfield 44406

(937) 865-4324 ..**DeFazio**, Judith D '80 Lexis/Nexis -Bx933 -Dayton 45401

(954) 563-3388 ..**DeFelice**, Salvatore D '70 -2637 N Andrews Av -Fort Lauderdale, FL 33311 **Fx:**561-9700

(937) 225-4652 ..**Deffet**, Michael E '91 Montgomery Cnty Pub Def -117 S Main -Ste 400 -Dayton 45422 **Fx:**225-3449

(330) 375-2030 ..**Defibaugh**, Michael J '00 Law Dept -161 S High -Ste 202 -Akron 44308

(216) 621-5300 ..**deFilippis**, Lisa M '86 (Buckingham D&B,LLP) -1375 E 9th -Ste 1700 -Cleveland 44114 **Fx:**621-5440

(216) 931-6000 ..**DeFlaun**, Claudia Rose '01 %Ulmer & B LLP -1300 E 9th -Ste 900 Penton Media Bldg -Cleveland 44114 **Fx:**931-6001

(330) 497-0700 ..**de Forest**, Benjamin B II '84 %Krugliak WG&D Co,LPA -4775 Munson NW -Bx36963 -Canton 44735 **Fx:**497-4020

(412) 227-3100 ..**DeForest**, Walter P III '01 (DeForest K&Y) -436 7th Av -3000 Koppers Bldg -Pittsburgh, PA 15219

(614) 224-8166 ..**Defossez**, Mark E '91 Twyford & D -495 S High -Ste 100 -Columbus 43215

(216) 771-1330 ..**DeFoy**, Ernest D '88 (Douglass & D) -526 Superior Av E -630 Leader Bldg -Cleveland 44114

DeFrance, Abigail L '04 -(Address Unavailable)

(216) 696-4600 ..**DeFranco**, Ralph T '73 (R DeFranco Co,LPA) -75 Pub Sq -Ste 1320 -Cleveland 44113 **Fx:**696-4606

(216) 696-4600 ..**DeFranco**, Thomas G '99 (T DeFranco Co,Inc) -75 Pub Sq -Ste 1320 -Cleveland 44113

(859) 344-1188 ..**DeFrank**, Michael E '88 Hemmer SPD&K -250 Grandvw Dr -Ste 200 -Ft Mitchell, KY 41017

(614) 466-2980 ..**DeFrank**, Stephen E Jr. '90 Atty Gen -30 E Broad -Columbus 43215 **Fx:**728-9470

(937) 865-6800 ..**DeFrench**, Melissa K '95 Lexis/Nexis -Bx933 -Dayton 45401

(440) 933-3231 ..**DeGeeter**, Pamela A '97 Smith & S Co,LPA -110 Moore Rd -Bx210 -Avon Lake 44012

(216) 485-7970 ..**DeGeeter**, Timothy J '98 -5454 State Rd -Parma 44134

(614) 785-6495 ..**DeGennaro**, Nicholas C '00 -445 Hutchnsn Av -Ste 800 -Columbus 43235

(216) 664-2858 ..**DeGennaro**, Susanne M '04 Dept of Law -601 Lakeside Av -Rm 106 City Hall -Cleveland 44114 **Fx:**664-2663

(330) 743-4116 ..**DeGenova**, Damian P '94 %Brennan FV&Y,Ltd -29 E Front -2nd Fl -Youngstown 44503

(614) 752-8683 ..**DeGenova**, Jacqueline F '92 State Auditor Ofc -88 E Broad -Bx1140 -Columbus 43216

(419) 382-9590 ..**DeGidio**, Anthony J Jr. '98 -3738 Treelawn Dr -Toledo 43614

(330) 588-9700 ..**DeGirolamo**, Anthony J '92 -116 Cleveland Av NW -Ste 625 -Canton 44702 **Fx:**588-9713

(440) 720-3301 ..**Degnan**, Martin J '74 Anthony & Sylvan Pools Corp -6690 Beta Dr -Ste 300 -Mayfield Village 44143

(513) 771-2676 ..**DeGraffenreid**, Stacey L '00 SL DeGraffenreid,LPA -260 Northland Blvd -Ste 312A -Cincinnati 45246

(440) 414-6001 ..**DeGrandis**, Fred M '78 St John Westshore Hsptl -29000 Ctr Ridge Rd -Westlake 44145

(216) 523-1900 ..**Degrandis**, Ronald L '73 Hausser & Taylor,LLP -1001 Lakeside Av E -Ste 1400 -Cleveland 44114

(513) 241-0400 .. **DeGregorio**, Edmonde P '77 %Aronoff R&H Co,LPA -425 Walnut
-Ste 2400 -Cincinnati 45202 **Fx**:241-2877

(216) 635-4340 .. **DeGross**, Charles M '94 CWA Local 4340 -1400 E Schaaf Rd
-Brooklyn Heights 44131

(216) 521-6363 .. **De Gross**, Louis G '83 -13317 Mad Av -Lakewood 44107

(216) 621-1312 .. **DeGulis**, Gregory J '90 (McMahon DH&L LLP) -812 Huron Rd
-Ste 650 The Caxton Bldg -Cleveland 44115 **Fx**:621-0577

(513) 721-3330 .. **DeHaan**, Elizabeth S '76 %Robbins KP&T -7 W 7th -Ste 1400
-Cincinnati 45202

(513) 489-7522 .. **DeHaan**, Peter R '74 (DeHaan & B) -11256 Cornell Park Dr
-Ste 500 -Bx429321 -Cincinnati 45242

(513) 381-2838 .. **Dehan**, Paula J '03 %Taft S&H LLP -425 Walnut -Ste 1800
-Cincinnati 45202 **Fx**:381-0205

(330) 699-6703 .. **DeHaven**, Darren W '95 %McNamara & F Co,LPA
-12370 Cleveland Av -Bx867 -Uniontown 44685 **Fx**:699-4803

(740) 374-5346 .. **Dehmlow**, Jonathan C '00 %W Fields -125 Putnam -Ste 300
-Bx710 -Marietta 45750

(614) 462-3194 .. **Dehnart**, Stephen D '87 Franklin Cnty Pub Def -373 S High
-12th Fl -Columbus 43215

(513) 777-2222 .. **Dehner**, Jeffrey A '90 %Lyons & L Co,LPA
-8310 Prnctn-Glendale Rd -Ste B -West Chester 45069

(513) 651-6800 .. **Dehner**, Joseph J '73 (Frost BT LLC) -201 E 5th -2200 PNC Ctr
-Cincinnati 45202 **Fx**:651-6981

(330) 478-4711 .. **DeHoff**, Harold E '50 -4325 20th NW -Canton 44708

Deibel, David L Jr. '76 -(Address Unavailable)

(330) 745-0006 .. **Deibel**, John W '63 -103 5th SE -Ste M -Barberton 44203

(216) 360-7200 .. **Deighton**, Eric T '99 Carlisle MRK&U Co,LPA -24755 Chagrin Blvd
-Ste 200 -Cleveland 44122 **Fx**:360-7210

(800) 227-9597 .. **Deininger**, Patrick J '04 Lexis-Nexis -9443 Springboro Pike
-Miamisburg 45342

(216) 579-1700 .. **Deioma**, David B '65 (Pearne & G LLP) -1801 E 9th -Ste 1200
-Cleveland 44114 **Fx**:579-6073

(614) 898-9305 .. **Deis**, Michelle D '85 Columbus State Cmmnty Cllg -550 E Spring
-Columbus 43215

(614) 487-7506 .. **Deisner**, Vicki L '92 OH Environmental Cncl -1207 Grandvw Av
-Ste 201 -Columbus 43212

(937) 898-7673 .. **Deitering**, Joyce M '84 (Oldham & D) -8801 N. Main -Ste 200
-Dayton 45414

(740) 453-2566 .. **Deitrick**, Robert L '90 -11 S 4th -Bx39 -Zanesville 43702

(614) 464-6400 .. **Dejelo**, P Jason '03 %Vorys SS&P LLP -52 E Gay -Bx1008
-Columbus 43216 **Fx**:464-6350

(216) 696-1448 .. **DeJohn**, John E '90 Compensation Cnsltnts,Inc
-614 Superior Av NW -Ste 601 Rckfllr Bldg -Cleveland 44114

DeJohn, Michael '03 -1360 W 9th -Ste 310 -Cleveland 44113

(216) 861-6282 .. **DeJohn**, Michael C '04 %K Toohig -1360 W 9th -Ste 310
-Cleveland 44113

(216) 241-2414 .. **DeJohn**, Stephen E '72 NOACA -1299 Superior Av
-Cleveland 44114

(312) 346-5500 .. **De Jong**, David J '03 (DJ De Jong & Assoc,Ltd) -20 N Clark
-Ste 2700 -Chicago, IL 60602 **Fx**:551-1154

(330) 364-1112 .. **De La Cruz**, Christopher P '79 -134 2nd NW -New
Philadelphia 44663 **Fx**:343-4111

(419) 421-4476 .. **De La Cruz**, Jaime J '00 Marathon Ashland Petroleum LLC
-539 S Main -Rm 871-M -Findlay 45840 **Fx**:421-3578

(440) 442-6677 .. **Delahunty**, Martin S III '87 Elk & E Co,LPA -6100 Parkland Blvd
-Mayfield Heights 44124 **Fx**:442-7944

(419) 433-3130 .. **DeLamatre**, Richard D '58 -74 Mill -Huron 44839 **Fx**:433-3130

(219) 925-4560 .. **DeLambo**, Robert J '71 Smith & S -12th & Jackson -Bx686
-Auburn, IN 46706

(419) 244-8351 .. **DeLand**, Jennifer L '02 Lucas Cnty Pub Def -555 N Erie
-Toledo 43624

(419) 243-6148 .. **DeLaney**, Cormac B '75 (Manahan PB&D) -414 N Erie -Bx2328
-Toledo 43603

(216) 861-2500 .. **Delaney**, John C '77 -614 Superior Av W -Rckfllr Bldg Rm 662
-Cleveland 44113

(216) 566-8500 .. **Delaney**, Kelly C '03 %KH Bauernschmidt Co,LPA
-700 W St Clair Av -Ste 214 -Cleveland 44113 **Fx**:566-0942

(859) 441-6918 .. **Delaney**, Michael B '83 -2125 N Ft Thomas Av -Fort
Thomas, KY 41075

(614) 645-6933 .. **Delaney**, Patricia A '90 City Atty -90 W Broad -Columbus 43215

(216) 861-2500 .. **Delaney**, Timothy J '76 (Scully & D) -614 Superior Av W
-Rckfllr Bldg Ste 662 -Cleveland 44113

(614) 221-5439 .. **deLanglade-Spriggs**, Elise M '97 OH Petroleum Cncl
-88 E Broad -Ste 1460 -Columbus 43215

(614) 693-6838 .. **DelaRosa**, Regina M '88 Defense Finance & Accounting Ofc
-3990 E Broad -Columbus 43213

(419) 354-9217 .. **de la Serna**, Arlen B '96 Wood Cnty Cmmn Pleas Ct -1 Cthse Sq
-Bowling Green 43402

(614) 574-2593 .. **Delatte**, Margaret L '04 Christian Legal Srvcs -1468 W 25th
-Cleveland 44113

(614) 851-8810 .. **DeLaughter**, Sharon D '93 -2545 Hilliard Rome Rd PMB212
-Hilliard 43026

(330) 965-8000 .. **DeLaurentis**, Dominic J Jr. '88 (Osborne D&S Co LPA)
-100 Marwood Cir -Boardman 44512 **Fx**:965-8005

(440) 333-3708 .. **Delay**, Brendan E '86 -619 Linda -Ste 101 -Rocky River 44116

(216) 241-5310 .. **Del Balso**, Colleen R '02 %Gallagher SF&N -1501 Euclid Av
-6th Fl -Cleveland 44115 **Fx**:241-1608

(216) 443-7800 .. **DelBalso**, Dominic J '72 Cuyahoga Cnty Pros -1200 Ontario
-8th Fl -Cleveland 44113 **Fx**:698-2270

(213) 894-2811 .. **Del Bene**, Charles A '63 US DOJ -606 S Olive -Ste 1500
-Los Angeles, CA 90014

(330) 392-4176 .. **Del Bene LaPolla & Thomas** -155 Pine Av NE -Bx353
-Warren 44482 **Fx**:392-5694

(330) 670-5213 .. **DelBene**, Louis J '91 Schulte & Co -600 S Cleveland-Massillon Rd
-Fairlawn 44333

(216) 479-8500 .. **Delchin**, Steven A '97 %Squire S&D LLP -127 Pub Sq
-4900 Key Twr -Cleveland 44114 **Fx**:479-8780

(216) 621-1113 .. **Del Col**, John J '98 %Renner OB&S,LLP -1621 Euclid Av -19th Fl
-Cleveland 44115 **Fx**:621-6165

(216) 443-5143 .. **DeLeon**, Jose E '93 Cuyahoga Cnty-CSE -1640 Superior Av
-Cleveland 44114

DeLeone, James F '51 -1225 Marlyn Dr -Columbus 43220

(440) 350-2683 .. **De Leone**, Michael L '01 Lake Cnty Pros -105 Main -Bx490
-Painesville 44077 **Fx**:350-2585

(513) 621-0930 .. **Delev**, Gregory D '91 (Delev & W,LLC) -432 Walnut
-800 Tri State Bldg -Cincinnati 45202 **Fx**:562-8822

(513) 621-0930 .. **Delev & Williams,LLC** -432 Walnut -800 Tri State Bldg
-Cincinnati 45202 **Fx**:562-8822

(614) 224-5294 .. **deLevie**, Raymond M '92 -81 S 4th -Ste 310 -Columbus 43215
Fx:224-5284

(614) 249-8510 .. **Deley-Shimer**, Julie A '91 SrCnsl Nationwide Ins Co
-1 Nationwide Plz -Columbus 43215

(419) 599-5590 .. **DelFavero**, Christopher D '95 -614 N Perry -Napoleon 43545

(312) 803-6250 .. **Del Greco**, Barbara T '97 %Sudekum C&S -20 N Clark -Ste 1400
-Chicago, IL 60602

(330) 434-1000 .. **Delgros**, Melissa R '99 %Bernlohr W,LLP -23 S Main -3rd Fl
-Akron 44308 **Fx**:434-1001

(330) 535-5711 .. **DelGrosso**, Lisa S '95 (Brouse M) -106 S Main -500 First Natl Twr
-Akron 44308 **Fx**:253-8601

(216) 502-0588 .. **Delguyd**, Joseph A '85 -1360 W 9th -Ste 400 -Cleveland 44113

(614) 457-5901 .. **De Libera**, John S '63 (DeLibera L&B) -3363 Tremont Rd -Ste 101
-Columbus 43221

(614) 228-1313 .. **De Libera Lyons & Bibbo** -336 S High -Columbus 43215

(614) 457-5901 .. **De Libera Lyons & Bibbo** -3363 Tremont Rd -Ste 101
-Columbus 43221

(614) 457-6101 .. **De Libera**, Malissa M '97 -3363 Tremont Rd -Ste 101
-Columbus 43221

(216) 781-8700 .. **Deliberato**, Matthew D '99 Novak RP&S,LLP -1660 W 2nd
-Ste 270 Skylight Ofc Twr -Cleveland 44113 **Fx**:781-9227

(330) 225-7220 .. **Delliman**, Scott M '98 R Tinl & Assoc -3695 Ctr Rd
-Brunswick 44212 **Fx**:225-9770

(330) 535-9330 .. **Delino**, Lawrence L Jr. '84 -1 Cascade Plz -Ste 705 -Akron 44308

(304) 233-3511 .. **Delk**, David L Jr. '02 Bachmann HB&G,PLLC -1226 Chapline
-Bx351 -Wheeling, WV 26003

(419) 447-6181 .. **Dell Burtis & Anspach,LLP** -60 Sycamore -Tiffin 44883
Fx:477-6332

(419) 447-6181 .. **Dell**, Jane C '90 (Dell B&A,LLP) -60 Sycamore -Tiffin 44883
Fx:477-6332

(414) 513-4047 .. **Della Penna**, Michael A '97 GE Medical Syst
-3000 N Grandvw Blvd -Ste W-710 -Waukesha, WI 53188

(216) 447-8500 .. **Dell'Aquila**, Richard P '78 -414 rockside Rd -Ste 230
-Seven Hills 44131

(419) 321-1378 .. **Deller**, Scott G '90 (Shumaker L&K,LLP) -1000 Jackson
-Toledo 43624 **Fx**:241-6894

(419) 241-9000 .. **Deller**, Stefanie E '99 Shumaker L&K,LLP -1000 Jackson
-Toledo 43624 **Fx**:241-6894

(330) 744-1111 .. **Dellick**, John T '85 Harrington H&M,Ltd -26 Market -Ste 1200
-Youngstown 44503 **Fx**:744-2029

(614) 221-2580 .. **Delligatti**, Michael J '88 -500 S Front -Ste 250 -Columbus 43215
Fx:221-2575

(216) 621-0200 .. **Dellinger**, Elizabeth A '87 (Baker & H LLP) -1900 E 9th -Ste 3200
-Cleveland 44114 **Fx**:696-0740

(330) 376-4558 .. **DelMedico**, Michael J '80 (Scanlon & G Co,LPA) -50 S Main
-Ste 1200 -Akron 44308 **Fx**:376-3550

(216) 931-6000 .. **Del Monaco**, Maria A '97 (Ulmer & B LLP) -1300 E 9th
-Ste 900 Penton Media Bldg -Cleveland 44114 **Fx**:931-6001

(216) 741-2365 .. **Del Monte**, Jordan S '72 UAW Legal Srvcs -707 Brookpark Rd
-Brooklyn Heights 44109

(937) 225-5765 .. **Delnicki**, Christopher R '93 Montgomery Cnty Pros -301 W 3rd
-Bx972 -Dayton 45422 **Fx**:225-3470

(330) 252-1266 .. **DeLoach**, Jana B '99 -611 W Market -Ste 8 -Akron 44303

(216) 367-7744 .. **Delon**, Evana C '04 %Babcock & W Co,LPA -55 Pub Sq -Ste 700
-Cleveland 44113

(419) 224-0400 .. **DeLong**, David C '83 Citizens Natl Bank of Bluffton -201 N Main
-Bx990 -Lima 45802

(513) 977-8200 .. **DeLong**, Deborah '75 (Dinsmore & S LLP) -255 E 5th -Ste 1900
-Cincinnati 45202 **Fx**:977-8141

(216) 443-8575 .. **DeLong**, Hallryn S '00 Cuyahoga Cnty Ct Cmmn Pleas
-1200 Ontario -Justice Ctr 11th Fl -Cleveland 44113

DeLong, James C '83 -Bx1441 -Toledo 43603

(330) 832-1853 .. **DeLong**, James C Sr. '57 -818 16th NE -Massillon 44646

(330) 796-8757 .. **DeLong**, John D '00 Goodyear Tire & Rubber Co -1144 E Market
-Akron 44316

DeLong, Mark E '73 -(Address Unavailable)

(740) 655-2002 .. **Delong**, Richard W '74 -Bx730 -Kingston 45644

(614) 466-5394 .. **Delos Santos**, Luis D '00 Pub Def -8 E Long -Columbus 43215

(330) 965-2323 .. **Delost**, Raymond M '80 -412 Boardman Canfld Rd
-Youngstown 44512

Delsander, Dominic C '64 -3809 Northwood Rd
-University Heights 44118

(216) 443-6350 .. **Deltorto**, Darci L '04 8th Dist Ct of Appls -1 Lakeside Av -#202
-Cleveland 44113 **Fx**:443-2044

(216) 443-9000 .. **DeLuca**, Amy L '03 %Porter WM&A LLP -925 Euclid Av -Ste 1700
-Cleveland 44115 **Fx**:443-9011

(513) 651-6800 .. **DeLuca**, Christopher '92 (Frost BT LLC) -201 E 5th -2200 PNC Ctr
-Cincinnati 45202 **Fx**:651-6981

(800) 543-5589 .. **DeLuca**, Donald R '94 R&L Carriers -600 Gillam Rd
-Wilmington 45177

(614) 890-3300 .. **DeLuca**, Gaither B '93 Charter Title -2602 Oakstone Dr
-Columbus 43231

(419) 255-8331 .. **Del Vecchio**, Susan P '91 -33 S Mich -Toledo 43602

(216) 206-1238 .. **Delventhal**, Thomas M '91 Metropolitan Bank & Trust
-30100 Chagrin Blvd -Ste 100 -Pepper Pike 44124

(216) 479-8500 .. **Demanelis**, Ernie K '81 (Squire S&D LLP) -127 Pub Sq -4900
Key Twr -Cleveland 44114 **Fx**:479-8780

(937) 898-3911 .. **DeMarco**, Alex U '61 (A DeMarco Co, LPA) -212 W Natl Rd
-Vandalia 45377 **Fx**:898-3311

(202) 739-3000 .. **Demarco**, Anthony J '95 Morgan L&B LLP -1111 Penn Av NW
-Washington, DC 20004

(216) 621-0150 .. **DeMarco**, Daniel A '87 (Hahn L&P LLP) -3300 BP Twr/200 Pub Sq
-Ste 3300 -Cleveland 44114 **Fx**:241-2824

(330) 929-9222 .. **DeMarco**, John C '92 -2332 Providence Blvd
-Cuyahoga Falls 44221

(330) 376-1600 .. **DeMarco**, Louis M '79 Cincinnati Ins Co -50 S Main -Ste 615
-Akron 44308

(513) 621-0267 .. **De Marco**, Paul M '89 Waite SB&C -1 W 4th -1513 4th & Vine Twr
-Cincinnati 45202

(614) 466-7447 ..**DeMarco**, Peter E '84 Atty Gen -150 E Gay -Columbus 43215
(440) 248-8811 ..**DeMarco**, Robert P '69 (R DeMarco & Assoc) -30505 Bainbrdg Rd -Ste 190 -Solon 44139
(732) 516-4200 ..**DeMarco**, Victor J '92 Ernst & Young LLP -99 Wood Av S -Bx751 -Iselin, NJ 08830
(740) 393-1122 ..**Demaree**, Duff D '79 -136 S Main -Mount Vernon 43050
(614) 895-3095 ..**Demaree**, Karin E '99 Cnsl Nationwide Ins -5900 Parkwood Dr -PW -01-08 -Dublin 43016
(904) 357-9176 ..**DeMarko**, Ken '91 Rayonier -50 N Laura -Ste 1900 -Jacksonville, FL 32202
(216) 736-6334 ..**Demarr**, Jean A '83 SrCnsl Dominion East Ohio Gas -1201 E 55th -Cleveland 44101 **Fx:**736-5308
(216) 274-1608 ..**Demaske**, Susan J '84 Chase Manhattan Trust -250 W Huron Rd -Ste 220 -Cleveland 44113
(330) 544-0424 ..**DeMatteis**, Martin D '80 (Witten & D) -465 Robbins Av -Niles 44446
(614) 793-5964 ..**DeMatteo**, Lucia Villari '00 Sterling Commerce -4600 Lakehurst Ct -Dublin 43016
(614) 466-1305 ..**Dembinski**, David M '84 Atty Gen -30 E Broad -Columbus 43215 **Fx:**466-8898
(330) 454-2136 ..**Demchak**, Michael D '77 -116 Cleveland Av NW -Ste 717 -Canton 44702
(330) 699-6703 ..**Demczyk**, Michael V '82 %McNamara & F Co,LPA -12370 Cleveland Av -Bx867 -Uniontown 44685 **Fx:**699-4803
(216) 771-1525 ..**DeMelto**, Vincent K '71 -425 W Lakeside Av -Ste 100 -Cleveland 44113
(440) 826-1560 ..**Demer**, Adrian J '74 -18660 E Bagley Rd -Phase II-Ste 203 -Cleveland 44130
(216) 621-5036 ..**Demer**, John A '71 (Demer W&M,LLC) -2 Berea Cmmns -Ste 200 -Berea 44017 **Fx:**(440) 891-1684
(216) 475-3655 ..**Demer**, Margaret E '59 -11429 Bradwell Rd -Garfield Heights 44125
(216) 621-5036 ..**Demer Weiner & Marniella,LLC** -2 Berea Cmmns -Ste 200 -Berea 44017 **Fx:**(440) 891-1684
(614) 628-6880 ..**Demers**, Andrew B '02 %Dinsmore & S LLP -175 S 3rd -10th Fl -Columbus 43215 **Fx:**628-6890
(614) 939-1235 ..**Demers & Cohen** -3 N High -Bx430 -New Albany 43054
(614) 939-1235 ..**Demers**, David J '91 (Demers & C) -3 N High -Bx430 -New Albany 43054
(740) 772-7466 ..**DeMers**, Karen D '96 Ross Cnty Job/Fam Srvcs -475 Wstrn Av -Ste B -Bx469 -Chillicothe 45601
(614) 466-7900 ..**Demers**, Stephanie Bostos '93 Atty Gen -30 E Broad -Columbus 43215 **Fx:**466-2437
(440) 350-0233 ..**Demeter**, Richard V '84 -9944 Johnny Cake Ridge Rd -Concord 44077
(216) 621-5980 ..**DeMetz**, Kathleen S '77 Legal Aid -1223 W 6th -Cleveland 44113
(614) 228-9550 ..**Demian**, Mark J '94 %Javitch B&R -33 N 3rd -Ste 300 -Columbus 43215 **Fx:**228-2818
(216) 642-3342 ..**Demian**, Simon P '92 %Wegman H&V,LPA -6055 Rockside Wds Blvd -Ste 200 -Cleveland 44131 **Fx:**642-8826
(216) 621-0200 ..**DeMinico**, Michael P '03 %Baker & H LLP -1900 E 9th -Ste 3200 -Cleveland 44114 **Fx:**696-0740
(216) 520-5527 ..**Demis-Young**, Elisa C '88 West Grp -6111 Oak Tree Blvd -Bx318063 -Cleveland 44131
(216) 586-3939 ..**Demitrack**, Thomas '79 (Jones D) -901 Lakeside Av -Cleveland 44114 **Fx:**579-0212
(937) 445-2701 ..**Demko**, Thomas A '00 NCR Corp -1611 S Main -Dayton 45479
(330) 723-6404 ..**Demlow**, Amy D '94 (Critchfield C&J Ltd) -3985 Medina Rd -Ste 100 -Medina 44256
(513) 621-2120 ..**Demmerle**, Daniel H II '73 Strauss & T,LPA -150 E 4th -4th Fl -Cincinnati 45202 **Fx:**241-8259
(419) 433-5006 ..**Demmitt**, Denise M '00 -Bx1417 -Sandusky 44871
(614) 365-2700 ..**DeMonte**, Jessica E '00 %Squire S&D LLP -41 S High -1300 Huntngtn Ctr -Columbus 43215 **Fx:**365-2499
deMoraes Crossman, Beatriz B '98 -(Address Unavailable)
(513) 932-2121 ..**Demos**, Gregory J '94 (Diehl & D) -304 E Warren -Lebanon 45036
(216) 443-7800 ..**Demosthenes**, Suzie '95 Cuyahoga Cnty Pros -1200 Ontario -8th Fl -Cleveland 44113 **Fx:**698-2270
(513) 946-9338 ..**DeMott**, Paul D Sr. '85 Hamilton Cnty Juv Ct -800 Bway -Cincinnati 45202 **Fx:**946-9217
(513) 794-5040 ..**Dempsey**, Joel L '00 Brown Publishing Co -10222 Alliance Rd -Cincinnati 45242
(216) 687-2300 ..**Dempsey**, Louise P '82 CSU-Marshall Cllg of Law -2121 Euclid Av -LB138 -Cleveland 44115 **Fx:**687-6881
(419) 627-6207 ..**Dempsey**, Timothy H '81 -158 E Market -Ste 205 -Sandusky 44870
(216) 621-2300 ..**Demsey**, Richard L '82 Nurenberg PH&M LPA -1370 Ontario -Ste 100 -Cleveland 44113 **Fx:**771-2242
(202) 205-0568 ..**Demske**, Gregory E '90 US Dept of HHS -330 Indpndnc Av SW -Rm 5527 -Washington, DC 20201
(330) 833-9736 ..**Demsky**, William E '76 -54 Fed Av NE -Massillon 44646
(419) 399-3801 ..**DeMuth**, John A '79 -110 E Jackson -Paulding 45879
(330) 554-1888 ..**Demyan**, John W '02 (JW Demyan,LLC) -72 N Main -Ste 204 -Hudson 44236
(937) 910-7550 ..**Denardo**, Thomas R '81 Dayton Metro Housing Auth -Bx8750 -Dayton 45401
(614) 262-5737 ..**Denbow-Hubbard**, Stefania A '84 -4388 Scenic Dr -Columbus 43214
(614) 224-0531 ..**Dendis**, Lorree L '00 %Williams & P Co,LLC -338 S High -2nd Fl -Columbus 43215 **Fx:**224-0553
(937) 223-6003 ..**Dendwick-Gordon**, Laurie N '02 %Dunlevey M&F -110 N Main -Ste 1000 -Dayton 45402 **Fx:**223-8550
(937) 547-7350 ..**Deneke**, Albert J Jr. '64 Darke Cnty Probate/Juv Ct -300 Garst Av -Greenville 45331
(330) 920-2620 ..**Dengg**, Edwin L '99 (Dengg & Assoc) -1623 Riverside Dr -Akron 44310
(614) 464-6400 ..**Dengler**, A Brian '85 OfCnsl Vorys SS&P LLP -52 E Gay -Bx1008 -Columbus 43216 **Fx:**464-6350
(610) 272-4222 ..**Dengler**, Cynthia L '94 Murphy OC&G PC -43 E Marshall -Norristown, PA 19401
Dengler, Mary M '86 -4168 Sudbrook Sq W -New Albany 43054
(859) 962-4300 ..**Denham**, Donna S '03 St Luke Hsptl West -7380 Turfway Rd -Florence, KY 41042

(202) 324-5701 ..**Denholm**, Richard M II '91 FBI -935 Penn Av NW -Washington, DC 20535
(513) 621-9660 ..**Denicola**, Ronald J '67 Denicola & Co,LPA -36 E 7th -Ste 2020 -Cincinnati 45202
(937) 382-1497 ..**Denier**, Charles P '03 %Peelle Law Ofcs Co,LPA -1929 Rombach Av -Bx950 -Wilmington 45177
(216) 566-5574 ..**Denkewalter**, Jack Kurt '90 (Thompson H LLP) -127 Pub Sq -3900 Key Ctr -Cleveland 44114 **Fx:**566-5800
(937) 653-7186 ..**Denkewalter**, William F '95 (Houston H&D) -1 Monument Sq -Ste 200 -Bx913 -Urbana 43078 **Fx:**653-3293
(513) 621-3440 ..**Denlinger Rosenthal & Greenberg Co, LPA** -425 Walnut -Ste 2310 -Cincinnati 45202 **Fx:**621-4449
(440) 951-6666 ..**Denman**, Alfred '70 Denman & L Co,LPA -8039 Broadmoor Rd -Mentor 44060
(440) 951-6666 ..**Denman & Lerner Co, LPA** -8039 Broadmoor Rd -Mentor 44060
(440) 352-5318 ..**Denman**, Patrice F '89 -48 Prentice Rd -Painesville 44077
(330) 742-2340 ..**Denman**, Sandra L '88 Youngstown State Univ -1 Univ Plz -209 Tod Hall -Youngstown 44555
(614) 228-5271 ..**Denmead**, Craig '72 (Denmead & M) -37 W Broad -Ste 1150 -Columbus 43215
(614) 228-5271 ..**Denmead & Maloney** -37 W Broad -Ste 1150 -Columbus 43215
(330) 545-4250 ..**Denney**, James A '77 -1631 S State -Girard 44420
(440) 338-8981 ..**Denney**, Jon E '64 -163 Chestnut Ln -South Russell 44022
(513) 852-6000 ..**Denney**, Mark A '95 %Wood & L LLP -600 Vine -Ste 2500 -Cincinnati 45202 **Fx:**852-6087
(614) 457-8260 ..**Denney**, Patti L '85 -1387 Portage Dr -Columbus 43235
(513) 671-0994 ..**Dennie**, Daryl T '97 -12025 Sprngdl Lk Dr -Cincinnati 45246
(419) 861-2300 ..**Dennis**, David A '85 Cnsl Fiduciary Solutions,Ltd -6135 Trust Dr -Ste 118 -Holland 43528 **Fx:**861-3804
(513) 651-6800 ..**Dennis**, Douglas R '95 %Frost BT LLC -201 E 5th -2200 PNC Ctr -Cincinnati 45202 **Fx:**651-6981
(937) 229-9999 ..**Dennis**, James D '76 (Ambrose & D) -130 W 2nd -Ste 999 -Dayton 45402 **Fx:**229-7898
(937) 382-3831 ..**Dennis**, Joseph H '86 (Dennis & W Co,LPA) -245 N South -Wilmington 45177
(614) 471-2900 ..**Dennis**, Keith A '84 Dennis Pontiac -2900 Morse Rd -Columbus 43231
(330) 434-1995 ..**Dennis**, Mark R '03 Arcadis FPS -520 S Main -Ste 2400 -Akron 44311
(330) 447-3613 ..**Dennis**, Michael W '95 Chemical Abstracts Srvc -2540 Olentangy Rvr Rd -Columbus 43202
Dennis, Shari E '87 -16860 Catsden Rd -Chagrin Falls 44023
(330) 643-2372 ..**Dennis**, Sharon '87 Summit Cnty Dom Rltns Ct -209 S High -Akron 44308
(937) 642-6297 ..**Dennison**, Judith L '96 Honda of Amer Mfg Inc -24000 Honda Pkwy -Leg Dept -Marysville 43040
(614) 228-3413 ..**Dennison**, Sallynda P '97 -500 S Front -Ste 102 -Columbus 43215
(216) 861-4533 ..**Denny**, Douglas R '74 (Ray RC&D PLL) -1717 E 9th -Cleveland 44114 **Fx:**861-4568
(419) 244-6788 ..**Denny**, Gregory B '73 (Bugbee & C) -405 Mad Av -Ste 1300 -Toledo 43604 **Fx:**244-7145
(937) 224-0039 ..**Denny**, Larry J '74 L Denny -371 W 1st -2nd Fl -Dayton 45402 **Fx:**222-1050
(937) 866-8454 ..**Denny**, Richard G '73 -110 E Central Av -Miamisburg 45342
(937) 445-5821 ..**Denny**, Simone M '99 NCR Corp Law Dept -101 W Schantz Av -ECD - 3 -Dayton 45409
(937) 225-4253 ..**Denslow**, Jeremiah J '02 Montgomery Cnty Pros -303 W 2nd -Rm 113 -Dayton 45402
(540) 510-3024 ..**Densmore**, Douglas W '76 (Flippin DMR&J) -Bx1200 -Roanoke, VA 24006
(216) 696-4700 ..**Dent**, Rebecca Holloway '91 %Spieth BM&N Co,LPA -925 Euclid Av -2000 Huntngtn Bldg -Cleveland 44115 **Fx:**696-2706
(614) 224-2428 ..**Dentinger**, David P '97 -500 S Front -Ste 1140 -Columbus 43215
(513) 579-6400 ..**Denton**, David B '00 %Keating M&K PLL -1 E 4th -1400 Provident Twr -Cincinnati 45202 **Fx:**579-6457
(419) 882-4707 ..**DeNune**, Ralph III '75 McHugh D&M,Ltd) -5580 Monroe -Sylvania 43560 **Fx:**885-3861
(216) 586-3939 ..**DeNuzzo**, Noreen '86 Jones D -901 Lakeside Av -Cleveland 44114 **Fx:**579-0212
(614) 298-8200 ..**DePascale**, Diane M '81 -786 Northwest Blvd -Columbus 43212
(614) 224-9207 ..**DePascale**, Paul A '87 Title First Agncy,Inc -555 S Front -Ste 400 -Columbus 43213
(614) 298-8200 ..**DePascale**, Vincent N '67 -786 Northwest Blvd -Columbus 43212
(330) 492-2511 ..**DePasquale**, David F '88 (Fitzpatrick & D) -4942 Higbee Av NW -Ste I -Canton 44718
(330) 492-2511 ..**DePasquale**, Lauren E '83 Fitzpatrick & D -4942 Higbee Av NW -Ste I -Canton 44718
(740) 474-7841 ..**DePaul**, Sara C '04 4th Dist Ct of Appls -121-A W Franklin -Circleville 43113 **Fx:**474-6870
(216) 575-0777 ..**DePerro**, Dayna M '04 %Kelley & F,LLP -1300 E 9th -Ste 1901 -Cleveland 44114 **Fx:**575-0799
(614) 227-2000 ..**DePew**, Lloyd G Jr. '81 (Porter WM&A LLP) -41 S High -Columbus 43215 **Fx:**227-2100
(216) 696-8860 ..**DePiero**, Daniel R '94 -1648 Hanna Bldg -1422 Euclid Av -Cleveland 44115
(216) 485-7970 ..**DePiero**, Dean E '94 -5454 State Rd -Parma 44134
(330) 545-4326 ..**DePietro**, Harry J '89 Harry J. DePietro -3 N State -Girard 44420
(440) 209-1600 ..**DePledge**, Laura A '97 -7372 Lk Shr Blvd -#8 -Mentor 44060 **Fx:**209-1275
(419) 347-7421 ..**Depler**, Thomas A '75 (Poland D&S Co,LPA) -6 Water -Shelby 44875
(937) 434-6040 ..**Depoorter**, Kent J '92 -7501 Paragon Rd -Dayton 45459
(937) 773-7621 ..**DePriest**, Roy H '59 -429 N Main -Bx1435 -Piqua 45356
(440) 483-3000 ..**DeRamus**, Monica D '01 Phillips Medical Sys -595 Miner Rd -Highland Heights 44143
(419) 663-6634 ..**Derby**, Charles P '91 -17 N. Hester -Bx24 -Norwalk 44857
(216) 363-4500 ..**Derenthal**, Jacob B '04 %Benesch FC&A LLP -200 Pub Sq -Ste 2300 -Cleveland 44114 **Fx:**363-4588
(312) 596-1900 ..**de Resendiz**, Susan Barnes '74 OfCnsl Gardner C&D -191 N Wacker Dr -Ste 3700 -Chicago, IL 60606
Derflinger, Candice L '04 -(Address Unavailable)

(330) 673-0114 ..DeRhodes, Jon M '88 (Flynn & D) -250 S Water -Bx762
　　　　　　　　-Kent 44240
(719) 634-6620 ..Derickson, Andrew L '97 (AL Derickson,PC) -128 S Tejon
　　　　　　　　-Ste 310 -Colorado Springs, CO 80903 Fx:634-3142
(216) 931-6000 ..DeRienzo, Elizabeth M '04 %Ulmer & B LLP -1300 E 9th
　　　　　　　　-Ste 900 Penton Media Bldg -Cleveland 44114 Fx:931-6001
(513) 422-1136 ..Derivan, Hubert T '67 HT Derivan,Co LPA -220 S Breiel Blvd
　　　　　　　　-Ste C -Middletown 45044
(330) 375-5834 ..Derivan, Sharon K '87 Hon DD Dowd Jr -2 S Main -#402
　　　　　　　　-Akron 44308
(216) 771-3336 ..Derkin, William S '73 Allstate Ins Co -113 St Clair Av -Ste 525
　　　　　　　　-Cleveland 44114
(614) 866-9999 ..Derksen, Tina M '02 Dynalab,Inc -555 Lncstr Av
　　　　　　　　-Reynoldsburg 43068
(740) 862-4191 ..Dern, Robert O '03 (Jackson KS&D) -719 W Market
　　　　　　　　-Baltimore 43105
(800) 397-8529 ..DeRoberts, David N '95 -1963 E 126th -Cleveland 44106
(216) 291-9905 ..DeRocco, Gary D '74 -4170 Silsby Rd -University Heights 44118
(440) 498-4000 ..DeRoche, James A '91 Stopol Inc -31875 Solon Rd -Ste 3
　　　　　　　　-Solon 44139 Fx:498-4001
(216) 987-3257 ..DeRosa, James D '95 Cuyahoga Comm Cllg -2415 Woodlnd Av
　　　　　　　　-Cleveland 44115 Fx:987-3198
(216) 621-8700 ..De Rosa, Joseph C '79 (Wincek & D Co,LPA) -1370 Ontario
　　　　　　　　-1500 Standard Bldg -Cleveland 44113
(216) 621-1742 ..DeRose, Carole A '63 Mancino M&M -75 Pub Sq -Ste 1016
　　　　　　　　-Cleveland 44113
(614) 221-4221 ..DeRose, Robert E II '91 Barkan + N -360 S Grant Av -Bx1989
　　　　　　　　-Columbus 43216 Fx:221-5423
(614) 464-6400 ..DeRousie, Charles S '73 (Vorys SS&P LLP) -52 E Gay -Bx1008
　　　　　　　　-Columbus 43216 Fx:464-6350
(740) 743-1669 ..Derr, Vicki B '79 Envirotech Cnsltnts Inc -5380 Twp Rd 143 NE
　　　　　　　　-Somerset 43783 Fx:743-1644
(216) 991-0800 ..Derrick, William A Jr. '69 (W Derrick & Co,Ltd)
　　　　　　　　-18550 S Woodlnd Rd -Shaker Heights 44122
(937) 223-8177 ..Derrien, Sylvie '00 %Coolidge WW&L -33 W 1st -Ste 600
　　　　　　　　-Dayton 45402 Fx:223-6705
(419) 227-5531 ..Derryberry, Glenn H '77 Allen Cnty Juv Ct -1000 Ward Hill Av
　　　　　　　　-Bx419 -Lima 45802
(419) 738-9678 ..Derryberry, Quentin M II '70 -4 E Auglaize -Bx2056
　　　　　　　　-Wapakoneta 45895
(513) 621-2100 ..Dershaw, Brian G '00 Beckman W&S LLC -120 E 4th
　　　　　　　　-1200 Mercantile Ctr -Cincinnati 45202 Fx:621-0106
(216) 621-7227 ..Dertouzos, Nicholas J '99 %Nicola G&C,LLC -25 W Prospect Av
　　　　　　　　-Republic Bldg Ste 1400 -Cleveland 44115 Fx:621-3999
(216) 861-5142 ..Dertouzos, Nicole B '99 Legal Aid -1223 W 6th -Cleveland 44113
　　　　　　　　Fx:687-0779
(513) 721-4450 ..Desai, Deepak K '93 %Santen & H -312 Walnut -Ste 3100
　　　　　　　　-Cincinnati 45202
(330) 747-2661 ..DeSalvo, Anthony R '69 Cafaro Co -2445 Belmont Av -Bx2186
　　　　　　　　-Youngstown 44504
(202) 879-5967 ..DeSanctis, Joseph J '83 OfCnsl Kirkland & E -655 15th NW
　　　　　　　　-Washington, DC 20005 Fx:879-5200
(216) 787-5299 ..DeSantis, Fedele '84 Atty Gen -615 W Superior Av -11th Fl
　　　　　　　　-Cleveland 44113 Fx:787-3480
(216) 566-5514 ..DeSantis, Frank R '83 (Thompson H LLP) -127 Pub Sq
　　　　　　　　-3900 Key Ctr -Cleveland 44114 Fx:566-5800
(216) 898-1800 ..DeSantis, Lynette S '84 White Consolidated Inc
　　　　　　　　-18013 Cleve Pkwy -Bx35920 -Cleveland 44135
(330) 376-4444 ..DeSantis, Vicki L '02 %Edminister & Assoc -159 S Main
　　　　　　　　-Akron 44308
(317) 276-2759 ..DeSanto, Anthony R '53 Eli Lilly & Co -Lilly Corp Ctr
　　　　　　　　-Indianapolis, IN 46285
(614) 444-8777 ..DeSanto, Debra J '83 (DeSanto & M) -887 S High
　　　　　　　　-Columbus 43206
(330) 758-3878 ..DeSanto, Donald J '81 DeSanto & D -807 Southwestern Run
　　　　　　　　-Youngstown 44514
(330) 758-3878 ..DeSanto, Jeanne Bitonte '87 -807 Southwestern Run
　　　　　　　　-Youngstown 44514
(330) 758-3878 ..DeSanto, Joseph D '68 (DeSanto & D) -807 Southwestern Run
　　　　　　　　-Youngstown 44514
(614) 444-8777 ..DeSanto & McNichols -887 S High -Columbus 43206
(419) 289-1710 ..DeSanto, Robert P '77 -935 Sandusky -Ashland 44805
(330) 575-5934 ..De Sario, Nicole J '03 Hon JS Gwin -Two S Main -510 US Cthse
　　　　　　　　-Akron 44308
　　　　　　　　DeSaussure, Ariane L '84 US Air Force 3AF/DSJA
　　　　　　　　-HQ 3AF Unit 4840 -APO, AE 09549
(330) 762-7377 ..DeSaussure, Hamilton Jr. '83 (Oldham & D) -195 S Main -Ste 300
　　　　　　　　-Akron 44308 Fx:762-7390
(216) 292-5807 ..Desberg, Gary S '85 (Singerman MD&K) -3401 Enterprise Pkwy
　　　　　　　　-Ste 200 -Beachwood 44122 Fx:292-5867
(937) 225-6103 ..Deschler, Robert C '92 Montgomery Cnty Pros -301 W 3rd -Bx972
　　　　　　　　-Dayton 45422 Fx:225-3470
(740) 432-6397 ..DeSelm & Baker -819 Steubenvll Av -Cambridge 43725
(740) 432-6397 ..DeSelm, David H '65 (DeSelm & B) -819 Steubenvll Av
　　　　　　　　-Cambridge 43725
(216) 781-1212 ..Deseran, Sophia M '92 %Walter & H LLP -1301 E 9th -Ste 3500
　　　　　　　　-Cleveland 44114 Fx:575-0911
(937) 865-6800 ..DeSerna, Alexander C '89 Lexis/Nexis -Bx933 -Dayton 45401
(609) 720-5608 ..Deshmukh, Jayadeep R '92 %Ranbaxy Pharm Inc -600 Cllg Rd E
　　　　　　　　-Ste 2100 -Princeton, NJ 08540 Fx:514-9779
(216) 642-3342 ..DeShon, A. M '96 %Wegman H&V,LPA -6055 Rockside Wds Blvd
　　　　　　　　-Ste 200 -Cleveland 44131 Fx:642-8826
(330) 262-3030 ..Desiderio, Jason B '02 Wayne Cnty Pros -115 W Lbrty
　　　　　　　　-Wooster 44691 Fx:287-5412
　　　　　　　　Desimone, John P '93 -(Address Unavailable)
(937) 223-8171 ..DeSio, Laura C '04 %Rogers & G -2160 Kettering Twr
　　　　　　　　-Dayton 45423 Fx:223-1649
(202) 638-5300 ..Desjardins, Douglas P '93 RJ Clapp & Assoc Co,LPA
　　　　　　　　-444 N Cptl NW -Ste 828 Hall of States -Washington, DC 20001
　　　　　　　　Fx:393-1725
(412) 765-2272 ..Desman, Robert J '74 Advanced Business Consultants,Inc
　　　　　　　　-2604 Giant Oaks Dr -Pittsburgh, PA 15241
(419) 242-5399 ..DeSmith, Amber R '00 -250 S Stadium Rd -Oregon 43616

(419) 946-2100 ..Desmond, Earl K '78 -75 S Main -Bx67 -Mount Gilead 43338
　　　　　　　　Fx:946-2195
(330) 740-2330 ..Desmond, Martin P '04 %Mahoning Cnty Pros -21 W Boardman
　　　　　　　　-6th Fl -Youngstown 44503 Fx:740-2008
(419) 470-1487 ..Desmond, Patrick J '97 -4626 Willys Pkwy -Toledo 43612
(513) 632-7600 ..Desmond, William J '78 Queen City Metro Lgl Affrs -1014 Vine
　　　　　　　　-Risk Mngmnt Dept/Ste 2000 -Cincinnati 45202
(937) 593-1020 ..DeSomma, Peter K '94 -720 N Main -Bx315 -Bellefontaine 43311
　　　　　　　　Fx:593-1021
(440) 356-0408 ..Despins, Martin P '72 -19510 Lorain Rd -Ste 303
　　　　　　　　-Cleveland 44126
(717) 791-0400 ..Desseyn, Donald M '94 Cincinnati Ins Co -4999 Louise Dr
　　　　　　　　-Ste 103 -Mechanicsburg, PA 17055
(419) 227-5862 ..DeStephens, Clifford R '75 (DeStephens & D) -232 N Main -Bx547
　　　　　　　　-Lima 45802
(513) 639-2834 ..DeStigter, Mitchell Lee '00 Catholic Hlthcre Prtnrs -615 Elsinore Pl
　　　　　　　　-Cincinnati 45202
(740) 532-9422 ..Destocki, Paul E '74 (Hampton & D Co,LPA) -336 Center
　　　　　　　　-Ironton 45638
(202) 319-5140 ..Destro, Robert A '76 Columbus School of Law
　　　　　　　　-3600 John McCormack Rd NE -Rm 456 -Washington, DC 20064
(330) 743-1171 ..Detec, David A '80 (Manchester BP&U) -201 E Commerce
　　　　　　　　-Atrium Level 2 Commerce Bldg -Youngstown 44503
　　　　　　　　Fx:743-1190
(614) 466-4705 ..DeTemple, Matthew J '82 OH Dept of Edu -25 S Front -7th Fl
　　　　　　　　-Columbus 43215
(513) 241-4110 ..Deters Benzinger & Lavelle,PSC -441 Vine -Ste 3500 Carew
　　　　　　　　Twr -Cincinnati 45202 Fx:241-4551
(513) 524-5000 ..Deters, Dennis P '00 %D Haughey,LLC -121 W High
　　　　　　　　-Oxford 45056 Fx:524-5001
(859) 426-5300 ..Deters, Eric C '87 E Deters & Assoc,PSC -300 Buttermilk Pike
　　　　　　　　-Ste 322 -Fort Mitchell, KY 41017
(859) 341-1881 ..Deters, Jeremy J '97 %Deters B&L,PSC -2701 Turkeyfoot Rd
　　　　　　　　-207 Thomas More Pkwy -Crestview Hills, KY 41017 Fx:341-1469
(513) 946-3000 ..Deters, Joseph T '82 Hamilton Cnty Pros -230 E 9th
　　　　　　　　-Cincinnati 45202 Fx:946-3017
(513) 421-2540 ..Deters, William M II '95 %Ennis R&F -121 W 9th -Cincinnati 45202
　　　　　　　　Fx:562-4986
(937) 548-1157 ..Detling, James S '89 (Hanes SCGG&D,Ltd) -507 S Bway
　　　　　　　　-Greenville 45331
(614) 246-1000 ..Detrick, Joanne F '89 %R Kelm -37 W Broad -Ste 860
　　　　　　　　-Columbus 43215 Fx:246-8110
(216) 861-6000 ..Dettelbach, Sally Marcia '83 -2000 E 9th -1100 Euclid Ninth Twr
　　　　　　　　-Cleveland 44115
(216) 696-6000 ..Dettelbach Sicherman & Baumgart, LPA -1801 E 9th
　　　　　　　　-1100 Ohio Svngs Plz -Cleveland 44114 Fx:696-3338
(216) 622-3600 ..Dettelbach, Steven M '91 %US Atty -801 W Superior -Ste 400
　　　　　　　　-Cleveland 44113 Fx:622-3370
(216) 831-3212 ..Dettelbach, Thomas L '66 -3733 Park E Dr -Ste 200
　　　　　　　　-Beachwood 44122 Fx:831-3216
(419) 243-6281 ..Dettinger, James F '74 (Shindler NH&S,LLP) -300 Mad Av
　　　　　　　　-Ste 1200 -Toledo 43604 Fx:243-0129
(330) 490-5037 ..Dettinger, Warren W '80 Cnsl Diebold,Inc -5995 Mayfair Rd
　　　　　　　　-Bx3077 -North Canton 44720 Fx:490-4450
(740) 286-1112 ..Detty, John L '81 -287 E Main -Bx642 -Jackson 45640
(330) 434-3000 ..Detweiler, William J '87 (Roderick & L) -One Cascade Plz
　　　　　　　　-Ste 1500 -Akron 44308 Fx:434-9220
(330) 745-0016 ..Deuber, Frederick J '61 -480 W Tuscarawas Av -Ste 208
　　　　　　　　-Barberton 44203
(770) 772-6282 ..Deupree, Darcie A '96 US Hlthwrks,Inc -3655 N Pnt Pkwy -Ste 150
　　　　　　　　-Alpharetta, GA 30005
(937) 449-8880 ..Deuser, Charles W II '81 Bank One Trust Co -40 N Main -6th Fl
　　　　　　　　-Bx1103 -Dayton 45401
(513) 793-5505 ..Deutch, Joel G '93 -9000 Plainfld Rd -Cincinnati 45236
(561) 483-7000 ..Deutch, Theodore E '94 (Broad & C) -7777 Glades Rd -Ste 300
　　　　　　　　-Boca Raton, FL 33434 Fx:483-7321
(614) 299-1008 ..Deutsch, Adam J '99 -53 E Prescott -Columbus 43215
(937) 223-7170 ..Deutsch, David M '69 DM Deutsch Co,LPA -208 W Monument Av
　　　　　　　　-Pollack Hse -Dayton 45402 Fx:223-7180
(330) 689-2700 ..Deutsch, Gary B '97 Stow Law Dept -3760 Darrow Rd
　　　　　　　　-Stow 44224 Fx:686-0219
(216) 781-5245 ..DeVan, Mark R '74 (Berkman GM&D) -55 Pub Sq -2121 The
　　　　　　　　Illuminating Bldg -Cleveland 44113 Fx:781-8207
(419) 241-6000 ..Devaney, Kevin D '91 (Eastman & S Ltd) -1 Seagate -24th Fl
　　　　　　　　-Bx10032 -Toledo 43699 Fx:247-1777
(330) 723-9540 ..Devanney, Katharina E '98 Medina Cnty Pros -72 Pub Sq
　　　　　　　　-Medina 44256
(330) 867-9242 ..Devany, David M '85 (DeCamp R&D) -3250 W Market -Ste 203
　　　　　　　　-Akron 44333 Fx:867-9282
(937) 252-2030 ..DeVeny, Dain N '74 (Thompson & D Co,LPA) -1340 Woodman Dr
　　　　　　　　-Dayton 45432
(937) 225-7233 ..DeVenzio, William A '85 SSA-OHA -110 N Main -Ste 800
　　　　　　　　-Dayton 45402
(216) 443-7800 ..Dever, Andrew Steven '85 Cuyahoga Cnty Pros -1200 Ontario
　　　　　　　　-8th Fl -Cleveland 44113 Fx:698-2270
(937) 834-2170 ..Dever, Jonathan T '02 -16 S Main -Mechanicsburg 43044
(412) 562-1637 ..Dever, Michael L '84 %Buchanan I,PC -301 Grant -20th Fl
　　　　　　　　-Pittsburgh, PA 15219
(740) 353-1157 ..Dever, Robert E '56 (Bannon H&D) -325 Masonic Bldg -Bx1384
　　　　　　　　-Portsmouth 45662
(740) 353-1157 ..Dever, Robert R '80 Bannon H&D -325 Masonic Bldg -Bx1384
　　　　　　　　-Portsmouth 45662
(419) 254-4858 ..Dever, Timothy J '88 Modern Bldrs Supply -3500 Phillips Av
　　　　　　　　-Toledo 43608
　　　　　　　　Dever, Veronica M '70 -21095 Parkwood Av -Fairview Park 44126
(330) 702-1960 ..DeVicchio, Mark A '91 -3680 Starrs Centre Dr -Canfield 44406
(330) 702-1747 ..DeVicchio, Matthew L '99 ML DeVecchio Co, LPA
　　　　　　　　-3680 Starr Ctr Dr -Canfield 44406 Fx:702-1755
(614) 466-2872 ..DeVictor, Audra O '96 Atty Gen -30 E Broad -Columbus 43215
　　　　　　　　Fx:728-7592
(419) 627-1371 ..Deville, Patrick L '80 Erie Cnty Cablevision -409 E Market -Bx5800
　　　　　　　　-Sandusky 44871
(614) 469-5715 ..DeVillers, David M '92 US Atty -303 Marconi Blvd -Ste 200
　　　　　　　　-Columbus 43215

(614) 221-1830 .. **DeVillers,** Sean P '96 (Christensen C&D) -401 N Front -Ste 350
　-Columbus 43215

(419) 448-9250 .. **DeVine,** Derek W '93 %Lange,LLC -174 S Wshngtn -Bx685
　-Tiffin 44883

(614) 228-1541 .. **Devine,** Joseph C '95 (Baker & H LLP) -65 E State -Ste 2100
　-Columbus 43215 **Fx:**462-2616

(614) 462-2238 .. **Devine,** Patrick A '80 (Schottenstein Z&D) -250 West -Bx165020
　-Columbus 43216 **Fx:**462-5135

(216) 861-1365 .. **Devine,** Sara C Clicquennoi '02 %Hawkins & Co,LPA -1267 W 9th
　ste 500 -Cleveland 44113 **Fx:**861-0714

(513) 632-5332 .. **DeVita,** David W '78 (DeVita & H) -117 E Court -Cincinnati 45202

(330) 761-2912 .. **DeVita,** Stephen L '83 Akron Pub Schools -10 N Bway
　-Akron 44308 **Fx:**761-3226

(216) 687-1212 .. **DeVito,** Christopher M '90 (Morganstern M&D Co,LPA)
　-623 W St Clair Av -Cleveland 44113 **Fx:**621-2951

(216) 861-4414 .. **DeVito,** Maureen M '98 Brown M LLC -1468 W 9th -Ste 210
　-Cleveland 44113

(216) 932-4680 .. **DeVito,** Ronald A '75 -3180 Chelsea Dr -Cleveland Heights 44118

(513) 737-6164 .. **Devney,** Denise L '91 -110 N 3rd -Hamilton 45011

(614) 761-0042 .. **DeVore,** Cheryl H '91 (CH Devore Co,LPA) -5148 Blazer Pkwy
　-Ste A -Dublin 43017

(216) 348-5400 .. **DeVore,** Tara C '02 %McDonald H Co,LPA -600 Superior Av E
　-Ste 2100 -Cleveland 44114 **Fx:**348-5474

(616) 632-8000 .. **DeVries,** John M '00 Mika MB&J,PLC -900 Monroe Av NW
　-Grand Rapids, MI 49503

(614) 228-1541 .. **deVyver,** K Issac '00 %Baker & H LLP -65 E State -Ste 2100
　-Columbus 43215 **Fx:**462-2616

(513) 558-5651 .. **DeWalt,** Marquel A '98 Univ of Cincinnati Intellectual Property Ofc
　-G09 Wherry Hall -Bx670829 -Cincinnati 45267

(513) 983-1549 .. **Dewan,** Margaret W '78 Procter & Gamble Co-Legal
　-1 Procter & Gamble Plz -Cincinnati 45202

(937) 225-4652 .. **Dewar,** Glen H '89 Montgomery Cnty Pub Def -117 S Main
　-Ste 400 -Dayton 45422 **Fx:**225-3449

(419) 530-7230 .. **Dewberry,** Charlon K '79 Univ of Toledo Law Schl
　-2801 W Bancroft -Toledo 43606

　　　　　　 DeWeese, James B '83 -(Address Unavailable)

(614) 848-6500 .. **DeWeese,** Stephen S '90 (Hill A&D) -7737 Olentangy Rvr Rd
　-Columbus 43235 **Fx:**848-6516

(412) 395-2566 .. **Dewey,** David K '93 Equitable Resources -200 Allegheny Ctr
　-Pittsburgh, PA 15212 **Fx:**395-3311

(419) 547-9471 .. **Dewey,** John P '72 (Dewey & D) -107 N Main -Bx28 -Clyde 43410
　Fx:547-0139

(419) 547-9471 .. **Dewey,** Thomas F Jr. '70 (Dewey & D) -107 N Main -Bx28
　-Clyde 43410 **Fx:**547-0139

(419) 243-6281 .. **Dewhirst,** Peter A '94 %Shindler NH&S,LLP -300 Mad Av
　-Ste 1200 -Toledo 43604 **Fx:**243-0129

(614) 221-0944 .. **Dewhirst,** Scot E '78 (Artz & D,LLP) -560 E Town
　-Columbus 43215 **Fx:**221-2340

(513) 579-6400 .. **DeWine,** Richard P '95 OfCnsl Keating M&K PLL -1 E 4th
　-1400 Provident Twr -Cincinnati 45202 **Fx:**579-6457

(614) 469-1301 .. **DeWitt,** Michael W '96 %Chorpenning G&P Co,LPA -585 S Front
　-Ste 250 -Columbus 43215

(262) 544-3011 .. **DeWitt,** Nancy D '92 GE Med Syst -3000 N Grandvw Blvd
　-Waukesha, WI 53188

(419) 254-3114 .. **DeWitt,** Theresa R '83 (Bunda S&D,PLL) -One SeaGate -Ste 650
　-Toledo 43604 **Fx:**241-4697

(937) 495-3143 .. **DeWolfe,** Gregory S '73 Mead Corp -Cthse Plz NE -Dayton 45463

(513) 946-3000 .. **Deye,** Thomas E '79 Hamilton Cnty Pros -230 E 9th
　-Cincinnati 45202 **Fx:**946-3017

(216) 261-0200 .. **Deyo,** Kenneth D '63 -27801 Euclid Av -Ste 500 -Euclid 44132

(330) 867-4891 .. **DeYoung,** Bruce R '85 -267 Hllywd Av -Akron 44313

(614) 224-1222 .. **DeYoung,** Kathleen A '99 %Maguire & S,LLP -250 Civic Ctr Dr
　-Ste 200 -Columbus 43215 **Fx:**221-2033

(937) 225-5795 .. **Dezarn,** Marcell N '83 Montgomery Cnty Pros -301 W 3rd -Bx972
　-Dayton 45422 **Fx:**225-3470

(440) 838-8800 .. **Dezort,** Robert E Jr. '92 (Millisor & N Co,LPA) -9150 S Hills Blvd
　-Ste 300 -Cleveland 44147 **Fx:**838-8805

(330) 535-2151 .. **Dhinojwala,** Duriya A '02 %Guy L&T -106 S Main -Ste 2210
　-Akron 44308 **Fx:**535-9048

(614) 899-1119 .. **DiAlbert,** John E '85 -483 Dempsey Rd -Westerville 43081

(216) 696-3311 .. **Diamant,** Michael H '71 (Kahn K) -1301 E 9th -2600 Erievw Twr
　-Cleveland 44114 **Fx:**623-4912

(513) 929-1108 .. **Diamond,** Barbara M '00 KnowledgeWorks Fdn -1 W 4th -Ste 200
　-Cincinnati 45202 **Fx:**929-1121

(216) 902-6010 .. **Diamond,** Clayton L '00 US Coast Guard -1240 E 9th
　-Cleveland 44199

(330) 253-5060 .. **Diamond,** John T '83 (Brennan M&D,LLC) -75 E Market
　-Akron 44308 **Fx:**253-1977

(513) 651-6800 .. **Dias,** Monica L '01 %Frost BT LLC -201 E 5th -2200 PNC Ctr
　-Cincinnati 45202 **Fx:**651-6981

(216) 621-0150 .. **Diaz,** Derek E '98 %Hahn L&P LLP -3300 BP Twr/200 Pub Sq
　-Ste 3300 -Cleveland 44114 **Fx:**241-2824

(937) 257-7143 .. **Diaz,** Norbert J '82 USAF -4225 Logistics Av -HQ-AFMC/JAG
　-Wright Patterson AFB 45433

(216) 621-0150 .. **Diaz,** Robert J '04 %Hahn L&P LLP -3300 BP Twr/200 Pub Sq
　-Ste 3300 -Cleveland 44114 **Fx:**241-2824

(216) 595-0071 .. **Diaz-Rex,** Julia '00 Roth B LLP -5196 Richmond Rd
　-Bedford Heights 44146 **Fx:**595-0073

(216) 621-0200 .. **DiBaggio,** Joseph E '02 Baker & H LLP -1900 E 9th -Ste 3200
　-Cleveland 44114 **Fx:**696-0740

(216) 813-0167 .. **DiBaggio,** Julie A '04 Key Bank -4910 Tiedeman Rd
　-Brooklyn 44144

(815) 654-5637 .. **Dibbin,** Edward J Jr. '89 Atwood Mobile -4750 Hiawatha Dr
　-Rockford, IL 61103

(419) 423-2035 .. **Dibble,** Barbara A '94 -Bx1741 -Findlay 45839

(412) 261-2900 .. **DiBella,** Richard V '02 (DiBella & G,PC) -312 Blvd of the Allies
　-3rd fl -Pittsburgh, PA 15222 **Fx:**261-3222

　　　　　　 Di Biase, Daniele Franco '04 -(Address Unavailable)

(330) 896-5209 .. **DiCato,** Edward M '91 -1475 Spring Wood Ln -Bx550
　-Green 44232

(330) 375-2730 .. **DiCaudo,** Thomas M '88 Pros -217 S High -Ste 203 -Akron 44308

(740) 393-2718 .. **Dice,** Daniel S '98 Folland & D,LPA -112 N Main
　-Mount Vernon 43050

(614) 224-8271 .. **DiCeglio,** Gary M '92 %OH AFL-CIO -395 E Broad -Ste 300
　-Columbus 43215

(440) 953-8888 .. **DiCello,** Mark Andrew '94 R DiCello Co,LPA -7556 Mentor Av
　-Mentor 44060 **Fx:**953-9138

(216) 696-3232 .. **DiCello,** Nicholas A '02 %Spangenberg S&L,LLP -1900 E 9th
　-2400 Natl City Ctr -Cleveland 44114 **Fx:**696-3924

(440) 953-8888 .. **DiCello,** Robert F '00 %R DiCello Co,LPA -7556 Mentor Av
　-Mentor 44060 **Fx:**953-9138

(440) 953-8888 .. **DiCello,** Robert J '71 (R DiCello Co,LPA) -7556 Mentor Av
　-Mentor 44060 **Fx:**953-9138

(212) 436-6144 .. **DiCenso,** Giovanni '96 Deloitte & Touche -2 World Fncl Ctr
　-New York, NY 10281 **Fx:**653-2493

(513) 621-4488 .. **DiCesare,** Francis J '87 Ofc of Chapter 13 Trustee -36 E 4th
　-Ste 700 -Cincinnati 45202 **Fx:**621-2643

(740) 702-3035 .. **DiCesare,** John C '86 Ross Cnty Ct -2 N Paint -Ste C
　-Chillicothe 45601

(216) 642-5353 .. **DiChiro,** Patrick '89 -5800 Lombardo Ctr -Ste 255
　-Seven Hills 44131

(937) 222-8091 .. **DiCicco,** Matthew D '00 (Lowe & D) -130 W 2nd -Ste 1600
　-Dayton 45402

(440) 585-5111 .. **DiCicco,** Richard D '66 -29435 Euclid Av -Ste 1 -Wickliffe 44092

　　　　　　 Dick, Bernard E '76 -4284 Huffman Rd -Medina 44256

(317) 833-3033 .. **Dick,** Steven K '81 W Tucker & Assoc LLC -429 N Penn -Ste 400
　-Indianapolis, IN 46204

　　　　　　 Dick, Trafford '83 -Bx3124 -Zanesville 43702

(210) 536-4061 .. **Dick,** William M '78 US Air Force -AFCEE/JA
　-Brooks AFB, TX 78235

(440) 284-0800 .. **Dickason,** Joyce M '97 -371 Broad -Elyria 44035

(419) 225-4055 .. **Dickason,** Miner O '67 Lima Prop Ltd -101 N Elizabeth -Ste 400
　-Lima 45801

(419) 225-4055 .. **Dickason,** Oren E '38 -101 N Elizabeth -Ste 400 -Lima 45801

(704) 759-0584 .. **Dickens,** Floyd III '94 21st Century Mgmt Srvcs Inc -Bx49291
　-Charlotte, NC 28277

(937) 333-4100 .. **Dickens,** Norma M '93 Law Dept -110 W 3rd -Bx22 -Dayton 45402

(614) 224-6488 .. **Dicker,** Gary H '87 -307 E Lvngstn Av -Columbus 43215

(614) 224-1222 .. **Dickerson,** Brian E '98 (Maguire & S,LLP) -250 Civic Ctr Dr
　-Ste 200 -Columbus 43215 **Fx:**224-1236

(859) 283-2200 .. **Dickerson,** Daniel L '84 -30 Shelby -Bx276 -Florence, KY 41042

(216) 928-2200 .. **Dickerson,** Denise A '95 Sutter OM&F -1301 E 9th
　-3600 Erievw Twr -Cleveland 44114 **Fx:**928-4400

(216) 696-5444 .. **Dickerson,** Emmanuel E '52 (Trivers & D LLC) -925 Euclid Av
　-Cleveland 44115

(513) 361-1200 .. **Dickerson,** James M Jr. '03 %Squire S&D LLP -312 Walnut
　-Ste 3500 -Cincinnati 45202 **Fx:**361-1201

(440) 821-6289 .. **Dickerson,** Susanne E '98 -Bx221193 -Beachwood 44122

(202) 564-3638 .. **Dickerson,** Thomas P '80 US EPA -1200 Penn Av NW -#1305A
　-Washington, DC 20460

(330) 452-1144 .. **Dickes,** Don D '64 Timken Foundation -200 Market Av N -Ste 210
　-Canton 44702

(330) 426-4121 .. **Dickey,** Larry M '70 (Hartford D&Y Co, LPA) -91 W Taggart -Bx85
　-East Palestine 44413

(513) 621-2260 .. **Dickey,** Patricia L '89 (Weber D&B) -813 Bway -1st Fl
　-Cincinnati 45202

(330) 336-6666 .. **Dickey,** Richard D '63 -126 King -Wadsworth 44281

(614) 466-4683 .. **Dickhaut,** Ellen A '79 Industrial Commssn of OH -30 W Spring
　-9th Fl -Columbus 43215 **Fx:**752-8785

(937) 228-1525 .. **Dickhaut,** William A '92 Nationwide Mutl Ins-Trail Div -130 W 2nd
　-Ste 410 -Dayton 45402

　　　　　　 Dickie, Erin A '94 -4117 Meadowleigh Way -Columbus 43230

(330) 535-5711 .. **Dickinson,** Clair E '77 (Brouse M) -106 S Main -500 First Natl Twr
　-Akron 44308 **Fx:**253-8601

(937) 255-6111 .. **Dickinson,** Diana S '89 HQ AFMC LO/JAB -2240 B -Rm C1
　-Wright Patterson AFB 45433 **Fx:**255-9570

(216) 621-7860 .. **Dickinson,** James G '73 (Cavitch FD&F) -1717 E 9th -14th Fl
　-Cleveland 44114 **Fx:**621-3415

(330) 352-6090 .. **Dickinson,** Joseph A '93 -6566 Beach Rd -Wadsworth 44281

(330) 643-8301 .. **Dickinson,** Matthew A '03 Summit Cnty Common Pleas Ct
　-209 S High -Akron 44308

(614) 540-4000 .. **Dickinson,** Richard J '70 OH Schl Brds Assn -8050 N High
　-Ste 100 -Columbus 43235

　　　　　　 Dickinson, Sandra J '97 -2570 Summit -Columbus 43202

(740) 452-2757 .. **Dickman,** James L '65 -604 Main -Bx159 -Zanesville 43702

(937) 440-5960 .. **Dicks,** James R Jr. '96 Miami Cnty Pros -201 W Main -Troy 45373
　Fx:440-5961

(216) 621-7743 .. **Dickson,** Blake A '92 (Schiff & D,LLC) -1370 Ontario
　-Standard Bldg 6th Fl -Cleveland 44113

(330) 477-9675 .. **Dickson,** William H '72 -1845 Glenmont Dr NW -Canton 44708

(330) 499-6000 .. **DiCola,** Renee N '03 %Baker DBW&M -400 S Main
　-Canton 44720 **Fx:**449-6423

(614) 221-3151 .. **DiCuccio,** Nicholas G '66 (Butler C&D) -50 W Broad -Ste 700
　-Columbus 43215

(614) 221-3151 .. **DiCuccio,** Nicole '99 %Butler C&D -50 W Broad -Ste 700
　-Columbus 43215

(614) 645-7483 .. **Diederick,** Melissa E '01 City Pros -375 S High -7th Fl
　-Columbus 43215

(248) 594-0600 .. **Diedrich,** Bradley J '00 %Rader F&G PLLC -39533 Woodward Av
　-Ste 140 -Bloomfield Hills, MI 48304 **Fx:**594-0610

(513) 871-1545 .. **Diedrichs,** Francis M '76 (Rice & D LLP) -3530 Edwards Rd
　-Cincinnati 45208 **Fx:**871-1545

(513) 621-2250 .. **Dieffenbach,** Roxann H '78 -13 E Court -Ste 100
　-Cincinnati 45202

(513) 932-2121 .. **Diehl & Demos** -304 E Warren -Lebanon 45036

(513) 932-2121 .. **Diehl,** Thomas J '88 (Diehl & D) -304 E Warren -Lebanon 45036

(614) 433-9612 .. **Diehl,** William D '66 (Kagay AD&G) -6877 N High -Ste 300
　-Worthington 43085

(614) 466-1288 .. **Diehm,** Paul C '69 Industrial Commssn of OH -30 W Spring -9th Fl
　-Columbus 43215 **Fx:**752-8785

(614) 273-0580 .. **Dieker,** Jeannie K '94 (Dieker & D) -Bx12143 -Columbus 43212

(614) 486-1428 .. **Dieker,** Lawrence L '72 -1885 Coventry Rd -Columbus 43212

(614) 273-0580 .. **Dieker,** Lawrence Leo Jr. '93 (Dieker & D) -Bx12143
　-Columbus 43212

(614) 469-6638 .. **Diem,** Lisa M '98 Hon D Calhoun Jr -170 N High
　-US Bankruptcy Ct -Columbus 43215

(216) 328-8700 ..Diemer, Dennis J '82 ICX Corp -2 Summit Park Dr -Ste 300
　　　　　　　　-Cleveland 44131
(440) 442-6800 ..Diemert, Joseph W Jr. '72 (JW Diemert Jr & Assoc Co,LPA)
　　　　　　　　-1360 SOM Center Rd -Mayfield Heights 44124 Fx:442-0825
(419) 259-8372 ..Diener, Erwin '74 Key Trust Co of OH -Bx10099 -Toledo 43699
(740) 233-1470 ..Diequez, Douglas B '02 %Collins & L -125 S Main -Marion 43302
　　　　　　　　Fx:223-1467
(513) 241-3100 ..Dierks, Mark N '88 %Lerner S&R -120 E 4th -8th Fl
　　　　　　　　-Cincinnati 45202
(513) 863-6700 ..Dierling, Thomas A '01 %Millikin & F -6 S 2nd -6th Fl -Bx598
　　　　　　　　-Hamilton 45012 Fx:863-0031
(740) 345-3411 ..Diernbach, Jonathan C '99 %Shapiro Legal Ctr -30 W Locust
　　　　　　　　-Newark 43055
(740) 363-1313 ..Diersing, Charles M '94 %Manos MP&D Co,LPA -50 N Sandusky
　　　　　　　　-Delaware 43015 Fx:363-1314
(513) 721-4256 ..Diersing, George A Jr. '76 -632 Vine -Ste 500 -Cincinnati 45202
　　　　　　　　Fx:721-1919
(419) 241-9000 ..Diesing, Gary R '75 (Shumaker L&K,LLP) -1000 Jackson
　　　　　　　　-Toledo 43624 Fx:241-6894
(614) 442-5539 ..Dieterich, Eric R '82 (Perry D & Assoc Co,LPA) -941 Chatham Ln
　　　　　　　　-Ste 217 -Columbus 43221 Fx:442-6682
(419) 252-5851 ..Diethelm, Joan P '84 HCR-Manorcare,Inc -333 N Summit
　　　　　　　　-Ste 1600 -Bx10086 -Toledo 43604
(513) 753-7277 ..Dietrich, Clifford A '03 %W Rapp -1 E Main -Amelia 45102
　　　　　　　　Fx:753-6984
　　　　　　　　Dietrich, Ellen E '91 -355 Candy Ln -Amherst 44001
(330) 376-2700 ..Dietrich, George A '68 (Roetzel & A,LPA) -222 S Main
　　　　　　　　-Akron 44308 Fx:376-4577
(614) 249-7638 ..Dietrich, Thomas W '76 Nationwide Ins Co -1 Nationwide Plz
　　　　　　　　-Columbus 43215
(216) 623-3688 ..Dietsch, Gary J '77 (Young & D) -1801 E 9th
　　　　　　　　-1425 Ohio Svngs Plz -Cleveland 44114 Fx:623-3692
(513) 946-3432 ..Dietz, Christopher P '79 US Ct of Appeals-1st Dist of OH
　　　　　　　　-230 E 9th -12th Fl Wm Howard Taft Law Ctr -Cincinnati 45202
(330) 929-4495 ..Dietz, David R '82 -527 Portage Trl -Cuyahoga Falls 44221
(859) 341-1881 ..Dietz, James A '02 Deters B&L,PSC -2701 Turkeyfoot Rd
　　　　　　　　-207 Thomas More Pkwy -Crestview Hills, KY 41017 Fx:341-1469
(330) 744-4137 ..Dietz, James B '91 (Friedman & R Co,LPA) -100 Fed Plz E
　　　　　　　　-Ste 300 City Centre One -Youngstown 44503 Fx:744-9962
(740) 363-1313 ..Dietz, James M '85 (Manos MP&D Co,LPA) -50 N Sandusky
　　　　　　　　-Delaware 43015 Fx:363-1314
(859) 394-6200 ..Dietz, Marc D '82 (Adams SW&D) -40 W Pike -Bx861
　　　　　　　　-Covington, KY 41012 Fx:291-7902
(313) 961-3234 ..Dietz, Richard A '91 (Foster M&B,PC) -607 Shelby -7th Fl
　　　　　　　　-Detroit, MI 48226 Fx:961-6184
(859) 331-8668 ..Dietz, Stephanie A '95 %Summe & L PLLC -3384 Madison Pike
　　　　　　　　-Ft Wright, KY 41017
(740) 587-4150 ..Diewald, Jodi S '99 Paramount Financial Group
　　　　　　　　-4009 Columbus Rd SW -Granville 43023
(440) 466-4624 ..DiFabio, Louis A '68 -299 S Bway -Bx187 -Geneva 44041
(330) 535-6644 ..DiFiore, David V '96 (DiFiore & D) -Bx9188 -Akron 44305
(330) 535-6644 ..DiFiore, Sandy A '70 (DiFiore & D) -Bx9188 -Akron 44305
(614) 224-9221 ..DiFranco, Brian C '03 %Bloomfield & K -199 S 5th
　　　　　　　　-Columbus 43215
(440) 357-6111 ..DiFranco, Carl L II '98 %Redmond W&M -174 N St Clair
　　　　　　　　-Painesville 44077
(216) 592-5000 ..DiFranco, Sandra M '03 %Tucker E&W LLP -925 Euclid Av
　　　　　　　　-1150 Huntngtn Bldg -Cleveland 44115 Fx:592-5009
(678) 247-7305 ..Digby, Bruce W '76 JM Huber Corp -1000 Parkwood Cir -Ste 1800
　　　　　　　　-Atlanta, GA 30339 Fx:247-7605
(216) 524-4673 ..DiGeronimo, Kellie L '00 Isaiahs Promise,NFP -6900 Granger Rd
　　　　　　　　-Ste 203 -Independence 44131
(440) 546-9200 ..Di Geronimo, Sergio I '89 -8748 Brecksvll Rd -Ste 130
　　　　　　　　-Brecksville 44141
(216) 566-9700 ..Digges, Randolph E III '92 (Rankin HP&C,LLP) -925 Euclid Av
　　　　　　　　-Ste 700 -Cleveland 44115 Fx:566-9711
(412) 434-2911 ..Diggs, James C '73 PPG Ind,Inc -1 PPG Pl -40th Fl
　　　　　　　　-Pittsburgh, PA 15067
(724) 933-3366 ..DiGiacobbe, Toni L '00 (DiGiacobbe & Assoc) -3500 Brooktree Rd
　　　　　　　　-Ste 100 -Wexford, PA 15090
(440) 998-1811 ..DiGiacomo, Laura M '94 SpclCnsl Children Srvc Bd -Bx1175
　　　　　　　　-Ashtabula 44005
(216) 621-5300 ..DiGirolamo, Alan P '89 (Buckingham D&B,LLP) -1375 E 9th
　　　　　　　　-Ste 1700 -Cleveland 44114 Fx:621-5440
　　　　　　　　Dikeman, James R '79 US Navy -Naval Forces Europe -Bx151
　　　　　　　　-FPO, AE 09499
(419) 843-9883 ..DiLabbio, Larry V '84 -3230 Cntrl Pk W -Ste 106 -Toledo 43617
(614) 752-2761 ..Dile, Madelyn M '84 OH Dept Hlth -246 N High -Bx118
　　　　　　　　-Columbus 43216
(216) 696-7600 ..Dileno, Jon M '88 (Duvin C&H) -1301 E 9th -20th Fl Erievw Twr
　　　　　　　　-Cleveland 44114 Fx:696-2038
(614) 221-3155 ..Dilenschneider, John J '59 OfCnsl Bailey C LLC -10 W Broad
　　　　　　　　-Columbus 43215 Fx:221-0479
(919) 791-0900 ..DiLeone, Ralph J '84 (DiLeone & Assoc,PC) -900 Rdgfld Dr
　　　　　　　　-Ste 350 -Raleigh, NC 27609
(216) 623-1155 ..Di Lisi, Richard A '89 Nationwide Ins -323 Lakeside Av W
　　　　　　　　-Ste 410 Lakeside Pl -Cleveland 44113
(614) 464-2572 ..Dill, Ralph E '75 (Harris MB&C,PLL) -37 W Broad -9th Fl
　　　　　　　　-Columbus 43215 Fx:464-2245
(513) 621-2120 ..Dill, Stephanie A '99 %Strauss & T,LPA -150 E 4th -4th Fl
　　　　　　　　-Cincinnati 45202 Fx:241-8259
(513) 381-2838 ..Diller, Edward D '76 (Taft S&H LLP) -425 Walnut -Ste 1800
　　　　　　　　-Cincinnati 45202 Fx:381-0205
(419) 384-3238 ..Diller, Jon N '75 -208 E Main -Bx297 -Pandora 45877
　　　　　　　　Fx:384-3239
(804) 527-7398 ..Diller, Kathleen L '80 Hamilton Beach/Proctor-Silex
　　　　　　　　-4421 Wtrfrnt Dr -Glen Allen, VA 23060
(419) 358-5606 ..Diller, Samuel W '60 -138 N Main -Bx46 -Bluffton 45817
(419) 238-6621 ..Diller, Steven L '80 -124 E Main -Van Wert 45891 Fx:238-4705
(336) 627-9501 ..Dilley, David M '77 (DD Dilley & Assoc) -168 Beaver Run
　　　　　　　　-Eden, NC 27288
(614) 466-3934 ..Dilling, Thomas A '87 State Med Brd -77 S High -17th Fl
　　　　　　　　-Columbus 43215

(216) 368-5136 ..Dillman, Jeffrey D '00 CWRU Law Schl -11075 East Blvd
　　　　　　　　-Cleveland 44106
(614) 469-3200 ..Dillman, Jennifer L '00 %Thompson H LLP -10 W Broad -Ste 700
　　　　　　　　-Columbus 43215 Fx:469-3361
(740) 385-2191 ..Dillon, Cornelius W '52 N Dillon Co,LPA -340 W Main -Bx816
　　　　　　　　-Logan 43138 Fx:385-2192
(614) 249-3077 ..Dillon, Cynthia L '89 Cnsl Nationwide Ins Co -1 Nationwide Plz
　　　　　　　　-Columbus 43215
(740) 533-2720 ..Dillon, David R '80 -112 S 3rd -Ironton 45638
(248) 646-5100 ..Dillon, Donald R Jr. '99 (Moffett & D PC) -255 E Brown
　　　　　　　　-Ste 340 Brown St Ctr -Birmingham, MI 48009 Fx:646-5332
(248) 457-7102 ..Dillon, Joseph F '75 (Cox H&G,PC) -101 W Big Beaver Rd
　　　　　　　　-10th Fl -Troy, MI 48084 Fx:457-7001
(614) 461-1551 ..Dillon, Julia B '04 %Barkan & B Co LPA -81 S 4th -Ste 300
　　　　　　　　-Columbus 43215
(513) 705-9000 ..Dillon, Martina M '96 %Pratt SP Co,LPA -301 N Breiel Blvd
　　　　　　　　-Middletown 45044 Fx:705-9001
(614) 463-9770 ..Dillon, Thomas A '74 (Roetzel & A,LPA) -155 E Broad
　　　　　　　　-Natl City Ctr 12th Fl -Columbus 43215 Fx:463-9792
(419) 241-9000 ..Dillon, Thomas P '92 (Shumaker L&K,LLP) -1000 Jackson
　　　　　　　　-Toledo 43624 Fx:241-6894
(419) 241-9770 ..Dills, Alan B '73 (Vassar DD&B,LLC) -420 Mad Av -Ste 1102
　　　　　　　　-Toledo 43604 Fx:241-9771
(614) 459-0047 ..DiLorenzo, John F Jr. '81 -2756 Elginfld Rd -Columbus 43220
(419) 525-0777 ..Dilts, John S '88 -28 Park S -Mansfield 44902
(513) 381-0656 ..Dilts, Joseph L '81 (Kohnen & P LLP) -201 E 5th -Ste 800
　　　　　　　　-Cincinnati 45202 Fx:381-5823
(859) 394-6200 ..Dilts, Robert D '95 %Adams SW&D -40 W Pike -Bx861
　　　　　　　　-Covington, KY 41012 Fx:291-7902
(216) 241-6602 ..DiMarco, Victor T '00 %Weston HFP&H LLP -50 Pub Sq
　　　　　　　　-2500 Trmnl Twr -Cleveland 44113 Fx:621-8369
(330) 758-7313 ..DiMartino, Dennis A '87 (D DiMartino LPA,Inc) -6004 Market
　　　　　　　　-Boardman 44512 Fx:758-4938
(330) 643-2765 ..DiMartino, Heaven R '01 Summit Cnty Pros-CSEA -171 S Main
　　　　　　　　-Akron 44308 Fx:643-2822
(513) 333-4076 ..Dimasi, Vincent A '91 %Weltman W&R Co,LPA -525 Vine
　　　　　　　　-Ste 800 -Cincinnati 45202 Fx:723-2239
(216) 621-0150 ..DiMassa, Pasquale Jr. '01 %Hahn L&P LLP -3300 BP
　　　　　　　　Twr/200 Pub Sq -Ste 3300 -Cleveland 44114 Fx:241-2824
(513) 579-6400 ..DiMauro, Caroline M '99 %Keating M&K PLL -1 E 4th
　　　　　　　　-1400 Provident Twr -Cincinnati 45202 Fx:579-6457
(330) 376-5300 ..Dimengo, Steven A '86 (Buckingham D&B,LLP) -50 S Main
　　　　　　　　-Bx1500 -Akron 44309 Fx:258-6559
(614) 365-2700 ..DiMickele, Susan M '95 (Squire S&D LLP) -41 S High
　　　　　　　　-1300 Huntngtn Ctr -Columbus 43215 Fx:365-2499
(405) 717-4335 ..Dimit, Richard W '87 Tuttle VoTech Centre -12772 N Rockwell
　　　　　　　　-Oklahoma City, OK 73142
(216) 348-5400 ..Dimitrijevs, James A '94 (McDonald H Co,LPA)
　　　　　　　　-600 Superior Av E -Ste 2100 -Cleveland 44114 Fx:348-5474
(937) 864-3000 ..Dimitry, Edward S '84 Speedway SuperAmer LLC -Bx1500
　　　　　　　　-Springfield 45501
(513) 241-3100 ..Dimitt, Jill L '00 Lerner S&R -120 E 4th -8th Fl -Cincinnati 45202
(513) 651-6800 ..Dimling, Robert A '66 (Frost BT LLC) -201 E 5th -2200 PNC Ctr
　　　　　　　　-Cincinnati 45202 Fx:651-6981
(216) 241-1909 ..Dimond, Douglas A '80 -50 Pub Sq -Ste400 -Cleveland 44113
(614) 228-4494 ..Dimond, Richard L '57 -601 S High -Columbus 43215
(513) 621-2888 ..DiMuzio, David C '77 -1014 Vine -Ste 1900 -Cincinnati 45202
(513) 241-9400 ..DiNardo, Nicholas J '98 Legal Aid -215 E 9th -Ste 200
　　　　　　　　-Cincinnati 45202
(513) 241-4722 ..Dine, Jennifer Dunlap '03 %Montgomery R&J,LPA -36 E 7th
　　　　　　　　-Ste 2100 -Cincinnati 45202 Fx:241-8775
(937) 433-8611 ..Dineen, Thomas M '87 -683 Miamisburg-Centervll Rd -Ste 20
　　　　　　　　-Dayton 45459
(253) 967-0830 ..Diner, David N '83 US Army JAG -HQ 1st Corps JAG
　　　　　　　　-Tacoma, WA 98433
(614) 462-2214 ..Dingledy, Jay R '72 (Schottenstein Z&D) -250 West -Bx165020
　　　　　　　　-Columbus 43216 Fx:462-5135
(614) 542-0220 ..Dingus, Michael S '98 -1141 S High -Columbus 43206
(330) 455-6112 ..Dingwell, David L '92 (Tzangas PM&R) -220 Market Av S -8th Fl
　　　　　　　　-Canton 44702 Fx:455-2108
(858) 674-1373 ..Dinklage, Ingolf R '78 -15643 Caldas De Reyes
　　　　　　　　-San Diego, CA 92128
(440) 446-1100 ..Dinn Hochman & Potter,LLC -5910 Landerbrook Dr -Ste 200
　　　　　　　　-Cleveland 44124 Fx:446-1240
(440) 446-1100 ..Dinn, Irwin J '64 (Dinn H&P,LLC) -5910 Landerbrook Dr -Ste 200
　　　　　　　　-Cleveland 44124 Fx:446-1240
(513) 943-7200 ..Dinnen, Jeffrey A '98 Midland Co -7000 Mdlnd Blvd -Amelia 45102
(216) 592-5000 ..Dinner, Gary L '73 Cnsl Tucker E&W LLP -925 Euclid Av
　　　　　　　　-1150 Huntngtn Bldg -Cleveland 44115 Fx:592-5009
(772) 462-1414 ..DiNovo, Joseph X '81 -Bx2565 -Fort Pierce, FL 34954
　　　　　　　　Dinsio, Melissa D '97 -3627 South Av -Youngstown 44502
(614) 462-5200 ..Dinsmore, Beth A '91 %Franklin Cnty CSEA -80 E Fulton
　　　　　　　　-Columbus 43215
(614) 466-7447 ..Dinsmore, James P '91 Atty Gen -150 E Gay -Columbus 43215
(513) 977-8200 ..Dinsmore & Shohl LLP -255 E 5th -Ste 1900 -Cincinnati 45202
　　　　　　　　Fx:977-8141
(937) 449-6400 ..Dinsmore & Shohl LLP -1 S Main -Ste 1300 One Dayton Centre
　　　　　　　　-Dayton 45402 Fx:449-6405
(614) 628-6880 ..Dinsmore & Shohl LLP -175 S 3rd -10th Fl -Columbus 43215
　　　　　　　　Fx:628-6890
(216) 685-9188 ..Dintaman, Robert E Jr. '98 %Swartz C LLC -55 Pub Sq -Ste 1120
　　　　　　　　-Cleveland 44113 Fx:685-9293
(330) 493-1570 ..DioGuardi, Anthony M II '86 %Macala BM&G,LLC -4150
　　　　　　　　Belden Vllg NW -Ste 604 -Canton 44718 Fx:493-7042
(740) 593-2626 ..Dioguardi, Nicolette '84 %Ohio Univ -10 E Union -Pilcher Hse
　　　　　　　　-Athens 45701
(330) 491-0900 ..Dionisio, Christopher '00 -4883 Dressler Rd NW -Canton 44718
(440) 230-0978 ..Dionisopoulos, Justine M '04 -6713 Drawbrdg Cir
　　　　　　　　-North Royalton 44133
(216) 621-7860 ..DiPalma, Douglas A '85 (Cavitch FD&F) -1717 E 9th -14th Fl
　　　　　　　　-Cleveland 44114 Fx:621-3415
(216) 378-9905 ..DiPalma, Joy A '00 %McGlinchey S PLLC -25550 Chagrin Blvd
　　　　　　　　-Ste 406 -Cleveland 44122 Fx:378-9910

(440) 639-9000 ..**DiPalma,** William J '77 -9853 Johnnycake Ridge Rd -Ste 207
 -Concord 44060

(330) 255-6419 ..**DiPaola,** Peggy R '82 GOJO Ind,Inc -Bx991 -Akron 44309

(614) 262-1704 ..**DiPasquale,** Anita A '88 OSU Moritz Cllg of Law -55 W 12th Av
 -Columbus 43210 Fx:292-1383

(216) 696-4441 ..**DiPetta,** Deanna L '87 Zashin & R Co,LPA -55 Pub Sq -Ste 1490
 -Cleveland 44113 Fx:696-1618

(440) 262-1429 ..**Di Piero,** Frank A '82 Goodrich Corp -9921 Brecksvll Rd
 -Brecksville 44141

(419) 221-5230 ..**DiPierro,** Rocco W '02 %Lima City Pros -109 N Union
 -Lima 45801

(703) 516-0101 ..**DiPlacido,** Carmen A '72 C DiPlacido & Assoc,Inc -2609 1st Rd S
 -Arlington, VA 22204

(216) 696-3311 ..**DiPuccio,** Dominic A '90 (Kahn K) -1301 E 9th -2600 Erievw Twr
 -Cleveland 44114 Fx:623-4912

(614) 466-2166 ..**Dirina,** John G '95 OH Dept Taxation -30 E Broad -22nd Fl
 -Columbus 43215

(330) 643-2230 ..**Dirksen,** Teresa L '02 Hon J Adams -209 S High -Ct of Cmmn
 Pleas -Akron 44308

(614) 466-9305 ..**Diroll,** David J '77 OH Sentencing Commssn -65 S Front -2nd Fl
 -Columbus 43215

(614) 761-2003 ..**DiRosario,** Lewis J '57 -5900 Sawmill Rd -Ste 220 -Dublin 43017

(419) 255-0675 ..**DiSalle,** Anthony B '66 -316 N Mich -501 Toledo Bldg
 -Toledo 43624

(419) 930-5600 ..**DiSalle,** John D '91 -405 Mad Av -Ste 2020 -Toledo 43604
 Fx:930-5601

(330) 726-0484 ..**DiSalvo-LaCivita,** Renee M '97 -1040 S Cmmns Pl -Ste 200
 -Youngstown 44514

(330) 562-9588 ..**Disantis,** John P '75 -105 Chesterton Ln -Aurora 44202

(614) 461-1156 ..**Disantis,** Paul V '96 %Webster & Assoc -2 Miranova Pl -Ste 310
 -Columbus 43215

(216) 363-1400 ..**Disantis,** Richard J '66 (Buckley K,LPA) -600 E Superior Av
 -Ste 1400 -Cleveland 44114 Fx:579-1020

(614) 575-3519 ..**Disantis,** Sandra M '91 Franklin Cnty Children Srvcs
 -855 W Mound -Columbus 43223 Fx:275-2589

(216) 771-2533 ..**Disbro,** Terry R '93 Ferry Cap & Set Screw Co -2151 Scranton Rd
 -Cleveland 44113

(216) 687-1311 ..**DiSilvio,** Marilena '95 (Reminger & R) -101 Prospect Av W
 -1400 Mdlnd Bldg -Cleveland 44115

(330) 562-6800 ..**Dismuke,** Daniel K '01 %D Benjamin -199 S Chillicothe Rd -Bx511
 -Aurora 44202

(412) 566-1998 ..**Dismukes,** Scott R '00 (Eckert SC&M,LLC) -600 Grant -44th Fl
 -Pittsburgh, PA 15219

(757) 436-2049 ..**Dissen,** Walter C '62 Norfolk Sthrn Corp -509 LasGaviotas Blvd
 -Chesapeake, VA 23322

(614) 236-6553 ..**Distelhorst,** Michael '76 Capital Univ Law Sch -303 E Broad
 -Columbus 43215

(440) 333-2508 ..**Distin,** John H '90 -3492 Middlepost Ln -Rocky River 44116

(937) 255-5270 ..**Ditalia,** Peter M '81 AFMCLO/JAN -1864 4th -Rm 130A
 -Wright Patterson AFB 45433

 Ditchey, Matthew J '97 -Bx15338 -Cleveland 44115

(216) 348-6384 ..**Ditchey,** Timothy J '00 -1148 Euclid Av -Ste 405 -Cleveland 44115

(216) 621-6138 ..**Ditko-Bevione,** Sharon R '04 %Abel & Z,LPA -1015 Superior Av
 -The Superior Bldg Ste 1915 -Cleveland 44114 Fx:241-5620

 Ditmer, Mary A '96 -107 Commerce -Bx28 -Lewisburg 45338

(561) 276-2900 ..**Dittman,** Robert A '73 (Spinner DF&D) -151 NW 1st Av
 -Delray Beach, FL 33444 Fx:276-5489

(304) 723-9670 ..**Dittmar,** David N '78 %Taylor & M,PLLC -Bx2827
 -Weirton, WV 26062

(614) 228-5822 ..**Dittmer,** Jeffrey A '89 (Rich C&D,LLC) -300 E Broad -Ste 300
 -Columbus 43215 Fx:228-2725

(614) 238-2828 ..**Ditullio,** Jessica K '87 Banc 1 Corp -100 E Broad -OH1-0152
 -Columbus 43215

(614) 461-1516 ..**Ditullio,** Mark A '85 -169 E Lvngstn Av -Columbus 43215

(216) 348-5400 ..**DiVenere,** Anthony J '67 (McDonald H Co,LPA) -600
 Superior Av E -Ste 2100 -Cleveland 44114 Fx:348-5474

(330) 258-6456 ..**Divine,** Phylip J '00 %Buckingham D&B,LLP -50 S Main -Bx1500
 -Akron 44309 Fx:258-6559

(440) 576-3662 ..**Divoky,** Rebecca K '99 Ashtabula Cnty Pros -25 W Jffrsn
 -Jefferson 44047

(203) 357-3401 ..**Dix,** Diane S '93 GE Captl -120 Long Ridge Rd
 -Stamford, CT 06927

(513) 241-3100 ..**Dix,** Robert C '01 %Lerner S&R -120 E 4th -8th Fl
 -Cincinnati 45202

(419) 255-4543 ..**Dixon,** Blondell '74 -316 N Mich -#514 -Toledo 43624
 Fx:324-0676

(513) 352-4715 ..**Dixon,** Gertrude P '97 Law Dept -801 Plum -Rm 214
 -Cincinnati 45202 Fx:352-1515

 Dixon, Harold V Jr. '77 -2349 Banbury Rd -Akron 44333

(419) 536-8600 ..**Dixon & Hayes,Ltd** -3361 Exec Pkwy -Ste 100 -Toledo 43606

(734) 622-1705 ..**Dixon,** James M '88 Pfizer,Inc -2800 Plymouth Rd
 -Ann Arbor, MI 48105

(216) 515-1660 ..**Dixon,** James T '04 %Frantz W LLP -127 Pub Sq -2500 Key Ctr
 -Cleveland 44114 Fx:515-1650

(330) 744-0202 ..**Dixon,** John J '76 -26 Market -Ste 610 -Youngstown 44503
 Fx:744-5147

(614) 221-7663 ..**Dixon,** Matthew R '02 %Luper N&L,LPA -50 W Broad
 -1200 LeVeque Twr -Columbus 43215 Fx:464-2425

(419) 536-8600 ..**Dixon,** Randall C '80 (Dixon & H,Ltd) -3361 Exec Pkwy -Ste 100
 -Toledo 43606

(216) 432-1992 ..**Dixon,** Robert A '81 -4403 St Clair Av -Cleveland 44103

(419) 536-8600 ..**Dixon,** Robert B '53 %Dixon & H,Ltd -3361 Exec Pkwy -Ste 100
 -Toledo 43606

(330) 369-1533 ..**Dixon,** Rodger L '89 Cnsl Trumbull Metro Housing Auth
 -4076 Youngstown Rd SE -Ste 101 -Warren 44484 Fx:369-1027

(419) 241-6000 ..**Dixon,** Thomas A '82 (Eastman & S Ltd) -1 Seagate -24th Fl
 -Bx10032 -Toledo 43699 Fx:247-1777

(309) 765-5159 ..**Dixon,** William M '94 Deere & Co -One John Deere Pl
 -Moline, IL 61265

(937) 339-1500 ..**Dixon,** William M Jr. '75 (Shipman D&L) -215 W Water -Bx310
 -Troy 45373 Fx:339-1519

(513) 336-2539 ..**Dizenhuz,** Robert S '91 Cnsl Anthem Blue Cross/Blue Shield
 -1351 William Howard Taft Rd -MB1-220 -Cincinnati 45206

(330) 376-6766 ..**Djordjevic,** Michael M '77 M Djordjevic Co,LPA -17 S Main
 -Ste 201 -Akron 44308 Fx:376-7344

(216) 689-3621 ..**Djulvezan,** Florentina G '95 Key Trust Natl Assn -127 Pub Sq
 -8th Fl -Cleveland 44114

(216) 875-4800 ..**DKW Law Group** -200 Pub Sq -26th Fl BP Twr -Cleveland 44114
 Fx:875-4809

(216) 696-5400 ..**Dlott,** Steven P '85 Crosby O & Assoc Co,LPA -55 Pub Sq
 -Ste 1475 -Cleveland 44113 Fx:696-2610

(440) 329-3264 ..**Dlugosz,** Robert W '85 First Merit Bank,NA -105 Court
 -Elyria 44035

(305) 530-7000 ..**Doakes,** Chantel R '95 Fed Pub Def Ofc -150 W Flagler -Ste 1700
 -Miami, FL 33130

 Doan, Amy Ingham '03 -20333 Detroit Rd -#110
 -Rocky River 44116

(513) 272-1200 ..**Doan,** Burgess L '65 (Doan K&B,LLC) -5710 Wooster Pike
 -Ste 212 -Cincinnati 45227

(513) 576-9579 ..**Doan,** Charles H '72 -698 Dorgene Ln -Cincinnati 45244

(216) 523-4109 ..**Doan,** James N '71 Eaton Corp -1111 Superior Av
 -Cleveland 44114

(513) 272-1200 ..**Doan Keith & Brokamp,LLC** -5710 Wooster Pike -Ste 212
 -Cincinnati 45227

(419) 223-1861 ..**Dobay,** Nikki E '03 3rd Dist Ct of Appeals -204 N Main
 -Lima 45801

 Dobbins, Angela A '03 -(Address Unavailable)

(330) 666-6400 ..**Dobbins,** Elizabeth A '03 %Dobbins & H
 -1000 S Cleveland-Massillon Rd -Ste 105 -Akron 44333

(330) 666-6400 ..**Dobbins & Henshaw** -1000 S Cleveland-Massillon Rd -Ste 105
 -Akron 44333

 Dobbins, Mark E '82 -5070 Shady Ridge Ln
 -Brooklyn Heights 44131

(330) 666-6400 ..**Dobbins,** Richard E '77 (Dobbins & H)
 -1000 S Cleveland-Massillon Rd -Ste 105 -Akron 44333

(614) 870-3000 ..**Dobbs,** James B '70 -4937 W Broad -Columbus 43228

 Dobbs, Melvin Keith '71 -6581 Forrester Way
 -Reynoldsburg 43068

(330) 451-7785 ..**Dobbs,** Shaunna L '01 Stark Cnty Cmmn Pleas Crt
 -115 Central Plz N -Ste 400 -Canton 44702

(216) 443-6344 ..**Dobeck,** Rochelle L '88 8th Dist Ct of Appls -1 Lakeside Av -#202
 -Cleveland 44113 Fx:443-2044

(440) 886-3800 ..**Dobeck,** Timothy G '86 Boyko & D -6741 Ridge Rd -Parma 44129

(216) 687-1900 ..**Dobos,** Dennis A '92 Legal Aid -1223 W 6th -Cleveland 44113
 Fx:687-0779

(573) 596-0624 ..**Dobosh,** William J Jr. '02 US Army JAGC -125 E 8th -SJA Ofc
 -Fort Leonard Wood, MO 65473

(330) 747-2661 ..**Dobran,** James M '82 Cafaro Co -2445 Belmont Av -Bx2186
 -Youngstown 44504

(216) 622-8200 ..**Dobrea,** Diane L '94 %Calfee H&G LLP -800 Superior Av
 -Ste 1400 -Cleveland 44114 Fx:241-0816

(614) 224-3838 ..**Dobres,** Jacob '99 %P Fulton & Assoc -89 E Nationwide Blvd
 -Ste 300 -Columbus 43215 Fx:224-3933

(216) 787-3083 ..**Dobronos,** Michael G '91 Industrial Commssn of OH
 -615 Superior Av NW -Cleveland 44113 Fx:787-3483

 Dobronos, Victoria '03 -(Address Unavailable)

(216) 443-7295 ..**Dobroshi,** Anduena '99 Cuyahoga Cnty Pub Def
 -1849 Prospect Av -Ste 222 -Cleveland 44115

(740) 833-2720 ..**Dobrovich,** Christine E '96 Delaware Cnty CSEA
 -140 N Sandusky -Delaware 43015

(614) 621-1500 ..**Dobrowski,** Stanley J '76 SrCnsl Calfee H&G LLP -21 E State
 -1100 Fifth Third Ctr -Columbus 43215 Fx:621-0010

(440) 603-3791 ..**Dobscha,** Stephen F '87 Progressive Ins -6671 Beta Dr -Leg Dept
 -Mayfield Village 44143

(419) 354-9250 ..**Dobson,** Paul A '94 %Wood Cnty Pros -One Cthse Sq
 -Bowling Green 43402 Fx:353-2904

(937) 224-7200 ..**Dobson,** Stephanie D '02 %Horenstein N&B -124 E 3rd -5th Fl
 -Dayton 45402 Fx:224-3353

(937) 382-2838 ..**Dobyns,** John M '80 (Rose & D Co,LPA) -97 N South
 -Wilmington 45177

(614) 464-6400 ..**Dobyns,** Timothy J '96 (Vorys SS&P LLP) -52 E Gay -Bx1008
 -Columbus 43216 Fx:464-6360

(216) 622-8416 ..**Docherty,** Pamela Ann '94 %Calfee H&G LLP -800 Superior Av
 -Ste 1400 -Cleveland 44114 Fx:241-0816

(330) 792-0827 ..**Dockry,** Michael B '82 -296 N Canfld-Niles Rd -Youngstown 44515

(740) 342-7324 ..**Dodd,** Daniel F '03 %R Dodd Jr Co,LPA -106 N Main
 -New Lexington 43764

(989) 496-4980 ..**Dodd,** Jeanne D '87 Dow Corning Corp -2200 W Salzburg Rd
 -Mail No. CO1222 -Midland, MI 48686

(740) 342-7324 ..**Dodd,** Maureen E '96 R Dodd Jr Co,LPA -106 N Main
 -New Lexington 43764

(740) 342-7324 ..**Dodd,** Robert J Jr. '65 (R Dodd Jr Co,LPA) -106 N Main
 -New Lexington 43764

(216) 292-3300 ..**Dodd,** Stephen D '00 %Conway MWK&K Co,LPA
 -30195 Chagrin Blvd -Ste 300 -Cleveland 44124

(614) 464-2572 ..**Dodd,** Stephen H '85 (Harris MB&C,PLL) -37 W Broad -9th Fl
 -Columbus 43215 Fx:464-2245

(412) 777-8307 ..**Dodero,** William B '04 Bayer -100 Bayer Rd -Pittsburgh, PA 15205

(330) 456-8341 ..**Dodez,** Richard D '69 (Black MS&A,LPA) -220 Market Av S
 -Ste 1000 -Canton 44702 Fx:456-5756

(602) 277-3000 ..**Dodge,** David D '65 (Lieberman DGK&A) -3003 N Central Av
 -Ste 1800 -Phoenix, AZ 85012

(614) 443-2494 ..**Dodgion,** Jeremy M '97 -1188 S High -Columbus 43206
 Fx:444-1501

(216) 443-7800 ..**Dodrill,** Joyce M '84 Cuyahoga Cnty Pros -1200 Ontario -8th Fl
 -Cleveland 44113 Fx:698-2270

 Dodson, David J '90 -121 E Walnut -Jefferson 44047

(330) 477-8535 ..**Dodson,** Irene Elizabeth '04 %Cross & R Co,LPA
 -2884 Whipple Av NW -Canton 44708 Fx:477-2611

(419) 999-9999 ..**Dodson,** James M Jr. '98 -1910 W Robb Av -Ste 6 -Drwr5171
 -Lima 45802

(330) 864-6611 ..**Dodson,** Jason D '04 %McCarty & P -1655 W Market -Ste 400
 -Akron 44313

(330) 244-8000 ..**Dodson,** Kara M '02 %RE Soles Jr -1401 S Main -Ste 202
 -North Canton 44720 Fx:244-8002

(330) 477-8535 ..**Dodson,** Richard S Jr. '77 (Cross & R Co,LPA)
 -2884 Whipple Av NW -Canton 44708 Fx:477-2611

(513) 856-8601 ..**Doellman**, Norbert M Jr. '76 -Bx475 -Hamilton 45012

(513) 860-2560 ..**Doerflein**, Angela L '04 LandAmerica Fncl Grp -8892 Beckett Rd
-West Chester 45069

(412) 288-3280 ..**Doerfler**, James M '92 %Reed S,LLP -435 Sixth Av
-Pittsburgh, PA 15219

(419) 861-7800 ..**Doerner**, David W '76 %Bahret & Assoc Co,LPA
-7050 Spring Meadow W Dr -Holland 43528

(216) 566-8816 ..**Doerner**, Maureen A '92 Charter One Bank,NA -1215 Superior Av
-SU530 -Cleveland 44114 **Fx:**566-0405

(440) 953-1771 ..**Doganiero**, John A III '78 -35104 Euclid Av -Ste 304
-Willoughby 44094

(216) 522-4373 ..**Doganiero**, Mara D '80 %Hon PE Morgenstern-Clarren
-127 Pub Sq -32nd Fl -Cleveland 44114

(513) 241-6116 ..**Doggett**, Robert I '58 -6740 Clough Pike -Ste 200
-Cincinnati 45244

(216) 592-5000 ..**Doheny**, John T '74 (Tucker E&W LLP) -925 Euclid Av
-1150 Huntngtn Bldg -Cleveland 44115 **Fx:**592-5009

(330) 643-2788 ..**Doherty**, Rebecca L '92 Summit Cnty Pros-Crim -53 Univ Av
-7th Fl -Akron 44308 **Fx:**643-8277

(919) 541-0818 ..**Doherty**, Thomas J '82 US EPA -79 TW Alxndr Dr -Mail Drop 31
-Durham, NC 27711

(330) 376-6300 ..**Dohner**, John M '86 -120 E Mill -Ste 407 -Akron 44304

(440) 247-2104 ..**Dolan**, Eva H '84 -516 E Wshngtn -Chagrin Falls 44022

Dolan, James H '50 -1301 Susan Dr -Hamilton 45013

(440) 285-2242 ..**Dolan**, Matthew J '90 Thrasher D&D,LPA -100 7th Av -Ste 150
-Chardon 44024 **Fx:**285-9423

(216) 579-4114 ..**Dolan**, Michael A '91 OfCnsl McIntyre K&K Co LPA -1301 E 9th
-Ste 1200 -Cleveland 44114

Dolan, Michael K '02 -7606 E Linden Ln -Parma 44130

(740) 695-0114 ..**Dolan**, Richard E '80 -67810 Brokaw Dr -Saint Clairsville 43950

(330) 723-8828 ..**Dolatowski**, John J '87 Largent BP&J Co,LPA -232 N Court
-Medina 44256 **Fx:**723-8898

(614) 462-3194 ..**Dolchin**, Marla R '89 Franklin Cnty Pub Def -373 S High -12th Fl
-Columbus 43215

(440) 729-2959 ..**Doles**, Edward A '84 -8130 Wedgewood Dr -Chesterland 44026

(419) 249-7100 ..**Dolgorukov**, D Edward '93 Marshall & M,LLC -Four Seagate
-8th Fl -Toledo 43604 **Fx:**249-7151

(614) 236-1545 ..**Dolin**, Jason M '89 -2369 E Main -Columbus 43209

(954) 522-3456 ..**Dolin**, Susan L '78 (Rothstein R) -300 SE 2nd -Ste 860
-Fort Lauderdale, FL 33301 **Fx:**527-8663

(513) 381-2838 ..**Dolive**, Devin C '02 %Taft S&H LLP -425 Walnut -Ste 1800
-Cincinnati 45202 **Fx:**381-0205

(937) 461-5310 ..**Doll Jansen & Ford** -111 W 1st -Ste 1100 -Dayton 45402
Fx:461-7219

(937) 461-5310 ..**Doll**, John R '78 (Doll J&F) -111 W 1st -Ste 1100 -Dayton 45402
Fx:461-7219

(513) 621-4849 ..**Dolle**, Robert H '73 (Dolle R&M Co,LPA) -817 Main -Ste 500
-Cincinnati 45202

(513) 621-4849 ..**Dolle Rueger & Mathews Co,LPA** -817 Main -Ste 500
-Cincinnati 45202

(440) 967-6136 ..**Dolyk**, Walter Z '78 Buckingham LM&Z Co,LPA -1513
State Route 60 -Vermilion 44089

(216) 241-1278 ..**Doman**, Paul M '95 1st Amer Equity Loan Srvcs -1228 Euclid Av
-Cleveland 44115

(216) 529-8400 ..**Domanovic**, Dieter '81 -14805 Detroit Rd -Ste 490
-Cleveland 44107

(216) 932-4978 ..**Domb**, Brian '93 -1895 Powell Av -Cleveland Heights 44118

Dombek, Arthur E '77 -(Address Unavailable)

(419) 874-3536 ..**Dombey**, Philip L '73 (Leatherman WD&H) -353 Elm
-Perrysburg 43551 **Fx:**874-3899

(440) 395-3679 ..**Domeck**, John W '88 Progressive Ins Co -6300 Wilson Mills Rd
-#N72A -Mayfield Village 44143

(216) 621-0070 ..**Domiano**, Joseph C '57 (Friedman D&S Co,LPA) -1370 Ontario
-Ste 600 -Cleveland 44113 **Fx:**621-4008

(216) 566-5771 ..**Dominguez**, Kathryn I '00 Thompson H LLP -127 Pub Sq
-3900 Key Ctr -Cleveland 44114 **Fx:**566-5800

(614) 469-5715 ..**Dominguez**, Salvador A '91 US Atty -303 Marconi Blvd -Ste 200
-Columbus 43215

(614) 644-1989 ..**Dominic**, Elizabeth Tsvetkoff '04 Legis Srvc Commssn -77 S High
-Columbus 43215

(614) 985-0556 ..**Dominy**, Shawn N '97 -500 W Wilson Bridge Rd -Ste 110
-Worthington 43085

(614) 462-3555 ..**Domis**, Christian B '98 Franklin Cnty Pros -373 S High
-Columbus 43215

(650) 615-4860 ..**Domozick**, Daniel D '84 %Simpson G&I -651 Gtwy Blvd -Ste 1050
-South San Francisco, CA 94080

(248) 851-4111 ..**Domzal**, David A '76 OfCnsl Fink Z&K,PC -31700 Middlebelt
-Ste 150 -Farmington Hills, MI 48334

Donachy, Nicole L '04 -(Address Unavailable)

(937) 548-6888 ..**Donadio**, Raymond M Jr. '80 -1400 N Bway -Greenville 45331

(614) 224-8166 ..**Donahey**, Richard S Jr. '68 (Twyford & D) -495 S High -Ste 100
-Columbus 43215

(440) 331-3232 ..**Donahue**, Charles B II '67 -827 Brick Mill Run Rd -Westlake 44145
Fx:331-5656

(440) 884-5538 ..**Donahue**, James R '57 -10780 Richard Dr -Parma 44130
Fx:884-5538

(419) 874-4604 ..**Donahue**, John P '83 -119 W 2nd -Bx526 -Perrysburg 43551

(937) 299-0893 ..**Donahue**, John W '66 -4466 Maplerdg Pl -Dayton 45429

(614) 761-0402 ..**Donahue**, Mary M '93 (Bellinger & D) -6065 Frantz Rd -Ste 106
-Dublin 43017

(216) 523-1500 ..**Donahue**, Mary E '94 %Mansour GG&M Co,LPA -55 Pub Sq
-Ste 2150 -Cleveland 44113 **Fx:**523-1705

(937) 228-8183 ..**Donahue**, Peter J '55 -120 W 2nd -Dayton 45402 **Fx:**228-7011

(614) 224-1222 ..**Donahue**, William C '70 %Maguire & S,LLP -250 Civic Ctr Dr
-Ste 200 -Columbus 43215 **Fx:**224-1236

(727) 539-4729 ..**Donald**, Gina C '91 Tech Data Corporation -5350 Tech Data Dr
-Clearwater, FL 33607

(419) 525-1984 ..**Donaldson**, John D '86 -233 Marion Av -Mansfield 44903

(937) 333-4100 ..**Donaldson**, Lynn R '89 Law Dept -101 W 3rd -Bx22
-Dayton 45402

(216) 351-3207 ..**Donaldson**, Michael R '85 -4330 E Bstn Rd -Brecksville 44141

Donaldson, Michael W '72 -(Address Unavailable)

(937) 372-3584 ..**Donatelli**, Mark J '79 %Peterson & P -87 S Progress Dr
-Xenia 45385 **Fx:**372-7218

(312) 269-8473 ..**Donati**, Victoria L '92 (Neal G&E) -2 N La Salle -Ste 2200
-Chicago, IL 60602 **Fx:**269-1747

(614) 228-6611 ..**Donchatz**, Kenneth R '93 OfCnsl Fuller & H,Ltd -35 N 4th -Ste 310
-Columbus 43215 **Fx:**228-6623

(216) 896-3295 ..**Donchess**, James M '89 Parker-Hannifin Corp
-6035 Parkland Blvd -Cleveland 44124

(513) 632-5311 ..**Donenfeld**, Jack A '76 -119 E Court -Cincinnati 45202

(937) 226-7501 ..**Donenfeld**, Richard D '93 -40 N Main -1812 Kettering Twr
-Dayton 45423

(419) 535-4739 ..**Doner**, Gary W '90 Dana Corp -4500 Dorr -Bx1000 -Toledo 43697

(614) 840-3698 ..**Doney**, Timothy J '85 Worthington Ind,Inc -1205 Dearborn Dr
-Columbus 43085

(419) 213-6819 ..**Dong**, Mui-Ling Y '92 Lucas Cnty Cmn Pleas Ct -429 N Mich
-Toledo 43624

Donham, Joy M '04 -(Address Unavailable)

(419) 241-1200 ..**Doniere**, Brandi L '04 %Cooper & W,LPA -900 Adams
-Toledo 43624 **Fx:**242-5675

(513) 474-1919 ..**Donithan**, Dayle E '88 (DE Donithan Co,LPA) -1231 Nagel Rd
-Cincinnati 45255

(330) 399-2632 ..**Donlin**, Patrick J Sr. '71 -308 Porter NE -Warren 44483

(616) 632-8000 ..**Donnell**, Douglas A '00 Mika MB&J,PLC -900 Monroe Av NW
-Grand Rapids, MI 49503

(513) 579-6400 ..**Donnellon**, Daniel J '86 (Keating M&K PLL) -1 E 4th
-1400 Provident Twr -Cincinnati 45202 **Fx:**579-6457

(513) 891-7087 ..**Donnellon Donnellon & Miller** -9079 Mntgmry Rd
-Cincinnati 45242

(513) 891-7087 ..**Donnellon**, Terrence M '79 (Donnellon D&M) -9079 Mntgmry Rd
-Cincinnati 45242

(513) 891-7087 ..**Donnellon**, Thomas E '76 (Donnellon D&M) -9079 Mntgmry Rd
-Cincinnati 45242

(937) 339-7181 ..**Donnelly**, Dennis M '76 -124 W Main -Troy 45373

(513) 398-4891 ..**Donnelly**, Karen S '90 %Peeler M&Z -423 Reading Rd
-Mason 45040

(216) 241-9628 ..**Donnelly**, Kathleen '89 -526 Superior Av E -Ste 1030
-Cleveland 44114 **Fx:**621-0408

(513) 721-4500 ..**Donnelly**, Matthew J '01 %Patsfall Y&P LLC -1 W 4th -Ste 1800
-Cincinnati 45202 **Fx:**639-7554

(216) 621-8484 ..**Donnelly**, Michael P '92 %Climaco LPW&G Co,LPA
-1228 Euclid Av -Ste 900 Halle Bldg -Cleveland 44115
Fx:771-1632

(440) 354-2600 ..**Donnelly**, Nancy A '91 Steris Corp -5960 Heisley Rd
-Mentor 44060

(513) 221-7722 ..**Donnelly**, Thomas C '85 -632 Riddle Rd -Cincinnati 45220

(419) 625-8373 ..**Donnelly**, Timothy J '77 Dist Petroleum Prdcts Inc -1814 Rvr Rd
-#100 -Huron 44839

(513) 241-0400 ..**Donnelly**, Tina M '00 %Aronoff R&H Co,LPA -425 Walnut
-Ste 2400 -Cincinnati 45202 **Fx:**241-2877

(513) 455-4366 ..**Donnelly**, William R '92 Fed Reserve Bank -150 E 4th
-Cincinnati 45202

(216) 685-1039 ..**Donnersbach**, Sara M '98 %Weltman W&R Co,LPA
-323 W Lakeside Av -Ste 200 -Cleveland 44113 **Fx:**363-4121

(513) 421-4000 ..**Donnett**, David D '80 -1212 Sycamore -Ste 36 -Cincinnati 45202

(937) 223-4400 ..**Donoff**, Marilyn R '81 (M Donoff & Assoc) -131 N Ludlow
-Ste 1313 -Dayton 45402

(330) 726-0484 ..**Donofrio**, Anthony '91 -1040 S Cmmns Pl -Ste 200
-Youngstown 44514

(614) 224-8374 ..**Donofrio**, Susan S '79 Legal Aid -40 W Gay -Columbus 43215

(330) 896-0300 ..**Donohew**, Monty Lee '92 (M Donohew & Assoc,LPA)
-3570 Exec Dr -Ste 106 -Uniontown 44685

(202) 307-6492 ..**Donohue**, Dennis M '69 US DOJ -555 4th NW
-Washington, DC 20001

(419) 229-4529 ..**Donohue**, Gregory W '80 -311 E Market -Ste 306 -Lima 45801

(440) 277-4444 ..**Donohue**, Paul C '84 -2815 Pearl Av -Lorain 44055

(202) 955-1704 ..**Donohue**, Sharon K '86 Natl Committee for Quality Assurance
-2000 L NW -Ste 500 -Washington, DC 20036

(740) 355-3283 ..**Donohue**, Stephen P '79 Shawnee State Univ -940 2nd
-Portsmouth 45662

(513) 723-4000 ..**Donovan**, Corey A '02 %Vorys SS&P LLP -221 E 4th
-Ste 2000 Atrium Two -Bx0236 -Cincinnati 45201 **Fx:**723-4056

(757) 836-6409 ..**Donovan**, Daniel G '83 US Navy JAG Corps
-US Joint Forces Command -1562 Mitscher Av Ste 200
-Norfolk, VA 23511

(202) 879-5174 ..**Donovan**, Daniel T '97 (Kirkland & E) -655 15th NW
-Washington, DC 20005 **Fx:**879-5200

Donovan, Erin J '04 -(Address Unavailable)

Donovan, Janet R '83 -(Address Unavailable)

(419) 213-4700 ..**Donovan**, Jennifer L '97 %Lucas Cnty Pros -Adams & Erie
-Lucas Cnty Cthse -Toledo 43624

(419) 599-1936 ..**Donovan**, John '83 -609 N Perry -Napoleon 43545

(513) 352-4706 ..**Donovan**, Kevin O '85 Law Dept -801 Plum -Rm 214
-Cincinnati 45202 **Fx:**352-1515

(440) 934-3700 ..**Donovan**, Kevin W '80 (Fauver K-W&D) -5333 Meadow Ln Ct
-Elyria 44035 **Fx:**934-3708

(419) 255-5990 ..**Donovan**, Kimberly A '02 %Kerger & K -33 S Mich -Ste 201
-Toledo 43602 **Fx:**255-5997

(216) 592-5000 ..**Donovan**, Larry B '99 Cnsl Tucker E&W LLP -925 Euclid Av
-1150 Huntngtn Bldg -Cleveland 44115 **Fx:**592-5009

(513) 651-5900 ..**Donovan**, Mary Jill '01 (Donovan Law) -910 Race
-Cincinnati 45202 **Fx:**651-4937

(614) 985-3651 ..**Donovan**, Richard J '93 (R Donovan & Assoc Co LPA)
-200 E Campus Vw Blvd -Ste 200 -Columbus 43235 **Fx:**985-3744

(513) 533-2996 ..**Donovan**, Sean P '98 %Finney SS&K Co,LPA -2623 Erie Av
-Bx8804 -Cincinnati 45208

Donovan, Zachary T '88 -2034 N Devon Rd -Columbus 43212

(614) 485-2010 ..**Donovsky**, Nicole M '00 %Means BB&B Co,LPA -2006 Kenny Rd
-Columbus 43221 **Fx:**485-2019

(513) 381-2838 ..**Donson**, G Jack Jr. '71 (Taft S&H LLP) -425 Walnut -Ste 1800
-Cincinnati 45202 **Fx:**381-0205

(216) 348-1700 ..**Donze**, Shannon M '04 %Davis & Y -101 Prospect Av W -Ste 1700
-Cleveland 44115 **Fx:**621-0602

(330) 860-2086 ..**Dool**, Carl D '71 Babcock & Wilcox Co -20 S Van Buren Av -Bx351
-Barberton 44203

(615) 632-7032 ..**Doolan**, Thomas C '75 Tennessee Valley Auth
-400 W Summit Hill Dr -Knoxville, TN 37902

(419) 936-5120 ..**Dooley**, Colleen M '84 -411 N Mich -Ste A -Toledo 43624
Dooley, Lloyd D '66 -1120 State Rt 131 -Ste C -Milford 45150

(513) 684-9975 ..**Doppes**, Michael J '83 -432 Walnut -1100 Tri-State Bldg
-Cincinnati 45202

(216) 685-4289 ..**Doran**, James M '98 %Weltman W&R Co,LPA
-323 W Lakeside Av -Ste 200 -Cleveland 44113 **Fx:**363-4121

(716) 884-2000 ..**Doran**, Michael '97 (Doran & M) -1234 Delaware Av
-Buffalo, NY 14209 **Fx:**884-2146

(614) 464-6305 ..**Doran**, Perry W II '00 %Vorys SS&P LLP -52 E Gay -Bx1008
-Columbus 43216 **Fx:**464-6350

(614) 464-6400 ..**Doran**, Scott M '86 (Vorys SS&P LLP) -52 E Gay -Bx1008
-Columbus 43216 **Fx:**464-6350
Dorcas, Carl F '51 -5239 Harroun Rd -Sylvania 43560

(440) 734-7600 ..**Dorchak**, Thomas J '66 Crombie Law Firm
-4615 Great Nrthrn Blvd -North Olmsted 44070 **Fx:**734-1054

(716) 566-2800 ..**Doren**, Robert A '02 Bond S&K,PLLC -40 Fountian Plz -Ste 600
-Buffalo, NY 14202 **Fx:**566-2808

(440) 505-0040 ..**Dorer**, William R Jr. '78 Cardinal Amer Corp -32111 Aurora Rd
-Solon 44139

(419) 244-4000 ..**Dorf & Kalniz** -Two Maritime Plz -2nd Fl -Bx952 -Toledo 43697
Fx:241-1900

(419) 244-4000 ..**Dorf**, Michael D '66 (Dorf & K) -Two Maritime Plz -2nd Fl -Bx952
-Toledo 43697 **Fx:**241-1900

(614) 462-2700 ..**Dorgan**, Brandi L '03 %Schottenstein Z&D -250 West -Bx165020
-Columbus 43216 **Fx:**462-5135

(614) 466-7250 ..**Dorgan**, James Q III '03 Atty Gen -30 E Broad -Columbus 43215
Fx:644-7634

(513) 579-6400 ..**Dorger**, Paul D '92 (Keating M&K PLL) -1 E 4th
-1400 Provident Twr -Cincinnati 45202 **Fx:**579-6457

(216) 650-2038 ..**Dori**, Aryeh I '03 -23951 Hermitage Rd -Shaker Heights 44122

(216) 479-8500 ..**Doris**, Alan S '72 (Squire S&D LLP) -127 Pub Sq -4900 Key Twr
-Cleveland 44114 **Fx:**479-8780
Dority, Erika N '04 -(Address Unavailable)

(440) 838-7600 ..**Dorman**, Andrew J '94 Janik & D,LLP -9200 S Hills Blvd -Ste 300
-Cleveland 44147 **Fx:**838-7601

(248) 945-0523 ..**Dorn**, Heather M '02 Consolidated Legal Srvcs -2000 Town Ctr
-Ste 2350 -Southfield, MI 48075

(614) 461-1234 ..**Dorner**, Nancy L '93 (Portman F&F LLP) -471 E Broad -Ste 1820
-Columbus 43215 **Fx:**461-9150

(419) 327-4303 ..**Dorner**, Renisa A '88 %Wise & D,Ltd -151 N Mich -Ste 333
-Toledo 43624 **Fx:**327-4302

(419) 524-8011 ..**Dorner**, Thomas M '74 (Knell D&G Co,LPA) -3 N Main -Ste 602
-Mansfield 44902 **Fx:**524-8011

(812) 537-2522 ..**Dornette**, John J '74 Ewbank & K -114 W High -Bx4200
-Lawrenceburg, IN 47025

(513) 381-2838 ..**Dornette**, W Stuart '75 (Taft S&H LLP) -425 Walnut -Ste 1800
-Cincinnati 45202 **Fx:**381-0205

(419) 332-1101 ..**Dorobek**, David A '85 -Bx1273 -Fremont 43420

(216) 351-2613 ..**Dorocak**, John R '77 -5954 Broadw Rd -Parma 44134

(513) 741-3939 ..**Dorr**, James W '55 -2638 Kipling Av -Cincinnati 45239

(216) 687-6264 ..**Dorrell**, John S '75 Med Mutual of OH -2060 E 9th
-Cleveland 44115

(614) 644-7233 ..**Dorris**, Tomi L '89 Atty Gen -150 E Gay -Columbus 43215
Fx:728-9327

(513) 421-6630 ..**Dorsey**, Edward S '87 Lindhorst & D Co,LPA -312 Walnut
-Ste 2300 -Cincinnati 45202

(440) 322-1329 ..**Dorsey**, Jennifer M '03 %Pulito & Assoc -230 3rd -2nd Fl
-Elyria 44035 **Fx:**322-6474

(216) 522-4373 ..**Dorsey**, Joseph D '03 US Bankruptcy Ct -127 Pub Sq -3205 Key
Twr -Cleveland 44102

(614) 228-1541 ..**Dortch**, Michael D '90 (Baker & H LLP) -65 E State -Ste 2100
-Columbus 43215 **Fx:**462-2616

(513) 241-2324 ..**Dorton**, David W '01 %Wood H&E LLP -441 Vine -Ste 2700
-Cincinnati 45202 **Fx:**421-7269

(216) 443-8549 ..**Dorton**, Jennifer M '01 Cuyahoga Cnty Ct Cmmn Pleas
-1200 Ontario -Justice Ctr 11th Fl -Cleveland 44113

(513) 621-2120 ..**Dosker**, Marshall K '91 Strauss & T,LPA -150 E 4th -4th Fl
-Cincinnati 45202 **Fx:**241-8259

(440) 239-8881 ..**Doslak**, William R '81 (Safeco P&C Ins) -18151 Jffrsn Park Rd
-Ste 104 -Middleburg Heights 44130 **Fx:**239-8882

(419) 662-9200 ..**Doss**, Cynthia A '02 -200 Superior -Rossford 43460

(330) 451-7709 ..**Dossi**, Jacquelyn M '98 Stark Cnty Cmmn Pleas Crt
-115 Central Plz N -Ste 400 -Canton 44702

(859) 224-7231 ..**Dostart**, Thomas J '81 SrCnsl Alliance Coal,LLC -771 Corp Dr
-Ste 1000 -Lexington, KY 40503 **Fx:**224-7211

(740) 373-4474 ..**Dotsenko**, Juliana C '88 Marietta Mun Ct -301 Putnam -Marietta
45750

(513) 897-9738 ..**Dotson**, Douglas C '74 -7791 Twp Line Rd -Waynesville 45068

(614) 466-5394 ..**Dotson**, Wendi L '99 Pub Def -8 E Long -Columbus 43215

(330) 769-4544 ..**Doty**, Joseph E '98 -6009 Sevll Rd -Seville 44273

(330) 643-8052 ..**Doty**, Karen M '81 Summit Cnty Law Dept -175 S Main -8th Fl
-Akron 44308 **Fx:**643-2507

(419) 530-7230 ..**Doty**, Robert L '90 Univ of Toledo Law Schl -2801 W Bancroft
-Toledo 43606

(216) 263-3405 ..**Doubrava**, Brenda W '78 FTC -1111 Superior Av E -Ste 200
-Cleveland 44114

(614) 444-5700 ..**Doucet**, Elizabeth H '86 (E Doucet & Assoc Co LPA) -895 S High
-Columbus 43206

(216) 861-6833 ..**Doucette**, Stephen B '93 Sonkin & K Co,LPA -55 Pub Sq
-Ste 1660 -Cleveland 44113

(614) 921-1080 ..**Doucher**, Kimberley A '96 -5582 Jennybrook Ln -Hilliard 43026

(614) 280-1100 ..**Doucher**, Paul M '80 (Keener DC&P,LPA) -88 E Broad -Ste 1750
-Columbus 43215

(202) 942-3811 ..**Douek**, Andre M '83 Cnsl FDIC -550 17th NW -PA1730 #300
-Washington, DC 20429

(330) 744-3196 ..**Dougan**, Patricia '94 Cmmnty Lgl Aid Srvcs,Inc
-11 Fed Plz Central -7th Fl -Youngstown 44503 **Fx:**744-2503

(440) 775-1903 ..**Dougan**, Thomas J '73 -20N E Cllg -Oberlin 44074

(216) 267-5600 ..**Dougher**, Kevin A '87 Rooney Optical,Inc -5440 W 164th
-Cleveland 44142

Dougherty, Diane L '88 -1655 W MArket -Ste 400 -Akron 44313

(614) 798-1933 ..**Dougherty**, Douglas A '80 -3010 Hayden Rd -Columbus 43235
Fx:798-1935

(937) 599-5834 ..**Dougherty**, Edwin '91 (Dougherty Law Ofc) -325 N Main -Bx186
-Bellefontaine 43311

(614) 461-6300 ..**Dougherty**, Gina M '82 -336 S High -Columbus 43215

(216) 586-3939 ..**Dougherty**, Jennifer L '95 %Jones D -901 Lakeside Av
-Cleveland 44114 **Fx:**579-0212

(866) 837-8847 ..**Dougherty**, Kathryn C '92 LAWO -20 S Limestone -Ste 220
-Springfield 45502 **Fx:**(937) 323-0291

(614) 224-8187 ..**Dougherty**, Kathy A '92 (Lamkin VTB&D) -500 S Front -Ste 200
-Columbus 43215 **Fx:**224-4943

(800) 799-1770 ..**Dougherty**, Patricia A '83 -3154 Eppleworth Dr -Dublin 43017

(330) 489-5057 ..**Dougherty**, Richard L '77 Nationwide Mutual Ins Co.
-1000 Market Av N -Canton 44711

(813) 875-2736 ..**Dougherty**, Robert A '62 -3314 Henderson Blvd. -#100
-Tampa, FL 33609

(330) 497-0700 ..**Dougherty**, Ronald W '60 (Krugliak WG&D Co,LPA)
-4775 Munson NW -Bx36963 -Canton 44735 **Fx:**497-4020

(614) 789-1086 ..**Dougherty**, Timothy R '95 Natl Century Financial Enterprises
-6125 Mem'l Dr -Dublin 43017

(216) 687-2348 ..**Dougherty**, Veronica M '87 CSU-Marshall Cllg of Law
-2121 Euclid Av -LB138 -Cleveland 44115 **Fx:**687-6881

(216) 361-1112 ..**Doughten**, David L '81 -4403 St Clair Av -Cleveland 44103

(614) 365-2700 ..**Doughty**, H Cort Jr. '66 OfCnsl Squire S&D LLP -41 S High
-1300 Huntngtn Ctr -Columbus 43215 **Fx:**365-2499

(937) 323-3705 ..**Doughty**, Jon A '78 Doughty & D -39 N Fountain Av -Springfield
45502

(614) 462-4679 ..**Doughty**, Tara L '01 Franklin Cnty Common Pleas Ct -369 S High
-Courtroom 6A -Columbus 43215 **Fx:**462-3868

(614) 221-7663 ..**Douglas**, Danyelle E '04 %Luper N&L,LPA -50 W Broad
-1200 LeVeque Twr -Columbus 43215 **Fx:**464-2425

(614) 221-0446 ..**Douglas**, David W '78 (Fisher & D) -122 E Main -Columbus 43215

(513) 831-6697 ..**Douglas**, Flach '57 (F Douglas & Co,LPA) -114 Main
-Milford 45150

(419) 242-7985 ..**Douglas**, Julie A '01 %Roetzel & A,LPA -One SeaGate -9th Fl
-Toledo 43604 **Fx:**242-0316

(440) 992-5891 ..**Douglas**, Malcolm S '89 -4920 State Rd -Ashtabula 44004

(330) 742-8857 ..**Douglas**, Robert A Jr. '80 Mun Ct Judge -26 S Phelps -Bx6047
-Youngstown 44501

(410) 962-3385 ..**Douglas**, Stephen A '87 Army Corps of Engineers -10 S Howard
-Baltimore, MD 21201

(216) 696-7600 ..**Douglas**, Sue M '84 (Duvin C&H) -1301 E 9th -20th Fl Erievw Twr
-Cleveland 44114 **Fx:**696-2038

(330) 676-5909 ..**Douglas**, Thomas C '74 -5820 State Route 241 -Millersburg 44654

(419) 882-2400 ..**Douglas**, Thomas S '75 -4930 N Holland-Sylvania Rd -#D
-Sylvania 43560

(330) 629-9030 ..**Douglass**, Anthony R '01 -1032 Boardman Canfld Rd
-Youngstown 44512 **Fx:**629-9036

(440) 808-4242 ..**Douglass**, David M '79 Douglass & Assoc Co,LPA
-551 Dover Ctr Rd -Bx40480 -Cleveland 44140 **Fx:**808-4215

(304) 485-4595 ..**Douglass**, Ernest M '86 -914 Market -Ste 300 -Bx472
-Parkersburg, WV 26102 **Fx:**485-5030

(216) 771-1330 ..**Douglass**, James R '80 (Douglass & D) -526 Superior Av E
-630 Leader Bldg -Cleveland 44114

(937) 224-1427 ..**Douple**, Daryl R '79 -130 W 2nd -Ste 1900 -Dayton 45402

(513) 542-8940 ..**Dourson**, Martha C '83 -4303 Kirby Av -Cincinnati 45223
Fx:542-7487

(419) 228-2091 ..**Doute**, Jerome R '88 -1045 MacKenzie Dr -Lima 45805

(216) 523-5465 ..**Douthett**, Breaden M '91 OfCnsl Bricker & E LLP -1375 E 9th
-Ste 1500 -Cleveland 44114 **Fx:**523-7071

(740) 349-6051 ..**Dove**, Dennis E '91 Licking Cnty Pros -20 S 2nd -4th Fl -Newark
43055

(614) 466-4929 ..**Dove**, Richard A '83 Supreme Ct of OH -30 E Broad -3rd Fl
-Columbus 43266

(317) 233-8993 ..**Dovenbarger**, Daniel B '83 Intelenet Comm -101 W Ohio -8th Fl
-Indianapolis, IN 46204

(216) 241-5310 ..**Dover**, Thomas E '80 (Gallagher SF&N) -1501 Euclid Av -6th Fl
-Cleveland 44115 **Fx:**241-1608

(419) 255-5111 ..**Dow**, Martin P '73 -520 Mad Av -1030 Spitzer Bldg -Toledo 43604
Fx:255-3231

(216) 849-8296 ..**Dow**, Tijuan M '03 Dow Law Firm -4925 Payne Av -Bx103
-Cleveland 44103

(937) 222-2333 ..**Dowd**, Edward J '83 (Surdyk D&T Co,LPA) -40 N Main
-1610 Kettering Twr -Dayton 45423 **Fx:**222-1970

(859) 491-5843 ..**Dowell**, Laurie B '89 %Twehues & V -331 York
-Newport, KY 41071

(740) 382-4445 ..**Dowler**, Harry L Jr. '61 -131 S Prospect -Marion 43302

(216) 410-1467 ..**Dowling**, Dawn M '91 -25935 Detroit -#162 -Westlake 44145

(212) 969-3000 ..**Dowling**, Donald C Jr. '85 SrCnsl Proskauer R LLP -1585 Bway
-New York, NY 10036 **Fx:**969-2900

(440) 331-1010 ..**Dowling**, Jerome E '82 -20800 Ctr Ridge Rd -Ste 222
-Rocky River 44116

(216) 221-1260 ..**Dowling**, John L '77 -14900 Detroit Av -Lakewood 44107

(216) 664-4946 ..**Dowling**, Joseph P '80 Cleveland Mun Ct -1200 Ontario -12th Fl
-Bx94894 -Cleveland 44101

(513) 946-3015 ..**Dowling**, Kerry B '91 Hamilton Cnty Pros -230 E 9th
-Cincinnati 45202 **Fx:**946-3017

(330) 762-7377 ..**Dowling**, William D Jr. '80 (Oldham & D) -195 S Main -Ste 300
-Akron 44308 **Fx:**762-7390

(614) 466-1055 ..**Dowling-Fitzpatrick**, Carla R '89 SrCnsl Dept of Aging
-50 W Broad -9th Fl -Columbus 43215 **Fx:**995-1049

(614) 221-1216 ..**Downes Hurst & Fishel** -400 S 5th -Ste 200 -Columbus 43215
Fx:221-8769

(614) 221-1216 ..**Downes**, Jonathan J '79 (Downes H&F) -400 S 5th -Ste 200
-Columbus 43215 **Fx:**221-8769

(614) 469-3939 ..**Downey**, Brian J '98 %Jones D -325 John H McConnell Blvd
-Ste 600 -Bx165017 -Columbus 43216 **Fx:**461-4198

(216) 696-6700 ..**Downey**, Brian P '89 (Schwartz D & Co,LPA) -200 Pub Sq
-Ste 2860 BP Twr -Cleveland 44114 **Fx:**696-6772
Downey, Carolyn M '95 -(Address Unavailable)

(614) 221-2121 ..**Downey**, Daniel T '94 %Isaac BL&T,LLP -250 E Broad
-Ste 900 Mdlnd Bldg -Columbus 43215 **Fx:**365-9516

(864) 836-6312 ..**Downey**, John P '68 (JP Downey Consulting) -3 Long Shadow Ln -Travelers Rest, SC 29690

(419) 724-2600 ..**Downey**, John J '93 Udell & A Ltd -5738 Main -Sylvania 43560

(614) 464-6400 ..**Downey**, Philip F '88 (Vorys SS&P LLP) -52 E Gay -Bx1008 -Columbus 43216 **Fx**:464-6350

(440) 967-2060 ..**Downie**, John P '59 -5300 Park Dr -Vermilion 44089

(440) 244-4809 ..**Downie**, Thomas A '78 Gary N&T,LLC -446 Bway -Lorain 44052 **Fx**:244-3462

(937) 667-4481 ..**Downing**, Joseph A '98 (Dysinger S&D) -249 S Garber Dr -Tipp City 45371 **Fx**:667-5393

(216) 861-9111 ..**Downing**, Michael J '83 (MJ Downing Co,LPA) -75 Pub Sq -Ste 920 -Cleveland 44113

Downing, Patricia J '89 -733 Dayton -Hamilton 45011

(216) 931-6000 ..**Downing**, Timothy J '89 (Ulmer & B LLP) -1300 E 9th -Ste 900 Penton Media Bldg -Cleveland 44114 **Fx**:931-6001

(216) 623-1155 ..**Downs**, James J '82 %Nationwide Ins -323 Lakeside Av W -Ste 410 Lakeside Pl -Cleveland 44113

(937) 333-4100 ..**Downs**, Timothy S '03 %Law Dept -101 W 3rd -Bx22 -Dayton 45402

(614) 292-3159 ..**Doyle**, Anne M '93 OSU Moritz Cllg of Law -55 W 12th Av -Columbus 43210 **Fx**:292-1383

(216) 589-9926 ..**Doyle**, Barry T '77 -21801 Lk Shr Blvd -Euclid 44123

Doyle, Brendan R '04 -(Address Unavailable)

(614) 462-4023 ..**Doyle**, David A '86 10th Dist Ct of Appls -373 S High -24th Fl -Columbus 43215

(330) 487-5151 ..**Doyle**, Duane L '71 -8413 Twr Dr -Twinsburg 44087

(513) 632-3170 ..**Doyle**, James R Jr. '72 -7265 Kenwood Rd -Ste 250 -Cincinnati 45236

(614) 229-3888 ..**Doyle**, Jon S '03 %Cheek & Z,LLP -471 E Broad -18th Fl -Bx15009 -Columbus 43215 **Fx**:241-5865

(419) 248-1500 ..**Doyle Lewis & Warner** -202 N Erie -Bx2168 -Toledo 43603 **Fx**:248-2002

(614) 469-3939 ..**Doyle**, Meghan E '01 %Jones D -325 John H McConnell Blvd -Ste 600 -Bx165017 -Columbus 43216 **Fx**:461-4198

(440) 323-6100 ..**Doyle**, Michael D '91 (Haynes & D) -134 Middle Av -Elyria 44035

(614) 249-4726 ..**Doyle**, Michael F '00 Cnsl Nationwide Ins Co -1 Nationwide Plz -Columbus 43215

(513) 946-3000 ..**Doyle**, Michael T '83 Hamilton Cnty Pros -230 E 9th -Cincinnati 45202 **Fx**:946-3017

(614) 228-1541 ..**Doyle**, R Christopher '79 (Baker & H LLP) -65 E State -Ste 2100 -Columbus 43215 **Fx**:462-2616

(216) 896-3000 ..**Doyle**, Raymond E '80 Parker-Hannifin Corp -6035 Parkland Blvd -Tax Dept -Mayfield Heights 44124

(216) 363-6048 ..**Doyle**, William T Jr. '72 -1370 Ontario Av -2000 Standard Bldg -Cleveland 44113

(614) 224-1222 ..**Dozer**, Jodi L '97 %Maguire & S,LLP -250 Civic Ctr Dr -Ste 200 -Columbus 43215 **Fx**:224-1236

(330) 758-1781 ..**Draa**, Charles M '81 -1315 Boardman-Canfld Rd -Ste 2 -Youngstown 44512

(614) 890-4770 ..**Drabick**, Thomas C Jr. '94 OAPSE -6805 Oak Crk Dr -Columbus 43229

(419) 530-1486 ..**Drabik**, Sandra A '80 Univ of Toledo Law Schl -2801 W Bancroft -Toledo 43606

(614) 249-6583 ..**Dracopoulos**, James J '80 Nationwide Ins Co -1 Nationwide Plz -Columbus 43215

(479) 277-0995 ..**Dragash**, Mickey R '01 Wal-Mart Stores,Inc -601 N Walton Blvd -MS-L20 -Bentonville, AR 72716

(248) 655-8318 ..**Drage**, Michelle S '94 Delphi Interior Syst -5725 Delphi Dr -Mail Code 483.400.404 -Troy, MI 48098

(216) 592-5000 ..**Drago**, Christian R '01 %Tucker E&W LLP -925 Euclid Av -1150 Huntngtn Bldg -Cleveland 44115 **Fx**:592-5009

(330) 668-6500 ..**Drago**, Michelle M '99 Spector & Saulino -4040 Embssy Pkwy -Ste 100 -Akron 44333

(330) 535-0124 ..**Drahovsky**, Timothy J '00 %Semple & E -One Cascade Plz -7th Fl -Akron 44308

(216) 621-3000 ..**Drain**, John Michael Jr. '70 -Bx6041 -Cleveland 44101 **Fx**:241-0839

(440) 356-7255 ..**Drain**, Joseph A '82 %Grady & Assoc -20950 Ctr Ridge Rd -Ste 100 -Rocky River 44116 **Fx**:356-7255

(614) 228-6453 ..**Drakatos**, Eleni A '03 %Colley S&A Co,LPA -536 S High -Columbus 43215 **Fx**:228-7122

(614) 466-3206 ..**Drake**, Carol Nolan '85 SERB -65 E State -Ste 1200 -Columbus 43215 **Fx**:466-3074

(740) 773-9000 ..**Drake**, Claire F '99 -78 E 2nd -Chillicothe 45601

(614) 645-7385 ..**Drake**, Daniel W '70 City Atty -90 W Broad -Columbus 43215

(440) 516-6000 ..**Drake**, Eric M '93 -30432 Euclid Av -Ste 204 -Wickliffe 44092

(859) 431-1340 ..**Drake**, Laura L '98 Nielson & S -639 Wshngtn Av -Newport, KY 41071

(419) 423-0242 ..**Drake Phillips Kuenzli & Clark** -301 S Main -Ste 3 -Findlay 45840 **Fx**:423-0186

(740) 345-3431 ..**Drake**, Robert N '72 (Reese PD&M,PLL) -36 N 2nd -Bx919 -Newark 43058 **Fx**:349-5116

(419) 423-0242 ..**Drake**, Robert W '48 (Drake PK&C) -301 S Main -Ste 3 -Findlay 45840 **Fx**:423-0186

(440) 247-7800 ..**Drake**, Therese Sweeney '84 (McSherry & Co) -178 E Wshngtn -Chagrin Falls 44022 **Fx**:247-7801

(419) 423-0242 ..**Drake**, Thomas D '77 (Drake PK&C) -301 S Main -Ste 3 -Findlay 45840 **Fx**:423-0186

(216) 861-8736 ..**Drake-Kinnear**, Alison L '94 Oglebay-Norton Co -1001 Lakeside Av -Ste 1500 -Cleveland 44114

(614) 267-9367 ..**Dranichak**, Michelle L '91 -2334 N 4th -Columbus 43202

(702) 294-4157 ..**Draper**, Gerald L '66 -2109 Cumberland Hill Dr -Henderson, NV 89052

(216) 443-7223 ..**Draper**, James A '75 (Cuyahoga Cnty Pub Def) -1200 W 3rd NW -100 Lakeside Pl -Cleveland 44113

(216) 357-7000 ..**Drasner**, Lawrence S '92 US Dist Ct -801 W Superior Av -Ste 17B -Cleveland 44113

(513) 977-8200 ..**Drasnin**, Lori '01 %Dinsmore & S LLP -255 E 5th -Ste 1900 -Cincinnati 45202 **Fx**:977-8141

(330) 972-7972 ..**Dratler**, Jay Jr. '01 Univ of Akron Law Schl -C Blake McDowell Law Ctr -231D -Akron 44325

(216) 479-8500 ..**Draucker**, Carl A '77 (Squire S&D LLP) -127 Pub Sq -4900 Key Twr -Cleveland 44114 **Fx**:479-8780

(513) 852-8200 ..**Draugelis**, Peter A '00 %Cors & B LLC -537 E Pete Rose Way -Ste 400 -Cincinnati 45202

(614) 443-6839 ..**Dray**, Michael G '99 -211½ E Whittier -Columbus 43206

(440) 352-4400 ..**Dray**, Sandra A '81 -270 E Main -Ste 200 -Painesville 44077

(863) 668-6707 ..**Drayer**, Lonnie R '76 Breed Technologies -5300 Allen K Breed Hwy -Lakeland, FL 33811

(216) 621-5300 ..**Drechsler**, David L '89 (Buckingham D&B,LLP) -1375 E 9th -Ste 1700 -Cleveland 44114 **Fx**:621-5440

(614) 628-1601 ..**Dreher**, Darrell L '74 (Dreher L&T LLP) -41 S High -2250 Huntngtn Ctr -Columbus 43215 **Fx**:628-1600

(216) 861-5582 ..**Dreher**, Joseph D '91 (Fay SFM&M LLP) -1100 Superior Av -7th Fl -Cleveland 44114 **Fx**:241-1666

Dreher, Joseph M '80 -405 Riverdale Dr -Rocky River 44116

(614) 628-8000 ..**Dreher Langer & Tomkies LLP** -41 S High -2250 Huntngtn Ctr -Columbus 43215 **Fx**:628-1600

(614) 481-8943 ..**Dreifke**, Stuart L '75 -1225 Dublin Rd -Columbus 43215

(216) 583-3692 ..**Dreis**, Michael E '97 Ernst & Young LLP -925 Euclid Av -Ste 1300 -Cleveland 44115

(614) 764-8459 ..**Dreitler**, Beth L '93 Wendys Intl -4288 W Dublin-Granvll Rd -Bx256 -Dublin 43017

(614) 469-3939 ..**Dreitler**, Joseph R '79 (Jones D) -325 John H McConnell Blvd -Ste 600 -Bx165017 -Columbus 43216 **Fx**:461-4198

(330) 376-1242 ..**Drenski**, Tama L '03 %Renner KGBT&W,LPA -106 S Main -4th Fl First Natl Twr -Akron 44308 **Fx**:376-9646

Drescher, Cathy S '83 -3560 Valley Pkwy -North Royalton 44133

(419) 885-7515 ..**Drescher**, Erich W '00 %W Drescher & Assoc Co,LPA -6611 Mplwd Av -Sylvania 43560 **Fx**:885-3265

(419) 885-7515 ..**Drescher**, Wolfgang '69 (W Drescher & Assoc Co,LPA) -6611 Mplwd Av -Sylvania 43560 **Fx**:885-3265

(216) 642-3342 ..**Dresp**, Donna M '95 %Wegman H&V,LPA -6055 Rockside Wds Blvd -Ste 200 -Cleveland 44131 **Fx**:642-8826

(937) 434-3556 ..**Dressel**, Frederick W '81 (Ruffolo SD&L) -7501 Paragon Rd -Dayton 45459

(937) 325-7365 ..**Dressel**, Quinton R '83 (Emerich W&P) -20 S Limestone -Ste 300 -Bx1087 -Springfield 45501

(513) 634-1452 ..**Dressel**, Sarah Ann '04 Procter & Gamble Co -6090 Ctr Hill Av -Rm CC2W10 -Cincinnati 45224

(513) 931-6800 ..**Dressing**, John W '70 -1172 W Galbraith Rd -Ste 211 -Cincinnati 45231

(513) 946-3000 ..**Dressing**, Patrick X '94 Hamilton Cnty Pros -230 E 9th -Cincinnati 45202 **Fx**:946-3017

(330) 489-5410 ..**Dressler**, Donald J '73 Key Bank NA -126 Central Plz N -Canton 44702

Dressler, Ronald L Jr. '97 -985 Lawrence -Medina 44256

(330) 678-3088 ..**Dressler**, Roy D '69 -502 Rellim Dr -Kent 44240

(859) 341-1881 ..**Dressman**, James A III '96 (Deters B&L,PSC) -2701 Turkeyfoot Rd -207 Thomas More Pkwy -Crestview Hills, KY 41017 **Fx**:341-1469

(513) 627-4132 ..**Dressman**, Marianne '99 Procter & Gamble -5299 Spring Grove Av -Cincinnati 45217

(330) 762-0080 ..**Drew**, David P '91 -611 W Market -Ste C -Akron 44303

(513) 621-8210 ..**Drew**, George R '50 OfCnsl Drew & W Co,LPA -1 W 4th -Ste 2400 -Cincinnati 45202 **Fx**:621-5444

(614) 621-1500 ..**Drew**, Joan N '01 %Calfee H&G LLP -21 E State -1100 Fifth Third Ctr -Columbus 43215 **Fx**:621-0010

(513) 621-8210 ..**Drew & Ward Co,LPA** -1 W 4th -Ste 2400 -Cincinnati 45202 **Fx**:621-5444

(614) 221-0922 ..**Drexel**, Ray P '74 Gamble HJ Co,LPA -1 E Lvngstn Av -Columbus 43215 **Fx**:365-9741

(419) 223-8511 ..**Drexler**, Deborah L '83 Allen Cnty Cmmn Pleas Ct -Cthse -Bx1243 -Lima 45802

(513) 469-1472 ..**Dreyer**, Kevin T '87 General Revenue Corp -11501 Northlake Dr -Cincinnati 45249

(904) 366-3741 ..**Dreyer**, Timothy C '78 Pricewaterhouse Coopers LLP -50 N Laura -Ste 3000 -Jacksonville, FL 32202

(216) 241-5300 ..**Dreyfuss**, Daniel W '78 (D Dreyfuss Co,LPA) -1801 E 9th -Ste 740 -Cleveland 44114

(440) 205-3600 ..**Driggs**, Charles M '51 (Driggs LB&H Co,LPA) -8522 East Av -Mentor 44060 **Fx**:205-3601

(440) 205-3600 ..**Driggs Lucas Brubaker & Hogg Co,LPA** -8522 East Av -Mentor 44060 **Fx**:205-3601

(859) 292-0100 ..**Drill**, Robert M '94 IRS -200 W 4th -Covington, KY 41011

(216) 241-5310 ..**Drinko**, Donald G '93 %Gallagher SF&N -1501 Euclid Av -6th Fl -Cleveland 44115 **Fx**:241-1608

(216) 621-0200 ..**Drinko**, John D '45 (Baker & H LLP) -1900 E 9th -Ste 3200 -Cleveland 44114 **Fx**:696-0740

(937) 254-2600 ..**Driscoll**, Brian C '01 Warden & D LLP -732 Watervliet Av -Dayton 45420

(937) 254-2600 ..**Driscoll**, Daniel P '02 Warden & D LLP -732 Watervliet Av -Dayton 45420

(216) 443-7800 ..**Driscoll**, Jennifer A '01 Cuyahoga Cnty Pros -1200 Ontario -8th Fl -Cleveland 44113 **Fx**:698-2270

(513) 558-5277 ..**Driscoll**, Kathleen M '82 Univ of Cincinnati Cllg of Nursing -248 Procter -Vine & Martin Luther King Dr -Cincinnati 45221

(419) 248-1432 ..**Driscoll**, Perry F '72 (Barone & D) -320 N Mich -4th Fl -Toledo 43624 **Fx**:244-0765

(740) 592-3061 ..**Driscoll**, Robert P '93 Athens Cnty Pros -Athens Cnty Cthse -Athens 45701 **Fx**:592-3291

(614) 461-4177 ..**Driscoll**, William P '76 Levin & Driscoll -60 E Broad -Ste 350 -Columbus 43215

(305) 448-7089 ..**Dritz**, Abby R '03 %Lott & F,PA -355 Alhambra Cir -Ste 1100 -Coral Gables, FL 33134 **Fx**:446-6191

(614) 464-4644 ..**Dritz**, Stanley B '73 -50 W Broad -Columbus 43215 **Fx**:464-0946

(216) 363-4500 ..**Drockton**, Leslie A '86 Benesch FC&A LLP) -200 Pub Sq -Ste 2300 -Cleveland 44114 **Fx**:363-4588

(513) 651-6800 ..**Droder**, Eugene J III '04 %Frost BT LLC -201 E 5th -2200 PNC Ctr -Cincinnati 45202 **Fx**:651-6981

(513) 721-1504 ..**Droder & Miller Co,LPA** -125 W Cntrl Pkwy -Cincinnati 45202 **Fx**:721-0310

(937) 225-3499 ..**Droessler**, Julie A '97 Montgomery Cnty Pros -301 W 3rd -Bx972 -Dayton 45422 **Fx**:225-3470

Dropko, Daniel G '03 -(Address Unavailable)

(440) 779-6722 ..**Drossis,** Deborah A '86 -23857 Mastick Rd -North Olmsted 44070

(740) 702-3100 ..**Drotleff,** Steven E '94 Nusbaum A&W -72 N Paint -Chillicothe 45601

(740) 393-2718 ..**Drown,** William T '98 (Folland & D,LPA) -112 N Main -Mount Vernon 43050

(216) 621-0150 ..**Drozdowski,** James M '95 (Hahn L&P LLP) -3300 BP Twr/200 Pub Sq -Ste 3300 -Cleveland 44114 **Fx:**241-2824

(216) 861-5777 ..**Drucker,** David H '84 -1370 Ontario -Ste 330 -Cleveland 44113

(212) 688-3819 ..**Drucker,** Jacquelin F '81 -432 E 58th -#2 -New York, NY 10022 **Fx:**935-1870

(216) 771-5356 ..**Drucker,** Marvin '56 -1370 Ontario -Ste 330 -Cleveland 44113

(216) 771-1900 ..**Drucker,** Richard H '81 (R Drucker LPA Inc) -700 W St Clair Av -Ste 100 -Cleveland 44113

(614) 444-7655 ..**Druen,** W Sidney '70 -85 E Deshler Av -Columbus 43206 **Fx:**444-5599

Drumm, Cynthia J '91 -Bx646 -Worthington 43085

(248) 258-6262 ..**Drumm,** John E '99 %O'Bryan B&C -401 S Old Woodward -Ste 320 -Birmingham, MI 48009

Drummond, Bonnie R '91 -557 S Grant Av -Columbus 43206

(330) 264-4444 ..**Drushal,** Bonnie C '82 OfCnsl Critchfield C&J Ltd -225 N Market -Bx599 -Wooster 44691 **Fx:**263-9278

(330) 264-4444 ..**Drushal,** Jeff D '77 (Critchfield C&J Ltd) -225 N Market -Bx599 -Wooster 44691 **Fx:**263-9278

(440) 546-7616 ..**Drushel,** Kelly E '90 -7000 Fitzwater Rd -Ste 202 -Cleveland 44141

(614) 227-2000 ..**Dryer,** Aaron A '98 %Porter WM&A LLP -41 S High -Columbus 43215 **Fx:**227-2100

(614) 462-3194 ..**Drzewiecki,** Stanley L '93 Franklin Cnty Pub Def -373 S High -12th Fl -Columbus 43215

(216) 228-6715 ..**D'Souza,** Gerard I '96 -15600 Mad Av -Lakewood 44107

(216) 241-5310 ..**Dub,** Stanley M '75 (Gallagher SF&N) -1501 Euclid Av -6th Fl -Cleveland 44115 **Fx:**241-1608

(440) 734-7858 ..**Dubelko,** James M '79 JM Dubelko Co,LPA -6051 Sandpiper Ln -North Olmsted 44070

(216) 787-3030 ..**Duber,** Jeffrey B '84 Atty Gen -615 W Superior Av -11th Fl -Cleveland 44113 **Fx:**787-3480

(216) 861-1234 ..**Duber,** Michael J '73 (Bentoff & D Co,LPA) -55 Pub Sq -Ste 1200 -Cleveland 44113

(330) 677-5298 ..**Dubetz,** Shirley A '54 -1511 Rvr Edge Dr -Kent 44240

(216) 241-6055 ..**Dubin,** Gary W '65 (Dubin J&S) -75 Pub Sq -Ste 650 -Cleveland 44113

(216) 623-0000 ..**Dubin,** Jeffrey E '97 (Javitch B&R) -1300 E 9th -14th Fl -Cleveland 44114 **Fx:**623-0190

(216) 241-6055 ..**Dubin Joseph & Shagrin** -75 Pub Sq -Ste 650 -Cleveland 44113

(216) 573-6174 ..**Dubin,** Lawrence D '91 Cnsl Cambell Telecom -23600 Mercantile Rd -Ste F -Beachwood 44122 **Fx:**274-9749

(330) 499-6000 ..**Dublikar,** Justin A '04 %Baker DBW&M -400 S Main -Canton 44720 **Fx:**449-6423

(330) 499-6000 ..**Dublikar,** Ralph F '74 (Baker DBW&M) -400 S Main -Canton 44720 **Fx:**449-6423

(937) 644-6639 ..**DuBoise,** Nancy F '00 Honda of Amer Mfg -24000 Honda Pkwy -Motorcycle Plant -Marysville 43040

(440) 998-6835 ..**Dubsky,** Duane J '73 Andrews & P LLC -4817 State Rd -Ste 100 -Bx10 -Ashtabula 44005

(216) 241-0300 ..**Dubyak,** Joseph A '69 -920 Trmnl Twr -Cleveland 44113 **Fx:**241-2731

(216) 896-5600 ..**Dubyak,** Robert J '92 (Levy & D) -25200 Chagrin Blvd -Ste 310 -Beachwood 44122 **Fx:**896-5601

(216) 586-3939 ..**Ducatman,** Robert P '80 (Jones D) -901 Lakeside Av -Cleveland 44114 **Fx:**579-0212

(419) 867-3946 ..**Ducey,** Ernest D '83 (Ducey & R) -5330 Heatherdowns Blvd -Ste 105 -Toledo 43614

(419) 867-3946 ..**Ducey & Reiwaldt** -5330 Heatherdowns Blvd -Ste 105 -Toledo 43614

Duchak, Kathleen E '89 -1862 E Lower Springboro Rd -Waynesville 45068

DuChene, Todd M '88 -11 Hunter Dr -Hampton, NH 03842

(216) 621-1113 ..**DuChez,** Neil A '72 (Renner OB&S,LLP) -1621 Euclid Av -19th Fl -Cleveland 44115 **Fx:**621-6165

Duck, Brandon C '03 -(Address Unavailable)

(937) 224-1006 ..**Ducker,** John T '67 (Talbot & D) -34 N Main -Ste 1400 -Dayton 45402

(513) 887-3257 ..**Duckett,** Douglas E '82 Cnty Commissioners -315 High -6th Fl -Bx515 -Hamilton 45012

(616) 392-1821 ..**Duckworth,** Vincent L '97 %Cunningham D,PC -321 Sttlrs Rd -Bx1767 -Holland, MI 49422 **Fx:**396-7106

(614) 466-0570 ..**Duco,** Michael P '92 %OH Ofc Collctv Barg -100 E Broad -18th Fl -Columbus 43215

(216) 443-7800 ..**Ducoff,** Ronni E '88 Cuyahoga Cnty Pros -1200 Ontario -8th Fl -Cleveland 44113 **Fx:**698-2270

(330) 270-1700 ..**Duda,** Donald A Jr. '94 -48 W Lbrty -Hubbard 44425

(216) 861-4020 ..**Duda,** John E '61 -2101 Richmond Rd -LaPlace 2nd Fl -Beachwood 44122

(419) 536-1708 ..**Dudda-Sworden,** Barbara '93 -2125 Brookdale Rd -Toledo 43606

(216) 931-6000 ..**Duddy,** Suzanne E '00 %Ulmer & B LLP -1300 E 9th -Ste 900 Penton Media Bldg -Cleveland 44114 **Fx:**931-6001

(440) 951-1525 ..**Dudley,** Celine M '87 -38021 Euclid Av -Willoughby 44094

(765) 640-2600 ..**Dudley,** Mark K '03 %Howard D&D -403 W 8th -Anderson, IN 46016

(513) 844-8515 ..**Dudley,** Mary K '83 -223 S Front -Bx1134 -Hamilton 45012

(216) 443-3178 ..**Dudley,** Vincent B '97 Domestic Relations Ct -1 Lakeside Av -Rm 187 -Cleveland 44113

(937) 309-9297 ..**Duell,** Mark E '94 SrCnsl Honda R&D Amer,Inc -21001 St Rt 739 -Raymond 43067 **Fx:**645-8677

(937) 548-1157 ..**Dues,** Gail M '03 %Hanes SCGG&D,Ltd -507 S Bway -Greenville 45331

(513) 241-2124 ..**Duesing,** Jerome A '62 -617 Vine -Rm 1315 Enquirer Bldg -Cincinnati 45202

(330) 762-2411 ..**Duff,** Andrew R '79 (Amer C Co,LPA) -159 S Main -6th Fl -Akron 44308 **Fx:**762-9918

Duff, David W '74 -601 N Ellsworth Av -Salem 44460

(304) 233-3390 ..**Duff,** Frank X III '81 Schrader B&C,PLLC -32-20th -Ste 500 -Wheeling, WV 26003

(740) 695-1444 ..**Duff,** Gerald P '71 Hanlon DE&M Co,LPA -46457 Natl Rd W -Saint Clairsville 43950 **Fx:**695-1563

(440) 244-2434 ..**Duff,** Michael J '80 -715 Bway Av -Lorain 44052

(216) 241-2838 ..**Duff,** Timothy J '90 (Taft S&H LLP) -200 Pub Sq -3500 BP Twr -Cleveland 44114 **Fx:**241-3707

(937) 294-2778 ..**Duff,** Trisha M '91 -424 Patterson Rd -Dayton 45419

(614) 221-6563 ..**Duffey,** David L '80 OH Democratic Party -271 E State -Columbus 43215

(513) 684-3646 ..**Duffey,** Jonathan D '98 NLRB -550 Main -Ste 3003 -Cincinnati 45202 **Fx:**684-3946

(614) 224-5205 ..**Duffey,** Mary S '87 Peck S&W,LLP -175 S 3rd -Ste 600 -Columbus 43215 **Fx:**224-0069

Duffey, Wendy K '03 -(Address Unavailable)

(419) 242-1400 ..**Duffin,** John P '77 -608 Mad Av -Ste 1400 -Toledo 43604

(330) 740-2330 ..**Duffrin,** Robert E '93 Mahoning Cnty Pros -21 W Boardman -6th Fl -Youngstown 44503 **Fx:**740-2008

(330) 430-3804 ..**Duffrin,** Vivianne W '93 Stark Cnty Sheriffs Ofc -4500 Atl Blvd NE -Canton 44705

(614) 227-4885 ..**Duffy,** Alan D '02 %Bricker & E LLP -100 S 3rd -Columbus 43215 **Fx:**227-2390

(614) 728-2845 ..**Duffy,** Drew M '86 Atty Gen -150 E Gay -Columbus 43215 **Fx:**728-2122

(937) 898-4941 ..**Duffy,** Edward J Jr. '51 -32 N Dixie Dr -Bx76 -Vandalia 45377

(216) 522-4169 ..**Duffy,** James M '82 US SBA -1111 Superior Av E -Ste 630 -Cleveland 44114

(440) 779-6636 ..**Duffy,** John J '78 (J Duffy & Assoc) -23823 Lorain Rd -Ste 270 -North Olmsted 44070

(614) 716-1617 ..**Duffy,** Kevin F '72 Amer Elec Pwr Co -1 Riverside Plz -Columbus 43215

(216) 222-8013 ..**Duffy,** Kevin T '76 Natl City Bank -1900 E 9th -Law Dept Loc 2174 -Cleveland 44114

(216) 696-3030 ..**Duffy,** Mary Beth '89 %Kadish H&W,LPA -1717 E 9th -Ste 2112 -Cleveland 44114 **Fx:**696-3492

(216) 447-9850 ..**Duffy,** Matthew M '99 The Hartford -7100 E Plsnt Vlly Rd -Ste 210 -Independence 44131

(614) 466-0122 ..**Duffy,** Paul J '74 PUCO -180 E Broad -Columbus 43266

(440) 556-0719 ..**Duffy,** Sheila A '86 Cleveland-West Mediation Srvcs -2273 Windward Dr -Westlake 44145

(440) 350-2683 ..**Dugan,** Joan E '80 Lake Cnty Pros -105 Main -Bx490 -Painesville 44077 **Fx:**350-2585

(216) 583-1455 ..**Dugan,** Joan E '93 Ernst & Young LLP -925 Euclid Av -Ste 1300 -Cleveland 44115

(513) 946-9222 ..**Dugan,** Leah A '78 Hamilton Cnty Juv Ct -800 Bway -11th Fl -Cincinnati 45202 **Fx:**946-9217

(513) 784-7209 ..**Dugan,** Matthew J '97 Deloitte & Touche,LLP -250 E 5th -Ste 1900 -Cincinnati 45202

(216) 861-5582 ..**Dugan,** Matthew P '00 %Fay SFM&M LLP -1100 Superior Av -7th Fl -Cleveland 44114 **Fx:**241-1666

(419) 228-0189 ..**Dugan,** Michael E '74 (Dugan & B) -138 W High -Lima 45801

(614) 365-2700 ..**Dugan,** Patrick J '82 (Squire S&D LLP) -41 S High -1300 Huntngtn Ctr -Columbus 43215 **Fx:**365-2499

Dugan, Thomas A '58 -7520 Dogwood Ln -Parma 44130

(419) 691-3051 ..**Dugan,** Thomas P '74 -2460 Navarre Av -Oregon 43616

Dugan, Thomas P '02 -2211 Sandston Rd -Columbus 43220

(614) 445-6161 ..**Dugan,** Vincent A Jr. '83 -52 W Whittier -Columbus 43206

(614) 249-1432 ..**Dugasz,** Erwin J '91 %National Invstmnt Srvcs Corp -One Nationwide Plz -1-07-11 -Columbus 43215 **Fx:**249-3812

(419) 636-2999 ..**Duggan,** Paul H '93 -1426 E High -Bryan 43506

(937) 484-2455 ..**Duggan,** Scott T '99 Allied Signal/Grimes Aero -550 Route #55 -Urbana 43078

(614) 221-4255 ..**Dugger,** Glen A '84 (Smith & H) -37 W Broad -Columbus 43215

(740) 373-5513 ..**Dugger,** Raymond E '99 Washington Cty Dept of Job & Family Srvc -1115 Gilman Av -Bx2005 -Marietta 45750

(216) 689-5882 ..**Dugovics,** Jill T '84 KeyBank NA -127 Pub Sq -17th Fl -Cleveland 44114

(216) 479-6100 ..**Duhamel,** Marcel C '93 %Vorys SS&P LLP -1375 E 9th -Ste 2100 One Cleve Ctr -Cleveland 44114 **Fx:**479-6060

(708) 596-8544 ..**Duhart,** Jake J '83 -14521 Myrtle -Harvey, IL 60426

(419) 244-3393 ..**Duhart,** Myron C II '97 -316 N Mich -Ste 600 -Toledo 43624

(330) 491-5230 ..**Dukat,** James C '69 Certified Title Agency Inc -4518 Fulton Dr NW -Canton 44718

(937) 642-9718 ..**Duke,** John E '03 Assurance Grp -Bx198 -Marysville 43040

(330) 489-5096 ..**Dukes,** Patrick M '91 Nationwide Enterprise Trial Div -1000 Market Av -Canton 44711

(216) 586-3939 ..**Dulabon,** David W '01 %Jones D -901 Lakeside Av -Cleveland 44114 **Fx:**579-0212

(513) 361-0200 ..**Dulaney,** William H III '87 (Roetzel & A,LPA) -250 E 5th -310 Chiquita Ctr -Cincinnati 45202 **Fx:**361-0335

(419) 782-2253 ..**Dulebohn,** Diana G '80 UAW Legal Srvcs -1500 Baltimore Rd -Defiance 43512

(513) 946-3176 ..**Dulemba,** Gerard A '89 Hamilton Cnty Pros -230 E 9th -Cincinnati 45202 **Fx:**946-3017

(330) 399-3544 ..**Dull,** David A Jr. '86 -808 N Park Av -Warren 44483

(330) 399-3544 ..**Dull,** David A Sr. '56 -808 N Park Av -Warren 44483

(330) 652-5006 ..**Dull,** Joseph T '76 -52 E Park Av -Niles 44446

(614) 466-7900 ..**Dull,** Patrick M '95 Atty Gen -30 E Broad -Columbus 43215 **Fx:**466-2437

(202) 616-5934 ..**Dulmage,** Claudia H '79 US DOJ-Antitrust Div -Rm 4016 CCB -Washington, DC 20530 **Fx:**307-5802

(330) 379-6582 ..**Dumas,** David M '91 Bridgestone/Firestone -1200 Firestone Pkwy -Akron 44317

(216) 696-3833 ..**Dumas,** Wesley A '80 -815 Superior Av NE -Ste 612 -Cleveland 44114

(513) 474-3495 ..**Dumbacher,** David A Jr. '67 -2804 Whitehouse Ln -Cincinnati 45244

(513) 425-7012 ..**Dumes,** Robert M '77 -1058 N Univ Blvd -Middletown 45042

(740) 474-6021 ..**Dumm,** Gary R '77 (Young T&D) -180 W Franklin -Circleville 43113

(330) 832-1597 ..**Dummermuth,** Karen S '93 -2137 Wales Av NW -Ste 2 -Massillon 44646

Dunbar, Brian D '91 -43 Greenbriar Dr -Aurora 44202

Dunbar, Erik S '04 -(Address Unavailable)

(614) 995-9566 ..**Dunbar**, Frank C III '64 Mstr Comm/Supreme Ct OH -65 S Front -Columbus 43215 **Fx:**995-9569

(937) 644-8151 ..**Dunbar**, Stephen C '03 %Coleman E&A -110 S Court -Bx266 -Marysville 43040

(216) 592-5000 ..**Duncan**, Ed E '74 (Tucker E&W LLP) -925 Euclid Av -1150 Huntngtn Bldg -Cleveland 44115 **Fx:**592-5009
Duncan, Julie L '97 -1034 Paxton Av -Cincinnati 45208
Duncan, Lane S '02 -1530 Willow Dr -Sandusky 44870

(330) 376-5300 ..**Duncan**, Matthew R '03 %Buckingham D&B,LLP -50 S Main -Bx1500 -Akron 44309 **Fx:**258-6559

(859) 426-1300 ..**Duncan**, Michael A '86 (Ziegler & S,PSC) -541 Buttermilk Pike -Ste 500 -Bx175710 -Covington, KY 41017

(937) 434-6040 ..**Duncan**, Richard L '73 (Little D&P) -7501 Paragon Rd -Dayton 45459

(614) 231-9086 ..**Duncan**, Robert M '52 -1397 Hddn Rd -Columbus 43209

(216) 696-3030 ..**Duncan**, William A '87 (Kadish H&W,LPA) -1717 E 9th -Ste 2112 -Cleveland 44114 **Fx:**696-3492

(937) 222-2500 ..**Duncombe**, Barbara A '00 OfCnsl Sebaly S&D -1900 Kettering Twr -Dayton 45423 **Fx:**222-6554

(513) 932-3145 ..**Dundes**, Raymond J '89 -7 S Mechanic -Lebanon 45036

(937) 438-3122 ..**Dundon**, Jeffrey R '85 (J Dundon Co,LPA) -156 E Sprng Vlly Rd -Centerville 45458

(216) 566-5500 ..**Dunford**, Oliver J '01 %Thompson H LLP -127 Pub Sq -3900 Key Ctr -Cleveland 44114 **Fx:**566-5800

(937) 339-0511 ..**Dungan & LeFevre Co,LPA** -210 W Main -Troy 45373 **Fx:**335-5802

(937) 773-8054 ..**Dungan & LeFevre Co,LPA** -111 W Ash -Bx1529 -Piqua 45356 **Fx:**773-3379

(513) 932-2871 ..**Duning**, James W '68 (Gray & D) -4 S Bway -Bx268 -Lebanon 45036

(419) 352-8222 ..**Dunipace**, John M '75 (Marcin & D) -440 E Poe Rd -Bowling Green 43402

(614) 899-9014 ..**Dunkerley**, Debra L '86 -1115 E Cllg Av -Westerville 43081

(740) 852-2746 ..**Dunkle**, Richard A '90 -2 N Main -London 43140

(614) 253-2740 ..**Dunlap**, B William '66 Amer Red Cross -995 E Broad -Columbus 43205 **Fx:**253-1544

(937) 783-2401 ..**Dunlap**, Brenda N '79 (Lyons M&D) -212 W Main -Blanchester 45107

(330) 702-0033 ..**Dunlap**, Charles E '77 -3855 Starrs Centre Dr -Ste A -Canfield 44406

(330) 733-7369 ..**Dunlap**, Jeffrey D '75 -370 Newton Cir -Akron 44305

(216) 931-6000 ..**Dunlap**, Jeffrey S '97 %Ulmer & B LLP -1300 E 9th -Ste 900 Penton Media Bldg -Cleveland 44114 **Fx:**931-6001
Dunlap, John H '94 -543 Fairway Park Ct -Ann Arbor, MI 48103

(937) 593-6065 ..**Dunlap**, Robert E '57 (Thompson DHMW&T) -1111 Rush Av -Bx68 -Bellefontaine 43311
Dunlap, William E III '68 -2559 Welsford Rd -Columbus 43221

(614) 462-2236 ..**Dunlay**, Catherine T '84 (Schottenstein Z&D) -250 West -Bx165020 -Columbus 43216 **Fx:**462-5135

(937) 223-3277 ..**Dunlevey**, Karen T '96 %Bieser G&L LLP -6 N Main -400 Natl City Ctr -Dayton 45402 **Fx:**223-6339

(937) 223-6003 ..**Dunlevey Mahan & Furry** -110 N Main -Ste 1000 -Dayton 45402 **Fx:**223-8550

(937) 223-6003 ..**Dunlevey**, Robert T '73 (Dunlevey M&F) -110 N Main -Ste 1000 -Dayton 45402 **Fx:**223-8550

(513) 412-1460 ..**Dunn**, Carol E '85 Great Amer Fncl Resrcs,Inc -525 Vine -11th Fl -Cincinnati 45202

(216) 479-6100 ..**Dunn**, Carrie M '03 %Vorys SS&P LLP -1375 E 9th -Ste 2100 One Cleve Ctr -Cleveland 44114 **Fx:**479-6060

(614) 228-5151 ..**Dunn**, Danielle R '02 %Gallagher GPT&L LLP -471 E Broad -19th Fl -Columbus 43215 **Fx:**228-0032

(937) 512-2935 ..**Dunn**, Darlene Efinger '03 Sinclair Comm College -444 W 3rd -Dayton 45402

(419) 536-2399 ..**Dunn**, Darlene J '77 -2945 Riva Ridge Rd -Toledo 43615

(513) 621-0397 ..**Dunn**, Dolores A '75 Lawriter LLC -121 W Cntrl Pkwy -Cincinnati 45202

(937) 322-0891 ..**Dunn**, Edward W '55 (Cole AH&D) -333 N Limestone -Bx1687 -Springfield 45501 **Fx:**322-9931

(937) 322-0891 ..**Dunn**, Elizabeth J '92 OfCnsl Cole AH&D -333 N Limestone -Bx1687 -Springfield 45501 **Fx:**322-9931

(513) 352-0500 ..**Dunn**, Elizabeth S '04 -602 Main -Ste 1010 -Cincinnati 45202 **Fx:**352-0555

(330) 792-7061 ..**Dunn**, Francis L Jr. '00 -Bx15175 -Austintown 44515

(216) 241-2838 ..**Dunn**, George J '60 OfCnsl Taft S&H LLP -200 Pub Sq -3500 BP Twr -Cleveland 44114 **Fx:**241-3707

(614) 462-2339 ..**Dunn**, Gregory J '78 (Schottenstein Z&D) -250 West -Bx165020 -Columbus 43216 **Fx:**462-5135

(614) 462-2212 ..**Dunn**, Harvey '66 (Schottenstein Z&D) -250 West -Bx165020 -Columbus 43216 **Fx:**462-5135

(216) 443-5834 ..**Dunn**, Howard A '78 Cuyahoga Cnty Juv Ct -1910 Carnegie -Cleveland 44115

(330) 629-8877 ..**Dunn**, James C '86 -8255 South Av -Ste A -Youngstown 44512
Dunn, James E Jr. '73 -201 Taplow Rd -Baltimore, MD 21212

(216) 241-7255 ..**Dunn**, James J '84 -2401 Superior Viaduct -Cleveland 44113

(513) 721-1311 ..**Dunn**, John M '04 %Reminger & R -7 W 7th -Ste 1990 -Cincinnati 45202 **Fx:**721-2553

(216) 586-3939 ..**Dunn**, John P '74 (Jones D) -901 Lakeside Av -Cleveland 44114 **Fx:**579-0212

(937) 322-0891 ..**Dunn**, Joseph A '92 (Cole AH&D) -333 N Limestone -Bx1687 -Springfield 45501 **Fx:**322-9931

(330) 834-3602 ..**Dunn**, Karen A '90 Fresh Mark,INL -188 S Way -Massillon 44648

(614) 722-3940 ..**Dunn**, Kathleen M '94 %Children's Hsptl -700 Children's Dr -Columbus 43205

(330) 723-6102 ..**Dunn**, Kevin W '91 K Dunn Co,LPA -600 E Smith Rd -Medina 44256

(330) 486-3100 ..**Dunn**, Leslie D '75 Cole Natl Corp -1925 Enterprise Pkwy -Twinsburg 44087

(614) 236-8000 ..**Dunn**, Marcus D '94 (Zacks Law Grp LLC) -33 S James Rd -3rd Fl -Columbus 43213

(513) 929-3400 ..**Dunn**, Martiné R '85 (Baker & H LLP) -312 Walnut -Ste 3200 -Cincinnati 45202 **Fx:**929-0303
Dunn, Owen B Jr. '02 -5340 Rambo Ln -Toledo 43623

(440) 449-6800 ..**Dunn**, Paul L '91 Skoda Minotti & Co -6685 Beta Dr -Mayfield Village 44143

(216) 252-3542 ..**Dunn**, Robert D '92 Key Bank NA -127 Pub Sq -OH-01-99-2014 -Cleveland 44114

(216) 634-7777 ..**Dunn**, Robert M '81 -3359 W 58th -Cleveland 44102

(614) 221-3155 ..**Dunn**, Robert R '91 (Bailey C LLC) -10 W Broad -Columbus 43215 **Fx:**221-0479
Dunn, Sean P '94 -7498 Alpath Rd -New Albany 43054

(419) 734-9009 ..**Dunn**, Terry J '88 -125 Jffrsn -Port Clinton 43452

(216) 363-1400 ..**Dunn**, Theodore M Jr. '82 (Buckley K,LPA) -600 E Superior Av -Ste 1400 -Cleveland 44114 **Fx:**579-1020

(216) 515-1660 ..**Dunn**, William P '03 %Frantz W LLP -127 Pub Sq -2500 Key Center -Cleveland 44114 **Fx:**515-1650

(440) 998-1202 ..**Dunne**, Robert W Jr. '82 Meese Oibition Dunne Co -Bx607 -Ashtabula 44005

(937) 222-3000 ..**Dunphy**, Patrick K '82 (Falke & D LLC) -30 Wyoming -Dayton 45409 **Fx:**222-1414

(330) 376-3304 ..**Dunseath**, Frances N '94 -441 Wolf Ledges Pkwy -#302 -Akron 44311

(614) 764-8486 ..**Dunsizer**, Jennifer B '93 Wendys Intl -4288 W Dublin-Granvll Rd -Bx256 -Dublin 43017

(937) 225-2910 ..**Dunsky**, Gregory P '77 US Atty -200 W 2nd -602 Fed Bldg -Dayton 45402

(440) 331-3191 ..**Dunson**, James A Jr. '79 (Dunson & D Co,LPA) -21851 Ctr Ridge Rd -Ste 410 -Rocky River 44116

(440) 331-3191 ..**Dunson**, Richard W '88 (Dunson & D Co,LPA) -21851 Ctr Ridge Rd -Ste 410 -Rocky River 44116
Duong, Vy T '02 -6777 Montpellier Blvd -Dayton 45459

(614) 464-4100 ..**DuPont**, Gregory S '92 (AuCoin DH&Y LLC) -495 S High -Ste 250 -Columbus 43215
Dupree, Randy H '02 -122 N Illinois Av -Wellston 45692

(614) 775-3827 ..**Duprey**, Mary E '85 TOO,Inc -8323 Walton Pkwy -New Albany 43054

(513) 381-9200 ..**Dupuis**, Charles T '68 OfCnsl Rendigs FK&D,LLP -One W 4th -Ste 900 -Cincinnati 45202 **Fx:**381-9206

(513) 352-3334 ..**Dupuis**, Mary F '69 City of Cincinnati -801 Plum -214 -Cincinnati 45202

(513) 381-2838 ..**Duran**, Samuel M '84 (Taft S&H LLP) -425 Walnut -Ste 1800 -Cincinnati 45202 **Fx:**381-0205

(614) 224-1222 ..**Duran**, Ysidro E '86 %Maguire & S,LLP -250 Civic Ctr Dr -Ste 200 -Columbus 43215 **Fx:**224-1236

(614) 481-3210 ..**Durban**, Lee E '78 -1335 Dublin Rd -Ste 200A -Columbus 43215

(330) 489-4430 ..**Durben**, Annette M '99 US Bankruptcy Ct -201 Cleveland Av SW -Canton 44702

(937) 461-9400 ..**Durden**, Aaron G '88 A Durden & Co,LPA -10 W Monument Av -Dayton 45402

(630) 875-5300 ..**Durden**, Mildred F '86 Enesco Grp Inc -225 Windsor Dr -Itasca, IL 60143

(937) 910-7530 ..**Durden**, Paula V '86 Dayton Metro Housing Auth -400 Wayne Av -Bx8750 -Dayton 45401

(614) 761-1733 ..**Duren**, David L '80 (Metcalf DMS&W,LLC) -655 Metro Pl S -Ste 210 -Dublin 43017

(937) 445-5522 ..**Duren**, Mark W '92 Gasper Corp -1700 S Patterson Blvd -#WHQ-3E -Dayton 45419

(330) 491-5289 ..**Dureska**, David P '87 (Buckingham D&B,LLP) -4518 Fulton Dr NW -Bx35048 -Canton 44735 **Fx:**492-9625

(614) 466-7788 ..**Durfey**, Miles C '70 OH Ct of Claims -65 E State -Ste 1100 -Columbus 43215

(937) 548-2122 ..**Durham**, Darrell T '96 2nd Natl Bk -499 S Bway -Bx 130 -Greenville 45331

(937) 854-6686 ..**Durham**, Joan D '82 Moto Photo,Inc -4444 Lk Ctr Dr -Dayton 45426

(614) 228-5822 ..**Durham**, Joseph R '91 OfCnsl Rich C&D,LLC -300 E Broad -Ste 300 -Columbus 43215 **Fx:**228-2725

(513) 632-5318 ..**Durham**, Leona L '83 -119 E Court -Cincinnati 45202

(513) 651-4900 ..**Durham**, Mark Freeman '83 -119 E Court -Ste 525 -Cincinnati 45202
Durham, Mary L '78 -19200 N Park Blvd -Shaker Heights 44122
Durham, Susan C '81 -74 E Kelso Rd -Columbus 43202

(330) 375-2730 ..**Durian**, Chad M '04 Pros -217 S High -Ste 203 -Akron 44308

(440) 888-0843 ..**Durica**, Terrence D '74 -3406 Norris Av -Parma 44134

(330) 373-1448 ..**Duricy**, Patrick B '89 Cmmnty Lgl Aid Srvcs,Inc -160 E Market -Ste 250 -Warren 44481 **Fx:**395-5227

(513) 732-2212 ..**Durkee & Uhle** -97 Main -Batavia 45103 **Fx:**732-3318

(330) 740-2330 ..**Durkin**, Dawn M '98 Mahoning Cnty Pros -21 W Boardman -6th Fl -Youngstown 44503 **Fx:**740-2008

(216) 621-7860 ..**Durkin**, George J '62 OfCnsl Cavitch FD&F -1717 E 9th -14th Fl -Cleveland 44114 **Fx:**621-3415

(614) 891-8422 ..**Durkin**, Kevin P '80 (Taylor & D) -471 E Broad -Ste 1100 -Columbus 43215

(330) 343-5585 ..**Durmann**, Glenn G '72 Miller & K,LPA -405 Chauncey Av NW -Bx668 -New Philadelphia 44663 **Fx:**343-7977

(440) 729-7181 ..**Durn**, Raymond J '53 -13088 W Geauga Trl -Chesterland 44026

(419) 353-2108 ..**Durney**, Ronda L '01 -13385 Dirlam Rd -Bowling Green 43402

(330) 393-1584 ..**Durniok**, Deborah S '95 %Guarnieri & S -151 E Market -Bx4270 -Warren 44482 **Fx:**395-3831

(407) 423-7656 ..**DuRose**, Richard A '62 (Foley & L LLP) -111 N Orange Av -Bx2193 -Orlando, FL 32802 **Fx:**648-1743

(330) 929-4002 ..**Durr**, Susan L '83 -2674 N Haven Blvd -Ste 18 -Cuyahoga Falls 44223

(614) 846-1081 ..**Durst**, Alan T '65 -1395 E Dublin Granvll Rd -Ste 406 -Columbus 43229

(614) 846-1126 ..**Durst**, Nathan A '88 -1395 E Dublin Granvll Rd -Ste 400 -Columbus 43229

(513) 929-3400 ..**Dusing**, Benjamin G '04 %Baker & H LLP -312 Walnut -Ste 3200 -Cincinnati 45202 **Fx:**929-0303

(513) 791-6500 ..**Dusterberg**, Richard B '66 -9157 Mntgmry Rd -Ste 203 -Cincinnati 45242

(419) 241-0767 ..**Dustin**, Ava M '92 US Atty -4 Seagate -Ste 308 -Toledo 43604 **Fx:**259-6360

(419) 243-6122 ..**Dustin**, David C '92 FBI -420 Mad Av -Ste 800 -Toledo 43604

(419) 626-3800 ..**Dusza**, Thomas M '90 (Reno B&F Co,LPA) -725 Sycamore Line -Sandusky 44870 **Fx:**626-3638

(513) 579-6400 ..**Dutro,** Daniel G Jr. '94 %Keating M&K PLL -1 E 4th
-1400 Provident Twr -Cincinnati 45202 **Fx:**579-6457

(330) 643-2248 .. **Dutt,** Janet L '92 Summit Cnty Cmmn Pleas Ct -209 S High
-Akron 44308

(513) 946-3700 ..**Dutta,** Soumyajit '03 %Hamilton Cnty Pub Def -230 E 9th -3rd Fl
-Cincinnati 45202 **Fx:**946-3707

(614) 583-7602 ..**Dutton,** F Mitchell '82 Amer Elec Pwr Co -1 Riverside Plz
-Columbus 43215

(614) 462-3555 ..**Dutton,** Jennifer D '97 Franklin Cnty Pros -373 S High
-Columbus 43215

(330) 744-1111 ..**Dutton,** Paul M '72 Harrington H&M,Ltd -26 Market -Ste 1200
-Youngstown 44503 **Fx:**744-2029

(614) 469-3939 ..**Dutton,** Thomas E '83 (Jones D) -325 John H McConnell Blvd
-Ste 600 -Bx165017 -Columbus 43216 **Fx:**461-4198

(614) 889-2531 ..**Duvall,** James '63 (Sanborn BD&B Co,LPA) -2515 W Granvll Rd
-Columbus 43235

(614) 462-3555 ..**Duvall,** Jennifer L '95 Franklin Cnty Pros -373 S High
-Columbus 43215

(440) 892-6896 ..**DuVall,** Michael A '75 -3226 Balsam Dr -Westlake 44145

(216) 696-3525 ..**Duvall,** Wendy E '03 %Cleveland Bar Assn -1301 E 9th
-Ste BU620 -Cleveland 44114 **Fx:**696-2413

(513) 695-1732 ..**Duvelius,** Carolyn A '88 Warren Cnty Probate-Juv Ct
-500 Justice Dr -Lebanon 45036 **Fx:**695-2948

(216) 696-7600 ..**Duvin Cahn & Hutton** -1301 E 9th -20th Fl Erievw Twr
-Cleveland 44114 **Fx:**696-2038

(440) 395-9599 ..**Duvin,** Deborah C '90 Progressive Ins Co -747 Alpha Dr -PLG-A31
-Highland Heights 44143

(216) 696-7600 ..**Duvin,** Robert P '63 (Duvin C&H) -1301 E 9th -20th Fl Erievw Twr
-Cleveland 44114 **Fx:**696-2038

(937) 297-1154 ..**Duwel,** David M '73 (%D Duwel & Assoc) -2310 Far Hills Av -Ste 5
-Dayton 45419 **Fx:**297-1152

(513) 421-2700 ..**Duwel,** David M '73 (Stethem & D) -11177 Reading Rd
-Cincinnati 45241 **Fx:**763-7694

(937) 297-1154 ..**Duwel,** Kyle C '02 %D Duwel & Assoc -2310 Far Hills Av -Ste 5
-Dayton 45419 **Fx:**297-1152

(937) 297-1154 ..**Duwel,** Todd T '98 %D Duwel & Assoc -2310 Far Hills Av -Ste 5
-Dayton 45419 **Fx:**297-1152
Dvorak, Beth L '93 -(Address Unavailable)

(574) 371-8040 ..**Dvorak,** David C '91 Zimmer,Inc -345 E Main -Warsaw, IN 46580

(216) 736-7224 ..**Dvorin,** David M '97 %Kohrman J&K PLL -1375 E 9th
-One Cleve Ctr 20th Fl -Cleveland 44114 **Fx:**621-6536

(513) 287-2643 ..**Dwight,** George II '93 Cinergy Corp -139 E 4th -25 Atrium II
-Bx960 -Cincinnati 45201

(440) 352-3391 ..**Dworken & Bernstein Co,LPA** -60 S Park Pl -Painesville 44077
Fx:352-3469

(440) 352-3391 ..**Dworken,** Marvin P '59 (Dworken & B Co,LPA) -60 S Park Pl
-Painesville 44077 **Fx:**352-3469

(419) 471-1489 ..**Dworkin,** David M '92 UAW Legal Srvcs -3360 W Laskey Rd
-Toledo 43606 **Fx:**471-0498

(614) 462-5400 ..**Dyas,** Charles R Jr. '86 OfCnsl Kegler BH&R -65 E State
-Ste 1800 -Columbus 43215 **Fx:**464-2634

(937) 461-1142 ..**Dybvig,** Roger S '60 Dybvig B D -22 Green -Dayton 45402

(216) 623-0150 ..**Dyczek,** Carl J '80 (Roetzel & A,LPA) -1375 E 9th
-One Cleve Ctr 9th Fl -Cleveland 44114 **Fx:**623-0134

(614) 461-1100 ..**Dye,** David A '85 (Swedlow BLL&D Co,LPA) -10 W Broad
-Ste 2400 -Columbus 43215 **Fx:**461-8178

(330) 656-3799 ..**Dye,** Edward R '73 -6021 Willow Lk Dr -Hudson 44236

(614) 927-9059 ..**Dye,** James L Jr. '93 -Bx161 -Pickerington 43147

(614) 224-7298 ..**Dye,** Lewis T '04 -555 S 3rd -Columbus 43215

(614) 224-7298 ..**Dye,** Lewis W '72 -555 S 3rd -Columbus 43215

(740) 962-4776 ..**Dye,** Ralph D Jr. '58 -Bx178 -McConnelsville 43756

(740) 454-8585 ..**Dye,** Scott A '02 %Graham M&R Co,LPA -11 N 4th -Bx340
-Zanesville 43702

(937) 223-8888 ..**Dyer Garofalo Mann & Schultz** -131 N Ludlow -Ste 1400
-Dayton 45402 **Fx:**223-0127

(937) 222-2500 ..**Dyer,** James A '80 (Sebaly S&D) -1900 Kettering Twr
-Dayton 45423 **Fx:**222-6554

(330) 673-8336 ..**Dyer,** James D '76 -123 N Water -Kent 44240

(216) 514-3127 ..**Dyer,** John J III '93 Competitive Title -23611 Chagrin Blvd -Ste 300
-Beachwood 44122

(937) 223-8888 ..**Dyer,** Michael E '80 (Dyer GM&S) -131 N Ludlow -Ste 1400
-Dayton 45402 **Fx:**223-0127

(216) 443-8612 ..**Dyke,** John T '01 Cuyahoga Cnty Ct Cmmn Pleas -1200 Ontario
-Justice Ctr 11th Fl -Cleveland 44113

(216) 443-7295 ..**Dyke,** Lorianne E '98 Cuyahoga Cnty Pub Def -1849 Prospect Av
-Ste 222 -Cleveland 44115

(614) 464-6400 ..**Dykes,** Robert G '81 (Vorys SS&P LLP) -52 E Gay -Bx1008
-Columbus 43216 **Fx:**464-6350

(330) 456-8341 ..**Dylewski,** Faith R '02 %Black MS&A,LPA -220 Market Av S
-Ste 1000 -Canton 44702 **Fx:**456-5756

(740) 283-3300 ..**Dylewski,** Mary C '92 Jefferson Cnty Job & Fam Srvcs -125 S 5th
-Bx367 -Steubenville 43952

(316) 676-8649 ..**Dymarkowski,** Daniel W '74 Raytheon Aircraft -Bx85
-Wichita, KS 67201

(419) 882-7100 ..**Dymarkowski,** Douglas A '94 %Lydy & M,Ltd
-4930 Holland Sylvania Rd -Sylvania 43560 **Fx:**882-1120

(440) 488-0287 ..**Dynes,** Brandon D '97 -2603 Riverside Dr -Ste 200
-Painesville 44077

(937) 692-5712 ..**Dynes,** Craig A '79 CA Dynes LLC -2840 Alt State Route 49N
-Ste B -Bx250 -Arcanum 45304

(216) 583-4884 ..**Dysert,** David C '90 Ernst & Young LLP -925 Euclid Av -Ste 1300
-Cleveland 44115

(614) 365-5575 ..**Dysert,** Jonita W '95 Columbus Pub Schls -420 E 19th Av
-Columbus 43201

(937) 667-4481 ..**Dysinger Stewart & Downing** -249 S Garber Dr -Tipp City 45371
Fx:667-5393

(937) 667-4481 ..**Dysinger,** Thomas E '77 (Dysinger S&D) -249 S Garber Dr
-Tipp City 45371 **Fx:**667-5393

(440) 461-9000 ..**Dyson Schmidlin & Foulds Co,LPA** -5843 Mayfld Rd
-Mayfield Heights 44124

(216) 621-5300 ..**Dzenitis,** Paul A '03 (Buckingham D&B,LLP) -1375 E 9th
-Ste 1700 -Cleveland 44114 **Fx:**621-5440

(513) 946-3000 ..**Dziech,** Robert W '96 Hamilton Cnty Pros -230 E 9th
-Cincinnati 45202 **Fx:**946-3017

(248) 754-0150 ..**Dziegielewski,** Gregory '75 BorgWarner Inc -3800 Automation Av
-Ste 100 -Auburn Hills, MI 48326

(419) 255-7300 ..**Dzienny,** Michael A '86 (Dzienny & Assoc,LPA) -500 Mad Av
-Ste 200 -Toledo 43604

(330) 860-6205 ..**Dziewisz,** John J '92 Babcock & Wilcox Co -20 S Van Buren Av
-Barberton 44203

(330) 343-6797 ..**Dzigiel,** Judith E '99 Municipal Ct -166 E High Av
-New Philadelphia 44663

(216) 694-4356 ..**Dzik,** Robert B '73 Hyatt Leg Plans Inc -1111 Superior Av
-Cleveland 44114

(740) 446-8575 ..**Eachus,** Michael N '03 %Eachus & F -431 2nd Av -Bx351
-Gallipolis 45631

(740) 446-8575 ..**Eachus,** William N '74 (Eachus & F) -431 2nd Av -Bx351
-Gallipolis 45631

(513) 977-8200 ..**Eagen,** Michael D '74 (Dinsmore & S LLP) -255 E 5th -Ste 1900
-Cincinnati 45202 **Fx:**977-8141

(513) 621-7600 ..**Eagen,** Thomas L Jr. '70 (Eagen W&H Co,LPA)
-2337 Victory Pkwy -Cincinnati 45206 **Fx:**455-8246

(513) 621-7600 ..**Eagen Wykoff & Healy Co,LPA** -2337 Victory Pkwy
-Cincinnati 45206 **Fx:**455-8246

(440) 942-8650 ..**Eager,** David T '01 WRG Srvcs,Inc -38585 Apollo Pkwy
-Willoughby 44094 **Fx:**954-3670

(703) 993-8054 ..**Eagle,** Steven Jay '76 George Mason Univ -3301 N Fairfax Dr
-Arlington, VA 22201

(937) 743-2545 ..**Eagle,** Thomas G '86 TG Eagle Co,LPA -3386 N State Route 123
-Lebanon 45036 **Fx:**704-9826

(616) 336-6537 ..**Eagle,** Timothy E '87 Varnum, RS&H LLP -Bx352
-Grand Rapids, MI 49501

(614) 565-2609 ..**Eagleson,** Freeman T III '91 -601 S High -Lwr Level
-Columbus 43215

(614) 228-6148 ..**Eakins,** Alan D '86 S Jaffy & Assoc Co,LPA -306 E Gay
-Columbus 43215 **Fx:**228-6140

(330) 650-0419 ..**Ealy,** Stephen T '90 -25 Milford Dr -Ste 2 -Hudson 44236

(440) 286-1907 ..**Eardley,** David J '57 -109 Court -Chardon 44024 **Fx:**286-4391

(937) 335-2928 ..**Earhart,** Scott W '95 %Earhart Petroleum,Inc -1494 Lytle Rd
-Bx39 -Troy 45373

(740) 349-7839 ..**Earl,** Kathleen A '81 K Ennen-Giwa -33 W Main -Ste 106 -Newark
43055
Earl, Lillian B '92 -3084 Berkshire Rd -Cleveland Heights 44118

(614) 464-2392 ..**Earl,** Ted L '60 (Earl WA&D,LPA) -136 W Mound
-Columbus 43215 **Fx:**464-0754

(614) 464-2392 ..**Earl Warburton Adams & Davis,LPA** -136 W Mound
-Columbus 43215 **Fx:**464-0754

(330) 296-8186 ..**Earle,** Paul M '84 -271 W Riddle Av -Ravenna 44266

(419) 624-3000 ..**Earle,** Vicki L '01 %Murray & M Co,LPA -111 E Shoreline Dr -Bx19
-Sandusky 44871

(937) 456-4104 ..**Earley,** Dirk E '00 (Earley & E) -112 N Barron -Bx58 -Eaton 45320

(937) 456-4104 ..**Earley,** George J '64 (Earley & E) -112 N Barron -Bx58
-Eaton 45320

(216) 443-7800 ..**Earley,** Michelle D '99 Cuyahoga Cnty Pros -1200 Ontario -8th Fl
-Cleveland 44113 **Fx:**698-2270

(513) 369-0222 ..**Earls,** William T Jr. '71 Earls Agency -550 E 4th -Cincinnati 45202
Early, Emily N '04 -(Address Unavailable)

(937) 222-2500 ..**Early,** Katherine L '02 %Sebaly S&D -1900 Kettering Twr
-Dayton 45423 **Fx:**222-6554

(303) 316-5644 ..**Early,** Thomas A '80 Janus -100 Fillmore -Denver, CO 80206

(330) 675-2426 ..**Earnhart,** Jason C '99 %Trumbull Cnty Pros -160 High NW
-Warren 44481

(216) 348-5400 ..**Earp,** Robert H III '96 (McDonald H Co,LPA) -600 Superior Av E
-Ste 2100 -Cleveland 44114 **Fx:**348-5474

(770) 248-3682 ..**Easley,** Leesa M '89 World Fncl Grp Inc -11315 Johns Creek Pkwy
-Duluth, GA 30097
Easley, Sue A '88 -5961 Torrey Pines Av -Westerville 43082

(614) 577-9970 ..**Eastep,** Kipley M '92 S Ames & Assoc -6100 Channingway Blvd
-Ste 301 -Columbus 43232

(330) 643-2788 ..**Easter,** Felicia '01 Summit Cnty Pros-Crim -53 Univ Av -7th Fl
-Akron 44308 **Fx:**643-8277

(937) 865-6800 ..**Easter,** Suzanne M '95 Lexis/Nexis -Bx933 -Dayton 45401

(614) 210-1840 ..**Easterday,** Jeffrey A '83 (Barrett EC&E LLP) -7269 Sawmill Rd
-Dublin 43016 **Fx:**210-1841

(419) 227-0061 ..**Easterday,** Jennifer S '00 OH Nrthrn Univ Pettit Cllg of Law
-306 N Main -Leg Clinic -Lima 45801 **Fx:**227-1826

(419) 259-6717 ..**Easterwood,** Cynthia A '89 Natl City Bank -Bx1688 -Toledo 43603

(614) 365-2700 ..**Eastham,** Ryan G '97 %Squire S&D LLP -41 S High
-1300 Huntngtn Ctr -Columbus 43215 **Fx:**365-2499

(614) 752-1300 ..**Eastman,** Brian J '89 OH Dept Rehab & Correction -968 Fwy Dr N
-Columbus 43229

(330) 745-2175 ..**Eastman,** David R '88 (Lombardi HHC&E) -2745 Nesbitt Av
-Akron 44319

(330) 745-2175 ..**Eastman,** Fred E '54 OfCnsl Lombardi HHC&E -2745 Nesbitt Av
-Akron 44319

(216) 766-5449 ..**Eastman,** Richard M '88 Genesis Prof Liability Underwriters
-25550 Chagrin Blvd -Ste 300 -Beachwood 44122

(419) 241-6000 ..**Eastman & Smith Ltd** -1 Seagate -24th Fl -Bx10032 -Toledo
43699 **Fx:**247-1777

(202) 626-6600 ..**Easton,** Amy L '98 %Squire S&D LLP -1201 Penn Av NW -Ste 500
-Washington, DC 20004

(513) 352-3794 ..**Eatmon,** Kristen A '01 Law Dept -801 Plum -Rm 214
-Cincinnati 45202 **Fx:**352-1515

(614) 462-3973 ..**Eaton,** Douglas W '92 10th Dist Ct of Appls -373 S High -24th Fl
-Columbus 43215

(740) 380-0332 ..**Eaton,** Jeffrey W '87 -974 W Hunter -Logan 43138

(419) 625-3957 ..**Eaton,** Melissa L '93 -3510 South Av -Sandusky 44870

(513) 581-0541 ..**Eaton,** Michael D '96 -318 Canyon Dr S -Columbus 43214

(513) 977-8200 ..**Eaton,** Shana N '04 %Dinsmore & S LLP -255 E 5th -Ste 1900
-Cincinnati 45202 **Fx:**977-8141

(513) 946-3800 ..**Eaves,** Kacy C '97 %Hamilton Cnty Pub Def -230 E 9th -3rd Fl
-Cincinnati 45202 **Fx:**946-3707

(502) 589-4200 ..**Eaves,** Mary H '83 Greenebaum D&M PLLC -101 S 5th -Ste 3300
-Louisville, KY 40202

(614) 868-0009 ..**Ebbeskotte,** Mark J '89 %Hallowes A&H -6445 E Lvngstn Av -Reynoldsburg 43068 Fx:868-0029

(937) 586-3100 ..**Ebenger,** Joseph R '77 (ES Gallon & Assoc) -40 W 4th -22nd Fl -Dayton 45402 Fx:586-3100

(614) 464-0082 ..**Eberhart,** Robert L '64 (Johrendt C&E) -471 E Broad -Ste 800 -Columbus 43215

(513) 576-5952 ..**Eberle,** Thomas F '80 Structural Dynamics Research Corp -2000 Eastman Dr -Milford 45150

(513) 533-9898 ..**Eberly,** David A '96 (Eberly MH,LLC) -3700 Eastern Av -Cincinnati 45226

(419) 448-0204 ..**Eberly,** Dennis J '85 (Eberly & E) -180 S Wshngtn -Tiffin 44883 Fx:448-8480

(513) 533-9898 ..**Eberly McMahon Hochscheid,LLC** -3700 Eastern Av -Cincinnati 45226

(513) 723-4000 ..**Eberly,** Stephen S '73 (Vorys SS&P LLP) -221 E 4th -Ste 2000 Atrium Two -Bx0236 -Cincinnati 45201 Fx:723-4056

(419) 448-0204 ..**Eberly,** Thomas J '65 (Eberly & E) -180 S Wshngtn -Tiffin 44883 Fx:448-8480

(937) 865-4637 ..**Ebersole,** John M '00 US DOE -1 Mound Rd -Miamisburg 45342

(740) 383-1151 ..**Ebert,** Douglas E '76 (Harris & E) -136 S Main -Marion 43302

(216) 566-8200 ..**Ebert,** Gary A '78 (Seeley S&E Co LPA) -600 Superior Av E -800 Bank One Ctr -Cleveland 44114 Fx:566-0213

(513) 732-6033 ..**Eberwein,** Thomas C '73 Southern Ohio Fabricators -2565 Batavia Wllmsbrg Pike -Batavia 45103

(843) 856-5234 ..**Eble,** Timothy E '81 (T Eble,PA) -Bx2313 -Mt Pleasant, SC 29465

(614) 221-3155 ..**Eblin,** Robert L '91 (Bailey C LLC) -10 W Broad -Columbus 43215 Fx:221-0479

(513) 455-7600 ..**Ebling,** Gretchen R '87 Greenebaum D&M PLLC -255 E 5th -2800 Chemed Ctr -Cincinnati 45202 Fx:455-8500

(513) 455-7600 ..**Ebling,** Louis K '95 Greenebaum D&M PLLC -255 E 5th -2800 Chemed Ctr -Cincinnati 45202 Fx:455-8500

(614) 224-6011 ..**Ebner,** Cynthia L '93 Ebner Law Ofc -3455 E Broad -Columbus 43213

(901) 495-1283 ..**Ebner,** Daniel S '04 Hon SH Mays Jr USDC -167 N Main -1111 Fed Bldg -Memphis, TN 38103

(513) 621-2888 ..**Ebner,** Drake W '73 (Ebner & R LLP) -1014 Vine -1900 Kroger Bldg -Cincinnati 45202

(513) 241-2324 ..**Eby,** Clyde R II '68 %Wood H&E LLP -441 Vine -Ste 2700 -Cincinnati 45202 Fx:421-7269

(513) 721-5525 ..**Eby,** Gary M '76 OfCnsl Manley B -225 W Court -Cincinnati 45202 Fx:721-4268

(614) 462-5875 ..**Eby,** James E '83 Franklin Cnty CSEA -80 E Fulton -Columbus 43215

(440) 350-2100 ..**Echols,** Kelly A '03 Lake Cnty Ct of Common Pleas -47 N Park Pl -Painesville 44077

(216) 443-8868 ..**Echols,** Sharon A '91 Cuyahoga Cnty Pros -1 Lakeside Av -Rm 49 -Cleveland 44115 Fx:443-3777

(614) 221-6766 ..**Eck,** Alice E '77 Firstlink -195 N Grant Av -Columbus 43215

(614) 228-4546 ..**Eck,** Franklin E Jr. '89 %Shuler P&B,LPA -145 E Rich -Ste 400 -Columbus 43215

Eck, Jamie R '04 -(Address Unavailable)

(216) 621-0200 ..**Eckart,** Dennis E '74 (Baker & H LLP) -1900 E 9th -Ste 3200 -Cleveland 44114 Fx:696-0740

(330) 785-9155 ..**Eckberg,** Barbara S '90 -Bx27171 -Akron 44319

(419) 874-9675 ..**Eckel,** Paul C '91 Adecco Employment Srvcs -845 Commerce Dr -Ste A -Perrysburg 43551

(614) 228-1541 ..**Eckelberry,** Rodger L '99 %Baker & H LLP -65 E State -Ste 2100 -Columbus 43215 Fx:462-2616

Eckels, Christopher R '95 -6895 Starfire Dr -Reynoldsburg 43068

(614) 221-7663 ..**Ecker,** Deborah P '80 %Luper N&L,LPA -50 W Broad -1200 LeVeque Twr -Columbus 43215 Fx:464-2425

(513) 651-6800 ..**Ecker,** Karen M '92 Cnsl Frost BT LLC -201 E 5th -2200 PNC Ctr -Cincinnati 45202 Fx:651-6981

(513) 831-1564 ..**Eckerson,** Mark D '77 -1 Crestvw Dr -Milford 45150

(513) 662-1818 ..**Eckert,** Charles A '55 OfCnsl Eckert E&E -3662 Glenmore Av -Bx11027 -Cincinnati 45211

(937) 748-5162 ..**Eckert & Eckert, Co LPA** -15 E Mill -Springboro 45066 Fx:748-5163

(740) 321-7173 ..**Eckert,** Inger H '96 Owens Corning -2790 Columbus Rd -Granville 43023

(513) 662-1818 ..**Eckert,** John C '92 (Eckert E&E) -3662 Glenmore Av -Bx11027 -Cincinnati 45211

(850) 222-7500 ..**Eckert,** Michael C '96 %Hopping G&S,PA -123 S Calhoun -Bx6526 -Tallahassee, FL 32314 Fx:224-8551

(330) 384-5289 ..**Eckert,** Phillip W '82 FirstEnergy Corp -76 S Main -Akron 44308

(937) 748-5162 ..**Eckert,** Roger C '91 (Eckert & E, Co LPA) -15 E Mill -Springboro 45066 Fx:748-5163

Eckert, Valerie L '00 -628 Hollendale Dr -Kettering 45429

(614) 248-5700 ..**Eckhart,** Anne E '93 Bank One Corp -1111 Polaris Pkwy -Ste 4P -Columbus 43271

(614) 461-0984 ..**Eckhart,** Henry W '58 -50 W Broad -Ste 2117 -Columbus 43215 Fx:221-7401

(937) 293-2392 ..**Eckhart,** Michael R '73 -580 Lincoln Park -Ste 244 -Dayton 45429

(312) 984-2162 ..**Eckhause,** Melissa M '00 %McDermott W&E -227 W Monroe -Chicago, IL 60606 Fx:984-7700

(330) 493-4877 ..**Eckinger,** Robert W '95 Eckinger Law Ofc,Ltd -1201 30th NW -Ste 101B -Canton 44709

(716) 473-3333 ..**Eckl,** James J '88 Cobblestone Capital -140 Allens Crk Rd -Rochester, NY 14618

(513) 421-4420 ..**Eckner,** Shannon F '03 %P Bossin Co,LPA -36 E 4th -Ste 1210 -Cincinnati 45202

(440) 329-5389 ..**Eckstein,** Ann C '97 Lorain Cnty Pros -225 Court -3rd Fl -Elyria 44035

(440) 774-4382 ..**Eckstein,** Barry S '71 -5 W Cllg -Bx387 -Oberlin 44074

(216) 621-3346 ..**Eckstein,** Georgia L '89 %Kendis & Assoc Co,LPA -614 Superior Av W -15th Fl Rckfllr Bldg -Cleveland 44113 Fx:621-3672

Eckstein, Scott M '98 -Bx39277 -North Ridgeville 44039

(740) 335-0888 ..**Eckstein,** Steven H '86 Fayette Cnty Pros -110 E Court -1st Fl -Washington Court House 43160

(330) 744-5029 ..**Economus,** Basil G '99 (Economus & E) -26 Market -Ste 508 -Youngstown 44503

(330) 468-3990 ..**Economus,** Dale S '77 -61 W Aurora Rd -Northfield 44067

(330) 744-5029 ..**Economus,** George C '64 (Economus & E) -26 Market -Ste 508 -Youngstown 44503

(216) 621-1500 ..**Eddington,** Isaac J '00 %Kehoe & Assoc LLP -1940 E 6th -900 Baker Bldg -Cleveland 44114 Fx:621-1551

(734) 483-9551 ..**Eddins,** Elizabeth W '93 (E Eddins,PLLC) -32 N Wshngtn -Ste 14 -Ypsilanti, MI 48197

Eddy, E R II '01 -620 Atalan Trl -Lima 45805

(513) 528-2850 ..**Eddy,** Marilyn M '88 -431 Ohio Pike -Ste 110 -Cincinnati 45255 Fx:528-8400

(216) 241-5310 ..**Eddy,** Robert H III '79 (Gallagher SF&N) -1501 Euclid Av -6th Fl -Cleveland 44115 Fx:241-1608

Eddy, Toni L '00 -280 Yocatangee Pkwy -Chillicothe 45601

(614) 227-2000 ..**Edelman,** Joyce D '83 (Porter WM&A LLP) -41 S High -Columbus 43215 Fx:227-2100

(216) 378-9905 ..**Edelman,** Mark S '86 (McGlinchey S PLLC) -25550 Chagrin Blvd -Ste 406 -Cleveland 44122 Fx:378-9910

(216) 522-4914 ..**Edelstein,** Joseph '84 SSA/OHA -1350 Euclid Av -7th Fl -Cleveland 44115

(937) 294-5800 ..**Edelstein,** Kimberly A '02 %LJ White -2533 Far Hills Av -2nd Fl -Dayton 45419 Fx:298-1503

(216) 514-4981 ..**Edelstein,** Robert '83 -23875 Commerce Pk Rd -Ste 105 -Beachwood 44122

(216) 447-8800 ..**Eder,** James R '89 Eder & Assoc Co,LPA -7100 E Plsnt Vlly Rd -Ste 155 -Independence 44131

(513) 851-3337 ..**Eder,** Robert F '93 -10236 Hmltn Av -Cincinnati 45231

(513) 852-6025 ..**Eder,** William H Jr. '63 (Wood & L LLP) -600 Vine -Ste 2500 -Cincinnati 45202 Fx:852-6087

(740) 689-3000 ..**Edgar,** Michelle L '00 %JA Price,LPA -126 E Chestnut -Lancaster 43130 Fx:689-3506

(916) 446-4656 ..**Edgar,** Peter S '80 Shaw Yoder,Inc -1414 K -Ste 320 -Sacramento, CA 95814

(216) 689-3894 ..**Edgehouse,** Gregory J '79 KeyBank NA -127 Pub Sq -2nd Fl, OH-01-27-0200 -Cleveland 44114

(650) 349-2727 ..**Edington,** Robert M '87 Webcor Builders -951 Mariners Isl Blvd -7th flr -San Mateo, CA 94404

(216) 991-2295 ..**Edison,** Glenn '83 Sixth Man LLC -22175 Rye Rd -Shaker Heights 44122

(812) 934-7500 ..**Edison,** Sheri H '83 Cnsl Hillenbrand Industries,Inc -1 Batesvll Blvd -Batesville, IN 47006 Fx:934-7613

(440) 323-8004 ..**Edleman,** Jeffrey G '94 -401 Broad -Ste 203 -Elyria 44035

Edminster, Joseph A '74 -2785 Goldleaf Dr -Akron 44333

(330) 376-4444 ..**Edminister,** Michael E '87 (Edminister & Assoc) -159 S Main -Akron 44308

(216) 523-5606 ..**Edmister,** Richard R '67 Washington Grp Intl Inc -1500 W 3rd -Cleveland 44113

(513) 632-5321 ..**Edmiston,** James P '75 -119 E Court -Ste 412 -Cincinnati 45202

Edmiston, Parker E '91 -110 E Pchtree -Scottsboro, AL 35768

(513) 721-5151 ..**Edmiston,** Robert G '82 R Edmiston,LLC -105 E 4th -4th Fl -Cincinnati 45202 Fx:621-9285

(330) 725-5297 ..**Edmonds,** Marie M '79 M Edmonds Co,LPA -807 E Wshngtn -Ste 200 -Medina 44256

(614) 227-2000 ..**Edmund,** Robert W '98 %Porter WM&A LLP -41 S High -Columbus 43215 Fx:227-2100

(513) 785-7184 ..**Edmunds,** Albert V '73 Al Edmunds -345 High -7th Fl -Hamilton 45011

(330) 225-2508 ..**Edmunds,** James Timothy '82 -1080 Substation Rd -Brunswick 44212

(937) 255-5270 ..**Edsall,** Richard L '82 AFMCLO/JANS -1864 4th -Rm 130A -Wright Patterson AFB 45433

(513) 732-7313 ..**Edwards,** Allan Lee '87 Clermont Cnty Pros -123 N 3rd -Batavia 45103

(216) 443-6350 ..**Edwards,** Amanda B '01 %8th Dist Ct of Appls -1 Lakeside Av -#202 -Cleveland 44113 Fx:443-2044

(606) 329-2929 ..**Edwards,** Carl D Jr. '89 (VanAntwerp MJ&E) -1544 Wnchstr Av -5th Fl -Bx1111 -Ashland, KY 41105

(740) 264-6960 ..**Edwards,** Charles W '51 -4204 Sunset Blvd -Steubenville 43952

(614) 469-3223 ..**Edwards,** Daniel F '92 (Thompson H LLP) -10 W Broad -Ste 700 -Columbus 43215 Fx:469-3361

(412) 488-8600 ..**Edwards,** Deborah L '75 Agnew Moyer Smith,Inc -3700 S Water -Ste 300 -Pittsburgh, PA 15203 Fx:488-8647

(614) 785-9958 ..**Edwards,** Delena '87 (D Edwards Co,LPA) -2021 E Dublin Granvll Rd -Ste 173 -Columbus 43229 Fx:785-9508

(740) 687-5803 ..**Edwards,** James A '76 (Edwards & E) -136 E Main -Lancaster 43130 Fx:687-5805

(614) 466-4328 ..**Edwards,** Jennifer L '00 Atty Gen -150 E Gay -Columbus 43215 Fx:995-0266

(614) 861-1916 ..**Edwards,** John B '00 -990 Gray -Pickerington 43147

(650) 739-3939 ..**Edwards,** John W II '74 (Jones DR&P) -2882 Sand Hill Rd -Ste 240 -Menlo Park, CA 94025

(740) 687-5803 ..**Edwards,** Judith L '78 (Edwards & E) -136 E Main -Lancaster 43130 Fx:687-5805

(614) 466-3379 ..**Edwards,** Judith T '97 Dept of Dvlpmnt -77 S High -Columbus 43215

(740) 532-4554 ..**Edwards Klein Anderson & Shope Co LPA** -211 Center -Ironton 45638

(212) 326-3939 ..**Edwards,** Lisa S '97 Jones D -222 E 41st -4th Fl -New York, NY 10017 Fx:755-7306

(216) 443-8868 ..**Edwards,** Michelle C '92 Cuyahoga Cnty Pros -1 Lakeside Av -Rm 49 -Cleveland 44115 Fx:443-3777

(216) 348-5400 ..**Edwards,** Paul N '79 (McDonald H Co,LPA) -600 Superior Av E -Ste 2100 -Cleveland 44114 Fx:348-5474

(614) 221-1306 ..**Edwards,** Robert D '00 %J Alden -1 E Lvngstn Av -Columbus 43215 Fx:221-3551

(513) 556-1590 ..**Edwards,** Ruth M '74 Univ of Cincinnati -2624 Clifton Av -#207 -Cincinnati 45221

(513) 381-2838 ..**Edwards,** Ryan C '02 %Taft S&H LLP -425 Walnut -Ste 1800 -Cincinnati 45202 Fx:381-0205

Edwards, Sally M '78 -4070 Stewartsvll Rd -Williamstown, KY 41097

(614) 875-6661 ..**Edwards,** Steve J '79 -4030 Bway -Grove City 43123

(513) 721-5151 ..**Edwards,** Tawanda J '00 %Katz G&N,LLP -105 E 4th -4th Fl -Cincinnati 45202 Fx:621-9285

(740) 353-1509 ..**Edwards,** Wallace E '82 -538 6th -Portsmouth 45662

(614) 462-3555 ..**Edwards**, Warren T '01 Franklin Cnty Pros -373 S High
-Columbus 43215

(216) 931-6000 ..**Edwards**, William A '62 (Ulmer & B LLP) -1300 E 9th
-Ste 900 Penton Media Bldg -Cleveland 44114 **Fx:**931-6001

(216) 931-6000 ..**Edwards**, William D '94 (Ulmer & B LLP) -1300 E 9th -Ste
900 Penton Media Bldg -Cleveland 44114 **Fx:**931-6001

(216) 622-3651 ..**Edwards**, William J '69 US Atty -801 W Superior -Ste 400
-Cleveland 44113 **Fx:**622-3370

(614) 224-8166 ..**Edwards**, William J '85 Twyford & D -495 S High -Ste 100
-Columbus 43215

Edwards-Smith, Karen L '81 -Bx23752 -Chagrin Falls 44023

(419) 244-7655 ..**Effler**, Fanny P II '79 -2830 Collingwood Blvd -Toledo 43610

(513) 785-5880 ..**Effler**, Julie K '98 Butler Cnty CSEA -315 High -7th Fl
-Hamilton 45011

(330) 456-8341 ..**Efremoff**, Anthony E '63 (Black MS&A,LPA) -220 Market Av S
-Ste 1000 -Canton 44702 **Fx:**456-5756

(330) 451-7453 ..**Efremoff**, Sarah A '63 Stark Cnty Fam Ct -110 Central Plz S
-Canton 44702

(614) 462-3194 ..**Efta**, Thomas J '87 %Franklin Cnty Pub Def -373 S High -12th Fl
-Columbus 43215

(614) 227-2000 ..**Eftimoff**, Katerina M '94 %Porter WM&A LLP -41 S High
-Columbus 43215 **Fx:**227-2100

(614) 262-3800 ..**Egan**, Daniel S '87 APSI -4110 N High SE -Columbus 43214

(410) 786-1007 ..**Egan**, Lynn E '99 US Dept of Hlth & Human Srvcs
-7500 Secuity Blvd -C2-05-23 -Baltimore, MD 21244

(216) 621-0200 ..**Egan**, Patrick J '01 %Baker & H LLP -1900 E 9th -Ste 3200
-Cleveland 44114 **Fx:**696-0740

Egbers, Mary E '94 -3029 Mapleleaf Av -Cincinnati 45213

(419) 448-4444 ..**Egbert**, Kenneth H Jr. '89 Seneca Cnty Pros -71 S Wshngtn
-Ste E -Bx667 -Tiffin 44883 **Fx:**448-7911

(614) 241-5550 ..**Egelhoff**, Rebecca L '03 %Brunner Law Firm Co,LPA
-545 E Town -Columbus 43215 **Fx:**241-5551

(440) 250-4400 ..**Egert Mayer & Hack** -1991 Crocker Rd -#550 -Westlake 44145

(419) 626-3871 ..**Egger**, Robert C '70 -189 E Market -Sandusky 44870

(734) 794-7100 ..**Eggertsen**, John H '75 -6270 Munger Rd -Ypsilanti, MI 48197
Fx:794-7104

(614) 221-5216 ..**Eggspuehler**, Jay B '90 (Wiles BB&B Co,LPA) -300 Spruce -1st Fl
-Columbus 43215 **Fx:**221-5692

(412) 263-3607 ..**Egleston**, Drew D '74 LTV Copperweld -Four Gtwy Ctr -22nd Fl
-Pittsburgh, PA 15222

(440) 835-0600 ..**Egleston**, James D '94 %Waldheger C,LPA -1991 Crocker Rd
-Ste 550 -Westlake 44145 **Fx:**835-1511

(937) 332-9300 ..**Ehinger**, Mark A '03 (Bucio & E,LLP) -10 N Market -Troy 45373
Fx:339-6549

(260) 423-9551 ..**Ehinger**, Ronald J '83 (Barrett & M LLP) -215 E Berry -Bx2263
-Fort Wayne, IN 46801 **Fx:**423-8920

(508) 549-6717 ..**Ehle**, Jay S '75 Invensys -33 Cmmrcial -B52-2Z -Foxboro,
MA 02035

(614) 464-6400 ..**Ehler**, Anthony L '87 (Vorys SS&P LLP) -52 E Gay -Bx1008
-Columbus 43216 **Fx:**464-6350

(216) 447-6297 ..**Ehlers**, Kristin M '94 Noveon,Inc -9911 Brecksvll Rd
-Cleveland 44141

(216) 443-3653 ..**Ehrbar**, Jeffrey J '97 Cuyahoga Cnty Pub Def -1849 Prospect Av
-Ste 222 -Cleveland 44115

Ehrbar, Kurt F '95 -3229 W 139th -Cleveland 44111

(914) 594-4495 ..**Ehren**, Judith A '96 NY Medical Cllg - Registrars Ofc
-Sunshine Cottage -Valhalla, NY 10595

(614) 920-4302 ..**Ehrenborg**, Carie A '93 -7774 E Bowling Grn Ln NW
-Lancaster 43130

(216) 861-1070 ..**Ehrenreich**, Leonard '73 (Ehrenreich & Assoc) -526 Superior Av E
-1130 Leader Bldg -Cleveland 44114 **Fx:**861-1131

(614) 257-3892 ..**Ehrie**, Dennis B Jr. '76 OH State Univ -1492 E Broad
-Talbot Univ Hosp East -Columbus 43205

(614) 728-6724 ..**Ehrle**, Kathryn C '93 OH Dept Rehab & Correction -1050 Fwy Dr N
-Columbus 43229

(216) 443-9000 ..**Ehrman**, James W '74 (Porter WM&A LLP) -925 Euclid Av
-Ste 1700 -Cleveland 44115 **Fx:**443-9011

(440) 835-0600 ..**Ehrnfelt**, Walter F III '88 (Waldheger C,LPA) -1991 Crocker Rd
-Ste 550 -Westlake 44145 **Fx:**835-1511

(937) 224-3724 ..**Ehrstine**, William H '79 Montgomery Cnty Pub Def -117 S Main
-Ste 400 -Dayton 45422 **Fx:**225-3449

(216) 830-6830 ..**Eiber**, Keven D '90 (Brouse M) -1001 Lakeside Av -Ste 1600
-Cleveland 44114 **Fx:**830-6807

(513) 887-3474 ..**Eichel**, Daniel G '76 Butler Cnty Pros -315 High -11th Fl -Bx515
-Hamilton 45012

(937) 258-3668 ..**Eichelman**, Nate '03 %Fox & Assoc Co,LPA -1344 Woodman Dr
-Ste F -Dayton 45432 **Fx:**258-3098

(614) 798-1600 ..**Eichenberger**, Jerry A '75 (Eichenberger & Assoc)
-6099 Frantz Rd -Dublin 43017

(614) 866-9327 ..**Eichenberger**, Raymond L III '80 -7620 Slate Ridge Blvd
-Reynoldsburg 43068

(330) 535-0124 ..**Eicher**, Geoffrey L '89 (Semple & E) -One Cascade Plz -7th Fl
-Akron 44308

(513) 229-0230 ..**Eichner**, Claire S '99 Eichner Invstmnt Plnng -7577 Cntrl Pke Blvd
-Ste 206 -Mason 45040

(614) 436-4200 ..**Eichner**, Kevin F '89 1st Amer Title Ins Co -8425 Pulsar Pl
-Ste 210 -Columbus 43240

(937) 449-6810 ..**Eichner**, Roland F '58 (Porter WM&A LLP) -1 S Main -Ste 1600
-Dayton 45402 **Fx:**449-6820

Eichorn, Philip A '04 -(Address Unavailable)

(740) 454-2591 ..**Eickelberger**, Scott D '91 (Kincaid T&G) -50 N 4th -Bx1030
-Zanesville 43702 **Fx:**454-6975

(419) 321-6444 ..**Eickholt**, William C '68 Cline C&W Co,LPA -300 Mad Av
-Ste 1100 -Toledo 43604 **Fx:**321-6430

(614) 228-8400 ..**Eidelberg**, David L '88 %Ulmer & B LLP -88 E Broad -Ste 1600
-Columbus 43215 **Fx:**228-8561

(216) 687-1900 ..**Eidenmiller**, David K '00 Legal Aid -1223 W 6th -Cleveland 44113
Fx:687-0779

(216) 479-8500 ..**Eidner**, Robert J '82 (Squire S&D LLP) -127 Pub Sq
-4900 Key Twr -Cleveland 44114 **Fx:**479-8780

(248) 693-7409 ..**Eidy**, Sam A '89 LSC,Inc -766 W Clarkston Rd
-Lake Orion, MI 48362

(513) 474-0028 ..**Eifrig**, Eric W '03 -8070 Beechmont Av -Cincinnati 45255

(440) 352-6200 ..**Eiger**, Marley F '74 Legal Aid -8 N State -#300 -Painesville 44077
Fx:352-0015

Eiler, Janis E '97 -1120 Halpin Av -Cincinnati 45208

(937) 228-8183 ..**Eilerman**, Robert J '57 -120 W 2nd -Ste 1406 -Dayton 45402
Fx:228-7011

(513) 852-6079 ..**Eilers**, John W '67 (Wood & L LLP) -600 Vine -Ste 2500
-Cincinnati 45202 **Fx:**852-6087

(216) 566-5593 ..**Eilers**, S Stuart '63 (Thompson H LLP) -127 Pub Sq -3900 Key Ctr
-Cleveland 44114 **Fx:**566-5800

(301) 342-1839 ..**Einboden**, Gregory J '76 Dept of the Navy -Naval Air Warfare Ctr
-Aircraft Div, Bldg 435 -Patuxent River, MD 20670

(216) 696-3311 ..**Einhorn**, Theodore '97 %Kahn K -1301 E 9th -2600 Erievw Twr
-Cleveland 44114

(304) 343-2343 ..**Einreinhofer**, John '91 -184 Summers -Cox Morton Bldg Ste 308
-Charleston, WV 25301 **Fx:**343-2362

(571) 227-2994 ..**Einsel**, Henry L Jr. '81 Transportation Chief Cnsl Ofc -601 S 12th
-Arlington, VA 22202

(614) 764-1444 ..**Einstein**, Dianne D '97 Mowery & Y -425 Metro Pl N -Ste 420
-Dublin 43017 **Fx:**760-8654

Eippert, Tonya L '98 -10611 Castle Pines Circle -Concord 44077

(419) 241-6000 ..**Eischen**, Heidi N '01 %Eastman & S Ltd -1 Seagate -24th Fl
-Bx10032 -Toledo 43699 **Fx:**247-1777

(216) 687-0900 ..**Eisen**, Brian N '92 (Greene & E Co,LPA) -1300 E 9th -Ste 1801
-Cleveland 44114

(216) 589-0600 ..**Eisen**, Hermine G '81 (Eisen & W) -75 Pub Sq -Ste 1005
-Cleveland 44113

(216) 522-7800 ..**Eisen**, Saul '60 US Trustees Ofc -200 Pub Sq -Ste 3300
-Cleveland 44114 **Fx:**522-4988

(216) 363-4500 ..**Eisenberg**, Gregg A '97 (Benesch FC&A LLP) -200 Pub Sq
-Ste 2300 -Cleveland 44114 **Fx:**363-4588

(202) 371-2600 ..**Eisenberg**, Jason D '01 %Sterne KG&F,PLLC -1100 NY Av
-Washington, DC 20005

(216) 291-2400 ..**Eisenberg**, Richard D '63 (Zimmerman CE&M) -5001 Mayfld Rd
-Ste 105 -Cleveland 44124

(216) 621-0200 ..**Eisenberg**, Steven A '95 (Baker & H LLP) -1900 E 9th -Ste 3200
-Cleveland 44114 **Fx:**696-0740

(330) 833-8700 ..**Eisenbrei**, Barbara Waltz '88 -820 Tanglewood Dr NE
-Massilon 44646

(216) 566-0356 ..**Eisenhardt**, Howard A '82 Chrtr One Bank,FSB -1215 Superior Av
-Ste 245 -Cleveland 44114

(330) 764-8399 ..**Eisenhower**, Anne E '96 Medina Cnty Pros -72 Pub Sq
-Medina 44256

(614) 222-0540 ..**Eisenman**, Susan G '74 -338 S High -Columbus 43215

(216) 687-1900 ..**Eisenstat**, Carol S '96 Legal Aid -1223 W 6th -Cleveland 44113
Fx:687-0779

(614) 486-8601 ..**Eisnaugle**, Ralph W '60 -2001 Cmbrdg Blvd -Columbus 43221

(216) 781-3533 ..**Eisner**, Gary W '73 -3241 Superior Av -Cleveland 44114

(216) 621-0070 ..**Eisner**, Michael L '95 Friedman D&S Co,LPA -1370 Ontario
-Ste 600 -Cleveland 44113 **Fx:**621-4008

Ekelman, Beth A '91 -101 E 272nd -Euclid 44132

Ekers, Patricia A '04 -(Address Unavailable)

(216) 781-2600 ..**Eklund**, Claudia Rieth '79 (Lowe EW&M Co,LPA) -1660 W 2nd
-610 Skylight Ofc Twr -Cleveland 44113 **Fx:**781-2610

(216) 622-8200 ..**Eklund**, John J '80 (Calfee H&G LLP) -800 Superior Av -Ste 1400
-Cleveland 44114 **Fx:**241-0816

(216) 348-1700 ..**Eklund**, Paul D '78 (Davis & Y) -101 Prospect Av W -Ste 1700
-Cleveland 44115 **Fx:**621-0602

(330) 684-3598 ..**Ekonomon**, Adam M '89 JM Smucker Co -One Strwbrry Ln
-Orrville 44667

(614) 255-9256 ..**Elam**, John W '82 Columbus Partnership -41 S High -Ste 1200
-Columbus 43215

(614) 227-2000 ..**El-Amin**, Taheerah K '02 %Porter WM&A LLP -41 S High
-Columbus 43215 **Fx:**227-2100

(440) 248-7906 ..**Elbert**, Kevin P '97 %Mazanec R&R Co,LPA -34305 Solon Rd
-Ste 100 -Cleveland 44139 **Fx:**248-8861

(216) 292-8116 ..**Elconin**, Eugene '66 -23240 Chagrin Blvd -Ste 600
-Beachwood 44122

(440) 967-0521 ..**Elden**, John A '57 -15008 Holiday Dr -Ste A -Vermilion 44089

(937) 399-9709 ..**Elder**, Andrew H '85 (Elder R&E) -2233 N Limestone
-Springfield 45503

(419) 334-6222 ..**Elder**, Benjamin R '98 Sandusky Cnty Pros -100 N Park Av
-Fremont 43420

(419) 897-6500 ..**Elder**, Gregory R '86 (Barkan & R Ltd) -1701 WoodInds Dr
-Maumee 43537 **Fx:**897-6200

(937) 399-9709 ..**Elder**, John M '68 (Elder R&E) -2233 N Limestone
-Springfield 45503

(937) 399-9709 ..**Elder**, Kenneth M '78 (Elder R&E) -2233 N Limestone
-Springfield 45503

(937) 399-9709 ..**Elder Roberts & Elder** -2233 N Limestone -Springfield 45503

(937) 382-8747 ..**Elder**, Steven E '81 (S Elder Co,LPA) -731 Fife Av -Wilmington
45177

(614) 213-0216 ..**Eldridge**, Brenda L '93 Bank 1 Corp -1111 Polaris Pkwy
-Columbus 43240

(614) 221-2400 ..**Eldridge**, Matthew A '84 -233 S High -Ste 222 -Columbus 43215

(614) 825-3539 ..**Eley**, James R '90 (Eley Law Firm) -7870 Olentangy Rvr Rd
-Ste 311 -Columbus 43235 **Fx:**825-9590

(513) 946-3000 ..**Elfers**, Kathleen M '82 Hamilton Cnty Pros -230 E 9th
-Cincinnati 45202 **Fx:**946-3017

(216) 382-2500 ..**Elfvin & Besser** -4070 Mayfld Rd -Cleveland 44121 **Fx:**381-0250

(216) 382-2500 ..**Elfvin**, Bruce B '72 (Elfvin & B) -4070 Mayfld Rd -Cleveland 44121
Fx:381-0250

(949) 251-8844 ..**Elgersma**, Lisa D '97 Hirson WP -4685 MacArthur -Ste 400
-Newport Beach, CA 92660

(216) 621-2034 ..**Elhamshari**, Muhammad K '01 %Margolius M & Assoc,LPA
-55 Pub Sq -Ste 1100 -Cleveland 44113 **Fx:**621-1908

(216) 464-6626 ..**Eli**, David A Jr. '79 Chase Properties -25825 Science Park Dr
-Ste 355 -Beachwood 44122

Elias, Eugene N '94 -Bx518 -Sharon Center 44274

(740) 592-3332 ..**Eliason**, Lisa A '87 Athens Pros -8 E Wshngtn -Ste 301
-Athens 45701

(513) 721-2120 ..**Eling**, Kenneth J '93 %Barrett & W -105 E 4th -Ste 500 -Cincinnati
45202

(937) 439-4400 ..**Elinger,** Abbey P '03 Cnsl Design Forum LLC -7575 Paragon Rd -Dayton 45459 Fx:439-4340

(614) 464-2200 ..**Eliot,** Adam S '94 -400 S 5th -Ste 102 -Columbus 43215

(440) 442-6677 ..**Elk,** Arthur M '73 (Elk & E Co,LPA) -6100 Parkland Blvd -Mayfield Heights 44124 Fx:442-7944

(440) 442-6677 ..**Elk,** David J '65 Elk & E Co,LPA -6100 Parkland Blvd -Mayfield Heights 44124 Fx:442-7944

(440) 442-6677 ..**Elk & Elk Co,LPA** -6100 Parkland Blvd -Mayfield Heights 44124 Fx:442-7944

(216) 522-1555 ..**El-Kamhawy,** Abdel H '00 -1701 E 12th -Ste 3G -Cleveland 44114

(614) 868-8718 ..**Elkin,** Joel K '85 -6119 E Main -Columbus 43213

(419) 946-7876 ..**Elkin,** Tom C '83 -19 E High -Bx189 -Mount Gilead 43338

(703) 292-7100 ..**Elkins,** Arthur A Jr. '93 Cnsl Natl Science Fndtn -4201 Wilson Blvd -Ste 1135 Ofc of Inspector Genl -Arlington, VA 22230 Fx:292-9158

(202) 927-2380 ..**Elkins,** John E '68 US Customs Srvc -1300 Penn Av NW -Washington, DC 20229

(440) 461-5000 ..**Elkins,** Otto E Jr. '01 Progressive Ins -5910 Landerbrook Dr -Mayfield Heights 44124

(330) 675-2426 ..**Elkins,** Stanley A '85 Trumbull Cnty Pros -160 High NW -Warren 44481

(614) 238-6738 ..**Ellard,** Steven M '04 (Ellard H & Assoc) -2388 E Main -Ste 105 -Columbus 43209 Fx:238-6740

(614) 464-1211 ..**Ellcessor,** Steven J '77 (Frost BT LLC) -10 W Broad -Ste 1000 -Columbus 43215 Fx:464-1737

(304) 424-5297 ..**Ellem,** John N '94 -500 Green -Bx322 -Parkersburg, WV 26102

(614) 272-1112 ..**Elleman,** James R '66 (Elleman & N) -2904 W Broad -Columbus 43204 Fx:272-1115

(937) 865-8868 ..**Elleman,** Jennifer N '98 Lexis/Nexis -Bx933 -Dayton 45401

(513) 977-8200 ..**Elleman,** Lawrence R '66 (Dinsmore & S LLP) -255 E 5th -Ste 1900 -Cincinnati 45202 Fx:977-8141

(937) 443-6838 ..**Elleman,** Steven J '96 (Thompson H LLP) -2000 Cthse Plz NE -Bx8801 -Dayton 45401 Fx:443-6635

(419) 246-5757 ..**Ellenberger,** Richard F '65 (Anspach M&N,LLP) -300 Mad Av -Ste 1600 -Toledo 43604 Fx:321-9070

(614) 728-7055 ..**Ellensohn,** Carol A '02 Atty Gen -30 E Broad -Columbus 43215 Fx:728-8600

(248) 646-1514 ..**Eller,** Gary S '97 (Hebert & E, PC) -30850 Telegraph -Ste 200 -Bingham Farms, MI 48025

(614) 486-6446 ..**Ellerbrock,** Donn G '75 Associated Genl Cntrctrs of OH -1755 Northwest Blvd -Columbus 43212

(937) 275-0944 ..**Ellerbrock,** Michael J '79 -4403 N Main -2nd Fl -Dayton 45405

(216) 696-4422 ..**Ellerin,** Jerome M '56 -1301 E 9th -Ste 1000 -Cleveland 44114

(859) 394-6200 ..**Ellerman,** Brian M '01 %Adams SW&D -40 W Pike -Bx861 -Covington, KY 41012 Fx:291-7902

(513) 381-2838 ..**Ellerman,** Paige L '99 %Taft S&H LLP -425 Walnut -Ste 1800 -Cincinnati 45202 Fx:381-0205

(513) 753-2300 ..**Elliff,** Brian E '95 Union Twp Zoning & Planning Bd -4312 Glen Este Withamsvll Rd -Cincinnati 45245

(614) 462-5452 ..**Ellinger,** Eve M '01 %Kegler BH&R -65 E State -Ste 1800 -Columbus 43215 Fx:464-2634

(513) 852-6026 ..**Ellington,** Sarah B '03 %Wood & L LLP -600 Vine -Ste 2500 -Cincinnati 45202 Fx:852-6087

Elliott, Angela M '04 -(Address Unavailable)

(419) 244-8336 ..**Elliott,** Brooke E '04 %Gressley K&P -608 Mad Av -Ste 930 -Toledo 43604 Fx:244-1914

(614) 875-0490 ..**Elliott,** Bryan K '95 J Hilt & Assoc -3793 Bway -Grove City 43123

(614) 210-9255 ..**Elliott,** Cynthia L '95 Safelite Glass Corp -2400 Farmers Dr -Columbus 43235

(216) 228-9400 ..**Elliott,** Daniel R III '89 United Trans Union -14600 Detroit Av -Lakewood 44107

(216) 861-3099 ..**Elliott,** Daniel R Jr. '70 Cnsl Lutheran Mtrpltn Ministry -1468 W 25th -Cleveland 44113 Fx:696-1779

(419) 843-2720 ..**Elliott,** Donna L '89 Nationwide Ins -7110 W Central Av -Ste 1007 -Bx351810 -Toledo 43635

(314) 772-9953 ..**Elliott,** Douglas R '85 TEQ Development -1410 Chesterfld Ests Dr -Chesterfield, MO 63005

(330) 650-4761 ..**Elliott,** Frances C '83 -83 Sussex Dr -Hudson 44236

(513) 423-3654 ..**Elliott,** George H '50 -500 Ken Ridge Dr -Middletown 45042 Fx:423-0766

(419) 422-7178 ..**Elliott,** Howard A II '86 %Christopher Law Ofc -330 S Main -Findlay 45840

(614) 227-2000 ..**Elliott,** Joseph F '82 (Porter WM&A LLP) -41 S High -Columbus 43215 Fx:227-2100

(919) 829-9600 ..**Elliott,** Joshua T '99 %Hutchison & M PLLC -3110 Edwards Mill Rd -Ste 100 -Raleigh, NC 27612 Fx:829-9696

(419) 424-3067 ..**Elliott,** Karen E '83 -744 Dayton Av -Findlay 45840

(216) 622-8200 ..**Elliott,** Linda U '91 Calfee H&G LLP -800 Superior Av -Ste 1400 -Cleveland 44114 Fx:241-0816

(513) 651-6946 ..**Elliott,** Lisa A '00 Hamilton Cnty Pub Def Guardian Ad Litem Div -230 E 9th -3rd Fl -Cincinnati 45202

(513) 241-9400 ..**Elliott,** Lori K '85 Legal Aid -10 Jrnl Sq -Hamilton 45011

(216) 592-5000 ..**Elliott,** Michael E '80 (Tucker E&W LLP) -925 Euclid Av -1150 Huntgtn Bldg -Cleveland 44115 Fx:592-5009

(330) 376-1440 ..**Elliott,** Michael J '98 (Scanlon & Co,LLC) -159 S Main -400 Key Bldg -Akron 44308 Fx:376-0257

(216) 363-4500 ..**Elliott,** Pete C '84 (Benesch FC&A LLP) -200 Pub Sq -Ste 2300 -Cleveland 44114 Fx:363-4588

(614) 481-6000 ..**Elliott,** Rex H '91 (Cooper & E LLC) -2175 Riverside Dr -Columbus 43221 Fx:481-6001

(330) 702-1800 ..**Elliott,** Rush E '68 -4590 Boardman-Canfld Rd -Ste B -Bx37 -Canfield 44406

(937) 228-1987 ..**Elliott,** Steven E '89 -130 W 2nd -Ste 2100 -Dayton 45402

(614) 221-5216 ..**Elliott,** Steven P '79 %Wiles BB&B Co,LPA -300 Spruce -1st Fl -Columbus 43215 Fx:221-5692

(330) 434-7733 ..**Elliott,** Steven S '03 %Eoff & E, LLC -12 E Exchange -8th Fl -Akron 44308 Fx:434-8629

(312) 269-4291 ..**Elliott,** Sue A '83 (Jones Day) -77 W Wacker Dr -Ste 3500 -Chicago, IL 60601 Fx:782-8585

(734) 426-5860 ..**Elliott,** Thomas B '96 Creative Solutions -7322 Newman Blvd -Dexter, MI 48130

(614) 481-9173 ..**Elliott,** Wiley J '93 -1967 Vllg Ct -Columbus 43212

(937) 264-8710 ..**Elliott,** William B '75 -7700 N Main -Dayton 45415

(216) 573-6000 ..**Elliott,** Zena B '91 %Licata & Assoc Co,LPA -6480 Rockside Wds Blvd S -Ste 390 -Independence 44131 Fx:573-6333

(216) 520-7172 ..**Ellis,** Brian R '73 IRS -5990 W Crk Rd -Independence 44131

(937) 865-6800 ..**Ellis,** Charles M '92 Lexis/Nexis -Bx933 -Dayton 45401

(419) 247-2500 ..**Ellis,** Daniel T '87 (Fuller & H,Ltd) -One SeaGate -Ste 1700 -Bx2088 -Toledo 43603 Fx:247-2665

(412) 355-8375 ..**Ellis,** Douglas J '96 %Kirkpatrick & LNG LLP -535 Smithfld -1500 Henry W Oliver Bldg -Pittsburgh, PA 15222 Fx:355-6501

(937) 562-5250 ..**Ellis,** Elizabeth A '01 Greene Cnty Pros -61 Greene -Xenia 45385

(740) 587-4682 ..**Ellis,** Gary E '81 -635 Mill Race Rd -Granville 43023

(614) 798-0511 ..**Ellis,** George M '74 -3008 Black Kettle Trl -Dublin 43017

(937) 226-1200 ..**Ellis,** James C '81 (Bogin P&B) -131 N Ludlow -1200 Talbot Twr -Dayton 45402

(216) 444-9234 ..**Ellis,** James D '98 Lerner Rsch Institute -9500 Euclid Av, NB21 -Cleveland 44195 Fx:444-3279

(419) 332-4722 ..**Ellis,** James H III '00 -802 Court -Fremont 43420

(440) 895-9700 ..**Ellis,** James W III '00 Battle & M PLL -1340 Depot -Ste 201 -Rocky River 44116

Ellis, Jay B '59 -4947 N Barton Rd -North Ridgeville 44039

(937) 652-2224 ..**Ellis,** Kirk D '91 Feinstein E Co,LPA -1052 S Main -Urbana 43078

(513) 721-5151 ..**Ellis,** Lisa M '91 %Katz G&N,LLP -105 E 4th -4th Fl -Cincinnati 45202 Fx:621-9285

(614) 225-9707 ..**Ellis,** Madry L '97 -233 S High -Ste 300 -Columbus 43215

(419) 294-3132 ..**Ellis,** Mark J '77 (Mason M&E) -110 S Sundusky Av -Bx8 -Upper Sandusky 43351

(216) 443-9000 ..**Ellis,** Michael A '77 (Porter WM&A LLP) -925 Euclid Av -Ste 1700 -Cleveland 44115 Fx:443-9011

(513) 423-0194 ..**Ellis,** Paris K '80 -1501 S Breiel Blvd -Middletown 45044

Ellis, Paul D '99 -Bx3184 -Charleston, WV 25332

(740) 373-8624 ..**Ellis,** Robert '77 Ellis & E,LPA -328 4th -Marietta 45750

(937) 910-4174 ..**Ellis,** Robert C '79 Natl City Bank -3232 Newmark Dr -Miamisburg 45342

(614) 505-0808 ..**Ellis,** Robert L '84 (Ellis & V) -8824 Commerce Loop Dr -Columbus 43240 Fx:985-6898

(440) 930-8085 ..**Ellis,** Robert P Jr. '75 Wickens HPC&B -35765 Chester Rd -Avon 44011 Fx:937-4466

Ellis, Ryan M '04 -(Address Unavailable)

(216) 592-5000 ..**Ellis,** Stephen C '72 (Tucker E&W LLP) -925 Euclid Av -1150 Huntgtn Bldg -Cleveland 44115 Fx:592-5009

(614) 505-0808 ..**Ellis & Venable** -8824 Commerce Loop Dr -Columbus 43240 Fx:985-6898

(513) 852-6067 ..**Ellis,** William R '85 (Wood & L LLP) -600 Vine -Ste 2500 -Cincinnati 45202 Fx:852-6087

(937) 222-1560 ..**Ellison,** Kathy L '79 -131 N Ludlow -265 -Dayton 45402 Fx:461-4494

(513) 721-7522 ..**Ellison,** Richard G '76 -22 W 9th -Cincinnati 45202

(304) 428-1899 ..**Ellison,** Robert A '79 -1222 Market -Bx1885 -Parkersburg, WV 26102 Fx:428-6638

(513) 732-7429 ..**Ellison,** Theresa B '92 Clermont Cnty CSEA -2400 Clermont Ctr Dr -Batavia 45103

(216) 221-1830 ..**Ellison,** Wildon V '93 -12020 Lk Av -Ste 205 -Lakewood 44107

(404) 581-8309 ..**Ellman,** Jeffrey B '91 (Jones Day) -303 Pchtree NE -3500 SunTrust Plz -Atlanta, GA 30308 Fx:581-8330

(216) 635-3243 ..**Ellsworth,** Gary L '91 Cleveland Metro Parks -4101 Fulton Pkwy -Cleveland 44144

(740) 349-6898 ..**Ellsworth,** Mary E '01 City Law Dir Ofc -40 W Main -4th Fl -Newark 43055

Ellsworth, Todd M '04 -(Address Unavailable)

(513) 559-0553 ..**Ellsworth,** Wilkes R '97 -817 Main -Ste 500 -Cincinnati 45202

(216) 382-1500 ..**Eloff,** Kathryn G '81 -3820 Monticello Blvd -Cleveland Heights 44121

(419) 241-1228 ..**Elrod,** Bradley C '82 -608 Mad Av -Ste 1400 -Bx1336 -Toledo 43603

(937) 492-6191 ..**Elsass,** Eugene P '57 (Elsass WES&Co) -100 S Main Av -Ste 102 -Bx499 -Sidney 45365 Fx:492-0876

Elsass, Timothy N '95 -(Address Unavailable)

(937) 492-6191 ..**Elsass Wallace Evans Schnelle & Co** -100 S Main Av -Ste 102 -Bx499 -Sidney 45365 Fx:492-0876

(614) 466-3445 ..**Elsass-Locker,** Jodi M '92 OH Alchl & Drug Addctn Srvcs -280 N High -Columbus 43215

(513) 381-4700 ..**Elsener,** Mark E '80 (Porter WM&A LLP) -250 E 5th -Ste 2200 -Cincinnati 45202 Fx:421-0991

(330) 908-4429 ..**Elsmore,** Venetia M '95 Charles Schwab & Co Inc -4150 Kinross Lks Pkwy -Richfield 44286

(216) 566-0415 ..**Elson,** Martin W '83 -1235 W 6th -Ste 4B -Cleveland 44113 Fx:574-4210

(304) 347-5050 ..**Elswick,** Samuel D '02 %J Humphreys & Assoc,LC -500 E VA -Ste 800 United Ctr -Charleston, WV 25301 Fx:347-5055

(513) 932-1836 ..**Elter,** Janina J '95 %J Hedges -24 N Bway -Lebanon 45036 Fx:932-2849

(309) 766-9831 ..**Elterich,** John P '76 Cnsl State Farm Ins Co -One State Farm Plz -E-3 -Bloomington, IL 61710 Fx:766-7423

(419) 464-6400 ..**Elvers,** Jason C '00 %Vorys SS&P LLP -52 E Gay -Bx1008 -Columbus 43216 Fx:464-6350

(216) 861-6645 ..**Elwell,** James N '83 -55 Pub Sq -Ste 2001 -Cleveland 44113

(440) 282-2121 ..**Elwell,** Thomas J Jr. '78 -4463 Oberlin Av -Lorain 44053

(614) 752-8983 ..**Elwing,** Alicia F '98 OH Supreme Ct -30 E Broad -2nd Fl -Columbus 43215

(614) 833-2531 ..**Elwing,** Thomas R '98 -60 W Columbus -Pickerington 43147

(614) 459-5200 ..**Ely,** Donald E '68 (Rance PBK&E Co,LPA) -1720 Zollinger Rd -Ste 200 -Columbus 43221 Fx:459-1151

(513) 732-2140 ..**Ely & True** -322 Main -Batavia 45103

(216) 861-0804 ..**Elzeer,** Bradley E II '91 %F Gallucci Jr Co,LPA -55 Pub Sq -Ste 2222 -Cleveland 44113

(216) 861-6191 ..**Elzeer,** Jeffrey M '91 %Rodgers & Co,LPA -45 Prospect Av W -1600 Guildhall Landmark Ofc Twrs -Cleveland 44115 Fx:861-4699

(216) 861-3086 ..**Elzeer,** Kimrey D '96 %Reid M&W -55 Pub Sq -Ste 2010 -Cleveland 44113 Fx:861-4409

(216) 523-1500 ..**Embleton,** Jeffrey M '75 Mansour GG&M Co,LPA -55 Pub Sq -Ste 2150 -Cleveland 44113 Fx:523-1705

(304) 757-0021 ..**Embree,** Eric A '95 -3058 Mt Vernon Rd -Hurricane, WV 25526

(614) 221-1314 ..**Embrey**, Elizabeth A '04 %P Robbins -175 S 3rd -Ste 360
-Columbus 43215

(216) 664-3671 ..**Embry**, Myra T '94 Cleveland Mun Ct -1200 Ontario -13th Fl
-Cleveland 44113

(419) 255-5900 ..**Emch**, Gregg W '85 (MacMillan S&T,LLC) -720 Water -4th Fl
-Toledo 43604 **Fx:**255-9639

(419) 243-1294 ..**Emch**, Richard D '63 Emch SS&P Co,LPA -One SeaGate
-Ste 1980 -Bx916 -Toledo 43697 **Fx:**243-8502

(419) 243-1294 ..**Emch Schaffer Schaub & Porcello Co,LPA** -One SeaGate
-Ste 1980 -Bx916 -Toledo 43697 **Fx:**243-8502

(614) 221-4000 ..**Emens**, John R II '64 (Chester W&S LLP) -65 E State -10th Fl
-Columbus 43215 **Fx:**221-4012

(937) 325-7365 ..**Emerich**, John D '64 (Emerich W&P) -20 S Limestone -Ste 300
-Bx1087 -Springfield 45501

(937) 325-7365 ..**Emerich Winks & Peifer** -20 S Limestone -Ste 300 -Bx1087
-Springfield 45501

(419) 229-1161 ..**Emerick**, Steven M '01 Lima Sheet Metal -1001 Bowman Rd
-Lima 45804

(419) 224-1353 ..**Emerick**, William C '00 %King & B -212 N Elizabeth -Lima 45801
Fx:224-5305

(203) 961-5674 ..**Emerling**, Sandra G '84 GE Captl Corp -777 Long Ridge Rd
-Stamford, CT 06927

(330) 376-5756 ..**Emershaw**, George J '68 Emershaw M&S -120 E Mill -#437
-Akron 44308 **Fx:**762-5980

(330) 376-5756 ..**Emershaw Mushkat & Schneier** -120 E Mill -#437 -Akron 44308
Fx:762-5980

(614) 227-2000 ..**Emerson**, Andrew C '00 %Porter WM&A LLP -41 S High
-Columbus 43215 **Fx:**227-2100

(419) 241-9000 ..**Emerson**, Edwin G '66 (Shumaker L&K,LLP) -1000 Jackson
-Toledo 43624 **Fx:**241-6894

(330) 535-5711 ..**Emerson**, Roger D '87 (Brouse M) -106 S Main -500 First Natl Twr
-Akron 44308 **Fx:**253-8601

(440) 498-0070 ..**Emery**, Marlene P '79 -6370 Som Center Rd -Ste 200
-Solon 44139

(419) 243-6281 ..**Emery**, Richard L '91 (Shindler NH&S,LLP) -300 Mad Av -Ste 1200
-Toledo 43604 **Fx:**243-0129

(216) 739-5647 ..**Emery**, Steven H '02 Weltman W&R Co,LPA
-323 W Lakeside Av -Ste 200 -Cleveland 44113 **Fx:**363-4121

(330) 491-5240 ..**Emley**, William W Sr. '71 (Buckingham D&B,LLP) -4518 Fulton Dr
NW -Bx35548 -Canton 44735 **Fx:**492-9625

(419) 755-1477 ..**Emmens**, David P '74 Gorman-Rupp Co -305 Bowman
-Mansfield 44903 **Fx:**755-1019

(330) 385-0419 ..**Emmerling**, Frederick C '78 -114 W 6th -Bx25
-East Liverpool 43920

(513) 852-8200 ..**Emmert**, Andrew C '88 Cors & B LLC -537 E Pete Rose Way
-Ste 400 -Cincinnati 45202

(513) 871-2459 ..**Emmert**, Marianne S '84 -2936 Alpine Ter -Cincinnati 45208

(202) 857-8254 ..**Emmert**, Steven M '82 Reed Elsevier Inc -1150 18th NW -Ste 600
-Washington, DC 20036 **Fx:**857-8294

(513) 946-3700 ..**Emmrich**, Joseph L '72 Hamilton Cnty Pub Def -230 E 9th -3rd Fl
-Cincinnati 45202 **Fx:**946-3707

(216) 781-3434 ..**Emoff**, Jerome M '74 -55 Pub Sq -Trmnl Twr Ste 1300
-Cleveland 44113

(216) 348-1666 ..**Emrick**, Charles R Jr. '58 TransAction Group -1422 Euclid Av
-Ste 500 -Cleveland 44115

(740) 423-9548 ..**Emrick**, Gregg M '77 (McCauley W&E) -1710 Wshngtn Blvd
-Bx196 -Belpre 45714

(937) 439-5642 ..**Emrick**, Nicky R '82 -6633 MeEwen Rd -Dayton 45459

(703) 693-1066 ..**Emswiler**, Thomas K '82 Ofc of the Secretary of Def
-4000 Defense Pentagon -Rm 2B279 -Washington, DC 20301

(215) 981-4000 ..**Endejann**, Nancy Nicole '02 %Pepper H LLP -3000 Two Logan Sq
-Philadelphia, PA 19103 **Fx:**981-4750

(419) 522-2733 ..**Enderle**, John R '74 (Inscore RW&E,LPA) -13 Park Av W -Ste 400
-Mansfield 44902 **Fx:**522-5165

(614) 461-1311 ..**Enders**, Warren M '76 (Reminger & R) -65 E State
-4th Fl Cptl Sq Ofc Bldg -Columbus 43215 **Fx:**232-2410

(606) 789-8232 ..**Endicott**, Michael S '89 -225 Court -Bx181 -Paintsville, KY 41240
Fx:789-0018

(614) 873-7171 ..**Endres**, Louis P III '78 -245 W Main -Plain City 43064

(216) 228-7550 ..**Endress**, Jeffrey C '80 (Endress & E Co,LPA) -17119 Mad Av
-Lakewood 44107

(513) 523-6369 ..**Engel**, Drew G '87 -31 W Church -Oxford 45056

(513) 695-1325 ..**Engel**, Joshua A '03 Warren Cnty Pros -500 Justice Dr
-Lebanon 45036 **Fx:**695-2962

(419) 530-8411 ..**Engel**, Lauri A '95 Univ of Toledo Law Schl -2801 W Bancroft
-Toledo 43606

(614) 227-2327 ..**Engel**, Mark A '79 (Bricker & E LLP) -100 S 3rd -Columbus 43215
Fx:227-2390

(513) 425-6609 ..**Engel**, Scott H '92 12th Dist Ct of Appls -1001 Reinartz Blvd
-Middletown 45042 **Fx:**425-8751

(859) 380-0378 ..**Engel**, William D '99 -492 Gerhard Dr -Edgewood, KY 41017
Fx:331-1545

(614) 548-0024 ..**England**, Dale R Jr. '72 -115 N Center -Pickerington 43147
Fx:837-2235

(330) 823-1190 ..**England**, Daniel L '80 -340 S Union Av -Bx3610 -Alliance 44601

(216) 363-1400 ..**Engle**, David C '81 (Buckley K,LPA) -600 E Superior Av -Ste 1400
-Cleveland 44114 **Fx:**579-1020

(513) 241-7332 ..**Engle**, John H '68 -7 W 7th -Ste 1800 -Cincinnati 45202

(330) 602-2833 ..**Engle**, Susan C '93 -707 N Wooster Av -Dover 44622

(513) 271-9026 ..**Englehart**, Andrew T '94 Construction Process Solutions
-3751 Eastern Av -Cincinnati 45226

(216) 696-7600 ..**Englehart**, Fredrick W '97 %Duvin C&H -1301 E 9th
-20th Fl Erievw Twr -Cleveland 44114 **Fx:**696-2038

(330) 729-9777 ..**Engler**, David L '85 (Engler & Assoc) -860 Boardman-Canfld Rd
-Ste 204 -Boardman 44512 **Fx:**758-9585

(937) 299-1914 ..**Engler**, Gregory T '88 -Bx49717 -Dayton 45449

(614) 871-5100 ..**Englert**, Christopher L '94 Solid Waste Auth of Cntrl OH
-6220 Young Rd -Grove City 43123

(330) 762-2255 ..**Englert**, Holly J '97 Stark Cnty Dept of Job & Family Srvcs
-220 E Tuscarawas -Canton 44702

(513) 381-9200 ..**Englert**, James J Jr. '90 (Rendigs FK&D,LLP) -One W 4th
-Ste 900 -Cincinnati 45202 **Fx:**381-9206

(937) 223-3001 ..**Engling**, Mark C '99 %Jenks P&O Co,LPA -10 N Ludlow -Ste 901
-Dayton 45402 **Fx:**223-3103

(216) 781-9917 ..**English**, Brent L '80 -1500 W 3rd -Ste 470 -Cleveland 44113
Fx:781-8113

(419) 213-4700 ..**English**, Ian B '01 %Lucas Cnty Pros -Adams & Erie
-Lucas Cnty Cthse -Toledo 43624

(614) 249-6096 ..**English**, John A '94 Nationwide Ins Co -1 Nationwide Plz
-Columbus 43215

(614) 566-5151 ..**English**, Katrina M '90 %OhioHealth -3722 Olentangy Rvr Rd
-Ste K -Columbus 43214

(216) 881-6600 ..**English**, Lawrence K '89 NEORSD -3826 Euclid Av
-Cleveland 44115 **Fx:**881-4407

(216) 479-6100 ..**English**, Matthew D '99 %Vorys SS&P LLP -1375 E 9th
-Ste 2100 One Cleve Ctr -Cleveland 44114 **Fx:**479-6060

(440) 743-4043 ..**English**, Monica L '89 Parma Community Gen Hospital
-7007 Powers Blvd -Parma 44129

English, Nicholas J '04 -(Address Unavailable)

(216) 661-4164 ..**Englund**, Joan M '88 Bridgeway,Inc -1708 Southpnt Dr
-Cleveland 44109

(419) 246-5757 ..**Engwert**, J Randall '99 %Anspach M&N,LLP -300 Mad Av
-Ste 1600 -Toledo 43604 **Fx:**321-6979

(419) 242-1400 ..**Engwert-Loyd**, Donna M '79 -608 Mad Av -Ste 1400
-Toledo 43606 **Fx:**246-5764

(740) 522-7106 ..**Ennen**, Bruce A '79 -Bx4461 -Newark 43058

(216) 642-3342 ..**Ennis**, Charles Roe '73 OfCnsl Wegman H&V,LPA
-6055 Rockside Wds Blvd -Ste 200 -Cleveland 44131
Fx:642-8826

(513) 421-2540 ..**Ennis Roberts & Fischer** -121 W 9th -Cincinnati 45202
Fx:562-4986

(513) 421-2540 ..**Ennis**, William J '66 (Ennis R&F) -121 W 9th -Cincinnati 45202
Fx:562-4986

(703) 903-2671 ..**Ennist**, Diane M '81 Fed Home Loan Mortgage Corp
-8200 Jones Brnch Dr -Mclean, VA 22102

(614) 292-9592 ..**Enns**, Terri L '96 OSU Moritz Cllg of Law -55 W 12th Av
-Columbus 43210 **Fx:**292-1383

(202) 514-1102 ..**Enos**, Anastasia M '96 US DOJ-Tax Div -Bx972 -Washington, DC
20044

(330) 384-7309 ..**Enright**, Timothy J '73 Firstmerit Trust Co -121 S Main -Ste 200
-Akron 44308

(800) 998-9454 ..**Enriquez**, Rick '87 Cmmnty Lgl Aid Srvcs,Inc -265 S Main -3rd Fl
-Akron 44308 **Fx:**(330) 535-0728

(740) 354-2300 ..**Enriquez**, Rick '87 -721 5th -Fifth St Law Bldg -Portsmouth 45662
Fx:354-5667

(216) 830-6830 ..**Ensign**, Cathryn R '86 (Brouse M) -1001 Lakeside Av -Ste 1600
-Cleveland 44114 **Fx:**830-6807

(216) 362-3818 ..**Ensign**, Gregory M '75 Kirkwood Industries,Inc -4855 W 130th
-Cleveland 44135

(614) 227-2300 ..**Ensign**, John A '03 %Bricker & E LLP -100 S 3rd
-Columbus 43215 **Fx:**227-2390

(419) 252-6225 ..**Entenmann**, Richard A '54 OfCnsl Spengler N PLL -608 Mad Av
-Ste 1000 -Toledo 43604 **Fx:**241-8599

(330) 434-7733 ..**Eoff**, Craig M '99 (Eoff & E, LLC) -12 E Exchange -8th Fl
-Akron 44308 **Fx:**434-8629

(330) 451-8964 ..**Eoff**, Cristina G '99 Stark Cnty CSEA -116 Cleveland Av -Bx21337
-Canton 44701

(330) 376-2700 ..**Ephlin**, Laura A '91 %Roetzel & A,LPA -222 S Main -Akron 44308
Fx:376-4577

(937) 228-7511 ..**Epley**, Christopher B '99 (Tolliver & E) -131 N Ludlow -Ste 1000
-Dayton 45402 **Fx:**228-9515

(513) 624-6204 ..**Epling**, John A '57 -7372 Ridgepoint Dr -#2 -Cincinnati 45230
Fx:624-6204

(216) 861-0026 ..**Epp**, Henry C '72 -55 Pub Sq -Ste 1350 -Cleveland 44113

(614) 297-6409 ..**Eppich**, Robert J '94 -252 W 5th Av -Columbus 43201

(614) 469-7404 ..**Eppler**, Rita S '81 SSA-OHA, Columbus -280 N High -3rd Fl
-Columbus 43215

(614) 457-6233 ..**Epps**, Richard M '76 -2820 Halstead Rd -Columbus 43221

(202) 226-1215 ..**Eppstein**, David M '96 US House of Reps -2129 HOB
-Washington, DC 20515

(513) 631-1501 ..**Eppstein**, Steven D '74 -4526 Mntgmry Rd -Cincinnati 45212
Fx:631-1502

(614) 481-6000 ..**Epstein**, Aaron D '94 Cooper & E LLC -2175 Riverside Dr
-Columbus 43221 **Fx:**481-6001

(614) 221-3966 ..**Epstein**, Barry W '77 -580 S High -Ste 130 -Columbus 43215

(330) 782-7000 ..**Epstein**, Bruce R '77 -Suite #101 -5500 Market -Boardman 44512

(419) 537-1954 ..**Epstein**, Robert '91 -4202 W Central Av -Bx352170 -Toledo 43635

(216) 464-1610 ..**Epstein**, Robert E '76 -2421 Allen Blvd -Beachwood 44122

(440) 466-7670 ..**Epstein**, Sherry Stein '86 Cnsl ATC Lighting & Plastics,Inc
-107 N Eagle -Geneva 44041 **Fx:**466-0186

Erb, James J '72 -(Address Unavailable)

(740) 373-5455 ..**Erb**, John E '69 (Theisen B,LPA) -424 2nd -Bx739 -Marietta 45750
Fx:373-4409

(216) 443-9000 ..**Erb**, L William '00 %Porter WM&A LLP -925 Euclid Av -Ste 1700
-Cleveland 44115 **Fx:**443-9011

(330) 744-1111 ..**Erb**, Shawna L '96 %Harrington H&M,Ltd -26 Market -Ste 1200
-Youngstown 44503 **Fx:**744-2000

(440) 349-5757 ..**Erdelack**, Wayne F '73 Nestle USA -30003 Bainbrdg Rd
-Solon 44139

(330) 343-0099 ..**Erdman**, Deborah L '95 Cnsl Tuscarawas Cnty CSEA -154 2nd NE
-Bx1016 -New Philadelphia 44663 **Fx:**364-4854

(614) 464-9112 ..**Erdy**, Pamela S '91 -518 N Park -Columbus 43215

(216) 241-2838 ..**Erenburg**, Kristin R '04 %Taft S&H LLP -200 Pub Sq
-3500 BP Twr -Cleveland 44114 **Fx:**241-3707

Erford, Katherine S '03 -(Address Unavailable)

(614) 469-1858 ..**Erfurt**, Edward W III '77 -85 E Gay -Ste 508 -Columbus 43215

(330) 453-0185 ..**Ergazos**, John W '52 -315 Tuscarawas W -Ste 300 -Canton 44702
Fx:453-5234

(216) 443-4939 ..**Ergun**, Serpil '84 Cuyahoga Cnty Cmmn Pleas Ct -1 Lakeside Av
-Rm 26 -Cleveland 44113

(740) 452-8485 ..**Erhard**, Gerald A Jr. '79 (Stubbins W&E Co LPA) -59 N 4th -Bx488
-Zanesville 43702

(740) 349-7262 ..**Erhard**, Robert T '77 (Morrow & E Co,LPA) -10 W Locust -Bx487
-Newark 43058

(513) 732-2332 ..**Erhardt**, Chris '62 -230 North -Batavia 45103 **Fx:**732-2332

(513) 732-2332 ..**Erhardt,** Christian IV '94 -230 North -Batavia 45103
(513) 732-1104 ..**Erhardt,** John D '52 -285 Main -Batavia 45103
(513) 579-6400 ..**Erhart,** Sue A '96 (Keating M&K PLL) -1 E 4th -1400 Provident Twr
-Cincinnati 45202 **Fx:**579-6457
(937) 443-6814 ..**Erickson,** Douglas E '89 Thompson H LLP -2000 Cthse Plz NE
-Bx8801 -Dayton 45401 **Fx:**443-6635
(614) 757-5000 ..**Erickson,** John C '03 SrCnsl Cardinal Hlth -7000 Cardinal Pl
-Dublin 43017
(513) 651-6800 ..**Erickson,** Richard J '71 (Frost BT LLC) -201 E 5th -2200 PNC Ctr
-Cincinnati 45202 **Fx:**651-6981
(513) 579-5324 ..**Erickson,** Robert M '74 Fifth 3rd Bk -38 Fountain Sq Plz -Trust Div
-Cincinnati 45263
Ericsson, John M '94 -167 E McMillan -#1 -Cincinnati 45219
(513) 287-2087 ..**Erisen,** Candace S '99 Cinergy Corp -139 E 4th -25 Atrium II
-Bx960 -Cincinnati 45201
(216) 222-2227 ..**Erkkila,** Linda K '99 Natl City Corp -1900 E 9th -Cleveland 44114
Fx:222-2336
(614) 228-1346 ..**Erkman,** Annemarie M '96 %OH Retirement Study Cncl
-88 E Broad -Ste 1175 -Columbus 43215
(614) 224-1222 ..**Erlenbach,** Thomas S '60 %Maguire & S,LLP -250 Civic Ctr Dr
-Ste 200 -Columbus 43215 **Fx:**224-1236
(614) 466-2766 ..**Erlewine,** Kristina L '99 Atty Gen -30 E Broad -Columbus 43215
Fx:644-1926
Erlichman, Sheryl D '85 -6994 Kindker Dr -New Albany 43054
(419) 468-6300 ..**Erlsten,** Steven J '68 -135 Hrdng Way W -Galion 44833
(614) 221-1111 ..**Ernest,** John T '99 %Shayne & G -221 S High -Columbus 43215
Fx:221-4070
(330) 364-5593 ..**Ernest,** Michael J '96 %Johnson U&R Co LPA -117 S Bway
-Bx1007 -New Philadelphia 44663 **Fx:**364-3714
(216) 575-7575 ..**Ernewein,** Michael E '73 (Kolick G&E Co,LPA) -55 Pub Sq
-1350 Illuminating Bldg -Cleveland 44113
(216) 566-5831 ..**Erney,** Jeffry J '88 (Thompson H LLP) -127 Pub Sq -3900 Key Ctr
-Cleveland 44114 **Fx:**566-5800
(614) 258-6100 ..**Erney,** Robert D '84 (R Erney & Assoc Co,LPA) -1654 E Broad
-Columbus 43203 **Fx:**258-6600
(614) 716-0500 ..**Ernsberger,** Todd A '04 %Onda L&R Co,LPA -266 N 4th -Ste 100
-Columbus 43215 **Fx:**716-0511
(216) 241-6602 ..**Ernst,** Christopher M '91 (Weston HFP&H LLP) -50 Pub Sq
-2500 Trmnl Twr -Cleveland 44113 **Fx:**621-8369
(937) 233-5555 ..**Ernst,** Daniel D '94 Ernst Entrprses,Inc -3361 Successful Way
-Bx13577 -Dayton 45413
(513) 932-2214 ..**Ernst,** David E '85 -11 S Bway -#2 -Lebanon 45036
(937) 223-2002 ..**Ernst,** Herbert Jr. '61 -120 W 3rd -Ste 308 -Dayton 45402
(513) 579-9500 ..**Ernst,** Matthew T '96 -114 E 8th -Cincinnati 45202
(513) 946-9200 ..**Ernst,** Tina I '91 Hamilton Cnty Juv Ct -800 Bway
-Cincinnati 45202 **Fx:**946-9217
(513) 977-8200 ..**Erny,** Frederick M '87 (Dinsmore & S LLP) -255 E 5th -Ste 1900
-Cincinnati 45202 **Fx:**977-8141
(419) 382-6888 ..**Errington,** Michael D '70 -3626 S Detroit Av -Toledo 43614
(440) 333-8088 ..**Ertle,** John B Jr. '87 -21300 Lorain Rd -Fairview Park 44126
(216) 445-7076 ..**Ertle,** Patrick Jay '90 Cleveland Clinic Fndtn -9500 Euclid Av
-#EE35 -Cleveland 44195
(513) 326-5555 ..**Erven,** Thomas P '83 (Young & A Co,LPA) -110 Boggs Ln
-Ste 350 -Cincinnati 45246
(614) 228-6885 ..**Ervin,** Amy J '96 %Lane A&H LLC -175 S 3rd -Ste 700
-Columbus 43215 **Fx:**228-0146
(937) 294-8420 ..**Ervin,** Joanne J '91 -135 W Dorothy Ln -Ste 101 -Dayton 45429
(513) 946-5200 ..**Erwin,** Anne B '81 Hamilton Cnty Mun Ct -1000 Main -Cincinnati
45202
(773) 525-0153 ..**Erwin,** James A '00 (Erwin & Assoc,LLC) -4048 N Hermitage Av
-Ste 101 -Chicago, IL 60613 **Fx:**525-0154
(614) 438-2648 ..**Erwin,** Joseph V '91 %CS Cobb -100 E Compus Vw Blvd -Ste 250
-Columbus 43235 **Fx:**438-2650
(614) 853-0294 ..**Erwin,** Van III '95 -809 Thorncrest Ct -Galloway 43119
(330) 644-2060 ..**Esber,** David M '75 -4584 Whyem Dr -Akron 44319
(440) 686-9000 ..**Esber,** Kevin J '04 OfCnsl Goodwin & B LLP -22050 Mastick Rd
-Fairview Park 44126 **Fx:**686-9001
(216) 348-5400 ..**Esborn,** Theodore J '79 (McDonald H Co,LPA) -600 Superior Av E
-Ste 2100 -Cleveland 44114 **Fx:**348-5474
(419) 247-2508 ..**Esch,** Raymond G Jr. '65 OfCnsl Fuller & H,Ltd -One SeaGate
-Ste 1700 -Bx2088 -Toledo 43603 **Fx:**247-2665
(216) 586-3939 ..**Eschbach-Hall,** Patricia L '99 %Jones D -901 Lakeside Av
-Cleveland 44114 **Fx:**579-0212
(614) 466-7447 ..**Eschbacher,** Lisa M '98 Atty Gen -150 E Gay -Columbus 43215
(614) 278-4795 ..**Eschbacher,** Timothy J '98 Big Lots Inc -300 Phillipi Rd
-Columbus 43228
(216) 621-0200 ..**Eschedor,** Jennifer L '93 Baker & H LLP -1900 E 9th -Ste 3200
-Cleveland 44114 **Fx:**696-0740
(614) 227-2000 ..**Eschleman,** Lisa L '87 OfCnsl Porter WM&A LLP -41 S High
-Columbus 43215 **Fx:**227-2100
(419) 668-4879 ..**Eschrich & Stoll Co,LPA** -130 Benedict Av -Bx465
-Norwalk 44857 **Fx:**663-0140
(440) 323-3456 ..**Eschrich & Stoll Co,LPA** -300 4th -Elyria 44035 **Fx:**323-3434
(419) 668-4879 ..**Eschrich,** T Craig '75 (Eschrich & S Co,LPA) -130 Benedict Av
-Bx465 -Norwalk 44857 **Fx:**663-0140
(216) 502-0600 ..**Eschweiler,** Thomas G '97 (Eschweiler & Assoc,LLC)
-629 Euclid Av -Ste 1210 -Cleveland 44114
(216) 771-8121 ..**Escovar,** Thomas J '69 (Steuer EB&B Co,LPA) -55 Pub Sq
-Ste 1828 -Cleveland 44113 **Fx:**771-8120
(614) 210-1840 ..**Eselgroth,** Carolyn D '92 (Barrett EC&E LLP) -7269 Sawmill Rd
-Dublin 43016 **Fx:**210-1841
(330) 376-3572 ..**Eshelman,** C Richard '68 Eshelman Lgl Grp
-263 Portage Trl Ext W -Cuyahoga Falls 44223 **Fx:**376-0199
Eshenbaugh, Robert N '04 -(Address Unavailable)
(614) 228-6647 ..**Eshman,** Patricia S '85 %OH Home Builders Assoc -17 S High
-Ste 700 -Columbus 43215
Eshman, Thomas H II '80 -11603 Old Hills Ln
-San Antonio, TX 78251
(330) 376-5300 ..**Esker,** Christopher C '88 %Buckingham D&B,LLP -50 S Main
-Bx1500 -Akron 44309 **Fx:**258-6559
(937) 298-0008 ..**Esler,** Charles M Jr. '87 (Scudder & E Co,LPA)
-2912 Springboro W -Ste 105 -Dayton 45439

(740) 593-6410 ..**Eslocker,** Thomas E '76 (Eslocker & O Co,LPA) -16 W State
-Athens 45701
(937) 865-6800 ..**Esparza,** Lorena '02 Lexis/Nexis -Bx933 -Dayton 45401
Espenschied, Diana L '86 -317 Donald Pl SW -Canton 44706
Espenschied, Erin R '03 -(Address Unavailable)
(440) 268-9212 ..**Esper,** Thomas L III '98 Stoughton D -Strongsville 44149
(614) 466-3180 ..**Espinoza,** David J '83 Atty Gen -150 E Gay -Columbus 43215
Fx:466-9788
(513) 474-3700 ..**Espohl,** Frank E '96 %K Mezher & Assoc -8075 Beechmont Av
-Cincinnati 45255
Esposito, Michael A '80 -Bx14133 -Columbus 43214
Esposito, Michael D '04 -(Address Unavailable)
(614) 228-2722 ..**Espy,** Bennie E '69 (B Espy Co,LPA) -43 Hmltn Pk
-Columbus 43203
(330) 744-1148 ..**Essad,** Scott C '96 %Henderson CMN&T Co,LPA -34 Fed Plz W
-Ste 600 Wick Bldg -Youngstown 44503 **Fx:**744-3807
(614) 728-6430 ..**Esselburne,** Peter C '75 Dept Agri -8995 E Main
-Reynoldsburg 43068 **Fx:**995-4585
(614) 462-3194 ..**Essex,** Robert D '93 Franklin Cnty Pub Def -373 S High -12th Fl
-Columbus 43215
(419) 782-6055 ..**Essex,** Troy A '00 %Clemens KL&W,Ltd -419 5th -Ste 2000
-Bx787 -Defiance 43512
(614) 486-9366 ..**Essey,** Norman A '86 Land America Fincl Grp Inc
-2845 Canterbury Ln -Columbus 43221
(216) 521-6552 ..**Essi,** Brian J '84 -15306 Edgewtr Dr -Lakewood 44107
Fx:521-6554
(513) 721-5151 ..**Essig,** Ellen '86 (Katz G&N,LLP) -105 E 4th -4th Fl
-Cincinnati 45202 **Fx:**621-9285
(330) 655-7000 ..**Essner,** Howard S '82 Automated Tracking Systms,Inc
-1140 Terex Rd -Hudson 44236
(740) 695-1444 ..**Estadt,** John R '83 Hanlon DE&M Co,LPA -46457 Natl Rd W
-Saint Clairsville 43950 **Fx:**695-1563
Estafanous, Katherine E '99 -135 Jackson Dr
-Chagrin Falls 44022
(513) 573-4880 ..**Estenfelder,** Regina L '95 Summer Hill Inc -6800 Cintas Blvd
-Mason 45040
(606) 564-5585 ..**Estill,** John F '96 (Fox WW&E) -24 W 3rd -Maysville, KY 41056
(800) 243-0210 ..**Estvanic,** Sally A '04 Westfield Grp -1 Park Cir -Bx5001
-Westfield Center 44251 **Fx:**(330) 887-2588
(216) 464-6901 ..**Etowski,** Earl J Jr. '74 Sterling Trust NCB -3550 Lander Rd
-Pepper Pike 44124
(614) 466-7964 ..**Etter,** Terry L '97 OH Consumers' Cnsl -10 W Broad -Ste 1800
-Columbus 43215 **Fx:**466-9475
(937) 296-2456 ..**Eubank,** David L '89 Law Dept -3600 Shroyer Rd -Kettering 45429
(614) 224-8374 ..**Eubanks,** Renee F '01 %Legal Aid -40 W Gay -Columbus 43215
(614) 466-2766 ..**Eubanks,** Robert A '01 Atty Gen -30 E Broad -Columbus 43215
Fx:644-1926
(937) 644-8151 ..**Eufinger,** John M '72 (Coleman E&A) -110 S Court -Bx266
-Marysville 43040
(330) 208-4520 ..**Evanchan,** Nicholas L Jr. '79 (Evanchan & P) -1 GOJO Plz
-Ste 300 -Akron 44311 **Fx:**208-4519
(330) 208-4520 ..**Evanchan & Palmisano** -1 GOJO Plz -Ste 300 -Akron 44311
Fx:208-4519
(216) 447-0814 ..**Evangelista,** James P '89 Allega Co -5585 Carol Rd
-Valley View 44125
(440) 322-5824 ..**Evanich,** Jeanette M '92 -401 Broad -Ste 311 -Elyria 44035
(216) 787-4381 ..**Evanick,** Barbara A '95 Workers Comp -615 W Superior
-Cleveland 44113 **Fx:**787-4487
(740) 264-6441 ..**Evans,** Augustus H Jr. '51 -Bx2003 -Wintersville 43953
(330) 305-6400 ..**Evans,** Cari F '93 %Pelini & F,Ltd -8040 Cleveland Av NW
-Ste 400 -North Canton 44720 **Fx:**305-0042
(513) 863-6700 ..**Evans,** Catherine L '96 (Millikin & F) -6 S 2nd -6th Fl -Bx598
-Hamilton 45012 **Fx:**863-0031
(216) 696-1448 ..**Evans,** Charles E III '68 Compensation Consultants Inc
-614 Superior Av NW -601 Rckfllr Bldg -Cleveland 44114
(216) 781-6166 ..**Evans,** Cheryl N '01 Roberts Law Ofc -323 Lakeside Av W
-Ste 450 -Cleveland 44113
(216) 621-0150 ..**Evans,** Christina D '91 (Hahn L&P LLP) -3300 BP Twr/200 Pub Sq
-Ste 3300 -Cleveland 44114 **Fx:**241-2824
(440) 338-3264 ..**Evans,** Clyde P Jr. '81 -14330 Caves Rd -Novelty 44072
(614) 841-1620 ..**Evans,** Craig E '73 -6660 N High -Ste 3A -Worthington 43085
(330) 287-5663 ..**Evans,** Dafydd W Jr. '73 Cnty Mun Ct Judge -538 N Market
-Wooster 44691
(740) 446-1737 ..**Evans,** David C '01 (Cherrington M&E) -Bx409 -Gallipolis 45631
Fx:446-1738
(202) 879-3772 ..**Evans,** David H '95 %Jones DR&P -51 Louisiana Av NW
-Washington, DC 20001
(513) 629-2529 ..**Evans,** David N '79 Eagle-Picher Industries, Inc -580 Walnut
-Bx779 -Cincinnati 45201
(419) 228-5111 ..**Evans,** David R '93 Northwestern Mutual Financial
-3745 Shawnee Rd -Ste 103 -Lima 45806
(419) 255-3948 ..**Evans,** Denise F '85 -1900 Monroe -Toledo 43624
(614) 464-2025 ..**Evans,** Dennis P '85 (Connor B LLP) -501 S High
-Columbus 43215 **Fx:**224-8708
(330) 926-9845 ..**Evans,** Diane K '97 -2253 Hoch Dr -Cuyahoga Falls 44221
(419) 624-3000 ..**Evans,** Donna Jean A '00 Murray & M Co,LPA -111 E Shoreline Dr
-Bx19 -Sandusky 44871
(740) 943-2325 ..**Evans Evans & Hoffman,LLP** -15 W Ottawa -Richwood 43344
Fx:943-2326
(513) 621-6033 ..**Evans,** Franklin R '99 %Richman Law Ofcs -906 Main -Ste 306
-Cincinnati 45202
(614) 462-6285 ..**Evans,** Gale A '99 Franklin Cnty Common Pleas Ct -369 S High
-Columbus 43215
(740) 773-2651 ..**Evans,** Gary L '93 Ross Cnty CSEA -475 Wstrn Av -Ste B
-Chillicothe 45601
(419) 625-5901 ..**Evans,** George M '94 Oglesby & O -1218 Cleveland Rd -Ste 2
-Sandusky 44870
(614) 224-8166 ..**Evans,** Gordon D II '01 %Twyford & D -495 S High -Ste 100
-Columbus 43215
(910) 333-5382 ..**Evans,** Helen O '79 Ofc of Hearings & Appls -101 S Edgeworth
-Ste 300 -Greensboro, NC 27401
(216) 664-4839 ..**Evans,** James D Jr. '04 Prosecutor -1200 Ontario Av
-8th Fl Justice Ctr -Cleveland 44113 **Fx:**664-4399

(513) 579-2536 ..**Evans**, James E '71 Amer Fncl Corp -One E Fourth -Ste 919 -Cincinnati 45202

(614) 475-9511 ..**Evans**, James M '67 (Blumenstiel HA&E,LLC) -261 W Johnstown Rd -Columbus 43230 **Fx:**475-0348

(614) 466-2980 ..**Evans**, James M '81 Atty Gen -30 E Broad -Columbus 43215 **Fx:**728-9470

(954) 384-0175 ..**Evans**, James P '86 Pediatrix Medical Grp Inc -1301 Concord Ter -Sunrise, FL 33323

(440) 350-2708 ..**Evans**, Janice S '78 Lake Cnty Cmmn Pleas Ct -Bx490 -Painesville 44077

(740) 943-2325 ..**Evans**, Jeffrey L '81 (Evans E&H,LLP) -15 W Ottawa -Richwood 43344 **Fx:**943-2326

(216) 443-7800 ..**Evans**, Jennifer '95 Cuyahoga Cnty Pros -1200 Ontario -8th Fl -Cleveland 44113 **Fx:**698-2270

Evans, Jeremy J '04 -(Address Unavailable)

(412) 393-3664 ..**Evans**, Jon E '92 AquaSource,Inc -411 7th Av -14th Flr -Pittsburgh, PA 15219 **Fx:**393-3715

(440) 395-1315 ..**Evans**, Joy M '92 Progressive Ins -300 N Columbus Blvd -OHF11 -Mayfield Heights 44143 **Fx:**395-0280

(513) 936-2012 ..**Evans**, Lisa M '94 Sara Lee Corp -10151 Carver Rd -Cincinnati 45242

(614) 227-4892 ..**Evans**, Mark E '01 %Bricker & E LLP -100 S 3rd -Columbus 43215 **Fx:**227-2390

(513) 336-4685 ..**Evans**, Marlene M '91 Anthem Blue Cross/BlueShield -4361 Irwin Simpson Rd -OH11C-151 -Mason 45040

(513) 241-1950 ..**Evans**, Marquette D '77 (Brown LH&E) -7 W 7th -Ste 1950 -Cincinnati 45202 **Fx:**241-4095

(330) 643-2617 ..**Evans**, Marvin D '91 Summit Cnty Pros-Tax -220 S Balch -Ste 118 -Akron 44302 **Fx:**643-8540

(614) 227-2000 ..**Evans**, Mason IV '77 (Porter WM&A LLP) -41 S High -Columbus 43215 **Fx:**227-2100

(330) 264-1222 ..**Evans**, Matthew C '00 Wayne Bancorp,Inc -112 W Lbrty -Bx757 -Wooster 44691

(937) 854-3788 ..**Evans**, Meg M '86 -Bx257 -Dayton 45405

(330) 455-0173 ..**Evans**, Merle D III '83 (Day KRW&R,Ltd) -200 Market Av N -Ste 300 -Bx24213 -Canton 44701 **Fx:**455-2633

(614) 890-4770 ..**Evans**, Michelle R '02 %OAPSE -6805 Oak Crk Dr -Columbus 43229

(216) 621-0150 ..**Evans**, Neil K '64 Cnsl Hahn L&P LLP -3300 BP Twr/200 Pub Sq -Ste 3300 -Cleveland 44114 **Fx:**241-2824

(937) 339-2627 ..**Evans**, Nika R '00 %Miller & L Co,LPA -314 W Main -Troy 45373

(614) 227-2000 ..**Evans**, R Leland '83 (Porter WM&A LLP) -41 S High -Columbus 43215 **Fx:**227-2100

(740) 373-3155 ..**Evans**, Robert E '67 Peoples Bancorp Inc -138 Putnam -Bx738 -Marietta 45750

(740) 943-2325 ..**Evans**, Robert E Jr. '55 OfCnsl Evans E&H,LLP -15 W Ottawa -Richwood 43344 **Fx:**943-2326

(330) 824-7725 ..**Evans**, Robert H '80 GM Corp -Bx1427 -Warren 44482

(216) 443-8299 ..**Evans**, Ronald M '99 %Cuyahoga Cnty Cmmn Pleas Crt -1 Lakeside Av -Leg Dept -Cleveland 44113

(614) 249-2983 ..**Evans**, Ronda L '89 Nationwide Ins Co -One Nationwide Plz -1-09-V2 -Columbus 43215

(513) 721-5151 ..**Evans**, Ross M '86 (Katz G&N,LLP) -105 E 4th -4th Fl -Cincinnati 45202 **Fx:**621-9285

Evans, Scott L '95 -859 Mosaic Ct -Gahanna 43230

Evans, Sharon L '83 -3549 Manor Hse Dr -Charlotte, NC 28270

(937) 492-6191 ..**Evans**, Stephen R '82 (Elsass WES&Co) -100 S Main Av -Ste 102 -Bx499 -Sidney 45365 **Fx:**492-0876

(419) 249-7100 ..**Evans**, Stephen P '98 Marshall & M,LLC -Four Seagate -8th Fl -Toledo 43604 **Fx:**249-7151

(216) 241-5735 ..**Evans**, Susan M '93 (Lustig E&L Co,LPA) -526 Superior Av E -Ste 615 -Cleveland 44114

(419) 421-3436 ..**Evans**, Thomas D '80 Marathon Ashland Petro LLC -539 S Main -Findlay 45840 **Fx:**421-8402

(513) 381-9200 ..**Evans**, Thomas M '86 (Rendigs FK&D,LLP) -One W 4th -Ste 900 -Cincinnati 45202 **Fx:**381-9206

(513) 868-7600 ..**Evans**, Timothy R '74 Holbrock & J Co,LPA -315 S Monument Av -Bx687 -Hamilton 45012 **Fx:**868-0909

(330) 643-3104 ..**Evans**, Todd W '93 OH Civ Rghts Cmmssn -161 S High -Ste 205 -Akron 44308

(330) 434-4050 ..**Evans**, William D II '92 Poly Tech -209 S Main -Ste 403 -Akron 44308

(419) 772-2208 ..**Evans**, William L '71 ONU-Pettit Clg of Law -525 S Main -Ada 45810 **Fx:**772-1875

(440) 329-5389 ..**Evard**, Mary R '96 Lorain Cnty Pros -225 Court -3rd Fl -Elyria 44035

Eve, Tanya '03 -(Address Unavailable)

(440) 237-1681 ..**Evenchik**, Aaron S '01 Gross Builders -14300 Ridge Rd -Ste 100 -North Royalton 44133 **Fx:**237-0706

(419) 999-4272 ..**Everett**, Bonnie E '86 Everett Law Co,LPA -3233 Spencervll Rd -Lima 45805

(513) 977-8200 ..**Everett**, Denise Mullen '02 %Dinsmore & S LLP -255 E 5th -Ste 1900 -Cincinnati 45202 **Fx:**977-8141

(937) 276-6565 ..**Everett**, John D '98 Montgomery Cnty Pros -301 W 3rd -Bx972 -Dayton 45422 **Fx:**225-3470

(614) 444-0016 ..**Everett**, John K '71 -1005 S High -Columbus 43206

(216) 479-6100 ..**Everett**, Margaret Dodane '85 Vorys SS&P LLP -1375 E 9th -Ste 2100 One Cleve Ctr -Cleveland 44114 **Fx:**479-6060

(440) 255-1522 ..**Everett**, P David II '85 -6988 Spinach Dr -Mentor 44060 **Fx:**255-1572

(651) 458-6458 ..**Everett**, Robert W '88 Marathon Ashland Petro -Bx9 -Saint Paul Park, MN 55071

(330) 535-5711 ..**Everett**, Stanley E '81 (Brouse M) -106 S Main -500 First Natl Twr -Akron 44308 **Fx:**253-8601

Everetts, Jason A '00 Hon Graham -85 Marconi Blvd -169 US Cthse -Columbus 43215

(219) 463-4949 ..**Everhardt**, Brad A '01 Beers MB&S,LLP -108 W Mich -Lagrange, IN 46761

(704) 366-6642 ..**Everman**, Gregory R '99 %Dougherty C&H -1901 Roxborough Rd -Ste 300 -Charlotte, NC 28211 **Fx:**366-9744

(937) 449-2800 ..**Evers**, Bradley W '85 (Chernesky H&K PLL) -10 Cthse Plz SW -Ste 1100 -Dayton 45402 **Fx:**449-2821

(212) 344-5680 ..**Evers**, Garrett D '98 %Thompson H LLP -1 Chase Manh Plz -58th Fl -New York, NY 10005 **Fx:**809-6890

(330) 668-9747 ..**Eversman**, Erica L '93 -846 N Cleveland-Massillon Rd -Akron 44333

(440) 933-4288 ..**Everson**, Anne M '86 -31781 Leeward Ct -Avon Lake 44012

(614) 249-0286 ..**Everson**, Deborah S '77 Nationwide Life Ins Co -2 Nationwide Plz -Columbus 43215

(440) 933-6188 ..**Everson**, John H '86 -31781 Leeward Ct -Avon Lake 44012

(513) 697-6999 ..**Ewald**, Brian A '98 -550 Wards Crnr Rd -Ste 102 -Loveland 45140

(330) 656-2600 ..**Ewald**, Michael J '96 Jo-Ann Stores Inc -5555 Darrow Rd -Hudson 44236

(614) 471-7424 ..**Ewald**, Shane W '00 -126 Walnut -Gahanna 43230

(704) 387-1053 ..**Ewald**, Stephen P '94 Bank of America,NA -100 N Tryon -20B Fl (NC-001-20-01) -Charlotte, NC 28255

Ewashinka, Heather E '95 -400 Tuscarawas W -Canton 44702

(937) 223-8177 ..**Ewers**, Gregory M '97 %Coolidge WW&L -33 W 1st -Ste 600 -Dayton 45402 **Fx:**223-6705

(440) 246-2317 ..**Ewers**, Raymond J '88 -2126 Hrbrvw Blvd. -Lorain 44052

(440) 244-2166 ..**Ewers**, Robert A '54 Lorain Mun Ct -100 W Erie Av -Lorain 44052

(502) 585-5800 ..**Ewing**, Charles D '80 (Gardner E&S) -462 S 4th Av -1600 Meidinger Twr -Louisville, KY 40202

(419) 252-5572 ..**Ewing**, Dana R '00 HCR Manor Care -333 N Summit -Bx10086 -Toledo 43699 **Fx:**254-5494

(317) 633-4090 ..**Ewing**, Kenneth A '93 Severns & B -41 E Wshngtn -Ste 300 -Indianapolis, IN 46204

(216) 522-2671 ..**Ext**, Traci L '98 US Dept of Ed-Civil Rights Ofc -600 Superior Av -Ste 750 -Cleveland 44114

(740) 432-7773 ..**Eyen**, Stephen P '80 -1300 Clark -Northstar Ctr -Bx1521 -Cambridge 43725

(614) 292-1882 ..**Eyerly**, Gloria A '76 -230 N Oval Mall -186 Univ Hall -Columbus 43210

(614) 436-3681 ..**Eyerman**, Philip L '81 -752 Olen Dr -Worthington 43085

(740) 474-5237 ..**Eyerman**, Susan E '84 4th Dist Ct of Appls -121-A W Franklin -Circleville 43113

(330) 963-7253 ..**Eyhusen**, Edward A '85 -10349 Sandalwood Dr -Twinsburg 44087

Eyler, Krista A '04 -(Address Unavailable)

(216) 486-2163 ..**Eyman**, Culver F III '80 -267 E 197th -Euclid 44119

Eynon, Ernest A II '69 -2592 Perkins Ln -Cincinnati 45208

(216) 621-0200 ..**Eyre**, Paul P '82 (Baker & H LLP) -1900 E 9th -Ste 3200 -Cleveland 44114 **Fx:**696-0740

(513) 621-2666 ..**Eyrich**, David J '73 (Statman HS&E LLC) -255 E 5th -Ste 2900 Chemed Ctr -Cincinnati 45202 **Fx:**587-4477

(614) 885-0123 ..**Eysser**, Dieter W '00 -Bx340316 -Columbus 43234

(419) 342-4261 ..**Eyster**, Gordon M '01 %McKown & M,LPA -10 Mansfld Av -Shelby 44875 **Fx:**347-5723

(419) 668-4896 ..**Eyster**, Kathryn M '02 %Freeman L&M -54 E Main -Norwalk 44857 **Fx:**663-7835

(614) 227-0306 ..**Ezell**, Larry A '98 -500 S Front -Ste 102 -Columbus 43215

(513) 977-4223 ..**Ezenagu**, Samuel O '98 -917 Main -Cincinnati 45202

(614) 221-8448 ..**Ezzie**, Joseph E '02 %Buckingham D&B,LLP -191 W Nationwide Blvd -Ste 300 -Bx151120 -Columbus 43215 **Fx:**221-8590

(440) 953-1310 ..**Ezzone**, Donald J '75 -4230 SR 306 -Ste 240 -Willoughby 44094 **Fx:**953-1427

(513) 721-5525 ..**Fabe**, George '81 OfCnsl Manley B -225 W Court -Cincinnati 45202 **Fx:**721-4268

(216) 566-5736 ..**Fabens**, Andrew L III '67 (Thompson H LLP) -127 Pub Sq -3900 Key Ctr -Cleveland 44114 **Fx:**566-5800

(419) 586-6886 ..**Faber**, Keith L '91 (K Faber & Assoc) -218 S Main -Ste B -Celina 45822

(937) 962-4341 ..**Faber**, Richard V Jr. '78 -200 N Commerce -Lewisburg 45338

(216) 621-0200 ..**Fabian**, Bethany L '02 %Baker & H LLP -1900 E 9th -Ste 3200 -Cleveland 44114 **Fx:**696-0740

(216) 586-3939 ..**Fabian**, John D '02 %Jones D -901 Lakeside Av -Cleveland 44114 **Fx:**579-0212

(808) 587-3057 ..**Fabrey**, Barbara A '81 Attorney General Ofc -465 S King -Rm 200 -Honolulu, HI 96813

(330) 726-0484 ..**Fabrizi**, Mary A '85 -1040 S Cmmns Pl -Ste 200 -Youngstown 44514

(215) 656-0641 ..**Facha**, Irene H '81 US Dept of Housing & Urban Dev -100 Penn Sq E -Philadelphia, PA 19107

(502) 587-5400 ..**Fadel**, Ronald B '97 Mapother & M -801 W Jffrsn -Louisville, KY 40202

(216) 781-7777 ..**Fadel**, William I '69 (Wuliger F&B) -1340 Sumner Ct -Brownell Bldg -Cleveland 44115 **Fx:**781-0621

(419) 868-1100 ..**Fadell**, Frederick J '59 -8021 N Shoreline Dr -Holland 43528

(937) 222-7777 ..**Fadia**, Jill D '04 %Stukey & Assoc -333 W 1st -Ste 400 -Dayton 45402 **Fx:**222-7772

(216) 696-3366 ..**Faeges**, Jay R '91 (Goodman WM LLP) -100 Erievw Plz -27th Fl -Cleveland 44114 **Fx:**363-5835

(614) 961-4848 ..**Faehnle**, Matthew C '00 -2280 W Henderson Rd -Ste 201 -Columbus 43220

(216) 621-1113 ..**Fafrak**, Kenneth W Jr. '03 %Renner OB&S,LLP -1621 Euclid Av -19th Fl -Cleveland 44115 **Fx:**621-6165

(216) 861-5582 ..**Fagan**, Christopher B '65 OfCnsl Fay SFM&M LLP -1100 Superior Av -7th Fl -Cleveland 44114 **Fx:**241-1666

(440) 260-6616 ..**Fagan**, Christopher P '03 CompliSource -7055 Engle Rd -Ste 403 -Cleveland 44130

(513) 421-6630 ..**Fagel**, Barry F '92 Lindhorst & D Co,LPA -312 Walnut -Ste 2300 -Cincinnati 45202

(513) 352-6214 ..**Fagel**, Stephen J '80 Law Dept -801 Plum -Rm 214 -Cincinnati 45202 **Fx:**352-1515

(614) 237-7634 ..**Fagin**, Marc K '85 -2388 E Main -Columbus 43209

(216) 348-1700 ..**Fagnilli**, David J '86 (Davis & Y) -101 Prospect Av W -Ste 1700 -Cleveland 44115 **Fx:**621-0602

(216) 521-8882 ..**Fagnilli**, Sara J '85 -13870 Edgewtr Dr -Lakewood 44107

(937) 223-8177 ..**Fague**, Terence L '78 (Coolidge WW&L) -33 W 1st -Ste 600 -Dayton 45402 **Fx:**223-6705

(330) 867-9998 ..**Fahey**, Bruce H '80 %Kastner W&W,LLC -3480 W Market -Ste 300 -Akron 44333 **Fx:**867-3786

(202) 606-8881 ..**Fahey**, Diane L '83 US Tax Ct -400 2nd NW -Washington, DC 20217

(216) 320-0976 ..**Fahey**, Melanie S '93 -Bx181463 -Cleveland Heights 44118

(614) 464-6400 .. **Fahey**, Richard P '73 (Vorys SS&P LLP) -52 E Gay -Bx1008 -Columbus 43216 **Fx:**464-6350
(614) 228-2605 .. **Fahnenbruck**, K Clarke '78 -50 W Broad -Columbus 43215
(216) 241-8004 .. **Failor**, Gary L '75 Port Auth -1375 E 9th -Ste 1650 -Cleveland 44114
(419) 634-0481 .. **Failor**, Kenneth G '66 -108 E Highland Av -Bx266 -Ada 45810
(614) 447-3600 .. **Faine**, Chris W '80 Chemical Abstracts Srvc -2540 Olentangy Rvr Rd -Bx3012 -Columbus 43210
(313) 225-3774 .. **Fair**, Kathryn E '83 Bank One Trust Co,NA -611 Woodward Av -Tax Dept -Detroit, MI 48226
(212) 854-0096 .. **Fairfield**, Joshua A T '01 Columbia Law Schl -435 W 116th -Rm 511 Jerome Green Hall -New York, NY 10027
(614) 464-6400 .. **Fairfield**, Mary Ellen '73 (Vorys SS&P LLP) -52 E Gay -Bx1008 -Columbus 43216 **Fx:**464-6350
(330) 535-5711 .. **Fairweather**, John C '77 (Brouse M) -106 S Main -500 First Natl Twr -Akron 44308 **Fx:**253-8601
(513) 621-6464 .. **Fairweather**, Neil '00 %Graydon H&R LLP -511 Walnut -1900 Fifth Third Ctr -Cincinnati 45202 **Fx:**651-3836
(513) 723-4000 .. **Fairweather**, Sarah Buzzee '02 %Vorys SS&P LLP -221 E 4th -Ste 2000 Atrium Two -Bx0236 -Cincinnati 45201 **Fx:**723-4056
(614) 645-7655 .. **Fais**, James J '70 Cnty Mun Ct Judge -375 S High -Court Room 14B -Columbus 43215
(614) 561-6775 .. **Fais**, Robert G '74 -6650 Wynwright Dr -Columbus 43016
(614) 475-6677 .. **Faist**, Julia A '78 -142 Granvll -Gahanna 43230
Fakhir, Ayana R '03 -1868 Hastings Av -East Cleveland 44112
(949) 888-8580 .. **Falck**, Robert D '00 Electronic Cash Systems -30052 Avntura -Ste B -Rancho Santa Margarita, CA 92688
Falcone, Juliet K '03 -540 Hilbish Av -Akron 44312
(330) 928-1040 .. **Falcone**, Vincent J '80 -2233 4th -Cuyahoga Falls 44221
(937) 226-0070 .. **Falconer**, Diane M '95 ClarkSchaeferHackett & Co -40 N Main -Ste 800 -Dayton 45423 **Fx:**226-1626
(440) 842-0455 .. **Falconi**, Ronald E '95 -5509 Ridge Rd -Parma 44129 **Fx:**888-7188
(513) 241-3111 .. **Fales**, Roy D '91 ClarkSchaeferHackett & Co -105 E 4th -16th Fl -Cincinnati 45202
(330) 759-4155 .. **Falgiani**, John D Jr. '85 (Dann & F,LLC) -4531 Belmont Av -Ste C Churchill Sq Plz -Youngstown 44505 **Fx:**759-9012
(216) 621-1000 .. **Falin**, William H '87 (Moscarino & T,LLP) -1422 Euclid Av -Hanna Bldg Ste 630 -Cleveland 44115 **Fx:**622-1556
(216) 348-5400 .. **Falk**, Bryan H '97 (McDonald H Co,LPA) -600 Superior Av E -Ste 2100 -Cleveland 44114 **Fx:**348-5474
(216) 622-8200 .. **Falk**, Ryan W '03 %Calfee H&G LLP -800 Superior Av -Ste 1400 -Cleveland 44114 **Fx:**241-0816
(614) 757-5000 .. **Falk**, Stephen T '94 Cardinal Hlth -7000 Cardinal Pl -Dublin 43017
(937) 222-3000 .. **Falke & Dunphy LLC** -30 Wyoming -Dayton 45409 **Fx:**222-1414
(937) 222-3000 .. **Falke**, Lee C '55 (Falke & D LLC) -30 Wyoming -Dayton 45409 **Fx:**222-1414
(216) 348-5400 .. **Falkowski**, Lynnette M '98 %McDonald H Co,LPA -600 Superior Av E -Ste 2100 -Cleveland 44114 **Fx:**348-5474
(937) 225-4652 .. **Fallang**, Dennis J '77 Montgomery Cnty Pub Def -117 S Main -Ste 400 -Dayton 45422 **Fx:**225-3449
(419) 891-6474 .. **Fallat**, Dale W '70 Andersons -1200 Dussel Dr -Maumee 43537
(513) 946-3700 .. **Fallat**, Kathryn A '00 Hamilton Cnty Pub Def -230 E 9th -3rd Fl -Cincinnati 45202 **Fx:**946-3707
(614) 227-2000 .. **Faller**, Bryan R '00 %Porter WM&A LLP -41 S High -Columbus 43215 **Fx:**227-2100
(419) 738-4578 .. **Faller**, Dennis P '79 -105 S Blackhoof -Bx413 -Wapakoneta 45895
(513) 579-1266 .. **Faller**, Raymond T '76 -1014 Vine -Ste 1450 -Cincinnati 45202
(513) 651-6800 .. **Faller**, Susan G '75 (Frost BT LLC) -201 E 5th -2200 PNC Ctr -Cincinnati 45202 **Fx:**651-6981
(330) 493-1570 .. **Falletta**, Salvatore J '67 Macala BM&G,LLC -4150 Belden Vllg NW -Ste 604 -Canton 44718 **Fx:**493-7042
(614) 326-1009 .. **Falleur**, Michael D '77 -1625 Bethel Rd -Ste 205 -Columbus 43220
(330) 375-2030 .. **Fallis**, Stephen A '74 Law Dept -161 S High -Ste 202 -Akron 44308
Fallon, Ann E '88 -(Address Unavailable)
(216) 241-1200 .. **Fallon**, Brian G '96 %D Fallon -1640 Standard Bldg -Cleveland 44113
(216) 621-0177 .. **Fallon**, Brian M '80 -1370 Ontario -Ste 410 -Cleveland 44113
(216) 241-1200 .. **Fallon**, Dominic J '59 -1640 Standard Bldg -Cleveland 44113
(216) 566-2000 .. **Fallon**, James C '94 Sherwin-Williams Co -101 Prospect Av NW -Cleveland 44115
(330) 493-4443 .. **Fallon**, Martin J '89 Emergency Med Physicians -4535 Dressler Rd NW -Canton 44718 **Fx:**491-4088
(216) 771-1760 .. **Fallsgraff**, Gary F '87 Smith & C LLP -1801 E Ninth -Ste 900 Ohio Svngs Plz -Cleveland 44114 **Fx:**771-3387
(937) 865-6800 .. **Fals**, Mary M '91 Lexis/Nexis -Bx933 -Dayton 45401
(513) 946-9200 .. **Falter**, Karen K '96 Hamilton Cnty Juv Ct -800 Bway -Cincinnati 45202 **Fx:**946-9217
(303) 978-4959 .. **Falter**, Lawrence S '71 Johns Manville Intl -Bx5108 -Denver, CO 80217
(330) 489-3216 .. **Falvey**, Mary Ann '79 Mun Ct Judge -218 Cleveland Av SW -Bx24218 -Canton 44701
(614) 475-9511 .. **Falvo**, Aaron R '03 %Blumenstiel HA&E,LLC -261 W Johnstown Rd -Columbus 43230 **Fx:**475-0348
(330) 678-3857 .. **Fanelly**, Richard M '67 -4913C Indpndnc Ctr -Stow 44224
(216) 479-6820 .. **Fanger**, Jeffrey J '92 -600 Superior Av E -Ste 1300 -Cleveland 44114 **Fx:**479-6801
(330) 297-7030 .. **Fankhauser**, Mark K '98 -224 W Main -Bx489 -Ravenna 44266
(330) 385-0850 .. **Fannin**, Thomas N '68 -Bx2226 -East Liverpool 43920
(937) 643-1920 .. **Fannon**, Patrick J '76 -1268 Westcliff Ct -Dayton 45409
(216) 689-4114 .. **Fanos**, William R '80 KeyBank NA -127 Pub Sq -18th Fl -Cleveland 44114 **Fx:**689-3545
(937) 465-5056 .. **Fansler**, Steven R '80 -212 N Detroit -Bx764 -West Liberty 43357
(440) 729-2258 .. **Fant**, John F Jr. '56 -13271 Caves Rd -Chesterland 44026
(734) 434-3800 .. **Fanta**, Anderson L '62 Washtenaw Legal Ctr -4930 Washtenaw Av -Ann Arbor, MI 48108
(330) 747-2661 .. **Fantauzzi**, David A '81 Cafaro Co -2445 Belmont Av -Bx2186 -Youngstown 44504
(216) 621-0200 .. **Fanter**, Guenther K '02 %Baker & H LLP -1900 E 9th -Ste 3200 -Cleveland 44114 **Fx:**696-0740
(513) 425-6609 .. **Fantetti**, James P '04 12th Dist Ct of Appls -1001 Reinartz Blvd -Middletown 45042 **Fx:**425-8751
(419) 626-3800 .. **Fantozzi**, Joseph M '04 %Reno B&F Co,LPA -725 Sycamore Line -Sandusky 44870 **Fx:**626-3638
(614) 761-2003 .. **Faoro**, Therese M '88 -5900 Sawmill Rd -Ste 220 -Dublin 43017
(216) 443-7800 .. **Faraglia**, Anna M '96 Cuyahoga Cnty Pros -1200 Ontario -8th Fl -Cleveland 44113 **Fx:**698-2270
(419) 474-9514 .. **Farah**, Asad S '96 (Farah & S) -3030 W Sylvania Av -Ste 106 -Toledo 43613 **Fx:**474-9522
(440) 331-0801 .. **Farah**, Benjamin F '81 -1154 Linda -Ste 175 -Rocky River 44116
(614) 462-3555 .. **Farbacher**, Marla H '93 Franklin Cnty Pros -373 S High -Columbus 43215
(614) 221-5200 .. **Farber**, Robert H Jr. '62 -42 E Gay -Ste 1300 -Columbus 43215
(216) 928-2200 .. **Farchione**, Joseph A Jr. '87 (Sutter OM&F) -1301 E 9th -3600 Erievw Twr -Cleveland 44114 **Fx:**928-4400
(614) 462-5290 .. **Fardal**, Patrick M '92 Cnty Coroners Ofc -520 King Av -Columbus 43201
(419) 843-1333 .. **Farell**, Gregory C '84 (Malone A&F) -7654 W Bancroft -Toledo 43617 **Fx:**843-3888
(614) 242-4333 .. **Fargo**, John Z '64 -471 E Broad -Ste 1303 -Columbus 43215
(513) 542-3469 .. **Farina**, Ciro P '82 -2233 Sweetbriar Ln -Cincinnati 45239
(330) 535-2220 .. **Farine**, Cheryl L '88 (Hudak S&F) -2020 Front -Ste 307 -Cuyahoga Falls 44221 **Fx:**535-1435
(513) 732-6871 .. **Faris**, Corinne M '80 -2110 Carriage Station Dr -Batavia 45103
(513) 732-1141 .. **Faris**, Dwight V '80 (Burreson B&H) -40 S 3rd -Batavia 45103
(614) 232-3088 .. **Faris**, Juliana M '89 NBBJ -1555 Lk Shr Dr -Columbus 43204
(216) 479-6100 .. **Farkas**, Bryan J '00 %Vorys SS&P LLP -1375 E 9th -Ste 2100 One Cleve Ctr -Cleveland 44114 **Fx:**479-6060
(216) 447-1551 .. **Farkas**, David S '03 %Ross B&S Co LPA -6000 Freedom Square Dr -Ste 540 -Cleveland 44131 **Fx:**447-1554
(216) 515-1660 .. **Farkas**, Gregory R '98 %Frantz W LLP -127 Pub Sq -2500 Key Center -Cleveland 44114 **Fx:**515-1650
(614) 222-2356 .. **Farkas**, Jeffrey W '93 Farkas Law Firm -303 E Lvngstn Av -Columbus 43215
(614) 466-8057 .. **Farkas**, Scott E '86 PUCO -180 E Broad -Columbus 43266
(330) 379-7000 .. **Farkas**, Toni Q '96 Bridgestone Americas Holding Inc -1200 Firestone Pky -Akron 44317 **Fx:**379-4064
(216) 621-1922 .. **Farley**, Betty C '88 -1836 Euclid Av -Ste 308 -Cleveland 44115
(513) 561-4602 .. **Farley**, Bobbie K W '80 -6075 Redbird Hllw Ln -Cincinnati 45243
(216) 241-7255 .. **Farley**, Donald W '57 -2401 Superior Viaduct -Cleveland 44113
(937) 339-2627 .. **Farley**, Jason R '02 %Miller & L Co,LPA -314 W Main -Troy 45373
(513) 381-8616 .. **Farley**, Katrina Z '92 %J Chalfie Co,LPA -36 E 7th -Ste 1600 -Cincinnati 45202
(937) 223-9133 .. **Farley**, Keri E '03 %Rion R&R Co,LPA -130 W 2nd -Ste 2150 -Bx1262 -Dayton 45402
(419) 535-0075 .. **Farley**, Larry D '77 (Allotta F&W Co,LPA) -2222 Centennial Rd -Toledo 43617 **Fx:**535-1935
Farley, Nicole Hatem '03 -20102 Ctr Ridge Rd -Rocky River 44116
(216) 357-3301 .. **Farling**, Harold E '91 (Kovach & F Co,LPA) -526 Superior Av E -Ste 925 -Cleveland 44114
(614) 734-1270 .. **Farlow**, Beverly J '85 (Farlow & Assoc LLC) -270 Bradenton Av -Dublin 43017 **Fx:**923-1031
(239) 262-2040 .. **Farmer**, Aaron A '93 -1415 Panther Ln -Ste 121 -Naples, FL 34109 **Fx:**262-2180
(419) 421-3344 .. **Farmer**, Clarence Eugene Jr. '86 Marathon Ashland Petro LLC -539 S Main -Findlay 45840 **Fx:**427-4188
(216) 921-0964 .. **Farmer**, Constance G '84 -2868 Torington Rd -Shaker Heights 44122
(937) 225-4640 .. **Farmer**, David M '81 Montgomery Cnty Probate Ct -41 N Perry -2nd Fl -Dayton 45402
(614) 759-0123 .. **Farmer**, Derek A '99 (D Farmer & Assoc,LPA) -800 Cross Pnte Rd -Ste Q -Columbus 43230 **Fx:**759-0125
(614) 221-2838 .. **Farmer**, James B '76 (Taft S&H LLP) -21 E State -12th Fl -Columbus 43215 **Fx:**221-2007
(216) 696-4200 .. **Farmer**, James P Jr. '81 (Schneider SR&L PLL) -1111 Superior Av -Ste 1000 -Cleveland 44114 **Fx:**696-7303
(330) 451-7910 .. **Farmer**, Kristin G '01 Stark Cnty Common Pleas Ct -115 Central Plz N -Canton 44702
(216) 931-6000 .. **Farnan**, Brian P '02 %Ulmer & B LLP -1300 E 9th -Ste 900 Penton Media Bldg -Cleveland 44114 **Fx:**931-6001
(216) 241-6602 .. **Farnan**, John G '87 (Weston HFP&H LLP) -50 Pub Sq -2500 Trmnl Twr -Cleveland 44113 **Fx:**621-8369
(614) 466-5394 .. **Farnbacher**, Barbara A '86 Pub Def -8 E Long -Columbus 43215
(330) 376-2700 .. **Farolino**, Shane A '88 (Roetzel & A,LPA) -222 S Main -Akron 44308 **Fx:**376-4577
(330) 364-6000 .. **Farone**, Eric V '00 Baerlocher USA -3676 Davis Rd NW -Dover 44622
(614) 248-6047 .. **Farquhar**, Christine M '81 JP Morgan Chase -1111 Polaris Pkwy -Ste OH1-0163 -Columbus 43271
(937) 643-1758 .. **Farquhar**, Harold R '75 -3723 Wilmngtn Pike -Dayton 45429 **Fx:**256-2801
(937) 223-1201 .. **Farquhar**, Robert N '61 (Altick & C Co,LPA) -1 S Main -1700 One Dayton Ctr -Dayton 45402 **Fx:**223-5100
(260) 426-0444 .. **Farr**, Melanie L '99 (Haller & C PC) -444 E Main -Fort Wayne, IN 46802 **Fx:**422-0274
(202) 307-6355 .. **Farragher**, Joan '73 DOJ-Lit Div -1401 H NW -Ste 4000 -Washington, DC 20530
(216) 687-1311 .. **Farrall**, William P '72 (Reminger & R) -101 Prospect Av W -1400 Mdlnd Bldg -Cleveland 44115 **Fx:**687-1841
(614) 464-6400 .. **Farrar**, Elizabeth T '82 (Vorys SS&P LLP) -52 E Gay -Bx1008 -Columbus 43216 **Fx:**464-6350
(419) 893-1444 .. **Farrar Naayers & Wilkinson,Ltd** -1605 Indn Wd Cir -Ste 200 -Maumee 43537
(419) 893-1444 .. **Farrar**, Richard G '66 (Farrar N&W,Ltd) -1605 Indn Wd Cir -Ste 200 -Maumee 43537
(614) 221-1827 .. **Farrell**, Clifford M '82 (Manring & F) -167 N High -Bx15037 -Columbus 43215
(513) 762-6200 .. **Farrell**, E Beth '90 %Ulmer & B LLP -600 Vine -Ste 2800 -Cincinnati 45202 **Fx:**762-6245
(440) 357-0939 .. **Farrell**, James K Jr. '77 -Bx1817 -Painesville 44077
(216) 621-2838 .. **Farrell**, Michael F '76 -614 W Superior Av -Ste 1300 -Cleveland 44113
(216) 621-0200 .. **Farrell**, Michael K '88 (Baker & H LLP) -1900 E 9th -Ste 3200 -Cleveland 44114 **Fx:**696-0740
(440) 333-3100 .. **Farrell**, Patrick M '83 -21430 Lorain Rd -Fairview Park 44126

(304) 292-9429 .. **Farrell,** Paul T Jr. '98 %Wilson FB&M,PLLC -151 Walnut -Morgantown, WV 26505 **Fx:**292-9427

(513) 721-1200 .. **Farrell,** Thomas M Jr. '92 %Young R&M Co,LPA -1014 Vine -Ste 2400 -Cincinnati 45202 **Fx:**721-7116

(513) 621-9921 .. **Farrell,** William I III '89 (Finkelmeier & F) -36 E 7th -Ste 1660 -Cincinnati 45202 **Fx:**621-9923

(216) 696-5297 .. **Farren,** Anthony S '96 Bilfield & S Co,LPA -1301 E 9th -Ste 1000 Erievw Twr -Cleveland 44114 **Fx:**696-2316

(440) 350-3200 .. **Farren,** David E '83 Lake Cnty Pub Def -125 E Erie -Painesville 44077

(440) 329-3255 .. **Farren,** John E '99 -105 Court -Elyria 44035

(800) 237-4148 .. **Farren,** Kristy E '97 Nationwide Ins -5525 Parkcenter Cir -Dublin 43017

(614) 466-5967 .. **Farrin,** Richard C '72 Atty Gen -30 E Broad -Columbus 43215 **Fx:**466-8226

(740) 387-9991 .. **Farrington,** Barbara J '87 -Bx1216 -Marion 43301

(330) 743-6004 .. **Farris,** Anthony J '91 -516 Redondo Rd -Youngstown 44504

(330) 253-3444 .. **Farris,** George L '81 -362 S Main -Akron 44311 **Fx:**253-6431

(513) 784-7319 .. **Farris,** Michael J '03 Deloitte & Touche,LLP -250 E 5th -Ste 1900 -Cincinnati 45202

(419) 247-2500 .. **Farris,** Ray A '75 (Fuller & H,Ltd) -One SeaGate -Ste 1700 -Bx2088 -Toledo 43603 **Fx:**247-2665

(330) 929-3777 .. **Farris,** Vincent G '93 (V Farris Co,LPA) -2050 6th -Cuyahoga Falls 44221

(513) 621-8700 .. **Farrish,** Kelly Jr. '79 K Farrish,LPA -601 Main -3rd Fl -Cincinnati 45202

(216) 586-3939 .. **Farroni,** Mark B '83 Jones D -901 Lakeside Av -Cleveland 44114 **Fx:**579-0212

(419) 249-4944 .. **Farthing,** Dana M '99 Mid Am Bank -519 Mad Av -Toledo 43604

(740) 474-3103 .. **Farthing,** John H '73 -233 S Scioto -Bx541 -Circleville 43113

(937) 227-3700 .. **Faruki,** Charles J '74 (Faruki I&C PLL) -10 N Ludlow -500 Cthse Plz SW -Dayton 45402 **Fx:**227-3717

(937) 227-3700 .. **Faruki Ireland & Cox PLL** -10 N Ludlow -500 Cthse Plz SW -Dayton 45402 **Fx:**227-3717

Farwell, Theresa M '88 -1001 S Water -Kent 44240

(513) 425-7990 .. **Fassler,** Bruce E '79 Middletown Law Dept -1 Donham Plz -Middletown 45042

(303) 277-3764 .. **Fast,** Harold J '81 Coors Brewing Co -311 10th -Golden, CO 80401

(614) 469-3939 .. **Fate,** Jennifer L '97 %Jones D -325 John H McConnell Blvd -Ste 600 -Bx165017 -Columbus 43216 **Fx:**461-4198

(614) 466-3596 .. **Fate,** Lisa Wu '93 State Auditor Ofc -88 E Broad -5th Fl -Bx1140 -Columbus 43216

(216) 696-2348 .. **Fatica,** John A '91 -55 Pub Sq -Ste 2200 -Cleveland 44113

(614) 228-6148 .. **Fauber,** Sue A '82 S Jaffy & Assoc Co,LPA -306 E Gay -Columbus 43215 **Fx:**228-6140

(216) 781-3600 .. **Faulkner,** David G '86 Faulkner M&P,LLP -820 W Superior Av -Ste 900 -Cleveland 44113 **Fx:**781-8839

(513) 695-1325 .. **Faulkner,** Derek B '99 Warren Cnty Pros -500 Justice Dr -Lebanon 45036 **Fx:**695-2962

(937) 492-1271 .. **Faulkner Garmhausen Keister & Shenk, LPA** -100 S Main Av -Ste 300 -Sidney 45365 **Fx:**498-1306

(937) 295-2983 .. **Faulkner Garmhausen Keister & Shenk, LPA** -31 S Main -Fort Loramie 45845 **Fx:**285-3633

(216) 781-3600 .. **Faulkner,** George H '80 Faulkner M&P,LLP -820 W Superior Av -Ste 900 -Cleveland 44113 **Fx:**781-8839

(937) 492-1271 .. **Faulkner,** Harry N '66 (Faulkner GK&S,LPA) -100 S Main Av -Ste 300 -Sidney 45365 **Fx:**498-1306

(937) 264-8710 .. **Faulkner,** Jonathan E '04 Elliott,LPA -7700 N Main -Dayton 45415

(513) 723-2210 .. **Faulkner,** Laura R '99 %Weltman W&R Co,LPA -525 Vine -Ste 800 -Cincinnati 45202 **Fx:**723-2239

(216) 781-3600 .. **Faulkner Muskovitz & Phillips, LLP** -820 W Superior Av -Ste 900 -Cleveland 44113 **Fx:**781-8839

(740) 574-4311 .. **Faulkner,** Rickey L '79 -8055 Hayport Rd -CB02-13 -Wheelersburg 45694 **Fx:**574-1129

(614) 228-1541 .. **Faulkner,** Sandra Parks '93 (Baker & H LLP) -65 E State -Ste 2100 -Columbus 43215 **Fx:**462-2616

(740) 657-1661 .. **Faulkner,** Steven L '93 -6800 Big Walnut Rd -Galena 43021

(513) 421-7500 .. **Faulkner & Tepe,LLP** -5 W 4th -2200 4th & Vine Twr -Cincinnati 45202

(614) 227-2000 .. **Faure,** David C '96 %Porter WM&A LLP -41 S High -Columbus 43215 **Fx:**227-2100

(216) 861-1365 .. **Faust,** Daniel M '02 Hawkins & Co,LPA -1267 W 9th -Ste 500 -Cleveland 44113 **Fx:**861-0714

(937) 335-8324 .. **Faust Harrelson Fulker McCarthy & Schlemmer** -12 S Cherry -Troy 45373 **Fx:**339-7155

(330) 376-2700 .. **Faust,** Laura M '92 (Roetzel & A,LPA) -222 S Main -Akron 44308 **Fx:**376-4577

(513) 381-2838 .. **Fausz,** Daniel E '94 (Taft S&H LLP) -425 Walnut -Ste 1800 -Cincinnati 45202 **Fx:**381-0205

(440) 934-3700 .. **Fauver Keyse-Walker & Donovan** -5333 Meadow Ln Ct -Elyria 44035 **Fx:**934-3708

(440) 934-3700 .. **Fauver,** Worth A Jr. '63 (Fauver K-W&D) -5333 Meadow Ln Ct -Elyria 44035 **Fx:**934-3708

(216) 479-6100 .. **Fauvie,** Lori L '03 %Vorys SS&P LLP -1375 E 9th -Ste 2100 One Cleve Ctr -Cleveland 44114 **Fx:**479-6060

(330) 253-8877 .. **Favalon,** Paul J '70 -50 S Main -Ste 502 -Akron 44308

(614) 478-3918 .. **Favor,** Hugh M Jr. '93 Favor Leg Srvcs & Co,LPA -4859 NorthTowne Blvd -Columbus 43229

(513) 871-8076 .. **Favret,** Bruce A '77 -2631 Erie Av -Cincinnati 45208

(614) 221-5151 .. **Fawley,** Darrell E Jr. '79 (Fawley & Assoc) -520 E Rich -Columbus 43215 **Fx:**221-1778

(216) 586-3939 .. **Faxon,** Robert S '92 (Jones D) -901 Lakeside Av -Cleveland 44114 **Fx:**579-0212

(216) 586-3939 .. **Fay,** Regan J '74 (Jones D) -901 Lakeside Av -Cleveland 44114 **Fx:**579-0212

(216) 861-5582 .. **Fay Sharpe Fagan Minnich & McKee LLP** -1100 Superior Av -7th Fl -Cleveland 44114 **Fx:**241-1666

(614) 464-1211 .. **Fay,** Terrence M '78 Cnsl Frost BT LLC -10 W Broad -Ste 1000 -Columbus 43215 **Fx:**464-1737

(513) 626-2408 .. **Fayette,** Thibault '00 Procter & Gamble Co -11510 Reed Hartman Hwy -SWTC, B1S08 -Cincinnati 45241

(216) 241-5310 .. **Fazio,** Catherine '04 Gallagher SF&N -1501 Euclid Av -6th Fl -Cleveland 44115 **Fx:**241-1608

(513) 946-3000 .. **Fazio,** Cynthia A '88 Hamilton Cnty Pros -230 E 9th -Cincinnati 45202 **Fx:**946-3017

(216) 381-4424 .. **Fazio,** John C '65 Justinian Publishing Co -2940 Noble Rd -Cleveland 44121

(216) 802-0077 .. **Fazio,** Mario J '89 -1801 E 9th -920 Ohio Svngs Plz -Cleveland 44114 **Fx:**621-7870

(412) 560-3319 .. **Fazio,** Mark F '03 %Morgan L&B LLP -One Oxford Centre -32nd Fl -Pittsburgh, PA 15219 **Fx:**560-7001

(216) 381-6400 .. **Fazio,** Ruth Morton '02 Jaynar Corp -2940 Noble Rd -Cleveland 44121

(216) 479-8500 .. **Fazio,** Stephen M '03 %Squire S&D LLP -127 Pub Sq -4900 Key Twr -Cleveland 44114 **Fx:**479-8780

(216) 589-5622 .. **Fazio,** Tyrone C '79 -55 Pub Sq -Ste 2200 -Cleveland 44113

(216) 937-2222 .. **Feagan,** Glenn D '89 -1280 W 3rd -Ste 3 -Cleveland 44113

(214) 812-6035 .. **Fease,** Kevin R '00 TXU Corp -1601 Bryan -6th Fl -Dallas, TX 75201

(614) 677-5932 .. **Featherstone,** James E '96 Nationwide Ins -280 N High -Ste 810 -Columbus 43215

(513) 852-8200 .. **Feazell,** Kevin R '92 Cors & B LLC -537 E Pete Rose Way -Ste 400 -Cincinnati 45202

(614) 466-2980 .. **Febus,** Charles E '94 Atty Gen -30 E Broad -Columbus 43215 **Fx:**728-9470

(419) 242-0461 .. **Fech & Fech, LLC** -405 N Huron -Ste 200 -Toledo 43604 **Fx:**242-0463

(419) 242-0461 .. **Fech,** Matthew N '01 (Fech & F,LLC) -405 N Huron -Ste 200 -Toledo 43604 **Fx:**242-0463

(419) 242-0461 .. **Fech,** Nicole Y '01 (Fech & F,LLC) -405 N Huron -Ste 200 -Toledo 43604 **Fx:**242-0463

(513) 621-2666 .. **Fecher,** William B '87 %Statman HS&E LLC -255 E 5th -Ste 2900 Chemed Ctr -Cincinnati 45202 **Fx:**587-4477

(440) 954-3111 .. **Feczko,** Christopher E '96 -38040 Euclid Av -Willoughby 44094

(661) 572-3063 .. **Fedak,** Laurence S '71 Lockheed Martin Corp -1011 Lockheed Way -Leg Dept -Palmdale, CA 93599

(614) 224-8187 .. **Federico,** John A '97 Lamkin VTB&D -500 S Front -Ste 200 -Columbus 43215 **Fx:**224-4943

(614) 292-9177 .. **Federle,** Katherine H '98 OSU Moritz Cllg of Law -55 W 12th Av -Columbus 43210 **Fx:**292-1383

(937) 382-2838 .. **Federle,** Richard L Jr. '93 Rose & D Co,LPA -97 N South -Wilmington 45177

(216) 781-0808 .. **Federman,** Jerry I '76 -526 Superior Av -Ste 350 -Cleveland 44114

(440) 250-9709 .. **Fedor,** Robert J Jr. '89 -1991 Crocker Rd -Ste 222 -Westlake 44145

(440) 442-5224 .. **Fedor,** Steven L '81 -6686 Sandalwood Dr -Gates Mills 44040

(216) 403-3388 .. **Fedor,** Victoria L '92 V Fedor Co LPA -628 W Market -Akron 44303

(216) 586-3939 .. **Feeling,** F Drexel '95 (Jones D) -901 Lakeside Av -Cleveland 44114 **Fx:**579-0212

(216) 221-8020 .. **Fegen,** David A '73 -14701 Detroit Av -#568 -Lakewood 44107

(216) 621-8484 .. **Fegen,** Joseph P '95 %Climaco LPW&G Co,LPA -1228 Euclid Av -Ste 900 Halle Bldg -Cleveland 44115 **Fx:**771-1632

(614) 462-5432 .. **Feheley,** Lawrence F '73 (Kegler BH&R) -65 E State -Ste 1800 -Columbus 43215 **Fx:**464-2634

(216) 566-5532 .. **Feher,** Thomas L '87 (Thompson H LLP) -127 Pub Sq -3900 Key Ctr -Cleveland 44114 **Fx:**566-5800

(248) 544-0888 .. **Fehn,** Amy K '98 %Wachler & Assoc -210 E 3rd -Royal Oak, MI 48067

(330) 740-2161 .. **Fehr,** Eugene J '78 Mahoning Cnty Cmmn Pleas Ct -120 Market -Youngstown 44503 **Fx:**740-2088

Fehr, Jill D '90 -5667 Huron -Vermilion 44089

(440) 734-3194 .. **Fehribach,** Michael R '92 -4367 Georgette Av -North Olmsted 44070

(937) 225-2910 .. **Fehrman,** Anne H '94 US Atty -200 W 2nd -602 Fed Bldg -Dayton 45402

(614) 223-9324 .. **Feibel,** James B '59 -88 E Broad -Ste 900 -Columbus 43215

(513) 977-8200 .. **Feichtner,** Douglas J '02 %Dinsmore & S LLP -255 E 5th -Ste 1900 -Cincinnati 45202 **Fx:**977-8141

(330) 471-4162 .. **Feielin,** Robert M '99 Timken Co -1835 Dueber Av SW -Canton 44706

(216) 664-4984 .. **Feighan,** Ann M '92 Mun Ct Judge -1200 Ontario -12th Fl -Cleveland 44113

(216) 651-9566 .. **Feighan,** Joseph E III '96 -1297 W 76th -Cleveland 44102

(216) 631-4740 .. **Feighan,** Joseph E Jr. '60 -11009 Edgewtr Dr -Cleveland 44102

(419) 422-4014 .. **Feighner,** Robert E Jr. '99 %Hackenberg B&R -314 W Crawford -Bx1544 -Findlay 45839

(216) 621-0200 .. **Feigi,** Diane L '98 Baker & H LLP -1900 E 9th -Ste 3200 -Cleveland 44114 **Fx:**696-0740

(313) 962-7777 .. **Feikens,** Robert H '99 Allen Bros,PLLC -400 Monroe -Ste 220 -Detroit, MI 48226

(513) 621-1660 .. **Feil,** Richard D III '92 -1029 Main -Cincinnati 45202

(614) 637-9994 .. **Fein,** Henry L '81 -75 E Wilson Bridge Rd -Ste C-1 -Worthington 43085

(216) 931-6000 .. **Fein,** Robert A '70 (Ulmer & B LLP) -1300 E 9th -Ste 900 Penton Media Bldg -Cleveland 44114 **Fx:**931-6001

(216) 875-2622 .. **Fein,** Robert U '88 Apollo Housing Capital -600 Superior Av -Ste 2300 -Cleveland 44114

(614) 469-3273 .. **Fein,** William S '71 (Thompson H LLP) -10 W Broad -Ste 700 -Columbus 43215 **Fx:**469-3361

(330) 896-2889 .. **Feinberg,** Kenneth S '87 (Miller & F,LLP) -3465 S Arlngtn Rd -Ste A -Akron 44312

(216) 522-3715 .. **Feinberg,** Melvin E '69 NLRB -1240 E 9th -1695 Celebrezze Bldg -Cleveland 44199 **Fx:**522-2418

(216) 621-0200 .. **Feinberg,** Paul H '79 (Baker & H LLP) -1900 E 9th -Ste 3200 -Cleveland 44114 **Fx:**696-0740

(216) 861-4000 .. **Feinleib,** Rachel C '93 -1300 E 9th -Ste 1600 -Cleveland 44114

(614) 463-9770 .. **Feinstein,** Donald L '70 OfCnsl Roetzel & A,LPA -155 E Broad -Natl City Ctr 12th Fl -Columbus 43215 **Fx:**463-9792

(937) 652-2224 .. **Feinstein,** Mark M '95 Feinstein E Co,LPA -1052 S Main -Urbana 43078

(412) 566-6000 .. **Feinstein,** Wendy W '95 %Eckert SC&M -600 Grant -44th Fl -Pittsburgh, PA 15219

(614) 882-1425 .. **Feister,** Ronald E '76 -3760 Lima Dr -Westerville 43081

(330) 451-7637 .. **Feisthamel,** Toni B '00 Stark Cnty Pros -110 Central Plz -Ste 510 -Canton 44702

Feiszli, William J '87 -21 Marina Pnt Dr -Sandusky 44870

(419) 241-6285 ..**Feit**, Elliot H '76 (Barry & F) -520 Mad Av -Ste 930 -Toledo 43604

(330) 758-4900 ..**Fekete**, Matthew T '83 -725 Boardman-Canfld Rd -Unit L1 -Boardman 44512

(216) 363-3900 ..**Felber**, Mark B '84 -526 Superior Av -Ste 1525 -Cleveland 44114

(847) 831-4800 ..**Felber**, Susan G '93 Solo Cup Co -1700 Old Deerfld Rd -Highland Park, IL 60035

(340) 774-5666 ..**Feld**, Joel M '69 Dept Justice -48B-50C Kronprindens Gade -GERS Bldg -Saint Thomas, VI 00802

(330) 761-4207 ..**Feld**, Stephen L '99 FirstEnergy -76 S Main -Akron 44308

(614) 229-4768 ..**Feldbauer**, Steven T '01 Deloitte & Touche LLP -155 E Broad -20th Flr -Columbus 43215

(513) 621-2100 ..**Feldhaus**, Joseph H '82 (Beckman W&S LLC) -120 E 4th -1200 Mercantile Ctr -Cincinnati 45202 **Fx:**621-0106

(614) 223-9300 ..**Feldkamp**, Janet K '90 (Benesch FC&A LLP) -88 E Broad -Ste 900 -Columbus 43215 **Fx:**223-9330

(513) 421-3323 ..**Feldkamp**, Joseph F Jr. '66 -14 Garfld Pl -Ste 200 -Cincinnati 45202

(216) 363-4500 ..**Feldman**, Irwin M '64 (Benesch FC&A LLP) -200 Pub Sq -Ste 2300 -Cleveland 44114 **Fx:**363-4588

(330) 873-9251 ..**Feldman**, James K '74 -1237 Weathervane Ln -#2D -Akron 44313

(216) 931-6000 ..**Feldman**, Marc H '02 %Ulmer & B LLP -1300 E 9th -Ste 900 Penton Media Bldg -Cleveland 44114 **Fx:**931-6001

(216) 781-6100 ..**Feldman**, Marvin J '55 -815 Superior Av NE -Ste 1104 -Cleveland 44114

(216) 523-1525 ..**Feldman**, Michael J '76 (Lallo & F Co,LPA) -55 Pub Sq -Ste 1616 -Cleveland 44113

(216) 902-8531 ..**Feldman**, Steven M '95 Capstone Rlty Advisors -1120 Chester Av -Ste 300 -Cleveland 44114

(614) 222-5924 ..**Feldman**, Toba J '74 Schl Employees Retirement Syst of OH -300 E Broad -Ste 100 -Columbus 43215

(614) 466-6750 ..**Feldman**, William B '73 OH Dept Taxation -30 E Broad -22nd Fl -Columbus 43215

(513) 985-3200 ..**Feldmann**, Donald J '75 Winton Assoc,Inc -8044 Mntgmry Rd -Ste 480 -Cincinnati 45236

(614) 644-3037 ..**Feldmann**, Stephen R '87 EPA -122 S Front -Bx1049 -Columbus 43216

(859) 344-3135 ..**Feldmann**, Steven M '89 Fischer Grp -2670 Chancellor Dr -Ste 300 -Crestview Hills, KY 41017

(513) 721-4876 ..**Feldmeier**, John P '91 %Sirkin P&S LLP -105 W 4th -920 4th & Race Twr -Cincinnati 45202 **Fx:**721-0876

(513) 287-3331 ..**Feldmeier**, Melissa M '97 Cnsl Cinergy Corp -139 E 4th -24th Fl AT 11 -Bx960 -Cincinnati 45201

(419) 243-5261 ..**Feldstein**, Eden S '67 -316 N Mich -Ste 210 -Toledo 43624 **Fx:**243-5262

(419) 537-1954 ..**Feldstein**, Jay E '79 Kalniz I&F,LPA -5550 W Central Av -Toledo 43615 **Fx:**535-7732

(513) 886-3829 ..**Felerski**, Heather A '91 -Bx181342 -Fairfield 45018

(419) 562-9782 ..**Felgenhauer**, Jack L '00 Crawford Cnty Pros -112 E Mansfld -Ste 305 -Bucyrus 44820 **Fx:**562-9533

(216) 621-0200 ..**Feliciano**, Jose C '75 (Baker & H LLP) -1900 E 9th -Ste 3200 -Cleveland 44114 **Fx:**696-0740

(513) 922-7700 ..**Felix**, Jeffrey A '91 (Lane F&R Co,LPA) -4931 Delhi Pike -Cincinnati 45238 **Fx:**922-4607

(412) 456-2200 ..**Felix**, Patrick J III '93 PJ Felix III,PC -213 E Main -Carnegie, PA 15106

(440) 605-6660 ..**Felker**, Nathan A '02 %Hurtuk & D Co,LPA -6120 Parkland Blvd -Ste 100 -Cleveland 44124 **Fx:**605-6666

(216) 449-8023 ..**Fell**, Gary R '85 Cleveland Schl Bd -7415 Bway -Rm 16 -Cleveland 44105

(419) 537-6610 ..**Fell**, George N '66 (Fell & M,LPA) -3425 Exec Pkwy -Ste 207 -Toledo 43606

(419) 537-6610 ..**Fell & Marcus,LPA** -3425 Exec Pkwy -Ste 207 -Toledo 43606

(216) 787-3030 ..**Fellenbaum**, Mark '78 Atty Gen -615 W Superior Av -11th Fl -Cleveland 44113 **Fx:**787-3480

(937) 225-5637 ..**Feller**, Gina A '98 Montgomery Cnty Pros -303 W 2nd -Rm 113 -Dayton 45402

(937) 223-3277 ..**Feller**, Joseph L '98 %Bieser G&L LLP -6 N Main -400 Natl City Ctr -Dayton 45402 **Fx:**223-6339

(513) 721-5525 ..**Fellerhoff**, Matthew W '94 (Manley B) -225 W Court -Cincinnati 45202 **Fx:**721-4268

(330) 837-4678 ..**Fellmeth**, Scott E '80 -46 Fed Av NW -Massillon 44646

Fellner, Amy L '81 -1360 E Hummingbird Ct -Gilbert, AZ 85296

(585) 327-6120 ..**Felman**, Philip A '94 -50 Broad St E -Rochester, NY 14694

(740) 283-1966 ..**Felmet**, Bryan H '76 Jefferson Cnty Pros -16001 State Route 7 -Steubenville 43952

(937) 225-4600 ..**Felsburg**, Timothy A '98 Montgomery Cnty CSEA -14 W 4th -Bx8744 -Dayton 45401

(513) 381-2838 ..**Felson**, Cynthia C '93 %Taft S&H LLP -425 Walnut -Ste 1800 -Cincinnati 45202 **Fx:**381-0205

(513) 721-2500 ..**Felson**, Edward J '89 -36 E 7th -Ste 1650 -Cincinnati 45202

(513) 721-4900 ..**Felson**, Stephen R '66 -617 Vine -Ste 1401 -Cincinnati 45202 **Fx:**639-7001

(313) 568-6700 ..**Felt**, J Kay '67 (Dykema G PLLC) -400 Renaissance Ctr -35th Fl -Detroit, MI 48243

(330) 492-8717 ..**Feltes**, Joseph J '78 (Buckingham D&B,LLP) -4518 Fulton Dr NW -Bx35548 -Canton 44735 **Fx:**492-9625

(330) 384-5778 ..**Feltner**, David Lee '76 FirstEnergy Corp -76 S Main -Akron 44308

Felton, Mary K '99 -Bx215 -Greenville 45331

(216) 621-1530 ..**Felty**, Kriss D '83 (Shapiro & F,LLP) -1500 W 3rd -Ste 400 -Cleveland 44113 **Fx:**621-1551

(440) 473-1025 ..**Feneli**, Dale C '75 -6690 Beta Dr -Ste 106 -Cleveland 44143

(937) 865-6800 ..**Fening**, Matthew B '94 Lexis/Nexis -Bx933 -Dayton 45401

(614) 222-3957 ..**Fenker**, Kristen K '94 Ernst & Young LLP -41 S High -Ste 1100 -Columbus 43215

Fenker, Steven M '94 -7441 Cody Ln -Delaware 43015

(614) 466-5394 ..**Fenlon**, John M '89 Pub Def -8 E Long -Columbus 43215

(614) 223-3302 ..**Fenlon**, Mary R '88 Cnsl Ameritech -150 E Gay -Columbus 43215

(440) 248-7906 ..**Fenn**, David R '98 %Mazanec R&R Co,LPA -34305 Solon Rd -Ste 100 -Cleveland 44139 **Fx:**248-8861

(214) 969-5130 ..**Fennell**, Thomas E '75 (Jones DR&P) -2727 N Harwood -Dallas, TX 75201 **Fx:**969-5100

(216) 689-5106 ..**Fenner**, Kathleen B '81 KeyBank NA -127 Pub Sq -2nd Fl, Leg Dept -Cleveland 44114 **Fx:**689-4121

(614) 863-3150 ..**Fennessey**, Dennis J '76 -5330 E Main -Ste 101 -Whitehall 43213

(216) 861-5000 ..**Fenske**, Audrey A '89 Ernst & Young -1300 Huntngtn Bldg -925 Euclid Av -Cleveland 44115

(305) 499-2165 ..**Fenske**, Kathryn F '95 AHCA -8355 NW 53rd -Fl 1 -Miami, FL 33166

(740) 594-3401 ..**Fenstermaker**, Eric B '75 -5466 Fox Lk Rd -Athens 45701

(440) 292-7060 ..**Fenton**, Gary H '80 Marlen Mfg & Devlpmnt Co -5150 Richmond Rd -Bedford 44146

(513) 218-7370 ..**Fenton**, John H '95 -5345 Moeller Av -Norwood 45212

(330) 296-3621 ..**Fenwick**, Timothy S '91 Courtesy Mgmt,Inc -1345 E Main -Ravenna 44266

(440) 888-8090 ..**Feola**, Dennis L '74 -6684 Fernhurst Av -Parma Heights 44130

(440) 446-1327 ..**Feran**, Amy R '83 -5650 Hawthorne Dr -Highland Heights 44143

(216) 622-3709 ..**Feran**, Edward F '87 US Atty -801 W Superior -Ste 400 -Cleveland 44113 **Fx:**622-3370

(239) 334-1555 ..**Ferber**, Charles T '99 C Ferber,PA -2125 1st -Ste 100 -Fort Myers, FL 33901 **Fx:**334-4855

(419) 626-3800 ..**Ferber**, Gary S '77 (Reno B&F Co,LPA) -725 Sycamore Line -Sandusky 44870 **Fx:**626-3638

(614) 463-4201 ..**Ferber**, James M '74 (Littler M,PC) -21 E State -Ste 1600 -Columbus 43215 **Fx:**221-3301

(404) 572-4600 ..**Ferber**, R Scott '98 %King & S,LLP -191 Pchtree NE -Atlanta, GA 30303

(775) 786-8000 ..**Ferchau**, Kimberly B '01 %Bible H&T -201 W Lrbty -3rd Fl -Reno, NV 89501

(513) 732-2140 ..**Ferenc**, Richard P '77 (Ely & T) -322 Main -Batavia 45103

(440) 333-8118 ..**Ferenczy-Furry**, Deborah S '95 Northern Title Agncy,Inc -20575 Ctr Ridge Rd -Ste 310 -Rocky River 44116

(513) 651-7222 ..**Ferestad**, Mark A '92 -30 Garfld Pl -Ste 430 Cincinnati Club Bldg -Cincinnati 45202

(614) 431-6006 ..**Fergus**, John C II '78 Fergus Companies -200 E Campus Vw Blvd -Ste 200 -Columbus 43235

(614) 451-7517 ..**Fergus**, Kevin B '61 -2134 Chardon Rd -Columbus 43220

(614) 644-8213 ..**Fergus**, Ronda H '80 PUCO -180 E Broad -Columbus 43266

(740) 363-1324 ..**Fergus**, William D Jr. '95 GS Miller -103 N Union -Ste A -Delaware 43015 **Fx:**548-5443

(513) 771-6768 ..**Ferguson**, Amy S '92 (Cuni F&L Co,LPA) -10655 Sprngfld Pike -Cincinnati 45215

(216) 443-7800 ..**Ferguson**, Anna B '01 %Cuyahoga Cnty Pros -1200 Ontario -8th Fl -Cleveland 44113 **Fx:**698-2270

(937) 865-6800 ..**Ferguson**, Candice H '02 Lexis/Nexis -Bx933 -Dayton 45401

(513) 887-3474 ..**Ferguson**, Danny L '86 Butler Cnty Pros -315 High -11th Fl -Bx515 -Hamilton 45012

(330) 762-9933 ..**Ferguson**, David H '70 (Ferguson & H) -120 E Mill -Ste 415 -Akron 44308

(440) 322-8236 ..**Ferguson**, George H '56 -359 Miami Av -Elyria 44035

(614) 464-6400 ..**Ferguson**, Gerald P '79 (Vorys SS&P LLP) -52 E Gay -Bx1008 -Columbus 43216 **Fx:**464-6350

(330) 762-9933 ..**Ferguson & Hanlon** -120 E Mill -Ste 415 -Akron 44308

Ferguson, Janet L '03 -(Address Unavailable)

(617) 742-2888 ..**Ferguson**, Jeffrey W '96 West Group -Exch Pl -53 State St 13th Fl -Boston, MA 02109

(513) 734-2283 ..**Ferguson**, Jeffry D '85 -424 W Plane -Bethel 45106

(614) 466-3664 ..**Ferguson**, Kathy A '91 %OH DOT -1980 W Broad -Columbus 43223

(419) 841-4294 ..**Ferguson**, Kevin M '86 (Schnorf F&G) -5217 Monroe -Ste A -Bx23156 -Toledo 43623

(937) 372-9963 ..**Ferguson**, Lester L '69 -Bx160 -Xenia 45385

(740) 264-0661 ..**Ferguson**, Lisa M '02 Lisa Kay Ferguson -131 Main -Wintersville 43953

(859) 824-6941 ..**Ferguson**, Margarita H '90 -141 N Main -Bx28 -Williamston, KY 41097

(440) 893-2327 ..**Ferguson**, Mark A '86 BearWare Inc -7160 Chagrin Rd -Ste 210 -Chagrin Falls 44023

(614) 481-4030 ..**Ferguson**, Melissa E '93 Natl Kidney Fdn of OH -1373 Grandvw Av -Columbus 43212

(614) 228-6885 ..**Ferguson**, Melissa M '98 %Lane A&H LLC -175 S 3rd -Ste 700 -Columbus 43215 **Fx:**228-0146

(614) 939-0590 ..**Ferguson**, Nancy H '80 -4789 Yantis Dr -New Albany 43054

(937) 456-8156 ..**Ferguson**, Rebecca J '75 Preble Cnty Pros -100 E Main -Cthse 1st Fl -Eaton 45320 **Fx:**456-8199

(216) 641-8580 ..**Ferguson**, Rhonda S '94 Ferro Corp -1000 Lakeside Av -Cleveland 44114 **Fx:**875-7275

(614) 692-3284 ..**Ferguson**, Richard D '88 US Dfnse Lgstcs Agncy -Bx3990 -Columbus 43218

(419) 213-3000 ..**Ferguson**, Twila R '94 Lucas Cnty CSEA -701 Adams -Toledo 43624

(614) 464-6400 ..**Ferguson**, Victor J '98 %Vorys SS&P LLP -52 E Gay -Bx1008 -Columbus 43216 **Fx:**464-6350

(740) 432-4502 ..**Ferguson**, William H '85 (Heine & F) -803 Steubenvll Av -Cambridge 43725 **Fx:**439-7712

(614) 466-3947 ..**Ferguson-Ramos**, Lisa A '94 OH Brd of Nursing -17 S High -Ste 400 -Columbus 43215

(440) 350-3000 ..**Ferkol**, Jeffrey C '86 Lake Co Juv Ct -53 E Erie -Painesville 44077

(614) 341-2645 ..**Fernald**, Willard T '93 Fifth Third Bank -21 E State -MD 4683840 -Columbus 43215

(419) 213-4775 ..**Fernandes**, Trevor N '95 Lucas Cnty Probate Ct -700 Adams -#200 -Toledo 43624

(513) 779-5516 ..**Fernandez**, Eric J '96 -7185 Lrbty Centre Dr -A -West Chester 45069 **Fx:**779-5519

(513) 751-6119 ..**Fernandez**, Justin E '94 -917 Main -4th Fl -Cincinnati 45202

(915) 747-5663 ..**Fernandez**, Myriam C '98 Univ of Texas/El Paso -306 E Union Bldg -El Paso, TX 79968

(216) 522-8191 ..**Fernandez**, Susan E '87 NLRB -1240 E 9th -1695 Celebrezze Bldg -Cleveland 44199 **Fx:**522-2418

(216) 579-1700 ..**Fernengel**, Gregory D '03 %Pearne & G LLP -1801 E 9th -Ste 1200 -Cleveland 44114 **Fx:**579-6073

(937) 443-6740 ..**Ferrante**, Francesco A '81 (Thompson H LLP) -2000 Cthse Plz NE -Bx8801 -Dayton 45401 **Fx:**443-6635

(216) 928-2200 ..**Ferrante**, Jason P '04 %Sutter OM&F -1301 E 9th -3600 Erievw Twr -Cleveland 44114 **Fx:**928-4400

(330) 533-0916 ..**Ferrante**, Joseph A '88 Nationwide Ins -6715 Tippecanoe Rd -Ste 201 -Canfield 44406

(216) 586-3939 ..**Ferraro**, Adrienne M '03 %Jones D -901 Lakeside Av -Cleveland 44114 **Fx:**579-0212

(216) 575-0777 ..**Ferraro**, James L '03 (Kelley & F,LLP) -1300 E 9th -Ste 1901 -Cleveland 44114 **Fx:**575-0799

(614) 365-9900 ..**Ferrell**, Bradley T '99 %Zeiger TL&L,LLP -41 S High -Ste 3500 Huntngtn Ctr -Columbus 43215 **Fx:**365-7900

(330) 452-7531 ..**Ferrell**, David B '78 Ferrell W&S -220 Market Av S -Ste 600 -Canton 44702

(419) 669-8500 ..**Ferrell**, Dennis L '79 -23151 Bays Rd -Custar 43511

(513) 381-2838 ..**Ferrell**, Richard L III '94 %Taft S&H LLP -425 Walnut -Ste 1800 -Cincinnati 45202 **Fx:**381-0205

(614) 466-5394 ..**Ferrell**, Stephen A '93 Pub Def -8 E Long -Columbus 43215

(614) 228-1541 ..**Ferrell**, Tara M '03 %Baker & H LLP -65 E State -Ste 2100 -Columbus 43215 **Fx:**462-2616

(304) 485-4452 ..**Ferrell**, Vernon P II '89 Badger Lumber Co,Inc -Bx367 -Parkersburg, WV 26102

Ferreri, Robert A '80 -10833 Fence Row Dr -Strongsville 44149

(330) 837-4678 ..**Ferrero**, John Dee Jr. '81 -46 Fed Av NW -Massillon 44647

(330) 837-4678 ..**Ferrero**, Thomas V '72 -46 Fed Av NW -Massillon 44647

(740) 594-8388 ..**Ferrier**, Lisbeth B '85 (Sowash C&F) -39 N Cllg -Bx2629 -Athens 45701

(859) 655-4200 ..**Ferrigno**, Nicholas W Jr. '02 Greenebaum D&M PLLC -50 E RiverCenter Blvd -Ste 1800 -Covington, KY 41011 **Fx:**655-4239

(614) 275-2672 ..**Ferriman**, David B '84 Franklin Cnty Children Srvcs -855 W Mound -Columbus 43223 **Fx:**275-2589

(614) 228-1541 ..**Ferris**, Andrew M '95 %Baker & H LLP -65 E State -Ste 2100 -Columbus 43215 **Fx:**462-2616

(614) 889-4777 ..**Ferris**, Boyd B '67 (Ferris & N LLP) -2733 W Dublin Granvll Rd -Columbus 43235

(513) 896-7722 ..**Ferris**, Carl D '80 -225 Ct -Hamilton 45011

(614) 889-4777 ..**Ferris**, David A '92 (Ferris & N LLP) -2733 W Dublin Granvll Rd -Columbus 43235

(330) 533-0052 ..**Ferris**, Dean F '51 -106 S Broad -Canfield 44406

(513) 896-7722 ..**Ferris**, Donald L '52 -225 Ct -Hamilton 45011

(614) 645-5849 ..**Ferris**, Jacqueline A '04 Franklin Cnty Municipal Ct -375 S High -Columbus 43215

(513) 231-1100 ..**Ferris**, James K '85 -6124 Corbly Rd -Cincinnati 45230

(330) 744-0202 ..**Ferris**, Ted A '79 -26 Market -Ste 610 Sky Bk Bldg -Youngstown 44503

(330) 426-9296 ..**Ferris**, Thomas A '82 -Bx421 -East Palestine 44413

(713) 652-7284 ..**Ferro**, Michael P '91 Equistar Chemicals,LP -1221 McKinney -Ste 1600 -Houston, TX 77010

(740) 283-1966 ..**Ferro**, Richard H '99 Jefferson Cnty Pros -16001 State Route 7 -Steubenville 43952

(614) 228-5225 ..**Ferron**, John W '85 (Ferron & Assoc,LPA) -580 N 4th -Ste 450 -Columbus 43215 **Fx:**228-3255

(330) 452-6400 ..**Ferruccio**, Samuel J Jr. '79 S Ferruccio Jr -220 Market Av S -Ste 400 -Canton 44702

(513) 579-6400 ..**Fershtman**, Alan S '94 (Keating M&K PLL) -1 E 4th -1400 Provident Twr -Cincinnati 45202 **Fx:**579-6457

(216) 416-3730 ..**Ferstman**, Jerome M '70 Forest City Enterprises -50 Pub Sq -Ste 1000-B -Cleveland 44113

(216) 696-4441 ..**Fertel**, Robert M '72 Zashin & R Co,LPA -55 Pub Sq -Ste 1490 -Cleveland 44113 **Fx:**696-1618

(614) 228-3822 ..**Fesenmyer**, Thomas M '01 (Sundberg & F,LLC) -5 E Long -Ste 609 -Columbus 43215 **Fx:**228-3882

(216) 241-9990 ..**Fesler**, Michael B '96 %J Jerome & Assoc -55 Pub Sq -Ste 2020 -Cleveland 44113 **Fx:**241-2920

(419) 524-4711 ..**Fesmier**, Raymond G '85 (Cole B&F) -28 Park Av -Mansfield 44902 **Fx:**522-8905

(516) 344-8629 ..**Fess**, Gregory H '71 Brookhaven Natl Lab -Bldg 450 -Upton, NY 11973

(440) 236-8412 ..**Fetchet**, Carl '54 -26091 Royalton Rd -Columbia Station 44028

(330) 364-9599 ..**Fete**, Marvin T '01 -138 2nd NW -New Philadelphia 44663 **Fx:**343-7511

(513) 785-4561 ..**Fette**, Glenn P '92 OH Bureau of Workers Comp -345 High -6th Fl -Hamilton 45011 **Fx:**785-4557

(513) 241-3630 ..**Fettner**, Saul A '65 -10 W 9th -Cincinnati 45202

(216) 621-7227 ..**Feudo**, Vincent A '65 OfCnsl Nicola G&C,LLC -25 W Prospect Av -Republic Bldg Ste 1400 -Cleveland 44115 **Fx:**621-3999

(440) 461-1054 ..**Feuer**, Charles E '89 -405 Longspur Rd -Highland Heights 44143

(937) 449-2800 ..**Feuer**, Mark S '78 (Chernesky H&K PLL) -10 Cthse Plz SW -Ste 1100 -Dayton 45402 **Fx:**449-2821

(216) 360-7200 ..**Feuerman**, Richard J '99 Carlisle MRK&U Co,LPA -24755 Chagrin Blvd -Ste 200 -Cleveland 44122 **Fx:**360-7210

(614) 462-2264 ..**Fewell**, Jennifer L '03 %Schottenstein Z&D -250 West -Bx165020 -Columbus 43216 **Fx:**462-5135

(614) 232-9100 ..**Fey**, Carol A '85 -454 E Main -Ste 218 -Columbus 43215

Feyko, James '90 -2591 Henthorn Rd -Columbus 43221

(614) 837-1870 ..**Feyko**, Jeffrey '85 -115 N Center -Pickerington 43147

(330) 832-9878 ..**Fichter**, Joel C '84 Stergios & K Co,LPA -2859 Aaronwood Av NE -Ste 101 -Massillon 44646

Fichter, Matthew N '03 -1003 2nd NE -Massillon 44646

(513) 961-1672 ..**Fichter**, Tawn A '79 %L Seiler -2056 Eastern Av -Cincinnati 45202

(513) 287-2660 ..**Ficke**, Gregory C '90 Cinergy Corp -139 E 4th -Rm 403-A MD EF402 -Cincinnati 45202 **Fx:**287-1592

(419) 259-6440 ..**Fickel**, David J '78 US Bnkrptcy Cts -1716 Spielbusch -Toledo 43624

(330) 497-0700 ..**Fickes**, Jeffrey A '01 %Krugliak WG&D Co,LPA -4775 Munson NW -Bx36963 -Canton 44735 **Fx:**497-4020

(330) 535-5711 ..**Fickes**, John C '85 (Brouse M) -106 S Main -500 First Natl Twr -Akron 44308 **Fx:**253-8601

(513) 579-7968 ..**Fiddes**, Richard C '80 Federated Dept Stores Inc -7 W 7th -Cincinnati 45202 **Fx:**579-7897

Fidel, Ann A '01 -531 Sprngwood Cir SW -New Philadelphia 44663

(614) 228-1541 ..**Fidler**, Christopher D '92 (Baker & H LLP) -65 E State -Ste 2100 -Columbus 43215 **Fx:**462-2616

(513) 621-5088 ..**Fidler**, Edward '37 -830 Main -Ste 200 -Cincinnati 45202

(330) 456-6200 ..**Fidler**, James G '95 FBI -220 Market Av S -Ste 602 -Canton 44702

(216) 696-4200 ..**Fidler**, John Paul '96 %Schneider SR&L PLL -1111 Superior Av -Ste 1000 -Cleveland 44114 **Fx:**696-7303

(513) 241-7600 ..**Fidler**, Mark W '84 %Scacchetti & S -601 Main -3rd Fl -Cincinnati 45202

(440) 350-2378 ..**Fiederer**, Barbara A '85 Lake Cnty Emplymnt & Training -125 E Erie -Painesville 44077

(419) 244-4304 ..**Fiedler**, Robert W Jr. '96 -1709 Spielbusch Av -Ste 100 -Toledo 43624 **Fx:**244-4306

(419) 333-4345 ..**Fiegl**, Christopher P '92 -416 W State -Ste 206 -Fremont 43420 **Fx:**333-4346

(513) 887-7300 ..**Fiehrer Lane & Copeland** -10 Jrnl Sq -Ste 400 -Hamilton 45011

(513) 887-7300 ..**Fiehrer**, Lawrence P '74 (Fiehrer L&C) -10 Jrnl Sq -Ste 400 -Hamilton 45011

(513) 684-9000 ..**Field**, Eileen K '82 (Field & H,Ltd) -36 E 4th -Ste 1304 -Cincinnati 45202

(440) 974-0099 ..**Field**, Harry E '71 -6988 Spinach Dr -Mentor 44060

(440) 992-5522 ..**Field**, Jon T '81 -4366 Main Av -Bx1276 -Ashtabula 44005

(419) 874-2261 ..**Field**, Peter F '96 Weiss & Assoc -330 Louisiana Av -Ste C -Perrysburg 43551

(614) 462-3555 ..**Fields**, Adria P '95 Franklin Cnty Pros -373 S High -Columbus 43215

(216) 696-7170 ..**Fields**, Darrell A '83 (Forbes F & Assoc Co,LPA) -614 W Superior Av -700 Rckflr Bldg -Cleveland 44113

(740) 689-1372 ..**Fields**, James A '88 Fields & I -112 E Main -Ste 202 -Lancaster 43130

Fields, Matthew H '99 -65 Shffld Rd -Columbus 43214

(614) 837-3980 ..**Fields**, Orval E II '75 O Fields II -660 Hill Rd N -Bx184 -Pickerington 43147

(937) 225-4600 ..**Fields**, Sarah E '01 Montgomery Cnty CSEA -14 W 4th -Bx8744 -Dayton 45401

(740) 374-5346 ..**Fields**, William A '64 (W Fields) -125 Putnam -Ste 300 -Bx710 -Marietta 45750

(859) 426-1300 ..**Fields-Lee**, Lori J '84 (Ziegler & S,PSC) -541 Buttermilk Pike -Ste 500 -Bx175710 -Covington, KY 41017

(513) 784-7338 ..**Fielman**, Tracey A '93 Deloitte & Touche -250 E 5th -Ste 1900 -Cincinnati 45202

(614) 865-4700 ..**Fiely**, Linda K '79 OCSEA -390 Worthngtn Rd -Ste A -Westerville 43082

(440) 460-0333 ..**Fierman**, Scott A '94 -6028 Mayfld Rd -#9 -Mayfield Heights 44124

(937) 254-3767 ..**Fierst**, David J '90 -205 Claypool Bldg -Dayton 45432

(937) 382-5509 ..**Fife**, David M '75 (Fife & F) -27 N South -Bx695 -Wilmington 45177

(937) 382-5509 ..**Fife**, Elaine H '75 (Fife & F) -27 N South -Bx695 -Wilmington 45177

(440) 871-5020 ..**Fifner**, Douglas K '79 (DK Fifner Co,LPA) -24441 Detroit Rd -Ste 300 -Westlake 44145

(440) 871-5020 ..**Fifner**, Elaine S '79 DK Fifner Co,LPA -24441 Detroit Rd -Ste 300 -Westlake 44145

(216) 623-1220 ..**Fifner**, Greta E '86 -2672 W 14th -Cleveland 44113

(614) 891-0336 ..**Fifner**, William F '73 (Fifner & J,LLC) -1001 Eastwind Dr -Ste 305 -Westerville 43081

(216) 696-7600 ..**Fiftal**, Emily C '04 %Duvin C&H -1301 E 9th -20th Fl Erievw Twr -Cleveland 44114 **Fx:**696-2038

Figelman, Jacob M '04 -(Address Unavailable)

(614) 248-6308 ..**Figetakis**, Frances L '87 Bank One Mgt Corp -100 E Broad -OH1-0158 -Columbus 43271

(330) 493-0040 ..**Figler**, Ronald G '71 OfCnsl Lesh C&M -4150 Belden Vllg NW -Ste 606 -Canton 44718

(330) 250-2746 ..**Figler**, Susan M '92 -Bx248 -Munroe Falls 44262

(804) 244-6259 ..**Figurski**, George A '84 US Army JAG School -600 Massie Rd -Charlottesville, VA 22903

(330) 762-2411 ..**Fike**, Lisa A '94 %Amer C Co,LPA -159 S Main -6th Fl -Akron 44308 **Fx:**762-9918

(216) 514-1100 ..**Fiktus**, Richard D '78 (Rolf & G Co,LPA) -30100 Chagrin Blvd -Ste 350 Corp Cir -Cleveland 44124 **Fx:**514-0030

(216) 221-1616 ..**Filak**, John J '56 -13979 Edgewtr Dr -Lakewood 44107

(216) 241-4554 ..**Filak**, John J Jr. '84 AFSCME OH Cncl 8 -1603 E 27th -Cleveland 44114

(937) 323-0093 ..**Filhart**, Eddie L '66 -451 Upper Valley Pike -Springfield 45504

(216) 443-7800 ..**Filiatraut**, Kevin R '02 %Cuyahoga Cnty Pros -1200 Ontario -8th Fl -Cleveland 44113 **Fx:**698-2270

(513) 352-6659 ..**Filiatraut**, Renee S '88 (Thompson H LLP) -312 Walnut -14th Fl -Cincinnati 45202 **Fx:**241-4771

(419) 427-9000 ..**Filkins**, John C III '90 -101 W Sandusky -Ste 204 -Findlay 45840 **Fx:**427-9887

(330) 394-6148 ..**Finamore**, Mark S '82 -258 Seneca Av NE -Warren 44481

(614) 871-5000 ..**Finan**, Nancy C '89 -31116 Carlton Dr -Bay Village 44140

(614) 621-1500 ..**Finan**, Richard H '59 (Calfee H&G LLP) -21 E State -1100 Fifth Third Ctr -Columbus 43215 **Fx:**621-0010

(937) 223-8177 ..**Finch**, Kristin A '95 %Coolidge WW&L -33 W 1st -Ste 600 -Dayton 45402 **Fx:**223-6705

(513) 684-3677 ..**Finch**, Linda B '80 NLRB -550 Main -Rm 3003 -Cincinnati 45202

(216) 241-6602 ..**Fincun**, Jeffrey D '73 (Weston HFP&H LLP) -50 Pub Sq -2500 Trmnl Twr -Cleveland 44113 **Fx:**621-8369

(419) 241-4400 ..**Findish**, Marie E '95 Munger W Co,LPA -626 Mad Av -Ste 400 -Toledo 43604

(419) 289-6888 ..**Findley**, Daniel G '97 (Harpster V&F) -60 W 2nd -Ashland 44805 **Fx:**281-2461

(614) 827-7300 ..**Findley**, Stephen C '80 (Freund F&A) -65 E State -Ste 800 -Columbus 43215 **Fx:**827-7303

(216) 514-6400 ..**Fine**, Michael L '03 %Zipkin W Co LPA -3637 S Green Rd -Zipkin Whiting Bldg -Cleveland 44122 **Fx:**514-6406

(216) 696-7525 ..**Fine**, Michael W '81 (Fine G & Assoc,LPA) -1370 W 6th -Ste 202 -Cleveland 44113

(216) 591-1455 ..**Fine**, Philip R '69 -3681 Green Rd -Room 410 -Beachwood 44122

(937) 438-2819 ..**Finefrock**, James L '75 (J Finefrock & Assoc Co,LPA) -5335 Far Hills Av -Bx4208 -Dayton 45401

Finefrock, Scott D '04 -(Address Unavailable)

(614) 466-0722 ..**Finegold**, Jordan '86 Atty Gen -150 E Gay -Columbus 43215 **Fx:**644-9973

(216) 621-2222 ..**Finelli**, Daniel M '93 (Finelli & M,PLL) -526 Superior Av -730 Leader Bldg -Cleveland 44114 **Fx:**621-1114

(330) 385-3900 ..**Fineman**, Bernard '58 Aronson F&D Co, LPA -124 E 5th -East Liverpool 43920

(513) 761-9300 .. **Finesman**, Theodore H '69 T Bear, Inc. -8405 Reading Rd
-Cincinnati 45215

(614) 466-2766 .. **Finfrock**, Teri Jo '87 Atty Gen -30 E Broad -Columbus 43215
Fx:644-1926

(513) 936-9300 .. **Fingerman**, Debra M '80 Attys Abstract Title Agncy -9352 Main
-Cincinnati 45242

(216) 241-3400 .. **Fini**, Rosalina M '94 Cnty Mental Health Bd -1400 W 25th -3rd Fl
-Cleveland 44113

(614) 228-0234 .. **Fink**, Andrew B '01 MidWest Comm & Media -57 E Gay
-Columbus 43215

(440) 887-7400 .. **Fink**, Edward J '76 Parma Mun Ct -5555 Powers Blvd
-Parma 44129

(513) 241-9400 .. **Fink**, Elaine E '85 Legal Aid -215 E 9th -Ste 200 -Cincinnati 45202

(330) 297-3850 .. **Fink**, Eric R '99 Portage Cnty Pros -466 S Chestnut
-Ravenna 44266

(216) 889-5530 .. **Fink**, Franklin E '04 Cnsl AG Interactive,Inc -1 Amer Rd
-Cleveland 44144 **Fx:**889-5531

(614) 227-2000 .. **Fink**, Howard P '70 OfCnsl Porter WM&A LLP -41 S High
-Columbus 43215 **Fx:**227-2100

(513) 381-2838 .. **Fink**, Jerold A '66 (Taft S&H LLP) -425 Walnut -Ste 1800
-Cincinnati 45202 **Fx:**381-0205

(614) 877-3333 .. **Fink**, Joan K '79 -Bx492 -Galloway 43119

(440) 846-3666 .. **Fink**, Joseph J '79 (J Fink Co,LPA) -11221 Pearl Rd
-Strongsville 44136

(216) 586-3939 .. **Fink**, Kevin H '04 %Jones D -901 Lakeside Av -Cleveland 44114
Fx:579-0212

(419) 530-4260 .. **Fink**, Maara A '96 Univ of Toledo Law Schl -2801 W Bancroft
-Toledo 43606

(330) 262-3030 .. **Fink**, Michelle Ann '89 Wayne Cnty Pros -115 W Lbrty
-Wooster 44691 **Fx:**287-5412

(216) 781-8700 .. **Fink**, Scott D '98 Novak RP&S,LLP -1660 W 2nd
-Ste 270 Skylight Ofc Twr -Cleveland 44113 **Fx:**781-9227

(334) 953-7931 .. **Fink**, Theodore J '77 USAF AU/JA -55 Lemay Plz -Ste 22
-Maxwell AFB, AL 36112

(859) 344-1262 .. **Finkbeiner**, Mae L '51 -149 Rossmoyne Av -Crestview
Hills, KY 41017

(513) 621-6464 .. **Finke**, Harry J IV '82 (Graydon H&R LLP) -511 Walnut
-1900 Fifth Third Ctr -Cincinnati 45202 **Fx:**651-3836

(513) 333-7528 .. **Finke**, Nicholas D '80 Natl Underground Railrd Freedom Ctr
-50 E Freedom Way -Cincinnati 45202

(937) 228-7104 .. **Finke**, R Peter '68 (Nolan SS&F) -40 N Main -Ste 1812
-Dayton 45423 **Fx:**226-1945

(419) 586-1334 .. **Finke**, Ross J '03 -110½ W Market -Ste 201 -Bx444 -Celina 45822
Fx:584-0120

(513) 621-9921 .. **Finkelmeier**, Louis J Jr. '68 (Finkelmeier & F) -36 E 7th -Ste 1660
-Cincinnati 45202 **Fx:**621-9923

(216) 464-3570 .. **Finkelstein**, Tracy K '92 RS Leiken -23611 Chagrin Blvd -Ste 225
-Beachwood 44122

(216) 241-0044 .. **Finkenthal**, Robert J '85 -101 W Prospect Av -Ste 1835
-Cleveland 44115

(937) 372-4411 .. **Finlay**, John A '66 (Brandabur FJW&B) -260 N Detroit
-Xenia 45385 **Fx:**372-4415

(216) 781-1212 .. **Finley**, Bonnie S '95 Walter & H LLP -1301 E 9th -Ste 3500
-Cleveland 44114 **Fx:**575-0911

(614) 249-6258 .. **Finley**, Cathy M '80 Nationwide Life Ins Co -1 Nationwide Plz
-Pub Comm Compliance -Columbus 43215

(216) 574-4814 .. **Finley**, David G '84 -25 W Prospect Av -Ste 704-R
-Cleveland 44115

(937) 222-2500 .. **Finley**, Gale S '81 (Sebaly S&D) -1900 Kettering Twr
-Dayton 45423 **Fx:**222-6554

(740) 446-8575 .. **Finley**, Jeffery L '98 (Eachus & F) -431 2nd Av -Bx351
-Gallipolis 45631

(415) 781-1788 .. **Finley**, Julie C '82 (Starr F LLP) -1 Calif -Ste 300
-San Francisco, CA 94111

(216) 941-0101 .. **Finley**, Kenneth W '81 -15008 Lorain Av -Ste 6 -Cleveland 44111

(614) 485-6207 .. **Finley**, Kim M '00 OH Insurance Liquidators Ofc -1366 Dublin Rd
-Columbus 43215 **Fx:**485-6316

(330) 375-8729 .. **Finley**, Michael J '81 Natl City Bnk-Trust Div -Bx2130 -Akron
44309

(614) 227-8897 .. **Finley**, Price D '90 (Bricker & E LLP) -100 S 3rd -Columbus 43215
Fx:227-2390

(406) 259-5024 .. **Finn**, Bradley J '77 -2812 1st Av N -Ste 300 -Billings, MT 59101

(330) 376-2700 .. **Finn**, Terrence S '87 (Roetzel & A,LPA) -222 S Main -Akron 44308
Fx:376-4577

(937) 225-5789 .. **Finn-DeLuca**, Valerie M '94 2nd Dist Ct of Appls -41 N Perry
-Rm 515 -Bx972 -Dayton 45422

(440) 808-8461 .. **Finnan**, Gabrielle A '95 Lexis Nexis -1235 Dellwood Dr
-Westlake 44145

(937) 548-3240 .. **Finnarn**, Theodore O '76 -201 E 5th -Greenville 45331

(330) 297-3850 .. **Finnegan**, Eric P '03 Portage Cnty Pros -466 S Chestnut
-Ravenna 44266

(734) 302-3233 .. **Finnegan**, John M '83 (Heberle & F) -2580 Craig Rd
-Ann Arbor, MI 48103

(614) 644-7741 .. **Finnegan**, Matthew L '86 Industrial Commssn of OH -30 W Spring
-9th Fl -Columbus 43215 **Fx:**752-8785

(740) 387-2020 .. **Finnegan**, William R '79 Mun Ct Judge -233 W Center
-Marion 43302
Finnen, George R '65 -212 Marvel Dr -Lancaster 43130

(614) 227-2000 .. **Finneran**, Mary Theresa '89 %Porter WM&A LLP -41 S High
-Columbus 43215 **Fx:**227-2100

(614) 846-1440 .. **Finneran**, Russell D '54 -5314 Woodglen Rd -Columbus 43214

(614) 457-6147 .. **Finneran**, Thomas J '54 -1073 Stanhope Dr -Columbus 43221

(614) 464-0776 .. **Finneran**, Todd G '81 -380 S 5th -Ste 4 -Columbus 43215

(216) 642-9200 .. **Finnerty**, Audrine P '92 -5700 Pearl Rd -Ste 202 -Cleveland 44129

(614) 466-4328 .. **Finnerty**, Beth A '91 Atty Gen -150 E Gay -Columbus 43215
Fx:995-0266

(216) 674-1400 .. **Finnerty**, David J '92 -5700 Pearl Rd -Ste 202 -Parma 44129
Fx:642-8780

(614) 221-4734 .. **Finnerty**, Gregory N '87 (Finnerty Law Ofc) -85 E Gay -Ste 702
-Columbus 43215

(937) 372-8055 .. **Finney**, Charles R '49 OfCnsl Miller FM&B -20 King Av -Bx610
-Xenia 45385

(330) 376-2600 .. **Finney**, Christopher N '03 %SK Pritchard -168 E Market -Ste 205
-Akron 44308

(513) 533-2996 .. **Finney**, Christopher P '87 (Finney SS&K Co,LPA) -2623 Erie Av
-Bx8804 -Cincinnati 45208

(513) 732-7327 .. **Finney**, Michael J '79 Clermont Cnty Dom Rltns Ct
-2340 Clermont Ctr Dr -Batavia 45103

(513) 533-2996 .. **Finney Stagnaro Saba & Klusmeier Co,LPA** -2623 Erie Av
-Bx8804 -Cincinnati 45208

(513) 287-3601 .. **Finnigan**, John J Jr. '79 SrCnsl Cinergy Srvcs Legal Dept
-139 E 4th -Rm 25 -Bx960 -Cincinnati 45201

(330) 497-2000 .. **Finnucan**, John C '93 Bruner Cox,LLP -4690 Munson NW
-Ste 201 -Bx35429 -Canton 44735

(513) 983-7190 .. **Finocharo**, John J '84 Procter & Gamble Co-Legal -1 Procter &
Gamble Plz -Cincinnati 45202

(513) 381-6810 .. **Finucane**, Michael E '88 Reisenfeld & Assoc -2355 Auburn Av
-Cincinnati 45219 **Fx:**381-0255

(614) 759-0123 .. **Finucane**, Sandra J '96 %D Farmer & Assoc,LPA
-800 Cross Pnte Rd -Ste Q -Columbus 43230 **Fx:**759-0125

(330) 339-3998 .. **Finzel**, Kristen A '01 SE OH Lgl Srvcs -332 W High Av
-New Philadelphia 44663

(330) 899-9335 .. **Fiocca**, Carl J '76 -304 N Cleveland-Massilon Rd -Akron 44333

(614) 469-7130 .. **Fiocca**, John A Jr. '75 %Smith R&S Co,LPA -50 W Broad
-Ste 3000 -Columbus 43215 **Fx:**469-7146

(614) 228-4201 .. **Fiore**, Anthonio C '04 Cnsl OH Chamber of Commerce
-230 E Town -Columbus 43215 **Fx:**228-6403

(216) 621-0150 .. **Fiore**, Rose Marie L '95 (Hahn L&P LLP)
-3300 BP Twr/200 Pub Sq -Ste 3300 -Cleveland 44114
Fx:241-2824

(216) 586-3939 .. **Fiorella**, Andrew G '03 %Jones D -901 Lakeside Av
-Cleveland 44114 **Fx:**579-0212

(513) 745-2050 .. **Fiorelli**, Paul E '81 Xavier Univ -3800 Victory Pkwy
-507 Schott Hall -Cincinnati 45207
Fiorenza, Robert O '98 -10490 Adventure Ln -Cincinnati 45242

(330) 376-2700 .. **Firca**, Patrick C '88 (Roetzel & A,LPA -222 S Main
-Akron 44308 **Fx:**376-4577

(330) 726-5518 .. **Fire**, Patrick C '88 -721 Boardman Poland Rd -Ste 201
-Youngstown 44512 **Fx:**726-7538

(440) 708-0720 .. **Firehammer**, Richard A Jr. '94 -8190 Carrington Pl Bainbrdg
-Chagrin Falls 44023

(614) 764-4840 .. **Fireman**, Steven H '92 Supreme Title Agency Ltd
-5880 Sawmill Rd -Ste 100 -Dublin 43017

(330) 665-5117 .. **Firestine**, David L '00 %Witschey & W Co,LPA
-300 N Cleveland-Missillon Rd -Ste 104 -Akron 44333

(740) 363-1213 .. **Firestone Brehm Hanson Nelson Wolf & Young,LLP**
-15 W Winter -Delaware 43015 **Fx:**369-0875

(330) 452-3762 .. **Firestone**, Eric A '78 -2800 Market Av N -Canton 44714

(216) 621-0200 .. **Firestone**, Julie E '96 Baker & H LLP -1900 E 9th -Ste 3200
-Cleveland 44114 **Fx:**696-0740

(614) 645-8946 .. **Firestone**, Lesley A '97 City Pros -375 S High -7th Fl
-Columbus 43215

(419) 592-3816 .. **Firestone**, Melissa P '93 Peper Law Firm -555 Monroe
-Napoleon 43545

(513) 632-8338 .. **Firm**, Christopher E '99 Hon N Nadel -1000 Main -Rm 560
-Cincinnati 45202

(419) 423-4321 .. **Firmin**, John C '41 OfCnsl Firmin S&H Co,LPA -220 W Sandusky
-Bx963 -Findlay 45839 **Fx:**423-8484

(419) 423-4321 .. **Firmin Sprague & Huffman Co,LPA** -220 W Sandusky -Bx963
-Findlay 45839 **Fx:**423-8484

(216) 991-6200 .. **Firstenberg**, Barbara A '81 (B Firstenberg & Assoc,LPA)
-20133 Farnsleigh Rd -Ohio Svngs Bldg -Shaker Heights 44122

(614) 228-6345 .. **Firstenberger**, Aaron C '00 %Strip HLM&T Co LPA -575 S 3rd
-Columbus 43215 **Fx:**228-6369

(740) 387-5854 .. **Firstenberger**, John P '59 (Firstenberger & M) -127 E Center
-Marion 43302

(614) 644-3037 .. **Fischbein**, William T '94 EPA -122 S Front -Bx1049
-Columbus 43216

(216) 932-2466 .. **Fischbein-Cohen**, Ruth R '89 -3552 Severn Rd -Cleveland 44118

(614) 221-8699 .. **Fischberg**, Jenna S '97 -500 S 4th -Columbus 43206

(330) 920-9920 .. **Fischer**, Cheryl A '93 -1799 Akron-Peninsula Rd -Ste 308
-Akron 44313

(513) 896-6623 .. **Fischer**, Daniel B '64 -308 N 2nd -Hamilton 45011

(202) 778-3000 .. **Fischer**, David T '99 %Porter WM&A LLP -1919 Penn Av NW
-Ste 500 -Washington, DC 20006

(419) 244-1680 .. **Fischer**, Edward J '84 -1900 Monroe -Bx353 -Toledo 43697

(216) 731-3535 .. **Fischer**, Henry B '64 (H Fischer Co,LPA) -26111 Brush Av
-400 Brush Bldg -Bx32644 -Cleveland 44132 **Fx:**261-5252

(614) 466-8600 .. **Fischer**, Holly R '91 %Atty Gen -30 E Broad -Columbus 43215
Fx:466-6090

(937) 227-3700 .. **Fischer**, John A '97 %Faruki I&C PLL -10 N Ludlow
-500 Cthse Plz SW -Dayton 45402 **Fx:**227-3717

(513) 421-2540 .. **Fischer**, John M '70 (Ennis R&F) -121 W 9th -Cincinnati 45202
Fx:562-4986

(513) 621-3440 .. **Fischer**, John W II '81 (Denlinger R&G Co,LPA) -425 Walnut
-Ste 2310 -Cincinnati 45202 **Fx:**621-4449

(513) 621-3394 .. **Fischer**, John W III '68 (Peck S&W,LLP) -201 E 5th -Ste 900
-Cincinnati 45202 **Fx:**621-3813

(513) 794-6442 .. **Fischer**, Joseph M '80 OH Natl Life Ins Co -One Fncl Way
-Cincinnati 45242

(419) 531-2514 .. **Fischer**, Karen M '91 -2655 Talmadge -Toledo 43606

(440) 526-4500 .. **Fischer**, Kathleen L '82 %RL Tuma & Assoc -8225 Brecksvll Rd
-Bldg 3 Ste 101 -Brecksville 44141 **Fx:**526-6362

(721) 850-9914 .. **Fischer**, Klaus P '76 -106 Univ Dr -Greensburg, PA 15601

(216) 586-3939 .. **Fischer**, Lynne C '96 Jones D -901 Lakeside Av -Cleveland 44114
Fx:579-0212

(330) 305-6400 .. **Fischer**, Mark F '91 (Pelini & F,Ltd) -8040 Cleveland Av NW
-Ste 400 -North Canton 44720 **Fx:**305-0042

(412) 261-6777 .. **Fischer**, Mark F '95 %Yukerich ML&Z -11 Stanwix -Ste #1024
-Pittsburgh, PA 15222

(419) 249-7100 .. **Fischer**, Matthew J '91 %Marshall & M,LLC -Four Seagate -8th Fl
-Toledo 43604 **Fx:**249-7151

(216) 586-3939 .. **Fischer**, Michelle K '89 (Jones D) -901 Lakeside Av
-Cleveland 44114 **Fx:**579-0212

(513) 579-6400 .. **Fischer**, Patrick F '88 (Keating M&K PLL) -1 E 4th
-1400 Provident Twr -Cincinnati 45202 **Fx:**579-6457

(419) 354-9250 .. **Fischer**, Raymond C '82 Wood Cnty Pros -One Cthse Sq
-Bowling Green 43402 **Fx:**353-2904

(216) 443-9000 .. **Fischer**, Rebecca K '99 %Porter WM&A LLP -925 Euclid Av -Ste 1700 -Cleveland 44115 Fx:443-9011
(216) 241-2838 .. **Fischer**, Robert H Jr. '99 %Taft S&H LLP -200 Pub Sq -3500 BP Twr -Cleveland 44114 Fx:241-3707
(513) 398-4646 .. **Fischer**, Robert S '99 (Sams F&S) -209 Reading Rd -Mason 45040 Fx:398-4608
Fischer, Sharon L '03 -(Address Unavailable)
(937) 225-2516 .. **Fischer**, Susan K '82 US Bankrptcy Ct -120 W 3rd -Dayton 45402
(330) 650-0551 .. **Fischer**, Thomas J '91 Commerce Title Co -581 Bstn Mills Rd -Ste 100 -Hudson 44236
(614) 645-4650 .. **Fischer**, Thomas M '89 Columbus Police Dept -120 Marconi Blvd -Training Bureau -Columbus 43215
(513) 533-0233 .. **Fischer**, Timothy A '71 -3507 Aultwoods Ln -Cincinnati 45208
(937) 264-8139 .. **Fischer**, William E '77 -2033 Waterfall Ln -Vandalia 45377
(419) 241-9000 .. **Fischer**, William G '73 (Shumaker L&K,LLP) -1000 Jackson -Toledo 43624 Fx:241-6894
(216) 731-3535 .. **Fischer-Doyle**, Julie Anne '99 %H Fischer Co,LPA -26111 Brush Av -400 Brush Bldg -Bx32644 -Cleveland 44132 Fx:261-5252
(330) 365-3269 .. **Fischer-Immke**, Andrea L '99 Tuscarawas Cnty Cmn Pleas Ct -101 E High Av -Ste 205 -New Philadelphia 44663 Fx:602-8811
(202) 835-6705 .. **Fischetti**, Lisa M '99 Riggs Bank -808 17th NW -Trust Dept -Washington, DC 20006 Fx:835-4380
(419) 673-1444 .. **Fischmann**, Garron R '97 -102 W Columbus -Ste E -Kenton 43326
(513) 771-8500 .. **Fischoff**, Alan H '73 -11499 Lippelman -Cincinnati 45246 Fx:771-8504
(415) 455-0300 .. **Fisco**, Dennis P '80 Seagate Properties,Inc -980 5th Av -San Rafael, CA 94901
(216) 441-7688 .. **Fisco**, Ernest B '78 -Bx602745 -Cleveland 44102
(419) 547-7770 .. **Fiser**, Mary E '86 (M Fiser Co,LPA) -Bx372 -Clyde 43410
(859) 491-1500 .. **Fiser**, Paul A '92 Lange Q&P,PSC -4 W 4th -Ste 400 -Newport, KY 41071
(513) 632-9595 .. **Fish**, Baruch D '73 -119 E Ct -Ste 510 -Cincinnati 45202
(330) 848-6728 .. **Fish**, David E '84 Barberton Law Dept -576 W Park Av -Barberton 44203
(614) 485-9300 .. **Fish**, Jeffrey D '91 (White & F,LPA Inc) -1335 Dublin Rd -Ste 201C -Columbus 43215 Fx:485-9462
(614) 865-2908 .. **Fish**, Stanley R '81 -3000 Corp Exchange Dr -6th Fl -Columbus 43231
(239) 649-6200 .. **Fishbane**, Jonathan D '88 (Roetzel & A) -850 Park Shore Dr -Trianon Centre 3rd Fl -Naples, FL 34103 Fx:261-3659
(614) 466-2766 .. **Fishel**, Joan I '87 %Atty Gen -30 E Broad -Columbus 43215 Fx:644-1926
(614) 221-1216 .. **Fishel**, Marc A '87 (Downes H&F) -400 S 5th -Ste 200 -Columbus 43215 Fx:221-8769
(419) 535-3247 .. **Fisher**, Allan S '72 -4115 Overlook Blvd -Toledo 43607
(740) 282-1911 .. **Fisher Brown & Peterson** -2017 Sunset Blvd -Steubenville 43952
(313) 965-7900 .. **Fisher**, Charles W '92 Kitch DWD&V -1 Woodward Av -10th Fl -Detroit, MI 48226
(216) 522-3380 .. **Fisher**, Christopher A '84 IRS -1375 E 9th -1200 -Cleveland 44114
(216) 931-6000 .. **Fisher**, Christopher P '97 %Ulmer & B LLP -1300 E 9th -Ste 900 Penton Media Bldg -Cleveland 44114 Fx:931-6001
(615) 742-7892 .. **Fisher**, Curtis L '01 %Bass B&S -315 Deaderick -Ste 2700 -Nashville, TN 37238
(216) 566-5502 .. **Fisher**, Damaris G '01 %Thompson H LLP -127 Pub Sq -3900 Key Ctr -Cleveland 44114 Fx:566-5800
(614) 469-1882 .. **Fisher**, David W '81 (Kephart & F LLP) -207 N 4th -Columbus 43215
(216) 464-2000 .. **Fisher**, Dennis J '93 Wald & Fisher,Inc -23825 Commerce Park Rd -Ste F -Beachwood 44122
(216) 443-9000 .. **Fisher**, Donald J '76 (Porter WM&A LLP) -925 Euclid Av -Ste 1700 -Cleveland 44115 Fx:443-9011
(614) 469-2455 .. **Fisher**, Donald P '96 %USDA -200 N High -#209 -Columbus 43215
(937) 456-4125 .. **Fisher**, Donnette A '97 City of Eaton -328 N Maple -Bx27 -Eaton 45320
(614) 221-0446 .. **Fisher & Douglas** -122 E Main -Columbus 43215
(513) 579-5479 .. **Fisher**, Francis J Jr. '75 Fifth 3rd Bank-Trust Div -38 Fountain Sq Plz -Cincinnati 45263
(740) 532-8744 .. **Fisher**, Frederick C Jr. '03 %McCown & D,LPA -311 Park Av -Ironton 45638
(614) 462-2277 .. **Fisher**, Fredrick L '76 Schottenstein Z&D -250 West -Bx165020 -Columbus 43216 Fx:462-5135
(614) 445-0372 .. **Fisher**, Gary E '85 -1141 S High -Columbus 43206
(614) 233-6950 .. **Fisher**, George V '53 (Fisher & S LLC) -400 E Town -Ste 210 -Columbus 43215 Fx:233-6960
(614) 221-8500 .. **Fisher**, J Matthew '96 Allen K&S LLP -21 W Broad -Ste 400 -Columbus 43215
(330) 376-5300 .. **Fisher**, James L III '71 (Buckingham D&B,LLP) -50 S Main -Bx1500 -Akron 44309 Fx:258-6559
(419) 228-8403 .. **Fisher**, James P '63 (Fisher V&F Co,LPA) -303 E High -Lima 45801
(330) 438-6360 .. **Fisher**, Jeanine M '99 Aultman Care Corp -2600 6th SW -Morrow Hse -Canton 44710
(440) 543-2664 .. **Fisher**, Jeffrey M '84 -8356 Canterbury Ct -Chagrin Falls 44023
(216) 586-3939 .. **Fisher**, Jo Ann '79 Jones D -901 Lakeside Av -Cleveland 44114 Fx:579-0212
(419) 843-2001 .. **Fisher**, John B '91 %Gallon & T Co,LPA -3516 Granite Cir -Bx352018 -Toledo 43635 Fx:843-6665
(419) 228-8403 .. **Fisher**, John H '85 (Fisher V&F Co,LPA) -303 E High -Lima 45801
(614) 248-6479 .. **Fisher**, Judith M '86 Bank One Mgt Corp -100 E Broad -OH1-0258 -Columbus 43271
(614) 221-8448 .. **Fisher**, Kenneth A Jr. '95 OfCnsl Buckingham D&B,LLP -191 W Nationwide Blvd -Ste 300 -Bx151120 -Columbus 43215 Fx:221-8590
(216) 696-7661 .. **Fisher**, Kenneth J '76 (Fisher & Assoc Co,LPA) -50 Pub Sq -1414 Trmnl Twr -Cleveland 44113
(614) 645-5150 .. **Fisher**, Lawrence L '67 Columbus Dwntwn Dvlpmnt Corp -20 E Broad -Columbus 43215
(216) 432-7200 .. **Fisher**, Lee I '76 Ctr for Families & Children -4500 Euclid Av -Cleveland 44103

(614) 227-2000 .. **Fisher**, Lloyd E Jr. '50 (Porter WM&A LLP) -41 S High -Columbus 43215 Fx:227-2100
(937) 237-9485 .. **Fisher**, Mara A '96 (Staton & F LLC) -5613 Brandt Pike -Huber Heights 45424
(614) 221-0446 .. **Fisher**, Mark R '80 (Fisher & D) -122 E Main -Columbus 43215
(614) 487-8210 .. **Fisher**, Mary B '89 -1500 W 3rd Av -Ste 127 -Columbus 43212
(330) 364-0088 .. **Fisher**, Michael R '96 -812 Kaderly NW -New Philadelphia 44663
(440) 617-1528 .. **Fisher**, Michael T '94 -55 Pub Sq -Ste 1010 -Cleveland 44113
(216) 373-7400 .. **Fisher**, Norman R Jr. '72 Graystone Properties,Inc -3615 Superior Av -Ste 3101-C -Cleveland 44114
(216) 261-0200 .. **Fisher**, Patricia A '88 -27801 Euclid Av -Ste 500 -Euclid 44132
(513) 325-9660 .. **Fisher**, Paul H '89 -5916 Ropes Dr -Cincinnati 45244
(419) 636-2596 .. **Fisher**, Rhonda L '91 Mun Ct Pros -Bx7076 -Bryan 43506
(419) 599-1010 .. **Fisher**, Richard A '74 (Hanna & F) -822 Oakwood Av -Bx605 -Napoleon 43545
(614) 365-2700 .. **Fisher**, Roberta Lee '76 Cnsl Squire S&D LLP -41 S High -1300 Huntngtn Ctr -Columbus 43215 Fx:365-2499
(216) 621-7905 .. **Fisher**, Ryan H '89 -75 Pub Sq #914 -Cleveland 44113 Fx:621-7261
(614) 233-6950 .. **Fisher & Skrobot LLC** -400 E Town -Ste 210 -Columbus 43215 Fx:233-6960
(216) 765-0123 .. **Fisher**, Stanley M '53 Budish & S Ltd -23240 Chagrin Blvd -Ste 450 Commerce Park 4 -Beachwood 44122 Fx:595-2787
(937) 390-9701 .. **Fisher**, Terry L '85 Affidavit Maker Sftwre -2219 Fountain Blvd -Springfield 45504
(614) 227-2000 .. **Fisher**, Theodore G '69 (Porter WM&A LLP) -41 S High -Columbus 43215 Fx:227-2100
(419) 228-8403 .. **Fisher Vandemark & Fisher Co,LPA** -303 E High -Lima 45801
(216) 595-0071 .. **Fisher**, Vincent E '99 %Roth B LLP -5196 Richmond Rd -Bedford Heights 44146 Fx:595-0073
(216) 787-3030 .. **Fisher**, Virginia E '82 Atty Gen -615 W Superior Av -11th Fl -Cleveland 44113 Fx:787-3480
(859) 394-6200 .. **Fisher**, William Thomas '00 %Adams SW&D -40 W Pike -Bx861 -Covington, KY 41012 Fx:291-7902
(614) 262-1605 .. **Fisher**, Windell F '61 -3692 N High -Columbus 43214
(216) 579-1700 .. **Fishman**, Aaron A '99 (Pearne & G LLP) -1801 E 9th -Ste 1200 -Cleveland 44114 Fx:579-6073
(216) 621-9181 .. **Fishman**, Gary S '82 -75 Pub Sq -Ste 1225 -Cleveland 44113
(216) 621-6060 .. **Fishman**, Lawrence R '69 Cnsl Forest City Enterprises -50 Pub Sq -1160 Trmnl Twr -Cleveland 44113
(216) 781-4800 .. **Fishman**, Mark S '81 -526 Superior Av E -#853 -Cleveland 44114
(216) 797-8780 .. **Fishman**, Martin A '68 Associated Estates Rlty Corp -5025 Swetland Ct -Richmond Heights 44143
(419) 245-1020 .. **Fiske**, Rex D '89 %Law Dept -One Govt Ctr -Ste 2250 -Toledo 43604 Fx:245-1090
(513) 732-3040 .. **Fisse**, Lawrence R '78 -34 N 3rd -Batavia 45103
(419) 241-6000 .. **Fissel**, Barry W '81 (Eastman & S Ltd) -1 Seagate -24th Fl -Bx10032 -Toledo 43699 Fx:247-1777
(216) 621-1113 .. **Fistek**, Thomas G '04 %Renner OB&S,LLP -1621 Euclid Av -19th Fl -Cleveland 44115 Fx:621-6165
(216) 241-5310 .. **Fister**, Anna S '03 %Gallagher SF&N -1501 Euclid Av -6th Fl -Cleveland 44115 Fx:241-1608
(614) 227-2640 .. **Fitch**, David A '82 Columbus State Cmmnty Cllg -Bx1609 -Columbus 43216
(614) 445-2661 .. **Fitch**, Glori E '89 Grange Mutual -650 S Front -Columbus 43206
(740) 354-3600 .. **Fitch**, James C '55 Miller S&F -806 6th -Ste 200 -Bx991 -Portsmouth 45662 Fx:354-1110
(614) 221-6969 .. **Fitch**, John K '79 Wolske & B,LPA -580 S High -Ste 300 -Columbus 43215
(330) 337-8761 .. **Fitch Kendall Cecil Robinson & Barry** -600 E State -Bx590 -Salem 44460 Fx:337-9453
(740) 354-3600 .. **Fitch**, Lee O '50 Miller S&F -806 6th -Ste 200 -Bx991 -Portsmouth 45662 Fx:354-1110
(513) 731-8460 .. **Fitch**, Mark R '87 (Fitch & S) -3752 Edwards Rd -Cincinnati 45209
(614) 221-4000 .. **Fitch**, Stephen C '73 (Chester W&S LLP) -65 E State -10th Fl -Columbus 43215 Fx:221-4012
(330) 535-4191 .. **Fitch**, Susan M '87 %Cmmnty Lgl Aid Srvcs,Inc -265 S Main -3rd Fl -Akron 44308 Fx:535-0728
(419) 522-7000 .. **Fithian**, William C III '81 W Fithian Co,LPA -111 N Main -Mansfield 44902
(614) 287-2482 .. **Fitrakis**, Robert J '03 Columbus State Comm Coll -550 E Spring -Columbus 43215
Fitten, Steven M '78 Dept of the Army -EAKC-OC Unit#15289 -APO, AP 96205
(202) 739-5019 .. **Fitterman**, Mark D '74 (Morgan L&B LLP) -1111 Penn Av NW -Washington, DC 20004
(513) 362-8217 .. **Fitton**, Jay S '97 Cnsl Integrated Fund Srvcs,Inc -221 E 4th -Ste 300 -Cincinnati 45202
(440) 395-0246 .. **Fitts**, John T '77 Progressive Ins Co -300 N Cmmns Blvd -OHF 11 -Mayfield Village 44143
(440) 892-3460 .. **Fitz**, Robert E '72 -1650 Xings Pkwy -Ste C -Westlake 44145 Fx:892-3608
(740) 452-8431 .. **Fitz**, Todd B '96 (Magaziner M&F) -44 S 6th -Zanesville 43701
(513) 629-1467 .. **FitzGerald**, Alice M '79 SrCnsl Western & Southern Life Ins Co -400 Bway -Cincinnati 45202
FitzGerald, Benjamin J '89 -10830 Mill Rd -Cincinnati 45240
(216) 687-1902 .. **FitzGerald**, Claudia P '80 %S Haygood & Assoc -1422 Euclid Av -Ste 1510 -Cleveland 44115 Fx:687-1906
(419) 420-9312 .. **FitzGerald**, Dennis M '76 (Fitzgerald Law Firm,LLC) -400 S Main -Findlay 45840 Fx:420-9314
FitzGerald, Janette M '84 -(Address Unavailable)
(216) 443-7800 .. **FitzGerald**, Michael P '00 Cuyahoga Cnty Pros -1200 Ontario -8th Fl -Cleveland 44113 Fx:698-2270
(330) 832-2918 .. **Fitzgerald**, Neal L '79 Bd of Trustees/Jackson Twp -5735 Wales Av -Massillon 44646
(216) 689-3292 .. **Fitzgerald**, Patricia E '82 KeyBank NA -127 Pub Sq -Cleveland 44114
(419) 227-5858 .. **Fitzgerald**, Robert B '82 (Baran PTF&T Co,LPA) -121 W High -Ste 905 -Bx568 -Lima 45802 Fx:227-4569
(614) 644-1768 .. **Fitzgerald**, Scott M '95 Workers Comp -30 W Spring -Level 26 -Columbus 43215
(419) 385-5704 .. **FitzGerald**, Sharon A '84 -2343 Old Stone Ct -#7 -Toledo 43614

(216) 241-5310 .. **Fitzgerald**, Timothy J '89 (Gallagher SF&N) -1501 Euclid Av -6th Fl -Cleveland 44115 **Fx:**241-1608

(513) 621-8267 .. **FitzGerald**, Timothy J '91 -5102 Carthage Av -Norwood 45212

(513) 421-4225 .. **Fitzgerald**, William F '62 (Burke FB&B,LLP) -817 Main -Ste 800 -Cincinnati 45202

Fitzhugh, Janel R '99 US DOL-PWBA -1885 Dixie Hwy -Ste 210 -Fort Wright, KY 41011

(216) 261-0200 .. **Fitzmaurice**, John P '91 -27801 Euclid Av -Ste 500 -Bx110902 -Cleveland 44111

(330) 424-4071 .. **Fitzpatrick**, Charles E Jr. '81 Columbiana Juv Ct -260 W Lincoln Way -Lisbon 44432

(440) 247-9200 .. **Fitzpatrick**, Jon D '77 -7181 Chargrin Rd -Ste 240 -Chagrin Falls 44023

(513) 634-4287 .. **Fitzpatrick**, Matthew P '96 Procter & Gamble -6090 Ctr Hill Av -Cincinnati 45224

(216) 696-6454 .. **Fitzpatrick**, Michael D '87 Cincinnati Ins Co -930 The 55 Bldg -55 Pub Sq -Cleveland 44113

(330) 364-1614 .. **Fitzpatrick Zimmerman & Rose Co LPA** -140 Fair Av NW -Bx1014 -New Philadelphia 44663 **Fx:**343-3077

(513) 977-8200 .. **Fitzsimmons**, Becky B '00 %Calfee H&G LLP -255 E 5th -Ste 1900 -Cincinnati 45202 **Fx:**977-8141

(216) 621-7227 .. **Fitzsimmons**, Matthew T '80 (Nicola G&C,LLC) -25 W Prospect Av -Republic Bldg Ste 1400 -Cleveland 44115 **Fx:**621-3999

(304) 277-1700 .. **Fitzsimmons**, Robert P '92 -1609 Warwood Av -Wheeling, WV 26003

(216) 622-8200 .. **FitzSimmons**, Thomas A '00 %Calfee H&G LLP -800 Superior Av -Ste 1400 -Cleveland 44114 **Fx:**241-0816

(216) 592-5000 .. **FitzSimons**, Brian W '74 (Tucker E&W LLP) -925 Euclid Av -1150 Huntngtn Bldg -Cleveland 44115 **Fx:**592-5009

(440) 247-2800 .. **Fixler**, Michael A '97 Candlewood Prtnrs,LLC -10½ E Wshngtn -Chagrin Falls 44022

(513) 852-3497 .. **Fixler**, Steven P '81 Atty Gen -441 Vine -1600 Carew Twr -Cincinnati 45202 **Fx:**852-3484

(513) 271-2482 .. **Fjord**, Hilliard J '54 -6725 Wooster Pike -Cincinnati 45227 **Fx:**271-5837

(937) 323-4004 .. **Flack**, Sanford H '70 (Flack & M) -101 N Fountain Av -Springfield 45502

(513) 381-9200 .. **Flacks**, Kenneth B '73 (Rendigs FK&D,LLP) -One W 4th -Ste 900 -Cincinnati 45202 **Fx:**381-9206

(330) 493-0460 .. **Fladen**, Sharon V '78 -1330 Mercy Dr NW -Ste 312 -Canton 44708

(513) 745-0400 .. **Flagel**, Todd J '96 (Furnier T,LLP) -1 Fncl Way -Ste 312 -Cincinnati 45242 **Fx:**792-6724

(614) 325-8525 .. **Flagler**, Harold G '78 -Bx1452 -Westerville 43086

(614) 794-9595 .. **Flaherty**, James G '84 (JG Flaherty Co,LPA) -575 Charring Cross Dr -Ste 100 -Westerville 43081 **Fx:**794-9590

(440) 942-2924 .. **Flaherty**, James T '71 -7187 Hodgson Rd -Mentor 44060

(330) 255-5012 .. **Flaherty**, Mary K '02 KEYCORP -222 S Main -Ste 200 -Akron 44308 **Fx:**255-5028

(937) 433-2411 .. **Flaherty**, Mimi K '91 -Bx752193 -Dayton 45475

(614) 469-3294 .. **Flahive**, Carolyn S '00 %Thompson H LLP -10 W Broad -Ste 700 -Columbus 43215 **Fx:**469-3361

(740) 369-4388 .. **Flahive**, Edward F '77 -314 Delaware Cnty Bk Bldg -Bx1040 -Delaware 43015

(614) 464-6400 .. **Flahive**, Shawn M '84 (Vorys SS&P LLP) -52 E Gay -Bx1008 -Columbus 43216 **Fx:**464-6350

(740) 363-1443 .. **Flahive**, Terrence P '86 -41 N Sandusky -Ste 314 -Bx1040 -Delaware 43015

(740) 363-1443 .. **Flahive**, Timothy I '83 -41 N Sandusky -Ste 314 -Bx1040 -Delaware 43015

(440) 286-9571 .. **Flaiz**, James R '02 %Svete M&C Co,LPA -100 Parker Ct -Chardon 44024

(216) 363-6031 .. **Flament**, Michael J '77 -1370 Ontario -Ste 2000 -Cleveland 44113

(513) 381-2838 .. **Flamm**, Justin D '99 %Taft S&H LLP -425 Walnut -Ste 1800 -Cincinnati 45202 **Fx:**381-0205

(216) 241-2838 .. **Flammang**, Donna M '75 (Taft S&H LLP) -200 Pub Sq -3500 BP Twr -Cleveland 44114 **Fx:**241-3707

(513) 946-3117 .. **Flanagan**, Anne S '83 Hamilton Cnty Pros -230 E 9th -Cincinnati 45202 **Fx:**946-3017

(740) 592-3208 .. **Flanagan**, Colleen Sue '95 Athens Cnty Pros -Athens Cnty Cthse -Athens 45701 **Fx:**592-3291

(330) 759-3232 .. **Flanagan**, Edward J '79 Flanagan & G Co,LPA -4350 Sampson Rd -Youngstown 44505

(614) 469-7404 .. **Flanagan**, Francis P '80 SSA-OHA -401 N Front -Ste 400 -Columbus 43215

(513) 621-6464 .. **Flanagan**, John A '77 (Graydon H&R LLP) -511 Walnut -1900 Fifth Third Ctr -Cincinnati 45202 **Fx:**651-3836

(304) 232-8100 .. **Flanagan**, John Kevin '94 %Cassidy MCV&T,LC -1413 Eoff -The 1st State Cptl -Wheeling, WV 26003 **Fx:**232-8200

(937) 223-5200 .. **Flanagan Lieberman Hoffman & Swaim** -318 W 4th -Dayton 45402 **Fx:**223-3335

(440) 329-5398 .. **Flanagan**, Martin R '84 Lorain Cnty Pros -225 Court -3rd Fl -Elyria 44035

(937) 223-5200 .. **Flanagan**, Patrick A '67 (Flanagan LH&S) -318 W 4th -Dayton 45402 **Fx:**223-3335

(440) 333-2755 .. **Flanagan**, Patrick M '73 (Flanagan LLC) -20102 Ctr Ridge Rd -Rocky River 44116

(330) 489-5258 .. **Flanagan**, Rosemary M '79 Nationwide Mutual Ins Co -1000 Market Av N -Bx8379 -Canton 44711

(614) 462-3194 .. **Flanigan**, Tanya D '03 Franklin Cnty Pub Def -373 S High -12th Fl -Columbus 43215

(304) 455-2180 .. **Flannery**, Carolyn G '93 %Snyder & H -Bx189 -New Martinsville, WV 26155

(330) 761-4206 .. **Flannery**, Harry A '00 Cnsl FirstEnergy/Lgl Dept -76 S Main -Akron 44308 **Fx:**384-3875

(414) 344-6565 .. **Flannery**, Michael J '02 -3111 W Wscnsn Av -Milwaukee, WI 53208

(216) 566-5500 .. **Flannery**, Sarah C '02 %Thompson H LLP -127 Pub Sq -3900 Key Ctr -Cleveland 44114 **Fx:**566-5800

(330) 762-2961 .. **Flannery**, Theresa '03 CYO & Comm Srvcs -812 Biruta -Akron 44307

(330) 645-4500 .. **Flasck**, Estelle D '88 Flasck Legal Srvcs -1650 S Arlngtn Rd -Ste 1 -Akron 44306

(216) 642-0797 .. **Flask**, John A '85 -6393 Oak Tree Blvd -Ste 110 -Independence 44131

(614) 837-8210 .. **Flaugher**, Robert A '96 (RA Flaugher,LLC) -38 E Columbus -Pickerington 43147 **Fx:**837-8228

(740) 342-3576 .. **Flautt**, Joseph A '80 (J Flautt,Ltd,LPA) -110 N Main -Bx569 -New Lexington 43764

(513) 471-5008 .. **Flax**, James A '04 Proffinn Real Estate Srvcs,Inc -5006 Rapid Run Rd -Cincinnati 45238

(740) 852-3000 .. **Flax**, Richard E '74 (Nichols S&F) -117 W High -Ste 105 -London 43140

(513) 381-6223 .. **Flax**, William E '59 -414 Walnut -Cincinnati 45202

(614) 851-9464 .. **Flecha**, Crucita '95 -Bx28427 -Columbus 43228

(330) 726-8700 .. **Fleck**, Jeffrey B '67 -845 Woodfld Ct -Youngstown 44512

(216) 687-1311 .. **Fleck**, Robert E '58 OfCnsl Reminger & R -101 Prospect Av W -1400 Mdlnd Bldg -Cleveland 44115 **Fx:**687-1841

(614) 224-0919 .. **Fleck**, William J Jr. '75 (Beauchamp & F) -118 E Main -Columbus 43215

Fleckinger, Vanita S '98 Lexis-Nexis -1942 Wedgewood Ln -Hebron, KY 41048

(513) 352-5858 .. **Fledderman**, Anne M '86 OfCnsl GR Wilson Co,LPA -1411 Sycamore -Ste 1500 -Cincinnati 45202

Fleetwood, Jessie H '04 -(Address Unavailable)

(513) 421-3494 .. **Flege**, John B Jr. '93 Crdvsclr & Thoracic Surgns,Inc -2123 Auburn Av -Ste 401 -Cincinnati 45219

(419) 562-5928 .. **Flegm**, Stanley E '73 -Bx786 -Bucyrus 44820

(614) 227-2000 .. **Fleischauer**, Marc L '95 (Porter WM&A LLP) -41 S High -Columbus 43215 **Fx:**227-2100

(614) 834-4340 .. **Fleischer**, David A '95 -Bx2533 -Westerville 43086

(513) 977-4209 .. **Fleischer**, Neil I '00 %R Fleischer & Assoc -917 Main -Cincinnati 45202

(513) 977-4209 .. **Fleischer**, Richard I '71 (R Fleischer & Assoc) -917 Main -Cincinnati 45202

(614) 466-4605 .. **Fleischman**, David A '93 OH Dept Job & Fam Srvcs -30 E Broad -32nd Fl -Columbus 43266

Fleischmann-Fellowes, Dagmar '93 Fellows Rsrch Grp,Inc -3299 Wllwbrk Dr -Cleveland 44124

(937) 223-3277 .. **Fleisher**, James P '92 %Bieser G&L LLP -6 N Main -400 Natl City Ctr -Dayton 45402 **Fx:**223-6339

Fleishman, Jill T '80 -2040 Inchcliff Rd -Columbus 43221

(513) 621-2666 .. **Flemer**, Lawrence A '80 OfCnsl Statman HS&E LLC -255 E 5th -Ste 2900 Chemed Ctr -Cincinnati 45202 **Fx:**587-4477

(330) 743-3232 .. **Fleming**, Alfred J '75 (A Fleming Co,LPA) -400 City Ctr One -Youngstown 44503

(216) 522-4856 .. **Fleming**, Charles E '90 Fed Pub Def -1660 W 2nd -Ste 750 -Cleveland 44113

(216) 566-5840 .. **Fleming**, Jennifer Lesny '93 (Thompson H LLP) -127 Pub Sq -3900 Key Ctr -Cleveland 44114 **Fx:**566-5800

(216) 621-0200 .. **Fleming**, Kyle B '95 (Baker & H LLP) -1900 E 9th -Ste 3200 -Cleveland 44114 **Fx:**696-0740

(734) 302-4898 .. **Fleming**, Kyra M '92 DTE Energy Srvcs Inc -414 S Main -Ste 600 -Ann Arbor, MI 48104

(812) 288-0211 .. **Fleming**, Lisa L '97 Amer Commrcl Lines Inc -1701 E Market -Jeffersonville, IN 47130

(740) 349-6575 .. **Fleming**, Mary E '88 Licking Cnty CSEA -65 E Main -Bx338 -Newark 43058

(513) 721-2120 .. **Fleming**, Mary M '79 (Barrett & W) -105 E 4th -Ste 500 -Cincinnati 45202

(216) 651-8484 .. **Fleming**, Nancy J '89 Domestic Violence Ctr -Bx5466 -Cleveland 44101 **Fx:**651-8575

(419) 372-2951 .. **Fleming**, Rodney A '91 Student Legal Srvc Inc -401 S Hall -Bowling Grn State Univ -Bowling Green 43403

(513) 745-3648 .. **Fleming**, Rose Ann '89 Xavier Univ -3800 Victory Pkwy -Cincinnati 45207

(614) 462-3194 .. **Fleming**, Tyson L '00 Franklin Cnty Pub Def -373 S High -12th Fl -Columbus 43215

(740) 773-9982 .. **Fleshman**, Gary A '94 -63 N Paint -Ste A -Chillicothe 45601

(513) 381-1234 .. **Flessa**, John H '82 -1019 Main -Cincinnati 45202

(513) 732-1420 .. **Flessa**, Thomas H '82 Nichols S&N -237 Main -Batavia 45103

(614) 443-4814 .. **Fletcher**, Daniel J '85 -761 S Front -Columbus 43206

Fletcher, Jackalynne A '95 -1368 Lakeshr Dr -#B -Columbus 43204

(513) 421-1313 .. **Fletcher**, Michael C '69 (Griffin-F,LLP) -3500 Redbank Rd -Cincinnati 45227 **Fx:**421-1118

(903) 592-0055 .. **Fletcher**, Natalie '91 -731 S Vine -Tyler, TX 75701

(419) 535-4652 .. **Fletcher**, Pamela W '76 Dana Corp -4500 Dorr -Bx1000 -Toledo 43697

(330) 468-6300 .. **Fletcher**, Peter F '82 -115 W Aurora Rd -Northfield 44067

(614) 228-6675 .. **Fletcher**, Robert E '76 %OH Assoc of Realtors -200 E Town -Columbus 43215

(513) 243-1645 .. **Fletcher**, Robert S '96 Cnsl GE Aircraft Engines -1 Neumann Way -F125 -Cincinnati 45215

(330) 545-9707 .. **Flevares**, William M '92 %J Thomas Co,LPA -42 E Wilson Av -Bx330 -Girard 44420

(330) 239-5041 .. **Flickinger**, Dare S '50 -5183 Boneta Dr -Medina 44256

(614) 944-5055 .. **Flickinger**, Russell N Jr. '82 -4200 Regent -Ste 200 -Columbus 43219

Fliehman, Travis L '00 -8338 Timber Ln -Mason 45040

(216) 831-3511 .. **Flinker**, Jon C '72 -25550 Chagrin Blvd -Ste 202 -Beachwood 44122

(937) 548-0324 .. **Flinn**, Gary L '78 (G Flinn Co,LPA) -429 Mem'l Dr -Greenville 45331

(614) 461-1234 .. **Flint**, Christopher A '95 (Portman F&F LLP) -471 E Broad -Ste 1820 -Columbus 43215 **Fx:**461-9150

(614) 227-2300 .. **Flint**, Jennifer A '92 %Bricker & E LLP -100 S 3rd -Columbus 43215 **Fx:**227-2390

(419) 524-3603 .. **Flippin**, Wilbur H Jr. '57 -30 S Mulberry -Mansfield 44902

(614) 449-2376 .. **Floetker**, Bernard M '78 -1295 S High -Columbus 43206

(419) 474-9623 .. **Flood**, Judy A '00 -Bx6625 -Toledo 43612

(937) 854-3047 .. **Flora**, Bruce J '81 Trotwood Corp -11 N Bway -Trotwood 45426

(412) 490-6921 .. **Florak**, Mark E '94 Shopping Cntr Law Assoc,PC -100 Cliff Mine Rd -Ste 530 -Pittsburgh, PA 15275

(513) 932-1515 .. **Florence**, Mark T '80 (Kaufman & F) -144 E Mulberry -Bx280 -Lebanon 45036

(513) 977-4777 .. **Florez**, Michael G '82 -119 E Court -Ste 5000 -Cincinnati 45202

(513) 946-5470 ..**Florez**, Rosalind C '89 Cnsl Hamilton Cnty Ct of Common Pleas -1000 Main -Rm 450 -Cincinnati 45202

(859) 971-8067 ..**Florian**, Stephen F '02 Lexington Fair Housing Council -205 E Reynolds Rd -Ste E -Lexington, KY 40517

(614) 871-5100 ..**Flory**, Paul D '04 Solid Waste Auth Cntrl OH -6220 Young Rd -Grove City 43123

(513) 684-3638 ..**Floth**, Kathleen A '01 NLRB -550 Main -Ste 3003 -Cincinnati 45202

(513) 751-4420 ..**Flottman**, Anne B '01 -2345 Ashland Av -Cincinnati 45206

(202) 857-6054 ..**Flowe**, Carol C '77 (Arent FKP&K) -1050 Conn Av NW -Washington, DC 20036

(330) 253-7171 ..**Flower**, Nancy J '92 Burdon & M -137 S Main -Ste 201 -Akron 44308 Fx:253-7174

(614) 879-9413 ..**Flowers**, Debra J '96 Self Insured Mgmt Co -29 W Main -Bx80 -West Jefferson 43162

(614) 860-9670 ..**Flowers**, Janice M '01 -7414 Bunker Ridge Ct -Blacklick 43004 Fx:860-9679

(513) 768-7416 ..**Flowers**, Laura J '02 Alderwoods Group,Inc -311 Elm -Ste 1000 -Cincinnati 45202 Fx:768-7401

(330) 451-7721 ..**Flowers**, Lori Ann '01 Stark Cnty Cmmn Pleas Ct -115 Central Plz N -Canton 44702

(614) 227-2340 ..**Flowers**, Michael E '79 (Bricker & E LLP) -100 S 3rd -Columbus 43215 Fx:227-2390

(216) 623-4143 ..**Flowers**, Michael J '04 AON Risk Srvcs -1660 W 2nd -Ste 650 -Cleveland 44113

(216) 344-9393 ..**Flowers**, Paul W '90 -50 Pub Sq -Ste 3500 -Cleveland 44113

(419) 255-0814 ..**Flowers**, Phyllis D '01 ABLE -520 Mad Av -740 Spitzer Bldg -Toledo 43604 Fx:259-2880

(419) 423-1644 ..**Flowers**, Richard W '96 -219 S Main -Findlay 45840

(740) 927-7933 ..**Floyd**, Dixie K '88 -3390 Watkins Rd -Pataskala 43062

(330) 747-4404 ..**Floyd**, James G '71 %Newman O&K,LPA -11 Fed Plz Central -Ste 1200 -Youngstown 44503 Fx:747-6056

(216) 689-2707 ..**Floyd**, Lawrence R '91 -3343 Comm Cllg -Cleveland 44115

Floyd, Marc L '00 Interim Legal -1051 Cedar Trace Blvd -Westerville 43081

(216) 566-5836 ..**Floyd**, Mark S '83 (Thompson H LLP) -127 Pub Sq -3900 Key Ctr -Cleveland 44114 Fx:566-5800

(216) 861-5582 ..**Floyd**, Patrick D '93 %Fay SFM&M LLP -1100 Superior Av -7th Fl -Cleveland 44114 Fx:241-1666

(419) 244-7596 ..**Flynn**, Abbey M '04 %LJ Weller -520 Mad Av -Ste 837 -Toledo 43604 Fx:255-5530

(330) 451-7200 ..**Flynn**, Beth A '04 Stark Cnty Pub Def -200 W Tuscarawas -Ste 200 -Canton 44702

(410) 981-1602 ..**Flynn**, Donald P Jr. '78 DoD Comp Invstgtns Training Pro -911 Elkrdg Lndng Rd -Ste 200 -Linthicum, MD 21090

(614) 227-8855 ..**Flynn**, James F '90 (Bricker & E LLP) -100 S 3rd -Columbus 43215 Fx:227-2390

(479) 464-6616 ..**Flynn**, John D '74 Bross Eagle Inc -1201 SE 30th -Bentonville, AR 72712

(330) 673-0114 ..**Flynn**, John J '74 (Flynn & D) -250 S Water -Bx762 -Kent 44240

(440) 285-2242 ..**Flynn**, John J '93 %Thrasher D&D,LPA -100 7th Av -Ste 150 -Chardon 44024 Fx:285-9423

(513) 762-4303 ..**Flynn**, John M '68 Kroger Co -1014 Vine -Cincinnati 45202

(513) 421-1313 ..**Flynn**, Kevin R '87 (Griffin-F,LLP) -3500 Redbank Rd -Cincinnati 45227 Fx:421-1118

(614) 734-9450 ..**Flynn**, Nicole A '01 OfCnsl Mason Law Firm Co,LPA -425 Metro Pl N -Ste 620 -Dublin 43017 Fx:734-9451

(216) 222-8014 ..**Flynn**, Patrick J '92 Natl City Bank -1900 E 9th -Locator 01-2174 -Cleveland 44114

(419) 625-8324 ..**Flynn Py & Kruse,LPA** -165 E Wshngtn Row -Sandusky 44870 Fx:625-9007

(419) 734-3174 ..**Flynn Py & Kruse,LPA** -115 W Perry -Port Clinton 43452 Fx:734-3175

(614) 228-1541 ..**Flynn**, Sean P '01 %Baker & H LLP -65 E State -Ste 2100 -Columbus 43215 Fx:462-2616

(513) 946-9200 ..**Flynn**, Thomas J '76 Hamilton Cnty Juv Ct -800 Bway -Cincinnati 45202 Fx:946-9217

(941) 748-5599 ..**Flynn**, Thomas P '78 (Legler & F) -2027 Manatee Av W -Bradenton, FL 34205 Fx:747-2371

(330) 925-9010 ..**Flynn**, Thomas T '69 (Flynn & C) -99 E Ohio Av -Bx116 -Rittman 44270

(513) 241-2324 ..**Flynn**, Thomas W '69 OfCnsl Wood H&E LLP -441 Vine -Ste 2700 -Cincinnati 45202 Fx:421-7269

(513) 621-2120 ..**Flynn**, William K '85 (Strauss & T,LPA) -150 E 4th -4th Fl -Cincinnati 45202 Fx:241-8259

(330) 746-5643 ..**Flynt**, Bobbie L '96 %Comstock S&W Co,LPA -100 Fed Plz E -Ste 926 -Youngstown 44503 Fx:746-4925

(330) 393-2519 ..**Fodor**, Jeffrey W '73 -269 Seneca Av NE -Bx1706 -Warren 44482

(313) 223-3022 ..**Foeller**, Ann-Jeannine '92 Dickinson-Wright,PLLC -500 Woodward Av -Detroit, MI 48226

(215) 665-4740 ..**Foerstner**, Georgia S '95 Cozen O -1900 Market -Philadelphia, PA 19103

(215) 592-1000 ..**Foerstner**, James E Jr. '89 %Beasley C&E -1125 Walnut -Philadelphia, PA 19107

(937) 228-5912 ..**Fogarty**, Canice J Jr. '83 (Allbery C&F) -137 N Main -Ste 500 -Dayton 45402

(216) 687-7625 ..**Fogarty**, David H '95 Medical Mutual of OH -2050 E 9th -Cleveland 44106

(216) 348-1700 ..**Fogarty**, Dennis R '91 (Davis & Y) -101 Prospect Av W -Ste 1700 -Cleveland 44115 Fx:621-0602

(216) 621-0150 ..**Fogarty**, Robert J '77 (Hahn L&P LLP) -3300 BP Twr/200 Pub Sq -Ste 3300 -Cleveland 44114 Fx:241-2824

(513) 241-3100 ..**Fogelman**, Adam R '01 %Lerner S&R -120 E 4th -8th Fl -Cincinnati 45202

(614) 529-9085 ..**Fogle**, Shawn C '90 -3900 Pinto Ct -Columbus 43221

(513) 424-2401 ..**Fogle**, Stephen R '93 Casper & C -1 N Main -Bx510 -Middletown 45042 Fx:424-0622

Fohlen, Adam S '03 -(Address Unavailable)

(614) 229-4808 ..**Foisset**, Chad A '02 Deloitte & Touche,LLP -155 E Broad -Ste 2000 -Columbus 43215

(336) 741-5162 ..**Folan**, McDara P III '85 RJ Reynolds Tobacco Holdings -401 N Main -Bx2866 -Winston Salem, NC 27102

(513) 424-4863 ..**Foley**, Darlene F '83 Meijer Store -3651 Towne Blvd -Franklin 45005

(614) 292-4288 ..**Foley**, Edward B '99 OSU Moritz Cllg of Law -55 W 12th Av -Columbus 43210 Fx:292-1383

(419) 252-5653 ..**Foley**, Elizabeth M '97 HCR ManorCare Inc -333 N Summit -Toledo 43604

(614) 464-6400 ..**Foley**, F James '77 (Vorys SS&P LLP) -52 E Gay -Bx1008 -Columbus 43216 Fx:464-6350

(614) 882-5980 ..**Foley**, J Edward '99 -299 S State -Westerville 43081 Fx:436-0347

(614) 466-5394 ..**Foley**, James R '98 Pub Def -8 E Long -Columbus 43215

(419) 241-1200 ..**Foley**, Janis E '86 Cooper & W,LPA -900 Adams -Toledo 43624 Fx:242-5675

(513) 785-4561 ..**Foley**, John P III '76 Workers Comp -125 E Court -Cincinnati 45202 Fx:361-8392

(937) 548-4132 ..**Foley**, Kandy H '89 Dept of Job & Family Srvcs -631 Wagner Av -Greenville 45331

(614) 469-7404 ..**Foley**, Kenneth M '64 SSA-OHA -401 N Front -Ste 400 -Columbus 43215

(614) 461-1311 ..**Foley**, Kevin P '92 (Reminger & R) -65 E State -4th Fl Cptl Sq Ofc Bldg -Columbus 43215 Fx:232-2410

(937) 324-6905 ..**Foley**, Margaret L '91 Sec Natl Bank &Trust Co -40 S Limestone -Springfield 45502

(440) 423-0154 ..**Foley**, Margaret R '85 -1280 SOM Center Rd -#370 -Cleveland 44124

(614) 461-1234 ..**Foley**, Mark A '69 (Portman F&F LLP) -471 E Broad -Ste 1820 -Columbus 43215 Fx:461-9150

(614) 752-8683 ..**Foley**, Mary B '93 State Auditor -88 E Broad -Bx1140 -Columbus 43216

(614) 898-5200 ..**Foley**, Megan C '97 %Pope & L Co,LPA -903 Eastwind Dr -Westerville 43081 Fx:898-5230

(937) 562-5250 ..**Foley**, Michael E '77 Greene Cnty Pros -61 Greene -Xenia 45385

(513) 381-9200 ..**Foley**, Michael P '93 (Rendigs FK&D,LLP) -One W 4th -Ste 900 -Cincinnati 45202 Fx:381-9206

(216) 251-9755 ..**Foley**, Michael P '95 -3525 Carrmunn Av -Cleveland 44111

(937) 836-4433 ..**Foley**, Patrick J '56 Montgomery Cnty Cmn Pleas Ct -41 N Perry -Dayton 45422

(330) 792-6611 ..**Foley**, Robert J Jr. '98 Heller MM&M Co LPA -54 Wstchstr Dr -Bx4144 -Youngstown 44515

(216) 696-0606 ..**Foley**, Stephen C '82 %RE Sweeney Co,LPA -55 Pub Sq -Ste 1500 -Cleveland 44113 Fx:696-0679

(937) 225-5769 ..**Folfas**, Paul A '72 Montgomery Cnty Pros -301 W 3rd -Bx972 -Dayton 45422 Fx:225-3470

Folger, Will R '85 -107 Sandusky Av -Huron 44839

(440) 333-8119 ..**Foliano**, Carrie A '89 -2922 Hmptn Rd -Rocky River 44116

(614) 227-2000 ..**Foliano**, Gregory B '90 (Porter WM&A LLP) -41 S High -Columbus 43215 Fx:227-2100

(517) 324-5600 ..**Folino**, Anita M '80 Plunkett & C,PC -325 E Grand Rvr Av -Ste 250 -East Lansing, MI 48823

(330) 762-8773 ..**Folk**, Alexander R '96 -Bx67128 -Cuyahoga Falls 44222

(419) 321-1226 ..**Folk**, Vivian C '76 (Shumaker L&K,LLP) -1000 Jackson -Toledo 43604 Fx:241-6894

(614) 466-7447 ..**Folkert**, Douglas R '82 Atty Gen -150 E Gay -Columbus 43215

(614) 227-2000 ..**Folkerth**, Andrew A '87 (Porter WM&A LLP) -41 S High -Columbus 43215 Fx:227-2100

(614) 228-2945 ..**Folkerth Haddow & Davis** -341 S 3rd -Columbus 43215

(614) 228-2945 ..**Folkerth Haddow & Davis** -250 Civic Ctr Dr -Ste 460 -Columbus 43215

(614) 466-7264 ..**Folkerth**, Jeffrey T '72 OH Legal Rghts Srvc -8 E Long -5th Fl -Columbus 43215

(937) 461-8656 ..**Folkerth**, John R Jr. '83 (Folkerth & F PLL) -1812 Kettering Twr -Dayton 45423

(937) 461-8656 ..**Folkerth**, Karen S '86 (Folkerth & F PLL) -1812 Kettering Twr -Dayton 45423

(937) 438-6848 ..**Folkerts**, Michael D '89 Stevens & S LLP -7019 Corp Way -Dayton 45459

(216) 522-3840 ..**Folkman**, Debra L '91 Dept of Veterans Affrs -1240 E 9th -Cleveland 44199

(239) 949-6989 ..**Folkman**, Jeffrey M '78 Hahn L&P LLP -3301 Bonita Beach Rd -Ste 308 -Bonita Springs, FL 34134 Fx:949-6687

(216) 566-5813 ..**Folland**, Robert C '95 (Thompson H LLP) -127 Pub Sq -3900 Key Ctr -Cleveland 44114 Fx:566-5800

(330) 456-9656 ..**Foltz**, Jeremy J '99 -122 Market Av N -Canton 44702

(614) 210-1840 ..**Foltz**, Terri H '91 OfCnsl Barrett EC&E LLP -7269 Sawmill Rd -Dublin 43016 Fx:210-1841

(740) 373-6604 ..**Folwell**, Norman L '91 -215 2nd -Marietta 45750

(216) 621-3247 ..**Fonda**, Charles W '81 -75 Pub Sq -Ste 650 -Cleveland 44113

(216) 781-8700 ..**Foos**, James R Jr. '80 -1660 W 2nd -Ste 270 Skylight Ofc Twr -Cleveland 44113

(937) 227-3700 ..**Foos**, Martin A '95 %Faruki I&C PLL -10 N Ludlow -500 Cthse Plz SW -Dayton 45402 Fx:227-3717

(513) 221-2345 ..**Foote**, Carl F '75 Univ of Cincinnati -Bx6129 -Cincinnati 45206

(937) 445-3265 ..**Foote**, Douglas A '85 NCR Corp -1700 S Patterson Blvd -WHQ5E -Dayton 45479

(513) 946-3000 ..**Foote**, Philip E '01 Hamilton Cnty Pros -230 E 9th -Cincinnati 45202 Fx:946-3017

(216) 991-6200 ..**Foote**, Richard C '76 -20133 Farnsleigh Rd -Ohio Svngs Bldg -Shaker Heights 44122

(419) 353-1062 ..**Foraker**, M Angela '00 %Twyman TH&S -519 W Wooster -Ctr Ste -Bowling Green 43402 Fx:353-6277

(740) 593-6909 ..**Foran**, Timothy J '76 -46141 Angel Ridge Rd -Athens 45701

(614) 444-3036 ..**Forbes**, Brian C '99 Saia & P,PLL -713 S Front -Columbus 43206

(216) 696-7170 ..**Forbes Fields & Associates Co, LPA** -614 W Superior Av -700 Rckfllr Bldg -Cleveland 44113

(216) 696-7170 ..**Forbes**, George L '62 (Forbes F & Assoc Co,LPA) -614 W Superior Av -700 Rckfllr Bldg -Cleveland 44113

(440) 357-6211 ..**Forbes**, Glenn E '79 (Cooper & F) -166 Main -Painesville 44077 Fx:357-1634

(216) 696-7170 ..**Forbes**, Helen M '85 (Forbes F & Assoc Co,LPA) -614 W Superior Av -700 Rckfllr Bldg -Cleveland 44113

(513) 852-6092 ..**Forbes**, Jeffrey D '01 %Wood & L LLP -600 Vine -Ste 2500 -Cincinnati 45202 Fx:852-6087

(216) 479-6100 ..**Forbes**, Lisa Babish '92 (Vorys SS&P LLP) -1375 E 9th -Ste 2100 One Cleve Ctr -Cleveland 44114 Fx:479-6060

(216) 696-7170 ..**Forbes**, Mildred O '98 %Forbes F & Assoc Co,LPA -614 W Superior Av -700 Rckfllr Bldg -Cleveland 44113

(504) 589-4612 .. **Forbes,** Nicole S '94 SSA-OHA -1 Gallaria Blvd -#2000
-Metairie, LA 70001

(216) 514-9500 .. **Forbes,** Steven Jay '89 Norchi & Assoc,LLC -23240 Chagrin Blvd
-Ste 600 -Beachwood 44122

(330) 489-3395 .. **Forchione,** Francis G '86 Pros -218 Cleveland Av SW -Bx24218
-Canton 44702

(419) 244-4277 .. **Forcht,** Melan M '01 -405 N Huron -Ste 201 -Toledo 43604

(216) 586-3939 .. **Ford,** Anne Owings '89 %Jones D -901 Lakeside Av
-Cleveland 44114 **Fx:**579-0212

(330) 535-5711 .. **Ford,** Brandon L '04 %Brouse M -106 S Main -500 First Natl Twr
-Akron 44308 **Fx:**253-8601

(614) 757-7713 .. **Ford,** Brendan A '86 Cardinal Hlth -7000 Cardinal Pl -Dublin 43017

(419) 243-1010 .. **Ford,** Claudia A '00 Leizerman & Assoc,LLC -717 Mad Av
-Toledo 43624

(330) 856-6888 .. **Ford,** Donald R Jr. '83 Ford Law Ofc -8501 E Market -Bx8806
-Warren 44484 **Fx:**856-7550

(216) 830-2770 .. **Ford,** Frank I '81 Neighborhood Progress Inc -1956 W 25th
-Ste 200 -Cleveland 44113

(614) 464-6400 .. **Ford,** Gail C '86 (Vorys SS&P LLP) -52 E Gay -Bx1008
-Columbus 43216 **Fx:**464-6350

(419) 668-7828 .. **Ford,** George C III '77 -9 Whittlesey Av -Norwalk 44857

(614) 464-6400 .. **Ford,** Jacklyn J '91 (Vorys SS&P LLP) -52 E Gay -Bx1008
-Columbus 43216 **Fx:**464-6350

(440) 998-6835 .. **Ford,** Jeffrey A '82 Andrews & P LLC -4817 State Rd -Ste 100
-Bx10 -Ashtabula 44005

(216) 787-3200 .. **Ford,** Jeffrey S '90 Cnsl OH Lottery Cmmssn -615 W Superior Av
-Cleveland 44113 **Fx:**787-3696

(216) 589-9030 .. **Ford,** Joan A '83 -1360 W 9th -Cleveland 44113

(937) 461-5310 .. **Ford,** Julie C '88 (Doll J&F) -111 W 1st -Ste 1100 -Dayton 45402
Fx:461-7219

(216) 622-3600 .. **Ford,** Laura M '02 US Atty -801 W Superior -Ste 400
-Cleveland 44113 **Fx:**622-3370

Ford, Leslie J '03 -(Address Unavailable)

(614) 583-5044 .. **Ford,** Regina M '93 City Hall -3600 Tremont Rd
-Upper Arlington 43221

(216) 566-5603 .. **Ford,** Robert B '68 (Thompson H LLP) -127 Pub Sq -3900 Key Ctr
-Cleveland 44114 **Fx:**566-5800

(513) 784-5561 .. **Ford,** William W III '85 Convergys Corp -201 E 4th
-Cincinnati 45202

Forejt, Christopher A '03 -1933 W Alexis Blvd -107 -Toledo 43613

(614) 464-6400 .. **Foreman,** Ivery D '78 (Vorys SS&P LLP) -52 E Gay -Bx1008
-Columbus 43216 **Fx:**464-6350

(330) 334-5255 .. **Foreman,** Joseph E '65 -122 Broad -Bx588 -Wadsworth 44282

(412) 281-4541 .. **Foreman,** Samuel H '95 %Weber GG&G -603 Stanwix -Ste #1450
-Pittsburgh, PA 15222

(330) 375-2030 .. **Forfia,** Deborah M '86 Law Dept -161 S High -Ste 202
-Akron 44308

(513) 889-0007 .. **Forg,** John H III '89 -6 S 2nd -Ste 208 -Hamilton 45011

(614) 825-3539 .. **Forhan,** Michael A '99 (Eley Law Firm) -7870 Olentangy Rvr Rd
-Ste 311 -Columbus 43235 **Fx:**825-9590

(304) 232-0008 .. **Forman,** Earl L II '88 -45 Eagle Av -Wheeling, WV 26003

(614) 463-9790 .. **Forman,** Edward R '03 %Marshall & M LLC -111 W Rich -Ste 430
-Columbus 43215 **Fx:**463-9780

(216) 696-7600 .. **Forman,** Jonathan S '94 %Duvin C&H -1301 E 9th
-20th Fl Erievw Twr -Cleveland 44114 **Fx:**696-2038

(513) 352-3340 .. **Forman,** Keith C '01 Law Dept -801 Plum -Rm 214
-Cincinnati 45202 **Fx:**352-1515

(614) 889-1493 .. **Forman,** Monica S '86 -7624 Worsley Ct -Dublin 43017

(614) 461-1551 .. **Forman,** Richard J '77 Barkan & B Co LPA -81 S 4th -Ste 300
-Columbus 43215

(216) 410-1456 .. **Forman,** Thomas M '82 FVC,Inc -22 Pepper Crk -Cleveland 44124

(513) 421-2881 .. **Forney,** Ferdinand A '54 -7725 Hartfld Pl -Cincinnati 45242

(614) 224-1500 .. **Fornia Luftman & Heck,LLP** -2 Miranova Pl -Ste 380
-Columbus 43215 **Fx:**224-2894

(614) 224-1500 .. **Fornia,** William J '03 (Fornia L&H,LLP) -2 Miranova Pl -Ste 380
-Columbus 43215 **Fx:**224-2894

(419) 213-6680 .. **Fornof,** Judith A '73 Lucas Co Juv Ct -429 Mich Av -Toledo 43624

(937) 653-7376 .. **Fornof-Lippencott,** Susan J '89 Cnty Mun Ct Judge -Bx85
-Urbana 43078 **Fx:**652-4333

(513) 977-8200 .. **Fornshell,** David P '99 %Dinsmore & S LLP -255 E 5th -Ste 1900
-Cincinnati 45202 **Fx:**977-8141

(216) 736-7226 .. **Fornshell,** Matthew L '93 (Kohrman J&K PLL) -1375 E 9th
-One Cleve Ctr 20th Fl -Cleveland 44114 **Fx:**621-6536

(330) 683-4981 .. **Forrer,** Carl E '72 -136 E Market -Orrville 44667

(216) 579-0800 .. **Forrest,** Audrey P '78 (A Forrest Co,LPA) -101 Prospect Av W
-1650 Mdlnd Bldg -Cleveland 44115

(216) 844-3777 .. **Forrest,** Carl L '04 Univeristy Anesthesologists Inc
-11100 Euclid Av -Cleveland 44106

(419) 447-9121 .. **Forrest,** Clair M Jr. '85 -140 Riverside Dr -Tiffin 44883

(216) 771-4050 .. **Forrest,** David A '79 (Jeffries KF&M Co,LPA) -101 W Prospect Av
-1650 Mdlnd Bldg -Cleveland 44115 **Fx:**771-0732

(330) 908-0229 .. **Forrestal,** Timothy J '93 (Forrestal Law Ofc,LPA)
-8570 Deep Cove Dr -Sagamore Hills 44067

(614) 644-6338 .. **Forrester,** Mary E '81 OH Dept of Edu -25 S Front -7th Fl
-Columbus 43215

Forrester, Steven R '04 -(Address Unavailable)

(440) 585-7968 .. **Forrester,** Traci L '02 ABB Inc -29801 Euclid Av -Wickliffe 44092

(973) 243-6273 .. **Forrester,** Wilbur G '77 Aventis Pharm,Inc
-300 Somerset Corp Blvd -Bridgewater, NJ 08807

(614) 462-2254 .. **Forry,** Steven '02 %Schottenstein Z&D -250 West -Bx165020
-Columbus 43216 **Fx:**462-5135

(740) 286-2223 .. **Forshey,** Timothy E '87 -212 Pearl -Ste D -Jackson 45640

(419) 282-4290 .. **Forsthoefel,** Ronald P '83 Ashland Cnty Cmmn Pleas Ct
-142 W 2nd -Ashland 44805

(440) 239-7767 .. **Forstner,** Gerald C Jr. '67 (Frost & F) -140 Sheldon Rd
-Berea 44017

(412) 566-2970 .. **Forsythe,** Dale K '96 (Wayman I&M) -437 Grant -1624 Frick Bldg
-Pittsburgh, PA 15219 **Fx:**391-1464

(614) 228-2345 .. **Forsythe,** Frank E '65 %Chicago Title Agncy -100 S 4th -Ste 100
-Columbus 43215

(419) 241-9000 .. **Fort,** Jeffrey E '82 (Shumaker L&K,LLP) -1000 Jackson
-Toledo 43624 **Fx:**241-6894

(330) 699-6703 .. **Fortado,** Matthew '77 OfCnsl McNamara & F Co,LPA
-12370 Cleveland Av -Bx867 -Uniontown 44685 **Fx:**699-4803

(216) 687-2342 .. **Forte,** David F '86 CSU-Marshall Cllg of Law -2121 Euclid Av
-LB138 -Cleveland 44115 **Fx:**687-6881

(330) 489-3395 .. **Forte,** Jennifer L '00 Pros -218 Cleveland Av SW -Bx24218
-Canton 44702

(614) 466-5337 .. **Fortkamp,** Jeffrey D '02 OH Legal Asst Fdn -42 E Gray -Ste 900
-Columbus 43215

(614) 752-6417 .. **Fortman,** Judith W '72 Atty Gen -30 E Broad -Columbus 43215
Fx:466-0013

(330) 665-5445 .. **Fortney & Klingshirn** -4040 Embssy Pkwy -Ste 280 -Akron 44333

(330) 665-5445 .. **Fortney,** Michael L '86 (Fortney & K) -4040 Embssy Pkwy -Ste 280
-Akron 44333

(216) 664-4825 .. **Fortunato,** Christopher R '87 -1200 Ontario -8th Fl
-Cleveland 44113

(330) 757-7171 .. **Fortunato,** Mark R '88 -3296 Stones Throw Av -Poland 44514

(216) 685-1105 .. **Fortunato,** Theresa A '92 (Weltman W&R Co,LPA)
-323 W Lakeside Av -Ste 200 -Cleveland 44113 **Fx:**363-4121

(614) 644-7233 .. **Fosnaught,** Jerri L '04 Atty Gen -150 E Gay -Columbus 43215

(216) 579-2861 .. **Fosnight,** William D '84 Fed Reserve Bk of Cleveland -1455 E 6th
-Bx6387 -Cleveland 44101

(216) 444-3619 .. **Foss,** Carolyn M '04 Cleveland Clinic Fndtn -9500 Euclid Av
-EE-35 -Cleveland 44195

(859) 292-2311 .. **Fossett,** John J '87 Cors & B -638 Mad Av -Covington, KY 41011

(740) 947-1026 .. **Fosson,** John L '75 -211 E 2nd -Waverly 45690

(937) 544-5251 .. **Foster,** Alan W '76 -228 N Market -West Union 45693

(937) 382-1000 .. **Foster,** Brett L '94 Liberty Capital,Inc -2251 Rombach Av -Bx1000
-Wilmington 45177

(440) 576-3489 .. **Foster,** David F '84 Ashtabula Cnty Pros -25 W Jffrsn
-Jefferson 44047

(330) 864-1335 .. **Foster,** Greta L '79 -205 Avondale Dr -Akron 44313

(216) 991-8325 .. **Foster,** Ivan V '76 Envirocycle Inc -3614 Tolland Rd
-Shaker Heights 44122

(614) 466-5640 .. **Foster,** Kelly L '99 OH Ofc of Collective Bargaining -106 N High
-7th Fl -Columbus 43215

Foster, Kimberley S '93 -968 Werner Way -Worthington 43085

(937) 278-0651 .. **Foster,** Mark S '80 -4428 N Dixie Dr -Dayton 45414

(304) 691-8354 .. **Foster,** Melissa G '95 (Huddleston BBP&C,LLP) -611 Third Av
-Bx2185 -Huntington, WV 25722 **Fx:**522-8142

(513) 579-5140 .. **Foster,** Philip A '00 Fifth 3rd Bank-Trust Div -38 Fountain Sq Plz
-ML1090C5 -Cincinnati 45263

Foster, Robert H '73 -6094 Endicott Rd -Columbus 43229

Foster, Robin W '00 -3009 Fairfld Av -Cincinnati 45206

(330) 972-6102 .. **Foster,** Sidney C Jr. '74 University of Akron -220 Buchtel Hall
-Akron 44325

(740) 622-1595 .. **Foster,** Susan M '84 Coshocton Cnty Cmmn Pleas Ct -318 Main
-Ct Hse -Coshocton 43812

(513) 241-3430 .. **Foster,** Thomas C '60 (Rich PWF&M) -830 Main -Ste 1115
-Cincinnati 45202 **Fx:**357-4392

(513) 421-4855 .. **Foster,** Ty L '81 -830 Main -Ste 1105 -Cincinnati 45202

(614) 833-0750 .. **Foster-Littlefield,** Deborah E '92 -4819 Hrbr Blvd -Columbus
43232

(440) 846-0000 .. **Foth,** Arthur E '03 (Foth & F Co,LPA) -11221 Pearl Rd
-Strongsville 44136

(440) 846-0000 .. **Foth,** Arthur F Jr. '74 (Foth & F Co,LPA) -11221 Pearl Rd
-Strongsville 44136

(216) 481-2020 .. **Foti,** Anthony L '88 Hose Master Inc -1233 E 222nd -Euclid 44117

(440) 461-9000 .. **Foulds,** Robert J '81 Dyson S&F Co,LPA -5843 Mayfld Rd
-Mayfield Heights 44124

(850) 414-3600 .. **Foulk,** Vincent L '90 Atty Gen -The Cptl PL-01
-Tallahassee, FL 32399 **Fx:**487-9475

(614) 228-5151 .. **Founds,** Mark J '98 %Gallagher GPT&L LLP -471 E Broad -19th Fl
-Columbus 43215 **Fx:**228-0032

(513) 983-3585 .. **Foureman,** William C '84 SrCnsl Procter & Gamble -Bx599
-Cincinnati 45201

(216) 689-0773 .. **Fourmas,** Thomas A '98 KeyBank NA -2025 Ontario -7th Fl
-Cleveland 44115

(419) 243-6281 .. **Fournier,** Heather J '02 %Shindler NH&S,LLP -300 Mad Av
-Ste 1200 -Toledo 43604 **Fx:**243-0129

Fournier, Jennifer E '91 USAF 11 WG/JA -20 MacDill Blvd
-Ste 240 -Bolling AFB, DC 20032

(313) 577-4283 .. **Fournier,** Robert J '86 Wayne State Univ -101 Manhaei
-Detroit, MI 48202

(740) 373-7572 .. **Fouss,** Daniel A '80 (Davidson HR&F) -311 4th -Bx567
-Marietta 45750 **Fx:**373-7081

(614) 227-3333 .. **Foust,** Hollie K '00 Abbott Laboratories, Ross Products Div
-625 Cleveland Av -Columbus 43215

(614) 447-3600 .. **Foust,** Jennifer A '00 Chem Abstrcts Srvcs
-2540 Olentangy Rvr Rd -Columbus 43202

(216) 621-9870 .. **Fout,** Karen Burke '04 -123 W Prospect Av -Ste 250
-Cleveland 44115

(440) 248-6700 .. **Fouts,** Douglas R '75 -30575 Bainbrdg Rd -Ste 160 -Solon 44139

Fowerbaugh, Andrew M '98 -Bx771331 -Lakewood 44107

(216) 622-8200 .. **Fowkes,** Joshua A '02 %Calfee H&G LLP -800 Superior Av
-Ste 1400 -Cleveland 44114 **Fx:**241-0816

(513) 579-7902 .. **Fowler,** Byron T '96 Federated Dept Stores,Inc -7 W 7th
-Cincinnati 45202

Fowler, Daniel B II '00 -Bx123 -Parkersburg, WV 26102

(330) 478-3833 .. **Fowler,** Douglas T '95 -316 Grandvw Av NW -Canton 44708

(330) 392-3991 .. **Fowler,** John E II '94 (Ivanchak & F) -119 W Market
-Warren 44481

(330) 533-4823 .. **Fowler,** Pamela P '85 -Bx425 -Canfield 44406

(419) 524-9811 .. **Fowler,** Richard R Jr. '53 OfCnsl Weldon H&K,LLP -28 Park Av W
-Bank One Bldg -Mansfield 44902 **Fx:**522-5758

(330) 329-3792 .. **Fowler,** Robert M '72 -560 Parkhill Dr -Ste 7 -Fairlawn 44333

(740) 427-5164 .. **Fowler,** Wendi M '01 Kenyon Cllg Dept of Athltcs -211 Duff
-Gambier 43022

(513) 932-7444 .. **Fowler,** William G '73 -12 W South -Lebanon 45036

(330) 746-5643 .. **Fowler,** William S '84 (Comstock S&W Co,LPA) -100 Fed Plz E
-Ste 926 -Youngstown 44503 **Fx:**746-4925

(216) 902-6010 .. **Fowles,** Ted R '00 US Coast Guard -1240 E 9th -Rm 2075
-Cleveland 44199

(419) 738-9688 .. **Fox,** Amy O '92 Auglaize Cnty Pros -201 Willipie -Ste G4 -Bx1992 -Wapakoneta 45895

(216) 357-5123 .. **Fox,** Angela '92 %A Isakoff -55 Pub Sq -Ste 1331 -Cleveland 44113 **Fx:**241-4591

(513) 961-6644 .. **Fox,** Bernard C '50 Fox & F Co,LPA -2407 Ashland Av -Cincinnati 45206

(513) 961-6644 .. **Fox,** Bernard C Jr. '78 (Fox & F Co,LPA) -2407 Ashland Av -Cincinnati 45206

(513) 564-0088 .. **Fox,** Bradley W '03 %Bleile & S -114 E 8th -Cincinnati 45202

(330) 482-4040 .. **Fox,** C Richard '52 -33 Pittsburgh -Bx244 -Columbiana 44408 **Fx:**482-1953

(614) 466-6750 .. **Fox,** Carolyn M '88 OH Dept Taxation -30 E Broad -22nd Fl -Columbus 43215

(937) 258-3668 .. **Fox,** Charles B '54 (Fox & Assoc Co,LPA) -1344 Woodman Dr -Ste F -Dayton 45432 **Fx:**258-3098

(614) 224-5209 .. **Fox,** Clenzo B '53 -209 S High -#511 -Columbus 43215

(419) 273-2730 .. **Fox,** Daniel C '50 Fox & F Co,LPA -2407 Ashland Av -Cincinnati 45206

(419) 273-2730 .. **Fox,** Daniel E '86 -12431 State Hwy 293 -Upper Sandusky 43351

(614) 466-1073 .. **Fox,** Daniel W '86 Supreme Ct of OH -30 E Broad -35th Fl -Columbus 43215

(330) 493-0040 .. **Fox,** Dennis J '71 Lesh C&M -4150 Belden Vllg NW -Ste 606 -Canton 44718

(614) 466-3615 .. **Fox,** Diana C '01 Legis Srvc Commssn -77 S High -Columbus 43215

(513) 357-9767 .. **Fox,** Elizabeth '92 Industrial Commssn of OH -125 E Court -Cincinnati 45202

Fox, Eric S '04 -(Address Unavailable)

(330) 744-5284 .. **Fox,** Eugene B '52 OfCnsl Harshman B&R -105 E Boardman -Youngstown 44503

(513) 961-6644 .. **Fox & Fox Co,LPA** -2407 Ashland Av -Cincinnati 45206

(740) 732-2222 .. **Fox,** Fred F '50 -406 North -Bx157 -Caldwell 43724

(740) 423-7569 .. **Fox,** Jim D '73 -2002 Wshngtn Blvd -Belpre 45714

(513) 844-8888 .. **Fox,** Jonathan N '88 -6 S 2nd -#720 -Hamilton 45011

(614) 463-8826 .. **Fox,** Karol C '89 Natl City Bank -155 E Broad -Columbus 43251

(440) 355-5297 .. **Fox,** Kathleen N '95 -98 N Center -Bx732 -LaGrange 44050

(614) 493-9730 .. **Fox,** Kelly J '95 Arshot Investment Corp -21 E State -16th Fl -Columbus 43215

(419) 483-3739 .. **Fox,** Kenneth P '67 -106 Northwest -Bellevue 44811

(419) 294-2336 .. **Fox,** Mary E '81 (Osborn & F,LPA) -116 E Wyandot Av -Upper Sandusky 43351 **Fx:**294-5669

(419) 586-8677 .. **Fox,** Matthew K '91 Mercer Cnty Pros -119 N Walnut -Celina 45822

(513) 381-3525 .. **Fox,** Peter M '85 %Kircher R&W -1014 Vine -Ste 2520 -Cincinnati 45202

(937) 791-8161 .. **Fox,** Randy E '87 Lexis/Nexis -Bx933 -Dayton 45401

(419) 999-3300 .. **Fox,** Rebecca S '83 -3951 Yellowood -Lima 45806

(330) 878-5535 .. **Fox,** Richard L '76 -122 S Wooster Av -Strasburg 44680

(330) 253-2227 .. **Fox,** Robert Roe '89 Parker LH&R,LLC -388 S Main -Ste 402 -Akron 44311 **Fx:**253-1261

(740) 452-9311 .. **Fox,** Rose M '98 -233 Main -Zanesville 43701

(330) 425-8520 .. **Fox,** Rosmarie T '86 Lerner S&R -8972 Darrow Rd -Ste A304 -Twinsburg 44087

(614) 462-3194 .. **Fox,** Steven T '99 Franklin Cnty Pub Def -373 S High -12th Fl -Columbus 43215

(440) 895-1234 .. **Fox,** Thomas C Jr. '92 OfCnsl Polito P&R -21300 Lorain Rd -Fairview Park 44126

(330) 364-6621 .. **Fox,** Thomas W '73 (Traver & F) -232 W 3rd -Ste 309 -Dover 44622

(614) 228-8400 .. **Fox,** Timothy M '87 (Ulmer & B LLP) -88 E Broad -Ste 1600 -Columbus 43215 **Fx:**228-8561

(440) 943-7080 .. **Foxx,** John E '65 (JE Foxx Co,LPA) -28601 Gilchrist Dr -Willowick 44095

(216) 241-5310 .. **Foy,** Patrick M '87 (Gallagher SF&N) -1501 Euclid Av -6th Fl -Cleveland 44115 **Fx:**241-1608

(614) 228-5331 .. **Fraas,** Henry C Jr. '94 %Don M Casto Org -191 W Nationwide Blvd -Ste 200 -Columbus 43215

(937) 335-8324 .. **Fraas,** Richard J '59 OfCnsl Faust HFM&S -12 S Cherry -Troy 45373 **Fx:**339-7155

(216) 583-4948 .. **Frabotta,** Craig M '96 Ernst & Young LLP -925 Euclid Av -Ste 1300 -Cleveland 44115

(216) 586-3939 .. **Fraelich,** Timothy P '93 (Jones D) -901 Lakeside Av -Cleveland 44114 **Fx:**579-0212

(740) 387-7438 .. **Fragale,** Robert D '82 (Nemo & F) -495 S State -Marion 43302

(740) 922-4795 .. **Fragasse,** Maria L '81 Cnty Ct -224 E 3rd -Uhrichsville 44683

(614) 337-8366 .. **Fraley,** Joseph A '91 (Pencheff & F) -2176A CityGate Dr -Columbus 43219

(440) 350-2708 .. **Fram,** Jeffrey W '77 Lake Cnty Cmmn Pleas Ct -47 N Park Pl -Bx490 -Painesville 44077

(937) 485-4088 .. **Frame,** Carla M '84 Reynolds & Reynolds Co -115 S Ludlow -Dayton 45402

(330) 438-0611 .. **Frame,** Gary J '93 Industrial Commssn of OH -400 3rd SE -Canton 44702

(330) 451-7200 .. **Frame,** Kenneth W '96 Stark Cnty Pub Def -200 W Tuscarawas -Ste 200 -Canton 44702

(330) 266-1931 .. **Framer,** Lee W '77 Leonard Ins Srvcs,Inc -4244 Mt Plsnt NW -Ste 200 -Bx9160 -Canton 44711 **Fx:**498-9946

(740) 622-6222 .. **France,** Timothy L '81 -442 Chestnut -Bx35 -Coshocton 43812

(419) 223-1861 .. **Franceschelli,** Anna M '03 Ct of Appeals 3rd Dist -204 N Main -Lima 45802

(937) 225-5783 .. **Franceschelli,** David M '79 Montgomery Cnty Pros -301 W 3rd -Bx972 -Dayton 45422 **Fx:**225-3470

(216) 621-3000 .. **Franceschini,** Antonio S '99 %JM Drain Jr -Bx6041 -Cleveland 44101 **Fx:**241-0839

(614) 752-4267 .. **Francis,** Caryn A '93 OH Dept Commerce -77 S High -Columbus 43266

(330) 764-8731 .. **Francis,** J Bruce '77 Medina/Wayne Cnty Ct of Cmmn Pleas -144 N Bway -Rm 306 -Medina 44256 **Fx:**764-8733

(937) 225-4987 .. **Francis,** Jessica L '02 Montgomery Cnty Pros/CSEA -14 W 4th -Ste 510 -Dayton 45402

(330) 829-3219 .. **Francis,** Philip Lee '83 United Natl Bank & Trust -2 W State -Bx3717 -Alliance 44601

(937) 644-6642 .. **Francis,** Stephen S '84 Honda of Amer Mfg -24000 Honda Pkwy -Marysville 43040

(415) 292-0330 .. **Francis,** Wanyee S '79 -2639 Hyde -San Francisco, CA 94109

(216) 752-4600 .. **Francis-Sable,** Kenneth J '04 -21825 Chagrin Blvd -Ste 320 -Beachwood 44122

(330) 490-5005 .. **Francis-Vogelsang,** Charee '88 Diebold,Inc -Bx3077 -North Canton 44720

(202) 273-3791 .. **Francke,** Claude R '88 NLRB -1099 14th NW -Div of Enforcement Lit -Washington, DC 20570

(513) 576-1060 .. **Franckewitz,** Stephanie P '01 %Calderhead Law Ofc,LLC -200 TechneCenter Dr -Ste 100 -Milford 45150 **Fx:**576-8792

(703) 248-4060 .. **Francois,** Constance H '81 CACI,Inc-Commercial -1100 N Glebe Rd -Arlington, VA

(615) 341-1062 .. **Francy,** David A '91 Caterpillar Fin Srvcs Corp -2120 W End Av -Nashville, TN 37203

(216) 522-7121 .. **Franczak,** Michael S '95 Fed Med & Conc Srvc -6161 Oak Tree Blvd -Ste 100 -Independence 44131

(216) 771-0157 .. **Franey,** Martin F '48 -1240 Standard Bldg -Cleveland 44113

(216) 579-1602 .. **Franey,** Martin T '78 (Rawlins G&F Co,LPA) -55 Pub Sq -Ste 850 -Cleveland 44113

(330) 621-9255 .. **Frangos,** Gus '82 -8062 Ravenna Rd -Hudson 44236

(513) 722-3617 .. **Frank,** Armin H '74 -1632 Woodvll Pike -Loveland 45140

(202) 337-7319 .. **Frank,** Carol R '83 -1247 30th NW -Washington, DC 20007

(614) 228-5931 .. **Frank,** David K '74 Mazanec R&R Co,LPA -250 Civic Ctr Dr -Ste 400 -Columbus 43215 **Fx:**228-5934

(330) 385-5595 .. **Frank,** Dominic A '92 -128 W 5th -East Liverpool 43920 **Fx:**385-7846

(202) 708-0340 .. **Frank,** Elizabeth '88 US Dept HUD -451 7th SW -Washington, DC 20410

(216) 515-1660 .. **Frank,** Ian H '96 (Frantz W LLP) -127 Pub Sq -2500 Key Center -Cleveland 44114 **Fx:**515-1650

(440) 446-1100 .. **Frank,** Irwin M '72 OfCnsl Dinn H&P,LLC -5910 Landerbrook Dr -Ste 200 -Cleveland 44124 **Fx:**446-1240

(216) 623-0000 .. **Frank,** John J '98 %Javitch B&R -1300 E 9th -14th Fl -Cleveland 44114 **Fx:**623-0190

(330) 493-6515 .. **Frank,** John R '91 -3930 Fulton Dr NW -Ste 102A -Canton 44718

(513) 852-6000 .. **Frank,** Kevin K '04 %Wood & L LLP -600 Vine -Ste 2500 -Cincinnati 45202 **Fx:**852-6087

(440) 232-9911 .. **Frank,** Louis S '69 (McDonald FH&H) -24262 Bway Av -Bx46390 -Oakwood Village 44146 **Fx:**439-2308

(216) 241-7226 .. **Frank,** Mark S '81 -55 Pub Sq -Ste 1400 -Cleveland 44113

(614) 469-3939 .. **Frank,** Marlene P '82 (Jones D) -325 John H McConnell Blvd -Ste 600 -Bx165017 -Columbus 43216 **Fx:**461-4198

(614) 645-7477 .. **Frank,** Melinda J '79 Columbus Income Tax Div -50 W Gay -Columbus 43215

(330) 493-4443 .. **Frank,** Michael '90 EMP Mgmt Group -4535 Dressler Rd NW -Canton 44718

(513) 722-3617 .. **Frank,** Rainer A '94 %A Frank -1632 Woodvll Pike -Loveland 45140

(419) 241-2200 .. **Frank,** Raymond M '71 Arnold & C,Ltd -1822 Cherry -Toledo 43608 **Fx:**255-7623

(740) 472-0708 .. **Frank,** William E Jr. '90 -122 N Main -Bx351 -Woodsfield 43793

(513) 598-4276 .. **Frank,** William N '78 -6470A Glenway Av -Ste 326 -Cincinnati 45202

(614) 221-1662 .. **Frank & Wooldridge Co LPA** -600 S Pearl -Columbus 43206

(614) 293-6500 .. **Frank-Scott,** Christine '03 OSU -410 W 10th Av -Columbus 43210

(614) 466-4605 .. **Frankart,** Robert J '78 OH Dept Job & Fam Srvcs -30 E Broad -32nd Fl -Columbus 43266

(513) 871-8855 .. **Franke,** Carolyn Mussio '83 -3411 Mich Av -Cincinnati 45208

(513) 564-9222 .. **Franke,** Gary F '85 (GF Franke Co,LPA) -120 E 4th -Ste 1040 -Cincinnati 45202

(513) 941-1850 .. **Franke,** Hal F '53 Motor Carriers Employers Conference, CS -6799 Rapid Run Rd -Cincinnati 45233

(513) 564-9222 .. **Franke,** Hal L '83 -120 E 4th -Ste 1040 -Cincinnati 45202

(614) 466-8288 .. **Franke,** Janice R '83 Mntl Hlth -30 E Broad -8th Fl -Columbus 43215

(513) 863-6700 .. **Franke,** John P '89 (Millikin & F) -6 S 2nd -6th Fl -Bx598 -Hamilton 45012 **Fx:**863-0031

(216) 363-1400 .. **Frankel,** Dov Y '04 %Buckley K,LPA -600 E Superior Av -Ste 1400 -Cleveland 44114 **Fx:**579-1020

(513) 761-9255 .. **Frankel,** Edward M '77 Standard Textile Co,Inc -1 Knollcrest Dr -Bx371805 -Cincinnati 45222

(513) 852-6045 .. **Frankel,** Jan M '78 (Wood & L LLP) -600 Vine -Ste 2500 -Cincinnati 45202 **Fx:**852-6087

(419) 627-0414 .. **Frankel,** John D '75 Buckingham LM&Z Co,LPA -414 Wayne -Bx929 -Sandusky 44870 **Fx:**627-0009

(440) 933-3231 .. **Frankel,** Kenneth P '75 Smith S Co,LPA -110 Moore Rd -Bx210 -Avon Lake 44012

(419) 255-5111 .. **Frankel,** Paul D '77 -520 Mad Av -1030 Spitzer Bldg -Toledo 43604 **Fx:**255-3231

(513) 621-1505 .. **Frankel,** Renee S '84 (Goodman & G) -123 E 4th -5th Fl -Cincinnati 45202

(330) 549-2497 .. **Franken,** Timothy E '79 -Bx3506 -Youngstown 44513

(614) 487-1488 .. **Franklin,** Charles E '77 -3068 Tremont Rd -Columbus 43221

(513) 651-6800 .. **Franklin,** David E '95 %Frost BT LLC -201 E 5th -2200 PNC Ctr -Cincinnati 45202 **Fx:**651-6981

(216) 523-4103 .. **Franklin,** Earl R '68 Eaton Corp -1111 Superior Av -Cleveland 44114

(419) 243-9005 .. **Franklin,** John D '91 (Franklin & G,LLC) -420 Mad Av -Ste 1101 -Toledo 43604 **Fx:**243-9404

(216) 476-7002 .. **Franklin,** Marlene A '91 Fairview Hospital -18101 Lorain Av -Cleveland 44111

(440) 998-0770 .. **Franklin,** Michael '81 -4510 Collins Blvd -Ste 3 -Ashtabula 44004

(419) 473-3916 .. **Franklin,** Pauline '00 -3601 Alexis Rd -Ste 102 -Toledo 43623 **Fx:**473-0613

(330) 668-5334 .. **Frankovich,** George S '80 Sterling,Inc -375 Ghent Rd -Akron 44333

(410) 649-2046 .. **Frankovich,** Jennifer R '98 %PG Angelos -100 N Charles -1 Charles Ctr 20th Fl -Baltimore, MD 21201

(304) 723-4400 .. **Frankovitch,** Carl N '93 (Frankovitch AC&S) -337 Penco Rd -Weirton, WV 26062

(304) 723-4400 .. **Frankovitch,** Marcus E '85 Frankovitch AC&S -337 Penco Rd -Weirton, WV 26062

(330) 637-4600 .. **Franks,** James D '84 -3637 State Route 5 -Ste 6 -Cortland 44410

(216) 621-1530 .. **Franks,** Jennifer R '02 %Shapiro & F,LLP -1500 W 3rd -Ste 400 -Cleveland 44113 **Fx:**621-1551

(330) 425-4201 .. **Franks**, Stephen R '02 %Reimer L&A Co,LPA -2450 Edison Blvd
-Bx968 -Twinsburg 44087 **Fx:**487-0923

(440) 843-5193 .. **Franks**, Steven L '94 Sears Credit -13200 Smith Rd
-Middleburg Heights 44130 **Fx:**843-5164

(937) 865-6800 .. **Frantz**, Deborah A '00 Lexis/Nexis -Bx933 -Dayton 45401

(501) 905-8111 .. **Frantz**, Francis X '78 Alltel Corp -1 Allied Dr
-Little Rock, AR 72202

(330) 262-3030 .. **Frantz**, Martin H '78 (Wayne Cnty Pros) -115 W Lbrty -Wooster
44691 **Fx:**287-5412

(216) 515-1660 .. **Frantz**, Michael J '76 (Frantz W LLP) -127 Pub Sq -2500 Key
Center -Cleveland 44114 **Fx:**515-1650

(216) 515-1660 .. **Frantz Ward LLP** -127 Pub Sq -2500 Key Center
-Cleveland 44114 **Fx:**515-1650

(330) 725-2348 .. **Frantz**, William G '80 Sandridge Food Corp -133 Commerce Dr
-Medina 44256

(513) 983-6064 .. **Franz**, Paul A '82 Procter & Gamble Co -1 Procter & Gamble Plz
-Cincinnati 45202

(216) 586-3939 .. **Franz**, Paul E '02 %Jones D -901 Lakeside Av -Cleveland 44114
Fx:579-0212

(614) 365-2700 .. **Franzmann**, Christopher J '98 (Squire S&D LLP) -41 S High
-1300 Huntngtn Ctr -Columbus 43215 **Fx:**365-2499

(937) 223-8378 .. **Frapwell**, William H '78 Chicago Title Ins Co -1 S Main -Ste 330
-Dayton 45402

(614) 326-5544 .. **Frasch**, Joseph F Jr. '74 -1550 Old Henderson Rd -#N-130
-Bx20387 -Columbus 43220 **Fx:**457-4151

(740) 622-6464 .. **Frase Weir Baker & McCullough Co,LPA** -305 Main -4th Fl
-Coshocton 43812 **Fx:**622-8107

(937) 644-9125 .. **Fraser**, Don W '79 (Cannizzaro FB&J) -302 S Main
-Marysville 43040 **Fx:**644-0754

(419) 874-1100 .. **Fraser**, Donald R '63 (Fraser MBM LLC) -132C W 2nd
-Perrysburg 43551 **Fx:**874-1130

(419) 874-1100 .. **Fraser Martin Buchanan Miller LLC** -132C W 2nd
-Perrysburg 43551 **Fx:**874-1130

(614) 227-2000 .. **Frasier**, Ralph K '76 OfCnsl Porter WM&A LLP -41 S High
-Columbus 43215 **Fx:**227-2100

(919) 680-4039 .. **Frasier**, Ralph K Jr. '94 (Frasier & A,PA) -100 E Parrish -Ste 350
-Durham, NC 27701 **Fx:**680-4390

(330) 492-8717 .. **Frasure**, Mark D '74 (Buckingham D&B,LLP) -4518 Fulton Dr NW
-Bx35548 -Canton 44735 **Fx:**492-9625

(216) 443-3429 .. **Fraunfelder**, William A Jr. '68 Ct of Common Pleas -2163 E 22nd
-Cleveland 44115

(330) 852-2513 .. **Frautschy**, Douglas D '99 -232 Factory NE -Bx462
-Sugarcreek 44681

(937) 224-0076 .. **Frayne**, Anne M '79 (Myers & F Co,LPA) -18 W 1st -Ste 200
-Dayton 45402

(937) 433-8985 .. **Frazee**, Willis H Jr. '53 -5400 Silbury Ln -Dayton 45429
Fx:433-8985

(614) 221-9400 .. **Frazier**, Jean M '87 (Habash R&F,LLP) -471 E Broad -Ste 800
-Columbus 43215

(216) 391-7700 .. **Frazier**, Linda M '96 McTech Corp -8100 Grand Av -Bx5270
-Cleveland 44101

(813) 985-9582 .. **Frazier**, Robert C '65 First Benefits,Inc -7930 US Hwy 301 N
-Tampa, FL 33637

(614) 466-2766 .. **Frazzini**, Cynthia K '96 Atty Gen -30 E Broad -Columbus 43215
Fx:644-1926

(740) 380-1704 .. **Frechette**, Monica A '95 -Bx851 -Logan 43138

(440) 461-3600 .. **Freda**, Joy C '79 -6009 Landerhaven Dr -#C-1 -Cleveland 44124

(419) 529-4560 .. **Freda**, Michael M '72 UAW Legal Srvcs Plan -1075 Natl Pkwy
-Bx2668 -Mansfield 44906 **Fx:**529-5350

.... **Fredenburg**, Gary C '85 -4868 Spruce Pine Way
-North Ridgeville 44039

(513) 737-5100 .. **Frederick**, Christopher P '03 -304 N 2nd -Hamilton 45011

(330) 743-4116 .. **Frederick**, Harry '51 (Brennan FV&Y,Ltd) -29 E Front -2nd Fl
-Youngstown 44503

(419) 732-1607 .. **Frederick**, Mark A '87 -125 Jffrsn -Port Clinton 43452

(614) 228-3372 .. **Frederick**, Michael A '00 %Comisford & P LLC -1243 S High
-Columbus 43206 **Fx:**228-3584

(216) 781-3434 .. **Frederick**, Ronald I '94 -55 Pub Sq -Ste 1300 -Cleveland 44113

(513) 737-5100 .. **Frederick**, Scott J '94 -304 N 2nd -Hamilton 45011

(330) 393-6400 .. **Fredericka**, James A '78 (Ambrosy & F) -144 N Park Av -Ste 200
-Warren 44481 **Fx:**392-5685

(419) 242-5100 .. **Frederickson**, Craig F '75 (Frederickson H&K Co,LPA)
-405 Mad Av -Ste 1212 -Toledo 43604 **Fx:**242-5556

(419) 242-5100 .. **Frederickson Heintschel & King Co,LPA** -405 Mad Av
-Ste 1212 -Toledo 43604 **Fx:**242-5556

(301) 214-9984 .. **Fredrickson**, Debra J '95 Lockhead Martin Corp -6901 Rockldg Dr
-Bethesda, MD 20817

(440) 946-9469 .. **Freeburg**, Antoinette E '99 %CP Kasunic Co,LPA
-38033 Euclid Av -#1 -Willoughby 44094

(216) 622-0850 .. **Freeburg**, David A '99 %McFadden & Assoc Co,LPA
-1370 Ontario -Ste 1700 -Cleveland 44113 **Fx:**622-0854

(202) 331-8800 .. **Freed**, Charles L '74 (Thompson H LLP) -1920 N NW -Ste 800
-Washington, DC 20036 **Fx:**331-8330

.... **Freed**, Irene K '93 -976 Lndngs Ct -Westerville 43082

(614) 442-4628 .. **Freed**, Robert P '03 McCloy Financial Srvcs -921 Chatham Ln
-#300 -Columbus 43221

(614) 235-6117 .. **Freed**, Ruth P '58 -464 E Main -Ste 275 -Columbus 43215
Fx:235-9222

(330) 670-0770 .. **Freedman**, Bruce R '81 (Corzin SU&F)
-304 N Cleveland-Massillon Rd -Akron 44333

(440) 247-0775 .. **Freedman**, Howard J '70 (Weiss & F LLP) -35 River
-Chagrin Falls 44022 **Fx:**893-9138

(202) 353-0527 .. **Freedman**, Lee J '97 DOJ-Civil Div Comm Lit -1100 L NW
-Washington, DC 20530

(216) 321-8284 .. **Freedman**, Leland S '56 -3797 Hillbrook Rd
-University Heights 44118

(216) 249-3199 .. **Freedman**, Steven A '76 -5525 Warrensvll Ctr Rd
-Cleveland 44137

(513) 977-8200 .. **Freedman**, William M '73 (Dinsmore & S LLP) -255 E 5th
-Ste 1900 -Cincinnati 45202 **Fx:**977-8141

(614) 466-7090 .. **Freel**, David E '77 Ethics Commssn -8 E Long -10th Fl
-Columbus 43215

(440) 255-9100 .. **Freeman**, Amy M '97 %McNamara HC&L -8440 Station
-Mentor 44060

(216) 696-7600 .. **Freeman**, Barry Y '93 (Duvin C&H) -1301 E 9th -20th Fl Erievw
Twr -Cleveland 44114 **Fx:**696-2038

(216) 621-7743 .. **Freeman**, Bryan S '99 %Schiff & D,LLC -1370 Ontario
-Standard Bldg 6th Fl -Cleveland 44113

(614) 221-2848 .. **Freeman**, Chester T '57 (Freeman & P) -50 W Broad
-Columbus 43215

(330) 497-2886 .. **Freeman**, Christopher J '91 %Zollinger DGT & Co
-6370 Mt Plsnt NW -Bx2985 -Canton 44720

(803) 849-1900 .. **Freeman**, Fleet '67 (Freeman & F) -941 Houston Northcutt Blvd
-Ste 204 -Bx1123 -Mt Pleasant, SC 29465

(330) 666-3973 .. **Freeman**, Gregory J '01 -3959 W Bath Rd -Akron 44333

(419) 668-4484 .. **Freeman**, Harold J '73 (Freeman & F) -12 Whittlesey Av
-Norwalk 44857

(513) 977-8200 .. **Freeman**, Harold S '60 OfCnsl Dinsmore & S LLP -255 E 5th
-Ste 1900 -Cincinnati 45202 **Fx:**977-8141

(513) 381-8115 .. **Freeman**, Herbert E '73 -114 E 8th -Cincinnati 45202 **Fx:**381-8153

(513) 684-3211 .. **Freeman**, John A '74 IRS Dist Cnsl -312 Elm -Ste 2300
-Cincinnati 45202

(803) 777-7224 .. **Freeman**, John P '70 USC Law Schl -Main & Greene
-Columbia, SC 29208

(937) 223-1201 .. **Freeman**, Jonathan B '97 (Altick & C Co,LPA) -1 S Main
-1700 One Dayton Ctr -Dayton 45402 **Fx:**223-5100

(216) 771-9980 .. **Freeman**, Kenneth J '81 -526 Superior Av -Ste 515
-Cleveland 44114

(419) 668-4896 .. **Freeman Laycock & McDaniel** -54 E Main -Norwalk 44857
Fx:663-7835

(216) 689-3851 .. **Freeman**, Mark T '97 Cnsl KeyBank Natl Assn -127 Pub Sq
-Law Dept -Cleveland 44114

(216) 566-2410 .. **Freeman**, Michelle M '99 Sherwin-Williams Co
-101 Prospect Av NW -Cleveland 44115

(740) 852-8383 .. **Freeman**, Robin R '59 Wildman S LLC -26 E 4th -London 43140

(419) 668-4896 .. **Freeman**, Ronald H '66 (Freeman L&M) -54 E Main
-Norwalk 44857 **Fx:**663-7835

(330) 699-6703 .. **Freeman**, Sidney N '77 OfCnsl McNamara & F Co,LPA
-12370 Cleveland Av -Bx867 -Uniontown 44685 **Fx:**699-4803

(478) 971-2000 .. **Freeman**, Tamara S '96 Grange Ins -3700 Crestwood Pkwy
-Duluth, GA 30096

(419) 668-4484 .. **Freeman**, Thomas H '75 (Freeman & F) -12 Whittlesey Av
-Norwalk 44857

(216) 685-1107 .. **Freeman**, Thomas J '82 %Weltman W&R Co,LPA
-323 W Lakeside Av -Ste 200 -Cleveland 44113 **Fx:**363-4121

(937) 222-2424 .. **Freeze**, Stephen V '74 (Freund F&A) -1 S Main -Ste 1800
-Dayton 45402 **Fx:**222-5369

(413) 567-2461 .. **Fregeau**, Jason D '91 -47 Lincoln Rd -Longmeadow, MA 01106
Fx:567-2932

(740) 635-0162 .. **Fregiato**, Francis A '77 (Thomas FMH&D) -320 Howard
-Bridgeport 43912 **Fx:**635-1601

(513) 241-2324 .. **Frei**, Donald F '65 (Wood H&E LLP) -441 Vine -Ste 2700
-Cincinnati 45202 **Fx:**421-7269

(216) 222-2272 .. **Frei**, Susan E '89 Natl City Bank -1900 E 9th -Bx5756
-Cleveland 44101

(937) 454-1468 .. **Freiberger**, Mary M '95 %Stocklin & S Co LPA -7825 N Dixie Dr
-Ste A -Dayton 45414

(614) 469-3280 .. **Freiburger**, Charles F IV '70 (Thompson H LLP) -10 W Broad
-Ste 700 -Columbus 43215 **Fx:**469-3361

(859) 428-3268 .. **Freihofer**, Victor J '86 -625 Flat Crk Rd -Dry Ridge, KY 41035

(201) 802-7706 .. **Freilich**, David J '83 Volvo Fncl Srvc,LLC -One Paragon Dr
-Montvale, NJ 07645 **Fx:**802-7740

(216) 479-8500 .. **Freimuth**, Marc W '71 OfCnsl Squire S&D LLP -127 Pub Sq
-4900 Key Twr -Cleveland 44114 **Fx:**479-8780

(513) 863-6700 .. **Freisthler**, Marlaina S '04 %Millikin & F -6 S 2nd -6th Fl -Bx598
-Hamilton 45012 **Fx:**863-0031

(513) 721-1975 .. **Freking & Betz** -215 E 9th -5th Fl -Cincinnati 45202 **Fx:**651-2570

(513) 721-1975 .. **Freking**, Randolph H '82 (Freking & B) -215 E 9th -5th Fl
-Cincinnati 45202 **Fx:**651-2570

(937) 667-4481 .. **French**, Andrew T '98 %Dysinger S&D -249 S Garber Dr
-Tipp City 45371 **Fx:**667-5393

(419) 772-2216 .. **French**, Bruce C '85 ONU-Pettit Clg of Law -525 S Main
-Ada 45810

(216) 621-0200 .. **French**, Charles J III '78 (Baker & H LLP) -1900 E 9th -Ste 3200
-Cleveland 44114 **Fx:**696-0740

(770) 788-8118 .. **French**, Dahlia M '94 -Bx1268 -Oxford, GA 30054

(419) 222-6266 .. **French**, Diane W '88 D French,LPA -1142 W North -Lima 45805

(513) 287-2136 .. **French**, Eric S '99 Cnsl Cinergy Corp -139 E 4th -25 Atrium II
-Bx960 -Cincinnati 45201

(513) 641-4692 .. **French**, Gregory S '85 -1244 Paddock Hills Av -Cincinnati 45229
Fx:242-5542

(216) 621-4260 .. **French**, James H '74 -820 W Superior Av -Ste 510
-Cleveland 44113

(216) 621-5090 .. **French**, Jo A '88 -1370 Ontario -Ste 330 -Cleveland 44113

(619) 524-7049 .. **French**, Joan M '02 Dept of Navy -4301 Pacific Hwy
-spawarsyscom -San Diego, CA 92110

(614) 644-0876 .. **French**, Judith L '88 Cnsl Governors Ofc -77 S High -30th Fl
-Columbus 43215

(888) 206-0161 .. **French**, Laverne A '00 Legal Nurse Insight -2924 Red Lion Ln
-Silver Spring, MD 20906

(216) 696-4200 .. **French**, Michael K '01 %Schneider SR&L PLL -1111 Superior Av
-Ste 1000 -Cleveland 44114 **Fx:**696-7303

(513) 887-3474 .. **French**, Rebecca S '01 %Butler Cnty Pros -315 High -11th Fl
-Bx515 -Hamilton 45012

(440) 826-1616 .. **French**, Richard H Jr. '84 (The French Firm Co,LPA)
-101 Seminary -Berea 44017 **Fx:**826-1617

(216) 622-3687 .. **French**, Richard J '73 US Atty -801 W Superior -Ste 400
-Cleveland 44114 **Fx:**622-3370

(440) 717-9850 .. **French-Scaggs**, Susan K '96 -8180 Brecksvll Rd
-Brecksville 44141

(216) 781-0636 .. **Frenden**, John A '64 Whalen & F -526 Superior Av E
-555 Leader Bldg -Cleveland 44114 **Fx:**781-0638

(216) 781-0636 .. **Frenden**, John B '03 %Whalen & F -526 Superior Av E
-555 Leader Bldg -Cleveland 44114 **Fx:**781-0638

(914) 633-1925 .. **Frenkel**, Michael '65 (M Frenkel Assoc) -17 Brwstr Ter
-New Rochelle, NY 10804

(501) 682-1314 .. **Freno-Engman**, Lori L '90 Atty Gen -323 Center -200 Twr Bldg
-Little Rock, AR 72201

Frentz, John C '50 -2367 Chatham Rd -Akron 44313

(740) 387-7384 .. **Frericks & Howard,LPA** -152 E Center -Marion 43302 **Fx:**382-2167

(740) 387-7384 .. **Frericks**, Theodore P '45 Frericks & H,LPA -152 E Center -Marion 43302 **Fx:**382-2167

(740) 387-7384 .. **Frericks**, Theodore P IV '70 Frericks & H,LPA -152 E Center -Marion 43302 **Fx:**382-2167

(740) 387-7384 .. **Frericks**, Thomas A '71 Frericks & H,LPA -152 E Center -Marion 43302 **Fx:**382-2167

(740) 387-7384 .. **Frericks**, Timothy M '74 %Frericks & H,LPA -152 E Center -Marion 43302 **Fx:**382-2167

(614) 461-1311 .. **Fresco**, Ronald A '92 (Reminger & R) -65 E State -4th Fl Cptl Sq Ofc Bldg -Columbus 43215 **Fx:**232-2410

(937) 848-9042 .. **Freudenberger**, Richard A '86 -3520 Big Tree Rd -Bellbrook 45305

(937) 222-2424 .. **Freudiger**, Ramon C '91 (Freund F&A) -1 S Main -Ste 1800 -Dayton 45402 **Fx:**222-5369

(937) 222-2424 .. **Freund Freeze & Arnold** -1 S Main -Ste 1800 -Dayton 45402 **Fx:**222-5369

(614) 827-7300 .. **Freund Freeze & Arnold** -65 E State -Ste 800 -Columbus 43215 **Fx:**827-7303

(513) 665-3500 .. **Freund Freeze & Arnold** -105 E 4th -Ste 1400 -Cincinnati 45202 **Fx:**665-3503

(937) 222-2424 .. **Freund**, Neil F '70 (Freund F&A) -1 S Main -Ste 1800 -Dayton 45402 **Fx:**222-5369

Frey, C David '70 -Bx206 -Athens 45701

(513) 732-1420 .. **Frey**, David J '75 (Nichols S&N) -237 Main -Batavia 45103

(419) 242-1400 .. **Frey**, Francis C '75 -608 Mad Av -Ste 1400 -Toledo 43604

(517) 423-8688 .. **Frey**, Hugh E Jr. '77 Tecumseh Prdcts Co -100 E Patterson -Tecumseh, MI 49286

(859) 344-5580 .. **Frey**, Lisa A '99 St Elizabeth Medical Ctr -One Med Vllg Dr -Edgewood, KY 41017

(419) 327-3324 .. **Frey**, Lou Ann '84 Lucas Cnty Chldrn Srvcs Brd -705 Adams -Toledo 43624

(216) 289-2746 .. **Frey**, Louis Christopher '87 Euclid Law Dept -585 E 222nd -Euclid 44123 **Fx:**289-2766

(937) 449-6400 .. **Frey**, Michael G '98 %Dinsmore & S LLP -1 S Main -Ste 1300 One Dayton Centre -Dayton 45402 **Fx:**449-6405

(859) 655-4200 .. **Frey**, Rhonda S '96 Greenebaum D&M PLLC -50 E RiverCenter Blvd -Ste 1800 -Covington, KY 41011 **Fx:**655-4239

(216) 928-7700 .. **Frey**, Ronald L II '04 I Friedman & Assoc -700 W St Clair Av -Ste 110 -Cleveland 44113 **Fx:**556-9779

(614) 480-5181 .. **Freye**, Deborah L '00 Huntington National Bank -41 S High -Columbus 43215 **Fx:**480-5404

(614) 365-9900 .. **Freytag**, Daniel R '75 OfCnsl Zeiger TL&L,LLP -41 S High -Ste 3500 Huntngtn Ctr -Columbus 43215 **Fx:**365-7900

(513) 765-6000 .. **Freytag**, David M '89 LensCrafters -4000 Luxottica Pl -Mason 45040

(614) 297-1000 .. **Frick**, Bradley N '78 (B Frick & Assoc) -1265 Neil Av -Columbus 43201 **Fx:**297-6666

(937) 223-8177 .. **Frick**, Dawn M '98 %Coolidge WW&L -33 W 1st -Ste 600 -Dayton 45402 **Fx:**223-6705

(614) 228-2678 .. **Frick**, James B '53 -261 S Front -Columbus 43215

(330) 670-7300 .. **Fricke**, Lori A '92 %Hanna C&P,LLP -3737 Embssy Pkwy -Bx5521 -Akron 44334 **Fx:**670-0977

(216) 696-4700 .. **Fricke**, Wade M '89 (Spieth BM&N Co,LPA) -925 Euclid Av -2000 Huntngtn Bldg -Cleveland 44115 **Fx:**696-2706

(937) 236-6444 .. **Fricker**, Keith A '86 -7460 Brandt Pike -Dayton 45424

(216) 687-1311 .. **Fried**, Adam M '95 (Reminger & R) -101 Prospect Av W -1400 Mdlnd Bldg -Cleveland 44115 **Fx:**687-1841

(440) 247-4765 .. **Fried**, Lorna J '92 %SG Thomas,LPA -35 River -Level B -Chagrin Falls 44022

Fried, Michele B '96 -(Address Unavailable)

(614) 415-7199 .. **Fried**, Samuel '92 The Limited,Inc -3 Limited Pkwy -Bx16000 -Columbus 43216

(312) 569-1000 .. **Fried**, Saundra N '94 %Gardner C&D LLC -191 N Wacker Dr -Ste 3700 -Chicago, IL 60606 **Fx:**569-3274

(216) 831-0042 .. **Friedberg**, Ronald P '91 Meyers RF&L LPA -28601 Chagrin Blvd -Ste 500 -Cleveland 44122 **Fx:**831-0542

(212) 935-3000 .. **Friedberg**, Stephen E '76 (Mintz LCFG&P,PC) -666 3rd Av -New York, NY 10017 **Fx:**983-3115

(216) 781-1212 .. **Friedell**, Katherine A '92 %Walter & H LLP -1301 E 9th -Ste 3500 -Cleveland 44114 **Fx:**575-0911

(812) 491-4000 .. **Friedeman**, Lawrence K '84 Vectren Retail LLC -20 NW 4th -Evansville, IN 47708

(419) 842-9902 .. **Friedes**, David E '84 (D Friedes & Assoc) -6545 W Central Av -Ste 209 -Toledo 43617

(513) 385-1505 .. **Friedhoff**, Gary E '86 -5752 Cheviot Rd -Cincinnati 45247

(216) 696-0600 .. **Friedland**, Dale R '76 (Rapoport SF&C) -55 Pub Sq -Ste 1750 -Cleveland 44113 **Fx:**696-2929

Friedlander, Betsy A '02 -7067 Society Ct -Dayton 45414

(216) 222-9473 .. **Friedlander**, Daniel A '83 Natl City Bank -1900 E 9th -17th Fl Loc 01-2174 -Cleveland 44114

(216) 631-0280 .. **Friedlander**, Jody E '01 Enterprise Social Invstmnt -3500 Lorain Av -#300 -Cleveland 44113 **Fx:**631-0450

(216) 615-7358 .. **Friedlander**, Lawrence H '65 OfCnsl Buckingham D&B,LLP -1375 E 9th -Ste 1700 -Cleveland 44114 **Fx:**621-5440

(614) 864-8210 .. **Friedman**, Alan P '76 -7110 E Lvngstn Av -Reynoldsburg 43068

(216) 621-9282 .. **Friedman**, Avery S '73 -850 Euclid Av -Ste 701 -Cleveland 44114

(513) 772-0740 .. **Friedman**, Benjamin S '01 -270 Northland Blvd -Ste 218 -Cincinnati 45246 **Fx:**(330) 772-1593

(216) 787-3030 .. **Friedman**, Betsey N '82 Atty Gen -615 W Superior Av -11th Fl -Cleveland 44113 **Fx:**787-3480

(313) 230-7777 .. **Friedman**, Bruce S '83 EDS -500 Renaissance Ctr -MS 20A -Detroit, MI 48243

(330) 762-7477 .. **Friedman**, David '58 (Hardesty K&Z) -520 S Main -Ste 500 -Akron 44311 **Fx:**762-8059

(216) 621-0070 .. **Friedman Domiano & Smith Co,LPA** -1370 Ontario -Ste 600 -Cleveland 44113 **Fx:**621-4008

(216) 241-1430 .. **Friedman & Gilbert** -1370 Ontario -1700 Standard Bldg -Cleveland 44113

(216) 241-1430 .. **Friedman**, Gordon S '68 (Friedman & G) -1370 Ontario -1700 Standard Bldg -Cleveland 44113

(216) 931-6000 .. **Friedman**, Harold E '59 (Ulmer & B LLP) -1300 E 9th -Ste 900 Penton Media Bldg -Cleveland 44114 **Fx:**931-6001

(419) 530-4131 .. **Friedman**, Howard M '65 Univ of Toledo Law Schl -2801 W Bancroft -Toledo 43606

(216) 928-7700 .. **Friedman**, Ian N '97 (I Friedman & Assoc) -700 W St Clair Av -Ste 110 -Cleveland 44113 **Fx:**556-9779

(216) 363-4500 .. **Friedman**, James M '66 (Benesch FC&A LLP) -200 Pub Sq -Ste 2300 -Cleveland 44114 **Fx:**363-4588

(216) 621-0070 .. **Friedman**, Jeffrey H '73 (Friedman D&S Co,LPA) -1370 Ontario -Ste 600 -Cleveland 44113 **Fx:**621-4008

(614) 292-3856 .. **Friedman**, Jerome E '77 OSU Medical Ctr -370 W 9th Av -Ste 200G -Columbus 43210 **Fx:**688-8644

Friedman, Kimberly J '89 -558 Haversham Dr -Gahanna 43230

(216) 781-5232 .. **Friedman**, Laurence A '93 OfCnsl M Levin Co,LPA -55 Pub Sq -Ste 940 -Cleveland 44113 **Fx:**696-8133

(419) 241-3101 .. **Friedman**, Lawrence M '84 Toledo Bldg Srvcs Co -Bx2223 -Toledo 43603

(216) 621-0580 .. **Friedman**, Lisa S '94 Schulman S&M,LPA -1370 Ontario -1700 Standard Bldg -Cleveland 44113 **Fx:**621-5428

(800) 977-7711 .. **Friedman**, Marc R '74 OH Dept of Taxation -800 Fwy Dr N -Estate Tax Div -Columbus 43229 **Fx:**(614) 387-1984

(937) 438-2828 .. **Friedman**, Mark J '79 -1163 Lyons Rd -Centerville 45459

(216) 883-8888 .. **Friedman**, Matthew S '93 Nrthrn Stamping,Inc -6600 Chapek Pkwy -Cuyahoga Heights 44125

(614) 221-0090 .. **Friedman & Mirman Co,LPA** -503 S Front -Ste 250 -Columbus 43215

(216) 651-6800 .. **Friedman**, Mitchell J '01 CVS -10022 Madison -Cleveland 44102

(202) 261-3300 .. **Friedman**, Paul H '78 (Dechert) -1775 I NW -Washington, DC 20006

(216) 241-1007 .. **Friedman**, Paul M '77 -1148 Euclid Av -Ste 300 -Cleveland 44115

(513) 421-9090 .. **Friedman**, Penny '77 BeneFactors,LLC -312 Walnut -Ste 3560 -Cincinnati 45202

(216) 781-8823 .. **Friedman**, Richard L '82 -614 W Superior Av -808 Rckfllr Bldg -Cleveland 44113

(216) 227-3340 .. **Friedman**, Robert E '80 Ganley Mgmt -13215 Detroit Av -Lakewood 44107

(216) 514-1180 .. **Friedman**, Robert G '94 (Krantz P&F,PLL) -23200 Chagrin Blvd -Ste 180 -Cleveland 44122 **Fx:**514-1185

(330) 456-8341 .. **Friedman**, Robert I '64 (Black MS&A,LPA) -220 Market Av S -Ste 1000 -Canton 44702 **Fx:**456-5756

(330) 744-4137 .. **Friedman & Rummell Co, LPA** -100 Fed Plz E -Ste 300 City Centre One -Youngstown 44503 **Fx:**744-9962

(614) 221-0090 .. **Friedman**, Scott N '98 (Friedman & M Co,LPA) -503 S Front -Ste 250 -Columbus 43215

(216) 479-8500 .. **Friedman**, Steven A '92 (Squire S&D LLP) -127 Pub Sq -4900 Key Twr -Cleveland 44114 **Fx:**479-8780

(440) 914-0287 .. **Friedman**, Susan L '96 Lexis Nexis -35695 Solon Rd -Solon 44139

(216) 295-2428 .. **Friedman**, Sydney S '50 -15520 Aldersyde Dr -Shaker Heights 44120 **Fx:**561-8199

(440) 349-3300 .. **Friedman**, Ted S '82 -32901 Station -Ste 105 -Solon 44139

(513) 721-4532 .. **Friedman**, Tedd M '92 (Katz TB&H) -255 E 5th -Ste 2400 -Cincinnati 45202

(614) 224-3814 .. **Friedman**, Thomas E '74 -502 S 3rd -Columbus 43215

(614) 221-9200 .. **Friedman**, Tod H '89 %Schottenstein Stores -1800 Moler Rd -Columbus 43207

(614) 221-0090 .. **Friedman**, William S '66 Friedman & M Co,LPA -503 S Front -Ste 250 -Columbus 43215

(216) 292-1148 .. **Friedman**, Zeev '78 Friedman Law Firm -23230 Chagrin Blvd -Ste 720 -Cleveland 44122

(216) 520-5516 .. **Friedmann**, Richard V '98 West Grp -6111 Oak Tree Blvd -Bx318063 -Cleveland 44131

(513) 579-1707 .. **Friedmann**, Roger E '76 (Loeb V&F) -1014 Vine -2150 Kroger Bldg -Cincinnati 45202

(419) 865-1251 .. **Friedmar**, Richard S '76 Wagoner & S,Ltd -7445 Airport Hwy -Holland 43528 **Fx:**866-8798

(440) 779-1400 .. **Friedrich**, Gordon R '73 Resenves Network -22021 Brookpark Rd -Fairview Park 44126

(330) 833-1734 .. **Frieg**, John H '82 -108 3rd NE -Massillon 44646 **Fx:**833-2547

(513) 626-2721 .. **Frieko**, Laura L '04 Procter & Gamble -11511 Reed Hartman Hwy -Cincinnati 45241

(513) 983-4187 .. **Friel**, Carol S '80 Procter & Gamble Co-Legal -1 Procter & Gamble Plz -Cincinnati 45202

(216) 781-1452 .. **Friel**, Thomas J '49 Friel & S -526 Superior Av E -448 Leader Bldg -Cleveland 44114

(614) 221-3355 .. **Friend**, Daniel K '73 OfCnsl Friend & H Co,LPA -118 E Main -Columbus 43215 **Fx:**221-3391

(216) 621-0200 .. **Frient**, Megan P '98 %Baker & H LLP -1900 E 9th -Ste 3200 -Cleveland 44114 **Fx:**696-0740

(513) 763-4315 .. **Fries**, Joseph C '91 Student Loan Funding Resrcs Inc -1 W 4th -Ste 300 -Cincinnati 45202

(740) 452-7555 .. **Fries**, Miles D '78 (Gottlieb JB&D,PLL) -320 Main -Bx190 -Zanesville 43702 **Fx:**452-2257

(513) 860-2560 .. **Fries**, Winifred G '91 LandAmerica -8892 Beckett Rd -West Chester 45069

(513) 523-1500 .. **Friesen**, Brendon P '03 %Mansour GG&M Co,LPA -55 Pub Sq -Ste 2150 -Cleveland 44113 **Fx:**523-1705

(937) 224-4128 .. **Friesinger**, Patricia J '00 %Rieser & Assoc LLC -130 W 2nd -Ste 1520 -Dayton 45402 **Fx:**224-3090

(813) 254-5100 .. **Frijouf**, Robert F '73 (Frijouf R&P) -201 E Davis Blvd -Tampa, FL 33606 **Fx:**254-5400

(440) 564-9350 .. **Frimel**, Michael P '96 -14392 Ravenna Rd -Newbury 44065

(248) 432-8000 .. **Frink**, Bryan M '01 Mazur & K -30665 Nrthwstrn Hwy -#175 -Farmington, MI 48334

(513) 977-8200 .. **Frink**, Neal A '99 %Dinsmore & S LLP -255 E 5th -Ste 1900 -Cincinnati 45202 **Fx:**977-8141

(330) 929-1195 .. **Frisby**, John D Jr. '80 J Frisby -135 Portage Trl -Bx374 -Cuyahoga Falls 44222

(614) 228-8111 .. **Friscoe**, Louis A '72 -520 N Park -Columbus 43215

(330) 376-2700 .. **Frisina**, Dominic A '04 %Roetzel & A,LPA -222 S Main -Akron 44308 **Fx:**376-4577

(513) 487-5979 .. **Friskney**, Stephen H '80 Milacron Inc -2090 Florence Av
-Cincinnati 45206

(330) 399-8500 .. **Fritz**, Andrew J '91 -135 Pine Av -Ste 212 -Warren 44481

(216) 664-4822 .. **Fritz**, Bryan J '78 Prosecutor -1200 Ontario Av -8th Fl Justice Ctr
-Cleveland 44113 Fx:664-4399

(440) 323-1203 .. **Fritz**, Joel D '91 Rothgery & Assoc -230 3rd -Ste 100 -Elyria 44035

(216) 328-1677 .. **Fritz**, Raymond N '78 -6678 Beechwd Dr -Independence 44131

(419) 624-8133 .. **Fritz-Gasteier**, Linda M '93 -1604 E Perkins Av -Ste 103
-Sandusky 44870

       Fritzsch, Sandra D '94 -995 Nob Hill Dr -Evergreen, CO 80439

(740) 676-2743 .. **Frizzi**, Daniel L Jr. '77 -224 32nd -Bx129 -Bellaire 43906

(216) 771-1525 .. **Froberg**, Steven C '75 -425 W Lakeside Av -1st Fl
-Cleveland 44113

(216) 586-3939 .. **Frodyma**, Scott F '98 %Jones D -901 Lakeside Av
-Cleveland 44114 Fx:579-0212

(614) 719-2850 .. **Froehle**, Thomas L '93 McNees W&N,LLC -21 E State -17th Fl
-Columbus 43215 Fx:469-4653

(614) 645-8849 .. **Froehlich**, Mark S '80 Cnty Mun Ct Judge -375 S High
-Columbus 43215

(937) 226-1776 .. **Froelich**, Gary L '68 (Froelich & W) -1812 Kettering Twr
-Dayton 45423 Fx:226-1945

(216) 464-6901 .. **Froelich**, Georgia A '84 Sterling Trust NCB -3550 Lander Rd -One
Cascade Plz -Pepper Pike 44124

(440) 835-5497 .. **Froelich**, Raymond R Jr. '73 -2100 Salem Pkwy -Westlake 44145

(937) 226-1776 .. **Froelich & Weprin** -1812 Kettering Twr -Dayton 45423
Fx:226-1945

(202) 962-2119 .. **Froelke**, Donald R Jr. '70 Washington Metro Area Transit
-600 5th NW -Washington, DC 20001

(513) 863-7600 .. **Froelke**, Frank J '66 -300 High -Ste 404 -Hamilton 45011

(513) 863-0083 .. **Froelke**, Gerald G '63 Wessel & F -6 S 2nd -315 Key Bldg
-Hamilton 45011

(614) 464-6400 .. **Froling**, David A '95 %Vorys SS&P LLP -52 E Gay -Bx1008
-Columbus 43216 Fx:464-6350

(614) 464-6400 .. **Froling**, Lynne M '03 %Vorys SS&P LLP -52 E Gay -Bx1008
-Columbus 43216 Fx:464-6350

(614) 466-0570 .. **Froment**, Jillian E '99 Ofc of Collective Bargaining -100 E Broad
-18th Fl -Columbus 43215

(216) 595-8222 .. **Fromet**, Avery H '72 -25550 Chagrin Blvd -Ste 403
-Cleveland 44122

(330) 562-2424 .. **Fromhercz**, Stephen P '82 -715 E Mennonite Rd -Aurora 44202

(614) 324-5955 .. **Fromm**, Barry H '80 Valve Recovery Grp Inc -919 Old
Henderson Rd -Columbus 43220

(850) 283-4681 .. **Frommeyer**, Todd A '97 USAF -445 Suwannee Rd -Ste 110
-Tyndall AFB, FL 32403

(216) 595-1300 .. **Fromson**, A Scott '87 (A Fromson & Assoc) -23240 Chagrin Blvd
-Ste 180 -Cleveland 44122

(614) 463-9770 .. **Fromson**, Jeffrey E '69 (Roetzel & A,LPA) -155 E Broad
-Natl City Ctr 12th Fl -Columbus 43215 Fx:463-9792

(216) 861-6833 .. **Fromson**, Richard A '55 Sonkin & K Co,LPA -55 Pub Sq -Ste 1660
-Cleveland 44113

(513) 241-5670 .. **Froncek**, Theodore J Jr. '80 Croswell & A Co,LPA
-1208 Sycamore -Cincinnati 45210

(513) 579-6400 .. **Fronduti**, John S '03 (Keating M&K PLL) -1 E 4th
-1400 Provident Twr -Cincinnati 45202 Fx:579-6457

(513) 421-6630 .. **Frooman**, James C '90 Lindhorst & D Co,LPA -312 Walnut
-Ste 2300 -Cincinnati 45202

(513) 754-3584 .. **Frooman**, Thomas E '94 Cintas Corp -6800 Cintas Blvd
-Bx625737 -Cincinnati 45262 Fx:754-3642

(513) 651-6800 .. **Frost Brown Todd LLC** -201 E 5th -2200 PNC Ctr
-Cincinnati 45202 Fx:651-6981

(513) 422-2001 .. **Frost Brown Todd LLC** -300 N Main -Ste 200 -Middletown 45042
Fx:422-3010

(614) 464-1211 .. **Frost Brown Todd LLC** -10 W Broad -Ste 1000 -Columbus 43215
Fx:464-1737

(216) 575-0777 .. **Frost**, Corey W '87 (Kelley & F,LLP) -1300 E 9th -Ste 1901
-Cleveland 44114 Fx:575-0799

(740) 354-3643 .. **Frost**, Daphne J '04 M Mearan,LLC -812 6th -Portsmouth 45662
Fx:354-5293

       Frost, Earl L '98 -500 W Wilson Bridge Rd -Ste 110
-Columbus 43085

(614) 221-6424 .. **Frost**, Earle R Jr. '69 (Frost & D LLP) -50 W Broad -Ste 1602
-Columbus 43215 Fx:221-7122

(513) 347-0861 .. **Frost**, Hugh O II '68 -140 Riverama Dr -Cincinnati 45238

(614) 228-1541 .. **Frost**, John J '03 %Baker & H LLP -65 E State -Ste 2100
-Columbus 43215 Fx:462-2616

(216) 622-8895 .. **Frost**, Kristin J '01 %Calfee H&G LLP -800 Superior Av -Ste 1400
-Cleveland 44114 Fx:241-0816

(614) 752-9496 .. **Frost**, Kristina D '84 OH Bd of Regents -30 E Broad -36th Fl
-Columbus 43215

(614) 224-0933 .. **Frost & Maddox Co,LPA** -400 S 5th -Ste 301 -Columbus 43215

(330) 426-3774 .. **Frost**, Mark A '74 Columbiana Cnty Municipal Ct -31 N Market
-East Palestine 44413

(440) 943-4700 .. **Frost**, Merrie M '92 -33579 Euclid Av -Willoughby 44094

(614) 224-0933 .. **Frost**, Robert E '64 (Frost & M Co,LPA) -400 S 5th -Ste 301
-Columbus 43215

(440) 239-3127 .. **Frost**, Robert R '70 (Frost & F) -140 Sheldon Rd -Berea 44017

(440) 871-8111 .. **Frost**, Robert S '94 (Huffman I&F LLC) -24441 Detroit Rd -Ste 200
-Westlake 44145

(703) 526-5155 .. **Frost**, Thomas E '79 The Mills Corp -1300 Wilson Blvd -Ste 400
-Arlington, VA 22209

       Froude, Jeffrey R '02 -12558 Clifton Blvd -Lakewood 44107

(513) 785-5880 .. **Froug**, Randi E '00 Butler Cnty Pros -315 High -11th Fl -Bx515
-Hamilton 45012

(513) 977-8200 .. **Fruechtemeyer**, A Scott '95 (Dinsmore & S LLP) -255 E 5th
-Ste 1900 -Cincinnati 45202 Fx:977-8141

(740) 654-4141 .. **Fruth**, Daniel J '02 %Stebelton A&S,LPA -109 N Broad -Bx130
-Lancaster 43130 Fx:654-2521

(419) 447-6181 .. **Fruth**, James W '95 %Dell B&A,LLP -60 Sycamore -Tiffin 44883
Fx:477-6332

(419) 531-4431 .. **Fruth**, Lynn L '76 -2655 Talmadge Rd -Toledo 43606

(216) 566-8200 .. **Frutig**, Patricia R '84 %Seeley S&E Co LPA -600 Superior Av E
-800 Bank One Ctr -Cleveland 44114 Fx:566-0213

       Frutig, Thomas R '69 -Bx173 -Gates Mills 44040

(216) 621-7860 .. **Frutkin**, Harvey L '72 (Cavitch FD&F) -1717 E 9th -14th Fl
-Cleveland 44114 Fx:621-3415

(202) 785-8100 .. **Frutkin**, Jonathan B '98 Doceus Inc -1016 16th NW -6th Fl
-Washington, DC 20036

(614) 228-2300 .. **Fry**, Carl B '74 (Fry W&M Co,LPA) -35 E Lvngstn Av
-Columbus 43215 Fx:228-6680

(740) 695-4412 .. **Fry**, Daniel P '79 Belmont Cnty Pros -147-A W Main
-Saint Clairsville 43950

(303) 623-9000 .. **Fry**, Joel C '97 %Rothgerber J&L LLP -1200 17th -Ste 3000
-Denver, CO 80202

(440) 473-3000 .. **Fry**, John J '91 Marconi Med Syst,Inc -595 Miner Rd
-Highland Heights 44143

(216) 861-5582 .. **Fry**, Jude A '91 (Fay SFM&M LLP) -1100 Superior Av -7th Fl
-Cleveland 44114 Fx:241-1666

(513) 684-3769 .. **Fry**, Patricia R '80 NLRB -550 Main -Rm 3003 -Cincinnati 45202

(419) 526-1131 .. **Fry**, Randall E '78 R Fry Co, LPA -10 W Newlon Pl
-Mansfield 44902 Fx:522-0416

(419) 424-7403 .. **Fry**, Robert A '78 (Hancock Cnty Pros) -222 Bway -#104
-Findlay 45840 Fx:424-7889

(513) 421-6000 .. **Fry**, Sallee M '89 -2345 Ashland Av -Cincinnati 45206

(216) 689-4663 .. **Fry**, Sherry L '97 KeyBank NA -127 Pub Sq -OH 01-27-1607
-Cleveland 44114

(614) 228-2300 .. **Fry Waller & McCann Co,LPA** -35 E Lvngstn Av
-Columbus 43215 Fx:228-6680

(513) 381-9200 .. **Fry**, William R '66 (Rendigs FK&D,LLP) -One W 4th -Ste 900
-Cincinnati 45202 Fx:381-9206

(937) 222-5992 .. **Frydman**, Joel M '79 Mdwst Iron & Metal Co -Bx546
-Dayton 45401

(740) 373-5455 .. **Frye**, Gary F '68 (Theisen B,LPA) -424 2nd -Bx739
-Marietta 45750 Fx:373-4409

(415) 492-4577 .. **Frye**, Hope L '78 -4040 Civic Ctr Dr -Ste 200
-San Rafael, CA 94903

(330) 379-5511 .. **Frye**, Michael T '02 Spherion -10 N Main -Bx3620 -Akron 44309

(202) 342-8878 .. **Frye**, Russell S '78 (Collier SS,PLLC) -3050 K NW -Ste 400
-Washington, DC 20007 Fx:342-8451

(216) 732-9250 .. **Frye**, Thomas E '72 -22034 Lk Shr Blvd -Euclid 44123

(513) 863-8270 .. **Fryman**, Robert E '53 (Parrish F&M Co,LPA) -300 High -Ste 704
-Bx747 -Hamilton 45012 Fx:863-9999

(513) 352-6741 .. **Fuchs**, Jack F '82 (Thompson H LLP) -312 Walnut -14th Fl
-Cincinnati 45202 Fx:241-4771

(513) 723-7043 .. **Fuchs**, Jill N '83 Cnsl Convergys Corp -201 E 4th
-Cincinnati 45202

       Fuchs, Lorrie E '86 -Bx35787 -Canton 44735

(330) 376-2700 .. **Fuchs**, Michael J '03 %Roetzel & A,LPA -222 S Main
-Akron 44308 Fx:376-4577

(216) 357-7270 .. **Fuchs**, Siegmund F '04 USFG -801 W Superior Av -Cleveland
44113

(937) 226-1996 .. **Fuchsman**, David H '83 -120 W 2nd -2000 Lbrty Twr
-Dayton 45402

(740) 775-2066 .. **Fuchsman**, Rita S '77 -26 W 4th -Bx6161 -Chillicothe 45601

(440) 951-5400 .. **Fudale**, William F '67 -38052 Euclid Av -Ste 105
-Willoughby 44094

(216) 522-1200 .. **Fuente**, Alan D '93 IMG -1360 E 9th -Ste 100 -Cleveland 44114

(216) 443-7950 .. **Fuerst**, Gerald E '59 Cuyahoga Cnty -1200 Ontario -Justice Ctr
-Cleveland 44113

(216) 766-5722 .. **Fuerst**, Harrison M '50 -3401 Enterprise Pkwy -Ste 340
-Beachwood 44122

(216) 696-3311 .. **Fuerst**, Robert A '79 (Kahn K) -1301 E 9th -2600 Erievw Twr
-Cleveland 44114 Fx:623-4912

(419) 242-7985 .. **Fugee**, Patricia Brown '99 (Roetzel & A,LPA) -One SeaGate
-9th Fl -Toledo 43604 Fx:242-0316

(216) 566-2961 .. **Fuhrer**, Eryn Ace '00 Sherwin-Williams Co -101 Prospect Av NW
-Cleveland 44115

(614) 462-5474 .. **Fuhrer**, Loriann E '97 %Kegler BH&R -65 E State -Ste 1800
-Columbus 43215 Fx:464-2634

(440) 834-4492 .. **Fuhry**, David L '77 -14537 Main -Bx345 -Burton 44021
Fx:834-0722

(330) 576-1234 .. **Fuhry**, Gigi H '99 ValMark Securities -130 Sprngside Dr -Ste 300
-Akron 44333

(440) 834-4492 .. **Fuhry**, Kenneth A '78 -14537 Main -Bx345 -Burton 44021
Fx:834-0722

(614) 752-2646 .. **Fulcher**, Laura P '91 OCRC -1111 E Broad -3rd Fl
-Columbus 43205 Fx:466-6250

(937) 298-7677 .. **Fulero**, Solomon M '80 -2705 Far Hills Av -Ste 4 -Dayton 45419

(937) 335-8324 .. **Fulker**, John E '53 (Faust HFM&S) -12 S Cherry -Troy 45373
Fx:339-7155

(937) 335-8324 .. **Fulker**, William J '82 (Faust HFM&S) -12 S Cherry -Troy 45373
Fx:339-7155

(614) 728-7055 .. **Fulkerson**, Jonathan R '97 Atty Gen -30 E Broad
-Columbus 43215 Fx:728-8600

(614) 414-0052 .. **Fulkerson**, Kimberly Loughry '01 -938 Barleycorn Pl
-Gahanna 43230

(614) 469-3939 .. **Fulkert**, Marc A '03 %Jones D -325 John H McConnell Blvd
-Ste 600 -Bx165017 -Columbus 43216 Fx:461-4198

(614) 224-6485 .. **Fullem**, Brett E '00 -360 S Grant Av -Columbus 43215

       Fullen, Craig M '92 -795 Jaeger -Columbus 43206

(513) 946-3000 .. **Fullen**, Kirstin T '02 %Hamilton Cnty Pros -230 E 9th
-Cincinnati 45202 Fx:946-3017

(937) 228-5151 .. **Fullenkamp**, James J '84 -131 N Ludlow -Ste 217 -Dayton 45402

(216) 566-5665 .. **Fuller**, Adam D '03 %Thompson H LLP -127 Pub Sq
-3900 Key Ctr -Cleveland 44114 Fx:566-5800

(740) 773-1875 .. **Fuller**, Don E '55 -19 W 2nd -Chillicothe 45601

(419) 247-2500 .. **Fuller & Henry,Ltd** -One SeaGate -Ste 1700 -Bx2088 -Toledo
43603 Fx:247-2665

(614) 228-6611 .. **Fuller & Henry,Ltd** -35 N 4th -Ste 310 -Columbus 43215
Fx:228-6623

(419) 422-7700 .. **Fuller & Henry,Ltd** -1995 Tiffin Av -Ste 312 -Findlay 45840
Fx:425-0042

(513) 422-2001 .. **Fuller**, Jennifer R '04 %Frost BT LLC -300 N Main -Ste 200
-Middletown 45042 Fx:422-3010

(305) 891-5199 .. **Fuller**, Lawrence A '03 (Fuller F & Assoc,PA)
-12000 Biscayne Blvd -#609 -North Miami Beach, FL 33181
Fx:893-9505

(740) 363-2600 ..**Fuller**, Randall D '95 (Burkam F&H) -43 E Central Av
-Delaware 43015

(614) 799-0898 ..**Fullerton**, Jacqueline D '93 Health Mgt Solutions
-2545 Farmers Dr -Ste 400 -Columbus 43235

(614) 221-6755 ..**Fullerton**, William D '86 Fullerton,PLL -975 S High
-Columbus 43206 **Fx:**445-6494

(614) 466-0457 ..**Fullin**, Daniel E '82 PUCO -180 E Broad -Columbus 43266

(614) 923-5800 ..**Fullin**, Francis X '85 Pure Title Agency -2545 Farmers Dr -Ste 270
-Columbus 43235

(216) 621-1111 ..**Fullmer**, Jerry A '69 -1831 W 30th -Cleveland 44113

(216) 348-5400 ..**Fullmer**, William A '84 (McDonald H Co,LPA) -600 Superior Av E
-Ste 2100 -Cleveland 44114 **Fx:**348-5474

(740) 363-7182 ..**Fulmer**, Amy M '97 (Thomas & F Co,LPA) -163 N Sandusky
-Ste 103 -Delaware 43015

(330) 854-4619 ..**Fulmer**, Claudia F '82 -8082 Bricker Rd NW -Massillon 44646

(419) 893-2195 ..**Fulop**, Louis J '61 -508 Dussel Dr -Maumee 43537

(419) 241-9000 ..**Fulop**, Sharon M '97 (Shumaker L&K,LLP) -1000 Jackson
-Toledo 43624 **Fx:**241-6894

(216) 931-6000 ..**Fulton**, Arlishea L '99 %Ulmer & B LLP -1300 E 9th
-Ste 900 Penton Media Bldg -Cleveland 44114 **Fx:**931-6001

(216) 241-5310 ..**Fulton**, Burt J '52 OfCnsl Gallagher SF&N -1501 Euclid Av -6th Fl
-Cleveland 44115 **Fx:**241-1608

(216) 221-5627 ..**Fulton**, Christopher L '74 Risk Sharing Auth -37 W Broad -Ste 650
-Columbus 43215

(360) 257-2011 ..**Fulton**, Marcus N '97 US Navy -3530 N Langley Blvd
-Oak Harbor, WA 98278

(513) 863-6700 ..**Fulton**, Michael A '70 (Millikin & F) -6 S 2nd -6th Fl -Bx598
-Hamilton 45012 **Fx:**863-0031

(614) 224-3838 ..**Fulton**, Philip J '80 (P Fulton & Assoc) -89 E Nationwide Blvd
-Ste 300 -Columbus 43215 **Fx:**224-3933

(330) 747-4404 ..**Fulton**, Robert S '72 Newman O&K,LPA -11 Fed Plz Central
-Ste 1200 -Youngstown 44503 **Fx:**747-6056

(216) 241-0707 ..**Fulton**, William H '73 -140 Pub Sq -Ste 512 -Cleveland 44114

(740) 992-7101 ..**Fultz**, Bernard V '56 -Bx723 -Pomeroy 45769

(419) 774-5727 ..**Fultz**, Lisa R '92 Richland Cnty CSEA -161 Park Av E
-Mansfield 44902

Fultz, Michael K '03 -(Address Unavailable)

(216) 566-8200 ..**Fumich**, William M Jr. '76 Seeley S&E Co LPA -600 Superior Av E
-800 Bank One Ctr -Cleveland 44114 **Fx:**566-0213

(847) 734-8811 ..**Funai**, Bryan Y '98 Masuda FE&M,Ltd -1475 E Woodfld Rd
-Ste 800 -Schaumburg, IL 60173 **Fx:**734-1089

(216) 689-1290 ..**Fung**, Mia M '96 Key Corp -2025 Ontario -7th Fl -Cleveland 44115

(614) 228-9550 ..**Funk**, Audra T '01 %Javitch B&R -33 N 3rd -Ste 300
-Columbus 43215 **Fx:**228-2818

(330) 499-6000 ..**Funk**, Daniel J '94 (Baker DBW&M) -400 S Main -Canton 44720
Fx:449-6423

(614) 228-1541 ..**Funk**, David R '98 Baker & H LLP -65 E State -Ste 2100
-Columbus 43215 **Fx:**462-2616

(419) 294-3533 ..**Funk**, James C '83 -18407 Twp Hwy 103 -Upper Sandusky 43351

(740) 373-6688 ..**Funk**, Rustin J '77 (Addison & F) -202 WesBanco Bldg
-Marietta 45750

(330) 376-2700 ..**Funk**, Stephen W '92 (Roetzel & A,LPA) -222 S Main
-Akron 44308 **Fx:**376-4577

(913) 315-9274 ..**Funk**, Steven J '84 Sprint Corp -6450 Sprint Pkwy -3A371
-Overland Park, KS 66251

(330) 722-9099 ..**Funk**, Susan L '88 (Jones D&F Co,LPA) -3995 Medina Rd
-Ste 200 -Bx447 -Medina 44258

(614) 443-5404 ..**Funkhouser**, Douglas A '95 -729 S 3rd -Columbus 43206

(614) 645-7385 ..**Furbee**, Jeffrey S '94 City Atty -90 W Broad -Columbus 43215

(330) 468-4984 ..**Furber**, Philip C '75 -839 Wdbrdg Trl -Sagamore Hills 44067
Fx:(443) 347-2292

(419) 473-1346 ..**Furey**, Thomas R '75 (Kroncke DS&F) -2255 W Laskey Rd
-Toledo 43613 **Fx:**473-0218

(330) 836-9302 ..**Furey-Ligan**, Amy J '04 -506 Letchworth Dr -Akron 44303

Furio, Catherine A '91 -1771 Century Oaks Dr -Westlake 44145

(513) 579-7762 ..**Furlong**, Kathleen A '80 Federated Dept Stores,Inc -7 W 7th
-Cincinnati 45202

(614) 416-5611 ..**Furman**, Sandra M '79 -1 Easton Oval -Ste 500 -Columbus 43219

(513) 745-0400 ..**Furnier**, Robert R '83 (Furnier T,LLP) -1 Fncl Way -Ste 312
-Cincinnati 45242 **Fx:**792-6724

(513) 745-0400 ..**Furnier Thomas,LLP** -1 Fncl Way -Ste 312 -Cincinnati 45242
Fx:792-6724

(678) 375-3711 ..**Furnish**, Davina M '98 Check Free Corp -4411 E Jones Brdg Rd
-Norcross, GA 30092

(513) 425-6609 ..**Furnish**, William B '04 12th Dist Ct of Appls -1001 Reinartz Blvd
-Middletown 45042 **Fx:**425-8751

(614) 227-8919 ..**Furniss**, John F III '00 %Bricker & E LLP -100 S 3rd
-Columbus 43215 **Fx:**227-2390

(740) 967-2261 ..**Furr**, Jeffrey M '93 -253 N Main -Johnstown 43031

(937) 223-6003 ..**Furry**, Richard L '64 OfCnsl Dunlevey M&F -110 N Main -Ste 1000
-Dayton 45402 **Fx:**223-8550

(614) 464-2025 ..**Fusco**, Daniel J '99 %Connor B LLP -501 S High
-Columbus 43215 **Fx:**224-8708

(216) 566-1600 ..**Fusco**, David M '84 (Schwarzwald & M) -1300 E 9th -Ste 616
-Cleveland 44114 **Fx:**566-1814

(614) 523-7575 ..**Fusco Mackey Mathews Smith & Watkins,LLP** -655 Cooper Rd
-Westerville 43081 **Fx:**523-7580

(440) 234-0662 ..**Fusco**, Mark S '88 %Wargo & W Co,LPA -Bx332 -Berea 44017
Fx:234-4179

(614) 523-7575 ..**Fusco**, Michael J '79 (Fusco MMS&W,LLP) -655 Cooper Rd
-Westerville 43081 **Fx:**523-7580

(614) 464-6400 ..**Fusonie**, Thomas H '01 %Vorys SS&P LLP -52 E Gay -Bx1008
-Columbus 43216 **Fx:**464-6350

(216) 443-4940 ..**Fuss**, Gregory C '78 Cuyahoga Cnty Cmmn Pleas Ct
-1200 Ontario -Cleveland 44113

(412) 281-5060 ..**Futey**, Daria S '93 (Houston H,PC) -401 Lbrty Av
-22nd Fl Three Gtwy Ctr -Pittsburgh, PA 15222 **Fx:**281-4499

(859) 291-9000 ..**Futscher**, David A '88 (Parry DF&S) -411 Garrard
-Covington, KY 41012 **Fx:**291-9300

(703) 846-2115 ..**Futterer**, Edward P '78 Exxon Mobil Global Srvcs Co
-3225 Gallows Rd -2B0203 -Fairfax, VA 22037

(440) 946-1380 ..**Futterer**, Stephen J '75 -38052 Euclid Av -Willoughby 44094

(419) 321-1290 ..**Fynes**, Jack G '77 (Shumaker L&K,LLP) -1000 Jackson
-Toledo 43624 **Fx:**241-6894

(614) 586-1586 ..**Gaba**, Elizabeth N '94 -1231 E Broad -Columbus 43205
Fx:586-0064

(937) 544-2831 ..**Gabbert**, Roy E Jr. '89 -301 N Market -West Union 45693

(937) 222-5335 ..**Gabel**, Alan D '84 -411 E 5th -Bx1423 -Dayton 45401 **Fx:**224-0811

(740) 363-1324 ..**Gabel**, Edna M '80 -103 N Union -Ste A -Delaware 43015

(614) 764-0681 ..**Gabel**, Jonathan M '85 Blaugrund H&M,Inc -5455 Rings Rd
-Ste 500 -Dublin 43017 **Fx:**764-0774

(202) 879-3939 ..**Gabel**, Louis P '02 %Jones D -51 Louisana Av NW
-Washington, DC 20001 **Fx:**626-1700

(513) 348-4813 ..**Gabelman**, Richard P '02 -Bx12005 -Cincinnati 45212

(513) 723-4000 ..**Gabelman**, Thomas L '84 (Vorys SS&P LLP) -221 E 4th
-Ste 2000 Atrium Two -Bx0236 -Cincinnati 45201 **Fx:**723-4056

(419) 423-8944 ..**Gaberman**, Robert N '79 -500 Bright Rd -Findlay 45840

(216) 368-3288 ..**Gabinet**, Leon '70 CWRU Law Schl -11075 East Blvd
-Cleveland 44106

(216) 736-7206 ..**Gabinet**, Sarah J '82 (Kohrman J&K PLL) -1375 E 9th
-One Cleve Ctr 20th Fl -Cleveland 44114 **Fx:**621-6536

(270) 926-4040 ..**Gabis**, Mark A '79 Daymar Learning,Inc -3361 Buckland Sq
-Owensboro, KY 42301

(216) 479-8500 ..**Gabriel**, D Bruce '80 (Squire S&D LLP) -127 Pub Sq -4900
Key Twr -Cleveland 44114 **Fx:**479-8780

(216) 443-5809 ..**Gabriel**, Gary V '84 Cuyahoga Cnty Pros -1910 Carnegie Av
-Whitlatch Bldg -Cleveland 44115 **Fx:**443-5815

(313) 237-6424 ..**Gabriel**, Grant E '84 IRS -477 Mich Av -1870 McNamara Bldg
-Detroit, MI 48226

(866) 794-7282 ..**Gabriele**, Linda C '94 LAWO -545 W Market -Ste 301 -Lima 45801
Fx:(419) 224-9947

(724) 598-8905 ..**Gacse**, Thomas M '80 Sky Bank -101 E Wshngtn
-New Castle, PA 16103

(704) 866-3194 ..**Gadd**, Kathleen M '98 Gaston Cnty -Bx1578 -Gastonia, NC 28053
Fx:866-3972

(503) 778-2130 ..**Gadon**, John H '87 (Lane PSL LLP) -601 SW 2nd Av -Ste 2100
-Portland, OR 97204

(330) 225-1491 ..**Gaeckle**, Matthew P '04 Laribee H&K -111 Pearl Rd -Bx839
-Brunswick 44212

Gaffield, Diane K '85 -8259 Paddington Ct -West Chester 45069

(937) 865-6800 ..**Gaffin**, Dana L '99 Lexis/Nexis -Bx933 -Dayton 45401

(330) 645-4866 ..**Gaffney**, Corina S '91 -3996 Bramblewood Dr -Akron 44319

(740) 635-0162 ..**Gagin**, Christopher J '94 %Thomas FMH&D -320 Howard
-Bridgeport 43912 **Fx:**635-1601

(419) 421-3112 ..**Gagle**, Suzanne J '92 Marathon Ashland Petroleum LLC
-539 S Main -Rm 890-M -Findlay 45840 **Fx:**421-3578

(216) 931-6000 ..**Gagliano**, Bill J '80 (Ulmer & B LLP) -1300 E 9th
-Ste 900 Penton Media Bldg -Cleveland 44114 **Fx:**931-6001

(330) 740-2330 ..**Gaglione**, Karen M '92 Mahoning Cnty Pros -21 W Boardman
-6th Fl -Youngstown 44503 **Fx:**740-2008

(937) 236-3020 ..**Gagnon**, Kathleen D '94 Megacity Fire Prtctn,Inc
-8210 Expansion Way -Dayton 45424

(216) 579-1700 ..**Gagnon**, Suzanne B '00 %Pearne & G LLP -1801 E 9th -Ste 1200
-Cleveland 44114 **Fx:**579-6073

(419) 245-1975 ..**Gaich**, Sharon D '96 %Pros -555 N Erie -4th Fl -Toledo 43624

(513) 721-3330 ..**Gaier**, Thomas M '75 (Robbins KP&T) -7 W 7th -Ste 1400
-Cincinnati 45202

(216) 566-5722 ..**Gaillard**, Clevonne M '02 %Thompson H LLP -127 Pub Sq
-3900 Key Ctr -Cleveland 44114 **Fx:**566-5800

(440) 951-4879 ..**Gainar**, Ronald A '96 -2515 Red Fox Pass -Willoughby Hills 44094

(513) 287-2633 ..**Gainer**, James B '86 Cinergy Corp -139 E 4th -25 Atrium II -Bx960
-Cincinnati 45201

(513) 475-0200 ..**Gaines**, Deborah K Brown '72 -527 Linton -Cincinnati 45219
Fx:475-0377

Gaines, George L '88 -(Address Unavailable)

Gaines, Jennifer C '04 -(Address Unavailable)

(937) 225-4652 ..**Gaines**, Kandis C '00 Montgomery Cnty Pub Def -117 S Main
-Ste 400 -Dayton 45422 **Fx:**225-3444

(513) 961-9900 ..**Gaines**, Leslie I '72 -229 E Court -Cincinnati 45202

(513) 271-0254 ..**Gaines**, Terry D '69 -6821 Hammerstone Way -Cincinnati 45227

(614) 249-7609 ..**Gainey**, Scott A '99 Cnsl Nationwide Ins Co -1 Nationwide Plz
-Columbus 43215

(330) 740-2330 ..**Gains**, Paul J '82 Mahoning Cnty Pros -21 W Boardman -6th Fl
-Youngstown 44503 **Fx:**740-2008

(614) 224-0761 ..**Gairing**, Ann F '86 Planned Parenthood -33 N 3rd
-Columbus 43215

(330) 456-6406 ..**Gaitanos**, Mario '84 -437 Market Av N -Canton 44702
Fx:456-1344

(216) 566-5931 ..**Gaj**, Brian L '85 OfCnsl Thompson H LLP -127 Pub Sq -3900
Key Ctr -Cleveland 44114 **Fx:**566-5800

(216) 830-6830 ..**Gajda**, Patricia A '90 (Brouse M) -1001 Lakeside Av -Ste 1600
-Cleveland 44114 **Fx:**830-6807

(216) 771-8038 ..**Galaska**, Edward J '82 -930 Leader Bldg -Cleveland 44114

(614) 235-4436 ..**Galasso**, John G '96 -2229 Bluebell Ln -Grove City 43123

(513) 721-3330 ..**Galasso**, Michael A '00 %Robbins KP&T -7 W 7th -Ste 1400
-Cincinnati 45202

(740) 593-5046 ..**Galbraith**, Randall L '98 Cnsl Athens Cnty CSEA -Bx37
-The Plains 45780 **Fx:**797-2447

(614) 469-3939 ..**Gale**, Erick D '02 %Jones D -325 John H McConnell Blvd -Ste 600
-Bx165017 -Columbus 43216 **Fx:**461-4198

(216) 363-4500 ..**Gale**, Gregory K '03 (Benesch FC&A LLP) -200 Pub Sq -Ste 2300
-Cleveland 44114 **Fx:**363-4588

(313) 961-3234 ..**Galea**, Paul D '93 Foster M&B,PC -607 Shelby -7th Fl
-Detroit, MI 48226

(614) 764-1444 ..**Galeano**, Judith E '90 Mowery & Y -425 Metro Pl N -Ste 420
-Dublin 43017 **Fx:**760-8654

(614) 836-9981 ..**Galeano**, Michael J '89 McGill Corp -1 Mission Park
-Groveport 43125

(937) 223-1113 ..**Galen**, Barry S '89 -111 W 1st -Ste 1000 -Dayton 45402

(419) 662-3100 ..**Galernik**, Gerald E '89 Heban & G -417 Superior -Ste A
-Rossford 43460 **Fx:**662-6533

(419) 662-3100 ..**Galernik**, Melissa M '03 (Heban & G) -417 Superior -Ste A
-Rossford 43460 **Fx:**662-6533

(412) 562-3927 ..**Galey**, Thomas S '01 (Buchanan I,PC) -301 Grant -20th Fl
-Pittsburgh, PA 15219 **Fx:**562-1041

(216) 621-1113 .. **Galin**, Morris David '96 (Renner OB&S,LLP) -1621 Euclid Av -19th Fl -Cleveland 44115 Fx:621-6165

(330) 726-5518 .. **Galip**, Ronald G '57 -721 Boardman-Poland Rd -Ste 201 -Youngstown 44512 Fx:726-7538

(614) 628-8000 .. **Gall**, Charles V '99 %Dreher L&T LLP -41 S High -2250 Huntngtn Ctr -Columbus 43215 Fx:628-1600

(740) 593-3357 .. **Gall**, Cherie H '83 (Mollica GS&S Co,LPA) -35 N Cllg -Drwr958 -Athens 45701

Gall, Christine C '02 -10020 Ridge Line Dr -North Royalton 44133

(937) 562-5250 .. **Gall**, Garrett T '77 Greene Cnty Pros -61 Greene -Xenia 45385

(614) 761-7701 .. **Gall**, Heather R '99 %T Thomas Co,LPA -5148 Blazer Pkwy -Ste A -Dublin 43017

Gall, Jacqueline M '04 -(Address Unavailable)

(419) 474-5678 .. **Gall**, Joanne F '79 -2828 W Central Av -Toledo 43606

(614) 365-2700 .. **Gall**, John R '71 (Squire S&D LLP) -41 S High -1300 Huntngtn Ctr -Columbus 43215 Fx:365-2499

(330) 670-7300 .. **Gall**, Juliana S '89 Hanna C&P,LLP -3737 Embssy Pkwy -Bx5521 -Akron 44334 Fx:670-0977

(513) 721-1200 .. **Gall**, Kenneth Z '97 %Young R&M Co,LPA -1014 Vine -Ste 2400 -Cincinnati 45202 Fx:721-7116

(614) 469-3939 .. **Gall**, Maryann B '70 (Jones D) -325 John H McConnell Blvd -Ste 600 -Bx165017 -Columbus 43216 Fx:461-4198

Gall, Michael K '04 -(Address Unavailable)

(740) 593-3357 .. **Gall**, Robert J '82 Mollica GS&S Co,LPA -35 N Cllg -Drwr958 -Athens 45701

(216) 443-7800 .. **Gall**, Steven E '91 Cuyahoga Cnty Pros -1200 Ontario -8th Fl -Cleveland 44113 Fx:698-2270

(216) 781-9440 .. **Gall**, Timothy L '79 Eastword Publications Devlpmnt inc -812 Huron Rd -Ste 401 -Cleveland 44115

(216) 241-8193 .. **Gallagher**, Candace M '75 %F Gallagher & Assoc -1801 E 12th -Ste 223 -Cleveland 44114

(216) 443-8509 .. **Gallagher**, Eileen T '96 Cuyahoga Cnty Cmmn Pleas Ct -1200 Ontario Av -Foreclosure Dept -Cleveland 44113

(216) 241-8193 .. **Gallagher**, Francis P '75 (F Gallagher & Assoc) -1801 E 12th -Ste 223 -Cleveland 44114

(614) 228-5151 .. **Gallagher Gams Pryor Talian & Littrell LLP** -471 E Broad -19th Fl -Columbus 43215 Fx:228-0032

(216) 443-7800 .. **Gallagher**, Hollie L '95 Cuyahoga Cnty Pros -1200 Ontario -8th Fl -Cleveland 44113 Fx:698-2270

(617) 854-8614 .. **Gallagher**, James D '79 Manulife Financial (USA) -73 Tremont -Boston, MA 02108

(440) 777-6500 .. **Gallagher**, James R '77 (Burke V&G) -22649 Lorain Rd -Fairview Park 44126 Fx:777-0507

(614) 228-5151 .. **Gallagher**, James R '81 (Gallagher GPT&L LLP) -471 E Broad -19th Fl -Columbus 43215 Fx:228-0032

(216) 443-7583 .. **Gallagher**, Jean M '86 Cuyahoga Cnty Pub Def -1200 W 3rd NW -100 Lakeside Pl -Cleveland 44113

(610) 478-2254 .. **Gallagher**, John F '02 %Stevens & L PC -111 N 6th -Bx679 -Reading, PA 19603

(216) 443-7800 .. **Gallagher**, John J '86 Cuyahoga Cnty Pros -1200 Ontario -8th Fl -Cleveland 44113 Fx:698-2270

(937) 225-4601 .. **Gallagher**, Joseph S '77 Montgomery Cnty Probate Ct -41 N Perry -Dayton 45422

(937) 445-4051 .. **Gallagher**, Julie D '93 NCR Corp -1700 S Patterson Blvd -Leg Dept -Dayton 45479

(419) 636-3166 .. **Gallagher**, Karen K '86 (Gallagher S&Y,Ltd) -216 S Lynn -Bryan 43506 Fx:636-5743

(216) 622-3600 .. **Gallagher**, Kathleen M '93 US Atty -801 W Superior -Ste 400 -Cleveland 44113 Fx:622-3370

(614) 221-3536 .. **Gallagher & Kavinsky,LPA** -400 S 5th Av -Ste 304 -Columbus 43215

(216) 689-0324 .. **Gallagher**, Kimberly A '94 Key Corp -127 Pub Sq -MC OH-01-27-1518 -Cleveland 44114

(330) 725-9709 .. **Gallagher**, Laura J '86 Medina Cnty Cmmn Pleas Ct -93 Pub Sq -Medina 44256

(440) 593-2309 .. **Gallagher**, Luke P '90 %Lafferty Law Ofc -365 Main -Conneaut 44030

(440) 333-1617 .. **Gallagher**, Mary C '85 -20942 Avalon Dr -Rocky River 44116

(614) 221-7614 .. **Gallagher**, Mary L '92 %OH Hospital Assoc -155 E Broad -Columbus 43215

(614) 397-8909 .. **Gallagher**, Michael J '01 (Gallagher & D) -1487 W 5th Av -Bx 226 -Columbus 43212

(216) 241-5310 .. **Gallagher**, Michael R '49 OfCnsl Gallagher SF&N -1501 Euclid Av -6th Fl -Cleveland 44115 Fx:241-1608

Gallagher, Nancy A '96 -2176 Burton Run Rd -High Point, NC 27262

(216) 377-0598 .. **Gallagher**, Patrick J '89 (Allan & G,LLP) -614 W Superior Av -Ste 1300 -Cleveland 44113

(330) 297-3850 .. **Gallagher**, Paul J '86 Portage Cnty Pros -466 S Chestnut -Ravenna 44266

(419) 636-3166 .. **Gallagher**, Ralph W '70 (Gallagher S&Y,Ltd) -216 S Lynn -Bryan 43506 Fx:636-5743

(216) 443-6350 .. **Gallagher**, Shannon M '04 8th Dist Ct of Appls -1 Lakeside Av -#202 -Cleveland 44113 Fx:443-2044

(216) 241-5310 .. **Gallagher Sharp Fulton & Norman** -1501 Euclid Av -6th Fl -Cleveland 44115 Fx:241-1608

(419) 241-4860 .. **Gallagher Sharp Fulton & Norman** -420 Mad Av -Ste 1250 -Toledo 43604 Fx:241-4866

(419) 636-3166 .. **Gallagher Stelzer & Yosick,Ltd** -216 S Lynn -Bryan 43506 Fx:636-5743

(614) 221-3536 .. **Gallagher**, Terence L '83 (Gallagher & K,LPA) -400 S 5th Av -Ste 304 -Columbus 43215

(614) 227-2384 .. **Gallagher**, Theodore J '91 Bricker & E LLP -100 S 3rd -Columbus 43215 Fx:227-2390

(614) 224-1222 .. **Gallagher**, Thomas J '85 %Maguire & S,LLP -250 Civic Ctr Dr -Ste 200 -Columbus 43215 Fx:224-1236

(419) 241-2122 .. **Gallagher**, Thomas W '75 (Williams JLG&S Co,LPA) -416 N Erie -Ste 500 -Toledo 43624 Fx:245-3849

(216) 566-1600 .. **Gallagher**, Timothy J '92 (Schwarzwald & M) -1300 E 9th -Ste 616 -Cleveland 44114 Fx:566-1814

(513) 651-6800 .. **Gallagher**, William E '01 Cnsl Frost BT LLC -201 E 5th -2200 PNC Ctr -Cincinnati 45202 Fx:651-6981

(513) 651-5666 .. **Gallagher**, William R '95 (Arenstein & G) -114 E 8th -Cincinnati 45202

(304) 242-3220 .. **Gallaway**, Michael G '86 (Burns W&H,LLC) -32 20th -Ste 200 -Wheeling, WV 26003

(216) 496-3427 .. **Gallick**, Donald M '01 -14837 Detroit Av #242 -Lakewood 44107

(859) 331-3300 .. **Galligan**, Kathleen M '85 Von Lehman & Co -250 Grandvw Dr -Ste 300 -Fort Mitchell, KY 41017

(330) 726-8700 .. **Gallitto**, Robyn R '01 J Fleck -845 Woodfld Ct -Youngstown 44512

(212) 894-8794 .. **Gallo**, Bruce S '82 CT Corp Syst -111 8th Av -13th Fl -New York, NY 10011

(216) 771-1081 .. **Gallo**, Charles J '55 (C Gallo Co,LPA) -55 Pub Sq -Ste 2222 -Cleveland 44113 Fx:771-5724

(216) 771-1081 .. **Gallo**, Charles J Jr. '89 C Gallo Co,LPA -55 Pub Sq -Ste 2222 -Cleveland 44113 Fx:771-5724

(203) 470-2313 .. **Gallo**, David R '85 GE Cmmrcl Fincl -10 Rivervw Dr -Danbury, CT 06810

(540) 977-4197 .. **Gallo**, Joseph J '73 JJ Gallo Consulting -140 Queen Regent Ct -Blue Ridge, VA 24064

(216) 771-1081 .. **Gallo**, Lori M '83 C Gallo Co,LPA -55 Pub Sq -Ste 2222 -Cleveland 44113 Fx:771-5724

(330) 744-0247 .. **Gallo**, Michael A Jr. '67 (Nadler N&B Co,LPA) -20 Fed Plz W -Ste 600 -Youngstown 44503 Fx:744-8690

(614) 227-2000 .. **Gallon**, Eric Benjamin '99 %Porter WM&A LLP -41 S High -Columbus 43215 Fx:227-2100

(937) 586-3100 .. **ES Gallon & Associates** -40 W 4th -22nd Fl -Dayton 45402 Fx:586-3100

(419) 843-2001 .. **Gallon**, Jack E '56 (Gallon & T Co,LPA) -3516 Granite Cir -Bx352018 -Toledo 43635 Fx:843-6665

(419) 843-2001 .. **Gallon & Takacs Co,LPA** -3516 Granite Cir -Bx352018 -Toledo 43635 Fx:843-6665

(440) 974-1173 .. **Gallovic**, John G '75 (Gallovic Granito &Co Ltd) -8518 Mentor Av -Ste A -Mentor 44060 Fx:951-8976

(419) 626-8630 .. **Galloway**, Duane L '77 (Galloway & Assoc) -538 Huron Av -Sandusky 44870

(904) 274-6200 .. **Galloway**, Elizabeth A '85 Ladies Pro Golf Assoc -100 Intl Golf Dr -Daytona Beach, FL 32124

(216) 621-0200 .. **Galloway**, Robert R '88 (Baker & H LLP) -1900 E 9th -Ste 3200 -Cleveland 44114 Fx:696-0740

(304) 748-7230 .. **Galloway**, William E '79 -3539 West -Weirton, WV 26062

(216) 575-0777 .. **Gallucci**, Anthony '96 (Kelley & F,LLP) -1300 E 9th -Ste 1901 -Cleveland 44114 Fx:575-0799

(216) 861-0804 .. **Gallucci**, Frank L III '00 %F Gallucci Jr Co,LPA -55 Pub Sq -Ste 2222 -Cleveland 44113

(330) 867-4013 .. **Gallucci**, Michael Jr. '80 Cornerstone Co -2841 Rivera Dr -Ste 320 -Akron 44333

(216) 621-4636 .. **Gallup Burns & Associates** -815 Superior Av E -Ste 1810 The Superior Bldg -Cleveland 44114

(216) 621-4636 .. **Gallup**, David B '79 (Gallup B & Assoc) -815 Superior Av E -Ste 1810 The Superior Bldg -Cleveland 44114

(216) 621-7860 .. **Gallup**, Jeffrey W '03 %Cavitch FD&F -1717 E 9th -14th Fl -Cleveland 44114 Fx:621-3415

(517) 458-1712 .. **Gallup**, Lynne H '89 -12253 Lime Crk Hwy -Morenci, MI 49256

(614) 575-1145 .. **Gallutia**, Christopher A '85 -7668 Slate Ridge Blvd -Reynoldsburg 43068

(305) 358-6300 .. **Gallwey**, William J III '72 (Shutts & B LLP) -201 S Biscayne Blvd -Ste 1500 -Miami, FL 33131 Fx:381-9982

(330) 643-2765 .. **Galonski**, John F '93 Summit Cnty Pros-CSEA -171 S Main -Akron 44308 Fx:643-2822

(330) 643-7528 .. **Galonski**, Tavia D '95 Summit Cnty Juv Ct -650 Dan -Akron 44310

(419) 424-7276 .. **Galose**, Michael C '90 Hancock Cnty Pub Def -316 Dorney Plz -Findlay 45840

(305) 944-9120 .. **Galvan-Blair**, Lisa M '99 %R Gelfman,PA -2020 NE 163rd -Ste 300 -North Miami Beach, FL 33162 Fx:948-3317

(937) 859-3628 .. **Galvas**, Walter W '89 Tracy & T -31 E Central Av -Bx156 -West Carrollton 45449

(937) 865-6800 .. **Galvin**, Gregory M '02 %Lexis/Nexis -Bx933 -Dayton 45401

(216) 622-3600 .. **Galvin**, Kelly L '93 US Atty -801 W Superior -Ste 400 -Cleveland 44113 Fx:622-3370

(216) 687-1311 .. **Galvin**, Martin T '94 (Reminger & R) -101 Prospect Av W -1400 Mdlnd Bldg -Cleveland 44115 Fx:687-1841

(330) 384-9000 .. **Gamache**, Elisa A '94 Roadway Express, Inc -1077 Gorge Blvd -Akron 44310

(216) 592-5000 .. **Gambaccini**, Janice R '03 %Tucker E&W LLP -925 Euclid Av -1150 Huntngtn Bldg -Cleveland 44115 Fx:592-5009

(216) 363-4500 .. **Gambaccini**, John S '00 %Benesch FC&A LLP -200 Pub Sq -Ste 2300 -Cleveland 44114 Fx:363-4588

(513) 287-2641 .. **Gambill**, Barbara F '97 SrCnsl Cinergy -139 E 4th -Bx960 -Cincinnati 45201

(937) 223-8177 .. **Gambill**, R Brent '97 (Coolidge WW&L) -33 W 1st -Ste 600 -Dayton 45402 Fx:223-6705

(440) 238-1070 .. **Gambino**, Joseph A '72 -11005 Pearl Rd -Strongsville 44136

(614) 228-5271 .. **Gamble**, Amanda D '01 %Denmead & M -37 W Broad -Ste 1150 -Columbus 43215

(614) 221-0922 .. **Gamble**, Eric B '02 %Gamble HJ Co,LPA -1 E Lvngstn Av -Columbus 43215 Fx:365-9741

(614) 221-0922 .. **Gamble Hartshorn Johnson Co,LPA** -1 E Lvngstn Av -Columbus 43215 Fx:365-9741

(330) 222-4315 .. **Gamble**, John E '89 -34909 Teagarden Rd -Salem 44460

(937) 241-9400 .. **Gamble**, Kathy L '73 Legal Aid -202 W Locust -Wilmington 45177

(614) 221-0922 .. **Gamble**, Kenneth A '72 Gamble HJ Co,LPA -1 E Lvngstn Av -Columbus 43215 Fx:365-9741

(216) 397-9180 .. **Gamble**, Ranelle A '72 -3370 Seaton Rd -Cleveland Heights 44118

(440) 350-2683 .. **Gambol**, Robert A '73 Lake Cnty Pros -105 Main -Bx490 -Painesville 44077 Fx:350-2585

(937) 449-6400 .. **Gambrel**, Kimberly '88 (Dinsmore & S LLP) -1 S Main -Ste 1300 One Dayton Centre -Dayton 45402 Fx:449-6405

(215) 569-5500 .. **Gamburg**, Donald D '96 %Blank RC&M -One Logan Sq -Philadelphia, PA 19103

(216) 289-3366 .. **Gamiere**, Dorothy S '75 Gamiere & Assoc -27004 Lakeshr Blvd -Cleveland 44132

(216) 357-7243 .. **Gamiere**, Jess E '02 Hon K O'Malley US Dist Ct -801 W Superior Av -#16A -Cleveland 44113

(216) 689-3241 .. **Gamin**, Dean D '87 KeyBank NA -127 Pub Sq -OH-01-27-0200 -Cleveland 44114

(440) 603-7558 .. **Gamin,** Mark A '83 Progressive Ins Co -5920 Landerbrook Rd
-#PLG-OHL33 -Mayfield Heights 44124
(937) 433-4090 .. **Gammell Hoshor Kendo & Ross LLP** -7925 Paragon Rd
-Dayton 45459 **Fx:**433-1510
(937) 433-4090 .. **Gammell,** Jeffrey W '91 (Gammell HK&R LLP) -7925 Paragon Rd
-Dayton 45459 **Fx:**433-1510
(216) 586-3939 .. **Gammie,** Sandra E '86 Cnsl Jones D -901 Lakeside Av
-Cleveland 44114 **Fx:**579-0212
(440) 984-2084 .. **Gammons,** Patrick E '71 -1610 Cooper Foster Park Rd
-Vermilion 44089
(614) 645-7385 .. **Gams,** Jennifer S '94 City Atty -90 W Broad -Columbus 43215
(614) 228-5151 .. **Gams,** Mark H '84 (Gallagher GPT&L LLP) -471 E Broad -19th Fl
-Columbus 43215 **Fx:**228-0032
(216) 472-2216 .. **Gamso,** Jeffrey M '90 ACLU of OH -4506 Chester Av
-Cleveland 44103 **Fx:**472-2210
(614) 870-9669 .. **Gander,** Van A '87 (Gander Law Ofc) -Bx106 -Galloway 43119
(419) 526-1622 .. **Gandert,** William F '50 Mansfield Metro Housing Auth
-150 Park Av -Bx1029 -Mansfield 44901
(513) 946-3800 .. **Gandert,** William T '98 Hamilton Cnty Pub Def -230 E 9th -3rd Fl
-Cincinnati 45202 **Fx:**946-3808
(440) 234-2662 .. **Gandola,** Paul D '69 -7456 Lewis Rd -Olmsted Township 44138
(440) 248-0240 .. **Ganger,** Milton E Jr. '62 Etched Metal Co
-30200 Solon Indstrl Pkwy -Bx391287 -Solon 44139
(606) 341-1256 .. **Gangwish,** Richard J II '78 (RJ Gangwish II,PSC) -3307 Dixie Hwy
-Erlanger, KY 41018
Ganim, Sandra M '95 -3218 Hwy 42 S -Delaware 43015
(513) 723-4000 .. **Gann,** Erica D '04 %Vorys SS&P LLP -221 E 4th -Ste 2000 Atrium
Two -Bx0236 -Cincinnati 45201 **Fx:**723-4056
(216) 687-1311 .. **Gannon,** Brian T '04 %Reminger & R -101 Prospect Av W
-1400 Mdlnd Bldg -Cleveland 44115 **Fx:**687-1841
(216) 696-6454 .. **Gannon,** John F '72 Cincinnati Ins Co -930 The 55 Bldg
-55 Pub Sq -Cleveland 44113
(614) 895-9619 .. **Gannon,** Patrick J '78 -15 Spring Creek Dr -Westerville 43081
(937) 382-3320 .. **Gano,** Judy A '86 -169 N South -Wilmington 45177
(813) 558-5510 .. **Ganobsik,** Keith J '97 DCF -9393 N Fla Av -Tampa, FL 33612
(440) 356-2828 .. **Ganor,** Stacey M '99 %Milano Law Ofc -2639 Wooster Rd
-Rocky River 44116 **Fx:**356-2873
(937) 865-6800 .. **Ganote,** David P '96 Lexis/Nexis -Bx933 -Dayton 45401
(216) 586-3939 .. **Ganske,** Lyle G '84 (Jones D) -901 Lakeside Av -Cleveland 44114
Fx:579-0212
(513) 721-2220 .. **Ganson,** Michael B '78 (M Ganson Co,LPA) -2306 park Av
-Ste 101 -Cincinnati 45206 **Fx:**721-5109
(419) 867-8900 .. **Gant,** Jim R '00 %Lyden L&C,Ltd -5565 Airport Hwy -Ste 101
-Toledo 43615 **Fx:**867-8909
(313) 871-3000 .. **Gant,** Norma M '99 (Bowman and B LLP) -50 W Big Beaver Rd
-Ste 600 -Troy, MI 48084
(216) 592-5000 .. **Gantous,** Anthony M '03 %Tucker E&W LLP -925 Euclid Av
-1150 Huntngtn Bldg -Cleveland 44115 **Fx:**592-5009
(937) 228-5912 .. **Gantt,** Gregory M '95 (Allbery C&F) -137 N Main -Ste 500
-Dayton 45402
(614) 228-6885 .. **Gantz,** Curtis F '68 (Lane A&H LLC) -175 S 3rd -Ste 700
-Columbus 43215 **Fx:**228-0146
(513) 651-6800 .. **Ganulin,** Neil '73 (Frost BT LLC) -201 E 5th -2200 PNC Ctr
-Cincinnati 45202 **Fx:**651-6981
(513) 352-3329 .. **Ganulin,** Richard '77 Law Dept -801 Plum -Rm 214
-Cincinnati 45202 **Fx:**352-1515
(614) 469-1990 .. **Garabis,** Francisco A '77 -155 W Main -Ste 200A
-Columbus 43215 **Fx:**469-4630
(202) 254-3661 .. **Garabis,** Maria S '03 US Ofc of Spcl Cnsl -1730 M NW
-Washington, DC 20036
(740) 354-2375 .. **Garaczkowski,** Joan M '93 (Garaczkowski & H) -602 Chillicothe
-Portsmouth 45662
(419) 698-4307 .. **Garand,** John D '71 -860 Ansonia -#113 -Oregon 43616
Fx:691-9583
(419) 691-0182 .. **Garand,** Richard C '64 -860 Ansonia -Ste 113 -Oregon 43616
Fx:691-9583
(216) 861-5000 .. **Garanich,** James G '84 (Ernst & Young) -1300 Huntngtn Bldg
-925 Euclid Av -Cleveland 44115
(814) 871-8002 .. **Garbarino,** Gwendolyn M '85 National Fuel -1100 State
-Erie, PA 16501
(513) 579-5472 .. **Garber,** David W '75 Fifth Third Bk -38 Fountain Sq Plz
-Trust Division-M.L. 1090C4 -Cincinnati 45263
(513) 922-3200 .. **Garber,** Deanna R '90 %Haverkamp BR&R Co,LPA
-5856 Glenway Av -Cincinnati 45238 **Fx:**922-8096
(614) 249-6816 .. **Garber,** Joseph F '91 Nationwide Ins Co -1 Nationwide Plz
-Columbus 43215
(614) 292-1315 .. **Garber,** Kathleen M '95 OSU -200 Rsrch Foundation
-1960 Kenny Rd -Columbus 43210
(614) 274-1107 .. **Garber,** Kenneth E '67 -3303 Sullivant Av -Columbus 43204
Garber, Valerie L '75 -6812 Miami Bluff Dr -Cincinnati 45207
(937) 692-5278 .. **Garbig & Blinn,LLC** -2840 Alt State Rt 49 N -Ste A -Bx100
-Arcanum 45304 **Fx:**692-6544
(937) 692-5278 .. **Garbig,** Phillip R '85 Garbig & B,LLC -2840 Alt State Rt 49 N
-Ste A -Bx100 -Arcanum 45304 **Fx:**692-6544
(614) 464-6400 .. **Garceau,** Mary L '97 (Vorys SS&P LLP) -52 E Gay -Bx1008
-Columbus 43216 **Fx:**464-6350
(859) 232-7846 .. **Garcia,** Christine K '01 Lexmark Intl Inc -740 W New Circle Rd
-IP Law Dept -Lexington, KY 40550
(614) 464-6400 .. **Garcia,** Daren S '03 %Vorys SS&P LLP -52 E Gay -Bx1008
-Columbus 43216 **Fx:**464-6350
(614) 228-6453 .. **Garcia,** Roger '96 OfCnsl Colley S&A Co,LPA -536 S High
-Columbus 43215 **Fx:**228-7122
(740) 349-3772 .. **Gard,** John S '81 Park Natl Bank -50 N 3rd -Bx3500
-Newark 43058 **Fx:**349-3704
(216) 687-2263 .. **Gard,** Stephen W '80 CSU-Marshall Cllg of Law -2121 Euclid Av
-LB138 -Cleveland 44115 **Fx:**687-6881
(440) 347-5094 .. **Gardiner,** Archibald T III '75 Lubrizol Corp -29400 Lakelnd Blvd
-Wickliffe 44092
(614) 459-1466 .. **Gardiner,** Donald B '67 -2645 Lane Rd -Columbus 43220
(216) 241-5310 .. **Gardner,** Abigail J '98 %Gallagher SF&N -1501 Euclid Av -6th Fl
-Cleveland 44115 **Fx:**241-1608
(937) 449-6400 .. **Gardner,** Ames Jr. '65 (Dinsmore & S LLP) -1 S Main
-Ste 1300 One Dayton Centre -Dayton 45402 **Fx:**449-6405

(937) 865-6800 .. **Gardner,** Ann M '94 Lexis/Nexis -Bx933 -Dayton 45401
(330) 655-5722 .. **Gardner,** Deborah F '83 (Gardner & G) -72 N Main -Ste 309
-Hudson 44236
(513) 579-6400 .. **Gardner,** Don R '60 SrCnsl Keating M&K PLL -1 E 4th
-1400 Provident Twr -Cincinnati 45202 **Fx:**579-6457
(727) 399-8300 .. **Gardner,** Drew A '93 Gibbs Law Firm,PA -5666 Seminole Blvd
-Ste 2 -Seminole, FL 33772 **Fx:**398-3907
(216) 687-1311 .. **Gardner,** Francis X '79 (Reminger & R) -101 Prospect Av W
-1400 Mdlnd Bldg -Cleveland 44115 **Fx:**687-1841
(216) 931-6000 .. **Gardner,** Gary T '97 %Ulmer & B LLP -1300 E 9th
-Ste 900 Penton Media Bldg -Cleveland 44114 **Fx:**931-6001
(216) 348-5400 .. **Gardner,** George Andrew '96 (McDonald H Co,LPA)
-600 Superior Av E -Ste 2100 -Cleveland 44114 **Fx:**348-5474
(513) 579-6400 .. **Gardner,** J Neal '71 (Keating M&K PLL) -1 E 4th
-1400 Provident Twr -Cincinnati 45202 **Fx:**579-6457
(330) 535-5757 .. **Gardner,** James E '91 -628 W Market -Akron 44303
Gardner, Jeffrey R '04 -(Address Unavailable)
(330) 533-1118 .. **Gardner,** Joseph W '77 JW Gardner Co LPA
-4280 Boardman-Canfld Rd -Canfield 44406
Gardner, Lauren A '93 -1260 Quillams Rd
-Cleveland Heights 44121
(740) 345-7955 .. **Gardner,** Mark D '82 -30 W Locust -Newark 43055
(216) 696-9800 .. **Gardner,** Mark J '93 (Gardner & K) -526 Superior Av E -Ste 1130
-Cleveland 44114
(513) 503-4998 .. **Gardner,** Matthew A '03 -20 Forest Hll Dr -Cincinnati 45208
(216) 283-2323 .. **Gardner,** Michael B '93 -22132 Wstchstr Rd
-Shaker Heights 44122
(440) 729-0296 .. **Gardner,** Robert E '65 -13178 W Geauga Trl -Chesterland 44026
(614) 221-0749 .. **Gardner,** Robert F '58 -601 S High -Columbus 43215 **Fx:**221-0749
(216) 348-5400 .. **Gardner,** Steven L '76 (McDonald H Co,LPA) -600 Superior Av E
-Ste 2100 -Cleveland 44114 **Fx:**348-5474
(614) 252-4010 .. **Gardner,** William A '79 -1258 E Lvngstn Av -Columbus 43205
(330) 629-7510 .. **Garea,** Stephen R '77 -8571 Foxwood Ct -Ste B -Youngstown
44514
(440) 777-1500 .. **Gareau,** David M '96 %MR Gareau & Assoc Co,LPA
-23823 Lorain Rd -Ste 200 -North Olmsted 44070
(440) 777-1500 .. **Gareau,** Michael R '67 (MR Gareau & Assoc Co,LPA)
-23823 Lorain Rd -Ste 200 -North Olmsted 44070
(440) 777-1500 .. **Gareau,** Michael R Jr. '96 %MR Gareau & Assoc Co,LPA
-23823 Lorain Rd -Ste 200 -North Olmsted 44070
(216) 664-4419 .. **Gareau,** William E Jr. '97 City Div of Taxation -1701 Lakeside Av
-Cleveland 44114
(614) 221-3155 .. **Garel,** Jules L '56 OfCnsl Bailey C LLC -10 W Broad
-Columbus 43215 **Fx:**221-0479
(615) 231-3524 .. **Garfield,** Gary A '81 Bridgestone/Firestone -1 Brdgstone Pk
-Nashville, TN 37214
(216) 574-2600 .. **Garfield,** Robert E '63 Lasko & L Co,LPA -1406 W 6th -Ste 200
-Cleveland 44113
Garfinkel, Gregg D '04 -(Address Unavailable)
(513) 352-6530 .. **Garfinkel,** Jane E '80 (Thompson H LLP) -312 Walnut -14th Fl
-Cincinnati 45202 **Fx:**241-4771
(440) 395-0257 .. **Garfunkel,** Steven B '72 Progressive Ins Co -300 N Cmmns Blvd
-OHF 11 -Mayfield Village 44143
(646) 496-1600 .. **Garg,** Anjula '02 %Baker & H LLP -666 5th Av
-New York, NY 10103 **Fx:**496-1601
(330) 393-3344 .. **Gargano,** John R '83 Trumbull Cnty Dept Human Srvcs
-175 Franklin SE -Bx1859 -Warren 44482
(440) 960-1670 .. **Gargasz,** Robert J '83 R Gargasz Co,LPA
-1670-C Cooper Foster Park Rd -Lorain 44053
(440) 285-2222 .. **Gargiulo,** Dawn M '92 Geauga Cnty Pros -231 Main -Cthse Annx
-Chardon 44024 **Fx:**286-4357
(216) 261-0200 .. **Gargiulo,** William C '69 -27801 Euclid Av -Ste 500 -Euclid 44132
(216) 621-0150 .. **Gariepy,** Stephen H '77 (Hahn L&P LLP)
-3300 BP Twr/200 Pub Sq -Ste 3300 -Cleveland 44114
Fx:241-2824
Garland, David E '02 -(Address Unavailable)
(937) 376-6333 .. **Garland,** John W '74 Cntrl State Univ -Bx1004 -Wilberforce 45384
(614) 228-6675 .. **Garland,** Lorie D '84 %OH Assoc of Realtors -200 E Town
-Columbus 43215
(412) 366-3333 .. **Garland,** Louis R '04 %Willaim & A,LLP -705 McKnight Park Dr
-Pittsburgh, PA 15237
(614) 228-1541 .. **Garling,** Ellen J '89 (Baker & H LLP) -65 E State -Ste 2100
-Columbus 43215 **Fx:**462-2616
(202) 225-5021 .. **Garlock,** Kirsti T '91 Cnsl House of Rep
-2170 Rayburn Hse Ofc Bldg -Washington, DC 20515
(330) 665-7200 .. **Garlock,** Paul R '75 Progressive Ins Co -190 Montrose W Av
-Ste 100 -Copley 44321
(703) 415-0780 .. **Garlock,** Vincent E '91 AIPLA -2001 Jeff Davis Hwy -Ste 203
-Arlington, VA 22202
(937) 435-8780 .. **Garman,** Richard K '57 -7501 Paragon Rd -Dayton 45459
Fx:436-0008
(937) 492-1271 .. **Garmhausen,** John M '73 (Faulkner GK&S,LPA) -100 S Main Av
-Ste 300 -Sidney 45365 **Fx:**498-1306
(419) 683-2214 .. **Garner & Berger** -211 N Seltzer -Bx29 -Crestline 44827
(513) 337-8559 .. **Garner,** Dean L '91 Johnson & Johnson -4545 Crk Rd
-Cincinnati 45242
(812) 539-2111 .. **Garner,** Douglas A '91 -15 W Center -Lawrenceburg, IN 47025
(513) 870-2000 .. **Garner,** Kimberly V '95 Cincinnati Ins Cos -Bx145496
-Cincinnati 45250 **Fx:**870-2097
(419) 535-0075 .. **Garner,** Mitchell E '04 %Allotta F&W Co,LPA -2222 Centennial Rd
-Toledo 43617 **Fx:**535-1935
(216) 348-1700 .. **Garner,** Richard M '93 (Davis & Y) -101 Prospect Av W -Ste 1700
-Cleveland 44115 **Fx:**621-0602
(614) 228-5151 .. **Garner,** Robika L '04 %Gallagher GPT&L LLP -471 E Broad
-19th Fl -Columbus 43215 **Fx:**228-0032
(513) 459-1745 .. **Garner-Stark,** Carol A '96 -4660 Duke Dr -Ste 300 -Mason 45040
Fx:459-1746
(937) 223-8888 .. **Garofalo,** Carmine M '74 (Dyer GM&S) -131 N Ludlow -Ste 1400
-Dayton 45402 **Fx:**223-0127
(216) 592-5000 .. **Garred,** John X '84 (Tucker E&W LLP) -925 Euclid Av
-1150 Huntngtn Bldg -Cleveland 44115 **Fx:**592-5009
(513) 863-6600 .. **Garretson,** John A '77 J Garretson Co,LPA -616 Dayton -Bx1166
-Hamilton 45012

(330) 762-9191 .. **Garretson**, Mark F '95 Garretson & Co,LPA -7 W Bowery -Ste 604 -Akron 44308 Fx:'762-4244

(513) 871-8900 .. **Garretson**, Matthew L '98 Little MG & Assoc -2651 Observatory Av -Cincinnati 45208

(513) 737-9900 .. **Garretson**, Patrick W '84 -924 Laurel Av -Hamilton 45015

(740) 833-2690 .. **Garrett**, Candace C '01 %Delaware Cnty Pros -140 N Sandusky -3rd Fl -Delaware 43015

(937) 433-2744 .. **Garrett**, Dawn S '91 -770 Congress Park Dr -Dayton 45459 Fx:433-2748

(513) 421-8888 .. **Garrett**, Edward J Jr. '83 -1014 Vine -Ste 1630 -Cincinnati 45202

(216) 781-5470 .. **Garrett**, Glen H '95 %Ziegler M&M LLP -925 Euclid Av -2020 Huntngtn Bldg -Cleveland 44115 Fx:781-0714

(419) 259-9459 .. **Garrett**, Laura A '88 Lucas Metro Housing Auth -435 Nebraska -Bx477 -Toledo 43697

Garrett, Lowell L '65 -912 Wescott Ln NE -Atlanta, GA 30319

(419) 471-1488 .. **Garrett**, Stanley J '92 -5249 Secor Rd -Unit 4 -Toledo 43623 Fx:255-4513

(734) 847-8080 .. **Garrett**, William A '70 (Garrett CS&R) -9042 Lewis Av -Bx490 -Temperance, MI 48182 Fx:847-1500

(614) 248-5700 .. **Garrett**, William A '87 Bank One Corp -1111 Polaris Pkwy -Ste 4P -Columbus 43271

(513) 241-7406 .. **Garrigan**, Terrence M '87 -3300 Royal Pl -Cincinnati 45208

(202) 942-1815 .. **Garris**, Dennis O '92 US SEC-Corp Fin -450 5th NW -Washington, DC 20549

(330) 392-2533 .. **Garris**, Joshua M '01 C Wern Jr,Ltd -210 Scott NE -Bx151 -Warren 44482 Fx:395-4304

(937) 512-2349 .. **Garrison**, Connie Lee '92 Sinclair Cmmnty Coll -444 W 3rd -Rm 9315 -Dayton 45402

(740) 592-3247 .. **Garrison**, Gary L '87 Ohio Fourth Dist Ct of Appeals -Athens Cnty Cthse -Athens 45701

(513) 791-1672 .. **Garrison**, Harold K '93 -8549 Mntgmry Rd -Cincinnati 45236

(330) 655-5722 .. **Garrison**, James E '84 (Gardner & G) -72 N Main -Ste 309 -Hudson 44236

(740) 373-2414 .. **Garrison**, Jennifer D '87 -205 Grant Edwards Dr -Marietta 45750

(202) 326-3043 .. **Garrison**, Loretta H '88 FTC -600 Penn Av NW -Stop S-4429 -Washington, DC 20580

(614) 221-4000 .. **Garrison**, W Travis '03 %Chester W&S LLP -65 E State -10th Fl -Columbus 43215 Fx:221-4012

(216) 696-8730 .. **Garritano**, Carlos P '04 %Amin & T LLP -1900 E 9th -24th Fl Natl City Ctr -Cleveland 44114 Fx:696-8731

(216) 592-5000 .. **Garritano**, Frank O '04 %Tucker E&W LLP -925 Euclid Av -1150 Huntngtn Bldg -Cleveland 44115 Fx:592-5009

(614) 327-2068 .. **Garrity**, Colleen M '04 Sup Ct of OH -65 S Front -Columbus 43215

Garrity, Rory E '04 -(Address Unavailable)

(513) 946-3000 .. **Garry**, Bruce S '71 Hamilton Cnty Pros -230 E 9th -Cincinnati 45202 Fx:946-3017

(513) 684-0339 .. **Garry**, Patrick J '91 -1019 Main -Ste 100 -Cincinnati 45202

(513) 579-6400 .. **Garry**, Timothy A '61 SrCnsl Keating M&K PLL -1 E 4th -1400 Provident Twr -Cincinnati 45202 Fx:579-6457

(513) 852-6035 .. **Garry**, Timothy A Jr. '86 (Wood & L LLP) -600 Vine -Ste 2500 -Cincinnati 45202 Fx:852-6087

(513) 852-3497 .. **Garry**, Victoria D '86 Atty Gen -441 Vine -1600 Carew Twr -Cincinnati 45202 Fx:852-3484

(216) 432-1800 .. **Garson**, Brent D '83 Vendors Exchnge,Inc -8700 Brookpark Rd -Cleveland 44129

(216) 696-9330 .. **Garson**, Stuart I '76 (Garson & Assoc Co,LPA) -614 Superior Av W -1600 Rckfllr Bldg -Cleveland 44113 Fx:696-8558

(614) 442-6601 .. **Gartland**, Frank A '89 %OH Ins Guaranty Assoc -1840 Mackenzie Dr -Columbus 43220

(614) 464-6400 .. **Gartland**, Sheila Nolan '86 (Vorys SS&P LLP) -52 E Gay -Bx1008 -Columbus 43216 Fx:464-6350

(440) 884-6800 .. **Gartman**, Thomas N '76 -6358 Pearl Rd -Parma Heights 44130

Gartner, Leonard S '77 -5290 Muskopf Rd -Fairfield 45014

(330) 364-1477 .. **Gartrell**, John A '03 -237 W 2nd -Dover 44622

(330) 364-1477 .. **Gartrell**, John M '88 -237 W 2nd -Dover 44622

(216) 391-1112 .. **Garver**, Jonathan N '74 -4403 St Clair Av -Cleveland 44103

(419) 468-4933 .. **Garverick**, Debra A '83 -112 W Church -Galion 44833

(419) 468-5044 .. **Garverick**, Grant B '88 (Hottenroth GT&G Co,LPA) -126 S Market -Bx477 -Galion 44833 Fx:468-1308

(419) 468-5044 .. **Garverick**, Lowell B '59 (Hottenroth GT&G Co,LPA) -126 S Market -Bx477 -Galion 44833 Fx:468-1308

(513) 665-3500 .. **Garvey**, John J III '92 (Freund F&A) -105 E 4th -Ste 1400 -Cincinnati 45202 Fx:665-3503

(216) 522-3873 .. **Garvey**, Mary A '80 US Dept of Labor -1240 E 9th -Rm 881 -Cleveland 44199

(216) 579-1700 .. **Garvey**, Michael W '91 (Pearne & G LLP) -1801 E 9th -Ste 1200 -Cleveland 44114 Fx:579-6073

(614) 225-9000 .. **Garvin & Hickey,LLC** -181 E Lvngstn Av -Columbus 43215 Fx:225-9080

(513) 241-1950 .. **Garvin**, James R '95 Brown LH&E -7 W 7th -Ste 1950 -Cincinnati 45202 Fx:241-4095

(216) 621-0150 .. **Garvin**, Michael J '84 (Hahn L&P LLP) -3300 BP Twr/200 Pub Sq -Ste 3300 -Cleveland 44114 Fx:241-2824

(614) 225-9000 .. **Garvin**, Preston J '74 (Garvin & H,LLC) -181 E Lvngstn Av -Columbus 43215 Fx:225-9080

(614) 228-6885 .. **Garvine**, Brian M '97 %Lane A&H LLC -175 S 3rd -Ste 700 -Columbus 43215 Fx:228-0146

(419) 841-1440 .. **Garwood**, John A '69 Atlas Tours & Trvl Srvcs -3139 N Republic -Toledo 43615

(216) 443-6376 .. **Gary**, Christina M '01 %8th Dist Ct of Appls -1 Lakeside Av -#202 -Cleveland 44113 Fx:443-2044

(330) 492-8717 .. **Gary**, Denise A '98 %Buckingham D&B,LLP -4518 Fulton Dr NW -Bx35548 -Canton 44735 Fx:492-9625

(440) 244-4809 .. **Gary Naegele & Theado, LLC** -446 Bway -Lorain 44052 Fx:244-3462

(440) 244-4809 .. **Gary**, Robert D '66 (Gary N&T,LLC) -446 Bway -Lorain 44052 Fx:244-3462

(614) 227-2300 .. **Gaschen**, Dane A '94 %Bricker & E LLP -100 S 3rd -Columbus 43215 Fx:227-2390

(330) 721-0000 .. **Gashel Dillon**, Amanda M '98 %Walker & J,LPA -231 S Bway -Medina 44256 Fx:722-6446

(614) 586-1586 .. **Gasior**, Charles V '03 -1231 E Broad -Columbus 43206

(614) 470-8000 .. **Gasior**, Joel C '92 Cnsl BISYS -3435 Stelzer Rd -Columbus 43219

(440) 934-7676 .. **Gasior**, John A '84 Stringer S&G -36815 Detroit Rd -Avon 44011

(614) 225-8593 .. **Gaskill**, Charles R II '76 Motorists Mutual Ins Co -471 E Broad -Columbus 43215

(614) 526-2581 .. **Gaskill**, Regina M '02 CompManagement Inc -6377 Emerald Pkwy -Dublin 43016

(330) 384-1717 .. **Gasparovic**, John J '82 Roadway Corp -1077 Gorge Blvd -Bx471 -Akron 44309

(330) 387-2954 .. **Gasper**, Carol L '88 -7877 N Burton -Hudson 44236

(216) 771-1900 .. **Gasper**, Frank C '68 -700 W St Clair Av -Ste 100 -Cleveland 44113

(937) 496-3226 .. **Gasper**, Margaret Lee '75 Montgomery Cnty Juv Ct -303 W 2nd -Dayton 45402

(614) 462-4017 .. **Gass**, Dorothy T '95 10th Dist Ct of Appeals -375 S High -24th Fl -Columbus 43215

(513) 241-2540 .. **Gast**, David M '98 -632 Vine -Ste 415 -Cincinnati 45202

(239) 598-0559 .. **Gast**, John D '83 %SunTrust Bk -801 Laurel Oak Dr -3rd Fl -Naples, FL 34108

(614) 462-3118 .. **Gast**, Melissa Moriarty '03 Franklin Cnty Cmn Pleas Ct -375 S High -Columbus 43215 Fx:462-6292

(513) 621-1414 .. **Gast**, Stephen P '86 %Butkovich SS&G Co,LPA -36 E 7th -Ste 2600 -Cincinnati 45202 Fx:977-5580

(419) 627-5851 .. **Gast-King**, Lynne A '90 Sandusky Law Dept -222 Meigs -Sandusky 44870

(513) 984-3587 .. **Gatch**, Lewis G '61 (LG Gatch Co,LPA) -8050 Hosbrook Rd -Ste 210 -Cincinnati 45236

(859) 341-1881 .. **Gates**, Angela M '03 %Deters B&L,PSC -2701 Turkeyfoot Rd -207 Thomas More Pkwy -Crestview Hills, KY 41017 Fx:341-1469

(513) 352-6676 .. **Gates**, Joan M '00 %Thompson H LLP -312 Walnut -14th Fl -Cincinnati 45202 Fx:241-4771

(216) 586-3939 .. **Gates**, Lisa B '88 %Jones D -901 Lakeside Av -Cleveland 44114 Fx:579-0212

(216) 348-5400 .. **Gates**, Martin S '88 (McDonald H Co,LPA) -600 Superior Av E -Ste 2100 -Cleveland 44114 Fx:348-5474

(513) 732-7327 .. **Gates**, Penny Ann '84 Clermont Cnty Dom Rltns Ct -2340 Clermont Ctr Dr -Batavia 45103

(513) 887-3478 .. **Gates**, Roger S '79 Butler Cnty Pros -315 High -11th Fl -Bx515 -Hamilton 45012

(330) 722-9070 .. **Gates**, Susan P '98 City of Medina -132 N Elmwood -Medina 44256

(614) 466-2118 .. **Gates**, Timothy L '97 Unemploymnt Comp Commssn -145 S Front -Bx182299 -Columbus 43218

(317) 353-9363 .. **Gath**, Neil E '84 Fillenwarth DG&T -1213 N Arlngtn Av -Ste 204 -Indianapolis, IN 46219

(614) 895-2000 .. **Gatherum**, Kristin L '93 Century Insurance Grp -465 Cleveland Av -Westerville 43082

(859) 578-1000 .. **Gatherwright**, Jennifer May '02 %Horwitz Law Firm PSC -541 Buttermilk Pike -Ste 305 -Crescent Springs, KY 41017

(330) 484-3302 .. **Gatien**, John M '84 -7794 Angel Dr NW -North Canton 44720

Gatskie, James M '74 -587 S Firestone Blvd -Akron 44301

(614) 224-9241 .. **Gatterdam**, Katherine N '92 Columbus Coal & Lime Co -Bx23156 -Columbus 43223

(614) 464-2000 .. **Gatterdam**, Kort W '88 %Kravitz & K -145 E Rich -Columbus 43215 Fx:464-2002

(513) 737-8000 .. **Gattermeyer**, Daniel J '83 (Gattermeyer & M LLC) -2 S 3rd -Ste 570 -Hamilton 45011

(513) 737-8000 .. **Gattermeyer & McCracken LLC** -2 S 3rd -Ste 570 -Hamilton 45011

(216) 464-2568 .. **Gatto**, Gregory D '95 Key Bank NA -2101 Richmond Rd -Beachwood 44122

(330) 792-3423 .. **Gattozzi**, Lisa M '84 Industrial Commssn of OH -242 Fed Plz W -Ste 303 -Youngstown 44503

(216) 622-8200 .. **Gattozzi**, Lynn M '87 (Calfee H&G LLP) -800 Superior Av -Ste 1400 -Cleveland 44114 Fx:241-0816

(216) 830-6830 .. **Gattozzi**, Thomas A '94 (Brouse M) -1001 Lakeside Av -Ste 1600 -Cleveland 44114 Fx:830-6807

(330) 762-1309 .. **Gatts**, Ronald T '98 -137 S Main -Ste 206 -Akron 44308

(480) 557-1926 .. **Gauby**, Karl M '99 Apollo Group Inc -4615 E Elwood -Phoenix, AZ 85040

(202) 879-3880 .. **Gauch**, James E '89 (Jones D) -51 Louisiana Av NW -Washington, DC 20001 Fx:626-1700

(614) 224-0220 .. **Gauer**, Philip J '91 -338 S High -Ste 302 -Columbus 43215

(513) 247-0082 .. **Gaugh**, Thomas B '02 NLPA -11331 Grooms Rd -Ste 1000 -Cincinnati 45242 Fx:247-9580

(330) 884-6264 .. **Gaughan**, Patrick H '89 -241 Fed Plz W -Youngstown 44503

(614) 462-3555 .. **Gaugler**, Scott J '04 Franklin Cnty Pros -373 S High -Columbus 43215

(216) 771-4444 .. **Gaul**, Patricia A '93 Playhouse Sq Fndtn -1501 Euclid Av -Ste 200 -Cleveland 44115

(513) 521-5344 .. **Gaulding**, Jerry M '88 -9604 Leebrook Dr -Cincinnati 45231

(330) 376-2700 .. **Gaum**, Karen D '01 %Roetzel & A,LPA -222 S Main -Akron 44308 Fx:376-4577

(330) 864-5550 .. **Gaum**, R Eric '96 (Hahn L&P LLP) -One GOJO Plz -Ste 300 -Akron 44311 Fx:864-7986

(513) 579-6400 .. **Gaunt**, Karen E '97 (Keating M&K PLL) -1 E 4th -1400 Provident Twr -Cincinnati 45202 Fx:579-6457

Gauntner, David M '04 -(Address Unavailable)

(216) 221-8474 .. **Gauntner**, Timothy J '70 T Gauntner Co,LPA -14701 Detroit Av -#757 -Lakewood 44107

(216) 443-8560 .. **Gauntner**, Timothy M '04 Cuyahoga Cnty Ct Cmmn Pleas -1200 Ontario -Justice Ctr 11th Fl -Cleveland 44113

(440) 329-5389 .. **Gauthier**, Peter J '91 Lorain Cnty Pros -225 Court -3rd Fl -Elyria 44035

(856) 482-9303 .. **Gavin**, James C '78 (Gavin & G) -1930 E Marlton Pk -Bldg Q -Cherry Hill, NJ 08003

(513) 629-1470 .. **Gavin**, Kevin K '95 Wstrn & Sthrn Life Ins -400 Bway -Cincinnati 45202

(216) 523-1500 .. **Gavin**, Michael T '55 (Mansour GG&M Co,LPA) -55 Pub Sq -Ste 2150 -Cleveland 44113 Fx:523-1705

(614) 232-3224 .. **Gavin**, Robert P '99 NBBJ,East Ltd Prtnrshp -1555 Lk Shr Dr -Columbus 43204

(440) 533-7585 .. **Gawell**, Lawrence E '75 Grtr Clvlnd Reg Trnst Auth -Bx360644 -Strongsville 44136

(216) 566-5908 .. **Gawlik**, Gregory J '00 %Thompson H LLP -127 Pub Sq -3900 Key Ctr -Cleveland 44114 Fx:566-5800

(216) 429-9493 .. **Gay**, James A '79 -3324 ML King Jr Dr -Cleveland 44104

(513) 852-8203 .. **Gay**, Michael L '77 Cors & B LLC -537 E Pete Rose Way -Ste 400 -Cincinnati 45202

(304) 258-1966 .. **Gay**, Richard G '74 -202 Congress -Berkeley Springs, WV 25411

(513) 287-6900 .. **Gay**, Steven F '82 (Marlow & G Co,LPA) -600 Vine -Ste 1810 -Cincinnati 45202 **Fx:**287-6903

(614) 792-5555 .. **Gayan**, Eric M '98 %Standley Law Grp LLP -495 Metro Pl S -Ste 210 -Dublin 43017 **Fx:**792-5536

(330) 745-1611 .. **Gayetsky-Ghadiri**, Marie T '91 Barberton Citizens Hosp -155 5th NE -Barberton 44203

Gaylord, Martha B '03 -5478 Uppr Mtn Rd -Lockport, NY 14094

(216) 696-3311 .. **Gaynor**, Bruce E '72 (Kahn K) -1301 E 9th -2600 Erievw Twr -Cleveland 44114 **Fx:**623-4912

(419) 885-3000 .. **Gaynor**, Christine M '96 %Brady C&S LLP -4052 Holland-Sylvania Rd -Toledo 43623 **Fx:**885-1120

(440) 442-9630 .. **Gaynor**, Donald A '50 -5150 Three Vllg Dr -Cleveland 44124

(440) 243-5000 .. **Gaynor**, Norman J III '74 Zahnow Cnsldtd,Inc -16900 Bagley Rd -Middleburg Heights 44130

(513) 412-2852 .. **Gaynor**, William T Jr. '99 Great American Life Ins Co -525 Vine -7th Fl -Cincinnati 45202

(614) 560-6279 .. **Gayton**, Charles W '72 -149 Piedmont Rd -Columbus 43214

(513) 977-5682 .. **Gazaway**, Joy E '95 Cincinnati Metro Housing Auth -16 W Cntrl Pkwy -Cincinnati 45210

(330) 702-0780 .. **Gazda**, Melody D '90 %Luckhart MZ&R -3810 Starrs Centre Dr -Canfield 44406

Gazivoda, Jelena '90 -2700 Fairfax Dr -#1 -Upper Arlington 43220

(440) 548-2312 .. **Gazley**, Lucinda '87 -16064 Tvrn Rd -Burton 44021

(330) 385-7702 .. **Gbur**, George A '94 -Bx2733 -East Liverpool 43920

(513) 381-2838 .. **Gearding**, Monica L '98 %Taft S&H LLP -425 Walnut -Ste 1800 -Cincinnati 45202 **Fx:**381-0205

(614) 249-2400 .. **Gearhardt**, Larry R '79 OH Farm Bureau Fed -2 Nationwide Plz -Bx182383 -Columbus 43218

(937) 339-0511 .. **Gearhardt**, Michelle J '80 (Dungan & L Co,LPA) -210 W Main -Troy 45373 **Fx:**335-5802

(312) 853-7000 .. **Gearhart**, Kurt '03 %Sidley AB&W,LLP -10 S Dearborn -Bank One Plz -Chicago, IL 60603 **Fx:**853-7036

(419) 421-2386 .. **Gearheart**, James W '03 Marathon Ashland Petro LLC -539 S Main -Findlay 45840 **Fx:**421-8402

(614) 221-5151 .. **Gearhiser**, Kurt O '83 Fawley & Assoc -520 E Rich -Columbus 43215 **Fx:**221-1778

(330) 376-4558 .. **Gearinger**, Bradford M '69 (Scanlon & G Co,LPA) -50 S Main -Ste 1200 -Akron 44308 **Fx:**376-3550

(513) 583-9221 .. **Geary**, Brett A '96 Clemans Nelson & Assoc -411 W Loveland Av -Ste 101 -Loveland 45140

(614) 692-1084 .. **Geary**, Matthew O '91 Defense Supply Ctr -3990 E Broad -Columbus 43213

(440) 576-3831 .. **Geary**, Michael P '89 (McNair & G Co,LPA) -35 W Jffrsn -Jefferson 44047 **Fx:**576-7167

(614) 227-2330 .. **Geary**, Susan E '89 (Bricker & E LLP) -100 S 3rd -Columbus 43215 **Fx:**227-2390

(614) 228-1968 .. **Geary**, William L '79 -155 W Main -Ste 101 -Columbus 43215 **Fx:**228-7630

(502) 573-2044 .. **Gebhardt**, Leigh A '95 Dept of Juvenile Justice -1025 Cptl Ctr Dr -Frankfort, KY 40601

(513) 221-1900 .. **Gebhart**, David E '61 -264 Ludlow Av -Cincinnati 45220

(330) 722-7171 .. **Gechter**, Maureen F '89 -5840 Deervw Ln -Medina 44256

(918) 661-7229 .. **Geczik**, Thomas F '93 Phillips Petroleum -790A Plz Ofc Bldg -Bartlesville, OK 74004

(440) 333-9001 .. **Gedeon**, Carol R '84 -19443 Lorain Rd -Fairview Park 44126

(216) 443-8979 .. **Gedeon**, Richard L '85 Cuyahoga Cnty Probate Ct -1 Lakeside Av -Cleveland 44113

Gedeon, Scott W '04 -(Address Unavailable)

(513) 868-7600 .. **Gedling**, James L '80 Holbrock & J Co,LPA -315 S Monument Av -Bx687 -Hamilton 45012 **Fx:**868-0909

(216) 861-1424 .. **Gedos**, Anthony A '73 -815 Superior Av NE -Ste 2010 -Cleveland 44114

(330) 723-4947 .. **Gedrock**, David V '80 -209 S Bway -Medina 44256

(937) 332-6836 .. **Gee**, Christopher M '78 Miami Cnty Probate Ct -201 W Main -Troy 45373

(513) 489-8787 .. **Gee**, John M '75 -11814 Tennyson Dr -Cincinnati 45241

(859) 291-4411 .. **Gee**, Judith T '82 -533 Pike -Ste 204 -Covington, KY 41011

(216) 621-1000 .. **Gee**, Kathleen E '02 %Moscarino & T,LLP -1422 Euclid Av -Hanna Bldg Ste 630 -Cleveland 44115 **Fx:**622-1556

(513) 241-6748 .. **Gee**, Rebecca C '03 %A Levine -324 Reading Rd -Cincinnati 45202

(614) 228-2678 .. **Geer**, Christopher J '78 (Matan G&W) -261 S Front -Columbus 43215

(724) 652-0511 .. **Geer**, Louise A '82 Geer & H,PC -2100 Wilmngtn Rd -New Castle, PA 16105

(419) 352-5164 .. **Geer**, Norman J '71 (Halleck & G) -105 N Main -Bowling Green 43402 **Fx:**352-6645

(513) 946-3000 .. **Geers**, Ronald M '97 Hamilton Cnty Pros -230 E 9th -Cincinnati 45202 **Fx:**946-3017

(216) 566-5666 .. **Geffert**, Alexandra J '03 %Thompson H LLP -127 Pub Sq -3900 Key Ctr -Cleveland 44114 **Fx:**566-5800

(216) 525-1998 .. **Geffert**, John J '01 Century Business Srvcs Inc -6050 Oak Tree Blvd -#500 -Cleveland 44131

(614) 424-4293 .. **Gegenheimer**, Charles M Jr. '85 Battelle Memorial Inst -505 King Av -Columbus 43201

(330) 761-7709 .. **Gegick**, Erik P '99 FirstEnergy Corp -76 S Main -Akron 44308

(440) 277-8146 .. **Gehlmann**, Donald E '60 -1860 E 34th -Lorain 44055

(202) 464-4300 .. **Gehlmann**, Gregory A '88 Cnsl Manatt P&P -1501 M NW -Ste 700 -Washington, DC 20005

(513) 737-4347 .. **Gehr**, Daniel W '98 -1400 Eaton Av -Hamilton 45013 **Fx:**863-5552

(937) 333-4460 .. **Gehres**, Daniel G '78 Mun Ct Judge -301 W 3rd -Dayton 45402

(419) 238-2057 .. **Gehres**, Stephen P '76 -316 W Main -Van Wert 45891

(937) 225-4892 .. **Gehres**, Virginia P '78 Montgomery Cnty Pros/CSEA -14 W 4th -Ste 510 -Dayton 45402

(513) 421-9010 .. **Gehrig**, Michael F '74 -36 E 4th -Ste 1140 -Cincinnati 45202

(419) 531-0507 .. **Gehring**, Edwin F '78 -5360 Dubois -Dublin 43615

(216) 241-2838 .. **Gehring**, Ronn J '03 %Taft S&H LLP -200 Pub Sq -3500 BP Twr -Cleveland 44114 **Fx:**241-3707

Gehrlein, Jennifer Girard '97 -(Address Unavailable)

(216) 592-5000 .. **Geib**, Richard P '95 %Tucker E&W LLP -925 Euclid Av -1150 Huntngtn Bldg -Cleveland 44115 **Fx:**592-5009

(704) 423-7086 .. **Geib**, Sally L '90 SrCnsl Goodrich Corp -2730 W Tyvola Rd -Charlotte, NC 28217

(937) 223-5200 .. **Geidner**, Charles F '73 (Flanagan LH&S) -318 W 4th -Dayton 45402 **Fx:**223-3335

(904) 366-4243 .. **Geiersbach**, Rachel E '80 CSX Corp -500 Water -J-160 -Jacksonville, FL 32202

Geiersbach, Ronald P '77 -1425 Burgandy Trl -Jacksonville, FL 32259

(419) 221-5183 .. **Geiger**, Anthony L '83 -209 N Main -6th Fl -Lima 45801

(614) 841-1000 .. **Geiger**, Franz A '91 NP Ltd Prtnrshp -8800 Lyra Dr -Ste 550 -Columbus 43240

(614) 716-3305 .. **Geiger**, Heather L '93 Amer Elec Pwr Co -1 Riverside Plz -Columbus 43215

(513) 621-6464 .. **Geiger**, Lee P '00 %Graydon H&R LLP -511 Walnut -1900 Fifth Third Ctr -Cincinnati 45202 **Fx:**651-3836

(419) 334-6211 .. **Geiger**, Michael R '72 Sandusky Cnty Probate/Juv Ct -100 N Park Av -Fremont 43420

(216) 586-3939 .. **Geiger**, Richard S '99 Jones D -901 Lakeside Av -Cleveland 44114 **Fx:**579-0212

(330) 821-1430 .. **Geiger Teeple Smith & Hahn** -1844 W State -Ste A -Alliance 44601 **Fx:**821-2217

(440) 816-1035 .. **Geiger**, Warren P '60 -18600 Main -Middleburg Heights 44130 **Fx:**816-0010

(513) 352-3338 .. **Geiler**, Geri H '89 Law Dept -801 Plum -Rm 214 -Cincinnati 45202 **Fx:**352-1515

(330) 834-2709 .. **Geis**, Raymond M '04 OH Dept of Youth Srvcs -Bx564 -Massillon 44648

(937) 492-6191 .. **Geise**, Steven J '94 %Elsass WES&Co -100 S Main Av -Ste 102 -Bx499 -Sidney 45365 **Fx:**492-0876

(216) 586-3939 .. **Geise**, Steven N '96 (Jones D) -901 Lakeside Av -Cleveland 44114 **Fx:**579-0212

(937) 836-8639 .. **Geisenfeld**, James R '64 -440 S Main -Bx40 -Englewood 45322

(513) 946-3000 .. **Geiser**, Edward J '89 Hamilton Cnty Pros -230 E 9th -Cincinnati 45202 **Fx:**946-3017

(330) 305-6400 .. **Geiser**, Julie A '94 %Pelini & F,Ltd -8040 Cleveland Av NW -Ste 400 -North Canton 44720 **Fx:**305-0042

(614) 221-1166 .. **Geiser**, Michael K '91 (Plymale & Assoc) -495 S High -Ste 400 -Columbus 43215 **Fx:**221-6633

(937) 335-7963 .. **Geisinger**, Bruce '66 -1619 Monroe-Concord Rd -Troy 45373

(330) 373-3316 .. **Geisler**, Brian T '03 Delphi Auto -North Rvr Rd -Larchmont Eng & Rsrch Bldg -Warren 44486

(440) 247-0003 .. **Geisse**, Timothy F '84 (Turner & G LLC) -100 N Main -Ste 350 -Chagrin Falls 44022 **Fx:**247-8903

(717) 849-4723 .. **Geitner**, Christopher W '89 Dentsply Intl Inc -570 W Cllg Av -York, PA 17405

(216) 781-9499 .. **Gelbman**, Alan G '64 -310 W Lakeside Av -Ste 550 -Cleveland 44113

(513) 870-2206 .. **Gelfand**, Eugene M '71 Cnsl Cincinnati Fin Corp -Bx145496 -Cincinnati 45250

(216) 228-8850 .. **Gelfand**, Martin D '97 Rep D Kucinich -14400 Detroit Av -Lakewood 44107

(513) 621-3440 .. **Gelhaus**, Emily J '03 %Denlinger R&G Co,LPA -425 Walnut -Ste 2310 -Cincinnati 45202 **Fx:**621-4449

(513) 762-4426 .. **Gellenbeck**, Lynne '77 Kroger Co-Law Dept -1014 Vine -9th Fl -Cincinnati 45202

(419) 255-5917 .. **Geller**, Paul L '71 (Scalzo & G) -520 Mad Av -Ste 434 -Toledo 43604 **Fx:**255-2030

(703) 433-4519 .. **Geller**, Shannon P '92 Nextel -Leg Dept -2001 Edmund Halley Dr -Reston, VA 20191

(304) 242-2900 .. **Gellner**, Gregory A '88 -1440 Natl Rd -Wheeling, WV 26003

(513) 381-9200 .. **Gelwicks**, Joseph W '76 (Rendigs FK&D,LLP) -One W 4th -Ste 900 -Cincinnati 45202 **Fx:**381-9206

(513) 421-6688 .. **Gelwicks**, Thomas A '82 -10945 Reed Hartman Hwy -Ste 212 -Cincinnati 45242

(440) 328-2207 .. **Gemelas**, James S '97 Lorain Cnty Cmmn Pleas Ct -225 Court -Elyria 44035

(330) 726-3736 .. **Gemma**, Anthony N '76 (Gemma & G) -1040 S Cmmns Pl -Ste 200 -Poland 44514

(330) 726-3736 .. **Gemma**, William A '46 (Gemma & G) -4636 New Eng Blvd -Boardman 44512

(612) 671-6870 .. **Gemmato**, Anthony J Jr. '87 Amer Exp Fin Advsrs -626 AXP Fncl Ctr -Minneapolis, MN 55474

(216) 750-4511 .. **Gemperline**, Richard B '80 Nationwide Ins Co -8200 Sweet Valley Dr -Valley View 44125

(813) 228-7411 .. **Gemunder**, David A '94 (Fowler WBB) -501 E Knndy Blvd -Ste 1700 -Bx1438 -Tampa, FL 33601 **Fx:**229-8313

(330) 972-6939 .. **Genetin**, Bernadette B '88 Univ of Akron Law Schl -LAW 303 -Akron 44325

(330) 451-8175 .. **Genetin**, Judee L '79 Stark Cnty Dept Job & Family Srvcs -220 E Tuscarawas -Canton 44702

(216) 831-0042 .. **Geneva**, Fount S '00 Meyers RF&L LPA -28601 Chagrin Blvd -Ste 500 -Cleveland 44122 **Fx:**831-0542

(216) 687-2346 .. **Geneva**, Louis B '73 CSU-Marshall Cllg of Law -2121 Euclid Av -LB138 -Cleveland 44115 **Fx:**687-6881

Gengler, Brenda J '02 -4050 N High -#30 -Columbus 43214

(970) 544-4628 .. **Genshaft**, Benjamin S '02 %Otten JRN&R,PC -420 E Main -Ste 210 -Aspen, CO 81611 **Fx:**544-4632

(614) 228-6345 .. **Genshaft**, Nelson E '73 Strip HLM&T Co LPA -575 S 3rd -Columbus 43215 **Fx:**228-6369

(614) 462-7648 .. **Genshock**, Lauren R '03 Franklin Cnty Ct of Common Pleas -369 S High -Ctrm 8D -Columbus 43202 **Fx:**462-2464

(330) 399-8801 .. **Gensler**, Robert L Jr. '02 %Turner M&S -185 High NE -Warren 44481 **Fx:**399-8805

(330) 376-1242 .. **Gentilcore**, Laura J '86 %Renner KGBT&W,LPA -106 S Main -4th Fl First Natl Twr -Akron 44308 **Fx:**376-9646

Gentile, Anthony M Jr. '80 -32349 S Woodlnd Rd -Cleveland 44124

(937) 224-5300 .. **Gentile**, Diane L '86 Cooper & G Co,LPA -118 W 1st -Ste 850 -Dayton 45402

(614) 431-1500 .. **Gentile**, Elisabeth D '96 %Perez & M LLC -8000 Ravines Edge Ct -Ste 300 -Columbus 43235 **Fx:**431-3885

(330) 746-5000 .. **Gentile**, James S '76 -44 Fed Plz Central -Ste 200A -Youngstown 44503

(440) 933-3231 .. **Gentile**, Leslie A '96 Smith & S Co,LPA -110 Moore Rd -Bx210 -Avon Lake 44012

(216) 875-3050 .. **Gentile**, Matthew D '04 %PricewaterhouseCoopers -200 Pub Sq -27th Fl BP Twr -Cleveland 44114

(614) 466-4328 .. **Gentile**, Mitchell L '81 Atty Gen -150 E Gay -Columbus 43215 **Fx**:995-0266

(740) 353-2187 .. **Gentner**, Susan Smith '01 Workers Comp -1005 4th -Bx1307 -Portsmouth 45662

(937) 222-2333 .. **Gentry**, Boyd W '99 %Surdyk D&T Co,LPA -40 N Main -1610 Kettering Twr -Dayton 45423 **Fx**:222-1970

(937) 449-6810 .. **Gentry**, Caroline H '96 %Porter WM&A LLP -1 S Main -Ste 1600 -Dayton 45402 **Fx**:449-6820

(937) 766-2020 .. **Gentry**, Daniel J '95 Applied Sciences, Inc -141 W Xenia Av -Cedarville 45314

(216) 221-0400 .. **Gentry**, Eldred A Jr. '59 (Gentry & G Co,LPA) -14701 Detroit Av -575 INA Bldg -Cleveland 44107

(216) 221-0400 .. **Gentry**, James E '78 (Gentry & G Co,LPA) -14701 Detroit Av -575 INA Bldg -Cleveland 44107

     Gentry, Stephen M '75 -55 S State Av -Indianapolis, IN 46201

(614) 799-1040 .. **Gentry**, Steven G '82 (SG Gentry,Ltd) -220 W Brdg -Dublin 43017

     Gentry, Vanessa L '82 -726 Burns Av -Wyoming 45215

(419) 663-5554 .. **Gentzel**, Robert W '78 -32 Benedict Av -Norwalk 44857

(513) 621-0267 .. **Geoppinger**, Jean M '90 Waite SB&C -1 W 4th -1513 4th & Vine Twr -Cincinnati 45202

(513) 762-6200 .. **Geoppinger**, Jeffrey D '01 %Ulmer & B LLP -600 Vine -Ste 2800 -Cincinnati 45202 **Fx**:762-6245

(216) 361-2273 .. **George**, Allen '73 A George & Assoc -1783 E 63rd -Cleveland 44103

(513) 932-3221 .. **George**, Andrew P '99 1st Natl Bank -730 E Main -Lebanon 45036

(248) 312-2800 .. **George**, Christopher R '99 %Vandeveer G,PC -1450 W Long Lk Rd -Ste 100 -Troy, MI 48098

(440) 322-4548 .. **George**, David C '56 -105 Court -Rm 715 -Elyria 44035

(513) 762-4538 .. **George**, Denis E '85 Kroger Co -1014 Vine -Cincinnati 45202

(614) 337-9000 .. **George**, Gary J Jr. '95 Autoville USA,Inc -3200 Morse Rd -Columbus 43231

(216) 861-4533 .. **George**, Gene B '74 (Ray RC&D PLL) -1717 E 9th -Cleveland 44114 **Fx**:861-4568

(216) 443-7800 .. **George**, George M '87 Cuyahoga Cnty Pros -1200 Ontario -8th Fl -Cleveland 44113 **Fx**:698-2270

(614) 224-5205 .. **George**, Jason L '98 %Peck S&W,LLP -175 S 3rd -Ste 600 -Columbus 43215 **Fx**:224-0069

(724) 658-8535 .. **George**, Joseph A '97 (Luxenberg, GK&G,PC) -315 N Mercer -New Castle, PA 16101

(330) 666-2226 .. **George**, Joyce J '66 -3597 Sparrow Pond Cir -Akron 44333

(850) 595-8057 .. **George**, Katie '87 %DCF -160 Gvrnmntl Ctr -601 -Pensacola, FL 32501 **Fx**:595-8232

(614) 466-7014 .. **George**, Lewis C '89 Pub Safety -1970 W Broad -Columbus 43223 **Fx**:752-6063

(216) 524-7100 .. **George**, Mark M '88 -5005 Rockside Rd -Ste 100 -Cleveland 44131

(440) 953-9180 .. **George**, Mark W '82 -35325 Vine -Eastlake 44095

(330) 535-9655 .. **George**, Michael E '91 (Lombardi G&J,Ltd) -7 W Bowery -Ste 507 -Akron 44308

(330) 376-3300 .. **George**, Michael E '95 %Stark & K Co,LPA -76 S Main -Ste 1512 -Akron 44308 **Fx**:376-6237

(614) 846-2001 .. **George**, Michael F '74 (M George Co,LPA) -575 Copeland Mill Rd -Ste 1B -Westerville 43081 **Fx**:(440) 895-7842

(330) 376-5300 .. **George**, Nicholas D '70 (Buckingham D&B,LLP) -50 S Main -Bx1500 -Akron 44309 **Fx**:258-6559

(419) 241-3213 .. **George**, Shannon J '97 Ritter RM&J -405 Mad Av -Ste 1850 -Toledo 43604 **Fx**:241-4925

(216) 348-5400 .. **George**, Susan Fenwick '04 %McDonald H Co,LPA -600 Superior Av E -Ste 2100 -Cleveland 44114 **Fx**:348-5474

(419) 247-2500 .. **George**, Thomas M '75 (Fuller & H,Ltd) -One SeaGate -Ste 1700 -Bx2088 -Toledo 43603 **Fx**:247-2665

(330) 652-8000 .. **George**, Timothy F '86 (Buckley & G Co,LPA) -5704 Youngstown-Warren Rd -Niles 44446

(216) 241-4100 .. **George**, Warren S '89 (Keis/G LLP) -55 Pub Sq -Ste 800 -Cleveland 44113 **Fx**:771-3111

(216) 575-7575 .. **Georgeadis**, Philip N '70 (Kolick G&E Co,LPA) -55 Pub Sq -1350 Illuminating Bldg -Cleveland 44113

(614) 337-2785 .. **Georgeff**, George C '82 -107 Granvll -Columbus 43230

     Georges, Samuel J '76 -2227 Cortina Cir -Escondido, CA 92029

(330) 456-8171 .. **Georges**, William H '69 (WH Georges Co,LPA) -Bx20407 -Canton 44701

(330) 373-1312 .. **Georgiadis**, Michael '82 -135 Pine Av -Ste 211 -Warren 44481

(513) 977-8200 .. **Georgiton**, Peter J '02 %Dinsmore & S LLP -255 E 5th -Ste 1900 -Cincinnati 45202 **Fx**:977-8141

(513) 336-2546 .. **Gephardt**, Stephanie M '88 Cnsl Anthem BCBS -4361 Irwin Simpson Rd -MBI-220 -Mason 45040

(513) 595-2200 .. **Gephart**, John F '79 Union Central Life Ins Co -Bx40888 -Cincinnati 45240

(513) 929-3400 .. **Geppert**, Eric J '98 (Baker & H LLP) -312 Walnut -Ste 3200 -Cincinnati 45202 **Fx**:929-0303

(419) 241-4900 .. **Gerace**, Ryan J '03 %Rauser & Assoc -316 N Mich -Ste 420 -Toledo 43624

(216) 771-2680 .. **Geraci & LaPerna Co, LPA** -1370 Ontario -Ste 1220 -Cleveland 44113

(216) 771-2680 .. **Geraci**, Rudolph J '62 (Geraci & L Co,LPA) -1370 Ontario -Ste 1220 -Cleveland 44113

(202) 767-5297 .. **Geraci**, Thomas A '69 Cnsl USAF -20 MacDill Blvd -Ste 300 -Bolling AFB, DC 20332 **Fx**:404-6763

(216) 623-0150 .. **Geraci**, Victor T '88 (Roetzel & A,LPA) -1375 E 9th -One Cleve Ctr 9th Fl -Cleveland 44114 **Fx**:623-0134

(614) 462-3555 .. **Geraghty**, Elizabeth A '00 Franklin Cnty Pros -373 S High -Columbus 43215

(216) 479-6100 .. **Gerak**, John '02 %Vorys SS&P LLP -1375 E 9th -Ste 2100 One Cleve Ctr -Cleveland 44114 **Fx**:479-6060

(740) 351-0499 .. **Gerard**, Christopher C '00 -500 Chillicothe -Ste 206 -Portsmouth 45662

(404) 464-2517 .. **Gerber**, Brian H '78 Army-HQ Forscom-OSJA -1301 Andrsn Way SW -Fort McPherson, GA 30330

(760) 380-2338 .. **Gerber**, Jason M '02 US Army -OSJA -Fort Irwin, CA 92310

(614) 221-5216 .. **Gerber**, Richard S '84 %Wiles BB&B Co,LPA -300 Spruce -1st Fl -Columbus 43215 **Fx**:221-5692

(216) 586-3939 .. **Gerber**, Susan M '99 %Jones D -901 Lakeside Av -Cleveland 44114 **Fx**:579-0212

(330) 375-7515 .. **Gerberry**, Robert A '97 Summa Health Sys -252 E Market -Akron 44304

(216) 586-3939 .. **Gerbick**, Amy E '02 %Jones D -901 Lakeside Av -Cleveland 44114 **Fx**:579-0212

(216) 676-7590 .. **Gerbino**, Perry L '76 Ford Motor Co -Bx9900 -Brook Park 44142

(419) 826-4866 .. **Gerbitz**, Clayton M '92 %TE Hallett -113 W Airport Hwy -Bx208 -Swanton 43558

(313) 965-7407 .. **Gerbitz**, Sara Mae '87 (Kitch DWD&V,PC) -One Woodward Av -10th FL -Detroit, MI 48226 **Fx**:965-7403

(937) 885-7272 .. **Gerbs**, Barbara L '85 PC Solutions -9090 N State Route 48 -#B -Centerville 45458

(303) 825-2700 .. **Gerbus**, David W '83 %Kennedy & C,PC -1050 17th -Ste 2500 -Denver, CO 80265 **Fx**:825-0434

(330) 726-3711 .. **Gerchak**, David J '98 -837 Boardman-Canfld Rd -Boardman 44512

(312) 353-8380 .. **Geren**, James B '98 SSA Ofc of Gen Cnsl -200 W Adams -30th Fl -Chicago, IL 60606 **Fx**:353-5876

(216) 586-0964 .. **Gerfen**, Chance N '02 -901 Lakeside Av -%Jones Day -Cleveland 44114 **Fx**:579-0212

(513) 621-9100 .. **Gerhardstein**, Alphonse A '76 (Laufman & G) -617 Vine -1409 Enquirer Bldg -Cincinnati 45202

(614) 461-4455 .. **Gerhardstein**, Walter J Jr. '73 (Cloppert LS&W) -225 E Broad -Columbus 43215 **Fx**:461-0072

(937) 224-7200 .. **Gerhardt**, Cassandra S '99 %Horenstein N&B -124 E 3rd -5th Fl -Dayton 45402 **Fx**:224-3353

(513) 579-6948 .. **Gerhardt**, Charles H III '86 KMK Consulting Co -One E 4th -1400 Provident Twr -Cincinnati 45202

(419) 524-5568 .. **Gerhardt**, Dan E '87 (Knell D&G Co,LPA) -3 N Main -Ste 602 -Mansfield 44902 **Fx**:524-8011

(614) 570-9949 .. **Gerhardt**, Richard L II '97 -2524 Andvr Rd -Columbus 43221 **Fx**:481-3241

(740) 474-7575 .. **Gerhardt**, Richard L '66 -143 W Franklin -Circleville 43113

(216) 295-9394 .. **Gerhart**, Ann T '72 -14400 Shaker Blvd -Shaker Heights 44120

(412) 298-5804 .. **Gerhold**, Wayne D '96 -One Gtwy Ctr -18th flr West -Pittsburgh, PA 15222 **Fx**:422-0308

(740) 593-3800 .. **Gerig**, Christian S '96 (Gerig & G) -3 W Stimson Av -Athens 45701

(740) 593-3800 .. **Gerig**, Paul J '68 (Gerig & G) -3 W Stimson Av -Athens 45701

(330) 399-3555 .. **Gerin**, Daniel N '78 -144 N Park Av -Ste 200 -Warren 44481

(216) 443-2059 .. **Gerity**, Eileen T '89 Cuyahoga Cnty Dom Rltns Ct -1 Lakeside Av -Cleveland 44113

(740) 385-2153 .. **Gerken**, Charles A '77 -59 E 2nd -Logan 43138

(419) 243-5552 .. **Gerken**, George E '97 -412 14th -Toledo 43624

(419) 861-7800 .. **Gerken**, Mandy M '04 %Bahret & Assoc Co,LPA -7050 Spring Meadow W Dr -Holland 43528

(440) 994-6012 .. **Gerken**, Philip D '79 Ashtabula Cnty Cmmn Pleas Ct -25 W Jffrsn -Jefferson 44047

(513) 891-8940 .. **Gerla**, Barbara Ullman '80 -9574 Heather Ct -Bx429111 -Cincinnati 45242 **Fx**:791-6246

(937) 229-3442 .. **Gerla**, Harry S '76 Univ of Dayton Schl of Law -300 Cllg Park -Dayton 45469

(513) 977-8200 .. **Gerlach**, Benjamin J '04 %Dinsmore & S LLP -255 E 5th -Ste 1900 -Cincinnati 45202 **Fx**:977-8141

(740) 354-7755 .. **Gerlach**, Cynthia K '85 Gerlach & G -814 17th -Portsmouth 45662 **Fx**:354-6496

(740) 354-7755 .. **Gerlach**, Franklin T '61 Gerlach & G -814 17th -Portsmouth 45662 **Fx**:354-6496

(740) 354-7755 .. **Gerlach & Gerlach** -814 17th -Portsmouth 45662 **Fx**:354-6496

(740) 354-7755 .. **Gerlach**, Valarie K '87 %Gerlach & G -814 17th -Portsmouth 45662 **Fx**:354-6496

(216) 523-1500 .. **Gerlack**, Julius R '62 (Mansour GG&M Co,LPA) -55 Pub Sq -Ste 2150 -Cleveland 44113 **Fx**:523-1705

(440) 395-3685 .. **Gerlack**, Robert J '94 Progressive Ins Co -6300 Wilson Mills Rd -#N72A -Mayfield Village 44143

(216) 241-4100 .. **Gerlack-George**, Lisa M '89 %Keis/G LLP -55 Pub Sq -Ste 800 -Cleveland 44113 **Fx**:771-3111

(614) 228-6885 .. **Gerling**, Joseph A '77 (Lane A&H LLC) -175 S 3rd -Ste 700 -Columbus 43215 **Fx**:228-0146

(513) 352-6527 .. **Germain**, Kenneth W '78 (Thompson H LLP) -312 Walnut -14th Fl -Cincinnati 45202 **Fx**:241-4771

(419) 537-1954 .. **German**, Bethany L '04 %Kalniz I&F,LPA -5550 W Central Av -Toledo 43615 **Fx**:535-7732

(937) 299-3576 .. **German**, Regina D '85 -112 Wisteria Dr -Dayton 45419

(314) 525-9264 .. **Germani**, Philip J '91 MetLife -13045 Tesson Ferry Rd -Saint Louis, MO 63128

(330) 753-1051 .. **Germano**, Jacqueline J '82 Germano R&C Co,LPA -2715 Mnchstr Rd -Akron 44319

(440) 942-6262 .. **Germano**, Michael P '88 (Wiles & R) -35350 Curtis Blvd -Ste 530 -Eastlake 44095 **Fx**:942-7211

(330) 753-1051 .. **Germano Rondy & Ciccolini Co,LPA** -2715 Mnchstr Rd -Akron 44319

(513) 241-7722 .. **Gerner**, David E '83 (Gerner & K Co,LPA) -215 W 9th -Cincinnati 45202

(419) 562-4075 .. **Gernert**, Terry L '79 (Kennedy PH&G) -111 Rensselaer -Bx191 -Bucyrus 44820 **Fx**:562-7850

(330) 762-7377 .. **Gerney**, Blake R '95 (Oldham & D) -195 S Main -Ste 300 -Akron 44308 **Fx**:762-7390

(419) 244-5831 .. **Gernot**, George III '74 -520 Mad Av -545 Spitzer Bldg -Toledo 43604

(440) 461-9661 .. **Gerred**, Michelle M '01 NCS -729 Miner Rd -Cleveland 44143 **Fx**:461-6252

(614) 224-8824 .. **Gerrity**, Timothy D '70 (Gerrity & B Ltd) -400 S 5th -Ste 302 -Columbus 43215 **Fx**:224-3810

(214) 777-4258 .. **Gerson**, Darlene R '86 Kane RC&L,PC -1601 Elm -Dallas, TX 75201

(970) 925-5278 .. **Gerson**, Elaine M '00 %Goldberg S&G,LLC -434 Cooper Av -Aspen, CO 81601

(330) 746-1712 .. **Gerson**, Rebecca M '94 -11 Fed Plz Central -600 Metro Twr -Youngstown 44503

(330) 336-3231 ..**Gerstenschlager**, Neal J '76 -315 Eric Ln -Wadsworth 44281
(440) 542-1900 ..**Gerstenslager**, William E '77 (Gerstenslager & O Co) -6500 Crkside Trl -Solon 44139
(202) 833-7481 ..**Gerster**, Mary A '89 Bureau of Natl Affrs -1231 25th NW -Washington, DC 20037
(740) 452-7555 ..**Gerstner**, Cole J '82 (Gottlieb JB&D,PLL) -320 Main -Bx190 -Zanesville 43702 **Fx:**452-2257
(419) 882-1144 ..**Gersz**, Theodore '73 -5800 Monroe -Bldg A -Sylvania 43560
(614) 833-5700 ..**Gerth**, Philip W '98 -3 S High -Canal Winchester 43110 **Fx:**834-9480
(614) 464-6400 ..**Gertmenian**, Russell M '72 (Vorys SS&P LLP) -52 E Gay -Bx1008 -Columbus 43216 **Fx:**464-6350
(614) 463-9393 ..**Gertner**, Michael H '66 Gertner & G -199 S 5th -Ste 302 -Columbus 43215
(216) 622-8200 ..**Gertsburg**, Alexander E '01 %Calfee H&G LLP -800 Superior Av -Ste 1400 -Cleveland 44114 **Fx:**241-0816
(513) 554-1868 ..**Gertz**, Anthony J '72 (Gertz Law Firm) -401 Pike -Reading 45215 **Fx:**554-1897
(513) 554-1868 ..**Gertz**, Anthony J II '02 (Gertz Law Firm) -401 Pike -Reading 45215 **Fx:**554-1897
(330) 376-8336 ..**Gertz**, Marc P '77 (Goldman & R,Ltd) -11 S Forge -Akron 44304 **Fx:**376-2522
(513) 554-1868 ..**Gertz**, Susan M '95 (Gertz Law Firm) -401 Pike -Reading 45215 **Fx:**554-1897
(614) 466-5394 ..**Gerus**, Wendie A '84 Pub Def -8 E Long -Columbus 43215
(330) 533-6565 ..**Gervelis**, Mark S '76 -6550 Sevll Dr #B -Canfield 44406
(614) 823-6246 ..**Gervers**, David '76 Century Ins Grp -465 N Cleveland Av -Westerville 43082
(330) 723-4656 ..**Gervinski**, Nancy L '78 Tomino & L,LLC -803 E Wshngtn -Ste 200 -Medina 44256
(513) 621-2120 ..**Gerwin**, Ann W '79 Strauss & T,LPA -150 E 4th -4th Fl -Cincinnati 45202 **Fx:**241-8259
(419) 241-2100 ..**Gess**, Thomas C '82 (Watkins B&C) -405 Mad Av -Ste 1900 -Toledo 43604 **Fx:**241-1960
(419) 724-6294 ..**Gessel**, Barbara F '87 Toledo Blade Co -541 N Superior -Toledo 43660
(330) 643-2788 ..**Gessner**, Brad L '86 Summit Cnty Pros-Crim -53 Univ Av -7th Fl -Akron 44308 **Fx:**643-8277
(330) 637-3906 ..**Gessner**, George E '69 (Gessner & P Co, LPA) -212 W Main -Cortland 44410
(330) 637-3906 ..**Gessner & Platt Co, LPA** -212 W Main -Cortland 44410
(216) 586-3939 ..**Gest**, Kristen Lau '03 %Jones D -901 Lakeside Av -Cleveland 44114 **Fx:**579-0212
(614) 462-5038 ..**Geswein**, Mary Frances '94 OfCnsl Schottenstein Z&D -250 West -Bx165020 -Columbus 43216 **Fx:**462-5135
(859) 655-3700 ..**Gettins**, Mary E '03 %Pearson & B PSC -1224 Hwy Av -Covington, KY 41011
         Gettler, Benjamin '49 -1 Filson Pl -Cincinnati 45202
(954) 931-2407 ..**Gettler**, Benjamin '04 Gold Coast Properties -4300 N Univ Dr -D103 -Lauderhill, FL 33351
(212) 688-8555 ..**Gettman**, Lowell J '69 (Fragomen DB&L,PC) -515 Mad Av -New York, NY 10022
(937) 436-0033 ..**Getty**, Daniel F '01 -7501 Paragon Rd -Lwr Level -Dayton 45459 **Fx:**436-0008
(614) 445-2923 ..**Getty**, Kathryn E '03 GrangeMutualCasualtyCo -650 S Front -Columbus 43216
(606) 259-1900 ..**Getty**, Richard A '74 (Getty K&M LLP) -250 W Main -1900 Lex Fncl Ctr -Lexington, KY 40507
(859) 491-2206 ..**Gettys**, Norbert P '77 -120 W 5th -Covington, KY 41011
(859) 581-0001 ..**Gettys**, Robert P '72 -216 E 4th -Covington, KY 41011
(216) 622-3840 ..**Getz**, Thomas E '88 %US Atty -801 W Superior -Ste 400 -Cleveland 44113 **Fx:**622-3370
(419) 241-5506 ..**Geudtner**, John A '75 -610 Adams -2nd Fl -Toledo 43604
(614) 464-4201 ..**Geyer**, Catherine C '90 OfCnsl McGrath & B LLP -140 E Town -Ste 1070 -Columbus 43215
(937) 325-2000 ..**Geyer**, Douglas W '68 (D Geyer & Assoc) -451 Upper Valley Pike -Springfield 45504 **Fx:**325-8800
(740) 454-2591 ..**Geyer**, Robert W '55 (Kincaid T&G) -50 N 4th -Bx1030 -Zanesville 43702 **Fx:**454-6975
(614) 221-3155 ..**Geyer**, Thomas E '90 OfCnsl Bailey C LLC -10 W Broad -Columbus 43215 **Fx:**221-0479
(513) 791-1673 ..**Geygan & Geygan Ltd** -8050 Hosbrook Rd -Ste 107 -Cincinnati 45236
(513) 791-1673 ..**Geygan**, Thomas J '63 (Geygan & G Ltd) -8050 Hosbrook Rd -Ste 107 -Cincinnati 45236
(513) 791-1673 ..**Geygan**, Thomas J Jr. '98 (Geygan & G Ltd) -8050 Hosbrook Rd -Ste 107 -Cincinnati 45236
(608) 388-6445 ..**Gfoeller**, Monica S '87 HQ USAG Attn OSJA -100 E Hdqrtrs Rd -Camp McCoy, WI 54656
(513) 455-7600 ..**Ghassomian**, Kevin R '02 %Greenebaum D&M PLLC -255 E 5th -2800 Chemed Ctr -Cincinnati 45202 **Fx:**455-8500
(216) 696-7777 ..**Ghaster**, Earl F Jr. '80 Musca & M -1300 E 9th -Ste 1202 -Cleveland 44114
(216) 621-0200 ..**Gherlein**, John M '80 (Baker & H LLP) -1900 E 9th -Ste 3200 -Cleveland 44114 **Fx:**696-0740
(419) 626-6781 ..**Ghezzi**, Karen A '89 Dept of Job & Fam Srvcs -221 W Parish -Sandusky 44870
(614) 488-4424 ..**Ghidotti**, Paul G '90 Daimler Grp Inc -1533 Lk Shr Dr -Columbus 43204
(513) 721-1975 ..**Ghiz**, Leslie E '94 %Freking & B -215 E 9th -5th Fl -Cincinnati 45202 **Fx:**651-2570
(513) 983-1100 ..**Ghuman**, Shiv P '01 Cnsl Procter & Gamble Co -1 Procter & Gamble Plz -Cincinnati 45202
(614) 757-7721 ..**Giacalone**, Robert P '02 Cardinal Hlth -7000 Cardinal Pl -Dublin 43017
(440) 473-2273 ..**Giaimo**, Frank P '79 -1392 SOM Center Rd -Mayfield Heights 44124
(216) 658-4729 ..**GiaMaria**, Melanie R '03 CWRU Milton Kramer Law Clinic -11075 East Blvd -Cleveland 44106 **Fx:**658-4727
(440) 365-8800 ..**Giamboi**, Frank C II '86 -1288 Abbe Rd -Elyria 44035
(614) 248-5700 ..**Giampapa**, Joseph A '83 Bank One Corp -1111 Polaris Pkwy -Ste 4P -Columbus 43271
(614) 224-9985 ..**Gianangeli**, Brian M '00 %C Mifsud,LLC -326 S High -Ste 201 -Columbus 43215 **Fx:**224-9986

(330) 867-8443 ..**Giancarli**, Mark A '85 Klais & Co Inc -1867 W Market -Akron 44313
(330) 384-5893 ..**Giannantonio**, Rickey C '85 FirstEnergy Co -76 S Main -Akron 44308
(513) 762-6200 ..**Giannella**, Andrew R '96 (Ulmer & B LLP) -600 Vine -Ste 2800 -Cincinnati 45202 **Fx:**762-6245
(216) 368-2098 ..**Giannelli**, Paul C '87 CWRU Law Schl -11075 East Blvd -Cleveland 44106
(330) 726-0484 ..**Giannini**, Matthew C '78 -1040 S Cmmns Pl -Ste 200 -Youngstown 44514
(216) 522-7800 ..**Giannirakis**, Maria D '87 US Trustees Ofc -200 Pub Sq -Ste 3300 -Cleveland 44114 **Fx:**522-4988
(440) 244-1811 ..**Giardini**, Anthony B '76 -520 Bway -3rd Fl -Lorain 44052
(412) 831-8300 ..**Giba**, Paul R '83 -20 Donati Rd -Ste 300 -Upper Saint Clair, PA 15241
(419) 248-8148 ..**Gibb**, James A '88 Owens Corning Fbrglss Corp -1 Owens Corning Pkwy -Toledo 43659
(216) 781-1212 ..**Gibbon**, Christopher L '77 (Walter & H LLP) -1301 E 9th -Ste 3500 -Cleveland 44114 **Fx:**575-0911
(216) 781-1212 ..**Gibbon**, John H '72 (Walter & H LLP) -1301 E 9th -Ste 3500 -Cleveland 44114 **Fx:**575-0911
(216) 621-2090 ..**Gibbons & Cullen LLP** -815 Superior Av -Ste 1210 -Cleveland 44114 **Fx:**621-2062
         Gibbons, Daniel J '96 -401 Broad -Ste 215 -Elyria 44035
(216) 622-3645 ..**Gibbons**, Gregory R '78 OH Industrial Comm -615 W Superior -Cleveland 44113
(216) 961-3500 ..**Gibbons**, Jason M '91 Arrow Intl Inc -9900 Clinton Rd -Cleveland 44144
(216) 363-6048 ..**Gibbons**, John B '75 -1370 Ontario Av -Ste 2000 -Cleveland 44113
(330) 792-1063 ..**Gibbons**, John D '83 %Industrial Commssn of OH -242 Fed Plz W -Ste 303 -Youngstown 44503
(216) 344-9220 ..**Gibbons**, Joseph P '79 (McGinty GH&S Co,LPA) -614 W Superior Av -Ste 1300 -Cleveland 44113
(419) 245-1060 ..**Gibbons**, Julie A '96 City Council -One Govt Ctr -Ste 2140 -Toledo 43604
(216) 443-5595 ..**Gibbons**, Katherine H '02 Cuyahoga Cnty Ct Cmmn Pleas -1200 Ontario -Justice Ctr 11th Fl -Cleveland 44113
(216) 664-2809 ..**Gibbons**, Kevin J '92 %Dept of Law -601 Lakeside Av -Rm 106 City Hall -Cleveland 44114 **Fx:**664-2663
(216) 394-5063 ..**Gibbons**, M Colette '76 (Schottenstein Z&D) -1350 Euclid Av -Ste 1400 -Cleveland 44115 **Fx:**621-6502
(216) 621-2090 ..**Gibbons**, Mark T '93 (Gibbons & C LLP) -815 Superior Av -Ste 1210 -Cleveland 44114 **Fx:**621-2062
(440) 878-9503 ..**Gibbons**, Timothy J '89 -17522 Hmptn Pl -Strongsville 44136
(216) 623-8000 ..**Gibbons**, William P '73 -526 Superior Av -Ste 1525 -Cleveland 44114
(216) 621-0150 ..**Gibbs**, Arthur E III '96 %Hahn L&P LLP -3300 BP Twr/200 Pub Sq -Ste 3300 -Cleveland 44114 **Fx:**241-2824
(727) 399-8300 ..**Gibbs**, David C Jr. '69 Gibbs & C Co,LPA -5666 Seminole Blvd -2 -Seminole, FL 33772
(614) 224-2366 ..**Gibbs**, Jack G Jr. '82 (Mann & G) -233 S High -Columbus 43215
(330) 497-0979 ..**Gibbs**, Richard P '79 -1001 S Main -North Canton 44720
(614) 221-3155 ..**Gibbs**, Rollyn C '59 OfCnsl Bailey C LLC -10 W Broad -Columbus 43215 **Fx:**221-0479
(216) 696-8070 ..**Gibel**, George R '96 -1276 W 3rd -Ste 411 -Cleveland 44113
(216) 586-3939 ..**Giblin**, Stephen Q '80 (Jones D) -901 Lakeside Av -Cleveland 44114 **Fx:**579-0212
(937) 372-4404 ..**Gibney Stephan Barrett & Root** -1354 N Monroe Dr -Ste B -Xenia 45385 **Fx:**372-5435
(419) 241-6000 ..**Gibney**, Thomas J '85 (Eastman & S Ltd) -1 Seagate -24th Fl -Bx10032 -Toledo 43699 **Fx:**247-1777
(216) 696-0800 ..**Gibson Brelo Ziccarelli & Martello** -55 Pub Sq -Ste 2075 -Cleveland 44113 **Fx:**696-0702
(440) 225-0500 ..**Gibson Brelo Ziccarelli & Martello** -8353 Mentor Av -Mentor 44060 **Fx:**225-8426
(513) 721-4532 ..**Gibson**, Cynthia L '89 (Katz TB&H) -255 E 5th -Ste 2400 -Cincinnati 45202
(937) 643-0600 ..**Gibson**, Gregory C '77 (G Gibson Co,LPA) -2810 Kettering Twr -Dayton 45423 **Fx:**586-9495
(614) 228-5000 ..**Gibson**, Janet D '81 WW Williams Co -835 Goodale Blvd -Columbus 43212
(312) 245-7500 ..**Gibson**, Jeremy A '99 Masuda FE&M,Ltd -203 N LaSalle -Ste 2500 -Chicago, IL 60601 **Fx:**245-7467
(216) 696-0800 ..**Gibson**, Joseph '72 (Gibson BZ&M) -55 Pub Sq -Ste 2075 -Cleveland 44113 **Fx:**696-0702
(937) 264-1122 ..**Gibson**, Joseph E '90 -545 Helke Rd -Vandalia 45377
(614) 445-5858 ..**Gibson**, Joseph Miles '78 (Gibson & R-P Co LPA) -673 Mohawk -4th Fl -Columbus 43206 **Fx:**445-5850
(330) 896-9172 ..**Gibson**, Joseph W '72 Area Agency on Aging 10B -1550 Corp Wds Pkwy -Uniontown 44685 **Fx:**896-6626
(330) 929-0507 ..**Gibson**, Kenneth L '79 -234 Portage Trl -Bx535 -Cuyahoga Falls 44222
(216) 479-8500 ..**Gibson**, L Todd '04 %Squire S&D LLP -127 Pub Sq -4900 Key Twr -Cleveland 44114 **Fx:**479-8780
(614) 221-7381 ..**Gibson**, Peter J '92 (Koltak & G,LLP) -5 E Long -Ste 100 -Columbus 43215
(202) 781-2870 ..**Gibson**, Randall K '98 US Dept of Navy -1333 Isaac Hull Av SE -2030 Wshngtn Navy Yd -Washington, DC 20376
(513) 946-3000 ..**Gibson**, Richard G '83 Hamilton Cnty Pros -230 E 9th -Cincinnati 45202 **Fx:**946-3017
(216) 766-5093 ..**Gibson**, Richard M '93 Genesis Ins Co -25550 Chagrin Blvd -Beachwood 44122
(614) 469-3939 ..**Gibson**, Rick J '96 %Jones D -325 John H McConnell Blvd -Ste 600 -Bx165017 -Columbus 43216 **Fx:**461-4198
(330) 864-5270 ..**Gibson**, Ruth Ann '83 (R Gibson Co LPA) -Bx22445 -Akron 44302
(614) 228-3566 ..**Gibson**, Stephanie L '97 -500 S 4th -Columbus 43215
(440) 729-7278 ..**Gibson**, Tammy G '96 (T Gibson Co LPA) -8228 Mayfld -Ste 6-B -Chesterland 44026 **Fx:**729-8132
(419) 249-7900 ..**Gibson**, Thomas A '86 (Robison C&O) -Four SeaGate -9th Fl -Toledo 43604 **Fx:**249-7911
(330) 864-4419 ..**Gibson**, Thomas H III '96 -175 Rentham Rd -Akron 44313
(216) 621-0200 ..**Gibson**, Wendy J '79 (Baker & H LLP) -1900 E 9th -Ste 3200 -Cleveland 44114 **Fx:**696-0740

(513) 723-4823 ..**Gibson**, Whitney C '04 %Vorys SS&P LLP -221 E 4th -Ste 2000
   Atrium Two -Bx0236 -Cincinnati 45201 **Fx**:852-7825

(419) 841-7416 ..**Gibson**, Willard L '73 -5415 Monroe -Ste 4 -Toledo 43623

(216) 241-5310 ..**Gibson**, William F '73 (Gallagher SF&N) -1501 Euclid Av -6th Fl
   -Cleveland 44115 **Fx**:241-1608

(804) 291-0069 ..**Gibson**, William M '81 SrCnsl SunTrust Mortgage,Inc
   -901 Semmes Av -Richmond, VA 23224 **Fx**:291-0276

(216) 281-2400 ..**Gicei**, Leslie L '85 ABL Products Inc -3726 Ridge Rd
   -Brooklyn 44144

(513) 784-9111 ..**Gick**, Kathleen M '91 -7 W 7th -1800 Federated Bldg
   -Cincinnati 45202

(216) 642-3342 ..**Gideon**, Antoinette F '87 %Wegman H&V,LPA
   -6055 Rockside Wds Blvd -Ste 200 -Cleveland 44131
   Fx:642-8826

(614) 430-3377 ..**Gideon**, John J '78 -250 E Stanton Av -Columbus 43214

(216) 443-7800 ..**Giegerich**, Laurence D '00 Cuyahoga Cnty Pros -1200 Ontario
   -8th Fl -Cleveland 44113 **Fx**:698-2270

(513) 721-4532 ..**Gierl**, John R '83 (Katz TB&H) -255 E 5th -Ste 200
   -Cincinnati 45202

(304) 233-0777 ..**Giertz**, Michael P '00 %Hartley A O,PLLC -2001 Main -Ste 600
   -Wheeling, WV 26003 **Fx**:233-0774

(202) 416-4008 ..**Gieseler**, Christian A '81 FDIC -801 17th NW -Rm 1027
   -Washington, DC 20434

(419) 624-1501 ..**Giesler**, E Ann S '77 -8 Hrbr Pkwy -Sandusky 44870 **Fx**:624-1500

(440) 899-8000 ..**Giesser**, Rosemary A '81 -28899 Ctr Ridge Rd -Ste 303
   -Westlake 44145

(216) 328-2037 ..**Giffels**, Thomas E II '87 (Flanagan & G Co,LPA) -6100
   Oak Tree Blvd -Ste 200 -Independence 44131 **Fx**:227-8952

(216) 621-5161 ..**Giffen & Kaminski, LLC** -1717 E 9th -Cleveland 44114
   Fx:621-2399

(216) 621-5161 ..**Giffen**, Karen L '89 (Giffen & K,LLC) -1717 E 9th
   -Cleveland 44114 **Fx**:621-2399

(513) 563-2992 ..**Giffin**, Patricia K '85 Giffin Dyer & Assoc Inc -4010 Exec Park Dr
   -Ste 115 -Cincinnati 45241

(614) 326-1222 ..**Giffin**, Robert E '73 (R Giffin Co,LPA) -4924B Reed Rd
   -Columbus 43220

(614) 469-3939 ..**Gifford**, Brian L '97 %Jones D -325 John H McConnell Blvd
   -Ste 600 -Bx165017 -Columbus 43215 **Fx**:461-4198

(440) 835-0600 ..**Giganti**, Mary J '91 %Waldheger C,LPA -1991 Crocker Rd
   -Ste 550 -Westlake 44145 **Fx**:835-1511

(330) 336-3330 ..**Gigiano**, Daniel F '99 -111 Broad -Wadsworth 44281 **Fx**:336-3331

(513) 352-3339 ..**Giglio**, Augustine '70 Law Dept -801 Plum -Rm 214
   -Cincinnati 45202 **Fx**:352-1515

(330) 762-0700 ..**Gigliotti**, Louis J Jr. '91 (Slater Z&G) -One Cascade Plz -Ste 2210
   -Akron 44308 **Fx**:762-3923

(419) 242-1400 ..**Giha**, Paul D '64 -608 Mad Av -Ste 1400 -Toledo 43604

(305) 557-0578 ..**Gil**, Bertha S '81 (Gil & G,PA) -4160 W 16th Av -Ste 501
   -Hialeah, FL 33012 **Fx**:557-3840

(703) 292-5055 ..**Gilanshah**, Bijan '02 Natl Science Fnd -4201 Wilson Blvd
   -Arlington, VA 22230

(419) 424-1085 ..**Gilb**, Michael E '85 -747 E Sandusky -Findlay 45840

(937) 833-5659 ..**Gilbert**, B. Eugene '92 -475 Arlington Rd -Bx28 -Brookville 45309

(937) 653-7174 ..**Gilbert**, Brett A '92 (Wagner MD&G) -117 W Court -Urbana 43078
   Gilbert, Deborah E '90 -Bx1398 -Madison, AL 35758

(330) 762-0700 ..**Gilbert**, Edward L '80 (Slater Z&G) -One Cascade Plz -Ste 2210
   -Akron 44308 **Fx**:762-3923

(614) 889-0500 ..**Gilbert**, James D '81 Immke Crestview Cadillac -6755 Sawmill Rd
   -Dublin 43017

(614) 466-3934 ..**Gilbert**, Lori S '93 State Med Brd -77 S High -17th Fl
   -Columbus 43215
   Gilbert, Louis H '03 -713 S Home Rd -Mansfield 44906

(937) 224-7311 ..**Gilbert**, Paul D '62 -120 W 2nd -Ste 503 -Dayton 45402

(614) 866-2510 ..**Gilbert**, Roland T '58 -5677 Plum Orchrd Dr -Columbus 43213

(513) 241-7722 ..**Gilbert**, Scott T '03 %Gerner & K Co,LPA -215 W 9th
   -Cincinnati 45202

(614) 462-3555 ..**Gilbert**, Seth L '00 %Franklin Cnty Pros -373 S High
   -Columbus 43215

(614) 985-1493 ..**Gilbert**, Stacey A '01 (Gilbert Law Ofc,LLC)
   -500 W Wilson Bridge Rd -Ste 110 -Worthington 43085

(440) 347-5072 ..**Gilbert**, Teresan W '83 Lubrizol Corp -29400 Lakelnd Blvd
   -Wickliffe 44092

(216) 241-1430 ..**Gilbert**, Terry H '73 (Friedman &) -1370 Ontario
   -1700 Standard Bldg -Cleveland 44113

(330) 447-4511 ..**Gilbertson**, Glen G '79 Canton Drop Forge -4575 Southway SW
   -Canton 44706

(216) 687-1311 ..**Gilbride**, Michael P '93 (Reminger & R) -101 Prospect Av W
   -1400 Mdlnd Bldg -Cleveland 44115 **Fx**:687-1841

(614) 466-4605 ..**Gilbride**, Thomas F '79 OH Dept Job & Fam Srvcs -30 E Broad
   -32nd Fl -Columbus 43266
   Gilchrist, Heather '97 -1701 Sulgrave Rd -Louisville, KY 40205

(614) 464-1919 ..**Gilchrist**, John '72 -341 S 3rd -Ste 300 -Columbus 43215
   Gilchrist, Luke A '04 -(Address Unavailable)

(216) 575-9272 ..**Gilchrist**, Thomas C '91 Natl City Bank -1900 E 9th -Loc 2020
   -Cleveland 44114

(614) 462-1055 ..**Gilcrest**, Roger A '85 (Schottenstein Z&D) -250 West -Bx165020
   -Columbus 43216 **Fx**:462-5135

(859) 578-1030 ..**Gilday**, Anne L '03 %Lawrence Firm -606 Phila
   -Covington, KY 41011 **Fx**:578-1032

(513) 651-4130 ..**Gilday**, Anne L '03 %Lawrence Firm -8044 Mntgmry Rd -Ste 700
   -Cincinnati 45236

(513) 621-5631 ..**Gilday**, Michael D '77 Indstrl Comm of OH -110 E 8th -Ste 200
   -Cincinnati 45202

(614) 469-3274 ..**Gildee**, Eva C '00 %Thompson H LLP -10 W Broad -Ste 700
   -Columbus 43215 **Fx**:469-3361

(614) 227-2000 ..**Gildehaus**, Ralph F III '90 (Porter WM&A LLP) -41 S High
   -Columbus 43215 **Fx**:227-2100

(937) 223-8177 ..**Gildner**, Lance A '91 (Coolidge WW&L) -33 W 1st -Ste 600
   -Dayton 45402 **Fx**:223-6705

(937) 223-1130 ..**Gilene**, Salvatore A '02 %Pickrel S&E -40 N Main
   -2700 Kettering Twr -Dayton 45423 **Fx**:223-0339

(513) 621-2666 ..**Giles**, Brian T '00 %Statman HS&E LLC -255 E 5th -Ste 2900
   Chemed Ctr -Cincinnati 45202 **Fx**:587-4477

(713) 750-2307 ..**Giles**, David L '79 Chase Manhattan Bank -1111 Fannin -7th Fl
   -Houston, TX 77002

(740) 397-5321 ..**Giles**, James A '81 -109 E High -Mount Vernon 43050

(703) 547-5282 ..**Gilker**, Robert J '83 Nextel Intl -10700 Parkrdg Blvd -Ste 600
   -Reston, VA 20191

(513) 923-5232 ..**Gilkey**, Sue E '00 %F Rosenacker Co,LPA -5537 Cheviot Rd
   -Cincinnati 45247

(216) 522-3380 ..**Gill**, Anita A '90 IRS -1375 E 9th -1200 -Cleveland 44114

(513) 745-7003 ..**Gill**, David L '82 -8044 Mntgmry Rd -#405 W -Cincinnati 45236

(513) 684-3655 ..**Gill**, Eric J '94 NLRB -550 Main -Rm 3003 -Cincinnati 45202

(330) 836-5373 ..**Gill**, James J '54 -273 Merriman Rd -Akron 44303

(216) 771-2680 ..**Gill**, John J '62 Geraci & L Co,LPA -1370 Ontario -Ste 1220
   -Cleveland 44113

(330) 498-4411 ..**Gill**, Lance D '89 -4096 Holiday NW -Canton 44718

(614) 228-1541 ..**Gill**, M Elizabeth '88 Baker & H LLP -65 E State -Ste 2100
   -Columbus 43215 **Fx**:462-2616

(513) 943-7500 ..**Gill**, Nancy Jo '79 Midland Co -7000 Mdlnd Blvd -Amelia 45102

(614) 397-7298 ..**Gill**, Sterling E II '78 -2599 E Main -Ste 171 -Columbus 43229

(216) 861-8000 ..**Gill**, Steven R '91 Ernst & Young LLP -925 Euclid Av -Ste 1300
   -Cleveland 44115

(216) 241-7255 ..**Gill**, Thomas P '73 -2401 Superior Viaduct -Cleveland 44113

(513) 241-9400 ..**Gillam**, Marcheta L '82 Legal Aid -215 E 9th -Ste 200
   -Cincinnati 45202

(513) 396-8787 ..**Gillan**, Brian P '85 United Dairy Farmers -3955 Mntgmry
   -Cincinnati 45212

(513) 455-7600 ..**Gillen**, Stephen E '80 Greenebaum D&M PLLC -255 E 5th
   -2800 Chemed Ctr -Cincinnati 45202 **Fx**:455-8500

(614) 718-6249 ..**Giller**, Victoria H '97 BMW Fncl Srvcs -5515 Parkcenter Cir
   -Dublin 43017

(407) 518-0023 ..**Gillespie**, John '85 (Leon G & Assoc,PA) -20 S Rose Av -Ste 2
   -Kissimmee, FL 34741 **Fx**:518-0046

(614) 857-2337 ..**Gillespie**, John D '94 Nationwide Rlty Invstrs,Ltd -1 Natiowide Plz
   -1-34-10 -Columbus 43215
   Gillespie, Ross A '03 -(Address Unavailable)

(419) 255-5900 ..**Gillespie**, Ted C '75 (MacMillan S&T,LLC) -720 Water -4th Fl
   -Toledo 43604 **Fx**:255-9639

(216) 451-8540 ..**Gillespie-Mobley**, Ricky L '89 -711 E 105th -Cleveland 44108

(614) 461-5600 ..**Gillett**, Gary A '85 (Buckley K,LPA) -10 W Broad -Ste 1300
   -Columbus 43215

(440) 286-7195 ..**Gillette**, James M '74 -117 South -Natl City Bk Bldg
   -Chardon 44024

(440) 329-5390 ..**Gillette**, Kimberly D '88 Lorain Cnty Pros -225 Court -3rd Fl
   -Elyria 44035

(614) 527-6762 ..**Gillette**, Nancy P '92 SrCnsl OH State Med Assoc
   -3401 Mill Run Dr -Hilliard 43026

(513) 870-2811 ..**Gilliam**, Scott A '86 Cincinnati Ins Co -Bx145496
   -Cincinnati 45250

(703) 546-4068 ..**Gilliam**, Theodore N '98 TeliaSonera AB -2201 Cooperative Way
   -Ste 302 -Herndon, VA 20171

(614) 462-2221 ..**Gilligan**, John P '81 (Schottenstein Z&D) -250 West -Bx165020
   -Columbus 43215 **Fx**:462-5135

(513) 579-6400 ..**Gilligan**, Louis F '68 (Keating M&K PLL) -1 E 4th
   -1400 Provident Twr -Cincinnati 45202 **Fx**:579-6457

(513) 621-2666 ..**Gilligan**, T Scott '82 (Statman HS&E LLC) -255 E 5th
   -Ste 2900 Chemed Ctr -Cincinnati 45202 **Fx**:587-4477

(440) 887-7458 ..**Gilligan**, Timothy P '87 Mun Ct Judge -5555 Powers Blvd
   -Parma 44129

(907) 269-1969 ..**Gillilan-Gibson**, Kelly E '94 AK Atty Gen -1031 W 4th Av -Ste 200
   -Anchorage, AK 99501

(740) 384-5440 ..**Gilliland**, Dana E '96 (Gilliland G&G) -23 E Bway -Bx284
   -Wellston 45692

(740) 384-5440 ..**Gilliland Gilliland & Gilliland** -23 E Bway -Bx284 -Wellston
   45692

(317) 704-2400 ..**Gilliland**, John C II '92 (Gilliland & C,LLP) -3905 Vincennes Rd
   -Ste 204 -Indianapolis, IN 46268 **Fx**:704-2410

(740) 384-5440 ..**Gilliland**, Kyle R '83 (Gilliland G&G) -23 E Bway -Bx284
   -Wellston 45692

(740) 384-5440 ..**Gilliland**, Roy J '52 (Gilliland G&G) -23 E Bway -Bx284
   -Wellston 45692

(614) 469-7404 ..**Gillingham**, John C '75 SSA-OHA -401 N Front -Ste 400
   -Columbus 43215

(330) 665-7200 ..**Gillis**, Eugene G '78 Progressive Ins Co -190 Montrose W Av
   -Ste 100 -Copley 44321

(614) 228-5822 ..**Gillis**, Mark H '96 %Rich C&D,LLC -300 E Broad -Ste 300
   -Columbus 43215 **Fx**:228-2725

(614) 227-2353 ..**Gillis**, Sylvia L '89 (Bricker & E LLP) -100 S 3rd -Columbus 43215
   Fx:227-2390

(304) 748-7116 ..**Gillison**, Edward L '04 H Jackson-Gillison -3139 West
   -Weirton, WV 26062

(216) 687-9413 ..**Gillombardo**, Carl F Jr. '67 -1370 Ontario -Ste 330 -Cleveland
   44113

(513) 241-3100 ..**Gillum**, Amy L '03 %Lerner S&R -120 E 4th -8th Fl
   -Cincinnati 45202

(419) 732-3135 ..**Gillum**, Richard R III '98 (Kocher & G) -101½ Madison
   -Port Clinton 43452 **Fx**:734-5644

(216) 289-4332 ..**Gilman**, Aimee E '84 -27900 Euclid Av -Euclid 44132

(216) 363-4500 ..**Gilman**, Jeremy '83 (Benesch FC&A LLP) -200 Pub Sq -Ste 2300
   -Cleveland 44114 **Fx**:363-4588

(502) 589-4215 ..**Gilman**, Sheldon D '67 (Lynch CG&M,PSC) -400 W Market
   -Aegon Ctr Ste 2200 -Louisville, KY 40202 **Fx**:589-4994

(419) 994-4892 ..**Gilman**, Thomas R '03 (Kick & G) -133 S Market
   -Loudonville 44842 **Fx**:994-4892

(330) 534-6275 ..**Gilmartin**, Gary M '76 City of Hubbard -220 W Lbrty
   -Hubbard 44425

(216) 485-0600 ..**Gilmartin**, Matthew T '82 -6148 Broadvw Rd -Parma 44134
   Fx:485-0800

(330) 744-3010 ..**Gilmartin**, Vincent E '54 -42 N Phelps -Youngstown 44503
   Fx:744-3165

(419) 241-6000 ..**Gilmer**, Robert J Jr. '75 (Eastman & S Ltd) -1 Seagate -24th Fl
   -Bx10032 -Toledo 43699 **Fx**:247-1777

(216) 896-0606 ..**Gilmore**, Alvin I '63 -23360 Chagrin Blvd -Ste 108
   -Cleveland 44122

(419) 586-8120 ..**Gilmore**, Matthew L '94 (Van Arsel & G Co,LPA) -118 W Market
   -Bx298 -Celina 45822

(202) 514-4024 ..**Gilmore**, Maureen E '80 US DOJ-US Attys -600 E -Rm 2200 -Washington, DC 20530

(216) 736-7240 ..**Gilmore**, Robert S '86 (Kohrman J&K PLL) -1375 E 9th -One Cleve Ctr 20th Fl -Cleveland 44114 Fx:621-6536

(440) 357-6129 ..**Gilson**, Gregory M '72 -6949 Morley Rd -Painesville 44077

(859) 261-9611 ..**Gilster**, Bruce K '87 -140 Bellpointe Cmmns -Bellevue, KY 41073

(216) 241-6602 ..**Gimbel**, Adam H '01 (Weston HFP&H LLP) -50 Pub Sq -2500 Trmnl Twr -Cleveland 44113 Fx:621-8369

(330) 674-1555 ..**Gindlesberger**, Thomas D '55 -127 E Adams -Unit B3 -Millersburg 44654

(330) 492-4249 ..**Ginella**, Andrea A '95 -4092 Holiday NW -Canton 44718

(330) 492-3636 ..**Ginella**, Stephen A Jr. '87 -3600 Cleveland Av NW -Ste 6 -Canton 44709

(937) 434-7114 ..**Ginger**, David S '70 (Cox & G) -267 Regency Ridge Dr -Dayton 45459

Gingo, Biagio '93 -3320 Pebble Bch Dr -Sierra Vista, AZ 85650

(330) 796-8299 ..**Gingo**, Joseph M '71 Goodyear Tire & Rubber Co -1144 E Market -Akron 44316

(330) 860-1522 ..**Gingo**, Michael J '81 Babcock & Wilcox Co -20 S Van Buren Av -Barberton 44203

(330) 253-7100 ..**Gingrich**, Mitchell L '88 -1 S Main -Ste 301 -Akron 44308 Fx:253-3500

(513) 564-7330 ..**Ginocchio**, Deborah N '79 US Ct of Appls 6th Circuit -100 E 5th -Rm 245 US PO & Cthse -Cincinnati 45202

(513) 872-7900 ..**Ginocchio**, James S '79 -2645 Erie Av -Ste 41 -Cincinnati 45208

(513) 977-5578 ..**Ginocchio**, Ralph P '77 (Butkovich SS&G Co,LPA) -36 E 7th -Ste 2600 -Cincinnati 45202 Fx:977-5580

(216) 443-7223 ..**Ginsberg**, Amy Jo '94 Cuyahoga Cnty Pub Def -1200 W 3rd NW -100 Lakeside Pl -Cleveland 44113

(216) 291-9200 ..**Ginsberg**, Melvin R '75 MR Ginsberg Co,LPA -2000 Warrensvll Ctr Rd -South Euclid 44121 Fx:291-2970

(216) 621-0200 ..**Ginsburg**, Edward S '75 (Baker & H LLP) -1900 E 9th -Ste 3200 -Cleveland 44114 Fx:696-0740

(440) 339-7607 ..**Ginsburg**, Janice R '99 Lexis-Nexis -2585 Butternut Ln -Pepper Pike 44124

(330) 674-5086 ..**Ginsburg**, Jeffrey M '90 Holmes Cnty Cmmn Pleas Ct -1 E Jackson -Ste 301 -Millersburg 44654

(513) 762-6200 ..**Ginsburg**, Pamela K '00 (Ulmer & B LLP) -600 Vine -Ste 2800 -Cincinnati 45202 Fx:762-6245

Ginter, Jonathon M '04 -(Address Unavailable)

(330) 929-0507 ..**Ginther**, Sharyl W '91 -234 Portage Trl -Bx535 -Cuyahoga Falls 44222

(419) 289-2555 ..**Ginty**, James R '50 Halligan & G,LLP -930 Claremont Av -Bx455 -Ashland 44805

(216) 771-1144 ..**Gioffre**, Joseph R '85 (Behrens G&S Co,LPA) -1360 W 9th -Ste 400 -Cleveland 44113 Fx:736-7136

(330) 253-0785 ..**Giordano**, Deena M '01 %Gorman MP&V -1 Cascade Plz -9th Fl -Akron 44308 Fx:253-7432

(614) 469-3295 ..**Giorgianni**, Paul '95 %Thompson H LLP -10 W Broad -Ste 700 -Columbus 43215 Fx:469-3361

(614) 462-3896 ..**Giorgione**, Edmund E '83 Franklin Cnty Probate Ct -373 S High -Fl 22 -Columbus 43215

(614) 457-8608 ..**Giovanetti**, Richard J '62 -1779 Ardleigh Rd -Columbus 43221

(330) 255-0716 ..**Gippin**, Robert M '73 (Goldman & R,Ltd) -11 S Forge -Akron 44304 Fx:(216) 274-9124

(330) 825-9991 ..**Gipson**, Thomas B '80 -580 W Tuscarawas Av -Ste 101 -Barberton 44203

(614) 227-2318 ..**Gire**, Michael K '77 (Bricker & E LLP) -100 S 3rd -Columbus 43215 Fx:227-2390

Gisser, Sheldon M '63 -3121 Kensdale Rd -Pepper Pike 44124

(404) 521-9900 ..**Gist**, Brian L '02 Southrn Environmntl Law Ctr -127 Pchtree -Ste 605 -Atlanta, GA 30303

(614) 221-4000 ..**Gitlitz**, Gary B '76 (Chester W&S LLP) -65 E State -10th Fl -Columbus 43215 Fx:221-4012

(614) 222-4735 ..**Gittes**, Frederick M '75 (Gittes & S) -723 Oak -Columbus 43205

(614) 222-4735 ..**Gittes & Schulte** -723 Oak -Columbus 43205

(330) 452-6400 ..**Giua**, John R '77 -220 S Market Av -Ste 400 -Canton 44702

(216) 522-4914 ..**Giuffre**, Susan G '83 SSA/OHA -1350 Euclid Av -7th Fl -Cleveland 44115

(216) 241-0520 ..**Giuliani**, Albert '83 -526 Superior Av -1540 Leader Bldg -Cleveland 44114

(614) 464-6400 ..**Giuliani**, Anthony J '88 (Vorys SS&P LLP) -52 E Gay -Bx1008 -Columbus 43216 Fx:464-6350

(513) 421-9222 ..**Giuliano**, Jeffrey P '83 Allstate Ins Co -1014 Vine -Ste 2322 -Cincinnati 45202 Fx:421-9555

(330) 296-3884 ..**Giulitto & Berger** -222 W Main -Bx350 -Ravenna 44266

(330) 296-3884 ..**Giulitto**, Michael A '88 %Giulitto & B -222 W Main -Bx350 -Ravenna 44266

(330) 296-3884 ..**Giulitto**, Paula C '92 %Giulitto & B -222 W Main -Bx350 -Ravenna 44266

(614) 227-8825 ..**Giumenti**, Katherine S '89 Bricker & E LLP -100 S 3rd -Columbus 43215 Fx:227-2390

(216) 289-4500 ..**Giunta**, Anthony J Jr. '88 -25000 Euclid Av -Ste 100 -Euclid 44117

(216) 348-9800 ..**Giusto**, Blaise C '73 -614 Superior Av NW -Ste 625 -Cleveland 44113

(740) 622-0166 ..**Given**, Jason W '02 Leech S&P -240 S 4th -Bx880 -Coshocton 43812

(740) 368-1865 ..**Givens**, Erin K '87 %Delaware Cnty Juv Crt -88 N Sandusky -Delaware 43015

(614) 462-3194 ..**Gjostein**, Thomas A '88 Franklin Cnty Pub Def -373 S High -12th Fl -Columbus 43215

(614) 469-3939 ..**Gladman**, Michael R '92 %Jones D -325 John H McConnell Blvd -Ste 600 -Bx165017 -Columbus 43216 Fx:461-4198

(216) 515-1660 ..**Gladstone**, Stephen F '81 (Frantz W LLP) -127 Pub Sq -2500 Key Center -Cleveland 44114 Fx:515-1650

(614) 645-8214 ..**Glaeden**, Carrie E '89 Franklin Cnty Mun Ct -375 High -10th Fl -Columbus 43215 Fx:645-8822

Glaeser, William P '03 -(Address Unavailable)

(937) 222-2500 ..**Glankler**, John R '88 (Sebaly S&D) -1900 Kettering Twr -Dayton 45423 Fx:222-6554

(330) 492-1800 ..**Glantz**, Arnold F '86 -4883 Dressler Rd NW -Canton 44718

(440) 498-1911 ..**Glanz**, David S '01 -34150 Ada Dr -Solon 44139

(614) 469-3939 ..**Glaros**, Christopher M '03 %Jones D -325 John H McConnell Blvd -Ste 600 -Bx165017 -Columbus 43216 Fx:461-4198

(330) 394-8333 ..**Glaros-King**, Koula E '83 -522 High -Warren 44483

(513) 672-8811 ..**Glaser**, Hermina M '84 Xerox Corp -4270 Glendale-Milford Rd -Cincinnati 45242

(216) 696-2938 ..**Glaser**, Robert E '60 -925 Euclid Av -1150 Hunttgtn Bldg -Cleveland 44115 Fx:592-5009

(937) 748-3838 ..**Glaser-Atkins**, Carol J '84 -144 Deer Trl Dr -Springboro 45066

(614) 225-1620 ..**Glasgow**, Aaron M '02 (Paolucci & G,LPA) -35 E Gay -Ste 406 -Columbus 43215

(614) 462-3555 ..**Glasgow**, Jeffrey L '75 Franklin Cnty Pros -373 S High -Columbus 43215

(937) 225-4892 ..**Glasper**, Thomas '81 Montgomery Cnty Pros/CSEA -14 W 4th -Ste 510 -Dayton 45402

(913) 758-9303 ..**Glass**, Andrew J '91 US Army JAG Corp -600 W Massie Rd -Charlottesville, VA 22903

(513) 352-6765 ..**Glass**, Gary M '89 (Thompson H LLP) -312 Walnut -14th Fl -Cincinnati 45202 Fx:241-4771

(614) 466-2434 ..**Glass**, Greg C '78 OH Dept of Hlth -246 N High -Columbus 43266

(513) 651-6800 ..**Glass**, Joanne W '94 (Frost BT LLC) -201 E 5th -2200 PNC Ctr -Cincinnati 45202 Fx:651-6981

(513) 701-3000 ..**Glass**, Robert P '83 Harvest Info -5412 Coursevw Dr -Ste 435 -Mason 45040

(440) 329-5455 ..**Glass**, Sherry L '98 Lorain Cnty Pros -225 Court -3rd Fl -Elyria 44035

(513) 621-2120 ..**Glass**, Thomas P '93 %Strauss & T,LPA -150 E 4th -4th Fl -Cincinnati 45202 Fx:241-8259

(216) 228-7250 ..**Glassman**, Alan B '78 J Saurman -14650 Detroit Av -Ste 450 -Lakewood 44107

(513) 361-1200 ..**Glassman**, Benjamin C '04 %Squire S&D LLP -312 Walnut -Ste 3500 -Cincinnati 45202 Fx:361-1201

(216) 464-6776 ..**Glassman**, Linda S '84 -23240 Chagrin Blvd -Ste 100 -Beachwood 44122

(513) 977-8200 ..**Glassman**, Michael S '76 (Dinsmore & S LLP) -255 E 5th -Ste 1900 -Cincinnati 45202 Fx:977-8141

(513) 564-7630 ..**Glassman**, Michelle C '03 Hon S Dlott -100 E 5th -829 Potter Stewart US Cthse -Cincinnati 45202 Fx:564-7638

(330) 535-1660 ..**Glassman**, Ronald R '79 %Mondello & L -106 S Main -#2302 -Akron 44308

(513) 579-0080 ..**Glassman**, Thomas F '93 (Smith R&S Co,LPA) -1014 Vine -Ste 2350 -Cincinnati 45202 Fx:579-0222

(513) 271-0075 ..**Glassmann**, Lawrence A '86 Resolution Cnsl,LLP -8005 Peregrine Rd -Cincinnati 45243

Glassmeyer, Sarah L '02 -(Address Unavailable)

(202) 942-5000 ..**Glatfelter**, Emily N '02 %Arnold & P,LLP -555 12th NW -Washington, DC 20004 Fx:942-5999

Glathofer, Katherine M '04 -(Address Unavailable)

(216) 579-7150 ..**Glavinos**, George Jr. '71 -1965 E 6th -Ste 507 -Cleveland 44114

Glavinos, Stephanie M '03 -(Address Unavailable)

(440) 846-6789 ..**Glaze**, Ryan A '96 -407 Front -Berea 44017 Fx:846-9678

(202) 393-7756 ..**Glazer**, Craig A '79 PJM Interconnection,LLC -1200 G NW -Ste 600 -Washington, DC 20005

(440) 248-5151 ..**Glazer**, Jeffrey S '71 (Glazer & C Co,LPA) -28815 Aurora Rd -Solon 44139

(513) 634-3244 ..**Glazer**, Julia A '96 Cnsl Procter & Gamble -6100 Ctr Hill Av -Cincinnati 45224

(440) 498-9010 ..**Glazer**, Neil T '85 -6762 Edgemoor Av -Solon 44139

(513) 489-7200 ..**Glazer**, Richard H '70 (R Glazer Co,LPA) -8180 Corp Park Dr -Ste 300 -Cincinnati 45242

(513) 422-2001 ..**Gleason**, Andrew D '00 %Frost BT LLC -300 N Main -Ste 200 -Middletown 45042 Fx:422-3010

(614) 223-9300 ..**Gleason**, John A '87 (Benesch FC&A LLP) -88 E Broad -Ste 900 -Columbus 43215 Fx:223-9330

(972) 813-7512 ..**Gleason**, Melissa W '94 Broadlane,Inc -13727 Noel Rd -Ste 1400 -Dallas, TX 75240

(216) 586-3939 ..**Gleason**, Michael J '01 %Jones D -901 Lakeside Av -Cleveland 44114 Fx:579-0212

(614) 222-4798 ..**Gleaves**, Mark M '78 OH Pub Employees Retrmnt Syst -277 E Town -Leg Dept -Columbus 43215

(740) 596-5583 ..**Gleeson**, Timothy P '90 Vinton Cnty Pros -100 E Main -McArthur 45651

(216) 622-8200 ..**Gleespen**, Melissa M '03 %Calfee H&G LLP -800 Superior Av -Ste 1400 -Cleveland 44114 Fx:241-0816

(216) 447-9000 ..**Gleespen**, Michael W '84 Century Bus Srvcs -6050 Oak Tree Blvd -Ste 500 -Cleveland 44131

Gleich, Caryn F '99 -2872 Alpine Ter -Cincinnati 45208

(216) 522-3715 ..**Gleine**, Gregory M '00 NLRB -1240 E 9th -1695 Celebrezze Bldg -Cleveland 44199 Fx:522-2418

(216) 496-3312 ..**Gleisser**, Brian S '88 -22162 Wstchstr Rd -Shaker Heights 44122

(216) 664-3567 ..**Glenn**, Cordelia A '83 Dept of Law -601 Lakeside Av -Rm 106 City Hall -Cleveland 44114 Fx:664-2663

(216) 431-8060 ..**Glenn**, Douglas H '71 -4403 St Clair Av -Cleveland 44103

(717) 241-3550 ..**Glenn**, Peter G '70 The Dickinson School of Law -150 S Cllg -Carlisle, PA 17013

(216) 416-3259 ..**Glenn-Katzakis**, Joan C '93 Forest City Enterprises,Inc -50 Pub Sq -Ste 1160 -Cleveland 44113

(513) 381-8430 ..**Glennon**, Thomas M '00 Immerman & T Co,LPA -632 Vine -Ste 1010 -Cincinnati 45202

(216) 241-6882 ..**Glesius**, Amy S '96 AS Glesius,LLC -1220 W 6th -Ste 307 -Cleveland 44113 Fx:937-1122

(330) 344-6005 ..**Glessner**, Daniel K '93 Akron Gen Hlth Syst-Legal -400 Wabash Av -Akron 44307

(937) 845-3878 ..**Glew**, James P '98 (Brichacek & G) -101 S Main -New Carlisle 45344

(740) 695-0532 ..**Glick**, Elizabeth L '88 (Thornburg B&G) -113 W Main -Bx96 -Saint Clairsville 43950

(216) 292-8108 ..**Glick**, Gregory R '73 (GR Glick,LLC) -147 Bell -Ste 302 -Chagrin Falls 44022

(419) 281-2556 ..**Glick**, Howard W '80 -23 W Main -Ashland 44805

(216) 361-4400 ..**Glick**, Nancy J '87 Bd of Ed -3100 Euclid -Cleveland 44115

(330) 644-0076 ..**Glick**, Sidney '91 -2666 S Arlngtn Rd -Akron 44319

(330) 867-8422 ..**Glick**, Sol Mark '57 -41 Merz Blvd -Akron 44333

(216) 931-6000 ..**Glickman**, Albert B '62 (Ulmer & B LLP) -1300 E 9th
-Ste 900 Penton Media Bldg -Cleveland 44114 Fx:931-6001
(216) 696-1422 ..**Glickman**, Robert T '92 (McCarthy LC&L Co,LPA)
-101 Prospect Av W -1800 Mdlnd Bldg -Cleveland 44115
Fx:696-1210
(330) 867-6600 ..**Glinsek**, Gerald J '67 (Glinsek & H) -88 S Portage Path -Ste 301
-Akron 44303 Fx:867-9720
(330) 867-6600 ..**Glinsek & Hingham** -88 S Portage Path -Ste 301 -Akron 44303
Fx:867-9720
(440) 953-1771 ..**Glinski**, Mark A '79 -35104 Euclid Av -Ste 304 -Willoughby 44094
(614) 462-3194 ..**Glisson**, David L '91 Franklin Cnty Pub Def -373 S High -12th Fl
-Columbus 43215
(216) 481-0020 ..**Glitzenstein**, Jonell R '93 -20050 Lakeshr Blvd -Euclid 44123
Fx:481-0554
(614) 847-8255 ..**Gloeckner**, George N '72 -Bx334 -Worthington 43085
(440) 886-4556 ..**Glorioso**, Russell J '67 -5851 Pearl Rd -Ste 201
-Parma Heights 44130 Fx:886-4556
(216) 861-3086 ..**Glover**, James T '89 Reid M&W -55 Pub Sq -Ste 2010
-Cleveland 44113 Fx:861-4409
(419) 673-1534 ..**Glover**, Teresa S '91 -131 S Detroit -Kenton 43326
(216) 696-7445 ..**Glowacki**, James L '80 (Glowacki & Assoc) -526 Superior Av E
-510 Leader Bldg -Cleveland 44114 Fx:696-0318
(216) 241-4300 ..**Gluck**, Jerry '79 -55 Pub Sq -Ste 1010 -Cleveland 44113
(614) 792-9358 ..**Gluck**, Myriam W '91 Gluck Law Ofc,Ltd -6111 St Mel Cir
-Dublin 43017 Fx:792-5358
(330) 264-6911 ..**Gluck**, Robert N '69 (Gluck & M,LPA) -231 N Buckeye
-Wooster 44691
Gluckin, Susan E '96 -200 Dixie Hwy -Rossford 43460
(513) 579-7339 ..**Glueck**, Neal J '80 Federated Dept Stores,Inc -7 W 7th
-Cincinnati 45202
(216) 515-1660 ..**Gluek**, Carl H '85 (Frantz W LLP) -127 Pub Sq -2500 Key Center
-Cleveland 44114 Fx:515-1650
(216) 696-4700 ..**Gluntz**, Kevin P '95 (Spieth BM&N Co,LPA) -925 Euclid Av
-2000 Huntngtn Bldg -Cleveland 44115 Fx:696-6569
(614) 948-0817 ..**Gluntz**, Paula S '98 -1475 Worthngtn Park Blvd -Westerville 43081
(304) 230-6600 ..**Glyptis**, Phillip T '04 %Flaherty S&B,PLLC -1225 Market -Bx6545
-Wheeling, WV 26003
(513) 892-8251 ..**Gmoser**, Michael T '73 OfCnsl Holcomb & H LLP -6 S 2nd -311
Key Bk Bldg -Hamilton 45011 Fx:737-6854
(614) 466-6298 ..**Gnann**, Deborah G '84 PUCO -180 E Broad -Columbus 43266
(203) 728-6484 ..**Gnazzo**, Patrick J '71 United Tech Corp -1 Fncl Plz
-Hartford, CT 06103
(216) 921-7589 ..**Gobel**, John H '76 -23911 Duffld Rd -Shaker Heights 44122
(614) 292-5899 ..**Gobey**, Nancilynn B '88 OSU-Ofc of Academic Affrs
-1121 Kinnear Rd -Columbus 43212
(614) 718-2517 ..**Goble**, Paula A '84 BMW Fincl Srvcs -5515 Parkcenter Cir
-Dublin 43017
(440) 954-9455 ..**Gockel**, Laura C '91 %Schraff & K Co,LPA -4230 SR 306 -#310
-Willoughby 44094
(713) 319-2428 ..**Gockerman**, Matthew F '95 KPMG -700 Louisiana
-Houston, TX 77002
(513) 651-6800 ..**Godar**, Mary M '02 %Frost BT LLC -201 E 5th -2200 PNC Ctr
-Cincinnati 45202 Fx:651-6981
(513) 241-6650 ..**Godbey**, Mark E '89 (M Godbey & Assoc) -914 Main -Ste 200
-Cincinnati 45202 Fx:241-6649
(614) 462-2700 ..**Godby**, Herbert R '73 (Schottenstein Z&D) -250 West -Bx165020
-Columbus 43216 Fx:462-5135
(513) 381-5700 ..**Godby**, Marissa L '94 Ritter & R,LLC -105 E 4th -Ste 1200
-Cincinnati 45202 Fx:381-0014
(614) 228-8833 ..**Goddard**, Gabriel Lee '98 Cincinnati Ins Co -140 E Town
-Ste 1015 -Columbus 43215
(216) 696-2719 ..**Goddard**, Lisa M '90 Long Term Care Ombudsman -2800
Euclid Av -Ste 200 -Cleveland 44115 Fx:696-6216
(216) 622-8200 ..**Goddard**, Richard P '79 (Calfee H&G LLP) -800 Superior Av
-Ste 1400 -Cleveland 44114 Fx:241-0816
(513) 352-6760 ..**Goderre**, Diane M '98 %Thompson H LLP -312 Walnut -14th Fl
-Cincinnati 45202 Fx:241-4771
(440) 323-0866 ..**Godles**, Michael J '89 -371 Broad -Elyria 44035
(513) 556-0107 ..**Godsey**, Mark A '01 Univ of Cincinnati Cllg of Law -Bx210040
-Cincinnati 45221 Fx:556-1236
(330) 376-5300 ..**Godshall**, Cathy C '76 (Buckingham D&B,LLP) -50 S Main
-Bx1500 -Akron 44309 Fx:258-6559
(330) 670-7300 ..**Godshall**, Douglas N '76 (Hanna C&P,LLP) -3737 Embssy Pkwy
-Bx5521 -Akron 44334 Fx:670-0977
(330) 929-3168 ..**Godward**, Eugene G '84 (Keith & G) -135 Portage Trl -Bx374
-Cuyahoga Falls 44222
(513) 621-8210 ..**Goeddel**, Frederic L '73 (Drew & W Co,LPA) -1 W 4th -Ste 2400
-Cincinnati 45202 Fx:621-8205
(513) 651-6800 ..**Goehler**, Richard M '82 (Frost BT LLC) -201 E 5th -2200 PNC Ctr
-Cincinnati 45202 Fx:651-6981
(313) 222-9501 ..**Goellnitz**, Michael J '80 Comerica Bank -Bx75000
-Detroit, MI 48275
(614) 841-0559 ..**Goelz**, Marilyn M '82 -Bx478 -Worthington 43085
(937) 223-5200 ..**Goelz**, Robert D '78 (Flanagan LH&S) -318 W 4th -Dayton 45402
Fx:223-3335
(513) 621-0912 ..**Goering**, Eric W '93 (Goering & G) -220 W 3rd -10th Fl
-Cincinnati 45202
(513) 621-0912 ..**Goering & Goering** -220 W 3rd -10th Fl -Cincinnati 45202
(513) 621-0912 ..**Goering**, Robert A '62 (Goering & G) -220 W 3rd -10th Fl
-Cincinnati 45202
(513) 621-0912 ..**Goering**, Robert A '86 (Goering & G) -220 W 3rd -10th Fl
-Cincinnati 45202
(513) 621-0912 ..**Goering**, Ruth F '59 (Goering & G) -220 W 3rd -10th Fl
-Cincinnati 45202
(216) 563-2009 ..**Goering**, Shelly A '87 McDonald Investments -800 Superior Av
-Cleveland 44114
(216) 621-7860 ..**Goetsch**, Alexander E '95 (Cavitch FD&F) -1717 E 9th -14th Fl
-Cleveland 44114 Fx:621-3415
Goetsch, Richard J '75 BP America Inc-Law Dept -4101 Winfld Rd
-5E -Warrenville, IL 60555
(937) 492-6125 ..**Goettemoeller**, Duane A '82 (Kerrigan BSG&B) -126 N Main Av
-Bx987 -Sidney 45365
(937) 783-2454 ..**Goettke**, Richard L '76 -213 N Bway -Blanchester 45107

(216) 781-1111 ..**Goetz**, Daniel P '95 %Weisman G&W Co,LPA -101 Prospect Av
-1600 Mdlnd Bldg -Cleveland 44115 Fx:781-6747
(239) 936-2841 ..**Goetz**, James L '72 (Goetz H&L) -2133 Winkler Av -Bx6844
-Fort Myers, FL 33911 Fx:936-4197
(330) 305-5565 ..**Goff**, Christopher V '00 Cmmnty Hlthcre -6263 Frank Av
-North Canton 44720
(419) 536-2066 ..**Goff**, Martin E '85 (Chase G&B) -2650 N Reynolds Rd -Ste 3
-Toledo 43615 Fx:536-2239
(859) 261-4200 ..**Goff**, Milton S '04 %M Goff III -2220 Grandvw Dr -Ste 190
-Fort Mitchell, KY 41017
(216) 241-6602 ..**Goff**, Robert E Jr. '98 %Weston HFP&H LLP -50 Pub Sq
-2500 Trmnl Twr -Cleveland 44113 Fx:621-8369
(440) 255-5998 ..**Goff**, Robert E Sr. '68 -7821 Hidden Hllw -Mentor 44060
(614) 227-4090 ..**Goff**, Tyler W '02 State Teachers Retirement Sys -275 E Broad
-Columbus 43215
(216) 514-1100 ..**Goffman**, Ira S '81 (Rolf & G Co,LPA) -30100 Chagrin Blvd
-Ste 350 Corp Cir -Cleveland 44124 Fx:514-0030
(330) 339-6322 ..**Goforth**, Richard E '47 R Goforth Co,LPA -219 W High
-New Philadelphia 44663
Goggin, Mary Ellen '02 -Bx876 -Homewood, CA 96141
(216) 931-6000 ..**Goggins**, Bari E '80 Ulmer & B LLP -1300 E 9th
-Ste 900 Penton Media Bldg -Cleveland 44114 Fx:931-6001
(440) 892-3344 ..**Gogul**, Ronald J '70 Gogul & Assoc -1991 Crocker Rd -Ste 600
-Westlake 44145 Fx:892-7972
(216) 931-6000 ..**Goheen**, John C '83 (Ulmer & B LLP) -1300 E 9th
-Ste 900 Penton Media Bldg -Cleveland 44114 Fx:931-6001
(410) 347-8700 ..**Going**, Kristin K '99 %Whiteford T&P LLP -7 St Paul
-Baltimore, MD 21202 Fx:752-7092
(614) 224-6000 ..**Goings**, Hope M '98 DP Meyer Co,LPA -401 N Front -Ste 350
-Columbus 43215 Fx:224-6066
(216) 931-6000 ..**Goins**, Frances Floriano '77 (Ulmer & B LLP) -1300 E 9th
-Ste 900 Penton Media Bldg -Cleveland 44114 Fx:931-6001
(614) 466-3615 ..**Gold**, David M '78 Legis Srvc Commssn -77 S High
-Columbus 43215
(847) 699-4701 ..**Gold**, Deidra D '84 United Stationers Inc -2200 E Golf Rd
-Des Plaines, IL 60016
(626) 793-4806 ..**Gold**, Edward I '51 -330 Cordova -Rm 142 -Pasadena, CA 91101
Fx:793-4806
(216) 687-1311 ..**Gold**, Erin R '99 (Reminger & R) -101 Prospect Av W
-1400 Mdlnd Bldg -Cleveland 44115 Fx:687-1841
(216) 696-6122 ..**Gold**, Gerald S '54 (Gold & P Co,LPA) -526 Superior Av E
-1140 Leader Bldg -Cleveland 44114 Fx:696-3214
(440) 247-4765 ..**Gold**, John W '04 %SG Thomas,LPA -35 River -Level B
-Chagrin Falls 44022
(216) 731-1529 ..**Gold**, Laura A '95 Srvcs for Indpndnt Living,Inc -25100 Euclid Av
-Ste 105 -Cleveland 44117
(330) 392-1541 ..**Gold**, Ned C Jr. '66 Harrington H&M,Ltd -108 Main Av SW
-Ste 500 -Bx1510 -Warren 44482 Fx:394-6890
(216) 696-6122 ..**Gold & Pyle Co, LPA** -526 Superior Av E -1140 Leader Bldg
-Cleveland 44114 Fx:696-3214
(216) 479-8500 ..**Gold**, Roger M '91 Squire S&D LLP -127 Pub Sq -4900 Key Twr
-Cleveland 44114 Fx:479-8780
(513) 651-6800 ..**Gold**, Ronald E '93 (Frost BT LLC) -201 E 5th -2200 PNC Ctr
-Cincinnati 45202 Fx:651-6981
(216) 593-0001 ..**Gold**, Rosemary G '82 -33000 Pine Tree Rd -Cleveland 44124
(312) 321-7664 ..**Gold**, Stephen '85 (Gordon & G LLC) -444 N Mich Av -Ste 3600
-Chicago, IL 60611 Fx:321-9324
(614) 644-9293 ..**Gold**, Yitzchak E '74 OH Supreme Ct -30 E Broad -2nd Fl
-Columbus 43266
(216) 391-5444 ..**Gold-Scott**, Lisa L '94 Housing Advocates Inc -3655 Prospect Av
-Cleveland 44115
(614) 466-2927 ..**Goldbaum**, Donald M '75 Legis Srvc Commssn -77 S High
-Columbus 43215
(513) 721-3111 ..**Goldberg**, Brian M '85 -441 Vine -Ste 4300 -Cincinnati 45202
(513) 946-6464 ..**Goldberg**, Brian T '04 Hamilton Cnty Mun Ct -1000 Main
-Cincinnati 45202
(937) 225-2910 ..**Goldberg**, Dale A '82 US Atty -200 W 2nd -602 Fed Bldg
-Dayton 45402
(216) 443-7800 ..**Goldberg**, Francine B '91 Cuyahoga Cnty Pros -1200 Ontario
-8th Fl -Cleveland 44113 Fx:698-2270
(216) 635-4275 ..**Goldberg**, Hillary Z '96 Brooklyn City Pros Ofc -7619 Memphis Av
-Brooklyn 44144
(440) 244-1640 ..**Goldberg**, Hyman S '54 -444 Bway -Lorain 44052
(440) 519-9900 ..**Goldberg**, J Michael '90 %S Goldberg Co,LPA -34055 Solon Rd
-Ste 103 -Solon 44139
(216) 781-1111 ..**Goldberg**, James R '64 (Weisman G&W Co,LPA)
-101 Prospect Av W -1600 Mdlnd Bldg -Cleveland 44115
Fx:781-6747
(513) 421-6630 ..**Goldberg**, John A '73 Lindhorst & D Co,LPA -312 Walnut
-Ste 2300 -Cincinnati 45202
(216) 831-6100 ..**Goldberg**, Jordan A '97 Goldberg Co,Inc -25101 Chagrin Blvd
-Ste 300 -Beachwood 44122
(614) 228-6345 ..**Goldberg**, Kenneth R '92 Strip HLM&T Co LPA -575 S 3rd
-Columbus 43215 Fx:228-6369
(419) 882-2889 ..**Goldberg**, Marvin E '84 -Bx8488 -Toledo 43623
(216) 696-4514 ..**Goldberg**, Michael J '88 (Goldberg & O) -323 Lakeside Av W
-Ste 450 -Cleveland 44113
(330) 468-5303 ..**Goldberg**, Mitchell B '68 -766 Valley Brook Cir
-Sagamore Hills 44067
(216) 241-0011 ..**Goldberg & O'Shea** -323 Lakeside Av W -Ste 450
-Cleveland 44113
(419) 843-5355 ..**Goldberg**, Paul S '77 (Goldberg W&H) -6800 W Central Av
-Toledo 43617
(614) 222-8686 ..**Goldberg**, Richard '83 Scott S&W LLP -50 W Broad
-2500 LeVeque Twr -Columbus 43215 Fx:222-8688
(513) 321-2662 ..**Goldberg**, Richard J '75 (Schuh & G,LLP) -2662 Madison Rd
-Cincinnati 45208 Fx:321-0855
(614) 764-7800 ..**Goldberg**, Scott D '90 Golden Title Agency,Inc -5500 Frantz Rd
-Ste 151 -Dublin 43017
(216) 351-7212 ..**Goldberg**, Scott E '85 Title Rlty Mgmt Co -5866 Broadvw Rd
-Cleveland 44134
(440) 519-9900 ..**Goldberg**, Steven M '89 -34055 Solon Rd -Ste 103 -Solon 44139
(419) 247-1623 ..**Goldberg**, Stuart J '85 (Eastman & S Ltd) -1 Seagate -24th Fl
-Bx10032 -Toledo 43699 Fx:247-1777

(614) 292-1536 .. **Goldberger,** David A '81 OSU Moritz Cllg of Law -55 W 12th Av
-Columbus 43210 Fx:292-1383

(419) 526-3177 .. **Goldberger,** Robert '76 -13 Park Av W -Ste 605 -Mansfield 44902
Fx:526-5515

(216) 881-5300 .. **Goldblatt,** Jay A '83 Pubco Corp -3830 Kelley Av
-Cleveland 44114

(304) 529-2443 .. **Goldcamp,** Maria T '96 Robinson & R -1032 6th Av -Bx407
-Huntington, WV 25708

(513) 624-3100 .. **Goldcamp,** Robert T '79 -5729 Dragon Way -Ste 13
-Cincinnati 45227

(513) 541-3900 .. **Golden,** Jason A '03 GTC FoodService Inc -1319 Hill Crest Rd
-Cincinnati 45224

(614) 258-1983 .. **Golden,** Keith E '84 (Golden & M Co,LPA) -923 E Broad
-Columbus 43205

(330) 746-5643 .. **Golden,** Kenneth L '04 %Comstock S&W Co,LPA -100 Fed Plz E
-Ste 926 -Youngstown 44503 Fx:746-4925

(513) 345-8291 .. **Goldenberg,** Jeffrey S '94 (Murdock GS&G) -35 E 7th -Ste 600
-Cincinnati 45202 Fx:345-8294

(216) 621-0150 .. **Goldenberg,** Warren '81 (Hahn L&P LLP)
-3300 BP Twr/200 Pub Sq -Ste 3300 -Cleveland 44114
Fx:241-2824

(419) 784-4699 .. **Goldenetz,** John P '69 -519 Perry -Defiance 43512

(216) 241-0300 .. **Goldense,** David W '77 -50 Pub Sq -Ste 920 -Cleveland 44113

(216) 696-0606 .. **Goldfarb,** Bernard S '40 SpclCnsl RE Sweeney Co,LPA
-55 Pub Sq -Ste 1500 -Cleveland 44113 Fx:696-0679

(216) 579-1117 .. **Goldfarb,** Gary M '72 -2000 Standard Bldg -Cleveland 44113

(216) 291-1155 .. **Goldfarb,** Joanne D '75 -2000 Auburn Dr -Ste 200
-Cleveland 44122

(937) 644-6634 .. **Goldfarb,** Lewis H '88 Cnsl Honda of America Mfg,Inc
-24000 Honda Pkwy -Marysville 43040

(216) 621-0150 .. **Goldfarb,** Steven A '85 (Hahn L&P LLP)
-3300 BP Twr/200 Pub Sq -Ste 3300 -Cleveland 44114
Fx:241-2824

(334) 395-8500 .. **Goldfinger,** Roy S '80 -Bx231555 -Montgomery, AL 36123

(440) 884-6500 .. **Goldhamer,** Stanley J '53 Precision Realty Co -6688 Pearl Rd
-Parma Heights 44130

(614) 418-3100 .. **Goldhand,** Joanne I '96 Skilken Prop -4270 Morse Rd
-Columbus 43230

(937) 376-7299 .. **Goldie,** Susan L '78 Mun Ct Judge -101 N Detroit -Xenia 45385
Fx:376-7288

(614) 224-5811 .. **Goldin,** Larry M '79 -85 E Gay -Ste 612 -Columbus 43215

(216) 514-9500 .. **Golding,** Michael L '93 Norchi & Assoc,LLC -23240 Chagrin Blvd
-Ste 600 -Beachwood 44122

(513) 651-8437 .. **Goldman,** Alan L '90 PNC Bank -201 E 5th -Cincinnati 45202

(419) 524-9811 .. **Goldman,** Catherine D '81 Weldon H&K,LLP -28 Park Av W
-Bank One Bldg -Mansfield 44902 Fx:522-5758

(614) 228-2325 .. **Goldman,** Dennis J '70 Plating Technology, Inc. -800 Frebis Av
-Columbus 43206

(216) 696-1122 .. **Goldman,** Donald L '60 Mgmt Recruiters Intl Inc -200 Pub Sq
-31st Fl -Cleveland 44114

(513) 381-9200 .. **Goldman,** Edward R '73 (Rendigs FK&D,LLP) -One W 4th
-Ste 900 -Cincinnati 45202 Fx:381-9206

Goldman, Elmer M '50 -6659 Vllgr Pl -Mason 45040

(513) 621-2666 .. **Goldman,** Fern E '81 %Statman HS&E LLC -255 E 5th
-Ste 2900 Chemed Ctr -Cincinnati 45202 Fx:587-4477

(513) 723-0400 .. **Goldman,** Gary S '94 -7 W 7th -Ste 1800 -Cincinnati 45202

Goldman, Jacqueline Meyer '02 -3365 Raymar Blvd
-Cincinnati 45208

(614) 864-4359 .. **Goldman,** Jerome S '73 (Goldman & R) -5350 E Main
-Columbus 43213 Fx:864-2818

(614) 365-2700 .. **Goldman,** Jessica '03 %Squire S&D LLP -41 S High
-1300 Huntngtn Ctr -Columbus 43215 Fx:365-2499

(216) 621-0200 .. **Goldman,** Matthew R '82 (Baker & H LLP) -1900 E 9th -Ste 3200
-Cleveland 44114 Fx:696-0740

(314) 523-3000 .. **Goldman,** Richard C '73 Deutsche Fin Srvcs Corp
-655 Maryvll Centre Dr -St. Louis, MO 63141

(330) 376-8336 .. **Goldman & Rosen,Ltd** -11 S Forge -Akron 44304 Fx:376-2522

(937) 254-4455 .. **Goldman Rubin & Shapiro** -1340 Woodman Dr -Dayton 45432

(216) 363-4500 .. **Goldner,** Allan '73 (Benesch FC&A LLP) -200 Pub Sq -Ste 2300
-Cleveland 44114 Fx:363-4588

(614) 227-2300 .. **Goldsand,** Corey A '04 %Bricker & E LLP -100 S 3rd
-Columbus 43215 Fx:227-2390

(412) 394-2500 .. **Goldsmith,** Frederick B '01 Burns W&H,LLC -120 5th Av
-Ste 2400 -Pittsburgh, PA 15222

(330) 225-7177 .. **Goldsmith,** Harvey S '66 -3698 Ctr Rd -Brunswick 44212
Fx:273-8468

(216) 931-6000 .. **Goldsmith,** James A '80 (Ulmer & B LLP) -1300 E 9th
-Ste 900 Penton Media Bldg -Cleveland 44114 Fx:931-6001

(513) 794-6849 .. **Goldsmith,** Katherine D '96 OH Natl Fin Srvcs -1 Fncl Way
-Cincinnati 45242

(817) 488-7645 .. **Goldsmith,** Martin N '69 -1331 Vllg Grn Dr -Southlake, TX 76092

(330) 434-3880 .. **Goldsmith,** Richard L Jr. '69 Laybourne & G -159 S Main -Ste 900
-Akron 44308 Fx:434-4661

(941) 955-4990 .. **Goldsmith,** Stanley Alan '80 -1605 Main -Ste 1001
-Sarasota, FL 34236

(419) 624-3000 .. **Goldsmith,** Sylvia M '95 Murray & M Co,LPA -111 E Shoreline Dr
-Bx19 -Sandusky 44871

(614) 297-1000 .. **Goldson,** Jennifer C '96 %B Frick & Assoc -1265 Neil Av
-Columbus 43201 Fx:297-6666

Goldstein, Amy R '82 -720 City Park Av -Columbus 43206

(440) 442-0022 .. **Goldstein,** Bruce S '83 (B Goldstein Co,LPA)
-1009 Ledgewood Trl -Lyndhurst 44124

Goldstein, Dana Ann '83 -3317 Ingleside Rd
-Shaker Heights 44122

(614) 839-5700 .. **Goldstein,** David A '95 (D Goldstein Co,LPA) -529 S 3rd
-Columbus 43215

(216) 566-5559 .. **Goldstein,** Heidi B '95 (Thompson H LLP) -127 Pub Sq
-3900 Key Ctr -Cleveland 44114 Fx:566-5800

(419) 255-0030 .. **Goldstein,** Jeffrey I '68 -520 Mad Av -804 Spitzer Bldg
-Toledo 43604

(216) 360-3737 .. **Goldstein,** Jerrold L '67 (Persky S&A Co,LPA)
-25101 Chagrin Blvd -Ste 350 Signature Sq II -Beachwood 44122
Fx:593-0921

(216) 341-7800 .. **Goldstein,** Joshua D '97 Amer Bronze Corp -2941 Bway Av
-Cleveland 44115

(216) 771-6633 .. **Goldstein,** Joyce '84 (Goldstein & O) -526 Superior Av E
-Ste 1040 Leader Bldg -Cleveland 44114 Fx:771-7559

(614) 221-9800 .. **Goldstein,** Judith B '98 Equal Justice Fndtn -88 E Broad
-Ste 1590 -Columbus 43215 Fx:221-9810

(216) 241-6677 .. **Goldstein,** Michael D '02 %WM Goldstein -55 Pub Sq -Ste 650
-Cleveland 44113 Fx:241-3748

(216) 295-2114 .. **Goldstein,** Michael S '74 (MS Goldstein Co,LPA)
-21625 Chagrin Blvd -Ste #240 -Beachwood 44122

(440) 259-5200 .. **Goldstein,** Noreen K '90 Mid-West Materials,Inc
-3687 Shepard Rd -Bx345 -Perry 44081 Fx:259-5204

(216) 771-6633 .. **Goldstein & O'Connor** -526 Superior Av E -Ste 1040 Leader Bldg
-Cleveland 44114 Fx:771-7559

(614) 274-0033 .. **Goldstein,** Robert R '92 (Goldstein & Assoc) -3649 W Broad
-Columbus 43228

(513) 651-6800 .. **Goldstein,** Steven J '75 (Frost BT LLC) -201 E 5th -2200 PNC Ctr
-Cincinnati 45202 Fx:651-6981

Goldstein, Stewart L '75 -630 River Gate Rd
-Chesapeake, VA 23322

(216) 241-6677 .. **Goldstein,** William M '69 -55 Pub Sq -Ste 650 -Cleveland 44113
Fx:241-3748

(330) 821-2516 .. **Goldthorpe,** Christopher J '72 (Lundgren G&Z) -526 E Main
-Bx2595 -Alliance 44601

(216) 658-9900 .. **Goldwasser,** Andrew S '97 (Ciano & G,LLP) -1500 W 3rd
-Ste 460 -Cleveland 44113

(513) 721-1311 .. **Goldwasser,** Brian D '93 (Reminger & R) -7 W 7th -Ste 1990
-Cincinnati 45202 Fx:721-2553

(216) 687-1311 .. **Goldwasser,** Gary H '67 (Reminger & R) -101 Prospect Av W
-1400 Mdlnd Bldg -Cleveland 44115 Fx:687-1841

(216) 592-5000 .. **Goldwood,** Jon J '98 Tucker E&W LLP -925 Euclid Av
-1150 Huntngtn Bldg -Cleveland 44115 Fx:592-5009

(216) 696-3366 .. **Goler,** Michael D '77 OfCnsl Goodman WM LLP -100 Erievw Plz
-27th Fl -Cleveland 44114 Fx:363-5835

(614) 258-6000 .. **Golian,** Joseph J '85 (Brenner BG&M Co,LPA) -2109 Stella Ct
-Columbus 43215 Fx:258-6006

(216) 443-7800 .. **Golish,** Matthew D '99 Cuyahoga Cnty Pros -1200 Ontario -8th Fl
-Cleveland 44113 Fx:698-2270

(330) 337-9529 .. **Goll,** Geoffrey S '73 -200 E Pershing -Bx92 -Salem 44460

(330) 782-6470 .. **Gollings,** Michael L '96 -4410 Market -Youngstown 44512

(513) 419-6982 .. **Gollomp,** Jeffrey A '01 Cinergy Corp -139 E 4th -Cincinnati 45202

(216) 831-6767 .. **Goloboff,** Barry D '63 -3659 Green Rd -#222 -Beachwood 44122

(614) 464-6400 .. **Golonka,** Kenneth A Jr. '86 (Vorys SS&P LLP) -52 E Gay -Bx1008
-Columbus 43216 Fx:464-6350

(216) 687-2737 .. **Golovan,** Kathleen R '94 Med Mutual of OH -2060 E 9th
-Cleveland 44115

Golowin, Russell C '03 -(Address Unavailable)

(614) 759-9590 .. **Golowin,** Serge A '79 -12347 Limerick Ln -Pickerington 43147

(216) 622-8200 .. **Golrick,** Mary E '85 Calfee H&G LLP -800 Superior Av -Ste 1400
-Cleveland 44114 Fx:241-0816

(317) 263-3580 .. **Golson-Dunlap,** Jenice R '77 J Golson-Dunlap,PC -1 VA Av
-Ste 850 -Indianapolis, IN 46204

(330) 452-8755 .. **Golub,** Gerald B '73 -1340 N Market Av -Ste 1 -Canton 44714

(440) 885-8073 .. **Golubovic,** Carla L '93 Cmmnty Dvlpmnt Program -5983 W 54th
-Rm 123 -Parma 44129

(216) 341-0940 .. **Golubski,** Robert J '81 -6500 Fullerton Av -Cleveland 44105

Gomez, Genevieve T '92 -Bx70203 -Rochester, MI 48307

(216) 481-0020 .. **Gonakis,** Spiros E '75 (S Gonakis Co,LPA) -20050 Lakeshr Blvd
-Euclid 44123

(216) 481-0020 .. **Gonakis,** Spiros E Jr. '03 -20050 Lk Shr Blvd -Euclid 44123

(216) 696-0440 .. **Gonda,** Diane M '92 (Gonda & Assoc) -75 Pub Sq -Ste 920
-Cleveland 44113 Fx:696-0075

Gonda, Douglas A '72 -261 N Mdwbrk Dr -Lakeside Marblehead
43440

(330) 965-8000 .. **Gongaware,** Aaron P '03 %Osborne D&S Co LPA
-100 Marwood Cir -Boardman 44512 Fx:965-8005

(614) 466-1305 .. **Gonidakis,** Michael L '99 Atty Gen -30 E Broad -Columbus 43215
Fx:466-8898

Gonsior, David S '85 -4601 Southrn Blvd -Kettering 45429

(216) 781-1212 .. **Gonyer,** Todd E '02 Walter & H LLP -1301 E 9th -Ste 3500
-Cleveland 44114 Fx:575-0911

(330) 494-1381 .. **Gonyias,** Drew '93 -6973 Promway Av -Ste 101 -North Canton
44720

(205) 970-7142 .. **Gonzales,** Arthur J '91 Vesta Ins Group,Inc -3760 Rvr Run Dr
-Bx43360 -Birmingham, AL 35243 Fx:970-7161

(205) 250-5000 .. **Gonzales,** Jacquelyn A '91 %Lange SR&S,LLP -417 20th North
-Ste 1700 -Birmingham, AL 35203

(614) 882-3443 .. **Gonzales,** John M '87 (J Gonzales,LLC) -140 Commerce Park Dr
-Westerville 43082

(419) 885-3597 .. **Gonzalez,** Alfonso J '00 %McHugh D&M,Ltd -5580 Monroe
-Sylvania 43560 Fx:885-3861

(740) 349-6195 .. **Gonzalez,** Jenny R '98 Licking Cnty Pros -20 S 2nd -4th Fl
-Newark 43055

(216) 664-2894 .. **Gonzalez,** Jose M '84 Dept of Law -601 Lakeside Av
-Rm 106 City Hall -Cleveland 44114 Fx:664-2663

(216) 621-5980 .. **Gonzalez,** Linda V '98 Legal Aid -1223 W 6th -Cleveland 44113

(419) 249-7100 .. **Gonzalez,** Mark M '98 Marshall & M,LLC -Four Seagate -8th Fl
-Toledo 43604 Fx:249-7151

(513) 651-3456 .. **Gonzalez Saggio & Harlan LLP** -441 Vine -Ste 3615
-Cincinnati 45202 Fx:651-3446

(216) 443-8556 .. **Gonzalez,** Tracey S '03 Cuyahoga Cnty Ct Cmmn Pleas
-1200 Ontario -Justice Ctr 11th Fl -Cleveland 44113

Gonzalez, Victor J '77 -17029 SE 115th Ter Rd
-Summerfield, FL 34491

(216) 651-1919 .. **Gonzalez,** Vincent J '74 -2159 West Blvd -Cleveland 44102

(614) 224-7291 .. **Gooch,** Rebecca A '93 -330 S High -Columbus 43215
Fx:224-7268

(216) 522-7800 .. **Good,** Amy L '91 US Trustees Ofc -200 Pub Sq -Ste 3300
-Cleveland 44114 Fx:522-4988

(972) 448-5463 .. **Good,** Andrew S '84 Nrth Amer Coal Corp -14785 Preston Rd
-Ste 1100 -Dallas, TX 75254

(216) 241-1200 .. **Good,** Christine F '91 %D Fallon -1640 Standard Bldg
-Cleveland 44113

(419) 227-4945 ..**Good,** Danielle A '97 C Nelson & Assoc,Inc -417 N West -Lima 45801

(216) 696-0650 ..**Good,** Darcy M '97 %Kaman & C -50 Pub Sq -Ste 600 Trmnl Twr -Cleveland 44113

(614) 469-1301 ..**Good,** Eliott R '81 (Chorpenning G&P Co,LPA) -585 S Front -Ste 310 -Columbus 43215

(440) 808-0163 ..**Good,** John D '92 Reniassance Mrtge & Fin Srvcs -25109 Detroit Rd -Ste 310 -Westlake 44145

(419) 207-0553 ..**Good,** John L '91 -930 Claremont Av -Ashland 44805

(216) 566-5500 ..**Good,** Jonathan A '95 %Thompson H LLP -127 Pub Sq -3900 Key Ctr -Cleveland 44114 **Fx:**566-5800

(513) 621-5252 ..**Good,** Martha H '85 (Clodfelter & G) -36 E 4th -Ste 1208 -Cincinnati 45202

(614) 885-0554 ..**Good,** William A '80 -5655 N High -Ste 202 -Worthington 43085

(937) 226-3525 ..**Goodall,** L S '93 -425 W Grand Av -Ste 3003 -Dayton 45405

(614) 463-4201 ..**Goodburn,** Paul R Jr. '98 %Littler M,PC -21 E State -Ste 1600 -Columbus 43215 **Fx:**221-3301

(614) 462-7242 ..**Goodburn,** Shannon E '98 Hon L Sadler Ct of Appeals -373 S High -24th Fl -Columbus 43215

Goode, Joshua '03 -(Address Unavailable)

(419) 255-0814 ..**Goode,** Victor L '98 ABLE -520 Mad Av -740 Spitzer Bldg -Toledo 43604 **Fx:**259-2880

(419) 249-6682 ..**Goodell,** Brian C '84 Lucas Cnty Juv Ct -429 Mich -Family Court Ctr -Toledo 43624

(216) 523-1100 ..**Gooden,** Deborah M '94 (Willis W&G) -113 St Clair Av -Ste 440 -Cleveland 44114

(614) 466-0114 ..**Gooden,** Robert R '78 PUCO -180 E Broad -Columbus 43266

(937) 339-0511 ..**Goodenough,** Wendy J '98 OfCnsl Dungan & L Co,LPA -210 W Main -Troy 45373 **Fx:**335-5802

(419) 634-0794 ..**Goodin,** David K '03 -722 S Main -Ada 45810

(614) 221-4221 ..**Goodin,** Eileen S '80 Barkan + N -360 S Grant Av -Bx1989 -Columbus 43216 **Fx:**221-5423

(513) 946-3000 ..**Goodin,** Steven P '99 Hamilton Cnty Pros -230 E 9th -Cincinnati 45202 **Fx:**946-3017

(419) 445-4511 ..**Gooding,** Jack D '69 (Gooding & W,Ltd) -201 Vine -Archbold 43502 **Fx:**445-2353

Goodlet, Charles William Jr. '75 -7 W Bowery -Ste 907 -Akron 44308

(216) 372-7104 ..**Goodluck,** James R '89 -3517 St Albans Rd -Cleveland Heights 44121

(216) 781-3434 ..**Goodman,** Alan I '69 (A Goodman Co,LPA) -55 Pub Sq -Ste 1300 -Cleveland 44113

(216) 523-1525 ..**Goodman,** Alan M '75 -55 Pub Sq -#1616 -Cleveland 44113 **Fx:**523-1487

Goodman, Amy O '01 -6072 Indpndnc Dr -Hudson 44236

(513) 561-9800 ..**Goodman,** Barry A '67 -5965 Stewart Rd -Ste 103 -Cincinnati 45227

(216) 363-4500 ..**Goodman,** Bernard D '60 (Benesck FC&A LLP) -200 Pub Sq -Ste 2300 -Cleveland 44114 **Fx:**363-4588

(216) 479-8500 ..**Goodman,** David S '77 (Squire S&D LLP) -127 Pub Sq -4900 Key Twr -Cleveland 44114 **Fx:**479-8780

(216) 586-3939 ..**Goodman,** Eric R '03 %Jones D -901 Lakeside Av -Cleveland 44114 **Fx:**579-0212

(513) 939-2439 ..**Goodman,** Farrell J '92 -5257 Cherry Mill Ct -Fairfield 45014

(216) 928-9990 ..**Goodman,** Grant A '95 -1300 E 9th -Ste 1717 -Cleveland 44114

(614) 757-5000 ..**Goodman,** Heather E '93 %Cardinal Hlth -7000 Cardinal Pl -Dublin 43017

(614) 466-8064 ..**Goodman,** J David '92 OH Senate -125 Statehse -Columbus 43215

(513) 621-1505 ..**Goodman,** Jeffrey S '93 Goodman & G -123 E 4th -5th Fl -Cincinnati 45202

(330) 393-3400 ..**Goodman,** Jeffrey V '91 -244 Seneca Av -Warren 44481

(216) 216-0606 ..**Goodman,** John L '70 -55 Pub Sq -Ste 1500 -Cleveland 44113

(216) 781-1212 ..**Goodman,** Jonathan H '99 Walter & H LLP -1301 E 9th -Ste 3500 -Cleveland 44113 **Fx:**575-0911

(202) 736-0313 ..**Goodman,** Larry Lee '73 Cnsl Fed Deposit Ins Corp -550 17th NW -Rm H-2118 -Washington, DC 20429

(740) 382-4445 ..**Goodman,** Malcolm L '74 -131 S Prospect -Marion 43302

(614) 223-9300 ..**Goodman,** Norton Victor '61 (Benesck FC&A LLP) -88 E Broad -Ste 900 -Columbus 43215 **Fx:**223-9330

(513) 533-0528 ..**Goodman,** Richard Lanahan '74 -3706 Broadvw Dr -Cincinnati 45208

(330) 652-8989 ..**Goodman,** Richard L '74 -720 Youngstown Warren Rd -Ste E -Niles 44446

(216) 696-3366 ..**Goodman,** Robert A '60 OfCnsl Goodman WM LLP -100 Erievw Plz -27th Fl -Cleveland 44114 **Fx:**363-5835

(513) 621-1505 ..**Goodman,** Ronald J '62 (Goodman & G) -123 E 4th -5th Fl -Cincinnati 45202

(513) 621-1505 ..**Goodman,** Stanley '55 (Goodman & G) -123 E 4th -5th Fl -Cincinnati 45202

(202) 879-7609 ..**Goodman,** Stephen J '85 Cnsl Jones DR&P -51 Louisiana Av NW -Washington, DC 20001 **Fx:**626-1700

(502) 589-4440 ..**Goodman,** Steven A '81 (Goldberg & S,PSC) -101 S 5th -Ste 3000 -Louisville, KY 40202

(513) 621-0267 ..**Goodman,** Terrence L '84 %Waite SB&C -1 W 4th -1513 4th & Vine Twr -Cincinnati 45202

(407) 206-6403 ..**Goodman,** Thomas A '83 Marriott Ownership Resorts,Inc -6649 Westwood Blvd -Ste 500 -Orlando, FL 32821

(202) 467-8800 ..**Goodman,** Timothy H '99 %Vorys SS&P LLP -1828 L NW -11th Fl -Washington, DC 20036

(216) 696-3366 ..**Goodman Weiss Miller LLP** -100 Erievw Plz -27th Fl -Cleveland 44114 **Fx:**363-5835

(732) 549-8600 ..**Goodrich,** David M '98 JM Huber Corp -333 Thornall -Edison, NJ 08837

(614) 436-8010 ..**Goodrich,** Kyle S '04 %WA Morse, ALPA -933 High -Ste 140 -Worthington 43085

(614) 462-5295 ..**Goodrich,** Mary W '92 Franklin Cnty Juv Ct -373 S High -5th Fl -Columbus 43215

(216) 621-1541 ..**Goodrich,** Paula J '80 %Newman & N -526 Superior Av -711 Leader Bldg -Cleveland 44114

(419) 627-7697 ..**Goodrum,** Cheryl Y '95 Erie Cnty Pros -247 Columbus Av -Ste 319 -Sandusky 44870 **Fx:**627-7567

(513) 621-5631 ..**Goodson,** Brett C '76 (Goodson & M,Ltd) -110 E 8th -Ste 200 -Cincinnati 45202

(513) 621-5631 ..**Goodson & Mullins,Ltd** -110 E 8th -Ste 200 -Cincinnati 45202

(513) 579-6400 ..**Goodson,** Stephen M '80 (Keating M&K PLL) -1 E 4th -1400 Provident Twr -Cincinnati 45202 **Fx:**579-6454

(330) 818-0131 ..**Goodson-Beal,** Amy E '03 -504 N Munroe Rd -Tallmadge 44278

(440) 686-9000 ..**Goodwin & Bryan LLP** -22050 Mastick Rd -Fairview Park 44126 **Fx:**686-9001

(937) 431-9700 ..**Goodwin,** Charles S '75 -3500 Plantation Pl -Dayton 45434 **Fx:**431-9703

(216) 575-7666 ..**Goodwin,** David J '82 -1836 Euclid Av -Ste 338 -Cleveland 44115

(440) 686-9000 ..**Goodwin,** Elizabeth A '95 (Goodwin & B LLP) -22050 Mastick Rd -Fairview Park 44126 **Fx:**686-9001

(330) 296-4451 ..**Goodwin,** Jerry A '81 -250 S Chestnut -Ste 17 -Ravenna 44266

Goodwin, Jonathon T '84 -2675 Herold Rd -Batavia 45103

(216) 241-3646 ..**Goodwin,** Paula R '77 %B Sheerer Co,LPA -820 Superior Av W -Ste 510 -Cleveland 44113

(216) 696-2719 ..**Goodwin,** Sally A '93 Long Term Care Ombudsman -2800 Euclid Av -Ste 200 -Cleveland 44115 **Fx:**696-6216

(419) 936-5120 ..**Goodwin,** Thomas P '90 -411 N Mich -Toledo 43624

(513) 785-7327 ..**Goodyear,** Brian E '98 City Law Dept -345 High -7th Fl -Hamilton 45011

(513) 946-3000 ..**Goolsby,** Henrietta L '94 Hamilton Cnty Pros -230 E 9th -Cincinnati 45202 **Fx:**946-3017

(216) 586-3939 ..**Goots,** Thomas R '96 %Jones D -901 Lakeside Av -Cleveland 44114 **Fx:**579-0212

(513) 381-9200 ..**Gora,** Felix J '80 (Rendigs FK&D,LLP) -One W 4th -Ste 900 -Cincinnati 45202 **Fx:**381-9206

(937) 225-4652 ..**Goraleski,** Carl G '83 Montgomery Cnty Pub Def -117 S Main -Ste 400 -Dayton 45422 **Fx:**225-3449

(419) 244-9500 ..**Goranson,** James E '78 (Goranson P&B) -405 Mad Av -Ste 2200 -Toledo 43604 **Fx:**(414) 244-9510

(419) 244-9500 ..**Goranson Parker & Bella** -405 Mad Av -Ste 2200 -Toledo 43604 **Fx:**(414) 244-9510

(419) 244-9500 ..**Goranson,** Roger W '76 (Goranson P&B) -405 Mad Av -Ste 2200 -Toledo 43604 **Fx:**(414) 244-9510

(330) 337-9515 ..**Gorby,** Jennifer A '01 -585 E State -Salem 44460

(216) 687-0404 ..**Gorczyca,** Francis A '81 -1370 Ontario -Ste 2000 -Cleveland 44113

(440) 846-5700 ..**Gordillo,** Gregory A '94 -1370 Ontario -Ste 2000 -Cleveland 44113

(216) 443-7800 ..**Gordillo,** Michael J '00 Cuyahoga Cnty Pros -1200 Ontario -8th Fl -Cleveland 44113 **Fx:**698-2270

(740) 363-1369 ..**Gordin,** Robert H '80 %Heald & L -125 N Sandusky -Delaware 43015

(513) 751-2145 ..**Gordon,** Abram S '87 Oncology/Hematology Care -2522 Highland Av -Cincinnati 45219

(330) 376-2700 ..**Gordon,** Amanda E '90 (Roetzel & A,LPA) -222 S Main -Akron 44308 **Fx:**376-4577

(216) 579-1700 ..**Gordon,** Charles B '52 (Pearne & G LLP) -1801 E 9th -Ste 1200 -Cleveland 44114 **Fx:**579-6073

(740) 653-7705 ..**Gordon,** Charles E '83 SE OH Lgl Srvcs -112 N Pearl -Lancaster 43130

(216) 226-8800 ..**Gordon,** Chester E '55 -14701 Detroit Av -Ste 700 -Lakewood 44107

(614) 299-4513 ..**Gordon,** Clarence T II '75 -394 W 2nd Av -Columbus 43201

(740) 363-8988 ..**Gordon,** David J '69 (Gordon & G) -40 N Sandusky -Delaware 43015

(216) 621-6060 ..**Gordon,** David J '78 Forest City Enterprises -50 Pub Sq -1160 Trmnl Twr -Cleveland 44113

(216) 674-7095 ..**Gordon,** Eric S '98 Bristol West Ins Grp -5990 W Crk Rd -Independence 44131

(937) 865-6800 ..**Gordon,** Erica J '04 Lexis/Nexis -Bx933 -Dayton 45401

(216) 621-2300 ..**Gordon,** Harlan M '68 Nurenberg PH&M LPA -1370 Ontario -Ste 100 -Cleveland 44113 **Fx:**771-2242

(216) 641-4701 ..**Gordon,** Heather A '94 (H Gordon,LLC) -4564 E 71st -Cleveland 44105

(216) 523-4134 ..**Gordon,** Howard D '71 Eaton Corp -1111 Superior Av -Cleveland 44114

(614) 228-0888 ..**Gordon,** James H '74 -21 E State -Ste 1700 -Columbus 43215

(614) 228-0888 ..**Gordon,** James H Jr. '97 -21 E State -Ste 1700 -Columbus 43215

(440) 871-4022 ..**Gordon,** Jeanne V '98 %Corsaro & Assoc Co,LPA -2001 Crocker Rd -Ste 400 -Westlake 44145

(412) 281-5060 ..**Gordon,** Jeffrey R '97 %Houston H,PC -401 Lbrty Av -22nd Fl Three Gtwy Ctr -Pittsburgh, PA 15222 **Fx:**281-4499

(614) 846-1767 ..**Gordon,** John P '78 Mindleaders.com,Inc -851 W 3rd Av -Columbus 43212

(216) 781-5245 ..**Gordon,** Larry S '56 (Berkman GM&D) -55 Pub Sq -2121 The Illuminating Bldg -Cleveland 44113 **Fx:**781-8207

(740) 345-9611 ..**Gordon,** Leland J '53 OfCnsl Morrow G&B,Ltd -33 W Main -Bx4190 -Newark 43058

(440) 951-9000 ..**Gordon,** Lesley A '99 CT Cnsltnts,Inc -35000 Kaiser Ct -Willoughby 44094

(740) 363-8988 ..**Gordon,** Linda M '86 (Gordon & G) -40 N Sandusky -Delaware 43015

(216) 861-5175 ..**Gordon,** Loren M '93 -75 Pub Sq -Ste 1300 -Cleveland 44113

(301) 340-1251 ..**Gordon,** Michael A '81 (Holmes S&G) -17 W Jffrsn -Ste 202 -Rockville, MD 20850

(216) 479-6100 ..**Gordon,** Michael Scot '99 %Vorys SS&P LLP -1375 E 9th -Ste 2100 One Cleve Ctr -Cleveland 44114 **Fx:**479-6060

(614) 621-4135 ..**Gordon,** Nathan '72 -2485 E Broad -Columbus 43209

(614) 645-7385 ..**Gordon,** Pamela J '85 City Atty -90 W Broad -Columbus 43215

(330) 364-4491 ..**Gordon,** Paul N '77 Mun Ct -166 E High Av -New Philadelphia 44663

(937) 865-6800 ..**Gordon,** Rachel E '03 LexisNexis -9393 Springboro Pike -Miamisburg 45342

(440) 282-1200 ..**Gordon,** Ronald H '63 R Gordon Co,LPA -5315 Oberlin Av -Lorain 44053

Gordon, Ryan A '04 -(Address Unavailable)

(941) 366-6660 ..**Gordon,** Scott E '78 (Abel BRCP&G) -240 S Pineapple Av -8th Fl -Bx49948 -Sarasota, FL 34230 **Fx:**366-3999

(419) 238-0114 ..**Gordon,** Scott R '88 -116 W Main -Van Wert 45891

(216) 566-5629 ..**Gordon,** Sean A '01 %Thompson H LLP -127 Pub Sq -3900 Key Ctr -Cleveland 44114 **Fx:**566-5800

(419) 447-3023 ..**Gordon,** Thomas J '68 -23 Court -Tiffin 44883

(614) 487-8887 .. **Gordon,** Thomas S '00 -1820 Northwest Blvd -Ste 100
 -Columbus 43212

(440) 349-1120 .. **Gordon,** William J Jr. '73 -30285 Bruce Indstrl Pkwy -Ste D
 -Solon 44139

(216) 592-5000 .. **Gore,** George F III '64 (Tucker E&W LLP) -925 Euclid Av
 -1150 Huntgtn Bldg -Cleveland 44115 **Fx:**592-5009

(216) 592-5000 .. **Gore,** Janet S '86 (Tucker E&W LLP) -925 Euclid Av
 -1150 Huntgtn Bldg -Cleveland 44115 **Fx:**592-5009

(330) 493-1570 .. **Gore,** William B '64 Macala BM&G,LLC -4150 Belden Vllg NW
 -Ste 604 -Canton 44718 **Fx:**493-7042

(248) 540-3100 .. **Goren,** Steven E '01 (Goren G&H,PC) -30400 Telegraph Rd
 -Ste 470 -Bingham Farms, MI 48025 **Fx:**540-3136

(330) 869-4262 .. **Gorenc,** William Jr. '81 GenCorp Inc -175 Ghent Rd
 -Fairlawn 44333

(216) 575-2253 .. **Gorensek,** Thomas F '85 Natl City Bank -1900 E 9th
 -Cleveland 44114

(513) 381-0656 .. **Gores,** Henrietta D '01 %Kohnen & P LLP -201 E 5th -Ste 800
 -Cincinnati 45202 **Fx:**381-5823

(513) 721-4532 .. **Goret,** Ronald J '64 (Katz TB&H) -255 E 5th -Ste 2400 -Cincinnati
 45202

(216) 357-7120 .. **Goretzke,** Cullen '04 US Dist Ct -801 W Superior Av -U.S. Ct Hse
 -Cleveland 44106

(216) 521-7525 .. **Gorie,** Leo F Jr. '76 -11732 Lk Av -#103 -Lakewood 44107

(216) 566-1778 .. **Gorjanc,** Laura T '04 Sherwin Williams Co -101 Prospect Av NW
 -Cleveland 44115

(740) 283-4781 .. **Gorman,** David D '99 %SE OH Lgl Srvcs -100 N 3rd
 -Steubenville 43952

(419) 245-1944 .. **Gorman,** Francis X '67 Mun Ct Judge -555 N Erie -Toledo 43624

(216) 931-7509 .. **Gorman,** Jennifer H '89 State Indstrl Products Corp
 -3100 Hmltn Av -Cleveland 44114

(330) 253-0785 .. **Gorman,** Joseph F '94 (Gorman MP&V) -1 Cascade Plz -9th Fl
 -Akron 44308 **Fx:**253-7432

(216) 475-8585 .. **Gorman,** Joseph T Jr. '87 Legendary Motorcars,Ltd
 -19950 Rockside Rd -Maple Heights 44137

(330) 562-2681 .. **Gorman,** Lisa M '94 Lexis/Nexis -Bx933 -Dayton 45401

(330) 253-0785 .. **Gorman Malarcik Pierce & Vuillemin** -1 Cascade Plz -9th Fl
 -Akron 44308 **Fx:**253-7432

(740) 282-6705 .. **Gorman,** Michelle L '96 Pietragallo B&G -100 N 4th
 -Steubenville 43952

Gorman, Patrick H '91 -5109 Lupine Ct -Rockville, MD 20853

(330) 264-4444 .. **Gorman,** Robert C '95 (Critchfield C&J Ltd) -225 N Market -Bx599
 -Wooster 44691 **Fx:**263-9278

(202) 778-3004 .. **Gorman,** Thomas O '73 (Porter WM&A) -1919 Penn Av NW
 -Ste 500 -Washington, DC 20006

(440) 350-2135 .. **Gorman,** Thomas R '92 Hon Collins -47 N Park Pl
 -Ct of Cmmn Pleas -Painesville 44077

(937) 325-7058 .. **Gorman Veskauf Henson & Wineberg** -4 W Main -Ste 723
 -Springfield 45502 **Fx:**325-9914

(216) 623-0000 .. **Gormley,** Darryl E '97 %Javitch B&R -1300 E 9th -14th Fl
 -Cleveland 44114 **Fx:**623-0190

(614) 387-9560 .. **Gormley,** David M '90 Cnsl Supreme Ct of OH -65 S Front
 -Columbus 43215 **Fx:**387-9569

(440) 392-9580 .. **Gornik,** David J '90 -7103 Brightwood Dr -Concord 44077

(440) 871-8288 .. **Gornik,** James T '73 Moore Stephens Apple -29550 Detroit Rd
 -Westlake 44145

(614) 566-5151 .. **Gorno,** Lorri A '91 %OhioHealth -3722 Olentangy Rvr Rd -Ste K
 -Columbus 43214

(216) 621-0150 .. **Gorom,** Stanley R III '93 (Hahn L&P LLP)
 -3300 BP Twr/200 Pub Sq -Ste 3300 -Cleveland 44114
 Fx:241-2824

(614) 469-3939 .. **Gorospe,** Gregory A '93 (Jones D) -325 John H McConnell Blvd
 -Ste 600 -Bx165017 -Columbus 43216 **Fx:**461-4198

(513) 946-5760 .. **Gorrasi-Dwenger,** Lisa M '03 Hamilton Cnty Ct of Common Pleas
 -1000 Main -495 -Cincinnati 45202 **Fx:**946-5757

(419) 399-2181 .. **Gorrell,** Brian S '02 %Cook T&B,Ltd -112 N Water
 -Paulding 45879

(614) 445-8416 .. **Gorrell,** Debra L '94 -52 W Whittier -Columbus 43206

(440) 247-5585 .. **Gorretta,** Laura J '86 Woodward & G -50 E Wshngtn -Chagrin
 Falls 44022 **Fx:**247-1031

(614) 228-5822 .. **Gorry,** James R Jr. '72 OfCnsl Rich C&D,LLC -300 E Broad
 -Ste 300 -Columbus 43215 **Fx:**228-2725

(216) 292-5807 .. **Gorski,** Jeffrey A '94 (Singerman MD&K) -3401 Enterprise Pkwy
 -Ste 200 -Beachwood 44122 **Fx:**292-5867

(440) 333-9800 .. **Gorski,** Pamela L '92 -19111 Detroit Rd -Ste 205 -Rocky
 River 44116

(513) 321-4238 .. **Gortsas,** Alex '58 -2444 Madison Rd -1910 -Cincinnati 45208

(614) 466-3615 .. **Goshay,** Pamela M '00 Legis Srvc Commssn -77 S High
 -Columbus 43215

(216) 687-2325 .. **Goshien,** David B '76 CSU-Marshall Cllg of Law -2121 Euclid Av
 -LB138 -Cleveland 44115 **Fx:**687-6881

(216) 932-5226 .. **Goshien,** Deborah P '70 (DP Goshien Co,LPA)
 -3391 Superior Park Dr -Cleveland Heights 44118

(330) 797-0086 .. **Goske,** Stephen Paul '81 Green H&S,Co LPA -120 Wstchstr Dr
 -Ste A -Bx3985 -Austintown 44515 **Fx:**797-2969

(937) 593-8075 .. **Goslee,** William T '89 (Goslee & G) -114 S Main -Bx416
 -Bellefontaine 43311

(419) 241-9000 .. **Gosline,** William H '70 (Shumaker L&K,LLP) -1000 Jackson
 -Toledo 43624 **Fx:**241-6894

(614) 221-4000 .. **Gosnell,** Gerhardt A II '95 %Chester W&S LLP -65 E State
 -10th Fl -Columbus 43215 **Fx:**221-4012

(216) 861-5582 .. **Goss,** Colleen Flynn '80 %Fay SFM&M LLP -1100 Superior Av
 -7th Fl -Cleveland 44114 **Fx:**241-1666

(614) 228-6438 .. **Goss,** Dianne '82 -632 N High -Columbus 43215

(614) 728-7055 .. **Gosselin,** Heather L '00 Atty Gen -30 E Broad -Columbus 43215
 Fx:728-8606

(513) 639-5421 .. **Gossett,** Deanna C '98 Provident Bank -1 E 4th -MS 198D
 -Cincinnati 45202

Gossett, Jay M '87 -608 W High -Uhrichsville 44683

(304) 234-3631 .. **Gossett,** Randy D '83 Marshall Cnty Pros Ofc -Cthse
 -Moundsville, WV 26041

(513) 734-7470 .. **Gossett,** Tresa '89 (Gossett & Assoc) -200 W Plane -Bx150
 -Bethel 45106

(440) 717-1680 .. **Gossick,** Lucius C '63 -8191 Broadvw Rd -Ste 201
 -Cleveland 44147

(513) 762-1384 .. **Gothard,** Jennifer K '92 Kroger Co -1014 Vine -Cincinnati 45202

(614) 221-4349 .. **Gotherman,** John E '61 Cnsl OH Mun League -175 S 3rd -Ste 510
 -Columbus 43215

(216) 696-7525 .. **Gottehrer,** Blaine L '80 (Fine G & Assoc,LPA) -1370 W 6th
 -Ste 202 -Cleveland 44113

(513) 651-2121 .. **Gottesman,** Zachary '92 -36 E 7th -2121 CBLD Ctr
 -Cincinnati 45202

(614) 297-1211 .. **Gottfried,** Gary J '73 (G Gottfried Co,LPA) -1265 Neil Av
 -Columbus 43201

(216) 348-2800 .. **Gottfried,** R. Mark Jr. '87 %Stefanski & Assoc,LLC
 -614 W Superior Av -Ste 1144 -Cleveland 44113 **Fx:**348-1557

(419) 255-3344 .. **Gottlieb,** Arnold N '78 -608 Mad Av -Ste 1523 -Toledo 43604

(727) 791-1977 .. **Gottlieb,** Jerry '76 (Gottlieb & G) -2475 Enterprise Rd -100
 -Clearwater, FL 33763 **Fx:**791-8090

(740) 452-7555 .. **Gottlieb Johnston Beam & Dal Ponte,PLL** -320 Main -Bx190
 -Zanesville 43702 **Fx:**452-2257

(419) 385-8002 .. **Gottlieb,** Judith B '81 -1241 Michele Rd -Toledo 43614

(727) 791-1977 .. **Gottlieb,** Richard '81 (Gottlieb & G) -2475 Enterprise Rd -100
 -Clearwater, FL 33763 **Fx:**791-8090

(937) 449-6810 .. **Gottman,** Andrew J '99 %Porter WM&A LLP -1 S Main -Ste 1600
 -Dayton 45402 **Fx:**449-6820

(937) 449-6400 .. **Gottman,** James F '74 (Dinsmore & S LLP) -1 S Main
 -Ste 1300 One Dayton Centre -Dayton 45402 **Fx:**449-6405

(937) 496-7609 .. **Gottman,** Virginia M '00 Montgomery Cnty Pros -301 W 3rd
 -Bx972 -Dayton 45422 **Fx:**225-3470

(419) 227-3423 .. **Gottschalk,** Craig A '97 %Huffman KB&B LLC -127-129 N Pierce
 -Bx546 -Lima 45802 **Fx:**228-1937

(614) 464-6400 .. **Gottschall,** Michael D '97 %Vorys SS&P LLP -52 E Gay -Bx1008
 -Columbus 43216 **Fx:**464-6350

(937) 913-0200 .. **Gottschlich,** Gary W '71 (Gottschlich & P LLP) -201 E 6th
 -Dayton 45402 **Fx:**824-2818

(937) 913-0200 .. **Gottschlich & Portune LLP** -201 E 6th -Dayton 45402
 Fx:824-2818

(440) 774-7722 .. **Gottschling,** Carol M '03 Oberlin Book Store -37 W Cllg
 -Oberlin 44074

(937) 548-2211 .. **Goubeaux,** James J '61 (Goubeaux & G) -100 Wshngtn Av
 -Bx158 -Greenville 45331

(614) 461-1100 .. **Gouhin,** Sean M '94 %Swedlow BLL&D Co,LPA -10 W Broad
 -Ste 2400 -Columbus 43215 **Fx:**461-8178

(304) 523-2100 .. **Gould,** Charles K '96 %Jenkins F PLLC -401 11th -Ste 1100
 -Bx2688 -Huntington, WV 25726

(614) 237-9802 .. **Gould,** Craigg E '93 City Attys Ofc -360 S Yearling Rd
 -Whitehall 43213

(937) 323-7531 .. **Gould,** John E '60 (J Gould Co,LPA) -649 E High -Bx1443
 -Springfield 45501

(419) 248-7448 .. **Gould,** Kenneth D '75 SrCnsl Owens Corning
 -1 Owens Corning Pkwy -Leg Dept -Toledo 43659

(216) 292-4261 .. **Goulder,** Herbert I '63 DOAN Capital -29525 Chagrin Blvd
 -Ste 103 -Beachwood 44122

(216) 676-6800 .. **Goulder,** Richard A '60 (Goulder & G) -15887 Snow Rd -Ste 301
 -Brook Park 44142 **Fx:**676-6885

(419) 243-6281 .. **Goulding,** Michael R '96 (Shindler NH&S,LLP) -300 Mad Av
 -Ste 1200 -Toledo 43604 **Fx:**243-0129

Goulet, Kathryn H '01 -4450 Belden Vllg NW -Ste 501
 -Canton 44718

(937) 226-1212 .. **Gounaris,** Nicholas G '95 Skelton MG&H -130 W 2nd -Ste 450
 -Dayton 45402

(216) 443-9000 .. **Gourash,** Daniel F '83 (Porter WM&A LLP) -925 Euclid Av
 -Ste 1700 -Cleveland 44115 **Fx:**443-9011

(330) 494-1015 .. **Goutras,** Gust '85 (Goutras & G) -4571 Stephen Cir NW
 -Canton 44718

(330) 494-1015 .. **Goutras,** Lora L '89 (Goutras & G) -4571 Stephen Cir NW -Canton
 44718

(419) 242-9900 .. **Gouttiere,** John P '74 (JP Gouttiere Co LPA) -520 Mad Av
 -Ste 1026 -Toledo 43604 **Fx:**244-8620

(614) 466-4882 .. **Govern,** Jodi A '89 OH Dept Hlth -246 N High -Bx118 -Columbus
 43216

(330) 384-7035 .. **Gow,** Robert M '92 FirstMerit Corp -III Cascade Plz -Akron 44308

(216) 241-5310 .. **Gowan,** James G '65 OfCnsl Gallagher SF&N -1501 Euclid Av
 -6th Fl -Cleveland 44115 **Fx:**241-1608

(216) 621-8744 .. **Gozdanovic,** Amy E '97 -920 E 9th -Ste 700 -Cleveland 44115

(216) 621-0200 .. **Graban,** Matthew D '97 %Baker & H LLP -1900 E 9th -Ste 3200
 -Cleveland 44114 **Fx:**696-0740

(513) 398-4891 .. **Graber,** Matthew J '02 Peeler M&Z -423 Reading Rd
 -Mason 45040

(513) 241-2324 .. **Graber,** Sarah Otte '97 %Wood H&E LLP -441 Vine -Ste 2700
 -Cincinnati 45202 **Fx:**421-7269

(937) 548-1157 .. **Graber,** Thomas H II '79 (Hanes SCGG&D,Ltd) -507 S Bway
 -Greenville 45331

(216) 241-5310 .. **Grable,** Jason P '03 %Gallagher SF&N -1501 Euclid Av -6th Fl
 -Cleveland 44115 **Fx:**241-1608

(614) 274-8100 .. **Grabovac,** Greg R '94 Cnsl Fishel Co -1810 Arlingate Ln
 -Columbus 43228 **Fx:**274-6794

(216) 479-6100 .. **Grabow,** Rachel J '97 %Vorys SS&P LLP -1375 E 9th
 -Ste 2100 One Cleve Ctr -Cleveland 44114 **Fx:**479-6060

(216) 447-4496 .. **Grabow,** Raymond J '58 R Grabow & Assoc -5005 Rockside Rd
 -Ste 425 -Independence 44131

(440) 899-7377 .. **Grace,** Charles H '71 -30803 Brcknrdg Trl -Westlake 44145
 Fx:808-9897

(713) 226-1200 .. **Grace,** Thomas H '72 Locke L&S LLP -600 Travis -Ste 2600
 -Houston, TX 77002 **Fx:**223-3717

(740) 592-5839 .. **Grace,** Todd L '01 (Grace & M) -19½ S Court -Athens 45701
 Fx:592-3764

(614) 462-3555 .. **Graceffo,** John P '96 Franklin Cnty Pros -373 S High -Columbus
 43215

(513) 651-6800 .. **Gracey,** Stephen M '03 %Frost BT LLC -201 E 5th -2200 PNC Ctr
 -Cincinnati 45202 **Fx:**651-6981

(419) 874-7188 .. **Grachek,** Ellen M '03 %Allotta F&W Co,LPA -27457 Holiday Ln
 -Ste W -Perrysburg 43551 **Fx:**874-7189

(614) 228-5225 .. **Graden,** Leslie B '91 Ferron & Assoc,LPA -580 N 4th -Ste 450
 -Columbus 43215 **Fx:**228-3255

(330) 535-5711 .. **Gradert,** Lisa Novosat '88 (Brouse M) -106 S Main
 -500 First Natl Twr -Akron 44308 **Fx:**253-8601

(330) 762-2411 ..**Gradisher,** Suzanne M '04 %Amer C Co,LPA -159 S Main -6th Fl
-Akron 44308 Fx:762-9918

(215) 699-6000 ..**Gradwohl,** David A '72 (Fox RO&F,LLP) -1250 S Broad -Ste 1000
-Lansdale, PA 19446

(513) 961-6200 ..**Gradwohl,** Samuel A '99 Markesbery & R Co,LPA
-2368 Victory Pkwy -Ste 200 -Bx6491 -Cincinnati 45206

(239) 337-3850 ..**Grady,** Beverly '76 (Roetzel & A) -2320 First -Ste 1000
-Fort Myers, FL 33901 Fx:337-0970

(440) 356-7255 ..**Grady,** Francis X '84 (Grady & Assoc) -20950 Ctr Ridge Rd
-Ste 100 -Rocky River 44116 Fx:356-7255

(216) 222-2000 ..**Grady,** Kathleen S '81 %Natl City Corp -1900 E 9th
-Cleveland 44114

(330) 860-1471 ..**Grady,** Michael J '86 Babcock & Wilcox Co -20 S Van Buren Av
-Barberton 44203

(937) 644-6545 ..**Grady,** Stephen L '97 Honda of America -24000 Honda Pkwy
-Marysville 43040

(614) 849-0378 ..**Grady,** Terrence A '82 (T Grady & Assoc Co,LPA) -100 E Broad
-Ste 2310 -Columbus 43215 Fx:849-0379

(614) 227-2000 ..**Grady,** Timothy E '79 (Porter WM&A LLP) -41 S High
-Columbus 43215 Fx:227-2100

(614) 226-5991 ..**Graeff,** David J '72 -Bx1948 -Westerville 43086

(419) 535-1840 ..**Graeff,** Scott M '02 %CC Covrett -2727 N Holland-Sylvania Rd
-Ste E -Toledo 43615

(513) 721-3323 ..**Graeter,** Richard A II '89 Graeters Inc -2145 Reading Rd
-Cincinnati 45202

(513) 421-1313 ..**Graf,** Andrew D '97 %Griffin-F,LLP -3500 Redbank Rd -Cincinnati
45227 Fx:421-1118

(614) 716-1649 ..**Graf,** Ann B '84 Amer Elec Pwr Co -1 Riverside Plz
-Columbus 43215

(614) 252-7108 ..**Graf,** Brenda J '96 Carington Hlth Systems -500 N Nelson Rd
-Columbus 43219

(216) 961-3500 ..**Graf,** Frederick L '79 Arrow Intl Inc -9900 Clinton Rd
-Brooklyn 44144

(614) 481-2020 ..**Graf,** Jack R Jr. '73 Graf & Sons Inc -2020 Builders Pl
-Columbus 43204

(937) 562-5041 ..**Graf,** Joseph C '75 Greene Cnty Pub Def -90 E Main -Xenia 45385

(513) 618-7800 ..**Graf Stiebel & Moyers, LPA** -425 Walnut -Ste 2400
-Cincinnati 45202 Fx:618-7801

(513) 618-7800 ..**Graf,** William R Jr. '76 (Graf S&M,LPA) -425 Walnut -Ste 2400
-Cincinnati 45202 Fx:618-7801

(614) 447-0314 ..**Graf-Caswell,** Mary L '96 -4469 Olentangy Blvd -Columbus 43214

(513) 579-2540 ..**Grafe,** Karl J '85 Amer Fncl Corp -One E 4th -Cincinnati 45202

(614) 228-5800 ..**Graff,** Douglas E '85 (Graff & Assoc) -604 E Rich
-Columbus 43215 Fx:228-8811

(419) 227-7193 ..**Graff,** Melinda J '87 OH Indstrl Commssn -2025 E 4th -Lima 45804

(419) 213-3030 ..**Graff,** Walter J '82 Lucas Cnty CSEA -701 Adams -Toledo 43624

(419) 294-1981 ..**Grafmiller,** Richard A '73 -Bx116 -Upper Sandusky 43351

(630) 428-0197 ..**Graft,** Maynard L Jr. '71 -1082 Whirlaway Av -Naperville, IL 60540

(405) 739-2692 ..**Grafton,** Jeanette A '86 USAF -7460 Arnold -OC-ALC/JAQ
-Tinker AFB, OK 73145

(216) 928-1010 ..**Gragel,** Susan L '80 (Rotatori BGS&A Co LPA) -526 Superior Av E
-800 Leader Bldg -Cleveland 44114 Fx:928-1007

(740) 962-2174 ..**Graham,** Amy S '02 -143 E Main -Bx537 -McConnelsville 43756
Fx:962-2174

(419) 447-7966 ..**Graham,** Arthur F '60 -716 Market -Bx38 -Tiffin 44883

(740) 454-8585 ..**Graham,** Clay P '80 Graham M&R Co,LPA -11 N 4th -Bx340
-Zanesville 43702

(740) 454-8585 ..**Graham,** David A '83 %Graham M&R Co,LPA -11 N 4th -Bx340
-Zanesville 43702

(614) 462-5455 ..**Graham,** David T '98 %Kegler BH&R -65 E State -Ste 1800
-Columbus 43215 Fx:464-2634

(614) 228-2300 ..**Graham,** Derek L '04 %Fry W&M Co,LPA -35 E Lvngstn Av
-Columbus 43215 Fx:228-6680

(216) 228-1166 ..**Graham,** Edward M '71 -13363 Mad Av -Lakewood 44107

(330) 296-3888 ..**Graham,** Gerald B '70 -204 S Meridian -Bx148 -Ravenna 44266

(202) 715-7749 ..**Graham,** Harry G '79 Watson Wyatt Worldwide -1717 H NW
-Washington, DC 20036

(216) 622-8200 ..**Graham,** James D '95 %Calfee H&G LLP -800 Superior Av
-Ste 1400 -Cleveland 44114 Fx:241-0816

(740) 454-8585 ..**Graham,** James F '52 (Graham M&R Co,LPA) -11 N 4th -Bx340
-Zanesville 43702

(937) 842-4258 ..**Graham,** Joseph V '90 -9450 State Rt 368 -Huntsville 43324

(614) 645-8730 ..**Graham,** Kathleen E '82 Franklin Cnty Mun Ct -375 S High
-Columbus 43215

..**Graham,** Kelly A '95 -(Address Unavailable)

(330) 297-3879 ..**Graham,** Kent M '82 Portage Cnty Cmmn Pleas Ct -203 E Main
-Ravenna 44266

(216) 263-6200 ..**Graham,** Maurice E '00 Rauser & Assoc,LPA -614 W Superior Av
-Ste 950 -Cleveland 44113 Fx:263-6202

(740) 454-8585 ..**Graham McClelland & Ransbottom Co,LPA** -11 N 4th -Bx340
-Zanesville 43702

..**Graham,** Michael P '04 -(Address Unavailable)

(330) 841-2538 ..**Graham,** Nicholas J '98 Pros -141 South SE -Warren 44483

(614) 221-0922 ..**Graham,** Richard C '68 Gamble HJ Co,LPA -1 E Lvngstn Av
-Columbus 43215 Fx:365-9741

(614) 436-3437 ..**Graham,** Richard E '78 -315 Blandford Av -Worthington 43085

(513) 474-0648 ..**Graham,** Richard K '92 -8070 Beechmont Rd -Cincinnati 45255

(216) 443-3584 ..**Graham,** Richard T '74 Cuyahoga Cnty Juv Ct -2163 E 22nd
-Cleveland 44115

(740) 454-8585 ..**Graham,** Robert P '79 Graham M&R Co,LPA -11 N 4th -Bx340
-Zanesville 43702

(440) 974-5752 ..**Graham,** Rondie M '87 City of Mentor -8500 Civic Ctr Blvd
-Mentor 44060

(216) 514-1180 ..**Graham,** Sarah S '99 %Krantz P&F,PLL -23200 Chagrin Blvd
-Ste 180 -Cleveland 44122 Fx:514-1185

..**Graham,** Sulaiman Roy '99 Buckeye Legal Aid Srvcs
-3250 E 116th -Cleveland 44120

(330) 499-1016 ..**Graham,** Wayne E Jr. '85 -4571 Stephen Cir NW -Canton 44718

(304) 529-5264 ..**Graham,** William G '76 US Army Corp of Engineers -502 8th
-Huntington, WV 25701

(330) 996-4099 ..**Graham-Hurd,** Melissa A '84 -7 W Bowery -704 Landmark Bldg
-Akron 44308

(202) 305-1334 ..**Graham-Oliver,** Heather D '84 US Attys Ofc -555 4th NW
-Judiciary Ctr -Washington, DC 20530

(419) 592-3503 ..**Grahn,** David M '90 City Law Director -255 W Rivervw -Bx151
-Napoleon 43545

(216) 766-6000 ..**Graines,** Stuart J '72 -4645 Richmond Rd -#101
-Warrensville Heights 44128

(304) 529-2391 ..**Graley,** James G '04 %Campbell WBEM&H,PLLC -Bx1835
-Huntington, WV 25719 Fx:529-1832

(614) 469-3939 ..**Gramann,** Margaret L '85 Cnsl Jones D
-325 John H McConnell Blvd -Ste 600 -Bx165017
-Columbus 43216 Fx:461-4198

(814) 459-8288 ..**Graml,** Michael J '88 -714 Sassafras -Erie, PA 16501

(937) 898-3975 ..**Gramza,** Jeffrey T '91 %Moore & Assoc -410 Corp Ctr Dr
-Vandalia 45377

(740) 349-8505 ..**Gramza,** Michelle L '91 %Schaller C&U -32 N Park Pl
-Newark 43055

(419) 252-2700 ..**Granata,** Eileen M '85 Regional Grwth Prtnrshp -300 Mad Av
-Ste 270 -Toledo 43604

(614) 464-6400 ..**Grande,** Monica E '04 %Vorys SS&P LLP -52 E Gay -Bx1008
-Columbus 43216 Fx:464-6350

(937) 393-1851 ..**Grandey,** James B '77 Pros -112 Governor Foraker Pl
-Hillsboro 45133

(202) 429-4560 ..**Grandinetti,** Paul '83 -1725 K NW -Ste 1401
-Washington, DC 20006

(937) 223-1201 ..**Grandjean,** Dalma C '77 (Altick & C Co,LPA) -1 S Main
-1700 One Dayton Ctr -Dayton 45402 Fx:223-5100

(614) 644-5312 ..**Grandon,** Jon D '87 Industrial Commssn of OH -30 W Spring
-9th Fl -Columbus 43215 Fx:752-8785

(614) 728-8400 ..**Grandon,** Pamela Jo '81 OH Dept Commerce -77 S High
-Columbus 43266

(614) 461-7799 ..**Graney,** Michael P '68 (Simpson T&B) -1 Riverside Plz -9th Fl
-Columbus 43215 Fx:461-0040

(614) 462-2312 ..**Granger,** Aaron L '97 %Schottenstein Z&D -250 West -Bx165020
-Columbus 43216 Fx:462-5135

(614) 854-0615 ..**Granger,** Mark S '97 (Granger Co,LPA) -132 Northwoods Blvd

(216) 382-9950 ..**Granito,** Michael B '84 -24400 Highland Rd -Ste 162
-Richmond Heights 44143 Fx:383-9946

(740) 432-2389 ..**Granitsas,** G '53 -123 W 8th -Cambridge 43725

(330) 889-2515 ..**Granitto,** Rhonda L '89 -6401 State Route 534
-West Farmington 44491

(216) 443-7800 ..**Grano,** Robert H Jr. '84 Cuyahoga Cnty Pros -1200 Ontario -8th Fl
-Cleveland 44113 Fx:698-2270

(216) 241-6868 ..**Grant,** David L '76 (Grant & Co,LPA) -1148 Euclid Av -Ste 300
-Cleveland 44115

(216) 771-1760 ..**Grant,** David R '95 %Smith & C LLP -1801 E Ninth
-Ste 900 Ohio Svngs Plz -Cleveland 44114 Fx:771-3387

(614) 221-3155 ..**Grant,** Dennis D '65 (Bailey C LLC) -10 W Broad -Columbus
43215 Fx:221-0479

(216) 443-8826 ..**Grant,** Garlandine J '86 Cuyahoga Cnty Dom Rltns Ct
-1 Lakeside Av -Cleveland 44113

..**Grant,** Holly J '98 -Bx276 -Damascus 44619

(513) 221-1745 ..**Grant,** James A '85 (Beirne & W Co,LPA) -1745 Madison Rd
-Bx6111 -Cincinnati 45206 Fx:221-6666

(513) 946-3700 ..**Grant,** Joan L '78 Hamilton Cnty Pub Def -230 E 9th -3rd Fl
-Cincinnati 45202 Fx:946-3707

(216) 721-3606 ..**Grant,** Joseph K '99 -10902 Wade Park Av -Cleveland 44106

(513) 684-3211 ..**Grant,** Joseph P '87 IRS Dist Cnsl -312 Elm -Ste 2300
-Cincinnati 45202

(419) 245-2747 ..**Grant,** Lloyd S '93 -Bx1883 -Toledo 43603

(703) 235-2307 ..**Grant,** Mario C '74 US DOJ/Immigration Ct -901 N Stuart
-Ste 1300 -Arlington, VA 22203

(513) 471-9405 ..**Grant,** Marvin F '55 -4123 Delhi Pike -Cincinnati 45204

(330) 762-0765 ..**Grant,** Paul M '95 -441 Wolf Ledges Pkwy -Ste 400 -Akron 44311
Fx:762-2255

(330) 253-4424 ..**Grant,** Priscilla A '97 Schlabig & Assoc -525 Wolf Ledges Pkwy
-Akron 44311

(617) 526-8402 ..**Grant,** Richard L '82 Tractebel LNG NA -One Lbrty Sq -11th Fl
-Boston, MA 02109

(518) 505-6263 ..**Grant,** Robert E '86 AIG Claims Srvc -1 Park Pl -Ste 3B
-Albany, NY 12205

(614) 792-5555 ..**Grant,** Stephen L '88 %Standley Law Grp LLP -495 Metro Pl S
-Ste 210 -Dublin 43017 Fx:792-5536

(216) 476-1299 ..**Granzier,** Paul A '59 -17508 Dartmth Av -Cleveland 44111

(330) 394-1539 ..**Graora,** David J '86 W Urban Co LPA -434 High NE
-Warren 44481

..**Grasham,** Matthew J '03 -Bx91 -Galloway 43119

(330) 374-6906 ..**Graske,** Leslie S '83 (Collins & G) -333 S Main -Ste 304
-Akron 44308

(937) 865-2012 ..**Grass,** Joseph J '72 Monarch Marking -Bx608 -Dayton 45401

(614) 224-5205 ..**Grassbaugh,** Stephen P '84 (Peck S&W,LLP) -175 S 3rd -Ste 600
-Columbus 43215 Fx:224-0069

(216) 348-5400 ..**Grassi,** Carl J '84 (McDonald H Co,LPA) -600 Superior Av E
-Ste 2100 -Cleveland 44114 Fx:348-5474

(216) 328-2600 ..**Grasso,** James A '83 1st Rlty Property Mgmt,Ltd
-6000 Rockside Wds Blvd -Ste 220 -Cleveland 44131

(513) 723-1121 ..**Grau,** Kenneth M '88 DuCharme McMillen & Assoc -312 Plum
-Ste 1100 -Cincinnati 45202

(216) 587-2120 ..**Grau,** Paul A '76 (Reddy G&M Co,LPA) -5306 Transportation Blvd
-Garfield Heights 44125

(614) 221-0240 ..**Grauel,** Dawn-Rae '01 %Hahn L&P LLP -65 E State -Ste 1400
-Columbus 43215 Fx:221-5909

(614) 365-2700 ..**Grauer,** David W '85 (Squire S&D LLP) -41 S High
-1300 Huntgtn Ctr -Columbus 43215 Fx:365-2499

(614) 236-6681 ..**Grauer,** Myron C '85 Capital Univ Law Sch -303 E Broad
-Columbus 43215

(859) 394-6200 ..**Graus,** Stacey L '92 (Adams SW&D) -40 W Pike -Bx861
-Covington, KY 41012 Fx:291-7902

(419) 242-1400 ..**Graven,** James P '90 -608 Mad Av -Ste 1400 -Toledo 43604

(330) 264-8161 ..**Graven,** Marion F III '69 -133 E Larwill -Wooster 44691

(440) 895-0062 ..**Gravens,** Maureen A '79 Mun Ct Judge -21012 Hilliard Blvd
-Rocky River 44116

(216) 579-1602 ..**Gravens,** Terrance P '77 (Rawlins G&F Co,LPA) -55 Pub Sq
-Ste 850 -Cleveland 44113

(614) 442-7903 .. **Graves,** Arthur C '64 -2929 Kenny Rd -Ste 295 -Columbus 43221
Graves, Christine C '02 -3721 Nicoya Ct -Lewis Center 43035
(440) 356-5700 .. **Graves,** David M '98 (Laubacher & G,LLP) -20525 Ctr Ridge Rd
-Ste 626 -Cleveland 44116
(216) 696-2022 .. **Graves,** Donet D '79 (Graves & H,LLC) -1111 Superior Av E
-Cleveland 44114 **Fx:**696-1995
(440) 886-1900 .. **Graves,** Harold D '61 -5788 Ridge Rd -Parma 44129
(216) 696-2022 .. **Graves & Horton, LLC** -1111 Superior Av E -Cleveland 44114
Fx:696-1995
(330) 836-7040 .. **Graves,** James R '57 -57 Baker Blvd -Fairlawn 44333
(513) 762-4252 .. **Graves,** Joan H '94 Kroger Co -1014 Vine -Cincinnati 45202
(419) 898-2671 .. **Graves Kohli & Christie** -142 W Water -Oak Harbor 43449
(440) 886-7901 .. **Graves,** Marco E '92 -4758 Ridge Rd PMB 116 -Brooklyn 44144
Fx:886-7901
(216) 831-2255 .. **Gray,** Brenda J '93 Beech Brook -3737 Lander Rd
-Cleveland 44124
(216) 622-8200 .. **Gray,** David E II '99 %Calfee H&G LLP -800 Superior Av -Ste 1400
-Cleveland 44114 **Fx:**224-1236
(419) 241-2777 .. **Gray,** David L '98 Bunda S&D,PLL -One SeaGate -Ste 650
-Toledo 43604 **Fx:**241-9601
(614) 224-1222 .. **Gray,** Deborah B '91 %Maguire & S,LLP -250 Civic Ctr Dr -Ste 200
-Columbus 43215 **Fx:**224-1236
(513) 932-2871 .. **Gray & Duning** -4 S Bway -Bx268 -Lebanon 45036
Gray, Edell R '96 -230 E 9th -2nd Fl -Cincinnati 45202
(216) 479-8500 .. **Gray,** James D '91 (Squire S&D LLP) -127 Pub Sq -4900 Key Twr
-Cleveland 44114 **Fx:**479-8780
(330) 856-7575 .. **Gray,** James E '74 (J Gray & Assoc) -8528 E Market
-Warren 44484
(614) 227-4834 .. **Gray,** James S '00 %Bricker & E LLP -100 S 3rd -Columbus 43215
Fx:227-2390
Gray, Jeffrey S '85 -10397 E Wood Dr -Scottsdale, AZ 85260
Gray, Jon F '86 -75 Rough Way -C -Lebanon 45036
(216) 781-5832 .. **Gray,** Louis '42 -330 Standard Bldg -Cleveland 44113
(419) 294-4991 .. **Gray,** Martha M '92 Wyandot Mem Hosp -885 N Sandusky Av
-Upper Sandusky 43351
(440) 327-9811 .. **Gray,** Robert W '65 (R Gray & Assoc) -35945 Ctr Ridge Rd
-Ste 203 -North Ridgeville 44039 **Fx:**327-7742
(513) 946-9200 .. **Gray,** Robin D '93 Hamilton Cnty Juv Ct -800 Bway
-Cincinnati 45202 **Fx:**946-9217
(216) 579-0800 .. **Gray,** Roland B '83 (R Gray & Co) -101 Prospect Av W
-1605 Mdlnd Bldg -Cleveland 44115
(440) 988-8786 .. **Gray,** Russell W '87 Moore Fin Enterprises -209 S Main -Ste 7
-Amherst 44001
(614) 227-2329 .. **Gray,** Stephen C '97 %Bricker & E LLP -100 S 3rd
-Columbus 43215 **Fx:**227-2390
(440) 331-3949 .. **Gray,** Susan M '93 -21330 Ctr Ridge Rd -Ste 11
-Rocky River 44116
(740) 833-2690 .. **Gray,** Thayne D '92 Delaware Cnty Pros -140 N Sandusky -3rd Fl
-Delaware 43015
(216) 831-8664 .. **Gray,** Thomas J '41 -4140 Brainard Rd -Chagrin Falls 44022
(216) 928-2200 .. **Gray,** Todd A '99 %Sutter OM&F -1301 E 9th -3600 Erievw Twr
-Cleveland 44114 **Fx:**928-4400
(513) 232-1700 .. **Gray,** Victoria M '93 Moore M&M -7416 Jager Ct -Cincinnati 45230
(727) 399-8300 .. **Gray,** Zachary S '90 Gibbs Law Firm,PA -5666 Seminole Blvd
-Ste 2 -Seminole, FL 33772 **Fx:**398-3907
(513) 621-6464 .. **Graydon Head & Ritchey LLP** -511 Walnut -1900 Fifth Third Ctr
-Cincinnati 45202 **Fx:**651-3836
(614) 462-2700 .. **Grayem,** Jeremy M '00 %Schottenstein Z&D -250 West
-Bx165020 -Columbus 43216 **Fx:**462-5135
(216) 522-0171 .. **Grays,** Winston '83 W Grays & Assoc Co,LPA -1422 Euclid Av
-Ste 1604 -Cleveland 44115
(859) 331-8883 .. **Grayson,** Carl E '97 (Sutton HLG&B PLC) -130 Dudley Rd
-Ste 250 -Edgewood, KY 41017 **Fx:**341-2777
(513) 345-4700 .. **Grayson,** Deborah R '94 (Meizlish & G) -830 Main -Ste 999
-Cincinnati 45202
(614) 841-1918 .. **Grayson,** R S '85 AFSCME OH Cnsl 8 -6800 N High
-Worthington 43085
(614) 463-9770 .. **Graziano,** Robert B '91 (Roetzel & A,LPA) -155 E Broad
-Natl City Ctr 12th Fl -Columbus 43215 **Fx:**463-9792
(202) 293-8090 .. **Grdina,** Elizabeth A '81 Heller HCLS&S -1730 M NW -Ste 412
-Washington, DC 20036
(614) 227-2000 .. **Greaney,** Constance M '92 (Porter WM&A LLP) -41 S High
-Columbus 43215 **Fx:**227-2100
(937) 333-4457 .. **Greaney,** Dennis J '79 Dayton Municipal Ct -301 W 3rd -Rm 127
-Dayton 45402
(216) 241-5310 .. **Greathouse,** Larry C '83 (Gallagher SF&N) -1501 Euclid Av -6th Fl
-Cleveland 44115 **Fx:**241-1608
(937) 865-6800 .. **Greathouse,** M Gregory '92 Lexis/Nexis -Bx933 -Dayton 45401
(330) 744-5139 .. **Greaves,** Elaine B '91 -34 Fed Plz W -810 Wick Bldg
-Youngstown 44503
Greco, Anthony W '93 -604 E Rich -Columbus 43215
(216) 433-2650 .. **Greco,** Frank J '86 NASA Lewis Research Ctr
-21000 Brookpark Rd -Cleveland 44135
(601) 951-8389 .. **Greco,** Fredrick T '96 -139 Murial -Clinton, MS 39056
(216) 696-8700 .. **Greco,** Karen L '82 (Kohrman J&K PLL) -1375 E 9th
-One Cleve Ctr 20th Fl -Cleveland 44114 **Fx:**621-6536
(216) 861-5000 .. **Greco,** Richard A Jr. '82 (Ernst & Young) -1300 Huntngtn Bldg
-925 Euclid Av -Cleveland 44115
(419) 243-4006 .. **Greeley,** Nancy P '86 %Kitch DWD&V,PC -405 Mad Av -Ste 1500
-Toledo 43604 **Fx:**243-7333
(859) 647-6981 .. **Green,** Andrew W '00 (AW Green,PLLC) -7430 US Hwy 42
-Ste 116 -Florence, KY 41042
(216) 831-5100 .. **Green,** Brian J '94 (Shapero & G LLC) -25101 Chagrin Blvd
-Ste 220 Signature Sq II -Beachwood 44122 **Fx:**831-9467
(513) 422-7665 .. **Green,** Bryan L '01 Pools & More,Inc -4420 S Dixie Hwy
-Franklin 45005
Green, Charles E '04 -(Address Unavailable)
(513) 651-6800 .. **Green,** Chelsea C '00 %Frost BT LLC -201 E 5th -2200 PNC Ctr
-Cincinnati 45202 **Fx:**651-6981
Green, Christopher C '03 -(Address Unavailable)
(330) 655-4980 .. **Green,** Cynthia L '87 Allstate -Bx337 -Hudson 44236
(513) 769-0840 .. **Green,** F Harrison '72 (FH Green Co,LPA) -4015 Exec Park Dr
-Ste 130 -Cincinnati 45241

(740) 654-5603 .. **Green,** Frank W '69 -123 S Broad -Ste 230 -Lancaster 43130
(440) 286-4770 .. **Green,** Frederick H '75 -207 Center -Ste J -Chardon 44024
Green, Frederick J '90 -1627 Sunnyacres Rd -Copley 44321
(614) 351-9827 .. **Green,** George M '94 -787 S Roys Av -Columbus 43204
(330) 743-5101 .. **Green Haines & Sgambati, Co LPA** -16 Wick Av -Ste 400
-Youngstown 44503 **Fx:**743-5451
(330) 797-0086 .. **Green Haines & Sgambati, Co LPA** -120 Wstchr Dr -Ste A
-Bx3985 -Austintown 44515 **Fx:**797-2969
(216) 491-1684 .. **Green-Howard,** Betty J '83 -3530 Warrensvll Ctr Rd -Beachwood
44122
Green, James S '02 -2089 Smokymill Rd -Dublin 43016
Green, Jason M '03 -(Address Unavailable)
(937) 547-7380 .. **Green,** Jesse J '88 Darke Cnty Pros -504 S Bway -Cthse, 3rd Fl
-Greenville 45331
(937) 223-8177 .. **Green,** John L '82 %Coolidge WW&L -33 W 1st -Ste 600
-Dayton 45402 **Fx:**223-6705
(248) 932-3500 .. **Green,** Jonathan A '01 (Green & G,PLLC) -30300 Nrthwstrn Hwy
-345 -Farmington Hills, MI 48334 **Fx:**932-3521
(513) 977-8200 .. **Green,** K C '84 (Dinsmore & S LLP) -255 E 5th -Ste 1900
-Cincinnati 45202 **Fx:**977-8141
(614) 462-4677 .. **Green,** Kelly A '02 Franklin Cnty Common Pleas Ct -369 S High
-Columbus 43215 **Fx:**462-3476
(330) 456-1112 .. **Green,** Lemuel R '72 -116 Cleveland Av NW -Ste 709
-Canton 44702
(216) 696-1275 .. **Green,** Linda M '82 Chicago Title Ins -1360 E 9th -Ste 500
-Cleveland 44114
(614) 462-1058 .. **Green,** Matthew T '02 %Schottenstein Z&D -250 West -Bx165020
-Columbus 43216 **Fx:**462-5135
(513) 651-6800 .. **Green,** Melissa D '04 %Frost BT LLC -201 E 5th -2200 PNC Ctr
-Cincinnati 45202 **Fx:**651-6981
(419) 241-2200 .. **Green,** Merritt W III '76 (Arnold & C,Ltd) -1822 Cherry
-Toledo 43608 **Fx:**255-7623
(419) 343-6952 .. **Green,** Michelle S '98 -1045 N Main -Ste 7B
-Bowling Green 43402
(312) 321-4222 .. **Green,** Raymond W '66 (Brinks HG&L,PC)
-455 N Cityfront Plaza Dr -Ste 3600 -Chicago, IL 60611
Fx:321-4299
(614) 410-1700 .. **Green,** Rebecca M '88 %M Hughes & Assoc
-150 E Wilson Bridge Rd -Ste 300 -Worthington 43085
(330) 375-0126 .. **Green,** Richard A '80 OfCnsl McMahon DH&L LLP -450 Grant
-Akron 44311 **Fx:**375-1590
(740) 349-7075 .. **Green,** Robin L '73 -33 W Main -Ste 103 -Newark 43055
(614) 879-4062 .. **Green,** Robin W '89 Green Havens -Bx253 -West Jefferson 43162
(216) 685-1154 .. **Green,** Stanley '69 OfCnsl Weltman W&R Co,LPA
-323 W Lakeside Av -Ste 200 -Cleveland 44113 **Fx:**363-4121
(614) 293-8446 .. **Green,** Sue Z '99 %OSU Hsptls -410 W 10th Av -Columbus 43210
(330) 867-9998 .. **Green,** Thomas E '02 %Kastner W&W,LLC -3480 W Market
-Ste 300 -Akron 44333 **Fx:**867-3786
(937) 224-3333 .. **Green,** Thomas M '76 (Green & G) -109 N Main -Ste 800
-Dayton 45402 **Fx:**224-4311
(330) 788-9174 .. **Green,** William Jr. '54 -4181 Lockwood Blvd -Boardman 44511
(216) 621-5112 .. **Greenberg,** Barbara C '94 Cnty Bar Assn -526 Superior Av E
-Ste 1240 -Cleveland 44114
(513) 946-3000 .. **Greenberg,** Bradley J '91 Hamilton Cnty Pros -230 E 9th
-Cincinnati 45202 **Fx:**946-3017
(513) 621-3440 .. **Greenberg,** Gary L '78 (Denlinger R&G Co,LPA) -425 Walnut
-Ste 2310 -Cincinnati 45202 **Fx:**621-4449
(513) 381-2838 .. **Greenberg,** Gerald S '88 (Taft S&H LLP) -425 Walnut -Ste 1800
-Cincinnati 45202 **Fx:**381-0205
(216) 781-1212 .. **Greenberg,** Jonathan D '83 (Walter & H LLP) -1301 E 9th
-Ste 3500 -Cleveland 44114 **Fx:**575-0911
Greenberg, Marc L '78 Eagle-Picher Ind,Inc -8260 Northcreek Dr
-Ste 100 -Cincinnati 45236
(937) 299-9607 .. **Greenberg,** Marc N '04 %Sherrets,LLC -580 Lincoln Park Blvd
-Ste 399 -Kettering 45459 **Fx:**299-9618
(513) 946-3695 .. **Greenberg,** Matthew L '00 Hamilton Cnty Pub Def -230 E 9th
-3rd Fl -Cincinnati 45202 **Fx:**946-3707
(419) 536-6168 .. **Greenberg,** Nathan '42 -3514 Orchrd Trl Dr -Toledo 43606
(216) 696-7533 .. **Greenberg,** Sheldon J '64 -1370 Ontario -Ste 1310
-Cleveland 44113
(740) 452-9311 .. **Greenberger,** Bruce L '74 -601 Main -Zanesville 43701
(513) 721-5151 .. **Greenberger,** Jeffrey J '92 %Katz G&N,LLP -105 E 4th -4th Fl
-Cincinnati 45202 **Fx:**621-9285
(513) 489-1633 .. **Greenberger,** Karen K '92 -11105 Brookbrdg Dr -Cincinnati 45249
(513) 721-5151 .. **Greenberger,** Mark A '66 (Katz G&N,LLP) -105 E 4th -4th Fl
-Cincinnati 45202 **Fx:**621-9285
(216) 831-8838 .. **Greenberger,** Paul M '75 (Berns O&G,LLC) -3733 Park East Dr
-Ste 200 -Beachwood 44122 **Fx:**464-4489
(614) 227-8848 .. **Greenberger,** Susan B '83 (Bricker & E LLP) -100 S 3rd
-Columbus 43215 **Fx:**227-2390
(847) 673-9668 .. **Greenblatt,** Mark L '86 -3820 W Touhy Av -Lincolnwood, IL 60712
(216) 566-9706 .. **Greenblatt,** Ronald H '74 -101 Prospect Av W -Ste 1835
-Cleveland 44115
(859) 525-0500 .. **Greene,** Angela L '89 -7415 Burlngtn Pike -Florence, KY 41042
Fx:525-0560
(216) 575-5200 .. **Greene,** Bradley L '89 -75 Pub Sq -Ste 920 -Cleveland 44113
Fx:696-0075
(330) 867-0215 .. **Greene,** Charles L '77 (Davison & G) -59 Shiawassee Av
-Akron 44333 **Fx:**867-0216
Greene, Christopher L '89 -1392 SOM Center Rd
-Mayfield Heights 44124
Greene, Dara L '99 -5691 Duchess Ct -Galloway 43119
(216) 687-0900 .. **Greene & Eisen Co, LPA** -1300 E 9th -Ste 1801
-Cleveland 44114
(513) 621-6464 .. **Greene,** Everett L '04 %Graydon H&R LLP -511 Walnut
-1900 Fifth Third Ctr -Cincinnati 45202 **Fx:**651-3836
(513) 362-2847 .. **Greene,** Gerald H Jr. '02 Legal Aid -215 E 9th -Ste 200
-Cincinnati 45202
(513) 381-9200 .. **Greene,** Gordon C '60 OfCnsl Rendigs FK&D,LLP -One W 4th
-Ste 900 -Cincinnati 45202 **Fx:**381-9206
(937) 225-3991 .. **Greene,** James F III '86 J Greene,III & Assoc -120 W 2nd
-Dayton 45402

(216) 573-7853 .. **Greene**, Joan E '94 Linde Gas,LLC -6055 Rockside Wds Blvd
-Cleveland 44131

(216) 443-7223 .. **Greene**, John F '85 Cuyahoga Cnty Pub Def -1200 W 3rd NW
-100 Lakeside Pl -Cleveland 44113

(937) 445-4276 .. **Greene**, Nelson F '88 NCR Corp -1700 S Patterson Blvd -WHQ-5
-Dayton 45479

(740) 477-6044 .. **Greene**, Patrick K '84 -Bx605 -Circleville 43113

(859) 371-0730 .. **Greene**, Robert F '59 -7415 Burlngtn Pike -Ste B
-Florence, KY 41042

(330) 497-0700 .. **Greene**, Stephanie M '99 %Krugliak WG&D Co,LPA
-4775 Munson NW -Bx36963 -Canton 44735 **Fx:**497-4020

(740) 345-9611 .. **Greene**, Steven T '73 (Morrow G&B,Ltd) -33 W Main -Bx4190
-Newark 43058

(216) 921-2011 .. **Greene**, Thornton R '52 -3732 E 147th -Cleveland 44120

(330) 364-6825 .. **Greene**, William C '92 -123 W High Av -Bx299
-New Philadelphia 44663

(216) 687-0900 .. **Greene**, William M '72 (Greene & E Co,LPA) -1300 E 9th
-Ste 1801 -Cleveland 44114

(513) 455-7600 .. **Greenebaum Doll & McDonald PLLC** -255 E 5th
-2800 Chemed Ctr -Cincinnati 45202 **Fx:**455-8500

(330) 492-8717 .. **Greenfelder**, Justin S '04 %Buckingham D&B,LLP
-4518 Fulton Dr NW -Bx35548 -Canton 44735 **Fx:**492-9625

(419) 865-5586 .. **Greenfield**, Donna J '74 -331 S King Rd -Holland 43528

(614) 221-9200 .. **Greenfield**, Gerald '94 %Schottenstein Stores -1800 Moler Rd
-Columbus 43207

(216) 363-1400 .. **Greenfield**, Harry W '70 (Buckley K,LPA) -600 E Superior Av
-Ste 1400 -Cleveland 44114 **Fx:**579-1020

(216) 464-2860 .. **Greenfield**, Mark R '81 Cnsl RL Stark Enterprises -28601
Chagrin Blvd -Ste 600 -Woodmere 44122 **Fx:**464-1458

(419) 243-9005 .. **Greenfield**, Richard Kevin '81 (Franklin & G,LLC) -420 Mad Av
-Ste 1101 -Toledo 43604 **Fx:**243-9404

(330) 339-9963 .. **Greenham**, Deborah E '95 -134 4th NW -Bx711
-New Philadelphia 44663

(614) 854-9150 .. **Greenlee**, David A '97 -7870 Olentangy Rvr Rd -Ste 304
-Columbus 43235

(216) 931-6000 .. **Greenlee**, Gary S '97 %Ulmer & B LLP -1300 E 9th
-Ste 900 Penton Media Bldg -Cleveland 44114 **Fx:**931-6001

(757) 838-0705 .. **Greenlee**, Harry '84 -1 Royal Oak Ct -Hampton, VA 23666

(216) 579-2163 .. **Greenlee**, Mark B '97 Cnsl Fed Reserve Bk of Cleveland
-1455 E 6th -Bx6387 -Cleveland 44101

(937) 645-8478 .. **Greeno**, Pamela E '00 Honda of Amer Mfg -19900 St Rt 739
-Support Ofc -Marysville 43040

(216) 292-6592 .. **Greenslade**, Victor F Jr. '53 -23700 S Woodlnd Rd
-Shaker Heights 44122

(216) 861-2588 .. **Greenspan**, Ronald B '74 -1370 Ontario -Ste 700
-Cleveland 44113

　　　　　　　　　 Greentree, Hugh A '85 -3111 E Broad -Columbus 43209

(937) 335-2121 .. **Greenwald**, Carol E '77 -22 N Short -Troy 45373

(614) 221-1111 .. **Greenwald**, Gary D '71 Shayne & G -221 S High
-Columbus 43215 **Fx:**221-4070

(216) 621-4411 .. **Greenwald**, Leonard S '68 (L Greenwald Co,LPA)
-526 Superior Av -Ste 1030 -Cleveland 44114 **Fx:**621-0408

(740) 354-7563 .. **Greenwald**, Tammy L '00 SE OH Lgl Srvcs -800 Gallia -Ste 700
-Portsmouth 45662

(703) 806-0685 .. **Greenway**, Curtis L '82 US Army Crim Invstgtn Command
-6010 6th -Attn:CISA-AAA -Fort Belvoir, VA 22060

(859) 815-4208 .. **Greenwood**, Frederick M III '82 Ashland Inc -Bx391
-Covington, KY 41012

(740) 942-2621 .. **Greenwood**, Rhonda L '95 Harrison Cnty Pros -111 W Warren
-Bx248 -Cadiz 43907

(513) 943-4200 .. **Greenwood**, Scott T '89 -1 Lbrty Hse -Bx54400 -Cincinnati 45254

(419) 252-6211 .. **Greenwood**, Truman A '79 (Spengler N PLL) -608 Mad Av
-Ste 1900 -Toledo 43604 **Fx:**241-8599

(937) 223-3277 .. **Greer**, David C '62 (Bieser G&L LLP) -6 N Main -400 Natl City Ctr
-Dayton 45402 **Fx:**223-6339

(614) 431-6358 .. **Greer**, David K '89 -1150 Morse Rd -Ste 106 -Columbus 43229

(513) 732-5888 .. **Greer**, Gary R '78 (GR Greer Co,LPA) -55 W Main -Batavia 45103

(937) 223-3277 .. **Greer**, James H '90 (Bieser G&L LLP) -6 N Main -400 Natl City Ctr
-Dayton 45402 **Fx:**223-6339

(901) 434-3108 .. **Greer**, Jeffery B '91 FedEx Corp -1715 Aaron Brenner Dr -Ste 600
-Memphis, TN 38120

(216) 241-5310 .. **Greer**, Mark A '86 (Gallagher SF&N) -1501 Euclid Av -6th Fl
-Cleveland 44115 **Fx:**241-1608

　　　　　　　　　 Grega, Richard J '92 -Bx513 -Sylvania 43560

　　　　　　　　　 Gregel, Robyn L '99 -8702 Infirmary Rd -Ravenna 44266

(937) 223-3153 .. **Greger**, Lawrence J '80 -120 W 2nd -Ste 1100 -Dayton 45402

(937) 223-4332 .. **Gregg**, Douglas B '72 -130 W 2nd -Ste 310 -Dayton 45402

(614) 469-3221 .. **Gregg**, Heather D '01 %Thompson H LLP -10 W Broad -Ste 700
-Columbus 43215 **Fx:**469-3361

(330) 499-0900 .. **Gregg**, James R '64 -4808 Munson NW -Canton 44718

(513) 487-5980 .. **Gregg**, John W '79 Milacron -2090 Florence Av -Cincinnati 45206

(419) 241-6000 .. **Gregg**, Joseph A '81 (Eastman & S Ltd) -1 Seagate -24th Fl
-Bx10032 -Toledo 43699 **Fx:**247-1777

(216) 589-8399 .. **Greggo**, Robert M '84 %Surety Title Agncy -1010 Leader Bldg
-Cleveland 44114

(419) 537-6610 .. **Grego**, Lisa A '94 %Fell & M,LPA -3425 Exec Pkwy -Ste 207
-Toledo 43606

(440) 585-0595 .. **Gregor**, Robert J '67 -29444 Euclid Av -Wickliffe 44092

(440) 808-9750 .. **Gregor**, Sean S '98 (S Gregor & Assoc Co,LPA) -842 Corp Way
-Ste 350 -Cleveland 44145 **Fx:**808-9785

(614) 264-0304 .. **Gregori**, Terri B '93 -250 E Broad -Ste 900 Mdlnd Bldg
-Columbus 43215 **Fx:**365-9516

(614) 462-5416 .. **Gregory**, Donald W '82 (Kegler BH&R) -65 E State -Ste 1800
-Columbus 43215 **Fx:**464-2634

(216) 586-3939 .. **Gregory**, Earnest B '04 %Jones D -901 Lakeside Av
-Cleveland 44114 **Fx:**579-0212

(216) 687-1900 .. **Gregory**, Herman E III '87 Legal Aid -1223 W 6th
-Cleveland 44113 **Fx:**687-0779

(614) 457-5990 .. **Gregory**, Janet K '82 -1375 Kirkley Rd -Columbus 43221

(713) 803-0551 .. **Gregory**, Michael W Jr. '90 Cnsl GE Aero Energy -1333 West
Loop S -Ste 1000 -Houston, TX 77027 **Fx:**803-0368

(419) 829-5297 .. **Gregory**, Michele L '99 -8657 Central Av -Sylvania 43560

(513) 734-0950 .. **Gregory**, Patrick L '79 -717 W Plane -Bx378 -Bethel 45106

(330) 688-9900 .. **Greif**, Carl '97 -Bx1554 -Stow 44224

(330) 364-3523 .. **Greig**, Gary L '89 Pub Def -153 N Bway -New Philadelphia 44663

(614) 644-0855 .. **Greim**, David M '88 Industrial Commssn of OH -30 W Spring
-9th Fl -Columbus 43215 **Fx:**752-8785

(513) 243-3329 .. **Greiner**, Carey A '00 GE Co Aircraft Engines -One Neuman Way
-J104 -Cincinnati 45215 **Fx:**243-6938

(513) 621-6464 .. **Greiner**, John C '83 (Graydon H&R LLP) -511 Walnut
-1900 Fifth Third Ctr -Cincinnati 45202 **Fx:**651-3836

(513) 665-9600 .. **Greiner**, Scott A '92 -1014 Vine -1919 Kroger Bldg
-Cincinnati 45202

(330) 376-1242 .. **Greive**, Edward G '67 Renner KGBT&W,LPA -106 S Main
-4th Fl First Natl Twr -Akron 44308 **Fx:**376-9646

(513) 977-4774 .. **Greiwe**, Nancy S '83 (Markovits & G Co,LPA) -119 E Court
-Ste 500 -Cincinnati 45202

(216) 831-5100 .. **Greller**, Renee Zaidenras '02 %Shapero & G LLC
-25101 Chagrin Blvd -Ste 220 Signature Sq II -Beachwood 44122
Fx:831-9467

(740) 349-6195 .. **Grenauer**, Regina M '92 Licking Cnty Pros -20 S 2nd -4th Fl
-Newark 43055

(216) 447-1161 .. **Grendel**, David S '80 -7111 Brecksvll Rd -Ste 4
-Independence 44131

(440) 922-5200 .. **Grendell**, Henry G '94 Family Heritage Life Ins Co
-6001 E Royalton Rd -Broadview Heights 44147

(440) 746-9600 .. **Grendell & Simon Co,LPA** -6638 Harris Rd
-Broadview Heights 44147

(440) 746-9600 .. **Grendell**, Timothy J '78 (Grendell & S Co,LPA) -6638 Harris Rd
-Broadview Heights 44147

(301) 424-3640 .. **Grendzynski**, Michael E '98 %Edell S&F,LLC -1901 Rsrch Blvd
-Ste 400 -Rockville, MD 20850

(440) 753-1490 .. **Grenell**, David J '87 Chart Industries,Inc -5885 Landerbrook Dr
-Cleveland 44124

(937) 378-4151 .. **Grennan**, Thomas F '75 Pros -200 E Cherry -Georgetown 45121

(614) 461-0734 .. **Gresham**, Cyane W '03 Sierra Club -36 W Gay -Ste 314
-Columbus 43215 **Fx:**461-0730

(440) 895-1510 .. **Gresko**, Gary E '97 -4079 Wooster Rd -Ste B
-Fairview Park 44126

(614) 469-3939 .. **Gresko**, Janice L '96 %Jones D -325 John H McConnell Blvd
-Ste 600 -Bx165017 -Columbus 43216 **Fx:**461-4198

(513) 337-3535 .. **Gressel**, Gerard S '92 -4545 Crk Rd -Rm H223 ML #93
-Cincinnati 45242

(417) 623-8000 .. **Gressel**, Lisa V '83 Eagle-Picher -Bx47 -Joplin, MO 64802

(513) 829-6700 .. **Gressel**, Michele M '78 (Millikin & F) -530 Wessel Dr -Ste 2A
-Fairfield 45014 **Fx:**829-0258

(419) 244-8336 .. **Gressley Kaplin & Parker** -608 Mad Av -Ste 930 -Toledo 43604
Fx:244-1914

(937) 865-6800 .. **Gressly**, Brian K '90 Lexis/Nexis -Bx933 -Dayton 45401

(216) 592-5000 .. **Gretter**, Craig T '02 %Tucker E&W LLP -925 Euclid Av
-1150 Huntngtn Bldg -Cleveland 44115 **Fx:**592-5009

(614) 462-3555 .. **Gretz**, Jennifer A '98 Franklin Cnty Pros -373 S High
-Columbus 43215

(614) 466-7447 .. **Greuel**, Tracy M '01 Atty Gen -150 E Gay -Columbus 43215

(216) 861-3366 .. **Greulich**, David P Jr. '96 L Solomon -1370 Ontario
-1800 Standard Bldg -Cleveland 44113

(513) 648-7067 .. **Greulich**, John E '69 Fluor Fernald Inc -Bx538704
-Cincinnati 45253

(216) 621-6570 .. **Greve**, Thomas F '81 (Rademaker MM&G) -55 Pub Sq -Ste 1775
-Cleveland 44113 **Fx:**621-1127

(330) 376-9260 .. **Greven**, John W '94 (Callahan GR&S LLC) -7 W Bowery -Ste 907
-Akron 44308 **Fx:**376-9807

(816) 292-2000 .. **Grever**, Thomas J '92 Lathrop & G -2345 Grand Blvd
-Kansas City, MO 64108 **Fx:**292-2001

　　　　　　　　　 Grevey, Bryan G '84 -202 Isl Pnt Ct -Mount Pleasant, SC 29464

(513) 632-8445 .. **Grey**, Billie J '97 Cincinnati Law Library Assn -1000 Main
-601 Cthse -Cincinnati 45202

(419) 884-9874 .. **Grey**, Lawrence A '69 -Bx3024 -Lexington 44904

(513) 891-2100 .. **Gribbell**, Frederick H '90 (Davidson & G LLP) -10250 Alliance Rd
-Ste 120 -Cincinnati 45242

(419) 278-7015 .. **Gribbell Sunderman & Collier** -114 E Main -Bx54
-Deshler 43516

(513) 287-3017 .. **Gribler**, Michael A '75 Cinergy Corp -139 E 4th -25 Atrium II
-Bx960 -Cincinnati 45201

(614) 466-0278 .. **Gridley**, Wendy H '84 Legis Srvc Commssn -77 S High
-Columbus 43215

(419) 562-9856 .. **Griebling**, Eric N '79 (Spurlock SPG&M,PLL) -120 N Lane
-Bucyrus 44820 **Fx:**562-9883

(216) 522-9000 .. **Grieco**, Paul '95 (Landskroner·G·M,Ltd) -1360 W 9th -Ste 200
-Cleveland 44113 **Fx:**522-9007

(614) 846-3378 .. **Grier**, Jerry '68 Jerry Grier -5311 Woodglen Rd -Columbus 43214

(614) 677-5410 .. **Grier**, Jill S '93 %Nationwide Ins Co -1 Nationwide Plz
-Columbus 43215

　　　　　　　　　 Grieselhuber, Pierre A '69 -17030 Greenbrier Dr
-Strongsvile 44136

(614) 475-9511 .. **Grieser**, Charles R '49 OfCnsl Blumenstiel HA&E,LLC
-261 W Johnstown Rd -Columbus 43230 **Fx:**475-0348

(440) 350-3200 .. **Grieshammer**, Charles R '81 Lake Cnty Pub Def -125 E Erie
-Painesville 44077

(440) 350-3200 .. **Grieshammer**, Susan C '88 Lake Cnty Pub Def -125 E Erie
-Painesville 44077

(614) 469-7404 .. **Griesheimer**, Jeffrey A '81 SSA-OHA -401 N Front -Ste 400
-Columbus 43215

(937) 223-5200 .. **Grieshop**, David B '71 (Flanagan LH&S) -318 W 4th
-Dayton 45402 **Fx:**223-3335

(614) 469-3939 .. **Griesmer**, Kelley M '93 (Jones D) -325 John H McConnell Blvd
-Ste 600 -Bx165017 -Columbus 43216 **Fx:**461-4198

(513) 651-6800 .. **Griess**, Murray W '95 Cnsl Frost BT LLC -201 E 5th
-2200 PNC Ctr -Cincinnati 45202 **Fx:**651-6981

(513) 551-1985 .. **Griest**, Shane E '00 Unemploymnt Comp Commssn
-225 Pictoria Dr -Pictoria Twr 5th Fl -Cincinnati 45246

(614) 464-6400 .. **Griffaton**, Michael C '93 %Vorys SS&P LLP -52 E Gay -Bx1008
-Columbus 43216 **Fx:**464-6350

　　　　　　　　　 Griffeth, Tobin C '97 USAF Trial Judiciary Cntrl Circ
-AFLSA/JAJT-3 -550 D St Ste 3 West -Randolph AFB, TX 78150

(330) 643-8124 .. **Griffin**, Alpha T '02 9th Dist Ct of Appeals -161 S High
-Akron 44308

(216) 689-0509 .. **Griffin,** Cathryn D '94 KeyBank NA -127 Pub Sq -2nd Fl
  -Cleveland 44114

(513) 621-6464 .. **Griffin,** Christopher A '03 %Graydon H&R LLP -511 Walnut
  -1900 Fifth Third Ctr -Cincinnati 45202 **Fx:**651-3836

(419) 422-2121 .. **Griffin,** Daniel A '96 Marathon Ashland Petroleum -539 S Main
  -Findlay 45840

(513) 530-0152 .. **Griffin,** Daniel W '87 (Griffin & G) -8180 Corp Park Dr -Ste 204
  -Cincinnati 45242

(850) 412-0300 .. **Griffin,** David '96 Griffin & H LLC -800½ N Calhoun
  -Tallahassee, FL 32302

(513) 421-1313 .. **Griffin-Fletcher,LLP** -3500 Redbank Rd -Cincinnati 45227
  Fx:421-1118

(937) 322-5242 .. **Griffin,** James N '76 -4 W Main -Ste 526 -Springfield 45502
  Fx:323-5061

(614) 228-1541 .. **Griffin,** Jeanne A '91 (Baker & H LLP) -65 E State -Ste 2100
  -Columbus 43215 **Fx:**462-2616

(614) 462-2720 .. **Griffin,** Kerri J '98 Ct of Common Pleas -373 S High -6th Fl
  -Columbus 43215

(440) 244-1811 .. **Griffin,** Paul A '01 -520 Bway -3rd Fl -Lorain 44052

(440) 243-5010 .. **Griffin,** Rae E '84 %D Briller Co,LPA -7379 Pearl Rd
  -Middleburg Heights 44130 **Fx:**243-0105

(614) 224-1222 .. **Griffin,** Robert H Jr. '85 %Maguire & S,LLP -250 Civic Ctr Dr
  -Ste 200 -Columbus 43215 **Fx:**224-1236

(305) 371-2700 .. **Griffin,** Scott A '00 %White & C LLP -200 S Biscayne Blvd
  -Ste 4900 -Miami, FL 33131 **Fx:**358-5744

(419) 255-8111 .. **Griffin,** Sharon L '83 -520 Mad Av -Ste 837 -Toledo 43604

(330) 491-5262 .. **Griffin,** Stephen P '88 (Buckingham D&B,LLP)
  -4518 Fulton Dr NW -Bx35548 -Canton 44735 **Fx:**492-9625

(614) 462-6087 .. **Griffin,** Vanessa M '98 Franklin Cnty Common Pleas Ct
  -369 S High -Columbus 43215

(216) 268-1126 .. **Griffin,** Willie L '87 -861 E 143rd -Cleveland 44110

(330) 322-8194 .. **Griffith,** Anne Marie '04 -3634 Oak Hill Rd -Peninsula 44264

(216) 586-3939 .. **Griffith,** Calvin P '88 (Jones D) -901 Lakeside Av
  -Cleveland 44114 **Fx:**579-0212

(419) 841-4294 .. **Griffith,** Carl D '85 Schnorf F&G -5217 Monroe -Ste A -Bx23156
  -Toledo 43623

(614) 890-4543 .. **Griffith,** Charles R '88 (Griffith & W) -575 Copeland Mill Rd
  -Ste 2C -Westerville 43081

(513) 943-7100 .. **Griffith,** Charles S III '97 Midland Co -7000 Mdlnd Blvd
  -Amelia 45102

(740) 653-6464 .. **Griffith,** D Joe '91 (Dagger JMO&H) -144 E Main -Bx667
  -Lancaster 43130 **Fx:**653-8522

(330) 456-8341 .. **Griffith,** Daniel R '02 %Black MS&A,LPA -220 Market Av S
  -Ste 1000 -Canton 44702 **Fx:**456-5756

(216) 348-5400 .. **Griffith,** James A '58 (McDonald H Co,LPA) -600 Superior Av E
  -Ste 2100 -Cleveland 44114 **Fx:**348-5474

(614) 488-7878 .. **Griffith,** Jeffrey A '99 Huddleston Law Ofcs
  -3650 Olentangy Rvr Rd -Ste 210 -Columbus 43214 **Fx:**246-7180

(740) 596-5291 .. **Griffith,** Jeffrey R '01 %Salyer & Assoc -114 W Main -Bx466
  -McArthur 45651

(513) 396-6117 .. **Griffith,** John B '71 -3810 Eileen Dr -Ste 1 -Cincinnati 45209
  Griffith, John T '76 -20 Rainbow Cir -Danville, CA 94506

(614) 227-2000 .. **Griffith,** Kevin E '86 (Porter WM&A LLP) -41 S High
  -Columbus 43215 **Fx:**227-2100

(330) 373-1035 .. **Griffith,** Lynn B III '82 Letson GWL&R -155 S Park Av -Ste 250
  -Bx151 -Warren 44482 **Fx:**392-5419

(419) 946-2001 .. **Griffith,** Matthew T '04 %McClelland,LLC -15 S Main
  -Mount Gilead 43338

(216) 231-7300 .. **Griffith,** Nancy L '90 Musical Arts Assn -11001 Euclid Av
  -Cleveland 44106

(440) 256-8806 .. **Griffith,** Pamela B '81 P Griffith Co LPA -7375 Reserve Dr
  -Kirtland 44094

(513) 381-2838 .. **Griffith,** Stephen M Jr. '81 (Taft S&H LLP) -425 Walnut -Ste 1800
  -Cincinnati 45870 **Fx:**381-0205

(419) 627-7697 .. **Griffith,** Terry R '88 Erie Cnty Pros -247 Columbus Av -Ste 319
  -Sandusky 44870 **Fx:**627-7567

(440) 729-7996 .. **Griffith,** Thomas J '90 Business Laws,Inc -11630 Chillicothe Rd
  -Bx185 -Chesterland 44026

(614) 890-4543 .. **Griffith & Worth** -575 Copeland Mill Rd -Ste 2C
  -Westerville 43081

(440) 247-5585 .. **Griffiths,** David E '57 (Woodward & G) -50 E Wshngtn
  -Chagrin Falls 44022 **Fx:**247-1031

(614) 841-9258 .. **Griffiths,** George K '78 -613 Glenrdg Pl -Columbus 43214

(513) 553-6286 .. **Griffiths,** Nancy K '84 -1075 Wilson Dunham Hill
  -New Richmond 45157

(330) 497-0700 .. **Griffiths,** Raymond E '57 (Krugliak WG&D Co,LPA)
  -4775 Munson NW -Bx36963 -Canton 44735 **Fx:**497-4020

(513) 765-6000 .. **Griffiths,** William D '80 LensCrafters,Inc -4000 Luxottica Pl
  -Mason 45040

(740) 687-6616 .. **Griggs,** Jason M '99 Pros -Bx1008 -Lancaster 43130

(202) 739-3000 .. **Griggs,** Linda L '74 (Morgan L&B LLP) -1111 Penn Av NW
  -Washington, DC 20004 **Fx:**739-3001

(937) 878-8649 .. **Griggs,** Peter N '01 %Martin MW&R -26 N Wright Av
  -Fairborn 45324 **Fx:**878-8479

(513) 263-4071 .. **Grigsby,** Donald E '69 US Treasury Dept -550 Main -Ste 7508
  -Cincinnati 45202

(937) 642-0515 .. **Grigsby,** Joseph B '48 -125 S Main -Marysville 43040

(330) 405-5061 .. **Grigsby,** Kelly N '96 %Williams S&S Co,LPA -2241 Pinnacle Pkwy
  -Twinsburg 44087 **Fx:**405-5586

(937) 642-0686 .. **Grigsby,** Michael J '80 -125 S Main -Marysville 43040

(419) 252-6261 .. **Grigsby,** Teresa L '85 (Spengler N PLL) -608 Mad Av -Ste 1000
  -Toledo 43604 **Fx:**241-8599

(419) 244-6700 .. **Grill,** Donna M '93 -1900 Monroe -Ste 108 -Toledo 43624

(937) 225-6379 .. **Grilliot-Murty,** Moira L '04 Hon GJ Davis -41 N Perry
  -Dayton 45422

(216) 696-8730 .. **Grillo,** David W '03 %Amin & T LLP -1900 E 9th
  -24th Fl Natl City Ctr -Cleveland 44114 **Fx:**696-8731

(614) 228-1541 .. **Grillo,** Mary Catherine P '94 (Baker & H LLP) -65 E State
  -Ste 2100 -Columbus 43215 **Fx:**462-2616

(330) 678-6595 .. **Grim,** Nancy E '84 -237 E Main -Kent 44240 **Fx:**678-6517

(740) 594-2241 .. **Grim,** William A '74 -8 N Court -Ste 203 -Athens 45701

(937) 392-4371 .. **Grimes,** David E '96 -112 Main -Ripley 45167 **Fx:**392-1365

(937) 208-2237 .. **Grimes,** Timothy M '89 Maimi Valley Hospital -1 Wyoming
  -Business Devlpmnt -Dayton 45409

(330) 677-0785 .. **Grimm,** Brian T '91 Emerald Envrnmntl Inc -Bx1953 -Kent 44240

(703) 697-9161 .. **Grimord,** David L '78 US Navy/JAG -1322 Patterson Av SE
  -Ste 1300 -Washington, DC 20374

(740) 574-4311 .. **Grimshaw,** Lynn A '75 -8055 Hayport Rd -Wheelersburg 45694
  Fx:574-1129

(419) 634-6646 .. **Grimslid,** Gregory A '81 (Grimslid & H) -231 N Main -Ada 45810

(740) 397-5262 .. **Grindle,** Larry J '86 (Zelkowitz B&C) -121 E High
  -Mount Vernon 43050

(419) 213-4791 .. **Grine,** Kathy J '89 Lucas Co Common Pleas Ct -700 Adams
  -Cnty Ct Hse -Toledo 43624

(216) 479-8500 .. **Grinham,** Jill A '02 %Squire S&D LLP -127 Pub Sq -4900 Key Twr
  -Cleveland 44114 **Fx:**479-8780

(330) 746-3251 .. **Grinstein,** Deborah L '85 Youngstown Jewish Fed -505 Gypsy Ln
  -Youngstown 44504

(330) 856-8800 .. **Grinstein,** Jeffrey M '85 Avalon Holdings Corp -1 Amer Way
  -Warren 44484

(330) 744-0247 .. **Grinstein,** Peter B '61 (Nadler N&B Co,LPA) -20 Fed Plz W
  -Ste 600 -Youngstown 44503 **Fx:**744-8690

(937) 325-1333 .. **Grinvalds,** Edwin A '83 -12 W Main -Springfield 45502

(614) 462-3555 .. **Gripshover,** John P '90 Franklin Cnty Pros -373 S High
  -Columbus 43215

(330) 535-8171 .. **Grisi,** Charles E '70 (Grisi & R) -159 S Main -Ste 1030
  -Akron 44308

(216) 447-9000 .. **Grisko,** Jerome P Jr. '87 Century Bus Srvcs -6050 Oak Tree Blvd
  -Ste 500 -Cleveland 44131

(330) 405-5440 .. **Grist,** Thomas '93 -1831 E Highland Rd -Twinsburg 44087

(440) 301-5206 .. **Griswold,** Desmond R '93 Attny Support Srvcs -4927 E Park Dr
  -North Olmsted 44070

(216) 621-0200 .. **Griswold,** James B '74 (Baker & H LLP) -1900 E 9th -Ste 3200
  -Cleveland 44114 **Fx:**696-0740
  Griswold, Jane W '75 -21210 Colby Rd -Shaker Heights 44122

(216) 771-5717 .. **Griveas,** Thomas '80 -1276 W 3rd -Ste 250 -Cleveland 44113

(419) 241-2000 .. **Grna,** Daniel H '76 (Adray & G) -709 Mad Av -Ste 209
  -Toledo 43624
  Grocki, Dale M '91 -233 W Wilson -Bryan 43506

(937) 341-9422 .. **Grodecki,** Paul A '90 Woolpert LLP -409 E Monument
  -Dayton 45402

(614) 466-2520 .. **Grodhaus,** D Michael '84 Atty Gen -30 E Broad -Columbus 43215
  Fx:728-7582

(312) 236-4600 .. **Grodsky,** Eric S '02 Maciorowsky S&U -221 N LaSalle -Ste 3600
  -Chicago, IL 60601

(614) 227-2332 .. **Grody,** Warren I '93 Bricker & E LLP -100 S 3rd -Columbus 43215
  Fx:227-2390

(614) 848-3400 .. **Groeber,** Anthony A '72 -6877 N High -Ste 300 -Columbus 43085

(937) 229-2919 .. **Groeber,** Claudette M '84 Univ of Dayton -300 Cllg Pk
  -Dayton 45469

(614) 433-9612 .. **Groeber,** John A '90 (Kagay AD&G) -6877 N High -Ste 300
  -Worthington 43085

(440) 544-1122 .. **Groedel,** Caryn M '92 -5910 Landerbrook Dr -Ste 200
  -Lyndhurst 44124

(216) 931-6000 .. **Groedel,** Howard M '92 (Ulmer & B LLP) -1300 E 9th
  -Ste 900 Penton Media Bldg -Cleveland 44114 **Fx:**931-6001

(216) 687-1311 .. **Groedel,** Marc W '79 (Reminger & R) -101 Prospect Av W
  -1400 Mdlnd Bldg -Cleveland 44115 **Fx:**687-1841

(513) 977-8200 .. **Groemminger,** Brian K '04 %Dinsmore & S LLP -255 E 5th
  -Ste 1900 -Cincinnati 45202 **Fx:**977-8141

(513) 723-4000 .. **Groenke,** David A '81 (Vorys SS&P LLP) -221 E 4th
  -Ste 2000 Atrium Two -Bx0236 -Cincinnati 45201 **Fx:**723-4056
  Groetzinger, Jon Jr. '91 -37455 Miles Rd -Moreland Hills 44022

(330) 493-1570 .. **Groff,** Shawn C '92 %Macala BM&G,LLC -4150 Belden Vllg NW
  -Ste 604 -Canton 44718 **Fx:**493-7042

(480) 344-7000 .. **Grogan,** James J '79 GW Holdings -6710 N Scttsdl Rd -Ste 100
  -Scottsdale, AZ 85253
  Grogan, Jerome J '03 -3317 S Sterling Way -Cincinnati 45209

(859) 341-4454 .. **Grogan,** Joanne F '92 -2493 Dixie Hwy -Fort Mitchell, KY 41017

(614) 486-6416 .. **Grogan,** Robert J Jr. '93 -1401 Friar Ln -Columbus 43221

(513) 345-8291 .. **Groh,** Theresa L '85 (Murdock GS&G) -35 E 7th -Ste 600
  -Cincinnati 45202 **Fx:**345-8294

(440) 243-2955 .. **Groh-Wargo,** Francis J '80 (Powers & G-W) -2 Berea Cmmns
  -Ste 215 -Bx1059 -Berea 44017 **Fx:**243-2967

(614) 486-2618 .. **Grohoske,** Donald E '00 -1500 W 3rd Av -Ste 222
  -Columbus 43212

(812) 377-3554 .. **Gron,** Gary M '66 Cummins Engine Co,Inc -Bx3005
  -Columbus, IN 47202

(407) 481-5800 .. **Gronek,** Robert J '78 (Gronek & L,LLP) -390 N Orange Av
  -Ste 600 -Bx3353 -Orlando, FL 32802 **Fx:**481-5801

(513) 946-3000 .. **Groneman,** Raymond C '73 Hamilton Cnty Pros -230 E 9th
  -Cincinnati 45202 **Fx:**946-3017

(330) 666-7765 .. **Groner,** Betty '85 -3584 Rdgwd Rd -Bx13514 -Akron 44334
  Fx:777-0067

(614) 221-3155 .. **Groner,** James M '91 (Bailey C LLC) -10 W Broad
  -Columbus 43215 **Fx:**221-0479

(513) 632-9595 .. **Groner,** Simon '75 -119 E Ct -Ste 510 -Cincinnati 45202

(513) 762-6200 .. **Gronotte,** Sharon E '99 %Ulmer & B LLP -600 Vine -Ste 2800
  -Cincinnati 45202 **Fx:**762-6245

(440) 329-5389 .. **Gronsky,** Richard A '86 Lorain Cnty Pros -225 Court -3rd Fl
  -Elyria 44035

(513) 425-6609 .. **Groom,** Kathy J '93 12th Dist Ct of Appls -1001 Reinartz Blvd
  -Middletown 45042 **Fx:**425-8751

(513) 985-3200 .. **Groshoff,** David A '96 Pacholder Assoc,Inc -8044 Mntgmry Rd
  -Ste 480 -Cincinnati 45236

(330) 425-4201 .. **Gross,** Adam L '91 Reimer L&A Co,LPA -2450 Edison Blvd -Bx968
  -Twinsburg 44087 **Fx:**487-0923

(216) 566-9200 .. **Gross,** Alan D '74 Jewish Cmmnty Fed -1750 Euclid Av
  -Cleveland 44115

(419) 609-5000 .. **Gross,** Gerhard R '00 Gross & G,LPA -231 W Wshngtn Row
  -Sandusky 44870 **Fx:**609-3650

(254) 287-3654 .. **Gross,** Gregory A '85 US Army OSJA -1001 761st Tank Battalion
  Av -Fort Hood, TX 76544
  Gross, J. Robert '53 -12250 S Potomac -Phoenix, AZ 85044

(614) 464-6400 ..**Gross**, James H '66 (Vorys SS&P LLP) -52 E Gay -Bx1008
-Columbus 43216 **Fx:**464-6350

(202) 496-0400 ..**Gross**, Jared '03 %Gebhardt & Assoc,LLP -1101 17th NW
-Ste 607 -Washington, DC 20036

(216) 621-0150 ..**Gross**, Joan M '76 OfCnsl Hahn L&P LLP
-3300 BP Twr/200 Pub Sq -Ste 3300 -Cleveland 44114
Fx:241-2824

(216) 397-4563 ..**Gross**, Joanne '86 John Carroll University -20700 N Park Blvd
-University Heights 44118

(216) 363-4500 ..**Gross**, Joseph N '91 (Benesch FC&A LLP) -200 Pub Sq -Ste 2300
-Cleveland 44114 **Fx:**363-4588

(216) 381-2162 ..**Gross**, Judd H '67 -2115 Campus Rd -South Euclid 44121

(216) 623-0150 ..**Gross**, Lynn A '00 %Roetzel & A,LPA -1375 E 9th
-One Cleve Ctr 9th Fl -Cleveland 44114 **Fx:**623-0134

(419) 609-5000 ..**Gross**, Mark R '95 Gross & G,LPA -231 W Wshngtn Row
-Sandusky 44870 **Fx:**609-3650

(216) 931-6000 ..**Gross**, Michael A '00 %Ulmer & B LLP -1300 E 9th
-Ste 900 Penton Media Bldg -Cleveland 44114 **Fx:**931-6001
Gross, Pamela A '97 -3710 Matthes Av -Sandusky 44870

(216) 991-6200 ..**Gross**, Robert E '79 (R Gross Co,LPA) -20133 Farnsleigh Rd
-Ohio Svngs Bldg -Shaker Heights 44122 **Fx:**991-6199

(216) 839-1111 ..**Gross**, Robert L '93 %S Gross Co,LPA -22901 Millcreek Blvd
-Ste 395 -Cleveland 44122

(216) 839-1111 ..**Gross**, Sanford '66 (S Gross Co,LPA) -22901 Millcreek Blvd
-Ste 395 -Cleveland 44122

(614) 466-6750 ..**Gross**, William F '81 OH Dept Taxation -30 E Broad -22nd Fl
-Columbus 43215

(614) 225-8505 ..**Gross**, William J '01 Motorists Mutual Ins Grp -471 E Broad
-Columbus 43215

(513) 357-9778 ..**Grosse**, Lisa L '77 Industrial Commssn of OH -125 E Court
-Cincinnati 45202

(513) 381-4700 ..**Grosser**, Theodore D '77 (Porter WM&A LLP) -250 E 5th
-Ste 2200 -Cincinnati 45202 **Fx:**421-0991

(513) 621-0550 ..**Grossheim**, Elmer R '60 Kelley & G -6000 Gaines Rd
-Cincinnati 45247 **Fx:**385-5375
Grossi, Kelly '03 -1574 Warren Rd -Lakewood 44107

(614) 221-7711 ..**Grossman**, Andrew S '96 %Grossman Law Ofcs -32 W Hoster
-Ste 100 -Columbus 43215 **Fx:**221-7145

(440) 446-0700 ..**Grossman**, Jack N '82 -6240 Mayfld Rd -#210
-Mayfield Heights 44124

(614) 221-7711 ..**Grossman**, Jeffrey A '72 Grossman Law Ofcs -32 W Hoster
-Ste 100 -Columbus 43215 **Fx:**221-7145

(513) 247-9094 ..**Grossman**, Joanne B '83 -8630 Twilight Tear Ln -Cincinnati 45249

(513) 241-2324 ..**Grossman**, Kurt L '83 (Wood H&E LLP) -441 Vine -Ste 2700
-Cincinnati 45202 **Fx:**421-7269

(614) 466-4314 ..**Grossman**, Lillian Y '84 OH DYS -51 N High -Columbus 43215

(216) 586-3939 ..**Grossman**, Theodore M '87 (Jones D) -901 Lakeside Av
-Cleveland 44114 **Fx:**579-0212

(513) 946-9000 ..**Grossmann**, David E '52 Hamilton Cnty Juv Ct -800 Bway
-Cincinnati 45202 **Fx:**946-9217

(615) 794-5829 ..**Grossmann**, Samuel W '97 Neo Gen Screening
-438 Forrest Park Cir -Franklin, TN 37064

(513) 381-2838 ..**Grossmann**, Thomas E '82 (Taft S&H LLP) -425 Walnut
-Ste 1800 -Cincinnati 45202 **Fx:**381-0205

(513) 241-3993 ..**Grote**, Jane M '76 -602 Main -Ste 307 -Cincinnati 45202

(513) 554-3000 ..**Grote**, Leo F '84 (L Grote,LPA) -4555 Lk Forest Dr
-Westlake Ctr #194 -Cincinnati 45242

(216) 696-2404 ..**Groth**, Mary C '83 Cleveland Bar Assn -1301 E 9th -2nd Fl
-Cleveland 44114 **Fx:**696-2413

(419) 930-3030 ..**Groth**, Stevin J '94 (SJ Groth & Assoc) -4032 Secor Rd -Ste A
-Toledo 43623

(513) 863-4015 ..**Groth**, William A '73 Natl Rtrmnt Consultants Inc -223 Ross Av
-Hamilton 45013

(317) 888-1000 ..**Grotke**, Allen E '73 (Grotke & B,PC) -420 Fry Rd -Ste A
-Greenwood, IN 46142

(937) 225-4652 ..**Grove**, Charles L III '81 Montgomery Cnty Pub Def -117 S Main
-Ste 400 -Dayton 45422 **Fx:**225-3449

(513) 829-2900 ..**Grove**, Jack F '79 -1251 Nilles Rd -Ste 10 -Fairfield 45014

(216) 621-7227 ..**Grove**, James H '88 (Nicola G&C,LLC) -25 W Prospect Av
-Republic Bldg Ste 1400 -Cleveland 44115 **Fx:**621-3999
Grove, Lance R '01 -7471 E Bowling -Lancaster 43130

(330) 399-4556 ..**Grove**, Michael E '78 (M Grove Co,LPA) -1125
Niles Crtland Rd SE -Warren 44484

(614) 443-1800 ..**Grove**, Raymond F '71 -25 Greenlawn Av -Columbus 43206

(517) 264-1477 ..**Grover**, Gregory W '77 -126 E Church -Adrian, MI 49221
Fx:264-1499

(281) 280-3741 ..**Groves**, Eileen A '82 SrCnsl United Space Alliance,LLC
-1150 Gemini -Houston, TX 77058 **Fx:**280-3754

(216) 664-4984 ..**Groves**, Emanuella D '81 Mun Ct Judge -1200 Ontario
-Cleveland 44113

(216) 491-1646 ..**Groves**, Gregory '80 -3530 Warrensvll Ctr Rd
-Shaker Heights 44122
Groves, Kevanne M '95 -4703 Orchrd Rd -Mentor 44060

(703) 693-9109 ..**Groves**, William A '82 USAF-Ofc of Secrtry
-1160 Air Force Pentagon -Washington, DC 20330

(937) 324-5541 ..**Groves**, William R '79 (Martin BH&H) -1 S Limestone -Ste 800
-Bx1488 -Springfield 45501 **Fx:**325-5432

(614) 645-8207 ..**Grubb**, Janet Ann '76 Cnty Mun Ct Judge -375 S High -13th Fl
-Columbus 43215

(216) 781-5515 ..**Grubb**, Natalie F '93 Hermann C&S,LLP -1301 E 9th -Ste 500
-Cleveland 44114 **Fx:**781-1030

(419) 626-0055 ..**Grubbe**, Richard E '65 (Tone GM&V) -1401 Cleveland Rd
-Sandusky 44870 **Fx:**626-0288

(614) 461-5600 ..**Grubbs**, Donell Roy '86 (Buckley K,LPA) -10 W Broad -Ste 1300
-Columbus 43215

(513) 721-7906 ..**Grubbs**, Gerald R '89 (McIlwain & G) -35 E 7th -510 Exec Bldg
-Cincinnati 45202 **Fx:**721-1555

(513) 651-6800 ..**Grubbs**, Kyle R '01 %Frost BT LLC -201 E 5th -2200 PNC Ctr
-Cincinnati 45202 **Fx:**651-6981

(859) 341-2500 ..**Grubbs**, Margo L '93 (ML Grubbs & Assoc) -Bx17808
-Covington, KY 41017

(216) 586-3939 ..**Grube**, Brian K '97 %Jones D -901 Lakeside Av -Cleveland 44114
Fx:579-0212

(440) 893-9686 ..**Gruber**, James P '89 -50 E Wshngtn -Chagrin Falls 44022
Fx:247-1031

(513) 412-1462 ..**Gruber**, John P '89 Great Amer Life Ins Co -Bx5420
-Cincinnati 45201

(513) 421-4646 ..**Gruber**, Joseph C '86 McCaslin I&M,LPA -632 Vine -Ste 900
-Cincinnati 45202 **Fx:**421-7929

(216) 642-8961 ..**Gruber**, Lynn F '82 Cigna HealthCare -5005 Rockside Rd -Ste 700
-Independence 44131

(614) 231-7090 ..**Gruber**, M Ellen '80 -471 E Broad -Ste 2001 -Columbus 43215

(330) 929-6212 ..**Gruber**, Michael J Jr. '79 -457 Portage Trl -Cuyahoga Falls 44221

(330) 497-2886 ..**Gruber**, Michael S '77 %Zollinger DGT & Co -6370 Mt Plsnt NW
-Bx2985 -Canton 44720

(513) 421-4646 ..**Gruber**, Thomas J '97 McCaslin I&M,LPA -632 Vine -Ste 900
-Cincinnati 45202 **Fx:**421-7929

(216) 371-3570 ..**Gruber**, William M Ondrey '82 -2714 Leighton Rd
-Shaker Heights 44120 **Fx:**(801) 697-4625

(614) 249-9001 ..**Grubler**, Gary L '85 -280 N High -Ste 810 -Columbus 43215
Fx:249-8752

(419) 472-9774 ..**Grude**, David G '79 -4253 Monroe Av -Toledo 43606

(614) 244-0874 ..**Gruenbaum**, Judith C '86 Bank 1 Trust Co NA -1111 Polaris Pkwy
-Ste 2N -Columbus 43240

(937) 223-8177 ..**Gruenberg**, Jonas J '70 (Coolidge WW&L) -33 W 1st -Ste 600
-Dayton 45402 **Fx:**223-6705

(419) 213-3115 ..**Gruenhagen**, Alan M '88 Lucas Cnty CSEA -701 Adams
-Toledo 43624

(513) 791-3558 ..**Gruenschlaeger**, Jeanne E '76 -9200 Mntgmry Rd -Ste 4A
-Cincinnati 45242

(216) 595-6300 ..**Gruenspan**, Charles '82 -23230 Chagrin Blvd -Ste 900
-Cleveland 44122

(330) 296-3868 ..**Grueschow**, Michael E '77 %Kane & K -101 E Main -Bx167
-Ravenna 44266 **Fx:**296-7100

(440) 248-8223 ..**Grugle**, Scott D '95 -33792 Hanover Wds Trl -Solon 44139

(216) 861-5555 ..**Gruhin**, Gloria S '93 (Gruhin & G) -1468 W 9th -Ste 750
-Cleveland 44113

(614) 224-4411 ..**Gruhin**, Lois A '73 Zashin & R Co,LPA -21 E State -Ste 1900
-Columbus 43215 **Fx:**224-4433

(216) 861-5555 ..**Gruhin**, Michael A '76 (Gruhin & G) -1468 W 9th -Ste 750
-Cleveland 44113

(216) 621-4244 ..**Grumbine**, Kylie L '03 %Morganstern M&D Co,LPA
-623 W St Clair Av -Cleveland 44113 **Fx:**621-2951

(216) 272-3918 ..**Grunberger**, Armand '77 (Grunberger Co,LPA) -Bx22321
-Beachwood 44122

(440) 326-1464 ..**Grunda**, Jay B '86 Solicitors Ofc -131 Court -Elyria 44035

(440) 244-1389 ..**Grunda**, Joseph C '79 (Grunda & G) -522 Bway -Lorain 44052
Fx:244-0154

(440) 244-1389 ..**Grunda**, Joseph R '58 (Grunda & G) -522 Bway -Lorain 44052
Fx:244-0154

(330) 637-9030 ..**Grundy**, John C '87 (J Grundy Co, LPA) -3333 State Route 46
-Bx46 -Cortland 44410

(202) 514-8338 ..**Grunes**, Allen P '83 US DOJ-Antitrust Div -325 7th NW -Ste 300
-Washington, DC 20530

(216) 689-4960 ..**Grunick**, Rebecca J '85 KeyBank NA -127 Pub Sq -2nd Fl
-Cleveland 44114

(513) 627-0079 ..**Grunzinger**, Laura R '01 Procter & Gamble
-11810 E Miami Rvr Rd -Bx 630 -Cincinnati 45252

(216) 228-6996 ..**Gruss**, Raymond S '91 %Murman & Assoc -14701 Detroit Av
-Lakewood 44107
Gruttadaurio, John J '89 -875 Cncrs Pkwy -Ste 150
-Maitland, FL 32751

(727) 323-5405 ..**Grybauskas**, Nyjola S '72 -3631 5th Av N
-Saint Petersburg, FL 33713

(419) 227-5531 ..**Grzybowski**, Robert A '90 Allen Cnty Juv Ct -1000 Wardhill Av
-Bx419 -Lima 45802

(330) 346-0674 ..**Guanciale**, Christopher M '85 Plan Member Srvcs
-2983 Wllmsbrg Cir -Stow 44224

(330) 489-3395 ..**Guardado**, Kristen D '95 Pros -218 Cleveland Av SW -Bx24218
-Canton 44702

(419) 529-7657 ..**Guarnera**, Anthony P '88 Workers Comp -240 Tappan Dr N
-Bx8051 -Mansfield 44906

(216) 932-1006 ..**Guarnieri**, Christine '80 -3150 Wshngtn Blvd
-Cleveland Heights 44118

(330) 742-8874 ..**Guarnieri**, Dana C '98 Law Dept -26 S Phelps -Youngstown 44503

(330) 393-7642 ..**Guarnieri**, Donald L '60 (D Guarnieri Co,LPA) -431 E Market
-Warren 44481

(330) 489-3374 ..**Guarnieri**, Lewis D '99 Pros -218 Cleveland Av SW -Bx24218
-Canton 44702

(330) 393-1584 ..**Guarnieri & Secrest** -151 E Market -Bx4270 -Warren 44482
Fx:395-3831

(216) 771-6464 ..**Guarnieri**, William T '62 -815 Superior Av -Ste 1711
-Cleveland 44114 **Fx:**771-0600

(614) 462-3949 ..**Gubola**, Michelle M '96 %Hon DJ Bowman -373 S High -24th Fl
-Columbus 43215

(513) 946-5238 ..**Guckenberger**, Guy C '69 Cnty Mun Ct Judge -1000 Main
-Cincinnati 45202

(419) 447-5132 ..**Gucker**, James R '88 (Meyer M&G,Ltd) -106 E Market -Bx400
-Tiffin 44883

(216) 621-7227 ..**Gudbranson**, Margaret A '83 Cleveland Botanical Garden
-11030 East Blvd -Cleveland 44106

(216) 621-7227 ..**Gudbranson**, Robert N '61 (Nicola G&C,LLC) -25 W Prospect Av
-Republic Bldg Ste 1400 -Cleveland 44115 **Fx:**621-3999
Gudgel, James R '02 -Bx254 -Jackson Center 45334

(305) 649-1553 ..**Gudorf**, Francis V '78 Jubilee Cmmnty Dev Corp -1800 SW 1st
-Ste 206 -Miami, FL 33135

(937) 223-5200 ..**Gudorf**, Theodore G '86 %Flanagan LH&S -318 W 4th
-Dayton 45402 **Fx:**223-3335

(330) 337-8235 ..**Guehl**, Robert L '73 -217 N Lincoln Av -Salem 44460

(614) 428-8555 ..**Gueli**, Christopher S '95 -2804 Johnstown Rd -Columbus 43219

(703) 305-1191 ..**Guendelsberger**, John W '77 DOJ-EOIR-BIA -5107 Leesburg Pk
-Ste 2400 -Falls Church, VA 22041

(202) 418-0634 ..**Guendelsberger**, Nese B '95 FCC -445 12th SW
-Washington, DC 20554

(812) 932-4545 ..**Guenther**, Katharine D '93 -976 Hwy 46 E -Ste D
-Batesville, IN 47006

(937) 833-2772 .. **Guenther,** Vanessa L '84 -475 Arlngtn Rd -Bx7 -Brookville 45309 **Fx:**833-9700

(513) 946-9200 .. **Guenthner,** Carla A '90 Hamilton Cnty Juv Ct -800 Bway -Cincinnati 45202 **Fx:**946-9217

(419) 242-7488 .. **Guerin,** Marshall W '92 Natl Mutual Ins -420 Mad Av -Ste 650 -Toledo 43604

(440) 327-5420 .. **Guerini,** David W '89 Plastics Components,Inc -38850 Taylor Pkwy -North Ridgeville 44035

(419) 435-1886 .. **Guernsey,** Donald J '77 (Guernsey & G) -142 W Tiffin -Bx310 -Fostoria 44830 **Fx:**435-8924

(216) 932-8109 .. **Guerra,** John B '57 -3104 Colerdg Rd -Cleveland Heights 44118

(205) 212-2100 .. **Guerrier,** Charles E '72 EEOC Birmingham Dist Ofc -1130 S 22nd -Ste 2000 -Birmingham, AL 35205

(937) 225-2910 .. **Guerrier,** Mona '96 US Atty -200 W 2nd -602 Fed Bldg -Dayton 45402

(614) 267-2871 .. **Guerrieri,** David D '02 (Hall G&C) -3763 N High -Ste C -Columbus 43214 **Fx:**267-2873

(757) 444-9461 .. **Guess,** Kyle A '99 Naval Legal Srvc Ofc -9620 Marylnd Av -Ste 100 -Norfolk, VA 23511

        Guest, David V '78 -Bx17097 -Baltimore, MD 21297

(407) 671-9700 .. **Guevara,** Gregory W '96 Great Comm Ministries -4037 Metric Dr -Ste 500 -Bx7101 -Winter Park, FL 32793

(513) 533-2996 .. **Gugino,** Julie M '01 Finney SS&K Co,LPA -2623 Erie Av -Bx8804 -Cincinnati 45208

(513) 887-3474 .. **Gugino,** R Paul '01 Butler Cnty Pros -315 High -11th Fl -Bx515 -Hamilton 45012

(614) 220-9100 .. **Gugle,** Kathryn R '92 %Oliver,Inc -471 E Broad -Ste 1303 -Columbus 43215 **Fx:**242-3948

(330) 253-5678 .. **Gugliotta,** John D '94 (Patent Cpyrt & Trdmrk Law Grp,LLC) -137 S Main -Ste 202 -Akron 44308 **Fx:**762-5063

(330) 742-8874 .. **Guglucello,** Iris T '82 Law Dept -26 S Phelps -Youngstown 44503

(330) 643-2374 .. **Gui,** Janice M '78 Summit Cnty Dom Rltns Ct -209 S High -Summit Cnty Cthse Annx -Akron 44308 **Fx:**643-2126

(216) 687-1311 .. **Guice,** Gregory G '03 %Reminger & R -101 Prospect Av W -1400 Mdlnd Bldg -Cleveland 44115 **Fx:**687-1841

(401) 456-1200 .. **Guida,** Patrick A '76 (Tillinghast LPS&C,LLP) -Ten Weybosset -Providence, RI 02903 **Fx:**456-1210

(973) 633-4839 .. **Guidry,** John R '92 Reckitt Benckiser -1655 Valley Rd -Bx943 -Wayne, NJ 07474

(216) 623-1123 .. **Guidubaldi,** David J '72 (Sindell YG&S,PLL) -55 Pub Sq -Ste 1020 -Cleveland 44113 **Fx:**623-1124

        Guiher, Virgil L '56 -4060 Morse Rd -Ste 10 -Columbus 43230

(407) 839-0866 .. **Guiley,** David D '75 (Maher G&M,PA) -631 W Morse Blvd -Ste 200 -Winter Park, FL 32789 **Fx:**425-7958

(330) 244-4200 .. **Guiley,** Richard R '85 Guiley & G Co,PA -4670 Douglas Cir NW -Bx35697 -Canton 44735

(330) 244-4200 .. **Guiley,** Rodney R '75 Guiley & G Co,PA -4670 Douglas Cir NW -Bx35697 -Canton 44735

(937) 498-7265 .. **Guillozet,** Melanie E '93 Shelby Cnty Probate/Juv Ct -Cthse -2nd Fl -Bx4187 -Sidney 45365 **Fx:**498-7260

(937) 548-1157 .. **Guillozet,** Thomas L '85 (Hanes SCGG&D,Ltd) -507 S Bway -Greenville 45331

(513) 946-3000 .. **Guinan,** Richard D '96 Hamilton Cnty Pros -230 E 9th -Cincinnati 45202 **Fx:**946-3017

(513) 425-6609 .. **Guinigundo,** Billy W '04 12th Dist Ct of Appls -1001 Reinartz Blvd -Middletown 45042 **Fx:**425-8751

(216) 622-8200 .. **Guinn,** Guy F '81 (Calfee H&G LLP) -800 Superior Av -Ste 1400 -Cleveland 44114 **Fx:**241-0816

(248) 203-0700 .. **Guise,** Clay A '93 (Dykema G PLLC) -39577 Woodward Av -Ste 300 -Bloomfield Hills, MI 48304 **Fx:**203-0763

(419) 734-4142 .. **Gulas,** Ruth M '87 (Gulas & K Co,LPA) -132 Madison -Port Clinton 43452

(614) 466-7014 .. **Guldin,** Theodore A '67 Pub Safety -1970 W Broad -Columbus 43223 **Fx:**752-6063

(440) 695-6500 .. **Gullia,** Theodore A Jr. '66 -Bx16400 -Cleveland 44116

(740) 454-1223 .. **Gullifer,** Amy E '01 SE OH Lgl Srvcs -27 N 6th -Ste B -Zanesville 43701

(440) 842-1313 .. **Gulyassy,** Victor J '50 Kinkela & K -1721 Carlton Rd -Cleveland 44134

(937) 854-4900 .. **Gump,** Dennis E '69 (Gump Assoc,LPA) -2541 Shiloh Sprngs Rd -Dayton 45426

(614) 469-3939 .. **Gunasekera,** Eva U '04 %Jones D -325 John H McConnell Blvd -Ste 600 -Bx165017 -Columbus 43216 **Fx:**461-4198

(513) 631-0022 .. **Gunderson,** Eric J '92 (Bailey & G Co,LPA) -5257 Mntgmry Rd -Cincinnati 45212

(805) 605-6226 .. **Gunderson,** John W '79 US Air Force -30th Space Wing -Ofc of Envrnmtl Mgmt -Vandenberg AFB, CA 93437

(216) 861-1070 .. **Gundy,** John M Jr. '92 %Ehrenreich & Assoc -526 Superior Av E -1130 Leader Bldg -Cleveland 44114 **Fx:**861-1131

(614) 466-7046 .. **Gunn,** Jeannette E '94 Personnel Brd of Review -65 E State -12th Fl -Columbus 43215

(502) 589-5400 .. **Gunn,** Matthew P '99 %Frost BT LLC -400 W Market -32nd FL -Louisville, KY 40202 **Fx:**581-1087

(614) 777-1203 .. **Gunner,** Michael T '73 -3535 Fishinger Blvd #220 -Hilliard 43026 **Fx:**777-4640

(216) 623-0150 .. **Gunning,** David H II '94 OfCnsl Roetzel & A,LPA -1375 E 9th -One Cleve Ctr 9th Fl -Cleveland 44114 **Fx:**623-0134

(216) 586-3939 .. **Gunning,** Gina K '95 %Jones D -901 Lakeside Av -Cleveland 44114 **Fx:**579-0212

(937) 435-4554 .. **Gunnoe,** Gerald E '73 (Gunnoe & Assoc) -2525 Miamisburg Centervll Rd -Centerville 45459

(614) 228-1541 .. **Gunsett,** Daniel J '74 (Baker & H LLP) -65 E State -Ste 2100 -Columbus 43215 **Fx:**462-2616

(513) 579-4328 .. **Gunter,** Stephanie A '99 Fifth 3rd Bank -38 Fountain Sq Plz -MD 1COM46 -Cincinnati 45263

(216) 623-0000 .. **Gupta,** Manju '03 %Javitch B&R -1300 E 9th -14th Fl -Cleveland 44114 **Fx:**623-0190

(330) 630-7908 .. **Guran,** John M '83 Time Warner Cable -530 S Main -Ste 1751 -Akron 44311

        Guran, Linda Sue '87 -1312 Cntry Clb Rd -Akron 44313

(330) 744-1111 .. **Gurbach,** Matthew D '03 Harrington H&M,Ltd -26 Market -Ste 1200 -Youngstown 44503 **Fx:**744-2029

(216) 479-8500 .. **Gurbst,** Richard S '71 (Squire S&D LLP) -127 Pub Sq -4900 Key Twr -Cleveland 44114 **Fx:**479-8780

(419) 259-0252 .. **Gurecky,** Marcia S '87 Fifth Third Bank -606 Mad Av -Leg Dept -Bx1868 -Toledo 43603

(614) 445-2646 .. **Gurian,** Jonathan G '85 Grange Mutual Cslty Co -650 S Front -Bx1218 -Columbus 43216

(614) 228-6885 .. **Gurile,** Melissa A '04 %Lane A&H LLC -175 S 3rd -Ste 700 -Columbus 43215 **Fx:**228-0146

(440) 460-3705 .. **Gurin,** Timothy B '87 Marconi Comm Inc -5900 Landerbrook Dr -Ste 300 -Cleveland 44124

(440) 354-3800 .. **Gurley,** Joanne G '81 Rand GH&K -270 E Main -Ste 300 -Painesville 44077

(440) 354-3800 .. **Gurley,** Joseph M '75 (Rand GH&K) -270 E Main -Ste 300 -Painesville 44077

(303) 830-0500 .. **Gurley,** Michael E '80 %Hamilton & F,PC -1600 Bway -Ste 500 -Denver, CO 80202

(513) 651-6800 .. **Gurney,** D Scott '86 (Frost BT LLC) -201 E 5th -2200 PNC Ctr -Cincinnati 45202 **Fx:**651-6981

(216) 621-3251 .. **Gurney Miller & Mamone** -75 Pub Sq -Ste 525 -Cleveland 44113 **Fx:**621-1332

(216) 931-6000 .. **Gurney,** Neil W '78 (Ulmer & B LLP) -1300 E 9th -Ste 900 Penton Media Bldg -Cleveland 44114 **Fx:**931-6001

(440) 236-5015 .. **Gurnick,** Raymond L '90 Seaway Bolt & Specials Corp -11561 Station Rd -Bx908 -Columbia Station 44028

(304) 723-3861 .. **Gurrera,** Vincent S '87 Cnsl Gurrera Law Ofcs,PLLC -3401 Penn Av -Bx2308 -Weirton, WV 26062 **Fx:**723-3871

(614) 224-5161 .. **Gurvis,** Anthony N '81 Crown Dielectric Indstrs -830 W Broad -Columbus 43222

(412) 562-1592 .. **Gurwin,** David A '85 (Buchanan I,PC) -301 Grant -20th Fl -Pittsburgh, PA 15219 **Fx:**562-1041

(248) 594-0600 .. **Gurwin,** Robert S '92 %Rader F&G PLLC -39533 Woodward Av -Ste 140 -Bloomfield Hills, MI 48304 **Fx:**594-0610

(616) 961-5397 .. **Gusching,** Gregory J '86 Defense Rev & Marketing Srvc -74 Wshngtn Av N -Battle Creek, MI 49017

(440) 888-1177 .. **Gusley,** Mark R '91 M Gusley & Assoc Co,LPA -6600 Park Av -Cleveland 44105

(419) 248-2419 .. **Gusses,** George '73 (G Gusses Co,LPA) -33 S Huron -Toledo 43602 **Fx:**321-6379

(614) 444-3900 .. **Gussler,** Stephanie G '92 -755 S High -Columbus 43206

(740) 983-2557 .. **Gussler,** Stephen S '66 (Margulis GH&H) -50 Bortz -Bx5 -Ashville 43103 **Fx:**983-2685

(763) 764-4169 .. **Gustaferro,** Mark P '93 General Mills -1 Gen Mills Blvd -Minneapolis, MN 55426

(740) 892-4444 .. **Gustafson,** Alan P '73 -Bx484 -Utica 43080

(330) 668-6501 .. **Gustafson,** Davin R '86 S&S Business Srvcs -4040 Embssy Pkwy -Ste 100 -Akron 44333

(513) 241-7880 .. **Gustafson,** Derek W '84 -1014 Vine -Ste 1919 -Cincinnati 45202

(513) 651-4130 .. **Gustafson,** Jill '90 %Lawrence Firm -8044 Mntgmry Rd -Ste 700 -Cincinnati 45236

(859) 578-1030 .. **Gustafson,** Jill '90 %Lawrence Firm -606 Phila -Covington, KY 41011 **Fx:**578-1032

(419) 255-3030 .. **Gustafson,** John P '85 -520 Mad Av -855 Spitzer Bldg -Toledo 43604

(513) 621-4477 .. **Gustavson,** William M '78 -1011 Paradrome -Cincinnati 45202 **Fx:**421-3043

(330) 384-5228 .. **Guster,** Christine M '84 First Energy Corp -76 S Main -Ste 1600 -Akron 44308

(513) 621-8200 .. **Gustin,** James W '55 (J Gustin & Assoc Co,LPA) -830 Main -Ste 609 -Cincinnati 45202

(937) 378-1072 .. **Gusweiler,** Scott T '90 -501 E State -Georgetown 45121 **Fx:**378-2311

(330) 825-2477 .. **Gutbrod,** James J '86 (Walkley K&G Co,LPA) -4071 S Cleveland-Massillon Rd -Bx1080 -Norton 44203 **Fx:**825-2029

(419) 885-3683 .. **Gutchess,** Allen D Jr. '60 -5741 Little Farms Ct -Sylvania 43560

(330) 255-6205 .. **Guten,** Sharon M '84 GoJo Ind -Bx991 -Akron 44309

(614) 221-2300 .. **Gutentag,** Mark S '93 -42 E Gay -Ste 1500 -Columbus 43215

(614) 568-0030 .. **Guthrie,** Graham D '93 (Akin G LLC) -100 Drchstr Sq Ln -Ste 202 -Westerville 43081 **Fx:**898-9685

(614) 466-2980 .. **Guthrie,** James M '71 Atty Gen -30 E Broad -Columbus 43215 **Fx:**728-9470

(614) 466-0722 .. **Guthrie,** John A '80 Atty Gen -150 E Gay -Columbus 43215 **Fx:**644-9973

(614) 431-1500 .. **Guthrie,** Maria C '97 %Perez & M LLC -8000 Ravines Edge Ct -Ste 300 -Columbus 43235 **Fx:**431-3885

(216) 443-7800 .. **Gutierrez,** James A '85 Cuyahoga Cnty Pros -1200 Ontario -8th Fl -Cleveland 44113 **Fx:**698-2270

(330) 477-6781 .. **Gutierrez,** Roy '61 Cnsl Stark Cnty Engineer -5165 Southway SW -Canton 44706 **Fx:**477-3926

(216) 739-2901 .. **Gutin,** Robert D '68 Safeguard Title & Escrow Agency,Inc -650 Safeguard Plz -Cleveland 44131 **Fx:**535-2245

(216) 621-1530 .. **Gutkoski,** Brian R '03 %Shapiro & F,LLP -1500 W 3rd -Ste 400 -Cleveland 44113 **Fx:**621-1551

(216) 363-4500 .. **Gutmacher,** Norman W '71 (Benesch FC&A LLP) -200 Pub Sq -Ste 2300 -Cleveland 44114 **Fx:**363-4588

(419) 228-3700 .. **Gutman,** Jana E '92 Allen Cnty Pros -204 N Main -#302 -Lima 45801

(412) 394-5425 .. **Gutman,** Michele M '76 (Babst CC&Z,PC) -Two Gtwy Ctr -8th Fl A -Pittsburgh, PA 15222

(937) 332-6971 .. **Gutmann,** Elizabeth S '84 Cnty Mun Ct Judge -201 W Main -Troy 45373

(937) 773-3212 .. **Gutmann,** Michael E '84 (McCulloch FF&G Co,LPA) -123 Market -Bx910 -Piqua 45356 **Fx:**773-9672

(212) 264-3449 .. **Gutridge,** Cheryl C '04 US Dept of Homeland Sec -26 Fed Plz -Rm 1130 -New York, NY 10278 **Fx:**264-1645

(703) 591-2664 .. **Guttag,** Eric W '79 Jagtiani & G -10363-A Democracy Ln -Fairfax, VA 22030 **Fx:**591-5907

(614) 236-6500 .. **Guttenberg,** Jack A '82 Capitol Univ Law Schl -303 E Broad -Columbus 43215 **Fx:**236-6972

(614) 228-1541 .. **Guttman,** Daniel J '97 %Baker & H LLP -65 E State -Ste 2100 -Columbus 43215 **Fx:**462-2616

(216) 696-4006 .. **Guttman,** Rubin '77 (R Guttman & Assoc,LPA) -55 Pub Sq -Ste 1860 -Cleveland 44113 **Fx:**696-2778

(614) 292-0611 .. **Guttman,** Todd G '96 OSU/Legal Affrs -33 W 11th Av -Ste 209 -Columbus 43201

(513) 621-5252 ..**Gutzwiller**, Robert H '78 (Clodfelter & G) -36 E 4th -Ste 1208
-Cincinnati 45202

(614) 752-1603 ..**Guy**, James R '03 OH Dept Rehab & Correction -1050 Fwy Dr N
-Columbus 43229

(330) 535-2151 ..**Guy**, John J '70 (Guy L&T) -106 S Main -Ste 2210 -Akron 44308
Fx:535-9048

(248) 436-5220 ..**Guy**, Kirk N '83 Barton Malow Co -26500 Amer Dr
-Southfield, MI 48034

(330) 535-2151 ..**Guy Lammert & Towne** -106 S Main -Ste 2210 -Akron 44308
Fx:535-9048

(419) 841-1571 ..**Guynes**, Marlene F '90 -4934 Rudgate Blvd -Toledo 43623

(212) 326-3739 ..**Guynn**, Steven D '84 (Jones DR&P) -222 E 41st
-New York, NY 10017 **Fx:**755-7306

(614) 462-3194 ..**Guzman**, Becky '01 Franklin Cnty Pub Def -373 S High -12th Fl
-Columbus 43215

(330) 374-1144 ..**Guzzo**, Diane R '89 Weisman & G -One Cascade Plz -Ste 1450
-Akron 44308

(216) 522-4914 ..**Guzzo**, Fred J '73 US ALJ - SSA Hearings & Appeals -US Bk Bldg
-7th Fl Ctrm 1 -Cleveland 44115

(440) 842-9328 ..**Gvozdenovic**, Milos '04 -3303 Norris Av -Parma 44134

(740) 594-8686 ..**Gwinn**, Susan L '79 -86 Columbus Rd -Ste 101 -Athens 45701

(419) 259-6217 ..**Gwinn**, Yolanda D '84 US Magistrates Ofc -1716 Spielbusch Av
-Rm 318 -Toledo 43624

(419) 874-3569 ..**Gwyn**, Peter D '68 -110 W 2nd -Perrysburg 43551 **Fx:**874-8547

(330) 841-2515 ..**Gysegem**, Thomas P '84 Mun Ct Judge -Bx1550 -Warren 44482
Gyurgyik, Peter F '04 -(Address Unavailable)

(330) 649-9102 ..**Haag**, Charles A '80 (Regas & H,Ltd) -3969 Convenience Cir NW
-Ste 101 -Canton 44718

(703) 456-8175 ..**Haag**, Charles T '96 %Cooley G LLP -11951 Freedom Dr
-Reston, VA 20190

(419) 248-5701 ..**Haak**, William H II '94 Owens Corning -1 Owens Corning Pkwy
-Leg Dept -Toledo 43659

(937) 443-6822 ..**Haaker**, Christine M '94 (Thompson H LLP) -2000 Cthse Plz NE
-Bx8801 -Dayton 45401 **Fx:**443-6635

(419) 898-0100 ..**Haar**, Dawn M '93 -139 E Water -Oak Harbor 43449

(202) 659-6946 ..**Haarz**, David R '90 Dickinson W PLLC -1901 L NW -Ste 800
-Washington, DC 20036

(513) 721-4532 ..**Haas**, Bradley G '86 (Katz TB&H) -255 E 5th -Ste 2400
-Cincinnati 45202

(513) 651-6800 ..**Haas**, Colleen M '97 %Frost BT LLC -201 E 5th -2200 PNC Ctr
-Cincinnati 45202 **Fx:**651-6981

(216) 363-4500 ..**Haas**, Douglas E '77 (Benesch FC&A LLP) -200 Pub Sq -Ste 2300
-Cleveland 44114 **Fx:**363-4588

(216) 472-1500 ..**Haas**, Gary C '69 OfCnsl O'Brien Law Firm,LLC -627 W St Clair Av
-Cleveland 44113 **Fx:**472-1600

(513) 721-1126 ..**Haas**, Herbert J '81 -114 E 8th -Cincinnati 45202

(440) 779-8300 ..**Haas**, John M '67 -26130 Lorain Rd -North Olmsted 44070

(740) 353-9805 ..**Haas**, John R '90 (Ruggiero & H) -800 Gallia -Ste 600 -Bx150
-Portsmouth 45662

(216) 623-0150 ..**Haas**, Michael J '94 (Roetzel & A,LPA) -1375 E 9th
-One Cleve Ctr 9th Fl -Cleveland 44114 **Fx:**623-0134

(513) 651-5651 ..**Haas**, Michael R '04 %Carr & S -817 Main -Ste 200
-Cincinnati 45202 **Fx:**651-5402

(216) 348-5400 ..**Haas**, Patricia J '99 %McDonald H Co,LPA -600 Superior Av E
-Ste 2100 -Cleveland 44114 **Fx:**348-5474

(330) 643-2040 ..**Haas**, Paula D '97 Cmn Pleas Ct/Probate Div -209 S High -Akron
44308

(330) 922-1771 ..**Haas**, Richard H '67 -1101 Aberdeen Cir -Stow 44224

(216) 689-4169 ..**Haas**, Robert M '75 KeyBank NA -127 Pub Sq -Cleveland 44114

(216) 861-5582 ..**Haas**, Steven M '94 (Fay SFM&M LLP) -1100 Superior Av -7th Fl
-Cleveland 44114 **Fx:**241-1666

(740) 452-4192 ..**Haas**, Susan J '85 -84 N 5th -Bx2323 -Zanesville 43702

(615) 937-1000 ..**Haase**, Glenn R '70 Bridgestone/Firestone -535 Marriott Dr
-Nashville, TN 37214

(614) 221-9400 ..**Habash Reasoner & Frazier,LLP** -471 E Broad -Ste 800
-Columbus 43215

(614) 221-9400 ..**Habash**, Stephen J '78 (Habash R&F,LLP) -471 E Broad -Ste 800
-Columbus 43215

(216) 595-0740 ..**Habat**, John L '83 -2686 Rocklyn Rd -Shaker Heights 44122

(419) 245-2740 ..**Habekost**, Carl E '90 Industrial Commssn of OH -One Govt Ctr
-Ste 1500 -Toledo 43604

(513) 651-6800 ..**Habel**, Christopher S '95 (Frost BT LLC) -201 E 5th -2200 PNC Ctr
-Cincinnati 45202 **Fx:**651-6981

(440) 349-4938 ..**Haber**, Harry L '70 -36065 Pepper Dr -Solon 44139

(216) 687-1311 ..**Haber**, Richard C '90 (Reminger & R) -101 Prospect Av W
-1400 Mdlnd Bldg -Cleveland 44115 **Fx:**687-1841

(330) 722-0330 ..**Haberman**, Ian S '82 -225 E Lbrty -Medina 44256

(440) 914-0400 ..**Habinski**, Amy K '99 %Suresite Cnsltng Grp,LLC
-6655 Parkland Blvd -Ste 200 -Solon 44139

(330) 562-3156 ..**Habowski**, Ronald J '85 (Christley H&P) -215 W Garfld -Ste 230
-Aurora 44202 **Fx:**562-9540

(440) 250-4400 ..**Hack**, Edward G '79 (Egert M&H) -1991 Crocker Rd -#550
-Westlake 44145

(419) 422-4014 ..**Hackenberg**, Alan D '94 (Hackenberg B&R) -314 W Crawford
-Bx1544 -Findlay 45839

(419) 422-4014 ..**Hackenberg Beutler & Rasmussen** -314 W Crawford -Bx1544
-Findlay 45839

(419) 429-7338 ..**Hackenberg**, David A '68 City of Findlay -318 Dorney Plz -Rm 310
-Findlay 45840

(440) 354-4364 ..**Hackenberg**, Isaac J '64 (Baker & H Co,LPA) -77 N St Clair
-Painesville 44077 **Fx:**639-8901

(330) 376-8336 ..**Hackenberg**, Stacey T '96 Goldman & R,Ltd -11 S Forge
-Akron 44304 **Fx:**376-2522

(614) 644-7250 ..**Hacker**, Cheryl R '88 Atty Gen -30 E Broad -Columbus 43215
Fx:644-7634

(216) 241-8282 ..**Hackerd**, Richard E '91 -2000 Standard Bldg -Cleveland 44113

(937) 443-6931 ..**Hackert**, Timothy J '88 (Thompson H LLP) -2000 Cthse Plz NE
-Bx8801 -Dayton 45401 **Fx:**443-6635

(614) 538-4256 ..**Hackett**, Andrew M '95 AOL Inc -5000 Arlngtn Centre Blvd
-Columbus 43220

(614) 221-3155 ..**Hackett**, Daniel R '88 (Bailey C LLC) -10 W Broad
-Columbus 43215

(614) 469-7447 ..**Hackett**, Lawrence J '85 US DOJ-Trustee Ofc -170 N High
-Ste 200 -Columbus 43215

(614) 621-9000 ..**Hackett**, Patricia A '93 %Glimcher Realty -150 E Gay
-Columbus 43215

(513) 333-0050 ..**Hackett**, Paul L III '88 -1014 Vine -Ste 1690 -Cincinnati 45202

(330) 740-2330 ..**Hackett**, Sharon K '84 %Mahoning Cnty Pros -21 W Boardman
-6th Fl -Youngstown 44503 **Fx:**740-2008

(330) 792-2336 ..**Hackett**, Timothy R '84 (Wellman JH&S Co,LPA)
-4990 Mahoning Av -Youngstown 44515 **Fx:**792-5403

(216) 623-0000 ..**Hacking**, Timothy J '01 %Javitch B&R -1300 E 9th -14th Fl
-Cleveland 44114 **Fx:**623-0190

(770) 469-8887 ..**Hackleman**, Tricia J '97 Hughes & Assoc PC
-2415BW Park Pl Blvd SW -Stone Mountain, GA 30087

(440) 350-2683 ..**Hackman**, David J Jr. '90 Lake Cnty Pros -105 Main -Bx490
-Painesville 44077 **Fx:**350-2685

(216) 586-3939 ..**Hackwelder**, Scott W '04 %Jones D -901 Lakeside Av -Cleveland
44114 **Fx:**579-0212

(419) 435-8139 ..**Hadacek**, John D '75 Mun Ct Judge -213 S Main -Bx985
-Fostoria 44830

(513) 737-1369 ..**Haddad**, Hanna B '03 -7099 Crown Pnt Dr -Hamilton 45011
Fx:737-1495

(727) 299-0449 ..**Haddad**, Royce C Jr. '95 (Haddad & S,PA)
-13555 Automobile Blvd -Ste 540 -Clearwater, FL 33762
Fx:299-9181

(216) 281-5210 ..**Haddad**, Tina R '89 (Haddad Law Ofc) -3155 W 33rd
-Cleveland 44109

(513) 732-7929 ..**Haddad**, Victor M '89 Cnty Mun Ct Judge -289 E Main
-Batavia 45103

(614) 431-2000 ..**Hadden**, E Bruce '60 Hadden Co LPA -132 Northwoods Blvd
-Columbus 43235 **Fx:**436-4500

(614) 227-2000 ..**Hadden**, James B '92 (Porter WM&A LLP) -41 S High
-Columbus 43215 **Fx:**227-2100

(513) 281-1040 ..**Hadden**, Richard Ray '76 -3900 Rose Hill Av -Ste 701B
-Cincinnati 45229

(937) 859-8026 ..**Haddick**, Reid J '84 -1129 Miamisburg Centervll Rd -Ste 305
-West Carrollton 45449 **Fx:**859-8279

(614) 228-2945 ..**Haddow**, Howard J '61 (Folkerth H&D) -341 S 3rd
-Columbus 43215

(614) 227-2320 ..**Haddox**, Craig A '82 (Bricker & E LLP) -100 S 3rd -Columbus
43215 **Fx:**227-2390

(740) 455-7123 ..**Haddox**, Dennis M '82 Muskingum Cnty Pros -27 N 5th
-Zanesville 43701

(614) 466-6696 ..**Haddox**, Kelley R '97 Atty Gen -150 E Gay -Columbus 43215
-Fx:752-2538

(513) 852-3497 ..**Haders**, William D '75 Atty Gen -441 Vine -1600 Carew Twr
-Cincinnati 45202 **Fx:**852-3484

(937) 222-2424 ..**Hadi**, Vaseem S Y '02 %Freund F&A -1 S Main -Ste 1800
-Dayton 45402 **Fx:**222-5369

(330) 761-4312 ..**Hadick**, Stephen N '94 FirstEnergy Corp -76 S Main -Akron 44308

(614) 764-3005 ..**Hadley**, Gregory A '88 Wendys Intl -4288 W Dublin-Granvll Rd
-Bx256 -Dublin 43017
Hadzinski, Kenneth W '96 -5840 Birdie Ln -Mentor 44060

(330) 689-2869 ..**Haefner**, Joseph P '96 Stow Law Dept -3760 Darrow Rd
-Stow 44224 **Fx:**686-0219

(216) 241-5310 ..**Haemmerle**, Todd M '93 (Gallagher SF&N) -1501 Euclid Av -6th Fl
-Cleveland 44115 **Fx:**241-1608

(614) 464-2025 ..**Hafenstein**, Kenneth S '94 (Connor B LLP) -501 S High
-Columbus 43215 **Fx:**224-8708

(513) 785-6548 ..**Haferkamp**, Shannon L '02 Butler Cnty Pros -315 High -11th Fl
-Bx515 -Hamilton 45012

(419) 421-3355 ..**Haffenden**, Philip E '84 Marathon Ashland Petro LLC -539 S Main
-Findlay 45840 **Fx:**427-3690

(513) 579-1500 ..**Haffer**, Gloria S '77 (Buechner HOM&H Co,LPA) -105 E 4th
-Ste 300 -Cincinnati 45202 **Fx:**977-4361

(937) 429-8595 ..**Haffey**, David A '73 -1195 Meadow Brdg Dr -Ste B -Dayton 45434
Fx:429-8590

(216) 291-3600 ..**Haffey**, James R Jr. '64 (Bernard & H Co,LPA) -5001 Mayfld Rd
-Ste 301 -Cleveland 44124 **Fx:**291-0159

(216) 291-3600 ..**Haffey**, Timothy P '89 (Bernard & H Co,LPA) -5001 Mayfld Rd
-Ste 301 -Cleveland 44124 **Fx:**291-0159

(513) 721-2120 ..**Haffner**, Karri K '94 Barrett & W -105 E 4th -Ste 500
-Cincinnati 45202

(513) 369-5947 ..**Haffner**, Paul F '94 Great Amer Ins Co -580 Walnut -10th Fl
-Cincinnati 45202

(419) 332-1670 ..**Hafford**, Roger W '77 -621 Croghan -Fremont 43420

(330) 740-2073 ..**Hafiz**, Ishraq A '83 %Mahoning Cnty CSEA -112 W Commerce
-Bx119 -Youngstown 44503
Hafner, Barbara A '87 -1932 Brim Dr -Toledo 43613

(419) 872-1272 ..**Hafner**, Mark A '87 Dewalt & Gallup,Inc -12855 Eckel Juncion Rd
-Bldg 1 Ste 201 -Perrysburg 43551

(513) 367-4861 ..**Haft**, James E '72 (Shank & H) -115 N Walnut -Harrison 45030

(440) 356-0062 ..**Hagan**, Brian F '81 (Rego C&H Co,LPA) -21270 Lorain Rd
-Fairview Park 44126

(937) 449-6400 ..**Hagan**, Timothy W '78 (Dinsmore & S LLP) -1 S Main
-Ste 1300 One Dayton Centre -Dayton 45402 **Fx:**449-6405

(419) 445-8815 ..**Hagans**, Mark D '94 (Plassman RHS&H) -302 N Defiance -Bx178
-Archbold 43502 **Fx:**445-1080

(216) 622-8200 ..**Hagedorn**, Gina K '04 %Calfee H&G LLP -800 Superior Av
-Ste 1400 -Cleveland 44114 **Fx:**241-0816

(937) 229-2423 ..**Hagel**, Thomas L '83 Univ of Dayton Schl of Law -300 Cllg Park
-Dayton 45469

(513) 762-6200 ..**Hageman**, Jennifer J '96 (Ulmer & B LLP) -600 Vine -Ste 2800
-Cincinnati 45202 **Fx:**762-6245

(216) 586-3939 ..**Hagen**, Daniel C '80 (Jones D) -901 Lakeside Av
-Cleveland 44114 **Fx:**579-0212

(614) 799-1788 ..**Hagen**, Theresa L '92 -4440 Hvrfrd Ct -Upper Arlington 43220

(614) 228-6888 ..**Hager**, Jackie L '00 %Havens W LLC -141 E Town -Ste 200
-Columbus 43215 **Fx:**228-6878

(440) 808-4242 ..**Hager**, Jason P '03 %Douglass & Assoc Co,LPA
-551 Dover Ctr Rd -Bx40480 -Cleveland 44140 **Fx:**808-4215

(216) 621-5300 ..**Hager**, Robert A '88 (Buckingham D&B,LLP) -1375 E 9th
-Ste 1700 -Cleveland 44114 **Fx:**621-5440

(614) 341-6233 ..**Hagerott**, Jacqueline C '99 Franklin Univ -201 S Grant
-Columbus 43215

(513) 774-0440 .. **Hagerstrand,** Eric C '74 Meridian Land Group, LTD -11310 Mntgmry Rd -Ste 100 -Cincinnati 45249

(216) 931-6000 .. **Haggerty,** John J '03 (Ulmer & B LLP) -1300 E 9th -Ste 900 Penton Media Bldg -Cleveland 44114 **Fx:**931-6001

(216) 515-1660 .. **Haggerty,** Patrick F '85 (Frantz W LLP) -127 Pub Sq -2500 Key Center -Cleveland 44114 **Fx:**515-1650

(937) 449-6810 .. **Haggerty,** Patrick H '02 %Porter WM&A LLP -1 S Main -Ste 1600 -Dayton 45402 **Fx:**449-6820

(513) 651-6800 .. **Haggerty,** Walter E Jr. '78 (Frost BT LLC) -201 E 5th -2200 PNC Ctr -Cincinnati 45202 **Fx:**651-6981

(216) 391-5110 .. **Haggins,** Edward T '66 -3030 Euclid Av -Ste 411 -Cleveland 44115

(513) 983-4282 .. **Hagopian,** Gary '76 Procter & Gamble Co-Legal -1 Procter & Gamble Plz -Cincinnati 45202

(845) 452-5900 .. **Hagstrom,** David D '71 (Van DeWater & Van D,LLP) -40 Grdn -Bx112 -Poughkeepsie, NY 12602 **Fx:**452-5848

(312) 782-3939 .. **Hagy,** James C '78 Jones DR&P -77 W Wacker Dr -Ste 3500 -Chicago, IL 60601

(330) 821-1430 .. **Hahn,** Brian Scott '80 (Geiger TS&H) -1844 W State -Ste A -Alliance 44601 **Fx:**821-2217

(937) 222-1800 .. **Hahn,** Douglas C '76 -130 W 2nd -Ste 201 -Dayton 45402

(614) 324-5959 .. **Hahn,** Halle B '94 Value Recovery Grp -919 Old Henderson -Columbus 43220

(614) 236-6425 .. **Hahn,** John V '91 Capital Univ -2199 E Main -Columbus 43209

(216) 991-6200 .. **Hahn,** Joseph A '95 R Gross Co,LPA -20133 Farnsleigh Rd -Ohio Svngs Bldg -Shaker Heights 44122 **Fx:**991-6199
Hahn, Joshua J '02 -1596 S Ludlow Rd -Urbana 43078
Hahn, Lesley W '77 -34 S Hmptn Pkwy -Rocky River 44116

(216) 432-9222 .. **Hahn,** Lisa A '94 -4403 St Clair Av -Cleveland 44103

(216) 621-0150 .. **Hahn Loeser & Parks LLP** -3300 BP Twr/200 Pub Sq -Ste 3300 -Cleveland 44114 **Fx:**241-2824

(614) 221-0240 .. **Hahn Loeser & Parks LLP** -65 E State -Ste 1400 -Columbus 43215 **Fx:**221-5909

(330) 864-5550 .. **Hahn Loeser & Parks LLP** -One GOJO Plz -Ste 300 -Akron 44311 **Fx:**864-7986

(614) 221-8448 .. **Hahn,** Peter W '98 %Buckingham D&B,LLP -191 W Nationwide Blvd -Ste 300 -Bx151120 -Columbus 43215 **Fx:**221-8590

(440) 930-1361 .. **Hahn,** Richard E '71 Poly One Corp -33587 Walker Rd -Avon Lake 44012

(614) 221-2223 .. **Hahn,** Susie Lin '98 %Leeseberg & V -175 S 3rd -PH 1 -Columbus 43215 **Fx:**221-3106

(216) 861-6160 .. **Hahn,** Victor H '50 -820 W Superior Av -Ste 510 -Cleveland 44113

(614) 469-5715 .. **Hahnert,** Robyn J '77 US Atty -303 Marconi Blvd -Ste 200 -Columbus 43215

(614) 249-7191 .. **Haid,** Amy E '01 Nationwide Mutual Ins Co -One Nationwide Plz -1-35-10 -Columbus 43215

(614) 644-2100 .. **Haight,** Karen M '87 EPA -122 S Front -Bx1049 -Columbus 43216

(210) 221-2282 .. **Haight,** Timothy J '02 US Army JAG -1306 Stanley Rd -Fort Sam Houston, TX 78234

(330) 867-1490 .. **Hail,** Gregory Lee '92 %Holland & M -55 S Miller Rd -Ste 103 -Akron 44333 **Fx:**865-1221

(216) 696-1422 .. **Haiman,** Irwin S '41 (McCarthy LC&L Co,LPA) -101 Prospect Av W -1800 Mdlnd Bldg -Cleveland 44115 **Fx:**696-1210

(216) 875-6226 .. **Haimes,** Rand S '84 Ferro Corp -1000 Lakeside Av -Cleveland 44114

(419) 843-2001 .. **Haims,** Bonnie E '00 %Gallon & T Co,LPA -3516 Granite Cir -Bx352018 -Toledo 43635 **Fx:**843-6665

(330) 743-5101 .. **Haines,** Dennis '62 (Green H&S,Co LPA) -16 Wick Av -Ste 400 -Youngstown 44503 **Fx:**743-3451

(216) 381-1881 .. **Haines,** Jacque M '58 -3820 Monticello Blvd -Cleveland Heights 44121 **Fx:**(440) 944-5873

(440) 256-2394 .. **Haines,** Jeffrey D '92 (J Haines & Assoc) -Bx630 -Willoughby 44096

(614) 227-4079 .. **Haines,** Kimberley K '90 State Teachers Retirmnt Sys -275 E Broad -Columbus 43015

(740) 369-1125 .. **Haines,** Quentin R '77 BSG Title Srvcs,LLC -15 N Franklin -Delaware 43015

(513) 381-0656 .. **Haines,** Richard M '76 (Kohnen & P LLP) -201 E 5th -Ste 800 -Cincinnati 45202 **Fx:**381-5823

(216) 622-8200 .. **Haines,** Warren M II '00 %Calfee H&G LLP -800 Superior Av -Ste 1400 -Cleveland 44114 **Fx:**241-0816

(419) 429-3500 .. **Hainley,** Sharon H '88 Owens Cmmnty Cllg -300 Davis -Findlay 45840

(614) 466-5394 .. **Haire,** Theresa G '82 Pub Def -8 E Long -Columbus 43215

(216) 861-2222 .. **Hairston,** Craig A '99 Rieth & A -200 Pub Sq -Ste 2940 -Cleveland 44114

(614) 228-1541 .. **Hairston,** George W '68 (Baker & H LLP) -65 E State -Ste 2100 -Columbus 43215 **Fx:**462-2616

(216) 664-2685 .. **Hajjar,** Joseph G '98 Dept of Law -601 Lakeside Av -Rm 106 City Hall -Cleveland 44114 **Fx:**664-2663

(216) 291-1117 .. **Haka,** Katherine M '90 -Bx18826 -Cleveland Heights 44118

(858) 202-7948 .. **Hake,** Richard A '97 Elan Pharmaceuticals -7475 Lusk Blvd -San Diego, CA 92121

(440) 282-5455 .. **Halasa,** Ghada K '87 -4642 Oberlin Av -Ste 204 -Lorain 44053

(330) 468-1056 .. **Halberg,** William S '70 (Halberg & Assoc Co,LPA) -198 E Aurora Rd -Northfield 44067 **Fx:**468-1068

(402) 245-4486 .. **Halbert,** Christopher C '03 %Halbert & D -111 E 17th -Bx447 -Falls City, NE 68355 **Fx:**245-4491

(513) 887-7300 .. **Halcomb,** Margot B '93 %Fiehrer L&C -10 Jrnl Sq -Ste 400 -Hamilton 45011

(614) 221-4255 .. **Hale,** Benjamin W Jr. '70 (Smith & H) -37 W Broad -Columbus 43215

(513) 352-0500 .. **Hale,** Jeffrey S '04 (Schmalz & H) -602 Main -Ste 1010 -Cincinnati 45202 **Fx:**352-0555

(740) 353-1629 .. **Hale,** Joseph L '83 -547 6th -Portsmouth 45662 **Fx:**355-3503

(330) 493-0272 .. **Hale,** Kathleen M '81 -3413 W Harvard Blvd NW -Canton 44709

(614) 228-1541 .. **Hale,** Mary A '96 Baker & H LLP -65 E State -Ste 2100 -Columbus 43215 **Fx:**462-2616

(937) 223-2200 .. **Hale,** Tarin S '92 %SG Caras Co,LPA -130 W 2nd -Ste 310 -Dayton 45402 **Fx:**223-8989

(513) 651-6800 .. **Halenkamp,** Erin Rieger '02 %Frost BT LLC -201 E 5th -2200 PNC Ctr -Cincinnati 45202 **Fx:**651-6981

(216) 348-5400 .. **Hales,** David K '96 (McDonald H Co,LPA) -600 Superior Av E -Ste 2100 -Cleveland 44114 **Fx:**348-5474

(419) 241-1200 .. **Hales,** Janet E '92 Cooper & W,LPA -900 Adams -Toledo 43624 **Fx:**242-5675

(419) 517-0090 .. **Hales,** Steven C '99 -5151 Monroe -Ste 105 -Toledo 43623

(419) 355-5374 .. **Haley,** Nancy E '89 Dept Job & Fam Srvcs -2511 Cntryside Dr -Fremont 43420

(330) 633-2069 .. **Haley,** Robert S '82 -867 Moe Dr -Ste G -Akron 44310

(216) 586-3939 .. **Halfon,** Ellen E '88 Cnsl Jones D -901 Lakeside Av -Cleveland 44114 **Fx:**579-0212

(216) 928-3474 .. **Halim,** Henny N '03 %Yormick & Assoc Co,LPA -127 Pub Sq -Ste 5200 -Cleveland 44114 **Fx:**566-0857

(330) 497-3000 .. **Halkias,** John W '88 Fisher Foods Mrktng Inc -4855 Frank Rd NW -North Canton 44720

(614) 462-5400 .. **Hall,** Adam J '00 %Kegler BH&R -65 E State -Ste 1800 -Columbus 43215 **Fx:**464-2634

(513) 651-6800 .. **Hall,** Adam P '89 (Frost BT LLC) -201 E 5th -2200 PNC Ctr -Cincinnati 45202 **Fx:**651-6981

(614) 463-4212 .. **Hall,** Alison Day '97 %Littler M,PC -21 E State -Ste 1600 -Columbus 43215 **Fx:**221-3301

(614) 228-6345 .. **Hall,** Andrew C '96 Strip HLM&T Co LPA -575 S 3rd -Columbus 43215 **Fx:**228-6369

(216) 622-8200 .. **Hall,** Arthur C III '95 (Calfee H&G LLP) -800 Superior Av -Ste 1400 -Cleveland 44114 **Fx:**241-0816

(216) 443-8800 .. **Hall,** Barbara S '79 Cuyahoga Co Cmmn Pleas Ct -1 Lakeside Av -Cleveland 44113

(216) 227-2000 .. **Hall,** Brian D '85 (Porter WM&A LLP) -41 S High -Columbus 43215 **Fx:**227-2100

(614) 249-7261 .. **Hall,** Carrie Ann '01 %Nationwide Ins Co -1 Nationwide Plz -Columbus 43215

(330) 453-2336 .. **Hall,** Charles D III '83 Hall Law Firm -610 Market Av N -Canton 44702 **Fx:**453-2919

(440) 914-9624 .. **Hall,** Charles M '79 -8 E Wshngtn -Ste 200 -Chagrin Falls 44022

(419) 443-9711 .. **Hall,** Charles R Jr. '03 -120½ Wshngtn -Ste 216 -Tiffin 44883

(614) 875-9619 .. **Hall,** Connie L '86 -3783 Bway -Grove City 43123

(614) 225-9000 .. **Hall,** Daniel M '93 %Garvin & H,LLC -181 E Lvngstn Av -Columbus 43215 **Fx:**225-9080

(937) 223-1201 .. **Hall,** David L '68 OfCnsl Altick & C Co,LPA -1 S Main -1700 One Dayton Ctr -Dayton 45402 **Fx:**223-5100

(937) 228-1111 .. **Hall,** Dennis L '69 (Hall & M,LPA) -51 Irongate Park Dr -Dayton 45459 **Fx:**912-8920

(937) 912-9810 .. **Hall,** Dennis L '69 (Hall & M,LPA) -3040 Prsdntl Dr -Ste 222 -Fairborn 45324 **Fx:**912-6920

(216) 696-1616 .. **Hall,** Edison H Jr. '79 -526 Superior Av -645 Leader Bldg -Cleveland 44114

(419) 891-6473 .. **Hall,** Elizabeth J '80 Cnsl The Andersons Inc -480 W Dussel Dr -Bx119 -Maumee 43537

(330) 723-2200 .. **Hall,** Eric D '97 %G Piszczek Co, LPA -412 N Court -Medina 44256

(216) 781-1212 .. **Hall,** Eric J '01 %Walter & H LLP -1301 E 9th -Ste 3500 -Cleveland 44114 **Fx:**575-0911

(513) 241-0400 .. **Hall,** Gary L '79 (Aronoff R&H Co,LPA) -425 Walnut -Ste 2400 -Cincinnati 45202 **Fx:**241-2877

(419) 524-9811 .. **Hall,** George '52 OfCnsl Weldon H&K,LLP -28 Park Av W -Bank One Bldg -Mansfield 44902 **Fx:**522-5758

(412) 762-1393 .. **Hall,** Hazel A '83 PNC Bank,NA -249 Fifth Av -P1-POPP-21-1 -Pittsburgh, PA 15222

(330) 384-7098 .. **Hall,** James A '76 FirstMerit Bank -III Cascade Plz -7th Fl -Akron 44308

(614) 885-3500 .. **Hall,** James A '79 -47 E Wilson Bridge Rd -Worthington 43085

(713) 615-8500 .. **Hall,** James M Jr. '75 (McGinnis L&K,LLP) -1221 McKinney -Ste 3200 -Houston, TX 77010 **Fx:**615-8585
Hall, Jeffrey L '91 -537 Weatherstone Dr -Wadsworth 44281

(740) 886-1616 .. **Hall,** John E '76 (Klein & H Co,LPA) -101 State -Bx844 -Proctorville 45669 **Fx:**886-1818

(419) 332-3800 .. **Hall,** John F '70 Hall Law Firm -707 Napoleon -Fremont 43420
Hall, Joshua E '03 -(Address Unavailable)

(614) 267-2871 .. **Hall,** Julie A '05 (Hall G&C) -3763 N High -Ste C -Columbus 43214 **Fx:**267-2873

(513) 534-4772 .. **Hall,** Kari K '03 Cnsl Fifth Third Bank -38 Fountain Sq Plz -MD 10AT76 -Cincinnati 45263

(937) 461-8800 .. **Hall,** Keith R '73 (Harker C&H) -130 W 2nd -Ste 2103 -Dayton 45402 **Fx:**449-1600

(216) 520-5554 .. **Hall,** Kenneth P '92 West Grp -6111 Oak Tree Blvd -Bx318063 -Cleveland 44131

(740) 383-6109 .. **Hall,** Kevin R '87 Hall & H -355 E Ctr -Ste 101 -Marion 43302

(614) 462-6641 .. **Hall,** Kimberly L '98 %Franklin Cnty Cmn Pleas Ct -375 S High -Columbus 43215 **Fx:**462-6292

(740) 983-2557 .. **Hall,** Leo J '65 Margulis GH&H -50 Bortz -Bx5 -Ashville 43103 **Fx:**983-2685

(330) 747-2661 .. **Hall,** Leonard D '85 Cafaro Co -2445 Belmont Av -Bx2186 -Youngstown 44504

(216) 623-0000 .. **Hall,** Lindsey I '02 %Javitch B&R -1300 E 9th -14th Fl -Cleveland 44114 **Fx:**623-0190

(216) 696-1616 .. **Hall,** Mary E '91 -526 Superior Av -645 Leader Bldg -Cleveland 44114

(800) 440-4284 .. **Hall,** Michael D '93 Bowling Trnsprtn Inc -5110 Defiance Pike -Wayne 43466

(216) 931-6000 .. **Hall,** Michael J '04 %Ulmer & B LLP -1300 E 9th -Ste 900 Penton Media Bldg -Cleveland 44114 **Fx:**931-6001

(513) 665-9333 .. **Hall,** Michael S '84 -432 Walnut -Ste 1000 -Cincinnati 45202

(614) 365-4100 .. **Hall,** Monique A '02 %Carpenter & L LLP -280 N High -Ste 1300 280 Plz -Columbus 43215 **Fx:**365-9165

(937) 228-1111 .. **Hall & Mueller, LPA** -51 Irongate Park Dr -Dayton 45459 **Fx:**912-8920

(937) 912-9810 .. **Hall & Mueller, LPA** -3040 Prsdntl Dr -Ste 222 -Fairborn 45324 **Fx:**912-6920

(419) 241-9000 .. **Hall,** Nathan A '03 %Shumaker L&K,LLP -1000 Jackson -Toledo 43624 **Fx:**241-6894

(614) 236-6719 .. **Hall,** Nicole K '01 %Capital Univ Law Schl -303 E Broad -Family Advocacy Clinic -Columbus 43215 **Fx:**236-6970

(614) 292-0748 .. **Hall,** Patrick J '92 OSU/Ofc Stdnt Affrs -1849 Cannon Dr -2050 Drake Union -Columbus 43210

(614) 247-7898 ..**Hall**, Peggy K '97 OSU-Dept of AEDE -2120 Fyffe Rd
-Columbus 43210

(419) 382-0111 ..**Hall**, Rhonda G '00 Intl Diamond Syst -5110 Angola Rd
-Toledo 43615

(916) 351-8582 ..**Hall**, Robert G '91 GenCorp Inc -Bx537012
-Sacramento, CA 95853

(330) 453-2336 ..**Hall**, Rosemarie A '92 Hall Law Firm -610 Market Av N
-Canton 44702 **Fx:**453-2919

(614) 480-3663 ..**Hall**, Sarah L '85 Huntington Banc Shares Inc -41 S High -HC0339
-Columbus 43215

(216) 443-5809 ..**Hall**, Stephanie N '01 Cuyahoga Cnty Pros -1910 Carnegie Av
-Whitlatch Bldg -Cleveland 44115 **Fx:**443-5815

(614) 458-0025 ..**Hall**, Stephen K '98 %McDonald H Co,LPA -41 S High -Ste 3650
-Columbus 43215 **Fx:**458-0028

(614) 418-8019 ..**Hall**, Timothy C Jr. '92 M/I Homes,Inc -3 Easton Oval -Ste 500
-Columbus 43219

(800) 621-3216 ..**Hall**, Timothy J '97 CT Corp -17 S High -Columbus 43215

(502) 852-6830 ..**Hall**, Timothy S '93 Brandeis Schl of Law -2301 S 3rd
-Univ of Louisvll -Louisville, KY 40292

(405) 552-2218 ..**Hall**, William D '90 OfCnsl McAfee & T -211 N Robnsn -10th Fl
-Two Leadership Sq -Oklahoma City, OK 73102 **Fx:**228-7418

(216) 363-1400 ..**Hallbauer**, John A '66 OfCnsl Buckley K,LPA -600 E Superior Av
-Ste 1400 -Cleveland 44114 **Fx:**579-1020

(440) 248-8448 ..**Hallberg**, Charles E '77 Member Hlth Inc -29100 Aurora Rd
-Ste 301 -Solon 44139

(419) 352-5164 ..**Halleck**, Michael J '71 (Halleck & G) -105 N Main
-Bowling Green 43402 **Fx:**352-6645

(419) 353-8491 ..**Halleck**, Peter T '73 (Halleck & H) -107 E Court
-Bowling Green 43402

(513) 424-2401 ..**Hallee**, Michael J '02 %Casper & C -1 N Main -Bx510
-Middletown 45042 **Fx:**424-0622

(513) 762-6200 ..**Hallenbeck**, Prentiss W Jr. '98 %Ulmer & B LLP -600 Vine
-Ste 2800 -Cincinnati 45202 **Fx:**762-6245

(513) 921-8433 ..**Haller**, Brad E '00 Wing Eyecare,Inc -5305 Glenway Av
-Cincinnati 45238

(216) 443-7295 ..**Haller**, Jason G '00 Cuyahoga Cnty Pub Def -1849 Prospect Av
-Ste 2 -Cleveland 44115

(614) 463-9441 ..**Haller**, John E '86 (Shumaker L&K,LLP) -41 S High -Ste 2210
-Columbus 43215 **Fx:**463-1108

(614) 292-5062 ..**Haller**, Kathryn '75 OSU Medical Ctr -370 W 9th Av
-200 Meiling Hall -Columbus 43210

..**Haller**, Sonja M '83 -2343 Fixler Rd -Medina 44256

(937) 562-5250 ..**Haller**, Stephen K '75 Greene Cnty Pros -61 Greene -Xenia 45385

(415) 371-1200 ..**Hallerud**, Michael C '73 (Thelen R&P LLP) -101 2nd -Ste 1800
-San Francisco, CA 94105

(419) 826-4866 ..**Hallett**, Christopher J '88 TE Hallett -113 W Airport Hwy -Bx208
-Swanton 43558

(419) 335-5011 ..**Hallett Hallett & Nagel** -132 S Fulton -Wauseon 43567
Fx:335-3187

(440) 933-3231 ..**Hallett**, Matthew H '98 %Smith & S Co,LPA -110 Moore Rd -Bx210
-Avon Lake 44012

(419) 335-5011 ..**Hallett**, Timothy W '72 (Hallett H&N) -132 S Fulton
-Wauseon 43567 **Fx:**335-3187

(614) 445-8416 ..**Halley**, Matthew S '99 -52 W Whittier -Columbus 43206

(614) 481-8608 ..**Halliburton-Cohen**, Kim M '82 (KM Halliburton-Cohen & Assoc)
-1776 W Lane Av -Ste B -Upper Arlington 43221 **Fx:**481-9795

(216) 623-2035 ..**Hallick**, Patricia J '79 IRS-Appls Ofc -1375 E 9th -Ste 815
-Cleveland 44114

(216) 771-5588 ..**Halliday**, Brian J '01 %Rosner & Assoc,LLC -812 Huron Rd
-Ste 601 Caxton Bldg -Cleveland 44115 **Fx:**771-5894

(740) 373-1155 ..**Halliday**, John M '93 (Bertram & H,LLC) -412 3rd -Marietta 45750

(419) 289-2555 ..**Halligan**, Brian J '83 (Halligan & G,LLP) -930 Claremont Av
-Bx455 -Ashland 44805

(312) 655-1500 ..**Halligan**, Robert Mark '78 (Welsh & K,Ltd) -120 S Riverside Plz
-22nd Fl -Chicago, IL 60606 **Fx:**655-1501

(937) 229-3031 ..**Hallinan**, Charles G '78 Univ of Dayton Schl of Law -300 Cllg Park
-Dayton 45469

(937) 449-6810 ..**Hallinan**, Paul G '80 (Porter WM&A LLP) -1 S Main -Ste 1600
-Dayton 45402 **Fx:**449-6820

(740) 266-2995 ..**Hallock**, Gary M '77 -4017A Sunset Blvd -Steubenville 43952
Fx:266-2998

..**Halloran**, Dennis E '81 -111 Pelican Ct -Edenton, NC 27932

(513) 852-8200 ..**Halloran**, James W '60 OfCnsl Cors & B LLC
-537 E Pete Rose Way -Ste 400 -Cincinnati 45202

(614) 868-0009 ..**Hallowes Allen & Haynes** -6445 E Lvngstn Av
-Reynoldsburg 43068 **Fx:**868-0029

(614) 868-0009 ..**Hallowes**, Donald B '89 (Hallowes A&H) -6445 E Lvngstn Av
-Reynoldsburg 43068 **Fx:**868-0029

..**Hallquist**, Kevin P '86 -1328 W 64th -Cleveland 44102

(330) 491-5221 ..**Halm**, Jeffrey A '73 (Buckingham D&B,LLP) -4518 Fulton Dr NW
-Bx35548 -Canton 44735 **Fx:**492-9625

(513) 793-4400 ..**Halper**, Steven D '75 (Katzman LH&B) -9000 Plainfld Rd
-Cincinnati 45236 **Fx:**793-4691

(216) 696-7550 ..**Halpern**, Marvin N '61 -815 Superior Av -Ste 1623
-Cleveland 44114

(614) 292-7480 ..**Halpern**, Sheldon W '97 OSU Moritz Cllg of Law -55 W 12th Av
-Columbus 43210 **Fx:**292-1383

(513) 977-8200 ..**Halpert**, Douglas J '94 (Dinsmore & S LLP) -255 E 5th -Ste 1900
-Cincinnati 45202 **Fx:**977-8141

(216) 946-5700 ..**Halpert**, Sanford A '57 -24985 Penhurst Dr -Beachwood 44122

(513) 241-3447 ..**Halpin**, John '04 -906 Main -Ste 405 -Cincinnati 45202

(513) 852-8210 ..**Halpin**, Victor C II '97 %Cors & B LLC -537 E Pete Rose Way
-Cincinnati 45202

(513) 867-1411 ..**Halverson**, Damon L '01 %Pater P&P Co,LPA -315 S Front
-Hamilton 45011

(419) 241-9000 ..**Halverson**, Micah J '01 %Shumaker L&K,LLP -1000 Jackson
-Toledo 43624 **Fx:**241-6894

(513) 956-6136 ..**Hamagami**, Monica Y '93 Fidelity Invstmnts -4445 Lk Forest Dr
-Cincinnati 45242

(614) 466-7264 ..**Hamalian**, Derek S '88 OH Legal Rghts Srvc -8 E Long -5th Fl
-Columbus 43215

(440) 365-8800 ..**Hamamey**, David A II '97 %MG Petroff -1288 Abbe Rd -Elyria
44035

(859) 655-7004 ..**Haman**, William D '98 Nelson & S,PLLC -639 Wshngtn Av
-Ste 200 -Newport, KY 41071

(513) 345-4160 ..**Hambley**, William C '87 Pro Seniors,Inc -7162 Redding Rd
-Ste 1150 -Cincinnati 45237

(216) 696-6700 ..**Hamed**, Michael R '98 (Kushner & R Co,LPA) -200 Pub Sq
-Ste 2860 BP Twr -Cleveland 44114 **Fx:**696-6772

(419) 252-5935 ..**Hamel**, Gregory J '94 HCR-Manor Care -333 N Summit
-Toledo 43604

(614) 486-6967 ..**Hamelberg**, William R '76 -1350 W 5th Av -Ste 124
-Columbus 43212

(330) 376-1600 ..**Hamer**, Kate M '03 %Cincinnati Ins Co -50 S Main -Ste 615
-Akron 44308

(937) 296-2456 ..**Hamer**, Theodore A III '89 Law Dept -3600 Shroyer Rd
-Kettering 45429

(937) 223-1100 ..**Hamilton**, Adelina E '04 %Slicer Law Ofc -111 W 1st -Ste 401
-Dayton 45402 **Fx:**223-8150

(614) 464-4532 ..**Hamilton**, Andrew P '79 -400 S 5th -Ste 103 -Columbus 43215

..**Hamilton**, Bethany J '02 -500 E 3rd -Apt 502 -Dayton 45402

..**Hamilton**, Brian K '98 -3725 Broadvw Dr -Cincinnati 45208

(270) 826-7200 ..**Hamilton**, Curtis J III '95 (Morton & B) -126 N Main -Bx883
-Henderson, KY 42419

(614) 885-0038 ..**Hamilton**, Elizabeth A '94 (Sinno & H,LLC) -8001 Ravines Edge Ct
-Ste 200 -Columbus 43235

(513) 558-4768 ..**Hamilton**, Frederick N '92 Univ of Cincinnati -3223 Eden AV
-Wherry Hall G-07 -Cincinnati 45267

(216) 621-0200 ..**Hamilton**, J Richard '56 (Baker & H LLP) -1900 E 9th -Ste 3200
-Cleveland 44114 **Fx:**696-0704

(440) 871-0026 ..**Hamilton**, James L '73 -24441 Detroit Rd -Ste 300
-Westlake 44145

(614) 443-7920 ..**Hamilton**, Karen E '95 -1021 S High -Columbus 43206
Fx:443-7922

(513) 793-3737 ..**Hamilton**, Louis G '82 Audible Elgnce -9464 Mntgmry Rd
-Montgomery 45242

(650) 874-5347 ..**Hamilton**, Michael A '96 GAP,Inc -900 Cherry Av
-San Bruno, CA 94066

(614) 464-6400 ..**Hamilton**, Nathan C '89 OfCnsl Vorys SS&P LLP -52 E Gay
-Bx1008 -Columbus 43216 **Fx:**464-6350

(614) 875-4114 ..**Hamilton**, Raymond K '96 (Hamilton & H) -3338 Columbus
-Grove City 43123

(419) 531-1734 ..**Hamilton**, Richard A '57 -Bx12558 -Toledo 43606

(513) 721-5672 ..**Hamilton**, Richard O Jr. '00 %Benjamin Y&H LLC -312 Elm
-Ste 1850 -Cincinnati 45202 **Fx:**562-4388

(216) 522-4107 ..**Hamilton**, Richard T Jr. '89 US DOJ-Antitrust Div -55 Erievw Plz
-Bldg 9-Ste 700 -Cleveland 44114

(937) 642-5877 ..**Hamilton**, Robert O '53 -116 S Ct -Marysville 43040

(614) 469-3939 ..**Hamilton**, Robert W '87 (Jones D) -325 John H McConnell Blvd
-Ste 600 -Bx165017 -Columbus 43216 **Fx:**461-4198

(513) 785-5880 ..**Hamilton**, Rodrick J '87 Butler Cnty CSEA -315 High -7th Fl
-Hamilton 45011

(419) 259-2891 ..**Hamilton**, Sandra A '88 %ABLE -520 Mad Av -740 Spitzer Bldg
-Toledo 43604

(440) 964-0236 ..**Hamilton**, Terry L '85 Lighthouse Legal Ministries -2929 Carpenter
Rd -Ashtabula 44004

(216) 586-3939 ..**Hamilton**, Thomas A '93 (Jones D) -901 Lakeside Av
-Cleveland 44114 **Fx:**579-0212

(614) 469-3939 ..**Hamilton McGranor**, AshLee M '00 Jones D
-325 John H McConnell Blvd -Ste 600 -Bx165017
-Columbus 43216 **Fx:**461-4198

(216) 574-8321 ..**Hamm**, George E Jr. '92 Cleveland Mun Sch Dist -1380 E 6th
-Cleveland 44114

(740) 354-2300 ..**Hamm**, George R '02 -721 5th -Portsmouth 45662 **Fx:**354-5667

(419) 354-9244 ..**Hamm**, Kathleen M '83 Wood Cnty Pub Def -123 N Summit
-Bowling Green 43402

(419) 223-8501 ..**Hamman**, Timothy C '73 Allen Cnty Probate Ct -Bx1243 -Lima
45802 **Fx:**221-3432

(513) 721-3242 ..**Hammelrath**, W S '65 (Siebold & H Co,LPA) -432 Walnut -Ste 850
-Cincinnati 45202

(419) 352-1581 ..**Hammer**, James A '86 (Mitchell S&H) -112 E Oak
-Bowling Green 43402

(216) 635-1705 ..**Hammer**, Lisa A '98 (Hammer & P) -4617 Denmark Av -Cleveland
44102

(513) 263-3906 ..**Hammer**, Vickie L '80 IRS -550 Main -Bx476 -Cincinnati 45201

(330) 376-5300 ..**Hammersmith**, Stephen M '81 (Buckingham D&B,LLP) -50 S Main
-Bx1500 -Akron 44309 **Fx:**258-6559

(614) 466-4395 ..**Hammerstein**, Anne L '82 Atty Gen -150 E Gay -Columbus 43215
Fx:644-8764

(330) 433-5349 ..**Hammond**, Elizabeth E '83 GE Consumer Fnc -4500 Munson NW
-Canton 44718

(614) 228-6061 ..**Hammond**, Gary W '80 (Hammond & S) -556 E Town
-Columbus 43215

(937) 327-9370 ..**Hammond**, John R '80 -4 W Main -#922 -Bx2646
-Springfield 45501 **Fx:**327-9370

(937) 223-1201 ..**Hammond**, Julie G '00 %Altick & C Co,LPA -1 S Main
-1700 One Dayton Ctr -Dayton 45402 **Fx:**223-5100

(614) 227-2000 ..**Hammond**, Karen K '94 %Porter WM&A LLP -41 S High
-Columbus 43215 **Fx:**227-2100

(216) 771-6500 ..**Hammond**, Kim M '93 K Weiner & Assoc Co,LPA -75 Pub Sq
-4th Fl -Cleveland 44113 **Fx:**771-6540

..**Hammond**, Mary M '97 -856 Doerdg Dr -Erlanger, KY 41018

(513) 381-2011 ..**Hammond**, Michael F '89 (Hammond Law Grp,LLC) -441 Vine
-3311 Carew Twr -Cincinnati 45202 **Fx:**381-2227

(937) 426-3310 ..**Hammond**, Richard H '68 (Hammond S&S)
-3836 Dayton-Xenia Rd -Beavercreek 45432 **Fx:**426-9328

(740) 335-8150 ..**Hammond**, Robert L '67 -129 N Hinde
-Washington Court House 43160

(614) 228-6061 ..**Hammond & Sewards** -556 E Town -Columbus 43215

(937) 426-3310 ..**Hammond Stier & Stadnicar** -3836 Dayton-Xenia Rd
-Beavercreek 45432 **Fx:**426-9328

(216) 664-2816 ..**Hammons-Brown**, Terri M '93 City of Cleveland -601 Lakeside Av
-Rm 106 -Cleveland 44114

(419) 241-2100 ..**Hamner**, Jessica R '03 %Watkins B&C -405 Mad Av -Ste 1900
-Toledo 43604 **Fx:**241-1960

(419) 255-1360 ..**Hamner**, Scott E '78 Findley Davies,Inc -300 Mad Av -Ste 1000
-Toledo 43604 **Fx:**259-5685

Hampl, Lisa S '96 -411 Grdn Rd -Columbus 43214

(440) 323-1145 .. Hampole, Gowri V '97 -401 Broad -Ste 211 -Elyria 44035

(216) 566-5257 .. Hampton, Bruce E '82 Grtr Clvlnd Reg Trans Auth -1240 W 6th
-Cleveland 44113

(740) 532-9422 .. Hampton, Carol J '69 (Hampton & D Co,LPA) -336 Center
-Ironton 45638

(614) 519-5817 .. Hampton, Kevin M '04 Hampton Law Firm,LLC -242 Trl Ct
-Newark 43055 Fx:(740) 321-3301

(740) 425-4020 .. Hampton, Thomas A '84 -160 E Main -Bx310 -Barnesville 43713
Fx:425-4021

(937) 223-4332 .. Hamrick, Winn C '50 -130 W 2nd -Ste 200 -Dayton 45402

(614) 365-2700 .. Han, Kyu Chang '04 %Squire S&D LLP -41 S High
-1300 Huntngtn Ctr -Columbus 43215 Fx:365-2499

(614) 462-2288 .. Han, Lisa Ge Shang '93 (Schottenstein Z&D) -250 West
-Bx165020 -Columbus 43216 Fx:462-5135

(937) 233-8194 .. Hanaghan, Dennis M '66 Hanaghan & H -34 N Main
-911 Key Bank -Dayton 45402

(440) 354-3800 .. Hanahan, Geoffrey C '79 (Rand GH&K) -270 E Main -Ste 300
-Painesville 44077

(606) 329-1919 .. Hanbury, John I '90 Hanbury PH&W,PSC -1401 Greenup Av
-Bx2008 -Ashland, KY 41105

(703) 696-0287 .. Hancock, George L Jr. '79 SrCnsl US Army JAGC -901 N Stuart
-Attn:DAJA-IM Rm 735 -Arlington, VA 22203 Fx:696-0376

(513) 561-6562 .. Hancock, John W '68 -7910 Shawnee Run Rd -Cincinnati 45243

(216) 844-3372 .. Hancock, Kathleen L '95 Univ Hospital -11100 Euclid Av
-Cleveland 44106

(419) 421-3687 .. Hancock, Paul D '78 Marathon Ashland Petroleum LLC
-539 S Main -Rm 864-M -Findlay 45840

(440) 442-6800 .. Hanculak, Thomas M '75 %JW Diemert Jr & Assoc Co,LPA
-1360 SOM Center Rd -Mayfield Heights 44124 Fx:442-0825

(740) 349-8371 .. Hand, James R '72 J Mantonya,LPA -3 N 3rd -Newark 43055

(513) 695-1325 .. Hand, Mary Kathleen '03 Warren Cnty Pros -500 Justice Dr
-Lebanon 45036 Fx:695-1775

(614) 241-5111 .. Handa, Charles Brent '85 -336 S High -Columbus 43215

(216) 831-2959 .. Handelman, James M '78 -23611 Chagrin Blvd -Ste 220
-Beachwood 44122

(614) 461-9212 .. Handelman & Kilroy -360 S Grant Av -Columbus 43215

(614) 252-2300 .. Handelman, Robert B '76 (Calig & H,LPA) -854 E Broad
-Columbus 43205

(614) 461-9212 .. Handelman, Robert K '72 (Handelman & K) -360 S Grant Av
-Columbus 43215

(614) 462-5471 .. Handlan, Allen L '72 (Kegler BH&R) -65 E State -Ste 1800
-Columbus 43215 Fx:464-2634

(513) 977-8200 .. Handler, Allyson B '03 %Dinsmore & S LLP -255 E 5th -Ste 1900
-Cincinnati 45202 Fx:977-8141

(614) 677-4456 .. Handley, Bobby J '98 Nationwide Life Ins -1 Nationwide Plz
-Columbus 43215

(513) 762-6200 .. Hands, John M '88 (Ulmer & B LLP) -600 Vine -Ste 2800
-Cincinnati 45202 Fx:762-6245

(419) 872-6600 .. Handwork, B Thomas Jr. '68 (Handwork & K)
-900 W South Boundary -Bldg 8-B -Perrysburg 43551

(419) 872-6600 .. Handwork & Kerscher -900 W South Boundary -Bldg 8-B
-Perrysburg 43551

(614) 794-9770 .. Hane, Wilbur H III '01 Amer Family Ins Grp -Bx6165
-Westerville 43086

(330) 867-9998 .. Haneline, Kenneth M '86 Kastner W&W,LLC -3480 W Market
-Ste 300 -Akron 44333 Fx:867-3786

(419) 354-9600 .. Hanes, Duncan L '03 Wood Cnty Ct of Common Pleas
-One Cthse Sq -Ctrm 4 -Bowling Green 43402

(713) 567-9375 .. Hanes, Richard D '86 US Atty -910 Travis -15th Fl -Bx61129
-Houston, TX 77208

(937) 548-1157 .. Hanes Schipfer Cooper Graber Guillozet & Detling, Ltd
-507 S Bway -Greenville 45331

(513) 232-8000 .. Hanessian, Edward J '77 River Downs -Bx30286
-Cincinnati 45230

(614) 444-4529 .. Haney, Andrew R '99 -673 Mohawk -Ste 200 -Columbus 43206

(859) 586-8494 .. Haney, Janell D '94 -1412 Stoneyhollow Ct -Hebron, KY 41048

(614) 876-8888 .. Haney, John L Jr. '76 -3544 Main -Hilliard 43026

(513) 651-6800 .. Haney, Maureen P '99 %Frost BT LLC -201 E 5th -2200 PNC Ctr
-Cincinnati 45202 Fx:651-6981

(330) 364-6553 .. Hanhart, David M '80 (Black MHD&B) -130 W 3rd -Bx2330
-Dover 44622 Fx:364-2739

(419) 213-4700 .. Hanible, Khary L '03 Lucas Cnty Pros -Adams & Erie
-Lucas Cnty Cthse -Toledo 43624

(419) 524-6682 .. Hanke, Chad P '03 %Baran PTF&T Co,LPA -3 N Main -Ste 500
-Mansfield 44902 Fx:525-4571

(614) 227-2000 .. Hanke, Paul A '61 (Porter WM&A LLP) -41 S High
-Columbus 43215 Fx:227-2100

(614) 463-4201 .. Hankerson, Cheryl R '97 %Littler M,PC -21 E State -Ste 1600
-Columbus 43215 Fx:221-3301

(513) 956-4620 .. Hanket, Mark J '68 Diversey Lever -3630 E Kemper Rd
-Sharonville 45241

(614) 451-9999 .. Hanks, John C '00 Homewood Corp -750 Northlawn Dr
-Columbus 43214

(330) 424-0550 .. Hanley, Cynthia A '85 -105 S Market -Lisbon 44432

(614) 885-4009 .. Hanley, Kathleen A '81 -120A N Woods Blvd -Columbus 43235

(859) 431-7077 .. Hanley, Patrick J '72 -214 E 4th -Covington, KY 41011

(330) 762-9933 .. Hanlon, Deidre A '79 (Ferguson & H) -120 E Mill -Ste 415
-Akron 44308

(740) 695-1444 .. Hanlon Duff Estadt & McCormick Co,LPA -46457 Natl Rd W
-Saint Clairsville 43950 Fx:695-1563

(330) 929-3324 .. Hanlon, Herbert J '85 -125 Portage Trl -Cuyahoga Falls 44221

(412) 456-2839 .. Hanlon, John R Jr. '93 (Meyer U&S,LLP) -1300 Oliver Bldg
-Pittsburgh, PA 15222

(740) 695-1444 .. Hanlon, Lodge L '58 OfCnsl Hanlon DE&M Co,LPA
-46457 Natl Rd W -Saint Clairsville 43950 Fx:695-1563

(937) 223-6211 .. Hann, Jennifer K '96 Crew & B -2580 Kettering Twr -Dayton 45423

(330) 670-7300 .. Hanna Campbell & Powell, LLP -3737 Embssy Pkwy -Bx5521
-Akron 44334 Fx:670-0977

(937) 593-6065 .. Hanna, Dane M '91 %Thompson DHMW&T -1111 Rush Av -Bx68
-Bellefontaine 43311

(513) 603-7176 .. Hanna, David B '00 OH Casualty Grp -9450 Seward Rd
-Fairfield 45014

(330) 670-7300 .. Hanna, David J '79 (Hanna C&P,LLP) -3737 Embssy Pkwy
-Bx5521 -Akron 44334 Fx:670-0977

(614) 466-6939 .. Hanna, Delbert P '93 OH Dept Taxation -30 E Broad -22nd Fl
-Columbus 43215

(419) 352-6501 .. Hanna, Drew A '72 (Hanna & H) -700 N Main -Bx25
-Bowling Green 43402 Fx:352-7008

(419) 599-1010 .. Hanna & Fisher -822 Oakwood Av -Bx605 -Napoleon 43545

(419) 352-6501 .. Hanna, Harold M '71 (Hanna & H) -700 N Main -Bx25
-Bowling Green 43402 Fx:352-7008

(419) 599-1010 .. Hanna, John H '72 (Hanna & F) -822 Oakwood Av -Bx605
-Napoleon 43545

(216) 344-8401 .. Hanna, John T '90 The Glidden Co -925 Euclid Av -Ste 900
-Cleveland 44115 Fx:344-8935

(330) 745-2175 .. Hanna, Joseph E '78 Lombardi HHC&E -2745 Nesbitt Av
-Akron 44319

(216) 514-7480 .. Hanna, Marcy J '04 Mortg Info Srvcs -4877 Galaxy Pkwy -Ste 1
-Cleveland 44128

(561) 738-1104 .. Hanna, Mark J '95 %Kaleel & C -555 N Congress Av -Ste 301
-Boynton Beach, FL 33426 Fx:738-1106

(216) 664-3739 .. Hanna, Mary N '03 Dept of Law -601 Lakeside Av
-Rm 106 City Hall -Cleveland 44114 Fx:664-2663

(216) 592-5000 .. Hanna, Robert J '86 (Tucker E&W LLP) -925 Euclid Av
-1150 Huntngtn Bldg -Cleveland 44115 Fx:592-5009

(937) 296-2543 .. Hanna, Thomas M '81 Mun Ct Judge -3600 Shroyer Rd
-Kettering 45429

(330) 253-2227 .. Hanna, Timothy H '85 Parker LH&R,LLC -388 S Main -Ste 402
-Akron 44311 Fx:253-2224

(216) 830-6830 .. Hanna, Valerie M '91 (Brouse M) -1001 Lakeside Av -Ste 1600
-Cleveland 44114 Fx:830-6807

(216) 479-8500 .. Hanna, W Michael '80 (Squire S&D LLP) -127 Pub Sq
-4900 Key Twr -Cleveland 44114 Fx:479-8780

(216) 781-1212 .. Hanna, William R '97 %Walter & H LLP -1301 E 9th -Ste 3500
-Cleveland 44114 Fx:575-0911

(216) 443-7800 .. Hannan, Charles E Jr. '86 Cuyahoga Cnty Pros -1200 Ontario
-8th Fl -Cleveland 44113 Fx:698-2270

(740) 774-1174 .. Hannan, Christine B '80 Ross Cnty Probate/Juv Ct -2 N Paint -#A
-Chillicothe 45601

(614) 621-1500 .. Hannan, Lori L '98 Calfee H&G LLP -21 E State
-1100 Fifth Third Ctr -Columbus 43215 Fx:621-0010

(216) 566-5723 .. Hannan, Tracy A '03 %Thompson H LLP -127 Pub Sq
-3900 Key Ctr -Cleveland 44114 Fx:566-5800

(419) 213-6850 .. Hanneman, Donna P '90 Lucas Cnty Dom Rltns Ct
-429 N Mich Av -Ste A -Toledo 43624

(614) 792-5170 .. Hanneman, James A '98 -3010 Hayden Rd -Columbus 43235
Fx:798-1935

Hannen, Robert J '91 -2108 Lumber Av -Ste 7
-Wheeling, WV 26003

(330) 484-3239 .. Hanner, Willard K Jr. '80 -2664 Cleveland Av SW -Canton 44707

(330) 746-6301 .. Hanni, Don L '53 -219 W Boardman -Youngstown 44503

Hanni, Mark A '04 -(Address Unavailable)

(330) 627-2191 .. Hannon, Richard C Jr. '79 Fusion Ceramics,Inc -160 Scio Rd SE
-Bx127 -Carrollton 44615

(513) 732-2214 .. Hannon, Richard D '77 -10 S 3rd -Batavia 45103

(412) 471-1180 .. Hannon, Sean P '98 (Gorr MD&L) -525 Wm Penn Pl -Ste 3700
-Pittsburgh, PA 15219 Fx:471-9012

(216) 479-8500 .. Hanover, Pamela I '80 (Squire S&D LLP) -127 Pub Sq
-4900 Key Twr -Cleveland 44114 Fx:479-8780

(440) 423-1259 .. Hanover, Stanley I '78 OH Dispute Resolution
-7031 Wilson Mills Rd -Chesterland 44026 Fx:423-1259

(202) 457-6000 .. Hanrahan, Colleen '00 %Patton B,LLP -2550 M NW
-Washington, DC 20037 Fx:457-6315

(440) 255-9100 .. Hanrahan, Patrick R '74 McNamara HC&L -8440 Station
-Mentor 44060

(330) 499-6000 .. Hanratty, James P '89 (Baker DBW&M) -400 S Main
-Canton 44720 Fx:449-6423

(412) 454-5000 .. Hansberry, John C '95 Pepper H LLP -500 Grant -50th Fl
-Pittsburgh, PA 15219

(216) 664-4504 .. Hansbrough, Keith '00 Dept of Law -601 Lakeside Av
-Rm 106 City Hall -Cleveland 44114 Fx:664-2663

(440) 943-4200 .. Hansell, Herbert J '49 Lubrizol Corp -29400 Lakelnd Blvd
-Wickliffe 44092

Hanselman, Aaron W '04 -(Address Unavailable)

Hanselman, John L Jr. '73 -5231 Hardisty Av -Cincinnati 45208

Hanselman, Lisa N '01 -5048 Dierker Rd -#D -Columbus 43220

(216) 621-0200 .. Hanselman, Suzanne K '91 (Baker & H LLP) -1900 E 9th
-Ste 3200 -Cleveland 44114 Fx:696-0740

(937) 222-2500 .. Hanseman, Robert G '00 %Sebaly S&D -1900 Kettering Twr
-Dayton 45423 Fx:222-6554

(216) 348-5400 .. Hansen, Bette E '01 %McDonald H Co,LPA -600 Superior Av E
-Ste 2100 -Cleveland 44114 Fx:348-5474

Hansen, Bowanne S '92 -1721 Deepwood Dr -Akron 44313

(937) 223-8177 .. Hansen, Chad D '02 %Coolidge WW&L -33 W 1st -Ste 600
-Dayton 45402 Fx:223-6705

Hansen, Curtis A '90 -5731 Heritage Lks Dr -Hilliard 43026

(216) 241-2880 .. Hansen, Glenn S '86 Cowden HN&L -50 Pub Sq -Ste 1414
-Cleveland 44113 Fx:241-2881

(614) 864-9971 .. Hansen, Jennifer B '94 IDEAS Intl,Inc
-1416 Reynoldsburg New Alban Rd N -Blacklick 43004

(937) 224-1427 .. Hansen, Thomas A '65 -130 W 2nd -Ste 1900 -Dayton 45402
Fx:228-5134

(740) 852-1576 .. Hansgen, Shirley C '79 (Tanner M&H) -2 S Main -London 43140

(330) 643-2724 .. Hanshaw, Regina S '04 Summit Cnty Cncl -175 S Main
-7th Fl Ohio Bldg -Akron 44308

(330) 609-5057 .. Hanshaw, William '78 Butler Wick Trust Co -Bx8803
-Warren 44484

(419) 241-2201 .. Hanson, Anastasia S '04 (Spengler N PLL) -608 Mad Av -Ste 1000
-Toledo 43604 Fx:241-8599

(614) 466-5394 .. Hanson, David F '92 Pub Def -8 E Long -Columbus 43215

(614) 462-3555 .. Hanson, Denise L '94 Franklin Cnty Pros -373 S High
-Columbus 43215

(937) 223-8888 .. Hanson, Diane E '93 Dyer GM&S -131 N Ludlow -Ste 1400
-Dayton 45402 Fx:223-0127

(216) 241-6602 .. **Hanson**, Jay S '85 (Weston HFP&H LLP) -50 Pub Sq -2500 Trmnl Twr -Cleveland 44113 Fx:621-8369

(419) 447-4912 .. **Hanson**, Kathryn E '97 Seneca Cnty Juv & Probate Cts -108 Jffrsn -Tiffin 44883

(612) 342-2880 .. **Hanson**, Kent B '93 Hanson MB&G Ltd -527 Marguette Av -Ste 2200 -Minneapolis, MN 55402

(740) 363-1213 .. **Hanson**, Lewis K III '95 (Firestone BHNW&Y,LLP) -15 W Winter -Delaware 43015 Fx:369-0875

(440) 239-9777 .. **Hanson**, Mary Jo '04 %Van Dress Law Ofc -46 Front -Berea 44017 Fx:(775) 521-5756

(614) 431-7200 .. **Hanson**, Robert E '79 (Scherner H&C,LLC) -130 Northwood Blvd -Columbus 43235 Fx:431-7262

(561) 659-7070 .. **Hanson**, Thomas A '76 (Carlton F,PA) -222 Lakevw Av -Ste 1400 -Bx150 -West Palm Beach, FL 33402 Fx:659-7368

(330) 379-2066 .. **Hanson-Estep**, Laurie B '92 Summit Cnty Chldrn Srvcs -264 S Arlngtn -Akron 44306 Fx:379-1897

(330) 375-2730 .. **Hanus**, Craig J '01 Pros -217 S High -Ste 203 -Akron 44308

(440) 285-3501 .. **Hanus**, Ronald B '74 -107 N Hambden -Bx94 -Chardon 44024

(330) 722-2144 .. **Hanwell**, Robert M '85 -52 Pub Sq -Medina 44256

(419) 734-4143 .. **Hany**, Frederick C II '84 Cnty Mun Ct Judge -1860 E Perry -Port Clinton 43452

Hanysh, Jennifer M '03 -544 S Front -#105 -Columbus 43215

(614) 469-7455 .. **Hanzel**, Dennis J '81 IRS -401 N Front -Ste 375 -Columbus 43215

(330) 867-4050 .. **Hanzel**, Donald C '77 Hanzel Cnsltng Grp Inc -1867 W Market -Akron 44313

(937) 443-6600 .. **Haper**, Cori R '04 %Thompson H LLP -2000 Cthse Plz NE -Bx8801 -Dayton 45401 Fx:443-6635

(937) 393-3487 .. **Hapner**, James D '51 (Hapner & H) -127 N High -Hillsboro 45133

(937) 393-3487 .. **Hapner**, Jon C '58 (Hapner & H) -127 N High -Hillsboro 45133

(937) 393-3487 .. **Hapner**, Mary K '96 %Hapner & H -127 N High -Hillsboro 45133

(614) 231-0381 .. **Hapner**, Priscilla L '96 -Bx91106 -Columbus 43209

(330) 723-7000 .. **Happ**, Gregory W '76 -238 W Lbrty -Medina 44256

(740) 653-6464 .. **Happeney**, Randy L '85 (Dagger JMO&H) -144 E Main -Bx667 -Lancaster 43130 Fx:653-8522

Happeny, Stephen R '03 -1129 East 174th -Cleveland 44119

Haque, Masarath N '99 -5995 Forestvw Dr -Columbus 43213

(513) 381-5552 .. **Hara**, Colin '98 Masuda FE&M,Ltd -312 Walnut -Ste 1750 -Cincinnati 45202 Fx:381-5559

(216) 566-5634 .. **Hara**, Halle B '98 %Thompson H LLP -127 Pub Sq -3900 Key Ctr -Cleveland 44114 Fx:566-5800

(216) 514-1100 .. **Haran**, Craig T '00 %Rolf & G Co,LPA -30100 Chagrin Blvd -Ste 350 Corp Cir -Cleveland 44124 Fx:514-0030

(614) 462-5523 .. **Harbage**, Amy E '03 Franklin Cnty Ct -373 S High -Domestic Div -Columbus 43215

(216) 623-0150 .. **Harbarger**, David R '75 (Roetzel & A,LPA) -1375 E 9th -One Cleve Ctr 9th Fl -Cleveland 44114 Fx:623-0134

(330) 494-7023 .. **Harbert**, Robert P II '95 -149 Wilbur Dr NE -North Canton 44720

(330) 643-7098 .. **Harbin**, Martha R '90 -86 E Ralston Av -Akron 44301

(614) 255-1140 .. **Harbold**, Robert C '75 (RC Harbold & Assoc) -500 S Front -Ste 1140 -Columbus 43215

(216) 689-4967 .. **Harbottle**, Scott A '89 Key Bank NA -127 Pub Sq -2nd Fl -Cleveland 44114

(248) 357-3010 .. **Harbour**, Randall L '00 (Raymond & P,PC) -26300 Nrthwstrn Hwy -4th Fl -Bx5058 -Southfield, MI 48086 Fx:357-2720

(740) 353-3113 .. **Harcha**, Howard H Jr. '52 -800 Gallia -Ste 800 -Portsmouth 45662

(440) 338-7141 .. **Hardacre**, Lynn L '93 Medical Protective Co -88 Bishop Dr -Chagrin Falls 44022

(216) 443-5809 .. **Hardaway**, Ayesha Bell '04 Cuyahoga Cnty Pros -1910 Carnegie Av -Whitlatch Bldg -Cleveland 44115 Fx:443-5815

(419) 241-6000 .. **Harden**, Gary M '80 (Eastman & S Ltd) -1 Seagate -24th Fl -Bx10032 -Toledo 43699 Fx:247-1777

(216) 431-5000 .. **Harden**, Regina '01 Cuyahoga Cnty Pros -1200 Ontario -8th Fl -Cleveland 44113

(216) 363-4500 .. **Harders**, Walter Scott '99 %Benesch FC&A LLP -200 Pub Sq -Ste 2300 -Cleveland 44114 Fx:363-4588

(614) 543-0369 .. **Hardesty**, Christian P '04 (Vidmar & H,Ltd) -100 E Campus Vw Blvd -Ste 250 -Columbus 43235 Fx:543-1306

(330) 762-7477 .. **Hardesty Kaffen & Zimmerman** -520 S Main -Ste 500 -Akron 44311 Fx:762-8059

(330) 489-6407 .. **Hardesty**, Lee P '98 Nationwide Ins -Bx8379 -Canton 44711

(614) 880-0883 .. **Hardesty**, Michael J '66 -933 High -Ste 140 -Worthington 43085 Fx:436-8330

(330) 762-7477 .. **Hardesty**, Stephen D '73 (Hardesty K&Z) -520 S Main -Ste 500 -Akron 44311 Fx:762-8059

(614) 864-5600 .. **Hardgrove**, James A '78 (Hardgrove & P) -7600 Slate Ridge Rd -Reynoldsburg 43068

(513) 737-4000 .. **Hardig**, Mark N '81 -245 Market -Bx656 -Hamilton 45012

(216) 502-0800 .. **Hardiman**, James L '68 -75 Pub Sq -Ste 333 -Cleveland 44113 Fx:502-7777

(216) 586-3939 .. **Hardin**, Charles W Jr. '87 (Jones D) -901 Lakeside Av -Cleveland 44114 Fx:579-0212

(513) 721-7300 .. **Hardin**, David E '96 Hardin LL&M LLC -30 Garfld Pl -915 Cincinnati Club Bldg -Cincinnati 45202

(513) 721-7300 .. **Hardin**, Donald E '63 (Hardin LL&M LLC) -30 Garfld Pl -915 Cincinnati Club Bldg -Cincinnati 45202

(614) 466-7090 .. **Hardin**, Jennifer A '89 Ethics Commssn -8 E Long -10th Fl -Columbus 43215

(513) 241-1334 .. **Hardin**, Jim L '91 -1014 Vine -Ste 1919 -Cincinnati 45202

(513) 721-7300 .. **Hardin Lefton Lazarus & Marks LLC** -30 Garfld Pl -915 Cincinnati Club Bldg -Cincinnati 45202

(513) 241-3685 .. **Hardin**, Leona B '01 %White G&M Co,LPA -1 W 4th -Ste 1700 -Cincinnati 45202 Fx:241-2399

(937) 778-0579 .. **Hardin**, Paulette D '00 -429 N Main -Piqua 45356 Fx:778-0645

(513) 352-1570 .. **Hardin**, Roshani D '90 Law Dept -801 Plum -Rm 214 -Cincinnati 45202 Fx:352-1515

(330) 364-9070 .. **Hardin & Schaffner, LPA** -132 Fair Av NW -New Philadelphia 44663 Fx:364-9073

(330) 364-9070 .. **Hardin**, Thomas W '81 Hardin & S,LPA -132 Fair Av NW -New Philadelphia 44663 Fx:364-9073

(216) 621-9767 .. **Hardin-Levine**, Peter S '84 (Thorman & H-L Co,LPA) -1220 W 6th -Ste 307 -Cleveland 44113 Fx:621-3422

(216) 831-2400 .. **Harding**, Frank I III '69 Chess Financial Corp -30050 Chagrin Blvd -Pepper Pike 44124 Fx:831-2401

(440) 232-2701 .. **Harding**, James N '73 (Melling H&M,LPA) -31 Columbus Rd -Bedford 44146 Fx:232-7995

(216) 687-1900 .. **Harding**, Sandra G '93 Legal Aid -1223 W 6th -Cleveland 44113 Fx:687-0779

(513) 946-3000 .. **Hardman**, Kevin M '96 Hamilton Cnty Pros -230 E 9th -Cincinnati 45202 Fx:946-3017

(330) 376-4558 .. **Hardman**, Kevin P '85 Scanlon & G Co,LPA -50 S Main -Ste 1200 -Akron 44308 Fx:376-3550

Hardwey, Angela M '04 -1493 Ridpath Av -Akron 44313

(614) 466-5394 .. **Hardwick**, Stephen P '94 Pub Def -8 E Long -Columbus 43215

(330) 438-0889 .. **Hardy**, Charlene S '96 Stark Cnty Pros -110 Central Plz -Ste 510 -Canton 44702

(740) 382-5781 .. **Hardy**, Charles T '84 OH Pub Def Commssn -BxF7 -Marion 43301

(859) 441-7404 .. **Hardy**, Kathleen S '96 -90 Alexabdria Pike PMB 227 -Fort Thomas, KY 41075 Fx:441-8404

(216) 566-5804 .. **Hardy**, Michael L '72 (Thompson H LLP) -127 Pub Sq -3900 Key Ctr -Cleveland 44114 Fx:566-5800

(419) 433-5798 .. **Hardy**, Richard B III '97 %S Shore Marine Srvcs -1605 Sawmill Pkwy -Bx25 -Huron 44839

(216) 931-6000 .. **Hardy**, Richard G '78 (Ulmer & B LLP) -1300 E 9th -Ste 900 Penton Media Bldg -Cleveland 44114 Fx:931-6001

(513) 621-4220 .. **Hardy**, William R '63 -432 Walnut -Ste 206 -Bx3398 -Cincinnati 45201 Fx:651-2217

(614) 464-6400 .. **Hardymon**, David W '76 (Vorys SS&P LLP) -52 E Gay -Bx1008 -Columbus 43216 Fx:464-6350

(412) 394-2500 .. **Hareza**, Randy K '99 (Burns W&H,LLC) -120 5th Av -Ste 2400 -Pittsburgh, PA 15222

Hargate, Edwin V III '83 -1055 Eastlawn Dr -Cleveland 44143

(440) 669-8855 .. **Hargitai**, Zoltan '04 -27643 Laurell Ln -North Olmsted 44070 Fx:779-7791

(740) 282-1900 .. **Hargrave**, Robert C '70 (King HS&J) -200 Sinclair Bldg -Bx249 -Steubenville 43952 Fx:282-5397

(419) 213-6850 .. **Hargreaves**, Carol J '78 Lucas Cnty Dom Rltns Ct -429 N Mich -Ste A -Toledo 43624

(513) 762-6200 .. **Hargreaves**, Jeanette '95 %Ulmer & B LLP -600 Vine -Ste 2800 -Cincinnati 45202 Fx:762-6245

(330) 869-9101 .. **Haridakis**, Paul M '84 -783 Newcastle Dr -Akron 44313

(614) 464-2770 .. **Harildstad**, Timothy N '91 -88 E Broad -Ste 1350 -Columbus 43215

(330) 929-2676 .. **Haring**, Brian J '99 %Hoover H&H Co,LPA -527 Portage Trl -Cuyahoga Falls 44221

(419) 525-1611 .. **Haring**, David N '94 (Brown BM&M) -70 Park Av W -Mansfield 44902 Fx:525-3810

Haring, Kimberly Koontz '02 -7321 Herrick Park Dr -Hudson 44236

(440) 329-5183 .. **Harkacz**, Myron '79 Lorain Cnty Probate Ct -226 Middle Av -Elyria 44035

(440) 322-4510 .. **Harkenrider**, Lawrence E '99 N Ohio Surgery Inc -210 E Broad -Elyria 44035

(937) 461-8800 .. **Harker Capizzi & Hall** -130 W 2nd -Ste 2103 -Dayton 45402 Fx:461-8818

(937) 461-8800 .. **Harker**, Donald F III '75 (Harker C&H) -130 W 2nd -Ste 2103 -Dayton 45402 Fx:461-8818

(804) 281-6910 .. **Harker**, Heather '94 GE Finl Assurance -6610 W Broad -Richmond, VA 23230

(740) 689-9007 .. **Harker**, John D '74 -123 S Broad -Ste 206 -Lancaster 43130

(937) 324-8482 .. **Harkins**, Daniel C '85 (D Harkins & Assoc) -333 N Limestone -Bx1125 -Springfield 45501

(216) 991-3940 .. **Harkins**, James L Jr. '54 -18590 Parkland Dr -Shaker Heights 44122

(330) 645-6282 .. **Harkins**, Lewis James '53 -3318 Mnchstr Rd -Akron 44319

(937) 298-1133 .. **Harlamert**, Irvin H Jr. '55 -330 Southvw Rd -Dayton 45419

(937) 643-0600 .. **Harlan**, Camille L '94 %G Gibson Co,LPA -2810 Kettering Twr -Dayton 45423 Fx:586-9495

(330) 684-3315 .. **Harlan**, M Ann '85 JM Smucker Co -One Strwbrry Ln -Bx280 -Orrville 44667

(330) 744-5284 .. **Harlan**, Michael D '98 Harshman B&R -105 E Boardman -Youngstown 44503

(330) 492-8717 .. **Harless**, Kristina M '99 %Buckingham D&B,LLP -4518 Fulton Dr NW -Bx35548 -Canton 44735 Fx:492-9625

(419) 353-3075 .. **Harlett**, William A '69 Louisville Title Co -100 S Main -Bowling Green 43402

Harley, Rachel M '91 -17877 Lk Rd -Lakewood 44107

(937) 324-5541 .. **Harley**, Robert E '57 (Martin BH&H) -1 S Limestone -Ste 800 -Bx1488 -Springfield 45501 Fx:325-5432

(614) 818-1100 .. **Harley**, Sean P '84 Stewart Title Grnty -259 W Schrock Rd -Westerville 43081

(216) 589-9615 .. **Harlow**, Kathryn '91 Towards Employment -1255 Euclid Av -Ste 300 -Cleveland 44115

(304) 232-6675 .. **Harman**, Anne D '95 (Bailey RB&H,LC) -900 Riley Bldg -53 14th -Bx631 -Wheeling, WV 26003 Fx:232-9897

(937) 485-4380 .. **Harman**, Daniel T '77 Reynolds & Reynolds Co -115 S Ludlow -Dayton 45402

(614) 837-0750 .. **Harman**, Kenneth C '69 -45 N High -Canal Winchester 43110 Fx:837-0756

(732) 845-1331 .. **Harmatz**, Hugo R '02 (HR Harmatz,PC) -Route 34 & Artisan Way -Bx500 -Colts Neck, NJ 07722 Fx:409-0008

(513) 977-8200 .. **Harmeyer**, John V '96 (Dinsmore & S LLP) -255 E 5th -Ste 1900 -Cincinnati 45202 Fx:977-8141

(513) 241-1991 .. **Harmon**, Arthur W Jr. '81 Harmon D & Assoc Co,LPA -1200 Cypress -Cincinnati 45206

(704) 344-8500 .. **Harmon**, David M '99 %Templeton & R,PA -1800 East Blvd -Charlotte, NC 28203

(216) 844-1686 .. **Harmon**, Heather M '00 Univ Hospital -11100 Euclid Av -Human Resources -Cleveland 44106

(513) 852-8200 .. **Harmon**, Jeffrey J '81 (Cors & B LLC) -537 E Pete Rose Way -Ste 400 -Cincinnati 45202

(614) 644-7257 .. **Harmon**, Jessica M '01 Atty Gen -150 E Gay -Columbus 43215 Fx:752-4677

(614) 249-7455 .. **Harmon**, John T '94 Cnsl Nationwide Ins Co -1 Nationwide Plz -Columbus 43215

(937) 865-6800 .. **Harmon**, Joseph P '86 Lexis/Nexis -Bx933 -Dayton 45401

(513) 579-1500 .. **Harmon**, Laurie M '92 %Buechner HOM&H Co,LPA -105 E 4th
　　　-Ste 300 -Cincinnati 45202 **Fx:**977-4361
(513) 352-2452 .. **Harmon**, Michael J '74 Law Dept -801 Plum -Rm 214
　　　-Cincinnati 45202 **Fx:**352-1515
(740) 366-7446 .. **Harmon**, Paul D '79 -964 N 21st -Ste A -Newark 43055
(614) 433-9502 .. **Harmon**, Phillip L '80 -6649 N High -Ste 105 -Worthington 43085
(937) 461-5980 .. **Harmon**, Sean H '97 Jablinski FR&M -214 W Monument Av
　　　-Bx1266 -Dayton 45402 **Fx:**461-4139
(614) 855-3220 .. **Harmon**, Vanessa R '98 -2993 Reynoldsburg-N Albany Rd
　　　-Blacklick 43004
(419) 353-1062 .. **Harms**, Robert G '77 (Twyman TH&S) -519 W Wooster -Ctr Ste
　　　-Bowling Green 43402 **Fx:**353-6277
(330) 434-3000 .. **Harnak**, Brian K '94 %Roderick & L -One Cascade Plz -Ste 1500
　　　-Akron 44308 **Fx:**434-9220
(330) 745-5995 .. **Harnden**, Thomas L '76 Barberton Comm Fdn -460 W Paige Av
　　　-Barberton 44203 **Fx:**745-3990
(312) 782-3939 .. **Harner**, Michelle M '95 %Jones DR&P -77 W Wacker Dr -Ste 3500
　　　-Chicago, IL 60601
(312) 782-3939 .. **Harner**, Paul E '90 (Jones DR&P) -77 W Wacker Dr -Ste 3500
　　　-Chicago, IL 60601
(205) 795-1511 .. **Harner**, Timothy M '94 US Army Judge Advocate
　　　-255 W Oxmoor Rd -Birmingham, AL 35209
(352) 335-2393 .. **Harness**, Melody L '96 %S Miller -311 NE 1st
　　　-Gainesville, FL 32601 **Fx:**375-0104
(614) 387-9090 .. **Harold**, David T '00 Supreme Ct of OH -65 S Front
　　　-Columbus 43215
(330) 262-3030 .. **Harp**, Bradley R '99 Wayne Cnty Pros -115 W Lbrty -Wooster
　　　44691 **Fx:**287-5412
　　　　　　　Harp, Malinda D '89 -4250 Lee Rd -Cleveland 44128
(740) 695-9202 .. **Harper & Hazlett** -185 W Main -Saint Clairsville 43950
　　　Fx:695-9211
(513) 946-3000 .. **Harper**, James W '74 Hamilton Cnty Pros -230 E 9th
　　　-Cincinnati 45202 **Fx:**946-3017
(614) 901-5700 .. **Harper**, John D '89 -570 Polaris Pkwy -Westerville 43082
(904) 357-8515 .. **Harper**, Lewis W '01 Brennan M&D -76 S Laura -Ste 1700
　　　-Jacksonville, FL 32202 **Fx:**791-3120
(740) 695-9202 .. **Harper**, Marlin J '75 (Harper & H) -185 W Main
　　　-Saint Clairsville 43950 **Fx:**695-9211
(419) 247-1822 .. **Harper**, Matthew D '92 (Eastman & S Ltd) -1 Seagate -24th Fl
　　　-Bx10032 -Toledo 43604 **Fx:**247-1777
(614) 485-2010 .. **Harper**, Michael Scott Jr. '99 %Means BB&B Co,LPA
　　　-2006 Kenny Rd -Columbus 43221 **Fx:**485-2019
(330) 758-9482 .. **Harper**, Paul R '92 -6758 West Blvd -Boardman 44512
(419) 524-1986 .. **Harper**, Roeliff E '91 -3 N Main -Ste 606 -Mansfield 44902
　　　Fx:524-1984
(216) 991-9122 .. **Harper**, Sara J '52 -13807 Drexmore Rd -Cleveland 44120
(614) 228-5331 .. **Harper**, Stephen L '81 Casto -191 W Nationwide Blvd -Ste 200
　　　-Columbus 43215
(513) 579-1414 .. **Harper**, Tessea M '01 %Schwartz M&R -441 Vine -Ste 2900
　　　-Cincinnati 45202 **Fx:**579-1418
(216) 622-8200 .. **Harper**, Walter G '74 (Calfee H&G LLP) -800 Superior Av
　　　-Ste 1400 -Cleveland 44114 **Fx:**241-0816
(440) 243-1058 .. **Harpst**, Ronald J '63 Inter-Continental Bus Cnsltng -14881
　　　Cherokee Trl -Middleburg Heights 44130
(330) 376-2700 .. **Harpst**, Todd A '96 %Roetzel & A,LPA -222 S Main -Akron 44308
　　　Fx:376-4577
(513) 558-7748 .. **Harpster**, Linda M '80 Univ of Cincinnati -Eden & Bethesda Avs
　　　-Bx670663 -Cincinnati 45267
(419) 289-6888 .. **Harpster**, Russell L '58 OfCnsl Harpster V&F -60 W 2nd
　　　-Ashland 44805 **Fx:**281-2461
(419) 289-6888 .. **Harpster Vanosdall & Findley** -60 W 2nd -Ashland 44805
　　　Fx:281-2461
(740) 387-1717 .. **Harraman**, Brent M '77 -399 E Church -Marion 43302
(614) 469-6638 .. **Harraway**, Andria M '04 US Bnkrptcy Ct-Sthrn Dist -170 N High
　　　-Columbus 43215
(513) 564-7051 .. **Harrell**, Dennis Ora '75 6th Dist Ct of Appls -100 E 5th -Cthse
　　　-Cincinnati 45202
(614) 644-6342 .. **Harrell**, Eric C '99 Atty Gen -30 E Broad -Columbus 43215
　　　Fx:752-5083
(740) 947-2171 .. **Harrell**, Kevin I '91 Cnty Jobs & Fam Srvcs -230 Waverly Plz
　　　-Ste 700 -Waverly 45690
(937) 393-1851 .. **Harrell**, Shari Lee '97 %Prosecutor Ofc -112 Govenor Foraker Pl
　　　-Hillsboro 45133
(937) 449-6400 .. **Harrelson**, Laura G '83 (Dinsmore & S LLP) -1 S Main
　　　-Ste 1300 One Dayton Centre -Dayton 45402 **Fx:**449-6405
(937) 335-8324 .. **Harrelson**, Robert M '82 (Faust HFM&S) -12 S Cherry
　　　-Troy 45373 **Fx:**339-7155
(330) 375-2037 .. **Harrill**, James F '84 Law Dept -161 S High -Ste 202 -Akron 44308
(419) 472-1900 .. **Harrington**, Dee A '00 %Bolotin Co,LPA -4349 Talmadge Rd
　　　-Toledo 43623
(740) 374-2629 .. **Harrington**, Dennis M '86 SE OH Lgl Srvcs -427 2nd
　　　-Marietta 45750
(786) 268-4160 .. **Harrington**, Donald F '63 %D Harrington,PA -1570 Madruga Av
　　　-Ste 200 -Coral Gables, FL 33146 **Fx:**268-4162
(330) 744-1111 .. **Harrington Hoppe & Mitchell, Ltd** -26 Market -Ste 1200
　　　-Youngstown 44503 **Fx:**744-2029
(330) 392-1541 .. **Harrington Hoppe & Mitchell, Ltd** -108 Main Av SW -Ste 500
　　　-Bx1510 -Warren 44482 **Fx:**394-6890
(330) 337-6586 .. **Harrington Hoppe & Mitchell, Ltd** -2235 E Pershing
　　　-Salem 44460 **Fx:**337-6662
(513) 561-5366 .. **Harrington**, John P '53 SpclCnsl J Harrington Co,LPA -8404
　　　Eustis Farm -Cincinnati 45243
(330) 339-3998 .. **Harrington**, Michael F '97 SE OH Lgl Srvcs -332 W High Av
　　　-New Philadelphia 44663
(440) 746-1500 .. **Harrington**, Patrick J '91 Grtr Cleveland Auto Dealers Assn
　　　-10100 Brecksvll Rd -Brecksville 44141
(202) 268-6029 .. **Harrington**, Paul Leo '00 US Postal Srvc -475 L'Enfant Plz SW
　　　-Rm 10802 -Washington, DC 20260
(616) 961-5808 .. **Harrington**, Reba M '91 Federal Center (DRMS)
　　　-74 Wshngtn Av N -Ste 6 -Battle Creek, MI 49017
(937) 223-1130 .. **Harrington**, Thomas J '60 OfCnsl Pickrel S&E -40 N Main
　　　-2700 Kettering Twr -Dayton 45423 **Fx:**223-0339
(216) 623-4900 .. **Harris**, Alan B '74 -614 W Superior Av -Ste 804 -Cleveland 44113

(216) 241-6602 .. **Harris**, Beverly A '78 (Weston HFP&H LLP) -50 Pub Sq
　　　-2500 Trmnl Twr -Cleveland 44113 **Fx:**621-8369
　　　　　　　Harris, Brad '03 -278 Ben Shaw -Aurora 44202
(513) 891-3270 .. **Harris & Burgin** -9545 Kenwood Rd -Ste 301 -Cincinnati 45242
(216) 621-2234 .. **Harris**, Christopher P '97 (Tarolli SC&T) -526 Superior Av
　　　-1111 Leader Bldg -Cleveland 44114 **Fx:**621-4072
(513) 861-3100 .. **Harris**, Demetrious A '98 Dept of Vet Affairs -3200 Vine
　　　-VA Med Ctr -Cincinnati 45220
(216) 696-5444 .. **Harris**, Eugenya Yvonne '92 -925 Euclid Av -Ste 1025
　　　-Cleveland 44115
(513) 558-5042 .. **Harris**, Gary R '84 Hlth Allnce of Grtr Cincinnati -3200 Burnet Av
　　　-Cincinnati 45229
(330) 645-4455 .. **Harris**, George B '48 -835 State Mill Rd -Akron 44319
(330) 833-3183 .. **Harris**, Henry G '70 St Timothys Episcopal Church -226 3rd SE
　　　-Massillon 44646
(513) 621-3333 .. **Harris**, Irving '51 -441 Vine -3801 Carew Twr -Cincinnati 45202
(740) 383-1151 .. **Harris**, James A '68 (Harris & E) -136 S Main -Marion 43302
(614) 464-2572 .. **Harris**, James B '76 (Harris MB&C,PLL) -37 W Broad -9th Fl
　　　-Columbus 43215 **Fx:**464-2245
(501) 204-0306 .. **Harris**, James J '89 Wal-Mart Stores -2001 SE 10th -Bentonville,
　　　AR 72712
(330) 451-7897 .. **Harris**, Jamila M '04 %Stark Cnty Pros -110 Central Plz -Ste 510
　　　-Canton 44702
　　　　　　　Harris, Jeffrey G '95 -164 Thompson Dr -Ste 101
　　　-Bridgeport, WV 26330
(513) 621-2666 .. **Harris**, Jeffrey P '76 (Statman HS&E LLC) -255 E 5th
　　　-Ste 2900 Chemed Ctr -Cincinnati 45202 **Fx:**587-4477
(513) 891-3270 .. **Harris**, Jeffrey W '03 %Harris & B -9545 Kenwood Rd -Ste 301
　　　-Cincinnati 45242
(614) 249-2300 .. **Harris**, Jeffry D '03 KPMG LLP -191 W Nationwide Blvd
　　　-Columbus 43215
(513) 891-3270 .. **Harris**, Jerald D '72 Harris & B -9545 Kenwood Rd -Ste 301
　　　-Cincinnati 45242
(330) 873-9931 .. **Harris**, Jo Ann '86 -1700 W Market -#140 -Akron 44313
(419) 243-1105 .. **Harris**, John A III '69 (Lackey NHR&T,LPA) -2 Maritime Plz -3rd Fl
　　　-Toledo 43604
(614) 224-7711 .. **Harris**, John A IV '00 Kitrick & L Co,LPA -515 E Main -Ste 515
　　　-Columbus 43215 **Fx:**225-8985
(216) 622-8200 .. **Harris**, Julie A '95 (Calfee H&G LLP) -800 Superior Av -Ste 1400
　　　-Cleveland 44114 **Fx:**241-0816
(937) 222-2424 .. **Harris**, Justin D '04 %Freund F&A -1 S Main -Ste 1800
　　　-Dayton 45402 **Fx:**222-5369
(513) 887-3474 .. **Harris**, Karl R '91 Butler Cnty Pros -315 High -11th Fl -Bx515
　　　-Hamilton 45012
(614) 457-9731 .. **Harris**, Kenneth E '75 (Harris & M) -941 Chatham Ln -Ste 201
　　　-Columbus 43221 **Fx:**457-3596
　　　　　　　Harris, Kysha L '03 -(Address Unavailable)
(216) 861-5542 .. **Harris**, Leodis '63 -745 Leader Bldg -526 Superior Av E
　　　-Cleveland 44114
(661) 284-7745 .. **Harris**, Lori P '86 -25239 Vis Sistine -Valencia, CA 91355
(614) 469-5715 .. **Harris**, Marcia J '79 US Atty -303 Marconi Blvd -Ste 200
　　　-Columbus 43215
　　　　　　　Harris, Mariel A '94 -(Address Unavailable)
(216) 432-7200 .. **Harris**, Marsha E '95 Ctr for Families & Children -4500 Euclid Av
　　　-Cleveland 44103
(614) 457-9731 .. **Harris & Mazza** -941 Chatham Ln -Ste 201 -Columbus 43221
　　　Fx:457-3596
(614) 464-2572 .. **Harris McClellan Binau & Cox,PLL** -37 W Broad -9th Fl
　　　-Columbus 43215 **Fx:**464-2245
(216) 592-5000 .. **Harris**, Michael F '77 (Tucker E&W LLP) -925 Euclid Av
　　　-1150 Huntngtn Bldg -Cleveland 44115 **Fx:**592-5009
(614) 645-8936 .. **Harris**, Natalia S '00 City Pros -375 S High -7th Fl
　　　-Columbus 43215
(216) 696-1545 .. **Harris**, Pamala S '02 %J Barrett -1370 Ontario -800 Standard Bldg
　　　-Cleveland 44113 **Fx:**696-2104
(216) 689-0350 .. **Harris**, Paul N '83 KeyCorp -127 Pub Sq -54th Fl
　　　-Cleveland 44114
(614) 227-2000 .. **Harris**, Polly J '85 (Porter WM&A LLP) -41 S High
　　　-Columbus 43215 **Fx:**227-2100
(330) 535-5711 .. **Harris**, Richard H III '80 (Brouse M) -106 S Main
　　　-500 First Natl Twr -Akron 44308 **Fx:**253-8601
(937) 653-7186 .. **Harris**, Richard O '58 (Houston H&D) -1 Monument Sq -Ste 200
　　　-Bx913 -Urbana 43078 **Fx:**653-3293
　　　　　　　Harris, Richard W '02 -13560 Exotica Ln -Wellington, FL 33414
(614) 464-6400 .. **Harris**, Robert A '92 (Vorys SS&P LLP) -52 E Gay -Bx1008
　　　-Columbus 43216 **Fx:**464-6350
(914) 641-2070 .. **Harris**, Robert D '76 ITT Industries -4 W Red Oak Ln
　　　-White Plains, NY 10604
(954) 725-7688 .. **Harris**, Robert G '74 -530 S Fed Hwy -Deerfield Beach, FL 33441
　　　Fx:725-7687
　　　　　　　Harris, Rodger C '87 -2202 Starboard Pl -Woodbridge, VA 22192
　　　　　　　Harris, Rodney J '97 -527 Linton -Cincinnati 45219
(513) 741-7888 .. **Harris**, Ronald C '78 -6218 Thompson Rd -Cincinnati 45247
(216) 228-7835 .. **Harris**, Russell W '75 -13215 Detroit Av -Lakewood 44107
(202) 467-3960 .. **Harris**, Steven D '75 KPMG LLP -2001 M NW
　　　-Washington, DC 20036
(614) 451-5300 .. **Harris**, Steven M '85 (Musser L&H) -3404 Riverside Dr
　　　-Columbus 43221
(614) 462-5466 .. **Harris**, Stuart W '96 %Kegler BH&R -65 E State -Ste 1800
　　　-Columbus 43215 **Fx:**464-2634
(440) 593-7410 .. **Harris**, Thomas E '82 Mun Ct Judge -290 Main -Conneaut 44030
(440) 943-4200 .. **Harris**, Tracy B '80 Lubrizol Corp -29400 Lakelnd Blvd
　　　-Wickliffe 44092
(210) 384-7100 .. **Harris**, William R '84 US DOJ -601 NW Loop 410 -Ste 600
　　　-San Antonio, TX 78216
(513) 988-6193 .. **Harrison**, Brian K '96 -240 E State -Trenton 45067
(216) 443-8746 .. **Harrison**, Gladys E '84 Hon JD Russo -1200 Ontario -22B
　　　-Cleveland 44113
(513) 977-8200 .. **Harrison**, Gregory A '85 (Dinsmore & S LLP) -255 E 5th -Ste 1900
　　　-Cincinnati 45202 **Fx:**977-8141
(513) 651-6800 .. **Harrison**, Jack B '93 (Frost BT LLC) -201 E 5th -2200 PNC Ctr
　　　-Cincinnati 45202 **Fx:**651-6981

(513) 852-6047 ..**Harrison,** James B '83 (Wood & L LLP) -600 Vine -Ste 2500
-Cincinnati 45202 **Fx:**852-6087

(614) 644-3374 ..**Harrison,** James M '93 Dept Ins -2100 Stella Ct -Columbus 43215

(972) 599-5600 ..**Harrison,** James W '81 S2 SYSTEMS -4965 Preston Park Blvd
-Ste 100 -Plano, TX 75093

(937) 461-4060 ..**Harrison,** John C '66 -130 W 2nd -Ste 604 -Dayton 45402

(614) 466-7264 ..**Harrison,** John R '95 OH Legal Rghts Srvc -8 E Long -5th Fl
-Columbus 43215

(330) 666-6900 ..**Harrison,** Joseph R '75 -310 N Cleveland-Massillon Rd
-Akron 44333

(614) 224-2428 ..**Harrison,** Kimberly E '03 %Shihab & Assoc -65 E State -Ste 1550
-Columbus 43215 **Fx:**224-5080

(614) 752-6291 ..**Harrison,** Lemuel E Jr. '90 Cnsl ODJFS -255 E Main -3rd Fl
-Columbus 43215 **Fx:**728-6803

(614) 469-3939 ..**Harrison,** Rebecca J '97 %Jones D -325 John H McConnell Blvd
-Ste 600 -Bx165017 -Columbus 43216 **Fx:**461-4198

(313) 983-7426 ..**Harrison,** Rosalie B '92 Butzel Long -150 W Jffrsn -Ste 900
-Detroit, MI 48226

(330) 453-1906 ..**Harrison,** Stephen J '80 -1400 Market Av N -Canton 44714

(614) 451-7066 ..**Harrison,** Wade E '93 -1570 Fishinger Rd -Columbus 43221

(513) 561-9229 ..**Harrison,** William K Jr. '59 -5495 Windrdg Ct -Cincinnati 45243

(724) 933-3100 ..**Harrison-Vogel,** Kathleen '96 %Sain Law,LLC
-12703-A Perry Hwy -Wexford, PA 15090

(216) 521-6556 ..**Harriston,** Michael A '96 Everstream,Inc -6001 Cochran Rd -4th Fl
-Solon 44139

(216) 696-7600 ..**Harrold,** Linda Hauserman '79 OfCnsl Duvin C&H -1301 E 9th
-20th Fl Erievw Twr -Cleveland 44114 **Fx:**696-2038

Harsch, Brett L '05 -(Address Unavailable)

(740) 474-6066 ..**Harsha,** Shelly R '86 Pros -118 E Main -Bx910 -Circleville 43113

(937) 496-3158 ..**Harshbarger,** Kimberly K '92 Montgomery Cnty Juv Ct
-117 S Main -Dayton 45422

(330) 744-5284 ..**Harshman Bernard & Ramage** -105 E Boardman
-Youngstown 44503

(330) 744-5284 ..**Harshman,** Michael S '66 (Harshman B&R) -105 E Boardman
-Youngstown 44503

(937) 443-6842 ..**Harson,** Linn S '96 (Thompson H LLP) -2000 Cthse Plz NE
-Bx8801 -Dayton 45401 **Fx:**443-6635

(419) 354-9244 ..**Hart,** Andrew P '02 %Wood Cnty Pub Def -123 N Summit
-Bowling Green 43402

Hart, April N '97 -2529 Canterbury Rd -Cleveland Heights 44118

(513) 651-6800 ..**Hart,** Douglas E '82 (Frost BT LLC) -201 E 5th -2200 PNC Ctr
-Cincinnati 45202 **Fx:**651-6981

(614) 231-9162 ..**Hart,** Douglas J '82 -2599 E Main #116 -Bexley 43209

(614) 238-6738 ..**Hart,** Elizabeth R '04 (Ellard H & Assoc) -2388 E Main -Ste 105
-Columbus 43209 **Fx:**238-6740

(419) 874-3536 ..**Hart,** James H '74 (Leatherman WD&H) -353 Elm
-Perrysburg 43551 **Fx:**874-3899

(419) 625-8324 ..**Hart,** James W '81 (Flynn P&K,LPA) -165 E Wshngtn Row
-Sandusky 44870 **Fx:**625-9007

(937) 229-4333 ..**Hart,** John E '86 Univ of Dayton Schl of Law -300 Cllg Park
-Dayton 45469

(513) 946-3000 ..**Hart,** Lashawn C '01 Hamilton Cnty Pros -230 E 9th
-Cincinnati 45202 **Fx:**946-3017

Hart, Lori B '93 -638 Miami Manor -Maumee 43537

(330) 376-4558 ..**Hart,** Patrick J '75 Scanlon & G Co,LPA -50 S Main -Ste 1200
-Akron 44308 **Fx:**376-3550

(216) 621-0150 ..**Hart,** Randy J '90 OfCnsl Hahn L&P LLP
-3300 BP Twr/200 Pub Sq -Ste 3300 -Cleveland 44114
Fx:241-2824

(440) 228-3010 ..**Hart,** Robert D '63 -20800 Ctr Ridge Rd -#222 -Rocky River 44116

(419) 332-5553 ..**Hart,** Robert G '84 -1710 McPherson Blvd -Fremont 43420

(614) 466-1305 ..**Hart,** Robert M '82 Atty Gen -30 E Broad -Columbus 43215
Fx:466-8898

(513) 381-0380 ..**Hart,** Robert R Jr. '85 -1019 Main -Cincinnati 45202

(740) 653-4259 ..**Hart,** Roy E '77 Fairfield Cnty Pros -201 S Broad -4th Fl
-Lancaster 43130

(937) 449-6810 ..**Hart,** Tami L '04 %Porter WM&A LLP -1 S Main -Ste 1600
-Dayton 45402 **Fx:**449-6820

(937) 224-1718 ..**Hart,** Terry R '97 Montgomery Cnty Pub Def -117 S Main -Ste 400
-Dayton 45422 **Fx:**225-3449

(614) 356-5000 ..**Hart,** Thomas L '94 Dominion Homes -Bx5000 -Dublin 43016

(330) 673-4181 ..**Hart,** Timothy J '80 Hart & H -136 N Water -Ste 209 -Kent 44240

(312) 904-2377 ..**Hart,** Tina M '98 LaSalle Bank NA -135 S LaSalle -Ste 2060
-Chicago, IL 60603

(937) 429-3841 ..**Hart,** Tracy L '94 -2828 Legend Falls Ct -Beavercreek 45431

(614) 462-3580 ..**Hartel,** Jeffry A '00 %Hon PL Bryant -373 S High -24th Fl
-Columbus 43215

(614) 276-8959 ..**Harter,** Brian W '91 OfCnsl Nein Law Ofcs -2291 Scioto Harper Dr
-Columbus 43204 **Fx:**276-8959

(614) 464-1211 ..**Harter,** William M '00 %Frost BT LLC -10 W Broad -Ste 1000
-Columbus 43215 **Fx:**464-1737

(330) 426-4121 ..**Hartford Dickey & Young Co, LPA** -91 W Taggart -Bx85
-East Palestine 44413

(330) 426-4121 ..**Hartford,** James T '79 (Hartford D&Y Co, LPA) -91 W Taggart
-Bx85 -East Palestine 44413

(330) 744-0247 ..**Hartford,** Robert S Jr. '74 (Nadler N&B Co,LPA) -20 Fed Plz W
-Ste 600 -Youngstown 44503 **Fx:**744-8690

(847) 405-3752 ..**Hartigan,** Michael J '04 Morgan Stanley Dean Witter
-2500 Lk Cook Rd -Riverwoods, IL 60015

(216) 787-3030 ..**Hartke,** Gregory T '84 Atty Gen -615 W Superior Av -11th Fl
-Cleveland 44113 **Fx:**787-3480

(513) 977-4210 ..**Hartke,** James R '73 -917 Main -Ste 400 -Cincinnati 45202

(614) 895-0575 ..**Hartlaub,** Joseph V '77 -12 Westervll Sq PMB 284
-Westerville 43081

(513) 241-4110 ..**Hartman,** Alan J '84 (Deters B&L,PSC) -441 Vine
-Ste 3500 Carew Twr -Cincinnati 45202 **Fx:**241-4551

(216) 831-6580 ..**Hartman,** Alan S '65 (Hartman & K Co,LPA) -27600 Chagrin Blvd
-Ste 340 -Woodmere 44122

(216) 781-5515 ..**Hartman,** Anthony J '68 (Hermann C&S,LLP) -1301 E 9th -Ste 500
-Cleveland 44114 **Fx:**781-1030

Hartman, Curt C '94 -3749 Foxpoint Ct -Amelia 45102

(216) 291-1554 ..**Hartman,** Dale M '87 -27600 Chagrin Blvd -Ste 340
-Cleveland 44122

(724) 652-4081 ..**Hartman,** Dallas W '98 (D Hartman,PC) -2815 Wilmngtn Rd
-New Castle, PA 16105

(330) 858-1375 ..**Hartman,** Dawn E '96 LD Carlson Co -6370 Mt Plsnt NW
-463 Portage Blvd -Kent 44240

(614) 227-2000 ..**Hartman,** Elizabeth A '04 %Porter WM&A LLP -41 S High
-Columbus 43215 **Fx:**227-2100

(216) 932-3976 ..**Hartman,** Franklin L '66 -1385 Burlngtn Rd
-Cleveland Heights 44118

(216) 831-6580 ..**Hartman & Kahn Co,LPA** -27600 Chagrin Blvd -Ste 340
-Woodmere 44122

(216) 443-7295 ..**Hartman,** Margaret A '04 %Cuyahoga Cnty Pub Def
-1849 Prospect Av -Ste 222 -Cleveland 44115

(614) 677-6367 ..**Hartman,** Mark E '93 Cnsl Nationwide Ins Co -1 Nationwide Plz
-Columbus 43215

(216) 771-3336 ..**Hartman,** Richard J '73 Allstate Ins Co -113 St Clair Av -Ste 525
-Cleveland 44114

(216) 696-4441 ..**Hartman,** Robert W '04 %Zashin & R Co,LPA -55 Pub Sq
-Ste 1490 -Cleveland 44113 **Fx:**696-1618

(740) 965-0746 ..**Hartman,** Ronald F '67 -11720 Gorsuch Rd -Galena 43021

(216) 689-5090 ..**Hartman,** Sheldon R '71 KeyBank NA -127 Pub Sq
-Mailcode: OHO1-27-0200 2nd Fl -Cleveland 44114

(419) 255-5990 ..**Hartman,** Stephen D '02 %Kerger & K -33 S Mich -Ste 201
-Toledo 43602 **Fx:**255-5997

(513) 381-4395 ..**Hartmann,** Dennis P '73 -1000 Provident Bk Bldg
-Cincinnati 45202

(513) 946-3000 ..**Hartmann,** Gregory P '99 Hamilton Cnty Pros -230 E 9th
-Cincinnati 45202 **Fx:**946-3017

Hartmann, Lora A '02 -1112 Brimfld Dr -Medina 44256

(216) 443-8831 ..**Hartmann,** Marie M '86 Cuyahoga Cnty Cmmn Pleas Ct
-1 Lakeside Av -Cleveland 44113

(614) 462-4941 ..**Hartmann,** Philip K '92 (Schottenstein Z&D) -250 West -Bx165020
-Columbus 43215 **Fx:**462-5135

(614) 463-8532 ..**Hartmann,** Robert G '88 Natl City Corp -155 E Broad
-Columbus 43251

(614) 443-7920 ..**Hartnell,** Molly Geyen '03 %KE Hamilton -1021 S High
-Columbus 43206 **Fx:**443-7922

(330) 438-0897 ..**Hartnett,** Chryssa N '95 Stark Cnty Pros -110 Central Plz -Ste 510
-Canton 44702

(330) 455-0173 ..**Hartnett,** Thomas E '93 (Day KRW&R,Ltd) -200 Market Av N
-Ste 300 -Bx24213 -Canton 44701 **Fx:**455-2633

(440) 951-6599 ..**Hartory,** Timothy P '72 T Hartory & Assoc -8320 Mentor Av
-Mentor 44060 **Fx:**974-1240

(614) 228-6885 ..**Hartranft,** Jeffrey B '97 (Lane A&H LLC) -175 S 3rd -Ste 700
-Columbus 43215 **Fx:**228-0146

(614) 227-2000 ..**Hartranft,** John C '67 (Porter WM&A LLP) -41 S High
-Columbus 43215 **Fx:**227-2100

(614) 227-2000 ..**Hartranft,** John C Jr. '00 %Porter WM&A LLP -41 S High
-Columbus 43215 **Fx:**227-2100

(614) 221-0922 ..**Hartshorn,** Michael W '72 (Gamble HJ Co,LPA) -1 E Lvngstn Av
-Columbus 43215 **Fx:**365-9741

(440) 930-4001 ..**Hartung,** Susan R '03 %Baumgartner & O
-5455 Detroit Rd (Rte 254) -Sheffield Village 44054 **Fx:**934-7205

Hartup, Bret R '04 -40 Severance Cir -Cleveland Heights 44118

(330) 792-2336 ..**Hartwig,** Edward J '98 %Wellman JH&S Co,LPA
-4990 Mahoning Av -Youngstown 44515 **Fx:**792-5403

(216) 566-5500 ..**Hartwig,** Jeffrey R '04 %Thompson H LLP -127 Pub Sq
-3900 Key Ctr -Cleveland 44114 **Fx:**566-5800

(614) 464-6400 ..**Harty,** Susan Barrett '91 (Vorys SS&P LLP) -52 E Gay -Bx1008
-Columbus 43216 **Fx:**464-6350

(216) 696-1080 ..**Hartzell,** Angelique M '99 D Seaman & Assoc Co,LPA -614
Superior Av W -Ste 1600 Rckflr Bldg -Cleveland 44113

(614) 466-3615 ..**Hartzell,** Julie C Kidwell '02 Legis Srvc Commssn -77 S High
-Columbus 43215

(419) 248-6330 ..**Harves,** Donald Scott '96 Owens Corning
-One Owens Corning Pkwy -Toledo 43659

(937) 439-5708 ..**Harvey,** Anne '91 -5335 Far Hills -Ste 313 -Dayton 45429

(216) 931-6000 ..**Harvey,** Elizabeth A '96 %Ulmer & B LLP -1300 E 9th
-Ste 900 Penton Media Bldg -Cleveland 44114 **Fx:**931-6001

(330) 535-5711 ..**Harvey,** Frank H Jr. '55 OfCnsl Brouse M -106 S Main
-500 First Natl Twr -Akron 44308 **Fx:**253-8601

(216) 447-5000 ..**Harvey,** Gregory S '95 Noveon Inc -9911 Brecksvll Rd
-Brecksville 44141

(740) 592-3240 ..**Harvey,** Karen M '89 Athens Cnty Cmmn Pleas Ct
-Athens Cnty Cthse -Athens 45701

(419) 636-2644 ..**Harvey,** Mary Ann '92 Williams Cnty Cmmn Pleas Ct -1 Cthse Sq
-Bryan 43506

(440) 356-9108 ..**Harvey,** Michael P '87 -311 Northcliff Dr -Rocky River 44116

(937) 335-3666 ..**Harvey,** Randal A '85 (R Harvey Co,LPA) -9 W Water -Troy 45373
Fx:335-3550

Harvey, Robert N Jr. '03 -(Address Unavailable)

(440) 838-8800 ..**Harvey,** Robert Scot '90 (Millisor & N Co,LPA) -9150 S Hills Blvd
-Ste 300 -Cleveland 44147 **Fx:**838-8805

(513) 929-3400 ..**Harvey,** Robin E '83 (Baker & H LLP) -312 Walnut -Ste 3200
-Cincinnati 45202 **Fx:**929-0303

(216) 368-6280 ..**Harvey,** Sara D '01 CaseWestern Univ/Alumni Relations
-10900 Euclid Av -Baker Bldg #331 -Cleveland 44106
Fx:368-2000

Harvey, Thomas F '64 -537 Manorbrook Dr -Chagrin Falls 44022

(330) 376-2272 ..**Harvey-Williams,** Lynda E '89 (Williams & Assoc) -106 S Main
-Ste 2300 -Akron 44308 **Fx:**376-5618

(419) 421-3173 ..**Harwick,** Cheryl L '91 Marathon Oil Co -539 S Main -Rm 4204
-Findlay 45840

(419) 935-0171 ..**Harwood,** David B '73 (Thornton T&H) -111 Myrtle Av -Bx207
-Willard 44890

(216) 348-0041 ..**Harwood,** Peter R '65 (Deacon H&A,Ltd) -127 Pub Sq -Ste 4110
-Cleveland 44114 **Fx:**348-0040

(419) 668-8101 ..**Harwood,** Sharon L '85 Fisher-Titus Med Ctr -272 Benedict Av
-Norwalk 44857

(419) 242-7985 ..**Hasbrook,** Denise M '84 (Roetzel & A,LPA) -One SeaGate -9th Fl
-Toledo 43604 **Fx:**242-0316

(937) 455-3352 ..**Hasbrook,** Jay T '94 -Bx50 -Germantown 45327

(419) 242-1400 ..**Hasbrook,** Richard C '77 -608 Mad Av -Ste 1400 -Toledo 43604

(740) 687-7155 ..**Haselberger,** Christina E '03 %Fairfield Cnty CSEA -239 W Main
-Lancaster 43130

(202) 226-8521 .. **Haseley**, John M '94 Cngrssmn T Strickland -336 Cannon HOB -Washington, DC 20515

(419) 249-7900 .. **Haselman**, Scott A '95 (Robison C&O) -Four SeaGate -9th Fl -Toledo 43604 **Fx:**249-7911

(305) 695-1122 .. **Hashmi**, Tarik '95 Int'l Law Grp,Inc -777 A Godfrey Rd -2nd Fl -Miami Beach, FL 33140

(440) 352-4484 .. **Haskell**, George B '75 -8 N State -Ste 376 -Painesville 44077 **Fx:**352-6729

(330) 762-9191 .. **Haskins**, Thomas F Jr. '76 (Daily & H) -7 W Bowery -Ste 604 -Akron 44308 **Fx:**762-4244

(937) 544-3600 .. **Haslam**, Aaron E '04 %Adams Cnty Prosecutor -110 W Main -Rm 112 -West Union 45693

(614) 221-1216 .. **Hass**, Cheri B '95 Downes H&F -400 S 5th -Ste 200 -Columbus 43215 **Fx:**221-8769

(614) 224-1222 .. **Hassay**, Wayne E '91 (Maguire & S,LLP) -250 Civic Ctr Dr -Ste 200 -Columbus 43215 **Fx:**224-1236

(513) 229-0383 .. **Hasse**, Donald E '78 (Hasse & N LLC) -7550 Cntrl Pke Blvd -Mason 45040 **Fx:**229-0683

(513) 229-0383 .. **Hasse & Nesbitt LLC** -7550 Cntrl Pke Blvd -Mason 45040 **Fx:**229-0683

(513) 684-3211 .. **Hassebrock**, Richard J '98 IRS Dist Cnsl -312 Elm -Ste 2300 -Cincinnati 45202

(937) 323-9739 .. **Hasselbach**, Kurt S '75 (Schmenk S&H) -20 N Limestone -Springfield 45502 **Fx:**323-9388

(513) 695-1459 .. **Hasselbach**, William A '91 Warren Cnty Cmmn Pleas Ct -500 Justice Dr -Lebanon 45036

(614) 891-3589 .. **Hasselback**, David G '85 (Bates & H LLP) -168 S State -Westerville 43081

(216) 586-3939 .. **Hassell**, Charles D '73 Cnsl Jones D -901 Lakeside Av -Cleveland 44114 **Fx:**579-0212

　　　　　　　　 Hasselschwert, Jay E '00 -(Address Unavailable)

(216) 771-1760 .. **Hassett**, Brian R '94 Smith & C LLP -1801 E Ninth -Ste 900 Ohio Svngs Plz -Cleveland 44114 **Fx:**771-3387

(615) 287-7339 .. **Hassmiller**, John H '74 Bridgestone Firestone Inc -1201 Firestone Pkwy -La Vergne, TN 37086

(678) 291-7422 .. **Hasten**, Bradley A '77 Rock-Tenn Co -504 Thrasher -Norcross, GA 30071

(513) 721-7500 .. **Hastings**, Deborah C '94 (Hastings & H) -22 W 9th -Cincinnati 45202

(216) 787-3030 .. **Hastings**, Jeffrey P '91 Atty Gen -615 W Superior Av -11th Fl -Cleveland 44113 **Fx:**787-3480

(513) 381-2838 .. **Hastings**, Kerry P '96 (Taft S&H LLP) -425 Walnut -Ste 1800 -Cincinnati 45202 **Fx:**381-0205

(239) 949-6989 .. **Hastings**, Kim M '86 (Hahn L&P LLP) -3301 Bonita Beach Rd -Ste 308 -Bonita Springs, FL 34134 **Fx:**949-6687

(216) 621-0150 .. **Hastings**, Kim M '86 (Hahn L&P LLP) -3300 BP Twr/200 Pub Sq -Ste 3300 -Cleveland 44114 **Fx:**241-2824

(216) 664-2665 .. **Hastings**, L Stewart Jr. '80 Dept of Law -601 Lakeside Av -Rm 106 City Hall -Cleveland 44114 **Fx:**664-2663

(216) 522-3877 .. **Hastings**, Linda M '94 US Dept of Labor -1940 E 9th -Rm 881 -Cleveland 44199

(513) 721-7500 .. **Hastings**, Robert R Jr. '73 (Hastings & H) -22 W 9th -Cincinnati 45202

(216) 479-8500 .. **Hastings**, Susan C '85 (Squire S&D LLP) -127 Pub Sq -4900 Key Twr -Cleveland 44114 **Fx:**479-8780

(614) 229-4822 .. **Hatch**, Colin K '80 Deloitte & Touche,LLP -155 E Broad -Columbus 43215 **Fx:**233-6217

(216) 771-6960 .. **Hatch**, Lawrence H '87 Private Trust Co,NA -1130 Hanna Bldg -Cleveland 44115

　　　　　　　　 Hatch, Michael E '89 US Dept Homeland Security -INS -425 I NW -Washington, DC 20536

(239) 949-7641 .. **Hatchadorian**, Matthew J '66 Source Interlink Cos -27500 Rivervw Ctr Blvd -Ste 400 -Bonita Springs, FL 34134

(513) 867-1856 .. **Hatcher**, Gregory E '83 -301 High -Ste 400 -Hamilton 45011

(419) 238-6621 .. **Hatcher**, John E '00 %WE Hatcher -124 E Main -Van Wert 45891

(513) 946-3263 .. **Hatcher**, John R '98 %Hamilton Cnty Pros -230 E 9th -Cincinnati 45202 **Fx:**946-3017

(614) 865-6680 .. **Hatcher**, Judi K '83 Cntrl OH Primary Care Physicians -570 Polaris Pkwy -Ste 250 -Westerville 43082

(404) 526-9440 .. **Hatcher**, Ronald B '75 -Bx161442 -Atlanta, GA 30321

(614) 628-0650 .. **Hatcher**, Steven J '73 -50 W Broad -Ste 1800 -Columbus 43215

(419) 238-6621 .. **Hatcher**, W Edward '74 -124 E Main -Van Wert 45891

(330) 841-0990 .. **Hatchner**, Jeffrey A '79 Second Natl Bank of Warren -Bx1311 -Warren 44482

(859) 431-0030 .. **Hatfield**, Curtis H '87 -1037 Mad Av -Covington, KY 41011

(614) 719-3300 .. **Hathaway**, Amy D '02 Hon G Frost US Dist Ct -85 Marconi Blvd -Rm 349 -Columbus 43215 **Fx:**719-3305

(513) 621-2100 .. **Hathaway**, David E '80 Beckman W&S LLC -120 E 4th -1200 Mercantile Ctr -Cincinnati 45202 **Fx:**621-0106

(419) 252-5602 .. **Hathaway**, Lisa A '89 HCR Manor Care -333 N Summit -Toledo 43604

(330) 725-4929 .. **Hathcock**, Alicia M '04 %Oberholtzer F&L -39 Pub Sq -Ste 201 -Bx220 -Medina 44258 **Fx:**723-4929

(216) 586-3939 .. **Hatina**, Joseph D '99 %Jones D -901 Lakeside Av -Cleveland 44114 **Fx:**579-0212

(614) 677-8754 .. **Hatler**, Patricia R '02 Nationwide Ins Co -1 Nationwide Plz -Columbus 43215

(614) 464-2392 .. **Hatten**, Steven A '78 (Earl WA&D,LPA) -136 W Mound -Columbus 43215 **Fx:**464-0754

(202) 898-5800 .. **Hatti**, Vivek K '99 %Spriggs & H -1350 I NW -Ste 900 -Washington, DC 20005

(419) 252-6229 .. **Hattner**, Louis J '68 OfCnsl Spengler N PLL -608 Mad Av -Ste 1000 -Toledo 43604 **Fx:**241-8599

(937) 224-0076 .. **Hatton**, Frederick W '00 %Myers & F Co,LPA -18 W 1st -Ste 200 -Dayton 45402

(614) 837-4238 .. **Hatton**, Jerry R '74 -8 Wshngtn -Canal Winchester 43110

(937) 225-5840 .. **Hatton**, Nicole K '00 2nd Dist Ct of Appls -41 N Perry -Rm 515 -Bx972 -Dayton 45422

(614) 228-6888 .. **Hatzifotinos**, Dimitrios G '04 %Havens W LLC -141 E Town -Ste 200 -Columbus 43215 **Fx:**228-6878

(216) 861-5582 .. **Hauber**, Karl W '01 %Fay SFM&M LLP -1100 Superior Av -7th Fl -Cleveland 44114 **Fx:**241-1666

(614) 278-6767 .. **Haubiel**, Charles W II '92 Big Lots,Inc -300 Phillipi Rd -Columbus 43228

(330) 454-3479 .. **Hauch**, Michael T '76 -2827 Heritage Av NW -Canton 44718

(513) 621-0800 .. **Hauck**, John W '78 -2406 Auburn Av -Cincinnati 45219

(513) 732-3200 .. **Hauck**, Stephen L '77 -285 Main -Batavia 45103

(216) 687-1311 .. **Haude**, Daniel R '97 (Reminger & R) -101 Prospect Av W -1400 Mdlnd Bldg -Cleveland 44115 **Fx:**687-1841

(216) 348-1700 .. **Haude**, Kristi L '02 %Davis & Y -101 Prospect Av W -Ste 1700 -Cleveland 44115 **Fx:**621-0602

　　　　　　　　 Hauenstein, Joan E '02 -7363 Burntwood Ln -Hudson 44236

(216) 622-8200 .. **Hauer**, Richard J Jr. '75 (Calfee H&G LLP) -800 Superior Av -Ste 1400 -Cleveland 44114 **Fx:**241-0816

(513) 422-4699 .. **Haugen**, Halver H '68 -4955 Rivervw Av -Middletown 45042

(513) 622-1822 .. **Haughey**, Angela K '03 Procter & Gamble -8700 Mason Mntgmry Rd -Mason 45040

(513) 524-5000 .. **Haughey**, Daniel E '00 (D Haughey,LLC) -121 W High -Oxford 45056 **Fx:**524-5001

(513) 651-6800 .. **Haughey**, Stephen N '84 (Frost BT LLC) -201 E 5th -2200 PNC Ctr -Cincinnati 45202 **Fx:**651-6981

(419) 472-9774 .. **Haughn**, James E II '96 -4253 Monroe -Toledo 43606

(813) 974-2131 .. **Haughney**, Jane '85 Univ S Fl -4202 E Fowler Av -ADM 250 -Tampa, FL 33620 **Fx:**974-5236

(614) 239-1801 .. **Haught**, Jack G '83 -2436 Bexley Park Rd -Columbus 43209

(304) 455-0172 .. **Haught**, Timothy E '89 -Bx268 -New Martinsville, WV 26155

(216) 692-3198 .. **Haumann**, Theresa R '88 BEM Srvcs Inc -17876 St Clair Av -Cleveland 44110

(216) 787-5329 .. **Haun**, Sharla R '99 Workers Comp -615 W Superior -Cleveland 44113 **Fx:**787-4487

　　　　　　　　 Haupt, Aimee N '03 -(Address Unavailable)

(614) 463-9770 .. **Haupt**, Erika L '94 (Roetzel & A,LPA) -155 E Broad -Natl City Ctr 12th Fl -Columbus 43215 **Fx:**463-9792

(330) 497-0700 .. **Haupt**, Fred J '67 (Krugliak WG&D Co,LPA) -4775 Munson NW -Bx36963 -Canton 44735 **Fx:**497-4020

(330) 497-0700 .. **Haupt**, Jason F '02 %Krugliak WG&D Co,LPA -4775 Munson NW -Bx36963 -Canton 44735 **Fx:**497-4020

(330) 492-3957 .. **Haupt**, Jeffrey D '85 -4884 Dressler Rd NW -Canton 44718

(330) 823-7411 .. **Haupt**, John E Jr. '83 -950 S Sawburg -Alliance 44601

(513) 241-2324 .. **Haupt**, Keith R '92 (Wood H&E LLP) -441 Vine -Ste 2700 -Cincinnati 45202 **Fx:**421-7269

(330) 297-3665 .. **Haupt**, Natalie Rogal '02 Portage Cnty Pub Def -209 S Chestnut -4th Fl -Ravenna 44266

(216) 781-4110 .. **Hauptman**, Nadine '99 C Kampinski Co,LPA -1370 Ontario -1530 Standard Bldg -Cleveland 44113 **Fx:**781-4178

(419) 241-9000 .. **Hauptman**, W Reed '98 %Shumaker L&K,LLP -1000 Jackson -Toledo 43624 **Fx:**241-6894

(330) 489-3395 .. **Hauritz**, Tyrone D '90 Pros -218 Cleveland Av SW -Bx24218 -Canton 44702

(216) 875-8221 .. **Haus**, Andrew M '92 KPMG LLP -1375 E 9th -One Cleve Ctr Ste 2600 -Cleveland 44114

(614) 460-4649 .. **Hauschild**, Neal T '03 %N Source, Inc -200 Civic Ctr Dr -Columbus 43215

(216) 479-8500 .. **Hauser**, Karen A '97 %Squire S&D LLP -127 Pub Sq -4900 Key Twr -Cleveland 44114 **Fx:**479-8780

(216) 566-5660 .. **Hauser**, Laura A '89 (Thompson H LLP) -127 Pub Sq -3900 Key Ctr -Cleveland 44114 **Fx:**566-5800

(419) 935-1681 .. **Hauser**, Richard B '73 -Bx68 -Willard 44890

(937) 592-8603 .. **Haushalter**, Barbara J '89 -228 Bent Pines Ct -Bellefontaine 43311

(216) 368-1797 .. **Hausman**, Thomas I '73 CWRU Law Schl -11075 East Blvd -Cleveland 44106

(513) 621-6787 .. **Haussler**, Jakki L '89 Opus Captl Advsrs,LLC -1 W 4th -Ste 415 -Cincinnati 45202

(614) 644-9278 .. **Hauswirth**, George M '68 Supreme Ct of OH -30 E Broad -35th Fl -Columbus 43266

(330) 494-6115 .. **Haut**, Annette R Ciavarella '03 -5656 Gray Fox Dr NW -Canton 44718

(419) 424-9889 .. **Hauter**, Gary M '88 -1941 N Main -Findlay 45840

(216) 696-4700 .. **Havach**, James M '74 (Spieth BM&N Co,LPA) -925 Euclid Av -2000 Huntngtn Bldg -Cleveland 44115 **Fx:**696-2706

(440) 356-9991 .. **Havemann**, Justin W '99 -19350 Laurel Av -Rocky River 44116

(937) 299-5530 .. **Havemann**, William L '70 -2049 Brandy Milll Ln -Dayton 45459

　　　　　　　　 Havener, Charles R '83 -3425 Lenox Dr -Kettering 45429

(614) 466-5589 .. **Havener**, John L '83 Industrial Commssn of OH -30 W Spring -9th Fl -Columbus 43215 **Fx:**752-8785

(216) 621-0150 .. **Havener**, Kathleen B '98 (Hahn L&P LLP) -3300 BP Twr/200 Pub Sq -Ste 3300 -Cleveland 44114 **Fx:**241-2824

(216) 479-8500 .. **Havener**, Thomas G '87 (Squire S&D LLP) -127 Pub Sq -4900 Key Twr -Cleveland 44114 **Fx:**479-8780

(216) 781-5515 .. **Havens**, Hunter S '84 (Hermann C&S,LLP) -1301 E 9th -Ste 500 -Cleveland 44114 **Fx:**781-1030

(614) 228-6888 .. **Havens**, James R '81 (Havens W LLC) -141 E Town -Ste 200 -Columbus 43215 **Fx:**228-6878

(614) 464-6400 .. **Havens**, Jolie N '00 %Vorys SS&P LLP -52 E Gay -Bx1008 -Columbus 43216 **Fx:**464-6350

(440) 729-2340 .. **Havens**, Patrick J '91 -12610 Caves Rd -Chesterland 44026

(614) 228-6888 .. **Havens Willis LLC** -141 E Town -Ste 200 -Columbus 43215 **Fx:**228-6878

(419) 782-7757 .. **Haver**, Mark L '90 (Haver & K) -118 Clinton -Defiance 43512

(330) 339-7791 .. **Haverfield**, David W '95 Cnty Job & Fam Srvcs -389 16th SW -New Philadelphia 44663

(513) 922-3200 .. **Haverkamp Brinker Rebold & Riehl Co,LPA** -5856 Glenway Av -Cincinnati 45238 **Fx:**922-8096

(513) 922-3200 .. **Haverkamp**, Gary J '63 (Haverkamp BR&R Co,LPA) -5856 Glenway Av -Cincinnati 45238 **Fx:**922-8096

(513) 794-6473 .. **Haverkamp**, Michael F '74 OH Natl Life Ins -1 Fncl Way -Cincinnati 45242

(614) 292-7970 .. **Haverkamp**, Robert J '71 OSU -190 N Oval Mall -108 Bricker Hall -Columbus 43210

(216) 479-8500 .. **Haverstick**, Rebecca Wistner '96 %Squire S&D LLP -127 Pub Sq -4900 Key Twr -Cleveland 44114 **Fx:**479-8780

(216) 292-8201 .. **Havighurst**, Alan W '77 -3071 Huntngtn Rd -Shaker Heights 44120

(937) 223-3277 .. **Haviland**, John F '85 (Bieser G&L LLP) -6 N Main -400 Natl City Ctr -Dayton 45402 **Fx:**223-6339

(216) 696-3232 .. **Hawal,** William '80 (Spangenberg S&L,LLP) -1900 E 9th -2400 Natl City Ctr -Cleveland 44114 **Fx:**696-3924

(303) 410-1809 .. **Hawk,** Beverly F '89 Hawk & H,PC -1333 W 120th Av -Ste 308 -Westminster, CO 80234

(216) 383-2061 .. **Hawk,** George W Jr. '87 Lincoln Elctrc Co -22801 St Clair Av -Cleveland 44117

(614) 644-9272 .. **Hawk,** Kristina P '96 Hon EL Stratton -30 E Broad -3rd Fl -Columbus 43266

(216) 781-1212 .. **Hawk,** Morris M '95 %Walter & H LLP -1301 E 9th -Ste 3500 -Cleveland 44114 **Fx:**575-0911

(216) 443-5809 .. **Hawk,** Sharon L '81 Cuyahoga Cnty Pros -1910 Carnegie Av -Whitlatch Bldg -Cleveland 44115 **Fx:**443-5815

(330) 672-2982 .. **Hawke,** Constance N '78 KSU-Exec Ofcs -2nd Fl Library -Bx5190 -Kent 44242

(216) 861-1365 .. **Hawkins,** Ann M '80 Hawkins & Co,LPA -1267 W 9th -Ste 500 -Cleveland 44113 **Fx:**861-0714

(419) 225-5706 .. **Hawkins,** Brandie L '04 -124 S Metcalf -Lima 45801 **Fx:**225-6003

(937) 599-6242 .. **Hawkins,** Bridget D '91 (Beck B&H) -709 N Main -Bx549 -Bellefontaine 43311

(614) 462-3555 .. **Hawkins,** Daniel R '01 Franklin Cnty Pros -373 S High -Columbus 43215

(513) 732-7313 .. **Hawkins,** Darrell C '89 Clermont Cnty Pros -123 N 3rd -Batavia 45103

(513) 684-6988 .. **Hawkins,** Douglas N '87 US DOJ -36 E 7th -Ste 2030 -Cincinnati 45202

(513) 352-6700 .. **Hawkins,** Heather MacGregor '04 %Thompson H LLP -312 Walnut -14th Fl -Cincinnati 45202 **Fx:**241-4771

(937) 433-2880 .. **Hawkins,** Homer D Jr. '53 -Bx955 -Dayton 45402

(513) 556-7040 .. **Hawkins,** Ilse Sue '77 Univ of Cincinnati -ML #211 -Cincinnati 45221

(419) 422-4089 .. **Hawkins,** Jeffrey Van '87 (Hawkins Law Ofc LLC) -103 E Sandusky -Findlay 45840 **Fx:**422-4655

(216) 861-1365 .. **Hawkins,** John T '87 Hawkins & Co,LPA -1267 W 9th -Ste 500 -Cleveland 44113 **Fx:**861-0714

(440) 951-6460 .. **Hawkins,** John W '85 -35350 Curtis Blvd -Ste 350 -Eastlake 44095

(440) 951-6460 .. **Hawkins,** Judson J '77 -35350 Curtis Blvd -Ste 350 -Eastlake 44095

(614) 875-4115 .. **Hawkins,** Laney J '97 (Hamilton & H) -3338 Columbus -Grove City 43123

(513) 887-3474 .. **Hawkins,** Lawrence C III '03 %Butler Cnty Pros -315 High -11th Fl -Bx515 -Hamilton 45012

(513) 984-4554 .. **Hawkins,** Lawrence C Jr. '75 (Hawkins & L) -7438 Mntgmry Rd -Cincinnati 45236

Hawkins, Mark E '00 -230 E Innis Av -Columbus 43207

(513) 621-3394 .. **Hawkins,** Melissa N '03 %Peck S&W,LLP -201 E 5th -Ste 900 -Cincinnati 45202 **Fx:**621-3813

(513) 977-8200 .. **Hawkins,** Michael W '72 (Dinsmore & S LLP) -255 E 5th -Ste 1900 -Cincinnati 45202 **Fx:**977-8141

(614) 341-6057 .. **Hawkins,** Monica E '00 Franklin Cnty Children Srvcs -855 W Mound -Columbus 43223 **Fx:**275-2589

(440) 484-2000 .. **Hawkins,** Pamela A '04 Litigation Mgt,Inc -300 Allen Bradley Dr -Ste 200 -Cleveland 44124

(216) 765-0123 .. **Hawkins,** Paula L '90 %Budish & S Ltd -23240 Chagrin Blvd -Ste 450 Commerce Park 4 -Beachwood 44122 **Fx:**595-2787

(513) 684-6018 .. **Hawkins,** Robert B '04 US Dept Labor ALJ Ofc -36 E 7th -Cincinnati 45202

(513) 621-2666 .. **Hawkins,** Tracy L '00 %Statman HS&E LLC -255 E 5th -Ste 2900 Chemed Ctr -Cincinnati 45202 **Fx:**587-4477

(513) 723-7049 .. **Hawkins,** William H II '78 Convergys Corp -600 Vine -Bx1638 -Cincinnati 45201

(614) 466-2980 .. **Hawkinson,** Cheryl Rae '91 Atty Gen -30 E Broad -Columbus 43215 **Fx:**728-9470

(216) 479-8500 .. **Hawley,** Barbara L '77 (Squire S&D LLP) -127 Pub Sq -4900 Key Twr -Cleveland 44114 **Fx:**479-8780

(513) 721-4505 .. **Hawley,** Kenneth G '79 Cnsl Holbrook & Assoc -105 W 4th -Ste 1400 4th & Race Twr -Cincinnati 45202 **Fx:**721-0519

(419) 221-5183 .. **Hawley,** Kevin M '02 City of Lima Law Dept -209 N Main -6th Fl -Lima 45801

Hawley, Matthew J '03 -56 E Main -Wakeman 44889

(614) 464-1877 .. **Hawley,** Robert B II '96 Sowald S&C -400 S 5th -Ste 101 -Columbus 43215

(330) 392-1541 .. **Hawley,** William L '79 Harrington H&M,Ltd -108 Main Av SW -Ste 500 -Bx1510 -Warren 44482 **Fx:**394-6890

(330) 740-2330 .. **Hawn,** Kerry L '03 Mahoning Cnty Pros -21 W Boardman -6th Fl -Youngstown 44503 **Fx:**740-2008

(440) 992-0647 .. **Hawn-Jackson,** Jane A '83 -4717 Park Av -Ashtabula 44004

(216) 689-4111 .. **Hawrylak,** Richard S '88 KeyBank NA -127 Pub Sq -Law Group 2nd Fl -Cleveland 44114

(202) 842-2345 .. **Haws,** Elizabeth A '00 %McLeod W&M -1 Mass Av NW -Ste 800 -Washington, DC 20001

(216) 514-3336 .. **Hawthorne,** Nathaniel '69 -27600 Chagrin Blvd -Ste 260 -Cleveland 44122

(937) 498-1311 .. **Hax,** Priscilla L '77 -108 W Poplar -Bx405 -Sidney 45365

(614) 248-5700 .. **Hay,** David S '74 Bank One Corp -1111 Polaris Pkwy -Ste 4P -Columbus 43271

Hay, Walter H '59 -719 Hadcock Rd -Brunswick 44212

(419) 627-7697 .. **Hayberger,** Trevor M '02 Erie Cnty Pros -247 Columbus Av -Ste 319 -Sandusky 44870 **Fx:**627-7567

(513) 929-3400 .. **Hayden,** Angela M '99 Baker & H LLP -312 Walnut -Ste 3200 -Cincinnati 45202 **Fx:**929-0303

(513) 621-2120 .. **Hayden,** Jeremy A '02 %Strauss & T,LPA -150 E 4th -4th Fl -Cincinnati 45202 **Fx:**241-8259

(513) 455-7600 .. **Hayden,** Mark T '96 (Greenebaum D&M PLLC) -255 E 5th -2800 Chemed Ctr -Cincinnati 45202 **Fx:**455-8500

(724) 745-5260 .. **Hayden,** Suzanne J '83 -38 W Pike -Canonsburg, PA 15317

(614) 228-2612 .. **Hayden,** William M '81 -35 E Lvngstn Av -Columbus 43215

(513) 721-4532 .. **Hayden,** William T '79 (Katz TB&H) -255 E 5th -Ste 2400 -Cincinnati 45202

(330) 253-2227 .. **Haydu,** Andrew T '02 %Parker LH&R,LLC -388 S Main -Ste 402 -Akron 44311 **Fx:**253-1261

(605) 385-2329 .. **Hayes,** Bryan M '99 USAF -1000 Ellsworth -Ste 2700 -Ellsworth AFB, SD 57706

(440) 777-6506 .. **Hayes,** Catherine K '94 -Bx238 -North Olmsted 44070

(740) 927-2927 .. **Hayes,** Chester D '01 Hayes Law Ofcs -195 E Broad -Bx958 -Pataskala 43062

(937) 562-5250 .. **Hayes,** David D '04 %Greene Cnty Pros -61 Greene -Xenia 45385

(614) 227-2000 .. **Hayes,** Jeffrey T '79 (Porter WM&A LLP) -41 S High -Columbus 43215 **Fx:**227-2100

Hayes, Josephine E '93 -4997 Skyline Dr -Cambridge 43725

Hayes, Kathleen E '82 -8480 Wethersfld Ln -Cincinnati 45236

Hayes, Kristine L '98 -(Address Unavailable)

(937) 981-4403 .. **Hayes,** Larry D '76 (Judkins & H) -303 W Jffrsn -Greenfield 45123 **Fx:**981-7256

(216) 566-2660 .. **Hayes,** Madeline M '81 Sherwin-Williams Co -101 Prospect Av -Cleveland 44115

(937) 548-8995 .. **Hayes,** Margaret B '89 -127 W 5th -Greenville 45331

(614) 280-9300 .. **Hayes,** Michael J '98 -575 S High -Columbus 43215

(614) 847-1660 .. **Hayes,** Susan N '92 %JC Deboard & Co,LPA -5878 N High -Worthington 43085

(513) 639-3876 .. **Hayes,** Thomas A '68 (KMK Cnsltng Co,LLC) -1 E 4th -1400 Provident Twr -Cincinnati 45202 **Fx:**579-6457

(614) 462-3194 .. **Hayes,** Thomas F '93 Franklin Cnty Pub Def -373 S High -12th Fl -Columbus 43215

(330) 761-4306 .. **Hayes,** Timothy A '87 First Energy -76 S Main -Akron 44307

(740) 927-2927 .. **Hayes,** William C '78 Hayes Law Ofcs -195 E Broad -Bx958 -Pataskala 43062

(513) 723-4000 .. **Hayes,** William D '86 (Vorys SS&P LLP) -221 E 4th -Ste 2000 Atrium Two -Bx0236 -Cincinnati 45201 **Fx:**723-4056

(740) 927-2927 .. **Hayes,** William S '93 %Hayes Law Ofcs -195 E Broad -Bx958 -Pataskala 43062

(419) 536-8600 .. **Hayes-Deckebach,** Jill L '90 (Dixon & H,Ltd) -3361 Exec Pkwy -Ste 100 -Toledo 43606

(216) 687-1902 .. **Haygood,** Sebraien M '90 (S Haygood & Assoc) -1422 Euclid Av -Ste 1510 -Cleveland 44115 **Fx:**687-1906

(513) 241-2025 .. **Hayhow,** Stephen F '70 -917 Main -2nd Fl -Cincinnati 45202

(216) 621-0200 .. **Haylor,** Jane T '86 (Baker & H LLP) -1900 E 9th -Ste 3200 -Cleveland 44114 **Fx:**696-0740

Hayman, Edward D '80 -28499 Orange Meadow Ln -Chagrin Falls 44022

(740) 283-3693 .. **Hayman,** Milton A '60 -700 Bank One Bldg -Bx4308 -Steubenville 43952 **Fx:**283-3824

(800) 544-7369 .. **Hayman-Weaner,** Pamela A '92 LAWO -201 E 2nd -Defiance 43512

(216) 566-5896 .. **Haymond,** Daniel M '93 (Thompson H LLP) -127 Pub Sq -3900 Key Ctr -Cleveland 44114 **Fx:**566-5800

(419) 241-9000 .. **Haynam,** Douglas G '80 (Shumaker L&K,LLP) -1000 Jackson -Toledo 43624 **Fx:**241-6894

(513) 765-4448 .. **Hayne,** April M '01 -4000 Luxottica Pl -Mason 45040

(330) 335-5961 .. **Hayne,** James R '94 -845 Akron Rd -Wadsworth 44281

(440) 239-8881 .. **Haynes,** Cheryl A '87 Safeco P&C Ins -18151 Jffrsn Park Rd -Ste 104 -Middleburg Heights 44130 **Fx:**239-8882

(216) 621-0150 .. **Haynes,** Dawn T '01 %Hahn L&P LLP -3300 BP Twr/200 Pub Sq -Ste 3300 -Cleveland 44114 **Fx:**241-2824

(614) 221-9500 .. **Haynes,** Douglas J '82 (Haynes & H) -399 E Main -Ste 200 -Columbus 43215

(614) 221-9500 .. **Haynes,** Eleanor E '84 (Haynes & H) -399 E Main -Ste 200 -Columbus 43215

(216) 875-6041 .. **Haynes,** Ernest M Jr. '97 Appollo Housing Captl LLC -600 Superior Av -Ste 2300 -Cleveland 44114

(440) 323-6100 .. **Haynes,** John S '68 (Haynes & D) -134 Middle Av -Elyria 44035

(614) 868-0009 .. **Haynes,** Samuel S '92 (Hallowes A&H) -6445 E Lvngstn Av -Reynoldsburg 43068 **Fx:**868-0029

(513) 735-0300 .. **Haynes,** Willard B '83 -196 E Main -Ste D -Batavia 45103

(740) 537-3827 .. **Haynes,** William Jr. '80 -806 Franklin -Toronto 43964

(724) 934-6888 .. **Hays,** Laura W '01 %Malone L&M -117 VIP Dr -Ste 310 -Wexford, PA 15090

(614) 466-4656 .. **Hays,** Mark E '76 Atty Gen -150 E Gay -Columbus 43215 **Fx:**466-1756

(614) 677-3463 .. **Hays,** Michelle L '93 Nationwide Ins Co -1 Nationwide Plz -Columbus 43215

(419) 213-4700 .. **Hays,** Patricia C '92 %Lucas Cnty Pros -Adams & Erie -Lucas Cnty Cthse -Toledo 43624

(614) 229-4955 .. **Hays,** Robert D '91 Morgan Stanley -41 S High -Ste 2700 -Columbus 43215

(419) 843-5355 .. **Hays,** Thomas R '94 (Goldberg W&H) -6800 W Central Av -Toledo 43617

(937) 434-8951 .. **Hayslip,** Michael W '94 NESTI -8951 Treeland Ln -Dayton 45458 **Fx:**434-7233

(419) 241-9000 .. **Hayward,** John F '66 (Shumaker L&K,LLP) -1000 Jackson -Toledo 43624 **Fx:**241-6894

(419) 241-2201 .. **Hayward,** John P '95 (Spengler N PLL) -608 Mad Av -Ste 1000 -Toledo 43604 **Fx:**241-8599

Haywood, Lisa M '99 -21 W Columbus -Pickerington 43147

(614) 466-4320 .. **Hazan,** Naomi B '04 Atty Gen -150 E Gay -Columbus 43215

(419) 249-7900 .. **Hazard,** Daniel G '01 %Robison C&O -Four SeaGate -9th Fl -Toledo 43604 **Fx:**249-7911

(419) 242-1400 .. **Hazard,** Elizabeth S '96 -608 Mad Av -Ste 1400 -Toledo 43604

(614) 249-5169 .. **Hazelbaker,** Elizabeth A '96 %Nationwide Ins Co -1 Nationwide Plz -Columbus 43215

(740) 594-8388 .. **Hazelbaker,** Joseph A '00 Sowash C&F -39 N Cllg -Bx2629 -Athens 45701

(330) 643-2788 .. **Hazelett,** Leonard W '87 Summit Cnty Pros-Crim -53 Univ Av -7th Fl -Akron 44308 **Fx:**643-8277

(216) 752-6811 .. **Hazelton,** Cynthia L '84 -3260 Green Rd -Beachwood 44122

(614) 901-2203 .. **Hazelton,** Peter M '92 ArcLight Syst -480 Olde Worthngtn Rd -Westerville 43082

(216) 861-4355 .. **Hazelwood,** James Michael '83 (Hazelwood & K) -1801 E 9th -Ste 730 -Cleveland 44114

(513) 421-8422 .. **Hazen,** Glen E Jr. '86 (Morgan H&G) -432 Walnut -Ste 1000 -Cincinnati 45202

(937) 461-6200 .. **Hazlett,** Jeffrey A '81 Cincinnati Ins Co -130 W 2nd -Ste 1850 -Dayton 45402 **Fx:**461-9338

(740) 695-9202 .. **Hazlett,** Thomas M '77 (Harper & H) -185 W Main -Saint Clairsville 43950 **Fx:**695-9211

(716) 200-5050 .. **Head,** Christopher A '77 OfCnsl Harris B LLP -726 Exchange -Ste 1000 -Buffalo, NY 14210 **Fx:**200-5201

(216) 739-5006 ..**Head,** David A '02 %Weltman W&R Co,LPA -323 W Lakeside Av -Ste 200 -Cleveland 44113 **Fx:**363-4121

(614) 459-8900 ..**Head,** Robert D '78 -3200 Riverside Dr -Ste 20 -Columbus 43221

(740) 965-1855 ..**Head,** Suzanne '89 K&H Consulting -4191 Harlem Rd -Galena 43021

(614) 462-2272 ..**Headen,** Raymond C '87 (Schottenstein Z&D) -250 West -Bx165020 -Columbus 43216 **Fx:**462-5135

(216) 394-5064 ..**Headen,** Raymond C '87 (Schottenstein Z&D) -1350 Euclid Av -Ste 1400 -Cleveland 44115 **Fx:**621-6502

(330) 825-2450 ..**Headley,** David L '58 -3571 Greenwich Rd -Norton 44203
Heagerty, Patrick J '04 -373 S High -12th Fl -Columbus 43215

(740) 363-1369 ..**Heald,** Anthony M '74 (Heald & L) -125 N Sandusky -Delaware 43015

(740) 363-1369 ..**Heald,** Chad A '02 %Heald & L -125 N Sandusky -Delaware 43015

(740) 363-1369 ..**Heald & Long** -125 N Sandusky -Delaware 43015

(740) 532-4169 ..**Heald,** Philip J '96 P Heald Co LPA -112 S 6th -Ironton 45638

(513) 579-1500 ..**Healey,** Roger W '76 (Buechner HOM&H Co,LPA) -105 E 4th -Ste 300 -Cincinnati 45202 **Fx:**977-4361

(812) 926-5689 ..**Healy,** Camille K '97 Aurora Casket Co,Inc -10944 Marsh Rd -Aurora, IN 47001 **Fx:**926-4886

(513) 621-7600 ..**Healy,** Jack S '73 (Eagen W&H Co,LPA) -2337 Victory Pkwy -Cincinnati 45206 **Fx:**455-8246

(216) 592-5000 ..**Healy,** Jeffrey A '92 %Tucker E&W LLP -925 Euclid Av -1150 Huntngtn Bldg -Cleveland 44115 **Fx:**592-5009

(513) 977-8200 ..**Healy,** Mary J '78 (Dinsmore & S LLP) -255 E 5th -Ste 1900 -Cincinnati 45202 **Fx:**977-8141

(614) 466-1818 ..**Heaphy,** William J III '75 Legis Srvc Commssn -77 S High -Columbus 43215

(937) 225-5757 ..**Heapy,** Jennifer N '03 Montgomery Cnty Pros -301 W 3rd -Bx972 -Dayton 45422 **Fx:**225-3470

(216) 561-6811 ..**Heard,** Arthur B '63 -17017 Miles Av -Cleveland 44128

(216) 696-4700 ..**Hearey,** Bruce G '82 (Spieth BM&N Co,LPA) -925 Euclid Av -2000 Huntngtn Bldg -Cleveland 44115 **Fx:**696-2706

(216) 696-4700 ..**Hearey,** Dianne Foley '85 (Spieth BM&N Co,LPA) -925 Euclid Av -2000 Huntngtn Bldg -Cleveland 44115 **Fx:**696-2706

(216) 622-3785 ..**Hearey,** Virginia D '84 US Atty -801 W Superior -Ste 400 -Cleveland 44113 **Fx:**622-3370

(419) 738-8171 ..**Hearn,** James F '87 -5 S Willipie -Wapakoneta 45895

(513) 326-1500 ..**Hearn,** Robert L '74 BHE Envrnmntl,Inc -11733 Chesterdale Rd -Cincinnati 45246

(440) 998-2628 ..**Heasley,** Phillip L '90 Ashtabula Cnty Pub Def -4817 State Rd -Ste 202 -Ashtabula 44004 **Fx:**998-2972

(513) 632-5132 ..**Heater,** Deborah Ann '94 Cincinnati Pub Sch -2651 Burnet Av -Cincinnati 45219

(740) 892-3443 ..**Heath,** F Richard '69 (Hite & H) -26 S Main -Bx457 -Utica 43080 **Fx:**892-3556

(937) 325-2492 ..**Heath,** James E '75 (Ronemus & H Co,LPA) -5 E Columbia -Springfield 45502

(513) 583-8888 ..**Heath,** James J '88 (Heath & Assoc) -8977 Columbia Rd -Ste A -Bx4770 -Maineville 45039

(513) 583-8888 ..**Heath,** James V '66 (Heath & Assoc) -8977 Columbia Rd -Ste A -Bx4770 -Maineville 45039

(740) 965-9697 ..**Heath,** John F '69 -599 Cheshire Rd -Sunbury 43074

(330) 456-7737 ..**Heath Cholley,** Taryn '82 -315 W Tuscarawas -Ste 307 -Canton 44702

(513) 721-5672 ..**Heather,** Timothy P '80 (Benjamin Y&H LLC) -312 Elm -Ste 1850 -Cincinnati 45202 **Fx:**562-4388

(937) 599-7272 ..**Heaton,** Gerald L '77 Logan Cnty Pros -117 E Columbus Av -Ste 200 -Bellefontaine 43311 **Fx:**599-7271

(419) 662-3100 ..**Heban,** Kevin A '85 (Heban & G) -417 Superior -Ste A -Rossford 43460 **Fx:**662-6533

(312) 269-4132 ..**Heban,** Linda A '85 Cnsl Jones DR&P -77 W Wacker Dr -Ste 3500 -Chicago, IL 60601 **Fx:**782-8585

(216) 431-5297 ..**Heben,** Edward J Jr. '75 Heben & Assoc -3740 Euclid Av -Cleveland 44115

(419) 724-0030 ..**Heben,** Mary Ellen '78 LAWO -520 Mad Av -Ste 640 -Toledo 43604 **Fx:**321-1582

(614) 481-6000 ..**Hebenstreit,** Stephen L '67 Cooper & E LLC -2175 Riverside Dr -Columbus 43221 **Fx:**481-6001

(734) 302-3233 ..**Heberle,** Denise M '95 (Heberle & F) -2580 Craig Rd -Ann Arbor, MI 48103

(440) 775-1751 ..**Heberling,** Martin M '65 Mun Ct Judge -85 S Main -Bx179 -Oberlin 44074

(248) 646-1514 ..**Hebert,** Dale L '97 Hebert & E, PC -30850 Telegraph -Ste 200 -Bingham Farms, MI 48025

(330) 762-7377 ..**Hebert,** Halle M '00 %Oldham & D -195 S Main -Ste 300 -Akron 44308 **Fx:**762-7300

(614) 292-0190 ..**Hébert,** L Camille '90 OSU Moritz Cllg of Law -55 W 12th Av -Columbus 43210 **Fx:**292-1383

(937) 435-7500 ..**Hébert,** Shireen J '04 %Botros B&S,LLC -5785 Far Hills Av -Dayton 45429 **Fx:**435-7511

(216) 991-5560 ..**Hecht,** Emanuel H '41 -3015 W Belvoir Oval -Shaker Heights 44122

(937) 228-6802 ..**Heck,** Cynthia M '79 (Heck & H Co,LPA) -1510 Hulman Bldg -Dayton 45402

(419) 525-1611 ..**Heck,** James J '88 (Brown BM&M) -70 Park Av W -Mansfield 44902 **Fx:**525-3810

(614) 224-1500 ..**Heck,** Jeremiah E '03 (Fornia L&H,LLP) -2 Miranova Pl -Ste 380 -Columbus 43215 **Fx:**224-2894

(937) 225-5757 ..**Heck,** Mathias H Jr. '72 Montgomery Cnty Pros -301 W 3rd -Bx972 -Dayton 45422 **Fx:**225-3470

(202) 224-7325 ..**Heck,** Patrick G '82 US Senate -219 Dirksen SOB -Committee on Finance -Washington, DC 20510 **Fx:**228-0483

(419) 259-8530 ..**Heck,** Richard W '91 KeyBank -Bx10099 -Toledo 43699

(614) 224-7700 ..**Heckert,** Christopher E '00 (Heckert & H Co,LPA) -495 S High -Ste 220 -Columbus 43215 **Fx:**224-7766

(614) 224-7700 ..**Heckert & Hockensmith Co,LPA** -495 S High -Ste 220 -Columbus 43215 **Fx:**224-7766

(202) 775-9800 ..**Heckman,** Annejanette K '98 Pillsbury W LLP -1133 Conn Av NW -Washington, DC 20036

(614) 228-0326 ..**Heckman,** Clarence L '69 -37 W Broad -Ste 1100 -Columbus 43215

(270) 781-5111 ..**Heckman,** Craig D '76 Cnsl Graves Gilbert Clinic -201 Park -Bowling Green, KY 42101

(937) 653-4478 ..**Heckman,** Darrell L '75 -107 N Main -Urbana 43078 **Fx:**653-8148

(614) 790-4265 ..**Hedden,** David L '74 Ashland Inc -Bx2219 -Columbus 43216 **Fx:**790-4268

(614) 464-6400 ..**Hedden,** Herbert A '90 (Vorys SS&P LLP) -52 E Gay -Bx1008 -Columbus 43216 **Fx:**464-6350

(216) 787-3934 ..**Heddesheimer,** Don J '74 Industrial Commssn of OH -615 Superior Av NW -Cleveland 44113 **Fx:**787-3483

(513) 932-1836 ..**Hedges,** Jackson C '63 (J Hedges) -24 N Bway -Lebanon 45036 **Fx:**932-2849

(740) 592-2435 ..**Hedges,** Richard H '95 -8 N Court -Ste 507 -Athens 45701 **Fx:**592-3724

(614) 538-5382 ..**Hedien,** Mark J '95 (Clark & H) -2000 Bethel Rd -Columbus 43220
Hedlund, Stephen D '73 -(Address Unavailable)

(216) 696-3030 ..**Hedman,** Kent S '97 %Kadish H&W,LPA -1717 E 9th -Ste 2112 -Cleveland 44114 **Fx:**696-3492

(614) 466-0000 ..**Hedman,** Sarah E '03 %OH Dept Taxation -30 E Broad -22nd Fl -Columbus 43215

(513) 887-3474 ..**Hedric,** Craig D '86 Butler Cnty Pros -315 High -11th Fl -Bx515 -Hamilton 45012

(614) 645-7483 ..**Hedrick,** Billy Ray '96 City Pros -375 S High -7th Fl -Columbus 43215

(937) 228-3889 ..**Hedrick,** James E '78 (Hedrick & J Co,LPA) -124 E 3rd -Ste 300 -Dayton 45402

(937) 228-3889 ..**Hedrick & Jordan Co,LPA** -124 E 3rd -Ste 300 -Dayton 45402

(937) 227-3700 ..**Hedrick,** R Holtzman '04 %Faruki I&C PLL -10 N Ludlow -500 Cthse Plz SW -Dayton 45402 **Fx:**227-3717

(419) 609-1311 ..**Heebsh,** Philip S '02 %Reminger & R -237 W Wshngtn Row -2nd Fl -Sandusky 44870 **Fx:**626-4805

(513) 651-6800 ..**Heekin,** Albert E III '65 Cnsl Frost BT LLC -201 E 5th -2200 PNC Ctr -Cincinnati 45202 **Fx:**651-6981

(513) 421-3399 ..**Heekin,** Christopher R '89 (Heekin & H) -817 Main -Ste 200 -Cincinnati 45202

(513) 381-2838 ..**Heekin,** Thomas D '62 (Taft S&H LLP) -425 Walnut -Ste 1800 -Cincinnati 45202 **Fx:**381-0205

(513) 421-3399 ..**Heekin,** Thomas D Jr. '88 (Heekin & H) -817 Main -Ste 200 -Cincinnati 45202

(513) 241-7644 ..**Heekin,** William C '84 -120 E 4th -Ste 425 -Cincinnati 45202

(513) 946-3227 ..**Heenan,** Scott M '02 Hamilton Cnty Pros -230 E 9th -Cincinnati 45202 **Fx:**946-3017

(614) 365-2700 ..**Heer,** Holly H '93 (Squire S&D LLP) -41 S High -1300 Huntngtn Ctr -Columbus 43215 **Fx:**365-2499

(216) 781-1212 ..**Heer,** John A II '91 %Walter & H LLP -1301 E 9th -Ste 3500 -Cleveland 44114 **Fx:**575-0911

(614) 224-9207 ..**Heer,** William C III '90 Title First Agncy,Inc -555 S Front -Ste 400 -Columbus 43213

(614) 428-2102 ..**Heeter,** Joseph L '88 Sky Fin Sltns Inc -2740 Airport Dr -Ste 300 -Columbus 43219

(859) 491-5297 ..**Heeter,** Sheryl E '93 -335 E 3rd -Newport, KY 41071

(216) 241-0040 ..**Heffernan,** Edward A '78 -1660 W 2nd -Ste 410 -Cleveland 44113

(216) 621-0200 ..**Heffernan,** John M '96 %Baker & H LLP -1900 E 9th -Ste 3200 -Cleveland 44114 **Fx:**696-0740

(614) 258-6000 ..**Heffernan,** Michael E '98 %Brenner BG&M Co,LPA -2109 Stella Ct -Columbus 43215 **Fx:**258-6006

(216) 875-2767 ..**Heffernan,** Michael V '02 %Bonezzi SM&P Co LPA -526 Superior Av -Ste 1400 -Cleveland 44114 **Fx:**875-1570

(614) 857-4390 ..**Heffernan,** Terrence R '82 (Weltman W&R Co,LPA) -175 S 3rd -Ste 900 -Columbus 43215 **Fx:**222-2193

(216) 464-5383 ..**Heffernan,** Thomas A '64 -2682 Rocklyn Rd -Shaker Heights 44122

(937) 842-2479 ..**Heffner,** Cynthia L '93 -7080 Arrowhead Ct -Huntsville 43324

(513) 887-4118 ..**Heffner,** Jann K '75 Butler Cnty Childrens Srvc -300 N Fair Av -Hamilton 45011

(440) 285-7750 ..**Heffter,** Sarah L '95 -151 Main -Chardon 44024

(614) 791-3243 ..**Hegedus,** Joseph M '91 Patrolmens Benevolent Assn -555 Metro Park Pl N -Ste 100 -Dublin 43017

(937) 492-6125 ..**Hegemann,** Heath H '93 %Kerrigan BSG&B -126 N Main Av -Bx987 -Sidney 45365

(859) 384-4300 ..**Hegge,** Colleen M '87 Noyes &M,PLLC -Bx437 -Union, KY 41091

(937) 548-2211 ..**Heggie,** Mark E '74 %Goubeaux & G -100 Wshngtn Av -Bx158 -Greenville 45331

(440) 951-1181 ..**Hegyes,** Bryan F '02 -38040 Euclid Av -Willoughby 44094

(440) 951-1181 ..**Hegyes,** Dean K '92 -38040 Euclid Av -Willoughby 44094

(216) 447-9105 ..**Hehr,** Albert G III '99 (Hehr & M Co,LPA) -4401 Rockside Rd -Ste 200 -Independence 44131 **Fx:**447-9171

(216) 449-3266 ..**Hehr,** Albert G Jr. '74 -4401 Rockside Rd -Ste 200 -Cleveland 44131

(330) 456-0061 ..**Heichel Craig & Prelac Co, LPA** -437 Market Av N -Canton 44702

(419) 524-6011 ..**Heichel,** William D '72 (Calhoun KH&C Co,LPA) -6 W 3rd -Ste 200 -Bx268 -Mansfield 44901 **Fx:**526-1431

(703) 714-3306 ..**Heick,** Kenneth W '78 Freddie Mac -8100 Jones Brnch Dr -MS # B2B -McLean, VA 22102

(614) 229-4431 ..**Heid,** Brigid E '90 (Luper N&L,LPA) -50 W Broad -1200 LeVeque Twr -Columbus 43215 **Fx:**464-2425

(740) 858-6991 ..**Heid,** Catherine S '83 -116 Poole -West Portsmouth 45663

(419) 332-8111 ..**Heid,** Robert C '64 -915 Croghan -Fremont 43420

(419) 332-8111 ..**Heid,** Sally R '54 %RC Heid -915 Croghan -Fremont 43420

(216) 586-3939 ..**Heidorf,** Travis M '03 %Jones D -901 Lakeside Av -Cleveland 44114 **Fx:**579-0212

(513) 530-4230 ..**Heidrich,** William A III '79 Equistar Chem,LP -11530 Northlake Dr -Cincinnati 45249

(614) 793-8470 ..**Heier,** David S '79 -2303-312 Vicente Ct -Columbus 43235

(614) 229-7596 ..**Heier,** Patricia W '79 Franklin Cnty Children Srvcs -855 W Mound -Columbus 43223 **Fx:**275-2589

(419) 732-3135 ..**Heigel,** Catherine Edwards '03 Kocher & G -101½ Madison -Port Clinton 43452 **Fx:**734-5644

(513) 336-9940 ..**Heil,** Michael F '87 -3469 Ketch Ct -Maineville 45039

(937) 324-5541 ..**Heil,** Richard F Jr. '86 (Martin BH&H) -1 S Limestone -Ste 800 -Bx1488 -Springfield 45501 **Fx:**325-5432

(440) 246-0045 ..**Heiland,** Eric K '91 -Bx553 -Lorain 44052

(513) 421-3940 .. **Heilbrun**, John L '77 -3536 Edwards Rd -Ste 100 -Cincinnati 45208 **Fx:**321-3929
(513) 241-1950 .. **Heile**, Charles D '62 (Brown LH&E) -7 W 7th -Ste 1950 -Cincinnati 45202 **Fx:**241-4095
(513) 946-3000 .. **Heile**, Jeffrey M '03 Hamilton Cnty Pros -230 E 9th -Cincinnati 45202 **Fx:**946-3017
(513) 946-3249 .. **Heile**, William P '70 Hamilton Cnty Pros -230 E 9th -Cincinnati 45202 **Fx:**946-3017
(216) 586-3939 .. **Heiman**, David G '71 (Jones D) -901 Lakeside Av -Cleveland 44114 **Fx:**579-0212
(330) 762-6001 .. **Heimbaugh**, Rebecca DiDonato '90 -333 S Main -Akron 44308
(859) 578-1000 .. **Heimkreiter**, Gregory W '02 Horwitz Law Firm -541 Buttermilk Pike -Ste 305 -Crescent Springs, KY 41017
(740) 362-1988 .. **Heimlich**, Michael M '84 -103 N Union -Ste E -Delaware 43015
(513) 732-7810 .. **Heimlich**, Rebecca S '94 %Clermont Cnty Mun Pros -4432 State Route 222 -Batavia 45103
(513) 425-6609 .. **Hein**, Jonathan A '98 12th Dist Ct of Appls -1001 Reinartz Blvd -Middletown 45042 **Fx:**425-8751
(937) 225-6308 .. **Hein**, Sara L '95 Montgomery Cnty Pros -303 W 2nd -Rm 113 -Dayton 45402
(330) 453-0458 .. **Heinbach**, Charles C Jr. '83 -128 Linwood Av NW -Canton 44708
(216) 621-4100 .. **Heindel**, Edward M '90 -1370 Ontario -# 450 -Cleveland 44113
Heindrichs, Carrie L '04 -(Address Unavailable)
(614) 771-7070 .. **Heine**, Bruce V '71 -7240 Muirfld Dr -Ste 140 -Dublin 43017
(740) 432-4502 .. **Heine**, Stephen C '74 (Heine & F) -803 Steubenvll Av -Cambridge 43725 **Fx:**439-7712
(216) 787-3663 .. **Heine**, William J '81 OH Industrial Comm -615 W Superior Av -7th Fl -Cleveland 44113
(216) 664-4224 .. **Heinert O'Leary**, Jennifer C '97 Dept of Law -601 Lakeside Av -Rm 106 City Hall -Cleveland 44114 **Fx:**664-2663
(513) 761-0011 .. **Heinichen**, Jeffrey K '78 Gen Polymers Corp -145 Caldwell Dr -Cincinnati 45216
(216) 579-1700 .. **Heinke**, Lowell L '60 OfCnsl Pearne & G LLP -1801 E 9th -Ste 1200 -Cleveland 44114 **Fx:**579-6073
(513) 579-0080 .. **Heinkel**, John C '81 %Smith R&S Co,LPA -1014 Vine -Ste 2350 -Cincinnati 45202 **Fx:**579-0222
(330) 253-5060 .. **Heinle**, Matthew A '95 (Brennan M&D,LLC) -75 E Market -Akron 44308 **Fx:**253-1977
(614) 228-8833 .. **Heinlein**, David J '88 Cincinnati Ins Co -140 E Town -Ste 1015 -Columbus 43215
(513) 651-6800 .. **Heinlen**, Ronald E '62 (Frost BT LLC) -201 E 5th -2200 PNC Ctr -Cincinnati 45202 **Fx:**651-6981
(330) 744-1148 .. **Heino**, John T '96 %Henderson CMN&T Co,LPA -34 Fed Plz W -Ste 600 Wick Bldg -Youngstown 44503 **Fx:**744-3807
(330) 747-2661 .. **Heinrich**, Julian '02 Cafaro Co -2445 Belmont Av -Bx2186 -Youngstown 44504
(216) 464-6153 .. **Heintel**, Robert C '96 Scott Tech Inc -2000 Auburn Dr -Ste 400 -Beachwood 44122
(419) 242-5100 .. **Heintschel**, Thomas W '79 (Frederickson H&K Co,LPA) -405 Mad Av -Ste 1212 -Toledo 43604 **Fx:**242-5556
(513) 381-9200 .. **Heintz**, Isaac T '01 %Rendigs FK&D,LLP -One W 4th -Ste 900 -Cincinnati 45202 **Fx:**381-9206
(330) 743-1171 .. **Heintz**, Jeffrey D '84 Manchester BP&U -201 E Commerce -Atrium Level 2 Commerce Bldg -Youngstown 44503 **Fx:**743-1190
(330) 535-5711 .. **Heintz**, Jeffrey T '75 (Brouse M) -106 S Main -500 First Natl Twr -Akron 44308 **Fx:**253-8601
(614) 227-2000 .. **Heintz**, Michael E '03 %Porter WM&A LLP -41 S High -Columbus 43215 **Fx:**227-2100
(603) 444-8000 .. **Heintz**, Ruth '97 NHLA -58 Main -Littleton, NH 03561 **Fx:**444-8804
Heinzerling, Barbara M '79 -166 E Market -Ste 205 -Akron 44308
(614) 337-8366 .. **Heinzerling**, Mark E '96 %Pencheff & F -2176A CityGate Dr -Columbus 43219
(614) 229-4722 .. **Heinzerling-Elkins**, Mary '94 Deloitte & Touche -155 E Broad -Columbus 43215
(513) 421-4225 .. **Heis**, Forest S '69 (Heis & W Co,LPA) -817 Main -Ste 800 -Cincinnati 45202
(513) 762-6200 .. **Heis**, Jennifer Snyder '03 %Ulmer & B LLP -600 Vine -Ste 2800 -Cincinnati 45202 **Fx:**762-6245
(513) 421-4225 .. **Heis & Wenstrup Co,LPA** -817 Main -Ste 800 -Cincinnati 45202
(330) 297-6460 .. **Heisa**, Mark H '78 -215 S Chestnut -Bx209 -Ravenna 44266
(216) 931-6000 .. **Heiser**, Donald E '63 (Ulmer & B LLP) -1300 E 9th -Ste 900 Penton Media Bldg -Cleveland 44114 **Fx:**931-6001
(330) 836-4141 .. **Heiser**, Edward N Jr. '55 -1999 Ganyard Rd -Akron 44313
(216) 523-5467 .. **Heiser**, Joel S '94 OfCnsl Bricker & E LLP -1375 E 9th -Ste 1500 -Cleveland 44114 **Fx:**523-7071
(740) 383-2446 .. **Heiser**, Larry N '02 -284 S State -Bx834 -Marion 43301 **Fx:**383-2471
(740) 384-2111 .. **Heiser**, Lawrence A '73 (Oths H&M) -16 E Bway -Bx309 -Wellston 45692
(513) 345-1532 .. **Heiser**, Stacey M '94 Kendle Intl Inc -441 Vine -1200 Carew Twr -Cincinnati 45202
(614) 802-2900 .. **Heiser**, Steven L '79 -100 E Wilson Bridge Rd -Ste 200 -Worthington 43085
(419) 215-5982 .. **Heisler**, Dwight Daniel '81 -17274 US Hwy 6 W -Bowling Green 43402
(513) 651-6800 .. **Heitchue**, Catherine A '03 %Frost BT LLC -201 E 5th -2200 PNC Ctr -Cincinnati 45202 **Fx:**651-6981
(740) 833-2593 .. **Hejmanowski**, David A '99 Delaware Cnty Juvenile Ct -88 N Sandusky -Delaware 43015 **Fx:**833-2599
(440) 331-0108 .. **Hejra**, Mary L '77 -1746 Walnut Ln -Rocky River 44116
(513) 946-5791 **Hekler**, Krista A '02 Hamilton Cnty Ct of Common Pleas -1000 Main -380 -Cincinnati 45202
(419) 882-0096 .. **Helberg**, Tom R '84 -5215 Monroe -Ste 4 -Toledo 43623
(330) 261-2486 .. **Helbley**, William C Jr. '89 -725 Boardman-Canfld Rd -Ste L-1 -Youngstown 44512
(513) 923-9740 .. **Helbling**, John J '90 -3672 Sprngdl Rd -Cincinnati 45251
(216) 781-1164 .. **Helbling**, Lauren Y '87 -1370 Ontatrio -Cleveland 44113
(513) 621-2120 .. **Heldman**, James G '81 Strauss & T,LPA -150 E 4th -4th Fl -Cincinnati 45202 **Fx:**241-8259
(513) 762-4421 .. **Heldman**, Paul W '77 Kroger Co -1014 Vine -Cincinnati 45202
(216) 241-2838 .. **Helfman**, Jill Friedman '87 (Taft S&H LLP) -200 Pub Sq -3500 BP Twr -Cleveland 44114 **Fx:**241-3707
(440) 250-9140 .. **Helfrich**, Karl S '86 -27350 Ctr Ridge Rd -Westlake 44145
(513) 946-3875 .. **Helfrich**, Kimberly Ann '97 Hamilton Cnty Pub Def -230 E 9th -3rd Fl -Cincinnati 45202 **Fx:**946-3707
(614) 469-3289 .. **Helfrich**, Kurt P '97 (Thompson H LLP) -10 W Broad -Ste 700 -Columbus 43215 **Fx:**469-3361
(513) 632-5317 .. **Helfrich**, Loretta Marie '89 -119 East Ct -Ste 304 -Cincinnati 45202
(614) 776-1000 .. **Helkowski**, Lawrence Scott '97 %Barren & M Co,LPA -110 Polaris Pkwy -Ste 302 -Westerville 43082 **Fx:**865-3396
(330) 792-6611 .. **Heller Maas Moro & Magill Co LPA** -54 Wstchstr Dr -Bx4144 -Youngstown 44515
(419) 255-0814 .. **Heller**, Mark R '82 ABLE -520 Mad Av -740 Spitzer Bldg -Toledo 43604 **Fx:**259-2880
(216) 374-7472 .. **Heller**, Michael A '01 -5047 Bristol Ct -Lyndhurst 44124
(216) 381-3400 .. **Heller**, Nancy J '96 (Petronzio S Co,LPA) -5001 Mayfld Rd -Ste 201 -Cleveland 44124
(212) 623-9117 .. **Heller**, Paul '76 %JP Morgan Chase -4 NY Plz -21st Fl -New York, NY 10004
(216) 591-0909 .. **Heller**, Renee P '94 -5525 Warrensvll Ctr Rd -Maple Heights 44137
(330) 792-6611 .. **Heller**, Robert L '81 (Heller MM&M Co LPA) -54 Wstchstr Dr -Bx4144 -Youngstown 44515
(216) 771-0811 .. **Heller**, Roger D '75 -614 Superior Av NW -Ste 625 -Cleveland 44113
(859) 431-7200 .. **Hellings**, Harry P Jr. '74 Hellings & P,PSC -214 E 4th -Covington, KY 41011
(202) 353-7172 .. **Hellman**, Matthew C '99 US DOJ -601 D NW -Washington, DC 20530
Hellmann, Barbara L '04 -(Address Unavailable)
(216) 696-3311 .. **Hellner-Cord**, Leigh A '04 (Kahn K) -1301 E 9th -2600 Erievw Twr -Cleveland 44114 **Fx:**623-4912
Hellstedt, Jonathan E '99 -238 Highgate Av -Worthington 43085
Helman, Lindsay A '04 -(Address Unavailable)
(614) 890-6696 .. **Helmer**, Elena V '02 -5482 Cypress Ct -Westerville 43082 **Fx:**890-6676
(513) 421-2400 .. **Helmer**, James B Jr. '75 (Helmer MR&P Co,LPA) -105 E 4th -Ste 1900 -Cincinnati 45202 **Fx:**421-7902
(513) 421-2400 .. **Helmer Martins Rice & Popham Co,LPA** -105 E 4th -Ste 1900 -Cincinnati 45202 **Fx:**421-7902
(513) 793-5297 .. **Helmes**, Andrew J '97 %Monnie & O Co,LPA -8035 Hosbrook Rd -Ste 200 -Cincinnati 45236
(513) 651-9666 .. **Helmick**, Bertha G '95 -1014 Vine -2525 Kroger Bldg -Cincinnati 45202
(419) 243-3800 .. **Helmick**, Jeffrey J '88 -1119 Adams -2nd Fl -Toledo 43624
(419) 213-4755 .. **Helmick**, Karen H '89 %Hon ML Pietrykowski -800 Jackson -Toledo 43624
(513) 563-2194 .. **Helmling**, Margaret R '59 -3939 Crk Rd -Cincinnati 45241
(614) 227-2000 .. **Helmreich**, Richard J '89 (Porter WM&A LLP) -41 S High -Columbus 43215 **Fx:**227-2100
(248) 203-0756 .. **Helms**, Ernest E '78 %Dykema G PLLC -39577 Woodward Av -Ste 300 -Bloomfield Hills, MI 48304
(937) 461-5980 .. **Helms**, Jeffrey R '02 %Jablinski FR&M -214 W Monument Av -Bx1266 -Dayton 45402 **Fx:**461-4139
(330) 683-0015 .. **Helmuth**, Ricky J '79 (Johnson & H) -343 S Crownhill Rd -Bx149 -Orrville 44667
(216) 241-2880 .. **Helon**, Phillip A '04 %Cowden HN&L -50 Pub Sq -Ste 1414 -Cleveland 44113 **Fx:**241-2881
(740) 587-4480 .. **Helser**, Gregory C '90 Helser Law Ofc -527 Newark Granvll Rd -Ste 4 -Granville 43023
(330) 392-4176 .. **Heltzel**, Paul E '82 DelBene L&T -155 Pine Av NE -Bx353 -Warren 44482 **Fx:**392-5694
(614) 875-1041 .. **Helvey**, Edward D '82 OH Edu Assn -5026 Pine Crk Dr -Westerville 43081
(513) 761-9393 .. **Helwig**, Nancy Coe '80 -272 Pkwy Av -Cincinnati 45216
(937) 224-9291 .. **Hemenway**, James K '88 Young & A Co,LPA -130 W 2nd -Ste 2000 -Dayton 45402 **Fx:**224-9679
(440) 826-9497 .. **Hemingway**, Christine A '94 Morsch Med Inc -9001 Fair Rd -Strongsville 44149
(513) 489-5495 .. **Hemingway**, Ronald Lee '68 -5366 Dickens Dr -Cincinnati 45241
(513) 634-2084 .. **Hemm**, Erich D '00 Procter & Gamble -6071 Ctr Hill Av -Bx 331 -Cincinnati 45224
(937) 773-8054 .. **Hemm**, John E '82 (Dungan & L Co,LPA) -111 W Ash -Bx1529 -Piqua 45356 **Fx:**773-3379
(937) 332-6965 .. **Hemm**, Michael W '74 Cnty Mun Ct Judge -201 W Main -Troy 45373
(859) 344-1188 .. **Hemmer**, Donald M '79 (Hemmer PDF) -250 Grandvw Dr -Ste 200 -Ft Mitchell, KY 41017
(614) 547-0350 .. **Hemmer**, Paul K '83 (Carroll U&H,LLC) -7100 N High -Ste 301 -Columbus 43085 **Fx:**547-0354
(919) 402-9100 .. **Hemmerich**, Michael R '85 Dilweg Companies,LLC -5310 S Alston Av -Ste 210 -Durham, NC 27713
(812) 438-5012 .. **Hemmerle**, Mark D '92 Grand Victoria Casino & Resort -600 Grand Victoria Dr -Rising Sun, IN 47040
(937) 435-2118 .. **Hemmert**, William F '73 -1340 E Stroop Rd -Kettering 45429
(740) 833-2690 .. **Hemmeter**, Marianne T '97 Delaware Cnty Pros -140 N Sandusky -3rd Fl -Delaware 43015
(614) 255-1140 .. **Hemminger**, Chad K '04 %RC Harbold & Assoc -500 S Front -Ste 1140 -Columbus 43215
(513) 831-5604 .. **Hemminger**, David G '65 -1105 Ctr -Milford 45150
(216) 241-7430 .. **Hemmons**, Willa M '77 -1276 W Third -Cleveland 44113
(937) 223-5200 .. **Hempfling**, Richard '85 %Flanagan LH&S -318 W 4th -Dayton 45402 **Fx:**223-3335
(330) 451-7152 .. **Hemphill**, Dwaine R '88 Stark Cnty Cmmn Pleas Crt -115 Central Plz N -Canton 44702
(614) 461-5955 .. **Hemphill**, John C '73 -370 S 5th -Ste G8 -Columbus 43215
(330) 287-5561 .. **Hemphill**, Joi E '87 Wayne Cnty Juv Ct -107 W Lbrty -Wooster 44691
(937) 592-9559 .. **Hemphill**, Richard A '85 -230 S Madriver -Bellefontaine 43311
(614) 757-7221 .. **Henchel**, Gregory J '95 Cardinal Health Inc -7000 Cardinal Pl -Dublin 43017
(216) 378-1579 .. **Henck**, John C '96 (J Henck & Assoc Co,LPA) -23240 Chagrin Blvd -Ste 535 -Beachwood 44122
(216) 443-7295 .. **Hencke**, Tiffany L '00 Cuyahoga Cnty Pub Def -1849 Prospect Av -Ste 222 -Cleveland 44115

(419) 874-5610 .. **Hendel,** Sharon S '94 (Croy & H,LLP) -801 W South Boundary
-Ste C -Perrysburg 43551

(614) 228-1541 .. **Hendershot,** Elizabeth L '95 %Baker & H LLP -65 E State
-Ste 2100 -Columbus 43215 **Fx:**462-2616

(440) 323-1808 .. **Hendershot,** Margaret A '98 St Marie Law Firm Co,LPA
-409 East Av -Ste A -Elyria 44035

(216) 360-9000 .. **Hendershott,** Howard E Jr. '53 %Ziegler M&M LLP -30100
Chagrin Blvd -Ste 301 -Pepper Pike 44122 **Fx:**360-0303

(419) 241-2222 .. **Hendershott,** Patrick D '93 -1900 Monroe -Ste 112 -Toledo 43624

(216) 774-0000 .. **Henderson,** Brandon J '02 (Browner & H,LLC) -526 Superior Av E
-Ste 545 -Cleveland 44114 **Fx:**774-0493

(937) 333-4450 .. **Henderson,** Carl S '85 Dayton Mun Ct -301 W 3rd -Dayton 45402

(414) 276-0200 .. **Henderson,** Charles I '74 (Davis & K,SC) -111 E Kilbourn Av
-Ste 1400 -Milwaukee, WI 53202 **Fx:**276-9369

(434) 948-5986 .. **Henderson,** Christal D '95 GE Fin Assurance -700 Main -3-040
-Lynchburg, VA 24504

(330) 744-1148 .. **Henderson Covington Messenger Newman
& Thomas Co, LPA** -34 Fed Plz W -Ste 600 Wick Bldg
-Youngstown 44503 **Fx:**744-3807

(440) 461-9000 .. **Henderson,** David B '92 %Dyson S&F Co,LPA -5843 Mayfld Rd
-Mayfield Heights 44124

(419) 243-7243 .. **Henderson,** David T '96 %Cubbon & Assoc Co,LPA -405 N Huron
-Ste 500 -Toledo 43604

(216) 566-5779 .. **Henderson,** Harold W '76 (Thompson H LLP) -127 Pub Sq
-3900 Key Ctr -Cleveland 44114 **Fx:**566-5800

(216) 241-2132 .. **Henderson,** Ivan L '98 WPS Energy Srvcs,Inc -600 Superior
-Ste 1300 -Cleveland 44114

(513) 732-2140 .. **Henderson,** James C '76 (Ely & T) -322 Main -Batavia 45103

(504) 299-9066 .. **Henderson,** Jennifer L '94 Cnsl Sun Belt Conference
-601 Poydras -Ste 2355 -New Orleans, LA 70130

(419) 213-2001 .. **Henderson,** Karlene D '03 Lucas Cnty Pros -Adams & Erie
-Lucas Cnty Cthse -Toledo 43624

(610) 270-6897 .. **Henderson,** Loretta J '92 GlaxoSmithKline -Bx1539
-King of Prussia, PA 19406

(216) 696-6555 .. **Henderson,** Louis G '82 -55 Pub Sq -Ste 2075 -Cleveland 44113
Fx:696-6121

(614) 255-2040 .. **Henderson,** Maurice M III '00 -336 S High -Columbus 43215

(206) 987-5220 .. **Henderson,** Pamela S '97 Childrens Hospital -S210 -Bx50020
-Seattle, WA 98145

(412) 551-1887 .. **Henderson,** Robert J '97 -Bx166 -Bethel Park, PA 15102
Fx:835-5633

(216) 861-4416 .. **Henderson,** Ronald E '80 -75 Pub Sq -Ste 1414 -Cleveland 44113

(419) 243-9876 .. **Henderson,** Ronald Roy '73 -520 Mad Av -Ste 524 -Toledo 43604

(440) 729-7374 .. **Henderson,** Susan S '84 -7940 Sherman Rd -Cleveland 44026
Fx:729-7483

(513) 241-3100 .. **Henderson,** Thomas L '88 Lerner S&R -120 E 4th -8th Fl
-Cincinnati 45202

(937) 222-2500 .. **Henderson,** Toby K '99 %Sebaly S&D -1900 Kettering Twr
-Dayton 45423 **Fx:**222-6554

(740) 385-5909 .. **Henderson,** William W '79 -30 W Hunter -Bx505 -Logan 43138
Fx:385-9664

(330) 376-8336 .. **Hendler,** Michael B '63 Goldman & R,Ltd -11 S Forge
-Akron 44304 **Fx:**376-2522

(330) 796-3151 .. **Hendricks,** Bruce J '81 Goodyear -1144 E Market -Akron 44316

(330) 722-9313 .. **Hendricks,** Connie G '88 Medina Cnty Job & Family Srvcs
-232 Northland Dr -Leg Dept -Medina 44256

(513) 621-6464 .. **Hendricks,** Jeffrey M '96 %Graydon H&R LLP -511 Walnut
-1900 Fifth Third Ctr -Cincinnati 45202 **Fx:**651-3836

(419) 526-2188 .. **Hendricks,** Richard E '69 -3 N Main -Rm 605 -Mansfield 44902

(513) 351-7599 .. **Hendricks,** Robert S '93 -4557 Mntgmry Rd -Cincinnati 45212

(330) 740-2180 .. **Hendrickson,** Jeffrey E '00 %7th Dist Ct of Appeals -120 Market
-4th Fl -Youngstown 44503 **Fx:**740-2182

(202) 514-2174 .. **Hendrickson,** Lori A '97 DOJ -Bx972 -Washington, DC 20044
Fx:514-9623

(513) 771-7449 .. **Hendrickson,** Nora C '86 -230 Northland Blvd -Ste 229
-Cincinnati 45246 **Fx:**771-7849

(513) 867-5070 .. **Hendrickson,** Robert A '84 Butler Cnty Area 3 Ct
-9577 Beckett Rd -Ste 300 -West Chester 45069
Hendrickson, Sharon M '99 -11689 Dunham Rd
-Mount Vernon 43050

(419) 668-6524 .. **Hendrixson,** Nancy E '83 Veterinary Phys & Srgns,Inc
-705 Route 20 E -Norwalk 44857

(937) 562-5250 .. **Hendrix,** Robert K '86 Greene Cnty Pros -61 Greene -Xenia 45385

(614) 791-2622 .. **Hendrix,** Robert S '86 -6065 Frantz Rd -Ste 103 -Bx1408
-Dublin 43017

(937) 222-1090 .. **Hendrixson,** Patricia L '00 %Statman HS&E LLC -110 N Main
-Ste 1520 -Dayton 45402 **Fx:**222-1046

(330) 503-5032 .. **Hendryx,** Bruce D '87 Key Corp -6575 Sevll Dr -2nd Fl
-Canfield 44406

(513) 651-6800 .. **Hendy,** Daniel J '04 %Frost BT LLC -201 E 5th -2200 PNC Ctr
-Cincinnati 45202 **Fx:**651-6981

(859) 578-4444 .. **Hendy,** Penny U '97 P Schachter & Assoc,PSC -250 Grandvw Dr
-#500 -Fort Mitchell, KY 41017

(614) 457-5600 .. **Henegar,** Charles S III '94 P Smith -5025 Arlngtn Centre Blvd
-Ste 250 -Columbus 43220

(216) 991-3574 .. **Henes,** Samuel E '62 -13605 Shaker Blvd -Cleveland 44120

(513) 381-9200 .. **Hengehold,** Steven D '85 (Rendigs FK&D,LLP) -One W 4th
-Ste 900 -Cincinnati 45202 **Fx:**381-9206

(513) 721-7295 .. **Hengelbrok,** James W '48 (Davis & H) -830 Main -Ste 200
-Cincinnati 45202

(330) 762-1935 .. **Henges,** John J '94 -628 W Market -Akron 44303

(775) 327-8270 .. **Hengstler,** Gary A '84 Natl Judicial Cllg -Univ of Nevada Bldg 358
-Reno, NV 89557

(614) 464-6400 .. **Henke,** Bruce R '79 (Vorys SS&P LLP) -52 E Gay -Bx1008
-Columbus 43216 **Fx:**464-6350

(937) 461-9330 .. **Henke,** Lawrence W III '70 -371 W 1st -Ste 100 -Dayton 45402
Fx:461-9331

(513) 723-4000 .. **Henkel,** Mary C '88 OfCnsl Vorys SS&P LLP -221 E 4th
-Ste 2000 Atrium Two -Bx0236 -Cincinnati 45201 **Fx:**723-4056

(216) 566-5806 .. **Henkel,** Oliver C Jr. '64 (Thompson H LLP) -127 Pub Sq
-3900 Key Ctr -Cleveland 44114 **Fx:**566-5800

(614) 466-8600 .. **Henkener,** Ann E '74 Atty Gen -30 E Broad -Columbus 43215
Fx:466-6090

(216) 781-8288 .. **Henkin,** Howard A '71 (Henkin & S) -310 W Lakeside Av -Ste 550
-Cleveland 44113 **Fx:**781-1273

(216) 771-8288 .. **Henkin,** Merrill H '78 -55 Pub Sq -Ste 1300 -Cleveland 44113

(330) 746-8491 .. **Henkin,** Robert A '73 (Henkin T&H) -6 Fed Plz Central -Ste 905
-Youngstown 44503

(614) 340-3444 .. **Henley,** Barron K '93 (Henley M&U Cnsltng,Inc)
-3300 Riverside Dr -Ste 350 -Columbus 43221 **Fx:**340-3443

(937) 222-5244 .. **Henley,** Elizabeth J '79 -131 N Ludlow -1205 Talbott Twr
-Dayton 45402
Henley, Walter G '90 Star Bank,NA -425 Walnut -ML KY-04-0105
-Cincinnati 45202

(614) 462-7450 .. **Hennebert,** Shaunna L '96 CASA Franklin Cnty -373 S High
-6th Fl -Columbus 43215 **Fx:**462-5070

(440) 544-2000 .. **Hennenberg,** Michael C '74 OfCnsl Dinn H&P,LLC
-5910 Landerbrook Dr -Ste 200 -Cleveland 44124 **Fx:**544-2002

(216) 523-4107 .. **Hennessey,** Joseph M '70 Eaton Corp -1111 Superior Av
-Cleveland 44114

(614) 224-8374 .. **Hennessey,** Molly A '88 Legal Aid -40 W Gay -Columbus 43215

(614) 248-6691 .. **Hennessey,** Thomas M '95 Bank One Corp -1111 Polaris Pkwy
-Ste 4P -Columbus 43271

(216) 222-2987 .. **Hennig,** Janet L '86 Natl City Bank -1900 E 9th
-17th Fl Loc 01-2174 -Cleveland 44114

(440) 354-4364 .. **Hennig,** Richard A '83 OfCnsl Baker & H Co,LPA -77 N St Clair
-Painesville 44077 **Fx:**639-8901

(740) 385-1078 .. **Henniger,** Louis Jackson II '73 (LJ Henniger & Assoc) -4 E Main
-Ste 200 -Logan 43138

(419) 242-1400 .. **Henning,** Frederick E '66 -608 Mad Av -Ste 1400 -Toledo 43604

(614) 227-2000 .. **Henning,** Harry L '71 (Porter WM&A LLP) -41 S High
-Columbus 43215 **Fx:**227-2100

(330) 479-9825 .. **Henning,** Richard L '76 -5022 Yukon NW -Ste D -Canton 44708

(330) 479-9825 .. **Henning,** Sally D '78 -5022 Yukon NW -Ste D -Canton 44708

(330) 860-6108 .. **Hennis,** Steven E '92 Babcock & Wilcox Co -20 S Van Buren
-Barberton 44203

(614) 478-5555 .. **Hennis,** Trina D '85 Gahanna-Jefferson Schls -515 Havens Crnr
-Gahanna 43230

(773) 235-3416 .. **Henretta,** David S '96 -908 N Wolcott Av -Unit 3
-Chicago, IL 60622

(330) 376-7800 .. **Henretta,** J T '75 -120 E Mill -Ste 401 -Akron 44308

(937) 228-5800 .. **Henrici,** Kelly A '94 Relizon Co -Bx2237 -Dayton 45401

(216) 621-6570 .. **Henrikson,** Kirk R '91 (Rademaker MM&G) -55 Pub Sq -Ste 1775
-Cleveland 44113 **Fx:**621-1127

(216) 382-1496 .. **Henry,** Alice K '65 -5001 Mayfld Rd -Ste 102 -Cleveland 44124
Henry, Cynthia L '85 -3856 Jones Rd -Diamond 44412

(937) 382-4559 .. **Henry,** David M '91 Clinton Cnty Pros -103 E Main
-Wilmington 45177 **Fx:**382-6278

(419) 448-4575 .. **Henry,** Dean C '90 (Behm & H) -187 S Wshngtn -Tiffin 44883
Fx:448-0543

(937) 748-5162 .. **Henry,** Deborah J '03 %Eckert & E, Co LPA -15 E Mill
-Springboro 45066 **Fx:**748-5163

(216) 241-6602 .. **Henry,** Deirdre G '77 (Weston HFP&H LLP) -50 Pub Sq
-2500 Trmnl Twr -Cleveland 44113 **Fx:**621-8369

(614) 224-9207 .. **Henry,** George L '72 Title First Agncy,Inc -555 S Front -Ste 400
-Columbus 43213

(740) 446-7889 .. **Henry,** James R '03 -21 Locust -Gallipolis 45631 **Fx:**446-3077

(614) 716-1612 .. **Henry,** Janet Jay '84 Amer Elec Pwr Co -1 Riverside Plz
-Columbus 43215

(317) 846-6514 .. **Henry,** Jolie B '00 %Campbell KP LLP -11595 N Meridian -Ste 701
-Carmel, IN 46032 **Fx:**843-8097

(336) 993-7958 .. **Henry,** Katherine Flynn '04 OfCnsl Anderson K & Assoc,PC
-233 W Mtn -Kernersville, NC 27284 **Fx:**993-7964

(216) 433-2313 .. **Henry,** Laura A '83 NASA -21000 Brookpark Rd -MS 500-118
-Cleveland 44135

(216) 830-2770 .. **Henry,** Lynn M '84 Neighborhood Progress Inc -1956 W 25th
-Ste 200 -Cleveland 44113

(419) 241-6000 .. **Henry,** Michael P '94 (Eastman & S Ltd) -1 Seagate -24th Fl
-Bx10032 -Toledo 43699 **Fx:**247-1777

(937) 456-4941 .. **Henry,** Paul D '81 Mun Ct Judge -Bx65 -Eaton 45320 **Fx:**456-4685

(330) 725-4929 .. **Henry,** Phillip J '99 %Oberholtzer F&L -39 Pub Sq -Ste 201 -Bx220
-Medina 44258 **Fx:**723-4929

(937) 226-1212 .. **Henry,** R Mark '93 (Skelton MG&H) -130 W 2nd -Ste 450
-Dayton 45402

(217) 785-9007 .. **Henry,** William C '81 Atty Gen -500 S 2nd -Pub Aid Div
-Springfield, IL 62706

(614) 486-4584 .. **Henry,** William D '53 -1830 Waltham -Columbus 43221

(419) 445-8815 .. **Hensal,** James E '71 (Plassman RHS&H) -302 N Defiance -Bx178
-Archbold 43502 **Fx:**445-1080

(330) 725-4929 .. **Hensal,** Jennifer L '93 (Oberholtzer F&L) -39 Pub Sq -Ste 201
-Bx220 -Medina 44258 **Fx:**723-4929

(614) 221-8448 .. **Hensel,** Jan E '88 (Buckingham D&B,LLP)
-191 W Nationwide Blvd -Ste 300 -Bx151120 -Columbus 43215
Fx:221-8590

(330) 666-6400 .. **Henshaw,** James M '81 (Dobbins & H) -1000 S
Cleveland-Massillon Rd -Ste 105 -Akron 44333

(330) 864-8866 .. **Henshaw,** Jean M '86 State Farm Ins -1653 Merriman Rd -Ste 108
-Akron 44313

(419) 517-7000 .. **Hensien,** Christopher J '03 %Kenney & N,Ltd -5470 Main -Ste 300
-Sylvania 43560 **Fx:**517-7001

(513) 243-6065 .. **Hensley,** Douglas L '93 GE Transportation -1 Neumann Way
-MD J104 -Cincinnati 45215

(937) 496-7231 .. **Hensley,** James A Jr. '87 Cnty Ct 2 Judge -6111 Taylorsvll Rd
-Huber Heights 45424

(937) 687-9099 .. **Hensley,** James A Sr. '78 Cnty Ct 1 Judge -195 S Clayton Rd
-New Lebanon 45345

(614) 249-6584 .. **Hensley,** Kimberly S '94 Atty Gen -1 Nationwide Plz -1-09-VO
-Columbus 43215

(740) 654-4141 .. **Hensley,** Paul R '97 %Stebelton A&S,LPA -109 N Broad -Bx130
-Lancaster 43130 **Fx:**654-2521
Hensley, William F '04 -(Address Unavailable)

(614) 217-1111 .. **Henson,** James J '79 Stonehenge Fincl Holdings,Inc
-191 W Nationwide Blvd -Ste 600 -Columbus 43215

(216) 348-1700 .. **Hentemann,** Henry A '63 (Davis & Y) -101 Prospect Av W
-Ste 1700 -Cleveland 44115 **Fx:**621-0602

(440) 942-5900 .. **Hentemann**, Paul H '62 -35000 Kaiser Ct -Ste 305
-Willoughby 44094 Fx:942-0451

(330) 797-1717 .. **Hepfner**, Donald C '89 -21 N Wickliffe Cir -Youngstown 44515

(614) 249-4420 .. **Herath**, Kirk Matthew '94 Nationwide Ins Co -One Nationwide Plz
-1-27-06 -Columbus 43215

(614) 873-8542 .. **Herb**, Wendy M '91 -7525 Cook Rd -Powell 43065
Herbaugh, Phillip L '95 -1655 W Market -Ste 400 -Akron 44313

(513) 539-3131 .. **Herbe**, Diana J '82 OH Edu Assoc -30 Overbrook Dr -Ste A
-Monroe 45050

(330) 744-4481 .. **Herberger**, Robert J Jr. '90 (McLauglin & M) -500 City Centre One
-Bx507 -Youngstown 44501 Fx:744-0444

(440) 243-2458 .. **Herbers**, Keith M '76 -7844 Normandie Blvd -Ste L-32
-Middleburg Heights 44130

(330) 499-1016 .. **Herbert & Benson** -4571 Stephen Cir NW -Canton 44718
Fx:499-0790

(330) 499-1016 .. **Herbert**, David L '74 (Herbert & B) -4571 Stephen Cir NW
-Canton 44718 Fx:499-0790

(419) 241-9000 .. **Herbert**, Edwin L III '75 (Shumaker L&K,LLP) -1000 Jackson
-Toledo 43624 Fx:241-6894

(937) 223-8177 .. **Herbert**, J Stephen '78 (Coolidge WW&L) -33 W 1st -Ste 600
-Dayton 45402 Fx:223-6705

(614) 764-0681 .. **Herbert**, John W '75 (Blaugrund H&M,Inc) -5455 Rings Rd
-Ste 500 -Dublin 43017 Fx:764-0774

(216) 623-0150 .. **Herbert**, Joseph E '92 (Roetzel & A,LPA) -1375 E 9th
-One Cleve Ctr 9th Fl -Cleveland 44114 Fx:623-0134

(513) 684-3201 .. **Herbert**, Nancy B '78 IRS Chief Cnsl -312 Elm -Ste 2350
-Cincinnati 45202

(614) 645-7657 .. **Herbert**, Paul M II '87 Franklin Cnty Mun Ct -375 S High -4th Fl
-Columbus 43215

(614) 464-6400 .. **Herbert**, Sarah L '04 %Vorys SS&P LLP -52 E Gay -Bx1008
-Columbus 43216 Fx:464-6350

(513) 946-5840 .. **Herberth**, Gretta M '03 Hamilton Cnty Common Pleas Ct
-1000 Main -#380 -Cincinnati 45202

(614) 443-4866 .. **Herd**, David A '92 %J Nemeth & Assoc -21 E Frankfort
-Columbus 43206 Fx:443-4860

(614) 444-5290 .. **Herder**, Mark A '93 -901 S High -Columbus 43206

(937) 228-0894 .. **Herdman**, Douglas '83 -130 W 2nd -Ste 2100 -Dayton 45402
Fx:461-2923

(513) 932-3221 .. **Herdman**, Paul N '51 -Bx 36 -Lebanon 45036

(740) 342-5511 .. **Herendeen**, Stephen R '85 Perry Cnty Pros -Bx569
-New Lexington 43764

(859) 291-0202 .. **Herfel**, Gary L '71 (Herfel & B) -100 E RiverCenter Blvd -Ste 250
-Covington, KY 41011

(937) 325-2000 .. **Herier**, David D '98 %D Geyer & Assoc -451 Upper Valley Pike
-Springfield 45504 Fx:325-8800

(419) 353-3886 .. **Heringhaus**, Pamela A '81 -124 E Court -Bowling Green 43402

(330) 562-3156 .. **Herington**, Leigh E '76 Christley H&P -215 W Garfld -Ste 230
-Aurora 44202 Fx:562-9540

(614) 464-6400 .. **Herlihy**, Kimberly Weber '97 (Vorys SS&P LLP) -52 E Gay
-Bx1008 -Columbus 43216 Fx:464-6350

(937) 449-2800 .. **Herman**, Carrie E '03 %Chernesky H&K PLL -10 Cthse Plz SW
-Ste 1100 -Dayton 45402 Fx:449-2821

(330) 364-3523 .. **Herman**, Christopher T '03 Tuscarawas Cnty Pub Def
-153 N Bway -New Philadelphia 44663

(202) 639-5900 .. **Herman**, David J '00 Natl Food Processors Assn -1350 I NW
-Ste 300 -Washington, DC 20005

(330) 535-2174 .. **Herman**, John F '68 (J Herman Co,LPA) -106 S Main -Ste 1800
-Akron 44308

(202) 572-8713 .. **Herman**, Kelly S '00 Bureau Cstms & Brdr Prtctn
-1300 Penn Av NW -Mint Annx -Washington, DC 20229
Fx:572-8727

(614) 292-2163 .. **Herman**, Lawrence '53 OSU Moritz Cllg of Law -55 W 12th Av
-Columbus 43210 Fx:292-1383

(614) 221-1191 .. **Herman**, Richard A '90 Don Castro Org -4200 Regent -Ste 200
-Columbus 43219

(216) 696-6170 .. **Herman**, Richard T '93 (RT Herman & Assoc) -815 Superior Av
-Ste 1910 -Cleveland 44114 Fx:696-0104

(440) 576-3662 .. **Herman**, Robert L '92 Ashtabula Cnty Pros -25 W Jffrsn
-Jefferson 44047

(419) 784-3700 .. **Herman**, Russell R '97 Defiance Cnty Pros -607 W 3rd
-Defiance 43512 Fx:782-0594

(614) 222-1889 .. **Herman**, Steven E '98 (S Herman Co,LPA) -529 S 3rd
-Columbus 43215
Hermanies, John H '48 -1201 Edgecliff Rd -Cincinnati 45206

(216) 781-5515 .. **Hermann Cahn & Schneider, LLP** -1301 E 9th -Ste 500
-Cleveland 44114 Fx:781-1030

(216) 781-5515 .. **Hermann**, Gary D '71 (Hermann C&S,LLP) -1301 E 9th -Ste 500
-Cleveland 44114 Fx:781-1030

(419) 523-5777 .. **Hermiller**, Gregory J '99 (Niese H&S,LLC) -1800 N Perry -Ste 104
-Ottawa 45875

(419) 228-9002 .. **Hermon**, Gary R '66 G Hermon Co,LPA -400 W North
-Lima 45801

(972) 906-8662 .. **Hernandez**, Carlos M '85 Fleming Co,Inc -1945 Lakepointe Dr
-Lewisville, TX 75057

(216) 443-7295 .. **Hernandez**, Juan C '87 Cuyahoga Cnty Pub Def -1849
Prospect Av -Ste 222 -Cleveland 44115

(419) 255-0814 .. **Hernandez**, Patricia Y '94 ABLE -520 Mad Av -740 Spitzer Bldg
-Toledo 43604 Fx:259-2880

(614) 221-8448 .. **Hernandez**, Richard A '86 (Buckingham D&B,LLP)
-191 W Nationwide Blvd -Ste 300 -Bx151120 -Columbus 43215
Fx:221-8590

(937) 236-6444 .. **Herndon**, John A '96 -7460 Brandt Pike -Huber Heights 45424

(502) 587-5427 .. **Herndon**, Lisa A '02 %Mapother & M,PSC -801 W Jffrsn
-Louisville, KY 40202 Fx:587-5444

(513) 421-1313 .. **Herndon**, Richard D '86 (Griffin-F,LLP) -3500 Redbank Rd
-Cincinnati 45227 Fx:421-1118

(937) 449-6810 .. **Heron**, John J '65 (Porter WM&A LLP) -1 S Main -Ste 1600
-Dayton 45402 Fx:449-6820

(937) 443-6615 .. **Herr**, James Michael '68 (Thompson H LLP) -2000 Cthse Plz NE
-Bx8801 -Dayton 45401 Fx:443-6635

(513) 423-1680 .. **Herr**, John W '66 -2 N Main -Ste 703 -Middletown 45042

(419) 213-4700 .. **Herr**, Mark T '89 %Lucas Cnty Pros -Adams & Erie
-Lucas Cnty Cthse -Toledo 43624

(513) 684-3211 .. **Herrell**, Robin L '84 IRS Dist Cnsl -312 Elm -Ste 2300
-Cincinnati 45202

(304) 733-1126 .. **Herrenkohl**, Amy M '92 -Bx554 -Barboursville, WV 25504

(717) 295-6561 .. **Herrera**, Carlos M '95 Thomson-Lancaster Patent Ops -1002 New
Holland Av -Lancaster, PA 17601

(440) 247-6060 .. **Herrick**, Craig W '91 -7181 Chagrin Rd -Ste 240
-Chagrin Falls 44023

(216) 682-0141 .. **Herrick**, John F '63 -3700 Park E Dr -Ofc 470 -Beachwood 44122

(419) 245-1020 .. **Herring**, Barbara E '84 Law Dept -One Govt Ctr -Ste 2250
-Toledo 43604 Fx:245-1090

(614) 890-4801 .. **Herrington**, Claudia S '97 Mark A Evans & Assoc -283 E State
-Ste 201 -Westerville 43081

(216) 642-3342 .. **Herrington**, David W '86 %Wegman H&V,LPA
-6055 Rockside Wds Blvd -Ste 200 -Cleveland 44131
Fx:642-8826

(330) 864-3840 .. **Herrington**, Linda M '75 -255 N Portage Path -#515 -Akron 44303

(330) 747-4404 .. **Herriott**, Donald P '74 Newman O&K,LPA -11 Fed Plz Central
-Ste 1200 -Youngstown 44503 Fx:747-6056
Herriott, Scott H '75 -1069 Carraway Ln -Milford 45150

(202) 514-4325 .. **Herriott**, Heide L '98 US DOJ -1100 L NW -Washington,
DC 20530 Fx:514-7969

(513) 768-7403 .. **Herrmann**, Julie R '93 Alderwood Grp Intl -311 Elm -Ste 1000
-Cincinnati 45202

(414) 287-1266 .. **Herrmann**, Leslye A '94 (von Briesen & R,SC) -411 E Wscnsn Av
-Ste 700 -Bx3262 -Milwaukee, WI 53201 Fx:276-6281

(216) 586-3939 .. **Herrmann**, Mark '90 (Jones D) -901 Lakeside Av
-Cleveland 44114 Fx:579-0212

(330) 972-6462 .. **Herrnstein**, Becky H '85 Univ of Akron -114 Buchtel Hall
-Akron 44325

(330) 929-2676 .. **Herrnstein**, John M '83 (Hoover H&H Co,LPA) -527 Portage Trl
-Cuyahoga Falls 44221

(513) 529-2945 .. **Herron**, Daniel J '78 Miami University -120 Upham Hall
-Dept of Finance -Oxford 45056

(513) 534-4900 .. **Herron**, David L '96 -38 Fountain Square Plz -MD 10907E
-Cincinnati 45263

(614) 232-7072 .. **Herron**, Katherine R '04 Ernst & Y,LLP -41 S High -Ste 1100
-Columbus 43215

(216) 621-9721 .. **Herron**, Mark P '91 -55 Pub Sq -Ste 650 -Cleveland 44113
Fx:621-6006

(937) 223-1201 .. **Herron**, Philip B '66 (Altick & C Co,LPA) -1 S Main
-1700 One Dayton Ctr -Dayton 45402 Fx:223-5100

(330) 420-0140 .. **Herron**, Robert L '77 Columbiana Cnty Pros -105 S Market
-Lisbon 44432 Fx:424-0944

(330) 722-1957 .. **Herron**, Sunny N '91 -209 S Bway -Medina 44256

(330) 467-5030 .. **Hersch**, John F '77 UAW Legal Srvc Plan -8536 Crow Dr -Ste 110
-Macedonia 44056

(216) 292-1880 .. **Hersch**, Marvin H '54 -24100 Chagrin Blvd -Ste 330
-Beachwood 44122 Fx:292-1876

(614) 469-3939 .. **Hersch**, Thomas J '01 %Jones D -325 John H McConnell Blvd
-Ste 600 -Bx165017 -Columbus 43216 Fx:461-4198

(419) 241-1150 .. **Herschel Accettola Bloom Mills & Manore** -615 Adams
-Toledo 43604 Fx:241-7825

(419) 241-1150 .. **Herschel**, Henry B '67 (Herschel ABM&M) -615 Adams
-Toledo 43604 Fx:241-7825

(513) 333-4020 .. **Hersh**, Gail C Jr. '92 %Weltman W&R Co,LPA -525 Vine -Ste 800
-Cincinnati 45202 Fx:723-2239

(614) 466-3998 .. **Hersh**, Jeffrey M '75 Unemploymnt Comp Commssn -145 S Front
-Bx182299 -Columbus 43218

(614) 461-1156 .. **Hershberger**, Eric B '91 %Webster & Assoc -2 Miranova Pl
-Ste 310 -Columbus 43215

(740) 264-1651 .. **Hershey**, Adrian V '75 (Blake H&B) -4110 Sunset Blvd
-Steubenville 43952

(202) 349-4186 .. **Hershey**, Loren W '76 -1725 I NW -Ste 300
-Washington, DC 20006

(419) 244-8336 .. **Hershman**, Howard B '78 %Gressley K&P -608 Mad Av -Ste 930
-Toledo 43604 Fx:244-1914

(513) 627-0633 .. **Hersko**, Bart S '86 Procter & Gamble Co -Miami Valley Labs
-Bx538707 -Cincinnati 45253

(614) 466-8240 .. **Hertel**, Kari B '96 Atty Gen -30 E Broad -Columbus 43215
Fx:728-2392

(614) 463-9770 .. **Hertenstein**, Edward C '76 (Roetzel & A,LPA) -155 E Broad
-Natl City Ctr 12th Fl -Columbus 43215 Fx:463-9792

(440) 331-4660 .. **Herthneck**, Richard E '73 -20220 Ctr Ridge Rd -Ste 160
-Rocky River 44116

(513) 977-8200 .. **Hertlein**, Charles F Jr. '80 (Dinsmore & S LLP) -255 E 5th
-Ste 1900 -Cincinnati 45202 Fx:977-8141

(614) 644-2658 .. **Hertlein**, Douglas L '88 Dept Ins -2100 Stella Ct -Columbus 43215

(330) 725-0531 .. **Hertrick**, Paul W '75 (Laribee H&K) -325 N Bway -Bx445
-Medina 44258

(859) 441-6840 .. **Hertz**, Giles T '01 -1125 Johns Hill Rd -Wilder, KY 41076

(415) 956-7700 .. **Hertzer**, J David '64 -611 Wshngtn -Ste 2204 -San
Francisco, CA 94111 Fx:956-7704

(202) 408-4600 .. **Hertzfeld**, Andrea Lynn '04 %Cohen MH&T,PLLC
-1100 NY Av NW -Ste 500 W Twr -Washington, DC 20005
Fx:408-4699

(513) 241-3685 .. **Hertzman**, Glenda M '79 (White G&M Co,LPA) -1 W 4th -Ste 1700
-Cincinnati 45202 Fx:241-2399

(216) 689-8328 .. **Herubin**, John F '87 McDonald Invstmnts,Inc -127 Pub Sq
-Mailcode-OH-01-27-1507 -Cleveland 44114

(216) 621-0200 .. **Hervey**, Michelle M '00 %Baker & H LLP -1900 E 9th -Ste 3200
-Cleveland 44114 Fx:696-0740

(330) 437-0026 .. **Hervey**, Paul B '84 -101 Central Plz S -300 Bank One Twr
-Canton 44702

(740) 942-2621 .. **Hervey**, Thomas S '97 Harrison Cnty Pros -111 W Warren -Bx248
-Cadiz 43907

(412) 553-4439 .. **Herwald**, Michelle L '92 Alcoa,Inc -201 Isabella
-Pittsburgh, PA 15212

(419) 245-1200 .. **Herwat**, Stephen J '03 Lucas Cnty Plan Comm -One Govt Ctr
-Ste 1620 -Toledo 43604

(513) 533-0888 .. **Hery**, Mary J '79 -2444 Madison Rd -#102 -Cincinnati 45208

(614) 837-6151 .. **Herzberger**, Brian L '82 (Herzberger & Assoc Co,LPA)
-125 W Waterloo -Canal Winchester 43110

(216) 586-3939 .. **Herzberger**, William A '87 (Jones D) -901 Lakeside Av
-Cleveland 44114 Fx:579-0212

(440) 930-8065 .. **Herzer**, David L '70 Wickens HPC&B -35765 Chester Rd -Avon 44011 **Fx**:937-4466

(513) 722-2441 .. **Herzner**, Richard S '01 Sax Rlty Grp,Inc -1785 State Route 28 -Goshen 45122

(740) 363-2600 .. **Herzog**, Louis H '98 (Burkam F&H) -43 E Central Av -Delaware 43015

(859) 781-8593 .. **Herzog**, Stephen B '89 -75 Bluegrass Av -Fort Thomas, KY 41075

(419) 468-1766 .. **Hesby**, Philip S '50 -Box 804 -Galion 44833

(513) 731-6601 .. **Hesch**, William E '80 (W Hesch Law Firm) -3047 Madison Rd -Ste 205 -Cincinnati 45209

(216) 522-3878 .. **Heslop**, Bruce C '72 Dept of Labor -1240 E 9th -Rm 881 -Cleveland 44199

(614) 442-5800 .. **Hess**, Charles W '81 -7211 Sawmill Rd -Ste 200 -Dublin 43016

(937) 223-1788 .. **Hess**, Douglas A '84 (Hess & D Co,LPA) -3946 Kettering Blvd -Kettering 45439 **Fx**:223-1789

(216) 687-1311 .. **Hess**, Erin S '05 %Reminger & R -101 Prospect Av W -1400 Mdlnd Bldg -Cleveland 44115 **Fx**:687-1841

(419) 865-8021 .. **Hess**, Harry R Jr. '70 %Balk H&M -5744 Southwyck Blvd -Toledo 43614 **Fx**:865-9105

(614) 827-7300 .. **Hess**, Kevin E '04 %Freund F&A -65 E State -Ste 800 -Columbus 43215 **Fx**:827-7303

(937) 427-4360 .. **Hess**, Loren H '92 Upper Mohawk,Inc -1321 Rsrch Park Dr -Beavercreek 45432

(614) 445-8287 .. **Hess**, Michael D '01 -825 S Front -Columbus 43206

(602) 216-6583 .. **Hess**, Otis R Jr. '64 Century Ins Grp -4722 N 24th -Ste 200 -Phoenix, AZ 85016 **Fx**:371-0113

(614) 225-9000 .. **Hess**, Paul J Jr. '81 %Garvin & H,LLC -181 E Lvngstn Av -Columbus 43215 **Fx**:225-9080

(614) 462-5441 .. **Hess**, Paul R '86 (Kegler BH&R) -65 E State -Ste 1800 -Columbus 43215 **Fx**:464-2634

(614) 857-9590 .. **Hess**, Rebecca J '84 MN Khorrami -115 W Main -Ste 400 -Columbus 43215 **Fx**:228-0701

(419) 354-9250 .. **Hess**, Renee E '92 %Wood Cnty Pros -One Cthse Sq -Bowling Green 43402 **Fx**:353-2904

(740) 774-6152 .. **Hess**, Robert C '74 -14 S Paint -Rm 2 Foulke Block -Chillicothe 45601 **Fx**:774-6153

(614) 462-5889 .. **Hess**, Stephanie E '01 Franklin Cnty Common Pleas Ct -369 S High -Ctrm 7A -Columbus 43215

(440) 350-3200 .. **Hess**, Terry E '02 Lake Cnty Pub Def -125 E Erie -Painesville 44077

(614) 221-8448 .. **Hess**, Thomas W '76 (Buckingham D&B,LLP) -191 W Nationwide Blvd -Ste 300 -Bx151120 -Columbus 43215 **Fx**:221-8590

(216) 292-4900 .. **Hess**, Timothy A '02 %Peltz & B -23230 Chagrin Blvd -Ste 715 -Beachwood 44122 **Fx**:292-4942

(513) 455-7600 .. **Hess**, W Ashley '03 %Greenebaum D&M PLLC -255 E 5th -2800 Chemed Ctr -Cincinnati 45202 **Fx**:455-8500

(330) 490-4522 .. **Hesse**, Chad F '00 Cnsl Diebold,Inc -5995 Mayfair Rd -Bx3077 -North Canton 44720 **Fx**:490-4450

(937) 222-2424 .. **Hesse**, Lisa A '89 %Freund F&A -1 S Main -Ste 1800 -Dayton 45402 **Fx**:222-5369

(330) 836-8523 .. **Hesske**, Constance A '93 -1655 W Market -#130 -Akron 44313

(216) 642-3342 .. **Hessler**, David J '68 (Wegman H&V,LPA) -6055 Rockside Wds Blvd -Ste 200 -Cleveland 44131 **Fx**:642-8826

(216) 368-2769 .. **Hessler**, Katherine M '96 CWRU Law Schl -11075 East Blvd -Cleveland 44106

(216) 642-3342 .. **Hessler**, Nathan E '95 %Wegman H&V,LPA -6055 Rockside Wds Blvd -Ste 200 -Cleveland 44131 **Fx**:642-8826

(216) 642-3342 .. **Hessler**, Peter A '78 (Wegman H&V,LPA) -6055 Rockside Wds Blvd -Ste 200 -Cleveland 44131 **Fx**:642-8826

(614) 764-3174 .. **Hessler**, Robert J '79 Wendys Intl -4288 W Dublin-Granvll Rd -Franchise Devlpmnt -Bx256 -Dublin 43017

(216) 443-8262 .. **Hessler**, Stephanie E '03 Probate Ct -1 Lakeside Av -Cleveland 44113

(602) 234-7800 .. **Hester**, Chad A '03 %Jennings H&C,LLP -2800 N Central Av -Ste 1800 -Phoenix, AZ 85004 **Fx**:277-5595

(336) 545-7300 .. **Hester**, Stephen M '77 Greensboro Assoc Inc -3300 Battleground Av -Ste 301 -Greensboro, NC 27410

(330) 666-6400 .. **Hete**, Emily M '97 %Dobbins & H -1000 S Cleveland-Massillon Rd -Ste 105 -Akron 44333

(614) 464-4100 .. **Hetterscheidt**, Robert C '76 (AuCoin DH&Y LLC) -495 S High -Ste 250 -Columbus 43215

(419) 882-5755 .. **Hetzer**, Nicholas W '78 (Hetzer & W) -5800 Monroe -Bldg C -Sylvania 43560

(513) 721-2220 .. **Heuck**, Kenneth Jr. '70 -36 E 7th -Ste 1540 -Cincinnati 45202

(513) 621-0267 .. **Heuck**, Robert II '91 Waite SB&C -1 W 4th -1513 4th & Vine Twr -Cincinnati 45202

(614) 987-1500 .. **Heuer**, Joseph Y '04 Big Lots Stores,Inc -300 Phillipi Rd -Columbus 43228

(419) 241-6000 .. **Heuerman**, Henry N '70 (Eastman & S Ltd) -1 Seagate -24th Fl -Bx10032 -Toledo 43699 **Fx**:247-1777

(614) 644-9529 .. **Heuerman**, Mark R '89 OH Dept Commerce -77 S High -Columbus 43266

(216) 241-1000 .. **Heutsche**, John V '73 J Heutsche Co,LPA -310 W Lakeside Av -500 Cthse Sq -Cleveland 44113

(216) 586-3939 .. **Hewitt**, Christopher J '98 (Jones D) -901 Lakeside Av -Cleveland 44114 **Fx**:579-0212

(216) 755-5500 .. **Hewitt**, Erin C '04 Developers Diversified Rlty Corp -3300 Enterprise Pkwy -Beachwood 44122

(513) 731-4247 .. **Hewitt**, Harry L '00 -7374 Reading Rd -Ste 117 -Cincinnati 45237

(216) 241-5700 .. **Hewitt**, James H III '80 (J Hewitt Co, LPA) -3043 Superior Av -Cleveland 44114

(212) 526-3533 .. **Hewitt**, John R '74 OfCnsl Mayer B&P -1675 Bway -New York, NY 10019

(937) 865-6800 .. **Hewitt**, Robin R '96 Lexis/Nexis -Bx933 -Dayton 45401

(330) 666-7250 .. **Hewitt**, William B '63 -4020 Stonebrdg -Copley 44321

(330) 666-7250 .. **Hewitt**, William W '84 -4020 Stonebrdg Blvd -Copley 44321

(513) 684-9700 .. **Hext**, Stephen R '72 -14 Garfld Pl -Ste 300 -Cincinnati 45202

(513) 621-6464 .. **Heyd**, Daniel C '86 (Graydon H&R LLP) -511 Walnut -1900 Fifth Third Ctr -Cincinnati 45202 **Fx**:651-3836

(513) 243-6678 .. **Heyd**, Joseph D '95 Cnsl GE Aircraft Engines -1 Neumann Way -MD J104 -Cincinnati 45215

(614) 410-6740 .. **Heydinger**, Mark C '83 %Contract Cnsl -470 Olde Worthngtn Rd -Ste 200 -Westerville 43082

(937) 593-6065 .. **Heydinger**, Thomas A '58 (Thompson DHMW&T) -1111 Rush Av -Bx68 -Bellefontaine 43311

(330) 929-2676 .. **Heydorn**, Robert W '75 (Hoover H&H Co,LPA) -527 Portage Trl -Cuyahoga Falls 44221

(202) 616-9931 .. **Heyer**, Michelle L '95 US DOJ -1301 NY Av NW -Ste 200 -Washington, DC 20530

(440) 942-6276 .. **Heyl**, Bonnie M '87 -2956 Sherbrooke Valley Ct -Willoughby Hills 44094

(614) 253-5411 .. **Heyman**, Ian A '98 BT Bingo -1300 Alum Crk Dr -Columbus 43209

(937) 449-2800 .. **Heyman**, Ralph E '56 (Chernesky H&K PLL) -10 Cthse Plz SW -Ste 1100 -Dayton 45402 **Fx**:449-2821

(419) 836-9955 .. **Heyman**, Richard A '98 -6601 Spring Beauty Ct -Curtice 43412

(216) 687-5508 .. **Heyward**, Carole O '93 CSU-Marshall Cllg of Law -2121 Euclid Av -LB138 -Cleveland 44115 **Fx**:687-6881

(419) 241-1200 .. **Heywood**, Susan M '02 %Cooper & W,LPA -900 Adams -Toledo 43624 **Fx**:242-5675

(419) 321-1262 .. **Heywood**, William H III '69 (Shumaker L&K,LLP) -1000 Jackson -Toledo 43624 **Fx**:241-6894

(216) 222-1087 .. **Hibbs**, Lisa A '98 Natl City Corp -1900 E 9th -Loc 01-3030 -Cleveland 44114

(216) 525-2626 .. **Hice**, Brooke M '00 Heidelberg Distributing Co -9101 E Plsnt Vlly Rd -Independence 44131 **Fx**:525-2620

(513) 946-3142 .. **Hickenlooper**, Smith D '00 Hamilton Cnty Pros -230 E 9th -Cincinnati 45202 **Fx**:946-3017

(864) 240-3246 .. **Hickey**, Bryan F '73 (Haynsworth SB PA) -75 Beattie Pl -Bx2048 -Greenville, SC 29602 **Fx**:250-5642

(419) 382-0292 .. **Hickey**, Charles J '88 -4354 Rvr Rd -Toledo 43614

(216) 241-1872 .. **Hickey**, Christopher J '95 SrCnsl B Coon & Assoc -1220 W 6th -Ste 303 -Cleveland 44113 **Fx**:241-1873

(937) 328-3741 .. **Hickey**, Christopher J '99 City Pros -50 E Columbia -Springfield 45502 **Fx**:328-3744

(419) 383-5533 .. **Hickey**, Daniel P '03 Mdcl College of OH -1015 Grdn Lk Pkwy -Toledo 43614

(216) 443-7800 .. **Hickey**, Elizabeth A '81 Cuyahoga Cnty Pros -1200 Ontario -8th Fl -Cleveland 44113 **Fx**:698-2270

(937) 452-7214 .. **Hickey**, Firmin A Jr. '01 -6871 Camden Rd -Camden 45311

(216) 861-6000 .. **Hickey**, Geoffrey S '01 %Miller S&B -2000 E 9th -Ste 1100 -Cleveland 44115

(937) 298-7584 .. **Hickey**, James P '68 -4 E Schantz Av -Dayton 45409

(216) 749-6556 .. **Hickey**, John W '63 -3794 Pearl Rd -Cleveland 44109

(614) 225-9000 .. **Hickey**, Michael J '68 (Garvin & H,LLC) -181 E Lvngstn Av -Columbus 43215 **Fx**:225-9080

(513) 651-6800 .. **Hickey**, Nicole Vickroy '95 (Frost BT LLC) -201 E 5th -2200 PNC Ctr -Cincinnati 45202 **Fx**:651-6981

(937) 775-3326 .. **Hickey**, Robert E Jr. '74 Wright State Univ -3640 Col Glenn Hwy -Dayton 45435 **Fx**:775-3696

(216) 749-6556 .. **Hickey**, Theresa A '86 %J Hickey -3794 Pearl Rd -Cleveland 44109

(513) 721-1904 .. **Hickey**, Timothy A '71 T Hickey Co,LPA -1014 Vine -2525 Kroger Bldg -Cincinnati 45202

(216) 861-0360 .. **Hickman**, Franklin J '73 (Hickman & L Co,LPA) -1370 Ontario -Ste 1620 -Cleveland 44113 **Fx**:861-3113

(419) 843-9883 .. **Hickman**, Gregg D '78 -3230 Cntrl Pk W -Ste 106 -Toledo 43617

(614) 764-3596 .. **Hickman**, Gregory A '88 Wendys Intl -4288 W Dublin-Granvll Rd -Bx256 -Dublin 43017

(513) 634-5395 .. **Hickman**, Ingrid N '02 Procter & Gamble -6110 Ctr Hill Av -Cincinnati 45224

(330) 434-3000 .. **Hickman**, Jason E '95 %Roderick & L -One Cascade Plz -Ste 1500 -Akron 44308 **Fx**:434-9220

(216) 861-0360 .. **Hickman & Lowder Co, LPA** -1370 Ontario -Ste 1620 -Cleveland 44113 **Fx**:861-3113

(513) 459-0492 .. **Hicks**, Andrea N '94 -224 Reading Rd -Mason 45040

(614) 644-7772 .. **Hicks**, Britton M '03 Legis Srvc Commssn -77 S High -Columbus 43215 **Fx**:644-1721

(513) 779-9850 .. **Hicks**, Bryan S '95 -7109 Hmltn Mason Rd -Unit C -West Chester 45069

(614) 644-1373 .. **Hicks**, Cassandra L '83 OH Sec of State -180 E Broad -Columbus 43215 **Fx**:466-5409

(419) 381-1148 .. **Hicks**, Cathy S '88 Metropolitan Title -3131 Exec Pkwy -Ste 100 -Toledo 43606

(330) 376-5756 .. **Hicks**, Donald R '83 Emershaw M&S -120 E Mill -#437 -Akron 44308 **Fx**:762-5980

(513) 579-6400 .. **Hicks**, Drew M '03 %Keating M&K PLL -1 E 4th -1400 Provident Twr -Cincinnati 45202 **Fx**:579-6457

(216) 685-1108 .. **Hicks**, George R Jr. '88 (Weltman W&R Co,LPA) -323 W Lakeside Av -Ste 200 -Cleveland 44113 **Fx**:363-4121

(330) 392-8397 .. **Hicks**, Gregory V '85 (GV Hicks Co,LPA) -Bx1068 -Warren 44482

(419) 354-9244 .. **Hicks**, James S '82 Wood Cnty Pub Def -123 N Summit -Bowling Green 43402

(304) 525-3201 .. **Hicks**, Kenneth P '01 Kenneth Paul Hicks -742 4th Av -Huntington, WV 25701

(304) 420-5510 .. **Hicks**, Paul L '03 %Bowles RMG&L PLLC -501 Avry -5th Fl -Bx49 -Parkersburg, WV 26102 **Fx**:420-5587

(440) 424-0058 .. **Hicks**, Robert C '99 Fidelity Natl -30825 Aurora Rd -Ste 140 -Solon 44139

(614) 487-5900 .. **Hicks**, Sharon A '03 %S Vourlis -1500 W 3rd Av -Ste 400 -Columbus 43212 **Fx**:481-7905

(513) 984-1899 .. **Hicks**, Steven R '90 (S Hicks,Inc) -10999 Reed Hartman Hwy -Ste 324 -Cincinnati 45242

(440) 285-2242 .. **Hicks**, Todd C '94 Thrasher D&D,LPA -100 7th Av -Ste 150 -Chardon 44024 **Fx**:285-9423

(937) 322-0891 .. **Hicks**, William C '74 Cole AH&D -333 N Limestone -Bx1687 -Springfield 45501 **Fx**:322-9931

(513) 352-3613 .. **Hicks**, William C '97 Law Dept -801 Plum -Rm 214 -Cincinnati 45202 **Fx**:352-1515

(419) 245-1060 .. **Hicks-Hudson**, Paula S '82 Law Dept -One Govt Ctr -Ste 2250 -Toledo 43604 **Fx**:245-1090

(419) 946-6055 .. **Hickson**, Robert C Jr. '83 -22 S Main -Bx 166 -Mount Gilead 43338

(330) 544-7818 ..**Hickton**, Dawne S '98 Cnsl RTI Intl Metals Inc -1000 Warren Av
-Bx269 -Niles 44446 **Fx:**544-7701

(216) 928-2200 ..**Hidek**, Christina T '00 %Sutter OM&F -1301 E 9th
-3600 Erievw Twr -Cleveland 44114 **Fx:**928-4400

(513) 785-5729 ..**Hider**, Patricia A '95 Butler Cnty Common Pleas Ct
-Old Ct Hse-1st Fl -101 High -Hamilton 45011

(937) 426-9564 ..**Hidy**, Joseph D '03 Hidy Honda -2300 Heller Dr
-Beavercreek 45434

(513) 946-3000 ..**Hidy**, Kathleen M '92 %Hamilton Cnty Pros -230 E 9th
-Cincinnati 45202 **Fx:**946-3017

(513) 632-4132 ..**Hidy**, Richard J '88 Firstar Corp -425 Walnut -Cincinnati 45202

(513) 984-0061 ..**Hieatt**, Jennifer F '96 Fraley Consulting -9309 Mntgmry Rd
-Cincinnati 45242

(513) 243-1025 ..**Hieatt**, Steven W '96 GE Aircraft Engineers -1 Neumann Way
-MD F17 -Cincinnati 45215

(937) 848-3461 ..**Hieber**, Raymond C '57 -3879 W Franklin -Bellbrook 45305

(440) 576-4166 ..**Hiener**, Michael A '86 -Bx1 -Jefferson 44047

(614) 462-3555 ..**Hiers**, Amy Lu '95 Franklin Cnty Pros -373 S High
-Columbus 43215

(937) 225-5770 ..**Hiett**, Teresa M '92 Montgomery Cnty Pros -301 W 3rd -Bx972
-Dayton 45422 **Fx:**225-3470

(614) 480-4282 ..**Higbee**, Michael A '85 Huntington Natl Bank -41 S High -HCO733
-Columbus 43215

(216) 360-2124 ..**Higerd**, Jeffrey Jay '75 (Moriarty & J,PLL) -30000 Chagrin Blvd
-Ste 200 -Pepper Pike 44124

(330) 707-0377 ..**Higgins**, Amy L '02 %C Carlin,LLC -62 S Main -Bx5369
-Poland 44514

(440) 350-9270 ..**Higgins**, Charles N Jr. '68 -9930 Johnnycake Ridge Rd -#3C
-Concord 44060

(513) 564-7200 ..**Higgins**, James A '69 6th Dist Ct of Appls -100 E 5th -Cthse
-Cincinnati 45202

(614) 460-4653 ..**Higgins**, Jenny L '91 NiSource Corp Srvcs Inc -200 Civic Ctr Dr
-Leg Dept -Bx117 -Columbus 43216 **Fx:**460-6986

(440) 845-9040 ..**Higgins**, John H '56 -5974 Deering Av -Parma Heights 44130

(513) 651-6800 ..**Higgins**, John S Jr. '97 %Frost BT LLC -201 E 5th -2200 PNC Ctr
-Cincinnati 45202 **Fx:**651-6981

(513) 852-6024 ..**Higgins**, Karen A '98 %Wood & L LLP -600 Vine -Ste 2500
-Cincinnati 45202 **Fx:**852-6087

(505) 222-9454 ..**Higgins**, Leah Straker '02 Atty Gen/CSED -1015 Tigeras NW
-Ste 100 -Albuquerque, NM 87112

(740) 349-6652 ..**Higgins**, Michael F '77 Cnty Mun Ct Judge -40 W Main
-Newark 43055

(419) 423-8746 ..**Higgins**, Patterson W '72 -117 S Main -Findlay 45840

(216) 515-1660 ..**Higgins**, Ralph P Jr. '80 (Frantz W LLP) -127 Pub Sq
-2500 Key Center -Cleveland 44114 **Fx:**515-1650

(614) 248-9727 ..**Higgins**, Thomas P '87 Banc 1 Ins Srvcs Corp -1111 Polaris Pkwy
-Columbus 43240

(330) 867-6600 ..**Higham**, Robert C '04 Glinsek & H -88 S Portage Path -Ste 301
-Akron 44303 **Fx:**867-7020

(330) 867-6600 ..**Higham**, Robert W '69 (Glinsek & H) -88 S Portage Path -Ste 301
-Akron 44303 **Fx:**867-7020

(216) 861-5582 ..**Highman**, Eric M '97 %Fay SFM&M LLP -1100 Superior Av -7th Fl
-Cleveland 44114 **Fx:**241-1666

(419) 246-5760 ..**Higley**, William E II '76 -520 Mad Av -Ste 1048 -Toledo 43604

(614) 224-1222 ..**Hiland**, Tammy L '97 %Maguire & S,LLP -250 Civic Ctr Dr
-Ste 200 -Columbus 43215 **Fx:**224-1236

(419) 321-1390 ..**Hilbert**, John W II '71 (Shumaker L&K,LLP) -1000 Jackson
-Toledo 43624 **Fx:**241-6894

(216) 586-3939 ..**Hilbert**, Peter G '03 %Jones D -901 Lakeside Av
-Cleveland 44114 **Fx:**579-0212

(614) 221-8889 ..**Hilbert**, Rebecca J '85 %Columbus Housing Prtnrshp -562 E Main
-Columbus 43215

(248) 642-8350 ..**Hilborn**, Craig E '01 %Hilborn & H -999 Haynes -Ste 205
-Birmingham, MI 48009

Hilbrands, Kirk A '93 -2619 E Broad -Columbus 43209

(614) 280-0570 ..**Hilburn**, Regina L '91 -118 E Main -Ste 204 -Columbus 43215

(513) 946-3000 ..**Hild**, Allison E '99 Hamilton Cnty Pros -230 E 9th
-Cincinnati 45202 **Fx:**946-3017

(513) 721-4532 ..**Hild**, Guy M '62 (Katz TB&H) -255 E 5th -Ste 2400
-Cincinnati 45202

(419) 946-3846 ..**Hildebrand**, Dale G '52 -23 E High -Bx15 -Mount Gilead 43338

(440) 333-3100 ..**Hildebrand**, John P Sr. '70 (Hildebrand & H) -21430 Lorain Rd
-Fairview Park 44126

(440) 333-3100 ..**Hildebrand**, John P Jr. '97 (Hildebrand & H) -21430 Lorain Rd
-Fairview Park 44126

(703) 614-8734 ..**Hildebrandt**, Arthur H '74 Ofc of the Genl Cnsl
-1000 Navy Pentagon -4D730 -Washington, DC 20350

(216) 621-1006 ..**Hildebrandt**, David W '87 D Hildebrandt Co, LPA
-323 Lakeside Av W -Cleveland 44113

(513) 852-3497 ..**Hildebrandt**, Dolores M '73 Atty Gen -441 Vine -1600 Carew Twr
-Cincinnati 45202 **Fx:**852-3484

(216) 222-9694 ..**Hildebrandt**, Thomas J '81 Natl City Ins Grp Inc -629 Euclid Av
-9th Fl Locator 01-3920 -Cleveland 44114

(614) 466-7264 ..**Hildebrant**, Kristin E '89 OH Legal Rghts Srvc -8 E Long -5th Fl
-Columbus 43215

(937) 222-2030 ..**Hilgeman**, John P '83 Cowan & H -12 W Monument Av
-Dayton 45402

(937) 257-5868 ..**Hilker**, Samuel R '76 AFMC/JA -4225 Logistics Av -Rm N237
-Wright Patterson AFB 45433

(330) 376-5300 ..**Hilkert**, David W '74 (Buckingham D&B,LLP) -50 S Main -Bx1500
-Akron 44309 **Fx:**258-6559

(330) 535-5122 ..**Hilkert**, Jennifer R '91 Botzum Bros Hrdwre,LLC -520 N Arlngtn
-Akron 44305

(330) 376-4558 ..**Hilkert**, Mark '76 Scanlon & G Co,LPA -50 S Main -Ste 1200
-Akron 44308 **Fx:**376-3550

(614) 848-6500 ..**Hill Allison & DeWeese** -7737 Olentangy Rvr Rd
-Columbus 43235 **Fx:**848-6516

(304) 233-4966 ..**Hill**, Barry M '78 (Hill & Assoc) -89 12th -Wheeling, WV 26003

(216) 368-0553 ..**Hill**, Beatrice Jessie '02 %CWRU Law Schl -11075 East Blvd
-Cleveland 44106

(703) 433-4216 ..**Hill**, Christie A '86 Nextel -2001 Edmund Halley Dr -Leg Dept
-Reston, VA 20191

(513) 684-9000 ..**Hill**, Christine B '88 Field & H,Ltd -36 E 4th -Ste 1304
-Cincinnati 45202

(330) 643-3347 ..**Hill**, Christine S '02 Summit Cnty Ct of Common Pleas -209 S High
-Akron 44308

(502) 226-6100 ..**Hill**, Christopher M '02 (Hill & Assoc,PSC) -609 Chmbrlin Av
-Bx4989 -Frankfort, KY 40604

(513) 984-2640 ..**Hill**, Constance A '79 UAW-Ford Legal Srvcs Plan
-4010 Exec Park Dr -Ste 225 -Cincinnati 45241

(937) 427-1747 ..**Hill**, Cynthia M '90 Cindys Cellars,Inc -4457 State Rt 725
-Bellbrook 45305

(216) 623-1400 ..**Hill**, David G '61 (D Hill & Assoc Co,LPA) -1422 Euclid Av
-Hanna Bldg Ste 248 -Cleveland 44115

(904) 346-0140 ..**Hill**, Debra '91 (Smith H Law Firm) -8810 Goodby's Exec Dr -Ste C
-Jacksonville, FL 32217 **Fx:**346-3933

(330) 373-1020 ..**Hill**, Donald W '74 -175 Franklin SE -Bx4120 -Warren 44482

(440) 646-3359 ..**Hill**, Edwin V Jr. '67 Rockwell Automation -1 Allen-Bradley Dr
-Mayfield Heights 44124

(330) 375-2730 ..**Hill**, Elisa B '98 Pros -217 S High -Ste 203 -Akron 44308

(216) 522-7792 ..**Hill**, James A '76 SSA/OHA -1350 Euclid Av -7th Fl
-Cleveland 44115

(740) 477-2173 ..**Hill**, James K '72 -408 E Main -Circleville 43113

(937) 427-2000 ..**Hill**, James M '85 -2371 Lakevw Dr -Beavercreek 45431
Fx:320-5393

(216) 363-4500 ..**Hill**, James M '88 (Benesch FC&A LLP) -200 Pub Sq -Ste 2300
-Cleveland 44115 **Fx:**363-4588

(419) 243-2100 ..**Hill**, Jason A '00 %Connelly J&C LLP -405 Mad Av -Ste 1600
-Toledo 43604 **Fx:**243-7119

(941) 778-4745 ..**Hill**, Jay '77 (J Hill,PA) -Bx516 -Anna Maria, FL 34216
Fx:778-5516

(937) 223-3277 ..**Hill**, Jennifer L '99 %Bieser G&L LLP -6 N Main -400 Natl City Ctr
-Dayton 45402 **Fx:**223-6339

(330) 376-4558 ..**Hill**, John F '88 Scanlon & G Co,LPA -50 S Main -Ste 1200
-Akron 44308 **Fx:**376-3550

(614) 848-6500 ..**Hill**, John W '52 (Hill A&D) -7737 Olentangy Rvr Rd
-Columbus 43235 **Fx:**848-6516

(614) 848-6500 ..**Hill**, John W Jr. '82 (Hill A&D) -7737 Olentangy Rvr Rd
-Columbus 43235 **Fx:**848-6516

(614) 227-2000 ..**Hill**, Kathleen B '98 %Porter WM&A LLP -41 S High
-Columbus 43215 **Fx:**227-2100

(513) 684-3211 ..**Hill**, Louis H '88 IRS Dist Cnsl -312 Elm -Ste 2300
-Cincinnati 45202

(302) 477-2123 ..**Hill**, Louise L '78 Widener Univ-Law Sch -4601 Concord Pike
-Bx7474 -Wilmington, DE 19803

(419) 625-8324 ..**Hill**, Mary J '84 Flynn P&K,LPA -165 E Wshngtn Row
-Sandusky 44870 **Fx:**625-9007

(412) 263-2000 ..**Hill**, Mary Margaret '92 %Pietragallo B&G -One Oxford Centre
-38th Fl -Pittsburgh, PA 15219 **Fx:**261-5295

(919) 715-5143 ..**Hill**, Meghan E '04 %Hon Wyn -1 W Morgan -NC Ct of Appls
-Raleigh, NC 27601

(740) 773-8119 ..**Hill Motes**, Laura J '00 -187 N High -Chillicothe 45601

(330) 535-4191 ..**Hill**, Patricia A '80 Cmmnty Lgl Aid Srvcs,Inc -265 S Main -3rd Fl
-Akron 44308 **Fx:**535-0728

(970) 249-9424 ..**Hill**, Robert J '87 Cnty Atty Ofc -161 S Townsend Av
-Montrose, CO 81401

Hill, Shauna M '02 -1490 Reid Av -Cincinnati 45224

(216) 566-9700 ..**Hill**, Stephen A '74 (Rankin HP&C,LLP) -925 Euclid Av -Ste 700
-Cleveland 44115 **Fx:**566-9711

(330) 426-3092 ..**Hill**, Stephen A '79 -284N N Market -Bx12 -East Palestine 44413

(614) 860-9249 ..**Hill**, Steven A '84 -Bx344 -Blacklick 43004

(330) 533-1828 ..**Hill**, Thomas A '84 Eric Petroleum Corp
-4206½ Boardman-Canfld Rd -Canfield 44406 **Fx:**533-2647

(513) 381-2838 ..**Hill**, Thomas C '73 (Taft S&H LLP) -425 Walnut -Ste 1800
-Cincinnati 45202 **Fx:**381-0205

(614) 462-5403 ..**Hill**, Thomas W '70 (Kegler BH&R) -65 E State -Ste 1800
-Columbus 43215 **Fx:**464-2634

(419) 241-9000 ..**Hiller**, Charles W '86 (Shumaker L&K,LLP) -1000 Jackson
-Toledo 43624 **Fx:**241-6894

(614) 221-2234 ..**Hiller**, David P '69 (Millisor & N Co,LPA) -300 E Broad -Ste 190
-Columbus 43215 **Fx:**221-1278

(216) 226-5000 ..**Hiller**, Deborah L '75 Eliza Jennings Grp -14650 Detroit Av
-Ste 710 -Lakewood 44107

(513) 583-4200 ..**Hiller**, Robert S '77 (Schroeder MB&P) -11935 Mason Rd -Ste 110
-Cincinnati 45249

(513) 381-9200 ..**Hillerich**, Laura I '02 %Rendigs FK&D,LLP -One W 4th -Ste 900
-Cincinnati 45202 **Fx:**381-9206

(440) 826-1250 ..**Hilliard**, Carol R '84 -7550 Lucerne Dr -Ste 401
-Middleburg Heights 44130

(937) 593-9015 ..**Hilliker**, Donald J '74 Better Food Sys,Inc -101 Columbus Av
-Bellefontaine 43311

(740) 455-3350 ..**Hillis**, Scott T '89 (Hillis & S Co,LLC) -825 Adair Av
-Zanesville 43701 **Fx:**455-3360

(859) 692-2221 ..**Hillman**, Bruce J '91 Natl Underwriter Co -5081 Olympic Blvd
-Erlanger, KY 41018

(216) 622-8200 ..**Hillman**, Jean M '94 Calfee H&G LLP -800 Superior Av -Ste 1400
-Cleveland 44114 **Fx:**241-0816

(573) 596-0629 ..**Hillman**, Kevin S '00 US Army-OSJA -HQ-Manlen &
Ft Leonard Wood -Fort Leonard Wood, MO 65473

(614) 766-6346 ..**Hillman**, Steven E '73 -425 Metro Pl N -Ste 460 -Dublin 43017

(614) 466-8544 ..**Hillmer**, Felicity M '89 Industrial Commssn of OH -30 W Spring
-9th Fl -Columbus 43215 **Fx:**752-8785

(614) 466-4086 ..**Hills**, William L '89 Joint Comm on Agncy Rule Review -77 S High
-Cncrs Lvl -Columbus 43215

(740) 922-4161 ..**Hillyer**, Bradley L '81 (Connolly H&W) -201 N Main -Bx272
-Uhrichsville 44683

(216) 622-8200 ..**Hillyer**, Shelly K '02 %Calfee H&G LLP -800 Superior Av
-Ste 1400 -Cleveland 44114 **Fx:**241-0816

(740) 922-4161 ..**Hillyer**, William H '53 (Connolly H&W) -201 N Main -Bx272
-Uhrichsville 44683

(216) 443-7800 ..**Hilow**, Eleanore E '91 Cuyahoga Cnty Pros -1200 Ontario -8th Fl
-Cleveland 44113 **Fx:**698-2270

(216) 344-9220 ..**Hilow**, Henry J '81 (McGinty GH&S Co,LPA) -614 W Superior Av
-Ste 1300 -Cleveland 44113

(216) 443-8989 ..**Hilow**, Roseanne '84 Cuyahoga Cnty Probate Ct -1 Lakeside Av
-Rm 35 -Cleveland 44113

(859) 344-0330 ..**Hils**, Lynda M '02 %K murphy & Assoc -207 Grandvw Dr -Bx17330
-Ft Mitchell, KY 41017

(513) 977-8200 ..**Hils,** M Gabrielle '84 (Dinsmore & S LLP) -255 E 5th -Ste 1900
-Cincinnati 45202 **Fx:**977-8141

(513) 579-2203 ..**Hils,** Mary E '80 Provident Bank -1 E 4th -Cincinnati 45202

(614) 462-5451 ..**Hilson,** Daniel G '86 (Kegler BH&R) -65 E State -Ste 1800
-Columbus 43215 **Fx:**464-2634

(330) 384-4803 ..**Hilston,** Thomas A '77 FirstEnergy -1910 W Market -Akron 44313

(614) 875-0490 ..**Hilt,** John F Jr. '75 (J Hilt & Assoc) -3793 Bway -Grove City 43123

(330) 833-3192 ..**Hilterbrand,** Charles M Jr. '94 -4775 Munson NW -Canton 44718

(248) 641-1600 ..**Hilton,** Michael E '89 Cnsl Harness D&P,PLC -5445 Corp Dr
-Ste 400 -Troy, MI 48098 **Fx:**641-0270

(740) 653-4259 ..**Hilty,** Julia C '98 Fairfield Cnty Pros -201 S Broad -4th Fl
-Lancaster 43130

(513) 651-6800 ..**Hiltz,** Allison L '03 %Frost BT LLC -201 E 5th -2200 PNC Ctr
-Cincinnati 45202 **Fx:**651-6981

(859) 431-5544 ..**Hiltz,** Lawrence T '70 -50 E Rivercenter Blvd -#620
-Covington, KY 41011

(419) 668-8211 ..**Hiltz Wiedemann Allton & Koch Co,LPA**
-401 Ctzns Natl Bk Bldg -Bx640 -Norwalk 44857 **Fx:**668-2813

(614) 462-4921 ..**Hilvert,** Kevin '02 %Schottenstein Z&D -250 West -Bx165020
-Columbus 43216 **Fx:**462-5135

(513) 621-2100 ..**Hilvert,** Margaret A '89 %Beckman W&S LLC -120 E 4th
-1200 Mercantile Ctr -Cincinnati 45202 **Fx:**621-0106

(614) 466-4882 ..**Himes,** Lance D '98 Ohio Dept of Health -246 N High -7th Fl
-Columbus 43215

Himes, Steven C '98 -8403 Bedlington Dr -Reynoldsburg 43068

(614) 224-7700 ..**Himes-Riley,** Jennifer M '02 %Heckert & H Co,LPA -495 S High
-Ste 220 -Columbus 43215 **Fx:**224-7766

(330) 374-1030 ..**Himmel,** Gary L '80 -80 S Summit -Ste 400 -Akron 44308

(614) 444-4455 ..**Himmelrick,** Amy D '00 %Talbott & R -1180 S High
-Columbus 43206

(614) 932-7000 ..**Himmelrick,** Matthew T '99 (Himmelrick & W,LLC)
-7215 Sawmill Rd -Ste 215 -Dublin 43016

(330) 492-8717 ..**Himmelspach,** Thomas R '87 (Buckingham D&B,LLP)
-4518 Fulton Dr NW -Bx35548 -Canton 44735 **Fx:**492-9625

(216) 694-5671 ..**Hindel,** Joanne E '84 First Merit-Bank -101 W Prospect Av
-Ste 350 -Cleveland 44115

(301) 713-2231 ..**Hindel,** Martin J '91 NOAA/Dept of Commerce -1315 E W Hwy
-Ste 15129 -Silver Spring, MD 20910

(419) 586-8677 ..**Hinders,** Andrew J '81 Mercer Cnty Pros -119 N Walnut
-Celina 45822

(419) 629-2311 ..**Hinders,** Rodney J '85 Crown Equip Corp -44 S Wshngtn
-New Bremen 45869

(614) 292-2694 ..**Hindes,** Thomas J '84 OSU -2650 Kenny Rd -Columbus 43210

(740) 772-6400 ..**Hine,** Katherine '77 -80 Wissler Av -Chillicothe 45601 **Fx:**775-0300

(513) 977-8200 ..**Hinebaugh,** Jeffrey P '92 (Dinsmore & S LLP) -255 E 5th
-Ste 1900 -Cincinnati 45202 **Fx:**977-8141

(513) 665-3500 ..**Hinegardner,** Charles L '95 (Freund F&A) -105 E 4th -Ste 1400
-Cincinnati 45202 **Fx:**665-3503

(513) 721-4532 ..**Hinegardner,** Laura A '97 (Katz TB&H) -255 E 5th -Ste 2400
-Cincinnati 45202 0

(304) 723-7201 ..**Hinerman,** Raymond A '84 Hinerman & Assoc,PLLC
-3203 Penn Av -Bx2465 -Weirton, WV 26062

(419) 625-7770 ..**Hines,** Adrienne M '96 %Calhoun KH&C Co,LPA -502 W Wshngtn
-Sandusky 44870 **Fx:**625-8552

(937) 439-5708 ..**Hines,** Dean E '94 (DE Hines Co,LPA) -5335 Far Hills Av -Ste 313
-Dayton 45429 **Fx:**439-5710

(513) 721-2525 ..**Hines,** Glenn R '75 -1014 Vine -2525 Kroger Bldg
-Cincinnati 45202

(513) 381-0656 ..**Hines,** Jeffrey M '99 %Kohnen & P LLP -201 E 5th -Ste 800
-Cincinnati 45202 **Fx:**381-5823

(207) 791-1236 ..**Hines,** Jonathan M '99 Pierce A -1 Monument Sq
-Portland, ME 04101

(614) 234-1287 ..**Hines,** Linda E '04 Mt Carmel Health -793 W State -Columbus
43222

(419) 245-2740 ..**Hines,** Richard S '83 Industrial Commssn of OH -One Govt Ctr
-Ste 1500 -Toledo 43604

(330) 674-1888 ..**Hines,** Robert B II '76 -19 W Jackson -Bx256 -Millersburg 44654

(330) 364-6665 ..**Hinig,** Richard W '79 -217 N Bway -New Philadelphia 44663

(216) 357-7100 ..**Hink,** Ralph M '85 %Hon PR Matia -801 W Superior Av
-Cleveland 44113

(216) 696-3030 ..**Hinkel,** Kevin M '80 (Kadish H&W,LPA) -1717 E 9th -Ste 2112
-Cleveland 44114 **Fx:**696-3492

(513) 556-4835 ..**Hinkel,** Rebecca A '04 Univ of Cincinnati Athletics Dept
-One Edwards Ctr -Ste 4146 -Bx210021 -Cincinnati 45221
Fx:556-2209

(330) 497-7815 ..**Hinkel,** Walter W '73 -6730 Hrbr Dr NW -Canton 44718

Hinkle, Gerald F '04 -(Address Unavailable)

(216) 689-0333 ..**Hinkle,** Steven D '84 Key Trust Co -127 Pub Sq -17th Fl
-Cleveland 44114

(513) 721-3330 ..**Hinners,** Jason R '03 %Robbins KP&T -7 W 7th -Ste 1400
-Cincinnati 45202

Hinners, Stacy A '03

(239) 549-5551 ..**Hino,** Roxanne M '91 -1420 SE 47th -Cape Coral, FL 33904

(513) 534-3165 ..**Hinshaw,** Steven A '77 Fifth 3rd Bank -38 Fountain Sq Plz
-MD 10AT5E -Cincinnati 45263

Hinson, Maureen Sullivan '03 -(Address Unavailable)

(330) 643-2925 ..**Hinton,** Belinda J '81 Summit Cnty Juv Ct -650 Dan -Akron 44310

(330) 666-8140 ..**Hinton,** James R '56 SrCnsl J Hinton Co LPA -4240 W Bath Rd
-Akron 44333 **Fx:**670-9028

(216) 241-6700 ..**Hinton,** Jennifer N '98 %Watts H Co,LPA -1100 Superior Av E
-Ste 1750 Diamond Bldg -Cleveland 44114 **Fx:**241-8151

(740) 321-1650 ..**Hinton,** Linda S '03 Paramount Finl Grp -4009 Columbus Rd SW
-Granville 43023

(614) 737-1358 ..**Hinze,** Keith W '03 Computer Sciences Corp -5200 Uppr Metro Pl
-Dublin 43017

(740) 695-4817 ..**Hinzey,** Gregory W '78 -276 E Main -Saint Clairsville 43950

(202) 626-6600 ..**Hipp,** Cheryl A '94 %Squire S&D LLP -1201 Penn Av NW -Bx407
-Washington, DC 20044 **Fx:**626-6780

(330) 343-2168 ..**Hipp,** David C '76 -108½ E High Av -Bx90
-New Philadelphia 44663

(202) 305-3091 ..**Hipp,** Roger A '95 US DOJ -1100 L NW -Rm 12072
-Washington, DC 20530

(202) 685-6974 ..**Hipple,** Richard D '74 Genl Cnsl of the Navy -720 Kennon SE
-Bldg 36-Lit Ofc -Washington, DC 20374

(202) 326-3285 ..**Hippsley,** Heather A '84 FTC -601 Penn NW -Rm 4606
-Washington, DC 20580

(614) 228-1541 ..**Hire,** Charles H '66 (Baker & H LLP) -65 E State -Ste 2100
-Columbus 43215 **Fx:**462-2616

(419) 884-3522 ..**Hire,** John S '82 Red Diamond Ltd -26 E Main -Ste 2
-Mansfield 44904

(513) 863-8270 ..**Hirka,** Sara C '97 (Parrish F&M Co,LPA) -300 High -Ste 704
-Bx747 -Hamilton 45012 **Fx:**863-9999

(614) 860-2000 ..**Hirn,** William E Jr. '88 Lucent Tech -5035 State -Medina 44256

(312) 861-8000 ..**Hirsberg,** David M '88 %Baker & M -130 E Randolph Dr
-Chicago, IL 60601

(614) 464-2392 ..**Hirsch,** Bruce L '79 Earl WA&D,LPA -136 W Mound
-Columbus 43215 **Fx:**464-0754

(740) 773-3660 ..**Hirsch,** Carl P Jr. '76 -Bx97 -Chillicothe 45601

(412) 355-2600 ..**Hirsch,** David J '80 (DKW Law Grp,LLC) -600 Grant -58th Fl
-Pittsburgh, PA 15219 **Fx:**355-2609

(614) 236-6685 ..**Hirsch,** Dennis D '03 %Capital Univ Law Schl -303 E Broad
-Columbus 43215

(419) 531-1021 ..**Hirsch,** Gordon H '72 (Hirsch & O) -2727 N Holland Sylvania Rd
-Ste K -Toledo 43615

(330) 722-9219 ..**Hirsch,** Susan L '91 -124 W Wshngtn -Ste B-4 -Medina 44256

Hirsch, William C '46 -5757 Cheviot Rd -Unit 3A -Cincinnati 45249

(513) 553-7740 ..**Hirschauer,** Gregory A '93 H Unlimited -1477 Fagins Run Rd
-New Richmond 45157 **Fx:**553-7740

(513) 621-6464 ..**Hirschfeld,** Michael A '77 (Graydon H&R LLP) -511 Walnut
-1900 Fifth Third Ctr -Cincinnati 45202 **Fx:**651-3856

(740) 376-9669 ..**Hirschi,** Helen '95 -703 Colegate Dr -Marietta 45750

(330) 675-2600 ..**Hirschi,** Rhonda S '01 Trumbull Cnty Fam Ct Ctr
-220 Main Av SW -Warren 44481

(216) 771-5800 ..**Hirshman,** Ellen H '82 Linton & H -700 W St Clair Av
-Hoyt Block Ste 300 -Cleveland 44113

(216) 771-5800 ..**Hirshman,** Tobias J '78 (Linton & H) -700 W St Clair Av
-Hoyt Block Ste 300 -Cleveland 44113

(330) 562-3156 ..**Hirt,** David S '94 (Christley H&P) -215 W Garfld -Ste 230
-Aurora 44202 **Fx:**562-9540

(330) 677-0506 ..**Hirt,** Lisa J '93 -Bx219 -Kent 44240

(216) 831-0042 ..**Hirth,** Alan N '73 Meyers RF&L LPA -28601 Chagrin Blvd -Ste 500
-Cleveland 44122 **Fx:**831-0542

(937) 228-8104 ..**Hirtle,** Stanley A '73 ABLE -333 W 1st -Ste 500B -Dayton 45402
Fx:449-8131

(330) 865-0153 ..**Hiscock,** Matthew G '97 -2295 W Market -Ste C -Akron 44313

(216) 586-3939 ..**Hiser,** Ted S '85 Cnsl Jones D -901 Lakeside Av -Cleveland 44114
Fx:579-0212

(330) 343-8834 ..**Hisrich,** Thomas H '66 -121 W 4th -Dover 44622

(614) 644-5281 ..**Hissom,** Heather L '97 OH Veterinary Med Lcnsng Bd -77 S High
-16th Fl -Columbus 43266

(614) 445-2582 ..**Histed,** Bradley J '81 Grange Mutual Cslty Co -650 S Front
-Bx1218 -Columbus 43216

(419) 255-5900 ..**Hitaffer,** Thedford I '00 %MacMillan S&T,LLC -720 Water -4th Fl
-Toledo 43604 **Fx:**255-9639

(419) 243-4006 ..**Hitaffer,** Tiffany J '00 %Kitch DWD&V,PC -405 Mad Av -Ste 1500
-Toledo 43604 **Fx:**243-7333

(214) 981-3311 ..**Hitchcock,** David L '76 SrCnsl Sidley AB&W -717 N Harwood
-Ste 3400 -Dallas, TX 75201 **Fx:**981-3400

(419) 782-5134 ..**Hitchcock,** James E '68 -650 W 1st -Defiance 43512

(904) 359-1192 ..**Hitchcock,** Paul R '76 CSX Trans,Inc -500 Water
-Jacksonville, FL 32202

(440) 998-0611 ..**Hitchcock,** Thomas '77 -217 Park Pl -Bx1308 -Ashtabula 44005

(419) 394-7432 ..**Hitchen,** Kenneth E '71 -510 W South -Saint Marys 45885

(419) 524-7400 ..**Hitchman,** Terry D '88 -16 W 2nd -Mansfield 44902

(330) 877-2613 ..**Hite,** Christopher E '69 McPherson & H Co,LPA -140 Sunnyside
-Bx667 -Hartville 44632 **Fx:**877-2614

(740) 366-1525 ..**Hite,** David L '46 -964D N 21st -Newark 43055 **Fx:**366-1655

(740) 892-3443 ..**Hite & Heath** -26 S Main -Bx457 -Utica 43080 **Fx:**892-3556

(330) 825-8670 ..**Hite,** Roger M '72 -3377 Grill Rd -Clinton 44216

(330) 723-2000 ..**Hiteman,** Carl G '83 -226 N Bway -Medina 44256

(330) 723-9546 ..**Hitsman,** David V '00 Medina Cnty Pros -72 Pub Sq
-Medina 44256

(614) 889-6600 ..**Hitsman,** Michael R '88 (Hitsman H&O) -6099 Riverside Dr
-Ste 200 -Dublin 43017

(440) 232-9911 ..**Hitzeman,** Janice L '98 (McDonald FH&H) -24262 Bway Av
-Bx46390 -Oakwood Village 44146 **Fx:**439-2308

(330) 740-2180 ..**Hively,** Aaron A '99 %Hon G Donofrio -120 Market
-Youngstown 44503

(614) 466-0211 ..**Hix,** John H Jr. '70 Dept of Agriculture -8995 E Main
-Reynoldsburg 43068 **Fx:**728-2622

(419) 249-7100 ..**Hixon,** Mark A '92 Marshall & M,LLC -Four Seagate -8th Fl
-Toledo 43604 **Fx:**249-7151

(216) 443-7800 ..**Hixson,** Traci M '90 Cuyahoga Cnty Pros -1200 Ontario -8th Fl
-Cleveland 44113 **Fx:**698-2270

(419) 829-2255 ..**Hizer,** Brian A '02 (Hizer & M,LLC) -8657 Central Av -Ste B
-Sylvania 43560

(614) 677-3700 ..**Hjeile,** Jennifer H '96 Gates McDonald -215 N Front
-Columbus 43215

(330) 856-7575 ..**Hlaudy,** Richard S '01 %J Gray & Assoc -8528 E Market
-Warren 44484

(216) 515-1660 ..**Hlavaty,** Joel R '83 (Frantz W LLP) -127 Pub Sq -2500 Key Center
-Cleveland 44114 **Fx:**515-1650

(216) 241-6700 ..**Hlavka,** John R '76 (Watts H Co,LPA) -1100 Superior Av E
-Ste 1750 Diamond Bldg -Cleveland 44114 **Fx:**241-8151

(216) 520-5638 ..**Hlucky,** Lori '95 West Grp -6111 Oak Tree Blvd -Bx318063
-Cleveland 44131

Ho, Jarling '04 -(Address Unavailable)

(216) 481-4815 ..**Hoag,** Joan '77 -15316 Shiloh Rd -Cleveland 44110

(614) 766-7000 ..**Hoag,** Wesley F '84 Meeder Fin,Inc -6125 Mem'l Dr -Dublin 43017

(614) 369-5297 ..**Hoague,** Michael C '83 -17 Carriage Dr -Ste 100 -Delaware 43015

(419) 522-7999 ..**Hoard,** JoAnn P '00 -13 Park Av W -Ste 309 -Mansfield 44902

(202) 544-0175 ..**Hoban,** Thomas M '99 -Bx15640 -Washington, DC 20003

(216) 622-8200 ..**Hoban,** Thomas M '99 SpclCnsl Calfee H&G LLP -800 Superior Av
-Ste 1400 -Cleveland 44114 **Fx:**241-0816

(440) 892-3670 .. **Hobar,** Susan G '92 DTC DesignTech -27005 Knckrbckr Rd -#126
-Bay Village 44140

(937) 962-2712 .. **Hobbs,** H Steven '83 -119 N Commerce -Bx489 -Lewisburg 45338
Fx:962-4296

(513) 287-1238 .. **Hobbs,** Jacqueline Schuster '97 Cinergy Corp -139 E 4th
-25 Atrium II -Bx960 -Cincinnati 45201
Hobday, John D '66 -1558 Waterstone Ct -Columbus 43235

(513) 381-2838 .. **Hoberg,** Timothy E '70 (Taft S&H LLP) -425 Walnut -Ste 1800
-Cincinnati 45202 **Fx:**381-0205

(419) 249-7100 .. **Hoblet,** Vaughn A '74 (Marshall & M,LLC) -Four Seagate -8th Fl
-Toledo 43604 **Fx:**249-7151

(513) 721-2744 .. **Hobson,** Anthony W '82 NA Prop -212 E 3rd -Ste 300
-Cincinnati 45202

(614) 469-2999 .. **Hobson,** Gordon G Jr. '80 Fed Pub Def -10 W Broad -Ste 1020
-Columbus 43215

(513) 321-8100 .. **Hobson,** Mary G '84 Dyer Realty -621 Wilmer Av
-Cincinnati 45226

(937) 225-5787 .. **Hobson,** Sandra K '78 Montgomery Cnty Pros -301 W 3rd -Bx972
-Dayton 45422 **Fx:**225-3470

(330) 253-2227 .. **Hobson,** Steven R II '98 %Parker LH&R,LLC -388 S Main -Ste 402
-Akron 44311 **Fx:**253-1261

(216) 771-4949 .. **Hobt,** Stephen D '78 -1370 Ontario -Ste 450 -Cleveland 44113

(419) 865-8021 .. **Hoch,** Brian J '82 (Balk H&M) -5744 Southwyck Blvd
-Toledo 43614 **Fx:**865-9105
Hochbein, Joseph J '80 -Bx12505 -Cincinnati 45212

(216) 771-3800 .. **Hochberg,** David Peter '76 (DP Hochberg Co,LPA) -1940 E 6th
-Baker Bldg 6th Fl -Cleveland 44114 **Fx:**771-3804

(216) 739-5649 .. **Hochheiser,** Alan C '89 (Weltman W&R Co,LPA)
-323 W Lakeside Av -Ste 200 -Cleveland 44113 **Fx:**363-4121

(440) 446-1100 .. **Hochman,** David B '74 (Dinn H&M,LLC) -5910 Landerbrook Dr
-Ste 200 -Cleveland 44124 **Fx:**446-1240

(937) 228-2666 .. **Hochman,** James B '66 (Hochman R&P Co,LPA) -118 W 1st
-Ste 650 -Dayton 45402 **Fx:**228-0508

(216) 586-3939 .. **Hochman,** Kenneth G '73 (Jones D) -901 Lakeside Av
-Cleveland 44114 **Fx:**579-0212

(937) 228-2666 .. **Hochman Roach & Plunkett Co,LPA** -118 W 1st -Ste 650
-Dayton 45402 **Fx:**228-0508

(513) 533-9898 .. **Hochscheid,** Tabitha M '95 (Eberly MH,LLC) -3700 Eastern Av
-Cincinnati 45226

(937) 297-1150 .. **Hochwalt,** Michael A '84 (Hochwalt & S,LLP)
-500 Lincoln Park Blvd -Ste 216 -Dayton 45429

(937) 297-1150 .. **Hochwalt & Schiff,LLP** -500 Lincoln Park Blvd -Ste 216
-Dayton 45429

(419) 352-5458 .. **Hock,** Jerome H '58 -130 E Wshngtn -Bx733
-Bowling Green 43402

(513) 752-8855 .. **Hock,** Thomas P '73 Pro Transit Mngmnt -907 E Legendary Run
-Cincinnati 45245

(614) 325-9144 .. **Hockenberry,** Rebecca K '02 -1427 Cottonwood Dr
-Columbus 43229

(614) 224-7700 .. **Hockensmith,** Mark L '97 (Heckert & H Co,LPA) -495 S High
-Ste 220 -Columbus 43215 **Fx:**224-7766

(859) 422-6000 .. **Hocker,** George B '94 (Clark & W) -333 W Vine -Ste 1100
-Lexington, KY 40507

(614) 481-3127 .. **Hockstad,** Karen S '93 -1459 Westwood Av -Columbus 43212

(937) 298-8191 .. **Hodapp,** Ruey F Jr. '58 -3490 S Dixie -Ste 114 -Dayton 45439

(513) 564-7053 .. **Hodesh,** Janine '82 6th Dist Ct of Appls -100 E 5th -Cthse
-Cincinnati 45202

(216) 355-5936 .. **Hodge,** Bruce E '95 -1187 Atwood Dr -Cleveland 44108

(614) 221-4255 .. **Hodge,** David L '02 Smith & H -37 W Broad -Columbus 43215

(203) 719-4903 .. **Hodge,** Jeffrey T '79 UBS Energy Inc -677 Wshngtn Blvd
-Stamford, CT 06901

(513) 579-6400 .. **Hodge,** Pamela M '89 (Keating M&K PLL) -1 E 4th
-1400 Provident Twr -Cincinnati 45202 **Fx:**579-6457

(937) 461-0009 .. **Hodge,** Victor A '81 -130 W 2nd -Ste 810 -Dayton 45402

(513) 489-7800 .. **Hodgeman,** Ronald L '98 Old Republic Exchange Co
-11300 Cornell Park Dr -Ste 100 -Cincinnati 45242

(513) 723-4000 .. **Hodges,** Jason L '00 %Vorys SS&P LLP -221 E 4th
-Ste 2000 Atrium Two -Bx0236 -Cincinnati 45201 **Fx:**723-4056

(330) 376-1242 .. **Hodgkiss,** Timothy A '03 %Renner KGBT&W,LPA -106 S Main
-4th Fl First Natl Twr -Akron 44308 **Fx:**376-9646

(216) 691-8472 .. **Hodgman,** Blair '78 (Allen & H) -1481 Warrensvll Ctr Rd
-South Euclid 44121

(440) 871-5151 .. **Hodous,** David F '76 %Childs M & Assoc,LPA -24600 Detroit Rd
-Ste 240 -WestLake 44145

(614) 888-7363 .. **Hodovanich,** Dina L '01 -2217 Castlebrook Dr -Powell 43065

(740) 376-4804 .. **Hodson,** Thomas S '73 Marietta Cllg -McKinney Media Ctr
-Marietta 45750

(614) 462-5454 .. **Hoeffel,** Melissa Rager '03 %Kegler BH&R -65 E State -Ste 1800
-Columbus 43215 **Fx:**464-2634

(419) 562-4075 .. **Hoeffel,** Paul E '73 (Kennedy PH&G) -111 Rensselaer -Bx191
-Bucyrus 44820 **Fx:**562-7850

(513) 241-2540 .. **Hoefle,** Henry F '65 -632 Vine -Ste 415 -Cincinnati 45202

(513) 574-4464 .. **Hoehne,** Jeffry M '70 Encon Assoc -6613 Powner Farm Dr
-Cincinnati 45248

(216) 685-1164 .. **Hoen,** Benjamin N '04 %Weltman W&R Co,LPA
-323 W Lakeside Av -Ste 200 -Cleveland 44113 **Fx:**363-4121

(419) 213-3000 .. **Hoenig-Navarette,** Kimberly S '97 Lucas Cnty CSEA -701 Adams
-Toledo 43624

(216) 956-3044 .. **Hoenigman,** Richard A '70 Permanent Grp Assrnc Corp
-9700 Rockside Rd -Ste 250 -Cleveland 44125

(419) 522-6242 .. **Hoerig,** Joseph P '95 %Sauter H&B -24 W 3rd -Ste 306
-Mansfield 44902

(972) 519-5143 .. **Hoersten,** Craig A '93 Alcatel USA -1000 Coit Rd -M/S LEGL2
-Plano, TX 75075

(202) 694-1011 .. **Hoersting,** Stephen M '96 Fed Election Comm -999 I NW
-Washington, DC 20403

(513) 621-1414 .. **Hof,** Robert E '92 Butkovich SS&G Co,LPA -36 E 7th -Ste 2600
-Cincinnati 45202 **Fx:**977-5580

(614) 466-7447 .. **Hofacker-Carr,** Velda K '88 Atty Gen -150 E Gay
-Columbus 43215

(937) 324-2224 .. **Hofbauer,** Lawrence J '96 (Hofbauer & M) -4 W Main -2nd Fl
-Springfield 45502

(216) 776-1000 .. **Hofelich,** James A '69 -600 Superior Av E -Bank One Ctr Ste 1300
-Cleveland 44114

(216) 443-7800 .. **Hofelich,** James J '00 Cuyahoga Cnty Pros -1200 Ontario -8th Fl
-Cleveland 44113 **Fx:**698-2270

(330) 745-2175 .. **Hofer,** Keith R '89 (Lombardi HHC&E) -2745 Nesbitt Av
-Akron 44319

(330) 264-6464 .. **Hoff,** George L '85 -529 Stratford Av -Akron 44303

(513) 241-0466 .. **Hoff,** Louis A '61 -1766 Churchwood Dr -Cincinnati 45238

(614) 752-1200 .. **Hoff,** Walter A '76 Parole Brd -1050 Fwy Dr N -Columbus 43229

(440) 350-4600 .. **Hoff,** Michele R '87 -6471 Hudson Av -Mentor 44060

(216) 515-4546 .. **Hoffer,** Christine S '87 Sherwin Williams -101 Prospect Av
-Cleveland 44115

(419) 242-1001 .. **Hoffer,** Jeremiah A II '83 (Szczepaniak & H) -1900 Monroe -Bx501
-Toledo 43697

(330) 706-1831 .. **Hoffer,** Paul R '85 -3067 Wadsworth Rd -Norton 44203

(859) 341-1881 .. **Hoffer,** Robert M '02 Deters B&L,PSC -2701 Turkeyfoot Rd
-207 Thomas More Pkwy -Crestview Hills, KY 41017 **Fx:**341-1469

(513) 381-2838 .. **Hoffheimer,** Daniel J '76 (Taft S&H LLP) -425 Walnut -Ste 1800
-Cincinnati 45202 **Fx:**381-0205

(513) 421-7666 .. **Hoffheimer,** Jon '65 -414 Walnut -Ste 1200 -Cincinnati 45202

(662) 915-6865 .. **Hoffheimer,** Michael H '84 Univ of Miss -Law Center
-University, MS 38677

(724) 743-7777 .. **Hoffman,** Annemarie '86 Centimark Corp -12 Grandvw Cir
-Canonsburg, PA 15317

(614) 421-2626 .. **Hoffman,** Bradley E '83 Container Mgmt Co
-1200 Corrugated Way -Columbus 43201

(513) 381-2838 .. **Hoffman,** Bridget C '02 %Taft S&H LLP -425 Walnut -Ste 1800
-Cincinnati 45202 **Fx:**381-0205

(513) 621-6464 .. **Hoffman,** Bruce A '75 (Graydon H&R LLP) -511 Walnut
-1900 Fifth Third Ctr -Cincinnati 45202 **Fx:**651-3836

(704) 383-5382 .. **Hoffman,** Carol A '80 Wachovia Bk -3 Wachovia
-Charlotte, NC 28288

(937) 449-6810 .. **Hoffman,** Craig A '02 %Porter WM&A LLP -1 S Main -Ste 1600
-Dayton 45402 **Fx:**449-6820

(614) 764-3214 .. **Hoffman,** Cynthia Jo '91 Wendys Intl -4288 W Dublin-Granvll Rd
-Tax Dept -Bx256 -Dublin 43017

(503) 696-2370 .. **Hoffman,** David A '94 Intel Corp -5200 NE Elam Young Pkwy
-Hillsboro, OR 97124

(202) 616-0341 .. **Hoffman,** David C '82 US DOJ -1100 L NW -Ste 12036
-Washington, DC 20005

(614) 645-8591 .. **Hoffman,** Deborah F '81 City of Columbus -757 Carolyn Av
-Bldg & Dvlpmnt -Columbus 43224

(419) 242-9281 .. **Hoffman,** Edward L '73 -450 W Delaware -Toledo 43610

(614) 222-0526 .. **Hoffman,** Eric J '84 -338 S High -Columbus 43215 **Fx:**358-0001

(440) 446-1100 .. **Hoffman,** Eric R '77 -5910 Landerbrook Dr -Ste 200
-Mayfield Heights 44124 **Fx:**446-1240

(216) 831-2552 .. **Hoffman,** Gary H '76 -27970 Chagrin Blvd -Ste 200
-Cleveland 44122

(614) 478-1975 .. **Hoffman,** George M '79 -261 W Johnstown Rd -Columbus 43230

(419) 693-0770 .. **Hoffman,** Glen R '81 -624 Main -Toledo 43605

(740) 425-2372 .. **Hoffman,** Grace L '91 -160 E Main -Bx310 -Barnesville 43713

(330) 448-1500 .. **Hoffman,** James E III '76 (Hoffman & W)
-7553 Warren-Sharon Rd -Bx316 -Brookfield 44403

(216) 781-3600 .. **Hoffman,** Joseph C Jr. '91 Faulkner M&P,LLP -820 W Superior Av
-Ste 900 -Cleveland 44113 **Fx:**781-8839

(614) 466-2585 .. **Hoffman,** Judith A '83 OH Sec of State -180 E Broad
-Columbus 43215 **Fx:**466-5409

(614) 719-3393 .. **Hoffman,** Kimberly E '95 US Dist Ct -85 Marconi Blvd
-140 US Cthse -Columbus 43215

(216) 621-0200 .. **Hoffman,** L Dennis '97 %Baker & H LLP -1900 E 9th -Ste 3200
-Cleveland 44114 **Fx:**696-0740
Hoffman, Linda G '89 -19984 Westover Av -Rocky River 44116

(937) 223-5200 .. **Hoffman,** Louis I '61 (Flanagan LH&S) -318 W 4th -Dayton 45402
Fx:223-3335

(216) 222-3495 .. **Hoffman,** Mark A '80 Nat'l City Bank -629 Euclid Av
-Cleveland 44114

(216) 991-6200 .. **Hoffman,** Mark L '76 -20133 Farnsleigh Rd -Shaker Heights 44122

(313) 965-6100 .. **Hoffman,** Marta J '93 %Rutledge MRT&T -4000 Penoloscot Bldg
-Detroit, MI 48226

(419) 447-2982 .. **Hoffman,** Randy F '80 Seneca Cnty Cmn Pleas Ct
-103 S Wshngtn -3rd Fl -Tiffin 44883

(614) 792-2565 .. **Hoffman,** Richard F '99 Local Govt Srvcs LLC -8832 Southwold Ct
-Powell 43065

(740) 943-2325 .. **Hoffman,** Scott L '96 (Evans E&H,LLP) -15 W Ottawa
-Richwood 43344 **Fx:**943-2326

(408) 527-9182 .. **Hoffman,** Sharon L '93 Cisco Systems,Inc -170 W Tasman Dr
-San Jose, CA 95134

(937) 223-8177 .. **Hoffman,** Timothy D '81 (Coolidge WW&L) -33 W 1st -Ste 600
-Dayton 45402 **Fx:**223-6705

(312) 641-1555 .. **Hoffman,** Timothy V '00 (Sanchez & D) -333 W Wacker Dr
-Ste 500 -Chicago, IL 60606 **Fx:**641-3004

(216) 292-5200 .. **Hoffman,** William A III '79 (Hoffman Lgl Grp,LLC)
-23230 Chagrin Blvd -Ste 232 -Cleveland 44122

(937) 328-2574 .. **Hoffman,** William D '90 Clark Cnty Pros -50 E Columbia -Bx1608
-Springfield 45501

(440) 498-7500 .. **Hoffmann,** Andrew W '75 Cnsl Cosmo Plastics Co
-30201 Aurora Rd -Solon 44139

(513) 732-7313 .. **Hoffmann,** David H '84 Clermont Cnty Pros -123 N 3rd -Batavia
45103

(216) 621-1312 .. **Hoffmann,** David S '85 (McMahon DH&L LLP) -812 Huron Rd
-Ste 650 The Caxton Bldg -Cleveland 44115 **Fx:**621-0577

(513) 677-0999 .. **Hoffmann,** Gary R '73 (G Hoffmann Co,LPA)
-11935 Mason-Mntgmry Rd -Ste 130 -Cincinnati 45249

(937) 208-2266 .. **Hoffmann,** John J '90 Miami Valley Hosp -1 Wyoming
-Dayton 45409

(330) 334-1536 .. **Hoffmann,** Linda '84 (Palecek MH&M Co LLP) -200 Smokerise Dr
-Ste 200 -Wadsworth 44281 **Fx:**334-7005

(757) 322-8020 .. **Hoffmann,** Theodore H '84
Cnsl Naval Facilities Engineering Command, Atlantic
-6506 Hmptn Blvd -US Dept of the Navy -Norfolk, VA 23508
Fx:322-8181

(513) 684-2572 .. **Hoffmann,** Timothy W '03 US Bankrptcy Ct -221 E 4th -Ste 800
-Cincinnati 45202

(513) 241-4722 .. **Hoffpauir,** Gregory T '95 %Montgomery R&J,LPA -36 E 7th
-Ste 2100 -Cincinnati 45202 **Fx:**241-8775

(513) 579-1500 ..**Hoffsis**, Stephen B '86 (Buechner HOM&H Co,LPA) -105 E 4th -Ste 300 -Cincinnati 45202 **Fx:**977-4361

(614) 837-0793 ..**Hofmeister**, Raymond E '72 -8310 Allen Rd -Canal Winchester 43110

(440) 285-2247 ..**Hofstetter**, William C '75 -155 Main -Chardon 44024 **Fx:**285-4140

(513) 388-2919 ..**Hoft**, Thomas W '89 Senco Prdcts,Inc -8485 Broadwell Rd -Cincinnati 45244

(513) 381-0656 ..**Hogan**, Andrew J '87 (Kohnen & P LLP) -201 E 5th -Ste 800 -Cincinnati 45202 **Fx:**381-5823

(614) 459-4140 ..**Hogan**, Christopher B '98 %Moots C&H -3600 Olentangy Rvr Rd -Ste 501 -Columbus 43214 **Fx:**459-4503

Hogan, Colleen S '04 -(Address Unavailable)

(614) 462-3555 ..**Hogan**, Dennis A '75 Franklin Cnty Pros -373 S High -Columbus 43215

(216) 378-2915 ..**Hogan**, Doris A '81 Glenmede Trust Co -25825 Science Park -Beachwood 44122

(440) 546-8614 ..**Hogan**, Douglas J '88 The Illuminating Co -6896 Miller Rd -Ste 210 -Brecksville 44141

(216) 479-6100 ..**Hogan**, James A '99 %Vorys SS&P LLP -1375 E 9th -Ste 2100 One Cleve Ctr -Cleveland 44113 **Fx:**479-6060

(419) 586-7171 ..**Hogan**, James P '72 -409 Myers Rd -Bx24 -Celina 45822

(614) 387-9831 ..**Hogan**, Lee '85 OH Ct of Claims -65 S Front -3rd flr -Columbus 43215

Hogan, Mark E '03 -3884 Pinto Ct -Columbus 43221

(216) 696-0606 ..**Hogan**, Michael W '85 RE Sweeney Co,LPA -55 Pub Sq -Ste 1500 -Cleveland 44113 **Fx:**696-0679

(513) 579-6400 ..**Hogan**, Patricia B '89 OfCnsl Keating M&K PLL -1 E 4th -1400 Provident Twr -Cincinnati 45202 **Fx:**579-6457

Hogan, Robert B '72 -2915 Portsmouth Av -Cincinnati 45208

(513) 744-9600 ..**Hogan**, Robert K '82 (Javitch B&R) -602 Main -Ste 500 -Cincinnati 45202 **Fx:**744-9602

(330) 334-1544 ..**Hogan**, Roy F '88 -8606 Hartman Rd -Wadsworth 44281

(513) 983-4374 ..**Hogan**, Tara C '01 Procter & Gamble Co-Legal -1 Procter & Gamble Plz -Cincinnati 45202

(330) 376-1600 ..**Hogan**, Thomas C '01 Cincinnati Ins Co -50 S Main -Ste 615 -Akron 44308

(216) 241-2880 ..**Hogg**, James S '85 Cowden HN&L -50 Pub Sq -Ste 1414 -Cleveland 44113 **Fx:**241-2881

(440) 205-3600 ..**Hogg**, William N '59 (Driggs LB&H Co,LPA) -8522 East Av -Mentor 44060 **Fx:**205-3601

(330) 296-9966 ..**Hogle**, James E Jr. '65 -202 S Prospect -Bx767 -Ravenna 44266 **Fx:**296-9967

(216) 523-4112 ..**Hogsett**, William F '73 Eaton Corp -1111 Superior Av -Cleveland 44114

(419) 725-0078 ..**Hohenberger**, Christopher E '88 Root EdVentures,Inc -461 Brdgwtr -Oregon 43616

(216) 241-5310 ..**Hohenberger**, Leah M '02 %Gallagher SF&N -1501 Euclid Av -6th Fl -Cleveland 44115 **Fx:**241-1608

(330) 683-5010 ..**Hohenberger**, Raymond W '74 (Kropf WH&L,LLP) -100 N Vine -Bx67 -Orrville 44667 **Fx:**683-5030

(419) 522-6242 ..**Hohenberger**, Wayne P '73 (Sauter H&B) -24 W 3rd -Ste 306 -Mansfield 44902

(937) 294-7400 ..**Hohl**, Lee E '84 Hohl Legal Srvcs Co,LPA -1839 E Stroop Rd -Kettering 45429

(614) 221-4670 ..**Hohl**, Ruth A '86 Rhiel & Assoc Co,LPA -124 S Wshngtn -Columbus 43215 **Fx:**232-9306

(216) 586-3939 ..**Hohler**, Kathleen '80 Cnsl Jones D -901 Lakeside Av -Cleveland 44114 **Fx:**579-0212

(419) 242-7985 ..**Hohman**, Teresa E '00 %Roetzel & A,LPA -One SeaGate -9th Fl -Toledo 43604 **Fx:**242-0316

(216) 696-1076 ..**Hohmann Boukis & Curtis Co, LPA** -1370 Ontario -Ste 520 Standard Bldg -Cleveland 44113 **Fx:**696-2317

(310) 479-2228 ..**Hohmann**, Christa M '97 Post Conviction Assist Ctr -1950 Sawtelle Blvd -Ste 310 -Los Angeles, CA 90025 **Fx:**479-2206

(216) 696-1076 ..**Hohmann**, William T '65 Hohmann B&C Co,LPA -1370 Ontario -Ste 520 Standard Bldg -Cleveland 44113 **Fx:**696-2317

(513) 721-1311 ..**Hojnoski**, Robert W '98 (Reminger & R) -7 W 7th -Ste 1990 -Cincinnati 45202 **Fx:**721-2553

(614) 466-8600 ..**Hoke**, Anne L '87 Atty Gen -30 E Broad -Columbus 43215 **Fx:**466-6090

(949) 475-0025 ..**Hoke**, Robert L Jr. '77 R Taylor Jr -4340 Campus Dr -Ste 100 -Newport Beach, CA 92660

(614) 757-5187 ..**Hoke**, Robin S '88 Cardinal Hlth -7000 Cardinal Pl -Dublin 43017

(216) 696-6525 ..**Hokky**, Naomi '89 Catholic Charities -7800 Detroit Av -Cleveland 44102

(614) 464-6400 ..**Holaday**, Rodney A '97 %Vorys SS&P LLP -52 E Gay -Bx1008 -Columbus 43216 **Fx:**464-6350

(614) 462-3194 ..**Holben**, Marla R '89 Franklin Cnty Pub Def -373 S High -12th Fl -Columbus 43215

(513) 868-7600 ..**Holbrock & Jonson Co,LPA** -315 S Monument Av -Bx687 -Hamilton 45012 **Fx:**868-0909

(216) 685-1141 ..**Holbrook**, Amy Clum '02 %Weltman W&R Co,LPA -323 W Lakeside Av -Ste 200 -Cleveland 44113 **Fx:**363-4121

(513) 721-4505 ..**Holbrook**, Lanny R '71 (Holbrook & Assoc) -105 W 4th -Ste 1400 4th & Race Twr -Cincinnati 45202 **Fx:**721-0519

(614) 221-0422 ..**Holbrook**, Michael J '83 -601 S High -Columbus 43215

(216) 621-0200 ..**Holbrook**, Scott C '00 %Baker & H LLP -1900 E 9th -Ste 3200 -Cleveland 44114 **Fx:**696-0740

(440) 934-6164 ..**Holcomb**, Craig A '83 -3075 Stoney Ridge Rd -Avon 44011

(513) 892-8251 ..**Holcomb & Hyde LLP** -6 S 2nd -311 Key Bk Bldg -Hamilton 45011 **Fx:**737-6854

(513) 863-6600 ..**Holcomb**, Jeffrey G '98 JG Holcomb Co,LPA -616 Dayton -Bx1166 -Hamilton 45012 **Fx:**887-4564

(330) 375-2052 ..**Holcomb**, John E '74 Mun Ct Judge -217 S High -Akron 44308

(513) 892-8251 ..**Holcomb**, John M '91 (Holcomb & H LLP) -6 S 2nd -311 Key Bk Bldg -Hamilton 45011 **Fx:**737-6854

(419) 591-1414 ..**Holcomb**, Victor H '99 -733 N Perry -Bx81 -Napoleon 43545 **Fx:**591-1416

(513) 929-3400 ..**Holcombe**, David G '81 (Baker & H LLP) -312 Walnut -Ste 3200 -Cincinnati 45202 **Fx:**929-0303

(330) 762-0765 ..**Holda**, Sheri L '01 -441 Wolf Ledges Pkwy -Ste 400 -Bx0079 -Akron 44309 **Fx:**762-2255

(330) 535-5711 ..**Holden**, Joseph M '52 OfCnsl Brouse M -106 S Main -500 First Natl Twr -Akron 44308 **Fx:**253-8601

(513) 894-2337 ..**Holden**, Kathryn L '86 -3561 Dawn Dr -Hamilton 45011

(330) 297-3850 ..**Holder**, Pamela J '00 Portage Cnty Pros -466 S Chestnut -Ravenna 44266

(614) 292-7755 ..**Holder**, Robert L '71 %OSU/Hlth Sci -370 W 9th Av -200 Meiling Hall -Columbus 43210

(216) 741-2365 ..**Holder**, Timothy D '77 UAW Legal Srvcs -707 Brookpark Rd -Brooklyn Heights 44109

(330) 964-1001 ..**Holder**, William P Jr. '66 -2311 W Market -Ste 1B -Akron 44313

(216) 363-4500 ..**Holderman**, Gretchen A '92 OfCnsl Benesch FC&A LLP -200 Pub Sq -Ste 2300 -Cleveland 44114 **Fx:**363-4588

(614) 792-1790 ..**Holderman**, Mark V '80 Securities Registration Depository -9437 Culross Ct -Dublin 43017

(216) 875-2767 ..**Holdsworth**, Peter A '02 %Bonezzi SM&P Co LPA -526 Superior Av -Ste 1400 -Cleveland 44114 **Fx:**875-1570

(216) 642-3342 ..**Holecek**, Christopher A '88 %Wegman H&V,LPA -6055 Rockside Wds Blvd -Ste 200 -Cleveland 44131 **Fx:**642-8826

(216) 642-3342 ..**Holecek**, Tanja M '89 %Wegman H&V,LPA -6055 Rockside Wds Blvd -Ste 200 -Cleveland 44131 **Fx:**642-8826

(216) 291-0143 ..**Holeski**, Walter L '77 -5001 Mayfld Rd #301 -Lyndhurst 44124 **Fx:**291-0159

(614) 469-0180 ..**Holfinger**, Alissa R '02 %M Shwartz -501 S High -Columbus 43215

(614) 464-4100 ..**Holfinger**, Jonathan L '02 %AuCoin DH&Y LLC -495 S High -Ste 250 -Columbus 43215

(330) 666-5550 ..**Holford**, Andrew M '01 %Cole Co,LPA -863 N Cleveland-Massillon Rd -Akron 44333

(513) 579-3153 ..**Holifield**, Johnathan M '96 Grtr Cincinnati Chmbr of Comm -441 Vine -300 Carew Twr -Cincinnati 45202

(614) 466-8330 ..**Holko**, Mark E '80 Industrial Commssn of OH -30 W Spring -9th Fl -Columbus 43215 **Fx:**752-8785

(859) 288-2613 ..**Hollaender**, David '79 Trane Co -1515 Mercer Rd -Lexington, KY 40511

(330) 493-6966 ..**Holland**, Darrell W Jr. '82 -4200 Munson NW -Bx35426 -Canton 44735

(216) 696-4009 ..**Holland**, David R '97 Kraig & K -614 Superior Av W -Ste 900 -Cleveland 44113 **Fx:**696-1835

(859) 341-2100 ..**Holland**, Gary E Jr. '99 (GE Holland Jr,PLL) -209 Thomas More Pkwy -Crestview Hills, KY 41017

(330) 239-4480 ..**Holland**, John J '88 (Holland & M) -1343 Sharon-Copley Rd -Bx345 -Sharon Center 44274 **Fx:**239-6224

(570) 819-2556 ..**Holland**, John J '88 PSEA -1188 Hwy 315 -Wilkes-Barre, PA 18702

(440) 729-7996 ..**Holland**, Mara J '98 Business Laws,Inc -11630 Chillicothe Rd -Bx185 -Chesterland 44026

(330) 239-4480 ..**Holland & Muirden** -1343 Sharon-Copley Rd -Bx345 -Sharon Center 44274 **Fx:**239-6224

(330) 867-1490 ..**Holland & Muirden** -55 S Miller Rd -Ste 103 -Akron 44333 **Fx:**865-1221

(330) 535-1202 ..**Holland Myers & Myers** -159 S Main -Ste 825 -Akron 44308

Holland, Patrick J '91 -22431 Fairlawn Cir -Fairview Park 44126

(937) 865-4772 ..**Holland**, Renee S '81 US DOE -1 Mound Rd -OSE-GC -Miamisburg 45343

(614) 457-4837 ..**Holland**, Robert J '63 -4837 Slate Run Ct -Columbus 43220

(216) 931-6000 ..**Hollander**, Jason S '99 %Ulmer & B LLP -1300 E 9th -Ste 900 Penton Media Bldg -Cleveland 44114 **Fx:**931-6001

(216) 881-6600 ..**Hollander**, Lisa E '84 NEORSD -3826 Euclid Av -Cleveland 44115 **Fx:**881-4407

(614) 466-6700 ..**Hollanshead**, Susan M '85 Tax Appeals -30 E Broad -Columbus 43215 **Fx:**644-5196

(614) 228-6135 ..**Hollenbaugh**, H Ritchey '73 (Carlile P&M LLP) -366 E Broad -Columbus 43215 **Fx:**221-0216

(937) 228-9179 ..**Hollencamp**, Arthur R '80 Hollencamp & H -130 W 2nd -Ste 2107 -Dayton 45402

(937) 449-6400 ..**Hollenkamp**, Nicholas C '64 (Dinsmore & S LLP) -1 S Main -Ste 1300 One Dayton Centre -Dayton 45402 **Fx:**449-6405

(210) 221-2282 ..**Hollering**, Kristen M '02 US Army JAGC -1306 Stanley Rd -San Antonio, TX 78234

(614) 839-5700 ..**Hollern**, Edwin J '88 -51 Drchstr Ln -Westerville 43081 **Fx:**839-4200

(216) 479-8500 ..**Hollern**, Pamela Ellinger '03 %Squire S&D LLP -127 Pub Sq -4900 Key Twr -Cleveland 44114 **Fx:**479-8780

(513) 765-6351 ..**Holley**, Cathy E '88 LensCrafters,Inc -4000 Luxottica Pl -Mason 45040

(614) 228-4141 ..**Holley**, Elisabeth M '01 RW Meeks Co LPA -511 S High -Columbus 43215

(513) 424-2401 ..**Hollifield**, Lisa S '03 %Casper & C -1 N Main -Bx510 -Middletown 45042 **Fx:**424-0622

(419) 636-6725 ..**Hollin**, Kimberly J '89 Williams Cnty CSEA -117 W Butler -Bryan 43506 **Fx:**636-8843

(330) 376-2700 ..**Hollinger**, Brandie N '03 %Roetzel & A,LPA -222 S Main -Akron 44308 **Fx:**376-4577

(937) 864-2924 ..**Hollingsworth**, David M '77 -7602 Dayton-Sprngfld Rd -Bx52 -Enon 45323 **Fx:**864-2312

Hollingsworth, Diana K '04 -(Address Unavailable)

(330) 456-0091 ..**Hollingsworth**, Jon M '76 -1400 Market Av N -Canton 44714

(937) 424-8556 ..**Hollingsworth**, Jonathan '83 (J Hollingsworth & Assoc LLC) -137 N Main -Ste 1002 -Dayton 45402

(513) 781-2626 ..**Hollingsworth**, Leigh A '88 -Bx19040 -Cleveland 44119

Hollingsworth, Michael M '80 -10538 Big Canoe -Jasper, GA 30143

(513) 852-8200 ..**Hollingsworth**, Robert J '73 Cors & B LLC -537 E Pete Rose Way -Ste 400 -Cincinnati 45202

(216) 621-0200 ..**Hollington**, Richard R Jr. '57 (Baker & H LLP) -1900 E 9th -Ste 3200 -Cleveland 44114 **Fx:**696-0740

(614) 882-2327 ..**Hollins**, Eugene L '88 (Metz & B) -33 E Schrock Rd -Westerville 43081

(937) 255-2838 ..**Hollins**, Gerald B '70 AFMC LO/JAZ -2240 B -Rm 100 -Wright Patterson AFB 45433

(440) 285-2222 ..**Hollins**, Marcia A '92 Magistrate/Ct of Common Pleas -100 Short Court -Cthse -Chardon 44024 **Fx:**285-2127

(419) 254-5107 .. **Hollins**, Sharon E '92 HCR ManorCare -333 N Summit -Bx10086
-Toledo 43699

(513) 721-5672 .. **Hollis**, Charles F III '97 %Benjamin Y&H LLC -312 Elm -Ste 1850
-Cincinnati 45202 **Fx**:721-4388

(330) 658-2960 .. **Hollis**, Cheryl A '96 -Bx201 -Doylestown 44230

(614) 221-2121 .. **Hollis**, Matthew T '01 %Isaac BL&T,LLP -250 E Broad
-Ste 900 Mdlnd Bldg -Columbus 43215 **Fx**:365-9516

(740) 373-5261 .. **Hollister**, Jeffrey L '74 Vanguard Paints & Finishes,Inc
-1409 Greene -Bx654 -Marietta 45750

(513) 553-2433 .. **Hollister**, Lisa H '87 -849 Ten Mile Rd -New Richmond 45157

(419) 422-8713 .. **Hollister**, Robert B '77 (Oxley MHO&W,PLL) -301 E Main Cross
-Bx1086 -Findlay 45840 **Fx**:422-6495

(330) 558-7107 .. **Hollister**, Terry R '74 MTD Products,Inc -Bx368022
-Cleveland 44136

(614) 466-2653 .. **Hollon**, Steven C '81 Supreme Ct of OH -30 E Broad -3rd Fl
-Columbus 43215

(330) 867-6147 .. **Holloway**, Donald P '55 -293 Delaware Pl -Akron 44303

(614) 221-2121 .. **Holloway**, James E '94 Isaac BL&T,LLP -250 E Broad
-Ste 900 Mdlnd Bldg -Columbus 43215 **Fx**:365-9516

.. **Hollowell**, Lyle A '04 -(Address Unavailable)

(937) 226-1973 .. **Holm**, Carol J '82 -130 W 2nd -Ste 1010 -Dayton 45402

(941) 778-5481 .. **Holm**, Duane T '81 -115 N 6th -Bradenton Beach, FL 34217

(419) 562-5771 .. **Holm**, Mary E '77 Crawford Cnty Common Pleas Ct
-112 E Mansfld -Ste 200 -Bucyrus 44820 **Fx**:562-8011

(330) 723-9536 .. **Holman**, Dean '80 Medina Cnty Pros -72 Pub Sq -Medina 44256

(614) 227-2348 .. **Holman**, Michael S '72 (Bricker & E LLP) -100 S 3rd
-Columbus 43215 **Fx**:227-2390

(440) 232-9911 .. **Holman**, Robert B '00 (McDonald FH&H) -24262 Bway Av
-Bx46390 -Oakwood Village 44146 **Fx**:439-2308

(216) 621-7860 .. **Holman**, Ronald D II '86 (Cavitch FD&F) -1717 E 9th -14th Fl
-Cleveland 44114 **Fx**:621-3415

(419) 478-1700 .. **Holmberg**, Claes S '67 -42 W Sylvania -Toledo 43612

(614) 848-4151 .. **Holmes**, Christy M '98 American Family Ins -8415 Pulsar Pl
-Ste 400 -Columbus 43240

(216) 991-0049 .. **Holmes**, Clarence H '53 -3048 Keswick Rd -Cleveland 44120

.. **Holmes**, David Michael '02 -13807 Chevy Oak
-San Antonio, TX 78247

(614) 644-9178 .. **Holmes**, Douglas J '79 Dept of Job & Fam Srvcs -145 S Front
-Columbus 43215

(419) 524-9811 .. **Holmes**, John A '94 (Weldon H&K,LLP) -28 Park Av W
-Bank One Bldg -Mansfield 44902 **Fx**:522-5758

(330) 796-7516 .. **Holmes**, Karen M '85 Goodyear Tire & Rubber Co -1144 E Market
-Dept 762 -Akron 44316

(614) 436-0346 .. **Holmes**, Leanne M '03 %Johnson S & Assoc,LLP -299 S State
-Westerville 43081 **Fx**:436-0347

(419) 354-9250 .. **Holmes**, Linda L '83 %Wood Cnty Pros -One Cthse Sq
-Bowling Green 43402 **Fx**:353-2904

(419) 424-1776 .. **Holmes**, Linda S '84 -200 W Sandusky -Ste 5 -Findlay 45840

(419) 243-6281 .. **Holmes**, Martin J '71 (Shindler NH&S,LLP) -300 Mad Av -Ste 1200
-Toledo 43604 **Fx**:243-0129

(419) 243-6281 .. **Holmes**, Martin J Jr. '95 (Shindler NH&S,LLP) -300 Mad Av
-Ste 1200 -Toledo 43604 **Fx**:243-0129

(937) 443-6820 .. **Holmes**, Nathan E '01 %Thompson H LLP -2000 Cthse Plz NE
-Bx8801 -Dayton 45401 **Fx**:443-6635

(513) 534-6030 .. **Holmes**, Richard W Jr. '00 Fifth Third Bank -38 Fountain Sq Plz
-MD10AT5G -Cincinnati 45263 **Fx**:534-7159

(614) 885-5112 .. **Holmes**, Robert D '49 -7100 N High -Ste 201 -Worthington 43085
Fx:848-5571

(513) 241-6650 .. **Holmes**, Robert F '01 %M Godbey & Assoc -914 Main -Ste 200
-Cincinnati 45202 **Fx**:241-6649

(614) 885-5112 .. **Holmes**, Scott D '80 -7100 N High -Ste 201 -Worthington 43085

(513) 852-8200 .. **Holmes**, Stephen S '82 Cors & B LLC -537 E Pete Rose Way
-Ste 400 -Cincinnati 45202

(419) 471-1489 .. **Holmes**, Terry S '96 UAW Legal Srvcs -3360 W Laskey Rd
-Toledo 43606 **Fx**:471-0498

(216) 520-0088 .. **Holmes**, Thomas C '01 Pepple & W Ltd -5005 Rockside Rd
-Ste 260 -Cleveland 44131 **Fx**:520-0044

(216) 586-3939 .. **Holmgren**, Cedar R '03 %Jones D -901 Lakeside Av
-Cleveland 44114 **Fx**:579-0212

(330) 744-1148 .. **Holmquist**, David K '61 (Henderson CMN&T Co,LPA)
-34 Fed Plz W -Ste 600 Wick Bldg -Youngstown 44503
Fx:744-3807

(614) 225-8516 .. **Holmquist**, Paul R '97 Motorists Mutual Ins Co -471 E Broad
-Columbus 43215

(614) 227-2300 .. **Holodnak**, Robert B '89 Bricker & E LLP -100 S 3rd
-Columbus 43215 **Fx**:227-2390

(513) 721-4450 .. **Holschuh**, John D Jr. '80 (Santen & H) -312 Walnut -Ste 3100
-Cincinnati 45202

.. **Holschuh**, Nathan W '02 -778 Morning -Worthington 43085

(800) 554-9406 .. **Holston**, Timothy L '77 Philip Morris Mgmt Corp
-400 Technecenter Dr -Ste 302 -Milford 45150

(216) 381-1902 .. **Holt**, Donald H '77 -23512 Cedar Rd -Beachwood 44122

(937) 865-6800 .. **Holt**, Jon D '96 Lexis/Nexis -Box933 -Dayton 45401

(216) 621-6570 .. **Holt**, Nicole M '02 %Rademaker MM&G -55 Pub Sq -Ste 1775
-Cleveland 44113 **Fx**:621-1127

(248) 851-9500 .. **Holt**, Robert B Jr. '00 (Secrest WLHT&M) -30903 Nrthwstrn Hwy
-Bx3040 -Farmington Hills, MI 48333 **Fx**:851-2158

(419) 727-7294 .. **Holt**, William J '77 -117 W Main -Ste 104 -Lancaster 43130
-Toledo 43608

(740) 687-0175 .. **Holt**, William J '77 -117 W Main -Ste 104 -Lancaster 43130

.. **Holt-Hudson**, Christine J '02 -787 Thornhill Dr -Cleveland 44108

(419) 738-6768 .. **Holthaus**, James H '81 Grain Production -12143 Infirmary Rd
-Wapakoneta 45895

(614) 461-1311 .. **Holthus**, Douglas P '86 (Reminger & R) -65 E State
-4th Fl Cptl Sq Ofc Bldg -Columbus 43215 **Fx**:232-2410

(330) 264-6115 .. **Holtman**, Ronald J '67 (Logee HS&L) -2171-B Eagle Pass
-Wooster 44691 **Fx**:262-5729

(513) 946-9000 .. **Holtmeier**, Denis G '75 Hamilton Cnty Juv Ct -800 Bway
-Cincinnati 45202 **Fx**:946-9217

(937) 449-6810 .. **Holton**, Thomas A '67 (Porter WM&A LLP) -1 S Main -Ste 1600
-Dayton 45402 **Fx**:449-6820

(740) 943-3739 .. **Holtschulte**, Jeffery M '85 -25 N Franklin -Bx56 -Richwood 43344

(216) 623-9274 .. **Holtz**, Gregory T '77 US Bank -Bx15174 -Cleveland 44115

(440) 746-9550 .. **Holtz**, Theodore S '52 -8180 Brecksvll Rd -Ste 153
-Brecksville 44141 **Fx**:746-9552

(513) 684-3711 .. **Holtzman**, Jan M '72 US Atty -221 E 4th -Ste 400
-Cincinnati 45202 **Fx**:684-6385

(330) 674-1111 .. **Holtzmann**, Cassandra A '99 Holmes Cnty Dept Job & Fam
-85 N Grant -Bx72 -Millersburg 44654

(937) 456-2819 .. **Holtzmuller**, Paul E '82 (PE Holtzmuller Co,LPA) -115 W Main
-Bx332 -Eaton 45320

(330) 762-8638 .. **Holub**, Jerome L '51 (J Holub & Assoc) -159 S Main -Ste 912
-Akron 44308

(814) 868-3900 .. **Holz**, Henry V II '89 The Holz Law Firm -4506 Miller Av
-Erie, PA 16509

(937) 299-8653 .. **Holz**, Michael H '68 -507 Wilmngtn Av -Dayton 45420

(614) 462-2296 .. **Holz**, Richard W '85 (Schottenstein Z&D) -250 West -Bx165020
-Columbus 43216 **Fx**:462-5135

(513) 852-6041 .. **Holzapfel**, Eric C '72 (Wood & L LLP) -600 Vine -Ste 2500
-Cincinnati 45202 **Fx**:852-6087

(937) 320-1047 .. **Holzer**, Richard J '75 -2251 Chrlstn Way -Dayton 45431

(216) 586-3939 .. **Holzer**, Walter S '95 (Jones D) -901 Lakeside Av
-Cleveland 44114 **Fx**:579-0212

(937) 293-2141 .. **Holzfaster Cecil McKnight & Mues** -1105 Wilmngtn Av
-Dayton 45420 **Fx**:293-0914

(614) 228-6885 .. **Holzhall**, Vincent I '02 %Lane A&H LLC -175 S 3rd -Ste 700
-Columbus 43215 **Fx**:228-0146

(513) 523-1900 .. **Holzheimer**, Edward T '69 Hausser & Taylor,LLP
-1001 Lakeside Av E -Ste 1400 -Cleveland 44114

(513) 761-6161 .. **Holzman**, Robert S '64 (Holzman & H) -31 E Galbraith Rd
-Cincinnati 45216

(513) 761-6161 .. **Holzman**, Wallace R Jr. '65 (Holzman & H) -31 E Galbraith Rd
-Cincinnati 45216

(440) 979-1030 .. **Hom**, Harold L '88 (H Hom & Assoc) -21418 Nottnghm Dr
-Fairview Park 44126

(330) 376-2272 .. **Hom**, Martha L '98 %Williams & Assoc -106 S Main -Ste 2300
-Akron 44308 **Fx**:376-5618

(937) 446-1734 .. **Homan**, Ruth E '92 Homan Consulting -Bx222 -Georgetown 45121

(614) 644-2657 .. **Hombach**, Stephen C '88 Dept Ins -2100 Stella Ct
-Columbus 43215

(919) 518-0418 .. **Homick**, Daniel J '78 American Invsco -8608 Cold Sprngs Rd
-Raleigh, NC 27615

(808) 473-4731 .. **Hommon**, Rebecca K '83 Cnsl Navy Region HI -850 Ticonderoga
-Ste 100 -Pearl Harbor, HI 96860

(216) 986-6656 .. **Homolak**, Diane I '89 Hewlett-Packard Co -6050 Oak Tree Blvd
-Ste 200 -Independence 44131

(440) 885-5559 .. **Homolak**, Gloria R '81 -6515 Olde York Rd -Parma Heights 44130
Fx:885-4983

(216) 443-8830 .. **Homolak**, John R '80 Cuyahoga Cnty Cmn Pleas Ct
-1 Lakeside Av -Cleveland 44113

(513) 863-0660 .. **Hon**, Michael D '00 -220 S Monument Av -Hamilton 45011

(419) 281-3409 .. **Honaker**, Jeffrey C '02 First Merit Bank -132 W Main
-Ashland 44805

.. **Hondorf**, Sherrill P '87 -4490 Hartman Ln -Batavia 45103

(614) 508-7204 .. **Hondros**, John G '72 -4140 Exec Pkwy -Westerville 43081

(330) 434-2113 .. **Honeck**, Richard D '79 %Armbruster KKH&B -159 S Main -Ste 720
-Akron 44308

(513) 931-2200 .. **Honerlaw**, Joseph S '80 (Honerlaw & H Co,LPA) -9227 Winton Rd
-Cincinnati 45231

(513) 931-2200 .. **Honerlaw**, Michael J '86 (Honerlaw & H Co,LPA) -9227 Winton Rd
-Cincinnati 45231

(859) 219-2255 .. **Honeycutt**, Kimberly C '00 Stidham & Assoc PSC
-401 Lewis Hargett Cir -Ste 250 -Lexington, KY 40503

(216) 586-7055 .. **Hong**, Karen G '04 %Jones D -901 Lakeside Av -Cleveland 44114
Fx:579-0212

(216) 479-8500 .. **Hong**, Laura K '86 (Squire S&D LLP) -127 Pub Sq -4900 Key Twr
-Cleveland 44114 **Fx**:479-8780

(937) 367-4784 .. **Hong**, Thomas S '01 -6077 Far Hills Av -Ste 200 -Dayton 45459
Fx:312-0334

.. **Honicky**, David A '94 -31312 Carlton Dr -Bay Village 44140

(419) 228-3300 .. **Honigford**, Robert J '91 (Rodabaugh & H) -234 N Main
-Lima 45801

(216) 222-3345 .. **Honohan**, Kathleen R '91 Natl City Bank -1900 E 9th
-17th Fl Loc 2030 -Bx5756 -Cleveland 44101

(440) 403-0628 .. **Honohan**, Michael T '61 -19425 Frazier Dr -Rocky River 44116

(419) 243-1239 .. **Honold**, David L '79 (Wasserman BL&H,LLP) -405 N Huron
-Ste 300 -Toledo 43604

(440) 808-9100 .. **Hood**, David R '93 SrCnsl TravelCenters of Amer
-24601 Ctr Ridge Rd -Ste 200 -Westlake 44145

(513) 621-2120 .. **Hood**, Gordon H '53 OfCnsl Strauss & T,LPA -150 E 4th -4th Fl
-Cincinnati 45202 **Fx**:241-8259

(614) 462-3194 .. **Hood**, James E '03 Franklin Cnty Pub Def -373 S High -12th Fl
-Columbus 43215

(419) 634-6646 .. **Hood**, James M '81 (Grimslid & H) -231 N Main -Ada 45810

(330) 336-3234 .. **Hood**, Terry W '85 -446 McEntee Dr -Wadsworth 44281

(972) 497-0458 .. **Hood**, William Benjamin II '93 Air Systems Components Dit
-1401 N Plano Rd -Richardson, TX 75081

(770) 991-8562 .. **Hoodin**, Daniel E '82 -11 Uppr Riverdale Rd SW
-Riverdale, GA 30274

(440) 835-2463 .. **Hook**, Kenneth A '72 -26123 Lk Rd -Bay Village 44140

(216) 566-5621 .. **Hooker**, David J '75 (Thompson H LLP) -127 Pub Sq -3900 Key
Ctr -Cleveland 44114 **Fx**:566-5800

(419) 448-4100 .. **Hool**, Mary L '98 -Bx29 -Findlay 45839

(419) 243-3800 .. **Hoolahan**, Catherine G '87 -1119 Adams -2nd Fl -Toledo 43624

(303) 233-4000 .. **Hooper**, Michael E '01 OfCnsl Jackson Kelly PLLC -1144 Market
-Wheeling, WV 26003 **Fx**:233-4077

(216) 363-4500 .. **Hooper**, Ryan P '01 %Benesch FC&A LLP -200 Pub Sq -Ste 2300
-Cleveland 44114 **Fx**:363-4588

(330) 343-6647 .. **Hoopingarner**, John M '79 Muskingum Wtrshd Cnsrvncy
-1319 3rd NW -Bx349 -New Philadelphia 44663

(513) 977-8200 .. **Hoops**, Michael W '03 %Dinsmore & S LLP -255 E 5th -Ste 1900
-Cincinnati 45202 **Fx**:977-8141

(330) 342-8203 .. **Hoose**, Robert R '02 J Clunk Co LPA -5061 Hudson Dr -Ste 400
-Hudson 44236 **Fx**:342-8205

(330) 854-3881 .. **Hoover**, Catherine J '92 -Bx483 -Canal Fulton 44614

(330) 342-4910 .. **Hoover**, Dean S '78 Hoover Legal Assoc -200 N Main -Bx1478
-Hudson 44236

(419) 524-9811 ..**Hoover**, Donald E '80 %Weldon H&K,LLP -28 Park Av W
-Bank One Bldg -Mansfield 44902 **Fx**:522-5758

(614) 436-1001 ..**Hoover**, Douglas E '73 -6660 N High -Ste 2E -Worthington 43085
Fx:436-2655

(216) 661-4668 ..**Hoover**, Garin C '93 -Bx34177 -Cleveland 44134

(216) 741-2365 ..**Hoover**, Gregory E '81 UAW Legal Srvcs -707 Brookpark Rd
-Brooklyn Heights 44109

(330) 929-2676 ..**Hoover Heydorn & Herrnstein Co,LPA** -527 Portage Trl
-Cuyahoga Falls 44221

(419) 562-2731 ..**Hoover**, James L '69 Cnty Mun Ct Judge -130 N Walnut -Bx550
-Bucyrus 44820

(330) 650-0525 ..**Hoover**, John E '94 Customer Driven Solutions,LLC -77 Milford Rd
-Ste 274 -Hudson 44236

(330) 971-8209 ..**Hoover**, Kim R '79 Mun Ct Judge -2310 2nd
-Cuyahoga Falls 44221

(614) 210-1848 ..**Hoover**, Larry E '96 OfCnsl Barrett EC&E LLP -7269 Sawmill Rd
-Dublin 43016 **Fx**:210-1841

(419) 241-9000 ..**Hoover**, Lynn M '90 Shumaker L&K,LLP -1000 Jackson
-Toledo 43624 **Fx**:241-6894

(740) 354-1000 ..**Hoover**, Marie Moraleja '94 (Hoover Law Grp) -621 7th
-Portsmouth 45662 **Fx**:353-0661

(773) 399-3659 ..**Hoover**, Mike J '78 Pechiney Plastic Packaging,Inc
-8770 W Bryn Mawr Av -Chicago, IL 60631

(330) 929-2676 ..**Hoover**, Orval Ray '59 (Hoover H&H Co,LPA) -527 Portage Trl
-Cuyahoga Falls 44221

(937) 547-7380 ..**Hoover**, Phillip D '86 Darke Cnty Pros -504 S Bway -Cthse, 3rd Fl
-Greenville 45331

(740) 354-1000 ..**Hoover**, Robert T '88 (Hoover Law Grp) -621 7th
-Portsmouth 45662 **Fx**:353-0661

(740) 354-2375 ..**Hoover**, Roxanne '96 (Garaczkowski & H) -602 Chillicothe
-Portsmouth 45662

(419) 448-4444 ..**Hoover**, Timothy J '04 Seneca Cnty Pros -71 S Wshngtn -Ste E
-Bx667 -Tiffin 44883 **Fx**:448-7911

(716) 551-3341 ..**Hoover**, Timothy W '97 Fed Pub Def -300 Pearl -Ste 450
-Buffalo, NY 14202 **Fx**:551-3346

(216) 736-7232 ..**Hoover**, Valoria C '92 (Kohrman J&K PLL) -1375 E 9th
-One Cleve Ctr 20th Fl -Cleveland 44114 **Fx**:621-6536

(419) 755-9659 ..**Hoovler**, Ryan M '01 Law Dir Ofc -30 N Diamond
-Mansfield 44902

(513) 563-3266 ..**Hopewell**, Craig S '80 Sentron Med,Inc -4445 Lk Forest Dr
-Ste 600 -Cincinnati 45242

(614) 889-1143 ..**Hopfinger**, John M '97 Northwest Capital Corp -5695 Avry Rd
-Dublin 43016

(513) 421-1313 ..**Hopkins**, Bruce G '90 (Griffin-F,LLP) -3500 Redbank Rd
-Cincinnati 45227 **Fx**:421-1118

Hopkins, Gregory L '89 -105 Edgewood Ct -Chagrin Falls 44022

(419) 228-3700 ..**Hopkins**, John J III '98 Allen Cnty Pros -204 N Main -#302
-Lima 45801

(216) 642-0030 ..**Hopkins**, Kathleen C '89 Kamalt Corp -5000 Rockside Rd
-Ste 130 -Independence 44131

(513) 533-3850 ..**Hopkins**, Rick A '84 -8044 Mntgmry Rd -Ste 700 -Cincinnati 45236

(330) 723-9536 ..**Hopkins**, Russell A '94 Medina Cnty Pros -72 Pub Sq
-Medina 44256

(440) 572-2919 ..**Hopkins**, William J '75 -9824 Parkvw Cir -Strongsville 44136

(260) 423-9440 ..**Hopkins**, William T Jr. '91 (Barnes & T) -600 One Summit Sq
-Fort Wayne, IN 46802 **Fx**:424-8316

(440) 843-1340 ..**Hopp**, Fred G '86 -7017 Pearl Rd -Ste 12
-Middleburg Heights 44130

(440) 835-0600 ..**Hoppe**, Herbert J Jr. '53 %Waldheger C,LPA -1991 Crocker Rd
-Ste 550 -Westlake 44145 **Fx**:835-1511

(330) 386-3640 ..**Hoppel**, Richard V '94 Hoppel & Y Co,LPA
-48938 Calcutta-Smith Ferry Rd -East Liverpool 43920

(330) 386-3640 ..**Hoppel & Yajko Co, LPA** -48938 Calcutta-Smith Ferry Rd
-East Liverpool 43920

Hopper, David M '98 -780 W Central Av -Springboro 45066

(513) 232-7578 ..**Hopper**, Kevin J '78 (K Hopper Co,LPA) -7434 Jager Ct
-Cincinnati 45230

(614) 728-6430 ..**Hopper**, William A Jr. '75 Dept Agri -8995 E Main
-Reynoldsburg 43068 **Fx**:995-4585

(614) 228-6345 ..**Hoppers**, John W '68 (Strip HLM&T Co LPA) -575 S 3rd
-Columbus 43215 **Fx**:228-6369

(614) 462-2305 ..**Hopple**, E James '63 (Schottenstein Z&D) -250 West -Bx165020
-Columbus 43216 **Fx**:462-5135

(513) 621-2100 ..**Hopple**, Richard M '73 Beckman W&S LLC -120 E 4th
-1200 Mercantile Ctr -Cincinnati 45202 **Fx**:621-0106

Hopple, Roy E Jr. '53 -Bx27475 -Columbus 43227

(216) 416-3419 ..**Hopps**, Lisa R '93 Forest City Enterprises, Inc -50 Pub Sq
-Ste 1160 -Cleveland 44113

(330) 489-5003 ..**Hopwood**, Arthur H Jr. '91 Nationwide Ins Co -1000 Market Av N
-Bx8379 -Canton 44711

(202) 312-5518 ..**Horbaly**, Jan '69 US Ct of Appls for the Fed Circ -717 Madison
Pl NW -Washington, DC 20439

(216) 781-1212 ..**Horbaly**, Robert S '70 (Walter & H LLP) -1301 E 9th -Ste 3500
-Cleveland 44114 **Fx**:781-5011

(330) 665-5117 ..**Horbus**, Craig S '04 %Witschey & W Co,LPA
-300 N Cleveland-Missillon Rd -Ste 104 -Akron 44333

(937) 645-4190 ..**Hord**, Terry Lee '82 Union Cnty Pros -221 W 5th -Ste 333
-Marysville 43040 **Fx**:645-4191

(513) 579-1414 ..**Hordes**, Donald B '82 (Schwartz M&R) -441 Vine -Ste 2900
-Cincinnati 45202 **Fx**:579-1418

(216) 696-1275 ..**Horejs**, Edward R Jr. '76 Chicago Title Ins -1360 E 9th -Ste 500
-Cleveland 44114

(419) 213-4789 ..**Horen**, Joanne E '96 Lucas Cnty Cmn Pleas Ct -700 Adams
-Toledo 43624

(937) 224-7200 ..**Horenstein Nicholson & Blumenthal** -124 E 3rd -5th Fl
-Dayton 45402 **Fx**:224-3353

(937) 224-7200 ..**Horenstein**, Steven B '72 (Horenstein N&B) -124 E 3rd -5th Fl
-Dayton 45402 **Fx**:224-3353

(216) 475-8497 ..**Horhn**, Ma'Rion D '99 -1370 Ontario Av -Ste 2000 Standard Bldg
-Cleveland 44113 **Fx**:475-5631

(330) 726-8939 ..**Horlick**, Chester W '58 (Horlick & Assoc) -5815 Market
-Youngstown 44512

(330) 726-8939 ..**Horlick**, Todd M '92 Horlick & Assoc -5815 Market
-Youngstown 44512

(216) 566-7992 ..**Horn**, Byron J '89 Thompson H LLP -127 Pub Sq -3900 Key Ctr
-Cleveland 44114 **Fx**:566-5800

(937) 293-6964 ..**Horn**, Charles F '54 -2185 S Dixie Av -Kettering 45409

(415) 391-7111 ..**Horn**, Charles H '75 Wright RO&T -44 Mntgmry -18th Fl
-San Francisco, CA 94104

(216) 431-1636 ..**Horn**, Christopher H '76 -3030 Euclid Av -Ste 406
-Cleveland 44115

(216) 221-3100 ..**Horn**, Dale H '73 -14701 Detroit Av -Ste 540 -Lakewood 44107

(513) 574-5100 ..**Horn**, David A '84 Old Town Title Agncy -4223 Harrison Av
-Cincinnati 45211

(513) 425-2690 ..**Horn**, David C '77 AK Steel Corp -703 Curtis -Middletown 45043

(216) 831-0042 ..**Horn**, Debra J '86 Meyers RF&L LPA -28601 Chagrin Blvd
-Ste 500 -Cleveland 44122 **Fx**:831-0542

(419) 478-6550 ..**Horn**, Gary E '82 -4325 Willys Pkwy -Toledo 43612

(216) 586-3939 ..**Horn**, Melissa E '03 %Jones D -901 Lakeside Av -Cleveland 44114
Fx:579-0212

(216) 443-7800 ..**Horn**, Michael D '77 Cuyahoga Cnty Pros -1200 Ontario -8th Fl
-Cleveland 44113 **Fx**:698-2270

(513) 984-2040 ..**Horn**, Stephanie D '92 %Scheuer M&B LLC
-11025 Reed Hartman Hwy -Cincinnati 45242 **Fx**:984-6590

(614) 846-2000 ..**Hornbeck**, David B '70 (Campbell HC&V,LLC) -7650 Rvrs Edge Dr
-Columbus 43235 **Fx**:846-2003

(231) 941-3445 ..**Hornberger**, Lee '80 -310 W Front -Ste 407
-Traverse City, MI 49684

(330) 456-0091 ..**Hornbrook**, John H '82 -1400 Market Av N -Canton 44714

(740) 345-0850 ..**Horne**, Benjamin D '00 SE OH Lgl Srvcs -12 W Locust Av
-Newark 43055

(313) 965-3900 ..**Horne**, Camille T '95 %Plunkett & C,PC -535 Griswald -Ste 2400
-Detroit, MI 48226

(419) 474-8377 ..**Horne**, Timothy J '85 (Horne & R) -4303 Talmadge Rd -Ste 102
-Toledo 43623 **Fx**:474-8377

Horne, William G '83 Social Security Admin -500 State Av
-Ste 380 -Kansas City, KS 66101

(937) 865-6800 ..**Horner**, Kurt F '91 Lexis/Nexis -Bx933 -Dayton 45401

(419) 244-7753 ..**Horner**, Patricia '88 -412 14th -Toledo 43624

Horner, Robert W III '91 -4907 Lytfld Dr -Dublin 43017

(404) 220-1314 ..**Horner**, Timothy J '92 Deloitte & Touche -191 Pchtree -Ste 1500
-Atlanta, GA 30303

(330) 379-4605 ..**Hornickel**, John H '78 Bridgestone/Firestone
-1200 Firestone Pkwy -Akron 44317

(307) 682-0133 ..**Horning**, David '90 %Lubnau B&D,PC -300 S Gillette Av -Ste 2000
-Bx1028 -Gillette, WY 82717 **Fx**:682-9340

(216) 241-2262 ..**Horning**, Gerald R '84 %Yulish T & Assoc -1419 W 9th
-Hilliard Bldg -Cleveland 44113

(307) 682-2500 ..**Horning**, Richard A '73 -400 S Kendrick Av -Ste 304
-Gillette, WY 82716 **Fx**:685-0527

(937) 773-3212 ..**Hornish-Schlosser**, Laura '00 %McCulloch FF&G Co,LPA
-123 Market -Bx910 -Piqua 45356 **Fx**:773-9672

(937) 378-4769 ..**Hornschemeier**, Patrick M '77 -104½ S Main -Georgetown 45121
Fx:378-6596

(513) 369-5009 ..**Horrell**, Karen H '77 Great Amer Ins Co -580 Walnut -10th Fl
-Cincinnati 45202

(216) 787-3030 ..**Horrigan**, Bruce D '90 Atty Gen -615 W Superior Av -11th Fl
-Cleveland 44113 **Fx**:787-3480

(419) 382-3270 ..**Horrigan**, Dean A '92 -3929 Woodhurst Dr -Toledo 43614

(440) 746-0707 ..**Horrigan**, John J '75 (Burke & H) -3505 E Royalton Rd -#218
-Broadview Heights 44147

(216) 861-5550 ..**Horrigan**, Suzanne K '75 -50 Pub Sq -Ste 400 -Cleveland 44113

(513) 451-0168 ..**Horsley**, William T '00 -Bx389067 -Cincinnati 45238 **Fx**:451-4581

(216) 523-4122 ..**Horst**, John R '68 Eaton Corp -1111 Superior Av -Cleveland 44114

(216) 443-8586 ..**Horst**, Rebecca Mathewson '03 Cuyahoga Cnty Ct Cmmn Pleas
-1200 Ontario -Justice Ctr 11th Fl -Cleveland 44113

(937) 227-3700 ..**Horstman**, Paul L '67 (Faruki IC& PLL) -10 N Ludlow
-500 Cthse Plz SW -Dayton 45402 **Fx**:227-3717

(216) 696-2022 ..**Horton**, Brett E '94 %Graves & H,LLC -1111 Superior Av E
-Cleveland 44114 **Fx**:696-1995

(216) 623-0150 ..**Horton**, Cathy B '86 (Roetzel & A,LPA) -1375 E 9th
-One Cleve Ctr 9th Fl -Cleveland 44114 **Fx**:623-0134

(216) 696-4345 ..**Horton**, Debbie K '86 -1370 Ontario -Ste 1328 Standard Bldg
-Cleveland 44113

(216) 696-2022 ..**Horton**, Earle C '69 (Graves & H,LLC) -1111 Superior Av E
-Cleveland 44114 **Fx**:696-1995

(330) 670-7300 ..**Horton**, Harland B Jr. '72 Hanna C&P,LLP -3737 Embssy Pkwy
-Bx5521 -Akron 44334 **Fx**:670-0977

(404) 639-7494 ..**Horton**, Heather H '99 Cntrs for Disease Control
-1600 Clifton Rd NE -M/S D-53 -Atlanta, GA 30333

(330) 675-2389 ..**Horton**, Monte Jay '92 Trumbull Cnty Juv Ct -220 S Main Av
-Warren 44481

(202) 339-8456 ..**Horton**, Thomas J '81 (Orrick H&S) -3050 K NW
-Washington, DC 20007 **Fx**:339-8500

(614) 221-4000 ..**Horton**, Timothy S '96 %Chester W&S LLP -65 E State -10th Fl
-Columbus 43215 **Fx**:221-4012

(440) 243-5010 ..**Horvath**, Carol D '81 %D Briller Co,LPA -7379 Pearl Rd
-Middleburg Heights 44130 **Fx**:243-0105

(216) 986-0860 ..**Horvath**, David J '91 -7100 E Plsnt Vlly -Independence 44131

(614) 449-8282 ..**Horvath**, Dennis E '01 %Joseph & J -931 S Front -Columbus
43206 **Fx**:449-8287

(330) 725-1962 ..**Horvath**, George '85 -200 Cntryside Dr -Medina 44256

(419) 782-2253 ..**Horvath**, Jeffrey J '01 UAW Legal Srvcs -1500 Baltimore Rd
-Defiance 43512

(650) 839-5070 ..**Horvath**, Katherine F '98 Fish & R PC -500 Arguello -Ste 500
-Redwood City, CA 94063

(330) 865-0021 ..**Horvath**, Michael L '85 -173 Waldorf Dr -Akron 44313

(330) 420-0019 ..**Horvath**, Peter G '81 -38294 Indstrl Park Rd -Lisbon 44432

(216) 664-2808 ..**Horvath**, Richard F '77 Dept of Law -601 Lakeside Av
-Rm 106 City Hall -Cleveland 44114 **Fx**:664-2663

(216) 751-7879 ..**Horvath**, Theodore J '52 -2843 Southington Rd
-Shaker Heights 44120

(202) 690-6013 ..**Horvath**, Thomas D '76 US Dept of H&HS -200 Indpndnc Av
-Rm 635D -Washington, DC 20201

(614) 253-2525 ..**Horvath**, Thomas L '73 -90 N Nelson Rd -Columbus 43219

(216) 586-3939 ..**Horvitz**, Michael J '75 OfCnsl Jones D -901 Lakeside Av
-Cleveland 44114 **Fx**:579-0212

(440) 995-5300 ..**Horvitz**, Richard A '78 Moreland Mgmt Co -6095 Parkland Blvd
-Ste 300 -Mayfield Heights 44124
Horwatt, deRicci T '01 -15 W Beau -Washington, PA 15301

(216) 664-4165 ..**Horwatt**, Robert F Jr. '00 City Empowerment Zone Ofc
-3634 Euclid Av -Ste 200 -Cleveland 44115

(513) 863-0664 ..**Horwitz**, Barbara L '94 %M Wolf -120 N 2nd -Bx741
-Hamilton 45012

(513) 852-8207 ..**Horwitz**, Elizabeth A '85 Cors & B LLC -537 E Pete Rose Way
-Ste 400 -Cincinnati 45202

(937) 278-5100 ..**Horwitz**, Jonathan A '75 (J Horwitz Co,LPA) -6927 N Main
-Ste 202 -Dayton 45415

(937) 225-4979 ..**Horwitz**, Jonathan A '97 Montgomery Cnty Pros -301 W 3rd
-Bx972 -Dayton 45422 Fx:225-3470

(859) 578-1000 ..**Horwitz**, Martin J '78 Horwitz Law Firm,PSC -541 Buttermilk Pike
-Ste 305 -Crescent Springs, KY 41017

(216) 831-0690 ..**Horwitz**, Martin S '79 -Bx22750 -Beachwood 44122

(216) 443-6350 ..**Horwitz**, Mary P '92 8th Dist Ct of Appls -1 Lakeside Av -#202
-Cleveland 44113 Fx:443-2044

(216) 408-3800 ..**Horwitz**, Stuart M '85 -130 Sprngside Dr -Ste 106 -Bath 44333

(216) 622-8200 ..**Horwitz**, Susan R '98 Calfee H&G LLP -800 Superior Av -Ste 1400
-Cleveland 44114 Fx:241-0816

(216) 579-4114 ..**Horwitz**, Thomas M '93 McIntyre K&K Co LPA -1301 E 9th
-Ste 1200 -Cleveland 44114

(202) 879-4000 ..**Horwood**, James N '61 (Spiegel & M) -1333 NH Av NW
-Washington, DC 20036

(614) 462-5310 ..**Hosafros**, Rexann M '85 Franklin Cnty Dom Rltns Ct -373 S High
-3rd Fl -Columbus 43215

(513) 248-0317 ..**Hoseus**, Edwin L Jr. '74 -741 Milford Hills Dr -Milford 45150

(804) 527-4000 ..**Hosey**, Lawrence P '89 Circuit City -9950 Mayland Dr
-Richmond, VA 23233

(937) 433-4090 ..**Hoshor**, Peter B '92 (Gammell HK&R LLP) -7925 Paragon Rd
-Dayton 45459 Fx:433-1510

(513) 362-8228 ..**Hosking**, Tina D '95 Cnsl Integrated Fund Srvcs,Inc -221 E 4th
-Ste 300 -Cincinnati 45202

(216) 622-8200 ..**Hoskins**, George R '98 %Calfee H&G LLP -800 Superior Av
-Ste 1400 -Cleveland 44114 Fx:241-0816

(937) 382-1000 ..**Hoskins**, Joseph C '93 Liberty Capital,Inc -2251 Rombach Av
-Bx1000 -Wilmington 45177

(859) 341-1881 ..**Hoskins**, Kevin F '04 %Deters B&L -207 Thomas More Pkwy
-Crestview Hills, KY 41017

(614) 466-8600 ..**Hoskins**, Patria V '86 Atty Gen -30 E Broad -Columbus 43215
Fx:466-6090

(513) 977-8200 ..**Hoskins**, Robert H '97 %Dinsmore & S LLP -255 E 5th -Ste 1900
-Cincinnati 45202 Fx:977-8141

(617) 742-8191 ..**Hoskins**, William K '62 (Hoskins & Assoc) -85 E India Row -20 A/B
-Boston, MA 02110

(501) 324-6381 ..**Hoskins-Hart**, Teresa L '77 SSA-OHA -700 W Cptl -Rm 2405
-Little Rock, AR 72201

(614) 751-9910 ..**Hoskinson**, Marla D '99 -1602 B Turnberry Dr -Pickerington 43147

(412) 433-5087 ..**Hosler**, Michael J '81 US Steel Corp -600 Grant
-Pittsburgh, PA 15219

(330) 456-7901 ..**Hossler**, Jerome H '49 -315 W Tuscarawas -Ste 305 -Canton
44702 Fx:456-7901

(740) 983-2557 ..**Hosterman**, John W '74 (Margulis GH&H) -50 Bortz -Bx5
-Ashville 43103 Fx:983-2685

(330) 264-6115 ..**Hostetler**, Daniel J '73 (Logee HS&L) -2171-B Eagle Pass
-Wooster 44691 Fx:262-5729

(740) 622-2871 ..**Hostetler**, David L '76 Mun Ct Judge -760 Chestnut
-Coshocton 43812

(740) 349-6663 ..**Hostetter**, James W '76 City Law Dept -40 W Main
-Newark 43055

(330) 296-5100 ..**Hostler**, Michael J '04 Portage Cnty Sheriff Ofc -8240 Infirmary Rd
-Ravenna 44266

(216) 443-8560 ..**Hostovich**, Julianne V '00 %Cuyahoga Cnty Crt Cmmn Pleas
-1200 Ontario -11th Fl -Cleveland 44113

(216) 621-0150 ..**Hotchkiss**, Herbert G '96 %Hahn L&P LLP
-3300 BP Twr/200 Pub Sq -Ste 3300 -Cleveland 44114
Fx:241-2824

(614) 488-2765 ..**Hotchkiss**, Lawrence J '79 -1241 Dublin Rd -Columbus 43215

(419) 468-5044 ..**Hottenroth**, Earl R '62 (Hottenroth GT&G Co,LPA) -126 S Market
-Bx477 -Galion 44833 Fx:468-1308

(419) 468-5044 ..**Hottenroth Garverick Tilson & Garverick Co,LPA**
-126 S Market -Bx477 -Galion 44833 Fx:468-1308

(740) 349-6575 ..**Hottensmith**, Mark H '89 Licking Cnty CSEA -65 E Main -Bx338
-Newark 43058

(440) 356-2600 ..**Hoty-Bliss**, Diane '82 (Bliss & H-B) -20899 Lorain Rd
-Fairview Park 44126

(614) 466-9563 ..**Hotz**, Ann M '91 OH Consumers' Cnsl -10 W Broad -Ste 1800
-Columbus 43215 Fx:466-9475

(440) 892-1990 ..**Hotz**, Gary A '77 -24461 Detroit Rd -Ste 209 -Westlake 44145

(614) 873-3421 ..**Houchard**, John E '64 -128 W Main -Plain City 43064

(614) 466-3947 ..**Houchen**, Betsy J '95 OH Brd of Nursing -17 S High -Ste 400
-Columbus 43215

(614) 480-5218 ..**Houck**, Annette M '98 Huntington National Bank -41 S High -5th Fl
-Columbus 43287

(614) 457-9731 ..**Houck**, Rachael A '04 %Harris & M -941 Chatham Ln -Ste 201
-Columbus 43221 Fx:457-3596

(304) 558-2036 ..**Houdyschell**, Charles P '94 WV Atty Gen/Div of Corrections
-112 Calif Av -Ste 300 -Charleston, WV 25305 Fx:558-5934

(304) 558-2021 ..**Houdyschell**, Jendonnae L '93 WV Atty Gen Ofc
-1900 Kanawha Blvd E -Rm E-26 State Cptl Cmplx
-Charleston, WV 25305

(614) 764-4346 ..**Houfek**, James T '69 OCLC Inc -6565 Frantz Rd -Dublin 43017

(440) 994-6000 ..**Hough**, Edith M '91 Ashtabula Cnty Juv Ct -3816 Donahoe Dr
-Ashtabula 44004

(330) 702-1869 ..**Hough**, Thomas E '73 -Bx111 -Greenford 44422

(502) 560-3679 ..**Houk**, Paul J '82 AEGON USA Inv Mgmt, LLC -400 W Market
-10th Fl -Louisville, KY 40202 Fx:560-3680

(330) 535-8771 ..**Houlihan**, Susan F '98 %Adgate & K -159 S Main -Ste 830
-Akron 44308 Fx:253-8578

(330) 762-2411 ..**Houlihan**, Thomas R '98 %Amer C Co,LPA -159 S Main -6th Fl
-Akron 44308 Fx:762-9918

(210) 255-6041 ..**Houliston-Otto**, Deborah '88 KCI -8023 Vantage Dr
-San Antonio, TX 78230

(202) 720-6110 ..**Houry**, Edward '67 USDA Bd of Contract Appls
-14th & Indpndnc Av SW -Washington, DC 20250

(614) 716-1630 ..**House**, David C '92 SrCnsl Amer Elec Pwr Co -1 Riverside Plz
-Columbus 43215

(440) 892-8430 ..**House**, Linda L '93 -24441 Detroit Rd -Ste 300 -Westlake 44145

(614) 461-1311 ..**House**, Lisa R '03 %Reminger & R -65 E State
-4th Fl Cptl Sq Ofc Bldg -Columbus 43215 Fx:232-2410

(314) 244-2889 ..**House**, Rachael K '99 US Ct of Appeals -111 S 10th -Ste 23.336
-Saint Louis, MO 63102

(216) 266-8216 ..**House**, Robert N '80 GE Lighting -1975 Noble Rd -Bldg 310D
-Cleveland 44112

(614) 223-9300 ..**House**, Ronald L Jr. '86 OfCnsl Benesch FC&A LLP -88 E Broad
-Ste 900 -Columbus 43215 Fx:223-9330

(419) 243-6148 ..**House**, Stephen E '98 Manahan PB&D -414 N Erie -Bx2328
-Toledo 43603

(614) 462-4010 ..**House**, Susan L '87 Franklin Cnty Juv Ct -399 S Front
-Columbus 43215
Householder, David K '92 -65 Parsons Av -Ste 205
-Columbus 43215

(216) 363-6038 ..**Housel**, Robert V Jr. '73 -55 Pub Sq -Ste 1600 -Cleveland 44113

(937) 444-2576 ..**Houser**, John B '71 -750 S High -Bx474 -Mount Orab 45154

(330) 743-1171 ..**Houser**, Joseph M '81 (Manchester BP&U) -201 E Commerce
-Atrium Level 2 Commerce Bldg -Youngstown 44503
Fx:743-1190

(330) 747-4404 ..**Houser**, Mary Beth M '82 Newman O&K,LPA -11 Fed Plz Central
-Ste 1200 -Youngstown 44503 Fx:747-6056

(330) 799-7711 ..**Housley**, Brett A '99 UAW Legal Srvcs -1570 S Canfld-Niles Rd
-Ste 101 -Youngstown 44515

(513) 931-7755 ..**Houston**, Daniel Ray '66 -8287 Winter Rd -Cincinnati 45231

(330) 455-6112 ..**Houston**, Denise M '95 %Tzangas PM&R -220 Market Av S -8th Fl
-Canton 44702 Fx:455-2108

(937) 879-9460 ..**Houston**, Douglas G '95 -1158 Kauffman Av -Fairborn 45324

(859) 341-1881 ..**Houston**, Ellen M '01 %Deters B&L,PSC -2701 Turkeyfoot Rd
-207 Thomas More Pkwy -Crestview Hills, KY 41017 Fx:341-1469

(937) 653-7186 ..**Houston Harris & Denkewalter** -1 Monument Sq -Ste 200
-Bx913 -Urbana 43078 Fx:653-3293

(513) 352-6700 ..**Houston**, James D '00 %Thompson H LLP -312 Walnut -14th Fl
-Cincinnati 45202 Fx:241-4771

(513) 852-8200 ..**Houston**, Janet L '89 Cors & B LLC -537 E Pete Rose Way
-Ste 400 -Cincinnati 45202

(937) 222-2424 ..**Houston**, M Cinamon '97 Freund F&A -1 S Main -Ste 1800
-Dayton 45402 Fx:222-5369

(440) 998-6835 ..**Houston**, Pamela D '99 %Andrews & P LLC -4817 State Rd
-Ste 100 -Bx10 -Ashtabula 44005

(254) 287-2797 ..**Hover**, Matthew R '03 US Army 4th Infantry Div -Ofc of SJAocate
-Fort Hood, TX 76544

(937) 224-7847 ..**Hovey**, Susan J '82 %Myers & F Co,LPA -18 W 1st -Ste 200
-Dayton 45402

(216) 241-6689 ..**Hovinen**, Jeffrey R '95 (HSA Law) -200 Pub Sq -Ste 4020
-Cleveland 44114

(419) 252-5523 ..**Hovland**, Valerie B '93 HCR ManorCare -333 N Summit
-Toledo 43604

(513) 934-0893 ..**Howard**, Anne K '01 -785 Lk Bluff Ct -Lebanon 45036
Fx:934-0895

(513) 421-7300 ..**Howard**, Barbara J '79 (Howard & B Co,LPA) -120 E 4th
-960 Mercantile Ctr -Cincinnati 45202

(513) 421-7300 ..**Howard & Bodnar Co,LPA** -120 E 4th -960 Mercantile Ctr
-Cincinnati 45202

(419) 447-2521 ..**Howard**, Brent T '87 (Supance & H) -84-88 S Wshngtn -Bx767
-Tiffin 44883 Fx:447-2310

(513) 381-2838 ..**Howard**, Catherine E '03 %Taft S&H LLP -425 Walnut -Ste 1800
-Cincinnati 45202 Fx:381-0205

(614) 766-9100 ..**Howard**, Charles C '94 OH Automobile Dealers Assn -655
Metro Pl S -Ste 270 -Dublin 43017

(330) 744-3198 ..**Howard**, Cherie H '82 NE OH Legal Srvcs -11 Fed Plz Central
-Ste 800 -Youngstown 44503

(419) 347-2573 ..**Howard**, David A '85 -4398 Plymouth-Springmill Rd -Shelby 44875

(727) 573-3800 ..**Howard**, Deborah J '86 Raymond James Fincl,Inc
-880 Carillon Pkwy -Bx12749 -Saint Petersburg, FL 33733
Howard, Donald E '77 -3530 Warrensvll Ctr Rd -Cleveland 44122

(937) 644-3849 ..**Howard**, Frank '75 (Schulze H&C) -110 S Main -Bx562
-Marysville 43040 Fx:644-1426

(703) 770-9300 ..**Howard**, James E '94 %Nixon P LLP -8180 Greensboro Dr
-Ste 800 -McLean, VA 22102

(513) 534-3167 ..**Howard**, Jerry R '01 Fifth Third Bank -38 Fountain Sq Plz
-MD 10AT5K -Cincinnati 45263 Fx:534-7296

(513) 868-3663 ..**Howard**, John G '87 -723 Dayton -Hamilton 45011

(740) 354-4200 ..**Howard**, Joshua D '04 %Johnson & O,LPA -701 6th -Bx1505
-Portsmouth 45662 Fx:353-2413

(419) 874-3536 ..**Howard**, Kay L '92 (Leatherman WD&H) -353 Elm
-Perrysburg 43551 Fx:874-3899

(937) 225-4652 ..**Howard**, Kelli R '01 Montgomery Cnty Pub Def -117 S Main
-Ste 400 -Dayton 45422 Fx:225-3449

(216) 348-5400 ..**Howard**, Kristin K '99 %McDonald H Co,LPA -600 Superior Av E
-Ste 2100 -Cleveland 44114 Fx:348-5474

(937) 644-6629 ..**Howard**, Lowell B Jr. '87 Cnsl Honda of Amer Mfg,Inc
-24000 Honda Pkwy -Leg Dept -Marysville 43040 Fx:644-6583

(585) 232-5300 ..**Howard**, Michael A '90 (Boylan BCV&W,LLP) -2400 Chase Sq
-Rochester, NY 14604 Fx:232-3528

(330) 451-7455 ..**Howard**, Michael L '79 Stark Cnty Fam Ct -110 Central Plz S
-#610 -Canton 44702

(740) 432-6990 ..**Howard**, Patrick J '89 -1032 Beatty Av -Ste 1 -Cambridge 43725
Fx:432-5528

(216) 475-4600 ..**Howard**, Randolph '95 Cuyahoga County Prosecutor
-12600 Rockside Rd -Ste 112 -Cleveland 44125

(937) 222-3000 ..**Howard**, Robert J '02 %Falke & D LLC -30 Wyoming
-Dayton 45409 Fx:222-1414

(216) 443-5809 ..**Howard**, Shataia G '01 Cuyahoga Cnty Pros -1910 Carnegie Av
-Whitlatch Bldg -Cleveland 44115 Fx:443-5815

(614) 464-6400 ..**Howard**, Stephen M '76 OfCnsl Vorys SS&P LLP -52 E Gay
-Bx1008 -Columbus 43216 Fx:464-6350
Howard, Steven W '85 -5498 Fawnbrook Ln -Dublin 43017

(419) 872-2600 ..**Howard**, Susan E '92 -900 W South Boundary -Ste 10
-Perrysburg 43551

Howard, Susan H '88 -32 Herrick Ct -Tiffin 44883
(614) 236-0011 .. Howard, Ted R '64 -227 S Broadleigh Rd -Columbus 43209
(513) 695-1548 .. Howard, Thomas E A '04 Warren Cnty CSEA -500 Justice Dr
-Lebanon 45036 Fx:695-2969
(216) 621-4244 .. Howard, Timothy J '68 -1406 W 6th -4th Fl -Cleveland 44113
(330) 376-3607 .. Howard, William E Jr. '68 (Howard & G Co,LPA) -50 S Main
-Ste 610 -Akron 44308
(215) 665-2173 .. Howard, William H '78 Cozen O -1900 Market
-Philadelphia, PA 19103
(614) 469-0100 .. Howarth, Robert F Jr. '70 (Shoemaker H&T LLP) -471 E Broad
-Ste 2001 -Columbus 43215 Fx:280-9675
(330) 860-1634 .. Howdyshell, Donald E '86 McDermott,Inc -20 S Van Buren Av
-Bx351 -Barberton 44203
(740) 342-3582 .. Howdyshell, Mark J '91 Howdyshell & O Ltd -113 N Main -Bx508
-New Lexington 43764
(740) 342-3582 .. Howdyshell & O'Neil Ltd -113 N Main -Bx508
-New Lexington 43764
(859) 572-0100 .. Howe, Albert B '70 -1407 Alexandria Pike -Fort Thomas, KY 41075
(216) 443-5829 .. Howe, Elizabeth '97 Cuyahoga Cnty Juv Ct -1910 Carnegie Av
-Cleveland 44115
(513) 632-5332 .. Howe, William D '77 (DeVita & H) -117 E Court -Cincinnati 45202
(419) 354-9250 .. Howe-Gebers, Gwendolyn K '89 %Wood Cnty Pros
-One Cthse Sq -Bowling Green 43402 Fx:353-2904
(859) 655-7000 .. Howell, Brittany L '04 %Nelson & S,PSC -639 Wshngtn Av
-Newport, KY 41071 Fx:655-8417
(513) 622-2184 .. Howell, John M '88 SrCnsl Procter & Gamble Co
-Health Care Rsrch Ctr -Bx8006 -Mason 45040
(616) 396-1265 .. Howell, Linda S '89 %Scholten & F -Bx9008 -Holland, MI 49422
Howell, Lynn A '89 -Bx66493 -Saint Petersburg, FL 33736
(419) 678-7111 .. Howell, Paul E '85 (PE Howell & Co,LPA) -420 S 1st
-Coldwater 45828
(937) 547-7380 .. Howell, Richard M '78 Darke Cnty Pros -504 S Bway
-Cthse, 3rd Fl -Greenville 45331
(614) 222-8686 .. Howenstein, C Bradley '91 %Scott S&W LLP -50 W Broad
-2500 LeVeque Twr -Columbus 43215 Fx:222-8688
Howery, Katrice M '02 -4408 W 173rd -Cleveland 44135
(330) 499-7453 .. Howes, Hubert A '53 -210 Summit SW -North Canton 44720
(330) 492-8717 .. Howes, Philip E '60 (Buckingham D&B,LLP) -4518 Fulton Dr NW
-Bx35548 -Canton 44735 Fx:492-9625
(330) 499-7453 .. Howes, Shirley E '96 -Bx2154 -North Canton 44720
(419) 947-4426 .. Howland, Charles S '83 (Howland & H) -58 N Main -Mount Gilead
43338 Fx:947-9926
(419) 947-4426 .. Howland, Hollis L '85 (Howland & H) -58 N Main
-Mount Gilead 43338 Fx:947-9926
(937) 225-5761 .. Howland, Linda L '80 Montgomery Cnty Pros -301 W 3rd -Bx972
-Dayton 45422 Fx:225-3470
(612) 333-7309 .. Howland, Naomi R '04 %FC Tyler,PA -331 2nd Av S
-230 TriTech Ofc Ctr -Minneapolis, MN 55408
(404) 885-3000 .. Howle, Joel P '95 %Troutman S LLP -600 Pchtree NE -Ste 5200
-Atlanta, GA 30308 Fx:885-3900
(937) 225-4053 .. Howley, Michael J '96 Montgomery Cnty Dom Rltns Ct -301 W 3rd
-Bx972 -Dayton 45422 Fx:496-7443
(216) 381-2900 .. Hoy, Kelly M '89 First Interstate Properties -25333 Cedar Rd
-Ste 300 -Lyndhurst 44124 Fx:381-2901
(415) 984-5607 .. Hoy, Michael G '85 Genesis Prof Liability Mgrs -160 Pine -Ste 350
-San Francisco, CA 94111
(614) 462-3714 .. Hoy, Suzanne H '88 %Franklin Cnty CSEA -80 E Fulton
-Columbus 43215 Fx:462-7185
(704) 523-2625 .. Hoying, Paul T '84 -1515 Mockingbird Ln -Ste 704
-Charlotte, NC 28209
(614) 644-0854 .. Hoylman, Barbara N '90 Industrial Commssn of OH -30 W Spring
-9th Fl -Columbus 43215 Fx:752-8785
(513) 218-5621 .. Hoyt, Bradley R '82 (B Hoyt CPA) -7900 Woodside -Landon 45039
(513) 425-2805 .. Hoyt, Lawrence K '87 AK Steel Corp -703 Curtis
-Middletown 45043
Hoyt, Marcia S '79 -407 Moore -Hackettstown, NJ 07840
(614) 228-1541 .. Hoyt, Matthew W '00 %Baker & H LLP -65 E State -Ste 2100
-Columbus 43215 Fx:462-2616
(330) 757-9293 .. Hoza, Michael L Jr. '94 -211 S Main -Poland 44514
(216) 736-7279 .. Hoza, Michele L '01 %Kohrman J&K PLL -1375 E 9th
-One Cleve Ctr 20th Fl -Cleveland 44114 Fx:621-6536
(614) 781-1400 .. Hrabcak, Michael '91 (Hrabcak & Co,LPA) -67 E Wilson Bridge Rd
-Worthington 43085
(614) 461-1551 .. Hrach, James A '91 Barkan & B Co LPA -81 S 4th -Ste 300
-Columbus 43215
Hrenko, Kimberly A '01 -7029 Austin Pnt Dr -Concord 44077
(216) 261-0200 .. Hribar, Joyce A '89 -27801 Euclid Av -Ste 500 -Euclid 44132
(216) 261-0200 .. Hribar, Paul J '41 -27801 Euclid Av -Ste 500 -Euclid 44132
(843) 720-3737 .. Hricik, Richard A '93 (Clekis & H) -Drwr1867
-Charleston, SC 29402
Hricko, Linda L '03 -(Address Unavailable)
(330) 643-0212 .. Hrina, David J '00 %Buckingham D&B,LLP -50 S Main -Bx1500
-Akron 44309 Fx:258-6559
(330) 565-5147 .. Hrina, Pamela S '01 (Villano & H Co,LPA) -1397 S Canfld-Niles Rd
-Austintown 44515 Fx:270-3696
(440) 888-7000 .. Hrisko, Paul A '69 Independence Capital -5579 Pearl Rd -Ste 100
-Parma 44129
(440) 282-8101 .. Hritsko, John J '54 -4642 Oberlin Av -Westlawn Pro Bldg
-Lorain 44053
(513) 425-5081 .. Hritz, John G '85 AK Steel Corp -703 Curtis -Middletown 45043
Hritz, Judith J '83 -Bx31149 -Independence 44131
(330) 864-5550 .. Hrivnak, Bret A '04 %Hahn L&P LLP -One GOJO Plz -Ste 300
-Akron 44311 Fx:864-7986
(440) 526-6722 .. Hronek, Christina M '02 %Wadsworth & B -8927 Brecksvll Rd
-Brecksville 44141
(937) 223-5200 .. Hruska, Gary M '80 (Flanagan LH&S) -318 W 4th -Dayton 45402
Fx:223-3335
(513) 534-0680 .. Hubanks, Tanya A '98 Fifth 3rd Bank -38 Fountain Sq Plz
-MD 10AT76-1060 -Cincinnati 45263
(614) 466-5967 .. Hubbard, Barton A '81 Atty Gen -30 E Broad -Columbus 43215
Fx:466-8226
(239) 540-3345 .. Hubbard, Cynthia J '04 -4427 SE 16th Pl -Ste 1
-Cape Coral, FL 33904 Fx:540-3346

(614) 228-6885 .. Hubbard, Edward G '97 Lane A&H LLC -175 S 3rd -Ste 700
-Columbus 43215 Fx:228-0146
(513) 744-6765 .. Hubbard, James R '91 Fifth 3rd Bank -38 Fountain Square Plz
-Cincinnati 45263
(216) 566-5562 .. Hubbard, Kenneth W '96 Thompson H LLP -127 Pub Sq
-3900 Key Ctr -Cleveland 44114 Fx:566-5800
(440) 323-7451 .. Hubbard, Neal E '69 Northern Savings & Loan Co -200 Middle Av
-Elyria 44035
(419) 782-3010 .. Hubbard, Stephen F '84 (Weaner ZBY&H,Ltd) -401 Wayne Av
-Defiance 43512 Fx:782-8426
(540) 375-8572 .. Hubbard, Timothy K '77 Yokohama Tire Corp -1500 Indna Av
-Salem, VA 24153 Fx:375-0230
(216) 566-5644 .. Hubbard, William J '03 Thompson H LLP -127 Pub Sq
-3900 Key Ctr -Cleveland 44114 Fx:566-5800
(419) 241-1200 .. Hubbell, Bradley F '02 %Cooper & W,LPA -900 Adams
-Toledo 43624 Fx:242-5675
(513) 932-2121 .. Hubbell, Martin E '01 %Diehl & D -304 E Warren -Lebanon 45036
(216) 736-7215 .. Hubbert, Christopher J '91 Kohrman J&K PLL -1375 E 9th
-One Cleve Ctr 20th Fl -Cleveland 44114 Fx:621-6536
(614) 469-1301 .. Hubble, Adam J '94 Chorpenning G&P Co,LPA -585 S Front
-Ste 250 -Columbus 43215
(740) 348-4533 .. Hubbuch, Carol A '99 Licking Mem Hlth Syst -1320 W Main
-Newark 43055
(904) 329-9660 .. Huber, Arlene B '77 -520 Oak -Palatka, FL 32177
(513) 481-1999 .. Huber, Giselle K '86 -3507 Glenmore Av -Cincinnati 45211
(330) 725-6666 .. Huber, Gregory A '84 (Williams & B,LLP) -105 W Lbrty -Bx394
-Medina 44258
(937) 225-4892 .. Huber, Janna L '02 Montgomery Cnty Pros/CSEA -14 W 4th
-Ste 510 -Dayton 45402
(937) 429-0577 .. Huber, John B '67 -2930 Stauffer Dr -Beavercreek 45434
(513) 744-8780 .. Huber, John C '94 Fifth 3rd Bank -38 Fountain Sq Plz -MD 1090VI
-Cincinnati 45263
(216) 586-3939 .. Huber, Mary Elizabeth '96 %Jones D -901 Lakeside Av
-Cleveland 44114 Fx:579-0212
(937) 445-6546 .. Huber, Matthew B '96 NCR Corp -1700 S Patterson Blvd -WHQ3
-Dayton 45479
(419) 499-4285 .. Huber, Michael J '95 -11 W Church -Bx1350 -Milan 44846
(859) 746-4191 .. Huber, Sigmund E '94 SrCnsl Toyota Motor Mfg NA -25 Atl Av
-Erlanger, KY 41018
(419) 394-7270 .. Huber, William E '68 -137 E Spring -Bx298 -Saint Marys 45885
Fx:394-5836
(330) 740-2208 .. Huberman, Mark A '76 Mahoning Cnty Dom Rltns Ct -120 Market
-Youngstown 44503
(937) 456-5581 .. Hubler, Charles D '69 C Hubler Co,LPA -201 S Barron -Bx349
-Eaton 45320
(614) 228-3125 .. Hubler, Julie P '86 -141 E Town -Ste 100 -Columbus 43215
(614) 228-3125 .. Hubler, Lloyd E III '85 -141 E Town -Ste 100 -Columbus 43215
Fx:228-3154
(614) 445-4455 .. Huckaby, Kristen J '95 OH Mulch Supply,Inc -2140 Advance Av
-Columbus 43207
(440) 461-4019 .. Hudacko, Andrew R '76 -6776 Seneca Rd -Mayfield Village 44143
Fx:461-0155
(330) 792-6612 .. Hudak, Ann C '71 -3400 White Beech Ln -Youngstown 44511
(614) 221-8800 .. Hudak, Clara J '74 (Hudak & R) -118 E Main -Columbus 43215
(330) 535-2220 .. Hudak, Daniel J '69 Hudak S&F -2020 Front -Ste 307
-Cuyahoga Falls 44221 Fx:535-1435
(330) 535-2220 .. Hudak, Daniel J Jr. '99 (Hudak S&F) -2020 Front -Ste 307
-Cuyahoga Falls 44221 Fx:535-1435
(216) 928-2200 .. Hudak, David J '99 %Sutter OM&F -1301 E 9th -3600 Erievw Twr
-Cleveland 44114 Fx:928-4400
(216) 292-3900 .. Hudak, James A '74 -29425 Chagrin Blvd -Ste 304
-Cleveland 44122
(614) 728-3053 .. Hudak, Kimberly Z '96 Workers Comp -30 W Spring -Level 26
-Columbus 43215
(330) 376-2700 .. Hudak, Michael J '87 (Roetzel & A,LPA) -222 S Main
-Akron 44308 Fx:376-4577
(330) 535-2220 .. Hudak Shunk & Farine -2020 Front -Ste 307
-Cuyahoga Falls 44221 Fx:535-1435
(614) 545-4118 .. Huddle, William G '81 Prospect Bk -6851 N High
-Worthington 43085
(513) 574-8900 .. Huddleson, William A '74 (Huddleson & Co,LPA)
-6061 Brdgtown Rd -Cincinnati 45248
(614) 488-7878 .. Huddleston, Charles L III '77 -3650 Olentangy Rvr Rd -Ste 210
-Columbus 43214 Fx:246-7180
(740) 353-8895 .. Huddleston, David M '77 -602 Chillicothe -Private Ofc
-Portsmouth 45662
(859) 371-1611 .. Huddleston, Marianne A '02 Rawlings & Assoc -8111 US Hwy 42
-Florence, KY 41042
(513) 241-3100 .. Hudec, Pamela A '96 %Lerner S&R -120 E 4th -8th Fl
-Cincinnati 45202
(978) 681-2404 .. Hudgens, Ronald C '75 Agilent Tech -40 Shattuck Rd
-Andover, MA 01810
(419) 251-0700 .. Hudgin, Barry F '84 Mercy Hlth Prtnrs -2200 Jffrsn Av
-Toledo 43624
(614) 464-6215 .. Hudok, Timothy D '02 %Vorys SS&P LLP -52 E Gay -Bx1008
-Columbus 43216 Fx:464-6350
(513) 929-4834 .. Hudson, Calvin B '93 Fed Pub Def -36 E 7th -2000 CBLD Ctr
-Cincinnati 45202
(513) 422-4015 .. Hudson, Eugene M Jr. '63 -4015 Grand Av -Middletown 45044
Hudson, Marcia M '01 -302 E 2nd -Perrysburg 43551
(614) 221-3155 .. Hudson, Mary Jo '89 (Bailey C LLC) -10 W Broad
-Columbus 43215 Fx:221-0479
(216) 241-0011 .. Hudson, Matthew C '04 %Goldberg & O -323 Lakeside Av W
-Ste 450 -Cleveland 44113
(614) 464-1211 .. Hudson, Nicolette R '99 %Frost BT LLC -10 W Broad -Ste 1000
-Columbus 43215 Fx:464-1737
(859) 655-4200 .. Hudson, Robert D '87 Greenebaum D&M PLLC
-50 E RiverCenter Blvd -Ste 1800 -Covington, KY 41011
Fx:655-4239
(941) 957-0500 .. Hudson, Thomas S '80 -1800 2nd -Ste 960 -Sarasota, FL 34236
(216) 586-3939 .. Hudson, Timothy M '04 %Jones D -901 Lakeside Av -Cleveland
44114 Fx:579-0212
(614) 462-4461 .. Hudson, Woodrow W '92 Franklin Cnty Dom Rltns Ct -373 S High
-5th Fl -Columbus 43215

(330) 792-1063 ..**Hudzik,** John C '83 Industrial Commssn of OH -242 Fed Plz W
-Ste 303 -Youngstown 44503

(216) 861-5582 ..**Hudzinski,** Michael E '89 (Fay SFM&M LLP) -1100 Superior Av
-7th Fl -Cleveland 44114 **Fx:**241-1666

(330) 375-5412 ..**Huebert,** Jacob H '04 Hon D Cook -2 S Main -433 US
Crthse & Fed Bldg -Akron 44308

(248) 945-3300 ..**Huebner,** Robert J '91 Allstate Insurance -2000 Town Ctr
-Ste 1800 -Southfield, MI 48075 **Fx:**945-3315

(937) 225-4652 ..**Huelsman,** Brian D '91 Montgomery Cnty Pub Def -117 S Main
-Ste 400 -Dayton 45422 **Fx:**225-3449

(614) 227-8791 ..**Huelsman,** Douglas L '04 Ernst & Young,LLP -41 S High -11th Fl
-Columbus 43215

(317) 614-4424 ..**Huelsman,** Kristopher M '94 US Customs & Border Protection
-6026 Lakeside Blvd -Asst Chief Cnsl Ofc -Indianapolis, IN 46208

(419) 535-4825 ..**Huelsman,** Lisa A '94 Dana Corp -4500 Dorr -Bx1000
-Toledo 43697

(502) 564-3940 ..**Huelsmann,** Martin J '70 KY Pub Srvcs -Bx615
-Frankfort, KY 40602

(412) 366-3333 ..**Huetter,** Glenn A Jr. '96 (Willman & A) -705 McKnight Park Dr
-Pittsburgh, PA 15237 **Fx:**366-3462

(216) 771-1330 ..**Huettner,** John A '87 -526 Superior Av E -630 Leader Bldg
-Cleveland 44114

(614) 487-8667 ..**Huey,** Donald Timothy '84 -2396 Wimbledon Rd -Columbus 43220

(614) 446-4470 ..**Huey,** Karen J '93 OH Criminal Justice Srvcs -140 E Town -14th Fl
-Columbus 43215 **Fx:**466-4516

(740) 593-5046 ..**Huff,** Debra K '83 Athens Cnty CSEA -Bx37 -The Plains 45780

(614) 387-0304 ..**Huff,** H Delmar '03 OH Sec of State -180 E Broad
-Columbus 43215 **Fx:**466-5409

(216) 241-2838 ..**Huff,** Kimberlie L '00 %Taft S&H LLP -200 Pub Sq -3500 BP Twr
-Cleveland 44114 **Fx:**241-3707

 Huff, Leslye M '99 -26717 Hurlingham Rd -Beachwood 44122

(740) 592-3208 ..**Huff,** Michael R '83 Athens Cnty Pros -Athens Cnty Cthse
-Athens 45701 **Fx:**592-3291

(614) 227-2000 ..**Huff,** Michael T '04 %Porter WM&A LLP -41 S High
-Columbus 43215 **Fx:**227-2100

(937) 228-2292 ..**Huffer,** Brian R '82 Mdwst Abstract Co -40 S Main -Ste 600
-Dayton 45402

(740) 474-2179 ..**Huffer & Huffer Co,LPA** -130 W Franklin -Bx464
-Circleville 43113

(740) 474-2179 ..**Huffer,** Robert H '56 (Huffer & H Co,LPA) -130 W Franklin -Bx464
-Circleville 43113

(740) 474-2179 ..**Huffer,** Roy H Jr. '64 Huffer & H Co,LPA -130 W Franklin -Bx464
-Circleville 43113

(317) 822-8010 ..**Huffer,** Steven K '87 (Huffer & W) -151 N Delaware
-1850 Market Square Ctr -Indianapolis, IN 46204

(440) 871-8111 ..**Huffman,** Charles S Jr. '52 Huffman I&F LLC -24441 Detroit Rd
-Ste 200 -Westlake 44145

(419) 352-2535 ..**Huffman,** Diane R '82 (Spitler HY&N,LLP) -131 E Court
-Bowling Green 43402 **Fx:**353-8728

(216) 227-3000 ..**Huffman,** Donald J '77 Huffman & T -14701 Detroit Av -Ste 450
-Lakewood 44107

(419) 423-4321 ..**Huffman,** Douglas A '87 (Firmin S&H Co,LPA) -220 W Sandusky
-Bx963 -Findlay 45839 **Fx:**423-8484

(614) 469-3939 ..**Huffman,** Fordham E '84 (Jones D) -325 John H McConnell Blvd
-Ste 600 -Bx165017 -Columbus 43216 **Fx:**461-4198

(440) 871-8111 ..**Huffman Isaac & Frost LLC** -24441 Detroit Rd -Ste 200
-Westlake 44145

(419) 227-3423 ..**Huffman,** John C '89 (Huffman KB&B LLC) -127-129 N Pierce
-Bx546 -Lima 45802 **Fx:**228-1937

(419) 242-8461 ..**Huffman,** John L '88 -520 Mad Av -Ste 520 -Toledo 43604

(419) 227-3423 ..**Huffman Kelley Becker & Brock LLC** -127-129 N Pierce -Bx546
-Lima 45802 **Fx:**228-1937

(937) 335-0550 ..**Huffman Landis & Weaks Co,LPA** -80 S Plum -Troy 45373

(419) 227-3423 ..**Huffman,** Lawrence A '81 %Huffman KB&B LLC
-127-129 N Pierce -Bx546 -Lima 45802 **Fx:**228-1937

(419) 227-3423 ..**Huffman,** Lawrence S '58 %Huffman KB&B LLC
-127-129 N Pierce -Bx546 -Lima 45802 **Fx:**228-1937

(419) 227-3423 ..**Huffman,** Matthew C '85 (Huffman KB&B LLC) -127-129 N Pierce
-Bx546 -Lima 45802 **Fx:**228-1937

(419) 352-2535 ..**Huffman,** Rex H '79 (Spitler HY&N,LLP) -131 E Court
-Bowling Green 43402 **Fx:**353-8728

(937) 335-0550 ..**Huffman,** Robert J Jr. '88 Huffman L&W Co,LPA -80 S Plum
-Troy 45373

(937) 335-0550 ..**Huffman,** Samuel L '95 Huffman L&W Co,LPA -80 S Plum
-Troy 45373

(440) 871-8111 ..**Huffman,** William C '80 Huffman I&F LLC -24441 Detroit Rd
-Ste 200 -Westlake 44145

(216) 381-8800 ..**Hufford,** Allen C '02 (Cocirteu H&S,LLC) -4040 Mayfld Rd
-Cleveland 44121

(419) 872-1998 ..**Huffstutler,** Rahn M '79 (Huffstutler & Assoc) -134 W
South Boundary -Perrysburg 43551

(614) 466-6696 ..**Hufstader,** Dennis L '75 Atty Gen -150 E Gay -Columbus 43215
Fx:752-2538

(216) 566-5500 ..**Huggins,** Emily S '04 %Thompson H LLP -127 Pub Sq
-3900 Key Ctr -Cleveland 44114 **Fx:**566-5800

(740) 373-5455 ..**Huggins,** James S '81 (Theisen B,LPA) -424 2nd -Bx739
-Marietta 45750 **Fx:**373-4409

(412) 227-2500 ..**Huggler,** Lyndall J '86 Blumling & G,LLP -1200 Koppers Bldg
-Pittsburgh, PA 15219

(513) 421-4020 ..**Hughes,** Angela M '04 %Cohen TK&S,LLC -250 E 5th -Ste 1200
-Cincinnati 45202 **Fx:**241-4922

(614) 227-2000 ..**Hughes,** Anne M '01 %Porter WM&A LLP -41 S High
-Columbus 43215 **Fx:**227-2100

(614) 410-6032 ..**Hughes,** Darrell A '99 Sequent Inc -222 E Campus Vw Blvd
-Columbus 43235

(216) 522-4856 ..**Hughes,** Debra M '87 Fed Pub Def -1660 W 2nd -Ste 750
-Cleveland 44113

(614) 224-1222 ..**Hughes,** Donald Timothy '84 Maguire & S,LLP -250 Civic Ctr Dr
-Ste 200 -Columbus 43215 **Fx:**224-1236

(614) 365-2700 ..**Hughes,** Donald W '97 (Squire S&D LLP) -41 S High
-1300 Huntngtn Ctr -Columbus 43215 **Fx:**365-2499

(859) 491-7000 ..**Hughes,** Gregory T '78 -243 Elm -Bx16167 -Ludlow, KY 41016

(614) 451-4824 ..**Hughes,** James E '72 -4021 Longhill Rd -Columbus 43220

(614) 227-2365 ..**Hughes,** James J III '86 (Bricker & E LLP) -100 S 3rd
-Columbus 43215 **Fx:**227-2390

(614) 221-5216 ..**Hughes,** James M '94 %Wiles BB&B Co,LPA -300 Spruce -1st Fl
-Columbus 43215 **Fx:**221-5692

(937) 865-6800 ..**Hughes,** Kathleen M '93 Lexis/Nexis -Bx933 -Dayton 45401

(216) 574-8210 ..**Hughes,** Kathleen M '95 School District -1380 E 6th
-Cleveland 44114

(937) 748-9447 ..**Hughes,** Kevin D '95 %C Cornyn Co,LPA -10 Fairway Dr
-Springboro 45066

(614) 227-2000 ..**Hughes,** Lawrence Bradfield '99 %Porter WM&A LLP -41 S High
-Columbus 43215 **Fx:**227-2100

(614) 410-1700 ..**Hughes,** Martin J '83 (M Hughes & Assoc) -150 E
Wilson Bridge Rd -Ste 300 -Worthington 43085

(513) 243-1412 ..**Hughes,** Matthew W '85 GE -1 Neumann Way -Cincinnati 45215

(216) 622-8200 ..**Hughes,** Maura L '93 (Calfee H&G LLP) -800 Superior Av
-Ste 1400 -Cleveland 44114 **Fx:**241-0816

(216) 515-1660 ..**Hughes,** Michael M '62 OfCnsl Frantz W LLP -127 Pub Sq
-2500 Key Center -Cleveland 44114 **Fx:**515-1650

(216) 595-1040 ..**Hughes,** Michael M Jr. '89 -27030 Cedar Rd -Ste 619
-Beachwood 44122

(614) 462-3555 ..**Hughes,** Michael T '01 Franklin Cnty Pros -373 S High
-Columbus 43215

(859) 341-1881 ..**Hughes,** Patrick R '97 Deters B&L,PSC -2701 Turkeyfoot Rd
-207 Thomas More Pkwy -Crestview Hills, KY 41017 **Fx:**341-1469

(614) 462-3194 ..**Hughes,** Paula S '96 Franklin Cnty Pub Def -373 S High -12th Fl
-Columbus 43215

(513) 983-0925 ..**Hughes,** Richard A '88 Procter & Gamble Co-Legal -1 Procter &
Gamble Plz -Cincinnati 45202

(513) 852-8200 ..**Hughes,** Richard Scott '99 %Cors & B LLC -537 E Pete Rose Way
-Ste 400 -Cincinnati 45202

(614) 451-7060 ..**Hughes,** Stephanie M '89 -Bx21041 -Columbus 43221

(614) 224-1222 ..**Hughes,** Steven R '83 %Maguire & S,LLP -250 Civic Ctr Dr
-Ste 200 -Columbus 43215 **Fx:**224-1236

(502) 852-5555 ..**Hughes,** Tom W '91 Univ of Louisville -222 Brigman Hall
-MS03-17 -Louisville, KY 40292

(937) 376-6629 ..**Hughey,** Andrew C '99 Cntrl State Univ -Bx1004
-Wilberforce 45384

(614) 475-9511 ..**Huhn,** Richard M '69 (Blumenstiel HA&E,LLC)
-261 W Johnstown Rd -Columbus 43230 **Fx:**475-0348

(330) 972-7331 ..**Huhn,** Wilson Ray '77 Univ of Akron Law Schl -302 E Buchtel Av
-Akron 44325

(843) 228-2568 ..**Hulbert,** Brian E '84 USMC -Depot Law Center MCRD
-Parris Island, SC 29902

(216) 751-1490 ..**Hulett,** W Michael '03 %B Caterino & Assoc
-3550 Warrensvll Ctr Rd -Ste 102N -Shaker Heights 44122
Fx:751-1492

(330) 762-6767 ..**Hull,** Alexandra '89 (A Hull Co,LPA) -362 S Main -Durkin Bldg
-Akron 44311

(412) 635-3167 ..**Hull,** Edwin J '83 -977 Perry Hwy -Pittsburgh, PA 15237

(513) 863-6700 ..**Hull,** Gregory E '83 (Millikin & F) -6 S 2nd -6th Fl -Bx598
-Hamilton 45012 **Fx:**863-0031

(440) 461-8880 ..**Hull,** Jonathan '78 -6505 Wilson Mills Rd -Mayfield Village 44143

(614) 875-0490 ..**Hull,** Joseph W '76 -3793 Bway -Grove City 43123

(216) 622-8200 ..**Hull,** Mark R '04 %Calfee H&G LLP -800 Superior Av -Ste 1400
-Cleveland 44114 **Fx:**241-0816

(614) 644-2640 ..**Hull,** Melissa L '98 Dept Ins -2100 Stella Ct -Columbus 43215

(440) 234-8811 ..**Hull,** Peter H '71 City of Middleburg Heights -15700 Bagley Rd
-Middleburg Heights 44130

(330) 679-2328 ..**Hull,** Rick L '81 Sky Bank -10 E Main -Salineville 43945

(330) 759-0102 ..**Hull,** Victor C '96 Petrarco Co -3055 Belmont Av
-Youngstown 44505 **Fx:**759-0199

(513) 870-2287 ..**Huller,** Mark J '82 Cincinnati Ins Co -Bx145496 -Cincinnati 45250

(216) 687-1311 ..**Hulme,** Roy A '79 (Reminger & R) -101 Prospect Av W
-1400 Mdlnd Bldg -Cleveland 44115 **Fx:**687-1841

(614) 222-4139 ..**Hulthen,** Amy M '88 CBC Cos,Inc -250 E Town -Columbus 43215

(614) 794-9770 ..**Hulthen,** Martin R '88 Amer Fam Ins Grp -550 Polaris Pkwy
-Ste 300 -Westerville 43082

(216) 696-1422 ..**Hultin,** Pamela N '89 (McCarthy LC&L Co,LPA)
-101 Prospect Av W -1800 Mdlnd Bldg -Cleveland 44115
Fx:696-1210

(330) 963-3939 ..**Hults,** Richard E '93 -2239 Enterprise E -Twinsburg 44087

(330) 482-1222 ..**Hum,** Robert W II '86 -117 Columbiana Shopping Plz -Bx394
-Columbiana 44408

(614) 462-4555 ..**Human,** Randy E '94 Franklin Cnty CSEA -80 E Fulton
-Columbus 43215

(513) 868-8721 ..**Humbach,** Thomas E '77 -723 Dayton -Hamilton 45011

(216) 583-4629 ..**Humbarger,** Michael L '96 Ernst & Young LLP -925 Euclid Av
-Ste 1300 -Cleveland 44115

(513) 768-4344 ..**Humbert,** Mark A '90 -1014 Vine -Ste 1919 -Cincinnati 45202

(330) 342-8203 ..**Humbert,** Ted A '81 %J Clunk Co LPA -5061 Hudson Dr -Ste 400
-Hudson 44236 **Fx:**342-8205

(440) 323-1019 ..**Hume,** Ernest E '71 -230 3rd -2nd Fl -Elyria 44035

(330) 746-8491 ..**Hume,** Martin S '81 (M Hume Co LPA) -6 Fed Plz Central -Ste 905
-Youngstown 44503

(740) 852-4085 ..**Hume,** Stephen L '87 -113 N Main -London 43140

(949) 798-5650 ..**Humenik,** Mark F '95 Athletes First,LLC -4695 Macarthur Ct
-11th Fl -Newport Beach, CA 92660

(304) 234-7144 ..**Hummel,** David W '03 -80 12th -Ste 303 -Wheeling, WV 26003

(614) 645-6945 ..**Hummel,** Gordon B '60 City Atty -90 W Broad -Columbus 43215

(614) 469-8000 ..**Hummel,** Gretchen J '79 Cnsl McNees W&N,LLC -21 E State
-17th Fl -Columbus 43215 **Fx:**469-4653

(216) 222-2967 ..**Hummel,** Jaqueline M '02 Cnsl Natl City Corp -1900 E 9th
-01-2174 -Cleveland 44114 **Fx:**222-3332

(614) 252-2300 ..**Hummel,** Terry Van '82 Calig & H,LPA -854 E Broad
-Columbus 43205

(614) 220-9200 ..**Hummer,** Brendan B '03 %Rourke & B,LLP -495 S High -Ste 450
-Columbus 43215 **Fx:**220-7900

(419) 486-9999 ..**Hummer,** Donal J '83 Cnsl Wineland Lgl Srvcs Corp -520 Mad Av
-Ste 915 -Toledo 43604 **Fx:**486-8939

(614) 645-6822 ..**Hummer,** Mark A '86 Franklin Cnty Mun Ct -375 S High
-Courtroom 10B -Columbus 43215

(859) 331-7900 ..**Humpert,** William A '71 (Kramer & H) -2493 Dixie Hwy
-Covington, KY 41017

(330) 492-8717 ..**Humphrey**, Christopher S '93 (Buckingham D&B,LLP)
-4518 Fulton Dr NW -Bx35548 -Canton 44735 Fx:492-9625

(614) 799-2800 ..**Humphrey**, David L '86 (Zaino & H LPA) -5775 Perimeter Dr
-Ste 275 -Dublin 43017 Fx:799-1500

(330) 337-7622 ..**Humphrey**, Don W Jr. '77 -562 E State -Salem 44460
Fx:337-9010

(614) 221-4000 ..**Humphrey**, Guy R '84 (Chester W&S LLP) -65 E State -10th Fl
-Columbus 43215 Fx:221-4012

Humphrey, Ian C '02 -Bx12451 -Columbus 43212

Humphrey, Laurie F '01 -585 Kenilworth -Bay Village 44140

(330) 668-3073 ..**Humphrey**, Michael B '85 -Bx13326 -Fairlawn 44334

(216) 241-2880 ..**Humphrey**, Robert M '82 (Cowden HN&L) -50 Pub Sq -Ste 1414
-Cleveland 44113 Fx:241-2881

(513) 241-2324 ..**Humphrey**, Thomas W '93 (Wood H&E LLP) -441 Vine -Ste 2700
-Cincinnati 45202 Fx:421-7269

(614) 241-5550 ..**Humphreys**, Kevin E '98 OfCnsl Brunner Law Firm Co,LPA
-545 E Town -Columbus 43215 Fx:241-5551

(330) 643-2234 ..**Humphrys**, Dawn A '98 Summit Cnty Cmmn Pleas Ct -209 S High
-Akron 44308

(440) 998-2628 ..**Humpolick**, Joseph A '79 Ashtabula Cnty Pub Def -4817 State Rd
-Ste 202 -Ashtabula 44004 Fx:998-2972

(810) 244-9252 ..**Hundley**, Seymour Jr. '85 (S Hundley Jr,PC) -Bx99207
-Troy, MI 48099

(937) 222-1285 ..**Hungerford**, Eric S '67 Beerman Realty Co -11 W Monument Bldg
-8th Fl -Dayton 45402

(216) 398-4100 ..**Hungerford**, James M '80 J Hungerford Co,LPA
-2424 Broadvw Rd -Cleveland 44109

(614) 488-7924 ..**Hunker**, Frederick '81 %OBLIC -1650 Lk Shr Dr -Bx2708
-Columbus 43216

(614) 451-1437 ..**Hunkins**, Blaine B '52 -4161 Rowanne Rd -Columbus 43214

(740) 374-6109 ..**Hunsaker**, Charles R '72 Peoples Bancorp Inc -138 Putman
-Marietta 45750

(330) 208-1000 ..**Hunsicker**, J Bruce '80 OfCnsl Vorys SS&P LLP -106 S Main
-First Natl Twr -Akron 44308

(330) 535-5711 ..**Hunsicker**, Oscar A Jr. '48 OfCnsl Brouse M -106 S Main
-500 First Natl Twr -Akron 44308 Fx:253-8601

(561) 832-5900 ..**Hunston**, Walter Jay Jr. '76 Cnsl Boose CCLMM&O
-515 N Flagler Dr -19th Fl -West Palm Beach, FL 33401
Fx:820-0381

(912) 267-2596 ..**Hunsucker**, Keith E '87 US Dept of the Treasury -Bldg 69 Leg Div
-Glynco, GA 31524

(859) 291-9000 ..**Hunt**, Amy L '02 %Parry DF&S -411 Garrard
-Covington, KY 41012 Fx:291-9300

(937) 562-5250 ..**Hunt**, Andrew J '01 Greene Cnty Pros -61 Greene -Xenia 45385

(614) 228-1541 ..**Hunt**, Ashanti T '02 %Baker & H LLP -65 E State -Ste 2100
-Columbus 43215 Fx:462-2616

(330) 489-3395 ..**Hunt**, Bernard L '84 Pros -218 Cleveland Av SW -Bx24218
-Canton 44702

(937) 335-7783 ..**Hunt**, Carroll E '51 -825 Charrington Way -Tipp City 45371

(419) 882-0518 ..**Hunt**, Charles N '58 (Hunt MD&O) -5808 Monroe -Bx370
-Sylvania 43560

(859) 252-3476 ..**Hunt**, Dean K '99 -520 W Short -Lexington, KY 40507

(937) 222-2500 ..**Hunt**, Deborah D '88 (Sebaly S&D) -1900 Kettering Twr
-Dayton 45423 Fx:222-6554

(614) 466-2872 ..**Hunt**, Holly J '02 Atty Gen -30 E Broad -Columbus 43215
Fx:728-7592

(513) 732-0770 ..**Hunt**, James A '74 (Hunt N&S) -97 Main -Batavia 45103
Fx:732-3423

(614) 466-6434 ..**Hunt**, James F Jr. '76 OH Dept Commerce -77 S High
-Columbus 43266

(419) 222-1040 ..**Hunt**, James Ira '48 (Hunt & J) -400 W North -Lima 45801

(614) 466-8911 ..**Hunt**, Jason M '98 Atty Gen -30 E Broad -Columbus 43215
Fx:728-7582

(419) 222-1040 ..**Hunt & Johnson** -400 W North -Lima 45801

(614) 415-7468 ..**Hunt**, Jonathan J '00 Limited Brands Inc -3 Limited Pkwy -DC3
-Columbus 43230

(202) 275-7041 ..**Hunt**, JuanCarlos M '97 EEOC -1400 L NW -Ste 200
-Washington, DC 20005

(216) 861-4104 ..**Hunt**, Judith S '84 -1370 Ontarop -Ste 600 -Cleveland 44113

Hunt, Karen S '84 Dept of Labor/Worker Comp Ofc
-200 Const Av NW -N4421i -Washington, DC 20210

(937) 222-1800 ..**Hunt**, Kevin M '01 %R Hunt Co,LPA -130 W 2nd -Ste 201
-Dayton 45402

(614) 444-3900 ..**Hunt**, Mark M '97 -755 S High -Columbus 43215

(513) 381-7399 ..**Hunt**, Marshall C Jr. '67 -66 E Hollister -Cincinnati 45219

(419) 882-0518 ..**Hunt Milliken DeVictor & O'Brien** -5808 Monroe -Bx370
-Sylvania 43560

(937) 443-6908 ..**Hunt**, Nathan C '01 %Thompson H LLP -2000 Cthse Plz NE
-Bx8801 -Dayton 45401 Fx:443-6635

(937) 865-6800 ..**Hunt**, Paul D '88 Lexis/Nexis -Bx933 -Dayton 45401

(330) 497-0700 ..**Hunt**, Randall C '78 (Krugliak WG&D Co,LPA) -4775 Munson NW
-Bx36963 -Canton 44735 Fx:497-4020

(937) 222-1800 ..**Hunt**, Richard M '66 (R Hunt Co,LPA) -130 W 2nd -Ste 201
-Dayton 45402

(330) 253-1111 ..**Hunt**, Robert C '76 Calhoun W&H -159 S Main -Ste 707
-Akron 44308

(216) 781-1212 ..**Hunt**, Robert Todd '84 (Walter & H LLP) -1301 E 9th -Ste 3500
-Cleveland 44114 Fx:575-0911

(513) 241-0400 ..**Hunt**, Stephen R '80 (Aronoff R&H Co,LPA) -425 Walnut
-Ste 2400 -Cincinnati 45202 Fx:241-2877

(216) 696-9555 ..**Hunt**, Thomas J '96 -526 Superior Av E -Leader Bldg Ste 1540
-Cleveland 44114

(513) 684-3711 ..**Hunt**, William E '72 US Atty -221 E 4th -Ste 400 -Cincinnati 45202
Fx:684-6385

(440) 892-0400 ..**Hunt**, William H '75 (Hunt & C,LLC) -2001 Crocker Rd -Ste 530
-Westlake 44145 Fx:892-1966

(513) 721-4532 ..**Hunter**, Bruce A '84 (Katz TB&H) -255 E 5th -Ste 2400
-Cincinnati 45202

(614) 442-5626 ..**Hunter Carnahan Shoub & Byard** -3360 Tremont Rd -2nd Fl
-Columbus 43221 Fx:442-5625

(248) 358-5645 ..**Hunter**, Christopher C '95 D Mitcham & Assoc
-25300 Telegraph Rd -Ste 360 -Bx2070 -Southfield, MI 48037

(216) 896-2461 ..**Hunter**, Christopher H '89 Parker Hannifin Corp
-6035 Parkland Blvd -Cleveland 44124

(614) 644-2658 ..**Hunter**, Daniel J '81 Dept Ins -2100 Stella Ct -Columbus 43215

(330) 535-5711 ..**Hunter**, David M '75 (Brouse M) -106 S Main -500 First Natl Twr
-Akron 44308 Fx:253-8601

(419) 994-3141 ..**Hunter**, David M '96 -244 W Main -Loudonville 44842

(937) 378-4151 ..**Hunter**, David Michael '03 %Brown Cnty Pros -200 E Cherry
-Georgetown 45121

(216) 292-5200 ..**Hunter**, Douglas S '00 %Hoffman Lgl Grp,LLC
-23230 Chagrin Blvd -Ste 232 -Cleveland 44122

(740) 592-5580 ..**Hunter**, Garry E '74 -26 S Congress -Athens 45701

(614) 221-2525 ..**Hunter**, James K III '73 -529 S 3rd -Columbus 43215

(614) 793-1770 ..**Hunter**, Jason C '01 %Kreiner & P Co,LPA -6047 Frantz Rd
-Ste 203 -Dublin 43017

(937) 562-5250 ..**Hunter**, Jeffrey D '93 Greene Cnty Pros -61 Greene -Xenia 45385

(419) 255-4300 ..**Hunter**, John J Jr. '86 %Hunter & S Co,LPA -1700 Canton Av
-One Canton Sq -Toledo 43624 Fx:255-9121

(614) 464-1969 ..**Hunter**, Kyle L '98 -601 S High -Columbus 43215

(614) 442-5626 ..**Hunter**, Michael J '85 (Hunter CS&B) -3360 Tremont Rd -2nd Fl
-Columbus 43221 Fx:442-5625

(740) 353-2155 ..**Hunter**, Richard S '50 -Bx1222 -Portsmouth 45662

(330) 823-1220 ..**Hunter**, Robert R '50 OfCnsl Hunter & H -520 E Main
-Alliance 44601 Fx:823-1232

(330) 823-1220 ..**Hunter**, Robert R Jr. '75 (Hunter & H) -520 E Main -Alliance 44601
Fx:823-1232

(216) 522-1900 ..**Hunter**, Sandra K '77 -600 Superior Av E -Ste 1300
-Cleveland 44114

(419) 255-4300 ..**Hunter & Schank Co,LPA** -1700 Canton Av -One Canton Sq
-Toledo 43624 Fx:255-9121

(330) 533-6119 ..**Hunter**, Scott D '88 (Hunter-Stevens) -6715 Tippecanoe Rd
-Canfield 44406

(937) 228-8080 ..**Hunter**, Stephen C '74 -226 Talbott Twr -Dayton 45402

(614) 461-1311 ..**Hunter**, Tracie M '93 (Reminger & R) -65 E State
-4th Fl Cptl Sq Ofc Bldg -Columbus 43215 Fx:232-2410

(859) 291-2255 ..**Hunter**, Tracie M '93 WCVG Radio -Bx15228
-Covington, KY 41015

(330) 438-8659 ..**Huntley**, Jacquelyn M '89 Stark Cnty CSEA -116 Cleveland Av
-Canton 44701

(614) 326-3399 ..**Huntley**, Jeffrey L '83 (Huntley & H) -3280 Riverside Dr -Ste 20
-Columbus 43221

(401) 841-1524 ..**Huntley**, Todd C '96 US Navy JAG Corps -360 Elliot
-Newport, RI 02841

(614) 944-5220 ..**Huntley**, Wendi R '92 The SPEC Group,Ltd -4200 Regent
-Ste 200 -Columbus 43219 Fx:245-6010

(216) 348-5400 ..**Huntsberger**, Jeffrey R '80 (McDonald H Co,LPA)
-600 Superior Av E -Ste 2100 -Cleveland 44114 Fx:348-5474

(304) 723-4442 ..**Huntzinger**, Keith R '01 %J Connolly,LLC -3071 Penn Av -Ste B
-Weirton, WV 26062

(419) 421-2948 ..**Hunziker**, Robin Morris '92 Marathon Ashland Petroleum
-539 S Main -Rm 885M -Findlay 45840

(216) 861-6556 ..**Hupertz**, Lawrence R '83 -25550 Chagrin Blvd -Ste 320
-Cleveland 44122

(216) 566-2504 ..**Hupp**, Diane H '89 Sherwin Williams Co -101 Prospect Av NW
-Cleveland 44115

(216) 875-2767 ..**Hupp**, Steven J '88 (Bonezzi SM&P Co LPA) -526 Superior Av
-Ste 1400 -Cleveland 44114 Fx:875-1570

(513) 763-3585 ..**Huprich**, Douglas L '58 Griffin-F,LLP -3500 Redbank Rd
-Cincinnati 45227 Fx:421-1118

(717) 849-4466 ..**Hura**, Douglas J '88 Cnsl DENTSPLY Intl Inc -570 W Cllg Av
-Bx872 -York, PA 17405

(330) 405-5061 ..**Hura**, Mark S '85 %Williams S&S Co,LPA -2241 Pinnacle Pkwy
-Twinsburg 44087 Fx:405-5586

(513) 867-1717 ..**Hurchanik**, Richard L '82 -110 N 3rd -Hamilton 45011

(216) 932-7331 ..**Hurd**, Calvin F Jr. '61 -3392 Ormond Rd -Cleveland Heights 44118

(614) 876-0480 ..**Hurd**, Dwight I '59 -4235 Westleton Ct -Columbus 43221

(216) 241-1000 ..**Hurd**, Gail A '85 -310 Lakeside Av W -Ste 500 -Cleveland 44113
Fx:241-1093

(513) 421-4646 ..**Hurd**, John K '74 McCaslin I&M,LPA -632 Vine -Ste 900
-Cincinnati 45202 Fx:421-7929

(614) 644-3037 ..**Hurdley**, Jeffery H '89 EPA -122 S Front -Bx1049
-Columbus 43216

(614) 621-8888 ..**Hurlbert**, Jay J '96 %S Schiff & Assoc -88 W Main
-Columbus 43215

(513) 421-6630 ..**Hurlburt**, Christopher H '00 %Lindhorst & D Co,LPA -312 Walnut
-Ste 2300 -Cincinnati 45202

(216) 566-2486 ..**Hurlbut**, Chris L '88 Sherwin-Williams Co -101 Prospect Av NW
-Cleveland 44115

(202) 514-6498 ..**Hurley**, Charles P '82 DOJ-Tax Div -Bx7238
-Washington, DC 20044

(440) 357-5558 ..**Hurley**, John J Jr. '68 (Nelson S&H) -8 N State -Ste 201
-Painesville 44077

(440) 237-1100 ..**Hurley**, Kenneth R '80 -6060 Royalton Rd -North Royalton 44133

(440) 357-5558 ..**Hurley**, Michael P '74 (Nelson S&H) -8 N State -Ste 201
-Painesville 44077

(216) 241-2838 ..**Hurley**, Nora L '89 OfCnsl Taft S&H LLP -200 Pub Sq
-3500 BP Twr -Cleveland 44114 Fx:241-3707

(216) 621-5980 ..**Hurley**, Scott R '94 Legal Aid -1223 W 6th -Cleveland 44113

(513) 381-2838 ..**Hurley**, Timothy J '76 (Taft S&H LLP) -425 Walnut -Ste 1800
-Cincinnati 45202 Fx:381-0205

Hurley, William H '01 -25008 Lk Rd -Bay Village 44140

(513) 863-0660 ..**Hurr**, Daniel J '86 (Masana M&H) -220 S Monument Av
-Hamilton 45011

(419) 674-2284 ..**Hursh**, Tammie K '95 Hardin Cnty Pros -1 Cthse Sq -Ste 50
-Kenton 43326

(440) 933-9884 ..**Hurst**, Bonita M '95 -18 WhitakerCove -Avon Lake 44012

(505) 827-4295 ..**Hurst**, Elizabeth C '86 NM Pub Regulation -224 E Palace Av
-Santa Fe, NM 87501

(309) 675-5525 ..**Hurst**, J Michael '99 Caterpillar Inc -100 NE Adams -Leg Dept
-Peoria, IL 61629 Fx:675-1711

(440) 395-0237 ..**Hurst**, John P '79 Progressive Ins Co -300 N Cmmns Blvd
-OHF 11 -Mayfield Village 44143

(216) 514-9999 ..**Hurst**, Jonathan R '01 Cornrich & C Co,LPA -2000 Auburn Dr
-Ste 315 -Cleveland 44122 Fx:514-8500

Hurst, Linda L '84 -145½ Gradolph -Toledo 43612

(614) 221-1216 .. **Hurst**, Rufus B '87 (Downes H&F) -400 S 5th -Ste 200 -Columbus
43215 **Fx:**221-8769

(614) 719-3200 .. **Hurst**, Sarah E '02 US Dist Ct SDOH -85 Marconi Blvd
-169 JP Kinnery US Cthse -Columbus 43215

(216) 696-5297 .. **Hurst**, Tricia L '04 Bilfield & S Co,LPA -1301 E 9th -Ste
1000 Erievw Twr -Cleveland 44114 **Fx:**696-2316

(614) 462-3194 .. **Hurt**, Emily '00 Franklin Cnty Pub Def -373 S High -12th Fl
-Columbus 43215

(330) 860-2702 .. **Hurt**, John P '79 Babcock & Wilcox Co -20 S Van Buren Av
-Barberton 44203

(216) 321-2775 .. **Hurt**, Marcia E '81 -18201 Shelburne Rd -Cleveland 44118

(440) 605-6660 .. **Hurtuk & Daroff Co,LPA** -6120 Parkland Blvd -Ste 100
-Cleveland 44124 **Fx:**605-6666

(440) 605-6660 .. **Hurtuk**, Edward A '79 (Hurtuk & D Co,LPA) -6120 Parkland Blvd
-Ste 100 -Cleveland 44124 **Fx:**605-6666

(651) 848-5835 .. **Hurwitz**, Joel A '93 West Group,Cleveland -610 Opperman Dr
-Eagan, MN 55123

(330) 455-6112 .. **Huryn**, Christopher M '93 (Tzangas PM&R) -220 Market Av S
-8th Fl -Canton 44702 **Fx:**455-2108

(513) 362-8700 .. **Huse**, William M '03 %Blank R -201 E 5th -Ste 1700
-Cincinnati 45202 **Fx:**362-8787

Husmann, Reinert W '75 -218 W Pearl -Union City, IN 47390

(248) 512-4126 .. **Huss**, Allan M '73 SrCnsl DaimlerChrysler Corp -1000 Chrysler Dr
-CIMS 485-13-65 -Auburn Hills, MI 48326 **Fx:**512-4202

(513) 523-6369 .. **Huss**, Dan E '65 -29 N Beech -Oxford 45056

(440) 687-1111 .. **Hussey**, Robert R '71 (R Hussey Co,LPA) -Bx700
-North Olmsted 44070

(513) 421-7700 .. **Hust**, Bruce K '86 -30 E Cntrl Pkwy -Ste 300 -Cincinnati 45202
Fx:421-7794

(513) 583-4200 .. **Hust**, John W '75 (Schroeder MB&P) -11935 Mason Rd -Ste 110
-Cincinnati 45249

(937) 644-6626 .. **Hust**, Robert L '86 Cnsl Honda of Amer Mfg -24000 Honda Pkwy
-Marysville 43040

(614) 265-6565 .. **Hustead**, Sherrie L '03 Dept of Natl Res -4435 Fountain Sq Dr
-Watercraft Invstgtr -Columbus 43224

Husted, Gerald E '75 -318 Sycamore Dr -Pickerington 43147

(937) 399-1429 .. **Husted**, Stanley N II '72 -1009 Moorefld Rd -Springfield 45503

(614) 818-9014 .. **Huston**, Catherine E '83 -12 Westervll Sq PMB 190
-Westerville 43081

(330) 376-8888 .. **Huston**, Charles M '70 -254 W Market -Akron 44303

(614) 644-2658 .. **Huston**, Daniel H '89 Dept Ins -2100 Stella Ct -Columbus 43215

(513) 634-9358 .. **Huston**, Larry L '87 Procter & Gamble -8611 Beckett Rd
-Beckett Ride Tech Ctr -West Chester 45069

(419) 227-7775 .. **Huston-Kinworthy**, Carlene '92 -211-215 N Elizabeth
-Lima 45801

(513) 753-2800 .. **Husvar**, Amy G '95 Advanced Land Title Agency
-4355 Ferguson Dr -Ste 190 -Cincinnati 45245

(513) 381-9200 .. **Hutcherson**, William H Jr. '54 OfCnsl Rendigs FK&D,LLP
-One W 4th -Ste 900 -Cincinnati 45202 **Fx:**381-9206

(419) 213-6685 .. **Hutcheson**, William G '83 Lucas Cnty Cmn Pleas Ct -429 N Mich
-Toledo 43624

(614) 340-5000 .. **Hutchins**, Antony Robert '85 -411 E Town -Columbus 43215

(513) 891-1530 .. **Hutchins**, Johanna B '98 %Keating R&S -8050 Hosbrook -Ste 200
-Cincinnati 45236 **Fx:**891-1537

(216) 443-8603 .. **Hutchins**, Sara E '03 Cuyahoga Cnty Ct Cmmn Pleas
-1200 Ontario -Justice Ctr 11th Fl -Cleveland 44113

(740) 369-0330 .. **Hutchins**, Shelby V '61 Hutchins Law Ofc -3491 Olentangy Rvr Rd
-Bx1056 -Delaware 43015

(614) 228-5331 .. **Hutchins**, William J III '71 %Don M Casto Org
-191 W Nationwide Blvd -Ste 200 -Columbus 43215

(202) 616-4126 .. **Hutchinson**, David V '70 US DOJ -1425 NY Av NW -Bx14271
-Washington, DC 20044

(216) 830-6830 .. **Hutchinson**, Joseph F Jr. '74 (Brouse M) -1001 Lakeside Av
-Ste 1600 -Cleveland 44114 **Fx:**830-6807

(419) 782-9881 .. **Hutchinson**, Matthew O '03 %Arthur OM&M Co,LPA
-901 Ralston Av -Bx781 -Defiance 43512

(440) 350-5060 .. **Hutchinson**, Trudy '83 Lake Cnty Bd of MR/DD
-8121 Deepwood Blvd -Mentor 44060

(440) 944-2736 .. **Hutchison**, Edward L '95 -213 E 327th -Willowick 44095

(330) 725-5233 .. **Huth**, Jeffrey A '89 J Huth Co,LPA -5035 State -Medina 44256

Huth, Lester C '51 -80 Northwood Dr -Tiffin 44883

(614) 466-3828 .. **Huth**, Sandra D '91 %OH Sup Ct -30 E Broad -2nd Fl
-Columbus 43215

(330) 832-8124 .. **Hutsell**, Randall A '84 Electra Cord,Inc -1320 Sanders Av -Bx875
-Massillon 44648

(614) 228-6885 .. **Hutson**, Jeffrey W '66 (Lane A&H LLC) -175 S 3rd -Ste 700
-Columbus 43215 **Fx:**228-0146

(513) 421-4020 .. **Hutson**, Joseph M '98 %Cohen TK&S,LLC -250 E 5th -Ste 1200
-Cincinnati 45202 **Fx:**241-4490

(330) 482-3356 .. **Hutson**, Mark A '83 (Stacey HS&P LPA) -20 S Main
-Columbiana 44408

(330) 887-6422 .. **Hutson**, William F '91 Westfield Grp -1 Park Cir -Bx5001
-Westfield Center 44251 **Fx:**887-2588

(440) 951-1848 .. **Hutton**, Bruce A '76 -38021 Euclid Av -Willoughby 44094
Fx:951-1815

(216) 696-7600 .. **Hutton**, Lee J '75 (Duvin C&H) -1301 E 9th -20th Fl Erievw Twr
-Cleveland 44114 **Fx:**696-2038

(740) 942-2936 .. **Hutyera**, Andrew '69 -105 Jamison Av -Stanton Bldg -Bx235
-Cadiz 43907

(513) 695-1325 .. **Hutzel**, Rachel A '91 Warren Cnty Pros -500 Justice Dr
-Lebanon 45036 **Fx:**695-2962

(614) 221-1000 .. **Huyghe**, Ryan K '99 Deloitte & Touche,LLP -155 E Broad
-Columbus 43215

(614) 227-4093 .. **Hvizdos**, Cynthia E '78 State Teachers Retirmnt Sys -275 E Broad
-Columbus 43215

(614) 464-2572 .. **Hvizdos**, John D '75 OfCnsl Harris MB&C,PLL -37 W Broad -9th Fl
-Columbus 43215 **Fx:**464-2245

(216) 595-1003 .. **Hyams**, Douglas K '90 -252001 Chagrin Blvd -Beachwood 44122

(419) 994-3269 .. **Hyde**, Andrew G '94 -144 N Water -Loudonville 44842

(937) 223-8888 .. **Hyde**, Henry III '94 Dyer GM&S -131 N Ludlow -Ste 1400
-Dayton 45402 **Fx:**223-0127

(513) 892-8251 .. **Hyde**, Richard A '89 (Holcomb & H LLP) -6 S 2nd
-311 Key Bk Bldg -Hamilton 45011 **Fx:**737-6854

(216) 514-7865 .. **Hyde**, William J '74 The Glenmede Trust Co
-25825 Science Park Dr -Ste 110 -Beachwood 44122

(614) 329-0732 .. **Hykes**, John E '75 -1865 Torch Wood Dr -Columbus 43229

(440) 930-7665 .. **Hyland**, John P '71 -225 Westwind Dr -#41 -Avon Lake 44012

(216) 443-7295 .. **Hyland**, John P '86 Cuyahoga Cnty Pub Def -1849 Prospect Av
-Ste 222 -Cleveland 44115

(513) 381-5700 .. **Hyland**, Robert G '72 Ritter & R,LLC -105 E 4th -Ste 1200
-Cincinnati 45202 **Fx:**381-0014

(330) 945-4234 .. **Hyland**, Scott A '99 %Chi Chi Rodriguez Mgt -3916 Clock Pnte Trl
-Ste 101 -Stow 44224

(513) 381-2838 .. **Hylander**, Brian R '03 %Taft S&H LLP -425 Walnut -Ste 1800
-Cincinnati 45202 **Fx:**381-0205

(513) 977-8200 .. **Hylander**, Jessica S '03 %Dinsmore & S LLP -255 E 5th -Ste 1900
-Cincinnati 45202 **Fx:**977-8141

(419) 255-0126 .. **Hylant**, Sandra M '81 Midland Title Sec Inc -420 Mad Av -Ste 1200
-Toledo 43604

(513) 481-9800 .. **Hyle**, Francis M '74 (Hyle & M Co,LPA) -3050 Harrison Av
-Cincinnati 45211 **Fx:**481-9592

(513) 481-9800 .. **Hyle & Mecklenborg Co,LPA** -3050 Harrison Av
-Cincinnati 45211 **Fx:**481-9592

(513) 421-9500 .. **Hylton**, Sheri L '96 Cinergy Corp -139 E 4th -MD EA503
-Cincinnati 45202

(419) 399-4916 .. **Hyman**, David A '78 (Hyman & H) -123 N Main -Paulding 45879

(216) 687-1311 .. **Hyman**, Jonathan T '97 %Reminger & R -101 Prospect Av W
-1400 Mdlnd Bldg -Cleveland 44115 **Fx:**687-1841

(304) 723-4400 .. **Hypes**, Bethsandra L '01 %Frankovitch AC&S -337 Penco Rd
-Weirton, WV 26062 **Fx:**723-5892

(740) 387-7799 .. **Hypes**, Maria L '91 -232 S Prospect -Marion 43302

(614) 207-2441 .. **Hyre**, John M III '96 -30 Dillmont Dr -#170 -Columbus 43235

(419) 248-1500 .. **Hyrne**, Michael E '80 (Doyle L&W) -202 N Erie -Bx2168
-Toledo 43603 **Fx:**248-2002

(614) 777-4411 .. **Hyslop**, Bruce A '66 (Hyslop & H Co,LPA) -3955 Brown Park Dr
-Ste B -Hilliard 43026

(614) 777-4411 .. **Hyslop**, Jean F '91 (Hyslop & H Co,LPA) -3955 Brown Park Dr
-Ste B -Hilliard 43026

(216) 664-2687 .. **Hyun**, Cecilia J '04 Cleveland Mncpl Ct-Housing -Bx94894
-Cleveland 44101

(513) 721-5672 .. **Iaciofano**, Anthony J '85 (Benjamin Y&H LLC) -312 Elm -Ste 1850
-Cincinnati 45202 **Fx:**562-4388

(419) 478-7078 .. **Iacoangeli**, James T '92 -2200 W Alexis -Toledo 43613

(330) 452-6400 .. **Iams**, Bradley R '81 -220 Market Av S -Ste 400 -Canton 44702

(614) 228-6345 .. **Iannotta**, Mark W '88 Strip HLM&T Co LPA -575 S 3rd
-Columbus 43215 **Fx:**228-6369

(614) 466-9511 .. **Iannotta**, Melissa J '87 Atty Gen -30 E Broad -Columbus 43215
Fx:466-5087

(330) 841-2566 .. **Iannucci**, Anthony
A Jr. '73 SpclCnsl Warren Redevlpmt & Planning Corp
-418 S Main Av -Ste 205 -Warren 44481 **Fx:**841-2738

(440) 593-6457 .. **Iarocci**, Nicholas A '89 Iarocci Law Firm,Ltd -213 Wshngtn
-Conneaut 44030 **Fx:**593-6458

(419) 475-9040 .. **Ibarra**, David H '88 -3809 Baybrook Ln -Toledo 43623

(859) 572-6578 .. **Ibarra-Burke**, Monica J '04 Nthrn Kentucky Univ -AC 505 Nunn Dr
-Highland Heights, KY 41099

(440) 473-2000 .. **Ibold**, Charles J '82 Things Remembered Inc -5500 Avion Park Dr
-Highland Heights 44143

(440) 285-3511 .. **Ibold**, Dennis J '73 (Petersen & I) -401 South -Chardon 44024
Fx:285-3363

(440) 285-3511 .. **Ibold**, Michael G '80 (Petersen & I) -401 South -Chardon 44024
Fx:285-3363

(330) 364-9070 .. **Iborra**, Jose A '94 %Hardin & S,LPA -132 Fair Av NW
-New Philadelphia 44663 **Fx:**364-9073

Ibos, Robert J '66 -3478 Mem'l Shoreway -Marblehead 43440

(513) 651-4226 .. **Ice**, Andrew G '96 (Zegarski & I Co,LPA) -917 Main -Ste 200
-Cincinnati 45202

(614) 443-4866 .. **Ice**, Matthew E '96 %J Nemeth & Assoc -21 E Frankfort
-Columbus 43206 **Fx:**443-4860

(330) 673-3444 .. **Ickes**, James C '00 %Williams W&K -11 S River -Bx396
-Kent 44240

(419) 332-4463 .. **Ickes**, Jon M '92 -114 N Wood -Fremont 43420

(419) 334-6446 .. **Ickes**, Leslie S '75 Cnty Jail -2323 Cntryside Dr -Fremont 43420

(216) 771-1760 .. **Icove**, Edward A '77 Smith & C LLP -1801 E Ninth
-Ste 900 Ohio Svngs Plz -Cleveland 44114 **Fx:**771-3387

(419) 627-5851 .. **Icsman**, Donald C '81 Sandusky Law Dept -222 Meigs
-Sandusky 44870

(330) 486-3000 .. **Icsman**, Robert D '94 ColeVision Corp -1925 Enterprise Pkwy
-Twinsburg 44087

(216) 781-1212 .. **Iddings**, Sarah L '03 %Walter & H LLP -1301 E 9th -Ste 3500
-Cleveland 44114 **Fx:**575-0911

(513) 961-1114 .. **Idinopulos**, Lea S '83 -3068 Taylor Av -Cincinnati 45220

(216) 692-0888 .. **Idzelis**, Augustine '90 -18021 Marcella Rd -Cleveland 44119

(614) 466-2766 .. **Idzkowski**, Michael E '94 Atty Gen -30 E Broad -Columbus 43215
Fx:644-1926

(513) 977-8200 .. **Iery**, Clare M '01 %Dinsmore & S LLP -255 E 5th -Ste 1900
-Cincinnati 45202 **Fx:**977-8141

(614) 677-8223 .. **Ifeduba**, Stephen E '97 Cnsl Nationwide Ins Co -1 Nationwide Plz
-Columbus 43215

(513) 534-8705 .. **Igel**, Nancy Hils '03 Fifth Third Bk -38 Fountain Sq Plz
-Cincinnati 45263

(216) 696-3311 .. **Igel**, Peter A '86 OfCnsl Kahn K -1301 E 9th -2600 Erievw Twr
-Cleveland 44114 **Fx:**623-4912

(219) 486-0864 .. **Ignasiak**, Robert L '87 Med Protective Co -5814 Reed Rd
-Fort Wayne, IN 46835

(440) 328-2250 .. **Ignatz-Hoover**, Gail M '81 Lorain Cnty Common Pleas Ct
-225 Court #301 -Civil Mediation Ofc -Elyria 44035 **Fx:**328-2252

(937) 223-8888 .. **Ignozzi**, Kenneth J '91 (Dyer GM&S) -131 N Ludlow -Ste 1400
-Dayton 45402 **Fx:**223-0127

(614) 261-9742 .. **Igo**, Richard B '70 (Igo & I) -3300 Indnola Av -Columbus 43214

(614) 464-3332 .. **Igoe**, Daniel J '68 (D Igoe & Assoc) -60 E Broad -Ste 400
-Columbus 43215

(513) 946-9000 .. **Igoe**, Elizabeth S '93 Hamilton Cnty Juv Ct -800 Bway -Cincinnati
45202 **Fx:**946-9217

(614) 228-6135 .. **Igoe**, Michael H '75 (Carlile P&M LLP) -366 E Broad
-Columbus 43215 **Fx:**221-0216

(614) 224-0100 ..**Ihlendorf,** Richard M '76 David J Glimcher Co -150 E Main
　　　-Ste 500 -Columbus 43215 Fx:224-8840

(419) 586-8677 ..**Ikerd,** Amy B '96 Mercer Cnty Pros -119 N Walnut -Celina 45822

(937) 332-9300 ..**Ikramuddin,** Asmina '03 OfCnsl Bucio & E,LLP -10 N Market
　　　-Troy 45373 Fx:339-6549

(216) 443-7800 ..**Ikuma,** Kaya A '99 Cuyahoga Cnty Pros -1200 Ontario -8th Fl
　　　-Cleveland 44113 Fx:698-2270

(954) 922-7877 ..**Ileana,** Dan V '01 (DV Ileana,PA) -2219 Hllywd Blvd -Ste 102
　　　-Hollywood, FL 33020 Fx:922-8688

(216) 696-5700 ..**Iler,** Don C '60 (DC Iler Co,LPA) -1370 Ontario
　　　-1640 Standard Bldg -Cleveland 44113

(216) 696-5700 ..**Iler,** Nancy C '87 %DC Iler Co,LPA -1370 Ontario
　　　-1640 Standard Bldg -Cleveland 44113

(941) 729-0000 ..**Illes,** Bruce H '88 Zirkelbach Construction Inc -1415 10th W
　　　-Palmetto, FL 34221 Fx:729-0007

(440) 324-5353 ..**Illner,** Michael D '85 %Spike & M,LLP -1551 W River Rd N
　　　-Elyria 44035 Fx:324-6529

(419) 704-4191 ..**Ilstrup,** Thomas G '89 -Bx5772 -Toledo 43613

(216) 664-4838 ..**Imbacuan,** Bruce D '00 Prosecutor -1200 Ontario Av
　　　-8th Fl Justice Ctr -Cleveland 44113 Fx:664-4399

(216) 696-7445 ..**Imbrigiotta,** James J '88 (Glowacki & Assoc) -526 Superior Av E
　　　-510 Leader Bldg -Cleveland 44114 Fx:696-0318

(614) 466-3615 ..**Imbrogno,** Andre R '99 Legis Srvc Commssn -77 S High
　　　-Columbus 43215

(513) 762-6200 ..**Imbus,** Karen L '96 %Ulmer & B LLP -600 Vine -Ste 2800
　　　-Cincinnati 45202 Fx:762-6245

(513) 894-9916 ..**Imfeld,** Bert C '55 Imfeld I&I -214 High -Hamilton 45011

(614) 365-4100 ..**Imhoff,** Caroline J '04 %Carpenter & L LLP -280 N High
　　　-Ste 1300 280 Plz -Columbus 43215 Fx:365-9145

(513) 423-3462 ..**Imhoff,** Don Jr. '72 -2 N Main -Ste 603 -Middletown 45042
　　　Fx:422-5141

(202) 326-2677 ..**Imhoff,** Tammy L '03 Fed Trade Comm -601 NJ Av NW -MD 5108
　　　-Washington, DC 20001 Fx:326-2655

(513) 721-5151 ..**Imm,** Stephen E '87 %Katz G&N,LLP -105 E 4th -4th Fl
　　　-Cincinnati 45202 Fx:621-9285

(513) 867-4502 ..**Immelt,** Mark W '76 First Fin Bank -300 High -Hamilton 45011
　　　Fx:867-5520

(513) 381-8430 ..**Immerman & Tobin Co,LPA** -632 Vine -Ste 1010
　　　-Cincinnati 45202

(216) 566-8099 ..**Immormino,** Mark '80 -1370 Ontario -Ste 1130 -Cleveland 44113
　　　Fx:771-1458

(713) 567-9000 ..**Imperato,** Ralph E '96 US Atty Ofc SDTX -910 Travis -Bx61129
　　　-Houston, TX 77208

(513) 708-1011 ..**Imwalle,** Mark A '02 -7207 Wooster Pike -Bx 242
　　　-Cincinnati 45227 Fx:271-8960

(614) 248-5656 ..**Imwalle,** Randall J '88 Bank One Corp -100 E Broad
　　　-Columbus 43271

(330) 659-8900 ..**Inama,** Tanya M '01 %Natl Interstate Corp -3250 Intrstate Dr
　　　-Richfield 44286

(330) 454-6555 ..**Inboden,** Marc B '73 Beese Fulmer Pincoe Inc
　　　-1150 United Bk Bldg -Canton 44702

(216) 328-1100 ..**Incorvaia,** Santo T '88 -5005 Rockside Rd -Ste 600
　　　-Independence 44131

(216) 787-4119 ..**Incorvati,** Nancy C '90 Workers Comp -615 W Superior
　　　-Cleveland 44113 Fx:787-3580

(330) 753-1051 ..**Incorvati,** Robert A '90 Germano R&C Co,LPA -2715 Mnchstr Rd
　　　-Akron 44319

(216) 369-2600 ..**Incze,** Norman E '95 -6100 Rockside Wds Blvd -Ste 305
　　　-Independence 44131

(787) 641-4545 ..**Indiano,** David C '81 (Indiano & W PSC) -207 Del Parque -3rd Fl
　　　-San Juan, PR 00912 Fx:641-4544

(513) 621-0267 ..**Infante,** Renee A '91 %Waite SB&C -1 W 4th -1513 4th & Vine
　　　Twr -Cincinnati 45202

(330) 726-0484 ..**Infante,** Thomas E '72 -1040 S Cmmns Pl -Ste 200 -Youngstown
　　　44514

(513) 887-3313 ..**Infantino,** Barbara M '89 Butler Cnty Juv Ct -280 N Fair Av
　　　-Hamilton 45011

(330) 489-3395 ..**Infantino,** Vernon M '03 %Pros -218 Cleveland Av SW -Bx24218
　　　-Canton 44702

(216) 363-6030 ..**Ingalls,** James D '91 -1370 Ontario -20th Fl -Cleveland 44113
　　　Ingersoll, Glenn N '94 -12461 Timber Ridge Trl -IDA, MI 48140

(216) 579-4111 ..**Ingersoll,** John D '85 -528 Superior Av -Ste 458 -Cleveland 44113

(216) 443-7583 ..**Ingersoll,** Robert M '81 Cuyahoga Cnty Pub Def -1200 W 3rd NW
　　　-100 Lakeside Pl -Cleveland 44113

(513) 793-0333 ..**Ingles,** Roxanne L '03 -9200 Mntgmry Rd -Ste 4-A
　　　-Cincinnati 45242

(216) 861-4000 ..**Inglis,** David S '82 Flashline Com,Inc -1300 E 9th -Ste 1600
　　　-Cleveland 44114

(330) 965-2000 ..**Inglis,** Patricia M '83 Cnsl The De Bartolo Corp -7620 Market
　　　-Youngstown 44512

(419) 244-7500 ..**Ingram,** Arthur C '83 (Mollenkamp & I) -411 N Mich -Ste 300
　　　-Toledo 43624 Fx:244-5238

(614) 464-6400 ..**Ingram,** Bruce L '78 (Vorys SS&P LLP) -52 E Gay -Bx1008
　　　-Columbus 43216 Fx:464-6350

(937) 225-3444 ..**Ingram,** Carley J '80 Montgomery Cnty Pros -301 W 3rd -Bx972
　　　-Dayton 45422 Fx:225-3470

(937) 229-3028 ..**Ingram,** Jefferson L '78 Univ of Dayton Schl of Law -300 Cllg Park
　　　-Dayton 45469

(330) 758-2308 ..**Ingram,** John Gerald Jr. '78 -7330 Market -Boardman 44512

(614) 469-3939 ..**Ingram,** Kasey T '02 %Jones D -325 John H McConnell Blvd
　　　-Ste 600 -Bx165017 -Columbus 43216 Fx:461-4198

(614) 466-8905 ..**Ingram,** Meribethe Richards '04 JCARR -77 S High -Cncrs Fl
　　　-Columbus 43215

(513) 423-8124 ..**Ingram,** Robert A '79 -2211 Central Av -Middletown 45044

(419) 255-5900 ..**Inks,** Allen W '92 (MacMillan S&T,LLC) -720 Water -4th Fl
　　　-Toledo 43604 Fx:255-9639

(614) 620-5754 ..**Inman,** Karl R '80 -5429 Aubrey Loop -Dublin 43016

(440) 329-5389 ..**Innes,** Gerald A '75 Lorain Cnty Pros -225 Court -3rd Fl
　　　-Elyria 44035

(614) 888-9611 ..**Innis,** Richard L '70 (Innis & B Co,LPA) -8415 Pulsar Pl -Ste 380
　　　-Columbus 43240 Fx:888-8499

(614) 818-4098 ..**Innocenti,** Trevor J '93 (Fields & I) -729 S Front -Columbus 43206

(419) 522-2733 ..**Inscore,** Larry Lee '59 (Inscore RW&E,LPA) -13 Park Av W
　　　-Ste 400 -Mansfield 44902 Fx:522-5165

(419) 522-2733 ..**Inscore,** Michael Lee '84 (Inscore RW&E,LPA) -13 Park Av W
　　　-Ste 400 -Mansfield 44902 Fx:522-5165

(419) 522-3398 ..**Inscore Rinehardt Whitney & Enderle,LPA** -13 Park Av W
　　　-Ste 400 -Mansfield 44902 Fx:522-5165

(513) 608-1247 ..**Inskeep,** Nancy Ann '93 O&G Consulting -9183 Kenwood Rd
　　　-Cincinnati 45201

(614) 462-3555 ..**Insley,** David W '81 Franklin Cnty Pros -373 S High -Columbus
　　　43215

(614) 224-0600 ..**Insley,** Susan J '77 Cochran Pub Rltns,Inc -14 E Gay
　　　-Columbus 43215

(419) 472-9774 ..**Intagliata,** John C '80 -4253 Monroe -Toledo 43606

(419) 242-9363 ..**Intagliata,** Patricia S '79 Toledo Bar Assoc -311 N Superior
　　　-Toledo 43604

(614) 227-2376 ..**Intihar,** Stephen '93 %Bricker & E LLP -100 S 3rd
　　　-Columbus 43215 Fx:227-2390

(440) 603-7630 ..**Intili,** Ann M '90 Progressive Ins Co -5920 Landerbrook Dr
　　　-PLG-OHL33 -Mayfield Heights 44124

(937) 222-3000 ..**Intili,** Thomas J '86 Falke & D LLC -30 Wyoming -Dayton 45409
　　　Fx:222-1414

(614) 764-6746 ..**Inzetta,** Mark S '80 Wendys Intl -4288 W Dublin-Granvll Rd -Bx256
　　　-Dublin 43017

(440) 329-5396 ..**Ioannidis,** Amy '03 %Lorain Cnty Pros -225 Court -3rd Fl
　　　-Elyria 44035 Fx:329-5430

(513) 946-9472 ..**Ionna,** Massimino M '00 Hamilton Cnty Juv Ct -800 Bway -7th Fl
　　　-Cincinnati 45202 Fx:946-9339

(330) 456-2300 ..**Ionno,** John M '72 -2223 Fulton Rd NW -Ste 206 -Canton 44709

(419) 537-1954 ..**Iorio,** Donato S '98 Kalniz I&F,LPA -5550 W Central Av -Toledo
　　　43615 Fx:535-7732

(616) 940-1911 ..**Iorio,** Theodore M '69 (Kalniz I&F) -4951 Cascade Rd SE
　　　-Grand Rapids, MI 49546

(216) 566-0371 ..**Ipavec,** Charles F '51 Laporte & I, LPA -1215 Superior Av
　　　-Charter One Bk Bldg Rm 245 -Cleveland 44114 Fx:566-0405

(513) 697-6999 ..**Ipsaro,** John R '93 -550 Wards Crnr Rd -Ste 102 -Loveland 45140
　　　Fx:697-8849

(937) 227-3700 ..**Ireland,** D Jeffrey '80 (Faruki I&C PLL) -10 N Ludlow
　　　-500 Cthse Plz SW -Dayton 45402 Fx:227-3717
　　　Ireland, William S '04 -(Address Unavailable)

(216) 696-5530 ..**Ireland-Phillips,** Karen S '96 -614 W Superior Av #1448
　　　-Cleveland 44113 Fx:696-5531

(614) 227-2000 ..**Ireton,** C Andrew Jr. '73 (Porter WM&A LLP) -41 S High
　　　-Columbus 43215 Fx:227-2100

(513) 721-1350 ..**Irey,** Kurt M '04 %Barron PB&S -3074 Madison Rd
　　　-Cincinnati 45209

(937) 865-6800 ..**Irizarry,** Francisco A '88 Lexis/Nexis -Bx933 -Dayton 45401

(419) 249-7100 ..**Irmen,** James H '86 Marshall & M,LLC -Four Seagate -8th Fl
　　　-Toledo 43604 Fx:249-7151

(440) 224-1606 ..**Irons,** David R '80 -Brdg Colonial Plz -Bx258
　　　-North Kingsville 44068

(440) 286-8887 ..**Irvin,** James D '74 Coldwell Banker Hunter Realty -106 Water
　　　-Chardon 44024

(614) 292-0611 ..**Irvine,** Joseph R '86 OSU/Legal Affrs -33 W 11th Av -Ste 209
　　　-Columbus 43201

(614) 799-9996 ..**Irwin,** Cynthia C '81 -339 Bear Woods Dr -Powell 43065
　　　Fx:799-2491

(513) 863-7771 ..**Irwin,** James S '61 -411 Walter Av -8 -Fairfield 45014

(440) 543-5001 ..**Irwin,** John R '76 -8401 Chagrin Rd -Ste 19 -Chagrin Falls 44023

(513) 579-6400 ..**Irwin,** Kevin E '77 (Keating M&K PLL) -1 E 4th
　　　-1400 Provident Twr -Cincinnati 45202 Fx:579-6457

(614) 891-7112 ..**Irwin,** Michael T '80 -280 S State -Westerville 43081

(216) 621-0200 ..**Irwin,** Scott D '92 (Baker & H LLP) -1900 E 9th -Ste 3200
　　　-Cleveland 44114 Fx:696-0740

(614) 221-2121 ..**Isaac Brant Ledman & Teetor,LLP** -250 E Broad
　　　-Ste 900 Mdlnd Bldg -Columbus 43215 Fx:365-9516

(336) 631-2866 ..**Isaac,** David J '86 SrCnsl Inmar,Inc -2650 Pilgrim Ct
　　　-Winston Salem, NC 27106 Fx:631-2888

(440) 871-8111 ..**Isaac,** Frank K '52 Huffman I&F LLC -24441 Detroit Rd -Ste 200
　　　-Westlake 44145

(614) 221-2121 ..**Isaac,** Frederick M '66 (Isaac BL&T,LLP) -250 E Broad
　　　-Ste 900 Mdlnd Bldg -Columbus 43215 Fx:365-9516

(419) 897-8200 ..**Isaac,** Lynn A '80 Isaac Prprty Co -1645 Indn Wd Cir -Maumee
　　　43537

(440) 234-2081 ..**Isaac,** Sharon D '84 OH Tpk Comm -682 Prospect -Berea 44017

(201) 395-4030 ..**Isaacs,** Betty B '79 Morgan Stanley -Hrbrsd Fincl Ctr -Plz 3/1st Fl
　　　-Jersey City, NJ 07311

(502) 458-1000 ..**Isaacs,** Darryl L '98 (Isaacs & I) -900 Cherokee Rd
　　　-Louisville, KY 40204

(216) 464-3570 ..**Isaacson,** Arnold M '87 %RS Leiken -23611 Chagrin Blvd -Ste 225
　　　-Beachwood 44122
　　　Isabell, Christiane M '04 -(Address Unavailable)

(216) 252-1700 ..**Isabella,** Joseph N '93 -15834 Edgecliff Av -Cleveland 44111

(216) 357-5123 ..**Isakoff,** Andrew H '86 -55 Pub Sq -Ste 1331 -Cleveland 44113
　　　Fx:241-4591

(216) 515-1660 ..**Isakoff,** Janice A '86 OfCnsl Frantz W LLP -127 Pub Sq
　　　-2500 Key Center -Cleveland 44114 Fx:515-1650

(513) 721-7522 ..**Isaly,** Charles W '77 -22 W 9th -Cincinnati 45202

(440) 352-8500 ..**Ischie,** Wilbur N '75 %LJ Talikka -2603 Riverside Dr -Ste 100
　　　-Painesville 44077

(614) 275-2692 ..**Isern,** Kathleen L '83 Franklin Cnty Children Srvcs -855 W Mound
　　　-Columbus 43223 Fx:275-2589

(330) 376-2700 ..**Isham,** Duane L '53 OfCnsl Roetzel & A,LPA -222 S Main
　　　-Akron 44308 Fx:376-4577

(619) 281-3327 ..**Isip,** Peter P '97 Stone & Young LLC -4350 LaJolla Vllg Dr
　　　-San Diego, CA 92108

(216) 687-1900 ..**Iskin,** Peter M '73 Legal Aid -1223 W 6th -Cleveland 44113
　　　Fx:687-0779

(740) 264-3700 ..**Isla,** Roger A '94 -4017A Sunset Blvd -Steubenville 43952

(213) 430-3400 ..**Isler,** Curtiss L '75 (Tucker E&W LLP) -725 S Figueroa -Ste 3400
　　　-Los Angeles, CA 90017

(614) 336-3083 ..**Ison,** David A '83 (Ison Law Ofc) -10 Vllg Pnte Dr -Bx1108
　　　-Powell 43065

(614) 464-6400 ..**Ison,** Richard G '53 OfCnsl Vorys SS&P LLP -52 E Gay -Bx1008
　　　-Columbus 43216 Fx:464-6350

(216) 443-7295 ..**Isquick,** Margaret O '85 Cuyahoga Cnty Pub Def -1849 Prospect
   Av -Ste 222 -Cleveland 44115

(412) 391-1114 ..**Israel,** James F '90 (Israel W&G,PC) -420 Ft Duquesne Blvd
   -Ste 700 -Pittsburgh, PA 15222

(801) 524-5796 ..**Israel,** Kenneth D Jr. '74 US SEC -50 S Main -Ste 500
   -Salt Lake City, UT 84144

(216) 696-6700 ..**Israel,** Rachael L '00 %Kushner & R Co,LPA -200 Pub Sq
   -Ste 2860 BP Twr -Cleveland 44114 **Fx:**696-6772

(216) 931-6000 ..**Isroff,** Ronald H '67 (Ulmer & B LLP) -1300 E 9th
   -Ste 900 Penton Media Bldg -Cleveland 44114 **Fx:**931-6001

(513) 421-3772 ..**Issenmann,** Jack K '67 -700 Walnut -Cincinnati 45202

(614) 365-2700 ..**Ita,** Amy R '02 %Squire S&D LLP -41 S High -1300 Huntngtn Ctr
   -Columbus 43215 **Fx:**365-2499

(216) 861-1400 ..**Ita,** Timothy A '85 RJ Clapp & Assoc Co,LPA -1375 E 9th
   -One Cleve Ctr #2420 -Cleveland 44114 **Fx:**861-1401

(740) 454-1223 ..**Itani,** Stuart Y '02 %SE OH Lgl Srvcs -27 N 6th -Ste B
   -Zanesville 43701

(614) 464-6400 ..**Iten,** Jonathan D '81 (Vorys SS&P LLP) -52 E Gay -Bx1008
   -Columbus 43216 **Fx:**464-6350

(330) 796-3084 ..**Ito,** Takashi '63 Goodyear Tire & Rubber Co -1144 E Market
   -Akron 44316

(216) 529-6090 ..**Ittu,** Yvette M '95 City of Lakewood -12650 Detroit Av
   -Lakewood 44107

(614) 461-1311 ..**Ivan,** Paulette M '94 (Reminger & R) -65 E State
   -4th Fl Cptl Sq Ofc Bldg -Columbus 43215 **Fx:**232-2410

(330) 841-2518 ..**Ivanchak,** Terry F '78 Mun Ct Judge -141 South -Warren 44483

(216) 444-2385 ..**Ivancic,** Robert J '75 Cleveland Clinic Fndtn -9500 Euclid Av
   -Cleveland 44195

(440) 546-1294 ..**Ivchenko,** Andrew '89 -9120 Brecksvll Rd -Brecksville 44141

(513) 695-1344 ..**Iversen,** Yvonne A '92 Warren Cnty Cmn Pleas Ct -500 Justice Dr
   -Lebanon 45036

(215) 564-8000 ..**Ives,** Kristin Hay '85 (Stradley RSY,LLP) -2600 One Commerce Sq
   -Philadelphia, PA 19103 **Fx:**564-8120

(614) 688-5683 ..**Iveson,** Mary A '91 OSU -2400 Olentangy Rvr Rd -401 Fawcett Ctr
   -Columbus 43210

(330) 376-2700 ..**Ivey,** Timothy C '87 (Roetzel & A,LPA) -222 S Main -Akron 44308
   Fx:376-4577

(513) 241-0400 ..**Ivy,** Christine J '86 Aronoff R&H Co,LPA -425 Walnut -Ste 2400
   -Cincinnati 45202 **Fx:**241-2877

(716) 566-5400 ..**Iyer,** Ramachandran B '00 %Goldberg S LLP -665 Main -Ste 400
   -Buffalo, NY 14203 **Fx:**566-5401

(216) 586-3939 ..**Izanec,** Peter E '04 %Jones D -901 Lakeside Av -Cleveland 44114
   Fx:579-0212

(513) 579-6400 ..**Izenson,** Daniel E '90 (Keating M&K PLL) -1 E 4th
   -1400 Provident Twr -Cincinnati 45202 **Fx:**579-6457

(937) 226-1996 ..**Izenson,** Fred M '59 -120 W 2nd -2000 Lbrty Twr -Dayton 45402

(937) 855-7111 ..**Izor,** David E '74 -52 N Main -Germantown 45327

(614) 728-8400 ..**Izzo,** John A '93 Cnsl Dept Commerce Div of Fncl Inst -77 S High
   -21st Fl -Columbus 43215

(513) 721-1350 ..**Jaap,** Joseph B '89 %Barron PB&S -3074 Madison Rd
   -Cincinnati 45209

(330) 762-2448 ..**Jaballas,** Roderick R '93 -450 Grant -Ste 104 -Akron 44311

(614) 462-2472 ..**Jabarin,** Nadia M '01 Franklin Cnty Domestic Relations Ct
   -373 S High -6th Fl -Columbus 43215

(614) 469-3939 ..**Jabe,** Daniel N '03 %Jones D -325 John H McConnell Blvd
   -Ste 600 -Bx165017 -Columbus 43216 **Fx:**461-4198

(937) 461-5980 ..**Jablinski,** David S '85 (Jablinski FR&M) -214 W Monument Av
   -Bx1266 -Dayton 45402 **Fx:**461-4139

(937) 461-5980 ..**Jablinski Folino Roberts & Martin** -214 W Monument Av
   -Bx1266 -Dayton 45402 **Fx:**461-4139

(440) 395-3692 ..**Jablonski,** Richard W '94 Progressive Ins Co
   -6300 Wilson Mills Rd -#N72A -Mayfield Village 44143

(614) 228-6107 ..**Jack,** Arnold L '64 (Jack & S) -572 E Rich -Columbus 43215

(330) 336-4455 ..**Jack,** David C '83 -145 Akron Rd -Wadsworth 44281

(304) 367-3423 ..**Jack,** Gary A '84 Monongahela Power Co -1310 Fairmont Av
   -Fairmont, WV 26554

(740) 282-1900 ..**Jack,** Otto A Jr. '74 (King HS&J) -200 Sinclair Bldg -Bx249
   -Steubenville 43952 **Fx:**282-5397

(440) 503-1795 ..**Jackel,** Katherine E '04 -21454 Greenfldf Pl -Strongsville 44149

(216) 687-1311 ..**Jackett,** Todd M '03 %Reminger & R -101 Prospect Av W
   -1400 Mdlnd Bldg -Cleveland 44115 **Fx:**687-1841

   Jacklitch, Thomas R Jr. '67 -1640 Turnberry Vllg Dr
   -Dayton 45458

(740) 852-0424 ..**Jackman,** David H '64 (Jackman & J) -60 S Main -London 43140
   Fx:852-0425

(727) 531-5555 ..**Jackman,** James D '90 OfCnsl Hilbert Law Grp
   -2963 Roosevelt Blvd -Clearwater, FL 33760 **Fx:**531-5520

(330) 673-5512 ..**Jackman,** Titus '54 -136 N Water -Bx513 -Kent 44240

   Jackman, Alice M '02 -296 Jackson -Medina 44256

(513) 564-7365 ..**Jackson,** Arthur L '91 6th Dist Ct of Appls -100 E 5th -Cthse
   -Cincinnati 45202

(513) 241-3100 ..**Jackson,** Brian S '97 Lerner S&R -120 E 4th -8th Fl -Cincinnati
   45202

(330) 972-7074 ..**Jackson,** Candace Campbell '95 Univ of Akron-Ofc of President
   -114 Buchtel Hall -Akron 44325

(937) 424-5390 ..**Jackson,** Christopher L '03 %Cicero & K,PLL -500 E 5th -Ste 100
   -Dayton 45402 **Fx:**424-5393

(724) 836-3848 ..**Jackson,** Deborah Lynn '85 -35 W Pittsburgh -Ste 110
   -Greensburg, PA 15601 **Fx:**837-7868

(216) 479-8500 ..**Jackson,** Denise A '94 %Squire S&D LLP -127 Pub Sq
   -4900 Key Twr -Cleveland 44114 **Fx:**479-8780

(440) 546-0100 ..**Jackson,** Dennis C '82 (DC Jackson Co,LPA) -20 Eagle Valley Ct
   -Broadview Heights 44147 **Fx:**546-0189

(614) 221-2702 ..**Jackson,** Douglas R '85 (Jackson & C Co,LPA) -171 E Lvngstn Av
   -Columbus 43215

(216) 664-2309 ..**Jackson,** Frank G '86 Cleveland City Cncl -601 Lakeside AVP
   -Cleveland 44114

(216) 932-2800 ..**Jackson,** Gary B '96 Bellefaire JCB -22001 Fairmount Blvd
   -Shaker Heights 44118

(216) 752-8000 ..**Jackson,** Gerald M '72 (Jackson Law Co,LPA) -3673 Lee Rd
   -Shaker Heights 44120

(216) 514-9500 ..**Jackson,** Iverson M '03 %Norchi & Assoc,LLC
   -23240 Chagrin Blvd -Ste 600 -Beachwood 44122

(614) 227-2700 ..**Jackson,** Janet E '78 United Way/Cntrl OH -360 S 3rd
   -Columbus 43215

(740) 922-4161 ..**Jackson,** Jason L '01 %Connolly H&W -201 N Main -Bx272
   -Uhrichsville 44683

(202) 305-2332 ..**Jackson,** Jennifer A '02 USDOJ/Environ Enfrcmnt Sec
   -Ben Franklin Sta -Bx7611 -Washington, DC 20044

   Jackson, Jennifer B '04 -(Address Unavailable)

(440) 603-7531 ..**Jackson,** Jennifer S '93 Progressive Ins Co -5920 Landerbrook Dr
   -PLG-L33 -Mayfield Heights 44124

(614) 757-5811 ..**Jackson,** John M '01 Cardinal Hlth -7000 Cardinal Pl
   -Dublin 43017

(216) 928-2200 ..**Jackson,** John V II '72 (Sutter OM&F) -1301 E 9th -3600
   Erievw Twr -Cleveland 44114 **Fx:**928-4400

(216) 707-2585 ..**Jackson,** Karen L '91 Museum of Art -11150 E Blvd
   -Cleveland 44106

(740) 862-4191 ..**Jackson Keller Shook & Dern** -719 W Market -Baltimore 43105

(513) 929-3400 ..**Jackson,** Kory A '00 %Baker & H LLP -312 Walnut -Ste 3200
   -Cincinnati 45202 **Fx:**929-0303

(513) 352-2417 ..**Jackson,** Lisa M '91 City of Cincinnati -805 Central Av -Ste 130
   -Cincinnati 45202

(419) 241-2201 ..**Jackson,** Louise A '77 (Spengler N PLL) -608 Mad Av -Ste 1000
   -Toledo 43604 **Fx:**241-8599

(419) 668-8403 ..**Jackson,** Michael B '91 (Lynch & W Co,LPA) -51 E Main -Ste B
   -Norwalk 44857 **Fx:**668-4172

(216) 566-1600 ..**Jackson,** Michael E '76 (Schwarzwald & M) -1300 E 9th -Ste 616
   -Cleveland 44114 **Fx:**566-1814

(419) 244-6788 ..**Jackson,** Michael W '03 %Bugbee & C -405 Mad Av -Ste 1300
   -Toledo 43604 **Fx:**244-7145

(330) 379-2041 ..**Jackson,** Montrella S '99 Summit Cnty Chldrn Srvcs
   -264 S Arlngtn -Akron 44306 **Fx:**379-1897

(419) 213-6951 ..**Jackson,** Natalie J '03 Lucas Cnty Pros-Juv Div
   -1801 Spielbusch Av -Toledo 43624

(614) 227-2000 ..**Jackson,** Patrick I '02 %Porter WM&A LLP -41 S High
   -Columbus 43215 **Fx:**227-2100

(330) 376-2700 ..**Jackson,** Paul L '88 (Roetzel & A,LPA) -222 S Main -Akron 44308
   Fx:376-4577

(513) 241-2324 ..**Jackson,** Randall S Jr. '98 %Wood H&E LLP -441 Vine -Ste 2700
   -Cincinnati 45202 **Fx:**421-7269

(419) 243-2100 ..**Jackson,** Reginald S Jr. '71 (Connelly J&C LLP) -405 Mad Av
   -Ste 1600 -Toledo 43604 **Fx:**243-7119

(614) 464-6400 ..**Jackson,** Reginald W '80 (Vorys SS&P LLP) -52 E Gay -Bx1008
   -Columbus 43216 **Fx:**464-6350

(205) 879-9948 ..**Jackson,** Richard L '58 -4225 Wilderness Rd
   -Birmingham, AL 35213

(216) 696-8700 ..**Jackson,** Robert H '61 (Kohrman J&K PLL) -1375 E 9th
   -One Cleve Ctr 20th Fl -Cleveland 44114 **Fx:**621-6536

(859) 291-8055 ..**Jackson,** Ruth B '92 -335 E 3rd -Newport, KY 41071

(216) 502-0800 ..**Jackson,** Stanley Jr. '03 -75 Pub Sq -Ste 333 -Cleveland 44113

(216) 687-1910 ..**Jackson,** Stephanie M '87 Legal Aid -1223 W 6th
   -Cleveland 44113

(614) 677-8212 ..**Jackson,** Stephen M-L '04 Nationwide Insurance
   -One Nationwide Plz -Columbus 43215

(740) 385-9611 ..**Jackson,** Steven F '89 -37 E Hunter -Bx602 -Logan 43138

(216) 622-3600 ..**Jackson,** Steven L '94 US Atty -801 W Superior -Ste 400
   -Cleveland 44113 **Fx:**622-3370

(513) 489-9191 ..**Jackson,** Thomas A '82 -12 Linden Ln -Cincinnati 45215

(973) 993-3443 ..**Jackson,** Thomas M '85 Gab Robins, Grp of Cos -9 Campus Dr
   -Parsippany, NJ 07054

(216) 241-6602 ..**Jackson,** Todd G '85 (Weston HFP&H LLP) -50 Pub Sq
   -2500 Trmnl Twr -Cleveland 44113 **Fx:**621-8369

   Jackson, Tracie J '95 -2030 Peniston -New Orleans, LA 70115

(216) 515-1660 ..**Jackson,** Travis F '99 %Frantz W LLP -127 Pub Sq
   -2500 Key Center -Cleveland 44114 **Fx:**515-1650

(216) 681-5020 ..**Jackson,** Warner Lee '71 E Cleveland Mun Ct -14340 Euclid Av
   -East Cleveland 44112

(614) 466-4397 ..**Jackson-Forbes,** Johnlander C '93 OH Dept Commerce
   -77 S High -Columbus 43266

(216) 241-3400 ..**Jackson-Winston,** Judy A '99 Cuyahoga Cnty Mental Health Bd
   -1400 W 25th -3rd Fl -Cleveland 44113

(330) 264-2216 ..**Jackwood,** Renee J '95 -132 E Lbrty -Wooster 44691
   Fx:264-6330

(740) 389-6283 ..**Jacob,** Dean L '86 -1138 Brook Park Rd -Marion 43302

(440) 349-3301 ..**Jacob,** Harry J III '81 Jacob & Assoc -30405 Solon Rd -Unit 14
   -Solon 44139

(513) 921-1400 ..**Jacob,** Nancy V '87 -4966 Glenway Av -Cincinnati 45238

(216) 991-1100 ..**Jacob,** Richard K '71 -3655 Lee Rd -Shaker Heights 44120

(330) 743-1171 ..**Jacob,** Timothy J '77 (Manchester BP&U) -201 E Commerce
   -Atrium Level 2 Commerce Bldg -Youngstown 44503
   Fx:743-1190

(419) 229-9800 ..**Jacobs,** Ann E '77 (Jacobs & V) -558 W Spring -Lima 45801

(614) 466-4605 ..**Jacobs,** Bobbi-Lynn '92 OH Dept Job & Fam Srvcs -30 E Broad
   -32nd Fl -Columbus 43266

(216) 621-1113 ..**Jacobs,** Christopher B '95 (Renner OB&S,LLP) -1621 Euclid Av
   -19th Fl -Cleveland 44115 **Fx:**621-6165

(937) 222-4059 ..**Jacobs,** Craig B '00 Montgomery Paper Co -400 E 4th
   -Dayton 45402

(937) 228-8104 ..**Jacobs,** Ellis '81 ABLE -333 W 1st -Ste 500B -Dayton 45402
   Fx:449-8131

(614) 718-9205 ..**Jacobs,** Francine I '80 -Bx705 -Dublin 43017

(419) 241-6000 ..**Jacobs,** Frank D '59 (Eastman & S Ltd) -1 Seagate -24th Fl
   -Bx10032 -Toledo 43699 **Fx:**247-1777

(937) 439-1189 ..**Jacobs,** Gary J '82 (G Jacobs,LPA) -330 Wellesley Way
   -Dayton 45459

(330) 941-2340 ..**Jacobs,** Holly A '91 Youngstown State Univ -1 Univ Plz
   -Gen Cnsl Ofc -Youngstown 44555

(216) 383-8055 ..**Jacobs,** Jacqueline A '91 -16009 Parkgrove -Cleveland 44110

(216) 831-5083 ..**Jacobs,** James K '80 -29555 Shaker Blvd -Cleveland 44124

(513) 621-4556 ..**Jacobs Jensen & Napolitano, LLC** -30 Garfld Pl -Ste 750
   -Cincinnati 45202 **Fx:**621-5563

(513) 721-7430 ..**Jacobs,** Jon H '62 (Jacobs & S Co,LPA) -432 Walnut
   -850 Tri-State Bldg -Cincinnati 45202

(216) 227-0900 ..**Jacobs,** Joseph J Jr. '96 Jacobs Legal Grp -15614 Detroit Av
   -Lakewood 44107

(513) 381-6600 ..**Jacobs Kleinman Seibel & McNally** -1014 Vine -Ste 2300 -Cincinnati 45202

(216) 566-5675 ..**Jacobs,** Leslie W '68 (Thompson H LLP) -127 Pub Sq -3900 Key Ctr -Cleveland 44114 **Fx:**566-5800

(614) 463-9790 ..**Jacobs,** Louis A '73 OfCnsl Marshall & M LLC -111 W Rich -Ste 430 -Columbus 43215 **Fx:**463-9780

(419) 248-3501 ..**Jacobs,** Mark I '84 -241 N Superior -Ste 200 -Toledo 43604

(216) 696-3311 ..**Jacobs,** Mark R '99 %Kahn K -1301 E 9th -2600 Erievw Twr -Cleveland 44114 **Fx:**623-4912

(419) 248-3501 ..**Jacobs,** Marvin K '53 SrCnsl M Jacobs Co,LPA -241 N Superior -Ste 200 -Toledo 43604 **Fx:**242-2021

(513) 381-5700 ..**Jacobs,** Mary Ann '82 Ritter R &R,LLC -105 E 4th -Ste 1200 -Cincinnati 45202 **Fx:**381-0014

(513) 844-2000 ..**Jacobs,** Michael E '97 (McGowan & J,LLC) -246 High -Hamilton 45011 **Fx:**868-1190

(513) 793-4684 ..**Jacobs,** Neal D '01 -7646 Trlwind Dr -Cincinnati 45242

(614) 228-8400 ..**Jacobs,** Rebecca B '97 %Ulmer & B LLP -88 E Broad -Ste 1600 -Columbus 43215 **Fx:**228-8561

(937) 865-7206 ..**Jacobs,** Richard E '80 Lexis/Nexis -Bx933 -Dayton 45401

(804) 788-1956 ..**Jacobs,** Robert D '86 -7 S Adams -Richmond, VA 23220 **Fx:**788-1982

(216) 464-0504 ..**Jacobs,** Thomas L '61 (TL Jacobs Co,LPA) -24700 Wimbledon Rd -Beachwood 44122

(419) 524-5568 ..**Jacobs,** Thomas L '86 %Knell D&G Co,LPA -3 N Main -Ste 602 -Mansfield 44902 **Fx:**524-8011

(513) 621-4556 ..**Jacobs,** Thomas W '89 (Jacobs J&N,LLC) -30 Garfld Pl -Ste 750 -Cincinnati 45202 **Fx:**621-5563

(419) 229-9800 ..**Jacobs & Von der Embse** -558 W Spring -Lima 45801

(513) 241-2324 ..**Jacobs,** Wayne L '90 (Wood H&E LLP) -441 Vine -Ste 2700 -Cincinnati 45202 **Fx:**421-7269

(216) 898-2343 ..**Jacobs,** William G '69 Electrolux NA -18013 Cleve Prkwy -Ste 100 -Cleveland 44135

(513) 621-2120 ..**Jacobs,** William R '73 Strauss & T,LPA -150 E 4th -4th Fl -Cincinnati 45202 **Fx:**241-8259

(216) 566-5533 ..**Jacobs,** William W '76 (Thompson H LLP) -127 Pub Sq -3900 Key Ctr -Cleveland 44114 **Fx:**566-5800

(614) 466-0632 ..**Jacobsen,** Lynda J '98 Legis Srvc Commssn -77 S High -Columbus 43215

(216) 831-1916 ..**Jacobson,** Aaron '59 -24395 Shaker Blvd -Beachwood 44122

(513) 723-4000 ..**Jacobson,** Barbara Bison '75 OfCnsl Vorys SS&P LLP -221 E 4th -Ste 2000 Atrium Two -Cincinnati 45201 **Fx:**723-4056

(937) 223-1130 ..**Jacobson,** James L '78 (Pickrel S&E) -40 N Main -2700 Kettering Twr -Dayton 45423 **Fx:**223-0339

(937) 461-1776 ..**Jacobson,** Jeffrey M '91 Montgomery Cnty Repub Prty -211 S Main -Ste 610 -Dayton 45402

(419) 837-9016 ..**Jacobson,** John L '75 -3450 W Central Av -Ste 124 -Toledo 43606

(614) 367-1493 ..**Jacobson,** Michael T '01 -546 Indn Mound Rd -Columbus 43213 **Fx:**367-1493

(216) 464-2289 ..**Jacobson,** Murray R '69 MR Jacobson & Assoc -28849 Edgedale Rd -Pepper Pike 44124

(330) 884-1046 ..**Jacobson,** Patricia F '80 Forum Health -3530 Belmont Av -Ste 7 -Youngstown 44505

(216) 621-2300 ..**Jacobson,** William S '84 Nurenberg PH&M LPA -1370 Ontario -Ste 100 -Cleveland 44113 **Fx:**771-2242

(330) 656-1572 ..**Jacobstein,** Pamela G '82 -6404 Canterbury Dr -Hudson 44236

(216) 586-3939 ..**Jacono,** Anthony T '00 %Jones D -901 Lakeside Av -Cleveland 44114 **Fx:**579-0212

(440) 460-3681 ..**Jacovetty,** Cynthia S '88 Marconi Communications -5900 Landerbrook Dr -Ste 300 -Cleveland 44124

(937) 298-2811 ..**Jacox Meckstroth & Jenkins** -2310 Far Hills Bldg -Dayton 45419 **Fx:**298-7418

(330) 434-1000 ..**Jacquemain,** Jennifer J '98 %Bernlohr W,LLP -23 S Main -3rd Fl -Akron 44308 **Fx:**434-1001

(614) 227-2000 ..**Jacques,** Laurie N '90 (Porter WM&A LLP) -41 S High -Columbus 43215 **Fx:**227-2100

(937) 228-9179 ..**Jacques,** Robert F '02 Hollencamp & H -130 W 2nd -Ste 2107 -Dayton 45402

(614) 223-1634 ..**Jadwin,** Jay E '87 Amer Elec Pwr Co -1 Riverside Plz -Columbus 43215

(937) 689-7360 ..**Jaeger,** Charles E '71 Nextech, Inc -63 Rhoades Ctr Dr -Dayton 45458

(610) 902-7237 ..**Jafery,** Farruq Z '94 Wyeth-Ayerst Phrmctcls -130-3 N Radnor Chester Rd -Saint Davids, PA 19087

(248) 746-2844 ..**Jaffa,** Jonathan M '02 Sullivan WBT&A -Bx222 -Southfield, MI 48037

(216) 736-7209 ..**Jaffe,** Ari H '87 (Kohrman J&K PLL) -1375 E 9th -One Cleve Ctr 20th Fl -Cleveland 44114 **Fx:**621-6536

(614) 443-7654 ..**Jaffe,** Brett H '78 -844 S Front -Columbus 43206

(614) 464-6400 ..**Jaffe,** Dan L '90 (Vorys SS&P LLP) -52 E Gay -Bx1008 -Columbus 43216 **Fx:**464-6350

(216) 479-8500 ..**Jaffe,** Daniel A '89 %Squire S&D LLP -127 Pub Sq -4900 Key Twr -Cleveland 44114 **Fx:**479-8780

(216) 360-3737 ..**Jaffe,** Donald N '61 OfCnsl Persky S&A Co,LPA -25101 Chagrin Blvd -Ste 350 Signature Sq II -Beachwood 44122 **Fx:**593-0921

(440) 684-1090 ..**Jaffe,** Michael A '93 %M Kusner Co,LPA -6151 Wilson Mills Rd -Ste 310 -Highland Heights 44143

(614) 228-6148 ..**Jaffy,** Lynn S '97 S Jaffy & Assoc Co,LPA -306 E Gay -Columbus 43215 **Fx:**228-6140

(614) 228-6148 ..**Jaffy,** Marc J '90 S Jaffy & Assoc Co,LPA -306 E Gay -Columbus 43215 **Fx:**228-6140

(614) 228-6148 ..**Jaffy,** Rachel B '94 S Jaffy & Assoc Co,LPA -306 E Gay -Columbus 43215 **Fx:**228-6140

(614) 228-6148 ..**Jaffy,** Stewart R '59 (S Jaffy & Assoc Co,LPA) -306 E Gay -Columbus 43215 **Fx:**228-6140

(614) 718-4434 ..**Jagers,** Susan M '93 Amer Cancer Society -5555 Frantz Rd -Dublin 43017

(212) 490-3000 ..**Jagodzinski,** Kimberly M '94 OfCnsl Wilson EME&D LLP -150 E 42nd -New York, NY 10017 **Fx:**490-3038

(216) 581-1481 ..**Jahn,** Frederick J '92 -16302 Turney Rd -Cleveland 44137

(513) 721-4532 ..**Jahnke,** Mark J '79 (Katz TB&H) -255 E 5th -Ste 2400 -Cincinnati 45202

(614) 728-2845 ..**Jaite,** Maura O'Neill '92 Atty Gen -150 E Gay -Columbus 43215 **Fx:**728-2122

(513) 361-8400 ..**Jakab,** Jill E '77 Workers Comp -125 E Court -Cincinnati 45202 **Fx:**361-8322

(513) 352-3343 ..**Jake,** Charles E IV '01 Law Dept -801 Plum -Rm 214 -Cincinnati 45202 **Fx:**352-1515

(216) 363-4500 ..**Jaketic,** Bryan J '04 %Benesch FC&A LLP -200 Pub Sq -Ste 2300 -Cleveland 44114 **Fx:**363-4588

(216) 621-0200 ..**Jakiel,** Kristin J '98 %Baker & H LLP -1900 E 9th -Ste 3200 -Cleveland 44114 **Fx:**696-0740

(330) 823-9757 ..**Jakmides,** Jeffrey Ray '81 -325 E Main -Alliance 44601

(440) 526-8018 ..**Jakubaitis,** Janis M '75 -Bx470275 -Broadview Heights 44147

(216) 523-5479 ..**Jakubaitis,** Jayne L '92 (Bricker & E LLP) -1375 E 9th -Ste 1500 -Cleveland 44114 **Fx:**523-7071

(330) 758-6422 ..**Jakubek,** John T '57 -5867 Tippecanoe Rd -Canfield 44406

(614) 462-3555 ..**Jakubow,** Michael R '90 Franklin Cnty Pros -373 S High -Columbus 43215

(419) 885-0234 ..**Jakubowski,** James D '97 -6019 Marshwood Dr -Sylvania 43560

(216) 696-4441 ..**Jakubs,** Michele L '99 %Zashin & R Co,LPA -55 Pub Sq -Ste 1490 -Cleveland 44113 **Fx:**696-1618

(216) 689-1761 ..**Jakyma,** Christopher P '94 KeyBank NA -127 Pub Sq -18th Fl -Cleveland 44114 **Fx:**689-0831

(330) 972-7712 ..**Jalbert,** Michael J '84 -2398 Fox Cir -Ravenna 44266

(216) 621-0200 ..**Jambe,** Suzanne M '93 (Baker & H LLP) -1900 E 9th -Ste 3200 -Cleveland 44114 **Fx:**696-0740

(949) 360-3039 ..**Jambor,** Margaret M '73 US DOJ/INS -2400 Avila Rd -6th Fl, Bx30080 -Laguna Niguel, CA 92607

(440) 352-3360 ..**Jambor,** Z Richard '67 -2136 Kingsborough Dr -Painesville 44077

(330) 643-8124 ..**James,** Amy Casner '03 9th Dist Ct of Appeals -161 S High -Ste 504 -Akron 44308

(330) 782-8301 ..**James,** Carl G III '77 -4450 Market -Youngstown 44512

(513) 721-1995 ..**James,** Daniel J '77 -Bx157 -North Bend 45052

(740) 289-2371 ..**James,** Darin C '96 Community Action Comm -Bx799 -Piketon 45661

(513) 721-1995 ..**James,** Diane M '80 -Bx157 -North Bend 45052

(614) 818-3800 ..**James,** Edmund G Jr. '75 James & Donohew Dvlpmnt Srvcs -635 Brooksedge Blvd -Westerville 43081

(330) 836-0374 ..**James,** Frances White '81 -2550 Addyston Rd -Akron 44313

(330) 535-9655 ..**James,** Jeffrey N '91 (Lombardi G&J,Ltd) -7 W Bowery -Ste 507 -Akron 44308

(203) 359-7479 ..**James,** Kenneth '80 Diageo -6 Landmark Sq -Stamford, CT 06901 **Fx:**359-7192

(419) 243-6200 ..**James,** Mary M '99 (Steltenpohl J&M Co,LPA) -421 N Mich -Toledo 43624 **Fx:**243-6280

(614) 252-0434 ..**James,** Peter K '84 Allied Healthcare Srvcs -1731 E Long -Columbus 43203

(419) 436-5613 ..**James,** Richard P '92 Honeywell -1600 N Union -Human Resources -Bx880 -Fostoria 44830

(330) 823-5100 ..**James,** Robert N '67 -Bx3753 -Alliance 44601 **Fx:**823-5515

(937) 438-5588 ..**James,** Stacey D '99 (Phillips & J) -7970 Clyo Rd -Dayton 45459

(614) 539-9994 ..**James,** Stephen A '93 -3902 Bway -Grove City 43123

(440) 734-1276 ..**James,** Teresa '81 -23556 Marion Rd -North Olmsted 44070

(513) 891-8900 ..**James,** Thomas C Jr. '01 %Sanders & Assoc,LPA -9122 Mntgmry Rd -Ste 201 -Cincinnati 45242

(419) 241-3213 ..**James,** Timothy C '80 (Ritter RM&J) -405 Mad Av -Ste 1850 -Toledo 43604 **Fx:**241-4925

(937) 439-1177 ..**James,** William K '83 -7965 Wshngtn Woods Dr -Ste B -Dayton 45459

(937) 496-7428 ..**James-Cox,** Mary E '91 Montgomery Cnty Pros/CSEA -14 W 4th -Ste 510 -Dayton 45402

(513) 621-1935 ..**Jameson,** Kenneth D '79 (Roeller R&J) -1029 Main -Cincinnati 45202

(216) 241-6988 ..**Jamieson,** Daniel J '80 -75 Pub Sq -Ste 1200 -Cleveland 44113

(614) 466-7900 ..**Jamieson,** Duffy W '89 Atty Gen -30 E Broad -Columbus 43215 **Fx:**466-2437

(614) 464-6400 ..**Jamieson,** J Scott '79 (Vorys SS&P LLP) -52 E Gay -Bx1008 -Columbus 43216 **Fx:**464-6350

(216) 931-6000 ..**Jamieson,** Sally A '00 %Ulmer & B LLP -1300 E 9th -Ste 900 Penton Media Bldg -Cleveland 44114 **Fx:**931-6001

(330) 375-1311 ..**Jamison,** Andrew D '98 %Reminger & R -80 S Summit -200 Courtyard Sq -Akron 44308 **Fx:**375-9075

Jamison, Melissa A '02 -4208 Benning Rd NE -Washington, DC 20019

(440) 816-0600 ..**Jamison,** Neal M '83 Largent BP&J Co,LPA -1 Berea Cmmns -Ste 216 -Berea 44017 **Fx:**816-0604

(740) 593-6400 ..**Jamison,** Patricia A '81 Pub Def -80 N Court -Athens 45701 **Fx:**591-2074

(614) 719-8792 ..**Jamison,** Terri B '04 Franklin Cnty Pub Def -373 S High -12th Fl -Columbus 43215

(513) 852-2584 ..**Jamison,** Tracy B '96 Cors & B LLC -537 E Pete Rose Way -Ste 400 -Cincinnati 45202

(419) 213-3000 ..**Jan,** Christopher M '87 Lucas Cnty CSEA -701 Adams -Toledo 43624

(440) 324-2409 ..**Janco,** David J '89 UAW Legal Srvcs -347 Midway Blvd -Ste 312 -Elyria 44035 **Fx:**324-4647

Jancura, Diana D '98 -689 Sunset Av -Sheffield Lake 44054

(440) 899-1551 ..**Jancura,** Scott E '95 JD Carney & Assoc,LLC -2001 Crocker Rd -440 Gemini Twr II -Westlake 44145

(614) 228-8400 ..**Janes,** Charles R '77 Ulmer & B LLP -88 E Broad -Ste 1600 -Columbus 43215 **Fx:**228-8561

(614) 236-6779 ..**Janes,** Kathryn B '00 Capital Univ Law Schl -303 E Broad -Fam Advocacy Clinic -Columbus 43215

(937) 461-6200 ..**Janes,** Robert J '85 Cincinnati Ins Co -130 W 2nd -Ste 1850 -Dayton 45402

(614) 224-7291 ..**Janes,** Ronald B '69 -330 S High -Columbus 43215

(614) 873-8227 ..**Janetzke,** Ronald H '67 -8189 State Route 736 -Plain City 43064

Janezic, Christopher B '96 -372 E 270th -Euclid 44132

(216) 621-8484 ..**Janice,** Christina M '91 %Climaco LPW&G Co,LPA -1228 Euclid Av -Ste 900 Halle Bldg -Cleveland 44115 **Fx:**771-1632

(612) 738-5004 ..**Janik,** Catherine J '84 Fortis Inc -500 Bielenberg Dr -Woodbury, MN 55125

(440) 838-7600 ..**Janik & Dorman,LLP** -9200 S Hills Blvd -Ste 300
-Cleveland 44147 **Fx:**838-7601

(440) 988-4172 ..**Janik,** Frank J III '90 -248 Park Av -Amherst 44001 **Fx:**988-4238

(440) 838-7600 ..**Janik,** Steven G '76 (Janik & D,LLP) -9200 S Hills Blvd -Ste 300
-Cleveland 44147 **Fx:**838-7601

(440) 892-1990 ..**Janis,** Edward M '76 (EM Janis Co,LPA) -34461 Detroit Rd
-Ste 209 -WestLake 44145

(937) 222-2424 ..**Janis,** Patrick J '82 (Freund F&A) -1 S Main -Ste 1800
-Dayton 45402 **Fx:**222-5369

(216) 566-5061 ..**Janis,** Paul A '86 Grtr Cleveland Regnl Transit Auth -1240 W 6th
-Cleveland 44113 **Fx:**781-4250

(216) 586-3939 ..**Janke,** Ronald R '74 (Jones D) -901 Lakeside Av
-Cleveland 44114 **Fx:**579-0212

(216) 521-2595 ..**Jankite,** Susan K '99 S Jankite Co,LPA -1253 Arlngtn Av
-Lakewood 44107

(614) 764-2007 ..**Jankowski,** Daniel R '01 %Stanley Steemer Intl
-5500 Stanley Steemer Pkwy -Dublin 43016

(412) 562-1417 ..**Jankowski,** Gretchen L '04 (Buchanan I,PC) -301 Grant
-One Oxford Ctr 20th Fl -Pittsburgh, PA 15219 **Fx:**562-1041

(304) 558-3570 ..**Jankowski,** Joseph J Jr. '74 WV Cnsldtd Pub Retirement Brd
-1900 Kanawha Blvd E -Cptl Cmplx Bldg 5 Ste 1000
-Charleston, WV 25305

(937) 845-9759 ..**Janning,** Charles W '67 -5255 Westland Dr -New Carlisle 45344

(513) 984-8989 ..**Janning,** Nancy M '96 -7616 Mntgmry Rd -Cincinnati 45236

(330) 253-5454 ..**Janos,** Peter P '92 Perantinides & N Co,LPA -80 S Summit
-300 Courtyard Sq -Akron 44308

(216) 687-1311 ..**Janovitz,** Barbara B '83 (Reminger & R) -101 Prospect Av W
-1400 Mdlnd Bldg -Cleveland 44115 **Fx:**687-1841

(440) 238-7373 ..**Janowski,** John T '94 Strongsville Police Dept
-18688 Royalton Rd -Strongsville 44136

(859) 431-8579 ..**Jansen,** Brian R '02 Woolpert LLP -525 W 5th -Ste 213
-Covington, KY 41011

(440) 826-3333 ..**Jansen,** Edward R '00 J Zalic -7550 Lucerne Dr -Ste 302
-Middleburg Heights 44130

(937) 461-5310 ..**Jansen,** Susan D '87 (Doll J&F) -111 W 1st -Ste 1100
-Dayton 45402 **Fx:**461-7219

(937) 748-1749 ..**Jansing,** Debra L '88 %R West & Assoc -195 E Central Av -Bx938
-Springboro 45066

(513) 579-6400 ..**Jansing,** James M '82 (Keating M&K PLL) -1 E 4th
-1400 Provident Twr -Cincinnati 45202 **Fx:**579-6457

(937) 228-3889 ..**Jansing,** John G '88 %Hedrick & J Co,LPA -124 E 3rd -Ste 300
-Dayton 45402

(513) 287-3025 ..**Janson,** Julia S '88 Cinergy Corp -139 E 4th -25 Atrium II -Bx960
-Cincinnati 45201

(419) 247-2500 ..**Janson,** Scott T '91 OfCnsl Fuller & H,Ltd -One SeaGate
-Ste 1700 -Bx2088 -Toledo 43603 **Fx:**247-2665

(513) 621-2120 ..**Janszen,** August T '93 Strauss & T,LPA -150 E 4th -4th Fl
-Cincinnati 45202 **Fx:**241-8259

(216) 241-6602 ..**Janusz,** John M '98 %Weston HFP&H LLP -50 Pub Sq
-2500 Trmnl Twr -Cleveland 44113 **Fx:**621-8369

(202) 512-8327 ..**Japikse,** Bert '70 SrCnsl US GAO -441 G NW
-Washington, DC 20548 **Fx:**512-7703

(216) 241-3114 ..**Jaquay,** Robert B '81 G Gund Fndn -45 Prospect Av -Ste 1845
-Cleveland 44115

(614) 466-5394 ..**Jaquith,** Craig M '91 Pub Def -8 E Long -Columbus 43215

(216) 781-1771 ..**Jarabek,** Timothy J '98 Women Helping Women
-1303 Prospect Av -Ste 100 -Cleveland 44115

(440) 473-9232 ..**Jarem,** Helen S '97 Preformed Line Prdctns Co -660 Beta Dr
-Mayfield Village 44143

(513) 932-5792 ..**Jarnicki,** Brent H '04 %H Jarnicki & Assoc -576 Mound Ct -Ste B
-Lebanon 45036

(513) 932-5792 ..**Jarnicki,** Harold '74 (H Jarnicki & Assoc) -576 Mound Ct -Ste B
-Lebanon 45036

(419) 724-5330 ..**Jaros,** James J '93 Cmmnty ISP,Inc -3035 Moffat Dr
-Toledo 43615

(216) 360-2124 ..**Jaros,** Stanley T '73 (Moriarty & J,PLL) -30000 Chagrin Blvd
-Ste 200 -Pepper Pike 44124

(614) 891-5923 ..**Jarosi,** Michael J '03 MJ Jarosi,LLC -140 Commerce Park Dr
-Westerville 43082 **Fx:**891-5870

(248) 338-8980 ..**Jarred,** Katherine A '03 %Ward AP&B -300 Enterprise Ct -Ste 100
-Bloomfield Hills, MI 48302 **Fx:**338-2732

Jarrett, Charles E '86 Progressive Ins Co -6300 Wilson Mills Rd
-#N72A -Mayfield Village 44143

(330) 262-9060 ..**Jarrett,** David L '93 Wstrn Rsrv Grp -1685 Cleveland Rd -Bx36
-Wooster 44691

(419) 249-7900 ..**Jarrett,** Evy M '93 %Robison C&O -Four SeaGate -9th Fl
-Toledo 43604 **Fx:**249-7911

(440) 333-1296 ..**Jarrett,** Rita M '92 -4251 W 212th -Fairview Park 44126

(330) 837-4678 ..**Jarvis,** Keith L '69 -46 Fed Av NW -Massillon 44647

(513) 631-6666 ..**Jarvis,** Robin Ann '98 -7374 Reading Rd -Cincinnati 45237

(215) 735-6876 ..**Jarvis,** Roland B '84 (R Jarvis Assoc) -1315 Walnut -Ste 1326
-Philadelphia, PA 19107 **Fx:**887-8205

(937) 865-6800 ..**Jarvis,** Ryan C '99 Lexis/Nexis -Bx933 -Dayton 45401

(513) 481-9800 ..**Jarvis,** Timothy P '03 -3050 Harrison Av -Cincinnati 45211

(419) 473-1350 ..**Jasin,** Christopher A '85 (Jasin S&M Co,LPA) -4303 Talmadge Rd
-Ste 201 -Toledo 43623 **Fx:**473-1929

(419) 473-1350 ..**Jasin Sallah & McHugh Co,LPA** -4303 Talmadge Rd -Ste 201
-Toledo 43623 **Fx:**473-1929

(937) 222-6090 ..**Jasinski,** James E '81 UAW-GM Legal Srvcs Plan -111 W 1st
-Ste 1045 -Dayton 45402

(614) 466-5394 ..**Jasiunas,** J Banning '01 Pub Def -8 E Long -Columbus 43215

Jasper, Joseph W Jr. '96 -(Address Unavailable)

(216) 664-4978 ..**Jasper,** Mabel M '77 Mun Ct Judge -1200 Ontario -Justice Ctr
-Cleveland 44113

(419) 738-9274 ..**Jauert,** Douglas S '72 -Fifth Third Bk Bldg -2nd Fl -Bx1957
-Wapakoneta 45895

(216) 623-0000 ..**Javitch Block & Rathbone** -1300 E 9th -14th Fl
-Cleveland 44114 **Fx:**623-0190

(513) 744-9600 ..**Javitch Block & Rathbone** -602 Main -Ste 500 -Cincinnati 45202
Fx:744-9602

(614) 228-9550 ..**Javitch Block & Rathbone** -33 N 3rd -Ste 300 -Columbus 43215
Fx:228-2818

(216) 623-0000 ..**Javitch,** Victor M '62 (Javitch B&R) -1300 E 9th -14th Fl
-Cleveland 44114 **Fx:**623-0190

Jay, David E '79 -5524 Glenhill NE -Canton 44718

(614) 466-8911 ..**Jean,** Martine '03 Atty Gen -30 E Broad -Columbus 43215
Fx:728-7582

(330) 725-4114 ..**Jeandrevin,** John T '59 J Jeandrevin Co,LPA -600 E Smith Rd
-Medina 44256

(614) 221-7711 ..**Jedinak,** Thomas J '74 %Grossman Law Ofcs -32 W Hoster
-Ste 100 -Columbus 43215 **Fx:**221-7145

(513) 241-2324 ..**Jefferies,** David E '98 %Wood H&E LLP -441 Vine -Ste 2700
-Cincinnati 45202 **Fx:**421-7269

(417) 358-8131 ..**Jefferies,** Robert A Jr. '66 Leggett & Platt,Inc -1 Leggett Rd
-Carthage, MO 64836

(740) 425-1023 ..**Jefferis,** Paul B '80 -58884 Wright Rd -Barnesville 43713

(800) 444-9950 ..**Jeffers,** James B '95 State Auto Ins Co -518 E Broad -Columbus
43215

(216) 241-6602 ..**Jeffers,** John W '64 (Weston HFP&H) -50 Pub Sq
-2500 Trmnl Twr -Cleveland 44113 **Fx:**621-8369

(614) 891-0336 ..**Jeffers,** Michael D '91 (Fifner & J,LLC) -1001 Eastwind Dr
-Ste 305 -Westerville 43081

(614) 855-5300 ..**Jeffers,** Michael K '88 -220 Market -Ste 201 -New Albany 43054

(216) 883-2671 ..**Jefferson,** Milton D '90 -11502 Nelson Av -Cleveland 44105

(513) 556-0075 ..**Jefferson,** Mina J '90 Univ of Cincinnati -Bx210040
-Cincinnati 45221

(937) 223-8177 ..**Jefferson,** My'chael D '03 %Coolidge WW&L -33 W 1st -Ste 600
-Dayton 45402 **Fx:**223-6705

Jefferson, Ollie '84 -212 S Mesquite -Ste 2F -Arlington, TX 76010

(202) 565-5200 ..**Jefferson,** William J '86 US Dept of Vet Affrs -811 VT Av
-Appls Bd -Washington, DC 20420

(419) 252-6226 ..**Jeffery,** James R '65 (Spengler N PLL) -608 Mad Av -Ste 1000
-Toledo 43604 **Fx:**241-8599

(614) 901-8380 ..**Jeffries,** Bryan L '87 (B Jeffries) -1091 Marie Lou Dr -Bx2969
-Westerville 43086 **Fx:**901-8381

(412) 473-4129 ..**Jeffries,** Gary A '00 Dominion Retail,Inc -1201 Pitt -Pittsburgh,
PA 15221

(614) 464-6400 ..**Jeffries,** Gretchen D '03 %Vorys SS&P LLP -52 E Gay -Bx1008
-Columbus 43216 **Fx:**464-6350

(937) 382-2838 ..**Jeffries,** Jacob M '04 Rose & D Co,LPA -97 N South
-Wilmington 45177

(216) 771-4050 ..**Jeffries Kube Forrest & Monteleone Co, LPA**
-101 W Prospect Av -1650 Mdlnd Bldg -Cleveland 44115
Fx:771-0732

(513) 381-2838 ..**Jeffries,** Lori E '97 %Taft S&H LLP -425 Walnut -Ste 1800
-Cincinnati 45202 **Fx:**381-0205

(330) 456-0061 ..**Jeffries,** Timothy J '00 %Heichel C&P Co,LPA -437 Market Av N
-Canton 44702

(440) 250-9709 ..**Jefson,** Thomas A '02 %R Fedor Jr -1991 Crocker Rd -Ste 222
-Westlake 44145

(614) 462-3194 ..**Jelen,** Scott Z '86 Franklin Cnty Pub Def -373 S High -12th Fl
-Columbus 43215

(440) 483-3798 ..**Jelenic,** Barbara A '96 Marconi Medical Sys -595 Miner Rd
-Highland Heights 44143

(513) 983-6388 ..**Jemison,** Steven W '75 Procter & Gamble Co-Legal -1 Procter
& Gamble Plz -Cincinnati 45202

(216) 681-1554 ..**Jencson,** Gary E '78 Cnsl Defense Logistics Agency -555 E 88th
-Cleveland 44108

(937) 865-6800 ..**Jeng,** Kathryn L '02 Lexis Nexis -9333 Springboro Pike
-Miamisburg 45342

(513) 241-9119 ..**Jenike,** David L '74 -1014 Vine -Ste 1919 -Cincinnati 45202

Jenkins, Anna Villarreal '04 -(Address Unavailable)

(513) 723-1600 ..**Jenkins,** Christian A '99 (Mezibov & J) -1726 Young
-Cincinnati 45202

(330) 375-7331 ..**Jenkins,** Donald M '64 Univ of Akron -302 E Buchtel Av
-Akron 44325

(216) 443-7800 ..**Jenkins,** George A Jr. '96 Cuyahoga Cnty Pros -1200 Ontario
-8th Fl -Cleveland 44113 **Fx:**698-2270

(614) 464-6400 ..**Jenkins,** George L '66 (Vorys SS&P LLP) -52 E Gay -Bx1008
-Columbus 43216 **Fx:**464-6350

(216) 363-6003 ..**Jenkins,** James A '85 -1370 Ontario -Ste 2000 -Cleveland 44113

(216) 622-8200 ..**Jenkins,** John J '86 (Calfee M&G LLP) -800 Superior Av -Ste 1400
-Cleveland 44114 **Fx:**241-0816

(216) 586-3939 ..**Jenkins,** Lindsay C '02 %Jones D -901 Lakeside Av
-Cleveland 44114 **Fx:**579-0212

(937) 298-2811 ..**Jenkins,** Matthew R '82 (Jacox M&J) -2310 Far Hills Bldg
-Dayton 45419 **Fx:**298-7418

(937) 223-8177 ..**Jenkins,** Peter L '03 %Coolidge WW&L -33 W 1st -Ste 600
-Dayton 45402 **Fx:**223-6705

(336) 733-2381 ..**Jenkins,** Rebecca J '76 Branch Banking & Trust Co -200 W 2nd
-3rd Fl -Bx1255 -Winston-Salem, NC 27102

(740) 446-2968 ..**Jenkins,** Robert W '61 Gallia Cnty Cmn Pleas Ct -Cthse
-Gallipolis 45631

(614) 644-7342 ..**Jenkins,** Vicki L '85 Dept Mntl Rtrdtn -1810 Sullivant Av
-Columbus 43266 **Fx:**752-8551

(614) 628-6880 ..**Jenkins,** Wayne A '78 (Dinsmore & S LLP) -175 S 3rd -10th Fl
-Columbus 43215 **Fx:**628-6890

(614) 645-8205 ..**Jenkins,** William B '52 Cnty Mun Ct Judge -375 S High
-Columbus 43215

(216) 586-3939 ..**Jenks,** Carl M '82 (Jones D) -901 Lakeside Av -Cleveland 44114
Fx:579-0212

(937) 223-3001 ..**Jenks Pyper & Oxley Co, LPA** -10 N Ludlow -Ste 901
-Dayton 45402 **Fx:**223-3103

(937) 223-3001 ..**Jenks,** Thomas E '53 (Jenks P&O Co,LPA) -10 N Ludlow -Ste 901
-Dayton 45402 **Fx:**223-3103

(216) 795-4117 ..**Jenner,** Simon '03 %Chilcote Law Firm -12434 Cedar Rd -Ste 1
-Cleveland Heights 44106 **Fx:**795-4245

(513) 860-2560 ..**Jennings,** Ann D '01 LandAmerica -8892 Beckett Rd
-West Chester 45069

(614) 764-9944 ..**Jennings,** Charles F '94 Natl Century Financial Enterprises
-6125 Mem'l Dr -Dublin 43017

(216) 479-8500 ..**Jennings,** Colin R '97 %Squire S&D LLP -127 Pub Sq
-4900 Key Twr -Cleveland 44114 **Fx:**479-8780

(614) 221-2121 ..**Jennings,** David G '88 (Isaac BL&T,LLP) -250 E Broad
-Ste 900 Mdlnd Bldg -Columbus 43215 **Fx:**365-9516

(419) 843-9921 ..**Jennings,** Debra M '92 -Bx351658 -Toledo 43635

(216) 763-1004 ..**Jennings,** James Kieran III '95 Siegel SJ&J Co,LPA
-25700 Science Park Dr -Ste 210 -Cleveland 44122 **Fx:**763-1016

(330) 297-1569 .. **Jennings**, Jonathan P '99 Cmmnty Lgl Aid Srvcs,Inc
-250 S Chestnut -Ste 22 -Ravenna 44266

(419) 244-2070 .. **Jennings**, Linda J '89 -413 N Mich -Toledo 43624

(614) 466-0461 .. **Jennings**, Lynn D '85 PUCO -180 E Broad -Columbus 43266

(419) 624-6882 .. **Jennings**, Nancy L '04 Erie Cnty Pub Def -220 Columbus Av
-Ste 37 -Sandusky 44870 **Fx:**627-6633

(513) 579-6400 .. **Jennings**, Robert W Jr. '82 OfCnsl Keating M&K PLL -1 E 4th
-1400 Provident Twr -Cincinnati 45202 **Fx:**579-6457

(614) 466-2872 .. **Jennings**, Sharon A '91 Atty Gen -30 E Broad -Columbus 43215
Fx:728-7592

(513) 984-8080 .. **Jennings**, Thomas M '86 -9000 Plainfld Rd -Cincinnati 45236

(859) 371-7581 .. **Jennings**, Thomas P '94 -606 Laurelwood Dr -Cleves 45002

(419) 244-2070 .. **Jennings**, William G '86 -413 N Mich -Toledo 43624

(216) 771-2680 .. **Jennrich**, Terry R '83 Geraci & L Co,LPA -1370 Ontario -Ste 1220
-Cleveland 44113

(216) 687-1311 .. **Jenny**, Leslie M '96 (Reminger & R) -101 Prospect Av W
-1400 Mdlnd Bldg -Cleveland 44115 **Fx:**687-1841

(919) 997-2350 .. **Jensen**, Eric P '91 Nortel Ntwrks -Bx13828 -Research
Triangle Park, NC 27709

(513) 241-3100 .. **Jensen**, Joel K '82 Lerner S&R -120 E 4th -8th Fl
-Cincinnati 45202

(419) 947-5515 .. **Jensen**, Jon L Jr. '00 Morrow Cnty Pros -60 E High
-Mount Gilead 43338

(614) 932-9884 .. **Jensen**, Judith K '94 -10070 Sylvian Dr -Dublin 43017

(419) 897-8456 .. **Jensen**, Julie A '98 St Lukes Hosp -5901 Monclova Rd
-Maumee 43537

(614) 995-1968 .. **Jensen**, Mitchell A '04 OH Tuition Trust Auth -580 S High -Ste 208
-Columbus 43215

(513) 621-4556 .. **Jensen**, Robert M '04 (Jacobs J&N,LLC) -30 Garfld Pl -Ste 750
-Cincinnati 45202 **Fx:**621-5563

.. **Jensen**, William A Jr. '96 -434 Hogarth Av -Niles 44446

(419) 995-8404 .. **Jenson-Schuck**, Margaret I '84 Rhodes State College
-4240 Campus Dr -Lima 45804

(330) 725-8816 .. **Jeppe**, Gerald L '69 %Brown & A,LPA -109 W Lbrty -Bx1117
-Medina 44258

(937) 224-1981 .. **Jerardi**, Peter J Jr. '65 (Young PL&J) -130 W 2nd -Ste 800
-Dayton 45402

(216) 931-6000 .. **Jerdonek**, Elizabeth A '97 %Ulmer & B LLP -1300 E 9th
-Ste 900 Penton Media Bldg -Cleveland 44114 **Fx:**931-6001

(216) 348-5400 .. **Jereb**, Brian J '83 (McDonald H Co,LPA) -600 Superior Av E
-Ste 2100 -Cleveland 44114 **Fx:**348-5474

(330) 792-2336 .. **Jeren**, John A Jr. '73 (Wellman JH&S Co,LPA) -4990 Mahoning Av
-Youngstown 44515 **Fx:**792-5403

(419) 756-7711 .. **Jerger**, Joseph L '90 (Bayer J&A) -362 Lex Av -Mansfield 44907
Fx:756-9566

(216) 664-4824 .. **Jerlstrom**, Stephanie L '95 Prosecutor -1200 Ontario Av
-8th Fl Justice Ctr -Cleveland 44113 **Fx:**664-4399

.. **Jermann**, Edmond L Jr. '56 -4659 Crestvw Dr -Sylvania 43560

(937) 276-6577 .. **Jermany**, Sharon A '02 Montgomery Cnty Pros -301 W 3rd -Bx972
-Dayton 45422 **Fx:**225-3470

(614) 469-3939 .. **Jernejcic**, Junxia Tang '02 %Jones D
-325 John H McConnell Blvd -Ste 600 -Bx165017
-Columbus 43216 **Fx:**461-4198

(216) 241-9990 .. **Jerome**, Joseph B '75 (J Jerome & Assoc) -55 Pub Sq -Ste 2020
-Cleveland 44113 **Fx:**241-2920

(216) 621-1000 .. **Jerse**, Edward S '83 Moscarino & T,LLP -1422 Euclid Av
-Hanna Bldg Ste 630 -Cleveland 44115 **Fx:**622-1556

(440) 350-5020 .. **Jerse**, Joseph J '81 Lake Cnty Bd of MR/DD -8121 Deewood Blvd
-Mentor 44060

(216) 430-8223 .. **Jerse**, Shannon F '88 Cleveland Clinic Health Syst
-17325 Euclid Av -Cleveland 44112

(440) 245-1160 .. **Jesensky**, Alex Jr. '71 Lorain Mun Ct -100 W Erie Av
-Lorain 44052

(440) 238-2601 .. **Jeske**, Kendra J '97 -Bx37 -Berea 44017

(216) 344-3838 .. **Jesse**, David A '82 %K Seminatore -815 Superior Av -Ste 1715
-Cleveland 44114

(216) 241-2838 .. **Jett**, Stephen H '90 (Taft S&H LLP) -200 Pub Sq -3500 BP Twr
-Cleveland 44114 **Fx:**241-3707

(513) 977-8200 .. **Jevicky**, John E '81 (Dinsmore & S LLP) -255 E 5th -Ste 1900
-Cincinnati 45202 **Fx:**977-8141

(440) 286-9549 .. **Jevnikar**, David W '81 %Newman & B -214 E Park
-Chardon 44024

(614) 583-0088 .. **Jewel**, Anne F '86 (Jewel & B,LLC) -230 E Town -1st Fl
-Columbus 43215

(513) 887-4221 .. **Jewett**, Bruce E '78 Cnty Human Srvcs Dept -315 High -Bx4000
-Hamilton 45012

(614) 268-8661 .. **Jewett**, James M '74 -2577 N High -Columbus 43202 **Fx:**268-8662

(937) 324-8481 .. **Jewett**, Reed P '60 (R Jewett Co LPA) -1345 W 1st
-Springfield 45504 **Fx:**324-8422

(937) 223-1130 .. **Jewson**, Matthew T '94 %Pickrel S&E -40 N Main
-2700 Kettering Twr -Dayton 45423 **Fx:**223-0339

(440) 442-7500 .. **Jiannetti**, Michael A '82 M Jiannetti Co,LPA -6449 Wilson Mills Rd
-Cleveland 44143 **Fx:**442-0007

(419) 241-2122 .. **Jilek**, Michael F '70 (Williams JLG&S Co,LPA) -416 N Erie
-Ste 500 -Toledo 43624 **Fx:**245-3849

(937) 644-9125 .. **Jillisky**, Donald R '93 (Cannizzaro FB&J) -302 S Main
-Marysville 43040 **Fx:**644-0754

(937) 644-9125 .. **Jillisky**, Nancy L '95 (Cannizzaro FB&J) -302 S Main
-Marysville 43040 **Fx:**644-0754

(937) 645-2316 .. **Jimenez**, Joseph V '02 Nestle R&D -809 Collins Av -Marysville
43040

(440) 729-7278 .. **Jimison**, Mark S '96 -8228 Mayfld Rd -Ste 6B -Chesterland 44026

(614) 221-7663 .. **Jinkens**, Jeffrey R '78 (Luper N&L,LPA) -50 W Broad
-1200 LeVeque Twr -Columbus 43215 **Fx:**464-2425

(937) 449-6400 .. **Jividen**, William A '99 %Dinsmore & S LLP -1 S Main
-Ste 1300 One Dayton Centre -Dayton 45402 **Fx:**449-6405

(216) 471-6865 .. **Jobe**, Lisa A '01 OfficeMax,Inc -Bx228070 -Cleveland 44122

.. **Jochim**, Erin '03 -(Address Unavailable)

(614) 444-1190 .. **Jochim**, Timothy C '76 (Jochim Co,LPA) -673 S Mohawk
-Columbus 43206 **Fx:**445-5850

(440) 585-4448 .. **Jochum**, F Eric '87 -7107 Wilson Mills Rd -Gates Mills 44040
Fx:423-0764

(330) 721-0000 ..**Jocke**, Ralph E '81 (Walker & J,LPA) -231 S Bway -Medina 44256
Fx:722-6446

(419) 478-1776 .. **Joelson**, Philip R '61 -1776 Tremainsvll Rd -Toledo 43613
Fx:478-5087

(615) 360-5604 ..**Joffe**, Matthew T '00 Kruse & Assoc -105 Continental Pl
-Brentwood, TN 37027

(614) 224-5700 .. **Johan**, Andrea H '85 %FOP/OH Labor Cncl -222 E Town
-Columbus 43215

(440) 835-2052 .. **Johanek**, Mary A '80 -1640 Queen Annes Gate -Westlake 44145

(419) 734-4928 .. **Johannsen**, Kyle J '90 Hartung Title -217 Madison
-Port Clinton 43452

(330) 665-7200 .. **Johanson**, David M '00 Progressive Ins Co -190 Montrose W Av
-Ste 100 -Copley 44321

(304) 233-4380 .. **John**, Joseph J '95 -80 12th -Ste 200 -Wheeling, WV 26003

(330) 633-1933 .. **John**, Michael L '83 (Marks & J) -1650 Home Av -Akron 44310

(614) 901-3676 .. **John**, Sidney C '65 -4594 Lakeside Ct -Westerville 43082
Fx:901-3686

.. **Johns**, Alan L '78 -1254 Fountaine Dr -Columbus 43221

(614) 752-6891 .. **Johns**, Brian E '91 Industrial Commssn of OH -30 W Spring -9th Fl
-Columbus 43215 **Fx:**752-8785

(585) 394-2665 .. **Johns**, David A '98 (Croucher J&J) -70 S Main -Ste 330
-Canandaigua, NY 14424 **Fx:**396-0247

(502) 227-1611 .. **Johns**, Elizabeth L '98 Farmers Bk & Capital Trust Co -Bx309
-Frankfort, KY 40602

(419) 255-0814 .. **Johns**, Jeanne D '82 ABLE -520 Mad Av -740 Spitzer Bldg
-Toledo 43604 **Fx:**259-2880

(330) 744-1311 .. **Johns**, Kelly A '00 %Reminger & R -11 Fed Plz Central -Ste 300
-Youngstown 44503 **Fx:**744-7500

(513) 977-8200 .. **Johns**, Michael D '97 %Dinsmore & S LLP -255 E 5th -Ste 1900
-Cincinnati 45202 **Fx:**977-8141

(740) 283-4781 .. **Johns**, Robert C '95 SE OH Lgl Srvcs -100 N 3rd
-Steubenville 43952

(937) 445-2968 .. **Johnsen**, Kirk D '87 NCR Corp -1700 S Patterson Blvd -WHQ-4W
-Dayton 45479

(412) 803-1196 .. **Johnson**, Alan E '79 %Marshall DWC&G -600 Grant -Ste 2900
-Pittsburgh, PA 15219 **Fx:**803-1188

(202) 353-1929 .. **Johnson**, Alicia D '97 US DOJ -Rm 4025 -Bx65968
-Washington, DC 20530

(330) 928-0307 .. **Johnson**, Allan Jr. '49 -1799 Akron Peninsula Rd -Akron 44313

(216) 851-0800 .. **Johnson**, Almeta A '71 (AA Johnson Co,LPA) -489 E 260th
-Euclid 44132

.. **Johnson**, Andrew L Jr. '60 -1205 W 110th -#16 -Cleveland 44102

(614) 442-8885 .. **Johnson**, Annrita S '76 (Siegel SJ&J Co,LPA) -3001 Bethel Rd
-Ste 208 -Columbus 43220 **Fx:**442-8880

(740) 622-8969 .. **Johnson**, Antonia K '84 Cnty Cmn Pleas Ct -426 Main -Cnty Cthse
-Coshocton 43812

(317) 838-1235 .. **Johnson**, Ariane S '04 Cinergy -1000 E Main -Plainfield, IN 46168

.. **Johnson**, Arthur C '04 -(Address Unavailable)

(216) 621-2300 .. **Johnson**, Brenda M '93 Nurenberg PH&M LPA -1370 Ontario
-Ste 100 -Cleveland 44113 **Fx:**771-2242

(614) 466-3379 .. **Johnson**, Bruce E '85 Dept of Dvlpmnt -77 S High
-Columbus 43215

(614) 464-1904 .. **Johnson**, Bryan B '83 (Gamble HJ Co,LPA) -1 E Lvngstn Av
-Columbus 43215 **Fx:**365-9741

(740) 354-4200 .. **Johnson**, C Clayton '70 (Johnson & O,LPA) -701 6th -Bx1505
-Portsmouth 45662 **Fx:**353-2413

(937) 449-6810 .. **Johnson**, C Terry '64 (Porter WM&A LLP) -1 S Main -Ste 1600
-Dayton 45402 **Fx:**449-6820

(614) 464-3563 .. **Johnson**, Calvin T Jr. '95 (Loveland & B) -50 W Broad -Ste 3300
-Columbus 43215

(330) 725-6666 .. **Johnson**, Carroll N Jr. '63 (Williams & B,LLP) -105 W Lbrty
-Bx394 -Medina 44258

(937) 224-1427 .. **Johnson**, Charles A '72 -130 W 2nd -Ste 1900 -Dayton 45402

(614) 249-3951 .. **Johnson**, Chris A '88 State Auto Ins Co -518 E Broad
-Columbus 43215

(330) 493-6966 .. **Johnson**, Christine A '99 -4200 Munson NW -Bx35426
-Canton 44735

(440) 356-2376 .. **Johnson**, Christopher A '78 -1340 Depot -Ste 104 -Rocky River
44116 **Fx:**356-2738

(937) 222-2424 .. **Johnson**, Christopher F '80 (Freund F&A) -1 S Main -Ste 1800
-Dayton 45402 **Fx:**222-5369

(216) 566-5911 .. **Johnson**, Christopher R '00 %Thompson H LLP -127 Pub Sq
-3900 Key Ctr -Cleveland 44114 **Fx:**566-5800

(216) 295-0826 .. **Johnson**, Clarence '60 -16115 Delrey Av -Cleveland 44128

(614) 299-8235 .. **Johnson**, Cleve M '79 -495 S High -Ste 400 -Columbus 43215

(317) 633-4884 .. **Johnson**, Clifton E '80 Halll RKH&L,PSC -1 Amer Sq -Ste 2000
-Indianapolis, IN 46282

(216) 696-5222 .. **Johnson & Colaluca,LLC** -1001 Lakeside Av
-Ste 1700 N Pnt Twr -Cleveland 44114 **Fx:**696-5288

(614) 873-9668 .. **Johnson**, Daniel E '84 -8175 McKitrick Rd -Plain City 43064

(314) 466-0247 .. **Johnson**, David C '69 Bank of Amer -7800 Forsyth Blvd
-M01-076-06-10 -Saint Louis, MO 63105

(513) 241-3100 .. **Johnson**, David E '99 Lerner S&R -120 E 4th -8th Fl
-Cincinnati 45202

(216) 861-5000 .. **Johnson**, David G '83 (Ernst & Young) -1300 Huntngtn Bldg
-925 Euclid Av -Cleveland 44115

(614) 221-2838 .. **Johnson**, David L '71 (Taft S&H LLP) -21 E State -12th Fl
-Columbus 43215 **Fx:**221-2007

(937) 848-7446 .. **Johnson**, DeAnna D '94 -90 N West -Bellbrook 45305

(937) 445-2928 .. **Johnson**, Debbie Watts '91 NCR Corp -1700 S Patterson Blvd
-Dayton 45479

(614) 466-6691 .. **Johnson**, Denise M '87 OH Civ Rghts Cmmssn -1111 E Broad
-Ste 301 -Columbus 43205

(419) 238-4469 .. **Johnson**, Donald J '74 -113 N Wshngtn -Van Wert 45891

(859) 441-3900 .. **Johnson**, Donald L '60 (Johnson & J,PLC) -50 N Ft Thomas Av
-Fort Thomas, KY 41075

(419) 843-2424 .. **Johnson**, Donald L Jr. '90 (D Johnson & Assoc) -3335 Meijer Dr
-Ste 200 -Toledo 43617

(614) 436-6812 .. **Johnson**, Doreen C '79 -1287 Beechlake Dr -Columbus 43235

(330) 665-4547 .. **Johnson**, Edward A '50 Johnson & Parrish Title Agncy
-1000 S Cleveland-Massillon Rd -Ste 3 -Akron 44321

(513) 533-8508 .. **Johnson**, Eileen A '79 Fed Aviation Admin -4240 Airport Rd
-Cincinnati 45226

(614) 222-0535 .. **Johnson**, Eric A '95 (Sabath & J Co,LPA) -338 S High
-Columbus 43215

(330) 533-1921 .. **Johnson**, Eric C '83 (Johnson & J) -12 W Main -Canfield 44406

(216) 479-8500 .. **Johnson**, Eric J '00 %Squire S&D LLP -127 Pub Sq
-4900 Key Twr -Cleveland 44114 **Fx**:479-8780

(614) 464-1877 .. **Johnson**, Eric W '95 %Sowald S&C -400 S 5th -Ste 101
-Columbus 43215

(513) 705-9000 .. **Johnson**, Eugene H '04 %Pratt SP Co,LPA -301 N Breiel Blvd
-Middletown 45044 **Fx**:705-9001

(614) 249-7187 .. **Johnson**, Freddie L '93 Nationwide Ins Enterprise
-One Nationwide Plz -1-01-18 -Columbus 43215

(937) 644-3691 .. **Johnson**, Frederick B '77 -214 S Ct -Marysville 43040

(216) 696-5222 .. **Johnson**, Gary C '80 (Johnson & C,LLC) -1001 Lakeside Av
-Ste 1700 N Pnt Twr -Cleveland 44114 **Fx**:696-5288

(614) 716-2827 .. **Johnson**, Gary L '98 Amer Elec Power Inc -1 Riverside Plz
-Regulating Specialist -Columbus 43215

(937) 372-4411 .. **Johnson**, Gary R '72 (Brandabur FJW&B) -260 N Detroit
-Xenia 45385 **Fx**:372-4415

(216) 241-6602 .. **Johnson**, Gary W '79 (Weston HFP&H LLP) -50 Pub Sq
-2500 Trmnl Twr -Cleveland 44113 **Fx**:621-8369

(614) 365-5673 .. **Johnson**, Giselle S '86 %Columbus Pub Sch -270 E State
-Columbus 43215

(614) 644-8878 .. **Johnson**, Gregory K '80 Workers Comp -30 W Spring -Level 26
-Columbus 43215

(330) 740-2330 .. **Johnson**, Greta L '04 %Mahoning Cnty Pros -21 W Boardman
-6th Fl -Youngstown 44503 **Fx**:740-2008

(330) 683-0015 .. **Johnson & Helmuth** -343 S Crownhill Rd -Bx149 -Orrville 44667

(614) 457-4026 .. **Johnson**, Jack L '61 -769 Marburn Dr -Columbus 43214
Fx:457-4026

(419) 293-2911 .. **Johnson**, Jack L '69 Cnsldtd Biscuit Co -312 Rader Rd
-McComb 45858

(216) 522-4856 .. **Johnson**, Jacqueline A '84 Fed Pub Def -1660 W 2nd -Ste 750
-Cleveland 44113

(513) 983-2069 .. **Johnson**, James Jay '74 Procter & Gamble Co-Legal
-1 Procter & Gamble Plz -Cincinnati 45202

(513) 352-6990 .. **Johnson**, James L '80 Law Dept -801 Plum -Rm 214
-Cincinnati 45202 **Fx**:352-1515

(216) 523-6354 .. **Johnson**, James M '84 -1280 W 3rd -Ste 2 -Cleveland 44113

(216) 696-9330 .. **Johnson**, Jeffrey D '04 %Garson & Assoc Co,LPA
-614 Superior Av W -1600 Rckfllr Bldg -Cleveland 44113
Fx:696-8558

(419) 249-7900 .. **Johnson**, Jennifer C '03 %Robison C&O -Four SeaGate -9th Fl
-Toledo 43604 **Fx**:249-7911

(614) 224-1373 .. **Johnson**, Jeremy W '02 -209 S High -301 -Columbus 43215

(419) 222-1040 .. **Johnson**, Jerry M '75 (Hunt & J) -400 W North -Lima 45801

(614) 241-2332 .. **Johnson**, Jessica L '04 %Maguire & S,LLP -250 Civic Ctr Dr
-Ste 200 -Columbus 43215 **Fx**:224-1236

(330) 683-0015 .. **Johnson**, John E '75 (Johnson & H) -343 S Crownhill Rd -Bx149
-Orrville 44667

(330) 683-0015 .. **Johnson**, John E Jr. '87 (Johnson & H) -343 S Crownhill Rd
-Bx149 -Orrville 44667

(614) 464-2025 .. **Johnson**, John P II '93 %Connor B LLP -501 S High
-Columbus 43215 **Fx**:224-8708

(212) 254-4152 .. **Johnson**, John W '69 -2 5th Av -Ste 53 -New York, NY 10011

(330) 533-1921 .. **Johnson & Johnson** -12 W Main -Canfield 44406
Johnson, Jonathan J '92 -Bx824 -Putney, VT 05346

(219) 724-2129 .. **Johnson**, Joseph M II '01 J Johnson,PC -147 S 2nd -Bx30
-Decatur, IN 46733

(419) 249-7100 .. **Johnson**, Justice G Jr. '64 (Marshall & M,LLC) -Four Seagate
-8th Fl -Toledo 43604 **Fx**:249-7151

(614) 444-4600 .. **Johnson**, Katherine A '04 Principle Title Agncy -673 Mohawk
-Ste 301 -Columbus 43206

(614) 475-6677 .. **Johnson**, Kathleen A '93 -142 Granvll -Gahanna 43230

(614) 436-0346 .. **Johnson**, Katryna L '99 (Johnson S & Assoc,LLP) -299 S State
-Westerville 43081 **Fx**:436-0347

(937) 339-2919 .. **Johnson**, Kay F '91 CSEA -2040 N Cnty Rd 25-A -Troy 45373

(614) 844-5208 .. **Johnson**, Keisha D '02 Special Cnsl -130 E Wilson Bridge Rd
-Ste 330 -Worthington 43085

(513) 651-8437 .. **Johnson**, Keith K '77 PNC Advsrs/PNC Bank -201 E 5th
-Cincinnati 45202 **Fx**:651-8766

(513) 636-1259 .. **Johnson**, Keith W '91 Childrens Hosptl -3333 Burnett Av
-MLC 7032 -Cincinnati 45229

(614) 227-2322 .. **Johnson**, Kenneth C '79 (Bricker & E LLP) -100 S 3rd
-Columbus 43215 **Fx**:227-2390

(216) 267-1985 .. **Johnson**, Kevin C '79 -19422 Marwood Av -Cleveland 44135

(513) 634-3849 .. **Johnson**, Kevin C '90 Procter & Gamble -6110 Ctr Hill Av
-Cincinnati 45224
Johnson, Kiehner '52 -291 S Columbia Av -Columbus 43209

(419) 424-7089 .. **Johnson**, Kristen K '93 Hancock Cnty Pros -222 Bway -#104
-Findlay 45840 **Fx**:424-7889

(216) 731-1080 .. **Johnson**, Lance B '69 -23420 Lakelnd Blvd -Cleveland 44132

(419) 433-3379 .. **Johnson**, Lawrence P '80 -401 Winona Av -Huron 44839

(614) 233-4710 .. **Johnson**, Leslie S '97 Lane A&H LLC -175 S 3rd -Ste 700
-Columbus 43215 **Fx**:228-0146

(513) 946-3446 .. **Johnson**, Linda F '88 1st Dist Ct of Appls -230 E 9th -12th Fl
-Cincinnati 45202 **Fx**:946-3412

(216) 523-1500 .. **Johnson**, Linda L '96 %Mansour GG&M Co,LPA -55 Pub Sq
-Ste 2150 -Cleveland 44113 **Fx**:523-1705

(216) 622-3600 .. **Johnson**, Lisa H '93 %US Atty -801 W Superior -Ste 400
-Cleveland 44113 **Fx**:622-3370

(330) 856-4115 .. **Johnson**, Lisa L '03 -8256 E Market -Ste 141 -Warren 44484

(202) 622-7550 .. **Johnson**, Lola L '94 Dept of Treasury -1111 Const Av
-CC:Corp:B05 -Washington, DC 20224

(614) 462-3194 .. **Johnson**, Lori A '04 Franklin Cnty Pub Def -373 S High -12th Fl
-Columbus 43215

(216) 622-3600 .. **Johnson**, Marcia W '76 US Atty -801 W Superior -Ste 400
-Cleveland 44113 **Fx**:622-3370
Johnson, Margaret L '02 -623 E Dominion Blvd -Columbus 43214

(614) 221-0984 .. **Johnson**, Margaret N '74 -620 City Park -Columbus 43206

(513) 579-4277 .. **Johnson**, Margaret S '95 Fifth 3rd Bank -38 Fountain Square Plz
-Mail Drop 1090C1 -Cincinnati 45202

(614) 228-1541 .. **Johnson**, Mark A '85 (Baker & H LLP) -65 E State -Ste 2100
-Columbus 43215 **Fx**:462-2616

(937) 865-6800 .. **Johnson**, Mark A '93 Lexis/Nexis -9443 Springboro Pike
-Miamisburg 45342

(216) 621-1113 .. **Johnson**, Mark C '00 %Renner OB&S,LLP -1621 Euclid Av
-19th Fl -Cleveland 44115 **Fx**:621-6165

(614) 722-3940 .. **Johnson**, Martha D '88 %Childrens Hssptl -700 Childrens Dr
-Columbus 43205

(330) 929-2838 .. **Johnson**, Mary D '91 -545 E Cuyahoga Falls Av -Akron 44310

(614) 462-3555 .. **Johnson**, Mary E '86 Franklin Cnty Pros -373 S High
-Columbus 43215

(740) 654-4141 .. **Johnson**, Matthew E '99 %Stebelton A&S,LPA -109 N Broad
-Bx130 -Lancaster 43130 **Fx**:654-2521

(513) 761-7585 .. **Johnson**, Maynard R '81 M Johnson Cnsltng
-449 Hidden Valley Rd -Cincinnati 45215

(216) 464-3570 .. **Johnson**, Melissa S '96 RS Leiken -23611 Chagrin Blvd -Ste 225
-Beachwood 44122

(216) 622-3689 .. **Johnson**, Michael Anne '78 US Atty -801 W Superior -Ste 400
-Cleveland 44113 **Fx**:622-3370

(330) 364-5593 .. **Johnson**, Michael C '73 Johnson U&R Co LPA -117 S Bway
-Bx1007 -New Philadelphia 44663 **Fx**:364-3714

(407) 420-1000 .. **Johnson**, Michele L '00 %Greenberg T LLP -450 S Orange Av
-Ste 650 -Orlando, FL 32801 **Fx**:420-5909

(216) 861-4076 .. **Johnson**, Nelli I '84 -140 Pub Sq -Ste 911 -Cleveland 44114

(330) 533-1921 .. **Johnson**, Nils P Jr. '76 (Johnson & J) -12 W Main -Canfield 44406

(614) 249-7918 .. **Johnson**, Olivia B '86 Nationwide Ins Co -One Nationwide Plz
-Compliance -Columbus 43215

(216) 566-2645 .. **Johnson**, Pamela M '91 Sherwin-Williams Co
-101 Prospect Av NW -Cleveland 44115

(859) 655-7000 .. **Johnson**, Patricia '03 %Nielson & S,PSC -639 Wshngtn Av
-Newport, KY 41071
Johnson, Patricia A '86 -(Address Unavailable)

(513) 381-2838 .. **Johnson**, Patrick G '03 %Taft S&H LLP -425 Walnut -Ste 1800
-Cincinnati 45202 **Fx**:381-0205

(419) 241-6000 .. **Johnson**, Patrick J '67 (Eastman & S Ltd) -1 Seagate -24th Fl
-Bx10032 -Toledo 43699 **Fx**:247-1777

(734) 847-1745 .. **Johnson**, Philip E '94 Nearpass & H -7008 Lewis Av -Bx F
-Temperance, MI 48182
Johnson, Ray E '00 -8199 Davington Dr -Dublin 43017

(216) 696-1000 .. **Johnson**, Richard G '90 (RG Johnson Co,LPA) -955 W St Clair Av
-220 Crittenden Ct Bldg -Cleveland 44113 **Fx**:696-0020

(513) 984-6672 .. **Johnson**, Richard H '68 -9902 Carver Rd -Cincinnati 45242

(419) 241-6000 .. **Johnson**, Richard L '78 %Eastman & S Ltd -1 Seagate -24th Fl
-Bx10032 -Toledo 43699 **Fx**:247-1777

(419) 241-6000 .. **Johnson**, Richard Lee '94 %Eastman & S Ltd -1 Seagate -24th Fl
-Bx10032 -Toledo 43699 **Fx**:247-1777

(216) 622-2700 .. **Johnson**, Rita R '96 (Saffold & J) -75 Pub Sq -Ste 1414
-Cleveland 44113 **Fx**:622-2714

(412) 234-8833 .. **Johnson**, Robert C '76 Mellon Bank -501 Grant -AIM 152-0581
-Pittsburgh, PA 15259

(419) 536-6038 .. **Johnson**, Robert G '81 -3425 Exec Pkwy -Ste 111 -Toledo 43606

(330) 373-6298 .. **Johnson**, Robert L '89 -269 Seneca Av NE -Warren 44481

(513) 352-6769 .. **Johnson**, Robert P '88 (Thompson H LLP) -312 Walnut -14th Fl
-Cincinnati 45202 **Fx**:241-4771

(419) 874-3203 .. **Johnson**, Robert W '78 Perrysburg Title Agncy,Inc -119
W Indna Av -Perrysburg 43551

(614) 466-5967 .. **Johnson**, Russel J '04 Atty Gen -30 E Broad -Columbus 43215
Fx:728-7582

(502) 587-7711 .. **Johnson**, Scott A '95 Conliffe S&S -325 W Main -Ste 2000
-Louisville, KY 40202
Johnson, Scott B '04 -3769 US Rte 30 -ADA 45810

(216) 787-3030 .. **Johnson**, Scott W '91 Atty Gen -615 W Superior Av -11th Fl
-Cleveland 44113 **Fx**:787-3480

(513) 946-3700 .. **Johnson**, Stephen D '84 Hamilton Cnty Pub Def -230 E 9th -3rd Fl
-Cincinnati 45202 **Fx**:946-3707

(614) 466-4656 .. **Johnson**, Stephen H '84 Atty Gen -150 E Gay -Columbus 43215
Fx:466-1756

(330) 451-7200 .. **Johnson**, Tammi R '85 Stark Cnty Pub Def -200 W Tuscarawas
-Ste 200 -Canton 44702

(614) 545-5555 .. **Johnson**, Terri Len '95 -788 Oak -Columbus 43205 **Fx**:545-5557

(216) 241-6602 .. **Johnson**, Timothy D '74 (Weston HFP&H LLP) -50 Pub Sq
-2500 Trmnl Twr -Cleveland 44113 **Fx**:621-8369

(216) 556-0858 .. **Johnson**, Tonya R '99 -Bx603783 -Cleveland 44103

(513) 241-3100 .. **Johnson**, Tracey M '97 %Lerner S&R -120 E 4th -8th Fl
-Cincinnati 45202

(216) 622-8200 .. **Johnson**, Tracy Scott '95 (Calfee H&G LLP) -800 Superior Av
-Ste 1400 -Cleveland 44114 **Fx**:241-0816

(330) 364-5593 .. **Johnson Urban & Range Co LPA** -117 S Bway -Bx1007
-New Philadelphia 44663 **Fx**:364-3714

(216) 621-0200 .. **Johnson**, Victoria A '91 OfCnsl Baker & H LLP -1900 E 9th
-Ste 3200 -Cleveland 44114 **Fx**:696-0740

(419) 241-3213 .. **Johnson**, Wendy C '96 %Ritter RM&J -405 Mad Av -Ste 1850
-Toledo 43604 **Fx**:241-4925

(419) 865-6586 .. **Johnson**, Willard A '54 (WA Johnson & Assoc) -7015
Spring Mdws Dr -Ste 106 -Holland 43528 **Fx**:865-7241

(614) 462-3203 .. **Johnson**, William C Jr. '91 Franklin Cnty Common Pleas Ct
-369 S High -Columbus 43215

(614) 716-1624 .. **Johnson**, William E '95 Amer Elec Pwr Co -1 Riverside Plz
-Columbus 43215

(513) 588-3055 .. **Johnson**, William E III '83 Progressive Ins Co -2722 E Kemper Rd
-Cincinnati 45236

(513) 732-7327 .. **Johnson**, Winslow W '80 Clermont Cnty Dom Rltns Ct
-2340 Clermont Ctr Dr -Batavia 45103

(513) 929-4834 .. **Johnson**, Winston K '86 Fed Pub Def -36 E 7th -2000 CBLD Ctr
-Cincinnati 45202

(937) 382-1200 .. **Johnson-Hebb**, Inza E '88 -3955 Antioch Rd -Wilmington 45177

(305) 673-7080 .. **Johnson-Wright**, Heidi '90 City of Miami Beach
-1700 Convntn Ctr Dr -4th Fl -Miami Beach, FL 33139

(248) 879-2000 .. **Johnson**, Amy M '01 SrCnsl Miller CP&S -840 W Long Lk
-Ste 200 -Troy, MI 48098 **Fx**:879-2001

(513) 723-4000 .. **Johnston**, Bradley K '98 %Vorys SS&P LLP -221 E 4th
-Ste 2000 Atrium Two -Bx0236 -Cincinnati 45201 **Fx**:723-4056

(330) 334-2520 .. **Johnston**, Charles F Jr. '54 -102 Main -Ste 201
-Wadsworth 44281

(614) 793-5163 ..**Johnston,** Craig E '83 Sterling Commerce Inc -4600 Lakehurst Ct
-Dublin 43017

(740) 385-8551 ..**Johnston,** Edwin C '56 -119 E Hunter -Logan 43138

(614) 227-2381 ..**Johnston,** Gordon W '76 (Bricker & E LLP) -100 S 3rd
-Columbus 43215 Fx:227-2390

(561) 391-3700 ..**Johnston,** Herbert J '86 %Kunmann & K,PA -300 E Palmetto
Park Rd -Boca Raton, FL 33432

(614) 466-5032 ..**Johnston,** Holly J '04 OH Dept Commerce -77 S High
-Columbus 43266

(614) 277-4577 ..**Johnston,** James E '97 Mahan Cnstrctn Co -3400 Southwest Blvd
-Grove City 43123

(419) 213-4700 ..**Johnston,** Jeffery B '81 Lucas Cnty Pros -Adams & Erie
-Lucas Cnty Cthse -Toledo 43624

(330) 264-4444 ..**Johnston,** John C III '75 (Critchfield C&J Ltd) -225 N Market
-Bx599 -Wooster 44691 Fx:263-0283

(614) 249-8613 ..**Johnston,** LeRoy III '90 Cnsl Nationwide Ins Co -1 Nationwide Plz
-Columbus 43215

(740) 286-2718 ..**Johnston,** Lorene G '82 Cnty Mun Ct Judge -350 Portsmouth -Ste
101 -Jackson 45640

(614) 464-6400 ..**Johnston,** Philip C '88 OfCnsl Vorys SS&P LLP -52 E Gay
-Bx1008 -Columbus 43216 Fx:464-6350

(513) 793-2992 ..**Johnston,** Robert A '60 -9403 Kenwood Rd -Ste B-203
-Cincinnati 45242

(937) 339-1500 ..**Johnston,** Robert C '78 (Shipman D&L) -215 W Water -Bx310
-Troy 45373 Fx:339-1519

(740) 653-6464 ..**Johnston,** Robert E '54 (Dagger JMO&H) -144 E Main -Bx667
-Lancaster 43130 Fx:653-8522

(216) 523-4132 ..**Johnston,** Roger A '68 Eaton Corp -1111 Superior Av
-Cleveland 44114

Johnston, Terry J '87 -65 Carrion Ln -#8A -Candler, NC 28715

(419) 241-1200 ..**Johnston,** Thomas S '70 Cooper & W,LPA -900 Adams
-Toledo 43624 Fx:242-5675

(614) 734-1270 ..**Johnston,** Vicki '04 %Farlow & Assoc LLC -270 Bradenton Av
-Dublin 43017 Fx:923-1031

(330) 334-9050 ..**Johnston,** Wesley A '93 -118 Main -Wadsworth 44281

(216) 622-8200 ..**Johnston,** William A '99 %Calfee H&G LLP -800 Superior Av
-Ste 1400 -Cleveland 44114 Fx:241-0816

(614) 466-0924 ..**Johnston,** William J '69 Industrial Commssn of OH -30 W Spring
-9th Fl -Columbus 43215 Fx:752-8785

(614) 880-9085 ..**Johnston,** William W '70 -94 Northwoods Blvd -#B1
-Columbus 43235

(304) 343-7100 ..**Johnstone,** Charles M II '00 (Thaxton & J,LLP) -1125 VA E
-Bx313 -Charleston, WV 25321 Fx:343-7107

(513) 946-3040 ..**Johnstone,** Robert H Jr. '71 Hamilton Cnty Pros -230 E 9th
-Cincinnati 45202 Fx:946-3017

(614) 464-0082 ..**Johrendt Cook & Eberhart** -471 E Broad -Ste 800
-Columbus 43215

(614) 464-0082 ..**Johrendt,** Michael J '77 (Johrendt C&E) -471 E Broad -Ste 800
-Columbus 43215

Joliat, Christina M '04 -(Address Unavailable)

Joliat, Amy Hathaway '03 -19970 Roslyn Dr -Rocky River 44116

(330) 833-2884 ..**Jollay,** Robert D Jr. '74 CorrChoice,Inc -777 3rd NW -Bx850
-Massillon 44648

(302) 477-7651 ..**Jolles,** Janet K '96 First Union Natl Bank -3 Beaver Valley Rd
-4th Fl,DE 5135 -Wilmington, DE 19803

(614) 628-6880 ..**Jolley,** John D '97 %Dinsmore & S LLP -175 S 3rd -10th Fl
-Columbus 43215 Fx:628-6890

(614) 251-4000 ..**Jolley,** Lisa M '97 %Columbus Fndtn -1234 E Broad
-Columbus 43205

(330) 759-4155 ..**Joltin,** Benjamin '00 %Dann & F,LLC -4531 Belmont Av -Ste
C Churchill Sq Plz -Youngstown 44505 Fx:759-9012

(419) 213-4775 ..**Jomantas,** Paul E '83 Lucas Cnty Probate Ct -700 Adams
-Ste 200 -Toledo 43624 Fx:212-4764

(330) 456-8341 ..**Jonas,** Daniel M '68 (Black MS&A,LPA) -220 Market Av S
-Ste 1000 -Canton 44702 Fx:456-5756

Jones, Andrea K '04 -(Address Unavailable)

(330) 782-5674 ..**Jones,** Anissa M '97 -Bx2915 -Youngstown 44511

(513) 721-1311 ..**Jones,** B Scott '98 (Reminger & R) -7 W 7th -Ste 1990
-Cincinnati 45202 Fx:721-2553

(440) 234-8745 ..**Jones,** Barbara L '89 City of Berea -11 Berea Cmmns
-Berea 44017

(614) 224-3855 ..**Jones,** Belinda M '94 Capitol Consulting -37 W Broad
-Columbus 43215

(614) 227-2000 ..**Jones,** Bernard M '04 %Porter WM&A LLP -41 S High
-Columbus 43215 Fx:227-2100

Jones, Beth C '02 -(Address Unavailable)

(419) 882-1718 ..**Jones,** Brian D '77 -5658 N Main -Sylvania 43560

(216) 479-8500 ..**Jones,** Bruce P '73 (Squire S&D LLP) -127 Pub Sq -4900 Key Twr
-Cleveland 44114 Fx:479-8780

(216) 621-0150 ..**Jones,** Candace M '92 (Hahn L&P LLP) -3300 BP Twr/200 Pub Sq
-Ste 3300 -Cleveland 44114 Fx:241-2824

(216) 687-1900 ..**Jones,** Carl Lyonel '63 Legal Aid -1223 W 6th -Cleveland 44113
Fx:687-0779

Jones, Carl W '64 -106 Starboard Cir -Oriental, NC 28571

(770) 992-5091 ..**Jones,** Catherine K '80 -595 4th Fairway Dr -Roswell, GA 30076

(614) 462-4427 ..**Jones,** Charles P Jr. '81 Franklin Cnty Cmn Pleas Ct -373 S High
-3rd Fl -Columbus 43215

(513) 587-2897 ..**Jones,** Christine Y '91 -114 E 8th -Ste 400 -Cincinnati 45202

(614) 621-1500 ..**Jones,** Christopher '90 SrCnsl Calfee H&G LLP -21 E State
-1100 Fifth Third Ctr -Columbus 43215 Fx:621-0010

(419) 241-6450 ..**Jones,** Christopher F '87 (Jones & S) -608 Mad Av -Toledo 43604

(330) 434-7988 ..**Jones,** Crystal L '89 -765 Stoner Av -Akron 44320

(513) 977-8200 ..**Jones,** Daniel L Jr. '99 %Dinsmore & S LLP -255 E 5th -Ste 1900
-Cincinnati 45202 Fx:977-8141

(614) 466-2980 ..**Jones,** Daniel P '89 Atty Gen -30 E Broad -Columbus 43215
Fx:728-7592

(614) 480-4258 ..**Jones,** David A '78 Huntington Natl Bank -41 S High
-Columbus 43215

Jones, David M '67 -5960 Rain Dance Trl -Littleton, CO 80125

(216) 226-4200 ..**Jones,** David W '87 Randolph & J -14701 Detroit Av -Ste 575
-Lakewood 44107

(330) 722-9099 ..**Jones Davies & Funk Co, LPA** -3995 Medina Rd -Ste 200
-Bx447 -Medina 44258

(216) 586-3939 ..**Jones Day** -901 Lakeside Av -Cleveland 44114 Fx:579-0212

(614) 469-3939 ..**Jones Day** -325 John H McConnell Blvd -Ste 600 -Bx165017
-Columbus 43216 Fx:461-4198

Jones, Dominic J '97 US Navy/JAGC -Naval Spcl Warfare Grp 1
-San Diego, CA 92155

(740) 373-7618 ..**Jones,** Donald L '63 (Redmond & J) -421 2nd -BxJ
-Marietta 45750 Fx:373-7626

(614) 229-4606 ..**Jones,** Donald J '82 Deloitte & Touche -155 E Broad -18th Fl
-Columbus 43215

(513) 241-5550 ..**Jones,** Donald T '80 -914 Main -Ste 200 -Cincinnati 45202

(330) 477-5570 ..**Jones,** Douglas D '80 (DD Jones Co,LPA) -2867 Sharonwood Av
-Canton 44708

(330) 971-8190 ..**Jones,** Dwayne K '87 Cuyahoga Falls Pros -2310 2nd
-Cuyahoga Falls 44221

(419) 345-2970 ..**Jones,** Ellen E G '80 Lucas Cnty Mntl Hlth Brd -642 Hmptn
-Toledo 43609 Fx:385-1532

(330) 297-3631 ..**Jones,** Erik E '02 Portage Cnty Pros -466 S Chestnut
-Ravenna 44266

(330) 376-7500 ..**Jones,** Erik M '00 Mentzer & M,Ltd -1 Cascade Plz -20th Fl
-Akron 44308 Fx:376-8018

(513) 910-8391 ..**Jones,** Erin Hogan '00 JIT Packaging Inc -6116 Oakbrdg Way
-Milford 45150

(440) 960-5970 ..**Jones,** Fred C '46 -4642 Oberlin Av -#200 -Lorain 44053

(740) 452-5403 ..**Jones Funk & Payne** -45 N 4th -Zanesville 43701

(732) 321-3866 ..**Jones,** Gary A '87 Siemens Corp -170 Wood Av S
-Iselin, NJ 08830

(614) 221-2300 ..**Jones,** Gary L '66 (G Jones Co,LPA) -42 E Gay -Ste 1500
-Columbus 43215

(216) 736-7231 ..**Jones,** Gary L '97 %Kohrman J&K PLL -1375 E 9th
-One Cleve Ctr 20th Fl -Cleveland 44114 Fx:621-6536

(740) 432-4030 ..**Jones,** Gerald L '76 -114 Southgate Pkwy -Cambridge 43725

(330) 722-9099 ..**Jones,** Glenn R '74 (Jones D&F Co,LPA) -3995 Medina Rd
-Ste 200 -Bx447 -Medina 44258

(740) 593-6400 ..**Jones,** Glenn T '97 %Pub Def -80 N Court -Athens 45701
Fx:591-2074

(334) 262-1245 ..**Jones,** Gregory M '01 Foundation for Moral Law Inc -2005
N Cntry Clb Dr -Montgomery, AL 36106

(216) 523-7200 ..**Jones,** Gretchen C '82 CSU-Planned Giving -2121 Euclid Av
-MM204 -Cleveland 44115

(614) 228-1398 ..**Jones,** Grey W '80 (Nelson LdL&H LLC) -280 N High -Ste 920
-Columbus 43215 Fx:221-7529

(937) 865-6800 ..**Jones,** Heather R '03 Lexis/Nexis -Bx933 -Dayton 45401

(330) 971-8190 ..**Jones,** Hope L '90 Cuyahoga Falls Pros -2310 2nd
-Cuyahoga Falls 44221

(614) 223-9300 ..**Jones,** James Allen III '00 %Benesch FC&A LLP -88 E Broad
-Ste 900 -Columbus 43215 Fx:223-9330

(419) 352-7537 ..**Jones,** James E '79 Poggemeyer Design Group -1168 N Main
-Bowling Green 43402

(412) 394-7230 ..**Jones,** James M '86 (Jones DR&P) -500 Grant
-31st Fl One Mellon Bk Ctr -Pittsburgh, PA 15219 Fx:394-7959

(330) 757-7700 ..**Jones,** James S '94 (J Jones,LPA) -10 Water -Poland 44514

(614) 462-2668 ..**Jones,** Janine H '01 %Baker & H LLP -65 E State -Ste 2100
-Columbus 43215 Fx:462-7616

(614) 469-3939 ..**Jones,** Jeffrey J '85 (Jones D) -325 John H McConnell Blvd
-Ste 600 -Bx165017 -Columbus 43216 Fx:461-4198

(216) 363-4500 ..**Jones,** Jeffrey P '01 OfCnsl Benesch FC&A LLP -200 Pub Sq
-Ste 2300 -Cleveland 44114 Fx:363-4588

(614) 466-0463 ..**Jones,** Jeffrey R '89 PUCO -180 E Broad -Columbus 43266

(513) 241-3100 ..**Jones,** Jeniece D '02 %Lerner S&R -120 E 4th -8th Fl
-Cincinnati 45202

(614) 644-7233 ..**Jones,** John H '91 Atty Gen -150 E Gay -Columbus 43215
Fx:728-9327

(614) 885-8118 ..**Jones,** John S '76 -867 High -Ste C -Worthington 43085

(330) 643-2250 ..**Jones,** Julie A '91 9th Dist Ct of Appls -161 S High -Ste 504
-Akron 44308

(513) 626-2127 ..**Jones,** Juliet A '04 Procter & Gamble Co
-11511 Reed Hartman Hwy -Cincinnati 45241

(513) 762-6200 ..**Jones,** Karen E '04 %Ulmer & B LLP -600 Vine -Ste 2800
-Cincinnati 45202 Fx:762-6245

(419) 525-1468 ..**Jones,** Kenneth D Jr. '96 K Jones Jr DDS -13 Park Av W -Ste 300
-Mansfield 44902

(513) 651-0505 ..**Jones,** Kevin P '74 -8035 Hosbrook Rd -#200 -Cincinnati 45236

(216) 664-4996 ..**Jones,** Larry A '78 Mun Ct Judge -1200 Ontario -Cleveland 44113

(216) 566-5500 ..**Jones,** Larry J '02 %Thompson H LLP -127 Pub Sq -3900 Key Ctr
-Cleveland 44114 Fx:566-5800

(216) 241-2838 ..**Jones,** Lessie Milton '85 (Taft S&H LLP) -200 Pub Sq
-3500 BP Twr -Cleveland 44114 Fx:241-3707

(419) 244-3888 ..**Jones,** Linda A '85 (Jones & L) -520 Mad Av -Ste 323
-Toledo 43604

Jones, Lori L '04 -(Address Unavailable)

(330) 225-1234 ..**Jones,** Lyle R '74 -Bx592 -Medina 44258

(330) 535-8116 ..**Jones,** Mary H '88 Oriana House,Inc -Bx1501 -Akron 44309

(216) 515-1437 ..**Jones,** Melissa A '02 Frantz W LLP -127 Pub Sq
-2500 Key Center -Cleveland 44114 Fx:515-1650

(937) 225-5437 ..**Jones,** Melissa L '98 Montgomery Cnty Pub Def -117 S Main
-Ste 400 -Dayton 45422 Fx:225-3449

(513) 634-6944 ..**Jones,** Melody A '98 Procter & Gamble -6071 Ctr Hill Av
-Cincinnati 45224

(330) 643-3550 ..**Jones,** Michael A '87 Industrial Commssn of OH -161 S High
-Ste 301 -Akron 44308

(419) 399-4911 ..**Jones,** Michael C '79 -308 N Main -Bx274 -Paulding 45879

Jones, Michael F '89 -6289 Freeman Rd -Westerville 43082

(419) 227-5858 ..**Jones,** Michael J '94 %Baran PTF&T Co,LPA -121 W High
-Ste 905 -Bx568 -Lima 45802 Fx:227-4569

(419) 882-7100 ..**Jones,** Michael S '91 %Lydy & M,Ltd -4930 Holland Sylvania Rd
-Sylvania 43560 Fx:882-1120

(513) 621-6464 ..**Jones,** Michael S '94 (Graydon H&R LLP) -511 Walnut
-1900 Fifth Third Ctr -Cincinnati 45202 Fx:651-3836

(513) 362-8700 ..**Jones,** Nathaniel R '57 SrCnsl Blank R -201 E 5th -Ste 1700
-Cincinnati 45202 Fx:362-8787

(740) 369-6812 ..**Jones,** Nicholas W '75 -2 W Winter -Ste 31 -Delaware 43015

(740) 345-9801 ..**Jones Norpell Miller & Howarth** -35 S Park Plz -Ste 35 -Bx4010
-Newark 43058 Fx:345-6031

(216) 623-0150 ..**Jones**, Peter Lawson '80 (Roetzel & A,LPA) -1375 E 9th
-One Cleve Ctr 9th Fl -Cleveland 44114 Fx:623-0134

(937) 335-8760 ..**Jones**, Phillip M '74 Peoples Svngs Bank -14 S Weston Rd
-Troy 45373

(419) 562-4986 ..**Jones**, Regis R '59 -Bx128 -Bucyrus 44820

(513) 684-2572 ..**Jones**, Richard B '96 US Bankrptcy Ct -221 E 4th -Ste 800
-Cincinnati 45202

(614) 466-2980 ..**Jones**, Richard M '92 Atty Gen -30 E Broad -Columbus 43215
Fx:728-7592

(216) 623-0150 ..**Jones**, Richard Mark '83 (Roetzel & A,LPA) -1375 E 9th
-One Cleve Ctr 9th Fl -Cleveland 44114 Fx:623-0134

(859) 578-1000 ..**Jones**, Rick A '96 Horwitz Law Firm PSC -541 Buttermilk Pike -Ste
305 -Crescent Springs, KY 41017

(419) 213-3000 ..**Jones**, Robert J Jr. '97 Lucas Cnty CSEA -701 Adams
-Toledo 43624

(513) 241-7111 ..**Jones**, Robert R '85 %O'Connor A&L Co,LPA -1014 Vine -22nd Fl
-Cincinnati 45202 Fx:241-7197

(937) 223-2175 ..**Jones**, Robert W '84 -12 W Monument Av -Ste 200 -Dayton 45402

(614) 221-2300 ..**Jones**, Robyn R '89 G Jones Co,LPA -42 E Gay -Ste 1500
-Columbus 43215

(419) 841-4400 ..**Jones**, Russell W '94 Contrada & Assoc -6641 Sylvania Av -Ste 8
-Sylvania 43560

(419) 241-6450 ..**Jones & Scheich** -608 Mad Av -Toledo 43604

(937) 449-6810 ..**Jones**, Scott K '98 %Porter WM&A LLP -1 S Main -Ste 1600
-Dayton 45402 Fx:449-6820

(216) 443-7800 ..**Jones**, Sean C '97 Cuyahoga Cnty Pros -1200 Ontario -8th Fl
-Cleveland 44113 Fx:698-2270

(614) 464-6400 ..**Jones**, Stacia Marie '00 %Vorys SS&P LLP -52 E Gay -Bx1008
-Columbus 43216 Fx:464-6350

(614) 463-9770 ..**Jones**, Stephen D '81 (Roetzel & A,LPA) -155 E Broad
-Natl City Ctr 12th Fl -Columbus 43215 Fx:463-9792

(513) 769-0007 ..**Jones**, Stephen R '00 Cnsl Gem City Tire Co -3680 E Kemper Rd
-Cincinnati 45241

(216) 382-0789 ..**Jones**, Steven D '80 -2164 Campus Rd -Beachwood 44122

(419) 248-3501 ..**Jones**, Stewart W '89 (Jones & S) -2 Maritime Plz -3rd Fl
-Toledo 43604

(419) 447-4999 ..**Jones**, Susan M '90 -159 S Wshngtn -Tiffin 44883 Fx:447-0371

(330) 420-0140 ..**Jones**, Tammie M '85 Columbiana Cnty Pros -105 S Market
-Lisbon 44432 Fx:424-0944

(859) 394-6200 ..**Jones**, Tara '03 %Adams SW&D -40 W Pike -Bx861
-Covington, KY 41012 Fx:291-7902

(937) 222-2841 ..**Jones**, Taylor Jr. '76 (Jones & W Co,LPA) -118 W 1st
-1308 Talbot Twr -Dayton 45402

(937) 443-6824 ..**Jones**, Teresa D '88 (Thompson H LLP) -2000 Cthse Plz NE
-Bx8801 -Dayton 45401 Fx:443-6635

(614) 562-6458 ..**Jones**, Terry T '90 J2 Consulting,LLC -829 Bethel Rd -#125
-Columbus 43214

(216) 861-7585 ..**Jones**, Theodore W '51 -1900 E 9th -Ste 3200 -Cleveland 44114

(202) 942-1927 ..**Jones**, Thomas A '89 SEC -450 5th NW -Washington, DC 20549

(614) 888-8500 ..**Jones Troyan Pappas & Perkins,LPA** -1472 Manning Pkwy
-Powell 43065 Fx:888-2560

(440) 333-9150 ..**Jones**, Vickie L '99 -20575 Ctr Ridge Rd -Ste 314
-Rocky River 44116

(330) 376-2700 ..**Jones**, Wayne M '89 (Roetzel & A,LPA) -222 S Main -Akron 44308
Fx:376-4577

(419) 354-1899 ..**Jones**, Wendell R '86 -1308 Bourgogne Av -Bowling Green 43402

(513) 241-3100 ..**Jones**, Wendy J '98 %Lerner S&R -120 E 4th -8th Fl
-Cincinnati 45202

Jones, Willis P Jr. '66 -1580 Clermont Dr -202 -Naples, FL 34109

(724) 983-6119 ..**Jones-Gibbs**, Marlene M '02 1st Natl Bk of PA -4140 E State
-Hermitage, PA 16148

(937) 276-1737 ..**Jones-Kelley**, Helen E '86 Cnty Chldrn Srvcs -3304 N Main
-Dayton 45405

(513) 241-4722 ..**Jonson**, George D '83 (Montgomery R&J,LPA) -36 E 7th
-Ste 2100 -Cincinnati 45202 Fx:241-8775

(513) 868-7600 ..**Jonson**, George N '58 Holbrock & J Co,LPA -315 S Monument Av
-Bx687 -Hamilton 45012 Fx:868-0909

(937) 461-6988 ..**Jonson**, Michele R '99 %A Patent Lwyr Corp PC -22 S St Clair
-Dayton 45402 Fx:461-6922

(216) 696-4700 ..**Jontz**, Jennifer Cook '94 (Spieth BM&N Co,LPA) -925 Euclid Av
-2000 Huntngtn Bldg -Cleveland 44115 Fx:696-2706

(330) 762-2600 ..**Joondeph & Bittel,LLP** -50 S Main -Ste 700 -Akron 44308
Fx:762-2604

(330) 762-2600 ..**Joondeph**, Jerome J '68 (Joondeph & B,LLP) -50 S Main -Ste 700
-Akron 44308 Fx:762-2604

(650) 856-6500 ..**Joondeph**, Jerome J Jr. '90 (Squire S&D) -600 Hansen Way
-Palo Alto, CA 94304 Fx:843-8777

(216) 861-5000 ..**Joranko**, David B '85 (Ernst & Young) -1300 Huntngtn Bldg
-925 Euclid Av -Cleveland 44115

(216) 664-2775 ..**Jordan**, Anthony D '96 Prosecutor -1200 Ontario Av
-8th Fl Justice Ctr -Cleveland 44113 Fx:664-4399

(937) 228-3889 ..**Jordan**, April A '87 (Hedrick & J Co,LPA) -124 E 3rd -Ste 300
-Dayton 45402

(216) 566-9477 ..**Jordan**, Bret '92 (Bruner & J Co LPA) -55 Pub Sq -Ste 1600
-Cleveland 44113

(219) 423-3525 ..**Jordan**, Denver C '96 (Blume CJ&S) -110 W Berry -Ste 1700
-Fort Wayne, IN 46802

(614) 227-2000 ..**Jordan**, Donald W '76 (Porter WM&A LLP) -41 S High
-Columbus 43215 Fx:227-2100

(419) 936-5120 ..**Jordan**, Douglas K '67 -411 N Mich -Ste A -Toledo 43624

(614) 890-2233 ..**Jordan**, James W '66 -80 Drchstr Sq -Westerville 43081

(614) 939-9822 ..**Jordan**, Jeffrey H '90 -Bx30863 -Columbus 43230

(614) 885-4828 ..**Jordan**, Jerry D '63 Jordan Energy Inc -795 Old Woods Rd
-Columbus 43235

(440) 234-5795 ..**Jordan**, Jill L '96 -17900 Main -Middleburg Heights 44130

(614) 798-2110 ..**Jordan**, Joan B '99 -4970 Chaddington Dr -Dublin 43017
Fx:798-2109

(419) 473-1300 ..**Jordan**, Joseph P '62 -4127 Monroe -Toledo 43606 Fx:473-0329

(513) 241-2324 ..**Jordan**, Joseph R '68 %Wood H&E LLP -441 Vine -Ste 2700
-Cincinnati 45202 Fx:421-7269

(740) 385-2181 ..**Jordan**, Laina Fetherolf '04 %R Lilley Co,LPA -9 E 2nd -Bx588
-Logan 43138 Fx:385-4531

(513) 721-4450 ..**Jordan**, Mark W '80 (Santen & H) -312 Walnut -Ste 3100
-Cincinnati 45202

(216) 781-1212 ..**Jordan**, Michael J '79 (Walter & H LLP) -1301 E 9th -Ste 3500
-Cleveland 44114 Fx:575-0911

(216) 462-2283 ..**Jordan**, Michael S '97 (Schottenstein Z&D) -250 West -Bx165020
-Columbus 43216 Fx:462-5135

(317) 226-6601 ..**Jordan**, Ronald T '83 IRS -Stop CN730 -Bx44010
-Indianapolis, IN 46244

(216) 432-7200 ..**Jordan**, Sharon Sobol '84 Ctr for Families & Children
-4500 Euclid Av -Cleveland 44103 Fx:432-7250

(216) 466-8109 ..**Jordan**, Suzanne S '97 Commerce/Div of Securities -77 S High
-22nd flr -Columbus 43215

(614) 462-3001 ..**Jordan**, Hanne M '85 Franklin Cnty Dom Rltns Ct -373 S High
-5th Fl -Columbus 43215

(216) 621-1500 ..**Jorgensen**, Matthew W '96 %Kehoe & Assoc LLP -1940 E 6th
-900 Baker Bldg -Cleveland 44114 Fx:621-1551

(216) 622-8200 ..**Jorgensen**, Thomas A '68 (Calfee H&G LLP) -800 Superior Av
-Ste 1400 -Cleveland 44114 Fx:241-0816

(216) 696-8730 ..**Jorgenson**, Eric D '02 Amin & T LLP -1900 E 9th
-24th Fl Natl City Ctr -Cleveland 44114 Fx:696-8731

(216) 479-8500 ..**Jorgenson**, Mary Ann '75 (Squire S&D LLP) -127 Pub Sq
-4900 Key Twr -Cleveland 44114 Fx:479-8780

(202) 408-7131 ..**Jorling**, James M '84 (Gardner C&D) -1301 K NW -Ste 900
-Washington, DC 20005

(513) 381-5500 ..**Jorling**, Jeffrey D '93 -906 Main -Ste 410 -Cincinnati 45202

(614) 459-4014 ..**Josenhans**, Paul J '72 -1280 Marlyn Dr -Columbus 43220
Fx:459-4014

Joseph, Ann L '00 -(Address Unavailable)

(216) 621-2505 ..**Joseph**, Edward L '82 -2403 St Clair Av -Cleveland 44114

(419) 531-9926 ..**Joseph**, G Christopher '79 -2104 Richmond Rd -Toledo 43607

(513) 721-3000 ..**Joseph**, Gregory G '87 Camargo Cadillac -250 E 5th -Ste 285
-Cincinnati 45202

(216) 522-3380 ..**Joseph**, James A '78 IRS -1375 E 9th -1200 -Cleveland 44114

(216) 241-6055 ..**Joseph**, James G '73 (Dubin J&S) -75 Pub Sq -Ste 650
-Cleveland 44113

(216) 921-9314 ..**Joseph**, Jane E '02 -2755 Attleboro Rd -Shaker Heights 44120

(330) 404-1901 ..**Joseph**, Jeffrey A '98 -6071 Deer Spring Run -Canfield 44406
Fx:702-1030

(614) 449-8282 ..**Joseph**, Jennifer J '91 (Joseph & J) -931 S Front
-Columbus 43206 Fx:449-8287

(330) 253-1555 ..**Joseph**, John E '01 %D Booher & Assoc Co,LPA -3180 W Market
-Fairlawn 44333

(614) 449-8282 ..**Joseph**, John J '81 (Joseph & J) -931 S Front -Columbus 43206
Fx:449-8287

(216) 522-1600 ..**Joseph**, Joseph T Jr. '99 -55 Pub Sq -Ste 650 -Cleveland 44113

(216) 765-8520 ..**Joseph**, Kathryn Theresa '86 (Aggers J&C Co,LPA)
-29565 Chagrin Blvd -Ste 306 Exec Cmmns E
-Pepper Pike 44122 Fx:765-8817

(330) 652-0630 ..**Joseph**, Michael D '73 -815 Robbins Av -Niles 44446

(419) 321-1435 ..**Joseph**, Regina M '79 (Shumaker L&K,LLP) -1000 Jackson
-Toledo 43624 Fx:241-6894

(513) 721-3000 ..**Joseph**, Richard S '91 Joseph Auto Grp -250 E 5th -Ste 285
-Cincinnati 45202

(513) 721-3000 ..**Joseph**, Robert G '67 -250 E 5th -Ste 285 -Cincinnati 45202

(513) 721-3000 ..**Joseph**, Ronald G '61 -250 E 5th -Ste 285 -Cincinnati 45202

(216) 621-1530 ..**Joseph**, Samantha S '99 %Shapiro & F,LLP -1500 W 3rd -Ste 400
-Cleveland 44113 Fx:621-1551

(216) 241-6602 ..**Joseph**, William R '72 (Weston HFP&H LLP) -50 Pub Sq
-2500 Trmnl Twr -Cleveland 44113 Fx:621-8369

(513) 241-2324 ..**Josephic**, David J '66 (Wood H&E LLP) -441 Vine -Ste 2700
-Cincinnati 45202 Fx:421-7269

(216) 696-8070 ..**Josselson**, Stanley L '66 (S Josselson Co,LPA) -1276 W 3rd
-Ste 411 -Cleveland 44113

(216) 391-0749 ..**Jovanovic**, Alex '84 -1625 E 49th -Cleveland 44103

(314) 935-6445 ..**Joy**, Peter A '77 Washington Univ Sch of Law -1 Brookings Dr
-Campus Bx 1120 -St. Louis, MO 63130

(440) 285-2222 ..**Joyce**, David P '82 Geauga Cnty Pros -231 Main -Cthse Annx
-Chardon 44024 Fx:286-4357

(614) 644-7435 ..**Joyce**, Deborah L '85 OH Dept Commerce -77 S High
-Columbus 43266

(216) 687-1244 ..**Joyce**, Eileen M '98 %Baughman & J LLC -2500 Brook Park Rd
-Ste E -Cleveland 44134

(419) 824-0636 ..**Joyce**, Kevin E '82 (K Joyce Co LLC) -Bx788 -Sylvania 43560

(216) 241-6602 ..**Joyce**, Therese P '99 %Weston HFP&H LLP -50 Pub Sq
-2500 Trmnl Twr -Cleveland 44113 Fx:621-8369

(513) 721-4532 ..**Jreisat**, Wijdan '94 (Katz TB&H) -255 E 5th -Ste 2400
-Cincinnati 45202

(419) 259-6197 ..**Juby**, Alyce R '87 Key Bank Natl Assoc -Three Seagate -Bx10099
-Toledo 43699

(517) 486-6209 ..**Juby**, Jeffrey J '89 -8651 E US 223 -Blissfield, MI 49228

(216) 241-7000 ..**Judge**, Beth A '04 %Landskroner & Assoc -55 Pub Sq -Ste 1040
-Cleveland 44113

Judge, Christopher P '03 -(Address Unavailable)

(614) 365-2700 ..**Judge**, Corie Marty '98 %Squire S&D LLP -41 S High
-1300 Huntngtn Ctr -Columbus 43215 Fx:365-2499

(937) 208-6395 ..**Judge**, Dianne D '93 Premier Hlth Prtnrs -1 Wyoming
-Dayton 45409

(614) 719-3300 ..**Judge**, Shawn K '98 US Dist Ct,Sthrn Dist of OH -85 Marconi Blvd
-Rm 349, Joseph P Kinneary Crthse -Columbus 43215
Fx:719-3305

(937) 981-4403 ..**Judkins**, Robert J '75 (Judkins & H) -303 W Jffrsn
-Greenfield 45123 Fx:981-7256

(440) 729-7279 ..**Judy**, Michael T '95 -8228 Mayfld Rd -Ste 6B -Chesterland 44026
Fx:729-8132

(614) 461-5600 ..**Judy**, Philip L '97 %Buckley K,LPA -10 W Broad -Ste 1300
-Columbus 43215

(803) 458-5952 ..**Juengel**, Lorin E '92 Michelin NA Inc -1 Pkwy S -Bx19001
-Greenville, SC 29602

(513) 241-9400 ..**Juenke**, Timothy R '93 Legal Aid -215 E 9th -Ste 200
-Cincinnati 45202

(937) 399-8180 ..**Juergens**, Carl E '54 (Juergens & J) -1504 N Limestone
-Springfield 45503

(937) 399-8180 ..**Juergens**, John C '86 (Juergens & J) -1504 N Limestone
-Springfield 45503

(937) 325-8214 ..**Juergens,** Joseph M '72 -39 N Fountain Av -Springfield 45502
(216) 241-5310 ..**Juergens,** Julie L '96 %Gallagher SF&N -1501 Euclid Av -6th Fl -Cleveland 44115 **Fx:**241-1608
(937) 325-1588 ..**Juergens Wilt & Strileckyi** -200 N Fountain Av -Springfield 45504
(330) 456-8341 ..**Juergensen,** John L '99 %Black MS&A,LPA -220 Market Av S -Ste 1000 -Canton 44702 **Fx:**456-5756
(330) 758-2308 ..**Juhasz,** John B Jr. '83 -7330 Market -Boardman 44512
(614) 436-7599 ..**Juhola,** Michael D '80 -867 High -Ste B -Worthington 43085 **Fx:**436-1662
(216) 621-5259 ..**Julian,** Christine M '93 (Julian & J LLC) -1836 Euclid Av -#308 -Cleveland 44115
(614) 462-3555 ..**Julian,** Christine S '92 Franklin Cnty Pros -373 S High -Columbus 43215
Julian, Christopher T '03 -7585 Andvr Ln -North Royalton 44133
(513) 579-7337 ..**Julian,** Frank G '82 Federated Dept Stores,Inc -7 W 7th -Tax Dept - 12th Fl -Cincinnati 45202
(216) 621-5259 ..**Julian,** Linda M '91 (Julian & J LLC) -1836 Euclid Av -#308 -Cleveland 44115
(614) 462-3555 ..**Julian,** Terry J '87 Franklin Cnty Pros -373 S High -Columbus 43215
(216) 621-7227 ..**Juliano,** Louis J Jr. '77 (Nicola G&C,LLC) -25 W Prospect Av -Republic Bldg Ste 1400 -Cleveland 44115 **Fx:**621-3999
(330) 668-7755 ..**Julius,** John C '01 First Union Sec -4040 Embssy Pk -Ste 400 -Akron 44333
(330) 283-6480 ..**Julius,** Thomas N '73 -265 Steeplechase Ln -Munroe Falls 44262
(703) 697-5357 ..**Jump,** Darren S '87 USMC -2 Navy Annx -Washington, DC 20380
(614) 645-7031 ..**Jump,** David S '81 Franklin Cnty Mun Ct -375 S High -11-C -Columbus 43215
Jump, James R '73 -143 Thresher -Granville 43023
(614) 481-4480 ..**Jump,** W Mark '94 (Koffel & J) -2130 Arlngtn Av -Columbus 43221
(202) 305-1457 ..**Jung,** Je Y '97 DOJ Civ Rghts Housing -950 Penn Av NW -Washington, DC 20530
(614) 227-2000 ..**Jung,** Jennifer L '00 %Porter WM&A LLP -41 S High -Columbus 43215 **Fx:**227-2100
(404) 607-4772 ..**Jung,** Laurie N '87 Bk of Amer Corp -600 Pchtree NE -17th Fl -Atlanta, GA 30308
(614) 462-3194 ..**Junga,** Christopher T '00 Franklin Cnty Pub Def -373 S High -12th Fl -Columbus 43215
(216) 586-3939 ..**Junge,** A Gregory '04 %Jones D -901 Lakeside Av -Cleveland 44114 **Fx:**579-0212
(508) 943-9000 ..**Jungeberg,** Thomas D '76 Cnsl Commerce Grp -211 Main -Webster, MA 01570
(248) 948-1196 ..**Junia,** Edward X '87 Mineral Sltns,Inc -4000 Town Ctr -Ste 2000 -Southfield, MI 48075
(740) 947-4323 ..**Junk,** Charles R Jr. '91 Pros -108 N Market -Waverly 45690
(740) 335-3231 ..**Junk,** William T '79 Junk & J -213 N Main -Washington Court House 43160
(812) 934-5578 ..**Junker,** Martha E '84 -79 Dogwood Trail -Batesville, IN 47006
(330) 796-3024 ..**Junod,** Scott K '02 Goodyear Tire & Rubber Co -1144 E Market -Human Resources Dept -Akron 44316
(216) 622-8200 ..**Jupin,** Seth M '96 %Calfee H&G LLP -800 Superior Av -Ste 1400 -Cleveland 44114 **Fx:**241-0816
(440) 871-1721 ..**Jurca,** Irene S '00 PDM Healthcare -24700 Ctr Ridge Rd -Ste 110 -Cleveland 44145
(614) 228-6885 ..**Jurca,** Jeffrey J '79 (Lane A&H LLC) -175 S 3rd -Ste 700 -Columbus 43215 **Fx:**228-0146
(614) 478-8616 ..**Jurca,** Melanie C '84 -458 Whitley Dr -Gahanna 43230
(614) 224-8374 ..**Jurcevich,** Laura M '03 Legal Aid -40 W Gay -Columbus 43215
(304) 233-3390 ..**Jurco,** John M '03 %Schrader B&C PLLC -32-20th -Ste 500 -Wheeling, WV 26003
(216) 771-4650 ..**Jurczenko,** Alexander '73 -1419 W 9th -2nd Fl -Cleveland 44113
(330) 722-8138 ..**Jurewicz,** Jessica Lynn '04 -650 Sturbrdg Dr -#7 -Medina 44256
(440) 951-6665 ..**Jurjans,** Peteris '72 -38021 Euclid Av -Willoughby 44094
(614) 221-5824 ..**Jurkovac,** Mark E '88 -24 N High -Columbus 43215
(513) 381-9200 ..**Jurs,** Peter B '97 %Rendigs FK&D,LLP -One W 4th -Ste 900 -Cincinnati 45202 **Fx:**381-9206
(614) 529-1742 ..**Jursek,** Stephanie J '86 -3983 Park Cir S -Hilliard 43026
(614) 486-0297 ..**Jurus,** Stanley R Jr. '54 -1375 Dublin Rd -Columbus 43215 **Fx:**486-8580
(419) 882-4686 ..**Justen,** Frank A '70 -4930 Holland-Sylvania Rd -Sylvania 43560
(216) 622-8200 ..**Juster,** Joseph K '89 (Calfee H&G LLP) -800 Superior Av -Ste 1400 -Cleveland 44114 **Fx:**241-0816
(937) 228-2838 ..**Justice,** J Steven '94 (Taft S&H LLP) -110 N Main -Ste 900 -Dayton 45402 **Fx:**228-2816
(614) 258-1133 ..**Justice,** Stewart III '01 TE Morgan & Assoc -906 E Broad -Columbus 43205
(937) 534-0500 ..**Justice,** Tabitha '02 %Subashi W&B -2305 Far Hills Av -Oakwood Bldg -Dayton 45419 **Fx:**534-0505
(513) 791-8800 ..**Jutze,** Robert G '92 Sr Impact Pblctns LLC -8041 Hosbrook Rd -Ste 130 -Cincinnati 45236
(513) 651-6800 ..**Kaake,** Andrew R '00 %Frost BT LLC -201 E 5th -2200 PNC Ctr -Cincinnati 45202 **Fx:**651-6981
(513) 424-2401 ..**Kabakoff,** Ronald M '77 (Casper & C) -1 N Main -Bx510 -Middletown 45042 **Fx:**424-0622
(216) 687-1311 ..**Kabat,** Andrew A '94 (Reminger & R) -101 Prospect Av W -1400 Mdlnd Bldg -Cleveland 44115 **Fx:**687-1841
(216) 595-8222 ..**Kabat,** Gary B '65 (Kabat M&S) -25550 Chagrin Blvd -Ste 403 -Beachwood 44122
(216) 595-8222 ..**Kabat Mielziner & Sobel** -25550 Chagrin Blvd -Ste 403 -Beachwood 44122
(216) 844-1252 ..**Kabb,** Marilyn S '91 University Hospital -11100 Euclid Av -Cleveland 44106
(216) 291-9126 ..**Kabb-Effron,** Rachel A '98 -3690 Oarnge Pl -Ste 370 -Cleveland 44122
(216) 444-3695 ..**Kaber,** Steven C '84 Cleveland Clinic Fndtn -9500 Euclid Av -Cleveland 44195
(330) 375-5630 ..**Kacarab,** Peter J '93 IRS -2 S Main -Akron 44308
(216) 398-9870 ..**Kacenjar,** Allen A '74 -5241 Broadvw Rd -#400 -Cleveland 44134
(216) 479-8500 ..**Kacenjar,** Allen A '99 %Squire S&D LLP -127 Pub Sq -4900 Key Twr -Cleveland 44114 **Fx:**479-8780
(216) 579-1700 ..**Kachmarik,** Ronald M '94 (Pearne & G LLP) -1801 E 9th -Ste 1200 -Cleveland 44114 **Fx:**579-6073

(614) 228-1346 ..**Kacic,** Glenn D '84 %OH Retirement Study Cncl -88 E Broad -Ste 1175 -Columbus 43215
(216) 348-5400 ..**Kacmar,** Donald E '97 (McDonald H Co,LPA) -600 Superior Av E -Ste 2100 -Cleveland 44114 **Fx:**348-5474
Kaczala, Larry A '83 -3723 Brookside Rd -Toledo 43606
(216) 348-5400 ..**Kaczka,** Michael J '03 %McDonald H Co,LPA -600 Superior Av E -Ste 2100 -Cleveland 44114 **Fx:**348-5474
(614) 466-6511 ..**Kaczmarek,** William F '89 Dept Admin Srvcs -30 E Broad -Columbus 43215
(216) 586-3939 ..**Kaczynski,** Stephen J '86 (Jones D) -901 Lakeside Av -Cleveland 44114 **Fx:**579-0212
(614) 463-4211 ..**Kadela,** David A '86 (Littler M,PC) -21 E State -Ste 1600 -Columbus 43215 **Fx:**221-3301
(419) 524-6011 ..**Kademenos,** Victor P '71 (Calhoun KH&C Co,LPA) -6 W 3rd -Ste 200 -Bx268 -Mansfield 44901 **Fx:**526-1431
(614) 466-2934 ..**Kades,** Liliya A '00 -5602 Feagan -Unit F -Houston, TX 77007
..**Kading,** Daniel J '87 Dept Job & Family Srvcs -30 E Broad -31st Fl -Columbus 43266
(216) 696-3030 ..**Kadish Hinkel & Weibel, LPA** -1717 E 9th -Ste 2112 -Cleveland 44114 **Fx:**696-3492
(216) 696-3030 ..**Kadish,** Matthew F '87 (Kadish H&W,LPA) -1717 E 9th -Ste 2112 -Cleveland 44114 **Fx:**696-3492
(513) 762-6200 ..**Kadish,** Scott P '85 (Ulmer & B LLP) -600 Vine -Ste 2800 -Cincinnati 45202 **Fx:**762-6245
(216) 696-3030 ..**Kadish,** Stephen L '65 (Kadish H&W,LPA) -1717 E 9th -Ste 2112 -Cleveland 44114 **Fx:**696-3492
(440) 331-8683 ..**Kadlec,** Georgia M '89 -20180 Kramer Dr -Ste 1 -Rocky River 44116
(216) 875-2767 ..**Kadlec,** Kevin O '87 %Bonezzi SM&P Co LPA -526 Superior Av -Ste 1400 -Cleveland 44114 **Fx:**875-1570
(513) 946-3000 ..**Kadon,** Karl P III '84 Hamilton Cnty Pros -230 E 9th -Cincinnati 45202 **Fx:**946-3017
(419) 243-7500 ..**Kadri,** Cherrefe A '93 -1109 Adams -Ste 202 -Toledo 43624
(937) 328-2640 ..**Kaech,** Noel E '71 Clark Cnty Pub Def -50 E Columbia -4th Fl -Springfield 45502 **Fx:**328-2715
(330) 225-2600 ..**Kaesgen,** Derek '93 MTD Products Inc -Bx368022 -Cleveland 44136
(330) 394-5455 ..**Kafantaris,** George N '81 -720 N Park Av -Warren 44483
(330) 762-7477 ..**Kaffen,** Ronald O '74 (Hardesty K&Z) -520 S Main -Ste 500 -Akron 44311 **Fx:**762-8059
(330) 253-0719 ..**Kaforey,** Ellen C '89 -159 S Main -Ste 1024 -Akron 44308 **Fx:**253-0722
(614) 433-9612 ..**Kagay Albert Diehl & Groeber** -6877 N High -Ste 300 -Worthington 43085
(216) 241-5310 ..**Kagels,** Edward G '63 (Gallagher SF&N) -1501 Euclid Av -6th Fl -Cleveland 44115 **Fx:**241-1608
Kagle, Barbara '03 -850 Willamette -Naval Legal Srvc Offic -Pearl Harbor, HI 96860
(513) 684-3211 ..**Kagy,** James E '81 IRS Dist Cnsl -312 Elm -Ste 2300 -Cincinnati 45202
Kahan, David D '64 -3486 Rolling Hills Dr -Cleveland 44124
(216) 696-5757 ..**Kahan,** Julian '59 -4069 Renaissance Pkwy -Cleveland 44128
(330) 887-0143 ..**Kahelin,** William J '74 Westfield Grp -1 Park Cir -Bx5001 -Westfield Center 44251 **Fx:**887-2588
(937) 644-6640 ..**Kahle,** John B '93 Honda of Amer Mfg -24000 Honda Pkwy -Marysville 43040
(304) 233-0000 ..**Kahle,** Karen E '97 (Steptoe & J PLLC) -Bx150 -Wheeling, WV 26003
(513) 929-3400 ..**Kahle,** Thomas W '75 (Baker & H LLP) -312 Walnut -Ste 3200 -Cincinnati 45202 **Fx:**929-0303
(419) 443-1121 ..**Kahler,** Jennifer L '97 (Kahler & K) -216 S Wshngtn -Ste A -Tiffin 44883
(419) 443-1121 ..**Kahler,** John M II '96 (Kahler & K) -216 S Wshngtn -Ste A -Tiffin 44883
(419) 447-2285 ..**Kahler,** Richard A '66 -210 S Wshngtn -Tiffin 44883
(513) 241-3100 ..**Kahmann,** Kathleen E '02 %Lerner S&R -120 E 4th -8th Fl -Cincinnati 45202
(614) 464-6400 ..**Kahn,** Benita A '82 (Vorys SS&P LLP) -52 E Gay -Bx1008 -Columbus 43216 **Fx:**464-6350
(330) 499-5104 ..**Kahn,** Bernard L '51 -4808 Ellinda Cir NW -Canton 44709
(216) 621-6101 ..**Kahn,** Craig A '94 (Kahn & Assoc,LLC) -55 Pub Sq -Ste 650 -Cleveland 44113 **Fx:**621-6006
(216) 696-3311 ..**Kahn Kleinman** -1301 E 9th -2600 Erievw Twr -Cleveland 44114 **Fx:**623-4912
(216) 292-2970 ..**Kahn,** Lawrence M '66 -24200 Chagrin Blvd -Ste 343 -Beachwood 44122
(513) 541-5410 ..**Kahn,** Marla J '01 -1639 N Bend Rd -Cincinnati 45224
(216) 931-6000 ..**Kahn,** Ronald L '73 (Ulmer & B LLP) -1300 E 9th -Ste 900 Penton Media Bldg -Cleveland 44114 **Fx:**931-6001
(216) 831-6580 ..**Kahn,** Ronald S '74 (Hartman & K Co,LPA) -27600 Chagrin Blvd -Ste 340 -Woodmere 44122
(216) 579-4114 ..**Kahn,** Scott H '82 (McIntyre K&K Co LPA) -1301 E 9th -Ste 1200 -Cleveland 44114
(740) 397-2443 ..**Kahrl,** Clyde C '80 -236 S Main -Ste 103 -Mount Vernon 43050 **Fx:**397-2208
(216) 586-3939 ..**Kahrl,** Robert C '75 (Jones D) -901 Lakeside Av -Cleveland 44114 **Fx:**579-0212
(740) 452-7555 ..**Kaido,** Mark E '91 Gottlieb JB&D,PLL -320 Main -Bx190 -Zanesville 43702 **Fx:**452-2257
(216) 295-8378 ..**Kaigler,** Lawrence M '77 -2826 E 119th -Up -Cleveland 44120
(614) 221-7548 ..**Kaikis,** Darla E '92 (Larrimer & L) -165 N High -Columbus 43206 **Fx:**221-8659
(330) 867-9998 ..**Kainec,** Lisa A '93 (Kastner W&W,LLC) -3480 W Market -Ste 300 -Akron 44333 **Fx:**867-3786
(216) 574-9500 ..**Kainski,** Dale F '75 -55 Pub Sq -Ste 2020 -Cleveland 44113
(302) 622-7000 ..**Kairis,** John C '87 %Grant & E,PA -1201 N Market -Ste 2100 -Wilmington, DE 19801
(614) 469-3939 ..**Kairis,** Matthew A '91 (Jones D) -325 John H McConnell Blvd -Ste 600 -Bx165017 -Columbus 43216 **Fx:**461-4198
(219) 665-8040 ..**Kaiser,** Brian W '83 -207 Hoosier Dr -Ste 6 -Angola, IN 46703
(216) 479-8500 ..**Kaiser,** Gordon S Jr. '73 (Squire S&D LLP) -127 Pub Sq -4900 Key Twr -Cleveland 44114 **Fx:**479-8780

(740) 867-3159 .. **Kaiser**, James Stewart '64 -411 Rockwood Av -Bx637
-Chesapeake 45619
    Kaiser, Jo E '00 -330 S High -Columbus 43215
(440) 357-5577 .. **Kaiser**, Mark A '85 -Bx632 -Painesville 44077
(740) 363-1931 .. **Kaiser**, R Lamont '69 (R Kaiser Co,LPA) -25 W Central Av
-Bx1340 -Delaware 43015
(716) 856-4000 .. **Kaiser**, Richard W '84 (Hodgson R LLP) -One M & T Plz -Ste 2000
-Buffalo, NY 14203 Fx:849-0349
(513) 684-3211 .. **Kaiser**, Robert D '74 IRS Dist Cnsl -312 Elm -Ste 2300
-Cincinnati 45202
(513) 474-5469 .. **Kaiser**, Robert S '87 -7434 Jager Ct -Cincinnati 45230
(937) 276-1900 .. **Kaiser**, Robert T '79 State Farm Ins Co -1436 Needmore Rd
-Dayton 45414
(216) 664-2852 .. **Kaiser**, Thomas J '82 Dept of Law -601 Lakeside Av -Rm 106
City Hall -Cleveland 44114 Fx:664-2663
    Kakascik, Karen C '91 -3302 N 7th -#269 -Phoenix, AZ 85014
(847) 734-8811 .. **Kakuda**, Eldon H '98 Masuda FE&M,Ltd -1475 E Woodfld Rd
-Ste 800 -Schaumburg, IL 60173 Fx:734-1089
(937) 238-9211 .. **Kalafatas**, Mark '02 -5450 Far Hills Av -Ste 203 -Kettering 45429
(513) 357-9750 .. **Kalafut**, Christopher M '87 Industrial Commssn of OH
-125 E Court -Cincinnati 45202
    Kalafut, George E '72 -1030 Andrsn Dr -Youngstown 44511
(216) 642-0323 .. **Kalail**, Karrie M '88 (Britton SP&K Co,LPA) -4700 Rockside Rd
-Ste 540 Summit One -Cleveland 44131 Fx:642-0747
(440) 234-6699 .. **Kalapos**, Michele A '90 M Kalapos Co,LPA -16600 Sprague Rd
-Ste 211 -Middleburg Heights 44130
(419) 517-7000 .. **Kalas**, Brian C '99 %Kenney & N,Ltd -5470 Main -Ste 300
-Sylvania 43560 Fx:517-7001
(330) 533-2617 .. **Kalasky**, William G '78 -106 S Broad -Canfield 44406
(201) 733-4244 .. **Kalb**, Ann L '94 FBI -Gtwy One -Market -Newark, NJ 07102
(440) 423-3420 .. **Kalberer**, Jean C '81 -1259 W Hill Dr -Gates Mills 44040
(216) 741-6334 .. **Kalbrunner**, Roger J '73 -3630 Trowbrdg Av -Cleveland 44109
(419) 254-5181 .. **Kale**, Connie E '92 HCR/ManorCare -333 N Summit
-Toledo 43604
(513) 961-6200 .. **Kaleda**, Jeffery A '98 %Markesbery & R Co,LPA
-2368 Victory Pkwy -Ste 200 -Bx6491 -Cincinnati 45206
(216) 592-5000 .. **Kaleps**, Krista L '04 %Tucker E&W LLP -925 Euclid Av
-1150 Huntngtn Bldg -Cleveland 44115 Fx:592-5009
(216) 881-5300 .. **Kalette**, Stephen R '74 Pubco Corp -3830 Kelley Av
-Cleveland 44114
(330) 729-9777 .. **Kalfas**, Plato J '87 %Engler & Assoc -860 Boardman-Canfld Rd
-Ste 204 -Boardman 44512 Fx:758-9585
(419) 668-2081 .. **Kalfs**, William D '83 Tucker Abstrct & Title Co -26 E Main -Bx738
-Norwalk 44857
(614) 213-7084 ..**Kalgreen**, Andrew J '79 Bank One Mgt Corp -1111 Polaris Pkwy
-OHI-1085 -Columbus 43240
(937) 472-3648 .. **Kalil**, Edmund H '89 -208 N Barron -Bx655 -Eaton 45320
(214) 871-6005 .. **Kalis**, Christopher A '83 -2512 Boll -Dallas, TX 75204
(740) 455-7123 .. **Kalis**, Maria N '01 Muskingum Cnty Pros -27 N 5th -Zanesville
43701
    Kalis, Perry M II '99 -Bx642 -Zanesville 43702
(216) 502-0570 .. **Kalish**, Daniel Scott '94 S Kalish Co,LLC -1360 W 9th -Ste 410
-Cleveland 44113
(440) 542-2901 .. **Kalk**, Daniel L '83 -32100 Solon Rd -Ste 203 -Solon 44139
(216) 523-4131 .. **Kalka**, Daniel S '86 Eaton Corp -1111 Superior Av
-Cleveland 44114
(216) 348-5400 ..**Kall**, David M '93 (McDonald H Co,LPA) -600 Superior Av E
-Ste 2100 -Cleveland 44114 Fx:348-5474
(513) 723-4000 .. **Kallas**, Hani R '94 (Vorys SS&P LLP) -221 E 4th -Ste 2000
Atrium Two -Bx0236 -Cincinnati 45201 Fx:723-4056
(260) 449-8096 .. **Kallas**, Rachel Y '04 Allen Superior Ct-Probation -2929 N Wells
-Fort Wayne, IN 46802
(216) 586-3939 .. **Kallergis**, Gus '99 %Jones D -901 Lakeside Av -Cleveland 44114
Fx:579-0212
(614) 415-7078 .. **Kallner**, Matthew G '90 The Limited,Inc -3 Limited Pkwy
-Columbus 43230
(419) 882-4707 ..**Kalmbach**, Frederick E '02 %McHugh D&M,Ltd -5580 Monroe
-Sylvania 43560 Fx:885-3861
(805) 989-8266 .. **Kalmbaugh**, David S '77 Naval Air Warfare Ctr -575 I Av
-Ste 1,Ofc of Couns-Code K00000E
-Point Mugu Nawc, CA 93042
(216) 348-5400 .. **Kalnay**, John T '98 (McDonald H Co,LPA) -600 Superior Av E
-Ste 2100 -Cleveland 44114 Fx:348-5474
(419) 537-1954 .. **Kalniz**, Burton A '67 (Kalniz I&F,LPA) -5550 W Central Av
-Toledo 43615 Fx:535-7732
(419) 537-1954 .. **Kalniz Iorio & Feldstein,LPA** -5550 W Central Av -Toledo 43615
Fx:535-7732
(330) 425-4201 .. **Kalniz**, Jeffrey T '96 %Reimer L&A Co,LPA -2450 Edison Blvd
-Bx968 -Twinsburg 44087 Fx:487-0923
(419) 244-4000 .. **Kalniz**, M '03 (Dorf & K) -Two Maritime Plz -2nd Fl -Bx952
-Toledo 43697 Fx:241-1900
(216) 348-9878 .. **Kalnoki**, Aniko T '91 (Sharon & K LLC) -55 Pub Sq -Ste 750
-Cleveland 44113 Fx:348-9879
    Kalski, Steven F '85 -6702 Silvermound Dr -Mentor 44060
(614) 792-9133 .. **Kalson**, Lisa S '95 -5911 Newbrdg Dr -Dublin 43017
(614) 224-1222 .. **Kaltenbach**, Jerry L II '02 %Maguire & S,LLP -250 Civic Ctr Dr
-Ste 200 -Columbus 43215 Fx:224-1236
(513) 761-5221 .. **Kaltman**, Sandra P '85 -4290 Glendale-Milford Rd
-Cincinnati 45242
(406) 328-4604 .. **Kalur**, Jerome S '69 -Bx72 -Fishtail, MT 59028
(216) 696-0650 .. **Kaman & Cusimano** -50 Pub Sq -Ste 600 Trmnl Twr
-Cleveland 44113
(216) 696-0650 .. **Kaman**, David W '80 (Kaman & C) -50 Pub Sq -Ste 600 Trmnl Twr
-Cleveland 44113
(419) 524-6011 .. **Kamarados**, John S '01 Calhoun KH&C Co,LPA -6 W 3rd
-Ste 200 -Bx268 -Mansfield 44901 Fx:526-1431
(216) 522-6103 .. **Kamat**, Deborah L '82 Defense Finance&AccountingSrvc
-1240 E 9th -2829 -Cleveland 44199
(614) 221-3151 .. **Kamb**, William T '03 %Butler C&D -50 W Broad -Ste 700
-Columbus 43215
(216) 685-4290 .. **Kamensky**, Fedor F '03 %Weltman W&R Co,LPA
-323 W Lakeside Av -Ste 200 -Cleveland 44113 Fx:363-4121

(859) 232-2632 .. **Kamer**, Joseph M '93 Lexmark Intl,Inc -740 W New Circle Rd
-Lexington, KY 40550
(614) 224-5205 .. **Kamer**, Marc T '98 %Peck S&W,LLP -175 S 3rd -Ste 600
-Columbus 43215 Fx:224-0069
(859) 226-2300 .. **Kamer**, Mauritia G '91 Stites & H,PLLC -250 W Main -Ste 2300
-Lexington, KY 40507
(614) 456-8341 .. **Kamerer**, James P '74 (Black MS&A,LPA) -220 Market Av S
-Ste 1000 -Canton 44702 Fx:456-5756
(614) 252-7221 .. **Kamin-Meyer**, Tamar '91 -2599 E Main -PMB #207 -Bexley 43209
(513) 721-6151 .. **Kamine**, Charles S '76 -602 Main -Ste 1309 -Cincinnati 45202
(513) 721-6151 .. **Kamine**, Darlene M '76 -602 Main -Ste 1309 -Cincinnati 45202
(330) 688-8484 .. **Kaminski**, Edward C '59 -3622 Oak Rd -Stow 44224 Fx:688-8484
(513) 684-3711 .. **Kaminski**, Gerald F '70 US Atty -221 E 4th -Ste 400
-Cincinnati 45202 Fx:684-6385
    Kaminski, Jill A '04 -(Address Unavailable)
(330) 455-0173 .. **Kaminski**, John S '03 %Day KRW&R,LLP -200 Market Av N
-Ste 300 -Bx24213 -Canton 44701 Fx:455-2633
(330) 656-2600 .. **Kaminski**, Karen D '00 JoAnn Stores,Inc -5555 Darrow Rd
-Hudson 44236
(216) 621-5161 .. **Kaminski**, Kerin Lyn '85 (Giffen & K,LLC) -1717 E 9th -Cleveland
44114 Fx:621-2399
    Kaminsky, Michael P '79 -Bx1006 -Medina 44258
(330) 634-8090 .. **Kamlowsky**, Lisa M '93 Summit Cnty Brd of MRDD
-89 E Howe Rd -Tallmadge 44278
(513) 241-8137 .. **Kammer**, David D '93 %Tobias K&T -414 Walnut -Ste 911
-Cincinnati 45202
(513) 241-0738 .. **Kammer**, Joseph C '55 -7 W 7th -Ste 1800 -Cincinnati 45202
(216) 696-5211 .. **Kammer**, Karl D '53 -75 Pub Sq -Ste 650 -Cleveland 44113
(513) 229-6536 .. **Kammer**, Richard E '90 Cnsl 409 Grp,Inc -5155 Fncl Way
-Mason 45040 Fx:229-6714
(216) 621-0200 .. **Kammer**, Sean M '04 %Baker & H LLP -1900 E 9th -Ste 3200
-Cleveland 44114 Fx:696-0740
(513) 241-3685 .. **Kamp**, David P '81 (White G&M Co,LPA) -1 W 4th -Ste 1700
-Cincinnati 45202 Fx:241-2399
(216) 251-8023 .. **Kampani**, Dharminder L '75 -17140 Lorain Av -Cleveland 44111
Fx:251-4400
(216) 781-4110 .. **Kampinski**, Charles I '74 (C Kampinski Co,LPA) -1370 Ontario
-1530 Standard Bldg -Cleveland 44113 Fx:781-4178
(216) 781-5470 .. **Kampman**, Joseph W '80 (Ziegler M&M LLP) -925 Euclid Av
-2200 Huntngtn Bldg -Cleveland 44115 Fx:781-0714
(614) 645-8896 .. **Kanai**, Matthew A '00 City Pros -375 S High -7th Fl
-Columbus 43215
(440) 333-1956 .. **Kanally**, John E Jr. '72 Suburban West Rlty Co -20800 Ctr Ridge
-Ste 416 -Rocky River 44116
(202) 955-3750 .. **Kananen**, Ronald P '64 (Rader F&G) -1233 20th NW -Ste 501
-Washington, DC 20036
(216) 363-4500 .. **Kancler**, Edward '64 (Benesch FC&A LLP) -200 Pub Sq -Ste 2300
-Cleveland 44114 Fx:363-4588
(614) 221-3155 .. **Kandawalla**, Darius N '96 (Bailey C LLC) -10 W Broad
-Columbus 43215 Fx:221-0479
(330) 456-8376 .. **Kandel**, James R '72 -101 Central Plz S -Ste 401 -Canton 44702
    Kandel, Stephen J '04 -(Address Unavailable)
(216) 736-2653 .. **Kane**, Gail R '83 -1275 Lakeside Av E -Cleveland 44114
    Kane, Ira O '73 -181 Stanbery Av -Columbus 43209
(419) 334-2232 .. **Kane**, Jeffrey A '87 -203 N Park Av -Fremont 43420
(937) 443-6816 .. **Kane**, John F '98 %Thompson H LLP -2000 Cthse Plz NE -Bx8801
-Dayton 45401 Fx:443-6635
(513) 621-6464 .. **Kane**, Joseph E '70 (Graydon H&R LLP) -511 Walnut
-1900 Fifth Third Ctr -Cincinnati 45202 Fx:651-3836
(614) 227-2371 .. **Kane**, Richard F '71 (Bricker & E LLP) -100 S 3rd
-Columbus 43215 Fx:227-2390
(513) 361-1200 .. **Kane**, Scott A '97 (Squire S&D LLP) -312 Walnut -Ste 3500
-Cincinnati 45202 Fx:361-1201
(937) 748-5162 .. **Kane**, Sherry L '98 %Eckert & E, Co LPA -15 E Mill
-Springboro 45066 Fx:748-5163
(330) 296-3868 .. **Kane**, Terrence G '77 (Kane & K) -101 E Main -Bx167 -Ravenna
44266 Fx:296-7100
(717) 861-8635 .. **Kane**, Thomas G '83 US Army Natl Guard -Ft Indntwn Gap
-Dep Military/Vets Affrs -Annville, PA 17003
(614) 645-7385 .. **Kane**, Wendy A '95 City Atty -90 W Broad -Columbus 43215
    Kanehailua, Sharoiha P '04 -(Address Unavailable)
(330) 425-4201 .. **Kanellis**, Dean W '94 Reimer L&A Co,LPA -2450 Edison Blvd
-Bx968 -Twinsburg 44087 Fx:487-0923
(330) 643-2788 .. **Kanellis**, Margaret A '94 Summit Cnty Pros-Crim -53 Univ Av
-7th Fl -Akron 44308 Fx:643-8277
(614) 559-9000 .. **Kang**, Catherine C '95 -601 S High -2nd Fl -Columbus 43215
Fx:221-8912
(419) 213-8803 .. **Kanios**, Peter N '82 Lucas Cnty Pros -Bx10007 -Toledo 43699
(330) 743-5181 .. **Kannensohn**, Fredric A '64 (Millstone & K) -11 Fed Plz Central
-1st Natl Bk Twr 3rd Fl -Youngstown 44503
(614) 224-1118 .. **Kanter**, Bernard E '57 -601 S High -Columbus 43215
(513) 469-6580 .. **Kanter**, Mark S '83 Rookwood Prop Inc -8160 Corp Park Dr
-Rm 220 -Cincinnati 45242 Fx:469-6584
(614) 834-7777 .. **Kantner**, John M '87 -5 W Waterloo -Canal Winchester 43110
(937) 225-4892 .. **Kantosky**, Dorothy A '77 Montgomery Cnty Pros/CSEA -14 W 4th
-Ste 510 -Dayton 45402
(937) 223-8378 .. **Kantosky**, William H '77 Chicago Title Ins Co -1 S Main -Ste 330
-Dayton 45402
(215) 496-9400 .. **Kantrowitz**, Steven B '92 (Kantrowitz & P,LLC)
-4210 Centre Square W -Ste 4210 -Philadelphia, PA 19102
(614) 466-6750 .. **Kantzer**, Joseph C '87 OH Dept Taxation -30 E Broad -22nd Fl
-Columbus 43215
(614) 645-4500 .. **Kanz**, Gayle E Jr. '99 Columbus Police Dept -120 Marconi Blvd
-Columbus 43215
    Kaper, Laura G '03 -(Address Unavailable)
(419) 822-3211 .. **Kaper**, Terry J '68 (Barber KS&R) -206 Main -Delta 43515
Fx:822-4593
(216) 520-0088 .. **Kapitan**, Robert B '01 Pepple & W Ltd -5005 Rockside Rd
-Ste 260 -Cleveland 44131 Fx:520-0044
(614) 526-4795 .. **Kapitan**, Robert J '64 OfCnsl Dreher L&T LLP -41 S High
-2250 Huntngtn Ctr -Columbus 43215 Fx:628-1600
(614) 228-4422 .. **Kaplan**, Aimee L '03 %Chappano W PLL -8 E Long -9th Fl
-Columbus 43215 Fx:228-4423

(847) 734-8811 .. **Kaplan**, Alan M '99 Masuda FE&M,Ltd -1475 E Woodfld Rd
-Ste 800 -Schaumburg, IL 60173 **Fx:**734-1089

(513) 723-4000 .. **Kaplan**, Andrew M '83 (Vorys SS&P LLP) -221 E 4th
-Ste 2000 Atrium Two -Bx0236 -Cincinnati 45201 **Fx:**723-4056

(513) 381-5552 .. **Kaplan**, Bradley D '88 Masuda FE&M,Ltd -312 Walnut -Ste 1750
-Cincinnati 45202 **Fx:**381-5559

(216) 363-4500 .. **Kaplan**, Ira C '79 (Benesch FC&A LLP) -200 Pub Sq -Ste 2300
-Cleveland 44114 **Fx:**363-4588

(330) 666-7922 .. **Kaplan**, Michael J '76 Kaplan & Assoc -395 Sprngside Dr
-Akron 44333

(216) 861-8888 .. **Kaplan**, Morton L '67 -1419 W 9th -2nd Fl -Cleveland 44113

(440) 350-2683 .. **Kaplan**, Paul E '91 Lake Cnty Pros -105 Main -Bx490
-Painesville 44077 **Fx:**350-2585

(614) 228-5151 .. **Kaplan**, Philip A '00 %Gallagher GPT&L LLP -471 E Broad
-19th Fl -Columbus 43215 **Fx:**228-0032

(202) 225-5074 .. **Kaplan**, Randall J '93 House of Rep -2157 Rayburn Hse Ofc Bldg
-Washington, DC 20515

(937) 434-2249 .. **Kaplan**, Richard L '81 -683 Miamisburg-Centervll Rd -Ste 202
-Dayton 45459 **Fx:**436-2179

(419) 241-6168 .. **Kaplan**, Robert Z '55 -520 Mad Av -Ste 830 -Toledo 43604

(419) 241-6168 .. **Kaplan**, Samuel Z '93 -520 Mad Av -Ste 830 -Toledo 43604

Kaplan, William '67 -18675 Parkland Dr -#406
-Shaker Heights 44122

(330) 643-2788 .. **Kaplan-Quinn**, Kimberly A '93 Summit Cnty Pros-Crim
-53 Univ Av -7th Fl -Akron 44308 **Fx:**643-8277

(330) 454-9960 .. **Kaplanis**, Anthony T '89 -116 Cleveland Av NW -Ste 808 -Canton
44702

(614) 252-5233 .. **Kaplin**, Thomas L Jr. '59 Ralston Indstrs Inc -600 N Cassady
-Columbus 43219

(216) 781-8823 .. **Kaplow**, Richard J '73 -614 W Superior Av -808 Rckfllr Bldg
-Cleveland 44113

(513) 721-2820 .. **Kapor**, David W '81 -2306 Park Av -Ste 102 -Cincinnati 45206

(216) 870-7500 .. **Kapp**, C Terrence '71 -30406 Crestvw Dr -Bx40447
-Bay Village 44140

(614) 469-3939 .. **Kapp**, Jeffrey L '93 (Jones D) -325 John H McConnell Blvd
-Ste 600 -Bx165017 -Columbus 43216 **Fx:**461-4198

(937) 339-0511 .. **Kappers**, Alan M '77 (Dungan & L Co,LPA) -210 W Main
-Troy 45373 **Fx:**335-5802

(513) 852-8208 .. **Kappers**, Stephen A '79 OfCnsl Cors & B LLC
-537 E Pete Rose Way -Ste 400 -Cincinnati 45202

(440) 247-5555 .. **Kaprosy**, David V '73 (Brenner K LLP) -50 E Wshngtn
-Chagrin Falls 44022 **Fx:**247-5551

(614) 764-4617 .. **Kaps**, Charles G '77 -Bx340256 -Columbus 43234

(614) 457-0635 .. **Kaps**, Dennis O '74 -5837 Kerric Square Dr -Dublin 43016

(513) 241-3447 .. **Kapsal**, Christopher P '01 -906 Main -Ste 405 -Cincinnati 45202
Fx:241-3553

(216) 586-3939 .. **Kapur**, Sanjiv K '92 (Jones D) -901 Lakeside Av -Cleveland 44114
Fx:579-0212

(216) 781-5515 .. **Kapusta-Dorogi**, Jonetta '92 %Hermann C&S,LLP -1301 E 9th
-Ste 500 -Cleveland 44114 **Fx:**781-1030

(614) 677-6335 .. **Kapustin**, Vladimir '89 Nationwide Ins Co -1 Nationwide Plz
-Columbus 43215

Karakoudas, Smaragda E '96 -3203 W 115th -Cleveland 44111

(216) 241-6602 .. **Karakul**, Kurt '79 (Weston HFP&H LLP) -50 Pub Sq
-2500 Trmnl Twr -Cleveland 44113 **Fx:**621-8369

(513) 852-8635 .. **Karam**, Ernest H '47 Hamilton Cnty Cmn Pleas Ct -800 Bway
-Cincinnati 45202

Karam, Gregory L '82 -Bx43070 -Cincinnati 45243

(724) 742-6757 .. **Karam**, James L '89 Marconi Comm Inc -1000 Marconi Dr
-Warrendale, PA 15086

(614) 294-0631 .. **Karam**, Joseph D '57 Cedar Entrprs,Inc -1328 Dublin Rd -Ste 300
-Columbus 43215 **Fx:**294-1648

(248) 258-6262 .. **Karamanian**, Kirk E '94 %O'Bryan B&C -401 S Old Woodward
-Ste 320 -Birmingham, MI 48009

(216) 696-1422 .. **Karas**, Kimon P '78 (McCarthy LC&L Co,LPA) -101 Prospect Av W
-1800 Mdlnd Bldg -Cleveland 44115 **Fx:**696-1210

(614) 764-3242 .. **Karasarides**, Shawn H '93 Wendys Intl
-4288 W Dublin-Granvll Rd -Bx256 -Dublin 43017

(216) 292-3300 .. **Karberg**, Bruce K '75 Conway MWK&K Co,LPA
-30195 Chagrin Blvd -Ste 300 -Cleveland 44124

(419) 255-1222 .. **Karcher**, Richard A '80 -421 N Mich -Toledo 43604

Kareth, James R '01 -613 Grandvw Av -Newport, KY 41071

(513) 632-5310 .. **Karl**, Kristie A '99 %Brinkman & Assoc -119 E Court
-Cincinnati 45202

(440) 891-8320 .. **Karl**, Margaret T '03 %Rooney & S -493 Front -Berea 44017
Fx:(866) 891-2844

(419) 529-1367 .. **Karl**, Melissa K '84 Industrial Commssn of OH -240 Tappen Dr N
-Bx8051 -Mansfield 44906 **Fx:**529-3084

(513) 721-1200 .. **Karl**, Robert D '92 %Young R&M Co,LPA -1014 Vine -Ste 2400
-Cincinnati 45202 **Fx:**721-7116

(614) 228-8400 .. **Karl**, Robert J '89 (Ulmer & B LLP) -88 E Broad -Ste 1600
-Columbus 43215 **Fx:**228-8561

(212) 512-4413 .. **Karle**, Thomas J '94 %McGraw-Hill -1221 Av of Amer
-New York, NY 10020 **Fx:**512-4415

(614) 252-2300 .. **Karlock**, Kenneth P '93 Calig & H,LPA -854 E Broad
-Columbus 43205

(216) 696-3344 .. **Karlovec**, Lucien B Jr. '62 Legal News Pub Co -2935 Prospect Av
-Cleveland 44115

(313) 226-3200 .. **Karmol**, Erikson C N '97 NLRB -477 Mich Av -Rm 300
-Detroit, MI 48226 **Fx:**226-2090

(216) 575-2383 .. **Karnatz**, William E Jr. '92 Natl City Bank -1900 E 9th -Loc 2030
-Bx5756 -Cleveland 44101

(216) 566-5748 .. **Karnatz**, William E Sr. '62 OfCnsl Thompson H LLP -127 Pub Sq
-3900 Key Ctr -Cleveland 44114 **Fx:**566-5800

(216) 941-7760 .. **Karnes**, William M '71 -13604 Lorain Av -Cleveland 44111

(937) 225-4652 .. **Karns**, Cynthia A '93 Montgomery Cnty Pub Def -117 S Main
-Ste 400 -Dayton 45422 **Fx:**225-3449

(419) 259-6376 .. **Karol**, Thomas A '78 US Atty -4 Seagate -Ste 308 -Toledo 43604
Fx:259-6360

(216) 622-1851 .. **Karon**, Daniel R '98 (Weinstein KSK&G Ltd) -55 Pub Sq -Ste 1500
-Cleveland 44113 **Fx:**622-1852

(216) 685-1360 .. **Karp & Camino, Ltd** -2000 E 9th -Ste 710 -Cleveland 44115
Fx:781-3130

(216) 685-1360 .. **Karp**, Harlan D '89 (Karp & C,Ltd) -2000 E 9th -Ste 710
-Cleveland 44115 **Fx:**781-3130

(216) 931-6000 .. **Karp**, Marvin L '58 (Ulmer & B LLP) -1300 E 9th
-Ste 900 Penton Media Bldg -Cleveland 44114 **Fx:**931-6001

(216) 696-3515 .. **Karp**, Sheldon '67 (S Karp Co,LPA) -101 Prospect Av W
-1835 Mdlnd Bldg -Cleveland 44115

(614) 764-8404 .. **Karpowicz**, Joseph R Jr. '81 Wendys Intl
-4288 W Dublin-Granvll Rd -Bx256 -Dublin 43017

(216) 348-5400 .. **Karr**, Bernard L '73 (McDonald H Co,LPA) -600 Superior Av E
-Ste 2100 -Cleveland 44114 **Fx:**348-5474

(614) 436-5466 .. **Karr**, Douglas B '80 -690 Shore Dr -Columbus 43229

(614) 848-3100 .. **Karr**, Glennon J '74 -1328 Oakview Dr -Columbus 43235

(412) 566-2452 .. **Karr**, Gwenn S '85 %Eckert SC&M,LLC -600 Grant -44th Fl
-Pittsburgh, PA 15219 **Fx:**566-6099

(614) 466-3998 .. **Karr**, Heather E '99 Unemploymnt Comp Commssn -145 S Front
-Bx182299 -Columbus 43218

(614) 478-6000 .. **Karr**, Keith M '83 (Karr & S Co,LPA) -1 Easton Oval -Ste 550
-Columbus 43219

(614) 478-6000 .. **Karr & Sherman Co,LPA** -1 Easton Oval -Ste 550
-Columbus 43219

(440) 274-2450 .. **Karris**, Tom J '82 -7835 Fwy Cir -Middleburg Heights 44130

(216) 621-3346 .. **Karson**, Jeffrey A '89 %Kendis & Assoc Co,LPA
-614 Superior Av W -15th Fl Rckfllr Bldg -Cleveland 44113
Fx:621-3672

(513) 347-1008 .. **Karsten**, Theresa S '90 Catholic Health Initiatives
-3900 Olympic Blvd -Erlanger, KY 41018

(216) 586-3939 .. **Karzmer**, Erin E '01 OfCnsl Jones D -901 Lakeside Av
-Cleveland 44114 **Fx:**579-0212

(216) 622-8526 .. **Karzmer**, Steven C '01 (Calfee H&G LLP) -800 Superior Av
-Ste 1400 -Cleveland 44114 **Fx:**241-0816

(614) 466-6290 .. **Kasai**, Jerry K '84 Ohio School Facilities Commission -10 W Broad
-14th Fl -Columbus 43215

(216) 443-7800 .. **Kasaris**, Daniel M '89 Cuyahoga Cnty Pros -1200 Ontario -8th Fl
-Cleveland 44113 **Fx:**698-2270

(330) 643-2788 .. **Kasay**, Richard S '77 Summit Cnty Pros-Crim -53 Univ Av -7th Fl
-Akron 44308 **Fx:**643-8277

(330) 456-2853 .. **Kaschak**, Bryan C '04 WR Kaschak Co,LPA -220 Market Av S
-Ste 1140 -Canton 44702

(330) 456-2853 .. **Kaschak**, Wayne R '72 (WR Kaschak Co,LPA) -220 Market Av S
-Ste 1140 -Canton 44702

(216) 621-7860 .. **Kasdan**, Howard P '69 OfCnsl Cavitch FD&F -1717 E 9th -14th Fl
-Cleveland 44114 **Fx:**621-3415

(216) 574-2600 .. **Kaselak**, Dennis J '74 Lasko & L Co,LPA -1406 W 6th -Ste 200
-Cleveland 44113

(513) 887-3474 .. **Kash**, David L '79 Butler Cnty Pros -315 High -11th Fl -Bx515
-Hamilton 45012

(513) 423-2609 .. **Kash**, Kevin '82 -1440 S Breiel Blvd -Middletown 45044

(216) 348-0652 .. **Kasicki**, Nancy M '95 -3191 W 14th -Cleveland 44109

(910) 396-2511 .. **Kaske**, Karen L '02 US Army JAGC
-XVIII Airborne Corp & Ft Bragg -Fort Bragg, NC 28310

(937) 449-6400 .. **Kaskey**, Gregory M '01 %Dinsmore & S LLP -1 S Main
-Ste 1300 One Dayton Centre -Dayton 45402 **Fx:**449-6405

(216) 861-4355 .. **Kasle**, Andrew R '89 (Hazelwood & K) -1801 E 9th -Ste 730
-Cleveland 44114

(440) 734-8092 .. **Kasler**, Carolyn J '89 -3946 Shelley Dr -North Olmsted 44070

(330) 723-6301 .. **Kasmer**, Richard J '94 -203 Timber Trl -Medina 44256

Kaspar, Johnny C '04 -(Address Unavailable)

(602) 532-5702 .. **Kasparek**, Timothy G '74 Sanders & P,PC -3030 N 3rd -Ste 1300
-Phoenix, AZ 85012

(419) 663-2320 .. **Kasper**, Daivia S '95 -10½ Benedict Av -Bx712 -Norwalk 44857

(216) 523-4138 .. **Kasper**, Leslie J '73 Eaton Corp -1111 Superior Av
-Cleveland 44114

(440) 891-9790 .. **Kasputis**, Edward F '88 -24545 Nobottom Rd
-Olmsted Township 44138

(614) 444-7841 .. **Kass**, Frederic R '72 -761 S Front -Columbus 43206

(330) 928-3373 .. **Kassinger**, John R '84 (Nehrer & K) -111 Stow Av -Ste 100
-Cuyahoga Falls 44221

(614) 461-1311 .. **Kasson**, Donald P '91 %Reminger & R -65 E State
-4th Fl Cptl Sq Ofc Bldg -Columbus 43215 **Fx:**232-2410

(513) 929-0254 .. **Kasson**, Henry C '69 (Kasson & W LLC) -441 Vine -Ste 3110
-Cincinnati 45202

(216) 523-4136 .. **Kastelic**, John A '90 Eaton Corp -1111 Superior Av
-Cleveland 44114

(216) 622-8200 .. **Kastelic**, Tara A '91 (Calfee H&G LLP) -800 Superior Av
-Ste 1400 -Cleveland 44114 **Fx:**241-0816

(216) 586-7307 .. **Kastelic**, Thomas J '82 -901 Lakeside Av -North Pnt %Jones Day
-Cleveland 44114

(202) 283-8620 .. **Kastl**, Robert J '78 IRS -1111 Const Av -M4-173
-Washington, DC 20224

(614) 462-4927 .. **Kastner**, Beth '01 %Schottenstein Z&D -250 West -Bx165020
-Columbus 43216 **Fx:**462-5135

Kastner, David L '04 -(Address Unavailable)

(330) 867-9998 .. **Kastner**, Harley M '73 (Kastner W&W,LLC) -3480 W Market
-Ste 300 -Akron 44333 **Fx:**867-3786

(513) 243-7410 .. **Kastner**, Richard G '82 GE Co -One Neumann Way
-Maildrop G408 -Cincinnati 45215

(859) 292-6596 .. **Kastner**, Stefanie L '98 KY Pub Def -333 Scott -Ste 400
-Covington, KY 41011

(330) 867-9998 .. **Kastner Westman & Wilkins,LLC** -3480 W Market -Ste 300
-Akron 44333 **Fx:**867-3786

(440) 946-9469 .. **Kasunic**, Carl P Jr. '86 (CP Kasunic Co,LPA) -38033 Euclid Av -#1
-Willoughby 44094

(440) 289-6213 .. **Kasunick**, Jason G '03 -35988 Reeves Rd -Eastlake 44095

(330) 375-2030 .. **Kaszowski**, Tammy L '00 Law Dept -161 S High -Ste 202
-Akron 44308

(412) 394-2388 .. **Katarincic**, Joseph A '01 (Thorp R&A,LLP) -301 Grant -14th Fl
-Pittsburgh, PA 15219

(937) 222-4301 .. **Katchman**, Steven C '89 -137 N Main -Ste 610 -Dayton 45402
Fx:222-4613

(937) 224-0036 .. **Katchmer**, George A Jr. '81 -175 St Clair -Ste 320 -Bx4235
-Dayton 45401

(513) 243-4475 .. **Kates**, Darryl M '91 GE Aircraft Engines -1 Neumann Way
-MD J104 -Cincinnati 45215

(513) 779-4601 .. **Kates**, Rick D '95 Kates & Co -Bx0724 -West Chester 45071

(513) 631-1300 ..**Kathman**, Edward T '91 -130 Silver Fox Ct -Loveland 45140
(859) 371-3600 ..**Kathman**, William J Jr. '89 Busald FZ -226 Main -Bx6910
 -Florence, KY 41022
(614) 728-3676 ..**Katko**, David P '90 State Med Brd -77 S High -17th Fl
 -Columbus 43215
(972) 664-9170 ..**Katosic**, George R '71 -300 N Coit Rd -Ste 1050
 -Richardson, TX 75080 **Fx:**664-9165
(513) 665-3500 ..**Katrus**, Ilona '03 %Freund F&A -105 E 4th -Ste 1400
 -Cincinnati 45202 **Fx:**665-3503
(513) 651-6800 ..**Katsanis**, James A '58 Cnsl Frost BT LLC -201 E 5th
 -2200 PNC Ctr -Cincinnati 45202 **Fx:**651-6981
(513) 731-6601 ..**Katt**, Angela G '99 %W Hesch Law Firm -3047 Madison Rd
 -Ste 205 -Cincinnati 45209
(419) 753-2967 ..**Katterheinrich**, Thomas H '78 -206 S Main -New Knoxville 45871
(330) 493-9149 ..**Kattman**, Jeffrey C '81 -4429 Fulton Dr NW -Canton 44718
(323) 932-3395 ..**Katz**, Bennett L '82 Farmers Ins -4680 Wilshire Blvd
 -Los Angeles, CA 90010
(216) 621-8550 ..**Katz**, Burton A '74 -55 Pub Sq -Ste 1010 -Cleveland 44113
(216) 696-5250 ..**Katz**, Daniel M '96 %DA Katz Co,LPA -842 Trmnl Twr -50 Pub Sq
 -Cleveland 44113 **Fx:**696-5256
(216) 696-5250 ..**Katz**, David A '65 (DA Katz Co,LPA) -842 Trmnl Twr -50 Pub Sq
 -Cleveland 44113 **Fx:**696-5256
(614) 227-4841 ..**Katz**, Deborah A '89 KMG Mgmt Grp,LLC -2625 Brandon Rd
 -Columbus 43221
 Katz, Garry Alan '67 -Bx1963 -Tijeras, NM 87059
(802) 878-0767 ..**Katz**, George W '73 -289 Southfld Dr -Williston, VT 05495
(513) 721-5151 ..**Katz Greenberger & Norton,LLP** -105 E 4th -4th Fl
 -Cincinnati 45202 **Fx:**621-9285
(216) 831-6721 ..**Katz**, Herbert R '69 -26106 Fairmount Blvd -Cleveland 44122
(419) 891-9999 ..**Katz**, Ian M '03 Delp Co -1440 Arrowhead Dr -Maumee 43537
(614) 466-5967 ..**Katz**, Jeremy C '89 Atty Gen -30 E Broad -Columbus 43215
 Fx:466-8226
(330) 375-5412 ..**Katz**, Jason M '03 Hon D Cook -2 S Main -433 US Cthse
 -Akron 44308
(216) 368-3287 ..**Katz**, Lewis R '73 CWRU Law Schl -11075 East Blvd
 -Cleveland 44106
(330) 757-0333 ..**Katz**, Louis E '75 -70 W McKinley Way -Poland 44514
(513) 721-5151 ..**Katz**, Louis H '73 (Katz G&N,LLP) -105 E 4th -4th Fl
 -Cincinnati 45202 **Fx:**621-9285
(216) 931-6000 ..**Katz**, Mark D '74 (Ulmer & B LLP) -1300 E 9th
 -Ste 900 Penton Media Bldg -Cleveland 44114 **Fx:**931-6001
(419) 241-4500 ..**Katz**, Michael S '84 -520 Mad Av -Ste 1055 -Toledo 43604
(419) 243-7281 ..**Katz**, Randolph S '79 (Katz & K) -1101 Monroe -Toledo 43624
(513) 241-3447 ..**Katz**, Raymond L '01 -906 Main -405 Schwartz Bldg
 -Cincinnati 45202
(513) 721-4532 ..**Katz**, Reuven J '50 (Katz TB&H) -255 E 5th -Ste 2400
 -Cincinnati 45202
(216) 360-0479 ..**Katz**, Richard B '77 -2745 Belviour Blvd -Shaker Heights 44122
(513) 721-3111 ..**Katz**, Richard J '74 -4300 Carew Twr -441 Vine -Cincinnati 45202
(800) 800-3106 ..**Katz**, Richard S '84 Hitachi Med Syst -1959
 Summit Commerce Park -Twinsburg 44087
(614) 227-2397 ..**Katz**, Robert H '75 OfCnsl Bricker & E LLP -100 S 3rd
 -Columbus 43215 **Fx:**227-2390
 Katz, Robert J '76 -2790 Ember Way -Ann Arbor, MI 48104
(216) 464-5130 ..**Katz**, Roger A '74 Consolidated Mgt Inc -24500 Chagrin Blvd
 -2nd Fl -Cleveland 44122
(216) 371-0568 ..**Katz**, Roger J '82 -14475 Wshngtn Blvd -University Heights 44118
(917) 902-2768 ..**Katz**, Susan S '79 -Bx26 -Hubbard 44425
(513) 721-4532 ..**Katz Teller Brant & Hild** -255 E 5th -Ste 2400 -Cincinnati 45202
(216) 595-3200 ..**Katzenmeyer**, Dale L '87 PPM Inc -23500 Merchantile Rd -Ste I
 -Cleveland 44122
(513) 793-4400 ..**Katzman**, Amy S '77 Katzman LH&B -9000 Plainfld Rd
 -Cincinnati 45236 **Fx:**793-4691
(513) 793-4400 ..**Katzman**, Irwin '49 (Katzman LH&B) -9000 Plainfld Rd -Cincinnati
 45236 **Fx:**793-4691
(513) 793-4400 ..**Katzman Logan Halper & Bennett** -9000 Plainfld Rd -Cincinnati
 45236 **Fx:**793-4691
(480) 948-0505 ..**Kaucheck**, David J '82 Scottsdale Ins Co -8877 N Gainey Ctr Dr
 -Scottsdale, AZ 85258
(614) 778-4414 ..**Kauffman**, Andrew M '79 -Bx9805 -Columbus 43209
(614) 864-1200 ..**Kauffman**, David E '95 (Betzel & K Co,LPA)
 -8100 Channingway Blvd -Ste 600 -Columbus 43232
 Fx:864-1284
(513) 829-0313 ..**Kauffman**, Giles F III '95 Proctech Cnsltng Grp,Inc -6671 Ross Ln
 -Mason 45040
(505) 242-5297 ..**Kauffman**, Gregory R '02 (G Kauffman,PC) -320 Gold SW
 -Ste 1218 -Albuquerque, NM 87102
(614) 719-1568 ..**Kauffman**, Kelly L '99 Ohio Dept Insurance -2100 Stella Ct
 -Columbus 43215
(330) 828-2288 ..**Kauffman**, Roland B '82 -40 W Main -Bx489 -Dalton 44618
(614) 846-1252 ..**Kauffman**, Ronald P '61 -10233 Southfork Ln -Powell 43065
 Fx:846-8287
(216) 621-0150 ..**Kaufman**, Arthur M '83 (Hahn L&P LLP)
 -3300 BP Twr/200 Pub Sq -Ste 3300 -Cleveland 44114
 Fx:241-2824
 Kaufman, Beth F '99 -(Address Unavailable)
(440) 349-3200 ..**Kaufman**, Craig I '81 -32675 Stony Brook Ln -Solon 44139
(330) 264-7355 ..**Kaufman**, Daniel W '02 D Kaufman,Ltd -248 N Walnut
 -Wooster 44691
(614) 464-8359 ..**Kaufman**, David Jacob '04 %Vorys SS&P LLP -52 E Gay -Bx1008
 -Columbus 43216 **Fx:**719-4626
(216) 363-1400 ..**Kaufman**, Elliot M '64 OfCnsl Buckley K,LPA -600 E Superior Av
 -Ste 1400 -Cleveland 44114 **Fx:**579-1020
(513) 932-1515 ..**Kaufman & Florence** -144 E Mulberry -Bx280 -Lebanon 45036
(513) 621-4899 ..**Kaufman**, Jacob M '93 -817 Main -#500 -Cincinnati 45202
 Kaufman, Jeffrey R '97 -3106 Griggsvw Ct -Columbus 43221
(419) 222-1395 ..**Kaufman**, Kurt A '92 -121 W High -Ste 1200 Bk One Twr
 -Lima 45801
(419) 626-6669 ..**Kaufman**, Michael D '98 (Kaufman K & Assoc Co,LPA)
 -422 E Monroe -Sandusky 44870
(216) 696-8200 ..**Kaufman**, Paul M '74 -50 Pub Sq -Ste 801 -Cleveland 44113
(614) 469-9650 ..**Kaufman**, Philip B '78 -341 S 3rd -Ste 300 -Columbus 43215

(419) 626-6669 ..**Kaufman**, Ronald G '66 Kaufman K & Assoc Co,LPA
 -422 E Monroe -Sandusky 44870
(216) 861-5542 ..**Kaufman**, Roy M '71 -745 Leader Bldg -526 Superior Av E
 -Cleveland 44114
(419) 841-4300 ..**Kaufman**, Steven R '82 Kaufman Captl Corp
 -3178 Republic Blvd N -Ste 10 -Toledo 43615
(216) 566-5528 ..**Kaufman**, Steven S '75 (Thompson H LLP) -127 Pub Sq
 -3900 Key Ctr -Cleveland 44114 **Fx:**566-5800
(513) 932-1515 ..**Kaufman**, William H '71 (Kaufman & F) -144 E Mulberry -Bx280
 -Lebanon 45036
(513) 932-1515 ..**Kaufman**, William R '01 %Kaufman & F -144 E Mulberry -Bx280
 -Lebanon 45036
(330) 740-2208 ..**Kaufmann**, Deborah A '97 Mahoning Cnty Dom Rltns Ct
 -120 Market -4th Fl -Youngstown 44503
(330) 762-7655 ..**Kaufmann**, Philip S '71 (Kaufmann & K) -106 S Main -Ste 1200
 -Akron 44308 **Fx:**762-7537
(330) 744-0291 ..**Kaufmann**, Walter '73 (Boyd RC&C Co LPA) -400 Sky Bk Bldg
 -Bx6565 -Youngstown 44501
 Kaune, Christopher J '04 -(Address Unavailable)
(216) 292-5807 ..**Kauntz**, Edmund G '87 (Singerman MD&K) -3401 Enterprise Pkwy
 -Ste 200 -Beachwood 44122 **Fx:**292-5867
(513) 422-6378 ..**Kaup**, Gerhard H '67 -2 N Main -Ste 703 -Middletown 45042
(954) 525-1000 ..**Kautz**, Thomas L '82 (Holland & K,LLP) -One E Broward Blvd
 -Ste 1300 -Fort Lauderdale, FL 33301 **Fx:**463-2030
(216) 443-4953 ..**Kavalec**, Marita L '89 Juv Ct -2163 E 22nd -Cleveland 44115
(248) 335-5000 ..**Kavalhuna**, Lisa M '94 %Hertz S&S,PC -1760 S Telegraph Rd
 -Ste 300 -Bloomfield Hills, MI 48302 **Fx:**335-3346
(937) 322-0891 ..**Kavanagh**, Paul J '95 Cole AH&D -333 N Limestone -Bx1687
 -Springfield 45501 **Fx:**322-9931
(614) 221-3536 ..**Kavinsky**, Keith A '92 (Gallagher & K,LPA) -400 S 5th Av -Ste 304
 -Columbus 43215
(513) 487-2008 ..**Kavouras**, Maria S '91 SrCnsl US EPA -26 W Martin Luther
 King Dr -OGC/FOLO -Cincinnati 45268 **Fx:**487-2132
(216) 479-8500 ..**Kavuru**, Joan A '92 %Squire S&D LLP -127 Pub Sq
 -4900 Key Twr -Cleveland 44114 **Fx:**479-8780
(740) 450-5167 ..**Kawalec**, Thomas C '68 State of OH -30 W Spring -7th Fl
 -Columbus 43215
(216) 579-6252 ..**Kay**, Abraham F '79 -55 Pub Sq -Ste 1200 -Cleveland 44113
(330) 533-4373 ..**Kay**, Charles J '93 %Davis & D -6715 Tippecanoe Rd -Bldg A-103
 -Canfield 44406 **Fx:**533-9954
(440) 248-7906 ..**Kay**, Jeffrey T '98 %Mazanec R&R Co,LPA -34305 Solon Rd
 -Ste 100 -Cleveland 44139 **Fx:**248-8861
(408) 376-6226 ..**Kay**, Kelly A '98 SrCnsl eBay Inc -2145 Hmltn Av -San
 Jose, CA 95125 **Fx:**376-7514
 Kay, Ryan M '04 -(Address Unavailable)
(513) 784-1532 ..**Kaye**, Rebecca Kay '78 -1014 Vine -Ste 2525 -Cincinnati 45202
(303) 400-8770 ..**Kaye**, Rhonda R '91 Lexis Nexis -1400 16th -Ste 400
 -Denver, CO 80202
(614) 462-3555 ..**Kaylor**, Jamie Z '90 Franklin Cnty Pros -373 S High
 -Columbus 43215
(614) 236-9900 ..**Kayne**, Daniel J '76 -2461 E Main -Columbus 43209
(216) 522-3530 ..**Kayton**, Jodee C '01 US DVA -1240 E 9th -Cleveland 44199
(330) 867-9998 ..**Kazaglis**, Ted N '88 OfCnsl Kastner W&W,LLC -3480 W Market
 -Ste 300 -Akron 44333 **Fx:**867-3786
(614) 462-3194 ..**Kazar**, Michelle L '99 Franklin Cnty Pub Def -373 S High -12th Fl
 -Columbus 43215
(216) 621-1375 ..**Kazdin**, Gary A '62 -75 Pub Sq -Ste 1020 -Cleveland 44113
(972) 718-6969 ..**Kazee**, Norman B '82 Verizon Srvc Grp -600 Hidden Rdg
 -Irving, TX 75038
(419) 691-2435 ..**Kazee**, Timothy S '02 %Schlageter & B Co,LPA -715 S Coy Rd
 -Oregon 43616
(216) 515-4338 ..**Kazimir**, James '95 Sherwin-Williams -101 Prospect Av -Ste 880
 -Cleveland 44115
(216) 621-9870 ..**Kealy**, John C '70 -123 W Prospect Av -Ste 250 Van
 Sweringen Arcade -Cleveland 44115
 Kean, Jason '03 -(Address Unavailable)
(419) 843-9101 ..**Kean**, John V '73 -3230 Cntrl Pk W -Ste 116 -Toledo 43617
(614) 365-9900 ..**Keane**, Aimee P '04 %Zeiger TL&L,LLP -41 S High
 -Ste 3500 Huntngtn Ctr -Columbus 43215 **Fx:**365-7900
(216) 443-7800 ..**Keane**, Martin J '02 Cuyahoga Cnty Pros -1200 Ontario -8th Fl
 -Cleveland 44113 **Fx:**698-2270
(513) 932-3931 ..**Kearin**, Kathy H '76 -730 E Main -Bx36 -Lebanon 45036
(513) 328-4100 ..**Kearney**, Eric H '89 J-ML Kearney,LPA -354 Hearne Av -100
 -Cincinnati 45229
(513) 961-3331 ..**Kearney**, Jan-Michele L '91 (J-ML Kearney,LPA) -354 Hearne Av
 -100 -Cincinnati 45229
(937) 223-8171 ..**Kearney**, Keith R '84 (Rogers & G) -2160 Kettering Twr
 -Dayton 45423 **Fx:**223-1649
(330) 392-7780 ..**Kearney**, Patricia A '91 Title Professionals,Inc -295 Harmon Av
 -Warren 44483
(937) 256-1449 ..**Kearney**, Philip F Jr. '75 -1158 Jeanette Dr -Dayton 45432
 Kearney, David B '02 -1388 Sackett Hills Dr -Akron 44313
(614) 365-2700 ..**Kearns**, Greta M '97 %Squire S&D LLP -41 S High
 -1300 Huntngtn Ctr -Columbus 43215 **Fx:**365-2499
(513) 977-8200 ..**Kearns**, Jerome H '66 (Dinsmore & S LLP) -255 E 5th -Ste 1900
 -Cincinnati 45202 **Fx:**977-8141
(419) 289-1600 ..**Kearns**, Joseph P Jr. '94 %Mason M&K -153 W Main -Bx345
 -Ashland 44805 **Fx:**289-6530
(513) 561-0900 ..**Kearns**, Michael A '94 (Kearns Co,LPA) -3028 Victory Pkwy
 -Cincinnati 45206
(513) 241-7722 ..**Kearns**, Michael S '93 (Gerner & K Co,LPA) -215 W 9th
 -Cincinnati 45202
(614) 272-6560 ..**Keating**, Bradley D '03 %Magelaner & Assoc -2975 W Broad
 -Columbus 43204
(330) 399-6847 ..**Keating**, Brendan J '98 -144 N Park Av -Ste 315 -Warren 44481
(513) 397-1480 ..**Keating**, Brian G '80 Cincinnati Bell Tlphne -201 E 4th
 -Cincinnati 45202
(330) 393-4611 ..**Keating**, Daniel G '82 (Keating K&K) -170 Monroe NW
 -Warren 44483 **Fx:**394-0101
(630) 692-8670 ..**Keating**, James A '77 Hartford Ins Grp -4245 Meridian Pkwy
 -Aurora, IL 60504
(330) 262-2916 ..**Keating**, John T '83 -141 E Lbrty -Wooster 44691 **Fx:**263-1738

(330) 393-4611 .. **Keating Keating & Kuzman** -170 Monroe NW -Warren 44483 Fx:394-0101

(513) 887-3690 .. **Keating**, Lori L '98 Butler Cnty Dom Rltns Ct -315 High -3rd Fl -Hamilton 45011

(330) 262-2916 .. **Keating**, Louise W '80 -141 E Lbrty -Wooster 44691 Fx:263-1738

(513) 579-4118 .. **Keating**, Michael K '80 Fifth 3rd Bank -38 Fountain Sq Plz -Cincinnati 45263

(513) 579-6400 .. **Keating Muething & Klekamp PLL** -1 E 4th -1400 Provident Twr -Cincinnati 45202 Fx:579-6457

(330) 376-5300 .. **Keating**, Patrick J '83 (Buckingham D&B,LLP) -50 S Main -Bx1500 -Akron 44309 Fx:258-6559

(330) 262-2916 .. **Keating**, Richard M '52 -141 E Lbrty -Wooster 44691 Fx:263-1738

(513) 891-1530 .. **Keating Ritchie & Swick** -8050 Hosbrook -Ste 200 -Cincinnati 45236 Fx:891-1537

(440) 930-4001 .. **Keating**, Susan E '02 %Baumgartner & O -5455 Detroit Rd (Rte 254) -Sheffield Village 44054 Fx:934-7205

(513) 891-1530 .. **Keating**, Thomas T '74 (Keating R&S) -8050 Hosbrook -Ste 200 -Cincinnati 45236 Fx:891-1537

(614) 540-4000 .. **Keating**, Van D '86 OH Schl Brds Assn -8050 N High -Ste 100 -Columbus 43235

(330) 393-4611 .. **Keating**, W Leo '50 (Keating K&K) -170 Monroe NW -Warren 44483 Fx:394-0101

(614) 481-4466 .. **Keating**, William H '72 -1289 Inglis Av -Columbus 43212

(513) 321-5357 .. **Keating**, William J '50 -2959 Alpine Ter -Cincinnati 45208 Fx:321-4010

(513) 579-6400 .. **Keating**, William J Jr. '79 (Keating M&K PLL) -1 E 4th -1400 Provident Twr -Cincinnati 45202 Fx:579-6457

(740) 653-3863 .. **Keaton**, Ronald L '69 Fairfield Fed Savings & Loan Assoc -111 E Main -Lancaster 43130

(937) 223-5200 .. **Keck**, Emerson R '75 (Flanagan LH&S) -318 W 4th -Dayton 45402 Fx:223-3335

(614) 645-7483 .. **Keck**, Heather L '99 City Pros -375 S High -7th Fl -Columbus 43215

(513) 868-7100 .. **Keck**, Jill A '99 %Davidson A&C Co,LPA -127 N 2nd -Hamilton 45011 Fx:868-9059

(513) 651-6800 .. **Keck**, Linda M '96 Cnsl Frost BT LLC -201 E 5th -2200 PNC Ctr -Cincinnati 45202 Fx:651-6981

(513) 863-6700 .. **Keck**, William C '70 (Millikin & F) -6 S 2nd -6th Fl -Bx598 -Hamilton 45012 Fx:863-0031

(216) 583-8236 .. **Keco**, Laurie A '96 Ernst & Young LLP -925 Euclid Av -Ste 1300 -Cleveland 44115

(216) 642-3342 .. **Kedzior**, John D '81 (Wegman H&V,LPA) -6055 Rockside Wds Blvd -Ste 200 -Cleveland 44131 Fx:642-8826

Keebaugh, Kristen N '04 -(Address Unavailable)

(513) 369-5057 .. **Keefe**, Daniel M '78 Great Amer Ins Co -580 Walnut -7W -Cincinnati 45202

(216) 479-8500 .. **Keefe**, F Barry '73 (Squire S&D LLP) -127 Pub Sq -4900 Key Twr -Cleveland 44114 Fx:479-8780

(216) 771-5800 .. **Keefe**, Stephen T Jr. '96 %Linton & H -700 W St Clair Av -Hoyt Block Ste 300 -Cleveland 44113

(513) 556-6932 .. **Keefe**, Thomas W '75 Univ of Cincinnati -0146 French-West -Cincinnati 45221

(614) 406-4399 .. **Keefer**, Stanislava '00 -Bx1606 -Westerville 43086

Keegan, Anne E '80 -130 Seneca Dr -Marietta 45750

(513) 651-9222 .. **Keegan**, John M '92 -414 Walnut -Ste 707 -Cincinnati 45202

(513) 752-3900 .. **Keegan**, Walter J '88 (C Keegan & Assoc) -4440 Glen Este-Withamsvll Rd -Ste 550 -Cincinnati 45245

(419) 213-3362 .. **Keeler**, Dianne L '80 Lucas Co Children Srvcs Brd -705 Adams -Toledo 43624

(513) 946-3000 .. **Keeling**, James M '97 Hamilton Cnty Pros -230 E 9th -Cincinnati 45202 Fx:946-3017

(614) 462-3194 .. **Keeling**, John W '75 Franklin Cnty Pub Def -373 S High -12th Fl -Columbus 43215

(513) 361-8310 .. **Keeling**, Julianne M '97 Workers Comp -125 E Court -Cincinnati 45202

(440) 878-2992 .. **Keenan**, Alexis G '03 Ceres Grp,Inc -17800 Royalton Rd -Strongsville 44136

(614) 460-4682 .. **Keenan**, David C '94 Columbia Gas -200 Civic Ctr Dr -Bx117 -Columbus 43216

(330) 455-0173 .. **Keenan**, J Sean '67 (Day KRW&R,Ltd) -200 Market Av N -Ste 300 -Bx24213 -Canton 44701 Fx:455-2633

(740) 282-5323 .. **Keenan**, Jane M '01 (Bruzzese & C) -300 Sinclair Bldg -Bx1506 -Steubenville 43952 Fx:282-5328

(216) 721-7700 .. **Keenan**, Martin J '77 (Buckeye Lgl Ctr) -11510 Buckeye Rd -Cleveland 44104 Fx:721-5261

(866) 794-7282 .. **Keenehan**, John C '78 LAWO -545 W Market -Ste 301 -Lima 45801 Fx:(419) 224-9947

(614) 280-1100 .. **Keener Doucher Curley & Patterson,LPA** -88 E Broad -Ste 1750 -Columbus 43215

(937) 327-3646 .. **Keener**, Kyle B '00 Clark Cnty CSEA -1346 Lagonda Av -Springfield 45503

(937) 687-1388 .. **Keener**, Ronald D '69 (R Keener Co,LPA) -129 W Main -New Lebanon 45345 Fx:687-1451

(614) 280-1100 .. **Keener**, Thomas J '75 (Keener DC&P,LPA) -88 E Broad -Ste 1750 -Columbus 43215

(513) 946-3443 .. **Keeney**, Kathleen B '83 1st Dist Ct of Appls -230 E 9th -12th Fl -Cincinnati 45202 Fx:946-3412

(216) 681-2214 .. **Keenon**, Una H '75 Mun Ct Judge -14340 Euclid Av -East Cleveland 44112

(513) 389-3700 .. **Keer**, Gregory A '81 -3907 N Bend Rd -Cincinnati 45211

(937) 223-1201 .. **Keeton**, Anne Pennington '03 %Altick & C Co,LPA -1 S Main -1700 One Dayton Ctr -Dayton 45402 Fx:223-5100

(216) 875-4800 .. **Keevican**, Leo A Jr. '78 (DKW Law Grp) -200 Pub Sq -26th Fl BP Twr -Cleveland 44114 Fx:875-4809

(937) 396-1269 .. **Kegelmeyer**, Jack M '03 -580 Lincoln Park Blvd -Ste 222 -Dayton 45429

Keggan, Cheryl L '04 -(Address Unavailable)

(614) 462-5400 .. **Kegler Brown Hill & Ritter** -65 E State -Ste 1800 -Columbus 43215 Fx:464-2634

(740) 387-1120 .. **Kegler Brown Hill & Ritter** -250 Exec Dr -Ste B -Marion 43302 Fx:387-3630

(614) 462-5446 .. **Kegler**, Charles J '68 (Kegler BH&R) -65 E State -Ste 1800 -Columbus 43215 Fx:464-2634

(614) 462-5409 .. **Kegler**, Todd M '97 (Kegler BH&R) -65 E State -Ste 1800 -Columbus 43215 Fx:464-2634

(614) 462-2279 .. **Keglewitsch**, Josef Jr. '96 (Schottenstein Z&D) -250 West -Bx165020 -Columbus 43218 Fx:462-5135

(614) 418-3100 .. **Keglewitsch**, Rebecca A '97 Skilken Prop -4270 Morse Rd -Columbus 43230

(440) 461-4150 .. **Kehn**, James M '71 -5555 Mayfld Rd -Lyndhurst 44124

Kehoe, John E '71 %Lawrence Cnty Cmn Pleas Ct -1 Veterans Sq -Cthse -Ironton 45638

(216) 621-1500 .. **Kehoe**, Robert D '82 (Kehoe & Assoc LLP) -1940 E 6th -900 Baker Bldg -Cleveland 44114 Fx:621-1551

(419) 738-5215 .. **Kehoe**, Robert W '89 -201 E Auglaize -Bx120 -Wapakoneta 45895

(330) 296-6742 .. **Kehres**, Douglas M '84 -638 W Main -Ravenna 44266

(513) 977-5579 .. **Kehres**, Julie Schimpf '92 Butkovich SS&G Co,LPA -36 E 7th -Ste 2600 -Cincinnati 45202 Fx:977-5580

(740) 593-9323 .. **Keifer**, John L '71 OH Univ -514B Copeland Hall -Athens 45701

(740) 593-2069 .. **Keifer**, Mary C '71 OH Univ -410A Copeland Hall -Athens 45701

(419) 213-4700 .. **Keiffer**, Lance M '89 Lucas Cnty Pros -Adams & Erie -Lucas Cnty Cthse -Toledo 43624

(419) 843-4499 .. **Keil**, Dennis M '85 (Camick & K Ltd) -3230 Cntrl Pk W -Ste 106 -Toledo 43617

(216) 515-1660 .. **Keim**, Christopher G '96 Frantz W LLP -127 Pub Sq -2500 Key Center -Cleveland 44114 Fx:515-1650

(216) 642-0323 .. **Keim**, Krista K '96 %Britton SP&K Co,LPA -4700 Rockside Rd -Ste 540 Summit One -Cleveland 44131 Fx:642-0747

(216) 348-5400 .. **Keiper**, Jeffrey B '94 (McDonald H Co,LPA) -600 Superior Av E -Ste 2100 -Cleveland 44114 Fx:348-5474

(216) 241-4100 .. **Keis / George LLP** -55 Pub Sq -Ste 800 -Cleveland 44113 Fx:771-3111

(216) 241-4100 .. **Keis**, William H Jr. '82 (Keis/G LLP) -55 Pub Sq -Ste 800 -Cleveland 44113 Fx:771-3111

(419) 825-1330 .. **Keiser**, Jed A '78 -110 W Airport Hwy -Bx154 -Swanton 43558

(937) 278-1543 .. **Keish**, Rodney D '72 -4428 N Dixie Dr -Dayton 45414 Fx:278-9059

(419) 841-1148 .. **Keisser**, Keith A '93 -5034 Hunters Grn -Toledo 43623

(614) 442-9200 .. **Keister**, David L '80 -1010 Old Henderson Rd -Ste 102 -Columbus 43220

(937) 492-1271 .. **Keister**, Ralph F '67 (Faulkner GK&S,LPA) -100 S Main Av -Ste 300 -Sidney 45365 Fx:498-1306

(419) 238-2488 .. **Keister**, Stephen E '74 -1175 Westwood Dr -Ste 200 -Van Wert 45891

(614) 876-1700 .. **Keith**, Charles L '80 Hi-Way Paving Inc -4343 Weaver Ct N -Bx550 -Hilliard 43026

(330) 644-9930 .. **Keith**, David A '80 -2775 S Arlngtn Rd -Akron 44312 Fx:644-9936

(330) 929-4293 .. **Keith**, George G '83 (Keith & G) -135 Portage Trl -Bx374 -Cuyahoga Falls 44222

(614) 466-7264 .. **Keith**, Harry B II '68 OH Legal Rghts Srvc -8 E Long -5th Fl -Columbus 43215

(614) 466-3014 .. **Keith**, James R '79 SERB -65 E State -Ste 1200 -Columbus 43215 Fx:466-3074

(740) 685-7611 .. **Keith**, Mary B '01 -254 Main -Bx82 -Byesville 43723

(216) 771-1760 .. **Keith**, Michele A '88 %Smith & C LLP -1801 E Ninth -Ste 900 Ohio Svngs Plz -Cleveland 44114 Fx:771-3387

(513) 272-1200 .. **Keith**, Robert F '97 (Doan K&B,LLC) -5710 Wooster Pike -Ste 212 -Cincinnati 45227

(614) 213-8510 .. **Kelbick**, Matt '02 Banc One Invstmnt Advsrs -1111 Polaris Pkwy -Ste B2 -Bx710211 -Columbus 43271 Fx:213-2292

(614) 445-2650 .. **Kelbley**, Jeffrey P '77 Grange Mutual Cslty Co -650 S Front -Bx1218 -Columbus 43216

(614) 442-1948 .. **Kelch**, Donald F Jr. '68 -1631 NW Prof Plz -Columbus 43220

(573) 564-6400 .. **Kell**, Scott K Jr. '63 (S Kell Jr,PC) -402 N Sturgeon -Ste 112 -Montgomery City, MO 63361 Fx:564-1500

(573) 564-6400 .. **Kell**, Scott K Jr. '63 (S Kell Jr,PC) -Bx91 -Hermann, MO 65041 Fx:564-1500

Kella, Archana S '04 -(Address Unavailable)

(419) 625-8735 .. **Kellam**, James R '68 (Catri & K Co,LPA) -1604 E Perkins Av -Ste 207 -Sandusky 44870

(330) 451-7911 .. **Kellar**, Cynthia A '86 5th Dist Ct of Appls -110 Central Plz Sq -Ste 320 -Canton 44702

(937) 223-1130 .. **Kelleher**, James W '79 Pickrel S&E -40 N Main -2700 Kettering Twr -Dayton 45423 Fx:223-0339

(216) 241-0520 .. **Kelleher**, Jeffry F '75 -526 Superior Av -1540 Leader Bldg -Cleveland 44114

(440) 843-5300 .. **Kelleher**, Sean F '92 -5579 Pearl Rd -Ste 203 -Parma 44129 Fx:842-1801

Kelleher, Vincent F '49 -516 Brandon Ct -Chardon 44024

(614) 841-1500 .. **Kelleher**, W Sean '74 -6797 N High -Ste 325 -Worthington 43085 Fx:841-9322

(513) 381-2838 .. **Keller**, Aimee L '93 (Taft S&H LLP) -425 Walnut -Ste 1800 -Cincinnati 45202 Fx:381-0205

(614) 444-5700 .. **Keller**, Amy E '01 E Doucet & Assoc Co LPA -895 S High -Columbus 43206

(281) 834-1978 .. **Keller**, Bradley A '91 Cnsl ExxonMobil Chemical Company -Law Tech -4500 Bayway Dr -Baytown, TX 77520

(216) 931-6000 .. **Keller**, C Reynolds Jr. '63 OfCnsl Ulmer & B LLP -1300 E 9th -Ste 900 Penton Media Bldg -Cleveland 44114 Fx:931-6001

(330) 376-5300 .. **Keller**, Clay K '00 %Buckingham D&B,LLP -50 S Main -Bx1500 -Akron 44309 Fx:258-6559

(216) 781-3366 .. **Keller**, Cleveland R '88 -200 Pub Sq -Ste 2940 -Cleveland 44114

(419) 468-7766 .. **Keller**, David W '82 (Keller Z&M) -659 Hrdng Way W -Galion 44833

Keller, Dennis F '75 -7445 Airport Hwy -Holland 43528

(614) 223-9300 .. **Keller**, Donald M '04 Benesch FC&A LLP -88 E Broad -Ste 900 -Columbus 43215 Fx:223-9330

(614) 227-2341 .. **Keller**, Donald R '74 (Bricker & E LLP) -100 S 3rd -Columbus 43215 Fx:227-2390

(937) 225-2910 .. **Keller**, Dwight K '02 US Atty -200 W 2nd -602 Fed Bldg -Dayton 45402

(513) 385-9080 .. **Keller**, Edward O '75 -5861 Cheviot Rd -Ste 101 -Cincinnati 45247

(216) 771-4830 .. **Keller**, Ellen H '79 -55 Pub Sq -Ste 2000 -Cleveland 44113

(513) 651-2121 .. **Keller**, James F '92 Z Gottesman -36 E 7th -2121 CBLD Ctr -Cincinnati 45202

(513) 579-1414 .. **Keller**, James K '94 (Schwartz M&R) -441 Vine -Ste 2900 -Cincinnati 45202 **Fx:**579-1418

(740) 862-4191 .. **Keller**, James L '75 (Jackson KS&D) -719 W Market -Baltimore 43105

(419) 242-8900 .. **Keller**, Jeffery B '88 -416 N Erie -Ste 200 -Toledo 43624

(877) 223-4633 .. **Keller**, Jennifer D '01 LAWO -35 N Park -Mansfield 44902

(614) 464-6400 .. **Keller**, John K '75 (Vorys SS&P LLP) -52 E Gay -Bx1008 -Columbus 43216 **Fx:**464-6350

(513) 872-5166 .. **Keller**, John T '75 -2345 Kemper Ln -Bx6129 -Cincinnati 45206

(330) 375-5900 .. **Keller**, Kerri L '02 Hon J Adams USDC -2 S Main -Rm 526 -Akron 44308

(513) 522-2000 .. **Keller**, Larry W '81 -7606 Hmltn Av -Cincinnati 45231

(614) 459-5200 .. **Keller**, Mark D '68 (Rance PBK&E Co,LPA) -1720 Zollinger Rd -Ste 200 -Columbus 43221 **Fx:**459-1151
           Keller, Mark J '04 -(Address Unavailable)

(419) 873-8660 .. **Keller**, Marvin E '75 -27457 Holiday Ln -Ste K -Perrysburg 43551

(216) 691-8888 .. **Keller**, Paul V '97 -4585 Lbrty Rd -South Euclid 44121

(616) 752-2479 .. **Keller**, R S '84 Warner N&J LLP -111 Lyon NW -Ste 900 -Grand Rapids, MI 49503

(732) 205-5937 .. **Keller**, Raymond F '85 Engelhard Corp -101 Wood Av -Iselin, NJ 08830

(937) 372-6921 .. **Keller**, Ronald P '83 (Cox K&R) -85 W Main -Xenia 45385
           Keller, Sandra L '99 -4230 Lyon Dr -Columbus 43220

(216) 566-7100 .. **Keller**, Stanley S '58 -1422 Euclid Av -330 The Hanna Bldg -Cleveland 44115 **Fx:**566-5430

(419) 893-3360 .. **Keller**, Stephen S '99 %Weber & S,LLC -1721 Indn Wd Cir -Ste 1 -Maumee 43537 **Fx:**893-7146

(614) 469-2999 .. **Keller**, Steven R '84 Fed Pub Def -10 W Broad -Ste 1020 -Columbus 43215

(419) 468-7766 .. **Keller Zeisler & Murphy** -659 Hrdng Way W -Galion 44833

(610) 270-5929 .. **Kellerman**, James C '97 GlaxoSmithKline -709 Swedeland Rd -King Of Prussia, PA 19406

(216) 443-8583 .. **Kelley**, Brendan P '04 Cmn Pleas Ct -1200 Ontario -Justice Ctr -Cleveland 44113

(614) 538-8155 .. **Kelley**, Brendan W '88 Franklin Research Grp,Inc -3518 Riverside Dr -Columbus 43221 **Fx:**538-8156

(513) 946-9000 .. **Kelley**, Catherine M '88 Hamilton Cnty Juv Ct -800 Bway -Cincinnati 45202 **Fx:**946-9217

(419) 227-3423 .. **Kelley**, Charles B '79 (Huffman KB&B LLC) -127-129 N Pierce -Bx546 -Lima 45802 **Fx:**228-1937

(937) 587-3119 .. **Kelley**, Christopher D '93 -115 Shaker Run Rd -Peebles 45660

(513) 946-3000 .. **Kelley**, David J '89 Hamilton Cnty Pros -230 E 9th -Cincinnati 45202 **Fx:**946-3017

(216) 523-1113 .. **Kelley**, Elizabeth '94 -1422 Euclid Av -Ste 1504 -Cleveland 44115

(216) 575-0777 .. **Kelley & Ferraro,LLP** -1300 E 9th -Ste 1901 -Cleveland 44114 **Fx:**575-0799

(440) 442-6677 .. **Kelley**, James M III '93 Elk & E Co,LPA -6100 Parkland Blvd -Mayfield Heights 44124 **Fx:**442-7944

(216) 902-4444 .. **Kelley Jasons McGuire & Spinelli LLP** -629 Euclid Av -Ste 1037 -Cleveland 44114 **Fx:**902-4447

(440) 895-9543 .. **Kelley**, John J III '93 (JJ Kelley Co,LPA) -19525 Hilliard Blvd -Bx16265 -Rocky River 44116 **Fx:**895-9583

(513) 321-4454 .. **Kelley**, John J Jr. '50 -3468 Forest Oak Ct -Cincinnati 45208

(513) 381-0656 .. **Kelley**, John J Jr. '60 (Kohnen & P LLP) -201 E 5th -Ste 800 -Cincinnati 45202 **Fx:**381-5823

(216) 937-1380 .. **Kelley**, Kevin E '77 Marsh Inc -200 Pub Sq -Ste 1100 -Cleveland 44114

(216) 443-9000 .. **Kelley**, Kevin J '04 %Porter WM&A LLP -925 Euclid Av -Ste 1700 -Cleveland 44115 **Fx:**443-9011

(614) 469-5715 .. **Kelley**, Kevin W '89 US Atty -303 Marconi Blvd -Ste 200 -Columbus 43215

(330) 654-5565 .. **Kelley**, L. P Jr. '73 -17019 Headland Av -Lake Milton 44429

(216) 941-1795 .. **Kelley**, Lawrence P '54 -16213 Marquis Av -Cleveland 44111

(216) 575-0777 .. **Kelley**, Lynn A '85 OfCnsl Kelley & F,LLP -1300 E 9th -Ste 1901 -Cleveland 44114 **Fx:**575-0799

(937) 855-6013 .. **Kelley**, Lynn M '63 -141 W Market -Germantown 45327
           Kelley, Michael B '03 -(Address Unavailable)

(614) 280-1100 .. **Kelley**, Michael J '81 (Keener DC&P,LPA) -88 E Broad -Ste 1750 -Columbus 43215

(330) 744-4137 .. **Kelley**, Michael J '89 (Friedman & R Co,LPA) -100 Fed Plz E -Ste 300 City Centre One -Youngstown 44503 **Fx:**744-9962

(216) 575-0777 .. **Kelley**, Michael V '82 (Kelley & F,LLP) -1300 E 9th -Ste 1901 -Cleveland 44114 **Fx:**575-0799

(216) 622-3600 .. **Kelley**, Nancy L '79 US Atty -801 W Superior -Ste 400 -Cleveland 44113 **Fx:**622-3370

(513) 651-2100 .. **Kelley**, Rebecca '97 Grtr Cincinnati YMCA -1105 Elm -Cincinnati 45202

(412) 355-2759 .. **Kelley**, Robert V Jr. '99 %DKW Law Grp -600 Grant -58th Fl -Pittsburgh, PA 15219

(216) 522-3530 .. **Kelley**, Shannon M '01 US DVA -1240 E 9th -Cleveland 44199

(216) 525-7392 .. **Kelley**, Steven K '84 -6133 Rockside Rd -Ste 208 -Independence 44131 **Fx:**643-3396

(513) 421-4225 .. **Kelley**, Terrence E '02 %Heis & W Co,LPA -817 Main -Ste 800 -Cincinnati 45202

(330) 434-2113 .. **Kelley**, Thomas '78 Armbruster KKH&B -159 S Main -Ste 720 -Akron 44308

(216) 241-5040 .. **Kelley**, Thomas G '72 -75 Pub Sq -Ste 700 -Cleveland 44113

(419) 321-6444 .. **Kelley**, Thomas J '82 (Cline C&W Co,LPA) -300 Mad Av -Ste 1100 -Toledo 43604 **Fx:**321-6430

(614) 228-5775 .. **Kelley**, Timothy M '83 -250 E Broad -Columbus 43215

(812) 933-1950 .. **Kelley**, William J II '00 (Craig K&F) -1305 Tekulve Rd -Batesville, IN 47006 **Fx:**933-1960

(574) 631-8646 .. **Kelley**, William K '90 Notre Dame Law Sch -BxR -Notre Dame, IN 46556

(940) 676-2442 .. **Kellhofer**, Jason M '02 US Air Force SJA -317 F Av Bldg 315 -Sheppard AFB, TX 76311

(330) 609-5045 .. **Kelligher**, William Chad '83 (Brutz & K,Ltd) -405 Niles Courtland Rd SE -Ste 203 -Warren 44484

(330) 253-2227 .. **Kelling**, Gilbert V Jr. '67 OfCnsl Parker LH&R,LLC -388 S Main -Ste 402 -Akron 44311 **Fx:**253-1261

(740) 654-6161 .. **Kellner**, George K Jr. '69 -419 E Main -Lancaster 43130

(937) 222-7600 .. **Kellner**, Jeffrey M '85 Chapter 13 Trustee -131 N Ludlow -Ste 900 -Dayton 45402

(216) 621-0200 .. **Kellogg**, Amy E '86 (Baker & H LLP) -1900 E 9th -Ste 3200 -Cleveland 44114 **Fx:**696-0740

(330) 674-0442 .. **Kellogg**, Jeffrey G '97 -5 S Wshngtn -Millersburg 44654

(212) 554-4240 .. **Kellogg**, John P '80 -1285 Av of Amer -35th Fl -New York, NY 10019

(419) 289-8857 .. **Kellogg**, Karen L '00 Ashland Cnty Pros -307 Orange -Ashland 44805 **Fx:**281-3865

(513) 381-9200 .. **Kellogg**, Paul J '93 OfCnsl Rendigs FK&D,LLP -One W 4th -Ste 900 -Cincinnati 45202 **Fx:**381-9206

(937) 325-1531 .. **Kellogg**, Scott K '92 Masonic Hlth Care,Inc -2655 W Natl Rd -Springfield 45504

(937) 599-7272 .. **Kellogg-Martin**, Kimberly J '84 Logan Cnty Pros -117 E Columbus Av -Ste 200 -Bellefontaine 43311 **Fx:**599-7271

(216) 443-7223 .. **Kellon**, Anthony J '89 Cuyahoga Cnty Pub Def -1200 W 3rd NW -100 Lakeside Pl -Cleveland 44113

(216) 687-6051 .. **Kelly**, Amy C '94 Medical Mtl-OH -2060 E 9th -01-10B-1900 -Cleveland 44115

(412) 434-0201 .. **Kelly**, Bernard J '02 Bashline & Hutton -210 6th Av -Ste 3500 -Pittsburgh, PA 15222

(216) 515-1660 .. **Kelly**, Brian J '94 %Frantz W LLP -127 Pub Sq -2500 Key Center -Cleveland 44114 **Fx:**515-1650

(513) 421-6630 .. **Kelly**, Charles J '65 Lindhorst & D Co,LPA -312 Walnut -Ste 2300 -Cincinnati 45202

(216) 586-3939 .. **Kelly**, Christopher M '01 (Jones D) -901 Lakeside Av -Cleveland 44114 **Fx:**579-0212

(740) 968-1800 .. **Kelly**, Claire R '03 Kelly Real Estate Appraisal -43029 Harrah -Flushing 43977

(216) 586-3939 .. **Kelly**, Dennis M '68 (Jones D) -901 Lakeside Av -Cleveland 44114 **Fx:**579-0212

(216) 696-5444 .. **Kelly**, Edwin '86 -925 Euclid Av -Huntngtn Bldg Ste 1025 -Cleveland 44115

(614) 469-1882 .. **Kelly**, Elizabeth M '94 Kephart & F LLP -207 N 4th -Columbus 43215

(614) 227-2308 .. **Kelly**, Emmett M '99 %Bricker & E LLP -100 S 3rd -Columbus 43215 **Fx:**227-2390

(513) 721-3330 .. **Kelly**, James M '76 (Robbins KP&T) -7 W 7th -Ste 1400 -Cincinnati 45202

(513) 396-6339 .. **Kelly**, Jeffrey B '78 -6319 Iris Av -Cincinnati 45213

(419) 213-4001 .. **Kelly**, Jill B '82 Lucas Cnty Brd of Elections -One Govt Ctr -Ste 300 -Toledo 43604

(937) 592-2776 .. **Kelly**, John B '51 -116 E Court -Bellefontaine 43311

(614) 280-1100 .. **Kelly**, John T '87 %Keener DC&P,LPA -88 E Broad -Ste 1750 -Columbus 43215

(614) 223-7928 .. **Kelly**, Jon F '76 Cnsl SBC -150 E Gay -Rm 4-A -Columbus 43215 **Fx:**223-5955

(614) 241-2174 .. **Kelly**, Joseph A '91 -118 E Main -Columbus 43215

(440) 333-0637 .. **Kelly**, Karen M '85 -20647 Beaconsfld Blvd -Rocky River 44116

(937) 444-2563 .. **Kelly**, Katherine M '02 %Kelly & W Co,LPA -108 S High -Mount Orab 45154

(937) 562-6249 .. **Kelly**, Kristen '95 Greene Cnty Dom Rltns Ct -595 Ledbetter Rd -Xenia 45385 **Fx:**562-6233

(330) 385-5595 .. **Kelly**, Kyde L '58 -128 W 5th -East Liverpool 43920 **Fx:**385-7846

(614) 466-5638 .. **Kelly**, Lori M '94 OH Dept of Educ -25 S Front -MS 104 -Columbus 43215

(216) 671-2888 .. **Kelly**, Mary W '87 -4367 Rocky Rvr Dr -Cleveland 44135

(216) 752-1022 .. **Kelly**, Michael F '78 Walter H Drane Co -20600 Chagrin Blvd -Ste 420 -Shaker Heights 44122 **Fx:**752-7935

(937) 444-2563 .. **Kelly**, Michael P '73 (Kelly & W Co,LPA) -108 S High -Mount Orab 45154

(216) 664-2887 .. **Kelly**, Nancy A '85 Dept of Law -601 Lakeside Av -Rm 106 City Hall -Cleveland 44114 **Fx:**664-2663

(216) 443-7800 .. **Kelly**, Patrick M '92 Cuyahoga Cnty Pros -1200 Ontario -8th Fl -Cleveland 44113 **Fx:**698-2270

(502) 0791 .. **Kelly**, R Patrick '73 -526 Superior Av -#530 -Cleveland 44114

(513) 603-7991 .. **Kelly**, Richard B '80 Ohio Casualty Corp -9450 Seward Rd -Fairfield 45014

(513) 531-3636 .. **Kelly**, Robert G '77 (R Kelly Co LPA) -4353 Mntgmry Rd -Norwood 45212

(216) 861-4533 .. **Kelly**, Sandra Maurer '86 (Ray RC&D PLL) -1717 E 9th -Cleveland 44114 **Fx:**861-4568

(216) 592-5000 .. **Kelly**, Scott J '98 %Tucker E&W LLP -925 Euclid Av -1150 Huntngtn Bldg -Cleveland 44115 **Fx:**592-5009

(216) 696-0606 .. **Kelly**, Sean S '02 RE Sweeney Co,LPA -55 Pub Sq -Ste 1500 -Cleveland 44113 **Fx:**696-0679
           Kelly, Shawn T '03 -(Address Unavailable)

(216) 622-8200 .. **Kelly**, Sheryl K '80 Calfee H&G LLP -800 Superior Av -Ste 1400 -Cleveland 44114 **Fx:**241-0816

(614) 478-6000 .. **Kelly**, Suzanne E '88 Karr & S Co,LPA -1 Easton Oval -Ste 550 -Columbus 43219

(440) 846-0000 .. **Kelly**, Thomas A III '74 (TA Kelly,LLC) -11221 Pearl Rd -Strongsville 44136 **Fx:**846-9770

(440) 846-0000 .. **Kelly**, Thomas J '02 OfCnsl TA Kelly,LLC -11221 Pearl Rd -Strongsville 44136 **Fx:**846-9770

(440) 442-6677 .. **Kelly**, Thomas R '88 Elk & E Co,LPA -6100 Parkland Blvd -Mayfield Heights 44124 **Fx:**442-7944

(937) 444-2563 .. **Kelly**, Timothy J '91 Kelly & W Co,LPA -108 S High -Mount Orab 45154

(330) 376-5756 .. **Kelly**, Timothy M '83 Emershaw M&S -120 E Mill -#437 -Akron 44308 **Fx:**762-5980

(937) 444-2563 .. **Kelly**, William B '84 Cuyahoga Cnty Pub Def -1200 W 3rd NW -100 Lakeside Pl -Cleveland 44113

(614) 227-2000 .. **Kelly**, William J Jr. '76 (Porter WM&A LLP) -41 S High -Columbus 43215 **Fx:**227-2100

(216) 566-5768 .. **Kelly Grasso**, Karen '94 %Thompson H LLP -127 Pub Sq -3900 Key Ctr -Cleveland 44114 **Fx:**566-5800

(513) 733-5683 .. **Kelly-Schilling**, Sandra '79 Glendale & Evendal Pros -3660 Sherbrooke Dr -Cincinnati 45241

(614) 246-1000 .. **Kelm**, Russell A '71 -37 W Broad -Ste 860 -Columbus 43215 **Fx:**246-8110
           Kelsey, Andrea M '85 -95 Tibet Rd -Columbus 43202

(614) 228-8662 .. **Kelsey**, Charles E '75 -155 W Main -#1706 -Columbus 43215

(614) 644-8390 .. **Kelsey,** Mark G '82 OH DOT Div of Contract Adm -1980 W Broad -Columbus 43223

(419) 625-7377 .. **Kelsey,** Robert T '82 -326 E Market -Sandusky 44870

(614) 228-1593 .. **Kelso,** Daniel J '76 OH Ins Inst -172 E State -Ste 201 -Columbus 43215

(706) 821-4024 .. **Kelsven,** Frederick D '78 MorganStanley -1301 Broad -Augusta, GA 30901

(937) 332-6920 .. **Kemmer,** Aubrey M '78 Miami Cnty Mun Ct -201 W Main -Troy 45373

(419) 245-4742 .. **Kemnitz,** Walter R Jr. '90 %Lucas Cnty Cmn Pleas Ct -700 Adams -Ste 110 -Toledo 43624

(419) 394-3341 .. **Kemp,** Barrett G '59 -Bx335 -Saint Marys 45885

(614) 846-5069 .. **Kemp,** Daniel W '70 -830 Gatehse Ln -Columbus 43235

(770) 925-0111 .. **Kemp,** Donna N '79 (Thompson OK&N,PC) -40 Tech Pkwy S -Ste 300 -Norcross, GA 30092 **Fx:**925-8597

(330) 996-3190 .. **Kemp,** Edward G '68 Akron Beacon Jrnl -44 E Exchange -Bx640 -Akron 44309

(614) 224-2678 .. **Kemp,** Harold R '74 Kemp SR&L Co,LPA -88 W Mound -Columbus 43215 **Fx:**469-7170

(614) 224-2678 .. **Kemp,** Jacqueline L '96 %Kemp SR&L Co,LPA -88 W Mound -Columbus 43215 **Fx:**469-7170

(602) 379-7108 .. **Kemp,** Raymond W '73 US HUD -1 N Central Av -6th Fl -Phoenix, AZ 85004

(614) 224-2678 .. **Kemp Schaeffer Rowe & Lardiere Co,LPA** -88 W Mound -Columbus 43215 **Fx:**469-7170

(419) 423-4321 .. **Kemp,** Thomas P '78 (Firmin S&H Co,LPA) -220 W Sandusky -Bx963 -Findlay 45839 **Fx:**423-8484

(801) 584-5761 .. **Kemper,** Kim R '81 -500 Huntsman Way -Salt Lake City, UT 84108

(513) 831-3223 .. **Kemper,** Richard J '57 -805 Wallace Av -Milford 45150

(614) 224-9221 .. **Kempf,** Christopher J '84 (Bloomfield & K) -199 S 5th -Columbus 43215

(513) 977-8200 .. **Kemphaus,** Nicholas J '04 %Dinsmore & S LLP -255 E 5th -Ste 1900 -Cincinnati 45202 **Fx:**977-8141

(888) 460-4332 .. **Kempic,** Mark R '91 Columbia Gas of PA -501 Tech Dr -Canonsburg, PA 15317

(412) 338-7884 .. **Kenawell,** Helen M '78 Deloitte & Touche -2500 One PPG Pk Ct -26th Fl -Pittsburgh, PA 15222

(513) 627-0081 .. **Kendall,** Dara M '97 Procter & Gamble -11810 E Miami Rvr Rd -Bx538707 -Cincinnati 45253

(614) 469-1301 .. **Kendall,** Darin G '82 Chorpenning G&P Co,LPA -585 S Front -Ste 250 -Columbus 43215

(216) 622-8200 .. **Kendall,** Laura K '04 %Calfee H&G LLP -800 Superior Av -Ste 1400 -Cleveland 44114 **Fx:**241-0816

(419) 229-4077 .. **Kendall,** William G '73 -212 N Elizabeth -Ste 410 -Lima 45801

(937) 440-5960 .. **Kendall,** Anthony E '96 Miami Cnty Pros -201 W Main -Troy 45373 **Fx:**440-5961

(216) 621-3346 .. **Kendis,** James D '66 (Kendis & Assoc Co,LPA) -614 Superior Av W -15th Fl Rckfllr Bldg -Cleveland 44113 **Fx:**621-3672

(216) 621-3346 .. **Kendis,** Robert D '69 (Kendis & Assoc Co,LPA) -614 Superior Av W -15th Fl Rckfllr Bldg -Cleveland 44113 **Fx:**621-3672

(937) 433-4090 .. **Kendo,** Thomas W Jr. '92 (Gammell HK&R LLP) -7925 Paragon Rd -Dayton 45459 **Fx:**433-1510

(513) 946-3877 .. **Kendrick,** Matthew J '79 Hamilton Cnty Pub Def -230 E 9th -3rd Fl -Cincinnati 45202 **Fx:**946-3707

(847) 634-9100 .. **Kendrick,** Matthew J '89 Mitsubishi -600 Barclay Blvd -Lincolnshire, IL 60069

(859) 578-2703 .. **Kenkel,** Stephen P '89 -626 Buttermilk Pike -Crescent Springs, KY 41017

(614) 469-3939 .. **Kennard,** J Todd '97 %Jones D -325 John H McConnell Blvd -Ste 600 -Bx165017 -Columbus 43216 **Fx:**461-4198

(440) 333-8960 .. **Kenneally,** Sean M '98 %Kenneally & Assoc Co -20525 Ctr Ridge Rd -Ste 505 -Rocky River 44116 **Fx:**333-8170

(440) 333-8960 .. **Kenneally,** Terrence J '78 (Kenneally & Assoc Co) -20525 Ctr Ridge Rd -Ste 505 -Rocky River 44116 **Fx:**333-8170

(740) 345-3431 .. **Kennedy,** Ann M '81 (Reese PD&M,PLL) -36 N 2nd -Bx919 -Newark 43058 **Fx:**349-5116

(330) 262-7555 .. **Kennedy,** Charles A '69 (Kennedy CK&B) -558 N Market -Wooster 44691

(419) 238-0180 .. **Kennedy,** Charles F III '79 (C Kennedy II Co,LPA) -101 E Main -Van Wert 45891

(216) 586-3939 .. **Kennedy,** Charles M '80 Cnsl Jones D -901 Lakeside Av -Cleveland 44114 **Fx:**579-0212

(330) 497-0389 .. **Kennedy,** Christopher P '02 Russell Law Ofcs -601 S Main -Canton 44720

(202) 879-3653 .. **Kennedy,** Christopher T '02 %Jones Day -51 Louisiana Av NW -Washington, DC 20001 **Fx:**626-1700

(330) 262-7555 .. **Kennedy Cicconetti Knowlton & Buytendyk** -558 N Market -Wooster 44691

(614) 221-8401 .. **Kennedy & Colasurd,LPA** -30 Spruce -3rd Fl -Columbus 43215 **Fx:**222-4799

(330) 825-2477 .. **Kennedy,** David R '86 (Walkley K&G Co,LPA) -4071 S Cleveland-Massillon Rd -Bx1080 -Norton 44203 **Fx:**825-2029

(614) 463-9770 .. **Kennedy,** Douglas M '80 (Roetzel & A,LPA) -155 E Broad -Natl City Ctr 12th Fl -Columbus 43215 **Fx:**463-9792

(330) 492-8717 .. **Kennedy,** Edward T '00 %Buckingham D&B,LLP -4518 Fulton Dr NW -Bx35548 -Canton 44735 **Fx:**492-9625

(440) 333-3949 .. **Kennedy,** Edwin A '56 -235 Yacht Club Dr -Rocky River 44116

.. **Kennedy,** Elizabeth N '03 -4806 High Oaks -Toledo 43623

(513) 579-2538 .. **Kennedy,** James C '76 Amer Fin Grp,Inc -1 E 4th -Ste 919 -Cincinnati 45202

(440) 546-0100 .. **Kennedy,** James D '91 %DC Jackson Co,LPA -20 Eagle Valley Ct -Broadview Heights 44147 **Fx:**546-0189

(412) 434-0201 .. **Kennedy,** James E '99 Bashline & Hutton -210 6th Av -Ste 3500 -Pittsburgh, PA 15222

(614) 464-6400 .. **Kennedy,** James P '60 OfCnsl Vorys SS&P LLP -52 E Gay -Bx1008 -Columbus 43216 **Fx:**464-6350

(614) 221-8401 .. **Kennedy,** Janice M '81 (Kennedy & C,LPA) -30 Spruce -3rd Fl -Columbus 43215 **Fx:**222-4799

(513) 489-4157 .. **Kennedy,** John T '79 (Kennedy & K Co,LPA) -10723 Mntgmry Rd -Ste 1 -Cincinnati 45242

(614) 451-9660 .. **Kennedy,** John W '89 -1570 Fishinger Rd -Columbus 43221

(216) 875-3568 .. **Kennedy,** Kathleen M '96 Pricewaterhouse Coopers -200 Pub Sq -27th Fl -Cleveland 44114

(614) 488-1161 .. **Kennedy & Knoll** -3040 Riverside Dr -Ste 103 -Columbus 43221

(313) 962-5909 .. **Kennedy,** L Neal '99 (Feikens SK&G PC) -660 Woodward Av -Ste 700 -Detroit, MI 48226 **Fx:**962-3125

(216) 363-4500 .. **Kennedy,** Margaret A '76 (Benesch FC&A LLP) -200 Pub Sq -Ste 2300 -Cleveland 44114 **Fx:**363-4588

(303) 292-2525 .. **Kennedy,** Mark F '77 (Wheeler T&K,PC) -1801 Calif -Ste 3600 -Denver, CO 80202 **Fx:**294-1879

(419) 562-7958 .. **Kennedy,** Michael A '66 -107 E Mansfld -Bx430 -Bucyrus 44820

(513) 732-2040 .. **Kennedy,** Michael A '78 (Rodenberg & K,Ltd) -70 N Riverside Dr -Batavia 45103

(614) 757-5000 .. **Kennedy,** Michael P '93 %Cardinal Hlth -7000 Cardinal Pl -Dublin 43017

(614) 488-1161 .. **Kennedy,** Nicholas E '98 (Kennedy & K) -3040 Riverside Dr -Ste 103 -Columbus 43221

(419) 337-9240 .. **Kennedy,** Paul N '95 Fulton Cnty Pros -123 Cthse Plz -Wauseon 43567

(419) 562-4075 .. **Kennedy Purdy Hoeffel & Gernert** -111 Rensselaer -Bx191 -Bucyrus 44820 **Fx:**562-7850

(740) 532-0814 .. **Kennedy,** Richard D '88 (Kennedy & K) -419 Center -Ironton 45638

(216) 781-1111 .. **Kennedy,** Robert Eric '80 Weisman G&W Co,LPA -101 Prospect Av -1600 Mdlnd Bldg -Cleveland 44115 **Fx:**781-6747

(614) 326-1222 .. **Kennedy,** Robert G '92 (R Kennedy Co,LPA) -4924B Reed Rd -Columbus 43220

(614) 644-7381 .. **Kennedy,** Robert S '90 OH Dept of Commerce -50 W Broad -Wage & Hour Bureau -Columbus 43266

(419) 537-2944 .. **Kennedy,** Robin M '70 Univ of Toledo Law Schl -2801 W Bancroft -Toledo 43606

(330) 376-2700 .. **Kennedy,** Ryan P '04 %Roetzel & A,LPA -222 S Main -Akron 44308 **Fx:**376-4577

(419) 734-0235 .. **Kennedy,** Shelly L '89 -318 Madison -Port Clinton 43452

(513) 489-4157 .. **Kennedy,** Sherri M '79 (Kennedy & K Co,LPA) -10723 Mntgmry Rd -Ste 1 -Cincinnati 45242

(216) 931-6000 .. **Kennedy,** Stephanie E '98 %Ulmer & B LLP -1300 E 9th -Ste 900 Penton Media Bldg -Cleveland 44114 **Fx:**931-6001

(216) 583-1504 .. **Kennedy,** Terence M '90 Ernst & Young LLP -925 Euclid Av -Ste 1300 -Cleveland 44115

(330) 434-3461 .. **Kennedy,** Traci F '84 Legal Def -One Cascade Plz -Ste 1940 -Akron 44308

(740) 532-0814 .. **Kennedy,** William D '57 (Kennedy & K) -419 Center -Ironton 45638

(419) 255-6252 .. **Kennedy,** William R '51 -520 Mad Av -506 Spitzer Bldg -Toledo 43604

(216) 433-2314 .. **Kennemuth,** Jerald J '78 NASA-Lewis Rsrch Ctr -21000 Brookpark Rd -Cleveland 44135

(330) 376-1242 .. **Kenner,** Phillip L '65 Renner KGBT&W,LPA -106 S Main -4th Fl Natl Twr -Akron 44308 **Fx:**376-9646

(937) 239-2711 .. **Kennett,** David H '82 -Bx41195 -Dayton 45441

(216) 752-1022 .. **Kenneweg,** William W '70 Walter H Drane Co -20600 Chagrin Blvd -Ste 420 -Shaker Heights 44122 **Fx:**752-7935

(216) 581-0500 .. **Kenney,** Carol A '85 Marymount Hsptl -12300 McCracken Rd -Garfield Heights 44125

(740) 345-5171 .. **Kenney,** Deborah L '83 -1 S Park Pl -Newark 43055

(216) 621-1500 .. **Kenney,** James Brian '01 %Kehoe & Assoc LLP -1940 E 6th -900 Baker Bldg -Cleveland 44114 **Fx:**621-1551

(513) 721-1504 .. **Kenney,** Jeffrey T '91 Droder & M Co,LPA -125 W Cntrl Pkwy -Cincinnati 45202 **Fx:**721-0310

(248) 355-5555 .. **Kenney,** Jeremiah J '91 Fieger FS&K -19390 W 10 Mile Rd -Southfield, MI 48075

(419) 517-7000 .. **Kenney,** Kevin J '81 (Kenney & N,Ltd) -5470 Main -Ste 300 -Sylvania 43560 **Fx:**517-7001

(216) 241-5300 .. **Kenney,** Mary A '87 %D Dreyfuss Co,LPA -1801 E 9th -Ste 740 -Cleveland 44114

(419) 517-7000 .. **Kenney & Niehaus,Ltd** -5470 Main -Ste 300 -Sylvania 43560 **Fx:**517-7001

(216) 622-0410 .. **Kenney,** Richard C Jr. '79 -55 Pub Sq -Ste 1550 -Cleveland 44113

(614) 481-8608 .. **Kenney-Pfalzer,** Susan M '03 %KM Halliburton-Cohen & Assoc -1776 W Lane Av -Ste B -Upper Arlington 43221 **Fx:**481-9795

(630) 420-2953 .. **Kenniff,** Thomas C '66 -1504 Maple Hills Ct -Naperville, IL 60563

(216) 368-2766 .. **Kenny,** Maureen Sheridan '98 CWRU Law Schl -11075 East Blvd -Cleveland 44106

(216) 443-7800 .. **Kenny,** Michael A Jr. '98 Cuyahoga Cnty Pros -1200 Ontario -8th Fl -Cleveland 44113 **Fx:**698-2270

(216) 765-1414 .. **Kenny,** Robert E III '82 -2367 Loyola Rd -University Heights 44118

(614) 461-0256 .. **Kent,** Joel S '87 Ofc Disciplinary Cnsl -250 Civic Ctr Dr -Ste 325 -Columbus 43215

(614) 248-7688 .. **Kent,** Megan V '94 Bank 1 -1111 Polaris Pkwy -OH1-0152 -Columbus 43271

(304) 485-8500 .. **Kent,** Robert J '80 Bowles RMG&L -501 Avry -5th Fl -Bx49 -Parkersburg, WV 26102

(216) 514-1413 .. **Kent,** Stanley B '50 -23351 Chagrin Blvd -#310 -Beachwood 44122

.. **Kentner,** David L '73 -(Address Unavailable)

(419) 738-1222 .. **Kentner,** Matthew J '92 -110 W Mechanic -Wapakoneta 45895

(419) 423-4676 .. **Kentris,** George L '76 (Kentris R&C,LLC) -2738 N Main -Ste A -Findlay 45840

(740) 477-2536 .. **Kenworthy,** Gary D '80 -443 N Court -Bx574 -Circleville 43113 **Fx:**477-6971

(515) 288-6440 .. **Kenworthy,** Martin J '89 %Duncan Law Firm -400 Locust -Ste 380 -Des Moines, IA 50309

(937) 225-7233 .. **Kenyon,** Gregory G '93 SSA-OHA -110 N Main -Ste 800 -Dayton 45402

(216) 363-1400 .. **Keogh,** Kevin R '83 (Buckley K,LPA) -600 E Superior Av -Ste 1400 -Cleveland 44114 **Fx:**579-1020

(216) 664-4990 .. **Keough,** Kathleen Ann '88 Mun Ct Judge -1200 Ontario -Cleveland 44113

(614) 469-1882 .. **Kephart & Fisher LLP** -207 N 4th -Columbus 43215

(740) 392-2900 .. **Kepko,** William J '86 (W Kepko Co LPA) -1 E Vine -Mount Vernon 43050

(614) 757-7992 ..**Kepner,** Kristina S '96 Cardinal Hlth -7000 Cardinal Pl
-Dublin 43017

(216) 621-0200 ..**Kepple,** Brandon E '03 %Baker & H LLP -1900 E 9th -Ste 3200
-Cleveland 44114 **Fx:**696-0740

(330) 864-3323 ..**Kepple,** Donald P '75 -1826 Breezewood Dr -Akron 44313

(304) 233-3100 ..**Kepple,** Mark '98 Bailey & W,PLLC -1219 Chapline
-Wheeling, WV 26003 **Fx:**233-0201

(216) 221-3100 ..**Kerber,** Anthony W '73 -14701 Detroit Av -Ste 540
-Lakewood 44107

(419) 223-8511 ..**Kerber,** Dennis S '91 Allen Cnty Dom Rltns Ct -301 N Main
-Bx1243 -Lima 45802

(937) 339-1500 ..**Kerber,** Grant D '97 (Shipman D&L) -215 W Water -Bx310
-Troy 45373 **Fx:**339-1519

(614) 221-5121 ..**Kerber,** Jacques C '75 OH League of Fncl Inst -37 W Broad
-Ste 1001 -Columbus 43215

(216) 687-2284 ..**Kerber,** Sandra J '82 CSU-Marshall Cllg of Law -2121 Euclid Av
-LB138 -Cleveland 44115 **Fx:**687-6881

(614) 227-2356 ..**Kerber,** Steven R '76 (Bricker & E LLP) -100 S 3rd
-Columbus 43215 **Fx:**227-2390

Kerek, Wayne L '83 -Bx991 -Brunswick 44212

(740) 373-7624 ..**Kerenyi,** Mark '96 Washington Cnty Pros -205 Putnam
-Marietta 45750

(440) 965-7520 ..**Keressi,** John S Jr. '79 Lorain Cnty Hlth Dept
-9880 S Murray Ridge Rd -Elyria 44035

(419) 255-5990 ..**Kerger,** Richard M '74 (Kerger & K) -33 S Mich -Ste 201
-Toledo 43602 **Fx:**255-5997

(216) 861-6191 ..**Kerka,** Kathryn A '85 %Rodgers & Co,LPA -45 Prospect Av W
-1600 Guildhall Landmark Ofc Twrs -Cleveland 44115
Fx:861-4699

(216) 771-1430 ..**Kern,** Anna M '98 %Masters & Assoc,LPA -1111 Superior Av
-Cleveland 44114 **Fx:**771-2070

(614) 223-9300 ..**Kern,** Benjamen E '03 %Benesch FC&A LLP -88 E Broad -Ste 900
-Columbus 43215 **Fx:**223-9330

(614) 466-5610 ..**Kern,** Charles D '00 Atty Gen -150 E Gay -Columbus 43215
Fx:752-2732

(330) 376-5300 ..**Kern,** David '90 (Buckingham D&B,LLP) -50 S Main -Bx1500
-Akron 44309 **Fx:**258-6559

(513) 381-0656 ..**Kern,** David G '00 %Kohnen & P LLP -201 E 5th -Ste 800
-Cincinnati 45202 **Fx:**381-5823

(513) 721-4500 ..**Kern,** David O '97 %Patsfall Y&P LLC -1 W 4th -Ste 1800
-Cincinnati 45202 **Fx:**639-7554

(216) 348-5400 ..**Kern,** Heather M '04 %McDonald H Co,LPA -600 Superior Av E
-Ste 2100 -Cleveland 44114 **Fx:**348-5474

(216) 344-1033 ..**Kern,** Keith W '75 -1301 E 9th -Ste 1420 -Cleveland 44114
Fx:344-9011

(513) 651-6800 ..**Kern,** Melissa A '01 %Frost BT LLC -201 E 5th -2200 PNC Ctr
-Cincinnati 45202 **Fx:**651-6981

(216) 622-3600 ..**Kern,** Robert W '82 US Atty -801 W Superior -Ste 400
-Cleveland 44113 **Fx:**622-3370

(614) 466-2766 ..**Kern,** Timothy J '86 Atty Gen -30 E Broad -Columbus 43215
Fx:644-7060

(330) 535-3882 ..**Kernan,** Joseph M '93 -333 S Main -Ste 401 -Akron 44308

(740) 385-2121 ..**Kernen,** Willard J '77 -158 E Main -Bx388 -Logan 43138
Fx:385-2122

(440) 933-6278 ..**Kerner,** James B '94 (JB Kerner Co,LPA) -525 Avon Belden Rd
-Avon Lake 44012 **Fx:**933-4309

(440) 395-3693 ..**Kerner,** William J Jr. '91 Progressive Ins Co -6300 Wilson Mills Rd
-#N72A -Mayfield Village 44143

(440) 933-6461 ..**Kerner,** William J Sr. '71 -525 Avon Belden Rd -Avon Lake 44012
Fx:933-4309

(440) 843-5320 ..**Kerns,** Brian D '86 Kerns H&P -7123 Pearl Rd -Ste 304
-Middleburg Heights 44130

(440) 843-5320 ..**Kerns Hurt & Proe** -7123 Pearl Rd -Ste 304
-Middleburg Heights 44130

(614) 486-2700 ..**Kerns,** Keith R '00 OH Dental Assn -1370 Dublin Rd
-Columbus 43215

(614) 462-5406 ..**Kerns,** R Kevin '83 (Kegler BH&R) -65 E State -Ste 1800
-Columbus 43215 **Fx:**464-2634

(614) 785-9420 ..**Kerns,** Ralph A '81 -6797 N High -Ste 325 -Worthington 43085
Fx:785-9490

(614) 268-7250 ..**Kerns-Bidwell,** Amy T '80 -4699 N High -Columbus 43214

(330) 376-7446 ..**Kerper,** Robert E Jr. '78 -One Cascade Plz -20th Fl -Akron 44308
Fx:376-1442

(614) 242-1000 ..**Kerpsack,** Robert W Jr. '89 -21 E State -Ste 300
-Columbus 43215

(513) 381-5700 ..**Kerr,** David L '73 Ritter & R,LLC -105 E 4th -Ste 1200
-Cincinnati 45202 **Fx:**381-0014

(330) 675-6682 ..**Kerr,** Dax W A '02 11th Dist Ct of Appeals -111 High NE
-Warren 44481

(216) 781-5515 ..**Kerr,** Henry V '74 Hermann C&S,LLP -1301 E 9th -Ste 500
-Cleveland 44114 **Fx:**781-1030

(330) 764-7253 ..**Kerr,** Lisa M '93 1st Merit Bk,NA -39 Pub Sq -Trust Dept -Medina
44256

(513) 241-7111 ..**Kerr,** Maggie '00 %O'Connor A&L Co,LPA -1014 Vine -22nd Fl
-Cincinnati 45202 **Fx:**241-7197

(937) 492-6125 ..**Kerrigan Boller Stevenson Goettemoeler & Biegel**
-126 N Main Av -Bx987 -Sidney 45365

(937) 492-6125 ..**Kerrigan,** Thomas W II '84 (Kerrigan BSG&B) -126 N Main Av
-Bx987 -Sidney 45365

(419) 872-6600 ..**Kerscher,** Jeffrey M '93 (Handwork & K) -900 W South Boundary
-Bldg 8-B -Perrysburg 43551

(614) 475-6440 ..**Kerscher,** Martin J '77 Bd of Mental Rtrdtn -2879 Johnstown Rd
-Columbus 43219

(614) 462-2229 ..**Kerschner,** Karl '01 %Schottenstein Z&D -250 West -Bx165020
-Columbus 43216 **Fx:**462-5135

(614) 459-4287 ..**Kersell,** Nancy S '85 -4794 Dierker Rd -Columbus 43220

(216) 241-3470 ..**Kersey,** James M '73 -1148 Euclid Av -Ste 300 -Cleveland 44115

(330) 535-5711 ..**Kersker,** Linda B '72 (Brouse M) -106 S Main -500 First Natl Twr
-Akron 44308 **Fx:**253-8601

(859) 746-4396 ..**Kersteiner,** James A '89 Toyota Motor Mfg NA -25 Atl Av
-Erlanger, KY 41018

(216) 831-9110 ..**Kertesz,** Ronnie M '81 -3439 W Brainard -Woodmere 44122

(440) 603-2301 ..**Kerwin,** Timothy L '91 Progressive Ins Co -6055 Parkland Blvd
-Mayfield Heights 44124

(440) 356-5775 ..**Keshock,** John P '89 -20325 Ctr Ridge Rd -Ste 512
-Rocky River 44116

(216) 755-5649 ..**Kessinger,** Kevin J '97 Developers Diversified Rlty Corp
-3300 Enterprise Pkwy -Beachwood 44122

(614) 764-0681 ..**Kessler,** David S '89 Blaugrund H&M,Inc -5455 Rings Rd -Ste 500
-Dublin 43017 **Fx:**764-0774

(614) 469-3939 ..**Kessler,** Elizabeth P '93 (Jones D) -325 John H McConnell Blvd
-Ste 600 -Bx165017 -Columbus 43216 **Fx:**461-4198

(513) 785-5805 ..**Kessler,** Eva D '73 Butler Cnty Dom Rltns Ct -315 High
-Butler Cnty Cthse -Hamilton 45011

(513) 361-0200 ..**Kessler,** Gregory S '96 %Roetzel & A,LPA -250 E 5th
-310 Chiquita Ctr -Cincinnati 45202 **Fx:**361-0335

(614) 221-0240 ..**Kessler,** Marc J '92 (Hahn L&P LLP) -65 E State -Ste 1400
-Columbus 43215 **Fx:**221-5909

(937) 449-6810 ..**Kessler,** Philip E '99 %Porter WM&A LLP -1 S Main -Ste 1600
-Dayton 45402 **Fx:**449-6820

Kessler, Robert S '61 -2483 E Erie Av -Lorain 44052

(614) 888-3185 ..**Kessler,** Russell W '80 (Kessler & B Co,LPA) -7650 Rvrs Edge Dr
-Ste 101 -Columbus 43235

(330) 456-8341 ..**Kessler,** Terrence P '75 (Black MS&A,LPA) -220 Market Av S
-Ste 1000 -Canton 44702 **Fx:**456-5756

(216) 621-0200 ..**Kestner,** R Steven '79 (Baker & H LLP) -1900 E 9th -Ste 3200
-Cleveland 44114 **Fx:**696-0740

(419) 865-1251 ..**Kestner,** Tara J '96 Wagoner & S,Ltd -7445 Airport Hwy
-Holland 43528 **Fx:**866-8798

Ketcham, Justin A '04 -(Address Unavailable)

(614) 444-3900 ..**Ketcham,** Richard S '74 (Ketcham & K) -755 S High
-Columbus 43206

(216) 479-8500 ..**Ketler,** Suzanne K '01 %Squire S&D LLP -127 Pub Sq
-4900 Key Twr -Cleveland 44114 **Fx:**479-8780

Ketron, Douglas L '04 -(Address Unavailable)

(330) 479-4371 ..**Kettler,** John Scott '76 FirstMerit Bank -4100 Dressler Rd NW
-Bx36059 -Canton 44735

(330) 830-1725 ..**Kettler,** Richard T '74 Mun Ct Judge -2 James Duncan Plz
-Massillon 44646

(330) 436-2750 ..**Kettlewell,** Charles J '00 C Kettlewell & Assoc
-150 E Wilson Bridge Rd -Ste 200 -Worthington 43085

Keune, Grant M '91 -25342 Appaloosa Ct -Perrysburg 43551

(312) 560-2148 ..**Key,** Jeffery A '82 -150 N Mich Av -Ste 1115 -Chicago, IL 60601

(216) 241-4525 ..**Keyes,** Robert L '54 -50 Pub Sq -Ste 3500 -Cleveland 44113

(513) 853-4841 ..**Keyes,** Royal M '72 Nrth Side Bank & Trust Co -4125 Hmltn Av
-Cincinnati 45223

(859) 291-9900 ..**Keys,** Alice G '02 (Taliaferro MSC&K,PLLC) -1005 Mad Av -Bx468
-Covington, KY 41012

(513) 349-1678 ..**Keys,** James G Jr. '76 (J Keys Co,LPA) -7442 Great Waters Ln
-West Chester 45069 **Fx:**759-9899

(440) 329-5725 ..**Keys,** John R '86 Lorain Co Common Pleas Ct -308 2nd
-Lorain Cnty Cthse -Elyria 44035

(440) 323-7946 ..**Keys,** Michael B '78 -263 Vassar Av -Elyria 44035

(216) 592-5000 ..**Keyse-Walker,** Irene C '82 (Tucker E&W LLP) -925 Euclid Av
-1150 Huntngtn Bldg -Cleveland 44115 **Fx:**592-5009

(440) 934-3700 ..**Keyse-Walker,** John L '81 (Fauver K-W&D) -5333 Meadow Ln Ct
-Elyria 44035 **Fx:**934-3708

(614) 338-0163 ..**Keyser,** Donald G '79 -3723 Birchtree Ln -Columbus 43232

(419) 526-2301 ..**Keyser,** George R '73 -44 Park Av W -Ste 20 -Mansfield 44902

(606) 259-1900 ..**Keyser,** Gregory A '86 (Getty K&M LLP) -250 W Main
-1900 Lex Fncl Ctr -Lexington, KY 40507

(610) 792-1695 ..**Keyser,** Polly M '88 -206 Springhaven Cir -Royersford, PA 19468

(614) 365-2700 ..**Keyser,** Raymond C '02 %Squire S&D LLP -41 S High
-1300 Huntngtn Ctr -Columbus 43215 **Fx:**365-2499

(440) 639-4494 ..**Khan,** Gulam A '93 US Endoscopy -5976 Heisley Rd
-Mentor 44060

(614) 462-5400 ..**Khan,** Rasheeda Z '02 %Kegler BH&R -65 E State -Ste 1800
-Columbus 43215 **Fx:**464-2634

(614) 459-6331 ..**Khasawneh,** Rateb M '00 (Rasul & K Co,LPA)
-1170 Old Henderson Rd -Ste 109 -Columbus 43220
Fx:538-1806

(330) 792-1063 ..**Khavari,** Bijan A '93 Industrial Commssn of OH -242 Fed Plz W
-Ste 303 -Youngstown 44503

Khayat, Saadideen I '69 -(Address Unavailable)

(614) 857-9590 ..**Khorrami,** Mina N '92 MN Khorrami -115 W Main -Ste 400
-Columbus 43215 **Fx:**228-0701

(304) 845-9750 ..**Khourey,** Louis H Jr. '74 Gold K&T LC -510 Tomlinson Av
-Moundsville, WV 26041

(216) 514-5997 ..**Khoury,** Alisa K '99 %Margulies & L -30100 Chagrin Blvd -Ste 250
-Pepper Pike 44124 **Fx:**514-5996

(216) 520-0088 ..**Khoury,** Lisa N '01 Pepple & W Ltd -5005 Rockside Rd -Ste 260
-Cleveland 44131 **Fx:**520-0044

Khoury, Nicole I '02 -3818 Frampton Dr -Toledo 43614

(614) 645-7483 ..**Khoury,** Paul T '99 City Pros -375 S High -7th Fl -Columbus 43215

Khoury, Tania M '02 -(Address Unavailable)

Khula, Bruce '03 -(Address Unavailable)

(212) 819-8200 ..**Khvesenya,** Victor '95 White & C -1155 Av of Amer -New
York, NY 10036

(419) 636-5951 ..**Kiacz,** Joseph R '73 -914 W High -Bryan 43506 **Fx:**633-9163

(614) 365-2700 ..**Kibbey,** Thomas F '02 %Squire S&D LLP -41 S High
-1300 Huntngtn Ctr -Columbus 43215 **Fx:**365-2499

(330) 424-9383 ..**Kibler,** Richard E '86 -37½ N Park Av -Lisbon 44432

(419) 994-4892 ..**Kick,** Erin R '98 (Kick & G) -133 S Market -Loudonville 44842
Fx:994-4892

(614) 469-3200 ..**Kidd,** Melissa L '99 %Thompson H LLP -10 W Broad -Ste 700
-Columbus 43215 **Fx:**469-3361

(330) 310-3802 ..**Kidd,** Michael Scott '02 -159 S Main -Ste 400 -Akron 44308

(440) 392-0147 ..**Kidd,** Patricia A '99 Fair Housing Resource Cntr Inc -54 S State
-Ste 303 -Painesville 44077

(419) 241-2900 ..**Kidd,** Tracy L '99 %Baran PTF&T Co,LPA -608 Mad Av -Ste 1620
-Toledo 43604 **Fx:**241-3002

(614) 278-7043 ..**Kidder,** Charles L '90 Consolidated Stores Corp -300 Phillipi Rd
-Bx28512 -Columbus 43228

(440) 943-4200 ..**Kidder,** Fred D '50 SpclCnsl Lubrizol Corp -29400 Lakelnd Blvd
-Wickliffe 44092

(216) 592-5000 ..**Kidder,** Richelle '03 %Tucker E&W LLP -925 Euclid Av
-1150 Huntngtn Bldg -Cleveland 44115 **Fx:**592-5009

(216) 896-9091 .. **Kidder,** Stephen J '91 -2692 Sulgrave Rd -Shaker Heights 44122 **Fx:**896-9083
(410) 296-6200 .. **Kidner,** Edward F '90 (McLean KS&H) -11311 McCormick Rd -Ste 100 -Hunt Valley, MD 21031 **Fx:**(443) 589-1165
(859) 261-4700 .. **Kidney,** James A '96 -40 E 10th -Newport, KY 41071
(937) 449-6810 .. **Kidwell,** Charles Y '85 (Porter WM&A LLP) -1 S Main -Ste 1600 -Dayton 45402 **Fx:**449-6820
(740) 590-3969 .. **Kieckhefer,** Frederick B Jr. '87 -63127 US 50 W -Bx315 -McArthur 45651 **Fx:**596-3811
(216) 586-3939 .. **Kiedrowski,** Carrie L '03 %Jones D -901 Lakeside Av -Cleveland 44114 **Fx:**579-0212
(937) 227-9382 .. **Kiefaber,** Robert W '02 %Faruki I&C PLL -10 N Ludlow -500 Cthse Plz SW -Dayton 45402 **Fx:**227-3717
(216) 771-6650 .. **Kiefer,** Daran P '94 %Kreiner & P Co,LPA -Bx6599 -Cleveland 44101
Kiefer, James C '58 -660 Buttercup Av -Vandalia 45377
(937) 427-1367 .. **Kieffaber,** Megan A '01 %McNamee & M,PLL -2625 Cmmns Blvd -Beavercreek 45431 **Fx:**427-1369
(513) 684-3935 .. **Kieffer-Dunn,** Aisa M '03 US Dept of Labor -36 E 7th -Ste 2550 -Cincinnati 45202
(513) 232-4449 .. **Kiel,** Frederick O '66 -1095 Nimitzvw Dr -Ste 103 -Cincinnati 45230
(614) 228-5151 .. **Kielkopf,** Andrew J '93 (Gallagher GPT&L LLP) -471 E Broad -19th Fl -Columbus 43215 **Fx:**228-0032
Kielkopf, Charles P '89 -7004 Arbor Ln -Mc Lean, VA 22101
(216) 621-9870 .. **Kieltsch-Packard,** Kristina M '00 %McNeal SA&B Co,LPA -123 W Prospect Av -Ste 250 Van Sweringen Arcade -Cleveland 44115 **Fx:**522-1112
(440) 603-5339 .. **Kienzl,** William P '83 -Bx43258 -Richmond Heights 44143
(419) 874-6048 .. **Kienzle,** David W '80 Kienzle Enterprises -28321 W River Rd -Perrysburg 43551
(330) 287-5560 .. **Kienzle,** Roger W Jr. '74 Cnty Juvenile Magistrate -107 W Lbrty -Wooster 44691
(419) 247-3758 .. **Kienzle,** Susan S '77 -28321 W River Rd -Perrysburg 43551
(202) 772-2482 .. **Kies,** Kenneth J '77 Clark/Bardes Consulting -101 Const Av -Ste 701E -Washington, DC 20001
(513) 887-3474 .. **Kiesey,** Cassandra E '90 Butler Cnty Pros -315 High -11th Fl -Bx515 -Hamilton 45012
Kiesling, C Mark '80 -9648 Busey Rd -Canal Winchester 43110
(513) 943-7100 .. **Kiessling,** Kurt M '92 Midland Co -7000 Mdlnd Blvd -Amelia 45102
(216) 348-5400 .. **Kiffner,** Kent C '04 %McDonald H Co,LPA -600 Superior Av E -Ste 2100 -Cleveland 44114 **Fx:**348-5474
(740) 335-5271 .. **Kiger,** David V '92 (Kiger & K) -132 S Main -Washington Court House 43160
(740) 335-5271 .. **Kiger,** James A '62 (Kiger & K) -132 S Main -Washington Court House 43160
(614) 227-2000 .. **Kiger,** Robert C '60 (Porter WM&A LLP) -41 S High -Columbus 43215 **Fx:**227-2100
(740) 695-5866 .. **Kigerl,** Jack J '74 -132 W Main -Bx248 -Saint Clairsville 43950
(330) 643-3540 .. **Kiggans,** Jeffrey M '03 OH Dept of Tax -161 S High -Ste 501 -Akron 44308
(419) 782-7757 .. **Kight,** Katrina Y '96 (Haver & K) -118 Clinton -Defiance 43512
(440) 327-6966 .. **Kikol,** John C '70 Cleve Realty Cnsltnts,Ltd -4937 Mills Ind Pkwy -Ste 200 -North Ridgeville 44039
(440) 871-4022 .. **Kikta,** Mark A '92 Corsaro & Assoc Co,LPA -2001 Crocker Rd -Ste 400 -Westlake 44145
(434) 977-3456 .. **Kilbane,** Brian P '73 SSA Ofc of Hearings -1 Morton Dr -3rd Fl -Charlottesville, VA 22903
(216) 252-7300 .. **Kilbane,** Catherine M '87 Amer Greetings Corp -1 Amer Rd -Cleveland 44144
(216) 687-1311 .. **Kilbane,** Thomas B '96 (Reminger & R) -101 Prospect Av W -1400 Mdlnd Bldg -Cleveland 44115 **Fx:**687-1841
(216) 479-8500 .. **Kilbane,** Thomas S '66 (Squire S&D LLP) -127 Pub Sq -4900 Key Twr -Cleveland 44114 **Fx:**479-8780
(614) 221-4221 .. **Kilbride,** Randall J '96 Barkan + N -360 S Grant Av -Bx1989 -Columbus 43216 **Fx:**221-5423
(937) 223-6035 .. **Kilby,** Kimberly A '98 Miami Valley Fair Housing Ctr,Inc -21-23 E Babbitt -Dayton 45405
(216) 221-3142 .. **Kilcoyne,** James F '62 -12700 Lk Av -#2409 -Lakewood 44107
(513) 421-4020 .. **Kilcoyne,** John W '34 OfCnsl Cohen TK&S,LLC -250 E 5th -Ste 1200 -Cincinnati 45202 **Fx:**241-4490
(513) 421-4020 .. **Kilcoyne,** Thomas C '84 OfCnsl Cohen TK&S,LLC -250 E 5th -Ste 1200 -Cincinnati 45202 **Fx:**241-4490
(304) 232-6810 .. **Kildow,** Todd M '93 %Phillips GK&A -61 14th -Wheeling, WV 26003 **Fx:**232-4918
(440) 323-8240 .. **Kile,** Carol A '91 Legal Aid -538 W Broad -Ste 300 -Elyria 44035
(513) 777-1545 .. **Kile,** Paul R '85 Vanguard Transportation -Bx609 -West Chester 45071
(513) 769-4040 .. **Kiley,** Robin O '89 Retirement Cptl Advsrs -11500 Northlake Dr -Ste 100 -Cincinnati 45249
(440) 322-3800 .. **Kilfoyle,** William E '56 -1004 Garford Av -Elyria 44035
(937) 226-2121 .. **Kilgo,** David M '78 Natl City Bank -Private Client Group -6 N Main -Dayton 45412
(614) 794-6992 .. **Kilgore,** Terry L '73 -3031 Birch Hllw Way -Columbus 43231 **Fx:**794-6993
Kilian, David P '83 -(Address Unavailable)
(419) 249-7100 .. **Killam,** Thomas P '76 Marshall & M,LLC -Four Seagate -8th Fl -Toledo 43604 **Fx:**249-7151
(330) 923-8758 .. **Kille,** Angela M '04 -232 Portage Trl -Ste H -Cuyahoga Falls 44221
(216) 592-5000 .. **Killeen,** Eugene M '88 (Tucker E&W LLP) -925 Euclid Av -1150 Huntngtn Bldg -Cleveland 44115 **Fx:**592-5009
(216) 752-3590 .. **Killian,** Karen L '97 -3530 Warrensvll Ctr Rd -Ste 110 -Shaker Heights 44122
(330) 375-2070 .. **Killian,** Laura A '90 Akron Municipal Ct -217 S High -Rm 939 -Akron 44308
(330) 494-1120 .. **Killian,** Robert R '77 -4495 Meadowvw Dr NW -Canton 44718
(330) 644-6746 .. **Killian,** Timothy J '76 Killian Latex,Inc -2064 Killian Rd -Akron 44312
(330) 724-4442 .. **Killinger,** Rebecca '82 Cook Law Ofcs -1350 Kelly Av -Bx7377 -Akron 44306
(614) 330-6844 .. **Killion,** Christopher L '01 -39 W North Bway -Columbus 43214
(614) 227-2334 .. **Killworth,** Allen R '97 %Bricker & E LLP -100 S 3rd -Columbus 43215 **Fx:**227-2390
(614) 249-1698 .. **Killworth,** Linda Klimas '97 Cnsl Nationwide Ins Co -1 Nationwide Plz -Columbus 43215
(614) 542-9000 .. **Killworth,** Melinda B '94 -789 S Front -Ste 201 -Columbus 43206
(937) 449-6400 .. **Killworth,** Richard A '73 (Dinsmore & S LLP) -1 S Main -Ste 1300 One Dayton Centre -Dayton 45402 **Fx:**449-6405
Kilo, Stephen F '02 -(Address Unavailable)
(440) 352-3003 .. **Kilpeck,** Lori R '02 Ziegler M&M LLP -152 Main -Painesville 44077 **Fx:**354-3299
(440) 244-2590 .. **Kilroy,** John P '78 -600 Bway -Lorain 44052
(310) 551-2210 .. **Kilroy,** Kenneth R '75 Davis Co -2121 Av of Stars -Ste 2800 -Los Angeles, CA 90067
(614) 461-9212 .. **Kilroy,** Mary J '81 (Handelman & K) -360 S Grant Av -Columbus 43215
(513) 946-3000 .. **Kim,** Donna L '99 Hamilton Cnty Pros -230 E 9th -Cincinnati 45202 **Fx:**946-3017
(216) 566-5948 .. **Kim,** Eduardo '00 %Thompson H LLP -127 Pub Sq -3900 Key Ctr -Cleveland 44114 **Fx:**566-5800
(614) 221-1216 .. **Kim,** Edward S '94 %Downes H&F -400 S 5th -Ste 200 -Columbus 43215 **Fx:**221-8769
(330) 434-2000 .. **Kim,** John Y '96 -80 S Summit -300 Courtyard Sq -Akron 44308
(937) 332-9300 .. **Kim,** Jonghoon James '03 (Bucio & E,LLP) -10 N Market -Troy 45373 **Fx:**339-6549
(646) 591-3272 .. **Kim,** Martha V '89 -350 5th Av -3304 Empire State Bldg -New York, NY 10118
(330) 376-9260 .. **Kim-Knox,** Candace A '03 -7 W Bowery -Ste 907 -Akron 44308
(614) 645-7547 .. **Kimball,** Dennis R '82 Franklin Cnty Mun Ct -375 S High -Chmbrs 11B -Columbus 43215
(216) 932-4961 .. **Kimball,** Maynerd A '59 -2375 Traymore Rd -University Heights 44118
(330) 633-0666 .. **Kimble,** Matthew '04 %R Maguire -190 East Av -Tallmadge 44278 **Fx:**633-0626
(330) 253-8877 .. **Kimbler,** Joyce V '82 -50 S Main -Ste 502 -Akron 44308
(513) 677-2667 .. **Kime,** Todd G '91 -550 Wards Crnr -Ste 102 -Loveland 45140
Kimes, Jessica Loomis '04 -(Address Unavailable)
(740) 596-9371 .. **Kimes-Brown,** Trecia M '98 -103 S Market -McArthur 45651
(614) 227-2000 .. **Kimm,** Lori-Lou '90 (Porter WM&A LLP) -41 S High -Columbus 43215 **Fx:**227-2100
(216) 363-4500 .. **Kimmel,** Lisa C '86 OfCnsl Benesch FC&A LLP -200 Pub Sq -Ste 2300 -Cleveland 44114 **Fx:**363-4588
(330) 995-0051 .. **Kimmel,** Roger A Jr. '72 SrCnsl R Kimmel Jr & Assoc -144 Barrington Town Sq -Ste 159 -Aurora 44202 **Fx:**562-1669
(419) 826-4866 .. **Kimmelman,** William C '87 TE Hallett -113 W Airport Hwy -Bx208 -Swanton 43558
(614) 644-0258 .. **Kimmet,** Kathryn A '91 OH Dept Hlth -246 N High -Bx118 -Columbus 43216
(330) 837-4251 .. **Kimmins,** Thomas W '63 -11 Lincoln Way E -Massillon 44646 **Fx:**837-4902
(216) 664-4845 .. **Kinast,** Aric H '98 Prosecutor -1200 Ontario Av -8th Fl Justice Ctr -Cleveland 44113 **Fx:**664-4399
(216) 623-0150 .. **Kinast,** Hugh S '04 %Roetzel & A,LPA -1375 E 9th -One Cleve Ctr 9th Fl -Cleveland 44114 **Fx:**623-0134
Kincade, Donald H '80 Merit Bank -411 Adams -Toledo 43604
(330) 832-1597 .. **Kincaid,** Dale B '67 -2137 Wales Av NW -Ste 2 -Massillon 44646
(513) 774-8500 .. **Kincaid,** Daniel E '95 Provider Synergies,LLC -5181 Natorp Blvd -Ste 205 -Mason 45040
(614) 224-7193 .. **Kincaid Randall & Craine** -2201 Riverside Dr -Columbus 43221 **Fx:**586-4051
(614) 228-1541 .. **Kincaid,** Robert M Jr. '77 (Baker & H LLP) -65 E State -Ste 2100 -Columbus 43215 **Fx:**462-2616
(740) 454-2591 .. **Kincaid Taylor & Geyer** -50 N 4th -Bx1030 -Zanesville 43702 **Fx:**454-6975
(614) 733-0720 .. **Kincaid,** Timothy J '96 -8079 McKitrick Rd -Plain City 43064
(513) 651-6800 .. **Kindel,** Frederick W '80 (Frost BT LLC) -201 E 5th -2200 PNC Ctr -Cincinnati 45202 **Fx:**651-6981
(513) 564-7054 .. **Kindel,** Patricia A '80 6th Dist Ct of Appls -100 E 5th -Cthse -Cincinnati 45202
(937) 773-8047 .. **Kindell,** Louie R '83 (L Kindell & Assoc) -419 N Wayne -Bx1454 -Piqua 45356
(304) 340-3800 .. **Kinder,** Eric E '94 Spilman T&B,PLLC -300 Kanawha Blvd E -Bx273 -Charleston, WV 25321
(216) 621-1113 .. **Kinder,** Gordon D II '77 (Renner OB&S,LLP) -1621 Euclid Av -19th Fl -Cleveland 44115 **Fx:**621-6165
(513) 852-2594 .. **Kinder,** Kenneth H II '00 %Cors & B LLC -537 E Pete Rose Way -Ste 400 -Cincinnati 45202
(260) 460-1736 .. **Kinder,** Martha M '93 Baker & D -111 E Wayne -Ste 800 -Fort Wayne, IN 46802
(330) 535-8771 .. **Kinder,** Richard A '93 (Adgate & K) -159 S Main -Ste 830 -Akron 44308 **Fx:**253-8578
(202) 312-5585 .. **Kinder,** Robert L Jr. '03 Ct of Appeals/Fed Circuit -717 Madison Pl -Washington, DC 20439
(513) 887-5643 .. **Kindley,** Zane E '88 CSEA -315 High -Hamilton 45011
(216) 623-6554 .. **Kindt,** Mark D '79 -16004 Detroit Av -Ste 3 -Lakewood 44107
(513) 421-4020 .. **Kindt,** Monica V '00 %Cohen TK&S,LLC -250 E 5th -Ste 1200 -Cincinnati 45202 **Fx:**241-4490
(937) 333-4400 .. **King,** Addie J '01 Dayton Pros -335 W 3rd -Ste 372 -Dayton 45402
(216) 771-9745 .. **King,** Alison M '95 S Moore Co,LPA -850 Euclid Av -Ste 701 -Cleveland 44114
(419) 224-1353 .. **King,** Andrew B '95 %King & B -212 N Elizabeth -Lima 45801 **Fx:**224-5305
(216) 443-3087 .. **King,** Barry '82 Cuyahoga Cnty Pub Def -1849 Prospect Av -Ste 222 -Cleveland 44115
(419) 224-1353 .. **King & Blair** -212 N Elizabeth -Lima 45801 **Fx:**224-5305
(513) 728-3700 .. **King,** Brad A '79 Finneytown Schl Dist Bd of Ed -8916 Fontainebleau Ter -Cincinnati 45224 **Fx:**931-0986
(330) 385-0576 .. **King,** Carl J '76 -101 E 6th -East Liverpool 43920
(614) 263-1810 .. **King,** Carl R '81 -3558 N High -Columbus 43214
(440) 995-5100 .. **King,** Charles H '92 -6140 Parkland Blvd -Mayfield Heights 44124
(216) 479-8500 .. **King,** Chaundra C '04 %Squire S&D LLP -127 Pub Sq -4900 Key Twr -Cleveland 44114 **Fx:**479-8780
(937) 328-9079 .. **King,** Courtney D '99 Community Hosp -2615 E High -Springfield 45505
King, David L '89 -5131 NE Cnty Road 340 -High Springs, FL 32643

(216) 360-0070 .. **King**, David M '72 -24500 Chagrin Blvd -Ste 340
-Beachwood 44122

(440) 954-9455 .. **King**, David M '84 (Schraff & K Co,LPA) -4230 SR 306 -#310
-Willoughby 44094

(216) 443-7223 .. **King**, David M '91 Cuyahoga Cnty Pub Def -1200 W 3rd NW
-100 Lakeside Pl -Cleveland 44113

(330) 972-8475 .. **King**, Dawn M '04 University of Akron -185 Carroll -Akron 44325

(972) 277-9623 .. **King**, Deborah Jenkins '80 Cnsl Ofc Thrift Supervision
-225 E John Carpenter Fwy -Ste 500 -Irving, TX 75062
Fx:277-9630

(330) 426-4121 .. **King**, Douglas A '91 Hartford D&Y Co, LPA -91 W Taggart -Bx85
-East Palestine 44413

(440) 247-4470 .. **King**, Douglas A Sr. '78 -34 S Main -Chagrin Falls 44022
Fx:247-1680

(513) 231-2699 .. **King**, Douglas E '73 -2862 Patterson Farms Rd -Cincinnati 45244

(419) 242-5100 .. **King**, Douglas W '91 Frederickson H&K Co,LPA -405 Mad Av
-Ste 1212 -Toledo 43604 **Fx:**242-5556

(614) 222-0068 .. **King**, Eric B '01 -Bx360874 -Columbus 43236

(614) 221-7201 .. **King**, Eugene R '83 OSLSA -555 Buttles Av -Columbus 43215

(419) 213-4755 .. **King**, Frances V '88 %6th Dist Crt Appeals -800 Jackson
-Toledo 43624

(703) 696-1601 .. **King**, Francis P '91 US Army Litigation Div -901 N Stuart -Ste 400
-Arlington, VA 22203

(513) 948-5072 .. **King**, Frederick G '91 Givaudan Flvrs/Frag Corp -1199 Edison Dr
-Bx371805 -Cincinnati 45222

(614) 469-3939 .. **King**, G Roger '71 (Jones D) -325 John H McConnell Blvd -Ste 600
-Bx165017 -Columbus 43216 **Fx:**461-4198

(513) 579-6400 .. **King**, Gail T '90 (Keating M&K PLL) -1 E 4th -1400 Provident Twr
-Cincinnati 45202 **Fx:**579-6457

(614) 846-2626 .. **King**, Gale R III '72 -870 High -Ste 16 -Worthington 43085
Fx:847-9669

(614) 784-8882 .. **King**, Gerald L '78 -3763 N High -Columbus 43214

(614) 889-2531 .. **King**, Hamlin C Jr. '67 Sanborn BD&B Co,LPA -2515 W Granvll Rd
-Columbus 43235

(740) 282-1900 .. **King Hargrave Scurti & Jack** -200 Sinclair Bldg -Bx249
-Steubenville 43952 **Fx:**282-5397

(216) 479-8500 .. **King**, Henry T Jr. '63 Squire S&D LLP -127 Pub Sq -4900 Key Twr
-Cleveland 44114 **Fx:**479-8780

(614) 227-2000 .. **King**, James A '88 (Porter WM&A LLP) -41 S High
-Columbus 43215 **Fx:**227-2100

(610) 591-4182 .. **King**, James A Jr. '83 Cnsl Boeing Co-Rotorcraft -MS P31-60
-Bx16858 -Philadelphia, PA 19142

(614) 469-3939 .. **King**, James R '74 (Jones D) -325 John H McConnell Blvd
-Ste 600 -Bx165017 -Columbus 43216 **Fx:**461-4198

(440) 892-3005 .. **King**, James R '80 Cnsl Scott Fetzer Co -28800 Clemens Rd
-Westlake 44145

(216) 664-6924 .. **King**, Joan M '83 Cleveland Mun Ct -1200 Ontario -Bx94894
-Cleveland 44101

(330) 394-3126 .. **King**, John E '56 -106 E Market -Warren 44481
King, John F '83 -28871 Ctr Ridge Rd -Ste 102 -Westlake 44145

(859) 283-0407 .. **King**, John K '95 Admin Law Judge -8120 Dream
-Dept Workers Claims -Florence, KY 41042

(216) 426-4304 .. **King**, Joseph D '96 Applied Industrial Tech, Inc -One Applied Plz
-Cleveland 44115

(740) 345-9801 .. **King**, Joseph Michael '79 (Jones NM&H) -35 S Park Plz -Ste 35
-Bx4010 -Newark 43058 **Fx:**345-6031

(216) 544-8888 .. **King**, Julie Mitrovich '94 -Bx23626 -Chagrin Falls 44023

(513) 852-8635 .. **King**, Kathleen C '75 Hamilton Cnty Cmn Pleas Ct -800 Bway
-Cincinnati 45202

(216) 621-0200 .. **King**, Kelly M '03 %Baker & H LLP -1900 E 9th -Ste 3200
-Cleveland 44114 **Fx:**696-0740

(770) 938-2250 .. **King**, Kimberly J '94 -2200 Northlake Pkwy -Ste 320
-Tucker, GA 30084

(304) 529-5531 .. **King**, Kristen B '95 SSA-OHA -1108 3rd Av -Ste 400
-Huntington, WV 25701

(440) 934-3700 .. **King**, Kristina M '01 %Fauver K-W&D -5333 Meadow Ln Ct -Elyria
44035 **Fx:**934-3708

(734) 622-6415 .. **King**, Lawrence E Jr. '75 Flint Ink Corp -4600 Arrowhead Dr
-Ann Arbor, MI 48105

(216) 443-7800 .. **King**, Matthew J '96 Cuyahoga Cnty Pros -1200 Ontario -8th Fl
-Cleveland 44113 **Fx:**698-2270

(614) 628-6880 .. **King**, Michael J '00 %Dinsmore & S LLP -175 S 3rd -10th Fl
-Columbus 43215 **Fx:**628-6890

(216) 643-2915 .. **King**, Michael L '84 -6100 Oak Tree Blvd -Ste 200
-Independence 44131

(937) 222-2424 .. **King**, Michele L '99 Freund F&A -1 S Main -Ste 1800 -Dayton
45402 **Fx:**222-5369

(614) 462-3194 .. **King**, Nancy B '80 Franklin Cnty Pub Def -373 S High -12th Fl
-Columbus 43215

(740) 773-3800 .. **King**, Nancy L '79 -66 N Walnut -Ste 3 -Chillicothe 45601

(513) 352-3336 .. **King**, Patricia M '93 Law Dept -801 Plum -Rm 214
-Cincinnati 45202 **Fx:**352-1515

(614) 644-7233 .. **King**, Philip A '00 Atty Gen -150 E Gay -Columbus 43215
Fx:728-9327

(440) 954-9455 .. **King**, Philip G '02 %Schraff & K Co,LPA -4230 SR 306 -#310
-Willoughby 44094

(859) 431-0170 .. **King**, Phillip E '60 (King & S) -3612 Caroline Av
-Covington, KY 41015

(614) 471-8181 .. **King**, Ray J '74 -107 W Johnstown Rd -Gahanna 43230

(419) 248-8000 .. **King**, Ricardo A '95 Owens Corning -One Owens Corning Pkwy
-Toledo 43659

(614) 469-7404 .. **King**, Robert C '75 SSA-OHA, Columbus -280 N High -Rm 300
-Columbus 43215

(419) 244-6788 .. **King**, Robert P '83 (Bugbee & C) -405 Mad Av -Ste 1300
-Toledo 43604 **Fx:**244-7145

(216) 271-8987 .. **King**, Russell W '90 BP Amoco Co -4850 E 49th -MBC1-L
-Cuyahoga Heights 44125

(937) 443-6560 .. **King**, Scott A '86 (Thompson H LLP) -2000 Cthse Plz NE -Bx8801
-Dayton 45401 **Fx:**443-6635

(859) 692-2242 .. **King**, Sonya E '94 Natl Underwriter Co -5081 Olympic Blvd
-Erlanger, KY 41018 **Fx:**692-2293

(513) 352-6746 .. **King**, Stephen M '85 (Thompson H LLP) -312 Walnut -14th Fl
-Cincinnati 45202 **Fx:**241-4771

(513) 793-2353 .. **King**, Stephen R '96 (King & M,LLC) -10999 Reed Hartman Hwy
-Ste 229 -Cincinnati 45242

(937) 339-2651 .. **King**, Stephen W '72 (Princi & K) -221 S Market -Troy 45373
King, Terri S '87 -Bx44735 -Middletown 45044

(419) 241-2000 .. **King**, Thomas R '55 -709 Mad Av -Ste 209 -Toledo 43624

(614) 716-1643 .. **King**, Timothy A '84 Amer Elec Pwr Co -1 Riverside Plz
-Columbus 43215

(216) 621-0200 .. **King**, Tom A Jr. '90 (Baker & H LLP) -1900 E 9th -Ste 3200
-Cleveland 44114 **Fx:**696-0740

(614) 621-0777 .. **King**, Tunney L '74 -380 S 5th -Ste 2 -Columbus 43215
Fx:464-0757

(419) 421-3370 .. **King**, Virginia M '03 Marathon Ashland Petroleum -539 S Main
-Findlay 45840

(513) 559-5299 .. **King**, William G '62 Frisch's Rstrnts,Inc -2800 Gilbert Av
-Cincinnati 45206

(941) 955-6832 .. **King**, William R '73 -2422 Juniper Pl -Sarasota, FL 34239

(216) 363-1400 .. **King**, Woods III '83 (Buckley K,LPA) -600 E Superior Av -Ste 1400
-Cleveland 44114 **Fx:**579-1020

(216) 622-8200 .. **King**, Zachary W '04 %Calfee H&G LLP -800 Superior Av
-Ste 1400 -Cleveland 44114 **Fx:**241-0816

(614) 466-8054 .. **Kingery**, Jeanne W '81 PUCO -180 E Broad -Columbus 43266

(216) 382-5454 .. **Kingsbury**, Dorothea J '81 -5031 Mayfld Rd -250 Hilltop Bldg
-Lyndhurst 44124

(330) 379-6851 .. **Kingsbury**, Thomas R '97 Bridgestone\Firestone
-1200 Fireston Pkwy -Akron 44317

(937) 223-8177 .. **Kingseed**, C Mark '86 (Coolidge WW&L) -33 W 1st -Ste 600
-Dayton 45402 **Fx:**223-6705

(740) 477-2546 .. **Kingsley**, James R '72 (Kingsley Law Ofc) -157 W Main
-Circleville 43113

(614) 644-8765 .. **Kingsley**, Kay A '80 SERB -65 E State -Ste 1200
-Columbus 43215 **Fx:**466-3074

(419) 358-5606 .. **Kingsley**, Mitchell L '93 %SW Diller Co,LPA -138 N Main -Bx46
-Bluffton 45817

(614) 221-4000 .. **Kington**, John A '80 (Chester W&S LLP) -65 E State -10th Fl
-Columbus 43215 **Fx:**221-4012

(214) 256-4444 .. **Kinkade**, Richard D '81 R Kinkade PC -2121 W Airport Fwy
-Ste 400 -Irving, TX 75062

(216) 446-0300 .. **Kinkaid**, Amy I '92 -5432 Mayfld Rd -Cleveland 44124

(440) 842-1313 .. **Kinkela**, Gabrielle G '69 (Kinkela & K) -1721 Carlton Rd
-Cleveland 44134
Kinkela, John F '83 -81 Keethler Dr S -Westerville 43081

(440) 842-1313 .. **Kinkela & Kinkela** -1721 Carlton Rd -Cleveland 44134

(440) 842-1313 .. **Kinkela**, Robert V '69 (Kinkela & K) -1721 Carlton Rd
-Cleveland 44134

(216) 621-6570 .. **Kinkopf**, Charles W '94 Rademaker MM&G -55 Pub Sq -Ste 1775
-Cleveland 44113 **Fx:**621-1127

(216) 623-0150 .. **Kinkopf**, Lauren K '92 %Roetzel & A,LPA -1375 E 9th
-One Cleve Ctr 9th Fl -Cleveland 44114 **Fx:**623-0134

(216) 623-0150 .. **Kinkopf-Zajac**, Ingrid A '96 (Roetzel & A,LPA) -1375 E 9th
-One Cleve Ctr 9th Fl -Cleveland 44114 **Fx:**623-0134

(937) 443-6922 .. **Kinlin**, Donald J '84 OfCnsl Thompson H LLP -2000 Cthse Plz NE
-Bx8801 -Dayton 45401 **Fx:**443-6635

(703) 696-9063 .. **Kinlin**, Karen J '86 USAF/JACN -1501 Wilson Blvd -Ste 606
-Arlington, VA 22209

(440) 329-5389 .. **Kinlin**, Michael J '98 Lorain Cnty Pros -225 Court -3rd Fl
-Elyria 44035

(713) 207-6986 .. **Kinman**, Lynn M '94 Reliant Energy -1111 Louisiana Av -REP 26
-Houston, TX 77002

(614) 225-4447 .. **Kinnan**, Brent E '74 Borden,Inc -180 E Broad -Columbus 43215

(614) 222-5853 .. **Kinnan**, Jimmie L '79 Sch Emplyees Rtrmnt Syst -300 E Broad
-Ste 100 -Columbus 43215
Kinnear, Kevin R '94 -6410 Wise Av -Canton 44720

(513) 352-6783 .. **Kinnen**, Jennifer L '02 %Thompson H LLP -312 Walnut -14th Fl
-Cincinnati 45202 **Fx:**241-4771

(513) 347-7260 .. **Kinney**, Ann J '01 Cincinnati Bell Tlphne -201 E 4th -102-890
-Cincinnati 45202

(330) 725-4365 .. **Kinney**, Jack M '58 -4134 E Normandy Park Dr -Medina 44256
Kinney, James D '04 -(Address Unavailable)

(937) 226-1990 .. **Kinney**, Winfield G III '61 (W Kinney III Co,LPA) -120 W 2nd
-1700 Lbrty Twr -Dayton 45402

(330) 799-0129 .. **Kinnick**, Paul G '92 -4613 Barrington Dr -Austintown 44515

(614) 227-2300 .. **Kinross**, Kevin M '00 %Bricker & E LLP -100 S 3rd
-Columbus 43215 **Fx:**227-2390

(800) 480-2265 .. **Kinross**, Shannon C '01 Huntington Natl Bank -41 S High -6th Fl
-Columbus 43215

(937) 323-9739 .. **Kinsler**, Christopher L '01 Schmenk S&H -20 N Limestone
-Springfield 45502 **Fx:**323-9388

(513) 721-4876 .. **Kinsley**, Jennifer M '99 %Sirkin P&S LLP -105 W 4th
-920 4th & Race Twr -Cincinnati 45202 **Fx:**721-0876

(513) 636-2725 .. **Kinsman**, Anne Marie '04 Cincinnati Childrens Hsptl
-3333 Burnet Av -MIC 4002 LOC W Rm 4-39 -Cincinnati 45229

(614) 466-6511 .. **Kinworthy**, Christine M '89 Dept Admin Srvcs -30 E Broad
-Columbus 43215

(614) 464-6400 .. **Kinzer**, Allen S '88 (Vorys SS&P LLP) -52 E Gay -Bx1008
-Columbus 43216 **Fx:**464-6350

(216) 520-5584 .. **Kipfstuhl**, Denise L '92 West Grp -6111 Oak Tree Blvd -Bx318063
-Cleveland 44131

(513) 651-6800 .. **Kipling**, James M '72 OfCnsl Frost BT LLC -201 E 5th -2200 PNC
Ctr -Cincinnati 45202 **Fx:**651-6981

(260) 426-9706 .. **Kiplinger**, Roy F '91 (Beers MB&S, LLP) -110 W Berry -Ste 1100
-Fort Wayne, IN 46802 **Fx:**420-1314

(330) 472-5796 .. **Kipp**, Jerald B '81 -2440 Remsen Rd -Medina 44256

(216) 696-8860 .. **Kipp**, Therese R '94 %Sheehan & S -1422 Euclid Av
-1648 Hanna Bldg -Cleveland 44115

(740) 622-9801 .. **Kiracofe**, Bruce H '81 Cmmnty Action Comm -120 N 4th
-Coshocton 43812 **Fx:**622-0165
Kirby, Charles A '04 -(Address Unavailable)

(614) 462-3979 .. **Kirby**, Edwin Lee Jr. '74 10th Dist Ct of Appls -373 S High -24th Fl
-Columbus 43215

(937) 748-1004 .. **Kirby**, Jeffrey T '88 (Kirby & T LPA) -4 Sycamore Crk Dr
-Springboro 45066 **Fx:**748-2390

(419) 213-4755 .. **Kirby**, JoAnne J '91 %Hon RW Knepper -800 Jackson
-Toledo 43624

(740) 286-3735 .. **Kirby**, Joseph D '91 -227 Main -Bx573 -Jackson 45640
(937) 748-1004 .. **Kirby**, Joseph W '95 (Kirby & T LPA) -4 Sycamore Crk Dr -Springboro 45066 **Fx:**748-2390
(419) 213-6850 .. **Kirby**, Michael D '84 Lucas Cnty Dom Rltns Ct -429 N Mich Av -Toledo 43624
(937) 748-1004 .. **Kirby**, Thomas B Jr. '68 (Kirby & T LPA) -4 Sycamore Crk Dr -Springboro 45066 **Fx:**748-2390
(937) 748-1004 .. **Kirby & Thomas. LPA** -4 Sycamore Crk Dr -Springboro 45066 **Fx:**748-2390
(614) 462-4477 .. **Kirby**, William J '80 Franklin Cnty Juv Ct -373 S High -5th Fl -Columbus 43215
(513) 229-7996 .. **Kircher**, Konrad '92 -4824 Socialville-Foster Rd -Ste 110 -Mason 45040
(513) 381-3525 .. **Kircher Robinson & Welch** -1014 Vine -Ste 2520 -Cincinnati 45202
(513) 381-3525 .. **Kircher**, Thomas J '70 (Kircher R&W) -1014 Vine -Ste 2520 -Cincinnati 45202
(216) 621-0200 .. **Kirchick**, Calvin B '72 (Baker & H LLP) -1900 E 9th -Ste 3200 -Cleveland 44114 **Fx:**696-0740
(513) 363-4500 .. **Kirchick**, Ross D '00 (Benesch FC&A LLP) -200 Pub Sq -Ste 2300 -Cleveland 44114 **Fx:**363-4588
(718) 340-4335 .. **Kirchmeier**, Jeffrey L '89 CUNY Schl of Law -65-21 Main -Flushing, NY 11367
(614) 236-6779 .. **Kirchner**, Lina Nizar '02 Capital Univ/Family Advoc Ctr -303 E Broad -Columbus 43215
(440) 871-6300 .. **Kirchner**, Lisa A '93 %D McIntyre & Co,LLC -2001 Crocker Rd -Ste 280 -Westlake 44145 **Fx:**871-6301
(614) 221-3318 .. **Kirchner**, Steven M '02 %Agee CM&L -89 E Nationwide Blvd -Ste 200 -Columbus 43215
(651) 344-3236 .. **Kirchstein**, Robert O '86 -Bx235 -Rosemount, MN 55068
(614) 365-2700 .. **Kirila**, Jill S '97 %Squire S&D LLP -41 S High -1300 Huntngtn Ctr -Columbus 43215 **Fx:**365-2499
(216) 227-0715 .. **Kirk**, Christopher S '98 -13317 Mad Av -Lakewood 44107
(614) 841-1620 .. **Kirk**, Edward R '73 -6660 N High -Ste 3A -Worthington 43085 **Fx:**841-1047
(614) 752-9039 .. **Kirk**, Margaret '89 Workers Comp -30 W Spring -Level 26 -Columbus 43215
(216) 787-3344 .. **Kirk**, Quan T '98 Ohio Lottery Commision -615 W Superior Av -Cleveland 44113
(203) 944-5310 .. **Kirk**, Richard H '97 Amer Skandia,Inc -1 Corp Dr -Bx883 -Shelton, CT 06484
(513) 272-1100 .. **Kirk**, Roger W '82 -114 E 8th -Cincinnati 45202
(614) 466-3180 .. **Kirk**, Samuel J III '04 %Atty Gen -150 E Gay -Columbus 43215 **Fx:**466-9788
(210) 221-8400 .. **Kirk**, William C '72 US Army Medical Comm -2050 Worth Rd -Ste 17 -Fort Sam Houston, TX 78234
(330) 683-5010 .. **Kirkbride**, Cheryl M '01 %Kropf WH&L,LLP -100 N Vine -Bx67 -Orrville 44667 **Fx:**683-5030
(513) 421-6630 .. **Kirkham**, William N '75 Lindhorst & D Co,LPA -312 Walnut -Ste 2300 -Cincinnati 45202
(614) 466-3998 .. **Kirkhope**, Anne M '97 Unemploymnt Comp Commssn -145 S Front -Bx182299 -Columbus 43218
(419) 291-2192 .. **Kirkhope**, Thomas G '91 -2150 W Central Av -Toledo 43606
(937) 223-0697 .. **Kirkland**, James R '69 (J Kirkland Co,LPA) -111 W 1st -Ste 518 -Dayton 45402 **Fx:**223-5318
(330) 337-9515 .. **Kirkland**, Samuel Lee '85 (Yeagley K&B) -585 E State -Salem 44460
(614) 466-7264 .. **Kirkman**, George M '80 OH Legal Rghts Srvc -8 E Long -5th Fl -Columbus 43215
(216) 621-0200 .. **Kirkpatrick**, Andrew W '03 %Baker & H LLP -1900 E 9th -Ste 3200 -Cleveland 44114 **Fx:**696-0740
(513) 665-3500 .. **Kirkpatrick**, Jennifer L '96 (Freund F&A) -105 E 4th -Ste 1400 -Cincinnati 45202 **Fx:**665-3503
　　　　　　　　 Kirkpatrick, Joel J '00 -4895 Monroe -Ste 201 -Toledo 43623
(937) 435-8780 .. **Kirkwood**, Lori E '91 -7501 Paragon Rd -Dayton 45459
(513) 352-6728 .. **Kirkwood**, Thomas J '74 (Thompson H LLP) -312 Walnut -14th Fl -Cincinnati 45202 **Fx:**241-4771
　　　　　　　　 Kirlin, Katherine West '03 -(Address Unavailable)
(216) 382-2394 .. **Kirn**, John J Jr. '71 -2004 S Belvoir -South Euclid 44121
(440) 884-4300 .. **Kirner & Boldt Co, LPA** -8025 Corp Cir -North Royalton 44133 **Fx:**884-4302
(440) 884-4300 .. **Kirner**, Paul T '73 (Kirner & B Co,LPA) -8025 Corp Cir -North Royalton 44133 **Fx:**884-4302
(419) 213-4755 .. **Kiroff**, Donna L '80 %6th Dist Crt Appeals -800 Jackson -Toledo 43624
(419) 259-6376 .. **Kiroff**, Lawrence J '83 US Atty -4 Seagate -Ste 308 -Toledo 43604 **Fx:**259-6360
(216) 363-4500 .. **Kirsanow**, Peter N '79 (Benesch FC&A LLP) -200 Pub Sq -Ste 2300 -Cleveland 44114 **Fx:**363-4588
(216) 621-0890 .. **Kirschenbaum**, Dan G '84 -1919 E 13th -Cleveland 44114
(614) 462-3555 .. **Kirschman**, Scott C '88 Franklin Cnty Pros -373 S High -Columbus 43215
(513) 241-3630 .. **Kirschner**, Leonard '50 -10 W 9th -Cincinnati 45202 **Fx:**241-3631
(513) 759-6346 .. **Kirschner**, Steven R '87 Behavioral Hlth Gnrtns -7372 Kingsgate Way -West Chester 45069
(781) 377-4078 .. **Kirschner**, William H III '96 USAF ESC/JA -35 Hmltn -Bldg 1436 -Hanscom AFB, MA 01731
(740) 322-5770 .. **Kirsh**, Andrea M '85 Longaberger Co -1500 E Main -Bx3400 -Newark 43055
(216) 691-8472 .. **Kirshner**, Adrienne B '02 %Allen & H -1481 Warrensvll Ctr Rd -South Euclid 44121
(419) 841-3311 .. **Kirshner**, Alan R '75 -6800 W Central Av -Ste G-2 -Toledo 43617
(614) 365-2700 .. **Kirsner**, John M '92 (Squire S&D LLP) -41 S High -1300 Huntngtn Ctr -Columbus 43215 **Fx:**365-2499
(214) 767-4996 .. **Kirsner**, William D '94 Fed Labor Rltns Auth -525 Griffin -Ste 926 -Dallas, TX 75202
(614) 246-4052 .. **Kirstein**, Gregory W '82 Columbus Blue Jackets -200 W Nationwide Blvd -Columbus 43215
(513) 723-8400 .. **Kirtley**, Emily A '03 %Coley & Assoc -9334 Union Centre Blvd -Ste 200 -West Chester 45069
(937) 226-9354 .. **Kirtley**, John F II '04 %Macey & C -40 W 4th -Ste 2160 -Dayton 45402 **Fx:**226-9359
(216) 664-4826 .. **Kirvel**, Brent C '01 Prosecutor -1200 Ontario Av -8th Fl Justice Ctr -Cleveland 44113 **Fx:**664-4399

(419) 626-1917 .. **Kirwan**, John F '71 -189 E Market -Sandusky 44870
(973) 492-1880 .. **Kirwin**, Martha A '83 Cnsl McKay Hochman Co Inc -10 Park Pl -Butler, NJ 07405
(513) 721-1350 .. **Kirzner**, Ryan D '00 %Barron PB&S -3074 Madison Rd -Cincinnati 45209
(330) 538-3863 .. **Kisan**, Peter J '87 -1130 N Duck Crk Rd -North Jackson 44451
(513) 458-4588 .. **Kiser**, Theodore E '99 Norwood Law Dept -4645 Mntgmry Rd -Norwood 45212
(330) 746-8484 .. **Kish**, Brian P '01 %Betras M&K LLC -6630 Sevll Dr -Bx129 -Canfield 44406 **Fx:**702-8280
(440) 967-9065 .. **Kish**, Robert A '90 -891 Vermilion Rd -Vermilion 44089
(614) 461-1311 .. **Kish**, Robert V III '03 %Reminger & R -65 E State -4th Fl Cptl Sq Ofc Bldg -Columbus 43215 **Fx:**232-2410
(330) 533-6821 .. **Kish**, William J '70 -73 N Broad -Canfield 44406 **Fx:**533-9968
(440) 967-8717 .. **Kishman**, Henry W '76 -555 Main -Vermilion 44089
(937) 222-2424 .. **Kislig**, Kimberly S '03 %Freund F&A -1 S Main -Ste 1800 -Dayton 45402 **Fx:**222-5369
　　　　　　　　 Kisling, Gary W '77 -3200 W Market -Ste 300 -Akron 44333
(513) 721-4532 .. **Kisling**, Stephen C '76 (Katz TB&H) -255 E 5th -Ste 2400 -Cincinnati 45202
(812) 537-1830 .. **Kisor**, Mark Joseph '80 M. Joseph Kisor -230 W High -Bx26 -Lawrenceburg, IN 47025
(216) 875-2767 .. **Kiss**, Lynette E '00 %Bonezzi SM&P Co LPA -526 Superior Av -Ste 1400 -Cleveland 44114 **Fx:**875-1570
(304) 347-1736 .. **Kiss**, Robert S '83 (Bowles RMG&L LLP) -600 Quarrier -Bx1386 -Charleston, WV 25325 **Fx:**343-3058
(513) 242-0600 .. **Kissel**, Larry E '69 Cntrl Insulation Syst,Inc -300 Murray Rd -Cincinnati 45217
(419) 424-1365 .. **Kissh**, John A Jr. '76 Hancock County CSEA -7814 Cnty Road 140 -Findlay 45840
(513) 381-9200 .. **Kissinger**, Curtis E '90 %Rendigs FK&D,LLP -One W 4th -Ste 900 -Cincinnati 45202 **Fx:**381-9206
(330) 629-8877 .. **Kissinger**, William J Jr. '92 -8255 South Av -Ste A -Youngstown 44512
(614) 280-4000 .. **Kissos**, Dean G '85 Pizzuti Dvlpmnt -2 Miranova Pl -Ste 800 -Columbus 43215
(954) 862-2288 .. **Kiszkiel**, Stanley '76 S Kiszkiel,PA -9000 Sheridan PMB 11 -Ste 100 -Pembroke Pines, FL 33024 **Fx:**517-1848
(419) 243-4006 .. **Kitch Drutchas Wagner DeNardis & Valitutti,PC** -405 Mad Av -Ste 1500 -Toledo 43604 **Fx:**243-7333
(614) 462-5400 .. **Kitch**, Thomas D '97 OfCnsl Kegler BH&R -65 E State -Ste 1800 -Columbus 43215 **Fx:**464-2634
(330) 375-5780 .. **Kitchell**, Marjorie H '90 %Hon ME Shea-Stonum -2 S Main -#240 -Akron 44308
(216) 621-0200 .. **Kitchen**, David E '04 %Baker & H LLP -1900 E 9th -Ste 3200 -Cleveland 44114 **Fx:**696-0740
(740) 474-6043 .. **Kitchen**, James D '70 -11841 State Route 56 E -Circleville 43113
(419) 534-6833 .. **Kitchen**, Margaret A '53 (Kitchen & K) -7209 Grenlock Dr -Sylvania 43560
(419) 534-6833 .. **Kitchen**, Margaret A '83 (Kitchen & K) -7209 Grenlock Dr -Sylvania 43560
(513) 421-4020 .. **Kite**, Matthew M '95 %Cohen TK&S,LLC -250 E 5th -Ste 1200 -Cincinnati 45202 **Fx:**241-4490
(614) 224-7711 .. **Kitrick & Lewis Co,LPA** -515 E Main -Ste 515 -Columbus 43215 **Fx:**225-8985
(614) 224-7711 .. **Kitrick**, Mark M '81 (Kitrick & L Co,LPA) -515 E Main -Ste 515 -Columbus 43215 **Fx:**225-8985
(248) 432-8000 .. **Kittel**, John I '00 (Mazur & K) -30665 Nrthwstrn Hwy -#175 -Farmington, MI 48334
(419) 524-8200 .. **Kitzler**, Benjamin D '00 (Anderson WO&K LLP) -3 N Main -Ste 703 -Mansfield 44902
(419) 524-8200 .. **Kitzler**, David L '76 (Anderson WO&K LLP) -3 N Main -Ste 703 -Mansfield 44902
(419) 524-8200 .. **Kitzler**, Patricia O '88 (Anderson WO&K LLP) -3 N Main -Ste 703 -Mansfield 44902
(330) 746-6301 .. **Kivlighan**, Michael O '03 -219 W Boardman -Youngstown 44503
(614) 224-7291 .. **Kizer**, Tanya J '01 -330 S High -Columbus 43215
(614) 221-8889 .. **Klaben**, Amy D '86 %Columbus Housing Prtnrshp -562 E Main -Columbus 43215
(216) 622-8200 .. **Klaben**, Matthew J '95 (Calfee H&G LLP) -800 Superior Av -Ste 1400 -Cleveland 44114 **Fx:**241-0816
(614) 464-6400 .. **Kladder**, Ronald A '79 OfCnsl Vorys SS&P LLP -52 E Gay -Bx1008 -Columbus 43216 **Fx:**464-6350
(419) 798-5203 .. **Klaehn**, John C '98 Mutachs Market -505 W Main -Marblehead 43440
(717) 593-5190 .. **Klaiber**, Mark J '86 Grove Worldwide -1565 Buchanan Trl E -Shady Grove, PA 17256
(513) 621-2120 .. **Klaine**, Franklin A Jr. '67 (Strauss & T,LPA) -150 E 4th -4th Fl -Cincinnati 45202 **Fx:**241-8259
(440) 974-8484 .. **Klammer**, Darya J '97 Klammer Law -6990 Lindsay Dr -Ste 7 -Mentor 44060
(440) 974-8484 .. **Klammer**, Joseph R '97 (Klammer Law Ofc,Ltd) -6990 Lindsay Dr -Ste 7 -Mentor 44060 **Fx:**255-6112
(440) 974-8484 .. **Klammer**, Lisa M '99 -6996 Lindsay Dr -Ste 7 -Mentor 44060
(440) 543-3879 .. **Klammer**, Martin A '85 -9744 Bainbrdg Rd -Chagrin Falls 44023
(419) 872-6808 .. **Klapp**, Austin F '00 Spore & Assoc,LLC -Bx906 -Perrysburg 43552
(330) 452-5781 .. **Klapp**, Victoria Z '75 Zwick Law Ofcs -1500 Market Av N -Bx8409 -Canton 44711
(770) 460-5061 .. **Klar**, Lawrence F '72 -345 E Lanier Av -Fayetteville, GA 30214
(216) 687-1900 .. **Klaric**, Betty '84 Legal Aid -1223 W 6th -Cleveland 44113 **Fx:**687-0779
(937) 222-2500 .. **Klasing**, Heather E '99 %Sebaly S&D -1900 Kettering Twr -Dayton 45423 **Fx:**222-6554
(440) 572-2100 .. **Klatka**, Edward J Jr. '81 -10950 Pearl Rd -Strongsville 44136
(614) 466-6416 .. **Klatt**, Andrew J '93 Industrial Commssn of OH -30 W Spring -9th Fl -Columbus 43215 **Fx:**752-8785
(614) 221-7548 .. **Klatt**, Courtney Larrimer '96 (Larrimer & L) -165 N High -Columbus 43206 **Fx:**221-8659
(304) 232-8888 .. **Klatt**, Wilbert N '97 %Jividen Law Ofc -729 Main -Wheeling, WV 26003
(419) 523-6200 .. **Klausing**, Jennifer L '04 Putnam Cnty Common Pleas Ct -245 E Main -Ste 302 -Ottawa 45875

(440) 349-3432 .. **Klausman**, Charles W III '67 Tradesmen Intl,Inc
-9760 Shepard Rd -Macedonia 44056

(614) 221-5216 ..**Klausman**, Charles W IV '94 (Wiles BB&B Co,LPA) -300 Spruce
-1st Fl -Columbus 43215 **Fx:**221-5692

(732) 980-3456 ..**Klausman**, David I '81 Amer Standard Co -One Centennial Av
-Bx6820 -Piscataway, NJ 08855

(614) 855-1867 ..**Klayman**, Elliot I '69 -5984 Hilltop Trl Dr -New Albany 43054
Fx:855-3616

(614) 462-3194 ..**Klecker**, Theodore L '00 Franklin Cnty Pub Def -373 S High
-12th Fl -Columbus 43215

(330) 643-5458 ..**Kleckner**, Janet Lee '84 %Summit Cnty Cmn Pleas Ct -209 S High
-Akron 44308

(419) 241-6000 ..**Klee**, Roger P '74 (Eastman & S Ltd) -1 Seagate -24th Fl
-Bx10032 -Toledo 43699 **Fx:**247-1777

(513) 721-4532 ..**Klee**, Tara A '98 %Katz TB&H -255 E 5th -Ste 2400 -Cincinnati
45202

(419) 885-3000 ..**Kleeberger**, Patricia J '98 (Brady C&S LLP)
-4052 Holland-Sylvania Rd -Toledo 43623 **Fx:**885-1120

(317) 881-5862 ..**Kleemann**, Matthew J '04 -125 Monticello Dr
-Greenwood, IN 46142

(312) 454-9580 ..**Kleffman**, Marsha L '84 American Appraisal Prop Tax Srvcs
-10 S Riverside Plz -Ste 300 -Chicago, IL 60606

(740) 354-2300 ..**Kleha**, Jeffrey A '03 -721 5th -Fifth St Law Bldg
-Portsmouth 45662 **Fx:**354-5667

(440) 974-9400 ..**Kleiman**, Michael M '79 -7200 Ctr -Polo Bldg,Ste 202
-Mentor 44060

Klein, Albert W Jr. '85 US Air Force SJAG
-CENTAF-AUAB/CAOC/JA -APO, AE 09309

(614) 299-6139 ..**Klein**, Andrew I '80 -13 W 1st Av -Columbus 43201

(216) 241-5300 ..**Klein**, Ann M Fitzpatrick '94 %D Dreyfuss Co,LPA -1801 E 9th
-Ste 740 -Cleveland 44114

(740) 532-4554 ..**Klein**, Charles C '49 Edwards KA&S Co LPA -211 Center
-Ironton 45638

(937) 255-5270 ..**Klein**, Charles M '86 AFMCLO/JAN -1864 4th -Rm 130A
-Wright Patterson AFB 45433

(614) 764-3228 ..**Klein**, Dana W '79 Wendys Intl -4288 W Dublin-Granvll Rd -Bx256
-Dublin 43017

(419) 861-1100 ..**Klein**, Daniel M '90 CB Richard Ellis Reichle Klein
-1695 Indn Wd Cir -Ste 100 -Maumee 43537

(937) 865-7947 ..**Klein**, Daniel P '92 Lexis/Nexis -Bx933 -Dayton 45401

(614) 323-5225 ..**Klein**, Jack A '76 -Bx21305 -Columbus 43221

(740) 363-3211 ..**Klein**, James H '83 -2 W Winter -Ste 201 -Delaware 43015

(419) 530-2948 ..**Klein**, James M '69 Univ of Toledo Law Schl -2801 W Bancroft
-Toledo 43606

(614) 645-7385 ..**Klein**, John C III '79 City Atty -90 W Broad -Columbus 43215

(614) 985-0527 ..**Klein**, John W '97 -101 Heather Ln -Powell 43065

(216) 561-6111 ..**Klein**, Jonathan I '80 -22899 Byron Rd -Shaker Heights 44122

(513) 762-6200 ..**Klein**, Joseph C '03 %Ulmer & B LLP -600 Vine -Ste 2800
-Cincinnati 45202 **Fx:**762-6245

(216) 861-0111 ..**Klein**, Larry S '80 (Klein & C Co,LPA) -55 Pub Sq -Ste 1200
-Cleveland 44113 **Fx:**861-8203

(202) 514-0458 ..**Klein**, Laura F '95 US DOJ -1325 Penn Av NW -Ste 500
-Washington, DC 20530

(859) 341-1881 ..**Klein**, Mathew R Jr. '92 (Deters B&L,PSC) -2701 Turkeyfoot Rd
-207 Thomas More Pkwy -Crestview Hills, KY 41017 **Fx:**341-1469

(419) 423-4321 ..**Klein**, Matthew L '01 %Firmin S&H Co,LPA -220 W Sandusky
-Bx963 -Findlay 45839 **Fx:**423-8484

Klein, Mattie M '02 -4239 Timber Valley Dr -Columbus 43230

(614) 225-8703 ..**Klein**, Michael A '80 PricewaterhouseCoopers -100 E Broad
-Columbus 43215 **Fx:**(813) 329-0624

Klein, Mitchell L '84 -Bx844 -Columbus 43216

Klein, Paul G '49 -1 Rose Hill Dr -#2 -Bluffton, SC 29910

(216) 696-5157 ..**Klein**, Richard C '64 -1111 Ohio Svngs Plz -Cleveland 44114

(216) 861-5582 ..**Klein**, Richard M '85 (Fay SFM&M LLP) -1100 Superior Av -7th Fl
-Cleveland 44114 **Fx:**241-1666

(440) 464-8388 ..**Klein**, Roger D '98 -33800 Jackson Rd -Moreland Hills 44022

(740) 532-4554 ..**Klein**, Sara B '83 Edwards KA&S Co LPA -211 Center
-Ironton 45638

(216) 566-5500 ..**Klein**, Shana F '01 %Thompson H LLP -127 Pub Sq -3900 Key Ctr
-Cleveland 44114 **Fx:**566-5800

(937) 890-5515 ..**Klein**, Stephen E '75 Klein Law Ofc -240 Bohanan Dr
-Vandalia 45377 **Fx:**890-6791

(740) 532-4554 ..**Klein**, Thomas L '81 Edwards KA&S Co LPA -211 Center
-Ironton 45638

(419) 223-1861 ..**Klein**, Zachary M '04 3rd Dist Ct of Appeals -204 N Main
-Lima 45805

(440) 239-2090 ..**Kleiner**, Stuart J '79 Estate Planning Team,Inc
-16570 Commerce Ct -Middleburg Heights 44130

(513) 721-8358 ..**Kleinhaus**, Ferdinand H Jr. '75 -830 Main -Ste 200
-Cincinnati 45202

(216) 363-4500 ..**Kleinman**, Allan D '52 OfCnsl Benesch FC&A LLP -200 Pub Sq
-Ste 2300 -Cleveland 44114 **Fx:**363-4588

(216) 736-7239 ..**Kleinman**, Kenneth W '74 OfCnsl Kohrman J&K PLL -1375 E 9th
-One Cleve Ctr 20th Fl -Cleveland 44114 **Fx:**621-6536

(216) 522-7800 ..**Kleinman**, Lenore '86 US Trustees Ofc -200 Pub Sq -Ste 3300
-Cleveland 44114 **Fx:**522-4988

(513) 489-9220 ..**Kleinman**, Marvin '53 -6310 E Kemper Rd -Ste100
-Cincinnati 45241 **Fx:**489-7960

(305) 367-3678 ..**Kleinman**, Richard E '56 -38A The Moorings
-Key Largo, FL 33037

(216) 348-5400 ..**Kleinman**, Roger L '84 (McDonald H Co,LPA) -600 Superior Av E
-Ste 2100 -Cleveland 44114 **Fx:**348-5474

(614) 224-0933 ..**Kleinman**, Seth K '02 %Frost & M Co,LPA -400 S 5th -Ste 301
-Columbus 43215

(614) 462-2700 ..**Kleinman**, Stephen R '95 (Schottenstein Z&D) -250 West
-Bx165020 -Columbus 43216 **Fx:**462-5135

(614) 586-1310 ..**Kleiser**, Christina M '98 %Nesbit Law Firm -447 E Main -Ste 200
-Columbus 43215

(513) 579-6400 ..**Klekamp**, Donald P '57 SrCnsl Keating M&K PLL -1 E 4th
-1400 Provident Twr -Cincinnati 45202 **Fx:**579-6457

(513) 579-6400 ..**Klekamp**, Jody T '92 (Keating M&K PLL) -1 E 4th
-1400 Provident Twr -Cincinnati 45202 **Fx:**579-6457

(740) 345-3431 ..**Klema**, Connie J '96 OfCnsl Reese PD&M,PLL -36 N 2nd -Bx919
-Newark 43058 **Fx:**349-5116

(614) 466-3998 ..**Klemann**, Michael A '72 Unemploymnt Comp Commssn
-145 S Front -Bx182299 -Columbus 43218

(216) 635-3980 ..**Klemenok**, Kimberly A '98 Asset Acceptance Corp -Bx318037
-Independence 44131

(614) 232-8134 ..**Klenk**, William C '90 Firstar Bank -175 S 3rd -OH-BR-0714
-Columbus 43215

(216) 931-6000 ..**Klepach**, Anne M '03 %Ulmer & B LLP -1300 E 9th
-Ste 900 Penton Media Bldg -Cleveland 44114 **Fx:**931-6001

(419) 448-4620 ..**Klepatz**, Mark A '84 -257 Ella -Tiffin 44883

(805) 372-8333 ..**Klepper**, Cheryl A '85 Verizon Srvcs Grp
-112 S Lakevw Canyon Rd -Westlake Village, CA 91362

(405) 948-6576 ..**Klepper**, Jim C '02 -1101 Sovereign Row
-Oklahoma City, OK 73108 **Fx:**948-7237

(216) 381-2880 ..**Kleri**, Patricia A '76 Mun Ct Judge -1349 S Green Rd
-South Euclid 44121

(513) 481-9800 ..**Klett**, Jerome R '85 %Hyle & M Co,LPA -3050 Harrison Av
-Cincinnati 45211 **Fx:**481-9592

(606) 344-9900 ..**Klette**, Virginia R '76 (Klette & K) -250 Grandvw Dr -Ste 250
-Fort Mitchell, KY 41017

(304) 233-5200 ..**Klie**, Erika H '04 %Robinson Law Ofc -77 12th
-Wheeling, WV 26003 **Fx:**233-2089

(440) 333-0099 ..**Klima**, Gregory K '86 (Title Access,LLC) -20006 Detroit Rd
-Ste 200 -Rocky River 44116 **Fx:**333-2665

(440) 356-9984 ..**Klima**, Ronald E '76 -40 Pond Dr -Ste 40 -Rocky River 44116

Klimek, Amy A '95 -(Address Unavailable)

(216) 348-5400 ..**Klimek**, Mark D '93 (McDonald H Co,LPA) -600 Superior Av E
-Ste 2100 -Cleveland 44114 **Fx:**348-5474

Kline, Carrie L '02 -2049 Water Crest Ln -Columbus 43209

Kline, Dale A '64 -259 N Elliston Trowbrdg Rd -Graytown 43432

Kline, Donald L '04 -(Address Unavailable)

(817) 858-3300 ..**Kline**, Gary A '81 Uniden America Corp -4700 Amon Carter Blvd
-Fort Worth, TX 76155

Kline, James E '66 -216 Treetop Pl -Holland 43528

(216) 931-6000 ..**Kline**, James N '84 (Ulmer & B LLP) -1300 E 9th -Ste 900
Penton Media Bldg -Cleveland 44114 **Fx:**931-6001

(614) 221-0090 ..**Kline**, Kenneth R '01 %Friedman & M Co,LPA -503 S Front
-Ste -250 -Columbus 43215

(216) 621-0200 ..**Kline**, Melinda M '04 %Baker & H LLP -1900 E 9th -Ste 3200
-Cleveland 44114 **Fx:**696-0740

(216) 328-2895 ..**Kline**, Paul J '02 IRS -5990 W Crk Rd -Independence 44131

(216) 363-4500 ..**Kline**, Rita E '00 %Benesch FC&A LLP -200 Pub Sq -Ste 2300
-Cleveland 44114 **Fx:**363-4588

(847) 317-8900 ..**Kline**, Sandra S '94 Fujisawa Hlthcre,Inc -3 Pkwy N -Deerfield, IL
60015

(614) 466-4320 ..**Kline**, Tiffany A '02 Atty Gen -150 E Gay -Columbus 43215

(440) 257-3060 ..**Kline**, William S III '99 WS Kline III & Assoc -9168 Lakeshr Blvd
-Mentor 44060

(513) 333-4075 ..**Klineman**, Susan B '01 %Weltman W&R Co,LPA -525 Vine
-Ste 800 -Cincinnati 45202 **Fx:**723-2239

(216) 525-4300 ..**Klinge**, Stephen D '01 Premier Farnell -7061 E Plesant Valley Rd
-Independence 44131

(440) 354-5923 ..**Klingenberg**, Donald H '73 -6695 Shannon Ln -Mentor 44060

(330) 494-4748 ..**Klingensmith**, Robert D '79 Lexis-Nexis
-7121 Cedar Grove Av NW -Canton 44720

(513) 665-9500 ..**Klingler**, Robert A '85 (R Klingler Co,LPA) -525 Vine -Ste 2320
-Cincinnati 45202

Klingshirn, Nancy P '86 -5785 Wllmsbrg Cir -Hudson 44236

(330) 665-5445 ..**Klingshirn**, Neil E '86 (Fortney & K) -4040 Embssy Pkwy -Ste 280
-Akron 44333

(216) 781-1212 ..**Klink**, Bradley J '04 %Walter & H LLP -1301 E 9th -Ste 3500
-Cleveland 44114 **Fx:**575-0911

(614) 488-9233 ..**Klitch**, Jennifer L '94 %Elite Recruiting -1435 Cmbrdg Blvd
-Columbus 43212

(440) 269-6246 ..**Klock**, Sally J '87 Geauga Hospital -13207 Ravenna Rd
-Chardon 44024

(513) 923-2120 ..**Klocke**, Dale W '73 -3572 Blue Rock Rd -Cincinnati 45247

(740) 349-5916 ..**Klockner**, Tricia M '04 Newark City Law Dept -40 W Main
-Newark 43055

(614) 466-4656 ..**Klodell**, Alan H '86 Atty Gen -150 E Gay -Columbus 43215
Fx:466-1756

(216) 241-0666 ..**Klonowski**, Daniel J '78 -50 Pub Sq -Ste 920 -Cleveland 44113

(216) 587-2120 ..**Klonowski**, Stephen M '74 Reddy G&M Co,LPA
-5306 Transportation Blvd -Garfield Heights 44125

(513) 352-6700 ..**Kloos**, Brenda M '82 (Thompson H LLP) -312 Walnut -14th Fl
-Cincinnati 45202 **Fx:**241-4771

(216) 771-4304 ..**Klopp**, Ralph M Jr. '75 -1157 Leader Bldg -Cleveland 44114

Klopsch, Diane K '96 -25 Grandon Rd -Dayton 45419

(614) 267-9581 ..**Klos**, Daniel H '84 -4591 Indnola Av -Columbus 43214

Kloss, Vincent J '85 -(Address Unavailable)

(614) 464-6400 ..**Kloss**, William D Sr. '58 OfCnsl Vorys SS&P LLP -52 E Gay
-Bx1008 -Columbus 43216 **Fx:**464-6350

(614) 464-6400 ..**Kloss**, William D Jr. '88 (Vorys SS&P LLP) -52 E Gay -Bx1008
-Columbus 43216 **Fx:**464-6350

(419) 213-4202 ..**Klosterman**, Julie A '98 OH Atty Gen -800 Jackson -Toledo 43624

(614) 480-4579 ..**Klosz**, Raymond T '88 Huntington Invstmnt & Co -41 S High
-7th Fl -Columbus 43215

(719) 262-5769 ..**Klubert**, Louise M '80 Progressive Ins Co -1110 Chapel Hills Dr
-Colorado Springs, CO 80920

(419) 255-1102 ..**Klucas**, David L '88 -1900 Monroe -Toledo 43624

(216) 515-6532 ..**Klucher**, Gregory W '86 Huntington Natl Bank -CM 24 -Bx5065
-Cleveland 44101

(513) 367-1999 ..**Kluener**, Thomas J '84 -1149 Stone Dr -Ste 200 -Harrison 45030

(304) 233-5599 ..**Klug**, Denise D '95 Thorp R&A,LLP -1233 Main -Ste 2001
-Wheeling, WV 26003

(216) 781-5470 ..**Klug**, Paul S '75 (Ziegler M&M LLP) -925 Euclid Av -2020
Huntngtn Bldg -Cleveland 44115 **Fx:**781-0714

(216) 402-9515 ..**Kluge**, Graig E '97 (GE Kluge Co,LPA) -955 W St Clair Av
-Ste 220 -Cleveland 44113

(419) 225-5706 ..**Kluge**, William F '76 -124 S Metcalf -Lima 45801

(419) 867-8900 ..**Klumb**, Marci A '89 OfCnsl Lyden L&C,Ltd -5565 Airport Hwy
-Ste 101 -Toledo 43615 **Fx:**867-8909

(513) 533-2996 ..**Klusmeier**, Mark H '83 Finney SS&K Co,LPA -2623 Erie Av
-Bx8804 -Cincinnati 45208

(216) 241-6602 .. **Kluznik**, Jack S '77 (Weston HFP&H LLP) -50 Pub Sq
-2500 Trmnl Twr -Cleveland 44113 **Fx:**621-8369

(216) 621-6570 .. **Klym**, Christopher J '93 %Rademaker MM&G -55 Pub Sq
-Ste 1775 -Cleveland 44113 **Fx:**621-1127

(504) 524-4162 .. **Klyza**, Stephen M '81 (Kullman Firm) -1100 Poydras -Ste 1600
-Bx60118 -New Orleans, LA 70160 **Fx:**596-4189

(303) 744-5706 .. **Kmentt**, Kimberly A '85 Gates Rubber Co/Tomkins Indust,Inc
-1551 Wewatta -Denver, CO 80202

(216) 861-5000 .. **Kmetich**, Victor G '84 Ernst & Young LLP -1300 Huntngtn Bldg
-925 Euclid Av -Cleveland 44115

(330) 744-5284 .. **Kmetz**, Kimberlee Jo '94 Harshman B&R -105 E Boardman
-Youngstown 44503

(216) 241-2838 .. **Kmetz**, Kristi J '03 %Taft S&H LLP -200 Pub Sq -3500 BP Twr
-Cleveland 44114 **Fx:**241-3707

Kmiec, Thomas D '71 -14886 Standish Av -Middlefield 44062

(216) 696-0650 .. **Kmiecik**, Robert E '84 Kaman & C -50 Pub Sq -Ste 600 Trmnl Twr
-Cleveland 44113

(513) 621-1767 .. **Knabe**, Arthur T '58 (Trenz M&K Co,LPA) -35 E 7th -Ste 400
-Cincinnati 45202

(513) 621-1767 .. **Knabe**, Bruce D '94 Trenz M&K Co,LPA -35 E 7th -Ste 400
-Cincinnati 45202

(216) 228-7200 .. **Knabe**, Kenneth J '79 Brown & S -14222 Mad Av
-Cleveland 44107

(330) 492-8717 .. **Knapic**, Barbara A '86 (Buckingham D&B,LLP)
-4518 Fulton Dr NW -Bx35548 -Canton 44735 **Fx:**492-9625

(419) 586-6444 .. **Knapke**, Henry J Jr. '72 -115 N Walnut -Bx504 -Celina 45822

(419) 586-6444 .. **Knapke**, Jeffrey P '93 -115 N Walnut -Bx504 -Celina 45822

(614) 547-0220 .. **Knapp**, Curtis H '89 Polaris Title Agency -8405 Pulsar Pl -Ste 125
-Columbus 43240

(614) 752-2045 .. **Knapp**, Derrick L '94 Atty Gen -150 E Gay -Columbus 43215

(614) 461-1551 .. **Knapp**, Ernestine M '91 Barkan & B Co LPA -81 S 4th -Ste 300
-Columbus 43215

(614) 462-3555 .. **Knapp**, Irene L '00 Franklin Cnty Pros -373 S High
-Columbus 43215

(614) 466-2766 .. **Knapp**, Jill L '03 Atty Gen -30 E Broad -Columbus 43215
Fx:644-1926

(614) 227-2000 .. **Knapp**, Kyle A '98 %Porter WM&A LLP -41 S High
-Columbus 43215 **Fx:**227-2100

(513) 936-0001 .. **Knapp**, William C '79 (Weber & K Co,LPA) -8044 Mntgmry Rd
-Ste 120 -Cincinnati 45236 **Fx:**936-0002

(937) 291-3400 .. **Knapp**, William G III '81 -848-C E Franklin -Centerville 45459

(440) 946-5155 .. **Knavel**, Randolph L '94 -7784 Reynolds Rd -Mentor 44060

(614) 461-1311 .. **Kneafsey**, Brian M Jr. '93 %Reminger & R -65 E State -4th Fl
Cptl Sq Ofc Bldg -Columbus 43215 **Fx:**232-2410

(216) 621-4882 .. **Knecht**, Denise J '81 -75 Pub Sq -#1300 -Cleveland 44113

(614) 249-6618 .. **Knecht**, Richard S '77 SrCnsl Nationwide Ins Co -1 Nationwide Plz
-Columbus 43215

(513) 946-3800 .. **Kneflin**, Mark C '00 Hamilton Cnty Pub Def -230 E 9th -3rd Fl
-Cincinnati 45202 **Fx:**946-3808

(419) 524-5568 .. **Knell Dorner & Gerhardt Co,LPA** -3 N Main -Ste 602
-Mansfield 44902 **Fx:**524-8011

Knepler, Carl W '94 -2115 Sea Isl Pl -San Marcos, CA 92069

(513) 732-3415 .. **Knepp**, Gary L '94 -65 N 2nd -Batavia 45103

(419) 249-7900 .. **Knepp**, James R II '92 (Robison C&O) -Four SeaGate -9th Fl
-Toledo 43604 **Fx:**249-7911

(419) 213-3191 .. **Knepp**, Linda M '92 Lucas Cnty CSEA -701 Adams -Toledo 43624

(330) 399-2649 .. **Knepp**, Patricia A '93 (J Leopardi Co,LPA) -409 Harmon Av
-Bx610 -Warren 44482

(216) 621-0150 .. **Knerly**, Stephen J Jr. '76 (Hahn L&P LLP) -3300
BP Twr/200 Pub Sq -Ste 3300 -Cleveland 44114 **Fx:**241-2824

(216) 348-0333 .. **Knevel**, Mark H '77 (Knevel & Asoc Co,LPA) -629 Euclid Av
-Ste 519 -Cleveland 44114 **Fx:**523-7801

(440) 322-4657 .. **Knezevic**, Samuel R Jr. '80 Elyria Foundry Co -120 Filbert
-Elyria 44035

(330) 758-0377 .. **Knickerbocker**, Ronald E '82 -725 Boardman-Canfld Rd -L-1
-Bx3202 -Youngstown 44513

Knickle, Lauren L '98 -(Address Unavailable)

(614) 248-7689 .. **Knight**, Barbara M '77 Bank 1 Corp -1111 Polaris Pkwy
-Columbus 43271

(740) 992-2090 .. **Knight**, Charles H '74 -109 W 2nd -Pomeroy 45769

(419) 547-9515 .. **Knight**, Christopher J '78 -422 E McPherson Hwy -Ste C -Bx36
-Clyde 43410

(513) 534-1964 .. **Knight**, M Michelle '93 -38 Fountain Sq -MD 10AT 76
-Cincinnati 45263

(937) 298-1988 .. **Knight**, Randal S '92 -427 Telford Av -Dayton 45419

Knippen, Steven T '04 -(Address Unavailable)

(216) 241-5310 .. **Knisely**, Joseph Colin '97 %Gallagher SF&N -1501 Euclid Av
-6th Fl -Cleveland 44115 **Fx:**241-1608

(614) 486-9503 .. **Knisley**, Daniel S '86 %Knisley Law Ofcs -1390 Dublin Rd
-Columbus 43216 **Fx:**486-7059

(614) 486-9503 .. **Knisley**, David L '89 Knisley Law Ofcs -1390 Dublin Rd
-Columbus 43216 **Fx:**486-7059

(614) 486-9503 .. **Knisley**, Dean A '86 Knisley Law Ofcs -1390 Dublin Rd
-Columbus 43216 **Fx:**486-7059

(614) 486-9503 .. **Knisley**, Douglas C '82 Knisley Law Ofcs -1390 Dublin Rd
-Columbus 43216 **Fx:**486-7059

(513) 701-5529 .. **Knisley**, Melinda E '84 -6860 Tylersvll Rd -Ste 1 -Mason 45040
Fx:701-5528

(614) 486-9503 .. **Knisley**, Scott M '53 Knisley Law Ofcs -1390 Dublin Rd
-Columbus 43216 **Fx:**486-7059

(419) 842-1333 .. **Knoblauch**, Diane J '94 -2354 Whsprng Pines Dr -Toledo 43617
Fx:842-1888

Knochelmann, Carl E Jr. '81 -3032 Belle Meade Ln -Edgewood,
KY 41017

(859) 491-2600 .. **Knoebber**, William T III '71 -319 York -Newport, KY 41071
Fx:491-5076

(330) 376-3300 .. **Knoll**, Jeffrey T '91 (Stark & K Co,LPA) -76 S Main -Ste 1512
-Akron 44308 **Fx:**376-6237

(614) 488-1161 .. **Knoll**, Laren E '99 (Kennedy & K) -3040 Riverside Dr -Ste 103
-Columbus 43221

(330) 376-3300 .. **Knoll**, Thomas G '65 (Stark & K Co,LPA) -76 S Main -Ste 1512
-Akron 44308 **Fx:**376-6237

(216) 928-7518 .. **Knopf**, Christopher D '89 Trust for Public Land -1422 Euclid Av
-Ste 446 -Cleveland 44115

(614) 466-4199 .. **Knopp**, Melissa Ann '95 OH Sup Crt -30 E Broad
-Columbus 43266

(937) 278-0651 .. **Knostman**, Richard G '72 -4428 N Dixie Dr -Dayton 45414

(216) 523-5484 .. **Knoth**, Richard M '89 (Bricker & E LLP) -1375 E 9th -Ste 1500
-Cleveland 44114 **Fx:**523-7071

(937) 443-6777 .. **Knoth**, Thomas A '86 (Thompson H LLP) -2000 Cthse Plz NE
-Bx8801 -Dayton 45401 **Fx:**443-6635

(216) 502-0350 .. **Knott**, Paul S '92 %Repicky & K -526 Superior Av
-530 Leader Bldg -Cleveland 44114

(216) 642-3342 .. **Knowles**, David R '74 (Wegman H&V,LPA)
-6055 Rockside Wds Blvd -Ste 200 -Cleveland 44131
Fx:642-8826

(216) 241-4100 .. **Knowles**, Scott T '03 %Keis/G LLP -55 Pub Sq -Ste 800
-Cleveland 44113 **Fx:**771-3111

(330) 674-9776 .. **Knowling**, Stephen D '75 (Rinfret & K) -184 E Jackson
-Millersburg 44654

(740) 439-2719 .. **Knowlton & Bennett** -126 N 9th -Cambridge 43725

(330) 262-7555 .. **Knowlton**, David C '92 (Kennedy CK&B) -558 N Market
-Wooster 44691

(937) 390-0695 .. **Knowlton**, Peter M '59 -3052 Bahia Dr -Bx1011 -Springfield 45501

(219) 428-7924 .. **Knox**, Noel H '83 Fifth 3rd Bank -132 E Berry
-Fort Wayne, IN 46802

(513) 241-3800 .. **Knox**, Scott E '85 -13 E Court -Ste 300 -Cincinnati 45202

(330) 684-3000 .. **Knudsen**, Jeannette L '98 JM Smucker Co -1 Strwbrry Ln
-Orrville 44667

(330) 471-4101 .. **Knudsen**, Nancy S '82 Timken Co -1835 Dueber Av -BIC-11
-Canton 44706

(614) 464-6400 .. **Knueve**, Mark A '96 (Vorys SS&P LLP) -52 E Gay -Bx1008
-Columbus 43216 **Fx:**464-6350

(614) 464-6400 .. **Knueve**, Meredith K '99 %Vorys SS&P LLP -52 E Gay -Bx1008
-Columbus 43216 **Fx:**464-6350

(216) 201-3504 .. **Knull**, Ralph E '92 SYSCO Food Srvcs of Clvlnd,Inc
-4747 Grayton Rd -Cleveland 44135 **Fx:**201-3531

(216) 363-4500 .. **Knuth**, Ann E '93 (Benesch FC&A LLP) -200 Pub Sq -Ste 2300
-Cleveland 44114 **Fx:**363-4588

(260) 484-4526 .. **Knuth**, Randall J '90 (R Knuth,PC) -4921 Desoto Dr
-Fort Wayne, IN 46815 **Fx:**484-0185

(330) 534-1481 .. **Knuth**, Richard L '84 -339-2 Viola Av -Hubbard 44425

(614) 466-7447 .. **Knutti**, Randall W '84 Atty Gen -150 E Gay -Columbus 43215

(216) 241-2500 .. **Koach**, Jules N '66 OfCnsl Monroe & Z -526 Superior Av
-Ste 1525 -Cleveland 44114

(216) 781-2258 .. **Kobal**, Cindy L '00 Stewart & D Co,LPA -1370 Ontario
-Ste 1440 Standard Bldg -Cleveland 44113 **Fx:**781-8210

(614) 466-4961 .. **Kobalka**, Walter S '76 %Sup Ct of OH -30 E Broad -2nd Fl
-Columbus 43215 **Fx:**644-4767

(216) 566-5833 .. **Kobasic**, Dena M '89 (Thompson H LLP) -127 Pub Sq
-3900 Key Ctr -Cleveland 44114 **Fx:**566-5800

(513) 381-2838 .. **Kobasuk**, Mark G '90 (Taft S&H LLP) -425 Walnut -Ste 1800
-Cincinnati 45202 **Fx:**381-0205

(614) 888-2600 .. **Kobe**, Robert F '62 -108 W Granvll Rd -Worthington 43085

(440) 997-9222 .. **Kobelak**, William A '80 -4366 Main Av -Bx1422 -Ashtabula 44005

(216) 781-5470 .. **Koberg**, Jeffrey L '90 %Ziegler M&M LLP -925 Euclid Av
-2020 Huntngtn Bldg -Cleveland 44115 **Fx:**781-0714

(216) 861-6833 .. **Koberna**, Mark R '87 (Sonkin & K Co,LPA) -55 Pub Sq -Ste 1660
-Cleveland 44113

(614) 236-6675 .. **Kobil**, Daniel T '83 Capital Univ Law Sch -303 E Broad
-Columbus 43215

(419) 874-3322 .. **Kobil**, Gerald M '75 -118 W S Boundary -Perrysburg 43551

(260) 489-0057 .. **Kobil**, Walter '56 -3425 Bramblewood Ln -Fort Wayne, IN 46818

(216) 621-3012 .. **Koblentz & Koblentz** -55 Pub Sq -Ste 1170 -Cleveland 44113
Fx:621-6567

(216) 621-3012 .. **Koblentz**, Richard S '75 (Koblentz & K) -55 Pub Sq -Ste 1170
-Cleveland 44113 **Fx:**621-6567

(614) 461-6666 .. **Koblentz**, Robert A '70 -35 E Lvngstn Av -Columbus 43215

(216) 292-7230 .. **Koblentz**, Steven B '81 -5910 Landerbrook Dr -Ste 300
-Cleveland 44124

(216) 621-0150 .. **Koblenz**, N Herschel '60 Cnsl Hahn L&P LLP
-3300 BP Twr/200 Pub Sq -Ste 3300 -Cleveland 44114
Fx:241-2824

(216) 292-6450 .. **Kobyljanec**, William '81 Entrust,Inc -24400 Hgh Pnt Rd -Ste 2
-Beachwood 44122

(216) 621-4244 .. **Kobylski**, Kimberly J '04 -623 W St Clair Av -% Michl Partlow
-Cleveland 44113

(330) 253-5060 .. **Kobzowicz**, Leigh A '03 %Brennan M&D,LLC -75 E Market
-Akron 44308 **Fx:**253-1977

(216) 781-5245 .. **Kocab**, Brooke F '85 (Berkman GM&D) -55 Pub Sq
-2121 The Illuminating Bldg -Cleveland 44113 **Fx:**781-8207

(419) 238-0014 .. **Koch**, Charles F '80 -106 W Main -Van Wert 45891

(419) 668-8211 .. **Koch**, Curtis J '85 (Hiltz WA&K Co,LPA) -401 Ctzns Natl Bk Bldg
-Bx640 -Norwalk 44857 **Fx:**668-2813

(513) 983-2630 .. **Koch**, Elizabeth M '97 %Proctor & Gamble
-1 Proctor & Gamble Plz -Cincinnati 45202 **Fx:**983-0911

(202) 778-9110 .. **Koch**, George W '67 OfCnsl Kirkpatrick & LNG LLP
-1800 Mass Av NW -Washington, DC 20036 **Fx:**778-9100

(702) 895-9584 .. **Koch**, Jan P '79 -712 S 8th -Las Vegas, NV 89101

(609) 518-4155 .. **Koch**, Kenneth H '79 Inrange Tech -100 Mt Holly By-Pass
-Lumberton, NJ 08048

(330) 253-2729 .. **Koch**, Matthew J '67 (Koch & R) -120 E Mill -Ste 405 -Akron 44308

(419) 626-1681 .. **Koch**, Richard D '80 -1604 E Perkins Av -Ste 104 -Bx372
-Sandusky 44871

(614) 288-4740 .. **Koch**, Ronald J '03 -140 E Town -Ste 1070 -Columbus 43215

(216) 443-9000 .. **Koch**, Suzana Krstevski '01 %Porter WM&A LLP -925 Euclid Av
-Ste 1700 -Cleveland 44115 **Fx:**443-9011

(614) 220-5611 .. **Kochalski**, Edward M '75 (Manley D&K,LLC) -495 S High -Ste 300
-Columbus 43215 **Fx:**220-5613

(202) 690-0390 .. **Kochan**, Gena R '99 USDA/Ofc of Gen Cnsl
-1400 Indpndnc Av SW -Washington, DC 20250

(419) 938-1740 .. **Kochensparger**, Andrea S '01 Mansfield Plumbing Prod,Inc
-150 1st -Bx620 -Perrysville 44864

(419) 732-3135 .. **Kocher**, John A '74 (Kocher & G) -101½ Madison
-Port Clinton 43452 **Fx:**734-5644

(614) 486-8905 ..**Kocher**, Walter W '75 -2245 Lane Woods Dr -Columbus 43221
Fx:486-8907

(740) 387-0970 ..**Kochheiser**, Keith A '78 (Wilson & K Co,LPA) -132 S Main
-Marion 43302

(216) 363-6050 ..**Kochis**, Joseph A '78 -1468 W 9th -Ste 425 -Cleveland 44113

(216) 781-9090 ..**Kochis**, Rob M '90 The Townsend Group -1660 W 2nd -Ste 450
-Cleveland 44113 Fx:781-1407

(440) 871-4858 ..**Kocian**, Jeffrey L '66 -25360 Westwood Rd -Westlake 44145
Fx:871-4850

(216) 443-7800 ..**Kocian**, Jeffrey V '03 %Cuyahoga Cnty Pros -1200 Ontario -8th Fl
-Cleveland 44113 Fx:698-2270

(216) 861-5582 ..**Kocovsky**, Thomas E Jr. '78 (Fay SFM&M LLP) -1100 Superior Av
-7th Fl -Cleveland 44114 Fx:241-1666

(614) 466-0605 ..**Kocsis**, Alexander S '77 Industrial Commssn of OH -30 W Spring
-9th Fl -Columbus 43215 Fx:752-8785

(440) 323-3456 ..**Kocsis**, Paul M '99 %Eschrich & S Co,LPA -300 4th -Elyria 44035
Fx:323-3434

(419) 472-9041 ..**Koder**, Stephen D '78 (Koder & S) -3361 Exec Pkwy -Ste 101
-Toledo 43606

(216) 977-0492 ..**Kodger**, Donald O '98 Analex Corp -1000 Apollo Dr
-Cleveland 44142

(216) 566-0580 ..**Kodish**, Joan A '79 -1015 Euclid Av -Ste 300 -Cleveland 44115

(330) 762-6474 ..**Kodish**, Joseph S '69 -411 Wolf Ledges Pkwy -Ste 300
-Akron 44311

(614) 443-7455 ..**Koeck**, Roger M '92 %Merullo R&S Co,LPA -772 S Front
-Columbus 43206

(703) 433-4634 ..**Koehler**, Alan W '86 Nextel Communications Inc
-2001 Edmund Halley Dr -Reston, VA 20191

(740) 345-9801 ..**Koehler**, Charles H '63 (Jones NM&H) -35 S Park Plz -Ste 35
-Bx4010 -Newark 43058 Fx:345-6031

(216) 515-1660 ..**Koehler**, Christopher C '92 Frantz W LLP -127 Pub Sq
-2500 Key Center -Cleveland 44114 Fx:515-1650

(216) 241-5310 ..**Koehler**, James F '73 (Gallagher SF&N) -1501 Euclid Av -6th Fl
-Cleveland 44115 Fx:241-1608

(419) 424-5847 ..**Koehler**, John H '79 (Lather & K) -725 S Main -Findlay 45840

(734) 827-8079 ..**Koehler**, Kathryn L '89 Ave Maria Sch of Law -3475 Plymouth Rd
-Ann Arbor, MI 48105

(614) 866-9154 ..**Koehler**, Mark W '93 -7662 Slate Ridge Blvd -Reynoldsburg 43068
Fx:866-3223

(513) 868-0008 ..**Koehler**, Richard N II '78 -6 S 2nd -Ste 205 -Hamilton 45011

(330) 644-3572 ..**Koehler**, Ronald J '86 -3522 Mnchstr Rd -Ste D -Akron 44319
Fx:644-5333

(419) 691-8889 ..**Koehn**, Richard W '79 -3015 Navarre Av -Ste 214 -Oregon 43616
Koenemann, Lynda '02 -2940 Lee Rd -Shaker Heights 44120

(614) 241-5902 ..**Koenig**, Charles A '78 (C Koenig,LPA) -326 S High
-Columbus 43215

(216) 443-8970 ..**Koenig**, Heidi M '86 Cuyahoga Cnty Probate Ct -1 Lakeside Av
-Cleveland 44113

(216) 566-5503 ..**Koenig**, James C '87 (Thompson H LLP) -127 Pub Sq
-3900 Key Ctr -Cleveland 44114 Fx:566-5800

(216) 522-6812 ..**Koenig**, John P '82 Defense Finance&AccountingSrvc -Bx998006
-Cleveland 44199
Koenig, Joseph A '75 -419 Lewiston Rd -Dayton 45429

(513) 241-8844 ..**Koenig**, Kenneth J '77 -441 Vine -4400 Carew Twr
-Cincinnati 45202

(513) 579-1500 ..**Koenig**, Peter E '81 (Buechner HOM&H Co,LPA) -105 E 4th
-Ste 300 -Cincinnati 45202 Fx:977-4361

(419) 241-9000 ..**Koenig**, Robert A '83 (Shumaker L&K,LLP) -1000 Jackson
-Toledo 43624 Fx:241-6894

(614) 466-6750 ..**Koenig**, Robert G Jr. '91 OH Dept Taxation -30 E Broad -22nd Fl
-Columbus 43215

(216) 861-5582 ..**Koenig**, Sandra M '87 (Fay SFM&M LLP) -1100 Superior Av
-7th Fl -Cleveland 44114 Fx:241-1666

(216) 566-6600 ..**Koenig**, William M '95 Mooney Grp -1301 E 9th -Ste 3330
-Cleveland 44114 Fx:566-6608

(419) 255-0814 ..**Koeninger**, Walter D '96 ABLE -520 Mad Av -740 Spitzer Bldg
-Toledo 43604 Fx:259-2880

(678) 947-9438 ..**Koepp**, Bryan P '01 AXA Distrbtrs,Inc -6435 Shiloh Rd -Ste A
-Alpharetta, GA 30005
Koepper, Engeline H '76 -Bx2143 -Painesville 44077

(440) 357-5577 ..**Koerner**, David E '85 -111 E Wshngtn -Ste 1 -Painesville 44077
Fx:357-1833

(440) 354-3800 ..**Koerner**, James P '75 (Rand GH&K) -270 E Main -Ste 300
-Painesville 44077

(614) 451-0713 ..**Koerner**, Nancy L '84 -3047 Wareham Rd -Columbus 43221

(614) 621-0200 ..**Koerwitz**, Deborah L '99 %Baker & H LLP -1900 E 9th -Ste 3200
-Cleveland 44114 Fx:696-0740

(216) 443-9000 ..**Koesel**, Margaret M '89 (Porter WM&A LLP) -925 Euclid Av
-Ste 1700 -Cleveland 44115 Fx:443-9011

(202) 687-4420 ..**Koester**, Anne Y '88 Georgetown Ctr for Liturgy -3510 N NW
-Washington, DC 20007 Fx:687-3728

(419) 227-2631 ..**Koester**, Mark A '93 OH-Adult Parole Auth -137 W North
-Lima 45801

(419) 678-2378 ..**Koesters**, Judy A '86 -201 E Vine -Coldwater 45828

(216) 696-1433 ..**Koeth Rice & Leo Co, LPA** -1280 W 3rd -Cleveland 44113
Fx:696-1439

(216) 696-1433 ..**Koeth**, Robert J '82 (Koeth R&L Co,LPA) -1280 W 3rd
-Cleveland 44113 Fx:696-1439

(216) 586-3939 ..**Koethe**, Paul D '86 (Jones D) -901 Lakeside Av -Cleveland 44114
Fx:579-0212

(614) 481-4480 ..**Koffel**, Bradley P '93 (Koffel & J) -2130 Arlngtn Av -Columbus
43221

(614) 481-4480 ..**Koffel & Jump** -2130 Arlngtn Av -Columbus 43221

(301) 718-2270 ..**Kohanek**, James J '77 TLI Systems -4340 E West Hwy -Ste 1120
-Bethesda, MD 20814

(937) 324-3000 ..**Kohler**, Anthony E '84 Kohler Legal Srvcs -210 N Fountain Av
-Springfield 45504

(937) 223-3001 ..**Kohler**, Chad M '01 %Jenks P&O Co,LPA -10 N Ludlow -Ste 901
-Dayton 45402 Fx:223-3103

(614) 438-4080 ..**Kohler**, Charles W '75 -100 E Campus Vw Blvd -Ste 250
-Columbus 43235 Fx:438-4081

(216) 529-2870 ..**Kohler**, John E '69 (Paynter K&W) -11740 Clifton Blvd -Ste 202
-Lakewood 44107 Fx:529-2883

(614) 888-4911 ..**Kohler**, Joseph E '75 (J Kohler & Assoc) -7650 Rvrs Edge Dr
-Ste 101 -Columbus 43235

(513) 852-8200 ..**Kohlhepp**, William G '69 Cors & B LLC -537 E Pete Rose Way
-Ste 400 -Cincinnati 45202

(419) 898-2671 ..**Kohli**, Gary A '71 (Graves K&C) -142 W Water -Oak Harbor 43449

(419) 868-1162 ..**Kohli**, Leslie A '00 -1236 Clark -Ste B -Holland 43528

(330) 527-7007 ..**Kohli**, Susan Kim '94 -8134 Main -Garrettsville 44231

(419) 223-1861 ..**Kohlrieser**, Terri L '01 %Hon SR Shaw -204 N Main -Lima 45801

(419) 228-2122 ..**Kohlrieser**, Todd E '02 -973 W North -Lima 45805 Fx:222-6718

(216) 694-4337 ..**Kohn**, Andrew '74 Hyatt Legal Plans,Inc -1111 Superior Av
-Cleveland 44114

(513) 631-6159 ..**Kohn**, Michael G '78 -2690 Madison Rd -Cincinnati 45208
Fx:351-1502

(312) 258-5500 ..**Kohn**, William I '76 Schiff H&W -233 S Wacker Dr -Ste 6600
-Chicago, IL 60606

(513) 621-6464 ..**Kohnen**, Monica Donath '85 (Graydon H&R LLP) -511 Walnut
-1900 Fifth Third Ctr -Cincinnati 45202 Fx:651-3836

(513) 381-0656 ..**Kohnen & Patton LLP** -201 E 5th -Ste 800 -Cincinnati 45202
Fx:381-5823

(513) 684-3711 ..**Kohnen**, Ralph W '86 US Atty -221 E 4th -Ste 400
-Cincinnati 45202 Fx:684-6385

(216) 696-8700 ..**Kohrman Jackson & Krantz PLL** -1375 E 9th
-One Cleve Ctr 20th Fl -Cleveland 44114 Fx:621-6536

(216) 696-8700 ..**Kohrman**, Soloman Lee '53 (Kohrman J&K PLL) -1375 E 9th
-One Cleve Ctr 20th Fl -Cleveland 44114 Fx:621-6536

(330) 643-2943 ..**Kohrs**, Brendon J '04 Summit Cnty Pros-Juv -650 Dan
-Akron 44310 Fx:379-3647

(614) 466-2413 ..**Kohrt**, Douglas H '74 Supreme Ct of OH -30 E Broad -35th Fl
-Columbus 43215

(330) 434-2713 ..**Kohut**, Eric T '02 LE Spragin -628 Payne Av -Akron 44302

(248) 680-8870 ..**Kohut**, Gary L '84 -Bx99187 -Troy, MI 48099
Kojetin, Erica A '04 -(Address Unavailable)

(614) 232-0424 ..**Kokensparger**, Steven J '94 -471 E Broad -Ste 2001
-Columbus 43215

(330) 448-1133 ..**Kokor**, Robert C '93 -394 State Route 7 SE -Bx236
-Brookfield 44403

(216) 328-2009 ..**Kola**, Arthur A '64 -6100 Oak Tree Blvd -Ste 200
-Independence 44131 Fx:328-2001

(614) 466-2766 ..**Koladin Plantz**, Summer '00 Atty Gen -30 E Broad
-Columbus 43215 Fx:644-1926

(330) 668-1050 ..**Kolarik**, Todd M '96 -3490 Rdgwd Rd -Akron 44333

(216) 443-7800 ..**Kolasinski**, Ralph A '83 Cuyahoga Cnty Pros -1200 Ontario
-8th Fl -Cleveland 44113 Fx:698-2270

(419) 882-2142 ..**Kolb**, Henry G '81 Morgan Stanley -7311 Crossleigh Ct -Ste 106
-Toledo 43617

(248) 512-4082 ..**Kolb**, Kim R '80 DamlerChrysler Corp -1000 Chrysler Dr
-CIMS 485-13-32 -Auburn Hills, MI 48326

(614) 466-6750 ..**Kolb**, Loretta R '74 OH Dept Taxation -30 E Broad -22nd Fl
-Columbus 43215

(419) 244-3006 ..**Kolb**, Richard L '67 (Kolb & Z) -405 Mad Av -Ste 2000
-Toledo 43604 Fx:246-4754

(937) 748-6700 ..**Kolb**, Stanley E '59 -95 Edgebrook Dr -Ste 201 -Bx142
-Springboro 45066 Fx:748-9030

(419) 244-3006 ..**Kolb & Zigray** -405 Mad Av -Ste 2000 -Toledo 43604
Fx:246-4754

(614) 466-4605 ..**Kolbash**, Ronn L '97 OH Dept Job & Fam Srvcs -30 E Broad
-32nd Fl -Columbus 43266

(718) 254-6039 ..**Kolbe**, Margaret M '96 US Atty-EDNY -One Pierrepont Plz
-Brooklyn, NY 11201

(937) 296-4153 ..**Kolberg**, John F '83 -3131 S Dixie Dr -Ste 107 -Dayton 45439

(440) 934-3590 ..**Kolczun**, Louis A '70 (LS Kolczun Co,LPA) -5060 Waterford Dr
-Sheffield Village 44035 Fx:934-3594

(216) 692-7200 ..**Kold**, Linda '01 Park-Ohio Ind,Inc -23000 Euclid Av -Euclid 44117

(713) 296-2535 ..**Kolencik**, Richard J '92 Marathon Oil Co -5555 San Felipe Rd
-Rm 2535 -Bx4813 -Houston, TX 77210 Fx:296-4227

(513) 352-6545 ..**Kolesar**, Andrew L '97 (Thompson H LLP) -312 Walnut -14th Fl
-Cincinnati 45202 Fx:241-4771

(847) 236-8454 ..**Kolesar**, Edward M '88 Deloitte & Touche -1751 Lk Cook Rd
-Tax Technologies -Deerfield, IL 60015

(419) 334-6222 ..**Kolesar**, John P '95 Sandusky Cnty Pros -100 N Park Av
-Fremont 43420

(330) 384-4580 ..**Kolich**, Kathy J '87 First Energy Corp -76 S Main -Akron 44308

(440) 835-1200 ..**Kolick**, Daniel J '75 (Kolick & K) -24500 Ctr Ridge Rd -Ste 175
-Westlake 44145

(216) 575-7575 ..**Kolick**, David '74 (Kolick G&E Co,LPA) -55 Pub Sq
-1350 Illuminating Bldg -Cleveland 44113

(216) 575-7575 ..**Kolick Georgeadis & Ernewein Co,LPA** -55 Pub Sq
-1350 Illuminating Bldg -Cleveland 44113

(440) 835-1200 ..**Kolick & Kondzer** -24500 Ctr Ridge Rd -Ste 175
-Westlake 44145

(513) 752-1300 ..**Koligian**, Helene '97 -325 W Ohio Pike -Amelia 45102
Fx:752-1305

(440) 930-8048 ..**Kolis**, William F Jr. '80 Wickens HPC&B -35765 Chester Rd
-Avon 44011 Fx:937-4466

(330) 374-1040 ..**Kolk**, Joseph M '86 Cohen & Co CPAs -121 S Main -Akron 44308

(702) 652-5548 ..**Kolkoski**, Richard R '73 Dep of the Air Force -4428 England Av
-AWFC/JA -Nellis AFB, NV 89191

(440) 254-8818 ..**Kolkowski**, Brian M '91 Kolkaski Law Ofc -6340 Taylor Rd
-Painesville 44077

(216) 522-3715 ..**Kollar**, John '56 NLRB -1240 E 9th -1695 Celebrezze Bldg
-Cleveland 44199 Fx:522-2418

(216) 441-5100 ..**Kollin**, Clement '75 (Kollin & Assoc) -4053 E 71st
-Cleveland 44105

(937) 424-5390 ..**Kollin**, Thomas M '96 (Cicero & K,PLL) -500 E 5th -Ste 100
-Dayton 45424 Fx:424-5393

(216) 443-7800 ..**Kollin**, Timothy J '85 Cuyahoga Cnty Pros -1200 Ontario -8th Fl
-Cleveland 44113 Fx:698-2270

(330) 746-6591 ..**Kolmacic**, Mark J '82 -26 Market -Ste 610 -Youngstown 44503
Fx:744-5147

(614) 462-5872 ..**Kolman**, Marya C '78 Franklin Cnty -373 S High -3rd Fl
-Columbus 43215

(614) 241-5550 ..**Kolman**, Michael S '81 %Brunner Law Firm Co,LPA -545 E Town
-Columbus 43215 Fx:241-5551

(614) 221-1000 .. **Kolnicki,** Shari A '00 Deloitte & Touche,LLP -155 E Broad -Columbus 43215

(216) 363-4500 .. **Kolocouris,** Gregory S '02 %Benesch FC&A LLP -200 Pub Sq -Ste 2300 -Cleveland 44114 **Fx:**363-4588

(216) 524-6207 .. **Koloda,** Richard J '98 -365 E Plsnt Vlly -Seven Hills 44131

(419) 241-5175 .. **Kolodgy,** Kathleen W '85 (Maloney M&K) -520 Mad Av -Ste 330 -Toledo 43604

(513) 821-1000 .. **Kolodny,** Victor M '62 First Amer Corp -2400 E Sharon Rd -Cincinnati 45241

(937) 461-5297 .. **Kolotkin,** Beth A '80 -1402 Lbrty Twr -Mid-City Station -Bx10134 -Dayton 45402

(440) 582-8180 .. **Kolozvary,** Stephen P '79 Nationwide Ins -6233 Bunker Rd -North Royalton 44133

(440) 349-0388 .. **Kolt,** Jeffrey A '70 -33840 Aurora Rd -Ste 200 -Solon 44139

(614) 462-3555 .. **Koltak,** Joseph A '04 %Franklin Cnty Pros -373 S High -Columbus 43215

(937) 492-1271 .. **Koltak,** Joshua A '04 %Faulkner GK&S,LPA -100 S Main Av -Ste 300 -Sidney 45365 **Fx:**498-1306

(614) 221-7381 .. **Koltak,** Ronald J '77 (Koltak & G,LLP) -5 E Long -Ste 100 -Columbus 43215

(407) 661-1177 .. **Koltun,** Jeffrey M '85 (Kane & K) -557 N Wymore Rd -Ste 100 -Maitland, FL 32751 **Fx:**660-6031

(440) 585-1441 .. **Komarjanski,** Stephen '71 -31809 Vine -Willowick 44095

(614) 365-2700 .. **Komasara,** Tiffany L '01 %Squire S&D LLP -41 S High -1300 Huntngtn Ctr -Columbus 43215 **Fx:**365-2499

(412) 355-6556 .. **Komoroski,** Kenneth S '00 (Kirkpatrick & LNG LLP) -535 Smithfld -Henry W Oliver Bldg -Pittsburgh, PA 15222 **Fx:**355-6501

(216) 341-5666 .. **Komorowski,** James J '71 -4105 E 71st -Cleveland 44105

Komp, Laurence E '94 -423 Madrina Ct -Ballwin, MO 63021

(614) 644-2782 .. **Koncelik,** Joseph P '93 EPA -122 S Front -Bx1049 -Columbus 43216

(216) 221-1215 .. **Konchan,** James E '73 -15203 Detroit Av -Lakewood 44107

(419) 241-2100 .. **Kondalski,** Kimberly Sue '87 (Watkins B&C) -405 Mad Av -Ste 1900 -Toledo 43604 **Fx:**241-1960

(216) 622-8200 .. **Kondas,** Brian E '95 %Calfee H&G LLP -800 Superior Av -Ste 1400 -Cleveland 44114 **Fx:**241-0816

(440) 350-2683 .. **Kondas,** Dale R '79 Lake Cnty Pros -105 Main -Bx490 -Painesville 44077 **Fx:**350-2585

(671) 472-7332 .. **Kondas,** Mark E '83 US DOJ -108 Hernan Cortez Av -Ste 500 -Hagatna, GU 96910

(330) 743-5101 .. **Kondela,** Joseph D '99 %Green H&S,Co LPA -16 Wick Av -Ste 400 -Youngstown 44503 **Fx:**743-3451

Kondik, Marie A '02 -3081 Wadsworth Rd -Norton 44203

(330) 338-1609 .. **Kondoleon,** Nicholas L '01 -3999 Cardinal Rd -Akron 44333

(440) 835-1200 .. **Kondzer,** Thomas A '75 (Kolick & K) -24500 Ctr Ridge Rd -Ste 175 -Westlake 44145

(216) 622-3600 .. **Konen,** Betty J '89 %US Atty -801 W Superior -Ste 400 -Cleveland 44113 **Fx:**622-3370

(216) 579-9740 .. **Konet,** Thomas J '72 -1370 Ontario -Ste 2000 -Cleveland 44113

(216) 575-2154 .. **Konfala,** John A '85 National City Corp -Natl City Ctr -Bx5756 -Cleveland 44101

(419) 249-7900 .. **Konieczny,** Timothy A '82 (Robison C&O) -Four SeaGate -9th Fl -Toledo 43604 **Fx:**249-7911

(520) 321-0424 .. **Konigsberg,** Neil J '78 (Konigsberg,PLLC) -2205 E Speedway Blvd -Tucson, AZ 85719 **Fx:**321-0585

(313) 961-4400 .. **Konkel,** John G '90 %McKeen & Assoc,PC -645 Griswold -42nd Fl Penobscot Bldg -Detroit, MI 48226

(440) 498-8237 .. **Konkol-Myers,** Kim R '85 -32906 Lisa Ln -Solon 44139

(216) 348-5400 .. **Konkoly,** Anthony D '86 (McDonald H Co,LPA) -600 Superior E -Ste 2100 -Cleveland 44114 **Fx:**348-5474

(202) 208-5134 .. **Konkoly-Thege,** Kaniah W '01 US Dept of the Interior -1849 C NW -MS 6456 -Washington, DC 20240

(312) 245-7500 .. **Kono,** Dayne O '98 Masuda FE&M,Ltd -203 N LaSalle -Ste 2500 -Chicago, IL 60601 **Fx:**245-7467

(419) 255-0571 .. **Konop,** Alan S '63 (Konop & C) -413 N Mich -Toledo 43624 **Fx:**255-6227

(330) 451-7897 .. **Konovsky,** Hope S '98 Stark Cnty Pros -110 Central Plz -Ste 510 -Canton 44702

(330) 497-8274 .. **Konovsky,** John T Jr. '98 %Lensman & Assoc,Ltd -6273 Frank Av NW -North Canton 44720 **Fx:**497-8269

(330) 253-2195 .. **Konstand,** Dean '79 -106 S Main -Ste 2500 -Akron 44308

(330) 253-2195 .. **Konstand,** Robert G '77 -106 S Main -Ste 2500 -Akron 44308 **Fx:**996-8174

(937) 645-8425 .. **Konstantacos,** Taso W '86 Honda of Amer Mfg -19900 St Rt 739 -Marysville 43040

(216) 623-0000 .. **Konstantinopoulos,** Theodore A '95 %Javitch B&R -1300 E 9th -14th Fl -Cleveland 44114 **Fx:**623-0190

(419) 691-2491 .. **Kontak,** James R '76 Fiske Bros Refining -1500 Oakdale -Toledo 43605

(330) 385-3900 .. **Kontnier,** Kellie S '91 Aronson F&D Co, LPA -124 E 5th -East Liverpool 43920

(937) 512-1532 .. **Konya,** Janice R '97 US Dist Ct/SD OH -200 W 2nd -Rm 902 -Dayton 45402

(937) 393-4600 .. **Koogler,** Lee D '01 -112 N High -Hillsboro 45133

(614) 227-2000 .. **Koogler,** Mark B '80 (Porter WM&A LLP) -41 S High -Columbus 43215 **Fx:**227-2100

(419) 447-2521 .. **Koop,** Martin D '98 Supance & H -84-88 S Wshngtn -Bx767 -Tiffin 44883 **Fx:**447-2310

(614) 461-1234 .. **Kooperman,** Brian T '04 Portman F&F LLP -471 E Broad -Ste 1820 -Columbus 43215 **Fx:**461-9150

(614) 280-1100 .. **Koorn,** Amy B '01 %Keener DC&P,LPA -88 E Broad -Ste 1750 -Columbus 43215

(937) 865-6800 .. **Koorndyk,** Jill A '95 Lexis/Nexis -Bx933 -Dayton 45401

(216) 696-2040 .. **Koosed,** Lee A '74 (Stotter & K Co,LPA) -75 Pub Sq -Ste 1200 -Cleveland 44113 **Fx:**696-2164

(330) 972-6793 .. **Koosed,** Margery B '74 Univ of Akron Law Schl -LAW 213 -Akron 44325

(419) 524-0471 .. **Kopcial,** Douglas J '87 -223 Reform -Mansfield 44902

(614) 242-5931 .. **Kopech,** David A '82 Kopech & Assoc -140 E Town -Columbus 43215 **Fx:**464-0572

(614) 469-3200 .. **Kopf,** John B III '02 %Thompson H LLP -10 W Broad -Ste 700 -Columbus 43215 **Fx:**469-3361

(216) 621-0150 .. **Kopit,** Alan S '77 (Hahn L&P LLP) -3300 BP Twr/200 Pub Sq -Ste 3300 -Cleveland 44114 **Fx:**241-2824

(216) 241-5735 .. **Kopkas,** Andrew J '59 Lustig E&L Co,LPA -526 Superior Av E -Ste 615 -Cleveland 44114

(216) 696-5211 .. **Koplow,** James B '56 -75 Pub Sq -Ste 650 -Cleveland 44113

(330) 746-8484 .. **Kopp,** Brian P '95 (Betras M&K LLC) -6630 Sevll Dr -Bx129 -Canfield 44406 **Fx:**702-8280

(216) 696-5400 .. **Kopp,** Rebecca A '04 %Crosby O & Assoc Co,LPA -55 Pub Sq -Ste 1475 -Cleveland 44113 **Fx:**696-2610

(330) 376-2700 .. **Kopp,** Ronald S '79 (Roetzel & A,LPA) -222 S Main -Akron 44308 **Fx:**376-4577

(216) 622-3600 .. **Kopp,** William J '80 US Atty -801 W Superior -Ste 400 -Cleveland 44113 **Fx:**622-3370

(614) 278-2305 .. **Koprucki,** Patricia J '81 -3965 Poplar Bend Dr -Columbus 43204

(216) 861-8888 .. **Koral,** Timothy J '67 -1419 W 9th -2nd Fl -Cleveland 44113

(513) 852-6082 .. **Korbee,** Harold G '65 (Wood & L LLP) -600 Vine -Ste 2500 -Cincinnati 45202 **Fx:**852-6087

(513) 651-4130 .. **Korbee,** Thomas C '77 %Lawrence Firm -8044 Mntgmry Rd -Ste 700 -Cincinnati 45236

(859) 578-1030 .. **Korbee,** Thomas C '77 %Lawrence Firm -606 Phila -Covington, KY 41011 **Fx:**578-1032

(216) 592-5000 .. **Kordas,** Anne M '95 Cnsl Tucker E&W LLP -925 Euclid Av -1150 Huntngtn Bldg -Cleveland 44115 **Fx:**592-5009

(216) 520-8400 .. **Kordel,** Douglas A '97 ProForma Inc -8800 E Plsnt Vlly Rd -Independence 44131

(216) 696-7600 .. **Kordeleski,** Kathleen M '86 (Duvin C&H) -1301 E 9th -20th Fl Erievw Twr -Cleveland 44114 **Fx:**696-2038

(216) 621-6684 .. **Kordic,** Gregory L '83 (Kordic & Assoc) -1422 Euclid Av -The Hanna Bldg Ste 350 -Cleveland 44115

(937) 223-8171 .. **Kordik,** James G '83 (Rogers & G) -2160 Kettering Twr -Dayton 45423 **Fx:**223-1649

(330) 725-3636 .. **Korduba,** Andrew M '98 -46 Pub Sq -Ste 210 -Medina 44256

(440) 735-1010 .. **Koreness,** Gregory B '99 Kronheims Furniture -23371 Aurora Rd -Bedford Heights 44146 **Fx:**735-1030

(216) 771-7030 .. **Korey,** Philip J '80 -526 Superior Av NE -Ste 410 -Cleveland 44114

Korff, Christopher J '03 -5494 Towbrdg Dr -Hudson 44236

(513) 977-8200 .. **Korfhage,** Melissa L '00 %Dinsmore & S LLP -255 E 5th -Ste 1900 -Cincinnati 45202 **Fx:**977-8141

(513) 732-1141 .. **Korfhagen,** John C '82 (Burreson B&H) -40 S 3rd -Batavia 45103

(419) 782-6055 .. **Korhn,** Stephen F '72 (Clemens KL&W,Ltd) -419 5th -Ste 2000 -Bx787 -Defiance 43512

(330) 384-5849 .. **Korkosz,** Arthur E '80 FirstEnergy Corp -76 S Main -Akron 44308

(216) 363-4500 .. **Korland,** Lee M '03 %Benesch FC&A LLP -200 Pub Sq -Ste 2300 -Cleveland 44114 **Fx:**363-4588

(937) 644-6630 .. **Korleski,** Christopher '88 Honda of Amer Mfg,Inc -24000 Honda Pkwy -Leg Dept -Marysville 43040 **Fx:**644-6583

(216) 363-4500 .. **Korman,** Jean Kerr '90 %Benesch FC&A LLP -200 Pub Sq -Ste 2300 -Cleveland 44114 **Fx:**363-4588

(330) 745-9927 .. **Kormanec,** Stephanie Rae '00 -712 Silvercrest Av -Akron 44314

(614) 224-4114 .. **Kormanik,** Paul S '79 -490 S High -Columbus 43215

(614) 224-1222 .. **Korn,** David G '76 %Maguire & S,LLP -250 Civic Ctr Dr -Ste 200 -Columbus 43215 **Fx:**224-1236

(216) 839-8500 .. **Kornblut,** Gerri L '88 Degussa Corp -23700 Chagrin Blvd -Leg Dept -Cleveland 44122 **Fx:**839-8813

(216) 696-0022 .. **Kornblut,** Russell D '86 Collins & S LLP -50 Pub Sq -3300 Trmnl Twr -Cleveland 44113 **Fx:**696-1166

(216) 368-3283 .. **Korngold,** Gerald '95 CWRU Law Schl -11075 East Blvd -Cleveland 44106

(937) 383-0050 .. **Kornman,** Sharon A '94 -283 N South -Wilmington 45177

(609) 987-6822 .. **Kornrumpf,** Doreen D '85 (Buchanan I,PC) -700 Alxndr Pk -Ste 300 -Princeton, NJ 08540 **Fx:**520-0360

(440) 729-5601 .. **Korosec,** Jason A '97 -11919 Caves Rd -Chesterland 44026 **Fx:(216)** 274-9717

(440) 729-1414 .. **Korosec,** Kenneth D '67 -12573 Chillicothe Rd -Chesterland 44026 **Fx:**729-7300

(216) 586-3939 .. **Korpics,** J Joseph '91 Cnsl Jones D -901 Lakeside Av -Cleveland 44114 **Fx:**579-0212

(614) 221-2226 .. **Kort,** Louis F '79 -338 S High -Columbus 43215

(216) 643-9331 .. **Kortan,** Katherine M '93 Comp Assoc -6150 Oak Tree Blvd -Cleveland 44131

(704) 423-7086 .. **Kortan-Sampson,** Maria A '94 Goodrich Corp -2730 W Tyvola Rd -Charlotte, NC 28217 **Fx:**423-3495

(937) 223-8177 .. **Korte,** David C '80 (Coolidge WW&L) -33 W 1st -Ste 600 -Dayton 45402 **Fx:**223-6705

(703) 617-8031 .. **Korte,** Edward J '71 Dept Army-Materiel Cmmnd -5001 Esnhwr Av -Alexandria, VA 22333

(614) 466-7090 .. **Korte,** Julie M '93 Ethics Commssn -8 E Long -10th Fl -Columbus 43215

(440) 542-1307 .. **Korte,** Peter B '93 Erico Intl Corp -30575 Bainbrdg Rd -Ste 300 -Solon 44139

(216) 642-0323 .. **Kosakowski,** Lori A '03 %Britton SP&K Co,LPA -4700 Rockside Rd -Ste 540 Summit One -Cleveland 44131 **Fx:**642-0747

(937) 291-9339 .. **Kosanovich,** Daniel N '77 -28 E Rahn Rd -Ste 100 -Dayton 45429

(216) 621-0200 .. **Kosanovich,** Laurie G '97 %Baker & H LLP -1900 E 9th -Ste 3200 -Cleveland 44114 **Fx:**696-0740

(216) 522-3380 .. **Kosar,** Katherine L '87 IRS -1375 E 9th -1200 -Cleveland 44114

(216) 830-6830 .. **Koschik,** Alan M '96 (Brouse M) -1001 Lakeside Av -Ste 1600 -Cleveland 44114 **Fx:**830-6807

(440) 845-0500 .. **Koscianski,** James P '88 %Koscianski & K -5700 Pearl Rd -Ste 201 -Parma 44129

(440) 845-0500 .. **Koscianski,** John P '90 (Koscianski & K) -5700 Pearl Rd -Ste 201 -Parma 44129

(440) 845-0500 .. **Koscianski,** Raymond A '58 Koscianski & K -5700 Pearl Rd -Ste 201 -Parma 44129

(216) 566-5732 .. **Kosek,** Kelly A '02 %Thompson H LLP -127 Pub Sq -3900 Key Ctr -Cleveland 44114 **Fx:**566-5800

(330) 535-5711 .. **Kosiewicz,** Joy D '98 %Brouse M -106 S Main -500 First Natl Twr -Akron 44308 **Fx:**253-8601

(614) 462-3262 .. **Kosinski,** Jeannie J '04 %Franklin Cnty Probate Ct -373 S High -22nd Fl -Columbus 43215

(216) 443-7800 .. **Kosko,** John R '81 Cuyahoga Cnty Pros -1200 Ontario -8th Fl
-Cleveland 44113 Fx:698-2270

(330) 405-5061 .. **Kosla,** Phillip C '98 %Williams S&S Co,LPA -2241 Pinnacle Pkwy
-Twinsburg 44087 Fx:405-5586

(216) 464-9967 .. **Kosmin,** Martin A '70 AL/KO -23715 Mercantile Rd -Ste 214
-Beachwood 44122

(614) 891-5133 .. **Kosmo,** Megan E '00 Midland Celtic Title -470 Olde Worthngtn Rd
-Ste 470 -Westerville 43082

(724) 342-6835 .. **Kosmowski,** Audra M '95 Evans GL&O -19 Jffrsn Av -Bx949
-Sharon, PA 16146

(614) 464-6400 .. **Kossoudji,** Scott A '00 %Vorys SS&P LLP -52 E Gay -Bx1008
-Columbus 43216 Fx:464-6350

(937) 222-2500 .. **Kost,** Susan S '92 OfCnsl Sebaly S&D -1900 Kettering Twr
-Dayton 45423 Fx:222-6554

(702) 245-3128 .. **Kostas,** Socrates J '89 -1350 E Flamingo Rd -Mailbox 490
-Las Vegas, NV 89119 Fx:396-2759

(614) 275-2460 .. **Kostelac,** Gregory M '81 -Bx365 -Columbus 43216

(216) 515-1660 .. **Kostelnik,** John F III '81 Frantz W LLP -127 Pub Sq
-2500 Key Center -Cleveland 44114 Fx:515-1650

(330) 643-2935 .. **Kostoff,** Maria V '95 Summit Cnty Juv Ct -650 Dan -Akron 44310

(330) 376-2700 .. **Kostoff,** Peter M '82 (Roetzel & A,LPA) -222 S Main -Akron 44308
Fx:376-4577

(330) 867-8422 .. **Kostoff,** Thomas W '80 -41 Merz Blvd -Fairlawn 44333

(614) 430-8885 .. **Kostreva,** David R II '03 %Curry RS&M Co,LLC
-8000 Ravines Edge Ct -Ste 103 -Columbus 43235 Fx:430-8890

(216) 696-3366 .. **Kostura,** Sarah Hauser '04 %Goodman WM LLP -100 Erievw Plz
-27th Fl -Cleveland 44114 Fx:363-5835

(216) 983-1262 .. **Kostyack,** Paul T '01 Univ Hosp Hlth Syst -10524 Euclid Av
-Ste 1100 WO Walker Ctr -Cleveland 44106 Fx:983-1057

(419) 422-7700 .. **Kostyo,** John F '81 -1100 E Main -Ste 200 -Findlay 45840
Fx:425-0042

(419) 244-5865 .. **Kosydar,** Walter J '73 -520 Mad Av -Ste 1020 -Toledo 43604
Fx:327-2540

(330) 434-2113 .. **Kot,** Thomas P '79 Armbruster KKH&B -159 S Main -Ste 720
-Akron 44308

(770) 667-2409 .. **Kota,** John M '87 Ryder Syst,Inc -6000 Windward Pkwy -5th Fl
-Alpharetta, GA 30005

(216) 696-7445 .. **Kotar,** William H III '01 %Glowacki & Assoc -526 Superior Av E
-510 Leader Bldg -Cleveland 44114 Fx:696-0318

(513) 683-1427 .. **Kothman,** David M '83 -1641 Lindenhall Dr -Loveland 45140
Fx:683-1427

(513) 651-1010 .. **Kotian,** Manisha B '93 -9200 Mntgmry Rd -Ste 17A
-Cincinnati 45242

(440) 293-6346 .. **Kotila,** Richard B '80 (McCombs & K) -100 Pub Sq -Bx217
-Andover 44003 Fx:293-5665

Kotlarsic, Liza Ann '89 -Bx62843 -Cincinnati 45262

(330) 535-6650 .. **Kotler,** Todd B '99 -611 W Market -Akron 44303 Fx:535-2205

(330) 493-0040 .. **Kotnik,** Donald P '90 %Lesh C&M -4150 Belden Vllg NW -Ste 606
-Canton 44718

Kotnik, Rhonda L '04 -(Address Unavailable)

(440) 684-9393 .. **Kotoch,** Norman A '90 Norcon Properties Ltd -355 Bishop Rd
-Ste 303 -Highland Heights 44143

(440) 886-1332 .. **Kotulic,** Irene M '55 -7425 Dartworth Dr -Parma 44129

(330) 458-2411 .. **Koukoutas,** Anthony '96 (Pitinii & K) -101 Central Plz S -Ste 1000
-Canton 44702

(614) 861-5362 .. **Kouns,** Mark E '76 -8674 Ashford Ln NW -Bx235
-Pickerington 43147

(419) 213-4700 .. **Kountouris,** Louis E '82 Lucas Cnty Pros -Adams & Erie
-Lucas Cnty Cthse -Toledo 43624

(440) 250-7015 .. **Koury,** Elias G '53 -835 Sharon Dr -Ste 200 -Westlake 44145

(440) 329-5389 .. **Koury,** George I Jr. '75 Lorain Cnty Pros -225 Court -3rd Fl
-Elyria 44035

(216) 965-5400 .. **Koury,** Laurice M '74 -Bx81678 -Cleveland 44181

(440) 250-7025 .. **Koury,** Lee M '97 SBN Magazine -835 Sharon Dr -Ste 200
-Westlake 44145

(513) 621-3616 .. **Koustmer,** Thomas R '81 -7 W 7th -Ste 1800 -Cincinnati 45202

(727) 864-3300 .. **Koutrodimos,** Demetrios P '02 Ceridian Rtrmnt Plan Srvcs,Inc
-3201 34th S -Saint Petersburg, FL 33711

(614) 644-3037 .. **Kovac,** Frances M '85 EPA -122 S Front -Bx1049
-Columbus 43216

(216) 771-5525 .. **Kovac,** James E '77 -1370 Ontario -Ste 2000 -Cleveland 44113

(216) 621-1530 .. **Kovach,** Christopher M '95 %Shapiro & F,LLP -1500 W 3rd
-Ste 400 -Cleveland 44113 Fx:621-1551

(228) 377-1320 .. **Kovach,** Diane L '85 USAF- 2AF/JA -721 Hangar Rd -Ste 102
-Keesler Afb, MS 39534

(216) 357-3301 .. **Kovach & Farling Co,LPA** -526 Superior Av E -Ste 925
-Cleveland 44114

(330) 668-2580 .. **Kovach,** John J '87 Stroud Engineering Srvcs
-4363 Colony Hills Dr -Akron 44333

(513) 942-7900 .. **Kovach,** Karen Sue '92 Powernet Communications
-100 Cmmrcial Dr -Fairfield 45014

(330) 471-1105 .. **Kovach,** Linda K '91 Industrial Commssn of OH -400 3rd SE
-Canton 44702

(216) 696-7600 .. **Kovach,** Lynda L '02 %Duvin C&H -1301 E 9th -20th Fl Erievw Twr
-Cleveland 44114 Fx:696-2038

(330) 643-2788 .. **Kovach,** Mary Ann '75 Summit Cnty Pros-Crim -53 Univ Av -7th Fl
-Akron 44308 Fx:643-8277

(330) 972-6794 .. **Kovach,** Richard J '74 Univ of Akron Law Schl -LAW 242
-Akron 44325

(216) 357-3301 .. **Kovach,** Thomas G '90 (Kovach & F Co,LPA) -526 Superior Av E
-Ste 925 -Cleveland 44114

(216) 348-7550 .. **Kovach,** William M '80 R Kuepper & Assoc -1660 W 2nd -Ste 480
-Cleveland 44113

Kovacik, Gerard J '79 -4561 Clague Rd -North Olmsted 44070

(419) 245-1893 .. **Kovacik,** Leslie A '98 %Law Dept -One Govt Ctr -Ste 2250
-Toledo 43604 Fx:245-1090

(614) 764-0681 .. **Kovacs,** Francis A Jr. '80 OfCnsl Blaugrund H&M,Inc
-5455 Rings Rd -Ste 500 -Dublin 43017 Fx:764-0774

Kovacs, George C '77 -445 Richmond Park W -#602B
-Cleveland 44143

(440) 322-5985 .. **Kovacs,** John J '77 -105 Court -Ste 522 -Elyria 44035
Fx:323-5350

(440) 526-5001 .. **Kovacs,** Julius E '67 (J Kovacs & Assoc Co,LPA)
-8221 Brecksvll Rd -4 Brecksvll Cmmns #202 -Brecksville 44141

(419) 843-2001 .. **Kovacs,** Louis S '88 %Gallon & T Co,LPA -3516 Granite Cir
-Bx352018 -Toledo 43635 Fx:843-6665

(419) 241-4050 .. **Kovacs,** Patricia A '93 -500 Mad Av -Ste 525 -Toledo 43604

(216) 696-5222 .. **Koval,** Joseph S '04 %M Schlachet -1001 Lakeside Av -Ste 1700
-Cleveland 44114

(330) 729-9000 .. **Koval,** Margaret '84 -412 Boardman-Canfld Rd
-Youngstown 44512

(440) 995-5110 .. **Koval,** William J Jr. '90 Evergreen/UNI -6140 Parkland Blvd
-Ste 300 -Mayfield Heights 44124

Kovalchik, Aaron '03 -(Address Unavailable)

(216) 621-2388 .. **Kovanda,** Ralph D '50 (Forrester & K) -140 Pub Sq -711 Park Bldg
-Cleveland 44114

(216) 621-6570 .. **Kovass,** David A '02 %Rademaker MM&G -55 Pub Sq -Ste 1775
-Cleveland 44113 Fx:621-1127

(937) 222-6926 .. **Koverman,** John R Jr. '59 -120 W 2nd -1300 Lbrty Twr
-Dayton 45402

(937) 224-1427 .. **Kovich,** Don E '78 -130 W 2nd -Ste 1900 -Dayton 45402

(330) 394-5500 .. **Kovoor,** Sarah T '98 -640 High NE -Warren 44483

Kowalczyk, Crystina M '93 -1616 Warren Rd -Lakewood 44107

(614) 466-7751 .. **Kowalczyk,** Elizabeth A '93 Dept Job & Family Srvcs -145 S Front
-1st Fl -Columbus 43215

(440) 357-2683 .. **Kowall,** Karen L '85 Lake Cnty Pros Ofc -47 N Park Pl
-Painesville 44077

(216) 766-5416 .. **Kowalski,** Alexandra M '98 Genesis Prof Liability Mngrs
-25550 Chagrin Blvd -Ste 300 -Beachwood 44122

(419) 241-1200 .. **Kowalski,** Gerald R '80 Cooper & W,LPA -900 Adams
-Toledo 43624 Fx:242-5675

Kowalski, Gregory J '83 Support Enfrcmnt Agncy -770 Skinner Av
-Painesville 44077

(216) 261-1529 .. **Kowalski,** Judith M '93 -22408 Lk Shr Blvd -Euclid 44123

(440) 331-2731 .. **Kowalski,** Kathiann '79 -21255 S Park Dr -Fairview Park 44126

(216) 687-4825 .. **Kowalski,** Kenneth J '81 CSU-Marshall Cllg of Law
-2121 Euclid Av -LB138 -Cleveland 44115 Fx:687-6881

(419) 861-0755 .. **Kowalski,** Lawrence W '75 -8528 Royal Birkdale Ln -Holland
43528

(513) 425-6609 .. **Kowalski,** Susan M '98 12th Dist Ct of Appls -1001 Reinartz Blvd
-Middletown 45042 Fx:425-8751

(440) 356-4400 .. **Kowalski,** Theodore R '67 -20777 Lorain Rd -Fairview Park 44126

(972) 448-5460 .. **Koza,** Thomas A '86 Nrth Amer Coal Corp -14785 Preston Rd
-Ste 1100 -Dallas, TX 75254

(937) 222-6764 .. **Kozar,** Ronald J '89 -40 N Main -Ste 2830 -Dayton 45423

(440) 979-0775 .. **Kozel,** Thomas '90 -B x534 -North Olmsted 44070

(614) 461-4014 .. **Kozelek,** Edward F '96 OH Cable Telecom Assn -50 W Broad
-Ste 1118 -Columbus 43215

(614) 801-2768 .. **Kozelek,** James G '01 %Weltman W&R Co,LPA -175 S 3rd
-Ste 900 -Columbus 43215 Fx:222-2193

(216) 524-4260 .. **Kozelka,** Frank J '71 -7223 Hemlock Rd -Independence 44131

(440) 526-7200 .. **Kozelka,** Kay J '78 -2207 E Wallings Rd
-Broadview Heights 44147

(937) 259-7215 .. **Koziar,** Stephen F Jr. '71 Dayton Power & Light Co -Bx1247
-Dayton 45401

(614) 464-2572 .. **Kozich,** John H '75 (Harris MB&C,PLL) -37 W Broad -9th Fl
-Columbus 43215 Fx:464-2245

Kozik, Mary Ann J '96 -1597 Jacoby Rd -Copley 44321

(513) 977-8200 .. **Kozlowski,** Holly D '96 (Dinsmore & S LLP) -255 E 5th -Ste 1900
-Cincinnati 45202 Fx:977-8141

(614) 336-2984 .. **Kozlowski,** John F '81 Ohio Credit Union League -5815 Wall
-Dublin 43017

(614) 228-1541 .. **Kozlowski,** Richard E '98 %Baker & H LLP -65 E State -Ste 2100
-Columbus 43215 Fx:462-2616

(614) 461-4455 .. **Kozlowski,** Susan H '80 (Cloppert LS&W) -225 E Broad
-Columbus 43215 Fx:461-0072

(330) 535-4191 .. **Kozlowski,** Timothy E Jr. '91 %Cmmnty Lgl Aid Srvcs,Inc
-265 S Main -3rd Fl -Akron 44308 Fx:535-0728

(216) 579-4114 .. **Kracht,** Robert Roy '83 (McIntyre K&K Co LPA) -1301 E 9th
-Ste 1200 -Cleveland 44114

(513) 777-2222 .. **Kraemer,** Bradley M '98 %Lyons & L Co,LPA
-8310 Prnctn-Glendale Rd -Ste B -West Chester 45069

(216) 464-2777 .. **Kraemer,** Lisa R '79 -23230 Chagrin Blvd -Ste 740
-Cleveland 44122 Fx:464-7990

(937) 227-3700 .. **Kraemer,** Thomas R '92 (Faruki I&C PLL) -10 N Ludlow
-500 Cthse Plz SW -Dayton 45402 Fx:227-3717

(440) 885-2854 .. **Krafcik,** Jamie R '95 -7200 Langerford Dr -Parma 44129

Kraft, Brian D '04 -(Address Unavailable)

(937) 512-1681 .. **Kraft,** Julie A '95 Montgomery Cnty Pros -301 W 3rd -Bx972
-Dayton 45422 Fx:225-3470

(614) 692-3284 .. **Kraft,** Michael J '73 US Dfnse Lgstcs Agncy -Bx3990
-Columbus 43218

(513) 455-7600 .. **Krafte,** Lori E '98 %Greenebaum D&M PLLC -255 E 5th
-2800 Chemed Ctr -Cincinnati 45202 Fx:455-8500

(330) 373-1035 .. **Kragalott,** Samuel R '82 Letson GWL&R -155 S Park Av -Ste 250
-Bx151 -Warren 44482 Fx:392-5419

(216) 348-5400 .. **Kraguljac,** Peter '94 (McDonald H Co,LPA) -600 Superior Av E
-Ste 2100 -Cleveland 44114 Fx:348-5474

(440) 247-2562 .. **Krahe,** Mitchell W '96 (M Krahe Co,LPA) -35 W Cottage
-Chagrin Falls 44022

(216) 861-6833 .. **Krahe,** Shawn Marie '96 %Sonkin & K Co,LPA -55 Pub Sq
-Ste 1660 -Cleveland 44113

(216) 696-6525 .. **Kraig,** Barbara A '03 Catholic Diocese of Cleveland -1404 E 9th
-Ste 800 -Cleveland 44114

(216) 696-4009 .. **Kraig,** Brian S '88 (Kraig & K) -614 Superior Av W -Ste 900
-Cleveland 44113 Fx:696-1835

Krainess, Gregory L '91 -(Address Unavailable)

(216) 861-4357 .. **Krainess,** Jonathan I '00 Krainess Law Firm -13882 Cedar Rd
-Rm 1 Lwr Level -Cleveland 44118

(216) 583-1273 .. **Krajcer,** Michael A '01 Ernst & Young LLP -925 Euclid Av
-Ste 1300 -Cleveland 44115

(404) 504-6115 .. **Krajec,** Phil '83 Royal Specialty Underwriting,Inc
-945 E Paces Ferry Rd -Atlanta, GA 30326

(216) 443-7295 .. **Krajenke,** Francis R Jr. '96 Cuyahoga Cnty Pub Def
-1849 Prospect Av -Ste 222 -Cleveland 44115

(216) 363-1400 .. **Krajewski,** Eric D '04 %Buckley K,LPA -600 E Superior Av
-Ste 1400 -Cleveland 44114 Fx:579-1020

(330) 376-3300 .. **Krajewski,** John K '85 (Stark & K Co,LPA) -76 S Main -Ste 1512
-Akron 44308 **Fx:**376-6237

(440) 442-6677 .. **Kral,** Donald J '89 Elk & E Co,LPA -6100 Parkland Blvd
-Mayfield Heights 44124 **Fx:**442-7944

(330) 740-2330 .. **Kralj,** Kevin M '92 Mahoning Cnty Pros -21 W Boardman -6th Fl
-Youngstown 44503 **Fx:**740-2008

(513) 629-2417 .. **Krall,** David G '86 Eagle-Picher Ind,Inc -8260 Northcreek Dr
-Ste 100 -Cincinnati 45236

(937) 264-5110 .. **Krall,** Michael F '81 Workers Comp -3401 Park Ctr Dr
-Dayton 45414 **Fx:**264-5088

(304) 242-2300 .. **Krall,** Robert J '91 (Herndon MH&Y) -83 Edgington Ln -Wheeling,
WV 26003

(330) 762-7655 .. **Krall,** Roy A '89 (Kaufmann & K) -106 S Main -Ste 1200
-Akron 44308 **Fx:**762-7537

(614) 227-2300 .. **Kram,** Elbert J '66 (Bricker & E LLP) -100 S 3rd -Columbus 43215
Fx:227-2390

(202) 879-4660 .. **Kramer,** Andrew M '90 (Jones DR&P) -51 Louisiana Av NW
-Washington, DC 20001 **Fx:**626-1700

(216) 522-2123 .. **Kramer,** Barbara L '91 US EEOC -1660 W 2nd -Ste 850
-Cleveland 44113

(336) 854-8291 .. **Kramer,** Douglas B '73 Greensboro Assoc Inc
-3300 Battleground Av -Ste 301 -Greensboro, NC 27410

(216) 431-5300 .. **Kramer,** Edward G '75 (Kramer & Assoc,LPA) -3214 Prospect Av
-Cleveland 44115

(216) 781-7956 .. **Kramer,** Ellen M '91 (Cohen R&K LLP) -1468 W 9th -Ste 705
-Cleveland 44113 **Fx:**781-8061

(216) 621-7974 .. **Kramer,** Eugene L '64 -1422 Euclid Av -Ste 706 -Cleveland 44115

(216) 621-9870 .. **Kramer,** Fredric E '62 (McNeal SA&B Co,LPA)
-123 W Prospect Av -Ste 250 Van Sweringen Arcade
-Cleveland 44115 **Fx:**522-1112

(937) 257-8189 .. **Kramer,** Gary M '91 USAF -4225 Logistics Av -Ste 23
-Wright Patterson AFB 45433

(216) 360-7200 .. **Kramer,** Herbert J '84 (Carlisle MRK&U Co,LPA)
-24755 Chagrin Blvd -Ste 200 -Cleveland 44122 **Fx:**360-7210

(859) 331-7900 .. **Kramer,** Herman H '68 (Kramer & H) -2493 Dixie Hwy
-Covington, KY 41017

(440) 461-3461 .. **Kramer,** Ivan '79 Victoria Fncl Corp -5915 Landerbrook Dr
-Bx94534 -Cleveland 44101 **Fx:**(866) 824-6764

(419) 522-7474 .. **Kramer,** Jeffrey N '93 -24 W 3rd -Ste 300 -Mansfield 44902
Fx:522-7478

(412) 456-1141 .. **Kramer,** John D Jr. '94 PrintCafe,Inc -40 24th
-Pittsburgh, PA 15222

(216) 566-1208 .. **Kramer,** John F '90 Sherwin-Williams -101 Prospect Av NW
-Cleveland 44115

(216) 321-3514 .. **Kramer,** Lawrence J Jr. '03 -2602 Prnctn Rd
-Cleveland Heights 44118

(440) 247-6167 .. **Kramer,** Nancy W '79 -57 E Wshngtn -Chagrin Falls 44022

(330) 721-0000 .. **Kramer,** Patricia S '97 %Walker & J,LPA -231 S Bway
-Medina 44256 **Fx:**722-6446

(330) 762-7377 .. **Kramer,** Reginald S '80 (Oldham & D) -195 S Main -Ste 300
-Akron 44308 **Fx:**762-7390

(216) 241-5358 .. **Kramer,** Roger S '77 -1370 Ontario -Ste 330 Standard Bldg
-Cleveland 44113

(614) 766-7243 .. **Kramer,** Ronald A '71 -8420 Kilbirnie Ct -Dublin 43017

(216) 522-3876 .. **Kramer,** Sandra B '80 US Dept of Labor -1240 E 9th -Ste 881
-Cleveland 44199

(937) 222-1700 .. **Kramer,** Scott A '00 -130 W 2nd -Ste 924 -Dayton 45402

(937) 878-3956 .. **Kramer,** Thomas G '83 Kramer & Assoc,Inc
-640 E Dayton Yellow Sprngs Rd -Fairborn 45324

(330) 487-6965 .. **Kramer,** Timothy E '69 CVS Pharmacy -1920 Enterprise Pkwy
-Twinsburg 44087

(312) 946-2628 .. **Kranjc,** Judith K '91 Deloitte & Touche -180 N Stetson
-Chicago, IL 60601

(614) 224-7771 .. **Kranstuber,** Charles W '79 %Livorno & A Co,LPA -280 N High
-Ste 1410 -Columbus 43215 **Fx:**224-7775

(216) 696-8700 .. **Krantz,** Brett S '98 (Kohrman J&K PLL) -1375 E 9th
-One Cleve Ctr 20th Fl -Cleveland 44114 **Fx:**621-6536

(216) 736-7210 .. **Krantz,** Byron S '62 (Kohrman J&K PLL) -1375 E 9th
-One Cleve Ctr 20th Fl -Cleveland 44114 **Fx:**621-6536

(216) 514-1180 .. **Krantz,** Howard J '86 (Krantz P&F,PLL) -23200 Chagrin Blvd
-Ste 180 -Cleveland 44122 **Fx:**514-1185

(216) 736-7204 .. **Krantz,** Marc C '93 (Kohrman J&K PLL) -1375 E 9th
-One Cleve Ctr 20th Fl -Cleveland 44114 **Fx:**621-6536

(440) 684-8753 .. **Krantz,** Michele L '93 Meridia Hlth Sys -6803 Mayfld Rd
-Hllcrst Med Bldg I #500 -Mayfield Heights 44124

(216) 514-1180 .. **Krantz Powers & Friedman,PLL** -23200 Chagrin Blvd -Ste 180
-Cleveland 44122 **Fx:**514-1185

(216) 514-1180 .. **Krantz,** Stuart W '93 Krantz P&F,PLL -23200 Chagrin Blvd
-Ste 180 -Cleveland 44122 **Fx:**514-1185

(216) 676-3897 .. **Krantz,** Timothy J '81 Ford Motor Co -5600 Engle Rd -Bx9900
-Brook Park 44142

(614) 415-8397 .. **Kranyak,** John T '97 LimitedBrands,Inc -3 Limited Pkwy
-Columbus 43230 **Fx:**415-7900

Kranz, Claire E '78 -2 Windsor Ct -Rocky River 44116

(419) 841-9623 .. **Kranz,** Michelle L '93 (Zoll & K) -6620 W Central Av -Ste 200
-Toledo 43617

(614) 462-3555 .. **Krapenc,** Robert F '88 Franklin Cnty Pros -373 S High
-Columbus 43215

Krash, Allan L '61 -1001 Parkside Dr -Alliance 44601

(216) 765-0123 .. **Krasovec,** Frank C Jr. '83 (Budish & S Ltd) -23240 Chagrin Blvd
-Ste 450 Commerce Park 4 -Beachwood 44122 **Fx:**595-2787

(216) 394-5074 .. **Krasovec,** Jay E '98 %Schottenstein Z&D -1350 Euclid Av
-Ste 1400 -Cleveland 44115 **Fx:**621-6502

(513) 983-3063 .. **Krass,** Marc S '81 Procter & Gamble Co-Legal
-1 Procter & Gamble Plz -Cincinnati 45202

(216) 523-5469 .. **Krassen,** Glenn S '80 (Bricker & E LLP) -1375 E 9th -Ste 1500
-Cleveland 44114 **Fx:**523-7071

(724) 935-6227 .. **Krassenstein,** Jonathan T '86 (Krassenstein & Assoc,PC)
-7500 Brooktree Dr -Wexford, PA 15090 **Fx:**935-0742

(330) 673-3444 .. **Kratcoski,** Peter C '88 (Williams W&K) -11 S River -Bx396
-Kent 44240

(216) 696-4700 .. **Kratus,** Eugene A '76 (Spieth BM&N Co,LPA) -925 Euclid Av
-2000 Huntngtn Bldg -Cleveland 44115 **Fx:**696-2706

(216) 831-8771 .. **Kraus,** Alan H '81 (Lazzaro & K) -25700 Science Park Dr -Ste 250
-Cleveland 44122

(513) 515-5210 .. **Kraus,** Christopher Eli '96 -414 Walnut -Ste 911 -Cincinnati 45202

(216) 556-1457 .. **Kraus,** David P '88 -Bx22154 -Beachwood 44122 **Fx:**252-3193

(216) 623-0000 .. **Kraus,** Edward H '86 (Javitch B&R) -1300 E 9th -14th Fl
-Cleveland 44114 **Fx:**623-0190

(330) 376-5300 .. **Kraus,** James D '83 (Buckingham D&B,LLP) -50 S Main -Bx1500
-Akron 44309 **Fx:**258-6559

(412) 288-4000 .. **Kraus,** James W '01 (Picadio MM&N) -600 Grant
-Pittsburgh, PA 15219

(440) 352-3391 .. **Kraus,** Keith R '84 (Dworken & B Co,LPA) -60 S Park Pl
-Painesville 44077 **Fx:**352-3469

(440) 238-5720 .. **Kraus,** Kenneth A '72 City Law Dir Ofc -16099 Foltz Indstrl Pkwy
-Strongsville 44149

(513) 241-8137 .. **Kraus,** Marvin H '54 (Tobias K&T) -414 Walnut -Ste 911
-Cincinnati 45202

(419) 249-7100 .. **Kraus,** Paul M '57 (Marshall & M,LLC) -Four Seagate -8th Fl
-Toledo 43604 **Fx:**249-7151

(440) 816-0600 .. **Kraus,** Thomas J '84 Largent BP&J Co,LPA -1 Berea Cmmns
-Ste 216 -Berea 44017 **Fx:**816-0604

(216) 381-0315 .. **Kraus,** William M '50 -4491 Univ Pkwy -University Heights 44118

(216) 642-3342 .. **Krause,** Christopher W '93 %Wegman H&V,LPA
-6055 Rockside Wds Blvd -Ste 200 -Cleveland 44131
Fx:642-8826

(216) 687-1311 .. **Krause,** David H '99 (Reminger & R) -101 Prospect Av W
-1400 Mdlnd Bldg -Cleveland 44115 **Fx:**687-1841

(440) 808-6322 .. **Krause,** Douglas R '93 Richard E Jacobs Grp,Inc
-25425 Ctr Ridge Rd -Cleveland 44145 **Fx:**808-6905

(216) 621-0890 .. **Krause,** Edward A '67 -1919 E 13th -Cleveland 44114

(313) 259-6258 .. **Krause,** Gregory M '99 %McGuire W LLP -400 Renaissance Ctr
-Ste 950 -Detroit, MI 48243 **Fx:**259-1840

(513) 621-5252 .. **Krause,** Joseph M '04 %Clodfelter & G -36 E 4th -Ste 1208
-Cincinnati 45202

Krause, Lauren '04 -(Address Unavailable)

(440) 835-6212 .. **Krause,** Marcella A '91 Far West Ctr -29133 Health Campus Dr
-Westlake 44145

(330) 742-8791 .. **Krause,** Michael J '97 City Pros -26 S Phelps -4th Fl
-Youngstown 44503

(614) 340-3444 .. **Krauss,** M Samuel '03 %Henley M&U Cnsltng,Inc
-3300 Riverside Dr -Ste 350 -Columbus 43221 **Fx:**340-3443

(513) 636-8074 .. **Kravetsky,** Lorie J '90 Cincinnati Chldrns Hosp -3333 Burnet Av
-Cincinnati 45229

(513) 942-6196 .. **Kravetz,** Andrea F '83 Elsevier Science -8080 Beckett Ctr Dr
-Ste 225 -West Chester 45069

(216) 357-7268 .. **Kravetz,** Cheryl L '02 US Dist Ct -801 W Superior Av -16B
-Cleveland 44113 **Fx:**357-7271

(513) 936-0800 .. **Kravetz,** Scott H '93 (J Stillpass,LLC) -9545 Kenwood Rd -Ste 103
-Cincinnati 45242 **Fx:**794-8800

(614) 466-2766 .. **Kravitz,** Brett A '98 Atty Gen -30 E Broad -Columbus 43215
Fx:644-1926

(330) 538-0066 .. **Kravitz,** Cynthia A '83 Kravitz Bagels -12485 Commissioner Dr
-Bx447 -North Jackson 44451

(614) 464-2000 .. **Kravitz,** Janet E '87 (Kravitz & K) -145 E Rich -Columbus 43215
Fx:464-2002

Kravitz & Kravitz -145 E Rich -Columbus 43215 **Fx:**464-2002

(216) 749-0808 .. **Kravitz,** Lee R '80 -4508 State Rd -Cleveland 44109

(614) 464-2000 .. **Kravitz,** Max '73 (Kravitz & K) -145 E Rich -Columbus 43215
Fx:464-2002

(330) 538-0066 .. **Kravitz,** Solomon J '82 Kravitz Bagels -12485 Commissioner Dr
-Bx447 -North Jackson 44451

(216) 685-9188 .. **Krawczak,** Kenneth F '77 (Swartz C LLC) -55 Pub Sq -Ste 1120
-Cleveland 44113 **Fx:**685-9293

(412) 456-8103 .. **Krawec,** Nicholas D '00 -707 Grant -Ste 2200
-Pittsburgh, PA 15219

(330) 225-1491 .. **Kray,** Paul J '91 (Laribee H&K) -111 Pearl Rd -Bx839
-Brunswick 44212

(216) 623-6614 .. **Kray,** Richard A '83 -1468 W 9th -Ste 425 -Cleveland 44113

(614) 529-5701 .. **Kreber,** John F '91 Kreber Graphics,Inc -2580 Westbelt Dr
-Columbus 43228 **Fx:**777-4890

(330) 336-9561 .. **Krebs,** Brian E '93 -7695 Boneta Rd -Wadsworth 44281

(513) 626-4856 .. **Krebs,** Jay A '95 Procter & Gamble -11450 Grooms Rd
-Cincinnati 45242

(614) 246-2515 .. **Krebs,** Kenneth J '84 Rockbridge Captl,Inc -191 W
Nationwide Blvd -Ste 600 -Columbus 43215

(937) 223-3277 .. **Krebs,** Leo F '66 (Bieser G&L LLP) -6 N Main -400 Natl City Ctr
-Dayton 45402 **Fx:**223-6339

(216) 771-2243 .. **Krebs,** Martha H '79 -55 Pub Sq -Cleveland 44113

(216) 241-2836 .. **Krebs,** Patrick J '00 %Taft S&H LLP -200 Pub Sq -3500 BP Twr
-Cleveland 44114 **Fx:**241-2837

(513) 897-5901 .. **Krebs,** Robert J Jr. '73 -4510 Laura Marie Dr -Waynesville 45068

(513) 785-6531 .. **Krebs,** Robert T '99 Butler Cnty Ct of Common Pleas -315 High
-3rd Fl -Hamilton 45011 **Fx:**785-6533

(440) 944-4580 .. **Krebs,** Scott T '89 -5463 Oak Rdg Dr -Willoughby 44094

(937) 512-2724 .. **Krebs,** William A '77 %Sinclair Cmmnty Coll -444 W 3rd
-Dayton 45402

(202) 647-5767 .. **Kreczko,** Alan J '77 State Dept Legal HR/MSA -2201 C NW
-#5824 -Washington, DC 20520

Kreek, Louis F Jr. '55 -2321 Stckbrdg Rd -Akron 44313

(513) 934-3200 .. **Krehbiel,** Anne E '80 -42 E Mulberry -Ste B -Lebanon 45036

(513) 579-6400 .. **Kreider,** Gary P '64 (Keating M&K PLL) -1 E 4th
-1400 Provident Twr -Cincinnati 45202 **Fx:**579-6457

(513) 579-6400 .. **Kreider,** Kenneth P '89 (Keating M&K PLL) -1 E 4th
-1400 Provident Twr -Cincinnati 45202 **Fx:**579-6457

(513) 621-6464 .. **Kreidler,** Robert L '62 (Graydon H&R LLP) -511 Walnut
-1900 Fifth Third Ctr -Cincinnati 45202 **Fx:**651-3836

(614) 249-6235 .. **Kreighbaum,** John S '01 Nationwide Finl Srvcs Inc
-1 Nationwide Plz -1-09-V3 -Columbus 43215

(970) 245-4601 .. **Kreiling,** Jamie B '89 LaCroix K&M,PC -725 Rood Av
-Grand Junction, CO 81501 **Fx:**243-7403

(440) 460-5000 .. **Kreiner,** Frederick J '96 Progressive Casualty Ins Co
-6300 Wilson Mills Rd -N-72 -Cleveland 44143

(330) 923-5315 .. **Kreiner,** Margaret H '85 -2020 Front -Ste 200
-Cuyahoga Falls 44221

(614) 793-1770 ..**Kreiner & Peters Co,LPA** -6047 Frantz Rd -Ste 203
-Dublin 43017

(216) 771-6650 ..**Kreiner & Peters Co,LPA** -Bx6599 -Cleveland 44101

(513) 367-5401 ..**Kreiner & Peters Co,LPA** -Bx1209 -Dublin 43017

(704) 686-3451 ..**Kreisa**, Renee M '94 Presbyterian Home for Children
-80 Lk Eden Rd -Black Mountain, NC 28711

(614) 466-7788 ..**Kreiter**, Robert D '87 OH Ct of Claims -65 E State -Ste 1100
-Columbus 43215
Kreitzer, Matthew P '04 -(Address Unavailable)

(614) 228-8400 ..**Krejci**, Matthew C '02 %Ulmer & B LLP -88 E Broad -Ste 1600
-Columbus 43215 Fx:228-8561

(216) 875-7500 ..**Krembs**, Andrew P '76 (Krembs & C Co,LPA) -55 Pub Sq
-Ste 1700 -Cleveland 44113 Fx:875-7501

(216) 781-5515 ..**Krembs**, Peter J '73 (Hermann C&S,LLP) -1301 E 9th -Ste 500
-Cleveland 44114 Fx:781-1030

(937) 586-7242 ..**Kremer**, Debra S '99 Key Private Bnkng & Invstng -34 N Main
-11th Fl -Dayton 45402

(330) 375-1311 ..**Kremer**, Stephan C '93 (Reminger & R) -80 S Summit
-200 Courtyard Sq -Akron 44308 Fx:375-9075

(937) 332-2112 ..**Kremmel**, Donn A '88 Hobart Corp -701 S Ridge Av -Troy 45374

(440) 838-7600 ..**Kremser**, Mark E '96 %Janik & D,LLP -9200 S Hills Blvd -Ste 300
-Cleveland 44147 Fx:838-7601

(216) 778-5174 ..**Krenek**, Robert F '84 Metro Hlth Med Ctr -2500 Metro Health Dr
-Cleveland 44109

(614) 644-7257 ..**Kreps**, Cavett R '02 Atty Gen -150 E Gay -Columbus 43215
Fx:752-4677

(440) 331-0422 ..**Kreps**, Robert C '75 -21400 Lorain Rd -Fairview Park 44126

(216) 622-8200 ..**Kresnye**, Stephen P '77 (Calfee H&G LLP) -800 Superior Av
-Ste 1400 -Cleveland 44114 Fx:241-0816

(330) 746-5643 ..**Kress**, Douglas J '94 (Comstock S&W Co,LPA) -100 Fed Plz E
-Ste 926 -Youngstown 44503 Fx:746-4925

(937) 449-2800 ..**Kress**, Edward M '74 (Chernesky H&K PLL) -10 Cthse Plz SW
-Ste 1100 -Dayton 45402 Fx:449-2821

(314) 231-0570 ..**Kress**, John C '01 %D Damick -211 N Bway -Ste 2450
-Saint Louis, MO 63102

(419) 321-1292 ..**Kress**, Kathleen A '85 (Shumaker L&K,LLP) -1000 Jackson
-Toledo 43624 Fx:241-6894

(937) 604-0488 ..**Kress**, Timothy S '03 -2314 Auburn Av -Cincinnati 45219

(330) 746-0171 ..**Kretzer**, Alan R '68 (AR Kretzer Co,LPA) -107 S Champion
-Youngstown 44503 Fx:746-4333

(757) 443-1086 ..**Kreutzberg**, Gregory D '04 Dept of Navy - Gen Cnsl Ofc
-1968 Gilbert -Ste 600 RM0611 -Norfolk, VA 23511

(859) 491-4300 ..**Kreutzer**, Jan K '85 -510 Wshngtn Av -Newport, KY 41071
Krevis, Noreen M '89 -26800 Morgan Run -Cleveland 44145

(216) 241-2838 ..**Krewson**, Patricia Fleming '03 %Taft S&H LLP -200 Pub Sq -3500
BP Twr -Cleveland 44114 Fx:241-3707

(216) 861-7994 ..**Kriedman**, Cynthia B '85 Baker & H LLP -1900 E 9th -Ste 3200
-Cleveland 44114 Fx:696-0740

(614) 415-7320 ..**Krier**, Peter C '95 The Limited Inc -3 Limited Pkwy
-Columbus 43230

(216) 831-0042 ..**Kriessler**, Lynn A '91 Meyers RF&L LPA -28601 Chagrin Blvd
-Ste 500 -Cleveland 44122 Fx:831-0542

(614) 462-2209 ..**Krimm**, John J '87 (Schottenstein Z&D) -250 West -Bx165020
-Columbus 43216 Fx:462-5155

(770) 667-7942 ..**Krinsky**, Arthur L '70 -1210 Lndngs Cove -Alpharetta, GA 30005

(614) 462-5316 ..**Krippel**, Darrolyn C '80 Franklin Cnty Dom Rltns Ct -373 S High
-3rd Fl -Columbus 43215

(740) 452-7555 ..**Krischak**, James R '77 (Gottlieb JB&D,PLL) -320 Main -Bx190
-Zanesville 43702 Fx:452-2257

(937) 223-3277 ..**Krisher**, Howard P II '75 (Bieser G&L LLP) -6 N Main
-400 Natl City Ctr -Dayton 45402 Fx:223-6339

(216) 696-7600 ..**Kristan**, Bonita L '01 %Duvin C&H -1301 E 9th -20th Fl Erievw Twr
-Cleveland 44114 Fx:696-2038

(216) 902-4444 ..**Kristan**, John A Jr. '01 Kelley JM&S LLP -629 Euclid Av -Ste 1037
-Cleveland 44114 Fx:902-4447

(614) 228-8995 ..**Krivda**, Pamela S '88 (Owens & K Co,LPA) -471 E Broad
-Ste 2100 -Columbus 43215 Fx:228-8996

(216) 586-3939 ..**Krivinskas**, Dainius A '03 %Jones D -901 Lakeside Av -Cleveland
44114 Fx:579-0212

(614) 688-3062 ..**Krivoshey**, Robert M '78 OSU Moritz Cllg of Law -55 W 12th Av
-Columbus 43210 Fx:292-1383

(617) 421-8080 ..**Krivulka**, Thomas G '95 The Gillette Co -Pru Twr Bldg
-Boston, MA 02199
Kriwinsky, Paul '04 -(Address Unavailable)

(216) 787-3030 ..**Kriynovich**, Wayne S '88 Atty Gen -615 W Superior Av -11th Fl
-Cleveland 44113 Fx:787-3480

(312) 353-6057 ..**Kriz**, Judith A '79 US EPA -77 W Jackson Blvd -De-9J
-Chicago, IL 60604

(202) 752-6836 ..**Krncevic**, Margarita Santos '97 Cnsl Fannie Mae
-3900 Wscnsn Av NW -Washington, DC 20016

(202) 898-5884 ..**Krncevic**, Raymond '98 %Spriggs & H -1350 I NW -9th Fl
-Washington, DC 20005

(937) 275-7170 ..**Krochmal**, Kenneth J '81 (Albert & K) -4403 N Main
-Dayton 45405

(419) 247-1679 ..**Krock**, David C '82 (Eastman & S Ltd) -1 Seagate -24th Fl
-Bx10032 -Toledo 43699 Fx:247-1717

(330) 456-8361 ..**Krocker**, Michelle L '02 Cmmnty Lgl Aid Srvcs,Inc
-306 Market Av N -Ste 730 -Canton 44702

(614) 644-3037 ..**Kroeger**, Susan C '92 EPA -122 S Front -Bx1049
-Columbus 43216

(330) 670-9777 ..**Kroeger**, Tia M '94 Kroeger Law Offices -334 Fieldcrest Dr
-Fairlawn 44333

(419) 734-4142 ..**Kroeger-Baum**, Linda Lee '93 Gulas & K Co,LPA -132 Madison
-Port Clinton 43452

(216) 676-2528 ..**Krogh**, Timothy R '92 GrafTech Intl Ltd -12900 Snow Rd
-Parma 44130

(330) 535-6868 ..**Krohn**, Mark E '96 White Hat Mgt -159 S Main -11th Fl
-Akron 44308 Fx:535-5055

(216) 566-7100 ..**Krohngold**, Walter H '83 %SS Keller -1422 Euclid Av
-330 The Hanna Bldg -Cleveland 44115 Fx:566-5430
Krol, Kenneth H '81 -4437 W 11th -Cleveland 44109

(216) 566-9399 ..**Kroll**, Catherine A '96 Arthur J Gallagher & Co -1500 W 3rd
-Ste 405 -Cleveland 44113

(440) 546-9200 ..**Kroll**, Thomas J II '04 %S Di Geronimo -8748 Brecksvll Rd
-Ste 130 -Brecksville 44141

(419) 473-1346 ..**Kroncke D'Arcangelo Sutter & Furey** -2255 W Laskey Rd
-Toledo 43613 Fx:473-0218

(419) 473-1346 ..**Kroncke**, William G '64 (Kroncke DS&F) -2255 W Laskey Rd
-Toledo 43613 Fx:473-0218

(513) 241-1234 ..**Krone**, Bruce A '82 (Eichel & K Co,LPA) -602 Main -Ste 302
-Cincinnati 45202

(614) 451-7159 ..**Krone**, Gilbert L '68 -2000 W Henderson Rd -Ste 255
-Columbus 43220

(216) 426-2970 ..**Kronenberg**, Jacob A '76 -4403 St Clair Av NE -Cleveland 44103

(216) 692-3312 ..**Kronenberg**, Janet L '79 -339 Claymore Blvd
-Richmond Heights 44143

(513) 984-2640 ..**Kronke**, Suzanne M '99 UAW-Ford Legal Srvcs Plan
-4010 Exec Park Dr -Ste 225 -Cincinnati 45241

(740) 653-2616 ..**Krooner**, Theresa M '01 -136½ W Mulberry -Lancaster 43130

(330) 683-5010 ..**Kropf**, John W '68 (Kropf WH&L,LLP) -100 N Vine -Bx67
-Orrville 44667 Fx:683-5030

(330) 683-5010 ..**Kropf Wagner Hohenberger & Lutz, LLP** -100 N Vine -Bx67
-Orrville 44667 Fx:683-5030

(304) 340-1199 ..**Kropp**, Edward L '79 Jackson K PLLC -1600 Laidley Twr -Bx553
-Charleston, WV 25322 Fx:340-1130

(513) 621-6464 ..**Kropp**, John J '72 (Graydon H&R LLP) -511 Walnut
-1900 Fifth Third Ctr -Cincinnati 45202 Fx:651-3836

(202) 303-5465 ..**Kropp**, Norman W '80 Amer Red Cross -2025 E NW -Washington,
DC 20006

(216) 566-7010 ..**Krosin**, Donald N '58 -1700 E 13th -#20S -Cleveland 44114

(216) 781-4680 ..**Krotinger**, Myron N '39 Van Aken W&W -629 Euclid Av
-1000 Natl City Bk Bldg -Cleveland 44114 Fx:241-1421

(330) 740-2330 ..**Krueger**, Dawn P '02 %Mahoning Cnty Pros -21 W Boardman
-6th Fl -Youngstown 44503 Fx:740-2008

(216) 642-3342 ..**Krueger**, Jeffrey W '85 %Wegman H&V,LPA
-6055 Rockside Wds Blvd -Ste 200 -Cleveland 44131
Fx:642-8826

(419) 691-3542 ..**Krueger**, Mary M '79 Lakewood Grnhse,Inc -909 LeMoyne Rd
-Northwood 43619

(216) 491-3628 ..**Krueger**, William J '93 OfficeMax Inc -3605 Warrensvll Ctr Rd
-Bx228070 -Cleveland 44122

(859) 291-6900 ..**Kruer**, David A '87 (Kruer & Assoc,PSC) -17 Cedar Pnt
-Cold Spring, KY 41076

(859) 394-6200 ..**Kruer**, James R '73 (Adams SW&D) -40 W Pike -Bx861
-Covington, KY 41012 Fx:291-7902

(513) 651-6800 ..**Krug**, John C '89 (Frost BT LLC) -201 E 5th -2200 PNC Ctr
-Cincinnati 45202 Fx:651-6981

(330) 796-3204 ..**Kruger**, Gary I '77 Goodyear Tire & Rubber Co -1144 E Market
-Akron 44316

(419) 249-7900 ..**Krugh**, Timothy D '78 (Robison C&O) -Four SeaGate -9th Fl
-Toledo 43604 Fx:249-7911

(330) 497-0700 ..**Krugliak Wilkins Griffiths & Dougherty Co,LPA**
-4775 Munson NW -Bx36963 -Canton 44735 Fx:497-4020

(330) 823-9262 ..**Krugliak Wilkins Griffiths & Dougherty Co,LPA** -960 W State
-Alliance 44601 Fx:821-2447

(330) 343-9578 ..**Krugliak Wilkins Griffiths & Dougherty Co,LPA** -158 N Bway
-New Philadelphia 44663 Fx:602-3187

(617) 534-1200 ..**Krull**, Kevin C '77 Intl Data Group -One Exeter Plz
-Boston, MA 02116

(330) 499-4059 ..**Krum**, Frederick J '80 Akron-Canton Airport -5430 Lauby Rd -Bx 9
-North Canton 44720

(614) 466-9378 ..**Krum**, Jean Amy '90 Workers Comp -30 W Spring -Level 26
-Columbus 43215

(513) 241-4480 ..**Krumbein**, Mark S '83 -36 E 7th -Ste 2020 -Cincinnati 45202

(614) 466-1285 ..**Krumenacker**, James R '76 Industrial Commssn of OH
-30 W Spring -9th Fl -Columbus 43215 Fx:752-8785

(937) 225-5781 ..**Krumholtz**, John F '76 Montgomery Cnty Pros -301 W 3rd -Bx972
-Dayton 45422 Fx:225-3470

(937) 223-3277 ..**Krumholtz**, Michael W '79 (Bieser G&L LLP) -6 N Main
-400 Natl City Ctr -Dayton 45402 Fx:223-6339

(614) 249-3586 ..**Krumm**, Nancy M '80 Cnsl Nationwide Ins Co -1 Nationwide Plz
-Columbus 43215

(614) 227-2000 ..**Krummen**, Robert J '03 %Porter WM&A LLP -41 S High
-Columbus 43215 Fx:227-2100

(513) 946-3124 ..**Krumpelbeck**, Gerald W '77 Hamilton Cnty Pros -230 E 9th
-Cincinnati 45202 Fx:946-3017

(614) 258-9300 ..**Krupman**, Victor S '59 -923 E Broad -Columbus 43205

(216) 479-8500 ..**Kruppa**, Andrew R '00 %Squire S&D LLP -127 Pub Sq
-4900 Key Twr -Cleveland 44114 Fx:479-8780

(513) 241-3676 ..**Kruse**, Daniel A '70 -1029 Main -Cincinnati 45202
Kruse, Daniel A Jr. '02 -951 Hutch -#2 -Cincinnati 45202

(513) 361-6955 ..**Kruse**, John A Jr. '78 Columbus Life Ins Co -400 E 4th
-Cincinnati 45202

(216) 579-4114 ..**Kruse**, Mark F '85 (McIntyre K&K Co LPA) -1301 E 9th -Ste 1200
-Cleveland 44114

(330) 673-6515 ..**Krutz**, Deborah A '88 Kent City Schl Dist -321 N DePeyster
-Kent 44240

(937) 333-4100 ..**Krygowski**, Walter J '96 Law Dept -101 W 3rd -Bx22
-Dayton 45402

(216) 479-8500 ..**Kryshtalowych**, Helen Z '80 (Squire S&D LLP) -127 Pub Sq
-4900 Key Twr -Cleveland 44114 Fx:479-8780

(440) 322-5441 ..**Kryszak**, Andrea C '03 %Lessing W&R Ltd -374 Broad -Ste A
-Elyria 44035

(216) 566-5642 ..**Kryszak**, Michele T '03 %Thompson H LLP -127 Pub Sq
-3900 Key Ctr -Cleveland 44114 Fx:566-5800

(330) 743-1171 ..**Krzys**, Jerry R II '04 %Manchester BP&U -201 E Commerce
-Atrium Level 2 Commerce Bldg -Youngstown 44503
Fx:743-1190

(216) 475-5484 ..**Kuban**, Noreen M '96 City of Garfield Hghts -5407 Turney Rd
-Garfield Heights 44125

(513) 421-6630 ..**Kubicki**, Margaret G '93 %Lindhorst & D Co,LPA -312 Walnut
-Ste 2300 -Cincinnati 45202

(330) 489-3210 ..**Kubilus**, Richard J '78 Mun Ct Judge -218 Cleveland Av SW
-Bx24218 -Canton 44701

(614) 466-3998 ..**Kubli**, David F '75 Unemploymnt Comp Commssn -145 S Front
-Bx182299 -Columbus 43218

(440) 350-1900 ..**Kubyn**, R R '84 (Kubyn & K) -100 S Park Pl -Ste 210
-Painesville 44077

(440) 350-1900 ..**Kubyn**, Stacey L '91 Kubyn & K -100 S Park Pl -Ste 210
-Painesville 44077

(440) 526-2428 ..**Kucha**, Helen A '77 -180 E Royalton Rd -Broadview Heights 44147

(440) 350-3200 ..**Kucharski**, Carolyn M '93 Lake Cnty Pub Def -125 E Erie
-Painesville 44077

(216) 696-9800 ..**Kucharski**, Timothy J '93 (Gardner & K) -526 Superior Av E
-Ste 1130 -Cleveland 44114

(216) 363-4500 ..**Kucharson**, Michael C '04 %Benesch FC&A LLP -200 Pub Sq
-Ste 2300 -Cleveland 44114 **Fx:**363-4588

(937) 228-8367 ..**Kuczak**, Konrad '69 -130 W 2nd -Ste 1010 -Dayton 45402

(216) 263-6593 ..**Kuderna**, Dawn M '97 Ameritech -45 Erievw Plz -#860
-Cleveland 44114

(800) 346-4497 ..**Kuebler**, Christopher D '82 -32565 Lk Rd -Avon Lake 44012

(216) — **Kuehn**, Kevin '03 -2485 Merrybell Ct -Grove City 43123

(614) 221-8500 ..**Kuehnle**, Kenton L '70 (Allen K&S LLP) -21 W Broad -Ste 400
-Columbus 43215

(216) 241-0040 ..**Kuenzi**, Hans C '83 (H Kuenzi Co,LPA) -1660 W 2nd -#410
-Cleveland 44113 **Fx:**241-4804

(419) 423-0242 ..**Kuenzli**, David P '64 (Drake PK&C) -301 S Main -Ste 3
-Findlay 45840 **Fx:**423-0186

(216) 348-7550 ..**Kuepper**, Richard R '80 (R Kuepper & Assoc) -1660 W 2nd
-Ste 480 -Cleveland 44113

(419) 394-2516 ..**Kuffner**, John F '55 (Kuffner & P) -201 W North
-Saint Marys 45885 **Fx:**394-1163

(216) 241-6770 ..**Kugelman**, Harvey '84 -1370 Ontario -Ste 450 -Cleveland 44113

(216) 592-5000 ..**Kuhar**, Deviani M '94 Cnsl Tucker E&W LLP -925 Euclid Av
-1150 Huntngtn Bldg -Cleveland 44115 **Fx:**592-5009

(440) 944-4470 ..**Kuhar**, Fred '71 -1951 Grdn Dr -Wickliffe 44092

(440) 392-7126 ..**Kuhel**, Anthony E Jr. '00 STERIS Corp -5960 Heisley Rd
-Mentor 44060

(419) 241-6000 ..**Kuhl**, David L '75 (Eastman & S Ltd) -1 Seagate -24th Fl -Bx10032
-Toledo 43699 **Fx:**247-1777

(419) 473-1431 ..**Kuhl**, John R '77 (JR Kuhl,LPA) -4127 Monroe -Toledo 43606
Fx:473-0329

(859) 669-8923 ..**Kuhl**, Shannon M '98 Shire US,Inc -One Rvrfrnt Pl -Newport,
KY 41071

(216) 696-5222 ..**Kuhlman**, Gina A '96 %Johnson & C,LLC -1001 Lakeside Av
-Ste 1700 N Pnt Twr -Cleveland 44114 **Fx:**696-5288

(859) 394-6200 ..**Kuhlman**, Jason C '01 %Adams SW&D -40 W Pike -Bx861
-Covington, KY 41012 **Fx:**291-7902

(440) 461-5000 ..**Kuhlman**, Kathleen L '95 Progressive Ins Co -6055 Parkland Blvd
-Mayfield Heights 44124

(419) 287-4618 ..**Kuhlman**, Robert A '79 (Kuhlman & B) -221 E Front -BxH
-Pemberville 43450

(614) 262-2539 ..**Kuhlmann**, Will '72 %Anadem Pblshng -3620 N High
-Columbus 43214

(614) 466-0182 ..**Kuhn**, Amy K '94 Dept of Dvlpmnt -77 S High -Columbus 43215

(740) 354-1454 ..**Kuhn**, David W '69 -612 6th -Ste A -Portsmouth 45662

(419) 471-2034 ..**Kuhn**, Jeffrey C '82 ProMedica Health Sys -2142 N Cove Blvd
-Toledo 43606

(330) 452-6400 ..**Kuhn**, John S '77 -220 Market Av S -Ste 400 -Canton 44702

(734) 847-8080 ..**Kuhn**, Kimberly B '96 %Garrett CSR&S,LLP -9042 Lewis Av -Bx7
-Temperance, MI 48182

(614) 224-8339 ..**Kuhn**, Kristie Campbell '03 %Britt CN&S -490 City Park Av
-Columbus 43215 **Fx:**224-2001

(740) 355-8215 ..**Kuhn**, Mark E '94 Scioto Cnty Pros -602 7th -Rm 310
-Portsmouth 45662 **Fx:**354-5546

(440) 366-9930 ..**Kuhn**, Paula A '99 %McCray MS&M Co,LPA -260 Burns Rd
-Ste 150 -Elyria 44035 **Fx:**366-1910

(330) 452-7334 ..**Kuhn**, Richard R '80 -1428 Market Av N -Canton 44714

(419) 228-2122 ..**Kuhn**, Thomas R '70 -973 W North -Lima 45805

(419) 244-8336 ..**Kuhn**, Todd J '02 %Gressley K&P -608 Mad Av -Ste 930
-Toledo 43604 **Fx:**244-1914

(513) 977-8200 ..**Kuhnell**, Clayton L '01 %Dinsmore & S LLP -255 E 5th -Ste 1900
-Cincinnati 45202 **Fx:**977-8141

(419) 865-1251 ..**Kuhnle**, Carl A '71 Wagoner & S,Ltd -7445 Airport Hwy
-Holland 43528 **Fx:**866-8798

(614) 466-6750 ..**Kuhns**, Keven J '89 OH Dept Taxation -30 E Broad -22nd Fl
-Columbus 43215

(419) 882-6528 ..**Kujawa**, Kenneth T '71 -7749 WestBourne Ct -Sylvania 43560

(216) 771-6500 ..**Kukovec-Krasnicki**, Suzana '01 %K Weiner & Assoc Co,LPA
-75 Pub Sq -4th Fl -Cleveland 44113 **Fx:**771-6540

(614) 464-6400 ..**Kulewicz**, John J '81 (Vorys SS&P LLP) -52 E Gay -Bx1008
-Columbus 43216 **Fx:**464-6350

(216) 337-3331 ..**Kulick**, Martina '91 -6000 Freedom Square Dr
-Freedom Square II, Ste 380 -Independence 44131

(313) 965-8300 ..**Kulick**, Stacee M '00 %Clark H,PLC -500 Woodward Av -Ste 3500
-Detroit, MI 48266

(513) 985-1524 ..**Kulick**, Susan G '92 Jewish Fed of Cincinnati -4380 Malsbary Rd
-Ste 200 -Cincinnati 45242

(440) 886-7700 ..**Kulig**, John J '60 -6325 York Rd -Ste 305 -Parma Heights 44130

(972) 982-4803 ..**Kulik**, Joseph P Jr. '72 Comp USA Inc -14951 Dallas Pkwy
-Dallas, TX 75254

— **Kulin**, Laszlo G '00 -1 Lbrty Plz -#3800 -New York, NY 10006

— **Kulka**, Amy M '04 -(Address Unavailable)

(614) 462-3580 ..**Kullman**, Jack R Jr. '77 %10th Dist Crt of Appeals -373 S High
-24th Fl -Columbus 43215

(216) 241-2600 ..**Kulwicki**, David A '88 %Becker & M Co,LPA -1660 W 2nd
-Ste 660 -Cleveland 44113 **Fx:**241-5757

(419) 469-3939 ..**Kulwicki**, Laura A '87 %Jones D -325 John H McConnell Blvd
-Ste 600 -Bx165017 -Columbus 43216 **Fx:**461-4198

(606) 341-0255 ..**Kummer**, John R '90 (Ware BW&K) -157 Barnwood Dr -Bx17718
-Edgewood, KY 41017

(210) 829-3136 ..**Kunczt**, Robert M '69 Univ of the Incarnate Word -4301 Bway
-San Antonio, TX 78209

(937) 255-2838 ..**Kundert**, Thomas L '87 AFMC LO/JAZ -2240 B -Rm 100
-Wright Patterson AFB 45433

(614) 888-4160 ..**Kundtz**, Alan J '81 SEA Inc -7349 Worth Galena Rd
-Columbus 43085

(440) 248-2027 ..**Kundtz**, John A '58 -30000 Aurora Rd -#250 -Solon 44139
Fx:248-2153

(412) 391-7299 ..**Kunkel**, Gregory T '88 (Kunkel & F,LLP) -429 Forbes Av
-Pittsburgh, PA 15219

(513) 946-3103 ..**Kunkel**, Jerome A '88 -230 E 9th -Ste 700 -Cincinnati 45202

(216) 586-3939 ..**Kunkle**, Lisa K '94 %Jones D -901 Lakeside Av -Cleveland 44114
Fx:579-0212

— **Kunkle**, Matthew S '04 -(Address Unavailable)

(937) 278-9399 ..**Kuns**, David E '91 -Bx60419 -Dayton 45406

(419) 893-7600 ..**Kuns**, Gary F '68 -99 Conant -Maumee 43537

(216) 696-3366 ..**Kunselman**, David A '01 %Goodman WM LLP -100 Erievw Plz
-27th Fl -Cleveland 44114 **Fx:**363-5835

(513) 977-8200 ..**Kunst**, John M Jr. '66 (Dinsmore & S LLP) -255 E 5th -Ste 1900
-Cincinnati 45202 **Fx:**977-8141

(216) 566-9477 ..**Kuntz**, Christine M '04 %Bruner & J Co LPA -55 Pub Sq -Ste 1600
-Cleveland 44113

(330) 497-0700 ..**Kuntz**, Leslie I '86 (Krugliak WG&D Co,LPA) -4775 Munson NW
-Bx36963 -Canton 44735 **Fx:**497-4020

— **Kunz**, MK '03 -6933 Chadbourne Dr -North Olmsted 44070

(740) 286-5008 ..**Kunze**, Mary B '50 -235 Pearl -Bx508 -Jackson 45640

(513) 977-3835 ..**Kuprionis**, Mary D '95 EW Scripps Co -312 Walnut -Ste 2800
-Cincinnati 45202

(216) 292-3300 ..**Kurant**, John '95 (Conway MWK&K Co,LPA) -30195 Chagrin Blvd
-Ste 300 -Cleveland 44124

(216) 664-4190 ..**Kurdila**, Julianne '89 Dept of Law -601 Lakeside Av
-Rm 106 City Hall -Cleveland 44114 **Fx:**664-2663

(419) 562-1896 ..**Kurek**, Edward L '94 Crawford Cnty Juv Ct -112 E Mansfld
-Ste 101 -Bucyrus 44820

(330) 376-2700 ..**Kurek**, James D '81 (Roetzel & A,LPA) -222 S Main -Akron 44308
Fx:376-4577

(850) 505-6618 ..**Kurek**, Matthew B '00 Naval Hospital -SJAG -6000 W Hwy 98
-Pensacola, FL 32512

(216) 221-2121 ..**Kurek**, Randy S '79 (Isaac BL&T,LLP) -250 E Broad
-Ste 900 Mdlnd Bldg -Columbus 43215 **Fx:**365-9516

(419) 242-8461 ..**Kurek-Maloney**, Kimberly C '98 -520 Mad Av -Ste 520
-Toledo 43604 **Fx:**242-6866

(614) 464-1610 ..**Kurgis**, Kevin F '82 (K Kurgis Co,LPA) -100 S 4th -Ste 300
-Columbus 43215 **Fx:**464-1616

— **Kuri**, Camille D '93 -2180 Hudson Aurora Rd -Hudson 44236

(330) 375-1311 ..**Kuri**, Phillip A '93 (Reminger & R) -80 S Summit -200 Courtyard Sq
-Akron 44308 **Fx:**375-9075

(614) 462-3194 ..**Kurila**, Mary C '85 Franklin Cnty Pub Def -373 S High -12th Fl
-Columbus 43215

(216) 696-3311 ..**Kurit**, Neil B '64 (Kahn K) -1301 E 9th -2600 Erievw Twr
-Cleveland 44114 **Fx:**623-4912

(216) 541-3311 ..**Kurland**, Gerald J '68 -One Bratenahl Pl -#704 -Cleveland 44108
Fx:541-3311

(513) 946-3700 ..**Kurlansky**, Amy L '98 Hamilton Cnty Pub Def -230 E 9th -3rd Fl
-Cincinnati 45202 **Fx:**946-3707

(216) 363-4500 ..**Kursh**, Deanna C '74 OfCnsl Benesch FC&A LLP -200 Pub Sq
-Ste 2300 -Cleveland 44114 **Fx:**363-4588

(419) 241-4288 ..**Kurt**, Patricia H '82 (Spengler N PLL) -608 Mad Av -Ste 1000
-Toledo 43604 **Fx:**241-8599

(419) 248-2600 ..**Kurt**, Ted '79 OfCnsl Rohrbachers LC&T Co,LPA -405 Mad Av
-8th Fl -Toledo 43604 **Fx:**248-2614

(614) 227-2000 ..**Kurtz**, Charles J III '65 Cnsl Porter WM&A LLP -41 S High
-Columbus 43215 **Fx:**227-2100

(937) 865-6800 ..**Kurtz**, Christy L '89 Lexis/Nexis -Bx933 -Dayton 45401

(216) 382-2249 ..**Kurtz**, John C '68 -4843 Gleeton Rd -Cleveland 44143

(330) 399-1891 ..**Kurtz**, John W '50 (Thomas & K) -Bx1268 -Warren 44482
Fx:399-1892

(937) 904-5041 ..**Kurtz**, Marcia L '81 US Air Force -2776 C -Ste 200, 5 SGL
-Wright Patterson AFB 45433

(513) 421-2255 ..**Kurtz**, Michael L '86 (Boehm K&L) -36 E 7th -2110 Society Bk Ctr
-Cincinnati 45202

(216) 443-8422 ..**Kurtz**, William A '72 US Bankruptcy Ct -127 Pub Sq
-Cleveland 44114

(513) 232-2600 ..**Kurtzer**, Jamey L '94 -7164 Beechmont -Ste 101
-Cincinnati 45230

(330) 832-9878 ..**Kurtzman**, John L '66 Stergios & K Co,LPA
-2859 Aaronwood Av NE -Ste 101 -Massillon 44646

— **Kuruc**, Carolyn J '04 -(Address Unavailable)

(330) 746-6301 ..**Kurz**, Jeffrey A '02 -219 W Boardman -Youngstown 44503
Fx:743-3559

(513) 844-2288 ..**Kusel**, Mary L '80 -118 S 2nd -Hamilton 45011

(216) 896-5600 ..**Kushkin**, Lauren M '98 %Levy & D -25200 Chagrin Blvd -Ste 310
-Beachwood 44122 **Fx:**896-5601

(202) 833-8833 ..**Kushner**, Gordon P '91 OfCnsl Sommer BA,PC -1666 K NW
-Ste 1010 -Washington, DC 20006 **Fx:**833-8831

(216) 696-6700 ..**Kushner**, Philip S '90 (Kushner & R Co,LPA) -200 Pub Sq
-Ste 2860 BP Twr -Cleveland 44114 **Fx:**696-6772

(216) 696-6700 ..**Kushner & Rendon Co, LPA** -200 Pub Sq -Ste 2860 BP Twr
-Cleveland 44114 **Fx:**696-6772

(216) 937-4000 ..**Kusner**, Andrew T '94 Watson Wyatt & Co -1001 Lakeside Av E
-Ste 1900 -Cleveland 44114

(440) 684-1090 ..**Kusner**, Mark '80 (M Kusner Co,LPA) -6151 Wilson Mills Rd
-Ste 310 -Highland Heights 44143

(614) 462-2252 ..**Kutell**, Russell J '97 (Schottenstein Z&D) -250 West -Bx165020
-Columbus 43216 **Fx:**462-5135

(216) 586-3939 ..**Kutik**, David A '80 (Jones D) -901 Lakeside Av -Cleveland 44114
Fx:579-0212

(330) 758-9525 ..**Kutlick**, Paula '94 -755 Boardman-Canfld Rd -Ste K4
-Youngstown 44512

(440) 333-9270 ..**Kutsko**, Douglas A '97 (Kutsko & Assoc) -19071 Old Detroit Rd
-Ste 200 -Rocky River 44116

(330) 762-1134 ..**Kutuchief**, Richard P '78 -159 S Main -Ste 807 -Akron 44308
Fx:762-2226

(614) 464-6400 ..**Kuykendall**, Laura G '78 (Vorys SS&P LLP) -52 E Gay -Bx1008
-Columbus 43216 **Fx:**464-6350

(440) 233-7626 ..**Kuzela**, Dennis M '72 -6645 Lemonwood -Lorain 44053

(202) 616-6070 ..**Kuzma**, Susan M '78 DOJ-Ofc of Pardon Atty -500 1st NW
-Ste 400 -Washington, DC 20530

(513) 425-5224 ..**Kuzman**, John J Jr. '86 AK Steel Corp -703 Curtis
-Middletown 45043

(440) 554-8588 ..**Kuzmickas**, Paul S '03 -27126 Cook Rd
-Olmsted Township 44138

(216) 443-7223 ..**Kuzmins**, Paul A '01 %Cuyahoga Cnty Pub Def -1200 W 3rd NW
-100 Lakeside Pl -Cleveland 44113

(419) 353-5073 ..**Kuzoff**, George D '62 -Bx212 -Bowling Green 43402

(216) 566-1144 ..**Kvale**, Craig P '91 (Webster WK LLP) -1220 W 6th -Ste 600
-Cleveland 44113 Fx:566-1221

(216) 831-5010 ..**Kwait**, Todd M '84 -23230 Chagrin Blvd -Ste 340
-Beachwood 44122

(614) 792-5555 ..**Kwak**, James L '96 (Standley Law Grp LLP) -495 Metro Pl S
-Ste 210 -Dublin 43017 Fx:792-5536

(847) 938-5864 ..**Kwakye**, Benjamin '93 Abbott Labs -100 Abbott Park Rd
-Dept 32L,Bldg AP6D -Abbott Park, IL 60064

(419) 241-2777 ..**Kwapich**, Christie M '99 Bunda S&D,PLL -One SeaGate -Ste 650
-Toledo 43604 Fx:241-4697

(216) 737-0000 ..**Kwarciak**, Richard F '94 (Reese & K) -1375 E 9th -Ste 610
-Cleveland 44114

(440) 871-5020 ..**Kwarciany**, Dale L '76 DK Fifner Co,LPA -24441 Detroit Rd
-Ste 300 -Westlake 44145

(513) 977-8680 ..**Kwiatkowski**, Andrew R '02 %Dinsmore & S LLP -255 E 5th
-Ste 1900 -Cincinnati 45202 Fx:977-8141

(216) 241-4664 ..**Kwiatkowski**, Peter S '91 -1370 Ontario -Ste 330
-Cleveland 44113

(330) 455-0173 ..**Kyhos**, Wayne C '69 (Day KRW&R,Ltd) -200 Market Av N
-Ste 300 -Bx24213 -Canton 44701 Fx:455-2633

(614) 645-8210 ..**Kyle-Reno**, Shelia Ann '83 Columbus Pblc Sfty -50 W Gay -2nd Fl
-Columbus 43215 Fx:645-8268

(330) 343-5585 ..**Kyler**, William A '64 Miller & K,LPA -405 Chauncey Av NW -Bx668
-New Philadelphia 44663 Fx:343-7977

(513) 870-2989 ..**Kyrios**, Helen '98 Cincinnati Ins Co -6200 S Gilmore Rd
-Fairfield 45014

(513) 651-6800 ..**Kyte**, Lawrence H Jr. '66 Cnsl Frost BT LLC -201 E 5th
-2200 PNC Ctr -Cincinnati 45202 Fx:651-6981

(740) 455-7123 ..**LaAsmar**, Ronald G '69 Muskingum Cnty Pros -27 N 5th
-Zanesville 43701

(330) 762-7477 ..**Laatsch**, Morris H III '75 (Hardesty K&Z) -520 S Main -Ste 500
-Akron 44311 Fx:762-8059

(212) 326-3600 ..**LaBarre**, Dennis W '68 (Jones DR&P) -222 E 41st -New York, NY
10017 Fx:755-7306

(513) 721-7500 ..**Laber**, Christopher T '79 -22 W 9th -Cincinnati 45202

(859) 431-6100 ..**Laber**, Stephen C '75 Arnzen & W,PSC -600 Greenup
-Covington, KY 41011 Fx:431-3778

(216) 479-8500 ..**Labes**, Robert D '88 (Squire S&D LLP) -127 Pub Sq
-4900 Key Twr -Cleveland 44114 Fx:479-8780

(513) 595-2470 ..**Labmeier**, John F '75 Union Cntrl Life Ins Co -1876 Waycross Rd
-Bx40888 -Cincinnati 45240

(216) 696-0022 ..**Labovitz**, Harvey '69 (Collins & S LLP) -50 Pub Sq
-3300 Trmnl Twr -Cleveland 44113 Fx:696-1166

(614) 221-1111 ..**LaBue**, Anne M '91 %Shayne & G -221 S High -Columbus 43215
Fx:221-4070

(614) 716-0500 ..**LaBuhn**, Matthew A '96 (Onda L&R Co,LPA) -266 N 4th -Ste 100
-Columbus 43215 Fx:716-0511

(440) 603-2378 ..**LaCava**, Robin K '90 Progressive Ins Co -6055 Parkland Blvd
-Mayfield Heights 44124

(216) 622-8200 ..**LaCerva**, Anthony J '86 (Calfee H&G LLP) -800 Superior Av
-Ste 1400 -Cleveland 44114 Fx:241-0816

(440) 285-2222 ..**LaChapelle**, Laura Ann '96 Geauga Cnty Pros -231 Main
-Cthse Annx -Chardon 44024 Fx:286-4357

(330) 535-5711 ..**Lacher**, Frederick K '50 OfCnsl Brouse M -106 S Main -500
First Natl Twr -Akron 44308 Fx:253-8601

(937) 223-5200 ..**Lachey**, Robert E '73 Flanagan LH&S -318 W 4th -Dayton 45402
Fx:223-3335

(937) 369-6288 ..**Lachman**, Marshall G '03 -75 N Pioneer Blvd -Springboro 45066

(216) 622-4363 ..**Lachman**, Roy E '80 OH Savings Bank -1801 E 9th
-Cleveland 44114

(330) 744-5211 ..**Lacich**, Christopher P '93 Roth BRS&L,LPA -100 Fed Plz E
-Ste 600 -Youngstown 44503 Fx:744-3184

(330) 534-3139 ..**LaCivita**, Richard J '75 -973 W Lbrty -Ste B -Hubbard 44425

(216) 621-1530 ..**LaCivita**, Richard J '00 %Shapiro & F,LLP -1500 W 3rd -Ste 400
-Cleveland 44113 Fx:621-1551

(216) 621-1530 ..**LaCivita**, Robert J '02 %Shapiro & F,LLP -1500 W 3rd -Ste 400
-Cleveland 44113 Fx:621-1551

(614) 242-4242 ..**Lackey**, David L '91 (Decker VSL&V Co LPA) -620 E Broad
-Columbus 43215 Fx:242-4243

(954) 929-5145 ..**Lackey**, Gerald B '62 -3111 N Ocean Dr -#1407
-Hollywood, FL 33019

               Lackey, Jane L '79 -2107 Central Grv -Toledo 43614

(419) 243-1105 ..**Lackey Nusbaum Harris Reny & Torzewski,LPA**
-2 Maritime Plz -3rd Fl -Toledo 43604

(330) 966-1866 ..**Lacki**, Ralph S '77 -6161 Lk O'Sprngs Av NW -Canton 44718

(614) 792-5703 ..**Lacksonen**, Todd A '92 -8732 Tayport Dr -Dublin 43017

               Lacy, David L '77 -819 Smith Rd -Wilmington 45177

(330) 788-2480 ..**Laczko**, John P '91 -4800 Market -Ste C -Youngstown 44512

(216) 831-2345 ..**Ladanyi**, Albert L II '83 Noral,Inc -2301 Hmltn Av
-Cleveland 44114 Fx:831-1315

(419) 353-2365 ..**Ladd**, Elisabeth S '91 -929 Melrose -Bowling Green 43402

(216) 520-5512 ..**Ladegaard**, Brenda Lee '94 West Grp -6111 Oak Tree Blvd
-Bx318063 -Cleveland 44131

(513) 369-0200 ..**LaDue**, Edna G '89 (Bazeley & L) -13 E Court -#400
-Cincinnati 45202

(216) 664-2569 ..**Lady**, Julie A '02 Dept of Law -601 Lakeside Av -Rm 106 City Hall
-Cleveland 44114 Fx:664-2663

(216) 522-1200 ..**Lafave**, Arthur J Jr. '60 IMG -1360 E 9th -Ste 100
-Cleveland 44114

(614) 228-2154 ..**LaFayette**, Eric L '04 %BL Potts & Co,LPA -415 E Broad -Ste 112
-Columbus 43215 Fx:228-2155

(614) 466-5707 ..**LaFayette**, Jennifer L '97 Legis Srvc Commssn -77 S High
-Columbus 43215

(614) 461-1311 ..**La Fayette**, Paul-Michael '96 %Reminger & R -65 E State
-4th Fl Cptl Sq Ofc Bldg -Columbus 43215 Fx:232-2410

(440) 347-1541 ..**Laferty**, Samuel B '83 Lubrizol Corp -29400 Lakelnd Blvd
-Wickliffe 44092

(440) 593-2309 ..**Lafferty**, Charles N Jr. '77 -365 Main -Conneaut 44030

(419) 241-2122 ..**Lafferty**, Jon A '73 (Williams JLG&S Co,LPA) -416 N Erie -Ste 500
-Toledo 43624 Fx:245-3849

(216) 766-5416 ..**Lafferty**, Michelle A '89 Genesis -25550 Chagrin Blvd -Ste 300
-Beachwood 44122

(216) 522-6104 ..**Lafferty**, Scott W '80 Dfnse Fin & Accntng Srvc -1240 E 9th
-Gen Cnsl Ofc -Cleveland 44199

(937) 225-2910 ..**Lafferty**, Sheila G '89 US Atty -200 W 2nd -602 Fed Bldg
-Dayton 45402

(440) 232-6288 ..**Laffin**, Keith A '88 (Acosta & L) -318 Solon Rd -Bedford 44146

(314) 621-8383 ..**Lafkas**, David M '01 Oliff & B,PLC -1010 Market -Ste 1520
-Saint Louis, MO 63101

(937) 644-6631 ..**LaFleur**, Joseph F '86 Honda of Amer Mfg -24000 Honda Pkwy
-Marysville 43040

(216) 696-4200 ..**LaFond**, Thomas J '66 (Schneider SR&L PLL) -1111 Superior Av
-Ste 1000 -Cleveland 44114 Fx:696-7303

(440) 352-0761 ..**LaForce**, Robert W '81 -10870 Tanglewood Trl -Painesville 44077

(614) 221-2121 ..**LaForge**, Steven G '86 (Isaac BL&T,LLP) -250 E Broad
-Ste 900 Mdlnd Bldg -Columbus 43215 Fx:365-9516

(937) 443-6600 ..**LaForte**, Rene '93 OfCnsl Thompson H LLP -2000 Cthse Plz NE
-Bx8801 -Dayton 45401 Fx:443-6635

(614) 692-3284 ..**Lagana**, Beth B '80 US Dfnse Lgstcs Agncy -Bx3990
-Columbus 43218

(614) 752-1767 ..**Lagana**, Vincent E '89 OH Dept Rehab & Correction
-1050 Fwy Dr N -Columbus 43229

(330) 297-3665 ..**Lager**, Dennis D '76 Portage Cnty Pub Def -209 S Chestnut -4th Fl
-Ravenna 44266

(937) 323-5555 ..**Lagos**, James H '73 (Lagos & L) -1 S Limestone -Ste 1000
-Springfield 45502

(937) 323-5555 ..**Lagos & Lagos** -1 S Limestone -Ste 1000 -Springfield 45502

(937) 323-5555 ..**Lagos**, Thomas M '72 (Lagos & L) -1 S Limestone -Ste 1000
-Springfield 45502

(216) 641-7575 ..**Lah**, Andrej N '89 Catholic Cemeteries Assn -10000 Miles Av
-Bx605310 -Cleveland 44105

(419) 248-2600 ..**Lah**, Jack J '04 %Rohrbachers LC&T Co,LPA -405 Mad Av -8th Fl
-Toledo 43604 Fx:248-2614

(330) 486-0950 ..**Lah-O'Brien**, Kristina I '94 Majestic Title Agncy LLC
-2132 Case Pkwy N -Unit C -Twinsburg 44087

(212) 980-0010 ..**Lahey**, John H '72 (Kozusko LH LLP) -575 Mad Av -Ste 7B
-New York, NY 10022 Fx:751-0084

(614) 222-0963 ..**Lahm**, Gunther K '87 (G Lahm,LLC) -155 W Main -Ste 101
-Columbus 43215

(937) 743-1500 ..**Lahmann**, Barbara A '87 %D Chicarelli Co,LPA -614 E 2nd
-Franklin 45005

               Lahmers, Nancy K '80 -447 E North Bway -Columbus 43214

               Lai, David C '03 -(Address Unavailable)

(330) 743-5101 ..**Laine**, Barry Robert '73 Green H&S,Co LPA -16 Wick Av -Ste 400
-Youngstown 44503 Fx:743-3451

(216) 664-3316 ..**Laine**, Robin L '77 Cleveland Mun Ct -Bx94894 -Cleveland 44101

(614) 716-2435 ..**Laing**, David A '81 Amer Elec Pwr Co -1 Riverside Plz
-Columbus 43215

(330) 945-7238 ..**Laing**, Matthew A '92 -2020 Front -Ste 104 -Cuyahoga Falls 44221

(513) 381-2838 ..**Laing**, Michael A '04 (Taft S&H LLP) -425 Walnut -Ste 1800
-Cincinnati 45202 Fx:381-0205

(216) 696-4200 ..**Laino**, Kenneth J '81 OfCnsl Schneider SR&L PLL -1111 Superior
Av -Ste 1000 -Cleveland 44114 Fx:696-7303

(937) 293-2392 ..**Lair**, Anthony R '54 (Lair O&M) -580 Lincoln Park Blvd -Ste 111
-Dayton 45429

(937) 293-2392 ..**Lair Owen & Meadows** -580 Lincoln Park Blvd -Ste 111 -Dayton
45429

(614) 443-6721 ..**Laird**, Eric M '98 EM Laird Co,LPA -673 Mohawk -Ste 200
-Columbus 43206 Fx:444-7788

(216) 622-3911 ..**Laisure**, Lori E '92 US Atty -801 W Superior -Ste 400
-Cleveland 44113 Fx:622-3370

(513) 241-1950 ..**Laite**, David A '90 Brown LH&E -7 W 7th -Ste 1950
-Cincinnati 45202 Fx:241-4095

(513) 684-3641 ..**Laite**, Theresa L '93 NLRB -550 Main -Rm 3003 -Cincinnati 45202

(513) 621-6464 ..**LaJeunesse**, Richard T '80 (Graydon H&R LLP) -511 Walnut
-1900 Fifth Third Ctr -Cincinnati 45202 Fx:651-3836

(330) 394-7580 ..**Lake**, David G '84 -154 Park Av NE -Bx1150 -Warren 44482

(513) 621-6464 ..**Lake**, Matthew B '99 %Graydon H&R LLP -511 Walnut
-1900 Fifth Third Ctr -Cincinnati 45202 Fx:651-3836

(312) 580-0100 ..**Lake**, Michael J '97 %Gessler HSPR&D,Ltd -70 W Madison
-Ste 2200 -Chicago, IL 60602

(216) 225-7572 ..**Lake**, Robert A '99 -11470 Euclid Av -Cleveland 44106

(412) 471-0677 ..**Lalama**, Jeffrey R '04 (Feldstein GS&M) -428 Blvd of the Allies
-Pittsburgh, PA 15219

(216) 586-7514 ..**Lalchandani**, Kabir A '04 %Jones D -901 Lakeside Av
-Cleveland 44114 Fx:579-0212

(614) 464-6400 ..**Laliberte**, Brian J '99 %Vorys SS&P LLP -52 E Gay -Bx1008
-Columbus 43216 Fx:464-6350

(614) 464-6400 ..**Laliberte**, Elizabeth A '02 %Vorys SS&P LLP -52 E Gay -Bx1008
-Columbus 43216 Fx:464-6350

(440) 428-1136 ..**Lalka**, Colman R '81 C Lalka Co,LPA -Bx813 -Madison 44057

(216) 523-1525 ..**Lallo**, Ernest A '79 (Lallo & F Co,LPA) -55 Pub Sq -Ste 1616
-Cleveland 44113

(216) 348-4809 ..**Lally**, Charles J '81 8th Dist Ct of Appls -1 Lakeside Av -#202
-Cleveland 44113 Fx:443-2044

(614) 263-7809 ..**Lally**, Mark S '75 -72 Grdn Rd -Columbus 43214

(216) 721-6650 ..**Lally**, Marlene N '89 -2351 N Park Blvd -Cleveland Heights 44106

(216) 579-4114 ..**Lally**, Robert J '92 %McIntyre K&K Co LPA -1301 E 9th -Ste 1200
-Cleveland 44114

(440) 788-5097 ..**Lally**, Sarah T '02 Hyland Software Inc -28500 Clemens Rd
-Westlake 44145

(330) 499-5474 ..**Lally**, Thomas W '73 -4571 Stephen Cir NW -Canton 44718
Fx:433-1313

(216) 479-8500 ..**Lally Spicer**, Meegan '93 Squire S&D LLP -127 Pub Sq
-4900 Key Twr -Cleveland 44114 Fx:479-8780

(412) 658-3758 ..**Lamancusa**, Carmen F '67 (C Lamancusa, PC) -414 N Jffrsn
-New Castle, PA 16101

(440) 708-0115 ..**Lamanna**, Michael A '91 -17119 Northbrook Trl
-Chagrin Falls 44023

(740) 282-5122 ..**Lamatrice**, Stephen B '82 -123 N 4th -Steubenville 43952

(216) 566-5590 ..**Lamb**, Brian J '91 (Thompson H LLP) -127 Pub Sq -3900 Key Ctr
-Cleveland 44114 Fx:566-5800

(440) 395-3698 ..**Lamb**, David C '90 Progressive Ins Co -6300 Wilson Mills Rd
-#N72A -Mayfield Village 44143
Lamb, Geoffrey R '95 -Bx491 -Gates Mills 44040

(216) 520-6400 ..**Lamb**, Jason C '02 %West Group -6111 Oak Tree Blvd -Bx318063
-Cleveland 44131

(440) 988-9000 ..**Lamb**, Joshua E '03 %Colella & W,PLL -6055 Park Square Dr
-Oak Pnt Prof Park -Lorain 44053 **Fx**:988-9002

(330) 823-9080 ..**Lamb**, Joyce A '90 -1610 S Union Av -Alliance 44601 **Fx**:823-1070

(513) 621-2100 ..**Lamb**, Laurie A '03 %Beckman W&S LLC -120 E 4th
-1200 Mercantile Ctr -Cincinnati 45202 **Fx**:621-0106

(330) 675-2650 ..**Lamb**, Matthew O '87 %11th Dist Ct of Appls -111 High NE
-Warren 44481

(513) 553-4713 ..**Lamb**, Robert M '89 -1247 Fagins Run Rd -New Richmond 45157
Lamb, William H '91 -(Address Unavailable)

(419) 213-4687 ..**Lambdin**, Jennifer M '98 %Lucas Cnty Pros-Juv Div
-1801 Spielbusch Av -Toledo 43624

(216) 443-5869 ..**Lambert**, David G '85 %Cuyahoga Cnty Pros -1200 Ontario -8th Fl
-Cleveland 44113 **Fx**:698-2270

(513) 421-2400 ..**Lambert**, Jennifer L '02 %Helmer MR&P Co,LPA -105 E 4th
-Ste 1900 -Cincinnati 45202 **Fx**:421-7902

(330) 434-5444 ..**Lambert**, John D '79 (Lambert & M Co,LPA) -265 S Main
-Akron 44308

(330) 856-6868 ..**Lambert**, Marc D '98 -144 N Park Av -Ste 101 -Warren 44481

(614) 469-1400 ..**Lambert**, Marnie C '00 %Clark PR&S Co,LPA -471 E Broad
-Ste 1400 -Columbus 43215 **Fx**:469-0900

(614) 229-7631 ..**Lambert**, Martha M '04 Franklin Cnty CSB -525 E Mound
-Columbus 43215

(740) 532-4333 ..**Lambert McWhorter & Bowling** -215 S 4th -Bx725
-Ironton 45638

(614) 236-6779 ..**Lambert**, Michelle R '01 Capital Univ Law Schl -303 E Broad
-Family Advocacy Clinic -Columbus 43215

(216) 621-8484 ..**Lambert**, Phillip Wesley '03 %Climaco LPW&G Co,LPA
-1228 Euclid Av -Ste 900 Halle Bldg -Cleveland 44115
Fx:771-1632

(740) 532-4333 ..**Lambert**, Randall L '79 (Lambert M&B) -215 S 4th -Bx725
-Ironton 45638

(937) 222-2500 ..**Lambert**, William W '81 OfCnsl Sebaly S&D -1900 Kettering Twr
-Dayton 45423 **Fx**:222-6554

(440) 816-0600 ..**Lambros**, David A '85 -1 Berea Cmmns -Ste 216 -Berea 44017

(440) 838-7600 ..**Lambros**, Thomas D '52 OfCnsl Janik & D,LLP -9200 S Hills Blvd
-Ste 300 -Cleveland 44147 **Fx**:838-7601

(440) 997-8130 ..**Lambros**, Thomas D '52 (T Lambros Co,LPA) -618 Holden Dr
-Ashtabula 44004

(513) 721-1350 ..**Lameier**, Richard D '68 (Barron PB&S) -3074 Madison Rd
-Cincinnati 45209

(440) 593-7413 ..**Lamer**, Lori B '83 -294 Main -Conneaut 44030

(216) 368-2696 ..**Lamis**, Alexander P '97 Case Wstrn Reserve Univ
-10900 Euclid Av -Dept Political Sci -Cleveland 44106

(614) 224-8187 ..**Lamkin Van Emin Trimble Beals & Dougherty** -500 S Front
-Ste 200 -Columbus 43215 **Fx**:224-4943

(614) 224-8187 ..**Lamkin**, William W '66 (Lamkin VTB&D) -500 S Front -Ste 200
-Columbus 43215 **Fx**:224-4943

(513) 777-7460 ..**Lamm**, Dennis J '84 -7237 Cincinnati-Dayton Rd -Ste 201A
-West Chester 45069 **Fx**:777-7542

(614) 267-6308 ..**Lamm**, Russell E Jr. '63 -3368 Olentangy Rvr Rd -Columbus
43202

(937) 221-1540 ..**Lamme**, Kathryn A '80 Std Register Co -600 Albany
-Dayton 45408

(419) 523-5400 ..**Lammers**, Gary L '89 -125 W Main -Ottawa 45875

(419) 586-6442 ..**Lammers**, Thomas D '77 (Purdy L&S) -113 E Market -Bx404
-Celina 45822 **Fx**:586-1948

(216) 447-4477 ..**Lammert**, Cynthia A '91 Smythe Cramer Co -Bx318006
-Cleveland 44131

(330) 535-2151 ..**Lammert**, Thomas E '76 (Guy L&T) -106 S Main -Ste 2210
-Akron 44308 **Fx**:535-9048

(419) 445-3015 ..**Lammy**, James E '78 Scott Port-A-Fold,Inc -100 Taylor Pkwy
-Archbold 43502

(312) 750-1215 ..**LaMonica**, Deneen J '01 %Matushek N&S,LLC -One N LaSalle
-Ste 2100 -Chicago, IL 60602 **Fx**:750-1273

(216) 621-4268 ..**Lamos**, Philip D '96 Ofc of Chptr 13 Trustees -200 Pub Sq
-Ste 3860 BP Twr -Cleveland 44114

(513) 421-2540 ..**Lampe**, David J '00 %Ennis R&F -121 W 9th -Cincinnati 45202
Fx:562-4986

(513) 922-5200 ..**Lampe**, Gerald A '71 -5115 Delhi Av -Cincinnati 45238

(614) 469-3939 ..**Lampe**, Matthew W '89 (Jones D) -325 John H McConnell Blvd
-Ste 600 -Bx165017 -Columbus 43216 **Fx**:461-4198

(513) 889-0400 ..**Lampe**, Misty L '92 -2 S 3rd -Ste 405 -Hamilton 45011

(513) 534-0681 ..**Lampe**, Molly Kay '00 Cnsl Fifth 3rd Bank -38 Fountain Square Plz
-Cincinnati 45202

(518) 884-8004 ..**Lampe**, Robert C Jr. '76 RCL Consulting -152 Charlton Rd
-Ballston Spa, NY 12020

(216) 622-8200 ..**Lampert**, Donald E '86 Calfee H&G LLP -800 Superior Av
-Ste 1400 -Cleveland 44114 **Fx**:241-0816

(740) 772-7472 ..**Lamphear**, Patricia J '89 Adena Regional Med Ctr -272 Hsptl Rd
-Chillicothe 45601

(614) 466-7447 ..**Lampke**, Matthew J '97 Atty Gen -150 E Gay -Columbus 43215

(614) 227-2000 ..**Lampke**, Monique B '97 %Porter WM&A LLP -41 S High
-Columbus 43215 **Fx**:227-2100

(614) 462-5295 ..**Lampkin-Crafter**, Odella '89 Franklin Cnty Cmn Pleas Ct
-375 S High -Columbus 43215 **Fx**:462-6292

(614) 790-3019 ..**Lampkin-Isabel**, Robin E '90 Ashland Inc -5200 Blazer Pkwy
-Law Dept -Bx2219 -Columbus 43215

(740) 349-6575 ..**Lampl**, Robert C '71 Licking Cnty CSEA -65 E Main -Bx338
-Newark 43058

(513) 723-4000 ..**Lampley**, Nathaniel Jr. '89 (Vorys SS&P LLP) -221 E 4th
-Ste 2000 Atrium Two -Bx0236 -Cincinnati 45201 **Fx**:723-4056

(208) 334-1211 ..**Lamprecht**, Lynne W '76 US Atty Ofc -877 W Main -Ste 200
-Bx32 -Boise, ID 83707

(440) 333-9000 ..**Lampus**, Robert W '73 Dawson Ins -1340 Depot
-Rocky River 44116

(614) 855-5079 ..**Lanahan**, Patrick M '96 (Hlth & Human Srvcs Consulting LLC)
-7626 Alpath Rd -New Albany 43054 **Fx**:283-5599

(304) 347-3350 ..**Lancaster**, George H Jr. '87 Fed Pub Def -300 VA E -Ste 3400
-Charleston, WV 25301

(330) 454-1674 ..**Lancaster**, Judith E '94 -111 2nd NW -Ste 505 -Canton 44702

(937) 328-4645 ..**Lancaster**, Katrine M '91 Clark Cnty Common Pleas Ct-Juv Div
-31 N Limestone -Springfield 45502

(614) 221-2400 ..**Lancaster**, Leonard T '76 -233 S High -Ste 300 -Columbus 43215

(937) 325-5500 ..**Lancaster**, Robert N Jr. '87 (Pavlatos C&L Co,LPA) -700 E High
-Springfield 45505

(208) 334-2400 ..**Lance**, Alan G '74 Ofc of Atty Gen -Statehse -210 -Bx83720
-Boise, ID 83720

(216) 881-9191 ..**Lanci**, Wallace J '02 Consolidated Graphics Grp,Inc -1614 E 40th
-Cleveland 44103

(330) 477-8535 ..**Lancianese**, Frank W '84 %Cross & R Co,LPA -2884
Whipple Av NW -Canton 44708 **Fx**:477-2611
Lancione, Bernard G '65 -1108 Acillom Dr -Westerville 43081

(614) 299-2100 ..**Lancione**, David '77 (D Lancione & Assoc) -1041 Summit
-Columbus 43201 **Fx**:299-2200

(216) 623-4949 ..**Lancione**, John A '88 (Lancione & L,PLL) -200 Pub Sq -Ste 2945
-Cleveland 44114 **Fx**:623-3975

(216) 623-4949 ..**Lancione**, John G '59 (Lancione & L,PLL) -200 Pub Sq -Ste 2945
-Cleveland 44114 **Fx**:623-3975

(740) 676-2034 ..**Lancione & Lloyd,LPA** -3800 Jffrsn -Bellaire 43906 **Fx**:676-3931

(740) 676-2034 ..**Lancione**, Richard L '66 (Lancione & L,LPA) -3800 Jffrsn
-Bellaire 43906 **Fx**:676-3931

(614) 228-6627 ..**Lancione**, Robert M '76 Lancione Law Ofc,LLC -875 Mt Vernon Av
-Columbus 43203

(419) 784-1072 ..**Land**, David A '89 Law Dept -324 Perry -City Bldg -Defiance 43512
Fx:784-0492

(513) 984-3030 ..**Land**, Gregory E '84 Comm Mgmt Corp
-10925 Reed Hartman Hwy -200 -Cincinnati 45242

(419) 424-7286 ..**Land**, Lucinda M '89 Hancock Cnty Pros -222 Bway -#104
-Findlay 45840 **Fx**:424-7889

(513) 455-7600 ..**Land**, Suzanne P '90 Greenebaum D&M PLLC -255 E 5th
-2800 Chemed Ctr -Cincinnati 45202 **Fx**:455-8500

(740) 558-9997 ..**Landaker**, Shawna M '02 -3140 Route 83 N -Beverly 45715

(863) 603-4822 ..**Landau**, Joel M '78 -Bx2393 -Lakeland, FL 33806 **Fx**:603-4922
Landefeld, Anne M '52 -2181 Ambleside Dr -814
-Cleveland 44106

(740) 653-4259 ..**Landefeld**, David L '76 (Fairfield Cnty Pros) -201 S Broad -4th Fl
-Lancaster 43130

(513) 421-8173 ..**Landen**, Everett E '73 -3450 Burch Av -Cincinnati 45208

(740) 593-9418 ..**Landen**, Frank Gifford '78 University Medical Assoc
-332 Parks Hall -Athens 45701

(513) 621-6464 ..**Landen**, J Jeffrey '82 (Graydon H&R LLP) -511 Walnut
-1900 Fifth Third Ctr -Cincinnati 45202 **Fx**:651-3836

(513) 425-7714 ..**Landen**, Leslie S '79 City Law Director's Ofc -1 City Centre Plz
-Middletown 45042

(859) 331-4880 ..**Landen**, Pennington P '86 -436 Larkspur Ct -Edgewood, KY 41017

(330) 673-0142 ..**Lander**, Byron G '74 -500 Harvey -Kent 44240

(740) 335-8060 ..**Lander**, Michael J '75 -134 W Court -Washington Court
House 43160

(216) 595-9828 ..**Lander**, Steven C '85 Levin Consulting -23550 Commerce Park Rd
-Beachwood 44122

(513) 381-2838 ..**Landers**, Dawn R '00 %Taft S&H LLP -425 Walnut -Ste 1800
-Cincinnati 45202 **Fx**:381-0205

(614) 847-0309 ..**Landers**, Mary M '86 (Landers & Assoc) -100 W New Eng Av
-Worthington 43085

(330) 925-1010 ..**Landers**, William D '91 -20 W Ohio Av -Bx398 -Rittman 44270

(614) 221-2121 ..**Landes**, Mark '82 Isaac BL&T,LLP -250 E Broad
-Ste 900 Mdlnd Bldg -Columbus 43215 **Fx**:365-9516

(216) 687-2331 ..**Landever**, Arthur R '81 CSU-Marshall Cllg of Law -2121 Euclid Av
-LB138 -Cleveland 44115 **Fx**:687-6881

(216) 781-1111 ..**Landever**, David C '95 Weisman G&W Co,LPA -101 Prospect Av
-1600 Mdlnd Bldg -Cleveland 44115 **Fx**:781-6747

(330) 688-8962 ..**Landi**, Albert J '54 -3672 Oak Rd -Stow 44224
Landis, David H '79 -246 High -Hamilton 45011

(937) 335-0550 ..**Landis**, Raymond L '67 Huffman L&W Co,LPA -80 S Plum
-Troy 45373

(513) 621-2888 ..**Landis**, Richard M '69 -1014 Vine -1900 Kroger Bldg
-Cincinnati 45202

(614) 464-6400 ..**Landolfi**, John L '89 (Vorys SS&P LLP) -52 E Gay -Bx1008
-Columbus 43216 **Fx**:464-6350

(440) 746-3600 ..**Landoll**, Richard W '95 -3505 E Royalton Rd -Ste 165 Ofc Atrium
-Broadview Heights 44147

(740) 397-4040 ..**Landon**, Adam B '01 %Critchfield C&J Ltd -10 S Gay
-Mount Vernon 43050 **Fx**:397-6775

(614) 221-1662 ..**Landon**, Laurence B '86 Frank & W Co LPA -600 S Pearl
-Columbus 43206

(513) 946-3557 ..**Landon**, Thomas W '97 Hamilton Cnty Probate Ct -230 E 9th
-10th Fl -Cincinnati 45202 **Fx**:946-3626

(614) 227-2000 ..**Landrum**, Jaime T '03 %Porter WM&A LLP -41 S High
-Columbus 43215 **Fx**:227-2100

(513) 651-6800 ..**Landrum**, Lori A '93 (Frost BT LLC) -201 E 5th -2200 PNC Ctr
-Cincinnati 45202 **Fx**:651-6981

(513) 762-4231 ..**Landrum**, Ricky J '93 Kroger Co -1014 Vine -Cincinnati 45202

(419) 243-1239 ..**Landry**, Francis J '76 (Wasserman BL&H,LLP) -405 N Huron
-Ste 300 -Toledo 43604

(419) 243-1239 ..**Landry**, John A '77 (Wasserman BL&H,LLP) -405 N Huron
-Ste 300 -Toledo 43604

(816) 474-6550 ..**Landsberg**, Donnamarie A '82 OfCnsl Shook H&B,LLP
-1200 Main -Kansas City, MO 64105

(216) 522-9000 ..**Landskroner**, Jack '92 (Landskroner·G·M,Ltd) -1360 W 9th
-Ste 200 -Cleveland 44113 **Fx**:522-9007

(216) 241-7000 ..**Landskroner**, Lawrence '51 (Landskroner & Assoc) -55 Pub Sq
-Ste 1040 -Cleveland 44113

(305) 891-5858 ..**Landsman**, Lisa Cortney '84 (Pomeranz & L)
-12955 Biscayne Blvd -Ste 202 -North Miami, FL 33181
Fx:891-5734

(312) 362-6647 ..**Landsman**, Stephan A '76 DePaul Univ Cllg of Law -25 E Jackson
Blvd -Chicago, IL 60604

(513) 946-3000 ..**Landthorn**, Tricia L '95 Hamilton Cnty Pros -230 E 9th
-Cincinnati 45202 **Fx**:946-3017

(614) 449-0449 ..**Landusky**, Joseph R II '86 -901 S High -Columbus 43206

(419) 241-6000 ..**Landwehr**, John T '74 (Eastman & S Ltd) -1 Seagate -24th Fl
-Bx10032 -Toledo 43699 **Fx**:247-1777

(440) 808-9138 ..**Landy,** Pamela S '81 -30628 Detroit Rd -Ste 285 -Westlake 44145

(216) 781-1212 ..**Lane,** Aimee W '99 %Walter & H LLP -1301 E 9th -Ste 3500
-Cleveland 44114 Fx:575-0911

(614) 228-6885 ..**Lane Alton & Horst LLC** -175 S 3rd -Ste 700 -Columbus 43215
Fx:228-0146

(216) 431-4500 ..**Lane,** Cheryl R '97 Cuyahoga Cnty Pros -3955 Euclid Av
-Jane Edna Hunter Bldg -Cleveland 44115 Fx:431-4113

(412) 243-9700 ..**Lane,** Christina L '95 %Andrews & P -1500 Ardmore Blvd -Ste 506
-Pittsburgh, PA 15221

(502) 584-1600 ..**Lane,** Christopher B '03 %Blackburn H&D -455 S 4th Av
-Louisville, KY 40202

(513) 922-7700 ..**Lane,** David C '82 (Lane F&R Co,LPA) -4931 Delhi Pike
-Cincinnati 45238 Fx:922-4607

(513) 721-1504 ..**Lane,** Donald A '87 Droder & M Co,LPA -125 W Cntrl Pkwy
-Cincinnati 45202 Fx:721-0310

(440) 998-2628 ..**Lane,** Dorothy M '91 Ashtabula Cnty Pub Def -4817 State Rd
-Ste 202 -Ashtabula 44004 Fx:998-2972

(513) 922-7700 ..**Lane Felix & Raisbeck Co,LPA** -4931 Delhi Pike
-Cincinnati 45238 Fx:922-4607

(440) 934-3700 ..**Lane,** Howard T '93 Fauver K-W&D -5333 Meadow Ln Ct
-Elyria 44035 Fx:934-3708

(216) 781-5515 ..**Lane,** James L '99 %Hermann C&S,LLP -1301 E 9th -Ste 500
-Cleveland 44114 Fx:781-1030

(614) 462-7450 ..**Lane,** Jessica L '03 CASA Franklin Cnty -373 S High -6th Fl
-Columbus 44215 Fx:462-5070

(330) 533-5447 ..**Lane,** Joseph D '84 (Lane & R Co,LPA) -55 N Broad
-Canfield 44406 Fx:553-3327

(740) 393-0110 ..**Lane,** Kenneth E '78 -31 Pub Sq -Bx888 -Mount Vernon 43050

(561) 622-6000 ..**Lane,** Matthew J '81 Prosperity Prtnrs Inc -1015 10th
-Lake Park, FL 33403

(513) 634-3617 ..**Lane,** Patrick D '80 Procter & Gamble -6090 Ctr Hill Av
-Cincinnati 45224

(614) 466-5394 ..**Lane,** Robert L '81 Pub Def -8 E Long -Columbus 43215

(614) 221-3155 ..**Lane,** Robert S '89 (Bailey C LLC) -10 W Broad -Columbus 43215
Fx:221-0479

(513) 983-5302 ..**Lane,** Sandra T '93 Procter & Gamble Co-Legal
-1 Procter & Gamble Plz -Cincinnati 45202

(513) 887-7300 ..**Lane,** Stephen C '86 (Fiehrer L&C) -10 Jrnl Sq -Ste 400
-Hamilton 45011

(614) 228-6885 ..**Lane,** William M '60 (Lane A&H LLC) -175 S 3rd -Ste 700
-Columbus 43215 Fx:228-0146

(231) 727-2699 ..**Lang,** Brian T '99 %Warner N&J -400 Terrace Plz -Bx900
-Muskegon, MI 49443

(440) 247-9660 ..**Lang,** Charles V '88 -3800 Chagrin Rvr Rd -Moreland Hills 44022

(440) 886-3000 ..**Lang,** Daniel P '86 Leary SN&L -5579 Pearl Rd -Ste 203
-Parma 44129 Fx:886-3171

(614) 462-3194 ..**Lang,** Heather D '02 Franklin Cnty Pub Def -373 S High -12th Fl
-Columbus 43215

(216) 622-8200 ..**Lang,** James F '92 (Calfee H&G LLP) -800 Superior Av -Ste 1400
-Cleveland 44114 Fx:241-0816

(757) 274-7000 ..**Lang,** James T '89 %Tanner MG&L,PC -5700 Lk Wright Dr
-Ste 102 -Norfolk, VA 23502

(216) 241-6602 ..**Lang,** Jeffrey R '02 %Weston HFP&H LLP -50 Pub Sq
-2500 Trmnl Twr -Cleveland 44113 Fx:621-8369

(330) 674-7070 ..**Lang,** Kimberly A '98 %Miller & M Ltd -88 S Monroe -Ste B
-Millersburg 44654

(330) 385-3137 ..**Lang,** Mary S '74 -517 Bway -Bx103 -East Liverpool 43920

(513) 621-0267 ..**Lang,** Melissa M '04 Waite SB&C -1 W 4th -1513 4th & Vine Twr
-Cincinnati 45202

(937) 339-7161 ..**Lang,** Michael L '79 (Vest & L) -406 W Main -Troy 45373

(740) 707-4740 ..**Lang,** Patrick J '03 -Bx382 -Athens 45701

Lang, Paul A '77 -12992 Sunset Cir -Uniontown 44685

(216) 514-1100 ..**Lang,** Paul A II '92 (Rolf & G Co,LPA) -30100 Chagrin Blvd
-Ste 350 Corp Cir -Cleveland 44124 Fx:514-0030

(614) 466-3636 ..**Lang,** Robert K '89 OH Dept Commerce -77 S High -Columbus
43266

(440) 720-1100 ..**Lang,** Ronald J '68 N Point Portfolio Mngrs Corp
-5910 Landerbrook Dr -Ste 160 -Mayfield Heights 44124

(412) 655-8500 ..**Lang,** Scott B '81 (S Lang & Assoc,PC) -619 Clairton Blvd
-Pittsburgh, PA 15236

(937) 223-5533 ..**Lang,** Wilbur S '58 -1060 Talbott Twr -Dayton 45402

(937) 492-1271 ..**Lang,** William E Jr. '59 %Faulkner GK&S,LPA -100 S Main Av
-Ste 300 -Sidney 45365 Fx:498-1306

(440) 933-8938 ..**Lang,** William P '79 -680 Moore Rd -Bx108 -Avon Lake 44012

(513) 577-7380 ..**Langdon,** David R '96 (Langdon & S LLC) -11175 Reading Rd
-Ste 103 -Cincinnati 45241 Fx:577-7383

(419) 448-9250 ..**Lange,** Anne M '00 %Lange,LLC -174 S Wshngtn -Bx685
-Tiffin 44883

(216) 839-0012 ..**Lange,** Frederick J Jr. '75 Aspen River Wood & Glass
-28700 Chagrin Blvd -Beachwood 44122 Fx:839-0014

(216) 687-1900 ..**Lange,** Jill J '87 Legal Aid -1223 W 6th -Cleveland 44113
Fx:687-0779

(859) 491-1500 ..**Lange,** John E III '70 Lange Q&P,PSC -4 W 4th -Ste 400
-Newport, KY 41071

(419) 674-4502 ..**Lange,** Keith A '81 -15 N Detroit -Ste 1000 -Kenton 43326

(419) 448-9250 ..**Lange,** Michael B '61 -174 S Wshngtn -Bx685 -Tiffin 44883

Lange, Paul T '04 -(Address Unavailable)

(614) 466-3998 ..**Lange,** Richard M '75 Unemploymnt Comp Commssn -145 S Front
-Bx182299 -Columbus 43218

(937) 496-3048 ..**Langemo,** Bree D '03 2nd Dist Ct of Appeals -41 N Perry -Rm 515
-Bx972 -Dayton 45422

(859) 394-6200 ..**Langen,** Jennifer L '98 Adams SW&D -40 W Pike -Bx861
-Covington, KY 41012 Fx:291-7902

(513) 421-6630 ..**Langenbahn,** Jay R '76 Lindhorst & D Co,LPA -312 Walnut
-Ste 2300 -Cincinnati 45202

(859) 371-3600 ..**Langendorf,** Gail M '95 Busald FZ -226 Main -Bx6910 -Florence,
KY 41022

(513) 705-4104 ..**Langendorf,** James P '91 -2 N Main -Ste 408 -Middletown 45042
Fx:705-4106

(513) 651-6800 ..**Langenkamp,** Max V '02 %Frost BT LLC -201 E 5th
-2200 PNC Ctr -Cincinnati 45202 Fx:651-6981

(216) 222-3339 ..**Langer,** Carlton E '79 Natl City Corp -1900 E 9th
-17th Fl Loc 01-2174 -Bx5756 -Cleveland 44101

(614) 628-1602 ..**Langer,** Jeffrey Ira '90 (Dreher L&T LLP) -41 S High
-2250 Huntngtn Ctr -Columbus 43215 Fx:628-1600

(216) 443-9000 ..**Langer,** Philip E '73 (Porter WM&A LLP) -925 Euclid Av -Ste 1700
-Cleveland 44115 Fx:443-9011

(440) 338-3097 ..**Langer,** Warren D '53 -9100 Kinsman Rd -Russell Township
44072

(818) 598-5191 ..**Langevin,** Mark E '82 Litton Industries,Inc -21240 Burbank Blvd
-Leg Dept -Woodland Hills, CA 91367

(614) 221-6969 ..**Langfelder,** John O '02 %Wolske & B,LPA -580 S High -Ste 300
-Columbus 43215

(937) 837-3302 ..**Langhals,** Joyce A '85 Sisters of the Precious Blood
-4000 Denlinger Rd -Dayton 45426

(216) 664-2893 ..**Langhenry,** Barbara A '87 Dept of Law -601 Lakeside Av
-Rm 106 City Hall -Cleveland 44114 Fx:664-2663

(614) 213-2316 ..**Langley,** Beverly J '91 Banc 1 Invstmnt Advsrs Corp -1111 Polaris
Pkwy -Columbus 43271

(614) 451-2210 ..**Langlois,** Jennifer L '97 %S Roberts & Assoc -1625 Bethel Rd
-Ste 102 -Columbus 43220

(513) 946-3415 ..**Langlois,** Thomas W '91 1st Dist Ct of Appls -230 E 9th -12th Fl
-Cincinnati 45202 Fx:946-3412

(513) 528-9350 ..**Langner,** Kevan K '75 Pentair Pool Prdcts Inc
-4030 Mt Carmel-Tobasco Rd -Ste 314 -Cincinnati 45255

(513) 381-0656 ..**Langston,** Malinda L '97 %Kohnen & P LLP -201 E 5th -Ste 800
-Cincinnati 45202 Fx:381-5823

(312) 886-5810 ..**Langston-Cox,** Pamela D '85 Cnsl Dept of Trea/Gen Lgl
Srvcs Div -200 W Adams -Ste 2400 -Chicago, IL 60606
Fx:886-8290

(330) 264-5141 ..**Lham,** James J '85 Taggart Law Firm -142 W Lbrty -Bx218
-Wooster 44691 Fx:262-1046

Lanham, Patrick C '04 -(Address Unavailable)

(216) 491-8170 ..**Lanham,** Verna J '84 -3001 Becket Rd -Cleveland 44120

(330) 725-4935 ..**Lanier,** J Matthew '98 -600 E Smith Rd -Medina 44256

Lanier, Janice Kay '94 -35 Berkshire Commons Dr
-Westerville 43082

(614) 486-0052 ..**Lanier,** Lorelei M '81 -1515 W Lane Av -#3 -Columbus 43221

(419) 592-0010 ..**Lankenau,** Jeffrey R '86 -105 W Main -Napoleon 43545

(614) 231-4440 ..**Lanker,** Lois L '57 -97 S Broadleigh Rd -Columbus 43209

(513) 263-3589 ..**Lanman,** Diana S '01 IRS -550 Main -Rm 4106 -Cincinnati 45202

(216) 696-3232 ..**Lansdowne,** Dennis R '81 (Spangenberg S&L,LLP) -1900 E 9th
-2400 Natl City Ctr -Cleveland 44114 Fx:696-3924

(859) 331-8668 ..**Lanter,** Edward C '95 (Summe & L,PLLC) -3384 Madison Pike
-Fort Wright, KY 41017 Fx:331-8690

(740) 654-7777 ..**Lantz,** James A '47 (Lantz & L) -123 S Broad -Bx2240
-Lancaster 43130

(937) 222-2333 ..**Lantz,** Kevin A '94 %Surdyk D&T Co,LPA -40 N Main
-1610 Kettering Twr -Dayton 45423 Fx:222-1970

(614) 228-2044 ..**Lantz,** Susan M '83 -150 E Mound -Ste 208 -Columbus 43215

(330) 743-1171 ..**Lanz,** Charles Scott '80 (Manchester BP&U) -201 E Commerce
-Atrium Level 2 Commerce Bldg -Youngstown 44503
Fx:743-1190

(513) 921-1555 ..**Lanzillotta,** Michael A '84 -4550 Carnation Av -Cincinnati 45238

(419) 245-2550 ..**Lanzinger,** Joshua W '98 %Atty Gen -One SeaGate -Ste 2150
-Toledo 43604 Fx:246-2520

(330) 782-8283 ..**Lanzo,** James E '98 -4126 Youngstown-Poland Rd
-Youngstown 44514

Lanzy, Patricia A '01 -16411 Nicholas Rd -Shaker Heights 44120

(614) 728-5599 ..**Lapczynski,** James '94 OH Alchl & Drug Addctn Srvcs
-280 N High -Columbus 43215

(859) 647-8400 ..**Lape,** Kathleen S '92 (Knight HL&A PSC) -18160 Dream -Ste D
-Florence, KY 41022

(513) 741-9738 ..**Lape,** Lynn Ann '97 -3533 Epley Ln -Cincinnati 45247

(614) 228-1541 ..**Lape,** Marcella L '04 %Baker & H LLP -65 E State -Ste 2100
-Columbus 43215 Fx:462-2616

(614) 469-3939 ..**Lape,** Rodd B '96 %Jones D -325 John H McConnell Blvd -Ste 600
-Bx165017 -Columbus 43216 Fx:461-4198

(330) 830-1718 ..**LaPenna,** Anthony '83 Massillon Law Dept -2 James Duncan Plz
-Massillon 44646 Fx:833-7144

(216) 771-2680 ..**LaPerna,** Anthony A '62 (Geraci & L Co,LPA) -1370 Ontario
-Ste 1220 -Cleveland 44113

(404) 851-0300 ..**Lapine,** Jay M '79 LaRoche Ind,Inc -1100 Johnson Ferry Rd NE
-Atlanta, GA 30342

(216) 623-0150 ..**Lapine,** Kenneth M '67 (Roetzel & A,LPA) -1375 E 9th
-One Cleve Ctr 9th Fl -Cleveland 44114 Fx:623-0134

(440) 329-9179 ..**LaPlaca,** Anthony C '84 Bendix Commercial Vehicle Systems
-901 Cleveland -Elyria 44035 Fx:329-9265

(440) 350-3200 ..**LaPlante,** Roland P '72 Lake Cnty Pub Def -125 E Erie
-Painesville 44077

(330) 392-4176 ..**LaPolla,** Thomas A '62 (DelBene L&T) -155 Pine Av NE -Bx353
-Warren 44482 Fx:392-5694

(216) 622-8200 ..**LaPorte,** Dale C '66 (Calfee H&G LLP) -800 Superior Av -Ste 1400
-Cleveland 44114 Fx:241-0816

(412) 262-6787 ..**LaPorte,** Daniel G '66 FedEx Grnd Pckge Syst -1000 FedEX Dr
-Moon Township, PA 15108

(937) 865-6800 ..**La Porte,** Justina M '95 Lexis/Nexis -Bx933 -Dayton 45401

(330) 945-7111 ..**LaPorte,** Mary C '85 -2754 Front -Cuyahoga Falls 44221

(704) 483-2578 ..**LaPorte,** Ted B '94 Nationwide Ins Co -9119 Grove Tree Ln
-Huntersville, NC 28078

(614) 644-3037 ..**Lapp,** Alan L '72 EPA -122 S Front -Bx1049 -Columbus 43216

Lapp, Deborah A '85 -3629 Trls End Dr -Medina 44256

(513) 946-3000 ..**Lapp,** Judith A '83 Hamilton Cnty Pros -230 E 9th
-Cincinnati 45202 Fx:946-3017

(440) 838-8800 ..**Lardakis,** Terry E '77 (Millisor & N Co,LPA) -9150 S Hills Blvd
-Ste 300 -Cleveland 44147 Fx:838-8805

(614) 224-2678 ..**Lardiere,** Christopher L '83 Kemp SR&L Co,LPA -88 W Mound
-Columbus 43215 Fx:469-7170

(614) 221-3318 ..**Laret,** Joffre S '84 Agee CM&L -89 E Nationwide Blvd -Ste 200
-Columbus 43215

(513) 695-1231 ..**Larez,** Michael P '03 Warren Cnty Ct of Common Pleas
-500 Justice Dr -Lebanon 45036

(330) 395-1490 ..**Large,** John H '97 -144 N Park Av -Ste 323 -Warren 44481

(440) 816-0600 ..**Largent Berry Preston & Jamison Co,LPA** -1 Berea Commns
-Ste 216 -Berea 44017 Fx:816-0604

(330) 723-8828 ..**Largent** Berry Preston & Jamison Co,LPA -232 N Court
-Medina 44256 **Fx:**723-8898

(330) 725-0531 ..**Laribee**, Gillian A '01 %Laribee H&K -325 N Bway -Bx445
-Medina 44258

(330) 725-0531 ..**Laribee Hertrick & Kray** -325 N Bway -Bx445 -Medina 44258

(330) 225-1491 ..**Laribee Hertrick & Kray** -111 Pearl Rd -Bx839 -Brunswick 44212

(330) 725-0531 ..**Laribee**, Michael L '96 %Laribee H&K -325 N Bway -Bx445
-Medina 44258

(330) 725-0531 ..**Laribee**, Ray E '68 (Laribee H&K) -325 N Bway -Bx445 -Medina
44258

(216) 443-8868 ..**Laribee**, Shirley S '96 Cuyahoga Cnty Pros -1 Lakeside Av -Rm 49
-Cleveland 44115 **Fx:**443-3777

(513) 244-6953 ..**Larimer**, John T '66 -4315 Redstar Ct -Cincinnati 45238

(440) 331-8747 ..**Larimer**, Leanne G '93 -21139 Lorain Rd -Ste 17
-Fairview Park 44126

Larissey, Michele L '01 -21380 Montclare Blvd -Strongsville 44149

Larkin, Anne W '00 -3613 Tyverton Ct -Richmond, VA 23233

(614) 221-4400 ..**Larkin**, Janet L '01 Volkema TMBS&M,LPA -140 E Town
-Ste 1100 -Columbus 43215 **Fx:**221-6010

(330) 929-0507 ..**Larko**, John '73 -234 Portage Trl -Cuyahoga Falls 44221

(330) 399-2216 ..**Larmi**, Allan R '51 -3056 E Market -Warren 44483

(937) 593-6591 ..**LaRoche**, Daniel J '98 %M Triplett -332 S Main
-Bellefontaine 43311

(440) 729-3770 ..**Larrick**, Scott A '96 -8442 Mayfld Rd -Chesterland 44026
Fx:729-3772

(440) 895-0041 ..**Larrick-Serrat**, Kelly Ann '81 Rocky River Mun Ct
-21012 Hilliard Blvd -Rocky River 44116

(614) 221-7548 ..**Larrimer**, Craig G '97 (Larrimer & L) -165 N High
-Columbus 43206 **Fx:**221-8659

(614) 221-7548 ..**Larrimer**, Gavin R '61 (Larrimer & L) -165 N High
-Columbus 43206 **Fx:**221-8659

(614) 221-7548 ..**Larrimer**, John H '97 (Larrimer & L) -165 N High -Columbus 43206
Fx:221-8659

(614) 221-7548 ..**Larrimer**, Kevin J '98 (Larrimer & L) -165 N High
-Columbus 43206 **Fx:**221-8659

(614) 221-7548 ..**Larrimer**, Terrence W '72 (Larrimer & L) -165 N High
-Columbus 43206 **Fx:**221-8659

Larrison, Anne M '86 -8900 Cruden Bay Ct -Dublin 43017

(513) 721-4555 ..**Larsen**, Beatrice V '69 -8 W 9th -Cincinnati 45202

(216) 515-1660 ..**Larsen**, Hans L '92 %Frantz W LLP -127 Pub Sq
-2500 Key Center -Cleveland 44114 **Fx:**515-1650

(216) 619-0072 ..**Larsen**, Lynn R '91 %T Sweeney -820 W Superior Av -Ste 430
-Cleveland 44113 **Fx:**241-3138

(216) 696-3311 ..**Larsen**, Stuart L '93 (Kahn K) -1301 E 9th -2600 Erievw Twr
-Cleveland 44114 **Fx:**623-4912

(440) 992-3120 ..**Larson**, Bernadette T '77 -4717 Park Av -Firstar Bk Bldg
-Ashtabula 44004

(937) 223-1201 ..**Larson**, David E '79 %Altick & C Co,LPA -1 S Main -1700
One Dayton Ctr -Dayton 45402 **Fx:**223-5100

(330) 375-2730 ..**Larson**, Gerald K '91 Pros -217 S High -Ste 203 -Akron 44308

(216) 479-8500 ..**Larson**, John S '77 (Squire S&D LLP) -127 Pub Sq -4900 Key Twr
-Cleveland 44114 **Fx:**479-8780

(440) 930-3827 ..**Larson**, Lee E '72 PolyOne Corp -One Geon Ctr
-Avon Lake 44012

(440) 779-6383 ..**Larson**, Patricia A '97 -4820 W 228th -Fairview Park 44126

(216) 696-3510 ..**Larson**, Paul E '98 (Robinette & L,LLP) -526 Superior Av
-Ste 1160 -Cleveland 44114

(513) 241-2540 ..**Larson**, Robert K Jr. '89 -632 Vine -Ste 415 -Cincinnati 45202

(614) 464-9112 ..**Larson**, Steven A '80 -518 N Park -Columbus 43215

(740) 284-1000 ..**LaRue**, David A '88 -2021 Sunset Blvd -Steubenville 43952

(216) 696-8995 ..**LaRue**, Edward R '92 -75 Pub Sq -Ste 800 -Cleveland 44113

(419) 843-5028 ..**LaRue**, Lawrence B '75 (L LaRue Co LPA) -Bx23271
-Toledo 43623

(212) 756-2000 ..**LaSalle**, Frank J '97 %Schulte R&Z LLP -919 3rd Av
-New York, NY 10022 **Fx:**593-5955

(614) 466-6700 ..**LaSalle**, Lawrence J '82 Tax Appeals -30 E Broad
-Columbus 43215 **Fx:**644-5196

(330) 972-6479 ..**LaSalvia**, Anthony J '72 Univ of Akron -Polsky Bldg
-Div of Pub Srvcs Tech -Akron 44325

(216) 621-0070 ..**LaSalvia**, Christine M '03 Friedman D&S Co,LPA -1370 Ontario
-Ste 600 -Cleveland 44113 **Fx:**621-4008

(513) 922-8100 ..**LaScalea**, Nicholas J '73 -4931 Delhi Pike -Cincinnati 45238

(216) 241-2880 ..**Lasch**, Debora S '88 Cowden HN&L -50 Pub Sq -Ste 1414
-Cleveland 44113 **Fx:**241-2881

Lash, David L '77 -23811 Chagrin Blvd -Ste 228
-Beachwood 44122

(614) 464-6400 ..**Lash**, Lester S '61 OfCnsl Vorys SS&P LLP -52 E Gay -Bx1008
-Columbus 43216 **Fx:**464-6350

(614) 227-2000 ..**Lashbrook**, April D '01 %Porter WM&A LLP -41 S High
-Columbus 43215 **Fx:**227-2100

(513) 621-6464 ..**Lasher**, Katherine M '99 %Graydon H&R LLP -511 Walnut
-1900 Fifth Third Ctr -Cincinnati 45202 **Fx:**651-3836

(614) 233-4766 ..**Lashuk**, Beth Anne S '94 Lane A&H LLC -175 S 3rd -Ste 700
-Columbus 43215 **Fx:**228-0146

(614) 677-4064 ..**Lashutka**, Gregory S '74 Nationwide Ins Co -One Nationwide Plz
-1-36-18 -Columbus 43215

(240) 686-2352 ..**Laskas**, Karl M '99 Smiths Aerospace -20501 Senca Mdws Pkwy
-Germantown, MD 20876

(740) 321-3080 ..**Laskiewicz**, Larry K '82 Owens Corning -2790 Columbus Rd
-Granville 43023

(216) 621-9646 ..**Lasko**, John J Jr. '77 -614 W Superior Av -Ste 1150
-Cleveland 44113

(216) 574-2600 ..**Lasko & Lind Co,LPA** -1406 W 6th -Ste 200 -Cleveland 44113

(937) 222-6699 ..**Lasky**, Laurence A '77 (Lasky & S) -130 W 2nd -#830
-Dayton 45402

(216) 222-8056 ..**Lasky**, Rebecca L '95 Natl City Corp -1900 E 9th
-Cleveland 44114

(937) 222-6699 ..**Lasky & Scharrer** -130 W 2nd -#830 -Dayton 45402

(614) 365-2700 ..**Lasley**, Aneca E '00 %Squire S&D LLP -41 S High
-1300 Huntngtn Ctr -Columbus 43215 **Fx:**365-2499

Laslo, Tracey A '99 -612 Center W -Warren 44481

(513) 556-0096 ..**Lassiter**, Harvey C '97 Univ of Cincinnati Law Schl -Clifton &
Calhoun -Bx210040 -Cincinnati 45221

(859) 572-5358 ..**Lassiter**, Sharlene W '94 Chase College of Law -545 Nunn Hall
-Highland Heights, KY 41099

(440) 617-1200 ..**Lastovka**, Terri A '96 Hillow Getsay & Connors -27476 Detroit Rd
-Ste 104 -Westlake 44145

(419) 213-4700 ..**Lastra**, Andrew J '98 %Lucas Cnty Pros -Adams & Erie
-Lucas Cnty Cthse -Toledo 43624

(216) 787-4183 ..**Laszcz**, Joseph S '81 Industrial Comm -615 Superior NW -7th Fl
-Cleveland 44114

(303) 292-2525 ..**Laszlo**, Theodore E Jr. '81 OfCnsl Wheeler TK,PC -1801 Calif
-Ste 3600 -Denver, CO 80202 **Fx:**294-1879

(330) 343-4540 ..**Latanich**, Gerald A '81 Joint Cnty Pub Def -153 N Bway
-New Philadelphia 44663

(614) 461-4455 ..**Latanick**, David G '74 (Cloppert LS&W) -225 E Broad
-Columbus 43215 **Fx:**461-0072

(330) 743-3988 ..**Latas**, Mark A '81 -26 Market -Ste 610 -Youngstown 44503

(614) 466-1283 ..**Latas**, Michael D '85 Industrial Commssn of OH -30 W Spring
-9th Fl -Columbus 43215 **Fx:**752-8785

(330) 743-3998 ..**Latas**, Milan '58 -26 Market -Ste 610 -Youngstown 44503

(330) 723-4656 ..**Latchney**, John D '90 (Tomino & L,LLC) -803 E Wshngtn -Ste 200
-Medina 44256

(330) 544-4002 ..**Latell**, Kurt D '93 (Blair & L Co,LPA) -724 Youngstown Rd
-Niles 44446

(937) 225-8871 ..**Latham**, Samuel S '95 -371 W 1st -Dayton 45402

(937) 325-7058 ..**Latham**, William D '88 (Gorman VH&W) -4 W Main -Ste 723
-Springfield 45502 **Fx:**325-9914

(419) 424-5847 ..**Lather**, Kenneth L '78 (Lather & K) -725 S Main -Findlay 45840

(606) 329-8300 ..**Latherow**, David F '96 (Hamburg WH&L) -1401 Greenup Av
-Ste 200 -Bx2008 -Ashland, KY 41105

(606) 329-2929 ..**Latherow**, Leigh G '96 %VanAntwerp MJ&E -1544 Wnchstr Av
-5th Fl -Bx1111 -Ashland, KY 41105

(216) 586-3939 ..**Lathrop**, Lisa S '01 %Jones D -901 Lakeside Av -Cleveland 44114
Fx:579-0212

(614) 644-6338 ..**Lathwell**, Kyle E '99 OH Dept of Edu -25 S Front -7th Fl
-Columbus 43215

(440) 329-5389 ..**Lathwell**, Lindsey C '04 Lorain Cnty Pros -225 Court -3rd Fl
-Elyria 44035

(937) 226-1900 ..**Latimore**, Caroll A '02 -Bx1711 -Dayton 45401

LaTour, Kathleen A '87 -6974 Berry Ln -Dublin 43017

(614) 464-6400 ..**LaTour**, Randall D '87 (Vorys SS&P LLP) -52 E Gay -Bx1008
-Columbus 43216 **Fx:**464-6350

(614) 462-2329 ..**Latsko**, John M '81 (Schottenstein Z&D) -250 West -Bx165020
-Columbus 43215 **Fx:**462-5135

(419) 352-8627 ..**Latta**, Delbert L '44 -516 Hllcrst Dr -Bowling Green 43402

(614) 255-4326 ..**Latta**, Jennifer E '03 Residential Finance Corp -401 N Front
-Ste 300 -Columbus 43215

(614) 466-8104 ..**Latta**, Robert E '81 OH House of Reps -77 S High
-Columbus 43215

(330) 456-4571 ..**Lattavo**, Philip E '67 Lattavo Bros Inc
-2230 Shepler Church Av SW -Canton 44706

(513) 421-8500 ..**Latter**, Bruce E '75 -830 Main -Ste 700 -Cincinnati 45202

(614) 466-7983 ..**Lau**, Edward Ho '88 OH Dept Taxation -30 E Broad -22nd Fl
-Columbus 43215

(513) 651-6800 ..**Laub**, Patricia D '83 (Frost BT LLC) -201 E 5th -2200 PNC Ctr
-Cincinnati 45202 **Fx:**651-6981

(440) 356-5700 ..**Laubacher**, Eric R '99 (Laubacher & G,LLP) -20525 Ctr Ridge Rd
-Ste 626 -Cleveland 44116

(419) 213-3000 ..**Lauback**, Mary D '79 Lucas Cnty CSEA -701 Adams
-Toledo 43624

(804) 520-8592 ..**Laube**, Gary L '69 -302 Norwood Dr -Colonial Heights, VA 23834

(216) 363-1400 ..**Laube-Haughton**, Emily '04 %Buckley K,LPA -600 E Superior Av
-Ste 1400 -Cleveland 44114 **Fx:**579-1020

(440) 322-5505 ..**Laubenthal**, Marilu '82 -633 Broad -Ste 200 -Elyria 44035

(440) 835-3889 ..**Lauber**, Richard E '81 Fidelity Natl Title Ins -30644 Mallard Cove
-Westlake 44145

(614) 752-9677 ..**Laubert**, Robert M '90 OH Dept of Aging -50 W Broad -9th Fl
-Columbus 43215

(216) 622-8200 ..**Lauderdale**, Jeffrey J '02 %Calfee H&G LLP -800 Superior Av
-Ste 1400 -Cleveland 44114 **Fx:**241-0816

(937) 228-2666 ..**Lauer**, Carla J '92 %Hochman R&P Co,LPA -118 W 1st -Ste 650
-Dayton 45402 **Fx:**228-0508

(703) 752-7091 ..**Lauer**, Laura A '85 Freddie Mac -8100 Jones Brnch Dr -MS B2B
-McLean, VA 22102

(513) 721-3330 ..**Lauer**, Richard T '94 Robbins KP&T -7 W 7th -Ste 1400
-Cincinnati 45202

(419) 213-5131 ..**Lauer**, Steven K '77 IRS -433 N Summit -226 -Toledo 43604
Fx:213-5120

(513) 621-9100 ..**Laufman & Gerhardstein** -617 Vine -1409 Enquirer Bldg
-Cincinnati 45202

(513) 621-9100 ..**Laufman**, Paul M '96 Laufman & G -617 Vine -1409 Enquirer Bldg
-Cincinnati 45202

(513) 621-9100 ..**Laufman**, Robert F '61 (Laufman & G) -617 Vine
-1409 Enquirer Bldg -Cincinnati 45202

Laughlin, David J '81 -2954 Arcola Rd -Madison 44057

(614) 292-2448 ..**Laughlin**, Stanley K Jr. '61 OSU Moritz Cllg of Law -55 W 12th Av
-Columbus 43210 **Fx:**292-1383

(614) 462-3194 ..**Laughlin-Schopis**, Susan K '82 Franklin Cnty Pub Def
-373 S High -Columbus 43215

(513) 481-8444 ..**Laumann**, John M '77 -3505 Glenmore Av -Cheviot 45211

(513) 632-5350 ..**Laurens**, Jesse S '01 -119 E Court -Cincinnati 45202

(440) 871-4022 ..**Lauricia**, Samuel J III '04 %Corsaro & Assoc Co,LPA
-2001 Crocker Rd -Ste 400 -Westlake 44145

(216) 579-1700 ..**Lauricia**, Una L '02 %Pearne & G LLP -1801 E 9th -Ste 1200
-Cleveland 44114 **Fx:**579-6073

(440) 526-2014 ..**Laurie**, Charles R Jr. '74 -8180 Brecksvll Rd -Brecksville 44141

(937) 743-4878 ..**Laurito**, Erin M '02 %Laurito & L LLC -35 Cmmrcial Way
-Springboro 45066 **Fx:**743-4877

(937) 743-4878 ..**Laurito**, Jeffrey V '73 (Laurito & L LLC) -35 Cmmrcial Way
-Springboro 45066 **Fx:**743-4877

(513) 771-5455 ..**Lausche**, Louis F '65 -9526 Winton Rd -Cincinnati 45231

(419) 692-0931 ..**Lause**, Glen D '73 Suever Stone Co -Bx10 -Delphos 45833

(419) 472-1900 ..**Lautar**, Brian F '87 %Bolotin Co,LPA -4349 Talmadge Rd
-Toledo 43623

(513) 723-4000 ..**Lautzenhiser**, Roger E Jr. '79 (Vorys SS&P LLP) -221 E 4th
-Ste 2000 Atrium Two -Bx0236 -Cincinnati 45201 **Fx:**723-4056

(513) 579-1414 ..**Laux**, Colleen B '94 %Schwartz M&R -441 Vine -Ste 2900
-Cincinnati 45202 **Fx:**579-1418

(440) 323-4460 ..**Laux**, Richard T '52 -154 Cleveland -Elyria 44035

(419) 249-7900 ..**Lavalette**, Peter N '94 (Robison C&O) -Four SeaGate -9th Fl
-Toledo 43604 **Fx:**249-7911

(419) 243-2100 ..**Lavalette**, Tammy G '99 %Connelly J&C LLP -405 Mad Av
-Ste 1600 -Toledo 43604 **Fx:**243-7119

La Vallee, Rebecca H '00 -30500 State Route 172
-East Rochester 44625

(419) 882-0081 ..**LaValley**, Daniel J '85 (LaValley LT&S Co,LPA) -5800 Monroe
-Bldg F -Sylvania 43560 **Fx:**882-4635

(419) 882-0081 ..**LaValley LaValley Todak & Schaefer Co,LPA** -5800 Monroe
-Bldg F -Sylvania 43560 **Fx:**882-4635

(419) 882-0081 ..**LaValley**, Richard G '53 OfCnsl LaValley LT&S Co,LPA
-5800 Monroe -Bldg F -Sylvania 43560 **Fx:**882-4635

(419) 882-0081 ..**LaValley**, Richard G Jr. '83 (LaValley LT&S Co,LPA)
-5800 Monroe -Bldg F -Sylvania 43560 **Fx:**882-4635

(828) 258-2991 ..**Lavelle**, Brian F '68 (VanWinkle BWS&D,PA) -11 N Market
-Bx7376 -Asheville, NC 28802 **Fx:**257-2773

(330) 373-1035 ..**Lavelle**, Edward L '73 Letson GWL&R -155 S Park Av -Ste 250
-Bx151 -Warren 44482 **Fx:**392-5419

(740) 593-3347 ..**Lavelle**, Francis A '82 (Lavelle Law Ofc,LPA) -8 N Court -2nd Fl
-Bx661 -Athens 45701

(330) 743-5101 ..**Lavelle**, Gregory J '75 Green H&S,Co LPA -16 Wick Av -Ste 400
-Youngstown 44503 **Fx:**743-3451

(740) 593-3348 ..**Lavelle**, John P '82 (Lavelle & Assoc) -207 Columbus Rd -Ste B
-Athens 45701

(330) 758-6900 ..**Lavelle**, Mark J '93 -7000 South Av -Ste 4 -Youngstown 44512

(216) 781-2787 ..**Lavelle**, Neal P '60 (Lavelle & L Co,LPA) -526 Superior Av E
-Ste 522 -Cleveland 44114

(216) 443-7800 ..**Lavelle**, Patrick J Jr. '93 Cuyahoga Cnty Pros -1200 Ontario
-8th Fl -Cleveland 44113 **Fx:**698-2270

(216) 621-9870 ..**Lavelle**, Patrick S '93 -123 W Prospect Av
-#250 Van Sweringen Arcade -Cleveland 44115

(740) 594-9625 ..**Lavelle**, William A '52 -449 E State -2nd Fl,Ste One
-Athens 45701 **Fx:**594-8155

(614) 228-6885 ..**Lavelle**, William S '80 (Lane A&H LLC) -175 S 3rd -Ste 700
-Columbus 43215 **Fx:**228-0146

(216) 931-6000 ..**Laven**, Stuart A '70 (Ulmer & B LLP) -1300 E 9th
-Ste 900 Penton Media Bldg -Cleveland 44114 **Fx:**931-6001

(216) 363-4500 ..**Laven**, Stuart A Jr. '99 %Benesch FC&A LLP -200 Pub Sq
-Ste 2300 -Cleveland 44114 **Fx:**363-4588

(419) 244-3888 ..**Lavender**, Barbara A '94 (Jones & L) -520 Mad Av -Ste 323
-Toledo 43604

(513) 579-0080 ..**Lavender-Che**, Joyce C '89 Smith R&S Co,LPA -1014 Vine
-Ste 2350 -Cincinnati 45202 **Fx:**579-0222

Laver, Gerald D '83 -Bx472 -Napoleon 43545

(216) 479-8500 ..**Lavey**, David B '87 OfCnsl Squire S&D LLP -127 Pub Sq
-4900 Key Twr -Cleveland 44114 **Fx:**479-8780

(937) 228-8088 ..**Lavey**, Debra A '01 LAWO -333 W 1st -Ste 500A -Dayton 45402
Fx:449-8131

(216) 479-8500 ..**Lavey**, Wendlene M '89 (Squire S&D LLP) -127 Pub Sq
-4900 Key Twr -Cleveland 44114 **Fx:**479-8780

(216) 261-0200 ..**Lavigna**, Michael P Jr. '74 -27801 Euclid Av -Ste 500
-Euclid 44132

(740) 625-5215 ..**Lavin**, Christopher '98 T Cooper Co,LPA -36 W Main -Bx747
-Centerburg 43011

(216) 443-8603 ..**Lavin**, Sean T '01 Hon R Suster -1200 Ontario -11th Fl
-Cleveland 44113

(614) 628-6880 ..**Lavinsky**, Rick A '69 (Dinsmore & S LLP) -175 S 3rd -10th Fl
-Columbus 43215 **Fx:**628-6890

(734) 457-2651 ..**LaVoy**, Jill M '96 -2 E 1st -Ste 207 -Monroe, MI 48161

Lavrisha, Anton M '79 -18975 Villavw Rd -Cleveland 44119

(614) 228-6717 ..**Law**, Sam S '99 -171 E Lvngstn Av -Columbus 43215

(216) 252-6555 ..**Lawko**, Susan M '84 (Lawko & L) -11711 Lorain Av
-Cleveland 44111

(216) 252-6555 ..**Lawko**, William A '50 (Lawko & L) -11711 Lorain Av
-Cleveland 44111

Lawler, John H '89 -Bx171 -West Union 45693

(440) 461-0866 ..**Lawley**, Patricia M '85 -797 Hanover Rd -Gates Mills 44040

(216) 622-8200 ..**Lawniczak**, James M '89 (Calfee H&G LLP) -800 Superior Av
-Ste 1400 -Cleveland 44114 **Fx:**241-0816

(614) 799-2800 ..**Lawrence**, James J '78 Zaino & H LPA -5775 Perimeter Dr
-Ste 250 -Dublin 43017 **Fx:**799-1500

(513) 651-6800 ..**Lawrence**, James K '65 (Frost BT LLC) -201 E 5th -2200 PNC Ctr
-Cincinnati 45202 **Fx:**651-6981

(513) 651-4130 ..**Lawrence**, Jennifer L '96 %Lawrence Firm -8044 Mntgmry Rd
-Ste 700 -Cincinnati 45236

(859) 578-1030 ..**Lawrence**, Jennifer L '96 %Lawrence Firm -606 Phila
-Covington, KY 41011 **Fx:**578-1032

(419) 255-5202 ..**Lawrence**, John H '81 -1700 Canton Av -Two Canton Sq
-Toledo 43624

(937) 592-2831 ..**Lawrence**, John T '67 Lawrence & L -110 E Court Av -Bx216
-Bellefontaine 43311

Lawrence, Joy '85 -159 Burns Av -Ste 1 -Cincinnati 45215

(216) 689-3692 ..**Lawrence**, Kimberly A '95 Keybank Natl Assn -127 Pub Sq -2nd Fl
-Cleveland 44114

(614) 228-3664 ..**Lawrence**, Linda J '90 Lawrence Law Ofc -496 S 3rd
-Columbus 43215

(606) 567-8500 ..**Lawrence**, Meredith L '77 -101 2nd -Bx1330 -Warsaw, KY 41095

(216) 858-6451 ..**Lawrence**, Michael J '91 School Dist -1380 E Sixth
-Cleveland 44114

(419) 255-5117 ..**Lawrence**, Morgan A '83 (M Lawrence & Assoc) -237 N Mich
-Toledo 43624

(513) 651-4130 ..**Lawrence**, Richard D '71 (Lawrence Firm) -8044 Mntgmry Rd
-Ste 700 -Cincinnati 45236

(859) 578-1030 ..**Lawrence**, Richard D '71 (Lawrence Firm) -606 Phila
-Covington, KY 41011 **Fx:**578-1032

(614) 228-3664 ..**Lawrence**, Rodd S '88 -496 S 3rd -Columbus 43215

(614) 677-2069 ..**Lawrence**, Stephanie D '00 Cnsl Nationwide Ins Co
-1 Nationwide Plz -Columbus 43215

(330) 630-9502 ..**Lawrence**, Walter R '85 -101 Northeast Av -Tallmadge 44278
Fx:630-3735

(614) 227-2000 ..**Lawrence**, Wayman C III '59 Cnsl Porter WM&A LLP -41 S High
-Columbus 43215 **Fx:**227-2100

(216) 621-9800 ..**Lawrence-Auten**, Deborah J '94 Land America -1300 E 9th
-Ste 1201 -Cleveland 44114

(330) 723-3287 ..**Lawrie**, Charles T '86 Medina Mun Ct -135 N Elmwood Av
-Medina 44256

(614) 249-5706 ..**Lawroski**, John P '82 Nationwide Ins Co -One Nationwide Plz
-Columbus 43215

(216) 443-8587 ..**Laws**, Meghan Graves '02 Cuyahoga Cnty Ct Cmmn Pleas
-1200 Ontario -Justice Ctr 11th Fl -Cleveland 44113

(937) 748-9155 ..**Lawson**, Eddie Jr. '66 -195 E Central Av -Bx104
-Springboro 45066

(513) 721-4466 ..**Lawson**, Jerry H '68 Ctr for Rsltn of Disputes -8 W 9th
-Cincinnati 45202 **Fx:**721-3383

(216) 881-3928 ..**Lawson**, John H '76 -4403 St Clair Av -Cleveland 44103

(440) 352-8700 ..**Lawson**, Karen D '82 -240N E Main -Painesville 44077

(513) 345-5000 ..**Lawson**, Kenneth L '89 (Lawson & Assoc) -808 Elm -Ste 100
-Cincinnati 45202

(501) 987-7886 ..**Lawson**, Marci A '95 USAF 314AW/JA -1250 Thomas Av -Ste 222
-Little Rock Air Force Base, AR 72099

(513) 381-2838 ..**Lawson**, Margaret A '82 (Taft S&H LLP) -425 Walnut -Ste 1800
-Cincinnati 45202 **Fx:**381-0205

(513) 241-9400 ..**Lawson**, Mark B '98 Legal Aid -215 E 9th -Ste 200
-Cincinnati 45202

(419) 626-3241 ..**Lawson**, Michael J '87 -Bx110 -Sandusky 44871

(513) 977-8200 ..**Lawson**, Nancy A '75 (Dinsmore & S LLP) -255 E 5th -Ste 1900
-Cincinnati 45202 **Fx:**977-8141

(502) 564-8100 ..**Lawson**, Norman W Jr. '68 Legislative Research Comm
-State Cptl Bldg -Frankfort, KY 40601

(440) 409-0135 ..**Lawson**, Scott E '94 Lawson Firm,LLC -2695 Hmptn Rd -Bx16355
-Cleveland 44116

(330) 296-4451 ..**Lawson**, Stephen C '90 -250 S Chestnut -#17 -Ravenna 44266

(419) 227-6506 ..**Lawson**, Walter M III '69 -119 N West -Ste 103 -Lima 45801

(419) 227-6506 ..**Lawson**, Walter M Jr. '48 -119 N West -Bx1255 -Lima 45802

Lawter, Jennifer K '90 -(Address Unavailable)

(216) 621-0794 ..**Lawther**, Jennifer Lee '96 %Taubman & Assoc -55 Pub Sq
-Ste 1670 -Cleveland 44113

(330) 745-1500 ..**Lax**, Susan J '96 -754 Kenmore Blvd -Akron 44314

(419) 421-4476 ..**Lay**, Lisa A '94 %Marathon Ashland Petro LLC -539 S Main
-Findlay 45840 **Fx:**421-8402

(419) 674-2245 ..**Lay**, Mark A '96 Hardin Cnty Juv Ct -1 Cthse Sq -Ste 200
-Kenton 43326

(330) 434-3880 ..**Laybourne**, Robert B '73 Laybourne & G -159 S Main -Ste 900
-Akron 44308 **Fx:**434-4661

(419) 668-4896 ..**Laycock**, Jeffrey P '69 (Freeman L&M) -54 E Main
-Norwalk 44857 **Fx:**663-7835

(614) 292-0611 ..**Layish**, Michael D '02 %OSU/Legal Affrs -33 W 11th Av -Ste 209
-Columbus 43201

(330) 497-2886 ..**Layman**, Brian C '00 %Zollinger DGT & Co -6370 Mt Plsnt NW
-Bx2985 -Canton 44720

(937) 296-0365 ..**Layman**, David L '83 -580 Lincoln Park Blvd -Ste 133
-Dayton 45429

(216) 586-3939 ..**Layman**, Richard P '80 (Jones D) -901 Lakeside Av
-Cleveland 44114 **Fx:**579-0212

(937) 322-6811 ..**Layman**, Steven R '85 Pub Def -Old Cthse -Troy 45373

(614) 469-3939 ..**Laymon**, Ronald E '97 %Jones D -325 John H McConnell Blvd
-Ste 600 -Bx165017 -Columbus 43216 **Fx:**461-4198

(216) 443-3377 ..**Layne**, Keith A '91 CCBA Juv Ct -2163 E 22nd -3rd Fl
-Cleveland 44115

(602) 564-7380 ..**Layton**, Mary '99 ReSolutions -3101 W Peoria Av -Ste B-310
-Phoenix, AZ 85029

(419) 241-6000 ..**Lazar**, Bruce D '95 (Eastman & S Ltd) -1 Seagate -24th Fl
-Bx10032 -Toledo 43699 **Fx:**247-1777

(330) 666-6900 ..**Lazar**, John P '83 -310 N Cleveland-Massillon Rd -Akron 44333

(216) 586-3939 ..**Lazar**, Kathy P '82 Cnsl Jones D -901 Lakeside Av
-Cleveland 44114 **Fx:**579-0212

(419) 213-3000 ..**Lazar**, Mary E '95 Lucas Cnty CSEA -701 Adams -Toledo 43624

(740) 852-9777 ..**Lazaroff**, Alan J '86 Madison Correctional Inst -1851 St Rt 56
-Bx740 -London 43140

(614) 236-6535 ..**Lazaroff**, Risa D '88 Capital Univ Law Sch -303 E Broad
-Columbus 43215

(513) 422-5407 ..**Lazarow**, Jeffrey W '77 Rogers Ltd,Inc -124 City Ctr
-Middletown 45042

(213) 894-2854 ..**Lazarow**, William S '72 Central Dist of CA -321 E 2nd
-Los Angeles, CA 90012

(513) 241-7460 ..**Lazarus**, David '82 -7 W 7th -Ste 1850 -Cincinnati 45202
Fx:684-7777

(216) 687-2347 ..**Lazarus**, Stephen R '74 CSU-Marshall Cllg of Law -2121 Euclid Av
-LB138 -Cleveland 44115 **Fx:**687-6881

(513) 721-7300 ..**Lazarus**, Stephen S '89 (Hardin LL&M LLC) -30 Garfld Pl
-915 Cincinnati Club Bldg -Cincinnati 45202

(614) 221-1616 ..**Lazear**, Bruce C '84 (Lazear-Simmons Cap Prtnrs,Ltd) -401 N
Front -Ste 350 -Columbus 43215

(614) 228-1541 ..**Lazear**, Sherri B '85 (Baker & H LLP) -65 E State -Ste 2100
-Columbus 43215 **Fx:**462-2616

(216) 931-6000 ..**Lazich**, Patricia D '91 %Ulmer & B LLP -1300 E 9th
-Ste 900 Penton Media Bldg -Cleveland 44114 **Fx:**931-6001

(614) 466-4605 ..**Lazorishak**, Karen L '85 OH Dept Job & Fam Srvcs -30 E Broad
-32nd Fl -Columbus 43266

(216) 515-1660 ..**Lazzaro**, Anthony J '04 %Frantz W LLP -127 Pub Sq -2500
Key Center -Cleveland 44114 **Fx:**515-1660

(440) 333-1445 ..**Lazzaro**, Lynn A '75 L Lazzaro -2639 Wooster Rd
-Rocky River 44116 **Fx:**356-2873

(216) 831-8771 ..**Lazzaro**, Michele M '81 (Lazzaro & K) -25700 Science Park Dr
-Ste 250 -Cleveland 44122

(216) 522-4916 ..**Lazzaro**, Patrick G '57 SSA/OHA -1350 Euclid Av -7th Fl
-Cleveland 44115

(216) 226-8241 ..**Lazzaro**, Robert E '78 (Costanzo & L) -13317 Mad Av
-Lakewood 44107

(513) 381-2011 ..**Le**, Peter L '03 %Hammond Law Grp,LLC -441 Vine
-3311 Carew Twr -Cincinnati 45202 **Fx:**381-2227

(614) 221-8448 ..**Leach**, Donald B Jr. '82 (Buckingham D&B,LLP)
-191 W Nationwide Blvd -Ste 300 -Bx151120 -Columbus 43215
Fx:221-8590

(614) 995-4198 ..**Leach,** Ellen C '92 PERS of OH -277 E Town -Columbus 43215
(614) 995-5287 ..**Leach,** George W Jr. '01 OH Dept of Edu -25 S Front -7th Fl -Columbus 43215
(304) 295-0766 ..**Leach,** James R '98 -821½ 23rd -Bx5502 -Vienna, WV 26105
(216) 928-2200 ..**Leach,** John C '02 %Sutter OM&F -1301 E 9th -3600 Erievw Twr -Cleveland 44114 **Fx:**928-4400
(513) 241-3100 ..**Leach,** Lori R '98 %Lerner S&R -120 E 4th -8th Fl -Cincinnati 45202
(440) 943-6800 ..**Leach,** Robert S '78 -29339 Euclid Av -Wickliffe 44092
(216) 515-1660 ..**Leader,** Edward J '99 Frantz W LLP -127 Pub Sq -2500 Key Center -Cleveland 44114 **Fx:**515-1650
(305) 373-0733 ..**Leaf,** Maralyn D '89 Leaf & Assoc,LLC -100 SE 2nd -Ste 2330 -Miami, FL 33131
(513) 751-6860 ..**Leahr,** David W '95 -111 Ehrman Av -Cincinnati 45220
(419) 227-9595 ..**Leahy,** John M '66 Daley B&L LLC -1728 Allentown Rd -Lima 45805 **Fx:**227-3177
(419) 227-9595 ..**Leahy,** John M '98 Daley B&L LLC -1728 Allentown Rd -Lima 45805 **Fx:**227-3177
(614) 249-4784 ..**Leahy,** Walter R '71 Nationwide Ins Co -1 Nationwide Plz -Columbus 43215
(216) 621-5300 ..**Leahy,** William B '68 (Buckingham D&B,LLP) -1375 E 9th -Ste 1700 -Cleveland 44114 **Fx:**621-5440
(614) 466-1305 ..**Leahy-Connolly,** Erin B '98 Atty Gen -30 E Broad -Columbus 43215 **Fx:**466-8898
(216) 623-0150 ..**Leak,** Douglas G '89 (Roetzel & A,LPA) -1375 E 9th -One Cleve Ctr 9th Fl -Cleveland 44114 **Fx:**623-0134
(513) 626-1597 ..**Leal,** George H '03 Procter & Gamble -11450 Grooms Rd -Cincinnati 45242
(216) 696-0900 ..**Lear,** Scott Michael '89 (Zukerman D&L,LPA) -2000 E 9th -Ste 700 -Cleveland 44115 **Fx:**696-8800
(513) 621-3394 ..**Learmonth,** Doloris F '78 (Peck S&W,LLP) -201 E 5th -Ste 900 -Cincinnati 45202 **Fx:**621-3813
(330) 929-3160 ..**Learner,** Edward C '84 -1200 Portage Trl -Cuyahoga Falls 44223 **Fx:**923-7975
(440) 285-5041 ..**Leary,** Arthur Pearch III '74 -401 South -Bldg 4A -Chardon 44024
(330) 670-8588 ..**Leary,** Jeffrey N '00 Tour Talent -843 N Cleveland-Massillon Rd -Akron 44333
(440) 886-3000 ..**Leary,** Lynn W '63 Leary SN&L -5579 Pearl Rd -Ste 203 -Parma 44129 **Fx:**886-3171
(216) 443-7800 ..**Leary,** Patrick S '00 Cuyahoga Cnty Pros -1200 Ontario -8th Fl -Cleveland 44113 **Fx:**698-2270
(440) 886-3000 ..**Leary Schifko Nobili & Lang** -5579 Pearl Rd -Ste 203 -Parma 44129 **Fx:**886-3171
(614) 358-8056 ..**Lease,** Charles H '85 Ricketts Co,LPA -580 S High -3rd Fl -Columbus 43215
(614) 628-8361 ..**Lease,** Diane M '86 OH Police & Fire Pension Fund -140 E Town -Columbus 43215
(216) 621-0200 ..**Lease,** Robert K '76 (Baker & H LLP) -1900 E 9th -Ste 3200 -Cleveland 44114 **Fx:**696-0740
(202) 693-6206 ..**Leasure,** Linda L '75 Dept of Labor -200 Const Av NW -Rm S-4309 -Washington, DC 20210
(216) 368-3585 ..**Leatherberry,** Wilbur C '68 CWRU Law Schl -11075 East Blvd -Cleveland 44106
(419) 232-2700 ..**Leatherman,** Jill T '02 -515 E Main -Van Wert 45891 **Fx:**232-2800
(419) 874-3536 ..**Leatherman,** Wayne M '50 (Leatherman WD&H) -353 Elm -Perrysburg 43551 **Fx:**874-3899
(419) 874-3536 ..**Leatherman Witzler Dombey & Hart** -353 Elm -Perrysburg 43551 **Fx:**874-3899
(330) 725-9729 ..**Leaver,** James R '90 Medina Cnty Cmn Pleas Ct -93 Pub Sq -Medina 44256
(216) 586-3939 ..**Leavitt,** Jeffrey S '73 (Jones D) -901 Lakeside Av -Cleveland 44114 **Fx:**579-0212
(330) 492-8717 ..**Leb,** Arthur S '55 OfCnsl Buckingham D&B,LLP -4518 Fulton Dr NW -Bx35548 -Canton 44735 **Fx:**492-9625
(330) 376-7800 ..**Leb,** Gerald P '82 -120 E Mill -401 Quaker Sq -Akron 44308
(216) 289-2888 ..**LeBarron,** Deborah A '84 Mun Ct Judge -555 E 222nd -Euclid 44123
(614) 782-8727 ..**Leber,** William E '75 -6606 Tussing Rd -Reynoldsburg 43068
Lebo, Franklin B '04 -(Address Unavailable)
(330) 762-9191 ..**LeBoeuf,** Bradley S '99 -7 W Bowery -Ste 604 -Akron 44308 **Fx:**762-4244
(937) 496-7959 ..**LeBoeuf,** Mary Carmichael '03 %Hon MK Huffman -41 N Perry -Cmmn Pleas Ct -Dayton 45422
(216) 566-2439 ..**Lebold,** John W '82 Sherwin-Williams Co -101 Prospect Av NW -Cleveland 44115
(216) 621-2300 ..**Lebovitz,** Jamie R '82 Nurenberg PH&M LPA -1370 Ontario -Ste 100 -Cleveland 44113 **Fx:**771-2242
(216) 621-0200 ..**Lebowitz,** Todd H '97 %Baker & H LLP -1900 E 9th -Ste 3200 -Cleveland 44114 **Fx:**696-0740
(614) 621-1500 ..**Lech,** Robert R '00 %Calfee H&G LLP -21 E State -1100 Fifth Third Ctr -Columbus 43215 **Fx:**621-0010
(614) 422-5046 ..**Lechnowsky,** Orest J '01 Chase Manhattan Mortgage Corp -3415 Vision Dr -2nd Fl -Columbus 43219
(216) 274-2354 ..**Lechowick,** Sonja M '01 French-Amer Chmbr of Comm -200 Pub Sq -Ste 3300 -Cleveland 44114
(614) 644-7257 ..**Lecklider,** Timothy A '83 Atty Gen -150 E Gay -Columbus 43215 **Fx:**752-4677
(440) 232-2223 ..**Lecso,** Madelene L '89 -21 Mapledale Av -Bedford 44146
(937) 228-2696 ..**Ledbetter,** Michael A '97 (Snyder R&S) -11 W Monument Bldg -Ste 307 -Dayton 45402
(216) 586-3939 ..**Leddy,** Patrick J '90 (Jones D) -901 Lakeside Av -Cleveland 44114 **Fx:**579-0212
(937) 832-1973 ..**Ledford,** George W '74 -23 N Main -Ste 4 -Bx242 -Englewood 45322
(440) 918-1850 ..**Ledman,** David E '87 -34950 Chardon Rd -Ste 105 -Willoughby Hills 44094
(614) 221-2121 ..**Ledman,** James H '65 (Isaac BL&T,LLP) -250 E Broad -Ste 900 Mdlnd Bldg -Columbus 43215 **Fx:**365-9516
(216) 445-6231 ..**Leduc,** Marie-Jeanne S '03 Cleveland Clinic Fndtn -9500 Euclid Av -EE-35 -Cleveland 44195

(703) 614-1097 ..**Ledvina,** Thomas N '78 US Navy -Genl Cnsl of the Navy Rm 5E677 -Washington, DC 20350
(513) 721-5672 ..**Lee,** Brian A '00 %Benjamin Y&H LLC -312 Elm -Ste 1850 -Cincinnati 45204 **Fx:**562-4388
(614) 462-3555 ..**Lee,** Catherine M '04 %Franklin Cnty Pros -373 S High -Columbus 43215
(330) 455-6112 ..**Lee,** Cheryl S '00 %Tzangas PM&R -220 Market Av S -8th Fl -Canton 44702 **Fx:**455-2108
(614) 466-3636 ..**Lee,** Denise C '94 OH Dept Commerce -77 S High -Columbus 43266
(440) 338-6117 ..**Lee,** Dennis J '73 -13683 Caves Rd -Novelty 44072 **Fx:**338-9827
(440) 285-2222 ..**Lee,** Dorothy H '94 Geauga Cnty Ct -100 Short Ct -Chardon 44024
(513) 946-3000 ..**Lee,** Ernest W Jr. '01 Hamilton Cnty Pros -230 E 9th -Cincinnati 45202 **Fx:**946-3017
(614) 236-4600 ..**Lee,** James C '84 -901F Robinwood Av -Columbus 43213
(419) 353-0311 ..**Lee,** Jerry W '78 -121 E Wooster -Ste 208 -Bx1001 -Bowling Green 43402
(513) 732-0443 ..**Lee,** Joan C '85 (Decatur & L Co,LPA) -350 E Main -Ste 4 -Bx605 -Batavia 45103
(440) 247-7800 ..**Lee,** Karen E '82 (McSherry & Co) -178 E Wshngtn -Chagrin Falls 44022 **Fx:**247-7801
(202) 691-3084 ..**Lee,** Kyu S '98 Dept of Vet Affrs-Ofc of Regl Cnsl -1120 VT Av NW -Ste 1013 -Washington, DC 20421
(216) 520-5559 ..**Lee,** Lori Ann '95 West Grp -6111 Oak Tree Blvd -Bx318063 -Cleveland 44131
(216) 752-8027 ..**Lee,** Martha C '76 -13800 Shaker Blvd -#808 -Cleveland 44120
(614) 248-5590 ..**Lee,** Matthew David '93 Banc 1 -Bx711273 -Columbus 43271
(614) 444-4999 ..**Lee,** Paul W '78 -705 E Lvngstn Av -Columbus 43205
(614) 249-2229 ..**Lee,** Philip W '93 Cnsl Nationwide Ins Co -1 Nationwide Plz -Columbus 43215
(614) 227-2300 ..**Lee,** Phillip H '03 %Bricker & E LLP -100 S 3rd -Columbus 43215 **Fx:**227-2390
(740) 392-8838 ..**Lee,** Robert D '79 -136 S Main -Mount Vernon 43050
Lee, Robert E '61 -9934 Plsnt Lk Blvd -#T408 -Cleveland 44130
(330) 644-6161 ..**Lee,** Robert E '74 (Mallo & L) -2483 S Main -Akron 44319 **Fx:**644-7926
(937) 433-5753 ..**Lee,** Roger A '76 -2249 Belloak -Dayton 45440
(330) 376-2700 ..**Lee,** Ronald B '78 (Roetzel & A,LPA) -222 S Main -Akron 44308 **Fx:**376-4577
(216) 271-8947 ..**Lee,** Stephen C '96 BP Oil Co -6585 Ridge Rd -Cleveland 44129
(440) 808-4472 ..**Lee,** Steven C '89 TravelCenters of Amer -24601 Ctr Ridge Rd -Ste 200 -Westlake 44145
(513) 983-9529 ..**Lee,** Tanya M '01 Procter & Gamble Co-Legal -1 Procter & Gamble Plz -Cincinnati 45202
(216) 241-2838 ..**Lee,** Thomas J '77 (Taft S&H LLP) -200 Pub Sq -3500 BP Twr -Cleveland 44114 **Fx:**241-3707
(614) 466-5394 ..**Lee,** Thomas K '95 Pub Def -8 E Long -Columbus 43215
(202) 693-0286 ..**Lee,** Tiffany Omolara '02 US Dept of Labor -200 Const Av NW -Washington, DC 20210
(740) 393-0405 ..**Lee,** William J '48 -704 Cntry Clb Dr -Howard 43028
(216) 631-4301 ..**Leece,** Wilson A II '69 -9840 Lorain Av -Cleveland 44102
Leech, Charles R Jr. '55 -20285 Zion Rd -Gambier 43022
(440) 247-7876 ..**Leech,** John D '64 Dynamis Hlthcr Advsrs,Inc -7227 Chagrin Rd -Chagrin Falls 44023
(740) 622-0166 ..**Leech Scherbel & Peddicord** -240 S 4th -Bx880 -Coshocton 43812
(740) 622-0166 ..**Leech,** Thomas B '46 (Leech S&P) -240 S 4th -Bx880 -Coshocton 43812
Leed, Carolyn E '04 -(Address Unavailable)
(440) 892-3315 ..**Leeders,** Lawrence D '80 -1991 Crocker Rd -Ste 600 -Cleveland 44145
(513) 381-0656 ..**Leeper,** Andrew R '85 (Kohnen & P LLP) -201 E 5th -Ste 800 -Cincinnati 45202 **Fx:**381-5823
(740) 373-5455 ..**Leeper,** Myron D Jr. '74 (Theisen B,LPA) -424 2nd -Bx739 -Marietta 45750 **Fx:**373-4409
(216) 623-0150 ..**Lees,** Tammi J '04 %Roetzel & A,LPA -1375 E 9th -One Cleve Ctr 9th Fl -Cleveland 44114 **Fx:**623-0134
(937) 438-6848 ..**Lees,** Thomas E '98 %Stevens & S LLP -7019 Corp Way -Dayton 45459
(614) 221-2223 ..**Leeseberg,** Gerald S '79 Leeseberg & V -175 S 3rd -PH 1 -Columbus 43215 **Fx:**221-3106
(614) 221-2223 ..**Leeseberg & Valentine** -175 S 3rd -PH 1 -Columbus 43215 **Fx:**221-3106
(937) 312-3614 ..**Leesman,** Michael G '03 Premier Hlth Care Srvcs,Inc -332 Congress Park Dr -Dayton 45459 **Fx:**312-3615
(330) 425-4501 ..**LeFaiver,** William A '69 W LeFaiver Co,LPA -8010 McGhee Ln -Hudson 44236
(440) 838-8800 ..**Lefelar,** Scott A '99 %Millisor & N Co,LPA -9150 S Hills Blvd -Ste 300 -Cleveland 44147 **Fx:**838-8805
(937) 864-3000 ..**LeFevre,** Deana L '83 Speedway SuperAmer LLC -Bx1500 -Springfield 45501
(937) 259-7115 ..**Leffak,** Ellen S '85 Dayton Power & Light Co -Bx8825 -Dayton 45401
(614) 221-4221 ..**Leffel,** Elizabeth C '89 Barkan + N -360 S Grant Av -Bx1989 -Columbus 43216 **Fx:**221-5423
(716) 512-8434 ..**Leffel,** Kevin L '95 Heidelberg Digital LLC -2600 Manitou Rd -Rochester, NY 14624
(216) 291-3806 ..**Lefferts,** Dale E '85 Cleveland Hts Mun Ct -40 Severance Cir -Cleveland Heights 44118
(216) 928-2200 ..**Lefferts,** Susan H '86 %Sutter OM&F -1301 E 9th -3600 Erievw Twr -Cleveland 44114 **Fx:**928-4400
(330) 535-5711 ..**Leffler,** Amanda M '02 %Brouse M -106 S Main -500 First Natl Twr -Akron 44308 **Fx:**253-8601
(330) 253-5996 ..**Leffler,** Daniel J '03 -190 N Union -Ste 201 -Akron 44304
(330) 376-2700 ..**Leffler,** Frederick W '90 (Roetzel & A,LPA) -222 S Main -Akron 44308 **Fx:**376-4577
(419) 668-8215 ..**Leffler,** Russell V '77 Huron Cnty Pros -12 E Main -Norwalk 44857
(216) 621-8484 ..**Lefkowitz,** Paul S '74 (Climaco LPW&G Co,LPA) -1228 Euclid Av -Ste 900 Halle Bldg -Cleveland 44115 **Fx:**771-1632
(330) 793-4610 ..**Lefoer,** Dominic S '65 -4374 Mahoning Av -Austintown 44515
(614) 466-8600 ..**Lefton,** David E '85 Atty Gen -30 E Broad -Columbus 43215 **Fx:**466-6090

(513) 721-7300 ..**Lefton,** David H '87 (Hardin LL&M LLC) -30 Garfld Pl
-915 Cincinnati Club Bldg -Cincinnati 45202

(513) 721-1350 ..**Lefton,** Jimmy J '94 %Barron PB&S -3074 Madison Rd
-Cincinnati 45209

(330) 996-3185 ..**Lefton,** Karen C '84 Cnsl Akron Beacon Jrnl -44 E Exchange
-Bx640 -Akron 44309 Fx:996-3678
Lefton, Stacy B '02 -2440 Vera Av -Cincinnati 45237

(513) 241-3100 ..**Legel,** Tracy M '03 %Lerner S&R -120 E 4th -8th Fl
-Cincinnati 45202

(216) 566-2478 ..**Legenza,** Richard A '84 Sherwin-Williams -101 Prospect Av NW
-Cleveland 44115 Fx:566-1708

(216) 778-5776 ..**Legerski,** Mary L '94 Metro Hlth Med Ctr -2500 Metro Health Dr
-Cleveland 44109

(440) 838-8585 ..**Legerski,** Steven A '94 WKNR -9446 Broadvw -Cleveland 44147

(216) 587-2120 ..**Leggett,** Linda A '91 %Reddy G&M Co,LPA
-5306 Transportation Blvd -Garfield Heights 44125

(941) 748-5599 ..**Legler,** Kennedy III '78 (Legler & F) -2027 Manatee Av W
-Bradenton, FL 34205 Fx:747-2371

(330) 744-3196 ..**Legow,** Christine Blair '79 Cmmnty Lgl Aid Srvcs,Inc -11 Fed Plz
Central -7th Fl -Youngstown 44503 Fx:744-2503

(330) 759-7988 ..**Legow,** Elliot P '78 -998 Colonial Dr -Youngstown 44505

(702) 222-2500 ..**LeGrand,** David G '79 Hale LPD&H -2300 W Sahara Av
-8th Fl,Bx 8 -Las Vegas, NV 89102

(419) 826-0055 ..**Lehenbauer,** Alan J '84 McQuades Co,LPA -Lincoln at Bway
-Bx237 -Swanton 43558

(330) 744-3198 ..**Lehere,** Allyson L '95 NE OH Legal Srvcs -11 Fed Plz Central
-Ste 200 -Youngstown 44503

(330) 364-4421 ..**Lehigh,** Daniel T '57 -158 N Bway -New Philadelphia 44663

(937) 885-3612 ..**Lehman,** Barbara L '93 -9515 Sheehan Rd -Centerville 45458

(614) 888-2033 ..**Lehman,** David B '74 -142 Park Blvd -Worthington 43085

(330) 463-5738 ..**Lehman,** David W '96 -1998 E Hines Hill Rd -Hudson 44236

(440) 356-9575 ..**Lehman,** Jeffrey K '84 -21270 Lorain Rd -Fairview Park 44126

(216) 431-3406 ..**Lehman,** Jeffrey T '89 Scripps Howard Corp -3001 Euclid Av
-Cleveland 44115

(937) 866-1629 ..**Lehman,** Joseph A '77 (Ruschau & L) -443 E Central Av
-Miamisburg 45342

(513) 579-0080 ..**Lehman,** Linda L '92 %Smith R&S Co,LPA -1014 Vine -Ste 2350
-Cincinnati 45202 Fx:579-0222

(419) 936-2290 ..**Lehman,** Mary J '03 City Div of Transportation
-110 N Westwood Av -Toledo 43607

(330) 264-6115 ..**Lehman,** Ralph E '79 (Logee HS&L) -2171-B Eagle Pass
-Wooster 44691 Fx:262-5729

(419) 659-2141 ..**Lehman,** Scott C '93 United Bancshares Inc -100 S High -Bx67
-Columbus Grove 45830

(419) 213-3000 ..**Lehman-Sentle,** Susan K '00 Lucas Cnty CSEA -701 Adams
-Toledo 43624

(614) 466-4605 ..**Lehmann,** Dale E III '95 OH Dept Job & Fam Srvcs -30 E Broad
-32nd Fl -Columbus 43266

(937) 322-2161 ..**Lehmkuhl,** Allen M '74 (A Lehmkuhl Co,LPA) -111 E Cecil
-Springfield 45504

(740) 393-2788 ..**Lehmkuhl,** Phillip D '78 -100 N Main -Ste 100
-Mount Vernon 43050

(513) 852-6013 ..**Lehner,** Lisa d '01 (Wood & L LLP) -600 Vine -Ste 2500
-Cincinnati 45202 Fx:852-6087

(440) 356-1219 ..**Lehnowsky,** Judith A '84 -20220 Ctr Ridge Rd
-Rocky River 44116

(440) 350-2683 ..**LeHoty-Ostry,** Randi '89 Lake Cnty Pros -105 Main -Bx490
-Painesville 44077 Fx:350-2585

(419) 625-3672 ..**Lehrer,** John W '40 (Smith & L,LPA) -308 W Adams
-Sandusky 44870

(614) 258-1955 ..**Lehv,** Michael S '94 -78 Park Dr -Columbus 43209

(937) 449-2800 ..**Leibold,** William J '82 (Chernesky H&K PLL) -10 Cthse Plz SW
-Ste 1100 -Dayton 45402 Fx:449-2821

(614) 823-6290 ..**Leibrock,** Robin D '93 Century Surety Co -465 Cleveland Av
-Westerville 43082

(330) 253-2227 ..**Leiby,** Stephen P '73 (Parker LH&R,LLC) -388 S Main -Ste 402
-Akron 44311 Fx:253-1261

(302) 992-3220 ..**Leichliter,** Van H Jr. '69 Dupont Co -1007 Market
-Wilmington, DE 19898

(513) 734-4848 ..**Leicht,** George P '72 -202 E Plane -Bethel 45106

(614) 475-5174 ..**Leickly,** James R '86 -114 Misty Oak Pl -Gahanna 43230

(614) 464-2020 ..**Leidner,** Ellen B '83 Prvnt Blindness OH -1500 W 3rd Av -Ste 200
-Columbus 43212

(843) 851-0072 ..**Leiendecker,** Mark A '83 (M Leiendecker,LLC) -610 N Cedar
-Summerville, SC 29483

(614) 220-5611 ..**Leier,** Rachel A '99 %Manley D&K,LLC -495 S High -Ste 300
-Columbus 43215 Fx:220-5613

(312) 474-7900 ..**Leigh,** Mari Henry '83 (Meckler B&T) -123 N Wacker Dr -Ste 1800
-Chicago, IL 60606 Fx:474-7898

(614) 236-1075 ..**Leighton,** Charles T '71 (Leighton & L) -261 S Hmltn Rd
-Columbus 43213

(440) 576-3662 ..**Leikala,** Brenda S '00 Ashtabula Cnty Pros -25 W Jffrsn
-Jefferson 44047

(216) 621-0200 ..**Leiken,** Earl M '67 (Baker & H LLP) -1900 E 9th -Ste 3200
-Cleveland 44114 Fx:696-0740

(216) 479-8500 ..**Leiken,** Jonathan B '97 %Squire S&D LLP -127 Pub Sq
-4900 Key Twr -Cleveland 44114 Fx:479-8780

(216) 464-3570 ..**Leiken,** Robert S '71 -23611 Chagrin Blvd -Ste 225
-Beachwood 44122

(216) 621-2300 ..**Leikin,** Jeffrey A '85 Nurenberg PH&M LPA -1370 Ontario
-Ste 100 -Cleveland 44113 Fx:771-2242

(330) 674-3055 ..**Leininger,** Mark E '95 (Critchfield C&J Ltd) -138 E Jackson -Ste A
-Millersburg 44654

(614) 920-2261 ..**Leininger,** Robert E '00 Waste Mgmt -1006 Walnut
-Canal Winchester 43110

(330) 923-2122 ..**Leipply,** Gerald R '59 (Leipply & A) -2101 Front -Ste 101
-Cuyahoga Falls 44221 Fx:923-8167
Leis, Craig L E '02 -(Address Unavailable)

(513) 946-6400 ..**Leis,** Simon L Jr. '66 Hamilton Cnty Sheriff -1000 Sycamore
-Rm 110 -Cincinnati 45202

(614) 228-7771 ..**Leist,** Darrin C '99 -400 S 5th -Ste 202 -Columbus 43215

(513) 931-8564 ..**Leist,** Nelson R '61 -8238 Winton Rd -Ste 200D -Cincinnati 45231

(614) 485-2010 ..**Leister,** Craig D '74 (Means BB&B Co,LPA) -2006 Kenny Rd
-Columbus 43221 Fx:485-2019

(937) 492-6125 ..**Leistner,** Ann K '00 %Kerrigan BSG&B -126 N Main Av -Bx987
-Sidney 45365

(440) 779-6922 ..**Leitch,** David B '94 -22021 Brookpark Rd -Ste 100
-Cleveland 44126

(614) 228-6345 ..**Leithart,** Paul W II '81 (Strip HLM&T Co LPA) -575 S 3rd
-Columbus 43215 Fx:228-6369

(740) 354-7563 ..**Leitzell,** Karyn J '00 SE OH Lgl Srvcs -800 Gallia -Ste 700
-Portsmouth 45662

(419) 243-1010 ..**Leizerman,** Erwin J '76 Leizerman & Assoc,LLC -717 Mad Av
-Toledo 43624

(419) 842-8200 ..**Leizerman,** Joseph-Jacques S '93 %GW Osborne
-7150 Granite Cir Dr -Toledo 43617

(419) 243-1010 ..**Leizerman,** Michael J '94 Leizerman & Assoc,LLC -717 Mad Av
-Toledo 43624

(216) 861-3550 ..**Leizman,** William S '51 -526 Superior Av E -Ste 833
-Cleveland 44114

(513) 665-9400 ..**Leksan,** Thomas J '82 -432 Walnut -Ste 1000 -Cincinnati 45202

(562) 904-6955 ..**Leland,** Judith S '73 (J Leland,APLC) -8345 E Firestone Av
-Ste 300 -Downey, CA 90241

(937) 438-9985 ..**Leland,** Robert G '64 -1210 Brittany Hills Dr -Dayton 45459

(216) 443-7800 ..**Leland,** William G '03 Cuyahoga Cnty Pros Ofc -1200 Ontario
-Justice Center, Courts Tower -Cleveland 44113

(614) 464-2819 ..**Lelli,** Craig T '81 -51 N High -Ste 400 -Columbus 43215

(919) 483-8247 ..**Lemanowicz,** John L '92 Glaxo SmithKline -5 Moore Dr -Bx13398
-Research Triangle Park, NC 27709

(937) 227-3700 ..**LeMar,** Andrew D '03 %Faruki I&C PLL -10 N Ludlow
-500 Cthse Plz SW -Dayton 45402 Fx:227-3717

(513) 651-6800 ..**Lemasters,** P R '72 (Frost BT LLC) -201 E 5th -2200 PNC Ctr
-Cincinnati 45202 Fx:651-6981

(513) 665-3500 ..**Lemasters,** Poul H '04 %Freund F&A -105 E 4th -Ste 1400
-Cincinnati 45202 Fx:665-3503

(330) 869-4250 ..**LeMay,** James C '82 Omnova Solutions -175 Ghent Rd
-Fairlawn 44333
Lemberg, Charles J '91 -1123 Park Av -Newport, KY 41071

(513) 381-2838 ..**Lembke,** Raymond W '84 %Taft S&H LLP -425 Walnut -Ste 1800
-Cincinnati 45202 Fx:381-0205

(216) 621-1530 ..**Lembright,** Mark R '89 (Shapiro & F,LLP) -1500 W 3rd -Ste 400
-Cleveland 44113 Fx:621-1551

(330) 434-3000 ..**Lembright,** Ronald K '73 (Roderick & L) -One Cascade Plz
-Ste 1500 -Akron 44308 Fx:434-9220

(440) 576-9104 ..**Lemieux,** James M '82 J Lemieux Co,LPA -531 E Beech -Bx243
-Jefferson 44047

(440) 576-9177 ..**Lemire,** Jerome A '76 -838 St Rt 46N -Bx346 -Jefferson 44047

(216) 781-3600 ..**Lemmerbrock,** Ryan J '03 %Faulkner M&P,LLP
-820 W Superior Av -Ste 900 -Cleveland 44113 Fx:781-8839

(513) 522-8111 ..**Lemmink,** Robert D '91 -7539 Greenfarms Dr -Cincinnati 45224

(419) 885-3597 ..**Lemon,** David B '94 %McHugh D&M,Ltd -5580 Monroe
-Sylvania 43560 Fx:885-3861

(740) 354-3600 ..**Lemons,** Richard A '85 Miller S&F -806 6th -Ste 200 -Bx991
-Portsmouth 45662 Fx:354-1110

(202) 408-4419 ..**Lemper,** Timothy A '02 Finnegan HFG&D,LLP -901 NY Av NW
-Washington, DC 20001

(216) 861-7200 ..**Lenahan,** Brian J '92 Colliers Intl -1100 Superior Av -8th Fl
-Cleveland 44114

(440) 930-5678 ..**Lenahan,** Christopher R '00 -32932 Durrell Av -Avon Lake 44012

(330) 972-6357 ..**Lenart,** Lynn M '00 Univ of Akron Law Schl -150 Univ Av
-Akron 44325

(419) 885-0805 ..**Lenavitt,** David J '95 -4032 N Holland-Sylvania Rd -Toledo 43623

(419) 885-0805 ..**Lenavitt,** Jack M '65 Lenavitt Law Ofc
-4032 N Holland-Sylvania Rd -Toledo 43623

(440) 247-1990 ..**Lencewicz,** Christopher A '95 Lencewicz Co,LPA -45 E Wshngtn
-Ste 303 -Chagrin Falls 44022

(216) 651-4600 ..**Leneghan,** Christine T '91 (Leneghan & L) -9500 Maywood Av
-Cleveland 44102 Fx:961-4111

(440) 223-4260 ..**Leneghan,** David M '93 -200 Treeworth Blvd -Ste 200
-Broadview Heights 44147

(216) 651-4600 ..**Leneghan,** Patrick P '89 (Leneghan & L) -9500 Maywood Av
-Cleveland 44102 Fx:961-4111

(937) 542-3007 ..**Lenehan,** John F '67 Dayton Brd of Edu -348 W 1st
-Dayton 45402

(216) 694-5470 ..**Lenhard,** John E '66 Cleveland-Cliffs Inc -1100 Superior Av
-Cleveland 44114

(216) 583-3371 ..**Lenhard,** Kevin J '93 Ernst & Young LLP -925 Euclid Av -Ste 1300
-Cleveland 44115

(216) 241-2880 ..**Lenhard,** Matthew J '99 %Cowden HN&L -50 Pub Sq -Ste 1414
-Cleveland 44113 Fx:241-2881

(216) 861-8888 ..**Lenhardt,** Fred P '94 -1419 W 9th -2nd Fl -Cleveland 44113

(513) 977-8200 ..**Lenhart,** Amanda L '00 %Dinsmore & S LLP -255 E 5th -Ste 1900
-Cincinnati 45202 Fx:977-8141

(513) 651-6800 ..**Lenhart,** Elizabeth A '04 %Frost BT LLC -201 E 5th -2200
PNC Ctr -Cincinnati 45202 Fx:651-6981

(216) 881-6600 ..**Lenhart,** Thomas E '88 NEORSD -3826 Euclid Av
-Cleveland 44115 Fx:881-4407

(937) 223-9133 ..**Lennen,** Kevin L '87 %Rion R&R Co,LPA -130 W 2nd -Ste 2150
-Bx1262 -Dayton 45402
Lennon, Cynthia A '81 -Bx68 -Xenia 45385

(216) 586-3939 ..**Lennox,** Heather '92 (Jones D) -901 Lakeside Av
-Cleveland 44114 Fx:579-0212

(513) 352-6675 ..**Lenox,** Bryce A '98 %Thompson H LLP -312 Walnut -14th Fl
-Cincinnati 45202 Fx:241-4771

(937) 496-7487 ..**Lenski,** Kathleen S '98 %Montgomery Cnty Pub Def -117 S Main
-Ste 400 -Dayton 45422 Fx:225-3449

(330) 497-8274 ..**Lensman,** Todd A '92 (Lensman & Assoc,Ltd) -6273 Frank Av NW
-North Canton 44720 Fx:497-8269

(216) 621-0070 ..**Lenson,** Kevin Lee '96 (Friedman D&S Co,LPA) -1370 Ontario
-Ste 600 -Cleveland 44113 Fx:621-4008

(216) 931-6000 ..**Lenson,** Murray K '68 (Ulmer & B LLP) -1300 E 9th
-Ste 900 Penton Media Bldg -Cleveland 44114 Fx:931-6001

(740) 446-1356 ..**Lentes,** John R '85 -537½ 2nd Av -Gallipolis 45631 Fx:446-1534

(216) 443-7800 ..**Lentz,** Edward G '93 Cuyahoga Cnty Pros -1200 Ontario -8th Fl
-Cleveland 44113 Fx:698-2270

(216) 689-4389 ..**Lentz,** James F '01 Key Bank -127 Pub Sq
-16th Fl OH-01-27-1614 -Cleveland 44114

(330) 963-5883 .. **Lentz,** John C '98 -1094 E Dunedin Rd -Columbus 43224
(216) 291-4983 .. **Lentz,** Karen C '95 -9461 Lawnfld Dr -Ste A -Twinsburg 44087
(440) 247-8701 .. **Lentz,** Martin G '68 Cleveland Heights Police Dept -40 Severance Circle -Cleveland Heights 44118
(937) 913-0200 .. **Lentz,** Mary A '73 (M Lentz Co,LPA) -100 N Main -Ste 310 -Chagrin Falls 44022
(330) 297-5718 .. **Lentz,** Mary E '90 Gottschlich & P LLP -201 E 6th -Dayton 45402 **Fx:**824-2818
(216) 696-1433 .. **Lentz,** William D '76 (Sandvoss & L) -228 W Main -Bx248 -Ravenna 44266
(614) 452-8963 .. **Leo,** Ann E '79 (Koeth R&L Co,LPA) -1280 W 3rd -Cleveland 44113 **Fx:**696-1439
(216) 523-4488 .. **Leo,** James J '91 Petroleum Underground Storage Tank Rel -Bx163188 -Columbus 43216
(513) 946-3000 .. **Leo,** Victor J '79 Eaton Corp -1111 Superior Av -Cleveland 44114 **Fx:**946-3017
Leon, Lori '95 -Bx5231 -Herndon, VA 20172
(614) 481-4480 .. **Leon,** Robert J '04 %Koffel & J -2130 Arlngtn Av -Columbus 43221
(513) 721-2180 .. **Leonard,** Amy J '88 %DD Altman Co,LPA -15 E 8th -Ste 200W -Cincinnati 45202
(614) 462-6707 .. **Leonard,** Edward J '91 Cnty Clerk of Cts -369 S High -Columbus 43215
(216) 586-3939 .. **Leonard,** Irvin A '70 (Jones D) -901 Lakeside Av -Cleveland 44114 **Fx:**579-0212
(614) 791-9112 .. **Leonard,** James K '87 %Wright Law Co,LPA -4266 Tuller Rd -Ste 101 -Dublin 43017 **Fx:**791-9116
(330) 376-2700 .. **Leonard,** Jeffrey W '83 (Roetzel & A,LPA) -222 S Main -Akron 44308 **Fx:**376-4577
(330) 287-5490 .. **Leonard,** John J '96 Wayne Cnty Pub Def -113 W Lbrty -Wooster 44691 **Fx:**287-5479
(513) 946-3489 .. **Leonard,** Margaret M '88 1st Dist Ct of Appls -230 E 9th -12th Fl -Cincinnati 45202 **Fx:**946-3412
(216) 621-0200 .. **Leonard,** Melissa A '95 (Baker & H LLP) -1900 E 9th -Ste 3200 -Cleveland 44114 **Fx:**696-0740
(937) 294-2778 .. **Leonard,** Paul R '69 -424 Patterson Rd -Dayton 45419
(419) 228-1020 .. **Leonard,** Robert K '69 (R Leonard Law Ofcs,LLC) -119 N West -Ste 101 -Lima 45801 **Fx:**228-5490
(412) 391-8510 .. **Leonard,** Roy E '83 (Stonecipher CB&S,PC) -125 1st Av -Pittsburgh, PA 15222
(614) 436-3211 .. **Leonard,** Tracey A '94 Cloud & O -5354 N High -Ste 3D -Columbus 43214
(513) 321-2250 .. **Leonard,** William L Jr. '50 -31 E Observatory Hill -Cincinnati 45208
(419) 535-4791 .. **Leonardi,** Robert M '74 Dana Corp -4500 Dorr -Bx1000 -Toledo 43697
(614) 424-6760 .. **Leonatti,** Adam H '97 Thompson M&D -929 Harrison Av -Ste 205 -Columbus 43215
Leone, Denio A '84 -1 Berea Cmmns -Ste 216 -Berea 44017
(330) 746-5652 .. **Leone,** Donald P '76 -24 W Boardman -Youngstown 44503
(216) 752-1000 .. **Leonetti,** Albert F '66 -13111 Shaker Sq -Ste 211 -Cleveland 44120
(216) 443-3454 .. **Leonetti,** Ellen M '86 Cuyahoga Cnty Juv Ct -2163 E 22nd -Cleveland 44115
(216) 752-1000 .. **Leonetti,** Frank Jr. '56 -13111 Shaker Sq -Ste 211 -Cleveland 44120
(216) 687-1311 .. **Leonetti,** Frank III '82 (Reminger & R) -101 Prospect Av W -1400 Mdlnd Bldg -Cleveland 44115 **Fx:**687-1841
(330) 643-7758 .. **Leong,** Joann M '99 Summit Cnty Juv Ct -650 Dan -Akron 44310
(859) 392-7907 .. **Leonhard,** Elaine Korb '04 US Dist Ct EDKY -Bx232 -Covington, KY 41012 **Fx:**392-7945
(419) 243-1010 .. **Leonhardt,** Ronald F '92 Leizerman & Assoc,LLC -717 Mad Av -Toledo 43624
(216) 592-5000 .. **Leonti,** Joseph R '00 %Tucker E&W LLP -925 Euclid Av -1150 Huntngtn Bldg -Cleveland 44115 **Fx:**592-5009
(330) 399-2649 .. **Leopardi,** John A '57 (J Leopardi Co,LPA) -409 Harmon Av -Bx610 -Warren 44482
(216) 696-4676 .. **Leopold,** David W '85 (DW Leopold & Assoc Co,LPA) -2000 E 9th -Ste 300 -Cleveland 44115
(419) 523-5015 .. **Leopold,** Lawrence E '74 (Leopold W&S) -321 E Main -Bx303 -Ottawa 45875
(419) 523-5015 .. **Leopold Wildenhaus & Sahloff** -321 E Main -Bx303 -Ottawa 45875
(216) 566-5520 .. **Lepene,** Alan R '71 (Thompson H LLP) -127 Pub Sq -3900 Key Ctr -Cleveland 44114 **Fx:**566-5800
(216) 443-9000 .. **Lepene,** Scott B '03 %Porter WM&A LLP -925 Euclid Av -Ste 1700 -Cleveland 44115 **Fx:**443-9011
(330) 643-7952 .. **Lepidi-Carino,** Madeline J '03 Summit Cnty Pros-Juv -650 Dan -Akron 44310 **Fx:**379-3647
(330) 376-3300 .. **Lepp,** Aaron G '95 (Stark & K Co,LPA) -76 S Main -Ste 1512 -Akron 44308 **Fx:**376-6237
(614) 866-5051 .. **Lepp,** Michael '74 -1798 Sawgrss Dr -Reynoldsburg 43068
(937) 294-5959 .. **Leppla,** Gary J '78 (Leppla Assoc) -2100 S Patterson Blvd -Wright Bros Station -Bx612 -Dayton 45409 **Fx:**294-4411
(419) 947-9111 .. **Leppo,** Erin L '03 Morrow Cnty Dpt of Job & Family Srvcs -619 W Marion Rd -Mount Gilead 43338
(330) 468-1000 .. **Lepri,** Attilio J '65 -8775 Olde Eight Rd -Northfield 44067
(513) 771-0771 .. **Lerman,** Murray '89 -1528 Spring Park Walk -Cincinnati 45215 **Fx:**771-9625
(513) 241-3100 .. **Lerner,** Donald M '60 (Lerner S&R) -120 E 4th -8th Fl -Cincinnati 45202
(614) 227-2346 .. **Lerner,** Marshall L '73 (Bricker & E LLP) -100 S 3rd -Columbus 43215 **Fx:**227-2390
(440) 951-6666 .. **Lerner,** Michael J '92 %Denman & L Co,LPA -8039 Broadmoor Rd -Mentor 44060
(614) 222-0526 .. **Lerner,** Michael J '03 %EJ Hoffman -338 S High -Columbus 43215 **Fx:**358-0001
(216) 889-5478 .. **Lerner,** Rachel D '96 AG Interactive,Inc -1 Amer Rd -Cleveland 44144
(513) 241-3100 .. **Lerner Sampson & Rothfuss** -120 E 4th -8th Fl -Cincinnati 45202
(330) 425-8520 .. **Lerner Sampson & Rothfuss** -8972 Darrow Rd -Ste A304 -Twinsburg 44087
(513) 361-1200 .. **Lerner,** Stephen D '91 (Squire S&D LLP) -312 Walnut -Ste 3500 -Cincinnati 45202 **Fx:**361-1201

(440) 951-6666 .. **Lerner,** Susan D '92 Denman & L Co,LPA -8039 Broadmoor Rd -Mentor 44060
(440) 808-3390 .. **Leroux,** Clayton G Jr. '71 -30400 Detroit Rd -Ste 401 -Westlake 44145
(513) 867-8200 .. **LeRoy,** Donald C '77 -304 N 2nd -Hamilton 45011
(216) 420-9000 .. **Lesco,** Richard A '61 -1370 Ontario -Ste 1640 -Cleveland 44113
(330) 493-0040 .. **Lesh Casner & Miller** -4150 Belden Vllg NW -Ste 606 -Canton 44718
(513) 939-3300 .. **Leshner,** Gerald R '77 -1244 Nilles Rd -Ste 9 -Fairfield 45014
(614) 224-0401 .. **Leshner,** Jay Harris '85 -336 S High -Columbus 43215
(614) 461-1178 .. **Leshy,** George V '73 -1390 Dublin Rd -Columbus 43215
(330) 725-4929 .. **Lesiak,** Theodore J '89 (Oberholtzer F&L) -39 Pub Sq -Ste 201 -Bx220 -Medina 44258 **Fx:**723-4929
(513) 860-2560 .. **Lesick,** John R II '71 LandAmerica -8892 Beckett Rd -West Chester 45069
(216) 763-2200 .. **Leska,** Abbie B '92 Title 2000 Agncy -27629 Chagrin Blvd -Ste 202 -Woodmere 44122
(440) 992-2499 .. **Lesko,** Jane L '96 -4717 Park -Bx1417 -Ashtabula 44005
(216) 896-5600 .. **Leskovec,** Mark E '86 %Levy & D -25200 Chagrin Blvd -Ste 310 -Beachwood 44122 **Fx:**896-5601
(614) 462-3194 .. **Lesley,** Jane E '78 Franklin Cnty Pub Def -373 S High -12th Fl -Columbus 43215
(614) 921-9487 .. **Leslie,** Mark A '78 -76 S Powell Av -Columbus 43204
(330) 376-3575 .. **Leslie,** Mary Ellen '01 -777 W Market -Akron 44303 **Fx:**762-1009
(606) 473-7303 .. **Leslie,** Phillip B '94 (McBrayer ML&K) -Bx280 -Greenup, KY 41144
(614) 923-7700 .. **Leslie,** Richard L Jr. '93 %Clemens Nelson & Assoc -5100 Park Ctr Blvd -Ste 120 -Dublin 43017
(216) 361-4169 .. **Leslie,** Timothy C '94 Premier Farnell Corp -7061 E Plsnt Vlly Rd -Independence 44131
(614) 228-2226 .. **Lesser,** Frances S '79 Cnty Auditors Assn of OH -66 E Lynn -Columbus 43215
(513) 621-9660 .. **Lesser,** Richard F '82 -36 E 7th -Ste 2020 -Cincinnati 45202
(954) 985-4137 .. **Lesser,** Steven B '79 (Becker & P,PA) -3111 Stirling Rd -Fort Lauderdale, FL 33312 **Fx:**985-4176
(614) 466-3191 .. **Lesser,** Steven D '78 PUCO -180 E Broad -Columbus 43266
(440) 322-5441 .. **Lessing,** Robert E Jr. '69 (Lessing W&R Ltd) -374 Broad -Ste A -Elyria 44035
(440) 322-5441 .. **Lessing White & Roig Ltd** -374 Broad -Ste A -Elyria 44035
(859) 344-9500 .. **Lester,** Amber A Porter '02 %TW Bosse,PLLC -2101 Chmbr Ctr Dr -Ft Mitchell, KY 41017
(859) 781-2406 .. **Lester,** Charles T Jr. '80 -Bx75069 -Fort Thomas, KY 41075 **Fx:**781-8391
(216) 931-6000 .. **Lester,** David L '83 (Ulmer & B LLP) -1300 E 9th -Ste 900 Penton Media Bldg -Cleveland 44114 **Fx:**931-6001
(216) 752-1488 .. **Lester,** Esther O '89 -3715 Warrensvll Ctr Rd -#307 -Shaker Heights 44122
(614) 466-5204 .. **Lestini,** Gregory J '03 Sen T Fedor -Statehse -Columbus 43215
(609) 441-4633 .. **LeTart,** Phyllis A '82 Great Bay Hotel & Casino,Inc -Indiana Av & Brighton Park -Atlantic City, NJ 08401
(614) 228-6885 .. **Letcher,** Barbara K '90 %Lane A&H LLC -175 S 3rd -Ste 700 -Columbus 43215 **Fx:**228-0146
(614) 424-6424 .. **Letizia,** Donald L '87 Battelle Memorial Inst -505 King Av -Columbus 43201
(330) 373-1035 .. **Letson,** Daniel B '86 Letson GWL&R -155 S Park Av -Ste 250 -Bx151 -Warren 44482 **Fx:**392-5419
(330) 373-1035 .. **Letson Griffith Woodall Lavelle & Rosenberg** -155 S Park Av -Ste 250 -Bx151 -Warren 44482 **Fx:**392-5419
(330) 373-1035 .. **Letson,** Thomas B '88 Letson GWL&R -155 S Park Av -Ste 250 -Bx151 -Warren 44482 **Fx:**392-5419
(330) 373-1035 .. **Letson,** William N '55 Letson GWL&R -155 S Park Av -Ste 250 -Bx151 -Warren 44482 **Fx:**392-5419
(614) 875-2301 .. **Lett,** Ellsworth jack '51 -3031 Columbus -Bx66 -Grove City 43123
(419) 289-1234 .. **Lett,** Robert W '38 (Lett & L) -273 Sandusky -Bx219 -Ashland 44805
(419) 289-1234 .. **Lett,** Sam J '77 Lett & L -273 Sandusky -Bx219 -Ashland 44805
(330) 253-5060 .. **Lettieri,** Paula A '74 (Brennan M&D,LLC) -75 E Market -Akron 44308 **Fx:**253-1977
(216) 623-1155 .. **Letts,** Laurel E '91 Nationwide Ins -323 Lakeside Av W -Ste 410 Lakeside Pl -Cleveland 44113
(614) 469-7404 .. **Letts,** Richard D '74 SSA-OHA, Columbus -280 N High -3rd Fl -Columbus 43215
(614) 273-1000 .. **Leuby,** William A III '83 Hamilton Capital Mgmt Inc -5025 Arlngtn Centre Blvd -Columbus 43220
(614) 224-1222 .. **Leuchtag,** Emery J '83 %Maguire & S,LLP -250 Civic Ctr Dr -Ste 200 -Columbus 43215 **Fx:**224-1236
(330) 430-1998 .. **Leuchtag,** Holly A '83 Workers Comp -400 3rd SE -Bx24801 -Canton 44701
(216) 586-3939 .. **Leukart,** Barbara J '75 (Jones D) -901 Lakeside Av -Cleveland 44114 **Fx:**579-0212
(216) 621-0200 .. **Leukart,** Richard H II '67 (Baker & H LLP) -1900 E 9th -Ste 3200 -Cleveland 44114 **Fx:**696-0740
(216) 566-5656 .. **Leung,** Diane S '92 %Thompson H LLP -127 Pub Sq -3900 Key Ctr -Cleveland 44114 **Fx:**566-5800
(513) 946-3000 .. **Leurck,** Brian F '97 Hamilton Cnty Pros -230 E 9th -Cincinnati 45202 **Fx:**946-3017
(419) 562-5560 .. **Leuthold,** Sean E '95 (Leuthold & L) -1317 E Mansfld -Bx769 -Bucyrus 44820
(419) 562-5560 .. **Leuthold,** Shane M '98 (Leuthold & L) -1317 E Mansfld -Bx769 -Bucyrus 44820
(614) 221-5627 .. **Leutz,** John R '79 %Cnty Commissrs Assoc of OH -37 W Broad -Ste 650 -Columbus 43215
(216) 274-2346 .. **Levasseur,** Eric B '02 %Hahn L&P LLP -3300 BP Twr/200 Pub Sq -Ste 3300 -Cleveland 44114 **Fx:**241-2824
(513) 771-6768 .. **LeVay,** Helen F '85 (Cuni F&L Co,LPA) -10655 Sprngfld Pike -Cincinnati 45215
Leve, Katherine E '04 -(Address Unavailable)
(937) 224-1427 .. **Leve,** Stephen '66 -130 W 2nd -Ste 1900 -Dayton 45402
(440) 899-5130 .. **Levenberg,** Jessica A '04 Cnsl Plantrex.com -802 Sharon Dr -Westlake 44145
(614) 227-2328 .. **LeVere,** T Earl '94 (Bricker & E LLP) -100 S 3rd -Columbus 43215 **Fx:**227-2390
(614) 449-8282 .. **Leveridge,** Julia L '00 %Joseph & J -931 S Front -Columbus 43206 **Fx:**449-8287

(614) 645-7483 .. **Levering**, Robert B '80 City Pros -375 S High -7th Fl
-Columbus 43215

Leveton, Morton E '55 -(Address Unavailable)

(216) 696-1111 .. **Levey**, Harold L '68 -526 Superior Av E -Ste 410 -Cleveland 44114

(614) 629-3002 .. **Levey**, Jack S '83 %Plunkett & C,PC -300 E Broad -Ste 590
-Columbus 43215 Fx:629-3019

(216) 241-3333 .. **Levey**, Scott I '78 Mondello & L -55 Pub Sq -Ste 1010
-Cleveland 44114 Fx:241-7435

(419) 213-6986 .. **Levin**, Anita '98 CASA -1801 Spielbusch Av -Toledo 43624

(216) 621-1543 .. **Levin**, Ann R '80 -526 Superior Av -Ste 711 -Cleveland 44114

(440) 949-5425 .. **Levin**, Arnold S '34 -5555 Lk Rd -Sheffield Lake 44054
Fx:949-5425

(859) 578-1000 .. **Levin**, Chad S '94 %Horwitz Law Firm PSC -541 Buttermilk Pike
-Ste 305 -Crescent Springs, KY 41017

(216) 781-5233 .. **Levin**, Daniel J '91 (M Levin Co,LPA) -55 Pub Sq -Ste 940
-Cleveland 44113 Fx:696-8133

(312) 578-9428 .. **Levin**, David B '92 Krohn & M -120 W Madison -Ste 1001
-Chicago, IL 60602

(513) 618-7800 .. **Levin**, Debbe A '79 (Graf S&M,LPA) -425 Walnut -Ste 2400
-Cincinnati 45202 Fx:618-7801

(216) 831-3939 .. **Levin**, Dennis P '78 -5910 Landerbrook Dr -Ste 200
-Cleveland 44124

(216) 281-3535 .. **Levin**, James A '79 -6415 Detroit Av -Cleveland 44102

(216) 928-0600 .. **Levin**, Joel L '84 (Levin & Assoc) -1301 E 9th -Ste 1100
-Cleveland 44114

(419) 535-4640 .. **Levin**, Marc S '80 Dana Corp -4500 Dorr -Bx1000 -Toledo 43697

(216) 781-5236 .. **Levin**, Morris '52 (M Levin Co,LPA) -55 Pub Sq -Ste 940
-Cleveland 44113 Fx:696-8133

(216) 771-2175 .. **Levin**, Morton Q '66 Levin Grp Inc -1801 E 9th -Ste 1505
-Cleveland 44114

(216) 464-5778 .. **Levin**, Paul F '74 -2705 Rocklyn Rd -Shaker Heights 44122

(330) 836-5297 .. **Levin**, Richard V '67 -3250 W Market -Ste 307 -Akron 44333

(202) 962-0322 .. **Levine**, Abby R '97 NCNA -1030 15th NW -Ste 870
-Washington, DC 20005 Fx:962-0321

(216) 696-1233 .. **Levine**, Alan S '79 -55 Pub Sq -1200 Illuminating Bldg
-Cleveland 44113

(614) 224-5291 .. **Levine**, Amy M '01 -85 E Gay -Ste 1006 -Columbus 43215

(419) 885-4461 .. **Levine**, Arleen R '82 Toledo Jewish Cmmnty Fndtn -6505 Sylvania
-Sylvania 43560

(513) 241-6748 .. **Levine**, Arnold S '67 -324 Reading Rd -Cincinnati 45202

(216) 321-4477 .. **Levine**, Barbara H '04 -2831 Fairmount Blvd -Cleveland 44118

(202) 694-1650 .. **Levine**, Brant S '00 Fed Election Comm -999 E NW
-Washington, DC 20463

(614) 235-4340 .. **Levine**, Cathy J '91 UHCAN OH -1015 E Main -Columbus 43205

(408) 535-5118 .. **Levine**, David A '00 US Bankruptcy Ct-Dist of MD -280 S 1st
-US Crths 3035 -San Jose, CA 95113

(614) 228-1541 .. **Levine**, David C '89 (Baker & H LLP) -65 E State -Ste 2100
-Columbus 43215 Fx:462-2616

(216) 696-1233 .. **Levine**, David L '53 -55 Pub Sq -1200 Illuminating Bldg
-Cleveland 44113

(216) 363-4500 .. **Levine**, David M '94 (Benesch FC&A LLP) -200 Pub Sq -Ste 2300
-Cleveland 44114 Fx:363-4588

(513) 369-3715 .. **Levine**, David S '78 Great Amer Ins Co -580 Walnut -10th Fl
-Cincinnati 45202

(216) 623-2110 .. **Levine**, Gary H '76 -55 Pub Sq -Ste 1350 -Cleveland 44113

(937) 222-7884 .. **Levine**, Jeffrey L '76 Larry Stein Realty -2 Riverplace -Ste 300
-Dayton 45405

(419) 252-6274 .. **Levine**, Joel A '63 OfCnsl Spengler N PLL -608 Mad Av -Ste 1000
-Toledo 43604 Fx:241-8599

(614) 463-9770 .. **Levine**, Judith D '79 (Roetzel & A,LPA) -155 E Broad
-Natl City Ctr 12th Fl -Columbus 43215 Fx:463-9792

Levine, Kenneth J '89 -7914 Gleason Dr -#1134
-Knoxville, TN 37919

(216) 522-1200 ..**Levine**, Lisa K '96 IMG -1360 E 9th -Ste 100 -Cleveland 44114

(419) 843-2001 .. **Levine**, Marilyn J Brenner '01 %Gallon & T Co,LPA
-3516 Granite Cir -Bx325018 -Toledo 43635 Fx:843-6665

(310) 208-2800 .. **Levine**, Mark S '97 Weiss & Y -10940 Wilshire Blvd -24th Fl
-Los Angeles, CA 90024

(216) 363-4500 .. **Levine**, Mary Beth '87 OfCnsl Benesch FC&A LLP -200 Pub Sq
-Ste 2300 -Cleveland 44114 Fx:363-4588

(614) 438-7000 .. **Levine**, Richard J '75 Natl Auto Care Corp -101 Green Mdws Dr S
-Westerville 43081

(614) 227-0300 .. **Levine**, Richard L '84 (Richard L Levine Co,LPA) -515 E Main
-Ste 500 -Columbus 43215

(312) 879-3031 .. **Levine**, Robert S '77 Ernst & Young LLP -233 S Wacker Dr
-Chicago, IL 60606 Fx:879-4000

(937) 444-2626 .. **Levine**, Robin J '90 -107 E Main -Bx478 -Mount Orab 45154

(937) 225-5602 .. **Levinson**, James R '73 Montgomery Cnty Pros -301 W 3rd -Bx972
-Dayton 45422 Fx:225-3470

(216) 514-5997 .. **Levinson**, Jeffrey M '90 (Margulies & L) -30100 Chagrin Blvd
-Ste 250 -Pepper Pike 44124 Fx:514-5996

(614) 228-4141 .. **Levinson**, Lawrence L '94 -511 S High -Columbus 43215

(740) 452-4574 .. **Levion**, Leon L '52 -Bx36 -Zanesville 43702

(513) 621-2666 .. **Levison**, Jill S '01 %Statman HS&E LLC -255 E 5th
-Ste 2900 Chemed Ctr -Cincinnati 45202 Fx:587-4477

(614) 252-1818 .. **Levy**, Barbara '90 -235 S Drexel Av -Columbus 43209

(513) 241-7111 .. **Levy**, Barry D '76 (O'Connor A&L Co,LPA) -1014 Vine -22nd Fl
-Cincinnati 45202 Fx:241-7197

(513) 241-2540 .. **Levy**, Barry R '89 -632 Vine -Ste 415 -Cincinnati 45202

(216) 241-0050 .. **Levy**, Donald M '65 -55 Pub Sq -Ste 2240 -Cleveland 44113

(216) 896-5600 .. **Levy & Dubyak** -25200 Chagrin Blvd -Ste 310 -Beachwood 44122
Fx:896-5601

(216) 896-5600 .. **Levy**, Gregg S '91 (Levy & D) -25200 Chagrin Blvd -Ste 310
-Beachwood 44122 Fx:896-5601

(216) 363-4500 .. **Levy**, Howard A '73 (Benesch FC&A LLP) -200 Pub Sq -Ste 2300
-Cleveland 44114 Fx:363-4588

(513) 985-2500 .. **Levy**, Howard S '89 Phillips Law Firm,Inc -9521 Mntgmry Rd
-Cincinnati 45242 Fx:985-2503

(419) 255-3360 .. **Levy**, Jeffrey D '77 (Wittenberg PL&N) -520 Mad Av -Ste 840
-Toledo 43604

(513) 621-2120 .. **Levy**, John M '04 Strauss & T,LPA -150 E 4th -4th Fl
-Cincinnati 45202 Fx:241-8259

(513) 946-9200 .. **Levy**, Judith Ann '89 Hamilton Cnty Cmn Pleas Ct -800 Bway
-Cincinnati 45202

(937) 443-6949 .. **Levy**, Mark P '81 (Thompson H LLP) -2000 Cthse Plz NE -Bx8801
-Dayton 45401 Fx:443-6635

(702) 367-1224 .. **Levy**, Michael K '77 Retirement Planning Co,Inc
-2920 S Jones Blvd -Ste 240 -Las Vegas, NV 89146

(614) 224-9550 .. **Levy**, Stefan C '60 -261 S Front -Columbus 43215

(847) 374-0150 .. **Levy**, Susan M '87 -95 Sequoia Ln -Deerfield, IL 60015

(614) 898-5200 .. **Levy**, Yale R '95 (Pope & L Co,LPA) -903 Eastwind Dr
-Westerville 43081 Fx:898-5230

(716) 633-1984 .. **Lew**, Marilyn E '86 %S Graziano -Bx1165
-Cheektowaga, NY 14225

(330) 643-2788 .. **Lewandowski**, Connie J '91 Summit Cnty Pros-Crim -53 Univ Av
-7th Fl -Akron 44308 Fx:643-8277

(216) 241-6336 .. **Lewandowski**, Joseph A Jr. '80 -705-709 Literary Rd
-Cleveland 44113

Lewandowski, Thomas P '70 -8004 Fayette Av NW
-Massillon 44646

(216) 241-2838 .. **Lewanski**, Christine A '96 %Taft S&H LLP -200 Pub Sq -3500 BP
Twr -Cleveland 44114 Fx:241-3707

(513) 684-3954 .. **Lewin**, Gail S '80 Defense Logistics Agency -550 Main
-Fed Bldg Rm 9104 -Cincinnati 45202

(937) 562-4000 .. **Lewis**, Amy H '92 Greene Cnty Juv Ct -2100 Greene Way Blvd
-Xenia 45385

(216) 522-3715 .. **Lewis**, Bert II '99 NLRB -1240 E 9th -1695 Celebrezze Bldg
-Cleveland 44199 Fx:522-2418

(614) 466-0570 .. **Lewis**, Beth A '98 %OH Ofc Collctv Barg -100 E Broad -18th Fl
-Columbus 43215

(937) 225-7687 .. **Lewis**, Beth G '93 Fed Pub Def -130 W 2nd -Ste 820
-Dayton 45402

(407) 423-5561 .. **Lewis**, Charles E '67 T Olsen,PA -2518 Edgewtr Dr
-Orlando, FL 32804 Fx:423-5563

(513) 977-8200 .. **Lewis**, Colleen P '89 (Dinsmore & S LLP) -255 E 5th -Ste 1900
-Cincinnati 45202 Fx:977-8141

(513) 531-0909 .. **Lewis**, Cornelius "Carl" '91 -6066 Stover Av -Ste 1
-Cincinnati 45237

(330) 376-5300 .. **Lewis**, David J '87 (Buckingham D&B,LLP) -50 S Main -Bx1500
-Akron 44309 Fx:258-6559

(937) 252-6683 .. **Lewis**, David M '85 Lewis & Michael,Inc -1827 Woodman Dr
-Dayton 45420

(216) 443-9000 .. **Lewis**, David M '00 %Porter WM&A LLP -925 Euclid Av -Ste 1700
-Cleveland 44115 Fx:443-9011

(216) 222-2227 .. **Lewis**, David P '87 Natl City Corp -1900 E 9th -Cleveland 44114

(513) 723-4000 .. **Lewis**, Donald B '77 OfCnsl Vorys SS&P LLP -221 E 4th
-Ste 2000 Atrium Two -Bx0236 -Cincinnati 45201 Fx:723-4056

(740) 687-5025 .. **Lewis**, Douglas A '01 OH Rehab & Diagnostic Ctr
-2405 N Columbus -Ste 140 -Lancaster 43130

(614) 734-6270 .. **Lewis**, Emily J '86 -270 Bradenton Av -Dublin 43017 Fx:734-7270

(614) 221-4000 .. **Lewis**, Eugene B '82 (Chester W&S LLP) -65 E State -10th Fl
-Columbus 43215 Fx:221-4012

(937) 865-6800 .. **Lewis**, Forrest R '98 LexisNexis -6800 Springboro Pike
-Miamisburg 45342

(513) 665-9222 .. **Lewis**, Gary R '78 (G Lewis Co,LPA) -30 Garfld Pl -Ste 915
-Cincinnati 45202

(513) 870-2118 .. **Lewis**, George G '79 Cincinnati Ins Co -Bx145496
-Cincinnati 45250

(419) 255-5111 .. **Lewis**, Gina M '02 -520 Mad Av -Ste 1030 -Toledo 43604

(614) 221-3938 .. **Lewis**, Gregg R '89 -625 City Park Av -Columbus 43206
Fx:221-3713

(440) 943-4200 .. **Lewis**, Gregory R '93 Lubrizol Corp -29400 Lakelnd Blvd
-Wickliffe 44092

(513) 863-6700 .. **Lewis**, Heather Sanderson '98 (Millikin & F) -6 S 2nd -6th Fl
-Bx598 -Hamilton 45012 Fx:863-0031

(614) 231-7513 .. **Lewis**, Jacqueline '80 -2735 Scottwood Rd -Columbus 43209

(301) 677-9023 .. **Lewis**, James A '90 %US Army JAG Corps -2257 Huber Rd
-Fort Meade, MD 20755 Fx:677-9940

(740) 380-2561 .. **Lewis**, James C III '79 Citizens Bank -1319 W Hunter -Bx591
-Logan 43138

(330) 393-7727 .. **Lewis**, James F '72 OH Pub Def Comm -328 Mahoning Av
-Warren 44483

(614) 228-6885 .. **Lewis**, James W '75 OfCnsl Lane A&H LLC -175 S 3rd -Ste 700
-Columbus 43215 Fx:228-0146

(614) 461-1100 .. **Lewis**, Jeffrey M '81 (Swedlow BLL&D Co,LPA) -10 W Broad
-Ste 2400 -Columbus 43215 Fx:461-8178

(513) 232-6959 .. **Lewis**, Jeffrey Roy '79 Signs on Site Inc -2710 Turpin Knoll Ct
-Cincinnati 45244

(216) 586-3939 .. **Lewis**, Jennifer C '95 %Jones D -901 Lakeside Av
-Cleveland 44114 Fx:579-0212

(216) 621-0200 .. **Lewis**, John B '80 (Baker & H LLP) -1900 E 9th -Ste 3200
-Cleveland 44114 Fx:696-0740

(216) 479-8500 .. **Lewis**, John F '58 SrCnsl Squire S&D LLP -127 Pub Sq
-4900 Key Twr -Cleveland 44114 Fx:479-8780

(614) 231-5531 .. **Lewis**, John F Jr. '87 889 Global Solutions Ltd
-2501 Brookwood Rd -Columbus 43209

(216) 586-3939 .. **Lewis**, John Q '96 %Jones D -901 Lakeside Av -Cleveland 44114
Fx:579-0212

(740) 362-2881 .. **Lewis**, Jonathan C '74 (Lewis & L Co,LPA) -31 W Winter
-Delaware 43015

(216) 436-3237 .. **Lewis**, Julie E '96 IMG -1360 E 9th -Ste 100 -Cleveland 44114

(216) 241-1074 .. **Lewis**, Kenneth J '00 %Stafford & S Co,LPA -323 Lakeside Av W
-Ste 380 -Cleveland 44113

(513) 412-4842 .. **Lewis**, Kevin C '95 Great Amer Ins Co -49 E 4th -700 Dixie N
-Cincinnati 45202

(513) 977-8200 .. **Lewis**, Kim Martin '89 (Dinsmore & S LLP) -255 E 5th -Ste 1900
-Cincinnati 45202 Fx:977-8141

(216) 622-8200 .. **Lewis**, Leonard L III '84 (Calfee H&G LLP) -800 Superior Av
-Ste 1400 -Cleveland 44114 Fx:241-0816

(513) 634-5649 .. **Lewis**, Leonard W '84 Procter & Gamble -8611 Beckett Rd
-Beckett Ridge tech Ctr -West Chester 45069

(330) 755-1414 .. **Lewis**, Lora L '89 AstroShapes -65 Main -Struthers 44471
Fx:755-6190

(614) 224-7711 .. **Lewis**, Mark D '94 (Kitrick & L Co,LPA) -515 E Main -Ste 515
-Columbus 43215 Fx:225-8985

(216) 592-5000 ..**Lewis,** Martin H '79 (Tucker E&W LLP) -925 Euclid Av -1150 Huntngtn Bldg -Cleveland 44115 **Fx:**592-5009

(937) 225-4652 ..**Lewis,** Michael V '81 Montgomery Cnty Pub Def -117 S Main -Ste 400 -Dayton 45422 **Fx:**225-3449

(614) 253-9737 ..**Lewis,** Milton E '95 J Recchie & Co,LPA -1349 E Broad -Columbus 43205

(216) 586-7078 ..**Lewis,** Nathan Thomas '04 %Jones D -901 Lakeside Av -Cleveland 44114 **Fx:**579-0212

(216) 592-5000 ..**Lewis,** Nicole E '01 %Tucker E&W LLP -925 Euclid Av -1150 Huntngtn Bldg -Cleveland 44115 **Fx:**592-5009

(216) 696-7600 ..**Lewis,** Patrick H '85 %Duvin C&H -1301 E 9th -20th Fl Erievw Twr -Cleveland 44114 **Fx:**696-2038

(216) 443-9000 ..**Lewis,** Patrick T '04 %Porter WM&A LLP -925 Euclid Av -Ste 1700 -Cleveland 44115 **Fx:**443-9011

(614) 466-4605 ..**Lewis,** Randi G '78 OH Dept Job & Fam Srvcs -30 E Broad -32nd Fl -Columbus 43266

(304) 353-8000 ..**Lewis,** Richard L II '90 (Steptoe & J) -Bank One Ctr -7th Fl -Bx1588 -Charleston, WV 25326

(740) 286-0071 ..**Lewis,** Richard M '82 (R Lewis) -295 Pearl -Bx664 -Jackson 45640 **Fx:**286-2988

(513) 651-4130 ..**Lewis,** Robert D Jr. '97 %Lawrence Firm -8044 Mntgmry Rd -Ste 700 -Cincinnati 45236

(859) 578-1030 ..**Lewis,** Robert D Jr. '97 %Lawrence Firm -606 Phila -Covington, KY 41011 **Fx:**578-1032

(216) 561-4437 ..**Lewis,** Robert J '90 -18668 Parkland Dr -Shaker Heights 44122

(216) 621-5980 ..**Lewis,** Robert L '73 Legal Aid -1223 W 6th -Cleveland 44113

(216) 566-5500 ..**Lewis,** Robert S '02 %Thompson H LLP -127 Pub Sq -3900 Key Ctr -Cleveland 44114 **Fx:**566-5800

(937) 376-7303 ..**Lewis,** Ronald C '93 Pros -101 N Detroit -Xenia 45385

(216) 664-2270 ..**Lewis,** Sandra R '91 Cleveland Mun Ct -1200 Ontario -Cleveland 44113

(513) 977-8200 ..**Lewis,** Sarah V '03 %Dinsmore & S LLP -255 E 5th -Ste 1900 -Cincinnati 45202 **Fx:**977-8141

(216) 831-0042 ..**Lewis,** Scott M '84 Meyers RF&L LPA -28601 Chagrin Blvd -Ste 500 -Cleveland 44122 **Fx:**831-0542

(513) 942-7900 ..**Lewis,** Stacy A '94 PNG TeleComm -100 Cmmrcial Dr -Fairfield 45014

(480) 648-8721 ..**Lewis,** Stephen '74 Vista Care Inc -4800 N Scttsdl Rd -Ste 5000 -Scottsdale, AZ 85251

(330) 643-2765 ..**Lewis,** Susana B '91 Summit Cnty Pros-CSEA -171 S Main -Akron 44308 **Fx:**643-2822

(937) 222-1234 ..**Lewis,** Terry L '79 (T Lewis Co,LPA) -111 W 1st -Ste 1000 -Dayton 45402 **Fx:**222-1990

(740) 342-4184 ..**Lewis,** Thomas A '77 (T Lewis Co,LPA) -121 S Main -Bx826 -New Lexington 43764

(937) 444-2563 ..**Lewis,** Val E '99 %Kelly & W Co,LPA -108 S High -Mount Orab 45154

(937) 461-1900 ..**Lewis,** Vincent A '99 %S Miles -18 W Monument Av -Dayton 45402

(614) 469-3317 ..**Lewis,** William Blair '98 %Thompson H LLP -10 W Broad -Ste 700 -Columbus 43215 **Fx:**469-3361

(216) 443-7800 ..**Lewis-Bevel,** Ellainna J '92 Cuyahoga Cnty Pros -1200 Ontario -8th Fl -Cleveland 44113 **Fx:**698-2270

(330) 489-3251 ..**L'Hommedieu,** Kevin R '96 Law Dept -218 Cleveland Av SW -Bx24218 -Canton 44702

(216) 595-0071 ..**L'Hommedieu,** Mary Louisa '96 Roth B LLP -5196 Richmond Rd -Bedford Heights 44146 **Fx:**595-0073

(614) 227-2000 ..**Li,** Christine D '04 %Porter WM&A LLP -41 S High -Columbus 43215 **Fx:**227-2100

(440) 878-8200 ..**Li,** Peter B '96 -10749 Pearl Rd -#1D -Strongsville 44136 **Fx:**878-8300

(513) 241-3100 ..**Li,** YanFang M '01 %Lerner S&R -120 E 4th -8th Fl -Cincinnati 45202

(216) 696-3232 ..**Liber,** John D '63 OfCnsl Spangenberg S&L,LLP -1900 E 9th -2400 Natl City Ctr -Cleveland 44114 **Fx:**696-3924

(440) 247-5078 ..**Liber,** John R II '92 -100 N Main -Ste 350 -Chagrin Falls 44022

(740) 633-5551 ..**Liberati,** David K '82 (Sommer L&B Co,LPA) -409 Walnut -Bx279 -Martins Ferry 43935 **Fx:**633-5660

(937) 223-1201 ..**Liberman,** Scott A '92 (Altick & C Co,LPA) -1 S Main -1700 One Dayton Ctr -Dayton 45402 **Fx:**223-5100

(740) 687-6082 ..**Libert,** Donald J '56 -2198 William T Cir -Lancaster 43130

(740) 383-2161 ..**Libster,** Mitchell A '76 Legal Aid -Bx6029 -Marion 43301

(216) 583-8266 ..**Licastro,** Gabriel M '83 (Ernst & Young LLP) -925 Euclid Av -Ste 1300 -Cleveland 44115

(216) 573-6000 ..**Licata,** Louis J '83 (Licata & Assoc Co,LPA) -6480 Rockside Wds Blvd S -Ste 390 -Independence 44131 **Fx:**573-6333

(216) 928-1503 ..**Lichko,** Gregory M '75 (Lichko & S) -55 Pub Sq -Ste 1600 -Cleveland 44113 **Fx:**619-9846

(330) 296-2851 ..**Lichtenberger,** Lisa K '95 Indpndnc of Portage Cnty -161 E Main -Ravenna 44266

(216) 902-4444 ..**Lichtig,** Steven M '92 Kelley JM&S LLP -629 Euclid Av -Ste 1037 -Cleveland 44114 **Fx:**902-4447

(330) 253-1555 ..**Lichtman,** Corey S '02 %D Booher & Assoc Co,LPA -3180 W Market -Fairlawn 44333

(216) 522-0562 ..**Lichtman,** Jeffrey E '71 US Dist Ct -801 Superior -Cleveland 44113

(914) 828-8842 ..**Licitra,** Lawrence J '87 SrCnsl Swiss Re America -175 King -Armonk, NY 10504 **Fx:**828-7842

.....................**Lick,** Fred Jr. '61 -3820 Clay Mtn Dr -Medina 44256

(419) 627-7696 ..**Lickfelt,** Gary A '73 Erie Cnty Pros -247 Columbus Av -Ste 319 -Sandusky 44870 **Fx:**627-7567

(216) 586-3939 ..**Licygiewicz,** Arthur P '97 %Jones D -901 Lakeside Av -Cleveland 44114 **Fx:**579-0212

(513) 579-4203 ..**Liddy,** J Patrick '96 Fifth Third Bank -38 Fountain Sq Plz -MD10AT68 -Cincinnati 45263 **Fx:**534-1960

(216) 861-0360 ..**Lidrbauch,** Elena A '99 %Hickman & L Co,LPA -1370 Ontario -Ste 1620 -Cleveland 44113 **Fx:**861-3113

(419) 867-8900 ..**Liebenthal,** Jon B '86 Lyden L&C,Ltd -5565 Airport Hwy -Ste 101 -Toledo 43615 **Fx:**867-8909

(440) 930-4001 ..**Lieberman,** Abraham '76 Baumgartner & O -5455 Detroit Rd (Rte 254) -Sheffield Village 44054 **Fx:**934-7205

(330) 972-6229 ..**Lieberman,** Alvin H '64 Univ of Akron -CBA 267 -Akron 44325

(513) 721-5700 ..**Lieberman,** Bernard '52 -216 E 9th -2nd Fl -Cincinnati 45202

(614) 462-4082 ..**Lieberman,** Brett H '97 Ct of Appeals 10th Dist -373 S High -24th Fl -Columbus 43215

(937) 223-5200 ..**Lieberman,** Dennis A '78 (Flanagan LH&S) -318 W 4th -Dayton 45402 **Fx:**223-3335

(440) 893-7700 ..**Lieberman,** Gary L '81 -35 River -Chagrin Falls 44022

(513) 241-3100 ..**Lieberman,** Jon J '92 Lerner S&R -120 E 4th -8th Fl -Cincinnati 45202

(513) 674-1111 ..**Lieberman Lipez & Berman** -415 Glensprings Dr -Ste 102 -Cincinnati 45246

(202) 261-4607 ..**Lieberman,** Michael L '81 ADL -1100 Conn Av NW -Washington, DC 20036 **Fx:**296-2371

(513) 674-1111 ..**Lieberman,** Sidney C '68 (Lieberman L&B) -415 Glensprings Dr -Ste 102 -Cincinnati 45246

(614) 480-4434 ..**Liebersbach,** John W '76 Huntington Natl Bank -41 S High -Bx1558 -Columbus 43287

(614) 469-3939 ..**Liebman,** Helen L '74 Cnsl Jones D -325 John H McConnell Blvd -Ste 600 -Bx165017 -Columbus 43216 **Fx:**461-4198

(513) 721-1904 ..**Liebman,** Robert L '73 -1014 Vine -2525 Kroger Bldg -Cincinnati 45202

(216) 566-5653 ..**Liebson,** Matthew E '99 %Thompson H LLP -127 Pub Sq -3900 Key Ctr -Cleveland 44114 **Fx:**566-5800

(419) 882-0081 ..**Liedel,** Deidre A '98 %LaValley LT&S Co,LPA -5800 Monroe -Bldg F -Sylvania 43560 **Fx:**882-4635

(216) 291-3600 ..**Liederbach,** Kirk W '92 %Bernard & H Co,LPA -5001 Mayfld Rd -Ste 301 -Cleveland 44124 **Fx:**291-0159

(440) 777-0478 ..**Liedtke,** William P '72 -27443 Linwood Cir -North Olmsted 44070

(937) 443-6958 ..**Lienesch,** Theodore D '80 (Thompson H LLP) -2000 Cthse Plz NE -Bx8801 -Dayton 45401 **Fx:**443-6635

(513) 241-3100 ..**Liepold,** Christina M '98 Lerner S&R -120 E 4th -8th Fl -Cincinnati 45202

(513) 939-3300 ..**Lierman,** Dale O '77 D Lierman Co,LPA -1244 Nilles Rd -Ste 9 -Fairfield 45014

(216) 987-4648 ..**Lietzke,** Jeffrey S '96 Cuyahoga Comm Cllg -700 Carnegie Av -Cleveland 44115

(440) 323-6180 ..**Lieux,** Kenneth M '84 -110 Middle Av -Elyria 44035

(216) 696-1422 ..**Liffman,** Kenneth B '79 (McCarthy LC&L Co,LPA) -101 Prospect Av W -1800 Mdlnd Bldg -Cleveland 44115 **Fx:**696-1210

(513) 530-9595 ..**Liggett,** Dennis A '64 -4725 Cornell Rd -Cincinnati 45241

(614) 227-2399 ..**Liggett,** Luther L '81 (Bricker & E LLP) -100 S 3rd -Columbus 43215 **Fx:**227-2390

(860) 285-9798 ..**Liggett,** Thomas E '76 Alstom Power Inc -2000 Day Hill Rd -Bx500 -Windsor, CT 06095

(330) 867-6600 ..**Liggins,** Jasper '75 Glinsek & H -88 S Portage Path -Ste 301 -Akron 44303 **Fx:**867-9720

(419) 248-2600 ..**Light,** C Randolph '66 (Rohrbachers LC&T Co,LPA) -405 Mad Av -8th Fl -Toledo 43604 **Fx:**248-2614

(216) 515-4361 ..**Light,** Jeffrey H '86 Sherwin-Williams -101 W Prospect Av -Cleveland 44115

(419) 242-1400 ..**Light,** Neil H '79 -608 Mad Av -Ste 1400 -Toledo 43604

(937) 294-1715 ..**Light,** Ronald A '82 -40 Southmoor Cir NE -Ofc #6 -Kettering 45429

(740) 892-3443 ..**Light,** Sara G '87 %Hite & H -26 S Main -Bx457 -Utica 43080 **Fx:**892-3556

(202) 616-9352 ..**Lightbody,** Jennifer L '92 US DOJ -1331 Penn Av NW -Rm 700 -Washington, DC 20530

(330) 675-2521 ..**Lightbody,** Susan M '87 %Trumbull Cnty Probate Ct -161 High NW -Warren 44481

(216) 621-7337 ..**Lightbody,** William S '77 -32600 Fairmount Blvd -Pepper Pike 44124

(216) 621-8484 ..**Lightner,** Terri A '04 %Climaco LPW&G Co,LPA -1228 Euclid Av -Ste 900 Halle Bldg -Cleveland 44115 **Fx:**771-1632

.....................**Ligibel,** Bradley T '04 -(Address Unavailable)

(419) 242-4055 ..**Ligibel,** Rebecca K '92 -607 Monroe -Toledo 43604

(216) 221-3079 ..**Liguore,** Maryann T '80 -17831 Lk Rd -Lakewood 44107

(330) 451-7705 ..**Lile,** Jennifer L '00 Stark Cnty Probate Ct -110 Central Plz S -Ste 501 -Canton 44702

.....................**Lile,** Levi W '72 -Bx102 -Bellefontaine 43311

(859) 252-0889 ..**Liles,** James D '74 OfCnsl King & S,PLLC -247 N Bway -Lexington, KY 40507 **Fx:**252-0889

.....................**Liles,** Joshua A '04 -(Address Unavailable)

(440) 646-9721 ..**Lilko,** Robert J '87 -1447 Summit Dr -Mayfield Heights 44124

(216) 781-1700 ..**Lill,** Abby K '04 %Shapero & R Co,LPA -1350 Euclid Av -Ste 1550 -Cleveland 44115 **Fx:**781-1972

(614) 764-1444 ..**Lillard,** Samuel N '88 (Mowery & Y) -425 Metro Pl N -Ste 420 -Dublin 43017 **Fx:**760-8654

(740) 385-2181 ..**Lilley,** Robert L '72 (R Lilley Co,LPA) -9 E 2nd -Bx588 -Logan 43138 **Fx:**385-4531

(843) 766-4700 ..**Lilley,** Robin B '00 -2408 Castlereagh Rd -Charleston, SC 29414

(216) 363-4500 ..**Lillie,** Richard G '79 (Benesch FC&A LLP) -200 Pub Sq -Ste 2300 -Cleveland 44114 **Fx:**363-4588

(330) 799-7711 ..**Lilly,** Jeffrey A '99 UAW Legal Srvcs -1570 S Canfld-Niles Rd -Ste 101 -Youngstown 44515

(216) 781-8435 ..**Lilly,** John C '77 Charter One Bank FSB -1215 Superior Av -Cleveland 44114

(614) 469-4778 ..**Lilly,** Phillip G '87 (Becker & L LLC) -100 E Broad -Ste 2320 -Columbus 43215 **Fx:**469-4779

(440) 838-7600 ..**Lilly,** Stacy N '00 %Janik & D,LLP -9200 S Hills Blvd -Ste 300 -Cleveland 44147 **Fx:**838-7601

(614) 644-2824 ..**Lim,** Edwin Y '77 EPA -122 S Front -Bx1049 -Columbus 43216

(216) 381-3400 ..**Lim,** Gene M '92 (Petronzio S Co,LPA) -5001 Mayfld Rd -Ste 201 -Cleveland 44124

(614) 462-6004 ..**Lim,** Lawrence S '92 Franklin Cnty Common Pleas Ct -369 S High -Columbus 43215

(330) 726-6999 ..**Limbian,** John J '90 -755 Boardman Canfld Rd -Ste P-4 -Youngstown 44512

(419) 674-2284 ..**Limerick,** Colleen P '93 Hardin Cnty Pros -1 Cthse Sq -Ste 50 -Kenton 43326

(419) 782-6055 ..**Liming,** John M '81 (Clemens KL&W,Ltd) -419 5th -Ste 2000 -Bx787 -Defiance 43512

(614) 488-2053 ..**Liming,** Roxi A '98 -1989 W 5th Av -Ste 13 -Columbus 43212

.....................**Limoli,** John K Jr. '92 -1402 Sunset Dr -Fairborn 45324

(614) 719-3355 ..**Lin**, Albert G '03 %Hon RG Cole -85 Marconi Blvd -US Ct Hse
-Columbus 43215

(614) 901-7100 ..**Linch**, Heather L '84 Toukan & Co,CPA -575 Charring Cross Dr
-Westerville 43081 **Fx:**901-7110

(614) 891-6363 ..**Linch**, M Jebb '77 -483 Dempsey Rd -Westerville 43081
Fx:891-6366

(860) 354-8144 ..**Lincicome**, David V '86 -26 North -Bx222 -Roxbury, CT 06783

(239) 262-8888 ..**Lind**, Gary D '81 %Northern Trust Bk -4001 Tamiami Trl N
-Naples, FL 34103 **Fx:**262-4276

(937) 525-0025 ..**Lind**, Gregory K '91 -4 W Main -Ste 415 -Springfield 45502

(513) 534-3719 ..**Lind**, Harry S '94 Fifth Third Bk -38 Fountain Sq Plz
-Cincinnati 45263

(216) 574-2600 ..**Lind**, John K Jr. '91 (Lasko & L Co,LPA) -1406 W 6th -Ste 200
-Cleveland 44113

(216) 687-5506 ..**Lind**, Kermit J '85 CSU-Marshall Cllg of Law -2121 Euclid Av
-LB138 -Cleveland 44115 **Fx:**687-6881
    Lind, Michael W '96 -10 Deshler Av -#8 -Columbus 43206

(216) 586-3939 ..**Lindahl**, Burkhart R '00 %Jones D -901 Lakeside Av
-Cleveland 44114 **Fx:**579-0212

(330) 499-6000 ..**Lindamood**, John B '66 (Baker DBW&M) -400 S Main
-Canton 44720 **Fx:**449-6423

(614) 466-0195 ..**Lindamood**, Suzanne '91 Legis Srvc Commssn -77 S High
-Columbus 43215

(513) 381-2838 ..**Lindberg**, Charles D '54 OfCnsl Taft S&H LLP -425 Walnut
-Ste 1800 -Cincinnati 45202 **Fx:**381-0205

(260) 449-7633 ..**Lindberg**, Jon L '03 -715 S Calhoun -Fort Wayne, IN 46802

(216) 621-0200 ..**Lindberg**, Lawrence V '73 (Baker & H LLP) -1900 E 9th -Ste 3200
-Cleveland 44114 **Fx:**696-0740

(419) 724-0030 ..**Lindberg**, Mark S '88 LAWO -520 Mad Av -Ste 640 -Toledo 43604
Fx:321-1582

(513) 361-8033 ..**Lindeman-Lorenz**, Laura '91 PricewaterhouseCoopers
-720 E Pete Rose Way -Cincinnati 45202

(614) 464-1211 ..**Lindemann**, Jeffrey N '91 (Frost BT LLC) -10 W Broad -Ste 1000
-Columbus 43215 **Fx:**464-1737

(216) 621-0590 ..**Linden**, Michael J '75 -1111 Chester Av -Ste 400
-Cleveland 44114

(440) 350-2683 ..**Linden**, Taylir K '94 Lake Cnty Pros -105 Main -Bx490
-Painesville 44077 **Fx:**350-2585

(330) 873-2518 ..**Lindenberger**, Jeffrey K '82 Nationwide Ins Co -809 White Pond
Dr -Akron 44320

(214) 880-9754 ..**Linder**, Herbert W '95 Dept of Justice -717 N Harwood -Ste 400
-Dallas, TX 75201

(614) 865-4700 ..**Linder**, Mark E '89 OCSEA -390 Worthngtn Rd -Ste A
-Westerville 43082

(513) 721-1129 ..**Lindgren**, Lawrence F '95 -114 E 8th -Cincinnati 45202

(614) 466-4395 ..**Lindgren**, Thomas G '87 Atty Gen -150 E Gay -Columbus 43215
Fx:644-8764

(614) 222-3924 ..**Lindholm**, Jason P '04 Ernst & Young -41 S High
-1100 Huntngtn Ctr -Columbus 43215

(513) 421-6630 ..**Lindhorst & Dreidame Co,LPA** -312 Walnut -Ste 2300
-Cincinnati 45202

(216) 363-5220 ..**Lindner**, Daniel F '94 (Lindner WC&B,LLP) -55 Pub Sq -Ste 1600
-Cleveland 44113

(216) 621-5300 ..**Lindner**, David J '01 %Buckingham D&B,LLP -1375 E 9th
-Ste 1700 -Cleveland 44114 **Fx:**621-5440

(216) 363-5220 ..**Lindner Weaver Crane & Brondou,LLP** -55 Pub Sq -Ste 1600
-Cleveland 44113

(440) 333-0011 ..**Lindon**, Elizabeth A '99 (Lindon & L) -1250 Linda -Ste 104
-Rocky River 44116 **Fx:**(419) 710-4925

(440) 333-0011 ..**Lindon**, James Lee '97 (Lindon & L) -1250 Linda -Ste 104
-Rocky River 44116 **Fx:**(419) 710-4925

(330) 865-9635 ..**Lindow**, Michael B '04 (Bednarski R&L) -159 S Main -Ste 300
-Akron 44308

(419) 867-5294 ..**Lindower**, Kurt J '90 Millar Elevator Srvc Co -1530 Timberwolf Dr
-Bx960 -Holland 43528

(216) 566-5500 ..**Lindquist**, David C '04 %Thompson H LLP -127 Pub Sq
-3900 Key Ctr -Cleveland 44114 **Fx:**566-5800

(330) 490-4726 ..**Lindroos**, Michael E '83 SrCnsl Diebold,Inc -5995 Mayfair Rd
-Bx3077 -North Canton 44720 **Fx:**490-4450

(215) 862-9096 ..**Lindsay**, C L III '97 Co-Star -Bx491 -Solebury, PA 18963

(614) 466-3998 ..**Lindsay**, George B '75 Unemploymnt Comp Commssn
-145 S Front -Bx182299 -Columbus 43218

(419) 248-4611 ..**Lindsay**, James M '86 -3513 Cedar Crk Ct -Maumee 43537

(937) 225-4464 ..**Lindsay**, Karen R '98 2nd Dist Ct of Appls -41 N Perry -Rm 515
-Bx972 -Dayton 45422

(330) 761-9960 ..**Lindsay**, Shawn P '04 State & Federal Communications,Inc
-80 S Summit -Ste 100 -Akron 44308
    Lindsay, Veronica D '04 -(Address Unavailable)

(330) 453-3999 ..**Lindsey**, James B Jr. '77 (JB Lindsey Jr Co,LPA)
-116 Cleveland Av NW -500 Courtyard Ctr -Canton 44702

(614) 466-3998 ..**Lindsey**, Kirk A '96 Unemploymnt Comp Commssn -145 S Front
-Bx182299 -Columbus 43218

(614) 442-5858 ..**Lindsey**, Scott T '96 Lindsey,LLC -1880 MacKenzie Dr -Bx20345
-Columbus 43220

(614) 442-5858 ..**Lindsey**, Thomas H '65 Lindsey,LLC -1880 MacKenzie Dr
-Bx20345 -Columbus 43220

(614) 583-5020 ..**Lindsey**, Thomas K '86 %City Atty -3600 Tremont Rd
-Columbus 43221

(419) 255-1222 ..**Lindsley**, William R Jr. '76 Lindsley & Assoc -421 N Mich -Ste D
-Toledo 43624

(614) 365-9900 ..**Lindsmith**, Quintin F '84 (Zeiger TL&L,LLP) -41 S High
-Ste 3500 Huntngtn Ctr -Columbus 43215 **Fx:**365-7900

(937) 456-5300 ..**Lindstrom**, Carol P '80 -121 E Main -Bx313 -Eaton 45320

(614) 882-9803 ..**Lindwall**, Robert R '73 -6491 Faircrest Rd -Columbus 43229

(304) 424-1933 ..**Line**, Mindi D '04 WV Supreme Ct of Appeals -2 Govt Sq -Rm 321
-Parkersburg, WV 26101

(513) 489-1040 ..**Lineback**, Charles S '78 -11427 Reed Hartman Hwy
-Cincinnati 45241

(216) 344-3944 ..**Lineberger**, Martha E '94 -75 Pub Sq -Ste 920 -Cleveland 44113

(740) 681-9290 ..**Linehan**, James M '88 (Linehan & Assoc,LPA) -120½ E Main
-Lancaster 43130

(216) 348-5400 ..**Linehan**, Paul W '98 %McDonald H Co,LPA -600 Superior Av E
-Ste 2100 -Cleveland 44114 **Fx:**348-5474

    Lines, John K '84 TriTech Sftwre Syst -9860 Mesa Rim Rd
-San Diego, CA 92121

(216) 621-0150 ..**Linetsky**, Yuri C '00 %Hahn L&P LLP -3300 BP Twr/200 Pub Sq
-Ste 3300 -Cleveland 44114 **Fx:**241-2824

(216) 621-1113 ..**Ling**, Daniel R '03 %Renner OB&S,LLP -1621 Euclid Av -19th Fl
-Cleveland 44115 **Fx:**621-6165

(216) 696-8730 ..**Ling**, John M '02 %Amin & T LLP -1900 E 9th -24th Fl Natl City Ctr
-Cleveland 44114 **Fx:**696-8731

(440) 395-0252 ..**Ling**, Raymond S '90 Progressive Casualty Ins Co -300 N Cmmns
-Mayfield Village 44143

(216) 443-6350 ..**Ling**, Wendy A '93 8th Dist Ct of Appls -1 Lakeside Av -#202
-Cleveland 44113 **Fx:**443-2044

(419) 213-4700 ..**Lingo**, Jeffrey D '90 %Lucas Cnty Pros -Adams & Erie
-Lucas Cnty Cthse -Toledo 43624

(614) 228-6888 ..**Linhart**, Brian E '99 Havens W LLC -141 E Town -Ste 200
-Columbus 43215 **Fx:**228-6878
    Linhart, Larry R '71 -4683 Yantis Dr -New Albany 43054

(216) 591-1599 ..**Linick**, David I '75 -26703 Hurlingham Rd -Beachwood 44122

(216) 621-0150 ..**Link**, Bradley C '04 %Hahn L&P LLP -3300 BP Twr/200 Pub Sq
-Ste 3300 -Cleveland 44114 **Fx:**241-2824

(216) 926-6305 ..**Link**, David M Jr. '04 -1244 Avondale Rd -South Euclid 44121
Fx:(440) 815-2015

(360) 476-2156 ..**Link**, James A '95 Naval Legal Srvcs Ofc NW -365 S Barclay
-Bldg 433 -Bremerton, WA 98314
    Link, Jeanette '03 -(Address Unavailable)

(330) 376-2700 ..**Link**, Terrence H II '99 %Roetzel & A,LPA -222 S Main
-Akron 44308 **Fx:**376-4577

(419) 530-3364 ..**Linker**, Carol W '80 Univ of Toledo Law Schl -2801 W Bancroft
-Toledo 43606

(239) 394-9246 ..**Linman**, Elmer K '72 KL Cnsltng -1250 Osprey Ct -Marco
Island, FL 34145 **Fx:**394-9246

(972) 605-5496 ..**Linn**, Charles A IV '87 EDS -5400 Legacy Dr -H3-3D-05
-Plano, TX 75024

(513) 381-8430 ..**Linn**, Cliff G '85 Immerman & T Co,LPA -632 Vine -Ste 1010
-Cincinnati 45202

(216) 263-8548 ..**Linn**, Martin P '82 McDonald Invstmnts -800 Superior Av
-Cleveland 44114

(216) 623-0000 ..**Linn**, Michael D '86 (Javitch B&R) -1300 E 9th -14th Fl
-Cleveland 44114 **Fx:**623-0190

(216) 491-5000 ..**Linn**, Michael S '69 -1370 Ontario -Ste 1520 -Cleveland 44113
    Linne, Sheryl M '86 -(Address Unavailable)

(513) 732-7385 ..**Linneman**, Daniel E '04 Clermont Cnty Cmn Pleas Ct -270 Main
-Batavia 45103

(513) 721-4450 ..**Linneman**, Jerome Robert '01 %Santen & H -312 Walnut
-Ste 3100 -Cincinnati 45202

(330) 258-8000 ..**Linnen**, Jerome T Jr. '87 (Linnen Co,LPA) -789 W Market -Akron
44303 **Fx:**253-8095
    Linnen, Stephen P '99 -Bx429 -Westfield Center 44251

(513) 607-4002 ..**Linnenberg**, John W '69 -5971 Beechtop -Cincinnati 45233

(704) 423-5520 ..**Linnert**, Terrence G '75 BF Goodrich Co -2730 W Tyvola Rd
-Charlotte, NC 28217

(770) 578-5736 ..**Linscott**, Walt A '90 Solvay Pharm,Inc -901 Sawyer Rd
-Marietta, GA 30062

(419) 774-5573 ..**Linsker**, Jeffrey A '76 Richland Cnty Cmn Pleas Ct -50 Park Av E
-Mansfield 44902

(216) 771-5800 ..**Linton & Hirshman** -700 W St Clair Av -Hoyt Block Ste 300
-Cleveland 44113

(330) 434-3000 ..**Linton**, Robert F '60 OfCnsl Roderick & L -One Cascade Plz
-Ste 1500 -Akron 44308 **Fx:**434-9220

(216) 771-5800 ..**Linton**, Robert F Jr. '84 (Linton & H) -700 W St Clair Av
-Hoyt Block Ste 300 -Cleveland 44113

(440) 543-6509 ..**Linton**, Thomas A '73 -19105 Snyder Rd -Chagrin Falls 44023

(614) 451-0206 ..**Linville**, James B '01 Integrated Title -4675 Winterset Dr
-Columbus 43220 **Fx:**451-0179

(614) 228-1541 ..**Linville**, Ronald G '80 (Baker & H LLP) -65 E State -Ste 2100
-Columbus 43215 **Fx:**462-2616

(216) 566-5596 ..**Linville**, Timothy H '03 %Thompson H LLP -127 Pub Sq
-3900 Key Ctr -Cleveland 44114 **Fx:**566-5800

(614) 734-3320 ..**Lipari**, Gretchen M '93 Progressive Ins -5500 Frantz Rd -Ste 157
-Dublin 43017 **Fx:**798-4858

(614) 464-4644 ..**Lipchak**, Melissa R '91 -50 W Broad -Ste 2200 -Columbus 43215

(937) 865-6800 ..**Lipchik**, Marie-Lise '93 Lexis/Nexis -Bx933 -Dayton 45401

(937) 222-2424 ..**Lipcius**, Jesse R '04 %Freund F&A -1 S Main -Ste 1800
-Dayton 45402 **Fx:**222-5369

(216) 621-2234 ..**Lipcsik**, Robert N '96 %Tarolli SC&T -526 Superior Av
-1111 Leader Bldg -Cleveland 44114 **Fx:**621-4072

(513) 674-1111 ..**Lipez**, Ronald A '70 (Lieberman L&B) -415 Glensprings Dr
-Ste 102 -Cincinnati 45246

(202) 653-7188 ..**Lipinski**, Michael L '03 US Ofc of Special Cnsl -1730 M NW
-Washington, DC 20036

(419) 243-9005 ..**Lipinski**, Tracy A '03 %Franklin & G,LLC -420 Mad Av -Ste 1101
-Toledo 43604 **Fx:**243-9404

(330) 743-1171 ..**Lipka**, Thomas J '96 (Manchester BP&U) -201 E Commerce
-Atrium Level 2 Commerce Bldg -Youngstown 44503
Fx:743-1190

(513) 523-4111 ..**Lipnickey**, Susan C '91 (Robinson & L Co,LPA) -Park Place W
-Fay Bldg -Oxford 45056

(216) 692-0577 ..**Lipold**, Albin '05 -24913 Plsnt Trl -Richmond Heights 44143

(614) 248-6508 ..**Lipovsek**, Kimberly J '93 Banc One Mgt Corp -100 E Broad
-OHI-0158 -Columbus 43215

(937) 436-0033 ..**Lipowicz**, Richard A '80 (Ruffolo SD&L) -7501 Paragon Rd
-Dayton 45459

(937) 435-2322 ..**Lipp**, Robert W III '00 (R Lipp II,LPA,Inc) -986 Marycrest Ln
-Dayton 45429 **Fx:**435-2342

(740) 654-7777 ..**Lipp**, Thomas C '78 (Lantz & L) -123 S Broad -Bx2240
-Lancaster 43130

(614) 462-3555 ..**Lippe**, Christine B '86 Franklin Cnty Pros -373 S High
-Columbus 43215

(614) 224-1979 ..**Lippe**, Jerry L '67 (J Lippe Co,LPA) -592 S 3rd -Columbus 43215

(216) 696-7666 ..**Lippe**, Stuart H '75 -1900 Pub Sq -Ste 930 -Cleveland 44114

(513) 621-6464 ..**Lippert**, Amy E '01 %Graydon H&R LLP -511 Walnut
-1900 Fifth Third Ctr -Cincinnati 45202 **Fx:**651-3836

(513) 563-6161 ..**Lippert**, Gary M '70 -11137 Main -Cincinnati 45241

(513) 241-1950 ..**Lippert,** James W '69 Brown LH&E -7 W 7th -Ste 1950
   -Cincinnati 45202 **Fx:**241-4095

(419) 627-7697 ..**Lippert,** Jeanne '92 Erie Cnty Pros -247 Columbus Av -Ste 319
   -Sandusky 44870 **Fx:**627-7567

(513) 241-1950 ..**Lippert,** Richard H '65 (Brown LH&E) -7 W 7th -Ste 1950
   -Cincinnati 45202 **Fx:**241-4095

(614) 937-1300 ..**Lippman,** Allison J '02 -545 E Town -Columbus 43213
   Fx:449-2191

(614) 365-4100 ..**Lipps,** Jeffrey A '81 (Carpenter & L LLP) -280 N High
   -Ste 1300 280 Plz -Columbus 43215 **Fx:**365-9145

(513) 381-2838 ..**Lips,** J Alan '68 OfCnsl Taft S&H LLP -425 Walnut -Ste 1800
   -Cincinnati 45202 **Fx:**381-0205

(216) 861-5000 ..**Lipski,** Christopher '89 (Ernst & Young) -1300 Huntgtn Bldg
   -925 Euclid Av -Cleveland 44115

(216) 241-7226 ..**Lipson,** Ronald M '58 -55 Pub Sq -Ste 1400 -Cleveland 44113

(937) 435-4554 ..**Liptock,** Thomas P '86 %Gunnoe & Assoc
   -2525 Miamisburg Centervll Rd -Centerville 45459

(419) 243-1088 ..**Lipton,** Andrew S '80 -412 14th -Toledo 43624

(216) 368-3318 ..**Lipton,** Judith P '80 CWRU Law Schl -11075 East Blvd
   -Cleveland 44106

(302) 577-8477 ..**Lisa,** James P Jr. '86 DE Economic Dvlpmnt Ofc -820 N French
   -10th Fl -Wilmington, DE 19801

(216) 241-0220 ..**Lisboa,** Kimberly A '93 ITX Corp -4400 Carnegie Av
   -Cleveland 44103

(330) 643-3554 ..**Lischner,** Anna E '90 Industrial Commssn of OH -161 S High
   -Ste 301 -Akron 44308

(440) 888-4220 ..**Liscynesky,** Marta L '93 -5907 State Rd -Parma 44134

(440) 888-4220 ..**Liscynesky,** Orest W '83 -5907 State Rd -Parma 44134
   Lisher, James R II '04 -(Address Unavailable)

(614) 227-2000 ..**Lisle,** Shawn G '01 %Porter WM&A LLP -41 S High
   -Columbus 43215 **Fx:**227-2100

(216) 787-3030 ..**Lisowski,** Sandra J '87 Atty Gen -615 W Superior Av -11th Fl
   -Cleveland 44113 **Fx:**787-3480

(614) 221-1771 ..**Liss,** Robert B '83 -145 N High -Ste 900 -Columbus 43215

(513) 421-6630 ..**Liss,** William Jay '97 %Lindhorst & D Co,LPA -312 Walnut
   -Ste 2300 -Cincinnati 45202

(440) 514-8694 ..**Lissauer,** Rick A '94 -15 Brandywood Dr -Pepper Pike 44124

(440) 327-5721 ..**Lissner,** Joan E '90 -Bx39267 -North Ridgeville 44039

(740) 344-2518 ..**List,** A David '58 -724 Snowdon Dr -Newark 43055 **Fx:**344-2518

(614) 469-1400 ..**List,** David Andrew '91 (Clark PR&S Co,LPA) -471 E Broad
   -Ste 1400 -Columbus 43215 **Fx:**469-0900

(440) 329-5389 ..**List,** Faye S '82 Lorain Cnty Pros -225 Court -3rd Fl -Elyria 44035

(216) 696-7600 ..**List,** Martin S '81 (Duvin C&H) -1301 E 9th -20th Fl Erievw Twr
   -Cleveland 44114 **Fx:**696-2038

(859) 491-4268 ..**List,** Robert E '82 -526 Greenup -Covington, KY 41011

(440) 329-5389 ..**List,** Stephen A '79 Lorain Cnty Pros -225 Court -3rd Fl
   -Elyria 44035

(216) 363-4500 ..**Listati,** Ezio A '90 (Benesch FC&A LLP) -200 Pub Sq -Ste 2300
   -Cleveland 44114 **Fx:**363-4588

(614) 224-1222 ..**Lister,** Kelli E '95 %Maguire & S,LLP -250 Civic Ctr Dr -Ste 200
   -Columbus 43215 **Fx:**224-1236

(440) 350-2098 ..**Lister,** Kevin S '86 Lake Cnty Ct of Common Pleas -Bx490
   -Painesville 44077

(614) 228-6131 ..**Liston,** Dennis D '74 (McNamara & M,LLP) -88 E Broad -Ste 1250
   -Columbus 43215 **Fx:**228-6126

(614) 221-1341 ..**Liston,** Jefferson E '78 (Tyack B&L Co,PA) -536 S High
   -Columbus 43215 **Fx:**228-0253

(614) 645-8255 ..**Liston,** Teresa Lea '82 Cnty Mun Ct Judge -375 S High -Columbus
   43215

(254) 287-1850 ..**Litka,** Timothy D '99 US Army JAG Corp -Bahalion Av
   -Fort Hood, TX 76544

(614) 469-3939 ..**Litle,** Jeffrey D '99 %Jones D -325 John H McConnell Blvd
   -Ste 600 -Bx165017 -Columbus 43216 **Fx:**461-4198

(614) 365-2700 ..**Litle,** T Bennett '04 %Squire S&D LLP -41 S High
   -1300 Huntgtn Ctr -Columbus 43215 **Fx:**365-2499
   Litt, Arthur M '56 -1440 Powers Way -Venice, FL 34292

(614) 227-2305 ..**Litt,** Gordon F '85 (Bricker & E LLP) -100 S 3rd -Columbus 43215
   Fx:227-2390

(216) 586-3939 ..**Litt,** Shoshana E '03 %Jones D -901 Lakeside Av
   -Cleveland 44114 **Fx:**579-0212

(614) 424-5071 ..**Litteral,** Malesa A '98 Battelle Memorial Inst -505 King Av
   -Rm A-1-89 -Columbus 43201

(740) 321-6013 ..**Little,** Anne C '95 Owens Corning -2790 Columbus Rd
   -Granville 43023

(479) 204-8111 ..**Little,** Arthur F '95 Wal-Mart Stores Inc -702 SW 8th
   -Bentonville, AR 72716

(239) 213-0402 ..**Little,** Catherine Cicchini '97 -4100 Corp Sq -Ste 160
   -Naples, FL 34104

(973) 385-4401 ..**Little,** Darryl C '94 Pfizer Inc -201 Tabor Rd
   -Morris Plains, NJ 07950

(740) 454-1223 ..**Little,** David A '67 SE OH Lgl Srvcs -27 N 6th -Ste B
   -Zanesville 43701

(937) 434-6040 ..**Little,** Don A '66 (Little D&P) -7501 Paragon Rd -Dayton 45459

(330) 456-4576 ..**Little,** Donald R '66 -1400 Market Av N -Canton 44714

(740) 992-6689 ..**Little,** Douglas W '79 (Little S&W,LLP) -211-213 E 2nd -Bx686
   -Pomeroy 45769 **Fx:**992-5168

(937) 434-6040 ..**Little Duncan & Pinchot** -7501 Paragon Rd -Dayton 45459

(614) 462-3555 ..**Little,** Elza M '91 Franklin Cnty Pros -373 S High
   -Columbus 43215

(937) 544-2581 ..**Little,** Jessica A '03 %D Bubp -307 N Market -West Union 45693
   Fx:544-1802

(330) 643-2250 ..**Little,** Jonathan D '04 9th Dist Ct of Appls -161 S High -Ste 504
   -Akron 44308

(304) 624-8147 ..**Little,** Kelly J '96 %Steptoe & J,PLLC -Bank One Ctr -6th Fl
   -Bx2190 -Clarksburg, WV 26302 **Fx:**624-8183

(614) 365-9900 ..**Little,** Marion H Jr. '89 (Zeiger TL&L,LLP) -41 S High
   -Ste 3500 Huntngtn Ctr -Columbus 43215 **Fx:**365-7900

(513) 871-8900 ..**Little Meyers Garretson & Associates** -2651 Observatory Av
   -Cincinnati 45208

(202) 296-2116 ..**Little,** Michael B '96 Consumers Energy Co -1016 16th NW
   -Ste 500 -Washington, DC 20036

(330) 923-5315 ..**Little,** Sarah L '04 MH Kreiner -2020 Front -Ste 200
   -Cuyahoga Falls 44221

(614) 885-4980 ..**Little,** Shawn A '91 -5655 N High -Ste 202 -Worthington 43085

(740) 992-2186 ..**Little Sheets & Warner, LLP** -211-213 E 2nd -Bx686
   -Pomeroy 45769 **Fx:**992-5168

(614) 466-2980 ..**Little,** Tamara S '83 Atty Gen -30 E Broad -Columbus 43215
   Fx:728-9470

(937) 333-4369 ..**Littlejohn,** Billy C '73 Mun Ct Judge -301 W 3rd -313
   -Dayton 45402

(937) 449-2800 ..**Littlejohn,** Gail H '83 OfCnsl Chernesky H&K PLL
   -10 Cthse Plz SW -Ste 1100 -Dayton 45402 **Fx:**449-2821

(614) 540-3940 ..**Littlejohn,** Glen E '95 Jordan West Cos -2000 Polaris Pkwy
   -Ste 200 -Columbus 43240

(614) 463-4201 ..**Littler Mendelson,PC** -21 E State -Ste 1600 -Columbus 43215
   Fx:221-3301

(937) 399-8415 ..**Littleton,** Charles D Jr. '51 -4900 Mechanicsburg Rd -Bx1368
   -Springfield 45501

(513) 724-2969 ..**Littman,** Donald F '65 -5014 Burdsall Rd -Williamsburg 45176

(513) 946-3000 ..**Littner,** Jay G '86 Hamilton Cnty Pros -230 E 9th -Cincinnati 45202
   Fx:946-3017

(219) 416-3700 ..**Litton,** Arthur C II '89 Triple Crown Srvcs Co -2720 Dupont
   Commerce Ct -Ste 200 -Fort Wayne, IN 46825

(775) 784-4879 ..**Litton,** Lauren J '94 Natl Cncl of Juvenile & Fam -Bx8970
   -Reno, NV 89507

(614) 228-5151 ..**Littrell,** Barry W '83 (Gallagher GPT&L LLP) -471 E Broad -19th Fl
   -Columbus 43215 **Fx:**228-0032

(614) 228-8400 ..**Littrell,** Rex A '89 (Ulmer & B LLP) -88 E Broad -Ste 1600
   -Columbus 43215 **Fx:**228-8561

(513) 357-9776 ..**Litts,** Norman W Jr. '91 Indstrl Commssn of OH -125 E Court
   -Cincinnati 45202

(937) 890-4787 ..**Litvin,** Joseph '73 Joseph Litvin ESQ -6460 Noranda Dr
   -Dayton 45415
   Litwin, Amy L '92 -283 Compton Rd -Cincinnati 45215
   Litwin, Erica N '99 HQ USAF/JAX -1420 Air Force Pentagon
   -Washington, DC 20330

(513) 721-8880 ..**Litz,** Stanley J '77 -1228 Louden -Cincinnati 45202

(513) 871-8812 ..**Litzinger,** Jerrold J '77 Sentron Med Inc -2134 Madison Rd
   -Cincinnati 45208

(216) 621-3344 ..**Litzow,** Joan M '84 -55 Pub Sq -Ste 2240 -Cleveland 44113

(202) 663-7950 ..**Liu,** Fang '02 %Sughrue M,PLLC -2100 Penn Av NW
   -Washington, DC 20037

(513) 961-6200 ..**Lively,** Michael E '96 %Markesbery & R Co,LPA
   -2368 Victory Pkwy -Ste 200 -Bx6491 -Cincinnati 45206

(330) 836-9111 ..**Livick,** Anthony '80 URS Corp -564 White Pond Dr -Akron 44320

(937) 339-1500 ..**Livingston,** James W '69 (Shipman D&L) -215 W Water -Bx310
   -Troy 45373 **Fx:**339-1519

(937) 222-0500 ..**Livingston,** Jeffrey D '93 -120 W 2nd -Ste 1717 -Dayton 45402

(513) 622-1962 ..**Livingston,** Jennifer Lyon '03 Procter & Gamble
   -8700 Mason-Mntgmry Rd -Mason 45040

(601) 949-4593 ..**Livingston-Wilson,** Karen E '90 Butler SOS&C -Bx22567
   -Jackson, MS 39225

(216) 241-2838 ..**Livingstone,** Fred J '50 OfCnsl Taft S&H LLP -200 Pub Sq
   -3500 BP Twr -Cleveland 44114 **Fx:**241-3707

(614) 224-7771 ..**Livorno & Arnett Co,LPA** -280 N High -Ste 1410
   -Columbus 43215 **Fx:**224-7775

(614) 224-7771 ..**Livorno,** John F '72 (Livorno & A Co,LPA) -280 N High -Ste 1410
   -Columbus 43215 **Fx:**224-7775

(440) 835-9535 ..**Liwosz,** John C Jr. '64 -27397 Detroit Rd -Westlake 44145

(440) 899-6776 ..**Ljubi,** Sharon J '81 %WE Reichard,LPA -25109 Detroit Rd
   -Ste 300 -Westlake 44145

(614) 292-9176 ..**Lloyd,** Angela M '04 OSU Moritz Cllg of Law -55 W 12th Av
   -Columbus 43210 **Fx:**292-1383

(614) 224-1222 ..**Lloyd,** John A '00 %Maguire & S,LLP -250 Civic Ctr Dr -Ste 200
   -Columbus 43215 **Fx:**224-1236

(614) 365-4100 ..**Lloyd,** Katheryn M '02 %Carpenter & L LLP -280 N High
   -Ste 1300 280 Plz -Columbus 43215 **Fx:**365-9145

(614) 462-5034 ..**Lloyd,** Melissa C '99 %Schottenstein Z&D -250 West -Bx165020
   -Columbus 43216 **Fx:**462-5155

(614) 645-7385 ..**Lloyd,** Paula J '85 City Atty -90 W Broad -Columbus 43215

(330) 208-1000 ..**Lloyd,** Philip A '72 OfCnsl Vorys SS&P LLP -106 S Main
   -First Natl Twr -Akron 44308
   Lloyd, Richard D '04 -(Address Unavailable)

(440) 285-0300 ..**Lloyd,** Scott A '90 Eltech Systms Corp -100 7th Av -Ste 300
   -Chardon 44024

(740) 676-2034 ..**Lloyd,** Scott A '93 (Lancione & L,LPA) -3800 Jffrsn -Bellaire 43906
   Fx:676-3931

(216) 831-0042 ..**Lloyd,** Thomas J '99 %Meyers RF&L LPA -28601 Chagrin Blvd
   -Ste 500 -Cleveland 44122 **Fx:**831-0542

(740) 432-7414 ..**Lloyd,** Thomas R '47 -1350 Edgeworth Av -Cambridge 43725

(740) 676-2034 ..**Lloyd,** Tracey L '99 (Lancione & L,LPA) -3800 Jffrsn
   -Bellaire 43906 **Fx:**676-3931

(216) 664-4287 ..**Loar,** Estella L '80 City of Cleveland -601 Lakeside Av
   -Project Manager -Cleveland 44114

(614) 752-2450 ..**Lobb,** Christopher M '91 OH Sec of State -180 E Broad
   -Columbus 43215 **Fx:**466-5409

(216) 861-6820 ..**Lobe,** Thomas G '79 -1280 W 3rd -Cleveland 44113

(216) 566-1661 ..**Lobo,** Alfred D '64 -526 Superior Av -Ste 933 -Cleveland 44114

(216) 696-7600 ..**Lobritz,** Meredith A '03 %Duvin C&H -1301 E 9th -20th Fl Erievw
   Twr -Cleveland 44114 **Fx:**696-2038

(440) 350-1616 ..**Lobur,** John S '01 %Black & Assoc Co,LPA -1501 Mad Av
   -Painesville 44077 **Fx:**350-1691

(330) 253-1101 ..**LoCascio,** Thomas J '88 -80 S Summit -400 Courtyard Sq
   -Akron 44308

(330) 425-4201 ..**Locke,** Faye D '02 %Reimer L&A Co,LPA -2450 Edison Blvd
   -Bx968 -Twinsburg 44087 **Fx:**487-0923

(419) 281-0171 ..**Locke,** Gregory F '78 (Nordstrom & L) -34 W 2nd -Bx366
   -Ashland 44805

(216) 520-0088 ..**Locke,** Kevin J '90 Pepple & W Ltd -5005 Rockside Rd -Ste 260
   -Cleveland 44131 **Fx:**520-0044

(419) 281-0171 ..**Locke,** Nancy N '77 (Nordstrom & L) -34 W 2nd -Bx366 -Ashland
   44805

(216) 689-3907 ..**Locke,** Susan S '78 KeyBank NA -127 Pub Sq
   -19th Fl, OH-01-127-0200 -Cleveland 44114 **Fx:**689-1709

(440) 323-6545 ..**Locke Graves,** Lisa A '91 Elyria Municipal Ct -328 Broad
   -Elyria 44035

(513) 569-9999 ..**Lockemeyer,** David S '92 (Triona & L,Ltd) -2909 Vernon Pl
-Cincinnati 45219 **Fx:**569-9998

(937) 225-2910 ..**Lockhart,** Gregory G '76 US Atty -200 W 2nd -602 Fed Bldg
-Dayton 45402

(330) 869-8149 ..**Lockhart,** John D '01 Summit Empire Prop -1700 W Market
-Ste 212 -Akron 44313

(419) 241-1200 ..**Lockhart,** Margaret J '88 Cooper & W,LPA -900 Adams
-Toledo 43624 **Fx:**242-5675

(317) 638-2922 ..**Lockman,** David M '89 (Maginot M&B LLP) -111 Monument Cir
-Ste 3000 -Indianapolis, IN 46204 **Fx:**638-2139

(419) 333-3552 ..**Lockshin,** Andrew C '02 -802 Court -Fremont 43420

(330) 376-3300 ..**Lockshin,** Mary Jo '81 (Stark & K Co,LPA) -76 S Main -Ste 1512
-Akron 44308 **Fx:**376-6237

(513) 556-0093 ..**Lockwood,** Bert B Jr. '81 Univ of Cincinnati -417 McAlpin Av
-Cincinnati 45220

(513) 853-2850 ..**Lockwood,** Thomas M '92 -5343 Hmltn Av -Cincinnati 45224

(216) 696-7170 ..**LoConti,** Dennis N '82 Forbes F & Assoc Co,LPA
-614 W Superior Av -700 Rckfllr Bldg -Cleveland 44113
..................**LoConti,** Joseph E '77 -6140 Parkland Blvd -Ste 300
-Cleveland 44124

(614) 644-3372 ..**Lodge,** Connie M '87 Dept Ins -2100 Stella Ct -Columbus 43215

(419) 241-9000 ..**Lodge,** Gregory T '82 (Shumaker L&K,LLP) -1000 Jackson
-Toledo 43624 **Fx:**241-6894

(419) 255-7552 ..**Lodge,** Terry J '79 -316 N Mich -Ste 520 -Toledo 43624
Fx:255-8582

(614) 469-3246 ..**Lodge,** Thomas E '81 (Thompson H LLP) -10 W Broad -Ste 700
-Columbus 43215 **Fx:**469-3361

(330) 744-5211 ..**Lodge,** Thomas J '77 (Roth BRS&L,LPA) -100 Fed Plz E -Ste 600
-Youngstown 44503 **Fx:**744-3184

(330) 454-9960 ..**Lo Dico,** Steven L '89 -116 Cleveland Av NW -Ste 808
-Canton 44702

(216) 378-9730 ..**Lodwick,** Sheila A '82 (Shapiro & L Co,LPA) -27600 Chagrin Blvd
-Ste 340 -Woodmere 44122

(954) 831-6955 ..**Loe,** W Anthony '85 State Atty -201 SE 6th
-Fort Lauderdale, FL 33301 **Fx:**831-6171

(216) 621-0200 ..**Loeb,** James A '88 (Baker & H LLP) -1900 E 9th -Ste 3200
-Cleveland 44114 **Fx:**696-0740

(216) 443-4947 ..**Loeb,** Lawrence R '72 -23130 Lyman Blvd -Shaker Heights 44122

(513) 579-1707 ..**Loeb Vollman & Friedmann** -1014 Vine -2150 Kroger Bldg
-Cincinnati 45202

(513) 367-2141 ..**Loechel,** Angela G '97 %D Meyer Jr -1005 Harrison Av
-Harrison 45030

(419) 732-1041 ..**Loeffler,** Donald B '85 -122 N Adams -Port Clinton 43452

(419) 244-8351 ..**Loeffler,** Joseph H '88 Toledo Legal Aid Soc -555 N Erie
-Toledo 43624

(330) 688-1806 ..**Loepp,** Thomas C '90 (Maistros & L) -3580 Darrow Rd
-Stow 44224 **Fx:**688-1103

(216) 621-0200 ..**Loesch,** Robert M '92 (Baker & H LLP) -1900 E 9th -Ste 3200
-Cleveland 44114 **Fx:**696-0740

(216) 241-6602 ..**Loesel,** Pamela E '95 (Weston HFP&H LLP) -50 Pub Sq
-2500 Trmnl Twr -Cleveland 44113 **Fx:**621-8369

(614) 365-2700 ..**Loewengart,** Steven M '87 (Squire S&D LLP) -41 S High
-1300 Huntngtn Ctr -Columbus 43215 **Fx:**365-2499

(415) 278-4434 ..**Loewenthal,** Marc S '74 Providian Finl Srvcs -201 Mission
-San Francisco, CA 94105

(304) 233-3390 ..**Lofstead,** Gerald E III '03 %Schrader B&C,PLLC -32 20th
-Ste 500 -Wheeling, WV 26003 **Fx:**233-2769

(513) 381-2838 ..**Loftus,** Matthew C '02 %Taft S&H LLP -425 Walnut -Ste 1800
-Cincinnati 45202 **Fx:**381-0205

(262) 260-4814 ..**Lofty,** Donald A '84 SC Johnson & Son,Inc -1525 Howe -MS 062
-Racine, WI 53403

(419) 241-4900 ..**Logan,** Amy M '04 %Rauser & Assoc,LPA -316 N Mich -Ste 420
-Toledo 43624 **Fx:**241-4920

(937) 333-4400 ..**Logan,** Deirdre E '91 Dayton Pros -335 W 3rd -Ste 372
-Dayton 45402

(614) 457-1010 ..**Logan,** John A '78 (Brooks & L Co,LPA) -4921 Dierker Rd
-Columbus 43220

(513) 793-4400 ..**Logan,** Philip A '72 (Katzman LH&B) -9000 Plainfld Rd
-Cincinnati 45236 **Fx:**793-4691

(937) 254-0054 ..**Logan,** Ronald G '58 -1336 Woodman Dr -Dayton 45432

(614) 221-7663 ..**Logan,** William B Jr. '74 (Luper N&L,LPA) -50 W Broad
-1200 LeVeque Twr -Columbus 43215 **Fx:**464-2425

(216) 592-5000 ..**Logan Melick,** Heather '97 %Tucker E&W LLP -925 Euclid Av
-1150 Huntngtn Bldg -Cleveland 44115 **Fx:**592-5009

(330) 264-6115 ..**Logee Hostetler Stutzman & Lehman** -2171-B Eagle Pass
-Wooster 44691 **Fx:**262-5729

(937) 433-0624 ..**Logothetis,** Sorrell '68 -930 Grants Trl -Dayton 45459

(216) 291-1159 ..**Lograsso,** Michael P '92 -1414 S Green Rd -Ste 101
-South Euclid 44121

(740) 387-6688 ..**Logsdon-Babich,** Sara E '84 CSEA -620 Leader -Marion 43302

(330) 971-8190 ..**Lohan,** Angela F '03 Cuyahoga Falls Pros -2310 2nd
-Cuyahoga Falls 44221 **Fx:**971-8296

(216) 622-8200 ..**Lohiser,** Kenneth L '88 %Calfee H&G LLP -800 Superior Av
-Ste 1400 -Cleveland 44114 **Fx:**241-0816

(216) 241-4100 ..**Lohr,** Carole A '00 %Keis/G LLP -55 Pub Sq -Ste 800
-Cleveland 44113 **Fx:**771-3111

(330) 643-2765 ..**Lohr,** Mary A '99 Summit Cnty Pros-CSEA -171 S Main -Akron
44308 **Fx:**643-2822

(330) 643-3100 ..**Lohr,** Richard A Jr. '99 OH Civ Rghts Cmmssn -161 S High
-Ste 205 -Akron 44308

(440) 357-5537 ..**Loiacono,** James V III '78 (Cannon SA&L Co,LPA) -41 E Erie
-Painesville 44077 **Fx:**357-9234

(937) 898-9440 ..**Loikoc,** Edmund G '70 -3814 Little York Rd -Dayton 45414

(419) 213-4700 ..**Loisel,** Michael J '98 Lucas Cnty Pros -Adams & Erie
-Lucas Cnty Cthse -Toledo 43624

(703) 518-6567 ..**Loizos,** Chrisanthy J '94 Natl Credit Union Admin -1775 Duke
-Alexandria, VA 22314 **Fx:**837-2780

(216) 830-9000 ..**Lojewski,** Jeffrey D '82 %Berger & Z Co,LPA -614 W Superior Av
-Ste 1425 Rckfllr Bldg -Cleveland 44113 **Fx:**830-4200
..................**Lokai,** Jeffery M '00 -4950 Cmmn Market Pl -Dublin 43016

(216) 520-5642 ..**Lokiec,** Benjamin K '01 Westgroup -6111 Oak Tree Blvd
-Bx318063 -Cleveland 44131

(330) 492-8717 ..**Lolli,** Richard J '76 (Buckingham D&B,LLP) -4518 Fulton Dr NW
-Bx35548 -Canton 44735 **Fx:**492-9625

(614) 221-8500 ..**Lomax,** Lisa A '93 Allen K&S LLP -21 W Broad -Ste 400
-Columbus 43215

(937) 223-8177 ..**Lombard,** John C '64 Coolidge WW&L -33 W 1st -Ste 600
-Dayton 45402 **Fx:**223-6705

(330) 535-9655 ..**Lombardi,** David G '89 (Lombardi G&J,Ltd) -7 W Bowery -Ste 507
-Akron 44308

(330) 745-2175 ..**Lombardi,** Donald E '68 Lombardi HHC&E -2745 Nesbitt Av
-Akron 44319

(330) 376-5300 ..**Lombardi,** Frederick M '62 (Buckingham D&B,LLP) -50 S Main
-Bx1500 -Akron 44309 **Fx:**258-6559

(330) 535-9655 ..**Lombardi George & James, Ltd** -7 W Bowery -Ste 507
-Akron 44308

(330) 745-2175 ..**Lombardi Hofer Hanna Conway & Eastman** -2745 Nesbitt Av
-Akron 44319

(216) 621-1312 ..**Lombardi,** Maria T '92 (McMahon DH&L LLP) -812 Huron Rd
-Ste 650 The Caxton Bldg -Cleveland 44115 **Fx:**621-0577

(330) 296-5252 ..**Lombardi,** Richard C '71 -240 S Chestnut -Ravenna 44266

(330) 454-9041 ..**Lombardi,** Robert M '55 -315 Tuscarawas W -Natl City Bldg
-Canton 44702

(330) 493-0040 ..**Lombardi,** Thomas J '66 Lesh C&M -4150 Belden Vllg NW
-Ste 606 -Canton 44718

(419) 242-1555 ..**Lombardo,** Carla A '92 %Spitler & W-Y Co,LPA -1000 Adams
-Ste 200 -Toledo 43624

(440) 953-7348 ..**Lombardo,** Catherine M '79 Lakeland Cmmnty Cllg
-7700 Clocktower Dr -Kirtland 44094

(216) 481-0020 ..**Lombardo,** David J '63 -20050 Lakeshr Blvd -Euclid 44123

(216) 241-9990 ..**Lombardo,** John J '71 OfCnsl J Jerome & Assoc -55 Pub Sq
-Ste 2020 -Cleveland 44113 **Fx:**241-2920
..................**Lombardo,** Margaret M '97 -1025 Birchmont Rd -Columbus 43220

(216) 621-0400 ..**Lombardo,** Vincent J '82 -614 Superior Av NW -Ste 1600
-Cleveland 44113

(216) 787-3030 ..**Lombardo,** Vincent T '81 Atty Gen -615 W Superior Av -11th Fl
-Cleveland 44113 **Fx:**787-3480
..................**Lombardy,** Kelly L M '03 -17822 Fox Hllw Dr -Strongsville 44136

(216) 771-6500 ..**Lombardy,** Matthew P '01 %K Weiner & Assoc Co,LPA
-75 Pub Sq -4th Fl -Cleveland 44113 **Fx:**771-6540

(216) 781-2550 ..**Lonardo,** Angelo F '79 (Yelsky & L Co,LPA) -75 Pub Sq -Ste 800
-Cleveland 44113 **Fx:**781-6688

(202) 467-8811 ..**Lonardo,** Joseph D '72 (Vorys SS&P) -1828 L NW -11th Fl
-Washington, DC 20036

(330) 493-9901 ..**Lonas McGonegal & Tsangeos** -1810 36th NW -Canton 44709
Fx:493-9338

(330) 493-9901 ..**Lonas,** Webster M Jr. '65 (Lonas M&T) -1810 36th NW
-Canton 44709 **Fx:**493-9338

(740) 852-1126 ..**Londergan,** Gary W '76 -27 E 4th -Bx190 -London 43140

(216) 621-5980 ..**London,** James D '67 Legal Aid -1223 W 6th -Cleveland 44113

(419) 865-5743 ..**Loney,** Brett A '00 St Johns Jesuit High Schl -5901 Airport Hwy
-Toledo 43615 **Fx:**867-9695

(216) 692-5934 ..**Loney,** David '77 Argo-Tech Corp -23555 Euclid Av
-Cleveland 44117

(412) 471-2822 ..**Long,** Christine M '78 (May L&S,PC) -600 Grant
-3030 US Steel Twr -Pittsburgh, PA 15219 **Fx:**261-0572

(614) 466-2166 ..**Long,** Clare N '83 OH Dept Taxation -30 E Broad -22nd Fl
-Columbus 43215

(440) 871-4022 ..**Long,** Clare S '84 Corsaro & Assoc Co,LPA -2001 Crocker Rd
-Ste 400 -Westlake 44145

(440) 323-1203 ..**Long,** David C '75 Rothgery & Assoc -230 3rd -Ste 100
-Elyria 44035

(513) 333-0050 ..**Long,** Edward III '95 %P Hackett -1014 Vine -Ste 1690
-Cincinnati 45202

(419) 947-9505 ..**Long,** Frank G '87 -7326 SR 19 -Unit 3005 -Mount Gilead 43338

(937) 296-2456 ..**Long,** James F '84 Law Dept -3600 Shroyer Rd -Kettering 45429

(614) 488-0681 ..**Long,** James M '76 1st Cmmnty Church -1320 Camrdg Blvd
-Columbus 43212

(614) 224-9207 ..**Long,** Kelly A '01 Title First Agncy,Inc -555 S Front -Ste 400
-Columbus 43215

(360) 385-0858 ..**Long,** Kenneth R '66 -100 Lands End Ln
-Port Townsend, WA 98368

(614) 466-4371 ..**Long,** Kristin Jo '01 OH Senate Mnrty Caucus -304 Statehse
-Columbus 43215

(937) 644-6645 ..**Long,** Mark A '87 Honda of Amer Mfg -24000 Honda Pkwy
-Marysville 43040

(614) 464-6400 ..**Long,** Michael G '69 (Vorys SS&P LLP) -52 E Gay -Bx1008
-Columbus 43216 **Fx:**464-6350

(740) 363-1369 ..**Long,** Oscar R '73 (Heald & L) -125 N Sandusky -Delaware 43015

(740) 477-1605 ..**Long,** Paul E II '74 -118 E Main -Bx910 -Circleville 43113

(614) 451-5300 ..**Long,** Richard S '76 (Musser L&H) -3404 Riverside Dr
-Columbus 43221

(937) 440-5960 ..**Long,** Robert E III '96 Miami Cnty Pros -201 W Main -Troy 45373
Fx:440-5961

(216) 696-4441 ..**Long,** Ryan L '04 %Zashin & R Co,LPA -55 Pub Sq -Ste 1490
-Cleveland 44113 **Fx:**696-1618

(216) 622-3600 ..**Long,** Sharon L '78 US Atty -801 W Superior -Ste 400
-Cleveland 44113 **Fx:**622-3370

(419) 241-2900 ..**Long,** Stephen D '94 %Baran PTF&T Co,LPA -608 Mad Av
-Ste 1620 -Toledo 43604 **Fx:**241-3002

(716) 853-5100 ..**Long,** Steven K '85 (Lippes MW&F LLP) -665 Main -Ste 300
-Buffalo, NY 14203 **Fx:**853-5199

(614) 228-1541 ..**Long,** Thomas L '76 (Baker & H LLP) -65 E State -Ste 2100
-Columbus 43215 **Fx:**462-2616
..................**Long,** Timothy C '88 -4877 Galway Dr -Dublin 43017

(419) 283-9888 ..**Longacre,** Timothy W '92 -6800 W Central Av -Ste C
-Toledo 43617

(513) 946-3000 ..**Longano,** Bernadette M '97 Hamilton Cnty Pros -230 E 9th
-Cincinnati 45202 **Fx:**946-3017

(513) 946-3000 ..**Longano,** Thomas P '74 Hamilton Cnty Pros -230 E 9th
-Cincinnati 45202 **Fx:**946-3017

(216) 771-3737 ..**Longauer,** Nicholas E '76 Continental Title Agncy -1300 E 9th
-Ste 1220 -Cleveland 44114

(330) 438-0767 ..**Longbrake,** Suzanne Trocki '95 Hon W Hoffman
-110 Central Plz S -5th Dist Ct of Appls Rm 320 -Canton 44702

(330) 744-1311 ..**Longbrake**, W Bradford '95 %Reminger & R -11 Fed Plz Central
-Ste 300 -Youngstown 44503 **Fx:**744-7500

(513) 455-7600 ..**Longenecker**, Mark H Jr. '79 (Greenebaum D&M PLLC)
-255 E 5th -2800 Chemed Ctr -Cincinnati 45202 **Fx:**455-5800

(216) 231-7936 ..**Longino**, Nicole C '83 -11811 Shaker Blvd -#420
-Cleveland 44120

(216) 514-1919 ..**Longo**, Charles V '85 (C Longo Co,LPA) -25550 Chagrin Blvd
-Ste 320 -Beachwood 44122 **Fx:**593-0914

(419) 499-8308 ..**Longo**, David J '86 -Bx2082 -Sandusky 44871

(937) 454-9458 ..**Longo**, James M '88 -612 Bright Av -Bx357 -Vandalia 45377

(614) 644-0731 ..**Longo**, Scott A '89 Atty Gen -30 E Broad -Columbus 43215
Fx:728-7582

(513) 381-9200 ..**Longtin**, Lynne M '99 %Rendigs FK&D,LLP -One W 4th -Ste 900
-Cincinnati 45202 **Fx:**381-9206

(800) 224-7914 ..**Longton**, Erik W '01 LAWO -125 W Water -Sandusky 44870
Fx:(419) 609-9173

(513) 229-6537 ..**Longwell**, Christopher D '00 409 Grp Inc -5155 Fncl Way
-Mason 45040

(440) 669-0876 ..**Longwell**, Donald E Jr. '93 -46962 Grafton Eastern Rd
-Grafton 44044

(216) 861-3444 ..**Lonjak**, George F '82 -1280 W 3rd -1st Fl -Cleveland 44113
Fx:696-1439

(614) 895-1234 ..**Lonn**, Thomas C '92 -833 Eastwind Dr -Westerville 43081

(740) 593-1643 ..**Lonsinger**, Linda Lee '87 OH Univ -McKee Hse -Athens 45701

(330) 785-3337 ..**Looney**, David A '74 (D Looney Co LPA) -1735 S Main
-Akron 44301 **Fx:**785-3337

(513) 853-5906 ..**Looney**, Kimberly G '99 Mercy Hlth Prtnrs -2446 Kipling Av
-Cincinnati 45239

(614) 644-7073 ..**Lopez**, A Ruben '92 Dept of Job & Fam Srvcs -Hearing Auth
-Bx1082825 -Columbus 43218 **Fx:**644-6674

(937) 298-7794 ..**Lopez**, Alvin J '86 -438 Patterson Rd -Dayton 45419

(419) 245-1198 ..**Lopez**, Anita L '99 Affirmative Action Dept -1 Govt Ctr -19th Fl
-Toledo 43624

(614) 227-3098 ..**Lopez**, Christopher A '88 OH Education Assn -225 E Broad
-Bx2550 -Columbus 43216

(513) 770-3801 ..**Lopez**, David B '63 Clopay Corp -8585 Duke Blvd -Mason 45040

(513) 852-5600 ..**Lopez Hodes Restaino Milman & Skikos** -312 Walnut
-Ste 2090 -Cincinnati 45202 **Fx:**852-5611

(202) 663-6264 ..**Lopez**, James C '98 %Wilmer C&P -1899 Penn Av
-Washington, DC 20006 **Fx:**663-6363

(937) 335-5658 ..**Lopez**, Jose M '79 (Lopez S&P Co,LPA) -18 E Water -Troy 45373
Fx:339-6446

(513) 585-7155 ..**Lopez**, Mary J '01 Hlth Alliance -3200 Burnet Av -Cincinnati 45229

(614) 462-3555 ..**Lopez**, Robert C '99 Franklin Cnty Pros -373 S High
-Columbus 43215

(937) 335-5658 ..**Lopez Severt & Pratt Co,LPA** -18 E Water -Troy 45373
Fx:339-6446

Lopina, David A '89 US Army/Dept of Defense
-25th Infantry Div Light -Ofc SJAocate
-Schofield Barracks, HI 96857

(216) 932-2902 ..**LoPresti**, Carl L '76 -2402 Eardley Rd -University Heights 44118

(216) 622-8200 ..**LoPresti**, Charles A '96 %Calfee H&G LLP -800 Superior Av
-Ste 1400 -Cleveland 44114 **Fx:**241-0816

(216) 348-5400 ..**LoPresti**, Joseph J Jr. '73 (McDonald H Co,LPA)
-600 Superior Av E -Ste 2100 -Cleveland 44114 **Fx:**348-5474

(216) 443-4945 ..**LoPresti**, Mary C '85 Cuyahoga Cnty Dom Rltns Ct -1 W Lakeside
Av -Cleveland 44113

(216) 241-7740 ..**LoPresti**, Salvatore J '73 (Willacy L&M) -1468 W 9th
-700 Wstrn Reserve Bldg -Cleveland 44113

(216) 928-2200 ..**LoPrinzi**, Brian V '96 Sutter OM&F -1301 E 9th -3600 Erievw Twr
-Cleveland 44114 **Fx:**928-4400

(330) 425-4201 ..**Lorber**, Michael F '73 (Reimer L&A Co,LPA) -2450 Edison Blvd
-Bx968 -Twinsburg 44087 **Fx:**487-0923

(216) 696-5673 ..**Lord**, Frank H '56 (Lord & L) -614 W Superior Av
-1100 Rckfllr Bldg -Cleveland 44113

(440) 582-2374 ..**Lord**, John A '00 -Bx33610 -North Royalton 44133

(216) 696-5673 ..**Lord**, Kimberly M '85 Lord & L -614 W Superior Av
-1100 Rckfllr Bldg -Cleveland 44113

(513) 423-9276 ..**Lord**, Mary C '51 -2120 Central Av -Middletown 45044

(614) 864-1117 ..**Lord**, Richard E '79 -7518 Slate Ridge Blvd -Reynoldsburg 43068

(614) 898-9522 ..**Lord**, Shannon R '04 %Sammons & Assoc,LPA
-635 Park Meadow Rd -Westerville 43081

(513) 634-2084 ..**Lorentz**, Bryn M Taylor '03 Procter & Gamble -6071 Ctr Hill Av
-Cincinnati 45224

(513) 977-8200 ..**Lorentz**, Joshua A '01 %Dinsmore & S LLP -255 E 5th -Ste 1900
-Cincinnati 45202 **Fx:**977-8141

(216) 689-4969 ..**Lorentzen**, Lee Ann '79 KeyBank NA -127 Pub Sq
-Cleveland 44114

(330) 364-2467 ..**Lorenz**, Charles E II '84 -114 E High Av -New Philadelphia 44663

(330) 673-2440 ..**Lorenz**, Peter P '00 -1012 Hudson Rd -Kent 44240

(847) 970-5112 ..**Lorenzen**, John M '70 USG Corp -700 N Hwy 45
-Libertyville, IL 60048

(330) 652-1111 ..**Lorenzetti**, Jack C Jr. '82 (J Lorenzetti Jr Co LPA)
-815 Youngstown Rd -Ste 2 -Niles 44446

Lorenzo, Paul S '94 -237 Tyler Crk Dr -Powell 43065

(216) 367-6260 ..**Loreta**, Daniel R '89 Middough Assoc -1901 E 13th
-Cleveland 44114

(937) 222-2424 ..**Loridas**, Heather M '01 %Freund F&A -1 S Main -Ste 1800
-Dayton 45402 **Fx:**222-5369

(614) 431-2600 ..**Lorimer**, James J '69 -1245 Worthngtn Wds Blvd
-Worthington 43085

(513) 721-1975 ..**Loring**, Elizabeth S '03 %Freking & B -215 E 9th -5th Fl
-Cincinnati 45202 **Fx:**651-2570

(216) 443-7800 ..**Loritts**, Lynn D '91 Cuyahoga Cnty Pros -1200 Ontario -8th Fl
-Cleveland 44113 **Fx:**698-2270

(419) 227-7193 ..**Lortie**, Daniel J '95 OH Indstrl Commssn -2025 E 4th -Lima 45804

(419) 698-9595 ..**Lorton**, Michael D '79 -2467 Woodvll Rd -Oregon 43616

Losekamp, Geoffrey M '96 -1345 Bruton Parish Way -Fairfield
45014

(202) 544-9614 ..**Losey**, Franklin W '64 Brown & Co Inc -600 Penn Av SE -Ste 304
-Washington, DC 20003

(614) 621-1500 ..**Losey**, Mark A '94 %Calfee H&G LLP -21 E State
-1100 Fifth Third Ctr -Columbus 43215 **Fx:**621-0010

(304) 697-8678 ..**Losey**, Robert M '84 -Bx2448 -Huntington, WV 25725

(614) 463-8251 ..**Lossing**, Roger A '83 Natl City Bank -155 E Broad -Ste 500
-Columbus 43209 **Fx:**463-8369

(440) 237-1679 ..**Lotenero**, Dale J '75 -11903 Royalton Rd -North Royalton 44133

Lotspeich, Michael D '93 -3506 Concord Dr -Erlanger, KY 41018

(216) 696-7600 ..**Louard**, Janette A '96 (Duvin C&H) -1301 E 9th
-20th Fl Erievw Twr -Cleveland 44114 **Fx:**696-2038

(216) 834-0400 ..**Loucas**, Cathryn N '01 G Loucas Co,LPA -6060 Rockside Wd Blvd
-Ste 250 -Cleveland 44131 **Fx:**834-0404

(216) 834-0400 ..**Loucas**, George E '85 (G Loucas Co,LPA)
-6060 Rockside Wd Blvd -Ste 250 -Cleveland 44131 **Fx:**834-0404

(216) 834-0400 ..**Loucas**, Penny E '87 G Loucas Co,LPA -6060 Rockside Wd Blvd
-Ste 250 -Cleveland 44131 **Fx:**834-0404

(614) 462-5996 ..**Loucks**, Nicole M '03 Ct of Common Pleas -369 S High -Ctrm 6C
-Columbus 43215

(614) 466-4961 ..**Loudenslagel**, Mark T '78 %Sup Crt of OH -30 E Broad -2nd Fl
-Columbus 43266

(513) 985-0110 ..**Loudermilk**, Timothy D '91 -311 Elm -Ste 200 -Cincinnati 45202

(216) 778-8475 ..**Loue**, Sana '96 Case Western Reserve Univ -10900 Euclid Av
-Cleveland 44106

(440) 930-4001 ..**Loughman**, Michael J '73 (Baumgartner & O) -5455 Detroit
Rd (Rte 254) -Sheffield Village 44054 **Fx:**934-7205

(614) 228-5931 ..**Loughry**, Michael S '01 %Mazanec R&R Co,LPA -250 Civic Ctr Dr
-Ste 400 -Columbus 43215 **Fx:**228-5934

(614) 466-2980 ..**Loughry**, Timothy C '04 %Atty Gen -30 E Broad -Columbus 43215
Fx:728-9470

(216) 241-5310 ..**Lougovskaia**, Elena N '00 %Gallagher SF&N -1501 Euclid Av -6th
Fl -Cleveland 44115 **Fx:**241-1608

(614) 221-3155 ..**Louis**, Harlan S '94 %Bailey C LLC -10 W Broad
-Columbus 43215 **Fx:**221-0479

(330) 721-0000 ..**Louke**, Marcella R '03 %Walker & J,LPA -231 S Bway
-Medina 44256 **Fx:**722-6446

(419) 245-1020 ..**Loukx**, Adam W '93 %Law Dept -One Govt Ctr -Ste 2250
-Toledo 43604 **Fx:**245-1090

(937) 223-8177 ..**Lounsbury**, Joshua R '04 %Coolidge WW&L -33 W 1st -Ste 600
-Dayton 45402 **Fx:**223-6705

(440) 331-2245 ..**Louth**, Richard P '73 -21580 Hilliard Blvd -Rocky River 44116

(740) 467-1308 ..**Louthen**, Constance S '98 -4105 Blacklick Eastern Rd
-Millersport 43046

(216) 525-1939 ..**Louttit**, Kathryn H '04 Century Business Srvcs,Inc
-6050 Oak Tree Blvd S -Ste 500 -Cleveland 44131

(614) 466-8181 ..**Loutzenhiser**, Charles F Jr. '77 PUCO -180 E Broad
-Columbus 43266

(216) 621-0200 ..**Loux**, Lloyd F Jr. '53 OfCnsl Baker & H LLP -1900 E 9th -Ste 3200
-Cleveland 44114 **Fx:**696-0740

(513) 345-5000 ..**Love**, Ayanna '01 %Lawson & Assoc -808 Elm -Ste 100
-Cincinnati 45202

(513) 534-4529 ..**Love**, David C '04 5th 3rd Bank -38 Fountain Square Plz
-MD 1090D2 -Cincinnati 45231

(614) 236-1075 ..**Love**, Donald P '70 (Leighton & L) -261 S Hmltn Rd
-Columbus 43213

(513) 621-3498 ..**Love**, Ellsworth '74 -119 E Court -Cincinnati 45202

(216) 586-3939 ..**Love**, Julia Ann '95 %Jones D -901 Lakeside Av -Cleveland 44114
Fx:579-0212

(330) 456-4308 ..**Love**, Kenyon D '52 -323 Court Av NW -Canton 44702

(513) 870-2288 ..**Love**, Lisa A '91 Cnsl Cincinnati Fin Corp -Bx145496
-Cincinnati 45250

(216) 586-3939 ..**Love**, Sheryl H '95 %Jones D -901 Lakeside Av -Cleveland 44114
Fx:579-0212

(330) 644-0607 ..**Love**, William E II '76 -739 W Rextur -Akron 44319

(304) 522-3038 ..**Lovejoy**, Chad S '98 Duffield Law Firm -Bx608
-Huntington, WV 25710

(513) 765-6340 ..**Lovejoy**, Wallace W '88 Luxottica Retail -4000 Luxottica Pl
-Mason 45040

(614) 464-3563 ..**Loveland & Brosius** -50 W Broad -Ste 3300 -Columbus 43215

(614) 227-2000 ..**Loveland**, Curtis A '73 (Porter WM&A LLP) -41 S High
-Columbus 43215 **Fx:**227-2100

Loveland, Daniel R '86 -37 N Rivervw -Dublin 43017

(614) 464-3563 ..**Loveland**, Richard L '57 (Loveland & B) -50 W Broad -Ste 3300
-Columbus 43215

(614) 464-3563 ..**Loveland**, William L '82 (Loveland & B) -50 W Broad -Ste 3300
-Columbus 43215

(216) 928-3474 ..**Lovequist**, Sarah E '01 %Yormick & Assoc Co,LPA -127 Pub Sq
-Ste 5200 -Cleveland 44114 **Fx:**566-0857

(614) 227-2307 ..**Lovering**, Richard S III '80 (Bricker & E LLP) -100 S 3rd
-Columbus 43215 **Fx:**227-2390

(734) 761-8358 ..**Lovernick**, Richard N '98 Lacey & Jones -220 E Huron -Ste 525
-Ann Arbor, MI 48104

(937) 667-8805 ..**Lovett**, George H '88 (Lovett & L Co,LPA) -1420 W Main
-Tipp City 45371

(216) 241-2880 ..**Lovett**, Mary F '85 (Cowden HN&L) -50 Pub Sq -Ste 1414
-Cleveland 44113 **Fx:**241-2881

(937) 667-8805 ..**Lovett**, Roselyn G '89 (Lovett & L Co,LPA) -1420 W Main
-Tipp City 45371

(216) 622-8200 ..**Lovett**, Ruth L '85 Calfee H&G LLP -800 Superior Av -Ste 1400
-Cleveland 44114 **Fx:**241-0816

(330) 722-0113 ..**Loving**, Deborah G '79 -203 N Bway -Medina 44256

(216) 621-7045 ..**Lovinger**, Daniel L '67 -1370 Ontario -Ste 2000 -Cleveland 44113
Lowder, Cristina D '03 -(Address Unavailable)

(216) 861-0360 ..**Lowder**, Janet L '92 (Hickman & L Co,LPA) -1370 Ontario
-Ste 1620 -Cleveland 44113 **Fx:**861-3113

(614) 462-3555 ..**Lowe**, Amanda J '02 Franklin Cnty Pros -373 S High
-Columbus 43215

(330) 499-9200 ..**Lowe**, Arnold B '75 Hoover Co -101 E Maple -North Canton 44720

(216) 241-2838 ..**Lowe**, Bruce A '79 (Taft S&H LLP) -200 Pub Sq -3500 BP Twr
-Cleveland 44114 **Fx:**241-3707

(937) 222-8091 ..**Lowe**, Charles D '64 (Lowe & D) -130 W 2nd -Ste 1600
-Dayton 45402

(937) 865-6800 ..**Lowe**, Christopher P '95 Lexis/Nexis -Bx933 -Dayton 45401

(513) 243-8993 ..**Lowe**, Cynthia Kay '00 GE Aircraft Engines -1 Neumann Way
-MD J104 -Cincinnati 45215

(440) 285-2242 ..**Lowe**, David E '70 Thrasher D&D,LPA -100 7th Av -Ste 150
-Chardon 44024 **Fx:**285-9423

(614) 340-3895 ..**Lowe**, David K '84 (Clark & L,LLC) -1500 W 3rd Av -Ste 310
-Bx12310 -Columbus 43212

(216) 781-2600 ..**Lowe Eklund Wakefield & Mulvihill Co, LPA** -1660 W 2nd
-610 Skylight Ofc Twr -Cleveland 44113 Fx:781-2610

(305) 536-7243 ..**Lowe**, Eve G '87 EEOC -2 S Biscayne Blvd -Ste 2700
-Miami, FL 33131

(614) 228-5331 ..**Lowe**, Gregory A '93 %Don M Casto Org -191 W Nationwide Blvd
-Ste 200 -Columbus 43215

(614) 784-0912 ..**Lowe**, Howard P '55 -227 E Blake Av -Columbus 43202

(216) 781-2600 ..**Lowe**, James A '72 (Lowe EW&M Co,LPA) -1660 W 2nd
-610 Skylight Ofc Twr -Cleveland 44113 Fx:781-2610

(614) 462-3555 ..**Lowe**, James L '94 Franklin Cnty Pros -373 S High
-Columbus 43215

(614) 462-5485 ..**Lowe**, John IV '98 %Kegler BH&R -65 E State -Ste 1800
-Columbus 43215 Fx:464-2634

(214) 768-2595 ..**Lowe**, John S '66 Sthrn Methodist Univ -3315 Daniel
-Dallas, TX 75275

(614) 793-7000 ..**Lowe**, Justin D '00 Sterling Commerce -4600 Lakehurst Ct
-Dublin 43016

(740) 962-3862 ..**Lowe**, Michael D '83 -100 S Kennebec Av -McConnelsville 43756

(614) 466-5394 ..**Lowe**, Robert K '00 Pub Def -8 E Long -Columbus 43215

(740) 345-3431 ..**Lowe**, William Douglas '85 (Reese PD&M,PLL) -36 N 2nd -Bx919
-Newark 43058 Fx:349-5116

(843) 836-3420 ..**Lowell**, James R '83 -74 Saw Timber Dr
-Hilton Head Island, SC 29926 Fx:836-3420

(440) 352-3391 ..**Lowell**, Staci D '04 %Dworken & B Co,LPA -60 S Park Pl
-Painesville 44077 Fx:352-3469

(440) 427-9760 ..**Lowenkamp**, Cynthia D '96 -9197 Wllwbrk Ct
-Olmsted Falls 44138 Fx:427-9761

(419) 522-3113 ..**Lowenkamp Cockley**, Heather M '91 -16 W 2nd
-Mansfield 44902

(323) 298-6979 ..**Lowenstam**, Susan Guggenheim '96 General Atomics -5140 W
Goldleaf Cir -Bx56901 -Los Angeles, CA 90056 Fx:298-2521

(419) 321-6444 ..**Lowenstein**, Jacob M '98 %Cline C&W Co,LPA -300 Mad Av
-Ste 1100 -Toledo 43604 Fx:321-6430

(419) 321-6444 ..**Lowenstein**, Jay J '75 Cline C&W Co,LPA -300 Mad Av -Ste 1100
-Toledo 43604 Fx:321-6430

(614) 224-8446 ..**Lowenstein**, Roy '76 Ohio Capital Corp -88 E Broad -Ste 1800
-Columbus 43215

(937) 865-1812 ..**Lowery**, Kermit F '84 Cnsl Lexis/Nexis -Bx933 -Dayton 45401

(513) 793-7737 ..**Lowery**, Robert R '63 (Lowery & R Co LPA) -1212 Sycamore
-Ste 35 -Cincinnati 45202 Fx:421-1119

(216) 787-3668 ..**Lowes**, Lawrence J '78 OH Indus Comm -615 Superior NW -#700
-Cleveland 44113

(330) 451-7213 ..**Lowman**, Catherine S '01 Stark Cnty Pub Def -200 W Tuscarawas
-Ste 200 -Canton 44702

(330) 867-2444 ..**Lowrey**, Robert W '74 Intl Chem Wrkrs Union Cncl
-1655 W Market -Akron 44313

(330) 896-6162 ..**Lowrie**, Scott R '84 -3700 Massillon Rd -Ste 360
-Uniontown 44685

(614) 229-4690 ..**Lowry**, Bruce R '77 (Deloitte & Touche) -155 E Broad
-Columbus 43215

(740) 587-2139 ..**Lowry**, Carla E '95 -75 Wexford Dr -Granville 43023

(330) 376-2004 ..**Lowry**, David M '82 -32 Edgerton -Akron 44303

..**Lowry**, Derek J '98 -101 Central Plz S -Ste 300 -Canton 44702

(330) 451-8659 ..**Lowry**, Jennifer T '99 Stark Cnty CSEA -116 Cleveland Av NW
-Canton 44702

(513) 421-2255 ..**Lowry**, John P '86 (Boehm K&L) -36 E 7th -2110 Society Bk Ctr
-Cincinnati 45202

(513) 381-2838 ..**Lowry**, Patricia O '85 (Taft S&H LLP) -425 Walnut -Ste 1800
-Cincinnati 45202 Fx:381-0205

(330) 929-0507 ..**Lowry**, Randal A '76 -234 W Portage Trl -Cuyahoga Falls 44221

(216) 274-0520 ..**Lowry**, Van M '83 -1422 Euclid Av -Ste 1604 -Cleveland 44115

(740) 233-1470 ..**Lowther**, David H '96 (Collins & L) -125 S Main -Marion 43302
Fx:223-1467

(614) 464-5052 ..**Lowther**, John R '76 State Auto Mutual Ins Co -518 E Broad
-Columbus 43215

(513) 695-1325 ..**Loxley**, Gary A '87 Warren Cnty Pros -500 Justice Dr
-Lebanon 45036 Fx:695-2962

(440) 255-9100 ..**Loxterman**, Kirk F '85 (McNamara HC&L) -8440 Station
-Mentor 44060

(330) 723-2400 ..**Loyer**, Richard A '78 -445 E Wshngtn -Medina 44256

(216) 592-5000 ..**Lu**, David S '96 %Tucker E&W LLP -925 Euclid Av
-1150 Huntngtn Bldg -Cleveland 44115 Fx:592-5009

(937) 645-8693 ..**Luang**, Hsin-Wei '04 Honda R&D Americas,Inc
-21001 State Route 739 -Raymond 43067

(216) 622-8200 ..**Luarde**, Sharon A '99 %Calfee H&G LLP -800 Superior Av
-Ste 1400 -Cleveland 44114 Fx:241-0816

(914) 328-0404 ..**Lubbe**, E Johannes '88 (Jackson L LLP) -1 N Bway -15th Fl
-White Plains, NY 10601 Fx:328-1882

(440) 329-5565 ..**Lubbe**, Timothy P '98 Lorain Co Common Pleas Ct -308 2nd
-Cnty Cthse -Elyria 44035

(937) 981-7318 ..**Lubbers**, Carol A '02 %Curren Law Ofc -330 Jffrsn -Bx149
-Greenfield 45123

(440) 285-2222 ..**Lubecky**, David '87 Geauga Cnty Cmn Pleas Ct -231 Main
-Ste 200 -Chardon 44024

..**Lubes**, Michael J '04 -(Address Unavailable)

(419) 829-5297 ..**Lublin**, Jeffery M '80 -8657 Central Av -Sylvania 43560

(614) 888-0040 ..**Lubow**, Barry L '83 DLZ Corp -6121 Huntley Rd -Columbus 43229

(614) 466-3934 ..**Lubow**, Lauren '83 State Med Brd -77 S High -17th Fl
-Columbus 43215

(614) 228-1541 ..**Lubow**, Susan N '95 %Baker & H LLP -65 E State -Ste 2100
-Columbus 43215 Fx:462-2616

(419) 627-0414 ..**Lucal**, Dean S '62 (Buckingham LM&Z Co,LPA) -414 Wayne
-Bx929 -Sandusky 44870 Fx:627-0009

(216) 696-7777 ..**Lucarelli**, Robert R '86 %Musca & M -1300 E 9th -Ste 1202
-Cleveland 44114

(614) 621-1500 ..**Lucas**, Albert J '84 (Calfee H&G LLP) -21 E State
-1100 Fifth Third Ctr -Columbus 43215 Fx:621-0010

..**Lucas**, Alfred V '68 -(Address Unavailable)

(614) 836-7593 ..**Lucas**, Barbara D '89 -5515 Ebright Rd -Groveport 43125

(614) 752-9740 ..**Lucas**, Cynthia G '81 Ofc of Child Support -30 E Broad -31st Fl
-Columbus 43266

(614) 221-1364 ..**Lucas**, George Robert II '68 The Jeffrey Trusts -88 E Broad
-Columbus 43215

(302) 774-9503 ..**Lucas**, Hinton J Jr. '80 Dupont Co -1007 Market
-Wilmington, DE 19898

(440) 205-3600 ..**Lucas**, James A '64 (Driggs LB&H Co,LPA) -8522 East Av
-Mentor 44060 Fx:205-3601

(614) 326-0818 ..**Lucas**, Jeffrey K '01 -1717 Bethel Rd -Columbus 43220

(614) 228-5711 ..**Lucas**, John C '76 (Lucas PAG&N) -600 S High -Columbus 43215
Fx:228-0982

(614) 248-6115 ..**Lucas**, Jonathan R '04 JP Morgan Chase -100 E Broad -3rd Fl
-Columbus 43215

(419) 774-5700 ..**Lucas**, Kelly L '91 Richland Cnty CSEA -161 Park Av E
-Mansfield 44902

(614) 923-7706 ..**Lucas**, Mark J '81 -5100 Parkcenter Av -Ste 120 -Dublin 43017

(216) 241-5735 ..**Lucas**, Matthew H '91 (Lustig E&L Co,LPA) -526 Superior Av E
-Ste 615 -Cleveland 44114

(440) 942-6262 ..**Lucas**, Michael C '80 (Wiles & R) -35350 Curtis Blvd -Ste 530
-Eastlake 44095 Fx:942-7211

(216) 443-6654 ..**Lucas**, Paul H '97 Cuyahoga Cnty Cmmn Pleas Ct -1200 Ontario
-10th Fl -Cleveland 44113

(614) 228-5711 ..**Lucas Prendergast Albright Gibson & Newman** -600 S High
-Columbus 43215 Fx:228-0982

(330) 659-0416 ..**Lucas**, Robert A '76 Smith & Nephew,Inc
-4418 Forest Brooke Ct N -Richfield 44286

(513) 977-8200 ..**Lucas**, Robert A '01 %Dinsmore & S LLP -255 E 5th -Ste 1900
-Cincinnati 45202 Fx:977-8141

(513) 891-2084 ..**Lucas**, Ronna S '94 -9245 Bluewing Ter -Cincinnati 45236

(216) 696-4200 ..**Lucas**, Sandra C '00 %Schneider SR&L PLL -1111 Superior Av
-Ste 1000 -Cleveland 44114 Fx:696-7303

(419) 627-0400 ..**Lucas**, Thomas R '00 Rengel Law Ofc -421 Jackson
-Sandusky 44870

(216) 621-5300 ..**Lucas**, Walter A '97 %Buckingham D&B,LLP -1375 E 9th
-Ste 1700 -Cleveland 44114 Fx:621-5440

(216) 771-8340 ..**Lucas**, William J '75 -1360 W 9th -Ste 200 -Cleveland 44113

(216) 621-0200 ..**Lucchesi**, Thomas R '84 (Baker & H LLP) -1900 E 9th -Ste 3200
-Cleveland 44114 Fx:696-0740

(216) 586-3939 ..**Lucci**, John Paul '03 %Jones D -901 Lakeside Av
-Cleveland 44114 Fx:579-0212

(330) 744-0247 ..**Lucci**, Joseph C '78 (Nadler N&B Co,LPA) -20 Fed Plz W -Ste 600
-Youngstown 44503 Fx:744-8690

(937) 498-8119 ..**Luce**, Donald G '76 Mun Ct Judge -201 W Poplar -Sidney 45365

(216) 621-0590 ..**Lucey**, James B '88 US Title -1111 Chester Av -400 Park Plz
-Cleveland 44114

(734) 847-9660 ..**Luchansky**, John E Jr. '77 -7431 Jackman Rd -Bx307
-Temperance, MI 48182 Fx:847-2113

(614) 462-6041 ..**Luchsinger**, Ann L '85 Franklin Cnty CSEA -80 E Fulton
-Columbus 43215

(330) 376-4558 ..**Lucht**, Gregory J '02 %Scanlon & G Co,LPA -50 S Main -Ste 1200
-Akron 44308 Fx:376-3550

(937) 335-5658 ..**Lucia**, Andrew D '96 %Lopez S&P Co,LPA -18 E Water
-Troy 45373 Fx:339-6446

(215) 981-4000 ..**Luciano**, Isla M '99 %Pepper H LLP -3000 Two Logan Sq
-18th & Arch -Philadelphia, PA 19103 Fx:981-4750

(614) 466-6700 ..**Luck**, Rebecca R '79 Tax Appeals -30 E Broad -Columbus 43215
Fx:644-5196

(614) 464-4414 ..**Luckage**, Eric J '97 Albers & A -88 N 5th -Columbus 43215
Fx:464-0604

(614) 221-9665 ..**Luckett**, Ermel R Jr. '89 -24 N High -Columbus 43215

(614) 466-4395 ..**Luckey**, Duane W '79 Atty Gen -150 E Gay -Columbus 43215
Fx:644-8764

(330) 702-0780 ..**Luckhart Mumaw Zellers & Robinson** -3810 Starrs Centre Dr
-Canfield 44406

(419) 471-2281 ..**Luckner**, Kleia R '91 Toledo Hosp -2142 N Cove Blvd
-Toledo 43606

(740) 474-7500 ..**Lucks**, Barbara J '76 -203 S Scioto -Bx828 -Circleville 43113

(614) 221-5265 ..**Luczkowski**, Jean M '78 OfCnsl Habash R&F,LLP -471 E Broad
-Ste 800 -Columbus 43215

(419) 321-1251 ..**Ludd**, Oksana M '80 (Shumaker L&K,LLP) -1000 Jackson
-Toledo 43624 Fx:241-6894

(419) 539-7449 ..**Ludd**, Steven O '82 -3326 Brookside Rd -Toledo 43606

(216) 844-4477 ..**Ludgin**, John R '87 Univ Hosp -11100 Euclid Av -HRV 6032
-Cleveland 44106

(330) 296-9654 ..**Ludick**, Timothy D '78 -231 S Chestnut -Ravenna 44266

(937) 865-7634 ..**Ludlow**, Vicki L '89 Lexis/Nexis -Bx933 -Dayton 45401

(330) 385-3900 ..**Ludovici**, Joseph L '86 Aronson F&D Co, LPA -124 E 5th
-East Liverpool 43920

(513) 621-6674 ..**Ludwig**, James D '95 %Mulvey & M LLC -35 E 7th -Ste 750
-Cincinnati 45202 Fx:621-0183

(330) 666-5550 ..**Ludwig**, Mark H '74 %Cole Co,LPA
-863 N Cleveland-Massillon Rd -Akron 44333

(513) 984-4554 ..**Ludwig**, Mina K '93 (Hawkins & L) -7438 Mntgmry Rd
-Cincinnati 45236

(614) 595-7500 ..**Ludwig**, William C '73 -970 Windham Ct -Boardman 44512

(513) 961-6644 ..**Luebbers**, Jody M '91 %Fox & F Co,LPA -2407 Ashland Av
-Cincinnati 45206

(513) 621-3394 ..**Luebbers**, Thomas A '66 (Peck S&W,LLP) -201 E 5th -Ste 900
-Cincinnati 45202 Fx:621-3813

(410) 772-3318 ..**Luebke**, Richard J '84 GSE Syst,Inc -9189 Red Brnch Rd
-Columbia, MD 21045

(330) 761-4207 ..**Luecken**, John J Jr. '90 FirstEnergy Corp -76 S Main -18th Fl
-Akron 44308

(216) 520-5600 ..**Luedeke**, Theresa '87 West Grp -6111 Oak Tree Blvd -Bx318063
-Cleveland 44131

(414) 271-2400 ..**Lueder**, Michael C '87 (Foley & L) -777 E Wscnsn Av
-Milwaukee, WI 53202

(419) 724-5240 ..**Luettke**, Thomas E '99 -1946 N 13th -Ste 169 -Toledo 43624

(216) 896-0707 ..**Luft**, Julie R '88 -3401 Enterprise Pkwy -Ste 200
-Beachwood 44122

(614) 224-1500 ..**Luftman**, Benjamin L '03 (Fornia L&H,LLP) -2 Miranova Pl
-Ste 380 -Columbus 43215 Fx:224-2894

(513) 784-1280 ..**Lugbill**, Ann '80 -2406 Auburn Av -Cincinnati 45219 Fx:784-1449

(630) 941-5377 ..**Lugibihl**, Carson E '77 Fifth Third Bank -109 S York
-Elmhurst, IL 60126

(216) 531-5390 .. **Luikart**, Loyal E Jr. '54 -18975 Villavw Dr -Cleveland 44119
(614) 223-1646 .. **Luis**, Michael R '69 AEP Srvc Corp -1 Riverside Plz -Columbus 43215
(216) 575-0777 .. **Luka**, Lori Ann '00 %Kelley & F,LLP -1300 E 9th -Ste 1901 -Cleveland 44114 **Fx**:575-0799
(216) 621-4244 .. **Lukacs**, Cheryl A '92 %Morganstern M&D Co,LPA -623 W St Clair Av -Cleveland 44113 **Fx**:621-2951
(440) 449-4200 .. **Lukas**, Anne L '86 Ursuline College -2550 Lander Rd -Pepper Pike 44124
Lukas, Henry F Jr. '60 -6600 Farview Rd -Cleveland 44141
(937) 746-9921 .. **Lukas**, James M '96 City of Franklin -35 E 4th -Franklin 45005
(440) 238-1070 .. **Lukcso**, Andrew J '69 -11005 Pearl Rd -Strongsville 44136
(513) 967-1857 .. **Luke**, Gregory C '90 -6902 Murray Av -Cincinnati 45227
(614) 228-5331 .. **Lukeman**, Paul G '77 %Don M Casto Org -191 W Nationwide Blvd -Ste 200 -Columbus 43215
(513) 352-3250 .. **Luken**, Charles J '76 Mayor -801 Plum -Rm 150 -Cincinnati 45202 **Fx**:352-5201
(513) 241-2324 .. **Luken**, Clement H Jr. '86 (Wood H&E LLP) -441 Vine -Ste 2700 -Cincinnati 45202 **Fx**:421-7269
(513) 977-8200 .. **Luken**, John D '81 (Dinsmore & S LLP) -255 E 5th -Ste 1900 -Cincinnati 45202 **Fx**:977-8141
(513) 984-2640 .. **Luken**, Joseph M '88 UAW-Ford Legal Srvcs Plan -4010 Exec Park Dr -Ste 225 -Cincinnati 45241
(513) 684-3686 .. **Luken**, Kevin P '98 NLRB -550 Main -3003 John Peck Fed Bldg -Cincinnati 45202
(513) 977-8380 .. **Luken**, Susan M '02 %Dinsmore & S LLP -255 E 5th -Ste 1900 -Cincinnati 45202 **Fx**:977-8141
(513) 352-3346 .. **Luken**, Thomas A '50 -5300 Hmltn Av -Cincinnati 45224
(313) 394-5582 .. **Lukes**, John P '97 Deloitte & Touche -600 Renaissance -Ste 900 -Detroit, MI 48243
(513) 591-2000 .. **Lukey**, Paul E '75 -1538 Cedar Av -Cincinnati 45224
(216) 522-4180 .. **Lukich**, Richard A '82 US SBA -1111 Superior Av -Ste 630 -Cleveland 44114
(440) 237-3554 .. **Lukuch**, Kollene '04 European Adoption Consultants,Inc -9800 Bstn Rd -North Royalton 44133
(216) 830-6830 .. **Lum**, David A '94 (Brouse M) -1001 Lakeside Av -Ste 1600 -Cleveland 44114 **Fx**:830-6807
(303) 930-6526 .. **Lummanick**, James F '80 Invesco Funds Grp,Inc -4350 S Monaco -Denver, CO 80237
(614) 221-5212 .. **Lumpe**, Joseph Richard '63 -37 W Broad -Ste 730 -Columbus 43215 **Fx**:221-6944
(216) 522-8179 .. **Lund**, Paul C '73 NLRB -1240 E 9th -1695 Celebrezze Bldg -Cleveland 44199 **Fx**:522-2418
(216) 621-0200 .. **Lundberg**, Arthur H '94 (Baker & H LLP) -1900 E 9th -Ste 3200 -Cleveland 44114 **Fx**:696-0740
(330) 821-2516 .. **Lundgren**, David J '76 (Lundgren G&Z) -526 E Main -Bx2595 -Alliance 44601
(330) 821-2516 .. **Lundgren Goldthorpe & Zumbar** -526 E Main -Bx2595 -Alliance 44601
(330) 343-5585 .. **Lundholm**, John K '85 Miller & K,LPA -405 Chauncey Av NW -Bx668 -New Philadelphia 44663 **Fx**:343-7977
(440) 483-4281 .. **Lundin**, Thomas M '98 Philips Med Syst -595 Miner Rd -Cleveland 44143
(414) 616-1852 .. **Lundquist**, Eric J '89 Harley-Davidson -11800 W Cptl Dr -Wauwatosa, WI 53222
(513) 621-2120 .. **Lundrigan**, Nicole M '02 %Strauss & T,LPA -150 E 4th -4th Fl -Cincinnati 45202 **Fx**:241-8259
(513) 721-5525 .. **Lundrigan**, William K '92 %Manley B -225 W Court -Cincinnati 45202 **Fx**:721-4268
(330) 451-7214 .. **Lunich**, Dana L '85 Stark Cnty Pub Def -200 W Tuscarawas -Ste 200 -Canton 44702
(513) 241-2324 .. **Lunn**, Gregory J '79 (Wood H&E LLP) -441 Vine -Ste 2700 -Cincinnati 45202 **Fx**:421-7269
Lunn, John P '78 -8498 Bowers Rd SW -Amanda 43102
(614) 221-7663 .. **Luper**, Frederick M '65 (Luper N&L,LPA) -50 W Broad -1200 LeVeque Twr -Columbus 43215 **Fx**:464-2425
(614) 221-7663 .. **Luper Neidenthal & Logan,LPA** -50 W Broad -1200 LeVeque Twr -Columbus 43215 **Fx**:464-2425
(419) 252-6298 .. **Lupica**, Thomas A '90 OfCnsl Spengler N PLL -608 Mad Av -Ste 1000 -Toledo 43604 **Fx**:241-8599
(313) 964-0110 .. **Lupo**, Kenneth L '02 %Lupo & K -660 Woodward Av -Ste 1000 -Detroit, MI 48226
(216) 321-5606 .. **Luria**, Neil F '92 -2344 Roxboro Rd -Cleveland Heights 44106
(216) 283-8970 .. **Luria**, Robert A '65 (Luria & B) -20600 Chagrin Blvd -#1111 -Beachwood 44122
(216) 921-7878 .. **Lurie**, Elana Turoff '92 Turoff & L -20320 Farmsleigh Rd -Shaker Heights 44122
(216) 514-6400 .. **Lurie**, Jeffrey K '89 %Zipkin W Co LPA -3637 S Green Rd -Zipkin Whiting Bldg -Cleveland 44122 **Fx**:514-6406
(216) 623-0000 .. **Lurie**, Robert N '94 (Javitch B&R) -1300 E 9th -14th Fl -Cleveland 44114 **Fx**:623-0190
(216) 443-7223 .. **Lurie-Licata**, Rochelle M '85 Cuyahoga Cnty Pub Def -1200 W 3rd NW -100 Lakeside Pl -Cleveland 44113
(937) 339-2627 .. **Luring**, Roger E '75 (Miller & L Co,LPA) -314 W Main -Troy 45373
(419) 332-7301 .. **Luse**, Barry F '85 Croghan Colonial Bk -323 Croghan -Fremont 43420
(614) 464-6400 .. **Lusenhop**, Peter A '98 %Vorys SS&P LLP -52 E Gay -Bx1008 -Columbus 43216 **Fx**:464-6350
(937) 223-8171 .. **Lush**, L Anthony '90 (Rogers & G) -2160 Kettering Twr -Dayton 45423 **Fx**:223-1649
(216) 781-2126 .. **Luskin**, John P '88 -4615 Mayfld Rd -Cleveland 44121
(216) 443-8423 .. **Lusnia**, Kenneth J '74 Juv Ct -2163 E 22nd -Cleveland 44115
(216) 443-7800 .. **Lusnia**, Kristen L '99 Cuyahoga Cnty Pros -1200 Ontario -8th Fl -Cleveland 44113 **Fx**:698-2270
(216) 241-5735 .. **Lustig**, Arthur F '60 (Lustig E&L Co,LPA) -526 Superior Av E -Ste 615 -Cleveland 44114
(216) 241-5735 .. **Lustig Evans & Lucas Co,LPA** -526 Superior Av E -Ste 615 -Cleveland 44114
(561) 479-3200 .. **Lustig**, Gregory J '73 Baron Capital Prtnrs -19227 Skyrdg Cir -Boca Raton, FL 33498 **Fx**:479-3230
(216) 241-5735 .. **Lustig**, Robert M '60 (Lustig E&L Co,LPA) -526 Superior Av E -Ste 615 -Cleveland 44114
(440) 256-9210 .. **Lustri**, Ralph R '87 R Lustri Co,LPA -9446 Chillicothe Rd -Kirtland 44094
(330) 499-6000 .. **Lute**, Melvin L Jr. '90 (Baker DBW&M) -400 S Main -Canton 44720 **Fx**:449-6423
(419) 586-6481 .. **Luth**, Thomas E '77 (Meikle T&L) -100 N Main -Bx485 -Celina 45822 **Fx**:586-2629
(937) 327-1767 .. **Luthe**, Suzanne M '93 Clark Cnty Pros -50 E Columbia -Bx1608 -Springfield 45501
(330) 821-9997 .. **Luther**, Brant A '02 -770 N Lincoln Av -Alliance 44601
(513) 674-4827 .. **Luther**, Dana R '04 Berkeley Premium Nutraceuticals -1661 Waycross Rd -Cincinnati 45240
Luther, Daniel V '04 -(Address Unavailable)
(419) 691-2150 .. **Luther**, Lynn A '02 %Eastman & S Ltd -1 Seagate -24th Fl -Bx10032 -Toledo 43699 **Fx**:247-1777
(330) 385-8144 .. **Luther**, Richard A '83 -49020 Ashland Pl -East Liverpool 43920
(216) 348-1700 .. **Lutjen**, George W '64 (Davis & Y) -101 Prospect Av W -Ste 1700 -Cleveland 44115 **Fx**:621-0602
(740) 382-6588 .. **Luton**, James P '76 -131 S Prospect -Ste 104 -Marion 43302 **Fx**:375-5372
(937) 865-6800 .. **Lutsch**, Eric C '95 Lexis/Nexis -Bx933 -Dayton 45401
(330) 856-3898 .. **Lutseck**, John P '84 -762 Youngstown-Kingsvll Rd -Vienna 44473
(513) 321-7728 .. **Luttenegger**, Jerry F '71 -653 Stanley Av -Cincinnati 45226 **Fx**:321-5638
(419) 842-0600 .. **Lutton**, Robert S '93 Pension Innov & Cnsltng,LLC -2254 Centennial Rd -Toledo 43617
(614) 462-3194 .. **Lutz**, Carroll W '74 Franklin Cnty Pub Def -373 S High -12th Fl -Columbus 43215
(513) 771-2444 .. **Lutz Cornetet Meyer & Rush Co,LPA** -130 Tri-Cnty Pkwy -Ste 208 -Cincinnati 45246 **Fx**:771-2447
(330) 683-5010 .. **Lutz**, Daniel R '87 (Kropf WH&L,LLP) -100 N Vine -Bx67 -Orrville 44667 **Fx**:683-5030
(513) 651-6800 .. **Lutz**, Douglas L '95 (Frost BT LLC) -201 E 5th -2200 PNC Ctr -Cincinnati 45202 **Fx**:651-6981
(513) 771-2444 .. **Lutz**, James G '60 (Lutz CM&R Co,LPA) -130 Tri-Cnty Pkwy -Ste 208 -Cincinnati 45246 **Fx**:771-2447
(440) 572-2100 .. **Lutz**, Jeffrey J '91 J Lutz Co,LPA -10950 Pearl Rd -Ste A-2 -Strongsville 44136 **Fx**:572-2170
(419) 578-9211 .. **Lutz**, Lonnie R '80 -4334 W Central Av -Ste 238 -Toledo 43615 **Fx**:536-7701
(513) 621-3440 .. **Lutz**, Mark E '81 (Denlinger R&G Co,LPA) -425 Walnut -Ste 2310 -Cincinnati 45202 **Fx**:621-4449
Lutz, Matthew D '99 -1500 Fair Av -Columbus 43205
(216) 586-3939 .. **Lutz**, Nathan L '02 %Jones D -901 Lakeside Av -Cleveland 44114 **Fx**:579-0212
(412) 281-7272 .. **Lutz**, Thomas P '03 %Dickie M&C -2 PPG Pl -Ste 400 -Pittsburgh, PA 15222
Lutz, Timothy R '89 -489 Eastwood Rd -Hinckley 44233
(216) 621-0200 .. **Lutzko**, Rebecca C '98 %Baker & H LLP -1900 E 9th -Ste 3200 -Cleveland 44114 **Fx**:696-0740
(937) 443-6600 .. **Lux**, Carl A '04 %Thompson H LLP -2000 Cthse Plz NE -Bx8801 -Dayton 45401 **Fx**:443-6635
(419) 663-6400 .. **Lux**, Paul G '81 -3 Stower Ln -Ste 6 -Norwalk 44857
(330) 535-5711 .. **Lux**, Sallie C '81 (Brouse M) -106 S Main -500 First Natl Twr -Akron 44308 **Fx**:253-8601
Luxenburg, Mitchel E '99 -4454 Silsby Rd -University Heights 44118
(440) 708-2000 .. **Lybarger**, Leonard F '63 -284 Twin Crks Dr -Bx23428 -Chagrin Falls 44023
(330) 264-4444 .. **Lycans**, Andrew P '04 %Critchfield C&J Ltd -225 N Market -Bx599 -Wooster 44691 **Fx**:263-9278
(330) 762-2600 .. **Lyden**, Kevin T '87 Joondeph & B,LLP -50 S Main -Ste 700 -Akron 44308 **Fx**:762-2604
(419) 867-8900 .. **Lyden Liebenthal & Chappell,Ltd** -5565 Airport Hwy -Ste 101 -Toledo 43615 **Fx**:867-8909
(419) 867-8900 .. **Lyden**, Patricia G '80 (Lyden L&C,Ltd) -5565 Airport Hwy -Ste 101 -Toledo 43615 **Fx**:867-8909
(330) 535-5711 .. **Lyden**, Shawn M '95 (Brouse M) -106 S Main -500 First Natl Twr -Akron 44308 **Fx**:253-8601
(614) 793-1246 .. **Lyden**, Terrence W '86 Lyle Mngmt Co,LLC -6347 Mem'l Dr -Dublin 43017
(513) 977-8200 .. **Lydon**, Deborah R '81 (Dinsmore & S LLP) -255 E 5th -Ste 1900 -Cincinnati 45202 **Fx**:977-8141
(419) 882-7100 .. **Lydy & Moan,Ltd** -4930 Holland Sylvania Rd -Sylvania 43560 **Fx**:882-1120
(419) 882-7100 .. **Lydy**, Robert J '72 Lydy & M,Ltd -4930 Holland Sylvania Rd -Sylvania 43560 **Fx**:882-1120
(330) 497-9455 .. **Lyke**, Trevor A '96 -1375 S Main -Ste 202 -North Canton 44720
(614) 292-2681 .. **Lyke-Catalano**, Heather R '97 OSU -1767 Barrington Rd -Columbus 43221
(513) 241-3100 .. **Lykins**, Susana E '02 %Lerner S&R -120 E 4th -8th Fl -Cincinnati 45202
(419) 247-2500 .. **Lyle**, Dennis A '84 (Fuller & H,Ltd) -One SeaGate -Ste 1700 -Bx2088 -Toledo 43603 **Fx**:247-2665
(614) 462-6418 .. **Lyle**, James K '00 Franklin Cnty CSEA -80 E Fulton -Columbus 43215
(937) 393-4731 .. **Lyle**, Jeffrey J '83 Lyle Law Ofc -139 E Beech -Hillsboro 45133
Lyle, Roxana R '81 -Bx532 -Kent 44240
(614) 466-3876 .. **Lyles**, Andrew E '87 OH DOT Advrtsng Device Cntrl -1980 W Broad -1st Fl -Columbus 43223
(614) 469-3939 .. **Lyles**, Kevin D '86 (Jones D) -325 John H McConnell Blvd -Ste 600 -Bx165017 -Columbus 43216 **Fx**:461-4198
(513) 241-2324 .. **Lyman**, Beverly A '96 %Wood H&E LLP -441 Vine -Ste 2700 -Cincinnati 45202 **Fx**:421-7269
(614) 252-0688 .. **Lyman**, Chester T Jr. '82 -1313 E Broad -Ste 17 -Columbus 43205
(614) 365-2700 .. **Lynch**, Chanda L '00 %Squire S&D LLP -41 S High -1300 Huntngtn Ctr -Columbus 43215 **Fx**:365-2499
(419) 525-1000 .. **Lynch**, Charles D '75 -6 W 3rd -Ste 200 -Mansfield 44902
(216) 261-4004 .. **Lynch**, David M '82 -216 Wells Ct -Euclid 44132
(216) 787-3653 .. **Lynch**, Debra P '83 OH Indus Comm-Hearing Ofc -615 Superior Av SW -Cleveland 44113
(216) 622-3600 .. **Lynch**, James C '68 US Atty -801 W Superior -Ste 400 -Cleveland 44113 **Fx**:622-3370
(937) 224-3333 .. **Lynch**, Jane M '82 (Green & G) -109 N Main -Ste 800 -Dayton 45402 **Fx**:224-4311

(281) 366-7733 ..**Lynch,** John E Jr. '80 BP Amoco -501 Westlake Park Blvd
-Bx3092 -Houston, TX 77253

(216) 771-2545 ..**Lynch,** John Kennedy '57 (Lynch & L Co,LPA) -526 Superior Av E
-Ste 410 -Cleveland 44114

(330) 564-4000 ..**Lynch,** Joseph M Jr. '80 Doyle Systems -284 7th NW
-Barberton 44203

(419) 609-7000 ..**Lynch,** Kula H '98 Hoty Enterprises,Inc -4918 Milan Rd
-Sandusky 44870

(330) 374-0066 ..**Lynch,** Margaret T '90 (M Lynch & Assoc) -665 W Exchange
-Akron 44302

(440) 543-6790 ..**Lynch,** Matthew J '80 (Lynch Assoc) -Bx23279
-Chagrin Falls 44023

(419) 248-8000 ..**Lynch,** Patricia Ann '75 Owens Corning -1 Owens Corning Pkwy
-Leg Dept -Toledo 43659

(419) 668-8403 ..**Lynch,** Richard S '74 (Lynch & W Co,LPA) -51 E Main -Ste B
-Norwalk 44857 **Fx:**668-4172

(417) 833-8200 ..**Lynch,** Robert A '87 (R Lynch,PC) -1360 E Bradford Pkwy -Ste 10
-Springfield, MO 65804

(216) 664-3579 ..**Lynch,** Robert P Jr. '00 Dept of Law -601 Lakeside Av
-Rm 106 City Hall -Cleveland 44114 **Fx:**664-2663

(216) 771-0999 ..**Lynch,** Robert T '75 Lynch Legal Srvcs -2900 Fairmont Blvd
-Cleveland Heights 44118

(440) 338-8935 ..**Lynch,** Stephen T '98 -5212 Maple Sprngs Dr
-Chagrin Falls 44022

(513) 946-3163 ..**Lynch,** Teresa P '91 Hamilton Cnty Pros -230 E 9th
-Cincinnati 45202 **Fx:**946-3017

(216) 621-4636 ..**Lynch,** Tiaon M '98 %Gallup B & Assoc -815 Superior Av E
-Ste 1810 The Superior Bldg -Cleveland 44114

(859) 344-1188 ..**Lynch,** Timothy A '01 %Hemmer SPD&K -250 Grandvw Dr
-Ste 200 -Fort Mitchell, KY 41017

(419) 668-8403 ..**Lynch & White Co,LPA** -51 E Main -Ste B -Norwalk 44857
Fx:668-4172

(216) 443-4292 ..**Lynch-King,** Joan M '95 USPS-Inspection Srvc -2400 Orange Av
-Bx5001 -Cleveland 44101

(330) 434-3000 ..**Lynett,** John J '61 OfCnsl Roderick & L -One Cascade Plz
-Ste 1500 -Akron 44308 **Fx:**434-9220

(330) 762-0700 ..**Lynett,** John J Jr. '93 (Slater Z&G) -One Cascade Plz -Ste 2210
-Akron 44308 **Fx:**762-3923

(330) 375-2285 ..**Lynett,** Thomas F Jr. '57 Akron Mun Ct -217 S High -Akron 44308

(614) 466-0451 ..**Lynn,** James M '98 PUCO -180 E Broad -Columbus 43266

(614) 221-3155 ..**Lynn,** Sarah E '92 OfCnsl Bailey C LLC -10 W Broad
-Columbus 43215 **Fx:**221-0479

(330) 971-8190 ..**Lynn,** Stacy L '97 Cuyahoga Falls Pros -2310 2nd
-Cuyahoga Falls 44221

(614) 466-1305 ..**Lynskey,** Sandra L '97 Atty Gen -30 E Broad -Columbus 43215
Fx:466-8898

(216) 622-8200 ..**Lyon,** Charles B '71 (Calfee H&G LLP) -800 Superior Av -Ste 1400
-Cleveland 44114 **Fx:**241-0816

(801) 323-2270 ..**Lyon,** David J '79 OfCnsl Fabian & C -215 S State -12th Fl
-Salt Lake City, UT 84111

(954) 752-3400 ..**Lyon,** James B '80 (JB Lyon,PA) -3300 N Univ Dr -Ste 802
-Coral Springs, FL 33065 **Fx:**752-3411

(513) 852-5600 ..**Lyon,** Joseph M '03 %Lopez HRM&S -312 Walnut -Ste 2090
-Cincinnati 45202 **Fx:**852-5611

(202) 273-0677 ..**Lyon,** Kathleen E '98 USDC-Northern Dist -1099 14th NW
-Rm 8407 -Washington, DC 20570

(513) 421-6630 ..**Lyon,** Michael F '75 Lindhorst & D Co,LPA -312 Walnut -Ste 2300
-Cincinnati 45202

    Lyonette, Desiree '01 -2113 Stirrup Ln -5 -Toledo 43613

(937) 255-5270 ..**Lyons,** Bridget E '98 AFMCLO/JAN -1864 Fourth -Bldg 15
-Wright Patterson AFB 45433

(614) 464-6271 ..**Lyons,** Christina M '04 %Vorys SS&P LLP -52 E Gay -Bx1008
-Columbus 43216 **Fx:**719-5253

    Lyons, David P '95 -(Address Unavailable)

(513) 621-6673 ..**Lyons & Fries Co,LPA** -35 E 7th -Ste 750 -Cincinnati 45202

(614) 228-1313 ..**Lyons,** Gary W '64 (DeLibera L&B) -336 S High -Columbus 43215

(614) 286-9690 ..**Lyons,** George A '84 -1150 Morse Rd -Ste 307 -Columbus 43229

(513) 621-6673 ..**Lyons,** James L '50 (Lyons & F Co,LPA) -35 E 7th -Ste 750
-Cincinnati 45202

(440) 357-5000 ..**Lyons,** James M '78 (Lyons & O Co LPA) -240 E Main
-Painesville 44077

(330) 670-7300 ..**Lyons,** James M Jr. '82 %Hanna C&P,LLP -3737 Embssy Pkwy
-Bx5521 -Akron 44334 **Fx:**670-0977

(513) 621-6673 ..**Lyons,** James W '75 (Lyons & F Co,LPA) -35 E 7th -Ste 750
-Cincinnati 45202

(513) 777-2222 ..**Lyons & Lyons Co,LPA** -8310 Prnctn-Glendale Rd -Ste B
-West Chester 45069

(937) 783-2401 ..**Lyons McHenry & Dunlap** -212 W Main -Blanchester 45107

(740) 284-8111 ..**Lyons,** Meeta Bass '87 -824 Oxford Blvd -Steubenville 43952

(330) 659-3296 ..**Lyons,** Michael K '85 Pros -3300 Broadvw Rd -Richfield 44286

(859) 371-9889 ..**Lyons,** Michael W '96 -7130 Price Pike -Florence, KY 41042

(513) 777-2222 ..**Lyons,** Robert H '80 (Lyons & L Co,LPA)
-8310 Prnctn-Glendale Rd -Ste B -West Chester 45069

(404) 581-8550 ..**Lyons,** Rory D '85 (Jones DR&P) -303 Pchtree -Ste 3500
-Atlanta, GA 30308

    Lyren, Philip S '93 -2947 Courtland Blvd -Shaker Heights 44122

    Lysenko, John '99 -Bx487 -Barberton 44203

(888) 955-2947 ..**Lytle,** Alicia M '98 (Lytle & Assoc,LLC) -Bx200494
-Cleveland 44120

(216) 664-4333 ..**Ma,** Catherine '98 Dept of Law -601 Lakeside Av -Rm 106 City Hall
-Cleveland 44114 **Fx:**664-2663

(513) 621-2120 ..**Maag,** Marilyn J '86 Strauss & T,LPA -150 E 4th -4th Fl
-Cincinnati 45202 **Fx:**241-8259

(330) 721-0000 ..**Maag,** Robert E Jr. '83 %Walker & J,LPA -231 S Bway
-Medina 44256 **Fx:**722-6446

(614) 228-5822 ..**Maas,** Brandy M '03 %Rich C&D,LLC -300 E Broad -Ste 300
-Columbus 43215 **Fx:**228-2725

(330) 373-1000 ..**Maas,** Paula D '87 %C Richards -159 E Market -Ste 300 -Warren
44481 **Fx:**394-5291

(330) 792-6611 ..**Maas,** Steven D '82 (Heller MM&M Co LPA) -54 Wstchstr Dr
-Bx4144 -Youngstown 44515

(330) 499-0049 ..**Maasz,** Philip Steven '91 -4571 Stephen Cir NW -Belpar Law Ctr
-Canton 44718

(614) 249-8438 ..**Mabe,** William E '76 Nationwide Ins Co -One Nationwide Plz
-(1-08-04) -Columbus 43215

(419) 524-1403 ..**Mabee & Mills** -24 W 3rd -Ste 300 -Mansfield 44902 **Fx:**522-4315

(419) 524-1403 ..**Mabee,** Robert E '50 (Mabee & M) -24 W 3rd -Ste 300
-Mansfield 44902 **Fx:**522-4315

(216) 621-4244 ..**MacAdams,** Pamela J '84 (Morganstern M&D Co,LPA)
-623 W St Clair Av -Cleveland 44113 **Fx:**621-2951

(330) 493-1570 ..**Macala Baasten McKinley & Gore,LLC** -4150 Belden Vllg NW
-Ste 604 -Canton 44718 **Fx:**493-7042

(330) 337-7934 ..**Macala,** Brian J '92 -192 S Lincoln Av -Salem 44460

(330) 493-1570 ..**Macala,** Ronald G '74 (Macala BM&G,LLC) -4150 Belden Vllg NW
-Ste 604 -Canton 44718 **Fx:**493-7042

(614) 443-1512 ..**Macali,** Virginia L '85 State of Ohio -Hgh Pnt Transitions
-287 Stewart Av -Columbus 43206

(216) 261-2800 ..**Macauda,** Vincent '91 (V Macauda Co,LPA)
-26301 Curtiss Wright Pkwy -Ste 210 -Richmond Heights 44143
Fx:261-4208

(937) 298-1054 ..**Macbeth,** William H '63 (Murr CC&M) -401 E Stroop Rd
-Kettering 45429 **Fx:**293-1766

(614) 278-6769 ..**Macbeth,** William H III '95 Big Lots -300 Phillipi Rd
-Leg Dept 10051 -Bx28512 -Columbus 43228

    Macce, Barbara R '78 -(Address Unavailable)

(513) 321-2334 ..**MacConnell,** Stephen T '72 -3095 Victoria Av -Cincinnati 45208

(440) 891-5019 ..**MacCracken,** Alan L III '00 Cleveland Browns -76 Lou Groza Blvd
-Berea 44017

(606) 473-7303 ..**MacDonald,** Bruce W '87 (McBrayer ML&K) -Main & Harrison
-Bx280 -Greenup, KY 41144

(216) 523-1400 ..**Macdonald,** George W '79 -614 Superior Av NW -Ste 848
-Cleveland 44113

(330) 434-5444 ..**MacDonald,** Ida Lyn '83 (Lambert & M Co,LPA) -265 S Main
-Akron 44308

(513) 665-3500 ..**MacDonald,** Mark A '80 (Freund F&A) -105 E 4th -Ste 1400
-Cincinnati 45202 **Fx:**665-3503

(937) 593-6065 ..**MacDonald,** Robert B Jr. '75 (Thompson DHMW&T)
-1111 Rush Av -Bx68 -Bellefontaine 43311

(330) 792-0439 ..**MacDonald,** Stewart D '72 -3143 Mahoning Av
-Youngstown 44509

(216) 443-9000 ..**MacDougall,** Irene M '83 (Porter WM&A LLP) -925 Euclid Av
-Ste 1700 -Cleveland 44115 **Fx:**443-9011

    MacDowell, Benjamin J '02 -227 W Nationwide Blvd -Ste 200
-Columbus 43215

(216) 443-5809 ..**Mace,** Birgit '90 Cuyahoga Cnty Pros -1910 Carnegie Av
-Whitlatch Bldg -Cleveland 44115 **Fx:**443-5815

(216) 479-8500 ..**Mace,** Damond R '84 (Squire S&D LLP) -127 Pub Sq
-4900 Key Twr -Cleveland 44114 **Fx:**479-8780

(202) 622-7830 ..**MacEachen,** John D '79 IRS -1111 Const Av NW
-Washington, DC 20224

(216) 360-9919 ..**Macedonio,** Rosemary A '80 (Macedonio T&B,PLL)
-29525 Chagrin Blvd -Ste 208 -Cleveland 44122

(216) 360-9919 ..**Macedonio Toerek & Box,PLL** -29525 Chagrin Blvd -Ste 208
-Cleveland 44122

(330) 740-2330 ..**Macejko,** Joseph R '98 %Mahoning Cnty Pros -21 W Boardman
-6th Fl -Youngstown 44503 **Fx:**740-2008

(330) 744-9007 ..**Macejko,** Melissa M '99 A Suhar & Assoc -11 Fed Plz Central
-Ste 1101 -Bx1497 -Youngstown 44501

(330) 746-1054 ..**Macejko,** Theodore T Jr. '63 (Macejko & M) -34 Fed Plz W
-808 Wick Bldg -Youngstown 44503

    Macek, Stephen G '82 -18780 Claridon-Troy Rd -Hiram 44234

(513) 621-2044 ..**Macey & Chern** -1014 Vine -2500 Kroger Bldg -Cincinnati 45202

(937) 226-9354 ..**Macey & Chern** -40 W 4th -Ste 2160 -Dayton 45402 **Fx:**226-9359

(740) 653-4259 ..**MacFadden,** Denise D '82 Fairfield Cnty Pros -201 S Broad -4th Fl
-Lancaster 43130

(937) 593-8725 ..**MacGillivray,** Douglas D '65 MacGillivray Law Ofc -325 N Main
-Bellefontaine 43311

(330) 478-2595 ..**Machan,** Mitchell A '81 -3810 Tuscarawas W -Mellett Plz
-Canton 44708

(330) 497-9700 ..**Machan,** Sandra J '91 (Machan & Assoc Co,LPA)
-6647 Frank Av NW -Ste 110 -North Canton 44720

(419) 936-5120 ..**MacHarg,** James C '75 -411 Mich -Toledo 43624

(419) 241-2777 ..**Machin,** Barbara E '78 OfCnsl Bunda S&D,PLL -One SeaGate
-Ste 650 -Toledo 43604 **Fx:**241-4697

(614) 888-4017 ..**Machle,** Kathi J '87 -286 Weydon Rd -Worthington 43085

(513) 946-3000 ..**Machol,** Melynda J '88 Hamilton Cnty Pros -230 E 9th
-Cincinnati 45202 **Fx:**946-3017

(330) 702-0033 ..**Machuga,** Richard W '87 -3855 Starr Centre Dr -Ste A
-Canfield 44406 **Fx:**702-1133

(216) 515-1660 ..**Maciak,** Brian A '00 %Frantz W LLP -127 Pub Sq
-2500 Key Center -Cleveland 44114 **Fx:**515-1650

(614) 719-3240 ..**Macias,** Lisa A '96 %Hon EA Sargus Jr -85 Marconi Blvd -Rm 301
-Columbus 43215

(937) 496-3158 ..**Maciorowski,** Michelle M '97 Montgomery Cnty Cmn Pleas Ct
Juv Div -14 W 4th -8th Fl -Dayton 45422 **Fx:**496-3157

(440) 247-5740 ..**Mac Iver,** Michael A '82 Case Western Reserve Univ -Bx505
-Chagrin Falls 44022

(216) 861-1700 ..**Mack,** David E '75 Stevens & M -75 Pub Sq -Ste 1450
-Cleveland 44113

(419) 241-9000 ..**Mack,** David J '00 %Shumaker L&K,LLP -1000 Jackson
-Toledo 43624 **Fx:**241-6894

(419) 524-4683 ..**Mack,** Deborah L '96 -34 Park S -Mansfield 44902

    Mack, Fernando O '94 -323 W Lakeside -Ste 450
-Cleveland 44113

(419) 729-3944 ..**Mack,** James R '67 -5198 Summit -Toledo 43611

(216) 566-7800 ..**Mack,** Jimmie Jr. '79 -526 Superior -Ste 716 -Cleveland 44114

    Mack, Kevin A '84 -117 Hidden Pnt -Hendersonville, TN 37075

(614) 716-1642 ..**Mack,** Kevin D '86 Amer Elec Pwr Co -1 Riverside Plz
-Columbus 43215

(216) 520-5502 ..**Mack,** Khara M Singer '02 West Grp -6111 Oak Tree Blvd
-Bx318063 -Cleveland 44131

(504) 885-9994 ..**Mack,** Lawrence E '93 Robein U&L,PLC -Bx6768
-Metairie, LA 70009

(216) 881-6600 ..**Mack,** Lisa A '86 NEORSD -3826 Euclid Av -Cleveland 44115
Fx:881-4407

(419) 354-9250 ..**Mack,** Mary L '90 Wood Cnty Pros -One Cthse Sq
-Bowling Green 43402 **Fx:**353-2904

(330) 865-9250 ..**Mack,** Michael R '73 (MR Mack Co,LPA) -34 Merz Blvd -Ste B -Fairlawn 44333

(216) 575-2708 ..**Mack,** Richard W '78 Natl City Bank -1900 E 9th -Bx5756 -Cleveland 44101

(216) 520-5508 ..**Mack,** Stephanie M '00 West Grp -6111 Oak Tree Blvd -Bx318063 -Cleveland 44131

(513) 931-1086 ..**Mack,** Thomas A '79 -954 N Hill Ln -Cincinnati 45224

(330) 747-2661 ..**Mackall,** Robert L III '00 Cafaro Co -2445 Belmont Av -Bx2186 -Youngstown 44504

(614) 462-5428 ..**Mackanos,** Jennifer L '02 %Kegler BH&R -65 E State -Ste 1800 -Columbus 43215 Fx:464-2634

MacKay, Grant W '04 -(Address Unavailable)

(419) 241-9000 ..**MacKay,** John J '75 (Shumaker L&K,LLP) -1000 Jackson -Toledo 43624 Fx:241-6894

(440) 886-4500 ..**Mackay,** Michael '77 -7017 Pearl Rd -Cleveland 44130

MacKay, Walter S '58 -3423 Nandale Dr -Cincinnati 45239

(614) 464-0011 ..**Macke,** Francis J '75 F Macke Co LPA -400 S 5th -Ste 303 -Columbus 43215

(614) 464-0011 ..**Macke,** Jason A '98 F Macke Co LPA -400 S 5th -Ste 303 -Columbus 43215

(614) 462-3580 ..**Macke,** Kenneth W '77 Franklin Cnty Ct of Apls -373 S High -Columbus 43215

(614) 221-2121 ..**MacKenzie,** Paul A '92 Isaac BL&T,LLP -250 E Broad -Ste 900 Mdlnd Bldg -Columbus 43215 Fx:365-9516

(740) 380-1555 ..**Mackey,** Carol A '80 CMC Real Estate Grp -48 W Main -Logan 43138

(216) 696-7177 ..**Mackey,** Cheryl A '95 %Teamor & Assoc -1301 E 9th -Ste 3110 -Cleveland 44114 Fx:696-7195

(330) 762-2411 ..**Mackey,** James F '98 %Amer C Co,LPA -159 S Main -6th Fl -Akron 44308 Fx:762-9918

(216) 781-1212 ..**Mackey,** James M '74 (Walter & H LLP) -1301 E 9th -Ste 3500 -Cleveland 44114 Fx:575-0911

(614) 523-7575 ..**Mackey,** Jeffrey D '81 (Fusco MMS&W,LLP) -655 Cooper Rd -Westerville 43081 Fx:523-7580

(330) 452-6567 ..**Mackey,** John N '71 -217 2nd NW -Bliss Twr Ste 610 -Canton 44702

(216) 443-7800 ..**Mackin,** Brendan J '96 Cuyahoga Cnty Pros -1200 Ontario -8th Fl -Cleveland 44113 Fx:698-2270

(440) 930-4103 ..**Mackin,** John F '61 Mun Ct Judge -32855 Walker Rd -Avon Lake 44012

(614) 221-8448 ..**Mackin,** Kerry McConaghy '02 %Buckingham D&B,LLP -191 W Nationwide Blvd -Ste 300 -Bx151120 -Columbus 43215 Fx:221-8590

(216) 522-4914 ..**Mackin,** Maura C '89 SSA/OHA -1350 Euclid Av -7th Fl -Cleveland 44115

(937) 898-1465 ..**Mackin,** Melanie R '84 (Scheuer M&B LLC) -8565 N Dixie Dr -Dayton 45414 Fx:898-1478

(440) 933-3177 ..**Mackin,** Patrick C '87 -33463 Lk Rd -Bx77 -Avon Lake 44012 Fx:933-7873

(419) 874-5610 ..**Mackin,** Thomas G '90 OfCnsl Croy & H,LLP -801 W South Boundary -Ste C -Perrysburg 43551

(614) 480-5120 ..**Mackin,** William J '94 Huntington Natl Bank -41 S High -HCO0220 -Columbus 43287

(937) 461-6200 ..**Mackinnon,** Douglas A '01 Cincinnati Fin Corp -130 W 2nd -Ste 1850 -Dayton 45402

(614) 224-1008 ..**MacKinnon,** John J '83 -501 S High -Columbus 43215

(937) 443-6730 ..**Macklin,** Crofford J Jr. '77 (Thompson H LLP) -2000 Cthse Plz NE -Bx8801 -Dayton 45401 Fx:443-6635

(614) 249-8720 ..**Macklin,** George K '84 Nationwide Ins Co -1 Nationwide Plz -Columbus 43215

(330) 848-6715 ..**Macko,** Gregory '93 Barberton Law Dept -576 W Park Av -Barberton 44203

(614) 864-5200 ..**Mackura,** Denise '82 Right to Life,Inc -2238 S Hmltn Rd -Columbus 43232

(330) 682-3000 ..**Mackus,** Eloise L '79 Smuckers -Bx280 -Orrville 44667

MacLaughlin, Lewis H III '73 -107 E Dunedin Rd -Columbus 43214

(513) 751-3600 ..**MacLeid,** Matthew T '63 -1348 Chapel -Bx6099 -Cincinnati 45206

(419) 255-5900 ..**MacMillan,** Richard S '80 (MacMillan S&T,LLC) -720 Water -4th Fl -Toledo 43604 Fx:255-9639

(419) 255-5900 ..**MacMillan Sobanski & Todd,LLC** -720 Water -4th Fl -Toledo 43604 Fx:255-9639

(614) 462-5462 ..**MacMurray,** Helen M '87 (Kegler BH&R) -65 E State -Ste 1800 -Columbus 43215 Fx:464-2634

(614) 466-5610 ..**Macon-Bruce,** Marcia J '90 Atty Gen -150 E Gay -Columbus 43215 Fx:752-2732

Macpherson, Catherine R '78 -91 Mtn Vw Dr -Phoenix, OR 97535

(513) 852-3497 ..**MacQueeney,** Vincent P '89 Atty Gen -441 Vine -1600 Carew Twr -Cincinnati 45202 Fx:852-3484

(330) 996-8585 ..**Macro,** Judith A '93 SummaCare Inc -400 W Market -Bx3620 -Akron 44309

(440) 243-2800 ..**Madachik,** Joseph M '96 -7530 Lucerne Dr -Ste 200 -Middleburg Heights 44130

(440) 998-6950 ..**Madden,** Daniel L '75 -Bx18 -Kingsville 44048

(330) 451-7200 ..**Madden,** Jean A '96 Stark Cnty Pub Def -200 W Tuscarawas -Ste 200 -Canton 44702

(216) 522-9000 ..**Madden,** Justin F '93 (Landskroner·G·M,Ltd) -1360 W 9th -Ste 200 -Cleveland 44113 Fx:522-9007

(614) 221-1216 ..**Madden,** Kathleen J '01 %Downes H&F -400 S 5th -Ste 200 -Columbus 43215 Fx:221-8769

(216) 696-1080 ..**Madden,** Michael I '85 D Seaman & Assoc Co,LPA -614 Superior Av W -Ste 1600 Rckfllr Bldg -Cleveland 44113

Madden, Michele A '03 -(Address Unavailable)

(513) 621-8700 ..**Madden,** Stephan D '80 S Madden Co,LPA -601 Main -3rd Fl -Cincinnati 45202

(614) 466-8911 ..**Madden,** Thomas E '03 Atty Gen -30 E Broad -Columbus 43215 Fx:728-7582

(813) 354-6960 ..**Madden,** Timothy M '83 Progressive Cslty Ins Co -3725 W Grace -Ste 300 -Tampa, FL 33607

(513) 241-3100 ..**Maddix,** Anita L '02 Lerner S&R -120 E 4th -8th Fl -Cincinnati 45202

(330) 467-5030 ..**Maddock,** Darrell D '82 UAW Legal Srvc Plan -8536 Crow Dr -Ste 110 -Macedonia 44056

(614) 224-0933 ..**Maddox,** Mark S '84 (Frost & M Co,LPA) -400 S 5th -Ste 301 -Columbus 43215

(216) 698-4785 ..**Madigan,** Holley M '97 Common Pleas Ct Juv Ct Div -2163 E 22nd -Cleveland 44115

(419) 245-1020 ..**Madigan,** John T '73 %Law Dept -One Govt Ctr -Ste 2250 -Toledo 43604 Fx:245-1090

(216) 522-5396 ..**Madigan,** Joseph P '76 Dfnse Fin & Accntng Srvc -1240 E 9th -Rm 2829 -Cleveland 44199

(216) 781-5470 ..**Madigan,** Kathleen A '04 %Ziegler M&M LLP -925 Euclid Av -2020 Huntngtn Bldg -Cleveland 44115 Fx:781-0714

(614) 461-1100 ..**Madison,** Timothy G '94 (Swedlow BLL&D Co,LPA) -10 W Broad -Ste 2400 -Columbus 43215 Fx:461-8178

(330) 376-2272 ..**Madison,** Walter T '99 Williams & Assoc -106 S Main -Ste 2300 -Akron 44308 Fx:376-5618

Madonna, Alfred P '95 -240 Sunnyrige Av #109 -Fairfield, CT 06824

Madorski, Harold A '81 -16500 Shaker Blvd -Cleveland 44120

(216) 292-4666 ..**Madorsky,** Larry I '67 L Madorsky & Assoc Co,LPA -2101 Richmond Rd -Ste 39 -Beachwood 44122

Madow, Paul B '80 -24601 Meldon Blvd -Beachwood 44122

(614) 466-1604 ..**Madriguera,** Christina M '00 OH Judicial Conf -65 S Front -Columbus 43215

(419) 243-6148 ..**Madrzykowski,** Jeffrey Jon '92 Manahan PB&D -414 N Erie -Bx2328 -Toledo 43603

(440) 826-5803 ..**Madzy,** Matthew J '99 City of Berea -11 Berea Cmmns -Berea 44017

(419) 424-7276 ..**Maekask,** Paul V '97 Hancock Cnty Pub Def -316 Dorney Plz -Findlay 45840

(216) 586-3939 ..**Maersch,** Karl M '02 %Jones D -901 Lakeside Av -Cleveland 44114 Fx:579-0212

(740) 779-6662 ..**Maerten-Moore,** Sharon A '98 4th Dist Ct Appeals -14 S Paint -Ste 38 -Chillicothe 45601

(216) 241-6602 ..**Maestle,** Shawn W '94 (Weston HFP&H LLP) -50 Pub Sq -2500 Trmnl Twr -Cleveland 44113 Fx:621-8369

(330) 796-1755 ..**Maffei,** Rocco J '77 Lockheed Martin -1210 Massillon Rd -Akron 44315

(937) 443-6804 ..**Maffett,** Jennifer L '02 %Thompson H LLP -2000 Cthse Plz NE -Bx8801 -Dayton 45401 Fx:443-6635

(513) 579-0080 ..**Magas,** Steven M '82 %Smith R&S Co,LPA -1014 Vine -Ste 2350 -Cincinnati 45202 Fx:579-0222

(740) 452-8431 ..**Magaziner,** Blair L '84 (Magaziner M&F) -44 S 6th -Zanesville 43701

(740) 452-8431 ..**Magaziner McGlade & Fitz** -44 S 6th -Zanesville 43701

(937) 225-4063 ..**Magee,** Christine L '70 Montgomery Cnty Dom Rltns Ct -301 W 3rd -Rm 204 -Bx972 -Dayton 45402

(216) 443-7223 ..**Magee,** David T '95 Cuyahoga Cnty Pub Def -1200 W 3rd NW -100 Lakeside Pl -Cleveland 44113

(513) 621-9660 ..**Magee,** James V Jr. '74 -36 E 7th -Ste 2020 -Cincinnati 45202

Magee, Linda L '73 -2184 Telegraph Ct -Cincinnati 45244

(513) 579-2861 ..**Magee,** Mark E '75 Provident Bank -1 E 4th -Cincinnati 45202

Magee, Neal H II '66 -(Address Unavailable)

(419) 422-7393 ..**Magee,** Timothy A '96 -130 Sherman Dr -Findlay 45840

(614) 272-6560 ..**Magelaner,** Thomas L '90 (Magelaner & Assoc) -2975 W Broad -Columbus 43204

(513) 241-7111 ..**Magenheim,** Alissa J '04 %O'Connor A&L Co,LPA -1014 Vine -22nd Fl -Cincinnati 45202 Fx:241-7197

(330) 723-9536 ..**Magensky,** Jill A '04 %Medina Cnty Pros -72 Pub Sq -Medina 44256

(330) 746-6301 ..**Mager,** Kevin D '91 -219 W Boardman -Youngstown 44503

(239) 334-8890 ..**Maggiano,** Molly A '03 %Aiken O & Assoc -2072 Victoria Av -Fort Myers, FL 33901

(614) 464-2236 ..**Maggied,** Pamela N '79 -50 W Broad -Ste 2250 -Columbus 43215

(513) 977-8306 ..**Maggio,** Margaret M '02 %Dinsmore & S LLP -255 E 5th -Ste 1900 -Cincinnati 45202 Fx:977-8141

(317) 276-2925 ..**Magid,** Terren B '90 Eli Lilly & Co -Lilly Corp Ctr DC 1074 -Indianapolis, IN 46285

(330) 792-6611 ..**Magill,** Terren A '87 (Heller MM&M Co LPA) -54 Wstchstr Dr -Bx4144 -Youngstown 44515

(614) 255-7552 ..**MaGinn,** Tara M '04 %Freund F&A -65 E State -Ste 800 -Columbus 43215 Fx:827-6552

(614) 527-6762 ..**Maglione,** Timothy I '93 %OH State Med Assoc -3401 Mill Run Dr -Hilliard 43026

(216) 771-5588 ..**Magner,** Caitlin E '02 Rosner & Assoc,LLC -812 Huron Rd -Ste 601 Caxton Bldg -Cleveland 44115 Fx:771-5894

(513) 621-8280 ..**Magner,** George E Jr. '85 -7 W 7th -Ste 1800 -Cincinnati 45202

(513) 721-0200 ..**Magnus,** Michele L '03 %McKinney & N Co,LPA -15 E 8th -Cincinnati 45202 Fx:632-5688

(513) 731-2889 ..**Magnus,** Richard A '82 -4526 Mntgmry Rd -Cincinnati 45212

(507) 934-6940 ..**Magnus,** Ryan B '97 %Brandt Law Ofc -219 W Nassau -Bx57 -St Peter, MN 56082 Fx:934-6909

(614) 371-1101 ..**Magnuson,** James A '76 (Magnuson & B) -1720 Zollinger Rd -Columbus 43221

(303) 672-2980 ..**Magnuson,** Kevin M '94 Qwest Srvcs Corp -1801 Calif -38th Fl -Denver, CO 80205

Magri, Joseph J '63 -653 Sandpiper Bay Dr SW -Sunset Beach, NC 28468

(419) 249-7900 ..**Maguire,** Edmund T '63 (Robison C&O) -Four SeaGate -9th Fl -Toledo 43604 Fx:249-7911

(419) 421-3277 ..**Maguire,** John K '83 Marathon Ashland Petro LLC -539 S Main -Findlay 45840 Fx:421-3578

(614) 224-1222 ..**Maguire,** Patrick D '76 (Maguire & S,LLP) -250 Civic Ctr Dr -Ste 200 -Columbus 43215 Fx:224-1236

(614) 436-0346 ..**Maguire,** Peggy L '00 %Johnson S & Assoc,LLP -299 S State -Westerville 43081 Fx:436-0347

(330) 633-0666 ..**Maguire,** Robert D '75 -190 East Av -Tallmadge 44278 Fx:633-0626

(614) 224-1222 ..**Maguire & Schneider, LLP** -250 Civic Ctr Dr -Ste 200 -Columbus 43215 Fx:224-1236

(800) 600-1222 ..**Maguire & Schneider, LLP** -1370 Ontario -Ste 1700 -Cleveland 44113

(440) 338-6338 ..**Magyaros,** Anne S '90 -1188 Bell Rd -Ste 105 -Chagrin Falls 44022

(614) 464-6400 ..**Mahaffey,** Carol '83 Vorys SS&P LLP -52 E Gay -Bx1008 -Columbus 43216 Fx:464-6350

(614) 462-3194 .. **Mahaffey**, John P '80 Franklin Cnty Pub Def -373 S High -12th Fl
-Columbus 43215

(614) 279-5360 .. **Mahaffey**, Morgan E '99 -439 Binns Blvd -Columbus 43204

(419) 829-2255 .. **Mahaffey**, Ty S '02 (Hizer & M,LLC) -8657 Central Av -Ste B
-Sylvania 43560

(440) 835-5620 .. **Mahall**, Stephen K '94 Trimark -564 Marvis Dr -Bay Village 44140

(937) 223-6003 .. **Mahan**, Charles W '71 (Dunlevey M&F) -110 N Main -Ste 1000
-Dayton 45402 **Fx:**223-8550

(216) 443-7800 .. **Mahaney**, Kimberly A '92 Cuyahoga Cnty Pros -1200 Ontario
-8th Fl -Cleveland 44113 **Fx:**698-2270

(216) 443-7295 .. **Maher**, Christopher S '91 Cuyahoga Cnty Pub Def -1849
Prospect Av -Ste 222 -Cleveland 44115

(614) 365-2700 .. **Maher**, Daniel M '72 (Squire S&D LLP) -41 S High
-1300 Huntngtn Ctr -Columbus 43215 **Fx:**365-2499

(330) 762-8691 .. **Maher**, Douglas B '77 -107 Rose Bldg -265 S Main -Akron 44308

(330) 923-2316 .. **Maher**, Edward C '49 -3071 8th -Cuyahoga Falls 44221

(216) 696-4161 .. **Maher**, Edward J '64 -1370 Ontario -Ste 1548 -Cleveland 44113

(330) 650-2200 .. **Maher**, Robert V '49 -15 Baldwin -Hudson 44236

(614) 728-7055 .. **Maher**, Stephen E '82 Atty Gen -30 E Broad -Columbus 43215
Fx:728-8600

(513) 721-6500 .. **Mahin**, John E '77 (Clements M&C) -35 E 7th -Ste 710
-Cincinnati 45202 **Fx:**763-6415

(330) 643-2250 .. **Mahlay**, Natalia B '03 Ct of Appeals 9th Dist -161 S High -Rm 504
-Akron 44308

(419) 529-1367 .. **Mahlay**, Oleh '95 Industrial Commssn of OH -240 Tappen Dr N
-Bx8051 -Mansfield 44906 **Fx:**529-3084

(412) 268-4387 .. **Mahler**, Carl P II '93 Carnegie Mellon Univ -5000 Forbes Av
-Pittsburgh, PA 15213

(614) 478-2302 .. **Mahler**, Eric A '95 Value City Dept Stores -3241 Westervll Rd
-Columbus 43224

(216) 443-7800 .. **Mahnic**, Lisa M '95 Cuyahoga Cnty Pros -1200 Ontario -8th Fl
-Cleveland 44113 **Fx:**698-2270

(330) 722-0836 .. **Mahon**, Brian P '93 -250 Halifax Ln -Medina 44256 **Fx:**722-0836

(440) 277-2538 .. **Mahon**, Richard J Jr. '92 Lorain Tubular Co,LLC -2199 E 28th
-Lorain 44055

(513) 784-7127 .. **Mahon**, Scott J '89 Deloitte & Touche LLP -250 E 5th -Ste 1900
-Cincinnati 45202

(513) 361-1200 .. **Mahon**, Stephen C '93 (Squire S&D LLP) -312 Walnut -Ste 3500
-Cincinnati 45202 **Fx:**361-1201

(937) 222-2424 .. **Mahoney**, Bryan J '99 %Freund F&A -1 S Main -Ste 1800
-Dayton 45402 **Fx:**222-5369

(513) 241-7111 .. **Mahoney**, Dennis C '90 %O'Connor A&L Co,LPA -1014 Vine
-22nd Fl -Cincinnati 45202 **Fx:**241-7197

(937) 227-6531 .. **Mahoney**, Joan A '95 Fifth 3rd Bank Wstrn OH -110 N Main
-Dayton 45402

(216) 621-1424 .. **Mahoney**, Lisa M '02 US Title Agency,Inc -1111 Chester Av -#400
-Cleveland 44114

(419) 223-1861 .. **Mahoney**, Luke D '02 3rd Dist Ct of Appeals -204 N Main
-Lima 45801

(937) 208-3195 .. **Mahoney**, Mark E '03 Miami Valley Hsptl -1 Wyoming
-Dayton 45409

(216) 443-7800 .. **Mahoney**, Mark J '89 Cuyahoga Cnty Pros -1200 Ontario -8th Fl
-Cleveland 44113 **Fx:**698-2270

(216) 687-1480 .. **Mahoney**, Michael J '79 CGI Group,Inc -1301 E 9th -Ste 3000
-Cleveland 44114 **Fx:**687-1488

(614) 221-3155 .. **Mahoney**, Michael P '72 (Bailey C LLC) -10 W Broad
-Columbus 43215 **Fx:**221-0479

(216) 443-8611 .. **Mahoney**, Molly C '98 Cuyahoga Cnty Ct Cmmn Pleas
-1200 Ontario -Justice Ctr 11th Fl -Cleveland 44113

(440) 234-0662 .. **Mahoney**, William F '75 OfCnsl Wargo & W Co,LPA -Bx332
-Berea 44017 **Fx:**234-4179

(614) 469-7404 .. **Mahood**, Margaret W '89 SSA-OHA -401 N Front -Ste 400
-Columbus 43215

(614) 233-7910 .. **Mahota**, John M '73 -341 S 3rd -Ste 300 -Columbus 43215

(650) 919-1111 .. **Mahota**, Timothy J '91 Integral Dvlpmnt Co -2027 Stierlin Ct
-Mountain View, CA 94043

(614) 645-8980 .. **Maia**, Elizabeth L '04 Franklin Cnty Pub Def -373 S High -12th Fl
-Columbus 43215

(513) 762-6200 .. **Maichl**, Linda E '89 (Ulmer & B LLP) -600 Vine -Ste 2800
-Cincinnati 45202 **Fx:**762-6245

(330) 832-9833 .. **Maier**, Erich J '96 -2200 Wales Rd NW -Massillon 44646

(937) 223-8888 .. **Maier**, Frank M '81 Dyer GM&S -131 N Ludlow -Ste 1400
-Dayton 45402 **Fx:**223-0127

(216) 361-0002 .. **Maier**, John P '01 Tenable Protective Srvcs -2423 Payne Av
-Cleveland 44114 **Fx:**361-8690

(614) 466-5967 .. **Maier**, Robert C '90 Atty Gen -30 E Broad -Columbus 43215
Fx:466-5967

(773) 665-1161 .. **Mailander**, Jennifer K '92 Lexis Nexis -135 S LaSalle
-Chicago, IL 60603

(330) 747-6548 .. **Maillis**, Michael J '95 -26 S Phelps -Youngstown 44503

(513) 352-6747 .. **Maiman**, Earle J '81 (Thompson H LLP) -312 Walnut -14th Fl
-Cincinnati 45202 **Fx:**241-4771

(216) 592-5000 .. **Maimbourg**, Rita A '81 Tucker E&W LLP -925 Euclid Av
-1150 Huntngtn Bldg -Cleveland 44115 **Fx:**592-5009

(216) 520-0088 .. **Maimona**, Cheryl L '75 Pepple & W Ltd -5005 Rockside Rd
-Ste 260 -Cleveland 44131 **Fx:**520-0044

(937) 502-4160 .. **Main**, Chad W '04 -5785 Far Hills Av -Dayton 45429 **Fx:**502-4161

(513) 631-8292 .. **Main**, David K '74 Hamilton Cnty Dvlpmnt Co -1776 Mentor Av
-Cincinnati 45212

(614) 221-1662 .. **Mains**, Donald Leo Jr. '69 %Frank & W Co LPA -600 S Pearl
-Columbus 43206

(513) 562-2971 .. **Maio**, Michael L '83 -125 E Court -Ste 200 -Cincinnati 45202

(216) 586-3939 .. **Maiorana**, David M '99 %Jones D -901 Lakeside Av
-Cleveland 44114 **Fx:**579-0212

(440) 323-2456 .. **Maiorca**, Philip R '97 -230 3rd -Ste 101 -Elyria 44035 **Fx:**322-5116

(419) 228-6365 .. **Maisch**, Victoria U '94 (Cory MWR&C,LPA) -101 N Elizabeth
-Ste 607 -Bx1217 -Lima 45802 **Fx:**228-5319

(248) 816-0315 .. **Maish**, Mark T '89 Bank One -2155 W Big Beaver -2nd Fl
-Troy, MI 48084 **Fx:**816-0340

(513) 721-5555 .. **Maislin**, Blake R '97 -906 Main -Ste 500 -Cincinnati 45202

(716) 631-4772 .. **Maislin**, Sam '72 -5684 Main -Williamsville, NY 14221

(419) 396-7691 .. **Maison**, Robert T '73 -3727 CR 96 -Bx45 -Carey 43316
Fx:396-3233

(440) 247-6862 .. **Maistros**, David M '90 -50 E Wshngtn -Chagrin Falls 44022

(330) 688-1806 .. **Maistros**, Georgia '90 (Maistros & L) -3580 Darrow Rd
-Stow 44224 **Fx:**688-1103

(330) 688-1806 .. **Maistros & Loepp** -3580 Darrow Rd -Stow 44224 **Fx:**688-1103

(216) 479-8500 .. **Maiwurm**, James J '74 (Squire S&D LLP) -127 Pub Sq
-4900 Key Twr -Cleveland 44114 **Fx:**479-8780

(513) 946-3500 .. **Majba**, Michael P '03 1st Dist Ct of Appls -230 E 9th -12th Fl
-Cincinnati 45202 **Fx:**946-3412

(419) 213-2001 .. **Majdalani**, Brenda J '89 Lucas Cnty Pros -Adams & Erie
-Lucas Cnty Cthse -Toledo 43624

(216) 443-3789 .. **Majer**, Mark R '92 Cuyahoga Cnty Juv Ct -2163 E 22nd
-Cleveland 44115

(216) 394-5072 .. **Majernik**, Meghan D '02 %Schottenstein Z&D -1350 Euclid Av
-Ste 1400 -Cleveland 44115 **Fx:**621-6502

(216) 443-7800 .. **Majeski**, Colleen A '97 Cuyahoga Cnty Pros -1200 Ontario -8th Fl
-Cleveland 44113 **Fx:**698-2270

(614) 693-6837 .. **Majeski**, Michael B '93 -Bx182317 -Columbus 43218

(216) 443-6393 .. **Majka**, Susan L '95 %8th Dist Ct of Appls -1 Lakeside Av -#202
-Cleveland 44113 **Fx:**443-2044

(216) 522-4086 .. **Majkrzak**, Theresa M '80 DOJ-Antitrust Div -55 Erievw -Ste 700
-Cleveland 44114

(440) 746-3700 .. **Major**, James L Jr. '89 (Major & Assoc) -3505 E Royalton Rd
-Ste 165 The Ofc Atrium -Broadview Heights 44147

(440) 395-0249 .. **Major**, Lynn N '90 Progressive Ins Co -300 N Cmmns Blvd
-OHF 11 -Mayfield Village 44143

(614) 775-5278 .. **Major**, Robert H '02 JP Morgan -6525 W Campus Oval
-New Albany 43054

Major, Roberta J '91 -8019 NE 71st Loop -Vancouver, WA 98662

(513) 621-2349 .. **Major**, Ronald D '74 -30 Garfld Pl -Ste 740 -Cincinnati 45202

(330) 477-1510 .. **Majors**, Shirley E '78 -5999 Canterbury NW -Canton 44708

(216) 348-5400 .. **Makee**, Dan L '85 (McDonald H Co,LPA) -600 Superior Av E
-Ste 2100 -Cleveland 44114 **Fx:**348-5474

(216) 241-2838 .. **Makee**, Joel A '69 (Taft S&H LLP) -200 Pub Sq -3500 BP Twr
-Cleveland 44114 **Fx:**241-3707

(614) 818-1100 .. **Makela**, Charity R '01 Stewart Title Agency -259 W Schrock Rd
-Westerville 43081

(216) 241-2838 .. **Makhlouf**, Majeed G '01 %Taft S&H LLP -200 Pub Sq
-3500 BP Twr -Cleveland 44114 **Fx:**241-3707

(937) 223-8177 .. **Makley**, Roger J '60 (Coolidge WW&L) -33 W 1st -Ste 600
-Dayton 45402 **Fx:**223-6705

(216) 348-5400 .. **Makofsky**, Michael D '99 %McDonald H Co,LPA
-600 Superior Av E -Ste 2100 -Cleveland 44114 **Fx:**348-5474

(405) 858-7220 .. **Makohin**, George M '78 -1140 NW 63rd -Ste 402
-Oklahoma City, OK 73116 **Fx:**858-8601

(513) 639-2832 .. **Makos**, Susan S '79 Catholic Hlthcre Prtnrs -615 Elsinore Pl
-Cincinnati 45202

(440) 729-7278 .. **Makowski**, Pamela A '81 -8228 Mayfld -#6B -Chesterland 44026

(216) 787-3030 .. **Makowski**, Richard J '77 Atty Gen -615 W Superior Av -11th Fl
-Cleveland 44113 **Fx:**787-3480

(304) 723-9670 .. **Makricostas**, Dean G '04 (Taylor & M,PLLC) -Bx2827
-Weirton, WV 26062

(330) 394-1587 .. **Makridis**, Irene K '81 -183 W Market -Warren 44481

(202) 263-4300 .. **Makuch**, Michael A '84 (Smith G&R) -1850 M NW -Ste 800
-Washington, DC 20036

(216) 579-9938 .. **Malaker**, Albert D '85 -622 Literary Rd -Cleveland 44113

(440) 329-5389 .. **Malanowski**, Stephanie '03 %Lorain Cnty Pros -225 Court -3rd Fl
-Elyria 44035

(330) 253-0785 .. **Malarcik**, Donald J Jr. '93 (Gorman MP&V) -1 Cascade Plz -9th Fl
-Akron 44308 **Fx:**253-7432

(513) 579-6400 .. **Malas**, Mary Ellen '91 (Keating M&K PLL) -1 E 4th
-1400 Provident Twr -Cincinnati 45202 **Fx:**579-6457

(216) 541-8200 .. **Malbasa**, Stephanie H '79 -13405 Lk Shr Blvd -Cleveland 44110

(513) 321-5816 .. **Malblanc**, Craig J '96 HC Nutting -611 Lunken Park Dr
-Cincinnati 45226

(440) 357-5537 .. **Malchesky**, Paul R '97 (Cannon SA&L Co,LPA) -41 E Erie
-Painesville 44077 **Fx:**357-9234

Malcolm, Mark W '04 -(Address Unavailable)

(513) 984-6100 .. **Male**, Gregory R '85 Schneider & Brown Co EA -7775 Cooper Rd
-Ste B -Cincinnati 45242

(614) 436-8338 .. **Malech**, Arnold M '80 -681 Maplerun Ln -Westerville 43081

(216) 987-4418 .. **Maleckar**, Rebecca J '91 Cuyahoga Cmmnty Cllg -2900 Comm
Cllg Av -207 Business & Adm Bldg -Cleveland 44115

(614) 469-5715 .. **Malek**, Andrew M '93 US Atty -303 Marconi Blvd -Ste 200
-Columbus 43215

(740) 397-7420 .. **Malek**, Bruce J '77 (McDevitt M&M,LPA) -1 Pub Sq
-Mount Vernon 43050 **Fx:**397-6611

(614) 444-7440 .. **Malek**, Edwin L '69 Malek & M -1227 S High -Columbus 43206

(614) 444-7440 .. **Malek**, James E '95 Malek & M -1227 S High -Columbus 43206

(330) 374-5540 .. **Malek**, Linda M '01 %Vasko R&E Co, LPA -137 S Main -Ste 206
-Akron 44308

(614) 444-7440 .. **Malek & Malek** -1227 S High -Columbus 43206

(216) 443-0450 .. **Malek**, Nader N '96 (Malek D & Assoc,LLC) -323 W Lakeside
-Ste 350 -Cleveland 44113

(216) 687-1311 .. **Malemud**, Franklin C '97 (Reminger & R) -101 Prospect Av W
-1400 Mdlnd Bldg -Cleveland 44115 **Fx:**687-1841

(216) 241-2863 .. **Malensek**, Jennifer L '98 -815 Superior Av -Ste 1915
-Cleveland 44114

(330) 497-0700 .. **Malesick**, Paul H II '81 %Krugliak WG&D Co,LPA
-4775 Munson NW -Bx36963 -Canton 44735 **Fx:**497-4020

(513) 721-7500 .. **Maley**, George S '81 -22 W 9th -Cincinnati 45202

(740) 653-0100 .. **Maley**, Lawrence M '91 -123 S Broad -Ste 234 -Lancaster 43130
Fx:653-9252

(937) 496-3220 .. **Malhotra**, Rajshree R '93 Montgomery County Juvenile Ct
-303 W 2nd -Rm 1142 -Dayton 45422

(216) 802-3664 .. **Malick**, Keith G '00 1st Amer Exch Co,LLC -1111 Superior Av E
-Ste 510 -Cleveland 44114

(216) 781-3434 .. **Malicki**, Jack A '04 %R Frederick -55 Pub Sq -Ste 1300
-Cleveland 44113

(440) 729-8260 .. **Malik**, David B '80 -8437 Mayfld Rd -Ste 103 -Chesterland 44026

(202) 626-3697 .. **Malik**, Rajeev V '98 White & C,LLP -601 13th -Ste 600 S
-Washington, DC 20005

(937) 323-3768 .. **Malina**, Paul D '62 (P Malina Co,LPA) -6 W High -Ste 806
-Springfield 45502

(216) 771-6500 ..**Malkin,** Jack S '81 %K Weiner & Assoc Co,LPA -75 Pub Sq -4th Fl
-Cleveland 44113 **Fx:**771-6540

(216) 222-3443 ..**Malkin,** Jennifer R '86 Natl City Bank -1900 E 9th
-17th Fl Loc 01-2174 -Cleveland 44114

(419) 674-2256 ..**Malkin,** Leslie N '86 Hardin Cnty Cmn Pleas Ct -1 Cthse Sq -3rd Fl
-Kenton 43326

(330) 740-2970 ..**Malkin,** Michael L '81 Phar-Mor Inc -20 Fed Plz W -Bx400
-Youngstown 44501

(614) 292-5062 ..**Malkoff,** Daniel A '85 OSU Medical Ctr -370 W 9th Av
-200 Meiling Hall -Columbus 43210

(330) 744-0291 ..**Malkoff,** Solomon '42 Boyd RC&C Co LPA -400 Sky Bk Bldg
-Bx6565 -Youngstown 44501

(614) 466-4882 ..**Malkoff,** Tamara L '85 OH Dept Hlth -246 N High -Bx118
-Columbus 43216

(419) 861-7800 ..**Malkoski,** Kathleen M '99 Bahret & Assoc Co,LPA
-7050 Spring Meadow W Dr -Holland 43528

(216) 621-2090 ..**Mallamad,** Shawn M '84 Gibbons & C LLP -815 Superior Av
-Ste 1210 -Cleveland 44114 **Fx:**621-2062

Mallett, David W '03 -(Address Unavailable)

(614) 895-9473 ..**Mallett,** Jacqueline S '92 Lexis-Nexis -4645 Cautela Dr
-Westerville 43081

(614) 299-8321 ..**Mallett,** Jeanne M '82 -1055H Neil Av -Columbus 43201

(740) 348-4000 ..**Mallett,** Renee M '99 Licking Mem Hlth Syst -1320 W Main
-Newark 43055

(614) 431-1763 ..**Malley,** Kingston E '72 -89 E Wilson Bridge Rd
-Worthington 43085

(216) 662-7711 ..**Mallin,** Christopher J '74 -21821 Libby Rd -Bedford Heights 44146

Mallitz, Elizabeth R '93 -9216 Highland Ridge Way
-Tampa, FL 33647

(330) 644-6161 ..**Mallo,** George D '74 (Mallo & L) -2483 S Main -Akron 44319
Fx:644-7926

(330) 972-7945 ..**Mallo,** Ted A '72 Univ of Akron -302 E Buchtel Av -Akron 44325

(614) 644-7233 ..**Mallory,** Diane D '80 Atty Gen -150 E Gay -Columbus 43215
Fx:728-9327

(513) 977-8200 ..**Mallory,** Donald W '99 %Dinsmore & S LLP -255 E 5th -Ste 1900
-Cincinnati 45202 **Fx:**977-8141

(513) 352-4712 ..**Mallory,** Dwane K '00 Law Dept -801 Plum -Rm 214
-Cincinnati 45202 **Fx:**352-1515

(740) 393-9562 ..**Mallory,** Heidi A '00 City Law Director -5 N Gay -Ste 222
-Mount Vernon 43050

(614) 228-9707 ..**Mallory,** Thomas H Jr. '95 (Mallory & T Co,LPA) -88 E Broad
-Ste 1560 -Columbus 43215

(614) 228-9707 ..**Mallory & Tsibouris Co,LPA** -88 E Broad -Ste 1560
-Columbus 43215

(513) 946-5112 ..**Mallory,** William L Jr. '86 Cnty Mun Ct Judge -1000 Main -Rm 240
-Cincinnati 45202

(440) 356-9789 ..**Malloy,** Anthony T '91 -23286 Maybelle Dr -Westlake 44145
Malloy, John R '56 -12550 Lk Av -Unit 411 -Lakewood 44107

(614) 462-5011 ..**Malloy,** Marie A '91 (Schottenstein Z&D) -250 West -Bx165020
-Columbus 43216 **Fx:**462-5135

(937) 586-3100 ..**Malloy,** Martin L '77 %ES Gallon & Assoc -40 W 4th -22nd Fl
-Dayton 45402 **Fx:**586-3100

(216) 521-7400 ..**Malloy,** Mary A '92 -1524 Grace Av -Lakewood 44107

(513) 622-5419 ..**Malloy,** Matthew M '95 Procter & Gamble Co-Legal
-1 Procter & Gamble Plz -Cincinnati 45202

(513) 852-6043 ..**Malloy,** Robert P '74 (Wood & L LLP) -600 Vine -Ste 2500
-Cincinnati 45202 **Fx:**852-6087

(216) 348-5400 ..**Malloy,** Sean D '00 (McDonald H Co,LPA) -600 Superior Av E
-Ste 2100 -Cleveland 44114 **Fx:**348-5474

(740) 592-3247 ..**Malloy,** Susan E '97 %Hon PB Abele -Athens Cnty Cthse
-Athens 45701

(216) 563-2146 ..**Malloy,** Timothy P '85 McDonald Invstmnts, Inc -800 Superior Av
-10th Fl -Cleveland 44114

(330) 740-2073 ..**Malmisur,** Joanna M '92 Mahoning Cnty CSEA -112 W Commerce
-Bx119 -Youngstown 44503

(216) 687-1311 ..**Malnar,** PattiJo '92 (Reminger & R) -101 Prospect Av W
-1400 Mdlnd Bldg -Cleveland 44115 **Fx:**687-1841

(937) 461-0000 ..**Malocu,** Frank A '91 -130 W 2nd -Ste 2100 -Dayton 45402

(513) 651-6800 ..**Malof,** Kevin K '00 %Frost BT LLC -201 E 5th -2200 PNC Ctr
-Cincinnati 45202 **Fx:**651-6981

(614) 469-7130 ..**Malone,** Andrew R '03 %Smith R&S Co,LPA -50 W Broad
-Ste 3000 -Columbus 43215 **Fx:**469-7146

(419) 843-1333 ..**Malone Ault & Farell** -7654 W Bancroft -Toledo 43617
Fx:843-3888

(330) 455-2222 ..**Malone,** Brian J '94 Chapter 13 Trustee -400 Tuscarawas W
-4th Fl Charter One Bk Bldg -Canton 44702

(216) 687-1311 ..**Malone,** James L '70 (Reminger & R) -101 Prospect Av W
-1400 Mdlnd Bldg -Cleveland 44115 **Fx:**687-1841

(216) 861-5511 ..**Malone,** John P Jr. '71 -614 W Superior Av -Ste 1150
-Cleveland 44113

(513) 241-9400 ..**Malone,** Kathleen A '87 Legal Aid -215 E 9th -Ste 200
-Cincinnati 45202

(440) 846-1556 ..**Malone,** Laurie A '97 -14493 Windsor Castle Ln
-Strongsville 44149

(614) 466-2766 ..**Malone,** Margaret A '75 Atty Gen -30 E Broad -Columbus 43215
Fx:644-1926

(419) 422-8716 ..**Malone,** Michael J '73 (Oxley MHO&W,PLL) -301 E Main Cross
-Bx1086 -Findlay 45840 **Fx:**422-6495

(419) 241-9000 ..**Malone,** Nicholas D '04 %Shumaker L&K,LLP -1000 Jackson
-Toledo 43624 **Fx:**241-6894

(216) 621-0200 ..**Malone,** Raymond M '82 (Baker & H LLP) -1900 E 9th -Ste 3200
-Cleveland 44114 **Fx:**696-0740

(937) 586-3100 ..**Malone,** Richard M '77 (ES Gallon & Assoc) -40 W 4th -22nd Fl
-Dayton 45402 **Fx:**586-3100

(419) 843-1333 ..**Malone,** Richard R '77 (Malone A&F) -7654 W Bancroft
-Toledo 43617 **Fx:**843-3888

Malone, Robert B '96 -9690 Highland Dr -Cleveland 44141

(330) 376-5300 ..**Malone,** Robert W '76 (Buckingham D&B,LLP) -50 S Main
-Bx1500 -Akron 44309 **Fx:**258-6559

(202) 879-7647 ..**Malone,** Sean P '03 %Jones Day -51 Louisiana Av
-Washington, DC 20001

(216) 522-4856 ..**Malone,** Vanessa F '96 Fed Pub Def -1660 W 2nd -Ste 750
-Cleveland 44113

(419) 241-5175 ..**Maloney,** Daniel J '98 Maloney M&K -520 Mad Av -Ste 330
-Toledo 43604

(513) 737-5473 ..**Maloney,** James P II '93 -4793 Willow Ridge Ct
-Liberty Township 45011

(614) 228-5271 ..**Maloney,** Kevin M '85 (Denmead & M) -37 W Broad -Ste 1150
-Columbus 43215

(216) 586-3939 ..**Maloney,** Mary D '87 (Jones D) -901 Lakeside Av
-Cleveland 44114 **Fx:**579-0212

(216) 523-1900 ..**Maloney,** Matthew J '91 Hausser & Taylor CPA -1001 Lakeside Av
-Ste 1400 -Cleveland 44114

(419) 241-5175 ..**Maloney McHugh & Kolodgy** -520 Mad Av -Ste 330
-Toledo 43604

(440) 716-8562 ..**Maloney,** Michael P '87 -24461 Detroit Rd -Ste 340
-Westlake 44145 **Fx:**716-8563

(216) 621-0200 ..**Maloney,** Ruth Ann '90 (Baker & H LLP) -1900 E 9th -Ste 3200
-Cleveland 44114 **Fx:**696-0740

(330) 740-2311 ..**Maloney,** Timothy P '85 Mun Ct Judge -120 Market -Youngstown
44503

(419) 241-5175 ..**Maloney,** William T '78 (Maloney M&K) -520 Mad Av -Ste 330
-Toledo 43604

(440) 234-8888 ..**Maloof,** George M '78 AmWare Distribution Warehouse
-19000 Holland Rd -Cleveland 44142
Maloof-Wolf, Faye J '89 -1804 Farrs Grdn Path -Westlake 44145

(614) 221-4400 ..**Maloon,** Jeffrey L '83 Volkema TMBS&M,LPA -140 E Town
-Ste 1100 -Columbus 43215 **Fx:**221-6010

(614) 462-3555 ..**Maloon,** Jerry L II '92 Franklin Cnty Pros -373 S High
-Columbus 43215

(614) 798-1616 ..**Maloon,** Jerry L '75 -9155 Moors Pl N -Dublin 43017

(513) 732-7220 ..**Malott,** Frank W '77 Clermont Cnty Cmn Pleas Ct
-2340 Clermont Ctr Dr -Batavia 45103

(312) 645-4223 ..**Malovany,** Howard '77 Wm Wrigley Jr Co -410 N Mich Av
-Law Dept -Chicago, IL 60611

(216) 357-7000 ..**Malumphy,** Christopher R '88 %US Dist Crt -801 W Superior Av
-Cleveland 44113

(216) 360-7200 ..**Malvasi,** Maurus G '94 Carlisle M -25200 Chagrin Blvd
-Cleveland 44122

(440) 498-9510 ..**Maly,** Michael P '92 Winncom Tech -30700 Carter -Solon 44139

(216) 621-5161 ..**Malynn,** Steven R '96 %Giffen & K,LLC -1717 E 9th
-Cleveland 44114 **Fx:**621-2399

(330) 929-9700 ..**Malyuk,** Michael A '75 -2020 Front -Ste 207
-Cuyahoga Falls 44221 **Fx:**929-9720

(216) 787-3030 ..**MaMana,** Frank J Jr. '78 Atty Gen -615 W Superior Av -11th Fl
-Cleveland 44113 **Fx:**787-3480

(216) 514-6400 ..**Mamich,** Samuel J '73 %Zipkin W Co LPA -3637 S Green Rd
-Zipkin Whiting Bldg -Cleveland 44122 **Fx:**514-6406

(216) 621-3251 ..**Mamone,** Edward J '87 %Gurney M&M -75 Pub Sq -Ste 525
-Cleveland 44113 **Fx:**621-1332

(216) 621-3251 ..**Mamone,** Joseph A '61 (Gurney M&M) -75 Pub Sq -Ste 525
-Cleveland 44113 **Fx:**621-1332

(202) 244-7435 ..**Mamone,** Russell B '65 -2610 Nrthmptn NW
-Washington, DC 20015

(216) 261-0200 ..**Mamrack,** Edward D '79 -27801 Euclid Av -Ste 500 -Euclid 44132

(419) 592-3283 ..**Manahan,** David A '87 -Bx531 -Napoleon 43545

(419) 259-6803 ..**Manahan,** Marsha A '81 Fifth 3rd Bank -Bx1868 -Toledo 43603

(419) 243-6148 ..**Manahan,** Michael J '79 (Manahan PB&D) -414 N Erie -Bx2328
-Toledo 43603

(419) 243-6148 ..**Manahan Pietrykowski Bamman & DeLaney** -414 N Erie
-Bx2328 -Toledo 43603

(419) 592-8300 ..**Manahan,** Thomas R '85 -614 N Perry -Napoleon 43545
Manak, Charles R '92 -21 Keswick Dr -Hudson 44236

(614) 466-4961 ..**Manchak,** John F III '74 %Sup Crt of OH -30 E Broad -2nd Fl
-Columbus 43266

(330) 743-1171 ..**Manchester Bennett Powers & Ullman** -201 E Commerce
-Atrium Level 2 Commerce Bldg -Youngstown 44503
Fx:743-1190

(216) 382-9150 ..**Mancini,** James M '69 -5001 Mayfld Rd -Ste 306 -Lyndhurst 44124

(614) 644-7233 ..**Mancini,** Joseph M '66 Atty Gen -150 E Gay -Columbus 43215
Fx:728-9327

(216) 696-5222 ..**Mancino,** Brett M '99 %Johnson & C,LLC -1001 Lakeside Av
-Ste 1700 N Pnt Twr -Cleveland 44114 **Fx:**696-5288

(513) 381-2838 ..**Mancino,** David A '94 (Taft S&H LLP) -425 Walnut -Ste 1800
-Cincinnati 45202 **Fx:**381-0205

(213) 551-9323 ..**Mancino,** Douglas M '74 (McDermott W&E) -2049 Century Pk E
-Ste 3400 -Los Angeles, CA 90067

(216) 575-0777 ..**Mancino,** Jennifer L '04 %Kelley & F,LLP -1300 E 9th -Ste 1901
-Cleveland 44114 **Fx:**575-0799

(216) 621-1742 ..**Mancino,** Paul A Jr. '63 (Mancino M&M) -75 Pub Sq -Ste 1016
-Cleveland 44113

(216) 687-2675 ..**Mancino,** Paul III '92 Med Mutual-OH -2060 E 9th -Ste 1900
-Cleveland 44115

(614) 475-7040 ..**Mancuso,** Anthony O '86 Mancuso Law Ofc -135 N Hmltn Rd
-Gahanna 43230 **Fx:**475-0214

(954) 563-9225 ..**Mancuso,** Charles A '00 %Thomas & P -2404 NE 9th
-Fort Lauderdale, FL 33304

(937) 223-8171 ..**Mancz,** Barry W '77 (Rogers & G) -2160 Kettering Twr
-Dayton 45423 **Fx:**223-1649

(216) 391-6680 ..**Mandel,** Bernard '68 -1775 E 45th -Cleveland 44103

(216) 931-6000 ..**Mandel,** Bruce P '76 (Ulmer & B LLP) -1300 E 9th -Ste
900 Penton Media Bldg -Cleveland 44114 **Fx:**931-6001
Mandel, Stewart I '69 -2534 Milton Rd -University Heights 44118

(216) 771-7080 ..**Mandell,** Ellen S '78 -55 Pub Sq -Ste 1717 -Cleveland 44113

(419) 578-6300 ..**Mandell,** Steven L '83 Heartland Info Srvcs -3103 Exec Pkwy
-Ste 600 -Toledo 43606
Mandell-Brown, Marianne '88 -7815 Hartford Hill Ln
-Cincinnati 45242

(859) 394-6200 ..**Mando,** Jeffrey C '90 (Adams SW&D) -40 W Pike -Bx861
-Covington, KY 41012 **Fx:**291-7902

(419) 213-4700 ..**Mandross,** Dean P '80 %Lucas Cnty Pros -Adams & Erie
-Lucas Cnty Cthse -Toledo 43624

(419) 213-4061 ..**Mandross,** Suzanne C '80 %Lucas Cnty Pros-Foreclosure
-One Govt Ctr -Ste 500 -Toledo 43604

(330) 425-8520 ..**Mandryk,** Susan E '97 %Lerner S&R -8972 Darrow Rd -Ste A304
-Twinsburg 44087

(330) 796-4908 ..**Manella**, Michael J '97 Aircraft Braking Sys Corp
-1204 Massillion Rd -Akron 44306

(330) 451-7203 ..**Manello**, James S '85 Stark Cnty Pub Def -200 W Tuscarawas
-Ste 200 -Canton 44702

(513) 579-1414 ..**Manes**, Dennis L '73 (Schwartz M&R) -441 Vine -Ste 2900
-Cincinnati 45202 **Fx:**579-1418

(330) 762-1199 ..**Manes**, Gregg A '84 -333 S Main -Ste 701 -Akron 44308

(513) 977-4214 ..**Manes**, Marlene P '70 -917 Main -Ste 400 -Cincinnati 45202

(614) 848-4300 ..**Maney**, Thomas P Jr. '83 (Maney & B) -92 Northwoods Blvd -Ste B
-Columbus 43235

(330) 208-1000 ..**Manfull**, Ashley M '99 %Vorys SS&P LLP -106 S Main
-First Natl Twr -Akron 44308

(614) 899-7477 ..**Mangan**, Patrick F '79 -2999 E Dublin-Granvll Rd -Ste 206
-Columbus 43231

(513) 618-7800 ..**Mangan**, Sean K '04 %Graf S&M,LPA -425 Walnut -Ste 2400
-Cincinnati 45202 **Fx:**618-7801

(440) 329-5389 ..**Mangan**, Thomas M '81 Lorain Cnty Pros -225 Court -3rd Fl
-Elyria 44035

(614) 645-7385 ..**Mangan**, Timothy J '82 City Atty -90 W Broad -Columbus 43215

(513) 419-6933 ..**Mangan**, Timothy S '98 SrCnsl Cinergy Corp -139 E 4th
-25 Atrium II -Bx960 -Cincinnati 45201 **Fx:**419-6955

(216) 771-1430 ..**Mangano**, Basil W '96 %Masters & Assoc,LPA -1111 Superior Av
-Cleveland 44114 **Fx:**771-2070

(513) 469-0470 ..**Mangels**, Alfred J '64 -4729 Cornell Rd -Cincinnati 45241

(216) 586-3939 ..**Manghillis**, Jeffrey R '00 %Jones D -901 Lakeside Av
-Cleveland 44114 **Fx:**579-0212

(216) 696-8700 ..**Manghillis**, Katherine G '04 %Kohrman J&K PLL -1375 E 9th
-One Cleve Ctr 20th Fl -Cleveland 44114 **Fx:**621-6536

(330) 726-1444 ..**Mangie**, Mark G '75 -945 Windham Ct -Ste 3 -Youngstown 44512

(614) 444-3036 ..**Mango**, Dominic L '99 Saia & P,PLL -713 S Front
-Columbus 43206

(330) 668-9696 ..**Mangon**, Brett J '01 SS & G Fin Srvcs -301 Sprngside Dr -Akron
44333

(330) 379-1796 ..**Mangon**, Elizabeth R '01 Summit Cnty Chldrn Srvcs -264 S Arlngtn
-Akron 44306 **Fx:**379-1897

(202) 639-7750 ..**Mani**, Lalitha P '86 Baker B LLP -1299 Penn Av NW -Ste 1300
-Washington, DC 20004

(614) 221-4000 ..**Maniace**, James V '81 (Chester W&S LLP) -65 E State -10th Fl
-Columbus 43215 **Fx:**221-4012

(330) 740-2600 ..**Manigault**, Kimberly A '93 Mahoning County Job & Family Svcs
-709 N Garland Av -Youngstown 44505

(216) 241-5094 ..**Maniker**, Howard B '68 (H Maniker Co LPA) -1370 Ontario
-Ste 330 -Cleveland 44113 **Fx:**621-4959

(812) 425-5200 ..**Manion**, Andrew J '01 Kinney K&B,LLP -20 NW 1st -Ste 200
-Evansville, IN 47708

(734) 847-9660 ..**Manion**, Robert A '73 -7431 Jackman Rd -Bx 307
-Temperance, MI 48182

(614) 466-5414 ..**Manken**, James T '94 OH Ofc of the State Auditor -88 E Broad
-5th flr -Bx1140 -Columbus 43215

(513) 721-5525 ..**Manley Burke** -225 W Court -Cincinnati 45202 **Fx:**721-4268

(614) 220-5611 ..**Manley Deas & Kochalski, LLC** -495 S High -Ste 300
-Columbus 43215 **Fx:**220-5613
Manley, James R '69 -Bx358 -Wickliffe 44092

(330) 643-2800 ..**Manley**, John F '88 Summit Cnty Pros-Civil -53 Univ Av -6th Fl
-Akron 44308 **Fx:**643-2137

(513) 721-5525 ..**Manley**, Robert E '60 (Manley B) -225 W Court -Cincinnati 45202
Fx:721-4268

(614) 220-5611 ..**Manley**, Theodore K '92 (Manley D&K,LLC) -495 S High -Ste 300
-Columbus 43215 **Fx:**220-5613

(216) 755-5667 ..**Manley-Dutton**, Maria C '00 Developers Diversified Rlty Corp
-3300 Enterprise Pkwy -Beachwood 44122

(330) 527-4351 ..**Manlove**, Mark L '74 -10864 North -Garrettsville 44231

(216) 687-1900 ..**Manly**, Cornelius A '73 Legal Aid -1223 W 6th -Cleveland 44113
Fx:687-0779

(216) 583-1258 ..**Manly**, Michael N '96 Ernst & Young LLP -925 Euclid Av -Ste 1300
-Cleveland 44115

(614) 224-2366 ..**Mann**, Daniel L '55 (Mann & G) -233 S High -Columbus 43215

(513) 621-2888 ..**Mann**, David S '68 (Mann & M LLC) -1014 Vine -1900 Kroger Bldg
-Cincinnati 45202

(937) 223-8888 ..**Mann**, Douglas A '84 (Dyer GM&S) -131 N Ludlow -Ste 1400
-Dayton 45402 **Fx:**223-0127

(216) 241-5310 ..**Mann**, Eric H '80 (Gallagher SF&N) -1501 Euclid Av -6th Fl
-Cleveland 44115 **Fx:**241-1608

(614) 462-3555 ..**Mann**, Frederick M '68 Franklin Cnty Pros -373 S High
-Columbus 43215

(740) 775-2222 ..**Mann**, James L '68 (Mann & P,LLP) -18 E 2nd -Chillicothe 45601
Fx:775-2627

(740) 687-9355 ..**Mann**, Jayne H '88 %Mann & M Co,LPA
-3006 Columbus-Lncstr Rd -Lancaster 43130

(614) 464-6400 ..**Mann**, Joseph B '04 %Vorys SS&P LLP -52 E Gay -Bx1008
-Columbus 43216 **Fx:**464-6350

(216) 566-5546 ..**Mann**, Kent L '76 (Thompson H LLP) -127 Pub Sq -3900 Key Ctr
-Cleveland 44114 **Fx:**566-5800

(740) 345-0850 ..**Mann**, Laura S '98 %SE OH Lgl Srvcs -12 W Locust Av -Newark
43055

(216) 696-7600 ..**Mann**, Lisa F '80 %Duvin C&H -1301 E 9th -20th Fl Erievw Twr
-Cleveland 44114 **Fx:**696-2038

(513) 621-2888 ..**Mann**, Michael T '01 (Mann & M LLC) -1014 Vine
-1900 Kroger Bldg -Cincinnati 45202

(937) 534-0500 ..**Mann**, Nikolas P '97 %Subashi W&B -2305 Far Hills Av
-Oakwood Bldg -Dayton 45419 **Fx:**534-0505

(614) 224-5427 ..**Mann**, Richard L '72 -555 S Front -Ste 400 -Columbus 43215

(614) 253-4090 ..**Mann**, Robert J '88 -800 E Broad -Columbus 43205
Mann, Robert K '84 Progressive Ins Co -5920 Landerbrook Dr
-#PLG-OHL33 -Mayfield Heights 44124

(216) 621-6147 ..**Mann**, Theodore M Jr. '76 -925 Euclid Av -Huntgntn Bldg Ste 644
-Cleveland 44115

(740) 687-9355 ..**Mann**, Toby J '81 (Mann & M Co,LPA) -3006 Columbus-Lncstr Rd
-Lancaster 43130

(614) 224-4114 ..**Mann**, William C '79 OfCnsl Mitchell AC&B Co,LPA -580 S High
-Ste 200 -Columbus 43215 **Fx:**224-3804

(330) 253-5060 ..**Manna**, Anthony S '86 (Brennan M&D,LLC) -75 E Market
-Akron 44308 **Fx:**253-1977

(440) 356-5775 ..**Manning**, Anthony L '89 -20325 Ctr Ridge Rd -Ste 512
-Rocky River 44116

(513) 425-6609 ..**Manning**, Bennett A '82 12th Dist Ct of Appls -1001 Reinartz Blvd
-Middletown 45042 **Fx:**425-8751

(440) 248-0135 ..**Manning**, Charles H '91 (C Manning Co,LPA) -30505 Bainbrdg Rd
-#225 -Solon 44139

(330) 334-2877 ..**Manning**, Elizabeth B '81 Wadsworth-Rittman Hosp
-195 Wadsworth Rd -Wadsworth 44281

(440) 269-8823 ..**Manning**, Francis P '90 (Manning & M Co,LPA) -7556 Mentor Av
-Mentor 44060

(937) 456-8156 ..**Manning**, Gractia S '98 Preble Cnty Pros -100 E Main
-Cthse 1st Fl -Eaton 45320 **Fx:**456-8199

(937) 687-9099 ..**Manning**, James L '74 Cnty Ct 1 Judge -195 S Clayton Rd
-New Lebanon 45345

(216) 241-5310 ..**Manning**, Jamie '80 Gallagher SF&N -1501 Euclid Av -6th Fl
-Cleveland 44115 **Fx:**241-1608

(216) 641-7500 ..**Manning**, Janice G '90 The Garland Co,Inc -3800 E 91st
-Cleveland 44105

(614) 462-3555 ..**Manning**, Jason P '01 Franklin Cnty Pros -373 S High -Columbus
43215
Manning, Jeffrey J '01 -2534 Glenshire Cir -Uniontown 44685

(440) 942-6405 ..**Manning**, Joseph J Jr. '77 -7310 Brownell Dr -Mentor 44060

(440) 269-8823 ..**Manning**, Karen T '95 (Manning & M Co,LPA) -7556 Mentor Av
-Mentor 44060

(740) 622-3911 ..**Manning**, Michael D '75 (Owens & M) -413 Main -2nd Fl -Bx787
-Coshocton 43812

(419) 885-2153 ..**Manning**, Pamela M '99 -5800 Monroe -Bldg C -Sylvania 43560

(937) 291-3400 ..**Manning**, Thomas J '92 T Manning Co,LPA -848-C E Franklin
-Centerville 45459

(216) 621-1113 ..**Manning**, Timothy E '98 %Renner OB&S,LLP -1621 Euclid Av
-19th Fl -Cleveland 44115 **Fx:**621-6165

(614) 677-8655 ..**Mannion**, Brian L '97 Cnsl Nationwide Ins Co -1 Nationwide Plz
-Columbus 43215

(614) 262-2300 ..**Mannion**, Laurel E '94 OH Legislative Comm -77 S High -9th Fl
-Columbus 43266

(216) 928-2200 ..**Mannion**, Thomas P '93 (Sutter OM&F) -1301 E 9th
-3600 Erievw Twr -Cleveland 44114 **Fx:**928-4400

(330) 455-6112 ..**Mannos**, James G '77 (Tzangas PM&R) -220 Market Av S -8th Fl
-Canton 44702 **Fx:**455-2108
Manolis, Chrysostomos E '03 -(Address Unavailable)

(216) 479-8500 ..**Manoloff**, Richard D '92 (Squire S&D LLP) -127 Pub Sq
-4900 Key Twr -Cleveland 44114 **Fx:**479-8780

(419) 245-1975 ..**Manon**, Lora L '86 %Pros -555 N Erie -4th Fl -Toledo 43624

(419) 241-1150 ..**Manore**, John J III '94 Herschel ABM&M -615 Adams
-Toledo 43604 **Fx:**241-7825

(330) 745-4477 ..**Manos**, Chris G '85 -2745 Nesbitt Av -Akron 44319

(216) 523-1500 ..**Manos**, Eli '58 (Mansour GG&M Co,LPA) -55 Pub Sq -Ste 2150
-Cleveland 44113 **Fx:**523-1705

(330) 535-1555 ..**Manos**, George T '54 (Teodosio M&W) -One Cascade Plz
-Ste 1000 -Akron 44308

(216) 681-1818 ..**Manos**, John M '84 Manos & Co -739 E 140th -Cleveland 44110

(740) 363-1313 ..**Manos Martin Pergram & Dietz Co,LPA** -50 N Sandusky
-Delaware 43015 **Fx:**363-1314

(614) 221-3155 ..**Manougian**, Nancy J '85 (Bailey C LLC) -10 W Broad
-Columbus 43215 **Fx:**221-0479

(937) 225-3322 ..**Manovich**, Mark E '83 Robins & Myers,Inc -40 N Main
-Dayton 45423

(614) 221-1827 ..**Manring**, Daniel Lee '76 (Manring & F) -167 N High -Bx15037
-Columbus 43215

(614) 221-1827 ..**Manring & Farrell** -167 N High -Bx15037 -Columbus 43215

(614) 469-3939 ..**Mansfield**, Douglas M '94 (Jones D) -325 John H McConnell Blvd
-Ste 600 -Bx165017 -Columbus 43216 **Fx:**461-4198

(419) 695-0097 ..**Mansfield**, Stephen J '77 -10100 Elida Rd -Bx84 -Delphos 45833

(954) 727-2600 ..**Manso**, Peter J '82 Cnsl Edwards & A,LLP -350 E Las Olas Blvd
-Ste 1150 -Fort Lauderdale, FL 33301 **Fx:**727-2601

(216) 983-1288 ..**Manson**, Marcie A '89 University Hospital -10524 Euclid Av
-Cleveland 44106

(440) 943-4200 ..**Manson**, William D '85 Cnsl Lubrizol Corp -29400 Lakelnd Blvd
-Wickliffe 44092

(513) 923-4647 ..**Mansoor**, Raeshon M '04 -2239 N Bend Rd -Cincinnati 45239

(216) 523-1500 ..**Mansour**, Ernest P '55 (Mansour GG&M Co,LPA) -55 Pub Sq
-Ste 2150 -Cleveland 44113 **Fx:**523-1705

(216) 523-1500 ..**Mansour Gavin Gerlack & Manos Co,LPA** -55 Pub Sq
-Ste 2150 -Cleveland 44113 **Fx:**523-1705

(216) 696-7661 ..**Mansour**, Robert G '86 %Fisher & Assoc Co,LPA -50 Pub Sq
-1414 Trmnl Twr -Cleveland 44113

(419) 535-7100 ..**Mansour-Ismail**, Linda N '81 (L Mansour-Ismail Co,LPA)
-2909 W Central Av -Ste 200 -Toledo 43606

(419) 243-0922 ..**Mantel**, Dianne Sue '93 -1709 Spielbusch Av -Ste 100
-Toledo 43624

(614) 471-8194 ..**Mantel**, James K '91 -107 W Johnstown Rd -Gahanna 43230

(937) 865-6800 ..**Mantel**, Kaila A '94 Lexis/Nexis -Bx933 -Dayton 45401

(800) 547-7369 ..**Mantel**, Lisa L '01 LAWO -201 E 2nd -Defiance 43512

(202) 874-5300 ..**Manthey**, Christopher C '80 Ofc of the Comptroller of Currency
-250 E SW -Washington, DC 20219

(202) 408-2585 ..**Mantini**, John C '79 Fed Housing Fin Bd -1777 F NW -Genl Cnsl
-Washington, DC 20006

(216) 479-8500 ..**Mantione**, Lianne R '03 %Squire S&D LLP -127 Pub Sq -4900
Key Twr -Cleveland 44114 **Fx:**479-8780

(330) 239-1230 ..**Mantkowski**, Gary T '82 %E Brannon Co,LPA -6294 Ridge Rd
-Bx189 -Sharon Center 44274

(740) 349-8371 ..**Mantonya**, John B '49 (J Mantonya,LPA) -3 N 3rd -Newark 43055

(216) 241-6277 ..**Mantz**, Allison M '04 %Carlozzi & Assoc Co,LPA -1382 W 9th
-Ste 215 -Cleveland 44113 **Fx:**241-6343

(614) 424-6198 ..**Manuel**, James C Jr. '83 Battelle Memorial Inst -505 King Av
-Columbus 43201

(734) 850-0392 ..**Manuelidis**, Emmanuel E '02 -7333 Sunvalley Ct
-Temperance, MI 48182

(216) 283-5575 ..**Manuszak**, Michael J '77 -2905 Paxton Rd -Shaker Heights 44120

(440) 461-9000 ..**Manway**, Celeste M '87 %Dyson S&F Co,LPA -5843 Mayfld Rd
-Mayfield Heights 44124

(513) 977-8200 ..**Manzler**, Michael A '92 (Dinsmore & S LLP) -255 E 5th -Ste 1900
-Cincinnati 45202 **Fx:**977-8141

(614) 837-1889 .. **Mapes,** Robert E '74 City of Pickerington -115 N Center -Pickerington 43147
(513) 381-4888 .. **Mapother & Mapother, PSC** -1014 Vine -Ste 2320 Kroger Bldg -Cincinnati 45202 **Fx:**381-3117
(513) 762-7674 .. **Mara,** Timothy G '78 -312 Walnut -Ste 1600 -Cincinnati 45202 **Fx:**762-7675
(513) 661-7790 .. **Maraan,** Benjamin M II '91 -5465 Northbend Rd -Ste 333 -Cincinnati 45247
(541) 948-0306 .. **Maragas,** Douglas J '96 -643 NW Colorado Av -Bend, OR 97701
(330) 392-1541 .. **Marando,** Michael G '74 (Harrington H&M,Ltd) -108 Main Av SW -Ste 500 -Bx1510 -Warren 44482 **Fx:**394-6890
(330) 702-9700 .. **Marando,** Michael P '77 (Pfau P&M) -6715 Tippecanoe Rd -Bx9070 -Youngstown 44513
Marazsky, Stanley P '99 -531 Evergreen Dr -Dover 44622
(614) 387-9390 .. **Marbley,** Janet Green '79 Client's Sec Fund -65 S Front -5th Fl -Columbus 43215
(216) 443-7838 .. **Marburger,** Barbara R '84 %Cuyahoga Cnty Pros -1200 Ontario -8th Fl -Cleveland 44113 **Fx:**698-2270
(216) 621-0200 .. **Marburger,** David L '84 (Baker & H LLP) -1900 E 9th -Ste 3200 -Cleveland 44114 **Fx:**696-0740
(937) 255-6111 .. **Marcey,** Thomas S '75 Air Force Contract Law Ofc -2240 B -C1 -Wright Patterson AFB 45433 **Fx:**255-9570
(419) 242-1959 **March,** Andrew G '96 -405 N High -Bx3353 -Toledo 43607
(937) 548-1125 .. **Marchal & Brown** -116 W 4th -Greenville 45331
(937) 548-1125 .. **Marchal,** John F '58 (Marchal & B) -116 W 4th -Greenville 45331
(937) 548-1125 .. **Marchal,** John F '96 %Marchal & B -116 W 4th -Greenville 45331
(216) 363-4500 .. **Marchant,** Robert A '01 %Benesch FC&A LLP -200 Pub Sq -Ste 2300 -Cleveland 44114 **Fx:**363-4588
(513) 629-2149 .. **Marchese,** Michael III '90 Wstrn & Sthrn Life Ins -400 Bway -MS 28 -Cincinnati 45202
(614) 224-2062 .. **Marchese,** Thomas J '85 (Marchese & M) -1017 Dublin Rd -Columbus 43215
(412) 553-4621 .. **Marchlen,** Louis T '72 Alcoa -201 Isabella -Pittsburgh, PA 15212
(440) 933-5442 .. **Marcie,** Jay C '92 -32730 Walker Rd -Ste I-6 -Avon Lake 44012
(419) 352-8222 .. **Marcin,** Chester H '69 (Marcin & D) -440 E Poe Rd -Bowling Green 43402
(513) 965-8012 .. **Marcin,** Edward W '97 (Marcin & M) -931 State Rt 28 -Ste 309 -Milford 45150
(513) 965-8012 .. **Marcin,** Melissa A '98 (Marcin & M) -931 State Rt 28 -Ste 309 -Milford 45150
(419) 213-3000 .. **Marciniak,** Douglas G '87 Lucas Cnty CSEA -701 Adams -Toledo 43624
(216) 692-1222 .. **Marcinkevicius,** Egidijus K '77 (A Sirvaitis & Assoc) -880 E 185th -Cleveland 44119 **Fx:**531-8687
(419) 734-1528 .. **Marcinko,** Christopher M '04 %T DeBacco & Assoc -537 W Lakeshr Dr -Ste 800 -Port Clinton 43452
(440) 871-0310 .. **Marcis,** Robert A '69 -339 Tanglewood Ln -Bay Village 44140
(216) 575-0777 .. **Marcis,** Robert A II '98 %Kelley & F,LLP -1300 E 9th -Ste 1901 -Cleveland 44114 **Fx:**575-0799
(480) 733-6800 .. **Marco,** Daniel J '87 Davis Miles,PLLC -1500 E McKellips Rd -Ste 101 -Mesa, AZ 85203
(330) 725-0030 .. **Marco,** Kenneth J '91 %Marco M&B -52 Pub Sq -Medina 44256 **Fx:**722-4888
(330) 725-0030 .. **Marco Marco & Bailey** -52 Pub Sq -Medina 44256 **Fx:**722-4888
(330) 725-0030 .. **Marco,** Richard J '57 Marco M&B -52 Pub Sq -Medina 44256 **Fx:**722-4888
(330) 725-0030 .. **Marco,** Richard J Jr. '81 (Marco M&B) -52 Pub Sq -Medina 44256 **Fx:**722-4888
(440) 734-7600 .. **Marcoguiseppe,** Joseph J '74 Crombie Law Firm -4615 Great Nrthrn Blvd -North Olmsted 44070 **Fx:**734-1054
(330) 384-5272 .. **Marconi,** John R '94 First Energy Corp -76 S Main -12th FL -Akron 44308
(216) 241-7740 .. **Marcovy,** Timothy A '77 (Willacy L&M) -1468 W 9th -700 Wstrn Reserve Bldg -Cleveland 44113
Marcum, Joshua D '02 -10565 Talbot Av -Huntington Woods, MI 48070
(513) 863-8270 .. **Marcum,** Stephen S '83 (Parrish F&M Co,LPA) -300 High -Ste 704 -Bx747 -Hamilton 45012 **Fx:**863-9999
(419) 537-6610 .. **Marcus,** Steven E '78 (Fell & M,LPA) -3425 Exec Pkwy -Ste 207 -Toledo 43606
(216) 464-6555 .. **Marcus,** Terry H '85 -3659 S Green Rd -Ste 200 -Cleveland 44122
(216) 566-5560 .. **Marcuz,** Denise L '01 %Thompson H LLP -127 Pub Sq -3900 Key Ctr -Cleveland 44114 **Fx:**566-5800
(216) 687-4614 .. **Marczely,** Bernadette A '95 Cleveland State Univ -Euclid at E 24th -Coll of Educ -Cleveland 44115
(330) 375-1390 .. **Marczely,** David W '91 Envrnmntl Design Grp -450 Grant -Ste 201 -Akron 44311
(740) 453-8900 .. **Marczewski,** Mitchell C '01 -2994 Maple Av -Ste 102 -Zanesville 43701 **Fx:**453-8988
(216) 781-0722 .. **Marein & Bradley** -526 Superior Av E -Ste 222 -Cleveland 44114
(216) 781-0722 .. **Marein,** Mark B '82 (Marein & B) -526 Superior Av E -Ste 222 -Cleveland 44114
(440) 461-9975 .. **Marek,** Edward F '65 -1100 Haverston Rd -Lyndhurst 44124
(440) 248-8873 .. **Marek,** Robert J '69 -5845 Elm Hill Dr -Solon 44139
(937) 913-0200 .. **Maresca,** Richard A '95 %Gottschlich & P LLP -201 E 6th -Dayton 45402 **Fx:**824-2818
(614) 466-4395 .. **Margard,** Werner L III '82 Atty Gen -150 E Gay -Columbus 43215 **Fx:**644-8764
(419) 244-4200 .. **Margelefsky,** Michael P '77 -709 Mad Av -Ste 301 -Toledo 43624
(216) 241-0011 .. **Margolis,** Daniel M '96 %Goldberg & O -323 Lakeside Av W -Ste 450 -Cleveland 44113
(216) 368-5160 .. **Margolis,** Kenneth R '78 CWRU Law Schl -11075 East Blvd -Cleveland 44106
(216) 363-4500 .. **Margolis,** Kevin D '89 (Benesch FC&A LLP) -200 Pub Sq -Ste 2300 -Cleveland 44114 **Fx:**363-4588
(216) 641-1071 .. **Margolis,** Loren J '83 -3920 E 91st -Cleveland 44105
(216) 363-4500 .. **Margolis,** Richard D '63 OfCnsl Benesch FC&A LLP -200 Pub Sq -Ste 2300 -Cleveland 44114 **Fx:**363-4588
(216) 621-2222 .. **Margolis,** Ronald A '83 (Finelli & M,PLL) -526 Superior Av -730 Leader Bldg -Cleveland 44114 **Fx:**621-1114
(216) 621-2034 .. **Margolius,** Andrew L '83 (Margolius M & Assoc,LPA) -55 Pub Sq -Ste 1100 -Cleveland 44113 **Fx:**621-1908
(216) 621-2034 .. **Margolius,** Marcia W '83 (Margolius M & Assoc,LPA) -55 Pub Sq -Ste 1100 -Cleveland 44113 **Fx:**621-1908
(216) 621-2034 .. **Margolius Margolius & Associates, LPA** -55 Pub Sq -Ste 1100 -Cleveland 44113 **Fx:**621-1908
(216) 514-5997 .. **Margulies,** James W '94 (Margulies & L) -30100 Chagrin Blvd -Ste 250 -Pepper Pike 44124 **Fx:**514-5996
(216) 479-8500 .. **Margulies,** Jeffrey J '73 (Squire S&D LLP) -127 Pub Sq -4900 Key Twr -Cleveland 44114 **Fx:**479-8780
(614) 466-8626 .. **Margulies,** Pamela L '76 Tax Appeals -30 E Broad -Columbus 43215 **Fx:**644-5196
(216) 514-5997 .. **Margulies,** Susan C '95 %Margulies & L -30100 Chagrin Blvd -Ste 250 -Pepper Pike 44124 **Fx:**514-5996
(740) 983-2557 .. **Margulis Gussler Hall & Hosterman** -50 Bortz -Bx5 -Ashville 43103 **Fx:**983-2685
(614) 644-7250 .. **Marhevka,** Donna M '84 Atty Gen -30 E Broad -Columbus 43215 **Fx:**644-7634
(216) 622-8200 .. **Marhofer,** Michael F '91 (Calfee H&G LLP) -800 Superior Av -Ste 1400 -Cleveland 44114 **Fx:**241-0816
(937) 225-5780 .. **Mariani,** Laura G '94 Montgomery Cnty Pros -301 W 3rd -Bx972 -Dayton 45422 **Fx:**225-3470
Maricco, Michael A '01 -2401 Calvert NW -310 -Washington, DC 20008
(330) 860-6606 .. **Marich,** Eric '85 Babcock & Wilcox Co -20 S Van Buren Av -Bx351 -Barberton 44203
(330) 675-2521 .. **Marik,** Deborah E '91 %Trumbull Cnty Probate Ct -161 High NW -Warren 44481
(614) 299-9466 .. **Marinakis,** Angela D '93 Marinakis Law Ofc -673 Mohawk -Ste 101 -Columbus 43206
(513) 684-9393 .. **Marinakis,** George S '91 (Marinakis & M) -605 Sycamore -Cincinnati 45202
(513) 684-9393 .. **Marinakis,** Marina '91 (Marinakis & M) -605 Sycamore -Cincinnati 45202
(740) 693-2063 .. **Marinelli,** Arthur J Jr. '67 Ohio Univ/Cllg of Business Admin -401 Copeland Hall -Athens 45701
(330) 253-1555 .. **Marinelli,** Deborah M '01 %D Booher & Assoc Co,LPA -3180 W Market -Fairlawn 44333
(718) 237-9913 .. **Marini,** Francis J '73 Eparchy of St Maron of Bklyn -109 Remsen -Brooklyn, NY 11201
(419) 625-8324 .. **Marinko,** Christopher M '88 Flynn P&K,LPA -165 E Wshngtn Row -Sandusky 44870 **Fx:**625-9007
(216) 443-7800 .. **Marino,** Carmen M '71 %Cuyahoga Cnty Pros -1200 Ontario -8th Fl -Cleveland 44113 **Fx:**698-2270
Marino, Lucien R '72 -2286 S Belvoir Blvd -University Heights 44118
Marino, Nicholas J '81 -89 Westover Dr -Akron 44313
(440) 350-1174 .. **Marinucci,** Daniel F '80 -260 Nelmar Dr -Painesville 44077
(216) 619-5223 .. **Mariotti,** Mark '97 -323 Lakeside Av -Ste 450 -Cleveland 44113
Mark, Brian D '04 -(Address Unavailable)
(419) 241-6000 .. **Markakis,** Maria Limbert '00 %Eastman & S Ltd -1 Seagate -24th Fl -Bx10032 -Toledo 43699 **Fx:**247-1777
(216) 292-3300 .. **Marken,** Howard A '50 (Conway MWK&K Co,LPA) -30195 Chagrin Blvd -Ste 300 -Cleveland 44124
(513) 961-6200 .. **Markesbery,** Glenn A '88 (Markesbery & R Co,LPA) -2368 Victory Pkwy -Ste 200 -Bx6491 -Cincinnati 45206
(513) 853-5642 .. **Markesbery,** Maria A '86 Mercy Hlth Prtnrs -2446 Kipling -Cincinnati 45239
(513) 961-6200 .. **Markesbery & Richardson Co,LPA** -2368 Victory Pkwy -Ste 200 -Bx6491 -Cincinnati 45206
(216) 443-8610 .. **Markey,** Daniel J '03 Cuyahoga Cnty Ct Cmmn Pleas -1200 Ontario -Justice Ctr 11th Fl -Cleveland 44113
(216) 621-0200 .. **Markey,** Robert G '64 (Baker & H LLP) -1900 E 9th -Ste 3200 -Cleveland 44114 **Fx:**696-0740
(606) 344-9910 .. **Markgraf,** Paul R '83 -100 Crisler Av -Fort Mitchell, KY 41017
(330) 492-7107 .. **Markijohn,** Darrell N '85 -4100 Holiday NW -Ste 101 -Canton 44718
Markijohn, Jayne L '89 -Bx35204 -Canton 44735
(419) 673-4176 .. **Markley,** Frederick E '61 (Wetherill SM&S) -109 E Franklin -Kenton 43326 **Fx:**673-8089
(330) 670-0005 .. **Markling,** Matthew J '97 (McGown & M) -1894 N Cleveland Massillon Rd -Akron 44333
(517) 241-7333 .. **Markman,** Mary K '74 MI Emplymnt Sec Bd of Review -611 W Ottawa -Bx30475 -Lansing, MI 48909 **Fx:**241-7326
(216) 586-3939 .. **Markovic,** Sasha '04 %Jones D -901 Lakeside Av -Cleveland 44114 **Fx:**579-0212
(440) 759-1420 .. **Markovich,** Anna '03 -18975 Villavw Rd -Ste 7 -Cleveland 44119
(330) 384-1623 .. **Markovich,** Edward P '97 -209 S Main -Ste 201 -Bx80130 -Akron 44308
(513) 977-4774 .. **Markovits,** Wilbert B '83 (Markovits & G Co,LPA) -119 E Court -Ste 500 -Cincinnati 45202
(440) 285-2242 .. **Markowitz,** Dale H '75 Thrasher D&D,LPA -100 7th Av -Ste 150 -Chardon 44024 **Fx:**285-9423
(216) 861-3086 .. **Markowski,** Anne M '98 %Reid M&W -55 Pub Sq -Ste 2010 -Cleveland 44113 **Fx:**861-4409
(937) 438-3122 .. **Markowski,** Joseph H '99 %J Dundon Co,LPA -156 E Sprng Vlly Rd -Centerville 45458
(937) 461-9330 .. **Markowski,** Kristen A '99 -371 W 1st -Dayton 45402
(330) 626-1118 .. **Markowski,** Lucille '89 -10145 Keith's Close -Streetsboro 44241
(740) 345-0850 .. **Marks,** Anna L '02 SE OH Lgl Srvcs -12 W Locust Av -Newark 43055
Marks, Bruce W '79 -(Address Unavailable)
(614) 387-9030 .. **Marks,** Caroline L '99 Hon T O'Donnell Supreme Ct -65 S Front -9th Fl -Columbus 43215
(330) 633-1933 .. **Marks,** Donald L '53 (Marks & J) -1650 Home Av -Akron 44310
(513) 421-4400 .. **Marks,** Edward G '67 (Hardin LL&M LLC) -30 Garfld Pl -915 Cincinnati Club Bldg -Cincinnati 45202
(216) 479-8500 .. **Marks,** Erin E '04 %Squire S&D LLP -127 Pub Sq -4900 Key Twr -Cleveland 44114 **Fx:**479-8780
(614) 258-9300 .. **Marks,** Irving B '71 -923 E Broad -Columbus 43205
(614) 462-2800 .. **Marks,** Janine M '88 %Bank First Natl -66 S 3rd -Columbus 43215
(513) 361-1200 .. **Marks,** Jeffrey A '81 OfCnsl Squire S&D LLP -312 Walnut -Ste 3500 -Cincinnati 45202 **Fx:**361-1201
(216) 664-2715 .. **Marks,** Jeffrey B '69 Dept of Law -601 Lakeside Av -Rm 106 City Hall -Cleveland 44114 **Fx:**664-2663

(216) 523-5405 .. **Marks,** Joshua M '96 %Bricker & E LLP -1375 E 9th -Ste 1500 -Cleveland 44114 **Fx:**523-7071

(419) 724-0030 .. **Marks,** R Edward '94 LAWO -520 Mad Av -Ste 640 -Toledo 43604 **Fx:**321-1582

(330) 677-9000 .. **Marks,** Richard S '94 Marks & C Co,LPA -1001 S Water -Kent 44240 **Fx:**677-1404

    Marks, Ronald A '75 -4765 Topper Hill Dr -Hubbard 44425

(216) 292-2600 .. **Marks,** Seth B '71 -3637 Green Rd -Beachwood 44122 **Fx:**464-4130

(513) 867-5001 .. **Markstein,** Peggy A '87 -441 Patterson Dr -Fairfield 45014

(440) 333-8603 .. **Markstrom,** Paul F Jr. '72 -22255 Ctr Ridge Rd -Ste 208 -Rocky River 44116

(216) 651-6100 .. **Marksz,** John A '65 -11200 Edgewtr Dr -Cleveland 44102

(216) 531-5898 .. **Markulin,** Katica K '89 -18975 Villavw Rd -Cleveland 44119

(614) 236-6545 .. **Markus,** Kent R '84 Capital Univ Law Sch -303 E Broad -Natl Ctr Adoption Law & Policy -Columbus 43215 **Fx:**236-6956

(440) 356-2728 .. **Markus,** Richard M '56 Private Judicial Svcs, Inc -3903 N Valley Dr -Fairview Park 44126

(216) 621-0150 .. **Markus,** Robert D '67 (Hahn L&P LLP) -3300 BP Twr/200 Pub Sq -Ste 3300 -Cleveland 44114 **Fx:**241-2824

(216) 931-6000 .. **Markus,** Stephen A '79 (Ulmer & B LLP) -1300 E 9th -Ste 900 Penton Media Bldg -Cleveland 44114 **Fx:**931-6001

(740) 653-4259 .. **Markwood,** Maureen L '03 %Fairfield Cnty Pros -201 S Broad -4th Fl -Lancaster 43130

(216) 523-1500 .. **Markworth,** Dale E '73 Mansour GG&M Co,LPA -55 Pub Sq -Ste 2150 -Cleveland 44113 **Fx:**523-1705

(330) 364-7421 .. **Markworth,** Lawrence '72 The Huntington Bank -232 W 3rd -Bx100 -Dover 44622 **Fx:**364-7492

(614) 241-2078 .. **Markworth,** Thomas '68 -900 Mich Av -Ste B -Columbus 43215

(614) 523-3575 .. **Marlatt,** Jonathan Scott '03 Mills & M -1935 W Schrock Rd -Westerville 43081

(513) 563-3525 .. **Marler,** Karen F '82 (Marler & Assoc) -Bx1036 -Milford 45150 **Fx:**833-9022

(419) 435-7786 .. **Marley,** Barbara L '73 (Marley & M) -100 N Popular -Drwr866 -Fostoria 44830

(419) 435-7786 .. **Marley,** Francis M Jr. '71 (Marley & M) -100 N Popular -Drwr866 -Fostoria 44830

(419) 321-7188 .. **Marley,** James W '96 Toledo Edison Co -300 Mad Av -Toledo 43652

(614) 227-2000 .. **Marlier,** Haimavathi V '04 %Porter WM&A LLP -41 S High -Columbus 43215 **Fx:**227-2100

(614) 442-0002 .. **Marlin,** James J Jr. '68 -2066 W Henderson Rd -Columbus 43220

(614) 864-4352 .. **Marlin,** Michael S '73 -5150 E Main -Ste 200 -Columbus 43213

(937) 325-7058 .. **Marlow,** Brandin D '03 %Gorman VH&W -4 W Main -Ste 723 -Springfield 45502 **Fx:**325-9914

(513) 287-6900 .. **Marlow,** James R '67 (Marlow & G Co,LPA) -600 Vine -Ste 1810 -Cincinnati 45202 **Fx:**287-6903

(440) 347-5487 .. **Marlowe,** Cecil '88 Lubnzol Corp -29400 Lakelnd Blvd -Wickliffe 44092

(216) 781-4900 .. **Marmaros,** Peter W '83 (P Marmaros Co,LPA) -323 Lakeside Pl W -Ste 450 -Cleveland 44113

(513) 76-4441 .... **Marmer,** Lynn '86 Kroger Co -1014 Vine -Corp Affairs Dept -Cincinnati 45202

(216) 696-0990 .. **Marnecheck,** Philip A '81 (Shapiro M&R) -1468 W 9th -Rm 425 -Cleveland 44113 **Fx:**696-7790

(513) 579-1500 .. **Marnell,** Francis X '82 (Buechner HOM&H Co,LPA) -105 E 4th -Ste 300 -Cincinnati 45202 **Fx:**977-4361

(216) 621-5036 .. **Marniella,** James A '01 (Demer W&M,LLC) -2 Berea Cmmns -Ste 200 -Berea 44017 **Fx:**(440) 891-1684

(440) 826-5860 .. **Marniella,** Marisa Ann '95 Berea Mun Ct -11 Berea Cmmns -Berea 44017

(330) 629-9030 .. **Maro,** Lynn A '91 -1032 Boardman-Canfld Rd -Youngstown 44512 **Fx:**629-9036

(216) 291-2807 .. **Marocco,** William '69 -2176 Fenway Dr -Beachwood 44122

(216) 781-8286 .. **Marolt,** Evelyn R '87 -1370 Ontario -Ste 1130 -Cleveland 44113

    Marosan, Joseph E '84 -7050 Engle Rd -Cleveland 44130

(614) 340-2699 .. **Marotta,** Joseph M '01 Schl Employees Retrmnt Syst of OH -300 E Broad -Ste 100 -Columbus 43215

(614) 466-4514 .. **Marotta,** Melissa L '01 State Auditor -88 E Broad -Bx1140 -Columbus 43216

(614) 462-5435 .. **Marotta,** Robert D '75 OfCnsl Kegler BH&R -65 E State -Ste 1800 -Columbus 43215 **Fx:**464-2634

(216) 241-7740 .. **Marotta,** Thomas P '81 OfCnsl Willacy L&M -1468 W 9th -700 Wstrn Reserve Bldg -Cleveland 44113

    Maroun, Anita S '97 -1160 Bway -Bedford 44146

(614) 469-5715 .. **Marous,** James M '79 US Atty -303 Marconi Blvd -Ste 200 -Columbus 43215

    Marquard, Robert J '54 -2284 Windward Dr -Westlake 44145

(614) 734-1270 .. **Marquardt,** Richard F '00 %Farlow & Assoc LLC -270 Bradenton Av -Dublin 43017 **Fx:**923-1031

(937) 223-8888 .. **Marquis,** David W '91 %Dyer GM&S -131 N Ludlow -Ste 1400 -Dayton 45402 **Fx:**223-0127

    Marquis, Stacie R '04 -(Address Unavailable)

(216) 623-0880 .. **Marra,** Joni L '91 West Group -600 Superior Av E -2550 Bk One Ctr -Cleveland 44114

(404) 572-2729 .. **Marrah,** Scott L '93 (King & S LLP) -191 Pchtree NE -Atlanta, GA 30303 **Fx:**572-5100

(941) 575-7497 .. **Marrazzo,** Dante '97 -1133 Bal Hrbr Blvd PMB203 -Ste 1139 -Punta Gorda, FL 33950

(216) 241-2838 .. **Marrer,** Steven A '83 (Taft S&H LLP) -200 Pub Sq -3500 BP Twr -Cleveland 44114 **Fx:**241-3707

(513) 762-6200 .. **Marrero,** Michael A '77 (Ulmer & B LLP) -600 Vine -Ste 2800 -Cincinnati 45202 **Fx:**762-6245

(740) 368-0111 .. **Marrocco,** Michael A '94 %Hrabcak & Co,LPA -5 W Winter -Ste 250 -Delaware 43015 **Fx:**367-0115

(614) 336-8575 .. **Marsalka,** Joseph P '58 Comel,Inc -6452 Fiesta Dr -Columbus 43235

(419) 893-4880 .. **Marsh,** Benjamin F '55 (Marsh M Ltd) -204 W Wayne -Maumee 43537

(330) 456-8105 .. **Marsh,** Bobbie L '89 -111 2nd NW -303 Granger Bldg -Canton 44702

(614) 227-2000 .. **Marsh,** John F '95 (Porter WM&A LLP) -41 S High -Columbus 43215 **Fx:**227-2100

(740) 373-4171 .. **Marsh,** John H Jr. '00 City of Marietta -301 Putnam -Marietta 45750

(614) 464-6400 .. **Marsh,** Judith L '00 %Vorys SS&P LLP -52 E Gay -Bx1008 -Columbus 43216 **Fx:**464-6350

(330) 467-7131 .. **Marsh,** Linda S '89 Nrthcst Behav Hlthcre Syst -1756 Sagamore Rd -Bx305 -Northfield 44067

(419) 893-4880 .. **Marsh McAdams Ltd** -204 W Wayne -Maumee 43537

(419) 352-2518 .. **Marsh,** Michael J '79 (Marsh & M) -249 S Main -Bx347 -Bowling Green 43402

(937) 866-8454 .. **Marsh,** Michael T '92 -110 E Central Av -Miamisburg 45342

(614) 228-6885 .. **Marsh,** Rick E '60 (Lane A&H LLC) -175 S 3rd -Ste 700 -Columbus 43215 **Fx:**228-0146

(330) 456-8341 .. **Marsh,** Victor R Jr. '66 (Black MS&A,LPA) -220 Market Av S -Ste 1000 -Canton 44702 **Fx:**456-5756

(937) 333-4400 .. **Marsh-Cook,** Stephanie L '96 Dayton Pros -335 W 3rd -Ste 372 -Dayton 45402

(954) 525-9900 .. **Marshall,** Adam D '99 %Berger S,PA -350 E Las Olas Blvd -Ste 1000 -Fort Lauderdale, FL 33301 **Fx:**525-2872

(216) 861-3086 .. **Marshall,** Bernadette '85 Reid M&W -55 Pub Sq -Ste 2010 -Cleveland 44113 **Fx:**861-4409

(216) 928-2200 .. **Marshall,** Christina J '98 Sutter OM&F -1301 E 9th -3600 Erievw Twr -Cleveland 44114 **Fx:**928-4400

(614) 227-2000 .. **Marshall,** Colleen L '04 %Porter WM&A LLP -41 S High -Columbus 43215 **Fx:**227-2100

(513) 621-5428 .. **Marshall,** Courtland E '49 (Chatfield & M) -7 W 7th -Ste 1800 -Cincinnati 45202

(330) 376-5300 .. **Marshall,** Craig S '86 (Buckingham D&B,LLP) -50 S Main -Bx1500 -Akron 44309 **Fx:**258-6559

(740) 335-4381 .. **Marshall,** Dallas B '97 (Butler & M) -200 E Market -Washington Court House 43160

(330) 255-0037 .. **Marshall Dennehey Warner Coleman & Goggin** -120 E Mill -Ste 240 -Akron 44308 **Fx:**255-0040

(330) 471-0187 .. **Marshall,** Donald D '78 Workers Comp -400 3rd SE -Bx24801 -Canton 44701 **Fx:**471-0075

(203) 968-3453 .. **Marshall,** Douglas H '81 Xerox Corp -800 Long Ridge Rd -Bx1600 -Stamford, CT 06904

(614) 888-6533 .. **Marshall,** Dwight A '69 -1159 Blind Brook Dr -Columbus 43235

    Marshall, Giles T '78 -1267 W 9th -Cleveland 44113

(937) 324-2224 .. **Marshall,** James D '83 (Hofbauer & M) -4 W Main -2nd Fl -Springfield 45502

(740) 353-1800 .. **Marshall,** John B Jr. '79 -717 Wshngtn -Portsmouth 45662

(614) 463-9790 .. **Marshall,** John S '83 (Marshall & M LLC) -111 W Rich -Ste 430 -Columbus 43215 **Fx:**463-9780

(614) 387-9370 .. **Marshall,** Jonathan W '70 Bd Comm on Grievances & Discipline -65 S Front -5th Fl -Columbus 43215 **Fx:**387-9379

(614) 469-0331 .. **Marshall,** Joy L '02 -336 S High -Columbus 43215

(850) 414-3400 .. **Marshall,** Marilyn J '85 Atty Gen -The Cptl PL-01 -Tallahassee, FL 32399 **Fx:**922-9429

(419) 526-2223 .. **Marshall,** Mark A '02 -Bx3651 -Mansfield 44907

(216) 443-7800 .. **Marshall,** Mark R '91 Cuyahoga Cnty Pros -1200 Ontario -8th Fl -Cleveland 44113 **Fx:**698-2270

(419) 249-7100 .. **Marshall & Melhorn,LLC** -Four Seagate -8th Fl -Toledo 43604 **Fx:**249-7151

(419) 254-4300 .. **Marshall & Melhorn,LLC** -420 Mad Av -Ste 1100 -Toledo 43604

(740) 282-7400 .. **Marshall,** Michael J '95 -339 Market -Rm 700 -Steubenville 43952

(614) 459-8106 .. **Marshall,** Michelle A '91 Settlement Consultants -1248 London Dr -Columbus 43221

(614) 538-1840 .. **Marshall,** Michelle L '03 %Balcerzak Law Ofc -4656 Exec Dr -Columbus 43220

(614) 463-9790 .. **Marshall & Morrow LLC** -111 W Rich -Ste 430 -Columbus 43215 **Fx:**463-9780

(513) 241-4722 .. **Marshall,** Pamela '04 %Montgomery R&J,LPA -36 E 7th -Ste 2100 -Cincinnati 45202 **Fx:**241-8775

(614) 466-3934 .. **Marshall,** Rebecca J '99 %State Med Brd -77 S High -17th Fl -Columbus 43215

(312) 762-3100 .. **Marshall,** Robert S '94 %Bates & C -333 W Wacker Dr -Ste 900 -Chicago, IL 60606 **Fx:**762-3200

(404) 525-8622 .. **Marshall,** Townsell G Jr. '75 (Constangy B&S,LLP) -230 Pchtree NW -Ste 2400 -Atlanta, GA 30303

(859) 231-0000 .. **Marshall,** Valerie M '01 %Frost B&T,LLC -250 W Main -Ste 2700 -Lexington, KY 40507 **Fx:**231-0011

(216) 781-4994 .. **Marshall,** Wentworth J Jr. '56 (Smith MW&V) -1965 E 6th -500 Natl City-E 6th Bldg -Cleveland 44114 **Fx:**781-9448

(330) 746-6301 .. **Marshall,** William M Jr. '74 -219 W Boardman -Youngstown 44503

(919) 843-7747 .. **Marshall,** William P '87 Univ of N Carolina Schl of Law -5132 Van Hecke-Wettach Hall -CB#3380 -Chapel Hill, NC 27599 **Fx:**962-1277

(740) 355-8301 .. **Marshall,** William T '83 Scioto Cnty Common Pleas Ct -602 7th -Portsmouth 45662

(216) 292-2913 .. **Marshek,** Ronald S '73 -27600 Chagrin Blvd -Ste 160 -Woodmere 44122 **Fx:**292-7564

(513) 421-4646 .. **Marsick,** Philip J Jr. '72 McCaslin I&M,LPA -632 Vine -Ste 900 -Cincinnati 45202 **Fx:**421-7929

(412) 667-7987 .. **Marsico,** Leonard J '99 (McGuireWoods LLP) -625 Lbrty Av -23rd Fl -Pittsburgh, PA 15222 **Fx:**667-6050

(937) 222-2424 .. **Marsico,** Lindsay N '04 %Freund F&A -1 S Main -Ste 1800 -Dayton 45402 **Fx:**222-5369

(330) 562-3156 .. **Marsilio,** Tommie Jo '98 %Christley H&P -215 W Garfld -Ste 230 -Aurora 44202 **Fx:**562-9540

(304) 522-1700 .. **Marsteller,** Derek W '98 (Marsteller & H) -622 7th -Huntington, WV 25701

(216) 523-5000 .. **Marsteller,** Marcia E '95 %Eaton Corp -1111 Superior Av -Cleveland 44114

(440) 934-3441 .. **Marta,** Wayne P '77 (W Marta Co,LPA) -37106 Hunters Trl -Avon 44011

(216) 566-5699 .. **Marthaus,** Craig R '79 (Thompson H LLP) -127 Pub Sq -3900 Key Ctr -Cleveland 44114 **Fx:**566-5800

(210) 246-8610 .. **Martaus,** Cecilia M '79 SBC Adv Solutions -300 Convent -18-B-50 -San Antonio, TX 78205

(216) 696-0800 .. **Martello,** James P '74 (Gibson BZ&M) -55 Pub Sq -Ste 2075 -Cleveland 44113 **Fx:**696-0702

(614) 279-8059 .. **Martello,** Suzanne E '90 (Martello & M) -3079 W Broad -Ste 3 -Columbus 43204 **Fx:**279-8146

(614) 279-8059 .. **Martello,** Thomas F Jr. '92 (Martello & M) -3079 W Broad -Ste 3 -Columbus 43204 **Fx:**279-8146

(614) 261-0143 .. **Martens,** Franklin A '67 -293 Ceramic Dr -Columbus 43214

(614) 644-7233 .. **Marti,** Todd R '83 Atty Gen -150 E Gay -Columbus 43215 **Fx:**728-9327

(216) 523-1500 .. **Martillotta,** Samuel R '80 %Mansour GG&M Co,LPA -55 Pub Sq -Ste 2150 -Cleveland 44113 **Fx:**523-1705

(216) 928-2200 .. **Martin,** Adam W '04 %Sutter OM&F -1301 E 9th -3600 Erievw Twr -Cleveland 44114 **Fx:**928-4400

(614) 224-1222 .. **Martin,** Andrea E '82 %Maguire & S,LLP -250 Civic Ctr Dr -Ste 200 -Columbus 43215 **Fx:**224-1236

(216) 514-1100 .. **Martin,** Aric D '95 (Rolf & G Co,LPA) -30100 Chagrin Blvd -Ste 350 Corp Cir -Cleveland 44124 **Fx:**514-0030

(513) 333-0990 .. **Martin & Bailey** -120 E 4th -Ste 420 -Cincinnati 45202 **Fx:**333-0066

(937) 225-4652 .. **Martin,** Barbara J '92 Montgomery Cnty Pub Def -117 S Main -Ste 400 -Dayton 45422 **Fx:**225-3449

(937) 324-5541 .. **Martin Browne Hull & Harper** -1 S Limestone -Ste 800 -Bx1488 -Springfield 45501 **Fx:**325-5432

(330) 471-6831 .. **Martin,** Byron D '94 Timken Co -1100 Cherry Av SE -Bx6929 -Canton 44706

(954) 463-0100 .. **Martin,** Carlos F '02 %Johnson AMB&G -2455 E Sunrise Blvd -Ste 1000 -Fort Lauderdale, FL 33304 **Fx:**463-2444

(513) 984-3940 .. **Martin,** Carol Ann '82 -7645 Trlwind Dr -Cincinnati 45242

(513) 831-6697 .. **Martin,** Charles R II '96 OfCnsl F Douglas & Co,LPA -114 Main -Milford 45150

(937) 848-8400 .. **Martin,** Cynthia G '92 -90 E Franklin -Bellbrook 45305

(440) 543-6498 .. **Martin,** Dallan W '74 -7765 Cntry Ln -Chagrin Falls 44023

(614) 466-2766 .. **Martin,** Daniel J '95 Atty Gen -30 E Broad -Columbus 43215 **Fx:**644-1926

(419) 224-1011 .. **Martin,** Danny N '85 D Martin & Assoc -Bx5185 -Lima 45802

(614) 424-5018 .. **Martin,** David A '89 Battelle Memorial Inst -505 King Av -Columbus 43201

(419) 248-3318 .. **Martin,** David L '88 -1119 Adams -2nd Fl -Toledo 43624

Martin, David L '73 -27 N 4th -Newark 43055

(937) 324-5000 .. **Martin,** David M '75 (D Martin Co LPA) -4 W Main -Ste 707 -Springfield 45502

(740) 387-1613 .. **Martin,** Denise '99 %J Armengau -208 S Main -Marion 43302

(937) 865-6800 .. **Martin,** Denise D '00 Lexis/Nexis -Bx933 -Dayton 45401

(614) 462-3396 .. **Martin,** Don W '77 Franklin Cnty Dom Rltns Ct -373 S High -3rd Fl -Columbus 43215

(330) 425-3500 .. **Martin,** Donald L '64 Whitlatch & Co -8848 Cmmns Blvd -Bx363 -Twinsburg 44087

(740) 455-7123 .. **Martin,** Eric D '95 Muskingum Cnty Pros -27 N 5th -Zanesville 43701

(330) 547-3327 .. **Martin,** Frances '99 -12151 Ellsworth Rd -Bx638 -North Jackson 44441

(513) 281-1544 .. **Martin,** Gary P '96 %W Snyder & Assoc -2115 Luray Av -Cincinnati 45206

(330) 868-1138 .. **Martin,** Jack E '80 -201 S Market -Bx89 -Minerva 44657

(614) 249-4217 .. **Martin,** James D '96 Nationwide Ins Co -One Nationwide Plz -Columbus 43215

(419) 964-0423 .. **Martin,** James J '74 -111B W Walton -Willard 44890

(586) 979-6500 .. **Martin,** James N '03 (Martin B&M,PC) -44 1st -Mount Clemens, MI 48043

(859) 386-5292 .. **Martin,** James V '87 Fidelity Invstmnts -100 Crosby Pkwy -Covington, KY 41015

(740) 775-5321 .. **Martin,** Jane Spring '78 -176 W Water -Chillicothe 45601

(503) 675-5700 .. **Martin,** Jeffrey A '98 Textron Fincl Corp -4949 Meadow Rd -Ste 500 -Lake Oswego, OR 97035

(330) 253-5060 .. **Martin,** John F '84 (Brennan M&D,LLC) -75 E Market -Akron 44308 **Fx:**253-1977

(614) 221-0944 .. **Martin,** John S '83 %Artz & D,LLP -560 E Town -Columbus 43215 **Fx:**221-2340

(216) 443-7583 .. **Martin,** John T '84 Cuyahoga Cnty Pub Def -1200 W 3rd NW -100 Lakeside Pl -Cleveland 44113

(216) 771-3033 .. **Martin,** John W '69 -614 Superior Av -Ste 800 -Cleveland 44113

(419) 248-4611 .. **Martin,** John W '76 Louisville Title Agncy -626 Mad Av -Toledo 43604

(513) 558-0057 .. **Martin,** Joyce M '03 Univ of Cincinnati -Envrnmtl Policy Ctr -Bx670056 -Cincinnati 45267

(614) 222-8686 .. **Martin,** Julie C '91 Scott S&W LLP -50 W Broad -2500 LeVeque Twr -Columbus 43215 **Fx:**222-8688

(614) 466-4656 .. **Martin,** Jutta E '87 Atty Gen -150 E Gay -Columbus 43215 **Fx:**466-1756

(614) 719-3200 .. **Martin,** Karen L '78 %Hon JL Graham -85 Marconi Blvd -Rm 69 -Columbus 43215

(216) 443-7800 .. **Martin,** Kathleen A '81 Cuyahoga Cnty Pros -1200 Ontario -8th Fl -Cleveland 44113 **Fx:**698-2270

(937) 865-6800 .. **Martin,** Kathleen A '91 Lexis/Nexis -Bx933 -Dayton 45401

(330) 467-3300 .. **Martin,** Kenneth C '87 -8536 Crow Dr -Ste 41 -Bx293 -Macedonia 44056

(937) 278-2612 .. **Martin,** Kenneth D '04 Premier Health Partners -2222 Phila Dr -Ste 225 Davve Bldg -Dayton 45406

(614) 464-1626 .. **Martin,** Kyle D '89 L Smith & Assoc -929 Harrison Av -Ste 300 -Columbus 43215

(937) 332-9300 .. **Martin,** Laura J '03 Bucio & E,LLP -10 N Market -Troy 45373 **Fx:**339-6549

(937) 249-2490 .. **Martin,** Lauren B '96 %Nationwide Ins Co -1 Nationwide Plz -Columbus 43215

(937) 223-8177 .. **Martin,** M Shannon '93 (Coolidge WW&L) -33 W 1st -Ste 600 -Dayton 45402 **Fx:**223-6705

(713) 276-5391 .. **Martin,** Mark R '92 Fulbright WS LLP -1000 Louisiana Av -Ste 3400 -Houston, TX 77002

(614) 462-3555 .. **Martin,** Mary J '96 Franklin Cnty Pros -373 S High -Columbus 43215

(614) 224-1222 .. **Martin,** Matthew F '91 %Maguire & S,LLP -250 Civic Ctr Dr -Ste 200 -Columbus 43215 **Fx:**224-1236

(937) 878-8649 .. **Martin McCarty Wright & Roach** -26 N Wright Av -Fairborn 45324 **Fx:**878-8479

(614) 577-0488 .. **Martin,** Paige A '78 -77 Outerbelt -Columbus 43213

(937) 445-2990 .. **Martin,** Paul W Jr. '91 NCR Corp -1700 S Patterson Blvd -Dayton 45479

Martin, Rachael J '03 -1832 S Green Rd -South Euclid 44121

(419) 874-1100 .. **Martin,** Richard G '90 (Fraser MBM LLC) -132C W 2nd -Perrysburg 43551 **Fx:**874-1130

(330) 686-1708 .. **Martin,** Richard P '77 (R Martin Co, LPA) -3603 Darrow Rd -Stow 44224

(513) 333-0990 .. **Martin,** Robert C '53 (Martin & B) -120 E 4th -Ste 420 -Cincinnati 45202 **Fx:**333-0066

(330) 868-6161 .. **Martin,** Robert D '69 -850 McDaniel Av -Minerva 44657

(330) 923-8297 .. **Martin,** Ronald M '69 -1615 Akron Peninsula Rd -#102 -Akron 44313

(513) 621-2666 .. **Martin,** S Scott '99 %Statman HS&E LLC -255 E 5th -Ste 2900 Chemed Ctr -Cincinnati 45202 **Fx:**587-4477

Martin, Sacara E '04 -(Address Unavailable)

(330) 453-8279 .. **Martin,** Sherri L '84 Canton Cntry Day Schl -3000 Demington Av NW -Canton 44718

(740) 363-1313 .. **Martin,** Stephen D '74 (Manos MP&D Co,LPA) -50 N Sandusky -Delaware 43015 **Fx:**363-1314

(614) 764-0681 .. **Martin,** Steven A '88 (Blaugrund H&M,Inc) -5455 Rings Rd -Ste 500 -Dublin 43017 **Fx:**764-0774

(859) 426-1300 .. **Martin,** Steven C '80 Ziegler & S,PSC -541 Buttermilk Pike -Ste 500 -Bx175710 -Covington, KY 41017

(614) 293-7149 .. **Martin,** Suzanne C '83 Arthur G James Cancer Hosp -300 W 10th Av -Rm 519 -Columbus 43210

(216) 889-5530 .. **Martin,** Tammy L '92 Amer Greetings.com Inc -3 Amer Rd -Cleveland 44144

(513) 929-3400 .. **Martin,** Ted T '82 (Baker & H LLP) -312 Walnut -Ste 3200 -Cincinnati 45202 **Fx:**929-0303

(513) 421-6630 .. **Martin,** Thomas E '79 Lindhorst & D Co,LPA -312 Walnut -Ste 2300 -Cincinnati 45202

(330) 877-0700 .. **Martin,** Thomas H '04 (Martin & F) -1557 Lk O'Pines NE -Hartville 44632

(937) 461-5980 .. **Martin,** Thomas P '75 (Jablinski FR&M) -214 W Monument Av -Bx1266 -Dayton 45402 **Fx:**461-4139

(502) 815-5000 .. **Martin,** Timothy D '02 (Alber C,PSC) -9300 Shelbyvll Rd -Ste 1300 Hurstbourne Pl -Louisville, KY 40222 **Fx:**815-5005

(330) 877-0700 .. **Martin,** Todd M '04 Martin & F,LLP -1557 Lk O'Pines NE -Hartville 44632

(740) 286-8054 .. **Martin,** William C '74 -141 Portsmouth -Bx926 -Jackson 45640

(513) 352-6764 .. **Martin,** William L Jr. '71 (Thompson H LLP) -312 Walnut -14th Fl -Cincinnati 45202 **Fx:**241-4771

(513) 563-4700 .. **Martin,** William P II '95 Cntrl Invstmnt Corp -10560 Ashview Pl -#250 -Cincinnati 45242

(202) 772-5939 .. **Martin,** William R '76 (Blank R LLP) -600 NH Av NW -12th Fl -Washington, DC 20037 **Fx:**572-8380

(614) 227-2000 .. **Martin-Jones,** Melanie '99 %Porter WM&A LLP -41 S High -Columbus 43215 **Fx:**227-2100

(216) 272-7750 .. **Martindale,** John E '62 -26031 Butternut Ridge Rd -North Olmsted 44070 **Fx:**(440) 779-4697

(419) 255-5900 .. **Martineau,** Catherine B '82 (MacMillan S&T,LLC) -720 Water -4th Fl -Toledo 43604 **Fx:**255-9639

(614) 298-6488 .. **Martineau,** Eric D '95 -22 E 4th Av -Ste 1A -Columbus 43201

(615) 244-6380 .. **Martineau,** Robert J Jr. '83 Waller LD&D -511 Union -Ste 2100 -Nashville, TN 37219

(216) 664-4503 .. **Martinek,** Steven '75 Dept of Law -601 Lakeside Av -Rm 106 City Hall -Cleveland 44114 **Fx:**664-2663

(216) 875-5555 .. **Martinez,** Hector G Jr. '97 -526 Superior Av -Ste 545 -Cleveland 44114

(513) 852-3497 .. **Martinez,** Jose A '93 Atty Gen -441 Vine -1600 Carew Twr -Cincinnati 45202 **Fx:**852-3484

(513) 420-5653 .. **Martinez,** Lisa A '91 Middletown Rgnl Hosp -105 McKnight Dr -Middletown 45044

(216) 226-1170 .. **Martinez,** Richard D '62 -14701 Detroit Av -Rm 757 -Lakewood 44107

(330) 670-7300 .. **Marting,** Margaret L '92 Hanna C&P,LLP -3737 Embssy Pkwy -Bx5521 -Akron 44334 **Fx:**670-0977

(216) 586-3939 .. **Marting,** Michael G '74 (Jones D) -901 Lakeside Av -Cleveland 44114 **Fx:**579-0212

(740) 474-7642 .. **Marting,** Rodger A '74 -414 S Court -Circleville 43113

(513) 595-2200 .. **Martini,** Elizabeth F '84 Cnsl Union Cntrl Life Ins Co -Union Central Bldg -Bx40888 -Cincinnati 45240

(513) 241-6600 .. **Martini,** James C '85 -830 Main -Ste 607 -Cincinnati 45202 **Fx:**621-4007

(937) 865-1653 .. **Martino,** Bruce F '82 Lexis/Nexis -Bx933 -Dayton 45401

(513) 421-2400 .. **Martins,** Paul B '79 (Helmer MR&P Co,LPA) -105 E 4th -Ste 1900 -Cincinnati 45202 **Fx:**421-7902

(216) 479-6100 .. **Martinsek,** Amanda J '92 (Vorys SS&P LLP) -1375 E 9th -Ste 2100 One Cleve Ctr -Cleveland 44114 **Fx:**479-6060

(937) 433-5513 .. **Martinson,** Charles L '76 -6385 Jason Ln -Centerville 45459

(216) 222-3495 .. **Martis,** Charles G '55 -Natl City Ctr -Bx5756 -Cleveland 44101

(216) 586-3939 .. **Martis,** Michael S '85 Jones D -901 Lakeside Av -Cleveland 44114 **Fx:**579-0212

(440) 543-2979 .. **Martorana,** Kim Gerette '92 -11289 Stafford Rd -Chagrin Falls 44023

(330) 489-3251 .. **Martuccio,** Joseph '81 Law Dept -218 Cleveland Av SW -Bx24218 -Canton 44702

(216) 861-4700 .. **Martyn,** Hartley B '86 (Martyn & Assoc Co,LPA) -820 Superior Av NW -Ste 920 -Cleveland 44113

(202) 965-3060 .. **Martyn,** Iden G '84 (Martyn L,PLLC) -1054 31st NW -Ste 415 -Washington, DC 20007 **Fx:**965-3063

(330) 673-4414 .. **Martyniuk,** Andrew O '95 Kent Free Library -312 W Main -Kent 44240

(859) 341-1881 .. **Martyniuk,** Lev K '87 (Deters B&L,PSC) -2701 Turkeyfoot Rd -207 Thomas More Pkwy -Crestview Hills, KY 41017 **Fx:**341-1469

(740) 549-6188 .. **Martz,** Gary R '82 Cnsl Greif Bros Corp -425 Winter Rd -Delaware 43015

(614) 464-6400 .. **Martz,** Michael D '91 (Vorys SS&P LLP) -52 E Gay -Bx1008 -Columbus 43216 **Fx:**464-6350

(330) 746-8484 .. **Maruca,** Christopher A '98 (Betras M&K LLC) -6630 Sevll Dr -Bx129 -Canfield 44406 **Fx:**702-8280

(330) 746-8484 .. **Maruca,** Susan Gaetano '95 (Betras M&K LLC) -6630 Sevll Dr -Bx129 -Canfield 44406 **Fx:**702-8280

(440) 835-5238 .. **Maruster,** Robert F '75 -2939 S Bay Dr -#G1 -Westlake 44145 **Fx:**835-9699

(216) 476-4002 .. **Marvar,** Raymond J '79 Cleveland Clinic Hlth Syst
-18101 Lorain Av -Cleveland 44111

(614) 466-3016 .. **Marvin,** Robert E Jr. '80 PUCO -180 E Broad -Columbus 43266

(248) 737-8400 .. **Marvin,** Ronald S '00 %S Bernstein -31100 Nrthwstrn Hwy
-Farmington Hills, MI 48334 **Fx:**737-4392

(216) 931-6000 .. **Marvinney,** Craig A '82 (Ulmer & B LLP) -1300 E 9th
-Ste 900 Penton Media Bldg -Cleveland 44114 **Fx:**931-6001

(216) 443-9000 .. **Marvinney,** Michelle Powe '84 %Porter WM&A LLP -925 Euclid Av
-Ste 1700 -Cleveland 44115 **Fx:**443-9011

(740) 653-2423 .. **Marx,** Carol S '79 -106 Starret -Ste 210 -Lancaster 43130
Marx, Denise M '03 -(Address Unavailable)

(937) 443-6810 .. **Marx,** Dianne F '82 (Thompson H LLP) -2000 Cthse Plz NE
-Bx8801 -Dayton 45401 **Fx:**443-6635

(740) 653-4259 .. **Marx,** Gregg '79 Fairfield Cnty Pros -201 S Broad -4th Fl
-Lancaster 43130

(440) 835-1800 .. **Marx,** James A '87 -835 Sharon Dr -Ste 350 -Westlake 44145

(513) 977-8200 .. **Marx,** James A '97 %Dinsmore & S LLP -255 E 5th -Ste 1900
-Cincinnati 45202 **Fx:**977-8141

(614) 466-2872 .. **Marziale,** Arthur J Jr. '85 Atty Gen -30 E Broad -Columbus 43215
Fx:728-7592

(614) 224-7291 .. **Mas,** Joseph L '79 -330 S High -Columbus 43215

(513) 863-0660 .. **Masana,** Michael P '74 (Masana M&H) -220 S Monument Av
-Hamilton 45011

(614) 249-5736 .. **Mascarin,** Paul E '95 Nationwide Ins Co -One Nationwide Plz
-Tax Dept -Columbus 43215

(440) 395-0400 .. **Mascaro,** Daniel P '88 (Progressive Ins Co) -300 N Cmmns Blvd
-OHF 11 -Mayfield Village 44143

(216) 687-1311 .. **Masch,** Clifford C '83 (Reminger & R) -101 Prospect Av W
-1400 Mdlnd Bldg -Cleveland 44115 **Fx:**687-1841

(937) 865-6800 .. **Maschino,** Lisa L '91 Lexis/Nexis -Bx933 -Dayton 45401
Mascio, David A '03 -(Address Unavailable)

(740) 282-1544 .. **Mascio,** John J '92 -329 N 4th -Steubenville 43952

(412) 366-3333 .. **Mascio,** Karen L '01 %Willman & A,LLP -705 McKnight Park Dr
-Pittsburgh, PA 15237 **Fx:**366-3462

(330) 643-2788 .. **Mascolo,** John A '93 Summit Cnty Pros-Crim -53 Univ Av -7th Fl
-Akron 44308 **Fx:**643-8277

(614) 466-0278 .. **Mase,** Elizabeth K '85 Legis Srvc Commssn -77 S High
-Columbus 43215

(440) 246-2202 .. **Mase,** Lawrence L II '81 -522 Bway -Lorain 44052

(330) 395-5297 .. **Masek,** Raymond J '77 -183 W Market -Ste 200 -Warren 44481
Fx:392-0125

(614) 466-5709 .. **Masek,** Richard E '80 Legis Srvc Commssn -77 S High
-Columbus 43215

(614) 462-3194 .. **Masello,** Dean J '03 Franklin Cnty Pub Def -373 S High -12th Fl
-Columbus 43215

(216) 643-6952 .. **Maser,** Douglas L '76 Workers Comp Mgmt Solutions
-5005 Rockside Rd -Ste 530 -Independence 44131

(614) 836-3124 .. **Mashburn,** John B '74 -518 Main -Bx45 -Groveport 43125

(330) 296-9642 .. **Masi,** James '89 (Wilson & M) -250 S Prospect -Ravenna 44266
Fx:296-9644

(614) 457-6549 .. **Maskas,** George P '72 -3361 Stonehenge Ct -Columbus 43221

(614) 224-8374 .. **Maskovyak,** Joseph V '85 Legal Aid -40 W Gay -Columbus 43215

(330) 278-2343 .. **Mason,** Chris '01 Clinical Rsrch Mgmt,Inc -1265 Ridge Rd -Ste A
-Hinckley 44233

(330) 434-4399 .. **Mason,** Cynthia Ann '93 -879 Home Av -Akron 44310

(440) 930-4001 .. **Mason,** Daniel D '91 (Baumgartner & O)
-5455 Detroit Rd (Rte 254) -Sheffield Village 44054 **Fx:**934-7205

(740) 828-4016 .. **Mason,** Danielle M '89 Longaberger Co -1500 E Main -Bx3400
-Newark 43055

(419) 294-3132 .. **Mason,** David C '61 (Mason M&E) -110 S Sundusky Av -Bx8
-Upper Sandusky 43351

(732) 537-6500 .. **Mason,** David W '91 Cardinal Hlth -14 Schlhse Rd
-Somerset, NJ 08873

(614) 466-3905 .. **Mason,** Donald L '89 PUCO -180 E Broad -Columbus 43266

(614) 621-1214 .. **Mason,** Doris D '86 -209 S High -Ste 512G -Columbus 43215
Mason, Emma J '79 -139 Sycamore Dr -Oberlin 44074

(330) 674-7070 .. **Mason,** Grant A III '94 (Miller & M Ltd) -88 S Monroe -Ste B
-Millersburg 44654

(513) 732-7313 .. **Mason,** Helen E '91 Clermont Cnty Pros -123 N 3rd
-Batavia 45103

(614) 418-8044 .. **Mason,** James Thomas '84 M/I Schottenstein -3 Eastern Oval
-Ste 500 -Columbus 43219

(614) 462-2275 .. **Mason,** Jennifer '96 %Schottenstein Z&D -250 West -Bx165020
-Columbus 43216 **Fx:**462-5135

(513) 489-0829 .. **Mason,** Jeremy R '00 %Mason S&M Co,LPA -11340 Mntgmry Rd
-Ste 210 -Cincinnati 45249 **Fx:**489-0834

(513) 489-0829 .. **Mason,** Jonathan A '79 (Mason S&M Co,LPA) -11340 Mntgmry Rd
-Ste 210 -Cincinnati 45249 **Fx:**489-0834

(419) 289-1600 .. **Mason,** Josiah L '60 (Mason M&K) -153 W Main -Bx345
-Ashland 44805 **Fx:**289-6530

(216) 621-0200 .. **Mason,** Lance T '96 OfCnsl Baker & H LLP -1900 E 9th -Ste 3200
-Cleveland 44114 **Fx:**696-0740
Mason, Marsha D '83 Lexmark -740 New Circle Rd NW
-Lexington, KY 40550

(419) 294-3132 .. **Mason Mason & Ellis** -110 S Sundusky Av -Bx8
-Upper Sandusky 43351

(419) 289-1600 .. **Mason Mason & Kearns** -153 W Main -Bx345 -Ashland 44805
Fx:289-6530

(513) 984-4172 .. **Mason,** Michael G '68 -7919 Plainfld Rd -Cincinnati 45236

(513) 943-7100 .. **Mason,** Natalie Ann '01 Midland Co -7000 Mdlnd Blvd
-Amelia 45102

(703) 696-4543 .. **Mason,** Paul J '75 US Dept of Defense -4015 Wilson Blvd
-#300 Twr 3 -Bx3627 -Arlington, VA 22203

(513) 489-0829 .. **Mason,** Rachel J '03 %Mason S&M Co,LPA -11340 Mntgmry Rd
-Ste 210 -Cincinnati 45249 **Fx:**489-0834

(513) 248-2820 .. **Mason,** Ronald A '85 -110 Main -Milford 45150

(614) 734-9450 .. **Mason,** Ronald L '78 (Mason Law Firm Co,LPA) -425 Metro Pl N
-Ste 620 -Dublin 43017 **Fx:**734-9451

(513) 489-0829 .. **Mason Schilling & Mason Co,LPA** -11340 Mntgmry Rd -Ste 210
-Cincinnati 45249 **Fx:**489-0834

(419) 289-1600 .. **Mason,** Thomas L '89 %Mason M&K -153 W Main -Bx345
-Ashland 44805 **Fx:**289-6530

(216) 443-7800 .. **Mason,** William D '86 (Cuyahoga Cnty Pros) -1200 Ontario -8th Fl
-Cleveland 44113 **Fx:**698-2270

(614) 222-3060 .. **Mass,** Amy '95 -500 S Front -Ste 870 -Columbus 43215

(937) 865-6800 .. **Massa,** Susan '93 Lexis/Nexis -Bx933 -Dayton 45401
Massa, Vincent J '69 -316 Whitetail Dr -Chagrin Falls 44022

(513) 528-2850 .. **Massa,** William G '92 -431 Ohio Pike -Ste 110 North
-Cincinnati 45255 **Fx:**528-8400

(330) 675-2650 .. **Massacci,** Shibani S '97 %11th Dist Ct of Appls -111 High NE
-Warren 44481

(216) 621-4859 .. **Massaro,** Peter T '91 -1235 W 6th -Ste 5B -Bx93532
-Cleveland 44101 **Fx:**621-4859

(419) 241-2122 .. **Masse,** Andrew R '84 %Williams JLG&S Co,LPA -416 N Erie
-Ste 500 -Toledo 43624 **Fx:**245-3849

(614) 841-1918 .. **Massengill,** Kimberly A '92 AFSCME OH Cnsl 8 -6800 N High
-Worthington 43085

(216) 771-3336 .. **Massetti,** Regina M '81 -113 St Clair Av NE -Ste 525 -Cleveland
44114

(606) 426-9000 .. **Massey,** Charles E '95 -2643 Erlanger-Crescent Springs
-Erlanger, KY 41017

(614) 227-2000 .. **Massey,** Daniel J '70 (Porter WM&A LLP) -41 S High
-Columbus 43215 **Fx:**227-2100

(614) 365-4100 .. **Massey,** Daniel M '03 %Carpenter & L LLP -280 N High -Ste 1300
280 Plz -Columbus 43215 **Fx:**365-9145
Massey, Gaye A '99 -11641 Tanglewood Dr
-Eden Prairie, MN 55347

(740) 453-5544 .. **Massey,** Jefferson H '75 -30 S 4th -Zanesville 43701

(419) 843-2001 .. **Massey,** Laura A '01 %Gallon & T Co,LPA -3516 Granite Cir
-Bx352018 -Toledo 43635 **Fx:**843-6665

(614) 466-2766 .. **Massey,** Lori A '90 Atty Gen -30 E Broad -Columbus 43215
Fx:644-1926

(937) 372-9981 .. **Massie,** Marshall J '51 -119 E 2nd -Xenia 45385

(419) 774-5676 .. **Massie,** Nancy H '88 Richland Cnty Pros -38 S Park -2nd Fl
-Mansfield 44902 **Fx:**774-5589

(614) 221-0944 .. **Massucci,** LeeAnn M '03 %Artz & D,LLP -560 E Town
-Columbus 43215 **Fx:**221-2340

(216) 586-3939 .. **Mast,** Bernadette Mihalic '88 (Jones D) -901 Lakeside Av
-Cleveland 44114 **Fx:**579-0212

(440) 937-5911 .. **Mast,** David L '88 -3276 Nagel Rd -Avon 44011

(330) 674-7070 .. **Mast,** Diane S '81 (Miller & M Ltd) -88 S Monroe -Ste B
-Millersburg 44654

(330) 262-2350 .. **Mast,** Thomas K '80 -111 S Buckeye -Ste 240 -Wooster 44691

(216) 932-0663 .. **Mastandrea,** Joseph M '87 -2520 Lee Rd
-Cleveland Heights 44118

(740) 549-2444 .. **Master,** John E '83 -3817 Nicoya Ct -Lewis Center 43035

(330) 545-2800 .. **Masternick,** John '55 Windsor House,Inc -20 E Lbrty
-Girard 44420

(330) 545-1550 .. **Masternick,** John J '91 Windsor House,Inc -101 W Lbrty
-Girard 44420

(216) 771-1430 .. **Masters,** John M '85 (Masters & Assoc,LPA) -1111 Superior Av
-Cleveland 44114 **Fx:**771-2070

(415) 774-2700 .. **Masters,** Joseph '82 URS Consultants -100 Calif -Ste 500
-San Francisco, CA 94111

(513) 528-1414 .. **Masters,** Robert L '71 (Masters & Co,LPA) -4760 Sandra Lee Ln
-Cincinnati 45244 **Fx:**528-0213

(216) 781-2822 .. **Masters,** William N '83 (Winters & M Co,LPA) -820 W Superior Av
-Ste 600 -Cleveland 44113 **Fx:**344-2720

(740) 587-4782 .. **Masterson,** Hugh A '89 -2292 Welsh Hills Rd -Granville 43023

(513) 831-6444 .. **Masterson,** Michael E '93 -1019 Main -Milford 45150

(216) 432-1992 .. **Masterson,** Nora M '02 %R Dixon -4403 St Clair Av -Cleveland
44103

(813) 874-0758 .. **Masterson,** Paul J '78 Cath Hlth E/SE Div
-4211 W Boy Scout Blvd -Ste 160 -Tampa, FL 33607

(330) 343-1614 .. **Mastin,** Joseph S '77 (Bowers & M) -108½ E High Av
-New Philadelphia 44663

(330) 643-2943 .. **Mastran,** Christine E '96 Summit Cnty Pros-Juv -650 Dan
-Akron 44310 **Fx:**379-3647

(330) 342-1080 .. **Mastrangelo,** Ellen L '89 Cnsl Clarke Automotive Grp
-5715 Darrow Rd -Hudson 44236 **Fx:**655-0803

(614) 466-6696 .. **Mastrangelo,** Joseph J '79 Atty Gen -150 E Gay
-Columbus 43215 **Fx:**752-2538

(216) 787-3030 .. **Mastrangelo,** Mark E '82 Atty Gen -615 W Superior Av -11th Fl
-Cleveland 44113 **Fx:**787-3480

(330) 434-3000 .. **Mastrantonio,** Steven W '93 (Roderick & L) -One Cascade Plz
-Ste 1500 -Akron 44308 **Fx:**434-9220

(330) 451-7881 .. **Mastriacovo,** Paul A '78 -Bx20428 -Canton 44701

(330) 726-8300 .. **Mastriana,** Richard J '79 -1006 Boardman-Canfld Rd -Ste 1
-Boardman 44512

(440) 743-4749 .. **Mastroianni,** Anthony '83 -2484 Stratford Rd
-Cleveland Heights 44118

(740) 283-3330 .. **Mastros,** Costa D '95 -Bank One Bldg -Ste 1210 -Bx608
-Steubenville 43952

(513) 421-6464 .. **Mastruserio,** Dominic J '73 (D Mastruserio Co,LPA) -306 E 14th
-Cincinnati 45210

(513) 421-1313 .. **Mastruserio,** Karen L '86 %Griffin-F,LLP -3500 Redbank Rd
-Cincinnati 45227 **Fx:**421-1118

(513) 381-5552 .. **Masuda Funai Eifert & Mitchell,Ltd** -312 Walnut -Ste 1750
-Cincinnati 45202 **Fx:**381-5559

(317) 237-3892 .. **Masur,** James D II '85 (Locke R LLP) -201 N Illinois -Ste 1000
-Bx44961 -Indianapolis, IN 46204

(614) 228-2678 .. **Matan,** Eugene L '58 (Matan G&W) -261 S Front -Columbus 43215

(614) 228-2678 .. **Matan Geer & Wright** -261 S Front -Columbus 43215

(216) 447-9850 .. **Matas,** Richard S '95 The Hartford -7100 E Plsnt Vlly Rd -Ste 210
-Independence 44131 **Fx:**986-6245

(216) 473-2530 .. **Matas,** Vytas R '71 Matas Associates -2412 Cedarwood Rd
-Pepper Pike 44124

(216) 622-8200 .. **Matasar,** Scott C '00 %Calfee H&G LLP -800 Superior Av
-Ste 1400 -Cleveland 44114 **Fx:**241-0816

(330) 376-5300 .. **Matasich,** Michael J '04 %Buckingham D&B,LLP -50 S Main
-Bx1500 -Akron 44309 **Fx:**255-6559

(330) 455-0173 .. **Matasich,** Stephen E '96 (Day KRW&R,Ltd) -200 Market Av N
-Ste 300 -Bx24213 -Canton 44701 **Fx:**455-2633

(330) 726-5888 .. **Matavich,** Alan J '76 -945 Windham Ct -Ste 3 -Youngstown 44512

(216) 241-6602 .. **Matchinga,** Walter R '73 OfCnsl Weston HFP&H LLP -50 Pub Sq -2500 Trmnl Twr -Cleveland 44113 **Fx:**621-8369

(216) 589-9939 .. **Mate,** James T '77 -614 Superior Av NW -Ste 650 -Cleveland 44113

(330) 837-4678 .. **Matecheck,** Vincent G '71 -46 Fed Av NW -Massillon 44647

(440) 746-0911 .. **Matejczyk,** David M '89 (Vozar R&M Co,LPA) -3505 E Royalton Rd -Ste 100 -Cleveland 44147

(216) 664-2678 .. **Matejka,** Dennis A '83 Dept of Law -601 Lakeside Av -Rm 106 City Hall -Cleveland 44114 **Fx:**664-2663

(330) 972-8243 .. **Matejkovic,** John E '79 Univ of Akron -302 Buchtel Mall -209 Bus Admin Bldg -Akron 44333

(513) 705-6000 .. **Matejkovic,** Joseph R '91 -2 N Main -Middletown 45042

(440) 838-8800 .. **Matejkovic,** Margaret Andreeff '92 %Millisor & N Co,LPA -9150 S Hills Blvd -Ste 300 -Cleveland 44147 **Fx:**838-8805

(740) 622-1051 .. **Mathay,** Charles E '72 -1687 Evergreen Park Dr -Coshocton 43812

(614) 692-3284 .. **Matheke,** Carol N '86 US Dfnse Lgstcs Agncy -Bx3990 -Columbus 43218

(216) 443-6371 .. **Matheney,** Bridey '99 %8th Dist Ct of Appls -1 Lakeside Av -#202 -Cleveland 44113 **Fx:**443-2044

(216) 515-1660 .. **Matheney,** Matthew H '98 %Frantz W LLP -127 Pub Sq -2500 Key Center -Cleveland 44114 **Fx:**515-1650

(513) 732-7313 .. **Mather,** James M '96 Clermont Cnty Pros -123 N 3rd -Batavia 45103

(330) 375-5934 .. **Mather,** Jason N '00 Hon J Gwin USDC -2 S Main -510 US Cthse -Akron 44308

(419) 255-4864 .. **Mather,** John G '83 -1018 Adams -Toledo 43624

(216) 689-4725 .. **Mather,** Laura M '93 KeyCorp -127 Pub Sq -Cleveland 44114

(419) 213-4719 .. **Mathew,** Anita '96 Lucas Cnty Pros -Adams & Erie -Lucas Cnty Cthse -Toledo 43624

(614) 228-6885 .. **Mathews,** Alvin E Jr. '87 %Lane A&H LLC -175 S 3rd -Ste 700 -Columbus 43215 **Fx:**228-0146

(614) 415-7457 .. **Mathews,** Colin A '96 Limited Brands,Inc -3 Limited Pkwy -Columbus 43230

(614) 645-8724 .. **Mathews,** Denise R '93 Franklin Cnty Mun Ct -375 S High -Columbus 43215

(440) 835-1531 .. **Mathews,** Eileen T '96 (D'Aurelio & M) -96 Church -Chagrin Falls 44022

(614) 523-7575 .. **Mathews,** Gregory B '88 (Fusco MMS&W,LLP) -655 Cooper Rd -Westerville 43081 **Fx:**523-7580

(614) 387-9010 .. **Mathews,** Gregory P '04 Supreme Ct of OH -65 S Front -9th Fl -Columbus 43215

(440) 350-3200 .. **Mathews,** James C '00 Lake Cnty Pub Def -125 E Erie -Painesville 44077

(330) 499-6000 .. **Mathews,** James F '88 (Baker DBW&M) -400 S Main -Canton 44720 **Fx:**449-6423

(703) 696-9124 .. **Mathews,** Lance E '94 USAF/JACL -1501 Wilson Blvd -7th Flr -Arlington, VA 22209

            Mathews, Larry D '83 -6 Kim Ct E -Westerville 43081

(937) 865-6800 .. **Mathews,** Maureen Ly '02 Lexis Nexis -9595 Springboro Pike -Miamisburg 45342

(513) 351-1525 .. **Mathews,** Stanley A '68 (Mathews & M) -4557 Mntgmry Rd -Cincinnati 45212

(513) 351-1525 .. **Mathews,** Stanley M '99 (Mathews & M) -4557 Mntgmry Rd -Cincinnati 45212

(740) 387-5854 .. **Mathews,** Thomas A '77 (Firstenberger & M) -127 E Center -Marion 43302

(216) 348-5400 .. **Mathews,** Tyler L '94 (McDonald H Co,LPA) -600 Superior Av E -Ste 2100 -Cleveland 44114 **Fx:**348-5474

(513) 621-4849 .. **Mathews,** William S II '77 (Dolle R&M Co,LPA) -817 Main -Ste 500 -Cincinnati 45202

(937) 376-5429 .. **Mathewson,** Thomas G '96 -987 US Route 35 E -Xenia 45385

(330) 674-3055 .. **Mathie,** Daniel L '83 (Critchfield C&J Ltd) -138 E Jackson -Ste A -Millersburg 44654

(614) 252-1333 .. **Mathless,** Steven A '83 -800 E Broad -Columbus 43205

(216) 755-5500 .. **Mathoslah,** Rachel K '04 Developers Diversified Rlty Corp -3300 Enterprise Pkwy -Beachwood 44122

(602) 528-4000 .. **Matia,** Robert L '66 (Squire S&D LLP) -40 N Central Av -Ste 2700 -Phoenix, AZ 85004 **Fx:**253-8129

(216) 621-1000 .. **Matile,** Michael W '00 %Moscarino & T,LLP -1422 Euclid Av -Hanna Bldg Ste 630 -Cleveland 44115 **Fx:**622-1556

(937) 225-4348 .. **Matis,** Michael M '97 Cnsl Combined Hlth Dist -117 S Main -Dayton 45402 **Fx:**496-3072

(614) 227-2000 .. **Matisziw,** Kristin E '04 %Porter WM&A LLP -41 S High -Columbus 43215 **Fx:**227-2100

(740) 395-8303 .. **Matlack,** Ross A III '01 Holzer Medical Ctr -500 Burlngtn Rd -Jackson 45640

(216) 475-3656 .. **Matlin,** Judith L '91 -18424 Maple Heights Blvd -Maple Heights 44137

(937) 461-9234 .. **Matlock,** Michael D '85 (Matlock & Assoc) -333 W 1st -Ste 525 -Dayton 45402

(440) 603-2064 .. **Matoh,** James E '85 Progressive Ins Co -6055 Parkland Blvd -Mayfield Heights 44124

(513) 671-6333 .. **Matre,** James A '75 (Matre & M Co,LPA) -225 Pictoria Dr -Ste 200 -Cincinnati 45246 **Fx:**671-1234

(513) 671-6333 .. **Matre,** Kerrie K '98 (Matre & M Co,LPA) -225 Pictoria Dr -Ste 200 -Cincinnati 45246 **Fx:**671-1234

            Matsa, Aristotle R '84 -Bx65 -Columbus 43216

(937) 427-2271 .. **Mattera,** Joseph P '03 -75 Harbert Dr -Ste B -Dayton 45440

(216) 443-7800 .. **Mattes,** Jay L '90 Cuyahoga Cnty Pros -1200 Ontario -8th Fl -Cleveland 44113 **Fx:**698-2270

(614) 628-6880 .. **Mattes,** William M '88 (Dinsmore & S LLP) -175 S 3rd -10th Fl -Columbus 43215 **Fx:**628-6890

(513) 634-7419 .. **Mattheis,** David K '01 Cnsl Procter & Gamble -6000 Ctr Hill Av -Cincinnati 45224

(612) 361-1409 .. **Mattheis,** Martha E '92 Carver Cnty Atty Ofc -600 E 4th -Carver Co Govt Ctr Justice Ctr -Chaska, MN 55318

(513) 626-0673 .. **Matthews,** Armina E '98 Procter & Gamble -11511 Reed Hartman Hwy -HB3n26, Bx 325 -Cincinnati 45241

(614) 466-5057 .. **Matthews,** Christina '87 Industrial Commssn of OH -30 W Spring -9th Fl -Columbus 43215 **Fx:**752-8785

(937) 434-9393 .. **Matthews,** Craig T '78 (CT Matthews & Assoc LPA) -376 Regency Ridge Dr -Centerville 45459

(614) 752-1200 .. **Matthews,** Dale E Jr. '78 Parole Brd -1050 Fwy Dr N -Columbus 43229

            Matthews, David W '59 -5520 Wasigo Dr -Mount Washington 45230

(614) 464-6400 .. **Matthews,** Douglas R '87 (Vorys SS&P LLP) -52 E Gay -Bx1008 -Columbus 43216 **Fx:**464-6350

(419) 354-4442 .. **Matthews,** Frederic E '80 (Rayle M&C) -100 S Main -Bowling Green 43402

(513) 579-6400 .. **Matthews,** James R '90 (Keating M&K PLL) -1 E 4th -1400 Provident Twr -Cincinnati 45202 **Fx:**579-6457

(614) 431-9912 .. **Matthews,** James S '88 -8310 Blackmore Ct -Westerville 43081 **Fx:**431-9912

(937) 285-6500 .. **Matthews,** Jason P '01 OH Civ Rghts Cmmssn -40 W 4th -Ste 1900 -Dayton 45402

(614) 462-5321 .. **Matthews,** Jill A '02 Franklin Cnty Common Pleas Ct -373 S High -3rd Fl Domestic Relations -Columbus 43215

(513) 243-8406 .. **Matthews,** Kevin G '95 GE Aircraft Engines -1 Neumann Way -MD J104 -Cincinnati 45215

(216) 781-4110 .. **Matthews,** Laurel Ann '94 %C Kampinski Co,LPA -1370 Ontario -1530 Standard Bldg -Cleveland 44113 **Fx:**781-4178

(513) 579-6400 .. **Matthews,** Timothy B '82 (Keating M&K PLL) -1 E 4th -1400 Provident Twr -Cincinnati 45202 **Fx:**579-6457

(614) 227-2000 .. **Mattimoe,** James M '89 (Porter WM&A LLP) -41 S High -Columbus 43215 **Fx:**227-2100

(419) 874-5610 .. **Mattimoe,** John I '89 Croy & H,LLP -801 W South Boundary -Ste C -Perrysburg 43551

(740) 335-4750 .. **Mattingly,** Dennis W '83 Fayette Cnty Cmn Pleas Ct -110 E Ct -Washington Court House 43160

(513) 632-8618 .. **Mattingly,** Elizabeth B '75 Cnty Mun Ct Judge -1000 Main -Cincinnati 45202

(513) 977-8200 .. **Mattingly,** Paul R '75 (Dinsmore & S LLP) -255 E 5th -Ste 1900 -Cincinnati 45202 **Fx:**977-8141

(304) 284-4110 .. **Mattingly,** William S '85 (Jackson & K PLLC) -150 Clay -Ste 500 -Morgantown, WV 26501 **Fx:**284-4156

(614) 486-5392 .. **Mattis Daniell Voltolini & Voltolini** -1350 W 5th Av -Columbus 43212

(937) 746-1010 .. **Mattis,** Scott W '81 Bros Trading Co -400 Victory Dr -Springboro 45066

(614) 464-6400 .. **Mattis,** Theodore P '91 (Vorys SS&P LLP) -52 E Gay -Bx1008 -Columbus 43216 **Fx:**464-6350

(937) 775-2475 .. **Mattison,** Gwen M '84 Wright State Univ -3640 Colonel Glenn Hwy -356 Univ Hall -Dayton 45435

(614) 227-2300 .. **Matto,** Edward A '66 (Bricker & E LLP) -100 S 3rd -Columbus 43215 **Fx:**227-2390

(216) 875-4008 .. **Matts,** Joseph J '92 HWHAEP, Inc. -1001 Lakeside Av -Ste 800 -Cleveland 44114

(216) 621-6570 .. **Matty,** David J '79 (Rademaker MM&G) -55 Pub Sq -Ste 1775 -Cleveland 44113 **Fx:**621-1127

            Matune, Elizabeth A '04 -(Address Unavailable)

(330) 744-0247 .. **Matune,** Frank J '98 (Nadler N&B Co,LPA) -20 Fed Plz W -Ste 600 -Youngstown 44503 **Fx:**744-8690

(330) 747-2661 .. **Matune,** Timothy J '84 Cnsl Cafaro Co -2445 Belmont Av -Bx2186 -Youngstown 44504

(937) 293-3890 .. **Matusoff,** Robert B '55 -3033 Kettering Blvd -Ste 202 -Dayton 45439

(419) 213-4700 .. **Matuszak,** Thomas A II '97 %Lucas Cnty Pros -Adams & Erie -Lucas Cnty Cthse -Toledo 43624

            Matuszynski, Charles A '69 -2270 Ruthanne Dr -Toledo 43611

(330) 725-7045 .. **Matyac,** Jennifer D '03 %SJ Brown Co,LPA -326 N Court -Medina 44256 **Fx:**722-5909

(330) 643-7954 .. **Matyjasik,** Robert E '81 -22049 Hillard Blvd -Rocky River 44116

            Matz, Deborah Sue '92 Summit Cnty Cmn Pleas Ct -209 S High -Akron 44308

            Matz, John A '04 -(Address Unavailable)

            Mauceri, Frank D '92 -774 Mays Blvd -Ste 10-454 -Incline Village, NV 89451

(724) 983-3591 .. **Mauch,** Dale L '93 FNB Corp -1 FNB Blvd -Hermitage, PA 16148

(202) 487-5460 .. **Mauer,** Jeffrey F '89 -2816 O NW -Washington, DC 20007

(419) 249-7100 .. **Mauer,** Kenneth J '85 Marshall & M,LLC -Four Seagate -8th Fl -Toledo 43604 **Fx:**249-7151

(513) 651-6800 .. **Mauer,** Kimberly K '87 Cnsl Frost BT LLC -201 E 5th -2200 PNC Ctr -Cincinnati 45202 **Fx:**651-6981

(513) 651-6800 .. **Mauer,** Vincent E '87 Cnsl Frost BT LLC -201 E 5th -2200 PNC Ctr -Cincinnati 45202 **Fx:**651-6981

(614) 241-2156 .. **Mauger,** Jud R '94 (Moore Y&M) -326 S High -Columbus 43215

            Maugeri, Beatrice '92 -2450 Goddard Rd -Toledo 43606

(517) 784-9122 .. **Mauldin,** Clyde W Jr. '78 Laflamme & M,PC -2540 Spring Arbor Rd -Jackson, MI 49203

(513) 583-4200 .. **Maundrell,** Michael E '74 OfCnsl Schroeder MB&P -11935 Mason Rd -Ste 110 -Cincinnati 45249

(859) 344-9966 .. **Mauntel,** Phyllis A '97 Klette & K -250 Grandvw Dr -Ste 250 -Fort Mitchell, KY 41017

(419) 247-2500 .. **Mauntler,** John E '88 (Fuller & H,Ltd) -One SeaGate -Ste 1700 -Bx2088 -Toledo 43603 **Fx:**247-2665

(614) 224-9223 .. **Maurer,** James '64 (Ward KBM&M) -199 S 5th -Columbus 43215

(614) 262-9002 .. **Maurer,** John W '79 Maurer Advsry -2744 Kensngtn Pl E -Columbus 43202 **Fx:**262-3315

(419) 352-4621 .. **Maurer Newlove & Bakies** -224 E Wooster -Bowling Green 43402

(419) 352-4621 .. **Maurer,** Robert W '68 (Maurer N&B) -224 E Wooster -Bowling Green 43402

(937) 291-3400 .. **Maurer,** Ronald J '94 (Maurer Law Ofc,LLC) -848C E Franklin -Centerville 45459

(330) 666-5550 .. **Maurer,** Steven A '88 %Cole Co,LPA -863 N Cleveland-Massillon Rd -Akron 44333

(937) 653-7174 .. **Maurice,** Allen R '70 (Wagner MD&G) -117 W Court -Urbana 43078

(704) 633-5244 .. **Mauriello,** Christopher D '00 %Wallace & G,PA -525 N Main -Salisbury, NC 28144

(614) 771-0597 .. **Mauro,** Carmen C '83 -3095 Scioto Trace Rd -Columbus 43221

            Maus, Richard A '04 -(Address Unavailable)

(216) 685-1037 .. **Mausar,** Donald A '95 (Weltman W&R Co,LPA) -323 W Lakeside Av -Ste 200 -Cleveland 44113 **Fx:**363-4121

(216) 787-4901 .. **Mausser**, Cynthia B '91 Div Parole & Comm Srvcs
-615 W Superior Av -#960 -Cleveland 44113

(580) 745-2622 .. **Mawer**, William T '73 Sthestrn OK State Univ -1405 N 4th -#202R
-Bx4185 -Durant, OK 74701 **Fx**:745-7485

(419) 629-2311 .. **Maxa**, John G '75 Crown Equip Corp -44 S Wshngtn -Leg Dept
-New Bremen 45869

(859) 781-6620 .. **Maxey**, Jeannette E '02 -1932 Highland Av -Cincinnati 45219

(216) 621-7860 .. **Maxfield**, Harold O Jr. '86 (Cavitch FD&F) -1717 E 9th -14th Fl
-Cleveland 44114 **Fx**:621-3415

(614) 269-4900 .. **Maxfield**, Michael L '84 (Bricker & M,LLC) -4100 Regent -Ste T
-Columbus 43219 **Fx**:269-4901

(614) 445-8287 .. **Maxfield**, Sean H '76 -825 S Front -Columbus 43206

(614) 466-8600 .. **Maxfield**, Sheryl C '84 Atty Gen -30 E Broad -Columbus 43215
Fx:466-6090

(330) 629-8977 .. **Maxin**, Joseph J '87 (Maxin & M) -945 Windham Ct -Ste 3
-Youngstown 44512

(330) 629-8977 .. **Maxin**, Joseph W '61 (Maxin & M) -945 Windham Ct -Ste 3
-Youngstown 44512

(312) 353-5392 .. **Maxse**, Paul J '73 US Gen Srvcs Admin -230 S Dearborn
-Ste 3786 -Chicago, IL 60604

(216) 696-5444 .. **Maxton**, Reginald N '93 -925 Euclid Av -Ste 1025
-Cleveland 44115

(614) 326-3960 .. **Maxwell**, Amanda P '80 -4773-A Olentangy Rvr Rd
-Columbus 43214

(216) 696-5750 .. **Maxwell**, Gary J '88 Towards Employment-Lgl Srvcs Dept
-1255 Euclid Av -Ste 300 -Cleveland 44115

(614) 231-8529 .. **Maxwell**, James Jr. '51 Maxwell Law -631-A Olde Towne Av
-Columbus 43214

(412) 262-6736 .. **Maxwell**, James M '74 FedEx Grnd Pckge Syst -1000 Fedex Dr
-Moon Twp, PA 15108

(330) 364-9070 .. **Maxwell**, John P '94 (Hardin & S,LPA) -132 Fair Av NW
-New Philadelphia 44663 **Fx**:364-9073

(330) 643-2930 .. **Maxwell**, Kristin Wardell '92 Summit Cnty Juv Ct -650 Dan
-Akron 44310

(216) 363-1400 .. **Maxwell**, Lindsay '93 %Buckley K,LPA -600 E Superior Av
-Ste 1400 -Cleveland 44114 **Fx**:579-1020

(614) 249-7822 .. **Maxwell**, Mark D '96 Cnsl Nationwide Ins Co -1 Nationwide Plz
-Columbus 43215

(330) 374-1334 .. **Maxwell**, MaryBeth G '82 -7 W Bowery -Ste 507 -Akron 44308

(330) 744-1111 .. **Maxwell**, Neil H '84 Harrington H&M,Ltd -26 Market -Ste 1200
-Youngstown 44503 **Fx**:744-2029

(513) 579-6400 .. **Maxwell**, Robert W II '68 (Keating M&K PLL) -1 E 4th
-1400 Provident Twr -Cincinnati 45202 **Fx**:579-6457

(330) 745-9027 .. **May**, Bruce J '85 (B May,LPA) -480 Tuscarawas Av
-Barberton 44203

(216) 875-9842 .. **May**, Claire C '96 CSU-Marshall Cllg of Law -2121 Euclid Av
-LB138 -Cleveland 44115 **Fx**:687-6881

(513) 333-0990 .. **May**, Douglas J '89 (Martin & B) -120 E 4th -Ste 420
-Cincinnati 45202 **Fx**:333-0066

(614) 527-7610 .. **May**, Gregory D '88 -3325 Scioto Run Blvd -Columbus 43026

(216) 431-4500 .. **May**, James D '01 Cuyahoga Cnty Pros -3955 Euclid Av
-Jane Edna Hunter Bldg -Cleveland 44115 **Fx**:431-4113

(216) 621-0150 .. **May**, James W '04 %Hahn L&P LLP -3300 BP Twr/200 Pub Sq
-Ste 3300 -Cleveland 44114 **Fx**:241-2824

(513) 588-3050 .. **May**, Jeffrey M '90 Progressive Ins -2722 E Kemper Rd
-Cincinnati 45241

(937) 223-8177 .. **May**, Jill A '00 %Coolidge WW&L -33 W 1st -Ste 600
-Dayton 45402 **Fx**:223-6705

(330) 399-8801 .. **May**, Joyce A '78 (Turner M&S) -185 High NE -Warren 44481
Fx:399-8805

(313) 496-7567 .. **May**, Julie B '96 %Miller CP&S,PLC -150 W Jffrsn Av -Ste 2500
-Detroit, MI 48226

(216) 241-2880 .. **May**, Karl E '74 (Cowden HN&L) -50 Pub Sq -Ste 1414
-Cleveland 44113 **Fx**:241-2881

(216) 348-5400 .. **May**, Katayoon Sadre '04 %McDonald H Co,LPA -600 Superior Av
E -Ste 2100 -Cleveland 44114 **Fx**:348-5474

(937) 498-2108 .. **May**, Kelli E '00 Shelby Cnty Pros -126 N Main -Sidney 45365

(937) 746-1010 .. **May**, Kenneth F '78 Bros Trading Co -400 Victory Dr
-Springboro 45066

May, Neal A '93 -(Address Unavailable)

(614) 249-7899 .. **May**, Randall W '90 SrCnsl Nationwide Ins Co -1 Nationwide Plz
-Columbus 43215

(216) 642-3133 .. **Maybaum**, Scott D '78 -6060 Rockside Wds Pkwy -250
-Independence 44131

(216) 937-1390 .. **Maybee**, Matthew E '04 Marsh & M -200 Pub Sq -Ste 1100
-Cleveland 44114

(414) 299-8053 .. **Mayberry-French**, Ann G '89 Fortis Hlthcre -501 W Mich -Bx3050
-Milwaukee, WI 53201

(419) 524-2444 .. **Mayer**, Cassandra J '99 %PA Mayer -564 Park Av W
-Mansfield 44906

(330) 376-5300 .. **Mayer**, Christine A '96 OfCnsl Buckingham D&B,LLP -50 S Main
-Bx1500 -Akron 44309 **Fx**:258-6559

(937) 878-8030 .. **Mayer & Cusack LLC** -510 W Main -Fairborn 45324 **Fx**:878-8031

(513) 897-9222 .. **Mayer**, Donald G '80 -581 North -Bx289 -Waynesville 45068

(614) 224-8374 .. **Mayer**, Donna C '80 Legal Aid -40 W Gay -Columbus 43215

(561) 683-2484 .. **Mayer**, Earl E '54 (Mayer & K) -1675 Plm Bch Lks Blvd -Ste 700
-West Palm Beach, FL 33401

(513) 381-2838 .. **Mayer**, James J '69 OfCnsl Taft S&H LLP -425 Walnut -Ste 1800
-Cincinnati 45202 **Fx**:381-0205

(614) 462-3555 .. **Mayer**, James J III '00 Franklin Cnty Pros -373 S High
-Columbus 43215

(419) 774-5676 .. **Mayer**, James J Jr. '77 Richland Cnty Pros -38 S Park -2nd Fl
-Mansfield 44902 **Fx**:774-5589

(312) 360-6474 .. **Mayer**, Jeffrey J '98 (Freeborn & P) -311 S Wacker Dr -Ste 3000
-Chicago, IL 60606 **Fx**:360-6520

(216) 901-4824 .. **Mayer**, John E '89 -6060 Rockside Wds Blvd -Ste 250
-Independence 44131

(330) 643-2788 .. **Mayer**, Kevin A '93 Summit Cnty Pros-Crim -53 Univ Av -7th Fl
-Akron 44308 **Fx**:643-8277

(513) 381-0656 .. **Mayer**, Kimberly A '96 %Kohnen & P LLP -201 E 5th -Ste 800
-Cincinnati 45202 **Fx**:381-5823

(216) 592-5000 .. **Mayer**, Kristen L '91 OfCnsl Tucker E&W LLP -925 Euclid Av
-1150 Huntngtn Bldg -Cleveland 44115 **Fx**:592-5009

(937) 878-8030 .. **Mayer**, Michael A '94 (Mayer & C LLC) -510 W Main
-Fairborn 45324 **Fx**:878-8031

Mayer, Michael P '94 -4472 W 215th -Fairview Park 44126

(302) 892-0680 .. **Mayer**, Nancy S '82 El Du Pont de Nemours & Co -1007 Market
-Leg Dept -Wilmington, DE 19898

(419) 524-2444 .. **Mayer**, Philip A '77 -564 Park Av W -Mansfield 44906

(219) 665-2606 .. **Mayer**, Steven C '81 -227 W Maumee -Angola, IN 46703

(804) 788-5484 .. **Mayer**, Steven M '68 Ethyl Corp -330 S 4th -Bx2189
-Richmond, VA 23218

(440) 250-4400 .. **Mayer**, Wallace J Jr. '70 (Egert M&H) -1991 Crocker Rd -#550
-Westlake 44145

(440) 225-0500 .. **Mayernik**, Thomas J '89 Gibson BZ&M -8353 Mentor Av
-Mentor 44060 **Fx**:225-8426

(937) 323-4004 .. **Mayhall**, Richard E '82 (Flack & M) -101 N Fountain Av
-Springfield 45502

(740) 397-7420 .. **Mayhew**, Frederick E II '70 (McDevitt M&M,LPA) -1 Pub Sq
-Mount Vernon 43050 **Fx**:397-6611

(937) 226-2118 .. **Mayhew**, Kimberly H '91 Natl City Bank -6 N Main -Loc 21-2320
-Dayton 45412

(330) 908-4512 .. **Mayland**, Gail B '92 Charles Schwab & Co Inc
-4150 Kinross Lks Pkwy -Bx5050 -Richfield 44286

(216) 621-7743 .. **Mayle**, Andrew R '02 %Schiff & D,LLC -1370 Ontario
-Standard Bldg 6th Fl -Cleveland 44113

(330) 489-5434 .. **Mayle**, Kimberly A '90 Key Trust Co -126 Central Plz N
-Canton 44702

(419) 334-8377 .. **Mayle**, Ronald J '74 -210 S Front -Bx429 -Fremont 43420

Mayle, Timothy L '99 -645 W Main -Geneva 44041

(304) 428-8900 .. **Mayle**, Virginia K '86 Jan Dils,LC -1037 Market -Parkersburg,
WV 26102

(816) 556-1870 .. **Maymir**, Javier A '89 Ofc Comptroller of Currency
-2345 Grand Blvd -Ste 700 -Kansas City, MO 64108 **Fx**:556-1892

(304) 340-3871 .. **Maynard**, Adam L '04 %Spilman T&B,PLLC -300 Kanawha Blvd E
-Charleston, WV 25301

(214) 220-3939 .. **Maynard**, Christopher S '01 %Jones D -2727 N Harwood
-Dallas, TX 75201

(614) 985-3670 .. **Maynard**, Jay W '88 -200 E Campus Vw Blvd -Ste 200
-Columbus 43235

(614) 258-6000 .. **Maynard**, Jeffery S '01 %Brenner BG&M Co,LPA -2109 Stella Ct
-Columbus 43215 **Fx**:258-6006

(440) 826-4100 .. **Maynard**, Jerry L '78 (Allen RM & Assoc) -7530 Lucerne Dr
-Ste 200 -Middleburg Heights 44130

(304) 529-2443 .. **Maynard**, Lora L '99 %Robinson & R, LC -1034 6th Av
-Huntington, WV 25701 **Fx**:529-0332

(330) 725-2116 .. **Maynard**, Patricia F '89 (P Maynard & Assoc) -246 W Lbrty
-Medina 44256

(330) 373-1000 .. **Maynard**, Robert C '63 %C Richards -159 E Market -Ste 300
-Warren 44481 **Fx**:394-5291

(614) 645-8286 .. **Maynard**, William D '86 Cnty Mun Ct Judge -375 S High
-Columbus 43215

(216) 363-4500 .. **Mayo**, David R '76 (Benesch FC&A LLP) -200 Pub Sq -Ste 2300
-Cleveland 44114 **Fx**:363-4588

(216) 292-3300 .. **Mays**, Alfred R '56 OfCnsl Conway MWK&K Co,LPA
-30195 Chagrin Blvd -Ste 300 -Cleveland 44114

(216) 522-4796 .. **Mays**, Lawrence '75 US EEOC -1160 W 2nd -Ste 850
-Cleveland 44113

(419) 241-8195 .. **Mays**, Richard D '78 NW Title Agncy -328 N Erie -Toledo 43624

(614) 236-6560 .. **Mays**, Shirley L '88 %Capital Univ Law Sch -303 E Broad
-Columbus 43215

(216) 696-4421 .. **Mays**, Thomas C '86 %M Obral -1370 Ontario -Ste 1520
-Cleveland 44113 **Fx**:696-3228

(614) 466-5415 .. **Mayton**, Craig R '80 State Auditor Ofc -88 E Broad -5th FL
-Bx1140 -Columbus 43216

(330) 762-8885 .. **Mazak**, Edward P Jr. '81 (Smith & M Co,LPA) -777 W Market
-Akron 44303 **Fx**:762-1009

(216) 479-8500 .. **Mazanec**, Daniel C '04 %Squire S&D LLP -127 Pub Sq
-4900 Key Twr -Cleveland 44114 **Fx**:479-8780

(440) 248-8844 .. **Mazanec**, David T '76 -34305 Solon Rd -Ste 40 -Solon 44139

(216) 621-0200 .. **Mazanec**, Mark R '88 (Baker & H LLP) -1900 E 9th -Ste 3200
-Cleveland 44114 **Fx**:696-0740

(440) 248-7906 .. **Mazanec Raskin & Ryder Co,LPA** -34305 Solon Rd -Ste 100
-Cleveland 44139 **Fx**:248-8861

(614) 228-5931 .. **Mazanec Raskin & Ryder Co,LPA** -250 Civic Ctr Dr -Ste 400
-Columbus 43215 **Fx**:228-5934

(216) 522-0800 .. **Mazanec**, Richard O '76 (Reed M&W,Ltd) -1801 E 9th
-Cleveland 44114

(440) 248-7906 .. **Mazanec**, Thomas S '76 (Mazanec R&R Co,LPA)
-34305 Solon Rd -Ste 100 -Cleveland 44139 **Fx**:248-8861

(614) 837-5077 .. **Mazel**, Joel M '90 -60 W Columbus -Pickerington 43147

(614) 766-8108 .. **Mazer**, Bernard D '87 Mazer & Co -340 Cramer Crk Ct
-Dublin 43017

(216) 586-3939 .. **Mazey**, John E '98 %Jones D -901 Lakeside Av -Cleveland 44114
Fx:579-0212

(330) 670-7300 .. **Mazgaj**, Frank G '87 %Hanna C&P,LLP -3737 Embssy Pkwy
-Bx5521 -Akron 44334 **Fx**:670-0977

(216) 787-3030 .. **Mazorow**, Laurel D '82 Atty Gen -615 W Superior Av -11th Fl
-Cleveland 44113 **Fx**:787-3480

(614) 228-8833 .. **Mazur**, Alan E '96 Cincinnati Ins Co -140 E Town -Ste 1015
-Columbus 43215

(419) 734-1969 .. **Mazur**, James A '68 -7597 E Hrbr Rd -Marblehead 43440
Fx:734-1712

(216) 447-0070 .. **Mazur**, Lloyd D '67 Norton Cnstrctn -6200 Rockside Wds Blvd
-Ste 105 -Independence 44131

(330) 666-5555 .. **Mazur**, Louise M '82 %Ruport Co,LPA -3700 Embssy Pkwy
-Ste 440 -Akron 44333

(330) 384-5570 .. **Mazurek**, Michelle Ann '85 FirstEnergy Corp -74 S Main
-Akron 44308

(216) 579-9800 .. **Mazurkiewcz**, Janice L '79 -Bx94189 -Cleveland 44101

(937) 497-0880 .. **Mazurowski**, Suellen P '83 -120 N Main Av -Ste 204
-Sidney 45365

(614) 457-9731 .. **Mazza**, John P '77 (Harris & M) -941 Chatham Ln -Ste 201
-Columbus 43221 **Fx**:457-3596

(216) 443-3432 .. **Mazza**, Margaret M '63 Juv Ct -2163 E 22nd -Cleveland 44115

(513) 721-1200 .. **Mazzei**, Stephen S '80 (Young R&M Co,LPA) -1014 Vine
-Ste 2400 -Cincinnati 45202 **Fx**:721-7116

(216) 623-0880 .. **Mazzella,** Michael J '99 West Group -600 Superior Av E -Bank One Ctr Ste 2550 -Cleveland 44114
(216) 781-5515 .. **Mazzi,** Alicia L '02 %Hermann C&S,LLP -1301 E 9th -Ste 500 -Cleveland 44114 **Fx:**781-1030
(419) 472-8213 .. **Mazziotti,** Mary L '67 -2252 Georgtwn Av -Bx5660 -Toledo 43613
(614) 289-5430 .. **Mazzitti,** Madeleine Linda '82 Garden City Grp,Inc -6525 W Campus Oval -Ste 175 -New Albany 43054
(330) 434-3000 .. **Mazzola,** Todd A '93 (Roderick & L) -One Cascade Plz -Ste 1500 -Akron 44308 **Fx:**434-9220
(614) 229-4602 .. **Mazzoli,** Joseph A '97 DeLoitte & Touche,LLP -155 E Broad -Ste 1700 -Columbus 43215
(216) 781-1180 .. **Mazzone,** Frank B '76 -925 Euclid Av -Ste 2010 -Cleveland 44115
(513) 352-3332 .. **McAdams,** Ernest F Jr. '79 Law Dept -801 Plum -Rm 214 -Cincinnati 45202 **Fx:**352-1515
(614) 221-2838 .. **McAdams,** Robert W Jr. '87 (Taft S&H LLP) -21 E State -12th Fl -Columbus 43215 **Fx:**221-2007
(419) 893-4880 .. **McAdams,** Sheilah H '78 Marsh M Ltd -204 W Wayne -Maumee 43537
(937) 462-8361 .. **McAdow,** Samuel J '64 Buckeye Recyclers,Inc -15 Sprague Rd -South Charleston 45368
(614) 464-6400 .. **McAfee,** Melinda R '95 (Vorys SS&P LLP) -52 E Gay -Bx1008 -Columbus 43216 **Fx:**464-6350
(330) 821-2130 .. **McAlister,** David C '82 Clem Distributing Co -Bx2238 -Alliance 44601
(330) 935-2359 .. **McAlister,** Don E '64 Clem Distributing Co -8421 Pontius NE -Alliance 44601
(614) 469-8000 .. **McAlister,** Lisa G '02 %McNees W&N,LLC -21 E State -17th Fl -Columbus 43215 **Fx:**469-4653
(330) 264-4444 .. **McAllister,** Kevin J '04 %Critchfield C&J Ltd -225 N Market -Bx599 -Wooster 44691 **Fx:**263-9278
McAllister, Ralph A '56 Ct Common Pleas -1200 Ontario -Courts Tower Bldg -Cleveland 44113
McAnaul, Matthew M '04 -(Address Unavailable)
(216) 520-7177 .. **McAndrew,** John A '69 IRS -5990 W Crk Rd -Independence 44131
(216) 589-9600 .. **McAndrew,** Moira A '00 %Wilsman & S,LLC -1301 E 9th -Ste 1420 -Cleveland 44114
(216) 363-4500 .. **McAndrews,** James P '74 Benesch FC&A LLP -200 Pub Sq -Ste 2300 -Cleveland 44114 **Fx:**363-4588
(614) 466-5394 .. **McAnespie,** Molly Jo '99 Pub Def -8 E Long -Columbus 43215
(866) 562-0700 .. **McArdle,** Elgine H '00 -1242 Kings Rd -Morgantown, WV 26508
(419) 243-7243 .. **McArdle,** Thomas J '87 Cubbon & Assoc Co,LPA -405 N Huron -Ste 500 -Toledo 43604
(503) 224-6655 .. **McArthur,** Douglas W '03 %Kolisch H -500 SW Yamhill -Ste 200 Pacific Bldg -Portland, OR 97204
(330) 723-1919 .. **McArtor,** David L '95 -209 W Lbrty -Bx1061 -Medina 44258
(203) 226-7866 .. **McBain,** Patricia M '98 Blazzard G&H,PC -943 Post Rd E -Westport, CT 06880
(248) 813-1235 .. **McBain,** Scott A '92 Delphi Auto Sys -5825 Delphi Dr -M/C 480-410-202 -Troy, MI 48098
(614) 227-2303 .. **McBeath,** Gretchen A '82 (Bricker & E LLP) -100 S 3rd -Columbus 43215 **Fx:**227-2390
(419) 321-6444 .. **McBee,** Clint M '79 Cline C&W Co,LPA -300 Mad Av -Ste 1100 -Toledo 43604 **Fx:**321-6430
(513) 946-3822 .. **McBeth,** Steven J '94 Hamilton Cnty Pub Def -230 E 9th -3rd Fl -Cincinnati 45202 **Fx:**946-3707
(407) 237-4659 .. **McBride,** Anne N '86 SunTrust Bank -200 S Orange Av -Orlando, FL 32801
(419) 252-6231 .. **McBride,** Benjamin G '67 (Spengler N PLL) -608 Mad Av -Ste 1000 -Toledo 43604 **Fx:**241-8599
(419) 893-5050 .. **McBride,** Beverly J '66 Andersons -480 W Dussel Dr -Bx119 -Maumee 43537
(216) 861-3448 .. **McBride,** Brian A '85 -2069 W 3rd -Cleveland 44113
(216) 765-1199 .. **McBride,** Danielle L '99 Collier S & Assoc Inc -30195 Chagrin Blvd -Ste 100 -Cleveland 44124
(419) 562-9856 .. **McBride,** Gordon S '86 (Spurlock SPG&M,PLL) -120 N Lane -Bucyrus 44820 **Fx:**562-9883
(513) 634-1402 .. **McBride,** James F '92 Procter & Gamble -6071 Ctr Hill Av -Cincinnati 45224
(440) 526-3759 .. **McBride,** Judith B '86 -7886 Cmbrdg Dr -Brecksville 44141
(513) 931-2100 .. **McBride,** Maria L '88 -8624-B Winton Rd -Cincinnati 45231
(419) 242-1400 .. **McBride,** Mark R '81 -608 Mad Av -Ste 1400 -Toledo 43604
(330) 743-6300 .. **McBride,** Michael J '02 Atway & C,LLC -19 E Front -Ste 1 -Youngstown 44503
(513) 931-2100 .. **McBride,** Michael L '87 -8624-B Winton Rd -Cincinnati 45231 **Fx:**521-2312
(330) 675-6687 .. **McBride,** Michele L '02 11th Dist Ct of Appls -111 High NE -Warren 44481
(216) 529-6242 .. **McBride,** Robert D '73 Kirby Co -1920 W 114th St -Cleveland 44102
(330) 455-0173 .. **McBride,** Robert J '95 (Day KRW&R,Ltd) -200 Market Av N -Ste 300 -Bx24213 -Canton 44701 **Fx:**455-2633
(614) 621-1500 .. **McBride,** Shelley A '82 SrCnsl Calfee H&G LLP -21 E State -1100 Fifth Third Ctr -Columbus 43215 **Fx:**621-0010
(513) 977-8200 .. **McBroom,** Christine L '81 %Dinsmore & S LLP -255 E 5th -Ste 1900 -Cincinnati 45202 **Fx:**977-8141
(440) 746-9740 .. **McCabe,** Daniel M '85 -8185 Brecksvll Rd -Ste 103 -Brecksville 44141
(513) 772-3962 .. **McCabe,** Penelope '79 -270 Northland Blvd -Cincinnati 45246
(216) 781-7011 .. **McCabe,** Peter J '88 Snider Blake Bus Srvcs, Inc -850 Euclid Av -Ste 405 -Cleveland 44114
(513) 553-1323 .. **McCachran,** Marshall T '79 -1769 Cedar Trl -New Richmond 45157 **Fx:**553-0596
(216) 861-6116 .. **McCafferty,** Joseph P '86 -2000 E Ninth -Ste 700 -Cleveland 44115
(513) 651-5900 .. **McCafferty,** Michael P '04 Donovan Law -910 Race -Cincinnati 45202 **Fx:**651-4937
(216) 771-0270 .. **McCafferty,** Owen J '55 (McCafferty & P Co,LPA) -614 W Superior Av -Ste 804 -Cleveland 44113
(216) 533-3301 .. **McCafferty,** Thomas M '02 -231 E 216th -Euclid 44123
(216) 623-0900 .. **McCaffrey,** John F '87 (McLaughlin & M,LLP) -1111 Superior Av E -Ste 1350 Eaton Ctr -Cleveland 44114 **Fx:**623-0935
(614) 258-6000 .. **McCaffrey,** Patrick Jr. '96 (Brenner BG&M Co,LPA) -2109 Stella Ct -Columbus 43215 **Fx:**258-6006
(412) 803-3690 .. **McCague,** John M Jr. '82 (Griffith M&F,PC) -707 Grant -Ste 3626 -Pittsburgh, PA 15219
(919) 333-3244 .. **McCain,** Christine A '87 -1323 Carlton -Clayton, NC 27520
(216) 241-5310 .. **McCain,** Kenneth W '98 %Gallagher SF&N -1501 Euclid Av -6th Fl -Cleveland 44115 **Fx:**241-1608
(330) 493-0040 .. **McCall,** John S Jr. '74 Lesh C&M -4150 Belden Vllg NW -Ste 606 -Canton 44718
(330) 453-9999 .. **McCallin,** Alfred D '82 -116 Cleveland Av NW -500 Courtyard Ctr -Canton 44702
(614) 466-7014 .. **McCallister,** Michael D '95 Pub Safety -1970 W Broad -Columbus 43223 **Fx:**752-6063
(216) 696-4700 .. **McCallum,** Allison '99 %Spieth BM&N Co,LPA -925 Euclid Av -2000 Huntngtn Bldg -Cleveland 44115 **Fx:**696-2706
(202) 282-8067 .. **McCament,** James W '01 Ofc of General Counsel -US Dept of Homeland Security -Washington, DC 20528
(304) 232-6750 .. **McCamic,** Jeffrey W '83 (McCamic & M) -56 14th -Wheeling, WV 26003
(216) 292-7355 .. **McCamley,** Janet S '81 (Rosenbaum & M Co,LPA) -24100 Chagrin Blvd -330 -Beachwood 44122
(614) 801-2714 .. **McCandlish,** Joseph M '01 %Weltman W&R Co,LPA -175 S 3rd -Ste 900 -Columbus 43215 **Fx:**222-2193
(614) 422-7866 .. **McCane,** Lisa A '99 Chase Manhattan Mrtg Corp -3415 Vision Dr -Columbus 43219 **Fx:**422-4084
(614) 424-6585 .. **McCann,** Dennis J '81 Battelle Meml Inst -505 King Av -Columbus 43201
(614) 228-2300 .. **McCann,** George R '73 (Fry W&M Co,LPA) -35 E Lvngstn Av -Columbus 43215 **Fx:**228-6680
(937) 220-4904 .. **McCann,** Gregory L Jr. '82 Danis Co -Bx725 -Dayton 45401
(606) 329-2929 .. **McCann,** Kimberly F '91 VanAntwerp MJ&E -1544 Wnchstr Av -5th Fl -Bx1111 -Ashland, KY 41105
(740) 454-8585 .. **McCann,** Stephen R '76 Graham M&R Co,LPA -11 N 4th -Bx340 -Zanesville 43702
McCann, Tricia A '00 -5514 Deer Hill Dr -Galloway 43119
(216) 520-7170 .. **McCarroll,** Elaine A '77 IRS -5990 W Crk Rd -Independence 44131
(216) 861-6655 .. **McCarroll,** John J '89 -1370 Ontario -Ste 330 -Cleveland 44113
(216) 586-3939 .. **McCartan,** Patrick F '60 (Jones D) -901 Lakeside Av -Cleveland 44114 **Fx:**579-0212
(419) 255-9100 .. **McCarter,** Charles T '71 -421 N Mich -Ste D -Toledo 43624 **Fx:**255-9190
(614) 358-0880 .. **McCarter,** Sean A '94 -471 E Broad -Ste 2001 -Columbus 43215
(440) 354-6242 .. **McCarter,** William K '67 -9720 Johnnycake Ridge Rd -Mentor 44060
(216) 566-5500 .. **McCarthy,** Brendan J '04 %Thompson H LLP -127 Pub Sq -3900 Key Ctr -Cleveland 44114 **Fx:**566-5800
(304) 842-0460 .. **McCarthy,** Christopher J '94 (Booth & M) -901 W Main -Ste 201 -Bx4669 -Bridgeport, WV 26330
(513) 721-5525 .. **McCarthy,** Daniel J '04 Manley B -225 W Court -Cincinnati 45202 **Fx:**721-4268
(216) 696-1422 .. **McCarthy,** Daniel R '54 (McCarthy LC&L Co,LPA) -101 Prospect Av W -1800 Mdlnd Bldg -Cleveland 44115 **Fx:**696-1210
(614) 222-6466 .. **McCarthy,** Deborah Beckerich '93 Pub Emplyees Retirement Sys -277 E Town -Columbus 43215 **Fx:**857-1114
(513) 651-9440 .. **McCarthy,** Dennis K '73 -7800 Cooper Rd -Ste 201 -Montgomery 45242
(216) 621-2300 .. **McCarthy,** Ellen M '90 Nurenberg PH&M LPA -1370 Ontario -Ste 100 -Cleveland 44113 **Fx:**771-2242
(740) 592-3332 .. **McCarthy,** George P '90 Athens Pros -8 E Wshngtn -Ste 301 -Athens 45701
(513) 721-4532 .. **McCarthy,** James F III '77 (Katz TB&H) -255 E 5th -Ste 2400 -Cincinnati 45202
(216) 696-1422 .. **McCarthy Lebit Crystal & Liffman Co, LPA** -101 Prospect Av W -1800 Mdlnd Bldg -Cleveland 44115 **Fx:**696-1210
(216) 592-5000 .. **McCarthy,** Mark F '76 (Tucker E&W LLP) -925 Euclid Av -1150 Huntngtn Bldg -Cleveland 44115 **Fx:**592-5009
(614) 791-7648 .. **McCarthy,** Mark M '89 Frank Gates Srvc Co -5000 Bradenton Av -Dublin 43017
(614) 846-1908 .. **McCarthy,** Michael J '80 -15 N Lbrty -Powell 43065 **Fx:**840-9202
(330) 675-2840 .. **McCarthy,** Patrick F '90 Trumbull Cnty Cmn Pleas Ct -160 High NW -Cthse -Warren 44481
(440) 543-8511 .. **McCarthy,** Patrick J '93 Chempak Intl LLC -10175 Qns Way -Chagrin Falls 44023
(937) 335-8324 .. **McCarthy,** Robert A '55 (Faust HFM&S) -12 S Cherry -Troy 45373 **Fx:**339-7155
(614) 462-3555 .. **McCarthy,** Sean V '00 Franklin Cnty Pros -373 S High -Columbus 43215
(937) 367-8697 .. **McCarthy,** Steven D '87 -Bx53524 -Cincinnati 45253
(216) 363-4500 .. **McCarthy,** Thomas Cormac '99 %Benesch FC&A LLP -200 Pub Sq -Ste 2300 -Cleveland 44114 **Fx:**363-4588
(419) 241-9000 .. **McCarthy,** Timothy C '79 (Shumaker L&K,LLP) -1000 Jackson -Toledo 43624 **Fx:**241-6894
(614) 462-4692 .. **McCarthy,** Timothy P '73 Franklin Cnty Cmn Pleas Ct -375 S High -Columbus 43215 **Fx:**462-6292
(513) 381-9200 .. **McCartney,** Paul W '88 (Rendigs FK&D,LLP) -One W 4th -Ste 900 -Cincinnati 45202 **Fx:**381-9206
(330) 375-2611 .. **McCarty,** Alison E '87 Mun Ct Judge -217 S High -Akron 44308
(614) 462-5469 .. **McCarty,** David M '92 (Kegler BH&R) -65 E State -Ste 1800 -Columbus 43215 **Fx:**464-2634
(216) 696-4009 .. **McCarty,** John M '04 Kraig & K -614 Superior Av W -Ste 900 -Cleveland 44113 **Fx:**696-1835
(330) 864-6611 .. **McCarty,** Justin D '82 (McCarty & P) -1655 W Market -Ste 400 -Akron 44313
(614) 836-1866 .. **McCarty,** Kevin R '92 -495 Main -Bx446 -Groveport 43125
(937) 865-6800 .. **McCarty,** Kimberly A '97 %Lexis/Nexis -Bx933 -Dayton 45401
(216) 586-3939 .. **McCarty,** Philip W '03 %Jones D -901 Lakeside Av -Cleveland 44114 **Fx:**579-0212
(330) 864-6611 .. **McCarty & Pry** -1655 W Market -Ste 400 -Akron 44313
(330) 643-2900 .. **McCarty,** Robert A '88 Summit Cnty Juv Ct -650 Dan -Akron 44310
(216) 228-9400 .. **McCarty,** Robert L '69 United Trans Union -14600 Detroit Av -Cleveland 44107
(614) 539-1480 .. **McCarty,** Robert L '50 -3783 Bway -Grove City 43123

(859) 594-3252 .. **McCarty**, Steven M '88 Catholic Health Initiatives
-3900 Olympic Blvd -Ste 400 -Erlanger, KY 41018

(330) 873-1199 .. **McCarty**, Thomas M '82 (T McCarty Co,LPA) -230 White Pond Dr
-Ste A -Akron 44313 **Fx:**869-0651

(216) 751-6000 .. **McCary**, Renee D '83 -16781 Chagrin Blvd -Ste 201
-Shaker Heights 44120

(614) 761-9321 .. **McCash**, Thomas M '92 -Bx3101 -Dublin 43016 -Fx:761-9321

(513) 421-4646 .. **McCaslin Imbus & McCaslin,LPA** -632 Vine -Ste 900
-Cincinnati 45202 **Fx:**421-7929

(614) 236-6245 .. **McCaughan**, Lorie L '96 %Capital Univ Law Sch -303 E Broad
-Columbus 43215

          McCaughey, Maura A '98 -5347 Wilshire Park Dr -Hudson 44236

(317) 684-6260 .. **McCaulay**, Paul M '76 Allstate Ins Co -135 N Penn -Ste 1375
-Indianapolis, IN 46204

(419) 241-2100 .. **McCauley**, Ann M '99 Watkins B&C -405 Mad Av -Ste 1900
-Toledo 43604 **Fx:**241-1960

(216) 861-6833 .. **McCauley**, Ann M '00 Sonkin & K Co,LPA -55 Pub Sq -Ste 1660
-Cleveland 44113

(216) 485-7970 .. **McCauley**, Christopher J '86 (McCauley & Assoc Co,LPA)
-5454 State Rd -Parma 44134 **Fx:**485-7979

(740) 423-9548 .. **McCauley**, James H '70 (McCauley W&E) -1710 Wshngtn Blvd
-Bx196 -Belpre 45714

(607) 257-0121 .. **McCauley**, James N '76 -701 W State -Ithaca, NY 14850

(216) 622-8200 .. **McCauley**, Stephen L '93 %Calfee H&G LLP -800 Superior Av
-Ste 1400 -Cleveland 44114 **Fx:**241-0816

(202) 418-2136 .. **McCauley**, Victoria M '83 FCC-Mass Media Bureau -445 12th SW
-Washington, DC 20554

(740) 423-9548 .. **McCauley Webster & Emrick** -1710 Wshngtn Blvd -Bx196
-Belpre 45714

(513) 867-4729 .. **McCauley-Myers**, Janie P '94 1st Finl Bancorp -Bx476
-Hamilton 45012

(513) 705-9000 .. **McCausland**, Patrick E '98 %Pratt SP Co,LPA -301 N Breiel Blvd
-Middletown 45044 **Fx:**705-9001

(646) 471-4531 .. **McClain**, Aaron M '02 PricewaterhouseCoopers,LLC
-1177 Av of Amer -New York, NY 10036

(330) 535-4450 .. **McClain**, Andrew B '97 -209 S Main -8th Fl -Akron 44308

(440) 871-0109 .. **McClain**, Bruce W '82 -28218 Knckrbckr -Bay Village 44140

(513) 369-3070 .. **McClain**, Elizabeth N '84 Great Amer Ins -49 E 4th -Ste 400 DTS
-Cincinnati 45202

(440) 322-0596 .. **McClain**, James M '75 -105 Court -Ste 321 -Elyria 44035

(419) 476-7210 .. **McClanahan**, Dawn M '95 -5510 San Paulo Dr -Toledo 43612

(440) 392-7105 .. **McClaning**, Kathy M '89 Steris Corp -5960 Heisley Rd
-Mentor 44060

(614) 275-2587 .. **McClaren**, Robert J '90 Franklin Cnty Children Srvcs
-855 W Mound -Columbus 43223 **Fx:**275-2589

(216) 523-1500 .. **McClatchey**, Christopher J '97 %Mansour GG&M Co,LPA
-55 Pub Sq -Ste 2150 -Cleveland 44113 **Fx:**523-1705

(614) 462-5463 .. **McClatchey**, Larry J '75 (Kegler BH&R) -65 E State -Ste 1800
-Columbus 43215 **Fx:**464-2634

(614) 224-1222 .. **McClatchey**, Ted P '94 %Maguire & S,LLP -250 Civic Ctr Dr
-Ste 200 -Columbus 43215 **Fx:**224-1236

(419) 241-9000 .. **McClay**, Susan D '76 (Shumaker L&K,LLP) -1000 Jackson
-Toledo 43624 **Fx:**241-6894

(707) 424-3251 .. **McClean**, Hugh B '02 %USAF -510 Mulheron
-Travis AFB, CA 94535 **Fx:**424-0991

          McCleese, Gary D '98 -706 Gee Hllw Rd -Waverly 45690

(614) 464-2572 .. **McClellan**, Edward T '75 (Harris MB&C,PLL) -37 W Broad -9th Fl
-Columbus 43215 **Fx:**464-2245

(614) 477-9844 .. **McClellan**, Sharon A '80 -900 Main -Groveport 43125

(740) 454-8585 .. **McClelland**, Jack J '73 (Graham M&R Co,LPA) -11 N 4th -Bx340
-Zanesville 43702

(614) 340-0440 .. **McClelland**, Jeffrey L '70 -1013 Dublin Rd -Columbus 43215

(419) 947-5045 .. **McClelland**, Lee W '74 -48 E High -Mount Gilead 43338

(216) 621-6570 .. **McClelland**, Robert C '80 (Rademaker MM&G) -55 Pub Sq
-Ste 1775 -Cleveland 44113 **Fx:**621-1127

(419) 946-2001 .. **McClelland**, Shawn R '01 -15 S Main -Mount Gilead 43338

(216) 443-7223 .. **McClelland**, Warren L Jr. '81 Cuyahoga Cnty Pub Def
-1200 W 3rd NW -100 Lakeside Pl -Cleveland 44113

(614) 252-0688 .. **McCleskey**, Harvey N Jr. '03 -1313 E Broad -Ste 17
-Columbus 43205

(216) 689-4690 .. **McClintic**, Janine M '02 Key Bank NA -127 Pub Sq
-Cleveland 44114

(216) 566-9700 .. **McClintic**, Shawn A '02 Rankin HP&C,LLP -925 Euclid Av
-Ste 700 -Cleveland 44115 **Fx:**566-9711

(614) 221-8448 .. **McCloskey**, Christopher L '00 %Buckingham D&B,LLP
-191 W Nationwide Blvd -Ste 300 -Bx151120 -Columbus 43215
Fx:221-8590

(513) 745-0400 .. **McCloskey**, Hugh P Jr. '00 %Furnier T,LLP -1 Fncl Way -Ste 312
-Cincinnati 45242 **Fx:**792-6724

(937) 890-0826 .. **McCloskey**, James B '94 -6100 Brantford Rd -Dayton 45414

(614) 228-1398 .. **McCloskey**, Kerri L '01 %Nelson LdL&H LLC -280 N High
-Ste 920 -Columbus 43215 **Fx:**221-7529

(614) 466-8081 .. **McCloud**, Bradley L '88 OH DOT -1980 W Broad -Columbus
43223

(614) 466-4656 .. **McCloud**, Stephanie B '96 Atty Gen -150 E Gay -Columbus 43215
Fx:466-1756

(330) 356-0314 .. **McClowry**, Derek C '04 -401 Bank One Twr -Canton 44702

(614) 227-2000 .. **McClure**, Anthony R '03 %Porter WM&A LLP -41 S High
-Columbus 43215 **Fx:**227-2100

(614) 421-7500 .. **McClure**, David L '64 -949 King Av -Columbus 43212

(740) 432-7844 .. **McClure**, Frank A '75 (FA McClure,LPA) -213 N 8th
-Cambridge 43725 **Fx:**439-4950

(513) 621-8280 .. **McClure**, John D '72 -7 W 7th -Ste 1800 -Cincinnati 45202

(614) 485-2010 .. **McClure**, Lisa M '01 %Means BB&B Co,LPA -2006 Kenny Rd
-Columbus 43221 **Fx:**485-2019

(440) 933-3231 .. **McClure**, Richard D '72 Smith & S Co,LPA -110 Moore Rd -Bx210
-Avon Lake 44012

(440) 684-1090 .. **McClure**, Thomas D Jr. '03 %M Kusner Co,LPA
-6151 Wilson Mills Rd -Ste 310 -Highland Heights 44143

(419) 222-5045 .. **McCluskey**, Holly Lee '93 (Siferd & M LPA) -212 N Elizabeth
-Ste 504 -Lima 45801

(513) 421-6630 .. **McCluskey**, Laurie A '02 %Lindhorst & D Co,LPA -312 Walnut
-Ste 2300 -Cincinnati 45202

(419) 592-5926 .. **McColley**, Denise A '81 Henry Cnty Cmn Pleas Ct -660 N Perry
-Cthse -Bx70 -Napoleon 43545 **Fx:**599-0803

(216) 861-5582 .. **McCollister**, Scott A '89 (Fay SFM&M LLP) -1100 Superior Av
-7th Fl -Cleveland 44114 **Fx:**241-1666

          McCollister, Sharon F '94 -Bx340066 -Columbus 43234

(216) 443-3344 .. **McCollough**, Heather C '03 Juvenile Ct -2209 Central Av
-Cleveland 44115

(937) 225-4400 .. **McCollum**, Alice O '72 Montgomery Cnty Probate Ct -41
N. Perry St. -Bx972 -Dayton 45402 **Fx:**496-3181

(202) 273-3841 .. **McCollum**, Carolyn B '77 NLRB -1099 14th NW -Div of Advice
-Washington, DC 20570

(330) 740-2278 .. **McCollum**, Donna J '85 Mahoning Cnty Juv Ct -300 E Scott
-Youngstown 44505

(614) 464-1266 .. **McCollum**, James E '87 InterUniversity Cncl of OH -10 W Broad
-Ste 450 -Columbus 43215 **Fx:**464-9281

(513) 424-2401 .. **McCollum**, Margaret H '92 (Casper & C) -1 N Main -Bx510
-Middletown 45042 **Fx:**424-0622

(937) 913-0200 .. **McComas**, Benjamin K '04 %Gottschlich & P LLP -201 E 6th
-Dayton 45402 **Fx:**824-2818

(216) 696-5400 .. **McComas**, Sherri N '86 %Crosby O & Assoc Co,LPA -55 Pub Sq
-Ste 1475 -Cleveland 44113 **Fx:**696-2610

(440) 293-6346 .. **McCombs**, David L '74 (McCombs & K) -100 Pub Sq -Bx217
-Andover 44003 **Fx:**293-5665

(248) 645-0800 .. **McConaghy**, Timothy K '00 (Hardy L&P,PC)
-401 S Old Woodward Av -Ste 400 -Birmingham, MI 48009
Fx:645-2602

(513) 634-9076 .. **McConihay**, Julie A '04 Cnsl Procter & G -8611 Beckett Rd
-Beckett Ridge Tech Cntr -West Chester 45069

(937) 378-6165 .. **McConn-Pirman**, Julie A '79 (McConn & C) -118 S Main
-Georgetown 45121 **Fx:**378-6567

(330) 653-9372 .. **McConnel**, Stewart P Jr. '74 -350 W Streetsboro -Hudson 44236

(404) 479-2841 .. **McConnell**, Daniel D '84 Invesco Retirement Inc -1315 Pchtree
-Atlanta, GA 30309

(216) 566-3741 .. **McConnell**, Donald J '90 Sherwin Williams Co
-101 Prospect Av NW -Cleveland 44115

(401) 457-7700 .. **McConnell**, John J Jr. '04 (Motley R LLC) -321 S Main -Bx6067
-Providence, RI 02940 **Fx:**457-7708

(419) 241-6282 .. **McConnell**, Karyn R '98 -316 N Mich -Ste 700 -Toledo 43624

(440) 329-5389 .. **McConnell**, Lucinda C '00 Lorain Cnty Pros -225 Court -3rd Fl
-Elyria 44035

(910) 346-5000 .. **McConnell**, Robert K '87 Tisdale & M,LLP -400 New Brdg
-Jacksonville, NC 28540

(440) 835-0600 .. **McConville**, Luke F '96 %Waldheger C,LPA -1991 Crocker Rd
-Ste 550 -Westlake 44145 **Fx:**835-1511

          McConville, Mary Cook '95 -(Address Unavailable)

(513) 421-2540 .. **McCord**, Charles B III '97 %Ennis R&F -121 W 9th
-Cincinnati 45202 **Fx:**562-4986

(513) 241-4722 .. **McCord**, Elizabeth A '82 OfCnsl Montgomery R&J,LPA -36 E 7th
-Ste 2100 -Cincinnati 45202 **Fx:**241-8775

(614) 443-4063 .. **McCord**, Lumumba T '96 (McCord & A,LLP) -844 S Front
-Columbus 43206

(216) 283-4385 .. **McCord**, Michael B '84 -19413 Lomond Blvd -Shaker Heights
44122

(614) 764-3210 .. **McCorkle**, Leon M Jr. '72 Wendys Intl -4288 W Dublin-Granvll Rd
-Bx256 -Dublin 43017

(216) 664-6791 .. **McCorkle**, Martha R '90 Cleveland Mun Ct -1200 Ontario
-Crtrm 3-B -Cleveland 44113

          McCormac, John W '61 -395 Longfllw Av -Worthington 43085

          McCormac, Orville T '73 -7411 15th Av NW -Bradenton, FL 34209

(216) 443-7181 .. **McCormack**, John T '72 Cnty Brd of Commissioners
-1219 Ontario -4th Flr -Cleveland 44113 **Fx:**443-6668

          McCormack, Thomas A '79 -148 Solon Rd -Chagrin Falls 44022

(513) 487-2047 .. **McCormick**, Charles D Jr. '83 US EPA
-26 W Martin Luther King Dr -Cincinnati 45268

(216) 241-8333 .. **McCormick**, Courtney M '04 %Ritzler C&S,LPA -1001 Lakeside Av
-1550 North Pnt Twr -Cleveland 44114 **Fx:**241-5890

(419) 829-2463 .. **McCormick**, Daniel J '83 -8340 W Bancroft -Toledo 43617

(412) 471-1180 .. **McCormick**, Donald J '99 (Dell ML&L LLC) -525 William Penn Pl
-Ste 3700 -Pittsburgh, PA 15219 **Fx:**471-9012

          McCormick, Grant S '04 -(Address Unavailable)

(614) 221-2718 .. **McCormick**, Jack E '69 -500 City Park Av -Columbus 43215

(412) 281-8541 .. **McCormick**, James F '01 (Cain A&M) -2 Chatham Ctr -Ste 1410
-Pittsburgh, PA 15219

(513) 934-0038 .. **McCormick**, Jeffrey A '02 -1073 Oregonia Rd -Ste C-2
-Lebanon 45036 **Fx:**297-4591

(440) 779-5815 .. **McCormick**, Keith L '91 -26760 Hyannis Port Dr
-North Olmsted 44070

(614) 444-9414 .. **McCormick**, Kerry L '01 %Solove Law Ofc -79 Thurman Av
-Columbus 43206 **Fx:**444-4494

(614) 818-1118 .. **McCormick**, Marshall S '93 Stewart Title -259 W Schrock Rd
-Westerville 43081

(740) 695-1444 .. **McCormick**, Michael P '89 Hanlon DE&M Co,LPA -46457 Natl
Rd W -Saint Clairsville 43950 **Fx:**695-1563

(614) 717-0768 .. **McCormick**, Nicole D '98 (McCormick & S) -3931 Inverness Cir
-Dublin 43016

(419) 252-5958 .. **McCormick**, Patricia A '95 HCR Manorcare -333 N Summit
-Bx10086 -Toledo 43699

(859) 331-6218 .. **McCormick**, Shawn '79 -Bx17354 -Ft Mitchell, KY 41017

(614) 464-6433 .. **McCormick**, Thomas N '02 %Vorys SS&P LLP -52 E Gay -Bx1008
-Columbus 43216 **Fx:**464-6350

(614) 464-1904 .. **McCormick**, Tristan A '95 (Gamble HJ Co,LPA) -1 E Lvngstn Av
-Columbus 43215 **Fx:**365-9741

          McCort, Melanie J '97 -5151 Pfeiffer Rd -Ste 120
-Cincinnati 45242

(804) 697-8472 .. **McCorvey**, William R Jr. '90 %Fed Reserve Bk of Richmond
-701 E Byrd -Richmond, VA 23219 **Fx:**697-8473

(419) 213-6850 .. **McCourt**, Ronald V '76 Lucas Cnty Dom Rltns Ct -429 N Mich
-Ste A -Toledo 43624

(740) 532-8744 .. **McCown**, David H '60 McCown & D,LPA -311 Park Av -Ironton
45638

(740) 532-8744 .. **McCown & Davis,LPA** -311 Park Av -Ironton 45638

(617) 523-6666 .. **McCown**, Keith H '94 (Morgan B&J) -200 State -11th Fl -Boston,
MA 02109 **Fx:**367-3125

(740) 532-8744 .. **McCown,** Mark K '97 McCown & D,LPA -311 Park Av -Ironton 45638

McCoy, Beth A '92 -2435 Yarmouth Ln -Crofton, MD 21114

(740) 345-4545 .. **McCoy,** Carl E Jr. '82 -195 Union -Newark 43055

(216) 622-8200 .. **McCoy,** Darlene E '79 (Calfee H&G LLP) -800 Superior Av -Ste 1400 -Cleveland 44114 **Fx:**241-0816

(513) 381-2838 .. **McCoy,** John J '77 (Taft S&H LLP) -425 Walnut -Ste 1800 -Cincinnati 45202 **Fx:**381-0205

McCoy, Karen C '99 -1630 Ardwick Rd -Columbus 43220

(614) 481-8106 .. **McCoy,** Steven J '74 %Natl Housing Corp -1225 Dublin Rd -Columbus 43215

(216) 931-6000 .. **McCracken,** Christopher C '77 (Ulmer & B LLP) -1300 E 9th -Ste 900 Penton Media Bldg -Cleveland 44114 **Fx:**931-6001

(419) 424-4333 .. **McCracken,** Jack J '90 Cooper Tire & Rubber -Lima & Wstrn Av -Findlay 45840

(513) 737-8000 .. **McCracken,** John J '89 (Gattermeyer & M LLC) -2 S 3rd -Ste 570 -Hamilton 45011

(216) 575-1002 .. **McCracken,** Matthew J '04 Simon Law Firm,LLC -1300 E 9th -Ste 1717 -Cleveland 44114

(937) 382-0581 .. **McCracken,** William B '72 Cnty Common Pleas Ct -46 S South -Wilmington 45177

(513) 556-3483 .. **McCrate,** Mitchell D '90 Univ of Cincinnati -305A Admin Bldg -Bx210623 -Cincinnati 45221

(859) 441-7571 .. **McCraw,** Robin '01 -20 Brandywine Ct -Highland Heights, KY 41076

(440) 366-9930 .. **McCray Muzilla Smith & Meyers Co,LPA** -260 Burns Rd -Ste 150 -Elyria 44035 **Fx:**366-1910

(937) 277-3984 .. **McCray,** Risa C '74 -827 W Grand Av -Dayton 45407

McCray, Scott R '90 -106 Tasman Ct -Cary, NC 27513

(419) 241-2122 .. **McCready,** Jennifer C '99 %Williams JLG&S Co,LPA -416 N Erie -Ste 500 -Toledo 43624 **Fx:**245-3849

(937) 324-5541 .. **McCready,** Steven J '83 (Martin BH&H) -1 S Limestone -Ste 800 -Bx1488 -Springfield 45501 **Fx:**325-5432

(419) 241-3213 .. **McCready,** William S '69 (Ritter RM&J) -405 Mad Av -Ste 1850 -Toledo 43604 **Fx:**241-4925

(614) 227-2387 .. **McCreary,** Charles H III '78 (Bricker & E LLP) -100 S 3rd -Columbus 43215 **Fx:**227-2390

(614) 899-9194 .. **McCreary,** David M '58 -338 Windemere Dr -Westerville 43082 **Fx:**899-9651

(614) 469-5614 .. **McCreary,** Marcee C '81 %Cngrsswmn D Pryce -500 S Front -Rm 1130 -Columbus 43215

(216) 443-7800 .. **McCreary,** Sherry M '78 Cuyahoga Cnty Pros -1200 Ontario -8th Fl -Cleveland 44113 **Fx:**698-2270

(304) 353-8147 .. **McCreery,** Charles N II '94 -707 VA E -7th Fl Bank One Ctr -Bx1588 -Charleston, WV 25326

(440) 503-6099 .. **McCreery,** Robert D Jr. '86 -8935 Elm -Brecksville 44141

(708) 352-4289 .. **McCrery,** Michael J '87 -411 W Hillsgrove Av -La Grange, IL 60525

McCright, Joseph E '92 -429 Tealwood Dr -Alexandria, LA 71303

McCrory, Dorothy B '65 -416 N Erie -Ste 200 -Toledo 43624

(419) 473-3916 .. **McCrory,** Paul A Jr. '65 -3601 W Alexis Rd -Toledo 43623

(301) 340-4862 .. **McCroskey,** Jeffrey A '88 GE Global Exchng Srvcs -100 Edison Park Dr -Gaithersburg, MD 20878

McCroskey, Maureen E '88 -(Address Unavailable)

(216) 586-3939 .. **McCrum,** Ryan B '99 %Jones D -901 Lakeside Av -Cleveland 44114 **Fx:**579-0212

(419) 471-1489 .. **McCrury,** Lowell D '76 UAW Legal Srvcs -3360 W Laskey Rd -Toledo 43606 **Fx:**471-0498

(216) 664-6900 .. **McCrystal,** James L Jr. '73 (Brzytwa Q&M LLC) -1660 W 2nd -900 Skylight Ofc Twr -Cleveland 44113 **Fx:**664-6901

McCrystal, Thomas W '80 -Bx551 -Chagrin Falls 44022

(614) 466-3998 .. **McCue,** Dana C '74 Unemploymnt Comp Commssn -145 S Front -Bx182299 -Columbus 43218

(330) 376-3572 .. **McCue,** Kevin L '03 %Eshelman Lgl Grp -263 Portage Trl Ext W -Cuyahoga Falls 44223 **Fx:**376-0199

(513) 752-2611 .. **McCue,** Richard G '68 (R McCue Co,LPA) -948 Old State Rt 74 -Ste 6 -Cincinnati 45245

(330) 376-1242 .. **McCue,** Shannon V '98 Renner KGBT&W,LPA -106 S Main -4th Fl First Natl Twr -Akron 44308 **Fx:**376-9646

(330) 875-8555 .. **McCue,** Thomas P '76 -824 W Main -Louisville 44641 **Fx:**875-3675

(847) 492-8314 .. **McCue,** William M '91 -Bx5729 -Evanston, IL 60204

(614) 461-7596 .. **McCuen,** Michael D '00 Columbus Dispatch -34 S 3rd -Columbus 43215

(419) 865-8021 .. **McCulley,** David C '83 %Balk H&M -5744 Southwyck Blvd -Toledo 43614 **Fx:**865-9105

(937) 773-3212 .. **McCulloch Felger Fite & Gutmann Co,LPA** -123 Market -Bx910 -Piqua 45356 **Fx:**773-9672

(513) 241-3685 .. **McCullough,** C. J '98 %White G&M Co,LPA -1 W 4th -Ste 1700 -Cincinnati 45202 **Fx:**241-2399

McCullough, George V '52 -1450 E Xings Pl -Westlake 44145

(740) 622-6464 .. **McCullough,** Michael P '74 (Frase WB&M Co,LPA) -305 Main -4th Fl -Coshocton 43812 **Fx:**622-8107

(216) 851-3304 .. **McCully,** Joanne '77 Virgil Brown Ins Agency -2136 Noble Rd -Cleveland 44112

(513) 248-4497 .. **McCune,** David S '79 -626 Main -Milford 45150

(614) 790-3787 .. **McCune,** Diana R '88 Ashland Inc -5200 Blazer Pkwy -Dublin 43017

(513) 629-2407 .. **McCune,** Francis P '83 Eagle-Picher Ind,Inc -250 E 5th -Ste 500 -Cincinnati 45202

(614) 889-5718 .. **McCurdy,** Gay L '88 -5148 Reserve Dr -Dublin 43017

(614) 249-7636 .. **McCutchan,** R. Lindsey '97 Cnsl Nationwide Ins Co -1 Nationwide Plz -Columbus 43215

(419) 668-4896 .. **McDaniel,** Herman F Jr. '72 (Freeman L&M) -54 E Main -Norwalk 44857 **Fx:**663-7835

(513) 684-0808 .. **McDaniel,** James F '78 -36 E 4th -1234 Bartlett Bldg -Cincinnati 45202

(614) 462-5009 .. **McDaniel,** Jennifer M '02 %Schottenstein Z&D -250 West -Bx165020 -Columbus 43216 **Fx:**462-5135

(513) 744-8944 .. **McDaniel,** John Lee Jr. '92 Fifth 3rd Bank -38 Fountain Sq Plz -ML 10 at 68 -Cincinnati 45263

(513) 936-5663 .. **McDaniel,** Sarah L '95 (Wood & M) -1101 St Gregory -Ste 345 -Cincinnati 45202

(859) 341-1936 .. **McDaniel,** Scott F '83 -Bx176625 -Covington, KY 41017

(513) 241-2225 .. **McDaniel,** Vernon W '41 -1101 St Gregory -Ste 345 -Cincinnati 45202

McDaniels, Jeaneen J '84 -2328 Raintree NE -Canton 44705

(937) 865-6800 .. **McDermond,** Lori A '00 Lexis/Nexis -Bx933 -Dayton 45401

(419) 627-0414 .. **McDermond,** Maurice L Jr. '71 Buckingham LM&Z Co,LPA -414 Wayne -Bx929 -Sandusky 44870 **Fx:**627-0009

(216) 522-7807 .. **McDermott,** Daniel M '78 US Trustee-DOJ -200 Pub Sq -20th Fl-Ste 3300 -Cleveland 44114

(419) 874-3177 .. **McDermott,** James A '96 %Pheils & W -410 Louisiana Av -Perrysburg 43551 **Fx:**874-0180

(440) 356-1650 .. **McDermott,** John M '71 -21851 Ctr Ridge Rd -Rocky River 44116

(440) 934-7676 .. **McDermott,** Kevin E '84 -36815 Detroit Rd -Avon 44011

(614) 462-5001 .. **McDermott,** Kevin R '77 (Schottenstein Z&D) -250 West -Bx165020 -Columbus 43216 **Fx:**462-5135

(513) 336-2702 .. **McDermott,** Maureen A '96 Anthem BCBS -4361 Irwin Simpson Rd -MB1-220 -Mason 45040

(859) 261-6400 .. **McDermott,** Ronald L '80 -27 E 4th -Covington, KY 41011 **Fx:**491-1343

(419) 352-5263 .. **McDevitt,** Thomas J '93 Bowling Green Mun Ct -711 S Dunbrdg Rd -Bx326 -Bowling Green 43402

(440) 585-0919 .. **McDevitt,** John F '57 -2255 Par Ln -Ste 626 -Willoughby Hills 44094 **Fx:**585-0919

(740) 397-7420 .. **McDevitt Mayhew & Malek,LPA** -1 Pub Sq -Mount Vernon 43050 **Fx:**397-6611

(937) 642-6297 .. **McDonald,** Alan T '00 Honda of Amer Mfg Inc -24000 Honda Pkwy -Leg Dept -Marysville 43040

(513) 977-8200 .. **McDonald,** Angelina N '04 Dinsmore & S LLP -255 E 5th -Ste 1900 -Cincinnati 45202 **Fx:**977-8141

(216) 348-1700 .. **McDonald,** Charles R '73 (Davis & Y) -101 Prospect Av W -Ste 1700 -Cleveland 44115 **Fx:**621-0602

(937) 428-9800 .. **McDonald,** Christine M '93 (McDonald & M) -683 Miamisburg Centervll Rd -Ste 210 -Dayton 45459 **Fx:**428-9811

(216) 921-8718 .. **McDonald,** Craig D '80 -3124 Warrington Rd -Shaker Heights 44120

(614) 899-1700 .. **McDonald,** Deborah A '84 Lawyers Title Ins Corp -921 Eastwide Dr -Ste 133 -Westerville 43081

(440) 232-9911 .. **McDonald Frank Hitzeman & Holman** -24262 Bway Av -Bx46390 -Oakwood Village 44146 **Fx:**439-2308

(937) 223-1130 .. **McDonald,** Gerald L '04 Pickrel S&E -40 N Main -2700 Kettering Twr -Dayton 45423 **Fx:**223-0339

(216) 348-5400 .. **McDonald Hopkins Co, LPA** -600 Superior Av E -Ste 2100 -Cleveland 44114 **Fx:**348-5474

(614) 458-0025 .. **McDonald Hopkins Co, LPA** -41 S High -Ste 3650 -Columbus 43215 **Fx:**458-0028

(740) 947-4323 .. **McDonald,** Jessica S '02 Pike Cnty Pros Ofc -100 E 2nd -Ste 100 -Waverly 45690

(614) 462-2201 .. **McDonald,** John C '61 (Schottenstein Z&D) -250 West -Bx165020 -Columbus 43216 **Fx:**462-5135

(937) 428-9800 .. **McDonald,** Joseph P '91 (McDonald & M) -683 Miamisburg Centervll Rd -Ste 210 -Dayton 45459 **Fx:**428-9811

(202) 879-3743 .. **McDonald,** Kevin D '78 (Jones DR&P) -51 Louisiana Av NW -Washington, DC 20001 **Fx:**626-1700

(440) 232-9911 .. **McDonald,** Michael J '82 (McDonald FH&H) -24262 Bway Av -Bx46390 -Oakwood Village 44146 **Fx:**439-2308

(216) 566-2432 .. **McDonald,** Robert E '79 Sherwin-Williams Co -101 Prospect Av NW -Cleveland 44115

(740) 283-4529 .. **McDonald,** Robert E '00 %D Scarpone & Assoc -2021 Sunset Blvd -Steubenville 43952

McDonald, Ryan P '02 -6604 South Cove Dr -Cincinnati 45233

(614) 228-4201 .. **McDonald,** Susan J '02 OH Chamber of Commerce -230 E Town -Bx15159 -Columbus 43215

(202) 861-1500 .. **McDonald,** Thomas A '81 (Baker & H LLP) -1050 Conn Av NW -Ste 1100 -Washington, DC 20036

(614) 466-6696 .. **McDonald,** William J '75 Atty Gen -150 E Gay -Columbus 43215 **Fx:**752-2538

(216) 781-2125 .. **McDonnell,** Daniel P '52 -75 Pub Sq -Ste 700 -Cleveland 44113

(216) 781-2125 .. **McDonnell,** James J '80 -75 Pub Sq -Ste 700 -Cleveland 44113

(937) 439-1083 .. **McDonnell,** Ronald H Jr. '52 -937 Pine Needles Dr -Dayton 45458

(989) 496-5020 .. **McDonnell,** Sue K '88 Dow Corning Corp -2200 W Salzburg Rd -Bx994 -Midland, MI 48686

(513) 352-3334 .. **McDonnell,** Ursula M '95 City Solicitors Ofc -801 Plum -214 -Cincinnati 45202 **Fx:**352-1575

(513) 946-6464 .. **McDonough,** Amy S '92 Hamilton Cnty Mun Ct -1000 Main -Cincinnati 45202

(216) 509-0140 .. **McDonough,** Brian M '00 -Bx16252 -Rocky River 44116

(937) 323-3441 .. **McDonough,** John P '54 -2100 E High -Ste 108 -Springfield 45505

(614) 716-1696 .. **McDonough,** Kenneth E '84 Amer Elec Pwr Co -1 Riverside Plz -Columbus 43215

(513) 421-4020 .. **McDonough,** Kevin C '89 (Cohen TK&S,LLC) -250 E 5th -Ste 1200 -Cincinnati 45202 **Fx:**241-4490

(513) 794-6428 .. **McDonough,** Therese S '88 OH Natl Life Ins Co -1 Fncl Way -Cincinnati 45242

(440) 327-1542 .. **McDonough,** William F '74 (McDonough S & Co) -35888 Ctr Ridge Rd -Ste 3 -North Ridgeville 44039

(608) 271-2202 .. **McDorman,** David M '80 (McDorman & G) -2901 W Beltline Hwy -Ste 302 -Madison, WI 53713 **Fx:**271-4009

(440) 356-8050 .. **McDougal,** Larry E '85 -21360 Ctr Ridge Rd -Ste 301 -Rocky River 44116

(614) 462-5839 .. **McDougall,** Ian '70 Dept of Job & Fam Srvc -80 E Fulton -Columbus 43215

(937) 224-7200 .. **McDougall,** Kevin T '97 %Horenstein N&B -124 E 3rd -5th Fl -Dayton 45402 **Fx:**224-3353

(330) 784-8800 .. **McDowall,** Laura K '87 (Young & M) -507 Canton Rd -Bx6210 -Akron 44312

(330) 929-4291 .. **McDowall,** Robert H '62 -130 Portage Trl -Bx8 -Cuyahoga Falls 44222

McDowall, Robert T Jr. '84 -3502 Curtis -Mogadore 44260

(513) 634-0102 .. **McDow-Dunham,** Kelly L '97 Cnsl Procter & Gamble -6071 Ctr Hill Av -Cincinnati 45224

(202) 225-7502 .. **McDowell,** Carter K '93 US House of Reps-Financial Srvcs -2129 Rayburn HOB -Washington, DC 20515

(513) 977-8200 .. **McDowell,** Christopher R '00 %Dinsmore & S LLP -255 E 5th
-Ste 1900 -Cincinnati 45202 **Fx:**977-8141

(440) 221-7238 .. **McDowell,** James M '58 -Bx161034 -Rocky River 44116

(210) 805-8166 .. **McDowell,** Jerry L '69 (McDowell & P,Ltd) -6104 Bway
-San Antonio, TX 78209

(513) 977-8200 .. **McDowell,** John E '52 OfCnsl Dinsmore & S LLP -255 E 5th
-Ste 1900 -Cincinnati 45202 **Fx:**977-8141

(216) 689-5707 .. **McDowell,** Robert F Jr. '99 Key Bank,NA -127 Pub Sq
-Cleveland 44114

(440) 899-8990 .. **McDowell,** Sharon L '86 -Bx40103 -Bay Village 44140

(502) 852-4827 .. **McDowell,** Wyatt '84 W McDowell Co,LPA -Bx3093 -Louisville, KY
40201

(216) 721-8903 .. **McDuffie,** Kenard '74 -12108 Bucknghm Av -Cleveland 44120

(216) 621-7860 .. **McEaneney,** Shannon L '98 %Cavitch BD&F -1717 E 9th -14th Fl
-Cleveland 44114 **Fx:**621-3415

(419) 539-6000 .. **Mc Elfresh,** Randall J '90 AFSCME OH Cncl 8
-420 S Reynolds Rd -Ste 108 -Toledo 43615

(614) 267-1306 .. **McElligott,** William W '88 -511 E Jeffrey Pl -Columbus 43214

(216) 382-3835 .. **McElrath,** Lenza Jr. '85 -1039 Quilliams Rd
-Cleveland Heights 44121

(440) 838-7600 .. **McElroy,** Brian T '01 %Janik & D,LLP -9200 S Hills Blvd -Ste 300
-Cleveland 44147 **Fx:**838-7601

(330) 796-3917 .. **McElroy,** James Jr. '97 Goodyear Tire & Rubber Co
-1144 E Market -Akron 44316

McElroy, Kenneth K '99 -3629 E 149th -Cleveland 44120

(419) 248-2600 .. **McElroy,** Neil S '03 %Eohrbachers LC&T Co -405 Mad Av -8th Flr
-Toledo 43604

(804) 775-1067 .. **McElroy,** Robert G '78 (McGuire W,LLP) -901 E Cary -Richmond,
VA 23219

(415) 954-0394 .. **McElwee,** Charles R II '81 (Squire S&D LLP) -1 Maritime Plz
-Ste 300 -San Francisco, CA 94111 **Fx:**393-9887

(614) 466-3998 .. **McElwee,** Donald L '75 Unemploymnt Comp Commssn
-145 S Front -Bx182299 -Columbus 43218

(513) 984-1811 .. **McElwee,** John L '77 -9902 Carver Rd -Bx42414 -Cincinnati 45242

(614) 431-0851 .. **McElwee,** Larry A '91 -369 E Clearvw -Worthington 43085

(937) 382-3640 .. **McElwee,** Mary H '77 Clinton Cnty Cmn Pleas Ct -46 S South
-Wilmington 45177

McEnaney, Erin J '03 -982 Hunter Av -Columbus 43201

(513) 369-0360 .. **McEvilley,** Chris '85 (McEvilley & M) -135 Garfld Pl -Ste 334
-Cincinnati 45202 **Fx:**369-0143

(513) 369-0360 .. **McEvilley,** Robert Michael '74 (McEvilley & M) -135 Garfld Pl
-Ste 334 -Cincinnati 45202 **Fx:**369-0143

(216) 622-0850 .. **McFadden,** Donald P '73 (McFadden & Assoc Co,LPA)
-1370 Ontario -Ste 1700 -Cleveland 44113 **Fx:**622-0854

(614) 221-8868 .. **McFadden,** Mary J '74 (McFadden W&S) -175 S 3rd -Ste 210
-Columbus 43215 **Fx:**221-3985

(614) 221-8868 .. **McFadden Winner & Savage** -175 S 3rd -Ste 210
-Columbus 43215 **Fx:**221-3985

(513) 791-2122 .. **McFall,** Tanner B '04 -10979 Reed Hartman Hwy -Ste 33AD
-Cincinnati 45242

(202) 879-3864 .. **McFalls,** Michael S '95 %Jones DR&P -51 Louisiana Av NW
-Washington, DC 20001 **Fx:**686-1700

(513) 241-6748 .. **McFarland,** Andrew D '00 A Levine -324 Reading Rd
-Cincinnati 45202

McFarland, Anne S '74 -12699 Cedar Rd -Cleveland 44106

McFarland, Chad M '03 -(Address Unavailable)

(502) 845-2754 .. **McFarland,** Charles E '79 -338 Jackson Rd
-New Castle, KY 40050

(740) 587-3633 .. **McFarland,** Jonathan Drew '87 McFarland Law Ofc -230 E Bway
-Ste 200 -Granville 43023

(740) 355-8306 .. **McFarland,** Matthew W '92 Scioto Cnty Juv Ct -602 7th
-Portsmouth 45662

(937) 544-2371 .. **McFarland,** Michelle Elrick '02 Adams Cnty CSEA -482 Rice Dr
-Bx386 -West Union 45144 **Fx:**544-5406

(304) 424-6400 .. **McFarland,** Patrick E '87 -615 Market -Bx736 -Parkersburg, WV
26102

(303) 277-0202 .. **McFarland,** Thomas D '76 -350 Indna -#603 -Golden, CO 80401

(330) 453-5302 .. **McFarren,** Randy '74 -220 Market Av S -Ste 1140 -Canton 44702
Fx:456-8578

(216) 586-9537 .. **McFaul,** Kevin T '86 -1566 E 36th -Cleveland 44114

(216) 481-4495 .. **McGaffick,** Jeffrey M '86 -571 E 185th -Cleveland 44119

(614) 885-4078 .. **McGaffick,** Timothy D '88 -85 Bywood Ln -Columbus 43214

(216) 622-8200 .. **McGann,** Amy B '01 %Calfee H&G LLP -800 Superior Av
-Ste 1400 -Cleveland 44114 **Fx:**241-0816

(216) 696-7883 .. **McGann,** Regis E Jr. '75 -1370 Ontario -Ste 410 -Cleveland 44113

(614) 466-8600 .. **McGann,** Steven C '02 Atty Gen -30 E Broad -Columbus 43215
Fx:466-6090

(330) 535-4191 .. **McGarrity,** Steven J '96 Cmmnty Lgl Aid Srvcs,Inc -265 S Main
-3rd Fl -Akron 44308 **Fx:**535-0728

(239) 945-3883 .. **McGarry,** Amy L '95 -2323 Del Prado Blvd -Ste 7-258
-Cape Coral, FL 33990

(216) 566-0500 .. **McGarry,** James J Jr. '63 (Deegan & M) -1468 W 9th -Ste 240
-Cleveland 44113

(505) 757-3989 .. **McGarry,** Kathleen '87 -Bx310 -Glorieta, NM 87535

(216) 621-7227 .. **McGarry,** Timothy L '91 OfCnsl Nicola G&C,LLC -25 W
Prospect Av -Republic Bldg Ste 1400 -Cleveland 44115
Fx:621-3999

(614) 224-8374 .. **McGarvey,** Kathleen C '03 Legal Aid -40 W Gay -Columbus 43215

(513) 398-4891 .. **McGary,** Bruce A '91 (Peeler M&Z) -423 Reading Rd
-Mason 45040

McGary, Ryan C '01 -2830 Victory Pkwy -Ste 201
-Cincinnati 45206

(216) 348-5400 .. **McGaughey,** George L Jr. '75 (McDonald H Co,LPA)
-600 Superior Av E -Ste 2100 -Cleveland 44114 **Fx:**348-5474

(513) 651-6800 .. **McGavran,** Frederick J '72 (Frost BT LLC) -201 E 5th
-2200 PNC Ctr -Cincinnati 45202 **Fx:**651-6981

(440) 286-9571 .. **McGee,** David A '82 (Svete M&C Co,LPA) -100 Parker Ct
-Chardon 44024

(513) 844-6100 .. **McGee,** Gary A '81 -332 S Front -Hamilton 45011

(614) 466-3559 .. **McGee,** Jonathon L '89 OH House of Reps -77 S High -14th Fl
-Columbus 43215

(513) 870-2000 .. **McGee,** Joseph A '88 Cincinnati Ins Co -6200 S Gilmore Rd
-Fairfield 45014

(216) 741-4486 .. **McGee,** Kathleen H '79 -4603 Brookpark Rd -Parma 44134

(330) 392-1541 .. **McGee,** Michael J '02 Harrington H&M,Ltd -108 Main Av SW
-Ste 500 -Bx1510 -Warren 44482 **Fx:**394-6890

(740) 592-5839 .. **McGee,** Patrick C '79 (Grace & M) -19½ S Court -Athens 45701
Fx:592-3764

(202) 514-2895 .. **McGee,** Ramona L '93 DOJ-Immigration -425 I NW -Ste 6100
-Washington, DC 20536

(304) 523-2100 .. **McGee,** William J Jr. '92 Jenkins F PLLC -401 11th -Ste 1100
-Bx2688 -Huntington, WV 25726

(937) 225-5773 .. **McGee-Cromartie,** Frances E '83 Montgomery Cnty Pros
-303 W 2nd -Rm 113 -Dayton 45402

(513) 948-1080 .. **McGehee,** John H '80 -Bx141453 -Cincinnati 45250

(513) 287-2781 .. **McGehee,** Julie Ann '92 Cinergy Corp -139 E 4th -25 Atrium II
-Bx960 -Cincinnati 45201

(440) 845-1666 .. **McGhee,** Shorain L '03 -6325 York Rd -Ste 305
-Parma Heights 44130

(513) 287-8768 .. **McGhghy,** Julie A '03 Mitsui Sumitomo Maurine Mgmt -49 E 4th
-Ste 500 -Cincinnati 45202

(216) 241-8333 .. **McGill,** Danielle M '03 %Ritzler C&S,Ltd -1001 Lakeside Av
-1550 North Pnt Twr -Cleveland 44114 **Fx:**241-5890

(419) 245-2740 .. **McGill,** David C '84 Industrial Commssn of OH -One Govt Ctr
-Ste 1500 -Toledo 43604

McGill, John G '77 -Bx79459 -Atlanta, GA 30357

(614) 276-6555 .. **McGinley,** John Michael '71 -1078 Hardesty Pl W
-Columbus 43204

(440) 392-7056 .. **McGinley,** Mark D '82 Steris Corp -5966 Heisley Rd
-Mentor 44060

(607) 273-4200 .. **McGinn,** Barbara A '97 True W&M,LLP -202 E State -Ste 700
-Ithaca, NY 14850 **Fx:**272-6694

(216) 241-5224 .. **McGinness,** Joseph T '69 -23811 Chagrin Blvd -Ste 36
-Cleveland 44122

(216) 696-8440 .. **McGinness,** Neil M '69 (McGinness P&M) -1900 Superior Av
-Ste 230 -Cleveland 44114

(937) 224-1981 .. **McGinnis,** Carlo C '79 (Young PL&J) -130 W 2nd -Ste 800
-Dayton 45402

(513) 721-1975 .. **McGinnis,** Charles T III '78 Freking & B -215 E 9th -5th Fl
-Cincinnati 45202 **Fx:**651-2570

(216) 518-2200 .. **McGinnis,** John P '78 (McGinnis & T LLC) -12395 McCracken Rd
-Ste A2 -Garfield Heights 44125 **Fx:**518-2246

McGinnis, Lori A '92 -1937 Claremont Av -Lot 35 -Ashland 44805

(614) 263-7000 .. **McGinnis,** Mark A '03 %D McTigue -3886 N High
-Columbus 43214 **Fx:**263-7078

(330) 458-0484 .. **McGinnis,** William F '91 (Puterbaugh & M) -111 2nd NW -Ste 505
-Canton 44702

(216) 344-9220 .. **McGinty Gibbons Hilow & Spellacy Co,LPA**
-614 W Superior Av -Ste 1300 -Cleveland 44113

McGinty, John P '58 -12901 Rexwood Av -Garfield Heights 44105

(216) 344-9220 .. **McGinty,** William T '80 (McGinty GH&S Co,LPA)
-614 W Superior Av -Ste 1300 -Cleveland 44113

(740) 452-8431 .. **McGlade,** Roger D '89 (Magaziner M&F) -44 S 6th
-Zanesville 43701

(440) 930-4001 .. **McGlamery,** Heidi K '98 %Baumgartner & O
-5455 Detroit Rd (Rte 254) -Sheffield Village 44054 **Fx:**934-7205

(216) 378-9905 .. **McGlinchey Stafford PLLC** -25550 Chagrin Blvd -Ste 406
-Cleveland 44122 **Fx:**378-9910

(614) 227-8879 .. **McGlone,** Sean M '02 %Bricker & E LLP -100 S 3rd
-Columbus 43215 **Fx:**227-2390

(412) 316-7054 .. **McGonagle,** Patrick J '80 Dominion Retail,Inc -625 Lbrty Av
-Pittsburgh, PA 15222

(330) 493-9901 .. **McGonegal,** Terrance J '77 (Lonas M&T) -1810 36th NW
-Canton 44709 **Fx:**493-9338

(419) 627-0414 .. **McGookey,** Daniel L '79 (Buckingham LM&Z Co,LPA) -414 Wayne
-Bx929 -Sandusky 44870 **Fx:**627-0009

(419) 625-4121 .. **McGookey,** James E '75 1st Citizens Bnk -100 E Water
-Sandusky 44870

(419) 627-7782 .. **McGory,** Gregory S '96 Erie Cnty Family Ct -323 Columbus Av
-4th Fl -Sandusky 44870

(419) 626-0055 .. **McGory,** Peter J '73 (Tone GM&V) -1401 Cleveland Rd
-Sandusky 44870 **Fx:**626-0288

(614) 221-5771 .. **McGough,** John T '81 (McGough & Assoc,Inc) -100 S 3rd -Ste 111
-Columbus 43215

(614) 228-6061 .. **McGovern,** James M '93 Hammond & S -556 E Town
-Columbus 43215

(614) 464-1969 .. **McGowan,** Charles W '96 -601 S High -Columbus 43215

(412) 391-9860 .. **McGowan,** David A '87 Caroselli BM&C -312 Blvd of the Allies
-8th Fl -Pittsburgh, PA 15222

(216) 451-4796 .. **McGowan,** Harvey J '83 -1245 E 135th -East Cleveland 44112

(513) 844-2000 .. **McGowan,** Jack C '74 (McGowan & J,LLC) -246 High
-Hamilton 45011 **Fx:**868-1190

(216) 621-0200 .. **McGowan,** John J Jr. '84 (Baker & H LLP) -1900 E 9th -Ste 3200
-Cleveland 44114 **Fx:**696-0740

(419) 213-6824 .. **McGowan,** Lisa D '93 %Hon DE Lewandowski -429 N Mich -Ste A
-Toledo 43624

(330) 864-2236 .. **McGowan,** Michael L '60 -646 Cliffside Dr -Akron 44313
Fx:835-4340

(419) 241-9000 .. **McGowan,** Michael S '82 (Shumaker L&K,LLP) -1000 Jackson
-Toledo 43624 **Fx:**241-6894

(419) 243-1105 .. **McGowan,** Paul D '89 Lackey NHR&T,LPA -2 Maritime Plz -3rd Fl
-Toledo 43604

(330) 929-4155 .. **McGowan,** Raymond J II '78 -1799 Akron-Peninsula Rd
-Stes 211-212 -Akron 44313

(440) 582-8080 .. **McGowan,** Stephen '77 -Bx33519 -North Royalton 44133

(440) 333-6300 .. **McGowan,** Thomas B III '69 McGowan & Co -20595 Lorain Rd
-Ste 300 -Cleveland 44126 **Fx:**333-3214

(440) 333-6300 .. **McGowan,** Thomas B IV '96 McGowan & Co -20595 Lorain Rd
-Ste 300 -Cleveland 44126 **Fx:**333-3214

McGown, Daniel J '77 -Bx4375 -Copley 44321

(330) 670-0005 .. **McGown,** Susan S '88 (McGown & M)
-1894 N Cleveland Massillon Rd -Akron 44333

(419) 249-3325 .. **McGrail,** Michael T '87 Sky Trust,NA -519 Mad Av -3rd Fl -Toledo
43604

McGrail, Thomas E '77 -941 Bexley Dr -Perrysburg 43551

(216) 787-3030 .. **McGrail,** Timothy X '81 Atty Gen -615 W Superior Av -11th Fl
-Cleveland 44113 **Fx:**787-3480

(614) 221-3155 .. **McGranor,** Timothy B '00 %Bailey C LLC -10 W Broad
    -Columbus 43215 **Fx:**221-0479

(614) 645-7531 .. **McGrath,** Barbara A '79 Columbus Civ Srvc Cmmssn -50 W Gay
    -Columbus 43215

(614) 464-4201 .. **McGrath & Breitfeller LLP** -140 E Town -Ste 1070
    -Columbus 43215

(716) 855-1553 .. **McGrath,** Dennis M '85 Legal Aid -50 Delaware Av -4th Fl
    -Buffalo, NY 14202

(859) 233-2012 .. **McGrath,** Gayle B '82 Wyatt T&C -250 W Main -1700 Lex Fin Ctr
    -Lexington, KY 40507

(216) 642-9494 .. **McGrath,** James J '67 -Bx31177 -Independence 44131

(216) 459-9040 .. **McGrath,** James J IV '89 -8748 Brecksvll Rd -Ste 130
    -Brecksville 44141

(513) 977-8200 .. **McGrath,** Jennifer L '02 %Dinsmore & S LLP -255 E 5th -Ste 1900
    -Cincinnati 45202 **Fx:**977-8141

(614) 462-3555 .. **McGrath,** Keith '92 Franklin Cnty Pros -373 S High
    -Columbus 43215

(440) 603-7079 .. **McGrath,** Kevin P '96 Progressive Ins Co -5920 Landerbrook Dr
    -PLG-OHL33 -Mayfield Heights 44124

(216) 443-7800 .. **McGrath,** Mary H '84 Cuyahoga Cnty Pros -1200 Ontario -8th Fl
    -Cleveland 44113 **Fx:**698-2270

(216) 443-3997 .. **McGrath,** Michele A '96 McDonald Invts -800 Superior Av
    -Cleveland 44114

(614) 464-4201 .. **McGrath,** Thomas R '74 (McGrath & B LLP) -140 E Town
    -Ste 1070 -Columbus 43215

(614) 228-6345 .. **McGrath,** Timothy J '69 (Strip HLM&T Co LPA) -575 S 3rd
    -Columbus 43215 **Fx:**228-6369

(513) 852-6066 .. **McGrath,** V Brandon '00 %Wood & L LLP -600 Vine -Ste 2500
    -Cincinnati 45202 **Fx:**852-6087

(216) 574-2516 .. **McGraw,** Brian R '86 (McGraw & M Co,LPA) -1280 W 3rd -3rd Fl
    -Cleveland 44113 **Fx:**696-1439

(513) 651-6800 .. **McGraw,** Bridget Gannon '03 %Frost BT LLC -201 E 5th
    -2200 PNC Ctr -Cincinnati 45202 **Fx:**651-6981

(216) 265-6009 .. **McGraw,** Candace S '88 Cleveland Hopkins Intl Airport
    -5300 Riverside Dr -Cleveland 44135

(614) 217-4436 .. **McGraw,** Christopher E '93 Bank One Invstmnt Advsrs
    -100 E Broad -3rd Fl -Columbus 43215

(941) 353-3372 .. **McGraw,** Doonan D '62 -245 St James Way -Naples, FL 34104

(513) 579-6400 .. **McGraw,** James J Jr. '74 (Keating M&K LLC) -1 E 4th
    -1400 Provident Twr -Cincinnati 45202 **Fx:**579-6457

(216) 566-3009 .. **McGraw,** Joseph E '88 Sherwin-Williams Co -101 Prospect Av NW
    -Cleveland 44115

(216) 566-8780 .. **McGraw,** Mark D '77 -1370 Ontario -Ste 800 -Cleveland 44113

(216) 574-2516 .. **McGraw,** Mary H '84 (McGraw & M Co,LPA) -15819 Stillwood Av
    -Cleveland 44111

(614) 899-7477 .. **McGraw,** Michael Scott '01 Goldstein & Assoc
    -2999 E Dublin-Granvll Rd -Ste 220 -Columbus 43231

(216) 787-3175 .. **McGraw,** Patrick A '66 Oh Civ Rghts Cmmssn -615 W Superior Av
    -Ste 885 -Cleveland 44113

(614) 225-8700 .. **McGraw,** Richard S '96 %PricewaterhouseCoopers LLP
    -100 E Broad -Columbus 43215

(216) 292-5015 .. **McGraw,** Shawn M '94 Tremco Inc -3735 Green Rd
    -Beachwood 44122

(937) 339-0511 .. **McGraw,** William J '73 (Dungan & L Co,LPA) -210 W Main -Troy
    45373 **Fx:**335-5802

(440) 285-4771 .. **McGregor,** Emanuel H '48 -203 Main -Chardon 44024

(216) 696-4700 .. **McGregor,** Erica E '98 %Spieth BM&N Co,LPA -925 Euclid Av
    -2000 Huntngtn Bldg -Cleveland 44115 **Fx:**696-2706

(440) 951-4679 .. **McGregor,** John T '76 -36851 Riviera Ridge
    -Willoughby Hills 44094

(216) 931-6000 .. **McGrew,** Steven D '01 %Ulmer & B LLP -1300 E 9th
    -Ste 900 Penton Media Bldg -Cleveland 44114 **Fx:**931-6001

(216) 623-0150 .. **McGrievy,** Mark P '93 (Roetzel & A,LPA) -1375 E 9th
    -One Cleve Ctr 9th Fl -Cleveland 44114 **Fx:**623-0134

(330) 643-5328 .. **McGuckin,** Denise M '86 Summit Cnty Juv Ct -650 Dan
    -Akron 44310

(330) 836-9200 .. **McGuckin,** Richard B '65 -315 S Miller Rd -Akron 44333

McGuigan, Leigh A '92 -4016 Glenda Pl -Columbus 43220

(440) 352-6200 .. **McGuinness,** Clare I '85 Legal Aid Society -8 N State
    -Painesville 44077

(216) 222-9708 .. **McGuire,** Daniel J '88 Natl City Bnk -1900 E 9th -3rd Fl
    -Cleveland 44114 **Fx:**222-3173

(937) 267-7625 .. **McGuire,** Dennis M '94 -4100 W 3rd -Bldg 408 -Dayton 45428

(937) 885-0871 .. **McGuire,** James C '80 -10748 Cntry Walk Ct -Centerville 45458

(440) 322-5770 .. **McGuire,** James J '74 -116 Clemson Ct -Elyria 44035

(614) 431-1133 .. **McGuire,** James W '60 -110B Northwoods Blvd -Columbus 43235

(513) 651-6800 .. **McGuire,** Joel F '01 %Frost BT LLC -201 E 5th -2200 PNC Ctr
    -Cincinnati 45202 **Fx:**651-6981

(216) 622-8200 .. **McGuire,** John J '98 %Calfee H&G LLP -800 Superior Av
    -Ste 1400 -Cleveland 44114 **Fx:**241-0816

(440) 366-9930 .. **McGuire,** Lisa J '01 %McCray MS&M Co,LPA -260 Burns Rd
    -Ste 150 -Elyria 44035 **Fx:**366-1910

(248) 354-0380 .. **McGuire,** Lynn F '00 %Novara T&M PLLC -2000 Town Ctr
    -Ste 2370 -Southfield, MI 48075

(573) 893-5600 .. **McGuire,** Megan B '98 Amer Family Ins Co -3600 Amazonas Dr
    -Jefferson City, MO 65109

(216) 348-5056 .. **McGuire,** Michael P '93 Cuyahoga Metro Housing Auth
    -1441 W 25th -Cleveland 44113

McGuire, Michelle K '03 -5267 Dana Pl -North Ridgeville 44039

(614) 466-5610 .. **McGuire,** Robin L '96 Atty Gen -150 E Gay -Columbus 43215
    Fx:752-2732

(216) 787-3030 .. **McGuire,** Thomas D '83 Atty Gen -615 W Superior Av -11th Fl
    -Cleveland 44113 **Fx:**787-3480

(419) 668-4879 .. **McGuire,** Thomas J '01 %Eschrich & S Co,LPA -130 Benedict Av
    -Bx465 -Norwalk 44857 **Fx:**663-0140

(740) 662-5503 .. **McGuire,** Thomas R '75 -3073 Glazier Rd -Guysville 45735

(614) 462-5408 .. **McGuire,** Traci A '99 %Kegler BH&R -65 E State -Ste 1800
    -Columbus 43215 **Fx:**464-2634

(330) 392-8800 .. **McGuire,** William P '80 (W McGuire Co,LPA) -106 E Market
    -Ste 705 -Bx1243 -Warren 44482

(937) 365-2080 .. **McGuire-Haines,** Kimberly J '96 -Bx793 -Hillsboro 45133
    Fx:365-2080

(216) 472-1500 .. **McHale,** Katharine N '84 O'Brien Law Firm,LLC -627 W St Clair Av
    -Cleveland 44113 **Fx:**472-1600

(216) 522-2675 .. **McHargh,** Kelly-Marie '98 US Dept of Ed/Civ Rghts
    -600 Superior Av E -Ste 750 -Cleveland 44114 **Fx:**522-2573

(740) 779-6662 .. **McHenry,** Aaron M '99 4th Dist Ct Appeals -14 S Paint -Rm 38
    -Chillicothe 45601

(937) 461-6200 .. **McHenry,** Brian R '96 Cincinnati Ins Co -130 W 2nd -Ste 1850
    -Dayton 45402

(614) 466-5394 .. **McHenry,** Jerry L '76 Pub Def -8 E Long -Columbus 43215

(740) 778-2982 .. **McHenry,** John K '87 -Bx240 -South Webster 45682

(614) 764-1801 .. **McHenry,** Linda F '82 -6519 Blickling Dr -Dublin 43017

(513) 922-3200 .. **McHenry,** Martin '83 OfCnsl Haverkamp BR&R Co,LPA
    -5856 Glenway Av -Cincinnati 45238 **Fx:**922-8096

(513) 977-8200 .. **McHenry,** Powell '51 OfCnsl Dinsmore & S LLP -255 E 5th
    -Ste 1900 -Cincinnati 45202 **Fx:**977-8141

(937) 783-2401 .. **McHenry,** Ronald J '72 (Lyons M&D) -212 W Main
    -Blanchester 45107

(419) 885-3597 .. **McHugh DeNune & McCarthy,Ltd** -5580 Monroe
    -Sylvania 43560 **Fx:**885-3861

(330) 455-6112 .. **McHugh,** James M '90 (Tzangas PM&R) -220 Market Av S -8th Fl
    -Canton 44702 **Fx:**455-2108

(419) 885-3597 .. **McHugh,** John J III '76 (McHugh D&M,Ltd) -5580 Monroe
    -Sylvania 43560 **Fx:**885-3861

(419) 473-1350 .. **McHugh,** Peter J '88 (Jasin S&M Co,LPA) -4303 Talmadge Rd
    -Ste 201 -Toledo 43623 **Fx:**473-1929

(419) 241-5175 .. **McHugh,** Sarah A '83 (Maloney M&K) -520 Mad Av -Ste 330
    -Toledo 43604

(937) 223-1201 .. **McHugh,** Stephen M '79 (Altick & C Co,LPA) -1 S Main
    -1700 One Dayton Ctr -Dayton 45402 **Fx:**223-5100

(216) 221-8023 .. **McHugh,** Terrence P '85 -13460 Lk Av -Lakewood 44107

(330) 334-1536 .. **McIlvaine,** Andrew S '96 %Palecek MH&M Co LLP
    -200 Smokerise Dr -Ste 200 -Wadsworth 44281 **Fx:**334-7005

(330) 334-1536 .. **McIlvaine,** James R '69 (Palecek MH&M Co LLP)
    -200 Smokerise Dr -Ste 200 -Wadsworth 44281 **Fx:**334-7005

(330) 335-1596 .. **McIlvaine,** Stephen B '78 Mun Ct Judge -120 Maple
    -Wadsworth 44281

(513) 852-3253 .. **McIlwain,** Carol N '77 Industrial Commssn of OH -125 E Court
    -Cincinnati 45202

(937) 544-7900 .. **McIlwain,** Douglas E '79 -217 W Main -West Union 45693

(513) 721-7906 .. **McIlwain,** Harry H Jr. '76 (McIlwain & G) -35 E 7th -510 Exec Bldg
    -Cincinnati 45202 **Fx:**721-1555

(513) 929-4040 .. **McIntosh,** Anthony B '96 (McIntosh & M) -15 E 8th -Ste 300W
    -Cincinnati 45202

(513) 929-4040 .. **McIntosh,** Bruce B '60 McIntosh & M -15 E 8th -Ste 300W
    -Cincinnati 45202

(513) 762-4425 .. **McIntosh,** Jill V '97 Kroger Co -1014 Vine -Law Dept
    -Cincinnati 45202

(513) 929-4040 .. **McIntosh,** Michael T '93 (McIntosh & M) -15 E 8th -Ste 300W
    -Cincinnati 45202

(614) 827-7300 .. **McIntosh,** Sandra R '04 %Freund F&A -65 E State -Ste 800
    -Columbus 43215 **Fx:**827-7303

(614) 645-8081 .. **McIntosh,** Stephen L '84 City Pros -375 S High -7th Fl -Columbus
    43215

(513) 762-6200 .. **McIntosh,** Thomas G '03 %Ulmer & B LLP -600 Vine -Ste 2800
    -Cincinnati 45202 **Fx:**762-6245

(513) 381-2838 .. **McInturf,** Lora N '03 %Taft S&H LLP -425 Walnut -Ste 1800
    -Cincinnati 45202 **Fx:**381-0205

(614) 464-2235 .. **McInturff,** Judith M '80 -50 W Broad -Ste 2600 -Columbus 43215

(440) 871-6300 .. **McIntyre,** Daniel M '90 (D McIntyre & Co,LLC) -2001 Crocker Rd
    -Ste 280 -Westlake 44145 **Fx:**871-6301

(216) 566-5261 .. **McIntyre,** John F III '96 Grtr Cleveland Regnl Transit Auth
    -1240 W 6th -Cleveland 44113

(216) 579-4114 .. **McIntyre Kahn & Kruse Co LPA** -1301 E 9th -Ste 1200
    -Cleveland 44114

(513) 579-6400 .. **McIntyre,** M Scott '02 %Keating M&K PLL -1 E 4th
    -1400 Provident Twr -Cincinnati 45202 **Fx:**579-6457

McIntyre, Patricia Ann '85 -535 Piccadilly Cir -Akron 44319

(216) 830-6830 .. **McIntyre,** Patrick J '89 (Brouse M) -1001 Lakeside Av -Ste 1600
    -Cleveland 44114 **Fx:**830-6807

(216) 579-4114 .. **McIntyre,** Robert W '75 (McIntyre K&K Co LPA) -1301 E 9th
    -Ste 1200 -Cleveland 44114

(216) 586-1292 .. **McIntyre,** Sharon R '82 -901 Lakeside Av
    -Jones Day-New Matter Srvcs -Cleveland 44114

(740) 322-5498 .. **McIntyre,** Teresa O '87 Longaberger Co -1500 E Main
    -Newark 43055

(419) 525-1611 .. **McIntyre,** William T '75 (Brown BM&M) -70 Park Av W
    -Mansfield 44902 **Fx:**525-3810

(614) 752-6417 .. **McIver,** Kevin M '80 Atty Gen -30 E Broad -Columbus 43215
    Fx:466-0013

(513) 651-6800 .. **McKay,** Bernard L '94 (Frost BT LLC) -201 E 5th -2200 PNC Ctr
    -Cincinnati 45202 **Fx:**651-6981

(216) 443-9000 .. **McKay,** Hugh E '82 (Porter WM&A LLP) -925 Euclid Av -Ste 1700
    -Cleveland 44115 **Fx:**443-9011

(513) 932-1414 .. **McKay,** Leroy F '83 Lebanon Citizens Natl Bank -2 N Bway
    -Lebanon 45036

(513) 621-1767 .. **McKay,** Timothy E '88 (Trenz M&K Co,LPA) -35 E 7th -Ste 400
    -Cincinnati 45202

(419) 898-3095 .. **McKean,** Alan R '85 (McKean & M) -161 W Water
    -Oak Harbor 43449

(419) 898-3095 .. **McKean,** Pamela A '85 (McKean & M) -161 W Water -Oak Harbor
    43449

(216) 861-5582 .. **McKee,** James W '69 (Fay SFM&M LLP) -1100 Superior Av -7th Fl
    -Cleveland 44114 **Fx:**241-1666

(216) 861-0360 .. **McKee,** Mary B '97 %Hickman & L Co,LPA -1370 Ontario
    -Ste 1620 -Cleveland 44113 **Fx:**861-3113

(614) 692-3284 .. **McKee,** Susan E '84 US Dfnse Lgstcs Agncy -Bx3990
    -Columbus 43218

(216) 622-8200 .. **McKee,** Thomas F '75 (Calfee H&G LLP) -800 Superior Av
    -Ste 1400 -Cleveland 44114 **Fx:**241-0816

(419) 241-1200 .. **McKee,** William M '90 Cooper & W,LPA -900 Adams
    -Toledo 43624 **Fx:**242-5675

(216) 241-5310 .. **McKeegan,** Jennifer L '97 %Gallagher SF&N -1501 Euclid Av
    -6th Fl -Cleveland 44115 **Fx:**241-1608

(740) 283-1966 .. **McKeegan,** Terrence L '04 Jefferson Cnty Pros
    -16001 State Route 7 -Steubenville 43952

(216) 875-3122 ..**McKeever,** Kelly L '98 PriceWaterhouse Coopers -200 Pub Sq -Ste 2700 -Cleveland 44114

(800) 456-2375 ..**McKellar,** Amy C '99 Besl Transfer Co -5550 Este Av -Cincinnati 45232

      McKelvey, Matthew I '02 -1624 Highland Ridge Blvd -Highland Heights, KY 41076

(513) 367-6133 ..**McKenery,** Deborah L '85 -106 Harrison Av -Harrison 45030 **Fx:**367-7801

(614) 227-2000 ..**McKenna,** Alvin J '67 (Porter WM&A LLP) -41 S High -Columbus 43215 **Fx:**227-2100

(937) 393-1814 ..**McKenna,** David H '92 -149 E Main -Bx760 -Hillsboro 45133 **Fx:**393-4498

(216) 586-7042 ..**McKenna,** Mary P '96 -901 Lakeside Av -%Jones Day -Cleveland 44114

(513) 791-8916 ..**McKenna,** Matthew C '93 -4710 Cooper Rd -Blue Ash 45242

(513) 241-9400 ..**McKenna,** Melissa A '03 %Legal Aid -215 E 9th -Ste 200 -Cincinnati 45202

(513) 946-3000 ..**McKenna,** Timothy J '02 Hamilton Cnty Pros -230 E 9th -Cincinnati 45202 **Fx:**946-3017

(216) 382-1370 ..**McKenna,** Todd J '84 -1572 Westdale Rd -South Euclid 44121

(330) 376-6400 ..**McKenney,** Todd M '89 The Chapel -135 Fir Hill -Akron 44304

(937) 333-4121 ..**McKenzie,** Brent L '97 Law Dept -101 W 3rd -Bx22 -Dayton 45402

(502) 589-4200 ..**McKenzie,** Jeffrey A '87 Greenebaum D&M PLLC -101 S 5th -Ste 3300 -Louisville, KY 40202

(330) 867-9998 ..**McKenzie,** John W '92 (Kastner W&W,LLC) -3480 W Market -Ste 300 -Akron 44333 **Fx:**867-3786

(513) 737-5180 ..**McKenzie,** Kyle B '94 (McKenzie & S) -315 Maple Av -Hamilton 45011

(614) 227-2000 ..**McKenzie,** Myra L '02 %Porter WM&A LLP -41 S High -Columbus 43215 **Fx:**227-2100

(740) 354-8602 ..**McKenzie,** Ronald E '75 -Bx1363 -Portsmouth 45662

(312) 347-7600 ..**McKenzie,** Steven Q '98 Lawyers Comm for Better Housing -220 S State -Ste 1700 -Chicago, IL 60604 **Fx:**347-7604

(614) 621-2605 ..**McKenzie,** William Locke Jr. '75 -380 S 5th -Ste 2 -Columbus 43215

(216) 241-5310 ..**McKeon,** Sheila A '84 (Gallagher SF&N) -1501 Euclid Av -6th Fl -Cleveland 44115 **Fx:**241-1608

(937) 372-8055 ..**McKeown,** Noel K '72 (Miller FM&B) -20 King Av -Bx610 -Xenia 45385

(614) 466-2980 ..**McKew,** Barry D '80 Atty Gen -30 E Broad -Columbus 43215 **Fx:**728-9470

(216) 523-8165 ..**McKew,** Walter M '72 -1500 W 3rd -Cleveland 44113

(740) 373-1441 ..**McKim,** Janet F '77 %Washington Cnty Pub Def -330 4th -Marietta 45750

(614) 255-1140 ..**McKinlay,** Amy M '96 RC Harbold & Assoc -500 S Front -Ste 1140 -Columbus 43215

(330) 493-1570 ..**McKinley,** Kathleen K '90 (Macala BM&G,LLC) -4150 Belden Vllg NW -Ste 604 -Canton 44718 **Fx:**493-7042

(614) 410-6740 ..**McKinley,** Kristen E '94 %Contract Cnsl -470 Olde Worthngtn Rd -Ste 200 -Westerville 43082

(419) 673-1128 ..**McKinley,** Paul N Jr. '75 McKinley & C -936 E Franklin -Bx207 -Kenton 43326

(216) 931-6000 ..**McKinley,** Stacey L '97 %Ulmer & B LLP -1300 E 9th -Ste 900 Penton Media Bldg -Cleveland 44114 **Fx:**931-6001

(419) 774-5573 ..**McKinley,** William S '98 Richland Cnty Dom Rltns Ct -50 Park Av E -Mansfield 44902

(937) 393-1102 ..**McKinney,** Carroll V '60 -131 E Beech -Bx675 -Hillsboro 45133

(937) 461-9000 ..**McKinney,** Charles A '87 -20 W Monument Av -Dayton 45402 **Fx:**461-9640

(513) 721-0200 ..**McKinney,** Daniel H III '59 McKinney & N Co,LPA -15 E 8th -Cincinnati 45202 **Fx:**632-5898

(330) 792-1063 ..**McKinney,** Debra J '92 Industrial Commssn of OH -242 Fed Plz W -Ste 303 -Youngstown 44503

(330) 273-9710 ..**McKinney,** Karin H '86 -4628 Dogwood Dr -Brunswick 44212

(216) 368-6360 ..**McKinney,** Louise E '78 CWRU Law Schl -11075 East Blvd -Cleveland 44106

(513) 721-0200 ..**McKinney & Namei Co,LPA** -15 E 8th -Cincinnati 45202 **Fx:**632-5898

(419) 447-1632 ..**McKinney,** Samuel R Jr. '75 Seneca Cnty CSEA -Bx377 -Tiffin 44883

(740) 387-1120 ..**McKinniss,** Ted M '76 OfCnsl Kegler BH&R -250 Exec Dr -Ste B -Marion 43302 **Fx:**387-3630

(330) 864-3100 ..**McKinzie,** Timothy D '93 T McKinzie -529 White Pond Dr -Akron 44320

(614) 764-7440 ..**McKirahan,** Jay F '72 OfCnsl Whann & Assoc -6300 Frantz Rd -Dublin 43017

(419) 586-7328 ..**McKirnan,** Kevin M '76 City Law Dir -110½ W Market -Rm 207 Wyckoff Bldg -Bx417 -Celina 45822

      McKnight, Brian J '84 -(Address Unavailable)

(740) 439-5900 ..**McKnight,** Charles E '89 -121 W 8th -Cambridge 43725

(216) 622-8200 ..**McKnight,** Douglas B '00 %Calfee H&G LLP -800 Superior Av -Ste 1400 -Cleveland 44114 **Fx:**241-0816

(513) 425-7899 ..**McKnight,** Patrick E '97 Middletown Law Dept -1 Donham Plz -Middletown 45042

(216) 765-1240 ..**McKown,** Michael O '77 The American Coal Co -29325 Chagrin -Ste 300 -Pepper Pike 44122

(419) 342-4261 ..**McKown,** Neil A '78 (McKown & M,LPA) -10 Mansfld Av -Shelby 44875 **Fx:**347-5723

(330) 393-8200 ..**McLain,** David H '92 -144 N Park Av -Ste 301 -Warren 44481

(608) 231-4000 ..**McLain,** Michael P '84 Cuna & Affiliates -5710 Mineral Pnt Rd -Madison, WI 53705

(330) 372-3483 ..**McLain,** William P '58 -2770 Dartmoor Dr NE -Warren 44483

(440) 248-7906 ..**McLandrich,** John T '83 (Mazanec R&R Co,LPA) -34305 Solon Rd -Ste 100 -Cleveland 44139 **Fx:**248-8861

(614) 228-8833 ..**McLane,** Michael J '87 Cincinnati Ins Co -140 E Town -Ste 1015 -Columbus 43215

(330) 364-1811 ..**McLane,** William G '69 -138 2nd NW -New Philadelphia 44663 **Fx:**343-7511

(312) 655-1500 ..**McLaren,** Richard W Jr. '73 (Welsh & K Ltd) -120 S Riverside Plz -22nd Fl -Chicago, IL 60606 **Fx:**655-1501

(770) 644-3228 ..**McLary,** Steve M '71 Graphic Packaging Intl,Inc -814 Lvngstn Ct SE -Marietta, GA 30067

(419) 327-3314 ..**McLaughlin,** Bruce D '73 Lucas Cnty Children Srvcs Brd -705 Adams -Toledo 43624

      McLaughlin, Christopher M '04 -(Address Unavailable)

(303) 399-6037 ..**McLaughlin,** George E '80 (McDermott H&M) -1890 Gaylord -Denver, CO 80206

(216) 241-8230 ..**McLaughlin,** John B '72 Bd Mntl Rtrdtn -1275 Lakeside Av -Cleveland 44114

(513) 381-9200 ..**McLaughlin,** John F '91 (Rendigs FK&D,LLP) -One W 4th -Ste 900 -Cincinnati 45202 **Fx:**381-9206

(513) 651-6800 ..**McLaughlin,** Karen M '81 Cnsl Frost BT LLC -201 E 5th -2200 PNC Ctr -Cincinnati 45202 **Fx:**651-6981

(330) 376-9691 ..**McLaughlin,** Kelly Lyn '87 -441 Wolf Ledges Pkwy -Ste 302 -Akron 44311

(216) 623-0900 ..**McLaughlin & McCaffrey, LLP** -1111 Superior Av E -Ste 1350 Eaton Ctr -Cleveland 44114 **Fx:**623-0935

(614) 583-7610 ..**McLaughlin,** Patricia A '99 Cnsl Amer Elec Pwr Co -1 Riverside Plz -Columbus 43215

(216) 623-0900 ..**McLaughlin,** Patrick M '76 (McLaughlin & M,LLP) -1111 Superior Av E -Ste 1350 Eaton Ctr -Cleveland 44114 **Fx:**623-0935

(330) 744-4481 ..**McLaughlin,** Richard P '62 (McLauglin & M) -500 City Centre One -Bx507 -Youngstown 44501 **Fx:**744-0444

(513) 752-2111 ..**McLaughlin,** Robert C '97 %D Moore Jr & Co,LPA -4355 Ferguson Dr -Ste 200 -Cincinnati 45245 **Fx:**753-2354

(216) 221-2323 ..**McLaughlin,** Ronald L '86 -14701 Detroit Av -Ste 757 -Lakewood 44107

(440) 930-4001 ..**McLaughlin,** Russell T '74 %Baumgartner & O -5455 Detroit Rd (Rte 254) -Sheffield Village 44054 **Fx:**934-7205

(614) 462-3194 ..**McLaughlin,** Tara L '00 Franklin Cnty Pub Def -373 S High -12th Fl -Columbus 43215

(614) 583-6731 ..**McLaughlin,** Tracy A '97 Amer Elec Pwr -Bx16036 -Columbus 43216

(330) 744-4481 ..**McLauglin & McNally** -500 City Centre One -Bx507 -Youngstown 44501 **Fx:**744-0444

(330) 376-5300 ..**McLean,** Hillary B '04 %Buckingham D&B,LLP -50 S Main -Bx1500 -Akron 44309 **Fx:**258-6559

(513) 381-9200 ..**McLean,** James E Jr. '90 Rendigs FK&D,LLP -One W 4th -Ste 900 -Cincinnati 45202 **Fx:**381-9206

(614) 462-3555 ..**McLean,** Michael J '99 Franklin Cnty Pros -373 S High -Columbus 43215

(614) 277-6598 ..**McLean,** Patricia A '00 Nationwide Ins -1 Nationwide Plz -Columbus 43215

(330) 688-7908 ..**McLeland,** Joseph C '64 -Bx336 -Munroe Falls 44262 **Fx:**688-8097

(740) 454-2545 ..**McLendon,** Jeremy M '02 %Micheli BN Co,LPA -3808 James Ct -Ste 2 -Bx788 -Zanesville 43702

(614) 466-6700 ..**McLennan,** Bruce A '87 Tax Appeals -30 E Broad -Columbus 43215 **Fx:**644-5196

(419) 224-0066 ..**McLeod,** Katy J '89 -Bx1032 -Lima 45802

(614) 228-1717 ..**McLeod,** Mark A '87 -471 E Broad -Ste 1900 -Columbus 43215

(937) 222-1242 ..**McLeran,** William T Jr. '49 -255 N Main -Dayton 45402 **Fx:**228-2165

(614) 232-9132 ..**McLeskey,** Waymon B II '81 -5 E Long -Ste 405 -Columbus 43215 **Fx:**232-9135

(614) 841-1918 ..**McLinden,** Peter M '97 Cnsl OH Cncl 8 AFSCME AFL-CIO -6800 N High -Worthington 43085 **Fx:**430-7960

(614) 882-2327 ..**McLoughlin,** William J '86 (Metz & B) -33 E Schrock Rd -Westerville 43081

(413) 744-2483 ..**McLymont,** Virginia B '83 MassMutual Fin Grp -1295 State -MIP N-205 -Springfield, MA 01111

(513) 870-2000 ..**McMackin,** Thomas K '80 Cincinnati Ins Co -Bx145496 -Cincinnati 45250

(216) 622-8660 ..**McMahon,** Brian A '94 (Calfee H&G LLP) -800 Superior Av -Ste 1400 -Cleveland 44114 **Fx:**241-0816

(419) 241-9000 ..**McMahon,** Brian N '78 (Shumaker L&K,LLP) -1000 Jackson -Toledo 43624 **Fx:**241-6894

(216) 241-8040 ..**McMahon,** Carl G '75 -526 Superior Av -Ste 410 -Cleveland 44114

(804) 845-0911 ..**McMahon,** David H '67 1st Colony Life Ins Co -700 Main -Lynchburg, VA 24504

(216) 621-1312 ..**McMahon DeGulis Hoffmann & Lombardi LLP** -812 Huron Rd -Ste 650 The Caxton Bldg -Cleveland 44115 **Fx:**621-0577

(330) 375-0126 ..**McMahon DeGulis Hoffmann & Lombardi LLP** -450 Grant -Akron 44311 **Fx:**375-1590

(202) 267-0096 ..**McMahon,** James D III '03 US Coast Guard -2100 2nd SW -Washington, DC 20593

(612) 605-4188 ..**McMahon,** John A '85 Defense Contract Mgmt -1 Fed Dr -Saint Paul, MN 55111

(419) 254-9000 ..**McMahon,** John W '94 -316 N Mich -#600 -Toledo 43624

(216) 566-5639 ..**McMahon,** Louis L '96 (Thompson H LLP) -127 Pub Sq -3900 Key Ctr -Cleveland 44114 **Fx:**566-5800

(513) 622-5502 ..**McMahon,** Mary P '92 SrCnsl Procter & Gamble -8700 Mason Mntgmry Rd -Mason 45040

      McMahon, Maureen B '99 -1777 Coventry Rd -Columbus 43212

(216) 621-1312 ..**McMahon,** Michael S '81 (McMahon DH&L LLP) -812 Huron Rd -Ste 650 The Caxton Bldg -Cleveland 44115 **Fx:**621-0577

(740) 774-2142 ..**McMahon,** Paige J '88 (Spetnagel & M) -42 E 5th -Chillicothe 45601

(513) 533-9898 ..**McMahon,** Robert A '95 (Eberly MH,LLC) -3700 Eastern Av -Cincinnati 45226

(216) 621-1000 ..**McMahon,** Seamus J '03 %Moscarino & T,LLP -1422 Euclid Av -Hanna Bldg Ste 630 -Cleveland 44115 **Fx:**622-1556

(859) 371-3600 ..**McMain,** Michael J '89 (Busald FZ) -226 Main -Bx6910 -Florence, KY 41022

(513) 241-3685 ..**McManus,** Barbara J '82 OfCnsl White G&M Co,LPA -1 W 4th -Ste 1700 -Cincinnati 45202 **Fx:**241-2399

(513) 946-9460 ..**McManus,** John F '80 Hamilton Cnty Juv Ct -800 Bway -Cincinnati 45202 **Fx:**946-9217

(614) 466-2766 ..**McManus,** John K '86 Atty Gen -30 E Broad -Columbus 43215 **Fx:**644-1926

(248) 646-5100 ..**McManus,** John M '99 (Moffett & D,PC) -255 E Brown -Ste 340 -Birmingham, MI 48009

(419) 242-1255 ..**McManus,** Kevin P '88 (McManus & M) -709 Mad Av -303 Bell Bldg -Toledo 43624

(419) 242-1255 ..**McManus,** Martin J '87 (McManus & M) -709 Mad Av -303 Bell Bldg -Toledo 43624

(216) 241-2838 .. **McManus,** Robert P '78 (Taft S&H LLP) -200 Pub Sq
-3500 BP Twr -Cleveland 44114 **Fx:**241-3707

(412) 281-8541 .. **McMaster,** Lori E '86 %Cain A&M,PC -2 Chatham Ctr -Ste 1410
-Pittsburgh, PA 15219

(216) 781-1212 .. **McMenamin,** Michael T '68 (Walter & H LLP) -1301 E 9th
-Ste 3500 -Cleveland 44114 **Fx:**575-0911

(440) 998-1110 .. **McMillan,** Debra S '85 %Ashtabula Cnty CSEA -Bx1650
-Ashtabula 44005 **Fx:**998-1538

(216) 595-8222 .. **McMillan,** Kevin R '98 %Kabat M&S -25550 Chagrin Blvd -Ste 403
-Beachwood 44122

(740) 587-4150 .. **McMillan,** Lori A '01 Paramount Finl Grp -4009 Columbus Rd SW
-Granville 43023

(216) 622-8200 .. **McMillan,** Ronald M '00 %Calfee H&G LLP -800 Superior Av
-Ste 1400 -Cleveland 44114 **Fx:**241-0816

(513) 721-1311 .. **McMillan,** Shelby M '97 %Reminger & R -7 W 7th -Ste 1990
-Cincinnati 45202 **Fx:**721-2553

(216) 522-7453 .. **McMillan,** Solvita A '78 EEOC-CLDO -1660 W 2nd -Ste 850
-Cleveland 44113

(216) 443-8400 .. **McMillen,** Nancy G '82 Cuyahoga Cnty Juv Ct -1910 Carnegie Av
-Cleveland 44115

(937) 225-4892 .. **McMillin,** Judson G '02 Montgomery Cnty Pros/CSEA -14 W 4th
-Ste 510 -Dayton 45402
McMillin, Larry H '76 -105 Rachel Dr -New Richmond 45157

(765) 647-4105 .. **McMillin,** Lowell C '74 (Mullin M&R) -814 Main -Bx68
-Brookville, IN 47012 **Fx:**647-6401

(216) 443-7800 .. **McMonagle,** Christopher N '97 Cuyahoga Cnty Pros -1200 Ontario
-8th Fl -Cleveland 44113 **Fx:**698-2270

(216) 479-6100 .. **McMonagle,** James J '70 OfCnsl Vorys SS&P LLP -1375 E 9th
-Ste 2100 One Cleve Ctr -Cleveland 44114 **Fx:**479-6060

(216) 575-0777 .. **McMonagle,** Matthew A '04 %Kelley & F,LLP -1300 E 9th
-Ste 1901 -Cleveland 44114 **Fx:**575-0799

(216) 622-8200 .. **McMullen,** Daniel J '83 (Calfee H&G LLP) -800 Superior Av
-Ste 1400 -Cleveland 44114 **Fx:**241-0816

(513) 946-9200 .. **McMullen,** Martin E '67 Hamilton Cnty Cmn Pleas Ct -800 Bway
-Cincinnati 45202

(937) 378-4151 .. **McMullen,** Mary G '96 Brown Cnty Pros -200 E Cherry
-Georgetown 45121

(856) 968-7263 .. **McMullen,** Robert G '81 Cooper Health Sys -3 Cooper Plz
-Ste 316 -Camden, NJ 08103

(973) 992-4800 .. **McMurdy,** Keith R '93 (Grotta G&H,PA) -75 Lvngstn Av
-Roseland, NJ 07068 **Fx:**992-9125

(513) 651-6800 .. **McMurray,** Kevin N '89 (Frost BT LLC) -201 E 5th -2200 PNC Ctr
-Cincinnati 45202 **Fx:**651-6981

(925) 924-2138 .. **McMurray,** Kevin S '95 Cnsl Shaklee Corp -4747 Willow Rd
-Pleasanton, CA 94588 **Fx:**924-2155

(937) 865-1464 .. **McMurry,** Donna M '88 Lexis/Nexis -Bx933 -Dayton 45401

(859) 341-1881 .. **McMurtry,** Todd V '93 %Deters B&L,PSC -2701 Turkeyfoot Rd
-207 Thomas More Pkwy -Crestview Hills, KY 41017 **Fx:**341-1469

(513) 977-8200 .. **McNabb,** Suzanne C '00 %Dinsmore & S LLP -255 E 5th
-Ste 1900 -Cincinnati 45202 **Fx:**977-8141

(513) 381-0656 .. **McNair,** Brian E '86 Kohnen & P LLP -201 E 5th -Ste 800
-Cincinnati 45202 **Fx:**381-5823

(614) 224-2678 .. **McNair,** Darren A '02 %Kemp SR&L Co,LPA -88 W Mound
-Columbus 43215 **Fx:**469-7170

(216) 566-1600 .. **McNair,** Eben O IV '83 (Schwarzwald & M) -1300 E 9th -Ste 616
-Cleveland 44114 **Fx:**566-1814

(440) 576-3831 .. **McNair,** Robert M '70 (McNair & G Co,LPA) -35 W Jffrsn
-Jefferson 44047 **Fx:**576-7167

(330) 744-4481 .. **McNally,** John A III '71 (McLauglin & M) -500 City Centre One
-Bx507 -Youngstown 44501 **Fx:**744-0444

(330) 742-8874 .. **McNally,** John A IV '96 Law Dept -26 S Phelps
-Youngstown 44503

(513) 381-6600 .. **McNally,** John W Jr. '74 (Jacobs KS&M) -1014 Vine -Ste 2300
-Cincinnati 45202

(216) 861-5225 .. **McNally,** Kimberly D '98 Guardian Title -1370 W 6th -Ste 300
-Cleveland 44113

(513) 752-5466 .. **McNally,** Robert A '66 -3631 Parfore Ct -Cincinnati 45245

(440) 333-1277 .. **McNally,** Thomas G '78 -19800 Ctr Ridge Rd -Rocky River 44116

(614) 464-2770 .. **McNamara,** Dennis W '76 -88 E Broad -Ste 1350
-Columbus 43215

(330) 699-6703 .. **McNamara & Freeman Co, LPA** -12370 Cleveland Av -Bx867
-Uniontown 44685 **Fx:**699-4803

(440) 255-9100 .. **McNamara Hanrahan Callender & Loxterman** -8440 Station
-Mentor 44060

(614) 461-5788 .. **McNamara,** James D '74 -326 S High -Ste 300 -Columbus 43215

(419) 241-1200 .. **McNamara,** Joseph V '03 %Cooper & W,LPA -900 Adams
-Toledo 43624 **Fx:**242-5675

(614) 228-6131 .. **McNamara,** Keith '53 OfCnsl McNamara & M,LLP -88 E Broad
-Ste 1250 -Columbus 43215 **Fx:**228-6126

(216) 515-1660 .. **McNamara,** Marislynn J '93 (Frantz W LLP) -127 Pub Sq
-2500 Key Center -Cleveland 44114 **Fx:**515-1650

(216) 621-0200 .. **McNamara,** Michael P Jr. '96 (Baker & H LLP) -1900 E 9th
-Ste 3200 -Cleveland 44114 **Fx:**696-0740

(330) 699-6703 .. **McNamara,** Robert F '77 McNamara & F Co,LPA
-12370 Cleveland Av -Bx867 -Uniontown 44685 **Fx:**699-4803

(603) 740-2840 .. **McNamara,** Sharon R '86 Wentworth Douglass Hospital
-Central Av -Dover, NH 03820

(216) 731-1400 .. **McNamara,** Thomas R '79 -22700 Shore Ctr Dr -Ste 206
-Cleveland 44123

(440) 255-9100 .. **McNamara,** Walter J III '69 (McNamara HC&L) -8440 Station
-Mentor 44060

(614) 466-2980 .. **McNamara,** Walter J IV '02 Atty Gen -30 E Broad -Columbus
43215 **Fx:**728-9470

(440) 282-6431 .. **McNamee,** Brian F '88 McNamee & M -5373 Oberlin Av
-Lorain 44053

(937) 427-1367 .. **McNamee,** Cynthia P '91 %McNamee & M,PLL
-2625 Cmmns Blvd -Beavercreek 45431 **Fx:**427-1369

(937) 427-9650 .. **McNamee,** David M '97 (Stone & M Co,LPA) -42 Woodcroft Trl
-Ste A -Beavercreek 45430 **Fx:**427-9659

(440) 572-3420 .. **McNamee,** Jeffrey M '94 (McNamee & Co) -13702 Pearl Rd
-Strongsville 44136 **Fx:**572-9493

(937) 427-1367 .. **McNamee,** Michael P '90 (McNamee & M,PLL) -2625 Cmmns Blvd
-Beavercreek 45431 **Fx:**427-1369

(614) 466-4395 .. **McNamee,** Thomas W '79 Atty Gen -150 E Gay -Columbus 43215
Fx:644-8764

(614) 224-7291 .. **McNeal,** Earl D '92 -330 S High -Columbus 43215

(419) 634-5791 .. **McNeal,** Jan C '66 CP VanDyne -Huber Bldg -Ada 45810

(614) 451-2151 .. **McNeal,** Kathleen K '82 Natl Church Residences -2335 N Bank Dr
-Columbus 43220

(216) 621-9870 .. **McNeal Schick Archibald & Biro Co, LPA** -123 W Prospect Av
-Ste 250 Van Sweringen Arcade -Cleveland 44115 **Fx:**522-1112

(614) 227-2000 .. **McNealey,** J Jeffrey '69 (Porter WM&A LLP) -41 S High
-Columbus 43215 **Fx:**227-2100

(614) 469-8000 .. **McNees Wallace & Nurick,LLC** -21 E State -17th Fl
-Columbus 43215 **Fx:**469-4653
McNeil, Christopher B '89 -Bx595 -Worthington 43085

(513) 352-3334 .. **McNeil,** Julia Rita '89 Law Dept -801 Plum -Rm 214
-Cincinnati 45202 **Fx:**352-1515

(330) 466-6103 .. **McNeil,** Keith P '81 OH Civ Rghts Cmmssn -161 S High
-205 Akron Govt Bldg -Akron 44308

(513) 621-8210 .. **McNeil,** Michael D '91 (Drew & W Co,LPA) -1 W 4th -Ste 2400
-Cincinnati 45202 **Fx:**621-5444

(505) 572-7217 .. **McNeil,** Robert C '98 USAF -490 1st -Ste 1940
-Holloman Air Force Base, NM 88330

(937) 773-3212 .. **McNeil,** William B '64 (McCulloch FF&G Co,LPA) -123 Market
-Bx910 -Piqua 45356 **Fx:**773-9672

(614) 228-1541 .. **McNellie,** Elizabeth A '90 (Baker & H LLP) -65 E State -Ste 2100
-Columbus 43215 **Fx:**228-1544

(216) 360-7200 .. **McNellie,** Richard L '75 (Carlisle MRK&U Co,LPA)
-24755 Chagrin Blvd -Ste 200 -Cleveland 44122 **Fx:**360-7210

(614) 837-2308 .. **McNemar,** Joseph G '78 CMS East,Inc -5802 Elder Rd
-Canal Winchester 43110
McNerney, Thomas '03 -(Address Unavailable)

(937) 461-5310 .. **McNew,** Michael A '99 %Doll J&F -111 W 1st -Ste 1100
-Dayton 45402 **Fx:**461-7219

(614) 444-8777 .. **McNichols,** David J '83 (DeSanto & M) -887 S High
-Columbus 43206

(330) 420-0140 .. **McNicol,** Timothy J '91 Columbiana Cnty Pros -105 S Market
-Lisbon 44432 **Fx:**424-0944

(614) 449-8282 .. **McNinch,** Deborah L '91 %Joseph & J -931 S Front -Columbus
43206 **Fx:**449-8287

(614) 224-1244 .. **McNitt,** Robert M '82 -465 Waterbury Ct -Ste A -Columbus 43230
Fx:583-1243

(330) 753-2261 .. **McNulty,** Michael J '74 Mun Ct Judge -576 W Park Av
-Barberton 44203

(202) 514-1210 .. **McNulty,** Michael J '83 US DOJ -Bx7611 -Washington, DC 20044

(419) 244-6864 .. **McNulty,** Michael S '94 -316 N Mich -Ste 600 -Toledo 43624
McNutt, Patrick T '04 -(Address Unavailable)

(937) 865-6800 .. **McPeek,** Anna L '85 Lexis/Nexis -Bx933 -Dayton 45401

(513) 421-6630 .. **McPeek,** Bradley D '99 %Lindhorst & D Co,LPA -312 Walnut
-Ste 2300 -Cincinnati 45202

(513) 651-6800 .. **McPeek,** Monica Hart '99 %Frost BT LLC -201 E 5th
-2200 PNC Ctr -Cincinnati 45202 **Fx:**651-6981

(704) 715-3536 .. **McPhee,** Joel E Jr. '93 First Union Corp -201 S Tryon
-Ste 300 NC1013 -Charlotte, NC 28288

(513) 651-6800 .. **McPherson,** David J '86 Cnsl Frost BT LLC -201 E 5th
-2200 PNC Ctr -Cincinnati 45202 **Fx:**651-6981

(614) 228-1128 .. **McPherson,** Joel S '93 J Wichman -500 S Front -Ste 970
-Columbus 43215

(614) 462-3118 .. **McPhillips,** Michael C '95 Franklin Cnty Cmn Pleas Ct -375 S High
-Columbus 43215 **Fx:**462-6292

(216) 481-6258 .. **McPhillips,** Michael D '90 -20531 Crystal Av -Ste 1300
-Euclid 44123

(419) 826-5636 .. **McQuade,** Colin J '80 Fulton Cnty Ct Estrn Div -204 S Main
-Swanton 43558

(419) 826-0055 .. **McQuade,** Daniel P '67 (McQuades Co,LPA) -Lincoln at Bway
-Bx237 -Swanton 43558

(216) 592-5000 .. **McQuade,** Rachel M '95 %Tucker E&W LLP -925 Euclid Av
-1150 Huntngtn Bldg -Cleveland 44115 **Fx:**592-5009
McQuade, Richard B Jr. '65 -2036 Cntry Rd -F -Swanton 43558

(513) 232-0903 .. **McQuade,** Shannon L '96 -973 Artwood Dr -Cincinnati 45230

(614) 461-1516 .. **McQuain,** Larry G '96 -169 E Lvngstn Av -Columbus 43215

(330) 376-2700 .. **McQueen,** Aaron E '97 %Roetzel & A,LPA -222 S Main
-Akron 44308 **Fx:**376-4577

(330) 455-0173 .. **McQueen,** Jill C '86 (Day KRW&R,Ltd) -200 Market Av N -Ste 300
-Bx24213 -Canton 44701 **Fx:**455-2633

(336) 475-3228 .. **McQueen,** Joetta I '87 -32 Trade -Thomasville, NC 27360
Fx:475-3230

(330) 497-0700 .. **McQueen,** Karen S '84 (Krugliak WG&D Co,LPA)
-4775 Munson NW -Bx36963 -Canton 44735 **Fx:**497-4020

(440) 331-2328 .. **McQuillan,** Jean M '80 -21612 Kenwood Av -Rocky River 44116

(937) 865-6800 .. **McQuillan,** Suzanne T '95 Lexis/Nexis -Bx933 -Dayton 45401

(937) 226-1212 .. **McQuiston,** Jeffrey R '76 Skelton MG&H -130 W 2nd -Ste 450
-Dayton 45402

(614) 901-8380 .. **McQuown,** Cara M '00 %B Jeffries -1091 Marie Lou Dr -Bx2969
-Westerville 43086 **Fx:**901-8381

(614) 227-2000 .. **McQuown,** Richard C '86 (Porter WM&A LLP) -41 S High
-Columbus 43215 **Fx:**227-2100

(937) 223-8177 .. **McQuown,** Terence P '00 %Coolidge WW&L -33 W 1st -Ste 600
-Dayton 45402 **Fx:**223-6705

(302) 739-4247 .. **McRae,** Arnetta '78 Public Srvc Comm -861 Silver Lk Blvd
-Ste 100 -Dover, DE 19904 **Fx:**739-4849

(614) 221-1919 .. **McShane,** Eugene F '71 -660 S High -Ste 200 -Columbus 43215

(937) 512-1572 .. **McShea,** Michael B '89 Us District Ct -200 W Second -#810
-Dayton 45402

(440) 247-7800 .. **McSherry,** James C '87 (McSherry & Co) -178 E Wshngtn
-Chagrin Falls 44022 **Fx:**247-7801

(513) 852-6087 .. **McSherry,** Jeffrey P '91 (Wood & L LLP) -600 Vine -Ste 2500
-Cincinnati 45202 **Fx:**852-6087

(937) 225-4464 .. **McSherry,** Shauna K '79 2nd Dist Ct of Appls -41 N Perry
-Rm 515 -Bx972 -Dayton 45422

(212) 952-0100 .. **McSwain,** William T '76 US Aviation Underwriters,Inc -199 Water
-New York, NY 10038

(815) 432-4450 .. **McTaggart,** Jane A '84 -123 S 4th -Watseka, IL 60970
Fx:432-4451

McTague, Jerome A '01 -19740 W State Rte 105 -Elmore 43416

(614) 263-7000 .. **McTigue,** Donald J '79 -3886 N High -Columbus 43214
Fx:263-7078

(513) 621-8700 .. **McTigue,** Edward J '79 -601 Main -3rd Fl -Cincinnati 45202

(937) 223-5200 .. **McTigue,** Terrence P Jr. '93 Flanagan LH&S -318 W 4th
-Dayton 45402 Fx:223-3335

(614) 444-3900 .. **McVay,** Kirk A '95 -755 S High -Columbus 43206 Fx:444-9086

(419) 247-1009 .. **McWeeny,** Philip '65 Owens-Illinois,Inc -One SeaGate -8 OSG
-Toledo 43666

(740) 532-4333 .. **McWhorter,** Donald L II '87 (Lambert M&B) -215 S 4th -Bx725
-Ironton 45638

McWilliam, John L '86 -333 N Summit -5th Fl -Toledo 43604

(216) 479-8500 .. **McWilliams,** Douglas A '94 (Squire S&D LLP) -127 Pub Sq
-4900 Key Twr -Cleveland 44114 Fx:479-8780

(419) 249-7100 .. **Meacham,** Ruth A '81 (Marshall & M,LLC) -Four Seagate -8th Fl
-Toledo 43604 Fx:249-7151

(614) 995-5618 .. **Mead,** Nancy L '87 OH Dept of Job & Fam Srvcs -145 S Front
-Columbus 43215

(419) 738-9688 .. **Meade,** Darren L '94 Auglaize Cnty Pros -201 Willipie -Ste G4
-Bx1992 -Wapakoneta 45895

(216) 696-3327 .. **Meade,** Karen K '83 -1370 W 6th -Ste 208 -Cleveland 44113

(412) 394-7932 .. **Meaden,** Laura A '87 Cnsl Jones DR&P -500 Grant
-Ste 3100 One Mellon Bk Ctr -Pittsburgh, PA 15219 Fx:394-7959

(419) 213-4700 .. **Meader,** Jevne C '00 %Lucas Cnty Pros -Adams & Erie
-Lucas Cnty Cthse -Toledo 43624

Meader, Robert H '04 -(Address Unavailable)

(330) 867-5310 .. **Meador,** Carl E '66 -2770 W Market -Akron 44333 Fx:867-8367

(216) 787-3094 .. **Meador,** Eugene B '82 %Atty Gen -615 W Superior Av -11th Fl
-Cleveland 44113 Fx:787-3480

(440) 461-9010 .. **Meador,** Garnett R '86 Fugen Capital Co -Bx24632
-Cleveland 44124

Meadows, Gene '89 -5761 Hubbards Brnch Rd
-Huntington, WV 25704

(513) 777-2222 .. **Meadows,** Jeffrey C '97 Lyons & L Co,LPA
-8310 Prnctn-Glendale Rd -Ste B -West Chester 45069

(937) 293-2392 .. **Meadows,** Jerry A '75 (Lair O&M) -580 Lincoln Park Blvd -Ste 111
-Dayton 45429

(404) 331-2829 .. **Meadows,** Kenneth D '69 NLRB -233 Pchtree NE
-Ste 1000 Harris Twr -Atlanta, GA 30303

(513) 281-2339 .. **Meadows,** Mary T '92 -1421 Locust -#1 -Cincinnati 45206

(513) 943-9278 .. **Meadows,** Perry '01 -841 Castlebay Dr -Cincinnati 45245

(216) 687-1311 .. **Meadows,** William A '86 (Reminger & R) -101 Prospect Av W
-1400 Mdlnd Bldg -Cleveland 44115 Fx:687-1841

(513) 381-9200 .. **Meagher,** James K '60 (Rendigs FK&D,LLP) -One W 4th -Ste 900
-Cincinnati 45202 Fx:381-9206

(336) 424-6145 .. **Meagher,** Laura C '89 VF Corp -105 Corp Ctr Blvd
-Greensboro, NC 27408

(614) 921-2070 .. **Meagher,** Stephen W '82 SrCnsl COA,Inc -3699 Paragon Dr
-Columbus 43228 Fx:921-2079

(505) 255-0202 .. **Meagle,** Shay E '96 (Puccini & M PA) -8015 Mtn Rd Pl NE
-Ste 200 -Albuquerque, NM 87110 Fx:255-8726

(216) 291-3441 .. **Meaker,** Mary A '84 -3621 Langton Rd -Cleveland 44121

(614) 752-1200 .. **Mealey,** Diane L '01 %Parole Brd -1050 Fwy Dr N
-Columbus 43229

(340) 773-3305 .. **Meaney,** James A '77 (Alkon M&H) -2115 Queen
-Christiansted, VI 00820 Fx:773-4491

(216) 348-5400 .. **Meaney,** Michael J '77 (McDonald H Co,LPA) -600 Superior Av E
-Ste 2100 -Cleveland 44114 Fx:348-5474

(440) 964-2700 .. **Meaney,** Michael P '87 C Altier -3503 Carpenter Rd
-Ashtabula 44004 Fx:964-7710

Meaney, Thomas P Jr. '53 -19551 Edgecliff Dr -Euclid 44119

(614) 485-2010 .. **Means** Bichimer Burkholder & Baker Co,LPA -2006 Kenny Rd
-Columbus 43221 Fx:485-2019

(740) 354-3643 .. **Mearan,** Michael H '71 (M Mearan,LLC) -812 6th
-Portsmouth 45662 Fx:353-5293

(216) 621-0200 .. **Mearns,** Geoffrey S '99 (Baker & H LLP) -1900 E 9th -Ste 3200
-Cleveland 44114 Fx:696-0740

(216) 687-2344 .. **Mearns,** Geoffrey S '99 CSU-Marshall Cllg of Law -2121 Euclid Av
-LB138 -Cleveland 44115 Fx:687-6881

(614) 791-5181 .. **Mears,** Rhonda L '01 Parsons Brinckerhoff Ohio,Inc
-6235 Enterprise Ct -Dublin 43016

(614) 466-3998 .. **Meas,** Loi L '00 Unemploymt Comp Commssn -145 S Front
-Bx182299 -Columbus 43218

(513) 721-3114 .. **Mebs,** Frederick W '52 -1210 Sycamore (rear) -Cincinnati 45202

(513) 353-1773 .. **Mechley,** Albert Jr. '65 (A Mechley Jr,Co LPA)
-7330 Eagle Creek Rd -Cincinnati 45247

(513) 475-9883 .. **Mechley,** Braden A '61 -670 Windings Ln -Cincinnati 45220

(614) 464-5754 .. **Mechling,** William C '83 Cntrl Benefits Mutual Ins -716
Mt Airyshire Blvd -Columbus 43235

(615) 298-8209 .. **Mecklenborg,** Daniel P '81 Ingram Barge Co -4400 Hrdng Rd
-1 Belle Meade Pl -Nashville, TN 37202

(513) 481-9800 .. **Mecklenborg,** Robert P '78 (Hyle & M Co,LPA) -3050 Harrison Av
-Cincinnati 45211 Fx:481-9592

(614) 236-1950 .. **Meckler,** Marcia L '75 -2369 E Main -Columbus 43209

(440) 324-5353 .. **Meckler,** Stephen G '65 (Spike & M,LLP) -1551 W River Rd N
-Elyria 44035 Fx:324-6529

(216) 397-8800 .. **Meckler,** Theodore E '75 -1991 Lee Rd -Ste 203
-Cleveland Heights 44118

(937) 298-2811 .. **Meckstroth,** Alan F '60 (Jacox M&J) -2310 Far Hills Bldg
-Dayton 45419 Fx:298-7418

(513) 721-8808 .. **Meckstroth,** James J '94 %J Meckstroth Jr -22 W 9th
-Cincinnati 45202

(513) 721-8808 .. **Meckstroth,** John R Jr. '81 -22 W 9th -Cincinnati 45202

(937) 865-6800 .. **Meder,** Frank C '99 Lexis/Nexis -Bx933 -Dayton 45401

(440) 439-1616 .. **Medford,** Cecil L '86 Halex Co -23901 Aurora Rd -Bedford Heights
44146

(412) 560-7017 .. **Medice,** Mark L '97 %Morgan L&B -1 Oxford Ctr -32nd Fl
-Pittsburgh, PA 15219

(216) 696-8730 .. **Medley,** Michael J '04 %Amin & T LLP -1900 E 9th
-24th Fl Natl City Ctr -Cleveland 44114 Fx:696-8731

(330) 297-3850 .. **Meduri,** Christopher J '95 Portage Cnty Pros -466 S Chestnut
-Ravenna 44266

(513) 891-3270 .. **Medven,** Ann-Dana '99 Harris & B -9545 Kenwood Rd -Ste 301
-Cincinnati 45242

(216) 479-8500 .. **Meehan,** Ellen K '92 %Squire S&D LLP -127 Pub Sq -4900
Key Twr -Cleveland 44114 Fx:479-8780

(216) 444-2340 .. **Meehan,** Michael Jan '82 Cleveland Clinic Fndtn -9500 Euclid Av
-Cleveland 44195

Meehan, Michael P '92 -3416 W 159th -Cleveland 44111

(419) 243-1294 .. **Meehan,** Thomas A '62 Emch SS&P Co,LPA -One SeaGate
-Ste 1980 -Bx916 -Toledo 43697 Fx:243-8502

(937) 432-9300 .. **Meehling,** John C '04 (Wilson & M) -4625 Far Hills Av
-Dayton 45429 Fx:432-9311

(216) 587-2120 .. **Meek,** David E '72 (Reddy G&M Co,LPA)
-5306 Transportation Blvd -Garfield Heights 44125

(513) 621-5252 .. **Meek,** Patricia S '98 Clodfelter & G -36 E 4th -Ste 1208
-Cincinnati 45202

(216) 687-1311 .. **Meeker,** Brian A '94 (Reminger & R) -101 Prospect Av W
-1400 Mdlnd Bldg -Cleveland 44115 Fx:687-1841

(330) 253-3337 .. **Meeker,** Robert C '69 (Blakemore M&B Co,LPA) -19 N High
-Akron 44308 Fx:253-4131

(419) 592-6801 .. **Meekison,** David F '72 (Meekison Law Firm) -123 W Wshngtn
-Napoleon 43545 Fx:592-6944

(419) 592-6801 .. **Meekison,** David P '36 (Meekison Law Firm) -123 W Wshngtn
-Napoleon 43545 Fx:592-6944

(614) 292-0943 .. **Meeks,** James E '63 OSU Moritz Cllg of Law -55 W 12th Av
-Columbus 43210 Fx:292-1383

(513) 639-7000 .. **Meeks,** Lisa T '93 (Newman & M Co,LPA) -617 Vine -Ste 1401
-Cincinnati 45202

(419) 246-5757 .. **Meeks,** Mark D '88 Anspach M&N,LLP -300 Mad Av -Ste 1600
-Toledo 43604 Fx:321-6979

(614) 228-4141 .. **Meeks,** Ralph W '75 (RW Meeks Co LPA) -511 S High
-Columbus 43215

(614) 267-2799 .. **Meena,** James W '81 -2310 Indnola Av -Columbus 43202

(724) 539-5485 .. **Meenan,** Larry R '92 SrCnsl Kennametal Inc -1600 Tech Way
-Bx231 -Latrobe, PA 15650

(216) 781-2770 .. **Meers,** Elizabeth A '84 -1370 Ontario -Ste 2000 -Cleveland 44113

Meftah, Diane M '89 -1909 Scioto Pnte Dr -Columbus 43221

(330) 677-0645 .. **Megargel,** Ralph C '92 (Megargel & Co LPA) -1001 S Water
-Kent 44240

(216) 363-4500 .. **Mehalko,** Megan L '90 (Benesch FC&A LLP) -200 Pub Sq
-Ste 2300 -Cleveland 44114 Fx:363-4588

(941) 461-2142 .. **Mehallo,** Danielle D '98 USDC of FL-Middle Dist -2110 1st
-Ste 6-109 -Fort Myers, FL 33901

(614) 644-7651 .. **Mehan,** Patrick J '04 %Atty Gen -150 E Gay -Columbus 43215
Fx:752-4677

(513) 871-7562 .. **Mehas,** Andrew G '41 -3680 Traskwood Cir -Cincinnati 45208

(513) 684-3678 .. **Mehas,** Mark G '84 NLRB -550 Main -Rm 3003 Fed Bldg
-Cincinnati 45202

(440) 838-7600 .. **Mehendale,** Ellyn B '94 OfCnsl Janik & D,LLP -9200 S Hills Blvd
-Ste 300 -Cleveland 44147 Fx:838-7601

(330) 425-4201 .. **Mehler,** Peter L '02 %Reimer L&A Co,LPA -2450 Edison Blvd
-Bx968 -Twinsburg 44087 Fx:487-0923

(859) 291-9900 .. **Mehling,** Christopher J '78 (Taliaferro MSC&K,PLLC)
-1005 Mad Av -Bx468 -Covington, KY 41012

(216) 368-3983 .. **Mehlman,** Maxwell J '88 CWRU Law Schl -11075 East Blvd
-Cleveland 44106

(330) 471-2097 .. **Mehosky,** Brian L '86 Timken -1835 Dueber Av -Bx6930
-Canton 44706

(513) 942-0224 .. **Mehrle,** Joseph P '95 SLWK PA -8080 Beckett Ctr Dr -Ste 104
-West Chester 45069 Fx:(612) 339-3061

(248) 209-3778 .. **Mehta,** Irene K '79 Siemens Corp -2400 Exec Hills Blvd
-Auburn Hills, MI 48326

(216) 696-4676 .. **Mehta,** Khorzad A '04 %DW Leopold & Assoc Co,LPA -2000 E 9th
-Ste 300 -Cleveland 44115

(513) 467-9903 .. **Meier,** Aimee D '97 (Meier & M) -7345 Southpnte Dr
-Cincinnati 45233

(614) 424-6760 .. **Meier,** Harold C '56 (Thompson M&D) -929 Harrison Av -Ste 205
-Columbus 43215

(513) 467-9903 .. **Meier,** Robert C '97 (Meier & M) -7345 Southpnte Dr
-Cincinnati 45233

(614) 424-6760 .. **Meier,** William A '78 (Thompson M&D) -929 Harrison Av -Ste 205
-Columbus 43215

(419) 586-6481 .. **Meikle Tesno & Luth** -100 N Main -Bx485 -Celina 45822
Fx:586-2629

(419) 586-6481 .. **Meikle,** William M '59 (Meikle T&L) -100 N Main -Bx485
-Celina 45822 Fx:586-2629

(937) 461-7000 .. **Meily,** William D '78 -22 Clay -Dayton 45402

(216) 696-3300 .. **Meimaris,** James G '87 -1801 E 9th -Ste 1710 -Cleveland 44114

(330) 376-1242 .. **Meinerding,** Wesley C '02 Renner KGBT&W,LPA -106 S Main
-4th Fl First Natl Twr -Akron 44308 Fx:376-9646

(513) 762-8022 .. **Meisenhelder,** Jamie L '00 Gradison McDonald Invstmnts
-580 Walnut -Cincinnati 45202

(513) 579-6400 .. **Meisenhelder,** John F '91 (Keating M&K PLL) -1 E 4th
-1400 Provident Twr -Cincinnati 45202 Fx:579-6457

(513) 921-5297 .. **Meiser,** Stephen M '86 (S Meiser Co,LPA) -4995 Glenway Av
-Cincinnati 45238

(216) 687-1900 .. **Meissner,** Joseph P '66 Legal Aid -1223 W 6th -Cleveland 44113
Fx:687-0779

(216) 479-8500 .. **Meissner,** Michael G '79 (Squire S&D LLP) -127 Pub Sq
-4900 Key Twr -Cleveland 44114 Fx:479-8780

(216) 289-8322 .. **Meister,** Brian H '96 Cnsl Euclid Law Dept -585 E 222nd
-Euclid 44123 Fx:289-2766

(614) 221-1644 .. **Meister,** Frederick '80 -150 E Mound -Ste 200 -Columbus 43215

(419) 822-4197 .. **Meister,** Joan B '61 (Meister & M) -321 Main -Bx39 -Delta 43515

(513) 381-2838 .. **Meister,** Julia B '95 (Taft S&H LLP) -425 Walnut -Ste 1800
-Cincinnati 45202 Fx:381-0205

(419) 865-9622 .. **Meister,** Marc J '79 MJ Meister & Assoc,Inc
-7050 Spring Meadow W Dr -Holland 43528

(419) 822-4197 .. **Meister,** Sheldon C '52 Meister & M -321 Main -Bx39 -Delta 43515

(419) 533-7701 .. **Meister,** Teckla H '87 Gerken Co -Bx607 -Napoleon 43545

(513) 345-4700 .. **Meizlish,** Bruce H '77 (Meizlish & G) -830 Main -Ste 999
-Cincinnati 45202

(614) 258-1983 .. **Meizlish,** Jodie M '87 (Golden & M Co,LPA) -923 E Broad
-Columbus 43205

(614) 221-4221 .. **Meizlish,** Sanford A '79 Barkan + N -360 S Grant Av -Bx1989
-Columbus 43216 Fx:221-5423

(614) 466-8911 .. **Mekhjian,** Ara G '97 Atty Gen -30 E Broad -Columbus 43215 **Fx:**728-7582

(502) 491-4737 .. **Meko,** Andrew C '75 Assoc Industries of KY -2303 Greene Way -Louisville, KY 40220

(216) 241-5310 .. **Meko,** Margaret M '84 (Gallagher SF&N) -1501 Euclid Av -6th Fl -Cleveland 44115 **Fx:**241-1608

(216) 831-4884 .. **Melamed,** Alan L '76 -24249 Lyman Blvd -Shaker Heights 44122

(216) 623-0000 .. **Melamed,** Marc A '77 (Javitch B&R) -1300 E 9th -14th Fl -Cleveland 44114 **Fx:**623-0190

(404) 652-4878 .. **Melampy,** Gary L '92 Georgia-Pacific Corp -133 Pchtree NE -Bx105605 -Atlanta, GA 30348

(740) 676-6503 .. **Melanko,** Richard E '74 -3892 Central Av -Shadyside 43947

(614) 566-5151 .. **Meldrum,** Terri W '94 %OhioHealth -3722 Olentangy Rvr Rd -Ste K -Columbus 43214

(419) 734-5700 .. **Melena,** Donald R '57 -201 Madison -Port Clinton 43452

(216) 443-7757 .. **Melena,** Timothy J '91 Cuyahoga Cnty Pros -1200 Ontario -8th Fl -Cleveland 44113 **Fx:**698-2270

(859) 594-3040 .. **Melfi,** Mitch H '84 Catholic Hlth Initiatives -3900 Olympic Blvd -Ste 400 -Erlanger, KY 41018

(317) 232-6350 .. **Melfi,** Richard C '71 Atty Gen Ofc -302 W Wshngtn -Indianapolis, IN 46204

(419) 249-7100 .. **Melhorn,** Donald F Jr. '60 Cnsl Marshall & M,LLC -Four Seagate -8th Fl -Toledo 43604 **Fx:**249-7151

(330) 451-7979 .. **Melia,** Patricia C '97 Stark Cnty Pros -110 Central Plz -Ste 510 -Canton 44702

(419) 421-3265 .. **Melin,** Douglas R '78 Marathon Ashland Petroleum LLC -539 S Main -Rm 824-M -Findlay 45840 **Fx:**427-4170

(614) 221-5216 .. **Melko,** Mark C '98 %Wiles BB&B Co,LPA -300 Spruce -1st Fl -Columbus 43215 **Fx:**221-5692

(614) 461-5600 .. **Melle,** James E '71 (Buckley K,LPA) -10 W Broad -Ste 1300 -Columbus 43215

(419) 332-8828 .. **Melle,** James F '94 -208 Justice -Fremont 43420

(513) 579-6400 .. **Mellen,** Joseph P '77 (Keating M&K PLL) -1 E 4th -1400 Provident Twr -Cincinnati 45202 **Fx:**579-6457

(614) 224-5205 .. **Melliere,** Michael J '97 (Peck S&W,LLP) -175 S 3rd -Ste 600 -Columbus 43215 **Fx:**224-0069

(440) 232-2701 .. **Melling,** Blair N '80 (Melling H&M,LPA) -31 Columbus Rd -Bedford 44146 **Fx:**232-7995

(440) 232-3420 .. **Melling,** Brian J '74 Mun Ct Judge -65 Columbus Rd -Bedford 44146

(440) 232-2701 .. **Melling Harding & Montello,LPA** -31 Columbus Rd -Bedford 44146 **Fx:**232-7995

(216) 621-8348 .. **Mellino,** Christopher M '84 -55 Pub Sq -Ste 1260 -Cleveland 44113

(216) 771-3800 .. **Mellino,** Sean F '02 %DP Hochberg Co,LPA -1940 E 6th -Baker Bldg 6th Fl -Cleveland 44114 **Fx:**771-3804

(440) 324-2409 .. **Mellion,** Paul J '72 UAW Legal Srvcs -347 Midway Blvd -Ste 312 -Elyria 44035 **Fx:**324-4647

Mellman, Nathan R '93 -846 N Elmwood Av -Oak Park, IL 60302

(614) 459-8912 .. **Mellon,** Howard J '77 -4823 Wynwood Ct -Columbus 43220

(740) 454-8585 .. **Mellor,** Adam K '99 Graham M&R Co,LPA -11 N 4th -Bx340 -Zanesville 43702

(412) 227-2500 .. **Mellor,** Kenneth B '88 (Blumling & G,LLP) -436 7th Av -Ste 1200 -Pittsburgh, PA 15219 **Fx:**227-2020

(216) 363-4500 .. **Mellott,** David W '78 (Benesch FC&A LLP) -200 Pub Sq -Ste 2300 -Cleveland 44114 **Fx:**363-4588

(513) 621-2666 .. **Mellott,** John Thomas '89 %Statman HS&E LLC -255 E 5th -Ste 2900 Chemed Ctr -Cincinnati 45202 **Fx:**587-4477

(440) 988-9500 .. **Mellott,** Richard R Jr. '84 Trigilio & S -5750 Cooper Foster Park Rd -Ste 102 -Lorain 44053

(216) 621-0150 .. **Mellyn,** John E Jr. '73 (Hahn L&P LLP) -3300 BP Twr/200 Pub Sq -Ste 3300 -Cleveland 44114 **Fx:**241-2824

(202) 307-0369 .. **Melnbrencis,** Velta A '68 US DOJ -1100 L NW -Ste 11048 -Washington, DC 20530

(312) 527-4000 .. **Melnick,** Jeffry A '72 (Shefsky & F,Ltd) -444 N Mich Av -Ste 2500 -Chicago, IL 60611 **Fx:**527-5921

(216) 642-6600 .. **Melnick,** Mark G '00 AGA Gas,Inc -6055 Rockside Woods -Cleveland 44131

(330) 744-8973 .. **Melnick,** Robert R '83 (Melnick & M) -18 N Phelps -Youngstown 44503

(412) 454-5812 .. **Melnik,** Warren J '94 Pepper H LLP -500 Grant -50th Fl -Pittsburgh, PA 15219

(216) 664-4304 .. **Melnyk,** Stephanie K '99 Dept of Law -601 Lakeside Av -Rm 106 City Hall -Cleveland 44114 **Fx:**664-2663

(330) 755-1437 .. **Melone,** James A '97 -700 5th -Struthers 44471

(614) 299-5522 .. **Meloun,** Grant J '00 Cnsl Durable Slate Co -1050 N 4th -Columbus 43201 **Fx:**299-7100

(614) 529-8988 .. **Meloun,** Stacy A '00 %Willis S&W Co LPA -5017 Cemetary Rd -Hilliard 43026 **Fx:**334-8989

(216) 685-9188 .. **Meloy,** Thomas C '70 OfCnsl Swartz C LLC -55 Pub Sq -Ste 1120 -Cleveland 44113 **Fx:**685-9293

(330) 757-1898 .. **Meloy,** William S '62 -211 S Main -Poland 44514

(216) 292-5807 .. **Melsher,** Gary W '64 OfCnsl Singerman MD&K -3401 Enterprise Pkwy -Ste 200 -Beachwood 44122 **Fx:**292-5867

(214) 969-8152 .. **Melson,** Robert S '92 Ernst & Young LLP -2121 San Jacinto -Ste 1500 -Dallas, TX 75201

(614) 644-2548 .. **Melton,** Katherine Jo '86 Dept Ins -2100 Stella Ct -Columbus 43215

(513) 621-2120 .. **Melville,** Charles H '62 Strauss & T,LPA -150 E 4th -4th Fl -Cincinnati 45202 **Fx:**241-8259

(530) 577-8922 .. **Melvin,** Beth A '85 -Bx624567 -South Lake Tahoe, CA 96154

(614) 729-4900 .. **Melvin,** Carolyn S '80 Alliance Data Syst -800 Tech Ctr Dr -Gahanna 43230

(440) 395-0303 .. **Melvin,** Eva Y '99 Progressive Casualty Ins Co -300 N Cmmns Blvd -#1006 -Mayfield Village 44143

(614) 464-5275 .. **Melvin,** John B '75 State Auto Mutual Ins Co -518 E Broad -Columbus 43215

(713) 918-3826 .. **Melvin,** John F '75 BMC Software,Inc -2101 City W Blvd -Houston, TX 77042

(513) 946-9000 .. **Melvin,** William H '83 Hamilton Cnty Juv Ct -800 Bway -Cincinnati 45202 **Fx:**946-9217

(614) 224-9223 .. **Melvin,** William J '58 OfCnsl Ward KBM&M -199 S 5th -Columbus 43215

(419) 242-1555 .. **Menacher,** William R '84 (Spitler & W-Y Co,LPA) -1000 Adams -Ste 200 -Toledo 43624

(614) 221-6500 .. **Menashe,** Diane M '98 -536 S Wall -Ste 300 -Columbus 43215

(440) 779-1430 .. **Menassa,** Alexander '87 Szarka Fin Mngmnt -29691 Lorain Rd -North Olmsted 44070

(216) 464-1626 .. **Mencer,** Jetta L '83 L Smith & Assoc -929 Harrison Av -Ste 300 -Columbus 43215

(614) 466-6750 .. **Mendel,** Janet J '87 OH Dept Taxation -30 E Broad -22nd Fl -Columbus 43215

(614) 464-6400 .. **Mendel,** Linda R '81 OfCnsl Vorys SS&P LLP -52 E Gay -Bx1008 -Columbus 43216 **Fx:**464-6350

(216) 566-5856 .. **Mendelsohn,** Clifford S '01 %Thompson H LLP -127 Pub Sq -3900 Key Ctr -Cleveland 44114 **Fx:**566-5800

(513) 352-6546 .. **Mendelsohn,** Donald S '75 (Thompson H LLP) -312 Walnut -14th Fl -Cincinnati 45202 **Fx:**241-4771

(440) 349-3300 .. **Mendelsohn,** Richard A '81 -32901 Station -Ste 105 -Solon 44139

(513) 793-0800 .. **Mendelsohn,** Robert N '93 -10979 Reed Hartman Hwy -Ste 201 -Cincinnati 45242 **Fx:**793-0888

Mendenhall, Audrey '83 -1165 Som Center Rd -#209 -Cleveland 44124

(330) 535-9160 .. **Mendenhall,** Warner D III '98 -190 N Union -Ste 201 -Akron 44304

(216) 765-7400 .. **Mendes,** Scott M '92 Cleveland Fncl Grove -28601 Chagrin Blvd -#300 -Cleveland 44122

(216) 622-8200 .. **Mendoza,** Matthew M '97 %Calfee H&G LLP -800 Superior Av -Ste 1400 -Cleveland 44114 **Fx:**241-0816

(440) 543-8445 .. **Menefee,** Donald R '01 -Bx23671 -Chagrin Falls 44023

(216) 861-4414 .. **Menefee,** M Terrell '99 (Brown M LLC) -1468 W 9th -Ste 210 -Cleveland 44113

(419) 354-9250 .. **Meneses,** Walter M '96 %Wood Cnty Pros -One Cthse Sq -Bowling Green 43402 **Fx:**353-2904

Mengel, Kathryn T '86 -295 Evergreen Dr -Springboro 45066

(614) 644-9316 .. **Mengel,** Marcia J '82 Supreme Ct of OH -30 E Broad -2nd Fl -Columbus 43215

(513) 932-2047 .. **Mengle,** John S '78 -42 E Silver -Lebanon 45036

(330) 762-1309 .. **Menicos,** Patrick L '76 -137 S Main -Ste 206 -Akron 44308

(503) 222-1125 .. **Menikoff,** Carrie '97 %JL Hoffman -1000 SW Bway -Ste 1500 -Portland, OR 97205 **Fx:**222-7589

(309) 766-3649 .. **Menke,** Christine M '84 State Farm Ins -One State Farm Plz -Bloomington, IL 61710

(513) 629-1471 .. **Menke,** David J '81 SrCnsl Wstrn Sthrn Life Ins Co -400 Bway -Cincinnati 45202

Menke, William C '76 -3884 Cotton Green Path Dr -Naples, FL 34114

(419) 435-2359 .. **Mennel,** Donald M '86 -1192 Pelton Rd -Fostoria 44830

(513) 852-6033 .. **Menninger,** Henry E Jr. '77 (Wood & L LLP) -600 Vine -Ste 2500 -Cincinnati 45202 **Fx:**852-6087

(614) 793-7600 .. **Mentel,** Michael C '88 Science App Intl -4400 Blazer Pkwy -Dublin 43017

(614) 227-2300 .. **Mentel,** Sean A '04 %Bricker & E LLP -100 S 3rd -Columbus 43215 **Fx:**227-2390

(216) 241-3272 .. **Mentrek,** Joseph M '85 Meaden-Moore,Ltd -1100 Superior Av E -Ste 1100 -Cleveland 44114

(513) 563-3271 .. **Mentrup,** Clifford C '01 Sentron Med,Inc -4445 Lk Forest Dr -Ste 600 -Cincinnati 45242

(614) 221-3329 .. **Mentser,** Barry A '84 -122 E Main -Ste 300W -Columbus 43215

(330) 376-7500 .. **Mentzer,** Howard E '69 Mentzer & M,Ltd -1 Cascade Plz -20th Fl -Akron 44308 **Fx:**376-8018

(330) 376-7500 .. **Mentzer,** Linda B '83 (Mentzer & M,Ltd) -1 Cascade Plz -20th Fl -Akron 44308 **Fx:**376-8018

(330) 376-7500 .. **Mentzer & Mygrant, Ltd** -1 Cascade Plz -20th Fl -Akron 44308 **Fx:**376-8018

(906) 458-2096 .. **Menucci,** William R '78 -Bx41 -Port Clinton 43452

(216) 928-2200 .. **Menuez,** Jonathan M '95 Sutter OM&F -1301 E 9th -3600 Erievw Twr -Cleveland 44114 **Fx:**928-4400

(702) 652-7528 .. **Menza,** Thomas J '04 Cnsl USAF -4428 England Av -Bldg 18 -Nellis AFB, NV 89191 **Fx:**652-2132

(216) 664-4285 .. **Menzalora,** William M '93 Dept of Law -601 Lakeside Av -Rm 106 City Hall -Cleveland 44114 **Fx:**664-2663

(216) 443-5830 .. **Menzies,** John W Jr. '75 Cuyahoga Cnty Juv Ct -1910 Carnegie Av -3rd Fl -Cleveland 44115

(330) 746-5643 .. **Meola,** Margo Stoffel '95 (Comstock S&W Co,LPA) -100 Fed Plz E -Ste 926 -Youngstown 44503 **Fx:**746-4925

(330) 373-1717 .. **Meola,** William Jack '84 (Davis & Y) -108 Main SW -10th Fl -Warren 44481 **Fx:**395-0610

(216) 687-1311 .. **Meraglio,** Russell J Jr. '83 (Reminger & R) -101 Prospect Av W -1400 Mdlnd Bldg -Cleveland 44115 **Fx:**687-1841

(330) 782-3000 .. **Meranto,** Anthony P '96 -4822 Market -#220 -Youngstown 44512

(513) 326-4675 .. **Meranus,** David '91 Sheakley Grp Inc -100 Merchant -Ste 100 -Cincinnati 45246

(216) 621-0150 .. **Mercer,** Harry D '67 (Hahn L&P LLP) -3300 BP Twr/200 Pub Sq -Ste 3300 -Cleveland 44114 **Fx:**241-2824

Mercer, Henry M III '76 -685-E Poore Farm Rd -Chocowinity, NC 27817

(330) 533-8315 .. **Mercer,** Jeralyn G '93 -6600 Summit Dr -Canfield 44406

(216) 368-2173 .. **Mercer,** Kathryn L '83 CWRU Law Schl -11075 East Blvd -Cleveland 44106

(419) 321-1436 .. **Mercer,** Mark E '02 %Shumaker L&K,LLP -1000 Jackson -Toledo 43624 **Fx:**241-6894

(440) 786-3229 .. **Merchant,** Charles E '62 -5661 Perkins Rd -Bedford Heights 44146

(513) 621-3394 .. **Merchant,** John C '92 Peck S&W,LLP -201 E 5th -Ste 900 -Cincinnati 45202 **Fx:**621-3813

(513) 977-8200 .. **Merchant,** Toby D '04 %Dinsmore & S LLP -255 E 5th -Ste 1900 -Cincinnati 45202 **Fx:**977-8141

(419) 241-1200 .. **Mercurio,** Michael J '99 Cooper & W,LPA -900 Adams -Toledo 43624 **Fx:**242-5615

(513) 258-7675 .. **Mercurio,** Michael T '00 -3127 Ferguson Rd -Cincinnati 45211

(330) 643-2788 .. **Mercurio,** Nancy L '96 Summit Cnty Pros-Crim -53 Univ Av -7th Fl -Akron 44308 **Fx:**643-8277

(216) 491-3850 .. **Meredith,** Colleen M '87 %R Schickler -21825 Chagrin Blvd -Ste 320 -Cleveland 44122

(419) 228-6365 .. **Meredith,** Robert J '88 (Cory MWR&C,LPA) -101 N Elizabeth -Ste 607 -Bx1217 -Lima 45802 **Fx:**228-5319

Mergl, Marija '01 -2054 Issaquah -Cuyahoga Falls 44221

(216) 222-9723 .. **Mericle**, Denise A '96 Natl City Bank -1900 E 9th -Locator 01-3979 -Cleveland 44114

(520) 621-1373 .. **Merico-Stephens**, Ana M '96 Univ of Ariz Cllg of Law -Bx210176 -Tucson, AZ 85721

(330) 643-3550 .. **Meriweather**, Lavonne A '78 Industrial Commssn of OH -161 S High -Ste 301 -Akron 44308

(614) 466-1797 .. **Merkel**, Richard L '73 Legis Srvc Commssn -77 S High -Columbus 43215

(614) 228-0068 .. **Merkle**, Howard T '79 (Winters & M) -500 S Front -Ste 900 -Columbus 43215 **Fx:**228-1660

(614) 227-2000 .. **Merkle**, Mark K Jr. '70 (Porter WM&A LLP) -41 S High -Columbus 43215 **Fx:**227-2100

(937) 642-4070 .. **Merklin**, Jeffrey A '85 (Allen Y&M) -233 W 5th -Bx391 -Marysville 43040

(330) 535-5711 .. **Merklin**, Marc B '84 (Brouse M) -106 S Main -500 First Natl Twr -Akron 44308 **Fx:**253-8601

(513) 564-7362 .. **Merling**, Joseph C '77 6th Dist Ct of Appls -100 E 5th -Cthse -Cincinnati 45202

(330) 253-7171 .. **Merlitti**, James A '74 (Burdon & M) -137 S Main -Ste 201 -Akron 44308 **Fx:**253-7174

(216) 621-0580 .. **Meros**, John C '80 (Schulman S&M,LPA) -1370 Ontario -1700 Standard Bldg -Cleveland 44113 **Fx:**621-5428

(937) 328-2640 .. **Merrell**, William N '77 Clark Cnty Pub Def -50 E Columbia -4th Fl -Springfield 45502 **Fx:**328-2715

(216) 931-6000 .. **Merriam**, Stephen C '85 (Ulmer & B LLP) -1300 E 9th -Ste 900 Penton Media Bldg -Cleveland 44114 **Fx:**931-6001

(216) 771-8121 .. **Merrick**, Patrick P '04 %Steuer EB&B Co,LPA -55 Pub Sq -Ste 1828 -Cleveland 44113 **Fx:**771-8120

(440) 323-1203 .. **Merrill**, Douglas W '00 Rothgery & Assoc -230 3rd -Ste 100 -Elyria 44035

(614) 227-8871 .. **Merrill**, Frank L '87 (Bricker & E LLP) -100 S 3rd -Columbus 43215 **Fx:**227-2390

(330) 458-2411 .. **Merrill**, Sandra L '86 -101 Central Plz S -Ste 1000 -Canton 44702

(614) 227-2000 .. **Merrill**, Tracy L '01 %Porter WM&A LLP -41 S High -Columbus 43215 **Fx:**227-2100

(419) 885-7152 .. **Merritt**, Daniel L '82 (Merritt & Assoc) -5933 Gillingham Dr -Sylvania 43560

Merritt, Diana B '97 -3343 Aberdeen Rd -Shaker Heights 44120

(419) 530-2949 .. **Merritt**, Frank S '68 Univ of Toledo Law Schl -2801 W Bancroft -Toledo 43606

(740) 852-2259 .. **Merritt**, Gregory T '71 Madison Cnty Pros -23 W High -London 43140 **Fx:**845-1649

(937) 339-1500 .. **Merritt**, Tom O '96 %Shipman D&L -215 W Water -Bx310 -Troy 45373 **Fx:**339-1519

(740) 454-8585 .. **Merry**, Joseph W '80 Graham M&R Co,LPA -11 N 4th -Bx340 -Zanesville 43702

(614) 776-1000 .. **Merry**, Thomas R '89 (Barren & M Co,LPA) -110 Polaris Pkwy -Ste 302 -Westerville 43082 **Fx:**865-3396

(614) 221-4400 .. **Merry**, Tony C '89 Volkema TMBS&M,LPA -140 E Town -Ste 1100 -Columbus 43215 **Fx:**221-6010

(330) 375-2730 .. **Merryweather**, Elizabeth A '97 Pros -217 S High -Ste 203 -Akron 44308

(740) 321-1212 .. **Mershon**, Steven W '81 -110 E Elm -Bx10 -Granville 43023

(216) 621-0200 .. **Mersol**, Gregory V '85 (Baker & H LLP) -1900 E 9th -Ste 3200 -Cleveland 44114 **Fx:**696-0740

(330) 666-4247 .. **Mertens**, Ernest A '86 -1887 Orchrd Dr -Bx18 -Bath 44210

(330) 456-8341 .. **Mertes**, Brian R '95 (Black MS&A,LPA) -220 Market Av S -Ste 1000 -Canton 44702 **Fx:**456-5756

(614) 293-4296 .. **Mertz**, Daniel T '92 OSU Hospitals -410 W 10th Av -151 Doan Hall -Columbus 43210

(419) 354-9244 .. **Mertz**, Elizabeth A '97 Wood Cnty Pub Def -123 N Summit -Bowling Green 43402

(419) 782-9881 .. **Mertz**, Eric A '79 Arthur OM&M Co,LPA -901 Ralston Av -Bx781 -Defiance 43512

(614) 365-2700 .. **Mertz**, Mary C '02 %Squire S&D LLP -41 S High -1300 Huntngtn Ctr -Columbus 43215 **Fx:**365-2499

(614) 443-7455 .. **Merullo Reister & Swinford Co,LPA** -772 S Front -Columbus 43206

(614) 443-7455 .. **Merullo**, Victor D '73 (Merullo R&S Co,LPA) -772 S Front -Columbus 43206

(614) 222-4327 .. **Merz**, Vincent P Jr. '98 CBCS -236 E Town -Columbus 43215

(937) 223-1201 .. **Mesaros**, David P '83 %Altick & C Co,LPA -1 S Main -1700 One Dayton Ctr -Dayton 45402 **Fx:**223-5100

(614) 227-2000 .. **Mescher**, Richard M '93 (Porter WM&A LLP) -41 S High -Columbus 43215 **Fx:**227-2100

(440) 878-2953 .. **Mesel**, Kathleen L '97 Ceres Group,Inc -17800 Royalton Rd -Cleveland 44136

(513) 221-8800 .. **Mesh**, Gene I '64 G Mesh & Assoc -2605 Burnet Av -Cincinnati 45219

(440) 684-1080 .. **Mesi**, Douglas P '88 -592 Strumbly Dr -Highland Heights 44143

(614) 792-1966 .. **Mesirow**, Christine T '78 -2537 Chiron Ct -Dublin 43016

(614) 645-7385 .. **Mesirow**, Keith S '78 City Atty -90 W Broad -Columbus 43215

(440) 871-0413 .. **Meslat**, Lanene M '01 -1515 Canterbury Rd -Westlake 44145 **Fx:**871-0513

(614) 846-4318 .. **Mess**, Michael A '79 %Quantum Hlth -125 Dillmont Dr -Ste 100 -Columbus 43235

(513) 983-1552 .. **Mess**, Thomas J '79 Procter & Gamble Co-Legal -1 Procter & Gamble Plz -Cincinnati 45202

(330) 744-1148 .. **Messenger**, James L '67 (Henderson CMN&T Co,LPA) -34 Fed Plz W -Ste 600 Wick Bldg -Youngstown 44503 **Fx:**744-3807

(419) 249-7900 .. **Messenger**, Michael S '83 (Robison C&O) -Four SeaGate -9th Fl -Toledo 43604 **Fx:**249-7911

(614) 444-7440 .. **Messenger**, Walter W Jr. '01 Malek & M -1227 S High -Columbus 43206

(330) 239-6095 .. **Messer**, Betty J '94 B Messer,CPA -4128 Beach Rd -Medina 44256

(513) 381-2838 .. **Messer**, Earl K '91 (Taft S&H LLP) -425 Walnut -Ste 1800 -Cincinnati 45202 **Fx:**381-0205

(937) 746-1010 .. **Messer**, Steven L '80 Inventory Hndlrs,Inc -400 Victory Dr -Springboro 45066

(330) 489-5411 .. **Messerly**, Edwin C '74 Key Trust Co -126 Central Plz N -Canton 44702

(216) 574-9990 .. **Messerman**, Gale S '71 (Messerman & M Co,LPA) -127 Pub Sq -Ste 4100 -Cleveland 44114

(216) 574-9990 .. **Messerman**, Gerald A '62 (Messerman & M Co,LPA) -127 Pub Sq -Ste 4100 -Cleveland 44114

(216) 861-8890 .. **Messerman**, Richard D '71 -925 Euclid Av -Ste 1940 -Cleveland 44115

(937) 866-2203 .. **Messham**, Robert E Jr. '72 Mun Ct Judge -10 N 1st -Miamisburg 45342

(216) 566-5571 .. **Messinger**, Donald H '68 (Thompson H LLP) -127 Pub Sq -3900 Key Ctr -Cleveland 44114 **Fx:**566-5800

(440) 605-1543 .. **Messinger-Rapport**, Kenneth H '84 -5600 Hawthorne Dr -Cleveland 44143

Messmer, Gail E '83 -440 Highmeadows Vllg Dr -Powell 43065

(614) 469-2999 .. **Messmer**, Jane S '98 Fed Pub Def -10 W Broad -Ste 1020 -Columbus 43215

(330) 489-3251 .. **Mestel**, Mariella '77 Law Dept -218 Cleveland Av SW -Bx24218 -Canton 44701

(216) 621-2300 .. **Mester**, Jonathan D '98 Nurenberg PH&M LPA -1370 Ontario -Ste 100 -Cleveland 44113 **Fx:**771-2242

(216) 621-2300 .. **Mester**, Thomas '69 (Nurenberg PH&M LPA) -1370 Ontario -Ste 100 -Cleveland 44113 **Fx:**771-2242

(614) 761-1733 .. **Metcalf Duren Morris Starkey & Waid,LLC** -655 Metro Pl S -Ste 210 -Dublin 43017

(216) 479-8500 .. **Metcalf**, J Seth '04 %Squire S&D LLP -127 Pub Sq -4900 Key Twr -Cleveland 44114 **Fx:**479-8780

(614) 761-1733 .. **Metcalf**, Richard B '51 Metcalf DMS&W,LLC -655 Metro Pl S -Ste 210 -Dublin 43017

(614) 469-1301 .. **Mets**, Anthony D '98 Chorpenning G&P Co,LPA -585 S Front -Ste 250 -Columbus 43215

(440) 243-8636 .. **Mettler**, Michelle D '96 SrCnsl Crawford & Co -7271 Engle Rd -Cleveland 44130 **Fx:**243-1111

(419) 242-2488 .. **Metusalem**, Mark J '87 Nationwide Ins -420 Mad Av -Ste 650 -Toledo 43604

(614) 882-2327 .. **Metz & Bailey** -33 E Schrock Rd -Westerville 43081

(216) 241-6602 .. **Metz**, Carol K '00 %Weston HFP&H LLP -50 Pub Sq -2500 Trmnl Twr -Cleveland 44113 **Fx:**621-8369

(419) 249-7900 .. **Metz**, Douglas E '65 (Robison C&O) -Four SeaGate -9th Fl -Toledo 43604 **Fx:**249-7911

(614) 225-8664 .. **Metz**, Douglas O '84 Motorists Mutual -471 E Broad -Columbus 43215

(513) 381-4700 .. **Metz**, Jerome J Jr. '80 (Porter WM&A LLP) -250 E 5th -Ste 2200 -Cincinnati 45202 **Fx:**421-0991

(513) 241-8844 .. **Metz**, John H '77 -441 Vine -4400 Carew Twr -Cincinnati 45202

Metz, William A III '04 -(Address Unavailable)

(937) 443-6841 .. **Metzcar**, Jeffrey C '00 %Thompson H LLP -2000 Cthse Plz NE -Bx8801 -Dayton 45401 **Fx:**443-6635

(202) 331-8777 .. **Metzenthin**, George A '95 Cahn & S,LLP -2000 P NW -Ste 200 -Washington, DC 20036

(216) 781-5470 .. **Metzger**, Robert L '62 (Ziegler M&M LLP) -925 Euclid Av -2020 Huntngtn Bldg -Cleveland 44115 **Fx:**781-0714

(614) 463-4201 .. **Metzger**, Thomas M '92 (Littler M,PC) -21 E State -Ste 1600 -Columbus 43215 **Fx:**221-3301

(216) 621-8484 .. **Metzinger**, Margaret M '95 %Climaco LPW&G Co,LPA -1228 Euclid Av -Ste 900 Halle Bldg -Cleveland 44115 **Fx:**771-1632

(614) 466-0722 .. **Metzler**, Jonathan L '94 Atty Gen -150 E Gay -Columbus 43215 **Fx:**644-9973

(419) 692-0060 .. **Metzner**, John A Jr. '57 (Marsh M&M) -302 W 1st -Bx363 -Delphos 45833

(330) 743-1171 .. **Meub**, Janet K '01 %Manchester BP&U -201 E Commerce -Atrium Level 2 Commerce Bldg -Youngstown 44503 **Fx:**743-1190

(513) 724-6111 .. **Meurer**, Gregory J '74 Diversified Glass,Inc -4175 Half Acre Rd -Batavia 45103

(616) 752-2448 .. **Meurlin**, Craig N '77 (Warner N&J LLP) -111 Lyon NW -Ste 900 -Grand Rapids, MI 49503

(419) 255-0126 .. **Mewhort**, Donald M III '91 Midland Title NW OH Inc -420 Mad Av -Toledo 43604

(419) 241-9000 .. **Mewhort**, Donald M Jr. '65 (Shumaker L&K,LLP) -1000 Jackson -Toledo 43624 **Fx:**241-6894

(216) 696-7600 .. **Meyer**, Andrew C '76 (Duvin C&H) -1301 E 9th -20th Fl Erievw Twr -Cleveland 44114 **Fx:**696-2038

(937) 259-7209 .. **Meyer**, Arthur G '82 Dayton Power and Light Co -1065 Woodman Dr -Dayton 45432

(513) 870-2207 .. **Meyer**, Barry A '76 Cincinnati Fin Corp -Bx145496 -Cincinnati 45250

(937) 461-5310 .. **Meyer**, Beverly A '94 OfCnsl Doll J&F -111 W 1st -Ste 1100 -Dayton 45402 **Fx:**461-7219

(419) 213-4700 .. **Meyer**, Brenda G '86 Lucas Cnty Pros -Adams & Erie -Lucas Cnty Cthse -Toledo 43624

(614) 444-2144 .. **Meyer**, Carl J '98 (C Meyer Co,LPA) -1243 S High -Columbus 43206

(513) 721-4450 .. **Meyer**, Charles M '78 (Santen & H) -312 Walnut -Ste 3100 -Cincinnati 45202

(859) 578-1000 .. **Meyer**, Cheryl A '95 Horwitz Law Firm PSC -541 Buttermilk Pike -Ste 305 -Crescent Springs, KY 41017

(740) 345-3431 .. **Meyer**, Christopher R '77 (Reese PD&M,PLL) -36 N 2nd -Bx919 -Newark 43058 **Fx:**349-5116

(513) 579-6400 .. **Meyer**, David A '96 %Keating M&K PLL -1 E 4th -1400 Provident Twr -Cincinnati 45202 **Fx:**579-6457

(614) 224-6000 .. **Meyer**, David P '95 (DP Meyer Co,LPA) -401 N Front -Ste 350 -Columbus 43215 **Fx:**224-6066

(404) 572-4707 .. **Meyer**, Donald E '81 Cnsl King & S LLP -191 Pchtree NE -Atlanta, GA 30303 **Fx:**572-5100

(937) 495-3660 .. **Meyer**, Donald E II '95 Mead Corp -Cthse Plz NE -Dayton 45463

(513) 367-2141 .. **Meyer**, Donald J Jr. '76 -1005 Harrison Av -Harrison 45030

(216) 444-2340 .. **Meyer**, Donna J '95 Cleveland Clinic Fndtn -9500 Euclid Av -Cleveland 44195

(800) 998-9454 .. **Meyer**, Elin S '88 Cmmnty Lgl Aid Srvcs,Inc -265 S Main -3rd Fl -Akron 44308 **Fx:**(330) 535-0728

(419) 244-4605 .. **Meyer**, Frederick C '81 Port Lwrnce Title & Trust Co -616 Mad Av -Toledo 43604

(216) 479-8500 .. **Meyer**, G Christopher '73 (Squire S&D LLP) -127 Pub Sq -4900 Key Twr -Cleveland 44114 **Fx:**479-8780

(419) 447-5132 ..**Meyer,** Gerald D '68 (Meyer M&G,Ltd) -106 E Market -Bx400
　　　　　　　-Tiffin 44883
(614) 469-3939 ..**Meyer,** H Theodore '62 SrCnsl Jones D
　　　　　　　-325 John H McConnell Blvd -Ste 600 -Bx165017
　　　　　　　-Columbus 43216 **Fx:**461-4198
(330) 343-8891 ..**Meyer,** Hank F III '99 J Patrick Co LPA -204 2nd NE -Bx191
　　　　　　　-New Philadelphia 44663
(419) 447-5132 ..**Meyer,** Jay A '96 (Meyer M&G,Ltd) -106 E Market -Bx400
　　　　　　　-Tiffin 44883
(614) 237-3525 ..**Meyer,** Jeffrey D '91 Hummel Title Agncy -2715 E Main
　　　　　　　-Columbus 43209
(202) 452-4489 ..**Meyer,** Jo-el J '99 Bureau of Natl Affrs -1231 25th NW -Rm N-519
　　　　　　　-Washington, DC 20037
(513) 357-9764 ..**Meyer,** Joseph W '93 -125 E Court -Ste 600 -Cincinnati 45202
(513) 771-2444 ..**Meyer,** Karen P '92 (Lutz CM&R Co,LPA) -130 Tri-Cnty Pkwy
　　　　　　　-Ste 208 -Cincinnati 45246 **Fx:**771-2447
(513) 381-0656 ..**Meyer,** Keith D '80 (Kohnen & P LLP) -201 E 5th -Ste 800
　　　　　　　-Cincinnati 45202 **Fx:**381-5823
(419) 243-6148 ..**Meyer,** Larry P '85 (Manahan PB&D) -414 N Erie -Bx2328
　　　　　　　-Toledo 43603
(513) 695-1325 ..**Meyer,** Leslie M '92 Warren Cnty Pros -500 Justice Dr
　　　　　　　-Lebanon 45036 **Fx:**695-2962
(216) 689-4633 ..**Meyer,** Lisa A '94 Key Bank -127 Pub Sq -4th Fl -Cleveland 44114
(513) 624-7300 ..**Meyer,** Marsha Rea '96 -8070 Beechmont Av -Cincinnati 45255
(513) 523-7722 ..**Meyer,** Martha P '79 %W Staton Co,LPA -110 N Beech
　　　　　　　-Oxford 45056
(216) 443-7800 ..**Meyer,** Matthew E '02 Cuyahoga Cnty Pros -1200 Ontario -8th Fl
　　　　　　　-Cleveland 44113 **Fx:**698-2270
(419) 447-5132 ..**Meyer Meyer & Gucker,Ltd** -106 E Market -Bx400 -Tiffin 44883
　　　　　　　Meyer, Patricia K '81 -(Address Unavailable)
(330) 869-6701 ..**Meyer,** Paul E '74 -1911 N Cleveland-Massillon Rd -Bx401 -Bath
　　　　　　　44210 **Fx:**475-1662
(513) 634-9359 ..**Meyer,** Peter D '01 Procter & Gamble -8611 Beckett Rd
　　　　　　　-West Chester 45069
(419) 241-2201 ..**Meyer,** Randy L '99 %Spengler N PLL -608 Mad Av -Ste 1000
　　　　　　　-Toledo 43604 **Fx:**241-8599
(937) 653-2744 ..**Meyer,** Richard A '74 Champaign Cnty Cmn Pleas Ct -200 N Main
　　　　　　　-Urbana 43078
(513) 521-2527 ..**Meyer,** Richard E '66 -1231 Hllywd Av -Cincinnati 45224
(614) 471-0085 ..**Meyer,** Richard F '80 Browning & M Co,LPA -8101 N High
　　　　　　　-Ste 370 -Columbus 43235 **Fx:**471-8132
(614) 761-6196 ..**Meyer,** Robert A Jr. '78 Dominion Homes,Inc -5501 Frantz Rd
　　　　　　　-Bx7166 -Dublin 43017
(330) 492-8717 ..**Meyer,** Robert C '78 (Buckingham D&B,LLP) -4518 Fulton Dr NW
　　　　　　　-Bx35548 -Canton 44735 **Fx:**492-9625
(513) 241-3685 ..**Meyer,** Ronald A '69 (White G&M Co,LPA) -1 W 4th -Ste 1700
　　　　　　　-Cincinnati 45202 **Fx:**241-2399
　　　　　　　Meyer, Scott A '89 -11620 Timber Ridge Ln -Cincinnati 45241
(513) 272-1940 ..**Meyer,** Stanley P '67 Columbia Rlty Grp,LLC -5710 Wooster Pike
　　　　　　　-Ste 307 -Cincinnati 45227
(419) 662-3113 ..**Meyer,** Stephen A '91 -200 Dixie Hwy -Rossford 43460
(216) 896-2809 ..**Meyer,** Thomas Lee '79 Parker Hannifin Corp -6035 Parkland Blvd
　　　　　　　-Cleveland 44124
(513) 561-4065 ..**Meyer,** William F '70 -5557 Maplerdg Dr -Cincinnati 45227
　　　　　　　Fx:561-4065
(419) 246-5722 ..**Meyer,** William G '77 -608 Mad Av -Ste 1400 -Toledo 43604
(216) 831-0042 ..**Meyers,** Anne J '77 Meyers RF&L LPA -28601 Chagrin Blvd
　　　　　　　-Ste 500 -Cleveland 44122 **Fx:**831-0542
　　　　　　　Meyers, Carl A '68 -109 Windward Way -Columbia, SC 29212
(440) 729-9621 ..**Meyers,** Edward F Jr. '65 Chagrin River Land Conservancy -Bx314
　　　　　　　-Novelty 44072
(513) 723-4000 ..**Meyers,** Eliot N '94 (Vorys SS&P LLP) -221 E 4th -Ste 2000 Atrium
　　　　　　　Two -Bx0236 -Cincinnati 45201 **Fx:**723-4056
(419) 424-4324 ..**Meyers,** Gregory E '77 Cooper Tire -701 Lima Av -Bx550 -Findlay
　　　　　　　45840
(614) 466-5394 ..**Meyers,** Gregory W '83 Pub Def -8 E Long -Columbus 43215
(419) 483-6748 ..**Meyers,** John E '69 -117 W Main -Bellevue 44811
(513) 871-8900 ..**Meyers,** Karen D '78 Little MG & Assoc -2651 Observatory Av
　　　　　　　-Cincinnati 45208
(440) 366-9930 ..**Meyers,** Kim R '84 (McCray MS&M Co,LPA) -260 Burns Rd
　　　　　　　-Ste 150 -Elyria 44035 **Fx:**366-1910
(513) 946-9200 ..**Meyers,** Paul W '78 Hamilton Cnty Cmn Pleas Ct -800 Bway
　　　　　　　-Cincinnati 45202
(740) 867-3166 ..**Meyers,** Richard B '67 Meyers & N,LLC -220 4th
　　　　　　　-Chesapeake 45619
(419) 529-4949 ..**Meyers,** Robert J '73 Lawyers Prprty Dev Corp
　　　　　　　-240 B Tappan Dr N -Mansfield 44906
(513) 579-1500 ..**Meyers,** Robert J '75 (Buechner HOM&H Co,LPA) -105 E 4th
　　　　　　　-Ste 300 -Cincinnati 45202 **Fx:**977-4361
(216) 831-0042 ..**Meyers Roman Friedberg & Lewis LPA** -28601 Chagrin Blvd
　　　　　　　-Ste 500 -Cleveland 44122 **Fx:**831-0542
　　　　　　　Meyers, Terri A '94 -10419 Roachton Rd -Perrysburg 43551
(216) 696-9330 ..**Meyerson,** David L '84 Garson & Assoc Co,LPA
　　　　　　　-614 Superior Av W -1600 Rckfllr Bldg -Cleveland 44113
　　　　　　　Fx:696-8558
(513) 221-7831 ..**Meyn,** Malcolm A Jr. '89 M Meyn,Jr,Inc -330 Straight -Ste 311
　　　　　　　-Cincinnati 45219
(216) 241-3377 ..**Mezacapa,** Victor A III '91 (Mezacapa & O Co,LPA) -55 Pub Sq
　　　　　　　-Ste 2200 -Cleveland 44113
(513) 474-3700 ..**Mezher,** Kathleen D '84 (K Mezher & Assoc) -8075 Beechmont Av
　　　　　　　-Cincinnati 45255
(513) 723-1600 ..**Mezibov & Jenkins** -1726 Young -Cincinnati 45202
(513) 723-1600 ..**Mezibov,** Marc D '74 (Mezibov & J) -1726 Young -Cincinnati 45202
(419) 244-4200 ..**Mezinko,** Vincent S '85 M Margelefsky LLC -709 Mad Av -Ste 301
　　　　　　　-Toledo 43624
(713) 839-9700 ..**Mgbaraho,** Uche J '88 (Okorafor & M) -2646 S Loop W -#565
　　　　　　　-Houston, TX 77054 **Fx:**666-6644
(513) 381-2838 ..**Miano,** Tamara A '01 %Taft S&H LLP -425 Walnut -Ste 1800
　　　　　　　-Cincinnati 45202 **Fx:**381-0205
(937) 382-7777 ..**Miars,** Mark J '78 %Bryant Law Ofc -21 N South
　　　　　　　-Wilmington 45177
(614) 221-9160 ..**Micciulla,** James '90 James Micciulla -85 E Gay -Ste 1004
　　　　　　　-Columbus 43215

(614) 466-8911 ..**Miceli,** Julie '04 Atty Gen -30 E Broad -Columbus 43215
　　　　　　　Fx:728-7582
(740) 286-4649 ..**Michael,** Aaron C '02 B Smith -233 E Main -Jackson 45640
(937) 223-8177 ..**Michael,** Allison D '99 %Coolidge WW&L -33 W 1st -Ste 600
　　　　　　　-Dayton 45402 **Fx:**223-6705
(614) 459-4840 ..**Michael,** Barbara J '91 (Michael & M) -3360 Tremont Rd
　　　　　　　-Columbus 43221
　　　　　　　Michael, Bonnie B '84 -6681 Markwood -Worthington 43085
(513) 523-3700 ..**Michael,** James E Jr. '73 (Millikin & F) -5020 B Cllg Crnr Pike
　　　　　　　-Oxford 45056 **Fx:**523-0463
(614) 443-6262 ..**Michael,** Jay E '85 -729 S Front -Columbus 43206
(330) 253-7800 ..**Michael,** Kathryn Ann '86 -106 S Main -Ste 2500 -Akron 44308
(614) 644-7250 ..**Michael,** Mark A '94 Atty Gen -30 E Broad -Columbus 43215
　　　　　　　Fx:644-7634
(614) 459-4840 ..**Michael,** Susan J '92 (Michael & M) -3360 Tremont Rd
　　　　　　　-Columbus 43221
(614) 596-1719 　**Michael,** Thomas P '68 -7652 Sawmill Rd-PMB 229 -Dublin 43016
　　　　　　　Fx:336-9086
(614) 621-1500 ..**Michael,** William J '99 %Calfee H&G LLP -21 E State
　　　　　　　-1100 Fifth Third Ctr -Columbus 43215 **Fx:**621-0010
(330) 668-1163 ..**Michaels,** Andrew '53 -840 S Medina Line Rd -Wadsworth 44281
(330) 342-8203 ..**Michaels,** Lisa M '96 J Clunk Co LPA -5061 Hudson Dr -Ste 400
　　　　　　　-Hudson 44236 **Fx:**342-8205
(216) 961-2313 ..**Michaels,** Thomas N '97 Michaels Leg Assoc -4204 Detroit Av
　　　　　　　-Ste 206 -Cleveland 44113
(419) 255-6171 ..**Michalak,** Alan J '91 -520 Mad Av -Ste 464 -Toledo 43604
(419) 255-6171 ..**Michalak,** Richard F '52 -520 Mad Av -Ste 464 -Toledo 43604
(216) 241-5310 ..**Michalec,** Daniel J '89 (Gallagher SF&N) -1501 Euclid Av -6th Fl
　　　　　　　-Cleveland 44115 **Fx:**241-1608
　　　　　　　Michalec, Mitchell J '03 -1059 Winhurst Dr -Akron 44313
(216) 622-8200 ..**Michals,** Thomas I '88 (Calfee H&G LLP) -800 Superior Av
　　　　　　　-Ste 1400 -Cleveland 44114 **Fx:**241-0816
(216) 621-0150 ..**Michalski,** David J '94 %Hahn L&P LLP
　　　　　　　-3300 BP Twr/200 Pub Sq -Ste 3300 -Cleveland 44114
　　　　　　　Fx:241-2824
(740) 653-6464 ..**Michalski,** Raymond R '76 (Dagger JMO&H) -144 E Main -Bx667
　　　　　　　-Lancaster 43130 **Fx:**653-8522
　　　　　　　Michalsky, Melissa F '01 -7446 Cummins Ct -New Albany 43054
(937) 866-6251 ..**Michaud,** Nancy A '80 Huffy Corp -901 Plsnt Vlly Dr
　　　　　　　-Springboro 45066
(419) 782-9881 ..**Michel,** Daniel R '96 (Arthur OM&M Co,LPA) -901 Ralston Av
　　　　　　　-Bx781 -Defiance 43512
(216) 831-9900 ..**Michel,** David S '84 %Shapero & G LLC -25101 Chagrin Blvd
　　　　　　　-Ste 220 Signature Sq II -Beachwood 44122 **Fx:**831-9467
(216) 689-5901 ..**Michel,** Lisa H '84 KeyBank NA -127 Pub Sq -18th Flr
　　　　　　　-Cleveland 44114
(513) 579-6400 ..**Michel,** Lisa Wintersheimer '88 (Keating M&K PLL) -1 E 4th
　　　　　　　-1400 Provident Twr -Cincinnati 45238 **Fx:**579-6457
(513) 922-3200 ..**Michel,** Timothy A '88 (Haverkamp BR&R Co,LPA) -5856
　　　　　　　Glenway Av -Cincinnati 45238 **Fx:**922-8096
(740) 454-2545 ..**Micheli Baldwin Northrup Co,LPA** -3808 James Ct -Ste 2
　　　　　　　-Bx788 -Zanesville 43702
(740) 454-2545 ..**Micheli,** Frank J '53 (Micheli BN Co,LPA) -3808 James Ct -Ste 2
　　　　　　　-Bx788 -Zanesville 43702
(216) 623-1155 ..**Micheli,** Mark V '84 Nationwide Ins -323 Lakeside Av W -Ste 410
　　　　　　　Lakeside Pl -Cleveland 44113
(740) 454-2545 ..**Micheli,** Michael J '80 (Micheli BN Co,LPA) -3808 James Ct -Ste 2
　　　　　　　-Bx788 -Zanesville 43702
(330) 725-5005 ..**Michelson,** Allan M '77 -225 E Lbrty -Medina 44256
(440) 466-6455 ..**Michelson,** Armand M '60 -677 E Main -Geneva 44041
(216) 696-3366 ..**Michelson,** Deborah J '92 %Goodman WM LLP -100 Erievw Plz
　　　　　　　-27th Fl -Cleveland 44114 **Fx:**363-5835
(216) 348-0700 ..**Michelson,** Michael B '79 (Stege & M Co,LPA) -200 Pub Sq
　　　　　　　-Ste 3220 -Cleveland 44114 **Fx:**348-0803
(410) 752-6030 ..**Michener,** Eric T '01 %Kramon & G,PA -One South -Ste 2600
　　　　　　　-Baltimore, MD 21202 **Fx:**539-1269
(330) 297-3850 ..**Michniak,** Stephen A '00 Portage Cnty Pros -466 S Chestnut
　　　　　　　-Ravenna 44266
(419) 242-8461 ..**Mickel,** Kenneth L '65 -520 Mad Av -Ste 520 -Toledo 43604
(419) 327-4336 ..**Mickel,** Marilyn D Miller '82 -608 Mad Av -Ste 940 -Toledo 43604
　　　　　　　Fx:243-4628
(330) 395-7405 ..**Mickens,** Charles G '91 -179 W Market -Warren 44481
(330) 875-7300 ..**Mickley,** Laurie A '02 -111 E Main -Louisville 44641
(937) 642-4618 ..**Mickley,** Richard S '71 -Bx731 -Marysville 43040
(508) 798-8621 ..**Miclat,** Joseph F '97 %Fletcher T&W,PC -370 Main -12th Fl
　　　　　　　-Worcester, MA 01608 **Fx:**791-1201
(440) 333-4431 ..**Miclau,** Daniel C '71 -20201 Lorain Rd -Ste 117
　　　　　　　-Fairview Park 44126
(513) 977-8200 ..**Middelhoff,** Mary-Jo '91 (Dinsmore & S LLP) -255 E 5th -Ste 1900
　　　　　　　-Cincinnati 45202 **Fx:**977-8141
(216) 566-8000 ..**Middleton,** Frederick D '73 -526 Superior Av -Ste 620 -Cleveland
　　　　　　　44114
(859) 581-6111 ..**Middleton,** John C '97 (Middleton & M,PLLC) -121 E 4th -Ste 1
　　　　　　　-Covington, KY 41011
(419) 352-7522 ..**Middleton Roebke & Nelson** -521 N Main -Bowling Green 43402
　　　　　　　Fx:353-4899
(419) 352-7522 ..**Middleton,** Staten T '93 (Middleton R&N) -521 N Main
　　　　　　　-Bowling Green 43402 **Fx:**353-4899
(419) 352-7522 ..**Middleton,** Thomas S '63 (Middleton R&N) -521 N Main
　　　　　　　-Bowling Green 43402 **Fx:**353-4899
(216) 622-3600 ..**Midian,** Kathleen L '82 US Atty -801 W Superior -Ste 400
　　　　　　　-Cleveland 44113 **Fx:**622-3370
(614) 466-0356 ..**Midlam-Mohler,** Tiffany J '04 JCARR -77 S High
　　　　　　　-Columbus 43215
　　　　　　　Miedema, Judith A '03 -(Address Unavailable)
(216) 588-5051 ..**Miehls,** Donald E '84 OH Savings Bnk -1801 E 9th -Ste 200
　　　　　　　-Cleveland 44114
(614) 462-1053 ..**Miele,** Philip R '84 %Schottenstein Z&D -250 West -Bx165020
　　　　　　　-Columbus 43216 **Fx:**462-5155
(419) 586-2323 ..**Mielke,** Steven P '95 -116 E Market -Celina 45822 **Fx:**586-2154
(216) 595-8222 ..**Mielziner,** Bruce L '66 (Kabat M&S) -25550 Chagrin Blvd -Ste 403
　　　　　　　-Beachwood 44122

(216) 621-0200 .. **Mierau**, Michael D Jr. '98 %Baker & H LLP -1900 E 9th -Ste 3200
-Cleveland 44114 **Fx:**696-0740

(419) 724-3499 .. **Miesle**, Gary E '81 -232 10th -Toledo 43624

(440) 238-5362 .. **Miesse**, Timothy S '79 Myers University -Main Campus -Bx1102
-Berea 44017

(248) 761-8607 .. **Mietty**, David R '84 UBS Fncl Srvcs Inc -3201 Big Beaver Rd
-Ste 800 -Troy, MI 48084

(614) 224-9985 .. **Mifsud**, Charles A II '99 -326 S High -Ste 201 -Columbus 43215
Fx:224-9986

(216) 522-4856 .. **Migdal**, Debra K '92 Fed Pub Def -1660 W 2nd -Ste 750
-Cleveland 44113

(330) 762-6474 .. **Migdal**, Kirk A '91 -411 Wolfe Ledges Pkwy -Ste 300 -Akron 44311
Fx:762-2127

(330) 867-5964 .. **Migdal**, Stanley B '56 -1769 Brookwood -Akron 44313

(614) 466-8574 .. **Migden**, Janine Lee '81 OH Consumers' Cnsl -10 W Broad
-Ste 1800 -Columbus 43215 **Fx:**466-9475

(440) 746-1177 .. **Miggins**, Janet L '81 (Baran PTF&T Co,LPA) -8748 Brecksvll Rd
-Ste 200 -Cleveland 44141 **Fx:**746-9637

(513) 784-0182 .. **Might**, Daniel P '96 -2357 Flora -#1 -Cincinnati 45219

(614) 644-7295 .. **Miglets**, Michael P '81 OH Dept Commerce -77 S High
-Columbus 43266

(216) 621-2030 .. **Miguel**, Melanie V '95 -614 Superior Av W -Rckfllr Bldg 15th Fl
-Cleveland 44113

(419) 420-9312 .. **Mihalik**, Drew Joseph '04 %Fitzgerald Law Firm,LLC -400 S Main
-Findlay 45840 **Fx:**420-9314

(330) 492-8888 .. **Mihalik**, Kathleen A '01 -4200 Munson NW -Canton 44718
Fx:493-1940

(614) 466-3186 .. **Mihaly**, Peter H '92 Workers Comp -30 W Spring -Level 26
-Columbus 43215

(216) 566-5752 .. **Mihet**, Horatio G '02 %Thompson H LLP -127 Pub Sq
-3900 Key Ctr -Cleveland 44114 **Fx:**566-5800

(330) 922-8060 .. **Mihiylov**, Robert L '75 -1251 N Howard -Akron 44310

(419) 229-5886 .. **Mihlbaugh**, Michael P '93 (Mihlbaugh & M) -Bx1141 -Lima 45802

(419) 229-5886 .. **Mihlbaugh**, Robert H '57 (Mihlbaugh & M) -Bx1141 -Lima 45802

(614) 719-3371 .. **Mihocik**, Eryn K '04 US Dist Ct -85 Marconi Blvd -Rm 208
-Columbus 43215

(440) 204-2159 .. **Mihok**, Mark J '82 Mun Ct Judge -100 W Erie -Lorain 44052
Fx:204-2162

(440) 350-2683 .. **Mijic-Barisic**, Katarina V '95 Lake Cnty Pros -105 Main -Bx490
-Painesville 44077 **Fx:**350-2585

(216) 687-5278 .. **Mika**, Karin '90 CSU-Marshall Cllg of Law -2121 Euclid Av -LB138
-Cleveland 44115 **Fx:**687-6881

(937) 339-0511 .. **Mikel**, David L '89 %Dungan & L Co,LPA -210 W Main
-Troy 45373 **Fx:**335-5802

(614) 462-5414 .. **Mikes**, Randall W '90 OfCnsl Kegler BH&R -65 E State -Ste 1800
-Columbus 43215 **Fx:**464-2634

(419) 893-9999 .. **Mikesell**, Alan D '84 -111 W Dudley -Maumee 43537

(330) 434-1211 .. **Mikesell**, William F '84 -7 W Bowery -10th Fl -Akron 44308

(216) 781-6166 .. **Mikhail**, Bishoy M '03 %Roberts Law Ofc -323 Lakeside Av W
-Ste 450 -Cleveland 44113

(216) 696-7600 .. **Mikhail**, Sherrie '01 %Duvin C&H -1301 E 9th -20th Fl Erievw Twr
-Cleveland 44114 **Fx:**696-2038

(513) 793-5297 .. **Mikita**, William H '83 Monnie & O Co,LPA -8035 Hosbrook Rd -Ste
200 -Cincinnati 45236

(419) 213-3000 .. **Mikkonen**, Michael P '88 Lucas Cnty CSEA -701 Adams
-Toledo 43624

(330) 747-2661 .. **Miklandric**, William J Jr. '01 Cafaro Co -2445 Belmont Av -Bx2186
-Youngstown 44504

(330) 329-6111 .. **Miklich**, Thomas R '74 Invacare Corp -1 Invacare Way
-Elyria 44035

(614) 466-9261 .. **Miko**, Matthew D '97 OH Civ Rghts Cmmssn -1111 E Broad
-Ste 301 -Columbus 43205 **Fx:**466-7742

(216) 575-8016 .. **Mikol**, Lisa M '04 Adelphia Communications -3400 Lakeside Av
-Cleveland 44114

(440) 998-5337 .. **Mikolay**, Joseph C '91 -355 W Prospect Rd -Ste 111
-Ashtabula 44004

(330) 792-6033 .. **Mikulka**, Angela J '84 (Anzellotti SP&S Co,LPA) -21 N Wickliffe Cir
-Youngstown 44515 **Fx:**793-3384

(330) 792-6033 .. **Mikulka**, Thomas L '98 Anzellotti SP&S Co,LPA
-21 N Wickliffe Cir -Youngstown 44515 **Fx:**793-3384

(330) 665-8519 .. **Milane**, Robert M '79 FedEx Ground -Bx5459 -Akron 44334

(440) 356-2828 .. **Milano**, Jerome A '81 Milano Law Ofc -2639 Wooster Rd
-Rocky River 44116 **Fx:**356-2873

(972) 548-4374 .. **Milasky**, Lisa '88 Collin Cnty DA -210 S McDonald -Ste 324
-Mc Kinney, TX 75069

(513) 852-8946 .. **Milazzo**, Charles C '82 Hamilton Cnty Juv Ct -800 Bway
-Cincinnati 45202 **Fx:**946-9217

(513) 887-3821 .. **Milbauer**, Jeffrey K '81 Butler Cnty Juv Ct -280 N Fair Av
-Hamilton 45011

(440) 842-2770 .. **Milenkovich**, Milosh D '75 -5851 Pearl Rd -# 302
-Parma Heights 44130

(937) 878-5266 .. **Miles**, David R '81 -125 W Main -Ste 201 -Fairborn 45324

(419) 626-4700 .. **Miles**, Gaye H '86 -121 W Water -Ste C -Sandusky 44870

(614) 644-9279 .. **Miles**, James R '61 Supreme Ct of OH -30 E Broad -35th Fl
-Columbus 43266

(513) 732-7313 .. **Miles**, Kevin T '99 Clermont Cnty Pros -123 N 3rd -Batavia 45103

(330) 750-9251 .. **Miles**, Sherman J Jr. '91 -861 Almasy Dr -Campbell 44405

(937) 461-1900 .. **Miles**, Stephen D '77 -18 W Monument Av -Dayton 45402

(440) 742-0241 .. **Miles**, Stephen L '88 -Bx26024 -Fairview Park 44126

(216) 443-6350 .. **Mileti**, Charlene R '91 %8th Dist Ct of Appls -1 Lakeside Av -#202
-Cleveland 44113 **Fx:**443-2044

(937) 223-8888 .. **Miley**, Douglas R '93 %Dyer GM&S -131 N Ludlow -Ste 1400
-Dayton 45402 **Fx:**223-0127

(216) 696-0808 .. **Miley**, Kathryn M '96 %Wilkerson & Assoc Co,LPA -1422 Euclid Av
-Ste 248 -Cleveland 44115 **Fx:**696-4970

(216) 263-3419 .. **Milgrom**, Michael '83 FTC -1111 E Superior -Ste 200
-Cleveland 44114

(330) 452-6180 .. **Milhoan**, Douglas A '01 -601 S Main -North Canton 44720

(216) 363-1400 .. **Milicic**, Heidi J '96 Buckley K,LPA -600 E Superior Av -Ste 1400
-Cleveland 44114 **Fx:**579-1020

(216) 431-4500 .. **Milkes**, Robert A '88 Cuyahoga Cnty Pros -3955 Euclid Av
-Jane Edna Hunter Bldg -Cleveland 44115 **Fx:**431-4113

(419) 627-0414 .. **Milkie**, Duffield E '91 Buckingham LM&Z Co,LPA -414 Wayne
-Bx929 -Sandusky 44870 **Fx:**627-0009

(937) 645-1973 .. **Millard**, Christen M '97 SrCnsl Honda R&D Amer,Inc
-21001 St Rt 739 -Raymond 43067

(614) 476-0554 .. **Millard**, William L '58 -467 Howland Dr -Columbus 43230

(330) 699-1129 .. **Millard**, William L '80 -1801 Buckeye NW -Mogadore 44260

(216) 431-4500 .. **Millas**, Gregory S '96 Cuyahoga Cnty Pros -3955 Euclid Av
-Jane Edna Hunter Bldg -Cleveland 44115 **Fx:**431-4113

(440) 243-2800 .. **Mille**, Dennis G '72 (Phillips M&C Co,LPA) -7530 Lucerne Dr
-Ste 200 -Middleburg Heights 44130 **Fx:**243-2852

(614) 224-1222 .. **Miller**, Adam C '94 %Maguire & S,LLP -250 Civic Ctr Dr -Ste 200
-Columbus 43215 **Fx:**224-1236

(206) 315-6358 .. **Miller**, Alaine Y '92 XO Comm -1633 Westlake Av -Ste 200
-Seattle, WA 98109

(614) 644-6347 .. **Miller**, Alan C '87 Industrial Commssn of OH -30 W Spring -9th Fl
-Columbus 43215 **Fx:**752-8785

(248) 952-2515 .. **Miller**, Alan J '81 Internet Corp -5445 Corp Dr -Ste 200
-Troy, MI 48098

(513) 852-8560 .. **Miller**, Allen R '72 Hamilton Cnty Juv Ct -800 Bway
-Cincinnati 45202 **Fx:**946-9217

(614) 221-7711 .. **Miller**, Alyson B '04 %Grossman Law Ofcs -32 W Hoster -Ste 100
-Columbus 43215 **Fx:**221-7145

(937) 222-2333 .. **Miller**, Amy '04 %Surdyk D&T Co,LPA -40 N Main
-1610 Kettering Twr -Dayton 45423 **Fx:**222-1970

(614) 365-2700 .. **Miller**, Andrew D M '02 %Squire S&D LLP -41 S High
-1300 Huntngtn Ctr -Columbus 43215 **Fx:**365-2499

Miller, Angela W '95 -1981 Andvr Rd -Columbus 43212

(513) 621-2666 .. **Miller**, Ann B '84 %Statman HS&E LLC -255 E 5th -Ste
2900 Chemed Ctr -Cincinnati 45202 **Fx:**587-4477

(330) 796-7975 .. **Miller**, Anthony E '77 Goodyear Tire & Rubber Co -1144 E Market
-Akron 44316

(614) 221-0240 .. **Miller**, Anthony J '00 %Hahn L&P LLP -65 E State -Ste 1400
-Columbus 43215 **Fx:**221-5909

(303) 772-0165 .. **Miller**, Arlene C '83 Miller & C PC -344 Main -Bx1259 -Longmont,
CO 80502

(513) 721-1504 .. **Miller**, Arthur D '73 Droder & M Co,LPA -125 W Cntrl Pkwy
-Cincinnati 45202 **Fx:**721-0310

(937) 229-1000 .. **Miller**, Arvin S III '84 Univ of Dayton Schl of Law -300 Cllg Park
-Dayton 45469

Miller, Barbara A '90 -904 Andee Ln -Fort Branch, IN 47648

(440) 543-8418 .. **Miller**, Barbara L '90 -7649 Cntry Ln -Chagrin Falls 44023

(216) 363-4500 .. **Miller**, Barry J '83 (Benesch FC&A LLP) -200 Pub Sq -Ste 2300
-Cleveland 44114 **Fx:**363-4588

(419) 473-9276 .. **Miller**, Bennet M '79 -124 N Summit -Ste 210 -Toledo 43604
Fx:255-2332

(614) 776-1000 .. **Miller**, Beth M '00 %Barren & M Co,LPA -110 Polaris Pkwy
-Ste 302 -Westerville 43081 **Fx:**865-3396

(412) 281-7272 .. **Miller**, Brant T '98 %Dickie M&C,PC -2 PPG Pl -Ste 400
-Pittsburgh, PA 15222

(216) 875-2767 .. **Miller**, Brett A '01 %Bonezzi SM&P Co LPA -526 Superior Av
-Ste 1400 -Cleveland 44114 **Fx:**875-1570

(614) 221-8448 .. **Miller**, Brett L '81 (Buckingham D&B,LLP) -191 W Nationwide Blvd
-Ste 300 -Bx151120 -Columbus 43215 **Fx:**221-8590

(614) 221-7791 .. **Miller**, Brian G '94 F Ray Co,LPA -175 S 3rd -Ste 350
-Columbus 43215 **Fx:**221-8957

(440) 329-6660 .. **Miller**, Bridget A '83 Invacare Corp -1 Invacare Way -Elyria 44035

(614) 462-5400 .. **Miller**, Camille A '04 %Kegler BH&R -65 E State -Ste 1800
-Columbus 43215 **Fx:**464-2634

(216) 889-5062 .. **Miller**, Carol J '97 Amer Greetings.com -3 Amer Rd
-Cleveland 44144

(216) 566-5635 .. **Miller**, Catherine L '01 %Thompson H LLP -127 Pub Sq
-3900 Key Ctr -Cleveland 44114 **Fx:**566-5800

(513) 579-8900 .. **Miller**, Charles M '89 Rothchild Law Ofcs -101 W Cntrl Pkwy
-Cincinnati 45202

(614) 466-1251 .. **Miller**, Charles M '01 %Hon M O'Connor-Supreme Ct -65 S Front
-9th Fl -Columbus 43215

Miller, Cherrie N '78 -4180 Chagrin Rvr Rd -Chagrin Falls 44022

(614) 462-5033 .. **Miller**, Christopher L '94 (Schottenstein Z&D) -250 West
-Bx165020 -Columbus 43216 **Fx:**462-5135

(614) 224-9223 .. **Miller**, Clifford W II '93 Ward KBM&M -199 S 5th
-Columbus 43215

(216) 228-9400 .. **Miller**, Clinton J III '75 United Trans Union -14600 Detroit Av
-2nd Fl -Cleveland 44107

(614) 621-1500 .. **Miller**, Courtney J '99 %Calfee H&G LLP -21 E State
-1100 Fifth Third Ctr -Columbus 43215 **Fx:**621-0010

(216) 931-6000 .. **Miller**, Craig S '77 (Ulmer & B LLP) -1300 E 9th
-Ste 900 Penton Media Bldg -Cleveland 44114 **Fx:**931-6001

(216) 875-8217 .. **Miller**, Dana C '97 KPMG -1375 E 9th -Cleveland 44115

Miller, David J '02 -3413 Heath Trace -Canal Winchester 43110

(614) 464-6400 .. **Miller**, Darrell A '03 %Vorys SS&P LLP -52 E Gay -Bx1008
-Columbus 43216 **Fx:**464-6350

(513) 732-8145 .. **Miller**, Darren Dee '97 Clermont Cnty Mun Ct -289 Main
-Batavia 45103

(800) 998-9454 .. **Miller**, David F Jr. '89 Cmmnty Lgl Aid Srvcs,Inc -265 S Main
-3rd Fl -Akron 44308 **Fx:**(330) 535-0728

(614) 878-9262 .. **Miller**, David L '80 %UAW Legal Srvc Plan -5212 W Broad
-Columbus 43228

Miller, Deena C '93 -1074 Lloyd Av -Aurora 44202

(614) 227-2241 .. **Miller**, Dixon F '76 (Porter WM&A LLP) -41 S High
-Columbus 43215 **Fx:**227-2100

(614) 462-3555 .. **Miller**, Donald L '88 Franklin Cnty Pros -373 S High
-Columbus 43215

(330) 456-9911 .. **Miller**, Donald M '74 -1400 Market Av N -Canton 44714

(614) 716-1645 .. **Miller**, Donald Michael '75 Amer Elec Pwr Co -1 Riverside Plz
-Columbus 43215

Miller, E Earl Jr. '04 -(Address Unavailable)

(330) 337-9587 .. **Miller**, Earl R '52 -300 E State -Bx419 -Salem 44460

(216) 622-8200 .. **Miller**, Ebony L '03 %Calfee H&G LLP -800 Superior Av -Ste 1400
-Cleveland 44114 **Fx:**241-0816

(412) 803-1183 .. **Miller**, Edward A '00 %Marshall DWC&G -600 Grant -Ste 2900
-Pittsburgh, PA 15219 **Fx:**803-1188

(212) 758-1625 .. **Miller**, Edward W '82 -950 3rd Av -8th Fl -New York, NY 10022

(440) 350-2708 .. **Miller,** Eileen N '86 %Lake Cnty Dom Rltns Ct -47 N Park Pl -Bx490 -Painesville 44077

(614) 644-3037 .. **Miller,** Elissa B '00 EPA -122 S Front -Bx1049 -Columbus 43216

(614) 485-2010 .. **Miller,** Elizabeth L '01 %Means BB&B Co,LPA -2006 Kenny Rd -Columbus 43221 **Fx:**485-2019

(614) 466-5394 .. **Miller,** Elizabeth R '04 %Pub Def -8 E Long -Columbus 43215

(330) 893-2600 .. **Miller,** Ellis Y '98 Hummel Ins Agncy -4585 State Route 39 -Bx250 -Berlin 44610

(419) 522-6262 .. **Miller,** Eric S '76 -13 Park Av W -Ste 608 -Mansfield 44902

(310) 445-4010 .. **Miller,** Erica J '97 Chanin Capital Prtnrs -11150 Santa Monica Blvd -Ste 600 -Los Angeles, CA 90025

(937) 372-8055 .. **Miller Finney McKeown & Baker** -20 King Av -Bx610 -Xenia 45385

(215) 861-8265 .. **Miller,** Floyd J '80 US Atty Ofc -615 Chestnut -Ste 1250 -Philadelphia, PA 19106

(614) 228-1541 .. **Miller,** Frank C V '99 %Baker & H LLP -65 E State -Ste 2100 -Columbus 43215 **Fx:**462-2616

(513) 868-2909 .. **Miller,** Fred S '79 -246 High -Hamilton 45011

(513) 977-8200 .. **Miller,** G Franklin '63 %Dinsmore & S LLP -255 E 5th -Ste 1900 -Cincinnati 45202 **Fx:**977-8141

(740) 363-1324 .. **Miller,** G Scott '84 GS Miller -103 N Union -Ste A -Delaware 43015 **Fx:**548-5443

(419) 247-1849 .. **Miller,** Gary L '99 %Eastman & S Ltd -1 Seagate -24th Fl -Bx10032 -Toledo 43699 **Fx:**247-1777

(513) 721-1504 .. **Miller,** Geoffrey M '02 Droder & M Co,LPA -125 W Cntrl Pkwy -Cincinnati 45202 **Fx:**721-0310

(330) 634-0220 .. **Miller,** George M '68 -143 Northwest Av -B-203 -Tallmadge 44278

(419) 223-1861 .. **Miller,** Gregory B '91 %3rd Dist Crt Appeals -204 N Main -Lima 45801

(216) 261-7792 .. **Miller,** Gregory J '78 -564 Babbitt Rd -Euclid 44123

(419) 244-6788 .. **Miller,** Harvey C Jr. '99 Bugbee & C -405 Mad Av -Ste 1300 -Toledo 43604 **Fx:**244-7145

(330) 535-4000 .. **Miller,** Harvey F '94 (Anderson M&L) -120 E Mill -Ste 315 -Akron 44308

(216) 586-3939 .. **Miller,** Heather Varley '03 %Jones D -901 Lakeside Av -Cleveland 44114 **Fx:**579-0212

(513) 785-7180 .. **Miller,** Hillary G '84 City of Hamilton -345 High -Ste 710 -Hamilton 45011

(614) 466-4705 .. **Miller,** Holly A '94 OH Dept of Edu -25 S Front -7th Fl -Columbus 43215

(419) 874-1100 .. **Miller,** J Douglas '00 %Fraser MBM LLC -132C W 2nd -Perrysburg 43551 **Fx:**874-1130

(330) 364-1614 .. **Miller,** J G '90 Fitzpatrick Z&R Co LPA -140 Fair Av NW -Bx1014 -New Philadelphia 44663 **Fx:**343-3077

(614) 895-8727 .. **Miller,** James D '87 Dandy Products,Inc -Bx1980 -Westerville 43086 **Fx:**895-8726

(216) 363-1400 .. **Miller,** James L '96 %Buckley K,LPA -600 E Superior Av -Ste 1400 -Cleveland 44114 **Fx:**579-1020

(740) 373-9447 .. **Miller,** James M '82 Washington Cnty CSEA -205 Putnam -Cthse -Marietta 45750

(937) 382-0946 .. **Miller,** James P '63 (Buckley M&W) -145 N South -Wilmington 45177

(740) 653-6464 .. **Miller,** James W '55 OfCnsl Dagger JMO&H -144 E Main -Bx667 -Lancaster 43130 **Fx:**653-8522

(614) 466-6114 .. **Miller,** James W Jr. '78 OH DOT Labor Relations -1980 W Broad -Columbus 43223

(614) 466-2479 .. **Miller,** Jane L '76 OH Dept of Edu -25 S Front -7th Fl -Columbus 43215

(216) 844-3817 .. **Miller,** Janet L '79 Univ Hosp Hlth Sys -11100 Euclid Av -Cleveland 44106 **Fx:**844-5010

(419) 673-4176 .. **Miller,** Jason M '01 %Wetherill SM&S -109 E Franklin -Kenton 43326 **Fx:**673-8089

(704) 523-1193 .. **Miller,** Jason S '98 (Miller E&B, PLLC) -4701 Hedgemore Dr -Ste 250 -Charlotte, NC 28209

(614) 464-6400 .. **Miller,** Jeffrey Allen '00 %Vorys SS&P LLP -52 E Gay -Bx1008 -Columbus 43216 **Fx:**464-6350

(216) 696-5222 .. **Miller,** Jeffrey C '97 %Johnson & C,LLC -1001 Lakeside Av -Ste 1700 N Pnt Twr -Cleveland 44114 **Fx:**696-5288

Miller, Jeffrey D '96 -62 Erie Rd -Columbus 43214

(419) 247-2729 .. **Miller,** Jeffrey H '88 Hlth Care Reit -One Seagate -Ste 1500 -Toledo 43604

(216) 443-5809 .. **Miller,** Jennifer L '97 Cuyahoga Cnty Pros -1910 Carnegie Av -Whitlatch Bldg -Cleveland 44115 **Fx:**443-5815

(419) 865-8021 .. **Miller,** Jim '76 (Balk H&M) -5744 Southwyck Blvd -Toledo 43614 **Fx:**865-9105

(419) 213-4755 .. **Miller,** Joann Kay '88 %Hon PM Handwork -800 Jackson -Toledo 43624

(216) 622-8200 .. **Miller,** John E '97 Calfee H&G LLP -800 Superior Av -Ste 1400 -Cleveland 44114 **Fx:**241-0816

(440) 247-8178 .. **Miller,** John F '58 Miller Capital Mgmt -14944 Hillbrook Cir -Novelty 44072

(440) 871-5151 .. **Miller,** John J '66 (Childs M & Assoc,LPA) -24600 Detroit Rd -Ste 240 -WestLake 44145

(614) 228-6131 .. **Miller,** John L '63 OfCnsl McNamara & M,LLP -88 E Broad -Ste 1250 -Columbus 43215 **Fx:**228-6126

(330) 873-1001 .. **Miller,** John R '76 -3250 W Market -#307 -Akron 44333

(419) 294-2232 .. **Miller,** Jonathan K '95 %Roth BY -50 Court -Upper Sandusky 43351 **Fx:**294-2488

(937) 228-5415 .. **Miller,** Joseph P '87 %Mdwst Abstract Co -40 S Main -Ste 600 -Dayton 45402

(614) 464-6400 .. **Miller,** Joseph R '97 (Vorys SS&P LLP) -52 E Gay -Bx1008 -Columbus 43216 **Fx:**464-6350

(304) 233-3519 .. **Miller,** Joshua D '02 (J Miller & Assoc) -44 16th -Wheeling, WV 26003

(937) 865-6800 .. **Miller,** Karen S '00 Lexis/Nexis -Bx933 -Dayton 45401

Miller, Kenneth M '90 -Bx599 -Georgetown 45121

(513) 554-1110 .. **Miller,** Kristi A '99 Phillips Edison & Co -11690 Grooms Rd -Cincinnati 45242

(614) 827-1465 .. **Miller,** Kristian M '01 US Dept of Defense -Bx3990 -Columbus 43218

(412) 394-2363 .. **Miller,** Kurt A '01 (Thorp R&A LLP) -301 Grant -One Oxford Ctr -Pittsburgh, PA 15219

(330) 343-5585 .. **Miller & Kyler, LPA** -405 Chauncey Av NW -Bx668 -New Philadelphia 44663 **Fx:**343-7977

(614) 882-2500 .. **Miller,** Larry B '86 Lifestyle Comm -2800 Corp Exchange Dr -Ste 400 -Columbus 43231

(302) 773-3622 .. **Miller,** Laurence L '69 El Du Pont de Nemours & Co -1007 Market -Leg Dept -Wilmington, DE 19898

(614) 267-1617 .. **Miller,** Linda D '86 -35 E Lvngstn Av -Columbus 43215

(419) 327-4303 .. **Miller,** Lisa A '02 %Wise & D,Ltd -151 N Mich -Ste 333 -Toledo 43624 **Fx:**327-4302

(330) 848-6710 .. **Miller,** Lisa O '91 Barberton Law Dept -576 W Park Av -Barberton 44203

(330) 643-2943 .. **Miller,** Lucy R '02 Summit Cnty Pros-Juv -650 Dan -Akron 44310 **Fx:**379-3647

(937) 339-2627 .. **Miller & Luring Co,LPA** -314 W Main -Troy 45373

(513) 945-5413 .. **Miller,** Lynne M '91 Proctor & Gamble -6090 Ctr Hill Av -Cincinnati 45224

(614) 221-5627 .. **Miller,** Maria G '81 %Cnty Risk Sharing Auth -37 W Broad -Ste 650 -Columbus 43215

(419) 424-7089 .. **Miller,** Mark C '91 Hancock Cnty Pros -222 Bway -#104 -Findlay 45840 **Fx:**424-7889

(440) 333-6239 .. **Miller,** Mark J '83 -1954 Clague Rd -Westlake 44145

(614) 227-0007 .. **Miller,** Mark J '03 (Shaw & M) -555 City Park Av -Columbus 43215 **Fx:**227-0001

(440) 774-5114 .. **Miller,** Mark N '84 -Bx343 -Oberlin 44074

(614) 253-5297 .. **Miller,** Mark S '81 -800 E Broad -Columbus 43205

(740) 636-4164 .. **Miller,** Mark S '99 Camco Title Ins -132½ E Court -Ste 217 -Washington Court House 43160

(614) 248-5936 .. **Miller,** Martha G '81 Bank 1 Invstmnt Mgmt Grp -100 E Broad -Columbus 43271

(513) 977-8200 .. **Miller,** Martin J '91 (Dinsmore & S LLP) -255 E 5th -Ste 1900 -Cincinnati 45202 **Fx:**977-8141

(513) 241-3430 .. **Miller,** Marvin A '66 (Rich PWF&M) -830 Main -Ste 1115 -Cincinnati 45202 **Fx:**357-4392

(740) 965-3991 .. **Miller,** Marvin C '64 -50 E Granvll -Bx1127 -Sunbury 43074 **Fx:**965-5272

(330) 674-7070 .. **Miller & Mast Ltd** -88 S Monroe -Ste B -Millersburg 44654

(614) 365-2700 .. **Miller,** Matthew J '03 %Squire S&D LLP -41 S High -1300 Huntngtn Ctr -Columbus 43215 **Fx:**365-2499

(330) 674-7070 .. **Miller,** Max A '81 (Miller & M Ltd) -88 S Monroe -Ste B -Millersburg 44654

(614) 225-0980 .. **Miller,** Melissa A '98 Southeast,Inc -16 W Long -Columbus 43215

(216) 241-6700 .. **Miller,** Michael A '02 %Watts H Co,LPA -1100 Superior Av E -Ste 1750 Diamond Bldg -Cleveland 44114 **Fx:**241-8151

(740) 592-3332 .. **Miller,** Michael D '02 Athens Pros -8 E Wshngtn -Ste 301 -Athens 45701

(614) 462-3896 .. **Miller,** Michael L '79 Franklin Cnty Probate Ct -373 S High -22th Fl -Columbus 43215

(330) 499-8223 .. **Miller,** Michael Lee '84 City of N Canton -145 N Main -Dir of Admin -North Canton 44720

(513) 621-6464 .. **Miller,** Michael P '83 (Graydon H&R LLP) -511 Walnut -1900 Fifth Third Ctr -Cincinnati 45202 **Fx:**651-3836

(614) 221-4400 .. **Miller,** Michael S '84 Volkema TMBS&M,LPA -140 E Town -Ste 1100 -Columbus 43215 **Fx:**221-6010

Miller, Michelle G '04 -(Address Unavailable)

(614) 228-6885 .. **Miller,** Monica L '99 Lane A&H LLC -175 S 3rd -Ste 700 -Columbus 43215 **Fx:**228-0146

(419) 213-4775 .. **Miller,** Nancy A '88 Lucas Cnty Probate Ct -700 Adams -Toledo 43624

(614) 292-7755 .. **Miller,** Nancy J '79 %OSU/Hlth Sci -370 W 9th Av -232 Meiling Hall -Columbus 43210

(216) 586-3939 .. **Miller,** Nicholas M '98 %Jones D -901 Lakeside Av -Cleveland 44114 **Fx:**579-0212

(330) 264-6911 .. **Miller,** Norman R Jr. '91 (Gluck & M,LPA) -231 N Buckeye -Wooster 44691

(513) 241-3430 .. **Miller,** Orville J '70 (Rich PWF&M) -830 Main -Ste 1115 -Cincinnati 45202 **Fx:**357-4392

(404) 236-6917 .. **Miller,** Pamela S '88 Cingular Wireless -5565 Glenrdg Connector NE -Ste 1720 -Atlanta, GA 30342

Miller, Patrick S '82 -5421 Lk Shr Av -Westerville 43082

(330) 674-1080 .. **Miller,** Paul A '72 -5797 Berlin Twp Rd 353 -Millersburg 44654

(614) 760-8119 .. **Miller,** Paul A '83 CompManagement Inc -6377 Emerald Pkwy -Dublin 43016

(440) 357-6211 .. **Miller,** Paul E '97 %Cooper & F -166 Main -Painesville 44077 **Fx:**357-1634

(330) 896-2889 .. **Miller,** Paul L '91 (Miller & F,LLP) -3465 S Arlngtn Rd -Ste A -Akron 44312

(440) 395-3751 .. **Miller,** Peter D '79 Progressive Ins Co -6300 Wilson Mills Rd -#N72A -Mayfield Village 44143

(513) 382-2059 .. **Miller,** Peter J '88 -Bx36306 -Cincinnati 45236

(216) 621-3251 .. **Miller,** Ralph A '48 (Gurney M&M) -75 Pub Sq -Ste 525 -Cleveland 44113 **Fx:**621-1332

(412) 454-5813 .. **Miller,** Raymond A '94 Pepper H LLP -500 Grant -50th Fl -Pittsburgh, PA 15219

(614) 883-7698 .. **Miller,** Regina A '96 American Electric Power -700 Morrison Rd -Gahanna 43230

(614) 466-3687 .. **Miller,** Regina B '86 Industrial Commssn of OH -30 W Spring -9th Fl -Columbus 43215 **Fx:**752-8785

(330) 493-0040 .. **Miller,** Rex W '70 Lesh C&M -4150 Belden Vllg NW -Ste 606 -Canton 44718

(513) 891-7087 .. **Miller,** Richard D '81 (Donnellon D&M) -9079 Mntgmry Rd -Cincinnati 45242

(614) 464-6400 .. **Miller,** Richard T '91 %Vorys SS&P LLP -52 E Gay -Bx1008 -Columbus 43216 **Fx:**464-6350

(419) 227-9595 .. **Miller,** Richard W III '96 Daley B&L LLC -1728 Allentown Rd -Lima 45805 **Fx:**227-3177

(216) 622-8200 .. **Miller,** Robert A '82 (Calfee H&G LLP) -800 Superior Av -Ste 1400 -Cleveland 44114 **Fx:**241-0816

(740) 342-1611 .. **Miller,** Robert A '89 -223A N Main -Bx716 -New Lexington 43764

(727) 894-0432 .. **Miller,** Robert A '99 JG Rothwell,PA -560 1st Av N -Saint Petersburg, FL 33701 **Fx:**894-0797

(216) 621-0040 .. **Miller,** Robert G '73 (Strachan MO&R Co LPA) -925 Euclid Av -Ste 1940 -Cleveland 44115

(614) 469-3939 .. **Miller,** Robert H '03 %Jones D -325 John H McConnell Blvd -Ste 600 -Bx165017 -Columbus 43216 **Fx:**461-4198

(513) 983-1100 .. **Miller,** Robert J '77 Procter & Gamble Co-Legal -1 Procter & Gamble Plz -Cincinnati 45202

(216) 241-0000 .. **Miller**, Robert L '71 (Miller & N) -25550 Chagrin Blvd -Ste 108 -Beachwood 44122

(614) 220-9200 .. **Miller**, Robert P '00 %Rourke & B,LLP -495 S High -Ste 450 -Columbus 43215 **Fx:**220-7900

(740) 384-2111 .. **Miller**, Robert R '90 (Oths H&M) -16 E Bway -Bx309 -Wellston 45692

(937) 865-1445 .. **Miller**, Robin F '93 Lexis-Nexis -9443 Springboro Pike -Miamisburg 45342

(419) 422-5565 .. **Miller**, Roger L '76 (Betts M&R) -101 W Sandusky -Findlay 45840 **Fx:**423-1868

(419) 738-8171 .. **Miller**, Ronald H '68 -5 S Willipie -Wapakoneta 45895

(216) 621-1530 .. **Miller**, Ross P '01 %Shapiro & F,LLP -1500 W 3rd -Ste 400 -Cleveland 44113 **Fx:**621-1551

(419) 242-7985 .. **Miller**, Russell R Sr. '78 (Roetzel & A,LPA) -One SeaGate -9th Fl -Toledo 43604 **Fx:**242-0316

(614) 462-5400 .. **Miller**, S Michael '63 OfCnsl Kegler BH&R -65 E State -Ste 1800 -Columbus 43215 **Fx:**464-2634

(740) 687-7087 .. **Miller**, Sandra Kay '93 Fairfield Cnty Dom Rltns Ct -224 E Main -Lancaster 43130

Miller, Sandy N '85 -3511 S Tudor Ln -Bloomington, IN 47401

(513) 361-0250 .. **Miller**, Sarah J '75 SSA-OHA -312 Elm -Ste 2100 -Cincinnati 45202

(216) 689-3691 .. **Miller**, Scott D '79 KeyBank NA -127 Pub Sq -Cleveland 44114

(216) 623-5646 .. **Miller**, Scott M '95 Police Forensic Lab -1300 Ontario -Rm #761 -Cleveland 44113

(216) 241-0622 .. **Miller**, Scott R '93 -55 Pub Sq -Ste 1300 -Cleveland 44113

(330) 497-0700 .. **Miller**, Scott R '97 (Krugliak WG&D Co,LPA) -4775 Munson NW -Bx36963 -Canton 44735 **Fx:**497-4020

(740) 354-3600 .. **Miller Searl & Fitch** -806 6th -Ste 200 -Bx991 -Portsmouth 45662 **Fx:**354-1110

(330) 438-0870 .. **Miller**, Sharon D '95 Stark Cnty Pros -110 Central Plz -Ste 510 -Canton 44702

(440) 895-9700 .. **Miller**, Sharon L '91 (Battle & M PLL) -1340 Depot -Ste 201 -Rocky River 44116

(614) 764-0681 .. **Miller**, Sharon Lou '79 Blaugrund H&M,Inc -5455 Rings Rd -Ste 500 -Dublin 43017 **Fx:**764-0774

Miller, Stanley R '66 -6835 Case Rd -North Ridgeville 44039

(216) 642-0931 .. **Miller**, Stephen C '93 -3360 Forest Overlook Dr -Sevvn Hills 44131

(216) 696-3366 .. **Miller**, Steven J '81 (Goodman WM LLP) -100 Erievw Plz -27th Fl -Cleveland 44114 **Fx:**363-5835

(513) 723-4000 .. **Miller**, Steven R '94 Vorys SS&P LLP -221 E 4th -Ste 2000 Atrium Two -Bx0236 -Cincinnati 45201 **Fx:**723-4056

(614) 242-4242 .. **Miller**, Steven V '95 %Decker VSL&V Co LPA -620 E Broad -Columbus 43215 **Fx:**242-4243

(513) 634-6332 .. **Miller**, Steven W '84 Procter & Gamble -6100 Ctr Hill Rd -Cincinnati 45224

(216) 861-6000 .. **Miller Stillman & Bartel** -2000 E 9th -Ste 1100 -Cleveland 44115

(330) 287-5663 .. **Miller**, Stuart K '74 Cnty Mun Ct Judge -215 N Grant -Wooster 44691

(216) 621-0200 .. **Miller**, Tanya F '99 %Baker & H LLP -1900 E 9th -Ste 3200 -Cleveland 44114 **Fx:**696-0740

(614) 227-2000 .. **Miller**, Terrance M '72 (Porter WM&A LLP) -41 S High -Columbus 43215 **Fx:**227-2100

(614) 464-6400 .. **Miller**, Terry M '75 (Vorys SS&P LLP) -52 E Gay -Bx1008 -Columbus 43216 **Fx:**464-6500

(937) 562-5250 .. **Miller**, Thomas C '03 %Greene Cnty Pros -61 Greene -Xenia 45385

(330) 364-2803 .. **Miller**, Thomas E '55 -1600 Crater Av -Dover 44622

(614) 221-3155 .. **Miller**, Tiffany C '00 %Bailey C LLC -10 W Broad -Columbus 43215 **Fx:**221-0479

(216) 443-7800 .. **Miller**, Timothy B '87 Cuyahoga Cnty Pros -1200 Ontario -8th Fl -Cleveland 44113 **Fx:**698-2270

(614) 221-2121 .. **Miller**, Timothy E '86 (Isaac BL&T,LLP) -250 E Broad -Ste 900 Midlnd Bldg -Columbus 43215 **Fx:**365-9516

(614) 443-4891 .. **Miller**, Timothy T '93 %Crane Plastics Co -2141 Fairwood Av -Columbus 43207

(937) 228-2666 .. **Miller**, Todd T '94 %Hochman R&P Co,LPA -118 W 1st -Ste 650 -Dayton 45402 **Fx:**228-0508

Miller, Verner B III '04 -(Address Unavailable)

(440) 576-9155 .. **Miller**, Virginia K '89 (Smith & M) -36 W Jffrsn -Ste 1 -Jefferson 44047

(513) 381-2838 .. **Miller**, W Timothy '92 (Taft S&H LLP) -425 Walnut -Ste 1800 -Cincinnati 45202 **Fx:**381-0205

Miller, Wayne D '92 -1121 Worthngtn Wds Blvd -Ste 132 -Columbus 43085

Miller, Wesley M Jr. '90 -Bx3021 -Kingman, AZ 86402

(937) 435-7500 .. **Miller**, William R '97 %Botros B&S,LLC -5785 Far Hills Av -Dayton 45429 **Fx:**435-7511

(614) 466-7264 .. **Miller-Coterel**, Vanessa K '03 %OH Legal Rghts Srvc -8 E Long -5th Fl -Columbus 43215

(330) 643-2158 .. **Miller-Leonard**, Allyson '92 Summit Cnty Sheriff's Ofc -53 Univ Av -4th Fl -Akron 44308

(614) 464-0011 .. **Milless**, Charles K '75 -400 S 5th -Ste 303 -Columbus 43215

(216) 765-7431 .. **Millet**, David G '98 Cleveland Fin Grp -28601 Chagrin Blvd -Ste 300 -Cleveland 44122

(216) 765-1188 .. **Millet**, Paul L '70 -25550 Chagrin Blvd -Ste 403 -Cleveland 44122

(216) 321-3897 .. **Millett**, Diane E '87 (DE Millett Co,LPA) -2504 Newbury Dr -Cleveland Heights 44118

(216) 621-0200 .. **Millette**, Ann G '98 %Baker & H LLP -1900 E 9th -Ste 3200 -Cleveland 44114 **Fx:**696-0740

Millhoan, Carol W '84 -5320 N Elyria Rd -West Salem 44287

(330) 535-6957 .. **Millhoff**, Patricia Ann '79 -3301 Easton Rd -Norton 44203

(216) 241-6602 .. **Millican**, James T II '67 OfCnsl Weston HFP&H LLP -50 Pub Sq -2500 Trmnl Twr -Cleveland 44113 **Fx:**621-8369

(419) 882-0518 .. **Millican**, Patrick R '87 (Hunt MD&O) -5808 Monroe -Bx370 -Sylvania 43560

(330) 742-4309 .. **Millich**, George P Jr. '00 National City Bank -20 Fed Plz -2nd Fl -Youngstown 44503

(614) 891-6363 .. **Milligan**, David T '68 -483 Dempsey Rd -Westerville 43081

(614) 891-6363 .. **Milligan**, Frederick J Jr. '67 -483 Dempsey Rd -Westerville 43081 **Fx:**891-6366

Milligan, John R Jr. '52 -1607 S Main -North Canton 44709

(330) 864-3100 .. **Milligan**, Kerry G '93 T McKinzie -529 White Pond Dr -Akron 44320

(202) 434-5000 .. **Milligan**, Luke M '04 %Williams & C,LLP -725 12th NW -Washington, DC 20005

(216) 928-7700 .. **Milligan**, Patrick J '04 l Friedman & Assoc -700 W St Clair Av -Ste 110 -Cleveland 44113 **Fx:**556-9779

(330) 492-8717 .. **Milligan**, Richard S '80 (Buckingham D&B,LLP) -4518 Fulton Dr NW -Bx35548 -Canton 44735 **Fx:**492-9625

Milligan, William W '51 -150 W Beechwold Blvd -Columbus 43214

Milliken, Christopher M '86 -6890 Woodvw Ct N -B -Reynoldsburg 43068

(614) 462-5310 .. **Milliken**, Olga Bosques '86 Franklin Cnty Dom Relatns Ct -373 S High -3rd Fl -Columbus 43215

(330) 830-1555 .. **Milliken**, Paul E '63 -9061 Wall NW -Massillon 44646 **Fx:**830-0266

(513) 863-6700 .. **Millikin & Fitton** -6 S 2nd -6th Fl -Bx598 -Hamilton 45012 **Fx:**863-0031

(513) 829-6700 .. **Millikin & Fitton** -530 Wessel Dr -Ste 2A -Fairfield 45014 **Fx:**829-0258

(513) 523-3700 .. **Millikin & Fitton** -5020 B Cllg Crnr Pike -Oxford 45056 **Fx:**523-0463

(740) 653-8050 .. **Millisor**, Kenneth C '94 -324 E Main -Lancaster 43130

(440) 838-8800 .. **Millisor**, Kenneth R '61 (Millisor & N Co,LPA) -9150 S Hills Blvd -Ste 300 -Cleveland 44147 **Fx:**838-8805

(440) 838-8800 .. **Millisor & Nobil Co,LPA** -9150 S Hills Blvd -Ste 300 -Cleveland 44147 **Fx:**838-8805

(614) 221-2234 .. **Millisor & Nobil Co,LPA** -300 E Broad -Ste 190 -Columbus 43215 **Fx:**221-1278

(330) 493-8525 .. **Millisor & Nobil Co,LPA** -4117 Whipple Av NW -Ste B -Canton 44718 **Fx:**493-8606

(440) 838-8800 .. **Millisor**, Richard A '94 (Millisor & N Co,LPA) -9150 S Hills Blvd -Ste 300 -Cleveland 44147 **Fx:**838-8805

(419) 893-4836 .. **Millon**, James W '76 -302 Conant -Maumee 43537

(937) 438-3977 .. **Millonig**, Michael J '81 (M Millonig Law Grp,LLC) -7601 Paragon Rd #103 -Dayton 45459

(440) 777-8497 .. **Mills**, Barbara A '94 -22465 Brookpark Rd -Fairview Park 44126

(440) 333-5700 .. **Mills**, Charles E '80 -22255 Ctr Ridge Rd -Ste 106 -Rocky River 44116

(330) 456-0506 .. **Mills**, Daniel M '86 (Mills MF&L) -Bx35656 -Canton 44735

(216) 586-3939 .. **Mills**, David E '02 %Jones D -901 Lakeside Av -Cleveland 44114 **Fx:**579-0212

(614) 464-6400 .. **Mills**, Frederick E '73 OfCnsl Vorys SS&P LLP -52 E Gay -Bx1008 -Columbus 43216 **Fx:**464-6350

(419) 241-1150 .. **Mills**, Gerald L '68 (Herschel ABM&M) -615 Adams -Toledo 43604 **Fx:**241-7825

(513) 621-3440 .. **Mills**, James A '80 (Denlinger R&G Co,LPA) -425 Walnut -Ste 2310 -Cincinnati 45202 **Fx:**621-4449

(216) 621-0200 .. **Mills**, Jennifer A '96 %Baker & H LLP -1900 E 9th -Ste 3200 -Cleveland 44114 **Fx:**696-0740

(614) 227-2000 .. **Mills**, Jennifer T '83 (Porter WM&A LLP) -41 S High -Columbus 43215 **Fx:**227-2100

(713) 296-4131 .. **Mills**, John T Jr. '73 Marathon Oil Co -5555 San Felipe Rd -Houston, TX 77056

(614) 794-9595 .. **Mills**, Julie S '98 %JG Flaherty Co,LPA -575 Charring Cross Dr -Ste 100 -Westerville 43081 **Fx:**794-9590

(614) 523-3575 .. **Mills**, Kathleen B '91 (Mills & M) -1935 W Schrock Rd -Westerville 43081

(330) 456-0506 .. **Mills**, Laura L '94 (Mills MF&L) -Bx35656 -Canton 44735

(330) 329-3170 .. **Mills**, Lori Ann '93 -47 Berkshire Ct -Apt 1-C -Akron 44313

(614) 523-3575 .. **Mills**, Luther J '89 (Mills & M) -1935 W Schrock Rd -Westerville 43081

(614) 299-6357 .. **Mills**, Melanie '93 -48 W Starr Av -Columbus 43201

(330) 456-0506 .. **Mills Mills Fiely & Lucas** -Bx35656 -Canton 44735

(216) 479-8500 .. **Mills**, Osborne Jr. '75 (Squire S&D LLP) -127 Pub Sq -4900 Key Twr -Cleveland 44114 **Fx:**479-8780

(419) 524-1403 .. **Mills**, Reese F '75 (Mabee & M) -24 W 3rd -Ste 300 -Mansfield 44902 **Fx:**522-4315

(440) 333-5700 .. **Mills**, Ronald H '72 -22255 Ctr Ridge Rd -Ste 106 -Rocky River 44116

(513) 425-7830 .. **Mills**, Sara E '01 Middletown Law Dept -One Donham Plz -Middletown 45042

(614) 848-4442 .. **Mills**, Steven B '85 Chicago Title -150 E Wilson Bridge Rd -Worthington 43085

(740) 453-1317 .. **Mills**, Thomas M '82 -1105 Maple Av -Zanesville 43701

(513) 732-9999 .. **Mills**, Tina R '99 -4351 Glen Este Withamsvll Rd -Cincinnati 45245 **Fx:**735-2455

(216) 292-5807 .. **Mills**, William M '75 (Singerman MD&K) -3401 Enterprise Pkwy -Ste 200 -Beachwood 44122 **Fx:**292-5867

(937) 328-2653 .. **Millspaugh**, Theodore E '79 2nd Dist Ct of Appls -101 N Limestone -Ste 315 -Springfield 45502

(216) 479-8500 .. **Millstone**, David J '71 (Squire S&D LLP) -127 Pub Sq -4900 Key Twr -Cleveland 44114 **Fx:**479-8780

Millward, Richard L '58 -1293 Smith Rd -Temperance, MI 48182

Milne, David M '90 -4347 Mumford Dr -Columbus 43220

(614) 466-9566 .. **Milne**, Susan E '94 OH Brd of Nursing -17 S High -Ste 400 -Columbus 43215

(315) 797-5200 .. **Milner**, David R '78 Commercial Trav Mutual Ins -70 Genesse -Utica, NY 13502

(216) 987-4856 .. **Miltner**, Lawrence J '78 Community College Dist -700 Carnegie Av -Cleveland 44115

(419) 568-5751 .. **Miltner**, Ryan K '02 BF Yale & Assoc,LPA -102 W Wapakoneta -Bx100 -Waynesfield 45896

(740) 747-0336 .. **Minadeo**, Joseph M '04 -1071 Worthngtn-New Haven Rd -Marengo 43334

(216) 706-9250 .. **Minahan**, Kathleen M '95 LESCO Inc -1301 E 9th -Ste 1300 -Cleveland 44114 **Fx:**706-5165

(937) 599-7260 .. **Minahan**, Wade T '88 Logan Cnty Cmn Pleas Ct -101 S Main -Rm 103 -Bellefontaine 43311

(513) 985-0390 .. **Minamyer**, William E '79 (W Minamyer,Co,LPA) -9690 Waterford Pl -103 -Loveland 45140

(330) 668-8243 .. **Minc**, David C '74 Flexsys Amer LP -260 Sprngside Dr -Akron 44333

(513) 241-9400 .. **Minch,** Christina L '03 %Legal Aid -215 E 9th -Ste 200
-Cincinnati 45202

(216) 622-8200 .. **Minchak,** JoEllen M '85 (Calfee H&G LLP) -800 Superior Av
-Ste 1400 -Cleveland 44114 Fx:241-0816

(614) 227-2000 .. **Minck,** Linda R '90 %Porter WM&A LLP -41 S High
-Columbus 43215 Fx:227-2100

(216) 357-5349 .. **Mindes,** Paula '97 US DOL Empl Standards Admin -Ofc of
Workers Comp Prog -1240 E 9th St -Rm 839 -Cleveland 44199

(216) 621-2030 .. **Mindlin,** Lewis B '75 (L Mindlin & Co,LPA) -614 Superior Av W
-15th Fl -Cleveland 44113

(614) 221-1125 .. **Mindzak,** Stephen E '92 (S Mindak,LLC) -51 N High -Ste 401
-Columbus 43215

(513) 735-0800 .. **Mineer,** Susan '97 -65 N 2nd -Ste 200 -Batavia 45103
Fx:735-2250

(216) 694-3930 .. **Mineff,** George Jr. '84 -1630 Standard Bldg -1370 Ontario
-Cleveland 44113

(407) 423-4246 .. **Minegar,** Craig A '96 Winderweedle HW&W -250 Park Av S
-Bx880 -Winter Park, FL 32790 Fx:645-3728

(937) 223-8888 .. **Minella,** Shirley L '92 Dyer GM&S -131 N Ludlow -Ste 1400
-Dayton 45402 Fx:223-0127

Miner, Deborah Ann '82 -Bx14367 -Cincinnati 45250

(412) 652-4081 .. **Minett,** Thomas W '96 %D Hartman,PC -2815 Wilmngtn Rd
-New Castle, PA 16105

Mingo, Clarence E II '99 -513 E Rich -Columbus 43215

(216) 687-1311 .. **Mingus,** Ronald A '90 (Reminger & R) -101 Prospect Av W
-1400 Mdlnd Bldg -Cleveland 44115 Fx:687-1841

(330) 666-0000 .. **Minichiello,** Alfred C '55 -1740 N Medina Line Rd -Akron 44333
Mininger, Lori L '04 -(Address Unavailable)

(614) 785-1122 .. **Minister,** Mark V '91 Mutual of Omaha Ins -8800 Lyra Dr -Ste 530
-Columbus 43240

(614) 228-1541 .. **Minister,** Michael E '74 (Baker & H LLP) -65 E State -Ste 2100
-Columbus 43215 Fx:462-2616

(740) 587-1900 .. **Minklei,** Lisa A '87 RE/MAX Excellence -124 S Main
-Granville 43023

(330) 455-0173 .. **Minkler,** Andrea D '79 (Day KRW&R,Ltd) -200 Market Av N
-Ste 300 -Bx24213 -Canton 44701 Fx:455-2633

Minkler, Patricia P '79 -(Address Unavailable)

(419) 229-5106 .. **Minnard,** Lawrence R '68 (Rizor M&R Co,LPA)
-1045 Mackenzie Dr -Lima 45805

(216) 520-0088 .. **Minney,** Ronzel B '78 Pepple & W Ltd -5005 Rockside Rd
-Ste 260 -Cleveland 44131 Fx:520-0044

(440) 238-0365 .. **Minni,** Dennis E '73 -14761 Pearl Rd -Ste 104 -Strongsville 44136

(937) 585-5165 .. **Minnich,** Michael G '87 -2 Rollicking Hills Ln -De Graff 43318

(216) 861-5582 .. **Minnich,** Richard J '65 OfCnsl Fay SFM&M LLP -1100 Superior Av
-7th Fl -Cleveland 44114 Fx:241-1666

(937) 592-2004 .. **Minnich,** Sheila E '87 -325 N Main -Bellefontaine 43311

(440) 835-3511 .. **Minnich,** William A '57 Echo Hlth,Inc -896 Corp Way -Ste 400
-Westlake 44145

(513) 248-0760 .. **Minniear,** Michael T '73 -626 Main -Milford 45150

(614) 481-7990 .. **Minnillo,** Christopher J '79 -1500 W 3rd Av -Ste 400 -Columbus
43212

Minnillo, Mary T '95 -1274 Herschel Av -Cincinnati 45208

(513) 752-3900 .. **Minnillo,** Paul J '95 %C Keegan & Assoc
-4440 Glen Este-Withamsvll Rd -Ste 550 -Cincinnati 45245

(330) 864-5550 .. **Minns,** Michael H '85 %Hahn L&P LLP -One GOJO Plz -Ste 300
-Akron 44311 Fx:864-7986

(216) 622-8200 .. **Mino,** John M '84 (Calfee H&G LLP) -800 Superior Av -Ste 1400
-Cleveland 44114 Fx:241-0816

(614) 899-0636 .. **Minor,** Anne E '97 Minor & Assoc -283 S State -Westerville 43081

(614) 464-6400 .. **Minor,** Daniel J '81 (Vorys SS&P LLP) -52 E Gay -Bx1008
-Columbus 43216 Fx:464-6350

(614) 464-6400 .. **Minor,** Robert A '75 (Vorys SS&P LLP) -52 E Gay -Bx1008
-Columbus 43216 Fx:464-6350

(216) 357-5900 .. **Minshall,** Kent R Jr. '79 -2189 Professor Av -#100
-Cleveland 44113

(740) 233-1470 .. **Minter,** John A '04 %Collins & L -125 S Main -Marion 43302
Fx:223-1467

(330) 562-2793 .. **Minton,** Andrea J '74 -311 E Garfld Rd -Aurora 44202

(614) 848-9600 .. **Minton,** Harvey S '62 (H Minton & Assoc) -6641 N High
-Worthington 43085

(202) 942-2844 .. **Minton,** Jeffrey J '96 US SEC -450 5th NW -MS 0312
-Washington, DC 20549

(202) 326-2479 .. **Minton,** Shira C '96 FTC -600 Penn Av -Washington, DC 20580

(216) 531-0311 .. **Mintz,** Gary L '79 -5533 State Rd -Cleveland 44134

(216) 696-1422 .. **Mintz,** Stuart A '78 (McCarthy LC&L Co,LPA) -101 Prospect Av W
-1800 Mdlnd Bldg -Cleveland 44115 Fx:696-1210

(513) 595-8800 .. **Minutolo,** James P '83 Jackson Rolfes Spurgeon & Co
-2090 Florence Av -Ste 201 -Cincinnati 45206

(419) 692-0060 .. **Minzing,** Paula A '50 (Marsh M&M) -302 W 1st -Bx363
-Delphos 45833

(202) 622-3050 .. **Miosi,** Dianna K '79 IRS -1111 Const Av NW
-Washington, DC 20001

(419) 474-5020 .. **Mira,** Charles J '83 (Mira & K Ltd) -4841 Monroe -Ste 350
-Toledo 43623

(703) 614-1513 .. **Miracle,** Charles A '97 USMC -2 Navy Annx -CMC JAR
-Washington, DC 20380

(440) 233-1100 .. **Miraldi & Barrett Co,LPA** -6061 S Bway -Lorain 44053

(440) 233-1100 .. **Miraldi,** David P '78 (Miraldi & B Co,LPA) -6061 S Bway
-Lorain 44053

(440) 233-1100 .. **Miraldi,** James L '77 (Miraldi & B Co,LPA) -6061 S Bway
-Lorain 44053

(440) 989-8080 .. **Miraldi,** John R '87 (J Miraldi Co,LPA) -4520 Oberlin Av
-Lorain 44053

(440) 245-1558 .. **Miraldi,** Karen K '88 -3060 W Erie Av -Lorain 44053

(216) 566-5508 .. **Miraldi,** Leslee W '78 (Thompson H LLP) -127 Pub Sq
-3900 Key Ctr -Cleveland 44114 Fx:566-5800

(216) 696-7777 .. **Miralia,** Benedict P Sr. '68 Musca & M -1300 E 9th -Ste 1202
-Cleveland 44114

(216) 696-7777 .. **Miralia,** Benedict P Jr. '88 %Musca & M -1300 E 9th -Ste 1202
-Cleveland 44114

(216) 443-7800 .. **Miranda de Ahrendt,** Myriam A '95 Cuyahoga Cnty Pros
-1200 Ontario -8th Fl -Cleveland 44113 Fx:698-2270

(513) 421-4020 .. **Mire,** Terrence A '73 (Cohen TK&S,LLC) -250 E 5th -Ste 1200
-Cincinnati 45202 Fx:241-4490

(513) 421-4855 .. **Mire,** William N '49 -830 Main -Ste 1105 -Cincinnati 45202

(330) 743-5101 .. **Mirkin,** Ira J '79 Green H&S,Co LPA -16 Wick Av -Ste 400
-Youngstown 44503 Fx:743-3451

(614) 221-0090 .. **Mirman,** Denise M '82 Friedman & M Co,LPA -503 S Front
-Ste 250 -Columbus 43215

(614) 221-0922 .. **Mirman,** Joel H '66 (Gamble HJ Co,LPA) -1 E Lvngstn Av
-Columbus 43215 Fx:365-9741

(614) 848-6611 .. **Mirras,** Thomas J '71 -1395 E Dublin-Granvll Rd -Ste 201
-Columbus 43229

(216) 931-6000 .. **Mischka,** Cash H '91 %Ulmer & B LLP -1300 E 9th
-Ste 900 Penton Media Bldg -Cleveland 44114 Fx:931-6001

(937) 293-1000 .. **Mischler,** Frederick F '94 -2323 W Schantz Av -Ste 216
-Kettering 45409 Fx:293-4707

Misciagna, Jennifer A '04 -(Address Unavailable)

(989) 631-2800 .. **Mishic,** Michael M '86 -711 Bayliss -Midland, MI 48640

(216) 241-2600 .. **Mishkind,** Howard D '80 (Becker & M Co,LPA) -1660 W 2nd
-Ste 660 -Cleveland 44113 Fx:241-5757

(440) 871-3131 .. **Mishler,** Howard V '73 (H Mishler Co,LLP) -30400 Detroit Rd
-Ste 108 -Westlake 44145

(330) 527-2335 .. **Mishler,** Robert E '60 -8121 Main -Bx326 -Garrettsville 44231

Misiewicz, Daniel J '04 -(Address Unavailable)

(414) 276-2850 .. **Miske,** Daniel J '04 %Petrie & S,SC -111 E Wscnsn Av -#1500
-Milwaukee, WI 53202

(614) 249-1948 .. **Miskell,** Jennifer L '98 KPMG LLP -191 W Nationwide Blvd
-Ste 500 -Columbus 43215

(330) 650-0088 .. **Mismas,** John D '04 %Bevan & Assoc LPA,Inc -10360 Nrthfld Rd
-Northfield 44067 Fx:467-4493

(440) 256-1395 .. **Misny,** Timothy P '81 -Bx1356 -Willoughby 44096

(330) 675-2426 .. **Misocky,** James J '78 Trumbull Cnty Pros -160 High NW
-Warren 44481

Misocky, Michael A '99 -706 Union -Warren 44485

(216) 752-3330 .. **Misra,** Anand N '97 -24220 Shaker Blvd -Shaker Heights 44122

(202) 273-3744 .. **Misra,** Polly '93 NLRB Cntmpt Lit Brnch -1099 14th NW
-Ste 10700 -Washington, DC 20570 Fx:273-4244

(440) 461-3461 .. **Misseldine,** Russell W '96 Victoria Ins Co -5915 Landerbrook Dr
-#101 -Bx93863 -Mayfield Heights 44124 Fx:(800) 884-4473

(740) 773-0012 .. **Missler,** Betsie L '98 SE OH Lgl Srvcs -11 E 2nd
-Chillicothe 45601

(419) 241-1200 .. **Mistry,** Jennifer S '01 %Cooper & W,LPA -900 Adams
-Toledo 43624 Fx:242-5675

(614) 463-7043 .. **Mitchell,** Albert A '75 Natl City Bank -155 E Broad -3rd Fl
-Columbus 43251

(614) 224-4114 .. **Mitchell Allen Catalano & Boda Co,LPA** -580 S High -Ste 200
-Columbus 43215 Fx:224-3804

(757) 851-8560 .. **Mitchell,** Alphonso '73 Al Mitchell Cnsltng -2 Deer Run Ln
-hampton, VA 23669

(937) 223-6003 .. **Mitchell,** Amy C '98 %Dunlevey M&F -110 N Main -Ste 1000
-Dayton 45402 Fx:223-8550

(216) 241-5310 .. **Mitchell,** Ann R '95 %Gallagher SF&N -1501 Euclid Av -6th Fl
-Cleveland 44115 Fx:241-1608

(513) 574-0606 .. **Mitchell,** Charles E '78 -6024 Harrison Av -Ste 14
-Cincinnati 45248

(202) 434-1500 .. **Mitchell,** Christopher P '04 %Staas & H LLP -1201 NY Av NW
-Ste 700 -Washington, DC 20005 Fx:434-1501

(502) 562-5350 .. **Mitchell,** Darryl '86 Fifth 3rd Bank KY -401 S 4th
-Louisville, KY 40202

(513) 243-9926 .. **Mitchell,** Darryl '93 GE Aircraft Engines -1 Neumann Way
-Mail Drop J-165 -Cincinnati 45215

(330) 297-7788 .. **Mitchell,** Donald P Jr. '73 -3766 Fishcreek Rd -#197 -Stow 44224

(419) 213-6762 .. **Mitchell,** Donna P '89 Lucas Cnty Juv Ct -1801 Spielbusch Av
-Toledo 43624

(513) 248-9300 .. **Mitchell,** Edward B Jr. '69 Supervalu Inc -25 Whitney Dr -Ste 122
-Milford 45150

(614) 221-3318 .. **Mitchell,** Gregory R '93 %Agee CM&L -89 E Nationwide Blvd
-Ste 200 -Columbus 43215

(937) 449-2800 .. **Mitchell,** James R '72 OfCnsl Chernesky H&K PLL
-10 Cthse Plz SW -Ste 1100 -Dayton 45402 Fx:449-2821

(513) 977-8200 .. **Mitchell,** Jennifer O '98 %Dinsmore & S LLP -255 E 5th -Ste 1900
-Cincinnati 45202 Fx:977-8141

(330) 762-0700 .. **Mitchell,** John A '98 %Slater Z&G -One Cascade Plz -Ste 2210
-Akron 44308 Fx:762-3923

(216) 566-5500 .. **Mitchell,** John R '96 %Thompson H LLP -127 Pub Sq
-3900 Key Ctr -Cleveland 44114 Fx:566-5800

(614) 466-0722 .. **Mitchell,** Keesha R '91 Atty Gen -150 E Gay -Columbus 43215
Fx:644-9973

(419) 255-4480 .. **Mitchell,** Keith L '87 -1700 Canton Av -Five Canton Sq
-Toledo 43624

(440) 256-4150 .. **Mitchell,** Kenneth L '82 Woodling K&R -9213 Chillicothe Rd
-Kirtland 44094

(216) 586-3939 .. **Mitchell,** Kimberley P '04 %Jones D -901 Lakeside Av
-Cleveland 44114 Fx:579-0212

(419) 213-4743 .. **Mitchell,** Kristina L '96 Lucas Co Common Pleas Ct -700 Adams
-Cnty Cthse -Toledo 43624

(419) 288-3025 .. **Mitchell,** L Snowden '60 -6401 Bays Rd -Wayne 43466
Fx:288-3245

(216) 486-0024 .. **Mitchell,** LuAnn '83 -Bx08531 -Cleveland 44108

(216) 443-8586 .. **Mitchell,** Mamie J '96 Cuyahoga Cnty Cmmn Pleas Ct
-1200 Ontario -11th Fl -Cleveland 44113

(330) 620-2642 .. **Mitchell,** Mary Gibbs '86 -716 Springwtr Dr -Akron 44333
Fx:666-7787

(419) 842-1166 .. **Mitchell,** Mary J '01 %Borgstahl & Z -6591 W Central Av -Ste 201
-Toledo 43617

(614) 464-6400 .. **Mitchell,** Melissa J '83 %Vorys SS&P LLP -52 E Gay -Bx1008
-Columbus 43216 Fx:464-6350

(614) 292-0611 .. **Mitchell,** Michael A '91 OSU Ofc of Legal Affairs -33 W 11th Av
-Ste 209 -Columbus 43201 Fx:292-8699

(937) 222-2424 .. **Mitchell,** Nicole A '97 Freund F&A -1 S Main -Ste 1800
-Dayton 45402 Fx:225-5369

(513) 381-2838 .. **Mitchell,** Patrick J '86 (Taft S&H LLP) -425 Walnut -Ste 1800
-Cincinnati 45202 Fx:381-0205

(513) 381-9200 .. **Mitchell**, Ralph F '51 (Rendigs FK&D,LLP) -One W 4th -Ste 900
-Cincinnati 45202 **Fx:**381-9206

(937) 384-6286 .. **Mitchell**, Richard J Jr. '90 SrCnsl Huffy Srvc 1st,Inc -225 Byers Rd
-Miamisburg 45342

(216) 381-2183 .. **Mitchell**, Richard N '60 -1775 Wrentford Rd -Cleveland 44121

(216) 623-0150 .. **Mitchell**, Richard S '84 (Roetzel & A,LPA) -1375 E 9th
-One Cleve Ctr 9th Fl -Cleveland 44114 **Fx:**623-0134

(614) 464-6400 .. **Mitchell**, Robert C '90 OfCnsl Vorys SS&P LLP -52 E Gay
-Bx1008 -Columbus 43216 **Fx:**464-6350

(937) 865-6800 .. **Mitchell**, Robert G II '91 Lexis/Nexis -Bx933 -Dayton 45401

(513) 721-5525 .. **Mitchell**, Robert H '86 (Manley B) -225 W Court -Cincinnati 45202
Fx:721-4268

(614) 236-6500 .. **Mitchell**, Roberta S '72 %Capital Univ Law Sch -303 E Broad
-Columbus 43215

(440) 483-4245 .. **Mitchell**, Sheila N '92 Philips Med Syst, Inc -595 Miner Rd
-Cleveland 44143

(419) 352-1581 .. **Mitchell Stearns & Hammer** -112 E Oak -Bowling Green 43402

(740) 432-6322 .. **Mitchell**, Stephanie L '01 Tribbie SP&P -139 Ct Hse Sq -Bx640
-Cambridge 43725 **Fx:**439-1795

Mitchell, Stephen D '78 -Bx91023 -Columbus 43209

(440) 423-0909 .. **Mitchell**, Thoral David '89 -1090 Cnty Lane Rd -Gates Mills 44040

(614) 221-2838 .. **Mitchell**, Timothy B '82 (Taft S&H LLP) -21 E State -12th Fl
-Columbus 43215 **Fx:**221-2007

(614) 462-3555 .. **Mitchell**, Timothy K '80 Franklin Cnty Pros -373 S High
-Columbus 43215

(216) 621-0200 .. **Mitchell**, Wade A '85 (Baker & H LLP) -1900 E 9th -Ste 3200
-Cleveland 44114 **Fx:**696-0740

(513) 677-0999 .. **Mitchell**, William J '97 %G Hoffmann Co,LPA
-11935 Mason-Mntgmry Rd -Ste 130 -Cincinnati 45249

(513) 566-0064 .. **Mitchell**, William Jr. '78 (Armstrong MD&Z) -101 Prospect Av W
-1725 The Mdlnd Bldg -Cleveland 44115 **Fx:**566-0224

(216) 431-4500 .. **Mitchell**, Willie L '95 Cuyahoga Cnty Pros -3955 Euclid Av
-Jane Edna Hunter Bldg -Cleveland 44115 **Fx:**431-4113

(703) 741-5098 .. **Mitra**, Surjya K '94 KPMG -1660 Int'l Dr -McLean, VA 22102

(513) 381-2838 .. **Mitroussia**, Antonia '91 %Taft S&H LLP -425 Walnut -Ste 1800
-Cincinnati 45202 **Fx:**381-0205

(330) 670-8400 .. **Mitsopoulos**, Sophia '97 H Tipping
-525 N Cleveland Massillon Rd -#207 -Akron 44333

(330) 452-4751 .. **Mittas**, William G '91 -1369 Market Av N -Canton 44714

(419) 248-4256 .. **Mittelstaedt**, David J '83 -520 Mad Av -920 Spitzer Bldg
-Toledo 43604

(419) 772-1933 .. **Mittendorf**, Allison A '99 ONU-Pettit Clg of Law -525 S Main
-Ada 45810

(513) 624-9276 .. **Mittendorf**, Richard K '50 -7128 Paddison Rd -Cincinnati 45230

(440) 892-8380 .. **Mittendorf**, William J '72 -24441 Detroit Rd -Ste 300
-Westlake 44145

(205) 934-5382 .. **Mittleman**, Linda S '86 Univ of Alabama/Birmingham
-1530 6th Av S -Ste 504B -Birmingham, AL 35294

(614) 221-5379 .. **Mittman**, Lee C '58 -502 S 3rd -Columbus 43215

(614) 443-8388 .. **Mix**, Carol P '90 -37 E Deshler Av -Columbus 43206

(216) 586-3939 .. **Mixter**, Stephen C '86 (Jones D) -901 Lakeside Av -Cleveland
44114 **Fx:**579-0212

(330) 263-2984 .. **Miyashita**, Monica L '00 (Miyashita & T,LLC) -111 S Buckeye
-Ste 270 -Wooster 44691

(614) 462-6033 .. **Mizelle**, Brian D '01 %Franklin Cnty Children Srvcs -855 W Mound
-Columbus 43223 **Fx:**462-5062

(216) 592-5000 .. **Mizer**, Susan L '93 %Tucker E&W LLP -925 Euclid Av
-1150 Huntgtn Bldg -Cleveland 44115 **Fx:**592-5009

(440) 842-1138 .. **Mizisin**, John '52 -7584 Dawn Haven Dr -Cleveland 44130

(216) 529-6030 .. **Mladek**, Jennifer L '98 Law Dept -12650 Detroit Av
-Lakewood 44107

(216) 363-4500 .. **Mlakar**, Ginger Fuller '92 OfCnsl Benesch FC&A LLP -200 Pub Sq
-Ste 2300 -Cleveland 44114 **Fx:**363-4588

(216) 687-1900 .. **Mlakar**, Thomas '92 Legal Aid -1223 W 6th -Cleveland 44113
Fx:687-0779

(419) 897-5295 .. **Mlcek**, Paula B '90 -1789 Indn Wd Cir -Ste 140 -Maumee 43537

(937) 323-3768 .. **Mlicki**, Teresa C '80 %P Malina Co,LPA -6 W High -Ste 806
-Springfield 45502

(330) 451-7897 .. **Mlinar**, Kristen L '96 Stark Cnty Pros -110 Central Plz -Ste 510
-Canton 44702

(419) 882-7100 .. **Moan**, James E '72 (Lydy & M,Ltd) -4930 Holland Sylvania Rd
-Sylvania 43560 **Fx:**882-1120

(614) 801-2767 .. **Moats**, Raymond F III '00 %Weltman W&R Co,LPA -175 S 3rd
-Ste 900 -Columbus 43215 **Fx:**222-2193

(440) 779-6613 .. **Mobberly**, Patricia H '88 %B Thompson -2156 Walter Rd
-Westlake 44145

(202) 514-7632 .. **Mobley**, Dawn K '92 US Atty Ofc -555 4th NW
-Washington, DC 20530

(614) 462-4556 .. **Mobley**, Laura J '93 Franklin Cnty CSEA -80 E Fulton -Columbus
43215

Mobydeen, Lana S '04 -(Address Unavailable)

(440) 257-4372 .. **Mocilnikar**, Frank C '76 -6442 Carter Blvd -Mentor 44060

(513) 563-6161 .. **Mock**, Russell J '96 -11137 Main -Cincinnati 45241

(216) 481-2350 .. **Mock**, Theron C '54 Clay Mock -20851 Edgecliff Dr -Euclid 44123

(419) 724-3499 .. **Mockensturm**, Mark M '93 -232 10th -Toledo 43624

(330) 793-2698 .. **Modarelli**, Nicholas E '83 -60 Wstchstr Dr -Ste 1
-Youngstown 44515

(419) 241-6000 .. **Modd**, Anthony R '02 %Eastman & S Ltd -1 Seagate -24th Fl
-Bx10032 -Toledo 43699 **Fx:**247-1777

Modderman, Geoffrey A '04 -(Address Unavailable)

(216) 522-3715 .. **Modic**, Catherine A '87 NLRB -1240 E 9th -1695 Celebrezze Bldg
-Cleveland 44199 **Fx:**522-2418

(216) 291-2400 .. **Modica**, Donald A '70 (Zimmerman CE&M) -5001 Mayfld Rd
-Ste 105 -Cleveland 44124

(216) 566-0835 .. **Modney**, Robert T '75 Chrtr One Bank,FSB -1215 Superior Av
-Cleveland 44114

Modrall, Gladys W '88 -(Address Unavailable)

Modugno, Vincent R '78 -706 Barbara Ct -Akron 44319

Mody, Shachi '03 -(Address Unavailable)

(513) 579-6400 .. **Moeddel**, Michael J '02 %Keating M&K PLL -1 E 4th
-1400 Provident Twr -Cincinnati 45202 **Fx:**579-6457

(614) 469-3206 .. **Moehring**, Boyd K '89 (Thompson H LLP) -10 W Broad -Ste 700
-Columbus 43215 **Fx:**469-3361

(937) 465-2002 .. **Moell**, Christopher J '96 (Brandt & M) -109 S Detroit -Bx910
-West Liberty 43357

(412) 394-7917 .. **Moellenberg**, Charles H Jr. '79 (Jones DR&P) -500 Grant
-31st Fl One Mellon Bk Ctr -Pittsburgh, PA 15219 **Fx:**394-7959

Moeller, Colin P '04 -(Address Unavailable)

(513) 721-5525 .. **Moeller**, George F '85 OfCnsl Manley B -225 W Court
-Cincinnati 45202 **Fx:**721-4268

(216) 781-5515 .. **Moeller**, Jeffrey S '02 Hermann C&S,LLP -1301 E 9th -Ste 500
-Cleveland 44114 **Fx:**781-1030

(513) 844-8515 .. **Moeller**, Patrick G '84 -223 S Front -Hamilton 45011

(419) 354-2727 .. **Moenich**, Terrence R '88 Wood Cnty Internet Council
-310 W Gypsy Ln -Bx207 -Bowling Green 43403

(419) 695-9925 .. **Moening**, Ronald S '73 Lakeview Farms,Inc -1700 Gressel Dr
-Delphos 45833

(440) 930-8068 .. **Moennich**, James W '77 Wickens HPC&B -35765 Chester Rd
-Avon 44011 **Fx:**937-4466

Moes, Stephanie '03 -(Address Unavailable)

(614) 501-1810 .. **Moesle**, Eric J '94 -4200 Regent -Ste 200 -Columbus 43219

Moffet, Beverly Lou '75 -17903 Drchstr Dr -Cleveland 44119

(419) 287-9307 .. **Moffett**, John J '72 -14555 New Rochester Rd -Pemberville 43450

(248) 646-5100 .. **Moffett**, Stephen T '98 (Moffett & D,PC) -255 E Brown
-Ste 340 Brown St Ctr -Birmingham, MI 48009 **Fx:**646-5332

(216) 479-8500 .. **Mog**, Cynthia C '93 %Squire S&D LLP -127 Pub Sq -4900 Key Twr
-Cleveland 44114 **Fx:**479-8780

(419) 255-0814 .. **Mogavero**, Mark N '97 ABLE -520 Mad Av -740 Spitzer Bldg
-Toledo 43604 **Fx:**259-2880

(212) 705-9817 .. **Moghal**, Saleem N '94 Gibney A&F -665 5th Av
-New York, NY 10022

(330) 759-8664 .. **Mogul**, Michael L '77 -17 Ruth Cir -Youngstown 44505

Mohammed, Kamala H '91 -3507 S Stafford -Arlington, VA 22206

(217) 421-2254 .. **Mohan**, Joseph P '77 AE Staley Mnfctrng Co -2200 E Eldorado
-Decatur, IL 62521

(513) 487-5610 .. **Mohan**, Patrick M '99 Milacron Inc -2090 Florence Av
-Cincinnati 45206

(859) 655-7004 .. **Mohan**, Theresa M '00 %Nielson & S,PSC -639 Wshngtn Av
-Ste 200 -Newport, KY 41071

(513) 241-0400 .. **Mohar**, Gregory J '92 (Aronoff R&H Co,LPA) -425 Walnut -Ste 2400
-Cincinnati 45202 **Fx:**241-2877

Mohl, Douglas C '71 -8514 29th E -Parrish, FL 34219

(419) 242-7488 .. **Mohler**, Edward T '89 -420 Mad Av -Ste 650 -Toledo 43604

(513) 721-3330 .. **Mohler**, Jarrod M '00 Robbins KP&T -7 W 7th -Ste 1400
-Cincinnati 45202

(419) 243-6281 .. **Mohler**, Martin E '73 (Shindler NH&S,LLP) -300 Mad Av -Ste 1200
-Toledo 43604 **Fx:**243-0129

(330) 864-5132 .. **Mohler**, Robert E '47 -321 Mull Av -Akron 44313

(419) 242-1400 .. **Mohr**, David M '66 -608 Mad Av -Ste 1400 -Toledo 43604

(937) 913-0200 .. **Mohr**, John R '72 %Gottschlich & P LLP -201 E 6th -Dayton 45402
Fx:824-2818

(419) 249-7900 .. **Mohr**, Kathryn M '87 (Robison C&O) -Four SeaGate -9th Fl
-Toledo 43604 **Fx:**249-7911

(419) 626-0055 .. **Moir**, Linda Tucker '87 %Tone GM&V -1401 Cleveland Rd
-Sandusky 44870 **Fx:**626-0288

(937) 382-6661 .. **Moke**, Paul F '82 Wilmington Cllg -1252 Pyle Ctr
-Wilmington 45177

(614) 461-1311 .. **Mokhtari**, Alvand A '00 %Reminger & R -65 E State
-4th Fl Cptl Sq Ofc Bldg -Columbus 43215 **Fx:**232-2410

(419) 213-4461 .. **Molaro**, Catherine M '93 6th Dist Crt of Appls -800 Jackson
-Toledo 43624

(419) 249-2707 .. **Molaro**, Salvatore C Jr. '87 -610 Adams -2nd Fl -Toledo 43604

Moldaver, Simon A '90 -28625 Bassett Rd -Westlake 44145

(216) 861-5582 .. **Moldovanyi**, Jay F '84 (Fay SFM&M LLP) -1100 Superior Av
-7th Fl -Cleveland 44114 **Fx:**241-1666

(630) 871-2614 .. **Molho**, Ross I '93 %Clingen CW&M LLC -2100 Mnchstr Rd
-Ste 1750 -Wheaton, IL 60187

(703) 312-6078 .. **Molina**, Joseph R '98 SAIC -4001 Fairfax Dr -Ste 850
-Arlington, VA 22203

(713) 296-3901 .. **Molina**, Richard Jr. '87 Marathon Oil Co -5555 San Felipe Rd
-Tax Dept -Houston, TX 77056

(513) 381-2838 .. **Molinsky**, George D '94 (Taft S&H LLP) -425 Walnut -Ste 1800
-Cincinnati 45202 **Fx:**381-0205

(330) 405-5061 .. **Moliterno**, Louis R '95 (Williams S&S Co,LPA)
-2241 Pinnacle Pkwy -Twinsburg 44087 **Fx:**405-5586

(419) 237-2661 .. **Molitierno**, Deanna S '82 -104 E Main -Bx40 -Fayette 43521

(740) 432-9252 .. **Moll**, Jeanette M '96 Guernsey Cnty Cmn Pleas Ct
-801 Wheeling Av -Cambridge 43725

(513) 721-5555 .. **Mollaun**, Terrance T '00 %B Maislin -906 Main -Ste 500
-Cincinnati 45202

(419) 244-7500 .. **Mollenkamp**, Alan L '74 (Mollenkamp & I) -411 N Mich -Ste 300
-Toledo 43624 **Fx:**244-5238

(740) 593-3357 .. **Mollica**, Andrew J '89 (Mollica GS&S Co,LPA) -35 N Cllg -Drwr958
-Athens 45701

(740) 797-4386 .. **Mollica**, Anthony C '83 -10695 Rosewood Ln -Athens 45701

(740) 593-3357 .. **Mollica Gall Sloan & Sillery Co,LPA** -35 N Cllg -Drwr958
-Athens 45701

(740) 593-3357 .. **Mollica**, Gerald A '63 Mollica GS&S Co,LPA -35 N Cllg -Drwr958
-Athens 45701

(248) 643-9494 .. **Mollicone**, David A '97 Munro & Z, PLLC -3250 W Big Beaver Rd
-Ste 520 -Troy, MI 48084

Mollohan, Brenda J '04 -(Address Unavailable)

(440) 899-1551 .. **Mollohan**, Bryan S '98 JD Carney & Assoc,LLC -2001 Crocker Rd
-440 Gemini Twr II -Westlake 44145

(859) 431-6100 .. **Molloy**, Mary K '81 Arnzen & W,PSC -600 Greenup
-Covington, KY 41011 **Fx:**431-3778

(937) 449-6400 .. **Molloy**, Matthew A '04 %Dinsmore & S LLP -1 S Main
-Ste 1300 One Dayton Centre -Dayton 45402 **Fx:**449-6405

(206) 553-4140 .. **Molloy**, Thomas P '83 DHS/ICE -1000 2nd -Ste 2900
-Seattle, WA 98104 **Fx:**553-5338

(216) 289-4500 .. **Molnar**, Bruce F '74 -25000 Euclid Av -Ste 100 -Euclid 44117

(216) 241-0300 .. **Molnar**, Edward S '64 -50 Pub Sq -Ste 920 -Cleveland 44113

(216) 443-8588 .. **Molnar**, Elizabeth A '03 Cuyahoga Cnty Ct Cmmn Pleas
-1200 Ontario -Justice Ctr 11th Fl -Cleveland 44113

(216) 586-3939 .. **Molnar**, Isaac A '03 %Jones D -901 Lakeside Av -Cleveland 44114
Fx:579-0212

(216) 896-2212 ..**Molnar,** John A '92 Parker Hannifin Corp -6035 Parkland Blvd -Cleveland 44124

(419) 255-5900 ..**Molnar,** John B '83 (MacMillan S&T,LLC) -720 Water -4th Fl -Toledo 43604 **Fx:**255-9639

(330) 665-5117 ..**Molnar,** Kelly A '00 %Witschey & W Co,LPA -300 N Cleveland-Missillon Rd -Ste 104 -Akron 44333

(740) 965-3900 ..**Molnar,** Kenneth J '74 -21 Middle -Galena 43021

(419) 448-4444 ..**Molnar,** Rhonda K '98 Seneca Cnty Pros/CSEA -81 Jffrsn -Bx377 -Tiffin 44883

(937) 361-6497 ..**Moloney,** Maureen A '82 -239 Green -Dayton 45402 **Fx:**222-7066

(937) 222-2500 ..**Moloney,** Michael P '80 (Sebaly S&D) -1900 Kettering Twr -Dayton 45423 **Fx:**222-6554

(614) 466-3180 ..**Moloney,** Monica A '78 Atty Gen -150 E Gay -Columbus 43215 **Fx:**466-9788

(614) 885-1901 ..**Moloney,** Thomas E '74 Amer Enrgy Srvcs -1105 Schrock Rd -Ste 602 -Columbus 43229

(216) 621-7860 ..**Molyneaux,** Rebecca S '02 %Cavitch FD&F -1717 E 9th -14th Fl -Cleveland 44114 **Fx:**621-3415

(216) 348-5400 ..**Monachino,** Grant A '03 %McDonald H Co,LPA -600 Superior Av E -Ste 2100 -Cleveland 44114 **Fx:**348-5474

(216) 348-5400 ..**Monachino,** Nicole M '03 %McDonald H Co,LPA -600 Superior Av E -Ste 2100 -Cleveland 44114 **Fx:**348-5474

(330) 643-8387 ..**Monaco,** Deborah J '97 Summit Cnty Dom Rltns Ct -209 S High -Akron 44308

(614) 224-2062 ..**Monast,** James P '85 (Marchese & M) -1017 Dublin Rd -Columbus 43215

(216) 574-9400 ..**Monastra,** Carl C '81 -75 Pub Sq -Ste 1000 -Cleveland 44113

(319) 295-7064 ..**Monclova,** Irma J '88 Rockwell Collins -400 Collins Rd NE -Cedar Rapids, IA 52498

(330) 869-4031 ..**Moncrief,** Cynthia Ann '88 -Bx13163 -Akron 44334

(216) 443-9000 ..**Mondalek,** Allyson J '04 %Porter WM&A LLP -925 Euclid Av -Ste 1700 -Cleveland 44115 **Fx:**443-9011

(937) 222-2500 ..**Monday,** Michael W '00 %Sebaly S&D -1900 Kettering Twr -Dayton 45423 **Fx:**222-6554

(937) 228-9000 ..**Mondock,** Joseph J III '02 %Thorson SW&S,LLP -130 W 2nd -Ste 1508 -Dayton 45402 **Fx:**228-3550

Mondon, Dana S '96 -796 Drummond Ct -Columbus 43214

(419) 243-5080 ..**Mondville,** Jeffrey J '95 -709 Mad Av -Ste 218 -Toledo 43624

(614) 752-9595 ..**Mone,** Maria L '88 OH Cmmssn on Dispute Rsltn -77 S High -24th Fl -Columbus 43215

(614) 469-3203 ..**Mone,** Robert P '59 (Thompson H LLP) -10 W Broad -Ste 700 -Columbus 43215 **Fx:**469-3361

(216) 664-4507 ..**Monegan,** Theodora M '87 Dept of Law -601 Lakeside Av -Rm 106 City Hall -Cleveland 44114 **Fx:**664-2663

(614) 848-7812 ..**Mong,** James F '84 -6641 N High -Worthington 43085

(513) 229-7996 ..**Mongenas-Handorf,** Jacqueline '92 %Kircher,LLC -4824 Socialville-Foster Rd -Ste 110 -Mason 45040

(740) 687-1450 ..**Mongold,** Jessica L '04 %TJ Corbin -842 N Columbus -Lancaster 43130

(216) 443-9000 ..**Monica,** John C Jr. '03 %Porter WM&A LLP -925 Euclid Av -Ste 1700 -Cleveland 44115 **Fx:**443-9011

Monick, Laura A '04 -(Address Unavailable)

(216) 696-4700 ..**Monihan,** M Elizabeth '84 (Spieth BM&N Co,LPA) -925 Euclid Av -2000 Huntngtn Bldg -Cleveland 44115 **Fx:**696-2706

(440) 356-1650 ..**Monjot,** James A '72 -21851 Ctr Ridge Rd -Rocky River 44116 **Fx:**356-0591

(513) 887-3474 ..**Monk,** James A '02 Butler Cnty Pros -315 High -11th Fl -Bx515 -Hamilton 45012

(412) 261-6400 ..**Monks,** Robert L '92 Jones GC&G,LLP -411 7th Av -Ste 1200 -Pittsburgh, PA 15219

(740) 369-8900 ..**Monnaville,** Robert H Jr. '73 -163 N Sandusky -Ste 206 -Delaware 43015

(513) 793-5297 ..**Monnie & O'Connor Co,LPA** -8035 Hosbrook Rd -Ste 200 -Cincinnati 45236

(513) 793-5297 ..**Monnie,** Terrance R '74 (Monnie & O Co,LPA) -8035 Hosbrook Rd -Ste 200 -Cincinnati 45236

(937) 548-8098 ..**Monnin,** Julie L '96 -771 Martin -Greenville 45331

(216) 566-5607 ..**Monnin,** Robert D '68 (Thompson H LLP) -127 Pub Sq -3900 Key Ctr -Cleveland 44114 **Fx:**566-5800

(859) 283-1140 ..**Monohan,** Edward S IV '90 (Monohan & B) -7711 Ewing Blvd -Bx157 -Florence, KY 41022

(859) 283-1140 ..**Monohan,** Edward S V '00 %Monohan & B -7711 Ewing Blvd -Bx157 -Florence, KY 41022

(419) 241-1200 ..**Monro,** Susan E '93 -900 Adams -Toledo 43624

(305) 253-2244 ..**Monroe,** Andromeda '80 %Assurant Grp -11222 Quail Roost Dr -Miami, FL 33157 **Fx:**252-7069

(513) 563-3031 ..**Monroe,** Dain T '92 -4555 Lk Forest Dr -650 Westlake Ctr -Cincinnati 45242

(216) 622-8200 ..**Monroe,** Gerald A '92 (Calfee H&G LLP) -800 Superior Av -Ste 1400 -Cleveland 44114 **Fx:**241-0816

Monroe, Jennifer '79 -(Address Unavailable)

(216) 781-1212 ..**Monroe,** John W '93 %Walter & H LLP -1301 E 9th -Ste 3500 -Cleveland 44114 **Fx:**575-0911

(216) 861-1365 ..**Monroe,** Robert W '85 %Hawkins & Co,LPA -1267 W 9th -Ste 500 -Cleveland 44113 **Fx:**861-0714

(216) 241-2500 ..**Monroe,** Thomas W '91 -526 Superior Av -Ste 1525 -Cleveland 44114

(937) 225-4652 ..**Monroe,** William J '75 Montgomery Cnty Pub Def -117 S Main -Ste 400 -Dayton 45422 **Fx:**225-3449

(216) 241-2500 ..**Monroe,** William T '53 (Monroe & Z) -526 Superior Av -Ste 1525 -Cleveland 44114

(216) 241-2500 ..**Monroe & Zucco** -526 Superior Av -Ste 1525 -Cleveland 44114

(937) 890-6921 ..**Monta,** Michael L '73 -3625 Old Salem Rd -Dayton 45415

Monta, Niki K '02 -3278 Columbus -Grove City 43123

(614) 692-3284 ..**Monta,** Vasso K '77 US Dfnse Lgstcs Agncy -Bx3990 -Columbus 43218

(419) 394-7441 ..**Montague,** Eldon E '49 OfCnsl Noble M&M -146 E Spring -Saint Marys 45885 **Fx:**394-7694

(419) 289-3777 ..**Montague,** Walter D '78 Law Director's Ofc -1213 E Main -Ashland 44805

(859) 655-4200 ..**Montague,** William L '86 Greenebaum D&M PLLC -50 E RiverCenter Blvd -Ste 1800 -Covington, KY 41011 **Fx:**655-4239

(216) 566-1600 ..**Montana,** Amy M '01 %Schwarzwald & M -1300 E 9th -Ste 616 -Cleveland 44114 **Fx:**566-1814

(317) 569-1680 ..**Montel,** Joseph J '00 (Montel Law Firm,PC) -Bx3970 -Carmel, IN 46082

(216) 771-4050 ..**Monteleone,** Joseph Michael '74 (Jeffries KF&M Co,LPA) -101 W Prospect Av -1650 Mdlnd Bldg -Cleveland 44115 **Fx:**771-0732

(440) 232-2701 ..**Montello,** John J '87 (Melling H&M,LPA) -31 Columbus Rd -Bedford 44146 **Fx:**232-7995

(740) 373-7674 ..**Montera,** Susan A '93 (Weaver & M) -227 3rd -Marietta 45750

Montfort, Donald G '51 -5652 Brdgtown Rd -Cincinnati 45248

(614) 466-4483 ..**Montgomery,** Betty D '76 Auditor of State -88 E Broad -5th Fl -Bx1140 -Columbus 43216

(513) 345-3832 ..**Montgomery,** David '79 -36 E 4th -Ste 1208 -Cincinnati 45202 **Fx:**345-3833

(937) 223-1130 ..**Montgomery,** David H Jr. '98 %Pickrel S&E -40 N Main -2700 Kettering Twr -Dayton 45423 **Fx:**223-0339

(513) 579-6400 ..**Montgomery,** David K '88 (Keating M&K PLL) -1 E 4th -1400 Provident Twr -Cincinnati 45202 **Fx:**579-6457

(513) 732-2900 ..**Montgomery,** George P '90 -45 N Market -Batavia 45103

(614) 228-1541 ..**Montgomery,** Henry P IV '79 (Baker & H LLP) -65 E State -Ste 2100 -Columbus 43215 **Fx:**462-2616

(513) 241-4722 ..**Montgomery,** James J '76 (Montgomery R&J,LPA) -36 E 7th -Ste 2100 -Cincinnati 45202 **Fx:**241-8775

(330) 535-5925 ..**Montgomery,** Jerry F '54 -560 Patterson Av -Akron 44310

(614) 291-3119 ..**Montgomery,** John J '76 -1207 N High -Bx8301 -Columbus 43201

(614) 469-7404 ..**Montgomery,** John R '81 SSA-OHA, Columbus -280 N High -3rd Fl -Columbus 43215

(216) 491-1442 ..**Montgomery,** K J '77 Mun Ct Judge -3355 Lee Rd -Shaker Heights 44120

(513) 574-1999 ..**Montgomery,** Kenneth A Jr. '99 -6564 Glen Way -Cincinnati 45211 **Fx:**574-8512

(513) 721-1975 ..**Montgomery,** Leanne R '01 Freking & B -215 E 9th -5th Fl -Cincinnati 45202 **Fx:**651-2570

(937) 225-5774 ..**Montgomery,** Mary E '98 Montgomery Cnty Pros -301 W 3rd -Bx972 -Dayton 45422 **Fx:**225-3470

(513) 574-8900 ..**Montgomery,** Matthew A '98 %Huddleson & Co,LPA -6061 Brdgtown Rd -Cincinnati 45248

(513) 651-6800 ..**Montgomery,** Mekesha H '01 %Frost BT LLC -201 E 5th -2200 PNC Ctr -Cincinnati 45202 **Fx:**651-6981

(614) 462-3194 ..**Montgomery,** Melissa A '00 Franklin Cnty Pub Def -373 S High -12th Fl -Columbus 43215

(216) 523-5482 ..**Montgomery,** Michael J '99 %Bricker & E LLP -1375 E 9th -Ste 1500 -Cleveland 44114 **Fx:**523-7071

(419) 629-2311 ..**Montgomery,** Ogden K '78 Crown Equip Corp -44 S Wshngtn -Leg Dept -New Bremen 45869

(513) 241-4722 ..**Montgomery Rennie & Jonson,LPA** -36 E 7th -Ste 2100 -Cincinnati 45202 **Fx:**241-8775

(330) 533-6821 ..**Montgomery,** Richard K '76 -73 N Broad -Canfield 44406

(614) 462-3378 ..**Montgomery,** Robert G '97 Franklin Cnty Recorder -373 S High -18th Fl -Columbus 43215

(202) 225-7502 ..**Montgomery,** Thomas C '80 SrCnsl US House of Reps-Financial Srvcs -2129 Rayburn HOB -Washington, DC 20515 **Fx:**225-9040

(312) 258-5672 ..**Montgomery,** Virgil R '92 (Schiff H&W) -6600 Sears Twr -233 S Wacker Dr -Chicago, IL 60606 **Fx:**258-5600

(937) 593-8510 ..**Montgomery,** William R '68 (Smith S&M) -112 N Main -Bellefontaine 43311

(216) 320-5800 ..**Montlack,** Kenneth R '67 -2835 Mayfld Rd -Ste 103 -Cleveland Heights 44118

(216) 421-8400 ..**Montlack,** Kirt A '92 -2590 N Moreland -#E1 -Shaker Heights 44120

(216) 566-5500 ..**Montville,** Julanne '02 %Thompson H LLP -127 Pub Sq -3900 Key Ctr -Cleveland 44114 **Fx:**566-5800

(216) 685-1136 ..**Monty,** Jennifer M '03 %Weltman W&R Co,LPA -323 W Lakeside Av -Ste 200 -Cleveland 44113 **Fx:**363-4121

(740) 345-1040 ..**Monty,** Michelle L '02 %Swank & Assoc,LPA -68 W Church -Ste 205 -Bx248 -Newark 43058

(419) 874-9500 ..**Montz,** Lane A '93 Cousino Construction Co -26901 Eckel Rd -Perrysburg 43551

(937) 328-3741 ..**Moody,** Denise L '90 Pros -50 E Columbia -Springfield 45502

(727) 562-7848 ..**Moody,** Lizabeth A '60 Stetson Univ Coll of Law -1401 S 61st -Saint Petersburg, FL 33707

(330) 701-2362 ..**Moody,** LoVeen Joy '03 -282 Grove -Akron 44302

(419) 254-4300 ..**Moody,** Nancy D '82 Marshall & M,LLC -420 Mad Av -Ste 1100 -Toledo 43604

(440) 248-7906 ..**Moody,** Steven J '02 %Mazanec R&R Co,LPA -34305 Solon Rd -Ste 100 -Cleveland 44139 **Fx:**248-8861

(908) 231-2356 ..**Moon,** Carolyn D '92 Hoechst Marion Roussel,Inc -Route 202-206 -Patent Dept -Bx6800 -Bridgewater, NJ 08807

(216) 443-7800 ..**Mooney,** Brian P '96 Cuyahoga Cnty Pros -1200 Ontario -8th Fl -Cleveland 44113 **Fx:**698-2270

Mooney, Christina K '81 -(Address Unavailable)

(614) 466-1291 ..**Mooney,** Colleen L '84 OH Consumers' Cnsl -10 W Broad -Ste 1800 -Columbus 43215 **Fx:**466-9475

(513) 762-6200 ..**Mooney,** Donald J Jr. '75 (Ulmer & B LLP) -600 Vine -Ste 2800 -Cincinnati 45202 **Fx:**762-6245

(248) 540-9636 ..**Mooney,** John M '00 %Foley & M,PLLP -24255 W 13 Mile Rd -Ste 200 -Bingham Farms, MI 48025

(216) 689-6176 ..**Mooney,** Kevin M '00 KeyBank NA -2025 Ontario -7th Fl -Cleveland 44115

(216) 830-9000 ..**Mooney,** Laura J '79 OfCnsl Berger & Z Co,LPA -614 W Superior Av -Ste 1425 Rckfllr Bldg -Cleveland 44113 **Fx:**830-4200

(513) 651-6800 ..**Mooney,** Martin E '78 (Frost BT LLC) -201 E 5th -2200 PNC Ctr -Cincinnati 45202 **Fx:**651-6981

(513) 977-4213 ..**Mooney,** Michael J '72 -917 Main -Ste 300 -Cincinnati 45202

(440) 286-5228 ..**Mooney,** Paul J '88 -107 Water -Chardon 44024

(202) 225-2248 ..**Mooney,** Thomas E '69 House Intl Relations Comm -2149 Rayburn HOB -Washington, DC 20515

(614) 466-5394 ..**Mooney,** William J '75 Pub Def -8 E Long -Columbus 43215

(614) 645-8576 ..**Moore,** Amy M '04 Franklin Cnty Municipal Ct -375 S High -16th Fl -Columbus 43215

(313) 596-0220 .. **Moore,** Andrew F '92 Univ of Detroit/Mercy Law Schl -651 E Jffrsn
-Detroit, MI 48226
(216) 586-3939 .. **Moore,** Anthony R '75 (Jones D) -901 Lakeside Av
-Cleveland 44114 **Fx:**579-0212
(330) 343-5585 .. **Moore,** Brent L '99 %Miller & K,LPA -405 Chauncey Av NW
-Bx668 -New Philadelphia 44663 **Fx:**343-7977
(330) 376-2700 .. **Moore,** Brian J '84 (Roetzel & A,LPA) -222 S Main -Akron 44308
Fx:376-4577
(614) 331-9556 .. **Moore,** Candada J '81 Huntington Natl Bank -7 Easton Oval
-EA4-E63 -Columbus 43219 **Fx:**331-5862
(330) 375-2053 .. **Moore,** Carla D '77 Mun Ct Judge -217 S High -Akron 44308
(919) 286-8000 .. **Moore,** Charles L Jr. '91 (Moore & V PLLC) -2200 W Main
-Ste 800 -Bx3843 -Durham, NC 27702 **Fx:**416-8312
(330) 899-0475 .. **Moore,** Christopher J '95 -3700 Massillion Rd -Ste 380
-Uniontown 44685
(513) 583-4200 .. **Moore,** Christopher L '93 Schroeder MB&P -11935 Mason Rd
-Ste 110 -Cincinnati 45249
(740) 286-0030 .. **Moore,** Christopher Michael '99 -266 E Main -Bx510
-Jackson 45640
(216) 363-4500 .. **Moore,** Craig L '94 %Benesch FC&A LLP -200 Pub Sq -Ste 2300
-Cleveland 44114 **Fx:**363-4588
(513) 752-2111 .. **Moore,** Daniel D %D Moore Jr & Co,LPA -4355 Ferguson Dr
-Ste 200 -Cincinnati 45245 **Fx:**753-2354
(330) 744-5211 .. **Moore,** David M '93 Roth BRS&L,LPA -100 Fed Plz E -Ste 600
-Youngstown 44503 **Fx:**744-3184
Moore, Donald C '63 -(Address Unavailable)
(513) 752-2111 .. **Moore,** Donald C Jr. '80 (D Moore Jr & Co,LPA)
-4355 Ferguson Dr -Ste 200 -Cincinnati 45245 **Fx:**753-2354
(614) 221-2505 .. **Moore,** Donald H Jr. '87 -5 E Long -Ste 100 -Columbus 43215
(330) 491-2222 .. **Moore,** Edgar M Jr. '77 (Bixler & M) -4200 Munson NW -Bx35426
-Canton 44735 **Fx:**493-1940
(216) 622-8200 .. **Moore,** Edward W '82 (Calfee H&G LLP) -800 Superior Av
-Ste 1400 -Cleveland 44114 **Fx:**241-0816
(614) 480-4435 .. **Moore,** Elizabeth B '86 Huntington Natl Bank -41 S High
-Columbus 43215
(330) 468-6333 .. **Moore,** Eric J '95 -61 W Aurora Rd -Northfield 44067
(937) 224-3333 .. **Moore,** Erin B '95 (Green & G) -109 N Main -Ste 800
-Dayton 45402 **Fx:**224-4311
(419) 893-0011 .. **Moore,** Everett D '77 -5714 Monclova Rd -Maumee 43537
(412) 232-0661 .. **Moore,** Francis M Jr. '97 Mansmann & M -220 Grant
-Pittsburgh, PA 15219
(513) 333-0050 .. **Moore,** Gregory A '93 %P Hackett -1014 Vine -Ste 1690
-Cincinnati 45202
(330) 666-5555 .. **Moore,** Gregory J '03 %Ruport Co,LPA -3700 Embssy Pkwy
-Ste 440 -Akron 44333
(313) 965-8826 .. **Moore,** Gregory L '81 (G Moore,PC) -65 Cadillac Sq -Ste #2200
-Detroit, MI 48226 **Fx:**961-6769
(513) 674-6000 .. **Moore,** Howard S '84 Jungle Jims Market Inc -5440 Dixie Hwy
-Fairfield 45014
(513) 421-6630 .. **Moore,** James M '72 Lindhorst & D Co,LPA -312 Walnut -Ste 2300
-Cincinnati 45202
(216) 579-1700 .. **Moore,** James M '88 (Pearne & G LLP) -1801 E 9th -Ste 1200
-Cleveland 44114 **Fx:**579-6073
(614) 462-3555 .. **Moore,** Jason A '96 Franklin Cnty Pros -373 S High
-Columbus 43215
(614) 462-5443 .. **Moore,** Jayme P '03 %Kegler BH&R -65 E State -Ste 1800
-Columbus 43215 **Fx:**464-2634
(513) 626-2238 .. **Moore,** Jeffrey R '00 Cnsl Procter & Gamble -11450 Grooms Rd
-Cincinnati 45242
Moore, Jeffrey R '01 -(Address Unavailable)
(248) 349-9002 .. **Moore,** Joan E '77 Arbor Cnslting Grp,Inc -186 E Main -Ste 201
-Northville, MI 48167
(937) 898-3975 .. **Moore,** Joseph P '74 (Moore & Assoc) -410 Corp Ctr Dr
-Vandalia 45377
(614) 227-2363 .. **Moore,** Karen M '75 (Bricker & E LLP) -100 S 3rd
-Columbus 43215 **Fx:**227-2390
(614) 728-4792 .. **Moore,** Karhlton F '98 OH Crim Jstc Srvcs -140 E Town -14th Fl
-Columbus 43215
Moore, Kathryn L '04 -(Address Unavailable)
(216) 443-7223 .. **Moore,** Kathy L '79 Cuyahoga Cnty Pub Def -1200 W 3rd NW
-100 Lakeside Pl -Cleveland 44113
(513) 924-0571 .. **Moore,** Keith D '93 Lexis Nexis -1910 Hopkins Av
-Cincinnati 45212
(561) 833-5787 .. **Moore,** Kelly P '02 Legal Aid-Foster Chldrns Prjct -315 S Dixie Hwy
-Ste 102 -West Palm Beach, FL 33401 **Fx:**833-5826
(513) 241-6748 .. **Moore,** Kellye N '03 %A Levine -324 Reading Rd
-Cincinnati 45202
(216) 479-8500 .. **Moore,** Kenneth C '73 (Squire S&D LLP) -127 Pub Sq
-4900 Key Twr -Cleveland 44114 **Fx:**479-8780
Moore, Larry W '69 -(Address Unavailable)
(330) 456-8361 .. **Moore,** Laureen M '84 Cmmnty Lgl Aid Srvcs,Inc -306 Market Av N
-Ste 730 -Canton 44702
(216) 696-7170 .. **Moore,** Leslie N '00 Forbes F & Assoc Co,LPA -614 W Superior Av
-700 Rckflr Bldg -Cleveland 44113
(614) 279-6626 .. **Moore,** Lillie B '83 -4280 Ongaro Dr -Columbus 43204
(859) 578-4444 .. **Moore,** Lisa A '98 %P Schachter & Assoc,PSC -250 Grandvw Dr
-#500 -Fort Mitchell, KY 41017
(216) 241-5310 .. **Moore,** Lynn L '84 (Gallagher SF&N) -1501 Euclid Av -6th Fl
-Cleveland 44115 **Fx:**241-1608
(614) 462-4511 .. **Moore,** Marchelle E '00 Franklin Cnty Cmn Pleas Ct -375 S High
-Columbus 43215 **Fx:**462-2462
(330) 683-9474 .. **Moore,** Marie L '98 -136 E Market -Orrville 44667
(216) 241-3400 .. **Moore,** Mary B '00 Cuyahoga Cnty Mental Health Bd -1400 W 25th
-3rd Fl -Cleveland 44113
(678) 287-2453 .. **Moore,** Melissa E '93 Microcoating Technologies
-5315 Pchtree Indstrl Blvd -Chamblee, GA 30341
(937) 865-7536 .. **Moore,** Michael E '88 Lexis/Nexis -Bx933 -Dayton 45401
(614) 481-0550 .. **Moore,** Michael G '79 -1301 S High -Columbus 43206
(614) 260-3797 .. **Moore,** Michael M '85 -1601A Turnberry Dr -Pickerington 43147
(614) 462-3555 .. **Moore,** Nancy D '89 Franklin Cnty Pros -373 S High
-Columbus 43215
(614) 224-1222 .. **Moore,** Patricia L '91 %Maguire & S,LLP -250 Civic Ctr Dr -Ste 200
-Columbus 43215 **Fx:**224-1236

(614) 227-2380 .. **Moore,** Randall E '78 (Bricker & E LLP) -100 S 3rd
-Columbus 43215 **Fx:**227-2390
(330) 376-2700 .. **Moore,** Randall J '84 (Roetzel & A,LPA) -222 S Main -Akron 44308
Fx:376-4577
(513) 345-4160 .. **Moore,** Rhonda Y '87 Pro Seniors,Inc -7162 Redding Rd -Ste 1150
-Cincinnati 45237
(317) 263-7942 .. **Moore,** Richard B '83 Simon Prop Gp -115 W Wshngtn
-Indianapolis, IN 46204
(513) 723-4000 .. **Moore,** Richard L '93 (Vorys SS&P LLP) -221 E 4th
-Ste 2000 Atrium Two -Bx0236 -Cincinnati 45201 **Fx:**723-4056
(937) 296-2466 .. **Moore,** Robert L '72 Mun Ct Judge -3600 Shroyer Rd
-Kettering 45429
(419) 626-3323 .. **Moore,** Robert M '84 (Muehlhauser & M) -422 Columbus Av
-Bx790 -Sandusky 44870
(330) 929-3337 .. **Moore,** Robert S '61 -111 Stow Av -Ste 100
-Cuyahoga Falls 44221
Moore, Robert S '86 -114 Neff Dr -Canfield 44406
(513) 651-6800 .. **Moore,** Rodger W '01 %Frost BT LLC -201 E 5th -2200 PNC Ctr
-Cincinnati 45202 **Fx:**651-6981
(859) 491-7487 .. **Moore,** Roger M '91 (Schletker H&M) -415 Garrard
-Covington, KY 41011
(216) 771-9745 .. **Moore,** Sarah J '95 (S Moore Co,LPA) -850 Euclid Av -Ste 701
-Cleveland 44114
(740) 372-0902 .. **Moore,** Steven A '99 -158 Dodds Rd -Otway 45657
(330) 497-0700 .. **Moore,** Terry A '80 (Krugliak WG&D Co,LPA) -4775 Munson NW
-Bx36963 -Canton 44735 **Fx:**497-4020
(513) 381-0656 .. **Moore,** Terry E '86 (Kohnen & P LLP) -201 E 5th -Ste 800
-Cincinnati 45202 **Fx:**381-5823
(614) 462-4551 .. **Moore,** Thomas A '90 Franklin Cnty CSEA -80 E Fulton
-Columbus 43215
(937) 643-1240 .. **Moore,** Thomas E '78 Systech Envrnmntl Corp
-3085 Woodman Dr -Dayton 45420
(614) 228-5711 .. **Moore,** Tonda L '95 %Lucas PAG&N -600 S High
-Columbus 43215 **Fx:**228-0982
(419) 698-1040 .. **Moore,** Troy L '85 (Ballenger & M Co,LPA) -3401 Woodvll Rd
-Northwood 43619
(216) 771-6776 .. **Moore,** William D '60 -526 Superior Av E -Ste 620
-Cleveland 44114
(614) 241-2156 .. **Moore,** William J '82 (Moore Y&M) -326 S High -Columbus 43215
(614) 241-2156 .. **Moore Yaklevich & Mauger** -326 S High -Columbus 43215
(216) 522-4914 .. **Moore,** Zoe Ann '86 SSA/OHA -1350 Euclid Av -7th Fl
-Cleveland 44115
(937) 544-2500 .. **Moore-Eiterman,** Barbara A '97 -106 S Cross -West Union 45693
Moore-Hewitt, Sheilarayne M '86 -(Address Unavailable)
(740) 452-9960 .. **Moorehead,** Douglas A '78 -58 N 5th -Zanesville 43701
(970) 328-8685 .. **Moorehead,** Robert T '75 Eagle Cnty -500 Bway -Bx850
-Eagle, CO 81631
(216) 344-3800 .. **Moorhead,** Russell A '85 -614 Superior Av NW -# 860
-Cleveland 44113 **Fx:**344-3869
(216) 622-8200 .. **Moorhead,** Sean T '93 (Calfee H&G LLP) -800 Superior Av
-Ste 1400 -Cleveland 44114 **Fx:**241-0816
(937) 333-4400 .. **Moorman,** Colette E '92 Dayton Pros -335 W 3rd -Ste 372
-Dayton 45402
(216) 622-8200 .. **Moorman,** Pauline L '89 Calfee H&G LLP -800 Superior Av
-Ste 1400 -Cleveland 44114 **Fx:**241-0816
(614) 459-4140 .. **Moots Carter & Hogan** -3600 Olentangy Rvr Rd -Ste 501
-Columbus 43214 **Fx:**459-4503
(614) 459-4140 .. **Moots,** Philip R '65 (Moots C&H) -3600 Olentangy Rvr Rd -Ste 501
-Columbus 43214 **Fx:**459-4503
(419) 609-1311 .. **Moracz,** Donald J '91 (Reminger & R) -237 W Wshngtn Row
-2nd Fl -Sandusky 44870 **Fx:**626-4805
(216) 591-0707 .. **Morad,** Rick J '95 Game One,Inc -5055 Richmond Rd
-Bedford Heights 44146
(740) 947-2099 .. **Moraleja,** Anthony A '92 -106 N High -Waverly 45690
(216) 443-6984 .. **Morales,** Egdilio J '94 Employee & Labor Relations -1255
Euclid Av -Ste 310 -Cleveland 44115
(202) 626-6600 .. **Morales,** Jennifer J '03 %Squire S&D LLP -1201 Penn Av NW
-Bx407 -Washington, DC 20044 **Fx:**626-6780
(419) 385-0765 .. **Moran,** James P '75 -2254 Townley Rd -Toledo 43614
(330) 723-5082 .. **Moran,** John D '84 Corrpro Co,Inc -1090 Enterprise Dr
-Medina 44256
(440) 354-3585 .. **Moran,** Mary A '83 Chicago Title Ins Co -168 N St Clair
-Painesville 44077
(419) 241-8171 .. **Moran,** Mary B '89 (Moran & M) -626 Mad Av -Ste 300
-Toledo 43604
(847) 559-0101 .. **Moran,** Mary E '83 Family Law Ctr -105 Revere Dr -Ste C
-Northbrook, IL 60062
(330) 929-0507 .. **Moran,** Michael J '78 -234 W Portage Trl -Cuyahoga Falls 44221
(614) 476-6453 .. **Moran,** Michael R '94 MR Moran Co,LPA -181 Granvll -Bx307437
-Gahanna 43230 **Fx:**476-4157
(513) 852-8200 .. **Moran,** Paul R '59 Cors & B LLC -537 E Pete Rose Way -Ste 400
-Cincinnati 45202
(419) 241-8171 .. **Moran,** Peter L '53 (Moran & M) -626 Mad Av -Ste 300
-Toledo 43604
(216) 348-1700 .. **Moran,** R Emmett '77 OfCnsl Davis & Y -101 Prospect Av W
-Ste 1700 -Cleveland 44115 **Fx:**621-0602
(440) 617-1528 .. **Moran,** Susan J '96 -55 Pub Sq -Ste 1010 -Cleveland 44113
(937) 431-0509 .. **Moran,** Timothy J '94 Lexi Nexis -1653 Oakwood Trl -Xenia 45385
(513) 241-4110 .. **Moran,** William J Jr. '92 (Deters B&L,PSC) -441 Vine
-Ste 3500 Carew Twr -Cincinnati 45202 **Fx:**241-4551
(513) 629-1479 .. **Morand,** Robert F '75 SrCnsl Wstrn & Sthrn Life Ins Co -400 Bway
-Cincinnati 45202
(440) 461-4980 .. **Moravick,** Robert J '70 -2042 Aldersgate Dr -Lyndhurst 44124
(513) 983-0004 .. **Mordan,** William R '97 Procter & Gamble Co-Legal
-1 Procter & Gamble Plz -Cincinnati 45202
(614) 365-4100 .. **Mordarski,** Daniel R '94 (Carpenter & L LLP) -280 N High
-Ste 1300 280 Plz -Columbus 43215 **Fx:**365-9145
(513) 421-7500 .. **Mordino,** Joseph T '95 Faulkner & T,LLP -5 W 4th
-2200 4th & Vine Twr -Cincinnati 45202
(703) 482-1100 .. **Morean,** Robert P '90 -Central Intelligence Agncy
-Washington, DC 20505
(513) 922-3200 .. **Morehart,** Douglas M '87 (Haverkamp BR&R Co,LPA)
-5856 Glenway Av -Cincinnati 45238 **Fx:**922-8096

(740) 653-4259 .. **Morehart,** Paul D '88 Fairfield Cnty Pros -201 S Broad -4th Fl
-Lancaster 43130

(865) 218-2282 .. **Morehous,** David L '96 CTI Molecular Imaging Inc -810 Innovation
Dr -Knoxville, TN 37932 **Fx:**218-3001

(740) 282-5323 .. **Moreland,** Carl C '62 OfCnsl Bruzzese & C -300 Sinclair Bldg
-Bx1506 -Steubenville 43952 **Fx:**282-5328

Moreland, Garnetta P '03 -9723 Foxhound Dr -Miamisburg 45342

(614) 836-3611 .. **Moreland,** Jay M '96 -5137 Phillips Run -Canal Winchester 43110

(419) 334-2909 .. **Moreland,** Ruth A '97 Sandusky Cnty/Job & Fam Srvcs
-2511 Cntryside Dr -Fremont 43420

(419) 447-5011 .. **Moreland,** Shannon A '03 Seneca Cnty Dept Job & Family Svcs
-3362 S Twp Rd 151 -Tiffin 44883 **Fx:**447-5345

(513) 887-3352 .. **Moreland,** Vickie G '77 Butler Cnty Cmn Pleas Ct -315 High
-2nd Fl -Hamilton 45011

(216) 573-6666 .. **Morell,** Dan A Jr. '86 D Morell & Assoc Co,LPA
-6060 Rockside Wds Blvd -250 Spectrum Bldg
-Independence 44131

(216) 348-1100 .. **Morell,** Karen M '88 -2913 Clinton Av -Cleveland 44113

(412) 369-9696 .. **Morella,** Jeffrey J '00 (Morella & Assoc) -8150 Perry Hwy -Ste 100
-Pittsburgh, PA 15237

(312) 673-0360 .. **Morella,** Timothy M '97 Baniak P&G -150 N Wacker Dr -Ste 1200
-Chicago, IL 60606

(419) 291-2419 .. **Morelli,** Deborah A '02 ProMedica Hlth Syst -2121 Hughes Dr
-Fl E -Toledo 43606

(216) 931-6000 .. **Morelli,** Matthew J '94 (Ulmer & B LLP) -1300 E 9th
-Ste 900 Penton Media Bldg -Cleveland 44114 **Fx:**931-6001

(724) 652-0821 .. **Morelli,** Richard R '95 -2625 Wilmngtn Rd -New Castle, PA 16105
Fx:652-7984

(216) 416-3114 .. **Morelli,** Theresa E '89 Forest City Enterprises -50 Pub Sq
-Ste 1200 -Cleveland 44113 **Fx:**619-9690

(615) 298-8244 .. **Morelli,** William P '78 Ingram Ind Inc -4400 Hrdng Rd
-One Belle Meade Pl -Nashville, TN 37205

(330) 454-9960 .. **Morello,** Herbert J '94 -116 Cleveland Av NW -Ste 808
-Canton 44702

(513) 651-6800 .. **Moreno,** Victor C '95 Cnsl Frost BT LLC -201 E 5th -2200 PNC Ctr
-Cincinnati 45202 **Fx:**651-6981

(216) 622-3600 .. **Morford,** James L '84 US Atty -801 W Superior -Ste 400
-Cleveland 44113 **Fx:**622-3370

(216) 592-5000 .. **Morford,** Joseph J '96 (Tucker E&W LLP) -925 Euclid Av
-1150 Huntngtn Bldg -Cleveland 44115 **Fx:**592-5009

(304) 562-5308 .. **Morford,** Warren N Jr. '80 -141 Wnchstr Dr -Culloden, WV 25510
Fx:562-2586

(513) 621-3418 .. **Morgan,** Amy T '99 (Morgan & M) -2692 Madison Rd -N-1#223
-Cincinnati 45208

(513) 721-7500 .. **Morgan,** Ann M '80 -22 W 9th -Cincinnati 45202

(440) 324-7607 .. **Morgan,** Brian D '86 Lorain Natl Bk -347 Midway Blvd -Ste 201
-Elyria 44035

(330) 451-7200 .. **Morgan,** Carl A '02 Stark Cnty Pub Def -200 W Tuscarawas
-Ste 200 -Canton 44702

(937) 335-7142 .. **Morgan,** Carol A '82 Miami Cnty Human Srvcs -2040 N Cnty Rd
#25A -Troy 45373

(216) 721-7700 .. **Morgan,** Charles M Jr. '86 -11510 Buckeye Rd -Cleveland 44104

(404) 249-2050 .. **Morgan,** Charles R '94 BellSouth Corp -1155 Pchtree NE -Atlanta,
GA 30309

(216) 371-0607 .. **Morgan,** Cynthia M '92 -2968 Mdwbrk Blvd
-Cleveland Heights 44118

(603) 356-5439 .. **Morgan,** Dennis L '94 %Cooper D&C,PA -2935 White Mtn Hwy
-North Conway, NH 03860 **Fx:**356-7975

(614) 621-1500 .. **Morgan,** Douglas S '82 (Calfee H&G LLP) -21 E State -1100 Fifth
Third Ctr -Columbus 43215 **Fx:**621-0010

(614) 462-3555 .. **Morgan,** Edward W '72 Franklin Cnty Pros -373 S High -Columbus
43215

(513) 651-4400 .. **Morgan,** Frederick M Jr. '83 Volkema TMBS&M,LPA -700 Walnut
-Ste 400 -Cincinnati 45202 **Fx:**651-4405

(419) 248-4611 .. **Morgan,** Frieda G '75 Louisville Title Agency -626 Madison
-Toledo 43604

(216) 663-8820 .. **Morgan,** Gerard R '02 M Neff Design Grp -5422 E 96th -Ste 120
-Cleveland 44125

Morgan, Harry W Jr. '71 -4040 W Bancroft -Toledo 43606

(216) 566-0064 .. **Morgan,** Hugh J '78 Armstrong MD&Z -101 Prospect Av W
-1725 The Mdlnd Bldg -Cleveland 44115 **Fx:**566-0224

Morgan, James A '66 -(Address Unavailable)

(419) 868-8150 .. **Morgan,** James E '76 -6912 Springvalley Dr -Ste 202-B
-Holland 43528

(216) 588-3788 .. **Morgan,** Jeffrey L '92 OH Savings Bnk -1801 E 9th -Ste 200
-Cleveland 44114

(330) 395-6444 .. **Morgan,** Jonathan P '01 (JP Morgan,Ltd) -173 W Market
-Warren 44481 **Fx:**394-6548

(614) 224-6488 .. **Morgan,** Kara A '92 -307 E Lvngstn Av -Columbus 43215

(513) 651-6800 .. **Morgan,** Katherine C '97 (Frost BT LLC) -201 E 5th -2200 PNC Ctr
-Cincinnati 45202 **Fx:**651-6981

Morgan, Kelly A '00 -Bx1325 -Medina 44258

(614) 221-6837 .. **Morgan,** Kelly M '77 (Morgan & P,LLP) -380 S 5th
-Columbus 43215 **Fx:**224-1537

(419) 213-4775 .. **Morgan,** Maria Q '76 Lucas Cnty Probate Ct -700 Adams
-Toledo 43624

(304) 231-0460 .. **Morgan,** Melanie A '01 %Steptoe & J -14th & Chapline -Bx150
-Wheeling, WV 26003

(513) 621-3418 .. **Morgan,** Michael D '99 (Morgan & M LLC)
-2692 Madison Rd N-1 #223 -Cincinnati 45208

(248) 948-2355 .. **Morgan,** Michael F '99 BASF Corp -26701 Telegraph Rd
-Patent Dept -Southfield, MI 48034

(614) 462-3194 .. **Morgan,** Michael W '92 Franklin Cnty Pub Def -373 S High
-12th Fl -Columbus 43215

(513) 241-9400 .. **Morgan,** Noel M '96 Legal Aid -215 E 9th -Ste 200
-Cincinnati 45202

(407) 629-5300 .. **Morgan,** Paul J '81 (P Morgan & Assoc,PA) -1099 W Morse Blvd
-Winter Park, FL 32789 **Fx:**629-9364

(330) 908-4149 .. **Morgan,** Richard A '01 Chas Schwab & Co,Inc -4150
Kinross Lks Pkwy -Richfield 44286

Morgan, Richard G '74 -1742 Karg Dr -Akron 44313

(803) 799-9800 .. **Morgan,** Richard J '77 McNair Law Firm -1301 Gervais
-Bk of Amer Twr -Bx11390 -Columbia, SC 29211

(614) 227-2000 .. **Morgan,** Robert J '01 %Porter WM&A LLP -41 S High
-Columbus 43215 **Fx:**227-2100

(513) 867-1731 .. **Morgan,** Ronald C '66 Morgan & Assoc -118 S 2nd
-Hamilton 45011

(336) 631-5297 .. **Morgan,** Ronald C '70 NLRB -4035 Univ Pkwy -Region 11 Ste 200
-Winston Salem, NC 27106

(614) 258-1133 .. **Morgan,** Thomas E '75 TE Morgan & Assoc -906 E Broad
-Columbus 43205

(440) 353-0848 .. **Morgan,** Toni L '96 -7307 Avon Belden Rd -N Ridgevll City Hall
-North Ridgeville 44039

(216) 621-4244 .. **Morganstern MacAdams & DeVito Co, LPA** -623 W St Clair Av
-Cleveland 44113 **Fx:**621-2951

(216) 621-4244 .. **Morganstern,** Stanley '67 (Morganstern M&D Co,LPA)
-623 W St Clair Av -Cleveland 44113 **Fx:**621-2951

(513) 893-6122 .. **Morgenstern,** Barbara L '86 Morgenstern & M -300 High -Ste 604
-Hamilton 45011

(513) 893-6122 .. **Morgenstern,** Carl '49 Morgenstern & M -300 High -Ste 604
-Hamilton 45011

(216) 241-2800 .. **Morgenstern,** Conrad J '49 Brown Gibbons Lang & Co
-1111 Superior Av -Ste 900 -Cleveland 44114 **Fx:**241-7417

(216) 696-3311 .. **Morgenstern,** Marc H '75 (Kahn K) -1301 E 9th -2600 Erievw Twr
-Cleveland 44114 **Fx:**623-4912

(216) 687-1900 .. **Morgenstern,** Susan E '86 Legal Aid -1223 W 6th
-Cleveland 44113 **Fx:**687-0779

(513) 721-1040 .. **Morgeson,** Junior A '69 Morgeson Law Ofc,LLC -105 W 4th
-Ste 1115 -Cincinnati 45202

(513) 721-1040 .. **Morgeson,** Philip J '00 -105 W 4th -Ste 1115 -Cincinnati 45202

(330) 742-8874 .. **Morgione,** Gregory G '98 Law Dept -26 S Phelps -Youngstown
44503

(330) 702-0230 .. **Morgione,** Vincent J '89 -3680 Starrs Centre Dr -Ste A
-Canfield 44406

(440) 461-6500 .. **Morhard,** Albert J '56 Lyndhurst Mun Ct -5301 Mayfld Rd
-Lyndhurst 44124

(216) 360-2124 .. **Moriarty & Jaros,PLL** -30000 Chagrin Blvd -Ste 200
-Pepper Pike 44124

(513) 421-9500 .. **Moriarty,** Kate E '96 Cnsl Cinergy Corp -139 E 4th -25 Atrium II
-Bx960 -Cincinnati 45201

(419) 624-3000 .. **Moriarty,** Mary M '00 Murray & M Co,LPA -111 E Shoreline Dr
-Bx19 -Sandusky 44871

(216) 592-5000 .. **Moriarty,** Matthew P '81 (Tucker E&W LLP) -925 Euclid Av
-1150 Huntngtn Bldg -Cleveland 44115 **Fx:**592-5009

(216) 360-2124 .. **Moriarty,** Richard J Jr. '49 (Moriarty & J,PLL) -30000 Chagrin Blvd
-Ste 200 -Pepper Pike 44124

(216) 566-8228 .. **Moriarty,** Robert B '94 -1370 Ontario -Ste 2000 -Cleveland 44113

(216) 621-3012 .. **Morice,** Craig J '95 %Koblentz & K -55 Pub Sq -Ste 1170
-Cleveland 44113 **Fx:**621-6567

Moritz, Larry G '68 -(Address Unavailable)

(614) 242-4242 .. **Morje,** Robert J '75 OfCnsl Decker VSL&V Co LPA -620 E Broad
-Columbus 43215 **Fx:**242-4243

(330) 726-5518 .. **Morley,** Michael J '81 -721 Boardman-Poland Rd -Ste 201
-Youngstown 44512

(330) 253-5060 .. **Morley,** Michael P '89 %Brennan M&D,LLC -75 E Market
-Akron 44308 **Fx:**253-1977

(216) 621-5300 .. **Morley,** Ryan J '04 %Buckingham D&B,LLP -1375 E 9th -Ste 1700
-Cleveland 44114 **Fx:**621-5440

(937) 223-3277 .. **Morman,** Carla J '96 (Bieser G&L LLP) -6 N Main
-400 Natl City Ctr -Dayton 45402 **Fx:**223-6339

(740) 589-7135 .. **Morman,** Todd A '03 -Bx2256 -Athens 45701

(330) 792-6611 .. **Moro,** Joseph A '85 (Heller MM&M Co LPA) -54 Wstchstr Dr
-Bx4144 -Youngstown 44515

(703) 693-8770 .. **Moro,** Roberta '84 USAF -1670 Air Force Pentagon -AFPAZ
-Washington, DC 20330

(330) 562-1339 .. **Moroney,** Carole J '64 -629 W Acadia Pnt -Aurora 44202

(216) 622-3600 .. **Moroney,** James V '82 US Atty -801 W Superior -Ste 400
-Cleveland 44113 **Fx:**622-3370

Moroney, John K '80 -2639 Wooster Rd -Ste 1
-Rocky River 44116

(419) 289-8857 .. **Moroney,** Melissa P '97 Ashland Cnty Pros -307 Orange
-Ashland 44805 **Fx:**281-3865

(330) 659-8900 .. **Moroney,** Michael J '85 %Natl Interstate Corp -3250 Intrstate Dr
-Richfield 44286

(216) 687-1200 .. **Moroscak,** John M '96 Palmer & Cay -1660 W 2nd -Ste 700
-Cleveland 44113 **Fx:**687-6775

(216) 951-8500 .. **Moroscak,** Richard J '70 (RJ Moroscak,Inc) -Bx24635 -Cleveland
44124

(216) 573-1223 .. **Moroz,** Nicholas M '75 Title 1st Agency -6060 Rockside Wds Blvd
-Ste 321 -Independence 44131

(216) 592-5000 .. **Morrical,** Glenn E '77 (Tucker E&W LLP) -925 Euclid Av
-1150 Huntngtn Bldg -Cleveland 44115 **Fx:**592-5009

Morris, Anissa K '94 -(Address Unavailable)

(773) 553-5937 .. **Morris,** Christopher B '98 Bd of Educ -125 S Clark -Ste 700
-Chicago, IL 60603

(216) 961-8116 .. **Morris,** Daniel G '88 -42205 Wdbrdg Av -Cleveland 44109

(740) 548-4231 .. **Morris,** David R '76 Whitney Ins Agncy,Inc -38 E Cherry -Bx387
-Sunbury 43074

(330) 376-5300 .. **Morris,** Duane '53 OfCnsl Buckingham D&B,LLP -50 S Main
-Bx1500 -Akron 44309 **Fx:**258-6559

(216) 529-0963 .. **Morris,** Edward L '90 Westpoint Title Agncy -3131 W 160th
-Cleveland 44111

(330) 823-4111 .. **Morris,** Evan W '65 -960 W State -Ste 130 -Alliance 44601

(614) 227-2000 .. **Morris,** Frank R Jr. '58 OfCnsl Porter WM&A LLP -41 S High
-Columbus 43215 **Fx:**227-2100

(937) 328-2574 .. **Morris,** Gregory M '89 Clark Cnty Pros -50 E Columbia -Bx1608
-Springfield 45501

(513) 744-7432 .. **Morris,** Gwen M '98 Cnsl Fifth 3rd Bank -38 Fountain Sq Plz
-MD 10AT76 -Cincinnati 45263

(614) 462-7585 .. **Morris,** James E '86 Franklin Cnty CSEA -80 E Fulton
-Columbus 43215

(859) 281-6981 .. **Morris,** James M '03 (Morris & M,PSC) -217 N Uppr -Bx394
-Lexington, KY 40588 **Fx:**233-7876

(937) 449-6810 .. **Morris,** Jeffrey W '93 OfCnsl Porter WM&A LLP -1 S Main
-Ste 1600 -Dayton 45402 **Fx:**449-6820

(740) 532-4333 .. **Morris,** Jeremy R '03 %Lambert M&B -215 S 4th -Bx725
-Ironton 45638

(330) 823-9080 ..**Morris**, John D '75 -1610 S Union -Bx2566 -Alliance 44601

(330) 453-0008 ..**Morris**, Jonathan E '94 (Redinger & M LLP)
-116 Cleveland Av NW -Ste 418 -Canton 44702

(330) 835-2323 ..**Morris**, Joseph R '96 Cnsl First Communications,LLC
-3340 W Market -Akron 44333

(614) 227-2057 ..**Morris**, Linda L '83 Porter WM&A -41 S High -28th flr
-Columbus 43215

(216) 623-0000 ..**Morris**, Melissa A '00 %Javitch B&R -1300 E 9th -14th Fl
-Cleveland 44114 **Fx:**623-0190

(419) 627-6620 ..**Morris**, Michael P '97 Erie Cnty Pub Def -220 Columbus Av
-Ste 37 -Sandusky 44870 **Fx:**627-6633

(330) 253-7100 ..**Morris**, Michele '84 -1 S Main -Ste 301 -Akron 44308 **Fx:**253-2500

(330) 533-9660 ..**Morris**, Patricia A '89 -4280 Boardman-Canfld Rd -Canfield 44406

(614) 476-5252 ..**Morris**, Richard L '90 (RL Morris Co,LPA) -4605 Morse Rd
-Ste 100 -Gahanna 43230 **Fx:**476-5255

(419) 536-2663 ..**Morris**, Robert G '51 -2823 Mnchstr Blvd -Toledo 43606
Fx:536-3464

(740) 345-3488 ..**Morris**, Robert L '85 Van Winkle & Assoc Co,LPA -8 Arcade Pl
-Newark 43055

(614) 761-1733 ..**Morris**, Robert V II '79 (Metcalf DMS&W,LLC) -655 Metro Pl S
-Ste 210 -Dublin 43017

(937) 328-2640 ..**Morris**, Ronald E '83 Clark Cnty Pub Def -50 E Columbia -4th Fl
-Springfield 45502 **Fx:**328-2715

(740) 432-4030 ..**Morris**, Roy L '54 -114 Southgate Pkwy -Cambridge 43725
Morris, Stacey A '04 -(Address Unavailable)

(330) 334-1536 ..**Morris**, Thomas J '98 %Palecek MH&M Co LLP
-200 Smokerise Dr -Ste 200 -Wadsworth 44281 **Fx:**334-7005

(850) 913-8035 ..**Morris**, Tim S '84 -3000 Fairmont Dr -Panama City, FL 32405

(614) 431-1500 ..**Morris**, Troy B '89 (Perez & M LLC) -8000 Ravines Edge Ct
-Ste 300 -Columbus 43235 **Fx:**431-3885

(216) 696-5400 ..**Morris**, William B '94 Crosby O & Assoc Co,LPA -55 Pub Sq
-Ste 1475 -Cleveland 44113 **Fx:**696-2610

(330) 823-3575 ..**Morris**, William F '71 -520 E Main -Ste 200 -Alliance 44601

(740) 472-0703 ..**Morrison**, C Mark '75 -117 N Main -Woodsfield 43793
Fx:472-9190

(614) 485-2010 ..**Morrison**, Dennis J '83 (Means BB&B Co,LPA) -2006 Kenny Rd
-Columbus 43221 **Fx:**485-2019
Morrison, Donald W '74 -60 Windrush Dr -Chagrin Falls 44022

(216) 687-0343 ..**Morrison**, Harvey S '62 -75 Pub Sq -Ste 1425 -Cleveland 44113

(330) 762-2411 ..**Morrison**, Jack Jr. '81 (Amer C Co,LPA) -159 S Main -6th Fl
-Akron 44308 **Fx:**762-9918

(419) 521-6222 ..**Morrison**, Jeffrey S '94 OH Edison Co -1717 Ashland Rd
-Mansfield 44905

(419) 244-4605 ..**Morrison**, Jennifer L '86 Port Lwrnce Title & Trust Co -616 Mad Av
-Toledo 43604

(216) 696-6900 ..**Morrison**, Jennifer L '89 Ctr-Health Affairs -1226 Huron Rd E
-Cleveland 44115

(330) 497-0700 ..**Morrison**, Jessica A '04 %Krugliak WG&D Co,LPA
-4775 Munson NW -Bx36963 -Canton 44735 **Fx:**497-4020

(330) 494-1815 ..**Morrison**, John W '96 Caterpillar Inc -101 E Maple
-North Canton 44720

(330) 744-1111 ..**Morrison**, Kelly J '85 Harrington H&M,Ltd -26 Market -Ste 1200
-Youngstown 44503 **Fx:**744-2029

(330) 744-1111 ..**Morrison**, Lance A '92 %Harrington H&M,Ltd -26 Market
-Ste 1200 -Youngstown 44503 **Fx:**744-2029

(614) 761-5001 ..**Morrison**, Melinda L '97 OCLC,Inc -6565 Frantz Rd -Dublin 43017

(413) 499-1950 ..**Morrison**, Meredith Horton '00 %WMLS -152 North -E-155
-Pittsfield, MA 01201 **Fx:**448-2715

(614) 221-3600 ..**Morrison**, Michael P '88 State St Cnsltnts -137 E State
-Columbus 43215 **Fx:**221-3600

(614) 487-0007 ..**Morrison**, Nancy E '83 -1170 Old Henderson Rd -Ste 109
-Columbus 43220 **Fx:**538-1806

(440) 838-8800 ..**Morrison**, Paul C '64 (Millisor & N Co,LPA) -9150 S Hills Blvd
-Ste 300 -Cleveland 44147 **Fx:**838-8805

(614) 469-6860 ..**Morrison**, Philip D '96 %US SBA -2 Nationwide Plz -Ste 1400
-Columbus 43215

(440) 944-7020 ..**Morrison**, Richard P '80 -30601 Euclid Av -Wickliffe 44092
Fx:943-3096

(770) 984-2707 ..**Morrison**, Samuel B '75 Cnsl Blimpie Intl,Inc
-180 Intrstate North Pkwy SE -Ste 500 -Atlanta, GA 30339
Fx:933-6098

(614) 221-4000 ..**Morrison**, Sarah D '97 (Chester W&S LLP) -65 E State -10th Fl
-Columbus 43215 **Fx:**221-4012

(513) 621-1505 ..**Morrisroe**, Donald P '79 (Goodman & G) -123 E 4th -5th Fl
-Cincinnati 45202

(727) 464-3354 ..**Morrissey**, Joseph A '81 %Cnty Atty -315 Court -6th Fl
-Clearwater, FL 33756 **Fx:**464-4147

(419) 251-2801 ..**Morrissey**, Martin B '92 St Vincent Mercy Med Ctr -2213 Cherry
-Toledo 43608

(614) 443-0352 ..**Morrissey**, Michael J '72 -34 W Whittier -Columbus 43206
Fx:445-8810

(440) 323-3335 ..**Morrisson**, John G '77 %J Morrison -105 Court -Ste 319
-Elyria 44035

(440) 329-5389 ..**Morrisson**, John G '77 Lorain Cnty Pros -225 Court -3rd Fl
-Elyria 44035

(330) 675-2426 ..**Morrow**, Charles L '88 (Trumbull Cnty Pros) -160 High NW
-Warren 44481

(740) 349-7262 ..**Morrow**, Clark A '71 (Morrow & E Co,LPA) -10 W Locust -Bx487
-Newark 43058

(937) 746-4997 ..**Morrow**, Edwin P III '98 Morrow Law Ofcs,LLC -780 W Central Av
-Springboro 45066

(740) 345-9611 ..**Morrow**, Elmer C '33 OfCnsl Morrow G&B,Ltd -33 W Main
-Bx4190 -Newark 43058

(740) 349-7262 ..**Morrow & Erhard Co,LPA** -10 W Locust -Bx487 -Newark 43058
(740) 345-9611 ..**Morrow Gordon & Byrd,Ltd** -33 W Main -Bx4190 -Newark 43058

(614) 485-2010 ..**Morrow**, Robert M '83 (Means BB&B Co,LPA) -2006 Kenny Rd
-Columbus 43221 **Fx:**485-2019

(330) 492-8717 ..**Morrow**, Tod T '89 (Buckingham D&B,LLP) -4518 Fulton Dr NW
-Bx35548 -Canton 44735 **Fx:**492-9625

(216) 941-5566 ..**Morscher**, Roy C '92 (Morscher & S) -11711 Lorain Av -Ste 56
-Cleveland 44111

(216) 861-2400 ..**Morse**, Andrew R '78 OH Awning & Manu Co -2658 Scranton Rd
-Cleveland 44113

(937) 879-2261 ..**Morse**, David R '00 %Brezine & B -188 W Hebble Av
-Fairborn 45324

(216) 241-0520 ..**Morse**, Joseph P '01 -526 Superior Av -1540 Leader Bldg
-Cleveland 44114

(614) 213-5355 ..**Morse**, Kerry L '90 Bank One Mngmnt Corp -1111 Polaris Pkwy
-Ste A-3 OH1-1085 -Columbus 43271

(330) 334-1536 ..**Morse**, Mary J '83 (Palecek MH&M Co LLP) -200 Smokerise Dr
-Ste 200 -Wadsworth 44281 **Fx:**334-7005

(216) 939-2065 ..**Morse**, Stephen S '75 Spectrum of Supportive Srvcs
-2900 Detroit Av -3rd Fl -Cleveland 44113

(216) 479-8500 ..**Morsek**, Leslie A '01 %Squire S&D LLP -127 Pub Sq
-4900 Key Twr -Cleveland 44114 **Fx:**479-8780

(937) 865-6800 ..**Mort**, Charles D '78 Lexis/Nexis -Bx933 -Dayton 45401

(513) 946-3000 ..**Morthorst**, Michael E '77 Hamilton Cnty Pros -230 E 9th
-Cincinnati 45202 **Fx:**946-3017

(740) 454-2545 ..**Mortimer**, David E '02 Micheli BN Co,LPA -3808 James Ct -Ste 2
-Bx788 -Zanesville 43702

(614) 844-5208 ..**Mortimer**, Pamela A '98 Special Counsel -130 E Wilson Bridge Rd
-Ste 330 -Worthington 43085

(614) 466-3934 ..**Mortland**, Karen H '79 State Med Brd -77 S High -17th Fl
-Columbus 43215

(330) 376-1242 ..**Morton**, Andrew B '93 Renner KGBT&W,LPA -106 S Main
-4th Fl First Natl Twr -Akron 44308 **Fx:**376-9646

(330) 483-3121 ..**Morton**, Christopher R '04 Mack's Inc -6760 Schl -Bx460
-Valley City 44280

(614) 480-5760 ..**Morton**, Daniel W '89 Huntington Natl Bank -41 S High
-Columbus 43287

(419) 247-2509 ..**Morton**, James M Jr. '67 (Fuller & H,Ltd) -One SeaGate -Ste 1700
-Bx2088 -Toledo 43603 **Fx:**247-2665

(216) 292-8117 ..**Morton**, John A '75 -2000 Auburn Dr -Ste 200 -Beachwood 44122

(419) 526-0050 ..**Morton**, Norman R '73 Morton Legal -55 S Diamond
-Mansfield 44902

(513) 983-2558 ..**Morton**, William S '74 Procter & Gamble Co-Legal
-1 Procter & Gamble Plz -Cincinnati 45202

(513) 929-3400 ..**Morwood**, Robert F '04 %Baker & H LLP -312 Walnut -Ste 3200
-Cincinnati 45202 **Fx:**929-0303

(614) 939-1948 ..**Mosbacher**, Linda F '89 -6381 Clark State Rd -Gahanna 43230
Fx:939-0856

(513) 665-3500 ..**Mosbaugh**, Jason A '04 %Freund F&A -105 E 4th -Ste 1400
-Cincinnati 45202 **Fx:**665-3503

(216) 586-3939 ..**Moscarino**, George J '58 SrCnsl Jones D -901 Lakeside Av
-Cleveland 44114 **Fx:**579-0212

(216) 621-1000 ..**Moscarino**, George M '83 (Moscarino & T,LLP) -1422 Euclid Av
-Hanna Bldg Ste 630 -Cleveland 44115 **Fx:**622-1556

(216) 621-1000 ..**Moscarino & Treu, LLP** -1422 Euclid Av -Hanna Bldg Ste 630
-Cleveland 44115 **Fx:**622-1556

(513) 771-2444 ..**Moschandreas**, John '03 %Lutz CM&R Co,LPA
-130 Tri-Cnty Pkwy -Ste 208 -Cincinnati 45246 **Fx:**771-2447

(216) 586-3939 ..**Moscioni**, Anna L '00 %Jones D -901 Lakeside Av
-Cleveland 44114 **Fx:**579-0212

Moseley, Adam H '03 US Navy -Address Unavailable

(440) 357-6211 ..**Moseman**, Heather L '03 %Cooper & F -166 Main
-Painesville 44077 **Fx:**357-1634

(216) 502-2002 ..**Moser**, Barbara J '82 -815 Superior Rd -Ste 1605
-Cleveland 44114

(216) 621-0200 ..**Moser**, Christina J '02 %Baker & H LLP -1900 E 9th -Ste 3200
-Cleveland 44114 **Fx:**696-0740
Moser, Devon L '92 -5131 Carter Ct -Mason 45040

(513) 844-1960 ..**Moser**, Donald K '87 (Moser Law Firm LLC) -1040 Symmes Rd
-Fairfield 45014

(513) 977-8200 ..**Moser**, Emerson C '02 %Dinsmore & S LLP -255 E 5th -Ste 1900
-Cincinnati 45202 **Fx:**977-8141

(614) 464-2200 ..**Moser**, Jack L Jr. '99 -400 S 5th -Ste 102 -Columbus 43215
Moser, John R '53 -(Address Unavailable)

(440) 285-3986 ..**Moser**, Lewis G '82 -11905 Fowlers Mill Rd -Chardon 44024

(614) 249-8226 ..**Moser**, Michael N '94 Nationwide Ins -1 Nationwide Plz -1-09-V3
-Columbus 43215

(614) 418-1729 ..**Moses**, Ambrose III '91 -2720 Airport Dr -Ste 100
-Columbus 43219
Moses, Barry W '81 -3330 Grenway Rd -Shaker Heights 44122

(740) 969-1101 ..**Moses**, Frederick T '02 -19538 Carroll Rd -Rockbridge 43149

(410) 244-7861 ..**Moses**, Gabrielle S '96 %Venable B&H,LLP -2 Hopkins Plz
-Ste 1800 -Baltimore, MD 21201

(440) 720-8169 ..**Moses**, Karen L '84 Sirva Relocation -6070 Parkland Blvd
-Mayfield Heights 44124

(216) 622-8200 ..**Moses**, Kimberly '85 (Calfee H&G LLP) -800 Superior Av
-Ste 1400 -Cleveland 44114 **Fx:**241-0816

(614) 224-7291 ..**Moses**, Michael A '77 -330 S High -Columbus 43215

(330) 533-1700 ..**Moses**, Norman A Jr. '97 -3870 Starrs Centre Dr -Canfield 44406

(740) 969-3171 ..**Moses**, Robert P '70 -20040 Carroll Rd -Rockbridge 43149

(216) 522-1424 ..**Mosher**, Louise H '74 Louise Mosher -1370 Ontario -Ste 600
-Cleveland 44113
Mosholder, Carol V '02 -(Address Unavailable)

(216) 586-3939 ..**Mosier**, Eric H '97 %Jones D -901 Lakeside Av -Cleveland 44114
Fx:579-0212

(858) 456-6022 ..**Mosier**, James F '73 PICA Holdings,Inc -875 Prospect -#301
-La Jolla, CA 92037

(419) 885-3597 ..**Mosier**, Stephen B '77 %McHugh D&M,Ltd -5580 Monroe
-Sylvania 43560 **Fx:**885-3861

(419) 255-9585 ..**Mosiniak**, Gary J '90 Rescue Mntl Hlth Srvcs
-3350 Collingwood Blvd -Toledo 43610

(216) 621-1000 ..**Moskowitz**, Carol J '02 %Moscarino & T,LLP -1422 Euclid Av
-Hanna Bldg Ste 630 -Cleveland 44115 **Fx:**622-1556

(513) 721-3111 ..**Moskowitz**, James H '94 Moskowitz & M -441 Vine -Ste 4300
-Cincinnati 45202

(216) 749-6300 ..**Moskowitz**, Jan S '68 -1703 Brookpark Rd -Cleveland 44109

(513) 721-3111 ..**Moskowitz**, Joel S '65 (Moskowitz & M) -441 Vine -Ste 4300
-Cincinnati 45202

(513) 721-3111 ..**Moskowitz**, Michael A '89 (Moskowitz & M) -441 Vine -Ste 4300
-Cincinnati 45202

(513) 721-3111 ..**Moskowitz & Moskowitz** -441 Vine -Ste 4300 -Cincinnati 45202

(216) 931-6000 ..**Moskowitz**, Suzann R '04 %Ulmer & B LLP -1300 E 9th
-Ste 900 Penton Media Bldg -Cleveland 44114 **Fx:**931-6001

(937) 865-6800 ..**Mosley**, Lynne R '93 Lexis/Nexis -Bx933 -Dayton 45401

(330) 384-7314 ..**Mosley**, Mark A '87 FirstMerit -121 S Main -#200 -Akron 44308

(330) 384-7060 ..**Moss**, A E '83 First Merit Bank,NA -121 S Main -Ste 200 -Akron 44308

(330) 670-7300 ..**Moss**, David T '82 (Hanna C&P,LLP) -3737 Embssy Pkwy -Bx5521 -Akron 44334 **Fx:**670-0977

(216) 447-0070 ..**Moss**, Debbie L '78 Dalad Grp -6200 Rockside Wds Blvd -Independence 44131

(330) 562-4404 ..**Moss**, Frank '57 (F Moss Co,LPA) -685 Elmwood Pt -Aurora 44202

(216) 443-7800 ..**Moss**, James E '93 Cuyahoga Cnty Pros -1200 Ontario -8th Fl -Cleveland 44113 **Fx:**698-2270

(216) 263-1715 ..**Moss**, Jerald L '83 Warwick Comm -2806 Payne Av -Cleveland 44114

(330) 334-4494 ..**Moss**, John P '88 -Bx155 -Wadsworth 44282

(614) 895-2302 ..**Moss**, Judith D '78 -275 Dogwood Ln -Westerville 43082 **Fx:**(866) 649-1834

(216) 771-5588 ..**Moss**, Karen Gabriel '89 Rosner & Assoc,LLC -812 Huron Rd -Ste 601 Caxton Bldg -Cleveland 44115 **Fx:**771-5894

(800) 693-7822 ..**Moss**, Liza C '91 West Bar Review -901 15th NW -#1010 -Washington, DC 20005

(614) 644-7257 ..**Moss**, Nicole S '94 Atty Gen -150 E Gay -Columbus 43215 **Fx:**752-4677

(614) 841-1918 ..**Moss**, Patricia A '81 AFSCME OH Cnsl 8 -6800 N High -Worthington 43085

(216) 696-3311 ..**Moss**, Steven M '91 (Kahn K) -1301 E 9th -2600 Erievw Twr -Cleveland 44114 **Fx:**623-4912

(614) 466-6700 ..**Moss-Edwards**, Linda A '80 Tax Appeals -30 E Broad -Columbus 43215 **Fx:**644-5196

(740) 942-2127 ..**Mosser**, Geoffrey B '71 -232 S Main -Bx265 -Cadiz 43907

(859) 371-3852 ..**Mossman**, Donald W II '79 -Bx17856 -Covington, KY 41017

(330) 296-5461 ..**Mostardi**, Sharon R '00 -3376 Summit Rd -Ravenna 44266 **Mosteller**, Brenda L '93 -5821 Fortrose Dr -Hudson 44236

(330) 744-3196 ..**Mostov**, Jan R '84 Cmmnty Lgl Aid Srvcs,Inc -11 Fed Plz Central -7th Fl -Youngstown 44503 **Fx:**744-2503

(419) 372-8364 ..**Mota**, Sue Ann '84 Bowling Green State Univ -275 BA Bldg -Dept of Leg Studies -Bowling Green 43403

(614) 488-7924 ..**Mote**, Gretchen J '78 %OBLIC -1650 Lk Shr Dr -Bx2708 -Columbus 43216

(614) 464-2572 ..**Mote**, Scott R '77 (Harris MB&C,PLL) -37 W Broad -9th Fl -Columbus 43215 **Fx:**464-2245

(740) 774-9421 ..**Motes**, Joseph E '96 -13 S Paint -Chillicothe 45601

(440) 526-1581 ..**Motiska**, Robert J '69 Small Business Dvlpmnt -9300 Mercer Ln -Brecksville 44141

(216) 443-7800 ..**Motley**, Bianca A '03 Cuyahoga Cnty Pros -1200 Ontario -8th Fl -Cleveland 44113 **Fx:**698-2270

(330) 702-8860 ..**Motosko**, Linda A '80 -3679 Mercedes Pl -Canfield 44406 **Motsch**, Barry B '76 -100 W Erie Av -Lorain 44052

(330) 468-3969 ..**Motsco**, Dwight P '87 -115 W Aurora Rd -Northfield 44067

(440) 439-4777 ..**Motsco**, Martha A '88 Bedford Bd of Educ -475 Nrthfld Rd -Bedford 44146

(216) 586-3939 ..**Mott**, Cassandra G '99 %Jones D -901 Lakeside Av -Cleveland 44114 **Fx:**579-0212

(513) 876-4160 ..**Motta**, Alan C '86 -2783 Bert Reed Mem'l Rd -Felicity 45120

(937) 225-7233 ..**Motta**, Elizabeth A '93 SSA-OHA -110 N Main -Ste 800 -Dayton 45402

(330) 643-6981 ..**Motter**, Allen H '93 Roadway Corp -1077 Gorge Blvd -Akron 44310

(419) 562-3007 ..**Motter**, John A '82 -1153 Rosedale Av -Bucyrus 44820

(614) 227-4810 ..**Motter**, Miranda C '01 %Bricker & E LLP -100 S 3rd -Columbus 43215 **Fx:**227-2390

(216) 749-7090 ..**Mottl**, Ronald M '57 -2525 Brookpark Rd -Parma 44134

(513) 381-2838 ..**Mottley**, J Donald '91 %Taft S&H LLP -425 Walnut -Ste 1800 -Cincinnati 45202 **Fx:**381-0205

(440) 746-1000 ..**Motylinski**, Michael '03 -1000 W Wallings Rd -Ste A -Broadview Heights 44147 **Fx:**746-1003

(330) 493-2685 ..**Motz**, Frank J '78 Start Cnty Fam Ct -2226 Harvard Av NW -Canton 44709

(614) 469-0400 ..**Moul**, Geoffrey J '99 (Murray MM&B LLP) -326 S High -Ste 400 -Columbus 43215 **Fx:**469-0402

(419) 394-7441 ..**Moul**, John F '69 (Noble M&M) -146 E Spring -Saint Marys 45885 **Fx:**394-7694

(614) 469-3220 ..**Moul**, William C '64 (Thompson H LLP) -10 W Broad -Ste 700 -Columbus 43215 **Fx:**469-3361

(216) 443-7800 ..**Moulin**, Darcy A '91 Cuyahoga Cnty Pros -1200 Ontario -8th Fl -Cleveland 44113 **Fx:**698-2270

(570) 775-9525 ..**Moulton**, Mark E '97 (Moulton & M PC) -HC8 Bet 83 84 -State Route 6 -Lords Valley, PA 18428

(740) 446-2922 ..**Moulton**, Thomas S Jr. '97 (Cherrington M&E) -Bx409 -Gallipolis 45631 **Fx:**446-1738

(440) 886-7878 ..**Moultrie**, Stuart C '91 State Farm Ins -7088 W 130th -Cleveland 44130

(937) 865-6800 ..**Mount**, Barbara A '80 Lexis/Nexis -Bx933 -Dayton 45401 **Mount**, Dick W Jr. '75 -Bx182 -Minerva 44657

(937) 225-4464 ..**Mount**, Ronald E '80 2nd Dist Ct of Appls -41 N Perry -Rm 515 -Bx972 -Dayton 45422

(614) 365-2700 ..**Mount**, Steven F '86 (Squire S&D LLP) -41 S High -1300 Huntngtn Ctr -Columbus 43215 **Fx:**365-2499

(216) 241-5310 ..**Mountcastle**, Colleen A '98 %Gallagher SF&N -1501 Euclid Av -6th Fl -Cleveland 44115 **Fx:**241-1608

(216) 566-5874 ..**Mountcastle**, Jennifer M '00 %Thompson H LLP -127 Pub Sq -3900 Key Ctr -Cleveland 44114 **Fx:**566-5800

(216) 781-1212 ..**Mounts**, Mia M '98 %Walter & H LLP -1301 E 9th -Ste 3500 -Cleveland 44114 **Fx:**575-0911

(330) 821-1430 ..**Moushey**, Thomas P '77 (Geiger TS&H) -1844 W State -Ste A -Alliance 44601 **Fx:**821-2217

(216) 348-5400 ..**Movius**, David T '98 %McDonald H Co,LPA -600 Superior Av E -Ste 2100 -Cleveland 44114 **Fx:**348-5474

(330) 376-2700 ..**Mowery**, Chad L '00 %Roetzel & A,LPA -222 S Main -Akron 44308 **Fx:**376-4577

(614) 764-1444 ..**Mowery**, James S Jr. '73 (Mowery & Y) -425 Metro Pl N -Ste 420 -Dublin 43017 **Fx:**760-8654

(740) 574-2521 ..**Mowery**, Steven L '79 (Mowery & B) -9050 Ohio Rvr Rd -Wheelersburg 45694

(614) 764-1444 ..**Mowery & Youell** -425 Metro Pl N -Ste 420 -Dublin 43017 **Fx:**760-8654

(614) 292-0160 ..**Mowoe**, Isaac J '82 OSU -230 N Oval Mall -486 Univ Hall -Columbus 43210

(740) 687-7155 ..**Mowry**, Kathy S '81 Fairfield Cnty CSEA -239 W Main -Lancaster 43130

(419) 213-4755 ..**Mowry**, Paula C '88 %Hon JR Sherck -800 Jackson -Toledo 43624

(614) 228-8400 ..**Mowry**, Sherry L '01 %Ulmer & B LLP -88 E Broad -Ste 1600 -Columbus 43215 **Fx:**228-8561

(330) 376-2700 ..**Moxon**, George W II '75 (Roetzel & A,LPA) -222 S Main -Akron 44308 **Fx:**376-4577

(330) 535-5711 ..**Moxon**, Joy A '99 %Brouse M -106 S Main -500 First Natl Twr -Akron 44308 **Fx:**253-8601

(216) 861-5582 ..**Moy**, Philip J Jr. '89 (Fay SFM&M LLP) -1100 Superior Av -7th Fl -Cleveland 44114 **Fx:**241-1666

(513) 983-3859 ..**Moyer**, David M '80 Procter & Gamble Co-Legal -1 Procter & Gamble Plz -Cincinnati 45202

(419) 539-6000 ..**Moyer**, Kevin J '84 AFSCME OH Cncl 8 -420 S Reynolds Rd -Ste 108 -Toledo 43615

(937) 382-4559 ..**Moyer**, Richard W '88 Clinton Cnty Pros -103 E Main -Wilmington 45177 **Fx:**382-6278

(614) 228-2552 ..**Moyer**, Stephen A '81 -400 S 5th -Ste 103 -Columbus 43215

(513) 618-7800 ..**Moyers**, Michael K '98 (Graf S&M,LPA) -425 Walnut -Ste 2400 -Cincinnati 45202 **Fx:**618-7801

(412) 281-1055 ..**Moyles**, James R '98 -310 Grant -Ste 1404 Grant Bldg -Pittsburgh, PA 15219 **Fx:**281-1058

(614) 790-8737 ..**Mozakis**, Lee W '98 Sterling Commerce,Inc -4600 Lakehurst Ct -Dublin 43016

(614) 855-7488 ..**Mozenter**, Michael J '84 -15 S High -New Albany 43054 **Mozola**, John M '77 -(Address Unavailable) **Mramor**, James P '03 -(Address Unavailable)

(248) 540-8500 ..**Mucha**, Robert A '88 (RA Mucha,PC) -1137 Holland -Birmingham, MI 48009 **Fx:**540-1400

(614) 761-9775 ..**Muchnicki**, Edward D '74 -5650 Blazer Pkwy -Ste 100 -Dublin 43017

(330) 494-6688 ..**Muckley**, Timothy R '97 Giltz & Assoc Inc -4835 Munson NW -Canton 44718

(330) 896-0450 ..**Mucklow**, David '00 First Place Bank -Bx18 -Green 44232 **Fx:**896-0450

(513) 772-3962 ..**Muehleisen**, Robert A Jr. '93 -270 Northland Blvd -Ste 226 -Cincinnati 45246 **Fx:**772-5060

(419) 626-3323 ..**Muehlhauser**, Eric M '93 %Muehlhauser & M -422 Columbus Av -Bx790 -Sandusky 44870

(419) 626-3323 ..**Muehlhauser**, George M III '55 (Muehlhauser & M) -422 Columbus Av -Bx790 -Sandusky 44870

(419) 626-3323 ..**Muehlhauser & Moore** -422 Columbus Av -Bx790 -Sandusky 44870

(330) 405-4736 ..**Mueller**, Caroline A '92 -2226 Enterprise Pkwy -Twinsburg 44087

(937) 912-9810 ..**Mueller**, Carolyn L '95 (Hall & M,LPA) -3040 Prsdntl Dr -Ste 222 -Fairborn 45324 **Fx:**912-6920

(937) 228-1111 ..**Mueller**, Carolyn L '95 (Hall & M,LPA) -51 Irongate Park Dr -Dayton 45459 **Fx:**912-8920

(419) 241-6000 ..**Mueller**, Denise A '00 Eastman & S Ltd -1 Seagate -24th Fl -Bx10032 -Toledo 43699 **Fx:**247-1777

(614) 436-0600 ..**Mueller**, Jerry K Jr. '73 (Mueller & S,LPA) -7700 Rvrs Edge Dr -Columbus 43235

(513) 621-3636 ..**Mueller**, John J '79 -632 Vine -Ste 800 -Cincinnati 45202 **Fx:**621-2550

(513) 381-2838 ..**Mueller**, John M '97 %Taft S&H LLP -425 Walnut -Ste 1800 -Cincinnati 45202 **Fx:**381-0205

(614) 221-8448 ..**Mueller**, Kevin M '02 %Buckingham D&B,LLP -191 W Nationwide Blvd -Ste 300 -Bx151120 -Columbus 43215 **Fx:**221-8590

(480) 715-2448 ..**Mueller**, Mark D '02 Intel Corp -4500 S Dobson Rd -OC2-157 -Chandler, AZ 85248

(330) 762-7377 ..**Mueller**, Raymond C '88 %Oldham & D -195 S Main -Ste 300 -Akron 44308 **Fx:**762-7390

(614) 436-0600 ..**Mueller & Smith,LPA** -7700 Rvrs Edge Dr -Columbus 43235

(216) 266-2487 ..**Mueller**, Wally M '90 GE Lighting -1975 Noble Rd -Bldg 310B -Cleveland 44112

(513) 887-3474 ..**Muench-McElfresh**, Jennifer R '97 Butler Cnty Pros -315 High -11th Fl -Bx515 -Hamilton 45012

(937) 225-5757 ..**Muennich**, Joshua M '01 Montgomery Cnty Pros -301 W 3rd -Bx972 -Dayton 45422 **Fx:**225-3470

(614) 885-2550 ..**Muenz**, Donald P '74 -132 W Rathbone Rd -Columbus 43214

(937) 293-2141 ..**Mues**, Robert L '78 (Holzfaster CM&M) -1105 Wilmngtn Av -Dayton 45420 **Fx:**293-0914

(513) 579-6400 ..**Muething**, Brian P '03 %Keating M&K PLL -1 E 4th -1400 Provident Twr -Cincinnati 45202 **Fx:**579-6457

(513) 579-6400 ..**Muething**, John L '48 SrCnsl Keating M&K PLL -1 E 4th -1400 Provident Twr -Cincinnati 45202 **Fx:**579-6457

(513) 333-5515 ..**Muething**, Mark F '84 Great Amer Fin Rsrces Inc -250 E 5th -10th Fl -Cincinnati 45202

(513) 579-6400 ..**Muething**, Paul V '77 (Keating M&K PLL) -1 E 4th -1400 Provident Twr -Cincinnati 45202 **Fx:**579-6457

(513) 471-4700 ..**Muething**, Thaddeus A '80 -Bx428843 -Cincinnati 45242

(614) 299-7700 ..**Muetzel**, Andrew T '99 Muetzel Plumbing & Heating -1661 Kenny Rd -Columbus 43212

(202) 606-0469 ..**Muetzel**, James '03 US Ofc Personnel Mgt -1900 E NW -Rm #7532 -Washington, DC 20415

(419) 243-6126 ..**Mufleh**, Ida B '95 -Bx5931 -Toledo 43613

(216) 443-9000 ..**Mugnano**, John A '01 %Porter WM&A LLP -925 Euclid Av -Ste 1700 -Cleveland 44115 **Fx:**443-9011

(440) 329-5389 ..**Muhek**, David P '82 Lorain Cnty Pros -225 Court -3rd Fl -Elyria 44035

(937) 449-6400 ..**Muhic**, Theresa M '88 %Dinsmore & S LLP -1 S Main -Ste 1300 One Dayton Centre -Dayton 45402 **Fx:**449-6405

(404) 338-9489 ..**Muhlbach**, James B '79 IRS -2888 Woodcock Blvd -MailStop 652-D -Atlanta, GA 30341 **Muhlberg**, Diana L '04 -(Address Unavailable)

(800) 274-7280 ..**Muir**, Herman S III '91 -6575 SW 86th Av -Portland, OR 97223

(330) 239-4480 ..**Muirden**, Marjorie A '89 Holland & M -1343 Sharon-Copley Rd -Bx345 -Sharon Center 44274 **Fx:**239-6224

(614) 464-6400 .. **Muklewicz**, Jacob T '01 %Vorys SS&P LLP -52 E Gay -Bx1008 -Columbus 43216 Fx:464-6350

(216) 896-2458 .. **Mulac**, Carol A '86 Parker Hannifin Corp -6035 Parkland Blvd -Cleveland 44124

(614) 471-8194 .. **Mularski**, Raymond J '84 -107 W Johnstown Rd -Gahanna 43230

(202) 767-1546 .. **Mulbarger**, Matthew J '96 US Air Force -112 Luke Av -AFLSA/JAJG,Rm 343 -Bolling AFB, DC 20332

(513) 241-9400 .. **Mulcahy**, Elizabeth A '02 Legal Aid -215 E 9th -Ste 200 -Cincinnati 45202

(216) 622-8200 .. **Mulcahy**, Michael T '76 Calfee H&G LLP -800 Superior Av -Ste 1400 -Cleveland 44114 Fx:241-0816

(614) 229-4429 .. **Mulchaey**, Rachel A '01 %Luper N&L,LPA -50 W Broad -1200 LeVeque Twr -Columbus 43215 Fx:464-2425

(419) 724-0030 .. **Mulder**, Kevin C '92 LAWO -520 Mad Av -Ste 640 -Toledo 43604 Fx:321-1582

     Muldoon, Andrea L '99 HQ USAF/JAX -1420 Air Force Pentagon -Rm 5B269 -Washington, DC 20330

(614) 233-4422 .. **Muldoon**, Damon P '98 Fifth 3rd Bank -21 E State -8th Fl -Columbus 43215

(614) 486-0297 .. **Muldoon**, Michael J '76 -1375 Dublin Rd -Columbus 43215 Fx:486-8580

(330) 296-4451 .. **Muldowney**, Eugene L '89 -250 S Chestnut -Ste 17 -Ravenna 44266

(330) 799-5940 .. **Muldowney**, Shawn R '92 Schiavoni S&B Co,LPA -87 Wstchstr Dr -Youngstown 44515

(740) 446-0603 .. **Mulford**, Eric R '04 %WD Conley -537 2nd Av -Gallipolis 45631 Fx:446-3411

(614) 486-2401 .. **Mulgrew**, Donald B '75 OH State Med Assoc -6401 Mill Run Dr -Hilliard 43026

     Mulhollan, John S '94 -7220 Northvw Dr -Wadsworth 44281

(516) 477-1673 .. **Mulholland**, John H '62 -725 Isl View Ln -Greenport, NY 11944

(419) 473-1431 .. **Mulkey**, Chad T '00 (JR Kuhl,LPA) -4127 Monroe -Toledo 43606 Fx:473-0329

(216) 523-1400 .. **Mull**, Donald P '52 -614 Superior Av NW -Ste 848 -Cleveland 44113

(419) 213-3168 .. **Mull**, Lawrence O '90 Lucas Cnty CSEA -701 Adams -Toledo 43624

(614) 644-2489 .. **Mull**, Sharon A '91 Dept Cmmrce/Liquor Cntrl -6606 Tussing Rd -Bx4005 -Reynoldsburg 43068 Fx:644-3740

(859) 581-5898 .. **Mullaney**, Darren '03 %Brooking M&H -1717 Dixie Hwy -Ste 920 -Covington, KY 41011 Fx:581-5164

(513) 852-8200 .. **Mullee**, Michelle A '85 OfCnsl Cors & B LLC -537 E Pete Rose Way -Ste 400 -Cincinnati 45202

(812) 934-8041 .. **Mullen**, David W '90 Forethought Fincl Srvcs -Forthought Ctr -Batesville, IN 47006

(330) 674-1900 .. **Mullen**, Jeffrey A '93 -46-A W Jackson -Millersburg 44654

(513) 946-3000 .. **Mullen**, Judith A '83 Hamilton Cnty Pros -230 E 9th -Cincinnati 45202 Fx:946-3017

(440) 395-3742 .. **Mullen**, Kristy M '03 Progressive -6300 Wilson Mills Rd -N72 -Mayfield Village 44143

(513) 684-6023 .. **Mullen**, M Holly '01 %US Dept of Labor -36 E 7th -Ste 2525 -Cincinnati 45202 Fx:684-6108

(330) 497-0700 .. **Mullen**, Matthew P '94 (Krugliak WG&D Co,LPA) -4775 Munson NW -Bx36963 -Canton 44735 Fx:497-4020

(330) 489-4414 .. **Mullen**, Robert K '97 %Rep R Regula -4150 Belden Vllg NW -Ste 408 -Canton 44718

(440) 286-9726 .. **Mullen**, Thomas J '66 -138 Center -Chardon 44024

(330) 666-6787 .. **Mullen**, Thomas T '87 -3500 W Market -Ste 4 -Fairlawn 44333

(513) 232-4200 .. **Mullenix**, Charles D '73 -1080 Nimitzvw Dr -Rm 303 -Cincinnati 45230

(513) 621-6674 .. **Muller**, Bradley K '78 (Mulvey & M LLC) -35 E 7th -Ste 750 -Cincinnati 45202 Fx:621-0183

(440) 997-6175 .. **Muller**, Carl F '72 (Warren & Y,PLL) -134 W 46th -Bx2300 -Ashtabula 44005 Fx:992-9114

(614) 221-3155 .. **Muller**, David A '00 %Bailey C LLC -10 W Broad -Columbus 43215 Fx:221-0479

(248) 645-2440 .. **Muller**, John F '84 (Muller MRHM&S) -33233 Woodward Av -Birmingham, MI 48009 Fx:645-5478

(248) 645-2440 .. **Muller**, John F Jr. '84 (Muller MRHM&S) -33233 Woodward Av -Birmingham, MI 48009 Fx:645-5478

(937) 298-2226 .. **Mulligan**, James J '54 (Mulligan & M) -812 Tmbrlk Ct -Dayton 45429

(216) 348-5400 .. **Mulligan**, John T '74 (McDonald H Co,LPA) -600 Superior Av E -Ste 2100 -Cleveland 44114 Fx:348-5474

(330) 747-2661 .. **Mulligan**, Joseph P '91 Cafaro Co -2445 Belmont Av -Bx2186 -Youngstown 44504

(937) 228-9790 .. **Mulligan**, Leo Patrick '84 (LP Mulligan & Assoc LPA,Co) -28 N Wilkinson -2nd Fl -Bx10838 -Dayton 45402

(419) 734-6845 .. **Mulligan**, Mark E '77 Ottawa Cnty Pros -315 Madison -2nd Fl -Port Clinton 43452 Fx:734-3862

(937) 298-2226 .. **Mulligan**, Patrick J '89 (Mulligan & M) -812 Tmbrlk Ct -Dayton 45429

(614) 463-9770 .. **Mulligan**, Richard S '79 (Roetzel & A,LPA) -155 E Broad -Natl City Ctr 12th Fl -Columbus 43215 Fx:463-9792

(202) 307-2438 .. **Mulligan**, Scott E '97 DOJ/Drug Enfrcmnt -2401 Jeff Davis Hwy -Ofc of Chief Cnsl -Alexandria, VA 22301

(216) 241-7700 .. **Mullin**, Edward M '88 -50 Pub Sq -Ste 558 -Cleveland 44113

(216) 443-7223 .. **Mullin**, Gregory K '86 Cuyahoga Cnty Pub Def -1200 W 3rd NW -100 Lakeside Pl -Cleveland 44113

(419) 609-1311 .. **Mullin**, Jeanne M '99 (Reminger & R) -237 W Wshngtn Row -2nd Fl -Sandusky 44870 Fx:626-4805

(937) 255-5270 .. **Mullin**, Michael J '75 AFMCLO/JAN -1864 4th -RM 130A -Wright Patterson AFB 45433

(614) 466-4280 .. **Mullin**, Philip A Jr. '74 Legis Srvc Commssn -77 S High -Columbus 43215

(513) 621-8210 .. **Mullin**, Sybil B '95 %Drew & W Co,LPA -1 W 4th -Ste 2400 -Cincinnati 45202 Fx:621-5444

(614) 466-4605 .. **Mullinax**, Robert L '74 OH Dept Job & Fam Srvcs -30 E Broad -32nd Fl -Columbus 43266

(937) 223-8177 .. **Mullins**, Jeffrey A '90 (Coolidge WW&L) -33 W 1st -Ste 600 -Dayton 45402 Fx:223-6705

(513) 621-5631 .. **Mullins**, Jeffrey S '87 (Goodson & M,Ltd) -110 E 8th -Ste 200 -Cincinnati 45202

(614) 777-4024 .. **Mullins**, Lawrence G '75 -3610 Oarlock Ct -Hilliard 43026

(614) 462-3194 .. **Mulrane**, Kevin P '75 Franklin Cnty Pub Def -373 S High -12th Fl -Columbus 43215

(614) 644-6803 .. **Mulrane-Meyers**, Toni E '81 OH Envrnmtl Brd of Review -309 S 4th -Ste 222 -Columbus 43215

     Mulrooney, Aaron L '90 -3064 W Edgerton Rd -Silver Lake 44224

(513) 721-5672 .. **Mulvaney**, Christopher J '97 %Benjamin Y&H LLC -312 Elm -Ste 1850 -Cincinnati 45202 Fx:562-4388

(513) 721-0001 .. **Mulvey**, John J '94 -2306 Park Av -Cincinnati 45206 Fx:721-5109

(513) 621-6674 .. **Mulvey & Muller LLC** -35 E 7th -Ste 750 -Cincinnati 45202 Fx:621-0183

(614) 430-8885 .. **Mulvey**, Thomas J '85 (Curry RS&M Co,LLC) -8000 Ravines Edge Ct -Ste 103 -Columbus 43235 Fx:430-8890

(513) 621-6674 .. **Mulvey**, William J Jr. '75 (Mulvey & M LLC) -35 E 7th -Ste 750 -Cincinnati 45202 Fx:621-0183

(216) 781-2600 .. **Mulvihill**, Dennis P '94 (Lowe EW&M Co,LPA) -1660 W 2nd -610 Skylight Ofc Twr -Cleveland 44113 Fx:781-2610

(330) 629-8860 .. **Mumaw**, Daniel J '86 -7178 West Blvd -Youngstown 44512

(440) 288-8192 .. **Mumford**, David M '77 -1213 Missouri Av -Lorain 44052

(216) 621-0200 .. **Mumford**, Michael E '01 %Baker & H LLP -1900 E 9th -Ste 3200 -Cleveland 44114 Fx:696-0740

(330) 972-5315 .. **Mumper**, John E '82 Univ of Akron -Polsky Bldg #166H -Akron 44325

(513) 983-1042 .. **Muncy**, Jason P '00 Procter & Gamble Co-Legal -1 Procter & Gamble Plz -Cincinnati 45202 Fx:983-7635

(614) 462-3555 .. **Muncy**, Rebecca L '04 Franklin Cnty Pros -373 S High -Columbus 43215

(513) 489-4988 .. **Mundy**, Ralph B '94 -11154 Centennial Av -Cincinnati 45242

(304) 525-1406 .. **Mundy**, William L '96 (Mundy & A) -422 9th -1 Plz S -Huntington, WV 25701

(419) 241-4400 .. **Munger**, Peter C '89 (Munger W Co,LPA) -626 Mad Av -Ste 400 -Toledo 43604

(419) 241-4400 .. **Munger Watkins Co,LPA** -626 Mad Av -Ste 400 -Toledo 43604

(859) 491-6141 .. **Mungo**, Frank M '01 -524 Greenup -Covington, KY 41011

(216) 523-1500 .. **Muniak**, William J '92 %Mansour GG&M Co,LPA -55 Pub Sq -Ste 2150 -Cleveland 44113 Fx:523-1705

(203) 961-5164 .. **Muniz**, Peter J '89 GE Captl Srvcs -120 Long Ridge Rd -2nd Fl -Stamford, CT 06927

(859) 655-2300 .. **Munninghoff**, Thomas J '77 Munninghoff L & Co -231 Scott Blvd -Covington, KY 41011

     Munoz, Charles R '96 -(Address Unavailable)

(651) 848-5359 .. **Munoz-Hurwitz**, Amy M '93 West Group -610 Opperman Dr -Eagan, MN 55123

(614) 228-6885 .. **Munsell**, Theodore M '79 (Lane A&H LLC) -175 S 3rd -Ste 700 -Columbus 43215 Fx:228-0146

(216) 586-3939 .. **Munson**, Adam D '01 %Jones D -901 Lakeside Av -Cleveland 44114 Fx:579-0212

(614) 462-3194 .. **Munson**, Sheryl K '94 Franklin Cnty Pub Def -373 S High -12th Fl -Columbus 43215

(330) 434-3461 .. **Muntean**, Christopher P '04 Legal Def -One Cascade Plz -Ste 1940 -Akron 44308

(330) 375-2030 .. **Muntean**, David A '87 Law Dept -161 S High -Ste 202 -Akron 44308

(937) 548-0324 .. **Muntean**, Susan M '78 %G Flinn Co,LPA -429 Mem'l Dr -Greenville 45331

(614) 752-1795 .. **Murch**, Elizabeth Z '97 OH Dept Rehab & Correction -1050 Fwy Dr N -Columbus 43229

(614) 462-2217 .. **Murch**, Kevin L '96 (Schottenstein Z&D) -250 West -Bx165020 -Columbus 43216 Fx:462-5135

(419) 213-3000 .. **Murd**, Pamela K '01 Lucas Cnty CSEA -701 Adams -Toledo 43624

     Murdoch, Randy P '04 -(Address Unavailable)

(216) 889-5190 .. **Murdoch**, Robert B '94 AG Interactive -One Amer Rd -Cleveland 44144

(330) 325-1145 .. **Murdock**, Chad E '91 -Bx334 -Rootstown 44272

(513) 946-9000 .. **Murdock**, Constance C '92 Hamilton Cnty Juv Ct -800 Bway -Cincinnati 45202 Fx:946-9217

(614) 272-7845 .. **Murdock**, Elizabeth A '02 Amer Commerce Ins Co -3590 Twin Crks Dr -Columbus 43204

(513) 345-8291 .. **Murdock Goldenberg Schneider & Groh** -35 E 7th -Ste 600 -Cincinnati 45202 Fx:345-8294

(513) 241-4042 .. **Murdock**, Jack A '57 (Murdock & Assoc Co,LPA) -615 Main -Cincinnati 45202

(513) 345-8291 .. **Murdock**, John C '94 (Murdock GS&G) -35 E 7th -Ste 600 -Cincinnati 45202 Fx:345-8294

(513) 345-8291 .. **Murdock**, Norman A '68 OfCnsl Murdock GS&G -35 E 7th -Ste 600 -Cincinnati 45202 Fx:345-8294

(216) 228-6996 .. **Murman**, Michael E '75 (Murman & Assoc) -14701 Detroit Av -Lakewood 44107

(216) 515-1660 .. **Murnane**, Colleen C '95 (Frantz W LLP) -127 Pub Sq -2500 Key Ctr -Cleveland 44114 Fx:515-1650

     Murnane, Linda S '81 US Air Force AFLSA/JUD -Unit 10305 Bx 390 -APO, AE 09094

     Murnane, Mary S '99 -(Address Unavailable)

(440) 838-7600 .. **Murner**, Barry R '98 %Janik & D,LLP -9200 S Hills Blvd -Ste 300 -Cleveland 44147 Fx:838-7601

(216) 241-0011 .. **Murner**, Brett F '01 %Goldberg & O -323 Lakeside Av W -Ste 450 -Cleveland 44113

(614) 442-8040 .. **Murphey**, David P '78 %Cantlon Assoc,Inc -4621 Reed Rd -Bx20950 -Columbus 43220

(614) 365-2700 .. **Murphey**, Richard R Jr. '50 Cnsl Squire S&D LLP -41 S High -1300 Huntngtn Ctr -Columbus 43215 Fx:365-2499

(419) 251-5263 .. **Murphree**, R K '95 Saint Vincent Mercy Med Ctr -2213 Cherry -Toledo 43608

     Murphy, Ann Marie '03 Major Legal Srvcs -1111 Chester Av -510 Park Plz -Cleveland 44114

(614) 445-2583 .. **Murphy**, Beth Williams '02 Grange Mutual Casualty Co -650 S Front -Bx1218 -Columbus 43216

(614) 469-0400 .. **Murphy**, Brian K '99 (Murray MM&B LLP) -326 S High -Ste 400 -Columbus 43215 Fx:469-0402

(513) 946-5138 .. **Murphy**, Carolyn S '87 Hamilton Cnty Mun Ct -1000 Main -Cincinnati 45202

     Murphy, Cathlyn S '93 -658 Charles Pl -Highland Heights 44143

     Murphy, Charles T Jr. '71 -9761 Bell Rd -Newbury 44065

(716) 884-2000 .. **Murphy**, Christopher M '02 (Doran & M) -1234 Delaware Av -Buffalo, NY 14209 Fx:884-2146

(419) 468-7766 .. **Murphy,** Clifford J '94 %Keller Z&M -659 Hrdng Way W
-Galion 44833

(216) 621-1113 .. **Murphy,** Cynthia S '88 (Renner OB&S,LLP) -1621 Euclid Av
-19th Fl -Cleveland 44115 **Fx:**621-6165

(216) 586-3939 .. **Murphy,** Dennis L '94 (Jones D) -901 Lakeside Av
-Cleveland 44114 **Fx:**579-0212

(216) 883-9220 .. **Murphy,** Donald R '72 OH Civil Rights Comm -24284 Halburton Rd
-Cleveland 44122

(440) 331-0266 .. **Murphy,** Eugene D '51 -18879 Timber Ln -Fairview Park 44126

(216) 479-8500 .. **Murphy,** James P '69 (Squire S&D LLP)
-4900 Key Twr -Cleveland 44114 **Fx:**479-8780

(216) 802-7571 .. **Murphy,** Jane C '96 Squire S&D,LLP -1500 W 3rd -Ste 4500
-Cleveland 44113

(614) 280-1100 .. **Murphy,** Jenifer J '99 %Keener DC&P,LPA -88 E Broad -Ste 1750
-Columbus 43215

(215) 761-6750 .. **Murphy,** John A Jr. '67 Cigna Corp -1601 Chestnut
-Philadelphia, PA 19192

(330) 455-0173 .. **Murphy,** John A Jr. '81 (Day KRW&R,Ltd) -200 Market Av N
-Ste 300 -Bx24213 -Canton 44701 **Fx:**455-2633

(614) 221-1266 .. **Murphy,** John E '72 OH Pros Attys Assoc -196 E State -Ste 200
-Columbus 43215

(440) 845-9110 .. **Murphy,** John F '80 (J Murphy Inc,LPA) -6856 Anthony Ln
-Parma Heights 44130

(513) 281-0346 .. **Murphy,** John J '76 -852 Clifton Hills Ter -Cincinnati 45220

(216) 575-0777 .. **Murphy,** John M '96 (Kelley & F,LLP) -1300 E 9th -Ste 1901
-Cleveland 44114 **Fx:**575-0799

(330) 262-9060 .. **Murphy,** John P Jr. '80 Wstrn Rsrv Grp -1685 Cleveland Rd -Bx36
-Wooster 44691

(216) 241-5310 .. **Murphy,** John T '90 (Gallagher SF&N) -1501 Euclid Av -6th Fl
-Cleveland 44115 **Fx:**241-1608

(614) 463-9770 .. **Murphy,** Katherine L '98 %Roetzel & A,LPA -155 E Broad
-Natl City Ctr 12th Fl -Columbus 43215 **Fx:**463-9792

(859) 344-0330 .. **Murphy,** Kevin L '84 (K Murphy & Assoc) -207 Grandvw Dr
-Ste 350 -Bx17330 -Covington, KY 41017

(704) 423-7102 .. **Murphy,** Kevin P '82 SrCnsl Goodrich Corp -2730 W Tyvola Rd
-Charlotte, NC 28217

(330) 392-1541 .. **Murphy,** Kevin P '85 Harrington H&M,Ltd -108 Main Av SW
-Ste 500 -Bx1510 -Warren 44482 **Fx:**394-6890

(440) 605-6660 .. **Murphy,** Kevin P '03 %Hurtuk & D Co,LPA -6120 Parkland Blvd
-Ste 100 -Cleveland 44124 **Fx:**605-6666

(513) 977-5576 .. **Murphy,** Laura Irving '86 %Butkovich SS&G Co,LPA -36 E 7th
-Ste 2600 -Cincinnati 45202 **Fx:**977-5580

(330) 643-7794 .. **Murphy,** Linda M '91 -175 S Main -Akron 44308

Murphy, Lynn G '95 -21352 Kenwood Av -Rocky River 44116

(216) 348-1700 .. **Murphy,** Martin J '63 OfCnsl Davis & Y -101 Prospect Av W
-Ste 1700 -Cleveland 44115 **Fx:**621-0602

Murphy, Matthew B '02 -(Address Unavailable)

(740) 382-1104 .. **Murphy,** Matthew P '92 General Machine & Saw Co
-740 W Center -Marion 43302

(859) 623-3728 .. **Murphy,** Melinda A '91 (Sword F&M,PLLC) -218 W Main -Bx300
-Richmond, KY 40476 **Fx:**623-4224

(440) 895-9970 .. **Murphy,** Michael H '94 -20325 Ctr Ridge Rd -Ste 512
-Rocky River 44116

(419) 609-1311 .. **Murphy,** Michael P '96 (Reminger & R) -237 W Wshngtn Row
-2nd Fl -Sandusky 44870 **Fx:**626-4805

(937) 227-3700 .. **Murphy,** Michele A '85 %Faruki I&C PLL -10 N Ludlow
-500 Cthse Plz SW -Dayton 45402 **Fx:**227-3717

(734) 827-8092 .. **Murphy,** Mollie A '80 Ave Maria Sch of Law -3475 Plymouth Rd
-Ann Arbor, MI 48105

(419) 562-4989 .. **Murphy,** Patrick J '74 (Bonezzi SM&P Co LPA) -526 Superior Av
-Ste 1400 -Cleveland 44114 **Fx:**875-1570

(216) 875-2767 .. **Murphy,** Patrick J '80 Euclid Law Dept -585 E 222nd
-Euclid 44123 **Fx:**289-2766

(216) 289-2746 .. **Murphy,** Patrick T '80 -153 Wshngtn Sq -Bucyrus 44820

(419) 562-4989 .. **Murphy,** Patrick T '86 (Dworken & B Co,LPA) -60 S Park Pl
-Painesville 44077 **Fx:**352-3469

(440) 352-3391 .. **Murphy,** Paul J '02 -Bx2 -New Knoxville 45871

(440) 473-1025 .. **Murphy,** Paul T '76 (Carbone & M Co,LPA) -6690 Beta Dr
-Ste 106 -Mayfield 44143

(440) 243-4600 .. **Murphy,** Rebecca Stubbs '82 Stubbs and Assoc -7055 Engle Rd
-Ste 1-101 -Cleveland 44130

(330) 456-8341 .. **Murphy,** Robert J '04 %Black MS&A,LPA -220 Market Av S
-Ste 1000 -Canton 44702 **Fx:**456-5756

(937) 865-6800 .. **Murphy,** Rosemary A '87 Lexis/Nexis -Bx933 -Dayton 45401

Murphy, Ross A '90 -7250 Gammwell Dr -Cincinnati 45255

(216) 520-4700 .. **Murphy,** Sandi R '91 Procare -4401 Rockside Rd -Ste 300
-Independence 44131

(614) 752-8211 .. **Murphy,** Sharon W '92 State Med Brd -77 S High -17th Fl
-Columbus 43215

(937) 328-2640 .. **Murphy,** Shawn P '93 Clark Cnty Pub Def -50 E Columbia -4th Fl
-Springfield 45502 **Fx:**328-2715

(202) 219-3031 .. **Murphy,** Silvia M '94 Dept of Interior Ofc of Solicitor -1849 C NW
-MS 6412 -Washington, DC 20240

(513) 634-4268 .. **Murphy,** Stephen T '02 Procter & Gamble -6100 Ctr Hill Rd
-Cincinnati 45224

(513) 723-7314 .. **Murphy,** Thomas J '98 Convergys Corp -201 E 4th -ML#1810
-Cincinnati 45202

(614) 847-3997 .. **Murphy,** Timothy E '73 -10 Valley Run Dr -Powell 43065

Murphy, Troy A '03 -(Address Unavailable)

(440) 888-0165 .. **Murphy,** William L '73 -8412 Sierra Oval -Cleveland 44130

(513) 946-9200 .. **Murphy,** William Leo '82 Hamilton Cnty Cmn Pleas Ct -800 Bway
-Cincinnati 45202

(216) 583-2896 .. **Murphy,** William P '95 Ernst & Young LLP -925 Euclid Av
-Ste 1300 -Cleveland 44115

Murphy-Allison, Maribeth V '03 -(Address Unavailable)

(937) 298-1054 .. **Murr Compton Claypoole & Macbeth** -401 E Stroop Rd
-Kettering 45429 **Fx:**293-1766

(937) 228-7277 .. **Murraine,** Fitzgerald T '01 Dayton Govt/HRC Ofc -130 W 2nd
-Ste 730 -Dayton 45402

(216) 621-0200 .. **Murray,** Andrew J '04 %Baker & H LLP -1900 E 9th -Ste 3200
-Cleveland 44114 **Fx:**696-0740

(614) 645-7483 .. **Murray,** Anne M '94 City Pros -375 S High -7th Fl -Columbus 43215

(614) 471-3113 .. **Murray,** Bernard M '69 -66 Mill -Gahanna 43230

(216) 622-8200 .. **Murray,** Brian M '99 %Calfee H&G LLP -800 Superior Av
-Ste 1400 -Cleveland 44114 **Fx:**241-0816

(419) 624-3000 .. **Murray,** Charles M '91 (Murray & M Co,LPA) -111 E Shoreline Dr
-Bx19 -Sandusky 44871

(937) 562-5250 .. **Murray,** Christopher A '92 Greene Cnty Pros -61 Greene -Xenia
45385

(202) 267-0055 .. **Murray,** Christopher F '03 US Coast Guard -2100 2nd SW
-Washington, DC 20593

(734) 302-6000 .. **Murray,** David D '77 Brinks HG&L -524 S Main -#200
-Ann Arbor, MI 48104

(419) 525-1611 .. **Murray,** David K '73 (Brown BM&M) -70 Park Av W
-Mansfield 44902 **Fx:**525-3810

(614) 462-3194 .. **Murray,** Deborah A '99 Franklin Cnty Pub Def -373 S High -12th Fl
-Columbus 43215

(419) 624-3000 .. **Murray,** Dennis E Jr. '87 (Murray & M Co,LPA)
-111 E Shoreline Dr -Bx19 -Sandusky 44871

(419) 624-3000 .. **Murray,** Dennis E Sr. '64 (Murray & M Co,LPA)
-111 E Shoreline Dr -Bx19 -Sandusky 44871

(330) 497-0700 .. **Murray,** Edward D '91 (Krugliak WG&D Co,LPA)
-4775 Munson NW -Bx36963 -Canton 44735 **Fx:**497-4020

(513) 721-4450 .. **Murray,** Elizabeth R '90 Santen & H -312 Walnut -Ste 3100
-Cincinnati 45202

(937) 865-1133 .. **Murray,** Erin '87 Lexis/Nexis -Bx933 -Dayton 45401

(419) 435-2284 .. **Murray,** Gene P '76 -227 W Center -Fostoria 44830

(419) 624-3000 .. **Murray,** James L '97 (Murray & M Co,LPA) -111 E Shoreline Dr
-Bx19 -Sandusky 44871

(419) 624-3000 .. **Murray,** James T '65 (Murray & M Co,LPA) -111 E Shoreline Dr
-Bx19 -Sandusky 44871

(216) 479-8500 .. **Murray,** Jan E '78 (Squire S&D LLP) -127 Pub Sq -4900 Key Twr
-Cleveland 44114 **Fx:**479-8780

(419) 525-1611 .. **Murray,** Jason B '95 (Brown BM&M) -70 Park Av W
-Mansfield 44902 **Fx:**525-3810

(216) 781-5245 .. **Murray,** John Michael '76 (Berkman GM&D) -55 Pub Sq
-2121 The Illuminating Bldg -Cleveland 44113 **Fx:**781-8207

(419) 624-3000 .. **Murray,** John T '79 (Murray & M Co,LPA) -111 E Shoreline Dr
-Bx19 -Sandusky 44871

(614) 469-0400 .. **Murray,** Joseph F '94 (Murray MM&B LLP) -326 S High -Ste 400
-Columbus 43215 **Fx:**469-0402

(614) 879-7606 .. **Murray,** Joseph M '83 (Culp P&M) -8 E Main
-West Jefferson 43162

(513) 946-3427 .. **Murray,** Katherine K '93 1st Dist Ct of Appls -230 E 9th -12th Fl
-Cincinnati 45202 **Fx:**946-3412

Murray, Kelly S '03 -1411 Fulton Rd NW -Canton 44703

(602) 382-2700 .. **Murray,** Kenneth F '84 %Federal Public Def -850 W Adams
-Ste 201 -Phoenix, AZ 85007

(216) 664-4329 .. **Murray,** Lynn A '89 Cleveland Mun Ct -1200 Ontario -12th Fl
-Cleveland 44113

(216) 522-1200 .. **Murray,** Margaret A '96 IMG -1360 E 9th -Ste 100
-Cleveland 44114

(419) 624-3000 .. **Murray,** Margaret M '96 (Murray & M Co,LPA) -111 E Shoreline Dr
-Bx19 -Sandusky 44871

(513) 241-2200 .. **Murray,** Michael C '89 FirstGroup Amer,Inc -705 Central Av
-One Centennial Plz -Cincinnati 45202

(440) 357-6111 .. **Murray,** Michael D '88 (Redmond W&M) -174 N St Clair
-Painesville 44077

(330) 829-7496 .. **Murray,** Michael F '69 McDermott Tech,Inc -1562 Beeson
-Alliance 44601

(419) 774-5676 .. **Murray,** Michael J '76 Richland Cnty Pros -38 S Park -2nd Fl
-Mansfield 44902 **Fx:**774-5589

(419) 624-3000 .. **Murray,** Michael T '70 Murray & M Co,LPA -111 E Shoreline Dr
-Bx19 -Sandusky 44871

(419) 784-3700 .. **Murray,** Morris J '85 Defiance Cnty Pros -607 W 3rd
-Defiance 43512 **Fx:**782-0594

(614) 469-0400 .. **Murray Murphy Moul & Basil LLP** -326 S High -Ste 400
-Columbus 43215 **Fx:**469-0402

(419) 289-3800 .. **Murray,** Oliver J '62 -10 E Main -Ashland 44805 **Fx:**289-6417

(216) 443-3431 .. **Murray,** Peter A '84 Cuyahoga Cnty Juv Ct -2163 E 22nd
-Cleveland 44115

(330) 253-2729 .. **Murray,** Philip W '64 (P Murray Co,LPA) -120 E Mill
-Ste 405 Quaker Sq -Akron 44308

(740) 397-7474 .. **Murray,** Richard B '77 (Murray & R) -305 E High
-Mount Vernon 43050

(614) 224-2678 .. **Murray,** Richard G II '00 Kemp SR&L Co,LPA -88 W Mound
-Columbus 43215 **Fx:**469-7170

(702) 259-8125 .. **Murray,** Ruthanne '89 Las Vegas Valley Water Dist
-1001 S Valley Vw Blvd -Finance Dept-Risk Mgmt
-Las Vegas, NV 89153

(614) 466-7788 .. **Murray,** Susan J '88 OH Ct of Claims -65 E State -Ste 1100
-Columbus 43215

(304) 233-4000 .. **Murray,** Teena Y '01 Jackson & K,PLLC -1144 Market -Ste 400
-Bx871 -Wheeling, WV 26003

(419) 624-3000 .. **Murray,** Thomas J Jr. '65 (Murray & M Co,LPA) -111 E Shoreline
Dr -Bx19 -Sandusky 44871

(419) 624-3000 .. **Murray,** William P '65 (Murray & M Co,LPA) -111 E Shoreline Dr
-Bx19 -Sandusky 44871

(614) 278-5902 .. **Murrell,** Julie L '02 Franklin Cnty Children Srvcs -855 W Mound
-Columbus 43223 **Fx:**275-2589

(614) 356-5564 .. **Murry,** Christine A '98 Dominion Homes,Inc -5000 Tuttle Xing Blvd
-Dublin 43016

(937) 461-0009 .. **Murry,** Michael K '83 -130 W 2nd -Ste 810 -Dayton 45402

(216) 521-5555 .. **Murtaugh,** Francis D Jr. '71 -1370 Ontario -Ste 2000
-Cleveland 44113

(804) 289-9635 .. **Murtaugh,** Genevieve K '77 Cnsl The Brink's Co
-1801 Bayberry Ct -Bx18100 -Richmond, VA 23226

(216) 579-1700 .. **Murtaugh,** John P '81 (Pearne & G LLP) -1801 E 9th -Ste 1200
-Cleveland 44114 **Fx:**579-6073

(216) 241-2838 .. **Murway,** Carl A '83 (Taft S&H LLP) -200 Pub Sq -3500 BP Twr
-Cleveland 44114 **Fx:**241-3707

(330) 659-1690 .. **Musacchia,** Jacqueline A '88 Bell & Howell PSC -3900
Kinross Lks Pkwy -Richfield 44286

(419) 535-5650 .. **Musachio,** Rosalie N '77 -4334 W Central Av -Ste 238
-Toledo 43615 **Fx:**536-7701

(216) 566-5943 .. **Musallam,** Samer M '04 %Thompson H LLP -127 Pub Sq
-3900 Key Ctr -Cleveland 44114 **Fx:**566-5800

Musallam-Martin, Yasmina T '01 -126 Leaview Ln -Chagrin Falls 44022

(330) 645-9399 ..**Musarra,** Thomas M '84 -4367 State Rd -Akron 44319

(216) 696-7777 ..**Musca & Miralia** -1300 E 9th -Ste 1202 -Cleveland 44114

(216) 898-2351 ..**Muscarella,** Lawrence G '83 White Consolidated Indus -18013 Cleve Parkway -Ste 100 -Bx35920 -Cleveland 44135

(330) 864-6611 ..**Muse,** Edward S '89 McCarty & P -1655 W Market -Ste 400 -Akron 44313

(843) 577-7700 ..**Musheff,** Todd M '86 SpclCnsl Barnwell WP&H,LLC -885 Isl Park Dr -DrwrH -Charleston, SC 29402 Fx:577-7708

(614) 466-3998 ..**Musheno,** Allen R '75 Unemploymnt Comp Commssn -145 S Front -Bx182299 -Columbus 43218

Mushett, Andrew C '03 Thomson West -610 Opperman Dr -Eagan, MN 55123

(330) 376-5756 ..**Mushkat,** Barbara S '70 Emershaw M&S -120 E Mill -#437 -Akron 44308 Fx:762-5980

(480) 951-0669 ..**Musial,** Jon S '87 -8230 E Gray Rd -Scottsdale, AZ 85260

(239) 542-8932 ..**Musial,** Lisa A '04 -3717 Del Prado Blvd S -Ste 1 -Cape Coral, FL 33904

(440) 892-2040 ..**Musial,** Lisa A '04 %Musial & M,LPA -28885 Ctr Ridge Rd -Ste 202 -Westlake 44145

(440) 892-2040 ..**Musial,** Mark N '85 (Musial & M,LPA) -28885 Ctr Ridge Rd -Ste 202 -Westlake 44145

(440) 892-2040 ..**Musial,** Norman T '61 (Musial & M,LPA) -28885 Ctr Ridge Rd -Ste 202 -Westlake 44145

(614) 221-3155 ..**Music,** Amanda M '03 %Bailey C LLC -10 W Broad -Columbus 43215 Fx:221-0479

(937) 642-3142 ..**Music,** Lisa W '98 -111 W 6th -Marysville 43040

(216) 520-5556 ..**Music-Biro,** Kristina E '83 Banks-Baldwin Law Pub -6111 Oaktree Blvd -Independence 44131

(216) 623-0150 ..**Musick,** Douglas S '92 (Roetzel & A,LPA) -1375 E 9th -One Cleve Ctr 9th Fl -Cleveland 44114 Fx:623-0134

(740) 286-4100 ..**Musick,** Mark T '86 M Musick Co,LPA -287 Pearl -Bx911 -Jackson 45640

(419) 524-6522 ..**Musilli,** Dale M '87 D Musilli Co,LPA -105 Sturges Av -Mansfield 44903 Fx:524-6522

(614) 464-6400 ..**Musilli,** Stephen C '00 Vorys SS&P LLP -52 E Gay -Bx1008 -Columbus 43216 Fx:464-6350

(513) 381-2011 ..**Musillo,** Christopher T '98 (Hammond Law Grp,LLC) -441 Vine -3311 Carew Twr -Cincinnati 45202 Fx:381-2227

(330) 535-5535 ..**Musitano,** Dominic A Jr. '60 (Manes & M) -411 Wolf Ledges Pkwy -Ste 300 -Akron 44311

(419) 243-7720 ..**Muska,** Susan Hartman '77 -608 Mad Av #1340 -Toledo 43604 Fx:243-9906

(216) 781-3600 ..**Muskovitz,** Susannah '84 Faulkner M&P,LLP -820 W Superior Av -Ste 900 -Cleveland 44113 Fx:781-8839

(216) 623-0150 ..**Musnuff,** Basil J '89 (Roetzel & A,LPA) -1375 E 9th -One Cleve Ctr 9th Fl -Cleveland 44114 Fx:623-0134

(614) 583-7608 ..**Musselman,** David T '86 SrCnsl AEP Srvc Corp -Bx16036 -Columbus 43216

(330) 264-5141 ..**Musselman,** Jeffrey D '97 Taggart Law Firm -142 W Lbrty -Bx218 -Wooster 44691 Fx:262-1046

(614) 451-5300 ..**Musser Long & Harris** -3404 Riverside Dr -Columbus 43221

(614) 451-5300 ..**Musser,** Philip S '75 (Musser L&H) -3404 Riverside Dr -Columbus 43221

(330) 869-0744 ..**Mussig,** Linda Mae '89 -1525 Sand Run Rd -Akron 44313

(330) 668-9696 ..**Mussig,** Mark L '87 Saltz Shamis & Goldfarb -301 Sprngside Dr -Akron 44333 Fx:668-2538

(440) 323-4903 ..**Musson,** John R '75 Mun Ct Judge -328 E Broad -Elyria 44035

(412) 918-1100 ..**Must,** Brian T '95 Metz L LLC -11 Stanwix -18th Fl -Pittsburgh, PA 15222

(614) 462-7450 ..**Must,** Jamie M '03 CASA Franklin Cnty -373 S High -6th Fl -Columbus 43215 Fx:462-5070

(937) 333-4400 ..**Musto,** Amy B '99 Dayton Pros -335 W 3rd -Ste 372 -Dayton 45402

(937) 333-4116 ..**Musto,** John C '99 Law Dept -101 W 3rd -Bx22 -Dayton 45402

(419) 213-6850 ..**Mutchler,** Alan D '76 Lucas Cnty Cmn Pleas Ct -429 N Mich -Ste A -Toledo 43624

(703) 295-2580 ..**Mutek,** Michael W '79 Raytheon Tech Srvcs Co -12160 Sunrise Valley Dr -Reston, VA 20191

(330) 762-7655 ..**Mutersbaugh,** Steven P '02 %Kaufmann & K -106 S Main -Ste 1200 -Akron 44308 Fx:762-7537

(513) 242-1541 ..**Muth,** Alison H '91 Frank Messer & Sons -5158 Fishwick Dr -Cincinnati 45216

(313) 481-8800 ..**Muth,** Andrew S '97 (Muth & S) -301 W Mich Av -Ste 302 -Ypsilanti, MI 48197

(513) 455-7600 ..**Muth,** Carl C '80 (Greenebaum D&M PLLC) -255 E 5th -2800 Chemed Ctr -Cincinnati 45202 Fx:455-8500

(330) 438-8811 ..**Muth,** Randall B '94 Stark Cnty Dept of Human Srvcs -220 E Tuscarawas -Canton 44702

(513) 388-2914 ..**Muto,** Anthony J '78 Senco Prdcts,Inc -8485 Broadwell Rd -Cincinnati 45244

(440) 366-9930 ..**Muzilla,** Raymond A '58 OfCnsl McCray MS&M Co,LPA -260 Burns Rd -Ste 150 -Elyria 44035 Fx:366-1910

(440) 366-9930 ..**Muzilla,** Thomas A '86 (McCray MS&M Co,LPA) -260 Burns Rd -Ste 150 -Elyria 44035 Fx:366-1910

(513) 721-5808 ..**Muzzo,** Albert L '70 FL Emmert Co,Inc -2007 Dunlap -Cincinnati 45214

(513) 977-8200 ..**Muzzo,** Christopher L '97 %Dinsmore & S LLP -255 E 5th -1900 -Cincinnati 45202 Fx:977-8141

(216) 566-5869 ..**Myer,** John D '01 %Thompson H LLP -127 Pub Sq -3900 Key Ctr -Cleveland 44114 Fx:566-5800

(614) 645-7483 ..**Myers,** Amy M '89 City Pros -375 S High -7th Fl -Columbus 43215

(513) 946-5102 ..**Myers,** Beth A '82 Common Pleas Ct -1000 Main -Ste 410 -Cincinnati 45202

(937) 225-4892 ..**Myers,** Beth L '99 %Montgomery Cnty Pros/CSEA -14 W 4th -Ste 510 -Dayton 45402

(614) 292-1556 ..**Myers,** Bradley A '80 OSU -1800 Cannon Dr -1200 Lincoln Twr -Columbus 43210

(614) 638-3993 ..**Myers,** Craig S '89 Myers Fincl Srvcs,LLC -941 Chatham Ln -Ste 305 -Columbus 43221

(419) 586-2396 ..**Myers,** Daniel '76 -90 N Ash -Bx230 -Celina 45822 Fx:586-2110

(440) 323-1111 ..**Myers,** David A '73 -374 Broad -Ste 2 -Elyria 44035

(513) 977-8200 ..**Myers,** David J '04 %Dinsmore & S LLP -255 E 5th -Ste 1900 -Cincinnati 45202 Fx:977-8181

(614) 227-2000 ..**Myers,** Eric C '02 %Porter WM&A LLP -41 S High -Columbus 43215 Fx:227-2100

(937) 224-0076 ..**Myers & Frayne Co,LPA** -18 W 1st -Ste 200 -Dayton 45402

(937) 224-0075 ..**Myers,** Jacob A '59 (Myers & F Co,LPA) -18 W 1st -Ste 200 -Dayton 45402

(216) 623-0150 ..**Myers,** James P '02 %Roetzel & A,LPA -1375 E 9th -One Cleve Ctr 9th Fl -Cleveland 44114 Fx:623-0134

(513) 891-9544 ..**Myers,** James Y '95 Loroco Ind,Inc -5000 Crk Rd -Cincinnati 45242

(330) 296-5920 ..**Myers,** Jeffery D '96 -409 S Prospect -Bx129 -Ravenna 44266

(937) 913-0200 ..**Myers,** Jeffrey R '99 Gottschlich & P LLP -201 E 6th -Dayton 45402 Fx:824-2818

(216) 621-5300 ..**Myers,** Jennifer L '02 %Buckingham D&B,LLP -1375 E 9th -Ste 1700 -Cleveland 44114 Fx:621-5440

(216) 696-0606 ..**Myers,** John C '87 OfCnsl RE Sweeney Co,LPA -55 Pub Sq -Ste 1500 -Cleveland 44113 Fx:696-0679

(330) 438-0422 ..**Myers,** John E '91 Stark Cnty Fam Ct -110 Central Plz S -Canton 44702

(330) 535-1202 ..**Myers,** John F '85 (Holland M&M) -159 S Main -Ste 825 -Akron 44308

Myers, Karen G '83 -1103 Chisolm Trl -Dayton 45458

(513) 721-1975 ..**Myers,** Kelly M '95 Freking & B -215 E 9th -5th Fl -Cincinnati 45202 Fx:651-2570

(216) 241-3900 ..**Myers,** Kenneth D '91 -75 Pub Sq -Ste 1300 -Cleveland 44113

(330) 866-4477 ..**Myers,** Kent J '95 -9090 Stallion Rd -Magnolia 44643

(513) 621-2100 ..**Myers,** Kristen M '04 %Beckman W&S LLC -120 E 4th -1200 Mercantile Ctr -Cincinnati 45202 Fx:621-0106

(740) 594-8178 ..**Myers,** Laura L '94 -11121 Vaughn Rd -Athens 45701

(330) 296-9199 ..**Myers,** Louis R '72 Myers & P -229½ S Chestnut -Ravenna 44266 Fx:296-4137

(614) 764-0681 ..**Myers,** Marc E '76 Blaugrund H&M,Inc -5455 Rings Rd -Ste 500 -Dublin 43017 Fx:764-0774

(513) 792-0792 ..**Myers,** Marcia J '85 (Schottenstein Z&D) -8044 Mntgmry Rd -Ste 630 -Cincinnati 45236 Fx:792-0803

Myers, Marcy J '97 -(Address Unavailable)

(216) 431-4500 ..**Myers,** Michelle A '94 Cuyahoga Cnty Pros -3955 Euclid Av -Jane Edna Hunter Bldg -Cleveland 44115 Fx:431-4113

(330) 535-1202 ..**Myers,** Nancy H '86 (Holland M&M) -159 S Main -Ste 825 -Akron 44308

(440) 602-5120 ..**Myers,** Neil '65 (N Myers Co,LPA) -35350 Curtis Blvd -#330 -Eastlake 44095

(216) 362-9212 ..**Myers,** O Lee '03 -19402 Ridgeland Av -Cleveland 44135

(757) 444-3657 ..**Myers,** Pamella A '92 US Navy -9620 Marylnd Av -Ste 100 -Norfolk, VA 23511

(757) 764-3278 ..**Myers,** Peter C '94 USAF 1FW/JA -33 Sweeney Blvd -Langley AFB, VA 23665

(216) 447-9105 ..**Myers,** Richard A Jr. '88 (Hehr & M Co,LPA) -4401 Rockside Rd -Ste 200 -Independence 44131 Fx:447-9171

(734) 827-8094 ..**Myers,** Richard S '81 Ave Maria Sch of Law -3475 Plymouth Rd -Ann Arbor, MI 48105

(440) 357-5134 ..**Myers,** Robert H Jr. '91 Mainstreet Title Agency -56 Lbrty -#201 -Painesville 44077

(216) 469-3275 ..**Myers,** Robert W '88 (Thompson H LLP) -10 W Broad -Ste 700 -Columbus 43215 Fx:469-3361

(614) 228-1432 ..**Myers,** Stanley L '67 -221 S High -Columbus 43215

(614) 873-0364 ..**Myers,** Susan M '89 -6500 Wynwright Dr -Dublin 43016

(740) 695-1350 ..**Myers,** Thomas M '80 Cassidy MCV&T,LC -126 E Main -Saint Clairsville 43950

(513) 723-2205 ..**Myers,** Thomas R '88 %Weltman W&R Co,LPA -525 Vine -Ste 800 -Cincinnati 45202 Fx:723-2239

(330) 788-2804 ..**Myers,** William A '93 -33 Melrose Av -Youngstown 44512

(614) 466-8600 ..**Myers,** William S '88 Atty Gen -30 E Broad -Columbus 43215 Fx:466-6090

(216) 687-1900 ..**Myerson,** Anita L '81 Legal Aid -1223 W 6th -Cleveland 44113 Fx:687-0779

(330) 376-7500 ..**Mygrant,** John W '77 Mentzer & M,Ltd -1 Cascade Plz -20th Fl -Akron 44308 Fx:376-8018

(216) 443-7800 ..**Myles,** Paul J '85 Cuyahoga Cnty Pros -1200 Ontario -8th Fl -Cleveland 44113 Fx:698-2270

Myles, Tina L '96 -(Address Unavailable)

(740) 635-0162 ..**Myser,** Richard A '78 (Thomas FMH&D) -320 Howard -Bridgeport 43912 Fx:635-1601

(419) 893-1444 ..**Naayers,** John A '86 (Farrar N&W,Ltd) -1605 Indn Wd Cir -Ste 200 -Maumee 43537

(330) 867-9242 ..**Nace,** R Bryan '85 (DeCamp R&D) -3250 W Market -Ste 203 -Akron 44333 Fx:867-9282

(859) 572-5340 ..**Nacev,** Adrienne N '00 Chase Coll of Law/NKU -Nunn Dr -Rm 508 -Highland Heights, KY 41099

(614) 221-9100 ..**Nacht,** Beth J '03 %Stein C & Assoc LLC -32 W Hoster -Ste 200 -Columbus 43215 Fx:221-9272

Nacht, Bradley J '04 -(Address Unavailable)

(419) 243-2100 ..**Nackowicz,** Timothy P '03 %Connelly J&C LLP -405 Mad Av -Ste 1600 -Toledo 43604 Fx:243-7119

Nacopoulos, Christina S '94 -1001 State -Ste 1400 -Erie, PA 16501

(502) 423-2291 ..**Nader,** Michelle M '94 Anthem BCBS -9901 Linn Station Rd -Louisville, KY 40223

(330) 395-7555 ..**Nader,** Paul G '53 (Nader & N) -155 S Park Av -Ste 123 -Warren 44481

(330) 373-1448 ..**Nader,** Rachel E '90 Cmmnty Lgl Aid Srvcs,Inc -160 E Market -Ste 250 -Warren 44481 Fx:395-5227

(330) 395-7555 ..**Nader,** Thomas C '87 (Nader & N) -155 S Park Av -Ste 123 -Warren 44481

(330) 744-0247 ..**Nadler Nadler & Burdman Co, LPA** -20 Fed Plz W -Ste 600 -Youngstown 44503 Fx:744-8690

(216) 592-5000 ..**Naeem,** Tariq M '00 Tucker E&W LLP -925 Euclid Av -1150 Huntngtn Bldg -Cleveland 44115 Fx:592-5009

(513) 621-1652 ..**Naegel,** Mark R '74 -414 Walnut -Ste 707 -Cincinnati 45202

(214) 368-1515 ..**Naegele,** Heather D '04 Savrick SJ&M -6440 N Central Expy -Ste 307 -Dallas, TX 75206

(440) 244-4809 ..**Naegele,** Jori Bloom '80 (Gary N&T,LLC) -446 Bway -Lorain 44052 Fx:244-3462

Naegele, Joseph J '64 -Bx16306 -Cleveland 44116
(440) 930-8074 .. **Naegele,** Richard A '79 Wickens HPC&B -35765 Chester Rd
-Avon 44011 **Fx:**937-4466
(216) 443-8838 .. **Naegele,** Sherry A '00 Ct Common Pleas-Dom Rel
-One Lakeside Av -Leg Dept -Cleveland 44113 **Fx:**443-4943
(216) 663-4552 .. **Naffah,** Eli Thomas '62 -15950 Libby Rd -Maple Heights 44137
(216) 663-4552 .. **Naffah,** Elias T Jr. '93 -15950 Libby Rd -Maple Heights 44137
(216) 566-5625 .. **Naftzinger,** David J '73 (Thompson H LLP) -127 Pub Sq
-3900 Key Ctr -Cleveland 44114 **Fx:**566-5800
(216) 621-5300 .. **Nagel,** Beth A '97 %Buckingham D&B,LLP -1375 E 9th -Ste 1700
-Cleveland 44114 **Fx:**621-5440
(419) 337-6116 .. **Nagel,** Dale J '80 -107 E Elm -Wauseon 43567
(513) 361-0250 .. **Nagel,** Ellen L '87 SSA-OHA -312 Elm -Ste 2100 -Cincinnati 45202
(419) 335-5011 .. **Nagel,** Eric K '01 %Hallett H&N -132 S Fulton -Wauseon 43567
Fx:335-3187
(513) 732-7313 .. **Nagel,** Jason E '99 Clermont Cnty Pros -123 N 3rd -Batavia 45103
(419) 335-5011 .. **Nagel,** Roger D '73 (Hallett H&N) -132 S Fulton -Wauseon 43567
Fx:335-3187
(614) 466-2022 .. **Nagel,** Susan K '90 Dept Admin Srvcs -30 E Broad
-Columbus 43215
(614) 224-8339 .. **Nagel,** Tom H '71 (Britt CN&S) -490 City Park Av
-Columbus 43215 **Fx:**224-2001
(513) 579-6400 .. **Nageleisen,** Christy M '03 %Keating M&K PLL -1 E 4th
-1400 Provident Twr -Cincinnati 45202 **Fx:**579-6457
(216) 228-4545 .. **Nageotte,** Edward C '99 Gold Coast Properties Inc -11740
Clifton Blvd -Lakewood 44107
(216) 241-0715 .. **Nager,** David E '90 (Nager & R) -425 W Lakeside Av -Ste 100
-Cleveland 44113 **Fx:**241-9434
(937) 298-8908 .. **Nagle,** Daniel A '59 D Nagle,Co LPA -3464 Southrn Blvd
-Kettering 45429
(440) 461-4433 .. **Nagle,** Jamie M '02 %Van Ness,LTD -6181 Mayfld Rd -Ste 104
-Mayfield Heights 44124
(419) 885-3229 .. **Nagle,** Robert T '86 -6503 Cornwall Ct -Sylvania 43560
(312) 759-1400 .. **Nagorka,** Frank W '79 (Mora BW&U,LLC) -55 W Monroe -Ste 600
-Chicago, IL 60603 **Fx:**759-0402
(216) 241-2880 .. **Nagorney,** Frank P '75 Cnsl Cowden HN&L -50 Pub Sq -Ste 1414
-Cleveland 44113 **Fx:**241-2881
(330) 869-4257 .. **Nagucki,** Robert E '93 Omnova Solutions Inc -175 Ghent Rd
-Fairlawn 44333
(513) 556-0113 .. **Nagy,** Donna M '00 Univ of Cincinnati/College of Law -Clifton &
Calhoun -Bx210040 -Cincinnati 45221
(440) 331-9998 .. **Nagy,** James E '91 -19120 Old Detroit Rd -Ste 7
-Rocky River 44116
Nagy, Joseph J '60 -(Address Unavailable)
(216) 222-2000 .. **Nagy,** Matthew E '99 Natl City Bank -1900 E 9th -Cleveland 44114
(419) 843-3168 .. **Nagy,** Ronald L '99 -3860 Clare Ridge -Unit B -Toledo 43623
(614) 221-2838 .. **Nagy,** Timothy P '74 (Taft S&H LLP) -21 E State -12th Fl
-Columbus 43215 **Fx:**221-2007
(248) 354-0380 .. **Nahat,** Nicholas R '02 Novara T&M,PLLC -2000 Town Ctr
-Ste 2370 -Southfield, MI 48075
(419) 241-6000 .. **Nahhas,** Fadi V '00 %Eastman & S Ltd -1 Seagate -24th Fl
-Bx10032 -Toledo 43699 **Fx:**247-1771
Nahra, Joseph A '98 NFL Players Assoc -2021 L NW
-Washington, DC 20036
(937) 225-4652 .. **Nailing,** Joyce E '94 %Montgomery Cnty Pub Def -117 S Main
-Ste 400 -Dayton 45422 **Fx:**225-3449
(216) 443-7800 .. **Naiman,** Deborah R '88 Cuyahoga Cnty Pros -1200 Ontario -8th Fl
-Cleveland 44113 **Fx:**698-2270
(404) 521-3939 .. **Najim,** Samuel J '86 (Jones DR&P) -3500 SunTrust Plz
-303 Pchtree NE -Atlanta, GA 30308 **Fx:**581-8330
(614) 866-0666 .. **Najjar,** Nina M '82 Cnsl J Banks -Bx40 -Dublin 43017 **Fx:**766-1203
(513) 381-2838 .. **Nakao,** Toshio '92 (Taft S&H LLP) -425 Walnut -Ste 1800
-Cincinnati 45202 **Fx:**381-0205
(614) 469-3939 .. **Nakasian,** William E '90 (Jones D) -325 John H McConnell Blvd
-Ste 600 -Bx165017 -Columbus 43216 **Fx:**461-4198
(440) 930-8051 .. **Nakon,** Matthew W '88 Wickens HPC&B -35765 Chester Rd
-Avon 44011 **Fx:**937-4466
(330) 491-5238 .. **Nalawadi,** Sushila J '01 %Buckingham D&B,LLP
-4518 Fulton Dr NW -Bx35548 -Canton 44735 **Fx:**492-9625
(740) 593-9844 .. **Nalazek,** Barbara U '99 OH Univ -10 E Union -Pilcher Hse
-Athens 45701
(513) 381-2838 .. **Nalbandian,** John B '00 (Taft S&H LLP) -425 Walnut -Ste 1800
-Cincinnati 45202 **Fx:**381-0205
(513) 871-8755 .. **Nalepka,** Paul M '88 %Richards & Assoc,LPA -3322 Erie Av
-Ste 101 -Cincinnati 45208 **Fx:**871-8744
(859) 344-0330 .. **Nalley,** David C '94 %Murphy & Assoc PSC -207 Grandvw Dr
-Ste 350 -Covington, KY 41017
(216) 621-5300 .. **Nam,** Brian K '04 %Buckingham D&B,LLP -1375 E 9th -Ste 1700
-Cleveland 44114 **Fx:**621-5440
(513) 621-6556 .. **Namanworth,** Elias '76 (Namanworth & S) -2306 Park Av -Ste 101
-Cincinnati 45206
(513) 721-0200 .. **Namei,** Firooz T '82 McKinney & N Co,LPA -15 E 8th
-Cincinnati 45202 **Fx:**632-5898
(216) 522-0183 .. **Nance,** Donald S '79 (DS Nance,LPA) -11811 Shaker Blvd
-Ste 420 -Cleveland 44120
(216) 479-8500 .. **Nance,** Frederick R Jr. '78 (Squire S&D LLP) -127 Pub Sq
-4900 Key Twr -Cleveland 44114 **Fx:**479-8780
(216) 586-3939 .. **Nandi,** Melissa J '98 %Jones D -901 Lakeside Av
-Cleveland 44114 **Fx:**579-0212
(216) 664-3774 .. **Nandi,** Neal R '99 Dept of Law -601 Lakeside Av -Rm 106 City Hall
-Cleveland 44114 **Fx:**664-2663
(740) 385-7611 .. **Nangle,** Patricia J '73 -30 W Main -Bx104 -Logan 43138
(800) 998-9454 .. **Nanni,** Thomas J '93 Cmmnty Lgl Aid Srvcs,Inc -265 S Main
-3rd Fl -Akron 44308 **Fx:**(330) 535-0728
(440) 331-8867 .. **Nanowsky,** Gail A '91 -2120 Seabury Av -Fairview Park 44126
(513) 868-8229 .. **Napier,** Clayton G '83 C Napier Co,LPA -29 North D -Hamilton
45013
(419) 673-1292 .. **Napier,** Jane A '93 %Tudor Law,LLC -22 N Main -Kenton 43326
Fx:675-2145
(513) 721-1975 .. **Napier,** Mark W '78 Freking & B -215 E 9th -5th Fl -Cincinnati
45202 **Fx:**651-2570
(614) 728-2845 .. **Napier,** Shawn P '01 Atty Gen -150 E Gay -Columbus 43215
Fx:728-2122

(216) 621-0200 .. **Napoli,** James R '95 %Baker & H LLP -1900 E 9th -Ste 3200
-Cleveland 44114 **Fx:**696-0740
(513) 621-4556 .. **Napolitano,** Gregory A '97 (Jacobs J&N,LLC) -30 Garfld Pl
-Ste 750 -Cincinnati 45202 **Fx:**621-5563
(330) 337-9578 .. **Naragon,** Frederic E '71 -248 E State -Bx317 -Salem 44460
(513) 887-3474 .. **Nardiello,** Mary A '89 Butler Cnty Pros -315 High -11th Fl -Bx515
-Hamilton 45012
(614) 458-0025 .. **Nardone,** Vincent J '96 %McDonald H Co,LPA -41 S High
-Ste 3650 -Columbus 43215 **Fx:**458-0028
(614) 291-9590 .. **Narens,** Mark E '98 -1438 N Wall -Ste 7 -Columbus 43201
(419) 213-4700 .. **Narges,** Michael E '94 Lucas Cnty Pros -Adams & Erie
-Lucas Cnty Cthse -Toledo 43624
(937) 440-5960 .. **Nasal,** Gary A '88 Miami Cnty Pros -201 W Main -Troy 45373
Fx:440-5961
Nasatir, Philippa H '84 -8 Bent Crk Xing -Sylvania 43560
Nash, C D '63 -(Address Unavailable)
(216) 291-1246 .. **Nash,** Carl '60 (Nash & N) -683 Parkside Blvd -Cleveland 44143
(216) 566-5774 .. **Nash,** David E '81 (Thompson H LLP) -127 Pub Sq -3900 Key Ctr
-Cleveland 44114 **Fx:**566-5800
(216) 291-1246 .. **Nash,** Jean K '77 (Nash & N) -683 Parkside Blvd -Cleveland 44143
(440) 395-0259 .. **Nash,** Jeffrey P '85 Progressive Casualty Ins Co
-300 N Cmmns Blvd -Mayfield Village 44143
(216) 691-3000 .. **Nash,** Joel A '93 -4325 Mayfld Rd -Cleveland 44121
(216) 443-2688 .. **Nash,** Kelly R '98 McDonald Invstmnts -800 Superior Av -18th Fl
-Cleveland 44114
(937) 865-6800 .. **Nash,** Nancy A '82 Lexis/Nexis -Bx933 -Dayton 45401
Nash, Richard M Jr. '04 -(Address Unavailable)
(216) 787-4186 .. **Nash,** Robin A '82 Industrial Commssn of OH
-615 Superior Av NW -Cleveland 44113 **Fx:**787-3483
(312) 886-9225 .. **Nasky,** Laurie A '03 IRS Chief Cnsl Ofc -200 W Adams -#2300
-Chicago, IL 60606
(216) 443-7800 .. **Naso,** Carmen '78 Cuyahoga Cnty Pros -1200 Ontario -8th Fl
-Cleveland 44113 **Fx:**698-2270
(330) 208-4520 .. **Nass,** Terri L '89 Evanchan & P -1 GOJO Plz -Ste 300
-Akron 44311 **Fx:**208-4519
(216) 515-1660 .. **Natale,** Andrew J '89 (Frantz W LLP) -127 Pub Sq -2500 Key Ctr
-Cleveland 44114 **Fx:**515-1650
(330) 675-2601 .. **Natale,** Anthony M '75 Trumball Cnty Dmstc Ct -220 S Main
-Warren 44481
(419) 609-9207 .. **Nath,** Michael J '76 -5000 Heywood Rd -Sandusky 44870
(419) 241-6168 .. **Nathan,** Daniel M '04 -520 Mad Av -Ste 830 -Toledo 43604
Fx:241-4215
(614) 227-2358 .. **Nathan,** Jerry E '73 (Bricker & E LLP) -100 S 3rd
-Columbus 43215 **Fx:**227-2390
(301) 610-7550 .. **Nathan,** Marian R '71 -8114 Jeb Stuart Rd -Potomac, MD 20854
(417) 223-7176 .. **Nathanson,** James '60 -Bx158 -Pineville, MO 64856
Naticchia, Alfred D '86 -4141 Rockside Rd -Ste 230
-Seven Hills 44131
(419) 734-6997 .. **Nation,** Sarah A '00 Ottawa Cnty Cmn Pleas Ct -315 Madison
-Rm 301 -Port Clinton 43452
Natkevicius, John R '02 -(Address Unavailable)
(212) 907-7300 .. **Natow,** Rebecca Spiro '00 %Golenbock EAB&P -437 Mad Av
-35th Fl -New York, NY 10022 **Fx:**754-0330
(419) 249-7100 .. **Natyshak,** Amy M '90 (Marshall & M,LLC) -Four Seagate -8th Fl
-Toledo 43604 **Fx:**249-7151
(937) 653-8338 .. **Nau,** Richard E '85 -300 N Main -Urbana 43078
(440) 886-6394 .. **Naughton,** John D '57 -8206 Sierra Oval -Parma 44130
(216) 241-5310 .. **Naughton,** Thomas F '00 %Gallagher SF&N -1501 Euclid Av
-6th Fl -Cleveland 44115 **Fx:**241-1608
(937) 643-0980 .. **Nauman,** Joseph G '53 -696 Renolda Woods Ct -Dayton 45429
(614) 365-2700 .. **Nauman,** Robert D '02 %Squire S&D LLP -41 S High
-1300 Huntngtn Ctr -Columbus 43215 **Fx:**365-2499
(513) 636-0800 .. **Nauman,** Stephen R '93 Chldrn's Hosp Med Ctr -5642 Hmltn Av
-Cincinnati 45224
(216) 861-5582 .. **Nauman,** Timothy E '83 (Fay SFM&M LLP) -1100 Superior Av
-7th Fl -Cleveland 44114 **Fx:**241-1666
(419) 524-3700 .. **Naumoff,** Annette R '95 (Naumoff & N) -358 Park Av W
-Mansfield 44906
(937) 865-7417 .. **Naumoff,** Cynthia S '00 Lexis/Nexis -Bx933 -Dayton 45401
(614) 865-2220 .. **Naumoff,** George '88 LandAmer Fin Grp -921 Eastwind Dr
-Ste 133 -Westerville 43081
(614) 464-6400 .. **Naumoff,** Jennifer A '01 %Vorys SS&P LLP -52 E Gay -Bx1008
-Columbus 43216 **Fx:**464-6350
(330) 753-6664 .. **Naumoff,** Mitchell A '76 -564 W Tuscarawas Av -Ste 306
-Barberton 44203 **Fx:**753-6665
(614) 227-2000 .. **Naumoff,** Mitchell A Jr. '04 %Porter WM&A LLP -41 S High
-Columbus 43215 **Fx:**227-2100
(614) 222-3142 .. **Naumoff,** Paul A '95 Ernst & Young -41 S High -11th Fl
-Columbus 43215
(419) 524-3700 .. **Naumoff,** Phillip S '94 Naumoff & N -358 Park Av W
-Mansfield 44906
(419) 524-3700 .. **Naumoff,** William K '94 (Naumoff & N) -358 Park Av W
-Mansfield 44906
(800) 837-8908 .. **Nava-Wade,** Nancy '93 LAWO -121 N Arch -Fremont 43420
Fx:(419) 334-9148
(937) 653-3501 .. **Navarre,** Mark A '96 -Bx537 -Urbana 43078
(614) 644-3037 .. **Navarre,** Mark J '80 EPA -122 S Front -Bx1049 -Columbus 43216
(202) 514-2895 .. **Navarro-Hamilton,** Cristina '86 DOJ-INS -425 I NW
-Washington, DC 20536
(440) 285-8311 .. **Navatsyk,** Donald A '80 -Bx798 -Chardon 44024
(216) 397-0420 .. **Nave,** Michele Garrick '82 -3374 Rumson Rd -Cleveland
Heights 44118 **Fx:**397-0933
(614) 221-7548 .. **Navin,** Joseph F '88 (Larrimer & L) -165 N High -Columbus 43206
Fx:221-8659
(513) 651-6800 .. **Naylor,** Beth S '89 (Frost BT LLC) -201 E 5th -2200 PNC Ctr
-Cincinnati 45202 **Fx:**651-6981
(440) 599-6708 .. **Naylor,** Robert E '72 -256 Lbrty -Bx203 -Conneaut 44030
Fx:599-6710
(419) 524-6011 .. **Naylor,** Robert S '93 (Calhoun KH&C Co,LPA) -6 W 3rd -Ste 200
-Bx268 -Mansfield 44901 **Fx:**526-1431
(513) 345-8291 .. **Naylor,** Todd B '97 %Murdock GS&G -35 E 7th -Ste 600
-Cincinnati 45202 **Fx:**345-8294

(216) 566-5500 ..**Nazette**, Adam R '03 %Thompson H LLP -127 Pub Sq
-3900 Key Ctr -Cleveland 44114 **Fx:**566-5800

(513) 272-0336 ..**Neagle**, Carolyn C '92 -8190 Beechmont Av -Ste 112
-Cincinnati 45255

(513) 732-5311 ..**Neal**, Catherine S '98 Univ of Cincinnati -4200 Cllg Dr
-Batavia 45103

(614) 221-8757 ..**Neal**, John G '77 -399 E Main -Ste 110 -Columbus 43215
Fx:246-8455

(216) 241-5310 ..**Neal**, John N '02 %Gallagher SF&N -1501 Euclid Av -6th Fl
-Cleveland 44115 **Fx:**241-1608

(330) 453-3709 ..**Neal**, Marianna D '77 Peoples Srvcs Inc -2207 Kimball Rd SE
-Bx20109 -Canton 44701

(614) 462-3998 ..**Neal**, Marianne '88 %Hon CC Lazarus -373 S High -24th Fl
-Columbus 43215

(937) 372-4411 ..**Neal**, Scott E '98 Brandabur FJW&B -260 N Detroit -Xenia 45385
Fx:372-4415

(513) 381-2011 ..**Neal**, Sherry L '94 (Hammond Law Grp,LLC) -441 Vine
-3311 Carew Twr -Cincinnati 45202 **Fx:**381-2227

(216) 515-1660 ..**Nealis**, Melanie Meyer '01 %Frantz W LLP -127 Pub Sq
-2500 Key Ctr -Cleveland 44114 **Fx:**515-1650

(216) 479-6418 ..**Nealis**, Peter S '00 %Kahn K -1301 E 9th -2600 Erievw Twr
-Cleveland 44114 **Fx:**623-4912

(614) 466-8600 ..**Nealon**, Dennis G '83 Atty Gen -30 E Broad -Columbus 43215
Fx:466-6090

(614) 365-9900 ..**Nealy**, Darren L '01 %Zeiger TL&L,LLP -41 S High
-Ste 3500 Huntngtn Ctr -Columbus 43215 **Fx:**365-7900

(614) 466-0722 ..**Nearhood**, Constance A '82 Atty Gen -150 E Gay
-Columbus 43215 **Fx:**644-9973

(216) 622-8200 ..**Neary**, Douglas A '85 (Calfee H&G LLP) -800 Superior Av
-Ste 1400 -Cleveland 44114 **Fx:**241-0816

(937) 898-1465 ..**Neary**, James G '82 Scheuer M&B LLC -8565 N Dixie Dr
-Dayton 45414 **Fx:**898-1478

(216) 696-2719 ..**Nebel**, Deborah J '88 Long Term Care Ombudsman
-2800 Euclid Av -Ste 200 -Cleveland 44115 **Fx:**696-6216

(407) 628-7077 ..**Nebel**, Michael E '85 (Nebel & B) -Bx533638 -Orlando, FL 32853
Fx:628-6072

(440) 886-6112 ..**Nebesh**, Eugene '71 -1949 W Plsnt Vlly Rd -Parma 44134

(513) 381-2838 ..**Nechemias**, Stephen M '69 (Taft S&H LLP) -425 Walnut
-Ste 1800 -Cincinnati 45202 **Fx:**381-0205

(865) 974-2261 ..**Neddenriep**, Gregory G '99 UnivTennessee -1001 McClung Twr
-Dept of Political Science -Knoxville, TN 37996

(937) 322-0891 ..**Nedelman**, Phyllis S '82 Cole AH&D -333 N Limestone -Bx1687
-Springfield 45501 **Fx:**322-9931

(614) 239-5033 ..**Nederveld**, Allen G '97 Regional Airport Auth -4600 Intl Gtwy
-Columbus 43219 -Bx238-7834

(419) 242-5485 ..**Nedom**, Francis P '89 Cnsl Area Title Agncy Inc -709 Mad Av
-Toledo 43624 **Fx:**242-8920

(703) 696-1511 ..**Neds**, Michael R '75 US Army Legal Srvcs Agency -901 N Stuart
-Ste 500 -Arlington, VA 22203

(440) 323-5646 ..**Nedwick**, Michelle D '93 Elyria City Solicitor's Ofc -328 Broad
-Elyria 44035

(440) 838-7600 ..**Nee**, Matthew M '00 %Janik & D,LLP -9200 S Hills Blvd -Ste 300
-Cleveland 44147 **Fx:**838-7601

(614) 529-8600 ..**Needleman**, Scott R '91 (Nobile N&T,LLC) -4511 Cemetery Rd
-Ste B -Hilliard 43026 **Fx:**529-8656

(614) 469-3939 ..**Needler-Turner**, Shawn M '04 %Jones D
-325 John H McConnell Blvd -Ste 600 -Bx165017
-Columbus 43216 **Fx:**461-4198

(419) 424-0202 ..**Needles**, John Stanley '69 -219 S Main -Findlay 45840

(703) 747-1000 ..**Needles**, Thayne T '92 Ernst & Young LLP -8484 Westpark Dr
-McLean, VA 22102

(937) 277-0175 ..**Neef**, James T '60 -299 Winding Ridge Dr -Dayton 45415

(216) 621-8484 ..**Neel**, David W '86 (Climaco LPW&G Co,LPA) -1228 Euclid Av
-Ste 900 Halle Bldg -Cleveland 44115 **Fx:**771-1632

Neeley, Paul L '93 -(Address Unavailable)

(614) 728-2849 ..**Neeley-See**, Greta M '94 PUCO -180 E Broad -Columbus 43266

(614) 854-5934 ..**Neely**, Demetries J '84 Nationwide Ins Co -One Nationwide Plz
-1-37-04 -Columbus 43215

(614) 249-7606 ..**Neely**, Sandra L '83 Nationwide Ins Co -1 Nationwide Plz
-Columbus 43215

(419) 243-6281 ..**Neff**, Carter P '68 (Shindler NH&S,LLP) -300 Mad Av -Ste 1200
-Toledo 43604 **Fx:**243-0129

(614) 221-4221 ..**Neff**, Frank J '60 Barkan + N -360 S Grant Av -Bx1989
-Columbus 43216 **Fx:**221-5423

(216) 751-8271 ..**Neff**, James A '86 -21625 Chagrin Blvd #250 -Beachwood 44122
Fx:751-9911

(614) 228-2345 ..**Neff**, Joseph H '90 %Chicago Title Agncy -100 S 4th
-Columbus 43215

(859) 291-6333 ..**Neff**, Kerry L '96 -526 Greenup -Covington, KY 41011

(216) 443-7800 ..**Neff**, Richard A Jr. '88 Cuyahoga Cnty Pros -1200 Ontario -8th Fl
-Cleveland 44113 **Fx:**698-2270

(419) 562-1951 ..**Neff**, Robert C Jr. '83 Neff Law Firm,Ltd -840 S Sandusky Av
-Bx406 -Bucyrus 44820

(513) 361-8013 ..**Neff**, Roger Lee IV '01 PricewaterhouseCoopers
-720 E Pete Rose Way -Ste 400 -Cincinnati 45202

(216) 529-6700 ..**Neff**, Terease Z '92 Lakewood Mun Ct -12650 Detroit Av
-Lakewood 44107

Neff, Theresa M '04 -5846 Winding Way -Sylvania 43560

(412) 392-2000 ..**Neft**, Bryan S '00 Klett RL&S -1 Oxford Ctr -40th Fl
-Pittsburgh, PA 15219

(440) 942-1144 ..**Negin**, Morton S '54 -9205 Idlewood Dr -Mentor 44060

(216) 741-2250 ..**Negrelli**, William E '66 Cnsl City Title -709 Brookpark Rdg
-Cleveland 44109

(440) 323-0687 ..**Nehr**, David W '04 (Berki & N,LLC) -124 Middle Av -Ste 800
-Elyria 44035 **Fx:**323-2332

(330) 928-3373 ..**Nehrer**, John A '66 Nehrer & K -111 Stow Av -Ste 100
-Cuyahoga Falls 44221

(330) 928-3373 ..**Nehrer & Kassinger** -111 Stow Av -Ste 100
-Cuyahoga Falls 44221

(330) 928-3373 ..**Nehrer**, Lori S '85 (Nehrer & K) -111 Stow Av -Ste 100
-Cuyahoga Falls 44221

(614) 221-7663 ..**Neidenthal**, Kenneth W '71 (Luper N&L,LPA) -50 W Broad
-1200 LeVeque Twr -Columbus 43215 **Fx:**464-2425

(614) 248-6037 ..**Neidenthal**, Randall C '79 Bank One Mngmnt Corp -100 E Broad
-5th Fl OHI-0152 -Columbus 43271

(858) 622-8060 ..**Neidert**, Karl O '93 Agouron Pharm,Inc -10350 N Torrey Pines Rd
-La Jolla, CA 92037

(937) 225-7233 ..**Neidhold**, Terri W '94 SSA-OHA -110 N Main -Ste 800
-Dayton 45402

(513) 556-3483 ..**Neiger**, Jan A '90 Univ of Cincinnati-Ofc Gen Cnsl -Bx210623
-Cincinnati 45221

(513) 579-1500 ..**Neiheisel**, Michael E '69 %Buechner HOM&H Co,LPA -105 E 4th
-Ste 300 -Cincinnati 45202 **Fx:**977-4361

(216) 622-8200 ..**Neill**, Ronald H '69 (Calfee H&G LLP) -800 Superior Av -Ste 1400
-Cleveland 44114 **Fx:**241-0816

(614) 469-8000 ..**Neilsen**, Daniel J '03 %McNees W&N,LLC -21 E State -17th Fl
-Columbus 43215 **Fx:**469-4653

(216) 522-7963 ..**Neilsen**, Karen N '95 NLRB -1240 E 9th -1695 Celebrezze Bldg
-Cleveland 44199 **Fx:**522-2418

(330) 873-1776 ..**Neiman**, Maurice P '53 -3200 W Market -Ste 104 -Akron 44333

(330) 643-2628 ..**Neiman**, Michelle M '96 Summit Cnty Cmn Pleas Ct -209 S High
-Akron 44308

(330) 869-0224 ..**Neiman**, Robert E '81 -3200 W Market -#104 -Fairlawn 44333

(614) 276-8959 ..**Nein**, James R '71 -2291 Scioto Harper Dr -Columbus 43204
Fx:276-8959

(513) 791-8600 ..**Neiswonger**, Garret S '98 Spherion -5151 Pfeiffer Rd -Ste 120
-Cincinnati 45242

(216) 861-5000 ..**Nejedlik**, David B '86 Ernst & Young -1300 Huntngtn Bldg
-925 Euclid Av -Cleveland 44115

Nelsen, Brian C '01 -(Address Unavailable)

(904) 641-0162 ..**Nelsen**, James D '72 -8558 Royal Lks Dr -Jacksonville, FL 32256
Fx:641-0935

Nelsen, Andrea M '99 -(Address Unavailable)

(740) 363-1213 ..**Nelson**, April D '90 (Firestone BHNW&Y,LLP) -15 W Winter
-Delaware 43015 **Fx:**369-0875

(513) 831-6660 ..**Nelson**, Barry E '84 BE Nelson,LLC -575 Chmbr Dr -Milford 45150
Fx:831-6010

(434) 924-7372 ..**Nelson**, Caleb E '93 Univ of Virginia Schl of Law -580 Massie Rd
-Charlottesville, VA 22903

(740) 622-2011 ..**Nelson**, Christie M '99 %Pomerene B&S -309 Main
-Coshocton 43812

(484) 530-1399 ..**Nelson**, Christopher A '98 Nationwide Fin/Villanova Captl
-1200 Rvr Rd -Conshohocken, PA 19428

(304) 525-1406 ..**Nelson**, Debra A '04 (Mundy & N) -422 9th -Bx2986
-Huntington, WV 25701

(216) 752-6965 ..**Nelson**, Delos T '48 -19901 Van Aken Blvd -Shaker Heights 44122

(216) 696-4700 ..**Nelson**, Douglas M II '96 %Spieth BM&N Co,LPA -925 Euclid Av
-2000 Huntngtn Bldg -Cleveland 44115 **Fx:**696-2706

(937) 882-9305 ..**Nelson**, Gordon R '03 (Baker & N,LLC) -926 Bischoff Rd
-New Carlisle 45344

(614) 224-7141 ..**Nelson**, Hugh W '59 %Lancaster Colony Corp -4865 Etrick Dr
-Ste 500 -Columbus 43220

(614) 864-5780 ..**Nelson**, James A '53 -4495 E Broad -Columbus 43213

Nelson, James E '53 -1125 Luray Dr -Ashland 44805

(614) 227-2000 ..**Nelson**, Janice A '92 %Porter WM&A LLP -41 S High
-Columbus 43215 **Fx:**227-2100

(513) 621-1771 ..**Nelson**, Jason M '99 -105 E 4th -Ste 600 -Cincinnati 45202

(419) 352-7522 ..**Nelson**, Jeffrey A '79 (Middleton R&N) -521 N Main
-Bowling Green 43402 **Fx:**353-4899

(440) 326-4399 ..**Nelson**, Jill E '00 EMH Regnl Healthcare Sys -630 E River
-Elyria 44035 **Fx:**326-4394

(419) 241-1200 ..**Nelson**, John K '79 Cooper & W,LPA -900 Adams -Toledo 43624
Fx:242-5675

(216) 272-8518 ..**Nelson**, Kenneth A II '03 -175 Inwood Blvd -Avon Lake 44012

(330) 665-3186 ..**Nelson**, Kimberly B '88 -Bx13873 -Akron 44334

(859) 586-0600 ..**Nelson**, Kristi R '95 Pomeroy Computer Rsrcs,Inc
-1020 Petersburg Rd -Hebron, KY 41048

(614) 228-1398 ..**Nelson Levine deLuca & Horst LLC** -280 N High -Ste 920
-Columbus 43215 **Fx:**221-7529

Nelson, Lisa V '99 -Bx755 -Willoughby 44096

(216) 472-0273 ..**Nelson**, Michael L '90 -3530 Warrensvll Ctr Rd -Ste 207
-Cleveland 44122

(614) 757-5000 ..**Nelson**, Michael R '86 %Cardinal Hlth -7000 Cardinal Pl
-Dublin 43017

(513) 421-4020 ..**Nelson**, Richard D '74 (Cohen TK&S,LLC) -250 E 5th -Ste 1200
-Cincinnati 45202 **Fx:**241-4490

(216) 621-7860 ..**Nelson**, Robert M '71 (Cavitch FD&F) -1717 E 9th -14th Fl
-Cleveland 44114 **Fx:**621-3415

(740) 345-3431 ..**Nelson**, Rodney A '92 (Reese PD&M,PLL) -36 N 2nd -Bx919
-Newark 43058 **Fx:**349-5116

(513) 946-3149 ..**Nelson**, Ryan L '97 Hamilton Cnty Pros -230 E 9th
-Cincinnati 45202 **Fx:**946-3017

(330) 425-2354 ..**Nelson**, Sidney G Jr. '90 Sorbent Tech Corp -1664 E Highland Rd
-Twinsburg 44087

(740) 687-6616 ..**Nelson**, Stephanie A '01 Pros -Bx1008 -Lancaster 43130

(513) 961-3111 ..**Nelson**, Steven A '77 -209 Hosea Av -Ste 3 -Cincinnati 45220

(804) 622-8950 ..**Nelson**, Steven S '75 Moody SKB&H -Bx1138
-Portsmouth, VA 23705

(419) 252-6217 ..**Nelson**, Susan B '81 (Spengler N PLL) -608 Mad Av -Ste 1000
-Toledo 43604 **Fx:**241-8599

(440) 357-5558 ..**Nelson Sweet & Hurley** -8 N State -Ste 201 -Painesville 44077

Nelson, Thomas E '97 -(Address Unavailable)

(614) 628-8000 ..**Nelson**, Vanessa A '00 Dreher L&T LLP -41 S High
-2250 Huntngtn Ctr -Columbus 43215 **Fx:**628-1600

(614) 227-4870 ..**Nelson Carney**, Jennifer M '04 %Bricker & E LLP -100 S 3rd
-Columbus 43215 **Fx:**227-2390

(937) 224-3333 ..**Neltner**, Michael M '94 %Green & G -109 N Main -Ste 800
-Dayton 45402 **Fx:**224-4311

(330) 864-3377 ..**Neman**, Patrick J '67 -133 Ghent Rd -Fairlawn 44333 **Fx:**836-2295

(614) 221-9790 ..**Nemann**, Adam Lee '03 %J Scott Co,LPA -35 E Lvngstn Av
-Columbus 43215 **Fx:**228-6680

(216) 621-1230 ..**Nemec**, Andrew '99 %G Walton & Assoc -2800 Euclid Av -Ste 320
-Cleveland 44115 **Fx:**621-3039

(614) 884-4800 ..**Nemecek**, Julia Carrie '04 %Slowik & R,LLC -250 E Broad
-Ste 250 -Columbus 43215 **Fx:**884-4801

(440) 526-6400 .. **Nemer**, Charles A '83 C Nemer Co,LPA -8180 Brecksvll Rd -Brecksville 44141

(216) 566-5552 .. **Nemer**, Laura Bancroft '99 %Thompson H LLP -127 Pub Sq -3900 Key Ctr -Cleveland 44114 **Fx:**566-5800

(330) 945-4234 .. **Nemer**, Robert J '95 %Chi Chi Rodriguez Mgt -3916 Clock Pnte Trl -Ste 101 -Stow 44224

(614) 443-4866 .. **Nemeth**, John C '71 (J Nemeth & Assoc) -21 E Frankfort -Columbus 43206 **Fx:**443-4860

(216) 479-8500 .. **Nemeth**, Laura D '89 (Squire S&D LLP) -127 Pub Sq -4900 Key Twr -Cleveland 44114 **Fx:**479-8780

(216) 502-1300 .. **Nemeth**, Richard H '84 Nemeth & Assoc Co, LPA -526 Superior Av NE -Ste 410 -Cleveland 44114

(330) 364-1614 .. **Nemitz**, Eugene H Jr. '73 Fitzpatrick Z&R Co LPA -140 Fair Av NW -Bx1014 -New Philadelphia 44663 **Fx:**343-3077

(740) 387-7438 .. **Nemo**, Robert C '79 (Nemo & F) -495 S State -Marion 43302

(513) 868-2731 .. **Nerenberg**, Jonathon O '77 Baden & J Co,LPA -246 High -Hamilton 45011 **Fx:**868-1190

(440) 350-2683 .. **Neroda**, Lisa A '91 Lake Cnty Pros -105 Main -Bx490 -Painesville 44077 **Fx:**350-2585

(216) 621-3801 .. **Nerren**, Guy V '71 -2401 Superior Viaduct -Cleveland 44113

(614) 586-1310 .. **Nesbit**, Mark M '95 (Nesbit Law Firm) -447 E Main -Ste 200 -Columbus 43215

(724) 662-3800 .. **Nesbit**, Tedd C '04 Hon Reed -Diamond Square -Mercer Cnty Cthse -Mercer, PA 16127

(513) 229-0383 .. **Nesbitt**, Daniel F '86 (Hasse & N LLC) -7550 Cntrl Pke Blvd -Mason 45040 **Fx:**229-0683

(513) 755-2600 .. **Nesbitt**, Patrick T '81 -8050 Beckett Ctr Dr -Ste 113 -West Chester 45069

(859) 394-6200 .. **Nesbitt**, Stephen G '04 Adams SW&D,PLLC -40 W Pike -Covington, KY 41011

(616) 833-1837 .. **Nesbitt**, Stephen L '85 Pharmacia Corp -301 Henrietta -Kalamazoo, MI 49007

(614) 798-0150 .. **Nesdore**, Bruce G '89 -100 Jerome Rd -Dublin 43017

(804) 289-3594 .. **Ness**, Christine A '95 GE Finl Assurance -6610 W Broad -Richmond, VA 23230

(614) 221-1934 .. **Nesser**, J Michael '83 Nesser Cnsltng Grp -495 S High -Ste 170 -Columbus 43215

(210) 652-1996 .. **Nesser**, Kathleen L '83 USAF -73 Main Cir -Ste 1-19AF/JA -Randolph AFB, TX 78150

(202) 293-3050 .. **Nestel**, Daniel A '93 NCAA -1 Dupont Cir NW -Ste 310 -Washington, DC 20036

(614) 442-2502 .. **Nester**, Elbert R '68 (E Nester & Assoc Co,LPA) -4621 Reed Rd -Ste 201 -Columbus 43220

(330) 376-3572 .. **Nestico**, Alberto '99 Eshelman Lgl Grp -263 Portage Trl Ext W -Cuyahoga Falls 44223 **Fx:**376-0199

(937) 208-2379 .. **Nestor**, Amy Bertke '99 Cnsl Miami Valley Hosp -1 Wyoming -Gen Cnsl Ofc -Dayton 45409 **Fx:**208-2871

(513) 352-3327 .. **Nestor**, Terrance A '95 Law Dept -801 Plum -Rm 214 -Cincinnati 45202 **Fx:**352-1515

(216) 368-3297 .. **Neth**, Spencer '64 CWRU Law Schl -11075 East Blvd -Cleveland 44106

(330) 832-9744 .. **Netzly**, Dwight H '52 -1237 Lincoln Way E -Massillon 44646

(614) 299-4975 .. **Neubauer**, David M '75 -334 W 3rd Av -Columbus 43201

(216) 522-3715 .. **Neubecker**, Mark F '78 NLRB -1240 E 9th -1695 Celebrezze Bldg -Cleveland 44199 **Fx:**522-2418

(330) 467-9776 .. **Neubert**, Eleanore S '54 -9555 Olde Eight Rd -Northfield 44067

(216) 767-1361 .. **Neubert**, William T '79 -23450 Hazelmere Rd -Shaker Heights 44122

(937) 227-3700 .. **Neudorfer**, Karl E '00 %Faruki I&C PLL -10 N Ludlow -500 Cthse Plz SW -Dayton 45402 **Fx:**227-3717

(937) 773-3212 .. **Neuenschwander**, Jack L '67 (McCulloch FF&G Co,LPA) -123 Market -Bx910 -Piqua 45356 **Fx:**773-9672

(216) 696-7660 .. **Neuger**, Charles J '54 -526 Superior Av E -Ste 1101 -Cleveland 44114

(937) 443-6775 .. **Neuhardt**, David A '79 (Thompson H LLP) -2000 Cthse Plz NE -Bx8801 -Dayton 45401 **Fx:**443-6635

(937) 443-6705 .. **Neuhardt**, Sharen S '76 (Thompson H LLP) -2000 Cthse Plz NE -Bx8801 -Dayton 45401 **Fx:**443-6635

(412) 281-7272 .. **Neuhart**, David M '04 Dickie M&C -2 PPG Pl -Ste 400 -Pittsburgh, PA 15222

(330) 372-2010 .. **Neuman**, Craig H '74 Trumbull Cnty Chldrn Srvcs -2282 Reeves Rd NE -Warren 44483

(330) 652-1749 .. **Neuman**, Douglas J '77 -761 N Cedar -Niles 44446 **Fx:**652-2356

Neuman, Edward B '66 -Bx41309 -Dayton 45441

(513) 621-2120 .. **Neuman**, Larry A '70 Strauss & T,LPA -150 E 4th -4th Fl -Cincinnati 45202 **Fx:**241-8259

(614) 889-4777 .. **Neuman**, Todd M '92 (Ferris & N LLP) -2733 W Dublin Granvll Rd -Columbus 43235

(216) 521-1418 .. **Neumann**, Arthur W '53 -11800 Edgewtr Dr -#1104 -Lakewood 44107

(216) 363-4500 .. **Neumann**, David M '97 %Benesch FC&A LLP -200 Pub Sq -Ste 2300 -Cleveland 44114 **Fx:**363-4588

(419) 522-5900 .. **Neumann**, James M '76 %Chicago Title Agncy -13 Park Av W -Ste 200 -Mansfield 44902

(513) 352-6772 .. **Neumark**, Michael H '70 (Thompson H LLP) -312 Walnut -14th Fl -Cincinnati 45202 **Fx:**241-4771

(419) 345-7122 .. **Neumeyer**, James D '04 -Bx351916 -Toledo 43635

(513) 651-6800 .. **Neusch**, Raymond D '78 (Frost BT LLC) -201 E 5th -2200 PNC Ctr -Cincinnati 45202 **Fx:**651-6981

(614) 923-7700 .. **Nevada**, Eugene P Jr. '76 %Clemens Nelson & Assoc -5100 Park Ctr Av -Ste 120 -Dublin 43017

(216) 696-7661 .. **Nevar**, Denis A '04 Fisher & Assoc Co,LPA -50 Pub Sq -1414 Trmnl Twr -Cleveland 44113

(937) 222-2333 .. **Nevherz**, Rebekah Sinnott '00 %Surdyk D&T Co,LPA -40 N Main -1610 Kettering Twr -Dayton 45423 **Fx:**222-1970

(740) 867-3217 .. **Neville**, Brenda K '93 Meyers & N,LLC -220 4th -Chesapeake 45619

(937) 212-3158 .. **Neville**, Jeffrey A '99 Sogeti USA -7735 Paragon Rd -Centerville 45459

(216) 687-1311 .. **Neville**, John A '68 (Reminger & R) -101 Prospect Av W -1400 Mdlnd Bldg -Cleveland 44115 **Fx:**687-1841

(419) 634-6646 .. **Neville**, John B '74 -229 N Main -Ada 45810

(614) 644-4133 .. **Neville**, William J Jr. '92 Pub Emplyees Rtrmnt Syst -277 E Town -Columbus 43215

(937) 328-3763 .. **Nevius**, Eugene S '72 Cnty Mun Ct Judge -50 E Columbia -Springfield 45502

(859) 344-1188 .. **Newbanks**, Ronal R '65 Hemmer SPD PLLC -250 Grandvw Dr -Ste 200 -Ft Mitchell, KY 41017

(513) 362-8248 .. **Newbauer**, Frank L '88 Integrated Fund Srvcs,Inc -221 E 4th -Ste 300 -Cincinnati 45202

(419) 242-3900 .. **Newberg**, Brian A '92 Cincinnati Ins Co -300 Mad Av -Ste 1406 -Toledo 43604

(937) 296-2456 .. **Newberry**, Forde J '73 Law Dept -3600 Shroyer Rd -Kettering 45429

(513) 541-0100 .. **Newberry**, Jeffrey S '82 -1538 Cedar Av -Bx24426 -Cincinnati 45224

Newberry, John F '04 -(Address Unavailable)

(513) 421-4225 .. **Newberry**, Peter C '88 OfCnsl Heis & W Co,LPA -817 Main -Ste 800 -Cincinnati 45202

(614) 466-6928 .. **Newbold**, Garold L '83 Workers Comp -30 W Spring -Level 26 -Columbus 43215

(330) 829-6560 .. **Newbold**, Pamela H '88 Mount Union Coll -1972 Clark Av -Alliance 44601

(216) 621-0200 .. **Newborn**, Karen B '76 (Baker & H LLP) -1900 E 9th -Ste 3200 -Cleveland 44114 **Fx:**696-0740

(937) 382-1316 .. **Newburger**, Craig A '01 Pub Def -39 E Locust -Wilmington 45177

(614) 462-2257 .. **Newcomb**, Angelique Paul '97 (Schottenstein Z&D) -250 West -Bx165020 -Columbus 43216 **Fx:**462-5135

(614) 464-6400 .. **Newcomb**, William S Jr. '69 (Vorys SS&P LLP) -52 E Gay -Bx1008 -Columbus 43216 **Fx:**464-6350

(614) 272-1112 .. **Newcome**, Ronald E '82 (Elleman & N) -2904 W Broad -Columbus 43204 **Fx:**272-1115

(419) 636-3196 .. **Newcomer**, David C '72 (Newcomer S&S) -117 W Maple -Bryan 43506 **Fx:**636-0867

(614) 752-6864 .. **Newcomer**, James D '64 OH Dept Taxation -30 E Broad -22nd Fl -Columbus 43215

(419) 872-2800 .. **Newcomer**, Ned S '68 -Drwr673 -Perrysburg 43552

(419) 636-3196 .. **Newcomer Shaffer & Spangler** -117 W Maple -Bryan 43506 **Fx:**636-0867

(419) 334-2909 .. **Newell**, Beverly S '96 Sandusky Cnty CSEA -2571 Cntryside Dr -Fremont 44818

(216) 371-7767 .. **Newell**, Evelyn B '84 -2429 Canterbury Rd -Cleveland Heights 44118

Newell, Janel M '94 -5965 Linder Cir NE -Canton 44721

(440) 243-2800 .. **Newell**, Monica M '01 %Phillips M&C Co,LPA -7530 Lucerne Dr -Ste 200 -Middleburg Heights 44130 **Fx:**243-2852

(216) 696-4700 .. **Newell**, Sterling Jr. '49 (Spieth BM&N Co,LPA) -925 Euclid Av -2000 Huntngtn Bldg -Cleveland 44115 **Fx:**696-2706

(330) 454-3508 .. **Newell**, William T '97 Top Echelon Contracting Inc -800 Market Av N -Canton 44702

(216) 621-2034 .. **Newendorp**, Paul W '82 %Margolius M & Assoc,LPA -55 Pub Sq -Ste 1100 -Cleveland 44113 **Fx:**621-1908

(740) 373-7674 .. **Newhart**, Anita L '83 (Newhart & M) -227 3rd -Marietta 45750

(614) 228-6885 .. **Newhouse**, D Wesley II '83 (Lane A&H LLC) -175 S 3rd -Ste 700 -Columbus 43215 **Fx:**228-0146

(614) 725-7055 .. **Newkirk**, Todd W '03 Atty Gen -30 E Broad -Columbus 43215 **Fx:**728-7582

(513) 887-9595 .. **Newland**, Michael A '89 -30 North D -Hamilton 45013 **Fx:**887-9608

(937) 434-2425 .. **Newlin**, John R '49 -420 Stoneybrook Dr -Dayton 45429

(513) 422-8443 .. **Newlin**, Joseph E '68 -1701 S Breiel Blvd -Middletown 45044

(330) 452-6400 .. **Newlon**, Clarence A '94 S Ferruccio Jr -220 Market Av S -Ste 400 -Canton 44702

(419) 352-4621 .. **Newlove**, John F '84 (Maurer N&B) -224 E Wooster -Bowling Green 43402

(419) 352-2535 .. **Newlove**, Megan E '95 (Spitler HY&N,LLP) -131 E Court -Bowling Green 43402 **Fx:**353-8728

(760) 743-5005 .. **Newman**, Barry I '58 -3308 Avnida Sierra -Escondido, CA 92029 **Fx:**743-8224

(440) 286-9549 .. **Newman & Brice** -214 E Park -Chardon 44024

(330) 744-1148 .. **Newman**, Christopher J '73 (Henderson CMN&T Co,LPA) -34 Fed Plz W -Ste 600 Wick Bldg -Youngstown 44503 **Fx:**744-3807

(216) 443-8824 .. **Newman**, Daniel M '01 Domestic Relations Ct -One W Lakeside Av -Cleveland 44113

(513) 721-1311 .. **Newman**, Danny M Jr. '02 %Reminger & R -7 W 7th -Ste 1990 -Cincinnati 45202 **Fx:**721-2553

(614) 221-2121 .. **Newman**, Dennis R '68 (Isaac BL&T,LLP) -250 E Broad -Ste 900 Mdlnd Bldg -Columbus 43215 **Fx:**365-9516

(330) 762-6474 .. **Newman**, Dianne M '79 (Sternberg NS & Assoc) -411 Wolf Ledges Pkwy -Ste 300 -Akron 44311 **Fx:**762-2127

(602) 271-7700 .. **Newman**, Donald J '72 OfCnsl Broening OWW&C -1122 E Jffrsn -Bx20527 -Phoenix, AZ 85036

(419) 254-1311 .. **Newman**, Emily Weaver '04 %Reminger & R -405 Mad Av -Ste 2300 -Toledo 43604 **Fx:**243-7830

(330) 535-7027 .. **Newman**, Herbert '65 (H Newman Co,LPA) -730 W Market -Akron 44303

Newman, Hilary J '03 -(Address Unavailable)

(513) 731-9888 .. **Newman**, James O '66 Newman Leather Corp -3924 VA Av -Cincinnati 45227

(216) 621-1541 .. **Newman**, Joel I '72 (Newman & N) -526 Superior Av -711 Leader Bldg -Cleveland 44114

(330) 747-4404 .. **Newman**, John M '42 Newman O&K,LPA -11 Fed Plz Central -Ste 1200 -Youngstown 44503 **Fx:**747-6056

(216) 586-3939 .. **Newman**, John M Jr. '76 (Jones D) -901 Lakeside Av -Cleveland 44114 **Fx:**579-0212

(412) 263-2000 .. **Newman**, Kenneth T '95 %Pietragallo B&G -1 Oxford Centre -38th Fl -Pittsburgh, PA 15219 **Fx:**261-5295

(317) 842-8000 .. **Newman**, Lawrence T '81 %RW York & Assoc -7212 N Shadeland Av -Ste 150 -Indianapolis, IN 46250 **Fx:**577-7321

(513) 241-7111 .. **Newman**, Mark L '89 %O'Connor A&L Co,LPA -1014 Vine -22nd Fl -Cincinnati 45202 **Fx:**241-7197

(513) 977-8200 .. **Newman**, Michael J '89 %Dinsmore & S LLP -255 E 5th -Ste 1900 -Cincinnati 45202 **Fx:**977-8141

(330) 747-4404 .. **Newman Olson & Kerr,LPA** -11 Fed Plz Central -Ste 1200 -Youngstown 44503 **Fx:**747-6056

(440) 286-9549 .. **Newman**, Paul A '77 (Newman & B) -214 E Park -Chardon 44024

(513) 455-7600 ..**Newman**, Peter K '80 (Greenebaum D&M PLLC) -255 E 5th -2800 Chemed Ctr -Cincinnati 45202 **Fx:**455-8500

(212) 797-3737 ..**Newman**, Randall S '99 (Newman & Assoc,PC) -80 Wall -Ste 815 -New York, NY 10005

(513) 639-7000 ..**Newman**, Robert B '73 (Newman & M Co,LPA) -617 Vine -Ste 1401 -Cincinnati 45202
Newman, Stephen C '91 -(Address Unavailable)

(740) 773-2105 ..**Newman**, Steven C '94 -41 N Paint -Bx1932 -Chillicothe 45601

(614) 228-5711 ..**Newman**, William F '55 (Lucas PAG&N) -600 S High -Columbus 43215 **Fx:**228-0982

(614) 464-5000 ..**Newman-Coleman**, Rosemarie '87 State Auto Ins Co -518 E Broad -Columbus 43215
Newmark, Lisa M '85 -7528 Fenway Rd -New Albany 43054

(419) 213-3169 ..**Newnham**, Gary C '79 Lucas Cnty CSEA -701 Adams -Toledo 43624

(727) 524-8486 ..**Newsom**, Jennifer R '82 %Goodman & N -14020 Roosevelt Blvd -Ste 808 -Clearwater, FL 33762 **Fx:**524-8786

(614) 228-5551 ..**Newsom**, Kimberly C '92 CSEA Directors Assoc -37 W Broad -Ste 1170 -Columbus 43215 **Fx:**228-5554

(419) 241-6000 ..**Newsom**, Scott D '96 %Eastman & S Ltd -1 Seagate -24th Fl -Bx10032 -Toledo 43699 **Fx:**247-1777
Newsome, David Jr. '89 US Army -USAEUR 7/A OSJA CMR 420 -APO, AE 09063

(614) 839-5700 ..**Newsome**, Romina P '03 %E Hollern Co,LPA -51 Drchstr Ln -Westerville 43081 **Fx:**839-4200

(702) 454-8244 ..**Newton**, Kathleen A '89 Wayne Newton Enterprises/Erin Miel Inc -6730 S Pecos Rd -Las Vegas, NV 89120

(513) 983-1100 ..**Newton**, Robert A '02 Procter & Gamble Co-Legal -1 Procter & Gamble Plz -Cincinnati 45202

(330) 427-2720 ..**Newton**, Walter L Jr. '85 -280 A Walnut -Leetonia 44431

(513) 983-4517 ..**Ney**, Carol J '87 Procter & Gamble Co-Legal -1 Procter & Gamble Plz -Cincinnati 45202

(513) 381-9200 ..**Ney**, Peter L '87 (Rendigs FK&D,LLP) -One W 4th -Ste 900 -Cincinnati 45202 **Fx:**381-9206

(513) 353-3439 ..**Neyer**, James P '95 -4895 State Route 128 -Cleves 45002

(614) 462-3194 ..**Neyerlin**, Amy L '88 Franklin Cnty Pub Def -373 S High -12th Fl -Columbus 43215

(440) 350-2683 ..**Neylon**, Benjamin J '99 Lake Cnty Pros -105 Main -Bx490 -Painesville 44077 **Fx:**350-2585

(330) 455-0935 ..**Niarchos**, Gust F P II '67 -1021 Rex Av NE -Canton 44704

(305) 251-5567 ..**Niarchos**, Julia E '80 Mains'L Florida,Inc -9900 SW 168th -Ste 6 -Miami, FL 33157

(216) 475-5045 ..**Nicastro**, Deborah J '79 Mun Ct Judge -5555 Turney Rd -Garfield Heights 44125
Niccum, Robert F '57 -8027 Meloria Ln -Mentor 44060

(614) 466-6750 ..**Nicely**, Fredrick J '92 OH Dept Taxation -30 E Broad -22nd Fl -Columbus 43215 **Fx:**466-7979

(740) 695-5263 ..**Nichelson**, James L '74 Belmont Cnty Pub Def -100 W Main -Lwr Level -Saint Clairsville 43950 **Fx:**695-5639

(614) 222-0050 ..**Nichelson**, Lauren R '00 OH Pub Empl Rtrmnt Sys -277 E Town -Columbus 43215

(216) 443-7800 ..**Nichol**, Andrew J '00 Cuyahoga Cnty Pros -1200 Ontario -8th Fl -Cleveland 44113 **Fx:**698-2270

(330) 434-3000 ..**Nichol**, David S '00 %Roderick & L -One Cascade Plz -Ste 1500 -Akron 44308 **Fx:**434-9220

(513) 946-3700 ..**Nicholas**, James A '80 Hamilton Cnty Pub Def -230 E 9th -3rd Fl -Cincinnati 45202 **Fx:**946-3707

(440) 248-7906 ..**Nicholas**, Joseph F Jr. '87 (Mazanec R&R Co,LPA) -34305 Solon Rd -Ste 100 -Cleveland 44139 **Fx:**248-8861

(740) 695-4331 ..**Nicholoff**, Sandra L '95 %Vavra Law Ofc -132 W Main -Bx430 -Saint Clairsville 43950

(740) 374-9000 ..**Nichols**, Curtis B '80 Nichols Law Ofc -324 Fourth -Ste 100 -Marietta 45750 **Fx:**374-9024

(513) 732-1420 ..**Nichols**, James G '68 (Nichols S&N) -237 Main -Batavia 45103

(312) 346-5486 ..**Nichols**, Jeannette E '99 Midwest Real Estate Investment Co -120 N LaSalle -Ste 2820 -Chicago, IL 60602

(614) 221-1111 ..**Nichols**, Philip R '96 Shayne & G -221 S High -Columbus 43215 **Fx:**221-4070

(614) 462-2234 ..**Nichols**, Robert H '92 (Schottenstein Z&D) -250 West -Bx165020 -Columbus 43216 **Fx:**462-5155

(614) 644-7784 ..**Nichols**, Robin M '02 Legis Srvc Commssn -77 S High -Columbus 43215

(513) 732-1420 ..**Nichols Speidel & Nichols** -237 Main -Batavia 45103

(740) 852-3000 ..**Nichols Stonecipher & Flax** -117 W High -Ste 105 -London 43140

(513) 983-3817 ..**Nichols**, Vanessa M '98 Procter & Gamble Co-Legal -1 Procter & Gamble Plz -Cincinnati 45202

(419) 248-2600 ..**Nicholson**, Brent B '79 OfCnsl Rohrbachers LC&T Co,LPA -405 Mad Av -8th Fl -Toledo 43604 **Fx:**248-2614

(937) 224-7200 ..**Nicholson**, Bruce I '77 (Horenstein N&B) -124 E 3rd -5th Fl -Dayton 45402 **Fx:**224-3353

(614) 466-0722 ..**Nicholson**, Claude V '91 Atty Gen -150 E Gay -Columbus 43215 **Fx:**644-9973

(216) 241-5310 ..**Nicholson**, Gary L '84 (Gallagher SF&N) -1501 Euclid Av -6th Fl -Cleveland 44115 **Fx:**241-1608

(740) 439-1430 ..**Nicholson**, John M '83 Mun Ct Judge -134 Southgate Pkwy -Cambridge 43725

(513) 564-7670 ..**Nicholson**, Laurie J '92 Hon S Beckwith US Dist Ct -100 E 5th -Ste 810 -Cincinnati 45202

(937) 865-7664 ..**Nicholson**, Mark W '85 Lexis/Nexis -Bx933 -Dayton 45401

(419) 562-8998 ..**Nicholson**, Thomas G '88 -438 E Lucas -Bucyrus 44820 **Fx:**562-2216

(740) 439-3077 ..**Nicholson**, William T '85 -217 N 8th -Cambridge 43725

(216) 902-8000 ..**Nici**, Anthony T '97 (AT Nici & Assoc,LLC) -24600 Aurora Rd -Bedford Heights 44146

(614) 466-7090 ..**Nick**, Paul M '90 Ethics Commssn -8 E Long -10th Fl -Columbus 43215
Nickel, Michelle D '96 -4141 N Braeswood Blvd -43 -Houston, TX 77025
Nickell, Angela R '94 -201 E Vine -Coldwater 45828

(614) 677-4251 ..**Nickell-Thomas**, Jennifer A '91 SrCnsl Nationwide Ins Co -1 Nationwide Plz -Columbus 43215

(304) 233-1220 ..**Nickerson**, Donald A Jr. '87 (Seibert & K,LC) -1217 Chapline -Bx311 -Wheeling, WV 26003

(614) 220-8900 ..**Nickerson**, George R '76 Amer Aprtmnt Comm -21 W Broad -11th Fl -Columbus 43215

(614) 757-5542 ..**Nickey**, Donald O '76 Cardinal Hlth -7000 Cardinal Pl -Dublin 43017

(740) 967-5555 ..**Nicks**, John M '01 %L Shafer -55 S Main -Ste C -Bx356 -Johnstown 43031

(330) 453-7045 ..**Nicodemo**, John L '72 -124 15th NW -Canton 44703

(330) 453-8261 ..**Nicodemo**, Richard A '84 Okey Law Firm,LPA -337 3rd NW -Canton 44702

(440) 989-4100 ..**Nicol**, Wayne R '04 %S Bradley,LPA -1958 Kresge Dr -Amherst 44001 **Fx:**989-4104

(216) 621-7227 ..**Nicola Gudbranson & Cooper, LLC** -25 W Prospect Av -Republic Bldg Ste 1400 -Cleveland 44115 **Fx:**621-3999

(740) 432-5648 ..**Nicolozakes**, William A '95 Nicolozakes Trucking & Construction,Inc -8555 Georgtwn Rd -Bx670 -Cambridge 43725

(216) 479-8500 ..**Nicols**, Howard J C '81 (Squire S&D LLP) -127 Pub Sq -4900 Key Twr -Cleveland 44114 **Fx:**479-8780

(440) 838-7600 ..**Nicosia**, Crystal L '04 %Janik & D,LLP -9200 S Hills Blvd -Ste 300 -Cleveland 44147 **Fx:**838-7601

(513) 821-0029 ..**Nidich**, Paul A '74 -1515 Corvallis Av -Cincinnati 45237

(513) 241-2226 ..**Nieberding**, James L '87 (Nieberding & N Co,LPA) -914 Main -Ste 500 -Cincinnati 45202

(513) 241-2226 ..**Nieberding**, James R '63 Nieberding & N Co,LPA -914 Main -Ste 500 -Cincinnati 45202

(513) 352-6700 ..**Nieberding**, Michael J '94 (Thompson H LLP) -312 Walnut -14th Fl -Cincinnati 45202 **Fx:**241-4771

(440) 930-8042 ..**Niederbaumer**, Michael R '00 Wickens HPC&B -35765 Chester Rd -Avon 44011 **Fx:**937-4466

(216) 674-0550 ..**Nieding**, Dean C '83 RC Alkire Co,LPA -6060 Rockside Wds Blvd -Ste 250 -Independence 44131 **Fx:**674-0104

(419) 245-1975 ..**Niedzielski**, Michael J '93 %Pros -555 N Erie -4th Fl -Toledo 43624

(513) 421-5999 ..**Niehaus**, Barron M '76 -914 Main -Ste 500 -Cincinnati 45202

(216) 515-1660 ..**Niehaus**, Bernard H Jr. '55 (Frantz W LLP) -127 Pub Sq -2500 Key Center -Cleveland 44114 **Fx:**515-1650

(419) 517-7000 ..**Niehaus**, Charles D '86 (Kenney & N,Ltd) -5470 Main -Ste 300 -Sylvania 43560 **Fx:**517-7001

(513) 251-4900 ..**Niehaus**, Francis J '78 -4820 Glenway Av -Cincinnati 45238

(216) 515-1660 ..**Niehaus**, James B '83 (Frantz W LLP) -127 Pub Sq -2500 Key Center -Cleveland 44114 **Fx:**515-1650

(513) 421-5999 ..**Niehaus**, Maurice A '41 -914 Main -Ste 500 -Cincinnati 45202

(513) 852-6062 ..**Niehaus**, Roccina S '81 %Wood & L LLP -600 Vine -Ste 2500 -Cincinnati 45202 **Fx:**852-6087

(216) 479-8500 ..**Niehaus**, Stephanie E '02 %Squire S&D LLP -127 Pub Sq -4900 Key Twr -Cleveland 44114 **Fx:**479-8780

(614) 469-9500 ..**Niehoff**, David O '66 Niehoff & S -501 S High -Columbus 43215 **Fx:**224-8708

(513) 621-3394 ..**Niehoff**, Harry C '73 (Peck S&W,LLP) -201 E 5th -Ste 900 -Cincinnati 45202 **Fx:**621-3813

(330) 434-1000 ..**Niekamp**, Christopher J '90 (Bernlohr W,LLP) -23 S Main -3rd Fl -Akron 44308 **Fx:**434-1001

(513) 684-3225 ..**Niekamp**, Thomas J '87 ATF -550 Main -Rm 1516 -Cincinnati 45202

(330) 373-1221 ..**Nielsen**, Dean E '89 First Place Bank -185 E Market -Warren 44481

(513) 665-4888 ..**Nielsen**, Jessica A '04 %J Brinker -414 Walnut -Ste 1220 -Cincinnati 45202

(415) 768-4452 ..**Nielson**, Mark K '80 Bechtel Enterprises,Inc -Bx193965 -San Francisco, CA 94119

(859) 655-7004 ..**Nielson**, Richard M '94 (Nielson & S,PLLC) -639 Wshngtn Av -Ste 200 -Newport, KY 41071

(513) 662-1818 ..**Nieman**, Joseph D '57 %Eckert E&E -3662 Glenmore Av -Bx11027 -Cincinnati 45211

(937) 492-1271 ..**Niemeyer**, Bryan A '97 %Faulkner GK&S,LPA -100 S Main Av -Ste 300 -Sidney 45365 **Fx:**498-1306

(513) 629-1472 ..**Niemeyer**, Jonathan D '98 Wstrn & Sthrn Life Ins -400 Bway -Cincinnati 45202

(440) 576-3667 ..**Niemi**, Ariana E '87 Ashtabula Cnty Pros -25 W Jffrsn -Jefferson 44047

(513) 569-6062 ..**Nienaber**, Donna S '82 TriHealth,Inc -619 Oak -Cincinnati 45206

(513) 558-5653 ..**Nienaber**, Douglas J '02 Univ of Cincinnati -Bx670829 -Cincinnati 45267

(440) 257-8329 ..**Nierenberg**, Alice S '87 -5829 Birchwood Dr -Mentor 44060

(216) 297-1040 ..**Niermann**, Dennis J '81 (D Niermann Co,LPA) -4070 Mayfld Rd -South Euclid 44121

(614) 222-4834 ..**Niermeyer**, Kurt L '89 -243 N 5th -3rd Fl -Columbus 43215

(419) 423-8055 ..**Niese**, Andrew J '03 %Whitman,LLC -101 W Sandusky -Findlay 45840 **Fx:**425-1508

(419) 523-5777 ..**Niese**, Chad C '97 (Niese H&S,LLC) -1800 N Perry -Ste 104 -Ottawa 45875

(419) 523-5777 ..**Niese Hermiller & Schierloh, LLC** -1800 N Perry -Ste 104 -Ottawa 45875

(859) 746-1259 ..**Nighswander**, Nicholas M '84 -7289 Burlngtn Pike -Florence, KY 41042
Nigolian, Nigol Stephen '76 -(Address Unavailable)

(216) 621-9870 ..**Nigro**, Suzanne M '83 -123 W Prospect Av -Ste 250 Van Sweringen Arcade -Cleveland 44115

(734) 827-4217 ..**Nigro-Nieber**, Laura A '83 Std Fed Bank,NA -777 E Esnhwr Pkwy -6th Fl Leg -Ann Arbor, MI 48108

(937) 255-5270 ..**Nihiser**, Nike '86 AFMCLO/JANO -1864 4th -Rm 130A -Wright Patterson AFB 45433

(216) 541-7000 ..**Nikiforovs**, Andris G '91 Lutheran Housing Corp -13944 Euclid Av -Ste 208 -East Cleveland 44112

(216) 621-1530 ..**Niklas**, Christian E '96 %Shapiro & F,LLP -1500 W 3rd -Ste 400 -Cleveland 44113 **Fx:**621-1551

(937) 525-9460 ..**Niles**, Lisa J '93 -14 N Lowry Av -Ste 16 -Springfield 45504 **Fx:**525-9933

(330) 535-5711 ..**Nilges**, Hans A '03 %Brouse M -106 S Main -500 First Natl Twr -Akron 44308 **Fx:**253-8601

(317) 236-2100 ..**Nill**, Andrew J '01 %Ice Miller -One Amer Sq Bx 82001 -Indianapolis, IN 46282

(937) 443-6808 ..**Nilles**, Victoria L '03 %Thompson H LLP -2000 Cthse Plz NE -Bx8801 -Dayton 45401 **Fx:**443-6635

(330) 384-5624 ..**Nilsson**, Nils E '86 OH Edison Co -76 S Main -Akron 44308

(216) 787-3030 ..**Nimrick**, Sandra L '89 Atty Gen -615 W Superior Av -11th Fl
-Cleveland 44113 **Fx:**787-3480

(216) 231-6121 ..**Nimrod**, Alfred F '57 -Bx10051 -Cleveland 44110
Nims, Ronald K '82 -10172 Windsor Way -Powell 43065

(216) 363-4500 ..**Ninneman**, Sheila M '89 Benesch FC&A LLP -200 Pub Sq
-Ste 2300 -Cleveland 44114 **Fx:**363-4588

(614) 227-2700 ..**Ninos**, Helen M '80 United Way -360 S 3rd -Columbus 43215

(216) 623-0150 ..**Nintcheff**, Peter C '99 %Roetzel & A,LPA -1375 E 9th
-One Cleve Ctr 9th Fl -Cleveland 44114 **Fx:**623-0134

(513) 772-7245 ..**Nippert**, Alfred K Jr. '76 (Nippert & N) -11 Vllg Sq
-Cincinnati 45246 **Fx:**772-7245

(513) 772-7245 ..**Nippert & Nippert** -11 Vllg Sq -Cincinnati 45246 **Fx:**772-7245

(614) 777-3420 ..**Nisbet**, Rebecca J '82 Gates McDonald & Co -3455 Mill Run Dr
-MR-09-06 -Hilliard 43026

(440) 247-6800 ..**Nischwitz**, Jeffrey L '84 -2080 Farmngtn Turn -Cleveland 44145

(513) 455-7600 ..**Nishizu**, Mikio '00 (Greenebaum D&M PLLC) -255 E 5th
-2800 Chemed Ctr -Cincinnati 45202 **Fx:**455-8500

(614) 225-4791 ..**Nissl**, Colleen K '75 Borden,Inc -180 E Broad -Columbus 43215

(330) 451-7305 ..**Nist**, David R '92 Stark Cnty Fam Ct -110 Central Plz S -Ste 601
-Canton 44702

(419) 247-1500 ..**Nitschke**, Drew A '00 %Stockwell & C,LPA -One Seagate
-Ste 1610 -Toledo 43604 **Fx:**247-1575

(440) 838-7600 ..**Nitschke**, Kathleen A '01 %Janik & D,LLP -9200 S Hills Blvd
-Ste 300 -Cleveland 44147 **Fx:**838-7601

(216) 381-0011 ..**Nittskoff**, David '70 Nittskoff & Co LPA -4491 Mayfld Rd
-South Euclid 44121 **Fx:**274-6278

(330) 643-3550 ..**Nitzsche**, Deborah A '90 Industrial Commssn of OH -161 S High
-Ste 301 -Akron 44308

(202) 861-1802 ..**Nix**, Clayton J '94 %Epstein B&G,PC -1227 25th NW -Ste 700
-Washington, DC 20037

(419) 337-5065 ..**Nixon**, Carrie J '00 %Barber KS&R -124 N Fulton
-Wauseon 43567 **Fx:**337-1136

(513) 695-1781 ..**Nixon**, Corwin K Jr. '99 Warren Cnty Pros -500 Justice Dr
-Lebanon 45036 **Fx:**695-2962
Nixon, James C '85 -1317 W 104th -Cleveland 44102

(440) 781-8440 ..**Nixon**, Patrick R '81 -21330 Ctr Ridge Rd -Ste 8
-Rocky River 44116

(216) 781-1212 ..**Noall**, Nancy A '81 (Walter & H LLP) -1301 E 9th -Ste 3500
-Cleveland 44114 **Fx:**575-0911

(513) 665-3500 ..**Nobbe**, Michelle L '01 %Freund F&A -105 E 4th -Ste 1400
-Cincinnati 45202 **Fx:**665-3503

(440) 838-8800 ..**Nobil**, Steven M '72 (Millisor & N Co,LPA) -9150 S Hills Blvd
-Ste 300 -Cleveland 44147 **Fx:**838-8805

(614) 529-8600 ..**Nobile**, James E '92 (Nobile N&T,LLC) -4511 Cemetery Rd -Ste B
-Hilliard 43026 **Fx:**529-8656

(614) 529-8600 ..**Nobile**, Martin C '94 %Nobile N&T,LLC -4511 Cemetery Rd -Ste B
-Hilliard 43026 **Fx:**529-8656

(614) 529-8600 ..**Nobile Needleman & Thompson, LLC** -4511 Cemetery Rd
-Ste B -Hilliard 43026 **Fx:**529-8656

(614) 575-1188 ..**Nobile Needleman & Thompson, LLC** -5300 E Main -Ste 109
-Columbus 43213

(614) 222-4220 ..**Nobile Needleman & Thompson, LLC** -341 S 3rd -Ste 11
-Columbus 43215

(440) 886-3000 ..**Nobili**, David L '71 Leary SN&L -5579 Pearl Rd -Ste 203
-Parma 44129 **Fx:**886-3171

(419) 243-6281 ..**Noble**, Catherine H '78 (Shindler NH&S,LLP) -300 Mad Av
-Ste 1200 -Toledo 43604 **Fx:**243-0129

(216) 781-1212 ..**Noble**, David J '68 (Walter & H LLP) -1301 E 9th -Ste 3500
-Cleveland 44114 **Fx:**575-0911
Noble, Deborah L '97 -(Address Unavailable)

(419) 394-7441 ..**Noble**, Edward S '47 (Noble M&M) -146 E Spring -Saint
Marys 45885 **Fx:**394-7694

(740) 283-4529 ..**Noble**, Frank W Jr. '95 %D Scarpone & Assoc -2021 Sunset Blvd
-Steubenville 43952

(419) 427-1355 ..**Noble**, John D '61 -101 Crystal Av -Findlay 45840

(216) 586-3939 ..**Noble**, Josephine S '04 %Jones D -901 Lakeside Av
-Cleveland 44114 **Fx:**579-0212

(419) 394-7441 ..**Noble**, Kraig E '74 (Noble M&M) -146 E Spring -Saint Marys 45885
Fx:394-7694

(614) 469-3254 ..**Noble**, Michele L '00 %Thompson H LLP -10 W Broad -Ste 700
-Columbus 43215 **Fx:**469-3361

(419) 394-7441 ..**Noble Montague & Moul** -146 E Spring -Saint Marys 45885
Fx:394-7694

(740) 474-5437 ..**Noble**, Ricky D '93 CSEA -110 Isl Rd -Bx439 -Circleville 43113

(614) 228-2678 ..**Noble**, Robert D '88 Matan G&W -261 S Front -Columbus 43215

(216) 451-8655 ..**Noble**, Scott A '88 Electrolizing Corp -1325 E 152nd
-Cleveland 44112

(419) 679-6050 ..**Noble-Haggy**, Laura L '01 -2834 Floex Dr -Toledo 43615

(419) 732-3145 ..**Noblitt**, Larry L '68 (Noblitt & B LPA) -318 Madison
-Port Clinton 43452 **Fx:**734-2123

(440) 350-2683 ..**Nocero**, Patricia A '80 Lake Cnty Pros -105 Main -Bx490
-Painesville 44077 **Fx:**350-2585

(440) 244-7374 ..**Nocjar**, David E '73 Lorain Natl Bank -457 Bway -Lorain 44052
Fx:245-4511

(330) 769-4470 ..**Noderer**, Eric W '94 -179 Center -Seville 44273

(602) 542-4250 ..**Nodes**, Dwight D '86 Arizona Corp Comm -1200 W Wshngtn
-Phoenix, AZ 85007

(419) 327-4303 ..**Noe**, Bernadette R '00 OfCnsl Wise & D,Ltd -151 N Mich -Ste 333
-Toledo 43624 **Fx:**327-4302

(513) 381-7333 ..**Noe**, Charles E '77 -2430 Cntrl Pkwy -Cincinnati 45214

(614) 466-0194 ..**Noel**, Gerald T Jr. '94 Legis Srvc Commssn -77 S High -Columbus
43215

(614) 469-3285 ..**Noel**, Mark A '03 %Thompson H LLP -10 W Broad -Ste 700
-Columbus 43215 **Fx:**469-3361

(513) 579-6400 ..**Noel**, W Keith '88 (Keating M&K PLL) -1 E 4th -1400 Provident Twr
-Cincinnati 45202 **Fx:**579-6457

(614) 834-1515 ..**Noethlich**, Keith A '77 -692 N Hill Rd -Pickerington 43147

(614) 857-4383 ..**Noga**, Ronald B '74 %Weltman W&R Co,LPA -175 S 3rd -Ste 900
-Columbus 43215 **Fx:**222-2193

(304) 723-1400 ..**Nogay**, Joseph G '85 (Sellitti N&M) -3125 Penn Av -Ste 7 -Bx2540
-Weirton, WV 26062

(304) 723-1400 ..**Nogay**, Michael E '84 (Sellitti N&M) -3125 Penn Av -Ste 7 -Bx2540
-Weirton, WV 26062

(419) 422-1887 ..**Noggle**, Michael C '86 -101 W Sandusky -Ste 200C
-Findlay 45840

(513) 243-1457 ..**Nogueira**, Mark W '98 GE Aircraft Engines -One Neumann Way
-Mail Drop F125 -Cincinnati 45215

(330) 742-0572 ..**Nohra**, Jude J '97 Home Savings & Loan Co -275 Fed Pl W
-Youngstown 44503

(330) 253-5454 ..**Nolan**, Chris T '73 (Perantinides & N Co,LPA) -80 S Summit
-300 Courtyard Sq -Akron 44308

(419) 586-2024 ..**Nolan**, Gary L '80 -445 Johnson Av -Celina 45822

(513) 481-8444 ..**Nolan**, Gregory M '78 -3505 Glenmore Av -Cheviot 45211

(513) 579-0080 ..**Nolan**, James P '91 %Smith R&S Co,LPA -1014 Vine -Ste 2350
-Cincinnati 45202 **Fx:**579-0222

(513) 272-3000 ..**Nolan**, John J '56 -7754 Camargo Rd -Ste 12 -Cincinnati 45243

(618) 262-7495 ..**Nolan**, John M '79 -Bx1055 -Mount Carmel, IL 62863

(513) 421-6630 ..**Nolan**, Joshua J '04 %Lindhorst & D Co,LPA -312 Walnut
-Ste 2300 -Cincinnati 45202
Nolan, Kelley T '03 -(Address Unavailable)
Nolan, Laura E '94 -(Address Unavailable)

(440) 329-5389 ..**Nolan**, Michael S '72 Lorain Cnty Pros -225 Court -3rd Fl -Elyria
44035

(440) 282-1616 ..**Nolan**, Quentin J '74 Q Nolan Co,LPA
-1700 Cooper Foster Park Rd -Lorain 44053

(937) 228-7104 ..**Nolan Sprowl Smith & Finke** -40 N Main -Ste 1812
-Dayton 45423 **Fx:**226-1945

(740) 753-1961 ..**Nolan**, T Michael '69 (M Nolan Co,LPA) -55 W Wshngtn
-Nelsonville 45764 **Fx:**753-3943
Nolan, Timothy P '84 -7754 Camargo Rd -12 -Cincinnati 45243

(614) 365-2700 ..**Nolan**, William A '89 (Squire S&D LLP) -41 S High
-1300 Huntngtn Ctr -Columbus 43215 **Fx:**365-2499

(216) 583-3688 ..**Nolan**, William G '96 Ernst & Young LLP -925 Euclid Av -Ste 1300
-Cleveland 44115

(937) 222-1090 ..**Noland**, Thomas R '70 (Statman HS&E LLC) -110 N Main
-Ste 1520 -Dayton 45402 **Fx:**222-1046

(614) 469-2999 ..**Nolder**, Steven A '87 Fed Pub Def -10 W Broad -Ste 1020
-Columbus 43215

(513) 948-2782 ..**Nolen**, Kay C '82 Drake Ctr Inc -151 W Galbraith Rd -CK3-220
-Cincinnati 45216
Nolfi, Edward A '83 -4965 State Route 14 -Ravenna 44266

(216) 621-0150 ..**Nolfi**, Gregory M '77 (Hahn L&P LLP) -3300 BP Twr/200 Pub Sq
-Ste 3300 -Cleveland 44114 **Fx:**241-2824

(330) 471-4363 ..**Nolin**, David B '91 Timken Co -1835 Dueber Av SW -GNE-03
-Bx6928 -Canton 44706

(419) 874-3536 ..**Noll**, Todd H '82 (Leatherman WD&H) -353 Elm
-Perrysburg 43551 **Fx:**874-3899

(419) 245-2740 ..**Nolte**, Lynne R '83 Industrial Commssn of OH -One Govt Ctr
-Ste 1500 -Toledo 43604

(330) 673-1535 ..**Nome**, William A '76 (Arthur & N) -1325 S Water -Kent 44240

(419) 241-6000 ..**Nooney**, James F '66 (Eastman & S Ltd) -1 Seagate -24th Fl
-Bx10032 -Toledo 43699 **Fx:**247-1777

(216) 514-9500 ..**Norchi**, Kevin M '86 Norchi & Assoc,LLC -23240 Chagrin Blvd
-Ste 600 -Beachwood 44122

(216) 781-5470 ..**Norcross**, Scott A '01 %Ziegler M&M LLP -925 Euclid Av
-2020 Huntngtn Bldg -Cleveland 44115 **Fx:**781-0714

(419) 443-9500 ..**Nord**, Kent D '93 -29 S Wshngtn -Bx340 -Tiffin 44883

(304) 529-2868 ..**Nord**, Steven K '85 (Offutt F&N) -949 3rd Av -Ste 300 -Bx2868
-Huntington, WV 25728 **Fx:**529-2999

(419) 447-2521 ..**Nordholt**, James S Jr. '74 Supance & H -84-88 S Wshngtn -Bx767
-Tiffin 44883 **Fx:**447-2310

(859) 491-9991 ..**Nordloh**, Christopher S '94 -28 W 5th -Covington, KY 41011

(513) 585-6453 ..**Nordlund**, Christa F '91 Hlth Allnce-Grtr Cincinnati
-3200 Burnet Av -Alliance Business Ctr -Cincinnati 45229

(614) 523-7506 ..**Nordman**, Eric R '80 -90 E Cllg Av -Westerville 43081

(419) 281-0171 ..**Nordstrom**, Kenneth J '46 (Nordstrom & L) -34 W 2nd -Bx366
-Ashland 44805

(419) 281-0171 ..**Nordstrom & Locke** -34 W 2nd -Bx366 -Ashland 44805

(937) 223-3001 ..**Nordstrom**, P Christian '95 %Jenks P&O Co,LPA -10 N Ludlow
-Ste 901 -Dayton 45402 **Fx:**223-3103

(614) 227-2000 ..**Nordstrom**, Robert J '56 OfCnsl Porter WM&A LLP -41 S High
-Columbus 43215 **Fx:**227-2100

(216) 479-8500 ..**Norfus**, Natalie E '04 %Squire S&D LLP -127 Pub Sq -4900 Key
Twr -Cleveland 44114 **Fx:**479-8780

(614) 224-0933 ..**Norman**, Arthur S '89 Frost & M Co,LPA -400 S 5th -Ste 301
-Columbus 43215

(614) 237-8050 ..**Norman**, Craig A '83 -4181 E Main -Columbus 43213

(216) 631-7774 ..**Norman**, Dennis O '69 -11216 Lk Av -Ste 700 -Cleveland 44102

(216) 241-5310 ..**Norman**, Forrest A III '92 (Gallagher SF&N) -1501 Euclid Av
-6th Fl -Cleveland 44115 **Fx:**241-1608

(216) 241-5310 ..**Norman**, Forrest A Jr. '54 OfCnsl Gallagher SF&N -1501 Euclid Av
-6th Fl -Cleveland 44115 **Fx:**241-1608

(410) 786-6256 ..**Norman**, Gary C '00 HCFA Centers -7500 Security Blvd
-Baltimore, MD 21244

(614) 464-6400 ..**Norman**, Jonathan M '76 (Vorys SS&P LLP) -52 E Gay -Bx1008
-Columbus 43216 **Fx:**464-6350

(330) 297-2241 ..**Norman**, Kelli Kay '97 Portage Cnty Cmn Pleas Ct -203 W Main
-Ravenna 44266

(513) 723-4000 ..**Norman**, Mark A '83 (Vorys SS&P LLP) -221 E 4th
-Ste 2000 Atrium Two -Bx0236 -Cincinnati 45201 **Fx:**723-4056

(216) 443-7800 ..**Norman**, Matthew T '99 Cuyahoga Cnty Pros -1200 Ontario -8th Fl
-Cleveland 44113 **Fx:**698-2270

(614) 246-2508 ..**Norman**, Nicole F '89 Rockbridge Cptl Inc -191 W Nationwide Blvd
-Ste 600 -Columbus 43215

(740) 654-9098 ..**Norman**, Roger H '70 -3265 Wheeling Rd NE -Lancaster 43130

(216) 566-2415 ..**Normington**, Dale A '69 Sherwin-Williams Co
-101 Prospect Av NW -Cleveland 44115

(937) 443-6815 ..**Norris**, Allen R '83 (Thompson H LLP) -2000 Cthse Plz NE
-Bx8801 -Dayton 45401 **Fx:**443-6635

(330) 644-0706 ..**Norris**, Andrea L '85 (Norris & N) -4367 State Rd -Akron 44319
Fx:645-1970

(513) 665-4040 ..**Norris**, Daniel W '87 DW Norris Co,LPA -2245 Gilbert Av -Ste 205
-Cincinnati 45206

(215) 250-1821 .. **Norris,** James A '76 Commonwealth of PA -220 Ferry
-Easton, PA 18042

(740) 397-4040 .. **Norris,** James R '76 %Critchfield C&J Ltd -10 S Gay
-Mount Vernon 43050 **Fx:**397-6775

(614) 792-5555 .. **Norris,** Jeffrey C '96 Standley Law Grp LLP -495 Metro Pl S
-Ste 210 -Dublin 43017 **Fx:**792-5536

(614) 757-7426 .. **Norris,** Jennifer R '96 Cardinal Hlth -7000 Cardinal Pl
-Dublin 43017

(937) 495-4341 .. **Norris,** Patricia C '87 Mead Corp -Cthse Plz NE -Dayton 45463

(330) 644-0706 .. **Norris,** Randolph C Jr. '53 (Norris & N) -4367 State Rd
-Akron 44319 **Fx:**645-1970

(614) 464-6400 .. **North,** Chris J '80 (Vorys SS&P LLP) -52 E Gay -Bx1008
-Columbus 43216 **Fx:**464-6350

(801) 359-6862 .. **North,** Edwin M '74 -1517 E Military Way
-Salt Lake City, UT 84103

North, Pricilla Kress '02 -2912 Clifton Rd -Columbus 43221

(614) 227-2000 .. **North,** Scott E '84 (Porter WM&A LLP) -41 S High
-Columbus 43215 **Fx:**227-2100

(740) 653-4259 .. **Northness,** Robert C '87 Fairfield Cnty Pros -201 S Broad -4th Fl
-Lancaster 43130

(614) 227-2000 .. **Northrop,** David E '73 OfCnsl Porter WM&A LLP -41 S High
-Columbus 43215 **Fx:**227-2100

(614) 291-7306 .. **Northrup,** Judith A '84 -365 W 5th Av -Columbus 43201

(740) 454-2545 .. **Northrup,** Michael A '79 (Micheli BN Co,LPA) -3808 James Ct
-Ste 2 -Bx788 -Zanesville 43702

(937) 293-2141 .. **Nortman,** Tammy C '01 %Holzfaster CM&M -1105 Wilmngtn Av
-Dayton 45420 **Fx:**293-0914

(330) 821-6648 .. **Norton,** Amy J '00 -40 N Arch Av -Alliance 44601 **Fx:**821-7288

(513) 946-9140 .. **Norton,** Barbara L '78 Hamilton Cnty Dom Rltns Ct -800 Bway
-#2-116 -Cincinnati 45202

(216) 696-1133 .. **Norton,** Eric E '99 %Chapman Law Firm Co,LPA
-123 W Prospect Av -Ste 150 -Cleveland 44115

(513) 721-3330 .. **Norton,** Esther M '00 %Robbins KP&T -7 W 7th -Ste 1400
-Cincinnati 45202

(440) 729-8100 .. **Norton,** John F '59 -8251 Mayfld Rd -Chesterland 44026

(216) 566-8200 .. **Norton,** John P '91 Seeley S&E Co LPA -600 Superior Av E
-800 Bank One Ctr -Cleveland 44114 **Fx:**566-0213

(216) 398-4100 .. **Norton,** Margaret M '83 -2424 Broadvw Rd -Cleveland 44109

(216) 566-0064 .. **Norton,** Maura '91 %Armstrong MD&Z -101 Prospect Av W
-1725 The Mdlnd Bldg -Cleveland 44115 **Fx:**566-0224

(216) 621-7292 .. **Norton,** Michele L '02 %S Schreiber & Assoc Co,LPA
-1224 Standard Bldg -1370 Ontario -Cleveland 44113

(216) 586-3939 .. **Norton,** Patrick J '98 %Jones D -901 Lakeside Av
-Cleveland 44114 **Fx:**579-0212

(513) 721-5151 .. **Norton,** Richard L '64 (Katz G&N,LLP) -105 E 4th -4th Fl
-Cincinnati 45202 **Fx:**621-9285

(216) 664-3513 .. **Norton,** Susan L '00 Dept of Law -601 Lakeside Av
-Rm 106 City Hall -Cleveland 44114 **Fx:**664-2663

(419) 893-4880 .. **Norton,** Suzanne Belot '84 (Marsh M Ltd) -204 W Wayne
-Maumee 43537

(330) 675-2521 .. **Norton,** Thomas F '69 %Trumbull Cnty Probate Ct -161 High NW
-Warren 44481

(440) 349-3432 .. **Norwillo,** Vincent T '90 Tradesmen Intl -9760 Shepard Rd
-Macedonia 44056

(513) 381-8213 .. **Norwine,** John C Jr. '76 Cincinnati Bar Assn -225 E 6th -2nd Fl
-Cincinnati 45202 **Fx:**381-0528

(440) 526-8018 .. **Nosan,** Bernard J '73 -Bx275 -Broadview Heights 44147

(614) 228-5151 .. **Nose,** Kevin R '79 -471 E Broad -19th Fl -Columbus 43215

(513) 381-2838 .. **Noser,** Patrick E '02 %Taft S&H LLP -425 Walnut -Ste 1800
-Cincinnati 45202 **Fx:**381-0205

(330) 638-1529 .. **Nosich,** Marty D '03 -143 W Main -Cortland 44410

Noss, Walter W '00 -(Address Unavailable)

(216) 621-8447 .. **Nosse,** Elizabeth A '88 Travelers Custom Case -2261 E 14
-Cleveland 44115

(614) 644-9292 .. **Noteman,** Jennifer L '99 Sup Ct of OH -30 E Broad -2nd Fl
-Columbus 43215 **Fx:**644-4767

(937) 225-7676 .. **Nothstine,** Roberta L '93 Montgomery Cnty Pros -301 W 3rd
-Bx972 -Dayton 45422 **Fx:**225-3470

(330) 643-8550 .. **Nott,** David L '92 Summit Cnty Exec Ofc -175 S Main
-Akron 44308

(614) 466-4395 .. **Nourse,** Steven T '90 Atty Gen -150 E Gay -Columbus 43215
Fx:644-8764

(614) 462-3418 .. **Novack,** Nancy A '88 Franklin Cnty Cmn Pleas Ct -375 S High
-Columbus 43215 **Fx:**462-6292

(614) 802-0150 .. **Novack,** Thomas J '87 (Bean & N) -85 E Wilson Bridge Rd
-Worthington 43085

(216) 443-5842 .. **Novak,** David M '76 Cuyahoga Cnty Juv Ct -2163 E 22nd
-Cleveland 44115

(716) 854-2620 .. **Novak,** Ellen A '83 %Brown & K,LLP -1500 Lbrty Bldg -424 Main
-Buffalo, NY 14202 **Fx:**854-0082

(216) 986-6144 .. **Novak,** Geoffrey '98 -6611 Rockside Rd -Rm 110
-Independence 44131 **Fx:**986-0976

(419) 224-2125 .. **Novak,** Gregory M '72 -128 W High -Lima 45801

(954) 351-1110 .. **Novak,** Henry '88 Coverall NA,Inc -500 Cypress Crk Rd -Ste 580
-Fort Lauderdale, FL 33309

(770) 303-2729 .. **Novak,** James P '85 ZC Sterling Ins Agency,Inc -210 Intrstate N
Pkwy NW -Atlanta, GA 30339

(216) 515-1660 .. **Novak,** Jenifer E '99 Frantz W LLP -127 Pub Sq -2500 Key Center
-Cleveland 44114 **Fx:**515-1650

(419) 241-3580 .. **Novak,** Karen A '84 -316 N Mich -8th Fl -Toledo 43624

(440) 572-3420 .. **Novak,** Karen J '83 (McNamee & Co) -13702 Pearl Rd
-Strongsville 44136 **Fx:**572-9493

(216) 664-4303 .. **Novak,** Katarina K '98 Dept of Law -601 Lakeside Av
-Rm 106 City Hall -Cleveland 44114 **Fx:**664-2663

(740) 681-1770 .. **Novak,** Lawrence J '88 -123 S Broad -Ste 234 -Lancaster 43130

(440) 845-4785 .. **Novak,** Richard P '93 City of Parma -6611 Ridge Rd
-Parma 44129

(216) 781-8700 .. **Novak Robenalt Pavlik & Scharf, LLP** -1660 W 2nd
-Ste 270 Skylight Ofc Twr -Cleveland 44113 **Fx:**781-9227

Novak, Scott J '98 Progressive Ins Co -6300 Wilson Mills Rd
-#N72A -Mayfield Village 44143

(216) 781-8700 .. **Novak,** William J '73 (Novak RP&S,LLP) -1660 W 2nd
-Ste 270 Skylight Ofc Twr -Cleveland 44113 **Fx:**781-9227

(859) 801-5828 .. **Novakov,** Linda S '02 (LS Novakov & Assoc,PLLC)
-653 Stevenson Rd -Erlanger, KY 41018 **Fx:**341-4111

November, Raymond R '62 -(Address Unavailable)

(440) 891-5000 .. **Novick,** Lorne J '00 Cleveland Browns -76 Lou Groza Blvd
-Berea 44017

(937) 436-2606 .. **Novick,** Wayne P '81 -2135 Miamisburg Centervll Rd
-Centerville 45459

(216) 241-6045 .. **Novinc,** Raymond C '76 1st Amer/Midland Tittle -1111 Superior Av
-Ste 700 -Cleveland 44114

(216) 348-0800 .. **Novotney,** George C Jr. '81 (Potts & N) -1370 Ontario -Ste 600
-Cleveland 44113

(216) 615-7319 .. **Nowak,** Dale A '80 (Buckingham D&B,LLP) -1375 E 9th -Ste 1700
-Cleveland 44114 **Fx:**621-5440

(419) 726-2605 .. **Nowak,** James S '76 -4808 N Summit -Toledo 43611

(614) 249-4669 .. **Nowak,** Joseph P '92 SrCnsl Nationwide Ins Co -1 Nationwide Plz
-Columbus 43215

(440) 354-3917 .. **Nowak,** Michael E '87 -7465 Hermitage Rd -Concord 44077

(216) 831-0042 .. **Nowak,** Stephen M '04 %Meyers RF&L LPA -28601 Chagrin Blvd
-Ste 500 -Cleveland 44122 **Fx:**831-0542

(937) 382-0201 .. **Nowel,** Lynne M '95 APA Local 1224 -1435 Rombach Av
-Wilmington 45177

(937) 222-1862 .. **Nowicki,** Griff M '00 -Bx1569 -Dayton 45401

(614) 422-5674 .. **Nowicki,** Ronald C '76 Chase Mortgage Corp -3415 Vision Dr
-Columbus 43219

(614) 462-3194 .. **Nowland,** Mahlon D '78 Franklin Cnty Pub Def -373 S High
-12th Fl -Columbus 43215

(859) 384-4300 .. **Noyes,** Timothy M '98 %A Frohlich,PSC -8660 Haines Dr -Bx396
-Florence, KY 41022

(614) 464-6400 .. **Nuber,** Anna K '04 %Vorys SS&P LLP -52 E Gay -Bx1008
-Columbus 43216 **Fx:**464-6350

(216) 771-4504 .. **Nuccio,** Anthony J '56 -1370 Ontario -Ste 2000 -Cleveland 44113

(513) 241-6748 .. **Nuckols,** Gerald L '79 A Levine -324 Reading Rd
-Cincinnati 45202

(216) 687-7874 .. **Nudelman,** Marc S '90 Medical Mutual -2060 E 9th
-Cleveland 44115

(216) 621-0150 .. **Nudelman,** Sidney '63 Cnsl Hahn L&P LLP -3300 BP Twr/200 Pub
Sq -Ste 3300 -Cleveland 44114 **Fx:**241-2824

(219) 925-3738 .. **Nugen,** John B '94 -221 S Main -Bx6067 -Auburn, IN 46706

(937) 229-8366 .. **Nugent,** Robert L '73 Fifth Third Bk -110 N Main -Dayton 45402
Fx:227-3060

(419) 245-1020 .. **Nugent,** Samuel J '78 %Law Dept -One Govt Ctr -Ste 2250
-Toledo 43604 **Fx:**245-1090

(216) 222-3638 .. **Nukes,** Elizabeth L '96 Natl City Bank -Bx94651 -Cleveland 44101

(330) 379-2727 .. **Nukes,** Sotir S '57 (S Nukes & Assoc) -1 Cascade Plz -12th Fl
-Akron 44308

(440) 204-2150 .. **Nunez,** Gustalo '67 Mun Ct Judge -100 W Erie Av -Lorain 44052

(301) 545-0459 .. **Nunez,** Ralph A '82 -11613 Paramus Dr
-North Potomac, MD 20878

(513) 241-3100 .. **Nunley,** Kerri L '01 %Lerner S&R -120 E 4th -8th Fl
-Cincinnati 45202

(419) 241-6000 .. **Nunn,** David W '91 (Eastman & S Ltd) -1 Seagate -24th Fl
-Bx10032 -Toledo 43699 **Fx:**247-1777

(716) 856-5012 .. **Nunn,** J Roy '88 (Anspach M&N,LLP) -2400 Main Pl Twr
-Buffalo, NY 14202 **Fx:**852-2485

(513) 651-6800 .. **Nunn,** Sandra L '95 (Frost BT LLC) -201 E 5th -2200 PNC Ctr
-Cincinnati 45202 **Fx:**651-6981

(614) 464-6400 .. **Nunnally,** Phillip L '71 OfCnsl Vorys SS&P LLP -52 E Gay
-Bx1008 -Columbus 43216 **Fx:**464-6350

(419) 578-9246 .. **Nunnari,** Jeffrey P '92 -3425 Exec Pkwy -Ste 111 -Toledo 43606

(330) 758-7992 .. **Nunziato,** Carl A '71 -5791 Sharon Dr -Boardman 44512

(216) 502-2000 .. **Nurczyk,** Jean A '01 -815 Superior Av -Ste 1605 -Cleveland 44114

(216) 621-2300 .. **Nurenberg Plevin Heller & McCarthy LPA** -1370 Ontario
-Ste 100 -Cleveland 44113 **Fx:**771-2242

(216) 586-3939 .. **Nurgaliyeva,** Aidana K '04 %Jones D -901 Lakeside Av
-Cleveland 44114 **Fx:**579-0212

(513) 721-3330 .. **Nurre,** Lawrence R '50 OfCnsl Robbins KP&T -7 W 7th -Ste 1400
-Cincinnati 45202

(216) 241-0000 .. **Nusbaum,** Alan H '71 (Miller & N) -25550 Chagrin Blvd -Ste 108
-Beachwood 44122

(740) 702-3100 .. **Nusbaum Ater & Wissler** -72 N Paint -Chillicothe 45601

(419) 255-6070 .. **Nusbaum,** James B '95 (Wittenberg PL&N) -520 Mad Av -Ste 840
-Toledo 43604

(419) 243-1105 .. **Nusbaum,** Melvin G '57 (Lackey NHR&T,LPA) -2 Maritime Plz -3rd
Fl -Toledo 43604

(740) 702-3100 .. **Nusbaum,** Scott W '78 (Nusbaum A&W) -72 N Paint
-Chillicothe 45601

(614) 228-8622 .. **Nusken,** Ralph E '70 -601 S High -Columbus 43215

(216) 241-4100 .. **Nussle,** Herbert L '94 %Keis/G LLP -55 Pub Sq -Ste 800
-Cleveland 44113 **Fx:**771-3111

(614) 572-0048 .. **Nussle,** Patricia A '93 -3149 S Drchstr -Bx21186 -Columbus 43221

(740) 373-4474 .. **Nuzum,** William M III '81 Mun Ct Judge -301 Putnam
-Marietta 45750

Nwabara, Chisara S '85 (C Nwabara Co,LPA) -3347 Central Av
-Cleveland 44115

(614) 246-6173 .. **Nyce,** Kinsley F '82 Nyce Co -1601 W 5th Av -#112
-Columbus 43212

(513) 621-6674 .. **Nye,** Darrin E '02 %Mulvey & M LLC -35 E 7th -Ste 750
-Cincinnati 45202 **Fx:**621-0183

(440) 899-1551 .. **Nye,** John R '89 JD Carney & Assoc,LLC -2001 Crocker Rd
-440 Gemini Twr II -Westlake 44145

(330) 644-0325 .. **Nye,** William B '60 -4538 Lahm Dr -Akron 44319

(419) 222-4100 .. **Nyers,** Athena J '92 -119 N West -Ste 102 -Lima 45801

(616) 396-3023 .. **Nyhof,** Jaron J '96 %Warner N&J LLP -85 E 8th -Ste 310
-Holland, MI 49423 **Fx:**494-3523

(513) 684-3711 .. **Nyktas,** Anthony W '71 US Atty -221 E 4th -Ste 400
-Cincinnati 45202 **Fx:**684-6385

(216) 443-6350 .. **Nykulak,** Nick A '03 8th Dist Ct of Appls -1 Lakeside Av -#202
-Cleveland 44113 **Fx:**443-2044

(937) 223-1011 .. **Nystrom,** Richard A '88 -120 W 2nd -Ste 1502 -Dayton 45402

(440) 746-1000 .. **Oakar,** Ann C '01 %Oakar & R -1000 W Wallings Rd -Ste A
-Broadview Heights 44147

(440) 746-1000 .. **Oakar,** James L '62 (Oakar & R) -1000 W Wallings Rd -Ste A
-Broadview Heights 44147

(440) 746-1000 ..**Oakar & Ruffa** -1000 W Wallings Rd -Ste A
-Broadview Heights 44147

(216) 431-5300 ..**Oakley**, David G '97 %Kramer & Assoc,LPA -3214 Prospect Av
-Cleveland 44115

(740) 593-5046 ..**Oakley**, Gregg V '81 Athens Cnty CSEA -Bx37 -The Plains 45780

(740) 753-3232 ..**Oakley**, Jack V '73 -17727 N Akron Av -Bx250 -Buchtel 45716

(513) 684-3711 ..**Oakley**, Timothy D '88 US Atty -221 E 4th -Ste 400
-Cincinnati 45202 Fx:684-6385

(513) 946-3872 ..**Oakley-Everson**, Karen '00 Hamilton Cnty Pub Def -230 E 9th
-3rd Fl -Cincinnati 45202 Fx:946-3707

(330) 678-5525 ..**Oates**, Ralph L '70 -217 E Main -Kent 44240

(216) 662-0430 ..**O'Bannon**, Pamela C '90 N Randall Mayors Ct -21937 Miles Rd
-North Randall 44128

(216) 431-4500 ..**Obed**, Debra A '88 Cuyahoga Cnty Pros -3955 Euclid Av
-Jane Edna Hunter Bldg -Cleveland 44115 Fx:431-4113

(216) 622-8200 ..**Oberdorff**, Marc L '80 (Calfee H&G LLP) -800 Superior Av
-Ste 1400 -Cleveland 44114 Fx:241-0816

(513) 977-8200 ..**Oberhaus**, Geoffrey L '98 %Dinsmore & S LLP -255 E 5th
-Ste 1900 -Cincinnati 45202 Fx:977-8141

Oberheu, Kristin M '99 -2229 Rexford Rd -Apt E
-Charlotte, NC 28211

(330) 725-4929 ..**Oberholtzer Filous & Lesiak** -39 Pub Sq -Ste 201 -Bx220
-Medina 44258 Fx:723-4929

(330) 725-4929 ..**Oberholtzer**, John C '67 (Oberholtzer F&L) -39 Pub Sq -Ste 201
-Bx220 -Medina 44258 Fx:723-4929

(330) 453-7874 ..**Oberholtzer**, Matheuw W '89 Oberholtzer & O
-116 Cleveland Av NW -Ste 650 -Canton 44702

(614) 249-0617 ..**Oberholtzer**, Todd L '95 %G Grubler -280 N High -Ste 810
-Columbus 43215 Fx:249-8752

(513) 381-2838 ..**Oberklein**, Daniel F '00 %Taft S&H LLP -425 Walnut -Ste 1800
-Cincinnati 45202 Fx:381-0205

Oberle, Daniel W '01 -(Address Unavailable)

(614) 462-2227 ..**Oberle**, John H '01 %Schottenstein Z&D -250 West -Bx165020
-Columbus 43216 Fx:462-5135

Oberle, Lori Kay '01 -(Address Unavailable)

(614) 249-7111 ..**Oberlin**, Janet S '04 Nationwide Ins Co -1 Nationwide Plz
-Columbus 43215

(419) 249-7100 ..**Oberlin**, Phillip S '59 OfCnsl Marshall & M,LLC -Four Seagate
-8th Fl -Toledo 43604 Fx:249-7151

(513) 651-6800 ..**Oberschmidt**, E Richard '78 (Frost BT LLC) -201 E 5th
-2200 PNC Ctr -Cincinnati 45202 Fx:651-6981

(330) 471-3937 ..**Oberster**, Alan C '93 Timken Co -1835 Dueber Av SW
-Canton 44706

(614) 798-1012 ..**Obert**, Carl R '95 Ernst & Young LLP -9488 Avmore Ct
-Dublin 43017

(440) 542-1900 ..**Obert**, Lisa M '87 (Gerstenslager & O Co) -6500 Crkside Trl -Solon
44139

(614) 464-6400 ..**Obetz**, Robin R '64 OfCnsl Vorys SS&P LLP -52 E Gay -Bx1008
-Columbus 43216 Fx:464-6350

(216) 586-3939 ..**Oblander**, R Jason '00 %Jones D -901 Lakeside Av
-Cleveland 44114 Fx:579-0212

(740) 345-6961 ..**Obora**, John H '85 -21 W Church -Ste 201 -Newark 43055

(216) 696-4421 ..**Obral**, Mark J '84 -1370 Ontario -Ste 1520 -Cleveland 44113
Fx:696-3228

(330) 376-1717 ..**O'Brien**, Ann M '91 (Davis & Y) -One Cascade Plz -Ste 800
-Akron 44308

(216) 443-6350 ..**O'Brien**, Bridget M '01 8th Dist Ct of Appls -1 Lakeside Av -#202
-Cleveland 44113 Fx:443-2044

(614) 644-7233 ..**O'Brien**, Carol A '83 Atty Gen -150 E Gay -Columbus 43215
Fx:728-9327

(440) 285-3511 ..**O'Brien**, Casey P '00 (Petersen & I) -401 South -Chardon 44024
Fx:285-3363

(216) 241-3377 ..**O'Brien**, Cheryl A '89 (Mezacapa & O Co,LPA) -55 Pub Sq
-Ste 2200 -Cleveland 44113

(859) 426-5700 ..**O'Brien**, Daniel B '96 -1984 Crescent Ter
-Crescent Springs, KY 41017

(937) 228-6001 ..**O'Brien**, Daniel J '61 -131 N Ludlow -Ste 1210 -Dayton 45402

(440) 838-8800 ..**O'Brien**, Daniel P '84 Millisor & N Co,LPA -9150 S Hills Blvd
-Ste 300 -Cleveland 44147 Fx:838-8805

(614) 538-0070 ..**O'Brien**, Dennis L '94 (O'Brien Law Firm Co,LPA)
-3366 Riverside Dr -Ste 207 -Columbus 43221

(419) 627-5920 ..**O'Brien**, Erich J '79 Mun Ct Judge -222 Meigs -Sandusky 44870

(216) 241-6602 ..**O'Brien**, George E '86 (Weston HFP&H LLP) -50 Pub Sq
-2500 Trmnl Twr -Cleveland 44113 Fx:621-8369

(216) 241-2838 ..**O'Brien**, Gregory J '94 (Taft S&H LLP) -200 Pub Sq -3500 BP Twr
-Cleveland 44114 Fx:241-3707

(419) 882-0518 ..**O'Brien**, Isobel T '89 (Hunt MD&O) -5808 Monroe -Bx370
-Sylvania 43560

(330) 448-6818 ..**O'Brien**, James A '65 -7337 Warren-Sharon Rd -Bx9
-Brookfield 44403

O'Brien, James E '84 -(Address Unavailable)

(419) 249-7900 ..**OBrien**, Jean M '89 (Robison C&O) -Four SeaGate -9th Fl
-Toledo 43604 Fx:249-7911

(614) 415-1676 ..**O'Brien**, Kathleen M '75 Limited Inc -2 Limited Pkwy
-Columbus 43230

(330) 762-5500 ..**O'Brien**, Kerry M '75 -159 S Main -Ste 423 -Akron 44308

(614) 224-3080 ..**O'Brien**, Kevin J '83 (K O'Brien & Assoc Co,LPA) -995 S High
-Columbus 43206

(216) 696-8700 ..**O'Brien**, Mark S '00 %Kohrman J&K PLL -1375 E 9th
-One Cleve Ctr 20th Fl -Cleveland 44114 Fx:621-6536

(440) 350-3200 ..**O'Brien**, Maryellen '01 Lake Cnty Pub Def -125 E Erie
-Painesville 44077

(304) 233-1022 ..**O'Brien**, Melvin F '94 Dickie M&C -1233 Main -Ste 2002
-Wheeling, WV 26003

(614) 464-6400 ..**O'Brien**, Michael F '93 %Vorys SS&P LLP -52 E Gay -Bx1008
-Columbus 43216 Fx:464-6350

(216) 472-1500 ..**O'Brien**, Michael J '83 (O'Brien Law Firm,LLC) -627 W St Clair Av
-Cleveland 44113 Fx:472-1600

(937) 225-7233 ..**O'Brien**, Mychael P '95 SSA-OHA -110 N Main -Ste 800
-Dayton 45402

(303) 879-6439 ..**O'Brien**, Patric M '88 -Bx770358 -Steamboat Springs, CO 80477

(740) 992-2381 ..**O'Brien**, Patrick H '77 (O'Brien & O) -102½ W Main
-Pomeroy 45769

(734) 854-5605 ..**O'Brien**, Richard E '70 -7043 S Rdgwd Dr -Lambertville, MI 48144

(614) 326-7987 ..**O'Brien**, Robert T '59 -1445 Fishinger Rd -Columbus 43221
Fx:326-7987

(614) 462-3555 ..**O'Brien**, Ronald J '74 Franklin Cnty Pros -373 S High
-Columbus 43215

(330) 675-2426 ..**O'Brien**, Sean J '98 %Trumbull Cnty Pros -160 High NW
-Warren 44481

(419) 841-0881 ..**O'Brien**, Shari L '87 -Bx8774 -Toledo 43623

(330) 434-3000 ..**O'Brien**, Tamara A '92 (Roderick & L) -One Cascade Plz
-Ste 1500 -Akron 44308 Fx:434-9220

(216) 696-5400 ..**O'Brien**, Terence K '88 (Crosby O & Assoc Co,LPA) -55 Pub Sq
-Ste 1475 -Cleveland 44113 Fx:696-2610

(412) 471-6226 ..**O'Brien**, Theresa Boland '94 (McKenna & C,PC)
-436 Blvd of the Allies -Ste 500 -Pittsburgh, PA 15219
Fx:471-6658

(614) 227-2335 ..**O'Brien**, Thomas J '96 OfCnsl Bricker & E LLP -100 S 3rd
-Columbus 43215 Fx:227-2390

O'Brien, Thomas P Jr. '74 -1457 Ida -Cincinnati 45202

(216) 696-1400 ..**O'Brien**, Timothy F '69 -700 W St Clair Av -Ste 210
-Cleveland 44113 Fx:696-4919

(513) 891-1066 ..**O'Brien**, William F '80 Winegardner & Hammons,Inc
-4243 Hunt Rd -Cincinnati 45242

(941) 575-1460 ..**O'Brien**, William S '80 -5058 La Costa Isl Ct
-Punta Gorda, FL 33950

(850) 386-4698 ..**O'Brien**, William S '72 -205 E Lakeshr Dr -Tallahassee, FL 32312

(248) 641-7600 ..**Obringer**, Robert A '99 Garan LM&S PC -1111 W Long Lk Rd
-Ste 300 -Troy, MI 48098

(440) 248-7906 ..**Obringer**, Timothy R '91 %Mazanec R&R Co,LPA
-34305 Solon Rd -Ste 100 -Cleveland 44139 Fx:248-8861

(614) 424-5400 ..**O'Bryan**, Daniel W '80 -505 King Av -Columbus 43201

(216) 566-5686 ..**O'Bryan**, Keely J '99 %Thompson H LLP -127 Pub Sq
-3900 Key Ctr -Cleveland 44114 Fx:566-5800

(216) 241-2838 ..**O'Bryan**, Stephen M '69 (Taft S&H LLP) -200 Pub Sq
-3500 BP Twr -Cleveland 44114 Fx:241-3707

(440) 930-4001 ..**O'Bryon**, Margaret A '93 Baumgartner & O
-5455 Detroit Rd (Rte 254) -Sheffield Village 44054 Fx:934-7205

(330) 762-7377 ..**Oby**, Thomas M '87 (Oldham & D) -195 S Main -Ste 300
-Akron 44308 Fx:762-7390

(330) 489-3395 ..**O'Byrne**, Eugene D IV '98 Pros -218 Cleveland Av SW -Bx24218
-Canton 44702

(614) 463-9441 ..**O'Callaghan**, Michael J '90 (Shumaker L&K,LLP) -41 S High
-Ste 2210 -Columbus 43215 Fx:463-1108

(440) 888-4888 ..**Ocampo**, Benjamin T '87 -5509 Ridge Rd -Parma 44129

(614) 466-7900 ..**O'Carroll**, Leah V Basobas '02 Atty Gen -30 E Broad
-Columbus 43215 Fx:466-2437

(330) 629-9030 ..**Ocasio**, Miriam M '00 -1032 Boardman-Canfld Rd
-Youngstown 44512 Fx:629-9036

(216) 464-7656 ..**Occhionero**, Michael J '74 (MJ Occhionero Co,LPA)
-28601 Chagrin Blvd -Ste 210 -Beachwood 44122

(614) 249-1941 ..**Ocheltree**, Alan J '01 KPMG LLP -191 W Nationwide Blvd
-Ste 500 -Columbus 43215

(330) 672-2982 ..**Ochmann**, David L '92 Kent State Univ-Exec Ofcs -2nd Fl Library
-Bx5190 -Kent 44242

(330) 208-1000 ..**Ochmann**, Patricia M '01 %Vorys SS&P LLP -106 S Main
-First Natl Twr -Akron 44308

(814) 461-5827 ..**Ochocki**, Gregory J '94 Rent-Way,Inc -One RentWay Pl
-Erie, PA 16505

(216) 830-2229 ..**Ochs**, Robert C '89 (R Ochs Co,LPA) -55 Pub Sq -Ste 1616
-Cleveland 44113 Fx:589-0180

(740) 384-2111 ..**Ochsenbein**, Mark A '77 OfCnsl Oths H&M -16 E Bway -Bx309
-Wellston 45692

(330) 376-2700 ..**Ochsenhirt**, Timothy J '71 (Roetzel & A,LPA) -222 S Main
-Akron 44308 Fx:376-4577

Ochu, Ann M '83 -4349 Eber Rd -Monclova 43542

(312) 832-4400 ..**Ockene**, Paul Bradford '03 Lovells -333 N Wabash -Ste 900
-Chicago, IL 60611

(330) 670-7300 ..**Ockerman**, Michael '91 %Hanna C&P,LLP -3737 Embssy Pkwy
-Bx5521 -Akron 44334 Fx:670-0977

(216) 831-4935 ..**Ockington**, William J '74 -29425 Chagrin Blvd -Ste 305
-Pepper Pike 44122

(216) 831-8838 ..**Ockner**, Benjamin J '86 (Berns O&G,LLC) -3733 Park East Dr
-Ste 200 -Beachwood 44122 Fx:464-4489

(216) 252-2936 ..**Ockuly**, Jane C '89 -4697 W 130th -Cleveland 44135

(513) 977-8200 ..**O'Connell**, Brian J '92 (Dinsmore & S LLP) -255 E 5th -Ste 1900
-Cincinnati 45202 Fx:977-8141

(419) 675-1297 ..**O'Connell**, Colleen M '90 Pros -111 W Franklin -Bx250
-Kenton 43326

(419) 249-7100 ..**O'Connell**, David L '84 (Marshall & M,LLC) -Four Seagate -8th Fl
-Toledo 43604 Fx:249-7151

(513) 579-1500 ..**O'Connell**, Edward M Jr. '73 (Buechner HOM&H Co,LPA)
-105 E 4th -Ste 300 -Cincinnati 45202 Fx:977-4361

(513) 621-6464 ..**O'Connell**, Gerald F Jr. '84 (Graydon H&R LLP) -511 Walnut
-1900 Fifth Third Ctr -Cincinnati 45202 Fx:651-3836

(513) 421-6630 ..**O'Connell**, James L '58 Lindhorst & D Co,LPA -312 Walnut
-Ste 2300 -Cincinnati 45202

(317) 656-6905 ..**O'Connell**, John K '83 (Deloitte & Touche) -111 Monument Cir
-Ste 2000 -Indianapolis, IN 46204

(419) 247-1500 ..**O'Connell**, Katherine R '84 OfCnsl Stockwell & C,LPA
-One Seagate -Ste 1610 -Toledo 43604 Fx:247-1575

(216) 389-0079 ..**O'Connell**, Martin James '03 -22626 Rye Rd
-Shaker Heights 44122

(216) 928-2200 ..**O'Connell**, Matthew C '83 (Sutter OM&F) -1301 E 9th
-3600 Erievw Twr -Cleveland 44114 Fx:928-4400

(419) 249-7900 ..**O'Connell**, Maurice D '56 OfCnsl Robison C&O -Four SeaGate
-9th Fl -Toledo 43604 Fx:249-7911

(614) 387-6118 ..**O'Connell**, Thomas C '02 Legis Srvc Commssn -77 S High
-Columbus 43215

(614) 461-6066 ..**O'Connell**, Thomas J '85 (Abramson & O,LLC) -695 Bryden Rd
-Columbus 43205 Fx:461-4524

(937) 225-4168 ..**O'Connell**, Timothy N '80 Montgomery Cnty Cmn Pleas Ct
-41 N Perry -Rm 3 -Dayton 45422

(330) 543-4732 ..**O'Connell-Burton**, Kathleen M '80 -7781 Lori Ln -Aurora 44202

(614) 227-2000 ..**O'Conner**, Adele E '76 (Porter WM&A LLP) -41 S High
-Columbus 43215 Fx:227-2100

(513) 241-7111 .. **O'Connor Acciani & Levy Co, LPA** -1014 Vine -22nd Fl
-Cincinnati 45202 **Fx:**241-7197

(216) 771-6633 .. **O'Connor**, Bryan P '96 (Goldstein & O) -526 Superior Av E
-Ste 1040 Leader Bldg -Cleveland 44114 **Fx:**771-7559

(214) 340-3567 .. **O'Connor**, Colleen A '83 -9131 Clayco Dr -Dallas, TX 75243
O'Connor, Debra L '95 -1010 Orchrd Ln
-Broadview Heights 44147

(216) 241-0033 .. **O'Connor**, Donald J '60 -614 Superior Av NW -820 Rckfllr Bldg
-Cleveland 44113

(937) 427-1367 .. **O'Connor**, Gregory B '04 %McNamee & M,PLL -2625 Cmmns
Blvd -Beavercreek 45431 **Fx:**427-1369

(216) 687-1311 .. **O'Connor**, James Jr. '94 %Reminger & R -101 Prospect Av W
-1400 Mdlnd Bldg -Cleveland 44115 **Fx:**687-1841
O'Connor, John P '67 -(Address Unavailable)

(513) 425-2669 .. **O'Connor**, John P Jr. '90 AK Steel Corp -703 Curtis
-Middletown 45043

(330) 643-2227 .. **O'Connor**, Kandi Sue '97 Summit Cnty Cmmn Pleas Ct
-209 S High -Akron 44308

(513) 621-2000 .. **O'Connor**, Kathleen A '03 %Seasongood & M -414 Walnut
-Ste 300 -Cincinnati 45208

(419) 252-5523 .. **O'Connor**, Kevin M '01 HCR ManorCare Inc -333 N Summit
-Toledo 43604

(216) 736-7213 .. **O'Connor**, Kevin T '77 (Kohrman J&K PLL) -1375 E 9th
-One Cleve Ctr 20th Fl -Cleveland 44114 **Fx:**621-6536

(513) 793-5297 .. **O'Connor**, Michael J '89 (Monnie & O Co,LPA)
-8035 Hosbrook Rd -Ste 200 -Cincinnati 45236

(513) 241-7111 .. **O'Connor**, Michael P '79 (O'Connor A&L Co,LPA) -1014 Vine
-22nd Fl -Cincinnati 45202 **Fx:**241-7197
O'Connor, Michael R '78 -Drwr1038 -Cincinnati 45201

(614) 751-2650 .. **O'Connor**, Robert F '79 Nationwide Ins -620 Morrison Rd
-Gahanna 43230 **Fx:**751-2350

(614) 621-1500 .. **O'Connor**, Thomas E Jr. '67 (Calfee H&G LLP) -21 E State
-1100 Fifth Third Ctr -Columbus 43215 **Fx:**621-0010

(216) 360-3737 .. **O'Daire**, Lacie L '03 %Persky S&A Co,LPA -25101 Chagrin Blvd
-Ste 350 Signature Sq II -Beachwood 44122 **Fx:**593-0921

(312) 321-4200 .. **Odar**, Helen A '93 Brinks HG&L -455 N Cityfront Plaza Dr
-Ste 3600 -Chicago, IL 60611
Oday, Edwin R '54 -6234 Edwards Av -Ashtabula 44004

(330) 675-2650 .. **O'Day**, Michael P '86 %11th Dist Ct of Appls -111 High NE
-Warren 44481
O'Day, Tracey K '88 Lexis Nexis -Bx933 -Dayton 45401

(216) 514-7480 .. **Oddi**, Joseph A '00 Mortgage Info Srvcs -4877 Galaxy Pkwy -Ste 1
-Cleveland 44128

(216) 520-5552 .. **O'Dell**, Kathy G '88 West Grp -6111 Oak Tree Blvd -Bx318063
-Cleveland 44131

(301) 757-6011 .. **Odell**, Valerie H '80 Naval Air Sys Cmmnd HQ/Unit IPT
-47123 Buse Rd -Bldg 2272 Ste 257 -Patuxent River, MD 20670

(937) 427-2271 .. **O'Diam**, Thomas M '85 (O'Diam & Assoc) -75 Harbert Dr -#B
-Dayton 45440

(614) 457-3453 .. **Odita**, Florence U '85 -3155 Wareham Rd -Columbus 43221
Fx:457-3298

(513) 977-8200 .. **Odmark**, Gwendolyn M '00 %Dinsmore & S LLP -255 E 5th
-Ste 1900 -Cincinnati 45202 **Fx:**977-8141

(419) 241-9000 .. **O'Doherty**, James H '99 %Shumaker L&K,LLP -1000 Jackson
-Toledo 43624 **Fx:**241-6894

(419) 272-2521 .. **O'Donnell**, Bruce V '86 Edon State Bk -101 N Mich -Edon 43518

(440) 777-6500 .. **O'Donnell**, Deanna '93 %Burke V&G -22649 Lorain Rd
-Fairview Park 44126 **Fx:**777-0507

(561) 393-5660 .. **O'Donnell**, Garry W '79 (Adorno & Y) -700 S Fed Hwy -Ste 200
-Boca Raton, FL 33432 **Fx:**338-8698

(513) 487-5982 .. **O'Donnell**, Hugh C '77 Milacron Inc -2090 Florence Av
-Cincinnati 45206

(419) 524-8200 .. **O'Donnell**, James J '54 Anderson WO&K LLP -3 N Main -Ste 703
-Mansfield 44902

(937) 473-3161 .. **O'Donnell**, James R '66 -9 N High -Bx98 -Covington 45318

(419) 524-5555 .. **O'Donnell**, John C III '80 -13 Park Av W -Ste 605 -Mansfield
44902

(440) 357-5000 .. **O'Donnell**, John P '87 (Lyons & O Co LPA) -240 E Main
-Painesville 44077

(614) 221-0888 .. **O'Donnell**, Laura S '93 -5 E Long -Ste 605 -Columbus 43215

(216) 830-6830 .. **O'Donnell**, Michael P '04 %Brouse M -1001 Lakeside Av
-Ste 1600 -Cleveland 44114 **Fx:**830-6807

(419) 882-7100 .. **O'Donnell**, Michael W '84 Lydy & M,Ltd -4930
Holland Sylvania Rd -Sylvania 43560 **Fx:**882-1120

(216) 621-0200 .. **O'Donnell**, Patricia J '82 (Baker & H LLP) -1900 E 9th -Ste 3200
-Cleveland 44114 **Fx:**696-0740

(513) 732-2254 .. **O'Donnell**, Priscilla S '77 -202 Main -Batavia 45103

(919) 732-8181 .. **O'Donnell**, Sheila M '92 Orange Cnty Human Rltns Dept
-110 S Churton -Bx8181 -Hillsborough, NC 27278

(614) 227-2345 .. **O'Donnell**, Terrence N '01 %Bricker & E LLP -100 S 3rd
-Columbus 43215 **Fx:**227-2390

(216) 283-4225 .. **O'Donnell**, Thomas P '84 -3700 Nrthfld Rd -Ste 11
-Cleveland 44122

(216) 622-8200 .. **O'Donnell**, Thomas R '96 %Calfee H&G LLP -800 Superior Av
-Ste 1400 -Cleveland 44114 **Fx:**241-0816

(513) 241-0391 .. **O'Dowd**, Jerome L '70 -216 E 9th -2nd Fl -Cincinnati 45202
O'Driscoll, Janet I '85 -Bx115 -Aurora 44202

(216) 443-7800 .. **Oebker**, Jon W '94 Cuyahoga Cnty Pros -1200 Ontario -8th Fl
-Cleveland 44113 **Fx:**698-2270
Oechsler, Michael C '78 -701 E Water -Charlottesville, VA 22902

(330) 262-5246 .. **Oehl**, Frank C '86 MB Stone,LPA -231 N Buckeye -Wooster 44691

(440) 808-0011 .. **Oehlenschlager**, James E '01 %Renner KGBT&W,LPA
-24500 Ctr Ridge Rd -Ste 280 -Westlake 44145 **Fx:**808-0657

(937) 223-3277 .. **Oehlers**, Joseph C '95 %Bieser G&L LLP -6 N Main
-400 Natl City Ctr -Dayton 45402 **Fx:**223-6339

(330) 725-5936 .. **Oehlhof**, Shayne M '01 %Skidmore & H -748 N Court
-Medina 44256

(614) 469-3939 .. **Oellermann**, Charles M '91 (Jones D)
-325 John H McConnell Blvd -Ste 600 -Bx165017
-Columbus 43216 **Fx:**461-4198

(614) 752-2438 .. **Oelslager**, W Scott '02 -77 S High -13th flr -Columbus 43215

(513) 352-6631 .. **Oestreicher**, Michael R '78 OfCnsl Thompson H LLP -312 Walnut
-14th Fl -Cincinnati 45202 **Fx:**441-4771

(330) 247-1057 .. **Oettinger**, Jennifer E '02 Eshelman Lgl Grp
-263 Portage Trl Ext W -Cuyahoga Falls 44223 **Fx:**376-0199

(937) 746-1010 .. **Office**, James R '82 Victory Wholesale Grocers -400 Victory Dr
-Springboro 45066

(216) 523-4117 .. **O'Flaherty**, Sharon L '82 Eaton Corp -1111 Superior Av
-Cleveland 44114

(440) 946-1743 .. **O'Flaherty**, Terence P '79 -7541 Mentor Av -Ste 105
-Mentor 44060

(330) 923-2211 .. **Ogden**, James R '79 -Bx3021 -Cuyahoga Falls 44223

(610) 372-4761 .. **Ogden**, W Edwin '02 (Ryan RO&S) -110 Berkshire Blvd -Ste 301
-Reading, PA 19610

(419) 627-6674 .. **Ogden-Dellisanti**, Nancy L '89 Erie Cnty Cmn Pleas Ct
-323 Columbus Av -Sandusky 44870

(614) 716-0500 .. **Ogg**, Benjamin W '03 %Onda L&R Co,LPA -266 N 4th -Ste 100
-Columbus 43215 **Fx:**716-0511

(740) 653-6464 .. **Ogilvie**, Norman J Jr. '68 (Dagger JMO&H) -144 E Main -Bx667
-Lancaster 43130 **Fx:**653-8522

(859) 578-4444 .. **Ogle**, Mark A '87 P Schachter & Assoc -250 Grandvw Dr -Ste 500
-Fort Mitchell, KY 41017

(614) 488-7373 .. **Oglesbee**, Carla E '99 (O'Malley & O) -4591 Indnola Av
-Columbus 43214

(419) 625-5901 .. **Oglesby**, Lurlia A '84 Oglesby & O -1218 Cleveland Rd -Ste 2
-Sandusky 44870

(330) 821-1430 .. **Ogline**, Michael A '78 (Geiger TS&H) -1844 W State -Ste A
-Alliance 44601 **Fx:**821-2217

(248) 362-3707 .. **Ogne**, Wayne L '89 (Ogne A&S,PC) -1869 E Maple Rd -Ste 100
-Troy, MI 48083 **Fx:**362-0422

(330) 342-0222 .. **Ognibene**, Michael A '81 -204 Monroe NW -Warren 44483

(513) 983-1648 .. **O'Grady**, Erin E '93 Procter & Gamble -SY-10 -Bx599
-Cincinnati 45201
O'Grady, James J '67 -(Address Unavailable)

(513) 651-6800 .. **O'Grady**, Michael J '95 (Frost BT LLC) -201 E 5th -2200 PNC Ctr
-Cincinnati 45202 **Fx:**651-6981
O'Grady, Michael P '79 -900 Litchfld Ct -Columbus 43235

(513) 651-6800 .. **O'Guinn**, Jennifer A '03 %Frost BT LLC -201 E 5th -2200 PNC Ctr
-Cincinnati 45202 **Fx:**651-6981

(513) 977-8200 .. **O'Guinn**, M Dave III '01 %Dinsmore & S LLP -255 E 5th -Ste 1900
-Cincinnati 45202 **Fx:**977-8141

(216) 623-0000 .. **Oh**, James W '99 %Javitch B&R -1300 E 9th -14th Fl -Cleveland
44114 **Fx:**623-0190

(312) 353-7390 .. **O'Hair**, Dea A '94 US SEC -175 W Jackson Blvd -Ste 900
-Chicago, IL 60604

(330) 792-6220 .. **O'Halloran**, Janice T '82 %Stefanski & Assoc,LLC
-5437 Mahoning Av -Ste 22 -Youngstown 44515 **Fx:**792-6250

(419) 354-9250 .. **Ohanian**, Aram M '94 %Wood Cnty Pros -One Cthse Sq
-Bowling Green 43402 **Fx:**353-2904

(330) 792-6220 .. **Ohanian**, Eric J '94 %Stefanski & Assoc,LLC -5437 Mahoning Av
-Ste 22 -Youngstown 44515 **Fx:**792-6250

(419) 663-6785 .. **O'Hara**, George S Jr. '79 Norwalk Law Dept -38 Whittlesey Av
-Norwalk 44857

(937) 449-2800 .. **O'Hara**, Lloyd H '42 OfCnsl Chernesky H&K PLL
-10 Cthse Plz SW -Ste 1100 -Dayton 45402 **Fx:**449-2821

(312) 822-2315 .. **O'Hara**, Margaret L '86 CNA Risk Mgmt -CNA Plz #295 -Law Dept
-Chicago, IL 60685 **Fx:**817-0885
O'Hara, Michael A '97 -7000 Houston Rd -Ste 9
-Florence, KY 41042

(859) 331-2000 .. **O'Hara**, Michael J '81 (O'Hara RTS&S) -25 Crestvw Hills Mall Rd
-Ste 201 -Bx17411 -Covington, KY 41017 **Fx:**578-3365

(216) 586-3939 .. **O'Hearn**, Timothy J '84 (Jones D) -901 Lakeside Av
-Cleveland 44114 **Fx:**579-0212

(330) 399-4554 .. **Ohlin**, Charles E '88 (Bluedorn & Co,LPA) -144 N Park Av
-Ste 310 -Warren 44481 **Fx:**399-5112

(330) 399-2070 .. **Ohlin**, Joseph D '85 Ohlin & S,LPA -309 Wshngtn NE
-Warren 44483 **Fx:**393-4344
Ohlrich, Holly A '04 -Bx472 -Mantua 44255

(440) 632-9090 .. **Ohly**, Robert S '85 -15985 E High -Ste 207 -Bx1236
-Middlefield 44062

(330) 740-2180 .. **O'Horo**, Kristen L '98 %Hon JJ Vukovich -120 Market
-Youngstown 44503

(216) 621-0200 .. **Okada**, Ronald S '85 (Baker & H LLP) -1900 E 9th -Ste 3200
-Cleveland 44114 **Fx:**696-0740

(614) 764-8407 .. **O'Kane**, Michael G '81 Wendys Intl -4288 W Dublin-Granvll Rd
-Bx256 -Dublin 43017

(614) 752-6417 .. **Okano**, Mary Lynne '78 Atty Gen -30 E Broad -Columbus 43215
Fx:466-0013

(614) 236-1011 .. **O'Keefe**, Bobbie C '92 -500 S Front -Ste 860 -Columbus 43215

(937) 324-6807 .. **O'Keefe**, Daniel M '69 Sec Natl Bank & Trust -Bx1408
-Springfield 45501 **Fx:**324-6861

(216) 621-0150 .. **O'Keefe**, F Ronald '77 (Hahn L&P LLP) -3300 BP Twr/200 Pub Sq
-Ste 3300 -Cleveland 44114 **Fx:**241-2824

(513) 887-5682 .. **O'Keefe**, Kelly A '03 Butler Cnty Cmn Pleas Ct -315 High -3rd Fl
-Hamilton 45011 **Fx:**785-6533

(937) 865-6800 .. **O'Keefe**, Kelly E '93 Lexis/Nexis -Bx933 -Dayton 45401

(937) 643-0600 .. **O'Keefe**, Stephen P '95 %G Gibson Co,LPA -2810 Kettering Twr
-Dayton 45423 **Fx:**586-9495

(440) 526-0430 .. **Oker**, Michael R '71 -9905 Tamarack Trl -Brecksville 44141
Fx:546-0680

(513) 621-6464 .. **Okerson**, Eric A '80 (Graydon H&R LLP) -511 Walnut
-1900 Fifth Third Ctr -Cincinnati 45202 **Fx:**651-3836

(330) 796-4827 .. **Okey**, Deborah A '87 Goodyear Tire & Rubber Co -1144 E Market
-Akron 44316

(330) 453-8261 .. **Okey**, Mark D '76 Okey Law Firm,LPA -337 3rd NW
-Canton 44702

(330) 453-8261 .. **Okey**, Steven P '87 Okey Law Firm,LPA -337 3rd NW
-Canton 44702

(440) 352-3391 .. **Okin**, Gary S '77 (Dworken & B Co,LPA) -60 S Park Pl
-Painesville 44077 **Fx:**352-3469

(614) 469-6638 .. **O'Korn**, Keith L '98 US Bankruptcy Ct -170 N High
-Columbus 43215

(513) 961-5311 .. **Okrzynski**, Sarah A '03 %Thomas & T -2323 Park Av
-Cincinnati 45206

(614) 436-0600 .. **Okuley**, John J '03 %Mueller & S,LPA -7700 Rvrs Edge Dr
-Columbus 43235

(216) 479-8500 ..**Okun**, Jill G '86 OfCnsl Squire S&D LLP -127 Pub Sq -4900
Key Twr -Cleveland 44114 **Fx:**479-8780

(330) 743-5101 ..**Okusewsky**, Stanley J III '03 %Green H&S,Co LPA -16 Wick Av
-Ste 400 -Youngstown 44503 **Fx:**743-3451
Olah, Michael J '85 -799 Weber Av -Akron 44303

(216) 241-5310 ..**Olarczuk-Smith**, Holly M '01 %Gallagher SF&N -1501 Euclid Av
-6th Fl -Cleveland 44115 **Fx:**241-1608

(330) 872-0302 ..**Old**, Thomas L '73 Mun Ct Judge -19 N Canal
-Newton Falls 44444

(202) 467-8800 ..**Oldach**, William H III '95 OfCnsl Vorys SS&P,LLP -1828 L NW
-11th Fl -Washington, DC 20036

(513) 241-9400 ..**Olden**, Stephen H '77 Legal Aid -215 E 9th -Ste 200
-Cincinnati 45202

(513) 887-3474 ..**Oldendick**, Lee A '80 Butler Cnty Pros -315 High -11th Fl -Bx515
-Hamilton 45012

(330) 675-6684 ..**Oldfield**, Charles W '99 11th Dist Ct of Appls -111 High NE
-Warren 44481

(330) 376-4558 ..**Oldfield**, Joy D '00 Scanlon & G Co,LPA -50 S Main -Ste 1200
-Akron 44308 **Fx:**376-3550

(859) 261-5777 ..**Oldfield**, Laura A '94 (Oldfield DR,PLLC) -213 E 4th -Bx1078
-Covington, KY 41012

(330) 762-7377 ..**Oldham & Dowling** -195 S Main -Ste 300 -Akron 44308
Fx:762-7390

(239) 262-8502 ..**Oldham**, Edwin W '66 SpclCnsl The Livingston Firm
-963 Trl Terrace Dr -Naples, FL 34103 **Fx:**261-3773

(330) 762-7377 ..**Oldham**, Jon A '02 %Oldham & D -195 S Main -Ste 300
-Akron 44308 **Fx:**762-7390

(330) 762-7377 ..**Oldham**, Joseph K '95 (Oldham & D) -195 S Main -Ste 300
-Akron 44308 **Fx:**762-7390

(330) 434-2113 ..**Oldham**, Peter D '72 -159 S Main -Ste 1111 -Akron 44308

(330) 928-9791 ..**Oldham**, Robert L '71 -126 Portgage Trl -#200
-Cuyahoga Falls 44221

(330) 864-5550 ..**Oldham**, Scott M '91 (Hahn L&P LLP) -One GOJO Plz -Ste 300
-Akron 44311 **Fx:**864-7986

(330) 762-7377 ..**Oldham**, William M '67 (Oldham & D) -195 S Main -Ste 300
-Akron 44308 **Fx:**762-7390

(614) 275-2620 ..**O'Leary**, Anne C '89 Franklin Cnty Children Srvcs -855 W Mound
-Columbus 43223 **Fx:**275-2589

(440) 974-8081 ..**O'Leary**, James R '96 (Sacerich & O) -6988 Spinach Dr
-Mentor 44060

(972) 308-7403 ..**O'Leary**, Mark E '75 IRS/Ofc Chief Cnsl -4050 Alpha Rd -13th Fl
-Dallas, TX 75244

(216) 664-3572 ..**O'Leary**, Ronald J '97 Dept of Law -601 Lakeside Av
-Rm 106 City Hall -Cleveland 44114 **Fx:**664-2663

(419) 524-9811 ..**Olecki**, Joseph T '94 %Weldon H&K,LLP -28 Park Av W
-Bank One Bldg -Mansfield 44902 **Fx:**522-5758

(563) 288-2204 ..**Oleksiak**, Edward M '91 Tire Dstrbtn Syst,Inc -1615 2nd Av
-Muscatine, IA 52761

(330) 491-9880 ..**Oleksy**, Lisa A '96 (Proctor-Donald & O) -4565 Dressler Rd NW
-LL-102 -Canton 44718

(419) 213-4700 ..**Olender**, Lori L '97 %Lucas Cnty Pros -Adams & Erie
-Lucas Cnty Cthse -Toledo 43624

(216) 621-0040 ..**Olender**, Robert J '76 (Strachan MO&R Co LPA) -925 Euclid Av
-Ste 1940 -Cleveland 44115

(330) 253-6121 ..**Olesh**, Kristen E '01 Chicago Title Insurance Co -1 Cascade Plz
-Ste 100 -Akron 44308

(513) 831-5250 ..**Olinger**, Philip S '55 -115 Fieldstone Dr -Terrace Park 45174

(614) 227-2000 ..**Oliphant**, James S '71 (Porter WM&A LLP) -41 S High
-Columbus 43215 **Fx:**227-2100

(216) 479-8500 ..**Oliss**, Philip M '96 %Squire S&D LLP -127 Pub Sq -4900 Key Twr
-Cleveland 44114 **Fx:**479-8780

(513) 867-8000 ..**Olivas**, Adolf '81 (A Olivas,LLC) -350 N 2nd -Hamilton 45011
Fx:867-0979

(513) 621-6464 ..**Oliver**, Christine E '99 %Graydon H&R LLP -511 Walnut
-1900 Fifth Third Ctr -Cincinnati 45202 **Fx:**651-3836

(513) 684-3642 ..**Oliver**, Eric V '83 NLRB -550 Main -Rm 3003 -Cincinnati 45202
Fx:684-3946

(216) 479-8500 ..**Oliver**, James P '69 (Squire S&D LLP) -127 Pub Sq -4900 Key Twr
-Cleveland 44114 **Fx:**479-8780

(614) 220-9100 ..**Oliver**, Jami S '93 -471 E Broad -Ste 1303 -Columbus 43215
Fx:242-3948

(330) 869-9944 ..**Oliver**, Joseph E '83 (J Oliver,Co) -230 White Pond Dr -Ste A
-Akron 44313

(800) 998-9454 ..**Oliver**, Kimberly L '03 Cmmnty Lgl Aid Srvcs,Inc -265 S Main
-3rd Fl -Akron 44308 **Fx:**(330) 535-0728

(513) 932-3452 ..**Oliver**, Lois A '76 -324 E Warren -Lebanon 45036

(216) 621-0150 ..**Oliver**, Nancy A '99 %Ulmer H&R LLP -3300 BP Twr/200 Pub Sq
-Ste 3300 -Cleveland 44114 **Fx:**241-2824

(513) 556-4361 ..**Oliver**, Nancy A '99 Univ of Cincinnati-Cllg of Law
-Clifton Av & Calhoun -Cincinnati 45221 **Fx:**556-1236
Oliver, Randall C '79 -27113 Brookpark Rd Ext
-North Olmsted 44070

(740) 354-4200 ..**Oliver**, Stephen L '81 (Johnson & O,LPA) -701 6th -Bx1505
-Portsmouth 45662 **Fx:**353-2413

(740) 282-4593 ..**Olivito**, Dominick E Jr. '78 -328 Market -Ste 606
-Steubenville 43952

(740) 283-3341 ..**Olivito**, Peter S '62 -328 Market -Ste 610 Sinclair Bldg
-Steubenville 43952 **Fx:**283-3588
Olivito, Richard A '89 -391 Westwood Dr -Steubenville 43953

(614) 559-1100 ..**Olix**, Thomas J '86 Chicago Title -5150 Reed Rd -Ste A
-Columbus 43220

(216) 621-0200 ..**Ollinger**, W James II '68 (Baker & H LLP) -1900 E 9th -Ste 3200
-Cleveland 44114 **Fx:**696-0740
Olminsky, Charles W Jr. '00 -209 S Main -8th Fl -Akron 44308

(513) 419-5770 ..**Olmstead**, Dina M '97 Cynergy Corp -139 E 4th -MD:EA503
-Cincinnati 45202

(216) 479-8500 ..**O'Loughlin**, Daniel J '51 (Squire S&D LLP) -127 Pub Sq
-4900 Key Twr -Cleveland 44114 **Fx:**479-8780

(216) 523-4111 ..**O'Loughlin**, David M '74 Eaton Corp -1111 Superior Av
-Cleveland 44114

(440) 838-7600 ..**Olsavsky**, Charles R Jr. '87 SrCnsl Janik & D,LLP
-9200 S Hills Blvd -Ste 300 -Cleveland 44147 **Fx:**838-7601

(973) 541-8867 ..**Olsen**, James S '80 Cnsl DeGussa Corp -379 Intrpace Pkwy
-Parsippany, NJ 07054 **Fx:**541-8850

(304) 347-4851 ..**Olsen**, Richard F '03 WV Ct of Claims -1900 Kanawha Blvd E
-W-334 -Charleston, WV 25305

(513) 621-3394 ..**Olson**, Carol D '90 (Peck S&W,LLP) -201 E 5th -Ste 900
-Cincinnati 45202 **Fx:**621-3813

(330) 722-8989 ..**Olson**, Conrad G '95 %J Cameron & Assoc -247 E Smith Rd
-Medina 44256

(513) 651-6800 ..**Olson**, David C '78 (Frost BT LLC) -201 E 5th -2200 PNC Ctr
-Cincinnati 45202 **Fx:**651-6981

(614) 424-6580 ..**Olson**, Kathy A '77 Battelle Memorial Inst -505 King Av
-Columbus 43201

(330) 747-4404 ..**Olson**, Leonard A '53 OfCnsl Newman O&K,LPA
-11 Fed Plz Central -Ste 1200 -Youngstown 44503 **Fx:**747-6056

(330) 699-5002 ..**Olson**, Martin L '73 -13312 Cleveland Av -Bx339
-Uniontown 44685

(216) 771-4055 ..**Olson**, Nancy L '80 -1419 W 9th -2nd Fl -Cleveland 44113
Fx:566-8810

(602) 528-4000 ..**Olson**, Robert H Jr. '69 (Squire S&D LLP) -40 N Central Av
-Ste 2700 -Phoenix, AZ 85004 **Fx:**253-8129

(216) 566-2587 ..**Olson**, Robert K '96 Sherwin-Williams Co -101 Prospect Av NW
-Cleveland 44115

(513) 784-8804 ..**Olson**, Robert W '91 Chiquita Brands Intl -250 E 5th
-Cincinnati 45202

(937) 461-7000 ..**Olsvig**, Josie '88 -22 Clay -Dayton 45402 **Fx:**461-3299

(724) 284-5294 ..**Olszewski**, Cheryl M '03 Cnty Ct of Common Pleas
-S Main Bx 1208A -Butler, PA 16001

(216) 685-1000 ..**Olsztyn**, Christopher E '04 %Weltman W&R Co,LPA
-323 W Lakeside Av -Ste 200 -Cleveland 44113 **Fx:**363-4121
Oluwole, Joseph O '03 -110 E Foster Av -#508
-State College, PA 16801

(216) 479-6100 ..**O'Malley**, Anthony J '84 (Vorys SS&P LLP) -1375 E 9th
-Ste 2100 One Cleve Ctr -Cleveland 44114 **Fx:**479-6060

(440) 734-1500 ..**O'Malley**, Bryan P '88 Pros -27243 Lorain Rd
-North Olmsted 44070

(216) 689-7638 ..**O'Malley**, Catherine M '98 Key Bank -127 Pub Sq -16th Fl
-Cleveland 44114

(216) 443-7800 ..**O'Malley**, Erin R '00 Cuyahoga Cnty Pros -1200 Ontario -8th Fl
-Cleveland 44113 **Fx:**698-2270

(216) 241-7255 ..**O'Malley**, Joseph P '92 -2401 Superior Viaduct -Cleveland 44113

(216) 485-7970 ..**O'Malley**, Michael C '92 -5454 State Rd -Parma 44134

(419) 523-6104 ..**O'Malley**, Michael E '68 (Oxley MHO&W,PLL) -814 N Locust
-Bx368 -Ottawa 45875 **Fx:**523-6447

(216) 241-6868 ..**O'Malley**, Michael P '80 (Grant & O Co,LPA) -1148 Euclid Av
-Ste 300 -Cleveland 44115

(216) 696-0606 ..**O'Malley**, Patrick J '92 RE Sweeney Co,LPA -55 Pub Sq
-Ste 1500 -Cleveland 44113 **Fx:**696-0679

(216) 241-4100 ..**O'Malley**, Patrick J '95 %Keis/G LLP -55 Pub Sq -Ste 800
-Cleveland 44113 **Fx:**771-3111

(216) 241-7255 ..**O'Malley**, Thomas F '57 T O'Malley Co,LPA
-2401 Superior Viaduct -Cleveland 44113

(216) 241-7255 ..**O'Malley**, Thomas F Jr. '86 -2401 Superior Viaduct
-Cleveland 44113

(216) 515-1300 ..**O'Malley**, William D '83 Medical Assurance Co
-113 St Clair Av NE -Ste 300 -Cleveland 44114

(614) 488-7373 ..**O'Malley**, William J '91 (O'Malley & O) -4591 Indnola Av
-Columbus 43214

(419) 423-0242 ..**Oman**, John D '82 (Drake PK&C) -301 S Main -Ste 3
-Findlay 45840 **Fx:**423-0186

(614) 464-6400 ..**Oman**, Richard Heer '51 OfCnsl Vorys SS&P LLP -52 E Gay
-Bx1008 -Columbus 43216 **Fx:**464-6350

(330) 364-5531 ..**O'Meara**, Douglas J '77 -128 N Bway -New Philadelphia 44663

(216) 341-7261 ..**O'Meara**, James E III '66 -4608 Beta Av -Cleveland 44105

(216) 479-8500 ..**Omerza**, Mark J '95 %Squire S&D LLP -127 Pub Sq
-4900 Key Twr -Cleveland 44114 **Fx:**479-8780

(614) 716-0500 ..**Onda LaBuhn & Rankin Co,LPA** -266 N 4th -Ste 100
-Columbus 43215 **Fx:**716-0511

(614) 716-0500 ..**Onda**, Robert J '83 (Onda L&R Co,LPA) -266 N 4th -Ste 100
-Columbus 43215 **Fx:**716-0511

(440) 605-6660 ..**Ondak**, Robert C Jr. '98 %Hurtuk & D Co,LPA -6120 Parkland Blvd
-Ste 100 -Cleveland 44124 **Fx:**605-6666
Onders, Kathleen D '94 -9994 Gatewood Dr -Brecksville 44141

(937) 241-9400 ..**Ondre**, Schaunette Marie '98 Legal Aid -202 W Locust
-Wilmington 45177

(440) 285-2242 ..**Ondrey**, David M '80 Thrasher D&D,LPA -100 7th Av -Ste 150
-Chardon 44024 **Fx:**285-9423

(330) 334-6345 ..**Ondrey**, Kevin P '99 -145 Akron Rd -Wadsworth 44281

(937) 222-7773 ..**O'Neal**, Raymond W Sr. '81 -11 W Monument Av -Ste 304
-Dayton 45402

(937) 224-0963 ..**O'Neal**, Robert M '84 (Breidenbach O&B) -131 N Ludlow -Ste 1060
-Dayton 45402

(330) 434-6687 ..**O'Neil**, Augustin F '82 -511 N Main -Akron 44310

(614) 249-8343 ..**O'Neil**, Bonnie Irvin '87 Nationwide Ins Co -One Nationwide Plz
-01-35-15 -Columbus 43215 **Fx:**249-2418

(740) 342-3582 ..**O'Neil**, Cindy M '99 (Howdyshell & O Ltd) -113 N Main -Bx508
-New Lexington 43764

(216) 622-8200 ..**O'Neil**, Colleen M '96 %Calfee H&G LLP -800 Superior Av
-Ste 1400 -Cleveland 44114 **Fx:**241-0816

(614) 792-2250 ..**O'Neil**, Dennis M '92 -4856 Sawmill Rd -#350 -Columbus 43235

(216) 687-1311 ..**O'Neil**, John P '97 (Reminger & R) -101 Prospect Av W
-1400 Mdlnd Bldg -Cleveland 44115 **Fx:**687-1841

(419) 782-9881 ..**O'Neil**, Joseph W '77 Arthur OM&M Co,LPA -901 Ralston Av
-Bx781 -Defiance 43512
O'Neil, Kelly R '99 -8830 Carnes Rd -Chagrin Falls 44023

(330) 761-6369 ..**O'Neil**, Kevin C '81 Cnsl Myers Ind,Inc -1293 S Main -Akron 44301
Fx:761-6166
O'Neil, Michael J '92 -(Address Unavailable)

(216) 861-4700 ..**O'Neil**, Michael W '94 %Martyn & Assoc Co,LPA
-820 Superior Av NW -Ste 920 -Cleveland 44113
O'Neil, Tamzin K '00 -(Address Unavailable)

(614) 235-1166 ..**O'Neil**, Thomas G '95 -231 S VA Lee Rd -Ste 228
-Columbus 43209

(216) 902-8803 ..**O'Neill**, Brian M '87 (Ulmer & B LLP) -1300 E 9th
-Ste 900 Penton Media Bldg -Cleveland 44114 **Fx:**931-6001

(614) 464-6400 ..**O'Neill,** C William '71 (Vorys SS&P LLP) -52 E Gay -Bx1008
-Columbus 43216 **Fx:**464-6350

(216) 241-2022 ..**O'Neill,** James P '79 (O'Neill & O) -50 Pub Sq -Ste 400
-Cleveland 44113

(330) 297-3622 ..**O'Neill,** John P '71 Portage Cnty Mun Ct -203 W Main -Bx823
-Ravenna 44266

(216) 241-2022 ..**O'Neill,** Keelin G '82 (O'Neill & O) -50 Pub Sq -Ste 400
-Cleveland 44113

(216) 687-5282 ..**O'Neill,** Kevin F '85 CSU-Marshall Cllg of Law -2121 Euclid Av
-LB138 -Cleveland 44115 **Fx:**687-6881

(216) 566-1144 ..**O'Neill,** Laura E '00 %Webster WK LLP -1220 W 6th -Ste 600
-Cleveland 44113 **Fx:**566-1221

(216) 241-6602 ..**O'Neill,** Mark P '52 (Weston HFP&H LLP) -50 Pub Sq
-2500 Trmnl Twr -Cleveland 44113 **Fx:**621-8369

(419) 624-3000 ..**O'Neill,** Mary S '97 Murray & M Co,LPA -111 E Shoreline Dr -Bx19
-Sandusky 44871

(440) 350-3200 ..**O'Neill,** Melissa A '04 Lake Cnty Pub Def -125 E Erie
-Painesville 44077

(513) 946-3243 ..**O'Neill,** Michael D '02 Hamilton Cnty Pros -230 E 9th
-Cincinnati 45202 **Fx:**946-3017

(614) 466-9858 ..**O'Neill,** Michael J '89 Legis Srvc Commssn -77 S High -Columbus
43215

(513) 241-0400 ..**O'Neill,** Patrick M '93 %Aronoff R&H Co,LPA -425 Walnut
-Ste 2400 -Cincinnati 45202 **Fx:**241-2877

(614) 462-3580 ..**O'Neill,** Shari W '89 %10th Dist Crt of Appeals -373 S High
-24th Fl -Columbus 43215

(216) 348-5400 ..**O'Neill,** William J '85 (McDonald H Co,LPA) -600 Superior Av E
-Ste 2100 -Cleveland 44114 **Fx:**348-5474

(614) 221-9055 ..**Onesto,** John L '72 -887 S High -Columbus 43206

(513) 626-3047 ..**Oney,** Lee Lee Jr. '01 Procter & Gamble
-11511 Reed Hartman Hwy -Cincinnati 45241

(216) 522-1200 ..**Oney,** John S '77 IMG -1360 E 9th -Ste 100 -Cleveland 44114

(330) 339-6444 ..**Ong,** James J '97 Stephenson S&C -206 W High Av
-New Philadelphia 44663 **Fx:**339-6228

(702) 242-3382 ..**Onufrieff,** Victor '73 Ryder System,Inc -9229 Whitetail Dr
-Las Vegas, NV 89134

(216) 479-6100 ..**Onusko,** Thomas J '77 OfCnsl Vorys SS&P LLP -1375 E 9th
-Ste 2100 One Cleve Ctr -Cleveland 44114 **Fx:**479-6060

(419) 247-2500 ..**Oostmeyer,** Melissa M '99 %Fuller & H,Ltd -One SeaGate
-Ste 1700 -Bx2088 -Toledo 43603 **Fx:**247-2665

(614) 764-8455 ..**Opelt,** Vivian Lee '85 Wendys Intl -4288 W Dublin-Granvll Rd
-Bx256 -Dublin 43017

(216) 566-5256 ..**Opett,** Edward J '75 SrCnsl Reg Trans Auth -1240 W 6th
-Cleveland 44113

(216) 348-5400 ..**Opincar,** Scott N '94 (McDonald H Co,LPA) -600 Superior Av E
-Ste 2100 -Cleveland 44114 **Fx:**348-5474

(216) 787-3030 ..**Oppenheimer,** David A '94 Atty Gen -615 W Superior Av -11th Fl
-Cleveland 44113 **Fx:**787-3480

(614) 227-8822 ..**Oppenheimer,** Susan L '94 Bricker & E LLP -100 S 3rd
-Columbus 43215 **Fx:**227-2390

(616) 456-1272 ..**Opper,** April L '04 %MI Ct of Appeals -350 Ottawa Av NW
-Grand Rapids, MI 49503

(419) 422-6486 ..**Opperman,** Raymond J '54 -951 W Lima -Findlay 45840
Oprisko, Brian S '84 -(Address Unavailable)

(513) 897-1310 ..**Opsahl,** Yvonne G '93 -4353 E State Route 73 -Bx579
-Waynesville 45068

(440) 243-2955 ..**Opsincs,** Katherine H '04 %Powers & G-W -2 Berea Cmmns
-Ste 215 -Bx1059 -Berea 44017 **Fx:**243-2967

(440) 937-4019 ..**Opsitnick,** Timothy M '85 JurInnov Ltd -34423 St Maron
-Avon 44011

(214) 855-4500 ..**O'Quinn,** Pamela M '89 (Jenkens & G PC) -1445 Ross Av
-Ste 3200 -Dallas, TX 75202

(303) 861-7400 ..**O'Quinn,** William L '70 -191 Univ Blvd -Ste 716 -Denver, CO
80206

(216) 443-7800 ..**Oradini,** Reno J Jr. '88 Cuyahoga Cnty Pros -1200 Ontario -8th Fl
-Cleveland 44113 **Fx:**698-2270

(413) 543-2400 ..**Orban,** Alex J Jr. '71 Friendly Restaurant Corp -1855 Bstn Rd
-Wilbraham, MA 01095

(651) 224-5074 ..**Orbovich,** Samuel D '78 Orbovich & G Chtd -408 St Peter
-Ste 417 -Saint Paul, MN 55102

(614) 469-3939 ..**Ording,** Michael K '80 (Jones D) -325 John H McConnell Blvd
-Ste 600 -Bx165017 -Columbus 43216 **Fx:**461-4198

(216) 987-5214 ..**O'Rear-Lassen,** Lisa E '85 Cugahoga Cmmnty Coll
-700 Carnegie Av -Cleveland 44115

(216) 896-0935 ..**Oreh,** John P '85 -25550 Chagrin Blvd -Ste 320 -Cleveland 44122
Fx:593-0914

(440) 286-9405 ..**O'Reilly,** David Kevin '68 DK O'Reilly Co,LPA -109 Court
-Chardon 44024

(513) 556-0062 ..**O'Reilly,** James T '74 Univ of Cincinnati -Bx210040
-Cincinnati 45221

(614) 461-9335 ..**O'Reilly,** Kelly C '96 Gvrnmntl Policy Grp -17 S High -Ste 245
-Columbus 43215

(330) 384-5224 ..**O'Reilly,** Mary E '84 FirstEnergy Corp -76 S Main -18th Fl
-Akron 44308

(614) 833-3777 ..**O'Reilly,** Michael J '84 -115 N Center -Pickerington 43147
O'Reilly, Patrick F '04 -6555 Lk of the Woods Pt -Galena 43021

(419) 289-8857 ..**O'Reilly,** Paul E '84 Ashland Cnty Pros -307 Orange
-Ashland 44805 **Fx:**281-3865

(520) 747-0999 ..**Oremland,** Lawrence R '74 -5055 E Bway Blvd -Ste C-214
-Tucson, AZ 85711

(740) 593-6410 ..**Oremus,** Frederick L '73 (Eslocker & O Co,LPA) -16 W State
-Athens 45701

(216) 664-2916 ..**Oren,** Cortney R '03 Dept of Law -601 Lakeside Av
-Rm 106 City Hall -Cleveland 44114 **Fx:**664-2663

(614) 457-6450 ..**Orenchuk,** Robert P '96 -1545 Scottsdale Av -Columbus 43235

(614) 227-2000 ..**Orensten,** David K '02 %Porter WM&A LLP -41 S High
-Columbus 43215 **Fx:**227-2100

(614) 469-3939 ..**Organ,** Shawn J '89 (Jones D) -325 John H McConnell Blvd
-Ste 600 -Bx165017 -Columbus 43216 **Fx:**461-4198

(307) 685-6141 ..**Orians,** Shane A '99 Kennecott Energy Corp -Bx3009
-Gillette, WY 82717

(910) 763-9925 ..**Oring,** Christopher L '03 -705 Princess -Wilmington, NC 28401

(614) 416-5120 ..**Orlandini,** David W '95 %BJ Bradigan,Inc -3948 Townfair Way
-Ste 230 -Columbus 43219

(937) 225-5757 ..**Orlando,** Elizabeth J '03 %Montgomery Cnty Pros -301 W 3rd
-Bx972 -Dayton 45422 **Fx:**225-3470

(216) 696-8730 ..**Orlando,** Gerardo C '90 OfCnsl Amin & T LLP -1900 E 9th
-24th Fl Natl City Ctr -Cleveland 44114 **Fx:**696-8731

(330) 747-2661 ..**Orlando,** Jacqueline A '98 Cafaro Co -2445 Belmont Av -Bx2186
-Youngstown 44504

(614) 236-6448 ..**Orlando,** Jacqueline M '88 Capital Univ Law Sch -303 E Broad
-Columbus 43215

(216) 696-7600 ..**Orlando,** Lisa A '02 %Duvin C&H -1301 E 9th -20th Fl Erievw Twr
-Cleveland 44114 **Fx:**696-2038

(740) 687-6725 ..**Orlando,** Michael E '88 Fairfield Cnty Job & Family Srvcs
-239 W Main -Lancaster 43130

(513) 381-8213 ..**Orlet,** Dimity V '97 Cincinnati Bar Assn -225 E 6th -2nd Fl
-Cincinnati 45202 **Fx:**381-0528

(937) 372-9236 ..**Orlins,** David A '75 (Silverberg Z&O Co,LPA) -100 E Market -Bx40
-Xenia 45385

(216) 522-1200 ..**Orloff,** Jeffrey K '89 IMG -1360 E 9th -Ste 100 -Cleveland 44114

(419) 213-6510 ..**Orlow,** Gary M '78 Lucas Cnty EMS -2144 Monroe -Toledo 43624

(713) 296-4051 ..**Orlowski,** Kenneth J '74 Marathon Oil Co -5555 San Felipe Rd
-Rm 4051 -Houston, TX 77056

(216) 857-2339 ..**Ormond,** Regina R '97 Cnsl Nationwide Mutual Ins Co
-375 N Front -Ste 200 -Columbus 43215

(937) 547-7380 ..**Ormsby,** Rowland K III '80 Darke Cnty Pros -504 S Bway
-Cthse, 3rd Fl -Greenville 45331

(440) 285-1710 ..**Orndorff,** Jeffrey T '77 -117 South -Ste 110 -Bx1137
-Chardon 44024 **Fx:**285-1723

(513) 772-1140 ..**Orner,** Danny R '78 (D Orner Co,LPA) -2463 Crowne Pnt Ct
-Cincinnati 45241

(216) 267-1200 ..**Ornstein,** Warren K '52 Forest City Entrprss,Inc -50 Pub Sq
-Trmnl Twr,Ste 1160 -Cleveland 44113

(513) 677-1008 ..**Ororokuma,** Inyeai E '84 -9435 Waterstone Blvd -Ste 140
-Cincinnati 45249

(614) 466-8911 ..**Orosz,** Nathaniel S '04 %Atty Gen -30 E Broad -Columbus 43215
Fx:728-7582

(440) 352-3324 ..**Orosz,** Richard T '71 -56 Lbrty -Ste 207 -Painesville 44077

(216) 447-9500 ..**O'Rourke,** R Russell '84 (O'Rourke & Assoc Co,LPA)
-2 Summit Park Dr -Ste 650 -Independence 44131 **Fx:**447-9501

(216) 696-4441 ..**Oroz,** Helen '02 %Zashin & K,LPA -55 Pub Sq -Ste 1490
-Cleveland 44113 **Fx:**696-1618

(216) 429-5047 ..**Orr,** Michelle F '91 Cnsl 3rd Fed Savings & Loan Assn
-7007 Bway Av -Cleveland 44105

(480) 948-0505 ..**Orr,** Randall L '80 Scottsdale Ins Co -8877 N Gainey Ctr Dr
-Scottsdale, AZ 85258

(757) 836-6411 ..**Orr,** Robert J III '84 US Navy JAG Corps -1562 Mitcher
-Comm US Atl Fleet -Norfolk, VA 23551

(330) 547-3722 ..**Orr,** Thomas T '81 -16320 Heiser Rd -Bx194 -Berlin Center 44401
Orr, Virginia A '86 -(Address Unavailable)

(202) 767-1550 ..**Orr,** William E Jr. '82 US Air Force -112 Luke Av -Ste 343
-Bolling AFB, DC 20332

(419) 244-7563 ..**Orra,** Said M '03 -Bx548 -Maumee 43537 **Fx:**242-4354

(614) 863-6220 ..**Ort,** Mark P '82 -12931 Edgewood Ct -Pickerington 43147

(330) 533-8304 ..**Ortenzio,** Albert J '51 -6800 Summit Dr -Canfield 44406

(212) 901-7311 ..**Ortiz,** Lillian '00 Jones D -222 E 41st -Latin Amer Bus Dev Mgr
-New York, NY 10017

(216) 771-5588 ..**Ortman,** Bradley L '96 Rosner & Assoc,LLC -812 Huron Rd
-Ste 601 Caxton Bldg -Cleveland 44115 **Fx:**771-5894

(440) 245-7000 ..**Ortner,** Kenneth N '98 -600 Bway Av -Lorain 44052

(440) 884-5015 ..**Oryshkewych,** George R '92 -5566 Pearl Rd -Parma 44129
Oryshkewych, George V '71 -8041 Royalvw Dr -Parma 44129

(419) 294-2336 ..**Osborn & Fox,LPA** -116 E Wyandot Av -Upper Sandusky 43351
Fx:294-5669

(614) 464-1999 ..**Osborn,** Larissa D '01 Andrew,LLC -454 E Main -Ste 200
-Columbus 43215

(513) 621-4612 ..**Osborn,** Marilyn J '77 Bartlett & Co -36 E 4th -Cincinnati 45202

(937) 324-5541 ..**Osborn,** Robert M '95 (Martin BH&H) -1 S Limestone -Ste 800
-Bx1488 -Springfield 45501 **Fx:**325-5432

(937) 225-5757 ..**Osborn,** Susan E '01 Montgomery Cnty Pros -301 W 3rd -Bx972
-Dayton 45422 **Fx:**225-3470

(419) 294-2336 ..**Osborn,** Thomas E '75 (Osborn & F,LPA) -116 E Wyandot Av
-Upper Sandusky 43351 **Fx:**294-5669

(330) 965-8000 ..**Osborne Delaurentis & Sontich Co LPA** -100 Marwood Cir
-Boardman 44512 **Fx:**965-8005

(614) 224-7747 ..**Osborne Delaurentis & Sontich Co LPA** -495 S High -Ste 200
-Columbus 43215

(513) 369-0200 ..**Osborne,** Frank E '72 Bazeley & L -13 E Court -#400
-Cincinnati 45202

(216) 592-5000 ..**Osborne,** Frank R '73 OfCnsl Tucker E&W LLP -925 Euclid Av
-1150 Huntngtn Bldg -Cleveland 44115 **Fx:**592-5009

(419) 842-8200 ..**Osborne,** Gary W '75 -7150 Granite Cir Dr -Toledo 43617

(330) 965-8000 ..**Osborne,** Glenn R '87 (Osborne D&S Co LPA) -100 Marwood Cir
-Boardman 44512 **Fx:**965-8005

(303) 295-8000 ..**Osborne,** Thomas J Jr. '94 %Holland & H -555 17th -Ste 3200
-Denver, CO 80202

(740) 363-9232 ..**Osborne,** Wesley W '00 Shade & S -41 N Sandusky -Ste 410
-Delaware 43015

(216) 621-0150 ..**Oscar,** Lawrence E '81 (Hahn L&P LLP) -3300 BP Twr/200 Pub Sq
-Ste 3300 -Cleveland 44114 **Fx:**241-2824

(513) 977-8200 ..**Ose,** Paul A '77 (Dinsmore & S LLP) -255 E 5th -Ste 1900
-Cincinnati 45202 **Fx:**977-8141

(614) 644-7342 ..**Oser,** Joseph M '76 Dept Mntl Rtrdtn -1810 Sullivant Av
-Columbus 43266 **Fx:**752-8551

(614) 224-3741 ..**Oser,** Michael N '78 -35 E Lvngstn Av -Columbus 43215

(419) 213-4700 ..**Osgood,** Mark R '78 %Lucas Cnty Pros -Adams & Erie
-Lucas Cnty Cthse -Toledo 43624

(614) 228-6885 ..**O'Shaughnessy,** Christopher T '98 %Lane A&H LLC -175 S 3rd
-Ste 700 -Columbus 43215 **Fx:**228-0146

(216) 348-5400 ..**O'Shaughnessy,** Lucy K '99 %McDonald H Co,LPA -600 Superior
Av E -Ste 2100 -Cleveland 44114 **Fx:**348-5474

(614) 464-6400 ..**O'Shaughnessy,** Margaret E '97 %Vorys SS&P LLP -52 E Gay
-Bx1008 -Columbus 43216 **Fx:**464-6350

(513) 287-2062 ..**O'Shea,** Jill T '86 SrCnsl Cinergy Corp -139 E 4th -25 Atrium II
-Bx960 -Cincinnati 45201

(513) 421-4020 ..**O'Shea**, John L '89 (Cohen TK&S,LLC) -250 E 5th -Ste 1200 -Cincinnati 45202 **Fx:**241-4490

(216) 241-0011 ..**O'Shea**, Michael J '87 %Goldberg & O -323 Lakeside Av W -Ste 450 -Cleveland 44113

(614) 469-3200 ..**Oshima**, June M '98 %Thompson H LLP -10 W Broad -Ste 700 -Columbus 43215 **Fx:**469-3361

(614) 898-9918 ..**Osif**, Thomas J '75 -496 Straiton Sq -Westerville 43082

(330) 489-3395 ..**Osler**, Tammie M '01 Pros -218 Cleveland Av SW -Bx24218 -Canton 44702

(330) 385-3900 ..**Osman**, Daniel P '01 Aronson F&D Co, LPA -124 E 5th -East Liverpool 43920

(513) 595-2200 ..**Osmond**, Charles D '84 Union Cntrl Life Ins Co -Bx40888 -Cincinnati 45240

(419) 531-1021 ..**Osnowitz**, Samuel '75 Hirsch & O -2727 N Holland Sylvania Rd -Ste K -Toledo 43615

(419) 245-1954 ..**Osowik**, Thomas J '82 Mun Ct Judge -555 N Erie -Toledo 43624

(216) 621-0040 ..**O'Stafy**, Stacey A '99 %Strachan MO&R Co LPA -925 Euclid Av -Ste 1940 -Cleveland 44115

(330) 364-3353 ..**Ostapuck**, John A '72 Knisely & Assoc -137 E Iron Av -Bx609 -Dover 44622 **Fx:**364-4888

(513) 732-2140 ..**Ostendarp**, Gary D '71 (Ely & T) -322 Main -Batavia 45103

(216) 674-7094 ..**Oster**, Alexis S '94 Bristol West Ins Grp -5990 W Creed Rd -Independence 44131

(513) 852-6071 ..**Oster**, E Wednesday '04 %Wood & L LLP -600 Vine -Ste 2500 -Cincinnati 45202 **Fx:**852-6087

(614) 480-4540 ..**Oster**, Jody M '89 Huntington Natl Bank -41 S High -HC1032 -Columbus 43215

(513) 887-3474 ..**Oster**, Michael A Jr. '03 Butler Cnty Pros -315 High -11th Fl -Bx515 -Hamilton 45012

(614) 463-9770 ..**Osterkamp**, Kevin J '74 (Roetzel & A,LPA) -155 E Broad -Natl City Ctr 12th Fl -Columbus 43215 **Fx:**463-9792

(440) 237-1100 ..**Osterland**, Charles E '69 -6060 Royalton Rd -North Royalton 44133

..**Osterland**, Holly A '94 -(Address Unavailable)

(513) 723-4000 ..**Osterlund**, Anthony L '99 %Vorys SS&P LLP -221 E 4th -Ste 2000 Atrium Two -Bx0236 -Cincinnati 45201 **Fx:**723-4056

(614) 262-7880 ..**Osterman**, Lewis N III '80 -1150 Morse Rd -Ste 331 -Columbus 43229

(614) 262-1269 ..**Osterman**, Linda W '80 OH Dept Natural Rsrces -1855 Fountain Square Ct -2nd Fl -Columbus 43224

(419) 872-7915 ..**Osterud**, S D '74 Mun Ct Judge -300 Walnut -Perrysburg 43551

..**Ostgaard**, Andrea M '03 -4921 Tanner Dr -Dayton 45424

(419) 695-8480 ..**Osting**, Clayton P '84 -1101 Krieft -Delphos 45833

(904) 542-2565 ..**Ostrom**, Donald '03 US Navy -Box 107 Naval Air Sta -Bldg 4 Rm 127 -Jacksonville, FL 32212

(216) 765-8888 ..**Ostrovsky**, Mark L '76 -1 Hmptn Ct -Beachwood 44122

..**Ostrowski**, Andrea G '02 -512 Orangewood Dr -Kettering 45429

(614) 849-3000 ..**Ostrowski**, Bernard A '83 (Plante & Moran PLLC) -65 E State -Ste 600 -Columbus 43215

(614) 222-8686 ..**Ostrowski**, Edward L Jr. '95 %Scott S&W LLP -50 W Broad -2500 LeVeque Twr -Columbus 43215 **Fx:**222-8688

(216) 316-3161 ..**Ostrowski**, Joseph T '97 -1475 Warren Rd -Lakewood 44107

(216) 931-6000 ..**Ostrowski**, Thomas W '93 (Ulmer & B LLP) -1300 E 9th -Ste 900 Penton Media Bldg -Cleveland 44114 **Fx:**931-6001

(216) 525-7392 ..**O'Sullivan**, Cornelius J Jr. '90 SK Kelley -6133 Rockside Rd -Ste 208 -Independence 44131 **Fx:**643-3396

(513) 243-5617 ..**O'Sullivan**, Daniel F '93 GE Aircraft Engines -1 Neumann Way -MD F-17 -Cincinnati 45215

(419) 893-3374 ..**Oswald**, Julie S '95 Appliance Ctr -321 Illinois Av -Maumee 43537

(216) 696-7600 ..**Oswald**, Suellen '90 (Duvin C&H) -1301 E 9th -20th Fl Erievw Twr -Cleveland 44114 **Fx:**696-2038

(740) 349-6195 ..**Oswalt**, Kenneth W '86 Licking Cnty Pros -20 S 2nd -4th Fl -Newark 43055

(330) 562-4076 ..**Oswick**, Barbara R '92 -506 Fox Run Trl -Aurora 44202

(440) 244-0826 ..**Otero**, John B Jr. '74 Otero & O Co,LPA -2100 Reid Av -Lorain 44052

(740) 384-2111 ..**Oths Heiser & Miller** -16 E Bway -Bx309 -Wellston 45692

(740) 384-2111 ..**Oths**, Joseph A '61 (Oths H&M) -16 E Bway -Bx309 -Wellston 45692

(937) 225-5910 ..**Otis**, Erin D Matre '03 Montgomery Cnty CSEA -14 W 4th -Bx8744 -Dayton 45410

(216) 592-5000 ..**O'Toole**, Charles J '64 OfCnsl Tucker E&W LLP -925 Euclid Av -1150 Huntngtn Bldg -Cleveland 44115 **Fx:**592-5009

..**O'Toole**, Colleen M '91 -3214 Prospect Av E -Cleveland 44115

(440) 930-4001 ..**O'Toole**, Dennis M '74 (Baumgartner & O) -5455 Detroit Rd (Rte 254) -Sheffield Village 44054 **Fx:**934-7205

(216) 443-6350 ..**O'Toole**, Erin M '97 %8th Dist Ct of Appls -1 Lakeside Av -#202 -Cleveland 44113 **Fx:**443-2044

(612) 540-2422 ..**O'Toole**, John A '76 General Mills,Inc -1 Gen Mills Blvd -Minneapolis, MN 55426

(216) 685-9940 ..**O'Toole**, John K '67 -1370 Ontario -Ste 1314 -Cleveland 44113 **Fx:**685-9942

(330) 764-8437 ..**O'Toole**, Linda A '99 Medina Cnty Pub Def -120 W Wshngtn -Ste 2D -Medina 44256

(216) 226-0166 ..**O'Toole**, Sean C '98 -13614 Detroit Av -Lakewood 44107

(216) 241-7255 ..**O'Toole**, Thomas E '78 -2401 Superior Viaduct -Cleveland 44113

(440) 843-3004 ..**Ott**, Arthur E '88 -2170 W Sprague Rd -Parma 44134

(216) 771-2600 ..**Ott**, Steven M '80 (Ott & Assoc Co,LPA) -55 Pub Sq -Ste 1008 -Cleveland 44113 **Fx:**830-8939

(202) 927-7405 ..**Ott**, Timothy J '87 IRS -N:C:SC:DOP -Washington, DC 20224

(937) 433-7755 ..**Otto**, Craig W '78 -6900 Normancrest Ct -Dayton 45429

(216) 621-1113 ..**Otto**, Donald L '64 (Renner OB&S,LLP) -1621 Euclid Av -19th Fl -Cleveland 44115 **Fx:**621-6165

(404) 817-5003 ..**Otto**, James M '86 Ernst & Young LLP -600 Pchtree -Ste 2800 -Atlanta, GA 30308

(419) 524-9811 ..**Otto**, Richard H '81 (Weldon H&K,LLP) -28 Park Av W -Bank One Bldg -Mansfield 44902 **Fx:**522-5758

(614) 462-2242 ..**Ouellette**, Robert R '91 (Schottenstein Z&D) -250 West -Bx165020 -Columbus 43216 **Fx:**462-5135

(216) 664-4969 ..**Ousley**, Bobette S '75 Cleveland Mun Ct -1200 Ontario -Bx94894 -Cleveland 44101 **Fx:**664-4949

(513) 946-5200 ..**Outcalt**, Peter L '78 Hamilton Cnty Mun Ct -1000 Main -Cincinnati 45202

(713) 521-3133 ..**Outlaw**, Wilbert J '74 -3401 Louisiana -Ste 115 -Houston, TX 77002

(216) 861-5582 ..**Overberger**, Erik J '00 %Fay SFM&M LLP -1100 Superior Av -7th Fl -Cleveland 44114 **Fx:**241-1666

(513) 983-4463 ..**Overbey**, Terry L '75 Procter & Gamble Co-Legal -1 Procter & Gamble Plz -Cincinnati 45202

(937) 228-0880 ..**Overholser**, James N '72 (Sutton O&S) -130 W 2nd -1628 1st Natl Plz -Dayton 45402

(937) 276-6568 ..**Overholt**, Matthew T '00 Montgomery Cnty Pros -301 W 3rd -Bx972 -Dayton 45422 **Fx:**225-3470

(419) 865-1251 ..**Overley**, Thomas G '84 Wagoner & S,Ltd -7445 Airport Hwy -Holland 43528 **Fx:**866-8798

(614) 793-8000 ..**Overly**, Niles C '88 Frank Gates Co -Bx182364 -Columbus 43218

(937) 456-8136 ..**Overmyer**, Jenifer K '98 Preble Cnty Probate/Juv Ct -101 E Main -Cthse 2nd Fl -Eaton 45320

(602) 266-0700 ..**Overstreet**, Eric L '91 -210 E Catalina -Ste B -Phoenix, AZ 85012

(330) 264-4444 ..**Oviatt**, Lincoln P '56 OfCnsl Critchfield C&J Ltd -225 N Market -Bx599 -Wooster 44691 **Fx:**263-9278

(216) 621-5045 ..**Oviatt**, Richard A '67 -1370 Ontario -Ste 2000 -Cleveland 44113

(614) 221-8448 ..**Owen**, Andrew W '92 (Buckingham D&B,LLP) -191 W Nationwide Blvd -Ste 300 -Bx151120 -Columbus 43215 **Fx:**221-8590

(330) 725-9132 ..**Owen**, Jackie L '88 Medina Cnty Cmn Pleas Ct -99 Pub Sq -Medina 44256

(614) 436-3211 ..**Owen**, James D '79 (Cloud & O) -5354 N High -Ste 3D -Columbus 43214

(707) 544-6947 ..**Owen**, Norman M '94 -115 4th -Santa Rosa, CA 95401

(216) 241-2838 ..**Owen**, Robert B '00 %Taft S&H LLP -200 Pub Sq -3500 BP Twr -Cleveland 44114 **Fx:**241-3707

(937) 293-2392 ..**Owen**, William J '73 (Lair O&M) -580 Lincoln Park Blvd -Ste 111 -Dayton 45429

(740) 833-2690 ..**Owen**, William J II '86 %Delaware Cnty Pros -140 N Sandusky -3rd Fl -Delaware 43015

(216) 586-3939 ..**Owendoff**, Michael S '96 %Jones D -901 Lakeside Av -Cleveland 44114 **Fx:**579-0212

(216) 621-0150 ..**Owendoff**, Stephen P '69 (Hahn L&P LLP) -3300 BP Twr/200 Pub Sq -Ste 3300 -Cleveland 44114 **Fx:**241-2824

(937) 275-6842 ..**Owens**, Alvarene N '77 (A Owens Co,LPA) -1101 Salem Av -Dayton 45406

(912) 877-2211 ..**Owens**, Amy L '94 %Osteen & O -Bx1309 -Hinesville, GA 31310

(419) 524-7788 ..**Owens**, Beth Allen '04 %Allen & Assoc -24 W 3rd -Ste 200 -Mansfield 44902 **Fx:**524-7789

(330) 262-2667 ..**Owens**, Clarke W '99 -132 S Market -Ste 204 -Wooster 44691

(614) 469-2004 ..**Owens**, David L '78 Dept of Labor/Inspector Gen -Bx15596 -Columbus 43216

(937) 255-4600 ..**Owens**, Jeffrey R '99 Modern Tech Corp -2275 D -Rm 101,Bldg 16,ASC/LUA -Wright Patterson AFB 45433

(937) 333-4300 ..**Owens**, Mark E '81 Municipal Ct Clerk -301 W 3rd -113 -Dayton 45402

(216) 696-3311 ..**Owens**, Mark E '97 %Kahn K -1301 E 9th -2600 Erievw Twr -Cleveland 44114 **Fx:**623-4912

(614) 438-4964 ..**Owens**, Matthew A '03 Mettler-Toledo,Inc -1900 Polaris Pkwy -Columbus 43240

(513) 946-3700 ..**Owens**, Robert E '74 Hamilton Cnty Pub Def -230 E 9th -3rd Fl -Cincinnati 45202 **Fx:**946-3707

(330) 644-9917 ..**Owens**, Robert E '78 (Singer & O) -2775 S Arlngtn Rd -Akron 44312

(740) 368-0008 ..**Owens**, Robert M '98 -46 N Sandusky -Ste 202 -Delaware 43015

(513) 241-9400 ..**Owens**, Ross C III '85 Legal Aid -215 E 9th -Ste 200 -Cincinnati 45202

(216) 592-5000 ..**Owens**, Susan E '04 %Tucker E&W LLP -925 Euclid Av -1150 Huntngtn Bldg -Cleveland 44115 **Fx:**592-5009

(614) 228-8995 ..**Owens**, Timothy J '84 (Owens & K Co,LPA) -471 E Broad -Ste 2001 -Columbus 43215 **Fx:**228-8996

(740) 622-3911 ..**Owens**, William M '72 (Owens & M) -413 Main -2nd Fl -Bx787 -Coshocton 43812

(419) 663-2871 ..**Owens**, William W '69 -2 Oak -Norwalk 44857

(937) 642-4070 ..**Owens-Ruff**, Tina L '99 %Allen Y&M -233 W 5th -Bx391 -Marysville 43040

..**Owings**, Daniel H '80 -(Address Unavailable)

(419) 281-3561 ..**Oxley**, Fred M '73 (Lutz & O Co,LPA) -930 Claremont Av -Bx0220 -Ashland 44805 **Fx:**281-6999

(419) 422-8713 ..**Oxley Malone Hollister O'Malley & Warren, PLL** -301 E Main Cross -Bx1086 -Findlay 45840 **Fx:**422-6495

(419) 523-6104 ..**Oxley Malone Hollister O'Malley & Warren, PLL** -814 N Locust -Bx368 -Ottawa 45875 **Fx:**523-6447

(304) 529-2868 ..**Oxley**, Perry W '02 %Offutt F&N -949 3rd Av -Ste 300 -Bx2868 -Huntington, WV 25728 **Fx:**529-2999

(937) 223-3001 ..**Oxley**, Scott G '87 (Jenks P&O Co,LPA) -10 N Ludlow -Ste 901 -Dayton 45402 **Fx:**223-3103

(216) 289-2746 ..**Oyaski**, Paul F '77 Euclid Law Dept -585 E 222nd -Euclid 44123 **Fx:**289-2766

(973) 236-4177 ..**Oyer**, Jay H '81 Pricewaterhouse Coopers LLP -400 Campus Rd -Florham Park, NJ 07932

(717) 237-5236 ..**Oyler**, John S '99 (McNees W&N) -100 Pine -Bx1166 -Harrisburg, PA 17108 **Fx:**237-5300

..**Ozan**, Paul H '59 -(Address Unavailable)

(973) 962-0673 ..**Ozello**, James M '87 Ozello Tax & Lgl Cnsltng -37 Kendall Dr -Ringwood, NJ 07456 **Fx:**962-0673

(614) 459-0561 ..**Ozier**, James M '84 -5447 Millington Rd -Columbus 43235

(419) 249-7900 ..**Ozimek**, Mark A '04 %Robison C&O -Four SeaGate -9th Fl -Toledo 43604 **Fx:**249-7911

(614) 645-6296 ..**Paat**, Antonio B Jr. '88 Franklin Cnty Mun Ct -375 S High -Chmbrs 11D -Columbus 43215

(330) 492-0010 ..**Pac-Urar**, Mary L '89 -100 30th NW -Ste 107 -Canton 44709 **Fx:**492-1055

(614) 252-4649 ..**Pacchino**, Carmine E '94 -1063 Bryden Rd -Columbus 43205

(513) 852-5600 ..**Pace**, Beverly H '86 %Lopez HRM&S -312 Walnut -Ste 2090 -Cincinnati 45202 **Fx:**852-5611

..**Pace**, Don H '64 -Bx10537 -Sedona, AZ 86339

(202) 514-7566 ..**Pace**, George A Jr. '90 US Attys Ofc -555 4th NW -Washington, DC 20001

(216) 574-8690 ..**Pace**, Gerald J '02 Cleveland Mun Sch Dist -1380 E 6th
-Cleveland 44114

(614) 221-2400 ..**Pace**, Richard W '82 -233 S High -Ste 222 -Columbus 43215

(609) 720-4348 ..**Pace**, Salvatore P '80 Tyco Intl Inc -9 Roszel Rd
-Princeton, NJ 08540

(216) 696-4700 ..**Pace**, Stanley Dan '75 (Spieth BM&N Co,LPA) -925 Euclid Av
-2000 Huntngtn Bldg -Cleveland 44115 **Fx**:696-2706

(419) 243-1294 ..**Pacella**, Patrick P '71 Emch SS&P Co,LPA -One SeaGate
-Ste 1980 -Bx916 -Toledo 43697 **Fx**:243-8502

(330) 376-5300 ..**Pacenta**, Patricia A '81 (Buckingham D&B,LLP) -50 S Main
-Bx1500 -Akron 44309 **Fx**:258-6559

(513) 977-8200 ..**Pacheco**, Bryan E '97 %Dinsmore & S LLP -255 E 5th -Ste 1900
-Cincinnati 45202 **Fx**:977-8141

(330) 666-3777 ..**Pachell**, James T '84 (Cooper & P) -525 N Cleveland-Massillon Rd
-Akron 44333

Paciorek, Bryan '04 -(Address Unavailable)

(513) 779-0111 ..**Packard**, Dwight A '77 -9319 Cincinnati Columbus Rd
-West Chester 45069

(513) 579-6400 ..**Packard**, Dwight A II '96 %Keating M&K PLL -1 E 4th
-1400 Provident Twr -Cincinnati 45202 **Fx**:579-6457

(330) 264-6115 ..**Packard**, Jerry S '77 Logee HS&L -2171-B Eagle Pass
-Wooster 44691 **Fx**:262-5729

(614) 466-0601 ..**Packer**, David R '77 Industrial Commssn of OH -30 W Spring
-9th Fl -Columbus 43215 **Fx**:752-8785

(513) 645-1400 ..**Packer**, Dennis M '92 Powernet Global Comm -100 Cmmrcial Dr
-Fairfield 45014

(937) 865-6800 ..**Paczelt**, Anna E '86 Lexis/Nexis -Bx933 -Dayton 45401

(740) 432-6322 ..**Padden**, Daniel G '87 (Tribbie SP&P) -139 Ct Hse Sq -Bx640
-Cambridge 43725 **Fx**:439-1795

(614) 839-0400 ..**Paddock**, Harold D III '73 H Paddock Co,LPA
-2600 Corp Exchange Dr -Ste 112 -Columbus 43231

(832) 239-3724 ..**Paddock**, William S '69 (Jones DR&P) -600 Travis -Ste 6500
-Houston, TX 77002

(513) 721-5555 ..**Padro**, Diego J III '99 %B Maislin -906 Main -Ste 500
-Cincinnati 45202

(614) 481-9792 ..**Padro**, Ruben E '00 -2538 Dorset Rd -Columbus 43221

(216) 622-3600 ..**Paffilas**, Steven J '86 US Atty -801 W Superior -Ste 400
-Cleveland 44113 **Fx**:522-4982

(513) 424-1823 ..**Pagan**, Christopher J '94 (Repper P&P,LTD) -1501 1st Av
-Middletown 45044

(216) 685-9940 ..**Pagano**, Joseph V '01 (Pagano WT&G) -1370 Ontario -Ste 1240
-Cleveland 44113 **Fx**:685-9942

(216) 685-9940 ..**Pagano Wilson Thomarios & Gillissie** -1370 Ontario -Ste 1240
-Cleveland 44113 **Fx**:685-9942

(937) 223-1130 ..**Page**, Gregory S '95 %Pickrel S&E -40 N Main -2700 Kettering Twr
-Dayton 45423 **Fx**:223-0339

(330) 923-0401 ..**Pagel**, Thomas R '79 DLZ Ohio,Inc -2162 Front
-Cuyahoga Falls 44221

(216) 382-0444 ..**Paghis**, Stacy D '91 -4577 Mayfld Rd -Cleveland 44121

(216) 241-8333 ..**Paglia**, Michael A '99 Ritzler C&S,Ltd -1001 Lakeside Av
-1550 North Pnt Twr -Cleveland 44114 **Fx**:241-5890

(513) 287-3075 ..**Pahutski**, Michael J '99 Cnsl Cinergy Corp -139 E 4th -25 Atrium II
-Bx960 -Cincinnati 45201

(614) 791-8215 ..**Pahwa**, Susan K '81 -5757 Richgrove Ln -Dublin 43016

(216) 529-0030 ..**Phys**, Thomas R '74 -18123 Sloane Av -Lakewood 44107

(614) 464-6359 ..**Paige**, Bruce P '02 %Vorys SS&P LLP -52 E Gay -Bx1008
-Columbus 43216 **Fx**:464-6350

(614) 262-2724 ..**Painter**, Dorothy S '96 -3391 N High -Columbus 43202

(513) 739-4013 ..**Painter**, John W '91 -5820 Graves Lk Dr -Cincinnati 45243

(216) 687-1900 ..**Painter**, Kevin R '94 Legal Aid -1223 W 6th -Cleveland 44113
Fx:687-0779

(614) 224-3838 ..**Painter**, Lori B '92 P Fulton & Assoc -89 E Nationwide Blvd
-Ste 300 -Columbus 43215 **Fx**:224-3933

(615) 377-4600 ..**Painter**, Mattison C '89 Lattimore Black Morgan & Cain,PC
-5250 VA Way -Bx1869 -Brentwood, TN 37024

(614) 462-3555 ..**Painter**, Nathan D '03 %Franklin Cnty Pros -373 S High
-Columbus 43215

(330) 342-8203 ..**Paisley**, Andrew A '89 J Clunk Co LPA -5061 Hudson Dr -Ste 400
-Hudson 44236 **Fx**:342-8205

(330) 747-2579 ..**Palagano**, Michael Jr. '79 -26 Market -#507 -Youngstown 44503
Palau, Lois V '88 -Bx442 -Tiffin 44883

(419) 448-5422 ..**Palau**, Richard H '88 Tiffin Pros Ofc -51 E Market -Rm A-21
-Tiffin 44883

(614) 644-6526 ..**Palazij**, Martha S '01 OH Dept Commerce -77 S High
-Columbus 43266

(703) 556-5338 ..**Palazzolo**, Catherine P '94 The Law Registry -1825 K NW
-Ste 1101 -Washington, DC 20006

(216) 621-2606 ..**Palda**, George W '76 -55 Pub Sq -Ste 2121 -Cleveland 44113

(330) 334-1536 ..**Palecek McIlvaine Hoffmann & Morse Co LLP**
-200 Smokerise Dr -Ste 200 -Wadsworth 44281 **Fx**:334-7005

(330) 334-1536 ..**Palecek**, Thomas E '69 (Palecek MH&M Co LLP)
-200 Smokerise Dr -Ste 200 -Wadsworth 44281 **Fx**:334-7005

(513) 762-9800 ..**Palermo**, Julia B '01 Justice Inst for Legal Prof -201 E 5th
-Ste 1310 PNC Ctr -Cincinnati 45202

(513) 381-8213 ..**Palermo**, Maria C '91 Cincinnati Bar Assn -225 E 6th -2nd Fl
-Cincinnati 45202 **Fx**:381-0528

(304) 292-6965 ..**Paletta-Davis**, Lori J '90 Gabriel Bros,Inc -55 Scott Av
-Morgantown, WV 26508

(740) 695-5034 ..**Paleudis**, John G '73 Belmnt Cnty Magistrate -100 W Main
-Ste 204 -Saint Clairsville 43950 **Fx**:699-2632

(614) 577-1330 ..**Paley**, Eileen Y '88 -5969 E Lvngstn Av -Ste 200 -Columbus 43232

(216) 751-9529 ..**Paley**, Rochelle L '89 -19606 Scottsdale Blvd
-Shaker Heights 44122

(202) 326-4020 ..**Paliga**, John R '89 Pension Benefit Guaranty Corp -1200 K NW
-Ste 340 -Washington, DC 20005

(216) 621-1312 ..**Palik**, Evan J '85 %McMahon DH&L LLP -812 Huron Rd
-Ste 650 The Caxton Bldg -Cleveland 44115 **Fx**:621-0577
Palinkas, Laura T '88 -4431 S Meadow Ln -Cleveland 44109

(513) 651-6800 ..**Paliobeis**, Bill J '96 %Frost BT LLC -201 E 5th -2200 PNC Ctr
-Cincinnati 45202 **Fx**:651-6981

(216) 771-3777 ..**Palkovitz**, Herbert '69 -1370 Ontario -1600 Standard Bldg
-Cleveland 44113 **Fx**:771-1950

(216) 383-6836 ..**Pallam**, John J '65 Brush Wellman,Inc -17876 St Clair Av
-Cleveland 44110

(614) 224-7747 ..**Pallante**, Jeffrey A '02 %Osborne D&S Co LPA -495 S High
-Ste 200 -Columbus 43215

(216) 928-1211 ..**Palm**, Edward O '98 -2000 E 9th -Ste 710 -Cleveland 44115
Fx:781-3130

(419) 242-7985 ..**Palm-Kuebler**, Lisa '01 %Roetzel & A,LPA -One SeaGate -9th Fl
-Toledo 43604 **Fx**:242-0316

(330) 744-4137 ..**Palma**, Robert M '75 Friedman & R Co,LPA -100 Fed Plz E
-Ste 300 City Centre One -Youngstown 44503 **Fx**:744-9962

(859) 394-6200 ..**Palmer**, Andrea M '04 Adams SW&D -40 W Pike -Bx861
-Covington, KY 41012 **Fx**:291-7902

(216) 241-7000 ..**Palmer**, Brian W '92 %Landskroner & Assoc -55 Pub Sq -Ste 1040
-Cleveland 44113
Palmer, Donna K '91 -(Address Unavailable)

(614) 462-7145 ..**Palmer**, Gina W '94 Franklin Cnty Cmn Pleas Ct -375 S High
-Columbus 43215 **Fx**:462-6292

(216) 241-6602 ..**Palmer**, Jeffrey W '99 %Weston HFP&H LLP -50 Pub Sq
-2500 Trmnl Twr -Cleveland 44113 **Fx**:621-8369

(216) 267-1144 ..**Palmer**, John A '76 Repko Machine,Inc -5081 W 164th
-Brook Park 44142

(614) 891-2109 ..**Palmer**, John W '63 -9270 Hawthorn Pnt -Westerville 43082

(614) 252-1780 ..**Palmer**, Mark J '82 (Joseph Grp) -1780 E Broad -Columbus 43203
Fx:253-5077

(216) 901-1072 ..**Palmer**, Matthew W '99 Northcoast Comm LLC -7165 E
Plsnt Vlly Rd -Independence 44131

(330) 379-6543 ..**Palmer**, Meredith E '01 Bridgestone/Firestone
-1200 Firestone Pkwy -Akron 44317

(614) 823-8577 ..**Palmer**, Richard D '73 (R Palmer Co,LPA)
-2550 Corp Exchange Dr -Ste 324 -Columbus 43231

(440) 774-3665 ..**Palmer**, Robert A '76 -281 N Prospect -Oberlin 44074

(419) 476-1411 ..**Palmer**, Robert C '78 Maumee Valley Fabricators
-4801 Bennett Rd -Toledo 43612

(614) 484-1200 ..**Palmer**, Robert G '76 (RG Palmer Co,LPA) -140 E Town
-Ste 1200 -Columbus 43215

(216) 566-5500 ..**Palmer**, Stacey A '04 %Thompson H LLP -127 Pub Sq
-3900 Key Ctr -Cleveland 44114 **Fx**:566-5800

(614) 224-6142 ..**Palmer**, Stephen E '95 (Yavitch & P Co,LPA) -511 S High
-Columbus 43215 **Fx**:228-6078

(419) 663-6785 ..**Palmer**, Steve Jr. '92 City Law Dir Ofc -38 Whittlesey Av -Bx30
-Norwalk 44857 **Fx**:660-9876

(231) 264-0616 ..**Palmer**, Thomas E '64 T Palmer & Co -11196 US 31
-Williamsburg, MI 49690 **Fx**:264-0685

(330) 872-1617 ..**Palmer**, Thomas H '69 Palmer & P -41 W Broad
-Newton Falls 44444 **Fx**:872-5289

(419) 462-7060 ..**Palmer**, Thomas N '92 -140 W Church -Galion 44833

(419) 249-7100 ..**Palmer**, Thomas W '72 Marshall & M,LLC -Four Seagate -8th Fl
-Toledo 43604 **Fx**:249-7151

(614) 469-4781 ..**Palmer**, Thomas W '00 %Thompson H LLP -10 W Broad -Ste 700
-Columbus 43215 **Fx**:469-3361

(216) 622-8200 ..**Palmer**, Todd F '90 (Calfee H&G LLP) -800 Superior Av -Ste 1400
-Cleveland 44114 **Fx**:241-0816

(419) 627-7697 ..**Palmer**, Vicki R '79 Erie Cnty Pros -247 Columbus Av -Ste 319
-Sandusky 44870 **Fx**:627-7567

(216) 831-7338 ..**Palmeri**, Charles J '77 (C Palmeri Co,LPA) -30100 Chagrin Blvd
-Ste 120 -Pepper Pike 44124

(216) 696-1400 ..**Palmieri**, Anthony G Jr. '75 M Amato Co,LPA -700 W St Clair Av
-Ste 210 -Cleveland 44113 **Fx**:696-4919

(410) 279-9700 ..**Palmiotto**, Vincent J '98 %Rubin & R -502 Wshngtn Av
-Towson, MD 21204

(330) 208-4520 ..**Palmisano**, Ralph J '73 (Evanchan & P) -1 GOJO Plz -Ste 300
-Akron 44311 **Fx**:208-4519

(504) 455-8890 ..**Palmisano**, Robin S '86 R Palmisano,LLC -4417 Lorino
-Metairie, LA 70006

(330) 725-4935 ..**Palmquist**, James B III '76 (JB Palmquist III Co,LPA) -5 Pub Sq
-Medina 44256

(352) 332-8800 ..**Palmquist**, Jonathon B '85 Tower Hill Ins Grp,Inc
-7201 NW 11th Pl -Gainesville, FL 32605

(216) 696-0990 ..**Palnik**, Matthew A '97 %Shapiro M&R -1468 W 9th -Rm 425
-Cleveland 44113 **Fx**:696-7790

(614) 224-8374 ..**Palof**, Marcia E '80 Legal Aid -40 W Gay -Columbus 43215

(330) 629-9030 ..**Palombaro**, Albert A '84 -1032 Boardman-Canfld Rd
-Youngstown 44512 **Fx**:629-9036

(412) 644-6394 ..**Palombizio**, Edward J Jr. '77 US Dept Housing & Urban Dvlpmnt
-339 6th Av -6th Fl -Pittsburgh, PA 15222

(216) 623-1123 ..**Palombo**, Antonio N '95 %Sindell YG&S,PLL -55 Pub Sq
-Ste 1020 -Cleveland 44113 **Fx**:623-1124

(216) 443-8800 ..**Palos**, Diane M '84 Cuyahoga Cnty Dom Rltns Ct -1 Lakeside Av
-Cleveland 44113

(216) 696-9555 ..**Paluf**, Timothy G '78 -526 Superior Av E -Leader Bldg Ste 1540
-Cleveland 44114

(216) 592-5000 ..**Palumbo**, John P '70 Cnsl Tucker E&W LLP -925 Euclid Av
-1150 Huntngtn Bldg -Cleveland 44115 **Fx**:592-5009
Palusak, Julie D '94 -625 Squirrel Hill Dr -Youngstown 44512

(614) 462-5041 ..**Pampush**, Thomas A '93 (Schottenstein Z&D) -250 West
-Bx165020 -Columbus 43216 **Fx**:462-5155

(330) 876-1583 ..**Panak**, Stephen D '86 -7444 Perkins Greenvll Rd -Kinsman 44428

(513) 241-5400 ..**Pandilidis**, Peter '65 -1029 Main -Cincinnati 45202

(614) 566-5151 ..**Pandora**, Frank T II '72 %OhioHealth -3722 Olentangy Rvr Rd
-Ste K -Columbus 43214

(614) 469-1301 ..**Pandora**, Gary J '78 (Chorpenning G&P Co,LPA) -585 S Front
-Ste 250 -Columbus 43215
Pandurevic, Branislav '87 -612 JoJoba Ct -Las Vegas, NV 89144

Panek, Jason M '04 -7684 Delaware Dr
-Middleburg Heights 44130

(859) 344-1188 ..**Pangburn**, Charles H III '90 (Hemmer SPD PLLC)
-250 Grandvw Dr -Ste 200 -Ft Mitchell, KY 41017

(419) 244-2201 ..**Pangle**, Laurie J '83 (Spengler N PLL) -608 Mad Av -Ste 1000
-Toledo 43604 **Fx**:241-8599

(216) 241-5310 ..**Pangrace**, Martin J '01 %Gallagher SF&N -1501 Euclid Av -6th Fl
-Cleveland 44115 **Fx**:241-1608

(614) 224-4004 ..**Panico**, Paul R '90 (P Panico,LPA) -155 W Main -Columbus 43215

(614) 221-3178 ..**Panitch**, Harry F '92 -454 E Main -st 275 -Columbus 43215

(330) 926-2483 ..**Pannell,** Linda L '86 -2525 State Rd -Cuyahoga Falls 44223
(614) 466-2739 ..**Pannett,** Thomas P '99 OH DOT -1980 W Broad
-Columbus 43223
(330) 376-6766 ..**Pantages,** Pamela E '90 M Djordjevic Co,LPA -17 S Main -Ste 201
-Akron 44308 **Fx:**376-7344
(513) 684-3711 ..**Pantel,** Nicholas J '72 US Atty -221 E 4th -Ste 400 -Cincinnati
45202 **Fx:**684-6385
(614) 624-7093 ..**Pantelakis,** Katherine J '93 Ross Prdcts Div -625 Cleveland Av
-Columbus 43215
(440) 930-8055 ..**Panza,** Richard D '73 Wickens HPC&B -35765 Chester Rd
-Avon 44011 **Fx:**937-4466
(740) 387-4998 ..**Panzer,** John W '70 -407 S Main -Ste 2C -Marion 43302
(614) 644-2489 ..**Panzera,** Dominic A Jr. '91 Dept Cmmrce/Liquor Cntrl
-6606 Tussing Rd -Bx4005 -Reynoldsburg 43068 **Fx:**644-3740
  Paolano, Mary J '74 -Erievw Station -Bx99101 -Cleveland 44199
(614) 466-2980 ..**Paoletti,** Paula L '94 Atty Gen -30 E Broad -Columbus 43215
Fx:728-9470
(513) 241-0400 ..**Paolo,** Richard A '82 (Aronoff R&H Co,LPA) -425 Walnut
-Ste 2400 -Cincinnati 45202 **Fx:**241-2877
(330) 678-0242 ..**Paoloni,** Robert J '74 -250 S Water -Kent 44240
(513) 946-3000 ..**Paolucci,** Krista R '91 Hamilton Cnty Pros -230 E 9th
-Cincinnati 45202 **Fx:**946-3017
(513) 651-1219 ..**Paolucci,** Michael A '91 -120 E 4th -Ste 425 -Cincinnati 45202
(216) 831-4935 ..**Papa,** Nicholas A '92 Carlin & C -29425 Chagrin Blvd -Ste 305
-Pepper Pike 44122
(419) 537-8524 ..**Papadimos,** Peter J '82 Univ of Toledo Law Schl
-2801 W Bancroft -Toledo 43606
(419) 213-4700 ..**Papadimos,** Steven J '83 %Lucas Cnty Pros -Adams & Erie
-Lucas Cnty Cthse -Toledo 43624
(216) 479-8500 ..**Papajcik,** Dale E '86 (Squire S&D LLP) -127 Pub Sq
-4900 Key Twr -Cleveland 44114 **Fx:**479-8780
  Papajcik, Daniel A '04 -21190 Erie Rd -Rocky River 44116
(513) 705-9000 ..**Papakirk,** James '94 (Pratt SP Co,LPA) -301 N Breiel Blvd
-Middletown 45044 **Fx:**705-9001
(513) 541-0061 ..**Papakirk,** Maria J '97 Camp Washington Chili Inc
-3005 Colerain Av -Cincinnati 45225
(440) 949-1500 ..**Papandreas,** George J '86 Profile Dvlpmnt Corp -5205 Edgewtr Dr
-Sheffield Lake 44054 **Fx:**949-6349
(216) 621-8600 ..**Papandreas,** John G '54 -1370 W 6th -Ste 208 -Cleveland 44113
Fx:621-8609
(440) 846-1661 ..**Papandreas,** Joyce M '91 -14193 Basswood Cir
-Strongsville 44136
(330) 643-2943 ..**Papanicolaou,** Vayia '03 Summit Cnty Pros-Juv -650 Dan
-Akron 44310 **Fx:**379-3647
(614) 334-3362 ..**Paparodis,** Chris O '82 -5275 Norwich -Hilliard 43026
Fx:334-3364
(330) 379-2083 ..**Papas,** Katerina C '89 Summit Cnty Chldrn Srvcs -264 S Arlngtn
-Akron 44306 **Fx:**379-1897
(419) 891-8884 ..**Papay,** Debbie J '85 (Bayer P&S Co,LPA) -1925 Indn Wd Cir
-Maumee 43537 **Fx:**891-8889
(440) 743-7000 ..**Papcke,** Mary E '84 -12936 Huffman Rd -Parma Heights 44130
Fx:743-7500
(440) 247-7800 ..**Papesh,** Amy L '00 %McSherry & Co -178 E Wshngtn
-Chagrin Falls 44022 **Fx:**247-7801
(513) 232-1111 ..**Papner,** Donald F '60 -7854 Kimbee Dr -Cincinnati 45244
(614) 466-3615 ..**Papp,** Dennis M '76 Legis Srvc Commssn -77 S High -Columbus
43215
(216) 621-0200 ..**Papp,** Edward D '97 %Baker & H LLP -1900 E 9th -Ste 3200
-Cleveland 44114 **Fx:**696-0740
(440) 526-4500 ..**Papp,** James E '72 %RL Tuma & Assoc -8225 Brecksvll Rd
-Bldg 3 Ste 101 -Brecksville 44141 **Fx:**526-6362
(216) 241-5310 ..**Pappalardo,** Joseph W '80 (Gallagher SF&N) -1501 Euclid Av
-6th Fl -Cleveland 44115 **Fx:**241-1608
(330) 864-0500 ..**Pappas,** Angela M '99 Boecker & P,LPA -55 S Miller Rd -Ste 200
-Fairlawn 44333 **Fx:**864-0520
(330) 643-3550 ..**Pappas,** Carol L '85 Industrial Commssn of OH -161 S High
-Ste 301 -Akron 44308
(330) 535-6185 ..**Pappas,** George C '86 -159 S Main -Ste 1002 -Akron 44308
Fx:996-4014
(937) 652-2700 ..**Pappas,** George Z '86 -115 N Main -Ste C -Bx321 -Urbana 43078
(614) 621-1500 ..**Pappas,** Leah '93 (Calfee H&G LLP) -21 E State
-1100 Fifth Third Ctr -Columbus 43215 **Fx:**621-0010
(720) 266-1040 ..**Pappas,** Lori C '00 %Gougér & F,LLC -400 Inverness Pkwy
-Englewood, CO 80112 **Fx:**266-1041
(937) 322-6655 ..**Pappas,** Panayotis F '67 -28 N Fountain Av -Springfield 45502
(614) 888-8500 ..**Pappas,** Robert T '84 (Jones TP&P,LPA) -1472 Manning Pkwy
-Powell 43065 **Fx:**888-2560
(360) 476-6597 ..**Pappas,** Stephanie E '74 Dept of Navy Shipyard Cnsl
-Puget Sound Nvl Shpyrd Code 1130 -Bremerton, WA 98314
(614) 621-2000 ..**Pappas,** Thomas P '87 -66 E Lynn -Ste 2000 -Columbus 43215
(937) 254-7312 ..**Pappayliou,** George S '90 Tomkins Indust,Inc -6450 Poe Av
-Ste 109 -Dayton 45414
(419) 475-7700 ..**Papurt,** Richard A '90 -2638 Latonia Blvd -Toledo 43606
(216) 741-2365 ..**Paradise,** Ramona E '79 UAW Legal Srvcs -707 Brookpark Rd
-Brooklyn Heights 44109
(614) 223-9300 ..**Paragas,** Conrado David '90 (Benesch FC&A LLP) -88 E Broad
-Ste 900 -Columbus 43215 **Fx:**223-9330
(614) 898-8795 ..**Paragas,** Leonore T '89 Mt Carmel Hlth Plan -495 Cooper Rd
-Ste 212 -Westerville 43081
(440) 356-0021 ..**Parasiliti,** Mary F '01 LexisNexis -4167 W 220th -Fairview
Park 44126
(734) 547-1153 ..**Paratto,** Yolanda M '92 Forest Hlth Srvcs -135 S Prospect
-Leg Dept -Ypsilanti, MI 48198
(216) 621-0200 ..**Paravano,** Jeffrey H '91 (Baker & H LLP) -1900 E 9th -Ste 3200
-Cleveland 44114 **Fx:**696-0740
(216) 443-6350 ..**Parchem,** David F '80 8th Dist Ct of Appls -1 Lakeside Av -#202
-Cleveland 44113 **Fx:**443-2044
(419) 475-6043 ..**Pardee,** John K III '74 -2828 W Central Av -Ste 10 -Toledo 43606
Fx:474-4654
(614) 221-2525 ..**Pardi,** James J II '92 -529 S 3rd -Columbus 43215
(216) 520-5600 ..**Paredes,** Marie-Joy L '01 West Grp -6111 Oak Tree Blvd
-Bx318063 -Cleveland 44131

(614) 459-8620 ..**Parello,** Raymond S '96 -3363 Tremont Rd -Ste 104-C
-Columbus 43221
(419) 247-8707 ..**Parikh,** Niravkumar D '91 Owens Illinois,Inc -One SeaGate
-25 LDP -Toledo 43666
(216) 621-2300 ..**Paris,** David M '78 Nurenberg PH&M LPA -1370 Ontario -Ste 100
-Cleveland 44113 **Fx:**771-2242
(216) 575-7500 ..**Paris,** E T '87 Paris & P -55 Pub Sq -Ste 1275 -Cleveland 44113
(216) 575-7500 ..**Paris,** John T '85 Paris & P -55 Pub Sq -Ste 1275
-Cleveland 44113
(216) 664-4955 ..**Paris,** Michelle L '84 Cleveland Mun Ct -1200 Ontario
-Cleveland 44113
(216) 687-1902 ..**Paris,** Scott W '03 %S Haygood & Assoc -1422 Euclid Av
-Ste 1510 -Cleveland 44115 **Fx:**687-1906
(216) 575-7500 ..**Paris,** Thomas '53 Paris & P -55 Pub Sq -Ste 1275
-Cleveland 44113
(216) 586-3939 ..**Paris,** Zachary T '73 (Jones D) -901 Lakeside Av
-Cleveland 44114 **Fx:**579-0212
(614) 466-0400 ..**Parise,** Rita R '85 OH Housing Finance Agncy -57 E Main
-Columbus 43215
(614) 253-1010 ..**Pariser,** David B '74 (Dana & P Co,LPA) -800 E Broad
-Columbus 43205 **Fx:**253-3310
(800) 224-7914 ..**Parish,** Elinor G '90 LAWO -125 W Water -Sandusky 44870
Fx:(419) 609-9173
(614) 217-2881 ..**Parisi,** Donna J '01 Bank One -100 E Broad -Columbus 43215
(937) 298-1961 ..**Parisi,** Georgianna I '82 -3430 S Dixie Dr -Ste 100
-Kettering 45439
(216) 360-9969 ..**Parisi,** Stephen T '66 -30800 Brookwood Dr -Pepper Pike 44124
Fx:360-9969
(614) 923-1000 ..**Parisi,** Vincent A '01 Interstate Gas Supply,Inc
-5020 Bradenton Av -Dublin 43017
(614) 459-3272 ..**Park,** Chan W '00 Sheet Metal Cntrctrs Assoc -3518 Riverside Dr
-Ste 203 -Columbus 43221
(330) 451-7716 ..**Park,** Dixilene T '92 Stark Cnty Cmn Pleas Crt -115 Central Plz N
-Canton 44702
(216) 443-8618 ..**Park,** Eliza J '02 Cuyahoga Cnty Ct Cmmn Pleas -1200 Ontario
-Justice Ctr 11th Fl -Cleveland 44113
(513) 977-4208 ..**Park,** Robert G '77 -917 Main -Cincinnati 45202
(216) 687-1311 ..**Parker,** Alan B '88 (Reminger & R) -101 Prospect Av W
-1400 Mdlnd Bldg -Cleveland 44115 **Fx:**687-1841
(330) 764-3101 ..**Parker,** Andrew M '03 -600 E Smith Rd -Medina 44256
(216) 928-7700 ..**Parker,** Anthony T '97 I Friedman & Assoc -700 W St Clair Av
-Ste 110 -Cleveland 44113 **Fx:**556-9779
(419) 244-9500 ..**Parker,** Christopher F '84 (Goranson P&B) -405 Mad Av -Ste 2200
-Toledo 43604 **Fx:**(414) 244-9510
(216) 621-5300 ..**Parker,** Christopher L '91 (Buckingham D&B,LLP) -1375 E 9th
-Ste 1700 -Cleveland 44114 **Fx:**525-5440
(740) 354-1000 ..**Parker,** Danielle M '03 %Hoover Law Grp -621 7th
-Portsmouth 45662 **Fx:**353-0661
(614) 445-3960 ..**Parker,** Darryl O '99 (D Parker Co,LPA) -786 S Front
-Columbus 43206
(513) 887-3778 ..**Parker,** Deborah L '90 Butler Cnty Dom Rltns Ct -315 High -2nd Fl
-Hamilton 45011
(216) 479-8500 ..**Parker,** Elton L '99 %Squire S&D LLP -127 Pub Sq -4900 Key Twr
-Cleveland 44114 **Fx:**479-8780
(419) 255-4300 ..**Parker,** Ericka S '97 %Hunter & S Co,LPA -1700 Canton Av
-One Canton Sq -Toledo 43624 **Fx:**255-9121
  Parker, Frederick B '64 -(Address Unavailable)
(513) 258-1991 ..**Parker,** George M '90 (Qucsai & P) -Bx432 -Mason 45040
(330) 884-4913 ..**Parker,** Gerald M '71 Forum Hlth Wstrn Resrv Care Syst
-500 Gypsy Ln -Youngstown 44504
(330) 867-6221 ..**Parker,** Harold G '69 -154 Birdwood Rd -Akron 44313
(440) 461-8500 ..**Parker,** Jason P '99 Basil Russo & Co,LPA -691 Richmond Rd
-Richmond Heights 44143
(614) 466-1156 ..**Parker,** Jennifer A '87 Legis Srvc Commssn -77 S High
-Columbus 43215
(216) 635-1705 ..**Parker,** Jennifer E '97 (Hammer & P) -4617 Denmark Av
-Cleveland 44102
(419) 244-8336 ..**Parker,** Jerome R '73 (Gressley K&P) -608 Mad Av -Ste 930
-Toledo 43604 **Fx:**244-1914
(216) 586-3939 ..**Parker,** Johanna Fabrizio '99 %Jones D -901 Lakeside Av
-Cleveland 44114 **Fx:**579-0212
(216) 621-0200 ..**Parker,** John D '83 (Baker & H LLP) -1900 E 9th -Ste 3200
-Cleveland 44114 **Fx:**696-0740
(216) 881-0900 ..**Parker,** John P '89 -4403 St Clair Av -Cleveland 44103
(330) 253-2227 ..**Parker Leiby Hanna & Rasnick,LLC** -388 S Main -Ste 402
-Akron 44311 **Fx:**253-1261
(419) 213-3270 ..**Parker,** Marilyn L '82 SrCnsl Lucas Co Children Srvcs -705 Adams
-5th Fl -Toledo 43624 **Fx:**327-3291
(216) 481-0020 ..**Parker,** Patrick R '93 -20050 Lakeshr Blvd -Euclid 44123
(513) 381-2838 ..**Parker,** R Joseph '69 (Taft S&H LLP) -425 Walnut -Ste 1800
-Cincinnati 45202 **Fx:**381-0205
(513) 529-6734 ..**Parker,** Robin L '82 Miami Univ -215 Roudebush Hall
-Oxford 45056
(614) 778-1695 ..**Parker,** Shinerr J '04 -Bx297805 -Columbus 43229
(614) 462-3555 ..**Parker,** Stacy '04 Franklin Cnty Pros -373 S High
-Columbus 43215
(513) 345-5000 ..**Parker,** Tamara R '04 %Lawson & Assoc -808 Elm -Ste 100
-Cincinnati 45202
(330) 253-2227 ..**Parker,** Thomas M '79 (Parker LH&R,LLC) -388 S Main -Ste 402
-Akron 44311 **Fx:**253-1261
(202) 225-7690 ..**Parker,** Wyndee M '95 House of Rep -H-405, US Cptl
-Washington, DC 20515
  Parkes, Wright C '83 -1932 Woodward Av
-Cleveland Heights 44118
(614) 469-3939 ..**Parkhill-Krein,** Gayle E '83 (Jones D) -325 John H McConnell
Blvd -Ste 600 -Bx165017 -Columbus 43216 **Fx:**461-4198
(216) 831-0042 ..**Parkins,** Matthew E '00 %Meyers RF&L LPA -28601 Chagrin Blvd
-Ste 500 -Cleveland 44122 **Fx:**831-0542
(214) 767-1590 ..**Parkinson,** William S '82 US Trustee -1100 Commerce -Rm 9C60
-Dallas, TX 75242
(513) 895-0044 ..**Parks,** Brenda B '91 Bruck Law Ofc -110 N 3rd -Hamilton 45011
(614) 255-2006 ..**Parks,** Edward Y '80 -336 S High -Columbus 43219
(614) 227-2386 ..**Parks,** Gregory T '95 %Bricker & E LLP -100 S 3rd
-Columbus 43215 **Fx:**227-2390

(937) 328-9055 ..**Parks,** Kimberly S '96 Cmmnty Hosp -2615 E High
-Springfield 45505

(814) 870-7754 ..**Parks,** Richard J '85 %McDonald IJ&B -100 State -Ste #700 -Erie, PA 16507

Parlier, Dawn Meyers '98 -(Address Unavailable)

(330) 721-0000 ..**Parmelee,** Christopher L '98 %Walker & J,LPA -231 S Bway
-Medina 44256 Fx:722-6446

(614) 229-5142 ..**Parmer,** Brandon J '03 Ernst & Young -41 S High
-1100 Huntgtn Ctr -Columbus 43215

(937) 323-3768 ..**Parmley,** Terri L '88 %P Malina Co,LPA -6 W High -Ste 806
-Springfield 45502

(330) 376-6136 ..**Parms,** Edwin L '65 -209 S Main -Akron 44308

(513) 621-2120 ..**Parnell,** John G Jr. '71 OfCnsl Strauss & T,LPA -150 E 4th -4th Fl
-Cincinnati 45202 Fx:241-8259

(216) 479-6100 ..**Parobek,** Drew T '84 (Vorys SS&P LLP) -175 E 9th
-Ste 2100 One Cleve Ctr -Cleveland 44114 Fx:479-6060

(440) 244-1681 ..**Parobek,** James J '52 -763 Bway -Lorain 44052 Fx:244-2101

(770) 394-8800 ..**Paronish,** Terry L '92 3M HIS Consulting Srvc -100 Ashford Ctr N
-Ste 200 -Atlanta, GA 30338

(330) 534-3103 ..**Paroz,** Roger C '80 -Bx67 -Brookfield 44403

Parra, Alan M '01 -(Address Unavailable)

(614) 464-4661 ..**Parrill,** Kenneth W Jr. '83 (Parrill & Assoc Co,LPA) -Bx06360
-Columbus 43206

(614) 462-3555 ..**Parris,** Selena D '95 Franklin Cnty Pros -373 S High
-Columbus 43215

(513) 248-1526 ..**Parrish,** Dawne M '96 -102 Laurel Av -Milford 45150

(513) 241-9400 ..**Parrish,** Donita S '01 Legal Aid -215 E 9th -Ste 200
-Cincinnati 45202

(513) 863-8270 ..**Parrish Fryman & Marcum Co,LPA** -300 High -Ste 704 -Bx747
-Hamilton 45012 Fx:863-9999

Parrish, Justin P '94 -Bx16805 -Rocky River 44116

(513) 863-8270 ..**Parrish,** Lee H '68 Parrish F&M Co,LPA -300 High -Ste 704
-Bx747 -Hamilton 45012 Fx:863-9999

(513) 455-5324 ..**Parrish,** Matthew S '94 Andrew Jergens Co
-2535 Spring Grove Av -Cincinnati 45214

(330) 665-4547 ..**Parrish,** Thomas E '77 Johnson & Parrish Title Agncy
-1000 N Cleveland-Massillon Rd -Ste 03 -Akron 44333

(937) 642-2950 ..**Parrott,** Robert W '85 Parrott Law Ofc -127 W 6th
-Marysville 43040

(330) 652-1749 ..**Parry,** Patrick E '94 -761 N Cedar -Niles 44446 Fx:652-2356

(614) 280-1804 ..**Parry,** Richard B '95 -5 E Long -Ste 902 -Columbus 43215

(859) 291-9000 ..**Parry,** Ronald R '87 (Parry DF&S,PSC) -411 Garrard
-Covington, KY 41012 Fx:291-9300

(239) 598-3176 ..**Parry,** Timothy R '80 SrCnsl HMA Hlth Mgmt Assoc
-5811 Pelican Bay Blvd -Ste 500 -Naples, FL 34108 Fx:594-7368

(614) 365-9900 ..**Parsell,** Stuart G '94 (Zeiger TL&L,LLP) -41 S High
-Ste 3500 Huntngtn Ctr -Columbus 43215 Fx:365-7900

(248) 813-3367 ..**Parshall,** Donald R Jr. '91 Delphi Auto Sys -5725 Delphi Dr
-M/C 483400 126 -Troy, MI 48098

(513) 621-6464 ..**Parsley,** Sharon S '04 %Graydon H&R LLP -511 Walnut
-1900 Fifth Third Ctr -Cincinnati 45202 Fx:651-3836

(937) 225-4987 ..**Parson,** Angela L '03 Montgomery Cnty Pros/CSEA -14 W 4th
-Ste 510 -Dayton 45402

(614) 462-5412 ..**Parsons,** Angela G '97 %Kegler BH&R -65 E State -Ste 1800
-Columbus 43215 Fx:464-2634

(614) 221-2838 ..**Parsons,** Benjamin J '03 %Taft S&H LLP -21 E State -12th Fl
-Columbus 43215 Fx:221-2007

(419) 257-2879 ..**Parsons,** Glenn C '52 -211 S Main -North Baltimore 45872

(330) 376-6611 ..**Parsons,** Joseph D '87 Albrecht Inc -17 S Main -Ste 401 -Bx1714
-Akron 44309

(937) 644-3144 ..**Parsons,** Perry N '95 -11 W 6th -Marysville 43040

(515) 280-4445 ..**Parsons,** Robert M '72 Allied Group Inc -701 5th Av
-Des Moines, IA 50391

(614) 879-7606 ..**Parsons,** Ronald C '67 (Culp P&M) -8 E Main
-West Jefferson 43162

(216) 586-3939 ..**Parsons,** Theodore C '98 %Jones D -901 Lakeside Av
-Cleveland 44114 Fx:579-0212

(513) 424-2401 ..**Partin,** Robin R '97 %Casper & C -1 N Main -Bx510
-Middletown 45042 Fx:424-0622

(216) 621-4244 ..**Partlow,** Michael A '86 %Morganstern M&D Co,LPA -623 W
St Clair Av -Cleveland 44113 Fx:621-2951

(617) 248-9480 ..**Pasalis,** Dean J '97 (Smith & P LLP) -100 State -Ste 500
-Boston, MA 02109 Fx:812-1256

Pasalis, Thano G '71 -75 Pub Sq -Ste 310 -Cleveland 44113

(440) 564-5525 ..**Paschke,** Carolyn J '95 -10808 Kinsman Rd -Bx141
-Newbury 44065

(412) 566-3520 ..**Pasciullo,** Nicholas A '02 (White and W LLP) -437 Grant
-Ste 1001 -Pittsburgh, PA 15219

(901) 525-2761 ..**Pascover,** Kathryn W '86 (Young & P) -1 Commerce Sq -Ste 2380
-Memphis, TN 38103

(210) 403-5600 ..**Pascucci,** Victor III '95 SecureInfo Corp
-211 North Loop 1604 East -San Antonio, TX 78232

(904) 301-6300 ..**Pashayan,** Donald J '99 US Atty -300 N Hogan -Ste 700
-Jacksonville, FL 32202

Pasiadis, Christopher F '86 -Bx241005 -Lyndhurst 44124

(612) 743-9002 ..**Pasko,** Brian S '02 -4020 Columbus Av S -Minneapolis, MN 55407

(216) 664-2692 ..**Paspek,** Andrea M '89 Dept of Law -601 Lakeside Av
-Rm 106 City Hall -Cleveland 44114 Fx:664-2663

Pasqua-Goldstein, Silvana D '85 -(Address Unavailable)

(440) 466-4818 ..**Pasqualone,** Gary L '74 -302 S Bway -Geneva 44041

(216) 696-0040 ..**Passalacqua,** Edele '90 Passalacqua & Assoc -2830 Franklin Blvd
-Cleveland 44113

(614) 221-2121 ..**Passella,** Michael V '00 %Isaac BL&T,LLP -250 E Broad
-Ste 900 Mdlnd Bldg -Columbus 43215 Fx:365-9516

(614) 645-6906 ..**Passmore,** Sherrie Jo '80 City Atty -90 W Broad -Columbus 43215

(412) 261-6600 ..**Passodelis,** Constantine J '02 (Meyer DBB&E,PLLC) -600 Grant
-Ste 4850 -Pittsburgh, PA 15219 Fx:471-2754

(216) 621-7905 ..**Passov,** Robert S '70 -75 Pub Sq -Ste 914 -Cleveland 44113

(614) 459-0118 ..**Pasternack,** Jacqueline B '94 -4347 Hrbrough Rd
-Columbus 43220

(216) 737-5000 ..**Pasternak,** Michael B '92 (Chernett WY&P) -1301 E 9th -Ste 3300
-Cleveland 44114 Fx:737-0011

Pastis, Alix G '85 -134 N Revere Rd -Akron 44333

(330) 497-2886 ..**Pastore,** Catherine A '87 %Zollinger DGT & Co -6370 Mt Plsnt NW
-Bx2985 -Canton 44720

(440) 572-3300 ..**Pasz,** David J '82 (D Pasz Co,LPA) -12001 Prospect Rd -Ste A1
-Strongsville 44149

(419) 321-1347 ..**Patberg,** William L '78 (Shumaker L&K,LLP) -1000 Jackson
-Toledo 43624 Fx:241-6894

(614) 466-7567 ..**Patchen,** Robert W '84 Dept Admin Srvcs -100 E Broad -15th Fl
-Columbus 43215

(614) 227-2000 ..**Pate,** Christina A '04 %Porter WM&A LLP -41 S High
-Columbus 43215 Fx:227-2100

Pate, Mary Ann '91 -327 Sterling Ct -Westerville 43082

(740) 282-2000 ..**Pate,** Samuel A '80 -328 Market -Ste 700 Sinclair Bldg
-Steubenville 43952 Fx:283-1111

(614) 469-3200 ..**Patel,** Akhil M '00 %Thompson H LLP -10 W Broad -Ste 700
-Columbus 43215 Fx:469-3361

(216) 348-1100 ..**Patel,** Ami J '04 %Schuster & S Co,LPA -2913 Clinton Av
-Cleveland 44113 Fx:348-0013

(513) 946-3700 ..**Patel,** Christine A '91 Hamilton Cnty Pub Def -230 E 9th -3rd Fl
-Cincinnati 45202 Fx:946-3707

Patel, Dipali R '01 -4110 N Lincoln Av -305 -Chicago, IL 60618

(513) 489-6678 ..**Patel,** Ken K '90 -8821 Weller Rd -Cincinnati 45249

(216) 658-3999 ..**Patel,** Ketan K '95 %Bio Enterprise Corp -11000 Cedar Av
-Ste 300 -Cleveland 44106

(216) 261-3500 ..**Patel,** Nirav A '03 Flight Optns -26180 Curtiss-Wright Pkwy
-Cuyahoga County Airport -Cleveland 44143

(513) 977-8200 ..**Patel,** Polly E '02 %Dinsmore & S LLP -255 E 5th -Ste 1900
-Cincinnati 45202 Fx:977-8141

(502) 561-0054 ..**Patel,** Sujyot S '91 (Peck S&W,LLP) -239 S 5th -Ste 1603
-Louisville, KY 40202 Fx:561-0058

(419) 435-5566 ..**Patel,** Upendra K '96 D Bennett & Assoc -125 S Main -Ste 301
-Fostoria 44830

(216) 586-3939 ..**Patel,** Vipul B '03 %Jones D -901 Lakeside Av -Cleveland 44114
Fx:579-0212

(513) 887-3277 ..**Pater,** Charles L '93 Butler Cnty Probate Ct -101 High
-Hamilton 45011

(513) 867-1411 ..**Pater,** Clement A III '69 (Pater P&P Co,LPA) -315 S Front
-Hamilton 45011

(513) 867-1411 ..**Pater,** Gerald L '68 (Pater P&P Co,LPA) -315 S Front
-Hamilton 45011

(513) 785-5880 ..**Pater,** Raymond C III '91 Butler Cnty CSEA -315 High -7th Fl
-Hamilton 45011

(419) 666-3116 ..**Paterson,** David G '82 -1016 Dixie Hwy -Ste A -Rossford 43460
Fx:662-8649

(440) 729-3930 ..**Patete,** Nancy Fioritto '86 -Bx895 -Chesterland 44026

(650) 739-3939 ..**Pathak,** Anand S '89 (Jones DR&P) -2882 Sand Hill Rd -Ste 240
-Menlo Park, CA 94025 Fx:739-3900

(419) 455-9508 ..**Patino,** Leticia G '82 -159 S Wshngtn -Tiffin 44883 Fx:455-9509

(614) 644-2489 ..**Patitsas,** Peter D '86 Dept Cmmrce/Liquor Cntrl -6606 Tussing Rd
-Bx4005 -Reynoldsburg 43068 Fx:644-3740

(614) 469-3939 ..**Patmon,** William W III '93 %Jones D -325 John H McConnell Blvd
-Ste 600 -Bx165017 -Columbus 43216 Fx:461-4198

(216) 696-9330 ..**Patno,** Christian R '90 Garson & Assoc Co,LPA
-614 Superior Av W -1600 Rckfllr Bldg -Cleveland 44113
Fx:696-8558

(734) 266-2648 ..**Paton,** Brian A '91 Cnsl TRW Automotive -12025 Tech Ctr Dr
-Livonia, MI 48150

(614) 248-6515 ..**Patrell,** Gregory S '99 Bank One Corp -100 E Broad -5th Fl
-Columbus 43215

(216) 523-1500 ..**Patrick,** Bradford J '99 Mansour GG&M Co,LPA -55 Pub Sq
-Ste 2150 -Cleveland 44113 Fx:523-1705

(614) 224-8374 ..**Patrick,** Gail D '79 Legal Aid -40 W Gay -Columbus 43215

(419) 227-3050 ..**Patrick,** James P '72 -1037 W Market -Lima 45805

(216) 687-1311 ..**Patrick,** John '93 (Reminger & R) -101 Prospect Av W
-1400 Mdlnd Bldg -Cleveland 44115 Fx:687-1841

(330) 744-4137 ..**Patrick,** Walter Terry '77 (Friedman & R Co,LPA) -100 Fed Plz E
-Ste 300 City Centre One -Youngstown 44503 Fx:744-9962

(937) 225-5601 ..**Patricoff,** George B '79 Montgomery Cnty Pros -301 W 3rd -Bx972
-Dayton 45422 Fx:225-3470

(330) 434-5118 ..**Patrino,** Anthony V '50 -265 S Main -1st Fl -Akron 44308

Patrizi, Judi A '04 -(Address Unavailable)

(937) 773-3212 ..**Patrizio,** Frank J '91 (McCulloch FF&G Co,LPA) -123 Market
-Bx910 -Piqua 45356 Fx:773-9672

(440) 951-3565 ..**Patronite,** Gerald J '73 (G Patronite Co,LPA) -34950 Chardon Rd
-#210 -Willoughby Hills 44094

(216) 442-1700 ..**Patsch,** Glenn F '75 -1144 Dorsh Rd -South Euclid 44121

(513) 721-4500 ..**Patsfall,** Stephen J '81 (Patsfall Y&P LLC) -1 W 4th -Ste 1800
-Cincinnati 45202 Fx:639-7554

(513) 721-4500 ..**Patsfall Yeager & Pflum LLC** -1 W 4th -Ste 1800
-Cincinnati 45202 Fx:639-7554

(216) 228-9400 ..**Patsouras,** Peter L '75 United Trans Union -14600 Detroit Av
-Cleveland 44107

(330) 725-5439 ..**Patsouras-Vukovich,** Rhonda '89 -5134 Fenn Rd -Medina 44256

(216) 228-7478 ..**Patta,** John D '88 -13317 Mad Av -Lakewood 44107

(859) 572-0100 ..**Patten,** John G '68 -1407 Alexandria Pike
-Fort Thomas, KY 41075

(614) 846-2000 ..**Patter,** Jeffrey J '81 Campbell HC&V,LLC -7650 Rvrs Edge Dr
-Columbus 43235 Fx:846-2003

(330) 670-8989 ..**Patterson,** Barbara J '85 -Bx8156 -Akron 44320

(260) 422-0800 ..**Patterson,** Craig R '92 (Beckman L LLP) -800 Standard Fed Plz
-Bx800 -Fort Wayne, IN 46801 Fx:420-1013

(614) 221-4799 ..**Patterson,** David C '75 (Readey & P) -37 W Broad -Ste 420
-Columbus 43215 Fx:221-2236

(440) 943-4700 ..**Patterson,** David N '64 -33579 Euclid Av -Willoughby 44094

(614) 280-1100 ..**Patterson,** David T '77 (Keener DC&P,LPA) -88 E Broad
-Ste 1750 -Columbus 43215

(330) 723-5082 ..**Patterson,** Denise K '88 Corrpro Co Inc -1090 Enterprise Dr
-Medina 44256

(937) 226-1200 ..**Patterson,** Dennis L '64 (Bogin P&B) -131 N Ludlow
-1200 Talbot Twr -Dayton 45402

(513) 381-8213 ..**Patterson,** Edwin W III '79 Cincinnati Bar Assn -225 E 6th -2nd Fl
-Cincinnati 45202 Fx:381-0528

(513) 272-3000 ..**Patterson,** George F Jr. '48 -7754 Camargo Rd -Ste 12
-Cincinnati 45243

(614) 228-2722 ..**Patterson**, Gregory L '79 -43 Hmltn Pk -Columbus 43203
(614) 466-2980 ..**Patterson**, James R '83 Atty Gen -30 E Broad -Columbus 43215 **Fx:**728-9470
(614) 228-7191 ..**Patterson**, Jay M '88 Cmmnty Mediation Srvcs -67 Jffrsn Av -Columbus 43215
(216) 241-6602 ..**Patterson**, Jill S '98 %Weston HFP&H LLP -50 Pub Sq -2500 Trmnl Twr -Cleveland 44113 **Fx:**621-8369
(614) 466-2980 ..**Patterson**, John E '82 Atty Gen -30 E Broad -Columbus 43215 **Fx:**728-9470
(216) 592-5000 ..**Patterson**, John P '03 %Tucker E&W LLP -925 Euclid Av -1150 Huntngtn Bldg -Cleveland 44115 **Fx:**592-5009
(513) 684-6022 ..**Patterson**, Karen A M '02 US Dept of Labor -36 E 7th -Ste 2525 -Cincinnati 45202
(205) 972-6133 ..**Patterson**, Kimberly S '92 BE&K Inc -2000 Intl Park Dr -Birmingham, AL 35243
(937) 228-2838 ..**Patterson**, Lisa L '96 %Taft S&H LLP -110 N Main -Ste 900 -Dayton 45402 **Fx:**228-2816
(513) 721-3330 ..**Patterson**, Mark C '79 (Robbins KP&T) -7 W 7th -Ste 1400 -Cincinnati 45202
(703) 696-9150 ..**Patterson**, Mark H '92 US Air Force Legal Srvcs -1501 Wilson Blvd -7th Fl -Arlington, VA 22209
(614) 790-3396 ..**Patterson**, Matthew T '82 Ashland Inc -5200 Blazer Pkwy -Dublin 43017
(419) 898-3688 ..**Patterson**, Michael P '90 Ottawa CDJFS -8043 W State Route 163 -Ste 200 -Oak Harbor 43449 **Fx:**898-2436
(740) 455-3448 ..**Patterson**, Ronald S '86 -2609 Bell -Zanesville 43701
(513) 241-3100 ..**Patterson**, Steven H '01 Lerner S&R -120 E 4th -8th Fl -Cincinnati 45202
(513) 533-2996 ..**Patterson**, William J '00 Finney SS&K Co,LPA -2623 Erie Av -Bx8804 -Cincinnati 45208
(440) 746-1177 ..**Patti**, Rose A '91 (Baran PTF&T Co,LPA) -8748 Brecksvll Rd -Ste 200 -Cleveland 44141 **Fx:**746-9637
(513) 732-3800 ..**Pattison**, George E '72 -285 Main -Batavia 45103
(740) 452-5403 ..**Pattison**, Jeff A '98 %Jones F&P -45 N 4th -Zanesville 43701
Patton, Anissa R '01 -Bx2389 -Peachtree City, GA 30269
(216) 231-9963 ..**Patton**, Charles L Jr. '83 -11811 Shaker Blvd -Ste 105 -Cleveland 44120 **Fx:**231-9965
(336) 631-8500 ..**Patton**, David V '99 %Robinson & L LLP -370 Knollwood -Ste 600 -Winston Salem, NC 27103
(440) 392-7169 ..**Patton**, Dennis P '77 STERIS Corp -5960 Heisley Rd -Mentor 44060
(419) 897-7439 ..**Patton**, Diana R '97 Dana Cmmrcl Credit -660 Beaver Crk -Maumee 43537
(216) 523-1500 ..**Patton**, Edward O '89 %Mansour GG&M Co,LPA -55 Pub Sq -Ste 2150 -Cleveland 44113 **Fx:**523-1705
(513) 221-2345 ..**Patton**, James W '72 -2345 Kemper Ln -Bx6129 -Cincinnati 45206 **Fx:**221-2375
(513) 583-4200 ..**Patton**, Jay D '97 %Schroeder MB&P -11935 Mason Rd -Ste 110 -Cincinnati 45249
Patton, John T '58 -(Address Unavailable)
(440) 899-1900 ..**Patton**, Joseph M '90 -25125 Detroit Rd -Ste 120 -Westlake 44145
(614) 462-7407 ..**Patton**, Kelly C '00 Franklin Cnty Probate Ct -373 S High -Columbus 43215
(513) 744-7146 ..**Patton**, Mona L '98 Fifth 3rd Bank -38 Fountain Sq Plz -MD1090V1 -Cincinnati 45263
(513) 412-1467 ..**Patton**, Nancy S '87 Great Amer Life Ins Co -525 Vine -11th Fl -Cincinnati 45202
(440) 734-9494 ..**Patton**, Richard F '54 -4573 W 221st -Cleveland 44126
(440) 350-2684 ..**Patton**, Robert J '96 Lake Cnty Pros -105 Main -Bx490 -Painesville 44077 **Fx:**350-2585
(216) 696-7600 ..**Patton**, Shannon K '98 %Duvin C&H -1301 E 9th -20th Fl Erievw Twr -Cleveland 44114 **Fx:**696-2038
(440) 247-7800 ..**Patton**, Steven E '84 (McSherry & Co) -178 E Wshngtn -Chagrin Falls 44022 **Fx:**247-7801
(330) 384-7033 ..**Patton**, Terry E '75 First Merit Corp -3 Cascade Plz -Akron 44308
(513) 381-0656 ..**Patton**, William A '68 (Kohnen & P LLP) -201 E 5th -Ste 800 -Cincinnati 45202 **Fx:**381-5823
(937) 225-5757 ..**Patzer**, Jeffrey M '96 Montgomery Cnty Pros -301 W 3rd -Bx972 -Dayton 45422 **Fx:**225-3470
(216) 241-7740 ..**Pauken**, Margaret M '90 -1468 W 9th -Ste 700 -Cleveland 44113
(419) 372-7377 ..**Pauken**, Patrick D '94 Bowling Green State Univ -508 Educ Bldg -Bowling Green 43403
(216) 621-0200 ..**Pauken**, Patrick J '78 (Baker & H LLP) -1900 E 9th -Ste 3200 -Cleveland 44114 **Fx:**696-0740
(614) 365-4100 ..**Paul**, Angela M '97 %Carpenter & L LLP -280 N High -Ste 1300 280 Plz -Columbus 43215 **Fx:**365-9145
(216) 928-0600 ..**Paul**, Aparesh '03 %Levin & Assoc -1301 E 9th -Ste 1100 -Cleveland 44114
(330) 725-6082 ..**Paul**, Dennis E '75 -211 S Court -Medina 44256
Paul, Diane F '94 -45038 Yorkshire Dr -Novi, MI 48375
(216) 621-5300 ..**Paul**, Douglas J '74 (Buckingham D&B,LLP) -1375 E 9th -Ste 1700 -Cleveland 44114 **Fx:**621-5440
(330) 562-3156 ..**Paul**, Douglas K '95 %Christley H&P -215 W Garfld -Ste 230 -Aurora 44202 **Fx:**562-9540
Paul, Jeffery J '98 -(Address Unavailable)
(614) 340-5000 ..**Paul**, Jephtha J '00 -411 E Town -Columbus 43215
(419) 483-2141 ..**Paul**, Roger D '72 (Aigler & P) -202½ W Main -Bellevue 44811
Paul, Ross R '90 -3860 Jeanne Dr -Parma 44134
(513) 744-7077 ..**Paul**, Therese M '96 Cnsl Fifth 3rd Bank -38 Fountain Sq Plz -ML 10AT76 -Cincinnati 45263
(216) 797-1796 ..**Paulett**, Harold K '82 Haskin Grp Ltd -24101 Lakeshr -#703A -Cleveland 44123
(440) 247-7800 ..**Paulett-Toumert**, Mary J '87 (McSherry & Co) -178 E Wshngtn -Chagrin Falls 44022 **Fx:**247-7801
(937) 653-5257 ..**Paulig**, Karl E '53 (Paulig S&T) -40 Monument Sq -Ste 300 -Urbana 43078
(937) 653-5257 ..**Paulig Singer & Talebi** -40 Monument Sq -Ste 300 -Urbana 43078
(614) 848-8411 ..**Paulino**, Harry R '59 -4980 Woodbriar Pl -Columbus 43229
(330) 455-0173 ..**Paulino**, Joanne G '96 %Day KRW&R,Ltd -200 Market Av N -Ste 300 -Bx24213 -Canton 44701 **Fx:**455-2633

(440) 895-1234 ..**Paulozzi**, Joseph G '92 (Polito P&R) -21300 Lorain Rd -Fairview Park 44126
(507) 454-6035 ..**Paulson**, Patrick G '91 -1415 Conrad Dr -Winona, MN 55987
Paulucci, Thomas S '03 -400 S 5th -Ste 101 -Columbus 43215
(256) 551-0300 ..**Paulus**, Craig R '01 -2317 Market Pl -Ste A -Huntsville, AL 35801
(937) 223-8177 ..**Paulus**, Janice M '85 (Coolidge WW&L) -33 W 1st -Ste 600 -Dayton 45402 **Fx:**223-6705
(317) 580-2290 ..**Paulus**, Sharon M '84 Sagamore Hlth Network,Inc -11555 N Meridian -Ste 400 -Carmel, IN 46032
(614) 462-7250 ..**Pausch**, Carma R '94 %Hon GG Tyack -373 S High -24th Fl -Columbus 43215
(614) 462-5016 ..**Pavarini**, Peter A '81 (Schottenstein Z&D) -250 West -Bx165020 -Columbus 43216 **Fx:**462-5135
(419) 255-5900 ..**Pavelko**, Douglas V '90 %MacMillan S&T,LLC -720 Water -4th Fl -Toledo 43604 **Fx:**255-9639
(330) 253-1131 ..**Pavick**, Dean G '80 Pavick & P,LPA -159 S Main -Ste 522 -Akron 44308
(330) 253-1131 ..**Pavick**, Michael J '50 Pavick & P,LPA -159 S Main -Ste 522 -Akron 44308
(614) 222-3137 ..**Pavkov**, Terracina '01 Ernst & Young LLP -41 S High -Ste 1100 -Columbus 43215 **Fx:**229-5127
(937) 325-2459 ..**Pavlatos Catanzaro & Lancaster Co,LPA** -700 E High -Springfield 45505
(937) 325-2459 ..**Pavlatos**, Robert B '49 Pavlatos C&L Co,LPA -700 E High -Springfield 45505
(937) 325-2459 ..**Pavlatos**, Stacey R '77 (Pavlatos C&L Co,LPA) -700 E High -Springfield 45505
(614) 224-7883 ..**Pavlic**, Paul V '70 -326 S High -Ste 100-Annx -Columbus 43215
(330) 376-5300 ..**Pavlidis**, Marietta M '97 %Buckingham D&B,LLP -50 S Main -Bx1500 -Akron 44309 **Fx:**258-6559
(440) 333-1445 ..**Pavlik**, Lisa A '02 %L Lazzaro -2639 Wooster Rd -Rocky River 44116 **Fx:**356-2873
(216) 781-8700 ..**Pavlik**, Thomas C '66 (Novak RP&S,LLP) -1660 W 2nd -Ste 270 Skylight Ofc Twr -Cleveland 44113 **Fx:**781-9227
(216) 623-0000 ..**Pavlovic**, Nevenka '00 %Javitch B&R -1300 E 9th -14th Fl -Cleveland 44114 **Fx:**623-0190
(919) 876-7800 ..**Pawl**, Debra C '83 Closure Medical Corp -5250 Greens Dairy Rd -Raleigh, NC 27616
(212) 559-2037 ..**Pawlicki**, Dana C '96 Citigroup Alternative Invstmnts -399 Park Av -Mezzanine Lvl -New York, NY 10022 **Fx:**793-8745
(419) 247-2500 ..**Pawlicki**, Sarah E '03 %Fuller & H,Ltd -One SeaGate -Ste 1700 -Bx2088 -Toledo 43603 **Fx:**247-2665
(216) 357-7182 ..**Pawlik**, James D '90 %Hon RB Krupansky -801 W Superior Av -Rm 21B -Cleveland 44113
(440) 930-8041 ..**Pawlukiewicz**, Charles J '83 Wickens HPC&B -35765 Chester Rd -Avon 44011 **Fx:**937-4466
Paxson, Debra D '93 -2866 Kipling Av NW -Massillon 44646
(303) 844-6694 ..**Paxton**, Beth A '99 Social Security Admin -1244 Speer Blvd -Ste 600 -Denver, CO 80204
(216) 736-8907 ..**Paxton**, Jeffrey C '90 Cnsl Dollar Bank -1301 E 9th -9th Fl -Cleveland 44114
(614) 221-3006 ..**Paxton**, Robert C II '72 (R Paxton & Assoc) -10 W Broad -Ste 1580 -Columbus 43215
(330) 896-6300 ..**Paxton**, William A '89 -567 E Turkeyfoot Lk Rd -Akron 44319
(614) 466-6696 ..**Payer**, Charissa D '95 Atty Gen -150 E Gay -Columbus 43215 **Fx:**752-2538
(513) 421-7300 ..**Payne**, April M '98 %Howard & B Co,LPA -120 E 4th -960 Mercantile Ctr -Cincinnati 45202
(330) 385-0351 ..**Payne**, Charles L '83 -617 St Clair Av -Bx114 -East Liverpool 43920 **Fx:**385-8852
(513) 475-0200 ..**Payne**, Darrell D '91 -527 Linton -Cincinnati 45219 **Fx:**475-0377
(330) 375-2030 ..**Payne**, James E '79 Law Dept -161 S High -Ste 202 -Akron 44308
(202) 514-3473 ..**Payne**, James O Jr. '84 US DOJ-ENR -Bx7611 -Washington, DC 20044
(740) 377-2120 ..**Payne**, James S '94 -604 4th E -South Point 45680
(216) 664-2868 ..**Payne**, Jerome A Jr. '97 Dept of Law -601 Lakeside Av -Rm 106 City Hall -Cleveland 44114 **Fx:**664-2663
(216) 241-5900 ..**Payne**, Kevin F '81 (Payne P&C) -6100 Oak Tree Blvd -200 Park Ctr I -Independence 44131
(614) 466-8911 ..**Payne**, Lori A '01 Atty Gen -30 E Broad -Columbus 43215 **Fx:**728-7582
(330) 535-4191 ..**Payne**, Paul D II '77 %Cmmnty Lgl Aid Srvcs,Inc -265 S Main -3rd Fl -Akron 44308 **Fx:**535-0728
(216) 241-5900 ..**Payne Payne & Cook** -6100 Oak Tree Blvd -200 Park Ctr I -Independence 44131
(330) 459-6587 ..**Payne**, Rex E III '97 -4337 State Rd -Peninsula 44264
(203) 351-4192 ..**Payne**, Robert T '81 (Cummings & L) -107 Elm -Four Stmfrd Plz -Stamford, CT 06902
(740) 452-5403 ..**Payne**, Thomas '52 (Jones F&P) -45 N 4th -Zanesville 43701
(513) 891-8261 ..**Payne**, Thomas F '94 -9726 Delray Dr -Montgomery 45242
(614) 466-5394 ..**Payne**, Timothy R '00 Pub Def -8 E Long -Columbus 43215
(570) 895-3413 ..**Payne**, Tracy H '93 Aventis Pasteur Inc -1 Discovery Dr -Swiftwater, PA 18370
(614) 898-8078 ..**Payne**, Walter R Jr. '78 State Farm -178 W Schrock Rd -Westerville 43081
(216) 241-5900 ..**Payne**, William A '84 (Payne P&C) -6100 Oak Tree Blvd -200 Park Ctr I -Independence 44131
(937) 382-5591 ..**Payne**, William J '92 Airborne Express -145 Hunter Dr -Wilmington 45177
(614) 221-4000 ..**Paynter**, Craig B '82 (Chester W&S LLP) -65 E State -10th Fl -Columbus 43215 **Fx:**221-4012
(614) 229-3221 ..**Paynter**, Donald G '71 (Bailey C LLC) -10 W Broad -Columbus 43215 **Fx:**221-0479
(216) 529-2870 ..**Paynter Kohler & Wagner** -11740 Clifton Blvd -Ste 202 -Lakewood 44107 **Fx:**529-2883
(330) 796-4503 ..**Payntor**, Carl S '82 Goodyear Tire & Rubber Co -1144 E Market -Akron 44316
(937) 222-4529 ..**Payson**, Frank M '91 (F Payson PC) -120 W 2nd -Ste 400 -Dayton 45402
(614) 466-7637 ..**Payton**, G Michael '84 OH Civ Rghts Cmmssn -1111 E Broad -Ste 301 -Columbus 43205
(440) 729-7996 ..**Payton**, Janet G '88 Business Laws,Inc -11630 Chillicothe Rd -Bx185 -Chesterland 44026
(419) 755-9616 ..**Payton**, Jeff '75 Mun Ct Judge -30 N Diamond -Mansfield 44902

(330) 792-6033 ..**Pazol,** James L '62 (Anzellotti SP&S Co,LPA) -21 N Wickliffe Cir
-Youngstown 44515 **Fx:**793-3384
(419) 251-3568 ..**Pazzo,** Michael P '00 St Vincent Mercy Medical Ctr -2213 Cherry
-Toledo 43608 **Fx:**251-4983
(513) 424-5000 ..**Peace,** Candice R '83 (Clark Schaefer Hackett & Co)
-160 N Breiel Blvd -Middletown 45042
(440) 232-5980 ..**Peace,** Christine M '93 T-Title Agncy,Inc -24748 Aurora Rd
-Bedford Heights 44146
(602) 207-8449 ..**Peach,** Roxanne O '89 IRS -210 E Earll Dr -MS 4207 PHX
-Phoenix, AZ 85012 **Fx:**207-8640
(216) 642-3342 ..**Peacock,** Bruce E '88 (Wegman H&V,LPA) -6055
Rockside Wds Blvd -Ste 200 -Cleveland 44131 **Fx:**642-8826
(330) 643-2788 ..**Peacock,** Gregory W '93 Summit Cnty Pros-Crim -53 Univ Av
-7th Fl -Akron 44308 **Fx:**643-8277
(330) 258-6565 ..**Peak,** Jack E '96 Roadway Exp -Bx471 -Akron 44309
(865) 774-0545 ..**Pealer,** Charles E '51 -1022 Valley Vw Cir -Sevierville, TN 37876
(502) 581-1630 ..**Pearce,** Stephanie J '95 O'Koon H -500 W Jffrsn -Louisville,
KY 40202
(419) 547-0553 ..**Pearce,** William D '72 (Homan & P) -135 W Maple -Bx88
-Clyde 43410
(330) 467-5002 ..**Pearl,** James R Jr. '96 -9391 Olde Eight Rd -Bx814
-Northfield 44067
(304) 723-4400 ..**Pearl,** Kevin M '02 %Frankovitch AC&S -337 Penco Rd
-Weirton, WV 26062 **Fx:**723-5892
(216) 731-3300 ..**Pearl,** Robert M '77 -26241 Lakeshr Blvd -Ste 1568 -Euclid 44132
Fx:731-3300
(914) 683-5599 ..**Pearlman,** Jay W '93 (JW Pearlman PC) -445 Hmltn Av -Ste 604
-White Plains, NY 10601 **Fx:**428-1660
(216) 479-8500 ..**Pearlman,** Samuel S '67 (Squire S&D LLP) -127 Pub Sq
-4900 Key Twr -Cleveland 44114 **Fx:**479-8780
(216) 579-1700 ..**Pearne & Gordon LLP** -1801 E 9th -Ste 1200 -Cleveland 44114
Fx:579-6073
(813) 843-2263 ..**Pearsall,** Wayne G '03 -Bx392 -Amherst 44001
(614) 461-4455 ..**Pearsol-Christie,** Erika L '98 %Cloppert LS&W -225 E Broad
-Columbus 43215 **Fx:**461-0012
(216) 622-3600 ..**Pearson,** Benita Y '95 %US Atty -801 W Superior -Ste 400
-Cleveland 44113 **Fx:**622-3370
(419) 213-4700 ..**Pearson,** Craig T '85 %Lucas Cnty Pros -Adams & Erie
-Lucas Cnty Cthse -Toledo 43624
(859) 655-3700 ..**Pearson,** Elizabeth A '90 Pearson & B,PSC -1224 Hwy Av
-Covington, KY 41011
(513) 621-6464 ..**Pearson,** Jennifer S '03 %Graydon H&R LLP -511 Walnut
-1900 Fifth Third Ctr -Cincinnati 45202 **Fx:**651-3836
(937) 667-8309 ..**Pearson,** John D '70 -23 W Main -Tipp City 45371
(603) 625-6464 ..**Pearson,** Michael T '93 %McLane GR&M -900 Elm Bx326
-Manchester, NH 03105 **Fx:**625-5650
(216) 623-1155 ..**Pearson,** Shawn R '90 Nationwide Ins -323 Lakeside Av W
-Ste 410 Lakeside Pl -Cleveland 44113
(913) 344-5405 ..**Pec,** Joseph J '96 Yellow Corp -10990 Roe Av
-Overland Park, KS 66211
(216) 621-8484 ..**Peca,** John A Jr. '77 (Climaco LPW&G Co,LPA) -1228 Euclid Av
-Ste 900 Halle Bldg -Cleveland 44115 **Fx:**621-1632
(216) 348-2800 ..**Pecchio,** Jennifer M '99 %Stefanski & Assoc,LLC
-614 W Superior Av -Ste 1144 -Cleveland 44113 **Fx:**348-1557
(330) 963-6600 ..**Pecchio,** Robert A '84 (R Pecchio Co,LPA) -2305 E Aurora Rd
-Ste A-1 -Twinsburg 44087 **Fx:**963-6650
(216) 685-1104 ..**Pecenka Cullen,** Danielle L '98 %Weltman W&R Co,LPA
-323 W Lakeside Av -Ste 200 -Cleveland 44113 **Fx:**363-4121
(740) 654-4141 ..**Pechar,** Todd D '98 %Stebelton A&S,LPA -109 N Broad -Bx130
-Lancaster 43130 **Fx:**654-2521
(202) 353-3459 ..**Pecinovsky,** Steven J '80 US Dept of Justice -950 Penn Av NW
-PHB Rm 4500 -Washington, DC 20530
(330) 753-3900 ..**Peck,** Andrew F '85 -507 W Park Av -Barberton 44203
(513) 381-2838 ..**Peck,** David Hamilton '92 (Taft S&H LLP) -425 Walnut -Ste 1800
-Cincinnati 45202 **Fx:**381-0205
(513) 381-9200 ..**Peck,** David W '66 (Rendigs FK&D,LLP) -One W 4th -Ste 900
-Cincinnati 45202 **Fx:**381-9206
(513) 721-1350 ..**Peck,** David W '70 (Barron PB&S) -3074 Madison Rd
-Cincinnati 45209
(513) 868-1113 ..**Peck,** Gregory L '88 -Bx187 -Hamilton 45012
(513) 762-6207 ..**Peck,** Jeffrey F '82 (Ulmer & B LLP) -600 Vine -Ste 2800
-Cincinnati 45202 **Fx:**762-6245
(216) 765-0123 ..**Peck,** Jennifer E '93 (Budish & S Ltd) -23240 Chagrin Blvd
-Ste 450 Commerce Park 4 -Beachwood 44122 **Fx:**595-2787
(740) 927-8790 ..**Peck,** Jimmy R '04 MPW Industrial Srvcs -9711 Lncstr Rd SE
-Bx10 -Hebron 43025
(513) 621-3394 ..**Peck,** John Weld '69 (Peck S&W,LLP) -201 E 5th -Ste 900
-Cincinnati 45202 **Fx:**621-3813
(585) 419-8800 ..**Peck,** Matthew J '99 %Harris B LLP -99 Garnsey Rd -Pittsford, NY
14534 **Fx:**419-8801
Peck, Michael N '03 -109 Court -% DK O'Reilly -Chardon 44024
(614) 462-4678 ..**Peck,** Richard A '96 Franklin Cnty Common Pleas Ct -369 S High
-Courtroom 8A -Columbus 43215
(513) 621-3394 ..**Peck Shaffer & Williams,LLP** -201 E 5th -Ste 900
-Cincinnati 45202 **Fx:**621-3813
(614) 224-5205 ..**Peck Shaffer & Williams,LLP** -175 S 3rd -Ste 600
-Columbus 43215 **Fx:**224-0069
(216) 292-8500 ..**Peckinpaugh,** Roger T '70 (Peckinpaugh & T,LLC)
-23230 Chagrin Blvd -Ste 605 -Beachwood 44122
(419) 241-6000 ..**Peckinpaugh,** Rudolph A Jr. '80 (Eastman & S Ltd) -1 Seagate
-24th Fl -Bx10032 -Toledo 43699 **Fx:**247-1777
(440) 930-4001 ..**Pecora,** Anthony R '98 Baumgartner & O
-5455 Detroit Rd (Rte 254) -Sheffield Village 44054 **Fx:**934-7205
(513) 621-2100 ..**Pecquet,** Janet E '81 Beckman W&S LLC -120 E 4th
-1200 Mercantile Ctr -Cincinnati 45202 **Fx:**621-0106
(216) 348-3840 ..**Pedace,** Theresa A '84 Cnty Engineer -2100 Superior Viaduct
-Cleveland 44113
(740) 622-0166 ..**Peddicord,** Randall H '82 (Leech S&P) -240 S 4th -Bx880
-Coshocton 43812
(614) 428-7867 ..**Peden,** John J '83 -146 Granvll -Gahanna 43230
(216) 932-3077 ..**Pederson,** Jeffrey W '80 -3305 Beechwd Av
-Cleveland Heights 44118

(513) 683-5666 ..**Pedicone,** Alfred J '97 Webster Packaging Corp -715 Riverside Dr
-Bx247 -Loveland 45140
(765) 494-6878 ..**Pedley,** Michael G '98 Purdue Univ -610 Purdue Mall
-Horde Hall, Rm 148 -West Lafayette, IN 47907
(419) 228-8989 ..**Pedlow,** Edward B IV '85 (Kilco Title Agency) -119 N West
-Ste 101 -Lima 45801 **Fx:**228-9111
(937) 323-1010 ..**Pedraza,** Miguel A Jr. '85 (Strozdas & P LLP) -20 S Limestone
-Ste 330 -Springfield 45502 **Fx:**323-1953
(330) 722-1234 ..**Pedro,** Cameron B '01 -215 W Wshngtn -Medina 44256
(619) 437-0921 ..**Pedrozo,** Raul A '84 US Navy -2000 Trident Way -San Diego,
CA 92155
(513) 626-2404 ..**Peebles,** Brent M '94 Cnsl Procter & Gamble -11511
Reed Hartman Hwy -Cincinnati 45241
(216) 861-6000 ..**Peebles,** David C '92 Miller S&B -2000 E 9th -Ste 1100
-Cleveland 44115
(216) 443-7800 ..**Peebles,** Tracy M '98 Cuyahoga Cnty Pros -1200 Ontario -8th Fl
-Cleveland 44113 **Fx:**698-2270
(513) 398-4891 ..**Peeler McGary & Zopff** -423 Reading Rd -Mason 45040
(513) 398-4891 ..**Peeler,** Robert W '83 (Peeler M&Z) -423 Reading Rd
-Mason 45040
(937) 382-1497 ..**Peelle,** Carol S '86 -1929 Rombach Av -Bx950 -Wilmington 45177
(937) 382-1497 ..**Peelle,** Chaley E '04 Peelle Law Ofcs Co,LPA -1929 Rombach Av
-Bx950 -Wilmington 45177
(937) 382-1497 ..**Peelle,** Robert C '76 -1929 Rombach Av -Bx950
-Wilmington 45177
(937) 382-1497 ..**Peelle,** William E '75 -1929 Rombach Av -Bx950
-Wilmington 45177
(614) 645-7385 ..**Peeples,** Andrea C '94 City Atty -90 W Broad -Columbus 43215
(216) 479-8500 ..**Peer,** Christina Henagen '99 %Squire S&D LLP -127 Pub Sq
-4900 Key Twr -Cleveland 44114 **Fx:**479-8780
(216) 621-0150 ..**Peer,** Christopher W '03 %Hahn L&P LLP
-3300 BP Twr/200 Pub Sq -Ste 3300 -Cleveland 44114
Fx:241-2824
(614) 228-6345 ..**Peer,** Jerry E Jr. '02 %Strip HLM&T Co LPA -575 S 3rd
-Columbus 43215 **Fx:**228-6369
(614) 759-1693 ..**Pehowic,** Shoshana R '02 -4486 Amesbury Rd -Columbus 43227
Peifer, Christopher S '00 USAF -PSC 41 -Bx5523 -APO, AE 09464
(937) 325-7365 ..**Peifer,** James F '72 (Emerich W&P) -20 S Limestone -Ste 300
-Bx1087 -Springfield 45501
(412) 281-7229 ..**Peirce,** Robert N III '01 (Peirce R&C,PC) -707 Grant
-2500 Gulf Twr -Pittsburgh, PA 15219 **Fx:**281-4229
Peitz, Mary E '03 -(Address Unavailable)
(216) 622-8835 ..**Pejic,** Nenad '96 %Calfee H&G LLP -800 Superior Av -Ste 1400
-Cleveland 44114 **Fx:**241-0816
(740) 355-8944 ..**Pekar,** Patricia R '92 Cnty CSE -Bx1347 -Portsmouth 45662
(440) 845-3030 ..**Pelagalli,** Rodger A '86 -6659 Pearl Rd -Ste 401
-Parma Heights 44130
(937) 642-5627 ..**Pelanda,** Dorothy K '82 -122 E 5th -Bx1 -Marysville 43040
(937) 642-8232 ..**Pelanda,** Kevin L '81 -581 Qualil Hllw Dr South -Marysville 43040
Fx:644-0511
(336) 931-2181 ..**Pelehash,** John A '79 Kay Chem Co -8300 Cptl Dr
-Greensboro, NC 27409
(330) 305-6400 ..**Pelini,** Craig G '84 (Pelini & F,Ltd) -8040 Cleveland Av NW
-Ste 400 -North Canton 44720 **Fx:**305-0042
(330) 305-6400 ..**Pelini & Fischer,Ltd** -8040 Cleveland Av NW -Ste 400
-North Canton 44720 **Fx:**305-0042
(440) 365-5000 ..**Pelka,** Karen M '94 Parole Authority -1131 E Broad -Elyria 44035
(216) 443-8856 ..**Pellegrin,** Joan K '80 Cuyahoga Cnty Cmn Pleas Ct -1
Lakeside Av -Cleveland 44113
(513) 621-0777 ..**Peller,** Kenneth E '76 -700 Walnut -Ste 313 -Cincinnati 45202
(216) 621-0200 ..**Pelliccioni,** Christopher D '03 %Baker & H LLP -1900 E 9th
-Ste 3200 -Cleveland 44114 **Fx:**696-0740
(614) 466-2765 ..**Pellitt,** Robert M '82 Industrial Commssn of OH -30 W Spring
-9th Fl -Columbus 43215 **Fx:**752-8785
Pellot, Anne B '93 -(Address Unavailable)
(440) 248-8622 ..**Pelsozy,** Dale F '78 -34535 Applevw Way -Solon 44139
Fx:248-8622
(239) 939-7855 ..**Pelstring,** R James '76 (Stephens LKLH&P,PA) -2891 Ctr Pnte Dr
-Ste 305 -Fort Myers, FL 33916 **Fx:**939-7850
(614) 224-3737 ..**Pelteson,** Edward F '60 (E Pelteson Co,LPA) -85 E Gay -Ste 400
-Columbus 43215
(937) 456-5544 ..**Peltier,** Paul E '77 Eaton Natl Bk & Trust -110 W Main
-Eaton 45320
(216) 292-4900 ..**Peltz & Birne** -23230 Chagrin Blvd -Ste 715 -Beachwood 44122
Fx:292-4942
(216) 292-4900 ..**Peltz,** Richard B '68 (Peltz & B) -23230 Chagrin Blvd -Ste 715
-Beachwood 44122 **Fx:**292-4942
(440) 248-4900 ..**Pelunis,** Robert N '99 -32286 S Roundhead Dr -Solon 44139
(740) 548-5654 ..**Pemberton,** David L '66 -2626 Lewis Ctr Rd -Lewis Center 43035
(440) 898-3098 ..**Pembridge,** Donald Timothy '82 Hyland Software Inc
-28500 Clemens Rd -Westlake 44145
(440) 331-2127 ..**Pempus,** Eric O '86 -1342 Elmwood Rd -Rocky River 44116
(440) 246-2665 ..**Pena,** Michelle Fernandez '04 %DC Cook -209 W 6th -Ste 10
-Lorain 44052
(419) 534-2304 ..**Penamon,** Alan W '95 -2125 Joffre Av -Bx3333 -Toledo 43607
(937) 393-4267 ..**Pence,** David W '73 -120 Govenor Trimble Pl -Hillsboro 45133
(859) 727-2222 ..**Pence,** John E '92 Answers in Genesis Ministries -Bx6330
-Florence, KY 41022
(614) 624-6300 ..**Pence-Lavy,** Mary M '98 Ross Products/Abbott Labs
-625 Cleveland Av -Columbus 43215
(614) 337-8366 ..**Pencheff & Fraley** -2176A CityGate Dr -Columbus 43219
(614) 337-8366 ..**Pencheff,** Peter M '52 (Pencheff & F) -2176A CityGate Dr
-Columbus 43219
(202) 939-3846 ..**Pendergrass,** John A III '79 Environmental Law Inst -1616 P NW
-Ste 200 -Washington, DC 20036 **Fx:**939-3868
(713) 844-3750 ..**Pendleton,** Dianna L '87 Blizzard & M -440 Louisiana -Ste 1710
-Houston, TX 77002
(937) 372-4919 ..**Pendry,** David L '80 (Smith & P) -133 E Market -Xenia 45385
(440) 333-2500 ..**Penfield,** George R '70 -19443 Lorain Rd -Fairview Park 44126
(216) 622-3600 ..**Penhallurick,** Kent W '76 US Atty -801 W Superior -Ste 400
-Cleveland 44113 **Fx:**622-3370
(937) 223-0122 ..**Penick,** Bryan K '99 %Boucher & B Co,LPA -12 W Monument Av
-Ste 200 -Dayton 45402

(513) 352-2732 .. **Penix,** Leonard N '85 Cincinnati Post -125 E Court
　　　-Cincinnati 45202
(216) 222-2189 .. **Penko,** Joseph C '87 Natl City Bank -1900 E 9th -Cleveland 44114
　　　　Penn, Ralph W '74 -1889 Royal Oak Dr -Lewis Center 43035
(740) 474-5407 .. **Penn,** Richard W '50 -503 Springhollow Rd -Circleville 43113
(202) 314-6838 .. **Penn,** Sonya J '87 USPS -400 VA Av SW -Ste 650
　　　-Washington, DC 20024
(513) 369-5059 .. **Pennekamp,** Lisa A '84 Great Amer Ins Co -580 Walnut -10th Fl
　　　-Cincinnati 45202
(419) 784-9982 .. **Penner,** Ted W '91 (Penner & S,Ltd) -101 Clinton -Ste 1500
　　　-Defiance 43512 **Fx:**784-9991
(513) 744-9600 .. **Penney,** Robert J '03 %Javitch B&R -602 Main -Ste 500
　　　-Cincinnati 45202 **Fx:**744-9602
(513) 984-2040 .. **Penney,** Todd D '92 (Scheuer M&B LLC)
　　　-11025 Reed Hartman Hwy -Cincinnati 45242 **Fx:**984-6590
(937) 325-4446 .. **Pennington,** Anthony B '77 -1107 Upper Valley Pike
　　　-Springfield 45504
(614) 445-3969 .. **Pennington,** Crysta R '04 -786 S Front -Columbus 43206
(614) 791-9112 .. **Pennington,** David S '83 Wright Law Co,LPA -4266 Tuller Rd
　　　-Ste 101 -Dublin 43017 **Fx:**791-9116
(419) 727-1040 .. **Pennington,** Stephen T '84 -5403 N Summit -Ste 3 -Toledo 43611
(216) 586-3939 .. **Penrod,** Stephen R '00 %Jones D -901 Lakeside Av -Cleveland
　　　44114 **Fx:**579-0212
(937) 223-8378 .. **Pensyl,** Michelle L '88 Chicago Title Ins Co -1 S Main -Ste 330
　　　-Dayton 45402
(937) 225-4652 .. **Pentecost,** Michael R '86 %Montgomery Cnty Pub Def
　　　-117 S Main -Ste 400 -Dayton 45422 **Fx:**225-3449
(216) 983-1051 .. **Penttila,** Jane E '92 Univ Hosp -10524 Euclid Av -Ste 1100
　　　-Cleveland 44106
(216) 737-5000 .. **Pentz,** Joel R '99 %Chernett WY&P -1301 E 9th -Ste 3300
　　　-Cleveland 44114 **Fx:**737-0011
(330) 393-3000 .. **Pentz,** Matthew A '84 -280 N Park Av -Ste 210 -Warren 44481
(216) 621-3012 .. **Penvose,** Bryan L '01 %Koblentz & K -55 Pub Sq -Ste 1170
　　　-Cleveland 44113 **Fx:**621-6567
(202) 879-3100 .. **Penzone,** David C '76 Deloitte & Touche -555 12th NW
　　　-Washington, DC 20004
(419) 592-3816 .. **Peper,** Edmund G Jr. '57 (Peper Law Firm) -555 Monroe
　　　-Napoleon 43545
(818) 729-8125 .. **Peper,** Robert C '75 CLH Foundation -2835 N Naomi -Ste 300
　　　-Burbank, CA 91504
(216) 479-8500 .. **Peppard,** Sean T '01 %Squire S&D LLP -127 Pub Sq
　　　-4900 Key Twr -Cleveland 44114 **Fx:**479-8780
(301) 951-1500 .. **Peppe,** James M '01 %West & F PC -4550 Mntgmry Av -Ste 775N
　　　-Bethesda, MD 20814 **Fx:**951-1525
(419) 249-7900 .. **Peppel,** Gregg A '99 (Robison C&O) -Four SeaGate -9th Fl
　　　-Toledo 43604 **Fx:**249-7911
　　　　Pepper, Anne K T '96 -(Address Unavailable)
(513) 361-1200 .. **Pepper,** David A '99 %Squire S&D LLP -312 Walnut -Ste 3500
　　　-Cincinnati 45202 **Fx:**361-1201
(202) 502-6556 .. **Pepper,** James A '83 FERC -888 1st NE -Washington, DC 20426
(937) 227-3700 .. **Pepper,** Timothy G '99 %Faruki I&C PLL -10 N Ludlow
　　　-500 Cthse Plz SW -Dayton 45402 **Fx:**227-3717
(614) 462-3896 .. **Peppers,** Samuel A III '93 Franklin Cnty Cmn Pleas Ct
　　　-373 S High -22nd Fl -Columbus 43215
(216) 520-0088 .. **Pepple & Waggoner Ltd** -5005 Rockside Rd -Ste 260
　　　-Cleveland 44131 **Fx:**520-0044
(216) 520-0088 .. **Pepple,** William C '82 (Pepple & W Ltd) -5005 Rockside Rd
　　　-Ste 260 -Cleveland 44131 **Fx:**520-0044
(513) 752-2111 .. **Pera,** Marc G '98 %D Moore Jr & Co,LPA -4355 Ferguson Dr
　　　-Ste 200 -Cincinnati 45245 **Fx:**753-2354
(513) 369-5611 .. **Peraino,** Vito C '81 Great Amer Ins Co -49 E 4th -Ste 700N
　　　-Cincinnati 45202
(330) 253-5454 .. **Perantinides & Nolan Co,LPA** -80 S Summit -300 Courtyard Sq
　　　-Akron 44308
(330) 253-5454 .. **Perantinides,** Paul G '69 (Perantinides & N Co,LPA)
　　　-80 S Summit -300 Courtyard Sq -Akron 44308
(704) 423-3464 .. **Percio,** David R '74 SrCnsl Goodrich Corp -2730 W Tyvola Rd
　　　-4 Coliseum Ctr -Charlotte, NC 28217
(440) 331-1850 .. **Percio,** Joseph M '75 -19111 Detroit Rd -Ste 302
　　　-Rocky River 44116
(330) 833-8521 .. **Percival,** Mark R '78 Brown & P Co,LPA -1231 Lincoln Way E
　　　-Massillon 44646
(216) 621-0200 .. **Perdion,** Jason P '98 %Baker & H LLP -1900 E 9th -Ste 3200
　　　-Cleveland 44114 **Fx:**696-0740
(614) 469-1400 .. **Perdue,** Dale K '80 (Clark PR&S Co,LPA) -471 E Broad -Ste 1400
　　　-Columbus 43215 **Fx:**469-0900
(440) 428-1258 .. **Per Due,** David W '86 -7547 N Ridge E -Bx207 -Unionville 44088
(330) 922-0934 .. **Perdue,** Stephen R '94 -2820 Norma -Cuyahoga Falls 44223
(330) 686-1708 .. **Perduk,** David C '96 OfCnsl R Martin Co, LPA -3603 Darrow Rd
　　　-Stow 44224
(330) 796-7082 .. **Perez,** Edward R '87 Goodyear Tire & Rubber Co -1144 E Market
　　　-Dept 616 -Akron 44316
(614) 221-9222 .. **Perez,** Jay G '97 (J Perez LLC) -5 E Long -Ste 404
　　　-Columbus 43215
(513) 852-8200 .. **Perez,** John X '04 %Cors & B LLC -537 E Pete Rose Way
　　　-Ste 400 -Cincinnati 45202
(614) 431-1500 .. **Perez,** Juan J '85 (Perez & M LLC) -8000 Ravines Edge Ct
　　　-Ste 300 -Columbus 43235 **Fx:**431-3885
(614) 431-1500 .. **Perez & Morris LLC** -8000 Ravines Edge Ct -Ste 300
　　　-Columbus 43235 **Fx:**431-3885
(205) 355-5007 .. **Perez,** Raymond W '87 Honda Mnfctrng of AL,LLC
　　　-1800 Honda Dr -Lincoln, AL 35096
(440) 953-1310 .. **Perez,** Richard J '74 (Rosplock & P) -4230 SR 306 -Ste 240
　　　-Willoughby 44094
(614) 221-3155 .. **Perez,** Rita A '04 %Bailey C LLC -10 W Broad -Columbus 43215
　　　Fx:221-0479
(513) 621-8256 .. **Perez,** Robert A Sr. '83 (Perez Law Firm Co LPA)
　　　-7672 Mntgmry Rd -Cincinnati 45236
(419) 447-5011 .. **Perez,** Victor H '02 Seneca Cnty Dept Jobs/Family Srvc
　　　-3362 S Twp Rd 151 -Tiffin 44883
(216) 664-2801 .. **Perez,** Victor R '01 Prosecutor -1200 Ontario Av -8th Fl Justice Ctr
　　　-Cleveland 44113 **Fx:**664-4399
(937) 255-6113 .. **Perfilio,** Anthony J '80 Air Force Material Cmmnd -1864 4th
　　　-Rm 130A,AFMC LO/JA -Wright Patterson AFB 45433

(740) 363-1313 .. **Pergram,** Dennis L '77 (Manos MP&D Co,LPA) -50 N Sandusky
　　　-Delaware 43015 **Fx:**363-1314
(614) 249-1447 .. **Perin,** Charles L Jr. '80 Cnsl Nationwide Ins Co -1 Nationwide Plz
　　　-Columbus 43215
(937) 645-6001 .. **Perin,** Douglas E '89 Honda R&D Amer,Inc
　　　-21001 State Route 739 -Raymond 43067
(513) 793-2222 .. **Perin,** Martha H '49 -6823 Kenwood Rd -Cincinnati 45243
(216) 566-2543 .. **Perisutti,** Stephen J '88 Sherwin-Williams Co
　　　-101 Prospect Av NW -Cleveland 44115
(216) 664-4982 .. **Perk,** Ralph J Jr. '83 Mun Ct Judge -1200 Ontario -Courtroom 14B
　　　-Cleveland 44113 **Fx:**664-4977
(513) 632-5335 .. **Perkins,** Bryan R '93 -119 E Court -Ste 314 -Cincinnati 45202
(614) 466-3664 .. **Perkins,** Catherine C '84 OH DOT -1980 W Broad
　　　-Columbus 43223
(937) 293-0810 .. **Perkins,** David C '93 -Bx340294 -Beavercreek 45434
(419) 243-6281 .. **Perkins,** Jeffrey J '82 (Shindler NH&S,LLP) -300 Mad Av
　　　-Ste 1200 -Toledo 43604 **Fx:**243-0129
(614) 888-8500 .. **Perkins,** John R Jr. '84 (Jones TP&P,LPA) -1472 Manning Pkwy
　　　-Powell 43065 **Fx:**888-2560
(415) 422-9501 .. **Perko,** Robert C '75 Lawrence Livermore Natl Lab -L-708 -Bx808
　　　-Livermore, CA 94551
(216) 781-6550 .. **Perl,** Warren R '78 -1836 Euclid Av -Ste 335 -Cleveland 44115
(440) 333-2503 .. **Perla,** Randall M '74 -19443 Lorain Rd -Fairview Park 44126
(419) 478-1776 .. **Perlman,** James M '80 -1776 Tremainsvll Rd -Toledo 43613
　　　Fx:478-5087
(330) 497-4604 .. **Perlman,** Marjorie R '77 -5502 Market Ave N -Ste B
　　　-Canton 44721
(614) 462-2253 .. **Perlmutter,** Jeffrey A '75 OfCnsl Schottenstein Z&D -250 West
　　　-Bx165020 -Columbus 43216 **Fx:**462-5135
(216) 621-6501 .. **Perlmutter,** Jeffrey A '75 OfCnsl Schottenstein Z&D
　　　-1350 Euclid Av -Ste 1400 -Cleveland 44115 **Fx:**621-6502
(216) 696-4009 .. **Perlmutter,** Joel A '87 Kraig & K -614 Superior Av W -Ste 900
　　　-Cleveland 44113 **Fx:**696-1835
(419) 241-4181 .. **Perlmutter,** Steven J '87 Peoples Jewelry Co -245 23rd
　　　-Toledo 43624
(614) 889-7567 .. **Permar,** David B II '85 Small Business Insights -Bx279
　　　-Dublin 43017
(216) 261-0200 .. **Perme,** Michael R '74 M Perme Co,LPA -27801 Euclid Av -Ste 500
　　　-Euclid 44132
(937) 229-4507 .. **Perna,** Richard P '83 Univ of Dayton Schl of Law -300 Cllg Park
　　　-Dayton 45469
(419) 243-4006 .. **Perne',** Lori L '01 %Kitch DWD&V,PC -405 Mad Av -Ste 1500
　　　-Toledo 43604 **Fx:**243-7333
(630) 690-2130 .. **Pernell,** Frances C '81 Prarie State Legal Srvcs
　　　-350 S Schmale Rd -Carol Stream, IL 60188
(815) 753-1380 .. **Pernell,** LeRoy '74 Nrthrn IL Univ/College of Law
　　　-270 Swen Parson -Dekalb, IL 60115
(614) 757-5427 .. **Pero,** Brian V '88 Cardinal Health,Inc -7000 Cardinal Pl
　　　-Dublin 43017
(937) 224-1518 .. **Pero,** Maureen '83 Dwntwn Dayton Prtnrshp -1360 Kettering Twr
　　　-Dayton 45423
(440) 352-3391 .. **Perotti,** Patrick J '82 (Dworken & B Co,LPA) -60 S Park Pl
　　　-Painesville 44077 **Fx:**352-3469
(440) 564-8282 .. **Perotti,** Thomas I '95 -100 Center -Ste 170 -Chardon 44024
(513) 723-2211 .. **Perr,** Karolina F '96 %Weltman W&R Co,LPA -525 Vine -Ste 800
　　　-Cincinnati 45202 **Fx:**723-2239
(419) 666-4974 .. **Perras,** Douglas L '78 -407 N Main -Walbridge 43465
(216) 222-8057 .. **Perrette,** John E '76 Natl City Bank -1900 E 9th -Cleveland 44114
(304) 234-0100 .. **Perri,** David J '95 %US Atty Ofc -Bx591 -Wheeling, WV 26003
(216) 928-2200 .. **Perrico,** Daniel E '99 %Sutter OM&F -1301 E 9th
　　　-3600 Erievw Twr -Cleveland 44114 **Fx:**928-4400
(740) 592-3236 .. **Perrin,** Jonathan M '92 Athens Cnty Cmn Pleas Ct -1 S Court
　　　-2nd Fl -Athens 45701
(216) 884-4436 .. **Perrin,** Ronald J '54 -2860 Bonny Blvd -Cleveland 44134
(513) 852-8634 .. **Perrino,** Dominic F '62 Hamilton Cnty Dom Rltns Ct -800 Bway
　　　-Cincinnati 45202
(513) 421-4855 .. **Perrino,** Nicholas A '69 -830 Main -Ste 1105 -Cincinnati 45202
(513) 870-9070 .. **Perrino,** Nicholas D '91 Prodigy Title Agncy,LLC
　　　-8080 Beckett Ctr Dr -Ste 318 -West Chester 45069
(330) 253-2195 .. **Perris,** Alexander C '94 -106 S Main -Ste 2500 -Akron 44308
(216) 479-8500 .. **Perris,** Terrence G '72 (Squire S&D LLP) -127 Pub Sq
　　　-4900 Key Twr -Cleveland 44114 **Fx:**479-8780
　　　　Perrucci, Christopher R '85 -6001 Cochran Rd -Ste 200
　　　-Cleveland 44139
(800) 243-0210 .. **Perry,** Alfred C Jr. '99 Westfield Grp -1 Park Cir -Bx5001
　　　-Westfield Center 44251 **Fx:**(330) 887-2588
(216) 348-5400 .. **Perry,** Andrew S '00 %McDonald H Co,LPA -600 Superior Av E
　　　-Ste 2100 -Cleveland 44114 **Fx:**348-5474
(216) 875-2767 .. **Perry,** Bret C '01 %Bonezzi SM&P Co LPA -526 Superior Av
　　　-Ste 1400 -Cleveland 44114 **Fx:**875-1570
(513) 977-8200 .. **Perry,** Brian P '93 (Dinsmore & S LLP) -255 E 5th -Ste 1900
　　　-Cincinnati 45202 **Fx:**977-8141
(513) 852-3311 .. **Perry,** David A '87 OH Dept of Taxation -1150 W 8th
　　　-Cincinnati 45203
(216) 472-3300 .. **Perry,** Dominic V '00 (D Perry & Assoc,LLC) -631 W St Clair Av
　　　-Cleveland 44113
(513) 621-0442 .. **Perry,** Edward C '91 -601 Main -3rd Fl -Cincinnati 45202
　　　　Perry, George W '53 -(Address Unavailable)
(614) 466-8600 .. **Perry,** Gregory A '95 Atty Gen -30 E Broad -Columbus 43215
　　　Fx:466-6090
(513) 621-0442 .. **Perry,** James N '62 -601 Main -3rd Fl -Cincinnati 45202
(614) 466-7264 .. **Perry,** Jane Pat '85 OH Legal Rghts Srvc -8 E Long -5th Fl
　　　-Columbus 43215
(419) 224-3828 .. **Perry,** Jennifer J '03 3rd Dist Ct of Appeals -204 N Main
　　　-Lima 45801
(216) 687-1900 .. **Perry,** Karla L '93 Legal Aid -1223 W 6th -Cleveland 44113
　　　Fx:687-0779
(419) 529-4560 .. **Perry,** Kathleen E '83 UAW Legal Srvcs Plan -1075 Natl Pkwy
　　　-Bx2668 -Mansfield 44906 **Fx:**529-5350
(972) 917-5338 .. **Perry,** Levis H Jr. '93 Texas Instrmnts Inc -7839 Churchill Way
　　　-MS 3999 -Dallas, TX 75251
(614) 629-3000 .. **Perry,** Paul E '76 %Plunkett & C,PC -300 E Broad -Ste 590
　　　-Columbus 43215 **Fx:**629-3019

(440) 395-9353 ..**Perry**, William F '03 Progressive Insurance -300 N Cmmns Blvd -Mayfield Village 44143

(513) 336-2544 ..**Pershern**, Judy L '84 -4361 Irwin Simpson Rd -MB1-220 -Mason 45040

(216) 241-5310 ..**Persia**, Stephen T '04 %Gallagher SF&N -1501 Euclid Av -6th Fl -Cleveland 44115 **Fx:**241-1608

(513) 977-8200 ..**Persiani**, John B '03 %Dinsmore & S LLP -255 E 5th -Ste 1900 -Cincinnati 45202 **Fx:**977-8141

(216) 689-5159 ..**Persing**, Brenda L '98 Key Private Bank -127 Pub Sq -16th Fl -Bx89464 -Cleveland 44101 **Fx:**689-7212

(419) 774-5751 ..**Persinger**, Kathleen M '90 Richland Cnty CSEA -161 Park Av -Mansfield 44906

(216) 360-3737 ..**Persky Shapiro & Arnoff Co,LPA** -25101 Chagrin Blvd -Ste 350 Signature Sq II -Beachwood 44122 **Fx:**593-0921

(513) 946-9200 ..**Persley**, Elisa M '94 Hamilton Cnty Juv Ct -800 Bway -Cincinnati 45202 **Fx:**946-9217

(937) 498-4981 ..**Pertee**, Lisa M '02 Shelby Cnty Job & Fam Srvcs -227 S Ohio Av -Sidney 45365

(419) 843-1010 ..**Pertz**, Frank E '83 -3230 Cntrl Pk W -Ste 200 -Toledo 43617

(440) 992-5561 ..**Pertz**, Julianne P '84 -4951 Rockwell Rd -Ashtabula 44004 **Pertz**, Linda M '79 -(Address Unavailable)

(513) 576-1060 ..**Peschke**, Joel L '00 %Calderhead Law Ofc,LLC -200 TechneCenter Dr -Ste 100 -Milford 45150 **Fx:**576-8792 **Peshek**, Linda M '86 -4775 Munson NW -Canton 44718

(419) 536-9708 ..**Pesin**, Donna K '92 St Lukes Hospital -5901 Monclova Rd -Maumee 43537

(440) 323-7070 ..**Peskin**, Lawrence F '92 %Becker & M Co,LPA -134 Middle Av -Elyria 44035 **Fx:**323-1879

(202) 622-3312 ..**Pesta**, Helen R '73 IRS -1111 Const Av NW -Washington, DC 20224

(614) 466-7447 ..**Pestello-Sharf**, Stephanie D '79 Atty Gen -150 E Gay -Columbus 43215

(216) 344-7908 ..**Pesuit**, Jo Ann Durk '95 -719 Natl City Bk Bldg -629 Euclid Av -Cleveland 44114

(513) 241-3100 ..**Petas**, Pamela S '92 Lerner S&R -120 E 4th -8th Fl -Cincinnati 45202

(804) 782-1422 ..**Peter**, James P '75 CSX Corp -One James Ctr -Richmond, VA 23219

(614) 732-0746 ..**Peter**, Jennifer M '04 PRH Consulting Grp,LLC -100 E Broad -Ste 2330 -Columbus 43215

(614) 280-0203 ..**Peterman**, Laura M '86 -221 S High -Columbus 43215

(440) 646-0222 ..**Peterman**, Michael J '73 N Pointe Realty,Inc -5915 Landerbrook Dr -Ste 120 -Mayfield Heights 44124 **Peters**, Craig M '90 -10150 Harrison Av -Harrison 45030

(614) 469-5715 ..**Peters**, Dana M '86 US Atty -303 Marconi Blvd -Ste 200 -Columbus 43215

(602) 379-4007 ..**Peters**, David L '71 INS -2035 N Central Av -260 -Phoenix, AZ 85004

(216) 579-9782 ..**Peters**, Deborah L '94 Major Legal Srvcs -1111 Chester Av -Ste 510 -Cleveland 44114

(513) 695-1168 ..**Peters**, Erik A '74 Warren Cnty Juv Ct -570 Justice Dr -Lebanon 45036

(614) 857-4324 ..**Peters**, Geoffrey J '94 %Weltman W&R Co,LPA -175 S 3rd -Ste 900 -Columbus 43215 **Fx:**222-2193

(216) 664-4331 ..**Peters**, George E IV '93 Dept of Law -601 Lakeside Av -Rm 106 City Hall -Cleveland 44114 **Fx:**664-2663

(614) 228-1541 ..**Peters**, Georgeann G '83 (Baker & H LLP) -65 E State -Ste 2100 -Columbus 43215 **Fx:**462-2616

(440) 930-8069 ..**Peters**, James E '97 Wickens HPC&B -35765 Chester Rd -Avon 44011 **Fx:**937-4466

(614) 793-1770 ..**Peters**, James M '76 (Kreiner & P Co,LPA) -6047 Frantz Rd -Ste 203 -Dublin 43017

(740) 472-1681 ..**Peters**, James W '81 -107 W Court -Woodsfield 43793

(440) 838-7600 ..**Peters**, Jeffrey Tim '99 %Janik & D,LLP -9200 S Hills Blvd -Ste 300 -Cleveland 44147 **Fx:**838-7601

(440) 350-2318 ..**Peters**, Jennifer L '99 %Hon V Culotta -47 N Park Pl -Cmmn Pleas Ct -Painesville 44077

(614) 221-2121 ..**Peters**, Joanne S '94 Isaac BL&T,LLP -250 E Broad -Ste 900 Mdlnd Bldg -Columbus 43215 **Fx:**365-9516

(740) 927-3859 ..**Peters**, John I '75 (J Peters Co,LPA) -26½ E Front -Bx48 -Pataskala 43062

(202) 638-1501 ..**Peters**, Joyce E '71 Ofc of Bar Cnsl -515 5th NW -Rm 127 Bldg A -Washington, DC 20001 **Peters**, Laura L '94 -(Address Unavailable)

(419) 213-4202 ..**Peters**, Lora D '97 Hon Lansinger -1 Const Av -6th Dist Ct of Appls -Toledo 43624

(614) 833-3804 ..**Peters**, Megan J '80 -5273 Mason Rd NW -Canal Winchester 43110

(216) 263-6200 ..**Peters**, Melissa L '00 Rauser & Assoc,LPA -614 W Superior Av -Ste 950 -Cleveland 44113 **Fx:**263-6202

(202) 693-6468 ..**Peters**, Pamela H '89 US Dept of Labor -200 Const Av NW -Rm C-2318 -Washington, DC 20210

(330) 468-0483 ..**Peters**, Saundra L '85 -7919 Chaffee Rd -Sagamore Hills 44067

(216) 642-0323 ..**Peters**, Scott C '92 (Britton SP&K Co,LPA) -4700 Rockside Rd -Ste 540 Summit One -Cleveland 44131 **Fx:**642-0747

(330) 668-3994 ..**Peters**, Suzanne '82 Acdmy of Ct Reporting -3675 Ira Rd -Akron 44333

(419) 242-5429 ..**Peters**, William J '73 -316 N Mich -Ste 422 -Toledo 43624

(614) 249-9001 ..**Peters**, William L '80 %Nationwide Ins Co -2 Nationwide Plz -Ste 810 -Columbus 43215

(419) 734-6840 ..**Petersen**, Barbara B '73 Ottawa Cnty Juv Ct -315 Madison -Port Clinton 43452

(440) 285-3511 ..**Petersen & Ibold** -401 South -Chardon 44024 **Fx:**285-3363

(330) 869-2177 ..**Petersen**, James Lee '81 -Bx13118 -Akron 44334 **Fx:**869-4922

(440) 285-3511 ..**Petersen**, Jerry A '66 (Petersen & I) -401 South -Chardon 44024 **Fx:**285-3363

(419) 732-2521 ..**Petersen**, Lowell S '52 -122 W 2nd -Port Clinton 43452

(800) 800-2000 ..**Petersen**, Mary B '79 Hartford -500 Bielenberg Dr -Woodbury, MN 55125

(614) 466-2766 ..**Petersen**, Shaun K '00 Atty Gen -30 E Broad -Columbus 43215 **Fx:**644-1926

(216) 696-3232 ..**Petersen**, Susan E '98 %Spangenberg S&L,LLP -1900 E 9th -2400 Natl City Ctr -Cleveland 44114 **Fx:**696-3924

(440) 285-3511 ..**Petersen**, Todd E '96 (Petersen & I) -401 South -Chardon 44024 **Fx:**285-3363

(513) 241-3100 ..**Petersmann**, Sara M '91 (Lerner S&R) -120 E 4th -8th Fl -Cincinnati 45202

(202) 267-6906 ..**Peterson**, Brenda M '83 Dept of Transportation -2100 2nd SW -Washington, DC 20593

(614) 462-5200 ..**Peterson**, Carolyn D '91 Franklin Cnty CSEA -80 E Fulton -Columbus 43215

(614) 645-7385 ..**Peterson**, David E '97 City Atty -90 W Broad -Columbus 43215

(937) 372-3584 ..**Peterson**, David S '84 (Peterson & P) -87 S Progress Dr -Xenia 45385 **Fx:**372-7218

(440) 734-7600 ..**Peterson**, Eric S '02 %Crombie Law Firm -4615 Great Nrthrn Blvd -North Olmsted 44070 **Fx:**734-1054

(216) 797-4489 ..**Peterson**, Grace M '94 Euclid City Schools -651 E 222nd -Euclid 44123

(614) 462-3555 ..**Peterson**, Gregory S '93 Franklin Cnty Pros -373 S High -Columbus 43215

(740) 282-1911 ..**Peterson**, Howard W III '91 (Fisher B&P) -2017 Sunset Blvd -Steubenville 43952

(304) 345-5667 ..**Peterson**, James C '79 (Hill PCB&D,PLLC) -500 Tracy Way -Charleston, WV 25311

(614) 325-0379 ..**Peterson**, Kathleen S '80 -5281 E Shore -Columbus 43231

(330) 342-3013 ..**Peterson**, Kenneth B '81 Cnsl FedEx Supply Chain Srvcs Inc -5455 Darrow Rd -Hudson 44236

(614) 791-4121 ..**Peterson**, Lauren M '82 (Peterson & Assoc) -5060 Bradenton Av -Ste D -Dublin 43017

(614) 228-4546 ..**Peterson**, Mark A '89 Shuler P&B,LPA -145 E Rich -Ste 400 -Columbus 43215

(937) 372-3584 ..**Peterson**, Marshall E '55 (Peterson & P) -87 S Progress Dr -Xenia 45385 **Fx:**372-7218

(330) 376-1600 ..**Peterson**, Mary J '87 Cincinnati Ins Co -50 S Main -Ste 615 -Akron 44308

(216) 771-1900 ..**Peterson**, Michael H '70 (M Peterson & Assoc) -700 W St Clair Av -Ste 100 -Cleveland 44113

(330) 796-4141 ..**Peterson**, Michael R '93 Goodyear Tire & Rubber Co -1144 E Market -Akron 44316

(614) 466-3664 ..**Peterson**, Michaela J '01 OH DOT -1980 W Broad -Columbus 43223

(216) 664-2807 ..**Peterson**, Natalie L '97 %Dept of Law -601 Lakeside Av -Rm 106 City Hall -Cleveland 44114 **Fx:**664-2663

(440) 564-9111 ..**Peterson**, Paul N '02 Kinetico,Inc -10845 Kinsmore Rd -Bx193 -Newbury 44065

(216) 265-2570 ..**Peterson**, Robert J '82 %Park Corp -6200 Riverside Dr -Cleveland 44135

(216) 642-9007 ..**Peterson**, Robin J '92 R Peterson Co,LLC -6060 Rockside Wds Blvd -Ste 250 -Independence 44131

(937) 382-0045 ..**Peterson**, Shaun D '91 (Peterson & D) -111 E Sugartree -Wilmington 45177

(937) 255-6111 ..**Peterson**, Sigurd R Jr. '87 AFMCLO/JAB -2240 B -Rm C1 -Wright Patterson AFB 45433

(614) 466-6511 ..**Peterson**, Sonni G '93 Dept Admin Srvcs -30 E Broad -Columbus 43215

(248) 399-8132 ..**Petit**, John M '94 Loyola House -2599 Harvard Rd -Berkley, MI 48072

(330) 265-8278 ..**Petit**, Matthew A '01 -101 Central Plz S -Ste 300 -Canton 44702

(614) 228-4422 ..**Petitjean**, David L '88 OfCnsl Chappano W PLL -8 E Long -9th Fl -Columbus 43215 **Fx:**228-4423

(419) 885-7515 ..**Petitjean**, David L '88 OfCnsl W Drescher & Assoc Co,LPA -6611 Mplwd Av -Sylvania 43560 **Fx:**885-3265 **Petkewitz**, Thomas G '69 -(Address Unavailable)

(740) 362-7729 ..**Petkovic**, Wayne E '71 -840 Brittany Dr -Delaware 43015

(419) 244-8396 ..**Petlow**, James J '67 -520 Mad Av -Ste 870 -Toledo 43604

(216) 931-6000 ..**Peto**, John G '78 Ulmer & B LLP -1300 E 9th -Ste 900 Penton Media Bldg -Cleveland 44114 **Fx:**931-6001

(216) 591-0927 ..**Peto**, Terri M '88 -25435 Wimbledon Rd -Beachwood 44122

(330) 740-2073 ..**Petraglia**, Catherine T '80 Mahoning Cnty CSEA -112 W Commerce -Bx119 -Youngstown 44503

(216) 621-8484 ..**Petralia**, Shelly R '04 %Climaco LPW&G Co,LPA -1228 Euclid Av -Ste 900 Halle Bldg -Cleveland 44115 **Fx:**771-1632

(954) 356-7314 ..**Petras**, Barbara L '75 %US Atty -500 E Broward Blvd -Fort Lauderdale, FL 33394 **Fx:**356-7180 **Petras**, David J '96 UUNET Technologies Inc -5000 Britton Rd -Hilliard 43026

(216) 621-0200 ..**Petras**, Stephen J Jr. '79 (Baker & H LLP) -1900 E 9th -Ste 3200 -Cleveland 44114 **Fx:**696-0704

(614) 225-8853 ..**Petrecca**, Michael A '85 PricewaterhouseCoopers -100 E Broad -Ste 2100 -Columbus 43215

(614) 436-1992 ..**Petrel**, David B '84 (D Petrel,Ltd) -352 Bailey Pl -Columbus 43235

(614) 466-4605 ..**Petrella**, Barbara Jo '89 OH Dept Job & Fam Srvcs -30 E Broad -32nd Fl -Columbus 43266

(937) 496-3147 ..**Petrella**, Jennifer A '04 Montgomery Cnty Juvenile Ct -303 W 2nd -Dayton 45403

(330) 726-6999 ..**Petrella**, Shelli E '99 -755 Boardman-Canfld Rd -Ste P-4 -Boardman 44512

(216) 928-2200 ..**Petrello**, Colleen H '89 %Sutter OM&F -1301 E 9th -3600 Erievw Twr -Cleveland 44114 **Fx:**928-4400

(216) 479-8500 ..**Petrey**, Katherine G '74 Cnsl Squire S&D LLP -127 Pub Sq -4900 Key Twr -Cleveland 44114 **Fx:**479-8780

(216) 371-9644 ..**Petrey**, Kenneth D '74 -2253 Chatfld Dr -Cleveland Heights 44106

(614) 464-6400 ..**Petricoff**, M Howard '74 (Vorys SS&P LLP) -52 E Gay -Bx1008 -Columbus 43216 **Fx:**464-6350

(513) 621-6464 ..**Petrie**, Bruce I Jr. '80 SrCnsl Graydon H&R LLP -511 Walnut -1900 Fifth Third Ctr -Cincinnati 45202 **Fx:**651-3836

(614) 227-2373 ..**Petrie**, James G '92 (Bricker & E LLP) -100 S 3rd -Columbus 43215 **Fx:**227-2390

(513) 579-2210 ..**Petrie**, Laura S '89 Provident Bank -1 E 4th -MS 652A -Cincinnati 45202

(440) 655-3543 ..**Petrinovic**, Peter A '79 -6576 Edgemore Av -Solon 44139 **Fx:**349-0609

(614) 466-8911 ..**Petro**, James M '73 Atty Gen -30 E Broad -Columbus 43215 **Fx:**728-7582

(614) 224-0531 ..**Petro**, John J '62 OfCnsl Williams & P Co,LLC -338 S High -2nd Fl -Columbus 43215 **Fx:**224-0553

(614) 224-0531 ..**Petro,** John P '92 (Williams & P Co,LLC) -338 S High -2nd Fl -Columbus 43215 **Fx:**224-0553

(614) 224-0531 ..**Petro,** Susan S '90 %Williams & P Co,LLC -338 S High -2nd Fl -Columbus 43215 **Fx:**224-0553

(216) 781-3600 ..**Petroff,** Dimitre James '89 Faulkner M&P,LLP -820 W Superior Av -Ste 900 -Cleveland 44113 **Fx:**781-8839

(440) 365-8800 ..**Petroff,** Mark G '79 -1288 Abbe Rd -Elyria 44035

(937) 323-5555 ..**Petroff,** Samuel J '80 %Lagos & L -1 S Limestone -Ste 1000 -Springfield 45502

(216) 696-5222 ..**Petronelli,** Jack L '80 %Johnson & C,LLC -1001 Lakeside Av -Ste 1700 N Pnt Twr -Cleveland 44114 **Fx:**696-5288

(330) 744-0247 ..**Petrony,** John F '93 (Nadler N&B Co,LPA) -20 Fed Plz W -Ste 600 -Youngstown 44503 **Fx:**744-8690

(216) 381-3400 ..**Petronzio,** Anna M '93 (Petronzio S Co,LPA) -5001 Mayfld Rd -Ste 201 -Cleveland 44124

(216) 381-3400 ..**Petronzio Schneier Co,LPA** -5001 Mayfld Rd -Ste 201 -Cleveland 44124

Petropouleas, Andreas '98 -(Address Unavailable)

(216) 573-6666 ..**Petropouleas,** Jim '02 %D Morell & Assoc Co,LPA -6060 Rockside Wds Blvd -250 Spectrum Bldg -Independence 44131

(330) 376-1242 ..**Petrosky,** Sylvia A '87 OfCnsl Renner KGBT&W,LPA -106 S Main -4th Fl First Natl Twr -Akron 44308 **Fx:**376-9646

(216) 241-5310 ..**Petrov,** Alan M '74 (Gallagher SF&N) -1501 Euclid Av -6th Fl -Cleveland 44115 **Fx:**241-1608

(216) 622-8200 ..**Petrov,** Daniel P '01 %Calfee H&G LLP -800 Superior Av -Ste 1400 -Cleveland 44114 **Fx:**241-0816

(937) 854-1137 ..**Petroziello,** Brian C '77 -1 Maple -Ste 100 -Trotwood 45426

(614) 466-0106 ..**Petrucci,** Gretchen L '90 PUCO -180 E Broad -Columbus 43266

(614) 221-6837 ..**Petrucci,** Mark C '90 (Morgan & P,LLP) -380 S 5th -Columbus 43215 **Fx:**224-1537

(513) 684-8740 ..**Petrucci,** Michael L '95 First Grp Amer -705 Central Av -Cincinnati 45202

(216) 689-3887 ..**Petrulis,** Richard D '77 KeyBank NA -127 Pub Sq -Cleveland 44114

(216) 621-0200 ..**Petrulis,** Robert C '88 (Baker & H LLP) -1900 E 9th -Ste 3200 -Cleveland 44114 **Fx:**696-0740

(330) 740-2208 ..**Petruska,** Heidi M '98 Mahoning Cnty Crt Cmmn Pleas -120 Market -Domestic Relations Div -Youngstown 44503

(216) 623-0900 ..**Petruzzi,** Anthony R '98 %McLaughlin & M,LLP -1111 Superior Av E -Ste 1350 Eaton Ctr -Cleveland 44114 **Fx:**623-0935

Petry, John L '69 -132 N Barron -Eaton 45320

(216) 523-4105 ..**Petry,** Samuel R II '67 Eaton Corp -1111 Superior Av -Cleveland 44114

(330) 963-0022 ..**Petsche,** John A III '89 J Petsche III & Assoc -2305 E Aurora Rd -Unit A9 -Twinsburg 44087

(740) 593-3348 ..**Pettey,** Sky '00 Lavelle & Assoc -207 Columbus Rd -Ste B -Athens 45701

(330) 762-0700 ..**Petti,** Gary M '95 %Slater Z&G -One Cascade Plz -Ste 2210 -Akron 44308 **Fx:**762-3923

(216) 664-6900 ..**Petticord,** Daniel F '92 (Brzytwa Q&M LLC) -1660 W 2nd -900 Skylight Ofc Twr -Cleveland 44113 **Fx:**664-6901

(419) 891-8662 ..**Pettiford,** Nadine S '95 Unemploymnt Comp Commssn -1684 WoodInds Dr -2nd Fl -Bx1298 -Maumee 43537

(614) 224-4357 ..**Pettigrew,** Grady L Jr. '71 (Cox S&P Co,LPA) -115 W Main -Ste 400 -Columbus 43215 **Fx:**228-0701

(614) 466-7788 ..**Pettigrew,** Lewis F '90 OH Ct of Claims -65 E State -Ste 1100 -Columbus 43215

(216) 781-7777 ..**Pettinelli,** Joan E '90 (Wuliger F&B) -1340 Sumner Ct -Brownell Bldg -Cleveland 44115 **Fx:**781-0621

(614) 221-1111 ..**Pettit,** Christopher R '98 %Shayne & G -221 S High -Columbus 43215 **Fx:**221-4070

(513) 946-4209 ..**Pettit,** Kenton K '00 Cnty Auditors Ofc -138 E Court -Rm 504 -Cincinnati 45202

(614) 228-3550 ..**Pettit,** Susan '97 -577 S High -Columbus 43215 **Fx:**228-3658

(614) 837-5700 ..**Pettorini,** John H '73 -Bx71 -Canal Winchester 43110

(330) 264-4444 ..**Pettorini,** Timothy B '98 (Critchfield C&J Ltd) -225 N Market -Bx599 -Wooster 44691 **Fx:**263-9278

(513) 946-5800 ..**Petty,** Kimberly A '02 Hamilton Cnty Cmn Pleas Ct -800 Bway -Cincinnati 45202

Petty, Robert C '98 -1322 W 7th Av -Apt A -Columbus 43212

(937) 426-0845 ..**Petty,** Timothy L '81 -3511 Swigert Rd -Beavercreek 45440

(614) 418-1810 ..**Pettys,** Jeffrey C '93 -2720 Airport Dr -Ste 100 -Columbus 43219

(614) 466-2166 ..**Petzinger,** John S '03 OH Dept Taxation -30 E Broad -22nd Fl -Columbus 43215

(937) 384-0079 ..**Petzold,** John P '62 Montgomery Cnty Common Pleas Ct -1767 Brandonhall Dr -Miamisburg 45342 **Fx:**384-0081

(614) 744-5070 ..**Peura,** David A '02 Fifth Third Bank -21 E State -8th Fl -Columbus 43215

(216) 348-0900 ..**Peyton,** Jennifer I '98 -2012 W 25th -Ste 701 -Cleveland 44113 **Fx:**348-0600

(304) 755-5556 ..**Peyton,** Thomas H '02 -2801 1st Av -Bx216 -Nitro, WV 25143

(216) 621-0112 ..**Pfaff,** Robert E '86 -1801 E 9th -Ste 1710 -Cleveland 44114

(404) 572-4600 ..**Pfahl,** Scott B '89 %King & S -191 Pchtree -Atlanta, GA 30303

(614) 583-5020 ..**Pfancuff,** Sharon L '83 %City Atty -3600 Tremont Rd -Columbus 43221

(937) 228-0894 ..**Pfarrer,** Stephen M '67 -130 W 2nd -Ste 2100 -Dayton 45402

(614) 228-8191 ..**Pfau,** Edward L '91 -987 S High -Columbus 43206

(330) 702-9700 ..**Pfau,** John C '80 (Pfau P&M) -6715 Tippecanoe Rd -Bx9070 -Youngstown 44513

(330) 702-9700 ..**Pfau Pfau & Marando** -6715 Tippecanoe Rd -Bx9070 -Youngstown 44513

(330) 702-9700 ..**Pfau,** William E III '79 (Pfau P&M) -6715 Tippecanoe Rd -Bx9070 -Youngstown 44513

(937) 392-4371 ..**Pfeffer,** Michael S '73 -112 Main -Ripley 45167

(614) 228-1541 ..**Pfefferle,** Ben L III '79 (Baker & H LLP) -65 E State -Ste 2100 -Columbus 43215 **Fx:**462-2616

(419) 433-4485 ..**Pfefferle,** John A '66 -332 Brnswck Dr -Huron 44839

(419) 294-1200 ..**Pfeifer,** Agnes A '86 (Pfeifer & P) -114 E Wyandot Av -Bx240 -Upper Sandusky 43351

(419) 294-1200 ..**Pfeifer,** Dennis E '79 (Pfeifer & P) -114 E Wyandot Av -Bx240 -Upper Sandusky 43351

(419) 294-2532 ..**Pfeifer,** E Michael '73 -Bx323 -Upper Sandusky 43351

(614) 466-8600 ..**Pfeiffer,** Barbara J '85 Atty Gen -30 E Broad -Columbus 43215 **Fx:**466-6090

(440) 286-4215 ..**Pfeiffer,** Donald E '74 -9650 Fox Meadow Ln -Chardon 44024

(419) 885-1819 ..**Pfeiffer,** James J '57 -Bx386 -Sylvania 43560

(412) 242-4400 ..**Pfeiffer,** Julie M '98 Maiello B&M,LLP -3301 McCrady Rd -One Churchill Pk -Pittsburgh, PA 15235

(614) 645-7385 ..**Pfeiffer,** Richard C Jr. '72 City Atty -90 W Broad -Columbus 43215

(614) 760-3502 ..**Pfeiffer,** William W '83 CareWorks -Bx182726 -Columbus 43218

(330) 376-1600 ..**Pfeister,** Alison J '85 Cincinnati Ins Co -50 S Main -Ste 615 -Akron 44308

(330) 493-9080 ..**Pfendler,** Christopher C '79 -4715 Fulton Dr NW -Canton 44718

(614) 469-2999 ..**Pfeuffer,** Alan J '00 Fed Pub Def -10 W Broad -Ste 1020 -Columbus 43215

(330) 384-6386 ..**Pfister,** Eugene W '95 -400 Wabash Av -Akron 44307

(703) 312-0140 ..**Pfizenmayer,** Rickard F '69 Cnsl McGinn Group,LLC -2300 Clarendon Blvd -Ste 901 -Arlington, VA 22201 **Fx:**312-0150

(513) 241-6748 ..**Pflanz,** David E '86 A Levine -324 Reading Rd -Cincinnati 45202

(216) 586-3939 ..**Pfleiderer,** Shane T '03 %Jones D -901 Lakeside Av -Cleveland 44114 **Fx:**579-0212

(513) 721-4500 ..**Pflum,** Joseph F '89 (Patsfall Y&P LLC) -1 W 4th -Ste 1800 -Cincinnati 45202 **Fx:**639-7554

(216) 839-4000 ..**Pfundstein,** Joseph A '91 -24100 Chagrin Blvd -Ste 330 -Beachwood 44122

(513) 684-6002 ..**Phalen,** Thomas F Jr. '67 Dept of Labor-OHA -36 E 7th -Ste 2525 -Cincinnati 45202

Pham, Hiep P '01 -59-071 Hakuola Rd -Haleiwa, HI 96712

Pheasant, Merle E Jr. '72 -4303 Bonnie Brook Rd -Toledo 43615

(419) 874-3177 ..**Pheils,** David R Jr. '74 (Pheils & W) -410 Louisiana Av -Perrysburg 43551 **Fx:**874-0180

(419) 874-3177 ..**Pheils & Wisniewski** -410 Louisiana Av -Perrysburg 43551 **Fx:**874-0180

(937) 526-3111 ..**Phelan,** Brent J '95 Phelan Ins Agncy,Inc -863 E Main -Bx1 -Versailles 45380 **Fx:**526-5178

(419) 530-4017 ..**Phelps,** Amy B '02 Univ of Toledo -2801 W Baneroft -VP's Ofc -Toledo 43606

(513) 381-9200 ..**Phelps,** Arthur E Jr. '85 (Rendigs FK&D,LLP) -One W 4th -Ste 900 -Cincinnati 45202 **Fx:**381-9206

(614) 462-4242 ..**Phelps-White,** Angela G '85 Franklin Cnty Cmn Pleas Ct -375 S High -Columbus 43215 **Fx:**462-6292

(419) 724-0030 ..**Phifer,** B Janelle Butler '75 LAWO -520 Mad Av -Ste 640 -Toledo 43604 **Fx:**321-1582

(614) 682-2049 ..**Philabaum,** Laura B '89 CSPC Ofc Shild Support -936 Eastwind Dr -Westerville 43081

(614) 466-5092 ..**Philabaun,** Michael A '83 Atty Gen -150 E Gay -Columbus 43215 **Fx:**644-9973

(614) 224-7883 ..**Philbrick,** Jon R '77 -326 S High -#100-Annx -Columbus 43215

(330) 758-9525 ..**Philibin,** Paul J '87 -755 Boardman-Canfld Rd -K-4 -Youngstown 44512

(440) 838-7600 ..**Philipp,** Jonathan W '89 Janik & D,LLP -9200 S Hills Blvd -Ste 300 -Cleveland 44147 **Fx:**838-7601

(513) 887-3305 ..**Phillabaum,** Jason R '00 Butler Cnty Pros -315 High -11th Fl -Bx515 -Hamilton 45012

(513) 941-6711 ..**Phillipps,** James E '66 -2985 Gilligan Av -Cincinnati 45233

(740) 452-7555 ..**Phillips,** Aaron B '00 %Gottlieb JB&D,PLL -320 Main -Bx190 -Zanesville 43702 **Fx:**452-2257

(216) 523-1500 ..**Phillips,** Amy L '98 %Mansour GG&M Co,LPA -55 Pub Sq -Ste 2150 -Cleveland 44113 **Fx:**523-1705

(614) 221-5216 ..**Phillips,** Christopher G '01 %Wiles BB&B Co,LPA -300 Spruce -1st Fl -Columbus 43215 **Fx:**221-5692

(330) 373-1639 ..**Phillips,** Clifford L '72 -1569 WoodInd Av -Ste 6 -Warren 44483

(202) 371-7283 ..**Phillips,** Daniel P '98 %Skadden ASM&F -1440 NY Av NW -Washington, DC 20005

(216) 523-1286 ..**Phillips,** David G '90 -2000 E Ninth -Ste 710 -Cleveland 44115

(740) 775-3300 ..**Phillips,** David M '52 (Phillips & S) -37 N Paint -Chillicothe 45601

(937) 645-4190 ..**Phillips,** David W III '84 Union Cnty Pros -221 W 5th -Ste 333 -Marysville 43040 **Fx:**645-4191

(330) 740-2330 ..**Phillips,** Elizabeth M '96 Mahoning Cnty Pros -21 W Boardman -6th Fl -Youngstown 44503 **Fx:**740-2008

Phillips, Elizabeth S '90 -1715 Bon Air Dr -Lexington, KY 40502

(440) 937-5545 ..**Phillips,** Gerald W '77 Phillips & Co,LPA -35955 Detroit Rd -Avon 44011 **Fx:**937-9142

(216) 622-8200 ..**Phillips,** Gregory J '04 %Calfee H&G LLP -800 Superior Av -Ste 1400 -Cleveland 44114 **Fx:**241-0816

(614) 464-6400 ..**Phillips,** James E '75 (Vorys SS&P LLP) -52 E Gay -Bx1008 -Columbus 43216 **Fx:**464-6350

(216) 687-8100 ..**Phillips,** James E '81 GPI Inc -812 Huron Rd -Cleveland 44115

(330) 471-6361 ..**Phillips,** James P A '02 Timken Co -1835 Dueber Av SW -Canton 44706

(614) 846-1700 ..**Phillips,** Janet L '97 (J Phillips Co LPA) -6660 N High -Ste 3-E -Worthington 43085

(419) 255-6070 ..**Phillips,** Jerome '69 (Wittenberg PL&N) -520 Mad Av -Ste 840 -Toledo 43604

(513) 985-2500 ..**Phillips,** John H '90 (Phillips Law Firm,Inc) -9521 Mntgmry Rd -Cincinnati 45242 **Fx:**985-2503

(513) 603-5082 ..**Phillips,** John P '04 Cincinnati Insurance Co -6200 S Gilmore Rd -Fairfield 45014

Phillips, John W '78 -(Address Unavailable)

Phillips, Kenneth W '89 -412 14th -Toledo 43624

(614) 656-0000 ..**Phillips,** Kimberly S '98 Columbus Mortg Brokers -6530 W Campus Oval -3rd flr -New Albany 43054

(216) 363-4500 ..**Phillips,** Mark A '90 (Benesch FC&A LLP) -200 Pub Sq -Ste 2300 -Cleveland 44114 **Fx:**363-4588

(614) 228-5822 ..**Phillips,** Mark E '84 -300 E Broad -Ste 300 -Columbus 43215

(513) 923-5232 ..**Phillips,** Mary K '99 %F Rosenacker Co,LPA -5537 Cheviot Rd -Cincinnati 45247

(216) 622-8200 ..**Phillips,** Michael D '77 (Calfee H&G LLP) -800 Superior Av -Ste 1400 -Cleveland 44114 **Fx:**241-0816

(440) 243-2800 ..**Phillips Mille & Costabile Co,LPA** -7530 Lucerne Dr -Ste 200 -Middleburg Heights 44130 **Fx:**243-2852

(440) 243-2800 ..**Phillips,** Nicholas E '73 (Phillips M&C Co,LPA) -7530 Lucerne Dr -Ste 200 -Middleburg Heights 44130 **Fx:**243-2852

(614) 462-7246 .. **Phillips**, Patricia M '93 %Hon CR Petree II -373 S High
-Columbus 43215

(937) 328-4557 .. **Phillips**, Patrick B '99 Clark Cnty Cmn Pleas Ct -31 N Limestone
-Juv Div -Springfield 45502

(216) 939-3000 .. **Phillips**, Paul R '89 Plating Prod & Manuf -1318 W 58th
-Cleveland 44102

(740) 452-7555 .. **Phillips**, Philip S '75 (Gottlieb JB&D,PLL) -320 Main -Bx190
-Zanesville 43702 **Fx:**452-2257

Phillips, R L Kelly III '02 -215 Ironclad Dr -Columbus 43213

(330) 650-4656 .. **Phillips**, Robert D '75 -Bx1148 -Hudson 44236

(216) 781-3600 .. **Phillips**, Robert M '71 Faulkner M&P,LLP -820 W Superior Av
-Ste 900 -Cleveland 44113 **Fx:**781-8839

Phillips, Robert W '51 -14317 Ovid Dr -Hudson, FL 34667

(216) 522-7451 .. **Phillips**, Ronald L '98 EEOC -1600 W 2nd -Ste 850
-Cleveland 44113

(513) 651-6800 .. **Phillips**, Scott D '89 (Frost BT LLC) -201 E 5th -2200 PNC Ctr
-Cincinnati 45202 **Fx:**651-6981

(419) 213-3000 .. **Phillips**, Shannon L '93 Lucas Cnty CSEA -701 Adams
-Toledo 43624

(614) 466-3180 .. **Phillips**, Sherry M '91 Atty Gen -150 E Gay -Columbus 43215
Fx:466-9788

(502) 627-2648 .. **Phillips**, Steven D '91 LG&E Energy Corp -220 W Main -11th Fl
-Louisville, KY 40202

(419) 947-5575 .. **Phillips**, Steven M '91 Morrow Cnty Probate Ct -48 E High
-Mount Gilead 43338

(740) 775-3300 .. **Phillips & Street** -37 N Paint -Chillicothe 45601

(216) 861-5582 .. **Phillips**, Sue Ellen '85 OfCnsl Fay SFM&M LLP -1100 Superior Av
-7th Fl -Cleveland 44114 **Fx:**241-1666

(419) 447-4952 .. **Phillips**, Susan J '90 -102 S Wshngtn -Tiffin 44883

(513) 651-6800 .. **Phillips**, T Stephen '66 (Frost BT LLC) -201 E 5th -2200 PNC Ctr
-Cincinnati 45202 **Fx:**651-6981

(614) 889-1425 .. **Phillips**, Thomas M '72 -5380 Dublin Rd -Dublin 43017

(937) 438-5588 .. **Phillips**, Thomas M '87 (Phillips & J) -7970 Clyo Rd
-Dayton 45459

(740) 452-7555 .. **Phillips**, Wayne W II '72 Gottlieb JB&D,PLL -320 Main -Bx190
-Zanesville 43702 **Fx:**452-2257

(614) 645-7385 .. **Phillips**, Westley M '04 %City Atty -90 W Broad -Columbus 43215

(216) 622-8200 .. **Phillips**, William M '83 (Calfee H&G LLP) -800 Superior Av
-Ste 1400 -Cleveland 44114 **Fx:**241-0816

(937) 372-4436 .. **Phipps**, David L '75 (Wead AP&A) -53 W Main -BxH -Xenia 45385

(717) 691-6019 .. **Phipps**, David M '91 Messiah College -1 Cllg Av
-Grantham, PA 17027

(419) 221-5234 .. **Phipps**, Heather L '02 City Prosecutors Ofc -109 N Union
-Lima 45801

(614) 469-1400 .. **Phipps**, Karen Held '03 Clark PR&S Co,LPA -471 E Broad
-Ste 1400 -Columbus 43215 **Fx:**469-0900

(937) 225-5778 .. **Phipps**, Michele D '98 Montgomery Cnty Pros -301 W 3rd -Bx972
-Dayton 45422 **Fx:**225-3470

(202) 616-8482 .. **Phipps**, Peter J '98 Dept of Justice -20 Mass Av
-Washington, DC 20001

(740) 387-6727 .. **Piacentino**, Charles M '73 Piacentino & P -198 E Center
-Marion 43302

(617) 570-1000 .. **Piacquad**, Joseph A '90 (Goodwin P LLP) -Exch Pl
-Boston, MA 02109 **Fx:**523-1231

(216) 664-4989 .. **Pianka**, Raymond Lee '78 Mun Ct Judge -1200 Ontario Av
-Cleveland 44113

(216) 621-0200 .. **Piatak**, Thomas J '89 (Baker & H LLP) -1900 E 9th -Ste 3200
-Cleveland 44114 **Fx:**696-0740

(614) 444-3036 .. **Piatt**, Richard A '93 (Saia & P,PLL) -713 S Front -Columbus 43206

(330) 743-5101 .. **Piatt**, Timothy R '88 %Green H&S,Co LPA -16 Wick Av -Ste 400
-Youngstown 44503 **Fx:**743-3451

(216) 696-6993 .. **Piazza**, Anthony M '77 -1370 Ontario -Ste 2000 -Cleveland 44113

(440) 365-8388 .. **Piazza**, Robert A '69 -10247 Dewhurst Dr -Elyria 44035
Fx:366-5265

(937) 485-9420 .. **Pica**, Mary R '79 Reynolds & Reynolds Co -1 Reynolds Way
-Kettering 45430

(440) 974-4014 .. **Picardini**, Joseph B '71 -8815 East Av -Mentor 44060

(216) 531-1766 .. **Picciano**, Mary B '89 -22551 Hadden -Euclid 44117

(614) 659-9616 .. **Piccin**, Joseph L '00 JL Piccin Co,LPA -3010 Hayden Rd
-Columbus 43235 **Fx:**798-1935

(614) 462-3555 .. **Piccininni**, Patrick J '91 Franklin Cnty Pros -373 S High
-Columbus 43215

(330) 965-7501 .. **Piccirillo**, Michael R '91 -7301 West Blvd -Ste C2
-Boardman 44512

(740) 852-1669 .. **Picken**, Robert D '74 Cnty Mun Ct Judge -Cthse -Bx646
-London 43140

(303) 397-8139 .. **Pickens**, Henry B '88 TeleTech Holdings Inc -9197 S Peoria
-Englewood, CO 80112

(614) 406-8548 .. **Pickens**, Jamie C '02 -Bx29366 -Columbus 43229 **Fx:**413-2813

Pickens, Joseph C '03 -(Address Unavailable)

(937) 328-2574 .. **Pickering**, Andrew P '97 Clark Cnty Pros -50 E Columbia -Bx1608
-Springfield 45501

Pickett, Gerald L '83 -(Address Unavailable)

(614) 221-2121 .. **Pickett**, Patrick M '89 Isaac BL&T,LLP -250 E Broad
-Ste 900 Mdlnd Bldg -Columbus 43215 **Fx:**365-9516

(614) 228-1541 .. **Pickrel**, Deborah A '04 %Baker & H LLP -65 E State -Ste 2100
-Columbus 43215 **Fx:**462-2616

(937) 333-4364 .. **Pickrel**, John S '70 Mun Ct Judge -301 W 3rd -Dayton 45402

(513) 705-7582 .. **Pickrel**, Patricia A '99 Contech Construction Products Inc
-1001 Grove -Middletown 45044

(937) 223-1130 .. **Pickrel Schaeffer & Ebeling** -40 N Main -2700 Kettering Twr
-Dayton 45423 **Fx:**223-0339

(502) 451-8821 .. **Pickrel**, Timothy R '74 -2121 Highland Av -Louisville, KY 40204

(330) 929-0161 .. **Pickut**, Sandra J '76 Performance Entrprses,Inc -4670 Allen Rd
-Stow 44224 **Fx:**929-0178

(330) 675-7037 .. **Pico**, John J '88 Trumbull Cnty Fam Ct -220 S Main -Bx1209
-Warren 44482

Pidala, Candice L '99 -(Address Unavailable)

(440) 232-1900 .. **Pidala**, Sherry A '85 (Pidala & P) -650 Bway Av -Bedford 44146

(330) 494-6611 .. **Pidcock**, William S '82 (Robertson Z&P) -4690 Munson NW
-Ste C -Canton 44718

(330) 643-2943 .. **Pience**, Jamie L '02 Summit Cnty Pros-Juv -650 Dan
-Akron 44310 **Fx:**379-3647

(440) 446-1100 .. **Pienta**, Renee S '01 %Dinn H&P,LLC -5910 Landerbrook Dr
-Ste 200 -Cleveland 44124 **Fx:**446-1240

(419) 399-3456 .. **Pieper**, Timothy R '86 Paulding Cnty Ct -201 E Caroline -Ste 2
-Paulding 45879

Piepho, Scott R '94 -719 Ecton Rd -Akron 44303

(513) 241-9400 .. **Pieples**, Gary J '96 Legal Aid -215 E 9th -Ste 200
-Cincinnati 45202

(614) 645-7385 .. **Pieplow**, Richard A '82 City Atty -90 W Broad -Columbus 43215

(513) 242-7591 .. **Piepmeier**, Mark E '81 -4344 Errun Ln -Cincinnati 45217

(330) 253-0785 .. **Pierce**, Brian M '94 (Gorman MP&V) -1 Cascade Plz -9th Fl
-Akron 44308 **Fx:**253-7432

(330) 740-2330 .. **Pierce**, Constance E '95 Mahoning Cnty Pros -21 W Boardman
-6th Fl -Youngstown 44503 **Fx:**740-2008

(937) 223-8177 .. **Pierce**, David P '93 %Coolidge WW&L -33 W 1st -Ste 600
-Dayton 45402 **Fx:**223-6705

(419) 394-2516 .. **Pierce**, Edwin A '80 (Kuffner & P) -201 W North
-Saint Marys 45885 **Fx:**394-1163

Pierce, Edwin C '64 -2338 Harrngtn Rd -Akron 44319

(740) 695-4412 .. **Pierce**, George F '76 Belmont Cnty Pros -147-A W Main
-Saint Clairsville 43950

(740) 886-2889 .. **Pierce**, James A '92 -1689 State Route 775 -Bx995
-Proctorville 45669

(513) 522-7700 .. **Pierce**, James R '81 -800 Compton Rd -Unit 37A
-Cincinnati 45231

(614) 221-7791 .. **Pierce**, Janica A '02 F Ray Co,LPA -175 S 3rd -Ste 350
-Columbus 43215 **Fx:**221-8957

(937) 449-2800 .. **Pierce**, Lisa S '95 (Chernesky H&K PLL) -10 Cthse Plz SW
-Ste 1100 -Dayton 45402 **Fx:**449-2821

(513) 474-9437 .. **Pierce**, Mary E '91 -8503 Corcoran Dr -Cincinnati 45255

(216) 621-0200 .. **Pierce**, Raymond C '89 (Baker & H LLP) -1900 E 9th -Ste 3200
-Cleveland 44114 **Fx:**696-0740

(304) 344-5800 .. **Pierce**, Robert N Jr. '77 %Robinson & M,PLLC -700 VA E -Bx1791
-Charleston, WV 25301 **Fx:**344-9566

(614) 462-3194 .. **Pierce**, Timothy E '89 Franklin Cnty Pub Def -373 S High -12th Fl
-Columbus 43215

Pierce, Walter R '74 -127 S Remngtn Rd -Bexley 43209

(937) 586-3100 .. **Piercy**, James R '73 (ES Gallon & Assoc) -40 W 4th -22nd Fl
-Dayton 45402 **Fx:**586-3100

(740) 859-2178 .. **Piergallini**, Lawrence T '80 -131 3rd -Bx7 -Tiltonsville 43963

(937) 233-8492 .. **Piergies**, James D '80 Bennington P&S -7229 Taylorsvll Rd
-Huber Heights 45424

Piero, Jeffrey D '00 -6742 Evening -Worthington 43085

(216) 479-8500 .. **Pierpont**, Christine Murphy '91 %Squire S&D LLP -127 Pub Sq
-4900 Key Twr -Cleveland 44114 **Fx:**479-8780

(440) 329-5389 .. **Pierre**, Christopher J '02 Lorain Cnty Pros -225 Court -3rd Fl
-Elyria 44035

(614) 249-3492 .. **Pierre**, Darrell M Jr. '96 Cnsl Nationwide Ins & Fncl Srvcs
-1 Nationwide Plz -Columbus 43215 **Fx:**249-2112

(513) 626-4055 .. **Pierre**, Kenya T '01 Cnsl Procter & Gamble -11511
Reed Hartman Hwy -Cincinnati 45241

(614) 224-6525 .. **Pierre-Louis**, Lloyd '97 -513 E Rich -Ste 300 -Columbus 43215

Piersall, Drew C '04 -(Address Unavailable)

(614) 462-2401 .. **Pierson**, Anthony D '03 %Schottenstein Z&D -250 West
-Bx165020 -Columbus 43216 **Fx:**462-5135

(330) 836-8159 .. **Pierson**, John C '82 -1221 W Market -Twin Oaks Estate -Bx7107
-Akron 44313

(937) 223-9133 .. **Pierson**, Steven T '84 %Rion R&R Co,LPA -130 W 2nd -Ste 2150
-Bx1262 -Dayton 45402

(216) 898-2350 .. **Pietch**, Richard S '80 White Cnsldtd Ind -18013 Cleve Pkwy
-Ste 100 -Cleveland 44135

(216) 622-8200 .. **Pietrafese**, Brent M '03 %Calfee H&G LLP -800 Superior Av
-Ste 1400 -Cleveland 44114 **Fx:**241-0816

(740) 282-6705 .. **Pietragallo Bosick & Gordon** -100 N 4th -Steubenville 43952

Pietrandrea, Beth L '85 -8044 Mntgmry Rd -Ste 470
-Cincinnati 45236

(315) 775-1440 .. **Pietrangelo**, James E II '97 US Army-OSJA -141 Lewis Av
-Fort Drum, NY 13602

Pietrangelo, Wendy D '95 -20232 Westover Av
-Rocky River 44116

(512) 617-3605 .. **Pietrantone**, Mark J '95 %Ernstmeyer & Assoc PC
-101 Westlake Dr -Ste 100 -Austin, TX 78746

(216) 587-8150 .. **Pietras**, John S '95 Marymount Hsptl -12300 McCracken Rd
-Garfield Heights 44125

(330) 364-6591 .. **Pietro**, Frank W II '78 -Bx337 -Dover 44622

(330) 376-2700 .. **Pietrowski**, Moira H '98 %Roetzel & A,LPA -222 S Main
-Akron 44308 **Fx:**376-4577

(419) 243-6148 .. **Pietrykowski**, William F '83 Manahan PB&D -414 N Erie -Bx2328
-Toledo 43603

(216) 515-1660 .. **Pietrzen**, Julie L '04 %Frantz W LLP -127 Pub Sq
-2500 Key Center -Cleveland 44114 **Fx:**515-1650

(216) 377-2604 .. **Pietz**, Lynne P '91 Amer Cancer Society -10501 Euclid Av
-Estate & Asset Srvcs -Cleveland 44106

(216) 731-0050 .. **Pigman**, Edwin P '82 -25000 Euclid Av -Euclid 44117

(614) 227-2000 .. **Pigman**, Jack R '69 (Porter WM&A LLP) -41 S High
-Columbus 43215 **Fx:**227-2100

(330) 376-5756 .. **Pignatelli**, Francis M '88 Emershaw M&S -120 E Mill -#437
-Akron 44308 **Fx:**762-5980

(216) 642-5353 .. **Pignatiello**, Richard A '82 -4141 Rockside Rd -Ste 230
-Independence 44131 **Fx:**642-5355

(216) 621-7860 .. **Pigott**, Stephen E '80 (Cavitch FD&F) -1717 E 9th -14th Fl
-Cleveland 44114 **Fx:**621-3415

(419) 776-4567 .. **Pigott**, Thomas D '94 -2828 W Central Av -Ste 207 -Toledo 43606

(502) 955-4400 .. **Pike**, David A '01 Pike Legal Grp,PLLC -1578 Hwy 44 E -Ste 6
-Bx369 -Shepherdsville, KY 40165

(216) 241-5310 .. **Pike**, Michael J '01 %Gallagher SF&N -1501 Euclid Av -6th Fl
-Cleveland 44115 **Fx:**241-1608

(731) 423-3300 .. **Pike**, Victoria J '01 Hill-Boren -1269 N Highland
-Jackson, TN 38301

(330) 971-8280 .. **Pike**, William B '58 Cuyahoga Falls Municipal Ct -2310 2nd
-Cuyahoga Falls 44221

(702) 382-3824 .. **Pikelny**, Julia E '78 J Osborne,PC -300 E Chrstn Blvd -Ste 123
-Las Vegas, NV 89104

(513) 852-6000 .. **Pikna,** Raymond J Jr. '79 %Wood & L LLP -600 Vine -Ste 2500
-Cincinnati 45202 **Fx:**852-6087

(614) 466-5146 .. **Pikosz,** Michael J '99 Industrial Commssn of OH -30 W Spring -9th
Fl -Columbus 43215 **Fx:**752-8785

(440) 259-3578 .. **Pikus,** James X '85 -4567 S Ridge Rd -Perry 44081

(216) 579-4114 .. **Pilat,** George V '87 McIntyre K&K Co LPA -1301 E 9th -Ste 1200
-Cleveland 44114

(216) 579-1602 .. **Pilawa,** Dennis M '78 (Rawlins G&F Co,LPA) -55 Pub Sq -Ste 850
-Cleveland 44113

(614) 752-8683 .. **Pilcher,** Emily J '04 B Montgomery -88 E Broad -5th Fl -Lgl Dvsn
-Columbus 43216

(330) 743-7000 .. **Pilcher,** Gary L '76 Butler Wick Trust Co -100 Fed Plz E -Bx149
-Youngstown 44503 **Fx:**744-7310

(419) 247-1600 .. **Pilkington,** Joseph H '59 (J Pilkington & Co,PC) -1 Seagate
-Ste 720 -Toledo 43604

(440) 264-5181 .. **Pilla,** Mary Lee '81 Nestle USA,Inc -30003 Bainbrdg Rd
-Solon 44139

(440) 930-8035 .. **Pillari,** Thomas '73 Wickens HPC&B -35765 Chester Rd
-Avon 44011 **Fx:**937-4466

(513) 621-5252 .. **Pillich,** Constance M '98 %Clodfelter & G -36 E 4th -Ste 1208
-Cincinnati 45202

(419) 245-1975 .. **Pilrose,** Daniel R Jr. '86 %Pros -555 N Erie -4th Fl -Toledo 43624

(216) 351-2643 .. **Pilwallis,** Clarence J '57 -4417 Milford Rd -Parma 44134

(937) 746-1010 .. **Pinales,** Ian M '94 Victory Wholesale Grocers -400 Victory Dr
-Springboro 45066

(513) 721-4876 .. **Pinales,** Martin S '68 (Sirkin P&S LLP) -105 W 4th
-920 4th & Race Twr -Cincinnati 45202 **Fx:**721-0876

(216) 241-6700 .. **Pinchak,** George L Jr. '91 (Watts H Co,LPA) -1100 Superior Av E
-Ste 1750 Diamond Bldg -Cleveland 44114 **Fx:**241-8151

(937) 434-6040 .. **Pinchot,** Pamela L '99 %Little D&P -7501 Paragon Rd
-Dayton 45459

(740) 942-2080 .. **Pincola,** Charles A '89 -112 N Main -Bx427 -Cadiz 43907

(440) 933-0674 .. **Pincura,** John D III '65 -158 Lear Rd -Ste A -Avon Lake 44012
Fx:930-2602

(614) 577-9898 .. **Pinder,** Dora P '89 -1228 Briarcliff Rd -Reynoldsburg 43068

(610) 503-7215 .. **Pindle,** Robert A '73 Vanguard Grp -W12 -Bx709
-Valley Forge, PA 19482

(216) 348-5400 .. **Pine Wood,** Jane '88 (McDonald H Co,LPA) -600 Superior Av E
-Ste 2100 -Cleveland 44114 **Fx:**348-5474

        Pines, Dennis S '73 -25 W 614 Summerfld Ct -Wheaton, IL 60187

(216) 696-8730 .. **Pingor,** James J '99 %Amin & T LLP -1900 E 9th -24th Fl
Natl City Ctr -Cleveland 44114 **Fx:**696-8731

(330) 452-7921 .. **Pinhard,** Richard B '85 -220 Market Av S -760 United Bk Bldg
-Canton 44702

(216) 622-3600 .. **Pinjuh,** Joseph M '99 US Atty -801 W Superior -Ste 400
-Cleveland 44113 **Fx:**622-3370

(216) 566-9908 .. **Pinjuh,** Lori A '99 M Wong & Assoc Co,LPA -3150 Chester Av
-Ste 200 -Cleveland 44114 **Fx:**566-1125

(614) 222-3062 .. **Pinkerton,** Sandra E '93 Allmerica Fincl/Citizens Ins -500 S Front
-Ste 870 -Columbus 43215

(216) 861-4416 .. **Pinkney,** Betty K '77 OfCnsl R Henderson -75 Pub Sq -Ste 1414
-Cleveland 44113

(219) 794-1888 .. **Pinkus,** Eugene A '89 (Kopka P&D) -5240 Fountain Dr -Suite E
-Crown Point, IN 46307 **Fx:**794-1892

(419) 385-8002 .. **Pinkus,** Fredric '83 -1241 Michele Dr -Toledo 43614

(513) 621-6464 .. **Pinney,** John B '74 (Graydon H&R LLP) -511 Walnut
-1900 Fifth Third Ctr -Cincinnati 45202 **Fx:**651-3836

(216) 696-8700 .. **Pinney,** Jon J '00 %Kohrman J&K PLL -1375 E 9th
-One Cleve Ctr -Cleveland 44114 **Fx:**621-6536

(614) 460-6383 .. **Pino,** Jovette S '84 Columbia Gas of OH,Inc -200 Civic Ctr Dr
-6th Fl -Columbus 43215

        Pinter, Jessica A '03 Murphy & P,LLC -1361 Granger Av
-Lakewood 44107

(216) 696-2900 .. **Pinto,** Libert '80 -50 Pub Sq -Ste 920 -Cleveland 44113

(216) 271-8254 .. **Pinzone,** Charles R Jr. '92 BP Prdcts NA -4850 E 49th -MBC3-157
-Cuyahoga Heights 44125

(330) 675-2650 .. **Pinzone,** John D '02 11th Dist Ct of Appls -111 High NE
-Warren 44481

(419) 424-4322 .. **Pinzone,** Scott R '95 Cooper Tire -701 Lima Av -Bx550
-Findlay 45840

(419) 474-3380 .. **Pioch,** Susan M '81 -4303 Talmadge Rd -Ste 201 -Toledo 43623

(614) 248-6041 .. **Pioli,** Robert J '85 Bank One Mgt Corp -100 E Broad -OH1-0158
-Columbus 43271

(412) 392-5452 .. **Pion,** John T '99 Dickie M&C -2 PPG Pl -Ste 400 -Pittsburgh,
PA 15222

(330) 753-7080 .. **Piotrowski,** Michael W '94 -2721 Mnchstr Rd -Akron 44319
Fx:753-8955

(937) 225-4652 .. **Piper,** Angela F '96 Montgomery Cnty Pub Def -117 S Main
-Ste 400 -Dayton 45422 **Fx:**225-3449

(614) 895-5500 .. **Piper,** Brian S '76 -555 W Schrock -Westerville 43081

(419) 524-6682 .. **Piper,** Gary A '75 (Baran PTF&T Co,LPA) -3 N Main -Ste 500
-Mansfield 44902 **Fx:**525-4571

(440) 466-5200 .. **Piper,** Kenneth L '75 -185 Water -Geneva 44041

(513) 887-3474 .. **Piper,** Robert N III '82 Butler Cnty Pros -315 High -11th Fl -Bx515
-Hamilton 45012

(330) 726-8177 .. **Pipino,** James D '85 Gallagher Pipino Inc -7600 Market -Bx3849
-Youngstown 44513

(614) 221-5216 .. **Pipino,** Samuel M '93 (Wiles BB&B Co,LPA) -300 Spruce -1st Fl
-Columbus 43215 **Fx:**221-5692

(800) 621-3216 .. **Pippin,** Laura B '98 CT Corp -17 S High -Columbus 43215

(216) 896-3000 .. **Piraino,** Thomas A Jr. '74 Parker Hannifin Corp
-6035 Parkland Blvd -Cleveland 44124

(614) 644-8955 .. **Pirik,** Christine M '85 PUCO -180 E Broad -Columbus 43266

        Pirnia, Abdol-Reza B '03 -(Address Unavailable)

(330) 666-5550 .. **Pirozzi,** Mark C '77 Cole Co,LPA -863 N Cleveland-Massillon Rd
-Akron 44333

(614) 538-5375 .. **Pirtle,** Timothy A '88 -1482 McCoy Rd -Columbus 43220

(859) 431-7200 .. **Pisacano,** Dean A '96 Hellings & P,PSC -214 E 4th
-Covington, KY 41011

(440) 603-2201 .. **Pisanelli,** Ernest C '90 Progressive Ins Co -6055 Parkland Blvd
-Mayfield Heights 44124

(419) 241-9000 .. **Pisanelli,** Mary Ellen '82 (Shumaker L&K,LLP) -1000 Jackson
-Toledo 43624 **Fx:**241-6894

(419) 433-3225 .. **Pisano,** Ralph C Sr. '51 (Pisano & P) -202 Cleveland Rd W
-Huron 44839

(419) 433-3225 .. **Pisano,** Ralph C Jr. '90 (Pisano & P) -202 Cleveland Rd W
-Huron 44839

(216) 241-8300 .. **Piscitelli,** Frank E Jr. '93 (TA Shimko & Assoc Co,LPA)
-925 Euclid Av -Ste 2010 -Cleveland 44115 **Fx:**241-2702

(330) 723-2200 .. **Piszczek,** Gerald D '77 (G Piszczek Co, LPA) -412 N Court
-Medina 44256

(513) 721-4532 .. **Pitcairn,** Robert A Jr. '73 (Katz TB&H) -255 E 5th -Ste 2400
-Cincinnati 45202

        Pitcher, Susan M '82 -(Address Unavailable)

(330) 376-2700 .. **Pitchford,** Marshal M '99 %Roetzel & A,LPA -222 S Main
-Akron 44308 **Fx:**376-4577

(216) 416-3268 .. **Pitcock,** Charles L '67 Forest City Entrprses,Inc -50 Pub Sq
-Ste 1160 -Cleveland 44113

(216) 573-1776 .. **Pitcock,** Danielle K '98 Cleary & Assoc Co,LPA
-6000 Lombardo Ctr Dr -Ste 635 -Independence 44131

(330) 458-2411 .. **Pitinii,** Fredrick M '96 (Pitinii & K) -101 Central Plz S -Ste 1000
-Canton 44702

(330) 458-2411 .. **Pitinii,** Melissa Voros '03 Pitinii & K -101 Central Plz S -Ste 1000
-Canton 44702

(419) 241-3031 .. **Pitkin,** Peter J '74 -608 Mad Av -Ste 1640 -Toledo 43604

(419) 255-0126 .. **Pitman,** Christopher '99 Midland Title Ins -420 Mad Av
-Toledo 43604

        Pitman, Roy V '04 -(Address Unavailable)

(513) 871-8812 .. **Pitocco,** Joseph A '77 -2134 Madison Rd -Cincinnati 45208

        Pitorak, Larry J '74 -9501 Pekin Rd -Novelty 44072

(513) 771-6768 .. **Pitstick,** Joseph V '93 -10655 Sprngfld Pike -Cincinnati 45215
Fx:771-6781

(740) 852-0112 .. **Pitstick,** Mark J '92 -26 N Main -Bx189 -London 43140

(606) 324-5136 .. **Pitt,** Ernest M Jr. '03 (Holbrook & P) -1500 Carter Av
-Ashland, KY 41101

(216) 291-1005 .. **Pittman,** Darryl E '73 -4929 Noble Rd -Ste 100 -Cleveland 44121

(972) 361-9880 .. **Pittman,** Francis P '75 Dresser,Inc -15455 Dallas Pkwy -Ste 1100
-Addison, TX 75001 **Fx:**361-9883

(513) 587-2888 .. **Pittman,** Geoffrey W '91 (G Pittman Co,LPA) -114 E 8th -4th Fl
-Cincinnati 45202

(330) 297-3628 .. **Pittman,** Laurie J '86 Cnty Mun Ct Judge -214 S Water
-Kent 44240

(216) 566-5500 .. **Pittman,** Lori A '04 Thompson H LLP -127 Pub Sq -3900 Key Ctr
-Cleveland 44114 **Fx:**566-5800

(419) 535-0311 .. **Pittman,** Raymond H III '91 Schuller Law Ofc -3450 W Central Av
-Ste 242 -Toledo 43606

(614) 227-8815 .. **Pittner,** Nicholas A '70 (Bricker & E LLP) -100 S 3rd
-Columbus 43215 **Fx:**227-2390

(419) 225-5706 .. **Pitts,** Jerry O '87 -124 S Metcalf -Lima 45801

(937) 372-3101 .. **Pitts,** Teddy L '78 -301 N Monroe Dr -Xenia 45385

(330) 762-0280 .. **Pitts,** Thomas R '79 -7 W Bowery -10th Fl -Akron 44308

(419) 248-1500 .. **Pituch,** Kevin A '88 (Doyle L&W) -202 N Erie -Bx2168
-Toledo 43603 **Fx:**248-2002

(513) 263-3634 .. **Pitula,** Julie M '97 IRS -550 Main -Rm 5106 -Cincinnati 45202

(216) 621-2234 .. **Pitzer,** Gary J '99 (Tarolli SC&T) -526 Superior Av
-1111 Leader Bldg -Cleveland 44114 **Fx:**621-4072

(419) 774-5676 .. **Pitzer,** Norma J '97 Richland Cnty Pros -38 S Park -2nd Fl
-Mansfield 44902 **Fx:**774-5589

(513) 621-4477 .. **Pitzer,** Philip E '71 -1011 Paradrome -Cincinnati 45202
Fx:421-3043

        Pivik, William T '98 -(Address Unavailable)

(216) 586-3939 .. **Pivonka,** Robert C II '96 %Jones D -901 Lakeside Av
-Cleveland 44114 **Fx:**579-0212

(202) 685-5295 .. **Pixa,** Rand R '79 USN-JAG -1322 Patterson Av SE
-Washington, DC 20374

(216) 766-5416 .. **Pizarro,** Robert T '97 Genesis Prof Liability Mngrs
-25550 Chagrin Blvd -Ste 300 -Beachwood 44122

(419) 865-4200 .. **Pizza,** Anthony G '50 -628 E Shoreline Dr -Holland 43528

(419) 252-6227 .. **Pizza,** Lisa E '81 (Spengler N PLL) -608 Mad Av -Ste 1000
-Toledo 43604 **Fx:**241-8599

        Pizzedaz, Gary J '72 -(Address Unavailable)

(330) 865-0100 .. **Pizzino,** Elisa P '89 Legal Cnsltng Srvcs,Inc -473 S Frank Blvd
-Akron 44313

(216) 522-1555 .. **Pla,** Jorge L '00 J Luis PLA LLC -1701 E 12th -Ste 3GW
-Cleveland 44114

(330) 747-2661 .. **Placanica,** Maria '97 Cafaro Co -2445 Belmont Av -Bx2186
-Youngstown 44504

(614) 228-3372 .. **Placzkiewicz,** James M '03 (Comisford & P LLC) -1243 S High
-Columbus 43206 **Fx:**228-3584

(330) 455-6112 .. **Plakas,** Leonidas E '76 (Tzangas PM&R) -220 Market Av S -8th Fl
-Canton 44702 **Fx:**455-2108

(513) 695-1325 .. **Planas,** William '01 Warren Cnty Pros -500 Justice Dr
-Lebanon 45036 **Fx:**695-2962

(614) 228-4546 .. **Plank,** Donald T '79 (Shuler P&B,LPA) -145 E Rich -Ste 400
-Columbus 43215

(513) 248-0317 .. **Plank,** Kevin D '79 -741 Milford Hills Dr -Milford 45150
Fx:248-0321

(614) 864-5600 .. **Plank,** Rhett A '82 (Hardgrove & P) -7600 Slate Ridge Rd
-Reynoldsburg 43068

(614) 293-8446 .. **Plant,** John F III '03 OSU Medical Ctr -410 W 10th Av
-Rm 151 Doan Hall -Columbus 43210

(216) 222-2112 .. **Plant,** Thomas A '74 Natl City Bank -1900 E 9th -17th Fl
Loc 01-2174 -Cleveland 44114

(330) 264-4444 .. **Plant,** Tricia L '02 %Critchfield C&J Ltd -225 N Market -Bx599
-Wooster 44691 **Fx:**263-9278

(513) 794-6278 .. **Plante,** Kimberly A '99 OH Natl Fincl Srvcs -1 Fncl Way
-Cincinnati 45242

(440) 255-8888 .. **Plasco,** Marvin R '69 -38040 Euclid Av -Willoughby 44094

(440) 639-0146 .. **Plassard,** Brett J '85 -1875 W Jackson -Painesville 44077

(419) 445-8815 .. **Plassman,** Harold H '59 (Plassman RHS&H) -302 N Defiance
-Bx178 -Archbold 43502 **Fx:**445-1080

(419) 445-8815 .. **Plassman Rupp Hensal Short & Hagans** -302 N Defiance
-Bx178 -Archbold 43502 **Fx:**445-1080

(614) 644-7233 .. **Plate,** Norman E '00 Atty Gen -150 E Gay -Columbus 43215
Fx:728-9327

Platenak, Frank '03 Delphi Packard Electric -Plant 12-North Rvr Rd -Warren 44483

(216) 696-3525 ..**Platfoot Lacey,** Denise L '01 Cleveland Bar Assn -1301 E 9th -Ste BU620 -Cleveland 44114 **Fx:**696-2413

(216) 696-3030 ..**Platko,** Jeffrey J '97 %Kadish H&W,LPA -1717 E 9th -Ste 2112 -Cleveland 44114 **Fx:**696-3492

(216) 621-1113 ..**Platt,** Jonathan A '97 (Renner OB&S,LLP) -1621 Euclid Av -19th Fl -Cleveland 44115 **Fx:**621-6165

Platt, Joseph J '92 -(Address Unavailable)

Platt, Marvin S '77 -3 Mdwbrk Vllg -#23 -West Lebanon, NH 03784

(330) 637-3906 ..**Platt,** Robert M Jr. '74 Gessner & P Co, LPA -212 W Main -Cortland 44410

(330) 637-3906 ..**Platt,** Robert M Sr. '54 (Gessner & P Co, LPA) -212 W Main -Cortland 44410

(216) 621-8348 ..**Platten,** Paige H '04 Mellino Law Firm -55 Pub Sq -Ste 1260 -Cleveland 44113

Platz, Sarah L '94 -3217 Escott Av -Toledo 43614

(216) 881-1950 ..**Plavac,** George N '54 -1375 E 40th -Cleveland 44103

(859) 426-1300 ..**Pleatman,** Debra S '93 (Ziegler & S,PSC) -541 Buttermilk Pike -Ste 500 -Bx175710 -Covington, KY 41017

(216) 586-3939 ..**Plesec,** William T '71 (Jones D) -901 Lakeside Av -Cleveland 44114 **Fx:**579-0212

(330) 923-8297 ..**Plesich,** Gregory T '73 -1615 Akron-Peninsula Rd -#101 -Akron 44313

(330) 643-2765 ..**Plesich,** Matthew J '03 %Summit Cnty Pros-CSEA -171 S Main -Akron 44308 **Fx:**643-2822

(440) 358-0534 ..**Pleska,** Kenneth W '81 -8348 Browning Ct -Concord 44060

(419) 241-6000 ..**Plessner,** Dirk P '87 (Eastman & S Ltd) -1 Seagate -24th Fl -Bx10032 -Toledo 43699 **Fx:**247-1777

(419) 241-9000 ..**Pletz,** Gregory Ta '71 (Shumaker L&K,LLP) -1000 Jackson -Toledo 43624 **Fx:**241-6894

Plevin, Leon M '57 -55 Pub Sq -Ste 2222 -Cleveland 44113

(216) 623-0150 ..**Plewacki,** Richard A '80 (Roetzel & A,LPA) -1375 E 9th -One Cleve Ctr 9th Fl -Cleveland 44114 **Fx:**623-0134

(614) 227-2000 ..**Plinke,** Eric J '92 (Porter WM&A LLP) -41 S High -Columbus 43215 **Fx:**227-2100

(614) 818-3222 ..**Pliskin,** Lawrence E '94 Cnsl Amer Hlth Holding,Inc -100 W Old Wilson Bridge Rd -3rd Fl -Bx6016 -Columbus 43085 **Fx:**818-3223

(216) 642-5812 ..**Plona,** Alexander '92 (A Plona & Assoc Co,LPA) -6000 Freedom Sq Dr -Ste 380 Freedom Sq II -Independence 44131 **Fx:**642-5813

(414) 273-2100 ..**Plotecher,** Gary R '88 (Whyte HD SC) -111 E Wscnsn Av -Ste 2100 -Milwaukee, WI 53202

(216) 696-4644 ..**Plotkin,** Patricia H '77 -55 Pub Sq -Ste 1330 -Cleveland 44113

(513) 985-2500 ..**Plotnick,** Harry B '77 %Phillips Law Firm,Inc -9521 Mntgmry Rd -Cincinnati 45242 **Fx:**985-2503

(330) 296-9199 ..**Plough,** John J '73 (Myers & P) -229½ S Chestnut -Ravenna 44266 **Fx:**296-4137

(330) 253-2227 ..**Plum,** Donald S '88 %Parker LH&R,LLC -388 S Main -Ste 402 -Akron 44311 **Fx:**253-1261

(330) 652-8000 ..**Pluma,** Richard S '92 %Buckley & G Co,LPA -5704 Youngstown-Warren Rd -Niles 44446

(330) 264-4444 ..**Plumly,** Daniel H '78 (Critchfield C&J Ltd) -225 N Market -Bx599 -Wooster 44691 **Fx:**263-9278

(614) 235-5747 ..**Plummer,** Angela K '92 Cmnty Refugee & Immig Srvcs -3624 Bexvie Av -Columbus 43227

(330) 332-0852 ..**Plummer,** Barbara J '85 -1265 E State -Salem 44460

(740) 432-6322 ..**Plummer,** Charles K '81 Tribbie SP&P -139 Ct Hse Sq -Bx640 -Cambridge 43725 **Fx:**439-1795

(614) 629-3000 ..**Plunkett & Cooney,PC** -300 E Broad -Ste 590 -Columbus 43215 **Fx:**629-3019

(937) 228-2666 ..**Plunkett,** Gary D '90 (Hochman R&P Co,LPA) -118 W 1st -Ste 650 -Dayton 45402 **Fx:**228-0508

(740) 349-3629 ..**Plunkett,** Jeffrey A '83 Licking Cnty Juv Ct -Cnty Cthse -Newark 43055

(304) 529-6181 ..**Plybon,** Christopher J '84 (Huddleston BBP&C,LLP) -611 3rd Av -Bx2185 -Huntington, WV 25722

(513) 425-5151 ..**Plye,** Joseph W '83 AK Steel Corp -703 Curtis -Middletown 45043

(614) 221-1166 ..**Plymale,** Ronald E '68 (Plymale & Assoc) -495 S High -Ste 400 -Columbus 43215 **Fx:**221-6663

(440) 324-5353 ..**Pocci,** Marisa A '04 %Spike & M,LLP -1551 W River Rd N -Elyria 44035 **Fx:**324-6529

(330) 793-3171 ..**Pochiro,** Patrick R '67 -2503 S Schenley Av -Youngstown 44511

(702) 388-8600 ..**Pocker,** Richard J '80 (Dickerson DC&P) -777 N Rainbow Blvd -Ste 350 -Las Vegas, NV 89101 **Fx:**388-0210

(614) 244-6505 ..**Pocorus,** Barbara '98 Bank One Trust Co -100 E Broad -3rd Fl -Columbus 43215 **Fx:**248-1934

(216) 861-7101 ..**Podboy,** Alvin M Jr. '72 -1900 E 9th #3200 -Ste 3200 -Cleveland 44114 **Fx:**696-0740

(440) 256-2990 ..**Podgurski,** John A '84 -9155 Chillicothe Rd -Kirtland 44094 **Fx:**256-2994

(419) 241-9000 ..**Podolsky,** Michael J '02 %Shumaker L&K,LLP -1000 Jackson -Toledo 43624 **Fx:**241-6894

(440) 914-5297 ..**Podor,** Kenneth C '78 (Podor & Assoc) -33565 Solon Rd -Solon 44139

(513) 621-0005 ..**Poe,** Harold F '72 (Uible & P) -7 W 7th -Ste 1920 -Cincinnati 45202

(614) 463-9770 ..**Poe,** Michael A '78 (Roetzel & A,LPA) -155 E Broad -Natl City Ctr 12th Fl -Columbus 43215 **Fx:**463-9792

(713) 215-4168 ..**Poe,** Paul A '95 Williams Co,Inc -2800 Post Oak Blvd -13th Fl -Houston, TX 77056

(216) 692-7076 ..**Poeppelman,** Robert L '89 Park-Ohio Ind,Inc -23000 Euclid Av -Euclid 44117

(513) 241-2324 ..**Poffenberger,** John D '61 (Wood H&E LLP) -441 Vine -Ste 2700 -Cincinnati 45202 **Fx:**421-7269

(513) 241-2324 ..**Poffenberger,** John D Jr. '94 %Wood H&E LLP -441 Vine -Ste 2700 -Cincinnati 45202 **Fx:**421-7269

(216) 687-4449 ..**Pofok,** Teresa R '94 Segal Co -1300 E 9th -Ste 1900 -Cleveland 44114

(330) 392-1541 ..**Pogue,** John L '69 Harrington H&M,Ltd -108 Main Av SW -Ste 500 -Bx1510 -Warren 44482 **Fx:**394-6890

(216) 586-7300 ..**Pogue,** Richard W '57 -901 Lakeside Av E -% Jones Day -Cleveland 44114 **Fx:**586-7960

(330) 456-8361 ..**Poh,** Jaime-Lyn '03 Cmmnty Lgl Aid Srvcs,Inc -306 Market Av N -Ste 730 -Canton 44702

(616) 336-7907 ..**Pohl,** Lisa M '96 Deloitte & Touche LLP -333 Brdg -Ste 700 -Grand Rapids, MI 49504

(239) 542-0700 ..**Pohl,** Michael A '68 (Warchol MRB&P,LLP) -1633 SE 47th Ter -Bx100767 -Cape Coral, FL 33910 **Fx:**542-8627

(412) 391-3939 ..**Pohl,** Paul M '76 (Jones DR&P) -500 Grant -31st Fl -Pittsburgh, PA 15219

(614) 466-4510 ..**Pohler,** Susan J '85 Atty Gen -150 E Gay -Columbus 43215 **Fx:**995-0501

(419) 647-6671 ..**Pohlman,** James D '79 Spencerville Title Agency -105 N Bway -Spencerville 45887 **Fx:**647-8028

(614) 227-2000 ..**Pohlman,** James E '57 OfCnsl Porter WM&A LLP -41 S High -Columbus 43215 **Fx:**227-2100

(937) 225-4228 ..**Pohlman,** Kenneth R '74 Montgomery Cnty Pros -301 W 3rd -Bx972 -Dayton 45422 **Fx:**225-3470

(614) 464-6400 ..**Pohlman,** William J '88 (Vorys SS&P LLP) -52 E Gay -Bx1008 -Columbus 43216 **Fx:**464-6350

(419) 471-1489 ..**Poirier,** Jennifer L '96 UAW Legal Srvcs -3360 W Laskey Rd -Toledo 43606 **Fx:**471-0498

(440) 951-4660 ..**Poklar,** Michael A '73 -34950 Chardon Rd -Ste 210 -Willoughby Hills 44094

(440) 746-1600 ..**Poklar,** Robert A '78 (R Poklar & Assoc,LLP) -10100 Brecksvll Rd -Brecksville 44141 **Fx:**746-1600

(614) 466-2980 ..**Pokorny,** Cheryl D '85 Atty Gen -30 E Broad -Columbus 43215 **Fx:**728-9470

(419) 433-5246 ..**Pokorny,** Donald '65 Spectra Wave,Inc -711 Mariner Vllg -Huron 44839

(216) 443-8820 ..**Pokorny,** Frank J '73 Ct of Common Pleas -1 W Lakeside Av -Domestic Relations Div -Cleveland 44113

(614) 462-3194 ..**Pokorski,** Rebecca R '87 Franklin Cnty Pub Def -373 S High -12th Fl -Columbus 43215

(330) 637-3906 ..**Polak,** Jenna Gessner '98 Gessner & P Co, LPA -212 W Main -Cortland 44410

(513) 871-1300 ..**Polanco,** Hector A '00 -2124 Madison Rd -Ste 2F -Cincinnati 45208

(419) 347-7421 ..**Poland Depler & Shepherd,Co,LPA** -6 Water -Shelby 44875

(330) 296-8552 ..**Poland,** Kevin T '86 -240 S Chestnut -Ravenna 44266

(216) 360-7200 ..**Poland,** Mark A '00 Carlisle MRK&U Co,LPA -24755 Chagrin Blvd -Ste 200 -Cleveland 44122 **Fx:**360-7210

(513) 793-5999 ..**Polaniecki,** Elliott '76 -9000 Plainfld Rd -Cincinnati 45236 **Fx:**793-4691

(812) 663-4923 ..**Polanski,** Margaret A '78 (Watts & P Corp) -125 W Wshngtn -Greensburg, IN 47240

(727) 822-6937 ..**Poley,** D S '94 Natl Assn of Pro Baseball -201 Bayshore Dr SE -Saint Petersburg, FL 33701

(937) 223-9790 ..**Poley,** John D '78 -46 Rogge -Dayton 45409

(703) 614-4075 ..**Polgar,** Matthew J '90 USAF/JAG -Rm 5-E279 1420 AF Pentagon -Washington, DC 20330

(614) 221-2848 ..**Polhamus,** William R '73 (Freeman & P) -50 W Broad -Columbus 43215

(216) 928-2200 ..**Poling,** Brant E '94 %Sutter OM&F -1301 E 9th -3600 Erievw Twr -Cleveland 44114 **Fx:**928-4400

(317) 684-6060 ..**Poling,** Christopher A '87 Kunz & O -135 N Penn -Ste 1750 -Indianapolis, IN 46204

(614) 764-1444 ..**Poling,** Karen L '98 Mowery & Y -425 Metro Pl N -Ste 420 -Dublin 43017 **Fx:**760-8654

(216) 621-1530 ..**Polinko,** John A '01 %Shapiro & F,LLP -1500 W 3rd -Ste 400 -Cleveland 44113 **Fx:**621-1551

(330) 759-2115 ..**Politi,** Jonathan D '93 -3040 Belmont Av -Bx5884 -Youngstown 44504

(216) 443-8979 ..**Polito,** John A '73 %Cuyahoga Cnty Probate Crt -1 Lakeside Av -Cleveland 44113

(216) 875-2767 ..**Polito,** John S '77 (Bonezzi SM&P Co LPA) -526 Superior Av -Ste 1400 -Cleveland 44114 **Fx:**875-1501

Polito, LuAnn A '91 -17206 Ernadale Av -Cleveland 44111

(440) 895-1234 ..**Polito,** Michael G '91 (Polito P&R) -21300 Lorain Rd -Fairview Park 44126

(440) 895-1234 ..**Polito Paulozzi & Rodstrom** -21300 Lorain Rd -Fairview Park 44126

(513) 238-5244 ..**Politsky,** Aleshia J '03 -119 E Court -Cincinnati 45202

(419) 291-3706 ..**Polizzi,** Arturo '97 ProMedica Hlth Syst -2121 Hughes Dr -Fl E -Toledo 43606

(216) 687-1311 ..**Polk,** Shannon J '00 %Reminger & R -101 Prospect Av W -1400 MdInd Bldg -Cleveland 44115 **Fx:**687-1841

(937) 775-2056 ..**Polk,** Simone G '96 Wright State Univ -3640 Colonel Glenn Hwy -118c Campus Srvcs Bldg -Dayton 45435

(216) 289-8304 ..**Polke,** Dennis J '81 -1370 Ontario -Ste 736 -Cleveland 44113

(216) 586-3939 ..**Pollack,** Joseph D '84 (Jones D) -901 Lakeside Av -Cleveland 44114 **Fx:**579-0212

(216) 931-6000 ..**Pollack,** Lawrence D '89 (Ulmer & B LLP) -1300 E 9th -Ste 900 Penton Media Bldg -Cleveland 44114 **Fx:**931-6001

(216) 514-1100 ..**Pollack,** Matthew I '03 %Rolf & G Co,LPA -30100 Chagrin Blvd -Ste 350 Corp Cir -Cleveland 44124 **Fx:**514-0030

(614) 222-0512 ..**Pollak,** Lawrence S '82 -338 S High -Bx09681 -Columbus 43209

(216) 875-8343 ..**Pollard,** Karen R '97 KPMG LLP -1375 E 9th -Ste 2600 One Cleve Ctr -Cleveland 44114

(814) 838-8258 ..**Pollard,** Malcolm L '75 -4845 W Lake Rd -Erie, PA 16505

(513) 868-2731 ..**Pollard,** Nellie R '76 Baden & J Co LPA -246 High -Hamilton 45011

Pollaro, John M '77 -(Address Unavailable)

(419) 245-2550 ..**Pollex,** Yvonne T '84 %Atty Gen -One SeaGate -Ste 2150 -Toledo 43604 **Fx:**246-2520

(412) 392-5306 ..**Polley,** Richard C '98 Dickie M&C,PC -2 PPG Pl -Ste 400 -Pittsburgh, PA 15222

(216) 589-1354 ..**Pollina,** Daniel T '94 Deloitte & Touche LLP -127 Pub Sq -25th Flr -Cleveland 44114

(216) 621-0150 ..**Pollis,** Andrew S '90 (Hahn L&P LLP) -3300 BP Twr/200 Pub Sq -Ste 3300 -Cleveland 44114 **Fx:**241-2824

(614) 645-7745 ..**Pollitt,** Harry W Jr. '74 Cnty Mun Ct Judge -375 S High -Columbus 43215

(216) 861-6160 ..**Pollock,** Candace M '87 -820 W Superior Av -Ste 510 -Cleveland 44113

(440) 528-0200 ..**Pollock,** Harold '76 -5900 Harper Rd -Ste 107 -Solon 44139

(419) 535-4653 ..**Pollock,** Robert E '71 Dana Corp -4500 Dorr -Bx1000
-Toledo 43697

(216) 348-5400 ..**Pollock,** Robert Jeffrey '76 (McDonald H Co,LPA)
-600 Superior Av E -Ste 2100 -Cleveland 44114 **Fx:**348-5474

(216) 471-3420 ..**Pollock,** Ross H '88 OfficeMax,Inc -Bx228070 -Cleveland 44122

(216) 861-4700 ..**Polly,** Steven C '99 %Martyn & Assoc Co,LPA
-820 Superior Av NW -Ste 920 -Cleveland 44113

(937) 382-8747 ..**Polly-Murphy,** Michelle L '00 %S Elder Co,LPA -731 Fife Av
-Wilmington 45177

(419) 241-7900 ..**Polofka,** John R '80 -500 Mad Av -Ste 605 -Toledo 43604
Polosky, John D III '87 -(Address Unavailable)

(216) 292-2711 ..**Polster,** Dorothea M '88 -2711 Landon Rd -Shaker Heights 44122

(440) 439-1040 ..**Polster,** Scott H '82 Mason Structural Steel,Inc -7500 Nrthfld Rd
-Walton Hills 44146

(614) 444-7822 ..**Pomerants,** Alex '98 -1141 S High -Columbus 43206

(216) 696-5959 ..**Pomerantz,** David I '85 (Pomerantz & Co,LPA)
-20676 Southgate Park Blvd -Ste 103 -Cleveland 44137

(740) 622-2011 ..**Pomerene Burns & Skelton** -309 Main -Coshocton 43812

(614) 944-5712 ..**Pomeroy,** Lisa K '01 -4200 Regent -Ste 200 -Columbus 43219

(614) 248-5654 ..**Pomeroy,** Mark C '87 Bank One Corp -1111 Polaris Pkwy -Ste 4P
-Columbus 43271

(614) 885-2101 ..**Pomeroy,** Rosemary E '88 -120 Northwoods Blvd -Ste A
-Columbus 43235 **Fx:**885-1783

(419) 352-8844 ..**Pomeroy,** Todd A '98 -113 N Main -Bowling Green 43402
Fx:352-8833

(419) 843-1333 ..**Pommeranz,** Milton E '02 %Malone A&F -7654 W Bancroft
-Toledo 43617 **Fx:**843-3888

(216) 443-9000 ..**Pompeani,** Fred J '82 (Porter WM&A LLP) -925 Euclid Av
-Ste 1700 -Cleveland 44115 **Fx:**443-9011

(614) 752-8855 ..**Pon,** Christopher E '84 Supreme Ct of OH -30 E Broad -35th Fl
-Columbus 43266

(216) 739-5001 ..**Pona,** Charles G '87 (Weltman W&R Co,LPA) -323 W Lakeside Av
-Ste 200 -Cleveland 44113 **Fx:**363-4121

(440) 259-0074 ..**Ponce de Leon,** Agustin '97 (Ponce de Leon & W LLC)
-3537 N Ridge Rd -Perry 44081

(330) 253-9747 ..**Pond,** Donald K Jr. '97 -190 N Union -Ste 201 -Akron 44304

(330) 392-5300 ..**Pond,** George S '82 -295 Harmon Av NW -Bx510 -Warren 44482
Fx:392-5827

(740) 437-7142 ..**Pontious,** Carole G '99 -5427 Wht Oak Rd -Bloomingburg 43106

(440) 998-6835 ..**Pontius,** David E '79 Andrews & P LLC -4817 State Rd -Ste 100
-Bx10 -Ashtabula 44005

(614) 224-2291 ..**Pontius,** Donald H '58 US Trotting Assoc -750 Mich Av -Columbus
43215

(513) 762-4503 ..**Pontius,** Erica S '98 Kroger Co -1014 Vine -Cincinnati 45202
Fx:762-4935

(513) 763-1978 ..**Pontius,** Jarrod B '98 %Kendle Intl Inc -441 Vine -Ste 1200
-Cincinnati 45202 **Fx:**562-1746

(216) 522-3380 ..**Poole,** Donza M '87 IRS -1375 E 9th -1200 -Cleveland 44114

(513) 352-5394 ..**Poole,** Jadene P '01 Law Dept -801 Plum -Rm 214 -Cincinnati
45202 **Fx:**352-1515

(216) 696-5444 ..**Poole,** Marcus L '78 -925 Euclid Av -1025 Huntngtn Bldg
-Cleveland 44115

(614) 466-5610 ..**Poole,** Mark R '01 Atty Gen -150 E Gay -Columbus 43215
Fx:752-2732

(216) 621-0200 ..**Poole,** Patricia A '91 (Baker & H LLP) -1900 E 9th -Ste 3200
-Cleveland 44114 **Fx:**696-0740

(859) 261-3400 ..**Poole,** Robert L '95 -2220 Grandvw Dr -Ste 190 -Bx17096
-Covington, KY 41017

(419) 891-1099 ..**Pooley,** Christopher J '97 -Bx4104 -Edwards, CO 81632

(216) 689-5105 ..**Poore,** Gregory R '72 KeyBank NA -127 Pub Sq -Law Dept
-Cleveland 44114

(419) 337-4300 ..**Poorman,** Gary L '84 -8520 Cnty Rd 16 -Wauseon 43567

(614) 898-5200 ..**Pope,** Elaine A '01 Pope & L Co,LPA -903 Eastwind Dr
-Westerville 43081 **Fx:**898-5230

(614) 898-5200 ..**Pope,** Gregory S '95 (Pope & L Co,LPA) -903 Eastwind Dr
-Westerville 43081 **Fx:**898-5230
Pope, Julie A '84 -3501 E Camelback Rd -204 -Phoenix, AZ 85018

(614) 898-5200 ..**Pope & Levy Co,LPA** -903 Eastwind Dr -Westerville 43081
Fx:898-5230

(216) 291-7680 ..**Pope,** Paul T '88 Northrop Grumman -1900 Richmond Rd
-Cleveland 44124

(216) 664-4918 ..**Pope,** Ruben E III '78 Cleveland Mun Ct -1200 Ontario -13th Fl
-Cleveland 44113

(330) 887-0560 ..**Popelmayer,** Richard A '86 Westfield Grp -1 Park Cir -Bx5001
-Westfield Center 44251 **Fx:**887-2588

(614) 225-8896 ..**Popelsky,** Steven P '81 Motorist Mutual Ins Co -471 E Broad
-Columbus 43215

(216) 896-2504 ..**Pophal,** Joseph J '93 Parker Hannifin Corp -6035 Parkland Blvd
-Cleveland 44124

(440) 835-8158 ..**Pophal,** Michael C '92 Eveready Battery Co,Inc -25225 Detroit Rd
-Westlake 44145

(513) 421-2400 ..**Popham,** Julie W '92 (Helmer MR&P Co,LPA) -105 E 4th
-Ste 1900 -Cincinnati 45202 **Fx:**421-7902

(614) 485-1800 ..**Popham,** Kevin W '96 %Arnold T&W -2075 Marble Cliff Ofc Park
-Columbus 43215 **Fx:**485-1944

(419) 242-3900 ..**Popil,** James J '86 Cincinnati Ins Co -300 Mad Av -Ste 1406
-Toledo 43604

(330) 740-2330 ..**Popio,** Kerry '03 Mahoning Cnty Pros -21 W Boardman -6th Fl
-Youngstown 44503 **Fx:**740-2008

(614) 898-5200 ..**Poplaski,** Leighann K '04 %Pope & L Co,LPA -903 Eastwind Dr
-Westerville 43081 **Fx:**898-5230

(440) 603-7525 ..**Popovich,** Elizabeth '97 Progressive Ins -5920 Landerbrook Dr
-3rd Fl -Cleveland 44124

(216) 443-8635 ..**Popovich,** Gregory M '89 Ct of Common Pleas -1200 Ontario
-Cleveland 44113

(859) 655-4200 ..**Popp,** M Pamela '84 Greenebaum D&M PLLC
-50 E RiverCenter Blvd -Ste 1800 -Covington, KY 41011
Fx:655-4239

(937) 222-8500 ..**Popp,** Vincent P '77 (Popp & T) -137 N Main -Ste 712
-Dayton 45402 **Fx:**222-0488

(419) 738-7180 ..**Poppe,** John A '72 -1100 W Auglaize -Wapakoneta 45895

(419) 738-7180 ..**Poppe,** Kris R '93 -1100 W Auglaize -Wapakoneta 45895

(216) 928-2200 ..**Popson,** James M '00 Sutter OM&F -1301 E 9th -3600 Erievw Twr
-Cleveland 44114 **Fx:**928-4400

(216) 687-1900 ..**Porath,** Ann M '82 Legal Aid -1223 W 6th -Cleveland 44113
Fx:687-0779

(216) 566-1600 ..**Porcaro,** James G '99 %Schwarzwald & M -1300 E 9th -Ste 616
-Cleveland 44114 **Fx:**566-1814

(419) 243-1294 ..**Porcello,** James F Jr. '77 (Emch SS&P Co,LPA) -One SeaGate
-Ste 1980 -Bx916 -Toledo 43697 **Fx:**243-8502

(213) 615-2673 ..**Pordan,** Jay J '88 Farmers Ins Grp of Co -700 S Flower -Ste 2700
-Los Angeles, CA 90017

(614) 566-5151 ..**Porembski,** Chester P '84 %OhioHealth -3722 Olentangy Rvr Rd
-Ste K -Columbus 43214

(513) 977-8200 ..**Porotsky,** Richard D Jr. '96 %Dinsmore & S LLP -255 E 5th
-Ste 1900 -Cincinnati 45202 **Fx:**977-8141

(419) 841-7211 ..**Porritt,** Russell W II '93 (Ward AP&B) -3230 Cntrl Pk W Dr
-Ste 202 -Toledo 43617 **Fx:**843-9850

(216) 622-8200 ..**Port,** Cynthia Krips '02 %Calfee H&G LLP -800 Superior Av
-Ste 1400 -Cleveland 44114 **Fx:**241-0816

(216) 621-0150 ..**Port,** Robert B '04 %Hahn L&P LLP -3300 BP Twr/200 Pub Sq
-Ste 3300 -Cleveland 44114 **Fx:**241-2824

(614) 645-7717 ..**Porte,** Stephen A '77 City Atty -90 W Broad -Columbus 43215

(216) 586-3939 ..**Porter,** David P '81 (Jones D) -901 Lakeside Av -Cleveland 44114
Fx:579-0212

(614) 466-2872 ..**Porter,** Elise W '91 Atty Gen -30 E Broad -Columbus 43215
Fx:728-7592

(216) 522-7425 ..**Porter,** Elliott V '76 US EEOC -1660 W 2nd -Ste 850
-Cleveland 44113

(440) 838-8883 ..**Porter,** Gerald M '63 -9100 S Hills Blvd -#300 -Cleveland 44147

(330) 208-1000 ..**Porter,** Jay P '78 OfCnsl Vorys SS&P LLP -106 S Main
-First Natl Twr -Akron 44308

(614) 462-5418 ..**Porter,** Jeffrey D '96 %Kegler BH&R -65 E State -Ste 1800
-Columbus 43215 **Fx:**464-2634

(216) 739-5003 ..**Porter,** John B C '02 %Weltman W&R Co,LPA
-323 W Lakeside Av -Ste 200 -Cleveland 44113 **Fx:**363-4121

(330) 225-7646 ..**Porter,** John N '75 -1212 Pearl Rd -Brunswick 44212

(937) 382-2838 ..**Porter,** John S '96 Rose & D Co,LPA -97 N South
-Wilmington 45177

(614) 865-2611 ..**Porter,** John T '86 OSEA/AFSCME -390 Worthngtn Rd
-Westerville 43082

(740) 574-4311 ..**Porter,** Kenneth W '81 -8055 Hayport Rd -Wheelersburg 45694
Fx:574-1129

(216) 227-2727 ..**Porter,** Leah B '01 Spooner,Inc -14725 Detroit Av -Ste 300
-Cleveland 44107

(216) 348-5400 ..**Porter,** Mark E '00 %McDonald H Co,LPA -600 Superior Av E
-Ste 2100 -Cleveland 44114 **Fx:**348-5474

(440) 240-1224 ..**Porter,** Mary R '89 NorthStar Title Srvcs,LLC -2173 N Ridge Rd E
-Ste H -Lorain 44055

(614) 466-5394 ..**Porter,** Randall L '77 Pub Def -8 E Long -Columbus 43215
Porter, Rhonda J '03 -(Address Unavailable)

(216) 696-7600 ..**Porter,** Richard D '02 %Duvin C&H -1301 E 9th
-20th Fl Erievw Twr -Cleveland 44114 **Fx:**696-2038

(614) 752-8211 ..**Porter,** Richard G '86 State Med Brd -77 S High -17th Fl
-Columbus 43215

(513) 621-3993 ..**Porter,** Robert C III '79 (Porter & P) -1 W 4th -2100 4th & Vine Twr
-Cincinnati 45202

(513) 621-3993 ..**Porter,** Robert C Jr. '52 (Porter & P) -1 W 4th -2100 4th &
Vine Twr -Cincinnati 45202

(614) 227-2000 ..**Porter,** Samuel H '53 (Porter WM&A LLP) -41 S High
-Columbus 43215 **Fx:**227-2100

(502) 589-4440 ..**Porter,** Sherry P '94 Goldberg & S,PSC -101 S 5th -Ste 3000
-Louisville, KY 40202 **Fx:**581-1344

(614) 462-2314 ..**Porter,** Susan '86 (Schottenstein Z&D) -250 West -Bx165020
-Columbus 43216 **Fx:**462-5135

(216) 566-9700 ..**Porter,** Wayne D Jr. '77 Rankin HP&C,LLP -925 Euclid Av
-Ste 700 -Cleveland 44115 **Fx:**566-9711

(614) 464-6400 ..**Porter,** William G II '84 (Vorys SS&P LLP) -52 E Gay -Bx1008
-Columbus 43216 **Fx:**464-6350

(614) 227-2000 ..**Porter Wright Morris & Arthur LLP** -41 S High
-Columbus 43215 **Fx:**227-2100

(513) 381-4700 ..**Porter Wright Morris & Arthur LLP** -250 E 5th -Ste 2200
-Cincinnati 45202 **Fx:**421-0991

(937) 449-6810 ..**Porter Wright Morris & Arthur LLP** -1 S Main -Ste 1600
-Dayton 45402 **Fx:**449-6820

(216) 443-9000 ..**Porter Wright Morris & Arthur LLP** -925 Euclid Av -Ste 1700
-Cleveland 44115 **Fx:**443-9011
Porterfield, Andrea J '99 -20926 W 117th -Olathe, KS 66061

(216) 241-2400 ..**Porterfield,** Michael C '76 -50 Pub Sq -Ste 627 -Cleveland 44113

(614) 461-1234 ..**Portman Foley & Flint LLP** -471 E Broad -Ste 1820
-Columbus 43215 **Fx:**461-9150

(614) 461-1234 ..**Portman,** Frederic A '73 (Portman F&F LLP) -471 E Broad
-Ste 1820 -Columbus 43215 **Fx:**461-9150

(330) 535-6185 ..**Portman,** Irving Abe '55 -159 S Main -Ste 1108 -Akron 44308

(440) 333-7704 ..**Portmann,** Richard W '50 -19111 Detroit Rd -Ste 302
-Rocky River 44116

(419) 666-5215 ..**Portnoy,** Michael D '88 -200 Dixie Hwy -Rossford 43460

(937) 913-0200 ..**Portune,** Robert E '73 (Gottschlich & P LLP) -201 E 6th
-Dayton 45402 **Fx:**824-2818

(419) 255-2366 ..**Porz,** Bonnie M '81 (Porz & P) -959 Spitzer Bldg -Toledo 43604

(419) 255-2366 ..**Porz,** Susan G '80 (Porz & P) -959 Spitzer Bldg -Toledo 43604

(330) 764-8736 ..**Porzio,** Barbara '79 Medina Common Pleas Ct -93 Pub Sq
-Medina 44256

(614) 891-9061 ..**Posani,** John P '78 Dome Finl Srvcs -68 Westervw Dr
-Westerville 43081

(850) 884-7821 ..**Posch,** Thomas E '93 Staff Judge Advocate Ofc -131 Bartley
-Ste 255 -Hurlburt Field, FL 32544

(937) 236-6444 ..**Posey,** Terry W '88 -7460 Brandt Pike -Huber Heights 45424

(937) 492-6191 ..**Posey,** Terry W Jr. '04 %Elsass WES&Co -100 S Main Av
-Ste 102 -Bx499 -Sidney 45365 **Fx:**492-0876

(513) 579-6400 ..**Posey,** William A '79 (Keating M&K PLL) -1 E 4th
-1400 Provident Twr -Cincinnati 45202 **Fx:**579-6457

(419) 213-4389 ..**Posner,** Curtis E '67 Lucas Co Sheriffs Ofc -1622 Spielbusch Av
-Toledo 43624

(216) 621-0200 .. **Posner**, David A '89 (Baker & H LLP) -1900 E 9th -Ste 3200 -Cleveland 44114 Fx:696-0740

(216) 360-3737 .. **Posner**, Jeffrey P '76 %Persky S&A Co,LPA -25101 Chagrin Blvd -Ste 350 Signature Sq II -Beachwood 44122 Fx:593-0921

(614) 227-2000 .. **Post**, Andrew R '03 %Porter WM&A LLP -41 S High -Columbus 43215 Fx:227-2100

(614) 279-1700 .. **Post**, Caris D '01 Amer Lung Assoc of OH -1950 Arlingate Ln -Columbus 43228

(419) 586-2915 .. **Post**, Donna M '86 -110½ N Main -Ste A -Bx126 -Celina 45822

(419) 865-1251 .. **Post**, Frederick R '74 OfCnsl Wagoner & S,Ltd -7445 Airport Hwy -Holland 43528 Fx:866-8798

(614) 559-2502 .. **Post**, Gerald R '71 White Castle Syst,Inc -555 W Goodale -Bx1498 -Columbus 43216

(216) 696-2118 .. **Post**, Rexford W '83 -1360 W 9th -Ste 200 -Cleveland 44113

(614) 457-2622 .. **Post**, Roger C '66 -2657 Woodstock Rd -Columbus 43221

(513) 482-3157 .. **Post**, Sharon L '85 Cognis Corp -5051 Estecreek Dr -Cincinnati 45232

(614) 228-1541 .. **Post**, William R '00 %Baker & H LLP -65 E State -Ste 2100 -Columbus 43215 Fx:462-2616

(614) 764-0681 .. **Postalakis**, Stephen P '94 %Blaugrund H&M,Inc -5455 Rings Rd -Ste 500 -Dublin 43017 Fx:764-0774

(216) 736-7218 .. **Posteraro**, David R '81 (Kohrman J&K PLL) -1375 E 9th -One Cleve Ctr 20th Fl -Cleveland 44114 Fx:621-6536

(614) 486-2111 .. **Postlewaite**, Charles C '82 (C Postlewaite,LLC) -3040 Riverside Dr -Ste 122 -Columbus 43221 Fx:486-8943

(907) 271-4131 .. **Postma**, Chandra R '94 US Dept of Interior -4230 Univ Dr -Ste 300 -Anchorage, AK 99508

(614) 837-5992 .. **Poston**, David W '82 FT Daniel & Assoc -49 Hill Rd N -Pickerington 43147

(859) 431-3200 .. **Poston**, James R Jr. '81 (Poston S&S) -525 W 5th -Ste 318 -Covington, KY 41011

(203) 333-9441 .. **Poston**, Sarah Wishard '95 %Zeldes N&C LLC -1000 Lafayette Blvd -Bx1740 -Bridgeport, CT 06601 Fx:333-1489

(513) 621-2120 .. **Postow**, Charles J '77 (Strauss & T,LPA) -150 E 4th -4th Fl -Cincinnati 45202 Fx:241-8259

(614) 738-2636 .. **Potash**, Arlene N '00 -399 E Main -Ste 200 -Columbus 43215

Potash, Erica L '04 -(Address Unavailable)

(216) 771-8400 .. **Potash**, Lester S '75 -55 Pub Sq -1717 Illuminating Bldg -Cleveland 44113

(216) 765-0038 .. **Potash**, Loree E '80 %MS Potash -1927 Temblethurst Rd -South Euclid 44121

(216) 765-0038 .. **Potash**, M. Steven '79 -1927 Temblethurst Rd -South Euclid 44121

(330) 609-9999 .. **Poteet**, Cherry L '85 %D Daniluk -1129 Niles-Crtland Rd SE -Warren 44484

(330) 670-7300 .. **Potenza**, Rocco D Jr. '92 (Hanna C&P,LLP) -3737 Embssy Pkwy -Bx5521 -Akron 44334 Fx:670-0977

(614) 227-2395 .. **Poth**, Christine M '95 (Bricker & E LLP) -100 S 3rd -Columbus 43215 Fx:227-2390

(614) 228-6885 .. **Poth**, Jeffery M '96 %Lane A&H LLC -175 S 3rd -Ste 700 -Columbus 43215 Fx:228-0146

(330) 643-2943 .. **Poth-Wypasek**, Angela K '01 Summit Cnty Pros-Juv -650 Dan -Akron 44310 Fx:379-3647

(419) 353-7547 .. **Potter**, Albert L II '82 -107 E Oak -Bowling Green 43402

(864) 367-9017 .. **Potter**, Andrew T '93 -Bx2722 -Anderson, SC 29622

(513) 248-1216 .. **Potter**, Carolyn A '91 -8 Curry Ln -Milford 45150

(513) 381-2838 .. **Potter**, John R '03 %Taft S&H LLP -425 Walnut -Ste 1800 -Cincinnati 45202 Fx:381-0205

Potter, Kimberly J '00 -(Address Unavailable)

(313) 792-4438 .. **Potter**, Michelle L '89 Masco Corp -21001 Van Born Rd -Taylor, MI 48180

(440) 446-1100 .. **Potter**, Steven B '81 (Dinn H&P,LLC) -5910 Landerbrook Dr -Ste 200 -Cleveland 44124 Fx:446-1240

(937) 325-9950 .. **Potter**, Wilfred L '78 -234 N Limestone Av -Springfield 45503

(513) 241-9400 .. **Potthast**, Elizabeth Shinkle '04 Legal Aid -215 E 9th -Ste 200 -Cincinnati 45202

(216) 751-9131 .. **Pottinger**, Albert A Jr. '60 -16106 Delrey Av -Cleveland 44128

(614) 228-2154 .. **Potts**, Byron L '88 (BL Potts & Co,LPA) -415 E Broad -Ste 112 -Columbus 43215 Fx:228-2155

(937) 444-2576 .. **Potts**, Cecelia J '86 -750 S High -Bx474 -Mount Orab 45154

Potts, John D '66 -(Address Unavailable)

(419) 255-2802 .. **Potts**, John F '78 -405 Mad Av -Ste 1010 -Toledo 43604

(740) 223-4290 .. **Potts**, Renee L '90 Marion Cnty Pros -134 E Center -Marion 43302 Fx:223-4299

(937) 492-1271 .. **Potts**, Thomas J '88 (Faulkner GK&S,LPA) -100 S Main Av -Ste 300 -Sidney 45365 Fx:498-1306

(419) 289-6888 .. **Potts**, Timothy E '97 %Harpster V&F -60 W 2nd -Ashland 44805 Fx:281-2461

(216) 348-0800 .. **Potts**, Timothy J '67 (Potts & N) -1370 Ontario -Ste 600 -Cleveland 44113

(419) 247-1500 .. **Poturalski**, Steven J '97 %Stockwell & C,LPA -One Seagate -Ste 1610 -Toledo 43604 Fx:247-1575

(614) 462-5427 .. **Pouget**, Anne D '03 %Kegler BH&R -65 E State -Ste 1800 -Columbus 43215 Fx:464-2634

(614) 644-3345 .. **Pouliot**, John A '00 Dept Ins -2100 Stella Ct -Columbus 43215

(614) 466-2766 .. **Poulos**, Gregory J '99 Atty Gen -30 E Broad -Columbus 43215 Fx:644-1926

(330) 489-3288 .. **Poulos**, John A '81 Mun Ct Judge -218 Cleveland Av SW -Bx24218 -Canton 44701

(440) 899-6317 .. **Poulos**, John D '88 -25849 Hidden Acres Dr -Westlake 44145

(330) 643-2336 .. **Poulos**, Larry G '73 Summit Cnty Cmn Pleas Ct -209 S High -Akron 44308

(216) 479-2500 .. **Poulos**, Maria A '95 Chase Financial Corp -250 W Huron -Cleveland 44113

(216) 241-2838 .. **Poulos**, Peter M '90 (Taft S&H LLP) -200 Pub Sq -3500 BP Twr -Cleveland 44114 Fx:241-3707

(937) 293-0900 .. **Poulton**, Thomas M '79 Miller-Valentine Grp -Bx744 -Dayton 45401

(330) 499-4121 .. **Pousoulides**, Dimitrios S '90 -931 N Main -Ste 201 -North Canton 44720

(503) 241-1320 .. **Poutasse**, Judith W '87 OfCnsl Parker B&L,PC -1400 SW 5th -Ste 670 -Portland, OR 97201 Fx:323-9058

Povtak, Andrew A '04 -(Address Unavailable)

(216) 261-0200 .. **Powall**, Constance A '91 -27801 Euclid Av -Ste 500 -Euclid 44132

(216) 621-0150 .. **Powar**, Lee D '63 (Hahn L&P LLP) -3300 BP Twr/200 Pub Sq -Ste 3300 -Cleveland 44114 Fx:241-2824

(937) 865-6800 .. **Powderly**, Melanie C '96 Lexis/Nexis -Bx933 -Dayton 45401

(330) 375-3954 .. **Powell**, William M III '92 Summa Hlth Syst -525 E Market -1st Fl -Bx2090 -Akron 44309

Powell, Aisha R '03 -(Address Unavailable)

(614) 466-5394 .. **Powell**, Amanda J '03 Pub Def -8 E Long -Columbus 43215

(330) 744-3198 .. **Powell**, Barbara E '83 NE OH Legal Srvcs -11 Fed Plz Central -Ste 800 -Youngstown 44503

(513) 721-1504 .. **Powell**, Bradley A '86 Droder & M Co,LPA -125 W Cntrl Pkwy -Cincinnati 45202 Fx:721-0310

(614) 444-4445 .. **Powell**, Bruce A '70 -58 W Riverglen Dr -Columbus 43085

(614) 464-6400 .. **Powell**, D Scott '92 (Vorys SS&P LLP) -52 E Gay -Bx1008 -Columbus 43216 Fx:464-6350

(614) 228-9550 .. **Powell**, David T '03 %Javitch B&R -33 N 3rd -Ste 300 -Columbus 43215 Fx:228-2818

(330) 670-7300 .. **Powell**, Donald A '65 Hanna C&P,LLP -3737 Embssy Pkwy -Bx5521 -Akron 44334 Fx:670-0977

(216) 696-1422 .. **Powell**, Eric C '01 %McCarthy LC&L Co,LPA -101 Prospect Av W -1800 Mdlnd Bldg -Cleveland 44115 Fx:696-1210

(513) 721-5525 .. **Powell**, Gary E '84 (Manley B) -225 W Court -Cincinnati 45202 Fx:721-4268

(330) 253-3900 .. **Powell**, Georgene S '79 (Powell & P) -655 S Bway -Akron 44311 Fx:253-3820

(513) 241-9400 .. **Powell**, Jessica L '01 Legal Aid -215 E 9th -Ste 200 -Cincinnati 45202

(440) 930-3317 .. **Powell**, Joe A '75 Polyone Corpartation -One Geon Ctr -Avon Lake 44012

(412) 456-2830 .. **Powell**, John W '77 (Meyer U&S,LLP) -1300 Oliver Bldg -Pittsburgh, PA 15222

(330) 253-3900 .. **Powell**, Joseph A '78 (Powell & P) -655 S Bway -Akron 44311 Fx:253-3820

(216) 443-7223 .. **Powell**, Noelle A '03 Cuyahoga Cnty Pub Def -1200 W 3rd NW -100 Lakeside Pl -Cleveland 44113

(330) 650-0088 .. **Powell**, Raymond M '91 %Bevan & Assoc LPA,Inc -10360 Nrthfld Rd -Northfield 44067 Fx:467-4493

(740) 283-6028 .. **Powell**, Richard L '53 %Municipal Court -123 S 3rd -Steubenville 43952

(614) 228-6107 .. **Powell**, Shane M '03 %Jack & S -572 E Rich -Columbus 43215

(419) 423-8668 .. **Powell**, Steven M '93 (SM Powell,LPA) -108 E Main Cross -Findlay 45840

(330) 455-0173 .. **Powell**, Tara A '76 (Day KRW&R,Ltd) -200 Market Av N -Ste 300 -Bx24213 -Canton 44701 Fx:455-2633

(216) 664-4800 .. **Powell**, Verlinda L '01 Prosecutor -1200 Ontario Av -8th Fl Justice Ctr -Cleveland 44113 Fx:664-4399

(513) 777-6009 .. **Powell**, Walter E '84 -6671 Wooden Shoe Dr -Middletown 45044

(513) 871-8915 .. **Powell**, Wallace M '48 -3664 Ashworth Dr -Cincinnati 45208

(330) 836-5110 .. **Powers**, Annette L '81 -1655 W Market -Akron 44313

(216) 496-3238 .. **Powers**, Brian E '88 -1085 Wilbert Rd -Lakewood 44107

(937) 208-2263 .. **Powers**, Cara W '98 Miami Valley Hospital -1 Wyoming -Dayton 45409 Fx:208-2871

(216) 781-3456 .. **Powers**, Dale D '60 -526 Superior Av E -Ste 720 -Cleveland 44114 Fx:566-1468

(513) 425-1370 .. **Powers**, Dallas P '68 Cnty Ct Judge -550 Justice Dr -Lebanon 45036

(330) 482-3356 .. **Powers**, David P '84 (Stacey HS&P LPA) -20 S Main -Columbiana 44408

(440) 243-2955 .. **Powers**, Donald H '64 (Powers & G-W) -2 Berea Cmmns -Ste 215 -Bx1059 -Berea 44017 Fx:243-2967

(440) 243-2955 .. **Powers**, Donna J '88 %Powers & G-W -2 Berea Cmmns -Ste 215 -Bx1059 -Berea 44017 Fx:243-2967

(440) 243-2955 .. **Powers & Groh-Wargo** -2 Berea Cmmns -Ste 215 -Bx1059 -Berea 44017 Fx:243-2967

Powers, Jeffrey W '04 -(Address Unavailable)

(248) 746-2718 .. **Powers**, Jeffry G '01 Sullivan WBT&A,PC -25800 Nrthwstrn Hwy -Southfield, MI 48075

(513) 271-0419 .. **Powers**, John A '92 Univ of Cincinnati -8180 Wooster Pk -#B -Cincinnati 45227

(216) 928-7700 .. **Powers**, John A '01 %I Friedman & Assoc -700 W St Clair Av -Ste 110 -Cleveland 44113 Fx:556-9779

(202) 514-2414 .. **Powers**, John J III '72 US DOJ -1401 H NW -Washington, DC 20530

(330) 757-1700 .. **Powers**, John W '49 -421 S Main -Poland 44514

(202) 761-8543 .. **Powers**, Kenneth R '69 US Army Corps of Engrs -441 G NW -Washington, DC 20001

(440) 237-7900 .. **Powers**, Kevin P '93 Ohio PBA -Bx338003 -North Royalton 44133

(216) 514-1180 .. **Powers**, Laurence J '87 (Krantz P&F,PLL) -23200 Chagrin Blvd -Ste 180 -Cleveland 44122 Fx:514-1185

(440) 326-1464 .. **Powers**, Linda M '93 City Law Dir Ofc -131 Court -Ste 201 -Elyria 44035

(419) 335-3971 .. **Powers**, Mark L '80 -142 N Fulton -Bx393 -Wauseon 43567

(216) 566-7100 .. **Powers**, Martin T '91 %SS Keller -1422 Euclid Av -330 The Hanna Bldg -Cleveland 44115 Fx:566-5430

(513) 421-6100 .. **Powers**, Melissa A '91 (M Powers,LPA) -306 E 14th -Cincinnati 45210 Fx:421-6478

(513) 424-1823 .. **Powers**, Noah E '80 (Repper P&P,LTD) -1501 1st Av -Middletown 45044

(937) 323-6120 .. **Powers**, Paula M '97 -4 W Main -Ste 630 -Springfield 45502

(513) 583-4200 .. **Powers**, Todd M '84 (Schroeder MB&P) -11935 Mason Rd -Ste 110 -Cincinnati 45249

(614) 462-5010 .. **Powers**, Victoria E '91 (Schottenstein Z&D) -250 West -Bx165020 -Columbus 43216 Fx:462-5135

(850) 561-3503 .. **Powers**, William E '68 OfCnsl Allen N&B,PA -906 N Monroe -Tallahassee, FL 32306 Fx:561-0332

(330) 451-7217 .. **Powers-Griffiths**, Kristina R '97 Stark Cnty Pub Def -200 W Tuscarawas -Ste 200 -Canton 44702

(330) 375-2730 .. **Powley**, Douglas J '79 Pros -217 S High -Ste 203 -Akron 44308

(302) 282-7833 .. **Powlus**, JoAnn Y '91 1st USA Bank,NA -201 N Walnut -3 Christina Ctr -Wilmington, DE 19801

(719) 333-9153 .. **Pozen**, Jeffrey M '98 HQ USAFA/DFL -2354 Fairchild Dr -Ste 1J100 -U S A F Academy, CO 80840

(216) 241-4244 ..**Pozzuto**, Bridgette D '94 %B Urban Co,LPA -1370 Ontario -600 Standard Bldg -Cleveland 44113

(513) 721-5525 ..**Prager**, Gerald D '00 OfCnsl Manley B -225 W Court -Cincinnati 45202 **Fx:**721-4268

(513) 569-7037 ..**Prahalad**, Punam K '03 US EPA -26 W ML King Dr -MS-498 -Cincinnati 45268

Pramuk, Daniel A '72 -1515 N Astor -Chicago, IL 60610

(216) 621-0150 ..**Prasse**, Richard T '81 (Hahn L&P LLP) -3300 BP Twr/200 Pub Sq -Ste 3300 -Cleveland 44114 **Fx:**241-2824

(330) 533-0916 ..**Prassinos**, Constant A '72 Nationwide Ins -6715 Tippecanoe Rd -Ste 201 -Canfield 44406

(937) 335-5658 ..**Pratt**, Andrew R '94 (Lopez S&P Co,LPA) -18 E Water -Troy 45373 **Fx:**339-6446

(513) 946-3700 ..**Pratt**, Charles A '66 Hamilton Cnty Pub Def -230 E 9th -3rd Fl -Cincinnati 45202 **Fx:**946-3707

(614) 224-5205 ..**Pratt**, Glendon B '82 (Peck S&W,LLP) -175 S 3rd -Ste 600 -Columbus 43215 **Fx:**224-0069

(513) 705-9000 ..**Pratt**, Gregory K '77 (Pratt SP Co,LPA) -301 N Breiel Blvd -Middletown 45044 **Fx:**705-9001

(937) 440-5960 ..**Pratt**, Jeannine N '95 Miami Cnty Pros -201 W Main -Troy 45373 **Fx:**440-5961

(614) 466-4328 ..**Pratt**, Jennifer L '87 Atty Gen -150 E Gay -Columbus 43215 **Fx:**995-0266

(614) 466-8600 ..**Pratt**, Lawrence D '73 Atty Gen -30 E Broad -Columbus 43215 **Fx:**466-6090

(937) 778-1770 ..**Pratt**, Robert A '61 (R Pratt Co,LPA) -312 N Wayne -Bx1720 -Piqua 45356

(614) 466-5394 ..**Pratt**, Shelley M '98 Pub Def -8 E Long -Columbus 43215

(513) 705-9000 ..**Pratt Singer Papakirk Co,LPA** -301 N Breiel Blvd -Middletown 45044 **Fx:**705-9001

(614) 224-7883 ..**Precario**, Peter A '70 -326 S High -Ste 100-Annx -Columbus 43215

(740) 334-1011 ..**Predieri**, Stephen Craig '01 Predieri Lgl Srvcs LLC -341 Granvw Rd -Granville 43023

(937) 222-2424 ..**Pregon**, Jamey T '02 %Freund F&A -1 S Main -Ste 1800 -Dayton 45402 **Fx:**222-5369

(216) 623-0000 ..**Prehn**, Diana J '02 %Javitch B&R -1300 E 9th -14th Fl -Cleveland 44114 **Fx:**623-0190

Preisch, James W '00 -1210 Aster Ct -Mishawaka, IN 46545

(216) 566-2370 ..**Prekop**, Joseph E '83 Sherwin-Williams Co -101 Prospect Av NW -Cleveland 44115

(330) 456-0061 ..**Prelac**, John M '84 Heichel C&P Co,LPA -437 Market Av N -Canton 44702

(513) 381-1234 ..**Prem**, David L '87 -1019 Main -Cincinnati 45202

Prendergast, Jon T '73 -(Address Unavailable)

(440) 892-1940 ..**Prendergast**, Kevin P '87 -27999 Clemens Rd -Ste 1 -Westlake 44145

(614) 258-6000 ..**Prendergast**, Melissa M '02 %Brenner BG&M Co,LPA -2109 Stella Ct -Columbus 43215 **Fx:**258-6006

(330) 666-3889 ..**Prentice**, Sally A '82 -2209 Round Rock Dr -Akron 44333

(419) 244-4697 ..**Prephan**, Michael Sr. '69 -520 Mad Av -Ste 310 -Toledo 43604 **Fx:**244-2782

(419) 874-2261 ..**Prephan**, Michael Jr. '87 -330 Louisiana Av -Perrysburg 43551

(614) 764-6056 ..**Presas**, Julie L '95 OCLC Online Comp Lib -6565 Frantz Rd -Dublin 43017

(614) 855-5223 ..**Prescott**, Gary M '76 -4157 Sudbrook Sq W -New Albany 43054

(513) 561-5900 ..**Prescott**, Karen C '83 -5725 Dragon Way -Ste 313 -Cincinnati 45227 **Fx:**561-5901

Prescott, Mary L '96 -(Address Unavailable)

(440) 930-8067 ..**Prescott**, William P '89 Wickens HPC&B -35765 Chester Rd -Avon 44011 **Fx:**937-4466

(614) 462-3555 ..**Press**, Katherine J '82 Franklin Cnty Pros -373 S High -Columbus 43215

(614) 221-5143 ..**Press**, Lawrence S '82 Lawyers Title -921 Eastwind Dr -Ste 133 -Westerville 43081

(513) 861-3200 ..**Pressler**, Frederick '03 -2170 Gilbert Av -Ste 300 -Cincinnati 45206

(614) 272-6951 ..**Pressler**, Timothy A '76 %Am Commerce Ins Co -3590 Twin Crks Dr -Columbus 43204

(614) 227-2000 ..**Pressley**, Fred G Jr. '78 (Porter WM&A LLP) -41 S High -Columbus 43215 **Fx:**227-2100

(513) 852-3497 ..**Pressman**, Marianne J '92 Atty Gen -441 Vine -1600 Carew Twr -Cincinnati 45202 **Fx:**852-3484

(216) 521-0771 ..**Presswala**, Rashi R '98 -15600 Mad Av -Lakewood 44107

(740) 283-3711 ..**Prest**, Joseph G '64 -328 Market -Ste 300 -Steubenville 43952

(216) 267-1200 ..**Presti**, Geralyn M '89 Forest City Entrprss,Inc -50 Pub Sq -Trmnl Twr,Ste 1160 -Cleveland 44113

(614) 480-5297 ..**Preston**, Carmen Kathryn '90 SrCnsl Huntington Natl Bk -41 S High -HC0523 -Columbus 43215 **Fx:**480-5404

(614) 297-1000 ..**Preston**, Charles A '97 %B Frick & Assoc -1265 Neil Av -Columbus 43201 **Fx:**297-6666

(614) 719-3240 ..**Preston**, Elizabeth A '94 %Hon EA Sargus Jr -85 Marconi Blvd -Rm 301 -Columbus 43215

(405) 348-7377 ..**Preston**, John R '01 -4216 Rimrdg Rd -Edmond, OK 73003

(937) 227-3700 ..**Preston**, K Lynn '04 %Faruki I&C PLL -10 N Ludlow -500 Cthse Plz SW -Dayton 45402 **Fx:**227-3717

(440) 816-0600 ..**Preston**, Kenneth G '60 Largent BP&J Co,LPA -1 Berea Cmmns -Ste 216 -Berea 44017 **Fx:**816-0604

(330) 974-8254 ..**Preston**, Kenneth G Jr. '65 Univ of Akron -170 Univ Cir -Akron 44325 **Fx:**972-2368

(440) 816-0600 ..**Preston**, Kevin M '81 Largent BP&J Co,LPA -1 Berea Cmmns -Ste 216 -Berea 44017 **Fx:**816-0604

(740) 775-2222 ..**Preston**, Mark A '80 (Mann & P,LLP) -18 E 2nd -Chillicothe 45601 **Fx:**775-2627

(740) 548-4802 ..**Preston**, Ralph W '76 -1900 Tmbrlk Dr -Delaware 43015

(330) 456-8341 ..**Preston**, Robert B III '04 %Black MS&A,LPA -220 Market Av S -Ste 1000 -Canton 44702 **Fx:**456-5756

(614) 221-8448 ..**Preston**, Robert C '58 (Buckingham D&B,LLP) -191 W Nationwide Blvd -Ste 300 -Bx151120 -Columbus 43215 **Fx:**221-8590

(419) 424-7144 ..**Preston**, Vernon L '80 Mun Ct Judge -206 Mncpl Bldg -Findlay 45840

(937) 223-8177 ..**Pretekin**, Ronald S '66 (Coolidge WW&L) -33 W 1st -Ste 600 -Dayton 45402 **Fx:**223-6705

(419) 634-9400 ..**Previte**, Peter A '78 -405 N Main -Ada 45810

(216) 479-6100 ..**Prewitt**, Jocelyn N '03 %Vorys SS&P LLP -1375 E 9th -Ste 2100 One Cleve Ctr -Cleveland 44114 **Fx:**479-6060

(513) 621-6464 ..**Prewitt**, Thomas A '93 (Graydon H&R LLP) -511 Walnut -1900 Fifth Third Ctr -Cincinnati 45202 **Fx:**651-3836

(412) 672-5444 ..**Pribanic**, Jeffrey A '90 (Pribanic & P,PC) -1735 Lincoln Way -White Oak, PA 15131

(614) 275-5927 ..**Pribich**, Dan T '82 Cntrl OH Transit Auth -1600 McKinley Av -Columbus 43222

(216) 696-3311 ..**Pribisko**, Patricia W '79 (Kahn K) -1301 E 9th -2600 Erievw Twr -Cleveland 44114 **Fx:**623-4912

(614) 865-1560 ..**Price**, Alise M '96 -168 S State -Westerville 43081

(216) 687-1900 ..**Price**, Andrea K '83 Legal Aid -1223 W 6th -Cleveland 44113 **Fx:**687-0779

(513) 852-3416 ..**Price**, Benjamin L '03 OH Dept of Tax -900 Dalton Av -Cincinnati 45203

(216) 830-6830 ..**Price**, Charles D '95 (Brouse M) -1001 Lakeside Av -Ste 1600 -Cleveland 44114 **Fx:**830-6807

(312) 755-2568 ..**Price**, Charles T '69 (Foley & L) -330 N Wabash Av -One IBM Plz Ste 3300 -Chicago, IL 60611 **Fx:**755-1925

(419) 747-9100 ..**Price**, Daniel E '02 -875 N Lex-Springmill Rd -Mansfield 44906 **Fx:**747-4150

(614) 217-0448 ..**Price**, Deborah E '93 Bank One Invstmnt Advsrs -Bx711216 -Columbus 43271

(216) 861-6000 ..**Price**, Donald C '58 -2000 E 9th -Ste 1100 -Cleveland 44115

(419) 242-3540 ..**Price**, Douglas R '75 -Bx8788 -Toledo 43623

(513) 661-3223 ..**Price**, Edwin C Jr. '57 Price Co,LPA -3249 Epworth Av -Cincinnati 45211

(614) 224-2319 ..**Price**, Gary P '73 (GP Price,LLC) -555 City Park Av -Columbus 43215

(614) 466-3191 ..**Price**, Gregory A '90 PUCO -180 E Broad -Columbus 43266

(216) 431-4500 ..**Price**, James M Jr. '01 Cuyahoga Cnty Pros -3955 Euclid Av -Jane Edna Hunter Bldg -Cleveland 44115 **Fx:**431-4113

(740) 689-3000 ..**Price**, Jason A '94 (JA Price,LPA) -126 E Chestnut -Lancaster 43130 **Fx:**689-3506

(216) 830-6830 ..**Price**, Jessica E '97 %Brouse M -1001 Lakeside Av -Ste 1600 -Cleveland 44114 **Fx:**830-6807

(216) 685-9710 ..**Price**, John T '73 -1370 Ontario -1218 Standard Bldg -Cleveland 44113 **Fx:**685-9714

(216) 363-4500 ..**Price**, Julie M '99 %Benesch FC&A LLP -200 Pub Sq -Ste 2300 -Cleveland 44114 **Fx:**363-4588

Price, Paul F '04 -(Address Unavailable)

(740) 852-2259 ..**Price**, Rachel M '95 Madison Cnty Pros -23 W High -London 43140 **Fx:**845-1649

(614) 462-5411 ..**Price**, Rebecca R '01 %Kegler BH&R -65 E State -Ste 1800 -Columbus 43215 **Fx:**464-2634

(330) 702-0780 ..**Price**, Robert W '01 %Luckhart MZ&R -3810 Starrs Centre Dr -Canfield 44406

(614) 644-7233 ..**Price**, Thelma T '76 Atty Gen -150 E Gay -Columbus 43215 **Fx:**728-9327

(513) 794-6078 ..**Price**, William C '90 OH Natl Life Ins Co -One Fncl Way -Cincinnati 45242

(614) 221-3155 ..**Price**, William E II '91 (Bailey C LLC) -10 W Broad -Columbus 43215 **Fx:**221-0479

(330) 376-7245 ..**Price**, William J '99 %Curtin & Assoc -159 S Main -920 Key Bldg -Akron 44305 **Fx:**376-8128

(937) 294-5959 ..**Price-Testerman**, Connie S '90 -2100 S Patterson Blvd -Dayton 45409

(614) 462-3555 ..**Prichard**, Sheryl L '95 Franklin Cnty Pros -373 S High -Columbus 43215

(614) 728-7055 ..**Prichard**, Timothy D '92 Atty Gen -30 E Broad -Columbus 43215 **Fx:**728-8600

(513) 946-3000 ..**Pridemore**, Katherine E '98 Hamilton Cnty Pros -230 E 9th -Cincinnati 45202 **Fx:**946-3017

(419) 255-0814 ..**Pridgeon**, Merritt J '02 ABLE -520 Mad Av -740 Spitzer Bldg -Toledo 43604 **Fx:**259-2880

(330) 744-5211 ..**Pridham**, Herbert H '55 OfCnsl Roth BRS&L,LPA -100 Fed Plz E -Ste 600 -Youngstown 44503 **Fx:**744-3184

(216) 522-6104 ..**Priest**, Charlie W Jr. '96 Dfnse Fin & Accntng Srvc -1240 E 9th -Cleveland 44199

(419) 243-2042 ..**Priestap**, Stephen T '92 (S Priestap & Assoc) -316 N Mich -Ste 300 -Toledo 43624

(614) 462-6281 ..**Prillo**, Jennifer A '01 %Franklin Cnty Cmmn Pleas Crt -369 S High -Columbus 43215

(216) 622-3600 ..**Primes**, Marlon A '90 US Atty -801 W Superior -Ste 400 -Cleveland 44113 **Fx:**622-3370

(216) 363-4500 ..**Primrose**, Michael A '89 (Benesch FC&A LLP) -200 Pub Sq -Ste 2300 -Cleveland 44114 **Fx:**363-4588

(214) 522-7900 ..**Prince**, Douglas C '80 Jojon Petroleum Co -3838 Oak Lawn Av -Dallas, TX 75219

(216) 531-4116 ..**Prince**, John J '55 -15613 Waterloo Rd -Cleveland 44110

(614) 876-2689 ..**Prince**, Stephanie N '04 OfCnsl S Craig -5251 Norwich -Hilliard 43026 **Fx:**876-0279

(216) 649-0399 ..**Prince**, Troy S '04 Orbitol Research,Inc -4415 Euclid Av -Ste 500 -Cleveland 44103

(216) 227-2302 ..**Princehorn**, Rebecca C '81 (Bricker & E LLP) -100 S 3rd -Columbus 43215 **Fx:**227-2390

(937) 339-2651 ..**Princi**, Paul R '72 (Princi & K) -221 S Market -Troy 45373

(330) 455-0173 ..**Princic**, Richard A '76 (Day KRW&R,Ltd) -200 Market Av N -Ste 300 -Bx24213 -Canton 44701 **Fx:**455-2633

(513) 340-7105 ..**Principe**, Julia K '04 Becker Gallagher Legal Publshng Inc -8790 Governors Hill Dr -Ste 102 -Cincinnati 45249

(330) 343-5585 ..**Pringle**, James J '79 Miller & K,LPA -405 Chauncey Av NW -Bx668 -New Philadelphia 44663 **Fx:**343-7977

(614) 227-2000 ..**Prior**, James H '85 (Porter WM&A LLP) -41 S High -Columbus 43215 **Fx:**227-2100

Prior, Kelly K '91 -1099 Marie Lou Dr -Westerville 43081

(937) 449-6400 ..**Prior**, Patricia L '86 OfCnsl Dinsmore & S LLP -1 S Main -Ste 1300 One Dayton Centre -Dayton 45402 **Fx:**449-6405

(614) 645-7483 ..**Prisley**, Michael A '91 City Pros -375 S High -7th Fl -Columbus 43215

(330) 375-1311 ..**Prislipsky**, Thomas A '97 (Reminger & R) -80 S Summit
-200 Courtyard Sq -Akron 44308 Fx:375-9075

(513) 241-2324 ..**Pritchard**, David E '93 %Wood H&E LLP -441 Vine -Ste 2700
-Cincinnati 45202 Fx:421-7269

Pritchard, Donnita C '87 -601 Bill France Blvd -801
-Daytona Beach, FL 32114

(614) 469-1400 ..**Pritchard**, Glen R '88 Clark PR&S Co,LPA -471 E Broad
-Ste 1400 -Columbus 43215 Fx:469-0900

(614) 466-2980 ..**Pritchard**, John J '01 Atty Gen -30 E Broad -Columbus 43215
Fx:728-9470

(330) 762-6474 ..**Pritchard**, Sheree T '97 %Sternberg NS & Assoc
-411 Wolf Ledges Pkwy -Ste 300 -Akron 44311 Fx:762-2127

(330) 376-2600 ..**Pritchard**, Susan K '80 -168 E Market -Ste 205 -Akron 44308

(614) 227-2000 ..**Pritchard**, W John '92 (Porter WM&A LLP) -41 S High
-Columbus 43215 Fx:227-2100

(330) 799-4311 ..**Pritchard**, Warren G '82 -296 N Niles-Canfld Rd
-Youngstown 44515

(614) 459-5200 ..**Pritchett**, Clark P Jr. '68 (Rance PBK&E Co,LPA)
-1720 Zollinger Rd -Ste 200 -Columbus 43221 Fx:459-1151

(239) 649-6200 ..**Pritt**, Robert D '74 (Roetzel & A) -850 Park Shore Dr
-Trianon Centre 3rd Fl -Naples, FL 34103 Fx:261-3659

(216) 642-3342 ..**Privitera**, Angela M '98 Wegman H&V,LPA
-6055 Rockside Wds Blvd -Ste 200 -Cleveland 44131
Fx:642-8826

(614) 224-2678 ..**Probst**, Erica A '01 Kemp SR&L Co,LPA -88 W Mound
-Columbus 43215 Fx:469-7170

(614) 464-2025 ..**Probst**, Michael S '99 %Connor B LLP -501 S High
-Columbus 43215 Fx:224-8708

(330) 492-5151 ..**Procario**, Gary J '69 -4450 Belden Vllg NW -Ste 800
-Canton 44718

(440) 248-7906 ..**Proctor**, Edward A '98 %Mazanec R&R Co,LPA -34305 Solon Rd
-Ste 100 -Cleveland 44139 Fx:248-8861

(330) 452-5781 ..**Proctor**, James P '80 %Zwick Law Ofcs -1500 Market Av N
-Bx8409 -Canton 44711

Proctor, James W '56 -6537 Dorr -#L-32 -Toledo 43615

(513) 241-3100 ..**Proctor**, Michael R '03 %Lerner S&R -120 E 14th -8th Fl
-Cincinnati 45202

(614) 566-5151 ..**Proctor**, Penelope A '80 %OhioHealth -3722 Olentangy Rvr Rd
-Ste K -Columbus 43214

(740) 349-4716 ..**Proctor**, Philip L '89 -Bx4803 -Newark 43058

(740) 385-5604 ..**Proctor**, Stephen E '82 %GD Rolston -61 N Market -Rear
-Logan 43138

(513) 381-5552 ..**Proctor**, Stephen M '98 Masuda FE&M,Ltd -312 Walnut -Ste 1750
-Cincinnati 45202 Fx:381-5559

(330) 491-9880 ..**Proctor-Donald**, Beverly P '98 (Proctor-Donald & O)
-4565 Dressler Rd NW -LL-102 -Canton 44718

(440) 843-5320 ..**Proe**, Stephen J '96 Kerns H&P -7123 Pearl Rd -Ste 304
-Middleburg Heights 44130

(937) 578-5509 ..**Proels**, Allayne W '96 Cnsl Scotts Co -14111 Scottslawn Rd
-Marysville 43041

(614) 464-6400 ..**Proels**, Sebastian E '99 %Vorys SS&P LLP -52 E Gay -Bx1008
-Columbus 43216 Fx:464-6350

(202) 879-4668 ..**Proger**, Phillip A '73 (Jones DR&P) -51 Louisiana Av NW
-Washington, DC 20001 Fx:626-1700

(513) 948-5402 ..**Proietti**, Louis D '91 Givaudan Flavors Corp -1199 Edison Dr
-Cincinnati 45216

(216) 778-6535 ..**Prokop**, Josephine V '85 -9700 Rockside Rd -Ste 250 -Valley View
44125

(740) 852-2259 ..**Pronai**, Stephen J '84 Madison Cnty Pros -23 W High
-London 43140 Fx:845-1649

(330) 264-4444 ..**Proper**, Roger D Jr. '97 (Critchfield C&J Ltd) -225 N Market
-Bx599 -Wooster 44691 Fx:263-9278

(614) 228-6885 ..**Prophater**, William H Jr. '93 %Lane A&H LLC -175 S 3rd -Ste 700
-Columbus 43215 Fx:228-0146

(614) 462-2333 ..**Prosek**, Bryan K '91 (Schottenstein Z&D) -250 West -Bx165020
-Columbus 43216 Fx:462-5135

(937) 449-6810 ..**Proud**, H John '04 Porter WM&A LLP -1 S Main -Ste 1600
-Dayton 45402 Fx:449-6820

(513) 946-3700 ..**Prouty**, Frank H Jr. '73 Hamilton Cnty Pub Def -230 E 9th -3rd Fl
-Cincinnati 45202 Fx:946-3707

(440) 244-6133 ..**Provenza**, Kenneth J '67 (Provenza & P) -218 8th -Lorain 44052

(440) 204-2250 ..**Provenza**, Mark R '85 City of Lorain -200 W Erie Av -7th Fl
-Lorain 44052

(440) 244-6133 ..**Provenza**, Michael K '92 -218 8th -Lorain 44052

(440) 244-6133 ..**Provenza**, Russell D '64 (Provenza & P) -218 8th -Lorain 44052

(614) 461-1311 ..**Proxmire**, Mickey L '01 %Reminger & R -65 E State
-4th Fl Cptl Sq Ofc Bldg -Columbus 43215 Fx:232-2410

(614) 466-5394 ..**Prucha**, Linda E '88 Pub Def -8 E Long -Columbus 43215

(614) 466-5394 ..**Prude-Smithers**, Pamela J '93 Pub Def -8 E Long
-Columbus 43215

(440) 930-2600 ..**Prudhoe**, Jeffrey R '98 OfCnsl K Brusnahan & Assoc
-158-A Lear Rd -Avon Lake 44012 Fx:930-2602

(419) 223-1861 ..**Prueter**, Susan M '92 Cnsl 3rd Dist Ct of Appeals -204 N Main
-Lima 45801 Fx:224-3828

(614) 387-9420 ..**Pruett**, Catherine Eileen '81 Supreme Ct of OH -65 S Front -6th Fl
- Dispute Resolution -Columbus 43215

Prugh, David C '49 -2176 N St James Pkwy
-Cleveland Heights 44106

(216) 265-6000 ..**Prugh**, Leigh S '00 Cleveland Hopkins Intl Airport
-5300 Riverside Dr -Law Dept -Cleveland 44135

(614) 444-7711 ..**Pruitt**, Jacob E Jr. '76 -66 Thurman Av -Columbus 43206

(216) 696-8730 ..**Prulhiere**, Jeffrey N '84 Amin & T LLP -1900 E 9th
-24th Fl Natl City Ctr -Cleveland 44114 Fx:696-8731

(330) 434-3000 ..**Pruneski**, Stephen J '85 (Roderick & L) -One Cascade Plz
-Ste 1500 -Akron 44308 Fx:434-9220

(614) 677-3452 ..**Prunte**, Thomas J '82 Nationwide Ins Co -1 Nationwide Plz
-Columbus 43215

(304) 529-4561 ..**Prunty**, Paul J '89 (Prunty Law Ofcs) -430 6th Av
-Huntington, WV 25701

(440) 244-2434 ..**Prusak**, John M '00 %MJ Duff -715 Bway Av -Lorain 44052

(216) 928-3474 ..**Prusinski**, Cathy C '03 %Yormick & Assoc Co,LPA -127 Pub Sq
-Ste 5200 -Cleveland 44114 Fx:566-0857

(419) 423-4481 ..**Pry**, C N '68 -551 Lk Cascades Pkwy -Bx1106 -Findlay 45839

(419) 562-9856 ..**Pry**, James W II '71 (Spurlock SPG&M,PLL) -120 N Lane
-Bucyrus 44820 Fx:562-9883

(330) 864-6611 ..**Pry**, Russell M '84 (McCarty & P) -1655 W Market -Ste 400
-Akron 44313

(330) 867-9998 ..**Pryatel**, Keith L '86 (Kastner W&W,LLC) -3480 W Market -Ste 300
-Akron 44333 Fx:867-3786

Pryatel, Mark R '83 -250 E 264th -Euclid 44132

(216) 642-3342 ..**Pryatel**, Steven E '86 (Wegman H&V,LPA)
-6055 Rockside Wds Blvd -Ste 200 -Cleveland 44131
Fx:642-8826

(614) 469-5614 ..**Pryce**, Deborah D '76 House of Reps -500 S Front -Ste 1130
-Columbus 43215

(614) 228-5151 ..**Pryor**, David W '84 (Gallagher GPT&L LLP) -471 E Broad -19th Fl
-Columbus 43215 Fx:228-0032

(937) 328-2574 ..**Pryor**, Johnny D '03 Clark Cnty Pros -50 E Columbia -Bx1608
-Springfield 45501

(513) 381-2838 ..**Pryor**, Patricia A '98 %Taft S&H LLP -425 Walnut -Ste 1800
-Cincinnati 45202 Fx:381-0205

Pryor, Richard E II '84 -551 Rockwell -Kent 44240

(513) 579-6400 ..**Pryse**, Gail Glassmeyer '88 (Keating M&K PLL) -1 E 4th
-1400 Provident Twr -Cincinnati 45202 Fx:579-6457

(216) 586-3939 ..**Przybysz**, Christine M '04 %Jones D -901 Lakeside Av -Cleveland
44114 Fx:579-0212

(513) 530-5357 ..**Przywara**, Kathryn K '90 -8652 Calumet Way -Cincinnati 45249

(216) 363-4500 ..**Psaropoulos**, Robert C '96 %Benesch FC&A LLP -200 Pub Sq
-Ste 2300 -Cleveland 44114 Fx:363-4588

(419) 774-5676 ..**Pscholka-Gartner**, Kirsten L '04 Richland Cnty Pros -38 S Park
-2nd Fl -Mansfield 44902 Fx:774-5589

(216) 928-3082 ..**P'Simer**, Irina '04 (Cheselka & P,LLC) -1940 E 6th
-8th Fl Baker Bldg -Cleveland 44114 Fx:619-7420

(216) 363-1400 ..**Psota**, Paul P '89 (Buckley K,LPA) -600 E Superior Av -Ste 1400
-Cleveland 44114 Fx:579-1020

(216) 621-0200 ..**Ptaszek**, Edward G Jr. '78 (Baker & H LLP) -1900 E 9th -Ste 3200
-Cleveland 44114 Fx:696-0740

(216) 522-3818 ..**Pubal**, Daniel J '03 US Dept of Labor/OSHA -1240 E 9th -899
-Cleveland 44199

(330) 497-1300 ..**Pucci-Sutton**, Susan '94 (Pucci & Q LLP) -4429 Fulton Dr NW
-Canton 44718

(330) 823-1970 ..**Puckett**, James P '69 -360 Overlook Dr -Alliance 44601

(216) 486-6500 ..**Puckett**, Kathryn '77 -2158 Belvoir Blvd -Cleveland 44121

(614) 224-2795 ..**Puckett**, Milton A '70 -155 W Main -Ste 200 -Columbus 43215

(216) 736-8907 ..**Pudner**, F Joseph '01 Dollar Bank FSB -1301 E 9th
-Cleveland 44114

(440) 423-1288 ..**Puette**, Thomas J '69 -675 Echo Dr -Gates Mills 44040

(520) 773-2006 ..**Puffenberger**, James A '86 Northern AZ Hlthcre -1200 Beaver
-Flagstaff, AZ 86001

(216) 586-3939 ..**Pugh**, Charles W '04 %Jones D -901 Lakeside Av
-Cleveland 44114 Fx:579-0212

(202) 707-2257 ..**Pugh**, Elizabeth A '78 Cnsl Library of Congress -101 Indpndnc
Av SE -LM 601 -Washington, DC 20540 Fx:707-1594

Pugh, Jason R '98 -11560 Georgtwn -Louisville 44641

(440) 356-7255 ..**Puglise**, Scott M '00 %Grady & Assoc -20950 Ctr Ridge Rd
-Ste 100 -Rocky River 44116 Fx:356-7255

(330) 745-0006 ..**Puglisi**, Salvatore P '75 -103 5th SE -Ste M -Barberton 44203
Fx:745-6286

(330) 747-4404 ..**Puhalla**, Leo J '96 Newman O&K,LPA -11 Fed Plz Central
-Ste 1200 -Youngstown 44503 Fx:747-6056

(440) 843-5320 ..**Puin**, Timothy J '95 %Kerns H&P -7123 Pearl Rd -Ste 304
-Middleburg Heights 44130

(859) 491-5114 ..**Puissegur**, Alma M '77 -321 W 6th -Covington, KY 41011

(937) 492-6191 ..**Pulfer**, Anthony R '88 %Elsass WES&Co -100 S Main Av -Ste 102
-Bx499 -Sidney 45365 Fx:492-0876

(419) 380-1330 ..**Puligandla**, Bertrand R '93 -2329 Airport Hwy -Toledo 43609

(419) 213-1330 ..**Puligandla**, Vijay K '88 -316 N Mich Av -Ste 514 -Toledo 43624

(440) 322-1329 ..**Pulito**, Gino '87 (Pulito & Assoc) -230 3rd -2nd Fl -Elyria 44035
Fx:322-6474

(330) 762-0700 ..**Pullekins**, Edward C '75 (Slater Z&G) -One Cascade Plz
-Ste 2210 -Akron 44308 Fx:762-3923

(216) 479-5085 ..**Pullen**, Cassandra '00 Kaiser Permanente -1001 Lakeside Av
-Ste 1200 -Cleveland 44114

(614) 224-3207 ..**Pullins**, Scott A '03 -50 W Broad -Ste 1328 -Columbus 43215

(703) 684-6885 ..**Pulsinelli**, Jennifer A '01 Breiner & B,LLC -115 N Henry
-Alexandria, VA 22314 Fx:684-8206

(419) 874-6173 ..**Pummill**, Brian S '89 -2062 Lex Dr -Perrysburg 43551

(937) 298-6105 ..**Puncer**, William O '80 i Manage Inc -401 Winding Way
-Kettering 45419

(513) 564-9999 ..**Pundzak**, Lynn D '86 -830 Main -Ste 999 -Cincinnati 45202

(419) 473-2322 ..**Purcel**, Jerry P '80 (J Purcell Co,LPA) -3425 Exec Pkwy #206
-Toledo 43606

(330) 562-2930 ..**Purcell**, Carl W '67 (Purcell & Assoc) -300-14 Wd Ridge Dr
-Aurora 44202

(614) 761-9990 ..**Purcell**, Cary W '85 (Purcell & S Co,LPA) -6035 Mem'l Dr
-Dublin 43017

(440) 331-5883 ..**Purcell**, Kevin '81 -19109 Old Detroit Rd -Rocky River 44116

(216) 479-6100 ..**Purcell**, Mary Eileen '94 Vorys SS&P LLP -1375 E 9th
-Ste 2100 One Cleve Ctr -Cleveland 44114 Fx:479-6060

(614) 761-9990 ..**Purcell & Scott Co,LPA** -6035 Mem'l Dr -Dublin 43017

(419) 531-0599 ..**Purdue**, David C '83 -2735 N Holland-Sylvania Rd -Ste B-2
-Toledo 43615

(419) 531-0599 ..**Purdue**, John C '49 Purdue Law Ofc -2735 N Holland-Sylvania Rd
-Ste B-2 -Toledo 43615

(440) 729-2378 ..**Purdy**, Dorrit W '78 -8970 Wilson Mills Rd -Chesterland 44026

(513) 851-3700 ..**Purdy**, Eugene K '53 (E Purdy Co LPA) -10776 Mill Rd
-Cincinnati 45240 Fx:851-3701

(419) 586-6442 ..**Purdy Lammers & Schiavone** -113 E Market -Bx404
-Celina 45822 Fx:586-1948

(937) 378-4119 ..**Purdy**, Stanley K '65 (Purdy & R) -318 W State
-Georgetown 45121

(440) 887-7400 ..**Purge**, Sherry M '00 Parma City Pros Ofc -5555 Powers Blvd
-Parma 44129

(312) 269-4368 ..**Purnell**, Edward A '90 (Jones DR&P) -77 W Wacker Dr
-Chicago, IL 60601 Fx:782-8585

(440) 951-2323 ..**Purola**, Albert L '70 -38108 3rd -Willoughby 44094

(614) 443-3860 ..**Pursglove**, Joseph II '75 -1295 S High -Columbus 43206

(614) 728-3300 ..**Pursley**, Gerald L '78 State Fire Marshal -8895 E Main
-Reynoldsburg 43068

(937) 544-2581 ..**Purtell**, Steven W '93 %D Bubp -307 N Market -West Union 45693
Fx:544-1802

(513) 241-3100 ..**Purtell**, William L '02 %Lerner S&R -120 E 4th -8th Fl
-Cincinnati 45202

(216) 781-1212 ..**Purtiman**, Teresa E '01 %Walter & H LLP -1301 E 9th -Ste 3500
-Cleveland 44114 **Fx:**575-0911

(614) 447-0100 ..**Pusateri**, Paul D '77 Kura & W Co LPA -26 W Henderson Rd
-Columbus 43214 **Fx:**447-0152

(330) 492-8717 ..**Pusateri**, Paul J '97 (Buckingham D&B,LLP) -4518 Fulton Dr NW
-Bx35548 -Canton 44735 **Fx:**492-9625

(513) 603-2209 ..**Pustinger**, David A '97 OH Casualty Ins Co -9450 Seward Rd
-Fairfield 45014

(216) 586-3939 ..**Pustulka**, Kimberly J '00 %Jones D -901 Lakeside Av
-Cleveland 44114 **Fx:**579-0212

(330) 458-0484 ..**Puterbaugh**, Michael R '89 (Puterbaugh & M) -111 2nd NW
-Ste 505 -Canton 44702

(954) 473-1001 ..**Puthoff**, Frank M '74 ProxyMed,Inc -2555 Davie Rd -Ste 110
-Fort Lauderdale, FL 33317

(513) 381-2838 ..**Puthoff**, Tracey A '95 (Taft S&H LLP) -425 Walnut -Ste 1800
-Cincinnati 45202 **Fx:**381-0205

(440) 331-5532 ..**Putka**, Andrew C '52 -28 Pond Dr -Rocky River 44116

(419) 238-2200 ..**Putman**, Shaun A '02 %CA Runser -111 E Main -Ste 105
-Van Wert 45891

(813) 661-7028 ..**Putman**, Susette C '87 Amer Nurses Assn -3917 Appletree Dr
-Valrico, FL 33594

(330) 498-9485 ..**Putman**, Timothy J '85 -3978 Fulton Rd NW -Canton 44718
Fx:498-3800

(614) 221-5627 ..**Putnam**, Douglas T '83 %Cnty Commssrs Assoc -37 W Broad
-Ste 650 -Columbus 43215

(216) 443-7223 ..**Puzin**, Gary W '75 Cuyahoga Cnty Pub Def -1200 W 3rd NW
-100 Lakeside Pl -Cleveland 44113

(412) 338-1100 ..**Puzzuole**, Bernadette L '91 (Rothman G,PC) -310 Grant -Ste 300
-Pittsburgh, PA 15219 **Fx:**281-7304

(419) 625-8324 ..**Py**, John D '73 (Flynn P&K,LPA) -165 E Wshngtn Row
-Sandusky 44870 **Fx:**625-9007

(216) 696-6122 ..**Pyle**, John S '74 (Gold & P Co,LPA) -526 Superior Av E
-1140 Leader Bldg -Cleveland 44114 **Fx:**696-3214

(440) 914-5297 ..**Pyle**, Thomas B '00 Podor & Assoc -33565 Solon Rd -Solon 44139

(614) 436-3701 ..**Pyles**, Clement W '75 -1405 Faltlander Dr N -Columbus 43229

(614) 463-4201 ..**Pyles**, Tracy Stott '01 Littler M,PC -21 E State -Ste 1600
-Columbus 43215 **Fx:**221-3301

(937) 223-3001 ..**Pyper**, Thomas H '81 (Jenks P&O Co,LPA) -10 N Ludlow -Ste 901
-Dayton 45402 **Fx:**223-3103

(419) 885-8920 ..**Pyzik**, Robert A '78 City Pros -6700 Monroe -Sylvania 43560

(216) 875-2767 ..**Quallich**, Patrick J '99 %Bonezzi SM&P Co LPA -526 Superior Av
-Ste 1400 -Cleveland 44114 **Fx:**875-1570

Qualls, John R '77 -7586 Keats Ln -Cincinnati 45224

(937) 981-4142 ..**Quance**, Peter D '84 (Smith & Q) -344 Jffrsn -Bx210
-Greenfield 45123

(561) 842-3000 ..**Quartell**, Jared N '96 %Ward D&P,PA -4420 Beacon Cir -Ste 100
-West Palm Beach, FL 33407 **Fx:**842-3626

Quartell, Robert J '98 -2602 Canterbury Rd -Cleveland 44118

(216) 443-9000 ..**Quathamer**, Nicole J '99 %Porter WM&A LLP -925 Euclid Av
-Ste 1700 -Cleveland 44115 **Fx:**443-9011

(419) 227-0506 ..**Quatman**, George B III '72 (Quatman & Q) -3090 Spencervll Rd
-Lima 45805

(419) 229-0023 ..**Quatman**, Janice A '91 -317 N Elizabeth -Lima 45801

(419) 227-0506 ..**Quatman**, Joseph E '79 (Quatman & Q) -3090 Spencervll Rd
-Lima 45805

(614) 221-5121 ..**Quayle**, Jeffrey D '78 OH Bankers Assoc -37 W Broad -#1001
-Columbus 43215

(513) 258-1991 ..**Qucsai**, Robert James III '04 (Qucsai & P) -Bx432 -Mason 45040

(614) 464-3563 ..**Quenemoen**, Helen M '85 %Loveland & B -50 W Broad -Ste 3300
-Columbus 43215

(330) 339-3998 ..**Query**, Callie S '04 SE OH Lgl Srvcs -332 W High Av
-New Philadelphia 44663

(216) 664-6900 ..**Quick**, Harry T '65 (Brzytwa Q&M LLC) -1660 W 2nd
-900 Skylight Ofc Twr -Cleveland 44113 **Fx:**664-6901

(317) 917-6326 ..**Quigg**, Stephanie L '01 NCAA -700 W Wshngtn
-Indianapolis, IN 46204

(937) 382-4559 ..**Quigley**, Deborah S '91 Clinton Cnty Pros -103 E Main
-Wilmington 45177 **Fx:**382-6278

(614) 292-1764 ..**Quigley**, John B Jr. '73 OSU Moritz Cllg of Law -55 W 12th Av
-Columbus 43210 **Fx:**292-1383

(419) 334-8444 ..**Quigley**, Richard W Jr. '73 -1101 Birchland Av -Fremont 43420

(972) 386-6664 ..**Quillin**, John G '85 %Quillin Law Firm,PC -4101 McEwen Rd
-Ste 540 -Dallas, TX 75244 **Fx:**386-6680

(330) 497-1300 ..**Quinlan**, Karen Ross '92 (Pucci & Q LLP) -4429 Fulton Dr NW
-Canton 44718

(513) 523-1500 ..**Quinlan**, Michael P '96 %Mansour GG&M Co,LPA -55 Pub Sq
-Ste 2150 -Cleveland 44113 **Fx:**523-1705

(440) 244-2120 ..**Quinn**, Alexander J '72 Cath Diocese of Cleveland -2500 Elyria Av
-Lorain 44055

Quinn, Charles R '79 -88 S Portage Path -Ste 303 -Akron 44303

(614) 644-7293 ..**Quinn**, David M '78 OH Dept Commerce -77 S High
-Columbus 43266

(614) 466-2585 ..**Quinn**, Gretchen A '87 OH Sec of State -180 E Broad
-Columbus 43215 **Fx:**466-5409

(937) 225-2910 ..**Quinn**, Margaret M '80 US Atty -200 W 2nd -602 Fed Bldg
-Dayton 45402

(216) 289-7600 ..**Quinn**, Patrick D '76 Cnsl Quinn Lgl Assoc,Inc
-21801 Lakeshr Blvd -Euclid 44123 **Fx:**289-7213

(937) 225-2910 ..**Quinn**, Patrick D '81 US Atty -200 W 2nd -602 Fed Bldg
-Dayton 45402

(419) 626-3323 ..**Quinn**, Patrick J '83 OfCnsl Muehlhauser & M -422 Columbus Av
-Bx790 -Sandusky 44870

(513) 381-2838 ..**Quinn**, Timothy J '75 (Taft S&H LLP) -425 Walnut -Ste 1800
-Cincinnati 45202 **Fx:**381-0205

(419) 245-1278 ..**Quintero**, Arturo M '79 City of Toledo -1 Govt Ctr -Ste 2200
-Toledo 43604

(216) 696-3622 ..**Quintrell**, Thomas A '48 -925 Euclid Av -1150 Huntngtn Bldg
-Cleveland 44115

(330) 535-5711 ..**Quirk**, Frank E '59 OfCnsl Brouse M -106 S Main
-500 First Natl Twr -Akron 44308 **Fx:**253-8601

(216) 589-8399 ..**Quirk**, Jamie Joy '93 %Surety Title Agncy -1010 Leader Bldg
-Cleveland 44114

(740) 695-4412 ..**Quirk**, Robert W '75 Belmont Cnty Pros -147-A W Main
-Saint Clairsville 43950

(513) 860-1555 ..**Quraishi**, Nadeem Z '00 -8050 Beckett Ctr Dr -Ste 104
-West Chester 45069

(614) 445-5858 ..**Rabaa**, Shareef S '03 %Gibson & R-P Co LPA -673 Mohawk
-4th Fl -Columbus 43206 **Fx:**445-5850

(513) 946-3132 ..**Rabanus**, Lisa '98 Hamilton Cnty Pros -230 E 9th
-Cincinnati 45202 **Fx:**946-3017

(440) 352-3391 ..**Rabb**, Howard S '86 (Dworken & B Co,LPA) -60 S Park Pl
-Painesville 44077 **Fx:**352-3469

(216) 696-1422 ..**Rabb**, Richard A '90 (McCarthy LC&L Co,LPA)
-101 Prospect Av W -1800 Mdlnd Bldg -Cleveland 44115
Fx:696-1210

Rabb, Sheldon E '62 -619 Magnolia Ln -Chagrin Falls 44023

(614) 766-5800 ..**Rabe**, Randall S '83 Employee Benefit Management Corp
-4789 Kings Rd -Dublin 43017

(513) 381-9697 ..**Rabenold**, Keith M '89 Intrieve,Inc -312 Plum -Bx5412
-Cincinnati 45201

(513) 221-5212 ..**Raber**, David A '92 %JR Lumpe -37 W Broad -Ste 730
-Columbus 43215 **Fx:**221-6944

(330) 761-9960 ..**Raber**, Megan E '02 City of Tallmadge -46 North Av
-Tallmadge 44278

(216) 771-8084 ..**Rabin**, Julie E '81 (Rabin & R Co,LPA) -55 Pub Sq -Ste 2000
-Cleveland 44113 **Fx:**771-4615

(781) 646-9905 ..**Rabin**, Kathy S '95 Rabin & R -144 Robbins Rd
-Arlington, MA 02476 **Fx:**646-0954

(216) 771-8084 ..**Rabin**, Mary Ann '78 (Rabin & R Co,LPA) -55 Pub Sq -Ste 2000
-Cleveland 44113 **Fx:**771-4615

Rabkin, Allyson B '94 -(Address Unavailable)

(513) 287-7428 ..**Rabkin**, Morton '61 -123 E 4th -Cincinnati 45202

(440) 989-8080 ..**Rabold**, Charles S '80 (CS Rabold Co,LPA) -4520 Oberlin Av
-Lorain 44053

(513) 621-0267 ..**Rabourn**, Dexter A '79 %Waite SB&C -1 W 4th -1513 4th
& Vine Twr -Cincinnati 45202

(513) 287-2089 ..**Raby**, Vivian M '86 Cinergy Corp -139 E 4th -25 Atrium II -Bx960
-Cincinnati 45201

(216) 592-5000 ..**Racey**, Susan L '89 (Tucker E&W LLP) -925 Euclid Av
-1150 Huntngtn Bldg -Cleveland 44115 **Fx:**592-5009

(859) 334-9091 ..**Rachlinski**, Irene L '97 -6170 1st Fncl Dr -Ste 303
-Burlington, KY 41005

(419) 885-4149 ..**Racine**, Charles E '67 -4149 Holland Sylvania Rd -#2
-Toledo 43623

Racioppi, Joseph G '04 -(Address Unavailable)

(330) 376-6222 ..**Rackoff**, Maryanne R '83 -Bx13653 -Fairlawn 44334

(212) 287-4962 ..**Racusin**, Robert O '96 Highbridge -9 W 57th -27th Fl
-New York, NY 10019

(937) 223-4101 ..**Radabaugh**, Tom B '63 -6 The Mall -Dayton 45402

Radanof, Richard G '69 -682 W Tuscarwas Av -Barberton 44203

(740) 774-2142 ..**Radcliffe**, Gerald E '50 Spetnagel & M -42 E 5th
-Chillicothe 45601

(614) 717-4444 ..**Radcliffe**, Michael T '73 DEC Investment Grp,Inc -255
Bradenton Av -Dublin 43017

(216) 586-3939 ..**Radefeld**, Mark B '03 %Jones D -901 Lakeside Av -Cleveland
44114 **Fx:**579-0212

(216) 737-5000 ..**Radel**, Victor D '02 %Chernett WY&P -1301 E 9th -Ste 3300
-Cleveland 44114 **Fx:**737-0011

(216) 621-6570 ..**Rademaker**, Dennis A '77 (Rademaker MM&G) -55 Pub Sq
-Ste 1775 -Cleveland 44113 **Fx:**621-1127

(216) 621-6570 ..**Rademaker Matty McClelland & Greve** -55 Pub Sq -Ste 1775
-Cleveland 44113 **Fx:**621-1127

(330) 405-9005 ..**Rader**, Clarence B III '89 (C Rader III,Ltd) -2112 Case Pkwy S
-Ste 9 -Twinsburg 44087

(216) 464-2125 ..**Rader**, Elizabeth A '87 LOCUM Med Grp -25825 Science Park Dr
-Ste 300 -Beachwood 44122

(513) 632-9521 ..**Rader**, James A '79 -119 E Court -Cincinnati 45202

(419) 422-5387 ..**Rader**, Roger L '79 Rader Law Ofc -330 S Main -Findlay 45840

(614) 464-6400 ..**Radnor**, Alan T '72 (Vorys SS&P LLP) -52 E Gay -Bx1008
-Columbus 43216 **Fx:**464-6350

(419) 897-6500 ..**Radon**, Paul A '81 (Barkan & R Ltd) -1701 Woodlnds Dr
-Maumee 43537 **Fx:**897-6200

(216) 222-2965 ..**Radonjich**, Rajko '86 Natl City Bank -1900 E 9th
-Cleveland 44114

(419) 213-4458 ..**Raduege**, Tammy J '89 OH Ct of Appls -800 Jackson
-Toledo 43624

(440) 234-0662 ..**Rady**, Marie M '90 %Wargo & W Co,LPA -Bx332 -Berea 44017
Fx:234-4179

(216) 687-3558 ..**Radzyminski**, Sharon G '03 Cleveland State Univ -2121 Euclid Av
-Cleveland 44115

(216) 443-4010 ..**Rae**, Michael T '84 USPS -Bx5726 -Cleveland 44101

Raemore, Emily E '03 -(Address Unavailable)

(937) 227-3700 ..**Raether**, Ronald I Jr. '97 (Faruki I&C PLL) -10 N Ludlow
-500 Cthse Plz SW -Dayton 45402 **Fx:**227-3717

(216) 443-7800 ..**Rafalski**, Lawrence '80 Cuyahoga Cnty Pros -1200 Ontario -8th Fl
-Cleveland 44113 **Fx:**698-2270

(740) 283-4781 ..**Raffaele**, Christine L '94 SE OH Lgl Srvcs -100 N 3rd
-Steubenville 43952

(513) 421-4020 ..**Rafferty**, Donald J '89 (Cohen TK&S,LLC) -250 E 5th -Ste 1200
-Cincinnati 45202 **Fx:**241-4490

(614) 227-2306 ..**Rafferty**, Robert C '84 (Bricker & E LLP) -100 S 3rd
-Columbus 43215 **Fx:**227-2390

(330) 788-5555 ..**Rafidi**, Joseph F '00 Rafidi Law Ofc -3627 South Av
-Youngstown 44502 **Fx:**782-2486

(330) 965-8000 ..**Rafidi**, Mark A '98 (Osborne D&S Co LPA) -100 Marwood Cir
-Boardman 44512 **Fx:**965-8005

(330) 744-4137 ..**Rafoth**, Carl D '68 (Friedman & R Co,LPA) -100 Fed Plz E
-Ste 300 City Centre One -Youngstown 44503 **Fx:**744-9962

(330) 758-0575 ..**Rafoth**, James '89 Beard Pension Srvcs -108 W Wstrn
Reserve Rd -Youngstown 44514

(419) 247-1225 ..**Ragan,** William A Jr. '94 Owens Illinois Inc -One SeaGate
-Toledo 43666

(614) 529-8988 ..**Rager,** Nicole E '04 Willis S&W Co LPA -5017 Cemetary Rd
-Hilliard 43026 **Fx:**334-8989

(513) 247-0082 ..**Ragiel,** Ronan C '02 Nat'l Legal Pro Assoc -11331 Grooms Rd
-Cincinnati 45242

(330) 451-7200 ..**Ragner,** John C '02 Stark Cnty Pub Def -200 W Tuscarawas
-Ste 200 -Canton 44702

(330) 376-2700 ..**Ragon,** Stacy A '96 (Roetzel & A,LPA) -222 S Main -Akron 44308
Fx:376-4577

(513) 528-9400 ..**Ragonesi,** Christopher '90 -4030 Mt Carmel-Tobasco Rd -Ste 311
-Cincinnati 45255

(330) 643-2788 ..**Ragsdale,** Susan L '91 Summit Cnty Pros-Crim -53 Univ Av -7th Fl
-Akron 44308 **Fx:**643-8277

(419) 474-8377 ..**Rahal,** Ronald Lee '92 (Horne & R) -4303 Talmadge Rd -Ste 102
-Toledo 43623 **Fx:**474-8377

(216) 685-1360 ..**Rahija,** Michelle A '92 Karp & C,Ltd -2000 E 9th -Ste 710
-Cleveland 44115 **Fx:**781-3130

(330) 455-6112 ..**Raies,** Elizabeth A '86 (Tzangas PM&R) -220 Market Av S -8th Fl
-Canton 44702 **Fx:**455-2108

(740) 397-5262 ..**Railsback,** David E '70 (Zelkowitz B&C) -121 E High
-Mount Vernon 43050

(513) 421-4420 ..**Raimey,** Kyra M '00 P Bossin Co,LPA -36 E 4th -Ste 1210
-Cincinnati 45202

(937) 775-4894 ..**Raines,** David A '90 Wright State Univ -3640 Col Glenn Hwy
-Ofc of Student Affairs -Dayton 45435

(330) 478-0755 ..**Raines,** Kimberly A '99 Fitness Quest Inc -1400 Raff Rd SW
-Canton 44710

(216) 515-1660 ..**Rains,** Merritt Neal '68 (Frantz W LLP) -127 Pub Sq
-2500 Key Center -Cleveland 44114 **Fx:**515-1650

(440) 892-4900 ..**Rains,** Robert N '70 -2001 Crocker Rd -Westlake 44145

(740) 772-4772 ..**Rainsberger,** Ben A '81 Ross Cnty Pub Def -14 S Paint -Ste 54
-Chillicothe 45601

(513) 922-7700 ..**Raisbeck,** Thomas E '92 (Lane F&R Co,LPA) -4931 Delhi Pike
-Cincinnati 45238 **Fx:**922-4607

Raish, Todd A '94 -1379 Hllywd Av -Columbus 43212

Raitano, Mary A '91 -(Address Unavailable)

(419) 891-8884 ..**Raitz,** Glenn N '63 OfCnsl Bayer P&S Co,LPA -1925 Indn Wd Cir
-Maumee 43537 **Fx:**891-8889

(937) 382-0946 ..**Raizk,** Lauren E '04 %Buckley M&W -145 N South
-Wilmington 45177

(440) 352-3391 ..**Raj,** Manav H '96 %Dworken & B Co,LPA -60 S Park Pl
-Painesville 44077 **Fx:**352-3469

(937) 228-2696 ..**Rakay,** Peter J '68 (Snyder R&S) -11 W Monument Bldg -Ste 307
-Dayton 45402

(216) 592-5000 ..**Raker,** Keith H '92 (Tucker E&W LLP) -925 Euclid Av
-1150 Huntngtn Bldg -Cleveland 44115 **Fx:**592-5009

(419) 422-9455 ..**Rakestraw,** Adam E '01 %Rakestraw & R -119 E Crawford
-Findlay 45840 **Fx:**422-2482

(419) 422-9455 ..**Rakestraw,** Gregory A '74 (Rakestraw & R) -119 E Crawford
-Findlay 45840 **Fx:**422-2482

(614) 457-7700 ..**Rakestraw,** W Vincent '68 -4930 Reed Rd -Columbus 43220
Fx:457-7878

(440) 230-0388 ..**Rakic,** Aleksandar '94 -8680 Greenwood Rd
-North Royalton 44133

(330) 463-3802 ..**Rakowsky,** Boris '68 Unemploymnt Comp Commssn -161 S High
-Ste 401-A Ocasek Bldg -Akron 44308

(608) 257-0257 ..**Rakvic,** Laure Burri '03 %Winner W&P -22 E Mifflin -Ste 702
-Madison, WI 53703

(561) 994-4499 ..**Raleigh,** Kerry A '98 %Sachs S&K -301 Yamato Rd -Ste 4150
-Bx810037 -Boca Raton, FL 33481 **Fx:**994-4985

(440) 248-3363 ..**Ralls,** Nancy E '86 -34805 Bridle Trl Ln -Solon 44139

(614) 793-7600 ..**Ralph,** Amanda S '83 %SAIC,Inc -4900 Blazer Pkwy
-Dublin 43017

(574) 246-8154 ..**Ralph,** Anne E '04 US Ct of Appeals -204 S Main -Rm 208
-South Bend, IN 46601

(614) 224-8178 ..**Ralston,** Jay C '72 -519 S 4th -Columbus 43206

(440) 323-8240 ..**Ramage,** Barbara K '80 Legal Aid -538 W Broad -Ste 300
-Elyria 44035

(330) 744-5284 ..**Ramage,** William C III '69 (Harshman B&R) -105 E Boardman
-Youngstown 44503

(412) 281-8000 ..**Ramaley,** Jeffrey A '95 Zimmer K,PLLC -600 Grant
-Pittsburgh, PA 15219

(610) 344-6940 ..**Ramanathan,** Chitra '03 Chester Cnty Pub Def Ofc -17 N Church
-Ste 313 -West Chester, PA 19380

(513) 243-2256 ..**Ramaswamy,** Vadakanchery G '98 GE Aircraft Engines
-1 Neumann Way -Cincinnati 45215

(330) 456-8341 ..**Rambacher,** John J '86 (Black MS&A,LPA) -220 Market Av S
-Ste 1000 -Canton 44702 **Fx:**456-5756

(609) 580-3700 ..**Rambert,** Michael A '89 SpclCnsl Archer & G -700 Alxndr Park
-Ste 102 -Princeton, NJ 08540 **Fx:**580-0051

Rambo, Brent E '03 -(Address Unavailable)

Rambo, Candi S '03 -(Address Unavailable)

(513) 768-8903 ..**Rambo,** Deborah P '87 -414 Walnute -Ste 508 -Cincinnati 45202

(419) 247-2524 ..**Rambo,** Glenn L '80 (Fuller & H,Ltd) -One SeaGate -Ste 1700
-Bx2088 -Toledo 43603 **Fx:**247-2665

(740) 594-8388 ..**Rambo,** Madeline A '91 Sowash C&F -39 N Cllg -Bx2629
-Athens 45701

(513) 768-8901 ..**Rambo,** William C '82 -414 Walnut -Ste 508 -Cincinnati 45202

(703) 481-5650 ..**Ramer,** Amelia L '97 -1516 Deer Pnt Way -Reston, VA 20194
Fx:481-5646

(937) 773-3212 ..**Ramer,** Daniel E '79 (McCulloch FF&G Co,LPA) -123 Market
-Bx910 -Piqua 45356 **Fx:**773-3217

(419) 885-8975 ..**Ramey,** Malcolm S '73 Mun Ct Judge -6700 Monroe
-Sylvania 43560

(413) 496-3175 ..**Ramey,** Stephen D Jr. '96 KB Toys -100 West
-Pittsfield, MA 01201

(513) 241-3100 ..**Ramirez,** Carlos S '97 %Lerner S&R -120 E 4th -8th Fl
-Cincinnati 45202

(202) 962-4800 ..**Ramirez,** Teddy L '77 Venable LLC -1201 NY Av NW -Ste 1000
-Washington, DC 20005

(216) 931-6000 ..**Ramm,** Brian N '87 (Ulmer & B LLP) -1300 E 9th
-Ste 900 Penton Media Bldg -Cleveland 44114 **Fx:**931-6001

(513) 922-5836 ..**Rammelsberg,** Sharri U '92 -Bx58181 -Cincinnati 45258

(513) 852-6051 ..**Rammes,** Lisa M '96 (Wood & L LLP) -600 Vine -Ste 2500
-Cincinnati 45202 **Fx:**852-6087

(216) 676-3898 ..**Ramon,** Anita M '91 Ford Motor Co -5600 Henry Ford Blvd
-Bx9900 -Brook Park 44142

(614) 466-4605 ..**Ramos,** Domingo '95 OH Dept Job & Fam Srvcs -30 E Broad
-32nd Fl -Columbus 43266

(440) 356-0775 ..**Ramos,** Edgar A '77 -2639 Wooster Rd -Rocky River 44116

(216) 642-1425 ..**Ramos,** Fred P '78 -4700 Rockside Rd -Ste 650
-Independence 44131

(513) 221-8383 ..**Ramos,** Gabriel E Jr. '77 -2115 Luray Av -Cincinnati 45206

(330) 434-5070 ..**Ramos,** George L '92 -Bx22388 -Akron 44302

(614) 466-0306 ..**Ramos-Reardon,** Diana L '97 OH Criminal Justice Srvcs
-140 E Town -14th Fl -Columbus 43215

(303) 986-2222 ..**Ramsay,** David E '81 (Alliance Comm Prtnrs LLC)
-165 S Union Blvd -Lakewood, CO 80228

Ramsburg, Cheryl L '96 -Bx746 -Hartville 44632

(216) 623-7300 ..**Ramsey,** Alison D '04 %Brunn Law Firm Co,LPA
-700 W St Clair Av -Ste 208 Hoyt Block -Cleveland 44113
Fx:623-7330

(513) 531-8725 ..**Ramsey,** Ann G '87 -6267 Kincaid Rd -Cincinnati 45213

(419) 843-6420 ..**Ramsey,** Brian M '91 -500 Mad Av -Ste 520 -Toledo 43604

(440) 238-3373 ..**Ramsey,** Bryan K '88 Ramsey C&R -13451 Pearl Rd
-Strongsville 44136

(440) 238-3373 ..**Ramsey Caputo & Ramsey** -13451 Pearl Rd -Strongsville 44136

Ramsey, Donald L '75 -247 Columbus Av -Sandusky 44870

(330) 499-3878 ..**Ramsey,** James Kevin '63 -5453 East Blvd NW -Canton 44718

(513) 579-6400 ..**Ramsey,** Jamie M '99 %Keating M&K PLL -1 E 4th
-1400 Provident Twr -Cincinnati 45202 **Fx:**579-6457

(440) 238-3373 ..**Ramsey,** Kenneth E '63 Ramsey C&R -13451 Pearl Rd
-Strongsville 44136

(440) 826-4100 ..**Ramsey,** Lloyd J '74 (Allen RM & Assoc) -7530 Lucerne Dr
-Ste 200 -Middleburg Heights 44130

(502) 589-5600 ..**Ramsey,** Nancy A '95 SalesT&W -325 W Main -Ste 1900
-Louisville, KY 40202

Ramsey, Reneé V '81 -(Address Unavailable)

(440) 989-5821 ..**Ramsey,** Richard S '03 -1812 Cooper Foster Park Rd W
-Lorain 44053 **Fx:**989-5821

(937) 276-6580 ..**Ramsey,** Sarah V '04 %Montgomery Cnty Pros -3304 N Main
-3rd Fl -Dayton 45405

(216) 696-1500 ..**Ramsey,** Wendle Scott '99 -1422 Euclid Av -Ste 1604
-Cleveland 44115

(440) 238-3373 ..**Ramsey-Caputo,** Donna J '84 Ramsey C&R -13451 Pearl Rd
-Strongsville 44136

(614) 227-2300 ..**Ramseyer,** Becky L '03 %Bricker & E LLP -100 S 3rd
-Columbus 43215 **Fx:**227-2390

(419) 258-2191 ..**Ramsier,** Floyd A '72 -120 S Main -Bx1 -Antwerp 45813

(937) 644-2626 ..**Ramsini,** Hope J '94 Quality Quest -19520 Bear Swamp Rd
-Marysville 43040

(513) 287-3020 ..**Ramundo,** Frank A II '95 Cinergy Corp -139 E 4th
-Cincinnati 45202

(513) 352-6656 ..**Ramundo,** Kimberly E '96 (Thompson H LLP) -312 Walnut -14th Fl
-Cincinnati 45202 **Fx:**241-4771

(513) 684-2496 ..**Ran,** Ronald S '69 IRS -550 Main -Bx476 -Cincinnati 45201

(312) 263-3600 ..**Ranallo,** Michael J '90 (Holland & K LLP) -55 W Monroe -8th Fl
-Chicago, IL 60603 **Fx:**578-6666

(440) 684-1600 ..**Ranallo,** Robert A '80 (Ranallo & A LLC) -6685 Beta Dr
-Cleveland 44143 **Fx:**684-1601

(419) 213-4700 ..**Ranazzi,** Andrew K '88 Lucas Cnty Pros -Adams & Erie
-Lucas Cnty Cthse -Toledo 43624

(614) 459-5200 ..**Rance Pritchett Brantner Keller & Ely Co,LPA** -1720 Zollinger
Rd -Ste 200 -Columbus 43221 **Fx:**459-1151

(614) 459-5200 ..**Rance,** William E '51 OfCnsl Rance PBK&E Co,LPA
-1720 Zollinger Rd -Ste 200 -Columbus 43221 **Fx:**459-1151

(614) 225-8325 ..**Ranck,** Stephen P '83 Motorists Mutual Ins Co -471 E Broad
-Columbus 43215

(440) 354-3800 ..**Rand Gurley Hanahan & Koerner** -270 E Main -Ste 300
-Painesville 44077

(419) 243-5581 ..**Randall,** Benjamin A '00 -238 10th -Toledo 43624

(419) 242-9405 ..**Randall,** Jane S '83 -608 Mad Av -Ste 1400 -Toledo 43604
Fx:246-5764

(216) 228-7250 ..**Randall,** Kerry L '84 J Saurman -14650 Detroit Av -Ste 450
-Lakewood 44107

(330) 456-8341 ..**Randall,** Mary E '83 (Black MS&A,LPA) -220 Market Av S
-Ste 1000 -Canton 44702 **Fx:**456-5756

(614) 227-2000 ..**Randall,** Nicole S '00 %Porter WM&A LLP -41 S High
-Columbus 43215 **Fx:**227-2100

(614) 224-7193 ..**Randall,** Samuel B '51 (Kincaid R&C) -2201 Riverside Dr
-Columbus 43221 **Fx:**586-4051

(614) 224-7193 ..**Randall,** Samuel B II '93 (Kincaid R&C) -2201 Riverside Dr
-Columbus 43221 **Fx:**586-4051

(330) 821-1430 ..**Randall,** Thomas K '68 Geiger TS&H -1844 W State -Ste A
-Alliance 44601 **Fx:**821-2217

Randazzo, Jana M '93 -(Address Unavailable)

(330) 425-9199 ..**Randazzo,** Joseph C '99 Fncl Network of America
-2214 Enterprise Pkwy E -Twinsburg 44087

(330) 272-2488 ..**Randazzo,** Mary E '98 -2212 Enterprise Pkwy E -Twinsburg 44087

(614) 469-8000 ..**Randazzo,** Samuel C '75 McNees W&N,LLC -21 E State -17th Fl
-Columbus 43215 **Fx:**469-4653

(216) 522-8188 ..**Randazzo,** Thomas M '88 NLRB -1240 E 9th
-1695 Celebrezze Bldg -Cleveland 44114 **Fx:**522-2418

(740) 588-6745 ..**Randles,** Steven G '89 First Fin Srvcs Grp,NA -422 Main -Bx2307
-Zanesville 43701

(513) 721-3290 ..**Randman,** Debra J '93 -10979 Reed Hartman Hwy -Ste 136B
-Cincinnati 45242

(513) 381-5700 ..**Randolph,** Daniel P '77 (Ritter & R,LLC) -105 E 4th -Ste 1200
-Cincinnati 45202 **Fx:**381-0014

(513) 381-5700 ..**Randolph,** Marc A '98 %Ritter & R,LLC -105 E 4th -Ste 1200
-Cincinnati 45202 **Fx:**381-0014

(215) 283-7714 ..**Randolph,** Mary Ann '88 Henkels & McCoy,Inc -985 Jolly Rd
-Blue Bell, PA 19422

(513) 241-8776 ..**Randolph,** Peter J '59 -644 Linn -Ste 1230 -Cincinnati 45203

(937) 382-4559 ..**Randolph,** William C '95 Clinton Cnty Pros -103 E Main
-Wilmington 45177 **Fx:**382-6278

(937) 433-7371 ..**Randolph,** William F '77 -56 Wythe Parish -Centerville 45459

(216) 241-6700 ..**Raney,** Linn J '68 OfCnsl Watts H Co,LPA -1100 Superior Av E -Ste 1750 Diamond Bldg -Cleveland 44114 **Fx:**241-8151

Ranft, Yvonne T '83 -(Address Unavailable)

(330) 253-7171 ..**Ranftl,** James R '76 Burdon & M -137 S Main -Ste 201 -Akron 44308 **Fx:**253-7174

(330) 364-5593 ..**Range,** James A '80 Johnson U&R Co LPA -117 S Bway -Bx1007 -New Philadelphia 44663 **Fx:**364-3714

(703) 696-1617 ..**Ranieri,** Steven M '98 US Army -901 N Stuart -Ste 442 -Arlington, VA 22203

(216) 575-7660 ..**Ranke,** Carolyn K '89 -1220 W 6th -Ste 303 -Cleveland 44113

(216) 787-3030 ..**Ranke,** Daniel R '90 Atty Gen -615 W Superior Av -11th Fl -Cleveland 44113 **Fx:**787-3480

(419) 242-4011 ..**Rankin,** Bonnie Rae '93 (Rakin Law Ofc,LLC) -1109 Adams -Ste 202 -Toledo 43624

(216) 566-9700 ..**Rankin,** Carl A '62 (Rankin HP&C,LLP) -925 Euclid Av -Ste 700 -Cleveland 44115 **Fx:**566-9711

(740) 452-2045 ..**Rankin,** D Scott '99 -975 Linden Av -Zanesville 43701 **Fx:**452-6187

(614) 228-6885 ..**Rankin,** Gregory D '77 (Lane A&H LLC) -175 S 3rd -Ste 700 -Columbus 43215 **Fx:**228-0146

(859) 655-4200 ..**Rankin,** Harry D '96 Greenebaum D&M PLLC -50 E RiverCenter Blvd -Ste 1800 -Covington, KY 41011 **Fx:**655-4239

(216) 566-9700 ..**Rankin Hill Porter & Clark,LLP** -925 Euclid Av -Ste 700 -Cleveland 44115 **Fx:**566-9711

(614) 221-3600 ..**Rankin,** Lisa V '91 %State St Cnsltnts -137 E State -Columbus 43215

(740) 772-4772 ..**Rankin,** Lori Jo '95 Ross Cnty Pub Def -14 S Paint -Ste 54 -Chillicothe 45601

(614) 241-5550 ..**Rankin,** Michael R '79 OfCnsl Brunner Law Firm Co,LPA -545 E Town -Columbus 43215 **Fx:**241-5551

(614) 628-8395 ..**Rankin,** Timothy J '01 OH Police & Fire Pnsn Fund -140 E Town -Columbus 43215

(614) 716-0500 ..**Rankin,** Timothy S '92 (Onda L&R Co,LPA) -266 N 4th -Ste 100 -Columbus 43215 **Fx:**716-0511

(330) 643-2617 ..**Rankins,** Milton C '91 Summit Cnty Pros-Tax -220 S Balch -Ste 118 -Akron 44302 **Fx:**643-8540

(216) 696-4200 ..**Ranney,** Phillip Allyn '61 (Schneider SR&L PLL) -1111 Superior Av -Ste 1000 -Cleveland 44114 **Fx:**696-7303

(740) 454-8585 ..**Ransbottom,** James W '77 (Graham M&R Co,LPA) -11 N 4th -Bx340 -Zanesville 43702

(614) 464-6400 ..**Ransier,** Frederick L '74 (Vorys SS&P LLP) -52 E Gay -Bx1008 -Columbus 43216 **Fx:**464-6350

(614) 464-6400 ..**Ransier,** Kathleen H '74 (Vorys SS&P LLP) -52 E Gay -Bx1008 -Columbus 43216 **Fx:**464-6350

(614) 466-6363 ..**Ransom,** Lenora S '99 OH Dept Taxation -30 E Broad -22nd Fl -Columbus 43215

(614) 227-2000 ..**Ransom,** Tracie N '04 %Porter WM&A LLP -41 S High -Columbus 43215 **Fx:**227-2100

(614) 221-7777 ..**Ranum,** Darrell B '86 %OHIC Ins Co -155 E Broad -13th Fl -Columbus 43215

(513) 651-5900 ..**Ranz,** David A '01 %Donovan Law -910 Race -Cincinnati 45202 **Fx:**651-4937

(513) 621-8688 ..**Ranz,** Robert J '80 -1071 Celestial -Ste 904 -Cincinnati 45202

(419) 423-0242 ..**Ranzau,** Christie L '02 %Drake PK&C -301 S Main -Ste 3 -Findlay 45840 **Fx:**423-0186

(512) 374-4500 ..**Rao,** Krishna S '93 Hoovers, Inc -5800 Airport Blvd -Austin, TX 78752

(216) 589-3932 ..**Rapacz,** Walter S '95 Deloitte & Touche -127 Pub Sq -Ste 2500 -Cleveland 44114

(859) 431-6100 ..**Raper,** Robert L '03 Arnzen & W,PSC -600 Greenup -Bx472 -Covington, KY 41012

(330) 675-6676 ..**Raphtis,** Harry T '01 11th Dist Ct of Appls -111 High NE -Warren 44481

(513) 381-2838 ..**Rapien,** Gerald J '68 (Taft S&H LLP) -425 Walnut -Ste 1800 -Cincinnati 45202 **Fx:**381-0205

(216) 696-0600 ..**Rapoport,** Alan J '75 (Rapoport SF&C) -55 Pub Sq -Ste 1750 -Cleveland 44113 **Fx:**696-2929

(216) 696-0600 ..**Rapoport Spitz Friedland & Courtney** -55 Pub Sq -Ste 1750 -Cleveland 44113 **Fx:**696-2929

(216) 931-6000 ..**Rapp,** Adrienne L '04 %Ulmer & B LLP -1300 E 9th -Ste 900 Penton Media Bldg -Cleveland 44114 **Fx:**931-6001

(216) 622-8200 ..**Rapp,** Robert N '72 (Calfee H&G LLP) -800 Superior Av -Ste 1400 -Cleveland 44114 **Fx:**241-0816

(513) 753-7277 ..**Rapp,** William J '87 -1 E Main -Amelia 45102 **Fx:**753-6984

(914) 273-4030 ..**Rappoport,** Ronald A '67 -11 Whippoorwill Rd -Armonk, NY 10504

(740) 432-2389 ..**Raptis,** Stamatios L '77 -123 W 8th -Cambridge 43725

(330) 497-0700 ..**Rarric,** Owen J '02 %Krugliak WG&D Co,LPA -4775 Munson NW -Bx36963 -Canton 44735 **Fx:**497-4020

(216) 685-1060 ..**Rasbach Yurechko,** Amanda '00 %Weltman W&R Co,LPA -323 W Lakeside Av -Ste 200 -Cleveland 44113 **Fx:**363-4121

Rashid, Lela P '04 -(Address Unavailable)

(216) 363-4500 ..**Raske,** Anna K '96 (Benesch FC&A LLP) -200 Pub Sq -Ste 2300 -Cleveland 44114 **Fx:**363-4588

(440) 248-7906 ..**Raskin,** Todd M '80 (Mazanec R&R Co,LPA) -34305 Solon Rd -Ste 100 -Cleveland 44139 **Fx:**248-8861

Raslan, Lila D '01 -2070 Valley Park Cir -Broadview Heights 44147

(419) 422-4014 ..**Rasmussen,** Donald J '84 (Hackenberg B&R) -314 W Crawford -Bx1544 -Findlay 45839

(216) 696-9100 ..**Rasmussen,** Jennifer A '00 KPMG LLP -1375 E 9th -One Cleve Ctr -Cleveland 44114

(216) 228-7250 ..**Rasmussen,** John V '85 J Saurman -14650 Detroit Av -Ste 450 -Lakewood 44107

(614) 764-0681 ..**Rasmussen,** Teri G '84 Blaugrund H&M,Inc -5455 Rings Rd -Ste 500 -Dublin 43017 **Fx:**764-0774

(419) 865-0251 ..**Rasmussen,** Deborah E '99 Sunshine Inc of NWO -7223 Maumee-Wstrn Rd -Maumee 43537

(330) 253-2227 ..**Rasnick,** John F '82 (Parker LH&R,LLC) -388 S Main -Ste 402 -Akron 44311 **Fx:**253-1261

(216) 861-4020 ..**Raso,** Frank A '98 -2101 Richmond Rd -LaPlace 2nd Fl -Beachwood 44122

(216) 566-5500 ..**Rassi,** Christopher M '03 %Thompson H LLP -127 Pub Sq -3900 Key Ctr -Cleveland 44114 **Fx:**566-5800

(440) 646-1677 ..**Rassin,** Julius '59 -6028 Mayfld Rd -Ste 7 -Mayfield Heights 44124

(937) 328-2574 ..**Rastatter,** Douglas M '94 Clark Cnty Pros -50 E Columbia -Bx1608 -Springfield 45501

Rastetter, Richard C Jr. '93 -5343 Castle Pines -Columbus 43235

(614) 459-6331 ..**Rasul,** Ronnie A '95 (Rasul & K Co,LPA) -1170 Old Henderson Rd -Ste 109 -Columbus 43220 **Fx:**538-1806

(330) 722-2222 ..**Ratajczak,** Michael P '93 -Bx41061 -Brecksville 44141

(614) 459-0364 ..**Ratchford,** Robert L Jr. '75 Dealers Allnce Corp -3518 Riverside Dr -Columbus 43221

(937) 335-7142 ..**Ratcliff,** Ann L '83 Miami Cnty Human Srvcs -2040 N Cnty Rd -#25A -Troy 45373

(419) 782-7284 ..**Rath,** Barbara A '83 Rath Construction & Builders Supply -07482 State Rt 66 -Bx811 -Defiance 43512

(216) 443-8872 ..**Rath,** Janet M '91 Cuyahoga Cnty Dom Rltns Ct -1 Lakeside Av -Rm 139 -Cleveland 44113

(847) 402-2532 ..**Rath,** Joseph P '74 Allstate Fincl Srvcs -3100 Sanders Rd -Ste J5B -Northbrook, IL 60062

(216) 623-0000 ..**Rathbone,** Joel H '79 (Javitch B&R) -1300 E 9th -14th Fl -Cleveland 44114 **Fx:**623-0190

(216) 623-0000 ..**Rathbone,** Kimberly L '01 %Javitch B&R -1300 E 9th -14th Fl -Cleveland 44114 **Fx:**623-0190

(419) 465-2534 ..**Rathbun,** Timothy J '89 Encore Plastics Corp -230 W Main -Bellevue 44811

(256) 842-0543 ..**Rathbun,** Willard R '85 US Army Aviation & Missile Command -Leg Ofc Brnch E -Redstone Arsenal, AL 35898

(614) 497-9918 ..**Rathburn,** Dennis A '91 (Rathburn & Assoc) -3700 S High -Ste 96 -Columbus 43207

(216) 479-8500 ..**Rathke,** Sarah K '01 %Squire S&D LLP -127 Pub Sq -4900 Key Twr -Cleveland 44114 **Fx:**479-8780

(216) 479-6100 ..**Ratliff,** Elizabeth A '02 %Vorys SS&P LLP -1375 E 9th -Ste 2100 One Cleve Ctr -Cleveland 44114 **Fx:**479-6060

(740) 383-6023 ..**Ratliff,** J C '78 -200 W Center -Marion 43302

(859) 344-1188 ..**Ratliff,** Janie M '01 Hemmer SPD&K -250 Grandvw Dr -Ste 200 -Ft Mitchell, KY 41017

(513) 469-7444 ..**Ratliff,** Robert A '97 -11331 Grooms Rd -Ste 2000 -Cincinnati 45242

(216) 791-0986 ..**Ratnoff,** Marian F '67 -1801 Chestnut Hills Dr -Cleveland Heights 44106

(614) 719-3240 ..**Rattan,** James E '62 %Hon EA Sargus Jr -85 Marconi Blvd -Rm 301 -Columbus 43215

(513) 946-3534 ..**Rattermann,** Paul D '85 Hamilton Cnty Probate Ct -230 E 9th -10th Fl -Cincinnati 45202 **Fx:**946-3626

(614) 466-2112 ..**Rau,** John E '97 Legis Srvc Commssn -77 S High -Columbus 43215

(216) 575-3105 ..**Rauch,** Je'anne M '98 Natl City Bank -Bx94651 -Cleveland 44101

(419) 238-6621 ..**Rauch,** Kelly J '98 Rice Law Ofcs -124 E Main -Van Wert 45891 **Fx:**238-4705

Rauch, Kelly Vaughn '94 -7805 N Hull Av -Kansas City, MO 64151

(937) 496-7291 ..**Rauch,** Thomas G '75 Montgomery Cnty Pros/CSEA -14 W 4th -Ste 510 -Dayton 45402

(513) 271-0800 ..**Rauchman,** Judith L '83 -7809 Laurel Av -Cincinnati 45243

(330) 262-7555 ..**Rauckhorst,** Robert J Jr. '99 (Kennedy CK&B) -558 N Market -Wooster 44691

Rauen, Mary E '99 -76 View Terrace Dr -Ste 8 -Southgate, KY 41071

(216) 443-9000 ..**Rauf,** Natalie H '01 %Porter WM&A LLP -925 Euclid Av -Ste 1700 -Cleveland 44115 **Fx:**443-9011

(513) 858-1258 ..**Rauh,** Leslie H '94 -5840 Winton Rd -Fairfield 45014

(202) 663-7386 ..**Raulerson,** Billy C '01 %Sughrue M,PLLC -2100 Penn Av NW -Washington, DC 20037

(440) 746-9602 ..**Rausch,** Edward W Jr. '74 -6640 Harris Rd -Broadview Heights 44147 **Fx:**746-9604

(614) 462-3555 ..**Rausch,** Jennifer M Gregg '02 Franklin Cnty Pros -373 S High -Columbus 43215

(614) 466-2980 ..**Rausch,** Monica L '03 Atty Gen -30 E Broad -Columbus 43215 **Fx:**728-9470

(216) 263-6200 ..**Rauser,** Victor P '93 (Rauser & Assoc,LPA) -614 W Superior Av -Ste 950 -Cleveland 44113 **Fx:**263-6202

(216) 736-7221 ..**Rauss,** Alan M '72 (Kohrman J&K PLL) -1375 E 9th -One Cleve Ctr 20th Fl -Cleveland 44114 **Fx:**621-6536

(216) 363-1400 ..**Rauzi,** Harold R '89 (Buckley K,LPA) -600 E Superior Av -Ste 1400 -Cleveland 44114 **Fx:**579-1020

(740) 397-7474 ..**Rauzi,** Robert L '72 (Murray & R) -305 E High -Mount Vernon 43050

(216) 781-2600 ..**Ravas,** Sara S '03 %Lowe EW&M Co,LPA -1660 W 2nd -610 Skylight Ofc Twr -Cleveland 44113 **Fx:**781-2610

Raven, Michael I '94 -(Address Unavailable)

(937) 435-3393 ..**Rawers,** Thomas G '69 -7920 Clyo Rd -Centerville 45459

(216) 586-3939 ..**Rawlin,** Dustin B '00 %Jones D -901 Lakeside Av -Cleveland 44114 **Fx:**579-0212

(216) 579-1602 ..**Rawlin,** Ronald V '72 (Rawlins G&F Co,LPA) -55 Pub Sq -Ste 850 -Cleveland 44113

(859) 371-1611 ..**Rawlings,** J S '89 (Rawlings & Assoc) -8111 US Route 42 -Bx908 -Florence, KY 41022

(614) 628-0818 ..**Rawlings,** Stephanie M '02 %Carlile P&M LLP -366 E Broad -Columbus 43215 **Fx:**221-0216

(330) 864-1183 ..**Rawlings,** Thomas E '77 -2411 Sourek Rd -Akron 44333

(216) 579-1602 ..**Rawlins Gravens & Franey Co,LPA** -55 Pub Sq -Ste 850 -Cleveland 44113

(602) 916-5393 ..**Rawlinson,** Melissa Wilson '04 %Fennemore C PC -3003 N Central Av -Ste 2600 -Phoenix, AZ 85012 **Fx:**916-5593

Rawn, Sonja L '04 -(Address Unavailable)

(614) 466-7090 ..**Rawski,** John '88 Ethics Commssn -8 E Long -10th Fl -Columbus 43215

(412) 566-6784 ..**Rawson,** Jennifer L '92 %Eckert SC&M -600 Grant -44th Fl -Pittsburgh, PA 15219

(216) 586-3939 ..**Rawson,** Rachel L '95 (Jones D) -901 Lakeside Av -Cleveland 44114 **Fx:**579-0212

(216) 586-3939 ..**Rawson,** Robert H Jr. '71 (Jones D) -901 Lakeside Av -Cleveland 44114 **Fx:**579-0212

(419) 861-1141 ..**Ray,** Brenda A '98 %Lyden L&C,Ltd -5565 Airport Hwy -Ste 101 -Toledo 43615 **Fx:**867-8909

(216) 586-3939 .. **Ray**, Brian E '01 %Jones D -901 Lakeside Av -Cleveland 44114 **Fx**:579-0212
(614) 466-4882 .. **Ray**, Carol L '87 OH Dept Hlth -246 N High -Bx118 -Columbus 43216
(614) 221-7791 .. **Ray**, Frank A '73 F Ray Co,LPA -175 S 3rd -Ste 350 -Columbus 43215 **Fx**:221-8957
(216) 521-8080 .. **Ray**, Jared S '98 %C Sumpter & Assoc,LLC -16927 Detroit Av -Ste 4 -Lakewood 44107
(419) 483-5744 .. **Ray**, Jeremiah S '02 -212 W Main -Bellevue 44811
Ray, Jeremy J '00 -3962 Orchrd Rd -Cleveland 44121
(513) 397-5420 .. **Ray**, Mary F '90 Cincinnati Bell -201 E 4th -Ste 102-620 -Cincinnati 45202
(330) 253-7171 .. **Ray**, Nathan A '89 Burdon & M -137 S Main -Ste 201 -Akron 44308 **Fx**:253-7174
(614) 227-2000 .. **Ray**, Nicholas M J '97 %Porter WM&A LLP -41 S High -Columbus 43215 **Fx**:227-2100
(216) 861-4533 .. **Ray Robinson Carle & Davies PLL** -1717 E 9th -Cleveland 44114 **Fx**:861-4568
(513) 977-8200 .. **Ray**, Steven H '88 (Dinsmore & S LLP) -255 E 5th -Ste 1900 -Cincinnati 45202 **Fx**:977-8141
(419) 864-6016 .. **Ray**, Thomas E '57 -107 S Marion -Bx100 -Cardington 43315
(614) 248-6038 .. **Raybuck**, David W '85 Bank One Corp -1111 Polaris Pkwy -Ste 4P -Columbus 43271
(713) 209-8409 .. **Rayl**, Brian D '80 Cooper Industries -Bx4446 -Houston, TX 77210
(419) 354-4442 .. **Rayle Mathews & Coon** -100 S Main -Bowling Green 43402
(419) 354-4442 .. **Rayle**, Max E '76 (Rayle M&C) -100 S Main -Bowling Green 43402
(330) 643-2788 .. **Raynes**, Kristina D '00 Summit Cnty Pros-Crim -53 Univ Av -7th Fl -Akron 44308 **Fx**:643-8277
(330) 535-5711 .. **Raynor**, David F '76 (Brouse M) -106 S Main -500 First Natl Twr -Akron 44308 **Fx**:253-8601
Razavi, Matthew K '96 -5201 Morning Song Dr -Medina 44256
(330) 832-4904 .. **Rea**, Brenda J '94 -5031 Highsaddle Av NW -Massillon 44646
(937) 225-6370 .. **Rea**, Darlene S '95 Montgomery Cnty CSEA -14 W 4th -Bx872 -Dayton 45422
(216) 664-4348 .. **Rea**, Raymond '97 Dept of Law -601 Lakeside Av -Rm 106 City Hall -Cleveland 44114 **Fx**:664-2663
(216) 566-5778 .. **Read**, Deborah Z '87 (Thompson H LLP) -127 Pub Sq -3900 Key Ctr -Cleveland 44114 **Fx**:566-5800
(216) 479-6100 .. **Read**, John Winship '85 (Vorys SS&P LLP) -1375 E 9th -Ste 2100 One Cleve Ctr -Cleveland 44114 **Fx**:479-6060
(216) 931-6000 .. **Reader**, Harold H III '74 (Ulmer & B LLP) -1300 E 9th -Ste 900 Penton Media Bldg -Cleveland 44114 **Fx**:931-6001
(330) 451-7765 .. **Reader**, Willard Donald Jr. '58 -110 Central Plz S -Ste 320 -Canton 44702
(614) 221-3377 .. **Readey**, James A '70 (Readey & P) -37 W Broad -Ste 420 -Columbus 43215 **Fx**:221-2236
(614) 466-7012 .. **Readey**, Mary Lynn '87 OH Schl Facilities Comm -10 W Broad -14th Fl -Columbus 43215 **Fx**:466-7749
(614) 469-3939 .. **Readler**, Chad A '97 %Jones D -325 John H McConnell Blvd -Ste 600 -Bx165017 -Columbus 43216 **Fx**:461-4198
(614) 462-5027 .. **Readler**, Jennifer Dutey '97 (Schottenstein Z&D) -250 West -Bx165020 -Columbus 43216 **Fx**:462-5135
(760) 322-8350 .. **Ready**, David H '93 City of Palm Springs -3200 E Tahquitz Canyon Way -Palm Springs, CA 92262
(216) 241-1000 .. **Ready**, John J '88 -310 W Lakeside Av -500 Cthse Sq -Cleveland 44113 **Fx**:241-1093
(216) 687-1311 .. **Reagan**, John J '96 (Reminger & R) -101 Prospect Av W -1400 Mdlnd Bldg -Cleveland 44115 **Fx**:687-1841
(614) 228-6400 .. **Real**, Mark J '77 KidsOhio.org -22 E Gay -Ste 600 -Columbus 43215
(860) 290-4070 .. **Reale**, Debra L '87 IRS/Ofc of Chief Cnsl -333 E River Dr -Ste 200 -East Hartford, CT 06108
(330) 373-1448 .. **Reale-Gottfried**, Elsa '92 Cmmnty Lgl Aid Srvcs,Inc -160 E Market -Ste 250 -Warren 44481 **Fx**:395-5227
(330) 689-2860 .. **Reali**, Brian A '98 Stow Law Dept -3760 Darrow Rd -Stow 44224 **Fx**:686-0219
(216) 443-7800 .. **Reali**, Colleen A '00 Cuyahoga Cnty Pros -1200 Ontario -8th Fl -Cleveland 44113 **Fx**:698-2270
(614) 470-8527 .. **Reall**, Christopher S '96 Bisys -3435 Stelzer Rd -Columbus 43219
(419) 342-4261 .. **Ream**, Jeffrey S '90 %McKown & M,LPA -10 Mansfld Av -Shelby 44875 **Fx**:347-5723
Reams, David A '84 -601 E Hudson Av -Madison Heights, MI 48071
(419) 666-2984 .. **Reams**, Frazier Jr. '55 -30120 Waterford Dr -Perrysburg 43551
(419) 537-1954 .. **Reardon**, Christine A '86 Kalniz I&F,LPA -5550 W Central Av -Toledo 43615 **Fx**:535-7732
(440) 286-9571 .. **Reardon**, James W '92 %Svete M&C Co,LPA -100 Parker Ct -Chardon 44024
(202) 273-1736 .. **Reardon**, Leigh A '82 NLRB -1099 14th NW -Washington, DC 20570
(937) 225-6070 .. **Reardon**, Melinda Barnett '04 Montgomery Cnty Ct of Cmn Pleas -41 N Perry -Bx972 -Dayton 45422
(440) 239-1109 .. **Reardon**, Michael E '93 M Reardon Co,LPA -7050 Engle Rd -Ste 100 -Middleburg Heights 44130
(330) 744-0247 .. **Reardon**, Timothy M '92 (Nadler N&B Co,LPA) -20 Fed Plz W -Ste 600 -Youngstown 44503 **Fx**:744-8690
(614) 221-4859 .. **Reasoner**, Willis Irl III '78 (Habash R&F,LLP) -471 E Broad -Ste 800 -Columbus 43215
(513) 721-0200 .. **Rebel**, John A '72 OfCnsl McKinney & N Co,LPA -15 E 8th -Cincinnati 45202 **Fx**:632-5898
(919) 466-5857 .. **Rebeor**, Daniel E '94 Spectrasite Communciations,Inc -100 Regency Forest Dr -Ste 400 -Cary, NC 27511
(614) 248-2517 .. **Reber**, Aaron J '97 JP Morgan -1111 Polaris Pkwy -MC OH1-1275 -Columbus 43240
(740) 387-5308 .. **Reber**, Frank K '73 -198 E Center -Bx1524 -Marion 43301
Reber, Susan G '91 -13942 Sheldon Rd -Brook Park 44142
(216) 566-5500 .. **Reblin**, Kelly L '97 %Thompson H LLP -127 Pub Sq -3900 Key Ctr -Cleveland 44114 **Fx**:566-5800
(513) 922-3200 .. **Rebold**, Peter M '68 (Haverkamp BR&R Co,LPA) -5856 Glenway Av -Cincinnati 45238 **Fx**:922-8096
(614) 253-9737 .. **Recchie**, Joseph J Jr. '82 (J Recchie & Co,LPA) -1349 E Broad -Columbus 43205
(804) 782-1593 .. **Recher**, Louis G '77 CSX Corp -901 E Cary -Richmond, VA 23219
(614) 221-1800 .. **Rechner**, Carl J Jr. '83 Continental Real Estate -150 E Broad -Columbus 43215
(216) 348-5400 .. **Rechner**, Matthew R '01 %McDonald H Co,LPA -600 Superior Av E -Ste 2100 -Cleveland 44114 **Fx**:348-5474
(304) 748-5850 .. **Recht**, Steven M '95 -3405 Main -Bx841 -Weirton, WV 26062
(614) 224-1222 .. **Recker**, Brice O '90 %Maguire & S,LLP -250 Civic Ctr Dr -Ste 200 -Columbus 43215 **Fx**:224-1236
(239) 642-4704 .. **Recker**, Frank R '81 (F Recker & Assoc Co,LPA) -267 N Collier Blvd -Ste 202 -Marco Island, FL 34145 **Fx**:642-5238
(614) 463-9441 .. **Reckless**, Walter W '69 OfCnsl Shumaker L&K,LLP -41 S High -Ste 2210 -Columbus 43215 **Fx**:463-1108
(937) 328-3741 .. **Reckley**, Kathryn A '86 City Pros -50 E Columbia -Springfield 45502 **Fx**:328-3744
(513) 852-6054 .. **Reckman**, Mark S '79 (Wood & L LLP) -600 Vine -Ste 2500 -Cincinnati 45202 **Fx**:852-6087
(513) 852-6019 .. **Reckman**, Robert F '48 OfCnsl Wood & L LLP -600 Vine -Ste 2500 -Cincinnati 45202 **Fx**:852-6087
(216) 522-3715 .. **Recko**, Nancy '78 NLRB -1240 E 9th -1695 Celebrezze Bldg -Cleveland 44199 **Fx**:522-2418
(419) 241-9000 .. **Rectenwald**, David J '86 (Shumaker L&K,LLP) -1000 Jackson -Toledo 43624 **Fx**:241-6894
(859) 371-1611 .. **Rectenwald**, Joseph A '94 %Rawlings & Assoc,PPLC -Bx908 -Florence, KY 41022
(513) 784-0357 .. **Rector**, Daniel G '84 -227 W 9th -Cincinnati 45202
(614) 224-6210 .. **Rector**, Neil K '83 (Rector & Assoc,Inc) -172 E State -Ste 305 -Columbus 43215
(614) 462-2219 .. **Rector**, Susan D '84 (Schottenstein Z&D) -250 West -Bx165020 -Columbus 43216 **Fx**:462-5135
(330) 492-3957 .. **Recupero**, James R '86 -4884 Dressler Rd NW -Canton 44718 **Fx**:492-7313
(513) 621-2100 .. **Redden**, Brian R '99 Beckman W&S LLC -120 E 4th -1200 Mercantile Ctr -Cincinnati 45202 **Fx**:621-0106
(937) 443-6833 .. **Redder**, Edward C '98 %Thompson H LLP -2000 Cthse Plz NE -Bx8801 -Dayton 45401 **Fx**:443-6635
(614) 462-3593 .. **Reddington**, William A '77 Franklin Cnty Probate Ct -373 S High -22nd Fl -Columbus 43215
(216) 587-2120 .. **Reddy**, Francis X Jr. '65 (Reddy G&M Co,LPA) -5306 Transportation Blvd -Garfield Heights 44125
(805) 447-3288 .. **Reddy**, Gade P '02 Amgen,Inc -One Amgen Ctr Dr -M/S 27-4-A -Thousand Oaks, CA 91320
(216) 587-2120 .. **Reddy Grau & Meek Co,LPA** -5306 Transportation Blvd -Garfield Heights 44125
(440) 933-8938 .. **Reddy**, James P Jr. '82 -680 Moore Rd -Ste 100 -Bx108 -Avon Lake 44012
(216) 781-5470 .. **Redeker**, John E '74 (Ziegler M&M LLP) -925 Euclid Av -2020 Huntngtn Bldg -Cleveland 44115 **Fx**:781-0714
(216) 621-5300 .. **Reder**, Henry I '79 (Buckingham D&B,LLP) -1375 E 9th -Ste 1700 -Cleveland 44114 **Fx**:621-5440
(937) 378-4151 .. **Reder**, Joseph M '02 Brown Cnty Pros -200 E Cherry -Georgetown 45121
(614) 645-7385 .. **Redick**, Glenn B '70 City Atty -90 W Broad -Columbus 43215
(330) 376-3572 .. **Redick**, Robert W '99 (Eshelman Lgl Grp) -263 Portage Trl Ext W -Cuyahoga Falls 44223 **Fx**:376-0199
(330) 453-0008 .. **Redinger**, Ivan L Jr. '85 (Redinger & M LLP) -116 Cleveland Av NW -Ste 418 -Canton 44702
(330) 972-6329 .. **Redle**, David A '80 Univ of Akron -College of Business -Finance Dept -Akron 44325
(330) 297-3850 .. **Redman**, Jennifer E '98 Portage Cnty Pros -466 S Chestnut -Ravenna 44266
(614) 336-3945 .. **Redman**, Timothy D '89 -7101 Wichita Ct -Dublin 43017
(614) 461-9300 .. **Redmon**, Ronald L '74 -520 S High -Ste 200 -Columbus 43215
(216) 522-4970 .. **Redmond**, Brenda '96 US Dept of Ed -660 Superior Av -Cleveland 44114
(740) 382-1121 .. **Redmond**, Dustin J Jr. '77 -284 S State -Marion 43302
(440) 357-6111 .. **Redmond**, Edward C '57 (Redmond W&M) -174 N St Clair -Painesville 44077
(216) 566-5820 .. **Redmond**, Hope E '01 %Thompson H LLP -127 Pub Sq -3900 Key Ctr -Cleveland 44114 **Fx**:566-5800
(216) 443-8581 .. **Redmond**, Ian M '02 Cuyahoga Cnty Ct Cmmn Pleas -1200 Ontario -Justice Ctr 11th Fl -Cleveland 44113
(440) 357-6111 .. **Redmond Walker & Murray** -174 N St Clair -Painesville 44077
(440) 893-0338 .. **Redmond**, William K '83 W Redmond Co LPA -16700 Brigadoon Dr -Chagrin Falls 44023
(937) 865-6800 .. **Reece**, Barbara W '96 Lexis/Nexis -Bx933 -Dayton 45401
(330) 255-0037 .. **Reece**, John C '89 Marshall DWC&G -120 E Mill -Ste 240 -Akron 44308 **Fx**:255-0040
(330) 643-2250 .. **Reece**, John W '61 Dist Ct of Appeals -161 S High -Akron 44308
(216) 621-0200 .. **Reece**, Lora M '02 %Baker & H LLP -1900 E 9th -Ste 3200 -Cleveland 44114 **Fx**:696-0740
(330) 865-9635 .. **Reece**, Richard A Jr. '03 (Bednarski R&L) -159 S Main -Ste 300 -Akron 44308
(740) 345-3431 .. **Reed**, Brian C '00 %Reese PD&M,PLL -36 N 2nd -Bx919 -Newark 43058 **Fx**:349-5116
(330) 745-2175 .. **Reed**, Carl L '66 OfCnsl Lombardi HHC&E -2745 Nesbitt Av -Akron 44319
(740) 687-1405 .. **Reed**, Charles E '51 -450 Mound -Lancaster 43130
(319) 292-6379 .. **Reed**, Cory J '95 John Deere Co -Bx8000 -Waterloo, IA 50704
(937) 223-8177 .. **Reed**, David N '91 (Coolidge WW&L) -33 W 1st -Ste 600 -Dayton 45402 **Fx**:223-6705
(216) 566-8200 .. **Reed**, David T '74 %Seeley S&E Co LPA -600 Superior Av E -800 Bank One Ctr -Cleveland 44114 **Fx**:566-0213
(740) 223-4060 .. **Reed**, David T '94 Marion Cnty Fam Crt -220 W Center -Marion 43302
(502) 580-2766 .. **Reed**, Donald G '74 Humann,Inc -500 W Main -Louisville, KY 40202
(614) 223-9300 .. **Reed**, Frank J Jr. '91 OfCnsl Benesch FC&A LLP -88 E Broad -Ste 900 -Columbus 43215 **Fx**:223-9330
(614) 734-2717 .. **Reed**, Frederick R '73 Dvlpmnt Specialists,Inc -6375 Riverside Dr -Ste 200 -Dublin 43017
(513) 887-3592 .. **Reed**, Harold M '01 Butler Cnty Cmn Pleas Ct -315 High -Hamilton 45011
(614) 466-7014 .. **Reed**, Heather S '98 Pub Safety -1970 W Broad -Columbus 43223 **Fx**:752-6063

(216) 928-2200 ..**Reed,** James E '01 Sutter OM&F -1301 E 9th -3600 Erievw Twr -Cleveland 44114 **Fx:**928-4400

(330) 375-2285 ..**Reed,** James K '88 Akron Mun Ct -217 S High -Akron 44308

(330) 762-2060 ..**Reed,** Joel D '96 -333 S Main -Ste 701 -Akron 44308 **Fx:**762-9446

(937) 449-6400 ..**Reed,** John D '97 %Dinsmore & S LLP -1 S Main -Ste 1300 One Dayton Centre -Dayton 45402 **Fx:**449-6405

(614) 221-5839 ..**Reed,** Joseph D '83 -713 S Front -Columbus 43206

(330) 364-8811 ..**Reed,** Joy E '77 Tuscarawas Cnty Prob/Juv Ct -101 E High Av -#103 -New Philadelphia 44663

(513) 943-7100 ..**Reed,** Kate E '99 Midland Co -7000 Mdlnd Blvd -Amelia 45102

(419) 530-3332 ..**Reed,** Kathleen M '93 Univ of Toledo -2801 W Bancroft -MS 400, Ofc FA124 -Toledo 43606 **Fx:**530-6205

(606) 331-4443 ..**Reed,** Kenneth R '85 -281 Buttermilk Pike -Fort Mitchell, KY 41017

(513) 946-9471 ..**Reed,** Kevin A '94 Hamilton Cnty Juv Ct -800 Bway -Cincinnati 45202 **Fx:**946-9217

(740) 474-5437 ..**Reed,** Kristen S '89 Job & Fam Srvcs -Bx439 -Circleville 43113

(419) 568-5751 ..**Reed,** Kristine H '96 %BF Yale & Assoc,LPA -102 W Wapakoneta -Bx100 -Waynesfield 45896

(330) 830-1718 ..**Reed,** Malynda M '97 Massillon Law Dept -2 James Duncan Plz -Massillon 44646 **Fx:**833-7144

(513) 946-9200 ..**Reed,** Mark H '91 Hamilton Cnty Juv Ct -800 Bway -Cincinnati 45202 **Fx:**946-9217

(513) 618-6732 ..**Reed,** Mark W '98 Intelliseek -1128 Main -Cincinnati 45210

(216) 522-0800 ..**Reed Mazanec & Wheeler,Ltd** -1801 E 9th -Cleveland 44114

(513) 381-4700 ..**Reed,** Michael G '81 (Porter WM&A LLP) -250 E 5th -Ste 2200 -Cincinnati 45202 **Fx:**421-0991

(614) 365-2700 ..**Reed,** Michael R '94 (Squire S&D LLP) -41 S High -1300 Huntngtn Ctr -Columbus 43215 **Fx:**365-2499

(330) 376-5300 ..**Reed,** Orville L '73 (Buckingham D&B,LLP) -50 S Main -Bx1500 -Akron 44309 **Fx:**258-6559

(216) 522-0800 ..**Reed,** Robert C Jr. '75 (Reed M&W,Ltd) -1801 E 9th -Cleveland 44114

(513) 721-7522 ..**Reed,** Robert F '64 -22 W 9th -Cincinnati 45202

(937) 464-5861 ..**Reed,** Robert G Jr. '60 -230 W Main -Bx337 -Belle Center 43310

(614) 443-9401 ..**Reed,** Robert R '52 (R Reed Co,LPA) -52 W Whittier -Columbus 43206

(937) 445-2109 ..**Reed,** Shelley A '80 NCR Corp -1700 S Patterson Blvd -WHQ - 5E -Dayton 45479

(614) 469-2455 ..**Reed,** Steven G '75 USDA -200 N High -Rm 209 -Columbus 43215

(740) 587-0733 ..**Reed,** Troy A '93 -3860 Raccoon Valley Rd -Alexandria 43001

(216) 231-7936 ..**Reed,** Tyrone E '76 -11811 Shaker Blvd -Ste 420 -Cleveland 44120

(740) 282-3019 ..**Reed,** William E II '76 -2321 Kragel Rd -Richmond 43944

(614) 888-2178 ..**Reeder,** Donald R '81 -Bx174 -Powell 43065

(216) 363-6033 ..**Reeder,** Harold C Jr. '82 -1370 Ontario -2000 Standard Bldg -Cleveland 44113

(817) 972-2935 ..**Reeder,** Linda M '95 NLRB -819 Taylor -Rm 8A24 Region 16 -Fort Worth, TX 76102

(212) 558-4000 ..**Reeder,** Robert W III '85 (Sullivan & C LLP) -125 Broad -New York, NY 10004 **Fx:**558-3588

(614) 785-1301 ..**Reedus,** Benita D '86 (B Reedus Co LPA) -2021 E Dublin Granvll Rd -Ste 171 -Columbus 43229

(614) 540-4000 ..**Reedy,** Hollie F '95 OH Schl Brds Assn -8050 N High -Ste 100 -Columbus 43235

(202) 616-0584 ..**Reedy,** Patricia J '87 DOJ -1301 NY Av NW -Rm 955 -Washington, DC 20005

(330) 643-2942 ..**Rees,** Christine '00 Summit Cnty Juv Ct -650 Dan -Akron 44310

(614) 488-8441 ..**Rees,** William J '81 -1332 Inglis Av -Columbus 43212

(440) 576-8120 ..**Reese,** Anne M '85 Legal Aid -121 E Walnut -Jefferson 44047 **Fx:**576-3021

..**Reese,** Brandon K '00 -(Address Unavailable)

(330) 643-2788 ..**Reese,** Holly E '99 Summit Cnty Pros-Crim -53 Univ Av -7th Fl -Akron 44308 **Fx:**643-8277

(330) 489-3395 ..**Reese,** Jason P '97 Pros -218 Cleveland Av SW -Bx24218 -Canton 44702

(740) 345-3431 ..**Reese,** John G '52 (Reese PD&M,PLL) -36 N 2nd -Bx919 -Newark 43058 **Fx:**349-5116

(513) 852-3497 ..**Reese,** Mary Anne '90 Atty Gen -441 Vine -1600 Carew Twr -Cincinnati 45202 **Fx:**852-3484

(216) 737-0000 ..**Reese,** Olan R '84 (Reese & K) -1375 E 9th -Ste 610 -Cleveland 44114

(740) 345-3431 ..**Reese Pyle Drake & Meyer,PLL** -36 N 2nd -Bx919 -Newark 43058 **Fx:**349-5116

..**Reese,** Richard C '03 -(Address Unavailable)

(419) 227-5858 ..**Reese,** Richard T '81 (Baran PTF&T Co,LPA) -121 W High -Ste 905 -Bx568 -Lima 45802 **Fx:**227-4569

(330) 491-9999 ..**Reese,** Robert G '93 -4450 Belden Vllg NW -Ste 704 -Canton 44718

(216) 689-3507 ..**Reese,** Veronica M '84 KeyBank NA -127 Pub Sq -Probate Administrator -Cleveland 44114

(614) 547-0370 ..**Reeve,** Gary A '95 (Reeve & W) -623 Hight -Worthington 43085

(513) 919-9429 ..**Reeve,** Kevin S '97 K Reeve Co,LPA -7804 Gail Dr -Cincinnati 45236

(216) 953-2856 ..**Reeve,** Mary E '82 Fed Reserve Bank -Bx6387 -Cleveland 44101

(216) 771-5511 ..**Reeve & Watts** -75 Pub Sq -Ste 1300 -Cleveland 44113

(614) 547-0370 ..**Reeve & Watts** -623 Hight -Worthington 43085

(440) 967-6565 ..**Reeves,** Gayle A '84 -1607 State Rd -Ste 103 -Vermilion 44089

(614) 716-2956 ..**Reeves,** James L '78 Amer Elec Pwr Co -1 Riverside Plz -Columbus 43215

(419) 784-1414 ..**Reeves,** John D '75 Defiance Clinic -1400 E 2nd -Defiance 43512

(330) 721-0000 ..**Reeves,** Nancy L '98 %Walker & J,LPA -231 S Bway -Medina 44256 **Fx:**722-6446

(419) 228-2122 ..**Reeves,** Randy L '80 (R Reeves Co,LPA) -973 W North -Lima 45805 **Fx:**222-6718

(330) 673-4515 ..**Reeves,** Troy A '98 -132 S Water -Kent 44240

(419) 435-1886 ..**Reffner,** Carol L '87 (Guernsey & G) -142 W Tiffin -Bx310 -Fostoria 44830 **Fx:**435-8924

(330) 535-5711 ..**Reffner,** Robert P '77 (Brouse M) -106 S Main -500 First Natl Twr -Akron 44308 **Fx:**253-8601

(330) 253-2729 ..**Regal,** Edwin M '70 (Koch & R) -120 E Mill -Ste 405 -Akron 44308

(330) 376-2700 ..**Regallis,** Caroline '02 %Roetzel & A,LPA -222 S Main -Akron 44308 **Fx:**376-4577

(740) 286-3601 ..**Regan,** Christopher J '87 Magistrate -226 E Main -Ct of Cmmn Pleas -Jackson 45640 **Fx:**286-5203

(304) 242-8410 ..**Regan,** Christopher J '01 Bordas & B,PLLC -1358 Natl Rd -Wheeling, WV 26003

(513) 241-3100 ..**Regan,** Robyn M '02 %Lerner S&R -120 E 4th -8th Fl -Cincinnati 45202

(330) 649-9102 ..**Regas & Haag, Ltd** -3969 Convenience Cir NW -Ste 101 -Canton 44718

(216) 621-2034 ..**Regas,** Jennifer H '92 %Margolius M & Assoc,LPA -55 Pub Sq -Ste 1100 -Cleveland 44113 **Fx:**621-1908

(330) 649-9102 ..**Regas,** John S '93 (Regas & H,Ltd) -3969 Convenience Cir NW -Ste 101 -Canton 44718

(330) 649-9102 ..**Regas,** Sharon S '93 OfCnsl Regas & H,Ltd -3969 Convenience Cir NW -Ste 101 -Canton 44718

(330) 875-5487 ..**Regas,** Steve G '64 -8131 Ravenna NE -Louisville 44641

(216) 443-7800 ..**Regas,** Tracy Allan '96 %Cuyahoga Cnty Pros -1200 Ontario -8th Fl -Cleveland 44113 **Fx:**698-2270

(513) 263-4823 ..**Regberg,** Neil S '76 IRS -Bx2026 -Cincinnati 45201 **Fx:**263-4800

(419) 354-6285 ..**Reger,** Matthew L '93 City Prosecutor Ofc -711 S Dunbrdg -Bx267 -Bowling Green 43402

(330) 793-2698 ..**Regginello,** John A '99 -60 Wstchsr Dr -Ste 1 -Austintown 44515

(330) 376-1242 ..**Reginelli,** Arthur M '95 Renner KGBT&W,LPA -106 S Main -4th Fl First Natl Twr -Akron 44308 **Fx:**376-9646

(419) 241-6000 ..**Regnier,** Michael W '93 (Eastman & S Ltd) -1 Seagate -24th Fl -Bx10032 -Toledo 43699 **Fx:**247-1777

(847) 272-8800 ..**Rego,** Charles A '96 Cnsl Underwriters Lab -333 Pfingsten Rd -Leg Dept -Northbrook, IL 60062

(440) 356-0062 ..**Rego Cullen & Hagan Co,LPA** -21270 Lorain Rd -Fairview Park 44126

(216) 586-3939 ..**Rego,** John A '88 (Jones D) -901 Lakeside Av -Cleveland 44114 **Fx:**579-0212

(440) 356-0062 ..**Rego,** Lucian C '71 (Rego C&H Co,LPA) -21270 Lorain Rd -Fairview Park 44126

(614) 837-3980 ..**Regoli,** Holly P '93 O Fields II -660 Hill Rd N -Bx184 -Pickerington 43147

(804) 819-2794 ..**Regulinski,** Michael C '86 Dominion Rsrcs Srvcs,Inc -120 Treder -Bx25632 -Richmond, VA 23261

(804) 267-8130 ..**Rehak,** Linda J '82 LandAmerica Exchg Co -101 Gtwy Centre Pkwy -6th Fl -Richmond, VA 23235

(513) 569-6805 ..**Rehbock,** Betty J '80 Trihealth Inc -619 Oak -Cincinnati 45206

(330) 345-7055 ..**Rehm,** Ronald L '79 -2922 Cleveland Rd -Wooster 44691

(513) 621-0267 ..**Rehme,** Thomas F '54 Waite SB&C -1 W 4th -1513 4th & Vine Twr -Cincinnati 45202

(440) 871-5072 ..**Rehor,** Daniel J '64 -3673 Prnctn Pl -Westlake 44145

(216) 696-6454 ..**Rehor,** Dennis G '94 -55 Pub Sq -Ste 930 -Cleveland 44113

(614) 221-0002 ..**Reibel,** Linda L '96 -39 Orchrd Dr -Worthington 43085

(513) 762-8215 ..**Reiber,** Kurt L '84 Keybank Natl Assoc -525 Vine -6th Fl/OH 18-17-0610 -Cincinnati 45202

(937) 322-0891 ..**Reich,** Barry P '70 (Cole AH&D) -333 N Limestone -Bx1687 -Springfield 45501 **Fx:**322-9931

(330) 758-2146 ..**Reich,** Jerry '55 -7120 Harrngtn Av -Youngstown 44512

(212) 891-7520 ..**Reich,** Stuart J '94 %Fragomen DB&L,PC -515 Mad Av -13th Fl -New York, NY 10022

(614) 766-9100 ..**Reich-Bruce,** Sara A '97 OH Auto Dealers Assn -655 Metro Pl S -Ste 270 -Dublin 43017

(216) 831-0042 ..**Reichard,** Jenifere M '03 %Meyers RF&L LPA -28601 Chagrin Blvd -Ste 500 -Cleveland 44122 **Fx:**831-0542

(440) 899-6776 ..**Reichard,** William E '68 (WE Reichard,LPA) -25109 Detroit Rd -Ste 300 -Westlake 44145

(216) 241-6930 ..**Reichek,** Edward R '57 -75 Pub Sq -Ste 1225 -Cleveland 44113 **Fx:**241-4279

(614) 462-3555 ..**Reichel,** Jeffrey L '89 Franklin Cnty Pros -373 S High -Columbus 43215

(614) 486-4311 ..**Reichelderfer,** Thomas S '99 EACA -2615 Chester Rd -Columbus 43211

(216) 431-4500 ..**Reichenbach,** Dorothy F '75 Cuyahoga Cnty Pros -3955 Euclid Av -Jane Edna Hunter Bldg -Cleveland 44115 **Fx:**431-4113

(419) 529-8300 ..**Reichenbach,** Gregory S '04 -3 N Main -Ste 800 -Mansfield 44902

(614) 228-1240 ..**Reichenbach,** Seth T '93 -35 E Lvngstn Av -Columbus 43215 **Fx:**228-6680

(513) 381-4700 ..**Reichert,** David '54 (Porter WM&A LLP) -250 E 5th -Ste 2200 -Cincinnati 45202 **Fx:**421-0991

(513) 241-2248 ..**Reichert,** James A '73 -14 Garfld Pl -Cincinnati 45202

(614) 466-7447 ..**Reichley,** John P '90 Atty Gen -150 E Gay -Columbus 43215

(614) 227-2000 ..**Reichwein,** Diane C '83 (Porter WM&A LLP) -41 S High -Columbus 43215 **Fx:**227-2100

(216) 687-1311 ..**Reid,** Christine S '93 (Reminger & R) -101 Prospect Av W -1400 Mdlnd Bldg -Cleveland 44115 **Fx:**687-1841

(614) 771-2785 ..**Reid,** David W '94 -2679 Willow Glen Rd -Hilliard 43026

(440) 998-2628 ..**Reid,** Dennis M '73 Ashtabula Cnty Pub Def -4817 State Rd -Ste 202 -Ashtabula 44004 **Fx:**998-2972

(216) 443-9000 ..**Reid,** Lisa A '88 OfCnsl Porter WM&A LLP -925 Euclid Av -Ste 1700 -Cleveland 44115 **Fx:**443-9011

(937) 225-5706 ..**Reid,** Lorine M '73 -531 Belmonte Pk N -#109 -Dayton 45405

(330) 375-2084 ..**Reid,** Margaret K '92 %City Planning Dept -166 S High -4th Fl -Akron 44308

(937) 426-5962 ..**Reid,** Marilyn J '66 -3866 Indn Ripple Rd -Beavercreek 45440

(216) 861-3086 ..**Reid Marshall & Wargo** -55 Pub Sq -Ste 2010 -Cleveland 44113 **Fx:**861-4409

..**Reid,** Mary E '90 -(Address Unavailable)

(614) 227-8812 ..**Reid,** Nelson M '97 (Bricker & E LLP) -100 S 3rd -Columbus 43215 **Fx:**227-2390

(937) 461-9400 ..**Reid,** Phillip A '79 -10 W Monument Av -Dayton 45402

(513) 977-8200 ..**Reid,** Robert J '93 (Dinsmore & S LLP) -255 E 5th -Ste 1900 -Cincinnati 45202 **Fx:**977-8141

(216) 787-3666 ..**Reid,** Sandra B '77 Industrial Commssn of OH -615 Superior Av NW -Cleveland 44113 **Fx:**787-3483

(440) 285-2222 ..**Reid,** Stacey '02 Geauga Cnty Pros -231 Main -Cthse Annx -Chardon 44024 **Fx:**286-4357

(216) 861-3086 ..**Reid,** Timothy T '71 (Reid M&W) -55 Pub Sq -Ste 2010 -Cleveland 44113 **Fx:**861-4409

(330) 744-5211 ..**Reid,** Wayne P '96 Roth BRS&L,LPA -100 Fed Plz E -Ste 600 -Youngstown 44503 **Fx:**744-3184

(937) 331-9227 ..**Reid**, Worrell A '92 -120 W 2nd -Ste 1717 -Dayton 45402

(330) 929-0507 ..**Reidy**, Jerome G '74 -234 Portage Trl -Cuyahoga Falls 44221

(216) 781-5470 ..**Reidy**, John J Jr. '57 OfCnsl Ziegler M&M LLP -925 Euclid Av
-2020 Huntngtn Bldg -Cleveland 44115 **Fx:**781-0714

(614) 462-2207 ..**Reidy**, Joseph M '85 (Schottenstein Z&D) -250 West -Bx165020
-Columbus 43216 **Fx:**462-5135

(440) 838-8800 ..**Reidy**, Michael J '78 Millisor & N Co,LPA -9150 S Hills Blvd
-Ste 300 -Cleveland 44147 **Fx:**838-8805

(740) 322-5137 ..**Reidy**, Thomas A '78 Longaberger Co -1500 E Main -Bx3400
-Newark 43055

(216) 781-5245 ..**Reiffer**, Erin L '04 %Berkman GM&D -55 Pub Sq -2121
The Illuminating Bldg -Cleveland 44113 **Fx:**781-8207

Reifin, Melvin H '62 -5955 McPicken Dr -Milford 45150

(419) 843-2001 ..**Reight**, Rachel M '04 Gallon & T Co,LPA -3516 Granite Cir
-Bx352018 -Toledo 43635 **Fx:**843-6665

(216) 622-8200 ..**Reil**, Mary M '82 (Calfee H&G LLP) -800 Superior Av -Ste 1400
-Cleveland 44114 **Fx:**241-0816

(937) 886-1151 ..**Reiling**, Richard B '96 -66 Remick Blvd -Springboro 45066

(330) 972-6197 ..**Reilly**, Elizabeth A '78 Univ of Akron Law Schl -LAW 136J
-Akron 44325

(216) 368-4286 ..**Reilly**, John J '89 Case Western Reserve Univ -10900 Euclid Blvd
-Cleveland 44106

(614) 466-4395 ..**Reilly**, Stephen A '75 Atty Gen -150 E Gay -Columbus 43215
Fx:644-8764

(330) 861-7193 ..**Reilly**, Susan K '03 Barberton Mun Ct -576 W Park Av -205
-Barberton 44203

(513) 381-2838 ..**Reilly**, Timothy P '78 (Taft S&H LLP) -425 Walnut -Ste 1800
-Cincinnati 45202 **Fx:**381-0205

(912) 267-2722 ..**Reim**, Jeffrey E '92 Bureau of Customs & Border Protection
-1131 Chapel Xing Rd -Townhse 374, FLETC -Glynco, GA 31524

(614) 225-9000 ..**Reim**, Sandee E '98 Garvin & H,LLC -181 E Lvngstn Av
-Columbus 43215 **Fx:**225-9080

(330) 425-4201 ..**Reimer**, Dennis '68 -2450 Edison Blvd -Twinsburg 44087

(330) 425-4201 ..**Reimer Lorber & Arnovitz Co, LPA** -2450 Edison Blvd -Bx968
-Twinsburg 44087 **Fx:**487-0923

(216) 687-0400 ..**Rein**, Thomas A '89 -526 Superior Av E -Ste 930
-Cleveland 44114

(419) 241-6000 ..**Reinbolt**, Steven D '85 (Eastman & S Ltd) -1 Seagate -24th Fl
-Bx10032 -Toledo 43699 **Fx:**247-1777

(330) 451-2040 ..**Reiners**, Paul R '78 -610 Market Av N -Canton 44702

Reinhard, Ann K '78 -(Address Unavailable)

(312) 394-3604 ..**Reinhard**, Constance W '77 Exelon Business Srvcs Co
-10 S Dearborn -35th Fl -Bx805379 -Chicago, IL 60680

(614) 621-1500 ..**Reinhard**, Daniel A '02 %Calfee H&G LLP -21 E State
-1100 Fifth Third Ctr -Columbus 43215 **Fx:**621-0010

(614) 228-7771 ..**Reinhart**, Harry R '78 -400 S 5th -Ste 202 -Columbus 43215
Fx:221-8601

(740) 833-2690 ..**Reinhart**, James G '03 %Delaware Cnty Pros -140 N Sandusky
-3rd Fl -Delaware 43015

(216) 522-5404 ..**Reinhart**, Lulita '97 Dept of Defense -1240 E 9th
-Rm 1429 Code L -Cleveland 44199

(419) 734-1723 ..**Reinheimer**, Frank W '65 (Reinheimer & R) -208 Madison -Bx638
-Port Clinton 43452

(419) 734-1723 ..**Reinheimer**, James L '92 Reinheimer & R -208 Madison -Bx638
-Port Clinton 43452

(248) 546-6784 ..**Reinhold**, Lawrence G '79 (L Reinhold,PC) -25211 E Roycourt
-Huntington Woods, MI 48070 **Fx:**544-9916

Reinicke, Daniel E '75 -880 Algonkin Trl -Lima 45805

(419) 246-5757 ..**Reinker**, Lisa M '03 %Anspach M&N,LLP -300 Mad Av -Ste 1600
-Toledo 43604 **Fx:**321-6979

(216) 771-2533 ..**Reinker**, Robb F '77 OfCnsl Ferry Cap & Set Screw Co
-2151 Scranton Rd -Cleveland 44113

(216) 875-2767 ..**Reinker**, Susan M '79 %Bonezzi SM&P Co LPA -526 Superior Av
-Ste 1400 -Cleveland 44114 **Fx:**875-1570

(614) 728-7171 ..**Reinoehl**, Erika M '00 State Auditor Ofc -88 E Broad -5th Fl
-Bx1140 -Columbus 43216

(216) 830-9000 ..**Reinshagen**, Amy L '04 %Berger & Z Co,LPA -614 W Superior Av
-Ste 1425 Rckflfl Bldg -Cleveland 44113 **Fx:**830-4200

(614) 801-2771 ..**Reis**, Allen J '76 (Weltman W&R Co,LPA) -175 S 3rd -Ste 900
-Columbus 43215 **Fx:**222-2193

(614) 466-6696 ..**Reis**, Kevin J '77 Atty Gen -150 E Gay -Columbus 43215
Fx:752-2538

(513) 241-0400 ..**Reis**, Mark W '83 (Aronoff R&H Co,LPA) -425 Walnut -Ste 2400
-Cincinnati 45202 **Fx:**241-2877

(330) 451-7200 ..**Reisch**, Steven A '97 Stark Cnty Pub Def -200 W Tuscarawas
-Ste 200 -Canton 44702

(513) 381-6810 ..**Reisenfeld**, Bradley A '90 %Reisenfeld & Assoc -2355 Auburn Av
-Cincinnati 45219 **Fx:**381-0255

(513) 381-6810 ..**Reisenfeld**, Sylvan P '60 (Reisenfeld & Assoc) -2355 Auburn Av
-Cincinnati 45219 **Fx:**381-0255

(419) 242-9501 ..**Reiser**, George K '87 Reiser & R -Bx2952 -Toledo 43606

(419) 244-8336 ..**Reiser**, Rosalind A '86 %Gressley K&P -608 Mad Av -Ste 930
-Toledo 43604 **Fx:**244-1914

(513) 352-4716 ..**Reising**, Melanie J '86 Law Dept -801 Plum -Rm 214
-Cincinnati 45202 **Fx:**352-1515

(614) 228-6888 ..**Reisinger**, Lori L '00 %Havens W LLC -141 E Town -Ste 200
-Columbus 43215 **Fx:**228-6878

(561) 585-0439 ..**Reisman**, Bernard E '53 -2600 S Ocean Blvd
-Palm Beach, FL 33480 **Fx:**585-0439

(419) 327-6313 ..**Reisner**, John R '81 Sky Fin Grp,Inc -221 S Church
-Bowling Green 43402

(513) 579-5688 ..**Reiss**, Anthony E '94 Fifth 3rd Bank -38 Fountain Sq Plz
-Cincinnati 45263

(614) 293-8446 ..**Reissland**, Gaibrelle M '89 %OSU Hsptls -410 W 10th Av
-151 Doan Hall -Columbus 43210

(937) 255-5270 ..**Reist**, Robert M '86 AFMCLO/JAN -1864 4th -Rm 130 -Wright
Patterson AFB 45433

(614) 443-7455 ..**Reister**, Frederick T '72 (Merullo R&S Co,LPA) -772 S Front
-Columbus 43206

(513) 863-6700 ..**Reister**, John J '78 (Millikin & F) -6 S 2nd -6th Fl -Bx598 -Hamilton
45012 **Fx:**863-0031

(614) 464-6400 ..**Reisz**, Lisa Pierce '92 (Vorys SS&P LLP) -52 E Gay -Bx1008
-Columbus 43216 **Fx:**464-6350

(330) 336-6405 ..**Reiter**, Carol C '80 Medina Cnty Cmn Pleas Ct -97 Pub Sq
-Medina 44256

(317) 383-2271 ..**Reiter**, Gary J '88 Fifth Third Bank -251 N Illinois -Ste 1200
-Indianapolis, IN 46204

(614) 464-6400 ..**Reitler**, Angela K '03 %Vorys SS&P LLP -52 E Gay -Bx1008
-Columbus 43216 **Fx:**464-6350

(440) 423-0792 ..**Reitman**, Robert S '58 Riverbend Advisors -2087 Chagrin Rvr Rd
-Gates Mills 44040

(740) 592-3208 ..**Reitmeier**, George J '95 Athens Cnty Pros -Athens Cnty Cthse
-Athens 45701 **Fx:**592-3291

(937) 227-3700 ..**Reitz**, Andrew J '03 %Faruki I&C PLL -10 N Ludlow
-500 Cthse Plz SW -Dayton 45402 **Fx:**227-3717

(513) 621-6464 ..**Reitz**, Daniel E '01 %Graydon H&R LLP -511 Walnut
-1900 Fifth Third Ctr -Cincinnati 45202 **Fx:**651-3836

(614) 466-2580 ..**Reitz**, Lili C '90 State Dental Brd -77 S High -18th Fl
-Columbus 43266

(614) 462-5425 ..**Reitz**, Mark R '96 %Kegler BH&R -65 E State -Ste 1800
-Columbus 43215 **Fx:**464-2634

(412) 456-5404 ..**Reitz**, Ronald E '88 (Swartz C LLP) -600 Grant
-Ste 4750 US Steel Twr -Pittsburgh, PA 15219 **Fx:**471-1106

(614) 221-7548 ..**Reitz**, Thomas L '97 %Larrimer & L -165 N High -Columbus 43206
Fx:221-8659

(330) 562-3156 ..**Reitz**, Thomas R '88 (Christley H&P) -215 W Garfld -Ste 230
-Aurora 44202 **Fx:**562-9540

(512) 251-5100 ..**Reitzel**, Michael H '77 Zebra Imaging -Bx81247 -Austin, TX 78708

(330) 864-7030 ..**Reitzes**, Jeffrey H '69 CCI Fin Grp,Inc -1653 Merriman Rd
-Ste 210 -Akron 44313

(216) 664-4918 ..**Reitzloff**, Barbara A '86 Cleveland Mun Ct -1200 Ontario -13th Fl
-Cleveland 44113

(480) 481-4007 ..**Rekate**, Mary W '81 Scottsdale Hlthcr Corp -3621 Wells Fargo Av
-Scottsdale, AZ 85251

(216) 479-8500 ..**Rekstis**, W Jack III '72 (Squire S&D LLP) -127 Pub Sq
-4900 Key Twr -Cleveland 44114 **Fx:**479-8780

(419) 248-6546 ..**Relation**, Alfred J '83 Owens Corning -1 Owens Corning Pkwy
-Leg Dept -Toledo 43659

(330) 225-5025 ..**Relic**, Grant D '78 (G Relic Co,LPA) -3511 Ctr Rd -#BD
-Brunswick 44212

(216) 991-3646 ..**Relic**, Marianne D '78 -3010 W Belvoir Oval
-Shaker Heights 44122

(513) 946-9000 ..**Rellahan**, Jacqueline J '90 Hamilton Cnty Juv Ct -800 Bway
-Cincinnati 45202 **Fx:**946-9217

(216) 514-4981 ..**Relman**, Craig W '90 (CW Relman Co,LPA) -23875 Commerce Pk
-Ste 105 -Beachwood 44122

(513) 241-2324 ..**Remaklus**, Theodore R '93 (Wood H&E LLP) -441 Vine -Ste 2700
-Cincinnati 45202 **Fx:**421-7269

(301) 654-6602 ..**Rembert**, LaToya D '04 Council for Mrktng & Opinion Res
-7475 Wscnsn Av -Ste 200 -Bethesda, MD 20814

(513) 723-4030 ..**Remesnitsky**, Jackie R '04 %Vorys SS&P LLP -221 E 4th
-Ste 2000 Atrium Two -Bx0236 -Cincinnati 45201 **Fx:**723-4056

(513) 721-1311 ..**Reminger & Reminger** -7 W 7th -Ste 1990 -Cincinnati 45202
Fx:721-2553

(614) 461-1311 ..**Reminger & Reminger** -65 E State -4th Fl Cptl Sq Ofc Bldg
-Columbus 43215 **Fx:**232-2410

(419) 609-1311 ..**Reminger & Reminger** -237 W Wshngtn Row -2nd Fl
-Sandusky 44870 **Fx:**626-4805

(419) 254-1311 ..**Reminger & Reminger** -405 Mad Av -Ste 2300 -Toledo 43604
Fx:243-7830

(330) 375-1311 ..**Reminger & Reminger** -80 S Summit -200 Courtyard Sq
-Akron 44308 **Fx:**375-9075

(330) 744-1311 ..**Reminger & Reminger** -11 Fed Plz Central -Ste 300
-Youngstown 44503 **Fx:**744-7500

(216) 687-1311 ..**Reminger & Reminger** -101 Prospect Av W -1400 Mdlnd Bldg
-Cleveland 44115 **Fx:**687-1841

(216) 687-1311 ..**Reminger**, Richard T '57 Reminger & R -101 Prospect Av W
-1400 Mdlnd Bldg -Cleveland 44115 **Fx:**687-1841

(216) 621-0150 ..**Remington**, Royce R '88 (Hahn L&P LLP)
-3300 BP Twr/200 Pub Sq -Ste 3300 -Cleveland 44114
Fx:241-2824

(216) 834-0400 ..**Remmert**, Danae K '03 %G Loucas Co,LPA
-6060 Rockside Wd Blvd -Ste 250 -Cleveland 44131 **Fx:**834-0404

(419) 755-9659 ..**Remy**, David L '75 Law Dir Ofc -30 N Diamond -Mansfield 44902

(330) 376-3300 ..**Rench**, James L '74 Stark & K Co,LPA -76 S Main -Ste 1512
-Akron 44308 **Fx:**376-6237

(614) 469-7404 ..**Rendar**, Gail M '92 SSA-OHA, Columbus -280 N High -3rd Fl
-Columbus 43215

(412) 281-5431 ..**Rende**, Bruce E '99 (Robb L&M) -2300 One Mellon Bk Ctr
-Pittsburgh, PA 15219

(216) 696-6700 ..**Rendon**, Carole O '99 (Kushner & R Co,LPA) -200 Pub Sq
-Ste 2860 BP Twr -Cleveland 44114 **Fx:**696-6772

(419) 627-0400 ..**Rengel**, D Jeffery '82 -421 Jackson -Sandusky 44870

(614) 466-7788 ..**Renick**, Anderson M III '97 OH Ct of Claims -65 E State -Ste 1100
-Columbus 43215

(614) 469-3939 ..**Renker**, Kerry M '02 %Jones D -325 John H McConnell Blvd
-Ste 600 -Bx165017 -Columbus 43216 **Fx:**461-4198

(216) 371-7632 ..**Renkert**, Richard C '50 -2722 Southington Rd -Cleveland 44120

(614) 469-3284 ..**Renne**, Michael A '87 Thompson H LLP -10 W Broad -Ste 700
-Columbus 43215 **Fx:**469-3361

(513) 932-5792 ..**Renneker**, Erin C '03 %H Jarnicki & Assoc -576 Mound Ct -Ste B
-Lebanon 45036

(330) 650-0452 ..**Renner**, Jack L '60 -250 Aurora -Hudson 44236

(216) 621-1113 ..**Renner**, John W '54 (Renner OB&S,LLP) -1621 Euclid Av -19th Fl
-Cleveland 44115 **Fx:**621-6165

(330) 376-1242 ..**Renner Kenner Greive Bobak Taylor & Weber, LPA**
-106 S Main -4th Fl First Natl Twr -Akron 44308 **Fx:**376-9646

(440) 808-0011 ..**Renner Kenner Greive Bobak Taylor & Weber, LPA**
-24500 Ctr Ridge Rd -Ste 280 -Westlake 44145 **Fx:**808-0657

(614) 644-0100 ..**Renner**, Michael J '73 Tobacco Use Prevention -300 E Broad
-Columbus 43215 **Fx:**995-4575

(216) 621-1113 ..**Renner Otto Boisselle & Sklar, LLP** -1621 Euclid Av -19th Fl
-Cleveland 44115 **Fx:**621-6165

(330) 364-9900 ..**Renner**, Richard R '81 (Tate & R) -505 N Wooster Av -Bx8
-Dover 44622 **Fx:**364-9901

(614) 466-8288 ..**Rennick**, Kyme W '82 Mntl Hlth -30 E Broad -8th Fl
-Columbus 43215

(513) 241-4722 ..**Rennie,** Douglas W '78 (Montgomery R&J,LPA) -36 E 7th
-Ste 2100 -Cincinnati 45202 **Fx:**241-8775

(216) 523-1313 ..**Rennillo,** Irene A '83 Rennillo Reporting Srvcs -1301 E Ninth
-Ste 2500 -Cleveland 44114

(216) 696-3232 ..**Rennillo,** Jennifer W '99 %Spangenberg S&L,LLP -1900 E 9th
-2400 Natl City Ctr -Cleveland 44114 **Fx:**696-3924

(937) 222-9687 ..**Reno,** Barbara E '86 -22 Brown -Bx3340 -Dayton 45401

(419) 626-3800 ..**Reno Bogden & Ferber Co,LPA** -725 Sycamore Line
-Sandusky 44870 **Fx:**626-3638

(419) 626-3800 ..**Reno,** Robert M '76 (Reno B&F Co,LPA) -725 Sycamore Line
-Sandusky 44870 **Fx:**626-3638

(419) 784-2123 ..**Renollet,** Tamara S '90 Defiance Cnty CSEA -500 Court -Bx246
-Defiance 43512

(330) 723-6120 ..**Renswick,** Julien C '48 -326 N Court -Medina 44256 **Fx:**722-5909

(513) 946-3000 ..**Rentz,** Margaret B '87 Hamilton Cnty Pros -230 E 9th
-Cincinnati 45202 **Fx:**946-3017

(650) 756-1228 ..**Rentz,** Mark E '96 Barnes & Noble,Inc -280 Metro Ctr
-Colma, CA 94014

(216) 664-2670 ..**Renwald Marquit,** Amy E '01 %Dept of Law -601 Lakeside Av
-Rm 106 City Hall -Cleveland 44114 **Fx:**664-2663

(419) 243-1105 ..**Reny,** Dennis M '77 (Lackey NHR&T,LPA) -2 Maritime Plz -3rd Fl
-Toledo 43604

(513) 621-6464 ..**Renz,** Karen J '97 (Graydon H&R LLP) -511 Walnut
-1900 Fifth Third Ctr -Cincinnati 45202 **Fx:**651-3836

(330) 244-4200 ..**Reolfi,** Michael L '92 M Reolfi Co -4670 Douglas Cir NW -Bx35697
-Canton 44735

(419) 242-5485 ..**Repass,** Michael D '84 Area Title Agncy Inc -709 Mad Av -Ste 101
-Toledo 43624

(330) 499-8648 ..**Repella,** Michael V II '04 Universal Syndicates,Inc
-5080 N Aultman Av -North Canton 44720

(740) 282-7929 ..**Repella,** Stephen G '79 -300 Market -Steubenville 43952

(859) 491-1800 ..**Repenning,** Dennis A '79 -467 Erlanger Rd -Ste 104 -Erlanger,
KY 41018

(216) 502-0350 ..**Repicky,** Thomas G '79 (Repicky & K) -526 Superior Av
-530 Leader Bldg -Cleveland 44114

(937) 223-2100 ..**Replogle,** Thomas J '89 -130 W 2nd -Ste 2110 -Dayton 45402

(513) 424-1823 ..**Repper Powers & Pagan,LTD** -1501 1st Av -Middletown 45044

(513) 424-1823 ..**Repper,** Theodore Jr. '55 OfCnsl Repper P&P,LTD -1501 1st Av
-Middletown 45044

(216) 586-3939 ..**Reppert,** Richard L '74 (Jones D) -901 Lakeside Av
-Cleveland 44114 **Fx:**579-0212

(937) 898-7673 ..**Requarth,** Justin S '04 Oldham & D -8801 N. Main -Ste 200
-Dayton 45414

(914) 345-7884 ..**Rerko,** Justin S '03 Regeneron Pharmaceuticals -777 Old
Saw Mill Rvr Rd -Tarrytown, NY 10591

(419) 241-9000 ..**Rerucha,** Cynthia L '84 (Shumaker L&K,LLP) -1000 Jackson
-Toledo 43624 **Fx:**241-6894

(440) 244-5214 ..**Resar,** Kenneth R '79 (Riley R & Assoc) -520 Bway -Ste 200
-Lorain 44052

(614) 760-1801 ..**Resch,** Frederick D '78 (Resch & R) -5060 Bradenton Av -Ste C
-Dublin 43017

(513) 946-3167 ..**Resler,** Mark L '82 Hamilton Cnty Pros -230 E 9th
-Cincinnati 45202 **Fx:**946-3017

(216) 241-6868 ..**Resnick,** Elliott I '77 (E Resnick & Co) -1148 Euclid Av -Ste 300
-Cleveland 44115

(513) 243-0506 ..**Resnick,** Kenneth S '81 GE Aircraft Engines -1 Neumann Way
-J104 -Cincinnati 45215

(216) 491-1323 ..**Resnick,** Lois S '82 Shaker Hts Mun Crt -3355 Lee Rd
-Shaker Heights 44120

(440) 352-3391 ..**Resnick,** Melvyn E '66 (Dworken & B Co,LPA) -60 S Park Pl
-Painesville 44077 **Fx:**352-3469

(440) 247-3666 ..**Resnick,** Ramie A '84 -46 Chagrin Plz -#215 -Chagrin Falls 44022

(614) 716-1606 ..**Resnik,** Marvin J '73 Amer Elec Pwr Co -1 Riverside Plz
-Columbus 43215

Ressing, Amy L '90 -(Address Unavailable)

(301) 757-6011 ..**Ressing,** Garrett L '90 Navy Ofc of Genl Cnsl -47123 Buse Rd
-Bldg 2272 Ste 257 -Patuxent River, MD 20670

(740) 397-0711 ..**Ressing,** T Garrett '66 -10 E Vine -Mount Vernon 43050

(216) 696-4994 ..**Ressler,** George E '74 -1370 Ontario -Ste 1548 -Cleveland 44113

(210) 403-5909 ..**Ressler,** George H '89 SBA -17319 San Pedro Av -Bldg 2 #200
-San Antonio, TX 78232

(330) 263-5333 ..**Ressler,** Jon H '97 (Roose & R PA) -243 E Lbrty -Ste 9
-Wooster 44691

(419) 878-8760 ..**Restivo,** Francis C '49 -7164 Venetian Bay -Maumee 43537

(419) 885-3000 ..**Restivo,** James B '96 (Brady C&S LLP)
-4052 Holland-Sylvania Rd -Toledo 43623 **Fx:**885-1120

(419) 249-6743 ..**Restivo,** Laura A '95 Lucas Cnty Juv Ct -429 Mich
-Family Court Ctr -Toledo 43624

(740) 283-1313 ..**Reszke,** Eric M '93 -2021 Sunset Blvd -Bx1571
-Steubenville 43952

(419) 882-0533 ..**Retske,** Robert A '70 (Retske & W) -5414 Monroe -Toledo 43623

(614) 237-9308 ..**Retter,** Erica E '87 -1064 S Cassingham Rd -Columbus 43209

(937) 855-4166 ..**Rettich,** Robert W III '78 -46 E Market -Germantown 45327

(513) 721-1975 ..**Reul,** George M Jr. '98 Freking & B -215 E 9th -5th Fl
-Cincinnati 45202 **Fx:**651-2570

(216) 227-9000 ..**Reulbach,** John L Jr. '86 -14701 Detroit Av -Ste 575
-Lakewood 44107

(614) 462-3555 ..**Reulbach,** Sue A '85 Franklin Cnty Pros -373 S High
-Columbus 43215

(216) 363-4500 ..**Reuscher,** Christopher P '02 %Benesch FC&A LLP -200 Pub Sq
-Ste 2300 -Cleveland 44114 **Fx:**363-4588

Reuscher, Tara S '03 -(Address Unavailable)

(614) 228-6885 ..**Reuss,** James K '79 Lane A&H LLC -175 S 3rd -Ste 700
-Columbus 43215 **Fx:**228-0146

(614) 575-8965 ..**Reusser,** Carl A '99 -Bx165 -New Albany 43054 **Fx:**575-8966

(513) 579-6400 ..**Reuter,** F Mark '96 (Keating M&K PLL) -1 E 4th
-1400 Provident Twr -Cincinnati 45202 **Fx:**579-6457

(513) 521-8400 ..**Reuter,** James E '78 -3025 W Galbrath Rd -Cincinnati 45239
Fx:521-8401

(937) 293-0110 ..**Reuther,** Albert H '53 -4489 Maplerdg Pl -Kettering 45429

(513) 791-6000 ..**Reutter,** Mary J '99 -6924 Plainfld Rd -Cincinnati 45236

(440) 914-5297 ..**Reuven,** David W '92 %Podor & Assoc -33565 Solon Rd
-Solon 44139

(517) 432-6882 ..**Revelos,** Constantine N '65 Michigan State Univ -353 Law Bldg
-East Lansing, MI 48824 **Fx:**432-6801

(513) 932-2300 ..**Revelson,** Jay D '76 -200 E Silver -Bx175 -Lebanon 45036

(513) 721-1200 ..**Reverman,** Richard E '80 (Young R&M Co,LPA) -1014 Vine
-Ste 2400 -Cincinnati 45202 **Fx:**721-7116

(614) 268-0534 ..**Reves,** Randal M '94 (Reves & W) -3207 N High -Columbus 43202

(216) 621-5980 ..**Rexford,** Kenneth J '95 Legal Aid -1223 W 6th -Cleveland 44113

(330) 841-9121 ..**Rexroad,** Jeffrey D '81 Trumbull Mem Hosp -1350 E Market
-Warren 44483

(330) 376-5300 ..**Reyes,** John L '78 (Buckingham D&B,LLP) -50 S Main -Bx1500
-Akron 44309 **Fx:**258-6559

(513) 868-2731 ..**Reyes,** Roger O '96 -246 High -Hamilton 45011

(330) 376-5300 ..**Reymann,** Patrick H '72 OfCnsl Buckingham D&B,LLP -50 S Main
-Bx1500 -Akron 44309 **Fx:**258-6559

(727) 299-1825 ..**Reymann,** T Gregory II '85 Aegon Transamerica Fund Adv
-570 Carillon Pkwy -Saint Petersburg, FL 33716

(937) 323-8643 ..**Reynard,** Jack P Jr. '64 -Bx1664 -Springfield 45501

(614) 221-8080 ..**Reynard,** Jeffrey D '99 -35 E Lvngstn Av -Columbus 43215

(740) 373-4171 ..**Reynolds,** Catherine I '92 City of Marietta -301 Putnam
-Marietta 45750

(614) 278-6800 ..**Reynolds,** Chadwick P '99 Big Lots,Inc -300 Phillipi Rd
-Columbus 43228

(513) 721-4450 ..**Reynolds,** Charles E '81 Santen & H -312 Walnut -Ste 3100
-Cincinnati 45202

(440) 892-1355 ..**Reynolds,** Corrine '79 -28012 Sites Rd -Bay Village 44140

(330) 264-1150 ..**Reynolds,** Craig R '86 (Reynolds & R) -441 W Lbrty
-Wooster 44691

(614) 863-9470 ..**Reynolds,** Cristyn G '92 -472 Hunt Valley Dr -Reynoldsburg 43068

(614) 221-2838 ..**Reynolds,** Diane D '85 (Taft S&H LLP) -21 E State -12th Fl
-Columbus 43215 **Fx:**221-2007

(330) 264-1150 ..**Reynolds,** Don L '57 Reynolds & R -441 W Lbrty -Wooster 44691

(419) 243-6610 ..**Reynolds,** Frank E '83 Williams & R -420 Mad Av -Toledo 43604

(937) 427-2000 ..**Reynolds,** George B '99 -3589 Timbrook Ct -Ste 100
-Beavercreek 45431

(614) 221-4255 ..**Reynolds,** Jackson B III '93 (Smith & H) -37 W Broad
-Columbus 43215

(513) 897-0525 ..**Reynolds,** Kimberly A '03 -209 W Ellis Dr -Waynesville 45068

(440) 347-5645 ..**Reynolds,** Leslie M '88 Lubrizol Corp -29400 Lakelnd Blvd
-Wickliffe 44092

(937) 865-7591 ..**Reynolds,** Lynn M '95 Lexis/Nexis -Bx933 -Dayton 45401

(614) 764-3387 ..**Reynolds,** Mark A '89 Wendys Intl -4288 W Dublin-Granvll Rd
-Bx256 -Dublin 43017

(216) 621-0200 ..**Reynolds,** Melinda L '97 OfCnsl Baker & H LLP -1900 E 9th
-Ste 3200 -Cleveland 44114 **Fx:**696-0740

(513) 579-4370 ..**Reynolds,** Paul L '86 Fifth Third Bk -38 Fountain Square Plz
-MD10AT76 -Cincinnati 45263

Reynolds & Richard -441 W Lbrty -Wooster 44691

(330) 264-1150 ..**Reynolds,** Robert J '82 (Reynolds & R) -441 W Lbrty
-Wooster 44691

Reynolds, Shannon M '93 -(Address Unavailable)

(419) 245-2550 ..**Reynolds,** Susan J '84 %Atty Gen -One SeaGate -Ste 2150
-Toledo 43604 **Fx:**246-2520

(419) 255-6810 ..**Reynolds,** Timothy R '79 -1107 Adams -Toledo 43624

(614) 677-6368 ..**Reynolds,** Tyla L '96 Nationwide Ins Co -One Nationwide Plz
-Columbus 43215

(937) 449-6810 ..**Reynolds,** Walter '79 (Porter WM&A LLP) -1 S Main -Ste 1600
-Dayton 45402 **Fx:**449-6820

(513) 248-2527 ..**Reynolds,** William J '93 -5772 Observation Ct -Milford 45150

(937) 222-1366 ..**Rezabek,** Jeffery S '98 -111 W 1st -Ste 519 -Dayton 45402
Fx:222-1399

(440) 350-2742 ..**Rezaee,** Alana A '04 %Lake Cnty Pros -105 Main -Bx490
-Painesville 44077 **Fx:**350-2585

(212) 612-8752 ..**Rezak,** Adam M '95 %Swiss Amer Securities -12 E 49th -40th Fl
-New York, NY 10017

(216) 241-5310 ..**Rezie,** Richard C '99 %Gallagher SF&N -1501 Euclid Av -6th Fl
-Cleveland 44115 **Fx:**241-1608

(216) 781-0383 ..**Reznick,** Morris M '51 -815 Superior Av -Cleveland 44114

(937) 599-7232 ..**Rhea,** Mark L '99 Logan County CSEA -120 E Sandusky -Bx517
-Bellefontaine 43311

(614) 462-2278 ..**Rhee,** Hansel H '03 %Schottenstein Z&D -250 West -Bx165020
-Columbus 43216 **Fx:**462-5135

Rhein, Clyde K '49 -21695 Kenwood Av -Rocky River 44116

(330) 533-6869 ..**Rheuban,** Norman A '48 -132 S Broad -Ste 101 -Canfield 44406

(614) 221-4670 ..**Rhiel,** Susan L '86 (Rhiel & Assoc Co,LPA) -124 S Wshngtn
-Columbus 43215 **Fx:**232-9306

(937) 222-2424 ..**Rhinehart,** Michael N '03 %Freund F&A -1 S Main -Ste 1800
-Dayton 45402 **Fx:**222-5369

(513) 351-8828 ..**Rhiney,** Sean L '95 -5915 Pandora Av -Cincinnati 45213

(614) 242-4242 ..**Rhoad,** Brant K '03 %Decker VSL&V Co LPA -620 E Broad
-Columbus 43215 **Fx:**242-4243

(614) 761-1010 ..**Rhoades,** Joel D '93 EPCON Grp,Inc -500 Stonehenge Pkwy
-Dublin 43017 **Fx:**761-1155

(614) 792-5212 ..**Rhoads,** Jennifer B '98 OH Petroleum Marketers Assn
-4242 Tuller Rd -Dublin 43017

(740) 947-7605 ..**Rhoads,** Joseph E '82 Rhoads Law Ofc -305 N Market
-Waverly 45690

(614) 644-3037 ..**Rhoads,** Kimberly A '93 EPA -122 S Front -Bx1049
-Columbus 43216

(419) 626-1915 ..**Rhode,** Edward W III '80 -231 E Adams -Sandusky 44870

(614) 466-9392 ..**Rhodebeck,** Larry D '80 Workers Comp -30 W Spring -Level 26
-Columbus 43215

(614) 228-6321 ..**Rhodehamel,** David R '90 Coldwell Banker Cmmrcl -81 S 5th
-Columbus 43215

Rhodes, Christopher R '00 -5747 Perimeter Dr -Ste 180
-Dublin 43017

(614) 365-2700 ..**Rhodes,** Keely J '03 %Squire S&D LLP -41 S High
-1300 Huntngtn Ctr -Columbus 43215 **Fx:**365-2499

(330) 451-7863 ..**Rhodes,** Ross A '00 Stark Cnty Pros -110 Central Plz -Ste 510
-Canton 44702

(216) 443-6350 ..**Rhodes,** Tina Y '86 Ct of Appeals 8th Dist -1 Lakeside Av
-Cleveland 44113

(216) 861-1100 ..**Rhyner,** Cynthia J '96 Lipson Group Inc -1422 Euclid Av -Ste 1500
-Cleveland 44115

(614) 298-8600 ..**Ribar,** Mark D '96 Itrac,Inc -1356 Norton Av -Columbus 43212

(419) 255-0814 ..**Ricaurte,** Eve K '93 ABLE -520 Mad Av -740 Spitzer Bldg
-Toledo 43604 Fx:259-2880

(513) 534-5958 ..**Riccardi,** John R '03 Fifth Third Bk -38 Fountain Sq Plz
-MD 1Com31 -Cincinnati 45263

(216) 664-3827 ..**Riccardi,** Richard M '85 -2808 Portman Av -Cleveland 44109

(216) 643-6991 ..**Ricchetti,** Eugene T '66 E Ricchetti & Assoc -5005 Rockside Rd
-Ste 500 -Independence 44131

(330) 743-1171 ..**Ricchiuti,** Doralice Tavolario '04 Manchester BP&U
-201 E Commerce -Atrium Level 2 Commerce Bldg
-Youngstown 44503 Fx:743-1190

(423) 265-8881 ..**Ricci,** Jane K '85 (Schumacker WG&W,PC)
-1100 SunTrust Bk Bldg -736 Market -Chattanooga, TN 37402
Fx:265-5298

(330) 297-3850 ..**Ricciardi,** Francis M '77 Portage Cnty Pros -466 S Chestnut
-Ravenna 44266

　　　　　　　　　Ricco, David C '04 -(Address Unavailable)

(937) 898-3996 ..**Rice,** Bonnie B '79 Vandalia Mun Ct
-245 James E Bohanan Mem'l Dr -Bx429 -Vandalia 45377

(614) 466-0722 ..**Rice,** Chelsea S '03 Atty Gen -150 E Gay -Columbus 43215
Fx:644-9973

(216) 696-1433 ..**Rice,** Clark D '80 (Koeth R&L Co,LPA) -1280 W 3rd
-Cleveland 44113 Fx:696-1439

(419) 531-5758 ..**Rice,** Darrel L '77 -3436 W Lincolnshire -Toledo 43606

(734) 847-8080 ..**Rice,** David L '77 (Garrett CS&R LLP) -9042 Lewis Av -Bx490
-Temperance, MI 48182

(513) 871-1545 ..**Rice & Diedrichs LLP** -3530 Edwards Rd -Cincinnati 45208
Fx:871-1545

(216) 664-4865 ..**Rice,** Donald '97 Mun Ct -1200 Ontario -Level 2 -Cleveland 44113

(419) 238-6621 ..**Rice,** Earl J '80 -124 E Main -Van Wert 45891 Fx:238-4705

(614) 559-2101 ..**Rice,** Frederick W '78 -250 Civic Ctr Dr -2nd Fl -Columbus 43215

　　　　　　　　　Rice, James F '89 -(Address Unavailable)

(513) 871-1545 ..**Rice,** James K '67 (Rice & D LLP) -3530 Edwards Rd
-Cincinnati 45208 Fx:871-1545

(216) 241-5310 ..**Rice,** Jay C '79 (Gallagher SF&N) -1501 Euclid Av -6th Fl
-Cleveland 44115 Fx:241-1608

(312) 346-8061 ..**Rice,** Joel W '86 OfCnsl Fisher & P LLP -140 S Dearborn
-Ste 420 Marquette Bldg -Chicago, IL 60603 Fx:346-3179

(513) 530-6563 ..**Rice,** John D '73 Millennium Petrochem Inc -11530 Northlake Dr
-Cincinnati 45249

(513) 887-3265 ..**Rice,** Kelli M '90 Butler Cnty Dom Rltns Ct -315 High -2nd Fl
-Hamilton 45011

(513) 243-2632 ..**Rice,** Kenneth C '94 GE Aircraft Engines -1 Neumann Way
-MD J104 -Cincinnati 45215

(202) 501-0496 ..**Rice,** Kevin J '94 GSA -1800 F NW -Rm 4129
-Washington, DC 20405

(419) 480-1900 ..**Rice,** Kollin L '96 (Rice & Co,LPA) -3730 Upton Av -Toledo 43613
Fx:480-1950

(513) 529-8759 ..**Rice,** Mackenzie L '02 Miami Univ -725 E Chestnut -Oxford 45056

(937) 865-6800 ..**Rice,** Martha E '01 Lexis/Nexis -Bx933 -Dayton 45401

(513) 768-5701 ..**Rice,** Michael D '86 Applied Business Tech -9370 Main -Ste E
-Cincinnati 45242

(419) 625-0536 ..**Rice,** Pamela D '97 UAW-GM Legal Srvc Plan -3116 Bardshar Rd
-Sandusky 44870

(513) 398-0820 ..**Rice,** Paul D '75 -5412 Coursevw Dr -Ste 140 -Mason 45040

(419) 243-1294 ..**Rice,** Philip M '62 Emch SS&P Co,LPA -One SeaGate -Ste 1980
-Bx916 -Toledo 43697 Fx:243-8502

(513) 421-2400 ..**Rice,** Robert M '93 (Helmer MR&P Co,LPA) -105 E 4th -Ste 1900
-Cincinnati 45202 Fx:421-7902

(330) 534-1901 ..**Rice,** Ronald J '85 -48 W Lbrty -Hubbard 44425

　　　　　　　　　Rice, Scott E '99 -2151 Firestone -Columbus 43228

(216) 621-0150 ..**Rice,** Sonja C '01 %Hahn L&P LLP -3300 BP Twr/200 Pub Sq
-Ste 3300 -Cleveland 44114 Fx:241-2824

(937) 225-4652 ..**Rice,** Ted W '67 Montgomery Cnty Pub Def -117 S Main -Ste 400
-Dayton 45422 Fx:225-3449

(937) 259-7103 ..**Rice,** Timothy G '79 SrCnsl Dayton Power & Light Co -Bx8825
-Dayton 45401

　　　　　　　　　Rice, Timothy S '01 -3537 Wenwood Dr -Hilliard 43026

(202) 482-6702 ..**Rice,** Tresa A '01 Fed Labor Relatns Auth -800 K NW
-Ste 910 Tech World Plz -Washington, DC 20001 Fx:482-6724

(330) 929-6000 ..**Rice,** Wayne M '76 Cuyahoga Falls Svngs Bank -2503 State Rd
-Cuyahoga Falls 44221

(216) 479-6100 ..**Rice,** Weldon H '03 Vorys SS&P LLP -1375 E 9th
-Ste 2100 One Cleve Ctr -Cleveland 44114 Fx:479-6060

　　　　　　　　　Rice, William K '65 -9314 Stockport Dr -Spring, TX 77379

(330) 337-9515 ..**Rice-Bartlett,** Kathleen J '94 (Yeagley K&B) -585 E State
-Salem 44460

　　　　　　　　　Rich, Aviva R '02 -2322 Delaware Dr -Cleveland Heights 44106

(614) 228-5822 ..**Rich Crites & Dittmer,LLC** -300 E Broad -Ste 300 -Columbus
43215 Fx:228-2725

(304) 529-2868 ..**Rich,** David Edward '00 %Offutt F&N -949 3rd Av -Ste 300
-Bx2868 -Huntington, WV 25728 Fx:529-2999

(330) 656-2702 ..**Rich,** Eric A '94 %Scheuer M&B LLC -110 W Streetsboro Rd
-Ste 2A -Hudson 44236 Fx:656-2755

(330) 394-6352 ..**Rich,** Gary R '81 -342 Mahoning Av NW -Bx4010 -Warren 44482

(740) 223-4290 ..**Rich,** J Anthony '96 Marion Cnty Pros -134 E Center
-Marion 43302 Fx:223-4299

(614) 228-5822 ..**Rich,** Jeffrey A '70 (Rich C&D,LLC) -300 E Broad -Ste 300
-Columbus 43215 Fx:228-2725

(216) 931-6000 ..**Rich,** Jodi B '00 %Ulmer & B LLP -1300 E 9th
-Ste 900 Penton Media Bldg -Cleveland 44114 Fx:931-6001

(216) 696-4441 ..**Rich,** Jonathan A '93 Zashin & R Co,LPA -55 Pub Sq -Ste 1490
-Cleveland 44113 Fx:696-1618

(404) 331-2896 ..**Rich,** Lawrence J '76 NLRB -233 Pchtree NE -Ste 1000
-Atlanta, GA 30303

(216) 696-4441 ..**Rich,** Lawrence J '67 Zashin & R Co,LPA -55 Pub Sq -Ste 1490
-Cleveland 44113 Fx:696-1618

(216) 289-4500 ..**Rich,** Linda M '77 -25000 Euclid Av -Ste 100 -Euclid 44117

(614) 227-8869 ..**Rich,** Matthew A '04 %Bricker & E LLP -100 S 3rd
-Columbus 43215 Fx:227-2390

　　　　　　　　　Rich, Matthew G '04 -(Address Unavailable)

(330) 758-2200 ..**Rich,** Michael J '95 -7000 South Av -Ste 4 -Boardman 44512

(513) 723-4000 ..**Rich,** Michael L '04 %Vorys SS&P LLP -221 E 4th
-Ste 2000 Atrium Two -Bx0236 -Cincinnati 45201 Fx:723-4056

(513) 241-3430 ..**Rich Pott Wetherell Foster & Miller** -830 Main -Ste 1115
-Cincinnati 45202 Fx:357-4392

(513) 381-2838 ..**Rich,** Robert E '70 (Taft S&H LLP) -425 Walnut -Ste 1800
-Cincinnati 45202 Fx:381-0205

(614) 457-9784 ..**Rich,** Sandra L '86 -3872 Patricia Dr -Columbus 43220

(614) 249-6201 ..**Rich-Barge,** Mario M '02 Nationwide Ins Co -One Nationwide Plz
-MC 1-26-17 -Columbus 43215 Fx:677-4188

(513) 551-4357 ..**Richard,** Arthur M III '93 -114 E 8th -Ste 400 -Cincinnati 45202

(330) 264-1150 ..**Richard,** James M '74 (Reynolds & R) -441 W Lbrty
-Wooster 44691

(937) 498-4810 ..**Richard,** Jonathan M '97 (J Richard Co,LPA) -108 E Poplar
-Sidney 45365

(216) 479-8500 ..**Richard,** Renee Tramble '88 %Squire S&D LLP -127 Pub Sq
-4900 Key Twr -Cleveland 44114 Fx:479-8780

(330) 735-2269 ..**Richards,** Allan R '70 -7145 Elgin Dr SW -Sherrodsville 44675

(330) 643-2944 ..**Richards,** Beverly J '98 Summit Cnty Juv Ct -650 Dan
-Akron 44310

(330) 373-1000 ..**Richards,** Charles L '69 -159 E Market -Ste 300 -Warren 44481
Fx:394-5291

(216) 241-6602 ..**Richards,** Daniel A '92 (Weston HFP&H LPA) -50 Pub Sq
-2500 Trmnl Twr -Cleveland 44113 Fx:621-8369

(440) 942-6262 ..**Richards,** Daniel F '65 (Wiles & R) -35350 Curtis Blvd -Ste 530
-Eastlake 44095 Fx:942-7211

(614) 476-2222 ..**Richards,** David J '77 OH Heart -765 N Hmltn -Gahanna 43230

(440) 352-3391 ..**Richards,** David J Jr. '71 (Dworken & B Co,LPA) -60 S Park Pl
-Painesville 44077 Fx:352-3469

(330) 864-1459 ..**Richards,** Donald '55 -565 Deering Dr -Akron 44313

　　　　　　　　　Richards, Dorothy Regas '94 -3742 W 169th -Cleveland 44111

(202) 736-6610 ..**Richards,** Douglas A '84 WorldCom -1133 19th NW
-Washington, DC 20036

(513) 621-1991 ..**Richards,** Gates T '69 (G Richards Co LPA) -5 Grandin Ln
-Cincinnati 45208

(330) 492-7107 ..**Richards,** Homer R '77 -4100 Holiday NW -Ste 101
-Canton 44718

(614) 781-1400 ..**Richards,** Jason W '98 Hrabcak & Co,LPA
-67 E Wilson Bridge Rd -Worthington 43085

(513) 695-1167 ..**Richards,** Jeffery E '83 Cnty Notary Pub Cmmssn -500 Justice Dr
-Lebanon 45036

(513) 723-8400 ..**Richards,** Jeremy D '01 Coley & Assoc -9334 Union Centre Blvd
-Ste 200 -West Chester 45069

(419) 784-9982 ..**Richards,** Jilene E '98 %Penner & S,Ltd -101 Clinton -Ste 1500
-Defiance 43512 Fx:784-9991

(614) 461-1156 ..**Richards,** John R '93 %Webster & Assoc -2 Miranova Pl -Ste 310
-Columbus 43215

(216) 861-5000 ..**Richards,** Joseph V Jr. '76 (Ernst & Young) -1300 Huntngtn Bldg
-925 Euclid Av -Cleveland 44115

(614) 221-7663 ..**Richards,** Kenneth M '88 (Luper N&L,LPA) -50 W Broad
-1200 LeVeque Twr -Columbus 43215 Fx:464-2425

(330) 743-3232 ..**Richards,** Lawrence H '76 (L Richards Co,LPA) -400 City Ctr One
-Youngstown 44503

(513) 424-2401 ..**Richards,** Megan '83 (Casper & C) -1 N Main -Bx510
-Middletown 45042 Fx:424-0622

(614) 764-8966 ..**Richards,** R L '75 RDT Ltd -5131 Post Rd -Ste 203 -Dublin 43017

(614) 228-1128 ..**Richards,** Robin S '01 J Wichman -500 S Front -Ste 970
-Columbus 43215

(440) 593-4900 ..**Richards,** Sally E '82 -215 Lbrty -Conneaut 44030

(513) 241-3447 ..**Richards,** Stuart L '62 -906 Main#405 -Cincinnati 45202

(614) 464-6400 ..**Richards,** Suzanne K '74 (Vorys SS&P LLP) -52 E Gay -Bx1008
-Columbus 43216 Fx:464-6350

(216) 469-3152 ..**Richards,** Terri M '94 Lexis-Nexis -13851 Lk Av -Lakewood 44107

(513) 871-8755 ..**Richards,** Thomas D '84 Richards & Assoc,LPA -3322 Erie Av
-Ste 101 -Cincinnati 45208 Fx:871-8744

(216) 621-0200 ..**Richards,** Timothy J '04 %Baker & H LLP -1900 E 9th -Ste 3200
-Cleveland 44114 Fx:696-0740

　　　　　　　　　Richards, Valencia D '97 -514 Wildwood Pkwy
-Cape Coral, FL 33904

(614) 424-5612 ..**Richards,** William B '99 Battelle Memorial Inst -505 King Av
-Intellectual Prop Law Dept -Columbus 43201

　　　　　　　　　Richards, Arthur W '02 -11663 Kiowa Av -#107
-Los Angeles, CA 90049

(513) 961-6200 ..**Richardson,** David G '93 %Markesbery & R Co,LPA
-2368 Victory Pkwy -Ste 200 -Bx6491 -Cincinnati 45206

(216) 931-6000 ..**Richardson,** Donald J '97 %Ulmer & B LLP -1300 E 9th
-Ste 900 Penton Media Bldg -Cleveland 44114 Fx:931-6001

(215) 222-8454 ..**Richardson,** Donna R '76 Comm on Graduates of Nurse Schl
-3600 Market -Ste 400 -Philadelphia, PA 19104

(513) 723-4000 ..**Richardson,** Eric W '96 (Vorys SS&P LLP) -221 E 4th
-Ste 2000 Atrium Two -Bx0236 -Cincinnati 45201 Fx:723-4056

(330) 743-1171 ..**Richardson,** Gina Agresta '99 (Manchester BP&U) -201 E
Commerce -Atrium Level 2 Commerce Bldg -Youngstown 44503
Fx:743-1190

(216) 861-1234 ..**Richardson,** Glen S '81 %Bentoff & D Co,LPA -55 Pub Sq
-Ste 1200 -Cleveland 44113

(614) 889-6008 ..**Richardson,** Herbert M III '86 -3809 Wedgewood Pl Dr
-Powell 43065 Fx:336-2864

(216) 619-9002 ..**Richardson,** Jeffrey S '93 -1419 W 9th -3rd Fl -Cleveland 44113

(412) 394-2470 ..**Richardson,** John J '02 %Thorp R&A,LLP -301 Grant -14th Fl
-Pittsburgh, PA 15219 Fx:394-2555

(419) 241-6168 ..**Richardson,** Jon D '73 -520 Mad Av -Ste 830 -Toledo 43604

　　　　　　　　　Richardson, Kristopher L '97 -5224 Southminster Rd
-Columbus 43221

(937) 865-6800 ..**Richardson,** Lisa A '01 Lexis/Nexis -Bx933 -Dayton 45401

(740) 373-8624 ..**Richardson,** Lynn M '77 Ellis & C,LPA -328 4th -Marietta 45750

(614) 464-6400 ..**Richardson,** Matthew J '03 %Vorys SS&P LLP -52 E Gay
-Bx1008 -Columbus 43216 Fx:464-6350

(216) 931-6000 ..**Richardson,** Nita Kay '94 %Ulmer & B LLP -1300 E 9th
-Ste 900 Penton Media Bldg -Cleveland 44114 Fx:931-6001

(614) 878-9262 ..**Richardson,** Randy '86 UAW Legal Srvc Plan -5212 W Broad
-Columbus 43228

(216) 592-5000 ..**Richardson,** Scott A '96 Cnsl Tucker E&W LLP -925 Euclid Av
-1150 Huntngtn Bldg -Cleveland 44115 Fx:592-5009

(513) 651-6800 ..**Richardson**, Scott M '02 %Frost BT LLC -201 E 5th -2200 PNC Ctr -Cincinnati 45202 **Fx:**651-6981

(330) 384-5272 ..**Richardson**, Tammy S '96 FirstEnergy Corp -76 S Main -12th Fl -Akron 44308

(859) 282-6220 ..**Richardson**, Tracy A '01 -1490 Flintrdg Rd -Florence, KY 41042

(216) 696-5250 ..**Richelson**, Murray '80 OfCnsl DA Katz Co,LPA -842 Trmnl Twr -50 Pub Sq -Cleveland 44113 **Fx:**696-5256

(440) 352-0716 ..**Richer**, Donald A '75 -270 Main -Ste 160 -Bx1575 -Painesville 44077

(330) 972-7447 ..**Richert**, Paul '77 Univ of Akron/Sch of Law -150 Univ Av -Library -Akron 44325 **Fx:**972-4948

(513) 352-6768 ..**Richey**, Stephen L '93 (Thompson H LLP) -312 Walnut -14th Fl -Cincinnati 45202 **Fx:**241-4771

(614) 228-5151 ..**Richie**, Crystal R '95 (Gallagher GPT&L LLP) -471 E Broad -19th Fl -Columbus 43215 **Fx:**228-0032

(440) 603-0066 ..**Richlak**, James D '73 -6501 Wilson Mills Rd -Ste A -Richmond Heights 44143

(440) 255-4838 ..**Richlak**, Susan P '94 -8000 Plz Blvd -#400 -Mentor 44060

(216) 623-1990 ..**Richman**, Brian H '69 (BH Richman & Co,Ltd) -1120 Chester Av -Ste 450 -Cleveland 44114

(216) 472-1500 ..**Richman**, Ellen J '90 O'Brien Law Firm,LLC -627 W St Clair Av -Cleveland 44113 **Fx:**472-1600

(513) 621-6033 ..**Richman**, Harvey A '95 -906 Main -Ste 306 -Cincinnati 45202

(202) 289-1800 ..**Richman**, Jessica R '02 %Ludwig & R,PLLC -818 Conn Av NW -Ste 750 -Washington, DC 20006 **Fx:**289-1804

(216) 556-0226 ..**Richman**, Stephen D '86 -29225 Chagrin Blvd -Ste 350 -Cleveland 44122

(740) 852-2221 ..**Richmond**, Charles D '50 -207 E High -Bx676 -London 43140 **Fx:**852-4331

(419) 882-0790 ..**Richmond**, Charles K Jr. '94 -6830 Fredrcksburg Dr -#347 -Sylvania 43560 **Fx:**882-0790

(954) 262-6102 ..**Richmond**, Gail Ayn '71 Nova SthEstrn Univ -3305 Cllg Av -Fort Lauderdale, FL 33314

(216) 881-0502 ..**Richmond**, Toni M '03 -4403 St Clair Av -Cleveland 44103

(513) 705-9000 ..**Richmond**, Vicki L '00 %Pratt SP Co,LPA -301 N Breiel Blvd -Middletown 45044 **Fx:**705-9001

(614) 365-2700 ..**Richner**, Kristin E '04 %Squire S&D LLP -41 S High -1300 Huntngtn Ctr -Columbus 43215 **Fx:**365-2499

(330) 425-2291 ..**Richner**, Robert A '76 -2305 E Aurora Rd -A-1 -Twinsburg 44087

(513) 621-2666 ..**Richshafer**, Howard L '75 (Statman HS&E LLC) -255 E 5th -Ste 2900 Chemed Ctr -Cincinnati 45202 **Fx:**587-4477

(440) 285-2222 ..**Richter**, Brian M '88 Geauga Cnty Pros -231 Main -Cthse Annx -Chardon 44024 **Fx:**286-4357

(614) 298-8150 ..**Richter**, Jody R '99 American Kidney Stone Mgmt -100 W 3rd Av -Ste 350 -Columbus 43201

(614) 728-9758 ..**Richter**, Michael P '90 Dept of Dvlpmnt -57 E Main -Columbus 43215

(614) 466-3205 ..**Richter**, Philip C '95 OH Elections Cmmssn -21 W Broad -Ste 600 -Columbus 43215 **Fx:**728-9408

(513) 229-0383 ..**Richter**, Ronald J '01 %Hasse & N LLC -7550 Cntrl Pke Blvd -Mason 45040 **Fx:**229-0683

(216) 241-5310 ..**Richthammer**, Theresa A '97 %Gallagher SF&N -1501 Euclid Av -6th Fl -Cleveland 44115 **Fx:**241-1608

(614) 365-2700 ..**Rickard**, Erik J '97 %Squire S&D LLP -41 S High -1300 Huntngtn Ctr -Columbus 43215 **Fx:**365-2499

(216) 831-1434 ..**Rickel**, Alice '77 (A Rickel & Assoc) -3690 Orange Pl -Ste 440 -Beachwood 44122 **Fx:**831-6376

(614) 464-6400 ..**Rickert**, Benjamin J '03 %Vorys SS&P LLP -52 E Gay -Bx1008 -Columbus 43216 **Fx:**464-6350

(937) 643-9999 ..**Rickert**, David M '78 (Weisbrod & D) -580 Lincoln Park Blvd -Ste 222 -Dayton 45429 **Fx:**643-0777

(216) 586-3939 ..**Rickert**, Jeanne M '80 (Jones D) -901 Lakeside Av -Cleveland 44114 **Fx:**579-0212

(330) 972-7189 ..**Rickett**, William G '86 Univ of Akron/Sch of Law -150 Univ Av -Rm 136-C -Akron 44325 **Fx:**258-2343

Ricketts, Anne E '93 -115470 Lakevw Pkwy -Findlay 45840

(937) 325-6221 ..**Ricketts**, Charles N '68 -302 N Plum -Springfield 45504

(614) 358-8056 ..**Ricketts**, Richard T '86 (Ricketts Co,LPA) -580 S High -3rd Fl -Columbus 43215 **Fx:**229-4111

(330) 796-3328 ..**Rickey**, June E '97 Goodyear Tire & Rubber Co -1144 E Market -Akron 44316

(513) 721-7500 ..**Rickey**, Robert E '02 %D Cook LLC -22 W 9th -Cincinnati 45202

(330) 796-6635 ..**Rickman**, Michael R '87 Goodyear Tire & Rubber Co -1144 E Market -Akron 44316

(740) 349-6215 ..**Rickrich**, C William II '79 Licking Cnty Dom Rltns Ct -75 E Main -Newark 43055 **Fx:**349-1485

(216) 241-0715 ..**Ricotta**, John J '80 -425 W Lakeside Av -Ste 100 -Cleveland 44113

(440) 842-4080 ..**Riczo**, John J Jr. '75 -7462 State Rd -Cleveland 44134

(513) 579-6400 ..**Riddell**, Brian A '04 %Keating M&K PLL -1 E 4th -1400 Provident Twr -Cincinnati 45202 **Fx:**579-6457

(614) 478-3676 ..**Riddell**, Peter H '74 (Riddell & Assoc) -194 W Johnstown Rd -Gahanna 43230

(330) 746-0171 ..**Ridder**, Bryan M '83 (B Ridder Co,LPA) -107 S Champion -Youngstown 44503

(440) 230-9230 ..**Riddle**, James C '96 -10710 Sherwood Trl -North Royalton 44133

(419) 894-6842 ..**Riddle**, Loretta A '02 -2070 Cnty Rd 18 -Arcadia 44804

(440) 414-5499 ..**Riddle**, Susan L '90 Nordson Corp -28601 Clemens Rd -Westlake 44145

(216) 664-4807 ..**Ridenour**, Marlene J '94 Prosecutor -1200 Ontario Av -8th Fl Justice Ctr -Cleveland 44113 **Fx:**664-4399

(740) 342-1109 ..**Ridenour**, Nancy N '96 -Bx827 -New Lexington 43764

(419) 241-9000 ..**Rideout**, Joseph A '76 (Shumaker L&K,LLP) -1000 Jackson -Toledo 43624 **Fx:**241-6894

(419) 535-4128 ..**Rider**, John A III '94 Dana Corp -4500 Dorr -Bx1000 -Toledo 43697

(216) 696-0800 ..**Rider**, William H Jr. '74 %Gibson BZ&M -55 Pub Sq -Ste 2075 -Cleveland 44113 **Fx:**696-0702

(419) 663-6771 ..**Ridge**, John S '79 Mun Ct Judge -45 N Linwood Av -Norwalk 44857

(614) 464-6400 ..**Ridgley**, Thomas B '68 (Vorys SS&P LLP) -52 E Gay -Bx1008 -Columbus 43216 **Fx:**464-6350

(216) 685-5000 ..**Riebe**, Radd L '78 Stout Risius Ross,Inc -600 Superior Av E -Ste 740 -Cleveland 44114

(219) 422-3900 ..**Riebenack**, Francis W '65 -110 W Berry -Ste 1910 -Fort Wayne, IN 46802

(614) 365-2700 ..**Rieck**, Kim A '77 OfCnsl Squire S&D LLP -41 S High -1300 Huntngtn Ctr -Columbus 43215 **Fx:**365-2499

(419) 424-7276 ..**Ried**, Aaron J '00 Hancock Cnty Pub Def -316 Dorney Plz -Findlay 45840

Riedel, Dale A '04 USAF -20 MacDill Blvd -Ste 240 - HQ 11WG/JA -Bolling AFB, DC 20032

(440) 997-6175 ..**Riedel**, Katherine S '00 %Warren & Y,PLL -134 W 46th -Bx2300 -Ashtabula 44005 **Fx:**992-9114

(614) 221-3155 ..**Riedel**, Timothy A '87 OfCnsl Bailey C LLC -10 W Broad -Columbus 43215 **Fx:**221-0479

(440) 997-6175 ..**Riedel**, William E '69 (Warren & Y,PLL) -134 W 46th -Bx2300 -Ashtabula 44005 **Fx:**992-9114

(614) 462-3555 ..**Riedl**, Daniel J '03 Franklin Cnty Pros -373 S High -Columbus 43215

(202) 293-5620 ..**Riedmiller**, Miriam B '94 -1901 L NW -Ste 670 -Washington, DC 20036

(440) 329-5397 ..**Riedthaler**, Jennifer M '01 Lorain Cnty Pros -225 Court -3rd Fl -Elyria 44035

Riedy, Elizabeth V '04 -(Address Unavailable)

(740) 653-6464 ..**Riegel**, Mark R '85 (Dagger JMO&H) -144 E Main -Bx667 -Lancaster 43130 **Fx:**653-8522

(440) 603-6335 ..**Riegel**, Sharon A '93 Progressive Ins Co -747 Alpha Dr -1st Fl -Highland Heights 44143

(859) 261-5777 ..**Rieger**, Brian C '84 (Oldfield DR,PLLC) -213 E 4th -Bx1078 -Covington, KY 41012

(330) 392-6171 ..**Rieger**, Gilbert L '70 Rieger SC&D -410 Mahoning Av -Bx1429 -Warren 44482 **Fx:**394-5507

(330) 392-6171 ..**Rieger Spencer Carpenter & Daugherty** -410 Mahoning Av -Bx1429 -Warren 44482 **Fx:**394-5507

(614) 799-2800 ..**Rieger**, Thaddeus T '89 Zaino & H LPA -5775 Perimeter Dr -Ste 275 -Dublin 43017 **Fx:**799-1500

Riegle, Phillip A '04 -(Address Unavailable)

(317) 633-4884 ..**Riegler**, Christopher L '93 (Hall RKH&L,PSC) -1 Amer Sq -Ste 2000 -Indianapolis, IN 46282

(330) 535-8171 ..**Riegler**, Edward J '74 (Grisi & R) -159 S Main -Ste 1030 -Akron 44308

(216) 781-1212 ..**Riehl**, Charles T '71 (Walter & H LLP) -1301 E 9th -Ste 3500 -Cleveland 44114 **Fx:**575-0911

(330) 273-3450 ..**Riehl**, David S '74 -3695 Ctr Rd -Brunswick 44212

(513) 922-3200 ..**Riehl**, Keith S '81 (Haverkamp BR&R Co,LPA) -5856 Glenway Av -Cincinnati 45238 **Fx:**922-8096

(614) 224-8160 ..**Riehl**, Lawrence A '79 (Vickery R&A) -500 S Front -Ste 200 -Columbus 43215 **Fx:**224-4943

(812) 934-1708 ..**Riehle**, Melanie A '78 Hillenbrand Industries -700 E State Rd 46 -Batesville, IN 47006

(216) 696-4240 ..**Riek**, F Benjamin III '78 Riek & Assoc,LPA -75 Pub Sq -Ste 1010 -Cleveland 44113

(216) 839-1111 ..**Rieke**, Michael K '00 S Gross Co,LPA -22901 Millcreek Blvd -Ste 395 -Cleveland 44122

(216) 621-5300 ..**Riemenschneider**, Dirk E '91 (Buckingham D&B,LLP) -1375 E 9th -Ste 1700 -Cleveland 44114 **Fx:**621-5440

(330) 434-3000 ..**Riemenschneider**, John K '69 %Roderick & L -One Cascade Plz -Ste 1500 -Akron 44308 **Fx:**434-9220

(440) 243-1222 ..**Riemenschneider**, Walter E Jr. '59 -31 E Brdg -Ste #302 -Berea 44017

(216) 696-0990 ..**Riemer**, Donald G '84 (Shapiro M&R) -1468 W 9th -Rm 425 -Cleveland 44113 **Fx:**696-7790

(703) 605-1922 ..**Riemer**, Steven R '74 Bd of Immig Appls -5107 Leesburg Pk -Ste 2600 -Falls Church, VA 22041

(614) 221-1216 ..**Riepenhoff**, David A '02 %Downes H&F -400 S 5th -Ste 200 -Columbus 43215 **Fx:**221-8769

(419) 247-4267 ..**Ries**, Deborah K '01 Pilkington Nrth Amer -811 Mad Av -Toledo 43624

(330) 393-0851 ..**Ries**, James R '75 -244 Seneca Av NE -Bx529 -Warren 44482 **Fx:**393-9943

(419) 246-5757 ..**Riesen**, Kent D '89 (Anspach M&N,LLP) -300 Mad Av -Ste 1600 -Toledo 43604 **Fx:**321-6979

(614) 466-7351 ..**Riesenberger**, William A '76 OH Dept Taxation -30 E Broad -22nd Fl -Columbus 43215 **Fx:**466-4977

(937) 224-4128 ..**Rieser & Associates LLC** -130 W 2nd -Ste 1520 -Dayton 45402 **Fx:**224-0900

(614) 444-6556 ..**Rieser**, David P '80 -844 S Front -Columbus 43206

(740) 349-6663 ..**Rieser**, Jack D '85 Newark Law Dir Ofc -40 W Main -Rm 404 -Newark 43055

(937) 224-4128 ..**Rieser**, John P '81 (Rieser & Assoc LLC) -130 W 2nd -Ste 1520 -Dayton 45402 **Fx:**224-0900

(614) 875-2371 ..**Rieser**, Richard E '89 Buckeye Ranch,Inc -5665 Hoover Rd -Grove City 43123

(216) 241-6602 ..**Riester**, Jennifer A '99 %Weston HFP&H LLP -50 Pub Sq -2500 Trmnl Twr -Cleveland 44113 **Fx:**621-8369

(216) 861-2222 ..**Rieth & Antonelli** -200 Pub Sq -Ste 2940 -Cleveland 44114

(216) 696-4200 ..**Rieth**, Janice Edgehouse '78 (Schneider SR&L PLL) -1111 Superior Av -Ste 1000 -Cleveland 44114 **Fx:**696-7303

(216) 861-2222 ..**Rieth**, Richard C '79 (Rieth & A) -200 Pub Sq -Ste 2940 -Cleveland 44114

(216) 464-8300 ..**Rieth**, Robert G '84 -30539 Pinetree Rd -#226 -Cleveland 44124

(740) 472-1158 ..**Riethmiller**, Lynn K '77 -110 N Main -Bx430 -Woodsfield 43793

(419) 251-3679 ..**Riethmiller**, Michael K '84 St Vincent Med Ctr -2213 Cherry -Toledo 43608

(419) 867-3946 ..**Riewaldt**, Martha L '80 (Ducey & R) -5330 Heatherdowns Blvd -Ste 105 -Toledo 43614

(937) 293-1000 ..**Rife**, Harry P '62 -2323 W Schantz Av -Dayton 45409

(419) 244-4000 ..**Rife**, Joan H '82 -Bx952 -Toledo 43607

(216) 861-6833 ..**Riffe**, George B '01 Sonkin & K Co,LPA -55 Pub Sq -Ste 1660 -Cleveland 44113

(440) 838-8883 ..**Rifici**, Anthony M '97 -9100 S Hills Blvd -Ste 300 -Cleveland 44147

(216) 357-7000 ..**Riga**, Lori B '96 District Ct -801 Superior Av -Cleveland 44114 **Fx:**357-7040

(614) 466-5394 ..**Rigby**, Kimberly S '04 %Pub Def -8 E Long -Columbus 43215

(212) 715-9100 .. **Rigel**, Blake A '00 %Kramer LN&F,LLP -919 3rd Av
-New York, NY 10022 **Fx:**715-8000

(510) 893-0921 .. **Rigelhaupt**, James L Jr. '67 -633 Santa Ray Av
-Oakland, CA 94610

(614) 248-6045 .. **Rigelman**, Bruce D '96 Bank One Mgt Corp -100 E Broad
-OHI-0158 -Columbus 43271

(614) 444-3900 .. **Rigg**, Brian J '87 -755 S High -Columbus 43206

(606) 563-8800 .. **Rigg**, Debra S '85 -210 Market -Maysville, KY 41056

(614) 228-6625 .. **Riggins**, Melissa K '88 -118 E Main -Columbus 43215
Fx:228-6640

(513) 977-8200 .. **Riggs**, Harry L Jr. '57 OfCnsl Dinsmore & S LLP -255 E 5th
-Ste 1900 -Cincinnati 45202 **Fx:**977-8141

(740) 373-7572 .. **Riggs**, Roland W III '72 (Davidson HR&F) -311 4th -Bx567
-Marietta 45750 **Fx:**373-7081

(614) 224-3208 .. **Riggs**, Warren G '53 -1 E Lvngstn -Ste B -Columbus 43215

(614) 268-1493 .. **Rigney**, Joseph K '74 -162 E North Bway -Columbus 43214

(937) 443-6586 .. **Rigot**, Joseph M '73 (Thompson H LLP) -2000 Cthse Plz NE
-Bx8801 -Dayton 45401 **Fx:**443-6635

(859) 233-4633 .. **Rigsby**, William F '80 (Rigsby Law Grp,PLC) -228 E High
-Bx34106 -Lexington, KY 40588 **Fx:**233-4642

(513) 621-2888 .. **Riker**, Jan T '77 (Ebner & R LLP) -1014 Vine -1900 Kroger Bldg
-Cincinnati 45202

(937) 223-1201 .. **Riley**, Adele M '82 OfCnsl Altick & C Co,LPA -1 S Main
-1700 One Dayton Ctr -Dayton 45402 **Fx:**223-5100

(216) 241-6602 .. **Riley**, Brian P '00 %Weston HFP&H LLP -50 Pub Sq
-2500 Trmnl Twr -Cleveland 44113 **Fx:**621-8369

(440) 808-8040 .. **Riley**, David J '97 -29932 Sycamore Oval -Westlake 44145
Fx:808-9656

(216) 360-2124 .. **Riley**, David R '80 (Moriarty & J,PLL) -30000 Chagrin Blvd
-Ste 200 -Pepper Pike 44124

(513) 241-4722 .. **Riley**, Kimberly V '97 %Montgomery R&J,LPA -36 E 7th -Ste 2100
-Cincinnati 45202 **Fx:**241-8775

(216) 348-5400 .. **Riley**, Michael G '87 (McDonald H Co,LPA) -600 Superior Av E
-Ste 2100 -Cleveland 44114 **Fx:**348-5474

(513) 831-2227 .. **Riley**, Michael J '83 -5854 Cinema Dr -Milford 45150

(440) 244-5214 .. **Riley**, Patrick D '79 (Riley R & Assoc) -520 Bway -Ste 200 -Lorain
44052

(216) 766-5486 .. **Riley**, Patrick G '98 Genesis Ins -25550 Chagrin Blvd -Ste 300
-Beachwood 44122

(513) 621-3394 .. **Riley**, R Patrick '69 OfCnsl Peck S&W,LLP -201 E 5th -Ste 900
-Cincinnati 45202 **Fx:**621-3813

(202) 893-9200 .. **Riley**, Robert F '85 Williams MC&D -1666 K NW -Ste 1200
-Washington, DC 20006

(216) 348-5400 .. **Riley**, Shawn M '86 (McDonald H Co,LPA) -600 Superior Av E
-Ste 2100 -Cleveland 44114 **Fx:**348-5474

(419) 243-6148 .. **Riley**, Ted B '88 (Manahan PB&D) -414 N Erie -Bx2328
-Toledo 43603

(614) 221-0240 .. **Riley**, Thomas J '69 (Hahn L&P LLP) -65 E State -Ste 1400
-Columbus 43215 **Fx:**221-5909

(216) 621-2771 .. **Riley**, Timothy J '89 -1370 Ontario -Ste 800 -Cleveland 44113

(419) 242-2251 .. **Riley**, Tyrone '85 -316 N Mich -Ste 700 -Toledo 43624

(440) 886-1900 .. **Riley**, Victoria J '98 -5788 Ridge Rd -Ste 4 -Parma 44129

Rill, Colleen K '00 -(Address Unavailable)

(614) 365-6034 .. **Rilley**, Karin W '90 Columbus Public Schls -270 E State
-Columbus 43215 **Fx:**365-6042

(330) 376-9260 .. **Rilley**, Scott A '93 (Callahan GR&S LLC) -7 W Bowery -Ste 907
-Akron 44308 **Fx:**376-9807

(330) 926-0404 .. **Rilley**, Sue A '93 Marconi Comm Inc -1000 Marconi Dr
-Warrendale, PA 15086

(513) 255-2345 .. **Rimedio**, James R '65 -810 Matson Pl -704 Queen's Twr
-Cincinnati 45204 **Fx:**244-2620

(614) 466-2872 .. **Rimelspach**, Rene L '01 Atty Gen -30 E Broad -Columbus 43215
Fx:728-7592

(419) 885-2153 .. **Rimelspach**, Ron L '73 -5800 Monroe -Bldg C -Sylvania 43560

(330) 376-2700 .. **Rimmel**, Brad A '99 %Roetzel & A,LPA -222 S Main -Akron 44308
Fx:376-4577

(330) 533-1990 .. **Rimmel**, James E '83 (J Rimmel Co,LPA) -44 N Broad -Bx477
-Canfield 44406

(216) 515-1040 .. **Rinaldi**, Anthony '02 (A Rinaldi & Co,LLC) -1360 W 9th -Ste 310
-Cleveland 44113

(248) 539-5050 .. **Rinaldo**, Amy E '97 Kohn & Assoc -30500 Nrthwstrn Hwy -Ste 410
-Farmington Hills, MI 48334

(734) 763-4319 .. **Rine**, Nicholas J '75 Univ of MI Law Sch -801 Monroe
-Ann Arbor, MI 48109

(513) 721-1504 .. **Rinear**, Richard J '84 Droder & M Co,LPA -125 W Cntrl Pkwy
-Cincinnati 45202 **Fx:**721-0310

(513) 244-5655 .. **Rinear**, Robert L '65 -4820 Glenway Av -Cincinnati 45238

(419) 424-7832 .. **Rinebolt**, Richard J '48 Cnty Law Library -Hancock County Cthse
-Findlay 45840

(937) 223-6003 .. **Rineer**, Donald B '99 %Dunlevey M&F -110 N Main -Ste 1000
-Dayton 45402 **Fx:**223-8550

(419) 522-3398 .. **Rinehardt**, John J '56 (Inscore RW&E,LPA) -13 Park Av W
-Ste 400 -Mansfield 44902 **Fx:**522-5165

(419) 529-2020 .. **Rinehardt**, John K '86 -2404 Park Av W -Mansfield 44906

(614) 444-4455 .. **Rinehart**, Adam R '89 (Talbott & R) -1180 S High
-Columbus 43206

Rinehart, Brenda L '88 -(Address Unavailable)

(614) 221-0717 .. **Rinehart**, Dana G '73 (Rinehart & R,Ltd) -300 E Broad -Ste 190
-Columbus 43215

(330) 744-5147 .. **Rinehart**, James P '80 Mahoning Cnty Probate Ct -110 Market
-Youngstown 44503

Rinehart, Melinda A '04 -(Address Unavailable)

(614) 221-0717 .. **Rinehart & Rishel,Ltd** -300 E Broad -Ste 190 -Columbus 43215

(614) 292-3694 .. **Rinehart-Thompson**, Laurie '94 Ohio State Univ -1583 Perry
-Ste 543 -Columbus 43210

(513) 352-6700 .. **Rines**, David A '04 %Thompson H LLP -312 Walnut -14th Fl
-Cincinnati 45202 **Fx:**241-4771

(330) 674-9776 .. **Rinfret**, Robert D '72 (Rinfret & K) -184 E Jackson
-Millersburg 44654

(937) 378-4119 .. **Ring**, Charles N '93 (Purdy & R) -318 W State -Georgetown 45121

(513) 381-2838 .. **Ringenbach**, Laura A '83 OfCnsl Taft S&H LLP -425 Walnut
-Ste 1800 -Cincinnati 45202 **Fx:**381-0205

(330) 497-0700 .. **Ringer**, Charles E '89 (Krugliak WG&D Co,LPA)
-4775 Munson NW -Bx36963 -Canton 44735 **Fx:**497-4020

(740) 373-7624 .. **Rings**, Kevin A '87 %Washington Cnty Pros -205 Putnam
-Marietta 45750

(440) 331-6671 .. **Rini**, Charles A Jr. '92 Rini Realty Co -19050 Lorain Rd
-Fairview Park 44126

(216) 362-6801 .. **Rini**, Denise N '03 -5255 Commerce Pkwy -Cleveland 44130
Fx:698-7202

(216) 687-1910 .. **Rini**, Gusty A '71 Legal Aid -1223 W 6th -Cleveland 44113

(216) 787-3030 .. **Rini**, Mary Ann '79 Atty Gen -615 W Superior Av -11th Fl
-Cleveland 44113 **Fx:**787-3480

(216) 360-7200 .. **Rini**, William T '75 (Carlisle MRK&U Co,LPA) -24755 Chagrin Blvd
-Ste 200 -Cleveland 44122 **Fx:**360-7210

(216) 363-0982 .. **Rinicella**, Randy D '86 Buchanan I PC -600 Superior Av E
-Ste 1300 -Cleveland 44114

(330) 455-3488 .. **Rinier**, Alton L '48 (AL Rinier,LLC) -116 Cleveland Av N -Ste 704
-Canton 44702 **Fx:**455-4772

(513) 863-9100 .. **Rink**, Martin D '03 (Yonas & R LLC) -9100 Centre Pnte Dr -Ste 250
-West Chester 45069 **Fx:**863-9110

(216) 622-8200 .. **Rink**, Robert P '86 (Calfee H&G LLP) -800 Superior Av -Ste 1400
-Cleveland 44114 **Fx:**241-0816

(513) 621-2120 .. **Rink**, Thomas C '70 Strauss & T,LPA -150 E 4th -4th Fl
-Cincinnati 45202 **Fx:**241-8259

(216) 523-1500 .. **Rinker**, Bruce G '77 %Mansour GG&M Co,LPA -55 Pub Sq
-Ste 2150 -Cleveland 44113 **Fx:**523-1705

(216) 687-1311 .. **Rinkes**, Jennifer K '04 %Reminger & R -101 Prospect Av W
-1400 Mdlnd Bldg -Cleveland 44115 **Fx:**687-1841

(937) 443-0121 .. **Rion**, James P '69 (J Rion & Assoc) -333 W 1st -Ste 550
-Dayton 45402

(937) 223-9133 .. **Rion**, John H '70 (Rion R&R Co,LPA) -130 W 2nd -Ste 2150
-Bx1262 -Dayton 45402

(937) 223-9133 .. **Rion**, Jon P '96 (Rion R&R Co,LPA) -130 W 2nd -Ste 2150
-Bx1262 -Dayton 45402

(317) 684-5116 .. **Riordan**, Sarah S '95 Bose M&E, LLP -135 N Penn -Ste 2700
-Indianapolis, IN 46204

(216) 443-6350 .. **Riordan**, Timothy P '87 8th Dist Ct of Appls -1 Lakeside Av -#202
-Cleveland 44113 **Fx:**443-2044

(513) 287-2929 .. **Rios**, Martin Jr. '99 Special Counsel Inc -201 E 5th -Ste 1400
-Cincinnati 45202

(212) 219-3360 .. **Rios**, Sara E '86 Puerto Rican Lgl Def & Educ Fund -99 Hudson
-14th Fl -New York, NY 10013

(740) 349-8714 .. **Ripko**, Cindy L '82 -35 S Park Pl -Ste 201 -Newark 43055

(216) 522-7800 .. **Rippy**, Derrick V '90 US Trustees Ofc -200 Pub Sq -Ste 3300
-Cleveland 44114 **Fx:**522-4988

(513) 421-4225 .. **Risch**, Dennis S '80 %Heis & W Co,LPA -817 Main -Ste 800
-Cincinnati 45202

(330) 650-0580 .. **Rischitelli**, Robert J Jr. '95 -5765 Argyle Dr -Hudson 44236

(614) 221-7548 .. **Riseling**, Jerry L '62 Larrimer & L -165 N High -Columbus 43206
Fx:221-8659

(614) 221-0717 .. **Rishel**, James R '72 Rinehart & R,Ltd -300 E Broad -Ste 190
-Columbus 43215

(614) 221-0717 .. **Rishel**, James R '02 %Rinehart & R,Ltd -300 E Broad -Ste 190
-Columbus 43215

(606) 248-5320 .. **Rising**, Donald A '82 SSA-OHA -3504 W Cumberland Av
-Middlesboro, KY 40965

(440) 326-4856 .. **Rising**, June K '89 Lorain Cnty Dom Rltns Ct -225 Court
-Elyria 44035

(440) 988-8455 .. **Riske**, Michelle L '92 Justice Rsrch & Advcy,Inc -849 Cleveland
-Amherst 44001

(614) 224-8374 .. **Risley**, Rebecca L '02 Legal Aid -40 W Gay -Columbus 43215

(419) 241-3565 .. **Risner**, Rick L '83 -316 N Mich -8th Fl -Toledo 43624

(423) 357-4867 .. **Risner**, Terry '85 -534 W Main -Mount Carmel, TN 37645
Fx:357-7067

(216) 241-6602 .. **Rispo**, Ronald A '67 (Weston HFP&H LLP) -50 Pub Sq
-2500 Trmnl Twr -Cleveland 44113 **Fx:**621-8369

(330) 626-1990 .. **Rissland**, Karl R '90 -9442 State Route 43 -Streetsboro 44241
Fx:626-1993

(847) 715-5224 .. **Rissover**, Lynne A '88 Ameritech/SBC -95 W Algonqin Rd
-Arlington Heights, IL 60005

(614) 227-4857 .. **Ristau**, Justin W '02 %Bricker & E LLP -100 S 3rd
-Columbus 43215 **Fx:**227-2390

(216) 241-6602 .. **Ristau**, Timothy P '66 (Weston HFP&H LLP) -50 Pub Sq
-2500 Trmnl Twr -Cleveland 44113 **Fx:**621-8369

(419) 258-1550 .. **Rister**, Suzanne S '00 -Bx100 -Antwerp 45813

(440) 943-6489 .. **Ristity**, Donald W '66 -27700 Bishop Park Dr -Ste 906
-Willoughby Hills 44092

(727) 842-9758 .. **Ristoff**, David R '81 (Williams R&P,PLC) -6131 US Hwy 19
-New Port Richey, FL 34652 **Fx:**848-2494

(216) 222-8016 .. **Ritchey**, John J '73 Natl City Bank -1900 E 9th -17th Fl
Loc 01-2174 -Cleveland 44114

(216) 472-4000 .. **Ritchie**, Alan S '94 American National Development -1220
Huron Rd E -Cleveland 44115

(330) 629-8371 .. **Ritchie**, Walter D '91 -725 Boardman Canfld Rd -Unit L-1
-Youngstown 44512

(513) 891-1530 .. **Ritchie**, Warren J '74 (Keating R&S) -8050 Hosbrook -Ste 200
-Cincinnati 45236 **Fx:**891-1537

(312) 269-4200 .. **Ritchie**, William P '71 (Jones D) -77 W Wacker
-Chicago, IL 60601 **Fx:**782-8585

(614) 228-6675 .. **Ritenour**, Margaret J '80 %OH Assoc of Realtors -200 E Town
-Columbus 43215

(419) 473-3450 .. **Ritson**, Douglas J '92 -Bx8969 -Toledo 43623 **Fx:**473-0949

(513) 361-0250 .. **Rittenhouse**, Roger P '75 SSA-OHA -312 Elm -Ste 2100
-Cincinnati 45202

(202) 778-9396 .. **Ritter**, Jeffrey B '83 (Kirkpatrick & LNG LLP) -1800 Mass Av NW
-Washington, DC 20036 **Fx:**778-9100

(740) 373-5455 .. **Ritter**, Khadine L '00 %Theisen B,LPA -424 2nd -Bx739
-Marietta 45750 **Fx:**373-4409

(216) 771-5588 .. **Ritter**, Marin K '96 %Rosner & Assoc,LLC -812 Huron Rd
-Ste 601 Caxton Bldg -Cleveland 44115 **Fx:**771-5894

(614) 462-5442 .. **Ritter**, Paul D Jr. '56 (Kegler BH&R) -65 E State -Ste 1800
-Columbus 43215 **Fx:**464-2634

(513) 763-1932 .. **Ritter**, Paul F '88 Kendle Intl Inc -441 Vine -1200 Carew Twr
-Cincinnati 45202

(513) 381-5700 ..**Ritter & Randolph,LLC** -105 E 4th -Ste 1200 -Cincinnati 45202
    Fx:381-0014

(740) 397-4040 ..**Ritter**, Richard F '69 OfCnsl Critchfield C&J Ltd -10 S Gay
    -Mount Vernon 43050 **Fx:**397-6775

(843) 681-3586 ..**Ritter**, Richard J '97 R Ritter & Assoc -28 Branford Ln
    -Hilton Head Island, SC 29926

(419) 421-2196 ..**Ritter**, Robert H '88 Marathon Ashland Petroleum LLC
    -539 S Main -Rm #4203 -Findlay 45840 **Fx:**421-4590

(419) 241-3213 ..**Ritter Robinson McCready & James** -405 Mad Av -Ste 1850
    -Toledo 43604 **Fx:**241-4925

(513) 425-6609 ..**Ritter**, Scot M '82 12th Dist Ct of Appls -1001 Reinartz Blvd
    -Middletown 45042 **Fx:**425-8751

(614) 794-0120 ..**Ritter**, Stacy J '00 -7226 Wallpepper Ct -Westerville 43082

(614) 224-9207 ..**Ritterspach**, Angela M '99 Title First Agncy,Inc -555 S Front
    -Ste 400 -Columbus 43213

(614) 462-3555 ..**Ritterspach**, Benjamin E '99 Franklin Cnty Pros -373 S High
    -Columbus 43215

(513) 932-2115 ..**Rittgers**, Charles H '78 (Rittgers & R) -12 E Warren
    -Lebanon 45036

(513) 932-2115 ..**Rittgers**, Ellen B '79 (Rittgers & R) -12 E Warren -Lebanon 45036

(216) 586-3939 ..**Ritts**, Geoffrey J '93 (Jones D) -901 Lakeside Av -Cleveland 44114
    Fx:579-0212

(216) 432-3384 ..**Ritz**, Steven W '88 Cuyahoga Cnty Pros -3955 Euclid Av
    -Jane Edna Hunter Bldg -Cleveland 44115 **Fx:**431-4113

(216) 696-3252 ..**Ritzenberg**, Marvin '52 Gen Title Agency -629 Euclid Av -Ste 1020
    -Cleveland 44114

(216) 360-3737 ..**Ritzert**, Patricia M '77 OfCnsl Persky S&A Co,LPA
    -25101 Chagrin Blvd -Ste 350 Signature Sq II -Beachwood 44122
    Fx:593-0921

(216) 241-8333 ..**Ritzler Coughlin & Swansinger, Ltd** -1001 Lakeside Av
    -1550 North Pnt Twr -Cleveland 44114 **Fx:**241-5890

(216) 241-8333 ..**Ritzler**, Joseph G '91 Ritzler C&S,Ltd -1001 Lakeside Av
    -1550 North Pnt Twr -Cleveland 44114 **Fx:**241-5890

(440) 446-1100 ..**Rivchun**, Ryan L '02 %Dinn H&P,LLC -5910 Landerbrook Dr
    -Ste 200 -Cleveland 44124 **Fx:**446-1240

(216) 586-3939 ..**Rivera**, Robert F '03 %Jones D -901 Lakeside Av
    -Cleveland 44114 **Fx:**579-0212

(440) 646-3098 ..**Rivera-Sanchez**, Kim M '94 Rockwell Automation
    -1 Allen-Bradley Dr -Mayfield Heights 44124

(216) 696-3311 ..**Rivitz**, Richard S '67 (Kahn K) -1301 E 9th -2600 Erievw Twr
    -Cleveland 44114 **Fx:**623-4912

(937) 259-7118 ..**Rizer**, Edward N '83 Dayton Power & Light Co -Bx8825
    -Dayton 45401

(419) 229-5106 ..**Rizor Minnard & Rizor Co,LPA** -1045 Mackenzie Dr -Lima 45805

(419) 229-5106 ..**Rizor**, Paul D '76 (Rizor M&R Co,LPA) -1045 Mackenzie Dr
    -Lima 45805

(513) 579-6400 ..**Roach**, Adrienne J '96 (Keating M&K PLL) -1 E 4th
    -1400 Provident Twr -Cincinnati 45202 **Fx:**579-6457

(740) 593-2013 ..**Roach**, Bonnie L '03 Ohio Univ -Coll of Business -Copeland Hall
    -Athens 45701

(937) 878-8649 ..**Roach**, Buddy R '95 %Martin MW&R -26 N Wright Av
    -Fairborn 45324 **Fx:**878-8479

(937) 228-2666 ..**Roach**, David G '83 (Hochman R&P Co,LPA) -118 W 1st -Ste 650
    -Dayton 45402 **Fx:**228-0508

(219) 424-8132 ..**Roach**, Dustin M '91 VanGilder & T -202 W Berry -Ste 200
    -Fort Wayne, IN 46802

(330) 674-3055 ..**Roach**, Garrett M '92 (Critchfield C&J Ltd) -138 E Jackson -Ste A
    -Millersburg 44654

(330) 867-1490 ..**Roach**, Jason R '96 %Holland & M -55 S Miller Rd -Ste 103
    -Akron 44333 **Fx:**865-1221

(216) 566-5885 ..**Roach**, Jennifer S '01 %Thompson H LLP -127 Pub Sq
    -3900 Key Ctr -Cleveland 44114 **Fx:**566-5800

(614) 221-8800 ..**Roach**, John R '74 (Hudak & R) -118 E Main -Columbus 43215

(216) 696-4009 ..**Roach**, Lawrence J '01 Kraig & K -614 Superior Av W -Ste 900
    -Cleveland 44113 **Fx:**696-1835

(513) 984-2040 ..**Roach**, Megan K '01 %Scheuer M&B LLC -11025 Reed Hartman
    Hwy -Cincinnati 45242 **Fx:**984-6590

(419) 242-3900 ..**Roach**, Stephen C '84 Cincinnati Ins Co -300 Mad Av -Ste 1406
    -Toledo 43604

(614) 445-2481 ..**Roark**, David T '80 Grange Mutual Cslty Co -650 S Front -Bx1218
    -Columbus 43216

(614) 487-0700 ..**Roark**, Sue D '80 (S Roark,Co,LPA) -1500 W 3rd -Ste 108
    -Columbus 43212

(330) 457-2820 ..**Robb**, Carol A '83 -46033 Hatcher Rd -New Waterford 44445

(937) 257-5728 ..**Robb**, Jeffrey L '84 US Air Force AFMC/JAQ -4225 Logistics Av
    -Wright Patterson AFB 45433 **Fx:**257-0537

(330) 305-6400 ..**Robbins**, Donald L Jr. '02 %Pelini & F,Ltd -8040 Cleveland Av NW
    -Ste 400 -North Canton 44720 **Fx:**305-0042

(513) 977-8200 ..**Robbins**, Eric M '01 %Dinsmore & S LLP -255 E 5th -Ste 1900
    -Cincinnati 45202 **Fx:**977-8141

(513) 721-3330 ..**Robbins**, Fredric J '74 (Robbins KP&T) -7 W 7th -Ste 1400
    -Cincinnati 45202

(330) 869-0263 ..**Robbins**, Howard S '77 -2521 Durand Rd -Fairlawn 44333

(330) 729-9777 ..**Robbins**, Jennifer R '03 %Engler & Assoc
    -860 Boardman-Canfld Rd -Ste 204 -Boardman 44512
    Fx:758-9585

(513) 721-3330 ..**Robbins Kelly Patterson & Tucker** -7 W 7th -Ste 1400
    -Cincinnati 45202

(513) 558-7380 ..**Robbins**, Mary K '80 Coll of Med -231 Albert Sabin Way
    -231 Bethesda M1 554 -Cincinnati 45267

(614) 221-1314 ..**Robbins**, Pamela S '97 -175 S 3rd -Ste 360 -Columbus 43215

(610) 328-8899 ..**Robbins**, Stephen A '80 Hlth Plex Assoc -194 W Sproul Rd
    -Springfield, PA 19064

(614) 445-5858 ..**Robbins-Penniman**, Gus E '78 (Gibson & R-P Co LPA)
    -673 Mohawk -4th Fl -Columbus 43206 **Fx:**445-5850

(740) 593-5576 ..**Robe**, Scott M '91 -14 W Wshngtn -Athens 45701

(614) 464-1211 ..**Robek**, Christine L '04 %Frost BT LLC -10 W Broad -Ste 1000
    -Columbus 43215 **Fx:**464-1737

(216) 566-5755 ..**Robenalt**, James D '81 (Thompson H LLP) -127 Pub Sq
    -3900 Key Ctr -Cleveland 44114 **Fx:**566-5800

(419) 229-0054 ..**Robenalt**, John A '48 -211-215 N Elizabeth -Lima 45801

(941) 966-7755 ..**Robenalt**, John F '79 Robenalt & R -Bx550 -Osprey, FL 34229
    Fx:966-6678

(614) 462-2294 ..**Robenalt**, Robert M '89 (Schottenstein Z&D) -250 West
    -Bx165020 -Columbus 43216 **Fx:**462-5135

(216) 781-8700 ..**Robenalt**, Thomas D '91 (Novak RP&S,LLP) -1660 W 2nd
    -Ste 270 Skylight Ofc Twr -Cleveland 44113 **Fx:**781-9227

(513) 579-6400 ..**Robenson**, Todd E '04 %Keating M&K PLL -1 E 4th
    -1400 Provident Twr -Cincinnati 45202 **Fx:**579-6457

(216) 443-7223 ..**Roberson**, Christopher W '92 Cuyahoga Cnty Pub Def
    -1200 W 3rd NW -100 Lakeside Pl -Cleveland 44113

(740) 593-2066 ..**Roberson**, Jessie C Jr. '80 Ohio Univ -330 Copeland Hall
    -Athens 45701

(315) 477-9107 ..**Roberson**, Michael L '84 Carlisle Co -250 S Clinton
    -Syracuse, NY 13202

(937) 643-2000 ..**Roberson**, Nancy A '82 N Roberson Co,LPA -2390 S Dixie Hwy
    -Kettering 45409

(330) 374-5540 ..**Roberto**, Carmen V '73 Vasko R&E Co, LPA -137 S Main -Ste 206
    -Akron 44308

(614) 645-6947 ..**Roberto**, Cheryl A '87 Columbus Dept Pub Utilities -910 Dublin Rd
    -Columbus 43215

(216) 573-6666 ..**Roberto**, Robert J '03 %D Morell & Assoc Co,LPA
    -6060 Rockside Wds Blvd -250 Spectrum Bldg
    -Independence 44131

(937) 461-5980 ..**Roberts**, Brian M '82 (Jablinski FR&M) -214 W Monument Av
    -Bx1266 -Dayton 45402 **Fx:**461-4139

(703) 491-7070 ..**Roberts**, Charles B '78 -1308 Devils Reach Rd -Ste 303
    -Woodbridge, VA 22192

(937) 223-1100 ..**Roberts**, Christopher D '00 %Slicer Law Ofc -111 W 1st -Ste 401
    -Dayton 45402 **Fx:**223-8150

(614) 885-8272 ..**Roberts**, Cynthia B '91 %Bailey & S -6877 N High -Ste 303
    -Columbus 43085

(614) 466-4100 ..**Roberts**, Daniel J '88 Ohio Dept of Commerce-Div of Real Estate
    -77 S High -20th Fl -Columbus 43215

(216) 431-5300 ..**Roberts**, David D '92 %Kramer & Assoc,LPA -3214 Prospect Av
    -Cleveland 44115

(216) 698-2820 ..**Roberts**, Dennis L '99 Cuyahoga Cnty Workforce Dvlpmnt
    -1275 Ontario -Cleveland 44113

(614) 224-8374 ..**Roberts**, Donald W '02 Legal Aid -40 W Gay -Columbus 43215

(513) 621-6464 ..**Roberts**, Douglas D '93 (Graydon H&R LLP) -511 Walnut
    -1900 Fifth Third Ctr -Cincinnati 45202 **Fx:**651-3836

(614) 451-2210 ..**Roberts**, Edward S '76 S Roberts & Assoc -1625 Bethel Rd
    -Ste 102 -Columbus 43220

(513) 421-6630 ..**Roberts**, Edward '95 %Lindhorst & D Co,LPA -312 Walnut
    -Ste 2300 -Cincinnati 45202

(513) 421-2540 ..**Roberts**, George E III '69 (Ennis R&F) -121 W 9th
    -Cincinnati 45202 **Fx:**562-4986

(440) 746-0911 ..**Roberts**, Glenna M '87 (Vozar R&M Co,LPA) -3505 E Royalton Rd
    -Ste 100 -Cleveland 44147

(419) 241-9000 ..**Roberts**, H Buswell Jr. '75 (Shumaker L&K,LLP) -1000 Jackson
    -Toledo 43624 **Fx:**241-6894

(440) 572-1151 ..**Roberts**, Jacqueline I K '03 (Kim R&S,LLC) -4070 Ctr Rd
    -Brunswick 44212

(614) 466-4328 ..**Roberts**, James C '04 %Atty Gen -150 E Gay -Columbus 43215
    Fx:995-0266

(330) 744-5211 ..**Roberts**, James E '74 (Roth BRS&L,LPA) -100 Fed Plz E -Ste 600
    -Youngstown 44503 **Fx:**744-3184

(614) 764-8486 ..**Roberts**, James E '92 Wendys Intl -4288 W Dublin-Granvll Rd
    -Bx256 -Dublin 43017

(614) 462-4010 ..**Roberts**, Janie D '85 Common Pleas Ct -399 S Front -Ctrm 3
    -Columbus 43215

(513) 867-4822 ..**Roberts**, Jeffrey C '98 1st Natl Bk of SW OH -Bx476
    -Hamilton 45012

(330) 438-1180 ..**Roberts**, Jeffrey D '90 Unizan Fncl Srvcs Grp -Bx24190
    -Canton 44701 **Fx:**438-1822

(614) 464-6400 ..**Roberts**, Jeffrey D '01 %Vorys SS&P LLP -52 E Gay -Bx1008
    -Columbus 43216 **Fx:**464-6350

(817) 421-4630 ..**Roberts**, Kathryn A '86 -612 Northwood Trl -Southlake, TX 76092

(513) 233-3666 ..**Roberts**, Kevin P '88 -7373 Beechmont Av -#3 -Cincinnati 45230
    Fx:233-3206

(440) 461-9000 ..**Roberts**, Kevin P '94 Dyson S&F Co,LPA -5843 Mayfld Rd
    -Mayfield Heights 44124

(216) 781-6166 ..**Roberts**, Kevin T '86 -323 Lakeside Av W -Ste 450
    -Cleveland 44113

(937) 399-9709 ..**Roberts**, Mark F '79 (Elder R&E) -2233 N Limestone
    -Springfield 45503

(740) 881-0888 ..**Roberts**, Mary A '81 -4808 Seven Lks Pl -Powell 43065

(216) 931-6000 ..**Roberts**, Megan K '02 %Ulmer & B LLP -1300 E 9th -Ste
    900 Penton Media Bldg -Cleveland 44114 **Fx:**931-6001

(513) 621-6464 ..**Roberts**, Michael A '90 (Graydon H&R LLP) -511 Walnut
    -1900 Fifth Third Ctr -Cincinnati 45202 **Fx:**651-3836

(330) 336-4111 ..**Roberts**, Nancy S '92 Amer Pro-Mold,Inc -350 State -Bldg 7
    -Bx325 -Wadsworth 44282

    Roberts, Neil E '73 -1615 Rosewood Av -Lakewood 44107

(513) 946-3391 ..**Roberts**, Norton B '93 Cnsl Cmn Pleas Mediation Srvc -230 E 9th
    -Ste 1150 -Cincinnati 45202 **Fx:**946-3388

(419) 244-4777 ..**Roberts**, Richard L Sr. '89 -1122 Adams -Toledo 43624

(513) 474-7900 ..**Roberts**, Richard S '70 Thermo Co -8076 Beechmont Av
    -Cincinnati 45255

(513) 723-8400 ..**Roberts**, Robert C '04 Coley & Assoc -9334 Union Centre Blvd
    -Ste 200 -West Chester 45069

(260) 426-9706 ..**Roberts**, Robert E '98 %Beers MB&S,LLP -110 W Berry -Ste 1100
    -Fort Wayne, IN 46802 **Fx:**420-1314

(972) 443-6537 ..**Roberts**, Robert L Jr. '83 Flowserve Corp -222 W Las Colinas Blvd
    -Ste 1500 -Irving, TX 75039

(937) 778-8000 ..**Roberts**, Roberta S '02 %T Buecker Co,LPA -306 W High
    -Bx1259 -Piqua 45356 **Fx:**778-1111

(614) 451-2210 ..**Roberts**, Scott R '79 (S Roberts & Assoc) -1625 Bethel Rd
    -Ste 102 -Columbus 43220

(937) 222-2424 ..**Roberts**, Shaun A '88 %Freund F&A -1 S Main -Ste 1800
    -Dayton 45402 **Fx:**222-5369

(614) 719-3410 ..**Roberts**, Stacy E '02 Hon T Kemp -US Dist Ct -85 Marconi Blvd
    -Columbus 43215

(614) 901-8178 ..**Roberts**, Stewart E '75 -1935 Schrock Rd -Bx298152
    -Columbus 43229

(216) 361-2500 ..**Roberts**, Tommy Jr. '84 Cnsl Roberts Cnsltnts,Inc
    -3611 Prospect Av -Cleveland 44115 **Fx:**361-2222

(248) 263-3721 ..**Roberts,** Wayne D '99 %Raymond & P,PC -26300 Nrthwstrn Hwy
-4th Fl -Bx5058 -Southfield, MI 48086

(216) 586-3939 ..**Roberts-Mamone,** Lisa A '88 (Jones D) -901 Lakeside Av
-Cleveland 44114 **Fx:**579-0212

(330) 823-1140 ..**Robertson,** Alex J '55 (AJ Robertson & Assoc) -2210 S Union Av
-Alliance 44601

(330) 823-1140 ..**Robertson,** Alex J '91 %AJ Robertson & Assoc -2210 S Union Av
-Alliance 44601

(513) 422-7184 ..**Robertson,** Charles S '95 -Bx948 -Middletown 45044

(216) 881-6600 ..**Robertson,** Darnella T '96 NEORSD -3826 Euclid Av
-Cleveland 44115 **Fx:**881-4407

(513) 563-6161 ..**Robertson,** David F Jr. '01 -11137 Main -Cincinnati 45241

(614) 466-4605 ..**Robertson,** David W '89 OH Dept Job & Fam Srvcs -30 E Broad
-32nd Fl -Columbus 43266

(216) 241-7255 ..**Robertson,** Deanna '91 -2401 Superior Viaduct -Cleveland 44113

(330) 823-1140 ..**Robertson,** Erin K '02 %AJ Robertson & Assoc -2210 S Union Av
-Alliance 44601

(216) 687-9264 ..**Robertson,** Heidi Gorovitz '97 CSU-Marshall Cllg of Law
-2121 Euclid Av -LB138 -Cleveland 44115 **Fx:**687-6881

(330) 494-6611 ..**Robertson,** James T '74 (Robertson Z&P) -4690 Munson NW
-Ste C -Canton 44718

(614) 462-3664 ..**Robertson,** Jan E '91 Hon D O'Neill Common Pleas -369 S High
-Ctrm 9A -Columbus 43215

(216) 348-5400 ..**Robertson,** Jean R '98 (McDonald H Co,LPA) -600 Superior Av E
-Ste 2100 -Cleveland 44114 **Fx:**348-5474

(626) 578-6906 ..**Robertson,** Jeffrey D '94 Jacobs Engineering Grp Inc
-1111 S Arroyo Pkwy -Pasadena, CA 91105
Robertson, Jeffrey H '03 -(Address Unavailable)

(419) 898-2921 ..**Robertson,** Jerry D '74 -132 W Water -Bx26 -Oak Harbor 43449

(440) 729-3488 ..**Robertson,** John B '61 -8251 Mayufld Rd -204 Cmbrdge Sq Bldg
-Chesterland 44026

(415) 836-2500 ..**Robertson,** Joseph M '78 -139 Townsend -Ste 400 -Bx77630
-San Francisco, CA 94107

(313) 465-7520 ..**Robertson,** Julie E '01 (Honigman MS&C,LLP) -660 Woodward Av
-Ste 2290 -Detroit, MI 48226

(216) 621-0200 ..**Robertson,** Kevin G '84 (Baker & H LLP) -1900 E 9th -Ste 3200
-Cleveland 44114 **Fx:**621-0216

(740) 345-5280 ..**Robertson,** Robert C '77 Cnsl Lwyrs Title Agncy -36 N 2nd -Bx919
-Newark 43058 **Fx:**349-9380

(330) 823-1140 ..**Robertson,** Shawn O '93 %AJ Robertson & Assoc
-2210 S Union Av -Alliance 44601

(330) 494-6611 ..**Robertson Zeglen & Pidlock** -4690 Munson NW -Ste C
-Canton 44718

(216) 581-8200 ..**Robey,** Gregory S '91 (Robey & R) -14402 Granger Rd
-Cleveland 44137

(412) 918-1100 ..**Robic,** Michael P II '94 Metz L LLC -11 Stanwix -18th Fl
-Pittsburgh, PA 15222

(216) 687-1976 ..**Robie,** Julie E '04 Legal Aid -1223 W 6th -Cleveland 44113

(614) 462-2218 ..**Robinett,** John D '82 (Schottenstein Z&D) -250 West -Bx165020
-Columbus 43216 **Fx:**462-5135

(216) 696-3510 ..**Robinette,** Burl C '87 (Robinette & L,LLP) -526 Superior Av
-Ste 1160 -Cleveland 44114

(419) 255-5900 ..**Robinette,** Gregory W '00 %MacMillan S&T,LLC -720 Water
-4th Fl -Toledo 43604 **Fx:**255-9639

(513) 396-5821 ..**Robinette,** Joseph A '87 US Playing Card Co -4590 Beech
-Cincinnati 45212 **Fx:**458-7565

(614) 228-1541 ..**Robins,** Harlan W '92 (Baker & H LLP) -65 E State -Ste 2100
-Columbus 43215 **Fx:**462-2616

(614) 464-6400 ..**Robins,** Ronald A Jr. '90 (Vorys SS&P LLP) -52 E Gay -Bx1008
-Columbus 43216 **Fx:**464-6350

(513) 762-6200 ..**Robins,** Teri E '02 %Ulmer & B LLP -600 Vine -Ste 2800
-Cincinnati 45202 **Fx:**762-6245

(216) 529-6030 ..**Robinson,** Andrew S Jr. '01 Law Dept -12650 Detroit Av
-Lakewood 44107

(513) 651-6800 ..**Robinson,** Ann G '94 (Frost BT LLC) -201 E 5th -2200 PNC Ctr
-Cincinnati 45202 **Fx:**651-6981

(614) 228-1541 ..**Robinson,** Barry R '72 (Baker & H LLP) -65 E State -Ste 2100
-Columbus 43215 **Fx:**462-2616

(419) 774-5676 ..**Robinson,** Brent N '94 Richland Cnty Pros -38 S Park -2nd Fl
-Mansfield 44902 **Fx:**774-5589

(419) 524-6000 ..**Robinson,** Charles T '66 -3 N Main -Ste 400 -Mansfield 44902

(859) 225-9625 ..**Robinson,** Clayton L '88 Jenkins PR&B -269 W Main -Ste 100
-Lexington, KY 40507

(937) 299-5098 ..**Robinson,** Constance M '90 -400 W Dorothy Ln -Kettering 45429

(216) 520-5518 ..**Robinson,** Craig A '92 %West Grp -6111 Oak Tree Blvd
-Bx318063 -Cleveland 44131

(330) 666-1650 ..**Robinson,** David J '76 -1615 Centervw Dr -Copley 44321
Fx:670-8010

(614) 462-5052 ..**Robinson,** David J '92 (Schottenstein Z&D) -250 West -Bx165020
-Columbus 43216 **Fx:**462-5135
Robinson, Denise A '03 -(Address Unavailable)

(440) 329-5286 ..**Robinson,** Donald G '89 Lorain Cnty Pros -225 Court -3rd Fl
-Elyria 44035

(937) 222-1440 ..**Robinson,** Eugene '71 -333 W 1st -Ste 420 -Dayton 45402

(614) 893-2514 ..**Robinson,** Evelyn R '82 Green Mountain Energy Co -5450
Frantz Rd -Dublin 43016

(513) 351-9112 ..**Robinson,** Gerald J '59 Kenko Corp -2250 Seymour Av
-Cincinnati 45212

(614) 462-3555 ..**Robinson,** Heather B '96 Franklin Cnty Pros -373 S High
-Columbus 43215

(330) 702-0780 ..**Robinson,** Henry C '49 OfCnsl Luckhart MZ&R
-3810 Starrs Centre Dr -Canfield 44406

(330) 337-8761 ..**Robinson,** Ian '79 Fitch KCR&B -600 E State -Bx590
-Salem 44460 **Fx:**337-9453

(513) 626-3356 ..**Robinson,** Ian S '03 Procter & Gamble -11450 Grooms Rd
-Cincinnati 45242

(513) 381-3525 ..**Robinson,** James B '75 (Kircher R&W) -1014 Vine -Ste 2520
-Cincinnati 45202

(513) 523-4111 ..**Robinson,** James G '74 (Robinson & L Co,LPA) -Park Place W
-Fay Bldg -Oxford 45056

(440) 323-5700 ..**Robinson,** James T '97 (Taylor B&R Co,LPA) -409 East Av -Ste B
-Elyria 44035
Robinson, Janet Y '99 -100 SE 9th -#600 -Topeka, KS 66612

(419) 337-5065 ..**Robinson,** Jeffrey L '77 (Barber KS&R) -124 N Fulton
-Wauseon 43567 **Fx:**337-1136

(703) 588-5291 ..**Robinson,** Jeremy W '96 US Army Legal Srvcs Agency
-901 N Stuart -Ste 340 -Arlington, VA 22203

(330) 376-2272 ..**Robinson,** Kandee S '04 %Williams & Assoc -106 S Main
-Ste 2300 -Akron 44308 **Fx:**376-5618

(216) 688-3737 ..**Robinson,** Kenneth F '86 -3886 Rocky Rvr Dr -Cleveland 44111

(614) 884-4800 ..**Robinson,** Kenneth J '98 (Slowik & R,LLC) -250 E Broad -Ste 250
-Columbus 43215 **Fx:**884-4801

(614) 854-3090 ..**Robinson,** Kerry L '98 SrCnsl Nationwide Ins -5900 Parkwood Dr
-PW 01-08 -Dublin 43016 **Fx:**854-8870

(330) 395-7405 ..**Robinson,** Learthon S Jr. '91 -179 W Market -Robnsn Prof Bldg
-Warren 44481

(330) 530-1620 ..**Robinson,** Lisa K '89 -Bx340 -Mc Donald 44437

(216) 781-3600 ..**Robinson,** Loreen M '88 Faulkner M&P,LLP -820 W Superior Av
-Ste 900 -Cleveland 44113 **Fx:**781-8839
Robinson, Mark A '79 -608 Mad Av -Ste 1400 -Toledo 43604

(216) 479-6100 ..**Robinson,** Marquettes D '01 %Vorys SS&P LLP -1375 E 9th
-Ste 2100 One Cleve Ctr -Cleveland 44114 **Fx:**479-6060

(330) 665-1117 ..**Robinson,** Michael L '77 -750 Springwtr Dr -Akron 44333

(614) 621-9000 ..**Robinson,** Michelle K '96 Glincher Dvlpmnt Corp -150 E Gay
-Columbus 43215

(304) 525-0320 ..**Robinson,** Monica L '00 Vital & V LC -536 5th Av
-Huntington, WV 25701

(614) 221-9800 ..**Robinson,** Rachel K '97 Equal Justice Fndtn -88 E Broad
-Ste 1590 -Columbus 43215 **Fx:**221-9810

(614) 221-8900 ..**Robinson,** Randal D '75 (Burman & R) -601 S High
-Columbus 43215 **Fx:**221-8912

(614) 221-3318 ..**Robinson,** Robert M '96 %Agee CM&L -89 E Nationwide Blvd
-Ste 200 -Columbus 43215

(216) 621-3839 ..**Robinson,** Ronald '85 -1276 W 3rd -#424 -Cleveland 44113

(330) 869-6121 ..**Robinson,** Saundra W '77 Robinson Legal Srvcs -Bx13144
-Akron 44334

(216) 696-0808 ..**Robinson,** Scott J '01 %Wilkerson & Assoc Co,LPA
-1422 Euclid Av -Ste 248 -Cleveland 44115 **Fx:**696-4970

(614) 365-2700 ..**Robinson,** Tim J '90 OfCnsl Squire S&D LLP -41 S High
-1300 Huntngtn Ctr -Columbus 43215 **Fx:**365-2499

(419) 724-0030 ..**Robinson,** Tonya M '99 LAWO -520 Mad Av -Ste 640
-Toledo 43604 **Fx:**321-1582

(330) 376-9225 ..**Robinson,** Virginia R '86 Akron Metro Housing Auth -100 W Cedar
-Akron 44307

(330) 337-8761 ..**Robinson,** Whitman '03 -255 N Union Av -Salem 44460

(513) 455-7600 ..**Robinson,** William T III '71 (Greenebaum D&M PLLC) -255 E 5th
-2800 Chemed Ctr -Cincinnati 45202 **Fx:**455-8500

(614) 466-5610 ..**Robinson-Bond,** Alice L '84 Atty Gen -150 E Gay
-Columbus 43215 **Fx:**752-2732

(937) 645-3029 ..**Robinson-Walls,** Sharon Kay '99 Union Cnty Juv Ct -215 W 5th
-Cthse -Marysville 43040

(757) 887-7641 ..**Robisch,** Thomas G '78 Cnsl Dept of Navy/Gen Cnsl Ofc
-Code OOL -Naval Weapons Station -Yorktown, VA 23691

(419) 249-7900 ..**Robison Curphey & O'Connell** -Four SeaGate -9th Fl -Toledo
43604 **Fx:**249-7911

(440) 324-2409 ..**Robison,** Deanne L '93 UAW Legal Srvcs -347 Midway Blvd
-Ste 312 -Elyria 44035 **Fx:**324-4647
Robison, Gary T '60 -3561 Kingsway Dr -Columbus 43221

(740) 345-9801 ..**Robison,** Joseph A '75 (Jones NM&H) -35 S Park Plz -Ste 35
-Bx4010 -Newark 43058 **Fx:**345-6031

(216) 381-4050 ..**Robison,** Nancy B '79 -4555 Wilburn Dr -South Euclid 44121

(513) 412-3483 ..**Robison,** Stephen L '86 -4500 Cooper Rd -Ste 305
-Cincinnati 45242

(614) 559-3839 ..**Robol,** Richard T '96 (Robol & W,LLC) -555 City Park Av
-Columbus 43215

(419) 897-6500 ..**Robon,** Marvin A '66 (Barkan & R Ltd) -1701 Woodlnds Dr
-Maumee 43537 **Fx:**897-6200

(513) 852-3497 ..**Robson-Higgins,** Yanna M '98 Atty Gen -441 Vine
-1600 Carew Twr -Cincinnati 45202 **Fx:**852-3484

(216) 741-2365 ..**Robusto,** Michael A '79 UAW Legal Srvcs -707 Brookpark Rd
-Brooklyn Heights 44109

(614) 430-8885 ..**Roby,** Robert S '96 (Curry RS&M Co,LLC) -8000 Ravines Edge Ct
-Ste 103 -Columbus 43235 **Fx:**430-8890

(419) 843-2001 ..**Roca,** John M '86 %Gallon & T Co,LPA -3516 Granite Cir
-Bx352018 -Toledo 43635 **Fx:**843-6665
Rocci, Melissa K '94 -(Address Unavailable)

(440) 617-4233 ..**Rocco,** Andrea F '93 Westlake Law Dept -27700 Hilliard Blvd
-City Hall -Westlake 44145

(614) 898-7100 ..**Rocco,** Gerald A '86 MS Cnsltnts,Inc -2221 Schrock Rd
-Columbus 43229

(216) 289-4500 ..**Rocco,** Patrick R '69 -25000 Euclid Av -Ste 100 -Euclid 44117

(614) 221-1111 ..**Rocco,** Thomas J '92 %Shayne & G -221 S High
-Columbus 43215 **Fx:**221-4070

(202) 295-4500 ..**Roche,** Marianne E '92 %Silver F&T LLP -1700 Wscnsn Av NW
-Washington, DC 20007 **Fx:**337-5502
Roche, Michael J '02 -16212 Ernadale Av -Cleveland 44111

(216) 348-1700 ..**Roche,** Patrick F '76 (Davis & Y) -101 Prospect Av W -Ste 1700
-Cleveland 44115 **Fx:**621-0602

(216) 348-1700 ..**Roche,** Patrick M '99 %Davis & Y -101 Prospect Av W -Ste 1700
-Cleveland 44115 **Fx:**621-0602

(216) 861-5582 ..**Roche,** Patrick R '78 (Fay SFM&M LLP) -1100 Superior Av -7th Fl
-Cleveland 44114 **Fx:**241-1666

(216) 671-0599 ..**Roche,** Peter M '03 Cleveland Mun Ct -6th Fl Justice Ctr Probation
-Cleveland 44113 **Fx:**671-4267

(614) 466-5394 ..**Roche,** Susan M '00 Pub Def -8 E Long -Columbus 43215

(216) 443-8195 ..**Roche,** Thomas J '84 Recorders Ofc -1219 Ontario Av
-Cleveland 44113

(330) 535-8116 ..**Rochford,** Bernard A '90 Oriana House -885 E Buchtel Av
-Bx1501 -Akron 44309

(330) 643-2963 ..**Rochford,** Rita M '85 Summit Cnty Juv Ct -650 Dan -Akron 44310

(937) 224-7625 ..**Rock,** William Randall '84 -32 N Main -Ste 911 -Dayton 45402
Fx:223-6967

(330) 497-4546 ..**Rockenfelder,** Wendy J '79 -5502 Market Av N -Ste B
-Canton 44721

(561) 776-0881 ..**Rocker,** Linda '83 -13864 Degas Dr E -Palm
Beach Gardens, FL 33410

(614) 457-9731 ..**Rocray,** John N '96 Harris & M -941 Chatham Ln -Ste 201
-Columbus 43221 **Fx:**457-3596

(614) 890-4543 ..**Roda,** Matthew J '93 Griffith & W -575 Copeland Mill Rd -Ste 2C
-Westerville 43081

(419) 228-3300 ..**Rodabaugh,** David A '77 (Rodabaugh & H) -234 N Main
-Lima 45801

(216) 443-6350 ..**Rodak,** Andrew N '83 8th Dist Ct of Appls -1 Lakeside Av -#202
-Cleveland 44113 **Fx:**443-2044

(937) 443-6825 ..**Roddy,** Joan H '81 (Thompson H LLP) -2000 Cthse Plz NE
-Bx8801 -Dayton 45401 **Fx:**443-6635

(419) 278-7015 ..**Rode,** James D '99 %Gribbell S&C -114 E Main -Bx54
-Deshler 43516

(216) 696-1122 ..**Rode,** Michael K '80 Mgmt Recruiters Intl,Inc -200 Pub Sq -31st Fl
-Cleveland 44114

(412) 338-7881 ..**Rodebush,** Curtis E '02 Deloitte & Touche,LLP -2500 One PPG Pl
-Pittsburgh, PA 15222

(740) 354-1300 ..**Rodeheffer,** Stephen C '76 -630 6th -Portsmouth 45662

(513) 352-4713 ..**Rodell,** Maria L '96 Law Dept -801 Plum -Rm 214
-Cincinnati 45202 **Fx:**352-1515

(513) 721-1200 ..**Rodenbeck,** Stephen P '82 %Young R&M Co,LPA -1014 Vine
-Ste 2400 -Cincinnati 45202 **Fx:**721-7116

(513) 732-2040 ..**Rodenberg,** Kathleen M '83 (Rodenberg & K,Ltd)
-70 N Riverside Dr -Batavia 45103

(937) 293-9189 ..**Roderer,** Paul B '67 Roderer Law Ofc -2090 S Patterson Blvd
-Bx897 -Dayton 45409 **Fx:**293-9372

(937) 293-9189 ..**Roderer,** Paul B Jr. '94 Roderer Law Ofc -2090 S Patterson Blvd
-Bx897 -Dayton 45409 **Fx:**293-9372

(614) 221-8651 ..**Roderick,** Gerald L '84 -5 E Long -Ste 605 -Columbus 43215

(330) 434-3000 ..**Roderick & Linton** -One Cascade Plz -Ste 1500 -Akron 44308
Fx:434-9220

(740) 446-8880 ..**Roderick,** Richard C Jr. '72 -21 Locust -Gallipolis 45631

(330) 965-9190 ..**Rodfong,** G Thomas '88 -965 Windham Ct -Ste 4
-Boardman 44512 **Fx:**965-9150

(937) 645-4190 ..**Rodger,** Lester R Jr. '89 Union Cnty Pros -221 W 5th -Ste 333
-Marysville 43040 **Fx:**645-4191

(419) 241-9000 ..**Rodgers,** Damian M P '94 %Shumaker L&K,LLP -1000 Jackson
-Toledo 43624 **Fx:**241-6894

(814) 451-6385 ..**Rodgers,** Daniel J '98 Erie Cnty Ct of Common Pleas -140 W 6th
-Cnty Cthse -Erie, PA 16501

(216) 621-1530 ..**Rodgers,** Jeffrey A '96 %Shapiro & F,LLP -1500 W 3rd -Ste 400
-Cleveland 44113 **Fx:**621-1551

(216) 479-8500 ..**Rodgers,** Joseph P '98 %Squire S&D LLP -127 Pub Sq
-4900 Key Twr -Cleveland 44114 **Fx:**479-8780

(513) 574-9264 ..**Rodgers,** Lori B '99 -4589 Hmptn Pnte Dr -Cincinnati 45248

(580) 481-7294 ..**Rodgers,** Michael A '85 US Air Force -97 AMW\JA -Altus, OK 73521

(202) 305-2795 ..**Rodgers,** Ronald L '83 US DOJ-Drug Sec -1400 NY Av NW
-Ste 11100 -Washington, DC 20005

(330) 497-0700 ..**Rodgers,** Susan C '91 (Krugliak WG&D Co,LPA)
-4775 Munson NW -Bx36963 -Canton 44735 **Fx:**497-4020

(937) 332-2114 ..**Rodgers,** Thomas H '70 Hobart Corp -701 S Ridge Av -Troy 45374

(513) 744-8537 ..**Rodgers,** Timothy A '99 Fifth 3rd Bank -38 Fountain Sq Plz
-Cincinnati 45263

(614) 221-4000 ..**Rodgers,** Todd M '93 %Chester W&S LLP -65 E State -10th Fl
-Columbus 43215 **Fx:**221-4012

(216) 861-6191 ..**Rodgers,** Walter A '70 (Rodgers & Co,LPA) -45 Prospect Av W
-1600 Guildhall Landmark Ofc Twrs -Cleveland 44115
Fx:861-4699

(614) 224-7754 ..**Rodier,** Ian H '89 -309 S 4th -Ste 200 -Columbus 43215
Fx:224-7760

(216) 515-1660 ..**Rodio,** Mark L '95 (Frantz W LLP) -127 Pub Sq -2500 Key Ctr
-Cleveland 44114 **Fx:**515-1650

(513) 887-3474 ..**Rodkey,** Jessica M '01 Butler Cnty Pros -315 High -11th Fl -Bx515
-Hamilton 45012

(216) 447-9850 ..**Rodman,** John D '87 -7100 Plesant Valley Rd -Ste 210
-Independence 44131

(937) 449-2800 ..**Rodman,** Rachael L '01 %Chernesky H&K PLL -10 Cthse Plz SW
-Ste 1100 -Dayton 45402 **Fx:**449-2821

(216) 932-4255 ..**Rodney,** David E '83 -1624 S Taylor Rd -Cleveland Heights 44118
Rodocker, Peter B '97 -209 Frankfort Sq -Columbus 43206

(216) 664-4802 ..**Rodriguez,** Angela L '01 Prosecutor -1200 Ontario Av
-8th Fl Justice Ctr -Cleveland 44113 **Fx:**664-4399

(319) 295-5938 ..**Rodriguez,** Bruno V '88 Rockwell Collins,Inc -350 Collins Rd NE
-Cedar Rapids, IA 52498

(614) 464-6400 ..**Rodriguez,** Joseph C '00 %Vorys SS&P LLP -52 E Gay -Bx1008
-Columbus 43216 **Fx:**464-6350

(216) 443-7800 ..**Rodriguez,** Oscar E '01 Cuyahoga Cnty Pros -1200 Ontario -8th Fl
-Cleveland 44113 **Fx:**698-2270

(407) 648-7500 ..**Rodriguez,** Roberto H Jr. '82 US Atty -501 W Church
-Orlando, FL 32805 **Fx:**648-7643
Rodriguez, Theodore F '91 -4 Niblick Rd -Shrewsbury, MA 01545

(979) 849-5741 ..**Rodriguez,** Christine M '91 -222 N Velasco -Bx1819
-Angleton, TX 77516

(440) 895-1234 ..**Rodstrom,** Derek N '96 (Polito P&R) -21300 Lorain Rd -Fairview
Park 44126

(317) 636-1600 ..**Rody,** Richard C Jr. '79 Simon Prop Grp -115 W Wshngtn
-Indianapolis, IN 46204

(412) 434-5544 ..**Roe,** Adrian N '98 (Watkins D&R PC) -603 Stanwix -Two
Gtwy Ctr 17E -Pittsburgh, PA 15222 **Fx:**434-5554

(216) 291-9215 ..**Roe,** Carol A '91 Ctrs for Dialysis Care -18720 Chagrin Blvd
-Shaker Heights 44122

(513) 977-8200 ..**Roe,** Clifford A Jr. '67 (Dinsmore & S LLP) -255 E 5th -Ste 1900
-Cincinnati 45202 **Fx:**977-8141

(614) 790-1556 ..**Roe,** Michael S '93 Ashland Inc -5200 Blazer Pkwy -Dublin 43017

(419) 352-7522 ..**Roebke,** Harry G '42 (Middleton R&N) -521 N Main
-Bowling Green 43402 **Fx:**353-4899
Roeder, James A '03 -(Address Unavailable)

(937) 252-2030 ..**Roedersheimer,** Charles J '68 %Thompson & D Co,LPA
-1340 Woodman Dr -Dayton 45432

(614) 361-6783 ..**Roeger,** Deborah L '89 Dr Mediation Srvcs -1689 Hardin Ln
-Powell 43065

(614) 365-2700 ..**Roehm,** Victor J III '01 %Squire S&D LLP -41 S High
-1300 Huntngtn Ctr -Columbus 43215 **Fx:**365-2499

(614) 469-3200 ..**Roehrenbeck,** Gabriel J '04 %Thompson H LLP -10 W Broad
-Ste 700 -Columbus 43215 **Fx:**469-3361
Roelker, Daniella A '97 -(Address Unavailable)

(513) 731-6601 ..**Roell,** Steven R '01 %W Hesch Law Firm -3047 Madison Rd
-Ste 205 -Cincinnati 45209

(614) 855-2292 ..**Roelle,** Robert H '57 -Bx399 -New Albany 43054

(513) 621-1935 ..**Roeller,** Robert K '62 (Roeller R&J) -1029 Main -Cincinnati 45202

(419) 475-5151 ..**Roemer,** Wellington F III '89 Wellington F Roemer Ins,Inc
-3912 Sunforest Ct -Toledo 43623

(419) 423-4321 ..**Roepke,** Stephen A '81 (Firmin S&H Co,LPA) -220 W Sandusky
-Bx963 -Findlay 45839 **Fx:**423-8484

(513) 977-8200 ..**Roesch,** Charles M '84 (Dinsmore & S LLP) -255 E 5th -Ste 1900
-Cincinnati 45202 **Fx:**977-8141

(513) 977-8200 ..**Roesch,** Lynda E '79 (Dinsmore & S LLP) -255 E 5th -Ste 1900
-Cincinnati 45202 **Fx:**977-8141

(614) 559-1188 ..**Roesch,** Robert C II '92 Chicago Title -100 S 4th -Columbus 43215

(216) 621-0040 ..**Roessler,** Kirk W '93 (Strachan MO&R Co LPA) -925 Euclid Av
-Ste 1940 -Cleveland 44115

(440) 350-3200 ..**Roessner,** Pamela L '01 Lake Cnty Pub Def -125 E Erie
-Painesville 44077

(330) 376-2700 ..**Roetzel & Andress,LPA** -222 S Main -Akron 44308 **Fx:**376-4577

(513) 361-0200 ..**Roetzel & Andress,LPA** -250 E 5th -310 Chiquita Ctr
-Cincinnati 45202 **Fx:**361-0335

(614) 463-9770 ..**Roetzel & Andress,LPA** -155 E Broad -Natl City Ctr 12th Fl
-Columbus 43215 **Fx:**463-9792

(216) 623-0150 ..**Roetzel & Andress,LPA** -1375 E 9th -One Cleve Ctr 9th Fl
-Cleveland 44114 **Fx:**623-0134

(419) 242-7985 ..**Roetzel & Andress,LPA** -One SeaGate -9th Fl -Toledo 43604
Fx:242-0316

(330) 294-1032 ..**Rogachefsky,** Barbara J '97 BJ Rogachefsky Co,LPA
-113 Portage Trl -Bx67128 -Cuyahoga Falls 44222 **Fx:**294-1032
Rogan, Michael J '83 -5710 Blair Dr -Highland Heights 44143
Rogers, Barbara A '97 -Bx251 -Blacklick 43004

(614) 789-5568 ..**Rogers,** Brent A '97 Sterling Commerce -4600 Lakehurst Ct
-Bx8000 -Dublin 43016

(513) 381-2838 ..**Rogers,** Brie S '02 %Taft S&H LLP -425 Walnut -Ste 1800
-Cincinnati 45202 **Fx:**381-0205

(614) 466-3101 ..**Rogers,** Clarence D '64 PUCO -180 E Broad -Columbus 43266

(330) 643-3550 ..**Rogers,** Clement H III '84 Industrial Commssn of OH -161 S High
-Ste 301 -Akron 44308

(614) 227-2367 ..**Rogers,** David A '76 (Bricker & E LLP) -100 S 3rd
-Columbus 43215 **Fx:**227-2390

(602) 528-4000 ..**Rogers,** David E '93 %Squire S&D LLP -40 N Central Av
-Ste 2700 -Phoenix, AZ 85004 **Fx:**253-8129

(623) 915-3394 ..**Rogers,** Donna M '87 -4625 W Desert Cove Av -Glendale, AZ 85304

(614) 464-6400 ..**Rogers,** Douglas L '71 (Vorys SS&P LLP) -52 E Gay -Bx1008
-Columbus 43216 **Fx:**464-6350

(419) 748-8041 ..**Rogers,** George C '74 -6884 State Route 110 -Napoleon 43545
Fx:748-8532

(937) 223-8171 ..**Rogers & Greenberg** -2160 Kettering Twr -Dayton 45423
Fx:223-1649

(513) 381-2838 ..**Rogers,** Gregory Parker '89 (Taft S&H LLP) -425 Walnut
-Ste 1800 -Cincinnati 45202 **Fx:**381-0205

(317) 226-6016 ..**Rogers,** James E Jr. '79 IRS -575 N Penn Av -Rm 558
-Indianapolis, IN 46204

(419) 241-6000 ..**Rogers,** James L '88 (Eastman & S Ltd) -1 Seagate -24th Fl
-Bx10032 -Toledo 43699 **Fx:**247-1777

(614) 863-6333 ..**Rogers,** James T '68 -1606 Lncstr Av -Reynoldsburg 43068

(740) 387-0800 ..**Rogers,** James W '62 -334 E Center -Bx544 -Marion 43301

(614) 462-3555 ..**Rogers,** Jeffrey C '98 Franklin Cnty Pros -373 S High
-Columbus 43215

(440) 350-2683 ..**Rogers,** John M '02 Lake Cnty Pros -105 Main -Bx490
-Painesville 44077 **Fx:**350-2585

(419) 245-4913 ..**Rogers,** Jon A '83 Lucas Co Sheriffs Dept -1622 Spielbusch Av
-Toledo 43624

(216) 622-8200 ..**Rogers,** Karla M '97 %Calfee H&G LLP -800 Superior Av
-Ste 1400 -Cleveland 44114 **Fx:**241-0816

(614) 462-7450 ..**Rogers,** Marilyn C '98 CASA Franklin Cnty -373 S High -6th Fl
-Columbus 43215 **Fx:**462-5070

(614) 292-0574 ..**Rogers,** Nancy Hardin '72 OSU Moritz Cllg of Law -55 W 12th Av
-Columbus 43210 **Fx:**292-1383

(216) 267-7100 ..**Rogers,** Niles P '86 Oatey Co -4700 W 106th -Bx35906
-Cleveland 44135

(419) 289-8857 ..**Rogers,** Ramona J '82 Ashland Cnty Pros -307 Orange
-Ashland 44805 **Fx:**281-3865

(937) 438-0555 ..**Rogers,** Richard H '74 -7333 Paragon Rd -Ste 200 -Dayton 45459

(781) 466-0700 ..**Rogers,** Samuel M '79 (Zelle Hoffman VM&G,LLP) -950 Winter
-Ste 1300 -Waltham, MA 02451 **Fx:**466-0701

(513) 564-7000 ..**Rogers,** Susan S '78 6th Dist Ct of Appls -100 E 5th -Cthse
-Cincinnati 45202

(937) 223-8171 ..**Rogers,** William A Jr. '60 (Rogers & G) -2160 Kettering Twr
-Dayton 45423 **Fx:**223-1649
Rogers-Barron, Sharon L '93 -2502A Av B
-Bradenton Beach, FL 34217

(216) 622-8410 ..**Rogge,** Gretchen H '97 %Calfee H&G LLP -800 Superior Av
-Ste 1400 -Cleveland 44114 **Fx:**241-0816

(216) 443-8578 ..**Rogo,** Patricia A '79 Common Pleas Ct -1200 Ontario
-Cleveland 44113

(440) 247-1452 ..**Rogoff,** Nancy H '85 -17 Water -Chagrin Falls 44022

(614) 464-1211 ..**Rogovin,** Richard D '68 (Frost BT LLC) -10 W Broad -Ste 1000
-Columbus 43215 **Fx:**464-1737

(216) 523-4515 ..**Rogozinski,** Lynn R '95 Eaton Corp -1111 Superior Av
-Cleveland 44114
Rogus, Claire V '95 -1180 McGuffey Ln -Batavia 45103

(513) 412-5400 ..**Rogus,** Timothy E '94 %Buckley K,LPA -201 E 5th -Ste 1420
-Cincinnati 45202 **Fx:**412-5401

(330) 744-5201 ..**Rohde,** R Keller '75 Unemploymnt Comp Commssn -Bx1198
-Youngstown 44501

(513) 723-2216 ..**Rohner,** Nicholas K '01 %Weltman W&R Co,LPA -525 Vine
-Ste 800 -Cincinnati 45202 **Fx:**723-2239

(513) 621-6464 ..**Rohr,** Jeffrey L '85 (Graydon H&R LLP) -511 Walnut
-1900 Fifth Third Ctr -Cincinnati 45202 **Fx:**651-3836

(216) 263-6200 ..**Rohr**, Nicole L '04 %Rauser & Assoc,LPA -614 W Superior Av
-Ste 950 -Cleveland 44113 **Fx:**263-6202

(419) 248-2600 ..**Rohrbacher**, David J '75 (Rohrbachers LC&T Co,LPA)
-405 Mad Av -8th Fl -Toledo 43604 **Fx:**248-2614

(419) 248-2600 ..**Rohrbacher**, Matthew J '80 (Rohrbachers LC&T Co,LPA)
-405 Mad Av -8th Fl -Toledo 43604 **Fx:**248-2614

(419) 248-2600 ..**Rohrbachers Light Cron & Trimble Co,LPA** -405 Mad Av -8th Fl
-Toledo 43604 **Fx:**248-2614

(330) 783-9222 ..**Rohrbaugh**, Robert J II '99 D'Apolito & D -4800 Market
-Youngstown 44512

(330) 456-8341 ..**Rohrer**, Amanda K '03 %Black MS&A,LPA -220 Market Av S
-Ste 1000 -Canton 44702 **Fx:**456-5756

(937) 228-9790 ..**Rohrer**, David A '89 %LP Mulligan & Assoc LPA,Co
-28 N Wilkinson -2nd Fl -Bx10838 -Dayton 45402

(740) 368-1545 ..**Rohrer**, Kyle E '96 City Pros -70 N Union -Delaware 43015

(330) 376-5300 ..**Rohrich**, Richard P '73 (Buckingham D&B,LLP) -50 S Main
-Bx1500 -Akron 44309 **Fx:**258-6559

Rohrkaste, William D '85 -439 S 2nd -Hamilton 45011

(216) 615-9100 ..**Rohrs**, Jeffrey K '94 Optiem -1330 Old River Rd -Cleveland 44113

(614) 387-9762 ..**Rohrs**, Kenneth A '73 OH Judicial Conf -65 S Front -4th Fl
-Columbus 43215

(614) 227-2000 ..**Rohyans**, John B '69 (Porter WM&A LLP) -41 S High
-Columbus 43215 **Fx:**227-2100

(440) 322-5441 ..**Roig**, Delbert L '92 (Lessing W&R Ltd) -374 Broad -Ste A
-Elyria 44035

(216) 622-3673 ..**Rokakis**, Alexander A '82 US Atty -801 W Superior -Ste 400
-Cleveland 44113 **Fx:**622-3370

(216) 443-7400 ..**Rokakis**, James '84 Cuyahoga Cnty Treasurer -1219 Ontario
-Cleveland 44113

(304) 748-3200 ..**Rokisky**, Jeffrey J '99 -3200 Main -Weirton, WV 26062

(740) 345-9183 ..**Roland**, Christian D '90 -30 W Locust -Newark 43055

(330) 759-9838 ..**Roland**, David K '86 -1406 W Lbrty -Hubbard 44425

(330) 451-7898 ..**Roland**, Deborah N '89 5th Dist Ct of Appls -110 Central Plz S
-Ste 320 -Canton 44702 **Fx:**451-7249

(330) 455-0173 ..**Roland**, Robert E '85 (Day KRW&R,Ltd) -200 Market Av N
-Ste 300 -Bx24213 -Canton 44701 **Fx:**455-2633

(513) 519-0766 ..**Rolcik**, Karen A '86 Law Offices of Karen Rolcik -Bx40634
-Cincinnati 45240

(216) 514-1100 ..**Rolf**, Carol '76 (Rolf & G Co,LPA) -30100 Chagrin Blvd
-Ste 350 Corp Cir -Cleveland 44124 **Fx:**514-0030

(216) 514-1100 ..**Rolf & Goffman Co,LPA** -30100 Chagrin Blvd -Ste 350 Corp Cir
-Cleveland 44124 **Fx:**514-0030

Rolf, Matthew W '02 -528 S Drexel Av -Bexley 43209

(740) 852-3094 ..**Rolfes**, James W Sr. '75 -17 S Main -Bx24 -London 43140

(513) 579-0080 ..**Rolfes**, Jerome F '89 (Smith R&S Co,LPA) -1014 Vine -Ste 2350
-Cincinnati 45202 **Fx:**579-0222

(513) 721-4185 ..**Rolfes**, Thomas A '95 -2117 Beechmont Av -Cincinnati 45230

(216) 622-8200 ..**Rolitsky**, Sandra G '82 (Calfee H&G LLP) -800 Superior Av
-Ste 1400 -Cleveland 44114 **Fx:**241-0816

(440) 918-2720 ..**Roll**, Kenneth R '80 Lake Cnty Cmn Pleas Ct -47 N Park Pl
-Painesville 44077

(216) 360-3737 ..**Roll**, Stewart D '87 (Persky S&A Co,LPA) -25101 Chagrin Blvd
-Ste 350 Signature Sq II -Beachwood 44122 **Fx:**593-0921

(440) 442-8383 ..**Rolla**, Dudley B '57 -31915 Cedar Rd -Mayfield Heights 44124

(216) 348-1700 ..**Roller**, Jan L '83 (Davis & Y) -101 Prospect Av W -Ste 1700
-Cleveland 44115 **Fx:**621-0602

(513) 579-0080 ..**Roller**, Pamela A '01 %Smith R&S Co,LPA -1014 Vine -Ste 2350
-Cincinnati 45202 **Fx:**579-0222

(614) 466-1305 ..**Roller**, Valerie A '87 Atty Gen -30 E Broad -Columbus 43215
Fx:466-8898

(937) 890-2110 ..**Rollert**, Joyce A '88 -150 W Natl Rd -Bx275 -Vandalia 45377

(614) 466-5091 ..**Rolletta**, Sandra M '83 Industrial Commssn of OH -30 W Spring
-9th Fl -Columbus 43215 **Fx:**752-8785

(419) 249-7100 ..**Rollison**, Gerardo R '80 %Marshall & M,LLC -Four Seagate -8th Fl
-Toledo 43604 **Fx:**249-7151

(513) 852-6057 ..**Rollman**, Jeffrey M '74 (Wood & L LLP) -600 Vine -Ste 2500
-Cincinnati 45202 **Fx:**852-6087

(216) 781-1700 ..**Roloff**, David E '78 (Shapero & R Co,LPA) -1350 Euclid Av
-Ste 1550 -Cleveland 44115 **Fx:**781-1972

(740) 385-5604 ..**Rolston**, George Drew '72 -61 N Market -Rear -Logan 43138

(614) 469-5715 ..**Rolwing**, Richard M '93 US DOJ-Tax Div -303 Marconi Blvd
-Ste 200 -Columbus 43215 **Fx:**469-5653

(216) 241-0715 ..**Romaine**, Daniel A '96 (Nager & R) -425 W Lakeside Av -Ste 100
-Cleveland 44113 **Fx:**241-9434

(740) 345-0850 ..**Romaker**, Robert R '90 SE OH Lgl Srvcs -12 W Locust Av
-Newark 43055

(216) 831-0042 ..**Roman**, Barbara Sue K '77 Meyers RF&L LPA
-28601 Chagrin Blvd -Ste 500 -Cleveland 44122 **Fx:**831-0542

(419) 424-4323 ..**Roman**, Bridgette C '88 SrCnsl Cooper Tire -701 Lima Av -Bx550
-Findlay 45840

(419) 241-6168 ..**Roman**, Jane E '02 -520 Mad Av -Ste 830 -Toledo 43604

(330) 253-8877 ..**Roman**, Kirk E '85 -50 S Main -Ste 502 -Akron 44308

(407) 835-4310 ..**Roman**, Laura J '97 US Dist Ct -80 N Hughey Av
-Orlando, FL 32801

(216) 479-8500 ..**Romancher**, Catherine Ziroli '03 %Squire S&D LLP -127 Pub Sq
-4900 Key Twr -Cleveland 44114 **Fx:**479-8780

(716) 512-8581 ..**Romanchik**, Richard A '87 Heidelberg Digital LLC
-2600 Manitou Rd -Rochester, NY 14653

(614) 461-1311 ..**Romanello**, George M '74 (Reminger & R) -65 E State
-4th Fl Cptl Sq Ofc Bldg -Columbus 43215 **Fx:**232-2410

Romano, Joseph M '02 -11431 State Rd -North Royalton 44133

(330) 726-8669 ..**Romano**, Karen M '00 -412 Boardman-Canfld Rd
-Boardman 44512

(216) 592-5000 ..**Romano**, Matthew '03 %Tucker E&W LLP -925 Euclid Av
-1150 Huntngtn Bldg -Cleveland 44115 **Fx:**592-5009

(614) 645-8287 ..**Romanoff**, Marvin S '67 Cnty Mun Ct Judge -375 S High
-Columbus 43215

(419) 842-1252 ..**Romanoff**, Rolland W '61 -6591 W Central Av -Ste 103
-Toledo 43617

(330) 762-0765 ..**Romanoski**, Janice Crossland '81 -441 Wolf Ledges Pkwy
-Ste 400 -Akron 44311 **Fx:**762-2255

(518) 384-7854 ..**Romanov**, Victor '83 Victor Romanov -116 Crane
-Scotia, NY 12302

(216) 522-4914 ..**Romanowski**, Esther B '79 SSA/OHA -1350 Euclid Av -7th Fl
-Cleveland 44115

(330) 761-2912 ..**Romans**, Clifford S '85 Akron Pub Schls -70 N Bway -Akron 44308

(513) 422-0158 ..**Romans**, Kathleen A '83 -Bx42572 -Middletown 45042

(216) 931-6000 ..**Rome**, Peter A '84 (Ulmer & B LLP) -1300 E 9th
-Ste 900 Penton Media Bldg -Cleveland 44114 **Fx:**931-6001

Romell, William C '61 -380 Elmwood Rd -Rocky River 44116

(216) 641-2400 ..**Romer**, James D '98 Romer & Co, LPA -5620 Bway Av -#300
-Cleveland 44127

(330) 743-1171 ..**Romero**, Edwin '78 (Manchester BP&U) -201 E Commerce
-Atrium Level 2 Commerce Bldg -Youngstown 44503
Fx:743-1190

(419) 225-2015 ..**Romey**, Steven A '79 (Romey & V) -330 N Main -Bx1256 -Lima
45802

(419) 225-2015 ..**Romey & Vandemark** -330 N Main -Bx1256 -Lima 45802

(330) 896-3023 ..**Romig**, Connie J '96 Green Chamber Of Commerce -Bx547
-Green 44232 **Fx:**896-3178

(817) 963-5942 ..**Romig**, Melissa A '96 American Airlines -4333 Amon Carter Blvd
-MD 567 -Fort Worth, TX 76155

(614) 248-8039 ..**Romohr**, Amy L '91 Banc One Accptnce Corp -100 E Broad
-Columbus 43215

(419) 241-1200 ..**Romp**, Janelle M '03 %Cooper & W,LPA -900 Adams
-Toledo 43624 **Fx:**242-5675

(419) 259-7633 ..**Romstadt**, Lori A '99 Fifth 3rd Bank -606 Mad Av -Toledo 43604

(937) 225-5964 ..**Rondy**, Anny Kraynanski '03 Montgomery Cnty CSEA -14 W 4th
-Bx8744 -Dayton 45401

(937) 325-2492 ..**Ronemus**, Thor G '55 Ronemus & H Co,LPA -5 E Columbia
-Springfield 45502

(614) 210-7616 ..**Ronnebaum**, Sherri L '94 Sterling Commerce -4600 Lakehurst Ct
-Dublin 43016

(440) 262-1423 ..**Ronyak**, David M '75 SrCnsl Goodrich Corp -9921 Brecksvll Rd
-Brecksville 44141 **Fx:**262-1421

(216) 515-1660 ..**Roof**, Brian E '99 %Frantz W LLP -127 Pub Sq -2500 Key Center
-Cleveland 44114 **Fx:**515-1650

(513) 634-5209 ..**Roof**, Carl J '92 Procter & Gamble -6071 Ctr Hill Rd -Ofc F3A14
-Cincinnati 45224

(419) 674-4031 ..**Roof**, Thomas A '79 (Roof & B) -218 W Columbus -Kenton 43326

(614) 628-0650 ..**Rook**, James E '93 -50 W Broad -Ste 1800 -Columbus 43215

(740) 335-0888 ..**Rooker**, Kristina M '01 Fayette Cnty Pros -110 E Court -1st Fl
-Washington Court House 43160

(216) 696-3030 ..**Rooney**, Dean M '83 (Kadish H&W,LPA) -1717 E 9th -Ste 2112
-Cleveland 44114 **Fx:**696-3492

(216) 763-1004 ..**Rooney**, Erin K '01 %Siegel SJ&J Co,LPA -25700 Science Park Dr
-Ste 210 -Cleveland 44122 **Fx:**763-1016

(216) 623-0150 ..**Rooney**, George W Jr. '74 (Roetzel & A,LPA) -1375 E 9th
-One Cleve Ctr 9th Fl -Cleveland 44114 **Fx:**623-0134

(440) 891-8320 ..**Rooney**, John J '84 (Rooney & S) -493 Front -Berea 44017
Fx:(866) 891-2844

(614) 221-5500 ..**Rooney**, Kevin G '85 -495 S High -Ste 120 -Columbus 43215

(513) 241-2324 ..**Rooney**, Kevin G '92 (Wood H&E LLP) -441 Vine -Ste 2700
-Cincinnati 45202 **Fx:**421-7269

(614) 486-7884 ..**Rooney**, Lisa A '85 -2070 Neil Av -153 Hithcock Hall
-Columbus 43210

(419) 423-0242 ..**Rooney**, Philip L '92 (Drake PK&C) -301 S Main -Ste 3
-Findlay 45840 **Fx:**423-0186

(440) 838-8800 ..**Rooney**, Thomas D '72 (Millisor & N Co,LPA) -9150 S Hills Blvd
-Ste 300 -Cleveland 44147 **Fx:**838-8805

(216) 635-0636 ..**Roosa**, James K '87 -3723 Pearl Rd -Cleveland 44109

(513) 362-2846 ..**Roosa**, Kathryn L '02 Legal Aid -10 Jrnl Sq -Hamilton 45011

(440) 774-7700 ..**Roose**, Kirk B '81 (Roose & R PA) -5 S Main -Ste 301
-Oberlin 44074

(440) 774-7700 ..**Roose & Ressler PA** -5 S Main Ste 301 -Oberlin 44074

(419) 242-1515 ..**Roose & Ressler PA** -Four SeaGate -Ste 600 -Toledo 43604

(330) 263-5333 ..**Roose & Ressler PA** -243 E Lbrty -Ste 9 -Wooster 44691

(937) 754-3040 ..**Root**, Beth W '92 Fairborn Mun Ct -44 W Hebble Av
-Fairborn 45324

(419) 249-7100 ..**Root**, Bridgett J '98 %Marshall & M,LLC -Four Seagate -8th Fl
-Toledo 43604 **Fx:**249-7151

(419) 447-8332 ..**Root**, Dawn D '87 -5219 N State Route 53 -Tiffin 44883

(614) 365-2700 ..**Root**, Emily E '03 %Squire S&D LLP -41 S High
-1300 Huntngtn Ctr -Columbus 43215 **Fx:**365-2499

(937) 433-2567 ..**Root**, Frank M Jr. '51 -6816 Cranford Dr -Dayton 45459

(937) 372-4404 ..**Root**, John A '92 (Gibney SB&R) -1354 N Monroe Dr -Ste B
-Xenia 45385 **Fx:**372-5435

(614) 760-1801 ..**Root**, William K '78 (Resch & R) -5060 Bradenton Av -Ste C
-Dublin 43017

(330) 376-2700 ..**Ropchock**, Mark A '85 (Roetzel & A,LPA) -222 S Main
-Akron 44308 **Fx:**376-4577

(614) 221-2121 ..**Roper**, James M '87 (Isaac BL&T,LLP) -250 E Broad -Ste
900 Mdlnd Bldg -Columbus 43215 **Fx:**365-9516

(614) 445-2744 ..**Rorapaugh**, Michael B '82 Grange Mutual Cslty Co -650 S Front
-Bx1218 -Columbus 43215

(513) 381-2838 ..**Rorer**, Sara S '88 %Taft S&H LLP -425 Walnut -Ste 1800
-Cincinnati 45202 **Fx:**381-0205

(330) 740-2180 ..**Rorick**, Christina M '99 %Hon MM DeGenaro -120 Market
-Youngstown 44503

(216) 586-3939 ..**Rorimer**, Louis '75 (Jones D) -901 Lakeside Av -Cleveland 44114
Fx:579-0212

(513) 482-5081 ..**Rosado**, Raul Jr. '89 Cnsl Cognis Corp -5051 Estecreek Dr
-Cincinnati 45232

(440) 461-8500 ..**Rosalina**, Gabriella M '98 BM Russo & Co,LPA -691 Richmond Rd
-Richmond Heights 44143

(440) 461-8500 ..**Rosalina**, Joseph K '01 BM Russo & Co,LPA -691 Richmond Rd
-Richmond Heights 44143

(813) 881-8638 ..**Rosamond**, Darrin M '99 CHASE Fncl -Indpndnc Pkwy
-MC FS1-4915 -Tampa, FL 33634

(614) 461-1100 ..**Rosan**, Kristin E '99 %Swedlow BLL&D Co,LPA -10 W Broad
-Ste 2400 -Columbus 43215 **Fx:**461-8178

(937) 225-5434 ..**Rosario**, Kay M '84 Montgomery Cnty Pub Def -117 S Main
-Ste 400 -Dayton 45422 **Fx:**225-3449

(440) 556-4926 ..**Rosati**, Flaviano P '79 -6001 Cochran Rd -Ste 202 -Solon 44139

(330) 533-3341 ..**Rosati**, Gary J '84 Farmers Natl Bank -20 S Broad -Canfield 44406

(614) 227-2321 .. **Rosati,** Jack R Jr. '89 (Bricker & E LLP) -100 S 3rd -Columbus 43215 **Fx:**227-2390

(614) 621-1500 .. **Rosato,** Peter A '97 %Calfee H&G LLP -21 E State -1100 Fifth Third Ctr -Columbus 43215 **Fx:**621-0010

(216) 991-8880 .. **Rosch,** Winn L '83 -20000 Shaker Blvd -% G Gehring -Shaker Heights 44122

(614) 221-6969 .. **Roscoe,** David A '01 Wolske & B,LPA -580 S High -Ste 300 -Columbus 43215

(216) 522-4914 .. **Roscoe,** George D '81 SSA/OHA -1350 Euclid Av -7th Fl -Cleveland 44115

Roscoe, Roberta J '02 -2535 McCoy Rd -Columbus 43220

(614) 225-9700 .. **Rose,** Bert L '92 -209 S High -Ste 212 -Columbus 43215

(330) 374-1144 .. **Rose,** Beverly J '74 -1 Cascade Plz -Ste 1450 -Akron 44308

(216) 397-9999 .. **Rose,** Bruce R '75 -1991 Lee Rd -Ste 203 -Cleveland Heights 44118

(440) 365-2880 .. **Rose,** Carl J '04 -246 Syracuse Ct -Elyria 44035

(216) 241-6602 .. **Rose,** Dana A '84 (Weston HFP&H LLP) -50 Pub Sq -2500 Trmnl Twr -Cleveland 44113 **Fx:**621-8369

(614) 415-7461 .. **Rose,** Daniel A '88 The Limited,Inc -3 Limited Pkwy -Bx16000 -Columbus 43216

(216) 861-8737 .. **Rose,** Daniel C '90 Oglebay Norton Co -1001 Lakeside Av -15th Fl -Cleveland 44114

(216) 642-0323 .. **Rose,** David A '01 %Britton SP&K Co,LPA -4700 Rockside Rd -Ste 540 Summit One -Cleveland 44131 **Fx:**642-0747

(614) 792-1188 .. **Rose,** David E '78 -Bx1357 -Dublin 43017

(216) 621-0150 .. **Rose,** Dennis R '87 (Hahn L&P LLP) -3300 BP Twr/200 Pub Sq -Ste 3300 -Cleveland 44114 **Fx:**241-2824

(937) 382-2838 .. **Rose & Dobyns Co,LPA** -97 N South -Wilmington 45177

(614) 889-8160 .. **Rose,** Donald G '66 -195 Stonefence Ln -Dublin 43017

Rose, Donald M '58 -(Address Unavailable)

Rose, Dora '04 -22475 McCauley Rd -Shaker Heights 44122

(330) 364-1614 .. **Rose,** Frank J Jr. '74 Fitzpatrick Z&R Co LPA -140 Fair Av NW -Bx1014 -New Philadelphia 44663 **Fx:**343-3077

(937) 382-2838 .. **Rose,** Gordon L '80 (Rose & D Co,LPA) -97 N South -Wilmington 45177

(713) 567-9360 .. **Rose,** Howard E '74 US Atty/Sthrn Dist TX -910 Travis -#1500 -Bx61129 -Houston, TX 77208 **Fx:**718-3301

(614) 444-8777 .. **Rose,** James V '58 DeSanto & M -887 S High -Columbus 43206

(513) 531-1197 .. **Rose,** Janet T '78 -2971 Rdgwd Av -Cincinnati 45213

(216) 241-7255 .. **Rose,** Jeri-ellen '93 -2401 Superior Viaduct -Cleveland 44113

(513) 621-7902 .. **Rose,** John W '81 -632 Vine -Ste 711 -Cincinnati 45202

(202) 879-3888 .. **Rose,** Jonathan C '78 (Jones DR&P) -51 Louisiana Av NW -Washington, DC 20001 **Fx:**626-1700

(216) 771-1777 .. **Rose,** Joseph B III '71 -55 Pub Sq -Ste 2200 -Cleveland 44113

(740) 397-4040 .. **Rose,** Kim M '81 (Critchfield C&J Ltd) -10 S Gay -Mount Vernon 43050 **Fx:**397-6775

(610) 282-3800 .. **Rose,** Mark E '96 Lutron Elctrncs Co,Inc -7200 Suter Rd -Coopersburg, PA 18036

(419) 249-7100 .. **Rose,** Mark H '87 (Marshall & M,LLC) -Four Seagate -8th Fl -Toledo 43604 **Fx:**249-7151

(330) 363-7463 .. **Rose,** Mark N '92 Aultman Hlth Fndtn -2600 6th SW -Canton 44710

(740) 687-1990 .. **Rose,** Martha A '79 -229 E Main -Lancaster 43130

(614) 292-8626 .. **Rose,** Michael D '63 OSU Moritz Cllg of Law -55 W 12th Av -Columbus 43210 **Fx:**292-1383

Rose, Pamela G '04 -(Address Unavailable)

(330) 535-5711 .. **Rose,** Paul A '82 (Brouse M) -106 S Main -500 First Natl Twr -Akron 44308 **Fx:**253-8601

(412) 562-8800 .. **Rose,** Richard D '00 (Buchanan I) -301 Grant -20th Fl -Pittsburgh, PA 15219 **Fx:**562-1041

(440) 255-4444 .. **Rose,** Ronald '91 Mentor High Schl -6477 Ctr -Mentor 44060

(614) 834-1200 .. **Rose,** Sara L '95 (S Rose,LLC) -Bx188 -Pickerington 43147

(208) 342-2552 .. **Rose,** Scott L '03 -300 W Main -Ste 153 -Boise, ID 83702

(216) 443-7800 .. **Rose,** Susan E '96 %Cuyahoga Cnty Pros -1200 Ontario -8th Fl -Cleveland 44113 **Fx:**698-2270

(216) 771-8420 .. **Rose,** Timothy F '82 -55 Pub Sq -# 2200 -Cleveland 44113

(330) 841-2605 .. **Rose,** Traci T '98 %City Law Dept -391 Mahoning Av -Warren 44483

(614) 268-8928 .. **Rose,** Waldo B '69 -592 E North Bway -Columbus 43214

(843) 785-5169 .. **Rose,** William S Jr. '77 (Mcnair Law Firm,PA) -Drwr7787 -Hilton Head Island, SC 29938 **Fx:**842-3310

(614) 645-7712 .. **Roseboro,** Anthony M '86 City Atty -90 W Broad -Columbus 43215

(419) 599-1010 .. **Rosebrook,** Amy C '98 Hanna & F -822 Oakwood Av -Bx605 -Napoleon 43545

(330) 262-2350 .. **Rosebrough-Schneider,** Christina A '94 -903 Douglas Dr -Wooster 44691

(513) 241-3100 .. **Roselle,** Cynthia M '01 %Lerner S&R -120 E 4th -8th Fl -Cincinnati 45202

(513) 621-0267 .. **Roselle,** Louise M '72 Waite SB&C -1 W 4th -1513 4th & Vine Twr -Cincinnati 45202

(614) 797-9700 .. **Roseman,** D Richard '95 -6016 Cleveland Av -Columbus 43231 **Fx:**797-9702

(216) 621-7227 .. **Roseman,** James D '72 OfCnsl Nicola G&C,LLC -25 W Prospect Av -Republic Bldg Ste 1400 -Cleveland 44115 **Fx:**621-3999

(937) 223-1130 .. **Rosemeyer,** Jon M '84 Pickrel S&E -40 N Main -2700 Kettering Twr -Dayton 45423 **Fx:**223-0339

(216) 781-3055 .. **Rosen,** Allard J '51 NCO Grp -1422 Euclid Av -Ste 510 -Cleveland 44115 **Fx:**781-1554

(513) 573-6606 .. **Rosen,** Arthur M '81 Mitsubishi Electric Auto Amer -4773 Bethany Rd -Mason 45040

(614) 466-8911 .. **Rosen,** Erin G '99 Atty Gen -30 E Broad -Columbus 43215 **Fx:**728-7582

(330) 376-8336 .. **Rosen,** Gary M '78 (Goldman & R,Ltd) -11 S Forge -Akron 44304 **Fx:**376-2522

(330) 607-7298 .. **Rosen,** Gerald M '99 -Bx13502 -Fairlawn 44334

(513) 241-0400 .. **Rosen,** Irving H '57 OfCnsl Aronoff R&H Co,LPA -425 Walnut -Ste 2400 -Cincinnati 45202 **Fx:**241-2877

(216) 579-4114 .. **Rosen,** Jonathan D '00 %McIntyre K&K Co LPA -1301 E 9th -Ste 1200 -Cleveland 44114

(513) 923-5232 .. **Rosenacker,** Frank B '83 F Rosenacker Co,LPA -5537 Cheviot Rd -Cincinnati 45247

(216) 595-0071 .. **Rosenbaum,** Beth Stoller '89 Roth B LLP -5196 Richmond Rd -Bedford Heights 44146 **Fx:**595-0073

(301) 469-7564 .. **Rosenbaum,** Greg A '78 Palisades Assoc,Inc -9140 Vendome Dr -Bethesda, MD 20817

(216) 592-5000 .. **Rosenbaum,** Jacob I '52 OfCnsl Tucker E&W LLP -925 Euclid Av -1150 Huntngtn Bldg -Cleveland 44115 **Fx:**592-5009

(216) 781-5245 .. **Rosenbaum,** Jeremy A '85 (Berkman GM&D) -55 Pub Sq -2121 The Illuminating Bldg -Cleveland 44113 **Fx:**781-8207

(440) 322-7972 .. **Rosenbaum,** Jonathan E '79 -230 3rd -Ste 104 -Elyria 44035

(716) 218-8620 .. **Rosenbaum,** Matthew A '98 (Gray, Feldman & Rosenbaum) -Bldg One, Ste 240 -625 panorama Trl -Rochester, NY 14625

(614) 249-7982 .. **Rosenbaum,** Melissa G '92 Nationwide -1 Nationwide Plz -1-26-09 -Columbus 43215

(216) 292-7355 .. **Rosenbaum,** Robert F '72 (Rosenbaum & M Co,LPA) -24100 Chagrin Blvd -330 -Beachwood 44122

(614) 461-1100 .. **Rosenberg,** Eric J '98 Swedlow BLL&D Co,LPA -10 W Broad -Ste 2400 -Columbus 43215 **Fx:**461-8178

(513) 564-7654 .. **Rosenberg,** Hilda '90 US Dist Ct -5th & Walnut -706 Cthse -Cincinnati 45202

(513) 579-6400 .. **Rosenberg,** J David '74 SrCnsl Keating M&K PLL -1 E 4th -1400 Provident Twr -Cincinnati 45202 **Fx:**579-6457

(513) 792-6729 .. **Rosenberg,** Jay A '66 (JA Rosenberg LPA) -1 Fncl Way -Ste 312 -Cincinnati 45242 **Fx:**(866) 611-0170

(614) 228-6885 .. **Rosenberg,** Karen Krisher '84 Lane A&H LLC -175 S 3rd -Ste 700 -Columbus 43215 **Fx:**228-0146

(216) 586-3939 .. **Rosenberg,** Martin Joseph '99 %Jones D -901 Lakeside Av -Cleveland 44114 **Fx:**579-0212

(330) 373-1035 .. **Rosenberg,** Michael W '66 Letson GWL&R -155 S Park Av -Ste 250 -Bx151 -Warren 44482 **Fx:**392-5419

(614) 464-2213 .. **Rosenberg,** Neil W '84 -400 S 5th -Ste 102 -Columbus 43215

(352) 395-6995 .. **Rosenberg,** Paul M '79 Shands Hlth Care -Bx100161 -Gainesville, FL 32610

(330) 296-3434 .. **Rosenberg,** Robert E '89 Stephens D&R -206 S Meridan -Ste A -Ravenna 44266 **Fx:**296-3435

(845) 354-1368 .. **Rosenberg,** Samuel L '71 -15 Astor Pl -Wesley Hills, NY 10952

(440) 442-6677 .. **Rosenberg,** Todd O '86 Elk & E Co,LPA -6100 Parkland Blvd -Mayfield Heights 44124 **Fx:**442-7944

Rosenberg, Victor R '02 -6543 Mplwd Dr -#104 -Mayfield Heights 44124

Rosenberg-Webster, Terri A '93 -Bx756 -Hudson 44236

(614) 224-1690 .. **Rosenberger,** John C '73 -804 City Park Av -Columbus 43206

(216) 360-3737 .. **Rosenberger,** Paul R '98 %Persky S&A Co,LPA -25101 Chagrin Blvd -Ste 350 Signature Sq II -Beachwood 44122 **Fx:**593-0921

(740) 947-2176 .. **Rosenberger,** Robert N '81 (Catanzaro & R) -112 W 3rd -Bx26 -Waverly 45690

(859) 578-6600 .. **Rosenberger,** Stephen M '88 %Buechel & C -25 Crestvw Hills Mall Rd -Ste 104 -Crestview Hills, KY 41017

(850) 769-1414 .. **Rosenblitt,** Jessica E '00 %Burke & B,PA -221 McKenzie Av -Panama City, FL 32401

Rosenblum, David M '79 -23 Col Conklin Dr -Stony Point, NY 10980

(330) 744-0247 .. **Rosenblum,** Donn D '79 %Nadler N&B Co,LPA -20 Fed Plz W -Ste 600 -Youngstown 44503 **Fx:**744-8690

(614) 464-6400 .. **Rosenfeld,** Aaron P '76 (Vorys SS&P LLP) -52 E Gay -Bx1008 -Columbus 43216 **Fx:**464-6350

(440) 446-9366 .. **Rosenfeld,** Robert T '58 -31853 Cedar Rd -Mayfield Heights 44124 **Fx:**(425) 699-4978

(216) 696-9300 .. **Rosenfield,** Ronald L '70 Spero & R Co,LPA -526 Superior Av -Ste 440 Leader Bldg -Cleveland 44114 **Fx:**696-9370

(513) 732-0300 .. **Rosenhoffer,** Gary A '79 G Rosenhoffer,LLC -190 Main -Batavia 45103

(513) 651-6800 .. **Rosenstiel,** Jeffrey S '96 (Frost BT LLC) -201 E 5th -2200 PNC Ctr -Cincinnati 45202 **Fx:**651-6981

(216) 662-1880 .. **Rosenthal,** Barbara S '87 N Coast Comm Homes -14221 Bway Av -Cleveland 44125

(614) 221-8448 .. **Rosenthal,** Brent D '84 (Buckingham D&B,LLP) -191 W Nationwide Blvd -Ste 300 -Bx151120 -Columbus 43215 **Fx:**221-8590

(513) 621-3440 .. **Rosenthal,** Daniel G '77 (Denlinger R&G Co,LPA) -425 Walnut -Ste 2310 -Cincinnati 45202 **Fx:**621-4449

(440) 975-1003 .. **Rosenthal,** Gary H '74 -353 S Curtis Blvd -Ste 340 -Eastlake 44095

(419) 885-4200 .. **Rosenthal,** James A '99 -6465 Monroe -Ste 213 -Sylvania 43560

(216) 781-7956 .. **Rosenthal,** James B '94 (Cohen R&K LLP) -1468 W 9th -Ste 705 -Cleveland 44113 **Fx:**781-8061

(614) 469-3245 .. **Rosenthal,** Janis B '81 (Thompson H LLP) -10 W Broad -Ste 700 -Columbus 43215 **Fx:**469-3361

(614) 644-7257 .. **Rosenthal,** Joseph N '84 Atty Gen -150 E Gay -Columbus 43215 **Fx:**752-4677

(614) 864-4359 .. **Rosenthal,** Lee S '82 (Goldman & R) -5350 E Main -Columbus 43213 **Fx:**864-2818

(614) 716-1646 .. **Rosenthal,** Martin S '85 Amer Elec Pwr Co -1 Riverside Plz -Columbus 43215

(330) 744-2667 .. **Rosenthal,** Patty B '81 Commonwealth,Inc -1221 Elm -Youngstown 44505

(412) 394-4463 .. **Rosenthal,** Richard M '98 E Snyder & Assoc -707 Grant -16th Fl -Pittsburgh, PA 15219

(216) 696-9936 .. **Rosenthal,** Sandra J '88 -75 Pub Sq -Ste 1300 -Cleveland 44113

(440) 998-5337 .. **Rosenthal,** Scott A '89 -355 W Prospect Rd -Ste 111 -Ashtabula 44004

(216) 589-9600 .. **Rosenthal,** Scott S '98 %Wilsman & S,LLC -1301 E 9th -Ste 1420 -Cleveland 44114

(513) 621-2257 .. **Rosenwald,** Peter '73 -114 E 8th -Cincinnati 45202

(216) 696-1422 .. **Rosenzweig,** David L '68 (McCarthy LC&L Co,LPA) -101 Prospect Av W -1800 Mdlnd Bldg -Cleveland 44115 **Fx:**696-1210

(513) 681-5617 .. **Roser,** Christopher P '90 Donnellon-McCarthy,Inc -4141 Turrill -Cincinnati 45223

(216) 491-1317 .. **Rosett,** Wendy Sue '91 Shaker Hts Mun Ct -3355 Lee Rd -Shaker Heights 44120

(419) 433-2525 .. **Roshong,** Alicia W '92 -28 Middle Av -Huron 44839

(330) 376-5300 .. **Rosin,** George H '76 (Buckingham D&B,LLP) -50 S Main -Bx1500 -Akron 44309 **Fx:**258-6559

(419) 625-8324 .. **Rosino,** John E '77 Flynn P&K,LPA -165 E Wshngtn Row -Sandusky 44870 **Fx:**625-9007

(440) 347-5099 ..**Rosko,** Christopher J '95 Lubrizol Corp -29400 Lakelnd Blvd
-Wickliffe 44092

(614) 464-6400 ..**Rosler,** Russell R '87 (Vorys SS&P LLP) -52 E Gay -Bx1008
-Columbus 43216 **Fx:**464-6350

(216) 831-7300 ..**Rosman,** Barbara Goldberg '88 -25700 Science Park Dr -Ste 360
-Beachwood 44122 **Fx:**831-7361

(216) 664-2788 ..**Rosman,** Debra Dee '82 Dept of Law -601 Lakeside Av -Rm 106
City Hall -Cleveland 44114 **Fx:**664-2663

(216) 241-6602 ..**Rosman,** Warren M '76 (Weston HFP&H LLP) -50 Pub Sq
-2500 Trmnl Twr -Cleveland 44113 **Fx:**621-8369

(513) 983-1100 ..**Rosnell,** Tara M '91 Cnsl Procter & Gamble -6071 Ctr Hill Av
-Cincinnati 45224

(440) 352-3391 ..**Rosner,** Irving '79 (Dworken & B Co,LPA) -60 S Park Pl
-Painesville 44077 **Fx:**352-3469

(513) 984-9098 ..**Rosner,** Lisa Miner '83 -9297 Witherbone Ct -Cincinnati 45242

(330) 796-6354 ..**Rosner,** Michael J '86 Goodyear -1144 E Market -Law Dept 822
-Akron 44316

(216) 696-3311 ..**Rosner,** Richard A '64 (Kahn K) -1301 E 9th -2600 Erievw Twr
-Cleveland 44114 **Fx:**623-4912

(216) 771-5588 ..**Rosner,** William R '83 (Rosner & Assoc,LLC) -812 Huron Rd
-Ste 601 Caxton Bldg -Cleveland 44115 **Fx:**771-5894

(216) 566-5861 ..**Rospert,** Anthony J '03 %Thompson H LLP -127 Pub Sq
-3900 Key Ctr -Cleveland 44114 **Fx:**566-5800

(440) 953-1310 ..**Rosplock,** Robert S '73 (Rosplock & P) -4230 SR 306 -Ste 240
-Willoughby 44094

(216) 447-1551 ..**Ross,** Alan G '75 (Ross B&S Co LPA) -6000 Freedom Square Dr
-Ste 540 -Cleveland 44131 **Fx:**447-1554

(216) 523-5405 ..**Ross,** Alan J '75 (Bricker & E LLP) -1375 E 9th -Ste 1500
-Cleveland 44114 **Fx:**523-7071

(937) 228-2465 ..**Ross,** Anne E '95 Metro Title Agncy,Inc -300 W Monument Av
-Ste 100 -Dayton 45402 **Fx:**228-4684
Ross, Anne H '93 -9241 Highland Dr -Brecksville 44141

(937) 472-0193 ..**Ross,** Augustus L III '75 -1614 US 35 E -Bx576 -Eaton 45320

(216) 447-1551 ..**Ross Brittain & Schonberg Co LPA** -6000 Freedom Square Dr
-Ste 540 -Cleveland 44131 **Fx:**447-1554

(937) 593-6065 ..**Ross,** Chad A '96 %Thompson DHMW&T -1111 Rush Av -Bx68
-Bellefontaine 43311

(937) 225-4464 ..**Ross,** Cheryl A '96 2nd Dist Ct of Appls -41 N Perry -Rm 515
-Bx972 -Dayton 45422

(330) 643-2617 ..**Ross,** Christopher C '01 Summit Cnty Pros-Tax -220 S Balch
-Ste 118 -Akron 44302 **Fx:**643-8540

(513) 459-1574 ..**Ross,** Clara S '88 Envir & Occptnl Health Cons Inc
-6331 Fireside Dr -Mason 45040

(216) 348-1000 ..**Ross,** Daryl B '93 -2012 W 25th -#812 -Cleveland 44113

(216) 687-1311 ..**Ross,** David '76 (Reminger & R) -101 Prospect Av W
-1400 Mdlnd Bldg -Cleveland 44115 **Fx:**687-1841

(937) 547-0218 ..**Ross,** Dean E '01 %S Rudnick,Ltd -121 W 3rd -Greenville 45331

(330) 395-9500 ..**Ross,** Douglas W '97 W Roux -106 E Market -Warren 44481

(330) 264-1213 ..**Ross,** Ford G '35 Ross Law Ofcs,PLL -406 N Market
-Wooster 44691 **Fx:**263-6054

(216) 861-1313 ..**Ross,** Harold A '56 Ross & K, LPA -1370 Ontario -Ste 1548
-Cleveland 44113

(440) 746-1600 ..**Ross,** Heather '99 %R Poklar & Assoc,LLP -10100 Brecksvll Rd
-Brecksville 44141 **Fx:**746-1600

(330) 264-1213 ..**Ross,** James H '81 Ross Law Ofcs,PLL -406 N Market
-Wooster 44691 **Fx:**263-6054
Ross, Jennifer K '03 -(Address Unavailable)

(513) 420-5755 ..**Ross,** JoAnn '93 Middletown Rgnl Hlth Sys -105 McKnight Dr
-Middletown 45044

(330) 492-8717 ..**Ross,** John C '82 (Buckingham D&B,LLP) -4518 Fulton Dr NW
-Bx35548 -Canton 44735 **Fx:**492-9625

(937) 599-6127 ..**Ross,** John L '74 Mun Ct Judge -226 W Columbus Av
-Bellefontaine 43311

(330) 643-2250 ..**Ross,** Karen E '01 9th Dist Ct of Appls -161 S High -Ste 504
-Akron 44308

(513) 621-7900 ..**Ross,** Kenneth L '74 Kenneth L. Ross -830 Main -Ste 999
-Cincinnati 45202

(216) 691-0112 ..**Ross,** Kenneth R '89 -2137 Halcyon Rd -Beachwood 44122

(937) 324-5541 ..**Ross,** Lauren M '84 Martin BH&H -1 S Limestone -Ste 800
-Bx1488 -Springfield 45501 **Fx:**325-5432

(513) 621-2120 ..**Ross,** Lori A '00 %Strauss & T,LPA -150 E 4th -4th Fl
-Cincinnati 45202 **Fx:**241-8259

(937) 224-0039 ..**Ross,** Marc T '99 %L Denny -371 W 1st -2nd Fl -Dayton 45402
Fx:222-1050

(614) 519-2488 ..**Ross,** Marcus A '97 -75 N Ohio Av -Columbus 43203 **Fx:**292-6940

(248) 362-3707 ..**Ross,** Michael A '92 %Ogne A&S,PC -1869 E Maple Rd -Ste 100
-Troy, MI 48083 **Fx:**362-0422

(401) 392-7737 ..**Ross,** Miriam A '79 GTech Corp -55 Tech Way
-West Greenwich, RI 02817

(216) 781-7777 ..**Ross,** Richard G '83 OfCnsl Wuliger F&B -1340 Sumner Ct
-Brownell Bldg -Cleveland 44115 **Fx:**781-0621

(740) 592-3208 ..**Ross,** Richard L '76 Athens Cnty Pros -Athens Cnty Cthse
-Athens 45701 **Fx:**592-3291

(614) 485-2010 ..**Ross,** Richard W '78 (Means BB&B Co,LPA) -2006 Kenny Rd
-Columbus 43221 **Fx:**485-2019

(216) 622-8200 ..**Ross,** Robert A '85 (Calfee H&G LLP) -800 Superior Av -Ste 1400
-Cleveland 44114 **Fx:**241-0816

(937) 433-4090 ..**Ross,** Robert D '94 (Gammell HK&R LLP) -7925 Paragon Rd
-Dayton 45459 **Fx:**433-1510

(330) 747-2661 ..**Ross,** Ronald J '65 Cafaro Co -2445 Belmont Av -Bx2186
-Youngstown 44504

(614) 475-4845 ..**Ross,** Ruth F '77 -2710 N Cassidy Av -Columbus 43219

(614) 457-4104 ..**Ross,** Stanley D '65 -1660 W Henderson Rd -Columbus 43220

(330) 643-2800 ..**Ross,** Susan Baker '91 Summit Cnty Pros-Civil -53 Univ Av -6th Fl
-Akron 44308 **Fx:**643-2137

(330) 264-1213 ..**Ross,** William F '75 Ross Law Ofcs,PLL -406 N Market
-Wooster 44691 **Fx:**263-6054

(614) 224-8374 ..**Ross,** William H '80 Legal Aid -40 W Gay -Columbus 43215

(330) 854-5177 ..**Ross,** William J '74 -8700 Foxglove Av NW -Clinton 44216

(216) 622-8200 ..**Ross,** William L '82 (Calfee H&G LLP) -800 Superior Av -Ste 1400
-Cleveland 44114 **Fx:**241-0816

(440) 684-0070 ..**Rossen,** Howard M '64 (Rossen & R) -16781 Chagrin Blvd
-Ste 108 -Cleveland 44120

(216) 522-5396 ..**Rossen,** Joel M '73 Dfnse Fin & Accntng Srvc -1240 E 9th -28th Fl
-Cleveland 44199

(440) 684-0070 ..**Rossen,** Marc D '94 (Rossen & R) -16781 Chagrin Blvd -Ste 108
-Cleveland 44120

(330) 393-1584 ..**Rossi,** Anthony G '61 (Guarnieri & S) -151 E Market -Bx4270
-Warren 44482 **Fx:**395-3831

(330) 393-1584 ..**Rossi,** Anthony G III '91 (Guarnieri & S) -151 E Market -Bx4270
-Warren 44482 **Fx:**395-3831

(330) 788-4922 ..**Rossi,** Armond V '56 Rossi Bros Funeral Home,Inc
-4442 South Av -Youngstown 44512

(800) 888-8424 ..**Rossi,** Assunta '89 Nationwide Mutual Ins -5915 Landerbrook Dr
-Cleveland 44124

(330) 744-8695 ..**Rossi,** Dan L '52 Rossi & R -26 Market -Ste 802
-Youngstown 44501 **Fx:**744-0334

(216) 231-5000 ..**Rossi,** David J '88 (DJ Rossi Co,LPA) -2025 Murray Hill Rd
-Cleveland 44106 **Fx:**231-5456

(330) 743-1191 ..**Rossi,** Eugene J '78 (E Rossi & Co) -201 E Commerce -Ste 337
-Youngstown 44503

(513) 887-3474 ..**Rossi,** Glenn J '01 Butler Cnty Pros -315 High -11th Fl -Bx515
-Hamilton 45012

(330) 744-8695 ..**Rossi,** Gregg A '90 (Rossi & R) -26 Market -Ste 802
-Youngstown 44501 **Fx:**744-0334

(330) 670-7300 ..**Rossi,** Gregory T '90 (Hanna C&P,LLP) -3737 Embssy Pkwy
-Bx5521 -Akron 44334 **Fx:**670-0977

(330) 393-1584 ..**Rossi,** Michael D '75 (Guarnieri & S) -151 E Market -Bx4270
-Warren 44482 **Fx:**395-3831

(330) 744-8695 ..**Rossi & Rossi** -26 Market -Ste 802 -Youngstown 44501 **Fx:**744-0334
Rossi, Sarah C '91 -(Address Unavailable)

(614) 888-1338 ..**Rossie,** Linda M '90 OH Cnsl for Exp Title Srvc
-2931 E Dublin Granvll Rd -Ste 250 -Columbus 43231

(216) 931-6000 ..**Rossiter,** Britt J '98 %Ulmer & B LLP -1300 E 9th
-Ste 900 Penton Media Bldg -Cleveland 44114 **Fx:**931-6001

(626) 302-3102 ..**Rosskopf,** Christine C '98 Sthrn CA Edison
-2244 Walnut Grove Av -Rm 359-GO1 -Rosemead, CA 91770

(216) 241-3658 ..**Rossman,** Alan C '81 -75 Pub Sq -Ste 1325 -Cleveland 44113

(614) 469-3939 ..**Rossman,** E Michael '98 %Jones D -325 John H McConnell Blvd
-Ste 600 -Bx165017 -Columbus 43216 **Fx:**461-4198

(614) 523-4159 ..**Rossman,** Jerry '87 -3592 Corp Dr -Columbus 43231

(614) 523-4145 ..**Rossman,** Kevin D '90 -3592 Corp Dr -#105 -Columbus 43231

(440) 442-6677 ..**Rost,** Grant M '01 Elk & E Co,LPA -6100 Parkland Blvd
-Mayfield Heights 44124 **Fx:**442-7944

(419) 241-6168 ..**Rost,** Peter G '77 -520 Madision Av -Ste 830 -Toledo 43604

(740) 382-2611 ..**Roston,** Timothy A '02 -117 E Center -Marion 43302
Roszman, Valerie Myers '89 -410 W Sandusky -#2 -Findlay 45840

(740) 335-8765 ..**Roszmann,** John H '73 -321 E Court
-Washington Court House 43160

(330) 373-2587 ..**Rotar,** Daniel R '90 Delphi Corp -Bx431 -Warren 44486

(216) 378-9905 ..**Rotatori,** Arthur J '81 (McGlinchey S PLLC) -25550 Chagrin Blvd
-Ste 406 -Cleveland 44122 **Fx:**378-9910

(216) 928-1010 ..**Rotatori Bender Gragel Stoper & Alexander Co LPA**
-526 Superior Av E -800 Leader Bldg -Cleveland 44114
Fx:928-1007

(216) 928-1010 ..**Rotatori,** Robert J '62 (Rotatori BGS&A Co LPA) -526
Superior Av E -800 Leader Bldg -Cleveland 44114 **Fx:**928-1007

(419) 294-2232 ..**Roth Bacon Young** -50 Court -Upper Sandusky 43351
Fx:294-2488

(216) 595-0071 ..**Roth Bierman LLP** -5196 Richmond Rd -Bedford Heights 44146
Fx:595-0073

(330) 744-5211 ..**Roth Blair Roberts Strasfeld & Lodge,LPA** -100 Fed Plz E
-Ste 600 -Youngstown 44503 **Fx:**744-3184

(330) 482-3825 ..**Roth Blair Roberts Strasfeld & Lodge,LPA** -11 S Main
-Columbiana 44408 **Fx:**482-0706

(614) 252-7824 ..**Roth,** Bruce I '74 -1620 E Broad -#708 -Columbus 43203
Roth, Carole A '78 -3162 Huntngtn Rd -Shaker Heights 44120

(419) 636-4411 ..**Roth,** Craig L '76 Williams Cnty Pros -1210 W High -Bryan 43506
Fx:636-3919

(330) 744-5211 ..**Roth,** Daniel B '56 (Roth BRS&L,LPA) -100 Fed Plz E -Ste 600
-Youngstown 44503 **Fx:**744-3184

(216) 623-9000 ..**Roth,** Daniel M '72 -1468 W 9th -Ste 425 -Cleveland 44113

(216) 595-0071 ..**Roth,** Dennis A '67 (Roth B LLP) -5196 Richmond Rd
-Bedford Heights 44146 **Fx:**595-0073
Roth, Henry A '66 -1319 Oakrdg Dr -Cleveland 44121

(419) 294-1971 ..**Roth,** Jeffrey P '72 (Roth BY) -50 Court -Upper Sandusky 43351
Fx:294-2488

(216) 622-8200 ..**Roth,** Jennifer Lawless '02 %Calfee H&G LLP -800 Superior Av
-Ste 1400 -Cleveland 44114 **Fx:**241-0816

(330) 379-3957 ..**Roth,** Kathleen E '97 Bridgestone Firestone Inc -1200
Firestone Pkwy -Akron 44317 **Fx:**379-4064

(614) 866-1195 ..**Roth,** Kelleen A '95 -7610 Slate Ridge Blvd -Reynoldsburg 43068

(216) 561-7419 ..**Roth,** Laddie J '50 -19303 Winslow Rd -Shaker Heights 44122

(614) 866-1195 ..**Roth,** Matthew N '90 -7610 Slate Ridge Blvd -Reynoldsburg 43068

(314) 694-1588 ..**Roth,** Michael J '78 Monsanto Company -800 N Lindbergh Blvd
-Saint Louis, MO 63167

(330) 879-9900 ..**Roth,** Michael J '97 -4268 Erie Av SW -Ste B -Navarre 44662

(513) 621-1652 ..**Roth,** Neil J '84 (Crowley A&R Co,LPA) -414 Walnut -Ste 707
-Cincinnati 45202 **Fx:**621-8430

(216) 642-8722 ..**Roth,** Randolph R '94 -6000 Freedom Sq Dr -Ste 380
-Independence 44131

(330) 456-4400 ..**Roth,** Stacie L '99 %A Schulman & Assoc, Co LPA -236 3rd SW
-Canton 44702

(419) 389-6413 ..**Roth,** Thomas J '85 -2424 Copland Blvd -Toledo 43614

(216) 241-5310 ..**Roth,** Timothy P '94 (Gallagher SF&N) -1501 Euclid Av -6th Fl
-Cleveland 44115 **Fx:**241-1608

(330) 867-9242 ..**Roth,** William J Jr. '83 (DeCamp R&D) -3250 W Market -Ste 203
-Akron 44333 **Fx:**867-9282

(330) 375-2030 ..**Rothal,** Max '57 Law Dept -161 S High -Ste 202 -Akron 44308
Rothbaum, Jennifer A '03 -5216 Calhoon Ct -Hilliard 43026

(513) 579-8900 ..**Rothchild,** Barry A '90 -101 W Cntrl Pkwy -Cincinnati 45202

(513) 579-8900 ..**Rothchild,** Eugene M '56 -101 W Cntrl Pkwy -Cincinnati 45202

(216) 685-1135 ..**Rothenberg,** Larry R '78 (Weltman W&R Co,LPA)
-323 W Lakeside Av -Ste 200 -Cleveland 44113 **Fx:**363-4121

(330) 656-2600 ..**Rothenberg,** Marc D '83 Jo-Ann Stores, Inc -5555 Darrow Rd
-Hudson 44236

(216) 394-5075 ..**Rothenbuecher**, H Alan '89 (Schottenstein Z&D) -1350 Euclid Av -Ste 1400 -Cleveland 44115 **Fx:**621-6502

(330) 493-1144 ..**Rothermel**, Nancy J '86 (Sponseller & R) -4180 Holiday NW -Canton 44718

(513) 241-3100 ..**Rothfuss**, Richard M '77 (Lerner S&R) -120 E 4th -8th Fl -Cincinnati 45202

(440) 323-1203 ..**Rothgery**, Eric J '99 %Rothgery & Assoc -230 3rd -Ste 100 -Elyria 44035

(440) 323-1203 ..**Rothgery**, Kenneth P '69 (Rothgery & Assoc) -230 3rd -Ste 100 -Elyria 44035

(813) 354-6446 ..**Rothman**, Howard E '73 OfCnsl Stewart Law Grp,PL -730 S Sterling Av -#304 -Tampa, FL 33609

(440) 930-8079 ..**Rothman**, Jason A '03 Wickens HPC&B -35765 Chester Rd -Avon 44011 **Fx:**937-4466

(216) 831-3171 ..**Rothschild**, Edmund W '58 -3681 S Green Rd -#410 -Cleveland 44122

(440) 323-5646 ..**Rothschild**, Honey '82 %Pros -328 Broad -Elyria 44035

(419) 241-9000 ..**Rothschild**, James I '93 (Shumaker L&K,LLP) -1000 Jackson -Toledo 43624 **Fx:**241-6894

(419) 241-9000 ..**Rothschild**, Stephen A '88 (Shumaker L&K,LLP) -1000 Jackson -Toledo 43624 **Fx:**241-6894

(513) 241-9400 ..**Rothstein**, Debra D '86 Legal Aid -10 Jrnl Sq -Hamilton 45011

(312) 855-4605 ..**Rothstein**, Lisa A '94 %Chuhak & T,PC -30 S Wacker Dr -Ste 2600 -Chicago, IL 60606 **Fx:**444-9027

(419) 243-7281 ..**Rothstein**, Scott D '91 Katz & K -1101 Monroe -Toledo 43624

(513) 721-5151 ..**Rothstein**, Steven M '77 (Katz G&N,LLP) -105 E 4th -4th Fl -Cincinnati 45202 **Fx:**621-9285

(216) 241-5152 ..**Rotman**, Dennis A '76 -1148 Euclid Av -#300 -Cleveland 44115

(419) 535-4655 ..**Rotman**, Phillip A II '93 Dana Corp -Bx906 -Toledo 43697

(614) 291-0826 ..**Rotondo**, Eric P '75 -1276 Neil Av -Columbus 43201

(513) 946-3500 ..**Rottinghaus**, Thomas J '73 1st Dist Ct of Appls -230 E 9th -12th Fl -Cincinnati 45202 **Fx:**946-3412

(614) 221-7791 ..**Roubanes**, Barbara A '97 F Ray Co,LPA -175 S 3rd -Ste 350 -Columbus 43215 **Fx:**221-8957

(330) 253-2195 ..**Roubenes**, Jerry G '65 -2500 First Natl Twr -Akron 44308

(330) 296-4336 ..**Roubic**, Melissa R V '96 Roubic Law Ofc,LLC -222 W Main -Ste 200 -Ravenna 44266 **Fx:**296-4339

(614) 841-9282 ..**Rouch**, Kevin C '85 -65 E Wilson Bridge Rd -Ste 200 -Worthington 43085

(614) 273-6004 ..**Rouda**, Harley E Jr. '87 HER,Inc -77 E Nationwide Blvd -Columbus 43215

(216) 781-9090 ..**Roules**, Daniel F '86 (Squire S&D LLP) -1 Guanghua Rd -2501 North Twr Chauyang Dist -Beijing 100020 China

(216) 781-9090 ..**Roulston**, Laurie L '82 The Townsend Group Inc -1500 W 3rd -Ste 410 -Cleveland 44113

(216) 522-4914 ..**Round**, Edmund B '75 %SSA/OHA -1350 Euclid Av -7th Fl -Cleveland 44115

(513) 621-8210 ..**Rounding**, Ruth I '79 (Drew & W Co,LPA) -1 W 4th -Ste 2400 -Cincinnati 45202 **Fx:**621-5444

(614) 220-9200 ..**Rourke & Blumenthal,LLP** -495 S High -Ste 450 -Columbus 43215 **Fx:**220-7900

(614) 220-9200 ..**Rourke**, Michael J '81 (Rourke & B,LLP) -495 S High -Ste 450 -Columbus 43215 **Fx:**220-7900

(513) 579-6400 ..**Rouse**, Joseph P '70 (Keating M&K PLL) -1 E 4th -1400 Provident Twr -Cincinnati 45202 **Fx:**579-6457

(859) 331-6440 ..**Rouse**, Thomas L '89 Cors & B,LLC -1881 Dixie Hwy -Ste 350 -Fort Wright, KY 41011

(419) 221-6712 ..**Roush**, Bradley C '79 -1110 Shawnee Rd -Lima 45805

(330) 376-3300 ..**Roush**, Carrie M '99 Stark & K Co,LPA -76 S Main -Ste 1512 -Akron 44308 **Fx:**376-6237

(216) 586-3939 ..**Roush**, Jeffrey D '02 Jones D -901 Lakeside Av -Cleveland 44114 **Fx:**579-0212

(419) 229-0023 ..**Roush**, William T '73 -317 N Elizabeth -Lima 45801

(937) 496-7646 ..**Rousseau**, Patricia E '90 Montgomery Cnty Pub Def -117 S Main -Ste 400 -Dayton 45422 **Fx:**225-3449

(740) 775-6254 ..**Roussey**, Vera G '00 -233 Maple Av -Chardon 44024

(740) 775-6254 ..**Rout**, Michele R '94 -137 S Paint -Ste 3 -Chillicothe 45601

(513) 706-5025 ..**Routh**, Jeffrey S '89 -407 Vine -Ste 184 -Cincinnati 45202 **Fx:**(208) 246-3719

(937) 296-0650 ..**Routh**, Paul J '86 -3931 S Dixie Dr -Dayton 45439

(216) 586-3939 ..**Routh**, Ryan T '00 %Jones D -901 Lakeside Av -Cleveland 44114 **Fx:**579-0212

(419) 228-3700 ..**Routson**, Jeffrey L '97 %Allen Cnty Pros -204 N Main -#302 -Lima 45801

(330) 395-9500 ..**Roux**, William M '83 W Roux -106 E Market -Warren 44481

(330) 637-9030 ..**Rouzzo**, David T '01 %J Grundy Co, LPA -3333 State Route 46 -Bx46 -Cortland 44410

(614) 475-0911 ..**Rovito**, Joel R '94 -7538 Slate Ridge Blvd -Reynoldsburg 43068

(614) 265-6883 ..**Rowan**, Charles G '89 Oh Dept Natrl Resources -1930 Belcher Drive D-3 -D-3 Fountain Sq -Columbus 43224

(216) 479-8500 ..**Rowan**, David W '78 (Squire S&D LLP) -127 Pub Sq -4900 Key Twr -Cleveland 44114 **Fx:**479-8780

(216) 685-1033 ..**Rowan**, Maria A '03 %Weltman W&R Co,LPA -323 W Lakeside Av -Ste 200 -Cleveland 44113 **Fx:**363-4121

(614) 224-9004 ..**Rowan**, Phyllis J '93 -336 S High -Columbus 43215

(216) 522-4856 ..**Rowan**, Sonja C '91 Fed Pub Def -1660 W 2nd -Ste 750 -Cleveland 44113

(216) 861-3810 ..**Rowan**, Stephen '83 Cleveland Fndtn -1422 Euclid Av -Ste 1300 -Cleveland 44115

(863) 682-8184 ..**Rowbotham**, Arthur J '74 Hall Communications,Inc -404 W Lime -Bx2038 -Lakeland, FL 33806 **Fx:**683-2409

(513) 732-7313 ..**Rowe**, Carol A '01 Clermont Cnty Pros -123 N 3rd -Batavia 45103

(513) 579-6400 ..**Rowe**, Rachael A '96 (Keating M&K PLL) -1 E 4th -1400 Provident Twr -Cincinnati 45202 **Fx:**579-6457

(614) 224-2678 ..**Rowe**, Steven D '74 Kemp SR&L Co,LPA -88 W Mound -Columbus 43215 **Fx:**469-7170

(859) 491-4444 ..**Rowekamp**, Leonard G '79 (Wolnitzek & R PSC) -502 Greenup -Bx352 -Covington, KY 41012 **Fx:**491-1001

(419) 241-8555 ..**Rowell**, Charles S Jr. '74 -520 Mad Av -864 Spitzer Bldg -Toledo 43604

(419) 252-6239 ..**Rowen**, Theodore M '70 (Spengler N PLL) -608 Mad Av -Ste 1000 -Toledo 43604 **Fx:**241-8599

(216) 663-9852 ..**Rowinski**, Gregory B '77 -13810 Carpenter Rd -Garfield Heights 44125

(216) 622-3847 ..**Rowland**, Ann C '76 US DOJ -801 Superior Av W -Ste 400 -Cleveland 44113

(740) 387-8916 ..**Rowland**, Brent A '80 -148 E Center -Marion 43302

(937) 372-6921 ..**Rowland**, Charles M II '95 (Cox K&R) -85 W Main -Xenia 45385

(614) 644-8912 ..**Rowland**, David L '85 OH State Brd of Pharm -77 S High -Rm 1702 -Columbus 43215

(419) 294-1200 ..**Rowland**, Douglas D '02 %Pfeifer & P -114 E Wyandot Av -Bx240 -Upper Sandusky 43351

Rowland, Gina C '00 -(Address Unavailable)

(614) 466-1826 ..**Rowland**, Jill M '93 Legis Srvc Commssn -77 S High -Columbus 43215

(412) 433-5077 ..**Rowland**, John R '78 USX Corp -600 Grant -Rm 2477 -Pittsburgh, PA 15219

(513) 723-8266 ..**Rowland**, Michelle L '01 Convergys Corp -201 E 4th -Cincinnati 45202

Rowland, Robert R '99 -2762 Martin Rd -#328 -Dublin 43017

(614) 464-6400 ..**Rowland**, Ronald L '72 (Vorys SS&P LLP) -52 E Gay -Bx1008 -Columbus 43216 **Fx:**464-6350

(614) 466-0641 ..**Rowland**, William G '93 Legis Srvc Commssn -77 S High -Columbus 43215

(937) 383-2067 ..**Rowlands**, Helen L '97 City of Wilmington -69 N South -Bx71 -Wilmington 45177

(330) 762-0287 ..**Rowlands**, Mary M '89 (Whitaker & R Co,LPA) -190 N Union -Ste 301 -Akron 44304

(216) 348-1100 ..**Rowles**, Kami D '99 %Schuster & S Co,LPA -2913 Clinton Av -Cleveland 44113 **Fx:**348-0013

(937) 778-3800 ..**Rowley**, Jamie P '01 -4259 Piqua Troy Rd -Troy 45373

(216) 696-3030 ..**Rownd**, James H '93 (Kadish H&W,LPA) -1717 E 9th -Ste 2112 -Cleveland 44114 **Fx:**696-3492

(216) 781-2787 ..**Rowthorn**, David L '76 Lavelle & L Co,LPA -526 Superior Av E -Ste 522 -Cleveland 44114

(614) 221-2400 ..**Roy**, Cynthia M '82 -233 S High -Ste 300 -Columbus 43215

(216) 381-2880 ..**Roy**, Debra E '85 Municipal Ct -1349 S Green Rd -Cleveland 44121

(859) 392-7907 ..**Royalty**, Grace Mowery '00 %Hon D Bunning -Bx232 -Covington, KY 41012

(614) 228-0704 ..**Royer**, Barth E '72 (Bell R&S Co,LPA) -33 S Grant Av -Columbus 43215

(216) 696-1422 ..**Royer**, Charles P '86 McCarthy LC&L Co,LPA -101 Prospect Av W -1800 Mdlnd Bldg -Cleveland 44115 **Fx:**696-1210

Royer, Christina M '01 -Bx217 -Peninsula 44264

(937) 390-7940 ..**Royer**, Etta S '95 Clark Cnty Cmn Pleas Ct -101 E Columbia -Springfield 45502

(419) 241-6612 ..**Royer**, George R '66 -316 N Mich -Ste 416 -Toledo 43624

(419) 252-5876 ..**Royer**, Jeffrey T '88 HCR Manor Care -333 N Summit -Bx10086 -Toledo 43699 **Fx:**(800) 321-0957

(330) 376-4558 ..**Royer**, Robert A '84 Scanlon & G Co,LPA -50 S Main -Ste 1200 -Akron 44308 **Fx:**376-3550

(440) 943-6888 ..**Rozanc**, Frank J '90 -240 Shoregate Mall -Ste 218 -Willowick 44095

Rozario, Charmaine C '99 -481 Sandhurst Dr -Highland Heights 44143

(614) 227-2000 ..**Rozelle**, Paul G '03 %Porter WM&A LLP -41 S High -Columbus 43215 **Fx:**227-2100

(513) 763-7700 ..**Rozic**, James P '92 %J Waite & Assoc Co,LPA -830 Main -Ste 500 -Cincinnati 45202

(419) 243-6281 ..**Rozic**, John W '78 (Shindler NH&S,LLP) -300 Mad Av -Ste 1200 -Toledo 43604 **Fx:**243-0129

Rozmajzl, Michael F '01 -463 Ely Rd -Akron 44313

(216) 771-4050 ..**Rua**, Mary Jane '86 (Jeffries KF&M Co,LPA) -101 W Prospect Av -1650 Mdlnd Bldg -Cleveland 44115 **Fx:**771-0732

(614) 460-4639 ..**Rubadue**, David W '84 Columbia Gas of OH Inc -200 Civic Ctr Dr -Columbus 43215

(216) 691-0369 ..**Rubadue**, Laura S '97 Lexis Nexis -2343 Lalemant Rd -University Heights 44118

(216) 687-2310 ..**Ruben**, Alan M '72 CSU-Marshall Cllg of Law -2121 Euclid Av -LB138 -Cleveland 44115 **Fx:**687-6881

(614) 228-5060 ..**Ruben**, Donald B '64 -165 E Lvngstn Av -Columbus 43215

(216) 464-4060 ..**Ruben**, Susan Grody '95 -30799 Pinetree Rd -Bx226 -Cleveland 44124 **Fx:**595-5274

(513) 352-4702 ..**Rubenstein**, Charles A '81 Law Dept -801 Plum -Rm 214 -Cincinnati 45202 **Fx:**352-1515

(513) 241-7460 ..**Rubenstein**, Jack C '67 (Rubenstein & T) -7 W 7th -Ste 1850 -Cincinnati 45202 **Fx:**684-7777

(513) 779-0237 ..**Rubenstein**, Jeffrey B '83 -9672 Tamarack Ter -Sharonville 45241

(440) 473-8944 ..**Rubenstein**, Kenneth D '91 -2112 Acacia Park Dr -Ste 505 -Lyndhurst 44124

(513) 241-7460 ..**Rubenstein**, Louis '78 -7 W 7th -Ste 1850 -Cincinnati 45202

(614) 365-2700 ..**Rubenstein**, Richard W '80 (Squire S&D LLP) -41 S High -1300 Huntngtn Ctr -Columbus 43215 **Fx:**365-2499

Rubenstein, Mandi M '57 -3503 Courtland Rd -Pepper Pike 44122

(513) 241-7460 ..**Rubenstein**, Scott A '99 (Rubenstein & T) -7 W 7th -Ste 1850 -Cincinnati 45202 **Fx:**684-7777

(513) 241-7460 ..**Rubenstein & Thurman** -7 W 7th -Ste 1850 -Cincinnati 45202 **Fx:**684-7777

(859) 331-2000 ..**Ruberg**, Michael K '93 (O'Hara RTS&S) -25 Crestvw Hills Mall Rd -Ste 201 -Bx17411 -Covington, KY 41017 **Fx:**578-3365

(440) 395-3760 ..**Rubesne**, Kellie M '97 Progressive Ins Co -6300 Wilson Mills Rd -#N72A -Mayfield Village 44143

(614) 719-3372 ..**Rubey**, Rachel A '03 US Dist Ct SDOH -85 Marconi Blvd -Rm 208 -Columbus 43215

(740) 594-3558 ..**Rubin**, Anne S '81 SE OH Lgl Srvcs -1005 E State -Athens 45701 **Fx:**594-3791

(614) 457-7700 ..**Rubin**, Daniel R '84 -4930 Reed Rd -Columbus 43220

(419) 244-7482 ..**Rubin**, Daryl F '82 (DK Rubin & Assoc) -2127 Monroe -Toledo 43624 **Fx:**244-7485

(937) 254-4455 ..**Rubin**, Ira '75 (Goldman R&S) -1340 Woodman Dr -Dayton 45432

(440) 942-2454 ..**Rubin**, Irl D '76 -35401 Euclid Av -Ste 101 -Willoughby 44094

(419) 241-7211 ..**Rubin**, Joanne '84 -520 Mad Av -Ste 610 -Toledo 43604 **Fx:**241-7229

(216) 566-5815 ..**Rubin**, Karen E '85 %Thompson H LLP -127 Pub Sq
-3900 Key Ctr -Cleveland 44114 **Fx:**566-5800

(419) 259-6470 ..**Rubin**, Kenneth J '04 US Dist Ct-NDOH -1716 Spielbusch Av
-Rm 203 -Toledo 43624

(513) 421-4020 ..**Rubin**, Marc W '74 (Cohen TK&S,LLC) -250 E 5th -Ste 1200
-Cincinnati 45202 **Fx:**241-4490

(216) 514-6400 ..**Rubin**, Neil S '98 %Zipkin W Co LPA -3637 S Green Rd
-Zipkin Whiting Bldg -Cleveland 44122 **Fx:**514-6406

(330) 456-0083 ..**Rubin**, Robert G '68 -315 W Tuscarawas -Ste 301 -Canton 44702

(513) 421-4020 ..**Rubin**, Robert S '79 (Cohen TK&S,LLC) -250 E 5th -Ste 1200
-Cincinnati 45202 **Fx:**241-4490

(330) 453-7104 ..**Rubin**, Rosemary G '74 Rubin & S -1428 Market N -Canton 44714

(216) 928-2200 ..**Rubin**, Ryan K '04 %Sutter OM&F -1301 E 9th -3600 Erievw Twr
-Cleveland 44114 **Fx:**928-4400

(419) 244-7482 ..**Rubin**, Sheldon '53 -2127 Monroe -Toledo 43624

(330) 455-5206 ..**Rubin**, Stanley R '76 -437 Market N -Canton 44702

(216) 464-2860 ..**Rubin**, Steven K '04 RL Stark Enterprises,Inc -28601 Chagrin Blvd
-Ste 600 -Woodmere 44122

(513) 351-9700 ..**Rubin**, Walter I '66 -3194 Dot Dr -Cincinnati 45213

(614) 752-8068 ..**Rubino**, Joseph D '88 Workers Comp -30 W Spring -Level 26
-Columbus 43215

(330) 643-2800 ..**Rubino**, Sandy J '78 Summit Cnty Pros-Civil -53 Univ Av -6th Fl
-Akron 44308 **Fx:**643-2137

(419) 241-2201 ..**Rubinoff**, Norman J '66 (Spengler N PLL) -608 Mad Av -Ste 1000
-Toledo 43604 **Fx:**241-8599

(216) 931-6000 ..**Rubinstein**, Richard E '64 (Ulmer & B LLP) -1300 E 9th
-Ste 900 Penton Media Bldg -Cleveland 44114 **Fx:**931-6001

(330) 376-5050 ..**Ruby**, Deborah L '99 %D'Andrea & Assoc -697 W Market -Ste 200
-Akron 44303

(513) 579-1414 ..**Ruby**, Stanley L '71 (Schwartz M&R) -441 Vine -Ste 2900
-Cincinnati 45202 **Fx:**579-1418

(614) 464-6400 ..**Ruby**, Thomas O '82 (Vorys SS&P LLP) -52 E Gay -Bx1008
-Columbus 43216 **Fx:**464-6350

(937) 223-1201 ..**Ruchman**, Marshall D '64 (Altick & C Co,LPA) -1 S Main
-1700 One Dayton Ctr -Dayton 45402 **Fx:**223-5100

(330) 762-6335 ..**Rucinski**, Keith Lee '94 Ofc of Chptr 13 Trustee -159 S Main
-Ste 930 -Akron 44308

(419) 287-3233 ..**Ruck**, John D '98 (Davies & R) -427 W Cllg Av -Bx412
-Pemberville 43450 **Fx:**287-3215

(440) 239-1790 ..**Ruck**, Theresa Nelson '00 %Baron & B,PC -7261 Engle Rd
-Ste 200 -Cleveland 44130 **Fx:**239-1794

(513) 721-4450 ..**Rucker**, Fanon A '96 %Santen & H -312 Walnut -Ste 3100
-Cincinnati 45202

(330) 392-8392 ..**Rucker**, Gilbert R III '86 -135 Pine Av -Ste 203 -Warren 44481

(614) 445-3971 ..**Rucker**, Retanio A '88 -786 S Front -Columbus 43206

Rucker, Susan K '95 -(Address Unavailable)

(216) 574-8232 ..**Ruda**, Lisa M '94 Cleveland Mun Sch Dist -1380 E 6th
-Cleveland 44114

(330) 345-4639 ..**Rudawsky**, Larry W '82 -1520 Wildwood Dr -Wooster 44691

(740) 420-8286 ..**Rudawsky**, Sandra E '00 Berger Hlth System -600 N Pickaway
-Circleville 43113

Rudd, Michael D '79 -(Address Unavailable)

(937) 225-4892 ..**Rudd**, Richard D '02 Montgomery Cnty Pros/CSEA -14 W 4th
-Ste 510 -Dayton 45402

(937) 396-0089 ..**Rudd**, Timothy R '02 %SL Braum & Assoc -3131 S Dixie Dr
-Ste 400 -Dayton 45439 **Fx:**396-1046

(330) 468-3990 ..**Rudder**, Verner R Jr. '83 -61 W Aurora Rd -Northfield 44067

(419) 213-3366 ..**Rudebock**, David T '91 Lucas Co Children Srvcs Brd -705 Adams
-Toledo 43624

(513) 961-6200 ..**Rudell**, Barry A '00 %Markesbery & R Co,LPA -2368 Victory Pkwy
-Ste 200 -Bx6491 -Cincinnati 45206

(216) 687-1900 ..**Ruden**, Alexandria M '80 Legal Aid -1223 W 6th -Cleveland 44113
Fx:687-0779

(419) 732-3000 ..**Rudes**, Terrence R '77 -216 Adams -Port Clinton 43452

(330) 643-2617 ..**Rudgers**, James A '73 Summit Cnty Pros-Tax -220 S Balch
-Ste 118 -Akron 44302 **Fx:**643-8540

(330) 393-1584 ..**Rudloff**, Randil J '73 (Guarnieri & S) -151 E Market -Bx4270
-Warren 44482 **Fx:**395-3831

(216) 931-6000 ..**Rudnick**, Elizabeth S '99 %Ulmer & B LLP -1300 E 9th
-Ste 900 Penton Media Bldg -Cleveland 44114 **Fx:**931-6001

(937) 547-0218 ..**Rudnick**, Scott D '79 -121 W 3rd -Greenville 45331

(330) 392-6171 ..**Rudnicki**, Susan E '83 -410 Mahoning Av NW -Bx1429
-Warren 44482 **Fx:**394-5507

Rudolph, Athena C '02 -Address Unavailable

(513) 388-2830 ..**Rudolph**, Glenn P '89 Senco Prdcts,Inc -8485 Broadwell Rd
-Cincinnati 45244

(330) 908-4276 ..**Rudolph**, Jennifer L '98 Charles Schwab -4150 Kinross Lks Pkwy
-Richfield 44286

(216) 447-5436 ..**Rudolph**, Richard Jay '92 Noveon Inc -9911 Brecksvll Rd
-Brecksville 44141

(937) 257-9996 ..**Rudolph**, Thomas E '83 US Air Force -4225 Logistics Av
-Wright Patterson AFB 45433

(614) 253-1010 ..**Rudolph**, Timothy J '99 Dana & P Co,LPA -800 E Broad
-Columbus 43205 **Fx:**253-3310

(937) 438-4601 ..**Rudwall**, David F '82 -500 E 3rd -239 -Dayton 45402

(440) 779-6330 ..**Rudy**, Donald M '68 -23201 Lorain Rd -North Olmsted 44070
Fx:779-6331

(216) 721-7700 ..**Rudy**, Mark T '90 -11510 Buckeye Rd -Cleveland 44104

(330) 287-5490 ..**Rudy**, Michael S '95 Wayne Cnty Pub Def -113 W Lbrty
-Wooster 44691 **Fx:**287-5479

(202) 458-3095 ..**Rudy**, Timothy D '91 Org of Amer States -19th & Const Av
-Washington, DC 20006

(617) 748-3260 ..**Rue**, Nancy B '90 US Atty -One Cthse Way -Ste 9200
-Boston, MA 02210

(513) 621-8210 ..**Ruebel**, Richard J '73 (Drew & W Co,LPA) -1 W 4th -Ste 2400
-Cincinnati 45202 **Fx:**621-5444

(513) 621-4849 ..**Rueger**, James M '77 (Dolle R&M Co,LPA) -817 Main -Ste 500
-Cincinnati 45202

(513) 381-4888 ..**Ruehle**, Ryan J '99 Mapother & M,PSC -1014 Vine
-Ste 2320 Kroger Bldg -Cincinnati 45202 **Fx:**381-3117

(513) 723-4000 ..**Ruehlmann**, Eugene P '50 OfCnsl Vorys SS&P LLP -221 E 4th
-Ste 2000 Atrium Two -Bx0236 -Cincinnati 45201 **Fx:**723-4056

(513) 361-1200 ..**Ruehlmann**, Gregory A '81 OfCnsl Squire S&D LLP -312 Walnut
-Ste 3500 -Cincinnati 45202 **Fx:**361-1201

(513) 361-1200 ..**Ruehlmann**, Mark J '87 (Squire S&D LLP) -312 Walnut -Ste 3500
-Cincinnati 45202 **Fx:**361-1201

(206) 622-9900 ..**Ruehr**, Frederick R '84 SP Investments,Inc -1201 3rd Av -Seattle,
WA 98101

Rueth, Joseph E '80 -1360 Apple Brook Ln -Dayton 45458

(216) 687-1999 ..**Ruf**, Mark W '90 -700 W St Clair Av -Ste 300 -Cleveland 44113

(937) 225-5609 ..**Ruf**, Walter F '82 Montgomery Cnty Pros -301 W 3rd -Bx972
-Dayton 45422 **Fx:**225-3470

(440) 746-1000 ..**Ruffa**, Vincenzo '96 (Oakar & R) -1000 W Wallings Rd -Ste A
-Broadview Heights 44147

(330) 670-0005 ..**Ruffin**, Sean P '98 OfCnsl McGown & M
-1894 N Cleveland Massillon Rd -Akron 44333

(740) 368-1545 ..**Ruffing**, Peter B '82 City Pros -70 N Union -Delaware 43015

(419) 499-4605 ..**Ruffing**, Vickie B '81 (V Ruffing Co,LPA) -16 W Church -Bx526
-Milan 44846

(937) 449-2800 ..**Ruffner**, James David II '94 OfCnsl Chernesky H&K PLL
-10 Cthse Plz SW -Ste 1100 -Dayton 45402 **Fx:**449-2821

(330) 535-7174 ..**Ruffner**, Keith C II '88 -209 S Main -#701 -Akron 44308

(937) 434-3556 ..**Ruffolo**, John M '82 (Ruffolo SD&L) -7501 Paragon Rd
-Dayton 45459

(937) 434-3556 ..**Ruffolo Stone Dressel & Lipowicz** -7501 Paragon Rd
-Dayton 45459

(330) 438-0838 ..**Rufo**, Alice F '87 Stark Cnty Fam Ct -110 Central Plz -Ste 604
-Canton 44702

(330) 456-8389 ..**Rufo**, Gregory J '83 Rufo Law Firm -1101 Bk One Twr
-Canton 44702 **Fx:**456-5328

(912) 267-2849 ..**Ruger**, James W '83 Ofc of Chief Cnsl -Bldg 69 3rd Fl
-FLETC-NCITA -Saint Simons Island, GA 31522

(216) 861-1940 ..**Ruggeri**, Robert A '68 -55 Pub Sq -Ste 1450 -Cleveland 44113

(740) 353-9805 ..**Ruggiero**, Daniel P '73 (Ruggiero & H) -800 Gallia -Ste 600
-Bx150 -Portsmouth 45662

(740) 353-9805 ..**Ruggiero & Haas** -800 Gallia -Ste 600 -Bx150 -Portsmouth 45662

(419) 668-8540 ..**Ruggles**, Warren W '65 -10½ Benedict Av -Norwalk 44857

(419) 660-8540 ..**Ruggles**, West M '02 -10½ Benedict Av -Norwalk 44857

(513) 621-2120 ..**Ruh**, Michael A Jr. '96 %Strauss & T,LPA -150 E 4th -4th Fl
-Cincinnati 45202 **Fx:**241-8259

(440) 871-1565 ..**Ruhe**, Linda J '83 -31044 Pinehurst Dr -Westlake 44145

(419) 294-2336 ..**Ruhlen**, James M '98 %Osborn & F,LPA -116 E Wyandot Av
-Upper Sandusky 43351 **Fx:**294-5669

(440) 247-8601 ..**Ruiter**, Paul J '98 -258 E Wshngtn -Chagrin Falls 44022

(216) 622-8200 ..**Ruiz**, David A '02 %Calfee H&G LLP -800 Superior Av -Ste 1400
-Cleveland 44114 **Fx:**241-0816

(513) 786-1518 ..**Ruiz**, Fernando A '96 GE Aircraft Engines -1 Neumann Way
-Mail Drop J104 -Cincinnati 45215

(216) 685-1182 ..**Ruiz-Bueno**, J Charles '90 %Weltman W&R Co,LPA
-323 W Lakeside Av -Ste 200 -Cleveland 44113 **Fx:**363-4121

(216) 443-7800 ..**Rukovena**, George '72 Cuyahoga Cnty Pros -1200 Ontario -8th Fl
-Cleveland 44113 **Fx:**698-2270

Rule, Hilary W '88 -68 Water -Chagrin Falls 44022

Rulli, Patricia G '86 -(Address Unavailable)

(513) 863-6700 ..**Rullman**, Stanley D '67 (Millikin & F) -6 S 2nd -6th Fl -Bx598
-Hamilton 45012 **Fx:**863-0031

(513) 863-6700 ..**Rulon**, Jeffrey L '83 (Millikin & F) -6 S 2nd -6th Fl -Bx598
-Hamilton 45012 **Fx:**863-0031

(330) 627-2918 ..**Rumbaugh**, Richard Lee '72 -63 E Main -Carrollton 44615

(513) 579-1414 ..**Rumberg**, Orly R '93 OfCnsl Schwartz M&R -441 Vine -Ste 2900
-Cincinnati 45202 **Fx:**579-1418

(330) 864-5369 ..**Rumel**, John E '75 -1832 Brookfld Dr -Akron 44313

(419) 228-6365 ..**Rumer**, Michael A '70 (Cory MWR&C,LPA) -101 N Elizabeth
-Ste 607 -Bx1217 -Lima 45802 **Fx:**228-5319

(440) 239-9376 ..**Rumes**, Kevin W '97 -23755 Cottage Trl -Olmsted Falls 44138

(216) 696-1080 ..**Rumizen**, Scott A '92 %D Seaman & Assoc Co,LPA
-614 Superior Av W -Ste 1600 Rckfllr Bldg -Cleveland 44113

(330) 744-0291 ..**Rummell**, Randall W '83 (Boyd RC&C Co LPA) -400 Sky Bk Bldg
-Bx6565 -Youngstown 44501

(513) 534-0803 ..**Rummer**, Keith A '01 Cnsl Fifth Third Bank
-38 Fountain Square Plz -MD# 10AT76 -Cincinnati 45263

(419) 385-5721 ..**Rump**, Deborah K '84 Toledo Zoo -Bx140130 -Toledo 43614

(513) 552-4377 ..**Rumpf**, John M '89 GE Aircraft Engines -1 Neumann Way
-Mail Drop T165A -Cincinnati 45215

Runco, Laryn D '02 -701 Northrdg Oval -Brooklyn 44144

(216) 622-8200 ..**Rundelli**, Raymond '85 (Calfee H&G LLP) -800 Superior Av
-Ste 1400 -Cleveland 44114 **Fx:**241-0816

(937) 746-6425 ..**Runge**, Steven M '75 (Runge Law Ofc) -401 S Main
-Franklin 45005

(419) 893-3798 ..**Runner**, George F '75 -1018 Rvr Rd -Maumee 43537

(419) 893-3798 ..**Runner**, Raymond A '76 -1018 Rvr Rd -Maumee 43537

(419) 238-2200 ..**Runser**, C Allan '67 -111 E Main -Ste 105 -Van Wert 45891

Ruocco, Davide R '02 -(Address Unavailable)

(216) 621-0200 ..**Rupert**, Aaron '02 %Baker & H LLP -1900 E 9th -Ste 3200
-Cleveland 44114 **Fx:**696-0740

(614) 848-4999 ..**Rupert**, David E '99 Bldng Mngmnt Corp -1148 Baumock Burn Dr
-Columbus 43235

(614) 464-1211 ..**Rupert**, Jeffrey G '95 (Frost BT LLC) -10 W Broad -Ste 1000
-Columbus 43215 **Fx:**464-1737

(614) 466-1305 ..**Rupert**, Rosemary E '89 Atty Gen -30 E Broad -Columbus 43215
Fx:466-8898

(216) 363-1400 ..**Ruple**, Jeffrey W '97 %Buckley K,LPA -600 E Superior Av
-Ste 1400 -Cleveland 44114 **Fx:**579-1020

(330) 666-5555 ..**Ruport**, Scott H '74 (Ruport Co,LPA) -3700 Embssy Pkwy
-Ste 440 -Akron 44333

(614) 249-7641 ..**Rupp**, Daniel P '69 Nationwide Ins Co -1 Nationwide Plz
-Columbus 43215

(419) 445-8815 ..**Rupp**, David P Jr. '65 (Plassman RHS&H) -302 N Defiance -Bx178
-Archbold 43502 **Fx:**445-1080

(614) 228-1541 ..**Rupp**, Robert K '82 (Baker & H LLP) -65 E State -Ste 2100
-Columbus 43215 **Fx:**462-2616

(513) 825-2492 ..**Rupp**, Susan C '80 -640 Northland Rd -Ste 33 -Cincinnati 45240

(888) 901-4647 ..**Rupp-Autero**, Margaret '98 Mortg Ifo Srvcs -4877 Galaxy Pkwy
-Ste 1 -Euclid 44123

(330) 626-2525 .. **Ruppelt,** Arthur G '89 (Ruppelt & R) -9294 State Route 43 -Streetsboro 44241

(440) 395-0256 .. **Ruppelt,** Ronna F '85 Progressive Casualty Ins Co -300 N Comomons Blvd -Mayfield Village 44143

(937) 746-2832 .. **Ruppert Bronson & Ruppert Co, LPA** -1063 E 2nd -Bx369 -Franklin 45005 **Fx:**746-2855

(937) 746-2832 .. **Ruppert,** James D '66 (Ruppert B&R Co,LPA) -1063 E 2nd -Bx369 -Franklin 45005 **Fx:**746-2855

(937) 746-2832 .. **Ruppert,** Jeffrey A '99 %Ruppert B&R Co,LPA -1063 E 2nd -Bx369 -Franklin 45005 **Fx:**746-2855

(216) 689-3937 .. **Ruppert,** Rebecca S '93 KeyBank NA -127 Pub Sq -2nd Fl -Cleveland 44114

(937) 746-2832 .. **Ruppert,** Ronald W '88 (Ruppert B&R Co,LPA) -1063 E 2nd -Bx369 -Franklin 45005 **Fx:**746-2855

(937) 746-2832 .. **Ruppert,** Rupert E '76 (Ruppert B&R Co,LPA) -1063 E 2nd -Bx369 -Franklin 45005 **Fx:**746-2855

Ruprecht, Samuel L '04 -(Address Unavailable)

(216) 221-3993 .. **Rus,** Vladimir M '81 -14600 Detroit Av -Ste 1365 -Lakewood 44107

(414) 282-7103 .. **Rusch,** Kenneth E '83 O'Hagan S&A LLC -4811 S 76th -Ste 306 -Milwaukee, WI 53220

(440) 243-2955 .. **Ruschak,** Melinda L '86 Powers & G-W -2 Berea Cmmns -Ste 215 -Bx1059 -Berea 44017 **Fx:**243-2967

(937) 866-1629 .. **Ruschau & Lehman** -443 E Central Av -Miamisburg 45342

(937) 866-1629 .. **Ruschau,** Steve J '77 (Ruschau & L) -443 E Central Av -Miamisburg 45342

(513) 242-7591 .. **Rusche,** Joseph F '49 -4344 Errun Ln -Cincinnati 45217

(216) 621-3370 .. **Ruschel,** Brian G '90 -925 Euclid Av -Ste 660 -Cleveland 44115

(614) 227-2000 .. **Ruscitti,** Donna M '86 (Porter WM&A LLP) -41 S High -Columbus 43215 **Fx:**227-2100

(330) 702-1436 .. **Ruse,** Linda S '85 Nationwide Ins -11 E Main -Canfield 44406

(419) 423-0242 .. **Ruse,** William E '72 -301 S Main -Ste 3 -Findlay 45840

(513) 771-2444 .. **Rush,** D Todd '97 (Lutz CM&R Co,LPA) -130 Tri-Cnty Pkwy -Ste 208 -Cincinnati 45246 **Fx:**771-2447

(614) 466-1560 .. **Rush,** Deanna D '83 Supreme Ct of OH -30 E Broad -23rd Fl -Columbus 43266

(513) 651-6800 .. **Rush,** Jeffery R '75 (Frost BT LLC) -201 E 5th -2200 PNC Ctr -Cincinnati 45202 **Fx:**651-6981

(937) 323-1007 .. **Rush,** Kenneth G '57 (K Rush Co) -4 W Main -Ste 707 -Springfield 45502

(440) 729-1848 .. **Rushworth,** Kim R '76 -8228 Mayfd Rd -Chesterland 44026

(614) 464-6400 .. **Rusie,** Jennifer A '03 %Vorys SS&P LLP -52 E Gay -Bx1008 -Columbus 43216 **Fx:**464-6350

(614) 464-6400 .. **Rusie,** Michael J '03 %Vorys SS&P LLP -52 E Gay -Bx1008 -Columbus 43216 **Fx:**464-6350

(440) 244-1827 .. **Ruskan,** Ronald J '77 -1623 Bway -Lorain 44052

(202) 366-4702 .. **Rusnak,** Allison Browns '02 US DOT Ofc Chief Cnsl -400 7th SW -Rm 5219 -Washington, DC 20590

(202) 778-9000 .. **Rusnak,** Eric C '04 %Kirkpatrick & LNG LLP -1800 Mass Av NW -Washington, DC 20036 **Fx:**778-9100

(614) 946-1966 .. **Russ,** Andrew E '02 -261 S Front -2nd Fl -Columbus 43215 **Fx:**221-5996

(440) 329-5521 .. **Russ,** Catherine A '96 -308 2nd -Elyria 44035

(216) 443-6022 .. **Russ,** Christopher J '83 Sheriffs Dept -1215 W 3rd -2nd Fl -Cleveland 44113

(614) 863-8880 .. **Russ,** Jason H '94 -6100 Channingway Blvd -Ste 706 -Columbus 43232

(513) 381-2838 .. **Russell,** Allison S '99 %Taft S&H LLP -425 Walnut -Ste 1800 -Cincinnati 45202 **Fx:**381-0205

Russell, Angela Y '04 -(Address Unavailable)

(440) 933-6377 .. **Russell,** Anson H '56 -32484 Lk Rd -Avon Lake 44012

(216) 592-5000 .. **Russell,** Carolyn C '01 %Tucker E&W LLP -925 Euclid Av -1150 Huntngtn Bldg -Cleveland 44115 **Fx:**592-5009

(614) 227-2000 .. **Russell,** Christopher C '88 (Porter WM&A LLP) -41 S High -Columbus 43215 **Fx:**227-2100

Russell, Diane P '02 -(Address Unavailable)

(614) 464-6400 .. **Russell,** Gregory D '92 (Vorys SS&P LLP) -52 E Gay -Bx1008 -Columbus 43216 **Fx:**464-6350

(216) 252-1100 .. **Russell,** James F '66 Sanders S&R -3400 W 123rd -Cleveland 44111

Russell, James R Jr. '02 -(Address Unavailable)

(919) 483-7870 .. **Russell,** John K '91 SrCnsl GlaxoSmithKline -Five Moore Dr -Bx13398 -Durham, NC 27709

(740) 387-3777 .. **Russell,** Mark D '90 M Russell,LPA -267 W Center -Ste 200 -Marion 43302

(937) 225-5799 .. **Russell,** Michael '71 Montgomery Cnty Pros -301 W 3rd -Bx972 -Dayton 45422 **Fx:**225-3470

(330) 497-0389 .. **Russell,** Michael S '77 Russell Law Ofcs -601 S Main -Canton 44720

(440) 842-3500 .. **Russell,** Monica E '02 %Carlisle-Kesling & Assoc LLC -7083 Pearl Rd -Middleburg Heights 44130

(614) 466-4656 .. **Russell,** Paul A '93 Atty Gen -150 E Gay -Columbus 43215 **Fx:**466-1756

Russell, Peter A '93 -8746 Barton Dr -Strongsville 44149

(216) 479-8500 .. **Russell,** Shawn R '86 OfCnsl Squire S&D LLP -127 Pub Sq -4900 Key Twr -Cleveland 44114 **Fx:**479-8780

(614) 222-5809 .. **Russell,** Susan L '88 Sch Employees Rtrmnt Syst -45 N 4th -Columbus 43215

(740) 687-6152 .. **Russell,** Theodore V '79 -130 E Chestnut -Bx625 -Lancaster 43130

(440) 734-3281 .. **Russell,** William H '74 -27397 Linwood -North Olmsted 44070

Russell, William S '04 -Bx30292 -Cincinnati 45230

(614) 228-6135 .. **Russell-Washington,** Necol D '01 %Carlile P&M LLP -366 E Broad -Columbus 43215 **Fx:**221-0216

(614) 462-5408 .. **Russi,** Steven R '84 Arctic Express,Inc -4277 Lyman Dr -Hilliard 43026

(216) 642-1425 .. **Russin,** Rodion J '60 (Rutter & R) -4700 Rockside Rd -Ste 650 -Cleveland 44131 **Fx:**(213) 642-0613

(216) 583-4538 .. **Russo,** Andrea '99 Ernst & Young LLP -925 Euclid Av -Ste 1300 -Cleveland 44115

Russo, Angelo '02 -24640 Surrey Cir -Westlake 44145

(440) 461-8500 .. **Russo,** Basil M '72 (BM Russo & Co,LPA) -691 Richmond Rd -Richmond Heights 44143

Russo, Dorcas A '81 Medina Cnty Common Pleas Ct -99 Pub Sq -Magistrate -Medina 44256

(614) 464-6400 .. **Russo,** Gina R '02 %Vorys SS&P LLP -52 E Gay -Bx1008 -Columbus 43216 **Fx:**464-6350

(216) 623-0150 .. **Russo,** Rachael L '99 %Roetzel & A,LPA -1375 E 9th -One Cleve Ctr 9th Fl -Cleveland 44114 **Fx:**623-0134

(419) 422-5565 .. **Russo,** Ralph D '78 (Betts M&R) -101 W Sandusky -Findlay 45840 **Fx:**423-1868

(513) 721-4532 .. **Russo,** William F '79 (Katz TB&H) -255 E 5th -Ste 2400 -Cincinnati 45202

(419) 476-0347 .. **Rust,** John G '48 -4628 Lewis Av -Toledo 43612

(513) 421-6555 .. **Rust,** Mary E '83 Prestige Title -914 Main -Ste 500 -Cincinnati 45202

(513) 381-2838 .. **Rust,** Mary L '87 %Taft S&H LLP -425 Walnut -Ste 1800 -Cincinnati 45202 **Fx:**381-0205

(513) 977-5681 .. **Rust,** Richard S IV '74 Cincinnati Housing Auth -16 W Cntrl Pkwy -Cincinnati 45202

(330) 533-5447 .. **Rusu,** Robert N Jr. '93 (Lane & R Co,LPA) -55 N Broad -Canfield 44406 **Fx:**553-3327

(703) 428-3028 .. **Rusyn,** Daria H '78 US Military Trffc Mngmnt Cmmnd -200 Stovall -Pffc of HQMTJA/Hoffman II 12n6 -Alexandria, VA 22332

(615) 254-1900 .. **Rutchow,** William S '99 OfCnsl Ogletree DNS&S -424 Church -Ste 800 -Nashville, TN 37219

(513) 983-2513 .. **Rutherford,** Elizabeth M '92 Procter & Gamble Co-Legal -1 Procter & Gamble Plz -Cincinnati 45202

(216) 621-0058 .. **Rutherford,** Guy D '96 (G Rutherford & Assoc) -614 Superior Av NW -940 Rckfllr Bldg -Cleveland 44113

(513) 636-4707 .. **Rutherford,** Melvin L Jr. '76 Chldrns Hosp -3333 Burnct Av -Cincinnati 45229

(740) 775-7434 .. **Rutherford,** Sherri K '98 -220 N Plz Blvd -Chillicothe 45601 **Fx:**775-3724

(216) 479-6100 .. **Rutigliano,** Barbara A '83 Vorys SS&P LLP -1375 E 9th -Ste 2100 One Cleve Ctr -Cleveland 44114 **Fx:**479-6060

(440) 789-3848 .. **Rutigliano,** Joseph E '82 (Rutigliano & Assoc Co LPA) -260 Meadowhill Ln -Moreland Hills 44022

(216) 739-5004 .. **Rutkowski,** Robert W '91 (Weltman W&R Co,LPA) -323 W Lakeside Av -Ste 200 -Cleveland 44113 **Fx:**363-4121

(419) 213-6907 .. **Rutledge,** Brenda I '88 Lucas Cnty Cmn Pleas Ct -1801 Spielbusch -Toledo 43624

(614) 227-8830 .. **Rutledge,** James A '78 (Bricker & E LLP) -100 S 3rd -Columbus 43215 **Fx:**227-2390

(330) 580-2568 .. **Rutledge,** James H '79 United Natl Bank&Trust -Bx24190 -Canton 44701

(937) 294-6000 .. **Rutledge,** Marybeth W '82 %Winwood C & Assoc -3077 Kettering Blvd -Ste 210 -Dayton 45439

Rutman, Gregory L '69 -(Address Unavailable)

(440) 930-8031 .. **Rutman,** Rennie C '01 Wickens HPC&B -35765 Chester Rd -Avon 44011 **Fx:**937-4466

Rutowski, Kimberly A '03 -(Address Unavailable)

(216) 381-3400 .. **Rutsky,** Bruce S '83 (Petronzio S Co,LPA) -5001 Mayfld Rd -Ste 201 -Cleveland 44124

(614) 466-8911 .. **Ruttan,** Mary Beth '93 Atty Gen -30 E Broad -Columbus 43215 **Fx:**728-7582

(216) 642-1425 .. **Rutter,** Robert P '79 (Rutter & R) -4700 Rockside Rd -Ste 650 -Cleveland 44131 **Fx:**(213) 642-0613

(513) 721-8822 .. **Ruttle,** Timothy M '80 Nationwide Ins Co -125 E Court -Ste 203 -Cincinnati 45202

(614) 464-6400 .. **Rutz,** Allen L '98 %Vorys SS&P LLP -52 E Gay -Bx1008 -Columbus 43216 **Fx:**464-6350

(513) 621-3394 .. **Ruwe,** Bradley N '97 Peck S&W,LLP -201 E 5th -Ste 900 -Cincinnati 45202 **Fx:**621-3813

(513) 489-0829 .. **Ruwe,** Joseph M '98 %Mason S&M Co,LPA -11340 Mntgmry Rd -Ste 210 -Cincinnati 45249 **Fx:**489-0834

(513) 381-2838 .. **Ruwe,** Katherine A '02 %Taft S&H LLP -425 Walnut -Ste 1800 -Cincinnati 45202 **Fx:**381-0205

(202) 606-8831 .. **Ruwe,** Robert P '70 US Tax Ct -400 2nd NW -Washington, DC 20217

(513) 271-0808 .. **Ruwe,** Thomas J '83 -5710 Wooster Rd -Ste 211 -Cincinnati 45227

(216) 586-3939 .. **Ruxin,** Paul T '77 (Jones D) -901 Lakeside Av -Cleveland 44114 **Fx:**579-0212

(410) 715-7622 .. **Ruygrok,** Alexander '93 (Bouland & B,LLC) -10025 Governer Whf -Columbia, MD 21044

(419) 259-6806 .. **Ruyle,** James P '79 Fifth 3rd Bank -606 Mad Av -Trust Div/MD292933 -Toledo 43604

(614) 447-2365 .. **Ruzicho,** Andrew J '67 -611 E Weber Rd -Ste 102 -Columbus 43211

(614) 447-2365 .. **Ruzicho,** Andrew J '94 Ruzicho & Assoc -611 E Weber Rd -Ste 102 -Columbus 43211

(330) 652-8387 .. **Ryan,** Allen L '97 (Ryan & Assoc) -701 Summit Av -#82 -Niles 44446

(330) 535-4191 .. **Ryan,** Anne J '97 %Cmmnty Lgl Aid Srvcs,Inc -265 S Main -3rd Fl -Akron 44308 **Fx:**535-0728

(513) 361-1200 .. **Ryan,** Carrie W '00 %Squire S&D LLP -312 Walnut -Ste 3500 -Cincinnati 45202 **Fx:**361-1201

(614) 228-1398 .. **Ryan,** Cheryl L '97 %Nelson LdL&H LLC -280 N High -Ste 920 -Columbus 43215 **Fx:**221-7529

(614) 228-6885 .. **Ryan,** Corinne N '96 %Lane A&H LLC -175 S 3rd -Ste 700 -Columbus 43215 **Fx:**228-0146

(614) 846-2000 .. **Ryan,** Daniel F '80 Campbell HC&V,LLC -7650 Rvrs Edge Dr -Columbus 43235 **Fx:**846-2003

(216) 363-6048 .. **Ryan,** Daniel J '73 -1370 Ontario Av -Ste 2000 -Cleveland 44113

(937) 433-9926 .. **Ryan,** Edwin L Jr. '71 -1974 Woodson Ct -Dayton 45459

(513) 423-5467 .. **Ryan,** James D '62 -4009 Central Av -Middletown 45044

(614) 221-3155 .. **Ryan,** James G '85 (Bailey C LLC) -10 W Broad -Columbus 43215 **Fx:**221-0479

(513) 381-2838 .. **Ryan,** James J '54 OfCnsl Taft S&H LLP -425 Walnut -Ste 1800 -Cincinnati 45202 **Fx:**381-0205

(513) 861-1544 .. **Ryan,** James J '58 -888 Rue De La Paix -Cincinnati 45220

(216) 573-6000 .. **Ryan,** Jody Le '91 %Licata & Assoc Co,LPA -6480 Rockside Wds Blvd S -Ste 390 -Independence 44131 **Fx:**573-6333

Ryan, John D '66 -20800 Ctr Ridge Rd -Rocky River 44116

(216) 591-9150 ..**Ryan,** John S '04 CSA -23240 Chagrin Blvd -Ste 805
　-Beachwood 44122

(614) 488-4880 ..**Ryan,** Joseph E Jr. '64 Ryan & R -1890 Northwest Blvd
　-Columbus 43212

(614) 227-2000 ..**Ryan,** Joseph W Jr. '78 (Porter WM&A LLP) -41 S High
　-Columbus 43215 Fx:227-2100

(216) 931-6000 ..**Ryan,** Kate E '97 %Ulmer & B LLP -1300 E 9th
　-Ste 900 Penton Media Bldg -Cleveland 44114 Fx:931-6001

(419) 947-5545 ..**Ryan,** Kathleen J '89 Morrow Cnty Cmn Pleas Ct -48 E High
　-Mount Gilead 43338 Fx:947-6341

(216) 327-2700 ..**Ryan,** Kevin M '98 -7064 Avon Belden Rd -North Ridgeville 44039

(513) 723-8261 ..**Ryan,** Laura A '92 Convergys Corp -201 E 4th -Cincinnati 45202

(414) 665-5240 ..**Ryan,** Laurence K '90 Nrthwstrn Mutual Trust Co
　-611 E Wscnsn Av -Ste 550 -Milwaukee, WI 53202

(614) 228-4546 ..**Ryan,** Michael F '88 %Shuler P&B,LPA -145 E Rich -Ste 400
　-Columbus 43215

(216) 664-4729 ..**Ryan,** Michael J '96 Municipal Ct -1200 Ontario -12th Fl
　-Cleveland 44113

(614) 249-0293 ..**Ryan,** Paige L '97 Nationwide Ins Co -1 Nationwide Plz
　-Compliance -Columbus 43215

(513) 946-3000 ..**Ryan,** Rae M '85 Hamilton Cnty Pros -230 E 9th -Cincinnati 45202
　Fx:946-3017

(614) 923-3300 ..**Ryan,** Robert S '96 Ruscilli Real Estate -5747 Perimeter Dr
　-Ste 130 -Dublin 43017

(937) 449-6810 ..**Ryan,** Robin D '01 %Porter WM&A LLP -1 S Main -Ste 1600
　-Dayton 45402 Fx:449-6820

(425) 867-4969 ..**Ryan,** Scott R '95 Physio-Control Corp -11011 Willows Rd NE
　-Redmond, WA 98052

(513) 381-6810 ..**Ryan,** Shawn R '89 %Reisenfeld & Assoc -2355 Auburn Av
　-Cincinnati 45219 Fx:381-0255

(740) 221-6211 ..**Ryan,** Sherman '91 -117 W Main -Ste 100 -Lancaster 43130

(740) 453-8737 ..**Ryan,** Sherry L '74 -309 Main -Zanesville 43701

(440) 930-8044 ..**Ryan,** Spencer A '01 Wickens HPC&B -35765 Chester Rd
　-Avon 44011 Fx:937-4466

(216) 363-1700 ..**Ryan,** Terrance Lee '76 Shanahan Law Firm,LLC -925 Euclid Av
　-Ste 1750 -Cleveland 44115

(614) 228-5151 ..**Ryan,** Timothy J '91 (Gallagher GPT&L LLP) -471 E Broad -19th Fl
　-Columbus 43215 Fx:228-0032

(440) 930-8075 ..**Rybarczyk,** John D '87 Wickens HPC&B -35765 Chester Rd
　-Avon 44011 Fx:937-4466

(216) 641-8265 ..**Rybka,** Edward W '81 -6302 Fleet Av -Cleveland 44105

(216) 641-5100 ..**Rybka,** Robert S '84 -6302 Fleet Av -Cleveland 44105

(765) 647-4105 ..**Rychener,** Ronald K '74 (Mullin M&R) -814 Main -Bx68
　-Brookville, IN 47012

(440) 241-1872 ..**Ryder,** Blanche S '98 -7861 Oakrdg Dr -Mentor 44060

(440) 248-7906 ..**Ryder,** Edward M Jr. '77 (Mazanec R&R Co,LPA) -34305 Solon Rd
　-Ste 100 -Cleveland 44139 Fx:248-8861

(513) 871-7090 ..**Ryder,** Ely M T '71 -2902 Alpine Ter -Cincinnati 45208
　Fx:871-7090

(605) 385-2329 ..**Ryder,** Ryan A '99 USAF -1000 Ellsworth -Ste 2700
　-Ellsworth AFB, SD 57706

(216) 586-3939 ..**Rydzel,** James A '72 (Jones D) -901 Lakeside Av
　-Cleveland 44114 Fx:579-0212

　Ryerson, John T Jr. '91 -Bx1824 -Columbus 43216

(216) 241-5310 ..**Ryhal,** James L Jr. '52 OfCnsl Gallagher SF&N -1501 Euclid Av
　-6th Fl -Cleveland 44115 Fx:241-1608

(216) 586-3939 ..**Ryland,** Joshua M '99 %Jones D -901 Lakeside Av
　-Cleveland 44114 Fx:579-0212

(614) 228-8833 ..**Rymers,** Beau K '99 Cincinnati Ins Co -140 E Town -Ste 1015
　-Columbus 43215

(216) 687-1311 ..**Rymond,** Richard J '82 (Reminger & R) -101 Prospect Av W
　-1400 Mdlnd Bldg -Cleveland 44115 Fx:687-1841

(740) 671-9300 ..**Ryncarz,** Thomas M '95 -3814 Central Av -Shadyside 43947

(440) 808-9494 ..**Ryser,** Elizabeth H '91 -24525 Detroit Rd -Westlake 44145

(614) 764-2007 ..**Ryser,** Philip P '78 %Stanley Steemer Intl
　-5500 Stanley Steemer Pkwy -Dublin 43016

(330) 869-4471 ..**Rywalski,** Robert F '68 Omnova Solutions Inc -175 Ghent Rd
　-Fairlawn 44333

(614) 466-3180 ..**Rzymek,** Michael A '88 Atty Gen -150 E Gay -Columbus 43215
　Fx:466-9788

(614) 457-5330 ..**Saad,** James A '77 (J Saad LLC) -2000 W Henderson Rd -Ste 400
　-Columbus 43220

(614) 365-2700 ..**Saad,** Michael D '66 (Squire S&D LLP) -41 S High
　-1300 Huntngtn Ctr -Columbus 43215 Fx:365-2499

(216) 586-3939 ..**Saada,** John M Jr. '93 (Jones D) -901 Lakeside Av -Cleveland
　44114 Fx:579-0212

(330) 747-1954 ..**Saadi,** Edward T '03 (ET Saadi,LLC) -1325 VA Trl
　-Youngstown 44505

(614) 464-6400 ..**Saalman,** Gary J '89 (Vorys SS&P LLP) -52 E Gay -Bx1008
　-Columbus 43216 Fx:464-6350

(513) 397-1333 ..**Saba,** Delia R '98 Broadwing Inc -201 E 4th -Bx2301
　-Cincinnati 45201

　Saba, Monica M '93 -(Address Unavailable)

(513) 533-2996 ..**Saba,** Paul T '94 %Finney SS&K Co,LPA -2623 Erie Av -Bx8804
　-Cincinnati 45208

(513) 533-2996 ..**Saba,** Peter A '91 (Finney SS&K Co,LPA) -2623 Erie Av -Bx8804
　-Cincinnati 45208

(216) 791-3800 ..**Saba,** Ruth H '80 Dept of Veterans Affairs -10000 Brecksvll Rd
　-Brecksville 44141

(330) 325-1790 ..**Sabarese,** Sharon A '89 -4139 Tallmadge Rd -Bx296
　-Rootstown 44272

(732) 594-1935 ..**Sabatelli,** Anthony D '94 Merck & Co -RYGO-30 -Bx2000
　-Rahway, NJ 07065

(614) 222-0535 ..**Sabath,** Mark K '92 (Sabath & J Co,LPA) -338 S High
　-Columbus 43215

(216) 416-3251 ..**Sabatine,** Jeffrey P '87 Cnsl Forest City Entrprs,Inc -50 Pub Sq
　-Ste 1360 Trmnl Twr -Cleveland 44113

(614) 229-3888 ..**Sabatino,** Alessandro Jr. '93 Cheek & Z,LLP -471 E Broad -18th Fl
　-Bx15069 -Columbus 43215 Fx:241-5865

(330) 742-7021 ..**Sabine,** John D '67 Sky Trust NA -Bx479 -Youngstown 44501

(440) 395-3762 ..**Sablack,** Michael A '96 Progressive Ins Co -6300 Wilson Mills Rd
　-#N72A -Mayfield Village 44143

　Sablotny, Dale A '92 -(Address Unavailable)

(216) 520-7176 ..**Sabo,** Aberdeen H '67 IRS -5990 W Crk Rd -Independence 44131
　Fx:520-7165

　Sabo, Kimberly '04 -(Address Unavailable)

(614) 462-5030 ..**Sabo,** Roger L '71 (Schottenstein Z&D) -250 West -Bx165020
　-Columbus 43216 Fx:462-5135

(216) 871-8970 ..**Sabol,** Garry A '82 -1419 Demorest Rd -Columbus 43228

(419) 224-2125 ..**Sabol,** John A '72 -128 W High -Lima 45801

(419) 772-2218 ..**Sabol,** Nancy P '87 ONU-Pettit Clg of Law -525 S Main
　-Ada 45810

(614) 445-0793 ..**Sabol,** Suzanne K '83 -820 S High -Columbus 43206

(440) 897-3180 ..**Sabrey,** James F '00 -Bx360376 -Strongsville 44136

(216) 360-0001 ..**Sabroff,** Brett M '77 -23230 Chagrin Blvd -Ste 720
　-Beachwood 44122

(216) 228-7200 ..**Saccany,** John C '83 Brown & S -14222 Mad Av -Cleveland 44107

(216) 443-8866 ..**Sacco,** Joel F '83 Cuyahoga Cnty Dom Rltns Ct -1 Lakeside Av
　-Cleveland 44113

(216) 566-5761 ..**Saccogna,** Patrick J '90 OfCnsl Thompson H LLP -127 Pub Sq
　-3900 Key Ctr -Cleveland 44114 Fx:566-5800

(440) 974-8081 ..**Sacerich,** Thomas J '80 (Sacerich & O) -6988 Spinach Dr
　-Mentor 44060

(216) 520-0077 ..**Sacha,** Laura J '97 Avid,Inc -4141 Rockside Rd -Ste 200
　-Seven Hills 44131

(419) 586-5669 ..**Sacher,** John W '68 Sacher Law Ofcs -112 W Market
　-Celina 45822 Fx:586-5669

(419) 586-5669 ..**Sacher,** Michael S '78 Sacher Law Ofcs -112 W Market
　-Celina 45822 Fx:586-5669

(248) 641-1292 ..**Sachs,** Jessica S '00 %Harness D&P,PLC -5445 Corp Dr
　-Troy, MI 48098 Fx:641-0270

(248) 457-7109 ..**Sachs,** Kenneth J '99 %Cox H&G, PC -101 W Big Beaver -10th Fl
　-Troy, MI 48084

(330) 656-2600 ..**Sachs,** Valerie G '81 Jo-Ann Stores Inc -5555 Darrow Rd
　-Hudson 44236

(216) 371-7121 ..**Sack,** Mark J '97 Taylor Academy -14780 Superior Rd
　-Cleveland Heights 44118

(513) 946-3000 ..**Sack,** Tamara S '99 Hamilton Cnty Pros -230 E 9th -Cincinnati
　45202 Fx:946-3017

(513) 977-8200 ..**Sackenheim,** Alison N '03 %Dinsmore & S LLP -255 E 5th
　-Ste 1900 -Cincinnati 45202 Fx:977-8141

(216) 781-7095 ..**Sackett,** Peter A '81 -55 Pub Sq -Ste 1350 -Cleveland 44113

(734) 242-9500 ..**Sacks,** Joshua J '95 %Lennard G&G PLC -222 Wshngtn
　-Monroe, MI 48161 Fx:242-9509

(513) 241-3100 ..**Sacks,** Steven L '03 %Lerner S&R -120 E 4th -8th Fl
　-Cincinnati 45202

(321) 222-2249 ..**Sadd,** George J '67 -4126 Bushnell Rd -Cleveland 44118

(641) 621-0340 ..**Sadler,** Julie D '00 Lexis Nexis -414 Lbrty -Pella, IA 50219

(631) 344-3435 ..**Sadler,** Louis F '79 US DOE -Brookhvn Group Ofc -Bx5000
　-Upton, NY 11973

(216) 696-8730 ..**Sadlowski,** Jeffrey R '90 %Amin & T LLP -1900 E 9th
　-24th Fl Natl City Ctr -Cleveland 44114 Fx:696-8731

(704) 386-9041 ..**Sadow,** Eric S '83 Bank of America Corp -101 S Tryon
　-NC1-002-29-01 -Charlotte, NC 28255

(630) 467-5000 ..**Sadowski,** Anthony '78 %NEC Tech, Inc -1250 Arlngtn Hghts Rd
　-500 -Itasca, IL 60143

(419) 517-7000 ..**Sadowski,** Stephen M '96 (Kenney & N,Ltd) -5470 Main -Ste 300
　-Sylvania 43560 Fx:517-7001

(614) 462-3555 ..**Saeger,** John S '89 Franklin Cnty Pros -373 S High
　-Columbus 43215

(513) 762-6200 ..**Saelinger,** Gina M '93 OfCnsl Ulmer & B LLP -600 Vine -Ste 2800
　-Cincinnati 45202 Fx:762-6245

(513) 621-6464 ..**Saelinger,** Robert R '88 (Graydon H&R LLP) -511 Walnut
　-1900 Fifth Third Ctr -Cincinnati 45202 Fx:651-3836

(216) 787-3030 ..**Saferin,** Stuart A '74 Atty Gen -615 W Superior Av -11th Fl
　-Cleveland 44113 Fx:787-3480

(419) 625-3672 ..**Saferstein,** Melvin A '86 Smith & L,LPA -308 W Adams
　-Sandusky 44870

(216) 622-2700 ..**Saffold,** Jeffrey P '96 (Saffold & J) -75 Pub Sq -Ste 1414
　-Cleveland 44113 Fx:622-2714

(216) 622-2700 ..**Saffold & Johnson** -75 Pub Sq -Ste 1414 -Cleveland 44113
　Fx:622-2714

(513) 381-2838 ..**Safier,** Kristen L '01 %Taft S&H LLP -425 Walnut -Ste 1800
　-Cincinnati 45202 Fx:381-0205

(248) 312-2800 ..**Safir,** Joel R '99 %Vandeveer G,PC -1450 W Long Lk Rd -Ste 100
　-Troy, MI 48098

(614) 466-3636 ..**Safko,** Sheldon R '84 OH Dept Commerce -77 S High
　-Columbus 43266

　Safos, Kristine A '02 -1209 St Charles Av -Lakewood 44107

(330) 395-1800 ..**Safos,** Robert P '77 -585 E Market -Warren 44481

(740) 592-5025 ..**Safranek,** William H III '72 -Bx2606 -Athens 45701

(614) 716-2430 ..**Sagan,** Fredric L '81 %Amer Elec Pwr Co -1 Riverside Plz
　-Columbus 43215

(216) 479-6100 ..**Saganich,** John M '98 (Vorys SS&P LLP) -1375 E 9th
　-Ste 2100 One Cleve Ctr -Cleveland 44114 Fx:479-6060

(216) 523-5405 ..**Saganich,** Suzanne Kleinsmith '98 (Bricker & E LLP) -1375 E 9th
　-Ste 1500 -Cleveland 44114 Fx:523-7071

(847) 850-4100 ..**Sagartz,** Andrew P '98 -5465 Grand Av -Ste 100
　-Gurnee, IL 60031

(440) 777-6500 ..**Sage,** Victoria M '88 -22649 Lorain Rd -Fairview Park 44126

　Sager, Barbara L '95 -8373 Wht Hill Ln -West Chester 45069

(970) 493-5959 ..**Sager,** Sheldon M '78 Lochland Mgmt Co -1 Old Town Sq -Ste 302
　-Bx481 -Fort Collins, CO 80524

(513) 721-3330 ..**Sager,** Stephen M '97 Robbins KP&T -7 W 7th -Ste 1400
　-Cincinnati 45202

(419) 841-9800 ..**Saggese,** Robert P '92 -Bx431 -Sylvania 43560

(440) 835-2232 ..**Saggio,** Joseph A '67 -1816 Halls Carriage Path -Westlake 44145

(419) 243-6450 ..**Saglioccolo,** Gaetano '92 -4231 Monroe -Toledo 43606

(614) 365-2700 ..**Sagone,** Matthew L '94 %Squire S&D LLP -41 S High
　-1300 Huntngtn Ctr -Columbus 43215 Fx:365-2499

(614) 460-4652 ..**Sagun,** Stanley J Jr. '92 Columbia Gas of OH,Inc -200 Civic Ctr Dr
　-Bx117 -Columbus 43216

(330) 405-5061 ..**Sah,** Perrin I '95 %Williams S&S Co,LPA -2241 Pinnacle Pkwy
　-Twinsburg 44087 Fx:405-5586

(330) 535-4191 ..**Sahl,** Joann M '86 %Cmmnty Lgl Aid Srvcs,Inc -265 S Main -3rd Fl
　-Akron 44308 Fx:535-0728

(330) 972-6753 ..**Sahl**, John P '92 Univ of Akron -LAW 243 -Akron 44325

(614) 853-2518 ..**Sahli**, Richard C '80 -5483 Runnymede Ln -Columbus 43228

(419) 523-5015 ..**Sahloff**, Kurt W '94 Leopold W&S -321 E Main -Bx303
-Ottawa 45875

(614) 444-3036 ..**Saia**, Jon J '87 (Saia & P,PLL) -713 S Front -Columbus 43206

(614) 444-3036 ..**Saia & Piatt,PLL** -713 S Front -Columbus 43206
Saiduddin, Shafi J '04 -(Address Unavailable)

(614) 469-3939 ..**Saigo**, Holly H '01 %Jones D -325 John H McConnell Blvd
-Ste 600 -Bx165017 -Columbus 43216 Fx:461-4198

(614) 863-1369 ..**Sain**, George R '98 (Sain Law Ofc) -6906 Starfire Dr
-Reynoldsburg 43068

(330) 535-4191 ..**Sain**, Gregory R '76 %Cmmnty Lgl Aid Srvcs,Inc -265 S Main
-3rd Fl -Akron 44308 Fx:535-0728

(216) 898-1800 ..**Saine**, Christian D '97 Electrolux -20445 Emerald Pkwy SW
-Ste 250 -Cleveland 44135

(304) 242-3220 ..**Saines**, William G '85 McDermott & B,PLLC -53 Wshngtn Av
-Wheeling, WV 26003 Fx:242-2907

(614) 224-4114 ..**St Clair & Bainter,LLP** -580 S High -Ste 200 -Columbus 43215
Fx:224-3804

(419) 471-1489 ..**St Clair**, Beverly J '93 UAW Legal Srvcs -3360 W Laskey Rd
-Toledo 43606 Fx:471-0498
St Clair, Donald D '92 -Bx23185 -Toledo 43623

(614) 224-4114 ..**St Clair**, Robert B '77 (St Clair & B,LLP) -580 S High -Ste 200
-Columbus 43215 Fx:224-3804

(216) 861-3086 ..**St George**, Jason M '01 %Reid M&W -55 Pub Sq -Ste 2010
-Cleveland 44113 Fx:861-4409

(216) 443-5100 ..**St John**, Janice L '95 Cuyahoga Cnty CSEA -1640 Superior Av
-Bx93318 -Cleveland 44114

(216) 621-2300 ..**St John**, Kathleen J '82 Nurenberg PH&M LPA -1370 Ontario
-Ste 100 -Cleveland 44113 Fx:771-2242

(440) 323-1808 ..**St Marie**, Paul R '81 St Marie Law Firm Co,LPA -409 East Av
-Ste A -Elyria 44035

(440) 323-1808 ..**St Marie**, Thomas A '75 (St Marie Law Firm Co,LPA) -409 East Av
-Ste A -Elyria 44035
St Onge, Susan P '92 -11100 Euclid Av -Cleveland 44106

(614) 716-1658 ..**St Pierre**, Thomas G '89 SrCnsl Amer Elec Pwr Co
-1 Riverside Plz -Columbus 43215

(404) 562-5461 ..**Saintvil**, Ledondria H '97 US Dept Educ OCR -61 Forsyth
-Ste 19T70 -Atlanta, GA 30303
Sakai, Michael H '78 -7677 Winding Way -Brecksville 44141
Saken, Elizabeta P '03 -5646 Blandon Run -Gahanna 43230

(330) 675-2426 ..**Saker**, James T '83 %Trumbull Cnty Pros -160 High NW
-Warren 44481

(614) 488-9900 ..**Saker**, Theodore R Jr. '84 -1374 King Av -Columbus 43212

(330) 783-1488 ..**Sakmar**, Michael A '93 -4410 Market -Boardman 44512
Fx:783-1489

(216) 586-3939 ..**Saks**, Jeffrey '99 %Jones D -901 Lakeside Av -Cleveland 44114
Fx:579-0212

(216) 321-7335 ..**Saks**, William M '91 -2511 Overlook Rd -Ste 8 -Cleveland Heights
44106 Fx:321-9733

(513) 385-0030 ..**Saksefski**, Louis M '76 -9910 Arborwood Dr -Cincinnati 45251

(440) 248-8437 ..**Salada**, Bernadette F '86 -5850 Briarhill Dr -Solon 44139

(216) 291-7392 ..**Salada**, Maurice R '82 Northrop Grumman -1900 Richmond Rd
-Cleveland 44124

(216) 781-5515 ..**Salamon**, Jay H '80 (Hermann C&S,LLP) -1301 E 9th -Ste 500
-Cleveland 44114 Fx:781-1030

(330) 376-1717 ..**Salamone**, James P '00 %Davis & Y -One Cascade Plz -Ste 800
-Akron 44308

(419) 255-0814 ..**Salas**, Jesus R '95 ABLE -520 Mad Av -740 Spitzer Bldg
-Toledo 43604 Fx:259-2880

(216) 348-5400 ..**Salata**, Robert Christopher '01 %McDonald H Co,LPA
-600 Superior Av E -Ste 2100 -Cleveland 44114 Fx:348-5474

(212) 545-4000 ..**Saldana**, Nicole D '95 %Jackson L LLP -59 Maiden Ln
-New York, NY 10038 Fx:972-3213

(937) 223-8888 ..**Saldanha**, Jason J '03 %Dyer GM&S -131 N Ludlow -Ste 1400
-Dayton 45402 Fx:223-0127

(216) 241-1074 ..**Saleh**, Abeer T '03 %Stafford & S Co,LPA -323 Lakeside Av W
-Ste 380 -Cleveland 44113

(513) 941-2668 ..**Salem**, David A '95 Salem Cptl Risk -3124 Triplecrown Dr
-North Bend 45052

(440) 951-6666 ..**Salem**, John S '96 Denman & L Co,LPA -8039 Broadmoor Rd
-Mentor 44060

(419) 475-8665 ..**Salem**, Nadeem S '96 Savage & Assoc -4427 Talmadge Rd
-Bx8526 -Toledo 43623

(419) 537-4236 ..**Salem**, Robert S '90 Univ of Toledo Law Schl -2801 W Bancroft
-Toledo 43606

(440) 285-2222 ..**Salem**, Sheila M '97 %Geauga Cnty Pros -231 Main -Cthse Annx
-Chardon 44024 Fx:286-4357

(614) 239-5034 ..**Saleme**, David W '97 Regional Airport Auth -4600 Intl Gtwy
-Columbus 43219 Fx:238-7834

(216) 781-8700 ..**Salerno**, Denise J '03 %Novak RP&S,LLP -1660 W 2nd
-Ste 270 Skylight Ofc Twr -Cleveland 44113 Fx:781-9227

(330) 673-7000 ..**Salerno**, Mark A '83 Glazing Syst Inc -Bx233 -Tallmadge 44278

(216) 348-5400 ..**Salerno**, Matthew A '99 %McDonald H Co,LPA -600 Superior Av E
-Ste 2100 -Cleveland 44114 Fx:348-5474

(513) 732-7573 ..**Sales**, Arrianna '03 Clermont Cnty Ct of Common Pleas -270 Main
-Batavia 45103

(419) 668-6162 ..**Sales**, Bradley E '87 Huron Cnty Cmn Pleas Ct -2 E Main
-Norwalk 44857
Sales, Gary N '80 -6491 Friarsgate Dr NW -Canton 44718

(513) 552-1400 ..**Salinas**, Vincent A '74 -100 Merchant -Ste 180 -Cincinnati 45246

(513) 946-9000 ..**Salinger**, Ann J '82 Hamilton Cnty Domestic Rel Ct -800 Bway
-Cincinnati 45202

(216) 566-5507 ..**Salisbury**, David W '84 (Thompson H LLP) -127 Pub Sq
-3900 Key Ctr -Cleveland 44114 Fx:566-5800

(216) 689-5736 ..**Salisbury**, Elizabeth W '84 KeyBank NA -127 Pub Sq
-17th Fl,Wealth Mngmnt -Cleveland 44114 Fx:689-3034

(440) 838-1222 ..**Salisbury**, Joyce A '93 (Salisbury & S) -8191 Broadvw Rd
-Broadview Heights 44147 Fx:838-0954

(740) 820-3145 ..**Salisbury**, Mark A '85 DGM,Inc -453 Salisbury Rd -Beaver 45613

(440) 838-1222 ..**Salisbury**, Richard L '79 (Salisbury & S) -8191 Broadvw Rd
-Broadview Heights 44147 Fx:838-0954

(330) 723-9536 ..**Salisbury**, Scott G '88 Medina Cnty Pros -72 Pub Sq
-Medina 44256

(419) 473-1350 ..**Sallah**, Charles H '81 (Jasin S&M Co,LPA) -4303 Talmadge Rd
-Ste 201 -Toledo 43623 Fx:473-1929

(740) 594-8093 ..**Sallah**, Margaret A '03 Ctr for Student Advocacy -8 N Court
-Ste 413 -Athens 45701

(216) 522-3240 ..**Sallee**, Brian C '97 IRS -1375 E 9th -1200 -Cleveland 44114

(513) 977-8200 ..**Sallee**, Jerry S '80 (Dinsmore & S LLP) -255 E 5th -Ste 1900
-Cincinnati 45202 Fx:977-8141

(513) 977-8200 ..**Sallee**, Joseph L Jr. '85 (Dinsmore & S LLP) -255 E 5th -Ste 1900
-Cincinnati 45202 Fx:977-8141

(330) 643-2788 ..**Sallerson**, Daniel F '95 Summit Cnty Pros-Crim -53 Univ Av -7th Fl
-Akron 44308 Fx:643-8277
Salman, Steven L '82 -6051 N Ocean Dr -#1401
-Hollywood, FL 33019

(513) 762-7648 ..**Salmen**, Gerald G '76 -250 E 5th -1500 Chiquita Ctr
-Cincinnati 45202

(513) 762-6200 ..**Salmon**, James L '00 %Ulmer & B LLP -600 Vine -Ste 2800
-Cincinnati 45202 Fx:762-6245

(440) 362-0775 ..**Salmon**, John G '65 -14340 Kingman Dr
-Middleburg Heights 44130

(419) 875-5474 ..**Salmon**, Joseph Michael '94 -8263 Woodbrier Ln
-Grand Rapids 43522

(419) 244-4605 ..**Salsberry**, Tam E '91 Port Lwrnce Title & Trust Co -616 Mad Av
-Toledo 43604

(216) 514-1100 ..**Salsbury**, Scott E '87 (Rolf & G Co,LPA) -30100 Chagrin Blvd
-Ste 350 Corp Cir -Cleveland 44124 Fx:514-0030

(440) 603-2367 ..**Salsbury**, Sue E '89 Progressive Casuality -6055 Parkland Blvd
-Mayfield Heights 44124 Fx:603-2580

(614) 207-0070 ..**Salters**, Woodrow W '02 -180 E Cllg Av -Westerville 43081

(703) 605-0335 ..**Saltsman**, Gary D '78 Board of Immigration Appeals
-5107 Leesburg Pk -19th Fl -Falls Church, VA 22041

(216) 696-1080 ..**Saltzer**, Michael A '88 %D Seaman & Assoc Co,LPA
-614 Superior Av W -Ste 1600 Rckfllr Bldg -Cleveland 44113

(216) 696-9290 ..**Saltzman**, Barbara E '77 -75 Pub Sq -Ste 920 -Cleveland 44113

(216) 861-0360 ..**Saltzman**, Judith C '98 %Hickman & L Co,LPA -1370 Ontario
-Ste 1620 -Cleveland 44113 Fx:861-3113

(216) 529-9377 ..**Saltzman**, Michael J '70 (Saltzman & Assoc Co,LPA)
-1370 Ontario -1000 Standard Bldg -Cleveland 44113
Fx:696-3228

(216) 623-0150 ..**Salvatore**, Albert N '82 (Roetzel & A,LPA) -1375 E 9th
-One Cleve Ctr 9th Fl -Cleveland 44114 Fx:623-0134

(937) 328-4557 ..**Salway**, Joel D '89 Clark Cnty Ct -101 N Limestone
-Springfield 45502

(937) 586-3100 ..**Salyer**, David R '91 %ES Gallon & Assoc -40 W 4th -22nd Fl
-Dayton 45402 Fx:586-3100

(904) 359-2000 ..**Salyer**, Hilary F '99 Foley & L -200 N Laura
-Jacksonville, FL 32202

(740) 596-5291 ..**Salyer**, James P '94 (Salyer & Assoc) -114 W Main -Bx466
-McArthur 45651
Salyer, Mary M '96 -226 Ft Mitchell Av -Covington, KY 41011

(513) 721-4500 ..**Salyer**, Susan M '03 %Patsfall Y&P LLC -1 W 4th -Ste 1800
-Cincinnati 45202 Fx:639-7554

(937) 225-6495 ..**Salyers**, Lance S '00 Montgomery Cnty Pros -301 W 3rd -Bx972
-Dayton 45422 Fx:225-3470

(330) 725-1199 ..**Salzgeber**, Joseph F Jr. '94 -229 W Lbrty -Bx1589 -Medina 44258

(937) 223-8821 ..**Salzler**, Mark J '76 Deloitte & Touche -1700 Cthse Plz NE
-Dayton 45402

(412) 261-0310 ..**Salzman**, David B '02 Campbell & L,LLC -310 Grant
-1700 Grant Bldg -Pittsburgh, PA 15219 Fx:261-5066

(440) 247-4765 ..**Samad**, Debra J '78 SG Thomas,LPA -35 River -Level B
-Chagrin Falls 44022

(614) 292-2019 ..**Samansky**, Michael J '95 OSU Moritz Cllg of Law -55 W 12th Av
-Columbus 43210 Fx:292-1383

(513) 626-2269 ..**Sambrook**, Michael J '03 Procter & Gamble
-11511 Reed Hartman Hwy -Bx 325 -Cincinnati 45241

(330) 565-5160 ..**Sammarone**, Christopher '99 -44 Fed Plz Central -Ste 204
-Youngstown 44503

(419) 447-5011 ..**Sammet**, Jenny L '02 Cnsl Seneca Cnty CSEA
-3362 S Twp Rd 151 -Tiffin 44883 Fx:447-5345

(216) 781-7990 ..**Sammon**, Albert C '85 Sammon & B Co,LPA -614 Superior Av NW
-1160 Rckfllr Bldg -Cleveland 44113

(216) 781-7990 ..**Sammon & Bolmeyer Co, LPA** -614 Superior Av NW
-1160 Rckfllr Bldg -Cleveland 44113

(216) 781-8700 ..**Sammon**, Colin P '03 %Novak RP&S,LLP -1660 W 2nd
-Ste 270 Skylight Ofc Twr -Cleveland 44113 Fx:781-9227

(419) 609-1311 ..**Sammon**, James P '94 (Reminger & R) -237 W Wshngtn Row
-2nd Fl -Sandusky 44870 Fx:626-4805

(216) 622-3600 ..**Sammon**, John D '86 US Atty -801 W Superior -Ste 400
-Cleveland 44113 Fx:622-3370

(216) 443-7800 ..**Sammon**, Thomas J '70 Cuyahoga Cnty Pros -1200 Ontario
-8th Fl -Cleveland 44113 Fx:698-2270

(614) 891-9522 ..**Sammons**, Jeffery D '82 (Sammons & Assoc Co,LPA)
-635 Park Meadow Rd -Ste 101 -Westerville 43081

(937) 865-7875 ..**Samonas**, Michael '86 Lexis/Nexis -Bx933 -Dayton 45401

(513) 946-3000 ..**Sampang**, Jocelyn M '94 Hamilton Cnty Pros -230 E 9th
-Cincinnati 45202 Fx:946-3017

(614) 221-3155 ..**Samples**, Todd J '01 %Bailey C LLC -10 W Broad
-Columbus 43215 Fx:221-0479

(216) 360-9720 ..**Sampsel**, Susan M '84 Guardian Natl Title -4920 Commerce Pkwy
-Ste 2 -Warrensville Heights 44128

(330) 438-0611 ..**Sampson**, Karen P '84 Industrial Commssn of OH -400 3rd SE
-Canton 44702

(513) 241-3100 ..**Sampson**, Kirk '75 (Lerner S&R) -120 E 4th -8th Fl
-Cincinnati 45202

(614) 688-0052 ..**Sampson**, Sara A '97 OSU - Moritz Law Library -55 W 12th Av
-Columbus 43210

(614) 879-8026 ..**Sams**, David A '91 -Bx40 -West Jefferson 43162

(513) 398-4646 ..**Sams Fischer & Schuessler** -209 Reading Rd -Mason 45040
Fx:398-4608

(614) 322-7923 ..**Sams**, Jeffrey B '88 (JB Sams LLC) -1579 Crosscreeks Blvd
-Pickerington 43147

(513) 398-4646 ..**Sams**, Jonathan D '96 (Sams F&S) -209 Reading Rd
-Mason 45040 Fx:398-4608

Sams, Mark A '99 -(Address Unavailable)

(419) 289-0509 .. **Samsel,** David A '72 -107 E Main -Rm 2 -Ashland 44805

(614) 466-5744 .. **Samsel,** Edward C '83 OH Dept Taxation -30 E Broad -22nd Fl
-Columbus 43215 Fx:752-9822

(937) 445-2908 .. **Samson,** Paul M '01 NCR Corp -1700 S Patterson Blvd
-Dayton 45479

(216) 443-8587 .. **Samson,** Shana A '00 Hon PF Jones -1200 Ontario
-Cleveland 44113

Samuel, Marcy B '83 -552 Westbury Woods Ct -Westerville 43081

(661) 276-3047 .. **Samuels,** David A '83 NASA Dryden Flight Ctr -Ofc of Chief Cnsl
-Mailstop:D-2016 -Bx273 -Edwards, CA 93523

(937) 445-4937 .. **Samuels,** Ellen J '86 NCR Corp -1700 S Patterson Blvd
-Law Dept WHQ-5 -Dayton 45479

(856) 810-5628 .. **Samuels,** Gregory A '01 American Water -701 Rte 73
-Bldg 1, Ste 300 -Marlton, NJ 08053

(614) 221-2580 .. **Samuels,** Harvey M '74 -529 S 3rd -Columbus 43215

(216) 453-3033 .. **Samuels,** James A '76 Grubb & E -1350 Euclid Av -#300
-Cleveland 44115

(330) 972-7898 .. **Samuels,** Jeffrey M '99 %Univ of Akron/Schl of Law -150 Univ Av
-Akron 44325

(614) 231-9134 .. **Samuels,** Margaret Ann '74 -787 Montrose Av -Columbus 43209

(614) 462-5021 .. **Samuels,** Stephen P '75 (Schottenstein Z&D) -250 West
-Bx165020 -Columbus 43216 Fx:462-5135

(614) 889-2531 .. **Sanborn Brandon Duvall & Bobbitt Co,LPA**
-2515 W Granvll Rd -Columbus 43235

(216) 479-8500 .. **Sanborn,** Elizabeth M '81 %Squire S&D LLP -127 Pub Sq
-4900 Key Twr -Cleveland 44114 Fx:479-8780

(614) 851-0200 .. **Sanborn,** Jeffrey W '91 -461 Round Up Dr -Galloway 43119

(216) 431-4131 .. **Sanchez,** Alexander M '93 Recovery Rsrcs -3950 Chester Av
-Cleveland 44114

(614) 462-5295 .. **Sanchez,** Lorenzo '92 Franklin Cnty Cmn Pleas Ct -375 S High
-Columbus 43215 Fx:462-6292

(216) 515-1660 .. **Sanchez,** Marc A '94 %Frantz W LLP -127 Pub Sq
-2500 Key Center -Cleveland 44114 Fx:515-1650

(330) 244-1174 .. **Sand,** Michael '69 OfCnsl Sand & S -4940 Munson NW -Ste 1100
-Canton 44718

(330) 244-1174 .. **Sand & Sebolt** -4940 Munson NW -Ste 1100 -Canton 44718

(216) 623-0150 .. **Sandacz,** Beverly A '94 (Roetzel & A,LPA) -1375 E 9th
-One Cleve Ctr 9th Fl -Cleveland 44114 Fx:623-0134

Sandalakis, Athanasia C '90 -25975 Newbury Dr -Westlake 44145

(614) 466-0284 .. **Sandberg,** Elisabet K '98 Legis Srvc Commssn -77 S High
-Columbus 43215

(330) 659-8900 .. **Sandel,** Kevin S '95 Natl Interstate Ins Co -3250 Intrstate Dr
-Richfield 44286 Fx:659-8909

(216) 696-5297 .. **Sandel,** Martin L '73 Bilfield & S Co,LPA -1301 E 9th
-Ste 1000 Erievw Twr -Cleveland 44114 Fx:696-2316

(614) 221-5216 .. **Sander,** Neil C '04 %Wiles BB&B Co,LPA -300 Spruce -1st Fl
-Columbus 43215 Fx:221-5692

(216) 651-4422 .. **Sander,** Richard W '75 St. Claire Cos -1216 W 65th
-Cleveland 44102

(859) 815-7105 .. **Sanders,** Clayton R Jr. '99 GEIT Solutions Inc -1101 Pacific Av
-Erlanger, KY 41018

(414) 297-1700 .. **Sanders,** Daniel H '91 Dept of Justice -517 E Wscnsn Av
-530 Fed Bldg -Milwaukee, WI 53202

(614) 469-5715 .. **Sanders,** Deborah F '89 US Atty -303 Marconi Blvd -Ste 200
-Columbus 43215

(614) 728-0849 .. **Sanders,** Howard M '75 Workers Comp -30 W Spring -Level 26
-Columbus 43215

(330) 399-8801 .. **Sanders,** James E '81 %Turner M&S -185 High NE
-Warren 44481 Fx:399-8805

Sanders, Joshua R '03 -(Address Unavailable)

(614) 228-0704 .. **Sanders,** Judith B '77 (Bell R&S Co,LPA) -33 S Grant Av
-Columbus 43215

(513) 891-8900 .. **Sanders,** Michael B '88 (Sanders & Assoc,LPA)
-9122 Mntgmry Rd -Ste 201 -Cincinnati 45242

(513) 352-5255 .. **Sanders,** Nicole '03 Law Dept -801 Plum -Rm 214
-Cincinnati 45202 Fx:352-1515

(740) 532-4333 .. **Sanders,** Patricia S '96 Lambert M&B -215 S 4th -Bx725
-Ironton 45638

(419) 868-5704 .. **Sanders,** Richard L '81 -Bx221 -Holland 43528

(859) 491-3000 .. **Sanders,** Robert E '72 -1017 Russell -Covington, KY 41011

(614) 864-8210 .. **Sanders,** Robert M '68 -7110 E Lvngstn Av -Reynoldsburg 43068

(330) 434-3000 .. **Sanders,** Rodd A '94 %Roderick & L -One Cascade Plz -Ste 1500
-Akron 44308 Fx:434-9220

(740) 345-0417 .. **Sanderson,** Andrew T '96 %K Burkett -21 W Church -Ste 201
-Newark 43055

(419) 872-5695 .. **Sanderson,** Dawn E '00 (Celley & S,LLP) -27457 Holiday Ln -#E
-Perrysburg 43551 Fx:872-4476

(419) 241-9000 .. **Sanderson,** Michael G '81 (Shumaker L&K,LLP) -1000 Jackson
-Toledo 43624 Fx:241-6894

(734) 747-7050 .. **Sanderson,** Richard L Jr. '96 OfCnsl Stevenson K Assoc
-444 S Main -Ann Arbor, MI 48104

(614) 466-5394 .. **Sandford,** Kathryn L '94 Pub Def -8 E Long -Columbus 43215

(800) 600-1222 .. **Sandhu,** Manbir S '02 %Maguire & S,LLP -1370 Ontario -Ste 1700
-Cleveland 44113

(412) 433-1117 .. **Sandman,** Dan D '73 USX Corp -600 Grant -Pittsburgh, PA 15219

(937) 229-4333 .. **Sandner,** Lisa A '94 Univ of Dayton Schl of Law -300 Cllg Park
-Dayton 45469

(937) 223-1130 .. **Sandner,** Michael W '94 Pickrel S&E -40 N Main
-2700 Kettering Twr -Dayton 45423 Fx:223-0339

(800) 243-0210 .. **Sandor,** Frank J III '91 Westfield Grp -1 Park Cir -Bx5001
-Westfield Center 44251 Fx:(330) 887-2588

(614) 225-8818 .. **Sandor,** Louis J Jr. '78 PricewaterhouseCoopers -100 E Broad
-Columbus 43215

(915) 595-0697 .. **Sandoval,** Jesus C '73 J Carruth Sandoval & Assoc
-1642 Lomaland -#1158 -El Paso, TX 79935

(440) 951-9246 .. **Sandrey,** Holly J '93 -4899 Waldamere Av -Willoughby 44094

(330) 456-8341 .. **Sandrock,** Scott P '78 (Black MS&A,LPA) -220 Market Av S
-Ste 1000 -Canton 44702 Fx:456-5756

(440) 888-5333 .. **Sands,** John F '56 (J Sands,LPA,Inc) -5001 Buttonbush Ln
-North Royalton 44133

(419) 891-5200 .. **Sandusky,** Barbara J '92 Burns Cnsltng Assoc -1755 Indn Wd Cir
-Ste 100 -Maumee 43537

(330) 297-5718 .. **Sandvoss,** Norman W '68 (Sandvoss & L) -228 W Main -Bx248
-Ravenna 44266

(419) 734-6511 .. **Sandwisch,** Michael W '82 -Bx129 -Port Clinton 43452

(202) 861-1626 .. **Sanford,** Bruce W '71 (Baker & H) -1050 Conn Av NW
-Washington, DC 20036

(312) 977-0200 .. **Sanford,** James M '87 Cochran & M -1 N LaSalle -Ste 2450
-Chicago, IL 60602

(614) 462-5319 .. **Sanford,** Jay H '72 Franklin Cnty Dom Rltns Ct -373 S High
-3rd Fl #35 -Columbus 43215

(202) 694-1650 .. **Sanford,** Paul S '91 Fed Election Comm-Ofc Genl Cnsl
-999 E NW -Washington, DC 20463

(330) 670-0770 .. **Sanislo,** Kevin R '79 (Corzin SU&F) -304 N
-Cleveland-Massillon Rd -Akron 44333

(216) 781-2258 .. **Sanislo,** Paul S '61 Stewart & D Co,LPA -1370 Ontario
-Ste 1440 Standard Bldg -Cleveland 44113 Fx:781-8210

(513) 579-6400 .. **Sanker,** Robert G '87 (Keating M&K PLL) -1 E 4th
-1400 Provident Twr -Cincinnati 45202 Fx:579-6457

(513) 421-7700 .. **Sanks,** Julius F '82 -30 E Cntrl Pkwy -Ste 100 -Cincinnati 45202
Fx:421-7794

(859) 472-1400 .. **Sanning,** Stacey S '98 -202 Colony Dr -Bx425 -Butler, KY 41006

(937) 227-3700 .. **Sanom,** Laura A '87 (Faruki I&C PLL) -10 N Ludlow
-500 Cthse Plz SW -Dayton 45402 Fx:227-3717

(513) 559-1160 .. **Sansalone,** Anthony M '87 -1008 Marshall Av -Cincinnati 45225

(216) 241-5310 .. **Sansalone,** Monica A '95 (Gallagher SF&N) -1501 Euclid Av
-6th Fl -Cleveland 44115 Fx:241-1608

(513) 336-2704 .. **Sansbury,** Amy Z '81 Cmmnty Ins Co -4361 Irwin Simpson Rd
-Mason 45040

(216) 861-4100 .. **Sanson,** Michael A '74 -1370 Ontario Av -Ste 1640 -Cleveland
44113

(614) 443-4866 .. **Sant,** Sanjeev J '01 %J Nemeth & Assoc -21 E Frankfort
-Columbus 43206 Fx:443-4860

(614) 227-2331 .. **Sant,** Thomas R '73 OfCnsl Bricker & E LLP -100 S 3rd
-Columbus 43215 Fx:227-2390

(216) 621-4268 .. **Santa,** Kevin J '86 Ofc of Chptr 13 Trustees -200 Pub Sq
-Ste 3860 BP Twr -Cleveland 44114

(513) 871-8755 .. **Santangelo,** Scott M '86 %Richards & Assoc,LPA -3322 Erie Av
-Ste 101 -Cincinnati 45208 Fx:871-8744

(614) 222-2172 .. **Santangelo,** Stephen A '78 (Weltman W&R Co,LPA) -175 S 3rd
-Ste 900 -Columbus 43215 Fx:222-2193

(614) 469-9500 .. **Santellani,** Lianne L '79 Niehoff & S -501 S High
-Columbus 43215 Fx:224-8708

(513) 241-9400 .. **Santen,** Edward E '88 Legal Aid -215 E 9th -Ste 200
-Cincinnati 45202

(513) 721-4450 .. **Santen,** Harry H '57 Santen & H -312 Walnut -Ste 3100
-Cincinnati 45202

(513) 721-4450 .. **Santen & Hughes** -312 Walnut -Ste 3100 -Cincinnati 45202

(513) 721-4450 .. **Santen,** William E '55 (Santen & H) -312 Walnut -Ste 3100
-Cincinnati 45202

(513) 721-4450 .. **Santen,** William E Jr. '84 (Santen & H) -312 Walnut -Ste 3100
-Cincinnati 45202

(513) 603-2221 .. **Santez,** David L '79 Ohio Casualty Ins Co -9450 Seward Rd
-Fairfield 45014 Fx:603-2208

(419) 245-1975 .. **Santiago,** Lourdes '79 Pros -555 N Erie -4th Fl -Toledo 43624

(937) 643-3770 .. **Santiago,** Miguel A '04 (Santiago & A,LLC) -2310 Far Hills Av
-Ste 3 -Dayton 45419 Fx:643-3704

(614) 424-4164 .. **Santilli,** Paul T '60 -1289 Fountaine Dr -Columbus 43221

(419) 225-5707 .. **Santo,** Maria '88 -124 S Metcalf -Lima 45801

(216) 241-0033 .. **Santoli,** David M '88 -614 Superior Av NW -820 Rckfllr Bldg
-Cleveland 44113

(703) 242-9224 .. **Santoli,** Dennis R '73 Campania Mngmnt Co,Inc -111 Berry SE
-Vienna, VA 22180

(216) 671-6975 .. **Santon,** Roger A '93 -3889 W 157th -Cleveland 44111

(419) 213-4700 .. **Santoro,** Jeremy J '01 %Lucas Cnty Pros -Adams & Erie
-Lucas Cnty Cthse -Toledo 43624

(216) 241-5310 .. **Santoro,** Joseph J '97 (Gallagher SF&N) -1501 Euclid Av -6th Fl
-Cleveland 44115 Fx:241-1608

(419) 673-1534 .. **Santoro,** Todd F '04 -216 W Columbus -Kenton 43326

(216) 443-6389 .. **Santosuosso,** Cara L '98 8th Dist Ct of Appls -1 Lakeside Av
-#202 -Cleveland 44113 Fx:443-2044

(513) 423-9291 .. **Sanzone,** Vincent A Jr. '75 (Bryant & S) -1600 1st Av
-Middletown 45044

(419) 243-8251 .. **Sapara,** Matthew A '99 Toledo-Lucas Cnty Port Authority
-1 Maritime Plz -Toledo 43604

(937) 586-3100 .. **Saphire,** David A '70 (ES Gallon & Assoc) -40 W 4th -22nd Fl
-Dayton 45402 Fx:586-3100

(937) 229-2820 .. **Saphire,** Richard B '71 Univ of Dayton Schl of Law -300 Cllg Park
-Dayton 45469

(513) 621-2666 .. **Sapinsley,** Thomas S '82 (Statman HS&E LLC) -255 E 5th
-Ste 2900 Chemed Ctr -Cincinnati 45202 Fx:587-4477

(440) 232-0505 .. **Sapir,** George R '75 -7140 Nrthfld -Walton Hills 44146

(216) 592-5000 .. **Saponaro,** Joseph M '99 %Tucker E&W LLP -925 Euclid Av -1150
Huntngtn Bldg -Cleveland 44115 Fx:592-5009

Sarady, Alexander V '02 -33803 Electric Blvd -Unit G-22
-Avon Lake 44012

(212) 282-5611 .. **Sarakatsannis,** Thomas J '91 Avon Prdcts,Inc -1345 Av of Amer
-New York, NY 10105

(216) 621-1113 .. **Saralino,** Mark D '90 (Renner OB&S,LLP) -1621 Euclid Av -19th Fl
-Cleveland 44115 Fx:621-6165

(843) 272-8902 .. **Saraniti,** Elizabeth J '98 Mullins Law Firm,PA -1312 Madison Dr
-Bx585 -North Myrtle Beach, SC 29597

(614) 433-0467 .. **Sarap,** George M '77 -Bx779 -Worthington 43085

(513) 241-7111 .. **Sarapata,** Michael A '04 %O'Connor A&L Co,LPA -1014 Vine
-22nd Fl -Cincinnati 45202 Fx:241-7197

(216) 348-1700 .. **Sardina,** Jennifer '00 %Davis & Y -101 Prospect Av W -Ste 1700
-Cleveland 44115 Fx:348-1830

(513) 579-0080 .. **Sarge,** Carmen C '00 %Smith R&S Co,LPA -1014 Vine -Ste 2350
-Cincinnati 45202 Fx:579-0222

(419) 241-6000 .. **Sargeant,** Richard T '75 (Eastman & S Ltd) -1 Seagate -24th Fl
-Bx10032 -Toledo 43699 Fx:247-1777

(410) 965-1695 .. **Sargent,** Gary E '76 Cnsl SSA -6401 Security Blvd
-Baltimore, MD 21235

(216) 522-7438 .. **Sargent,** John D '71 EEOC -1660 W 2nd -Ste 850
-Cleveland 44113

(216) 831-0042 .. **Sarkar,** Neil S '97 Meyers RF&L LPA -28601 Chagrin Blvd
-Ste 500 -Cleveland 44122 **Fx:**831-0542

(216) 931-6000 .. **Sarkar,** Richik '98 %Ulmer & B LLP -1300 E 9th
-Ste 900 Penton Media Bldg -Cleveland 44114 **Fx:**931-6001

(330) 376-2700 .. **Sarkis,** George R '80 (Roetzel & A,LPA) -222 S Main
-Akron 44308 **Fx:**376-4577

(216) 574-4421 .. **Sarkisian,** Susan A '82 Travelers Ins -1660 W 2nd -Ste 850
-Cleveland 44113

(614) 995-4399 .. **Sarko,** Thomas L '91 OH Div of Securities -77 S High -22nd Fl
-Columbus 43215

(216) 623-0150 .. **Sarlson,** Mark L '86 (Roetzel & A,LPA) -1375 E 9th
-One Cleve Ctr 9th Fl -Cleveland 44114 **Fx:**623-0134

(330) 744-3196 .. **Sarna,** Wayne W '83 Cmmnty Lgl Aid Srvcs,Inc
-11 Fed Plz Central -7th Fl -Youngstown 44503 **Fx:**744-2503

(614) 275-2650 .. **Saros,** John '74 Franklin Cnty Children Srvcs -855 W Mound
-Columbus 43223 **Fx:**275-2589

(513) 762-4592 .. **Sarra,** Martha C '88 Kroger Co -1014 Vine -Cincinnati 45202

(440) 775-1471 .. **Sarringhaus,** Kurt G '76 (KG Sarringhaus Co,LPA) -Five S Main
-Ste 310 -Oberlin 44074

(847) 484-4446 .. **Sarris,** Chrysso S '91 Cnsl Fortune Brands,Inc -300 Twr Pkwy
-Lincolnshire, IL 60069

(614) 644-2489 .. **Sarris,** Michael J '84 Dept Cmmrce/Liquor Cntrl -6606 Tussing Rd
-Bx4005 -Reynoldsburg 43068 **Fx:**644-3740

(440) 992-8322 .. **Sartini,** James J '91 -4717 Park Av -Bx1247 -Ashtabula 44005

(440) 576-3694 .. **Sartini,** Thomas L '75 (Ashtabula Cnty Pros) -25 W Jffrsn
-Jefferson 44047

(614) 575-1188 .. **Sarver,** Eden R '02 Nobile N&T,LLC -4511 Cemetery Rd -Ste B
-Hilliard 43026 **Fx:**529-8656

(614) 469-3939 .. **Sarver,** Todd L '93 (Jones D) -325 John H McConnell Blvd
-Ste 600 -Bx165017 -Columbus 43216 **Fx:**461-4198

(216) 861-5070 .. **Sasala,** Kathleen M '87 Cleveland Law Library -1 W Lakeside Av
-4th Fl -Cleveland 44113

(419) 843-3545 .. **Sass,** James C '73 -3230 Cntrl Pk W -Ste 200 -Toledo 43617

(419) 424-7276 .. **Sass,** Kenneth J '94 Hancock Cnty Pub Def -316 Dorney Plz
-Findlay 45840

(440) 708-2626 .. **Sass,** Lorrie A '90 -17850 Geauga Lk Rd -Chagrin Falls 44023

(216) 360-7200 .. **Sassano,** James L '93 Carlisle MRK&U Co,LPA
-24755 Chagrin Blvd -Ste 200 -Cleveland 44122 **Fx:**360-7210

(216) 592-5000 .. **Sassé,** Benjamin C '00 %Tucker E&W LLP -925 Euclid Av
-1150 Huntngtn Bldg -Cleveland 44115 **Fx:**592-5009

(440) 974-8194 .. **Sassé,** Cynthia A '89 -6642 Silvermound Dr -Mentor 44060

(216) 622-3600 .. **Sasse,** Gregory C '76 %US Atty -801 W Superior -Ste 400
-Cleveland 44113 **Fx:**622-3370

(740) 349-6131 .. **Sassen,** Douglas E '86 Licking Cnty Prob/Juv Ct -Cnty Cthse
-Newark 43055

(216) 479-8500 .. **Satola,** James W '89 Squire S&D LLP -127 Pub Sq -4900 Key Twr
-Cleveland 44114 **Fx:**479-8780

(937) 257-3851 .. **Satterfield,** Carol A '79 USAF -5135 Pearson Rd -Ste 2,
88 ABW JA -Wright Patterson AFB 45433

(513) 353-3287 .. **Satterfield,** Clarence R '74 -8220 E Miami Rvr Rd
-Cincinnati 45247

(614) 995-2096 .. **Satterwhite,** Matthew J '00 PUCO -180 E Broad -Columbus 43266

(216) 687-1311 .. **Satullo,** Nick '85 (Reminger & R) -101 Prospect Av W
-1400 Mdlnd Bldg -Cleveland 44115 **Fx:**687-1841

(513) 785-5880 .. **Sauer,** Gregory J '86 Butler Cnty CSEA -315 High -7th Fl
-Hamilton 45011

(216) 586-3939 .. **Sauer,** Joseph M '02 %Jones D -901 Lakeside Av
-Cleveland 44114 **Fx:**579-0212

(614) 466-1312 .. **Sauer,** Larry S '87 OH Consumers' Cnsl -10 W Broad -Ste 1800
-Columbus 43215 **Fx:**466-9475

(216) 621-0200 .. **Sauer,** McKinley H III '87 (Baker & H LLP) -1900 E 9th -Ste 3200
-Cleveland 44114 **Fx:**696-0740

(937) 748-0066 .. **Sauer,** Rena G '95 -85 E Waterbury Dr -Springboro 45066

(513) 946-3172 .. **Sauers,** Mark E '79 Hamilton Cnty Pros -230 E 9th
-Cincinnati 45202 **Fx:**946-3017

(937) 278-4858 .. **Saul,** Irving I '52 -113 Bethpolamy Ct -Dayton 45415

Sauline, Albert J III '04 -(Address Unavailable)

(202) 662-5471 .. **Saulino,** Jennifer L '01 %Covington & B -1201 Penn Av NW
-Washington, DC 20004

(419) 243-1144 .. **Saum,** Scott J '75 (Zyndorf & S) -320 N Mich -2nd Fl
-Toledo 43624

(740) 446-1652 .. **Saunders,** Brent A '83 (Halliday S&S) -19 Locust -Bx325
-Gallipolis 45631

(614) 462-2260 .. **Saunders,** Charles Jr. '72 (Schottenstein Z&D) -250 West
-Bx165020 -Columbus 43216 **Fx:**462-5135

(937) 372-4919 .. **Saunders,** Craig W '00 %Smith & P -133 E Market -Xenia 45385

(216) 577-0166 .. **Saunders,** James D '97 -16210 Shaker Blvd
-Shaker Heights 44120

(513) 744-9600 .. **Saunders,** Karen A '04 %Javitch B&R -602 Main -Ste 500
-Cincinnati 45202 **Fx:**744-9602

(440) 323-3570 .. **Saunders,** Kenneth G '96 -134 Lindsay Ct -Elyria 44035

(330) 746-5000 .. **Saunders,** Linda Sue '82 -44 Fed Plz Central -Ste 204
-Youngstown 44503

(412) 232-0125 .. **Saunders,** Martin J '02 (Jackson LS&K) -1 PPG Pl -28th Fl
-Pittsburgh, PA 15222

(614) 644-6342 .. **Saunders,** O'Neal '93 Atty Gen -30 E Broad -Columbus 43215
Fx:752-5083

(614) 719-8766 .. **Saunders,** Tyanna L '00 Franklin Cnty Pub Def -373 S High
-12th Fl -Columbus 43215

(216) 228-7250 .. **Saurman,** Jan A '78 -14650 Detroit Av -Ste 450 -Lakewood 44107

(419) 422-9693 .. **Sausser,** John C '61 -230 Crystal -Findlay 45840

(513) 946-3447 .. **Sauter,** Harold K '91 1st Dist Ct of Appls -230 E 9th -12th Fl
-Cincinnati 45202 **Fx:**946-3412

(419) 522-6242 .. **Sauter Hohenberger & Beddow** -24 W 3rd -Ste 306
-Mansfield 44902

(740) 965-3570 .. **Sauter,** John L '68 -4625 N Shore Dr -Westerville 43082

(614) 461-4455 .. **Sauter,** Robert W '77 (Cloppert LS&W) -225 E Broad
-Columbus 43215 **Fx:**461-0072

(513) 665-9500 .. **Sauter,** Susan M '91 %R Klingler Co,LPA -525 Vine -Ste 2320
-Cincinnati 45202

(216) 464-0008 .. **Sauvain,** Timothy W '70 -27900 Chagrin -Ste 203
-Cleveland 44122

(440) 356-6108 .. **Sava,** Michael F '82 -2720 Horseshoe Blvd -Westlake 44145

Savage, Barry E '65 -6512 Anthony Dr -Maumee 43537

Savage, Douglas J '76 -(Address Unavailable)

(614) 221-8868 .. **Savage,** James S III '81 (McFadden W&S) -175 S 3rd -Ste 210
-Columbus 43215 **Fx:**221-3985

(216) 566-5721 .. **Savage,** Jennifer A '90 (Thompson H LLP) -127 Pub Sq
-3900 Key Ctr -Cleveland 44114 **Fx:**566-5800

(330) 743-1171 .. **Savage,** John T '01 %Manchester BP&U -201 E Commerce
-Atrium Level 2 Commerce Bldg -Youngstown 44503
Fx:743-1190

(989) 894-8810 .. **Savage,** Kelly J '99 %US District Ct -1000 Wshngtn Av -#414
-Bay City, MI 48707

(216) 479-8500 .. **Savage,** Mark J '98 %Squire S&D LLP -127 Pub Sq -4900 Key Twr
-Cleveland 44114 **Fx:**479-8780

(239) 481-8388 .. **Savage,** Stewart W '77 -6719 Winkler Rd -Ste 218 -Fort Myers, FL
33919

(330) 675-2317 .. **Savakis,** Alexander J '78 Trumbull Cnty Dom/Juv Ct -220 S Main
Av -Bx1350 -Warren 44482

(330) 865-1937 .. **Savalan,** Thomas L '61 -1700 W Market -Ste 317 -Akron 44313

(502) 589-4200 .. **Savarise,** Jeffrey A '86 Greenebaum D&M PLLC -101 S 5th
-Ste 3300 -Louisville, KY 40202

(216) 566-8200 .. **Savidge,** Keith A '72 (Seeley S&E Co LPA) -600 Superior Av E
-800 Bank One Ctr -Cleveland 44114 **Fx:**566-0213

(616) 363-7272 .. **Savidge,** Marilyn R '90 Adv Radiology Srvc
-3264 N Evergreen Dr NE -Grand Rapids, MI 49525

(614) 249-8537 .. **Savini,** Steven R '91 Nationwide Financial -1 Nationwide Plz
-Columbus 43215

Savino, Adam M '03 -(Address Unavailable)

(614) 431-1500 .. **Savino,** Angela M '88 Perez & M LLC -8000 Ravines Edge Ct
-Ste 300 -Columbus 43235 **Fx:**431-3885

Savino, Elizabeth Reeves '03 -(Address Unavailable)

(440) 323-1650 .. **Savoy,** Jerome J '83 (Savoy & B) -595 W Broad -Elyria 44035

(216) 771-6597 .. **Savren,** Joy B '82 -1422 Euclid Av -Ste 717 -Cleveland 44115

Savula, Marta L '91 -Bx2975 -Akron 44309

(419) 242-8900 .. **Sawan,** Dennis P '88 -416 N Erie -Ste 200 -Toledo 43624

(330) 253-3444 .. **Sawan,** Edmund M '76 -362 S Main -Akron 44311 **Fx:**253-6431

(419) 243-5581 .. **Sawers,** Mary Lou '01 -238 10th -Toledo 43624 **Fx:**243-2159

(334) 269-2343 .. **Sawyer,** Jon P '02 Beasley ACMP&M,PC -218 Commerce
-Montgomery, AL 36104

Sawyer, Joseph A '70 -(Address Unavailable)

Sawyer, Kristina Sterrett '02 -(Address Unavailable)

(216) 241-6655 .. **Sawyer,** Robert J '61 -815 Superior Av -Cleveland 44114

(859) 431-6100 .. **Sawyers,** Jacqueline S '88 (Arnzen & W,PSC) -600 Greenup
-Bx472 -Covington, KY 41012 **Fx:**431-3778

(330) 643-2943 .. **Sawyers,** Paula M '93 Summit Cnty Pros-Juv -650 Dan
-Akron 44310 **Fx:**379-3647

(614) 221-4000 .. **Saxbe,** Charles R '75 (Chester W&S LLP) -65 E State -10th Fl
-Columbus 43215 **Fx:**221-4012

(330) 762-2411 .. **Saxer,** Thomas M '91 (Amer C Co,LPA) -159 S Main -6th Fl
-Akron 44308 **Fx:**762-9918

(614) 249-3572 .. **Saxon,** Anne D '89 Nationwide Ins Co -1 Nationwide Plz
-Columbus 43215

(813) 224-9000 .. **Saxon,** Bernice S '73 (Salem Law Grp PA) -101 E Knndy Blvd
-Bk of Amer Plz Ste 3220 -Bx3399 -Tampa, FL 33601
Fx:221-8811

(513) 381-9200 .. **Saxton,** Jonathan P '89 (Rendigs FK&D,LLP) -One W 4th -Ste 900
-Cincinnati 45202 **Fx:**381-9206

(502) 585-1880 .. **Say,** Margaret T '00 %Lloyd & M,PLC -11405 Park Rd -Ste 200
-Bx23200 -Louisville, KY 40223 **Fx:**585-3054

(614) 734-1270 .. **Sayers,** Michelle R '04 %Farlow & Assoc LLC -270 Bradenton Av
-Dublin 43017 **Fx:**923-1031

(513) 556-4200 .. **Sayers,** Steven E '89 Univ of Cincinnati -123 W Univ Av
-Cincinnati 45219

(216) 586-3939 .. **Sayler,** Richard H '85 OfCnsl Jones D -901 Lakeside Av
-Cleveland 44114 **Fx:**579-0212

(330) 471-5755 .. **Saylor,** Caroline A '00 Timken Co -1835 Dueber Av SW
-MD GNE-03 -Canton 44706

(614) 445-2623 .. **Saylor,** Lyle R '74 Grange Mutual Cslty Co -650 S Front -Bx1218
-Columbus 43216

(330) 456-4400 .. **Saylor,** Timothy B '89 %A Schulman & Assoc, Co LPA
-236 3rd SW -Canton 44702

(216) 292-5807 .. **Sayoc,** Jeffrey A '00 %Singerman MD&K -3401 Enterprise Pkwy
-Ste 200 -Beachwood 44122 **Fx:**292-5867

(440) 284-2883 .. **Sayre,** James G '95 -401 Broad -215 Robnsn Bldg -Elyria 44035

(919) 836-4274 .. **Sayre,** Jeremy R '98 Ward & S,PA -2400 Two Hannover Sq
-Fayettevll St Mall -Bx2091 -Raleigh, NC 27602

(216) 621-7227 .. **Sayre,** John D '77 (Nicola G&C,LLC) -25 W Prospect Av
-Republic Bldg Ste 1400 -Cleveland 44115 **Fx:**621-3999

(513) 381-2838 .. **Sayre,** Russell S '90 (Taft S&H LLP) -425 Walnut -Ste 1800
-Cincinnati 45202 **Fx:**381-0205

(513) 241-7600 .. **Scacchetti,** David J '82 (Scacchetti & S) -601 Main -3rd Fl
-Cincinnati 45202

(513) 421-3033 .. **Scacchetti,** Marcia E '83 -1009 Paradrome -Ste 900
-Cincinnati 45202

(937) 424-0041 .. **Scaccia,** John J '83 -104 E 3rd -4th Fl -Dayton 45402

(216) 696-7600 .. **Scadden,** Kathy J '03 %Duvin C&H -1301 E 9th
-20th Fl Erievw Twr -Cleveland 44114 **Fx:**696-2038

(513) 241-3430 .. **Scahill,** John P '52 -830 Main -Ste 1115 -Cincinnati 45202

(330) 297-3850 .. **Scahill,** Sean P '00 Portage Cnty Pros -466 S Chestnut
-Ravenna 44266

(330) 297-3850 .. **Scahill,** Theresa M '04 Portage Cnty Pros -466 S Chestnut
-Ravenna 44266

Scaia, Alan D '01 -(Address Unavailable)

(330) 393-0851 .. **Scala,** Michael A '76 -244 Seneca Av -Warren 44481

(216) 514-1919 .. **Scalise,** Justin T '03 %C Longo Co,LPA -25550 Chagrin Blvd
-Ste 320 -Beachwood 44122 **Fx:**593-0914

(216) 216-2840 .. **Scalish,** Rachel N '90 City Council -601 Lakeside Av
-Cleveland 44114

Scally, Erin L '82 -7308 Dunston -Springfield, VA 22151

(419) 255-5917 .. **Scalzo,** Joseph R Jr. '77 (Scalzo & G) -520 Mad Av -Ste 434
-Toledo 43604 **Fx:**255-2030

(419) 249-7100 .. **Scalzo,** Michael S '79 (Marshall & M,LLC) -Four Seagate -8th Fl
-Toledo 43604 **Fx:**249-7151

(513) 241-4722 ..**Scandy,** Kelly C '86 (Montgomery R&J,LPA) -36 E 7th -Ste 2100
-Cincinnati 45202 **Fx:**241-8775

(937) 225-4464 ..**Scanlon,** Erin E '94 2nd Dist Ct of Appls -41 N Perry -Rm 515
-Bx972 -Dayton 45422
Scanlon, Gary '03 -(Address Unavailable)

(330) 376-4558 ..**Scanlon & Gearinger Co, LPA** -50 S Main -Ste 1200
-Akron 44308 **Fx:**376-3550

(330) 376-4558 ..**Scanlon,** John T '94 %Scanlon & G Co,LPA -50 S Main -Ste 1200
-Akron 44308 **Fx:**376-3550

(330) 376-1440 ..**Scanlon,** Lawrence J '78 (Scanlon & Co,LLC) -159 S Main
-400 Key Bldg -Akron 44308 **Fx:**376-0257

(330) 376-4558 ..**Scanlon,** Maura E '88 Scanlon & G Co,LPA -50 S Main -Ste 1200
-Akron 44308 **Fx:**376-3550

(330) 535-2174 ..**Scanlon,** Michael C '66 -106 S Main -Ste 1800 -Akron 44308

(440) 892-3000 ..**Scanlon,** Patricia M '85 Scott Fetzer Co -28800 Clemens Rd
-Westlake 44145

(216) 586-3939 ..**Scanlon,** Stephen D '85 Cnsl Jones D -901 Lakeside Av
-Cleveland 44114 **Fx:**579-0212

(330) 836-9441 ..**Scanlon,** Terence E '76 -1198 Garman Rd -Akron 44313

(216) 696-0022 ..**Scanlon,** Thomas J '63 (Collins & S LLP) -50 Pub Sq
-3300 Trmnl Twr -Cleveland 44113 **Fx:**696-1166

(330) 376-4558 ..**Scanlon,** Timothy F '62 Scanlon & G Co,LPA -50 S Main
-Ste 1200 -Akron 44308 **Fx:**376-3550

(216) 861-5582 ..**Scarbrough,** James E '97 (Fay SFM&M LLP) -1100 Superior Av
-7th Fl -Cleveland 44114 **Fx:**241-1666

(216) 687-0290 ..**Scarcella,** Nancy '91 -815 Superior Av NE -Ste 2025
-Cleveland 44114

(216) 621-1530 ..**Scarlato,** Antonio J '01 %Shapiro & F,LLP -1500 W 3rd -Ste 400
-Cleveland 44113 **Fx:**621-1551

(740) 944-1925 ..**Scarnecchia,** Dan B '91 -154 Twp Rd 200 -Bloomingdale 43910

(330) 762-7377 ..**Scarpitti,** Mark J '02 %Oldham & D -195 S Main -Ste 300
-Akron 44308 **Fx:**762-7390

(740) 283-4529 ..**Scarpone,** David J '87 (D Scarpone & Assoc) -2021 Sunset Blvd
-Steubenville 43952

(330) 758-2308 ..**Scarsella,** Paul L '97 -7330 Market -Youngstown 44512

(330) 297-5778 ..**Scavdis,** Antonios C '74 Scavdis & S,LLC -261 W Spruce -Bx978
-Ravenna 44266 **Fx:**297-5770

(330) 297-5778 ..**Scavdis,** Antonios C Jr. '01 Scavdis & S,LLC -261 W Spruce
-Bx978 -Ravenna 44266 **Fx:**297-5770

(330) 451-7200 ..**Scavelli,** John A '04 Stark Cnty Pub Def -200 W Tuscarawas
-Ste 200 -Canton 44702

(937) 255-2838 ..**Scearce,** Bobby D '72 USAF Materiel Command Law Ofc -2240 B
-Rm 100 Bldg 11 AFMC LO/JAZ -Wright Patterson AFB 45433

(513) 595-2811 ..**Schaaf,** Mary E '97 Union Cntrl Life Ins Co -1876 Waycross Rd
-Bx40888 -Cincinnati 45240
Schaaf, Michael J '81 -3825 Mariners Walk -#614
-Cortez, FL 34215

(216) 363-4500 ..**Schabes,** Alan E '81 (Benesch FC&A LLP) -200 Pub Sq -Ste 2300
-Cleveland 44114 **Fx:**363-4588
Schacht, Cheryl B '84 -(Address Unavailable)

(859) 578-4444 ..**Schachter,** Paul J '90 (P Schachter & Assoc,PSC)
-250 Grandvw Dr -Ste 500 -Fort Mitchell, KY 41017

(781) 829-1800 ..**Schacter,** Stacey J '88 Cnsl EMCC,Inc -33 Riverside Dr
-Pembroke, MA 02359 **Fx:**829-1802

(312) 899-4460 ..**Schad,** Brian J '98 Gleeson SS&C LLP -225 W Wshngtn Av
-Chicago, IL 60606

(513) 870-4980 ..**Schad,** Kevin M '93 (Schad & C) -8240 Beckett Park Dr -Ste A
-Indian Springs 45011
Schad, Mildred P '68 -1031 Dustin Pl -Trinity, FL 34655

(216) 321-9144 ..**Schade,** Nancy V '87 -2891 Mdwbrk Blvd
-Cleveland Heights 44118

(614) 488-8930 ..**Schadek,** Michael A '93 -2566 Brandon Rd -Columbus 43221

(419) 668-2552 ..**Schaechterle,** Gordon E Jr. '80 Payne HN&Co -257 Benedict Av
-Bldg D -Norwalk 44857

(513) 241-2880 ..**Schaefer,** Barbara B '97 Grtr Cincinnati Fndtn -200 W 4th
-Cincinnati 45202

(614) 644-2640 ..**Schaefer,** Carol L '75 Dept Ins -2100 Stella Ct -Columbus 43215
(614) 644-2520 ..**Schaefer,** Carol S '87 Dept Ins -2100 Stella Ct -Columbus 43215
(216) 781-1212 ..**Schaefer,** Charles R '69 (Walter & H LLP) -1301 E 9th -Ste 3500
-Cleveland 44114 **Fx:**575-0911

(513) 946-3000 ..**Schaefer,** Christian J '76 Hamilton Cnty Pros -230 E 9th
-Cincinnati 45202 **Fx:**946-3017

(216) 696-1422 ..**Schaefer,** David A '74 (McCarthy LC&L Co,LPA) -101
Prospect Av W -1800 Mdlnd Bldg -Cleveland 44115 **Fx:**696-1210

(419) 843-2777 ..**Schaefer,** Debra G '80 Debra G. Schaefer & Associates, LLC
-7730 Big Bend Ct -Sylvania 43560

(513) 424-1660 ..**Schaefer,** Edward B '01 %Combs & S -1081 N Univ Blvd -Ste B
-Middletown 45042

(513) 424-1660 ..**Schaefer,** Gene E '64 (Combs & S) -1081 N Univ Blvd -Ste B
-Middletown 45042
Schaefer, Gerald J '03 -943 Woodvw Dr -Ashland 44805

(513) 946-3000 ..**Schaefer,** James J '89 Hamilton Cnty Pros -230 E 9th
-Cincinnati 45202 **Fx:**946-3017

(513) 621-8210 ..**Schaefer,** James R '92 %Drew & W Co,LPA -1 W 4th -Ste 2400
-Cincinnati 45202 **Fx:**621-5444

(513) 381-5700 ..**Schaefer,** Jeffrey R '93 Ritter & R,LLC -105 E 4th -Ste 1200
-Cincinnati 45202 **Fx:**381-0014

(513) 723-4000 ..**Schaefer,** Kimberly J '98 %Vorys SS&P LLP -221 E 4th
-Ste 2000 Atrium Two -Bx0236 -Cincinnati 45201 **Fx:**723-4056

(513) 619-5041 ..**Schaefer,** Lesley N '03 Phillips Edison & Co -11690 Grooms Rd
-Cincinnati 45242

(614) 451-3771 ..**Schaefer,** Philip S '72 -2685 Hvrfrd Rd -Upper Arlington 43220
(614) 229-4766 ..**Schaefer,** Robert B '87 Deloitte & Touche LLP -155 E Broad
-Columbus 43215

(419) 893-4880 ..**Schaefer,** Stephen A '73 OfCnsl Marsh M Ltd -204 W Wayne
-Maumee 43537

(614) 249-1748 ..**Schaefer,** Theresa R '85 Cnsl Nationwide Ins Co
-1 Nationwide Plz -Columbus 43215
Schaefer, William E '99 -Bx823 -Mukilteo, WA 98275

(937) 449-6400 ..**Schaeff,** B Joseph '75 (Dinsmore & S LLP) -1 S Main
-Ste 1300 One Dayton Centre -Dayton 45402 **Fx:**449-6405

(937) 223-1130 ..**Schaeffer,** Alan B '74 (Pickrel S&E) -40 N Main
-2700 Kettering Twr -Dayton 45423 **Fx:**223-0339

(937) 222-0410 ..**Schaeffer,** Beth W '75 The Dayton Fdn -2300 Kettering Twr
-Dayton 45423

(513) 752-1350 ..**Schaeffer,** Earl R '72 Clermont Distributing Co
-1155 Cincinnati-Batavia Pike -Batavia 45103

(330) 264-4444 ..**Schaeffer,** John H '89 %Critchfield C&J Ltd -225 N Market -Bx599
-Wooster 44691 **Fx:**263-9278

(614) 221-3155 ..**Schaeffer,** Matthew T '96 %Bailey C LLC -10 W Broad
-Columbus 43215 **Fx:**221-0479

(614) 224-2678 ..**Schaeffer,** Michael N '75 Kemp SR&L Co,LPA -88 W Mound
-Columbus 43215 **Fx:**469-7170

(513) 946-3416 ..**Schaen,** Susan D '99 1st Dist Ct of Appls -230 E 9th -12th Fl
-Cincinnati 45202 **Fx:**946-3412

(937) 228-8183 ..**Schaengold,** Gary C '82 -120 W 2nd -Dayton 45402 **Fx:**228-7011

(216) 822-3973 ..**Schafer,** Cynthia C '86 Ameritech -45 Erievw Plz -#1400
-Cleveland 44114

(614) 475-9511 ..**Schafer,** Dale C '49 Blumenstiel HA&E,LLC -261 W Johnstown Rd
-Columbus 43230 **Fx:**475-0348

(614) 221-1000 ..**Schafer,** Jennifer L '02 Deloitte & Touche, LLP -155 E Broad
-Columbus 43215

(330) 864-2003 ..**Schafer,** Julie A '02 (Schafer & C Co,LPA) -1745 W Market
-Akron 44313 **Fx:**864-7157

(937) 225-4652 ..**Schafer,** Mary L '02 Montgomery Cnty Pub Def -117 S Main
-Ste 400 -Dayton 45422 **Fx:**225-3449

(440) 428-6226 ..**Schafer,** Scott P '95 -1954 Hubbard Rd -Madison 44057
Fx:428-2666

(614) 488-4484 ..**Schafer,** Stephen E '73 -1474 Grandvw Av -Ste 400
-Columbus 43212

(330) 899-9335 ..**Schafer,** Victoria E '83 -1003 E Turkeyfoot Lk Rd -Ste C
-Akron 44312

(816) 531-5777 ..**Schaffer,** Eric S '01 IMG -700 W 47th -Ste 810
-Kansas City, MO 64112 **Fx:**753-2332

(440) 967-5695 ..**Schaffer,** Gail M '77 (Schaffer & S) -612 Main -Vermilion 44089
(614) 464-2392 ..**Schaffer,** Grier D '88 Earl WA&D,LPA -136 W Mound
-Columbus 43215 **Fx:**464-0754

(330) 285-1563 ..**Schaffer,** Lee A '90 -2910 Wdbrdg Ln -Stow 44224
(419) 243-1294 ..**Schaffer,** Mark C '69 (Emch SS&P Co,LPA) -One SeaGate
-Ste 1980 -Bx916 -Toledo 43697 **Fx:**243-8502

(440) 967-5695 ..**Schaffer,** Michael V '65 (Schaffer & S) -612 Main -Vermilion 44089
(937) 228-0880 ..**Schaffer,** Thomas A '72 (Sutton O&S) -130 W 2nd
-1628 1st Natl Plz -Dayton 45402

(419) 843-2001 ..**Schaffer,** Thomas J '90 (Gallon & T Co,LPA) -3516 Granite Cir
-Bx352018 -Toledo 43635 **Fx:**843-6665

(330) 364-9070 ..**Schaffner,** David K '88 Hardin & S,LPA -132 Fair Av NW
-New Philadelphia 44663 **Fx:**364-9073

(207) 780-3271 ..**Schaffner,** Jefferson N '74 SSA/OHA -1 Portlnd Sq -Ste 600
-Portland, ME 04101

(614) 466-3998 ..**Schaffner,** Jeffery O '84 Unemploymnt Comp Commssn
-145 S Front -Bx182299 -Columbus 43218

(330) 723-6024 ..**Schaffrath,** Kurt A '73 -3202 Rustic Valley Dr -Medina 44256
(740) 349-8505 ..**Schaller Campbell & Untied** -32 N Park Pl -Newark 43055
(419) 243-6281 ..**Schaller,** James F II '03 %Shindler NH&S,LLP -300 Mad Av
-Ste 1200 -Toledo 43604 **Fx:**243-0129

(740) 349-8505 ..**Schaller,** Stephen E '73 (Schaller C&U) -32 N Park Pl
-Newark 43055

(513) 229-6777 ..**Schaller,** Stephen J '95 CNG Fin Corp -5155 Fncl Way
-Mason 45040

(513) 651-6800 ..**Schalnat,** Eleanor Maria F '99 %Frost BT LLC -201 E 5th
-2200 PNC Ctr -Cincinnati 45202 **Fx:**651-6981

(440) 350-5020 ..**Schaltenbrand,** Eric J '95 Lake Cnty Bd of MR/DD
-8121 Deepwood Blvd -Mentor 44060

(216) 664-6436 ..**Schaltenbrand,** Rebecca K '95 SpclCnsl Cleveland City Council
-601 Lakeside Av -Rm 216 City Hall -Cleveland 44114

(216) 381-0454 ..**Schamovic,** Arthur '89 -24195 Wendover Dr -Beachwood 44122
(330) 456-1112 ..**Schandel,** Phillip D '67 P Schandel Co,LPA
-116 Cleveland Av NW -Ste 709 -Canton 44702

(419) 245-2740 ..**Schank,** Laura J '93 Industrial Commssn of OH -One Govt Ctr
-Ste 1500 -Toledo 43604

(419) 255-4300 ..**Schank,** Thomas J '77 (Hunter & S Co,LPA) -1700 Canton Av
-One Canton Sq -Toledo 43624 **Fx:**255-9121

(614) 223-9300 ..**Schantz,** Roger L '91 (Benesch FC&A LLP) -88 E Broad -Ste 900
-Columbus 43215 **Fx:**223-9330

(740) 382-2277 ..**Scharer,** Ronald J '73 -444 E Center -Bx406 -Marion 43301
(216) 781-8700 ..**Scharf,** Scott H '90 (Novak RP&S,LLP) -1660 W 2nd
-Ste 270 Skylight Ofc Twr -Cleveland 44113 **Fx:**781-9227

(330) 743-5101 ..**Scharf,** Shawn D '98 Green H&S,Co LPA -16 Wick Av -Ste 400
-Youngstown 44503 **Fx:**743-3451

(216) 252-7300 ..**Scharf,** Stephen L '99 Amer Greetings Corp -1 Amer Rd
-Cleveland 44144
Scharfeld, Leonard B '51 -16695 Chillicothe Rd -#110
-Chagrin Falls 44023

(513) 381-4700 ..**Scharff,** Daniel W '91 OfCnsl Porter WM&A LLP -250 E 5th
-Ste 2200 -Cincinnati 45202 **Fx:**421-0991
Scharff, Marisa M '00 -4111 Story Rd -Cleveland 44126
Scharff, Martin '59 -825 Deerhurst Dr -Vandalia 45377

(216) 765-8520 ..**Scharon,** John V '78 OfCnsl Aggers J&C Co,LPA
-29565 Chagrin Blvd -Ste 306 Exec Cmmns E
-Pepper Pike 44122 **Fx:**765-8817

(216) 621-6101 ..**Scharville,** James D '99 %Kahn & Assoc,LLC -55 Pub Sq
-Ste 650 -Cleveland 44113 **Fx:**621-6006

(859) 431-0522 ..**Schatteman,** Sally A '81 Campbell Cnty Chld Spprt Agncy
-515 Mnmth -2nd Fl -Newport, KY 41071

(513) 241-2324 ..**Schatz,** Brett A '00 %Wood H&E LLP -441 Vine -Ste 2700
-Cincinnati 45202 **Fx:**421-7269

(216) 881-6600 ..**Schatz,** William B '73 NEORSD -3826 Euclid Av -Cleveland 44115
Fx:881-4407

(419) 243-1294 ..**Schaub,** Charles R '73 (Emch SS&P Co,LPA) -One SeaGate
-Ste 1980 -Bx916 -Toledo 43697 **Fx:**243-8502

(313) 226-3210 ..**Schaub,** William C Jr. '68 NLRB -477 Mich Av -Rm 300
-Detroit, MI 48226 **Fx:**226-2090
Schauer, Melodie G '96 -(Address Unavailable)

(614) 469-3397 .. **Scheaf,** Oral Judson III '88 (Thompson H LLP) -10 W Broad
-Ste 700 -Columbus 43215 **Fx:**469-3361

(614) 224-8374 .. **Schear,** Kathi L '78 Legal Aid -40 W Gay -Columbus 43215

(330) 376-2700 .. **Scheatzle,** Kyle S '02 %Roetzel & A,LPA -222 S Main
-Akron 44308 **Fx:**376-4577

(313) 568-6672 .. **Schebor,** Todd C '02 %Dykema G PLLC -400 Renaissance Ctr
-Detroit, MI 48243

(216) 928-1503 .. **Schechter,** Roy J '86 (Lichko & S) -55 Pub Sq -Ste 1600
-Cleveland 44113 **Fx:**619-9846

(419) 294-5701 .. **Scheck,** Frederick L III '73 (Stansbery S&S) -106 E Wyandot Av
-Upper Sandusky 43351 **Fx:**294-5608

(419) 294-5701 .. **Scheck,** Laurie A '97 (Stansbery S&S) -106 E Wyandot Av
-Upper Sandusky 43351 **Fx:**294-5608

(216) 781-4994 .. **Schedlbauer,** Kara M '03 %Smith MW&V -1965 E 6th
-500 Natl City-E 6th Bldg -Cleveland 44114 **Fx:**781-9448

(614) 466-7447 .. **Schedler,** Karl W '76 Atty Gen -150 E Gay -Columbus 43215

(419) 243-2283 .. **Scheer Green & Burke Co,LPA** -520 Mad Av -Bx1335
-Toledo 43603

(419) 223-1861 .. **Scheeser,** Amanda L '01 %Hon SR Shaw -204 N Main
-Lima 45801

(330) 722-2636 .. **Scheetz,** Stanley D '74 S Scheetz Co,LPA -225 E Lbrty
-Medina 44256

(330) 643-2250 .. **Scheffler,** Bethany R '02 9th Dist Ct of Appls -161 S High -Ste 504
-Akron 44308

(419) 241-6450 .. **Scheich,** Richard A '84 (Jones & S) -608 Mad Av -Toledo 43604

(216) 441-5100 .. **Scheid,** Katherine A '87 %Kollin & Assoc -4053 E 71st
-Cleveland 44105

(419) 241-9000 .. **Scheidel,** Rolf H '65 (Shumaker L&K,LLP) -1000 Jackson
-Toledo 43624 **Fx:**241-6894

(614) 628-8000 .. **Scheiderer,** Judith M '91 Dreher L&T LLP -41 S High
-2250 Huntngtn Ctr -Columbus 43215 **Fx:**628-1600

(513) 579-6400 .. **Scheier,** Michael L '91 (Keating M&K PLL) -1 E 4th
-1400 Provident Twr -Cincinnati 45202 **Fx:**579-6457

(216) 621-7227 .. **Scheiman,** Becky M '00 %Nicola G&C,LLC -25 W Prospect Av
-Republic Bldg Ste 1400 -Cleveland 44115 **Fx:**621-3999

(513) 241-3100 .. **Scheimann,** Mary M '04 %Lerner S&R -120 E 4th -8th Fl
-Cincinnati 45202

(614) 462-4513 .. **Schelb,** Jon E '99 Franklin Cnty Common Pleas Ct -369 S High
-Courtroom 7D -Columbus 43215

(309) 789-0415 .. **Schell,** Nancy A '94 -26582 N M&M Rd -Canton, IL 61520
Schell, Thomas T '68 -1001 Clusterwood Dr -Yalaha, FL 34797

(216) 696-4400 .. **Schellenberger,** Anna Marie '91 -526 Superior Av E -901
-Cleveland 44114 **Fx:**696-4401

(614) 228-6885 .. **Schellhaas,** Kim M '93 %Lane A&H LLC -175 S 3rd -Ste 700
-Columbus 43215 **Fx:**228-0146

(419) 586-6886 .. **Schemenaur,** Wesley A '04 %K Faber & Assoc -218 S Main
-Ste B -Celina 45822

(419) 755-5725 .. **Schemine,** Bryan A '95 GM -2525 W 4th -Mansfield 44906

(419) 354-9244 .. **Schemrich,** LeAnn R '03 %Wood Cnty Pub Def -123 N Summit
-Bowling Green 43402

(330) 499-9200 .. **Schenck,** Brett A '04 Maytag Corp -101 E Maple -Canton 44720

(513) 284-8361 .. **Schenck,** Donald A '23 -2829 Whitehouse Ln -Cincinnati 45244

(937) 562-5250 .. **Schenck,** William F Jr. '70 Greene Cnty Pros -61 Greene
-Xenia 45385

(440) 603-2738 .. **Schenk,** Jeffrey A '91 Progressive Casualty Ins Co
-6055 Parkland Blvd -Mayfield Heights 44124

(513) 651-6800 .. **Schenk,** Mary Ann '76 Cnsl Frost BT LLC -201 E 5th
-2200 PNC Ctr -Cincinnati 45202 **Fx:**651-6981

(513) 665-3500 .. **Schenkel,** Timothy B '93 (Freund F&A) -105 E 4th -Ste 1400
-Cincinnati 45202 **Fx:**665-3503

(908) 437-4189 .. **Schenker,** Michael D '78 Aerostructures -3 Werner Way -Ste 210
-Lebanon, NJ 08833

(216) 739-5644 .. **Schenz,** Beth A '01 %Weltman W&R Co,LPA -323 W Lakeside Av
-Ste 200 -Cleveland 44113 **Fx:**363-4121

(513) 621-8333 .. **Scheper,** James H '68 %Shea & Assoc -250 E 5th -Ste 444
-Cincinnati 45202

(513) 552-1400 .. **Scheper,** Norbert J '74 -100 Merchant -Ste 180 -Cincinnati 45246

(440) 442-9500 .. **Schepis,** Nicholas '84 -6181 Mayfld Rd -Ste 302 -Mayfield Heights
44124

(330) 393-3200 .. **Scher,** James R '91 Burkey B&S Co,LPA -200 Chestnut Av NE
-Warren 44483 **Fx:**393-6436

(440) 244-0122 .. **Scherach,** Michael J '71 -814 Reid Av -Lorain 44052 **Fx:**244-6132

(740) 622-0166 .. **Scherbel,** Paul R '73 (Leech S&P) -240 S 4th -Bx880 -Coshocton
43812

(330) 253-1555 .. **Scherf,** Holly L '99 %D Booher & Assoc Co,LPA -3180 W Market
-Fairlawn 44333

(740) 772-4772 .. **Scherff,** John M '89 Ross Cnty Pub Def -14 S Paint -Ste 54
-Chillicothe 45601

(330) 471-4226 .. **Scherff,** Scott A '79 Timken Co -1835 Dueber Av SW -GNE-01
-Canton 44706

(614) 793-1770 .. **Scherger,** Scott C '02 %Kreiner & P Co,LPA -6047 Frantz Rd
-Ste 203 -Dublin 43017

(614) 785-1700 .. **Scherner,** Benjamin '97 (Scherner & S,LLC) -153 S Lbrty
-Powell 43065 **Fx:**785-0700

(614) 431-7200 .. **Scherner,** Hans '79 (Scherner H&C,LLC) -130 Northwood Blvd
-Columbus 43235 **Fx:**431-7262

(614) 431-7200 .. **Scherner Hanson & Cornwell,LLC** -130 Northwood Blvd
-Columbus 43235 **Fx:**431-7262

(419) 222-1155 .. **Scherner Hanson & Cornwell,LLC** -714 W North -Lima 45801
Fx:227-3131

(216) 623-0150 .. **Scherzer,** Donald S '75 (Roetzel & A,LPA) -1375 E 9th
-One Cleve Ctr 9th Fl -Cleveland 44114 **Fx:**623-0134

(513) 984-2040 .. **Scheuer,** Edna V '80 (Scheuer M&B LLC)
-11025 Reed Hartman Hwy -Cincinnati 45242 **Fx:**984-6590

(513) 984-2040 .. **Scheuer Mackin & Breslin LLC** -11025 Reed Hartman Hwy
-Cincinnati 45242 **Fx:**984-6590

(330) 656-2702 .. **Scheuer Mackin & Breslin LLC** -110 W Streetsboro Rd -Ste 2A
-Hudson 44236 **Fx:**656-2755

(937) 898-1465 .. **Scheuer Mackin & Breslin LLC** -8565 N Dixie Dr -Dayton 45414
Fx:898-1478

(216) 931-6000 .. **Scheufler,** Alan W '83 (Ulmer & B LLP) -1300 E 9th
-Ste 900 Penton Media Bldg -Cleveland 44114 **Fx:**931-6001

(440) 816-6704 .. **Scheutzow,** Susan O '82 SW General Hlth Ctr -18697 Bagley Rd
-Middleburg Heights 44130

(513) 946-3049 .. **Scheve,** Thomas J '78 Hamilton Cnty Pros -230 E 9th
-Cincinnati 45202 **Fx:**946-3017

(216) 861-5338 .. **Schiau,** Daniel L '91 Colliers Intl -1100 Superior Av -Ste 800
-Cleveland 44114

(330) 744-4137 .. **Schiavone,** Christopher J '01 Friedman & R Co,LPA
-100 Fed Plz E -Ste 300 City Centre One -Youngstown 44503
Fx:744-9962

(513) 863-4200 .. **Schiavone,** Frank J III '78 -520 Rentschler Bldg -Hamilton 45011

(330) 744-4137 .. **Schiavone,** Leonard D '77 (Friedman & R Co,LPA) -100 Fed Plz E
-Ste 300 City Centre One -Youngstown 44503 **Fx:**744-9962

(419) 586-6442 .. **Schiavone,** Louis J '84 (Purdy L&S) -113 E Market -Bx404
-Celina 45822 **Fx:**586-1948

(330) 799-5940 .. **Schiavoni,** Louis J '83 (Schiavoni S&B Co,LPA) -87 Wstchstr Dr
-Youngstown 44515

(330) 799-5940 .. **Schiavoni Schiavoni & Bush Co, LPA** -87 Wstchstr Dr
-Youngstown 44515

(440) 684-1164 .. **Schick,** Brian S '91 -1516 Sunview Rd -Lyndhurst 44124

(513) 287-3427 .. **Schick,** William W Jr. '86 Cincinnati Gas & Elec Co -Bx960
-Cincinnati 45201

(513) 677-9865 .. **Schickel,** Joseph '91 -200 W Loveland Av -Ste A -Loveland 45140

(216) 491-3850 .. **Schickler,** Ronald S '91 -21825 Chagrin Blvd -Ste 320
-Cleveland 44122

(216) 687-1902 .. **Schieman,** Nancy E '91 %S Haygood & Assoc -1422 Euclid Av
-Ste 1510 -Cleveland 44115 **Fx:**687-1906

(440) 442-5550 .. **Schiemann,** Jeffrey J '88 -845 Hanover Rd -Gates Mills 44040
Fx:442-5789

(614) 466-2801 .. **Schierholt,** Steven W '03 Atty Gen Criminal Investigation Bur
-30 E Broad -Columbus 43215 **Fx:**728-7582
Schiering, Geoffrey D '95 -301 Hidden Pines Rd
-Del Mar, CA 92014

(941) 931-7275 .. **Schiering,** George D '70 Radiation Thrpy Assoc
-2234 Colonial Blvd -Fort Myers, FL 33907

(937) 225-5757 .. **Schierloh,** Joshua R '04 %Montgomery Cnty Pros -301 W 3rd
-Bx972 -Dayton 45422 **Fx:**225-3470

(419) 523-5777 .. **Schierloh,** Keith H '99 (Niese H&S,LLC) -1800 N Perry -Ste 104
-Ottawa 45875

(216) 621-7743 .. **Schiff & Dickson, LLC** -1370 Ontario -Standard Bldg 6th Fl
-Cleveland 44113
Schiff, Jonathan E '81 -5465 Kenwood Rd -#502
-Cincinnati 45227

(614) 224-1484 .. **Schiff,** Lynda Z '88 -471 E Broad -Ste 1100 -Columbus 43215

(216) 621-7743 .. **Schiff,** Marvin R '84 (Schiff & D,LLC) -1370 Ontario
-Standard Bldg 6th Fl -Cleveland 44113

(812) 424-7575 .. **Schiff,** Mary L '89 Ziemer SW&S -20 NW 1st -Bx916
-Evansville, IN 47706

(614) 449-4313 .. **Schiff,** Michael S '86 Schottenstein Mngmnt Co -1800 Moler Rd
-Columbus 43207

(513) 421-4000 .. **Schiff,** Phyllis B '92 -1212 Sycamore -Ste 36 -Cincinnati 45202

(614) 621-8888 .. **Schiff,** Scott W '82 (S Schiff & Assoc) -88 W Main
-Columbus 43215

(937) 297-1150 .. **Schiff,** Thomas R '88 (Hochwalt & S,LLP) -500 Lincoln Park Blvd
-Ste 216 -Dayton 45429

(440) 886-3000 .. **Schifko,** Robert F '64 Leary SN&L -5579 Pearl Rd -Ste 203
-Parma 44129 **Fx:**886-3171

(740) 965-3991 .. **Schilder,** Joseph W '64 -50 E Granvll -Sunbury 43074

(216) 696-8700 .. **Schildhouse,** Mark B '80 (Kohrman J&K PLL) -1375 E 9th
-One Cleve Ctr 20th Fl -Cleveland 44114 **Fx:**621-6536

(440) 895-5000 .. **Schill,** William T '95 (Schill & S,LLC) -1250 Linda -Ste 201
-Rocky River 44116 **Fx:**730-3130

(216) 226-9530 .. **Schillawski,** Philip C '87 -2366 Woodward Av -Lakewood 44107

(330) 762-0080 .. **Schiller,** Glenn M '98 (G Schiller Co,LLC) -611 W Market -Ste C
-Akron 44303 **Fx:**762-0720

(216) 781-1212 .. **Schiller,** John E '84 %Walter & H LLP -1301 E 9th -Ste 3500
-Cleveland 44114 **Fx:**575-0911

(440) 543-8059 .. **Schiller,** Mary Sharon '77 -17240 Red Fox Trl -Chagrin
Falls 44023

(330) 337-3105 .. **Schiller,** Royal A '73 -861 S Lincoln Av -Salem 44460

(859) 261-6811 .. **Schiller,** Steven L '87 -4 W 4th -#200 -Newport, KY 41071
Fx:261-6826

(216) 579-1700 .. **Schiller,** Thomas P '60 (Pearne & G LLP) -1801 E 9th -Ste 1200
-Cleveland 44114 **Fx:**579-6073

(440) 449-9636 .. **Schilling,** Kenneth C '85 NACCO Ind,Inc -5875 Landerbrook Dr
-Ste 300 -Mayfield Heights 44124
Schilling, Nancy A '89 -301 W Spring -Eaton 45320

(513) 489-0829 .. **Schilling,** Richard D '77 (Mason S&M Co,LPA)
-11340 Mntgmry Rd -Ste 210 -Cincinnati 45249 **Fx:**489-0834

(513) 721-6151 .. **Schilling,** Ronald D '77 -602 Main -Ste 1309 -Cincinnati 45202

(513) 248-2580 .. **Schilling,** William H '75 -5714 Signal Hill Ct -Ste B -Milford 45150

(513) 241-7715 .. **Schimanski,** James R '91 -7 W 7th -1800 Federated Bldg
-Cincinnati 45202

(330) 325-2511 .. **Schimer,** Maria R '84 NE OH Univ Cllg of Medicine
-4209 State Route 44 -Rootstown 44272
Schimmel, Edward L '03 -(Address Unavailable)

(614) 464-6400 .. **Schimmer,** Alexandra T '02 %Vorys SS&P LLP -52 E Gay
-Bx1008 -Columbus 43216 **Fx:**464-6350

(513) 474-3309 .. **Schimpf,** Jerome L '66 -3861 Mt Carmel Rd -Cincinnati 45244

(513) 977-5585 .. **Schimpf,** Joseph M '01 %Butkovich SS&G Co,LPA -36 E 7th
-Ste 2600 -Cincinnati 45202 **Fx:**977-5580

(513) 977-5577 .. **Schimpf,** Richard J '67 (Butkovich SS&G,LPA) -36 E 7th
-Ste 2600 -Cincinnati 45202 **Fx:**977-5580

(614) 239-9980 .. **Schindler,** Jerome R '68 -395 S Chesterfld Rd -Columbus 43209
Fx:239-9981

(937) 689-3529 .. **Schindler,** Melissa K '00 -Bx13651 -Dayton 45413

(216) 583-3128 .. **Schindler,** Michael D '03 Ernst & Young LLP -925 Euclid Av
-Cleveland 44115

(330) 253-1555 .. **Schinker-Kuharich,** Dynele L '98 %D Booher & Assoc Co,LPA
-3180 W Market -Fairlawn 44333

(216) 265-0856 .. **Schiopota,** Eugene '64 -5723 Gtwy Ln -Cleveland 44142

(937) 548-1157 .. **Schipfer,** Daniel C Jr. '70 (Hanes SCGG&D,Ltd) -507 S Bway
-Greenville 45331

(614) 464-6400 .. **Schira,** David M '90 (Vorys SS&P LLP) -52 E Gay -Bx1008
-Columbus 43216 **Fx:**464-6350

(330) 743-1040 .. **Schiraldi**, Richard J '81 (Cohen & Co) -201 E Commerce
-400 Commerce Bldg -Youngstown 44503

(513) 977-8200 .. **Schisler**, H Toby II '97 %Dinsmore & S LLP -255 E 5th -Ste 1900
-Cincinnati 45202 Fx:977-8141

(513) 381-9200 .. **Schisler**, Heather M '03 %Rendigs FK&D,LLP -One W 4th
-Ste 900 -Cincinnati 45202 Fx:381-9206

(740) 354-3283 .. **Schisler**, Richard T '68 Mun Ct Judge -728 2nd
-Portsmouth 45662

(216) 781-3434 .. **Schlachet**, Jaye M '79 -55 Pub Sq -Ste 1300 -Cleveland 44113

(216) 696-5222 .. **Schlachet**, Mark '69 -1001 Lakeside Av -Ste 1700
-Cleveland 44114

(419) 841-9113 .. **Schlachter**, Thomas L '70 -7862 W Central Av -Toledo 43617

(440) 285-2222 .. **Schlag**, Rebecca F '93 Geauga Cnty Pros -231 Main -Cthse Annx
-Chardon 44024 Fx:286-4357

(419) 691-2435 .. **Schlageter & Bryce Co,LPA** -715 S Coy Rd -Oregon 43616
Schlageter, Derek C '01 -533 Sioux Trl -Rossford 43460

(419) 243-6281 .. **Schlageter**, John J III '97 (Shindler NH&S,LLP) -300 Mad Av
-Ste 1200 -Toledo 43604 Fx:243-0129

(419) 243-6281 .. **Schlageter**, John J Jr. '73 (Shindler NH&S,LLP) -300 Mad Av
-Ste 1200 -Toledo 43604 Fx:243-0129

(419) 691-2435 .. **Schlageter**, Thomas G '75 (Schlageter & B Co,LPA)
-715 S Coy Rd -Oregon 43616

(859) 394-6200 .. **Schlarman**, Lori A '95 %Adams SW&D -40 W Pike -Bx861
-Covington, KY 41012 Fx:291-7902

(419) 241-1261 .. **Schlatter**, Donald A '56 Art Iron,Inc -860 Curtis -Bx964
-Toledo 43697

(614) 466-4656 .. **Schlatter**, Robert L '83 Atty Gen -150 E Gay -Columbus 43215
Fx:466-1756

(419) 241-7371 .. **Schlaudecker**, David G '76 Leadership Toledo -316 Adams
-Toledo 43604

(614) 297-1211 .. **Schlaufman**, Darice L '01 %G Gottfried Co,LPA -1265 Neil Av
-Columbus 43201
Schleeter, Andrea R '97 -7734 Sutton Pl -New Albany 43054

(216) 621-0200 .. **Schlegelmilch**, Stephan J '00 %Baker & H LLP -1900 E 9th
-Ste 3200 -Cleveland 44114 Fx:696-0740

(440) 842-3848 .. **Schleicher**, Albert G '56 -3200 Augustina Dr -Parma 44134

(216) 579-1554 .. **Schleifer**, Karin F '87 -1370 Ontario -Ste 600 -Cleveland 44113

(216) 360-3737 .. **Schleimer**, Mary A '02 %Persky S&A Co,LPA
-25101 Chagrin Blvd -Ste 350 Signature Sq II -Beachwood 44122
Fx:593-0921

(513) 721-1350 .. **Schlemmer**, Arthur H '76 (Barron PB&S) -3074 Madison Rd
-Cincinnati 45209

(740) 397-7177 .. **Schlemmer**, Michael D '74 Knox Cnty Pros -117 E High -Ste 234
-Mount Vernon 43050

(937) 335-8324 .. **Schlemmer**, Robert N '69 (Faust HFM&S) -12 S Cherry
-Troy 45373 Fx:339-7155

(614) 249-4169 .. **Schleppi**, William J '79 Nationwide Ins Co -1 Nationwide Plz
-Columbus 43215

(412) 338-4750 .. **Schleppy**, Marian P '95 (Gaca MB&R) -444 Lbrty Av -Ste 300
-Pittsburgh, PA 15222 Fx:338-4742

(216) 696-1433 .. **Schlesinger**, Shawn W '98 %Koeth R&L Co,LPA -1280 W 3rd
-Cleveland 44113 Fx:696-1439

(859) 491-7487 .. **Schletker**, Steven C '92 Schletker H&M -415 Garrad
-Covington, KY 41011

(859) 431-3200 .. **Schloemer**, Douglas B '87 (Poston S&S) -2039 Dixie Hwy
-Fort Mitchell, KY 41011

(513) 381-2838 .. **Schloemer**, Jeffrey S '83 (Taft S&H LLP) -425 Walnut -Ste 1800
-Cincinnati 45202 Fx:381-0205

(614) 278-6807 .. **Schlonsky**, Michael A '91 Big Lots,Inc -300 Phillipi Rd
-Columbus 43228

(216) 561-3278 .. **Schloss**, John P '89 -3078 Huntngtn Rd -Shaker Heights 44120

(216) 696-1422 .. **Schloss**, Richard A '02 %McCarthy LC&L Co,LPA -101 Prospect
Av W -1800 Mdlnd Bldg -Cleveland 44115 Fx:696-1210

(513) 762-6200 .. **Schloss**, Stuart A Jr. '72 (Ulmer & B LLP) -600 Vine -Ste 2800
-Cincinnati 45202 Fx:762-6245

(614) 878-7251 .. **Schlosser**, Jacob A '62 (Wilcox S&B Co LPA) -4937 W Broad
-Columbus 43228
Schlosser, John E '73 -(Address Unavailable)

(614) 249-3606 .. **Schlosser**, Nicole A '00 Nationwide Ins Co -One Nationwide Plz
-4-4-3 -Columbus 43215

(513) 381-4700 .. **Schlosser**, R Jeffrey '84 (Porter WM&A LLP) -250 E 5th -Ste 2200
-Cincinnati 45202 Fx:421-0991
Schlotman, Edy C '90 -(Address Unavailable)

(513) 872-7505 .. **Schlotman**, James T '78 -3481 Cntrl Pkwy -Ste 100
-Cincinnati 45223

(216) 566-8703 .. **Schloz**, Jo A '85 Chrtr One Bank -1215 Superior Av NE
-Cleveland 44114

(330) 376-2700 .. **Schlue**, Daniel J '01 %Roetzel & A,LPA -222 S Main -Akron 44308
Fx:376-4577

(513) 591-6501 .. **Schlueter**, Daniel J '74 Greater Cincinnati Water Works
-4747 Spring Grove Av -Cincinnati 45232

(937) 544-2101 .. **Schlueter**, James W '74 -505 Walt Alsgood Rd -Bx305
-West Union 45693
Schlueter, Michael H '03 -(Address Unavailable)

(812) 432-9150 .. **Schmaltz**, Kimberly A '99 -10037 Wstrn Row -Bx545
-Dillsboro, IN 47018

(513) 352-0500 .. **Schmalz**, Anna '04 (Schmalz & H) -602 Main -Ste 1010
-Cincinnati 45202 Fx:352-0555

(614) 268-4993 .. **Schmalz**, Kurt J '89 -3316 N High -Columbus 43202

(606) 485-1765 .. **Schmalzl**, Mary W '87 -Bx162 -Union, KY 41091

(513) 621-6464 .. **Schmalzl**, Richard G '87 (Graydon H&R LLP) -511 Walnut
-1900 Fifth Third Ctr -Cincinnati 45202 Fx:651-3836

(740) 833-2534 .. **Schmansky**, Joseph E '00 Delaware Cnty Ct of Common Pleas
-91 N Sandusky -Delaware 43015

(614) 229-5260 .. **Schmarr**, John M '76 Ernst & Young LLP -41 S High -Ste 1100
-Columbus 43215 Fx:229-5127

(216) 283-2376 .. **Schmedlen**, George W '93 -17415 Winslow Rd -Cleveland 44120

(216) 781-3400 .. **Schmelzer Caterino & Helfgott** -55 Pub Sq -Ste 2200
-Cleveland 44113

(859) 815-3981 .. **Schmelzer**, Nicholas H '03 Ashland,Inc -50 E RiverCenter Blvd
-Law Dept -Covington, KY 41012

(216) 781-3400 .. **Schmelzer**, Thomas '77 (Schmelzer C&H) -55 Pub Sq -Ste 2200
-Cleveland 44113

(937) 644-7606 .. **Schmenk**, Christiane W '84 Scotts Co -14111 Scottslawn Rd
-Marysville 43041

(937) 323-9739 .. **Schmenk**, Gerald E '66 (Schmenk S&H) -20 N Limestone
-Springfield 45502 Fx:323-9388

(937) 323-9739 .. **Schmenk Spencer & Hasselbach** -20 N Limestone
-Springfield 45502 Fx:323-9388

(513) 922-3861 .. **Schmerber**, Donald E '74 -1043 Hickok Ln -Cincinnati 45238

(216) 573-1800 .. **Schmid**, Gordon E '76 -6000 Freedom Sq Dr -Ste 380
-Independence 44131

(330) 674-6264 .. **Schmid**, Laurel J '76 -34 S Clay -Bx268 -Millersburg 44654

(330) 535-4000 .. **Schmid**, Mora Lowry '99 (Anderson M&L) -120 E Mill -Ste 315
-Akron 44308

(513) 241-4110 .. **Schmid**, Peter A '04 %Deters B&L,PSC -441 Vine
-Ste 3500 Carew Twr -Cincinnati 45202 Fx:241-4551

(216) 378-9905 .. **Schmidley**, Eugenia M '85 Cnsl McGlinchey S PLLC
-25550 Chagrin Blvd -Ste 406 -Cleveland 44122 Fx:378-9910

(440) 461-9000 .. **Schmidlin**, Raymond J '65 (Dyson S&F Co,LPA) -5843 Mayfld Rd
-Mayfield Heights 44124

(440) 461-9000 .. **Schmidlin**, Raymond J Jr. '89 Dyson S&F Co,LPA
-5843 Mayfld Rd -Mayfield Heights 44124

(513) 852-6052 .. **Schmidt**, Carl J III '83 (Wood & L LLP) -600 Vine -Ste 2500
-Cincinnati 45202 Fx:852-6087

(513) 721-4450 .. **Schmidt**, Charles Gregory '80 (Santen & H) -312 Walnut
-Ste 3100 -Cincinnati 45202

(440) 914-0400 .. **Schmidt**, Courtney C '99 Sure Site Cnsltng Grp,LLC
-6655 Parkland Blvd -Solon 44139

(513) 621-8688 .. **Schmidt**, Dale G '65 -1071 Celestial -Ste 904 -Cincinnati 45202

(216) 621-6752 .. **Schmidt**, David G '71 (Schmidt Legal Grp) -614 Superior Av
-#1500 -Cleveland 44113 Fx:621-6474

(937) 299-1895 .. **Schmidt**, David R '84 -1200 E Dorothy Ln -Dayton 45419

(708) 450-3262 .. **Schmidt**, Gary P '77 Alberto-Culver Co -2525 Armitage
-Melrose Park, IL 60160

(614) 621-9000 .. **Schmidt**, George A '72 %Glimcher Realty -20 S 3rd
-Columbus 43215

(216) 291-3783 .. **Schmidt**, Georgeann R '78 Cleveland Hts Mun Ct -40 Severance
Cir -Cleveland Heights 44118

(412) 667-7946 .. **Schmidt**, Gordon W '99 McGuire W,LLP -625 Lbrty Av -23rd Fl
-Pittsburgh, PA 15222

(952) 593-9943 .. **Schmidt**, James M '85 Buffalo Wild Wings,Inc -1600 Utica Av S
-Ste 700 -Minneapolis, MN 55416

(937) 372-5591 .. **Schmidt**, James W '73 (Schmidt & S) -63½ E Main -Xenia 45385
Fx:376-2550

(513) 595-2879 .. **Schmidt**, Jerome C '73 Union Cntrl Life Ins Co -1876 Waycross
Rd -Bx40888 -Cincinnati 45240

(216) 523-1525 .. **Schmidt**, Jesse M '04 OfCnsl Lallo & F Co,LPA -55 Pub Sq
-Ste 1616 -Cleveland 44113 Fx:523-1487

(513) 977-8200 .. **Schmidt**, John J '92 (Dinsmore & S LLP) -255 E 5th -Ste 1900
-Cincinnati 45202 Fx:977-8141

(704) 887-1607 .. **Schmidt**, Joseph J '95 DeLoitte & Touche,LLP -227 W Trade
-Ste 1100 -Charlotte, NC 28202

(757) 455-7114 .. **Schmidt**, Laura B '90 Sentara Hlthcre -6015 Poplar Hall Dr
-Ste 308 -Norfolk, VA 23502

(937) 461-6200 .. **Schmidt**, Matthew M '00 Cincinnati Ins Co -130 W 2nd -Ste 1850
-Dayton 45402

(740) 702-3100 .. **Schmidt**, Matthew S '02 %Nusbaum A&W -72 N Paint
-Chillicothe 45601

(513) 533-2996 .. **Schmidt**, Michael C '01 %Finney SS&K Co,LPA -2623 Erie Av
-Bx8804 -Cincinnati 45208

(513) 421-4020 .. **Schmidt**, Michael R '81 (Cohen TK&S,LLC) -250 E 5th -Ste 1200
-Cincinnati 45202 Fx:241-4490

(937) 865-6800 .. **Schmidt**, Michele H '91 Lexis/Nexis -Bx933 -Dayton 45401

(419) 885-3000 .. **Schmidt**, Philip L '74 (Brady C&S LLP) -4052 Holland-Sylvania Rd
-Toledo 43623 Fx:885-1120

(419) 353-0152 .. **Schmidt**, Richard A '86 -133 N Prospect -Bowling Green 43402

(513) 621-8688 .. **Schmidt**, Richard L '83 -1071 Celestial -Ste 904 -Cincinnati 45202

(614) 227-2000 .. **Schmidt**, Robert J Jr. '93 %Porter WM&A LLP -41 S High
-Columbus 43215 Fx:227-2100

(216) 619-5925 .. **Schmidt**, Robert N '81 Orbital Rsrch Inc -4415 Euclid -Cleveland
44103

(614) 466-7900 .. **Schmidt**, Stefan J '90 Atty Gen -30 E Broad -Columbus 43215
Fx:466-2437

(937) 298-0399 .. **Schmidt**, Steven P '74 -4017 Stonehaven Rd -Kettering 45429

(937) 562-5250 .. **Schmidt**, Suzanne M '79 Greene Cnty Pros -61 Greene
-Xenia 45385

(614) 476-1596 .. **Schmidt**, Thomas F '83 -172 Granvll -Gahanna 43230

(513) 521-0651 .. **Schmidt**, Timothy J '92 (T Schmidt Co,LPA) -8617 Zenith Ct
-Cincinnati 45231

(202) 293-1382 .. **Schmidt**, William A Jr. '68 Universities Rsrch Assn -1111 19th NW
-Ste 400 -Washington, DC 20036 Fx:293-5012

(614) 466-3934 .. **Schmidt**, William J '81 State Med Brd -77 S High -17th Fl
-Columbus 43215

(513) 831-1200 .. **Schmieg**, Michael M '78 -110 Main -Milford 45150 Fx:831-1201

(513) 651-6800 .. **Schmit**, David E '75 (Frost BT LLC) -201 E 5th -2200 PNC Ctr
-Cincinnati 45202 Fx:651-6981

(330) 264-4500 .. **Schmitt**, Christopher A '94 -105 E Lbrty -Wooster 44691
Fx:264-5797

(513) 852-8200 .. **Schmitt**, David J '91 Cors & B LLC -537 E Pete Rose Way
-Ste 400 -Cincinnati 45202

(614) 744-2217 .. **Schmitt**, Grace E '96 CASTO -191 W Nationwide Blvd
-Columbus 43215

(937) 223-3001 .. **Schmitt**, J Jason '01 %Jenks P&O Co,LPA -10 N Ludlow -Ste 901
-Dayton 45402 Fx:223-3103

(304) 233-3390 .. **Schmitt**, Lisa M '03 %Schrader B&C,PLLC -32 20th -Ste 500
-Wheeling, WV 26003 Fx:233-2769

(740) 272-1723 .. **Schmitz**, Elizabeth S '91 -3254 Hrbr Dr -Lewis Center 43035
Fx:657-1354

(216) 622-3758 .. **Schmitz**, Joseph P '79 US Atty -801 W Superior -Ste 400
-Cleveland 44113 Fx:622-3370

(216) 443-8615 .. **Schmitz**, Michael F '95 Cuyahoga Cnty Ct Cmmn Pleas -1200
Ontario -Justice Ctr 11th Fl -Cleveland 44113

(614) 540-4000 .. **Schmitz**, Patrick J '91 OH Schl Brds Assn -8050 N High -Ste 100
-Columbus 43235

(330) 264-4444 .. **Schmitz**, Peggy Jo '78 (Critchfield C&J Ltd) -225 N Market -Bx599
-Wooster 44691 Fx:263-9278

(330) 535-2220 .. **Schmitz**, Thomas M '67 %Hudak S&F -2020 Front -Ste 307
-Cuyahoga Falls 44221 **Fx:**535-1435

(216) 696-5222 .. **Schmitz**, William F '85 %Johnson & C,LLC -1001 Lakeside Av
-Ste 1700 N Pnt Twr -Cleveland 44114 **Fx:**696-5288

Schmollinger, Mark S '82 -(Address Unavailable)

Schmotzer, Edward J '84 -(Address Unavailable)

Schnabel, Cynthia L '90 -2106 Green Briar Pl -Union, KY 41091

(213) 430-3400 .. **Schnaitman**, Peter E '99 %Tucker E&W LLP -725 S Figueroa
-Ste 3400 -Los Angeles, CA 90017

Schnalcer, Theresa '02 -1725 Southbend Dr -Rocky River 44116

(513) 651-6800 .. **Schnapp**, Karlyn A '00 %Frost BT LLC -201 E 5th -2200 PNC Ctr
-Cincinnati 45202 **Fx:**651-6981

(330) 497-4501 .. **Schnars**, Richard T '93 -3205 Bretton NW -Ste 300
-Canton 44720

(937) 222-1232 .. **Schneble**, Alfred William III '81 (Schneble C & Assoc Co,LPA)
-111 W Monument Av -Ste 402 -Dayton 45402

(216) 348-5400 .. **Schnee**, Douglas B '94 (McDonald H Co,LPA) -600 Superior Av E
-Ste 2100 -Cleveland 44114 **Fx:**348-5474

(216) 241-4740 .. **Schneiberg**, Jerald A '93 -425 W Lakeside Av -Ste 100
-Cleveland 44113

(216) 591-0727 .. **Schneider**, Albert E III '69 Summers & V Co,LPA
-23240 Chagrin Blvd -Ste 525 -Cleveland 44122 **Fx:**591-0740

(513) 421-7500 .. **Schneider**, Ann E '99 %Faulkner & T,LLP -5 W 4th
-2200 4th & Vine Twr -Cincinnati 45202

(513) 579-6400 .. **Schneider**, Benjamin A '00 %Keating M&K PLL -1 E 4th
-1400 Provident Twr -Cincinnati 45202 **Fx:**579-6457

Schneider, Betty T '89 -(Address Unavailable)

(614) 462-3194 .. **Schneider**, Carole B '79 Franklin Cnty Pub Def -373 S High
-12th Fl -Columbus 43215

(614) 645-8206 .. **Schneider**, Charles A '76 Cnty Mun Ct Judge -375 S High
-Columbus 43215

(859) 426-1300 .. **Schneider**, David A '63 (Ziegler & S,PSC) -541 Buttermilk Pike
-Ste 500 -Bx175710 -Covington, KY 41017

(513) 333-0013 .. **Schneider**, Donald E '75 -1101 St Gregory -Ste 350
-Cincinnati 45202

(330) 643-5456 .. **Schneider**, Edward M '95 Summit Cnty Cmn Pleas Ct -209 S High
-Domestic Relations Div -Akron 44308

Schneider, Gregory A '97 -18201 Falling Leaves Rd
-Strongsville 44136

(513) 579-1414 .. **Schneider**, Hallie L '03 %Schwartz M&R -441 Vine -Ste 2900
-Cincinnati 45202 **Fx:**579-1418

(513) 984-0300 .. **Schneider**, Harry R '80 Hills Dvlprs,Inc -4901 Hunt Rd -Ste 300
-Cincinnati 45242

(740) 373-7624 .. **Schneider**, James E '75 Washington Cnty Pros -205 Putnam
-Marietta 45750

(216) 671-9840 .. **Schneider**, James J '56 -17521 Oxford Av -Cleveland 44111

(216) 621-1230 .. **Schneider**, John J '01 %G Walton & Assoc -2800 Euclid Av
-Ste 320 -Cleveland 44115 **Fx:**621-3039

(216) 258-0996 .. **Schneider**, Joseph G '57 -1900 E 9th -Ste 2400 -Cleveland 44114

(614) 224-1222 .. **Schneider**, Karl H '82 (Maguire & S,LLP) -250 Civic Ctr Dr
-Ste 200 -Columbus 43215 **Fx:**224-1236

(614) 224-1222 .. **Schneider**, Keith W '89 (Maguire & S,LLP) -250 Civic Ctr Dr
-Ste 200 -Columbus 43215 **Fx:**224-1236

(513) 852-6021 .. **Schneider**, Kenneth J '66 (Wood & L LLP) -600 Vine -Ste 2500
-Cincinnati 45202 **Fx:**852-6087

(216) 781-5515 .. **Schneider**, Kent B '78 (Hermann C&S,LLP) -1301 E 9th -Ste 500
-Cleveland 44114 **Fx:**781-1030

(513) 381-0656 .. **Schneider**, Louis C '03 %Kohnen & P LLP -201 E 5th -Ste 800
-Cincinnati 45202 **Fx:**381-5823

(216) 443-7800 .. **Schneider**, Mark A '00 Cuyahoga Cnty Pros -1200 Ontario -8th Fl
-Cleveland 44113 **Fx:**698-2270

(614) 292-0611 .. **Schneider**, Mary F '89 OSU/Legal Affrs -33 W 11th Av -Ste 209
-Columbus 43201

(330) 296-9654 .. **Schneider**, Oliver J '51 -231 S Chestnut -Bx608 -Ravenna 44266

(216) 241-5310 .. **Schneider**, Paul Kohl '92 %Gallagher SF&N -1501 Euclid Av
-6th Fl -Cleveland 44115 **Fx:**241-1608

(937) 653-5259 .. **Schneider**, Philip S '68 -108 S Main -Bx357 -Urbana 43078

(513) 946-3164 .. **Schneider**, Richard J '77 Hamilton Cnty Pros -230 E 9th
-Cincinnati 45202 **Fx:**946-3017

(937) 644-9488 .. **Schneider**, Russell Larry '69 -111 W 6th -Marysville 43040

(216) 696-4200 .. **Schneider Smeltz Ranney & LaFond PLL** -1111 Superior Av
-Ste 1000 -Cleveland 44114 **Fx:**696-7303

(513) 345-8291 .. **Schneider**, Theodore J '92 (Murdock GS&G) -35 E 7th -Ste 600
-Cincinnati 45202 **Fx:**345-8294

(606) 291-9075 .. **Schneider**, Timothy E '88 (Fessler S&G) -14 N Grand Av
-Fort Thomas, KY 41075

(513) 621-2120 .. **Schneiderman**, Diane T '89 OfCnsl Strauss & T,LPA -150 E 4th
-4th Fl -Cincinnati 45202 **Fx:**241-8259

Schneiderman, Karen R '84 -2943 E Derbyshire Rd -#2
-Cleveland 44118

(330) 836-8777 .. **Schneiderman**, Stanley B '54 -585 White Pond Dr -Ste D
-Akron 44320

(330) 214-4202 .. **Schneiderman-Welch**, Ellen L '88 -Bx8776 -Canton 44711

(330) 376-5756 .. **Schneier**, Bernard '62 Emershaw M&S -120 E Mill -#437
-Akron 44308 **Fx:**762-5980

(216) 381-3400 .. **Schneier**, Jamie B '93 (Petronzio S Co,LPA) -5001 Mayfld Rd
-Ste 201 -Cleveland 44124

(513) 829-1590 .. **Schnell**, James M '73 -1251 Nilles Rd -Ste 15 -Fairfield 45014

(937) 492-6191 .. **Schnelle**, Keith M '81 (Elsass WES&Co) -100 S Main Av -Ste 102
-Bx499 -Sidney 45365 **Fx:**492-0876

(513) 946-9000 .. **Schnieders**, Joseph A '82 Hamilton Cnty Dom Rltns Ct -800 Bway
-Rm 301 -Cincinnati 45202

(419) 599-0212 .. **Schnitkey**, Mark D '84 -118 W Wshngtn -Napoleon 43545

Schnittke, Priscilla A '88 -(Address Unavailable)

(740) 342-2033 .. **Schnittke**, Steven P '75 (Schnittke & S) -Bx542
-New Lexington 43764

Schnittke, Teresa D '89 -(Address Unavailable)

(216) 586-3939 .. **Schnopp**, Stefan K '97 %Jones D -901 Lakeside Av
-Cleveland 44114 **Fx:**579-0212

(419) 841-4294 .. **Schnorf**, Brandon G Jr. '58 (Schnorf F&G) -5217 Monroe -Ste A
-Bx23156 -Toledo 43623

(419) 248-2646 .. **Schnorf**, David M '64 (Schnorf & S Co,LPA) -405 Mad Av
-1400 Natl City Bk Bldg -Toledo 43604

(419) 841-4294 .. **Schnorf Ferguson & Griffith** -5217 Monroe -Ste A -Bx23156
-Toledo 43623

(330) 670-7300 .. **Schobert**, Jeffrey E '85 %Hanna C&P,LLP -3737 Embssy Pkwy
-Bx5521 -Akron 44334 **Fx:**670-0977

(859) 431-0170 .. **Schoborg**, Teresa J '86 (King & S) -3612 Caroline Av -Covington,
KY 41015

(704) 423-7564 .. **Schoch**, Alexander C '83 BF Goodrich Corp -2730 W Tyvola Rd
-Charlotte, NC 28217

(614) 466-4656 .. **Schoch**, Frederick C '80 Atty Gen -150 E Gay -Columbus 43215
Fx:466-1756

(972) 233-6611 .. **Schochet**, William A '79 Overhead Door Corp -6750 LBJ Fwy
-Dallas, TX 75240

(614) 836-3242 .. **Schockling**, Scott D '94 Lexis-Nexis -5073 Bixby Rd
-Groveport 43125

(614) 233-4742 .. **Schockman**, Douglas J '94 Lane A&H LLC -175 S 3rd -Ste 700
-Columbus 43215 **Fx:**228-0146

(614) 464-6400 .. **Schoedinger**, Daniel H '69 (Vorys SS&P LLP) -52 E Gay -Bx1008
-Columbus 43216 **Fx:**464-6350

(216) 741-2365 .. **Schoen**, James S '79 UAW Legal Srvcs -707 Brookpark Rd
-Brooklyn Heights 44109

(419) 244-8336 .. **Schoenberger**, Bruce S '83 (Gressley K&P) -608 Mad Av -Ste 930
-Toledo 43604 **Fx:**244-1914

(513) 651-8486 .. **Schoenberger**, Jeanne L '91 PNC Bank, Ohio, N.A. -Bx1198
-Cincinnati 45241

(614) 224-0531 .. **Schoenberger**, Josh Logan '04 %Williams & P Co,LLC
-338 S High -2nd Fl -Columbus 43215 **Fx:**224-0553

(419) 294-5701 .. **Schoenberger**, Loren C '49 (Stansbery S&S) -106 E Wyandot Av
-Upper Sandusky 43351 **Fx:**294-5608

(330) 643-8800 .. **Schoenewald**, Michael A '88 Talon Grp -50 S Main -Ste 705
-Akron 44308

(513) 421-2540 .. **Schoenfeld**, Emily A '03 %Ennis R&F -121 W 9th
-Cincinnati 45202 **Fx:**562-4986

(513) 241-5005 .. **Schoenfeld**, Thomas R '80 -36 E 7th -Ste 2420 -Cincinnati 45202

(216) 621-0200 .. **Schoenfield**, Nichol M '96 Baker & H LLP -1900 E 9th -Ste 3200
-Cleveland 44114 **Fx:**696-0740

(513) 381-0656 .. **Schoeni**, Kenneth R '83 (Kohnen & P LLP) -201 E 5th -Ste 800
-Cincinnati 45202 **Fx:**381-5823

(330) 965-9910 .. **Schoenike**, Jonathan K '91 Am Archtctrl Prdcts
-860 Boardman Canfld Rd -Ste 107 -Youngstown 44512

(859) 341-1881 .. **Schoening**, Kelleene A '96 Deters B&L,PSC -2701 Turkeyfoot Rd
-207 Thomas More Pkwy -Crestview Hills, KY 41017 **Fx:**341-1469

(614) 430-8885 .. **Schoenling**, Karin K '91 (Curry RS&M Co,LLC)
-8000 Ravines Edge Ct -Ste 103 -Columbus 43235 **Fx:**430-8890

(513) 651-6800 .. **Schoeny**, James D '03 %Frost BT LLC -201 E 5th -2200 PNC Ctr
-Cincinnati 45202 **Fx:**651-6981

(202) 521-2200 .. **Schoeppe**, Michele M '97 UMWA-Hlth & Rtrmnt Funds
-2121 K NW -Rm 350 -Washington, DC 20037

(859) 491-5843 .. **Schoettelkotte**, William H '78 Cnty Atty -331 York -Newport,
KY 41071

(513) 946-9000 .. **Schoettmer**, Sara Ann '82 Hamilton Cnty Juv Ct -800 Bway
-Cincinnati 45202 **Fx:**946-9217

Schohl, John M '83 -(Address Unavailable)

(513) 241-2324 .. **Scholer**, Douglas A '00 %Wood H&E LLP -441 Vine -Ste 2700
-Cincinnati 45202 **Fx:**421-7269

(614) 249-9005 .. **Scholl**, Joseph M '79 Nationwide Ins Co -One Nationwide Plz
-Casualty Claims Ofc -Columbus 43215

(614) 466-7046 .. **Scholl**, Marcie M '80 Personnel Brd of Review -65 E State -12th Fl
-Columbus 43215

(216) 241-2200 .. **Scholl**, Mary J '90 (Zoller & S) -812 Huron Rd
-Caxton Bldg, Ste 490 -Cleveland 44115

(614) 466-2765 .. **Scholl**, Michael R '93 Industrial Commssn of OH -30 W Spring
-9th Fl -Columbus 43215 **Fx:**752-8785

(614) 462-7245 .. **Scholl**, Thomas W III '96 10th Dist Ct of Appls -373 S High
-24th Fl -Columbus 43215

(513) 422-2001 .. **Scholler**, Warren J III '00 %Frost BT LLC -300 N Main -Ste 200
-Middletown 45042 **Fx:**422-3010

(513) 729-3198 .. **Scholles**, James R '77 (Scholles & S) -8970 Winton Rd
-Cincinnati 45231

(513) 729-3198 .. **Scholles**, Jeffrey J '86 (Scholles & S) -8970 Winton Rd
-Cincinnati 45231

(216) 621-0200 .. **Scholz**, Karin M '03 %Baker & H LLP -1900 E 9th -Ste 3200
-Cleveland 44114 **Fx:**696-0740

(513) 579-0080 .. **Schomaker**, John P '03 %Smith R&S Co,LPA -1014 Vine
-Ste 2350 -Cincinnati 45202 **Fx:**579-0222

(330) 253-5060 .. **Schomer**, John B '91 (Brennan M&D,LLC) -75 E Market
-Akron 44308 **Fx:**253-1977

(216) 447-1551 .. **Schonberg**, Evelyn P '81 (Ross B&S Co LPA)
-6000 Freedom Square Dr -Ste 540 -Cleveland 44131
Fx:447-1554

(216) 363-4500 .. **Schonberg**, William E '79 (Benesch FC&A LLP) -200 Pub Sq
-Ste 2300 -Cleveland 44114 **Fx:**363-4588

(216) 621-5680 .. **Schonfeld**, Jay M '70 -1660 W 2nd -Ste 310 -Cleveland 44113

(216) 696-7170 .. **Schooler**, Scott H '84 Forbes F & Assoc Co,LPA
-614 W Superior Av -700 Rckfllr Bldg -Cleveland 44113

(513) 621-6464 .. **Schooley**, Ann K '99 %Graydon H&R LLP -511 Walnut
-1900 Fifth Third Ctr -Cincinnati 45202 **Fx:**651-3836

(740) 852-8383 .. **Schooley**, Eric M '97 (Wildman S LLC) -26 E 4th -London 43140

Schooley, Ruth K '86 -2235 Picket Post Ln
-Upper Arlington 43220

(713) 870-5516 .. **Schoolfield**, Bruce W Jr. '86 SrCnsl JR McDermott,Inc
-757 N Eldrdg -Houston, TX 77079

(419) 517-7000 .. **Schoonmaker**, Laurie A '99 %Kenney & N,Ltd -5470 Main
-Ste 300 -Sylvania 43560 **Fx:**517-7001

(216) 589-9600 .. **Schoonover**, John E '84 (Wilsman & S,LLC) -1301 E 9th
-Ste 1420 -Cleveland 44114

(513) 524-1177 .. **Schoonover**, Paul E '88 -115 W High -Oxford 45056

(614) 462-3194 .. **Schopis**, Robert O '85 Franklin Cnty Pub Def -373 S High -12th Fl
-Columbus 43215

(330) 744-1111 .. **Schor**, Neil D '89 Harrington H&M,Ltd -26 Market -Ste 1200
-Youngstown 44503 **Fx:**744-2029

(419) 774-5676 .. **Schoren**, James A '84 Richland Cnty Pros -38 S Park -2nd Fl
-Mansfield 44902 **Fx:**774-5589

(937) 372-7243 .. **Schornak**, Donald G '56 -85 W 2nd -Xenia 45385

(216) 514-7480 .. **Schorr,** Brian D '86 Mortgage Info Srvcs -4877 Galaxy Pkwy -Ste I
-Cleveland 44128

Schorr, Diane J '86 -(Address Unavailable)

(330) 337-3769 .. **Schory,** Earl A II '75 -288 E State -Salem 44460

(937) 644-7888 .. **Schostek,** Richard M '86 Honda of Amer Mfg,Inc -24000 Honda
Pkwy -Marysville 43040

Schott, Donald L '67 -1830 Neeb Rd -Cincinnati 45233

(330) 835-4523 .. **Schott,** Lyn M '79 -43 E Fairlawn Blvd -Akron 44313

(913) 551-1006 .. **Schott,** Richard W '93 US DOJ-Bureau of Prisons -400 State
-Twr I,8th Fl -Kansas City, KS 66101

(614) 462-2266 .. **Schottenstein,** Edwin E '82 -100 E Broad -Ste 1400
-Columbus 43215 **Fx:**462-2406

(614) 464-1880 .. **Schottenstein,** James M '72 (Schottenstein Legal Srvcs)
-341 S 3rd -Ste 300 -Columbus 43215 **Fx:**464-3004

(614) 462-2700 .. **Schottenstein Zox & Dunn** -250 West -Bx165020
-Columbus 43216 **Fx:**462-5135

(216) 621-6501 .. **Schottenstein Zox & Dunn** -1350 Euclid Av -Ste 1400
-Cleveland 44115 **Fx:**621-6502

(513) 792-0792 .. **Schottenstein Zox & Dunn** -8044 Mntgmry Rd -Ste 630
-Cincinnati 45236 **Fx:**792-0803

(330) 762-0765 .. **Schrader,** Alfred E '78 -441 Wolf Ledges Pkwy -Ste 400 -Bx0079
-Akron 44311 **Fx:**762-2255

(330) 376-2700 .. **Schrader,** Bruce R II '87 (Roetzel & A,LPA) -222 S Main
-Akron 44308 **Fx:**376-4577

(937) 843-3152 .. **Schrader,** Chris A '76 (Shirk & S) -185 S Main -Bx246 -Lakeview
43331

(614) 461-1311 .. **Schrader,** Matthew L '01 %Reminger & R -65 E State
-4th Fl Cptl Sq Ofc Bldg -Columbus 43215 **Fx:**232-2410

Schrader, Ryan C '02 -(Address Unavailable)

(216) 781-1212 .. **Schrader,** Thomas C '68 Walter & H LLP -1301 E 9th -Ste 3500
-Cleveland 44114 **Fx:**575-0911

(440) 930-8081 .. **Schrader,** Todd A '96 Wickens HPC&B -35765 Chester Rd
-Avon 44011 **Fx:**937-4466

(614) 227-2000 .. **Schraff,** Christopher R '72 (Porter WM&A LLP) -41 S High
-Columbus 43215 **Fx:**227-2100

(440) 954-9455 .. **Schraff & King Co,LPA** -4230 SR 306 -#310 -Willoughby 44094

(440) 954-9455 .. **Schraff,** Patricia J '80 (Schraff & K Co,LPA) -4230 SR 306 -#310
-Willoughby 44094

(808) 524-8000 .. **Schraff,** Paul A '77 Dwyer S&M -900 Fort St Mall -Ste 1800
-Honolulu, HI 96813

(513) 887-6400 .. **Schraffenberger,** Mark D '90 Dixon Builders LLC
-7924 Jessies Way -Hamilton 45011

(614) 464-6400 .. **Schrag,** Edward A Jr. '61 OfCnsl Vorys SS&P LLP -52 E Gay
-Bx1008 -Columbus 43216 **Fx:**464-6350

(937) 228-2735 .. **Schram,** Deborah C '78 -11 W Monument Av -Ste 408
-Dayton 45402

Schramm, David E '79 -8538 Forrester Blvd
-Springfield, VA 22152

(740) 695-1444 .. **Schramm,** Erik A '99 Hanlon DE&M Co,LPA -46457 Natl Rd W
-Saint Clairsville 43950 **Fx:**695-1563

(419) 222-4100 .. **Schramski,** Nancy S '87 -119 N West -Ste 102 -Lima 45801

(216) 932-8344 .. **Schreck,** Richard A '53 -3616 Berkeley Rd
-Cleveland Heights 44118

Schreckinger, Linda I '77 -26010 Hendon Rd -Beachwood 44122

(614) 228-9707 .. **Schreibeis,** George Dennis '98 %Mallory & T Co,LPA -88 E Broad
-Ste 1560 -Columbus 43215

(800) 997-7805 .. **Schreiber,** Jeffrey D '89 Fidelity Investments -82 Devonshr -L12A
-Boston, MA 02109

(513) 977-8200 .. **Schreiber,** Steven H '81 (Dinsmore & S LLP) -255 E 5th -Ste 1900
-Cincinnati 45202 **Fx:**977-8141

(216) 621-7292 .. **Schreiber,** Svetlana J '82 (S Schreiber & Assoc Co,LPA)
-1224 Standard Bldg -1370 Ontario -Cleveland 44113

(216) 687-0900 .. **Schreibman,** Eric M '97 %Greene & E Co,LPA -1300 E 9th
-Ste 1801 -Cleveland 44114

(202) 535-1255 .. **Schreibman,** Jack L '00 DC DMV Adjudication Srvcs -66 K NE
-Washington, DC 20002

(419) 213-3000 .. **Schreibman,** Sydney A '94 Lucas Cnty CSEA -701 Adams
-Toledo 43624

(740) 498-6254 .. **Schreiner,** Bernard J '76 -73443 Mill Rd -Kimbolton 43749

(440) 838-8800 .. **Schreiner,** David E '73 (Millisor & N Co,LPA) -9150 S Hills Blvd
-Ste 300 -Cleveland 44147 **Fx:**838-8805

(513) 977-8200 .. **Schreiner,** Joanne M '80 (Dinsmore & S LLP) -255 E 5th
-Ste 1900 -Cincinnati 45202 **Fx:**977-8141

(440) 838-8800 .. **Schreiner,** Melanie Webber '99 %Millisor & N Co,LPA
-9150 S Hills Blvd -Ste 300 -Cleveland 44147 **Fx:**838-8805

(216) 583-8340 .. **Schreiner,** Thomas E '82 Ernst & Young -1660 W 2nd -Ste 1000
-Cleveland 44113

(216) 241-5310 .. **Schremp,** Pamela S '98 %Gallagher SF&N -1501 Euclid Av -6th Fl
-Cleveland 44115 **Fx:**241-1608

(937) 228-8158 .. **Schriber,** Kenneth L '70 Natl Schriber Corp -973 S Perry
-Dayton 45402

(513) 241-9400 .. **Schrider,** John E Jr. '74 Legal Aid -215 E 9th -Ste 200
-Cincinnati 45202

(216) 623-0150 .. **Schriner,** John J '99 %Roetzel & A,LPA -1375 E 9th
-One Cleve Ctr 9th Fl -Cleveland 44114 **Fx:**623-0134

(330) 335-2749 .. **Schrock,** Page C III '78 Wadsworth Law Dept -120 Maple
-Wadsworth 44281 **Fx:**335-2711

(513) 621-2044 .. **Schroeck,** Rebecca L '00 %Macey & C -1014 Vine
-2500 Kroger Bldg -Cincinnati 45202

(614) 466-3578 .. **Schroeder,** Anthony D '91 %Hon AR Resnick -30 E Broad
-Columbus 43266

(419) 523-5658 .. **Schroeder Blankemeyer & Schroeder** -315 E Main -Bx110
-Ottawa 45875 **Fx:**523-6500

(419) 244-3344 .. **Schroeder,** Charles F '57 Cnsl C Schroeder & Assoc -608 Mad Av
-Ste 1630 -Toledo 43604 **Fx:**244-3344

(419) 523-5658 .. **Schroeder,** Clyde A '70 OfCnsl Schroeder B&S -315 E Main
-Bx110 -Ottawa 45875 **Fx:**523-6500

(440) 974-1433 .. **Schroeder,** David A '81 -9634 Brayes Mnr -Mentor 44060

(419) 478-1776 .. **Schroeder,** Jeffery A '94 -1776 Tremainsvll Rd -Toledo 43613
Fx:478-5087

(419) 422-8111 .. **Schroeder,** Jerome B '78 Knueven S & Co -1035 N Main
-Findlay 45840

(419) 523-5658 .. **Schroeder,** Joseph C '91 (Schroeder B&S) -315 E Main -Bx110
-Ottawa 45875 **Fx:**523-6500

(419) 421-2598 .. **Schroeder,** Kimberly B '92 Marathon Ashland Petro LLC
-539 S Main -Findlay 45840 **Fx:**421-3578

(419) 523-5688 .. **Schroeder,** Lee R '02 Putnam Cnty Econ Devlpmt Dir -240 E Main
-Ottawa 45875

(513) 583-4200 .. **Schroeder Maundrell Barbiere & Powers** -11935 Mason Rd
-Ste 110 -Cincinnati 45249

Schroeder, Michael A '91 -271 Bucknghm Rd -Cleveland 44116

(216) 771-1144 .. **Schroeder,** Michael S '95 (Behrens G&S Co,LPA) -1360 W 9th
-Ste 400 -Cleveland 44113 **Fx:**736-7136

(614) 224-6220 .. **Schroeder,** Sarah W '84 Rector & Assoc,Inc -172 E State
-Ste 305 -Columbus 43215

(419) 523-5658 .. **Schroeder,** Todd C '02 %Schroeder B&S -315 E Main -Bx110
-Ottawa 45875 **Fx:**523-6500

(513) 583-4200 .. **Schroeder,** William P '68 (Schroeder MB&P) -11935 Mason Rd
-Ste 110 -Cincinnati 45249

(513) 651-6800 .. **Schroer,** Charles E '79 (Frost BT LLC) -201 E 5th -2200 PNC Ctr
-Cincinnati 45202 **Fx:**651-6981

(513) 744-7260 .. **Schroer,** Dianna L '97 Fifth 3rd Bank -38 Fountain Sq Plz
-MD 1090V1 -Cincinnati 45263

(216) 486-2100 .. **Schron,** Jack H Jr. '75 Jergens Inc -15700 S Waterloo Rd
-Cleveland 44110

(330) 399-5469 .. **Schubert,** Thomas E '70 -138 E Market -Warren 44481

(513) 232-0922 .. **Schuch,** Paul W '53 -7591 Forest Rd -Cincinnati 45255

(419) 244-3808 .. **Schuchmann,** John J '54 -520 Mad Av -9 Spitzer Arcade
-Toledo 43604

(614) 227-8839 .. **Schuck,** James P '00 %Bricker & E LLP -100 S 3rd
-Columbus 43215 **Fx:**227-2390

(419) 422-2864 .. **Schuck,** Robert E '83 -101½ W Sandusky -Findlay 45840

(513) 381-2838 .. **Schuck,** Thomas R '76 (Taft S&H LLP) -425 Walnut -Ste 1800
-Cincinnati 45202 **Fx:**381-0205

Schuck, William B '82 -2353 McCauley Ct -Columbus 43220

(614) 221-8448 .. **Schuckmann,** Frank '97 %Buckingham D&B,LLP
-191 W Nationwide Blvd -Ste 300 -Bx151120 -Columbus 43215
Fx:221-8590

(614) 764-3339 .. **Schuerman,** Robert E '76 Wendys Intl -4288 W Dublin-Granvll Rd
-Bx256 -Dublin 43017

(614) 462-5440 .. **Schuermann,** Richard W Jr. '83 (Kegler BH&R) -65 E State
-Ste 1800 -Columbus 43215 **Fx:**464-2634

(513) 398-4646 .. **Schuessler,** Dolores C '89 (Sams F&S) -209 Reading Rd
-Mason 45040 **Fx:**398-4608

(513) 321-2662 .. **Schuh & Goldberg,LLP** -2662 Madison Rd -Cincinnati 45208
Fx:321-0855

(513) 321-2662 .. **Schuh,** John A '77 (Schuh & G,LLP) -2662 Madison Rd
-Cincinnati 45208 **Fx:**321-0855

(513) 321-2662 .. **Schuh,** Stephen J '78 (Schuh & G,LLP) -2662 Madison Rd
-Cincinnati 45208 **Fx:**321-0855

(513) 867-4838 .. **Schul,** David D '79 1st Natl Bk of SW OH -Bx476 -Hamilton 45012

(304) 760-2345 .. **Schulberg,** Arnold L '95 -39 Cedar Dr -Hurricane, WV 25526
Fx:760-2346

(513) 946-9000 .. **Schulcz,** Mary C '87 Hamilton Cnty Juv Ct -800 Bway
-Cincinnati 45202 **Fx:**946-9217

(863) 619-4112 .. **Schuler,** Cynthia A '81 FL Dept of Children & Families
-4720 Old Hwy 37 -Lakeland, FL 33813

(513) 553-4049 .. **Schuler,** Richard P '69 -97 E Main -Batavia 45103

(614) 224-1222 .. **Schuler,** Robert C '91 OfCnsl Maguire & S,LLP -250 Civic Ctr Dr
-Ste 200 -Columbus 43215 **Fx:**224-1236

(614) 462-5410 .. **Schuler,** Robert G '87 (Kegler BH&R) -65 E State -Ste 1800
-Columbus 43215 **Fx:**464-2634

(419) 782-2253 .. **Schuller,** Elizabeth J '96 UAW Legal Srvcs -1500 Baltimore Rd
-Defiance 43512

(419) 535-0311 .. **Schuller,** James L '77 -3450 W Central Av -Ste 242
-Toledo 43606

(513) 521-7430 .. **Schulman,** Alan A '72 Schulman Assoc -206 Hilltop
-Cincinnati 45215

(330) 456-4400 .. **Schulman,** Allen Jr. '75 (A Schulman & Assoc, Co LPA)
-236 3rd SW -Canton 44702

(216) 621-0580 .. **Schulman,** Howard A '78 (Schulman S&M,LPA) -1370 Ontario
-1700 Standard Bldg -Cleveland 44113 **Fx:**621-5428

(216) 621-0580 .. **Schulman,** Jack M '67 (Schulman S&M,LPA) -1370 Ontario
-1700 Standard Bldg -Cleveland 44113 **Fx:**621-5428

(419) 634-3666 .. **Schulman,** Jeffrey M '78 -215 E Lehr Av -Ada 45810

(216) 621-0580 .. **Schulman Schulman & Meros, LPA** -1370 Ontario
-1700 Standard Bldg -Cleveland 44113 **Fx:**621-5428

(614) 222-4735 .. **Schulte,** Kathaleen B '82 (Gittes & S) -723 Oak -Columbus 43205

(859) 291-9181 .. **Schulte,** Marcy A '91 -127 E 3rd -Covington, KY 41011

(859) 291-9181 .. **Schulte,** Michael J '87 -127 E 3rd -Covington, KY 41011

(937) 435-7500 .. **Schulte,** Richard W '96 (Botros B&S,LLC) -5785 Far Hills Av
-Dayton 45429 **Fx:**435-7511

(330) 721-0900 .. **Schultz,** Beau A '01 -107 N Court -Ste 7 -Medina 44256
Fx:721-1818

(614) 224-1500 .. **Schultz,** David B '04 Fornia L&H,LLP -2 Miranova Pl -Ste 380
-Columbus 43215 **Fx:**224-2894

(216) 622-8200 .. **Schultz,** Lawrence N '79 (Calfee H&G LLP) -800 Superior Av
-Ste 1400 -Cleveland 44114 **Fx:**241-0816

(216) 520-5600 .. **Schultz,** Richard F '91 West Grp -6111 Oak Tree Blvd -Bx318063
-Cleveland 44131

(216) 241-6700 .. **Schultz,** Stephen J '78 (Watts H Co,LPA) -1100 Superior Av E
-Ste 1750 Diamond Bldg -Cleveland 44114 **Fx:**241-8151

(513) 561-3907 .. **Schultz,** Susan E '99 -4523 Hector Av -Cincinnati 45227

(419) 774-1430 .. **Schulz,** Alicia A '86 Richland Cnty Juv Ct -411 S Diamond
-Mansfield 44902 **Fx:**774-5555

(216) 931-6000 .. **Schulz,** Isaac '71 (Ulmer & B LLP) -1300 E 9th
-Ste 900 Penton Media Bldg -Cleveland 44114 **Fx:**931-6001

(216) 696-9696 .. **Schulz,** James H Jr. '83 -1370 Ontario -Ste 1520
-Cleveland 44114

(216) 222-2536 .. **Schulz,** Martin C '92 National City Bk -1900 E 9th -Loc #2220
-Cleveland 44114

(480) 563-6283 .. **Schulz,** Mary E '93 GE Capital Franchise Fin
-17207 N Perimeter Dr -Scottsdale, AZ 85255

(202) 898-6627 .. **Schulz,** Thomas A '70 FDIC -550 17th NW
-Washington, DC 20429

(216) 771-1760 .. **Schulz,** William J '83 %Smith & C LLP -1801 E Ninth
-Ste 900 Ohio Svngs Plz -Cleveland 44114 **Fx:**771-3387

(937) 644-3849 .. **Schulze**, Dennis A '68 (Schulze H&C) -110 S Main -Bx562
-Marysville 43040 **Fx:**644-1426

(937) 644-3849 .. **Schulze Howard & Cox** -110 S Main -Bx562 -Marysville 43040
Fx:644-1426

(614) 444-3900 .. **Schumacher**, Donald C '74 -755 S High -Columbus 43206

(216) 514-6400 .. **Schumacher**, James T '90 %Zipkin W Co LPA -3637 S Green Rd
-Zipkin Whiting Bldg -Cleveland 44122 **Fx:**514-6406

(606) 564-9066 .. **Schumacher**, Jeffrey L '00 (McNeill & S) -217 Wall
-Maysville, KY 41056

(330) 262-3030 .. **Schumacher**, Jodie M '04 Wayne Cnty Pros -115 W Lbrty
-Wooster 44691 **Fx:**287-5412

(513) 777-9800 .. **Schumacher**, Lynn M '85 Schumacher Dugan Cnstrctn,Inc
-6355 Centre Park Dr -West Chester 45069

(614) 827-7300 .. **Schumacher**, Mark L '81 (Freund F&A) -65 E State -Ste 800
-Columbus 43215 **Fx:**827-7303

(216) 241-5310 .. **Schumacher**, Paul J Jr. '83 (Gallagher SF&N) -1501 Euclid Av
-6th Fl -Cleveland 44115 **Fx:**241-1608

(614) 777-9908 .. **Schumacher**, Stacy M '02 -5251 Norwich -Hilliard 43026
Schumaker, Kenneth B '68 -3655 Albright Rd -Newark 43056

(937) 328-2574 .. **Schumaker**, Stephen A '78 Clark Cnty Pros -50 E Columbia
-Bx1608 -Springfield 45501

(419) 354-9250 .. **Schuman**, Andrew R '00 %Wood Cnty Pros -One Cthse Sq
-Bowling Green 43402 **Fx:**353-2904

(614) 481-6900 .. **Schuman**, John D '93 Budros & Ruhlin -1650 Lk Shr Dr
-Columbus 43204

(216) 587-2120 .. **Schuman**, Kenneth A '97 -5306 Transportation Blvd
-Garfield Heights 44125

(614) 462-3194 .. **Schumann**, George M '94 Franklin Cnty Pub Def -373 S High
-12th Fl -Columbus 43215

(937) 255-5270 .. **Schumann**, Ronald G '92 AFMCLO/JAV -1864 4th -Rm 130A
-Wright Patterson AFB 45433

(614) 891-6920 .. **Schumann**, William M '67 -1001 Eastwind Dr -Ste 203
-Westerville 43081

(505) 665-5445 .. **Schumsky**, Shari L '81 Los Alamos Natl Lab -MS M992
-Envrnmtl Restoration Proj -Bx1663 -Los Alamos, NM 87545

(330) 633-0859 .. **Schunk**, Richard A '74 City Law Director -46 North Av
-Tallmadge 44278

(972) 334-3822 .. **Schur**, Thomas P '81 Frito-Lay,Inc -7701 Legacy Dr
-Plano, TX 75024

(330) 830-1718 .. **Schurer**, Laura A '98 Massillon Law Dept -2 James Duncan Plz
-Massillon 44646 **Fx:**833-7144
Schurowliew, Valentine G '00 -(Address Unavailable)

(419) 249-7100 .. **Schurr**, Donald A '89 (Marshall & M,LLC) -Four Seagate -8th Fl
-Toledo 43604 **Fx:**249-7151

(217) 893-3322 .. **Schurter**, Brian T '97 -425 E Champaign Av -Rantoul, IL 61866

(614) 644-0876 .. **Schuster**, Elizabeth L '97 Governors Ofc -77 S High -30th Fl
-Columbus 43215

(216) 831-1434 .. **Schuster**, Linda B '93 %A Rickel & Assoc -3690 Orange Pl
-Ste 440 -Beachwood 44122 **Fx:**831-6376

(216) 348-1100 .. **Schuster**, Nancy C '68 (Schuster & S Co,LPA) -2913 Clinton Av
-Cleveland 44113 **Fx:**348-0013

(614) 436-2022 .. **Schuster**, Richard C '81 Lee Hecht Harrison Inc -8101 N High -Ste
300 -Columbus 43235

(614) 464-6400 .. **Schuster**, Richard D '81 (Vorys SS&P LLP) -52 E Gay -Bx1008
-Columbus 43216 **Fx:**464-6350

(513) 981-6280 .. **Schuster**, Richard L '88 Mercy Hlth Prtnrs-SWO -4600 McAuley Pl
-6th Fl,Leg Serv -Cincinnati 45242 **Fx:**981-6101

(614) 644-7250 .. **Schuster**, Saundra D '97 Atty Gen -30 E Broad -Columbus 43215
Fx:644-7634

(216) 348-1100 .. **Schuster & Simmons Co,LPA** -2913 Clinton Av
-Cleveland 44113 **Fx:**348-0013

(513) 221-1745 .. **Schutte**, Michael J '94 Beirne & W Co,LPA -1745 Madison Rd
-Bx6111 -Cincinnati 45206 **Fx:**221-6666

(937) 324-4442 .. **Schutte**, Stephen E '73 -31 E High -#325 -Springfield 45502
Schutter, Keith J '01 -(Address Unavailable)

(859) 344-0828 .. **Schutzman**, Thomas J '91 -2890 Chancellor Dr -Ste 200
-Crestview Hills, KY 41017

(614) 466-4489 .. **Schwab**, Gregory B '92 Legis Srvc Commssn -77 S High
-Columbus 43215

(330) 665-5178 .. **Schwab**, Harry W '54 -1021 Bunker Dr -Akron 44333

(216) 222-2984 .. **Schwab**, Richard B '76 Natl City Bank -1900 E 9th -Law Dept,
17th Fl -Cleveland 44114

(419) 241-9999 .. **Schwab**, Stuart S '78 -316 N Mich -Ste 600 -Toledo 43624
Schwachter, Richard H '69 -156 Hrbr Cir -Delray Beach, FL 33483

(614) 466-4510 .. **Schwade**, Joseph A '98 Atty Gen -150 E Gay -Columbus 43215
Fx:995-0501

(614) 228-3727 .. **Schwager**, Richard A '88 -536 S 3rd -Columbus 43215

(216) 573-9700 .. **Schwallie**, Daniel P '91 Hewitt Assoc -5005 Rockside Rd
-Independence 44131

(513) 584-5042 .. **Schwallie**, David F '84 Univ of Cincinnati -Ofc of Risk Mgmt/Ins
-Bx670785 -Cincinnati 45267

(614) 224-5205 .. **Schwallie**, Dennis G '78 (Peck S&W,LLP) -175 S 3rd -Ste 600
-Columbus 43215 **Fx:**224-0069

(614) 488-6005 .. **Schwart**, Charles J '82 Schwart,LLC -1620 W 1st Av
-Columbus 43212

(440) 350-3200 .. **Schwartz**, Aaron A '02 Lake Cnty Pub Def -125 E Erie
-Painesville 44077

(716) 853-5100 .. **Schwartz**, Blaine S '82 %Lippes MW&F LLP -665 Main -Ste 300
-Buffalo, NY 14203 **Fx:**853-5199
Schwartz, Brenda S '94 -4690 Remngtn Av -Copley 44321

(216) 622-8200 .. **Schwartz**, Bryan A '04 OfCnsl Calfee H&G LLP -800 Superior Av
-Ste 1400 -Cleveland 44114 **Fx:**241-0816

(216) 277-0283 .. **Schwartz**, Craig H '95 Charter One Bank -1215 Superior Av
-Cleveland 44114

(216) 664-4958 .. **Schwartz**, Diane S '79 Cleveland Mun Ct -1200 Ontario
-Cleveland 44113

(216) 696-6700 .. **Schwartz Downey & Co, LPA** -200 Pub Sq -Ste 2860 BP Twr
-Cleveland 44114 **Fx:**696-6772

(216) 397-0111 .. **Schwartz**, Fred P '78 -13967 Cedar Rd -Ste 200
-South Euclid 44118

(330) 744-5211 .. **Schwartz**, Glenn J '74 OfCnsl Roth BRS&L,LPA -100 Fed Plz E
-Ste 600 -Youngstown 44503 **Fx:**783-3184

(440) 395-3764 .. **Schwartz**, Gregory E '94 Progressive Ins Co
-6300 Wilson Mills Rd -#N72A -Mayfield Village 44143

(216) 363-4500 .. **Schwartz**, H Jeffrey '80 (Benesch FC&A LLP) -200 Pub Sq
-Ste 2300 -Cleveland 44114 **Fx:**363-4588

(614) 451-2191 .. **Schwartz**, Heidi S '99 Saga Comm -4401 Carriage Hill Ln
-Columbus 43220

(513) 721-4876 .. **Schwartz**, Howard M '75 (Sirkin P&S LLP) -105 W 4th
-920 4th & Race Twr -Cincinnati 45202 **Fx:**721-0876

(216) 696-6700 .. **Schwartz**, Jennifer E '91 (Schwartz D & Co,LPA) -200 Pub Sq
-Ste 2860 BP Twr -Cleveland 44114 **Fx:**696-6772
Schwartz, Joel L '83 -2388 E Main -#103 -Columbus 43209

(216) 696-7600 .. **Schwartz**, Kenneth D '99 (Duvin C&H) -1301 E 9th
-20th Fl Erievw Twr -Cleveland 44114 **Fx:**696-2038

(440) 564-7528 .. **Schwartz**, Lynn B '91 -15750 Auburn Rd -Newbury 44065

(513) 579-1414 .. **Schwartz Manes & Ruby** -441 Vine -Ste 2900 -Cincinnati 45202
Fx:579-1418

(216) 360-0440 .. **Schwartz**, Mark B '67 -30100 Chagrin Blvd -Ste 110
-Cleveland 44124

(513) 579-1414 .. **Schwartz**, Michael G '92 (Schwartz M&R) -441 Vine -Ste 2900
-Cincinnati 45202 **Fx:**579-1418

(513) 241-3447 .. **Schwartz**, Michael S '71 -906 Main -405 Schwartz Bldg
-Cincinnati 45202

(216) 696-6700 .. **Schwartz**, Niki Z '64 (Schwartz D & Co,LPA) -200 Pub Sq
-Ste 2860 BP Twr -Cleveland 44114 **Fx:**696-6772

(513) 420-8774 .. **Schwartz**, Peter J '77 Rogers Jewelry Co -1000 Central Av
-Middletown 45044

(937) 223-8177 .. **Schwartz**, Richard A '78 (Coolidge WW&L) -33 W 1st -Ste 600
-Dayton 45402 **Fx:**223-6705

(502) 485-9200 .. **Schwartz**, Richard A '83 (Kruger S&M) -6040 Dutchmans Ln
-#220 -Louisville, KY 40205

(330) 394-7445 .. **Schwartz**, Richard F '83 -Bx1150 -Warren 44482

(440) 323-1774 .. **Schwartz**, Richard K '85 Elyria Mun Ct -328 Broad -Elyria 44035

(513) 579-1414 .. **Schwartz**, Richard M '68 (Schwartz M&R) -441 Vine -Ste 2900
-Cincinnati 45202 **Fx:**579-1418

(330) 799-7711 .. **Schwartz**, Richard N '82 UAW Legal Srvcs
-1570 S Canfld-Niles Rd -Ste 101 -Youngstown 44515

(216) 696-1422 .. **Schwartz**, Robert Dov '97 %McCarthy LC&L Co,LPA
-101 Prospect Av W -1800 Mdlnd Bldg -Cleveland 44115
Fx:696-1210

(513) 361-0250 .. **Schwartz**, Robert H '93 SSA-OHA -312 Elm -Ste 2100
-Cincinnati 45202

(513) 241-3447 .. **Schwartz**, Robert L '64 -906 Main -405 Schwartz Bldg
-Cincinnati 45202

(614) 252-7906 .. **Schwartz**, Robert S '86 -268 N Parkvw Av -Bexley 43209

(513) 792-0606 .. **Schwartz**, Ronald E '91 -8041 Hosbrook -Ste 230
-Cincinnati 45236

(330) 452-2889 .. **Schwartz**, Steven '86 -202 6th NW -Canton 44702

(248) 626-7500 .. **Schwartz**, Steven H '01 (S Schwartz & Assoc,PLC)
-31600 W 13 Mile Rd -Ste 125 -Farmington Hills, MI 48334

(330) 971-8260 .. **Schwartz**, Steven J '73 Cuyahoga Falls Mun Ct -2310 2nd
-Cuyahoga Falls 44221

(513) 771-2444 .. **Schwartz**, Steven L '97 %Lutz CM&R Co,LPA -130 Tri-Cnty Pkwy
-Ste 208 -Cincinnati 45246 **Fx:**771-2447

(202) 783-8400 .. **Schwartz**, Victor E '74 (Shook H&B LLP) -600 14th NW -#800
-Washington, DC 20005 **Fx:**783-4211

(216) 787-3030 .. **Schwartz**, Ying-yu Janice '00 %Atty Gen -615 W Superior Av
-11th Fl -Cleveland 44113 **Fx:**787-3480

(973) 325-1500 .. **Schwartzman**, Arnold I '69 %Wolff & S,PC -One Boland Dr
-West Orange, NJ 07052 **Fx:**325-1501

(513) 533-3495 .. **Schwarz**, Douglas A '98 -3414 Edwards Rd -Ste 7
-Cincinnati 45208 **Fx:**533-3498

(216) 623-0000 .. **Schwarz**, Harold M III '04 %Javitch B&R -1300 E 9th -14th Fl
-Cleveland 44114 **Fx:**623-0190

(614) 833-6033 .. **Schwarz**, Jerrold W '90 -660 Hill Rd N -Bx482 -Pickerington 43147

(513) 632-4292 .. **Schwarz**, Paul E '92 US Bank -425 Walnut -CN-OH W7PT
-Cincinnati 45202

(216) 566-1600 .. **Schwarzwald & McNair** -1300 E 9th -Ste 616 -Cleveland 44114
Fx:566-1814

(216) 566-1600 .. **Schwarzwald**, Melvin S '62 (Schwarzwald & M) -1300 E 9th
-Ste 616 -Cleveland 44114 **Fx:**566-1814

(614) 645-8828 .. **Schwarzwalder**, Alan M '70 %Mayors Ofc -90 W Broad -Rm 232
-Columbus 43215

(216) 522-4058 .. **Schwegler**, Mary B '80 US Dept of HUD -1350 Euclid Av -Ste 500
-Cleveland 44115

(513) 412-8260 .. **Schwegman**, Jennifer L '01 Deloitte & Touche -250 E 5th
-Ste 1900 -Cincinnati 45202

(513) 489-0881 .. **Schweiger**, Scott M '83 -11085 Mntgmry Rd -Ste 202
-Cincinnati 45249

(216) 761-7387 .. **Schweighoefer**, David E '04 Cleveland Clinic Hlth Sys
-13951 Terrace Rd -Cleveland 44112

(419) 255-5900 .. **Schweikert**, James D '03 %MacMillan S&T,LLC -720 Water
-4th Fl -Toledo 43604 **Fx:**255-9639

(419) 255-5900 .. **Schweikert**, Staci E '02 %MacMillan S&T,LLC -720 Water -4th Fl
-Toledo 43604 **Fx:**255-9639

(202) 225-4158 .. **Schweiter**, Henry J '81 Comm on Armed Srvcs
-2120 Rayburn HOB -Washington, DC 20515

(937) 223-1130 .. **Schweller**, Donald G '57 OfCnsl Pickrel S&E -40 N Main
-2700 Kettering Twr -Dayton 45423 **Fx:**223-0339

(513) 977-8200 .. **Schweller**, Stephen G '84 (Dinsmore & S LLP) -255 E 5th
-Ste 1900 -Cincinnati 45202 **Fx:**977-8141

(419) 673-4176 .. **Schwemer**, David J '70 (Wetherill SM&S) -109 E Franklin
-Kenton 43326 **Fx:**673-8089

(419) 673-4176 .. **Schwemer**, John A '01 (Wetherill SM&S) -109 E Franklin
-Kenton 43326 **Fx:**673-8089

(419) 673-4176 .. **Schwemer**, Mark B '02 (Wetherill SM&S) -109 E Franklin
-Kenton 43326 **Fx:**673-8089

(330) 535-5711 .. **Schwemler**, John A '54 OfCnsl Brouse M -106 S Main
-500 First Natl Twr -Akron 44308 **Fx:**253-8601

(614) 488-5008 .. **Schwenker**, Charles V '40 -2631 Berwyn Rd -Columbus 43221

(419) 787-6360 .. **Schwenning**, Lynn E '98 Alticor Inc -7575 Fulton -Ada, MI 49355

(614) 466-8600 .. **Schwepe**, Alan P '81 Atty Gen -30 E Broad -Columbus 43215
Fx:466-6090

(216) 241-2880 .. **Schwieg**, Frederic P '85 Cowden HN&L -50 Pub Sq -Ste 1414
-Cleveland 44113 **Fx:**241-2881

(513) 381-5700 .. **Schwierling**, John T '57 Ritter & R,LLC -105 E 4th -Ste 1200
-Cincinnati 45202 **Fx:**381-0014

(419) 241-1200 ..**Schwieterman**, Nicole K '99 Cooper & W,LPA -900 Adams -Toledo 43624 **Fx**:242-5675

(513) 455-7600 ..**Schworer**, Philip J '86 Greenebaum D&M PLLC -255 E 5th -2800 Chemed Ctr -Cincinnati 45202 **Fx**:455-8500

(216) 443-8579 ..**Schwotzer**, Tracy R '02 Cuyahoga Cnty Ct Cmmn Pleas -1200 Ontario -Justice Ctr 11th Fl -Cleveland 44113

(440) 248-7906 ..**Scialdone**, Frank H '02 %Mazanec R&R Co,LPA -34305 Solon Rd -Ste 100 -Cleveland 44139 **Fx**:248-8861

(440) 835-8200 ..**Sciangula**, Francis A '63 (Sciangula & D) -24500 Ctr Ridge Rd -Ste 175 -Westlake 44145

(419) 530-1472 ..**Sciarini**, James M '81 Univ of Toledo -2801 W Bancroft -Toledo 43606

(814) 464-9610 ..**Scibetta**, Kathleen A '92 Hon S McLaughlin -617 State -Erie, PA 16501

(330) 729-9777 ..**Sciortino**, Michael '03 %Engler & Assoc -860 Boardman-Canfld Rd -Ste 204 -Boardman 44512 **Fx**:758-9585

(330) 468-4096 ..**Sciortino**, Steven D '90 -8536 Crow Dr -Ste 215 -Macedonia 44056

(972) 960-7693 ..**Scislowski**, Richard J '96 Intl Risk Mgmt Inst,Inc -12222 Merit Dr -Ste 1450 -Dallas, TX 75251 **Fx**:371-5120

(513) 651-6800 ..**Scoggins**, Samuel M '75 (Frost BT LLC) -201 E 5th -2200 PNC Ctr -Cincinnati 45202 **Fx**:651-6981

(216) 321-3562 ..**Scola**, Ralph J '69 -2628 Courtland Blvd -Cleveland 44118 **Fx**:371-2093

(614) 221-7161 ..**Scoliere**, Michael E '86 (Scoliere & Assoc,Inc) -57 E Main -Ste 501 -Columbus 43215

               Scollard, Rosemary E '88 -(Address Unavailable)

(614) 224-7844 ..**Scopetti**, Nina P '80 -155 W Main -Ste 100B -Columbus 43215

(614) 792-5555 ..**Scotney**, Cheryl S '98 Standley Law Grp LLP -495 Metro Pl S -Ste 210 -Dublin 43017 **Fx**:792-5536

(513) 851-0600 ..**Scott**, Alexis Z '86 Nationwide Ins Co -11915 Kemper Sprngs Dr -Cincinnati 45240

(440) 576-3662 ..**Scott**, Angela M '99 Ashtabula Cnty Pros -25 W Jffrsn -Jefferson 44047

(740) 351-0981 ..**Scott**, Christine M '00 -842 Gallia -Portsmouth 45662

(614) 221-4400 ..**Scott**, Craig P '89 Volkema TMBS&M,LPA -140 E Town -Ste 1100 -Columbus 43215 **Fx**:221-6010

               Scott, Curtis Jr. '79 -6724 Larch -Oakwood Village 44146

(800) 998-9454 ..**Scott**, David A '88 Cmmnty Lgl Aid Srvcs,Inc -265 S Main -3rd Fl -Akron 44308 **Fx**:(330) 535-0728

(614) 229-4455 ..**Scott**, David M '97 %Luper N&L,LPA -50 W Broad -1200 LeVeque Twr -Columbus 43215 **Fx**:464-2425

(713) 552-1234 ..**Scott**, David M '02 %Zimmerman AMS&W,PC -3040 Post Oak Rd -Ste 1300 -Houston, TX 77056

(937) 223-1201 ..**Scott**, Donald K '86 (Altick & C Co,LPA) -1 S Main -1700 One Dayton Ctr -Dayton 45402 **Fx**:223-5100

(740) 927-9195 ..**Scott**, Elaine R '84 -5513 Headleys Mill Rd SW -Pataskala 43062

(614) 466-4034 ..**Scott**, Elizabeth A '91 Ofc Budget & Mngmnt -30 E Broad -Columbus 43215 **Fx**:466-3813

(937) 225-5757 ..**Scott**, Elizabeth Chapin '03 Montgomery Cnty Pros -301 W 3rd -Bx972 -Dayton 45422 **Fx**:225-3470

(330) 452-9255 ..**Scott**, Frederic R '92 -1428 Market Av N -Canton 44714

(614) 764-0681 ..**Scott**, Geoffrey P '97 %Blaugrund H&M,Inc -5455 Rings Rd -Ste 500 -Dublin 43017 **Fx**:764-0774

(614) 222-8686 ..**Scott**, Gregory B '76 (Scott S&W LLP) -50 W Broad -2500 LeVeque Twr -Columbus 43215 **Fx**:222-8688

(216) 781-2600 ..**Scott**, Gregory S '96 (Lowe EW&M Co,LPA) -1660 W 2nd -610 Skylight Ofc Twr -Cleveland 44113 **Fx**:781-2610

(937) 225-4829 ..**Scott**, Gregory T '84 Montgomery Cnty Juv Ct -303 W 2nd -Rm 1139 -Bx972 -Dayton 45422 **Fx**:496-7270

(216) 623-0150 ..**Scott**, James C '91 (Roetzel & A,LPA) -1375 E 9th -One Cleve Ctr 9th Fl -Cleveland 44114 **Fx**:623-0134

(740) 432-6322 ..**Scott**, James R '62 (Tribbie SP&P) -139 Ct Hse Sq -Bx640 -Cambridge 43725 **Fx**:439-1795

(513) 564-0088 ..**Scott**, James R '99 (Bleile & S) -114 E 8th -Cincinnati 45202

               Scott, James T '02 -2758 Clublane Dr -Columbus 43219

(513) 621-6464 ..**Scott**, Jamie D '87 (Graydon H&R LLP) -511 Walnut -1900 Fifth Third Ctr -Cincinnati 45202 **Fx**:651-3836

(513) 421-7500 ..**Scott**, John C '85 (Faulkner & T,LLP) -5 W 4th -2200 4th & Vine Twr -Cincinnati 45202

(937) 496-7265 ..**Scott**, John M Jr. '95 Montgomery Cnty Pros -303 W 2nd -Rm 113 -Dayton 45402

(419) 283-5444 ..**Scott**, John N '84 -3651 Chesterton Dr -Toledo 43615

(216) 687-1311 ..**Scott**, John R '86 (Reminger & R) -101 Prospect Av W -1400 Mdlnd Bldg -Cleveland 44115 **Fx**:687-1841

(614) 221-9790 ..**Scott**, Joseph E '93 (J Scott Co,LPA) -35 E Lvngstn Av -Columbus 43215 **Fx**:228-6680

(216) 664-3727 ..**Scott**, Joseph F '85 Dept of Law -601 Lakeside Av -Rm 106 City Hall -Cleveland 44114 **Fx**:664-2663

               Scott, Karla D '87 -(Address Unavailable)

(614) 995-2170 ..**Scott**, Keith A '97 OH Sec of State -180 E Broad -Columbus 43215 **Fx**:466-5409

(859) 525-0500 ..**Scott**, Kenneth W '81 -7415 Burlngtn Pike -Florence, KY 41042 **Fx**:525-0560

               Scott, Lori M '03 -(Address Unavailable)

               Scott, Michael H '04 -(Address Unavailable)

(216) 781-0083 ..**Scott**, Michael J '78 OM Grp,Inc -3800 Trmnl Twr -Cleveland 44113

(614) 464-0011 ..**Scott**, Paul A '57 F Macke Co LPA -400 S 5th -Ste 303 -Columbus 43215

(614) 221-1578 ..**Scott**, Paul A Jr. '92 (P Scott Co,LPA) -536 S High -Columbus 43215

(202) 712-0444 ..**Scott**, Paul M '72 US Agncy for Intl Dvlpmnt -1300 Penn Av NW -Washington, DC 20523

(614) 469-1400 ..**Scott**, Paul O '74 (Clark PR&S Co,LPA) -471 E Broad -Ste 1400 -Columbus 43215 **Fx**:469-0900

(614) 761-9930 ..**Scott**, Peggy A '91 (Purcell & S Co,LPA) -6035 Mem'l Dr -Dublin 43017

(614) 644-1773 ..**Scott**, Richard A '88 Dept Admin Srvcs -30 E Broad -Columbus 43215

(419) 241-5454 ..**Scott**, Robert B '01 -1700 Canton Av -Ste 2 -Toledo 43624

(419) 241-2122 ..**Scott**, Robert M '84 (Williams JLG&S Co,LPA) -416 N Erie -Ste 500 -Toledo 43624 **Fx**:245-3849

(419) 213-4700 ..**Scott**, Rose M '00 %Lucas Cnty Pros -Adams & Erie -Lucas Cnty Cthse -Toledo 43624

(614) 463-1299 ..**Scott**, Ryan M '97 -115 W Main -Ste 400 -Columbus 43215

(614) 222-8686 ..**Scott Scriven & Wahoff LLP** -50 W Broad -2500 LeVeque Twr -Columbus 43215 **Fx**:222-8688

(202) 408-4231 ..**Scott**, Steven J '97 %Finnegan HFG&D -1300 I NW -Washington, DC 20005

(216) 696-3232 ..**Scott**, Stuart E '95 (Spangenberg S&L,LLP) -1900 E 9th -2400 Natl City Ctr -Cleveland 44114 **Fx**:696-3924

(614) 471-7197 ..**Scott**, Theodore Jr. '84 (T Scott Jr Co,LPA) -1465 E Broad -Columbus 43205

(937) 225-4892 ..**Scott**, Thomas B '02 Montgomery Cnty Pros -303 W 2nd -Rm 113 -Dayton 45402

(914) 701-8000 ..**Scott**, Thomas G Sr. '90 Atlas Air,Inc -2000 Wstchstr Av -Purchase, NY 10577

(216) 664-4828 ..**Scott**, W Mona '03 Prosecutor -1200 Ontario Av -8th Fl Justice Ctr -Cleveland 44113 **Fx**:664-4399

(419) 473-1300 ..**Scouten**, John D '71 -4127 Monroe -Toledo 43606

(513) 732-7313 ..**Scovanner**, Thomas W '86 Clermont Cnty Pros -123 N 3rd -Batavia 45103

               Scovill, Kim R '81 -1 Radburn Ln -Newark, DE 19711

(614) 462-3555 ..**Scozzie**, Nicole M '01 Franklin Cnty Pros -373 S High -Columbus 43215

(513) 583-4200 ..**Scranton**, Derek W '02 %Schroeder MB&P -11935 Mason Rd -Ste 110 -Cincinnati 45249

(419) 334-9723 ..**Scranton**, Nancy M '73 -204 Justice -Fremont 43420

(216) 623-0150 ..**Screen**, Donald P '90 OfCnsl Roetzel & A,LPA -1375 E 9th -One Cleve Ctr 9th Fl -Cleveland 44114 **Fx**:623-0134

(216) 443-9000 ..**Screen**, Patricia A '85 (Porter WM&A LLP) -925 Euclid Av -Ste 1700 -Cleveland 44115 **Fx**:443-9011

(330) 836-5500 ..**Scribner**, Theodore '03 %Aronson & Assoc -3085 W Market -Ste 130 -Akron 44333

(703) 684-7550 ..**Scrimenti**, Belinda J '81 (Pattishall MNH&G) -1700 Diagnl Rd -Ste 550 -Alexandria, VA 22314

(614) 222-8686 ..**Scriven**, Donald C '74 (Scott S&W LLP) -50 W Broad -2500 LeVeque Twr -Columbus 43215 **Fx**:222-8688

(513) 584-5042 ..**Scrivens**, Kathleen M '88 Univ of Cincinnati Med Ctr -Ofc of Risk Mgmt -Bx670785 -Cincinnati 45267

(216) 781-5661 ..**Scrivens**, Scott L '81 (Falk & S) -2628 Detroit Av -Cleveland 44113

(513) 621-4886 ..**Scrofano**, Salvatore G '74 -Bx62860 -Cincinnati 45262 **Fx**:733-0852

(513) 771-7070 ..**Scroggins**, Robert C '96 Clayton L Scroggins Assoc -200 Northland Blvd -Cincinnati 45246

(614) 464-6400 ..**Scrutton**, Suzanne J '90 (Vorys SS&P LLP) -52 E Gay -Bx1008 -Columbus 43216 **Fx**:464-6350

(937) 298-0008 ..**Scudder & Esler Co,LPA** -2912 Springboro W -Ste 105 -Dayton 45439

               Scudder, Michael Y Jr. '01 -1465 Fireside Trl -Broadview Heights 44147

(937) 298-0008 ..**Scudder**, Steven C '90 (Scudder & E Co,LPA) -2912 Springboro W -Ste 105 -Dayton 45439

(614) 466-3998 ..**Scull**, John M '75 Unemploymnt Comp Commssn -145 S Front -Bx182299 -Columbus 43218

(216) 932-4724 ..**Scully**, Daniel G '94 -2816 Edgehill Rd -Cleveland Heights 44118

(202) 861-1698 ..**Scully**, Elizabeth A '97 %Baker & H LLP -1050 Conn Av NW -Ste 1100 -Washington, DC 20036

(216) 621-2110 ..**Scully**, William F Jr. '75 (Williams S&S Co,LPA) -55 Pub Sq -Ste 1850 -Cleveland 44113 **Fx**:621-2164

(316) 831-4201 ..**Scurfield**, Robert M '76 Cessna Aircraft -Bx7704 -Wichita, KS 67277

(740) 852-4133 ..**Scurry**, Fred L '72 -229 Toland -London 43140

(740) 282-1900 ..**Scurti**, Adam E '66 (King HS&J) -200 Sinclair Bldg -Bx249 -Steubenville 43952 **Fx**:282-5397

(614) 480-4393 ..**Scurti-Swain**, Tiffany '01 Huntington National Bank -41 S High -5th Fl -Columbus 43215

               Sczesny, Daniel J '03 -(Address Unavailable)

(216) 687-1311 ..**Seacrist**, Susan M '92 (Reminger & R) -101 Prospect Av W -1400 Mdlnd Bldg -Cleveland 44115 **Fx**:687-1841

(937) 324-5736 ..**Seall**, Elizabeth A '00 Home City Fed Svngs Bank -2454 N Limestone -Springfield 45503

(937) 434-7218 ..**Seall**, William H '68 RG Prop,Inc -8163 Old Yankee Rd -Ste B -Dayton 45458

               Seals, Thomas C '89 -501 Cotton Crk Dr -#803 -Gulf Shores, AL 36542

(216) 696-1080 ..**Seaman**, Dennis M '67 (D Seaman & Assoc Co,LPA) -614 Superior Av W -Ste 1600 Rckfllr Bldg -Cleveland 44113

(937) 748-2409 ..**Seaman**, Edward G '67 -28 Pinehurst Pl -Springboro 45066

(704) 594-8300 ..**Seaman**, Kenneth A '74 -8501 IBM Dr -Dept. QPZ/M590 -Charlotte, NC 28262

(614) 365-2700 ..**Seamon**, Aaron A '99 %Squire S&D LLP -41 S High -1300 Huntngtn Ctr -Columbus 43215 **Fx**:365-2499

(440) 247-8200 ..**Searby**, Edmund W '97 Scott + S -33 River -Chagrin Falls 44022

(419) 562-9856 ..**Sears**, John D Jr. '50 (Spurlock SPG&M,PLL) -120 N Lane -Bucyrus 44820 **Fx**:562-9883

(513) 241-5670 ..**Sears**, Julia A '86 Croswell & A Co,LPA -1208 Sycamore -Cincinnati 45210

(513) 946-3082 ..**Sears**, Pamela J '84 Hamilton Cnty Pros -230 E 9th -Cincinnati 45202 **Fx**:946-3017

(216) 579-1535 ..**Sears**, Ronald A '75 -55 Pub Sq -2240 -Cleveland 44113

(515) 288-3667 ..**Sease**, Edmund J '69 (Zarley MTV&S) -801 Grand Av -Ste 3200 -Des Moines, IA 50309

(216) 621-0150 ..**Seasly**, Steven E '99 %Hahn L&P LLP -3300 BP Twr/200 Pub Sq -Ste 3300 -Cleveland 44113 **Fx**:241-2824

(513) 361-1200 ..**Seaton**, Kim D '97 %Squire S&D LLP -312 Walnut -Ste 3500 -Cincinnati 45202 **Fx**:361-1201

(216) 491-0161 ..**Seballos**, Sandra K '86 -3340 Glencarin Rd -Shaker Heights 44122

(937) 222-2500 ..**Sebaly**, Jon M '65 (Sebaly S&D) -1900 Kettering Twr -Dayton 45423 **Fx**:222-6554

(937) 222-2500 ..**Sebaly Shillito & Dyer** -1900 Kettering Twr -Dayton 45423 **Fx**:222-6554

(513) 579-6400 .. **Sebastian**, Steven W '00 %Keating M&K PLL -1 E 4th
-1400 Provident Twr -Cincinnati 45202 Fx:579-6457
(330) 747-4404 .. **Sebastiano**, Patrick A '82 OfCnsl Newman O&K,LPA
-11 Fed Plz Central -Ste 1200 -Youngstown 44503 Fx:747-6056
(216) 875-2767 .. **Sebaugh**, Beth A '80 %Bonezzi SM&P Co LPA -526 Superior Av
-Ste 1400 -Cleveland 44114 Fx:875-1570
Sebesy, Douglas A '04 -(Address Unavailable)
(216) 586-3939 .. **Sebold**, Edward J '94 (Jones D) -901 Lakeside Av
-Cleveland 44114 Fx:579-0212
(804) 279-4815 .. **Sebold**, Robert E '90 Cnsl Dept of Defense/DLA -8000 Jeff Davis
Hwy -Ofc of Cnsl -Richmond, VA 23297 Fx:279-4137
(330) 244-1174 .. **Sebolt**, Joseph A '92 Sand & S -4940 Munson NW -Ste 1100
-Canton 44718
(614) 365-4100 .. **Sechler**, Joel E '03 %Carpenter & L LLP -280 N High
-Ste 1300 280 Plz -Columbus 43215 Fx:365-9145
(614) 889-0234 .. **Sechler**, Kenneth R '74 -425 Metro Pl N -Ste 640 -Dublin 43017
(419) 254-3121 .. **Sechrist**, Rebecca C '86 Bunda S&D,PLL -One SeaGate -Ste 650
-Toledo 43604 Fx:241-4697
(614) 645-7483 .. **Seckerson**, Cynthia L '95 City Pros -375 S High -7th Fl -Columbus
43215
(419) 259-6376 .. **Secor**, Thomas O '77 US Atty -4 Seagate -Ste 308 -Toledo 43604
Fx:259-6360
(513) 933-1278 .. **Secrest**, Elizabeth A '94 Warren Cnty CSEA -500 Justice Dr
-Lebanon 45036
(614) 224-1222 .. **Secrest**, Jonathan R '02 %Maguire & S,LLP -250 Civic Ctr Dr
-Ste 200 -Columbus 43215 Fx:224-1236
(513) 419-3248 .. **Secrest**, Thomas A '94 First Grp Amer -705 Central Av -Ste 500
-Cincinnati 45202
(216) 444-3126 .. **Secrist**, Robert V Jr. '72 Cleveland Clinic Fndtn -9500 Euclid Av
-Cleveland 44195
(330) 296-3599 .. **Sed**, David A '77 -269 W Main -Bx672 -Ravenna 44266
(216) 464-6744 .. **Seders**, Julianne M '97 Galt Enterprises Inc -28601 Chagrin Blvd
-Ste #400 -Woodmere 44122
(740) 983-3336 .. **Sedlak**, Alan F '75 -35 E Main -Ashville 43103
(330) 825-6089 .. **Sedmack**, Jane P '78 -4620 Roop Av -Norton 44203
(440) 238-3209 .. **Sedory**, Allen R '61 -17178 Woodleaf Rd -Strongsville 44136
(614) 728-2759 .. **See**, Charles W '91 OH Dept of Edu -25 S Front -7th Fl
-Columbus 43215
(419) 625-0536 .. **See**, Daniel E '81 UAW Legal Srvcs -3116 Bardshar Rd
-Sandusky 44870
(614) 365-2700 .. **See**, P Brian '00 %Squire S&D LLP -41 S High -1300 Huntngtn Ctr
-Columbus 43215 Fx:365-2499
(614) 365-4100 .. **See**, Shana Y '04 %Carpenter & L LLP -280 N High
-Ste 1300 280 Plz -Columbus 43215 Fx:365-9145
(937) 224-0076 .. **Seeberger**, Sheryl S '92 Myers & F Co,LPA -18 W 1st -Ste 200
-Dayton 45402
(330) 456-8341 .. **Seeberger**, Terrence L '79 (Black MS&A,LPA) -220 Market Av S
-Ste 1000 -Canton 44702 Fx:456-5756
(216) 642-0323 .. **Seed**, David H '96 %Britton SP&K Co,LPA -4700 Rockside Rd
-Ste 540 Summit One -Cleveland 44131 Fx:642-0747
(740) 349-6169 .. **Seeds**, Melinda G '94 Licking Cnty Pros -20 S 2nd -4th Fl
-Newark 43055
(513) 241-9400 .. **Seel**, Thomas R '89 Legal Aid -10 Jrnl Sq -Hamilton 45011
(216) 566-8200 .. **Seeley**, Glenn J '55 %Seeley S&E Co LPA -600 Superior Av E
-800 Bank One Ctr -Cleveland 44114 Fx:566-0213
(216) 566-8200 .. **Seeley**, Gregory D '72 (Seeley S&E Co LPA) -600 Superior Av E
-800 Bank One Ctr -Cleveland 44114 Fx:566-0213
(216) 566-8200 .. **Seeley**, Matthew K '97 %Seeley S&E Co LPA -600 Superior Av E
-800 Bank One Ctr -Cleveland 44114 Fx:566-0213
(740) 687-3339 .. **Seeley**, Robert H '47 -123 S Broad -Ste 310 -Lancaster 43130
(740) 687-3339 .. **Seeley**, Robert L '53 -123 S Broad -Ste 310 -Lancaster 43130
(216) 566-8200 .. **Seeley Savidge & Ebert Co LPA** -600 Superior Av E
-800 Bank One Ctr -Cleveland 44114 Fx:566-0213
(216) 696-7600 .. **Seeley**, Stephanie L '01 %Duvin C&H -1301 E 9th
-20th Fl Erievw Twr -Cleveland 44114 Fx:696-2038
(216) 583-2791 .. **Seeley**, William B '04 Ernst & Young LLP -925 Euclid Av -Ste 1300
-Cleveland 44115
(860) 747-7093 .. **Seeley**, William S '84 Ge Transportation Systems
-41 Woodford Av -Plainville, CT 06062
(440) 333-1000 .. **Seelie**, John F '68 (J Sellie Co,LPA) -19111 Detroit Av -Ste 205
-Rocky River 44116
(330) 688-8821 .. **Seeling**, Paul H '83 -44 Monroe Falls Av -Munroe Falls 44262
(330) 758-8369 .. **Seely**, Donald R '65 -8166 Market -Ste N -Youngstown 44512
(216) 416-3281 .. **Seewald**, Amanda M '95 Cnsl Forest City Enterprise -50 Pub Sq
-Ste 1160 -Cleveland 44113
(216) 781-8288 .. **Seewald**, Jerome Gary '71 (Henkin & S) -310 W Lakeside Av
-Ste 550 -Cleveland 44113 Fx:781-1273
(614) 365-2700 .. **Sefcovic**, Paul F '71 (Squire S&D LLP) -41 S High
-1300 Huntngtn Ctr -Columbus 43215 Fx:365-2499
(937) 222-2500 .. **Sefton**, Warren J '02 %Sebaly S&D -1900 Kettering Twr
-Dayton 45423 Fx:222-6554
(513) 564-9222 .. **Segal**, Andrew L '98 -120 E 4th -Ste 1040 -Cincinnati 45202
(614) 224-7141 .. **Segal**, David M '76 %Lancaster Colony Corp -37 W Broad
-Ste 500 -Columbus 43215
(216) 291-5775 .. **Segebarth**, Kim T '73 -40 Severance Cir
-Cleveland Heights 44118
(330) 434-1166 .. **Segedy**, Alan G '72 -105 E Market -Ste 204 -Akron 44308
(614) 785-6461 .. **Segel**, Benjamin B '79 -445 Hutchnsn Av -Ste 800
-Columbus 43235
(614) 227-2000 .. **Segelken**, Edward M '84 (Porter WM&A LLP) -41 S High
-Columbus 43215 Fx:227-2100
(216) 621-0200 .. **Seger**, Paula Friedman '79 (Baker & H LLP) -1900 E 9th -Ste 3200
-Cleveland 44114 Fx:696-0740
(216) 621-0200 .. **Seger**, Thomas M '72 (Baker & H LLP) -1900 E 9th -Ste 3200
-Cleveland 44114 Fx:696-0740
(614) 221-8868 .. **Segerman**, Douglas J '95 %McFadden W&S -175 S 3rd -Ste 210
-Columbus 43215 Fx:221-3985
(937) 439-0386 .. **Segreti**, A Mark Jr. '70 -1405 Streamside Dr -Dayton 45459
Segroves, Garth R '02 -1113 Wilson Av -Tullahoma, TN 37388
(614) 242-4242 .. **Seguin**, James P '84 OfCnsl Decker VSL&V Co LPA -620 E Broad
-Columbus 43215 Fx:242-4243
(216) 696-3311 .. **Segulin**, Mary R '04 %Kahn K -1301 E 9th -2600 Erievw Twr
-Cleveland 44114 Fx:623-4912

(513) 946-3000 .. **Seibel**, Adam F '00 Hamilton Cnty Pros -230 E 9th
-Cincinnati 45202 Fx:946-3017
(859) 926-1375 .. **Seibel**, John N '89 Corona Rsrces, LLC -176 Barnwood Dr -A
-Edgewood, KY 41017
(513) 381-6600 .. **Seibel**, Kenneth F '69 (Jacobs KS&M) -1014 Vine -Ste 2300
-Cincinnati 45202
(513) 381-6600 .. **Seibel**, Paul K '04 %Jacobs KS&M -1014 Vine -Ste 2300
-Cincinnati 45202
(419) 784-0002 .. **Seibel**, Peter R '71 -621 W 2nd -Defiance 43512
(513) 721-1975 .. **Seibel**, Ronald E '04 %Freking & B -215 E 9th -5th Fl
-Cincinnati 45202 Fx:651-2570
(513) 381-6600 .. **Seibel**, Scott K '98 Jacobs KS&M -1014 Vine -Ste 2300
-Cincinnati 45202
(330) 963-1015 .. **Seibert**, Darrel L II '91 %Seibert Entrprs Ltd -2241 Pinnacle Pkwy
-Ste B -Twinsburg 44087
(216) 696-4700 .. **Seibert**, Henry E IV '68 (Spieth BM&N Co,LPA) -925 Euclid Av
-2000 Huntngtn Bldg -Cleveland 44115 Fx:696-2706
(216) 822-3504 .. **Seibert**, Mark E '97 SBC Comm,Inc -45 Erievw Plz -950
-Cleveland 44114
(216) 696-1422 .. **Seich**, John S '82 (McCarthy LC&L Co,LPA) -101 Prospect Av W
-1800 Mdlnd Bldg -Cleveland 44115 Fx:696-1210
Seide, Apryl A '01 -(Address Unavailable)
(614) 451-0694 .. **Seidel**, Edward F Jr. '74 -4660 Stonehaven Dr -Columbus 43220
(703) 588-6787 .. **Seidel**, Michael G '94 US Army JAG -1777 N Kent
-Arlington, VA 22209
(606) 441-2700 .. **Seidenfaden**, Jann '77 (Bertelsman KS) -122 N Ft Thomas Av
-Fort Thomas, KY 41075
(614) 716-1638 .. **Seidensticker**, John W '90 SrCnsl Amer Elec Pwr Co
-1 Riverside Plz -Columbus 43215
(317) 916-1300 .. **Seidler**, Robert F '01 %Ogletree DNS&S,PC -One Indna Sq
-Ste 2300 -Indianapolis, IN 46204 Fx:916-9076
(614) 469-3939 .. **Seidt**, Andrea L '98 %Jones D -325 John H McConnell Blvd
-Ste 600 -Bx165017 -Columbus 43216 Fx:461-4198
(937) 229-3801 .. **Seielstad**, Andrea M '98 Univ of Dayton Schl of Law
-300 Cllg Park -Dayton 45469
(740) 947-7277 .. **Seif**, D Dale Jr. '03 (Seif & S LLC) -110 E Emmitt Av
-Waverly 45690 Fx:947-1815
(740) 947-7232 .. **Seif**, David D '74 -110 E Emmitt -Waverly 45690
(203) 961-7400 .. **Seifert**, Brit K '95 Paul HJ&W -1055 Washington Blvd -9th Fl
-Stamford, CT 06901
(216) 222-3584 .. **Seifert**, Jason L '99 National City Bank -1900 E 9th
-3rd Fl LOC 01-2030 -Cleveland 44114
(614) 461-4455 .. **Seifert**, Kristin L '04 %Cloppert LS&W -225 E Broad
-Columbus 43215 Fx:461-0072
(440) 255-8000 .. **Seifert**, Patricia L '89 Cleveland Cnstrctn,Inc -8620 Tyler Blvd
-Mentor 44060
(216) 431-4500 .. **Seifert**, Patricia L '99 Cuyahoga Cnty Pros -3955 Euclid Av
-Jane Edna Hunter Bldg -Cleveland 44115 Fx:431-4113
(859) 431-3200 .. **Seifried**, Kent W '77 (Poston S&S) -2039 Dixie Hwy
-Fort Mitchell, KY 41011
(614) 258-4401 .. **Seigerst**, Edward G '93 Professionals Guild of Ohio -Bx7139
-Columbus 43205
(513) 961-1672 .. **Seiler**, Lewis H '79 -2056 Eastern Av -Cincinnati 45202
(302) 282-3019 .. **Seiler**, Thomas G '98 Bk 1 Mgmt Corp -201 N Walnut
-10th Fl-DEI-1057 -Wilmington, DE 19801
(440) 546-0483 .. **Seink**, Daniel P '92 DP Seink Co,Ltd -8180 Brecksvll Rd
-Brecksville 44141 Fx:526-4548
(614) 460-4648 .. **Seiple**, Stephen B '81 Columbia Gas of OH,Inc -200 Civic Ctr Dr
-Bx117 -Columbus 43216
(216) 781-0150 .. **Seitz**, Brian J '03 %Turoff & T -629 Euclid Av -Ste 727
-Cleveland 44114 Fx:781-0416
(216) 514-9999 .. **Seitz**, Charles R '92 %Cornrich & C Co,LPA -2000 Auburn Dr
-Ste 315 -Cleveland 44122 Fx:514-8500
(859) 594-3013 .. **Seitz**, Julie Lyn '95 Catholic Hlth Initiatives -3900 Olympic Blvd
-Ste 400 -Erlanger, KY 41018
(513) 381-2838 .. **Seitz**, William J III '78 (Taft S&H LLP) -425 Walnut -Ste 1800
-Cincinnati 45202 Fx:381-0205
(419) 241-3213 .. **Seitzinger**, Mark P '89 %Ritter RM&J -405 Mad Av -Ste 1850
-Toledo 43604 Fx:241-4925
(301) 816-7225 .. **Seiver**, Dinah '93 Kaiser Permanente -2101 E Jffrsn
-Rockville, MD 20852
(330) 799-7711 .. **Sekerak**, Diane M '95 UAW Legal Srvcs -1570 S Canfld-Niles Rd
-Ste 101 -Youngstown 44515
(330) 490-5038 .. **Sekula**, John W '73 Diebold,Inc -5995 Mayfair Rd -Bx3077
-North Canton 44720
(330) 452-4005 .. **Sekula**, Mary Lou '96 -220 Market Av S -610 United Bk Plz
-Canton 44702
(513) 352-6663 .. **Selak**, Robert A '79 (Thompson H LLP) -312 Walnut -14th Fl
-Cincinnati 45202 Fx:241-4771
(330) 453-7104 .. **Selby**, Joan P '78 Rubin & S -1428 Market N -Canton 44714
(440) 816-0600 .. **Selby**, Matthew J '03 %Largent BP&J Co,LPA -1 Berea Cmmns
-Ste 216 -Berea 44017 Fx:816-0604
(440) 352-3391 .. **Selby**, Richard N '92 %Dworken & B Co,LPA -60 S Park Pl
-Painesville 44077 Fx:352-3469
(614) 469-3939 .. **Selden**, Brian G '95 (Jones D) -325 John H McConnell Blvd
-Ste 600 -Bx165017 -Columbus 43216 Fx:461-4198
(513) 421-4020 .. **Selden**, Heidi A '96 %Cohen TK&S,LLC -250 E 5th -Ste 1200
-Cincinnati 45202 Fx:241-4490
(330) 453-7377 .. **Selegean-Dostal**, Sue E '96 -116 Cleveland Av NW -Ste 309
-Canton 44702
(216) 931-6000 .. **Seleman**, Fred N '97 (Ulmer & B LLP) -1300 E 9th
-Ste 900 Penton Media Bldg -Cleveland 44114 Fx:931-6001
(513) 241-4722 .. **Self**, Janet A '88 (Montgomery R&J,LPA) -36 E 7th -Ste 2100
-Cincinnati 45202 Fx:241-8775
Selhorst, Angela J '96 -429 Kemper Av -Lancaster 43130
(614) 224-2428 .. **Seliavski**, Lioubov I '03 %Shihab & Assoc -65 E State -Ste 1550
-Columbus 43215 Fx:224-5080
(937) 454-1038 .. **Seligman**, William S '93 -4227 Linchmere Dr -Dayton 45415
(419) 248-2600 .. **Selis**, Tracy B '01 %Rohrbachers LC&T Co,LPA -405 Mad Av
-8th Fl -Toledo 43604 Fx:248-2614
(440) 248-7906 .. **Selker**, Eugene I '53 OfCnsl Mazanec R&R Co,LPA
-34305 Solon Rd -Ste 100 -Cleveland 44139 Fx:248-8861
(937) 339-1500 .. **Sell**, Charles H II '73 (Shipman D&L) -215 W Water -Bx310
-Troy 45373 Fx:339-1519

(330) 645-0431 .. **Sell**, Linda G '94 -500 Portage Lks Dr -Akron 44319

(937) 492-9191   **Sell**, Timothy S '83 Cnsl T Sell & Co,LPA -108 E Poplar
-Sidney 45365 **Fx:**492-6957

(740) 373-5455 .. **Sellers**, Abraham '97 (Theisen B,LPA) -424 2nd -Bx739
-Marietta 45750 **Fx:**373-4409

(513) 946-4280 .. **Sellers**, David L '83 Hamilton Cnty Engineer -138 E Court
-Rm 700 -Cincinnati 45202

  Sellers, Gary E '90 -(Address Unavailable)

(513) 946-3417 .. **Sellers**, John P III '82 1st Dist Ct of Appls -230 E 9th -12th Fl
-Cincinnati 45202 **Fx:**946-3412

(740) 833-2690 .. **Sellers**, Leah J '00 %Delaware Cnty Pros -140 N Sandusky -3rd Fl
-Delaware 43015

(513) 721-1504 .. **Sellins**, Warren John '76 Droder & M Co,LPA -125 W Cntrl Pkwy
-Cincinnati 45202 **Fx:**721-0310

(304) 723-1400 .. **Sellitti**, James J '80 (Sellitti N&M) -3125 Penn Av -Ste 7 -Bx2540
-Weirton, WV 26062

(614) 463-1986 .. **Sellman**, Jerry B '75 -88 E Broad -Ste 220 -Columbus 43215

(740) 472-1647 .. **Selmon**, Julie R '99 %Smith & C -316 S Main -Bx599
-Woodsfield 43793

(425) 451-3104 .. **Selover**, L Ann '78 -11000 NE 10th -Ste 221 -Bellevue, WA 98004

(610) 372-4761 .. **Seltzer**, Alan M '02 (Ryan RO&S) -1100 Berkshire Blvd -Ste 301
-Reading, PA 19610

(614) 227-2000 .. **Seltzer**, Martin S '77 (Porter WM&A LLP) -41 S High
-Columbus 43215 **Fx:**227-2100

(937) 652-1555 .. **Selvaggio**, Nicola A '91 Champaign Cnty Pros -200 N Main
-Urbana 43078

(216) 696-9100 .. **Selzer**, Lynn K '92 KPMG LLP -1900 E 9th -1500 Natl City Ctr
-Cleveland 44114

  Seman, Lawrence A '90 -1795 Crtland Ln -Cleveland 44147

(440) 205-0539 .. **Seman**, Richard T Jr. '94 -8320 Mentor Av -Mentor 44060

(216) 431-4500 .. **Semanco**, Tammy L '00 Cuyahoga Cnty Pros -3955 Euclid Av
-Jane Edna Hunter Bldg -Cleveland 44115 **Fx:**431-4113

(419) 332-2221 .. **Semer**, Jerry W '74 -617 Croghan -Fremont 43420

(216) 344-3838 .. **Seminatore**, Kenneth F '71 -815 Superior Av -Ste 1715
-Cleveland 44114

(216) 623-0880 .. **Semmelroth**, Cindy A '01 %Westgroup -600 Superior Av E
-Bank One Ctr -Cleveland 44114

(614) 228-1930 .. **Semons**, Tad A '98 (Semons & S) -42 E Gay -Ste 802
-Columbus 43215

(614) 228-1930 .. **Semons**, William A '66 (Semons & S) -42 E Gay -Ste 802
-Columbus 43215

(937) 865-7605 .. **Sempeles**, Leigh A '83 Lexis/Nexis -Bx933 -Dayton 45401

(330) 535-0124 .. **Semple & Eicher** -One Cascade Plz -7th Fl -Akron 44308

  Semple, Kathleen M '83 -5494 Boehm Dr -Fairfield 45014

(330) 535-0124 .. **Semple**, Neil M '02 Semple & E -One Cascade Plz -7th Fl
-Akron 44308

(330) 535-0124 .. **Semple**, Thomas P '88 (Semple & E) -One Cascade Plz -7th Fl
-Akron 44308

(419) 882-0081 .. **Semro**, Timothy J '99 %LaValley LT&S Co,LPA -5800 Monroe
-Bldg F -Sylvania 43560 **Fx:**882-4635

(330) 297-3880 .. **Sendry**, Douglas J '74 Portage Cnty Probate Ct -203 W Main
-Ravenna 44266

(614) 854-3437 .. **Senecal**, Theodore F '72 Nationwide Ins Co -5525 Parkcenter Cir
-CO-02-35 -Dublin 43017 **Fx:**854-3444

(864) 224-7436 .. **Senerius**, Gordon A '79 -609 N Murray Av -Bx4125
-Anderson, SC 29622

(614) 228-1541 .. **Senff**, Mark D '71 (Baker & H LLP) -65 E State -Ste 2100
-Columbus 43215 **Fx:**462-2616

(216) 661-6468 .. **Senich**, Kevin J '84 -4438 Pearl Rd -Cleveland 44109

(805) 781-6116 .. **Senn**, Charles L '66 Senn Cmmrcl Real Estate -860 Osos
-San Luis Obispo, CA 93401 **Fx:**781-6099

(440) 845-1900 .. **Senn**, Richard A '66 -6325 York Rd -Ste 305
-Parma Heights 44130

(330) 405-5061 .. **Sennett**, James A '80 (Williams S&S Co,LPA)
-2241 Pinnacle Pkwy -Twinsburg 44087 **Fx:**405-5586

(937) 223-1130 .. **Senney**, Jeffrey S '86 Pickrel S&E -40 N Main -2700 Kettering Twr
-Dayton 45423 **Fx:**223-0339

(216) 621-7860 .. **Senra**, Matthew E '00 %Cavitch FD&F -1717 E 9th -14th Fl
-Cleveland 44114 **Fx:**621-3415

(216) 479-8500 .. **Senturia**, Harris A '93 (Squire S&D LLP) -127 Pub Sq
-4900 Key Twr -Cleveland 44114 **Fx:**479-8780

(614) 221-1444 .. **Sentz**, Barbara A '83 -5 E Long -Ste 100 -Columbus 43215

(440) 930-4001 .. **Serazin**, Scott F '77 (Baumgartner & O) -5455 Detroit Rd (Rte 254)
-Sheffield Village 44054 **Fx:**934-7205

(216) 896-2430 .. **Serbin**, Daniel S '89 Parker Hannifin Corp -6035 Parkland Blvd
-Cleveland 44124

(703) 838-2700 .. **Serbin**, David J '82 -1423 Powhatan -Unit 2 -Alexandria, VA 22314

(216) 579-1700 .. **Serbinowski**, Paul A '95 (Pearne & G LLP) -1801 E 9th -Ste 1200
-Cleveland 44114 **Fx:**579-6073

(513) 684-3211 .. **Serena**, Terry '78 IRS Dist Cnsl -312 Elm -Ste 2300
-Cincinnati 45202

(216) 586-3939 .. **Serevitch**, Katherine M '04 %Jones D -901 Lakeside Av
-Cleveland 44114 **Fx:**579-0212

(216) 621-0200 .. **Sergent**, Douglas R '99 %Baker & H LLP -1900 E 9th -Ste 3200
-Cleveland 44114 **Fx:**696-0740

(859) 331-2000 .. **Sergent**, Gary J '80 (O'Hara RTS&S) -25 Crestvw Hills Mall Rd
-Ste 201 -Bx17411 -Covington, KY 41017

(614) 466-9565 .. **Serio**, Joseph P '86 OH Consumers' Cnsl -10 W Broad -Ste 1800
-Columbus 43215 **Fx:**466-9475

(614) 462-3580 .. **Serio**, Kimberly K '86 Ct of Appls 10th Dist -373 S High -24th Fl
-Columbus 43215

(216) 444-8657 .. **Serkey**, Janet M '94 Cleveland Clinic Fndtn -9500 Euclid Av
-Cleveland 44195

(330) 972-6018 .. **Sermersheim**, Michael D '73 Univ of Akron -Ofc of Gen Cnsl
-BH 69 -Akron 44325

(440) 997-6175 .. **Sernik**, Craig F '97 %Warren & Y,PLL -134 W 46th -Bx2300
-Ashtabula 44005 **Fx:**992-9114

(937) 436-6886 .. **Serr**, Willis O II '75 Lutheran Soc Srvcs -6430 Inner Mission Way
-Dayton 45459

(330) 452-6400 .. **Serra**, Jeffry V '03 %S Ferruccio Jr -220 Market Av S -Ste 400
-Canton 44702

(330) 497-7247 .. **Serra**, Rosemary C '84 -2624 Cottington Cir NW
-North Canton 44720

(216) 696-8730 .. **Serra**, Wayne M '02 %Amin & T LLP -1900 E 9th -24th Fl Natl City
Ctr -Cleveland 44114 **Fx:**696-8731

(419) 262-9898 .. **Serraino**, Stephen R '81 -2046 Carriage Hill Dr -Toledo 43606

(216) 622-3873 .. **Serrano**, Blas E Jr. '76 US Atty -801 W Superior -Ste 400
-Cleveland 44113 **Fx:**622-3370

(440) 891-8389 .. **Serrano**, Mariela F '80 -5530 State Rd -Ste 9 -Parma 44134

(216) 696-2150 .. **Serrat**, Jaime P '83 -1370 Ontario Av -2000 Standard Bldg
-Cleveland 44113

(614) 221-3311 .. **Serrott**, Mark A '79 Mark A Serrott Co,LPA -502 S 3rd
-Columbus 43215

(330) 742-8823 .. **Sertick**, Anthony Jr. '91 Youngstown Mun Ct -26 S Phelps
-Bx6047 -Youngstown 44501

(313) 496-7501 .. **Seryak**, Richard J '75 (Miller CP&S) -150 W Jffrsn
-Detroit, MI 48226

(216) 621-5300 .. **Sesek**, Deborah '76 (Buckingham D&B,LLP) -1375 E 9th
-Ste 1700 -Cleveland 44114 **Fx:**621-5440

(614) 469-1400 .. **Seskes**, Brandi R '04 %Clark PR&S Co,LPA -471 E Broad
-Ste 1400 -Columbus 43215 **Fx:**469-0900

(216) 931-6000 .. **Sesnowitz**, Douglas K '94 (Ulmer & B LLP) -1300 E 9th
-Ste 900 Penton Media Bldg -Cleveland 44114 **Fx:**931-6001

(330) 650-5444 .. **Sesny**, Thomas A Jr. '92 -1521 Georgtwn Rd -Ste 300
-Hudson 44236

(740) 259-6222 .. **Sesser**, Stephen K '01 Taylor Lumber -18253 State Route 73
-Mc Dermott 45652

  Sestak, James Christopher '92 -Bx19441 -Cleveland 44119

(614) 227-2000 .. **Sestile**, Lindsay M '02 %Porter WM&A LLP -41 S High
-Columbus 43215 **Fx:**227-2100

(513) 793-0710 .. **Sestito**, John P '83 -9846 Vllg Vw Ct -Cincinnati 45241

(513) 946-3000 .. **Seta**, Emma L '00 Hamilton Cnty Pros -230 E 9th
-Cincinnati 45202 **Fx:**946-3017

(614) 224-1222 .. **Seth**, Nivita '03 %Maguire & S,LLP -250 Civic Ctr Dr -Ste 200
-Columbus 43215 **Fx:**224-1236

(614) 436-3564 .. **Sethi**, Neil K '99 %Landis Prop -77 E Wilson Bridge Rd
-Columbus 43085

(330) 376-6766 .. **Sethna**, Farhad B '91 -17 S Main -Ste 201 -Akron 44308
Fx:376-7344

(513) 733-1759 .. **Setterberg**, Richard A '86 (R Setterberg Co,LPA)
-9872 Fawnrun Ct -Cincinnati 45241

(614) 445-0240 .. **Settina**, William A '97 (W Settina Co LPA) -729 S 3rd
-Columbus 43206

(614) 464-6400 .. **Settineri**, Michael J '01 %Vorys SS&P LLP -52 E Gay -Bx1008
-Columbus 43216 **Fx:**464-6350

(513) 381-2838 .. **Settles**, Brian S '04 %Taft S&H LLP -425 Walnut -Ste 1800
-Cincinnati 45202 **Fx:**381-0205

(615) 344-5950 .. **Seufert**, Carla M '92 HCA Inc -1 Park Plz -Nashville, TN 37203

(317) 636-6481 .. **Sever**, Philip '95 %Cohen & M,LLP -One Indna Sq -Ste 1400
-Indianapolis, IN 46204 **Fx:**636-2593

(614) 466-4656 .. **Severance**, Gregory S '81 Atty Gen -150 E Gay -Columbus 43215
Fx:466-1756

(614) 644-2186 .. **Severns**, William C '75 OH Dept Job & Fam Srvcs
-4300 Kimberly Pkwy -4th Fl -Columbus 43232 **Fx:**644-2217

(216) 523-4909 .. **Severs**, Deborah R '81 Eaton Corp -1111 Superior Av
-Cleveland 44114

(440) 774-1278 .. **Severs**, Eric R '75 (E Severs Co,LPA) -5 S Main -1st Flr
-Oberlin 44074

(937) 332-6993 .. **Severt**, Katherine K '91 Miami Cnty Prob/Juv Ct -201 W Main
-Troy 45373

(937) 335-5658 .. **Severt**, Todd D '92 (Lopez S&P Co,LPA) -18 E Water -Troy 45373
Fx:339-6446

(330) 767-3401 .. **Severtis**, Sarah A '03 Wheeling & Lk Erie Railway -100 E 1st
-Brewster 44613

(216) 746-0776 .. **Severyn**, Myra S '90 -5005 Rockside Rd -Ste 600
-Independence 44131

(614) 224-0370 .. **Sevis**, Chris S '97 -600 S High -Ste 201 -Columbus 43215

(614) 336-3322 .. **Sewalk**, Karen M '94 Merck-Medco Mngd Care,LLC
-495 Metro Pl S -Ste 350 -Columbus 43017

(513) 345-4160 .. **Sewall**, Grace C '86 Pro Seniors,Inc -7162 Redding Rd -Ste 1150
-Cincinnati 45237

(614) 228-6061 .. **Sewards**, Frederick A '90 (Hammond & S) -556 E Town
-Columbus 43215

(740) 345-6015 .. **Sewards**, William B Jr. '86 -30 W Locust -Newark 43055

(216) 896-5600 .. **Sexton**, Aileen S '99 %Levy & D -25200 Chagrin Blvd -Ste 310
-Beachwood 44122 **Fx:**896-5601

(937) 333-4400 .. **Sexton**, Andrew D '99 Dayton Pros -335 W 3rd -Ste 372
-Dayton 45402

(614) 221-4788 .. **Sexton**, Robert E '61 -580 S High -Ste 130 -Columbus 43215

(440) 729-9677 .. **Sexton**, Sheila M '97 -9092 Wyandot Rd -Chesterland 44026

(614) 221-4788 .. **Sexton**, Thomas P '99 -580 S High -Ste 130 -Columbus 43215

(216) 621-0500 .. **Sexton**, William J '58 W Sexton Co,LPA -1370 Ontario -#800
-Cleveland 44113

(817) 478-9861 .. **Seybold**, David B '82 -Bx172605 -Arlington, TX 76003

(614) 478-1540 .. **Seyfang**, Matthew G '04 -3997 Silver Sprngs Ln -Columbus 43230

(216) 696-7600 .. **Seymour**, Carolyn K '85 (Duvin C&H) -1301 E 9th
-20th Fl Erievw Twr -Cleveland 44114 **Fx:**696-2038

  Seymour, Gretchen T '03 -(Address Unavailable)

(330) 860-1477 .. **Seymour**, Michael J '04 Babcock & Wilcox Co -20 S Van Buren Av
-Barberton 44203

(440) 576-3003 .. **Sezon**, Marianne '98 Ashtabula Cnty Ct of Commn Pleas
-25 W Jffrsn -Jefferson 44047

(216) 696-7600 .. **Sferra**, Stephen J '86 (Duvin C&H) -1301 E 9th
-20th Fl Erievw Twr -Cleveland 44114 **Fx:**696-2038

(614) 469-7404 .. **Sferrella**, Nino A '64 SSA-OHA, Columbus -280 N High -3rd Fl
-Columbus 43215

(440) 327-1542 .. **Sfiscko**, Johanna M '74 (McDonough S & Co)
-35888 Ctr Ridge Rd -Ste 3 -North Ridgeville 44039

(614) 462-5995 .. **Sgalla-McClure**, Cynthia J '01 Franklin Cnty Common Pleas Ct
-369 S High -Courtroom 7C -Columbus 43215

(216) 566-2642 .. **Sgambellone**, James J '83 Sherwin-Williams Co
-101 Prospect Av NW -Cleveland 44115

(216) 283-2309 .. **Sgro**, Valentina '80 SGRO Cnsltng -3718 Normandy Rd
-Shaker Heights 44120

(740) 927-8000 .. **Shackelford**, Margaret O'Connor '87 %Allen Refractories
-131 Shackelford Rd -Pataskala 43062 **Fx:**927-9404

(330) 399-2070 .. **Shackelford**, William M '96 Ohlin & S,LPA -309 Wshngtn NE
-Warren 44483 **Fx:**393-4344

(513) 398-8911 .. **Shackelford**, Thomas D '68 -224 Reading Rd -Mason 45040
Fx:398-8927

(614) 462-5630 .. **Shad**, Matthew E '01 Cnty Dept Econ Dvlpmnt -373 S High -25th Fl
-Columbus 43215 **Fx:**462-5549

(740) 363-9232 .. **Shade**, David C '73 (Shade & S) -41 N Sandusky -Ste 410
-Delaware 43015

Shade, Jerry H '01 -(Address Unavailable)

(740) 363-9232 .. **Shade**, Michael R '80 (Shade & S) -41 N Sandusky -Ste 410
-Delaware 43015

(513) 762-6200 .. **Shadley**, Frederic X '81 (Ulmer & B LLP) -600 Vine -Ste 2800
-Cincinnati 45202 **Fx:**762-6245

Shady, Jason M '04 -(Address Unavailable)

(614) 436-5424 .. **Shady**, John M D '73 -132 Northwoods Blvd -Ste 100
-Columbus 43235

(304) 233-6290 .. **Shafer**, Amy P '96 %D Eddy -1144 Market -Ste 300
-Wheeling, WV 26003 **Fx:**233-6295

(304) 231-0444 .. **Shafer**, Bradley K '96 %Steptoe & J -14th & Chapline -Bx150
-Wheeling, WV 26003

(513) 723-4000 .. **Shafer**, Cynthia A '86 OfCnsl Vorys SS&P LLP -221 E 4th
-Ste 2000 Atrium Two -Bx0236 -Cincinnati 45201 **Fx:**723-4056

(513) 577-7380 .. **Shafer**, Jeffrey A '97 (Langdon & S LLC) -11175 Reading Rd
-Ste 103 -Cincinnati 45241 **Fx:**577-7383

(740) 967-5555 .. **Shafer**, Larry F '80 -55 S Main -Ste C -Bx356 -Johnstown 43031

(419) 289-3800 .. **Shafer**, Philip H '65 -10 E Main -Ashland 44805

(614) 462-2270 .. **Shaffer**, Anthony D '95 (Schottenstein Z&D) -250 West -Bx165020
-Columbus 43216 **Fx:**462-5135

Shaffer, Charles A '04 -(Address Unavailable)

(330) 668-1893 .. **Shaffer**, David H '73 -807 Wallwood Dr -Akron 44321

(513) 455-7600 .. **Shaffer**, Elizabeth Monroe '03 %Greenebaum D&M PLLC
-255 E 5th -2800 Chemed Ctr -Cincinnati 45202 **Fx:**455-8500

(614) 464-6400 .. **Shaffer**, Jody G '04 %Vorys SS&P LLP -52 E Gay -Bx1008
-Columbus 43216 **Fx:**464-6350

(740) 282-2676 .. **Shaffer**, John R '81 (Shaffer & S) -316 N 4th -Steubenville 43952

(419) 636-3196 .. **Shaffer**, John S '81 (Newcomer S&S) -117 W Maple -Bryan 43506
Fx:636-0867

(309) 766-0797 .. **Shaffer**, John S Jr. '81 State Farm Ins -One State Farm Plz
-Bloomington, IL 61710

(419) 636-3196 .. **Shaffer**, Michael A '90 (Newcomer S&S) -117 W Maple
-Bryan 43506 **Fx:**636-0867

(513) 723-4000 .. **Shaffer**, Robert M '96 %Vorys SS&P LLP -221 E 4th
-Ste 2000 Atrium Two -Bx0236 -Cincinnati 45201 **Fx:**723-4056

(419) 242-1400 .. **Shaffer**, Russel E '72 -608 Mad Av -Ste 1400 -Toledo 43604

(619) 524-9511 .. **Shaffer**, Russell L '87 US Navy -COM THIRD FLT
-FPO, AP 96601

(419) 636-3196 .. **Shaffer**, Wayne E '49 (Newcomer S&S) -117 W Maple
-Bryan 43506 **Fx:**636-0867

(216) 696-1545 .. **Shafran**, John '60 %J Barrett -1370 Ontario -800 Standard Bldg
-Cleveland 44113 **Fx:**696-2104

(216) 781-5245 .. **Shafron**, Steven D '87 (Berkman GM&D) -55 Pub Sq
-2121 The Illuminating Bldg -Cleveland 44113 **Fx:**781-8207

(216) 241-6055 .. **Shagrin**, Michael B '64 (Dubin J&S) -75 Pub Sq -Ste 650
-Cleveland 44113

(330) 759-6711 .. **Shagrin**, Steven S '81 Salomon Smith Barney Inc
-5048 Belmont Av -Youngstown 44505

(440) 946-3946 .. **Shah**, Indrawadan K '74 -577 St Lawrence Blvd -Eastlake 44095

(972) 466-6856 .. **Shah**, Nainesh P '95 ST Microelectronics -1310 Electronic Dr
-Carrollton, TX 75006

(614) 462-2331 .. **Shah**, Parag H '00 %Schottenstein Z&D -250 West -Bx165020
-Columbus 43216 **Fx:**462-5135

(419) 255-5900 .. **Shah**, Shital A '97 %MacMillan S&T,LLC -720 Water -4th Fl
-Toledo 43604 **Fx:**255-9639

(740) 927-9225 .. **Shaheen**, Arnold E Jr. '74 -365 S Main -Bx49 -Pataskala 43062

(216) 621-2234 .. **Shaheen**, Matthew M '97 %Tarolli SC&T -526 Superior Av
-1111 Leader Bldg -Cleveland 44114 **Fx:**621-4072

(740) 695-4448 .. **Shaheen**, Michael J '89 -227 E Main -Saint Clairsville 43950

(614) 274-0033 .. **Shaid**, Brett A '99 %Goldstein & Assoc -3649 W Broad
-Columbus 43228

(614) 466-8054 .. **Shailer**, John L '81 PUCO -180 E Broad -Columbus 43266

(216) 861-5217 .. **Shakarian**, Melanie A '03 Legal Aid -1223 W 6th
-Cleveland 44113 **Fx:**687-0779

(216) 586-7799 .. **Shakelton**, Paula G '04 %Jones D -901 Lakeside Av
-Cleveland 44114 **Fx:**579-0212

(330) 652-2762 .. **Shaker**, Christopher J '83 (Shaker & S,LLP) -2 S Main -5th Fl
-Niles 44446

(330) 652-2762 .. **Shaker**, Robert I '87 (Shaker & S,LLP) -2 S Main -5th Fl
-Niles 44446

(614) 466-2766 .. **Shaklee**, William V '02 %Atty Gen -30 E Broad -Columbus 43215
Fx:644-1926

(440) 331-8850 .. **Shalala**, Edna C '52 (Shalala & B) -2600 Wooster Rd
-Rocky River 44116

(937) 294-6000 .. **Shale**, Rebecca A '88 %Winwood C & Assoc -3077 Kettering Blvd
-Ste 210 -Dayton 45439

(330) 762-6224 .. **Shama**, Cynthia Lou '89 -333 S Main -7th Fl -Akron 44308

(614) 223-9300 .. **Shamansky**, Robert N '50 Benesch FC&A LLP -88 E Broad
-Ste 900 -Columbus 43215 **Fx:**223-9330

(614) 224-9078 .. **Shamansky**, Ronda S '88 -245 E Gay -Columbus 43215

(614) 228-4141 .. **Shamansky**, Samuel H '85 (S Shamansky Co,LPA) -511 S High
-Columbus 43215

(614) 469-3939 .. **Shambaugh**, Phyllis J '93 Jones D -325 John H McConnell Blvd
-Ste 600 -Bx165017 -Columbus 43216 **Fx:**461-4198

(216) 391-7111 .. **Shamberg**, Stefen K '00 %Silver & Assoc -3421 Prospect Av
-Cleveland 44115

(216) 621-0200 .. **Shamsi**, Azfar Bin '03 Baker & H LLP -1900 E 9th -Ste 3200
-Cleveland 44114 **Fx:**696-0740

(216) 357-5123 .. **Shanabruch**, Michael R '94 %A Isakoff -55 Pub Sq -Ste 1331
-Cleveland 44113 **Fx:**241-4591

(216) 687-7492 .. **Shanahan**, Brien W '79 -2060 E 9th -Ste 1900 -Cleveland 44115

(216) 363-1700 .. **Shanahan**, J K '72 Shanahan Law Firm,LLC -925 Euclid Av
-Ste 1750 -Cleveland 44115

(513) 985-3200 .. **Shanahan**, James P Jr. '84 Pacholder Assoc,Inc
-8044 Mntgmry Rd -Ste 480 -Cincinnati 45236

Shanahan, John T '99 %Squire S&D LLP
-Ebisu Prime Sq Twr 16F -1-1-39 Hiroo Shibuya-ku
-Tokyo 150-0012 Japan

(216) 297-7000 .. **Shanahan**, Karen F '72 Cleveland Clinic Fndtn
-1950 Richmond Rd -TR38 -Cleveland 44124

(513) 946-3000 .. **Shanahan**, Megan E '00 Hamilton Cnty Pros -230 E 9th
-Cincinnati 45202 **Fx:**946-3017

(614) 470-2664 .. **Shanahan**, Thomas G '82 -931 Euclaire Av -Bexley 43209

(330) 455-0173 .. **Shandor**, Steven D '04 %Day KRW&R,Ltd -200 Market Av N
-Ste 300 -Bx24213 -Canton 44701 **Fx:**455-2633

(937) 512-2935 .. **Shane**, Bonnie S '82 Sinclair Cmmnty Coll -444 W 3rd
-Dayton 45402

(937) 223-3277 .. **Shane**, Charles F '93 (Bieser G&L LLP) -6 N Main
-400 Natl City Ctr -Dayton 45402 **Fx:**223-6339

(859) 431-7800 .. **Shane**, Steven C '73 -321 Fairfld Av -Bx73067
-Bellevue, KY 41073

(614) 462-3555 .. **Shaner**, Nellie J '81 Franklin Cnty Pros -373 S High
-Columbus 43215

(937) 222-1090 .. **Shaneyfelt**, Paul H '95 %Statman HS&E LLC -110 N Main
-Ste 1520 -Dayton 45402 **Fx:**222-1046

(614) 227-2000 .. **Shank**, Aaron M '98 %Porter WM&A LLP -41 S High
-Columbus 43215 **Fx:**227-2100

(937) 865-6800 .. **Shank**, Anne L '88 Lexis/Nexis -Bx933 -Dayton 45401

Shank, Diane S '89 -975 Hill -Cincinnati 45202

(937) 223-3277 .. **Shank**, Edward L '56 (Bieser G&L LLP) -6 N Main
-400 Natl City Ctr -Dayton 45402 **Fx:**223-6339

(513) 651-6800 .. **Shank**, Robert D '98 (Frost BT LLC) -201 E 5th -2200 PNC Ctr
-Cincinnati 45202 **Fx:**651-6981

(614) 326-1217 .. **Shank**, Shirley A '80 -Bx8053 -Columbus 43201

(216) 368-3292 .. **Shanker**, Morris G '52 CWRU Law Schl -11075 East Blvd
-Cleveland 44106

(619) 296-6693 .. **Shankle**, Jessica A '01 %Nazimova & D -330 Brookes Av
-San Diego, CA 92103

(216) 443-8995 .. **Shankman**, Alan D '79 Cuyahoga Cnty Probate Ct -1 Lakeside Av
-Cleveland 44113

(513) 868-7600 .. **Shanks**, Michael D '76 Holbrock & J Co,LPA -315 S Monument Av
-Bx687 -Hamilton 45012 **Fx:**868-0909

(513) 381-2838 .. **Shanley**, Sharon I '99 %Taft S&H LLP -425 Walnut -Ste 1800
-Cincinnati 45202 **Fx:**381-0205

(614) 466-6600 .. **Shannon**, Ann M '92 Workers Comp -30 W Spring -Level 26
-Columbus 43215

(330) 486-4058 .. **Shannon**, Colleen M '89 Cole Managed Vision
-1925 Enterprise Pkwy -Twinsburg 44087

(614) 752-5374 .. **Shannon**, Desiree T '89 OH Dept Commerce -77 S High
-Columbus 43266

(216) 241-5040 .. **Shannon**, James F '74 -75 Pub Sq -Ste 700 -Cleveland 44113

(614) 866-1195 .. **Shannon**, Kevin C '92 -7610 Slate Ridge Blvd
-Reynoldsburg 43068

(937) 498-3777 .. **Shannon**, Michael K '01 Copeland Corp -1675 W Campbell Rd
-Bx669 -Sidney 45365

(513) 946-9006 .. **Shannon**, Raymond E '48 Hamilton Cnty Cmn Pleas Ct -800 Bway
-Cincinnati 45202

Shanov, Diana V '04 -(Address Unavailable)

(614) 466-4585 .. **Shantz**, Arthur W Jr. '71 Industrial Commssn of OH -30 W Spring
-9th Fl -Columbus 43215 **Fx:**752-8785

Shaper, Thomas O '82 -170 Canyon Rd -Chagrin Falls 44022

(216) 831-5100 .. **Shapero & Green LLC** -25101 Chagrin Blvd
-Ste 220 Signature Sq II -Beachwood 44122 **Fx:**831-9467

(216) 831-5100 .. **Shapero**, Michael I '71 (Shapero & G LLC) -25101 Chagrin Blvd
-Ste 220 Signature Sq II -Beachwood 44122 **Fx:**831-9467

(216) 781-1700 .. **Shapero**, Neal E '84 (Shapero & R Co,LPA) -1350 Euclid Av
-Ste 1550 -Cleveland 44115 **Fx:**781-1972

(216) 781-1700 .. **Shapero & Roloff Co, LPA** -1350 Euclid Av -Ste 1550 -Cleveland
44115 **Fx:**781-1972

(216) 927-2030 .. **Shapiro**, Alan J '62 Shapiro S&S Co,LPA
-4469 Renaissance Pkwy -Warrensville Heights 44128
Fx:763-2620

(216) 927-2030 .. **Shapiro**, Daniel L '92 Shapiro S&S Co,LPA
-4469 Renaissance Pkwy -Warrensville Heights 44128
Fx:763-2620

(216) 621-1530 .. **Shapiro & Felty, LLP** -1500 W 3rd -Ste 400 -Cleveland 44113
Fx:621-1551

(216) 378-9730 .. **Shapiro**, Fred D '54 (Shapiro & L Co,LPA) -27600 Chagrin Blvd
-Ste 340 -Woodmere 44122

(216) 927-2030 .. **Shapiro**, Geoffrey J '93 Shapiro S&S Co,LPA
-4469 Renaissance Pkwy -Warrensville Heights 44128
Fx:763-2620

(740) 345-3411 .. **Shapiro**, Harvey H '71 (Shapiro Legal Ctr) -30 W Locust
-Newark 43055

(216) 685-1106 .. **Shapiro**, Jeffrey A '93 %Weltman W&R Co,LPA
-323 W Lakeside Av -Ste 200 -Cleveland 44113 **Fx:**363-4121

(937) 254-4455 .. **Shapiro**, Joel S '67 (Goldman R&S) -1340 Woodman Dr
-Dayton 45432

(513) 381-2838 .. **Shapiro**, Joshua A '99 %Taft S&H LLP -425 Walnut -Ste 1800
-Cincinnati 45202 **Fx:**381-0205

(937) 866-6719 .. **Shapiro**, Kenneth H '78 -Mid City Station -Bx371 -Dayton 45402

(216) 522-3380 .. **Shapiro**, Marc A '87 IRS -1375 E 9th -1200 -Cleveland 44114

(216) 696-0990 .. **Shapiro Marnecheck & Riemer** -1468 W 9th -Rm 425
-Cleveland 44113 **Fx:**696-7790

(330) 375-2007 .. **Shapiro**, Marvin A '65 Mun Ct Judge -217 S High -Akron 44308

(614) 644-3037 .. **Shapiro**, Michael A '74 EPA -122 S Front -Bx1049
-Columbus 43216

(216) 360-3737 .. **Shapiro**, Michael J '94 (Persky S&A Co,LPA) -25101 Chagrin Blvd
-Ste 350 Signature Sq II -Beachwood 44122 **Fx:**593-0921

(216) 360-3737 .. **Shapiro**, Paul Y '63 (Persky S&A Co,LPA) -25101 Chagrin Blvd
-Ste 350 Signature Sq II -Beachwood 44122 **Fx:**593-0921

(513) 695-1325 .. **Shapiro**, Peggy A '04 %Warren Cnty Pros -500 Justice Dr
-Lebanon 45036 **Fx:**695-2962

Shapiro, Philip '75 -(Address Unavailable)

(614) 716-2927 .. **Shapiro**, Rick J '94 SrCnsl Amer Elec Pwr Co -1 Riverside Plz
-Columbus 43215

Shapiro, Robert M '68 -(Address Unavailable)

(216) 241-7442 .. **Shapiro**, Shia N '64 -1370 Ontario -600 Standard Bldg
-Cleveland 44113

(216) 479-8500 ..**Sharb**, Michael L '97 (Squire S&D LLP) -127 Pub Sq -4900 Key Twr -Cleveland 44114 Fx:479-8780

(614) 221-9400 ..**Sharett**, Anthony M '03 %Habash R&F,LLP -471 E Broad -Ste 800 -Columbus 43215

(614) 227-2300 ..**Sharett**, Hope M '03 %Bricker & E LLP -100 S 3rd -Columbus 43215 Fx:227-2390

(419) 255-8260 ..**Sharfman**, Mervin S '67 (Sharfman & C) -626 Madison -Ste 711 -Toledo 43604 Fx:255-4240

(513) 695-1759 ..**Sharkey**, Bartholomew B '01 Warren Cnty CSEA -500 Justice Dr -Lebanon 45036 Fx:695-2969

(703) 661-0597 ..**Sharkey**, Beverly J '89 FAA -13873 Park Ctr Rd -Ste 165 -Herndon, VA 20171

(937) 227-3700 ..**Sharkey**, Gerald S Jr. '97 %Faruki I&C PLL -10 N Ludlow -500 Cthse Plz SW -Dayton 45402 Fx:227-3717

(740) 587-6293 ..**Sharkey**, Gregory J '95 Denison Univ -Senior Development Ofcr -BxD -Granville 43023

(419) 865-6586 ..**Sharkey**, Susan K '93 %WA Johnson & Assoc -7015 Spring Mdws Dr -Ste 100 -Holland 43528 Fx:865-7241

Sharkin, Brian W '02 -15515 Lk Av -Bx770824 -Lakewood 44107

(614) 436-1240 ..**Sharma**, Constance L '78 Sharma Law Ofcs,LLC -853 Pipestone Dr -Columbus 43235 Fx:436-0220

(216) 696-1076 ..**Sharma**, Jandhyala L '83 -1370 Ontario -520 Standard Bldg -Cleveland 44113 Fx:696-2317

(937) 298-0067 ..**Sharma**, Meenu '97 -438 Patterson Rd -Dayton 45419

(312) 201-4000 ..**Sharma**, Sanjay '97 %Goldberg KBBR&M,Ltd -55 E Monroe -Ste 3700 -Chicago, IL 60603 Fx:322-2196

(216) 348-9878 ..**Sharon & Kalnoki LLC** -55 Pub Sq -Ste 750 -Cleveland 44113 Fx:348-9879

(216) 348-9878 ..**Sharon**, Michael H '82 (Sharon & K LLC) -55 Pub Sq -Ste 750 -Cleveland 44113 Fx:348-9879

(614) 469-3939 ..**Sharp**, Autumn L '03 %Jones D -325 John H McConnell Blvd -Ste 600 -Bx165017 -Columbus 43216 Fx:461-4198

(310) 827-2001 ..**Sharp**, Barbara '91 SpclCnsl J Gillen -4300 Promenade Way -Ste 118 -Marina Del Rey, CA 90292 Fx:827-4293

(419) 353-1062 ..**Sharp**, James M '83 (Twyman TH&S) -519 W Wooster -Ctr Ste -Bowling Green 43402 Fx:353-6277

Sharp, Jeffrey L '03 -(Address Unavailable)

(216) 696-7600 ..**Sharp**, Jeremy J '99 %Duvin C&H -1301 E 9th -20th Fl Erievw Twr -Cleveland 44114 Fx:696-2038

(330) 650-4436 ..**Sharp**, John M '81 (Umbaugh & S) -110 W Streetsboro Rd -Ste 3A -Hudson 44236

(513) 561-3347 ..**Sharp**, Timothy H '97 Timothy H. Sharp -6655 Drake Rd -Cincinnati 45243

(216) 579-1700 ..**Sharpe**, Richard A '92 (Pearne & G LLP) -1801 E 9th -Ste 1200 -Cleveland 44114 Fx:579-6073

(614) 424-4971 ..**Sharpe**, Thomas E '89 Battelle Memorial Inst -505 King Av -11-8-132 -Columbus 43201

(330) 725-5755 ..**Sharratt**, Thomas W '52 -860 Lindenwood Ln -Medina 44256

(937) 748-2761 ..**Sharts**, John E '74 -310 W Central Av -Bx350 -Springboro 45066

(419) 523-9600 ..**Shartzer**, D Jean '86 -145 Court -Bx408 -Ottawa 45875 Fx:523-5901

(614) 462-3194 ..**Shartzer**, Donald R '82 Franklin Cnty Pub Def -373 S High -12th Fl -Columbus 43215

(513) 621-2888 ..**Shartzer**, Sharon M '04 %Ebner & R LLP -1014 Vine -1900 Kroger Bldg -Cincinnati 45202

(216) 898-8399 ..**Sharvit**, Eliav '04 Legacy Hlth Srvcs -12380 Plz Dr -Parma 44130

(214) 706-9105 ..**Shatteen**, Joyce A '85 -8117 Preston Rd -Ste 300 -Dallas, TX 75225

Shaughnessy, Michael P '02 -4518 Ardendale Rd -South Euclid 44121

(216) 721-7700 ..**Shaughnessy**, Thomas E '90 -11510 Buckeye Rd -Cleveland 44104

(513) 763-4329 ..**Shaut**, Michael H '80 -1 W 4th -Ste 200 -Cincinnati 45202

(614) 837-8433 ..**Shaver**, David B '86 -27 W Columbus -Pickerington 43147

(216) 766-6432 ..**Shaver**, Elizabeth A '92 Genesis Ins -25550 Chagrin Blvd -Ste 300 -Beachwood 44122

(614) 466-7788 ..**Shaver**, Holly T '96 OH Ct of Claims -65 E State -Ste 1100 -Columbus 43215

(937) 562-5134 ..**Shaver**, Mark A '98 Greene Cnty Cmn Pleas Ct -45 N Detroit -Xenia 45385

(937) 456-8156 ..**Shaw**, Byron K '00 Preble Cnty Pros -100 E Main -Cthse 1st Fl -Eaton 45320 Fx:456-8199

(216) 228-1888 ..**Shaw**, Christopher J '85 -15203 Detroit Av -Cleveland 44107

(614) 227-0007 ..**Shaw**, Douglas W '76 (Shaw & M) -555 City Park Av -Columbus 43215 Fx:227-0001

(614) 221-6327 ..**Shaw**, Elwin S '76 -500 S Front -Ste 130 -Columbus 43215

Shaw, Gene R '75 -Bx2327 -Covington, KY 41012

(937) 795-0036 ..**Shaw**, Gerald W '69 -89 Market Pl -Drwr615 -Aberdeen 45101

(216) 621-0200 ..**Shaw**, Hewitt B Jr. '80 (Baker & H LLP) -1900 E 9th -Ste 3200 -Cleveland 44114 Fx:696-0740

(614) 223-3070 ..**Shaw**, James C '80 -2505 Dorset Rd -Columbus 43221

(216) 291-7286 ..**Shaw**, Karen C '97 Progressive Ins Co -6300 Wilson Mills Rd -#N72A -Mayfield Village 44143

(330) 856-2922 ..**Shaw**, Kenneth N '80 (KN Shaw,LPA) -145 Niles-Crtland Rd NE -Warren 44484 Fx:856-2922

(614) 227-2000 ..**Shaw**, Kyle T '04 %Porter WM&A LLP -41 S High -Columbus 43215 Fx:227-2100

(216) 689-5104 ..**Shaw**, Laura J '97 KeyBank NA -127 Pub Sq -2nd Fl -Cleveland 44114

(937) 229-2218 ..**Shaw**, Lori E '87 Univ of Dayton Schl of Law -300 Cllg Park -Dayton 45469

(614) 228-6611 ..**Shaw**, Mark A '92 (Fuller & H,Ltd) -35 N 4th -Ste 310 -Columbus 43215 Fx:228-6623

(614) 891-4158 ..**Shaw**, Melissa J '97 -7970 Chateau Ln S -Westerville 43082

(216) 291-7286 ..**Shaw**, Nancy A '80 Northrop Grumman -1900 Richmond Rd -Cleveland 44124

(419) 423-5172 ..**Shaw**, Patricia W '93 Blanchard Valley Hlth Assn -145 W Wallace -Findlay 45840

(614) 462-3981 ..**Shaw**, Richard T '81 Franklin Cnty Dom Rltns Ct -373 S High -3rd Fl -Columbus 43215

Shaw, Ronald R Jr. '91 -2625 Chmbrlain Rd -Fairlawn 44333

(216) 781-1212 ..**Shaw**, Russell C '65 (Walter & H LLP) -1301 E 9th -Ste 3500 -Cleveland 44114 Fx:575-0911

(202) 606-8806 ..**Shaw**, Stanley S Jr. '74 US Tax Ct -400 2nd NW -Rm 418 -Washington, DC 20217

(513) 651-2121 ..**Shaw**, Stephen K '79 OfCnsl Z Gottesman -36 E 7th -2121 CBLD Ctr -Cincinnati 45202

(301) 838-6771 ..**Shaw**, Terence L '80 BAE Systems NA -1601 Rsrch Blvd -Rockville, MD 20850

(312) 385-1500 ..**Shaw**, Vincent E '98 Dept of Justice -71 W Van Buren -Chicago, IL 60605

(740) 353-5191 ..**Shaw**, William K Jr. '76 -1306 Offnere -Portsmouth 45662 Fx:354-2028

(718) 765-7026 ..**Shay**, Madeline L '81 US Army Corps of Engineers -302 Gen Lee Av -Ft Hmltn Military Comm -Brooklyn, NY 11209

(202) 628-8000 ..**Shay**, Matthew R '87 Intl Franchise Assn -1350 NY Av NW -Ste 900 -Washington, DC 20005

(614) 457-2029 ..**Shay**, William M '75 -1010 Old Henderson Rd -Ste 102 -Columbus 43220

(313) 962-8255 ..**Shaye**, Marc K '96 %Riley R&C -615 Griswold -7th Fl -Detroit, MI 48226

Shaynak-Diaz, Christina L '02 -4950 Harvest Meadow Rd -Hilliard 43026

(614) 221-1111 ..**Shayne & Greenwald** -221 S High -Columbus 43215 Fx:221-4070

(614) 221-1111 ..**Shayne**, Stanley H '69 Shayne & G -221 S High -Columbus 43215 Fx:221-4070

(216) 479-8500 ..**Shea**, Christopher R '93 %Squire S&D LLP -127 Pub Sq -4900 Key Twr -Cleveland 44114 Fx:479-8780

(513) 651-6800 ..**Shea**, Jane H '79 Cnsl Frost BT LLC -201 E 5th -2200 PNC Ctr -Cincinnati 45202 Fx:651-6981

(513) 621-8333 ..**Shea**, Joseph W III '74 (Shea & Assoc) -250 E 5th -Ste 444 -Cincinnati 45202

(513) 579-2010 ..**Shea**, Kevin M '79 Provident Bank -1 E 4th -860 A -Cincinnati 45202

(217) 698-8500 ..**Shea**, Patrick T '81 Diocese of Springfield -1615 W Wshngtn -Bx3187 -Springfield, IL 62708

(614) 462-3194 ..**Shea**, Robert E '03 %Franklin Cnty Pub Def -373 S High -12th Fl -Columbus 43215

(216) 586-3939 ..**Sheaffer**, Jenny L '98 %Jones D -901 Lakeside Av -Cleveland 44114 Fx:579-0212

(513) 771-4557 ..**Shear**, Donald '53 -52 Evergreen Ct -Cincinnati 45215 Fx:771-0551

Sheard, Elizabeth K '02 -2788 Goldleaf Dr -Akron 44333

(513) 665-3500 ..**Shearer**, David A Jr. '99 (Freund F&A) -105 E 4th -Ste 1400 -Cincinnati 45202 Fx:665-3503

(440) 717-1580 ..**Shearer**, Mark S '96 -8193 Avry Rd -Ste 201 -Broadview Heights 44147

(937) 237-0112 ..**Shearer**, Robert B '68 -5585 Brandt Pike -Dayton 45424

(614) 228-1541 ..**Shearer**, William B '94 (Baker & H LLP) -65 E State -Ste 2100 -Columbus 43215 Fx:462-2616

(304) 252-5321 ..**Sheatsley**, James R '78 Gorman S & Co,LC -343 Prince -Bx5518 -Beckley, WV 25801

(330) 879-5017 ..**Shedlarz**, Robert J '73 -4 Wooster NE -Bx2 -Navarre 44662 Fx:879-3160

(216) 443-7800 ..**Sheehan**, Brendan J '94 Cuyahoga Cnty Pros -1200 Ontario -8th Fl -Cleveland 44113 Fx:698-2270

(330) 455-5379 ..**Sheehan**, Earl C '52 -220 Market Av S -Ste 1140 -Canton 44702 Fx:456-8578

(440) 329-5389 ..**Sheehan**, Erin M '03 Lorain Cnty Pros -225 Court -3rd Fl -Elyria 44035

(614) 466-3998 ..**Sheehan**, George M II '75 Unemploymnt Comp Commssn -145 S Front -Bx182299 -Columbus 43218

(216) 696-8860 ..**Sheehan**, John J Jr. '67 (Sheehan & S) -1422 Euclid Av -1648 Hanna Bldg -Cleveland 44115

(216) 687-1311 ..**Sheehan**, Michelle J '93 (Reminger & R) -101 Prospect Av W -1400 Mdlnd Bldg -Cleveland 44115 Fx:687-1841

(216) 696-8860 ..**Sheehan**, Thomas F '72 (Sheehan & S) -1422 Euclid Av -1648 Hanna Bldg -Cleveland 44115

(216) 771-3239 ..**Sheehan**, Thomas J '98 Bashein & B Co,LPA -50 Pub Sq -Ste 3500 Trmnl Twr -Cleveland 44113 Fx:781-5876

(216) 622-0850 ..**Sheehan**, William J '99 %McFadden & Assoc Co,LPA -1370 Ontario -Ste 1700 -Cleveland 44113 Fx:622-0854

(216) 522-7840 ..**Sheehe**, Barbara W '80 SSA/OHA -1350 Euclid Av -7th Fl -Cleveland 44115

(440) 846-0900 ..**Sheehe**, Lawrence G Jr. '83 -11925 Pearl Rd -Ste 402-A -Strongsville 44136

(614) 228-1541 ..**Sheely**, Sommer L '03 %Baker & H LLP -65 E State -Ste 2100 -Columbus 43215 Fx:462-2616

(614) 728-0742 ..**Sheeran**, Ellen J '81 Workers Comp -30 W Spring -Level 26 -Columbus 43215

(614) 462-3555 ..**Sheeran**, Patrick E '76 Franklin Cnty Pros -373 S High -Columbus 43215

(513) 731-8014 ..**Sheeran**, Thomas M '51 -5781 Pandora Av -Bx37085 -Cincinnati 45222

(216) 479-8500 ..**Sheeran**, Timothy J '75 (Squire S&D LLP) -127 Pub Sq -4900 Key Twr -Cleveland 44114 Fx:479-8780

(216) 241-3646 ..**Sheerer**, Benjamin B '65 (B Sheerer Co,LPA) -820 Superior Av W -Ste 510 -Cleveland 44113

(513) 737-1540 ..**Sheets**, Gary L '80 -1731 Cleveland Av -Hamilton 45013

(740) 992-2151 ..**Sheets**, Jennifer L '82 (Little S&W,LLP) -211-213 E 2nd -Bx686 -Pomeroy 45769 Fx:992-5168

(937) 376-3548 ..**Sheets**, Kenneth R '84 -46 S Detroit -Xenia 45385

(614) 466-2995 ..**Sheets**, Kerry K '84 PUCO -180 E Broad -Columbus 43266

(740) 446-1652 ..**Sheets**, Mark E '87 (Halliday S&S) -19 Locust -Bx325 -Gallipolis 45631

(937) 256-5252 ..**Sheets**, Michael A '91 -1343 Woodman Dr -Ste A -Dayton 45432

(304) 529-6181 ..**Sheets**, Scott K '97 (Huddleston BBP&C,LLP) -611 3rd Av -Bx2185 -Huntington, WV 25722

(614) 462-3555 ..**Sheets**, Scott O '03 Franklin Cnty Pros -373 S High -Columbus 43215

(740) 446-1652 ..**Sheets**, Warren F '50 -19 Locust -Bx325 -Gallipolis 45631

Shefcik, Patricia R '87 -(Address Unavailable)

(614) 944-5134 ..**Sheffer**, Brent A '90 -4200 Regent -Ste 200 -Columbus 43219 Fx:818-9334

(614) 228-1541 ..**Sheffer**, Karen E '79 Baker & H LLP -65 E State -Ste 2100 -Columbus 43215 Fx:462-2616

Sheffer, Sandra J '86 -(Address Unavailable)
Sheffield, Douglas M '76 -5000 Horizons Dr -Columbus 43220
(330) 799-7711 ..**Sheftel**, Lynn A '66 UAW Legal Srvcs -1570 S Canfld-Niles Rd -Ste 101 -Youngstown 44515
(614) 221-1800 ..**Sheidlower**, David T '86 Continental Real Estate -150 E Broad -Ste 800 -Columbus 43215
(937) 328-3741 ..**Sheils**, Michael F '84 City Pros -50 E Columbia -Springfield 45502 **Fx:**328-3744
(312) 655-1500 ..**Shekleton**, Gerald T '73 (Welsh & K Ltd) -120 S Riverside Plz -22nd Fl -Chicago, IL 60606 **Fx:**655-1501
(330) 427-2303 ..**Shelar**, Richard C '69 -710 Columbia -Leetonia 44431
Shelby, James D '73 -3153 Fairmont Blvd -Cleveland 44118
(440) 998-6923 ..**Sheldon**, David C '73 -4109 Lk Av -Bx1152 -Ashtabula 44005
(330) 722-8989 ..**Sheldon**, David C '88 %J Cameron & Assoc -247 E Smith Rd -Medina 44256
(513) 721-5100 ..**Sheldon**, Henry E III '03 %H Sheldon & Assoc -1618 Sycamore -Cincinnati 45202
(513) 421-8338 ..**Sheline**, Miriam H '84 -602 Main -307 Gwynne Bldg -Cincinnati 45202
(614) 237-5414 ..**Shelko**, Susan L '91 OH Nurses Assn -4000 E Main -Columbus 43213
(419) 663-1605 ..**Shell**, Gregory A '91 -111 Benedict Av -Norwalk 44857
(216) 371-0534 ..**Shelley**, Howard A Jr. '66 -2329 Walden Rd -East Cleveland 44112
(216) 479-8500 ..**Shelley**, John F '68 (Squire S&D LLP) -127 Pub Sq -4900 Key Twr -Cleveland 44114 **Fx:**479-8780
(216) 623-0000 ..**Shelley**, John S '03 %Javitch B&R -1300 E 9th -14th Fl -Cleveland 44114 **Fx:**623-0190
(216) 802-3601 ..**Shellhaas**, Samuel D '92 OH Bar Title Ins Co -1111 Superior Av E -Ste 700 -Cleveland 44114
(440) 498-4120 ..**Shellito**, Christopher J '97 Nextel Comm -31200 Carter -Solon 44139
(330) 740-2330 ..**Shells-Conne**, Lori Lei '91 Mahoning Cnty Pros -21 W Boardman -6th Fl -Youngstown 44503 **Fx:**740-2008
(412) 361-7916 ..**Shelly**, Carl H '96 Creo & S -1807 Jancey -Pittsburgh, PA 15206
Shelton, Brett D '99 -(Address Unavailable)
(513) 634-1148 ..**Shelton**, Kristy L '01 Procter & Gamble -6090 Ctr Hill Av -Cincinnati 45224
(216) 363-4500 ..**Shelton**, Peter K '93 (Benesch FC&A LLP) -200 Pub Sq -Ste 2300 -Cleveland 44114 **Fx:**363-4588
(216) 523-1300 ..**Shelton**, William R '86 Medimetrix Cnsltng -25 W Prospect Av -Ste 1100 -Cleveland 44115
(419) 865-8021 ..**Shemas**, James F '47 OfCnsl Balk H&M -5744 Southwyck Blvd -Toledo 43614 **Fx:**865-9105
(216) 689-3851 ..**Shemisa**, Jenann O '99 KeyBank Natl Assn -127 Pub Sq -2nd Fl Law Dept -Cleveland 44114
(330) 784-2292 ..**Shenise**, Larry D '97 -740 Canton Rd -Akron 44312
(740) 349-6195 ..**Shenk**, Brent W '76 Licking Cnty Pros -20 S 2nd -4th Fl -Newark 43055
(937) 492-1271 ..**Shenk**, James R '75 (Faulkner GK&S,LPA) -100 S Main Av -Ste 300 -Sidney 45365 **Fx:**498-1306
(419) 229-3044 ..**Shenk**, Robert E '80 Huntington Natl Bank -101 N Elizabeth -Bx1218 -Lima 45801 **Fx:**224-5959
Shenk, William A '68 -7675 La Jolla Blvd -Unit 206 -La Jolla, CA 92037
(724) 652-8000 ..**Shenkan**, Virginia L '99 (V Shenkan Law Ctr PC) -Bx1130 -New Castle, PA 16103
Shenker, Dina '04 -6811 Mayfld Rd -#993 -Mayfield Heights 44124
(216) 522-1555 ..**Shenyey**, Peter F '76 -1701 E 12th -Ste 3G -Cleveland 44114
(614) 227-2000 ..**Shepard**, Darrell R '81 (Porter WM&A LLP) -41 S High -Columbus 43215 **Fx:**227-2100
(614) 920-3941 ..**Shepard**, Gene A '78 -7667 Laurelwood Dr -Canal Winchester 43110
(614) 237-5414 ..**Shepard**, Laura J '98 OH Nurses Assn -4000 E Main -Columbus 43213
(614) 464-1211 ..**Shepard**, Noel C '96 %Frost BT LLC -10 W Broad -Ste 1000 -Columbus 43215 **Fx:**464-1737
(216) 426-2276 ..**Shepard**, Robert '80 Minute Men,Inc -3740 Carnegie Av -Cleveland 44115
Shepard, Susan A '00 -(Address Unavailable)
(614) 448-1035 ..**Shepardson**, Cathleen B '96 OH Nurses Assoc -4000 E Main -Columbus 43213
(614) 621-8888 ..**Shepardson**, Keith J '95 S Schiff & Assoc -88 W Main -Columbus 43215
(513) 621-2100 ..**Shepardson**, Warren P Jr. '71 (Beckman W&S LLC) -120 E 4th -1200 Mercantile Ctr -Cincinnati 45202 **Fx:**621-0106
(419) 825-5285 ..**Sheperak**, Thomas J '66 -102 Oak -Swanton 43558
(614) 228-1541 ..**Shepherd**, Amy M '89 (Baker & H LLP) -65 E State -Ste 2100 -Columbus 43215 **Fx:**462-2616
(330) 399-8801 ..**Shepherd**, David A '81 (Turner M&S) -185 High NE -Warren 44481 **Fx:**399-8805
(440) 899-9990 ..**Shepherd**, John B Jr. '78 (Short S&S) -24461 Detroit Rd -Ste 340 -Westlake 44145
(440) 331-2505 ..**Shepherd**, John E '61 -4180 Leona Dr -Bx16151 -Rocky River 44116
Shepherd, Matthew W '01 US Army -Mannheim Law Ctr -CMR 435 Bx 1217 -APO, AE 09086
(419) 347-7421 ..**Shepherd**, Richard L '77 (Poland D&S Co,LPA) -6 Water -Shelby 44875
(614) 692-9503 ..**Shepler**, Marc A '77 Dfnse Cnstrctn Supply Ctr -Bx3990 -Columbus 43216
(614) 273-3300 ..**Sheppard**, Alan W '70 -1900 Crown Park Ct -Columbus 43235
(216) 206-1239 ..**Sheppard**, James F '82 Metro Bank & Trust Co -30100 Chagrin Blvd -Ste 100 -Pepper Pike 44124
(419) 874-9300 ..**Sheppard**, Kenneth L Jr. '03 Barefoot Wealth Mgmt -885 Commerce Dr -Ste A -Perrysburg 43551
Sheppard, Linda M '04 -(Address Unavailable)
(312) 474-7900 ..**Sheppard**, Mary J '97 %Meckler B&T -123 N Wacker Dr -Ste 1800 -Chicago, IL 60606 **Fx:**474-7898
(615) 259-9080 ..**Sheppard**, Michael G '82 Spicer F&R PLLC -211 7th Av N -Ste 500 -Nashville, TN 37219
(330) 253-3128 ..**Sheppard**, Raymond C '55 Erickson & S Law Firm -583 Grant -Akron 44311
Shepperd, Frederick M '79 -Bx145 -New Philadelphia 44663

(440) 350-2683 ..**Sheppert**, Karen A '89 Lake Cnty Pros -105 Main -Bx490 -Painesville 44077 **Fx:**350-2585
(614) 233-6950 ..**Sheraw**, Brett R '01 %Fisher & S LLC -400 E Town -Ste 210 -Columbus 43215 **Fx:**233-6960
(216) 961-4530 ..**Sherban**, Diane L '79 Lexis/Nexis -9823 Lk Av -Ste 402 -Cleveland 44102
(734) 663-6535 ..**Shere**, Joel M '00 Cooper & W -206 S 5th Av -Ste 400 -Ann Arbor, MI 48104
(419) 332-8293 ..**Sherick**, Sara J '91 -206 N Clover -Fremont 43420 **Fx:**332-8269
(313) 465-7662 ..**Sherick**, Tricia A '97 %Honigman MS&C,LLP -660 Woodward Av -Ste 2290 -Detroit, MI 48226
(216) 589-0088 ..**Sheridan**, James P '99 (JP Sheridan,LLC) -75 Pub Sq -Ste 1225 -Cleveland 44113
(614) 644-9267 ..**Sheridan**, James W '89 %Hon PE Pfeifer -30 E Broad -3rd Fl -Columbus 43215
Sheridan, Michael P '01 -7691 Mary Ln -Mentor 44060
(614) 221-2001 ..**Sheridan**, Philip H Jr. '73 -915 S High -Columbus 43206
(614) 221-8448 ..**Sheridan**, Susan G '89 (Buckingham D&B,LLP) -191 W Nationwide Blvd -Ste 300 -Bx151120 -Columbus 43215 **Fx:**221-8590
(614) 221-5216 ..**Sheriff**, Mark J '70 %Wiles BB&B Co,LPA -300 Spruce -1st Fl -Columbus 43215 **Fx:**221-5692
(513) 665-3500 ..**Sheriff-MacDonald**, Dee C '84 (Freund F&A) -105 E 4th -Ste 1400 -Cincinnati 45202 **Fx:**665-3503
(937) 443-6757 ..**Sherk**, Arik A '84 (Thompson H LLP) -2000 Cthse Plz NE -Bx8801 -Dayton 45401 **Fx:**443-6635
(937) 225-4652 ..**Sherlock**, Karen M '82 Montgomery Cnty Pub Def -117 S Main -Ste 400 -Dayton 45422 **Fx:**225-3449
(440) 352-3391 ..**Sherlock**, Kristen A '01 %Dworken & B Co,LPA -60 S Park Pl -Painesville 44077 **Fx:**352-3469
(937) 227-3700 ..**Sherman**, Adam C '03 %Faruki I&C PLL -10 N Ludlow -500 Cthse Plz SW -Dayton 45402 **Fx:**227-3717
(216) 696-7600 ..**Sherman**, Bradley A '94 %Duvin C&H -1301 E 9th -20th Fl Erievw Twr -Cleveland 44114 **Fx:**696-2038
(614) 716-0979 ..**Sherman**, Bradley E '97 Cincinnati Ins Co -140 E Town -Ste 1015 -Columbus 43215
(216) 479-8500 ..**Sherman**, Charna E '90 (Squire S&D LLP) -127 Pub Sq -4900 Key Twr -Cleveland 44114 **Fx:**479-8780
(440) 871-2122 ..**Sherman**, David C '72 -1840 Newbury Ct -Westlake 44145
(216) 831-3181 ..**Sherman**, Dennis H '66 -3681 Green Rd -Ste 411 -Cleveland 44122 **Fx:**831-2135
(419) 673-3167 ..**Sherman**, Dorothy J '83 -10733 Twp Rd 215 -Kenton 43326
(614) 757-5000 ..**Sherman**, J Daniel '89 Cardinal Health -7000 Cardinal Pl -Dublin 43017
(614) 466-2166 ..**Sherman**, Jeffrey P '77 OH Dept Taxation -30 E Broad -22nd Fl -Columbus 43215
(614) 365-2700 ..**Sherman**, Kendra S '97 %Squire S&D LLP -41 S High -1300 Huntngtn Ctr -Columbus 43215 **Fx:**365-2499
Sherman, Lawrence C '63 -3329 St Malo Ct -Palm Beach Gardens, FL 33410
(614) 946-2259 ..**Sherman**, Michael C '03 -214 Medick Way -Columbus 43085
(740) 983-0155 ..**Sherman**, Richard B '03 (Sherman Law Ofc) -Bx166 -Ashville 43103
(614) 478-6000 ..**Sherman**, Robert P '76 (Karr & S Co,LPA) -1 Easton Oval -Ste 550 -Columbus 43219
(614) 227-2000 ..**Sherman**, Ryan P '02 %Porter WM&A LLP -41 S High -Columbus 43215 **Fx:**227-2100
(317) 238-6233 ..**Sherman**, Steven M '74 (Kreig D LLP) -1 Indna Sq -Ste 2800 -Indianapolis, IN 46204
Sherman, Susan E '94 -111 Wood -Westerville 43081
(513) 381-7971 ..**Sherman**, Terrie A '91 (T Sherman Co,LPA) -119 E Court -Ste 411 -Cincinnati 45202
(614) 444-8800 ..**Sherman**, Terry K '71 -52 W Whittier -Columbus 43206
(513) 977-8200 ..**Sherman**, Thomas J '69 (Dinsmore & S LLP) -255 E 5th -Ste 1900 -Cincinnati 45202 **Fx:**977-8141
(614) 995-3717 ..**Sherman**, Thomas L '79 -277 E Town -4th Fl -Columbus 43215
(513) 977-8200 ..**Sherman**, William A '87 (Dinsmore & S LLP) -255 E 5th -Ste 1900 -Cincinnati 45202 **Fx:**977-8141
(513) 721-3330 ..**Sherman**, William D '94 (Robbins KP&T) -7 W 7th -Ste 1400 -Cincinnati 45202
(440) 350-2683 ..**Sheroke**, William L '71 Lake Cnty Pros -105 Main -Bx490 -Painesville 44077 **Fx:**350-2585
(614) 459-5582 ..**Sherowski**, Elizabeth M '96 OSU Moritz Cllg of Law -55 W 12th Av -Columbus 43210 **Fx:**292-1383
(937) 299-9607 ..**Sherrets**, Carl D '88 -580 Lincoln Park Blvd -Ste 399 -Kettering 45459 **Fx:**299-9618
(330) 486-3403 ..**Sherriff**, David J '70 Cole Vision Corp -1925 Enterprise Pkwy -Twinsburg 44087
(330) 264-9454 ..**Sherrin**, Michele P '92 Cmmnty Lgl Aid Srvcs,Inc -121 W North -Ste 100 -Wooster 44691
(330) 376-1717 ..**Sherrod**, John P '04 %Davis & Y -One Cascade Plz -Ste 800 -Akron 44308
(513) 422-4488 ..**Sherron**, James E '86 Pros -280 N Fair Av -Hamilton 45011
(740) 472-1255 ..**Sherry**, Henry A '54 -4368 Highbone Dr NE -Marietta, GA 30066
(859) 655-7004 ..**Sherry**, Jeffrey S '95 (Nielson & S,PSC) -639 Wshngtn Av -Ste 200 -Newport, KY 41071
Sherry, Kathryn E '95 -4368 Highborne Dr -Marietta, GA 30066
(614) 462-3194 ..**Sherwin**, Dietra K '04 Franklin Cnty Pub Def -373 S High -12th Fl -Columbus 43215
(513) 241-4722 ..**Sherwood**, Elizabeth Poe '87 (Montgomery R&J,LPA) -36 E 7th -Ste 2100 -Cincinnati 45202 **Fx:**241-8775
(312) 269-1537 ..**Sheshadri**, Archana '98 %Jones DR&P -77 W Wacker Dr -Chicago, IL 60601 **Fx:**782-8585
(216) 566-5616 ..**Sheth**, Mili K '03 %Thompson H LLP -127 Pub Sq -3900 Key Ctr -Cleveland 44114 **Fx:**566-5800
(330) 823-2226 ..**Shetler**, William B '73 (Shetler & S) -950 S Sawburg Av -Bx2146 -Alliance 44601
(614) 227-4803 ..**Shevelow**, Douglas L '04 %Bricker & E LLP -100 S 3rd -Columbus 43215 **Fx:**227-2390
(513) 422-4861 ..**Shew**, James C '69 -16 N Main -Middletown 45042
(937) 225-5600 ..**Shia**, Johnna M '97 Montgomery Cnty Pros -301 W 3rd -Bx972 -Dayton 45422 **Fx:**225-3470

(216) 991-6200 ..**Shibley**, Cathy M '82 B Firstenberg & Assoc Co,LPA
-20133 Farnsleigh Rd -Ohio Svngs Bldg -Shaker Heights 44122

(727) 823-7400 ..**Shibley**, Jeffery L '75 -3204 Gulf Blvd
-Saint Pete Beach, FL 33706

(513) 595-2823 ..**Shick**, Daniel S '83 Union Cntrl Life Ins Co -1876 Waycross Rd
-Bx40888 -Cincinnati 45240

Shidel, Kasey C '99 US Marine Corps -3217 Eden
-Camp LeJeune, NC 28547

(216) 221-2889 ..**Shields**, Daniel E '85 -1501 Westwood Av -Lakewood 44107

(330) 764-3582 ..**Shields**, Jim A '91 Medina City Schls -120 W Wshngtn -Bx408
-Medina 44258

(704) 386-8878 ..**Shields**, Randal D '83 Bank of America Legal Dept -101 S Tryon
-NC1-002-29-01 -Charlotte, NC 28255

Shields, William S '78 -3137 Parkvw Av -Cincinnati 45213

(216) 351-5300 ..**Shiffra**, Robert '66 Tempo Securities Corp -4712 State Rd
-Ste 200 -Cleveland 44109

(440) 992-8211 ..**Shiflet**, Hobart M '82 -217 Park Pl -Bx1442 -Ashtabula 44005

(330) 456-8341 ..**Shifman**, Arnold R '64 (Black MS&A,LPA) -220 Market Av S
-Ste 1000 -Canton 44702 **Fx**:456-5756

(513) 531-4088 ..**Shifman**, Julie C '87 (Shifman & Assoc) -7431 E Aracoma Dr
-Cincinnati 45237

(216) 831-3366 ..**Shifrin**, David B '87 -23240 Chagrin Blvd -Ste 515
-Beachwood 44122

(330) 762-6474 ..**Shifrin**, Debra Sue '81 (Sternberg NS & Assoc) -411 Wolf Ledges
Pkwy -Ste 300 -Akron 44311 **Fx**:762-2127

(614) 224-2428 ..**Shihab**, Gus M '93 Shihab & Assoc -65 E State -Ste 1550
-Columbus 43215 **Fx**:224-5080

(614) 224-2428 ..**Shihab**, Sam M '94 Shihab & Assoc -65 E State -Ste 1550
-Columbus 43215 **Fx**:224-5080

(513) 946-3171 ..**Shilling**, Karen R '91 Hamilton Cnty Pros -230 E 9th
-Cincinnati 45202 **Fx**:946-3017

(614) 466-8950 ..**Shilling**, Melissa M '94 Envirnmntl Review Appls Comm -309 S 4th
-Rm 222 -Columbus 43215

(440) 322-1329 ..**Shilling**, Terry S '68 -230 3rd -Ste 200 -Elyria 44035

(614) 644-8763 ..**Shillington**, Beth C '90 SERB -65 E State -Ste 1200
-Columbus 43215 **Fx**:466-3074

(937) 222-2500 ..**Shillito**, Beverly F '78 (Sebaly S&D) -1900 Kettering Twr
-Dayton 45423 **Fx**:222-6554

(916) 978-5671 ..**Shillito**, Daniel G '73 US Dept of Interior/Regional Solicitor
-2800 Cottage Way -Ste E-1712 -Sacramento, CA 95825

(216) 781-0070 ..**Shillman**, David B '61 (D Shillman Co,LPA) -720 Leader Bldg
-526 Superior Av E -Cleveland 44114 **Fx**:566-1468

(801) 625-9598 ..**Shimabukuro**, Richard K '77 Autoliv ASP,Inc -3305 Airport Rd
-Ogden, UT 84405

(614) 466-2872 ..**Shimeall**, Kent M '82 Atty Gen -30 E Broad -Columbus 43215
Fx:7-7592

Shimko, John A '69 -19251 Briarwood Ln -Strongsville 44149

(216) 241-8300 ..**Shimko**, Timothy A '76 (TA Shimko & Assoc)
-925 Euclid Av -Ste 2010 -Cleveland 44115 **Fx**:241-2702

(216) 579-1700 ..**Shimola**, Howard G '70 (Pearne & G LLP) -1801 E 9th -Ste 1200
-Cleveland 44114 **Fx**:579-6073

(216) 363-4500 ..**Shin**, William J '02 %Benesch FC&A LLP -200 Pub Sq -Ste 2300
-Cleveland 44114 **Fx**:363-4588

(888) 550-9555 ..**Shinaberry**, Shannon L '96 JM Smucker Co -One Strwbrry Ln
-Orrville 44667

(419) 243-6281 ..**Shindler**, James V Jr. '66 (Shindler NH&S,LLP) -300 Mad Av
-Ste 1200 -Toledo 43604 **Fx**:243-0129

(419) 243-6281 ..**Shindler Neff Holmes & Schlageter,LLP** -300 Mad Av -Ste 1200
-Toledo 43604 **Fx**:243-0129

(859) 341-2707 ..**Shinkle**, Karen L '85 KY Trans Cabinet -Bx17711
-Covington, KY 41017

(614) 461-0256 ..**Shinn**, Brian E '96 Ofc Dscplnry Cnsl -250 Civic Ctr Dr -#325
-Columbus 43215 **Fx**:461-7205

(330) 297-3665 ..**Shinn**, Charles R Jr. '01 Portage Cnty Pub Def -209 S Chestnut
-4th Fl -Ravenna 44266

(419) 242-7985 ..**Shinn**, Jason M '01 %Roetzel & A,LPA -One SeaGate -9th Fl
-Toledo 43604 **Fx**:242-0316

(216) 228-4791 ..**Shinn**, Maria L '97 -2164 Glenbury Av -Lakewood 44107

(412) 521-3234 ..**Shipkovitz**, Samuel '79 -5829 Nicholson -Pittsburgh, PA 15217

(937) 328-6970 ..**Shipley**, Alma H '86 Fulton Elmntry Schl -631 S Yellow Sprngs
-Springfield 45506

(740) 349-6195 ..**Shipley**, Rachel C '02 Licking Cnty Pros -20 S 2nd -4th Fl -Newark
43055

(937) 339-1500 ..**Shipman Dixon & Livingston** -215 W Water -Bx310 -Troy 45373
Fx:339-1519

Shipp, Bradley W '04 -(Address Unavailable)

(513) 381-0656 ..**Shipp**, Jeffrey C '87 (Kohnen & P LLP) -201 E 5th -Ste 800
-Cincinnati 45202 **Fx**:381-5823

(937) 426-7010 ..**Shira**, William A III '67 -432 Silvercrest Ter -Beavercreek 45440
Fx:426-7010

Shirer, Albert D '94 -1033 Sunhaven Dr -Medina 44256

(812) 421-6080 ..**Shirey**, Daniel R '69 American Cancercare -611 Harriet -L-100
-Evansville, IN 47710 **Fx**:421-6088

(614) 469-1301 ..**Shirey**, Van R '76 Chorpenning G&P Co,LPA -585 S Front
-Ste 250 -Columbus 43215

(937) 843-3152 ..**Shirk**, William E '57 (Shirk & S) -185 S Main -Bx246
-Lakeview 43331

(949) 863-4670 ..**Shirley**, Robert B '81 Taco Bell Corp -17901 Von Karman
-Irvine, CA 92614

Shirokawer, Leo '03 -323 Elm -Oberlin 44074

(859) 291-9900 ..**Shirooni**, Lucinda C '92 (Taliaferro MSHC&K,PLLC)
-1005 Mad Av -Bx468 -Covington, KY 41012

(740) 773-1141 ..**Shively**, Arlene T '98 VA Ofc of Reg Cnsl -17273 State Route 104
-538/02 -Chillicothe 45601

(216) 443-6350 ..**Shively**, David A '90 8th Dist Ct of Appls -1 Lakeside Av -#202
-Cleveland 44113 **Fx**:443-2044

(216) 221-3100 ..**Shively**, Jeffrey A '77 -14701 Detroit Av -Ste 540
-Lakewood 44107

(513) 651-5651 ..**Shiverdecker**, Merlyn D '72 (Carr & S) -817 Main -Ste 200
-Cincinnati 45202 **Fx**:651-5402

(216) 931-6000 ..**Shlonsky**, Patricia A '84 (Ulmer & B LLP) -1300 E 9th -Ste 900
Penton Media Bldg -Cleveland 44114 **Fx**:931-6001

(330) 253-5060 ..**Shoaff**, Joseph A '99 %Brennan M&D,LLC -75 E Market
-Akron 44308 **Fx**:253-1977

(614) 365-4100 ..**Shoaff**, Shannon M '01 %Carpenter & L LLP -280 N High
-Ste 1300 280 Plz -Columbus 43215 **Fx**:365-9145

(330) 723-9536 ..**Shockley**, Carol '87 Medina Cnty Pros -72 Pub Sq -Medina 44256

(614) 229-5072 ..**Shockley**, John L '95 Ernst & Young LLP -41 S High -Ste 1100
-Columbus 43215 **Fx**:229-5127

(330) 875-3288 ..**Shockling**, Robert J '49 -920 S Mill -Louisville 44641

(614) 469-5715 ..**Shoemaker**, Brenda S '89 US Atty -303 Marconi Blvd -Ste 200
-Columbus 43215

(614) 462-4485 ..**Shoemaker**, Douglas Lyn '85 Franklin Cnty Dom Rltns Ct
-373 S High -5th Fl -Columbus 43215

(614) 890-0834 ..**Shoemaker**, Fred J '51 -5500 Ulry Rd -Westerville 43081

(513) 732-7327 ..**Shoemaker**, Gitte K '94 Clermont Cnty Dom Rltns Ct
-2340 Clermont Ctr Dr -Batavia 45103

(614) 469-0100 ..**Shoemaker Howarth & Taylor LLP** -471 E Broad -Ste 2001
-Columbus 43215 **Fx**:280-9675

(330) 643-2397 ..**Shoemaker**, John H '71 Summit Cnty Cmn Pleas Ct -209 S High
-Akron 44308

(513) 552-5838 ..**Shoemaker**, Kent A '94 Cnsl GE -1 Newman Way -MD 5150
-Cincinnati 45215

(614) 469-0100 ..**Shoemaker**, Kevin L '79 (Shoemaker H&T LLP) -471 E Broad
-Ste 2001 -Columbus 43215 **Fx**:280-9675

(614) 799-2144 ..**Shoemaker**, Larry B '90 -1737 Woodbluff Dr -Powell 43065

(216) 363-4500 ..**Shofar**, Nick D '87 %Benesch FC&A LLP -200 Pub Sq -Ste 2300
-Cleveland 44114 **Fx**:363-4588

(740) 653-6464 ..**Shonk**, Brian D '88 (Dagger JMO&H) -144 E Main -Bx667
-Lancaster 43130 **Fx**:653-8522

(216) 661-6468 ..**Shonk**, Paul W '03 -4438 Pearl Rd -%Kevin Senich
-Cleveland 44109

(440) 777-0639 ..**Shook**, Ann J '56 (Shook & S) -5130 Devon Dr
-North Olmsted 44070

(937) 223-3277 ..**Shook**, Charles D '52 (Bieser G&L LLP) -6 N Main -400 Natl City
Ctr -Dayton 45402 **Fx**:223-6339

(419) 254-3104 ..**Shook**, David C '90 %Bunda S&D,PLL -One SeaGate -Ste 650
-Toledo 43604 **Fx**:241-4697

(440) 777-0639 ..**Shook**, Gene E Sr. '56 (Shook & S) -5130 Devon Dr
-North Olmsted 44070

(614) 464-1211 ..**Shook**, Kevin T '01 %Frost BT LLC -10 W Broad -Ste 1000
-Columbus 43215 **Fx**:464-1737

(740) 862-4191 ..**Shook**, Stephanie K '00 (Jackson KS&D) -719 W Market
-Baltimore 43105

(513) 983-4225 ..**Shook**, Susan M '97 Procter & Gamble Co-Legal
-1 Procter & Gamble Plz -Cincinnati 45202

(843) 576-2255 ..**Shoop**, John E '71 JK Harris &Co -4995 LaCrosse Rd -#1800
-North Charleston, SC 29406

(740) 532-4554 ..**Shope**, Dru A '93 (Edwards KA&S Co LPA) -211 Center
-Ironton 45638

(419) 241-9000 ..**Shope**, Gregory J '01 %Shumaker L&K,LLP -1000 Jackson
-Toledo 43624 **Fx**:241-6894

(216) 621-4268 ..**Shopneck**, Craig H '84 Ofc of Chptr 13 Trustees -200 Pub Sq
-Ste 3860 BP Twr -Cleveland 44114

(216) 464-7000 ..**Shore**, Michael A '59 (MA Shore Co,LPA) -23230 Chagrin Blvd
-Beachwood 44122 **Fx**:464-6503

(216) 906-1300 ..**Shorey**, James D '96 -2952 Fairmount Blvd -Cleveland 44118

(330) 562-3156 ..**Shorr**, Alan I '70 (Christley H&P) -215 W Garfld -Ste 230
-Aurora 44202 **Fx**:562-9540

(573) 893-4336 ..**Shorr**, David A '84 (Lathrop & G LC) -314 E High
-Jefferson City, MO 65101 **Fx**:893-5398

(216) 631-1221 ..**Shorr**, Randall B '86 -6314 Franklin Blvd NW -Cleveland 44102

(440) 899-9990 ..**Short**, Dale W '77 Short S&S -24461 Detroit Rd -Ste 340
-Westlake 44145

(513) 932-2047 ..**Short**, Jane A '00 %J Mengle -42 E Silver -Lebanon 45036

(216) 771-1760 ..**Short**, Jeffrey R '91 -1801 E 9th -Ste 900 -Cleveland 44114

(614) 469-3209 ..**Short**, Jennifer E '98 %Thompson H LLP -10 W Broad -Ste 700
-Columbus 43215 **Fx**:469-3361

(614) 464-4100 ..**Short**, Jennifer E '04 %AuCoin DH&Y LLC -495 S High -Ste 250
-Columbus 43215

(419) 221-5230 ..**Short**, Michael J '94 City of Lima -109 N Union -Lima 45801

(614) 462-5037 ..**Short**, Michael T '98 %Schottenstein Z&D -250 West -Bx165020
-Columbus 43216 **Fx**:462-5135

(419) 445-8815 ..**Short**, Peter D '78 (Plassman RHS&H) -302 N Defiance -Bx178
-Archbold 43502 **Fx**:445-1080

Short, Randall L '88 -6601 Dixie Hwy -Florence, KY 41042

(440) 899-9990 ..**Short Shepherd & Stanton** -24461 Detroit Rd -Ste 340
-Westlake 44145

(330) 675-2521 ..**Shorts**, John T '00 %Trumbull Cnty Probate Ct -161 High NW
-Warren 44481

(513) 361-0200 ..**Shoskin**, Jeffrey S '83 (Roetzel & A,LPA) -250 E 5th
-310 Chiquita Ctr -Cincinnati 45202 **Fx**:361-0335

(740) 593-5828 ..**Shostak**, Robert J '90 -18 W State -Athens 45701 **Fx**:594-6446

(513) 621-2120 ..**Shott**, Andrew M '81 (Strauss & T,LPA) -150 E 4th -4th Fl
-Cincinnati 45202 **Fx**:241-8259

(513) 381-2838 ..**Shotten**, Melvin S '68 (Taft S&H LLP) -425 Walnut -Ste 1800
-Cincinnati 45202 **Fx**:381-0205

(614) 442-5626 ..**Shoub**, Grant D '77 (Hunter CS&B) -3360 Tremont Rd -2nd Fl
-Columbus 43221 **Fx**:442-5625

(419) 213-4775 ..**Shousher**, Eileen S '90 Lucas Cnty Probate Ct -700 Adams
-Toledo 43624

(419) 241-8885 ..**Shousher**, Mohamed Y '80 -618 Adams -2nd Fl -Toledo 43604

(614) 227-2000 ..**Shouvlin**, David P '96 (Porter WM&A LLP) -41 S High
-Columbus 43215 **Fx**:227-2100

(954) 525-1000 ..**Showalter**, Donald S '85 (Holland & K,LLP) -One E Broward Blvd
-Ste 1300 -Fort Lauderdale, FL 33301 **Fx**:463-2030

(937) 438-6848 ..**Showalter**, Robert L '89 (Stevens & S LLP) -7019 Corp Way
-Dayton 45459

(513) 932-2115 ..**Showen**, Jason A '00 %Rittgers & R -12 E Warren
-Lebanon 45036

(843) 971-4960 ..**Shpigler**, Debra R '85 (D Shpigler Co,LPA)
-1041 Johnnie Dodds Blvd -#2C -Mt Pleasant, SC 29464

(614) 461-1311 ..**Shrader**, Rebecca R '03 %Reminger & R -65 E State
-4th Fl Cptl Sq Ofc Bldg -Columbus 43215 **Fx**:232-2410

(440) 395-3765 ..**Shrallow**, Dane A '71 Progressive Ins Co -6300 Wilson Mills Rd
-#N72A -Mayfield Village 44143

(317) 271-6192 .. **Shrewsbury,** Paul R '93 Keystone Engineering -9786 E Cnty Rd -200 N -Avon, IN 46123

(330) 287-5542 .. **Shriner,** Rosanne K '02 Wayne Cnty Cmmn Pleas Ct -107 W Lbrty -Wooster 44691

(740) 286-0071 .. **Shriver,** Jill H '03 %R Lewis -295 Pearl -Bx664 -Jackson 45640 **Fx:**286-2988

(330) 674-3055 .. **Shrock,** Steven J '92 (Critchfield C&J Ltd) -138 E Jackson -Ste A -Millersburg 44654

(216) 687-1311 .. **Shroge,** Michael D '00 %Reminger & R -101 Prospect Av W -1400 Mdlnd Bldg -Cleveland 44115 **Fx:**687-1841

(614) 228-6453 .. **Shroyer,** David I '80 (Colley S&A Co,LPA) -536 S High -Columbus 43215 **Fx:**228-7122

(614) 464-1610 .. **Shroyer,** Gary S '84 K Kurgis Co,LPA -100 S 4th -Ste 300 -Columbus 43215 **Fx:**464-1616

Shroyer, Melisa S '85 -2259 Hvrfrd Rd -Columbus 43220

(440) 944-7020 .. **Shryock,** John W '79 (J Shryock Co LPA) -30601 Euclid Av -Wickliffe 44092 **Fx:**943-3096

(419) 245-4944 .. **Shuba,** John H '90 Lucas Co Sheriffs Dept -1622 Spielbusch Av -Toledo 43624

(614) 283-6393 .. **Shubitowski,** John K '80 Abercrombie & Fitch Co -6301 Fitch Path -New Albany 43054

(216) 241-2500 .. **Shucofsky,** Joseph F '86 -526 Superior Av -Ste 1525 -Cleveland 44114

(614) 529-8988 .. **Shufeldt,** Matthew D '01 (Willis S&W Co LPA) -5017 Cemetary Rd -Hilliard 43026 **Fx:**334-8989

(972) 443-6543 .. **Shuff,** Ronald F '77 Flowserve Corp -5215 N O'Connor Blvd -Ste 2300 -Irving, TX 75039

(937) 295-2983 .. **Shuffelton,** David B '69 %Faulkner GK&S,LPA -31 S Main -Fort Loramie 45845 **Fx:**285-3633

(740) 947-7277 .. **Shugart,** Jason V '02 (Seif & S LLC) -110 E Emmitt Av -Waverly 45690 **Fx:**947-1815

(330) 702-0033 .. **Shugart,** Ursula P '03 -3855 Starrs Centre Dr -Ste A -Canfield 44406 **Fx:**702-1133

(330) 643-2788 .. **Shuki,** Jennie R '98 Summit Cnty Pros-Crim -53 Univ Av -7th Fl -Akron 44308 **Fx:**643-8277

(513) 684-3211 .. **Shuler,** Gary R Jr. '98 IRS Dist Cnsl -312 Elm -Ste 2300 -Cincinnati 45202

(614) 251-1700 .. **Shuler,** Gordon P '73 Community Housing Network,Inc -957 E Broad -Columbus 43205

(513) 977-8200 .. **Shuler,** Matthew D '98 %Dinsmore & S LLP -255 E 5th -Ste 1900 -Cincinnati 45202 **Fx:**977-8141

(614) 228-4546 .. **Shuler Plank & Brahm,LPA** -145 E Rich -Ste 400 -Columbus 43215

(614) 228-4546 .. **Shuler,** Samantha A '96 %Shuler P&B,LPA -145 E Rich -Ste 400 -Columbus 43215

(513) 723-4000 .. **Shuller,** Donald J '76 (Vorys SS&P LLP) -221 E 4th -Ste 2000 Atrium Two -Bx0236 -Cincinnati 45201 **Fx:**723-4056

(202) 624-2964 .. **Shulman,** Darren M '02 %Crowell & M -1001 Penn Av NW -Washington, DC 20004

(330) 725-8685 .. **Shulman,** Gary A '90 -110 S Huntngtn -Medina 44256

(937) 222-2500 .. **Shulman,** Jeffrey B '63 (Sebaly S&D) -1900 Kettering Twr -Dayton 45423 **Fx:**222-6554

(216) 931-6000 .. **Shultz,** David E '02 %Ulmer & B LLP -1300 E 9th -Ste 900 Penton Media Bldg -Cleveland 44114 **Fx:**931-6001

(216) 664-4820 .. **Shultz,** Jaclyn R '03 %Prosecutor -1200 Ontario Av -8th Fl Justice Ctr -Cleveland 44113 **Fx:**664-4399

(419) 354-9250 .. **Shultz,** Jacqueline M '97 %Wood Cnty Pros -One Cthse Sq -Bowling Green 43402 **Fx:**353-2904

(616) 772-1800 .. **Shultz,** James E Jr. '00 Gentex Corp -600 N Centennial -Zeeland, MI 49464

(330) 782-3000 .. **Shultz,** John F '76 -4822 Market -Ste 220 -Boardman 44512

(330) 750-1333 .. **Shultz,** Michael W '95 Healthridge Medical Ctr,Inc -315 Struthers-Lbrty Rd -Campbell 44505

Shumaker, Dennis K '03 -6916 Morley Ln -Dayton 45424

(419) 241-9000 .. **Shumaker,** Gregory S '73 (Shumaker L&K,LLP) -1000 Jackson -Toledo 43624 **Fx:**241-6894

(419) 241-9000 .. **Shumaker Loop & Kendrick,LLP** -1000 Jackson -Toledo 43624 **Fx:**241-6894

(614) 463-9441 .. **Shumaker Loop & Kendrick,LLP** -41 S High -Ste 2210 -Columbus 43215 **Fx:**463-1108

(216) 348-5400 .. **Shumaker,** Roger L '76 (McDonald H Co,LPA) -600 Superior Av E -Ste 2100 -Cleveland 44114 **Fx:**348-5459

(614) 261-6331 .. **Shuman,** Dennis L '77 Speer Ind,Inc -600 Oaklnd Park Av -Columbus 43214

(614) 365-2700 .. **Shumate,** Alex '75 (Squire S&D LLP) -41 S High -1300 Huntngtn Ctr -Columbus 43215 **Fx:**365-2499

(859) 655-4200 .. **Shumate,** Gregory S '88 (Greenebaum D&M PLLC) -50 E RiverCenter Blvd -Ste 1800 -Covington, KY 41011 **Fx:**655-4239

(248) 258-1616 .. **Shumate,** Jack D '62 (Butzel L) -100 Blmfld Hills Pkwy -Ste 200 -Bloomfield Hills, MI 48304 **Fx:**258-1439

(614) 365-2700 .. **Shumate,** Keith '91 (Squire S&D LLP) -41 S High -1300 Huntngtn Ctr -Columbus 43215 **Fx:**365-2499

(614) 292-0611 .. **Shumate,** Kimberly A '92 OSU/Legal Affrs -33 W 11th Av -Ste 209 -Columbus 43201

(216) 228-2900 .. **Shumay,** Robert G '89 The Kirby Co -1920 W 114th -Cleveland 44102

(330) 535-2220 .. **Shunk,** Laura F '83 (Hudak S&F) -2020 Front -Ste 307 -Cuyahoga Falls 44221 **Fx:**535-1435

(216) 621-0200 .. **Shunk,** Thomas H '79 (Baker & H LLP) -1900 E 9th -Ste 3200 -Cleveland 44114 **Fx:**696-0740

(440) 746-2116 .. **Shurell,** Carolyn J '80 VA Ofc of Regional Cnsl -10000 Brecksvll Rd -Bldg 1 Fl 5 -Brecksville 44141

(614) 469-3939 .. **Shurte,** Matthew R '98 %Jones D -325 John H McConnell Blvd -Ste 600 -Bx165017 -Columbus 43216 **Fx:**461-4198

(216) 621-0150 .. **Shuster,** Michael P '95 (Hahn L&P LLP) -3300 BP Twr/200 Pub Sq -Ste 3300 -Cleveland 44114 **Fx:**241-2824

(614) 462-5400 .. **Shuster,** Michele Ann '93 OfCnsl Kegler BH&R -65 E State -Ste 1800 -Columbus 43215 **Fx:**464-2634

(330) 499-7946 .. **Shuttleworth,** William L Jr. '51 -5851 Carlew NW -North Canton 44720

(614) 469-0180 .. **Shwartz,** Myron '67 -501 S High -Columbus 43215

(614) 451-1580 .. **Sibbring,** Donald A '55 -4314 Camborne Rd -Columbus 43220

(216) 696-6000 .. **Sicherman,** Marvin A '60 (Dettelbach S&B,LPA) -1801 E 9th -1100 Ohio Svngs Plz -Cleveland 44114 **Fx:**696-3338

(330) 726-8700 .. **Siciliano,** Anthony '89 %J Fleck -845 Woodfld Ct -Youngstown 44512

(614) 466-2980 .. **Siciliano,** Anthony D '01 %Atty Gen -30 E Broad -Columbus 43215 **Fx:**728-9470

(216) 771-1760 .. **Siciliano,** Dennis J '89 Smith & C LLP -1801 E Ninth -Ste 900 Ohio Svngs Plz -Cleveland 44114 **Fx:**771-3387

(419) 321-1377 .. **Siciliano,** John J '78 (Shumaker L&K,LLP) -1000 Jackson -Toledo 43624 **Fx:**241-6894

(330) 580-5229 .. **Siciliano,** Patrick S '84 -457 Vandalia Dr -Tallmadge 44278

(859) 669-2148 .. **Sicking,** Albert G Jr. '60 IRS -201 W Rivercenter Blvd -Stop 824-T -Covington, KY 41019

(740) 732-5685 .. **Sickler,** Clifford N '77 Noble Cnty Pros -409 Poplar -Ste A -Caldwell 43724

(813) 225-3020 .. **Sickles,** Robert E '98 %Broad & C -100 N Tampa -Ste 3500 -Tampa, FL 33602 **Fx:**225-3039

(614) 466-6968 .. **Sico,** Thomas '78 Workers Comp -30 W Spring -Level 26 -Columbus 43215

(330) 296-9999 .. **Sicuro,** Thomas J '68 Sicuro & S -213 S Chestnut -Ravenna 44266

(216) 595-1631 .. **Sidaway,** Linda D '93 Citizens Ins -23240 Chagrin Blvd -Ste 102 -Beachwood 44122

(740) 852-1576 .. **Siddiqi,** Zahid Haq '97 Tanner M&H -2 S Main -London 43140

(859) 491-4444 .. **Sidebottom,** Shane C '00 %Wolnitzek & R,PSC -502 Greenup -Bx352 -Covington, KY 41012 **Fx:**491-1001

(937) 376-9454 .. **Sidell,** Arthur L III '73 -330 N Detroit -Xenia 45385

Sidloski, Robert A '96 -25047 Lorain Rd -North Olmsted 44070

(614) 464-6400 .. **Sidman,** Robert J '68 (Vorys SS&P LLP) -52 E Gay -Bx1008 -Columbus 43216 **Fx:**464-6350

(703) 433-4231 .. **Sidman,** Thomas J '80 Nextel Comm,Inc -2001 Edmund Halley Dr -5th Fl -Reston, VA 20191

(614) 865-8263 .. **Sidor,** David S '72 %Exel -570 Polaris Pkwy -Westerville 43082

(216) 357-3305 .. **Sidoti,** Marcus S '04 (Sidoti & S,LPA) -55 Pub Sq -Ste 1600 -Cleveland 44113

(216) 357-3305 .. **Sidoti,** Nicholas R II '03 (Sidoti & S,LPA) -55 Pub Sq -Ste 1600 -Cleveland 44113

(216) 861-5582 .. **Sidoti,** Robert A '98 %Fay SFM&M LLP -1100 Superior Av -7th Fl -Cleveland 44114 **Fx:**241-1666

(440) 808-0011 .. **Sidoti,** Salvatore A '99 %Renner KGBT&W,LPA -24500 Ctr Ridge Rd -Ste 280 -Westlake 44145 **Fx:**808-0657

(859) 294-0277 .. **Sidun,** Charles A '75 (KPMG) -3500 Antilles Dr -Lexington, KY 40509

Siebels, Scott A '80 -(Address Unavailable)

(216) 357-7214 .. **Siebenschuh,** Ellen A '95 US Dist Ct -801 W Superior Av -Cleveland 44113

(513) 831-5700 .. **Sieber,** Steven J '82 Sieber Cnstrctn Inc -5827 Happy Hllw Rd -#2B2C -Milford 45150

(614) 464-6400 .. **Sieck,** William A '00 %Vorys SS&P LLP -52 E Gay -Bx1008 -Columbus 43216 **Fx:**464-6350

(614) 644-8329 .. **Sieg,** Gary L '94 OH Dept Hlth -246 N High -Bx118 -Columbus 43216

(586) 447-3700 .. **Siegan,** Renee S '93 Saurbier & S,PC -400 Maple Park Dr -Ste 402 -Saint Clair Shores, MI 48081

(614) 227-2000 .. **Siegel,** Bradd N '78 (Porter WM&A LLP) -41 S High -Columbus 43215 **Fx:**227-2100

(513) 241-3100 .. **Siegel,** Christopher J '98 Lerner S&R -120 E 4th -8th Fl -Cincinnati 45202

(216) 763-1004 .. **Siegel,** Daniel S '93 Siegel SJ&J Co,LPA -25700 Science Park Dr -Ste 210 -Cleveland 44122 **Fx:**763-1016

(440) 544-1107 .. **Siegel,** Edward F '74 Siegel & Assoc -5910 Landerbrook Dr -Ste 200 -Mayfield Heights 44124 **Fx:**446-1240

(216) 763-1004 .. **Siegel,** Fred '55 Siegel SJ&J Co,LPA -25700 Science Park Dr -Ste 210 -Cleveland 44122 **Fx:**763-1016

(419) 383-3898 .. **Siegel,** Gregory B '84 Med Coll of OH -3000 Arilington Av -Toledo 43614

(216) 763-1004 .. **Siegel,** Jay P '97 %Siegel SJ&J Co,LPA -25700 Science Park Dr -Ste 210 -Cleveland 44122 **Fx:**763-1016

(941) 365-0550 .. **Siegel,** Michael E '92 (Livingston P&S,PA) -46 N Wshngtn Blvd -Ste 1 -Sarasota, FL 34236 **Fx:**366-0826

(216) 595-0944 .. **Siegel,** Neil W '91 -23220 Chagrin Blvd -#360 -Beachwood 44122 **Fx:**595-1350

(216) 291-1300 .. **Siegel,** Nessa G '86 (N Siegel Co,LPA) -4070 Mayfld Rd -Cleveland 44121

(513) 579-6400 .. **Siegel,** Richard D '71 (Keating M&K PLL) -1 E 4th -1400 Provident Twr -Cincinnati 45202 **Fx:**579-6457

(513) 621-2666 .. **Siegel,** Robert H '75 (Statman HS&E LLC) -255 E 5th -Ste 2900 Chemed Ctr -Cincinnati 45202 **Fx:**587-4477

(216) 763-1004 .. **Siegel Siegel Johnson & Jennings Co, LPA** -25700 Science Park Dr -Ste 210 -Cleveland 44122 **Fx:**763-1016

(614) 442-8885 .. **Siegel Siegel Johnson & Jennings Co, LPA** -3001 Bethel Rd -Ste 208 -Columbus 43220 **Fx:**442-8880

Siegel, Sindy J '99 -(Address Unavailable)

(513) 977-8200 .. **Siegel,** Steve N '97 %Dinsmore & S LLP -255 E 5th -Ste 1900 -Cincinnati 45202 **Fx:**977-8141

(954) 713-8119 .. **Siegel,** Tamara L '97 %L Mayersohn -515 Seabreeze Blvd -Ste 301 -Fort Lauderdale, FL 33316 **Fx:**713-8153

(419) 524-9811 .. **Siegenthaler,** John H '64 (Weldon H&K,LLP) -28 Park Av W -Bank One Bldg -Mansfield 44902 **Fx:**522-5758

(440) 885-8173 .. **Siegfried,** Elayne M '94 City of Parma -6611 Ridge Rd -Purchasing & Personnel -Parma 44129

(614) 227-2000 .. **Siegfried,** Erin Freund '96 %Porter WM&A LLP -41 S High -Columbus 43215 **Fx:**227-2100

(614) 752-1765 .. **Siegfried,** Gregory M '03 OH Dept Rehab & Correction -1050 Fwy Dr N -Columbus 43229

(614) 227-2000 .. **Siegfried,** Jeremy David '99 %Porter WM&A LLP -41 S High -Columbus 43215 **Fx:**227-2100

(440) 449-1320 .. **Siegfried,** John P '73 -674 Dvdsn Dr -Highland Heights 44143

(216) 931-6000 .. **Siegfried,** Mark S '94 %Ulmer & B LLP -1300 E 9th -Ste 900 Penton Media Bldg -Cleveland 44114 **Fx:**931-6001

Siegfried, Ruth L '72 -206 Guard -Rockford, IL 61103

(937) 456-6818 .. **Siehl,** Andrew F '95 (AF Siehl Co,LPA) -113 S Barron -Eaton 45320

(513) 361-1200 .. **Siehl,** Jeffrey D '98 %Squire S&D LLP -312 Walnut -Ste 3500
-Cincinnati 45202 **Fx:**361-1201

(614) 228-1541 .. **Siehl,** Richard W '77 (Baker & H LLP) -65 E State -Ste 2100
-Columbus 43215 **Fx:**462-2616

(216) 663-7991 .. **Siekierski,** Diane M '83 -14517 Wheeler Rd -Maple Heights 44137

(419) 249-7900 .. **Sieler,** Jean A '87 (Robison C&O) -Four SeaGate -9th Fl
-Toledo 43604 **Fx:**249-7911

(614) 734-1270 .. **Sieloff,** William L '01 %Farlow & Assoc LLC -270 Bradenton Av
-Dublin 43017 **Fx:**923-1031

Siemen, Christopher W '86 -(Address Unavailable)

(216) 622-3754 .. **Sierleja,** David A '82 US Atty -801 W Superior -Ste 400
-Cleveland 44113 **Fx:**622-3370

(859) 572-5321 .. **Sies,** Dennis E '83 NKU-Pol Sci -217 Landrum
-Highland Heights, KY 41099

(419) 738-7427 .. **Siesel,** Gerald F '76 -119 W Auglaize -Bx2006
-Wapakoneta 45895

(513) 695-1325 .. **Sievers,** Andrew L '94 Warren Cnty Pros -500 Justice Dr
-Lebanon 45036 **Fx:**695-2962

(213) 990-7810 .. **Sievers,** Ora J '49 -1716 Vineyard Av -Los Angeles, CA 90019

(614) 224-6488 .. **Siewert,** Michael H '84 -307 E Lvngstn Av -Columbus 43215

(419) 222-5045 .. **Siferd & McCluskey LPA** -212 N Elizabeth -Ste 504 -Lima 45801

(419) 222-5045 .. **Siferd,** Richard E '73 (Siferd & M LPA) -212 N Elizabeth -Ste 504
-Lima 45801

(330) 869-0522 .. **Siff,** Alan L '63 Widmann Siff & Co -3401 Stanley Rd -Akron 44333

(614) 466-4656 .. **Sigal,** Marc A '84 Atty Gen -150 E Gay -Columbus 43215
Fx:466-1756

(614) 781-7686 .. **Sigall,** Herschel M '65 %State Troopers Assoc -6161 Busch Blvd
-Ste 130 -Columbus 43229

(614) 866-4025 .. **Sigall,** Leonard S '59 -6470 E Main -Reynoldsburg 43068

(513) 731-1402 .. **Sigalov,** Vlad '99 -1717 Section Rd -Ste 222 -Cincinnati 45237

(216) 586-3939 .. **Sigalow,** Steven E '75 (Jones D) -901 Lakeside Av -Cleveland
44114 **Fx:**579-0212

(513) 352-4707 .. **Sigman,** Gloria J '95 Law Dept -801 Plum -Rm 214
-Cincinnati 45202 **Fx:**352-1515

(614) 854-5226 .. **Sigman,** Timothy E '95 Nationwide -5900 Parkwood Pl -PW 01-08
-Dublin 43016

(216) 241-6602 .. **Sigmier,** Harry T '80 (Weston HFP&H LLP) -50 Pub Sq
-2500 Trmnl Twr -Cleveland 44113 **Fx:**621-8369

(614) 221-8448 .. **Sigmund,** Thomas J '78 (Buckingham D&B,LLP)
-191 W Nationwide Blvd -Ste 300 -Bx151120 -Columbus 43215
Fx:221-8590

(614) 716-1556 .. **Signet,** Bradford R '81 Amer Elec Pwr Co -1 Riverside Plz
-Columbus 43215

(614) 227-2333 .. **Signoracci,** Diane M '81 (Bricker & E LLP) -100 S 3rd
-Columbus 43215 **Fx:**227-2390

(614) 462-3555 .. **Sika,** Warren J '75 Franklin Cnty Pros -373 S High
-Columbus 43215

(419) 252-6214 .. **Sikkema,** Gary D '75 (Spengler N PLL) -608 Mad Av -Ste 1000
-Toledo 43604 **Fx:**241-8599

(419) 241-2777 .. **Sikkema,** Sue A '82 Bunda S&D,PLL -One SeaGate -Ste 650
-Toledo 43604 **Fx:**241-4697

(614) 236-6889 .. **Sikora,** Alison D '99 Capital Univ Law Sch -303 E Broad
-Columbus 43215

(614) 827-7300 .. **Sikora,** Charity Seabrook '02 %Freund F&A -65 E State -Ste 800
-Columbus 43215 **Fx:**827-7303

(614) 466-8911 .. **Sikora,** Damian W '02 Atty Gen -30 E Broad -Columbus 43215
Fx:728-7582

(216) 433-2318 .. **Sikora,** John W '76 NASA Glenn Research Ctr
-21000 Brookpark Rd -Mail Stop LE-LAW -Cleveland 44135

(440) 266-7777 .. **Sikora,** Michael J III '98 (Sikora Law,LLC) -7340 Ctr
-Mentor 44060 **Fx:**255-9207

(216) 443-8582 .. **Sikorski,** Paul A '03 Cuyahoga Cnty Ct Cmmn Pleas
-1200 Ontario -Justice Ctr 11th Fl -Cleveland 44113

(330) 456-0900 .. **Silagy,** Anne Piero '85 -220 Market Av S -Ste 300 -Canton 44702
Fx:456-1981

(440) 354-2212 .. **Silakoski,** Linda G '97 (LG Silakoski,LPA) -8 N State -Ste 400
-Painesville 44077

(202) 514-7276 .. **Silas,** Adrien L '84 US DOJ -950 Penn Av NW
-Washington, DC 20530

(330) 867-3545 .. **Silas-Butler,** Jacqueline A '84 -2081 Larchmont Rd -Akron 44313

(216) 241-3033 .. **Silberman,** Marc N '80 Thomas & T -629 Euclid Av -Ste 740
-Cleveland 44114

(513) 977-8200 .. **Silbersack,** Mark L '71 (Dinsmore & S LLP) -255 E 5th -Ste 1900
-Cincinnati 45202 **Fx:**977-8141

(440) 347-5781 .. **Silbiger,** Mark C '88 Lubrizol Corp -29400 Lakelnd Blvd
-Wickliffe 44092

(740) 772-4772 .. **Silcott,** Daniel L '84 Ross Cnty Pub Def -14 S Paint -Ste 54
-Chillicothe 45601

(740) 385-1078 .. **Silcott,** Lori L '94 %LJ Henniger & Assoc -4 E Main -Ste 200
-Logan 43138

(330) 762-2411 .. **Silfani,** Daniel L '99 %Amer C Co,LPA -159 S Main -6th Fl
-Akron 44308 **Fx:**762-9918

(419) 252-6282 .. **Silk,** James P '62 OfCnsl Spengler N PLL -608 Mad Av -Ste 1000
-Toledo 43604 **Fx:**241-8599

(419) 252-6210 .. **Silk,** James P Jr. '93 (Spengler N PLL) -608 Mad Av -Ste 1000
-Toledo 43604 **Fx:**241-8599

(614) 461-1311 .. **Silk,** Richard J Jr. '01 %Reminger & R -65 E State -4th Fl Cptl
Sq Ofc Bldg -Columbus 43215 **Fx:**232-2410

(216) 696-6500 .. **Silk,** Thomas J '85 Caravona & C,PLL -50 Pub Sq -Ste
1900 Trmnl Twr -Cleveland 44113 **Fx:**696-1411

(740) 593-3357 .. **Sillery,** James D '73 (Mollica GS&S Co,LPA) -35 N Cllg -Drwr958
-Athens 45701

(216) 241-5250 .. **Silliman,** Kenneth G '88 -2920 Brdg Av -Cleveland 44113

(216) 321-8033 .. **Sills,** Alan J '82 -13882 Cedar Rd -University Heights 44118

(412) 366-3333 .. **Silvaggio,** Joseph D '01 %Willman & A,LLP
-705 McKnight Park Dr -Pittsburgh, PA 15237

(614) 781-7686 .. **Silveira,** Elaine N '00 %State Troopers Assoc -6161 Busch Blvd
-Ste 130 -Columbus 43229

(937) 865-6800 .. **Silver,** Harry R '88 Lexis/Nexis -Bx933 -Dayton 45401

(614) 221-2718 .. **Silver,** Howard D '76 -500 City Park Av -Columbus 43215

(330) 562-3156 .. **Silver,** James R '80 (Christley H&P) -215 W Garfld -Ste 230
-Aurora 44202 **Fx:**562-9540

(606) 344-8135 .. **Silver,** John A '91 CSX Trans,Inc -1717 Dixie Hwy -Ste 400
-Fort Wright, KY 41011

(614) 466-4605 .. **Silver,** Joseph J '84 OH Dept Job & Fam Srvcs -30 E Broad
-32nd Fl -Columbus 43266

(440) 324-2409 .. **Silver,** Michael D '88 UAW Legal Srvcs -347 Midway Blvd -Ste 312
-Elyria 44035 **Fx:**324-4647

(216) 371-5220 .. **Silver,** Paul Jay '87 -2000 Lee Rd -Ste 23
-Cleveland Heights 44118 **Fx:**371-5220

(415) 665-2346 .. **Silver,** Robert E '73 -419 Fredrck -San Francisco, CA 94117

(513) 946-4046 .. **Silver,** Susan '81 Hamilton Cnty Auditor -138 E Court -Rm 304A
-Cincinnati 45202

(440) 449-6800 .. **Silver,** Terry L '77 %Skoda Minotti & Co -6685 Beta Dr
-Mayfield Village 44143

(937) 372-9236 .. **Silverberg,** Eric '69 (Silverberg Z&O Co,LPA) -100 E Market -Bx40
-Xenia 45385

(614) 227-4812 .. **Silverberg,** Karl J '04 %Bricker & E LLP -100 S 3rd
-Columbus 43215 **Fx:**227-2390

(937) 372-9236 .. **Silverberg Zaharieff & Orlins Co,LPA** -100 E Market -Bx40
-Xenia 45385

(513) 241-9844 .. **Silverman,** Beth I '84 -30 Garfld Pl -Ste 920 -Cincinnati 45202
Fx:241-9908

(216) 687-1311 .. **Silverman,** Brent S '94 (Reminger & R) -101 Prospect Av W
-1400 Mdlnd Bldg -Cleveland 44115 **Fx:**687-1841

(201) 393-5254 .. **Silverman,** Charles '73 Cnsl Quest Diag, Inc -1 Malcolm Av
-Teterboro, NJ 07608 **Fx:**393-5771

(614) 249-7015 .. **Silverman,** Karen L '03 Nationwide -One Nationwide Plz
-Ofc of Gen Cnsl -Columbus 43215

(419) 243-3261 .. **Silverman,** Nathan Leo '61 -520 Mad Av -864 Spitzer Bldg
-Toledo 43604

(419) 241-9000 .. **Silverman,** Peter R '84 (Shumaker L&K,LLP) -1000 Jackson
-Toledo 43624 **Fx:**241-6894

(216) 898-2344 .. **Silveroli,** Genevieve A '97 Electrolux -18013 Cleve Pkwy -Ste 100
-Cleveland 44135

(513) 624-6720 .. **Silvers,** Jane E '86 (JF Silvers Co Ltd) -1080 Nimitzvw Dr
-Ste 400-A -Cincinnati 45230

(419) 474-9514 .. **Silvers,** Kyle A '97 (Farah & S) -3030 W Sylvania Av -Ste 106
-Toledo 43613 **Fx:**474-9522

(937) 228-3731 .. **Silverstein,** Jeffrey M '80 (Silverstein & Assoc) -130 W 2nd
-1616 1st Natl Plz -Dayton 45402

(614) 464-2233 .. **Silverstein,** Jerry '85 -Bx14906 -Columbus 43214

(216) 586-3939 .. **Silverstein,** Marc A '89 Cnsl Jones D -901 Lakeside Av
-Cleveland 44114 **Fx:**579-0212

(614) 466-3417 .. **Silverstein,** Michael L '84 %Hon AR Resnick -30 E Broad -3rd Fl
-Columbus 43215

(216) 586-3939 .. **Silversten,** Matthew P '02 %Jones D -901 Lakeside Av
-Cleveland 44114 **Fx:**579-0212

(815) 227-0700 .. **Silvestri,** Amy L '92 (Lyon & S) -4615 E State -Ste 203
-Rockford, IL 61108

(614) 237-8050 .. **Silvestri,** Ralph S Jr. '92 -4181 E Main -Columbus 43213

(614) 249-7618 .. **Simaitis,** David E '89 SrCnsl Nationwide Ins Co -1 Nationwide Plz
-Columbus 43215

Simak, Margaret L '88 -(Address Unavailable)

(216) 443-6654 .. **Simek,** Douglas R '03 Cuyahoga Cnty Ct of Cmn Pleas
-1200 Ontario -11th Fl Justice Cntr -Cleveland 44113

Simeri, Jane A '81 -(Address Unavailable)

(330) 497-0700 .. **Simele,** David L '63 %Krugliak WG&D Co,LPA -4775 Munson NW
-Bx36963 -Canton 44735 **Fx:**497-4020

(440) 871-0234 .. **Simiele,** Thomas C '71 -30080 Persimmon Dr -Westlake 44145

(740) 881-3131 .. **Simile,** Belinda H '87 -8933 Filiz Ln -Powell 43065

(419) 243-6281 .. **Simko,** David J '75 (Shindler NH&S,LLP) -300 Mad Av -Ste 1200
-Toledo 43604 **Fx:**243-0129

(419) 213-6951 .. **Simko,** Megan E '04 Lucas Cnty Pros-Juv Div
-1801 Spielbusch Av -Toledo 43624

(330) 497-0700 .. **Simmerman,** Sam O '79 (Krugliak WG&D Co,LPA)
-4775 Munson NW -Bx36963 -Canton 44735 **Fx:**497-4020

(513) 745-0400 .. **Simmonds,** Rasheed A '97 (Furnier T,LLP) -1 Fncl Way -Ste 312
-Cincinnati 45242 **Fx:**792-6724

(440) 526-2067 .. **Simmons,** Adele O '89 -6572 Thorntree Dr -Brecksville 44141

(330) 675-2659 .. **Simmons,** Cameron F '01 %11th Dist Ct of Appls -111 High NE
-Warren 44481

(330) 499-8899 .. **Simmons & Cleaver** -4690 Munson NW -Canton 44718

(330) 499-8899 .. **Simmons,** David J '82 (Simmons & C) -4690 Munson NW -Canton
44718

(419) 874-9145 .. **Simmons,** Donald D '58 -Bx5 -Perrysburg 43552

(330) 972-6979 .. **Simmons,** Franklin B III '87 Univ of Akron/Dept of Mngmnt
-CBA 334 -Akron 44325

(614) 224-7291 .. **Simmons,** Gerald G '71 -330 S High -Columbus 43215

(513) 352-6782 .. **Simmons,** Gerald W '67 (Thompson H LLP) -312 Walnut -14th Fl
-Cincinnati 45202 **Fx:**241-4771

(216) 443-7295 .. **Simmons,** Jennifer L '03 %Cuyahoga Cnty Pub Def
-1849 Prospect Av -Ste 222 -Cleveland 44115

(419) 421-3261 .. **Simmons,** Joe A '80 Marathon Ashland Petroleum LLC
-539 S Main -Rm 863-M -Findlay 45840 **Fx:**421-3578

(216) 694-4888 .. **Simmons,** Kenneth D '74 Cleveland Cliffs,Inc -1100 Superior Av
-Cleveland 44114

(614) 249-8480 .. **Simmons,** Kent N '85 Nationwide Ins Co -1 Nationwide Plz
-Columbus 43215

(440) 603-7530 .. **Simmons,** Laura M '92 Progressive Ins Co -5920 Landerbrook Dr
-#PLG-OHL33 -Mayfield Heights 44124

(330) 345-5340 .. **Simmons,** Lisa M '95 Wayne Cnty Chldrns Srvcs
-2534 Burbank Rd -Wooster 44691 **Fx:**345-7082

(740) 335-0640 .. **Simmons,** Melissa J '96 Fayette Cnty Probate/Juv Ct -110 E Court
-Washington Court House 43160

(216) 689-5834 .. **Simmons,** Michael A '00 Key Trust Co of Ohio -127 Pub Sq
-17th Fl -Cleveland 44114

(216) 526-2067 .. **Simmons,** Milton L '59 -Bx31637 -Independence 44131

Simmons, Nancy H '71 -(Address Unavailable)

(614) 258-4267 .. **Simmons,** Pamela J '83 -2581 E 5th Av -Columbus 43219

(614) 292-2829 .. **Simmons,** Ric Lee '04 OSU Moritz Cllg of Law -55 W 12th Av
-Columbus 43210 **Fx:**292-1383

(614) 527-7563 .. **Simmons,** Robert M '99 -3468 Fairway Cmmns Dr -Bx208
-Hilliard 43026

(937) 865-6800 .. **Simmons,** Stacy M '96 Lexis/Nexis -Bx933 -Dayton 45401

(216) 592-5000 ..**Simmons,** Thomas R '93 (Tucker E&W LLP) -925 Euclid Av
-1150 Huntngtn Bldg -Cleveland 44115 **Fx:**592-5009

(330) 425-2825 ..**Simms,** Andrew E '01 Plyrs Rep Sports Mngmnt -34208 Aurora Rd
#250 -Cleveland 44139

(614) 462-3555 ..**Simms,** Brian E '94 Franklin Cnty Pros -373 S High
-Columbus 43215

(216) 931-6000 ..**Simms,** Edward P '98 %Ulmer & B LLP -1300 E 9th
-Ste 900 Penton Media Bldg -Cleveland 44114 **Fx:**931-6001

(216) 931-6000 ..**Simms,** Joseph S '96 %Ulmer & B LLP -1300 E 9th
-Ste 900 Penton Media Bldg -Cleveland 44114 **Fx:**931-6001

(440) 946-8990 ..**Simms,** Michael A '73 Willoughby Iron & Waste Matls
-3884 Church -Willoughby 44094

(202) 685-6299 ..**Simms,** Michelle C '97 USN-Military Sealift Com
-914 Charles Morris Ct SE -210 Wshngtn Navel Yard
-Washington, DC 20398

(937) 431-3170 ..**Simms,** Thomas W '72 Unvrsl 1 Credit Union -2450 Esquire Dr
-Bx341090 -Beavercreek 45434

(440) 526-8818 ..**Simon,** Andrew J '86 -500 E Royalton Rd -Ste 180
-Broadview Heights 44147

(440) 333-5370 ..**Simon,** Charles T '77 -21220 Ctr Ridge Rd -Ste 250
-Rocky River 44116

(216) 583-2952 ..**Simon,** Christie L '01 Ernst & Young LLP -925 Euclid Av -Ste 1300
-Cleveland 44115

(845) 928-7604 ..**Simon,** Craig F '75 -11 Van Buren Ct -Highland Mills, NY 10930
Simon, Daniel E '99 -(Address Unavailable)

(216) 621-6201 ..**Simon,** David O '75 -1370 Ontario -Ste 450 -Cleveland 44113
(216) 664-9800 ..**Simon,** Debra P '89 -1468 W 9th -Ste 425 -Cleveland 44113
(216) 575-1002 ..**Simon,** Ellen S '81 Simon Law Firm,LLC -1300 E 9th -Ste 1717
-Cleveland 44114

(216) 696-3311 ..**Simon,** Eric M '87 (Kahn K) -1301 E 9th -2600 Erievw Twr
-Cleveland 44114 **Fx:**623-4912

(614) 846-4100 ..**Simon,** Frederick J '59 -75 E Wilson Bridge Rd -Ste C1
-Worthington 43085

(440) 746-9600 ..**Simon,** George T '99 (Grendell & S Co,LPA) -6638 Harris Rd
-Broadview Heights 44147

(216) 241-5310 ..**Simon,** John A '90 (Gallagher SF&N) -1501 Euclid Av -6th Fl
-Cleveland 44115 **Fx:**241-1608

(937) 449-2800 ..**Simon,** Kevin V '96 %Chernesky H&K PLL -10 Cthse Plz SW
-Ste 1100 -Dayton 45402 **Fx:**449-2821

(440) 247-0606 ..**Simon,** Lynn B '80 -3130 Topping Ln -Chagrin Falls 44022
(304) 723-4400 ..**Simon,** Michael G '97 (Frankovitch AC&S) -337 Penco Rd
-Weirton, WV 26062

(561) 447-0017 ..**Simon,** Michael W '89 (Simon S&S,PA) -120 E Palmetto Park Rd
-Ste 100 -Boca Raton, FL 33432 **Fx:**447-0018

(412) 281-5060 ..**Simon,** Samuel H '93 (Houston H,PC) -401 Lbrty Av -22nd Fl
3 Gtwy Ctr -Pittsburgh, PA 15222 **Fx:**281-4499

(513) 579-2542 ..**Simon,** Samuel J '82 American Fincl Group,Inc -1 E 4th -9th Fl
-Cincinnati 45202

(330) 630-5077 ..**Simon,** Shirley A '95 -12 Southwest Av -Tallmadge 44278
(610) 248-4896 ..**Simon,** Soma G '93 GlaxoSmithKline -709 Swedeland Rd -Bx1539
-King of Prussia, PA 19406

(513) 721-7500 ..**Simon,** Stephen A '97 %D Cook LLC -22 W 9th -Cincinnati 45202
(513) 229-0479 ..**Simon,** Steven E '75 -7577 Cntrl Pk Blvd -Ste 135 -Mason 45040
(216) 241-0040 ..**Simon,** Sunny M '88 -1660 W 2nd -Ste 410 -Cleveland 44113
Fx:241-4804

(440) 964-2200 ..**Simon,** Thomas J '81 (TJ Simon Co,LPA) -1105 Brdg -Bx3048
-Ashtabula 44005 **Fx:**964-6967

(330) 296-9999 ..**Simon,** William G Jr. '72 %Sicuro & S -213 S Chestnut
-Ravenna 44266

(614) 227-0091 ..**Simon,** William S '91 -37 W Broad -Ste 710 -Columbus 43215
(440) 285-3123 ..**Simon-Seymour,** Christine M '90 (Bond & S,LPA) -109 Main
-Chardon 44024
Simonelli, Mark M '96 -1501 Mad Av -Painesville 44077

(216) 520-5572 ..**Simonetta,** Paulette '89 Banks-Baldwin Publishing -Bx318063
-Cleveland 44131

(216) 523-4525 ..**Simonetti,** John A '76 Eaton Corp HR -1111 Superior Av
-Cleveland 44114

(440) 989-2755 ..**Simonoff,** Zachary B '98 (Simonoff & S Co,LPA) -4463 Oberlin Av
-Lorain 44053

(412) 288-7294 ..**Simons,** Robert P '04 (Reed Smith,LLP) -435 6th Av
-Pittsburgh, PA 15219 **Fx:**288-3063

(513) 684-9922 ..**Simons,** Thomas A Jr. '71 -120 E 4th -Ste 1240 -Cincinnati 45202
(330) 865-4904 ..**Simonton,** Stacey R '89 Sanctuary Software Studio Inc
-50 Baker Blvd -Ste 12 -Fairlawn 44333
Simpkins, Joshua M '04 -(Address Unavailable)

(216) 621-8484 ..**Simpkins,** Scott D '96 %Climaco LPW&G Co,LPA -1228 Euclid Av
-Ste 900 Halle Bldg -Cleveland 44115 **Fx:**771-1632

(614) 324-5959 ..**Simpson,** Carol '04 Value Recover Group -919 Old Henderson Rd
-Ste 203 -Columbus 43220

(937) 890-2889 ..**Simpson,** Charles J '60 -9020 N Dixie Dr -Ste B -Dayton 45414
(202) 514-9641 ..**Simpson,** Donald B '99 US DOJ -227 Ben Franklin Station
-Washington, DC 20044

(330) 384-7863 ..**Simpson,** Helen Mae '89 FirstMerit Corp -3 Cascade Plz -7th Fl
-Akron 44308

(216) 522-1200 ..**Simpson,** Jacqueline '77 IMG -1360 E 9th -Ste 100 -Cleveland
44114

(937) 454-1468 ..**Simpson,** Jay M '81 (Stocklin & S Co LPA) -7825 N Dixie Dr
-Ste A -Dayton 45414

(330) 837-4678 ..**Simpson,** John H '85 -46 Fed Av NW -Massillon 44647
(419) 321-1389 ..**Simpson,** Joseph S '88 (Shumaker L&K,LLP) -1000 Jackson
-Toledo 43624 **Fx:**241-6894
Simpson, Phebe A '04 -(Address Unavailable)

(614) 227-2354 ..**Simpson,** Richard C '72 (Bricker & E LLP) -100 S 3rd -Columbus
43215 **Fx:**227-2390

(440) 942-6262 ..**Simpson,** Robert A '97 (Wiles & R) -35350 Curtis Blvd -Ste 530
-Eastlake 44095 **Fx:**942-7211

(614) 628-8232 ..**Simpson,** William F '82 Police & Fire Pension Fnd -140 E Town
-Columbus 43215

(513) 852-6512 ..**Simpson,** Yvette R '04 %Frost BT LLC -201 E 5th -2200 PNC Ctr
-Cincinnati 45202 **Fx:**651-6981

(216) 931-6000 ..**Sims,** Alan S '58 (Ulmer & B LLP) -1300 E 9th -Ste 900 Penton
Media Bldg -Cleveland 44114 **Fx:**931-6001

(740) 927-7145 ..**Sims,** August C '84 -7010 Gale Rd SW -Pataskala 43062

(330) 643-2788 ..**Sims,** Colleen M '98 Summit Cnty Pros-Crim -53 Univ Av -7th Fl
-Akron 44308 **Fx:**643-8277

(330) 376-8019 ..**Sims,** David L '97 Allstate Ins Co -50 So Main -Ste 620
-Akron 44308 **Fx:**376-5713

(440) 576-6015 ..**Sims,** Donald C '84 Ashtabula Cnty Joint Voc Schl
-1565 State Rt 167 -Jefferson 44047

(513) 977-8200 ..**Sims,** Jason B '94 (Dinsmore & S LLP) -255 E 5th -Ste 1900
-Cincinnati 45202 **Fx:**977-8141

(513) 651-6800 ..**Sims,** Jud B '99 %Frost BT LLC -201 E 5th -2200 PNC Ctr
-Cincinnati 45202 **Fx:**651-6981

(614) 717-0768 ..**Sims,** Leigh-Ann M '98 (McCormick & S) -3931 Inverness Cir
-Dublin 43016

(513) 621-6464 ..**Sims,** Mark E '81 (Graydon H&R LLP) -511 Walnut
-1900 Fifth Third Ctr -Cincinnati 45202 **Fx:**651-3836

(216) 502-0800 ..**Sims,** Rufus '88 -75 Pub Sq -#333 -Cleveland 44113
(513) 651-2009 ..**Sims,** Victor D '89 -895 Central Av -Centennial Plaza III
-Cincinnati 45202

(614) 224-8374 ..**Simunic,** Nancy H '76 Legal Aid -40 W Gay -Columbus 43215
(800) 998-9454 ..**Sin,** Nancy P '96 Cmmnty Lgl Aid Srvcs,Inc -265 S Main -3rd Fl
-Akron 44308 **Fx:**(330) 535-0728

(216) 752-7400 ..**Sin,** Nancy P '96 -2854 Litchfld Rd -Shaker Heights 44120
(216) 221-2323 ..**Sinagra,** Anthony C '67 -14701 Detroit Av -Ste 757
-Lakewood 44107

(216) 586-3939 ..**Sinatra,** John L Jr. '98 %Jones D -901 Lakeside Av
-Cleveland 44114 **Fx:**579-0212

(301) 986-7900 ..**Sinay,** Michael P '93 %Paradiso DT&O -3 Bethesda Metro Ctr
-Ste 640 -Bethesda, MD 20814

(513) 621-3200 ..**Sinclair,** Jonathan R '96 -617 Vine -Ste 1401 -Cincinnati 45202
Sindelar, Raymond J '73 -206 N 4th Av -#168
-Sandpoint, ID 83864
Sindell, Rachel '04 -(Address Unavailable)

(216) 623-1123 ..**Sindell,** Steven A '68 (Sindell YG&S,PLL) -55 Pub Sq -Ste 1020
-Cleveland 44113 **Fx:**623-1124

(216) 623-1123 ..**Sindell Young Guidubaldi & Sucher, PLL** -55 Pub Sq -Ste 1020
-Cleveland 44113 **Fx:**623-1124

(937) 255-2872 ..**Sinder,** Fredric L '75 US Air Force -AFMC LO\JAZ WPAFR
-Rm 100 -Wright Patterson AFB 45433

(440) 230-1700 ..**Sindyla Anthony & Sindyla** -7425 Royalton Rd
-North Royalton 44133 **Fx:**230-1699

(440) 230-1700 ..**Sindyla,** John R '02 %Sindyla A&S -7425 Royalton Rd
-North Royalton 44133 **Fx:**230-1699

(440) 230-1700 ..**Sindyla,** Robert J '71 (Sindyla A&S) -7425 Royalton Rd
-North Royalton 44133 **Fx:**230-1699

(513) 705-9000 ..**Singer,** Andrew N '74 (Pratt SP Co,LPA) -301 N Breiel Blvd
-Middletown 45044 **Fx:**705-9001

(419) 245-1942 ..**Singer,** Arlene '76 Mun Ct Judge -555 N Erie -Toledo 43624
(937) 653-5257 ..**Singer,** Bradley C '89 (Paulig S&T) -40 Monument Sq -Ste 300
-Urbana 43078

(614) 457-9655 ..**Singer,** Lawrence A '70 -4265 Camborne Rd -Columbus 43220
(216) 621-9870 ..**Singer,** Marilyn J '79 (McNeal SA&B Co,LPA) -123 W Prospect Av
-Ste 250 Van Sweringen Arcade -Cleveland 44115 **Fx:**522-1112

(330) 644-9917 ..**Singer,** Paul Jay '71 (Singer & O) -2775 S Arlngtn Rd
-Akron 44312

(513) 977-8200 ..**Singer,** Peter S '03 %Dinsmore & S LLP -255 E 5th -Ste 1900
-Cincinnati 45202 **Fx:**977-8141

(216) 291-7949 ..**Singer,** Scott M '96 TRW Inc -1900 Richmond Rd
-Cleveland 44124

(513) 721-0778 ..**Singer,** William B '67 -621 Mehring Way -Ste 1609
-Cincinnati 45202 **Fx:**721-0778

(216) 360-9312 ..**Singerman,** Egon P '88 -3681 Green Rd -Ste 410
-Beachwood 44122

(216) 292-5807 ..**Singerman Mills Desberg & Kauntz** -3401 Enterprise Pkwy
-Ste 200 -Beachwood 44122 **Fx:**292-5867

(216) 292-5807 ..**Singerman,** Paul J '83 (Singerman MD&K) -3401 Enterprise Pkwy
-Ste 200 -Beachwood 44122 **Fx:**292-5867

(614) 221-4000 ..**Singh,** Bobby '00 %Chester W&S LLP -65 E State -10th Fl
-Columbus 43215 **Fx:**221-4012

(330) 670-7300 ..**Singletary,** Gary S '86 Hanna C&P,LLP -3737 Embssy Pkwy
-Bx5521 -Akron 44334 **Fx:**670-0977

(513) 421-1108 ..**Singleton,** David A '02 PRAC -617 Vine -Ste 1301
-Cincinnati 45202 **Fx:**562-3200

(937) 264-5116 ..**Singleton,** Vicki C '87 Industrial Commssn of OH -3401 Park Ctr
Dr -Ste 300 -Dayton 45414

(616) 726-4857 ..**Siniger,** William R '80 (Williams HC&S) -120 W Apple Av -Bx599
-Muskegon, MI 49443

(937) 225-4987 ..**Sink,** Jill R '03 %Montgomery Cnty Pros/CSEA -14 W 4th -Ste 510
-Dayton 45402

(614) 890-7004 ..**Sinkhorn,** Mark W '74 Lawyers Title Ins Corp -4111 Exec Pkwy
-Ste 304 -Westerville 43081

(937) 227-3700 ..**Sinkovits,** Angela M '03 %Faruki I&C PLL -10 N Ludlow
-500 Cthse Plz SW -Dayton 45402 **Fx:**227-3717

(248) 362-2030 ..**Sinkula,** Cheryl F '99 Stone B&O, PLLC -2701 Troy Ctr Dr
-Ste 400 -Troy, MI 48084

(330) 376-5300 ..**Sinn,** Deanna N '98 Summit Cnty Cmn Pleas Ct -209 S High
-Bx1500 -Akron 44309

(330) 376-9260 ..**Sinn,** Jonathan T '94 (Callahan GR&S LLC) -7 W Bowery -Ste 907
-Akron 44308 **Fx:**376-9807
Sinn, Valerie W '97 -166 Carlton Seitz Rd -Dahlonega, GA 30533

(419) 673-8188 ..**Sinn-Bailey,** Holly A '79 Bailey Law Ofc -28 N Main
-Kenton 43326

(614) 885-0038 ..**Sinno,** Sheila M '87 (Sinno & H,LLC) -8001 Ravines Edge Ct
-Ste 200 -Columbus 43235

(614) 464-6400 ..**Sinnott,** Bradley K '86 (Vorys SS&P LLP) -52 E Gay -Bx1008
-Columbus 43216 **Fx:**464-6350

(229) 544-5400 ..**Sinnott,** John P '61 OfCnsl Langdale & V,LLP -1007 N Patterson
-Bx1547 -Valdosta, GA 31603 **Fx:**244-0453

(330) 869-5297 ..**Sinopoli,** Debra L '92 (Sinopoli & S Co) -1717 Sandlewood Av
-Akron 44313

(330) 869-5297 ..**Sinopoli,** Vito F '92 (Sinopoli & S Co) -1717 Sandlewood Av
-Akron 44313

(440) 446-1529 ..**Sintsirmas,** George '84 -6212 Coldstrm Dr -Cleveland 44143
(419) 627-8075 ..**Sipe,** David Lee '73 -602 Jackson -Sandusky 44870
(740) 373-3219 ..**Sipe,** Dennis L '73 (Buell & S Co,LPA) -322 3rd -Marietta 45750
Fx:373-2892

(330) 283-6950 ..**Sipplen**, Eddie M '03 -Bx5373 -Fairlawn 44334

(440) 248-7906 ..**Sipusic**, David J '01 %Mazanec R&R Co,LPA -34305 Solon Rd
-Ste 100 -Cleveland 44139 Fx:248-8861

(330) 478-1947 ..**Sirak**, Norman L '72 -Bx7468 -Canton 44705

(513) 821-1510 ..**Sirkin**, Alan L '70 -8075 Reading Rd -Ste 400 -Cincinnati 45237

(513) 721-4876 ..**Sirkin**, H Louis '65 (Sirkin P&S LLP) -105 W 4th
-920 4th & Race Twr -Cincinnati 45202 Fx:721-0876

(513) 721-4876 ..**Sirkin Pinales & Schwartz LLP** -105 W 4th -920 4th & Race Twr
-Cincinnati 45202 Fx:721-0876

(614) 387-5600 ..**Sirkle**, Rebecca Haggar '04 %Atty Gen -30 E Broad
-Columbus 43215 Fx:387-5597

(216) 692-1222 ..**Sirvaitis**, Algis '66 (A Sirvaitis & Assoc) -880 E 185th
-Cleveland 44119 Fx:531-8687

(330) 743-7000 ..**Sisek**, James H '74 Butler Wick Trust Co -Bx149
-Youngstown 44501

(216) 502-0591 ..**Siskovic**, Carole N '83 -1360 W 9th -Ste 420 -Cleveland 44113

(330) 598-1062 ..**Sisson**, Edwin A '04 -2845 Woodhvn Dr -Medina 44256
Fx:598-1067

(614) 365-2700 ..**Sisto**, James E P '84 OfCnsl Squire S&D LLP -41 S High
-1300 Huntngtn Ctr -Columbus 43215 Fx:365-2499

(614) 221-7614 ..**Sites**, Richard L '75 %OH Hosp Assoc -155 E Broad -Columbus
43215

(330) 255-0041 ..**Sitler**, Martin H '04 Marshall DWC&G -120 E Mill -Ste 240
-Akron 44308 Fx:255-0040

(740) 653-0461 ..**Sitterley & Vandervoort Ltd** -123 S Broad -Ste 211
-Lancaster 43130

(740) 653-0461 ..**Sitterley**, William J '73 (Sitterley & V Ltd) -123 S Broad -Ste 211
-Lancaster 43130

(859) 572-8890 ..**Siverd**, Robert J '90 General Cable Corp -4 Tesseneer Dr
-Highland Heights, KY 41076

(216) 575-0777 ..**Sivinski**, John A '86 (Kelley & F,LLP) -1300 E 9th -Ste 1901
-Cleveland 44114 Fx:575-0799

(330) 463-5024 ..**Siwik**, Lori L '87 Risk Intl Srvcs,Inc -4199 Kinross Lks Pkwy
-Ste 220 -Richfield 44286

(330) 463-5000 ..**Siwik**, Mark R '88 Risk Intl Srvcs,Inc -4199 Kinross Lks Pkwy
-Ste 220 -Richfield 44286

(216) 522-3713 ..**Sizemore**, Cheryl A '01 NLRB -1240 E 9th -1695 Celebrezze Bldg
-Cleveland 44199 Fx:522-2418

(513) 563-4131 ..**Sizemore**, Gregory L '92 Construction Owners Assn -4100
Exec Park Dr -Ste 210 -Cincinnati 45241

(614) 469-3939 ..**Sjoberg-Witt**, Kerstin E '03 %Jones D -325 John H
McConnell Blvd -Ste 600 -Bx165017 -Columbus 43216
Fx:461-4198

(419) 874-3536 ..**Skaff**, Paul A '98 Leatherman WD&H -353 Elm -Perrysburg 43551
Fx:874-3899

(614) 221-9800 ..**Skaggs**, Kimberly M '93 Equal Justice Fndtn -88 E Broad
-Ste 1590 -Columbus 43215 Fx:221-9810

(330) 376-5300 ..**Skakun**, Mark J III '74 (Buckingham D&B,LLP) -50 S Main
-Bx1500 -Akron 44309 Fx:258-6559

Skaljac, Stella K '00 -9472 Sherwood Trl -Brecksville 44141

(216) 928-2200 ..**Skall**, David W '97 Sutter OM&F -1301 E 9th -3600 Erievw Twr
-Cleveland 44114 Fx:928-4400

(216) 241-8333 ..**Skaryd**, Drue Marie '99 Ritzler C&S,Ltd -1001 Lakeside Av
-1550 North Pnt Twr -Cleveland 44114 Fx:241-5890

(513) 579-0080 ..**Skavdahl**, Duane R '93 (Smith R&S Co,LPA) -1014 Vine
-Ste 2350 -Cincinnati 45202 Fx:579-0222

(614) 274-4700 ..**Skeeles**, Rebecca L '99 Skeeles Mfg,Inc -4180 Perimeter Dr
-Columbus 43228

(614) 462-4281 ..**Skeens**, Edwin L Jr. '87 Franklin Cnty Cmn Pleas Ct -375 S High
-Columbus 43215 Fx:462-6292

(740) 351-1243 ..**Skeens**, Marcia S '87 -Bx1602 -Portsmouth 45662

(513) 621-0267 ..**Skeens**, Troy W Jr. '81 %Waite SB&C -1 W 4th
-1513 4th & Vine Twr -Cincinnati 45202

(440) 256-1361 ..**Skeggs**, David C '89 -10371 Blair Ln -Kirtland 44094

(740) 622-2011 ..**Skelton**, James R '92 Pomerene B&S -309 Main
-Coshocton 43812

(330) 434-4000 ..**Skelton**, James R '97 -789 W Market -Akron 44303 Fx:434-4003

(740) 622-2011 ..**Skelton**, Joseph R '74 (Pomerene B&S) -309 Main
-Coshocton 43812

(937) 226-1212 ..**Skelton McQuiston Gounaris & Henry** -130 W 2nd -Ste 450
-Dayton 45402

(937) 226-1212 ..**Skelton**, Richard S '88 Skelton MG&H -130 W 2nd -Ste 450
-Dayton 45402

(740) 622-2011 ..**Skelton**, Robert A '90 Pomerene B&S -309 Main
-Coshocton 43812

(614) 462-3194 ..**Skendelas**, Paul '81 Franklin Cnty Pub Def -373 S High -12th Fl
-Columbus 43215

(330) 535-5711 ..**Skeriotis**, John M '98 (Brouse M) -106 S Main -500 First Natl Twr
-Akron 44308 Fx:253-8601

(216) 861-5582 ..**Skerry**, Ann M '97 (Fay SFM&M LLP) -1100 Superior Av -7th Fl
-Cleveland 44114 Fx:241-1666

(859) 394-6200 ..**Sketch**, Michael W '80 (Adams SW&D) -40 W Pike -Bx861
-Covington, KY 41012 Fx:291-7902

Skibbens, David W '81 -(Address Unavailable)

(330) 253-1550 ..**Skidmore**, Archie W '55 Skidmore & Assoc -1 Cascade Plz
-12th Fl -Akron 44308

(330) 253-1550 ..**Skidmore**, Brian K '84 Skidmore & Assoc -1 Cascade Plz -12th Fl
-Akron 44308

(513) 421-6630 ..**Skidmore**, Charles G '92 %Lindhorst & D Co,LPA -312 Walnut
-Ste 2300 -Cincinnati 45202

(330) 725-5936 ..**Skidmore**, Claudia M '96 %Skidmore & H -748 N Court
-Medina 44256

(513) 651-6800 ..**Skidmore**, David A Jr. '91 (Frost BT LLC) -201 E 5th
-2200 PNC Ctr -Cincinnati 45202 Fx:651-6981

(330) 253-1550 ..**Skidmore**, Eric E '89 (Skidmore & Assoc Co,LPA)
-One Cascade Plz -12th flr -Akron 44308 Fx:253-9657

(330) 725-5936 ..**Skidmore & Hall** -748 N Court -Medina 44256

(614) 466-4605 ..**Skidmore**, James R '84 OH Dept Job & Fam Srvcs -30 E Broad
-32nd Fl -Columbus 43266

(330) 725-5936 ..**Skidmore**, Lee T '85 (Skidmore & H) -748 N Court -Medina 44256

(330) 725-5936 ..**Skidmore**, Robert C '01 %Skidmore & H -748 N Court
-Medina 44256

(330) 379-2745 ..**Skidmore**, Thomas A '88 (T Skidmore Co,LPA) -1 Cascade Plz
-Akron 44308

(513) 381-2121 ..**Skilken**, Lynne E '75 Brown Firm Inc,LPA -2199 Victory Pkwy
-Cincinnati 45206

(937) 223-2214 ..**Skilken**, Ralph A Jr. '68 Cnsl R Skilken Jr Co,LPA
-580 Lincoln Park Blvd -Ste 222 -Dayton 45429 Fx:224-1402

(937) 223-6677 ..**Skilken**, Thomas E '78 -130 2nd -Ste 310 -Dayton 45402

(440) 333-0106 ..**Skillen**, Richard Jr. '61 -2 River Pnte Dr -Rocky River 44116

Skindell, Michael J '87 -(Address Unavailable)

(614) 469-3939 ..**Skingle**, Denise L '96 %Jones D -325 John H McConnell Blvd
-Ste 600 -Bx165017 -Columbus 43216 Fx:461-4198

(216) 861-3327 ..**Skingle**, Ronald A '94 -2450 St Clair Av -Cleveland 44114

(513) 651-6800 ..**Skinkiss**, Ralph J '73 Cnsl Frost BT LLC -201 E 5th -2200
PNC Ctr -Cincinnati 45202 Fx:651-6981

(937) 748-9771 ..**Skinn**, Bryce W '87 EDL,Inc -4391 Dayton-Xenia Rd
-Dayton 45432

(740) 833-2690 ..**Skinner**, Alison M '02 Delaware Cnty Pros -140 N Sandusky
-3rd Fl -Delaware 43015

(330) 762-7377 ..**Skinner**, Colin G '95 OfCnsl Oldham & D -195 S Main -Ste 300
-Akron 44308 Fx:762-7390

(614) 227-2000 ..**Skinner**, Karen R '99 %Porter WM&A LLP -41 S High
-Columbus 43215 Fx:227-2100

(513) 603-5097 ..**Skinner**, Matthew R '91 The Cincinnati Ins Co -6200 S Gilmore Rd
-Fairfield 45014

(216) 363-1313 ..**Skirbunt**, James R '74 (Skirbunt & S Co,LPA) -55 Pub Sq
-Ste 1310 -Cleveland 44113

(216) 363-1313 ..**Skirbunt**, Sharon A '86 (Skirbunt & S Co,LPA) -55 Pub Sq
-Ste 1310 -Cleveland 44113

(513) 721-5494 ..**Skirvin**, Rae '60 -830 Main -Ste 1201 -Cincinnati 45202

(419) 666-3417 ..**Skiver**, Stephen A '89 -30025 E River Rd -Perrysburg 43551

(216) 621-1113 ..**Sklar**, Warren A '73 (Renner OB&S,LLP) -1621 Euclid Av -19th Fl
-Cleveland 44115 Fx:621-6165

(440) 333-0653 ..**Skoch**, Gerald '84 -20826 Morewood Pkwy -Rocky River 44116

(216) 642-3342 ..**Skoczen**, Danielle A '99 %Wegman H&V,LPA
-6055 Rockside Wds Blvd -Ste 200 -Cleveland 44131
Fx:642-8826

(216) 443-7326 ..**Skoczen**, Stacey L '02 Cuyahoga Cnty Ct Cmmn Pleas
-1200 Ontario -Justice Ctr 11th Fl -Cleveland 44113

(330) 376-1242 ..**Skoglund**, Rodney L '91 Renner KGBT&W,LPA -106 S Main
-4th Fl First Natl Twr -Akron 44308 Fx:376-9646

(937) 322-6611 ..**Skogstrom**, James W '80 -10 W Columbia -Bx1885
-Springfield 45501

(937) 328-2626 ..**Skogstrom**, Janie O '80 Clark Cnty Juv Ct -101 E Columbia
-Springfield 45502

(216) 685-9991 ..**Skolnick**, Howard E '93 -1220 W 6th -Ste 600 -Cleveland 44114

(330) 744-0247 ..**Skolnick**, Jay M '67 (Nadler N&B Co,LPA) -20 Fed Plz W -Ste 600
-Youngstown 44503 Fx:744-8690

(440) 356-1910 ..**Skonce**, Ralph T Jr. '79 -1154 Linda -Ste 175 -Rocky River 44116

(513) 792-2942 ..**Skoog**, Norma '83 Growth Mgmt Advrs Inc -8044 Mntgmry Rd
-Ste 700 -Cincinnati 45236

(740) 695-4448 ..**Skorich**, Elaine L '98 %M Shaheen -227 E Main
-Saint Clairsville 43950

(419) 241-8811 ..**Skotynsky**, Walter J '76 -1018 Adams -Toledo 43624

(330) 792-2336 ..**Skoufatos**, Nikitas '88 (Wellman JH&S Co,LPA)
-4990 Mahoning Av -Youngstown 44515 Fx:792-5403

(216) 623-0150 ..**Skove**, Thomas M Jr. '77 (Roetzel & A,LPA) -1375 E 9th
-One Cleve Ctr 9th Fl -Cleveland 44114 Fx:623-0134

(614) 466-3998 ..**Skovron**, Richard C '74 Unemploymnt Comp Commssn
-145 S Front -Bx182299 -Columbus 43218

(440) 285-0337 ..**Skrabec**, David J '75 Eltech Systms Corp -100 7th Av -Ste 300
-Chardon 44024

(614) 233-6950 ..**Skrobot**, David A '77 (Fisher & S LLC) -400 E Town -Ste 210
-Columbus 43215 Fx:233-6960

(419) 683-3800 ..**Skropits**, Amy E '96 Magistrate-City of Crestline -100 N Seltzer
-Crestline 44827

(419) 213-2001 ..**Skrzyniecki**, Duane J '77 Lucas Cnty Pros -Adams & Erie
-Lucas Cnty Cthse -Toledo 43624

(513) 579-6400 ..**Skufca**, Christopher J '94 %Keating M&K PLL -1 E 4th
-1400 Provident Twr -Cincinnati 45202 Fx:579-6457

(419) 372-2951 ..**Skulina**, Michael S '92 Student Legal Srvc Inc -401 S Hall
-Bowling Grn State Univ -Bowling Green 43403

(440) 899-1911 ..**Skulina**, Thomas R '59 -24803 Detroit Rd -Westlake 44145

(216) 443-7800 ..**Skutnik**, Carol M '92 Cuyahoga Cnty Pros -1200 Ontario -8th Fl
-Cleveland 44113 Fx:698-2270

(216) 383-1637 ..**Slabaugh**, Susan K '88 -17525 Harland Av -Cleveland 44119

(330) 863-9455 ..**Slabaugh**, Vincent L '98 Schafer & S -209 Brdg -Bx836
-Malvern 44644

(216) 861-5582 ..**Slaby**, Scott M '03 %Fay SFM&M LLP -1100 Superior Av -7th Fl
-Cleveland 44114 Fx:241-1666

(330) 332-8101 ..**Slack**, Mark R '83 Slack Law Ofcs -Bx765 -Salem 44460
Fx:332-2856

(419) 784-3700 ..**Slade**, Carson L '94 Defiance Cnty Pros -607 W 3rd
-Defiance 43512 Fx:782-0594

(216) 363-4500 ..**Sladek**, Todd L '04 %Benesch FC&A LLP -200 Pub Sq -Ste 2300
-Cleveland 44114 Fx:363-4588

(740) 774-3300 ..**Sladoje**, Douglas S '88 -38 S Paint -Chillicothe 45601

(216) 521-7922 ..**Slaga**, John M '82 Chalfant Manufacturing -11525 Mad Av
-Cleveland 44102

(412) 257-4033 ..**Slage**, Lisa C '87 Ardent Resources, Inc. -1814 Tyris Dr
-Pittsburgh, PA 15241

(614) 227-8826 ..**Slagle**, Christopher N '04 %Bricker & E LLP -100 S 3rd
-Columbus 43215 Fx:227-2390

(614) 228-1144 ..**Slagle**, Ehren W '02 %P Collins & Assoc -21 E State -Ste 1130
-Columbus 43215

(740) 223-4290 ..**Slagle**, Jim '80 Marion Cnty Pros -134 E Center -Marion 43302
Fx:223-4299

(937) 286-2360 ..**Slagle**, John W '76 -Bx90362 -Dayton 45490

(330) 832-9833 ..**Slagle**, Larry V '77 (Rosenblithe & S) -2200 Wales Rd NW
-Massillon 44646

(216) 621-5300 ..**Slagter**, John P '91 (Buckingham D&B,LLP) -1375 E 9th -Ste 1700
-Cleveland 44114 Fx:621-5440

Slain, Roger S '93 -11560 Somerset Dr -211
-North Royalton 44133

(513) 771-7800 ..**Slap**, Albert J '02 -20 Erie Av -Glendale 45246

(216) 621-0200 .. **Slater,** James A Jr. '02 %Baker & H LLP -1900 E 9th -Ste 3200
-Cleveland 44114 **Fx:**696-0740

(330) 762-0700 .. **Slater,** James W '70 (Slater Z&G) -One Cascade Plz -Ste 2210
-Akron 44308 **Fx:**762-3923

(330) 493-8525 .. **Slater,** John R '81 (Millisor & Co,LPA) -4117 Whipple Av NW
-Ste B -Canton 44718 **Fx:**493-8606

(616) 459-0556 .. **Slater,** Michael W '98 Kluczynski G&V -648 Monroe Av NW
-Ste 900 -Grand Rapids, MI 49503

(513) 621-6464 .. **Slater,** Peter M '93 (Graydon H&R LLP) -511 Walnut
-1900 Fifth Third Ctr -Cincinnati 45202 **Fx:**651-3836

(973) 660-6535 .. **Slater,** Timothy T '72 Amer Home Prdcts Corp -5 Giralda Farms
-Madison, NJ 07940

(330) 762-0700 .. **Slater Zurz & Gilbert** -One Cascade Plz -Ste 2210 -Akron 44308
Fx:762-3923

(937) 226-1200 .. **Slaton,** Curtis F '86 (Bogin P&B) -131 N Ludlow -1200 Talbot Twr
-Dayton 45402

(513) 946-3700 .. **Slattery,** James J Jr. '71 Hamilton Cnty Pub Def -230 E 9th -3rd Fl
-Cincinnati 45202 **Fx:**946-3707

(703) 205-8000 .. **Slattery,** James M '76 (Birch SK&B,LLP) -8110 Gatehse Rd
-Ste 500 E -Falls Church, VA 22042

(440) 285-2242 .. **Slattery,** Kelly A '02 %Thrasher D&D,LPA -100 7th Av -Ste 150
-Chardon 44024 **Fx:**285-9423

(440) 953-2870 .. **Slattery,** Lisa J '86 -38033 Euclid Av -Ste 1 -Willoughby 44094

(440) 892-1580 .. **Slattery,** Raymond J III '83 Nordson Corp -28601 Clemens Rd
-Westlake 44145

(513) 632-5315 .. **Slauson,** John G '66 -119 E Court -Cincinnati 45202

(937) 228-9179 .. **Slavens,** John M '70 Hollencamp & H -130 W 2nd -Ste 2107
-Dayton 45402

(330) 742-8800 .. **Slavens,** Kathleen M '92 -26 S Phelps -5th Fl -Youngstown 44503

(216) 589-0669 .. **Slavin,** Jeffrey F '74 -55 Pub Sq -Ste 2200 -Cleveland 44113

(203) 368-0211 .. **Slavin,** Richard '77 (Cohen & W,PC) -1115 Broad
-Bridgeport, CT 06604 **Fx:**394-9901

(614) 885-8272 .. **Slavin,** Richard C '79 (Bailey & S) -6877 N High -Ste 303
-Columbus 43085

(949) 475-2822 .. **Slavin-Cosel,** Judith A '77 -5 Corp Park -Ste 210
-Irvine, CA 92606

Slawinski, Shari A '99 -(Address Unavailable)

(419) 255-3153 .. **Slaybod,** Sheldon M '75 (Casey & S) -520 Mad Av
-727 Spitzer Bldg -Toledo 43604

Slayton, Thomas F '75 IRS -433 N Summit -2nd Fl -Toledo 43604

(614) 462-5047 .. **Slazyk,** Denise R '01 %Schottenstein Z&D -250 West -Bx165020
-Columbus 43216 **Fx:**462-5135

(614) 487-2050 .. **Slee,** Richard A '84 %OH State Bar Assn -1700 Lk Shr Dr
-Columbus 43204

(216) 771-8990 .. **Sleggs,** Todd W '88 (T Sleggs & Assoc) -820 W Superior Av
-Ste 410 -Cleveland 44113

(216) 381-8800 .. **Sleibi,** Jalal T '03 (Cocirteu H&S,LLC) -4040 Mayfld Rd
-Cleveland 44121

(614) 444-1500 .. **Slemmer,** Greggory D '95 -1188 S High -Columbus 43206
Fx:444-1501

(330) 497-9644 .. **Slesnick,** Elizabeth M '92 -4804 Tanglewood Cir NE
-Canton 44714

(330) 528-3616 .. **Sley,** Benjamin H '99 -828 Rdgwd Blvd -Hudson 44236

(440) 684-6940 .. **Slezak,** David G '85 DentalCare Partners,Inc
-5900 Landerbrook Dr -Mayfield Heights 44124 **Fx:**684-6941

(937) 223-1100 .. **Slicer,** Charles W III '92 Slicer Law Ofc -111 W 1st -Ste 401
-Dayton 45402 **Fx:**223-8150

(937) 223-1100 .. **Slicer,** Charles W Jr. '66 Slicer Law Ofc -111 W 1st -Ste 401
-Dayton 45402 **Fx:**223-8150

(330) 492-8136 .. **Slick,** Mary J '84 Stark Cnty Educational Srvc Ctr -2100 38th NW
-Canton 44709

(216) 696-4200 .. **Slifko,** Jessica Flickinger '98 %Schneider SR&L PLL
-1111 Superior Av -Ste 1000 -Cleveland 44114 **Fx:**696-7303

(330) 725-4929 .. **Slimak,** Michelle L '99 %Oberholtzer F&L -39 Pub Sq -Ste 201
-Bx220 -Medina 44258 **Fx:**723-4929

(330) 797-0086 .. **Slipski,** Ronald Edward '79 (Green H&S,Co LPA)
-120 Wstchtr Dr -Ste A -Bx3985 -Austintown 44515 **Fx:**797-2969

(216) 566-1111 .. **Slive,** Harriet W '84 OfCnsl Slive & S Co,LPA -526 Superior Av
-Ste 935 -Cleveland 44114 **Fx:**566-7111

(216) 566-1111 .. **Slive,** Steven H '76 (Slive & S Co,LPA) -526 Superior Av -Ste 935
-Cleveland 44114 **Fx:**566-7111

(216) 696-4700 .. **Slivka,** John M '81 (Spieth BM&N Co,LPA) -925 Euclid Av
-2000 Huntngtn Bldg -Cleveland 44115 **Fx:**696-2706

Slivka, William J '60 -(Address Unavailable)

Sliwinski, Michael R '03 -(Address Unavailable)

(216) 641-9191 .. **Sliwinski,** Teddy '76 -5800 Fleet Av -Cleveland 44105

(419) 841-0221 .. **Sloan,** Aaron P '98 (Tareyton Homes) -6725 W Central Av -Ste R1
-Toledo 43617

(513) 861-5065 .. **Sloan,** Ayana L '91 -1420 E McMillan -Cincinnati 45206

(859) 331-2000 .. **Sloan,** David B '03 (O'Hara RTS&S) -25 Crestvw Hills Rd -Ste 201
-Covington, KY 41017 **Fx:**578-3365

(216) 586-3939 .. **Sloan,** David W '74 (Jones D) -901 Lakeside Av -Cleveland 44114
Fx:579-0212

(330) 643-2663 .. **Sloan,** Jerry Kay '71 Summit Cnty Treasurer -175 S Main
-Akron 44308

(740) 593-3357 .. **Sloan,** Steven T '73 (Mollica GS&S Co,LPA) -35 N Cllg -Drwr958
-Athens 45701

(614) 466-2765 .. **Slocum,** Cynthia D '93 Industrial Commssn of OH -30 W Spring
-9th Fl -Columbus 43215 **Fx:**752-8785

(513) 946-3000 .. **Slocum,** Lee R '78 %Hamilton Cnty Pros -230 E 9th
-Cincinnati 45202 **Fx:**946-3017

(216) 623-0000 .. **Slodov,** Michael D '91 %Javitch B&R -1300 E 9th -14th Fl
-Cleveland 44114 **Fx:**623-0190

(419) 729-5448 .. **Sloma,** Anthony P '97 Perstorp Polyols,Inc -600 Matzinger Rd
-Toledo 43612

(216) 360-4247 .. **Slomak,** Michael J '76 Hair Care Harmony Inc
-23500 Mercantile Rd -Beachwood 44122

Slominski, Zygmunt G '73 -4038 Carlyle Lks Blvd
-Palm Harbor, FL 34685

(937) 775-2796 .. **Slonaker,** William M Sr. '72 Wright State Univ -3640
Colonel Glenn Hwy -270 Rike Hall -Dayton 45435

(937) 222-9687 .. **Slone,** Lee A '02 %R Slone-Stiver -22 Brown -Bx3340
-Dayton 45401

Slone, Thomas J Sr. '79 -7624 Hedgewood Cir -Mason 45040

(937) 222-9687 .. **Slone-Stiver,** Ruth A '85 -22 Brown -Bx3340 -Dayton 45401

(216) 241-3400 .. **Slone-Young,** Tava D '99 Community Mental Hlth Bd
-1400 W 25th -3rd Fl -Cleveland 44113 **Fx:**241-3887

(614) 461-1516 .. **Slotnick,** Lisa M '99 -169 E Lvngstn Av -Columbus 43215

(614) 466-4605 .. **Slotnick,** Marcia T '82 OH Dept Job & Fam Srvcs -30 E Broad
-32nd Fl -Columbus 43266

(513) 683-9000 .. **Slovin,** Randy T '83 (Slovin & C) -9435 Waterstone Blvd -Ste 270
-Cincinnati 45249

(513) 579-1414 .. **Slovin,** Scott M '77 (Schwartz M&R) -441 Vine -Ste 2900
-Cincinnati 45202 **Fx:**579-1418

(513) 241-9844 .. **Slovin,** Sherri G '79 -30 Garfld Pl -Ste 920 -Cincinnati 45202
Fx:241-9908

Slowey, Suzanne L '01 -2096 Longfllw NE -Canton 44721

(614) 884-4800 .. **Slowik,** Donald C '80 (Slowik & R,LLC) -250 E Broad -Ste 250
-Columbus 43215 **Fx:**884-4801

(817) 390-6416 .. **Slugg,** Ramsay H '78 Bk of Amer -500 W 7th -Bx1317
-Fort Worth, TX 76101

(440) 564-9111 .. **Slusarz,** George V '81 Kinetico Inc -10845 Kinsman Rd -Bx193
-Newbury 44065

(513) 793-5560 .. **Slutsky,** June C '91 (Slutsky & S Co,LPA) -4153 U Crossgate Dr
-Cincinnati 45236

(513) 793-5560 .. **Slutsky,** Norman L '70 (Slutsky & S Co,LPA)
-4153 U Crossgate Dr -Cincinnati 45236

(513) 561-6277 .. **Slutz,** Leonard D '37 -3939 Erie Av -Hyde Park 45208

(937) 454-5544 .. **Slyman,** Jeffrey D '79 -575 S Dixie Dr -Vandalia 45377

(937) 653-7186 .. **Smack,** LeAnna D '02 %Houston H&D -1 Monument Sq -Ste 200
-Bx913 -Urbana 43078 **Fx:**653-3293

(216) 685-9500 .. **Smaili,** Jihad M '98 (JM Smaili,LLC) -1468 W 9th -Ste 330
-Cleveland 44113 **Fx:**685-9685

(216) 861-3086 .. **Smakula,** Michael J '76 Reid M&W -55 Pub Sq -Ste 2010
-Cleveland 44113 **Fx:**861-4409

(440) 286-6177 .. **Smalheer,** Bruce C '90 (Zulandt & S) -114 E Park -Chardon 44024
Fx:286-6158

(330) 376-2700 .. **Small,** Janis L '83 (Roetzel & A,LPA) -222 S Main -Akron 44308
Fx:376-4577

(614) 466-1292 .. **Small,** Jeffrey L '93 OH Consumers' Cnsl -10 W Broad -Ste 1800
-Columbus 43215 **Fx:**466-9475

(216) 451-1437 .. **Small,** Robert E '61 (R Small Co,LPA) -16249 Oak Hill Rd
-Cleveland Heights 44112

(740) 455-3350 .. **Small,** Susan E '96 (Hillis & S Co,LLC) -825 Adair Av
-Zanesville 43701 **Fx:**455-3360

(415) 848-4860 .. **Smalley,** Byron D '86 IRS -333 Market -Ste 1200
-San Francisco, CA 94105

(937) 223-8888 .. **Smalley,** John A '85 (Dyer GM&S) -131 N Ludlow -Ste 1400
-Dayton 45402 **Fx:**223-0127

(202) 857-4696 .. **Smalley,** Mark J '94 Lexis-Nexis Corp -1150 18th NW -Ste 600
-Washington, DC 20036

(614) 464-6400 .. **Smallwood,** Carl D '80 (Vorys SS&P LLP) -52 E Gay -Bx1008
-Columbus 43216 **Fx:**464-6350

Smallwood, Connie H '81 -4121 Edgehill Dr -Columbus 43220

(614) 224-5209 .. **Smallwood,** Howard '73 -209 S High -Ste 511 -Columbus 43215

(619) 661-3940 .. **Smallwood,** Joseph D '91 Hitachi,Inc -900 Hitachi Way
-Chula Vista, CA 91914

(614) 221-7201 .. **Smalz,** Michael R '89 OSLSA -555 Buttles Av -Columbus 43215

(614) 466-9581 .. **Smart,** John R '89 OH Consumers' Cnsl -10 W Broad -Ste 1800
-Columbus 43215 **Fx:**466-9475

(216) 664-2767 .. **Smayda,** Emily A '01 Dept of Law -601 Lakeside Av
-Rm 106 City Hall -Cleveland 44114 **Fx:**664-2663

(216) 781-4994 .. **Smearman,** Ralph Eric '93 (Smith MW&V) -1965 E 6th
-500 Natl City-E 6th Bldg -Cleveland 44114 **Fx:**781-9448

(216) 696-4200 .. **Smeltz,** John E '48 (Schneider SR&L PLL) -1111 Superior Av
-Ste 1000 -Cleveland 44114 **Fx:**696-7303

(216) 443-7800 .. **Smerillo,** John J '88 Cuyahoga Cnty Pros -1200 Ontario -8th Fl
-Cleveland 44113 **Fx:**698-2270

Smialek, Arthur D '77 -10402 Lk Shr Blvd -Cleveland 44108

(216) 363-4500 .. **Smidansky,** Kurt J '84 (Benesch FC&A LLP) -200 Pub Sq
-Ste 2300 -Cleveland 44114 **Fx:**363-4588

(216) 443-7800 .. **Smilanick,** Diane M '83 Cuyahoga Cnty Pros -1200 Ontario -8th Fl
-Cleveland 44113 **Fx:**698-2270

(317) 521-3295 .. **Smiler,** Brian L '01 Roche Diagnstcs Operatns,Inc
-9115 Hague Rd -Bx50416 -Indianapolis, IN 46250

(614) 486-3909 .. **Smiles,** Terri-Lynne B '86 (Collis S&C,LLC) -1650 Lk Shr Dr
-Ste 225 -Columbus 43204 **Fx:**486-2129

Smiley, Deborah A '02 -(Address Unavailable)

(770) 779-3900 .. **Smirnoff,** George III '97 PRG Schultz Intl,Inc -600 Galleria Pkwy
-Ste 100 -Atlanta, GA 30339

(614) 466-6700 .. **Smiseck,** Steven L '93 Tax Appeals -30 E Broad
-Columbus 43215 **Fx:**644-5196

(330) 434-7167 .. **Smith,** A Russell '61 -159 S Main -Akron 44308

(614) 462-2247 .. **Smith,** Adam L '99 %Schottenstein Z&D -250 West -Bx165020
-Columbus 43216 **Fx:**462-5135

(614) 249-4323 .. **Smith,** Alan B '69 Nationwide Ins Entrprse -One Nationwide Plz
-1-27-6 -Columbus 43215

(303) 312-6574 .. **Smith,** Alfred C '75 US EPA -999 18th -Ste 500 -Denver,
CO 80202

(216) 931-6000 .. **Smith,** Aliceia J '04 %Ulmer & B LLP -1300 E 9th
-Ste 900 Penton Media Bldg -Cleveland 44114 **Fx:**931-6001

(304) 624-8000 .. **Smith,** Amy M '87 (Steptoe & J) -6th Fl-Bank One Ctr -Bx2190
-Clarksburg, WV 26302

(614) 464-6400 .. **Smith,** Andrew C '84 (Vorys SS&P LLP) -52 E Gay -Bx1008
-Columbus 43216 **Fx:**464-6350

(216) 274-4556 .. **Smith,** Ann K '86 McKinsey & Co Inc -200 Pub Sq -Ste 3900
-Cleveland 44114

(216) 331-1110 .. **Smith,** Anne M '91 -12550 Lk Av -Ste 409 -Lakewood 44107

(330) 671-5226 .. **Smith,** Anne E '00 -511 N Main -Akron 44310

(513) 333-4012 .. **Smith,** Anne M '89 %Weltman W&R Co,LPA -525 Vine -Ste 800
-Cincinnati 45202 **Fx:**723-2239

(440) 891-8320 .. **Smith,** Anthony J '84 (Rooney & S) -493 Front -Berea 44017
Fx:(866) 891-2844

(614) 228-8943 .. **Smith,** Aria D '89 -209 S High -Ste 507 -Columbus 43215

(419) 325-2111 .. **Smith,** Arthur H '60 Libbey Inc -300 Mad Av -Toledo 43604

(440) 256-9213 .. **Smith,** Arthur L '72 -10750 Beechwd Dr -Kirtland 44094

(216) 394-5067 ..**Smith,** Barbara J '77 (Schottenstein Z&D) -1350 Euclid Av -Ste 1400 -Cleveland 44115 **Fx:**621-6502

(419) 624-3000 ..**Smith,** Barbara Q '91 Murray & M Co,LPA -111 E Shoreline Dr -Bx19 -Sandusky 44871

(740) 286-4649 ..**Smith,** Barry L '81 (B Smith) -233 E Main -Jackson 45640

(216) 622-3600 ..**Smith,** Bernard A '82 US Atty -801 W Superior -Ste 400 -Cleveland 44113 **Fx:**622-3370

(216) 592-5000 ..**Smith,** Bernard J '85 Cnsl Tucker E&W LLP -925 Euclid Av -1150 Huntgtn Bldg -Cleveland 44115 **Fx:**592-5009

(937) 223-5200 ..**Smith,** Bradley C '78 (Flanagan LH&S) -318 W 4th -Dayton 45402 **Fx:**223-3335

(419) 332-0550 ..**Smith,** Bradley J '96 -617 Croghan -Fremont 43420 **Fx:**332-0660

(216) 875-6512 ..**Smith,** Bradley S '91 Parkwood Corp -2829 Euclid Av -Cleveland 44115

(513) 651-6800 ..**Smith,** Brett A '04 %Frost BT LLC -201 E 5th -2200 PNC Ctr -Cincinnati 45202 **Fx:**651-6981

(614) 644-6429 ..**Smith,** Brian L '85 Industrial Commssn of OH -30 W Spring -9th Fl -Columbus 43215 **Fx:**752-8785

(330) 821-1430 ..**Smith,** Bruce E '75 (Geiger TS&H) -1844 W State -Ste A -Alliance 44601 **Fx:**821-2217

(419) 241-6000 ..**Smith,** Bruce L '66 (Eastman & S Ltd) -1 Seagate -24th Fl -Bx10032 -Toledo 43699 **Fx:**247-1777

Smith, Burke E '54 -11913 Park Lane Dr -Kenton 43326

(419) 625-0536 ..**Smith,** C Ross III '78 UAW Legal Srvcs -3116 Bardshar Rd -Sandusky 44870

(859) 392-7907 ..**Smith,** Candace J '92 Hon D Bunning USDC-EDKY -Bx232 -Covington, KY 41012 **Fx:**392-7945

(440) 458-4381 ..**Smith,** Catherine K '96 Delta Theta Phi Law Frtrnty,Intl -38640 Butternut Ridge Rd -Elyria 44035 **Fx:**458-4380

(508) 828-3709 ..**Smith,** Catherine W '90 Cnsl J&J -325 Paramount Dr -Raynham, MA 02767 **Fx:**828-3789

(614) 463-9770 ..**Smith,** Charles D '83 (Roetzel & A,LPA) -155 E Broad -Natl City Ctr 12th Fl -Columbus 43215 **Fx:**463-9792

(614) 276-8959 ..**Smith,** Charles J '84 OfCnsl Nein Law Ofcs -2291 Scioto Harper Dr -Columbus 43204 **Fx:**276-8959

(330) 643-2250 ..**Smith,** Christina I '03 9th Dist Ct of Appls -161 S High -Ste 504 -Akron 44308

(617) 248-9480 ..**Smith,** Christina N '97 (Smith & P LLP) -100 State -Ste 500 -Boston, MA 02109 **Fx:**812-1256

(216) 771-1760 ..**Smith & Condeni LLP** -1801 E Ninth -Ste 900 Ohio Svngs Plz -Cleveland 44114 **Fx:**771-3387

(330) 453-8788 ..**Smith,** Corey L '01 -349 Hmltn Av NE -Canton 44704

(740) 472-1647 ..**Smith & Coury** -316 S Main -Bx599 -Woodsfield 43793

(614) 221-0922 ..**Smith,** Craig A '84 Gamble HJ Co,LPA -1 E Lvngstn Av -Columbus 43215 **Fx:**365-9741

Smith, Craig E '02 -2512 Middle Bellvll Rd -Mansfield 44904

(216) 752-0612 ..**Smith,** Craig I '75 -2824 Coventry Rd -Cleveland 44120

(419) 244-8384 ..**Smith,** Craig J '04 Pub Def -555 N Erie -Ste 248 -Toledo 43624

(614) 621-8888 ..**Smith,** Craig T '00 %S Schiff & Assoc -88 W Main -Columbus 43215

(440) 230-9643 ..**Smith,** Csilla E '88 -1485 Royalwood Rd -Broadview Heights 44147

(419) 874-3569 ..**Smith,** Cynthia B '88 -110 W 2nd -Perrysburg 43551

(216) 791-1900 ..**Smith,** Cynthia D '83 -11811 Shaker Blvd -Ste #321 -Cleveland 44120

(404) 587-8635 ..**Smith,** Cynthia E '78 Kimberly Clark Corp -1400 Holcomb Brdg Rd -Roswell, GA 30076

(614) 487-1510 ..**Smith,** Daniel S '85 -1820 Northwest Blvd -Ste 100 -Columbus 43212 **Fx:**487-1599

(513) 621-8688 ..**Smith,** Darlene S M '03 (Smith Law Ofcs,LLC) -1071 Celestial -9th Fl Highland Twrs -Cincinnati 45202 **Fx:**621-3873

(937) 328-2574 ..**Smith,** David E '75 Clark Cnty Pros -50 E Columbia -Bx1608 -Springfield 45501

(419) 472-1720 ..**Smith,** David E '90 -3938 Bellevue Rd -MESA Bldg -Toledo 43613

(216) 642-0323 ..**Smith,** David Kane '84 (Britton SP&K Co,LPA) -4700 Rockside Rd -Ste 540 Summit One -Cleveland 44131 **Fx:**642-0747

(330) 456-4793 ..**Smith,** David L '97 -116 Cleveland Av NW -Ste 305 -Canton 44702

(513) 621-0442 ..**Smith,** David S '71 -601 Main -3rd Fl -Cincinnati 45202

(330) 762-8885 ..**Smith,** Dean E '72 (Smith & M Co,LPA) -777 W Market -Akron 44303 **Fx:**762-1009

(513) 361-0250 ..**Smith,** Deborah '82 SSA-OHA -312 Elm -Ste 2100 -Cincinnati 45202

(440) 786-1910 ..**Smith,** Deborah A '88 (Smith B & Co,LPA) -934 Archer Rd -Bedford 44146

(330) 253-2729 ..**Smith,** Deborah L '96 -120 E Mill -Ste 405 -Akron 44308

(859) 578-4680 ..**Smith,** Debra J '86 US Dept of Labor -1885 Dixie Hwy -Covington, KY 41011

(330) 297-3850 ..**Smith,** Denise L '84 Portage Cnty Pros -466 S Chestnut -Ravenna 44266

(513) 762-6200 ..**Smith,** Denise M '97 %Ulmer & B LLP -600 Vine -Ste 2800 -Cincinnati 45202 **Fx:**762-6245

(312) 201-2000 ..**Smith,** Derek C '98 Wildman HA&D -225 W Wacker Dr -Ste 3000 -Chicago, IL 60606

(937) 339-4257 ..**Smith,** De Wayne '72 -606 Ridge Av -Troy 45373

(740) 383-2161 ..**Smith,** Donald B Jr. '97 Legal Aid -Bx6029 -Marion 43301

(614) 692-3284 ..**Smith,** Donald L Jr. '86 US Dfnse Lgstcs Agncy -Bx3990 -Columbus 43218

(937) 593-8510 ..**Smith,** Douglas M '92 (Smith S&M) -112 N Main -Bellefontaine 43311

(216) 443-7800 ..**Smith,** Drew A '98 Cuyahoga Cnty Pros -1200 Ontario -8th Fl -Cleveland 44113 **Fx:**698-2270

(330) 744-0247 ..**Smith,** Edward F '88 (Nadler N&B Co,LPA) -20 Fed Plz W -Ste 600 -Youngstown 44503 **Fx:**744-8690

(859) 291-1808 ..**Smith,** Edward L Jr. '80 Govt Relations Consultants,Inc -831 Aberdeen Rd -Park Hills, KY 41011 **Fx:**291-3688

(937) 228-7104 ..**Smith,** Edward M '73 (Nolan SS&F) -40 N Main -Ste 1812 -Dayton 45423 **Fx:**226-1945

(330) 376-2272 ..**Smith,** Edward T '92 %Williams & Assoc -106 S Main -Ste 2300 -Akron 44308 **Fx:**376-5618

(937) 323-4641 ..**Smith,** Elbert G '58 -200 N Fountain Av -Springfield 45504

(614) 464-6400 ..**Smith,** Elizabeth Hanning '03 Vorys SS&P LLP -52 E Gay -Bx1008 -Columbus 43216 **Fx:**464-6350

(614) 728-6069 ..**Smith,** Elizabeth T '84 Atty Gen -30 E Broad -Columbus 43215 **Fx:**466-5087

(304) 485-9661 ..**Smith,** Ellen L '98 -331 Juliana -Bx2148 -Parkersburg, WV 26102

(513) 361-1200 ..**Smith,** Elliot M '04 %Squire S&D LLP -312 Walnut -Ste 3500 -Cincinnati 45202 **Fx:**361-1201

(614) 466-2980 ..**Smith,** Emily A '02 %Atty Gen -30 E Broad -Columbus 43215 **Fx:**728-9470

(614) 764-2007 ..**Smith,** Eric M '96 Stanley Steemer Intl -5500 Stanley Steemer Pkwy -Dublin 43016

(216) 621-1312 ..**Smith,** Erick C '88 %McMahon DH&L LLP -812 Huron Rd -Ste 650 The Caxton Bldg -Cleveland 44115 **Fx:**621-0577

(330) 549-2609 ..**Smith,** Eugene R '56 (E Smith & Assoc) -Bx253 -North Lima 44452

Smith, Florence H '87 -(Address Unavailable)

(614) 873-4511 ..**Smith,** Frank S '76 -366 Gay -Plain City 43064

(614) 365-2700 ..**Smith,** Fredric L '63 (Squire S&D LLP) -41 S High -1300 Huntgtn Ctr -Columbus 43215 **Fx:**365-2499

(614) 228-1233 ..**Smith,** G Rand '74 GR Smith Co,LPA -1349 E Broad -Columbus 43205 **Fx:**358-9814

(440) 238-1070 ..**Smith,** Gary D '79 -11005 Pearl Rd -Strongsville 44136 **Fx:**572-0757

(419) 825-2318 ..**Smith,** Gary Lee '89 -138 N Main -Swanton 43558

(740) 454-8585 ..**Smith,** Gary M '77 Graham M&R Co,LPA -11 N 4th -Bx340 -Zanesville 43702

(740) 472-1647 ..**Smith,** Gary W '82 (Smith & C) -316 S Main -Bx599 -Woodsfield 43793

(440) 323-2201 ..**Smith,** Geoffrey R '83 Geoffrey R Smith & Co,LPA -124 Middle Av -Ste 800 -Elyria 44035

(937) 865-6800 ..**Smith,** Georgeana G '94 Lexis/Nexis -Bx933 -Dayton 45401

(513) 946-3700 ..**Smith,** Gerald A '74 Hamilton Cnty Pub Def -230 E 9th -3rd Fl -Cincinnati 45202 **Fx:**946-3707

(614) 436-0600 ..**Smith,** Gerald L '76 (Mueller & S,LPA) -7700 Rvrs Edge Dr -Columbus 43235

(440) 933-3231 ..**Smith,** Gerald M '61 Smith & S Co,LPA -110 Moore Rd -Bx210 -Avon Lake 44012

(216) 357-7000 ..**Smith,** Geri M '81 US Dist Crt -801 W Superior Av -Cleveland 44113

(585) 338-6142 ..**Smith,** Glenn D '92 Bausch & Lomb -1 Bausch & Lomb Pl -Rochester, NY 14604 **Fx:**338-8706

(513) 861-7100 ..**Smith,** Gloria L '93 (Cross S & Assoc Co,LPA) -3460 Reading Rd -Cincinnati 45229 **Fx:**861-7101

(216) 523-4081 ..**Smith,** Gregory A '87 Eaton Corp -1111 Superior Av -Cleveland 44114

(614) 559-1185 ..**Smith,** Gregory D '96 Chicago Title Agency -100 S 4th -Columbus 43215

(513) 984-8313 ..**Smith,** Gregory E '04 %J Arnold & Assoc -9737 Loveland-Madeira Rd -Loveland 45140 **Fx:**984-8040

(614) 221-4255 ..**Smith & Hale** -37 W Broad -Columbus 43215

(954) 771-1850 ..**Smith,** Harold D '72 H Smith PA -701 E Cmmrcial Blvd -Ste 100 -Fort Lauderdale, FL 33334 **Fx:**491-3689

(419) 251-0714 ..**Smith,** Harold T '93 Mercy Hlth Prtnrs -2200 Jffrsn Av -Toledo 43624

(614) 221-4255 ..**Smith,** Harrison W Jr. '50 (Smith & H) -37 W Broad -Columbus 43215

Smith, Heather A '02 -8237 Overwood Av NW -North Canton 44720

(614) 781-1400 ..**Smith,** Heidi A '03 %Hrabcak & Co,LPA -67 E Wilson Bridge Rd -Worthington 43085

(513) 241-4722 ..**Smith,** Hope A '02 %Montgomery R&J,LPA -36 E 7th -Ste 2100 -Cincinnati 45202 **Fx:**241-8775

(513) 421-4646 ..**Smith,** Ian R '97 %McCaslin I&M,LPA -632 Vine -Ste 900 -Cincinnati 45202 **Fx:**421-7929

(937) 578-5237 ..**Smith,** Ivan C '94 The Scotts Co -14111 Scottslawn Rd -Marysville 43041

(614) 228-8400 ..**Smith,** J Gregory '93 %Ulmer & B LLP -88 E Broad -Ste 1600 -Columbus 43215 **Fx:**228-8561

(419) 244-0991 ..**Smith,** J P '97 -412 14th -Toledo 43624 **Fx:**244-1119

(859) 331-2838 ..**Smith,** J Stephen '95 %Taft S&H LLP -1717 Dixie Hwy -Ste 340 -Covington, KY 41011 **Fx:**(513) 381-6613

(614) 464-6400 ..**Smith,** J Theodore '98 %Vorys SS&P LLP -52 E Gay -Bx1008 -Columbus 43216 **Fx:**464-6350

(419) 228-6365 ..**Smith,** James A '89 Cory MWR&C,LPA -101 N Elizabeth -Ste 607 -Bx1217 -Lima 45802 **Fx:**228-5319

(513) 424-2600 ..**Smith,** James C '84 -4000 Roosevelt Blvd -Middletown 45044

(513) 421-6630 ..**Smith,** James H III '75 Lindhorst & D Co,LPA -312 Walnut -Ste 2300 -Cincinnati 45202

(440) 933-3231 ..**Smith,** James J '88 %Smith & S Co,LPA -110 Moore Rd -Bx210 -Avon Lake 44012

(216) 696-7600 ..**Smith,** James P '01 %Duvin C&H -1301 E 9th -20th Fl Erievw Twr -Cleveland 44115 **Fx:**696-2038

(304) 697-2400 ..**Smith,** James R II '90 -6 Norway Av -Huntington, WV 25705

(740) 353-1509 ..**Smith,** James S '79 -538 6th -Portsmouth 45662

Smith, Jarren L '04 -(Address Unavailable)

(740) 532-4911 ..**Smith,** Jason P '99 -413 Center -Ironton 45638

(614) 469-3204 ..**Smith,** Jeffery E '79 (Thompson H LLP) -10 W Broad -Ste 700 -Columbus 43215 **Fx:**469-3361

(440) 838-8800 ..**Smith,** Jeffrey D '04 %Millisor & N Co,LPA -9150 S Hills Blvd -Ste 300 -Cleveland 44147 **Fx:**838-8805

(740) 532-9000 ..**Smith,** Jeffrey M '84 -411 Center -Ironton 45638

(859) 594-4200 ..**Smith,** Jeffrey S '02 %Jones D&S,PLLC -51 Cavalier Blvd -Ste 260 -Bx0095 -Florence, KY 41022 **Fx:**594-4248

(614) 228-6647 ..**Smith,** Jeffrey S '02 OH Home Builders Assn -17 S High -Ste 700 -Columbus 43215

(419) 882-4131 ..**Smith,** Jeffrey T '93 (Smith & S) -4149 Holland-Sylvania -Ste 7 -Toledo 43623

(513) 621-6556 ..**Smith,** Jenny N '92 (Namanworth & S) -2306 Park Av -Ste 101 -Cincinnati 45206

(317) 266-8888 ..**Smith,** Jess M III '93 M Norris -22 E Wshngtn -Ste 114 -Indianapolis, IN 46204

(704) 388-7153 ..**Smith,** Jill A '82 Bank of America -101 S Tryon -Charlotte, NC 28255

(937) 748-2522 ..**Smith,** John D '80 (J Smith Co,LPA) -130 N Main -Springboro 45066 **Fx:**748-2712

(937) 593-8510 .. **Smith,** John M '66 (Smith S&M) -112 N Main -Bellefontaine 43311
(513) 541-0207 .. **Smith,** Jonathan K '97 -2467 Hearthstead -Cincinnati 45239
(513) 984-3320 .. **Smith,** Joseph A '70 -9403 Oakhurst Ct -Cincinnati 45241
(216) 696-6525 .. **Smith,** Joseph H '89 Catholic Diocese of Cleveland -1404 E 9th -8th Fl Diocese Finance Ofc -Cleveland 44114 **Fx:**696-1230
(614) 221-4221 .. **Smith,** Julie A '91 Barkan + N -360 S Grant Av -Bx1989 -Columbus 43216 **Fx:**221-5423
Smith, Julie L '01 -(Address Unavailable)
(614) 365-2700 .. **Smith,** Julie Rinehart '04 %Squire S&D LLP -41 S High -1300 Huntngtn Ctr -Columbus 43215 **Fx:**365-2499
(216) 696-1133 .. **Smith,** Justin M '00 Chapman Law Firm Co,LPA -123 W Prospect Av -Ste 150 -Cleveland 44115
(614) 227-2313 .. **Smith,** Karen D '91 (Bricker & E LLP) -100 S 3rd -Columbus 43215 **Fx:**227-2390
(614) 850-9472 .. **Smith,** Karen Fuller '99 -Bx21283 -Columbus 43221
Smith, Katherine C '88 -Bx13876 -Akron 44334
(513) 241-2324 .. **Smith,** Kathryn E '96 %Wood H&E LLP -441 Vine -Ste 2700 -Cincinnati 45202 **Fx:**421-7269
(419) 425-1110 .. **Smith,** Kelton K '86 -608 Lima Av -Bx213 -Findlay 45839
(216) 622-8200 .. **Smith,** Kenneth J '00 %Calfee H&G LLP -800 Superior Av -Ste 1400 -Cleveland 44114 **Fx:**241-0816
(860) 547-8289 .. **Smith,** Kenneth P '79 The Hartford Ins Co -690 Asylum Av -Hartford, CT 06105
(216) 443-7800 .. **Smith,** Kestra J '90 Cuyahoga Cnty Pros -1200 Ontario -8th Fl -Cleveland 44113 **Fx:**698-2270
(419) 424-7144 .. **Smith,** Kevin C '83 Mun Ct Judge -206 & 208 Mncpl Bldg -Findlay 45840
(216) 357-7130 .. **Smith,** Kevin M '04 US Dstrct Ct-Nthn OH -801 W Superior Av -Chmbrs 10B -Cleveland 44113
(513) 651-8317 .. **Smith,** Kimberly A '90 PNC Bank NA -201 E 5th -Bx1198 -Cincinnati 45201
(216) 378-9905 .. **Smith,** Kimberly Y '96 %McGlinchey S PLLC -25550 Chagrin Blvd -Ste 406 -Cleveland 44122 **Fx:**378-9910
(614) 466-8600 .. **Smith,** Kristin S '94 Atty Gen -30 E Broad -Columbus 43215 **Fx:**466-6090
(440) 576-9155 .. **Smith,** Kyle B '80 Smith & M -36 W Jffrsn -Ste 1 -Jefferson 44047
(937) 224-1981 .. **Smith,** Larry A '67 (Young PL&J) -130 W 2nd -Ste 800 -Dayton 45402
(740) 687-7087 .. **Smith,** Laura B '94 Fairfield Cnty Dom Rltns Ct -224 E Main -Lancaster 43130
(330) 376-9121 .. **Smith,** Lawrence R '72 -One Cascade Plz -Ste 710 -Akron 44308
(614) 464-1626 .. **Smith,** Lee M '78 (L Smith & Assoc) -929 Harrison Av -Ste 300 -Columbus 43215
(419) 625-3672 .. **Smith & Lehrer,LPA** -308 W Adams -Sandusky 44870
(740) 342-2033 .. **Smith,** Linda Loy '76 (Schnittke & S) -Bx542 -New Lexington 43764
Smith, Lindsay A '03 -(Address Unavailable)
(614) 466-5394 .. **Smith,** M Kathryn '99 %Pub Def -8 E Long -Columbus 43215
(614) 486-7182 .. **Smith,** Mara C '96 -Bx12202 -Columbus 43212
(614) 888-4911 .. **Smith,** Marc D '98 %J Kohler & Assoc -7650 Rvrs Edge Dr -Ste 101 -Columbus 43235
(513) 381-2838 .. **Smith,** Marcella Kay '04 %Taft S&H LLP -425 Walnut -Ste 1800 -Cincinnati 45202 **Fx:**381-0205
(740) 681-9499 .. **Smith,** Margaret A '98 -136½ W Mulberry -Lancaster 43130
(216) 687-1900 .. **Smith,** Maria A '84 Legal Aid -1223 W 6th -Cleveland 44113 **Fx:**687-0779
(216) 566-5915 .. **Smith,** Mark A '00 %Thompson H LLP -127 Pub Sq -3900 Key Ctr -Cleveland 44114 **Fx:**566-5800
(513) 287-7447 .. **Smith,** Mark B '84 -123 E 4th -Ste 400 -Cincinnati 45202
(513) 752-5350 .. **Smith,** Mark F '85 (Smith B&N) -905 Ohio Pike -Cincinnati 45245
Smith, Marsha D '77 -5050 Gabriels Lndng Rd -Oxford, MD 21654
(216) 781-4994 .. **Smith Marshall Weaver & Vergon** -1965 E 6th -500 Natl City-E 6th Bldg -Cleveland 44114 **Fx:**781-9448
Smith, Mary C '77 -(Address Unavailable)
(614) 879-5754 .. **Smith,** Mary E '53 -2333 Gardner Rd -Galloway 43119
(419) 243-6281 .. **Smith,** Mary E '85 (Shindler NH&S,LLP) -300 Mad Av -Ste 1200 -Toledo 43604 **Fx:**243-0129
Smith, Mary J '98 -(Address Unavailable)
(614) 424-7554 .. **Smith,** Mary K '91 Battelle Memorial Inst -505 King Av -Columbus 43201
(513) 579-0080 .. **Smith,** Matthew J '84 (Smith R&S Co,LPA) -1014 Vine -Ste 2350 -Cincinnati 45202 **Fx:**579-0222
(703) 308-1323 .. **Smith,** Matthew S '88 USPTO -Crystal Plz 3 Rm 2C02 -Washington, DC 20231
(740) 636-4164 .. **Smith,** Matthew T '85 Camco Title Ins Agncy -132½ E Court -Washington Court House 43160
(216) 621-0070 .. **Smith,** Maurice D '70 (Friedman D&S Co,LPA) -1370 Ontario -Ste 600 -Cleveland 44113 **Fx:**621-4008
(330) 376-4558 .. **Smith,** Melinda E '99 Scanlon & G Co,LPA -50 S Main -Ste 1200 -Akron 44308 **Fx:**376-3550
(614) 221-9200 .. **Smith,** Melita L '02 Schottenstein Stores Corp -1800 Moler Rd -Columbus 43207
(410) 783-2800 .. **Smith,** Michael D '92 Constellation Power Source -111 Market Pl -Ste 500 -Baltimore, MD 21202
(216) 515-1660 .. **Smith,** Michael E '89 (Frantz W LLP) -127 Pub Sq -2500 Key Center -Cleveland 44114 **Fx:**515-1650
(440) 835-4831 .. **Smith,** Michael K '87 -31382 St Andrews -Westlake 44145
(216) 292-3430 .. **Smith,** Michael L '76 -23611 Chagrin Blvd -Ste 229 -Beachwood 44122
(937) 492-4191 .. **Smith,** Michael L '73 (M Smith Co,LPA) -Bx496 -Sidney 45365
(419) 626-0055 .. **Smith,** Michele A '97 %Tone GM&V -1401 Cleveland Rd -Sandusky 44870 **Fx:**626-0288
(440) 244-2776 .. **Smith,** Nancy A '83 -811 Parkvw Av -Lorain 44052
(614) 462-3555 .. **Smith,** Nathan T '99 %Franklin Cnty Pros -373 S High -Columbus 43215
(216) 771-1760 .. **Smith,** Ned Lindsey '76 (Smith & C LLP) -1801 E Ninth -Ste 900 Ohio Svngs Plz -Cleveland 44114 **Fx:**771-3387
(937) 327-3687 .. **Smith,** Nichol R '01 Clark Cnty CSEA -1346 Lagonda Av -Springfield 45503
(937) 227-3700 .. **Smith,** Nicholas M '03 %Faruki I&C PLL -10 N Ludlow -500 Cthse Plz SW -Dayton 45402 **Fx:**227-3717
(214) 871-8419 .. **Smith,** Norma L '93 BSM Fncl LP -16479 Dallas Pkwy -Ste 700 -Addison, TX 75001
(216) 752-6401 .. **Smith,** Orlando E '91 -3922 E 149th -Cleveland 44128
(614) 466-1814 .. **Smith,** Patricia A '79 Workers Comp -30 W Spring -Level 26 -Columbus 43215
Smith, Patricia A '04 -(Address Unavailable)
(440) 576-3662 .. **Smith,** Patricia J '92 Ashtabula Cnty Pros -25 W Jffrsn -Jefferson 44047
(614) 457-5600 .. **Smith,** Patrick F '79 -5025 Arlngtn Centre Blvd -Ste 250 -Columbus 43220
(513) 564-7616 .. **Smith,** Patrick F '97 US Dist Ct-SD -100 E 5th -Rm 810 -Cincinnati 45202
(614) 227-2000 .. **Smith,** Patrick J '65 (Porter WM&A LLP) -41 S High -Columbus 43215 **Fx:**227-2100
(937) 222-6926 .. **Smith,** Patrick K '78 -120 W 2nd -1300 Lbrty Twr -Dayton 45402
(216) 443-7223 .. **Smith,** Paul '91 Cuyahoga Cnty Pub Def -1200 W 3rd NW -100 Lakeside Pl -Cleveland 44113
(513) 621-2120 .. **Smith,** Pete A '94 Strauss & T,LPA -150 E 4th -4th Fl -Cincinnati 45202 **Fx:**241-8259
(513) 723-4000 .. **Smith,** Phillip J '94 (Vorys SS&P LLP) -221 E 4th -Ste 2000 Atrium Two -Bx0236 -Cincinnati 45201 **Fx:**723-4056
(513) 556-6805 .. **Smith,** Rachel Jay '00 Univ of Cincinnati Cllg of Law -Bx210040 -Cincinnati 45221
(937) 910-7500 .. **Smith,** Randall J '82 Dayton Metropolitan Housing -400 Wayne Av -Dayton 45410
(614) 466-5394 .. **Smith,** Raymond H Jr. '90 Pub Def -8 E Long -Columbus 43215
(614) 221-0446 .. **Smith,** Rebecca Ann '96 Fisher & D -122 E Main -Columbus 43215
(937) 274-2313 .. **Smith,** Rebecca B '80 -4133 N Dixie Dr -Dayton 45414
(216) 685-9940 .. **Smith,** Rebecca R '01 SrCnsl Pagano WT&G -1370 Ontario -Ste 1240 -Cleveland 44113 **Fx:**685-9942
(216) 574-6300 .. **Smith,** Rene' D '93 Morse Diesel Intl -1111 Superior Av -Ste 1111 -Cleveland 44114
(440) 333-2551 .. **Smith,** Richard F Jr. '85 R Smith Jr,LPA -21330 Cedar Ridge Rd -Cleveland 44116
(614) 644-2658 .. **Smith,** Robert F III '78 Dept Ins -2100 Stella Ct -Columbus 43215 **Fx:**387-0092
(216) 502-0800 .. **Smith,** Robert III '84 -75 Pub Sq -Ste 333 -Cleveland 44113
(740) 455-7123 .. **Smith,** Robert L '83 Muskingum Cnty Pros -27 N 5th -Zanesville 43701
(614) 728-5448 .. **Smith,** Robin C '97 OH House/Rep-Mnrty Caucas -77 S High -11th Fl -Columbus 43215
(202) 616-4289 .. **Smith,** Robin D '88 US DOJ -Bx888 -Washington, DC 20044
(330) 492-0101 .. **Smith,** Roger Louis '75 -4450 Belden Vllg NW -Ste 404 Belden Vllg Twr -Canton 44718
(513) 579-0080 .. **Smith Rolfes & Skavdahl Co,LPA** -1014 Vine -Ste 2350 -Cincinnati 45202 **Fx:**579-0222
(614) 469-7130 .. **Smith Rolfes & Skavdahl Co,LPA** -50 W Broad -Ste 3000 -Columbus 43215 **Fx:**469-7146
(513) 762-6200 .. **Smith,** Ronald G '98 %Ulmer & B LLP -600 Vine -Ste 2800 -Cincinnati 45202 **Fx:**762-6245
(614) 466-7264 .. **Smith,** Ronald L '83 SrCnsl OH Legal Rghts Srvc -8 E Long -5th Fl -Columbus 43215
(419) 483-7724 .. **Smith,** Ronald R '74 -203 Northwest -Bx34 -Bellevue 44811 **Fx:**483-7724
(937) 865-6800 .. **Smith,** Rosemary E '94 Lexis/Nexis -Bx933 -Dayton 45401
(937) 223-5200 .. **Smith,** Roy Todd '87 Flanagan LH&S -318 W 4th -Dayton 45402 **Fx:**223-3335
(202) 273-6374 .. **Smith,** Royce E '78 US VA -810 VT Av NW -Rm 024I -Washington, DC 20420
(614) 792-0777 .. **Smith,** Ruth A '77 Scherer Co -5131 Post Rd -Dublin 43017
(216) 225-7972 .. **Smith,** Samuel R II '03 Cnty Pros Ofc -1463 E 173rd -Cleveland 44110
(614) 462-3555 .. **Smith,** Scott A '88 (Franklin Cnty Pros) -373 S High -Columbus 43215
(216) 241-6602 .. **Smith,** Scott C '88 (Weston HFP&H LLP) -50 Pub Sq -2500 Trmnl Twr -Cleveland 44113 **Fx:**621-8369
(513) 732-7360 .. **Smith,** Scott C '02 %Hon JR McBride -270 Main -Batavia 45103
(202) 533-3096 .. **Smith,** Scott D '87 KPMG Peat Marwick -2001 M Street, NW -Washington, DC 20036
(614) 224-4424 .. **Smith,** Scott E '82 (S Smith Co,LPA) -6660 N High -Ste 3-F -Columbus 43085
(330) 762-6474 .. **Smith,** Scott F '98 (Sternberg NS & Assoc) -411 Wolf Ledges Pkwy -Ste 300 -Akron 44311 **Fx:**762-2127
(330) 627-4770 .. **Smith,** Sean R H '81 (Childers & S) -70 Pub Sq -Bx252 -Carrollton 44615
(417) 873-5032 .. **Smith,** Shawn E '84 Bass Pro Shops -2500 E Kearney -Springfield, MO 65898
(513) 721-1975 .. **Smith,** Sheila M '95 (Freking & B) -215 E 9th -5th Fl -Cincinnati 45202 **Fx:**651-2570
(330) 270-7041 .. **Smith,** Shirley J '97 The Vansickle Corp -3666 Mahoning Av -Austintown 44515
(937) 593-8510 .. **Smith Smith & Montgomery** -112 N Main -Bellefontaine 43311
(614) 875-9640 .. **Smith,** Stanley S '64 -3697 Bway -Grove City 43123
(412) 995-4978 .. **Smith,** Stephen C '04 Carmeuse Nrth America -11 Stanwix -11th Fl -Pittsburgh, PA 15222
(614) 462-2249 .. **Smith,** Stephen J '71 (Schottenstein Z&D) -250 West -Bx165020 -Columbus 43216 **Fx:**462-5135
(330) 673-5015 .. **Smith,** Stephen J '91 -132 S Water -Kent 44240
(614) 462-2308 .. **Smith,** Stephen J Jr. '99 %Schottenstein Z&D -250 West -Bx165020 -Columbus 43216 **Fx:**462-5135
(419) 629-3681 .. **Smith,** Stephen L '72 S Smith Co,LPA -209 E Monroe -Bx22 -New Bremen 45869 **Fx:**629-3017
Smith, Stephen L '89 -3050 Rice Rd -Edinboro, PA 16412
(614) 228-6040 .. **Smith,** Steven L '73 (Smith & C) -261 S Front -Columbus 43215
(513) 684-0336 .. **Smith,** Steven L '92 -621 Mehring Way -Cincinnati 45202
(419) 243-2100 .. **Smith,** Steven R '80 (Connelly J&C LLP) -405 Mad Av -Ste 1600 -Toledo 43604 **Fx:**243-7119
(513) 455-7600 .. **Smith,** Steven R '84 (Greenebaum D&M PLLC) -255 E 5th -2800 Chemed Ctr -Cincinnati 45202 **Fx:**455-8500
(619) 239-0391 .. **Smith,** Steven R '93 CA Western Schl of Law -225 Cedar -San Diego, CA 92101
(216) 520-5600 .. **Smith,** Steven S '82 West Grp -6111 Oak Tree Blvd -Bx318063 -Cleveland 44131
(216) 344-9339 .. **Smith,** Stourton S '95 (SS Smith,Co LPA) -75 Pub Sq -Ste 800 -Cleveland 44113

(513) 977-8200 .. **Smith**, Susan A '03 %Dinsmore & S LLP -255 E 5th -Ste 1900
-Cincinnati 45202 Fx:977-8141

(440) 835-0600 .. **Smith**, Susan F '88 %Waldheger C,LPA -1991 Crocker Rd
-Ste 550 -Westlake 44145 Fx:835-1511

(614) 466-6750 .. **Smith**, Susan L '93 OH Dept Taxation -30 E Broad -22nd Fl
-Columbus 43215

(419) 247-8699 .. **Smith**, Susan L '00 Owens Illinois,Inc -1 SeaGate -25LDP
-Toledo 43666

(859) 426-1300 .. **Smith**, Thomas C '72 Ziegler & S,PSC -541 Buttermilk Pike
-Ste 500 -Bx175710 -Covington, KY 41017

(216) 382-3447 .. **Smith**, Thomas E '72 US Dept of Vet Affairs -1240 E 9th
-Cleveland 44199

(440) 366-9930 .. **Smith**, Thomas J '66 (McCray MS&M Co,LPA) -260 Burns Rd
-Ste 150 -Elyria 44035 Fx:366-1910

(513) 922-3200 .. **Smith**, Thomas R '57 OfCnsl Haverkamp BR&R Co,LPA
-5856 Glenway Av -Cincinnati 45238 Fx:922-8096

(513) 632-5333 .. **Smith**, Timothy A '77 -119 E Court -Cincinnati 45202

(330) 672-2572 .. **Smith**, Timothy D '77 Kent State University -130 Taylor Hall
-Schl of Jrnlism -Kent 44242 Fx:672-4064

(440) 933-3231 .. **Smith**, Timothy T '69 (Smith & S Co,LPA) -110 Moore Rd -Bx210
-Avon Lake 44012

(216) 566-1600 .. **Smith**, Todd M '91 (Schwarzwald & M) -1300 E 9th -Ste 616
-Cleveland 44114 Fx:566-1814

(614) 898-9900 .. **Smith**, Todd W '03 Akin G LLC -100 Drchstr Sq Ln -Ste 202
-Westerville 43081 Fx:898-9685

(859) 491-9100 .. **Smith**, Tracy A '95 %Morgan & G -335 E 3rd -Drwr928 -Newport,
KY 41072 Fx:491-9178

(304) 697-2400 .. **Smith**, Tyler B '04 %JR Smith II -6 Norway Av
-Huntington, WV 25705

(419) 245-1978 .. **Smith**, Victoria L '87 %Pros -555 N Erie -4th Fl -Toledo 43624

(440) 686-9000 .. **Smith**, Victoria N '95 %Goodwin & B LLP -22050 Mastick Rd
-Fairview Park 44126 Fx:686-9001

(330) 758-3075 .. **Smith**, Wade W Jr. '82 -725 Boardman-Canfld -#K-2
-Youngstown 44512

(216) 851-0799 .. **Smith**, Walterio S '60 -1284 Melbourne Rd -East Cleveland 44112

(614) 228-6148 .. **Smith**, Warren J '59 S Jaffy & Assoc Co,LPA -306 E Gay
-Columbus 43215 Fx:228-6140

(740) 393-9562 .. **Smith**, William D '75 -5 N Gay -Mount Vernon 43050

(216) 621-0058 .. **Smith**, William H '77 (W Smith Co LPA) -614 Superior Av NW
-940 Rckfllr Bldg -Cleveland 44113

(419) 625-3672 .. **Smith**, William H Jr. '69 Smith & L,LPA -308 W Adams
-Sandusky 44870

(216) 931-6000 .. **Smith**, William K '81 OfCnsl Ulmer & B LLP -1300 E 9th
-Ste 900 Penton Media Bldg -Cleveland 44114 Fx:931-6001

(419) 249-7100 .. **Smith Gorski**, Clare K '94 Marshall & M,LLC -Four Seagate
-8th Fl -Toledo 43604 Fx:249-7151

Smith-Johnston, Glenda A '99 -Bx1084 -Hamilton 45012

(304) 340-3800 .. **Smith-Kastick**, Dennise R '01 %Spilman T&B,PLLC
-300 Kanawha Blvd E -Bx273 -Charleston, WV 25321

(606) 327-6104 .. **Smith-Kemper**, Gina N '00 Kings Daughter Medical Ctr
-2201 Lex Av -Risk Mgt -Ashland, KY 41101

Smith-Monahan, Connie '96 -1674 Cherry Blossom Ct
-Hebron, KY 41048

(513) 929-4834 .. **Smith-Monahan**, Richard '95 Fed Pub Def -36 E 7th
-2000 CBLD Ctr -Cincinnati 45202

(440) 350-2394 .. **Smither**, Wendy J '91 Lake Cnty Domestic Relatns Ct
-47 N Park Pl -Painesville 44077

(330) 376-5300 .. **Smithern**, Michelle A '86 (Buckingham D&B,LLP) -50 S Main
-Bx1500 -Akron 44309 Fx:258-6559

(513) 785-6549 .. **Smithson**, Nicole M '02 Common Pleas Ct -315 High -3rd Fl
-Hamilton 45011

(216) 479-8500 .. **Smits**, Anthony M '99 %Squire S&D LLP -127 Pub Sq
-4900 Key Twr -Cleveland 44114 Fx:479-8780

(513) 352-6731 .. **Smitson**, Patricia M '77 (Thompson H LLP) -312 Walnut -14th Fl
-Cincinnati 45202 Fx:241-4771

Smoktonowicz, Andrea B '04 -(Address Unavailable)

(614) 210-9259 .. **Smolik**, Mark A '87 Safe Lite Group Inc -2400 Farmers Dr
-Columbus 43235

(205) 726-2418 .. **Smolin**, David M '86 Samford Univ/Cumberland Schl of Law
-800 Lakeshr Dr -Birmingham, AL 35229

(216) 348-5400 .. **Smolin**, Michele A '92 (McDonald H Co,LPA) -600 Superior Av E
-Ste 2100 -Cleveland 44114 Fx:348-5474

(330) 633-4865 .. **Smolk**, Edward C '58 -388 East Av -Tallmadge 44278

(216) 228-9191 .. **Smolka**, Monica '79 -14701 Detroit Av -Ste 575 -Lakewood 44107

(614) 253-9000 .. **Smoot**, Dana Dior '03 Smoot Construction -1907 Leonard Av
-Columbus 43219

(216) 771-7322 .. **Smrdel**, Patricia A '91 -1419 W 9th -3rd Fl -Cleveland 44113

(216) 566-5830 .. **Smyers**, Robyn Minter '01 %Thompson H LLP -127 Pub Sq
-3900 Key Ctr -Cleveland 44114 Fx:566-5800

(513) 621-8210 .. **Smyth**, Robert M '94 (Drew & W Co,LPA) -1 W 4th -Ste 2400
-Cincinnati 45202 Fx:621-5444

(210) 820-3500 .. **Smyth**, Vito S '96 Grtr San Antonio Hospital Council
-8610 N New Braunfels Av -Ste 105 -San Antonio, TX 78217

(216) 241-6868 .. **Smythe**, Marie T '93 %E Resnick & Co -1148 Euclid Av -Ste 300
-Cleveland 44115

(937) 592-2827 .. **Snapp**, Jeffrey C '90 -5346 Twp Rd -55E -Bellefontaine 43311

(419) 865-0852 .. **Snavely**, David A '74 Trust Co of Toledo, NA -6135 Trust Dr
-Ste 206 -Holland 43528

(419) 247-1662 .. **Snavely**, Jeffrey D '96 %Eastman & S Ltd -1 Seagate -24th Fl
-Bx10032 -Toledo 43699 Fx:247-1777

(419) 782-8846 .. **Snavely**, Stephen K '73 (SK Snavely Co,LPA) -505 4th
-Defiance 43512

(937) 492-5592 .. **Snavley**, James T '91 -7543 Baker Rd -Sidney 45365

(937) 324-5260 .. **Snead**, Cozette '95 -20 S Limestone -Ste 120A -Springfield 45502

(937) 228-9000 .. **Snead**, Jeffrey W '94 (Thorson SW&S,LLP) -130 W 2nd -Ste 1508
-Dayton 45402 Fx:228-3550

(614) 799-8899 .. **Snedaker**, Robert H III '81 -3010 Hayden Rd -Columbus 43235
Fx:798-1935

(216) 861-3086 .. **Sneiderman**, Lisa N '94 Reid M&W -55 Pub Sq -Ste 2010
-Cleveland 44113 Fx:861-4409

(216) 621-0150 .. **Sneiderman**, Steven H '91 (Hahn L&P LLP)
-3300 BP Twr/200 Pub Sq -Ste 3300 -Cleveland 44114
Fx:241-2824

(330) 467-9600 .. **Snell**, Jeffrey J '88 -253 W Aurora Rd -Bx569
-Sagamore Hills 44067

(937) 224-5297 .. **Snell**, Richard G '56 -120 W 2nd -Ste 506 -Dayton 45402

(513) 852-3344 .. **Snelling**, Angela '99 OH Civil Rts Cmmssn -7162 Reading Rd
-Ste 1001 -Cincinnati 45237

(614) 464-6400 .. **Snider**, Blake A '99 %Vorys SS&P LLP -52 E Gay -Bx1008
-Columbus 43216 Fx:464-6350

(440) 349-3700 .. **Snider**, Harvey A '61 (Kenen & S Co,LPA) -33595 Bainbrdg Rd
-Ste 105 -Solon 44139

(740) 654-4141 .. **Snider**, John M '82 (Stebelton A&S,LPA) -109 N Broad -Bx130
-Lancaster 43130 Fx:654-2521

(614) 227-2150 .. **Snider**, Mark A '04 %Porter WM&A LLP -41 S High
-Columbus 43215 Fx:227-4499

(740) 654-4141 .. **Snider**, Rick L '79 (Stebelton A&S,LPA) -109 N Broad -Bx130
-Lancaster 43130 Fx:654-2521

(419) 530-2418 .. **Snider**, Stephen J '02 Univ of Toledo -2801 W Bancroft
-Toledo 43606

(419) 213-4700 .. **Sniderhan**, James T '76 %Lucas Cnty Pros -Adams & Erie
-Lucas Cnty Cthse -Toledo 43624

(614) 221-2121 .. **Sniderman**, Jeffery J '95 Isaac BL&T,LLP -250 E Broad
-Ste 900 Mdlnd Bldg -Columbus 43215 Fx:365-9516

(216) 751-2877 .. **Snipes**, Alonzo Jr. '68 -3815 Lee Rd -Cleveland 44128

(614) 340-2035 .. **Snitcher McQuain**, Jill '99 Columbus Bar Assn -175 S 3rd -Ste 11
-Columbus 43215

(330) 376-3300 .. **Snitchler**, Todd '02 %Stark & K Co,LPA -76 S Main -Ste 1512
-Akron 44308 Fx:376-6237

(330) 837-4251 .. **Snively**, James D '66 -11 Lincoln Way E -Massillon 44646

(330) 945-4800 .. **Snoderly**, John A '59 -2044 E Bailey Rd -Cuyahoga Falls 44221
Fx:945-4225

(216) 771-1760 .. **Snodgrass**, Cristin R '03 %Smith & C LLP -1801 E Ninth
-Ste 900 Ohio Svngs Plz -Cleveland 44114 Fx:771-3387

(740) 653-6464 .. **Snoke**, Carrie S '02 %Dagger JMO&H -144 E Main -Bx667
-Lancaster 43130 Fx:653-8522

(513) 891-1373 .. **Snouffer**, Gary H '75 -6033 St Regis Dr -Cincinnati 45236

(216) 621-4666 .. **Snow**, David A '73 -1310 Standard Bldg -Cleveland 44113

(440) 603-2007 .. **Snow**, Gina D '96 Progressive Ins Co -6055 Parkland Blvd
-Mayfield Heights 44124

Snow, Jamie Lyn '04 -(Address Unavailable)

(330) 456-8341 .. **Snow**, Randolph L '71 (Black MS&A,LPA) -220 Market Av S
-Ste 1000 -Canton 44702 Fx:456-5756

(216) 443-7800 .. **Snow**, Renee L '97 Cuyahoga Cnty Pros -1200 Ontario -8th Fl
-Cleveland 44113 Fx:698-2270

(740) 349-7262 .. **Snow**, William P '81 %Morrow & E Co,LPA -10 W Locust -Bx487
-Newark 43058

(419) 422-8906 .. **Snyder Alge & Welch,LPA** -233 S Main -Findlay 45840

(216) 586-3939 .. **Snyder**, Amanda M '03 %Jones D -901 Lakeside Av
-Cleveland 44114 Fx:579-0212

(740) 349-6215 .. **Snyder**, Ann E '92 Licking Cnty Cmn Pleas Ct -75 E Main
-Newark 43055

(330) 643-2326 .. **Snyder**, Ann L '83 Summit Cnty Probate Ct -209 S High
-Akron 44308

(614) 463-9770 .. **Snyder**, Bradley L '81 (Roetzel & A,LPA) -155 E Broad
-Natl City Ctr 12th Fl -Columbus 43215 Fx:463-9792

(419) 666-1088 .. **Snyder**, Bruce T '76 -30072 Waterford Dr E -Perrysburg 43551

(937) 843-9297 .. **Snyder**, Cheryl Wright '81 -7310 Twp Rd 94 -Lewistown 43333

(513) 737-5180 .. **Snyder**, Christopher J '88 (McKenzie & S) -315 Maple Av
-Hamilton 45011

(330) 762-7488 .. **Snyder**, Christopher R '02 -137 S Main -Ste 206 -Akron 44308
Fx:762-2633

(419) 243-3800 .. **Snyder**, Constance A '83 -1119 Adams -2nd Fl -Toledo 43624

(614) 466-3947 .. **Snyder**, Cynthia R '84 OH Brd of Nursing -17 S High -Ste 400
-Columbus 43215

(727) 797-6878 .. **Snyder**, D James '74 -2790 Sunset Pnt Rd -Clearwater, FL 33759
Fx:799-1621

(419) 422-8906 .. **Snyder**, Daniel M '59 (Snyder A&W,LPA) -233 S Main
-Findlay 45840

(513) 583-9565 .. **Snyder**, David B '92 -154 Thorobred Rd -Loveland 45140

Snyder, Dawn E '04 -(Address Unavailable)

(734) 647-6095 .. **Snyder**, Donna J '80 Univ of MI/Gen Cnsl Ofc -3003 S State
-#9000 -Ann Arbor, MI 48109

(614) 794-0221 .. **Snyder**, Douglas A '81 -1001 Eastwind Dr -Ste 106
-Westerville 43081

(419) 867-8090 .. **Snyder**, Edward L '83 -6910 Airport Hwy -Ste 11 -Holland 43528

(330) 545-4326 .. **Snyder**, Emmor F '70 -3 N State -Girard 44420

(937) 228-2696 .. **Snyder**, Gary A '60 (Snyder R&S) -11 W Monument Bldg -Ste 307
-Dayton 45402

(330) 922-0342 .. **Snyder**, Gayle L '94 -2754 Front -Ste 109 -Cuyahoga Falls 44221
Fx:923-9710

(937) 439-3811 .. **Snyder**, Jeffrey D '94 -7925 Paragon Rd -Dayton 45459
Fx:433-1510

(216) 621-0200 .. **Snyder**, Kenneth F '66 (Baker & H LLP) -1900 E 9th -Ste 3200
-Cleveland 44114 Fx:696-0740

Snyder, Larry H '52 -5600 Morse Rd -Gahanna 43230

(216) 787-4740 .. **Snyder**, Laurence R '86 OH Lottery Cmmssn -615 W Superior Av
-Cleveland 44113

(419) 333-9918 .. **Snyder**, Lisa M '98 -714 Court -Fremont 43420 Fx:333-9054

(216) 687-3889 .. **Snyder**, Lloyd B '70 CSU-Marshall Cllg of Law -2121 Euclid Av
-LB138 -Cleveland 44115 Fx:687-6881

(614) 834-9879 .. **Snyder**, Luann K '89 -1039 Hill Rd N -Ste 105 -Pickerington 43147
Fx:834-1577

(419) 241-1200 .. **Snyder**, Lucy M '96 %Cooper & W,LPA -900 Adams -Toledo
43624 Fx:242-5675

(937) 865-6800 .. **Snyder**, Mark E '98 Lexis/Nexis -Bx933 -Dayton 45401

(419) 294-9744 .. **Snyder**, Mary F '97 -107 N Sandusky Av -Upper Sandusky 43351

(614) 466-8600 .. **Snyder**, Melinda Ryans '04 %Atty Gen -30 E Broad
-Columbus 43215 Fx:728-7582

(614) 228-6107 .. **Snyder**, Meredith A '95 (Jack & S) -572 E Rich -Columbus 43215

(614) 463-9441 .. **Snyder**, Michael A '98 %Shumaker L&K,LLP -41 S High -Ste 2210
-Columbus 43215 Fx:463-1108

(216) 348-5400 .. **Snyder**, Michael L '88 (McDonald H Co,LPA) -600 Superior Av E
-Ste 2100 -Cleveland 44114 Fx:348-5474

(937) 222-7777 .. **Snyder**, Monte K '85 Stukey & Assoc -333 W 1st -Ste 400
-Dayton 45402 Fx:222-7772

(216) 361-0102 ..**Snyder,** Patricia A '80 -4403 St Clair Av -Cleveland 44103
(614) 466-3013 ..**Snyder,** Patricia E '78 SERB -65 E State -Ste 1200
  -Columbus 43215 **Fx:**466-3074
  Snyder, Philip M '99 -13007 Heath Rd -Chesterland 44026
(937) 449-6810 ..**Snyder,** R Bruce '73 (Porter WM&A LLP) -1 S Main -Ste 1600
  -Dayton 45402 **Fx:**449-6820
(937) 228-2696 ..**Snyder Rakay & Spicer** -11 W Monument Bldg -Ste 307
  -Dayton 45402
(513) 241-7460 ..**Snyder,** Richard '64 -7 W 7th -Ste 1850 -Cincinnati 45202
(513) 868-1500 ..**Snyder,** Richard D '88 -5127 Plsnt Av -Fairfield 45014
(937) 222-2424 ..**Snyder,** Robert N '85 (Freund F&A) -1 S Main -Ste 1800
  -Dayton 45402 **Fx:**222-5369
(440) 392-7410 ..**Snyder,** Ronald E '73 Steris Corp -5960 Heisley Rd -Mentor 44060
(614) 461-4455 ..**Snyder,** Ronald H '80 (Cloppert LS&W) -225 E Broad
  -Columbus 43215 **Fx:**461-0072
(607) 974-3054 ..**Snyder,** Ronald J '82 Corning Inc -SP-TI-3-1 -IP Dept
  -Corning, NY 14831 **Fx:**974-3848
(775) 588-5757 ..**Snyder,** Stephanie J '76 Peak Development Sys -Bx11707
  -Zephyr Cove, NV 89448
(614) 436-0346 ..**Snyder,** Tamie I '99 (Johnson S & Assoc,LLP) -299 S State
  -Westerville 43081 **Fx:**436-0347
(513) 735-0300 ..**Snyder,** Terrell B '83 -196 E Main -Ste D -Batavia 45103
(440) 834-5000 ..**Snyder,** Timothy H '96 -13796 W Spring -Bx386 -Burton 44021
  Snyder, Timothy J '95 -80 Thuman Av -Columbus 43206
(513) 281-1544 ..**Snyder,** William D '76 (W Snyder & Assoc) -2115 Luray Av
  -Cincinnati 45206
(440) 895-4000 ..**Snyder,** William F '50 (Snyder Assoc) -21081 Aberdeen Rd
  -Rocky River 44116
(614) 222-8686 ..**Soards,** Karla S '98 Scott S&W LLP -50 W Broad
  -2500 LeVeque Twr -Columbus 43215 **Fx:**222-8688
(330) 456-8341 ..**Soares,** Bruce M '80 (Black MS&A,LPA) -220 Market Av S
  -Ste 1000 -Canton 44702 **Fx:**456-5756
(419) 255-5900 ..**Sobanski,** Mark J '82 (MacMillan S&T,LLC) -720 Water -4th Fl
  -Toledo 43604 **Fx:**255-9639
(513) 745-0400 ..**Sobecki,** Judi L '96 %Furnier T,LLP -1 Fncl Way -Ste 312
  -Cincinnati 45242 **Fx:**792-6724
(212) 258-4000 ..**Sobecki,** Mark S '86 Cnsl Siemens Corp -153 E 53rd -Leg Div
  -New York, NY 10022
(419) 242-9908 ..**Sobecki,** Thomas A '81 -520 Mad Av -811 Spitzer Bldg
  -Toledo 43604
(216) 595-8222 ..**Sobel,** Jonathan F '79 (Kabat M&S) -25550 Chagrin Blvd -Ste 403
  -Beachwood 44122
(262) 377-5506 ..**Sobel,** Ronald M Jr. '88 Sobel Law Ofc -1650 9th Av -Ste 2 -Bx397
  -Grafton, WI 53024
(216) 621-9767 ..**Sobel,** Ryan A '04 %Thorman & H-L Co,LPA -1220 W 6th -Ste 307
  -Cleveland 44113 **Fx:**621-3422
(513) 533-2723 ..**Sobers,** Sharon J '85 %Finney SS&K Co,LPA -2623 Erie Av
  -Bx8804 -Cincinnati 45208
(440) 382-5054 ..**Sobieski,** Ernest F '75 -6329 W 130th -Ste 660
  -Parma Heights 44130
(216) 583-3819 ..**Sobieski,** Jeffrey S '98 Ernst & Young -1660 W 2nd
  -1000 Skylight Ofc Twr -Cleveland 44113
(216) 443-8768 ..**Sobieski,** Ralph P '81 Cuyahoga Cnty Probate Ct -1 Lakeside Av
  -Cleveland 44113
(614) 436-8879 ..**Sobnosky,** Edward N '56 -Bx1650 -Powell 43065
(216) 426-4976 ..**Sobnosky,** Mary T '84 Applied Industrial Tech -One Applied Plz
  -Cleveland 44115
(216) 586-3939 ..**Sobolewski,** Brad A '00 %Jones D -901 Lakeside Av
  -Cleveland 44114 **Fx:**579-0212
(216) 464-5990 ..**Soclof,** Richard L '98 Soclof Enterprises -3659 S Green Rd
  -Ste 100 -Beachwood 44122
(202) 273-1714 ..**Socoloff,** Jane Ballenger '78 NLRB -1099 14th NW -Rm 9518
  -Washington, DC 20570
(216) 378-7570 ..**Socrates,** Christine S '93 -2000 Auburn Dr -Ste 200
  -Beachwood 44122
(804) 771-2977 ..**Soddy,** Susan J '96 SSA OHA -801 E Main -4th Fl
  -Richmond, VA 23219
  Sodeman, William A Jr. '97 -2017 Shenandoah Rd -Toledo 43607
(614) 249-7610 ..**Soden,** Glenn W '77 Nationwide Ins & Fincl Srvcs -One
  Nationwide Plz -1-38-04 -Columbus 43215
(440) 871-3300 ..**Soeder,** Robin L '93 City of Westlake -24216 Hilliar Blvd
  -Westlake 44145
(330) 477-4515 ..**Soehnlen,** Emil A '96 Superior Dairy Inc -4719 Navarre Rd SW
  -Canton 44706
  Soellner, Jon D '04 -(Address Unavailable)
(419) 213-4754 ..**Sofia-Cerilli,** Tamara L '97 Lucas Cnty Ct Common Pleas
  -700 Adams -Toledo 43624
(330) 743-9509 ..**Sofranko,** George B Jr. '83 Mahoning Cnty Msdmnr Drug Ct
  -20 Fed Plz W -2nd Fl -Youngstown 44503
(440) 684-8740 ..**Sogg,** Nancy W '75 Meridia Hlth Sys -6803 Mayfld Rd
  -Bldg 1 Ste 500 -Mayfield Heights 44124
(216) 696-1422 ..**Sogg,** Wilton S '60 OfCnsl McCarthy LC&L Co,LPA
  -101 Prospect Av W -1800 Mdlnd Bldg -Cleveland 44115
  Fx:696-1210
(937) 428-0540 ..**Soifer,** Stacey M '93 -Bx751704 -Dayton 45475
(440) 519-0113 ..**Sokell,** James C '87 -35425 Miles Rd -Moreland Hills 44022
(440) 442-6800 ..**Sokolowski,** Jeffrey J '00 %JW Diemert Jr & Assoc Co,LPA
  -1360 SOM Center Rd -Mayfield Heights 44124 **Fx:**442-0825
(330) 499-8899 ..**Sokolowski,** Sue A '01 %Simmons & C -4690 Munson NW
  -Canton 44718
(330) 643-2800 ..**Sokolowski-Craft,** Arlene '01 Summit Cnty Pros-Civil -53 Univ Av
  -6th Fl -Akron 44308 **Fx:**643-2137
(425) 873-1342 ..**Solberg,** Reese S '97 Classmates Online Inc -2001 Lind Av SW
  -#500 -Renton, WA 98055
(216) 586-3939 ..**Solecki,** Michael J '01 %Jones D -901 Lakeside Av
  -Cleveland 44114 **Fx:**579-0212
(330) 244-8000 ..**Soles,** Robert E Jr. '90 -1401 S Main -Ste 202
  -North Canton 44720 **Fx:**244-8002
(216) 622-4364 ..**Solganik,** Vivian L '70 Ohio Savings Bk -1801 E 9th -Ste 200
  -Cleveland 44114
(513) 352-6784 ..**Solimine,** Louis F '76 (Thompson H LLP) -312 Walnut -14th Fl
  -Cincinnati 45202 **Fx:**241-4771
(513) 556-0102 ..**Solimine,** Michael E '81 UC Cllg of Law -Clifton & Calhoun
  -Cincinnati 45221

(937) 496-3013 ..**Sollars,** Karen L '94 2nd Dist Ct of Appls -41 N Perry -Rm 515
  -Bx972 -Dayton 45422
(937) 449-2800 ..**Solle,** Susan D '99 %Chernesky H&K PLL -10 Cthse Plz SW
  -Ste 1100 -Dayton 45402 **Fx:**449-2821
  Sollitto, Sharmon '77 -2849 Fairfax Rd -Cleveland Heights 44118
(513) 421-3494 ..**Sollmann,** William J '74 Cardiovascular & Thoracic Surgns,Inc.
  -2123 Auburn Av -Ste 401 -Cincinnati 45219
  Solomon, Aurel '52 -3901 Martindale Rd NE -Canton 44714
(216) 416-3273 ..**Solomon,** Douglas H '83 Forest City Enterprises,Inc -50 Pub Sq
  -Ste 1000B -Cleveland 44113
(412) 434-4395 ..**Solomon,** Jeffrey D '72 PPG Ind,Inc -1 PPG Pl
  -Pittsburgh, PA 15272
(330) 208-1000 ..**Solomon,** John W '73 OfCnsl Vorys SS&P LLP -106 S Main
  -First Natl Twr -Akron 44308
(419) 248-3501 ..**Solomon,** Joseph J Jr. '84 (Jones & S) -2 Maritime Plz -3rd Fl
  -Toledo 43604
(216) 861-3366 ..**Solomon,** Lanny M '76 -1370 Ontario -1800 Standard Bldg
  -Cleveland 44113
(216) 765-0123 ..**Solomon,** Michael L '76 (Budish & S Ltd) -23240 Chagrin Blvd
  -Ste 450 Commerce Park 4 -Beachwood 44122 **Fx:**595-2787
  Solomon, Paul F '86 -6423 Visitation Dr -Cincinnati 45248
(216) 621-0200 ..**Solomon,** Randall L '73 (Baker & H LLP) -1900 E 9th -Ste 3200
  -Cleveland 44114 **Fx:**696-0740
(614) 292-5354 ..**Solomon,** Robert Lee Jr. '89 %OSU Moritz Cllg of Law -55 W
  12th Av -Columbus 43210 **Fx:**292-1383
(702) 458-8855 ..**Solomon,** Robert W '74 Amer Nevada Corp
  -901 N Green Valley Pkwy -Henderson, NV 89074
(216) 579-1700 ..**Solomon,** Steven J '03 %Pearne & G LLP -1801 E 9th -Ste 1200
  -Cleveland 44114 **Fx:**579-6073
(614) 469-5715 ..**Solove,** Deborah A '81 US Atty -303 Marconi Blvd -Ste 200
  -Columbus 43215
(614) 444-9414 ..**Solove,** Ronald L '70 -79 Thurman Av -Columbus 43206
  Fx:444-4494
(419) 244-6788 ..**Solt,** Robert L III '84 (Bugbee & C) -405 Mad Av -Ste 1300
  -Toledo 43604 **Fx:**244-7145
(937) 438-1001 ..**Soltau,** Hans H '73 H Soltau Co,LPA -6776 Loop Rd
  -Centerville 45459
(614) 221-2121 ..**Soltis,** Steve M '68 (Isaac BL&T,LLP) -250 E Broad
  -Ste 900 Mdlnd Bldg -Columbus 43215 **Fx:**365-9516
(216) 431-4500 ..**Solyn,** Melissa L '00 Cuyahoga Cnty Pros -3955 Euclid Av
  -Jane Edna Hunter Bldg -Cleveland 44115 **Fx:**431-4113
(419) 334-9725 ..**Solze,** Norman P '70 -617 Croghan -Fremont 43420
(513) 241-6748 ..**Somers,** Blake P '04 A Levine -324 Reading Rd -Cincinnati 45202
(703) 569-0400 ..**Somers,** Christopher A '97 (Altman & S,LLC) -7015
  Old Keene Mill Rd -Ste 204 -Springfield, VA 22150
(615) 886-6649 ..**Somers,** Heather M '94 CNA Ins Co -10 CNA Dr
  -Nashville, TN 37214
(678) 258-4237 ..**Somers,** Kirk L '91 Concurrent Computer Corp
  -4375 Rvr Green Pkwy -Ste 100 -Duluth, GA 30096
(937) 325-1588 ..**Sommer,** Eric M '96 %Juergens W&S -200 N Fountain Av
  -Springfield 45504
(419) 241-2100 ..**Sommer,** Gary O '84 (Watkins B&C) -405 Mad Av -Ste 1900
  -Toledo 43604 **Fx:**241-1960
(614) 752-9038 ..**Sommer,** Joseph C '83 Workers Comp -30 W Spring -Level 26
  -Columbus 43215
(740) 633-2954 ..**Sommer,** Karl W Jr. '63 -12 N 5th -Bx69 -Martins Ferry 43935
(740) 633-5551 ..**Sommer,** Keith A '66 (Sommer L&B Co,LPA) -409 Walnut -Bx279
  -Martins Ferry 43935 **Fx:**633-5660
(740) 633-5551 ..**Sommer Liberati & Berhalter Co,LPA** -409 Walnut -Bx279
  -Martins Ferry 43935 **Fx:**633-5660
(937) 224-7200 ..**Sommer,** Louis F III '99 %Horenstein N&B -124 E 3rd -5th Fl
  -Dayton 45402 **Fx:**224-3353
(513) 563-3003 ..**Sommer,** Rick J '99 -4555 Lk Forest Dr -Ste 650 -Cincinnati 45242
(330) 996-1087 ..**Sommerfeld,** Barbara I '99 Summit Cnty Chldrn Srvcs
  -264 S Arlngtn -Akron 44306 **Fx:**379-1897
(937) 435-7500 ..**Sommers,** Brian A '00 %Botros B&S,LLC -5785 Far Hills Av
  -Dayton 45429 **Fx:**435-7511
(401) 421-3060 ..**Sommers,** Eric M '99 %Vetter & W -20 Wshngtn Pl
  -Providence, RI 02903 **Fx:**272-6803
(440) 350-2707 ..**Sommers,** JoAnne V '73 Lake Cnty Juv Ct -53 E Erie -Bx490
  -Painesville 44077 **Fx:**350-2724
(216) 575-0777 ..**Sommers,** Sandra Becher '85 (Kelley & F,LLP) -1300 E 9th
  -Ste 1901 -Cleveland 44114 **Fx:**575-0799
(216) 241-0040 ..**Somogyi,** Robert E '93 -1660 W 2nd -Ste 410 -Cleveland 44113
(614) 258-6100 ..**Somos,** Tom '99 R Erney & Assoc Co,LPA -1654 E Broad
  -Columbus 43203 **Fx:**258-6600
  Somrak, Noreen H '82 -1801 E 12th -801 -Cleveland 44114
(419) 784-9982 ..**Sondergaard,** Steven J '91 (Penner & S,Ltd) -101 Clinton
  -Ste 1500 -Defiance 43512 **Fx:**784-9991
(614) 460-4640 ..**Sonderman,** Andrew J '79 Columbia Gas of OH,Inc
  -200 Civic Ctr Dr -Columbus 43215
(859) 581-4529 ..**Sondgerath,** Van L '83 -2101 Chmbr Ctr Dr -Chmbr Ofc Park
  -Fort Mitchell, KY 41017 **Fx:**344-4952
(216) 861-8844 ..**Sondik,** Kenneth I '90 -1370 Ontario -Ste 1640 -Cleveland 44113
(513) 868-8229 ..**Songer,** Diana L '93 -29 North D -Hamilton 45013
(216) 861-6833 ..**Sonkin,** Jeffrey M '92 %Sonkin & K Co,LPA -55 Pub Sq -Ste 1660
  -Cleveland 44113
(216) 861-6833 ..**Sonkin & Koberna Co, LPA** -55 Pub Sq -Ste 1660 -Cleveland
  44113
(216) 321-9494 ..**Sonkin,** Loren M '89 -2637 Ashton Rd -Cleveland Heights 44118
(216) 861-6833 ..**Sonkin,** Rick D '87 %Sonkin & K Co,LPA -55 Pub Sq -Ste 1660
  -Cleveland 44113
(216) 861-6833 ..**Sonkin,** Shale S '53 Sonkin & K Co,LPA -55 Pub Sq -Ste 1660
  -Cleveland 44113
(216) 861-6833 ..**Sonkin,** Yvette B '90 %Sonkin & K Co,LPA -55 Pub Sq -Ste 1660
  -Cleveland 44113
(614) 466-3998 ..**Sonnen,** Craig A '75 Unemploymnt Comp Commssn -145 S Front
  -Bx182299 -Columbus 43218
(212) 326-3939 ..**Sonnie,** Marilyn Weaver '93 (Jones D) -222 E 41st -4th Fl
  -New York, NY 10017 **Fx:**755-7306
(330) 965-8000 ..**Sontich,** Joseph P Jr. '86 (Osborne D&S Co LPA)
  -100 Marwood Cir -Boardman 44512 **Fx:**965-8005

(330) 965-8000 .. **Sontich**, Joseph P Sr. '49 OfCnsl Osborne D&S Co LPA
-100 Marwood Cir -Boardman 44512 Fx:965-8005

Soon, Christopher L '03 -(Address Unavailable)

(214) 651-5383 .. **Sooter**, Lisa S '93 OfCnsl Haynes & B,LLP -901 Main -Ste 3100
-Dallas, TX 75201 Fx:200-0773

(216) 579-1700 .. **Sopko**, Jeffrey J '75 (Pearne & G LLP) -1801 E 9th -Ste 1200
-Cleveland 44114 Fx:579-6073

(330) 394-9692 .. **Sopkovich**, Carol A '83 %M White Co,LPA -156 Park Av NE
-Bx1150 -Warren 44482 Fx:394-8589

(419) 693-4433 .. **Sorah**, Linda A '96 -101 Main -Bx8076 -Toledo 43605

(610) 941-7907 .. **Sorce**, Adam M '01 %Marshall DWC&G -620 W Grmntwn Pike
-Ste 350 -Plymouth Meeting, PA 19462 Fx:941-8133

(614) 728-7189 .. **Sorem**, Peter R '78 State Auditor -88 E Broad -Bx1140
-Columbus 43216

(513) 887-3795 .. **Sorey**, Roger L '86 Butler Cnty Cmn Pleas Ct -315 High -2nd Fl
-Hamilton 45011

(419) 213-4700 .. **Sorg**, Bruce J '92 %Lucas Cnty Pros -Adams & Erie
-Lucas Cnty Cthse -Toledo 43624

(937) 339-0511 .. **Sorg**, Matthew C '94 %Dungan & L Co,LPA -210 W Main
-Troy 45373 Fx:335-5802

(513) 241-3100 .. **Sorg**, Steven V '92 %Lerner S&R -120 E 4th -8th Fl
-Cincinnati 45202

(216) 514-9665 .. **Sorin**, Marvin '59 (M Sorin & Assoc,Inc) -26200 George Zeiger Dr
-Ste 506 -Beachwood 44122

(614) 901-3376 .. **Sornabala**, Jasmine '93 -5910 Cleveland Av -Columbus 43231

(937) 225-5565 .. **Sorrell**, Janet R '81 Montgomery Cnty Pub Def -117 S Main
-Ste 400 -Dayton 45422 Fx:225-3449

(440) 729-1252 .. **Sos**, Emil F Jr. '70 -12690 Opalocka Dr -Chesterland 44026

(216) 566-5500 .. **Sosin**, Jeremy S '04 %Thompson H LLP -127 Pub Sq
-3900 Key Ctr -Cleveland 44114 Fx:566-5800

(614) 855-2292 .. **Soska**, Christine V '97 -Bx399 -New Albany 43054

(216) 696-0022 .. **Sosnowski**, Kristie M '01 %Collins & S LLP -50 Pub Sq
-3300 Trmnl Twr -Cleveland 44113 Fx:696-1166

(330) 253-5060 .. **Sossi**, Frank T '78 (Brennan M&D,LLC) -75 E Market -Akron
44308 Fx:253-1977

(419) 485-0255 .. **Sostoi**, Martin W '82 -116 Broad -Montpelier 43543

(937) 278-8275 .. **Soter**, Mary K '75 -5518 N Main -Dayton 45415

Sotera, Mary C '86 -323 W Lakeside Av -Cleveland 44113

Soteriou, Michael J '87 US Dist Ct -7006 Tree Line Dr
-Harrison, TN 37341

(614) 891-2560 .. **Soto**, Michael '88 -5595 St Andrews Dr -Westerville 43082
Fx:891-6827

(202) 622-3769 .. **Sotos**, David J '94 IRS -1111 Const Av NW
-Washington, DC 20224

(937) 226-9354 .. **Sottile**, Derrick A '02 %Macey & C -40 W 4th -Ste 2160
-Dayton 45402 Fx:226-9359

(216) 623-0000 .. **Soucie**, Michele P '82 (Javitch B&R) -1300 E 9th -14th Fl
-Cleveland 44114 Fx:623-0190

(216) 443-7800 .. **Soucie**, Paul M '82 Cuyahoga Cnty Pros -1200 Ontario -8th Fl
-Cleveland 44113 Fx:698-2270

(419) 327-6304 .. **Souder**, William G Jr. '86 Sky Fin Grp,Inc -221 S Church
-Bowling Green 43402

(419) 841-2073 .. **Souders**, Kenneth M '78 -3236 Zone Av -Toledo 43617

(330) 455-0345 .. **Souers**, Loren E Jr. '74 -220 Market Av S -United Bk Plz Ste 600
-Canton 44702

(202) 347-0300 .. **Soukenik**, John P Jr. '76 Elias MT&H -734 15th NW -8th Fl
-Washington, DC 20005

(216) 781-5470 .. **Soukup**, Christopher E '75 %Ziegler M&M LLP -925 Euclid Av
-2020 Huntngtn Bldg -Cleveland 44115 Fx:781-0714

(614) 462-3555 .. **Soulas**, Nick A Jr. '93 Franklin Cnty Pros -373 S High
-Columbus 43215

Sourek, Michael J '02 -6586 Barton Rd -North Olmsted 44070

(937) 865-7786 .. **Southam**, Sharon L '00 Lexis/Nexis -Bx933 -Dayton 45401

(513) 241-6748 .. **Southard**, Mark M '88 A Levine -324 Reading Rd
-Cincinnati 45202

(513) 421-8686 .. **Southard**, Terence J '83 -36 E 4th -Ste 1140 -Cincinnati 45202

(937) 225-4652 .. **Souther**, Susan F '92 Montgomery Cnty Pub Def -117 S Main
-Ste 400 -Dayton 45422 Fx:225-3449

(614) 577-1050 .. **Southern**, James E '93 -7538 Slate Ridge Blvd
-Reynoldsburg 43068

(937) 222-1366 .. **Southern**, Patrick A '04 -111 W 1st -Ste 519 -Dayton 45402

(937) 324-5541 .. **Southward**, Wayne R '83 %Martin BH&H -1 S Limestone -Ste 800
-Bx1488 -Springfield 45501 Fx:325-5432

(216) 348-5400 .. **Southworth**, Glenn D '93 (McDonald H Co,LPA)
-600 Superior Av E -Ste 2100 -Cleveland 44114 Fx:348-5474

(216) 861-1100 .. **Southworth**, John D '98 Lipson Group -1422 Euclid Av -Ste 1500
-Cleveland 44115 Fx:861-6562

(937) 228-8104 .. **Souvé**, Todd W '86 ABLE -333 W 1st -Ste 500B -Dayton 45402
Fx:449-8131

(330) 376-2700 .. **Souza**, Jennifer L '98 %Roetzel & A,LPA -222 S Main
-Akron 44308 Fx:376-4577

Sova, Gregory '76 -38 Fountain Sq Plz -MD 10AT76
-Cincinnati 45263

(614) 228-5822 .. **Sova**, Rosemary L '84 OfCnsl Rich C&D,LLC -300 E Broad
-Ste 300 -Columbus 43215 Fx:228-2725

(614) 464-1877 .. **Sowald**, Beatrice K '66 (Sowald S&C) -400 S 5th -Ste 101
-Columbus 43215

(614) 464-1877 .. **Sowald**, Heather Gay '79 (Sowald S&C) -400 S 5th -Ste 101
-Columbus 43215

(614) 464-1877 .. **Sowald Sowald & Clouse** -400 S 5th -Ste 101 -Columbus 43215

(937) 221-1940 .. **Sowar**, Gerard D '87 Standard Register Co -600 Albany
-Dayton 45408 Fx:221-3431

Sowash, Allan D '02 -122 St Julien -Worthington 43085

(740) 594-8388 .. **Sowash Carson & Ferrier** -39 N Cllg -Bx2629 -Athens 45701

(740) 594-8388 .. **Sowash**, Jonathan B '80 (Sowash C&F) -39 N Cllg -Bx2629
-Athens 45701

(513) 977-8200 .. **Sowder**, Trenna K '03 %Dinsmore & S LLP -255 E 5th -Ste 1900
-Cincinnati 45202 Fx:977-8141

(614) 466-6696 .. **Sowell**, Lasheyl N '03 Atty Gen -150 E Gay -Columbus 43215

(614) 466-3615 .. **Sowers**, Amber D '04 Legis Srvc Commssn -77 S High
-Columbus 43215

Sowul, Kerry A '03

(216) 586-3939 .. **Sozio**, Stephen G '83 (Jones D) -901 Lakeside Av
-Cleveland 44114 Fx:579-0212

(330) 364-4491 .. **Space**, Mary E '81 Mun Ct Judge -166 E High Av
-New Philadelphia 44663

(330) 364-5505 .. **Space**, Socrates J '59 (Space & S Co,LPA) -714 N Wooster Av
-Dover 44622

(330) 364-5505 .. **Space**, Zachary T '86 (Space & S Co,LPA) -714 N Wooster Av
-Dover 44622

(216) 443-5809 .. **Spackman**, Timothy G '90 Cuyahoga Cnty Pros
-1910 Carnegie Av -Whitlatch Bldg -Cleveland 44115
Fx:443-5815

(216) 443-7223 .. **Spadaro**, Mark A '92 Cuyahoga Cnty Pub Def -1200 W 3rd NW
-100 Lakeside Pl -Cleveland 44113

(215) 563-0500 .. **Spade**, Eric F '95 %Frey PDBB&M,PC -1601 Market -26th Fl
-Philadelphia, PA 19103 Fx:563-5532

(513) 721-3330 .. **Spaeth**, Barry A '94 %Robbins KP&T -7 W 7th -Ste 1400
-Cincinnati 45202

(419) 420-9312 .. **Spaeth**, Bret A '97 %Fitzgerald Law Firm,LLC -400 S Main
-Findlay 45840 Fx:420-9314

(937) 865-8820 .. **Spaeth**, Edward J '89 Lexis/Nexis -9443 Springboro Pike
-Miamisburg 45342

(404) 233-7000 .. **Spaeth**, Juliana M '89 Morris M&M,LLP -3343 Peach Tree Rd NE
-Atlanta, GA 30326

(937) 223-1655 .. **Spaeth**, Paul H '83 (P Spaeth Co,LPA) -12 W Monument Av
-Ste 100 -Dayton 45402

Spaeth, Sara Bardon '03 -(Address Unavailable)

Spagna, Vincent A '97 -(Address Unavailable)

(440) 838-7600 .. **Spagnoli**, Charles C '02 %Janik & D,LLP -9200 S Hills Blvd
-Ste 300 -Cleveland 44147 Fx:838-7601

(614) 466-4510 .. **Spahia-Carducci**, Mary L '86 Atty Gen -150 E Gay
-Columbus 43215 Fx:995-0501

(740) 282-6028 .. **Spahn**, G Daniel '82 Mun Ct Judge -123 S 3rd -Steubenville 43952

(330) 643-2341 .. **Spahr**, Kenneth G Jr. '74 Summit Cnty Cmn Pleas Ct -209 S High
-Probate Div -Akron 44308

(740) 373-7624 .. **Spahr**, Michael G '74 Washington Cnty Pros -205 Putnam
-Marietta 45750

(216) 222-2976 .. **Spain**, Charles H Jr. '82 Natl City Bank -1900 E 9th -17th Fl
Loc 01-2174 -Cleveland 44114

(614) 331-9104 .. **Spainhoward**, Rebecca A '89 Huntington Natl Bank
-7 Easton Oval -EA4CO2 -Columbus 43219

(513) 731-3927 .. **Spaite**, Paul W '64 -6315 Grand Vista Av -Cincinnati 45213

(330) 823-2226 .. **Spalding**, David B '80 (Shetler & S) -950 S Sawburg Av -Bx2146
-Alliance 44601

(614) 624-7359 .. **Spalding**, Jennifer M '97 %Abbott Labs -625 Cleveland Av
-Columbus 43215

(614) 644-7257 .. **Spalding**, Sloan T '97 Atty Gen -150 E Gay -Columbus 43215
Fx:752-4677

(440) 835-8200 .. **Spalding**, Walter T Jr. '56 -24500 Ctr Ridge Rd -Westlake 44145

(561) 622-2700 .. **Spall**, Thomas L '82 -11891 US Hwy 1 -105 -Bx14127
-North Palm Beach, FL 33408 Fx:622-2841

(216) 621-0200 .. **Spallino**, James Jr. '93 (Baker & H LLP) -1900 E 9th -Ste 3200
-Cleveland 44114 Fx:696-0740

Spanagel, George W '50 -5871 Wickfld Dr -Parma Heights 44130

(216) 621-1530 .. **Spaner**, Martha R '02 %Shapiro & F,LLP -1500 W 3rd -Ste 400
-Cleveland 44113 Fx:621-1551

(216) 696-3232 .. **Spangenberg Shibley & Liber, LLP** -1900 E 9th
-2400 Natl City Ctr -Cleveland 44114 Fx:696-3924

Spangler, Craig D '79 -Bx 261 -Berea 44017

(740) 653-6464 .. **Spangler**, Jeffrey J '04 %Dagger JMO&H -144 E Main -Bx667
-Lancaster 43130 Fx:653-8522

(440) 942-6262 .. **Spangler**, Mathew E '02 (Wiles & R) -35350 Curtis Blvd -Ste 530
-Eastlake 44095 Fx:942-7211

(740) 345-0417 .. **Spangler**, Melanie A '01 %K Burkett -21 W Church -Ste 201
-Newark 43055

(614) 248-0463 .. **Spangler**, Melissa D '97 Bank One -1111 Polaris Pkwy -Ste 1N
-Columbus 43240

(419) 636-3196 .. **Spangler**, Michael W '86 (Newcomer S&S) -117 W Maple
-Bryan 43506 Fx:636-0867

Spanja, Stephanie G '04 -2804 Deerhaven Dr -Cincinnati 45244

(440) 269-8823 .. **Spano**, Lisa M '93 Manning & M Co,LPA -7556 Mentor Av
-Mentor 44060

(216) 522-7548 .. **Spanos**, Paul G '98 US Dept of Labor -1240 E 9th
-Cleveland 44199

(216) 241-6689 .. **Sparacia**, Andrew J '92 HSA Law Grp -200 Pub Sq -Ste 4020
-Cleveland 44114

(614) 645-8739 .. **Sparks**, Danielle R '91 Hon A Taylor -375 S High -15th Fl
-Columbus 43215

(859) 291-9000 .. **Sparks**, Robert R '01 (Parry DF&S,PSC) -411 Garrard
-Covington, KY 41012 Fx:291-9300

(330) 493-7211 .. **Sparks**, William R '77 -3930 Fulton Dr NW -Ste 106
-Canton 44718

(419) 242-1400 .. **Sparrow**, Keithley B '79 -608 Mad Av -Ste 1400 -Toledo 43604

(614) 469-5715 .. **Spartis**, Gary L '79 US Atty -303 Marconi Blvd -Ste 200
-Columbus 43215

(614) 222-4734 .. **Spater**, Alexander M '73 -565 E Town -Columbus 43215
Fx:222-4738

(513) 421-0300 .. **Spaulding**, Frederick D '91 -830 Main -Ste 700 -Cincinnati 45202

(419) 525-1811 .. **Spaulding**, Jonathon W '00 -13 Park Av W -Ste 305
-Mansfield 44902 Fx:526-5515

(407) 648-6208 .. **Spaulding**, Karla Rae '80 US Dist Ct -80 N Hughey Av -5th Fl
-Orlando, FL 32801

(216) 566-9700 .. **Spaw**, David E '91 (Rankin HP&C,LLP) -925 Euclid Av -Ste 700
-Cleveland 44115 Fx:566-9711

(614) 644-6338 .. **Speakman**, Claudia J '76 OH Dept of Edu -25 S Front -7th Fl
-Columbus 43215

(614) 462-5530 .. **Speaks**, George E '92 Franklin Cnty Admin Ofc -373 S High
-26th Fl -Columbus 43215 Fx:462-5999

(740) 532-6913 .. **Spears**, David R '78 Spears & Assoc Co,LPA -122 S 4th
-Ironton 45638

(937) 222-3000 .. **Spears**, Gregory P '82 %Falke & D LLC -30 Wyoming -Dayton
45409 Fx:222-1414

(740) 532-5815 .. **Spears**, Harold D '48 (Spears & Assoc Co,LPA) -122 S 4th
-Ironton 45638

(614) 868-0009 .. **Spears**, Jessica L '04 %Hallowes A&H -6445 E Lvngstn Av -Reynoldsburg 43068 Fx:868-0029

(330) 725-0030 .. **Spears**, Ronald S '98 Marco M&B -52 Pub Sq -Medina 44256 Fx:722-4888

(317) 488-6263 .. **Spears**, Timothy P '90 Anthem Inc -120 Monument Cir -M2SD -Indianapolis, IN 46204

(216) 732-9250 .. **Spechalske**, Richard A '80 -22034 Lk Shr Blvd -Euclid 44123 Fx:732-9252

(440) 576-3662 .. **Specht**, Harold E Jr. '00 Ashtabula Cnty Pros -25 W Jffrsn -Jefferson 44047

(330) 264-8956 .. **Spector**, David N '83 Wooster Iron & Metal Co. -972 Columbus Rd -Bx 1289 -Wooster 44691

(703) 415-1500 .. **Spector**, Eric S '62 Jones T&C,PC -2001 Jeff Davis Hwy -Ste 1002 -Arlington, VA 22202

(215) 597-9619 .. **Spector**, Jennifer R '97 %NLRB -615 Chestnut -7th Fl -Philadelphia, PA 19106

(216) 332-9280 .. **Spector**, Robert S '73 -5706 Turney Rd -Ste 101 -Cleveland 44125

(216) 486-4808 .. **Speece**, Janet L '87 -2016 Natona Rd -Euclid 44117

(614) 792-5555 .. **Speed**, Fred M Jr. '97 %Standley Law Grp LLP -495 Metro Pl S -Ste 210 -Dublin 43017 Fx:792-5536

(614) 466-3627 .. **Speelman**, Eleanor L '78 %Hon TJ Moyer -30 E Broad -3rd Fl -Columbus 43266

(419) 678-2378 .. **Speelman**, Kathryn W '98 JA Koesters -201 E Vine -Coldwater 45828

(312) 701-8605 .. **Speer**, Richard A '57 Cnsl Mayer BR&M -190 S LaSalle -Chicago, IL 60603

(513) 731-8460 .. **Spegal**, Karen L '93 (Fitch & S) -3752 Edwards Rd -Cincinnati 45209

(614) 939-1235 .. **Speidel**, Jamison S '01 %Demers & C -3 N High -Bx430 -New Albany 43054

(216) 241-0520 .. **Spellacy**, John J '95 -526 Superior Av -1540 Leader Bldg -Cleveland 44114

(216) 344-9220 .. **Spellacy**, Kevin M '89 (McGinty GH&S Co,LPA) -614 W Superior Av -Ste 1300 -Cleveland 44113

(216) 443-2025 .. **Spellacy**, Leo M '59 Ct of Appeals 8th Dist -1 Lakeside Av NW -Cleveland 44113

(216) 443-9000 .. **Spellacy**, Leo M Jr. '96 %Porter WM&A LLP -925 Euclid Av -Ste 1700 -Cleveland 44115 Fx:443-9011

(310) 395-1236 .. **Spellerberg**, Jeffrey K '83 -1541 Ocean Av -Ste 200 -Santa Monica, CA 90401

(937) 224-4600 .. **Spells**, Yashmin W '87 -5 N Williams -Dayton 45407

(202) 756-8340 .. **Spenard**, David A '93 (McDermott W&E) -600 13th NW -Washington, DC 20005 Fx:756-8087

(937) 544-3900 .. **Spencer**, Brett M '89 -231 N Cross -West Union 45693

(614) 249-3671 .. **Spencer**, Gilda L '93 SrCnsl Nationwide Ins Co -1 Nationwide Plz -Columbus 43215

(419) 241-1200 .. **Spencer**, Jodi D '01 Cooper & W,LPA -900 Adams -Toledo 43624 Fx:242-5675

(937) 325-8822 .. **Spencer**, John M '83 (Spencer & B) -30 Warder -Ste 250 -Springfield 45504

(614) 227-2300 .. **Spencer**, Maria E '94 Bricker & E LLP -100 S 3rd -Columbus 43215 Fx:227-2390

(937) 962-9320 .. **Spencer**, Maria L '00 (M Spencer,Inc) -120 N Commerce -Bx221 -Lewisburg 45338

(330) 392-6171 .. **Spencer**, Patricia L '79 Rieger SC&D -410 Mahoning Av -Bx1429 -Warren 44482 Fx:394-5507

(937) 323-9739 .. **Spencer**, Richard A '72 (Schmenk S&H) -20 N Limestone -Springfield 45502 Fx:323-9388

(614) 729-4921 .. **Spencer**, Robert W Jr. '98 Alliance Data Sys Corp -800 Techcenter Dr -Gahanna 43230

(623) 856-6801 .. **Spencer**, Ronald L Jr. '99 US Air Force -56 FW/JA -Luke AFB, AZ 85309

(419) 242-8214 .. **Spencer**, Scott E '79 -520 Mad Av -Ste 545 -Toledo 43604

(216) 755-5500 .. **Spencer**, William W '86 Developers Diversified Rlty Corp -3300 Enterprise Pkwy -Beachwood 44122

(419) 241-2201 .. **Spengler Nathanson PLL** -608 Mad Av -Ste 1000 -Toledo 43604 Fx:241-8599

(440) 326-4835 .. **Spenzer**, Sherry N '78 Lorain Cnty Domstc Relatns Ct -225 Court -2nd Fl -Elyria 44035

(561) 655-5050 .. **Speranzini**, Andrew P '00 %Foley & L LLP -777 S Flagler Dr -Ste 901 W Twr -West Palm Beach, FL 33401 Fx:655-6925

(614) 228-9707 .. **Sperl**, Kenneth J '02 Mallory & T Co,LPA -88 E Broad -Ste 1560 -Columbus 43215

(330) 792-6033 .. **Sperling**, Adam L '94 %Anzellotti SP&S Co,LPA -21 N Wickliffe Cir -Youngstown 44515 Fx:793-3384

(330) 792-6033 .. **Sperling**, Victor '60 (Anzellotti SP&S Co,LPA) -21 N Wickliffe Cir -Youngstown 44515 Fx:793-3384

(216) 696-9300 .. **Spero**, Keith E '56 Spero & R Co,LPA -526 Superior Av -Ste 440 Leader Bldg -Cleveland 44114 Fx:696-9370

(216) 861-9899 .. **Spero**, Scott A '89 Bentoff & S Co,LPA -526 Superior Av E -440 Leader Bldg -Cleveland 44114

(440) 646-3009 .. **Speroff**, Scott R '92 Rockwell Automation -1 Allen-Bradley Dr -Mayfield Heights 44124

(516) 626-5000 .. **Speros**, James M '80 VA Healthcare Ntwrk/Upstate NY -113 Holland Av -Albany, NY 12208 Fx:626-5500

(216) 383-1500 .. **Speros**, John W '84 -17310 Harland Av -Cleveland 44119

(740) 774-2142 .. **Spetnagel & McMahon** -42 E 5th -Chillicothe 45601

(740) 774-2142 .. **Spetnagel**, Thomas M '75 (Spetnagel & M) -42 E 5th -Chillicothe 45601

(330) 253-8877 .. **Spetrino**, Michael J '80 -50 S Main -Ste 502 -Akron 44308

(216) 583-3269 .. **Speyer**, Paul H '87 Ernst & Young LLP -925 Euclid Av -Ste 1300 -Cleveland 44115

(419) 249-4956 .. **Speyer**, Sharon S '85 Sky Bank -519 Mad Av -Bx1987 -Toledo 43603

(513) 737-5100 .. **Sphar**, Kristen L '98 %S Frederick,LLC -304 N 2nd -Hamilton 45011

(614) 227-2342 .. **Spialter**, David C '82 (Bricker & E LLP) -100 S 3rd -Columbus 43215 Fx:227-2390

(216) 692-2227 .. **Spiccia**, John C '84 -24400 Highland -Richmond Heights 44143

(937) 228-2696 .. **Spicer**, Jerry A '78 (Snyder R&S) -11 W Monument Bldg -Ste 307 -Dayton 45402

(419) 897-5295 .. **Spidel**, Douglas A '97 -1789 Indn Wd Cir -Ste 140 -Maumee 43537

(419) 245-3016 .. **Spidel**, Mara L '99 Workers Comp -1 Govt Ctr -Toledo 43604 Fx:245-2666

(419) 562-6624 .. **Spiegel**, John L '75 -222 W Charles -Bx1024 -Bucyrus 44820

(617) 951-2929 .. **Spiegel**, Robert M '93 %McCormack & E -1 Intl Pl -Boston, MA 02110 Fx:951-2672

(513) 761-9255 .. **Spiegel**, Walter E '02 Standard Textile Co,Inc -1 Knollcrest Dr -Bx371805 -Cincinnati 45222

(216) 475-5045 .. **Spiegelberg**, Wilhelm G II '82 Municipal Ct -5555 Turney Rd -Garfield Heights 44125

(216) 592-5000 .. **Spielman**, Michael A '02 Cnsl Tucker E&W LLP -925 Euclid Av -1150 Huntngtn Bldg -Cleveland 44115 Fx:592-5009

(513) 381-1500 .. **Spiering**, Kevin J '94 -119 E Court -Cincinnati 45202

(614) 221-7272 .. **Spiert**, Kenneth R '87 -85 E Gay -Ste 507 -Columbus 43215

(216) 696-4700 .. **Spieth Bell McCurdy & Newell Co, LPA** -925 Euclid Av -2000 Huntngtn Bldg -Cleveland 44115 Fx:696-2706

(440) 324-5353 .. **Spike**, Allen S '64 (Spike & M,LLP) -1551 W River Rd N -Elyria 44035 Fx:324-6529

(440) 324-5353 .. **Spike & Meckler, LLP** -1551 W River Rd N -Elyria 44035 Fx:324-6529

(440) 324-5353 .. **Spike**, Neil H '97 %Spike & M,LLP -1551 W River Rd N -Elyria 44035 Fx:324-6529

(419) 242-7985 .. **Spiker**, Douglas E '86 (Roetzel & A,LPA) -One SeaGate -9th Fl -Toledo 43604 Fx:242-0316

(239) 949-4686 .. **Spiker**, Kimberly A '93 -3688 Tomlinson -Bonita Springs, FL 34134

(740) 942-8181 .. **Spiker**, William E '60 Eagle Fuels,Inc -330 Oak Park Rd -Bx291 -Cadiz 43907

(513) 287-2094 .. **Spiller**, Amy B '90 Cinergy Corp -139 E 4th -25 Atrium II -Bx960 -Cincinnati 45201

(513) 352-6722 .. **Spiller**, Keith P '89 (Thompson H LLP) -312 Walnut -14th Fl -Cincinnati 45202 Fx:241-4771

(614) 719-1565 .. **Spina**, Anthony '98 Dept Ins -2100 Stella Ct -Columbus 43215

(419) 882-7100 .. **Spinazze**, Anthony P '00 %Lydy & M,Ltd -4930 Holland Sylvania Rd -Sylvania 43560 Fx:882-1120

(419) 882-7100 .. **Spinazze**, Dominic J '92 %Lydy & M,Ltd -4930 Holland Sylvania Rd -Sylvania 43560 Fx:882-1120

(330) 723-5450 .. **Spink**, Prudence C '81 -316 W Lbrty -Medina 44256

(440) 842-0770 .. **Spinks**, Thomas F '74 -5700 Pearl Rd -Ste 202 -Cleveland 44129

(216) 363-4500 .. **Spira**, Robert M '72 OfCnsl Benesch FC&A LLP -200 Pub Sq -Ste 2300 -Cleveland 44114 Fx:363-4588

(740) 687-5535 .. **Spires**, Jeremiah J '89 -735 Franklin Av -Bx2618 -Lancaster 43130 Fx:687-0092

(216) 781-4680 .. **Spirgen**, Dennis R '96 Van Aken W&W -629 Euclid Av -1000 Natl City Bk Bldg -Cleveland 44114 Fx:241-1421

(614) 485-1800 .. **Spirito**, Maryellen C '83 %Arnold T&W -2075 Marble Cliff Ofc Park -Columbus 43215 Fx:485-1944

(216) 621-1530 .. **Spirko**, Daniel M '00 %Shapiro & F,LLP -1500 W 3rd -Ste 400 -Cleveland 44113 Fx:621-1551

(216) 443-6350 .. **Spirko**, Nicole M '99 8th Dist Ct of Appls -1 Lakeside Av -#202 -Cleveland 44113 Fx:443-2044

(216) 621-5300 .. **Spirko**, Timothy A '99 %Buckingham D&B,LLP -1375 E 9th -Ste 1700 -Cleveland 44114 Fx:621-5440

(614) 224-2104 .. **Spiroff**, Christopher J '89 -329 E Broad -Columbus 43215

(734) 856-4880 .. **Spiros**, Michael J '72 (Spiros & S) -8160 Secor Rd -Bx336 -Lambertville, MI 48144

(216) 363-1400 .. **Spisak**, Michael J '94 (Buckley K,LPA) -600 E Superior Av -Ste 1400 -Cleveland 44114 Fx:579-1020

(330) 287-5663 .. **Spitler**, Corey E '88 Wayne Cnty Mun Ct -538 N Market -Wooster 44691

(419) 352-2535 .. **Spitler**, Daniel T '65 (Spitler HY&N,LLP) -131 E Court -Bowling Green 43402 Fx:353-8728

(419) 352-2535 .. **Spitler Huffman Yoon & Newlove,LLP** -131 E Court -Bowling Green 43402 Fx:353-8728

(419) 352-2535 .. **Spitler**, Robert E '74 (Spitler HY&N,LLP) -131 E Court -Bowling Green 43402 Fx:353-8728

(419) 352-2535 .. **Spitler**, Steven L '96 (Spitler HY&N,LLP) -131 E Court -Bowling Green 43402 Fx:353-8728

(419) 242-1555 .. **Spitler**, Steven M '81 (Spitler & W-Y Co,LPA) -1000 Adams -Ste 200 -Toledo 43624

(419) 242-1555 .. **Spitler & Williams-Young Co,LPA** -1000 Adams -Ste 200 -Toledo 43624

(440) 838-7600 .. **Spitz**, Brian D '97 %Janik & D,LLP -9200 S Hills Blvd -Ste 300 -Cleveland 44147 Fx:838-7601

(513) 631-7455 .. **Spitz**, Gregory G '72 -6670 Meadowrdg Ln -Cincinnati 45237

(216) 696-0600 .. **Spitz**, James E '69 (Rapoport SF&C) -55 Pub Sq -Ste 1750 -Cleveland 44113 Fx:696-2929

(513) 765-6000 .. **Spitz**, Mark A '89 LensCrafters,Inc -4000 Luxottica Dr -Mason 45040

(419) 241-9000 .. **Spitzer**, Lyman F '76 (Shumaker L&K,LLP) -1000 Jackson -Toledo 43624 Fx:241-6894

(513) 587-3403 .. **Splain**, John F '85 Ultimus Fund Solutions,LLC -225 Pictoria Dr -Ste 450 -Cincinnati 45246

(419) 472-0535 .. **Spohler**, Norman G '81 -2551 Oak Grove Pl -Toledo 43613

(740) 387-0900 .. **Spohn**, Clifford C '68 (Spohn S&Z) -144 E Center -Marion 43302

(513) 524-2453 .. **Spohn**, Monica L '96 (ML Spohn Co,LPA) -15 N Beech -Oxford 45056

(740) 387-0900 .. **Spohn Spohn & Zeigler** -144 E Center -Marion 43302

(412) 562-1836 .. **Spolar**, Stephen B '82 Buchanan I,PC -301 Grant -20th Fl -Pittsburgh, PA 15219

(419) 524-6011 .. **Spon**, John R Jr. '73 (Calhoun KH&C Co,LPA) -6 W 3rd -Ste 200 -Bx268 -Mansfield 44901 Fx:526-1431

(330) 836-9971 .. **Sponseller**, Alan W '80 Cedarwood Co -1765 Merriman Rd -Akron 44313

(419) 247-1731 .. **Sponseller**, Carrie L '01 %Eastman & S Ltd -1 Seagate -24th Fl -Bx10032 -Toledo 43699 Fx:247-1777

(440) 826-4114 .. **Sponseller**, Gregory M '82 -43 E Brdg -Ste 101 -Berea 44017

(419) 399-2217 .. **Sponseller**, James M '74 -200 N Williams -Paulding 45879

(330) 493-1144 .. **Sponseller**, John N '65 (Sponseller & R) -4180 Holiday NW -Canton 44718

(614) 764-0423 .. **Sponseller**, Nancy L '77 -425 Metro Pl N -Ste 640 -Dublin 43017

(216) 574-2600 .. **Spoonster**, Joseph R III '99 %Lasko & L Co,LPA -1406 W 6th -Ste 200 -Cleveland 44113

(513) 579-6400 .. **Spoor**, Richard D '72 (Keating M&K PLL) -1 E 4th -1400 Provident Twr -Cincinnati 45202 Fx:579-6457

(419) 872-6808 ..**Spore**, John S '86 (Spore & Assoc,LLC) -Bx906 -Perrysburg 43552
(419) 874-5850 ..**Spore**, Judson P Jr. '62 -345 Coventry Ct -Perrysburg 43551
(440) 964-6466 ..**Spotts**, David M '75 -Bx3046 -Ashtabula 44005
(216) 443-6396 ..**Spotts**, Mercedes H '81 OH 8th Dist Ct of Appeals -1 Lakeside Av
-Cleveland 44113
(216) 781-5470 ..**Spotz**, Richard T Jr. '73 (Ziegler M&M LLP) -925 Euclid Av
-2020 Huntngtn Bldg -Cleveland 44115 **Fx:**781-0714
(614) 227-2315 ..**Sprader**, Bobbie S '94 (Bricker & E LLP) -100 S 3rd
-Columbus 43215 **Fx:**227-2390
(513) 852-8200 ..**Spraetz**, Deborah L '88 Cors & B LLC -537 E Pete Rose Way
-Ste 400 -Cincinnati 45202
(330) 434-2713 ..**Spragin**, Lydia E '94 -628 Payne Av -Akron 44302
(216) 443-3425 ..**Sprague**, Charles E '82 Cuyahoga Cnty Juv Ct -2163 E 22nd
-Cleveland 44115
(614) 466-7046 ..**Sprague**, James R '89 Personnel Brd of Review -65 E State
-12th Fl -Columbus 43215
(216) 752-4200 ..**Sprague**, Madelon '78 (Zamore & S) -20600 Chagrin Blvd
-Shaker Heights 44122 **Fx:**752-0042
(606) 344-5968 ..**Sprague**, Marvin L '77 Fischer Dvlpmnt Co -2670 Chancellor Dr
-Ste 300 -Crestview Hills, KY 41017
(419) 423-4321 ..**Sprague**, Robert F '68 (Firmin S&H Co,LPA) -220 W Sandusky
-Bx963 -Findlay 45839 **Fx:**423-8484
(216) 241-4100 ..**Sprague**, Timothy L '99 %Keis/G LLP -55 Pub Sq -Ste 800
-Cleveland 44113 **Fx:**771-3111
(202) 616-5458 ..**Sprang**, Ethan J '00 US DOJ -1310 6th NW -Rm 570
-Washington, DC 20530
(202) 273-1476 ..**Sprang**, Kenneth A '75 SrCnsl NLRB -1099 14th NW -Rm 9122
-Washington, DC 20570
(614) 224-1222 ..**Sprankle**, Tricia A '99 %Maguire & S,LLP -250 Civic Ctr Dr
-Ste 200 -Columbus 43215 **Fx:**224-1236
(614) 847-1007 ..**Spratley**, William A '73 -7940 Fairway Dr -Columbus 43235
(513) 721-8210 ..**Spraul**, Daniel G '82 Spraul V&D -830 Main -Ste 200
-Cincinnati 45202
(513) 721-8210 ..**Spraul**, Holly Doan '88 (Spraul V&D) -830 Main -Ste 200
-Cincinnati 45202
(513) 721-8210 ..**Spraul Veith & Doan** -830 Main -Ste 200 -Cincinnati 45202
(614) 327-4636 ..**Sprayberry**, Brad A '95 -1487 W 5th Av -#312 -Columbus 43212
Fx:488-9244
(513) 651-6800 ..**Sprecher**, Christina M '96 %Frost BT LLC -201 E 5th
-2200 PNC Ctr -Cincinnati 45202 **Fx:**651-6981
(513) 651-6800 ..**Sprecher**, Kevin S '95 (Frost BT LLC) -201 E 5th -2200 PNC Ctr
-Cincinnati 45202 **Fx:**651-6981
(216) 831-4935 ..**Spremulli**, Leonard A '75 -29425 Chagrin Blvd -Ste 305
-Pepper Pike 44122
(216) 536-9619 ..**Spreng**, Michael R '87 -4315 Dogwood Trail -North Olmsted 44070
(419) 842-1035 ..**Sprenger**, George F '74 -6800 W Central Av -Unit C
-Toledo 43617
(216) 292-5048 ..**Sprenger**, Michael T '98 Tremco Inc -3735 Green Rd
-Beachwood 44122
(419) 399-4911 ..**Spriggs**, James P '73 -308 N Main -Bx387 -Paulding 45879
(330) 376-2700 ..**Spring**, Gary W '79 (Roetzel & A,LPA) -222 S Main -Akron 44308
Fx:376-4577
(513) 345-4160 ..**Spring**, Jean M '98 Pro Seniors,Inc -7162 Redding Rd -Ste 1150
-Cincinnati 45237
(216) 781-5470 ..**Spring**, William L '67 (Ziegler M&M LLP) -925 Euclid Av
-2020 Huntngtn Bldg -Cleveland 44115 **Fx:**781-0714
Springel, Barry L '69 -(Address Unavailable)
(513) 684-3711 ..**Springer**, Anthony '97 US Atty -221 E 4th -Ste 400
-Cincinnati 45202 **Fx:**684-6385
(614) 224-8374 ..**Springer**, Jennifer L '01 Legal Aid -40 W Gay -Columbus 43215
(330) 746-5643 ..**Springer**, Lawrence R '61 (Comstock S&W Co,LPA)
-100 Fed Plz E -Ste 926 -Youngstown 44503 **Fx:**746-4925
Springer, Robert J '04 -(Address Unavailable)
(216) 566-5894 ..**Springfield**, Delisa Y '01 %Thompson H LLP -127 Pub Sq
-3900 Key Ctr -Cleveland 44114 **Fx:**566-5800
(440) 329-5389 ..**Springfield**, Freddie M '81 Lorain Cnty Pros -225 Court -3rd Fl
-Elyria 44035
(513) 946-3000 ..**Springman**, Ronald W Jr. '89 Hamilton Cnty Pros -230 E 9th
-Cincinnati 45202 **Fx:**946-3017
(210) 841-5665 ..**Sprink**, Jeffrey L '74 (J Sprink,PC) -909 NE Loop 410 -Ste 300
-San Antonio, TX 78209
(614) 224-8339 ..**Sproat**, John W Jr. '87 (Britt CN&S) -490 City Park Av
-Columbus 43215 **Fx:**224-2001
(513) 721-5525 ..**Sprong**, Nathan W '04 %Manley B -225 W Court
-Cincinnati 45202 **Fx:**721-4268
(937) 439-0281 ..**Sprowl**, John O '93 Midland Title Sec,Inc -10 Prestige Plz Dr
-Miamisburg 45342
Sprowls, David E '82 US Air Force -AFLSA Bolling-AFB
-Washington, DC 20336
(419) 621-7999 ..**Sprunk**, Thomas R '97 -326 E Market -Sandusky 44870
Fx:621-7511
Spryszak, Frank H '04 -(Address Unavailable)
(216) 397-7820 ..**Spurgeon**, Roberta Kaye '77 -2660 Edgehill Rd -Cleveland
Heights 44106 **Fx:**397-7830
(614) 228-8575 ..**Spurlock**, Michael '74 (Beery & S Co,LPA) -275 E State
-Columbus 43215 **Fx:**228-1408
(419) 562-9856 ..**Spurlock Sears Pry Griebling & McBride,PLL** -120 N Lane
-Bucyrus 44820 **Fx:**562-9883
(859) 431-3313 ..**Spurlock**, Shanda L '03 Childrens Law Ctr -104 E 7th
-Covington, KY 41011
(419) 243-9424 ..**Spychalski**, Deborah K '93 -1709 Spielbusch -Ste 107
-Toledo 43624
(614) 227-2396 ..**Squeglia**, Elisabeth A '79 (Bricker & E LLP) -100 S 3rd
-Columbus 43215 **Fx:**227-2390
(513) 719-1100 ..**Squeri**, Donna M '84 Gateway Invstmnt Advsrs -3805 Edward Rd
-Ste 600 -Cincinnati 45209
(216) 586-3939 ..**Squeri**, Stephen J '79 (Jones D) -901 Lakeside Av
-Cleveland 44114 **Fx:**579-0212
Squeri, Therese V '82 -3047 Waterfall Way -Westlake 44145
(614) 628-6880 ..**Squillace**, Michael L '80 (Dinsmore & S LLP) -175 S 3rd -10th Fl
-Columbus 43215 **Fx:**628-6890
(614) 723-2022 ..**Squillace**, Vincent J III '02 %Roetzel & A,LPA -155 E Broad
-Natl City Ctr 12th Fl -Columbus 43215 **Fx:**463-9792

(419) 243-8003 ..**Squillante**, David G '82 -608 Mad Av -Ste 1523 -Toledo 43604
(419) 394-7441 ..**Squire**, Jeffrey P '93 (Noble M&M) -146 E Spring
-Saint Marys 45885 **Fx:**394-7694
(614) 224-6528 ..**Squire**, Percy '81 (P Squire Co LLP) -65 E State -Ste 200
-Columbus 43215
(216) 479-8500 ..**Squire Sanders & Dempsey LLP** -127 Pub Sq -4900 Key Twr
-Cleveland 44114 **Fx:**479-8780
(513) 361-1200 ..**Squire Sanders & Dempsey LLP** -312 Walnut -Ste 3500
-Cincinnati 45202 **Fx:**361-1201
(614) 365-2700 ..**Squire Sanders & Dempsey LLP** -41 S High -1300 Huntngtn Ctr
-Columbus 43215 **Fx:**365-2499
(614) 469-5715 ..**Squires**, Douglas W '01 US Atty -303 Marconi Blvd -Ste 200
-Columbus 43215
(330) 882-2920 ..**Squires**, Thomas B '90 -451 S Messner Rd -Akron 44319
(313) 628-8111 ..**Squires**, Trisha C '95 Ernst & Young LLP -500 Woodward Av
-Ste 1700 -Detroit, MI 48226
(216) 681-1553 ..**Srail**, Donald J '79 DCMA Cleveland -555 E 88th -Ofc of Cnsl
-Bratenahl 44108
(330) 972-1923 ..**Srail**, Roger A '69 BankOne, NA -528 S Main -Akron 44311
(330) 644-0061 ..**Sremack**, William M '75 (W Sremack Co LPA) -2745 S Arlngtn Rd
-Akron 44312
(216) 771-2600 ..**Srinivasan**, Latha M '98 %Ott & Assoc Co,LPA -55 Pub Sq
-Ste 1008 -Cleveland 44113 **Fx:**830-8939
(323) 954-9600 ..**Sroufe**, Gordon L '61 Wasserman Law Ofc -5750 Wilshire Blvd
-Ste 570 -Los Angeles, CA 90036
Srp, Karen M '04 -(Address Unavailable)
(614) 463-4212 ..**Srsic**, Daniel W '94 %Littler M,PC -21 E State -Ste 1600
-Columbus 43215 **Fx:**221-3301
(330) 643-2371 ..**Stabler**, Rhonda L '87 Summit Cnty Dom Rltns Ct -209 S High
-Akron 44308
(330) 482-3356 ..**Stacey Hutson Stacey & Powers LPA** -20 S Main -Columbiana
44408
(419) 626-0728 ..**Stacey**, James A '52 -1407 Julianne Cir -Sandusky 44870
(330) 253-0719 ..**Stacey**, Kelly M '95 -159 S Main -Ste 1024 -Akron 44308
Fx:253-0722
(765) 747-7523 ..**Stacey**, Kim T '73 Old Natl Trust Co -320 S High
-Muncie, IN 47305
(330) 482-3356 ..**Stacey**, Lawrence W '59 (Stacey HS&P LPA) -20 S Main
-Columbiana 44408
(330) 482-3356 ..**Stacey**, Lawrence W II '91 (Stacey HS&P LPA) -20 S Main
-Columbiana 44408
(216) 447-0500 ..**Stachewicz**, Gerald R '79 -4141 Rockside Rd -Ste 230
-Seven Hills 44131
(937) 461-5980 ..**Stachler**, John H '94 (Jablinski FR&M) -214 W Monument Av
-Bx1266 -Dayton 45402 **Fx:**461-4139
(770) 933-9500 ..**Stachler**, Robert E II '90 OfCnsl Thomas KH&R,LLP
-100 Galleria Pkwy NW -Ste 1750 -Atlanta, GA 30339
(513) 381-2838 ..**Stachler**, Robert G '57 OfCnsl Taft S&H LLP -425 Walnut
-Ste 1800 -Cincinnati 45202 **Fx:**381-0205
(513) 621-2120 ..**Stachler**, Thomas L '89 Strauss & T,LPA -150 E 4th -4th Fl
-Cincinnati 45202 **Fx:**241-8259
(330) 644-2940 ..**Stachowiak**, Robert W '69 -1685 Far View Rd -Akron 44312
(216) 522-2526 ..**Stack**, Brian J '98 US DOJ/Antitrust Div -55 Erievw Blvd
-Cleveland 44114
(330) 373-1035 ..**Stack**, Dene M '00 Letson GWL&R -155 S Park Av -Ste 250
-Bx151 -Warren 44482 **Fx:**392-5419
(740) 397-7177 ..**Stacker**, Jean Lou '84 Knox Cnty Pros -117 E High -Ste 234
-Mount Vernon 43050
(513) 352-3350 ..**Stackpole**, Peter J '00 Law Dept -801 Plum -Rm 214
-Cincinnati 45202 **Fx:**352-1515
(216) 241-8333 ..**Stadler**, David P III '01 %Ritzler C&S,Ltd -1001 Lakeside Av
-1550 North Pnt Twr -Cleveland 44114 **Fx:**241-5890
(937) 426-3310 ..**Stadnicar**, Joseph W '90 (Hammond S&S)
-3836 Dayton-Xenia Rd -Beavercreek 45432 **Fx:**426-9328
Staffe, Jeffrey C '82 -6644 Merritt -Whitehouse 43571
(419) 255-0814 ..**Stafford**, Ellen M '81 ABLE -520 Mad Av -740 Spitzer Bldg
-Toledo 43604 **Fx:**259-2880
(216) 241-1074 ..**Stafford**, Joseph G '85 (Stafford & S Co,LPA) -323 Lakeside Av W
-Ste 380 -Cleveland 44113
(937) 865-6800 ..**Stafford**, Mary J '81 Lexis/Nexis -Bx933 -Dayton 45401
(614) 485-2010 ..**Stafford**, Robert G '68 (Means BB&B Co,LPA) -2006 Kenny Rd
-Columbus 43221 **Fx:**485-2019
(937) 426-6633 ..**Stafford**, Thomas R '77 -968 Mound Ct -Xenia 45385
(216) 241-1074 ..**Stafford**, Vincent A '92 (Stafford & S Co,LPA) -323 Lakeside Av W
-Ste 380 -Cleveland 44113
(407) 306-8148 ..**Stage**, Betty R '98 -2506 Windsorgate Ln -Orlando, FL 32828
(513) 621-8755 ..**Stagnaro**, Eugene J Jr. '63 (EJ Stagnaro Jr Co,LPA) -808 Main
-Cincinnati 45202
(513) 241-0662 ..**Stagnaro**, Gene A '86 -906 Main -Ste 405 -Cincinnati 45202
(513) 533-2996 ..**Stagnaro**, Jeffrey G '89 (Finney SS&K Co,LPA) -2623 Erie Av
-Bx8804 -Cincinnati 45208
(513) 241-3447 ..**Stagnaro**, Michaela M '92 -906 Main -Ste 403 -Cincinnati 45202
(419) 242-9393 ..**Stahlbush**, Kristin A '94 -312 N Mich -Ste 800 -Toledo 43624
(216) 621-0150 ..**Staib**, Mark E '73 (Hahn L&P LLP) -3300 BP Twr/200 Pub Sq
-Ste 3300 -Cleveland 44114 **Fx:**241-2824
(513) 621-6464 ..**Stainton**, Jeffrey L '97 %Graydon H&R LLP -511 Walnut
-1900 Fifth Third Ctr -Cincinnati 45202 **Fx:**651-3836
(216) 241-5310 ..**Stakes**, Jennifer N '02 Gallagher SF&N -1501 Euclid Av -6th Fl
-Cleveland 44115 **Fx:**241-1608
(419) 244-8000 ..**Staler**, John J Jr. '99 Ernst & Young -1 Seagate -12th Fl
-Toledo 43604
(440) 285-2222 ..**Staley**, Anita C '93 Geauga Cnty Pros -231 Main -Cthse Annx
-Chardon 44024 **Fx:**286-4357
(330) 762-7377 ..**Staley**, Cara L '04 %Oldham & D -195 S Main -Ste 300
-Akron 44308 **Fx:**762-7390
(513) 831-2255 ..**Staley**, James A '76 J Staley Co,LPA -1 Crestvw Dr -Milford 45150
Fx:831-8561
(513) 574-8899 ..**Staley**, Jeffrey J '77 -5510 W Fork Rd -Cincinnati 45247
(419) 358-5606 ..**Staley-Burley**, Gina C '92 %SW Diller Co,LPA -138 N Main -Bx46
-Bluffton 45817
(513) 412-5400 ..**Stalf**, Dale A '83 (Buckley K,LPA) -201 E 5th -Ste 1420
-Cincinnati 45202 **Fx:**412-5401
(513) 965-2900 ..**Stall**, Mark G '88 XPEDX -6285 Tri Ridge Rd -Loveland 45140

(513) 241-2324   **Stallard,** David S '71 (Wood H&E LLP) -441 Vine -Ste 2700 -Cincinnati 45202 Fx:421-7269

(419) 241-2777 .. **Stallings,** Douglas E '94 Bunda S&D,PLL -One SeaGate -Ste 650 -Toledo 43604 Fx:241-4697

(419) 624-6369 .. **Stallkamp,** Christopher A '97 Erie Cnty Pros -247 Columbus Av -Ste 319 -Sandusky 44870 Fx:627-7567

(614) 469-3939 .. **Stalnaker,** R Alan '04 %Jones D -325 John H McConnell Blvd -Ste 600 -Bx165017 -Columbus 43216 Fx:461-4198

(216) 687-1311 .. **Stalzer,** John B '01 %Reminger & R -101 Prospect Av W -1400 Mdlnd Bldg -Cleveland 44115 Fx:687-1841

(614) 252-7601 .. **Stamatakos,** John C '74 -800 E Broad -Columbus 43205

(440) 937-6266 .. **Stamatis,** John N '85 -Bx175 -Avon 44011

(419) 337-5065 .. **Stamm,** Jan H '78 (Barber KS&R) -124 N Fulton -Wauseon 43567 Fx:337-1136

(419) 947-5515 .. **Stamolis,** David J '02 Morrow Cnty Pros -60 E High -Mount Gilead 43338

(614) 387-9030 .. **Stamp,** Jennifer L '03 Sup Ct of OH -65 S Front -9th Fl -Columbus 43215

(614) 229-4753 .. **Stamp,** Matthew E '98 Deloitte & Touche -155 E Broad -Columbus 43215

(513) 977-8200 .. **Stamp,** Vincent B '69 (Dinsmore & S LLP) -255 E 5th -Ste 1900 -Cincinnati 45202 Fx:977-8141

(937) 898-9440 .. **Stamps,** Dana A '77 -3814 Little York Rd -Dayton 45414

(937) 898-9440 .. **Stamps,** Eric A '99 -3814 Little York Rd -Dayton 45414

(216) 241-7660 .. **Stanard & Corsi Co,LPA** -1370 Ontario -Ste 748 -Cleveland 44113 Fx:241-7661

(216) 443-7223 .. **Stanard,** John P '87 Cuyahoga Cnty Pub Def -1200 W 3rd NW -100 Lakeside Pl -Cleveland 44113

(216) 241-7660 .. **Stanard,** Margaret E '81 (Stanard & C Co,LPA) -1370 Ontario -Ste 748 -Cleveland 44113 Fx:241-7661

(419) 891-7909 .. **Stancati,** Joseph A '72 Dana Corp -1745 Indn Wd Cir -Ste 210 -Maumee 43537

      Stanceu, James T '79 -700 W St Clair -#210 -Cleveland 44113

(617) 223-8590 .. **Stancliff,** Steven M '96 US Coast Guard -408 Atl Av -Rm 832 -Boston, MA 02110

(614) 792-5555 .. **Standley,** Jeffrey S '90 Standley Law Grp LLP -495 Metro Pl S -Ste 210 -Dublin 43017 Fx:792-5536

(419) 427-4182 .. **Standley,** Thomas R '81 Marathon Ashland Petro LLC -539 S Main -Findlay 45840 Fx:421-3578

(330) 545-6252 .. **Standohar,** Mark M '92 -626 E Prospect -Girard 44420

(216) 621-3346 .. **Stanek,** Carl J '80 %Kendis & Assoc Co,LPA -614 Superior Av W -15th Fl Rckfllr Bldg -Cleveland 44113 Fx:621-3672

(937) 225-2910 .. **Stanek,** Pamela M '85 US Atty -200 W 2nd -602 Fed Bldg -Dayton 45402

(419) 898-0400 .. **Stanfa,** Lori A '88 Clearwater Council of Govts -8200 W SR 163 -Oak Harbor 43449

(513) 421-4020 .. **Stanford,** Stanley L '58 (Cohen TK&S,LLC) -250 E 5th -Ste 1200 -Cincinnati 45202 Fx:241-4490

(419) 247-2500 .. **Stanford,** Stephen J '75 (Fuller & H,Ltd) -One SeaGate -Ste 1700 -Bx2088 -Toledo 43603 Fx:247-2665

(330) 689-2869 .. **Stanford,** Tamara J '01 Stow Law Dept -3760 Darrow Rd -Stow 44224 Fx:686-0219

(216) 228-7250 .. **Stanford,** Teresa G '85 J Saurman -14650 Detroit Av -Ste 450 -Lakewood 44107

(216) 586-3939 .. **Stanger,** Nicole D '98 %Jones D -901 Lakeside Av -Cleveland 44114 Fx:579-0212

(614) 431-6436 .. **Stanger,** Philip C '77 -Bx51 -Worthington 43085

(330) 841-0234 .. **Stanitz,** Christopher '74 Second Bancorp, Inc. -108 Main Av SW -Warren 44481

(614) 221-2121 .. **Stankunas,** Jeffrey A '00 %Isaac BL&T,LLP -250 E Broad -Ste 900 Mdlnd Bldg -Columbus 43215 Fx:365-9516

      Stanley, Devon A '02 -6854 Mill Rd -Brecksville 44141

(614) 466-3998 .. **Stanley,** Dina R '92 Unemploymnt Comp Commssn -145 S Front -Bx182299 -Columbus 43218

(216) 689-4107 .. **Stanley,** Forrest F '78 KeyBank NA -127 Pub Sq -2nd Fl 01-127-0200 -Cleveland 44114

(216) 592-5000 .. **Stanley,** Hugh M Jr. '69 (Tucker E&W LLP) -925 Euclid Av -1150 Huntngtn Bldg -Cleveland 44115 Fx:592-5009

(703) 720-7800 .. **Stanley,** Jennifer A '00 %Squire S&D LLP -8000 Towers Crescent Dr -14th Fl -Tysons Corner, VA 22182 Fx:720-7801

(706) 896-4118 .. **Stanley,** Kris-Ann '95 K-A Stanley,PC -231 Chatuge Way -Hiawassee, GA 30546

(937) 223-5200 .. **Stanley,** Lu Ann '85 Flanagan LH&S -318 W 4th -Dayton 45402 Fx:223-3335

(216) 623-0150 .. **Stanley,** Mitchell A '92 %Roetzel & A,LPA -1375 E 9th -One Cleve Ctr 9th Fl -Cleveland 44114 Fx:623-0134

(440) 285-3511 .. **Stanley,** Robin L '03 %Petersen & I -401 South -Chardon 44024 Fx:285-3363

(330) 723-3830 .. **Stanley,** Ronald R '74 -Bx571 -Medina 44258 Fx:723-3830

(440) 350-2683 .. **Stano,** Brian W '03 Lake Cnty Pros -105 Main -Bx490 -Painesville 44077 Fx:350-2585

(440) 888-6448 .. **Stano,** Paul J '81 (PJ Stano Co,LPA) -6650 Pearl Rd -Ste 202 -Cleveland 44130

      Stano, Susan L '96 -10770 Silver Tree Trl -Cleveland 44133

(330) 783-9222 .. **Stanos,** Steve P '58 OfCnsl D'Apolito & D -4800 Market -Youngstown 44512

(440) 843-8800 .. **Stanovic,** James M '79 -6020 State Rd -Ste 1 -Parma 44134

(419) 294-5701 .. **Stansbery Schoenberger & Scheck** -106 E Wyandot Av -Upper Sandusky 43351 Fx:294-5608

(740) 345-0417 .. **Stansbury,** David N '99 %K Burkett -21 W Church -Ste 201 -Newark 43055

(216) 622-8200 .. **Stansbury,** Ronald C '74 (Calfee H&G LLP) -800 Superior Av -Ste 1400 -Cleveland 44114 Fx:241-0816

(513) 961-8464 .. **Stansel,** Teresa L '88 -3347 Sherlock Av -Ste 3 -Cincinnati 45220

(502) 425-8148 .. **Stanton,** David W '89 -7321 New LaGrange Rd -Ste 106 -Louisville, KY 40222

(614) 221-4000 .. **Stanton,** Elizabeth M '82 (Chester W&S LLP) -65 E State -10th Fl -Columbus 43215 Fx:221-4012

(419) 243-2042 .. **Stanton,** Kristen A '01 S Priestap & Assoc -316 N Mich -Ste 300 -Toledo 43624

(440) 899-9990 .. **Stanton,** Mark A '77 Short S&S -24461 Detroit Rd -Ste 340 -Westlake 44145

(216) 479-8500 .. **Stanton,** R Thomas '69 (Squire S&D LLP) -127 Pub Sq -4900 Key Twr -Cleveland 44114 Fx:479-8780

(440) 838-7600 .. **Stanuszek,** Michael J '04 %Janik & D,LLP -9200 S Hills Blvd -Ste 300 -Cleveland 44147 Fx:838-7601

(606) 678-4230 .. **Stanziano,** Mark J '04 -310 W Columbia -Somerset, KY 42501

(216) 378-0140 .. **Staph,** Jack A '73 (JA Staph & Assoc) -29525 Chagrin Blvd -Ste 215 -Pepper Pike 44122

(330) 664-6524 .. **Staples,** Elizabeth A '85 -659 N Hametown Rd -Akron 44333

(678) 684-4112 .. **Staples,** Jason H '01 %Stewart & Assoc,PC -3950 Johns Creek Ct -Ste 100 -Suwanee, GA 30024

(419) 724-3499 .. **Starbird,** Debra L '93 -232 10th -Toledo 43624 Fx:724-3495

(740) 455-7146 .. **Starcher,** Gregory A '91 Muskingum Cnty Dept Job/Fam Srvcs -1830 E Pike -Bx9 -Zanesville 43702

(419) 251-3568 .. **Starcher,** John M '01 St Vincent Mercy Med Ctr -2213 Cherry -Toledo 43608

(513) 946-3571 .. **Stargel,** Rogena D '82 Hamilton Cnty Probate Ct -230 E 9th -10th Fl -Cincinnati 45202 Fx:946-3626

(614) 339-0171 .. **Stark,** Andrew W '98 Macloud Fincl Inc -6221 Riverside Dr -Ste 1 North -Dublin 43017

(216) 426-8400 .. **Stark,** J Norman '73 -1310 E 49th -Cleveland 44114 Fx:426-8411

(614) 469-5715 .. **Stark,** John J '03 US Atty -303 Marconi Blvd -Ste 200 -Columbus 43215

(216) 696-4200 .. **Stark,** Jonathan L '91 (Schneider SR&L PLL) -1111 Superior Av -Cleveland 44114 Fx:696-7303

(216) 696-7600 .. **Stark,** Kenneth B '79 (Duvin C&H) -1301 E 9th -20th Fl Erievw Twr -Cleveland 44114 Fx:696-2038

(330) 376-3300 .. **Stark & Knoll Co,LPA** -76 S Main -Ste 1512 -Akron 44308 Fx:376-6237

(614) 228-1541 .. **Stark,** Lisa R '02 %Baker & H LLP -65 E State -Ste 2100 -Columbus 43215 Fx:462-2616

(330) 376-3300 .. **Stark,** Michael L '67 (Stark & K Co,LPA) -76 S Main -Ste 1512 -Akron 44308 Fx:376-6237

(440) 350-1327 .. **Stark,** Paul S '92 -9040 Aileen Dr -Mentor 44060

(419) 625-0536 .. **Stark,** Roger S '01 UAW Legal Srvcs Plans -3116 Bardshar Rd -Sandusky 44870

(330) 761-4207 .. **Stark,** Wendy E '97 %FirstEnergy -76 S Main -18th Fl -Akron 44308

(216) 464-6666 .. **Starke,** Sheldon P '71 -23200 Chagrin Blvd -Ste 200 -Cleveland 44122

(419) 562-4529 .. **Starkey,** Bradley S '87 (Starkey & S,Ltd) -208 S Walnut -Bucyrus 44820

(614) 761-1733 .. **Starkey,** David H '77 (Metcalf DMS&W,LLC) -655 Metro Pl S -Ste 210 -Dublin 43017

(513) 977-8200 .. **Starkey,** Denise M '04 %Dinsmore & S LLP -255 E 5th -Ste 1900 -Cincinnati 45202 Fx:977-8141

      Starkey, Erin A '94 -(Address Unavailable)

(513) 352-6737 .. **Starkey,** James Shane '96 (Thompson H LLP) -312 Walnut -14th Fl -Cincinnati 45202 Fx:241-4771

      Starkey, Rachel E '04 -(Address Unavailable)

(304) 485-8091 .. **Starkey,** Richard L '78 -914 Market -Ste 302 -Parkersburg, WV 26101

(330) 376-3300 .. **Starkey,** Ronald K '92 (Stark & K Co,LPA) -76 S Main -Ste 1512 -Akron 44308 Fx:376-6237

(614) 462-4938 .. **Starkoff,** Alan G '75 (Schottenstein Z&D) -250 West -Bx165020 -Columbus 43216 Fx:462-5135

(216) 622-8200 .. **Starkoff,** Jack R '94 Calfee H&G LLP -800 Superior Av -Ste 1400 -Cleveland 44114 Fx:241-0816

(937) 496-3033 .. **Starline,** Tyler D '04 Hon D Langer -41 N Perry -Cmmn Pleas Ct -Bx972 -Dayton 45422

(419) 424-7818 .. **Starn,** Jonathan P '93 Hancock Cnty Cmn Pleas Ct -300 S Main -Findlay 45840

(419) 241-6000 .. **Starr,** Kimberly A '99 %Eastman & S Ltd -1 Seagate -24th Fl -Bx10032 -Toledo 43699 Fx:247-1777

(216) 368-8523 .. **Starr,** Mark R '04 -10900 Euclid Av -Yost 4 -Cleveland 44106

(740) 852-2114 .. **Starr,** Wendy J '96 -15 S Main -2nd Fl, Ste F -Bx615 -London 43140

(216) 241-2200 .. **Starrett,** Kevin L '84 -812 Huron Rd -Caxton Bldg, Ste 490 -Cleveland 44115

(513) 721-7430 .. **Startsman,** Daniel B Jr. '73 (Jacobs & S Co,LPA) -432 Walnut -850 Tri-State Bldg -Cincinnati 45202

(513) 785-5880 .. **Startzman,** Jeffrey P '79 Butler Cnty CSEA -315 High -7th Fl -Hamilton 45011

(614) 575-8440 .. **Stasiewicz,** Suzanne M '88 -5969 E Lvngstn Av -Ste 200 -Columbus 43232

(330) 762-2411 .. **Stasitis,** Mark G '01 %Amer C Co,LPA -159 S Main -6th Fl -Akron 44308 Fx:762-9918

(513) 621-2666 .. **Statman,** Alan J '83 (Statman HS&E LLC) -255 E 5th -Ste 2900 Chemed Ctr -Cincinnati 45202 Fx:587-4477

(513) 621-2666 .. **Statman Harris Siegel & Eyrich LLC** -255 E 5th -Ste 2900 Chemed Ctr -Cincinnati 45202 Fx:587-4477

(937) 222-1090 .. **Statman Harris Siegel & Eyrich LLC** -110 N Main -Ste 1520 -Dayton 45402 Fx:222-1046

(937) 237-9485 .. **Staton,** James C '97 (Staton & F LLC) -5613 Brandt Pike -Huber Heights 45424

(513) 934-0522 .. **Staton,** Roger D '75 -101 Dave Av E -Ste B1 -Lebanon 45036

(513) 523-7722 .. **Staton,** Wayne C '76 (W Staton Co,LPA) -110 N Beech -Oxford 45056

      Staub, Stacey S '90 -19416 Teibir Av -Rocky River 44116

(407) 281-2415 .. **Staudt,** Daniel J '92 Siemens Corp -4400 Alafaya Trl -Orlando, FL 32826 Fx:281-5048

(330) 456-0663 .. **Staudt,** Elmer Roman III '74 -940 Monument Rd NW -Canton 44703

(937) 492-1271 .. **Staudt,** Michael A '84 (Faulkner GK&S,LPA) -100 S Main Av -Ste 300 -Sidney 45365 Fx:498-1306

(330) 996-2037 .. **Stauffenger,** Leonard W '83 -460 White Pond Dr -Ste 1000 -Akron 44320

(419) 625-8324 .. **Stauffer,** Melvyn J '51 %Flynn P&K,LPA -165 E Wshngtn Row -Sandusky 44870 Fx:625-9007

(216) 687-1900 .. **Stauffer,** Susan P '70 Legal Aid -1223 W 6th -Cleveland 44113 Fx:687-0779

(614) 466-2166 .. **Stauffer,** Timothy D '82 OH Dept Taxation -30 E Broad -22nd Fl -Columbus 43215

(513) 636-4069 .. **Stautberg,** Elizabeth Ann '92 Chldrns Hosp Med Ctr -3333 Burnet Av -Cincinnati 45229

(513) 632-7077 .. **Stautberg**, Julia A '95 Bd of Elections -824 Bway
-Cincinnati 45202

(513) 977-8200 .. **Stautberg**, Lee A '93 (Dinsmore & S LLP) -255 E 5th -Ste 1900
-Cincinnati 45202 Fx:977-8141

(513) 579-6400 .. **Stautberg**, Peter J '93 %Keating M&K PLL -1 E 4th
-1400 Provident Twr -Cincinnati 45202 Fx:579-6457

(330) 757-4347 .. **Stavick**, Margaret A '74 -2415 Renwick Dr -Youngstown 44514

(216) 292-5807 .. **Stavnicky**, Michael R '94 %Singerman MD&K
-3401 Enterprise Pkwy -Ste 200 -Beachwood 44122 Fx:292-5867

(440) 886-0001 .. **Stavole**, C Anthony '61 (Stavole & M) -5700 Pearl Rd -Ste 202
-Cleveland 44129 Fx:886-0001

(216) 241-2838 .. **Stavole**, William J '88 (Taft S&H LLP) -200 Pub Sq -3500 BP Twr
-Cleveland 44114 Fx:241-3707

(614) 644-8340 .. **Stavridis**, John D '85 Industrial Commssn of OH -30 W Spring
-9th Fl -Columbus 43215 Fx:752-8785

(859) 394-6200 .. **Stavros**, Catherine D '97 %Adams SW&D -40 W Pike -Bx861
-Covington, KY 41012 Fx:291-7902

(614) 462-3555 .. **Stead**, Douglas P '84 Franklin Cnty Pros -373 S High
-Columbus 43215

(614) 644-2438 .. **Stead**, Susan T '84 Dept Ins -2100 Stella Ct -Columbus 43215

(217) 544-8491 .. **Steahly**, Taylor R '96 %Brown H&S -Bx2459 -Springfield, IL 62705

(216) 651-9500 .. **Stealey**, Patricia A '80 HKM Direct Market Communications
-5501 Cass Av -Cleveland 44102

(419) 352-1581 .. **Stearns**, Jodie L '84 (Mitchell S&H) -112 E Oak
-Bowling Green 43402

(216) 521-0200 .. **Stearns**, Roger S '67 -1387 Marlowe Av -Lakewood 44107

(513) 732-1691 .. **Stearns**, William A '71 -202 Main -Batavia 45103

(740) 393-3339 .. **Stebbins**, Carol G '90 -118 E Gambier -Mount Vernon 43050

(614) 228-9058 .. **Stebbins**, David C '78 -400 S 5th -Ste 202 -Columbus 43215

(614) 221-1000 .. **Stebbins**, Steven C '00 %Deloitte & Touche,LLP -155 E Broad
-Columbus 43215

(419) 936-5120 .. **Stebbins**, Thomas R '80 -411 N Mich -Toledo 43624

(740) 654-4141 .. **Stebelton Aranda & Snider,LPA** -109 N Broad -Bx130
-Lancaster 43130 Fx:654-2521

(740) 654-4141 .. **Stebelton**, Gerald L '70 (Stebelton A&S,LPA) -109 N Broad
-Bx130 -Lancaster 43130 Fx:654-2521

(330) 746-3291 .. **Stebelton**, Richard A '59 Cmmnwlth Land Title Agncy
-24 N Phelps -Youngstown 44503

(330) 253-5060 .. **Stecz**, Eric J '96 %Brennan M&D,LLC -75 E Market -Akron 44308
Fx:253-1977

Stedman, Richard R '64 -2665 Lane Rd -Columbus 43220

(216) 875-6529 .. **Steeb**, Cynthia L '01 Parkwood Corp -2829 Euclid Av
-Cleveland 44115

Steehler, Laura S '04 -(Address Unavailable)

(330) 376-8336 .. **Steel**, Frank E Jr. '63 Goldman & R,Ltd -11 S Forge -Akron 44304
Fx:376-2522

(937) 855-2376 .. **Steel**, Jennifer M '96 -26 Main -Germantown 45327

(330) 376-8336 .. **Steel**, Michael A '00 Goldman & R,Ltd -11 S Forge -Akron 44304
Fx:376-2522

(216) 241-2880 .. **Steel**, Terrence J '71 (Cowden HN&L) -50 Pub Sq -Ste 1414
-Cleveland 44113 Fx:241-2881

(614) 445-8870 .. **Steele**, Athornia '77 Capital Univ Law Sch -303 E Broad
-Columbus 43215

(513) 621-7600 .. **Steele**, Christine C '91 Eagen W&H Co,LPA -2337 Victory Pkwy
-Cincinnati 45206 Fx:455-8246

(419) 241-9000 .. **Steele**, Cynthia L K '98 %Shumaker L&K,LLP -1000 Jackson
-Toledo 43624 Fx:241-6894

(419) 241-9000 .. **Steele**, Jared B S '02 %Shumaker L&K,LLP -1000 Jackson
-Toledo 43624 Fx:241-6894

(614) 891-1041 .. **Steele**, Lucinda G '00 Ron Lykins,Inc -45 W Main -Westerville 43081

(513) 533-2996 .. **Steele**, Matthew C '03 %Finney SS&K Co,LPA -2623 Erie Av
-Bx8804 -Cincinnati 45208

(614) 462-3194 .. **Steele**, Rebecca S '89 Franklin Cnty Pub Def -373 S High -12th Fl
-Columbus 43215

(859) 359-4669 .. **Steele**, Sandra L '93 -6273 Stallion Ct -Independence, KY 41051

(614) 224-9223 .. **Steele**, Thomas L '78 (Ward KBM&M) -199 S 5th
-Columbus 43215

(614) 461-4455 .. **Steele**, William J '83 (Cloppert LS&W) -225 E Broad
-Columbus 43215 Fx:461-0072

(713) 785-6262 .. **Steelman**, Laura A '03 Steelman Law Firm -2400 Augusta Dr
-#367 -Houston, TX 77057

(740) 477-2502 .. **Steely**, Melody L '78 -151 W Franklin -Bx546 -Circleville 43113

(440) 717-1010 .. **Steely**, Robert L '71 -8227 Brecksvll Rd -Bldg 4 Ste 202
-Brecksville 44141

(646) 366-1890 .. **Steen**, Carla A '93 Phy for Rprdctve Choice\Hlth -55 W 39th
-10th Fl -New York, NY 10018

Steen, Daniel V '72 -76 S Main -Akron 44308

(330) 270-9016 .. **Steen**, Jon R '82 -5437 Mahoning Av -Ste 21 -Austintown 44515

(216) 443-7223 .. **Stefan**, Mark A '93 Cuyahoga Cnty Pub Def -1200 W 3rd NW
-100 Lakeside Pl -Cleveland 44113

(330) 650-0088 .. **Stefancik**, Christopher J '96 Bevan & Assoc LPA,Inc
-10360 Nrthfld Rd -Northfield 44067 Fx:467-4493

(330) 262-3030 .. **Stefancin**, Jocelyn '90 Wayne Cnty Pros -115 W Lbrty
-Wooster 44691 Fx:287-5412

(216) 394-5068 .. **Stefancin**, Robert M '90 (Schottenstein Z&D) -1350 Euclid Av -Ste
1400 -Cleveland 44115 Fx:621-6502

(937) 227-3700 .. **Stefanec**, Erin E '04 %Faruki I&C PLL -10 N Ludlow
-500 Cthse Plz SW -Dayton 45402 Fx:227-3717

(614) 279-9348 .. **Stefanelli**, Luisa V '79 -3099 Sullivant Av -2nd Fl
-Columbus 43204

(309) 671-7088 .. **Stefanik**, Debra L '83 NLRB -300 Hmltn Blvd -Ste 200
-Peoria, IL 61602

(440) 930-8056 .. **Stefanik**, Thomas J Jr. '96 Wickens HPC&B -35765 Chester Rd
-Avon 44011 Fx:937-4466

Stefaniuk, Joseph P '03 -(Address Unavailable)

(216) 696-6170 .. **Stefanova**, Vania T '96 %RT Herman & Assoc -815 Superior Av
-Ste 1910 -Cleveland 44114 Fx:696-0104

(330) 792-6220 .. **Stefanski**, Dale Kim '80 (Stefanski & Assoc,LLC)
-5437 Mahoning Av -Ste 22 -Youngstown 44515 Fx:792-6250

(419) 695-9080 .. **Steffan**, Christina L '02 %Shenk CW&C,LLC -214 W 2nd -Bx304
-Delphos 45833

(425) 348-2600 .. **Steffan**, Frederick V '78 Intermec Tech Corp -6001 36th Av W
-Everett, WA 98203

(513) 381-5700 .. **Steffen**, Carey K '00 Ritter & R,LLC -105 E 4th -Ste 1200
-Cincinnati 45202 Fx:381-0014

(614) 757-7861 .. **Steffensmeier**, Michael D '93 Cardinal Hlth,Inc -7000 Cardinal Pl
-Dublin 43017

(614) 225-8757 .. **Steffes**, James B '01 %PricewaterhouseCoopers -100 E Broad
-Ste 2100 -Columbus 43215

Stefl, Scott R '82 -7844 Lakeshr Blvd -Hrbr Hse Pro Bldg
-Mentor 44060

(513) 983-7738 .. **Stegbauer**, Joseph A '96 Procter & Gamble Co-Legal
-1 Procter & Gamble Plz -Cincinnati 45202

(216) 348-0700 .. **Stege**, Edward Richard Jr. '68 (Stege & M Co,LPA) -200 Pub Sq
-Ste 3220 -Cleveland 44114 Fx:348-0803

(216) 348-0700 .. **Stege & Michelson Co, LPA** -200 Pub Sq -Ste 3220
-Cleveland 44114 Fx:348-0803

(859) 491-3000 .. **Stegeman**, Christian B '83 %Sanders T & Assoc PSC
-1017 Russell -Covington, KY 41011

(614) 462-5495 .. **Steger**, S Martijn '83 (Kegler BH&R) -65 E State -Ste 1800
-Columbus 43215 Fx:464-2634

Stegman, David W II '01 -4426 S Mallard Cove -Mason 45040

Stegman, Melissa A '96 -(Address Unavailable)

(513) 762-7800 .. **Stegman**, Michael J '83 -250 E 5th -Ste 1500 -Cincinnati 45202

(513) 381-5700 .. **Stegman**, Monty T '01 %Ritter & R,LLC -105 E 4th -Ste 1200
-Cincinnati 45202 Fx:381-0014

(937) 322-2161 .. **Stegner**, Dennis E '72 -111 E Cecil -Springfield 45504

Stehle, William J '04 -(Address Unavailable)

(614) 337-0354 .. **Stehle**, William L '64 -136 N Hmltn Rd -Ste 104 -Gahanna 43230

(440) 777-1500 .. **Stehlik**, Elizabeth A '04 %MR Gareau & Assoc Co,LPA -23823
Lorain Rd -Ste 200 -North Olmsted 44070

(440) 238-5468 .. **Stehman**, Thomas E '77 -14751 Regency Dr -Strongsville 44149

(614) 228-7888 .. **Stehura**, Paul A '82 -115 W Main -Columbus 43215

(216) 696-6454 .. **Steiber Harbaugh**, Molly '83 Cincinnati Ins Co -930 The 55 Bldg
-55 Pub Sq -Cleveland 44113

(410) 224-3074 .. **Steich**, Thomas J '70 -2652 Shadow Cove -Annapolis, MD 21401

(513) 684-9900 .. **Steiden**, Eric A '94 -830 Main -Ste 1101 -Cincinnati 45202

(419) 947-8075 .. **Steiger**, Amy '00 %Morrow Cnty Pros -60 E High
-Mount Gilead 43338

(440) 234-7000 .. **Steiger**, Daniel N '87 -7530 Lucerne Dr -Ste 101 -Middleburg
Heights 44130

(216) 696-3515 .. **Steiger**, David J '92 S Karp Co,LPA -101 Prospect Av W
-1835 Mdlnd Bldg -Cleveland 44115

(216) 771-8104 .. **Steiger**, Sheldon G '72 -75 Pub Sq -Ste 650 -Cleveland 44113
Fx:241-4851

(440) 572-1151 .. **Steiger**, William E II '03 (Kim R&S,LLC) -4070 Ctr Rd
-Brunswick 44212

(330) 723-1889 .. **Steigerwald**, Dean R '73 -106 Highland Dr -Bx82 -Medina 44258

(937) 299-2899 .. **Steigerwald**, Jean M '86 -130 W 2nd -Ste 1508 -Dayton 45402

(330) 674-0001 .. **Steimel**, Samuel M '83 -111 S Clay -Millersburg 44654

(614) 221-9100 .. **Stein Chapin & Associates LLC** -32 W Hoster -Ste 200
-Columbus 43215 Fx:221-9272

(216) 445-4009 .. **Stein**, David J '02 Cleveland Clinic Fndtn -9500 Euclid Av
-Cleveland 44195

(614) 221-9100 .. **Stein**, David K '89 (Stein C & Assoc LLC) -32 W Hoster -Ste 200
-Columbus 43215 Fx:221-9272

(440) 461-6767 .. **Stein**, Elizabeth A '94 E Stein Co,LPA -6005 Landerhaven Dr -#B1
-Cleveland 44124

(330) 253-7070 .. **Stein**, Ernest R '51 -209 S Main -Ste 300 -Akron 44308

(907) 564-4039 .. **Stein**, Geoffrey E '78 BP Explrtn Alaska Inc -900 E Benson Blvd
-MB 6-4 -Anchorage, AK 99508

(216) 621-4244 .. **Stein**, Laurel G '00 %Morganstern M&D Co,LPA
-623 W St Clair Av -Cleveland 44113 Fx:621-2951

(614) 469-5737 .. **Stein**, Lesley E '03 US HUD -200 N High -Columbus 43215
Fx:469-2163

(330) 744-0247 .. **Stein**, Marc S '79 (Nadler N&B Co,LPA) -20 Fed Plz W -Ste 600
-Youngstown 44503 Fx:744-8690

(216) 831-8828 .. **Stein**, Paul N '73 -25550 Chagrin Blvd -#403 -Beachwood 44122

(216) 781-8040 .. **Stein**, Robert N '86 -614 Superior Av NW -Ste 1450
-Cleveland 44113

(216) 696-7449 .. **Stein**, Sheldon '76 -400 Trmnl Twr -Bx5606 -Cleveland 44101

(216) 621-2424 .. **Stein**, Stanley E '62 (SE Stein & Assoc Co,LPA) -75 Pub Square
-#714 -Cleveland 44113

(614) 224-7077 .. **Stein**, Stanley R '71 -280 N High -Ste 220 -Columbus 43215

(614) 221-1166 .. **Stein**, Sydney DeWitt '03 %Plymale & Assoc -495 S High -Ste 400
-Columbus 43215 Fx:221-6633

(513) 946-5133 .. **Stein-Russell**, Heather E '83 Cnty Mun Ct Judge -1000 Main
-#142 -Cincinnati 45202 Fx:946-3017

(216) 360-7500 .. **Stein-Sapir**, Leonard Roy '63 Morgans Foods,Inc -24200
Chargrin Blvd -Ste 126 -Beachwood 44122

(216) 696-9900 .. **Steinberg**, Gerald L '76 (Cohen & S) -1370 Ontario
-1020 Standard Bldg -Cleveland 44113

(419) 865-1251 .. **Steinberg**, Harold M '66 Wagoner & S,Ltd -7445 Airport Hwy
-Holland 43528 Fx:866-8798

(313) 962-3738 .. **Steinberg**, Richard L '72 (RL Steinberg,PC) -615 Griswold
-Ste 1724 -Detroit, MI 48226

(513) 621-0267 .. **Steinberg**, Robert A '67 Waite SB&C -1 W 4th
-1513 4th & Vine Twr -Cincinnati 45202

(419) 245-1975 .. **Steinberg**, Stephen J '97 %Pros -555 N Erie -4th Fl -Toledo 43624

(440) 519-3500 .. **Steinbock**, Mark A '84 Symax Ltd -30575 Bainbrdg Rd -Ste 130
-Solon 44139

Steinbrink, William H '67 -(Address Unavailable)

(216) 363-4500 .. **Steindler**, Howard A '67 (Benesch FC&A LLP) -200 Pub Sq
-Ste 2300 -Cleveland 44114 Fx:363-4588

(216) 751-4918 .. **Steiner**, Carolyn L '91 -Bx20649 -Cleveland 44120

(419) 891-8884 .. **Steiner**, Chris E '78 (Bayer P&S Co,LPA) -1925 Indn Wd Cir
-Maumee 43537 Fx:891-8889

(440) 544-1122 .. **Steiner**, David J '02 %C Groedel & Assoc -5910 Landerbrook Dr
-Ste 200 -Lyndhurst 44124

(513) 579-6400 .. **Steiner**, Edward E '83 (Keating M&K PLL) -1 E 4th
-1400 Provident Twr -Cincinnati 45202 Fx:579-6457

(440) 395-2269 .. **Steiner**, Eric J '00 SrCnsl Progressive Cslty Ins Co
-6300 Wilson Mills Rd -OHN72 -Mayfield Village 44143

(440) 234-2081 .. **Steiner**, James T '83 OH Tpk Comm -682 Prospect -Berea 44017

(330) 384-7287 .. **Steiner**, Judith A '87 FirstMerit Corp -3 Cascade Plz -7th Fl
-Akron 44308

(216) 765-0123 .. **Steiner**, Laurie G '89 (Budish & S Ltd) -23240 Chagrin Blvd
-Ste 450 Commerce Park 4 -Beachwood 44122 **Fx:**595-2787

(614) 466-3930 .. **Steiner**, Paul J '81 Treasury Dept-Sinking Fund Comm
-30 E Broad -9th Fl -Columbus 43266 **Fx:**752-8461

(216) 771-1310 .. **Steiner**, William F '51 Steiner & S Co,LPA -75 Pub Sq -Ste 1400
-Cleveland 44113 **Fx:**771-1312

(513) 579-7872 .. **Steines**, Ann M '90 Federated Dept Stores,Inc -7 W 7th -Cincinnati
45202

(216) 586-3939 .. **Steines**, Charles M '77 Cnsl Jones D -901 Lakeside Av
-Cleveland 44114 **Fx:**579-0212

(330) 725-6666 .. **Steingass**, Jonathan M '87 %Williams & B,LLP -105 W Lbrty
-Bx394 -Medina 44258

(216) 687-2300 .. **Steinglass**, Steven H '81 CSU-Marshall Cllg of Law
-2121 Euclid Av -LB138 -Cleveland 44115 **Fx:**687-6881

(330) 535-1010 .. **Steinhauer**, John S '69 -159 S Main -530 Key Bldg -Akron 44308

(330) 643-8457 .. **Steinhauer**, Susan K '98 Summit Cnty Common Pleas Ct
-209 S High -Akron 44308

(800) 544-7369 .. **Steinhauser**, Rebecca J '96 LAWO -201 E 2nd -Defiance 43512

(281) 518-6943 .. **Steinheiser**, Sylvia E '91 HP -20555 SH 249 -MS 110701
-Houston, TX 77070

(410) 573-2001 .. **Steinhilber**, August W '62 OfCnsl Reese and C LLP
-170 Jennifer Rd -Ste 245 -Annapolis, MD 21401

(614) 224-8374 .. **Steinhoff**, Rainer E '92 Legal Aid -40 W Gay -Columbus 43215

(614) 719-8770 .. **Steinkamp**, Amy D '01 Franklin Cnty Pub Def -373 S High -12th Fl
-Columbus 43215

(614) 292-2631 .. **Steinke**, Matthew R '00 OSU Moritz Cllg of Law -55 W 12th Av
-Library -Columbus 43210

(330) 699-4094 .. **Steinle**, Richard J '81 -219 Woodside Dr -Mogadore 44260

(513) 983-4349 .. **Steinmanis**, Karl S '73 Procter & Gamble Co-Legal
-1 Procter & Gamble Plz -Cincinnati 45202

(216) 781-1212 .. **Steinmetz**, Arthur P '51 OfCnsl Walter & H LLP -1301 E 9th
-Ste 3500 -Cleveland 44114 **Fx:**575-0911

(330) 722-3246 .. **Steinmetz**, Robert F '76 -3246 Granger Rd -Medina 44256

(325) 655-4700 .. **Steinsapir**, Laurence D '59 Schwartz SD&S -6300 Wilshire Blvd
-Ste 2000 -Los Angeles, CA 90048

(330) 799-9977 .. **Steiskal**, Arthur R '70 -4431 Mahoning Av -Youngstown 44515

(330) 494-2970 .. **Stelea**, Barbara J '89 -1030 N Main -Ste B -North Canton 44720

(216) 566-2648 .. **Steltenkamp**, Gerald L '73 Sherwin-Williams Co
-101 Prospect Av NW -Cleveland 44115

(419) 243-6200 .. **Steltenpohl**, Darrell D '99 (Steltenpohl J&M Co,LPA) -421 N Mich
-Toledo 43624 **Fx:**243-6280

(419) 243-6200 .. **Steltenpohl James & Menacher Co,LPA** -421 N Mich
-Toledo 43624 **Fx:**243-6280

(513) 791-2945 .. **Steltenpohl**, Robert H '76 -4100 Mntgmry Rd -Cincinnati 45212

(513) 248-6000 .. **Stelter**, Daniel C '97 Intl Paper -6285 Tri-Ridge Blvd
-Loveland 45140

(419) 636-3166 .. **Stelzer**, John T '81 (Gallagher S&Y,Ltd) -216 S Lynn -Bryan 43506
Fx:636-5743

(614) 221-7833 .. **Stelzer**, Lawrence J Jr. '91 %OH Cnsl of Retail Mrchnts
-50 W Broad -Ste 2020 -Columbus 43215

(614) 932-6010 .. **Stelzer**, Lorraine M '87 Duke Realty Corp -5600 Blazer Pkwy
-Dublin 43017

(614) 227-2000 .. **Stemm**, Mark S '84 (Porter WM&A LLP) -41 S High
-Columbus 43215 **Fx:**227-2100

(317) 964-6271 .. **Stemmer**, Linda S '78 -218 W Pearl -Union City, IN 47390

(614) 466-3379 .. **Stempfer**, Robert P '87 Dept of Dvlpmnt -77 S High
-Columbus 43215

(614) 577-9005 .. **Stempien**, James H Jr. '87 -6100 Channingway Blvd -Ste 301
-Columbus 43232

(216) 692-1222 .. **Stempuzis**, Almis J '00 A Sirvaitis & Assoc -880 E 185th
-Cleveland 44119 **Fx:**531-8687

(440) 352-3391 .. **Stender**, Jonathan T '99 %Dworken & B Co,LPA -60 S Park Pl
-Painesville 44077 **Fx:**352-3469

(859) 692-2222 .. **Stenken**, Joseph F '97 Natl Underwriter Co -5081 Olympic Blvd
-Erlanger, KY 41018

(937) 225-3981 .. **Stenson**, David E '89 D Stenson & Assoc -120 W 2nd -Ste 1210
-Dayton 45402

(216) 687-1311 .. **Stepan**, Linda L '91 (Reminger & R) -101 Prospect Av W
-1400 Mdlnd Bldg -Cleveland 44115 **Fx:**687-1841

(513) 381-2838 .. **Stepaniak**, Mark J '80 (Taft S&H LLP) -425 Walnut -Ste 1800
-Cincinnati 45202 **Fx:**381-0205

(216) 621-0200 .. **Stepanovic**, Ronald A '88 (Baker & H LLP) -1900 E 9th -Ste 3200
-Cleveland 44114 **Fx:**696-0740

(513) 381-2838 .. **Stephan**, Charles Michael '79 (Taft S&H LLP) -425 Walnut
-Ste 1800 -Cincinnati 45202 **Fx:**381-0205

(202) 225-5261 .. **Stephan**, John M '01 Cngrsmn T Ryan -222 Canon HOB
-Washington, DC 20515

(330) 364-4450 .. **Stephan**, Nicole R '02 Tuscarawas Cnty Title Co -203 Fair Av NE
-New Philadelphia 44663

(937) 372-4404 .. **Stephan**, Peter D '74 (Gibney SB&R) -1354 N Monroe Dr -Ste B
-Xenia 45385 **Fx:**372-5435

(614) 444-5604 .. **Stephan**, Randall L '88 -412 Forest -Columbus 43206

(937) 833-6326 .. **Stephan**, Rodney L '83 -245 Sycamore -Ste 200 -Brookville 45309

(937) 372-4404 .. **Stephan**, Stephanie B '03 OfCnsl Gibney SB&R -1354
N Monroe Dr -Ste B -Xenia 45385 **Fx:**372-5435

(937) 223-5200 .. **Stephan**, Wayne P '74 (Flanagan LH&S) -318 W 4th
-Dayton 45402 **Fx:**223-3335

(513) 556-0130 .. **Stephani**, Andrew J '00 Univ Cincinnati Law Schl -Bx210040
-Cincinnati 45221

(216) 685-9195 .. **Stephanoff**, Susan M '83 -1370 W 6th -Ste #208
-Cleveland 44113

(614) 227-2000 .. **Stephen**, John M '79 (Porter WM&A LLP) -41 S High
-Columbus 43215 **Fx:**227-2100

(216) 241-5310 .. **Stephens**, Alton L Jr. '75 (Gallagher SF&N) -1501 Euclid Av
-6th Fl -Cleveland 44115 **Fx:**241-1608

(202) 223-2620 .. **Stephens**, Arlus J '96 %Davis C&B,LLP -1701 K NW -Ste 210
-Washington, DC 20006

(330) 296-3434 .. **Stephens**, Craig M '74 (Stephens D&R) -206 S Meridan -Ste A
-Ravenna 44266 **Fx:**296-3435

(614) 466-9537 .. **Stephens**, Eric B '94 OH Consumers' Cnsl -10 W Broad -Ste 1800
-Columbus 43215 **Fx:**466-9475

(513) 887-3305 .. **Stephens**, Gregory S '95 Butler Cnty Pros -315 High -11th Fl
-Bx515 -Hamilton 45012

(614) 227-2594 .. **Stephens**, Lawrence G Jr. '81 -550 E Spring -Columbus 43215

(513) 762-6968 .. **Stephens**, Mark W '82 Chemed Corp -255 E 5th -Ste 2600
-Cincinnati 45202

(330) 758-2308 .. **Stephens**, Mary Jane '83 -7330 Market -Boardman 44512

(513) 946-3419 .. **Stephens**, Philip W '00 1st Dist Ct of Appls -230 E 9th -12th Fl
-Cincinnati 45202 **Fx:**946-3412

(330) 375-2285 .. **Stephens**, Suzanne L '88 Akron Mun Ct -217 S High -Akron 44308

(216) 479-8500 .. **Stephenson**, Dale E '82 (Squire S&D LLP) -127 Pub Sq
-4900 Key Twr -Cleveland 44114 **Fx:**479-8780

(330) 365-3299 .. **Stephenson**, Elizabeth W '89 Tuscarawas Cnty Cmn Pleas Ct
-101 E High Av -Ste 205 -New Philadelphia 44663 **Fx:**602-8811

(614) 227-2000 .. **Stephenson**, H Grant '79 (Porter WM&A LLP) -41 S High
-Columbus 43215 **Fx:**227-2100

(216) 861-3086 .. **Stephenson**, James E '01 Reid M&W -55 Pub Sq -Ste 2010
-Cleveland 44113 **Fx:**861-4409

(740) 354-3761 .. **Stephenson**, Marilee '91 Stephenson Law Ofc -530 6th
-Portsmouth 45662

(440) 988-9500 .. **Stephenson**, Mark E '80 (Trigilio & S)
-5750 Cooper Foster Park Rd -Ste 102 -Lorain 44053

(513) 887-9595 .. **Stephenson**, Nicole M '98 -30 North D -Hamilton 45013

(330) 339-6444 .. **Stephenson**, Richard L '58 (Stephenson S&C) -206 W High Av
-New Philadelphia 44663 **Fx:**339-6228

(330) 339-6444 .. **Stephenson**, Robert R II '86 Stephenson S&C -206 W High Av
-New Philadelphia 44663 **Fx:**339-6228

(330) 339-6444 .. **Stephenson Stephenson & Carrothers** -206 W High Av
-New Philadelphia 44663 **Fx:**339-6228

(419) 354-9244 .. **Stephenson**, William V '87 Wood Cnty Pub Def -123 N Summit
-Bowling Green 43402

(859) 394-6200 .. **Stepner**, Donald L '92 (Adams SW&D) -40 W Pike -Bx861
-Covington, KY 41012 **Fx:**291-7902

(859) 394-6200 .. **Stepner**, Jeffrey A '97 %Adams SW&D -40 W Pike -Bx861
-Covington, KY 41012 **Fx:**291-7902

(614) 463-9790 .. **Stepter**, Rayl L '90 -111 W Rich -Ste 430 -Columbus 43215
Fx:463-9877

(606) 767-3870 .. **Sterba**, Deborah A '96 Delta Airlines -Attn:In Flight Srvcs/Dept 610
-Atlanta, GA 30320

(330) 832-9878 .. **Stergios**, John F '69 Stergios & K Co,LPA
-2859 Aaronwood Av NE -Ste 101 -Massillon 44646

(330) 832-9878 .. **Stergios & Kurtzman Co,LPA** -2859 Aaronwood Av NE -Ste 101
-Massillon 44646

(330) 832-9878 .. **Stergios**, Paul J '61 Stergios & K Co,LPA
-2859 Aaronwood Av NE -Ste 101 -Massillon 44646

(330) 832-9878 .. **Stergios**, Pericles G '86 (P Stergios,LLC) -2859 Aaronwood Av NE
-Ste 101 -Massillon 44646

(216) 291-1050 .. **Sterkel**, Timothy R '94 -1414 S Green Rd -Cleveland 44121

(419) 228-3700 .. **Sterling**, Alissa M '98 %Allen Cnty Pros -204 N Main -#302
-Lima 45801

(216) 586-3939 .. **Sterling**, John L '68 OfCnsl Jones D -901 Lakeside Av
-Cleveland 44114 **Fx:**579-0212

(419) 893-3360 .. **Sterling**, Robert V '71 (Weber & S,LLC) -1721 Indn Wd Cir -Ste 1
-Maumee 43537 **Fx:**893-7146

(330) 887-0162 .. **Sterling**, William Fisher '83 Westfield Grp -1 Park Cir -Bx5001
-Westfield Center 44251 **Fx:**887-2588

(304) 233-5599 .. **Stern**, Aimee M '97 Thorp R&A,LLP -1233 Main -Ste 2001
-Wheeling, WV 26003

(740) 284-1211 .. **Stern**, Gary M '78 (Stern S&S Co,LPA) -502 Bank One Bldg
-Steubenville 43952

(614) 462-5457 .. **Stern**, Geoffrey '68 (Kegler BH&R) -65 E State -Ste 1800
-Columbus 43215 **Fx:**464-2634

(216) 781-1700 .. **Stern**, Harold S '52 OfCnsl Shapero & R Co,LPA -1350 Euclid Av
-Ste 1550 -Cleveland 44115 **Fx:**781-1972

(216) 771-1310 .. **Stern**, Howard S '56 Steiner & S Co,LPA -75 Pub Sq -Ste 1400
-Cleveland 44113 **Fx:**771-1312

(740) 282-5336 .. **Stern**, James A '77 (Stern S&S) -102 N 3rd -Steubenville 43952

(216) 522-7458 .. **Stern**, Jeffrey A '77 US EOC -1660 W 2nd -#850
-Cleveland 44113

(216) 861-0006 .. **Stern**, Mitchell A '77 -55 Pub Sq -Ste 1717 -Cleveland 44113

(513) 977-8200 .. **Stern**, Noah J '99 %Dinsmore & S LLP -255 E 5th -Ste 1900
-Cincinnati 45202 **Fx:**977-8141

(513) 936-2011 .. **Stern**, Steven D '04 SrCnsl Sara Lee Corp -10151 Carver Rd
-Cincinnati 45242 **Fx:**936-2020

(713) 686-6961 .. **Sternat**, Christian M '79 -2190 N Loop W -Ste 101
-Houston, TX 77018

(440) 942-6267 .. **Sternberg**, David J '73 (Sternberg & Z Co,LPA) -7547 Mentor Av
-Mentor 44060 **Fx:**942-6504

(330) 762-6474 .. **Sternberg Newman Shifrin & Associates**
-411 Wolf Ledges Pkwy -Ste 300 -Akron 44311 **Fx:**762-2127

(330) 762-6474 .. **Sternberg**, Richard '52 (Sternberg NS & Assoc) -411 Wolf
Ledges Pkwy -Ste 300 -Akron 44311 **Fx:**762-2127

(216) 360-7200 .. **Sternberg**, Sandor W '84 Carlisle MRK&U Co,LPA
-24755 Chagrin Blvd -Ste 200 -Cleveland 44122 **Fx:**360-7210

(330) 643-3550 .. **Sterner**, Steven L '85 Industrial Commssn of OH -161 S High
-Ste 301 -Akron 44308

(513) 421-2700 .. **Stethem & Duwel** -11177 Reading Rd -Cincinnati 45241
Fx:763-7694

(330) 761-9960 .. **Stetson**, Scott V '03 State & Federal Communications
-80 S Summit -Ste 100 -Akron 44308

(216) 781-0005 .. **Steuer**, Arlene B '52 (Cozza & S) -1420 Standard Bldg
-1370 Ontario -Cleveland 44113

(216) 771-8121 .. **Steuer Escovar Berk & Brown Co, LPA** -55 Pub Sq -Ste 1828
-Cleveland 44113 **Fx:**771-8120

(614) 466-8600 .. **Steuk**, Sally A '74 Atty Gen -30 E Broad -Columbus 43215
Fx:466-6090

(419) 625-8324 .. **Steuk**, William C '66 Flynn P&K,LPA -165 E Wshngtn Row
-Sandusky 44870 **Fx:**625-9007

(419) 625-8324 .. **Steuk**, William R '96 %Flynn P&K,LPA -165 E Wshngtn Row
-Sandusky 44870 **Fx:**625-9007

(216) 522-0564 .. **Stevens**, Anne M '00 USDC/NDOH -801 Superior Av
-Cleveland 44114

(513) 233-2525 .. **Stevens**, Annette K '90 -7312 Waterpoint Ln -Cincinnati 45255

(419) 352-7522 .. **Stevens**, Bruce B '99 %Middleton R&N -521 N Main
-Bowling Green 43402 **Fx:**353-4899

(216) 696-4700 .. **Stevens**, Eugene E '58 Spieth BM&N Co,LPA -925 Euclid Av
-2000 Huntngtn Bldg -Cleveland 44115 **Fx:**696-2706

(216) 861-1700 .. **Stevens,** Fred A '73 Stevens & M -75 Pub Sq -Ste 1450 -Cleveland 44113
(614) 466-8911 .. **Stevens,** Lori M '02 %Atty Gen -30 E Broad -Columbus 43215 **Fx:**728-7582
(937) 438-6848 .. **Stevens,** Richard C '82 (Stevens & S LLP) -7019 Corp Way -Dayton 45459
(440) 466-6026 .. **Stevens,** Richard Lee '77 -27 W Main -Geneva 44041
(330) 533-6119 .. **Stevens,** Robert L '74 (Hunter-Stevens) -6715 Tippecanoe Rd -Canfield 44406
(937) 438-6848 .. **Stevens & Showalter LLP** -7019 Corp Way -Dayton 45459
(216) 689-3196 .. **Stevens,** Thomas C '74 KeyBank NA -127 Pub Sq -Cleveland 44114
Stevens-Walther, Marylouise '99 -(Address Unavailable)
(313) 665-3897 .. **Stevenson,** Allan J '87 General Motors Corp -300 Renaissance Ctr -MC 482-C13-C96 -Detroit, MI 48265
(740) 653-0961 .. **Stevenson,** Andrew H '92 Stevenson & S -301 E Main -Lancaster 43130 **Fx:**653-4342
Stevenson, Anthony M '96 -3214 Prospect Av E -Cleveland 44115
(513) 946-3120 .. **Stevenson,** David T '81 Hamilton Cnty Pros -230 E 9th -Cincinnati 45202 **Fx:**946-3017
(330) 643-2326 .. **Stevenson,** Diana M '92 Summit Cnty Probate Ct -209 S High -Akron 44308
(614) 466-7046 .. **Stevenson,** Elaine K '99 Personnel Brd of Review -65 E State -12th Fl -Columbus 43215
(740) 653-0961 .. **Stevenson,** H James '66 (Stevenson & S) -301 E Main -Lancaster 43130 **Fx:**653-4342
(937) 492-6125 .. **Stevenson,** James F '75 (Kerrigan BSG&B) -126 N Main Av -Bx987 -Sidney 45365
(614) 451-6313 .. **Stevenson,** James S '95 Northwest Title -5055 Dierker Rd -Columbus 43220
(740) 858-6654 .. **Stevenson,** John R '81 -116 Wshngtn Blvd -West Portsmouth 45663
(860) 945-3032 .. **Stevenson,** Joseph John '72 -265 Cutler -Watertown, CT 06795
(440) 350-2683 .. **Stevenson,** Leah J '99 Lake Cnty Pros -105 Main -Bx490 -Painesville 44077 **Fx:**350-2585
(614) 469-6860 .. **Stevenson,** Louis '75 %US SBA -2 Nationwide Plz -Ste 1400 -Columbus 43215
(800) 864-4253 .. **Stevenson,** Marisa F '02 Cnsl Bulldog Ofc Prdcts,Inc -500 Glass Rd -Pittsburgh, PA 15205 **Fx:**430-8539
(614) 644-1422 .. **Stevenson,** Mary D '75 Industrial Commssn of OH -30 W Spring -9th Fl -Columbus 43215 **Fx:**752-8785
(330) 376-2700 .. **Stevenson,** Roger J '81 (Roetzel & A,LPA) -222 S Main -Akron 44308 **Fx:**376-4577
(330) 762-0765 .. **Stevenson,** Scot A '92 -441 Wolf Ledges Pkwy -Ste 400 -Akron 44311 **Fx:**762-2255
(614) 837-2486 .. **Stevenson,** William W '56 -20 S High -Canal Winchester 43110
(941) 365-3040 .. **Steves,** David A '72 (Muirhead G&S,LLP) -1800 2nd -Ste 918 -Sarasota, FL 34236 **Fx:**365-3333
(419) 241-1200 .. **Steves,** Jennifer W '02 %Cooper & W,LPA -900 Adams -Toledo 43624 **Fx:**242-5675
(614) 221-3938 .. **Steward,** Anne C '04 G Lewis,LPA -625 City Park Av -Columbus 43206
(937) 328-3758 .. **Stewart,** Albert Jr. '73 Clark Cnty Mun Ct -50 E Columbia -Springfield 45502
(937) 667-4481 .. **Stewart,** Andrew B '99 %Dysinger S&D -249 S Garber Dr -Tipp City 45371 **Fx:**667-5393
(419) 288-2989 .. **Stewart,** Beryl W '64 -116 E Main -Bx256 -Wayne 43466 **Fx:**288-3766
(937) 443-0416 .. **Stewart,** Beverly J '87 Cnsl Mntgmry Cnty Alchl&Drug Addctn -409 E Monument Av -Ste 102 -Dayton 45402
(937) 667-4481 .. **Stewart,** Bryan K '89 (Dysinger S&D) -249 S Garber Dr -Tipp City 45371 **Fx:**667-5393
(440) 439-4240 .. **Stewart,** Charles C '66 -714 Bway -Bedford 44146
(216) 831-1125 .. **Stewart,** Cheryl R '99 Harborside Healthcare Corp -3800 Park East -Ste 250 -Beachwood 44122
(615) 736-5151 .. **Stewart,** Darryl A '76 US Attys Ofc -110 9th Av -Ste A-961 -Nashville, TN 37203
(216) 781-2258 .. **Stewart & DeChant Co, LPA** -1370 Ontario -Ste 1440 Standard Bldg -Cleveland 44113 **Fx:**781-8210
(216) 696-1422 .. **Stewart,** Enos Roger '98 %McCarthy LC&L Co,LPA -101 Prospect Av W -1800 Mdlnd Bldg -Cleveland 44115 **Fx:**696-1210
(937) 599-7272 .. **Stewart,** Eric C '99 Logan Cnty Pros -117 E Columbus Av -Ste 200 -Bellefontaine 43311 **Fx:**599-7271
(513) 381-2838 .. **Stewart,** Frank H '59 OfCnsl Taft S&H LLP -425 Walnut -Ste 1800 -Cincinnati 45202 **Fx:**381-0205
(614) 221-7663 .. **Stewart,** Jackie L '80 (Luper N&L,LPA) -50 W Broad -1200 LeVeque Twr -Columbus 43215 **Fx:**464-2425
(513) 671-6333 .. **Stewart,** Jay T '02 %Matre & M Co,LPA -225 Pictoria Dr -Ste 200 -Cincinnati 45246 **Fx:**671-1234
(937) 443-6859 .. **Stewart,** Jeffry C '02 %Thompson H LLP -2000 Cthse Plz NE -Bx8801 -Dayton 45401 **Fx:**443-6635
(419) 478-1776 .. **Stewart,** John C '89 -1776 Tremainsvll Rd -Toledo 43613 **Fx:**478-5087
(614) 864-1054 .. **Stewart,** John Douglas '79 -7518 Slate Ridge Blvd -Reynoldsburg 43068
(419) 525-8705 .. **Stewart,** John P '91 Richland Trust Co -3 N Main -Mansfield 44902
(614) 220-8625 .. **Stewart,** Joseph R '73 United Tlphne Co of OH -50 W Broad -Ste 3600 -Columbus 43215
(734) 856-4880 .. **Stewart,** Julia L '91 (Spiros & S) -8160 Secor Rd -Bx336 -Lambertville, MI 48144
(216) 881-2690 .. **Stewart,** Kirk '76 -3631 Perkins Av -Cleveland 44114
(216) 781-2258 .. **Stewart,** Lawrence E '50 Stewart & D Co,LPA -1370 Ontario -Ste 1440 Standard Bldg -Cleveland 44113 **Fx:**781-8210
(614) 278-5815 .. **Stewart,** Lynne L '84 Franklin Cnty Children Srvcs -855 W Mound -Columbus 43223 **Fx:**275-2589
(419) 241-9000 .. **Stewart,** Mark C '76 (Shumaker L&K,LLP) -1000 Jackson -Toledo 43624 **Fx:**241-6894
(859) 394-6200 .. **Stewart,** Mary A '89 %Adams SW&D -40 W Pike -Bx861 -Covington, KY 41012 **Fx:**291-7902
(216) 687-4692 .. **Stewart,** Melody J '89 CSU-Marshall Cllg of Law -2121 Euclid Av -LB138 -Cleveland 44115 **Fx:**687-6881
(440) 269-1900 .. **Stewart,** Michael J '86 Walton & Stewart Inc,CPAs -7660 Tyler Blvd -Mentor 44060
Stewart, Michele E '89 -(Address Unavailable)
(330) 864-1923 .. **Stewart,** Richard M '50 -327 Asbury Rd -Fairlawn 44333
(512) 322-2584 .. **Stewart,** Robert T '77 (Baker & B) -98 San Jacinto Blvd -Ste 1600 -Austin, TX 78701
(216) 781-2258 .. **Stewart,** Scott E '76 (Stewart & D Co,LPA) -1370 Ontario -Ste 1440 Standard Bldg -Cleveland 44113 **Fx:**781-8210
(740) 264-6060 .. **Stewart,** Susan P '77 -4130 Sunset Blvd -Steubenville 43952
(513) 362-8700 .. **Stewart,** Thomas H '92 %Blank R -201 E 5th -Ste 1700 -Cincinnati 45202 **Fx:**362-8787
(614) 424-4692 .. **Stewart,** Todd A '02 -505 King Av -Columbus 43201
(216) 566-5580 .. **Stewart,** William R '68 (Thompson H LLP) -127 Pub Sq -3900 Key Ctr -Cleveland 44114 **Fx:**566-5800
(216) 398-2000 .. **Stibich,** Paul R Sr. '78 Watt Printers -4544 Hinckley Indstrl Pkwy -Cleveland 44109
(216) 581-2600 .. **Stibley,** Michael R '04 XLO Group -4495 Cranwood Pkwy -Cleveland 44128
(513) 241-3685 .. **Stich,** Carl J Jr. '80 (White G&M Co,LPA) -1 W 4th -Ste 1700 -Cincinnati 45202 **Fx:**241-2399
(330) 864-0117 .. **Stich,** Janet I '86 -1700 W Market -#104 -Akron 44313
(614) 341-2393 .. **Stichter,** Philip W '66 Griffith Fndtn for Ins Edu -172 E State -Ste 305A -Columbus 43215
(216) 622-3600 .. **Stickan,** Christian H '75 US Atty -801 W Superior -Ste 400 -Cleveland 44113 **Fx:**622-3370
(614) 466-4320 .. **Stickan,** Lisa M '01 Atty Gen -150 E Gay -Columbus 43215
(614) 462-3555 .. **Stickel,** Paul M '79 Franklin Cnty Pros -373 S High -Columbus 43215
(216) 241-0140 .. **Stickney,** John M '51 -50 Pub Sq -3300 Trmnl Twr -Cleveland 44113
(216) 241-0140 .. **Stickney,** Melissa Wiley '03 -50 Pub Sq -3300 Trmnl Twr -Cleveland 44113
(216) 241-0140 .. **Stickney,** Thomas Moore '95 -50 Pub Sq -3300 Trmnl Twr -Cleveland 44113
(513) 618-7800 .. **Stiebel,** Mark A '80 (Graf S&M,LPA) -425 Walnut -Ste 2400 -Cincinnati 45202 **Fx:**618-7801
(216) 348-5400 .. **Stief,** James E '97 (McDonald H Co,LPA) -600 Superior Av E -Ste 2100 -Cleveland 44114 **Fx:**348-5474
(216) 573-1776 .. **Stiefvater,** Robert G III '03 %Cleary & Assoc Co,LPA -6000 Lombardo Ctr Dr -Ste 635 -Independence 44131
(216) 241-6602 .. **Stienecker,** C Andrew '00 %Weston HFP&H LLP -50 Pub Sq -2500 Trmnl Twr -Cleveland 44113 **Fx:**621-8369
(513) 421-2400 .. **Stiens,** Donald G Jr. '03 %Helmer MR&P Co,LPA -105 E 4th -Ste 1900 -Cincinnati 45202 **Fx:**421-7902
(202) 767-1546 .. **Stiens,** Kevin P '97 Air Force -112 Luke Av -Rm 343 -Washington, DC 20032
(937) 426-3310 .. **Stier,** Charles H Jr. '77 (Hammond S&S) -3836 Dayton-Xenia Rd -Beavercreek 45432 **Fx:**426-9328
(513) 946-3425 .. **Stier,** Mary A '94 1st Dist Ct of Appeals -230 E 9th -12th flr -Cincinnati 45202
(419) 334-8937 .. **Stierwalt,** Thomas L '75 -617 Croghan -Fremont 43420
(216) 696-6122 .. **Stifel,** Orville E II '88 (Gold & P Co,LPA) -526 Superior Av E -1140 Leader Bldg -Cleveland 44114 **Fx:**696-3214
(513) 561-5444 .. **Stigler,** Margaret M '83 -5725 Dragon Way -Ste 306 -Cincinnati 45227
(216) 416-3771 .. **Stile,** David M '94 Forest City Land Group -50 Pub Sq -Ste 1050 -Cleveland 44113 **Fx:**263-4809
(614) 469-3939 .. **Stiles,** Kelli Jones '03 %Jones D -325 John H McConnell Blvd -Ste 600 -Bx165017 -Columbus 43216 **Fx:**461-4198
(614) 246-8257 .. **Still,** Nan M '87 OH Farm Bureau Fed -280 N High -2 Nationwide Plz, 6th Fl -Bx182383 -Columbus 43218
(216) 771-1760 .. **Stiller,** Robin R '00 Smith & C LLP -1801 E Ninth -Ste 900 Ohio Svngs Plz -Cleveland 44114 **Fx:**771-3387
(513) 936-0800 .. **Stillpass,** John E '81 (J Stillpass,LLC) -9545 Kenwood Rd -Ste 103 -Cincinnati 45242 **Fx:**794-8800
(740) 886-5402 .. **Stillpass,** Marty J '83 -116 State -Bx791 -Proctorville 45669
(614) 221-0240 .. **Stiltner,** Jeffrey W '95 (Hahn L&P LLP) -65 E State -Ste 1400 -Columbus 43215 **Fx:**221-5909
(513) 621-0267 .. **Stilz,** Fay E '78 Waite SB&C -1 W 4th -1513 4th & Vine Twr -Cincinnati 45202
(859) 578-4444 .. **Stilz,** William K Jr. '02 %P Schachter & Assoc -250 Grandvw Dr -Ste 500 -Ft Mitchell, KY 41017
(330) 252-0300 .. **Stimler,** James T '77 Stimler Law Ofc -50 S Main -Ste 703 -Akron 44308
(330) 252-0300 .. **Stimler,** Kathleen E '80 OfCnsl Stimler Law Ofc -50 S Main -Ste 703 -Akron 44308
Stimmel, Andrew H '03 -(Address Unavailable)
(614) 462-2332 .. **Stine,** Joshua N '03 %Schottenstein Z&D -250 West -Bx165020 -Columbus 43216 **Fx:**462-5135
(513) 241-2324 .. **Stinebruner,** Scott A '98 (Wood H&E LLP) -441 Vine -Ste 2700 -Cincinnati 45202 **Fx:**421-7269
(513) 533-0020 .. **Stineman,** Jerome P '91 -2101 Grandin Rd -Ste 601 -Cincinnati 45208
(216) 642-0323 .. **Stinn,** Michael E '84 OfCnsl Britton SP&K Co,LPA -4700 Rockside Rd -Ste 540 Summit One -Cleveland 44131 **Fx:**642-0747
(614) 221-3155 .. **Stinson,** Dane '81 (Bailey C LLC) -10 W Broad -Columbus 43215 **Fx:**221-0479
Stinson, Robert C '71 -(Address Unavailable)
(937) 415-3211 .. **Stipancich,** John K '93 Evenflo Co,Inc -707 Crssrds Ct -Vandalia 45377
(937) 443-6806 .. **Stirling,** Scott T '93 %Thompson H LLP -2000 Cthse Plz NE -Bx8801 -Dayton 45401 **Fx:**443-6635
(260) 423-9551 .. **Stites,** Anthony M '89 (Barrett & M LLP) -215 E Berry -Bx2263 -Fort Wayne, IN 46801 **Fx:**423-8920
(513) 381-4700 .. **Stith,** John S '64 (Porter WM&A LLP) -250 E 5th -Ste 2200 -Cincinnati 45202 **Fx:**421-0991
(330) 643-2850 .. **Stith,** Michael R '79 Summit Cnty Engineer -538 E South -Akron 44311 **Fx:**762-7829
(614) 445-6700 .. **Stith,** Robin S '80 -13 E Kossuth -Columbus 43206
(513) 863-7600 .. **Stitsinger,** Steven M '97 -300 High -Ste 404 -Hamilton 45011
(513) 579-6400 .. **Stitt,** Jason V '04 %Keating M&K PLL -1 E 4th -1400 Provident Twr -Cincinnati 45202 **Fx:**579-6457

(614) 221-1111 .. **Stitt,** Scott J '01 Shayne & G -221 S High -Columbus 43215 **Fx:**221-4070
(614) 275-5871 .. **Stitt,** Willie C '79 Cntrl OH Transit Auth -1600 McKinley Av -Columbus 43222
(513) 683-3221 .. **Stiver,** Shawn A '91 %R Bauer -501 W Loveland Av -Loveland 45140
Stobart, William M '98 -220 Main -9J -New Hartford, CT 06057
(614) 864-5292 .. **Stobbs,** Brent C '89 -7658 Slate Ridge Blvd -Reynoldsburg 43068
(614) 387-9033 .. **Stock,** Christopher D '02 Hon T O'Donnell Supreme Ct -65 S Front -Ste 900 -Columbus 43215 **Fx:**387-9039
(614) 227-2323 .. **Stock,** Elizabeth C '02 %Bricker & E LLP -100 S 3rd -Columbus 43215 **Fx:**227-2390
(614) 223-9300 .. **Stock,** John F '81 (Benesch FC&A LLP) -88 E Broad -Ste 900 -Columbus 43215 **Fx:**223-9330
(614) 469-3939 .. **Stock,** Jonathan Kent '95 %Jones D -325 John H McConnell Blvd -Ste 600 -Bx165017 -Columbus 43216 **Fx:**461-4198
(937) 443-1000 .. **Stock,** Otto F Jr. '66 Standard Register Co -600 Albany -Bx1167 -Dayton 45401
(614) 764-7440 .. **Stockamp,** Deanna L '96 Whann & Assoc -6300 Frantz Rd -Dublin 43017
(513) 946-5160 .. **Stockdale,** David C '76 Cnty Mun Ct Judge -1000 Main -Rm 170 -Cincinnati 45202
(513) 381-7333 .. **Stocker,** David E '79 -2430 Cntrl Pkwy -Cincinnati 45214
Stocker, Gretchen L '04 -(Address Unavailable)
(330) 452-8640 .. **Stocker,** Steven E '76 -437 Market Av N -Canton 44702
(216) 589-0302 .. **Stocker,** Suzanne '86 -2200 Illuminating Bldg -55 Pub Square -Cleveland 44113
(330) 255-5854 .. **Stocker,** Wendall W '85 -222 S Main -3rd Fl -Akron 44308
(937) 454-1468 .. **Stocklin & Simpson Co LPA** -7825 N Dixie Dr -Ste A -Dayton 45414
(937) 454-1468 .. **Stocklin,** Valerie '81 Stocklin & S Co LPA -7825 N Dixie Dr -Ste A -Dayton 45414
(216) 736-3333 .. **Stockman,** Mark J '96 %Kahn K -1301 E 9th -2600 Erievw Twr -Cleveland 44114 **Fx:**623-4912
(216) 696-4006 .. **Stockmaster,** Ann Marie '96 (R Guttman & Assoc,LPA) -55 Pub Sq -Ste 1860 -Cleveland 44113 **Fx:**696-2778
(419) 448-3321 .. **Stockner,** Jeffry J '85 Tiffin Univ -155 Miami -Tiffin 44883
(216) 621-6501 .. **Stockslager,** Matthew J '92 (Schottenstein Z&D) -1350 Euclid Av -Ste 1400 -Cleveland 44115 **Fx:**621-6502
(513) 243-7384 .. **Stockton,** Susan M '91 GE Aircraft Engines -One Neumann Way -MD J104 -Cincinnati 45201
(703) 747-7172 .. **Stockton,** Tracey M '99 Bearing Point,Inc -1676 Intl Dr -Mc Lean, VA 22102
(419) 247-1500 .. **Stockwell & Cooperman,LPA** -One Seagate -Ste 1610 -Toledo 43604 **Fx:**247-1575
(419) 247-1500 .. **Stockwell,** John P '73 (Stockwell & C,LPA) -One Seagate -Ste 1610 -Toledo 43604 **Fx:**247-1575
(859) 223-3400 .. **Stockwell,** Todd E '04 Stockwell & Assoc -861 Corp Dr -Ste 201 -Lexington, KY 40503 **Fx:**224-1399
(937) 225-4063 .. **Stoermer,** Elaine M '81 Montgomery Cnty Dom Rltns Ct -301 W 3rd -Rm 204 -Bx972 -Dayton 45422
(502) 583-8633 .. **Stoess,** Ray H Jr. '87 -235 S 5th -Louisville, KY 40202
(513) 870-2480 .. **Stofel,** Steven F '01 Cincinnati Ins Co -6200 S Gilmore Rd -Fairfield 45014
(513) 732-1420 .. **Stoffel,** Todd S '89 Nichols S&N -237 Main -Batavia 45103
(614) 228-5931 .. **Stoffers,** Robert H '82 (Mazanec R&R Co,LPA) -250 Civic Ctr Dr -Ste 400 -Columbus 43215 **Fx:**228-5934
(740) 332-1352 .. **Stohs,** Daniel J '77 -24525 Goose Crk Rd -Bx305 -South Bloomingville 43152
(937) 426-5497 .. **Stokely,** Elizabeth S '93 -299 Redwood Blvd -Beavercreek 45440
(937) 223-1201 .. **Stokely,** Matthew D '93 %Altick & C Co,LPA -1 S Main -1700 One Dayton Ctr -Dayton 45402 **Fx:**223-5100
(440) 845-4140 .. **Stoken,** Henry A '81 -7229 Parma Park -Parma 44130
(216) 664-4986 .. **Stokes,** Angela R '84 Mun Ct Judge -1200 Ontario Av -Cleveland 44113
(740) 349-7266 .. **Stokes,** David B '79 -21 W Church -Ste 206 -Newark 43055 **Fx:**345-9630
(616) 942-8090 .. **Stokes,** James R '84 -429 Turner Av NW -Grand Rapids, MI 49504
(216) 479-8500 .. **Stokes,** Louis '53 OfCnsl Squire S&D LLP -127 Pub Sq -4900 Key Twr -Cleveland 44114 **Fx:**479-8780
(419) 245-2550 .. **Stokes,** Michael L '95 %Atty Gen -One SeaGate -Ste 2150 -Toledo 43604 **Fx:**246-2520
(614) 628-8000 .. **Stolar,** Margaret M '93 Dreher L&T LLP -41 S High -2250 Huntngtn Ctr -Columbus 43215 **Fx:**628-1600
(216) 694-3987 .. **Stolarsky,** Lon D '84 -1370 Ontario -Ste 1630 -Cleveland 44113
(216) 363-4500 .. **Stoll,** Edward J Jr. '94 %Benesch FC&A LLP -200 Pub Sq -Ste 2300 -Cleveland 44114 **Fx:**363-4588
(419) 562-4529 .. **Stoll,** Geoffrey L '87 (Starkey & S,Ltd) -208 S Walnut -Bucyrus 44820
(216) 694-3846 **Stoll,** Myron S '60 Comm Tech -1422 Euclid Av -Ste 706 -Cleveland 44115
(937) 865-6800 .. **Stoll,** Sandra J '99 Lexis/Nexis -Bx933 -Dayton 45401
(614) 464-6400 .. **Stoll,** Sheryl Clark '98 OfCnsl Vorys SS&P LLP -52 E Gay -Bx1008 -Columbus 43216 **Fx:**464-6350
(419) 668-4879 .. **Stoll,** Thomas J '94 (Eschrich & S Co,LPA) -130 Benedict Av -Bx465 -Norwalk 44857 **Fx:**663-0140
(614) 225-2024 .. **Stoll,** William F Jr. '73 Borden,Inc -180 E Broad -Columbus 43215
(937) 324-5553 .. **Stoll,** William J '50 -22 S Limstone -360 Edison Ctr -Springfield 45502
(513) 583-8888 .. **Stolle,** Linda K '87 %Heath & Assoc -8977 Columbia Rd -Ste A -Bx4770 -Maineville 45039
Stoller, Brenda '91 -(Address Unavailable)
(614) 462-2255 .. **Stoller,** Eric M '99 %Schottenstein Z&D -250 West -Bx165020 -Columbus 43216 **Fx:**462-5135
(513) 621-7474 .. **Stoller,** Harry '58 -105 E 4th -Ste 1200 -Cincinnati 45202
(216) 687-1900 .. **Stoller,** Jennifer R '00 Legal Aid -1223 W 6th -Cleveland 44113 **Fx:**687-0779
(912) 236-0261 .. **Stolley,** Briana Becker '01 %Hunter ME&D,PC -200 E St Julian -Bx9848 -Savannah, GA 31412 **Fx:**236-4936
(937) 547-0218 .. **Stollings,** Jerry C '01 %S Rudnick,Ltd -121 W 3rd -Greenville 45331
(937) 593-6065 .. **Stolly,** Terrence G '01 %Thompson DHMW&T -1111 Rush Av -Bx68 -Bellefontaine 43311
(513) 651-6800 .. **Stolper,** Rita Mannheimer '91 %Frost BT LLC -201 E 5th -2200 PNC Ctr -Cincinnati 45202 **Fx:**651-6981
(216) 750-4529 .. **Stone,** Alesia M '89 Nationwide Ins Co -8200 Sweet Valley Dr -Valley View 44125
(614) 461-0256 .. **Stone,** Amy C '92 Ofc Dscplnry Cnsl -250 Civic Ctr Dr -#325 -Columbus 43215 **Fx:**461-7205
(330) 492-3957 .. **Stone,** Angela D '96 %J Haupt -4884 Dressler Rd NW -Canton 44718
(513) 634-9397 .. **Stone,** Angela M '99 Procter & Gamble -8611 Beckett Rd -West Chester 45069
(614) 866-4025 .. **Stone,** Deborah J '96 L Sigall -6470 E Main -Reynoldsburg 43068
(330) 823-0696 .. **Stone,** Donald S Jr. '73 (Stone & S) -981 W State -Alliance 44601
(216) 348-5400 .. **Stone,** James M '86 (McDonald H Co,LPA) -600 Superior Av E -Ste 2100 -Cleveland 44114 **Fx:**348-5474
(614) 466-5394 .. **Stone,** Jill E '79 Pub Def -8 E Long -Columbus 43215
(216) 433-8855 .. **Stone,** Kent N '77 NASA Glenn Research Ctr -21000 Brookpark Rd -Cleveland 44135
Stone, Lori L '03 Staffwise Legal Inc -1150 Conn Av NW -Washington, DC 20036
(330) 792-1063 .. **Stone,** Marc D '79 %Industrial Commssn of OH -242 Fed Plz W -Ste 303 -Youngstown 44503
(937) 427-9650 .. **Stone,** Mark E '82 (Stone & M Co,LPA) -42 Woodcroft Trl -Ste A -Beavercreek 45430 **Fx:**427-9659
(650) 858-8088 .. **Stone,** Martin L '86 -260 El Verano Av -Palo Alto, CA 94306
(330) 262-5246 .. **Stone,** Meredith Blake '73 (MB Stone,LPA) -231 N Buckeye -Wooster 44691
(248) 723-0435 .. **Stone,** Nancy K '97 %Howard & H,PC -39400 Woodward Av -Ste 101 -Bloomfield Hills, MI 48304
(216) 765-1130 .. **Stone,** Richard E '75 (RE Stone Co,LPA) -24100 Chagrin Blvd -Beachwood 44122
(513) 421-4020 .. **Stone,** Richard M '77 (Cohen TK&S,LLC) -250 E 5th -Ste 1200 -Cincinnati 45202 **Fx:**241-4490
(330) 823-0740 .. **Stone,** Robert H Jr. '91 (Bair & S) -643 W State -Alliance 44601
Stone, Robert S '67 -(Address Unavailable)
(440) 246-2800 .. **Stone,** Russell B '83 -814 Reid Av -Lorain 44052
(937) 436-0033 .. **Stone,** Scot A '82 (Ruffolo SD&L) -7501 Paragon Rd -Dayton 45459
(614) 866-4025 .. **Stone,** Steven D '96 -6470 E Main -Reynoldsburg 43068 **Fx:**866-6055
(614) 462-3896 .. **Stone,** Thomas A '85 Franklin Cnty Probate Ct -373 S High -22nd Fl -Columbus 43215
(614) 792-5555 .. **Stonebrook,** Michael R '02 %Standley Law Grp LLP -495 Metro Pl S -Ste 210 -Dublin 43017 **Fx:**792-5536
(740) 852-3000 .. **Stonecipher,** Timothy R '75 (Nichols S&F) -117 W High -Ste 105 -London 43140
(614) 280-8769 .. **Stonecipher Price,** Sheryl '75 IRS -200 N High -Rm 404 -Columbus 43215 **Fx:**280-8761
(513) 632-9555 .. **Stonehill,** David N '80 (D Stonehill Co,LPA) -400 Oliver Rd -Wyoming 45215
(304) 242-8410 .. **Stoneking,** James B '93 Bordas & B,PLLC -1358 Natl Rd -Wheeling, WV 26003
(614) 466-6849 .. **Stoneking,** Janet K '96 PUCO -180 E Broad -Columbus 43266
(330) 627-6642 .. **Stoneman,** Kathleen A '82 (Stoneman & A) -63 2nd SW -Bx235 -Carrollton 44615
(419) 242-8214 .. **Stoner,** Amy E '00 %Zaner & C -520 Mad Av -Ste 545 -Toledo 43604 **Fx:**242-8658
Stoner, Andrea H '92 -Bx84 -Baltimore 43105
Stoner, Carol M '79 -325 N High -Yellow Springs 45387
(937) 593-8725 .. **Stoner,** Linda C '89 %MacGillivray Law Ofc -325 N Main -Bellefontaine 43311
(513) 621-2120 .. **Stoner,** Michael B '97 %Strauss & T,LPA -150 E 4th -4th Fl -Cincinnati 45202 **Fx:**241-8259
(330) 643-2082 .. **Stoner,** Tracy D '91 Summit Cnty Dom Rltns Ct -209 S High -Annx -Akron 44308
(513) 732-6740 .. **Stoner-Barone,** Denise '92 -385 North -Batavia 45103
(614) 888-3560 .. **Stonerock,** Bobbie J '93 -1625 Bethel Rd -Columbus 43220
(614) 480-5181 .. **Stopa,** John R '94 Huntington Natl Bank -41 S High -HC1032 -Columbus 43287
(419) 241-6000 .. **Stopar,** Jeffrey M '96 %Eastman & S Ltd -1 Seagate -24th Fl -Bx10032 -Toledo 43699 **Fx:**247-1777
(216) 928-1010 .. **Stoper,** Richard L Jr. '84 (Rotatori BGS&A Co LPA) -526 Superior Av E -800 Leader Bldg -Cleveland 44114 **Fx:**928-1007
(937) 223-1130 .. **Storar,** Andrew C '81 Pickrel S&E -40 N Main -2700 Kettering Twr -Dayton 45423 **Fx:**223-0339
(614) 249-9001 .. **Storck,** Gail L '99 Nationwide Ins Co -2 Nationwide Plz -Ste 810 -Columbus 43215
(330) 263-9011 .. **Storck,** Jason '03 Cntr for Restorative Justice -201 Lbrty -Ste 3 -Wooster 44691
(330) 896-6250 .. **Storey,** Harlan G '79 Cornerstone Capital Advsrs -1507 Boettler Rd -Ste G -Bx769 -Green 44232
(614) 885-2066 .. **Storey,** Robert '80 -737 Enterprise Dr -Westerville 43081
(216) 771-5588 .. **Storie,** Lloyd F Jr. '73 Rosner & Assoc,LLC -812 Huron Rd -Ste 601 Caxton Bldg -Cleveland 44115 **Fx:**771-5894
(440) 593-6120 .. **Storm,** Laverne Frederick '93 (LF Storm Co,LPA) -308 Main -Conneaut 44030 **Fx:**593-4708
(440) 593-6120 .. **Storm,** Mary E '91 (LF Storm Co,LPA) -308 Main -Conneaut 44030 **Fx:**593-4708
(360) 257-6718 .. **Stormer,** Ryan '03 US Navy-JAGC -3530 N Longley Blvd -Oak Harbor, WA 98277
(614) 249-9086 .. **Storts,** Mark E '04 Nationwide Insurance -One Nationwide Plz -Columbus 43215
Story, Garlinn H '80 -Bx5576 -Cincinnati 45201
(740) 992-6371 .. **Story,** Patrick R '91 -117 W 2nd -Pomeroy 45769
(740) 992-6624 .. **Story,** Steven L '79 -236 W 2nd -Pomeroy 45769
(216) 696-2040 .. **Stotter,** Robert H '73 (Stotter & K Co,LPA) -75 Pub Sq -Ste 1200 -Cleveland 44113 **Fx:**696-2164
Stottner, Joseph L '03 -14615 Alger Rd -Cleveland 44111
(419) 228-8989 .. **Stotts,** Kevin J '98 %Kilco Title Agency -119 N West -Ste 101 -Lima 45801 **Fx:**228-9111
(419) 435-0606 .. **Stotzer,** Jonathan G '83 -111 W Center -Bx309 -Fostoria 44830

(216) 902-8880 ..**Stouffer**, Christine M '00 Ulmer & B,LLP -1300 E 9th
-Cleveland 44114

(419) 472-1900 ..**Stough**, Andrew J '01 Bolotin Co,LPA -4349 Talmadge Rd
-Toledo 43623

(740) 687-5962 ..**Stoughton**, Ronald C Sr. '79 Stoughton Law Ofc -121 N High
-Lancaster 43130

(304) 529-6181 ..**Stout**, Bruce A '95 (Huddleston BBP&C,LLP) -611 3rd Av -Bx2185
-Huntington, WV 25722

(937) 562-5250 ..**Stout**, Cheri L '01 Greene Cnty Pros -61 Greene -Xenia 45385

(740) 773-3660 ..**Stout**, Cherita E '94 -Bx97 -Chillicothe 45601

(513) 791-1673 ..**Stout**, Gregory A '02 %Geygan & G Ltd -8050 Hosbrook Rd
-Ste 107 -Cincinnati 45236

(614) 227-8861 ..**Stout**, Matthew L '99 %Bricker & E LLP -100 S 3rd
-Columbus 43215 **Fx:**227-2390

(937) 222-7600 ..**Stout**, Scott G '82 Chapter 13 Trustee -131 Ludlow -Ste 900
-Dayton 45402

(614) 752-1769 ..**Stout**, Thomas A '77 OH Dept Rehab & Correction -1050 Fwy Dr N
-Columbus 43229

Stout, William A Jr. '81 -2648 Lytham Ct -Cincinnati 45233

(614) 221-8500 ..**Stovall**, Richard K '85 (Allen K&S LLP) -21 W Broad -Ste 400
-Columbus 43215

(614) 487-4464 ..**Stover**, Stephan W '75 OH State Bar Assoc -1700 Lk Shr Dr
-Columbus 43204

(614) 792-5555 ..**Stovsky**, Carol G '94 (Standley Law Grp LLP) -495 Metro Pl S -Ste
210 -Dublin 43017 **Fx:**792-5536

(216) 931-6000 ..**Stovsky**, Michael D '91 (Ulmer & B LLP) -1300 E 9th
-Ste 900 Penton Media Bldg -Cleveland 44114 **Fx:**931-6001

(216) 875-3000 ..**Stovsky**, Richard P '83 (PricewaterhouseCoopers LLP)
-200 Pub Sq -27th Fl -Cleveland 44114

(216) 621-0040 ..**Strachan Miller Olender & Roessler Co LPA** -925 Euclid Av
-Ste 1940 -Cleveland 44115

(216) 696-8440 ..**Strachan**, Shannon C '89 -16712 Edgewtr Dr -Lakewood 44107

(216) 621-0040 ..**Strachan**, William R '72 (Strachan MO&R Co LPA) -925 Euclid Av
-Ste 1940 -Cleveland 44115

Stracker, Patricia Parker '04 -(Address Unavailable)

(740) 594-3558 ..**Strader**, Rekha S '04 SE OH Lgl Srvcs -1005 E State
-Athens 45701 **Fx:**594-3791

(513) 424-2401 ..**Strady**, Barbara L '91 Casper & C -1 N Main -Bx510
-Middletown 45042 **Fx:**424-0622

(937) 276-3990 ..**Strahorn**, Derrick A '86 -2 Redlands -Dayton 45407 **Fx:**276-3885

(513) 621-2889 ..**Strain**, Charles E '81 -830 Main -Ste 500 -Cincinnati 45202

(216) 443-9000 ..**Strain**, Howard G '98 %Porter WM&A LLP -925 Euclid Av
-Ste 1700 -Cleveland 44115 **Fx:**443-9011

(614) 466-7447 ..**Strait**, Anne B '83 Atty Gen -150 E Gay -Columbus 43215

(614) 462-3194 ..**Strait**, David L '81 Franklin Cnty Pub Def -373 S High -12th Fl
-Columbus 43215

(440) 329-5246 ..**Strait**, Gerald E '78 Lorain Cnty Juv Ct -226 Middle Av -5th Fl
-Elyria 44035

(216) 941-5566 ..**Straka**, Joseph J '92 (Morscher & S) -11711 Lorain Av -Ste 56
-Cleveland 44111

(216) 524-7499 ..**Stralka**, Gregory T '87 -5005 Rockside Rd -Ste 600
-Cleveland 44131

(513) 424-1660 ..**Strand**, Sheldon A '75 -1081 N Univ Blvd -Ste B
-Middletown 45042

(216) 592-5000 ..**Strang**, Carter E '84 (Tucker E&W LLP) -925 Euclid Av
-1150 Huntngtn Bldg -Cleveland 44115 **Fx:**592-5009

(614) 242-4242 ..**Stranges**, Jodelle N '01 Decker VSL&V Co LPA -620 E Broad
-Columbus 43215 **Fx:**242-4243

(513) 651-6800 ..**Strangfeld**, William C '84 (Frost BT LLC) -201 E 5th
-2200 PNC Ctr -Cincinnati 45202 **Fx:**651-6981

(216) 692-1172 ..**Stranke**, Terry L '78 -18975 Villavw -Ste 8 -Cleveland 44119

Strapp, Erin E '04 -(Address Unavailable)

(937) 653-8200 ..**Strapp**, Robert M '76 -112 E Court -Bx177 -Urbana 43078
Fx:653-8876

(330) 744-5211 ..**Strasfeld**, Stuart A '77 (Roth BRS&L,LPA) -100 Fed Plz E
-Ste 600 -Youngstown 44503 **Fx:**744-3184

(513) 352-6725 ..**Strasser**, JoAnn M '94 (Thompson H LLP) -312 Walnut -14th Fl
-Cincinnati 45202 **Fx:**241-4771

(513) 723-2889 ..**Strasser**, Peter J '74 -200 E Main -Batavia 45103

(614) 847-9843 ..**Strasser**, Thomas F '84 (T Strasser Co,LPA) -Bx163263
-Columbus 43216

(216) 297-7000 ..**Strassfeld**, Anne F '91 Cleveland Clinic Fndtn -1950 Richmond Rd
-TR-38 -Cleveland 44124

(440) 838-8800 ..**Strassman**, Carol D '80 Millisor & N Co,LPA -9150 S Hills Blvd
-Ste 300 -Cleveland 44147 **Fx:**838-8805

(330) 740-2330 ..**Stratford**, Linette M '90 Mahoning Cnty Pros -21 W Boardman
-6th Fl -Youngstown 44503 **Fx:**740-2008

(216) 586-3939 ..**Stratford**, Tracy K '98 %Jones D -901 Lakeside Av
-Cleveland 44114 **Fx:**579-0212

(513) 929-3400 ..**Stratigeas**, Eleni V '01 %Baker & H LLP -312 Walnut -Ste 3200
-Cincinnati 45202 **Fx:**929-0303

(216) 577-5021 ..**Stratman**, John W '84 -2540 N Moreland Blvd -#306
-Shaker Heights 44120

(614) 539-6550 ..**Stratman**, Michelle D '03 Buckeye Ranch -5665 Hoove Rd
-Grove City 43123

(330) 535-4191 ..**Strattan**, Sara E '76 %Cmmnty Lgl Aid Srvcs,Inc -265 S Main
-3rd Fl -Akron 44308 **Fx:**535-0728

(330) 937-1367 ..**Stratton**, Robert B '92 Marsh,Inc -200 Pub Sq -Ste 1100
-Cleveland 44114

(615) 902-0311 ..**Stratton**, Robert H '85 -4811 Lebanon Rd -Hermitage, TN 37076
Fx:902-0413

(419) 246-5757 ..**Straub**, Jessica Wilson '03 %Anspach M&N,LLP -300 Mad Av
-Ste 1600 -Toledo 43604 **Fx:**321-6979

(419) 241-9000 ..**Straub**, John L '70 (Shumaker L&K,LLP) -1000 Jackson
-Toledo 43624 **Fx:**241-6894

(216) 586-3939 ..**Strauch**, John L '64 (Jones D) -901 Lakeside Av -Cleveland 44114
Fx:579-0212

(513) 863-5888 ..**Straus**, Stephen M '78 -633 High -Ste 201 -Hamilton 45011

(513) 852-3497 ..**Straus**, Thomas J '78 Atty Gen -441 Vine -1600 Carew Twr
-Cincinnati 45202 **Fx:**852-3484

(740) 283-1966 ..**Straus**, Thomas R '78 Jefferson Cnty Pros -16001 State Route 7
-Steubenville 43952

(419) 784-3700 ..**Strausbaugh**, Erin S '02 Strausbaugh Law Ofc -607 W 3rd
-Defiance 43512

(419) 784-3700 ..**Strausbaugh**, Jeffrey A '86 Defiance Cnty Pros -607 W 3rd
-Defiance 43512 **Fx:**782-0594

(614) 464-6400 ..**Strause**, Edgar A III '54 OfCnsl Vorys SS&P LLP -52 E Gay
-Bx1008 -Columbus 43216 **Fx:**464-6350

(614) 462-5048 ..**Strause**, Catherine L '00 %Schottenstein Z&D -250 West
-Bx165020 -Columbus 43216 **Fx:**462-5135

(216) 621-0200 ..**Strauss**, David J '67 (Baker & H LLP) -1900 E 9th -Ste 3200
-Cleveland 44114 **Fx:**696-0740

(513) 946-3511 ..**Strauss**, Gordon M '75 Hamilton Cnty Probate Ct -230 E 9th
-10th Fl -Cincinnati 45202 **Fx:**946-3626

(216) 736-7234 ..**Strauss**, Marc I '86 OfCnsl Kohrman J&K PLL -1375 E 9th
-One Cleve Ctr 20th Fl -Cleveland 44114 **Fx:**621-6536

(419) 472-9041 ..**Strauss**, Robert D '92 %Koder & S -3361 Exec Pkwy -Ste 101
-Toledo 43606

(513) 768-8900 ..**Strauss**, Stephen D '66 -414 Walnut -Ste 508 -Cincinnati 45202

(513) 621-2120 ..**Strauss & Troy, LPA** -150 E 4th -4th Fl -Cincinnati 45202
Fx:241-8259

(513) 621-2120 ..**Strauss**, William V Jr. '67 Strauss & T,LPA -150 E 4th -4th Fl
-Cincinnati 45202 **Fx:**241-8259

(614) 221-8401 ..**Strautz**, Elizabeth M '97 %Kennedy & C,LPA -30 Spruce -3rd Fl
-Columbus 43215 **Fx:**222-4799

(847) 885-2250 ..**Straw**, Gerald K '79 Global Aerospace,Inc -1721 Moon Lk Blvd
-Ste 420 -Hoffman Estates, IL 60194 **Fx:**885-2249

(330) 456-8341 ..**Strawn**, James R '76 (Black MS&A,LPA) -220 Market Av S
-Ste 1000 -Canton 44702 **Fx:**456-5756

(614) 332-1632 ..**Strawser**, Eric J '00 -1654 Brice Rd -Reynoldsburg 43068

(614) 438-4962 ..**Strayer**, Brian S '90 Mettler-Toledo,Inc -1900 Polaris Pkwy
-Columbus 43240

(614) 228-4480 ..**Strayer**, Herbert N Jr. '03 %Rauser & Assoc -145 N High
-Columbus 43215

(614) 880-1907 ..**Strayer**, Susan L '96 MindLeaders.com, Inc -851 W 3rd Av -Bldg 3
-Columbus 43212

(614) 224-0200 ..**Streb**, Joseph S '84 -736 Neil Av -Columbus 43215

(330) 499-6000 ..**Streb**, Jude B '99 %Baker DBW&M -400 S Main -Canton 44720
Fx:449-6423

(513) 683-7539 ..**Street**, Gary D '83 -244 Shadow Wood Ct -Loveland 45140

(740) 775-3300 ..**Street**, John S Jr. '54 (Phillips & S) -37 N Paint -Chillicothe 45601

(440) 895-5000 ..**Streeter**, David A Jr. '01 (Schill & S,LLC) -1250 Linda -Ste 201
-Rocky River 44116 **Fx:**730-3130

(740) 349-6169 ..**Strefelt**, Christopher A '94 Licking Cnty Pros -20 S 2nd -4th Fl
-Newark 43055

(740) 364-3537 ..**Strefelt**, Kari A '94 State Farm Ins Co -1440 Granvll Rd
-Newark 43055

Strehl, Christine E '04 -(Address Unavailable)

(216) 622-8200 ..**Streicher**, James F '66 (Calfee H&G LLP) -800 Superior Av
-Ste 1400 -Cleveland 44114 **Fx:**241-0816

(614) 466-6750 ..**Strelou**, Karen L '84 OH Dept Taxation -30 E Broad -22nd Fl
-Columbus 43215

Stremski, Janet R '93 -3875 Poplar Bend Dr -Columbus 43204

(937) 644-9125 ..**Streng**, Michael J '00 %Cannizzaro FB&J -302 S Main
-Marysville 43040 **Fx:**644-0754

(513) 745-0713 ..**Stretcher**, Brian N '98 -10999 Reed Hartman Hwy -Ste 326
-Cincinnati 45242 **Fx:**745-0715

(216) 443-9000 ..**Streza**, Ralph '82 (Porter WM&A LLP) -925 Euclid Av -Ste 1700
-Cleveland 44115 **Fx:**443-9011

(513) 946-3000 ..**Stricker**, George Jr. '73 Hamilton Cnty Pros -230 E 9th
-Cincinnati 45202 **Fx:**946-3017

(407) 691-5600 ..**Strickland**, Joshua J '03 Noram Equities,Ltd -875 Cncrs Parking S
-Ste 1500 -Maitland, FL 32751

(419) 499-3000 ..**Strickler**, Randal L '86 (RL Strickler Co,LPA) -16 W Chruch
-Bx543 -Milan 44846

(513) 977-4211 ..**Stridsberg**, Roger C '49 -917 Main -Ste 400 -Cincinnati 45202

(216) 566-5733 ..**Striefsky**, Linda A '77 (Thompson H LLP) -127 Pub Sq
-3900 Key Ctr -Cleveland 44114 **Fx:**566-5800

(614) 466-2872 ..**Strigari**, Frank M '04 %Atty Gen -30 E Broad -Columbus 43215
Fx:728-7582

(513) 946-3700 ..**Strigari**, Louis F '73 Hamilton Cnty Pub Def -230 E 9th -3rd Fl
-Cincinnati 45202 **Fx:**946-3707

(937) 325-1588 ..**Strileckyj**, Wolodymyr '79 (Juergens W&S) -200 N Fountain Av
-Springfield 45504

(216) 621-0200 ..**Strimbu**, Victor Jr. '60 (Baker & H LLP) -1900 E 9th -Ste 3200
-Cleveland 44114 **Fx:**696-0740

(907) 452-1666 ..**Strines**, Joseph G '98 %Borgeson & B,PC -100 Cushman
-Ste 311 -Fairbanks, AK 99701

(216) 464-7986 ..**String**, Cynthia M '91 -3175 Northwood Dr -Pepper Pike 44124

(440) 247-6100 ..**String**, Kevin L '91 (KL String Co,LPA) -23 N Franklin -Ste 11
-Chagrin Falls 44022

(216) 622-8214 ..**Stringer**, Anthony F '99 %Calfee H&G LLP -800 Superior Av
-Ste 1400 -Cleveland 44114 **Fx:**241-0816

(440) 934-7676 ..**Stringer**, Anthony R '67 (Stringer S&G) -36815 Detroit Rd
-Avon 44011

(440) 934-7676 ..**Stringer**, Daniel P '63 (Stringer S&G) -36815 Detroit Rd -Avon
44011

(440) 934-7676 ..**Stringer Stringer & Gasior** -36815 Detroit Rd -Avon 44011

(440) 934-7676 ..**Stringer**, Thomas C '03 %Stringer S&G -36815 Detroit Rd
-Avon 44011

(614) 228-6345 ..**Strip**, Asriel C '60 (Strip HLM&T Co LPA) -575 S 3rd
-Columbus 43215 **Fx:**228-6369

(614) 228-6345 ..**Strip Hoppers Leithart McGrath & Terlecky Co LPA** -575 S 3rd
-Columbus 43215 **Fx:**228-6369

(313) 884-2317 ..**Stroad**, Charles S '65 -431 Lex Rd -Grosse Pointe
Farms, MI 48236

(614) 755-2424 ..**Strobl**, Derrick B '93 Conservatory of Piano -209 N Hmltn Rd
-Whitehall 43213

(513) 759-4403 ..**Strobl**, Lori A '01 -9753 Crescent Park Dr -West Chester 45069
Fx:759-6150

(419) 738-4417 ..**Stroebel**, George E '42 -108 W Auglaize -Wapakoneta 45895

(216) 443-6632 ..**Stroh**, Gary E '92 Cuyahoga Cnty Adult Probation Dept
-1200 Ontario -7th Fl -Cleveland 44113

(614) 882-2327 ..**Stroh**, Kyle J '99 Metz & B -33 E Schrock Rd -Westerville 43081

(215) 299-4342 ..**Stroh**, Robert M '84 %Swartz C LLC -1601 Market -34th Fl
-Philadelphia, PA 19103 **Fx:**299-4301

(216) 529-0300 ..**Stroh**, Thomas M '79 -18123 Sloane Av -Lakewood 44107

(216) 433-6679 ..**Strohbehn,** Karl '00 NASA -21000 Brookpart Rd -Mail Stop 501-9 -Cleveland 44135

(614) 228-0207 ..**Strohm,** Robin L '04 %CT Williams -555 S Front -Ste 320 -Columbus 43215 Fx:228-3102

(972) 506-9311 ..**Strohmann,** LeeAnne R '02 -116 St James -Irving, TX 75063

(216) 622-8200 ..**Strom,** Susan '90 OfCnsl Calfee H&G LLP -800 Superior Av -Ste 1400 -Cleveland 44114 Fx:241-0816

(202) 565-6730 ..**Strommen,** Gayle E '91 Bd of Vets Appls -811 VT Av NW -Washington, DC 20420

(216) 621-0200 ..**Stronczer,** Michelle P '96 %Baker & H LLP -1900 E 9th -Ste 3200 -Cleveland 44114 Fx:696-0740

(419) 885-8877 ..**Strong,** Dennis P '80 -5600 Monroe -Bldg B,Ste 202 -Sylvania 43560

(513) 241-2090 ..**Strong,** Michael H '92 -917 Main -2nd Fl -Cincinnati 45202

(330) 376-2700 ..**Strong,** Richard R '80 (Roetzel & A,LPA) -222 S Main -Akron 44308 Fx:376-4577

(937) 927-0154 ..**Stroop,** Richele M '96 Stroop Law Ofc -2822 US 62 -Hillsboro 45133

(614) 644-3037 ..**Stroup,** Catherine A '89 EPA -122 S Front -Bx1049 -Columbus 43216

(937) 323-1010 ..**Strozdas,** Jerome M '80 (Strozdas & P LLP) -20 S Limestone -Ste 330 -Springfield 45502 Fx:323-1953

(937) 323-1010 ..**Strozdas & Pedraza LLP** -20 S Limestone -Ste 330 -Springfield 45502 Fx:323-1953

(513) 621-4775 ..**Strubbe,** William B '79 (W Strubbe & Assoc) -1014 Vine -Ste 1525 -Cincinnati 45202

(614) 890-2900 ..**Struble,** Carla I '84 -855 S Sunbury Rd -Westerville 43081

(816) 356-8400 ..**Strugalski,** Greg '85 BHA Tech,Inc -8800 E 63rd -Kansas City, MO 64133

(216) 771-5777 ..**Struger,** Marlene S '80 -15203 Detroit Av -Cleveland 44107

(330) 493-9901 ..**Struhar,** Steven A '84 %Lonas M&T -1810 36th NW -Canton 44709 Fx:493-9338

(216) 348-4487 ..**Strunk,** Wayne E '80 Cuyahoga Cnty Cmn Pleas Ct -2163 E 22nd -Cleveland 44115

(419) 241-1200 ..**Strup,** David P '86 Cooper & W,LPA -900 Adams -Toledo 43624 Fx:242-5675

(517) 684-4111 ..**Stryker,** Gordon J '98 Maximus -2343 Delta Rd -Bay City, MI 48706

(304) 232-7333 ..**Stryker,** Kevin A '83 Legg Mason Wood Walker,Inc -1233 Main -Ste 1000 -Wheeling, WV 26003

(330) 633-7373 ..**Strzala-Peters,** Sheri A '91 (Williger & P) -323C S Main -Bx368 -Munroe Falls 44262 Fx:633-6353

(419) 213-4745 ..**Strzesynski,** Michelle A '96 Lucas Co Common Pleas Ct -700 Adams -Cnty Cthse -Toledo 43624

(419) 255-7300 ..**Strzyinski,** Kathy J '96 %Dzienny & Assoc,LPA -500 Mad Av -Ste 200 -Toledo 43604

(440) 930-2600 ..**Stuart,** Richard P '90 -158-A Lear Rd -Avon Lake 44012

(513) 336-2541 ..**Stubbers,** Edward L '95 Cnsl Anthem BCBS -4361 Irwin Simpson Rd -Mail # MB1-220 -Mason 45040

(740) 452-8484 ..**Stubbins,** Brent A '78 Stubbins W&E Co LPA -59 N 4th -Bx488 -Zanesville 43702

(740) 452-8484 ..**Stubbins,** James B '43 OfCnsl Stubbins W&E Co LPA -59 N 4th -Bx488 -Zanesville 43702

(740) 452-8484 ..**Stubbins,** Mark W '83 Stubbins W&E Co LPA -59 N 4th -Bx488 -Zanesville 43702

(740) 452-8484 ..**Stubbins Watson & Erhard Co LPA** -59 N 4th -Bx488 -Zanesville 43702

(509) 372-0479 ..**Stubblebine,** Scott D '78 SrCnsl US Dept of Energy -Ofc of River Prtctn -MSIN H6-60 -Bx450 -Richland, WA 99352 Fx:372-2784

(513) 241-4722 ..**Stubbs,** Matthew E '96 %Montgomery R&J,LPA -36 E 7th -Ste 2100 -Cincinnati 45202 Fx:241-8715

(740) 349-6575 ..**Stubbs,** SaKeya M '99 Licking Cnty CSEA -65 E Main -Bx338 -Newark 43058

(662) 680-3148 ..**Stuber,** John D '92 Comm ElderCare Srvcs, LLC -2844 Traceland Dr -Bx3667 -Tupelo, MS 38803

(330) 297-3850 ..**Stuck,** Michele A '94 Portage Cnty Pros -466 S Chestnut -Ravenna 44266

(440) 322-5441 ..**Stucke,** Agnes C '02 %Lessing W&R Ltd -374 Broad -Ste A -Elyria 44035

(419) 249-7900 ..**Stuckey,** David W '75 (Robison C&O) -Four SeaGate -9th Fl -Toledo 43604 Fx:249-7911

(614) 324-5929 ..**Stuckey,** Kent D '82 -919 Old Henderson Rd -Columbus 43220

(419) 335-2015 ..**Stuckey,** Kurt A '87 Cnty Hlth Ctr -725 S Shoop Av -Wauseon 43567

(419) 627-7723 ..**Stuckey,** Mark A '85 Erie Cnty Cmn Pleas Ct -323 Columbus Av -4th Fl -Sandusky 44870

(312) 715-5773 ..**Stucki,** Hans U '74 (Holland & K LLP) -131 S Dearborn -30th Fl -Chicago, IL 60603 Fx:578-6666

(614) 222-8686 ..**Stucko,** James K Jr. '93 Scott S&W LLP -50 W Broad -2500 LeVeque Twr -Columbus 43215 Fx:222-8688

(440) 338-1718 ..**Studen,** Greg E '77 -7675 Squires Ln -Novelty 44072

(419) 774-5676 ..**Studenmund,** John D '93 Richland Cnty Pros -38 S Park -2nd Fl -Mansfield 44902 Fx:774-5589

Studeny, Nathan F '04 -(Address Unavailable)

(614) 466-2766 ..**Studer,** Raymond J '76 Atty Gen -30 E Broad -Columbus 43215 Fx:644-1926

(216) 623-2004 ..**Studly,** Paul A '70 USTreasury-IRS -1375 E 9th -Ste 815 -Cleveland 44114 Fx:522-7910

(216) 583-2363 ..**Studnicha,** Cynthia H '92 Ernst & Young,LLP -1000 Skylight Ofc Twr -Cleveland 44113

(216) 383-2890 ..**Stueber,** Frederick G '82 Lincoln Electric -22801 St Clair Av -Cleveland 44117

(216) 621-8484 ..**Stueber,** Jennifer L '96 %Climaco LPW&G Co,LPA -1228 Euclid Av -Ste 900 Halle Bldg -Cleveland 44115 Fx:771-1632

(216) 269-0803 ..**Stuehr,** Eric W '03 -3820 Monticello Blvd -Cleveland 44121

(513) 932-7444 ..**Stueve,** Jeffrey W '00 WG Fowler -12 W South -Lebanon 45036

(937) 223-3277 ..**Stueve,** Jennifer L '02 %Bieser G&L LLP -6 N Main -400 Natl City Ctr -Dayton 45402 Fx:223-6339

(216) 586-3939 ..**Stuhan,** Richard G '86 (Jones D) -901 Lakeside Av -Cleveland 44114 Fx:579-0212

(513) 807-7510 ..**Stuhlbarg,** Steven F '92 -7809 Shadowhill Way -Cincinnati 45242 Fx:891-0929

(216) 241-5310 ..**Stuhldreher,** George W '51 OfCnsl Gallagher SF&N -1501 Euclid Av -6th Fl -Cleveland 44115 Fx:241-1608

(304) 720-2352 ..**Stuhr,** Richard W '78 (Colombo & S,PLLC) -1206 E VA -Ste 200 -Charleston, WV 25301

(937) 438-6848 ..**Stukenborg,** Charlene L '95 %Stevens & S LLP -7019 Corp Way -Dayton 45459

(937) 222-7777 ..**Stukey,** Linda S '78 Stukey & Assoc -333 W 1st -Ste 400 -Dayton 45402 Fx:222-7772

(740) 363-7182 ..**Stults,** Loran K '01 Thomas & F Co,LPA -163 N Sandusky -Ste 103 -Delaware 43015

(614) 487-8210 ..**Stumler,** Rebecca J '90 -1500 W 3rd Av -Ste 127 -Grandview 43212 Fx:487-8212

(419) 241-6000 ..**Stump,** Alexandra M '03 %Eastman & S Ltd -1 Seagate -24th Fl -Bx10032 -Toledo 43699 Fx:247-1777

(216) 479-6100 ..**Stump,** Kenneth A '94 Vorys SS&P LLP -1375 E 9th -Ste 2100 One Cleve Ctr -Cleveland 44114 Fx:479-6060

(937) 562-5249 ..**Stump,** Kimberly Metzler '96 Green Cnty Domestic Relations Div -45 N Detroit -Basement -Xenia 45385 Fx:562-5139

(937) 226-1200 ..**Stump,** Randall L '84 (Bogin P&B) -131 N Ludlow -1200 Talbot Twr -Dayton 45402

(440) 930-4001 ..**Stumphauzer,** Kenneth S '76 (Baumgartner & O) -5455 Detroit Rd (Rte 254) -Sheffield Village 44054 Fx:934-7205

(305) 582-5923 ..**Stumphauzer,** Ryan '03 US Dst Ct-Sthrn FL -99 NE 4th -Ste 1061 -Miami, FL 33132

(440) 729-3040 ..**Stupica,** Terri L '88 T Stupica Co,LPA -6449 Wilson Mills Rd -Cleveland 44143

(440) 446-0300 ..**Stuplinski,** Linda A '94 -5432 Mayfld Rd -Ste 103 -Lyndhurst 44124

(419) 248-3563 ..**Stupsker,** Charles A '65 -626 Mad Av -Ste 711 -Toledo 43604

(330) 782-3000 ..**Sturgeon,** Edward F '79 -4822 Market -#220 -Youngstown 44512

(304) 342-6000 ..**Sturgeon,** James M Jr. '03 (Pauley CS&V,PLLC) -100 Kanawha Blvd W -Charleston, WV 25302

(419) 241-6000 ..**Sturgeon,** Margaret M '90 (Eastman & S Ltd) -1 Seagate -24th Fl -Bx10032 -Toledo 43699 Fx:247-1777

(614) 228-6131 ..**Sturges,** Scott F '82 (McNamara & M,LLP) -88 E Broad -Ste 1250 -Columbus 43215 Fx:228-6126

(419) 755-4778 ..**Sturgill,** Judith L '85 N Cntrl State Coll -2441 Kenwood Cir -Bx698 -Mansfield 44901

(419) 626-2709 ..**Sturgill,** Russell I '53 -29610 Gleneagles Rd -Unit F -Perrysburg 43551

(216) 475-0725 ..**Sturik,** Mark M '83 -5706 Turney Rd -Ste 307 -Garfield Heights 44125

(614) 365-2700 ..**Sturtz,** Craig A '92 %Squire S&D LLP -41 S High -1300 Huntngtn Ctr -Columbus 43215 Fx:365-2499

(717) 293-5800 ..**Sturtz,** Kenneth H '75 Burham Corp -Bx3205 -Lancaster, PA 17604

Sturtz, Laurence E '67 -8474 Stonewoods Ln -Powell 43065

(419) 241-2777 ..**Stutz,** Barbara J '83 (Bunda S&D,PLL) -One SeaGate -Ste 650 -Toledo 43604 Fx:241-4697

(614) 365-2706 ..**Stutz,** Heather L '04 %Squire S&D LLP -41 S High -1300 Huntngtn Ctr -Columbus 43215 Fx:365-2499

(419) 241-4211 ..**Stutz,** Paul F '56 -520 Mad Av -Ste 964 -Toledo 43604 Fx:241-4212

(330) 264-6115 ..**Stutzman,** Morris '75 (Logee HS&L) -2171-B Eagle Pass -Wooster 44691 Fx:262-5729

(419) 242-3989 ..**Styblo,** Jennifer F '99 -Bx4592 -Toledo 43610

(614) 464-6400 ..**Styduhar,** Robert J '79 (Vorys SS&P LLP) -52 E Gay -Bx1008 -Columbus 43216 Fx:464-6350

(304) 529-2391 ..**Styer,** Bryan L '03 %Campbell WBEM&H -517 9th -Ste 1000 -Huntington, WV 25701

(330) 343-0449 ..**Styer,** Daniel M '94 -114 E High Av -New Philadelphia 44663

(330) 343-0449 ..**Styer,** Ryan D '98 -114 E High Av -New Philadelphia 44663

(614) 365-2700 ..**Stype,** Gregory W '82 (Squire S&D LLP) -41 S High -1300 Huntngtn Ctr -Columbus 43215 Fx:365-2499

(937) 298-7794 ..**Suarez,** Isabel '84 -438 Patterson Rd -Dayton 45419

(513) 983-4194 ..**Suarez,** Joseph P '82 Procter & Gamble Co-Legal -1 Procter & Gamble Plz -Cincinnati 45202

(937) 228-1525 ..**Subashi,** Deborah J '87 Nationwide Mutl Ins-Trail Div -130 W 2nd -Ste 410 -Dayton 45402

(937) 534-0500 ..**Subashi,** Nicholas E '86 (Subashi W&B) -2305 Far Hills Av -Oakwood Bldg -Dayton 45419 Fx:534-0505

(937) 534-0500 ..**Subashi Wildermuth & Ballato** -2305 Far Hills Av -Oakwood Bldg -Dayton 45419 Fx:534-0505

(513) 412-5400 ..**Subit,** Melissa C '99 %Buckley K,LPA -201 E 5th -Ste 1420 -Cincinnati 45202 Fx:412-5401

(614) 464-1880 ..**Subramaniam,** Radha '01 %Schottenstein Legal Srvcs -341 S 3rd -Ste 300 -Columbus 43215 Fx:464-3004

(216) 623-1123 ..**Sucher,** Daniel M '91 (Sindell YG&S,PLL) -55 Pub Sq -Ste 1020 -Cleveland 44113 Fx:623-1124

Suchta, Arthur M '73 -12485 Jerome Rd -Plain City 43064

(513) 639-3924 ..**Suder,** Sean S '04 %Keating M&K PLL -1 E 4th -1400 Provident Twr -Cincinnati 45202 Fx:579-6457

(216) 241-7255 ..**Sudilovsky,** Ariel '93 -2401 Superior Viaduct -Cleveland 44113

(513) 579-1414 ..**Sudman,** Harry S '72 (Schwartz M&R) -441 Vine -Ste 2900 -Cincinnati 45202 Fx:579-1418

Sudyk, Bradford A '96 -(Address Unavailable)

(513) 762-6200 ..**Suffern,** Michael J '93 (Ulmer & B LLP) -600 Vine -Ste 2800 -Cincinnati 45202 Fx:762-6245

(614) 462-3830 ..**Suffron,** Benjamin F III '78 Franklin Cnty Probate Ct -373 S High -22nd Fl -Columbus 43215

(614) 221-3155 ..**Sugar,** Anthony J '91 OfCnsl Bailey C LLC -10 W Broad -Columbus 43215 Fx:221-0479

(614) 761-6078 ..**Sugar,** Joseph A III '94 %Dominion Homes -5501 Frantz Rd -Bx7166 -Dublin 43017

(740) 455-7190 ..**Sugar,** Susan N '92 Muskingum Cnty Cmn Pleas Ct -22 N 5th -Zanesville 43701

(614) 462-5422 ..**Sugarman,** Roger P '75 (Kegler BH&R) -65 E State -Ste 1800 -Columbus 43215 Fx:464-2634

(330) 376-8336 ..**Sugerman,** Irving B '82 Goldman & R,Ltd -11 S Forge -Akron 44304 Fx:376-2522

(216) 371-4306 ..**Sugerman,** Martin A '58 -2381 Charney Rd -University Heights 44118

(614) 462-5476 ..**Suh,** Jean Hinte '96 %Kegler BH&R -65 E State -Ste 1800
-Columbus 43215 Fx:464-2634

(440) 717-9370 ..**Suh,** Luke K '96 -8787 Pnte Dr -Broadview Heights 44147

(330) 744-9007 ..**Suhar,** Andrew W '92 (A Suhar & Assoc) -11 Fed Plz Central
-Ste 1101 -Bx1497 -Youngstown 44501

(330) 744-2161 ..**Suhar,** Kandis W '94 Yngstwn Metro Housing Auth
-131 W Boardman -Youngstown 44503

(614) 449-1200 ..**Suhr,** Robert W '70 -755 S High -Columbus 43206

(513) 333-0014 ..**Suhre,** Joseph B IV '99 -1014 Vine -Ste 1525 -Cincinnati 45202
Fx:333-0032

(937) 427-1367 ..**Suich,** David P '97 %McNamee & M,PLL -2625 Cmmns Blvd
-Beavercreek 45431 **Fx:**427-1369

(440) 543-8868 ..**Suit,** Edward K '67 (Weiner S&C) -17370 Hawksvw Ln -Chagrin
Falls 44023

(440) 395-9729 ..**Sukel,** Christine H '87 Progressive Ins Co -300 N Cmmns Blvd
-OHF 11 -Mayfield Village 44143

(440) 461-5000 ..**Sukel,** Timothy M '85 Progressive Ins Co -6055 Parkland Blvd
-Mayfield Heights 44124

Sukenik, Rosalyn K '79 -18020 S Woodlnd Rd -Cleveland 44120

(614) 462-3194 ..**Sukienik,** Harvey '91 Franklin Cnty Pub Def -373 S High -12th Fl
-Columbus 43215

(419) 755-4869 ..**Sukys,** Paul A '80 N Centrl State Cllg -2441 Kenwood Cir
-284 Bromfld Hall -Mansfield 44901 **Fx:**755-5649

(513) 621-8210 ..**Sulau,** William C '81 (Drew & W Co,LPA) -1 W 4th -Ste 2400
-Cincinnati 45202 **Fx:**621-5444

(419) 243-6281 ..**Sulewski,** James A '87 (Shindler NH&S,LLP) -300 Mad Av
-Ste 1200 -Toledo 43604 **Fx:**243-0129

(440) 356-4165 ..**Sulin,** Alton G '82 Sulin Co -21130 Aberdeen Rd
-Rocky River 44116

(614) 462-4680 ..**Sullivan,** Angela M '02 Franklin Cnty Ct of Common Pleas
-369 S High -Ctrm 6D -Columbus 43215

(937) 640-5030 ..**Sullivan,** Anthony W '93 -130 W 2nd -Ste 2050 -Dayton 45402

(216) 687-1311 ..**Sullivan,** Brian D '94 (Reminger & R) -101 Prospect Av W
-1400 Mdlnd Bldg -Cleveland 44115 **Fx:**687-1841

(513) 977-8200 ..**Sullivan,** Brian S '88 (Dinsmore & S LLP) -255 E 5th -Ste 1900
-Cincinnati 45202 **Fx:**977-8141

(614) 466-6541 ..**Sullivan,** Christine A '79 Industrial Commssn of OH -30 W Spring
-9th Fl -Columbus 43215 **Fx:**752-8785

Sullivan, Claire '03 -(Address Unavailable)

(614) 460-4689 ..**Sullivan,** Cynthia L '97 Columbia Gas of OH,Inc -200 Civic Ctr Dr
-Columbus 43215

(419) 215-3194 ..**Sullivan,** Daniel J '02 DJ Sullivan LLC -6020 Bancroft -Bx351088
-Toledo 43635 **Fx:**885-0076

(419) 755-5376 ..**Sullivan,** Daniel W '87 GM Corp -2525 W 4th -Mansfield 44906

(513) 977-8200 ..**Sullivan,** David S '00 %Dinsmore & S LLP -255 E 5th -Ste 1900
-Cincinnati 45202 **Fx:**977-8141

(513) 522-5575 ..**Sullivan,** James P '77 (Sullivan & S) -7184 Pippin Rd
-Cincinnati 45239

(614) 777-8170 ..**Sullivan,** James T '78 (Sullivan Law Ofc) -4615 Leap Ct
-Hilliard 43026

(216) 621-0200 ..**Sullivan,** John E '84 (Baker & H LLP) -1900 E 9th -Ste 3200
-Cleveland 44114 **Fx:**696-0740

(216) 241-8111 ..**Sullivan,** John E III '86 (Sullivan & S Ltd) -815 Superior Av E
-Ste 2016 -Cleveland 44114

(513) 522-5575 ..**Sullivan,** John J '51 (Sullivan & S) -7184 Pippin Rd
-Cincinnati 45239

(614) 365-2700 ..**Sullivan,** Johnathan E '00 %Squire S&D LLP -41 S High
-1300 Huntngtn Ctr -Columbus 43215 **Fx:**365-2499

(216) 241-8111 ..**Sullivan,** Julia R '86 (Sullivan & S Ltd) -815 Superior Av E
-Ste 2016 -Cleveland 44114

(216) 622-8200 ..**Sullivan,** K James '01 %Calfee H&G LLP -800 Superior Av
-Ste 1400 -Cleveland 44114 **Fx:**241-0816

(216) 491-7158 ..**Sullivan,** Kerry H '88 Southside Radiology,Inc
-4110 Warrensvll Ctr Rd -Warrensville Heights 44122

(513) 983-9787 ..**Sullivan,** Lisa A '93 Procter & Gamble Co -1 Procter & Gamble Plz
-Cincinnati 45202

(216) 566-9909 ..**Sullivan,** Mark E '82 -75 Pub Square -Ste #1016
-Cleveland 44113

(216) 479-8500 ..**Sullivan,** Martha S '94 %Squire S&D LLP -127 Pub Sq
-4900 Key Twr -Cleveland 44114 **Fx:**479-8780

(419) 213-4758 ..**Sullivan,** Mary A '89 6th Dist Ct of Appls -800 Jackson
-Toledo 43624

(440) 395-3769 ..**Sullivan,** Mary B '01 Progressive Insurance Co
-6300 Wilson Mills Rd -N72 -Mayfield Village 44143

(216) 522-3530 ..**Sullivan,** Mary C '89 US DVA -1240 E 9th -Cleveland 44199

(513) 621-3394 ..**Sullivan,** Mary W '80 (Peck S&W,LLP) -201 E 5th -Ste 900
-Cincinnati 45202 **Fx:**621-3813

(614) 224-8374 ..**Sullivan,** Megan L '03 %Legal Aid -40 W Gay -Columbus 43215

(216) 443-7800 ..**Sullivan,** Michael A '95 Cuyahoga Cnty Pros -1200 Ontario -8th Fl
-Cleveland 44113 **Fx:**698-2270

(614) 227-2337 ..**Sullivan,** Michael F '67 (Bricker & E LLP) -100 S 3rd
-Columbus 43215 **Fx:**227-2390

(419) 289-3800 ..**Sullivan,** Michael P '87 -10 E Main -Ashland 44805

(419) 535-0075 ..**Sullivan,** Michelle T '99 %Allotta F&W Co,LPA
-2222 Centennial Rd -Toledo 43617 **Fx:**535-1935

Sullivan, Pamela J '04 -(Address Unavailable)

(216) 875-6530 ..**Sullivan,** Patrick F '87 Parkwood Corp -2829 Euclid Av
-Cleveland 44115

Sullivan, Sean '03 -500 Sewall -Bldg 150 -Brunswick, ME 04011

(614) 466-7447 ..**Sullivan,** Susan M '77 Atty Gen -150 E Gay -Columbus 43215

(216) 443-4022 ..**Sullivan,** Terrence C '89 US Postal Inspection Srvc -2400 Orange
Av -Bx5726 -Cleveland 44101

(216) 781-1452 ..**Sullivan,** Terrence P '86 %Friel & S -526 Superior Av E
-448 Leader Bldg -Cleveland 44114

(937) 222-2424 ..**Sullivan,** Thomas P '04 %Freund F&A -1 S Main -Ste 1800
-Dayton 45402 **Fx:**222-5369

(513) 381-2838 ..**Sullivan,** Timothy C '85 (Taft S&H LLP) -425 Walnut -Ste 1800
-Cincinnati 45202 **Fx:**381-0205

(440) 572-1540 ..**Sullivan,** Timothy M '93 Hy-Level Ind Inc -15400 Foltz Indstrl Pkwy
-Bx368015 -Strongsville 44136

(513) 474-5020 ..**Sullivan,** Wendall '50 -8006 Beechmont Av -Cincinnati 45255

(614) 443-3930 ..**Sully,** Ira B '74 -844 S Front -Columbus 43206

(740) 774-6320 ..**Sulzer,** Joseph P '82 -38 S Paint -Chillicothe 45601

(614) 464-6400 ..**Sumi,** Christopher E '02 %Vorys SS&P LLP -52 E Gay -Bx1008
-Columbus 43216 **Fx:**464-6350

(616) 787-6000 ..**Sumihiro,** Gary Kan '82 Amway Corp -7575 Fulton -MC 78-1X
-Ada, MI 49355

(859) 491-4093 ..**Summe,** Gabrielle A '00 Kenton Cnty Atty -333 Scott -Ste 300
-Covington, KY 41011

(513) 241-2324 ..**Summe,** Kurt A '91 (Wood H&E LLP) -441 Vine -Ste 2700
-Cincinnati 45202 **Fx:**421-7269

(614) 365-2700 ..**Summer,** Fred A '74 Cnsl Squire S&D LLP -41 S High
-1300 Huntngtn Ctr -Columbus 43215 **Fx:**365-2499

(312) 407-0700 ..**Summerhill,** Michael J '98 %Skadden ASM&F LLP
-333 W Wacker Dr -Ste 2100 -Chicago, IL 60606 **Fx:**407-0411

(513) 522-7700 ..**Summers,** Cynthia L '81 -800 Compton Rd -Unit 37A
-Cincinnati 45231

(419) 238-1010 ..**Summers,** Jeffrey A '82 Cntrl Mutual Ins Co -800 S Wshngtn
-Van Wert 45891 **Fx:**238-7626

(513) 932-3221 ..**Summers,** Jillora H '83 -730 E Main -Bx781 -Lebanon 45036

(216) 479-8500 ..**Summers,** Kelly L '02 %Squire S&D LLP -127 Pub Sq
-4900 Key Twr -Cleveland 44114 **Fx:**479-8780

(216) 931-6000 ..**Summers,** Linda DelaCourt '96 %Ulmer & B LLP -1300 E 9th
-Ste 900 Penton Media Bldg -Cleveland 44114 **Fx:**931-6001

(216) 696-9300 ..**Summers,** Lisa D '87 -526 Superior Av E -Ste 440 Leader Bldg
-Cleveland 44114

(216) 436-3449 ..**Summers,** Lorraine A '92 IMG -One Erievw Plz -Ste 1300
-Cleveland 44114

(513) 424-2401 ..**Summers,** Mark A '85 (Casper & C) -1 N Main -Bx510
-Middletown 45042 **Fx:**424-0622

(330) 867-6600 ..**Summers,** Patrick M '88 %Glinsek & H -88 S Portage Path
-Ste 301 -Akron 44303 **Fx:**867-9720

(216) 348-5400 ..**Summers,** Richard D '98 %McDonald H Co,LPA
-600 Superior Av E -Ste 2100 -Cleveland 44114 **Fx:**348-5474

(216) 292-4742 ..**Summers,** Richard M '80 -29400 Harvard Rd -Beachwood 44122

(513) 794-6287 ..**Summers,** Stuart G '68 OH Natl Finl Srvcs -Bx237 -Cincinnati
45201

(216) 791-3137 ..**Summers,** Sylvester Jr. '89 -7804 Linvwood Av -Cleveland 44103

(216) 591-0727 ..**Summers & Vargas Co,LPA** -23240 Chagrin Blvd -Ste 525
-Cleveland 44122 **Fx:**591-0740

(304) 420-0975 ..**Summers,** William B '03 -3301 Dudley Av -Parkersburg, WV
26104

(216) 591-0727 ..**Summers,** William L '69 (Summers & V Co,LPA)
-23240 Chagrin Blvd -Ste 525 -Cleveland 44122 **Fx:**591-0740

(610) 292-2572 ..**Sumner,** David W '86 -618 Swede -Norristown, PA 19401
Fx:292-4645

(614) 645-7385 ..**Sumner,** John H '80 City Atty -90 W Broad -Columbus 43215

(216) 521-8080 ..**Sumpter,** Chester L '85 (C Sumpter & Assoc,LLC)
-16927 Detroit Av -Ste 4 -Lakewood 44107

(614) 227-2300 ..**Sun,** Chuan '04 %Bricker & E LLP -100 S 3rd -Columbus 43215
Fx:227-2390

(212) 678-3258 ..**Sun,** Jeffrey C '98 Columbia Univ/Teachers Cllg -525 W 120th
-Bx 175 -New York, NY 10027

(614) 228-1200 ..**Sunbury,** Gerald T '74 (Sunbury & Y) -495 S High
-Columbus 43215

(614) 228-3822 ..**Sundberg & Fesenmyer,LLC** -5 E Long -Ste 609
-Columbus 43215 **Fx:**228-3882

(614) 228-3822 ..**Sundberg,** Steven D '99 (Sundberg & F,LLC) -5 E Long -Ste 609
-Columbus 43215 **Fx:**228-3882

(614) 469-3207 ..**Sunderland,** John T '83 (Thompson H LLP) -10 W Broad -Ste 700
-Columbus 43215 **Fx:**469-3361

(740) 368-1575 ..**Sunderman,** David P '77 Mun Ct Judge -70 N Union
-Delaware 43015 **Fx:**368-1583

(419) 278-2896 ..**Sunderman,** John D '80 (Gribbell S&C) -114 E Main -Bx54
-Deshler 43516

(513) 583-6921 ..**Sunderman,** Robert E '80 LensCrafters Inc
-8650 Governors Hill Dr -Cincinnati 45249

(513) 946-3000 ..**Sundermann,** David A '03 Hamilton Cnty Pros -230 E 9th
-Cincinnati 45202 **Fx:**946-3017

(216) 621-2234 ..**Sundheim,** Robert B '64 (Tarolli SC&T) -526 Superior Av
-1111 Leader Bldg -Cleveland 44114 **Fx:**621-4072

(216) 664-2444 ..**Sundheimer,** Marlene '79 City of Cleveland -1201 Lakeside Av
-Cleveland 44114

(513) 232-1004 ..**Sunyak,** Nicholas E III '91 -2484 Concordgreen Dr
-Cincinnati 45244

(419) 447-2521 ..**Supance & Howard** -84-88 S Wshngtn -Bx767 -Tiffin 44883
Fx:447-2310

(419) 447-2521 ..**Supance,** James D '72 (Supance & H) -84-88 S Wshngtn -Bx767
-Tiffin 44883 **Fx:**447-2310

(513) 721-5525 ..**Supinger,** Emily T '01 %Manley B -225 W Court -Cincinnati 45202
Fx:721-4268

(419) 259-6524 ..**Suplica,** Marie E '98 Natl City Bank -405 Mad Av -Toledo 43604

(513) 723-4000 ..**Suprock,** Mary E '04 %Vorys SS&P LLP -221 E 4th
-Ste 2000 Atrium Two -Bx0236 -Cincinnati 45201 **Fx:**723-4056

Surber, Nell D '55 -(Address Unavailable)

(937) 222-2333 ..**Surdyk Dowd & Turner Co,LPA** -40 N Main -1610 Kettering Twr
-Dayton 45423 **Fx:**222-1970

(937) 222-2333 ..**Surdyk,** Robert J '72 (Surdyk D&T Co,LPA) -40 N Main
-1610 Kettering Twr -Dayton 45423 **Fx:**222-1970

(216) 621-0200 ..**Suri,** Sunil '04 %Baker & H LLP -1900 E 9th -Ste 3200
-Cleveland 44114 **Fx:**696-0740

(513) 489-0404 ..**Surkamp,** Richard E Jr. '89 Midland Title Security,Inc
-4665 Cornell Rd -Cincinnati 45241

(216) 520-5677 ..**Surovy,** Thomas J '02 Thomas West -6111 Oak Tree Blvd
-CLeveland 44131

(513) 621-6464 ..**Surrey,** Michael C '98 %Graydon H&R LLP -511 Walnut
-1900 Fifth Third Ctr -Cincinnati 45202 **Fx:**651-3836

(614) 462-5448 ..**Susalla,** Malinda L '01 %Kegler BH&R -65 E State -Ste 1800
-Columbus 43215 **Fx:**464-2634

(330) 376-3300 ..**Susany,** John P '87 (Stark & K Co,LPA) -76 S Main -Ste 1512
-Akron 44308 **Fx:**376-6237

Susco, Michael E '82 -7718 Horizon Hills Dr -Springboro 45066

(614) 466-2872 ..**Susec,** Martin D '96 Atty Gen -30 E Broad -Columbus 43215
Fx:728-7592

(740) 345-3431 ..**Suskind,** Ira R '71 (Reese PD&M,PLL) -36 N 2nd -Bx919 -Newark
43058 **Fx:**349-5116

(513) 762-6200 ..**Susskind,** Stuart R '69 (Ulmer & B LLP) -600 Vine -Ste 2800 -Cincinnati 45202 **Fx:**762-6245

(216) 621-0150 ..**Sussman,** Cathryn A '98 %Hahn L&P LLP -3300 BP Twr 200 Pub Sq -Ste 3300 -Cleveland 44114 **Fx:**241-2824

(440) 347-5793 ..**Sussman,** Jason R '99 Lubrizol Corp -29400 Lakelnd Blvd -Wickliffe 44092

(740) 635-0347 ..**Sustersic,** Edward G '69 -894 Natl Rd -Bridgeport 43912

Sustin, Kenneth S '71 -3146 Richmond Rd -Beachwood 44122

Suter, Carol J '81 -7233 N Bellefontaine Av -Kansas City, MO 64119

(248) 641-1600 ..**Suter,** David L '81 (Harness D&P,PLC) -5490 Corp Dr -Ste 400 -Troy, MI 48098 **Fx:**641-0270

(614) 221-2121 ..**Suter,** Douglas J '88 (Isaac BL&T,LLP) -250 E Broad -Ste 900 Mdlnd Bldg -Columbus 43215 **Fx:**365-9516

(216) 464-6776 ..**Sutherland,** Robert B '94 -23240 Chagrin Blvd -Ste 100 -Beachwood 44122

(614) 461-1551 ..**Sutker,** Dory A '78 Barkan & B Co LPA -81 S 4th -Ste 300 -Columbus 43215

(216) 621-2234 ..**Sutkus,** Richard A '99 %Tarolli SC&T -526 Superior Av -1111 Leader Bldg -Cleveland 44114 **Fx:**621-4072

(614) 248-6478 ..**Sutter,** Andrew I '83 Bank One Mgt Corp -100 E Broad -OHI-0158 -Columbus 43271

(419) 255-5900 ..**Sutter,** Gary M '84 %MacMillan S&T,LLC -720 Water -4th Fl -Toledo 43604 **Fx:**255-9639

(419) 473-1346 ..**Sutter,** Jude F '59 %Kroncke DS&F -2255 W Laskey Rd -Toledo 43613 **Fx:**473-0218

(614) 227-2000 ..**Sutter,** Karl J '82 (Porter WM&A LLP) -41 S High -Columbus 43215 **Fx:**227-2100

(216) 771-2600 ..**Sutter,** Kimberly M '03 %Ott & Assoc Co,LPA -55 Pub Sq -Ste 1008 -Cleveland 44113 **Fx:**830-8939

(216) 928-2200 ..**Sutter,** Lawrence A III '89 (Sutter OM&F) -1301 E 9th -3600 Erievw Twr -Cleveland 44114 **Fx:**928-4400

(614) 466-4510 ..**Sutter,** Michelle T '81 Atty Gen -150 E Gay -Columbus 43215 **Fx:**995-0501

(216) 928-2200 ..**Sutter O'Connell Mannion & Farchione** -1301 E 9th -3600 Erievw Twr -Cleveland 44114 **Fx:**928-4400

(216) 579-2164 ..**Sutter-Hodgins,** Grace A '91 Cnsl Fed Reserve Bk of Cleveland -1455 E 6th -Bx6387 -Cleveland 44101

Suttle, Robert C '00 -(Address Unavailable)

Suttles, Celestine '81 -(Address Unavailable)

(216) 781-3600 ..**Sutton,** Betty S '91 Faulkner M&P,LLP -820 W Superior Av -Ste 900 -Cleveland 44113 **Fx:**781-8839

(330) 376-3607 ..**Sutton,** Charlotte A '04 %Howard & G Co,LPA -50 S Main -Ste 610 -Akron 44308

(614) 248-6080 ..**Sutton,** Gregory E '92 Bank One Corp -1111 Polaris Pkwy -Ste 4P -Columbus 43271

(513) 977-8200 ..**Sutton,** James T '04 %Dinsmore & S LLP -255 E 5th -Ste 1900 -Cincinnati 45202 **Fx:**977-8141

Sutton, Jerome P '77 -(Address Unavailable)

(614) 486-0297 ..**Sutton,** Joseph R '95 %S Jurus -1375 Dublin Rd -Columbus 43215 **Fx:**486-8580

(216) 523-4358 ..**Sutton,** Lisa D '94 Eaton Corp -1111 Superior Av -Cleveland 44114

(614) 462-3194 ..**Sutton,** Maximillian C '98 Franklin Cnty Pub Def -373 S High -12th Fl -Columbus 43215

(859) 331-8883 ..**Sutton,** Michael T '83 (Sutton HLG&B PLC) -130 Dudley Rd -Ste 250 -Edgewood, KY 41017 **Fx:**341-2777

(937) 228-0880 ..**Sutton Overholser & Schaffer** -130 W 2nd -1628 1st Natl Plz -Dayton 45402

(937) 228-0880 ..**Sutton,** Richard S '72 (Sutton O&S) -130 W 2nd -1628 1st Natl Plz -Dayton 45402

(216) 621-0200 ..**Sutton,** Stephen C '91 (Baker & H LLP) -1900 E 9th -Ste 3200 -Cleveland 44114 **Fx:**696-0740

(216) 328-1531 ..**Sutula,** Mark C '90 -6100 Oak Tree Blvd -Ste 200 -Cleveland 44131

(606) 329-4764 ..**Suver,** Jami K '88 SrCnsl Ashland Inc -Bx391 -Ashland, KY 41114

(513) 381-2838 ..**Suwanski,** Jillian M '02 %Taft S&H LLP -425 Walnut -Ste 1800 -Cincinnati 45202 **Fx:**381-0205

(202) 418-7069 ..**Svab,** Stephen '83 FCC -445 12th SW -Rm 2-A824 -Washington, DC 20554

(216) 861-5582 ..**Svat,** Mark S '89 (Fay SFM&M LLP) -1100 Superior Av -7th Fl -Cleveland 44114 **Fx:**241-1666

(216) 696-4441 ..**Svec,** Jennifer S '99 Zashin & R Co,LPA -55 Pub Sq -Ste 1490 -Cleveland 44113 **Fx:**696-1618

(440) 461-8500 ..**Svec,** Matthew J '00 %BM Russo & Co,LPA -691 Richmond Rd -Richmond Heights 44143

(440) 286-9571 ..**Svete,** Joseph T '64 (Svete M&C Co,LPA) -100 Parker Ct -Chardon 44024

(440) 286-9571 ..**Svete McGee & Carrabine Co,LPA** -100 Parker Ct -Chardon 44024

(650) 225-1489 ..**Svoboda,** Craig G '94 Genentech Inc -1 DNA Way -South San Francisco, CA 94080

(330) 373-1035 ..**Swader,** David S '02 %Letson GWL&R -155 S Park Av -Ste 250 -Bx151 -Warren 44482 **Fx:**392-5419

(937) 223-5200 ..**Swaim,** James E '71 (Flanagan LH&S) -318 W 4th -Dayton 45402 **Fx:**223-3335

(614) 469-1963 ..**Swaim,** Stephen '79 -118 E Main -Columbus 43215

(216) 589-5435 ..**Swain,** Maureen R '96 Deloitte & Touche LLP -127 Pub Square -Ste 2500 -Cleveland 44114

Swain, Paul A '02 -788 Lauraland Dr -Columbus 43214

(440) 974-5750 ..**Swain,** Richard A '63 Mentor Mun Ct -8500 Civic Ctr Blvd -Mentor 44060

(216) 752-9978 ..**Swain,** William L '84 -15705 Van Aken Blvd -4 -Cleveland 44120

(513) 867-5962 ..**Swaine,** David A '85 -155 Donald Dr -Fairfield 45014

(216) 447-1551 ..**Swanda,** Danielle D '02 %Ross B&S Co LPA -6000 Freedom Square Dr -Ste 540 -Cleveland 44131 **Fx:**447-1554

(614) 716-1691 ..**Swaneck,** Anthony J III '96 SrCnsl Amer Elec Pwr Co -1 Riverside Plz -Columbus 43215

(937) 323-0488 ..**Swaney,** Charles D '76 -515 N Fountain Av -Springfield 45504

(614) 227-4895 ..**Swank,** Christopher N '02 %Bricker & E LLP -100 S 3rd -Columbus 43215 **Fx:**227-2390

(740) 345-1040 ..**Swank,** James G '74 (Swank & Assoc,LPA) -68 W Church -Ste 205 -Bx248 -Newark 43058

(216) 241-8333 ..**Swansinger,** John '89 Ritzler C&S,Ltd -1001 Lakeside Av -1550 North Pnt Twr -Cleveland 44114 **Fx:**241-5890

(440) 329-5389 ..**Swansinger,** Laura Ann '92 Lorain Cnty Pros -225 Court -3rd Fl -Elyria 44035

Swanson, Charles A '75 -1370 Ontario -Rm 1800 -Cleveland 44113

(614) 459-1355 ..**Swanson,** Daniel T '86 -2757 Elginfld Rd -Columbus 43220

(614) 246-2511 ..**Swanson,** Kim L '72 Rockbridge Capital,LLC -4100 Regent -Ste G -Columbus 43219

(937) 449-6400 ..**Swanson,** Kristina E '04 %Dinsmore & S LLP -1 S Main -Ste 1300 One Dayton Centre -Dayton 45402 **Fx:**449-6405

(419) 706-1645 ..**Swanson,** Laura P '00 -3099 W SR 113 -Norwalk 44857

(419) 936-5120 ..**Swanson,** Mary S '82 -411 N Mich -Toledo 43624

(330) 375-5465 ..**Swanson,** Michael P '80 %Hon JS Gallas -2 S Main -Rm 480 -Akron 44308

(937) 255-4915 ..**Swanton,** Sandra L '86 -1636 Sunnington Grove -Centerville 45458

(614) 644-7342 ..**Swart,** Gregory W '80 Dept Mntl Rtrdtn -1810 Sullivant Av -Columbus 43266 **Fx:**752-8551

Swartwout, Daniel A '00 -5273 Frisco Dr -Hilliard 43026

(330) 394-1586 ..**Swartz,** Albert F '54 -149 E Market -Bx112 -Warren 44482 **Fx:**394-1586

(216) 685-9188 ..**Swartz Campbell LLC** -55 Pub Sq -Ste 1120 -Cleveland 44113 **Fx:**685-9293

(216) 479-8500 ..**Swartz,** Catherine M '02 %Squire S&D LLP -127 Pub Sq -4900 Key Twr -Cleveland 44114 **Fx:**479-8780

(330) 399-2306 ..**Swartz,** Charles I '68 (C Swartz Co,LPA) -1286 Elm Rd NE -Warren 44483

(614) 775-5000 ..**Swartz,** Dean E '74 The Swartz Law Firm -220 Market -Ste 208 -Bx709 -New Albany 43054

Swartz, Donald K '97 -3738 Hutton -Cincinnati 45226

(513) 977-8200 ..**Swartz,** Jennifer N '00 %Dinsmore & S LLP -255 E 5th -Ste 1900 -Cincinnati 45202 **Fx:**977-8141

(216) 241-6602 ..**Swartz,** Joseph B '70 (Weston HFP&H LLP) -50 Pub Sq -2500 Trmnl Twr -Cleveland 44113 **Fx:**621-8369

(703) 696-4001 ..**Swartz,** Marc L '79 Ofc of Naval Research -800 N Quincy -Rm 207 -Arlington, VA 22217

(440) 835-0600 ..**Swartz,** Scott S '92 %Waldheger C,LPA -1991 Crocker Rd -Ste 550 -Westlake 44145 **Fx:**835-1511

(216) 588-4365 ..**Swartz,** Steven S '82 OH Savings Bnk -1801 E 9th -Ste 200 -Cleveland 44114

(216) 586-3939 ..**Swartzbaugh,** Marc L '61 Jones D -901 Lakeside Av -Cleveland 44114 **Fx:**579-0212

(216) 621-0150 ..**Swary,** Mark F '73 (Hahn L&P LLP) -3300 BP Twr/200 Pub Sq -Ste 3300 -Cleveland 44114 **Fx:**241-2824

(614) 469-3939 ..**Swatsler,** Todd S '81 (Jones D) -325 John H McConnell Blvd -Ste 600 -Bx165017 -Columbus 43216 **Fx:**461-4198

(330) 395-9500 ..**Swauger,** Terry A '95 %W Roux -106 E Market -Warren 44481

(614) 469-7130 ..**Sway,** M Andrew '96 (Smith R&S Co,LPA) -50 W Broad -Ste 3000 -Columbus 43215 **Fx:**469-7146

(216) 363-4500 ..**Swearengen,** Michael K '89 (Benesch FC&A LLP) -200 Pub Sq -Ste 2300 -Cleveland 44114 **Fx:**363-4588

(330) 535-5711 ..**Swearingen-Hilker,** NiCole A '03 %Brouse M -106 S Main -500 First Natl Twr -Akron 44308 **Fx:**253-8601

(614) 923-7989 ..**Sweat,** Katherine D '03 %E Lewis -270 Bradenton Av -Dublin 43017 **Fx:**734-7270

(630) 836-5916 ..**Sweda,** Kip M '87 BP Prdcts NA Inc -28100 Torch Pkwy -312D -Warrenville, IL 60555

(614) 461-1100 ..**Swedlow Butler Levine Lewis & Dye Co,LPA** -10 W Broad -Ste 2400 -Columbus 43215 **Fx:**461-8178

(614) 461-1100 ..**Swedlow,** Gerald H '61 (Swedlow BLL&D Co,LPA) -10 W Broad -Ste 2400 -Columbus 43215 **Fx:**461-8178

(216) 931-6000 ..**Sweebe,** Richard D '79 (Ulmer & B LLP) -1300 E 9th -Ste 900 Penton Media Bldg -Cleveland 44114 **Fx:**931-6001

(440) 352-6200 ..**Sweeney,** Anne K '04 Legal Aid -8 N State -#300 -Painesville 44077 **Fx:**352-0015

Sweeney, Colleen A '89 -(Address Unavailable)

(440) 461-6000 ..**Sweeney,** David M '75 Nesco,Inc -6140 Parkland Blvd -Ste 110 -Mayfield Heights 44124 **Fx:**449-3111

(216) 622-3600 ..**Sweeney,** Emily M '81 US Atty -801 W Superior -Ste 400 -Cleveland 44113 **Fx:**622-3370

(216) 928-9288 ..**Sweeney,** Francis E Jr. '92 -323 Lakeside Av -Ste 450 -Cleveland 44113 **Fx:**928-9289

(419) 248-4677 ..**Sweeney,** Frederick J '78 -413 N Mich -Toledo 43624 **Fx:**255-6227

(216) 241-5310 ..**Sweeney,** James F '59 OfCnsl Gallagher SF&N -1501 Euclid Av -6th Fl -Cleveland 44115 **Fx:**241-1608

(216) 348-7550 ..**Sweeney,** Kathleen M '85 R Kuepper & Assoc -1660 W 2nd -Ste 480 -Cleveland 44113

(216) 787-3030 ..**Sweeney,** Kelley A '97 Atty Gen -615 W Superior Av -11th Fl -Cleveland 44115 **Fx:**787-3480

(216) 443-7295 ..**Sweeney,** Kristin W '95 Cuyahoga Cnty Pub Def -1849 Prospect Av -Ste 222 -Cleveland 44115

Sweeney, Mark L '03 -Bx172 -Munroe Falls 44262

(216) 696-0606 ..**Sweeney,** Mary B '89 RE Sweeney Co,LPA -55 Pub Sq -Ste 1500 -Cleveland 44113 **Fx:**696-0679

Sweeney, Mary F '01 -7424 Shaker Run Ln -West Chester 45069

(330) 726-1654 ..**Sweeney,** Maureen A '93 -120 Marwood Cir -Bx3965 -Boardman 44513 **Fx:**726-5608

(440) 350-9273 ..**Sweeney,** Maureen A '86 -11805 Girdled Rd -Concord 44077 **Fx:**354-7394

(330) 535-5711 ..**Sweeney,** Michael A '76 (Brouse M) -106 S Main -500 First Natl Twr -Akron 44308 **Fx:**253-8601

(216) 481-4753 ..**Sweeney,** Patrick J '70 -104 E 207th -Euclid 44123

(216) 566-5793 ..**Sweeney,** Patrick J '86 %Thompson H LLP -127 Pub Sq -3900 Key Ctr -Cleveland 44114 **Fx:**566-5800

(216) 696-0606 ..**Sweeney,** Robert E '51 (RE Sweeney Co,LPA) -55 Pub Sq -Ste 1500 -Cleveland 44113 **Fx:**696-0679

(330) 438-1223 ..**Sweeney,** Robert M '67 United Natl Bank&Trust -Bx24190 -Canton 44701

(216) 696-0606 ..**Sweeney,** Robert P '76 RE Sweeney Co,LPA -55 Pub Sq -Ste 1500 -Cleveland 44113 **Fx:**696-0679

(216) 363-1400 .. **Sweeney**, Rosemary '87 (Buckley K,LPA) -600 E Superior Av
-Ste 1400 -Cleveland 44114 **Fx**:579-1020

(216) 621-1000 .. **Sweeney**, Sean M '99 %Moscarino & T,LLP -1422 Euclid Av
-Hanna Bldg Ste 630 -Cleveland 44115 **Fx**:622-1556

(216) 443-7223 .. **Sweeney**, Suzan M '91 Cuyahoga Cnty Pub Def -1200 W 3rd NW
-100 Lakeside Pl -Cleveland 44113

(859) 246-2690 .. **Sweeney**, Thomas A '80 (Sweeney & F,PLLC) -2519 Ritchie Av
-Crescent Springs, KY 41017

(216) 619-0071 .. **Sweeney**, Timothy F '87 -820 W Superior Av -Ste 430
-Cleveland 44113 **Fx**:241-3108

(216) 875-2767 .. **Sweeney**, Timothy G '84 %Bonezzi SM&P Co LPA
-526 Superior Av -Ste 1400 -Cleveland 44114 **Fx**:875-1570

(216) 664-2853 .. **Sweeney**, William A '89 Dept of Law -601 Lakeside Av
-Rm 106 City Hall -Cleveland 44114 **Fx**:664-2663

(216) 289-5100 .. **Sweet**, Barry L '82 -22408 Lakeshr Blvd -Euclid 44123
Fx:289-0655

(314) 234-9531 .. **Sweet**, Jeffrey T '96 Boeing Co -Mail Code S270-1350 -Bx516
-Saint Louis, MO 63166

              Sweet, Joy A '83 -800 Brick Mill Run -Cleveland 44145

(614) 466-3033 .. **Sweet**, Sherry L '95 Industrial Commssn of OH -30 W Spring
-9th Fl -Columbus 43215 **Fx**:752-8785

(317) 818-5580 .. **Sweetin**, Doris L '95 Tyra & C,PC -10401 N Meridian -Ste 300
-Indianapolis, IN 46290

(513) 872-2290 .. **Swehla**, Marcia A '93 TriHealth,Inc -375 Dixmyth Av
-Cincinnati 45220

(513) 891-1530 .. **Swehla**, Nathaniel L '02 %Keating R&S -8050 Hosbrook -Ste 200
-Cincinnati 45236 **Fx**:891-1537

(703) 905-2000 .. **Sweigart**, Raymond L '73 (Pillsbury W,LLP) -1600 Tysons Blvd
-Mc Lean, VA 22102 **Fx**:905-2500

(412) 341-9300 .. **Sweitzer**, David E '88 Riley MH&S,PC -650 Wshngtn Rd -Ste 300
-Pittsburgh, PA 15228

(419) 247-1789 .. **Swemba**, Connie S '03 %Eastman & S Ltd -1 Seagate -24th Fl
-Bx10032 -Toledo 43699 **Fx**:247-1777

(216) 621-6400 .. **Swencki**, Ronald C '69 -2000 Standard Bldg -Cleveland 44113

(440) 989-2755 .. **Swenski**, Lisa I '99 Simonoff & S Co,LPA -4463 Oberlin Av
-Lorain 44053

              Swenson, Craig A '04 -(Address Unavailable)

(216) 397-4434 .. **Swenson**, Elizabeth v '86 John Carroll University
-20700 N Park Blvd -Dept of Psychology
-University Heights 44118

              Swenty, Peter W '55 -630 Vine -Ste 415 -Cincinnati 45202

(614) 223-9300 .. **Sweterlitsch**, Martha J '83 OfCnsl Benesch FC&A LLP
-88 E Broad -Ste 900 -Columbus 43215 **Fx**:223-9330

(216) 222-9892 .. **Swetlin**, Seema H '94 Natl City Bank -1900 E 9th
-10th Fl, Loc 2101 -Cleveland 44114

(614) 462-2225 .. **Swetnam**, Daniel R '82 (Schottenstein Z&D) -250 West -Bx165020
-Columbus 43216 **Fx**:462-5135

(330) 762-7655 .. **Swett**, Loma L '80 %Kaufmann & K -106 S Main -Ste 1200
-Akron 44308 **Fx**:762-7537

(212) 250-9031 .. **Swiader**, Michael C '99 %Deutsche Bk -60 Wall -NYC60-2204
-New York, NY 10005

(614) 463-9770 .. **Swick**, Jeffrey D '85 (Roetzel & A,LPA) -155 E Broad
-Natl City Ctr 12th Fl -Columbus 43215 **Fx**:463-9792

(513) 891-1530 .. **Swick**, Kevin L '81 (Keating R&S) -8050 Hosbrook -Ste 200
-Cincinnati 45236 **Fx**:891-1537

(251) 621-3485 .. **Swickard**, Dawn A '96 %Sears Law Firm -816-A Manci Av
-Daphne, AL 36526

(937) 222-7477 .. **Swift**, Ben M '95 %Wright & V,LPA -32 N Main -Ste 801
-Dayton 45404

(614) 227-8850 .. **Swift**, Betsy A '88 (Bricker & E LLP) -100 S 3rd -Columbus 43215
Fx:227-2390

(216) 621-0200 .. **Swift**, Christopher J '80 (Baker & H LLP) -1900 E 9th -Ste 3200
-Cleveland 44114 **Fx**:696-0740

(614) 464-6400 .. **Swift**, David A '78 (Vorys SS&P LLP) -52 E Gay -Bx1008
-Columbus 43216 **Fx**:464-6350

(330) 487-6520 .. **Swift**, Dean A '78 Nrth Coast Energy,Inc -1993 Case Pkwy N
-Twinsburg 44087

              Swift, James E '93 -(Address Unavailable)

(419) 337-9240 .. **Swigart**, William R '76 (Fulton Cnty Pros) -123 Cthse Plz
-Wauseon 43567

(937) 879-2261 .. **Swigert**, Daniel L '79 Brezine & B -188 W Hebble Av
-Fairborn 45324

(513) 381-2838 .. **Swigert**, J Mack '37 OfCnsl Taft S&H LLP -425 Walnut -Ste 1800
-Cincinnati 45202 **Fx**:381-0205

(740) 397-4040 .. **Swihart**, Kathy L '96 %Critchfield C&J Ltd -10 S Gay
-Mount Vernon 43050 **Fx**:397-6775

(219) 420-0625 .. **Swihart**, Thomas D '87 -202 W Berry -Ste 010
-Fort Wayne, IN 46802

(513) 721-1125 .. **Swillinger**, Bradley M '01 -1014 Vine -Ste 1650 -Cincinnati 45202

(937) 223-6211 .. **Swillinger**, Jeffrey A '79 (Crew & B) -2580 Kettering Twr
-Dayton 45423

(513) 721-1125 .. **Swillinger**, Steven R '74 -1014 Vine -Ste 1650 -Cincinnati 45202

(614) 227-2000 .. **Swinerton**, Jenny T '04 %Porter WM&A LLP -41 S High
-Columbus 43215 **Fx**:227-2100

(614) 443-7455 .. **Swinford**, Leslie B Jr. '75 (Merullo R&S Co,LPA) -772 S Front
-Columbus 43206

(330) 535-5711 .. **Swing**, Christopher F '91 (Brouse M) -106 S Main
-500 First Natl Twr -Akron 44308 **Fx**:253-8601

(937) 492-6148 .. **Swinger**, Welza L '60 -111 East Ct -Sidney 45365

(216) 831-0200 .. **Swirsky**, Judith R '91 %W Wohl -23230 Chagrin Blvd -Ste 800
-Beachwood 44122 **Fx**:831-5064

(800) 362-4500 .. **Swisher**, Danielle M '99 Thomson West -Bx318063
-Cleveland 44131

(216) 741-2365 .. **Swisher**, Helane J '77 UAW Legal Srvcs -707 Brookpark Rd
-Brooklyn Heights 44109

(800) 686-0025 .. **Swisher**, John R '95 Grange Mutual Ins Co -690 Taylor Rd
-Ste 100 -Gahanna 43230

(614) 462-3555 .. **Swisher**, Laura Rayce '99 Franklin Cnty Pros -373 S High
-Columbus 43215

(513) 531-2900 .. **Swisher**, Sarah E '93 Amer Para Prof Systems -6056 Mntgmry Rd
-Cincinnati 45213

(614) 221-3536 .. **Swisher**, Sarah J '99 %Gallagher & K,LPA -400 S 5th Av -Ste 304
-Columbus 43215

(614) 462-3555 .. **Swisher**, Zachary M '03 Franklin Cnty Pros -373 S High
-Columbus 43215

(937) 228-9000 .. **Switala**, Gilbert B '91 (Thorson SW&S,LLP) -130 W 2nd -Ste 1508
-Dayton 45402 **Fx**:228-3550

(216) 875-2767 .. **Switzer**, Donald H '78 (Bonezzi SM&P Co LPA) -526 Superior Av
-Ste 1400 -Cleveland 44114 **Fx**:875-1570

(216) 586-3939 .. **Switzer**, H Duane '64 Cnsl Jones D -901 Lakeside Av
-Cleveland 44114 **Fx**:579-0212

(216) 831-0042 .. **Switzer**, Kennee '88 %Meyers RF&L LPA -28601 Chagrin Blvd
-Ste 500 -Cleveland 44122 **Fx**:831-0542

(216) 444-2340 .. **Switzer**, Stephanie N '94 Cleveland Clinic Fndtn -9500 Euclid Av
-Cleveland 44195

(614) 233-4765 .. **Switzer**, Thomas E '97 Lane A&H LLC -175 S 3rd -Ste 700
-Columbus 43215 **Fx**:228-0146

(800) 592-8422 .. **Swob**, Jay D '81 -9525 Kenwood Rd -Ste 16 FC -Cincinnati 45242

(937) 393-4534 .. **Swonger**, Ronald L '60 -120 S West -Hillsboro 45133

(330) 497-0700 .. **Swope**, Gregory D '95 %Krugliak WG&D Co,LPA
-4775 Munson NW -Bx36963 -Canton 44735 **Fx**:497-4020

(614) 866-1492 .. **Swope**, Kristy J '86 (Swope & S) -6504 E Main
-Reynoldsburg 43068

(330) 497-5303 .. **Swope**, Raymond A Jr. '71 -Bx2548 -North Canton 44720

(614) 866-1492 .. **Swope**, Richard F '56 (Swope & S) -6504 E Main -Reynoldsburg
43068

(513) 422-2001 .. **Swope**, Thomas A '78 (Frost BT LLC) -300 N Main -Ste 200
-Middletown 45042 **Fx**:422-3010

(419) 422-0288 .. **Swope**, William L '85 %R Reeves Co,LPA -221 S Main
-Findlay 45840

(330) 666-6400 .. **Swyrydenko**, Nicholas '89 %Dobbins & H
-1000 S Cleveland-Massillon Rd -Ste 105 -Akron 44333

(614) 785-1700 .. **Sybert**, Curtis J '87 (Scherner & S,LLC) -153 S Lbrty
-Powell 43065 **Fx**:785-0700

(440) 995-2027 .. **Syby**, Craig W '93 Tower City Title Agncy,LLC
-6151 Wilson Mills Rd -#110 -Highland Heights 44143

(419) 259-6376 .. **Sydlow**, Holly T '75 US Atty -4 Seagate -Ste 308 -Toledo 43604
Fx:259-6360

(614) 854-6680 .. **Sydney**, Kristen J '87 Sagemark Cnsltng Inc -7650 Rvrs Edge Dr
-Ste 103 -Columbus 43235

(614) 462-5483 .. **Sykes**, Kevin L '79 (Kegler BH&R) -65 E State -Ste 1800
-Columbus 43215 **Fx**:464-2634

(937) 225-4063 .. **Sylvain**, Nicholas P '93 Montgomery Cnty Dom Rltns Ct
-301 W 3rd -2nd Fl -Bx972 -Dayton 45422

              Sylvester, Beverly E '67 -(Address Unavailable)

(216) 432-0306 .. **Sylvester**, Edward T '01 Professional Flair, Inc -3615 Euclid Av
-3rd Fl -Cleveland 44115

(216) 622-2727 .. **Synenberg**, Roger M '77 (R Synenberg,LLC) -55 Pub Sq
-Ste 1200 -Cleveland 44113 **Fx**:622-2707

(216) 731-2266 .. **Syracuse**, Vetus '04 -26250 Euclid Av -Euclid 44132

(216) 731-2266 .. **Syracuse**, Vetus J '70 -26250 Euclid Av -Euclid 44132

(419) 245-1020 .. **Syring**, Paul F '90 %Law Dept -One Govt Ctr -Ste 2250
-Toledo 43604 **Fx**:245-1090

(920) 727-5382 .. **Syroney**, David J '94 Associated Trust Co -100 W Wscnsn Av
-Neenah, WI 54956

(330) 869-4200 .. **Syrvalin**, Kristine C '93 Omnava Solutions Inc -175 Ghent Rd
-Fairlawn 44333

(216) 696-0650 .. **Sysack**, Russell '01 %Kaman & C -50 Pub Sq -Ste 600 Trmnl Twr
-Cleveland 44113

(330) 744-5145 .. **Szabados**, Lester M '86 -26 Market -Ste 610 -Youngstown 44503

(216) 446-0300 .. **Szabo**, Gabriel S Jr. '53 -5432 Mayfld Rd -Ste 103
-Cleveland 44124

(440) 282-2079 .. **Szabo**, Jeffrey S '78 -1700 Cooper Foster Pk Rd -Lorain 44053

(440) 446-0300 .. **Szabo**, John Z '69 -5432 Mayfld Rd -Ste 103 -Cleveland 44124

(216) 622-8200 .. **Szabo**, Magda B '77 Calfee H&G LLP -800 Superior Av -Ste 1400
-Cleveland 44114 **Fx**:241-0816

(216) 622-8200 .. **Szabo**, Paul E '79 Calfee H&G LLP -800 Superior Av -Ste 1400
-Cleveland 44114 **Fx**:241-0816

(216) 228-7200 .. **Szaller**, James F '75 (Brown & S) -14222 Mad Av
-Cleveland 44107

(419) 242-1001 .. **Szczepaniak**, Richard J Jr. '77 (Szczepaniak & H) -1900 Monroe
-Bx501 -Toledo 43697

(216) 522-3380 .. **Szczepanik**, Carol A '81 IRS -1375 E 9th -1200 -Cleveland 44114

(440) 323-7433 .. **Szekely**, Michael E '74 -230 3rd -Ste 200 -Elyria 44035
Fx:322-6474

(937) 382-1316 .. **Szelagiewicz**, Steven N '01 Clinton Co Pub Def -32 E Sugartree
-2nd Fl -Wilmington 45177 **Fx**:382-8670

(440) 354-4364 .. **Szeman**, Joseph P '95 Baker & H Co,LPA -77 N St Clair
-Painesville 44077 **Fx**:639-8901

(513) 794-6389 .. **Szeremet**, David M '97 Ohio Natl Financial Srvcs -1 Fncl Way
-Dept 64 -Cincinnati 45202

(216) 621-0200 .. **Szilvas**, Alexander J '87 (Baker & H LLP) -1900 E 9th -Ste 3200
-Cleveland 44114 **Fx**:696-0740

(614) 575-2500 .. **Szluzer**, Cheryl E '01 -8633 Ashford Ln -Pickerington 43147

(440) 358-4948 .. **Szmagala**, Taras G Jr. '91 Avery Dennison Corp -7590 Auburn Rd
-Painesville 44077

(419) 244-8989 .. **Szollosi**, Matthew A '98 (Cosme D&S) -202 N Erie -Toledo 43624

(419) 535-0075 .. **Szollosi**, Wednesday M '02 %Allotta F&W Co,LPA
-2222 Centennial Rd -Toledo 43617 **Fx**:535-1935

(614) 228-6131 .. **Szolosi**, Michael R Sr. '69 OfCnsl McNamara & M,LLP
-88 E Broad -Ste 1250 -Columbus 43215 **Fx**:228-6126

(614) 792-5555 .. **Szolosi**, Michael Roy Jr. '95 %Standley Law Grp LLP
-495 Metro Pl S -Ste 210 -Dublin 43017 **Fx**:792-5536

              Szonert-Binienda, Maria '90 -(Address Unavailable)

(216) 443-7229 .. **Szorady**, Ernest A '82 Labor & Employment Relatns Ofc
-1255 Euclid Av -Rm 310 -Cleveland 44115

(419) 893-4880 .. **Szozda**, Veronica L '88 Marsh M Ltd -204 W Wayne
-Maumee 43537

(216) 623-2008 .. **Szpalik**, Peter R '91 IRS -1375 E 9th -Ste 815 -Cleveland 44114

(419) 252-6270 .. **Szuberla**, Joan C '83 (Spengler N PLL) -608 Mad Av -Ste 1000
-Toledo 43604 **Fx**:241-8599

(216) 696-9330 .. **Szubski**, Grace A '82 Garson & Assoc Co,LPA
-614 Superior Av W -1600 Rckfllr Bldg -Cleveland 44113
Fx:696-8558

(419) 245-2465 .. **Szuch**, David P '82 Workers Comp -1 Govt Ctr -Toledo 43604
Fx:245-2666

(513) 784-6402 .. **Szucsik**, Barbara R '93 Convergys Corp -201 E 4th
-Cincinnati 45202

(614) 644-1614 .. **Szudy**, Katherine A '03 %Pub Def -8 E Long -Columbus 43215

(312) 419-6900 .. **Szura**, Louis C '03 Novack & M -303 W Madison
-Chicago, IL 60606

(216) 861-0503 .. **Szuter**, Gregory P '73 -1801 E 9th -Ste 730 -Cleveland 44114

(513) 708-3106 .. **Szydlowski**, Christine H '91 Emcee Properties LLC
-8147 Foxdale Ct -West Chester 45069

(614) 464-6400 .. **Szykowny**, Thomas E '82 (Vorys SS&P LLP) -52 E Gay -Bx1008
-Columbus 43216 **Fx:**464-6350

Szymanski, Duane A '94 -5721 N High -Worthington 43085

(330) 297-0881 .. **Szymanski**, Joseph '90 Portage Cnty Juv Ct -8000 Infirmary Rd
-Ravenna 44266

(419) 248-2419 .. **Szyperski**, Joseph T '04 %G Gusses Co,LPA -33 S Huron
-Toledo 43602 **Fx:**321-6379

(419) 248-2419 .. **Szyperski**, Thomas J '70 -33 S Huron -Toledo 43602

(740) 942-3130 .. **Tabacchi**, John O '76 -145 S Main -Bx284 -Cadiz 43907
Fx:942-8878

(724) 654-5537 .. **Tabak**, Kendra A '02 CD Ambrosia Trucking Co -Bx422
-Edinburg, PA 16116

(859) 428-3700 .. **Tabar**, Mary Patia '98 -Bx260 -Crittenden, KY 41030

(614) 249-7840 .. **Tabb**, Kimberly B '00 Cnsl Nationwide Ins Co -1 Nationwide Plz
-Columbus 43215

(216) 592-5000 .. **Taber**, Edward E '96 (Tucker E&W LLP) -925 Euclid Av
-1150 Huntngtn Bldg -Cleveland 44115 **Fx:**592-5009

Taber, Timothy J '75 -38241 Lk Shr Blvd -#511 -Willoughby 44094

Taboada, Frank J '96 -59 Bainton Rd -West Hartford, CT 06117

(304) 529-5265 .. **Tabor**, Debra L '83 US Army Corp of Engineers -502 8th
-Huntington, WV 25701

Tackett, Brian '02 -3179 Palmer Rd NE -New Lexington 43764

(330) 394-4488 .. **Tackett**, Dennis W '91 -106 E Market -Ste 308 -Warren 44481
Fx:394-4433

Tackett, Joe L Jr. '03 -300 4th -Elyria 44035

(713) 623-4844 .. **Tackett**, Keith M '84 Thomason M&P -3040 Post Oak Blvd
-Ste 1500 -Houston, TX 77056

(419) 324-2407 .. **Tackett**, Kevin A '95 -1709 Spielbusch Av -Ste 110 -Toledo 43624

Tackett, Natalie J '88 -11115 Collins Arbogast Rd
-South Vienna 45369

(216) 382-4848 .. **Taddeo**, Joseph H '69 -2000 Auburn Dr -Ste 200 -Cleveland 44122

(412) 288-7102 .. **Taddonio**, Gregory Lee '96 %Reed S,LLP -435 Sixth Av
-Pittsburgh, PA 15219

(330) 707-4000 .. **Tadla**, James A '90 -1310 Ohio Av -Mc Donald 44437

(202) 616-6789 .. **Tadross**, Shahira M '93 US DOJ -600 E NW -Ste 7600
-Washington, DC 20530

(414) 287-1409 .. **Taebel**, Scott W '86 von Briesen & R,SC -411 E Wscnsn Av
-Ste 700 -Milwaukee, WI 53202

(513) 381-0656 .. **Tafaro**, John P '83 OfCnsl Kohnen & P LLP -201 E 5th -Ste 800
-Cincinnati 45202 **Fx:**381-5823

(419) 255-0814 .. **Tafelski**, Joseph R '71 ABLE -520 Mad Av -740 Spitzer Bldg
-Toledo 43604 **Fx:**259-2880

(513) 627-1888 .. **Taffy**, Frank '01 Procter & Gamble -11810 E Miami Rvr Rd
-Cincinnati 45252

(216) 363-4500 .. **Taft**, Clare R '03 %Benesch FC&A LLP -200 Pub Sq -Ste 2300
-Cleveland 44114 **Fx:**363-4588

(216) 696-4700 .. **Taft**, Frederick I '72 (Spieth BM&N Co,LPA) -925 Euclid Av
-2000 Huntngtn Bldg -Cleveland 44115 **Fx:**696-2706

(440) 333-1333 .. **Taft**, Homer S Jr. '70 -Bx16216 -Rocky River 44116

(202) 263-3293 .. **Taft**, Jeffrey P '94 %Mayer BR&M -1909 K NW
-Washington, DC 20006

(513) 621-2120 .. **Taft**, Richard Guy '76 Strauss & T,LPA -150 E 4th -4th Fl
-Cincinnati 45202 **Fx:**241-8259

(513) 381-2838 .. **Taft Stettinius & Hollister LLP** -425 Walnut -Ste 1800
-Cincinnati 45202 **Fx:**381-0205

(614) 221-2838 .. **Taft Stettinius & Hollister LLP** -21 E State -12th Fl
-Columbus 43215 **Fx:**221-2007

(216) 241-2838 .. **Taft Stettinius & Hollister LLP** -200 Pub Sq -3500 BP Twr
-Cleveland 44114 **Fx:**241-3707

(937) 228-2838 .. **Taft Stettinius & Hollister LLP** -110 N Main -Ste 900
-Dayton 45402 **Fx:**228-2816

(216) 685-1103 .. **Taft-Milby**, Rosemary '91 (Weltman W&R Co,LPA) -323 W
Lakeside Av -Ste 200 -Cleveland 44113 **Fx:**363-4121

(614) 464-6400 .. **Taggart**, Brent C '88 (Vorys SS&P LLP) -52 E Gay -Bx1008
-Columbus 43216 **Fx:**464-6350

(513) 381-9200 .. **Taggart**, Carolyn A '78 (Rendigs FK&D,LLP) -One W 4th -Ste 900
-Cincinnati 45202 **Fx:**381-9206

(513) 381-5700 .. **Taggart**, Georgana '81 OfCnsl Ritter & R,LLC -105 E 4th
-Ste 1200 -Cincinnati 45202 **Fx:**381-0014

(614) 464-6400 .. **Taggart**, Thomas M '65 OfCnsl Vorys SS&P LLP -52 E Gay
-Bx1008 -Columbus 43216 **Fx:**464-6350

(304) 684-3400 .. **Taggart**, Thomas P '74 7 Ranges Radio Co,Inc -201 N 4th Av
-Paden City, WV 26159

(216) 781-0070 .. **Taich**, Harry H '73 -720 Leader Bldg -526 Superior Av E
-Cleveland 44114

(513) 721-8822 .. **Tailer**, Christine D '84 Nationwide Ins Co -125 E Ct -Ste 203
-Cincinnati 45202

(614) 466-0570 .. **Tait**, Amy C '98 Dept Admin Srvcs Ofc Collective Bargaining
-100 E Broad -18th Fl -Columbus 43215

(216) 622-8200 .. **Tait**, Christina '96 Calfee H&G LLP -800 Superior Av -Ste 1400
-Cleveland 44114 **Fx:**241-0816

(614) 469-3939 .. **Tait**, Mary E '99 %Jones D -325 John H McConnell Blvd -Ste 600
-Bx165017 -Columbus 43216 **Fx:**461-4198

(614) 464-6400 .. **Tait**, Robert E '73 (Vorys SS&P LLP) -52 E Gay -Bx1008
-Columbus 43216 **Fx:**464-6350

(419) 843-2001 .. **Takacs**, William E '76 (Gallon & T Co,LPA) -3516 Granite Cir
-Bx352018 -Toledo 43635 **Fx:**843-6665

(216) 685-1137 .. **Talaganis**, Dean S '89 %Weltman W&R Co,LPA
-323 W Lakeside Av -Ste 200 -Cleveland 44113 **Fx:**363-4121

(843) 280-5784 .. **Talbert**, Bonford R II '57 -1827 Spinnaker Dr -North Myrtle
Beach, SC 29582

(440) 331-1053 .. **Talbert**, Richard C '65 -18950 Colahan Dr -Rocky River 44116

(216) 621-0200 .. **Talbot**, Kevin R '01 %Baker & H LLP -1900 E 9th -Ste 3200
-Cleveland 44114 **Fx:**696-0740

(937) 224-1006 .. **Talbot**, Thomas B Jr. '74 (Talbot & D) -34 N Main -Ste 1400
-Dayton 45402

(419) 249-7900 .. **Talbott**, D Casey '90 (Robison C&O) -Four SeaGate -9th Fl
-Toledo 43604 **Fx:**249-7911

(614) 488-7590 .. **Talbott**, Harold B '52 -1917 Suffolk Rd -Columbus 43221

(614) 444-4455 .. **Talbott**, Harold B '85 (Talbott & R) -1180 S High -Columbus 43206

(419) 483-7330 .. **Talbott**, Jacquie F '83 -7353 Cnty Road 29 -Bx1 -Flat Rock 44828

(614) 444-4455 .. **Talbott & Rinehart** -1180 S High -Columbus 43206

(216) 875-4800 .. **Talcott**, Thomas J '76 (DKW Law Grp) -200 Pub Sq
-26th Fl BP Twr -Cleveland 44114 **Fx:**875-4809

(937) 223-8177 .. **Talda**, Richard A '82 (Coolidge WW&L) -33 W 1st -Ste 600
-Dayton 45402 **Fx:**223-6705

(614) 719-3719 .. **Talebi**, Denise J '93 US Fed Dist Ct -85 Marconi -Columbus 43215

(937) 653-5257 .. **Talebi**, Kevin S '98 (Paulig S&T) -40 Monument Sq -Ste 300
-Urbana 43078

Taliaferro, George W Jr. '93 -1 W 4th -Ste 2100 -Cincinnati 45202

(859) 291-9900 .. **Taliaferro**, Philip III '91 (Taliaferro MS&C PLLC) -1005 Mad Av
-Bx468 -Covington, KY 41012

(440) 352-8500 .. **Talikka**, Leo J '68 -2603 Riverside Dr -Ste 100 -Painesville 44077

(202) 254-3600 .. **Tall**, Christopher Taliferro '92 US Ofc Special Cnsl -1730 M NW
-Ste 300 -Washington, DC 20036

(614) 228-5151 .. **Tallan**, Mitchell M '84 (Gallagher GPT&L LLP) -471 E Broad
-19th Fl -Columbus 43215 **Fx:**228-0032

(216) 443-7800 .. **Talley**, Debra L '93 Cuyahoga Cnty Pros -1200 Ontario -8th Fl
-Cleveland 44113 **Fx:**698-2270

(330) 463-5000 .. **Talley**, Douglas L '84 Risk Intl Srvcs -4199 Kinross Lks Pkwy
-Ste 220 -Richfield 44286

Tallos, Edmund G '01 -11030 Mitchell Rd -Columbia Station 44028

(440) 356-9400 .. **Talty**, Patrick E '87 -20325 Ctr Ridge Rd -Ste 512 -Rocky River
44116

(513) 381-6555 .. **Tamarkin**, Ivan L '67 -830 Main -Ste 999 -Cincinnati 45202

(216) 443-5809 .. **Tamas**, Barbara A '00 Cuyahoga Cnty Pros -1910 Carnegie Av
-Whitlatch Bldg -Cleveland 44115 **Fx:**443-5815

(513) 695-1325 .. **Tamashasky**, Anne L '95 Warren Cnty Pros -500 Justice Dr
-Lebanon 45036 **Fx:**695-2962

(216) 664-4506 .. **Tamayo-Sarver**, Maritza '02 Dept of Law -601 Lakeside Av
-Rm 106 City Hall -Cleveland 44114 **Fx:**664-2663

(513) 874-4422 .. **Tamborski**, Peter E '82 Sugar Creek Packing Co
-4585 Muhlhauser Rd -Hamilton 45011

(216) 566-2360 .. **Tamburino**, Ronnie M '83 Sherwin-Williams Co
-101 Prospect Av NW -Cleveland 44115

(216) 664-2220 .. **Tame**, Craig A '91 Ofc of the Mayor -601 Lakeside Av E -202
-Cleveland 44114

(513) 533-4416 .. **Tami**, Molly T '93 -7 Forest Hll Dr -Cincinnati 45208

(614) 469-3200 .. **Tammaro**, Bradford L '85 OfCnsl Thompson H LLP -10 W Broad
-Ste 700 -Columbus 43215 **Fx:**469-3361

Tammisaar, Eric J '77 -32397 Lk Rd -Avon Lake 44012

Tan, Steven W '86 -(Address Unavailable)

(216) 241-5080 .. **Tancredi**, Dara A '92 TW Grogan Co -1442 Euclid Av
-Cleveland 44115

(419) 627-6620 .. **Tandon**, Harsh '99 Erie Cnty Pub Def -220 Columbus Av -Ste 37
-Sandusky 44870 **Fx:**627-6633

(859) 431-3313 .. **Tandy**, Kimberly Brooks '03 Childrens Law Ctr -104 E 7th
-Covington, KY 41011

(614) 241-2181 .. **Taneff**, Thomas N '88 -600 S High -Ste 201 -Columbus 43215

(330) 821-5330 .. **Tangi**, Thomas J '86 -2040 S Union Av -Alliance 44601

(859) 291-9900 .. **Tankersley**, Howard L '97 Taliaferro MSC&K,PLLC -1005 Mad Av
-Bx468 -Covington, KY 41012

(513) 721-4450 .. **Tankersley**, Sarah B '97 Santen & H -312 Walnut -Ste 3100
-Cincinnati 45202

(847) 864-4164 .. **Tann**, Joseph S Jr. '75 -1307 Seward -Evanston, IL 60202

(216) 443-8800 .. **Tanner**, James R Jr. '92 Cuyahoga Cnty Dom Rltns Ct
-1 W Lakeside Av -Cleveland 44113

(740) 852-1576 .. **Tanner Mathewson & Hansgen** -2 S Main -London 43140

(614) 239-4017 .. **Tanner**, Robert E Jr. '89 Regional Airport Auth -4600 Intl Gtwy
-Columbus 43219 **Fx:**238-7834

(740) 732-7667 .. **Tanner**, Sharon L '83 -421 West -Caldwell 43724

(614) 644-9402 .. **Tannous**, Marlo B '88 Dept of Dvlpmnt -77 S High
-Columbus 43215

(614) 227-2000 .. **Tannous**, Robert '87 (Porter WM&A LLP) -41 S High
-Columbus 43215 **Fx:**227-2100

(614) 447-1698 .. **Tanoury**, John L '77 (Ball & T) -700 Ackerman -Ste 450
-Columbus 43202 **Fx:**447-1673

(216) 889-3658 .. **Tansler**, Vicki S '96 Key Corp -127 Pub Square -8th Fl
-Cleveland 44114

(419) 321-6444 .. **Tantari**, Mark R '86 Cline C&W Co,LPA -300 Mad Av -Ste 1100
-Toledo 43604 **Fx:**321-6430

(614) 677-0281 .. **Tantra**, Dina A '94 SrCnsl Nationwide Ins Entrprse
-1 Nationwide Plz -Gen Cnsl Ofc -Columbus 43215 **Fx:**249-2418

(419) 248-2009 .. **Taoka**, Leslie M '79 -405 Mad Av -Natl City Bk NW -Toledo 43604

(216) 348-5056 .. **Taoras**, Bronius K '74 Cuyahoga Metro Housing Auth
-1441 W 25th -Cleveland 44113

(440) 720-7610 .. **Taormina**, Robert A '89 Pioneer-Standard Elec,Inc
-6065 Parkland Blvd -Cleveland 44124

(614) 443-8000 .. **Taps**, Richard T '78 -713 S Front -Columbus 43206

(216) 621-8484 .. **Tarantino**, Thomas J '90 (Climaco LPW&G Co,LPA)
-1228 Euclid Av -Ste 900 Halle Bldg -Cleveland 44115
Fx:771-1632

(440) 899-9161 .. **Tararin**, Alexander A '99 -Drwr936 -North Olmsted 44070

(330) 726-1654 .. **Tarasuck**, Raymond M Jr. '95 -120 Marwood Cir -Bx3965
-Boardman 44513

(740) 454-2591 .. **Tarbert**, David J '93 Kincaid T&G -50 N 4th -Bx1030
-Zanesville 43702 **Fx:**454-6975

(740) 452-5403 .. **Tarbert**, Molly J '93 Jones F&P -45 N 4th -Zanesville 43701

(614) 277-1000 .. **Tarbox**, Eric J '89 Atty Gen-OOCIC -Bx968 -Grove City 43123
Fx:277-1010

Tarbox, Jonathan A '71 -2691 NW 107th Av -Coral
Springs, FL 33065

(330) 762-2411 .. **Tarchinski**, Theresa A '89 (Amer C Co,LPA) -159 S Main -6th Fl
-Akron 44308 **Fx:**762-9918

(330) 783-1488 .. **Tareshawty**, Brian J '90 -4410 Market -Boardman 44512

(614) 463-9770 .. **Tarian**, Brian A '82 %Roetzel & A,LPA -155 E Broad
-Natl City Ctr 12th Fl -Columbus 43215 **Fx:**463-9792

(330) 492-7505 .. **Tarian**, Romain Joseph '77 (RJ Tarian Co,LPA)
-4773 Higbee Av NW -Canton 44718

(216) 621-7500 .. **Taricska**, Richard C '77 -602 Rckfllr Bldg -614 Superior Av NW
-Cleveland 44113

(419) 241-6000 .. **Tarini**, Mary Jo '91 %Eastman & S Ltd -1 Seagate -24th Fl
-Bx10032 -Toledo 43699 **Fx:**247-1777

(440) 838-7600 .. **Tark**, Lori Ross '03 %Janik & D,LLP -9200 S Hills Blvd -Ste 300
-Cleveland 44147 **Fx:**838-7601

(216) 787-3030 .. **Tarka**, Dawn M '92 Atty Gen -615 W Superior Av -11th Fl
-Cleveland 44113 **Fx:**787-3480

(859) 344-6420 .. **Tarkington**, James M '85 Credible Sltns,PLC -Bx175766
-Crescent Springs, KY 41017

(419) 524-6682 .. **Tarkowsky**, John '78 (Baran PTF&T Co,LPA) -3 N Main -Ste 500
-Mansfield 44902 **Fx:**525-4571

(202) 764-2101 .. **Tarlano**, John P '68 USN -3801 Nebraska Av NW
-Bldg 1 Rm 12056 -Washington, DC 20016

(216) 443-8609 .. **Tarnow**, Sara E '00 %Ct of Common Pleas -1200 Ontario
-Justice Ctr 11th Fl -Cleveland 44113

(216) 621-2234 .. **Tarolli**, James L '91 (Tarolli SC&T) -526 Superior Av
-1111 Leader Bldg -Cleveland 44114 **Fx:**621-4072

(216) 621-2234 .. **Tarolli Sundheim Covell & Tummino** -526 Superior Av
-1111 Leader Bldg -Cleveland 44114 **Fx:**621-4072

(216) 621-2234 .. **Tarolli**, Thomas L '61 (Tarolli SC&T) -526 Superior Av
-1111 Leader Bldg -Cleveland 44114 **Fx:**621-4072

(937) 227-3700 .. **Taronji**, Ian A '03 %Faruki I&C PLL -10 N Ludlow -500 Cthse
Plz SW -Dayton 45402 **Fx:**227-3717

(614) 464-6400 .. **Tarpy**, Thomas M '69 (Vorys SS&P LLP) -52 E Gay -Bx1008
-Columbus 43216 **Fx:**464-6350

(330) 456-4503 .. **Tarr**, David T '66 -1400 Market Av N -Canton 44714

(740) 498-7860 .. **Tarr**, Patricia L '75 (PL Tarr Co,LPA) -223 N Brdg
-Newcomerstown 43832

(614) 462-2304 .. **Tarullo**, Michael D '89 (Schottenstein Z&D) -250 West -Bx165020
-Columbus 43216 **Fx:**462-5135

Tarver, Michaele L '96 -(Address Unavailable)

(513) 381-2838 .. **Tarvin**, Julia E '02 %Taft S&H LLP -425 Walnut -Ste 1800
-Cincinnati 45202 **Fx:**381-0205

(202) 267-0096 .. **Tasikas**, Vasilios '99 USCG-Maritime & Intl Law -2100 2nd SW
-Washington, DC 20593

Tasse, James L '80 -26000 Newbury Dr -Westlake 44145

(216) 664-6900 .. **Tasse**, Jeffrey L '81 (Brzytwa Q&M LLC) -1660 W 2nd
-900 Skylight Ofc Twr -Cleveland 44113 **Fx:**664-6901

(216) 621-9091 .. **Tassi**, Arthur J '79 -75 Pub Square -Ste 1230 -Cleveland 44113

(440) 946-7450 .. **Tassi**, M Elaine '79 -34900 Chardon Rd -Ste 207
-Willoughby Hills 44094 **Fx:**946-7653

(419) 471-0211 .. **Tassie**, Deborah S '79 -5151 Monroe -Ste 207 -Toledo 43623
Fx:407-4400

(614) 644-0876 .. **Tassie**, James G '95 Cnsl Governors Ofc -77 S High -30th Fl
-Columbus 43215 **Fx:**995-1767

(216) 787-3030 .. **Tassie**, Sharon D '85 Atty Gen -615 W Superior Av -11th Fl
-Cleveland 44113 **Fx:**787-3480

(513) 533-0633 .. **Tassone**, Gregory J '88 -1203 Hayward Av -Cincinnati 45208

(937) 226-5725 .. **Tassone**, Joseph V '62 Dayco Prod,LLC -1 Prestige Pl
-Miamisburg 45342

(330) 456-7780 .. **Tatarsky**, Kathleen M '79 -236 3rd SW -Ste 100 Carnegie Bldg
-Canton 44702

(352) 543-6090 .. **Tataru**, Terry L '75 (T Tataru,PA) -Bx630 -Cedar Key, FL 32625
Fx:543-5030

(513) 333-4065 .. **Tate**, Charles L '00 %Weltman W&R Co,LPA -525 Vine -Ste 800
-Cincinnati 45202 **Fx:**723-2239

Tate, Davie Jr. '83 -3336 Sycamore Knoll Dr -Columbus 43219

(419) 629-2311 .. **Tate**, John E '80 Crown Equip Corp -44 SWshngtn -Leg Dept
-New Bremen 45869

(513) 784-6306 .. **Tate**, John M '72 Chiquita Brands Intl -250 E 5th -Cincinnati 45202

(513) 762-6200 .. **Tate**, Mary L '02 %Ulmer & B LLP -600 Vine -Ste 2800
-Cincinnati 45202 **Fx:**762-6245

(614) 469-3939 .. **Tate**, Tracy C '03 %Jones D -325 John H McConnell Blvd -Ste 600
-Bx165017 -Columbus 43216 **Fx:**461-4198

(614) 466-3180 .. **Tate**, Vivian P '92 Atty Gen -150 E Gay -Columbus 43215
Fx:466-9788

(216) 518-2200 .. **Tater**, Steve W '96 (McGinnis & T LLC) -12395 McCracken Rd
-Ste A2 -Garfield Heights 44125 **Fx:**518-2246

(216) 566-5602 .. **Tatter**, Rachel J '01 %Thompson H LLP -127 Pub Sq
-3900 Key Ctr -Cleveland 44114 **Fx:**566-5800

(740) 382-2153 .. **Taube**, Donald H '73 Wiedemann & T -117 E Center -Bx218
-Marion 43301

(513) 621-3440 .. **Tauber**, Jill Stanforth '01 %Denlinger R&G Co,LPA -425 Walnut
-Ste 2310 -Cincinnati 45202 **Fx:**621-4449

(216) 621-0794 .. **Taubman**, Bruce D '76 (Taubman & Assoc) -55 Pub Sq -Ste 1670
-Cleveland 44113

(513) 891-8900 .. **Taulbee**, Matthew A '04 %Sanders & Assoc,LPA
-9122 Mntgmry Rd -Ste 201 -Cincinnati 45242

(513) 946-3700 .. **Taunton**, Leigh Kimbrough '02 Hamilton Cnty Pub Def -230 E 9th
-3rd Fl -Cincinnati 45202 **Fx:**946-3707

Tauro, Frank C '58 -Bx235 -Girard 44420

(330) 539-4490 .. **Tauro**, Lori A '93 -Bx356 -Girard 44420

Tavaglione, Barbara A '94 -9191 Paulding NW -Massillon 44646

Tavares-di Meglio, Miranda '04 -(Address Unavailable)

(216) 363-6020 .. **Tavens**, James E '87 (JE Tavens Co,LPA) -1370 Ontario
-Ste 2000 -Cleveland 44113

(216) 696-3311 .. **Tavolier**, David R '86 (Kahn K) -1301 E 9th -2600 Erievw Twr
-Cleveland 44114 **Fx:**623-4912

(440) 953-7077 .. **Tawil**, Linda E '86 Lakeland Cmmnty Cllg -7700 Clock Twr Dr
-Kirtland 44094

(740) 681-9290 .. **Tawney**, David A '92 Linehan & Assoc,LPA -120½ E Main
-Lancaster 43130

(216) 787-3298 .. **Tayek**, Richard W '82 Industrial Commssn of OH
-615 Superior Av NW -Cleveland 44113 **Fx:**787-3483

(216) 696-0800 .. **Tayfel**, Eric W '97 Gibson BZ&M -55 Pub Sq -Ste 2075
-Cleveland 44113 **Fx:**696-0702

(419) 535-0311 .. **Taylor**, Allison M '02 %Schuller Law Ofc -3450 W Central Av
-Ste 242 -Toledo 43606

(614) 224-2426 .. **Taylor**, Amy S '83 (A Taylor Co,LPA) -505 S High
-Columbus 43215

(440) 323-5700 .. **Taylor Breunig & Robinson Co,LPA** -409 East Av -Ste B
-Elyria 44035

(703) 691-4626 .. **Taylor**, Bruce A '75 Natl Law Ctr for Children/Families -3819 Plz Dr
-Fairfax, VA 22030

(513) 721-6500 .. **Taylor**, Catharin R '92 (Clements M&C) -35 E 7th -Ste 710
-Cincinnati 45202 **Fx:**763-6415

(702) 269-7309 .. **Taylor**, Clarence B '62 -367 Bermuda Crk Rd
-Las Vegas, NV 89123 **Fx:**269-8020

(513) 785-7183 .. **Taylor**, Colleen H '99 Hamilton City Law Dir Ofc -345 High -7th Fl
-Hamilton 45011

(937) 226-5642 .. **Taylor**, Countess R '88 Montgomery Cnty Pub Def -117 S Main
-Ste 400 -Dayton 45422 **Fx:**225-3449

(614) 462-3555 .. **Taylor**, Cynthia L '88 Franklin Cnty Pros -373 S High
-Columbus 43215

(614) 228-8833 .. **Taylor**, Daniel P '89 Cincinnati Ins Co -140 E Town -Ste 1015
-Columbus 43215

(304) 723-2827 .. **Taylor**, Daniel P '98 (Taylor & M,PLLC) -Bx2827
-Weirton, WV 26062

(216) 241-1400 .. **Taylor**, Daniel W '79 D Taylor Co,LPA -55 Pub Sq -Ste 2200
-Cleveland 44113

(937) 446-2523 .. **Taylor**, David J '96 Sardinia Ready Mix,Inc -9 Oakdale Av -Bx53
-Sardinia 45171

(419) 244-1000 .. **Taylor**, David R III '76 -316 N Mich -Ste 514 -Toledo 43624

(419) 248-3503 .. **Taylor**, Douglas A '01 -241 N Mich -Ste B -Toledo 43624

(330) 542-0114 .. **Taylor**, Douglas B '90 -11490 Youngstown-Pittsburgh Rd
-New Middletown 44442

(513) 287-2929 .. **Taylor**, Douglas C '86 Cinergy Corp-IB Unit -139 E 4th
-Cincinnati 45202

(330) 535-2151 .. **Taylor**, E Jane '81 (Guy L&T) -106 S Main -Ste 2210 -Akron 44308
Fx:535-9048

(937) 278-2723 .. **Taylor**, Edward M Jr. '51 (Taylor & T) -7417 N Main -Dayton 45415

(330) 376-1112 .. **Taylor**, Elizabeth G '91 %Whalen & C,LPA
-565 Wolf Ledges Pkwy -Bx2020 -Akron 44309 **Fx:**376-3200

(614) 757-5680 .. **Taylor**, Ellisa A '93 SrCnsl Cardinal Hlth -7000 Cardinal Pl -Dublin
43017

(214) 397-4300 .. **Taylor**, Emily D '02 %Epstein BGW&H -500 N Akard -27th Fl
-Dallas, TX 75201 **Fx:**297-0702

(513) 684-3660 .. **Taylor**, Eric A '93 NLRB -550 Main -Ste 3003 -Cincinnati 45202

(419) 245-1020 .. **Taylor**, Gary R '88 %Law Dept -One Govt Ctr -Ste 2250
-Toledo 43604 **Fx:**245-1090

(330) 385-3990 .. **Taylor**, Hayes '82 -1250 Erie -East Liverpool 43920

(216) 664-6271 .. **Taylor**, Heather Ann '00 Cleveland Mun Ct -Bx94894
-Cleveland 44101

(614) 227-2000 .. **Taylor**, Heather N '03 %Porter WM&A LLP -41 S High
-Columbus 43215 **Fx:**227-2100

(216) 241-6602 .. **Taylor**, Hilary S '77 (Weston HFP&H LLP) -50 Pub Sq
-2500 Trmnl Twr -Cleveland 44113 **Fx:**621-8369

(216) 575-0777 .. **Taylor**, Jaeson L '01 %Kelley & F,LLP -1300 E 9th -Ste 1901
-Cleveland 44114 **Fx:**575-0799

(440) 323-5700 .. **Taylor**, James N '81 (Taylor B&R Co,LPA) -409 East Av -Ste B
-Elyria 44035

(614) 891-8422 .. **Taylor**, James R '00 (Taylor & D) -471 E Broad -Ste 1100
-Columbus 43215

(419) 654-0199 .. **Taylor**, Jayson A '04 -6044 N Chanticleer -Maumee 43537

(614) 222-8686 .. **Taylor**, Jodie M '95 Scott S&W LLP -50 W Broad
-2500 LeVeque Twr -Columbus 43215 **Fx:**222-8688

(614) 228-9707 .. **Taylor**, Josefina B '00 Mallory & T Co,LPA -88 E Broad -Ste 1560
-Columbus 43215

(614) 227-2000 .. **Taylor**, K Michael '69 (Porter WM&A LLP) -41 S High
-Columbus 43215 **Fx:**227-2100

Taylor, Kenya M '99 -(Address Unavailable)

(419) 238-1166 .. **Taylor**, Kevin H '77 (Young T&Y) -120 W Main -Bx525
-Van Wert 45891

(937) 865-6800 .. **Taylor**, Kevin M '01 Lexis/Nexis -Bx933 -Dayton 45401

(513) 636-1288 .. **Taylor**, Lisa A '00 Cincinnati Chldrns Hosp Med Ctr
-3333 Burnet Av -ML#9010 -Cincinnati 45229

(614) 227-2000 .. **Taylor**, M Todd '00 %Porter WM&A LLP -41 S High
-Columbus 43215 **Fx:**227-2100

(937) 278-2723 .. **Taylor**, Mary J '51 (Taylor & T) -7417 N Main -Dayton 45415

(937) 842-6159 .. **Taylor**, Mary L '97 Taylor Cnsltnts -9118 Hickory Ln
-Huntsville 43324

(614) 221-5216 .. **Taylor**, Mary TenCyck '85 %Wiles BB&B Co,LPA -300 Spruce
-1st Fl -Columbus 43215 **Fx:**221-5692

(216) 241-5700 .. **Taylor**, Matthew W '03 C Williams -Bx94062 -Cleveland 44101

(614) 227-2317 .. **Taylor**, Maureen P '97 Bricker & E LLP -100 S 3rd
-Columbus 43215 **Fx:**227-2390

(330) 633-0859 .. **Taylor**, Penelope K '87 Pros -46 North Av -Tallmadge 44278

(440) 244-2727 .. **Taylor**, Phillip D '62 -3530 Oberlin Av -Lorain 44053

(216) 241-6602 .. **Taylor**, Randy L '98 %Weston HFP&H LLP -50 Pub Sq
-2500 Trmnl Twr -Cleveland 44113 **Fx:**621-8369

(419) 241-8195 .. **Taylor**, Richard P '75 NW Title Agncy -328 N Erie -Toledo 43624

Taylor, Robert E '75 -17878 Front Beach Rd -A-5 -Panama City
Beach, FL 32413

(614) 469-0100 .. **Taylor**, Robert H '74 (Shoemaker H&T LLP) -471 E Broad
-Ste 2001 -Columbus 43215 **Fx:**280-9675

(757) 498-7035 .. **Taylor**, Robert P '04 %Lentz S&B,PLC -448 Viking Dr -Ste 370
-Virginia Beach, VA 23452 **Fx:**486-6127

(317) 635-9000 .. **Taylor**, Rodney V '91 (Christopher & T) -Bx 2850 -Indianapolis,
IN 46206

Taylor, Rosalind V '79 -2548 Treeside Way -Richmond, CA 94806

(513) 791-8600 .. **Taylor**, Sharon G '80 Spherion -5151 Pfeiffer Rd -Ste 120
-Cincinnati 45242

(937) 322-8600 .. **Taylor**, Shawn M '96 Benjamin Steel Co -777 Benjamin Dr
-Springfield 45502

(937) 865-6800 .. **Taylor**, Steven D '02 Lexis/Nexis -Bx933 -Dayton 45401

(614) 462-3555 .. **Taylor**, Steven L '90 Franklin Cnty Pros -373 S High -Columbus
43215

(440) 250-9709 .. **Taylor**, Susan Parker '04 %R Fedor Jr -1991 Crocker Rd -Ste 222
-Westlake 44145

(440) 701-1253 .. **Taylor**, Suzanne S '89 SourceOne Healthcare Technologies
-8020 Tyler Blvd -Mentor 44060

Taylor, Thomas E '72 -4202 Seven Lks W
-Seven Lakes, NC 27376

(440) 331-4441 .. **Taylor,** Timothy A '70 -20800 Ctr Ridge Rd -Ste 220
    -Rocky River 44116
(440) 930-7529 .. **Taylor,** Tyra L '94 -Bx196 -Avon Lake 44012
(513) 487-5977 .. **Taylor,** Wayne F '70 -2090 Florence Av -Cincinnati 45206
(440) 323-8240 .. **Taylor,** William D '79 -538 W Broad -Elyria 44035
(740) 454-2591 .. **Taylor,** William J '73 (Kincaid T&G) -50 N 4th -Bx1030
    -Zanesville 43702 **Fx:**454-6975
    Taylor, William W '95 -140 E Carlton Rd -Steubenville 43953
(216) 621-0070 .. **Taylor-Kolis,** Donna J '84 (Friedman D&S Co,LPA) -1370 Ontario
    -Ste 600 -Cleveland 44113 **Fx:**621-4008
(614) 443-3848 .. **Teaford,** Hamilton J '66 -91 E Deshler Av -Columbus 43206
(614) 263-4205 .. **Teaford,** Murray R '89 -302 Chatham Rd -Columbus 43214
(614) 462-5200 .. **Teague,** Rodney B '74 Franklin Cnty CSEA -80 E Fulton
    -Columbus 43215
(216) 696-7177 .. **Teamor,** Ricardo B '77 Teamor & Assoc -1301 E 9th -Ste 3110
    -Cleveland 44114 **Fx:**696-7195
(513) 352-4710 .. **Teass,** Lura I '91 Law Dept -801 Plum -Rm 214 -Cincinnati 45202
    Fx:352-1515
(440) 331-3410 .. **Teater,** Christopher C '84 -1325 Chatham Pl -Rocky River 44116
(775) 882-0724 .. **Teegardin,** Dwight A '67 -2505 Old Ranch Rd
    -Carson City, NV 89704
(419) 424-4318 .. **Teeple,** Richard D '67 Cooper Tire -701 Lima Av -Bx550
    -Findlay 45840
(614) 358-8056 .. **Teeples,** M Brandon '03 %Ricketts Co,LPA -580 S High -3rd Fl
    -Columbus 43215 **Fx:**229-4111
(419) 354-8787 .. **Teet,** Thomas E '88 -Bx523 -Bowling Green 43402
(937) 865-2810 .. **Teeters,** Bruce A '91 Huffy Corp -225 Byers Rd
    -Miamisburg 45342
(513) 651-6800 .. **Teeters,** Jeffrey R '93 (Frost BT LLC) -201 E 5th -2200 PNC Ctr
    -Cincinnati 45202 **Fx:**651-6981
(614) 221-2121 .. **Teetor,** John S '77 (Isaac BL&T,LLP) -250 E Broad
    -Ste 900 Mdlnd Bldg -Columbus 43215 **Fx:**365-9516
(614) 827-7676 .. **Teeven,** William G '85 Risk Mngmnt Alt,Inc -4000 E 5th Av
    -Columbus 43219
(513) 701-7300 .. **Tefend,** Mark B '93 Intelligrated Inc -7901 Innovation Way
    -Mason 45040
(419) 524-6211 .. **Teffner,** Donald R '77 -119 Park Av E -Mansfield 44902
(216) 363-8100 .. **Tegreene,** Joseph G '84 (Benesch FC&A LLP) -200 Pub Sq
    -Ste 2300 -Cleveland 44114 **Fx:**363-4588
    Teilans, Arkadijs A '91 -(Address Unavailable)
(216) 595-3234 .. **Teitelbaum,** Michael J '87 -23220 Chagrin Blvd -Ste 360
    -Cleveland 44122
(440) 918-6363 .. **Tekavec,** James W '72 -35350 Curtis Blvd -Ste 320 -Eastlake
    44095 **Fx:**602-5126
(513) 752-0001 .. **Tekulve,** Charles J '58 -785 Ohio Pike -Cincinnati 45245
(513) 752-0001 .. **Tekulve,** Mark J '87 -785 Ohio Pike -Cincinnati 45245
(972) 917-4434 .. **Telecky,** Frederick J Jr. '79 Texas Instrmnts,Inc -MS 3999
    -Bx655474 -Dallas, TX 75265
(330) 643-2365 .. **Teleis,** Kenneth R '93 Summit Cnty Dom Rltns Ct -209 S High
    -Akron 44308
(216) 443-5837 .. **Telep,** Michael B '89 Cuyahoga Cnty Cmn Pleas Ct -2163 E 22nd
    -Cleveland 44115
(216) 692-2010 .. **Telich,** Leslie A '84 MJ Chrzanowski DDS,Inc -782 E 185th
    -Cleveland 44119
(216) 531-4470 .. **Telich,** Mark S '82 -782 E 185th -Cleveland 44119
(513) 721-4532 .. **Teller,** Jerome S '53 (Katz TB&H) -255 E 5th -Ste 2400
    -Cincinnati 45202
(440) 899-1285 .. **Tellerd,** Craig M '87 Tellerd Org -896 Corp Way -Ste 440
    -Westlake 44145
(859) 815-7171 .. **Tellez,** Raul E '92 GE IT Solutions,Inc -1101 Pacific Av
    -Erlanger, KY 41018
(440) 895-3511 .. **Telzrow,** William J III '84 -619 Linda -Ste 101 -Rocky River 44116
    Fx:333-3779
(216) 351-8244 .. **Temas,** Jeffery D '88 -Bx44123 -Cleveland 44144
(513) 868-2838 .. **Temin,** Andrew M '82 -301 High -Ste 300 -Hamilton 45011
(513) 361-0250 .. **Temin,** Larry A '80 SSA-OHA -312 Elm -Ste 2100
    -Cincinnati 45202
(513) 721-3330 .. **Temming,** Daniel J '79 (Robbins KP&T) -7 W 7th -Ste 1400
    -Cincinnati 45202
(419) 353-1062 .. **Ten Brink,** Victor N '83 (Twyman TH&S) -519 W Wooster -Ctr Ste
    -Bowling Green 43402 **Fx:**353-6277
(614) 258-1969 .. **Tenenbaum,** Lee J '78 -325 S Dawson Av -Columbus 43209
    Fx:258-1970
(202) 797-8700 .. **Tenenbaum,** Marc A '89 OfCnsl Slevin & H,PC -1625 Mass Av
    NW -Ste 450 -Washington, DC 20036 **Fx:**234-8231
(216) 621-0200 .. **Tenerowicz,** Matthew A '98 %Baker & H LLP -1900 E 9th
    -Ste 3200 -Cleveland 44114 **Fx:**696-0740
(877) 223-4633 .. **Tenison,** Dennis C '79 LAWO -35 N Park -Mansfield 44902
(304) 232-8100 .. **Tennant,** Donald James Jr. '86 (Cassidy MCV&T,LC) -1413 Eoff
    -The 1st State Cptl -Wheeling, WV 26003 **Fx:**232-8200
(202) 789-4589 .. **Tenoever,** Kathleen M '87 AMA -1101 VT Av
    -Washington, DC 20005
(740) 992-6368 .. **Tenoglia,** Christopher '91 -200 E 2nd -Pomeroy 45769
(513) 561-0883 .. **Tent,** Brian A '03 Lambda Research -5521 Fair Ln
    -Cincinnati 45227
(202) 767-5297 .. **Tentman,** Devonnia M '94 US Air Force -7 AR/JA Unit 2047
    -APO, AP 96278
(614) 761-1991 .. **Tenuta,** Luigia '81 -6400 Riverside Dr -Dublin 43017
(937) 964-8974 .. **Tenwick,** David A '63 ADCARE -5057 Troy Rd -Springfield 45502
(440) 333-8153 .. **Tenwick,** Thomas J '72 -3511 Wooster Rd -Rocky River 44116
(330) 971-8256 .. **Teodosio,** Linda T '82 Mun Ct Judge -2310 2nd
    -Cuyahoga Falls 44221
(330) 535-1555 .. **Teodosio Manos & Ward** -One Cascade Plz -Ste 1000
    -Akron 44308
(330) 535-1555 .. **Teodosio,** Thomas A '82 (Teodosio M&W) -One Cascade Plz -Ste
    1000 -Akron 44308
(513) 721-7500 .. **Tepe,** Thomas M '72 -22 W 9th -Cincinnati 45202
(513) 579-6400 .. **Tepe,** Thomas M Jr. '99 %Keating M&K PLL -1 E 4th
    -1400 Provident Twr -Cincinnati 45202 **Fx:**579-6457
(513) 977-8200 .. **Tepe,** Timothy A '87 (Dinsmore & S LLP) -255 E 5th -Ste 1900
    -Cincinnati 45202 **Fx:**977-8141
(513) 934-5512 .. **Tepe,** Timothy N '84 -16 W Mulberry -Lebanon 45036

(216) 363-4500 .. **Teplitzky,** Ronald J '87 (Benesch FC&A LLP) -200 Pub Sq
    -Ste 2300 -Cleveland 44114 **Fx:**363-4588
    Tepper, Maury M '63 -15 Hickory Knoll Pl
    -Hilton Head Island, SC 29926
(614) 621-1500 .. **Terakedis,** J Troy '96 OfCnsl Calfee H&G LLP -21 E State
    -1100 Fifth Third Ctr -Columbus 43215 **Fx:**621-0010
(614) 462-5002 .. **Terakedis,** John Jr. '70 (Schottenstein Z&D) -250 West -Bx165020
    -Columbus 43216 **Fx:**462-5135
(614) 227-2000 .. **Terapak,** Richard G '72 (Porter WM&A LLP) -41 S High
    -Columbus 43215 **Fx:**227-2100
(614) 273-0448 .. **Terbeek,** Jeffrey L '73 -1010 Old Henderson Rd -Columbus 43220
(330) 665-5117 .. **Teresczuk,** Timothy G '94 %Witschey & W Co,LPA
    -300 N Cleveland-Missillon Rd -Ste 104 -Akron 44333
(216) 522-4856 .. **Terez,** Dennis G '85 Fed Pub Def -1660 W 2nd -Ste 750
    -Cleveland 44113
(513) 239-4244 .. **Terhune,** Charles P Jr. '78 -2301 Runway -Middletown 45042
(740) 636-1830 .. **Terhune-Olaker,** Landis L '01 -Bx895
    -Washington Court House 43160
(330) 929-0507 .. **Terilla,** John A '73 -234 Portage Trl -Bx535 -Cuyahoga Falls 44222
(330) 670-8588 .. **Terjesen,** Barry E '73 Tour Talent LLC
    -843 N Cleveland-Massillon Rd -Ste 6 -Akron 44333
(614) 228-6345 .. **Terlecky,** Myron N '84 (Strip HLM&T Co LPA) -575 S 3rd
    -Columbus 43215 **Fx:**228-6369
(440) 717-1517 .. **Termini,** Mark M '84 (M Termini Assoc,Inc) -8934 Brecksvll Rd
    -#417 -Brecksville 44141
(614) 644-9280 .. **Termuhlen,** Maureen A '83 Supreme Ct of OH -30 E Broad
    -23rd Fl -Columbus 43215
(614) 462-3555 .. **Termuhlen,** Richard A II '83 Franklin Cnty Pros -373 S High
    -Columbus 43215
(513) 381-2838 .. **Terp,** Thomas T '73 (Taft S&H LLP) -425 Walnut -Ste 1800
    -Cincinnati 45202 **Fx:**381-0205
(419) 241-1200 .. **Terpinski,** Kimberly '98 Cooper & W,LPA -900 Adams
    -Toledo 43624 **Fx:**242-5675
(216) 621-0200 .. **Terrion,** Halle F '93 (Baker & H LLP) -1900 E 9th -Ste 3200
    -Cleveland 44114 **Fx:**696-0740
(301) 827-7138 .. **Terry,** Douglas A '01 Food & Drug Admin -5600 Fishers Ln
    -Rockville, MD 20857
(216) 687-1910 .. **Terry,** Margaret L '72 Legal Aid -1223 W 6th -Cleveland 44113
(440) 748-2115 .. **Terry,** Robert M '95 -32822 Woodsprng Cir -North Ridgeville 44039
(216) 587-6500 .. **Terry,** Steven J '89 City Law Dept/Pros Ofc -4301 Warrensvll
    Ctr Rd -Warrensville Heights 44128
(216) 928-2200 .. **Terry,** Thomas H III '79 OfCnsl Sutter OM&F -1301 E 9th
    -3600 Erievw Twr -Cleveland 44114 **Fx:**928-4400
(330) 208-1000 .. **Tersigni,** Vincent J '88 OfCnsl Vorys SS&P LLP -106 S Main
    -First Natl Twr -Akron 44308
(614) 677-9352 .. **Terveer,** Thomas B '83 %Nationwide Ins -1 Nationwide Plz -35th Fl
    -Columbus 43215
(614) 222-4735 .. **Terzian,** Barbara A '75 Gittes & S -723 Oak -Columbus 43205
(330) 376-2700 .. **Terzola,** Mark C '96 (Roetzel & A,LPA) -222 S Main -Akron 44308
    Fx:376-4577
(248) 354-0380 .. **Tesija,** John I '86 (Novara T&M, PLLC) -2000 Town Ctr -Ste 2370
    -Southfield, MI 48075
(419) 586-6481 .. **Tesno,** James A '75 (Meikle T&L) -100 N Main -Bx485
    -Celina 45822 **Fx:**586-2629
(216) 566-7744 .. **Tessler,** Harvey E '71 -850 Euclid Av -Ste 801 -Cleveland 44114
(216) 575-0777 .. **Testa,** Catherine J '04 %Kelley & F,LLP -1300 E 9th -Ste 1901
    -Cleveland 44114 **Fx:**575-0799
(419) 691-6356 .. **Testa,** Charles R '42 -3922 Pickle Rd -Oregon 43616
(216) 486-6888 .. **Testa,** Paul A '88 -580 E 200th -Ste 208 -Euclid 44119
    Testa, Susan C '01 -(Address Unavailable)
(419) 897-6500 .. **Tesznar,** Cynthia G '84 %Barkan & R Ltd -1701 Woodlnds Dr
    -Maumee 43537 **Fx:**897-6200
(614) 227-2000 .. **Teteris,** Jean Y '75 (Porter WM&A LLP) -41 S High
    -Columbus 43215 **Fx:**227-2100
(216) 271-8047 .. **Tetlak,** Thomas E '76 BP Amer,Inc -4850 E 49th
    -Cuyahoga Heights 44125
(513) 321-6988 .. **Tewksbury,** Linn A '87 -3314 Monteith Av -Cincinnati 45208
(305) 982-5325 .. **Tews,** Scott A '90 IRS -51 SW 1st Av -Ste 1114 -Miami, FL 33130
(419) 241-1200 .. **Thacker,** Joseph P '78 Cooper & W,LPA -900 Adams
    -Toledo 43624 **Fx:**242-5675
(216) 689-7112 .. **Thacker,** Michael J '84 KeyBank NA -127 Pub Sq -OH 01-27-0200
    -Cleveland 44114
(734) 214-7646 .. **Thacker,** William M '97 %Dykema G,PLLC -2723 S State -Ste 400
    -Ann Arbor, MI 48104 **Fx:**214-7696
    Thackeray, Jonathan E '61 -15 Bates Farm Ln -Darien, CT 06820
(419) 242-8900 .. **Thakur,** Nirakar C Jr. '95 -416 N Erie -Ste 200 -Toledo 43624
    Thal, Michael L '65 -10607 Xings Dr -Reminderville 44202
(513) 732-7302 .. **Thaler,** Andrew R '03 Clermont Cnty Ct of Common Pleas
    -270 E Main -Batavia 45103
    Thalman, Alfred J '78 -(Address Unavailable)
(859) 692-2237 .. **Thamann,** David D '82 Natl Underwriter Co -5081 Olympic Blvd
    -Erlanger, KY 41018
(614) 466-4605 .. **Thambuswamy,** Ramesh '93 OH Dept Job & Fam Srvcs
    -30 E Broad -32nd Fl -Columbus 43266
(513) 946-3000 .. **Tharp,** Clay '03 Hamilton Cnty Pros -230 E 9th -Cincinnati 45202
    Fx:946-3017
(740) 393-6720 .. **Thatcher,** John C '89 Knox Cnty Pros -117 E High -Ste 234
    -Mount Vernon 43050
(740) 354-5800 .. **Thatcher,** John W '64 -309 Wshngtn -Portsmouth 45662
(513) 741-2651 .. **Thaxton,** James E '88 Rumpke Consolidated Co
    -10795 Hughes Rd -Leg Dept -Cincinnati 45251
(614) 224-9221 .. **Thaxton,** Larry R '97 %Bloomfield & K -199 S 5th
    -Columbus 43215
(513) 621-3394 .. **Thayer,** Abbot A II '80 Peck S&W,LLP -201 E 5th -Ste 900
    -Cincinnati 45202 **Fx:**621-3813
(440) 593-6255 .. **Thayer,** Walter E '50 -171 Broad -Bx460 -Conneaut 44030
    Fx:593-1206
(440) 244-4809 .. **Theado,** Thomas R '79 (Gary N&T,LLC) -446 Bway -Lorain 44052
    Fx:244-3462
(419) 255-3035 .. **Thebes,** John B '89 -413 N Mich -Konop & Cameron Bldg
    -Toledo 43624
(937) 461-5980 .. **Theibert,** Jennifer D '03 %Jablinski FR&M -214 W Monument Av
    -Bx1266 -Dayton 45402 **Fx:**461-4139

(513) 946-9200 .. **Theile,** Gregory R '79 Hamilton Cnty Cmn Pleas Ct -800 Bway -Cincinnati 45202

(419) 241-2900 .. **Theis,** Donald E '79 (Baran PTF&T Co,LPA) -608 Mad Av -Ste 1620 -Toledo 43604 **Fx:**241-3002

         Theis, Stuart H '70 -8705 Whitetail Rd -Kirtland 44060

(202) 879-3939 .. **Theis,** Virginia C '99 %Jones DR&P -51 Louisiana Av NW -Washington, DC 20001

(740) 373-5455 .. **Theisen Brock,LPA** -424 2nd -Bx739 -Marietta 45750 **Fx:**373-4409

(740) 373-5455 .. **Theisen,** Paul T '57 OfCnsl Theisen B,LPA -424 2nd -Bx739 -Marietta 45750 **Fx:**373-4409

(330) 856-7575 .. **Theisler,** Charles W '93 %J Gray & Assoc -8528 E Market -Warren 44484

(614) 249-9847 .. **Theiss,** Douglas J '81 Nationwide Ins Co -One Nationwide Plz -Columbus 43215

(330) 220-5200 .. **Theiss,** Raymond E '85 Litehouse Products Inc -1120 W 130th -Brunswick 44212

(513) 621-2120 .. **Theissen,** Timothy B '87 Strauss & T,LPA -150 E 4th -4th Fl -Cincinnati 45202 **Fx:**241-8259

(614) 462-3643 .. **Theller,** Robert T '98 Cnty Treasurer -373 S High -17th Fl -Columbus 43215

(419) 524-9811 .. **Them,** Jerod M '04 %Weldon H&K,LLP -28 Park Av W -Bank One Bldg -Mansfield 44902 **Fx:**522-5758

(513) 236-0166 .. **Theobald,** Jason M '04 -742 Fleming Rd -Cincinnati 45231

(937) 376-1937 .. **Theodor,** Christ '77 -1721 Ireland Rd -Xenia 45385

(740) 852-5420 .. **Theodotou,** Pamela I '89 -2108 Palouse Dr NW -London 43140

(330) 746-6612 .. **Theofilos,** Gus K '77 -910 Metro Twr -Youngstown 44503

(216) 445-7176 .. **Theofrastous,** Theodore C '99 Cleveland Clinic Fndtn -9500 Euclid Av -D 20 -Cleveland 44195

(614) 466-9939 .. **Thernes,** Linda J '89 Mntl Hlth -30 E Broad -8th Fl -Columbus 43215

(606) 261-0464 .. **Thesing,** James D '79 -330 Division -Bellevue, KY 41073

(713) 625-8100 .. **Thesing,** Patrick R '86 Stewart Title Grnty Co -1980 Post Oak Blvd -Houston, TX 77056

(440) 886-9999 .. **Thesling,** William H '76 (W Thesling,LPA) -5566 Pearl Rd -Parma 44129

(703) 696-8751 .. **Theurer,** Kenneth M '94 USAF/AFLSA -1501 Wilson Blvd -629 -Arlington, VA 22209

(513) 629-1939 .. **Theurich,** David E '91 Wstrn & Sthrn Life Ins -400 Bway -Cincinnati 45202

(419) 321-6325 .. **Thie,** Christopher J '00 Ernst & Young LLP -1 Seagate -Ste 1200 -Toledo 43604

         Thieken, Andrew J '97 -731 Hunt Clb Way -Avon Lake 44012

(440) 347-5792 .. **Thiele,** Terry V '96 Lubrizol Corp -29400 Lakelnd Blvd -Wickliffe 44092

(937) 492-1271 .. **Thieman,** James L '80 (Faulkner GK&S,LPA) -100 S Main Av -Ste 300 -Sidney 45365 **Fx:**498-1306

(937) 498-8118 .. **Thieman,** Tonya K '81 Sidney Cnty Mun Ct -201 W Poplar -Sidney 45365

(513) 897-3055 .. **Thiemann,** Charles L Jr. '01 OH Dept of Natural Rsrcs -8570 E State Route 73 -Waynesville 45068

(614) 227-2000 .. **Thien,** John Kenneth '99 %Porter WM&A LLP -41 S High -Columbus 43215 **Fx:**227-2100

(614) 462-3555 .. **Thies,** Arnold P '02 Franklin Cnty Pros -373 S High -Columbus 43215

(216) 623-0150 .. **Thimmig,** Diana M '83 (Roetzel & A,LPA) -1375 E 9th -One Cleve Ctr 9th Fl -Cleveland 44114 **Fx:**623-0134

(937) 220-9139 .. **Thinnes,** Mary A '82 -241 W Riverww Av -Dayton 45405

(419) 629-8108 .. **This,** Jason E '92 -Bx42 -New Bremen 45869

(513) 235-3902 .. **Thole,** Lori D '93 -2763 Orchrd Pk Dr -Cincinnati 45239

(513) 231-4900 .. **Thole,** Thomas J '74 -7803 Outlookrdg Ln -Cincinnati 45244

(614) 213-5832 .. **Tholt,** Rita E '89 Banc One Inv Advsrs -1111 Polaris Pkwy -Bx710211 -Columbus 43271

(330) 343-8864 .. **Thomakos,** Steven G '87 -158 N Bway -Bx944 -New Philadelphia 44663

(513) 576-1590 .. **Thoman,** Henry N '82 Kendle -Bx51 -Terrace Park 45174 **Fx:**831-3246

         Thomarios, Christopher G '03 -(Address Unavailable)

(216) 685-9940 .. **Thomarios,** Elizabeth A '99 (Pagano WT&G) -1370 Ontario -Ste 1240 -Cleveland 44113 **Fx:**685-9942

(614) 461-1311 .. **Thomas,** Amy S '01 (Reminger & R) -65 E State -4th Fl Cptl Sq Ofc Bldg -Columbus 43215 **Fx:**232-2410

(216) 360-9485 .. **Thomas,** Andrew R '02 -3201 Enterprise Pkwy -Ste 200 -Beachwood 44122

(937) 865-6800 .. **Thomas,** Angela M '94 Lexis/Nexis -Bx933 -Dayton 45401

(216) 443-8560 .. **Thomas,** Angela T '00 Cuyahoga Cnty Crt Comm Pleas -1200 Ontario -Cleveland 44113

(440) 247-1227 .. **Thomas,** Anne B '94 -590 Solon Rd -Bentleyville 44022

(614) 846-5080 .. **Thomas,** Arthur H Jr. '64 -6649 N High -Worthington 43085

(614) 464-6400 .. **Thomas,** Bethany R '02 %Vorys SS&P LLP -52 E Gay -Bx1008 -Columbus 43216 **Fx:**464-6350

(216) 443-7800 .. **Thomas,** Blaise D '85 Cuyahoga Cnty Pros -1200 Ontario -8th Fl -Cleveland 44113 **Fx:**698-2270

(330) 376-8019 .. **Thomas,** Bradley J '97 Allstate Ins Co -50 So Main -Ste 620 -Akron 44308 **Fx:**376-5713

(513) 621-6464 .. **Thomas,** Brian C '01 %Graydon H&R LLP -511 Walnut -1900 Fifth Third Ctr -Cincinnati 45202 **Fx:**651-3836

(513) 336-4628 .. **Thomas,** Brian J '98 Cnsl Anthem BCBS -4361 Irwin Simpson Rd -MB1-220 -Mason 45040

(330) 494-8700 .. **Thomas,** Christopher J '91 -811 Hllcrst Av SW -North Canton 44720

(513) 381-2838 .. **Thomas,** Cindy-Ann L '99 %Taft S&H LLP -425 Walnut -Ste 1800 -Cincinnati 45202 **Fx:**381-0205

(216) 929-0700 .. **Thomas,** Clyde E '56 Thomas & C Inc,LPA -1440 Snow Rd -315 Rockside Plz -Cleveland 44134

(614) 280-1860 .. **Thomas,** Collin N '95 -341 S 3rd -Ste 300 -Columbus 43215

         Thomas, Corrie D '00 -Bx2332 -Buckeye Lake 43008

(513) 241-3100 .. **Thomas,** Craig A '86 Lerner S&R -120 E 4th -8th Fl -Cincinnati 45202

(330) 392-4176 .. **Thomas,** Daniel A '93 DelBene L&T -155 Pine Av NE -Bx353 -Warren 44482 **Fx:**392-5694

(440) 835-1200 .. **Thomas,** Daniel J '89 %Kolick & K -24500 Ctr Ridge Rd -Ste 175 -Westlake 44145

(330) 392-4176 .. **Thomas,** Daniel P '66 (DelBene L&T) -155 Pine Av NE -Bx353 -Warren 44482 **Fx:**392-5694

(330) 255-4200 .. **Thomas,** David A '64 Bridgestone/Firestone Tech Co -1200 Firestone Pkwy -Akron 44317

(614) 228-4141 .. **Thomas,** David H '99 %RW Meeks Co LPA -511 S High -Columbus 43215

(330) 497-2886 .. **Thomas,** David M '88 (Zollinger DGT & Co) -6370 Mt Plsnt NW -Bx2985 -Canton 44720

(216) 621-9110 .. **Thomas,** David P '93 -801 Trmnl Twr -Cleveland 44113

(614) 464-6400 .. **Thomas,** Duke W '64 (Vorys SS&P LLP) -52 E Gay -Bx1008 -Columbus 43216 **Fx:**464-6350

(216) 479-8500 .. **Thomas,** Dynda A '86 (Squire S&D LLP) -127 Pub Sq -4900 Key Twr -Cleveland 44114 **Fx:**479-8780

(513) 961-5311 .. **Thomas,** Ernest V III '82 (Thomas & T) -2323 Park Av -Cincinnati 45206

(513) 961-5311 .. **Thomas,** Ernest V Jr. '68 (Thomas & T) -2323 Park Av -Cincinnati 45206

(330) 633-2300 .. **Thomas,** Esther L '98 -12 Southwest Av -Tallmadge 44278 **Fx:**634-0096

(513) 961-5311 .. **Thomas,** Evan D '00 Thomas & T -2323 Park Av -Cincinnati 45206

(614) 252-2141 .. **Thomas,** Fred Jr. '77 -875 Mt Veron Av -Columbus 43203

(740) 635-0162 .. **Thomas Fregiato Myser Hanson & Davies** -320 Howard -Bridgeport 43912 **Fx:**635-1601

(216) 696-1500 .. **Thomas,** Gregory S '93 Cnsl G Thomas LLC -1422 Euclid Av -Ste 1604 -Cleveland 44115 **Fx:**696-6930

(614) 252-8788 .. **Thomas,** Isabella D '88 -1058 Mt Vernon Av -Columbus 43203

(614) 221-2331 .. **Thomas,** J Patrick '77 -211 E Lvngstn Av -Columbus 43215 **Fx:**221-4525

(330) 345-7949 .. **Thomas,** James A '76 Christian Chldrns Home of OH -Bx765 -Wooster 44691

(216) 479-8500 .. **Thomas,** James D '87 (Squire S&D LLP) -127 Pub Sq -4900 Key Twr -Cleveland 44114 **Fx:**479-8780

(614) 227-0366 .. **Thomas,** James D '88 -5 E Long -Ste 1209 -Columbus 43215 **Fx:**224-0913

(330) 545-9707 .. **Thomas,** James W '60 (J Thomas Co,LPA) -42 E Wilson Av -Bx330 -Girard 44420

(937) 456-4103 .. **Thomas,** James W '74 Thomas Law Ofc -112 N Barron -Eaton 45320

(937) 456-4103 .. **Thomas,** James W Jr. '01 Thomas Law Ofc -112 N Barron -Eaton 45320

(440) 871-4040 .. **Thomas,** Joan Jacobs '84 -23850 Ctr Ridge Rd -Ste 3 -Westlake 44145 **Fx:**871-3004

(614) 719-8813 .. **Thomas,** Jodi L '02 Franklin Cnty Pub Def -373 S High -12th Fl -Columbus 43215

(216) 929-0700 .. **Thomas,** John E '89 Thomas & C Inc,LPA -1440 Snow Rd -315 Rockside Plz -Cleveland 44134

(972) 931-7612 .. **Thomas,** John L '66 -Bx796322 -Dallas, TX 75379

(614) 462-5453 .. **Thomas,** John R '68 (Kegler BH&R) -65 E State -Ste 1800 -Columbus 43215 **Fx:**464-2634

(513) 762-6200 .. **Thomas,** Joseph P '88 (Ulmer & B LLP) -600 Vine -Ste 2800 -Cincinnati 45202 **Fx:**762-6245

         Thomas, Karen Astrid '04 -(Address Unavailable)

(216) 443-8355 .. **Thomas,** Kathryn A '84 Cuyahoga Cnty Pub Def -1200 W 3rd NW -100 Lakeside Pl -Cleveland 44113

(216) 696-6454 .. **Thomas,** Keith D '87 %Cincinnati Ins Co -930 The 55 Bldg -55 Pub Sq -Cleveland 44113

(216) 875-2767 .. **Thomas,** Kimberly A '04 %Bonezzi SM&P Co LPA -526 Superior Av -Ste 1400 -Cleveland 44114 **Fx:**875-1570

(419) 249-7900 .. **Thomas,** Kimberly M '03 %Robison C&O -Four SeaGate -9th Fl -Toledo 43604 **Fx:**249-7911

(614) 252-8788 .. **Thomas,** Larry W '87 -1058 Mt Vernon Av -Columbus 43203

(513) 895-4200 .. **Thomas,** Lawrence R III '00 -526 Main -Hamilton 45013 **Fx:**895-4800

(513) 221-0007 .. **Thomas,** Leslie F '95 -1420 E McMillan -Ste Two -Cincinnati 45206

(740) 695-9335 .. **Thomas,** Mark A '87 Thomas Law Ofcs,LLC -118 W Main -Saint Clairsville 43950

(440) 237-2800 .. **Thomas,** Mary A '84 -12800 York Rd -Ste 2 -North Royalton 44133

(216) 931-6000 .. **Thomas,** Max W '03 %Ulmer & B LLP -1300 E 9th -Ste 900 Penton Media Bldg -Cleveland 44114 **Fx:**931-6001

(440) 356-6900 .. **Thomas,** Michael A '75 -1154 Linda -Ste 250 -Cleveland 44116

(513) 241-1950 .. **Thomas,** Michael E '97 %Brown LH&E -7 W 7th -Ste 1950 -Cincinnati 45202 **Fx:**241-4095

(937) 748-1004 .. **Thomas,** Michael R '81 (Kirby & T LPA) -4 Sycamore Crk Dr -Springboro 45066 **Fx:**748-2390

(614) 464-6400 .. **Thomas,** Michael R '85 OfCnsl Vorys SS&P LLP -52 E Gay -Bx1008 -Columbus 43216 **Fx:**464-6350

(440) 998-1110 .. **Thomas,** Nicholas K '89 %Ashtabula Cnty CSEA -Bx1650 -Ashtabula 44005 **Fx:**998-1538

(937) 225-5757 .. **Thomas,** Nolan C '04 %Montgomery Cnty Pros -301 W 3rd -Bx972 -Dayton 45422 **Fx:**225-3470

(216) 698-6410 .. **Thomas,** Patrick J '02 Cuyahoga Cnty Prosecutor's Ofc -The Justice Ctr -Courts Tower 9th Fl -Cleveland 44113

(614) 462-5430 .. **Thomas,** Patsy A '94 OfCnsl Kegler BH&R -65 E State -Ste 1800 -Columbus 43215 **Fx:**464-2634

(859) 594-3156 .. **Thomas,** Paulette M '99 Catholic Hlth Initiatives -3900 Olympic Blvd -Ste 400 -Erlanger, KY 41018

(614) 466-2980 .. **Thomas,** Peter M '88 Atty Gen -30 E Broad -Columbus 43215 **Fx:**728-9470

(440) 237-2800 .. **Thomas,** Phillip E '81 -12800 York Rd -Ste 2 -North Royalton 44133

(513) 529-4151 .. **Thomas,** Randi M '93 Miami University -203 Roudebush Hall -Oxford 45056

(614) 466-8600 .. **Thomas,** Rebecca L '96 Atty Gen -30 E Broad -Columbus 43215 **Fx:**466-6090

(419) 529-8672 .. **Thomas,** Rebecca M '92 -2294 Park Av W -Mansfield 44906 **Fx:**529-8659

(412) 454-5826 .. **Thomas,** Richard I '02 (Pepper H LLP) -500 Grant -50th Fl -Pittsburgh, PA 15219 **Fx:**281-0717

(330) 744-1148 .. **Thomas,** Richard J '87 (Henderson CMN&T Co,LPA) -34 Fed Plz W -Ste 600 Wick Bldg -Youngstown 44503 **Fx:**744-3807

(440) 498-5363 .. **Thomas,** Rita A '91 Pioneer-Standard Elec,Inc -6675 Parkland Blvd -Solon 44139

(512) 691-6120 .. **Thomas**, Robert P '81 Green Mtn Energy Co
-3815 Cptl of TX Hwy S -Ste 100 -Austin, TX 78704

(330) 535-0505 .. **Thomas**, Robert S II '97 %K Belfance & Assoc -One Cascade Plz
-Ste 2100 -Akron 44308

(216) 830-9000 .. **Thomas**, Sam III '97 OfCnsl Berger & Z Co,LPA
-614 W Superior Av -Ste 1425 Rckfllr Bldg -Cleveland 44113
Fx:830-4200

(513) 745-0400 .. **Thomas**, Scott R '93 (Furnier T,LLP) -1 Fncl Way -Ste 312
-Cincinnati 45242 **Fx:**792-6724

(740) 653-7678 .. **Thomas**, Scott S '93 Buckeye Honda -2055 Columbus-Lncstr Rd
-Bx189 -Lancaster 43130

(937) 328-2640 ..**Thomas**, Shawn A '88 Clark Cnty Pub Def -50 E Columbia -4th Fl
-Springfield 45502 **Fx:**328-2715

(740) 383-2161 .. **Thomas**, Staci K '00 Legal Aid -Bx6029 -Marion 43301

(440) 247-4765 .. **Thomas**, Stephen G '77 (SG Thomas,LPA) -35 River -Level B
-Chagrin Falls 44022

(440) 576-3665 .. **Thomas**, Susan R '96 Ashtabula Cnty -25 W Jffrsn -Cthse
-Jefferson 44047

(212) 632-3000 .. **Thomas**, Suzan Barnes '72 %Fiduciary Trust -600 5th Av
-New York, NY 10020 **Fx:**632-3002

(216) 479-8500 .. **Thomas**, Terence L '94 %Squire S&D LLP -127 Pub Sq
-4900 Key Twr -Cleveland 44114 **Fx:**479-8780

(614) 761-7701 .. **Thomas**, Terry L '85 (T Thomas Co,LPA) -5148 Blazer Pkwy
-Ste A -Dublin 43017

(513) 961-5311 .. **Thomas & Thomas** -2323 Park Av -Cincinnati 45206

(216) 241-3033 .. **Thomas & Thomas** -629 Euclid Av -Ste 740 -Cleveland 44114

(330) 296-3804 .. **Thomas**, Timothy R '77 -206 S Meridian -Ste B -Ravenna 44266

(513) 961-5311 .. **Thomas**, Vincent E '87 Thomas & T -2323 Park Av -Cincinnati
45206

(614) 221-4400 .. **Thomas**, Warner M Jr. '79 Volkema TMBS&M,LPA -140 E Town
-Ste 1100 -Columbus 43215 **Fx:**221-6010

(740) 363-7182 .. **Thomas**, William R '91 (Thomas & F Co,LPA) -163 N Sandusky
-Ste 103 -Delaware 43015

(330) 659-2578 .. **Thomas-Boehnlein**, Karen M '91 -Bx366 -Richfield 44286

(330) 643-7638 .. **Thomason**, Jacqueline '89 Cnsl Summit Cnty Dept Job & Fam
Srvcs -47 N Main -Ste 614 -Akron 44308 **Fx:**643-2424

(330) 762-6223 .. **Thomasson**, James S '69 -159 S Main -317 Key Bldg
-Akron 44308 **Fx:**762-8148

(440) 777-6332 .. **Thomay**, John S '70 -26777 Lorain Rd -707 Community Bldg
-North Olmsted 44070

(216) 222-3164 .. **Thomay**, Mark L '83 Natl City Bk -1900 E 9th -Locator No. 01-2174
-Cleveland 44114

(216) 292-3300 .. **Thomey**, H Charles '03 %Conway MWK&K Co,LPA
-30195 Chagrin Blvd -Ste 300 -Cleveland 44124

(216) 574-8279 .. **Thompson**, Adrian D '86 Cleveland Mun Sch -138 E 6th
-Cleveland 44114

(513) 241-3111 .. **Thompson**, Allan R II '80 ClarkSchaeferHackett & Co -105 E 4th
-16th Fl -Cincinnati 45202

(859) 226-2369 .. **Thompson**, Amanda J '95 (Stites & H) -250 W Main -Ste 2300
-Lexington, KY 40507 **Fx:**253-9144

(740) 373-4171 .. **Thompson**, Amy L '99 Law Dept -301 Putnam -Marietta 45750

(216) 348-0700 .. **Thompson**, Andrew J '99 %Stege & M Co,LPA -200 Pub Sq
-Ste 3220 -Cleveland 44114 **Fx:**348-0803

(216) 732-2854 .. **Thompson**, Barbara A '54 Unemploymnt Comp Commssn
-26301 Curtiss Wright Pkwy -Horizon Bldg 3rd Fl
-Cleveland 44143

(440) 779-6613 .. **Thompson**, Brian '75 -2156 Walter Rd -Westlake 44145

(513) 946-3700 .. **Thompson**, Bruce F '72 Hamilton Cnty Pub Def -230 E 9th -3rd Fl
-Cincinnati 45202 **Fx:**946-3707

(614) 249-6768 .. **Thompson**, Bruce R '85 Nationwide Ins Co -1 Nationwide Plz
-Columbus 43215

(419) 522-5297 .. **Thompson**, Charles R '76 -13 Park Av -Ste 300 -Mansfield 44902

(614) 728-7443 .. **Thompson**, Christine E '91 Dept Admin Srvcs -30 E Broad
-Columbus 43215

(937) 227-3310 .. **Thompson**, Christopher W '91 -130 W 2nd -Ste 2050
-Dayton 45402

(513) 961-6200 .. **Thompson**, Cory D '04 %Markesbery & R Co,LPA
-2368 Victory Pkwy -Ste 200 -Bx6491 -Cincinnati 45206

(937) 562-4000 .. **Thompson**, Cynthia L '87 Greene Cnty Juv Ct
-2100 Greene Way Blvd -Xenia 45385

Thompson, Dale A '75 -649 Westvw Blvd -Mansfield 44907

(937) 492-6101 .. **Thompson**, Daniel K '79 (Monnier & Co) -1055 Fairington Dr
-Sidney 45365

(216) 443-7583 .. **Thompson**, Darin G '96 Cuyahoga Cnty Pub Def -1200 W 3rd NW
-100 Lakeside Pl -Cleveland 44113

Thompson, David P '00 -2145 Bentwood Cir -1D
-Columbus 43235

(216) 378-9905 .. **Thompson**, David W '98 (McGlinchey S PLLC)
-25550 Chagrin Blvd -Ste 406 -Cleveland 44122 **Fx:**378-9910

(703) 767-6523 .. **Thompson**, Delores E '87 Dept of the Interior -1849 C NW
-Ste 5359 -Washington, DC 20240

(330) 753-6874 .. **Thompson**, Dennis Ray '85 -2719 Mnchstr Rd -Akron 44319

(614) 466-3934 .. **Thompson**, Diann K '84 State Med Brd -77 S High -17th Fl
-Columbus 43215

(937) 593-6065 .. **Thompson Dunlap Heydinger MacDonald Watkins & Traul**
-1111 Rush Av -Bx68 -Bellefontaine 43311

(937) 294-5959 .. **Thompson**, Eric S '99 Leppla Assoc -2100 S Patterson Blvd
-Wright Bros Station -Bx612 -Dayton 45409 **Fx:**294-4411

(419) 257-3121 .. **Thompson**, George G '76 (Bechtel & T) -119 E Bway
-North Baltimore 45872

(513) 829-7400 .. **Thompson**, Grace H '86 -1116-B Hicks Blvd -Fairfield 45014

(440) 331-8026 .. **Thompson**, Gregory L '00 (Thompson & T LLC) -19120 Detroit Rd
-Ste 6 -Rocky River 44116 **Fx:**331-8046

(614) 461-9000 .. **Thompson**, Harold Lee '75 (Thompson Law Firm) -85 E Gay
-Ste 810 -Columbus 43215 **Fx:**461-9334

(330) 263-2984 .. **Thompson**, Heather Walters '03 (Miyashita & T,LLC)
-111 S Buckeye -Ste 270 -Wooster 44691

(216) 771-6650 .. **Thompson**, Helen A '96 %Kreiner & P Co,LPA -Bx6599
-Cleveland 44101

(216) 566-5500 .. **Thompson Hine LLP** -127 Pub Sq -3900 Key Ctr -Cleveland
44114 **Fx:**566-5800

(937) 443-6600 .. **Thompson Hine LLP** -2000 Cthse Plz NE -Bx8801 -Dayton 45401
Fx:443-6635

(614) 469-3200 ..**Thompson Hine LLP** -10 W Broad -Ste 700 -Columbus 43215
Fx:469-3361

(513) 352-6700 .. **Thompson Hine LLP** -312 Walnut -14th Fl -Cincinnati 45202
Fx:241-4771

(614) 866-1436 .. **Thompson**, James C '61 -7509 E Main -Reynoldsburg 43068

(513) 232-7576 .. **Thompson**, James W '68 (Thompson & Co,LPA) -7434 Jager Ct
-Cincinnati 45230 **Fx:**232-7654

(614) 221-7777 .. **Thompson**, Janice C '86 %OHIC Ins Co -155 E Broad
-Columbus 43215

(216) 522-3875 .. **Thompson**, Janice L '85 US Dept of Labor -1240 E 9th
-881 Fed Ofc Bldg -Cleveland 44199

(215) 357-3300 .. **Thompson**, Jason L '02 %Leventhal S&G -3600 Horizon Blvd
-Ste 150 -Trevose, PA 19053

(614) 280-1500 .. **Thompson**, Jeffrey G '94 -601 S High -Columbus 43215

(614) 236-6245 .. **Thompson**, Jenifer S '02 Capital Univ Law Schl -303 E Broad
-Columbus 43215

(312) 431-1333 .. **Thompson**, Jennifer L '95 FBI -219 S Dearborn -Ste 905
-Chicago, IL 60604

(740) 965-9317 .. **Thompson**, Jerry L '92 -2260 Blayney Rd -Sunbury 43074

(419) 755-9659 .. **Thompson**, Jerry W '01 Law Dir Ofc -30 N Diamond
-Mansfield 44902

(202) 267-2310 .. **Thompson**, John A '81 USCG-Ofc of Chief Cnsl -2100 2nd
-Ste 3306 -Washington, DC 20593

(305) 762-3331 .. **Thompson**, John T '85 Dept Homeland Security
-7880 Biscayne Blvd -Miami, FL 33138

(330) 743-1171 .. **Thompson**, Jon M '04 %Manchester BP&U -201 E Commerce
-Atrium Level 2 Commerce Bldg -Youngstown 44503
Fx:743-1190

(330) 965-7507 .. **Thompson**, Kathleen '03 -412 Boardman-Canfld Rd
-Boardman 44512 **Fx:**965-7508

(937) 865-7606 .. **Thompson**, Kenneth R II '85 Lexis/Nexis -Bx933 -Dayton 45401

(740) 695-5263 .. **Thompson**, Kirk M '81 Belmont Cnty Pub Def -100 W Main
-Saint Clairsville 43950

(740) 653-4400 .. **Thompson**, Lee A '83 Calig & H,LPA -204 N Columbus
-Lancaster 43130

(937) 252-2030 .. **Thompson**, Lester R II '74 (Thompson & D Co,LPA)
-1340 Woodman Dr -Dayton 45432

(614) 462-3555 .. **Thompson**, Lisa F '97 Franklin Cnty Pros -373 S High
-Columbus 43215

(216) 522-3870 .. **Thompson**, Marcella L '79 US Dept of Labor/Ofc of Solicitor
-1240 E 9th -881 -Cleveland 44199

(614) 529-8600 .. **Thompson**, Matthew J '88 (Nobile N&T,LLC) -4511 Cemetery Rd
-Ste B -Hilliard 43026 **Fx:**529-8656

Thompson, Maurice A '04 Wood Cnty Ct of Cmn Pleas
-1 Cthse Sq -Bowling Green 43402

(614) 424-6760 .. **Thompson Meier & Dersom** -929 Harrison Av -Ste 205
-Columbus 43215

(330) 497-0700 .. **Thompson**, Michael A '74 (Krugliak WG&D Co,LPA)
-4775 Munson NW -Bx36963 -Canton 44735 **Fx:**497-4020

(937) 224-4600 .. **Thompson**, Michael C '89 -5 N Williams -Dayton 45407

(216) 479-8500 .. **Thompson**, Mitchell S '94 OfCnsl Squire S&D LLP -127 Pub Sq
-4900 Key Twr -Cleveland 44114 **Fx:**479-8780

(513) 891-1867 .. **Thompson**, Molly M '95 Liberty Hill Devlpmnt Grp
-10118 Humphrey Rd -Cincinnati 45242

(614) 462-3118 .. **Thompson**, Myron A '96 Franklin Cnty Cmn Pleas Ct -375 S High
-Columbus 43215 **Fx:**462-6292

(937) 378-3188 .. **Thompson**, Nathan A '80 Brown Cnty Cmn Pleas Ct -303
E Cherry -Cherry St Sta,Ste 102 -Georgetown 45121
Fx:378-3318

Thompson, Oliver A '52 -24800 Chagrin Blvd -#310
-Beachwood 44122

(763) 783-4000 .. **Thompson**, Patrick J '95 Aveda Corp -4000 Pheasant Ridge Dr
-Minneapolis, MN 55449

(614) 224-9207 .. **Thompson**, Paul C '02 Title First Agncy,Inc -555 S Front -Ste 400
-Columbus 43213

(440) 331-8026 .. **Thompson**, Rebecca A '99 (Thompson & T LLC)
-19120 Detroit Rd -Ste 6 -Rocky River 44116 **Fx:**331-8046

(734) 281-6464 .. **Thompson**, Ronald S '01 Thompson M,PC -1800 Biddle
-Wyandotte, MI 48192

(419) 636-5666 .. **Thompson**, Ryan S '04 %Bish B&T,Ltd -1210 W High -Bryan
43506 **Fx:**636-3919

(216) 283-9289 .. **Thompson**, Siobhan R '87 -2986 Glengary Rd
-Shaker Heights 44120

(440) 243-2500 .. **Thompson**, Stephen F '00 OH Equity Grp,LLC -6777 Engle Rd
-Ste E -Cleveland 44130

(513) 632-5330 .. **Thompson**, Stephen G '83 (Wade T & Co) -119 E Court -Ste 407
-Cincinnati 45202

(330) 334-5258 .. **Thompson**, Steven Forrest '94 -One Park Centre -Ste 107
-Wadsworth 44281

(614) 645-8226 .. **Thompson**, Susan E '01 City Pros -375 S High -7th Fl
-Columbus 43215

(419) 636-5666 .. **Thompson**, Thomas A '97 (Bish B&T,Ltd) -1210 W High -Bryan
43506 **Fx:**636-3919

(614) 424-6760 .. **Thompson**, Thomas D '71 (Thompson M&D) -929 Harrison Av
-Ste 205 -Columbus 43215

(937) 885-9860 .. **Thompson**, Thomas L '93 -91 Patton Dr -Springboro 45066

(614) 752-8200 .. **Thompson**, Timothy C '93 Div Fire Mrshl -8895 E Main
-Reynoldsburg 43068

(614) 825-4835 .. **Thompson**, Toby G '82 Pivot -400 Lazelle Rd -Ste 16
-Columbus 43240

(513) 721-1975 .. **Thompson**, Tod J '03 %Freking & B -215 E 9th -5th Fl
-Cincinnati 45202 **Fx:**651-2570

(614) 508-7240 .. **Thompson**, William A '81 -4140 Exec Pkwy -Ste 246
-Westerville 43081

(216) 831-0698 .. **Thompson**, William H '84 Seagate Investment Co Ltd
-30195 Chagrin Blvd -Ste 210 -Pepper Pike 44124

(216) 261-5680 .. **Thompson**, William J '62 Skylight Fncl Grp -1660 W 2nd -Ste 310
-Cleveland 44113

Thompson, William M '90 -(Address Unavailable)

(216) 443-7223 .. **Thompson**, William W IV '80 Cuyahoga Cnty Pub Def
-1200 W 3rd NW -100 Lakeside Pl -Cleveland 44113

(937) 748-5001 .. **Thomsen**, Ira H '79 -515 S Main -Bx639 -Springboro 45066

(614) 644-3490 .. **Thomson**, Anne E '92 Dept Ins -2100 Stella Ct -Columbus 43215

Thomson, Constance S '80 -4948 Skelly -Toledo 43623

(330) 535-5711 ..**Thomson**, Daniel A '99 %Brouse M -106 S Main
　　　-500 First Natl Twr -Akron 44308 **Fx:**253-8601

(513) 651-6800 ..**Thomson**, Douglas D '86 (Frost BT LLC) -201 E 5th -2200 PNC
　　　Ctr -Cincinnati 45202 **Fx:**651-6981

(513) 831-3373 ..**Thomson**, Douglas W '78 (Thomson & Z Co,LPA)
　　　-400 TechneCenter Dr -Ste 400 -Milford 45150 **Fx:**831-3402

(419) 865-8021 ..**Thomson**, Joseph M '80 %Balk H&M -5744 Southwyck Blvd
　　　-Toledo 43614 **Fx:**865-9105

(412) 562-1695 ..**Thomson**, Robert W '70 Buchanan I,PC -301 Grant -20th Fl
　　　-Pittsburgh, PA 15219

　　　　　Thomson, Stephanie Schrimpf '87 -1199 Edison Dr
　　　-Cincinnati 45216

(614) 227-2000 ..**Thomson**, Terry L '03 %Porter WM&A LLP -41 S High
　　　-Columbus 43215 **Fx:**227-2100

(937) 322-3330 ..**Thoresen**, Alice D '93 -28 N Fountain Av -Springfield 45502
　　　Fx:322-6655

(330) 875-3255 ..**Thorley**, David A '84 -Bx65 -Louisville 44641

(216) 621-9767 ..**Thorman**, Christopher P '91 (Thorman & H-L Co,LPA)
　　　-1220 W 6th -Ste 307 -Cleveland 44113 **Fx:**621-3422

(614) 224-3838 ..**Thorman**, William A III '88 P Fulton & Assoc
　　　-89 E Nationwide Blvd -Ste 300 -Columbus 43215 **Fx:**224-3933

(740) 695-0532 ..**Thornburg Bean & Glick** -113 W Main -Bx96
　　　-Saint Clairsville 43950

　　　　　Thornburgh, Nancy C '80 -(Address Unavailable)

　　　　　Thornbury, Lee A '90 -(Address Unavailable)

(312) 501-0007 ..**Thorne**, Christopher M '95 EFS Network,Inc -1555 W Schl -C
　　　-Chicago, IL 60657

(574) 262-5517 ..**Thorne**, William D '86 Elkhart Community Schools -2720 Calif Rd
　　　-Elkhart, IN 46514

(330) 723-9536 ..**Thorne**, William L '73 Medina Cnty Pros -72 Pub Sq
　　　-Medina 44256

(216) 292-8500 ..**Thornton**, Arthur C Jr. '69 (Peckinpaugh & T,LLC)
　　　-23230 Chagrin Blvd -Ste 605 -Beachwood 44122

(614) 227-2000 ..**Thornton**, Brett P '01 %Porter WM&A LLP -41 S High
　　　-Columbus 43215 **Fx:**227-2100

(513) 489-1955 ..**Thornton**, Charles W Jr. '72 The Beck Group -8534 E Kemper Rd
　　　-Cincinnati 45249

(330) 747-4404 ..**Thornton**, Edward C Jr. '71 Newman O&K,LPA -11
　　　Fed Plz Central -Ste 1200 -Youngstown 44503 **Fx:**747-6056

(614) 644-9110 ..**Thornton**, Gregg B '91 Insp Gen -30 E Broad -Ste 1820
　　　-Columbus 43215

(859) 422-6000 ..**Thornton**, Gregg E '95 Clark & W -333 W Vine -Ste 1100
　　　-Lexington, KY 40507

(513) 891-1222 ..**Thornton**, Jack F '69 -8280 Mntgmry Rd -Ste 102
　　　-Cincinnati 45236

(419) 935-0171 ..**Thornton**, Kenneth Alec '85 Thornton T&H -111 Myrtle Av -Bx207
　　　-Willard 44890

(216) 732-2854 ..**Thornton**, Kevin W '74 Unemploymnt Comp Commssn
　　　-26301 Curtiss Wright Pkwy -Horizon Bldg 3rd Fl
　　　-Cleveland 44143

(513) 932-4931 ..**Thornton**, Kevin W '95 -301 E Silver -Bx5 -Lebanon 45036

(419) 935-0171 ..**Thornton**, Robert F '58 (Thornton T&H) -111 Myrtle Av -Bx207
　　　-Willard 44890

(419) 935-0171 ..**Thornton Thornton & Harwood** -111 Myrtle Av -Bx207
　　　-Willard 44890

(937) 228-9000 ..**Thorson**, James M Jr. '90 (Thorson SW&S,LLP) -130 W 2nd
　　　-Ste 1508 -Dayton 45402 **Fx:**228-3550

(937) 228-9000 ..**Thorson Switala Wilkins & Snead, LLP** -130 W 2nd -Ste 1508
　　　-Dayton 45402 **Fx:**228-3550

(330) 471-4094 ..**Thouvenin**, Scott G '96 Timken Co -1835 Dueber Av SW -BIC-17
　　　-Bx6927 -Canton 44706

(440) 285-2242 ..**Thrasher Dinsmore & Dolan,LPA** -100 7th Av -Ste 150
　　　-Chardon 44024 **Fx:**285-9423

(330) 665-0916 ..**Thrasher**, Michael L '96 Gates McDonald Ins Co
　　　-150 Sprngside Dr -Ste B-240 -Akron 44333

(606) 824-3302 ..**Threlkeld**, John B '91 (Threlkeld & T,PSC) -144 N Main -Bx277
　　　-Williamstown, KY 41097

(216) 357-7000 ..**Throckmorton**, Keith A '93 US Dist Ct -801 W Superior Av
　　　-Nrthrn Dist of Ohio -Cleveland 44113

(419) 522-0004 ..**Thrush**, Douglas L '75 -13 Park Av -Ste 314 -Mansfield 44902

(513) 381-9200 ..**Thumann**, Robert J '02 %Rendigs FK&D,LLP -One W 4th
　　　-Ste 900 -Cincinnati 45202 **Fx:**381-9206

(202) 326-7900 ..**Thunder**, James M '90 Kellogg HHT&E -1615 M NW -Ste 400
　　　-Washington, DC 20036

(248) 879-2000 ..**Thurber**, John A '65 (Miller CP&S,PLC) -840 W Long Lk Rd
　　　-Ste 200 -Troy, MI 48098 **Fx:**879-2001

(216) 771-3777 ..**Thurman**, Adam J '97 %H Palkovitz -1370 Ontario
　　　-1600 Standard Bldg -Cleveland 44113 **Fx:**771-1950

(937) 225-7306 ..**Thurman**, Brett L '85 Dayton Newspaper,Inc -45 S Ludlow
　　　-Dayton 45402

(513) 241-7460 ..**Thurman**, Milton Jr. '61 (Rubenstein & T) -7 W 7th -Ste 1850
　　　-Cincinnati 45202 **Fx:**684-7777

(412) 553-2216 ..**Thurman**, Thomas D '75 Alcoa -201 Isabella -Pittsburgh,
　　　PA 15212

(937) 229-8257 ..**Thurston**, Heather L '95 Cnsl Fifth 3rd Bank -110 N Main -7th Fl
　　　-Dayton 45402

(614) 365-2700 ..**Thurston**, Pamela H '87 %Squire S&D LLP -41 S High
　　　-1300 Huntngtn Ctr -Columbus 43215 **Fx:**365-2499

(540) 510-3056 ..**Thweatt**, James W III '00 %Flippin DM&J -1800 Wachovia Twr
　　　-Drwr1200 -Roanoke, VA 24006

(513) 721-1200 ..**Thye**, Kelly W '01 %Young R&M Co,LPA -1014 Vine -Ste 2400
　　　-Cincinnati 45202 **Fx:**721-7116

(212) 455-2000 ..**Tibbets**, Mark S '89 SrCnsl Simpson T&B LLP -425 Lex Av
　　　-New York, NY 10017 **Fx:**455-2502

　　　　　Tibbetts, Michelle M '04 -(Address Unavailable)

(216) 226-4700 ..**Tibbetts**, Roger D '69 -14701 Detroit Av -Ste 555
　　　-Lakewood 44107

(740) 454-2591 ..**Tiberio**, Gerald J '04 Cnsl Kincaid T&G -50 N 4th -Bx1030
　　　-Zanesville 43702 **Fx:**454-6975

(330) 792-2336 ..**Tiberio**, Marian A '93 %Wellman JH&S Co,LPA
　　　-4990 Mahoning Av -Youngstown 44515 **Fx:**792-5403

(216) 443-7800 ..**Tiburzio**, Terese M '92 Cuyahoga Cnty Pros -1200 Ontario -8th Fl
　　　-Cleveland 44113 **Fx:**698-2270

(419) 241-6000 ..**Tice**, Ronald J '73 (Eastman & S Ltd) -1 Seagate -24th Fl
　　　-Bx10032 -Toledo 43699 **Fx:**247-1777

(614) 469-3225 ..**Ticknor**, Charles E III '89 %Thompson H LLP -10 W Broad
　　　-Ste 700 -Columbus 43215 **Fx:**469-3361

(216) 781-3858 ..**Ticktin Baron Co, LPA** -1621 Euclid Av -Ste 1700
　　　-Cleveland 44115

(216) 781-3858 ..**Ticktin**, Daniel S '85 Ticktin B Co,LPA -1621 Euclid Av -Ste 1700
　　　-Cleveland 44115

(216) 781-3858 ..**Ticktin**, Harold '53 Ticktin B Co,LPA -1621 Euclid Av -Ste 1700
　　　-Cleveland 44115

(216) 771-6633 ..**Tidball**, Emily A '02 %Goldstein & O -526 Superior Av E
　　　-Ste 1040 Leader Bldg -Cleveland 44114 **Fx:**771-7559

(212) 455-3647 ..**Tiedt**, Jacob C '03 %Simpson T&B LLP -425 Lex Av -New York,
　　　NY 10017 **Fx:**455-2502

(513) 946-3125 ..**Tieger**, Seth S '78 -230 E 9th -Ste 4000 -Cincinnati 45202

(419) 354-9270 ..**Tiell**, Gene V '88 Wood Cnty CSEA -Bx1028
　　　-Bowling Green 43402

(614) 728-6335 ..**Tiell**, Jennifer R '77 Dept of Agriculture -8995 E Main
　　　-Reynoldsburg 43068

(740) 355-8306 ..**Tieman**, Shane A '98 Scioto Cnty Probate/Juv Ct -602 7th
　　　-Rm 202 -Portsmouth 45662

(216) 292-5156 ..**Tierney**, James L II '93 Tremco Inc -3735 Green Rd
　　　-Beachwood 44122

(513) 946-3000 ..**Tierney**, Kevin M '00 %Hamilton Cnty Pros -230 E 9th
　　　-Cincinnati 45202 **Fx:**946-3017

(513) 946-3000 ..**Tierney**, Mark R '95 Hamilton Cnty Pros -230 E 9th
　　　-Cincinnati 45202 **Fx:**946-3017

(513) 629-1470 ..**Tierney**, Selena M '99 Western & Southern Financial Group
　　　-400 Bway -Cincinnati 45202 **Fx:**629-1044

(614) 365-9900 ..**Tigges**, Steven W '81 (Zeiger TL&L,LLP) -41 S High -Ste
　　　3500 Huntngtn Ctr -Columbus 43215 **Fx:**365-7900

　　　　　Tighe, James M '77 -4217 Dudley Rd -Mantua 44255

(216) 267-3044 ..**Tighe**, Robert F '73 -4517 W 172nd -Cleveland 44135

(216) 447-4496 ..**Tiktin**, Roger D '74 R Grabow & Assoc -5005 Rockside Rd
　　　-Ste 425 -Independence 44131

(513) 761-2958 ..**Tillar**, Mark T '85 -240 Clark Rd -Cincinnati 45215

(513) 631-3481 ..**Tillery**, Dwight '73 -1724 Brkly Av -Cincinnati 45237

(440) 423-6805 ..**Tillman**, John C '89 Alcan Aluminum Corp -6060 Parkland Blvd
　　　-Mayfield Heights 44124

(419) 468-5044 ..**Tilson**, Stephen F '74 (Hottenroth GT&G Co,LPA) -126 S Market
　　　-Bx477 -Galion 44833 **Fx:**468-1308

(513) 721-7522 ..**Tilton**, Fredric '73 -22 W 9th -Cincinnati 45202

(614) 932-6369 ..**Tilton**, Jerry E '75 -5998 Kirkwall Ct W -Dublin 43017

(614) 728-4639 ..**Tilton**, Richard J '85 Industrial Commssn of OH -30 W Spring
　　　-9th Fl -Columbus 43215 **Fx:**752-8765

(330) 725-4929 ..**Timer**, Kimberly J '03 %Oberholtzer F&L -39 Pub Sq -Ste 201
　　　-Bx220 -Medina 44258 **Fx:**723-4929

(330) 451-7931 ..**Timken**, Jane M '94 %Hon SE Lioi -115 Central Plz N
　　　-Canton 44702

(614) 466-5394 ..**Timken**, Kyle E '99 Pub Def -8 E Long -Columbus 43215

(440) 871-8048 ..**Timken**, Richard M Jr. '95 SrCnsl Chemtron Corp
　　　-35850 Schneider Ct -Avon 44011

(513) 870-2116 ..**Timmel**, Timothy L '76 Cincinnati Ins Co -Bx145496
　　　-Cincinnati 45250

(419) 624-3000 ..**Timmerberg**, James S '97 Murray & M Co,LPA
　　　-111 E Shoreline Dr -Bx19 -Sandusky 44871

　　　　　Timmers, Carol L '93 -(Address Unavailable)

(614) 853-1047 ..**Timmins**, Patrick F Jr. '67 -3435 Rolling Hills Ln -Grove City 43123

(330) 527-4882 ..**Timmons**, Dann S '87 -8118 Main -Bx3143 -Garrettsville 44231

(216) 566-2575 ..**Timmons**, Joseph F '87 Sherwin-Williams Co -101 Prospect
　　　-Cleveland 44115

(904) 670-8998 ..**Timmons**, Joyce T '81 -Bx726 -Eastpoint, FL 32328

(614) 734-9450 ..**Timms**, David S '99 OfCnsl Mason Law Firm Co,LPA
　　　-425 Metro Pl N -Ste 620 -Dublin 43017 **Fx:**734-9451

(614) 728-0449 ..**Timms**, Lisa H '99 Treasurer of State-Cnsls Ofc -30 E Broad
　　　-9th Fl -Columbus 43215 **Fx:**644-7313

(440) 576-8406 ..**Timonere**, Jane '01 -4 Lawyers Row -Jefferson 44047
　　　Fx:576-2072

(419) 248-1500 ..**Timonere**, Steven '55 Doyle L&W -202 N Erie -Bx2168
　　　-Toledo 43603 **Fx:**248-2002

(513) 631-2112 ..**Tincher**, James R '04 Teds Pawn Shop -4028 Forest Av
　　　-Cincinnati 45212

(412) 880-5070 ..**Tindall**, Marshall Jeff '92 Tindall & B PC -3 Gtwy Ctr -Ste 15W
　　　-Pittsburgh, PA 15222

(513) 983-4661 ..**Ting**, Jennifer J '00 Procter & Gamble Co -2 Procter & Gamble Plz
　　　-TN-7 Bx 28 -Cincinnati 45202

(614) 224-3303 ..**Tinianow**, Jerome C '80 Natl Audubon Scty -692 N High -Ste 208
　　　-Columbus 43215

(937) 773-9290 ..**Tinkler**, Cornelia E '96 Peoples Savings Bk -317 N Wayne
　　　-Bx1473 -Piqua 45356

(513) 621-6464 ..**Tinkler**, Hans M '02 %Graydon H&R LLP -511 Walnut
　　　-1900 Fifth Third Ctr -Cincinnati 45202 **Fx:**651-3836

(440) 357-3428 ..**Tinkler**, Timothy E '73 Ricerca,LLC -7528 Auburn Rd
　　　-Painesville 44077

(330) 225-7220 ..**Tinl**, Robert T '75 R Tinl & Assoc -3695 Ctr Rd -Brunswick 44212
　　　Fx:225-9770

(419) 241-1200 ..**Tinsley**, Dusty R '00 Cooper & W,LPA -900 Adams -Toledo 43624
　　　Fx:242-5675

　　　　　Tintor, Sarah A '63 -2927 Avnida Valera -Carlsbad, CA 92009

(330) 670-8400 ..**Tipping**, Christopher A '95 H Tipping
　　　-525 N Cleveland Massillon Rd -#207 -Akron 44333

(330) 670-8400 ..**Tipping**, Harry A '71 H Tipping -525 N Cleveland Massillon Rd
　　　-#207 -Akron 44333

(216) 781-0722 ..**Tipping**, Mary Jo '91 Marein & B -526 Superior Av E -Ste 222
　　　-Cleveland 44114

(614) 501-8012 ..**Tippins**, Adria M '02 -Bx13049 -Columbus 43213 **Fx:**501-8012

　　　　　Tipton, Susan D '93 -3006 N High -Ste A -Columbus 43202

(216) 357-5123 ..**Tira**, Joseph R '77 %A Isakoff -55 Pub Sq -Ste 1331
　　　-Cleveland 44113 **Fx:**241-4591

(216) 566-2000 ..**Tirey**, Arthi K '00 %Sherwin-Williams Co -101 Prospect Av NW
　　　-Cleveland 44115

(219) 424-1333 ..**Tirpak**, Ronald J '78 (Schenkel T&K) -520 S Calhoun
　　　-Fort Wayne, IN 46802

(859) 491-3000 .. **Tismo**, J. P '97 -1017 Russell -Covington, KY 41011

(330) 369-1200 .. **Tisone**, Raymond J '72 (RJ Tisone & Assoc Co,LPA) -4087 Youngstown Rd SE -Warren 44484

(513) 875-3511 .. **Tissandier**, Stephen J '90 -73 Pike & E Sts -Bx277 -Fayetteville 45118

(440) 930-1318 .. **Titas**, Francis G '73 Polyone Corp -33587 Walker Rd -Ste 36-5000 -Avon Lake 44012

(614) 644-5441 .. **Titchell**, Alan L '71 Industrial Commssn of OH -30 W Spring -9th Fl -Columbus 43215 Fx:752-8785

(216) 696-1422 .. **Titlebaum**, Ellen R '98 %McCarthy LC&L Co,LPA -101 Prospect Av W -1800 Mdlnd Bldg -Cleveland 44115 **Fx:**696-1210

(513) 241-2324 .. **Tittel**, Bruce '64 (Wood H&E LLP) -441 Vine -Ste 2700 -Cincinnati 45202 Fx:421-7269

(216) 755-5665 .. **Titterington**, Camilla '00 Developers Diversified Rlty Corp -3300 Enterprise Pkwy -Beachwood 44122

(440) 777-6500 .. **Tittle**, Donald S '75 Burke V&G -22649 Lorain Rd -Fairview Park 44126 Fx:777-0507

(614) 221-2838 .. **Titus**, Frank A '79 OfCnsl Taft S&H LLP -21 E State -12th Fl -Columbus 43215 Fx:221-2007

(937) 225-3449 .. **Titus**, Gary L '84 Montgomery Cnty Pub Def -117 S Main -Ste 400 -Dayton 45422 Fx:225-3449

(216) 522-3380 .. **Tkacik**, John M Jr. '93 IRS -1375 E 9th -1200 -Cleveland 44114

(614) 466-5394 .. **Tkacz**, Ruth L '93 Pub Def -8 E Long -Columbus 43215

(513) 241-8137 .. **Tobias Kraus & Torchia** -414 Walnut -Ste 911 -Cincinnati 45202

(614) 645-7483 .. **Tobias**, Melanie R '99 City Pros -375 S High -7th Fl -Columbus 43215

(513) 241-8137 .. **Tobias**, Paul H '62 (Tobias K&T) -414 Walnut -Ste 911 -Cincinnati 45202

(614) 645-8940 .. **Tobias**, Robert S '95 City Pros -375 S High -7th Fl -Columbus 43215

(216) 881-8030 .. **Tobik**, Robert L '70 -4403 St Clair -Cleveland 44103

(330) 668-6500 .. **Tobin**, Alan J '81 %C-Bus S&S -4040 Embssy Pkwy -Ste 100 -Akron 44333

(330) 535-5149 .. **Tobin**, Alfred S '82 Daywalt Tobin & Co -137 S Main -Ste 300 -Akron 44308

(216) 369-0100 .. **Tobin**, Christine M '82 -4141 Rockside Rd -Ste 230 -Seven Hills 44131 Fx:642-5355

(440) 353-3101 .. **Tobin**, Mary L '84 -34100 Ctr Ridge Rd -Ste 105 -North Ridgeville 44039

(513) 381-8430 .. **Tobin**, Stuart '69 (Immerman & T Co,LPA) -632 Vine -Ste 1010 -Cincinnati 45202

(614) 466-7264 .. **Tobin**, Susan G '81 OH Legal Rghts Srvc -8 E Long -5th Fl -Columbus 43215

(216) 787-3030 .. **Tobocman**, Marilyn '83 Atty Gen -615 W Superior Av -11th Fl -Cleveland 44113 Fx:787-3480

(216) 566-2492 .. **Tocci**, Dennis M '85 Sherwin-Williams Co -101 Prospect Av NW -Cleveland 44115

(216) 479-6100 .. **Tocco**, David J '86 (Vorys SS&P LLP) -1375 E 9th -Ste 2100 One Cleve Ctr -Cleveland 44114 Fx:479-6060

(419) 882-0081 .. **Todak**, Michael J '82 (LaValley LT&S Co,LPA) -5680 Monroe -Bldg F -Sylvania 43560 Fx:882-4635

(330) 659-2519 .. **Todaro**, David M '03 -4615 W Streetsboro Rd -Richfield 44286

(614) 242-4333 .. **Todaro**, Frank E '87 -471 E Broad -Ste 1303 -Columbus 43215

(614) 485-1800 .. **Todaro**, Gerald J '74 (Arnold T&W) -2075 Marble Cliff Ofc Park -Columbus 43215 Fx:485-1944

(614) 224-0933 .. **Todd**, Adam R '04 %Frost & M Co,LPA -400 S 5th -Ste 301 -Columbus 43215

(513) 421-4020 .. **Todd**, David H '63 OfCnsl Cohen TK&S,LLC -250 E 5th -Ste 1200 -Cincinnati 45202 Fx:241-4490

(412) 232-1642 .. **Todd**, Glenn D '96 KPMG LLP -One Mellon Bk Ctr -Pittsburgh, PA 15219

(219) 294-1499 .. **Todd**, James L '79 (Sanders & P LLP) -300 Rvrwalk Dr -Elkhart, IN 46516 Fx:294-7277

(419) 255-5900 .. **Todd**, Oliver E Jr. '67 (MacMillan S&T,LLC) -720 Water -4th Fl -Toledo 43604 Fx:255-9639

(740) 321-1741 .. **Todd**, Sara L '81 Paramount Financial Group,Inc -4009 Columbus Rd SW -Granville 43023 Fx:321-9741

(330) 869-9421 .. **Todd**, Tamara J '03 -311 Alden Av -Akron 44313

(419) 697-9672 .. **Todd**, Virginia L '97 -1215 Eastland Dr -Oregon 43616

(440) 338-1169 .. **Todd**, Walker F '95 -1164 Sheerbrook Dr -Chagrin Falls 44022

(904) 277-4406 .. **Todd**, William M '70 -26 Sea Marsh Rd -Amelia Island, FL 32034

(614) 365-2700 .. **Todd**, William M '76 (Squire S&D LLP) -41 S High -1300 Huntngtn Ctr -Columbus 43215 Fx:365-2499

(404) 521-3939 .. **Toddy**, Matthew J '85 (Jones DR&P) -303 Pchtree NE -Atlanta, GA 30308

(202) 371-7000 .. **Todor**, John J '98 Skadden ASM&F,LLP -1440 NY Av NW -Washington, DC 20005

(216) 621-0890 .. **Todt**, Robert W '86 %Kirschenbaum Co,LPA -1919 E 13th -Cleveland 44114

(330) 675-2426 .. **Toepfer**, David M '97 %Trumbull Cnty Pros -160 High NW -Warren 44481

Toepfer, Robert A '43 -304 Apple Blossom Ln -Bay Village 44140

(216) 360-9919 .. **Toerek**, Sharon L '91 (Macedonio T&B,PLL) -29525 Chagrin Blvd -Ste 208 -Cleveland 44122

(440) 843-5300 .. **Toetz**, David W '83 -5579 Pearl Rd -Ste 203 -Parma 44129 Fx:842-1801

(216) 378-2810 .. **Tognetti**, Edward J '96 Sky Trust NA -30050 Chagrin Blvd -Ste 150 -Pepper Pike 44124

(513) 946-3000 .. **Tolbert**, Steven M '78 Hamilton Cnty Pros -230 E 9th -Cincinnati 45202 Fx:946-3017

(330) 497-2886 .. **Tolbert**, Valerie L '97 %Zollinger DGT & Co -6370 Mt Plsnt NW -Bx2985 -Canton 44720

(202) 942-1891 .. **Tolbert**, William L Jr. '89 SEC -450 5th NW -Washington, DC 20549

Toler, Lynn C '84 -1267 Oakrdg Dr -Cleveland 44121

(412) 297-4960 .. **Tolhurst**, Frederick L '83 Cohen & G -11 Stanwix -15th Fl -Pittsburgh, PA 15222

(330) 343-5585 .. **Tolhurst**, Harry C III '00 %Miller & K,LPA -405 Chauncey Av NW -Bx668 -New Philadelphia 44663 Fx:343-7977

Tollefsen, Scott B '79 -60 Truman Av -Princeton, NJ 08540

(937) 255-2838 .. **Tollefson**, Gina S '94 AFMC LO/JAZ -2240 B -Rm 100 -Wright Patterson AFB 45433

(419) 352-1776 .. **Tolles**, Mark D '81 -920 N Main -Bowling Green 43402

(937) 228-7511 .. **Tolliver**, George W II '01 (Tolliver & E) -131 N Ludlow -Ste 1000 -Dayton 45402 Fx:228-9515

(419) 249-2703 .. **Tolliver**, Lafayette E '77 -316 N Mich -#514 -Toledo 43624

(918) 488-8922 .. **Tolliver**, Sandra L '93 -Bx14271 -Tulsa, OK 74159

(216) 231-8440 .. **Tolliver**, Stanley E Sr. '53 -1464 E 105th -Ste 404 -Cleveland 44106

(330) 332-4147 .. **Tolson**, Theresa T '97 -731 W State -Ste 103 -Salem 44460

(216) 251-6655 .. **Tolt**, Lester T '63 -3730 Rocky Rvr Dr -Ste 8 -Cleveland 44111 Fx:251-6657

(216) 261-0200 .. **Toma**, Timothy N '87 T Toma Co,LPA -27801 Euclid Av -Ste 500 -Cleveland 44132

(513) 651-6800 .. **Tomain**, Joseph A '03 %Frost BT LLC -201 E 5th -2200 PNC Ctr -Cincinnati 45202 Fx:651-6981

(216) 227-3913 .. **Tomallo**, Ronald P Jr. '96 Lake Erie Screw Corp -13001 Athens Av -Lakewood 44107

(216) 622-0850 .. **Toman**, Bradley P '89 %McFadden & Assoc Co,LPA -1370 Ontario -Ste 1700 -Cleveland 44113 Fx:622-0854

(847) 700-6228 .. **Toman**, Richard J '81 SrCnsl United Airlines -Leg Dept -Bx66100 -Chicago, IL 60666

(216) 592-5000 .. **Tomaro**, Robert B '74 (Tucker E&W LLP) -925 Euclid Av -1150 Huntngtn Bldg -Cleveland 44115 Fx:592-5009

(216) 664-3776 .. **Tomasello**, Shirley A '92 Dept of Law -601 Lakeside Av -Rm 106 City Hall -Cleveland 44114 Fx:664-2663

(330) 562-7277 .. **Tomasko**, Elizabeth S '91 -240 Harmon Rd -Aurora 44202

(440) 934-1425 .. **Tomassi**, John A '90 -2334 Candlewood Dr -Avon 44011

(440) 352-3391 .. **Tomaszewski**, Jodi L '99 %Dworken & B Co,LPA -60 S Park Pl -Painesville 44077 Fx:352-3469

(216) 520-5566 .. **Tomazic**, Mary E '84 West Grp-Cleveland Ofc -6111 Oak Tree Cir -Independence 44131

Tomblin, Kelly A '03 -351 Ocean Blvd -Atlantic Highlands, NJ 07716

(419) 213-4305 .. **Tomczak**, Thomas N '68 Lucas Cnty Treasurer Ofc -One Govt Ctr -Ste 500 -Toledo 43604

(614) 228-4141 .. **Tome**, Lisa M '01 -511 S High -Columbus 43215

(724) 495-7746 .. **Tomec**, John L '68 -446 Ridgemont Dr -Industry, PA 15052

(330) 643-2765 .. **Tomer**, Michele A '92 Summit Cnty Pros-CSEA -171 S Main -Akron 44308 Fx:643-2822

(203) 238-8949 .. **Tomich**, John A '83 Cuno Inc -400 Rsrch Pkwy -Meriden, CT 06450

(330) 723-4656 .. **Tomino**, Nick '78 (Tomino & L,LLC) -803 E Wshngtn -Ste 200 -Medina 44256

(614) 628-8000 .. **Tomkies**, Michael C '86 (Dreher L&T LLP) -41 S High -2250 Huntngtn Ctr -Columbus 43215 Fx:628-1600

(614) 262-9940 .. **Tomko**, Carole W '81 Customized Orgnztnl Solutions -3478 N High -Ste 200 -Columbus 43214 Fx:262-8850

(740) 695-8347 .. **Tomlan**, John R '83 -108 E Main -Saint Clairsville 43950

(937) 233-8605 .. **Tomlinson**, Jon S '99 -5689 Troy Villa Blvd -Huber Heights 45424

(330) 742-7032 .. **Tomlinson**, Kimberly A '94 Sky Trust NA -23 Fed Plz -Bx479 -Youngstown 44501 Fx:742-7091

(904) 359-3674 .. **Tomola**, James D '79 SrCnsl CSX Trans -500 Water -Jacksonville, FL 32202

(216) 749-7466 .. **Tomon**, Bert R '72 Tomon Funeral Home -4772 Pearl Rd -Cleveland 44109

(216) 479-8500 .. **Tompkins**, Catherine C '95 %Squire S&D LLP -127 Pub Sq -4900 Key Twr -Cleveland 44114 Fx:479-8780

(330) 273-8883 .. **Tompkins**, Paul K '81 RPM,Inc -2628 Pearl Rd -Bx777 -Medina 44258

(937) 653-3467 .. **Tompkins**, Ronald C '85 -19 Pearce Pl -Urbana 43078 Fx:653-3375

(740) 455-7190 .. **Tompkins**, Thomas Jay '85 Muskingum Cnty Cmn Pleas Ct -27 N 5th -Zanesville 43701

(216) 241-2838 .. **Tomsick**, Richard D '84 OfCnsl Taft S&H LLP -200 Pub Sq -3500 BP Twr -Cleveland 44114 Fx:241-3707

(440) 243-1458 .. **Tomsik**, Donald M '59 -14961 Cherokee Trl -Middleburg Heights 44130

(440) 846-3686 .. **Tomson**, William L Jr. '71 -14400 Pearl Rd -Strongsville 44136

(419) 626-0055 .. **Tone Grubbe McGory & Vermeeren** -1401 Cleveland Rd -Sandusky 44870 Fx:626-0288

(419) 626-0055 .. **Tone**, Tygh M '89 (Tone GM&V) -1401 Cleveland Rd -Sandusky 44870 Fx:626-0288

(419) 272-2521 .. **Toner**, John G '62 Edon State Bk -101 N Mich -Edon 43518

(330) 253-5060 .. **Toney**, Darrin R '95 %Brennan M&D,LLC -75 E Market -Akron 44308 Fx:253-1977

(614) 258-1476 .. **Tongren**, Robert S '72 -433 N Drexel Av -Columbus 43209

(330) 480-3203 .. **Tonies**, Theresa M '95 Humility of Mary Hlth Prtnrs -1044 Belmont Av -Youngstown 44504

(215) 297-0607 .. **Tonkonow**, Sherry R '81 -4130 Street Rd -Doylestown, PA 18901

(614) 431-1500 .. **Tonks**, Paul H '96 %Perez & M LLC -8000 Ravines Edge Ct -Ste 300 -Columbus 43235 Fx:431-3885

(740) 474-7588 .. **Tonn**, Jason W '01 Cnty Job & Family Srvcs -110 Isl Rd -Bx439 -Circleville 43113

(513) 621-2120 .. **Tonne**, Jason D '03 %Strauss & T,LPA -150 E 4th -4th Fl -Cincinnati 45202 Fx:241-8259

(440) 323-3335 .. **Tonry**, Eugene A '57 OfCnsl J Morrison -105 Court -Ste 319 -Elyria 44035

(216) 241-2838 .. **Tonsing**, Heather L '98 %Taft S&H LLP -200 Pub Sq -3500 BP Twr -Cleveland 44114 Fx:241-3707

(440) 244-1811 .. **Tony**, Michael J '89 -520 Bway -3rd Fl -Lorain 44052

(216) 586-3939 .. **Toohey**, Brian F '80 (Jones D) -901 Lakeside Av -Cleveland 44114 Fx:579-0212

(216) 586-3939 .. **Toohey**, Meagan E '03 %Jones D -901 Lakeside Av -Cleveland 44114 Fx:579-0212

(216) 861-6282 .. **Toohig**, Kevin T '96 -1360 W 9th -Ste 310 -Cleveland 44113

(216) 363-1400 .. **Toole**, Jeffrey C '95 (Buckley K,LPA) -600 E Superior Av -Ste 1400 -Cleveland 44114 Fx:579-1020

(216) 621-0200 .. **Toomajian**, William M '78 (Baker & H LLP) -1900 E 9th -Ste 3200 -Cleveland 44114 Fx:696-0740

(513) 863-6700 .. **Tooman**, Steven A '96 %Millikin & F -6 S 2nd -6th Fl -Bx598 -Hamilton 45012 Fx:863-0031

(703) 588-7954 .. **Toomey**, Allan A '72 US Army/Ct of Crim Appls -901 N Stuart -Arlington, VA 22203

(614) 487-1630 .. **Toomey**, Michael J '98 -1500 W 3rd Av -Ste 231 -Columbus 43212

(330) 533-9810 .. **Toot**, Douglas M '73 -106 S Broad -Canfield 44406

(614) 336-4401 .. **Tootle**, Heather W '96 -3010 Hayden Rd -Columbus 43235
-Fx:798-1935

(614) 228-7747 .. **Tootle**, Thomas C '93 (T Tootle Co LPA) -85 E Gay -Ste 900
-Columbus 43215

(740) 474-6021 .. **Tootle**, Thomas F '73 (Young T&D) -180 W Franklin -Circleville
43113

(513) 241-3100 .. **Top**, Andrew M '98 Lerner S&R -120 E 4th -8th Fl
-Cincinnati 45202

(440) 992-5891 .. **Topalof**, Dean F '96 -4920 State Rd -Ashtabula 44004

(859) 386-4065 .. **Topazio**, Bernadine C '94 Fidelity Inst Rtrmnt Srvc
-200 Magellan Way -Covington, KY 41015

(330) 796-4456 .. **Toppen**, Timothy R '92 Goodyear -1144 E Market -Akron 44316

(614) 486-4805 .. **Topper**, Richard D Jr. '79 -1500 W 3rd Av -Ste 400
-Columbus 43212

(202) 942-3863 .. **Topping**, Catherine R '84 FDIC -550 17th NW
-Washington, DC 20429

(330) 743-5101 .. **Torba**, Carla Jo '92 %Green H&S,Co LPA -16 Wick Av -Ste 400
-Youngstown 44503 **Fx**:743-3451

(202) 879-5562 .. **Torborg**, David S '98 %Jones DR&P -51 Louisiana Av NW
-Washington, DC 20001 **Fx**:626-1700

(216) 689-5086 .. **Torch**, Glenn F '74 -127 Pub Sq -OH-01-27-0200 -Cleveland
44114

(513) 241-8137 .. **Torchia**, David G '84 (Tobias K&T) -414 Walnut -Ste 911
-Cincinnati 45202

(419) 897-6500 .. **Torda**, Joseph R '90 Barkan & R Ltd -1701 Woodlnds Dr
-Maumee 43537 **Fx**:897-6200

(216) 241-6602 .. **Torgerson**, Kenneth A '66 (Weston HFP&H LLP) -50 Pub Sq
-2500 Trmnl Twr -Cleveland 44113 **Fx**:621-8369

(606) 325-8709 .. **Torian**, Miriam A '04 US Dist Ct-NDKY -1405 Greenup Av -Rm 210
-Ashland, KY 41101

(440) 984-3782 .. **Torma**, Mary D '92 -6464 Balsam Dr -Amherst 44001

(614) 644-3037 .. **Tormey**, Edmund J '90 EPA -122 S Front -Bx1049
-Columbus 43216

(513) 246-0034 .. **Tormey**, Randolph T '79 US Dept of Energy -175 Tri Cnty Pkwy
-Springdale 45246

(616) 336-6628 .. **Tornga**, Timothy J '76 (Varnum RS&H) -333 Brdg NW -Bx352
-Grand Rapids, MI 49501

(937) 562-5250 .. **Tornichio**, Adolfo A '99 Greene Cnty Pros -61 Greene
-Xenia 45385

(614) 261-7400 .. **Tornstrom**, Megan M '00 (DeFourny & T) -4840 N High
-Columbus 43214 **Fx**:263-1699

(216) 361-0002 .. **Torok**, Rosemary '86 Tenable Protective Srvcs -2423 Payne Av
-Cleveland 44114

(513) 569-9999 .. **Torok**, Ruth M '85 Triona & L,Ltd -2909 Vernon Pl
-Cincinnati 45219 **Fx**:569-9998

(513) 412-8336 .. **Toron**, Moses J '99 Deloitte & Touche -250 E 5th -Ste 1900
-Bx5340 -Cincinnati 45201

(610) 867-7568 .. **Torrence**, Samuel L '82 Just Born,Inc -1300 Stefko Blvd
-Bethlehem, PA 18017

(330) 898-5680 .. **Torres**, Cindy J '01 Lexis Nexis -5202 Nelson Mosier Rd
-Southington 44470

(216) 781-6450 .. **Torres-Lugo**, Jazmin G '94 -2012 W 25th -Ste 918
-Cleveland 44113

(216) 771-6303 .. **Torres-Ramirez**, José A '94 (Torres W Co,LPA) -75 Pub Sq
-Ste 800 -Cleveland 44113 **Fx**:771-6993

(216) 961-2100 .. **Torres-Waldo**, Rosa '96 Spanish Amer Comm -4407 Lorain Av
-Cleveland 44113

(614) 221-1216 .. **Torriero**, Dolores F '95 Downes H&F -400 S 5th -Ste 200
-Columbus 43215 **Fx**:221-8769

(419) 243-1105 .. **Torzewski**, Joan M '77 (Lackey NHR&T,LPA) -2 Maritime Plz
-3rd Fl -Toledo 43604

(480) 419-3986 .. **Toscano**, Randolph D '81 -7339 E Williams -Bx25434
-Scottsdale, AZ 85255 **Fx**:563-1509

(740) 928-3696 .. **Tosi**, James G '71 -117 E Main -Bx658 -Hebron 43025

(419) 241-9000 .. **Tosi**, Louis E '74 (Shumaker L&K,LLP) -1000 Jackson
-Toledo 43624 **Fx**:241-6894

(419) 255-5900 .. **Toska**, Anita S '03 %MacMillan S&T,LLC -720 Water -4th Fl
-Toledo 43604 **Fx**:255-9639

(419) 245-1975 .. **Toska**, David L '83 Pros -555 N Erie -4th Fl -Toledo 43624

(216) 514-1100 .. **Tost**, Christopher M '99 %Rolf & G Co,LPA -30100 Chagrin Blvd
-Ste 350 Corp Cir -Cleveland 44124 **Fx**:514-0030

(740) 439-2842 .. **Tostenson**, Neal S '58 -7077 Glenn Hwy -Bx1376
-Cambridge 43725 **Fx**:439-9086

(216) 241-2600 .. **Tosti**, Jeanne M '92 (Becker & M Co,LPA -1660 W 2nd -Ste 660
-Cleveland 44113 **Fx**:241-5757

(216) 491-8398 .. **Toth**, Barbara B '86 -21831 Wstchstr Rd -Shaker Heights 44122
Fx:491-8398

(248) 649-6000 .. **Toth**, Edward S '86 %Driggers S&H, PC -2600 W Big Beaver Rd
-Ste 550 -Troy, MI 48084

(440) 576-3009 .. **Toth**, Jason M '01 Ashtabula Cnty Pros -25 W Jffrsn
-Jefferson 44047

(313) 647-9595 .. **Toth**, John M '91 (Toth BV&F,PC) -30100 Telegraph Rd -Ste 250
-Bingham Farms, MI 48025

(302) 594-2942 .. **Toth**, Kathleen M '93 AIG -600 King -Leg Dept
-Wilmington, DE 19801

(216) 227-8623 .. **Toth**, Kathryn Ellen '91 -17405 Lk Av -Lakewood 44107

(614) 214-6720 .. **Toth**, Timothy J '96 CompManagement,Inc -6377 Emerald Pkwy
-Ste 280 -Dublin 43016

(410) 547-9040 .. **Totin**, Michael V '84 Sieira Military Health Srvc -111 Market Pl
-Ste #410 -Baltimore, MD 21202

Totten, Mark S '82 -1045 Parkleigh Rd -Columbus 43220

(614) 464-6400 .. **Tour**, Jeffrey H '93 OfCnsl Vorys SS&P LLP -52 E Gay -Bx1008
-Columbus 43216 **Fx**:464-6350

(614) 466-6859 .. **Touris**, Jaimee L '91 Industrial Commssn of OH -30 W Spring
-9th Fl -Columbus 43215 **Fx**:752-8785

(202) 616-7956 .. **Tournay**, Frederick H '88 US DOJ-INS -425 I NW -Rm 6040
-Washington, DC 20536

(614) 463-9441 .. **Tournoux**, Katie L '02 %Shumaker L&K,LLP -41 S High -Ste 2210
-Columbus 43215 **Fx**:463-1108

Tourville, Jennifer P '01 -(Address Unavailable)

(330) 364-9900 .. **Touschner**, Anthony J '73 %Tate & R -505 N Wooster Av -Bx8
-Dover 44622 **Fx**:364-9901

(614) 249-6184 .. **Towarnicky**, John M '92 Nationwide Ins Co -One Nationwide Plz
-1-1-10 -Columbus 43215

(330) 535-5711 .. **Towell**, Jennifer D '03 %Brouse M -106 S Main -500 First Natl Twr
-Akron 44308 **Fx**:253-8601

(614) 475-3493 .. **Tower**, Jessie M '95 -3100 Pittston Ct -Columbus 43231

(330) 535-2151 .. **Towne**, Ronald N '69 (Guy L&T) -106 S Main -Ste 2210
-Akron 44308 **Fx**:535-9048

(330) 652-5863 .. **Townley**, Thomas W '75 Mun Ct Judge -15 E State -Niles 44446

Townsend, Andrea C '86 -1703 Caminito Ardiente
-La Jolla, CA 92037

Townsend, Danielle D '03 -6467 Dorset Ln -Solon 44139

(304) 422-5449 .. **Townsend**, Gerald W '70 (Fluharty & T) -5th & Green -Bx201
-Parkersburg, WV 26102 **Fx**:485-0560

(419) 448-4444 .. **Townsend**, Matthew J '00 Seneca Cnty Pros -71 S Wshngtn
-Ste E -Bx667 -Tiffin 44883 **Fx**:448-7911

(614) 825-4029 .. **Townsend**, Maureen M '00 OH Bar Title Ins Co -8425 Pulsar Pl
-Ste 210 -Columbus 43240

(513) 381-2838 .. **Townsend**, Robert J '84 (Taft S&H LLP) -425 Walnut -Ste 1800
-Cincinnati 45202 **Fx**:381-0205

(740) 593-3187 .. **Toy**, Kerry R '77 -50½ S Court -Athens 45701

(419) 242-1400 .. **Traband**, Charles M Jr. '78 -608 Mad Av -Ste 1400 -Toledo 43604

(312) 230-2561 .. **Trabaris**, Douglas W '91 SrCnsl AT&T Corp -222 W Adams
-Ste 1500 -Chicago, IL 60606 **Fx**:230-8210

(216) 363-4500 .. **Tracanna**, Richard F '87 (Benesch FC&A LLP) -200 Pub Sq
-Ste 2300 -Cleveland 44114 **Fx**:363-4588

(513) 745-3129 .. **Tracey**, Ann M '75 Xavier Univ -3800 Victory Pkwy
-611 Schott Hall -Cincinnati 45207

(419) 241-6000 .. **Tracey**, Shawn M '01 %Eastman & S Ltd -1 Seagate -24th Fl
-Bx10032 -Toledo 43699 **Fx**:247-1777

(859) 282-3600 .. **Trachsel**, Gregory A '85 Hennegan Co -7455 Empire Dr
-Florence, KY 41042

(419) 291-5959 .. **Trachsel**, Kenneth R '89 ProMedica Hlth Syst -2121 Hughes Dr
-Toledo 43606

(440) 835-1800 .. **Traci**, Robert V '75 (RV Traci Co,LPA) -835 Sharon Dr -Ste 350
-Westlake 44145

(937) 859-3628 .. **Tracy**, Bridget A '84 (Tracy & T) -31 E Central Av -Bx156
-West Carrollton 45449

(937) 859-3628 .. **Tracy**, John P '84 Tracy & T -31 E Central Av -Bx156
-West Carrollton 45449

Tracy, Jonathan E '01 US Army JAG Corp -CMR 405 Bx 1032
-APO, AE 09034

(740) 354-5098 .. **Tracy**, Larry A '82 -460 Brown -Portsmouth 45662

(937) 859-3628 .. **Tracy**, Louis E '52 Tracy & T -31 E Central Av -Bx156
-West Carrollton 45449

(614) 466-7046 .. **Tracy**, Roger W '64 Personnel Brd of Review -65 E State -12th Fl
-Columbus 43215

(216) 861-2424 .. **Traeger**, Kenneth '73 (K Traeger Co,LPA) -1370 Ontario -Ste 450
-Cleveland 44113

(614) 227-2000 .. **Trafford**, Kathleen McManus '79 (Porter WM&A LLP) -41 S High
-Columbus 43215 **Fx**:227-2100

(614) 227-2000 .. **Trafford**, Robert W '77 (Porter WM&A LLP) -41 S High
-Columbus 43215 **Fx**:227-2100

(937) 443-6600 .. **Trahan**, Jeremy L '96 (Thompson H LLP) -2000 Cthse Plz NE
-Bx8801 -Dayton 45401 **Fx**:443-6635

(614) 213-7643 .. **Trail**, Christopher D '81 Bank One Leasing Corp
-1111 Polaris Pkwy -Ste A3 -Columbus 43240

(614) 248-7597 .. **Trail**, Judith D '82 Banc One Corp -100 E Broad -OHI-0158
-Columbus 43271

(216) 363-4500 .. **Trainer**, Mark D '02 %Benesch FC&A LLP -200 Pub Sq -Ste 2300
-Cleveland 44114 **Fx**:363-4588

(202) 223-6667 .. **Trainer**, Timothy P '87 Intl Anticounter-feiting Coalition
-1725 K NW -Ste 1101 -Washington, DC 20006

(859) 581-2822 .. **Trainor**, Robert N '78 -216 E 4th -Covington, KY 41011

(216) 765-8110 .. **Tramer**, Neil M '83 (Tramer & Z) -23775 Commerce Park
-Cleveland 44122

(231) 439-9493 .. **Trammel**, Kirk D '90 -Bx2058 -Petoskey, MI 49770

(513) 595-2328 .. **Trammell**, Dennis L '77 Union Cntrl Life Ins Co
-1876 Waycross Rd -Bx40888 -Cincinnati 45240

(330) 535-3103 .. **Tramonte**, Michael A '76 -1267 S Main -Akron 44301

(513) 983-1100 .. **Tramonte**, Tracy M '01 Cnsl Procter & Gamble Co
-1 Procter & Gamble Plz -Cincinnati 45202

(614) 466-3947 .. **Tran**, Terry D '04 OH Brd of Nursing -17 S High -Ste 400
-Columbus 43215

(513) 946-3000 .. **Tranter**, Amy L '00 %Hamilton Cnty Pros -230 E 9th
-Cincinnati 45202 **Fx**:946-3017

(513) 621-9204 .. **Tranter**, Michael L '02 Tranter Law Ofc -830 Main -Ste 806
-Cincinnati 45202

(513) 977-8200 .. **Tranter**, Richard B '85 (Dinsmore & S LLP) -255 E 5th -Ste 1900
-Cincinnati 45202 **Fx**:977-8141

(513) 621-9204 .. **Tranter**, Terence M '69 Tranter Law Ofc -830 Main -Ste 806
-Cincinnati 45202

(513) 621-9204 .. **Tranter**, Terry W '99 Tranter Law Ofc -830 Main -Ste 806
-Cincinnati 45202

(216) 696-3550 .. **Trapp**, Mary Jane '81 (Apicella & T) -1300 E 9th
-1200 Penton Media Bldg -Cleveland 44114 **Fx**:696-3830

(513) 665-9500 .. **Trapp**, Michael J '97 %R Klingler Co,LPA -525 Vine -Ste 2320
-Cincinnati 45202

(216) 771-4700 .. **Trattner**, Barry A '68 -1370 Ontario -Ste 1300 -Cleveland 44113

(216) 321-4608 .. **Trattner**, Douglas L '93 Anderson Publishing Co
-3373 E Fairfax Rd -Cleveland Heights 44118

(216) 771-4700 .. **Trattner**, Mary Lou '74 -1370 Ontario -Ste 1300 (% B Trattner)
-Cleveland 44113 **Fx**:771-4701

(330) 535-0505 .. **Trattner**, Robert B '93 K Belfance & Assoc -One Cascade Plz
-Ste 2100 -Akron 44308

(330) 305-6400 .. **Traub**, Randall M '99 %Pelini & F,Ltd -8040 Cleveland Av NW
-Ste 400 -North Canton 44720 **Fx**:305-0042

(937) 593-6065 .. **Traul**, Howard A II '76 (Thompson DHMW&T) -1111 Rush Av
-Bx68 -Bellefontaine 43311

(216) 771-6650 .. **Traut**, Ted M '00 %Kreiner & P Co,LPA -Bx6599 -Cleveland 44101

(513) 579-6400 .. **Trauth**, Joseph L Jr. '73 (Keating M&K PLL) -1 E 4th
-1400 Provident Twr -Cincinnati 45202 **Fx**:579-6457

(513) 421-7500 .. **Trautmann**, Richard S '74 -5 W 4th -2200 4th & Vine Twr
-Cincinnati 45202

(216) 443-7800 .. **Travaglini**, Kristine R '97 Cuyahoga Cnty Pros -1200 Ontario -8th Fl -Cleveland 44113 **Fx:**698-2270

(614) 292-2689 .. **Travalio**, Gregory M '85 OSU Moritz Cllg of Law -55 W 12th Av -Columbus 43210 **Fx:**292-1383

(330) 364-6621 .. **Traver**, Dennis D '73 (Traver & F) -232 W 3rd -Ste 309 -Dover 44622

(330) 533-1700 .. **Travers**, Thomas J Jr. '76 (TJ Travers LLC) -3870 Starrs Centre Dr -Canfield 44406

(216) 241-5310 .. **Travis**, D John '76 (Gallagher SF&N) -1501 Euclid Av -6th Fl -Cleveland 44115 **Fx:**241-1608

(412) 471-5055 .. **Travis**, Dennis L '65 Metlife Sec,Inc -320 Duquesne Blvd -Pittsburgh, PA 15222

(216) 664-2673 .. **Travis**, Gary N '82 Dept of Law -601 Lakeside Av -Rm 106 City Hall -Cleveland 44114 **Fx:**664-2663

(216) 443-7800 .. **Travis**, Linda R '79 Cuyahoga Cnty Pros -1200 Ontario -8th Fl -Cleveland 44113 **Fx:**698-2270

(614) 644-8969 .. **Travis**, Michael '93 Workers Comp -30 W Spring -Level 26 -Columbus 43215

(614) 326-3200 .. **Travis**, Paul D '73 -2929 Kenny Rd -Ste 290 -Columbus 43221

(513) 531-2889 .. **Travis**, Philip C '72 -3040 Madison Rd -Ste 201 -Bx9696 -Cincinnati 45209 **Fx:**531-2889

(330) 376-2700 .. **Treadon**, Thomas A '75 (Roetzel & A,LPA) -222 S Main -Akron 44308 **Fx:**376-4577

(440) 974-5750 .. **Trebets**, John '82 Mun Ct Judge -8500 Civic Ctr Blvd -Mentor 44060

Treece, Roger '03 -(Address Unavailable)

Trefethern, Randall J '95 -630 S Lazelle -Columbus 43206

(330) 687-5324 .. **Trefethern**, Thomas N '01 -2045 Chapel Hill Dr -Youngstown 44511

(513) 852-5600 .. **Tregre**, Calvin S Jr. '01 %Lopez HRM&S -312 Walnut -Ste 2090 -Cincinnati 45202 **Fx:**852-5611

(937) 223-3277 .. **Treherne**, Gretchen M '01 %Bieser G&L LLP -6 N Main -400 Natl City Ctr -Dayton 45402 **Fx:**223-6339

(937) 836-3296 .. **Treherne**, James E '73 -633 W Natl Rd -Englewood 45322

(937) 222-2424 .. **Treherne**, Jason E '01 %Freund F&A -1 S Main -Ste 1800 -Dayton 45402 **Fx:**222-5369

(330) 208-1000 .. **Treier**, Arthur R '92 Chicago Title Ins -106 S Main -First Natl Twr -Akron 44308

(513) 489-9200 .. **Treinen**, Arthur H '82 Chicago Title Ins -7890 E Kemper Rd -Ste 210 -Cincinnati 45249

(216) 566-7022 .. **Treinish**, Alan J '74 (A Treinish Co,LPA) -1370 Ontario -700 Standard Bldg -Cleveland 44113 **Fx:**861-2622

(216) 861-3000 .. **Treister**, William R '76 -800 Standard Bldg -1370 Ontario -Cleveland 44113

(216) 443-6350 .. **Trejbal**, Amy '98 8th Dist Ct of Appls -1 Lakeside Av -#202 -Cleveland 44113 **Fx:**443-2044

(212) 859-5059 .. **Tremiti**, Joseph F '78 Tremiti LLC -67 Wall -Ste 221, 22nd Fl -New York, NY 10005

(216) 368-4286 .. **Treml**, Colleen G '91 Case Western Univ -10900 Euclid Av -#311 -Cleveland 44106

(734) 677-7900 .. **Tremonti**, Leah G '95 -2008 Hogback Rdd -Ste 3A -Ann Arbor, MI 48105

(937) 328-2574 .. **Trempe**, Thomas E '80 Clark Cnty Pros -50 E Columbia -Bx1608 -Springfield 45501

(440) 285-2222 .. **Tremsyn**, John P '76 Geauga Cnty Pros -231 Main -Cthse Annx -Chardon 44024 **Fx:**286-4357

(740) 345-9611 .. **Treneff**, Alexander T '72 (Morrow G&B,Ltd) -33 W Main -Bx4190 -Newark 43058

(614) 228-3715 .. **Treneff**, Craig P '81 -555 S Front -Ste 320 -Columbus 43215

(216) 621-0200 .. **Trent**, Niesa R '03 %Baker & H LLP -1900 E 9th -Ste 3200 -Cleveland 44114 **Fx:**696-0740

(307) 721-2552 .. **Trent**, Peggy A '89 Cnty Atty -525 Grand Av -Ste 304 -Laramie, WY 82070

(216) 241-5310 .. **Trenta**, Melinda B '99 %Gallagher SF&N -1501 Euclid Av -6th Fl -Cleveland 44115 **Fx:**241-1608

(216) 481-4960 .. **Trentes**, John H '87 -866 E 185th -Cleveland 44119

(513) 621-1767 .. **Trenz**, Alan R '81 (Trenz M&K Co,LPA) -35 E 7th -Ste 400 -Cincinnati 45202

(513) 621-1767 .. **Trenz McKay & Knabe Co,LPA** -35 E 7th -Ste 400 -Cincinnati 45202

(216) 241-2600 .. **Tresl**, Jacqueline D '03 %Becker & M Co,LPA -1660 W 2nd -Ste 660 -Cleveland 44113 **Fx:**241-5757

(614) 292-0582 .. **Trethewey**, Virginia M '77 %OSU -190 N Oval Mall -103 Bricker Hall -Columbus 43210

(317) 842-5235 .. **Trettin**, Richard T '70 -6350 N Shadeland Av -Ste 4 -Indianapolis, IN 46220

(216) 621-1000 .. **Treu**, Kris H '83 (Moscarino & T,LLP) -1422 Euclid Av -Hanna Bldg Ste 630 -Cleveland 44115 **Fx:**622-1556

Treu, Nancy J '84 -(Address Unavailable)

Treuhaft, Joel S '85 OfCnsl Vorys SS&P LLP -1 Bayonet Point, FL 34667

(740) 852-0112 .. **Treynor**, Shannon M '00 %Pitstick Law Ofcs -26 N Main -Bx189 -London 43140

(717) 264-1996 .. **Trgovac**, Thomas J '89 -3221 Muirfld Dr -Chambersburg, PA 17201

(740) 432-6322 .. **Tribbie Scott Plummer & Padden** -139 Ct Hse Sq -Bx640 -Cambridge 43725 **Fx:**439-1795

(740) 432-6322 .. **Tribbie**, Thomas L '52 (Tribbie SP&P) -139 Ct Hse Sq -Bx640 -Cambridge 43725 **Fx:**439-1795

(614) 781-8896 .. **Tribble**, Judith E '01 Union Savings Bank -1330 Morse Rd -Columbus 43229

(330) 759-7499 .. **Tribby**, Alfred G Jr. '81 -1393 Youngstown Cntry Clb -Youngstown 44505

(216) 861-6677 .. **Tricarichi**, Carla M '83 (Tricarichi & C) -614 Superior Av NW -Rckfllr Bldg Ste 620 -Cleveland 44113

(216) 621-5980 .. **Tricarichi**, Tina L '96 Legal Aid -1223 W 6th -Cleveland 44113

Trieu, Vinh C '03 -(Address Unavailable)

(330) 456-6000 .. **Trifelos**, George H '54 -236 3rd SW -Carnegie Bldg -Canton 44702

(740) 344-6885 .. **Trifelos**, James N '83 -36 McMillen Dr -Newark 43055

(513) 946-5180 .. **Triggs**, Alan C '96 Hamilton Cnty Mun Ct -1000 Main -Rm 401 -Cincinnati 45202

(440) 988-9500 .. **Trigilio & Stephenson** -5750 Cooper Foster Park Rd -Ste 102 -Lorain 44053

(440) 988-9500 .. **Trigilio**, Timothy S '80 (Trigilio & S) -5750 Cooper Foster Park Rd -Ste 102 -Lorain 44053

(303) 224-1010 .. **Triguba**, Gregory A '98 Qwest Communications -1801 Calif -Ste 3800 -Denver, CO 80202

(216) 586-3939 .. **Trilling**, Jessica E '03 %Jones D -901 Lakeside Av -Cleveland 44114 **Fx:**579-0212

(216) 621-0200 .. **Trim**, Roger G '03 %Baker & H LLP -1900 E 9th -Ste 3200 -Cleveland 44114 **Fx:**696-0740

(440) 247-1428 .. **Trimble**, David L '90 Wetlands Prsrvtns Ltd -150 Hunting Trl -Moreland Hills 44022

(419) 248-2600 .. **Trimble**, J Mark '90 (Rohrbachers LC&T Co,LPA) -405 Mad Av -8th Fl -Toledo 43604 **Fx:**248-2614

Trimble, Kathy M '01 -4470 Raccoon Valley Rd -Alexandria 43001

(614) 224-8187 .. **Trimble**, Thomas W '83 (Lamkin VTB&D) -500 S Front -Ste 200 -Columbus 43215 **Fx:**224-4943

(419) 782-2253 .. **Trimboli**, Dennis B '79 UAW Legal Srvcs -1500 Baltimore Rd -Defiance 43512

Trimboli, Jon A '89 Asset Recovery Team,LLC -4700 Ashwood Dr -Ste 404 -Cincinnati 45241

(419) 245-1940 .. **Trimboli**, Mary G '78 Mun Ct Judge -555 N Erie -Toledo 43624

(740) 687-6616 .. **Trimmer**, David A '93 Pros -Bx1008 -Lancaster 43130

(513) 569-9999 .. **Triona**, James P '78 (Triona & L,Ltd) -2909 Vernon Pl -Cincinnati 45219 **Fx:**569-9998

(513) 569-9999 .. **Triona & Lockemeyer,Ltd** -2909 Vernon Pl -Cincinnati 45219 **Fx:**569-9998

(216) 664-4992 .. **Triozzi**, Robert J '82 Mun Ct Judge -1200 Ontario -Cleveland 44113

(216) 881-4243 .. **Tripi**, Joseph M '03 Genl Bldg Products Corp -1281 E 38th -Cleveland 44114

Tripi, Phillip G '57 -600 Wllmsbrg Dr -Highland Heights 44143

(216) 622-3600 .. **Tripi**, Phillip J Jr. '78 US Atty -801 W Superior -Ste 400 -Cleveland 44113 **Fx:**622-3370

(740) 353-8111 .. **Triplett**, Aaron R '83 -4705 Old Scioto Trl -Portsmouth 45662

(740) 373-5455 .. **Triplett**, John E Jr. '84 (Theisen B,LPA) -424 2nd -Bx739 -Marietta 45750 **Fx:**373-4409

(937) 593-6591 .. **Triplett**, Marc S '77 -332 S Main -Bellefontaine 43311

(330) 343-0212 .. **Tripodi**, Joseph I '67 (JI Tripodi Co,LPA) -114 E High Av -New Philadelphia 44663 **Fx:**364-4337

(513) 723-4000 .. **Tripp**, Douglas S '92 OfCnsl Vorys SS&P LLP -221 E 4th -Ste 2000 Atrium Two -Bx0236 -Cincinnati 45201 **Fx:**723-4056

(614) 475-2233 .. **Tripp**, Thomas N '67 -5420 Clark State Rd -Gahanna 43230

(614) 227-8918 .. **Trishman**, Natalie C '02 %Bricker & E LLP -100 S 3rd -Columbus 43215 **Fx:**227-2390

(937) 898-5870 .. **Trissell**, Stanley L Jr. '92 -7535 Turtle Crk Dr -Dayton 45414 **Fx:**898-5875

(330) 796-5019 .. **Tritt**, William C '88 Goodyear Tire & Rubber Co -1144 E Market -Akron 44316

Trivelli, Annette C '89 -57 E Wshngtn -#3 -Chagrin Falls 44022

(216) 696-5444 .. **Trivers**, Oscar '60 (Trivers & D LLC) -925 Euclid Av -Cleveland 44115

(419) 872-6808 .. **Troendle**, Janelle M '03 %Spore & Assoc,LLC -Bx906 -Perrysburg 43552

(216) 621-7227 .. **Troia**, Anthony R '66 OfCnsl Nicola G&C,LLC -25 W Prospect Av -Republic Bldg Ste 1400 -Cleveland 44115 **Fx:**621-3999

(513) 939-3300 .. **Trokhan**, Cynamon T '96 -1244 Nilles Rd -Ste 9 -Fairfield 45014

(440) 349-2110 .. **Trombetta**, I Bernard '63 -30505 Bainbrdg Rd -#190 -Solon 44139

(513) 579-0080 .. **Trombetta**, Patricia J '82 %Smith R&S Co,LPA -1014 Vine -Ste 2350 -Cincinnati 45202 **Fx:**579-0222

(440) 248-7906 .. **Trombetto**, Julius E '02 %Mazanec R&R Co,LPA -34305 Solon Rd -Ste 100 -Cleveland 44139 **Fx:**248-8861

Trost, Ericca L '04 -(Address Unavailable)

(419) 399-2181 .. **Troth**, Glenn H '82 (Cook T&B,Ltd) -112 N Water -Paulding 45879

(858) 824-9072 .. **Trotier**, Brian L '80 Johnson Capital -4225 Exec Square -Ste 250 -La Jolla, CA 92037

(937) 449-6400 .. **Trott**, Merideth A '75 (Dinsmore & S LLP) -1 S Main -Ste 1300 One Dayton Centre -Dayton 45402 **Fx:**449-6405

(740) 687-7176 .. **Trotter**, Kevin Jay '82 Fairfield Cnty Cmn Pleas Ct -224 E Main -Lancaster 43130

(330) 376-5300 .. **Trotter**, Thomas R '75 (Buckingham D&B,LLP) -50 S Main -Bx1500 -Akron 44309 **Fx:**258-6559

(937) 226-9354 .. **Trout**, Douglas M '00 Macey & C -40 W 4th -Ste 2160 -Dayton 45402 **Fx:**226-9359

(614) 752-1773 .. **Trout**, Gregory C '78 OH Dept Rehab & Correction -1050 Fwy Dr N -Columbus 43229

(888) 371-6763 .. **Trout**, Paula J '87 -589 Locust Ct -Westerville 43082

(740) 695-9202 .. **Trouten**, David S Jr. '93 %Harper & H -185 W Main -Saint Clairsville 43950 **Fx:**695-9211

(513) 684-2572 .. **Troutman**, Jane M '97 US Bankrptcy Ct -221 E 4th -Ste 800 -Cincinnati 45202

(614) 466-8600 .. **Troutman**, Mark H '03 %Atty Gen -30 E Broad -Columbus 43215 **Fx:**466-6090

(614) 466-5394 .. **Troutman**, Rachel G '03 %Pub Def -8 E Long -Columbus 43215

Troxell, Elizabeth O M '90 AirTouch Communications -5175 Emerald Pkwy -Dublin 43017

(216) 479-8500 .. **Troxell**, James D '76 (Squire S&D LLP) -127 Pub Sq -4900 Key Twr -Cleveland 44114 **Fx:**479-8780

(614) 445-9293 .. **Troxell**, Richard H '96 -681 S Front -Columbus 43206

Troy, Bartley J '81 -(Address Unavailable)

(614) 888-8500 .. **Troyan**, Gary M '78 (Jones TP&P,LPA) -1472 Manning Pkwy -Powell 43065 **Fx:**888-2560

(216) 781-4454 .. **Troyan**, Gregory M '91 -1276 W 3rd -419 Marion Bldg -Cleveland 44113

(216) 566-5654 .. **Troyer**, Brian A '92 (Thompson H LLP) -127 Pub Sq -3900 Key Ctr -Cleveland 44114 **Fx:**566-5800

Troyer, Edgar A '76 -(Address Unavailable)

(317) 636-4341 .. **Troyer**, Glenn T '75 (Krieg D LLP) -One Indna Sq -Ste 2800 -Indianapolis, IN 46204

(614) 221-1511 .. **Truax**, William H Jr. '76 -171 E Lvngstn Av -Columbus 43215

(216) 621-7860 .. **Trubiano**, Mark A '88 (Cavitch FD&F) -1717 E 9th -14th Fl -Cleveland 44114 **Fx:**621-3415

(330) 434-3000 .. **Truby**, Timothy J '72 (Roderick & L) -One Cascade Plz -Ste 1500 -Akron 44308 **Fx:**434-9220

(216) 931-6000 .. **Trudeau**, Stephanie E '82 (Ulmer & B LLP) -1300 E 9th
-Ste 900 Penton Media Bldg -Cleveland 44114 **Fx:**931-6001
(419) 243-4006 .. **Trudel**, Valerie A '97 %Kitch DWD&V,PC -405 Mad Av -Ste 1500
-Toledo 43604 **Fx:**243-7333
(513) 732-2140 .. **True**, James R '63 (Ely & T) -322 Main -Batavia 45103
(614) 469-3939 .. **True**, Mary R '90 %Jones D -325 John H McConnell Blvd -Ste 600
-Bx165017 -Columbus 43216 **Fx:**461-4198
(513) 868-3663 .. **Truesdell**, Gwendolyn A '93 -723 Dayton -Hamilton 45011
(614) 443-7000 .. **Truitt**, Kevin J '04 %Abroms Law Ofcs -753 S Front
-Columbus 43206
Truitt, Susan '84 -2338 Abngtn Rd -Upper Arlington 43221
(330) 722-8290 .. **Truman**, Kathryn M '96 -865 W Lbrty -Ste 120 -Medina 44256
(330) 722-8877 .. **Truman**, Vance P '93 -319 S Court -Medina 44256
(216) 991-9122 .. **Trumbo**, George W '53 -13807 Drexmore Rd -Cleveland 44120
(513) 794-6443 .. **Trumbo**, Steven H '88 OH Natl Life Ins Co -1 Fncl Way
-Cincinnati 45242
(404) 962-6411 .. **Trumpeter**, William G '76 (Miller & M LLP) -1275 Pchtree NE
-7th Fl -Atlanta, GA 30309 **Fx:**962-6300
(716) 551-4811 .. **Trusiak**, Robert G '86 %US Atty -138 Delaware Av -6th Fl
-Buffalo, NY 14202
(216) 443-9000 .. **Tryon**, David C '85 (Porter WM&A LLP) -925 Euclid Av -Ste 1700
-Cleveland 44115 **Fx:**443-9011
(216) 566-2487 .. **Tsang**, Vivien Y '96 Sherwin-Williams Co -101 Prospect Av NW
-1100 Mdlnd Bldg -Cleveland 44115
(330) 493-9901 .. **Tsangeos**, Angelo J '85 (Lonas M&T) -1810 36th NW
-Canton 44709 **Fx:**493-9338
(330) 376-8336 .. **Tsarnas**, George P '63 (Goldman & R,Ltd) -11 S Forge
-Akron 44304 **Fx:**376-2522
(330) 533-0916 .. **Tsarnas**, Nomiki P '03 %Nationwide Ins -6715 Tippecanoe Rd
-Bldg B Ste 201 -Canfield 44405 **Fx:**533-1043
(330) 376-8336 .. **Tsarnas**, Peter G '03 %Goldman & R,Ltd -11 S Forge
-Akron 44304 **Fx:**376-2522
(330) 253-5454 .. **Tsarouhas**, Antonios P '94 Perantinides & N Co,LPA
-80 S Summit -300 Courtyard Sq -Akron 44308
(330) 345-8100 .. **Tschantz**, David E '89 Wayne Mutual Ins Co -3873 Cleveland Rd
-Wooster 44691
Tschantz, Mary Myers '78 -336 Melbourne Av -Akron 44313
(937) 748-4080 .. **Tschanz**, Bryan M '03 -15 S Main -Springboro 45066 **Fx:**748-4839
(330) 456-4576 .. **Tscholl**, John A '74 -1400 Market Av N -Canton 44714
(330) 456-7702 .. **Tscholl**, Robert J '76 -220 Market Av S -Ste 1120 -Canton 44702
(330) 376-5300 .. **Tschugunov**, Eleanor J '79 (Buckingham D&B,LLP) -50 S Main
-Bx1500 -Akron 44309 **Fx:**258-6559
(212) 908-6243 .. **Tsevdos**, Estelle J '82 (Kenyon & K) -1 Bway -New York,
NY 10004
(440) 234-2081 .. **Tsevdos**, Noelle T '89 OH Tpk Comm -682 Prospect -Berea 44017
(614) 228-9707 .. **Tsibouris**, Dino '94 (Mallory & T Co,LPA) -88 E Broad -Ste 1560
-Columbus 43215
(614) 891-5555 .. **Tsiliacos**, Narcus J '64 -647 Park Meadow Rd -Ste I
-Westerville 43081
(216) 479-8500 .. **Tsilimos**, Jonathan S '02 %Squire S&D LLP -127 Pub Sq
-4900 Key Twr -Cleveland 44114 **Fx:**479-8780
(440) 449-9692 .. **Tsipis**, Constantine E '91 NACCO Industries,Inc
-5875 Landerbrook Dr -Mayfield Heights 44124
(614) 462-3570 .. **Tsitouris**, Anne K '75 Franklin Cnty Cmn Pleas Ct -375 S High
-Columbus 43215 **Fx:**462-6292
(614) 464-2211 .. **Tsitouris**, Chris C '72 (C Tsitouris Co,LPA) -50 W Broad -Ste 1715
-Columbus 43215
(614) 464-2211 .. **Tsitouris**, Chris C '03 -50 W Broad -Ste 1715 -Columbus 43215
Tsonis, Isidora '04 -(Address Unavailable)
(704) 665-3109 .. **Tucci**, Christopher J '94 Equifirst Corp -500 Forest Point Cir
-Charlotte, NC 28273
(440) 350-2683 .. **Tucci**, Christopher P '03 Lake Cnty Pros -105 Main -Bx490
-Painesville 44077 **Fx:**350-2585
(216) 696-3311 .. **Tucci**, Michael R '99 %Kahn K -1301 E 9th -2600 Erievw Twr
-Cleveland 44114 **Fx:**623-4912
(330) 253-1900 .. **Tuccillo**, Anthony '59 (A Tuccillo Co,LPA) -159 S Main -Ste 1000
-Akron 44308
(513) 721-0060 .. **Tuch**, Gayle G '89 Goldsmith & G -7 W 7th -Ste 1800
-Cincinnati 45202
(614) 466-4882 .. **Tuch**, Socrates H '95 OH Dept Hlth -246 N High -Bx118
-Columbus 43216
(440) 233-7232 .. **Tucholski**, Karen L '96 The Nord Ctr -6140 S Bway -Lorain 44053
(734) 354-5583 .. **Tucker**, Albert M '86 -47690 E Anchor Ct -Plymouth, MI 48170
(330) 379-2002 .. **Tucker**, Catherine P '93 Summit Cnty Chldrn Srvcs -264 S Arlngtn
-Akron 44306 **Fx:**379-1897
(513) 425-0180 .. **Tucker**, Curtis C '98 Sorg Opera Co -65 S Main -Ste 205
-Middletown 45044
(216) 592-5000 .. **Tucker Ellis & West LLP** -925 Euclid Av -1150 Huntngtn Bldg
-Cleveland 44115 **Fx:**592-5009
(440) 449-6482 .. **Tucker**, Howard J '89 -6801 Mayfld Rd -#348
-Mayfield Heights 44124
(513) 721-3330 .. **Tucker**, Jack L '83 (Robbins KP&T) -7 W 7th -Ste 1400
-Cincinnati 45202
(614) 464-6400 .. **Tucker**, Jennifer L '04 %Vorys SS&P LLP -52 E Gay -Bx1008
-Columbus 43216 **Fx:**464-6350
(202) 263-3913 .. **Tucker**, Jim S '80 William M Mercer,Inc -1255 23rd NW -Ste 250
-Washington, DC 20037
(614) 466-5038 .. **Tucker**, Jo-Ellyn H '02 %OH Sec of State -180 E Broad -Columbus
43215 **Fx:**466-5409
(330) 253-7100 .. **Tucker**, John A '91 J Tucker Co,LPA -1 S Main -Ste 301
-Akron 44308 **Fx:**253-2500
(330) 497-0700 .. **Tucker**, John M '96 (Krugliak WG&D Co,LPA) -4775 Munson NW
-Bx36963 -Canton 44735 **Fx:**497-4020
(330) 762-9191 .. **Tucker**, Jon D '97 (Daily & H) -7 W Bowery -Ste 604 -Akron 44308
Fx:762-4244
Tucker, Karen E '80 -(Address Unavailable)
(215) 568-8040 .. **Tucker**, Leon W '99 -42 S 15th -Ste 1300 -Philadelphia, PA 19102
Fx:568-7719
(614) 223-9300 .. **Tucker**, Mark D '86 (Benesch FC&A LLP) -88 E Broad -Ste 900
-Columbus 43215 **Fx:**223-9330
(317) 852-3291 .. **Tucker**, Mary Ann '92 -61 Ridgeway Dr -Brownsburg, IN 46112
(216) 931-6000 .. **Tucker**, Michael S '86 (Ulmer & B LLP) -1300 E 9th
-Ste 900 Penton Media Bldg -Cleveland 44114 **Fx:**931-6001

(216) 831-3140 .. **Tucker**, Peter C '93 Industrial Timber & Lumber Co
-23925 Commerce Park -Beachwood 44122
(216) 592-5000 .. **Tucker**, Robert C '76 (Tucker E&W LLP) -925 Euclid Av
-1150 Huntngtn Bldg -Cleveland 44115 **Fx:**592-5009
(330) 670-7300 .. **Tucker**, Robert L '84 %Hanna C&P,LLP -3737 Embssy Pkwy
-Bx5521 -Akron 44334 **Fx:**670-0977
(419) 255-0814 .. **Tucker**, Robert P '70 ABLE -520 Mad Av -740 Spitzer Bldg -Toledo
43604
(513) 946-3451 .. **Tucker**, Stacy L '00 OH Ct of Appls-1st Dist -230 E 9th -12th Fl
-Cincinnati 45202
(419) 248-3503 .. **Tucker**, Theodore B III '76 -421 N Mich -Ste B -Toledo 43624
(216) 621-1113 .. **Tucker**, Todd R '95 (Renner OB&S,LLP) -1621 Euclid Av -19th Fl
-Cleveland 44115 **Fx:**621-6165
(216) 321-8789 .. **Tuckerman**, John L '54 -3120 Corydon Rd -Cleveland 44118
(419) 673-1292 .. **Tudor**, John M '62 (Tudor Law,LLC) -22 N Main -Kenton 43326
Fx:675-2145
(502) 425-7200 .. **Tuemler**, Barry J '91 First American -9600 Brownsboro Rd
-Ste 304 -Louisville, KY 40241 **Fx:**425-7003
(216) 561-0566 .. **Tuffin**, Paul J '57 -3637 Sutherland Rd -Shaker Heights 44122
(614) 336-4020 .. **Tugend**, Stephen E '91 Farmers Ins -2500 Farmers Dr -Ste 120
-Columbus 43235
(216) 566-5500 .. **Tuggle**, Curtis L '04 %Thompson H LLP -127 Pub Sq
-3900 Key Ctr -Cleveland 44114 **Fx:**566-5800
(740) 349-6663 .. **Tuhy**, Elena V '95 City Law Dir Ofc -40 W Main -Newark 43055
(614) 227-2000 .. **Tulencik**, Aaron T '00 %Porter WM&A LLP -41 S High
-Columbus 43215 **Fx:**227-2100
(216) 931-6000 .. **Tulley**, Patrick J '94 %Ulmer & B LLP -1300 E 9th
-Ste 900 Penton Media Bldg -Cleveland 44114 **Fx:**931-6001
(614) 462-5464 .. **Tullis**, Timothy T '89 (Kegler BH&R) -65 E State -Ste 1800
-Columbus 43215 **Fx:**464-2634
(440) 244-3955 .. **Tully**, Michael D '80 M Tully Co,LPA -600 Bway -Lorain 44052
Tulman, Elizabeth E '82 -7619 Beechlake Dr -Columbus 43235
(440) 526-4500 .. **Tuma**, Brian G '91 %RL Tuma & Assoc -8225 Brecksvll Rd
-Bldg 3 Ste 101 -Brecksville 44141 **Fx:**526-6362
(440) 526-4500 .. **Tuma**, Jeffrey A '01 %RL Tuma & Assoc -8225 Brecksvll Rd
-Bldg 3 Ste 101 -Brecksville 44141 **Fx:**526-6362
(440) 526-4500 .. **Tuma**, Robert L '64 (RL Tuma & Assoc) -8225 Brecksvll Rd
-Bldg 3 Ste 101 -Brecksville 44141 **Fx:**526-6362
(440) 526-4500 .. **Tuma**, Scott M '99 %RL Tuma & Assoc -8225 Brecksvll Rd
-Bldg 3 Ste 101 -Brecksville 44141 **Fx:**526-6362
(513) 896-4411 .. **Tumblison**, Joan M '99 Housing Auth -4110 Hmltn Mddltwn Rd
-Hamilton 45011
(614) 227-2000 .. **Tumen**, David A '81 (Porter WM&A LLP) -41 S High
-Columbus 43215 **Fx:**227-2100
(216) 687-3595 .. **Tumeo**, Mark A '02 Cleveland State Univ -1983 E 24th -KB 1154
-Cleveland 44115
Tumlin, Thomas J '03 -(Address Unavailable)
(216) 621-2234 .. **Tummino**, Barry L '80 (Tarolli SC&T) -526 Superior Av
-1111 Leader Bldg -Cleveland 44114 **Fx:**621-4072
(419) 289-8857 .. **Tunnell**, Christopher R '00 Ashland Cnty Pros -307 Orange
-Ashland 44805 **Fx:**281-3865
(614) 227-8837 .. **Tunnell**, Kurtis A '87 (Bricker & E LLP) -100 S 3rd
-Columbus 43215 **Fx:**227-2390
(989) 753-6486 .. **Tunney**, Jason P '03 Duro-Last Roofing,Inc -525 Morley Dr
-Saginaw, MI 48601
(334) 386-7536 .. **Tuomala**, Jeffrey C '76 Thomas Goode Jones Law Sch
-5345 Atlanta Hwy -Montgomery, AL 36109
(216) 292-4932 .. **Tura**, James V '77 (Tura & Assoc) -31850 S Woodlnd Rd -101
-Pepper Pike 44124 **Fx:**292-4932
(614) 469-0100 .. **Turano**, David A '71 OfCnsl Shoemaker H&T LLP -471 E Broad
-Ste 2001 -Columbus 43215 **Fx:**280-9675
(216) 881-7939 .. **Turbow**, Laurence A '76 (L Turbow,LPA,Inc) -4403 St Clair Av
-Ste 300 -Cleveland 44103 **Fx:**881-6682
(216) 687-1311 .. **Turek**, James J '82 (Reminger & R) -101 Prospect Av W
-1400 Mdlnd Bldg -Cleveland 44115 **Fx:**687-1841
(330) 995-8663 .. **Turell**, Russell B '70 -529 Treetop Ct -Aurora 44202
(440) 943-5222 .. **Turi**, Louis A Jr. '50 -30432 Euclid Av -Bx325 -Wickliffe 44092
(419) 536-5110 .. **Turin**, John C '70 -3425 Exec Pkwy -Ste 206 -Toledo 43606
Fx:536-2464
(216) 391-4000 .. **Turk**, Edmund J '55 -Bx19085 -Cleveland 44103 **Fx:**391-7550
(614) 223-9300 .. **Turk**, Jennifer M '01 %Benesch FC&A LLP -88 E Broad -Ste 900
-Columbus 43215 **Fx:**223-9330
(614) 890-0093 .. **Turk**, Thomas E '66 -4843 Smoketalk Ln -Westerville 43081
(419) 243-2100 .. **Turley**, Anthony E '98 (Connelly J&C LLP) -405 Mad Av -Ste 1600
-Toledo 43604 **Fx:**243-7119
(609) 452-1558 .. **Turlik**, John A '81 (Segal MS&M Ltd) -5 Vaughn Dr -Ste 115
-Princeton, NJ 08540 **Fx:**452-1559
(419) 525-1611 .. **Turlo**, Emily M '04 %Brown BM&M -70 Park Av W -Mansfield
44902 **Fx:**525-3810
(216) 443-9000 .. **Turnbull**, Tracey L '96 %Porter WM&A LLP -925 Euclid Av
-Ste 1700 -Cleveland 44115 **Fx:**443-9011
(216) 566-5604 .. **Turnell**, Roy L '74 (Thompson H LLP) -127 Pub Sq -3900 Key Ctr
-Cleveland 44114 **Fx:**566-5800
(937) 492-6191 .. **Turner**, Allison Scherger '04 %Elsass WES&Co -100 S Main Av
-Ste 102 -Bx499 -Sidney 45365 **Fx:**492-0876
Turner, Amy J '01 -4742 Bridle Path Ct -Dublin 43017
Turner, Anne D '87 -3448 Rvr Narrows Rd -Hilliard 43026
(440) 233-1283 .. **Turner**, Deborah M '99 -7825 Regency Dr -Walton Hills 44146
(937) 229-2529 .. **Turner**, Dennis J '70 Univ of Dayton Schl of Law -300 Cllg Park
-Dayton 45469
(216) 664-4942 .. **Turner**, Franzetta D '87 Cleveland Mun Ct -Justice Ctr -12th Fl
-Bx94894 -Cleveland 44101
(937) 228-2838 .. **Turner**, Gregory '01 %Taft S&H LLP -110 N Main -Ste 900
-Dayton 45402 **Fx:**228-2816
(216) 586-3939 .. **Turner**, Henry G '03 %Jones D -901 Lakeside Av
-Cleveland 44114 **Fx:**579-0212
(216) 621-0200 .. **Turner**, Jack '02 %Baker & H LLP -1900 E 9th -Ste 3200
-Cleveland 44114 **Fx:**696-0740
(614) 221-3155 .. **Turner**, Jameel S '04 %Bailey C LLC -10 W Broad
-Columbus 43215 **Fx:**221-0479
(937) 299-9900 .. **Turner**, James D '84 -2555 S Dixie Dr -Ste 101A -Dayton 45409
(419) 213-4700 .. **Turner**, James D '72 %Lucas Cnty Pros -Adams & Erie
-Lucas Cnty Cthse -Toledo 43624

(614) 752-4260 .. **Turner,** James N '78 OH Dept Commerce -77 S High
-Columbus 43266

(937) 222-2333 .. **Turner,** Jeffrey C '94 (Surdyk D&T Co,LPA) -40 N Main
-1610 Kettering Twr -Dayton 45423 **Fx:**222-1970

(937) 461-6200 .. **Turner,** Jonathan C '95 Cincinnati Insurance Co -130 W 2nd
-Ste 1850 -Dayton 45402

(937) 222-2424 .. **Turner,** Julia A '03 %Freund F&A -1 S Main -Ste 1800
-Dayton 45402 **Fx:**222-5369

(330) 399-8801 .. **Turner,** Lawrence S '66 (Turner M&S) -185 High NE -Warren
44481 **Fx:**399-8805

(248) 355-1727 .. **Turner,** Lee I '69 Turner & T PC -26000 W 12 Mile Rd
-Southfield, MI 48034

(330) 426-2241 .. **Turner,** Leevesta J '28 -432 Wstrn Av -East Palestine 44413

(937) 383-2067 .. **Turner,** Lynn W '92 Wilmington Law Dept -69 N South -Bx71
-Wilmington 45177

(216) 241-5310 .. **Turner,** Mark M '02 %Gallagher SF&N -1501 Euclid Av -6th Fl
-Cleveland 44115 **Fx:**241-1608

(330) 399-8801 .. **Turner May & Shepherd** -185 High NE -Warren 44481
Fx:399-8805

(859) 431-6100 .. **Turner,** Michelle F '98 Arnzen & W,PSC -600 Greenup
-Covington, KY 41011 **Fx:**431-3778

(614) 225-8700 .. **Turner,** Pete S '01 %PricewaterhouseCoopers LLP -100 E Broad
-Ste 2100 -Columbus 43215 **Fx:**(813) 329-4349

(216) 292-3300 .. **Turner,** Peter '81 Conway MWK&K Co,LPA -30195 Chagrin Blvd
-Ste 300 -Cleveland 44124

(713) 831-5064 .. **Turner,** Richard A '91 Variable Annty Life Ins -2929 Allen Pkwy
-Houston, TX 77019

(513) 984-8700 .. **Turner,** Richard P '98 Title Resolutions LLC -10979
Reed Hartman Hwy -Ste 110 -Cincinnati 45242

(330) 726-8669 .. **Turner,** Roklyn M '01 -412 Boardman-Canfld Rd
-Youngstown 44512

(330) 399-8801 .. **Turner,** Stephen A '04 %Turner M&S -185 High NE
-Warren 44481 **Fx:**399-8805

(440) 247-0003 .. **Turner,** Thomas M '73 (Turner & G LLC) -100 N Main -Ste 350
-Chagrin Falls 44022 **Fx:**247-8903

(614) 221-9400 .. **Turner,** Tracy L '98 %Habash R&F,LLP -471 E Broad -Ste 800
-Columbus 43215

(216) 378-9905 .. **Turner-Bautista,** Brooke D '00 %McGlinchey S PLLC
-25550 Chagrin Blvd -Ste 406 -Cleveland 44122 **Fx:**378-9910

(216) 696-8730 .. **Turocy,** Gregory '91 (Amin & T LLP) -1900 E 9th
-24th Fl Natl City Ctr -Cleveland 44114 **Fx:**696-8731

(216) 921-7878 .. **Turoff,** Carole R '70 Turoff & L -20320 Farmsleadp Rd
-Shaker Heights 44122

(216) 561-8000 .. **Turoff,** Daniel C '63 -13224 Shaker Sq -Ste 201 -Cleveland 44120

(440) 352-3391 .. **Turoff,** Geoffrey H '88 %Dworken & B Co,LPA -60 S Park Pl
-Painesville 44077 **Fx:**352-3469

(216) 781-0150 .. **Turoff,** Jack N '60 (Turoff & T) -629 Euclid Av -Ste 727
-Cleveland 44114 **Fx:**781-0416

(216) 781-0150 .. **Turoff,** Robert S '63 (Turoff & T) -629 Euclid Av -Ste 727
-Cleveland 44114 **Fx:**781-0416

(614) 469-3939 .. **Turoff,** S James '04 %Jones D -325 John H McConnell Blvd
-Ste 600 -Bx165017 -Columbus 43216 **Fx:**461-4198

(216) 621-5161 .. **Turoff,** Tracy A '02 %Giffen & K,LLC -1717 E 9th
-Cleveland 44114 **Fx:**621-2399

(330) 836-2292 .. **Turowski,** Kenneth Lee '83 -88 S Portage Path -Ste 306
-Akron 44303

(937) 687-1388 .. **Turrell,** Claudia J '84 -129 W Main -New Lebanon 45345

(740) 282-1131 .. **Turrentine,** Samuel M '96 -2017 Sunset Blvd -Steubenville 43952

(216) 566-5617 .. **Turscak,** Andrew L Jr. '01 %Thompson H LLP -127 Pub Sq
-3900 Key Ctr -Cleveland 44114 **Fx:**566-5800

(216) 861-5582 .. **Turung,** Brian E '91 (Fay SFM&M LLP) -1100 Superior Av -7th Fl
-Cleveland 44114 **Fx:**241-1666

(419) 241-2300 .. **Turvey-Albert,** Michelle S '92 -316 N Mich -Ste 800 -Toledo 43624

(412) 561-6949 .. **Turzak,** Rose M '91 -3754 Willow Av -Castle Shannon, PA 15234

(419) 241-2122 .. **Tuschman,** Chad M '02 %Williams JLG&S Co,LPA -416 N Erie
-Ste 100 -Toledo 43624 **Fx:**245-3849

(419) 897-6500 .. **Tuschman,** James M '66 OfCnsl Barkan & R Ltd
-1701 WoodInds Dr -Maumee 43537 **Fx:**897-6200

(330) 629-8882 .. **Tusek,** Tim '83 -945 Windham Ct -Ste 3 -Boardman 44512

(216) 771-4600 .. **Tushman,** Sol '53 (S Tushman Co,LPA) -55 Pub Square -Ste 1717
-Cleveland 44113

(937) 222-8500 .. **Tuss,** Mark A '81 (Popp & T) -137 N Main -Ste 712 -Dayton 45402
Fx:222-0488

(727) 572-4444 .. **Tuthill,** John E '72 -3300 49th N -Saint Petersburg, FL 33710
Fx:528-4214

(614) 292-0611 .. **Tuttle,** Amanda L '02 Ohio State Univ -33 W 11th Av
-Columbus 43201

(734) 668-0321 .. **Tuttle,** Chauncey W Jr. '61 -5963 Judd Silo Ridge -Ann Arbor,
MI 48108

(614) 644-9274 .. **Tuttle,** Cheryl L '86 %Hon FE Sweeney Sr -30 E Broad -3rd Fl
-Columbus 43266

Tuttle, John R '91 Federal Express Corp -Bx727
-Memphis, TN 38194

(336) 370-8800 .. **Tuttle,** Melanie S '85 Schell BAA&L PLLC -230 N Elm -Ste 1500
-Greensboro, NC 27401

(260) 461-7127 .. **Tutwiler,** William J '90 %Natl City Bank of IN -110 W Berry
-Ste 900 -Fort Wayne, IN 46802 **Fx:**461-7433

(330) 468-0599 .. **Tuzi,** Louis A '56 -761 Stoney Brook Rd -Sagamore Hills 44067

(440) 233-8463 .. **Tweed,** Guy E II '74 UAW Legal Srvcs -347 Midway Blvd -Ste 312
-Elyria 44035 **Fx:**324-4647

(937) 449-2800 .. **Tweel,** Donna S '90 (Chernesky H&K PLL) -10 Cthse Plz SW
-Ste 1100 -Dayton 45402 **Fx:**449-2821

(216) 241-2262 .. **Twohig,** Catherine B '96 %Yulish T & Assoc -1419 W 9th
-Hilliard Bldg -Cleveland 44113

(216) 241-2262 .. **Twohig,** Mark M III '73 (Yulish T & Assoc) -1419 W 9th
-Hilliard Bldg -Cleveland 44113

(614) 224-8166 .. **Twyford & Donahey** -495 S High -Ste 100 -Columbus 43215

(614) 224-8166 .. **Twyford,** Thomas L '65 (Twyford & D) -495 S High -Ste 100
-Columbus 43215

(973) 622-4444 .. **Twyman,** Carmen M '02 %McCarter & E LLP -100 Mulberry
-4 Gtwy Ctr -Bx652 -Newark, NJ 07101 **Fx:**624-7070

(419) 353-1062 .. **Twyman TenBrink Harms & Sharp** -519 W Wooster -Ctr Ste
-Bowling Green 43402 **Fx:**353-6277

(614) 221-1341 .. **Tyack Blackmore & Liston Co,PA** -536 S High -Columbus 43215
Fx:228-0253

(614) 445-0793 .. **Tyack,** David B '82 -820 S High -Columbus 43206 **Fx:**445-7948

(614) 221-1341 .. **Tyack,** James P '00 %Tyack B&L Co,PA -536 S High -Columbus
43215 **Fx:**228-0253

(614) 221-1341 .. **Tyack,** Jonathan T '96 Tyack B&L Co,PA -536 S High
-Columbus 43215 **Fx:**228-0253

(614) 466-6858 .. **Tyack,** Matthew J '98 Industrial Commssn of OH -30 W Spring
-9th Fl -Columbus 43215 **Fx:**752-8785

(614) 221-1341 .. **Tyack,** Thomas M '65 Tyack B&L Co,PA -536 S High
-Columbus 43215 **Fx:**228-0253

(330) 456-8341 .. **Tyburski,** Charles J '64 OfCnsl Black MS&A,LPA -220 Market Av
S -Ste 1000 -Canton 44702 **Fx:**456-5756

(513) 352-4718 .. **Tye,** Elizabeth A '03 Law Dept -801 Plum -Rm 214
-Cincinnati 45202 **Fx:**352-1515

(216) 324-7893 .. **Tye,** Russell W '96 (Tye & Assoc,LPA) -75 Pub Sq -Ste 1414
-Cleveland 44113

(937) 291-8646 .. **Tye,** Timothy N '78 Tye & T,LPA -5975 Kentshire Dr
-Kettering 45440

(216) 443-7223 .. **Tylee,** David C '85 Cuyahoga Cnty Pub Def -1200 W 3rd NW
-100 Lakeside Pl -Cleveland 44113

(216) 687-5166 .. **Tyler,** Barbara J '89 CSU-Marshall Cllg of Law -2121 Euclid Av
-LB138 -Cleveland 44115 **Fx:**687-6881

(440) 843-5320 .. **Tyler,** Charles Sr. '01 Kerns H&P -7123 Pearl Rd -Ste 304
-Middleburg Heights 44130

(216) 621-0200 .. **Tyler,** Corinne M '98 %Baker & H LLP -1900 E 9th -Ste 3200
-Cleveland 44114 **Fx:**696-0740

(513) 585-0647 .. **Tyler,** June S '86 Christ Hospital -2139 Auburn Av -Christ Hsptl
-Cincinnati 45219

(216) 681-1551 .. **Tyler,** Thomas S '88 DCMA Cleveland -555 E 88th -Ofc of Cnsl
-Bratenahl 44108

(440) 576-3662 .. **Tylman,** Stephen J '04 Ashtabula Cnty Pros -25 W Jffrsn
-Jefferson 44047

Tymcio, Deborah '00 -Bx360413 -Strongsville 44136

(216) 241-5310 .. **Tyminski,** James T Jr. '99 %Gallagher SF&N -1501 Euclid Av
-6th Fl -Cleveland 44115 **Fx:**241-1608

(216) 241-8333 .. **Tyminski,** Michael J '01 Ritzler C&S,Ltd -1001 Lakeside Av
-1550 North Pnt Twr -Cleveland 44114 **Fx:**241-5890

(440) 717-9925 .. **Tyner,** Michaele '76 -8180 Brecksvll Rd -#151 -Brecksville 44141

(419) 524-4402 .. **Tyree,** James A '83 -13 Park Av W -609 Barrington One Bldg
-Mansfield 44902

(937) 325-2459 .. **Tyree,** Sherry L '04 %Pavlatos C&L Co,LPA -700 E High
-Springfield 45505

(216) 621-1113 .. **Tyrpak,** Michele M '96 %Renner OB&S,LLP -1621 Euclid Av
-19th Fl -Cleveland 44115 **Fx:**621-6165

Tyson, Marqueta N '98 -7 Mimosa Cres -Hampton, VA 23661

(614) 253-7800 .. **Tyson,** Renny J '81 (R Tyson Co,LPA) -1465 E Broad
-Columbus 43205 **Fx:**253-7855

(512) 823-1004 .. **Tyson,** Thomas E '80 IBM -11400 Burnet Rd -Austin, TX 78758

(330) 744-4495 .. **Tzagournis,** George A '60 -101 Market -Ste 302
-Youngstown 44503 **Fx:**744-7291

(330) 455-6112 .. **Tzangas,** George J '57 (Tzangas PM&R) -220 Market Av S -8th Fl
-Canton 44702 **Fx:**455-2108

(330) 455-6112 .. **Tzangas Plakas Mannos & Raies** -220 Market Av S -8th Fl
-Canton 44702 **Fx:**455-2108

(216) 830-6830 .. **Ubbing,** Thomas J '85 (Brouse M) -1001 Lakeside Av -Ste 1600
-Cleveland 44114 **Fx:**830-6807

(216) 586-3939 .. **Ubersax,** Jeffery D '88 (Jones D) -901 Lakeside Av
-Cleveland 44114 **Fx:**579-0212

(216) 696-4700 .. **Ubersax,** Kristin L '87 (Spieth BM&N Co,LPA) -925 Euclid Av
-2000 Huntngtn Bldg -Cleveland 44115 **Fx:**696-2706

(614) 547-0350 .. **Ucker,** Timothy J '67 (Carroll U&H,LLC) -7100 N High -Ste 301
-Columbus 43085 **Fx:**547-0354

(513) 459-3622 .. **Ucros,** Nancy '99 Harris Corp -4393 Digital Way -Mason 45040

(419) 724-2600 .. **Udell & Abramson Ltd** -5738 Main -Sylvania 43560

(419) 213-6753 .. **Udell,** Judith L '84 Lucas Co Juvenile Ct (CASA)
-1801 Spielbusch Av -Toledo 43624

(419) 724-2600 .. **Udell,** Louis '83 Udell & A Ltd -5738 Main -Sylvania 43560

(216) 292-6757 .. **Udisky,** Warren L '65 -2738 Sulgrave Rd -Shaker Heights 44122
Fx:292-6757

Uebel, Susan K '86 -(Address Unavailable)

(330) 670-0770 .. **Ufholz,** Louis T '74 (Corzin SU&F) -304 N Cleveland-Massillon Rd
-Akron 44333

(513) 561-3313 .. **Uhl,** Jay J '74 Oxford Title Agency Inc -3814 West -Ste 217
-Cincinnati 45227 **Fx:**561-7804

(513) 868-8900 .. **Uhl,** John W '70 -2 S 3rd -Ste 520 -Hamilton 45011

(513) 665-3500 .. **Uhl,** Judd R '99 Freund F&A -105 E 4th -Ste 1400
-Cincinnati 45202 **Fx:**665-3503

(513) 723-8400 .. **Uhl,** Leslee M '98 %Coley & Assoc -9334 Union Centre Blvd
-Ste 200 -West Chester 45069

(513) 732-2212 .. **Uhle,** D'Anne D '83 (Durkee & U) -97 Main -Batavia 45103
Fx:732-3318

(513) 732-2212 .. **Uhle,** Richard B Jr. '83 (Durkee & U) -97 Main -Batavia 45103
Fx:732-3318

(614) 527-8979 .. **Uhlmann,** Beth A '97 Cnsl Nationwide Ins Co -1 Nationwide Plz
-Columbus 43215

(330) 376-2700 .. **Uhlmann,** David C '00 -222 S Main -Ste 400 -Akron 44308

(614) 899-6868 .. **Uhrich,** Jeffrey P '90 -Bx1977 -Westerville 43086

(513) 345-6772 .. **Uhrig,** Robert F '92 Fifth Third Bk -38 Fountain Sq Plz
-Midwest Payment Systems -Cincinnati 45263

(937) 987-2612 .. **Uible,** Harold H '50 -280 W Main -New Vienna 45159

(330) 746-7830 .. **Ujczo,** Daniel D '02 %Hon PC Economus -125 Market
-US Fed Bldg -Youngstown 44503

(330) 399-3229 .. **Ujczo,** Dennis E '76 -689 N Park Av -Bx1033 -Warren 44482
Fx:395-6632

(440) 835-8200 .. **Ujczo,** Joseph E '81 -24500 Ctr Ridge Rd -Ste 175
-Westlake 44145

Ujvagi, Matthew K '00 -Bx23182 -Toledo 43623

(513) 388-9222 .. **Ulbrich,** Channing L '00 %Ulbrich & U -7801 Beechmont Av -Ste 1
-Cincinnati 45255

(513) 388-9222 .. **Ulbrich,** Peter '72 (Ulbrich & U) -7801 Beechmont Av -Ste 1
-Cincinnati 45255

(513) 388-9222 .. **Ulbrich,** Wayne E '00 %Ulbrich & U -7801 Beechmont Av -Ste 1 -Cincinnati 45255

(614) 781-6500 .. **Uldricks,** David M '99 Pharm Horizons -7100 N High -Ste 305 -Worthington 43085

(202) 371-7327 .. **Ulery,** Christopher J '97 %Skadden ASM&F LLP -1440 NY Av NW -Washington, DC 20005

Ulinski, Linda C '91 -(Address Unavailable)

(513) 241-3100 .. **Ullman,** Alan J '83 (Lerner S&R) -120 E 4th -8th Fl -Cincinnati 45202

(415) 773-5652 .. **Ullman,** Howard M '92 Orrick H&S,LLP -400 Sansome -San Francisco, CA 94111

(216) 447-1551 .. **Ullman,** Meredith L '02 %Ross B&S Co LPA -6000 Freedom Square Dr -Ste 540 -Cleveland 44131 **Fx:**447-1554

(614) 253-2532 .. **Ullmann,** Victoria E '77 -1135 Bryden Rd -Columbus 43205

(513) 489-0881 .. **Ullner,** Jonathan M '81 -11085 Mntgmry Rd -Ste 202 -Cincinnati 45249

(770) 763-1133 .. **Ullner,** Kimberlee S '95 SrCnsl Assurant Grp -260 Intrst North Cir NW -Atlanta, GA 30339

(215) 575-4200 .. **Ullom,** Marc F '72 %Rawle H,LLP -1339 Chestnut -16th Fl -Philadelphia, PA 19107 **Fx:**563-2583

(614) 895-7962 .. **Ullom-Morse,** Norman J '79 -575 Copeland Mill Rd -Ste 1B -Westerville 43081

(513) 651-6800 .. **Ulmer,** Andrew B '03 %Frost BT LLC -201 E 5th -2200 PNC Ctr -Cincinnati 45202 **Fx:**651-6981

(216) 931-6000 .. **Ulmer & Berne LLP** -1300 E 9th -Ste 900 Penton Media Bldg -Cleveland 44114 **Fx:**931-6001

(513) 762-6200 .. **Ulmer & Berne LLP** -600 Vine -Ste 2800 -Cincinnati 45202 **Fx:**762-6245

(614) 228-8400 .. **Ulmer & Berne LLP** -88 E Broad -Ste 1600 -Columbus 43215 **Fx:**228-8561

(513) 887-3474 .. **Ulreich,** Jacqueline M '01 Butler Cnty Pros -315 High -11th Fl -Bx515 -Hamilton 45012

(440) 352-8977 .. **Ulrich,** Joseph R '69 J Ulrich Co,LPA -1959 Mentor Av -Painesville 44077

(937) 222-2500 .. **Ulrich,** Karl R '91 (Sebaly S&D) -1900 Kettering Twr -Dayton 45423 **Fx:**222-6554

(614) 462-7450 .. **Ulrich,** Matthew E '03 CASA Franklin Cnty -373 S High -6th Fl -Columbus 43215 **Fx:**462-5070

(937) 449-6400 .. **Ulrich,** Paul M '99 %Dinsmore & S LLP -1 S Main -Ste 1300 One Dayton Centre -Dayton 45402 **Fx:**449-6405

(216) 360-7200 .. **Ulrich,** Phyllis A '91 (Carlisle MRK&U Co,LPA) -24755 Chagrin Blvd -Ste 200 -Cleveland 44122 **Fx:**360-7210

(513) 922-8836 .. **Ultsch,** William F '50 -3001 Ebenezer Rd -Cincinnati 45233

(617) 248-5032 .. **Uluer,** Deborah B '96 %Choate H&S -Exch Pl -Boston, MA 02109 **Fx:**248-4000

(330) 650-4436 .. **Umbaugh,** David G '74 (Umbaugh & S) -110 W Streetsboro Rd -Ste 3A -Hudson 44236

(440) 350-2708 .. **Umholtz,** Marie L '89 Lake Cnty Dom Relatns Ct -47 N Park Pl -Painesville 44077

Umholtz, Raymond Robert '84 -211 Main -Chardon 44024

(614) 475-4493 .. **Umpleby,** John I '74 -2444 Ottawa Dr -Columbus 43229

(516) 869-7135 .. **Umpleby,** Kimberly A '94 Kimco Realty Corp -3333 New Hyde Pk Rd -Ste 100 -Bx5020 -New Hyde Park, NY 11042

(317) 488-6659 .. **Umstead,** Raymond L Jr. '78 Anthem Ins Co -120 Monument Cir -Indianapolis, IN 46204

(704) 348-5314 .. **Underdown,** Ezell H '98 Cadwalader W&T -227 W Trade -Ste 2400 -Charlotte, NC 28202

(614) 466-4425 .. **Underhill,** Aaron L '00 %Hon FE Sweeney Sr -30 E Broad -3rd Fl -Columbus 43215

(614) 214-0459 .. **Underwood,** Charles D Jr. '80 -731 Fairway Blvd -Columbus 43213 **Fx:**358-6633

(937) 255-6111 .. **Underwood,** Denise A '85 USAF AFMCLO/JAN -1864 4th -Bldg 15 -Wright Patterson AFB 45433

(419) 756-7711 .. **Underwood,** Jeffrey A '96 (Bayer J&A) -362 Lex Av -Mansfield 44907 **Fx:**756-9566

(614) 227-2000 .. **Underwood,** Michael Joseph '80 (Porter WM&A LLP) -41 S High -Columbus 43215 **Fx:**227-2100

(614) 866-1195 .. **Underwood,** William F Jr. '74 -7610 Slate Ridge Blvd -Reynoldsburg 43068

Underwood-Faison, Wendy R '97 -1947 Chatham Dr -Troy, MI 48084

(216) 931-6000 .. **Ungar,** Michael N '84 (Ulmer & B LLP) -1300 E 9th -Ste 900 Penton Media Bldg -Cleveland 44114 **Fx:**931-6001

Unger, Mary Ann '84 -3606 Medinah Ct -Augusta, GA 30907

(614) 340-3444 .. **Unger,** Paul J '95 (Henley M&U Cnsltng,Inc) -3300 Riverside Dr -Ste 350 -Columbus 43221 **Fx:**340-3443

(609) 896-9060 .. **Unger,** Scott I '96 %Stark & S -993 Lenox Dr -Bldg 2 -Lawrenceville, NJ 08648 **Fx:**896-0629

(937) 223-8177 .. **Ungerman,** Fred A Jr. '80 (Coolidge WW&L) -33 W 1st -Ste 600 -Dayton 45402 **Fx:**223-6705

(216) 523-4126 .. **Union,** Marvin L '69 Eaton Corp -1111 Superior Av -Cleveland 44114

(614) 462-5487 .. **Union,** Stephanie P '99 %Kegler BH&R -65 E State -Ste 1800 -Columbus 43215 **Fx:**464-2634

Untener, David J '76 -4601 Eastwood Rd -Minnetonka, MN 55345

(419) 238-5252 .. **Unterbrink,** Gregory W '81 -614 High St -Van Wert 45891

(440) 354-1969 .. **Unterweiser,** Carl H '84 Lake Hospital Syst Inc -10 E Wshngtn -Painesville 44077

(740) 349-8505 .. **Untied,** Wesley K '85 (Schaller C&U) -32 N Park Pl -Newark 43055

(740) 549-2089 .. **Unver,** Douglas R '91 -439 Slate Run Dr -Powell 43065

Unver, Karen A '91 Lexis Nexis -439 Slate Run Dr -Powell 43065

(513) 622-1825 .. **Upite,** David V '00 Porter & Gamble Co -8700 Mason Mntgmry Rd -Bx8006 -Mason 45040

(212) 790-9200 .. **Urban,** Alexandra B '98 %Cowan L&L,PC -1133 Av of Amer -New York, NY 10036 **Fx:**575-0671

(216) 241-4244 .. **Urban,** Brian M '79 (B Urban Co,LPA) -1370 Ontario -600 Standard Bldg -Cleveland 44113

(440) 930-8082 .. **Urban,** Daniel C '96 Wickens HPC&B -35765 Chester Rd -Avon 44011 **Fx:**937-4466

(330) 437-0101 .. **Urban,** George '94 -101 Central Plz S -300 Bank One Twr -Canton 44702 **Fx:**452-2014

Urban, Jennifer L '04 -(Address Unavailable)

(440) 846-0000 .. **Urban,** John J '75 -11221 Pearl Rd -Strongsville 44136

(216) 222-2934 .. **Urban,** Margaret N '83 Natl City Bank -1900 E 9th -Tax Dept -Cleveland 44114

(330) 762-2411 .. **Urban,** Michael S '87 (Amer C Co,LPA) -159 S Main -6th Fl -Akron 44308 **Fx:**762-9918

(740) 881-4689 .. **Urban,** Raymond T '86 -2170 Wingate Dr -Delaware 43015

(330) 364-5593 .. **Urban,** Robert C Jr. '85 Johnson U&R Co LPA -117 S Bway -Bx1007 -New Philadelphia 44663 **Fx:**364-3714

(330) 394-1539 .. **Urban,** William J Jr. '69 (W Urban Co LPA) -434 High NE -Warren 44481

(216) 486-8200 .. **Urbancic,** Brano '56 -18975 Villavw Rd -Cleveland 44119

(216) 687-1900 .. **Urbanek,** Jerry R '04 Legal Aid -1223 W 6th -Cleveland 44113 **Fx:**687-0779

(843) 722-5526 .. **Urbanic,** Geraldine H '81 Trident College -66 Columbus -Bx118067 -Charleston, SC 29423

(216) 498-5397 .. **Urbank,** Donna E '95 Penton Media Inc -1300 E 9th -Penton Media Bldg -Cleveland 44114

(419) 841-8584 .. **Urenovitch,** Joseph J '96 Albrechta & C -3230 Cntrl Pk W Dr -Ste 200 -Toledo 43617

(513) 721-8822 .. **Urling,** James P '99 Nationwide Ins Co -125 E Ct -Ste 203 -Cincinnati 45202

(216) 781-3700 .. **Urse,** Michael F '84 PriceWaterhouse Coopers LLP -200 Pub Sq -27th Flr BP Twr -Cleveland 44114

(804) 916-2933 .. **Ursic,** Joseph '03 US Dist Ct of Appeals-4th Cir -600 E Main -Ste 2200 -Richmond, VA 23219

(440) 362-4820 .. **Ursu,** Daniel J '86 Factory Mutual Ins Co -25050 Cntry Clb Blvd -Ste 400 -North Olmsted 44070

(614) 469-8000 .. **Urvan,** Sean J '03 %McNees W&N,LLC -21 E State -17th Fl -Columbus 43215 **Fx:**469-4653

(216) 522-2683 .. **Ussery,** Karla K '97 US Dept of Educ/OfcCivilRights -600 Superior Av E -Ste 750 -Cleveland 44114

(937) 333-4400 .. **Utacht,** Edward C II '74 Dayton Pros -335 W 3rd -Ste 372 -Dayton 45402

(513) 563-4555 .. **Utaski,** Thomas J '87 -4555 Lk Forrest Dr -Ste 365 -Cincinnati 45242

(440) 395-3771 .. **Uth,** Michael M '87 Progressive Ins Co -6300 Wilson Mills Rd -#N72A -Mayfield Village 44143

(330) 376-1717 .. **Utley,** David G '87 (Davis & Y) -One Cascade Plz -Ste 800 -Akron 44308

(330) 467-3575 .. **Utley,** Sue E '70 -8509 Waterside Dr -Sagamore Hills 44067

Utpadel-Mandt, Deborah J '04 -(Address Unavailable)

(216) 228-1523 .. **Utrata,** Carl I '72 -1506 Arthur Av -Lakewood 44107

(937) 335-2622 .. **Utrecht,** James D '77 (Utrecht & Y) -12 S Plum -Troy 45373

(513) 721-4532 .. **Utt,** Daniel P '86 (Katz TB&H) -255 E 5th -Ste 2400 -Cincinnati 45202

(513) 579-6400 .. **Utter,** Gregory M '81 (Keating M&K PLL) -1 E 4th -1400 Provident Twr -Cincinnati 45202 **Fx:**579-6457

(202) 457-4266 .. **Uttrich,** Donald L '85 Jackson & C,PC -1120 20th NW -Ste 300S -Washington, DC 20036

(740) 966-5866 .. **Utz,** Dorothy A '95 -6655 Harmony Church Rd -Johnstown 43031

Utz, Eugene J '53 -7865 Shawnee Run Rd -Cincinnati 45243

(740) 967-3644 .. **Utz,** Nancy A '89 -55 S Main -Ste B -Johnstown 43031

(614) 464-2704 .. **Utz,** Richard A '77 OH Title Corp -155 W Main -Unit 200 -Columbus 43215

(216) 575-0777 .. **Uzl,** William E '90 %Kelley & F,LLP -1300 E 9th -Ste 1901 -Cleveland 44114 **Fx:**575-0799

(614) 281-3985 .. **Vaas,** Jonathan M '04 %Jones D -325 John H McConnell Blvd -Ste 600 -Bx165017 -Columbus 43216 **Fx:**461-4198

(216) 685-1157 .. **Vaccarelli,** Julie A '03 %Weltman W&R Co,LPA -323 W Lakeside Av -Ste 200 -Cleveland 44113 **Fx:**363-4121

(330) 451-8796 .. **Vaccaro,** Michael B '95 Stark Cnty Job/Fam Srvcs -220 E Tuscarawas -Canton 44702

(440) 974-8091 .. **Vaci,** Elizabeth D '83 -9512 Pilgrim Dr -Mentor 44060

(330) 670-7300 .. **Vadas,** Kathryn A '99 %Hanna C&P,LLP -3737 Embssy Pkwy -Bx5521 -Akron 44334 **Fx:**670-0977

(440) 954-3744 .. **Vadnal,** Richard A '88 (RA Vadnal Co,LPA) -35350 Curtis Blvd -Ste 330 -Eastlake 44095

(216) 664-4971 .. **Vagi,** Jolan B '82 Cleveland Mun Ct -1200 Ontario -Cleveland 44113

(513) 622-4433 .. **Vago,** James C '95 Procter & Gamble Co -8700 Mason Mntgmry Rd -Mason 45040

(330) 456-4122 .. **Vagotis,** Angela T '90 (AT Vagotis Co,LPA) -220 Market Av S -Ste 940 -Canton 44702

(513) 852-8200 .. **Vahlsing,** Joseph H '72 (Cors & B LLC) -537 E Pete Rose Way -Ste 400 -Cincinnati 45202

(216) 696-4200 .. **Vail,** James D '79 (Schneider SR&L PLL) -1111 Superior Av -Ste 1000 -Cleveland 44114 **Fx:**696-7303

(419) 472-2179 .. **Vail,** James E Jr. '76 Lucas Cnty Pros -Adams & Erie -Lucas Cnty Cthse -Toledo 43624

(216) 896-2734 .. **Vail,** Julia B '84 SrCnsl Parker Hannifin Corp -6035 Parkland Blvd -Cleveland 44124

(740) 681-4759 .. **Vail,** Madge E '83 Lancaster Bingo Co,Inc -200 Quarry Rd -Lancaster 43130

Vaile, George Q '68 -776 Worthngtn New Haven Rd -Marengo 43334

(202) 693-5300 .. **Valdez,** Rolando N '96 Dept of Labor -200 Const Av NW -Rm N-2464 -Washington, DC 20210

(412) 434-7958 .. **Valecko,** James P '93 (Weltman W&R Co,LPA) -436 7th Av -Ste 2718 -Pittsburgh, PA 15219 **Fx:**338-7101

(513) 984-8700 .. **Valencia,** Louis E '04 (Turner & V,LLP) -10979 Reed Hartman Hwy -Ste 110 -Cincinnati 45242

(312) 855-1010 .. **Valencic,** Michelle R '96 %Clausen M PC -10 S LaSalle -Ste 1600 -Chicago, IL 60603 **Fx:**606-7777

(937) 325-9000 .. **Valente,** Paul R '67 -10 S Spring -Springfield 45502

(216) 241-5310 .. **Valenti,** John A '80 (Gallagher SF&N) -1501 Euclid Av -6th Fl -Cleveland 44115 **Fx:**241-1608

(330) 643-2765 .. **Valenti,** Kimberly A '02 Summit Cnty Pros-CSEA -171 S Main -Akron 44308 **Fx:**643-2822

Valentin, Alina M '02 -(Address Unavailable)

(614) 221-2223 .. **Valentine,** Anne M '82 Leeseberg & V -175 S 3rd -PH 1 -Columbus 43215 **Fx:**221-3106

(614) 873-3421 .. **Valentine,** Clifton G Jr. '82 -128 W Main -Plain City 43064

(216) 241-8471 .. **Valentine,** James E '86 -323 Lakeside Av -Ste 450 -Cleveland 44113 **Fx:**781-6242

(614) 461-1311 .. **Valentine**, Matthew R '04 -(Address Unavailable)
(614) 461-1311 .. **Valentine**, Michael J '87 %Reminger & R -65 E State
-4th Fl Cptl Sq Ofc Bldg -Columbus 43215 **Fx**:232-2410
(216) 621-0150 .. **Valentine**, Nancy A '98 %Hahn L&P LLP
-3300 BP Twr/200 Pub Sq -Ste 3300 -Cleveland 44114
Fx:241-2824
(216) 363-6489 .. **Valentino**, Nicholas '77 Advisory Srvcs Inc -1422 Euclid Av
-1010 Hanna Bldg -Cleveland 44115
Valento, James J '89 -4536 Pond Mdws Ct -Mason 45040
(216) 696-3311 .. **Valerian**, Robert J '76 (Kahn K) -1301 E 9th -2600 Erievw Twr
-Cleveland 44114 **Fx**:623-4912
(336) 821-4760 .. **Valitutto**, Richard E '84 New Breed Transfer Corp -Bx18367
-Greensboro, NC 27419
(513) 852-8200 .. **Valleau**, Richard J '62 Cors & B LLC -537 E Pete Rose Way
-Ste 400 -Cincinnati 45202
(937) 225-5608 .. **Valley**, Theodore D '99 Montgomery Cnty Pros -301 W 3rd -Bx972
-Dayton 45422 **Fx**:225-3470
(216) 696-1400 .. **Valli**, Richard A '85 -700 W St Calir Av -Ste 210 -Cleveland 44113
(937) 278-0022 .. **Vallone**, Sean J '94 (Berry & V) -4612 Salem Av -Dayton 45440
(216) 689-4467 .. **Vallorz**, Ernest L Jr. '84 McDonald Investments -127 Pub Square
-Cleveland 44114
(216) 271-8983 .. **Vallorz**, Sonia C '84 BP Oil Co -6585 Ridge Rd -Cleveland 44129
(440) 333-7330 .. **Valore & Cruse Co,LPA** -23550 Ctr Ridge Rd -Westlake 44145
(216) 443-7800 .. **Valore**, Dean M '00 Cuyahoga Cnty Pros -1200 Ontario -8th Fl
-Cleveland 44113 **Fx**:698-2270
(440) 333-7330 .. **Valore**, Joseph A '70 (Valore & C Co,LPA) -23550 Ctr Ridge Rd
-Westlake 44145
(937) 653-1729 .. **Valore**, Joseph P '62 -120B N Main -Urbana 43078
(440) 333-0066 .. **Valponi**, Barbara D '79 Rocky River Mun Ct -21012 Hilliard Blvd
-Rocky River 44116
(216) 241-2838 .. **Valponi**, Mark J '77 (Taft S&H LLP) -200 Pub Sq -3500 BP Twr
-Cleveland 44114 **Fx**:865-9105
(419) 865-8021 .. **Valtin**, James D '03 %Balk H&M -5744 Southwyck Blvd -Toledo
43614 **Fx**:865-9105
(513) 579-1500 .. **Valz**, David R '94 (Buechner HOM&H Co,LPA) -105 E 4th -Ste 300
-Cincinnati 45202 **Fx**:977-4361
(614) 644-2640 .. **Vamos**, Stephen J III '81 Dept Ins -2100 Stella Ct
-Columbus 43215
(817) 978-2947 .. **Van**, Nam C '01 NLRB -819 Taylor -Rm 8AZY
-Fort Worth, TX 76102
(216) 566-5348 .. **Vana**, Robert J '77 Chrtr One Bank,FSB -1215 Superior Av
-Cleveland 44114
(330) 491-5235 .. **Van Abel**, John P '59 (Buckingham D&B,LLP) -4518 Fulton Dr NW
-Bx35548 -Canton 44735 **Fx**:492-9625
(216) 781-4680 .. **Van Aken Withers & Webster** -629 Euclid Av -1000 Natl City
Bk Bldg -Cleveland 44114 **Fx**:241-1421
(419) 586-8120 .. **Van Arsdel**, Peter R '82 Van Arsel & G Co,LPA -118 W Market
-Bx298 -Celina 45822
VanAtta, Nancy L '92 -(Address Unavailable)
(312) 928-1236 .. **VanAuken**, Bradley A '83 Equity Residential Properties
-2 N Riverside Plz -Ste 400 -Chicago, IL 60606
Van Ausdall, Erika M '00 -(Address Unavailable)
(415) 554-1296 .. **VanBergen**, James J '84 SF Housing Auth -440 Turk
-San Francisco, CA 94102
(419) 244-5000 .. **VanBerkom**, Trevor P '99 -500 Mad Av -Ste 525 -Toledo 43604
(440) 838-7600 .. **Van Blargan**, Christopher J '96 %Janik & D,LLP -9200 S Hills Blvd
-Ste 300 -Cleveland 44147 **Fx**:838-7601
(330) 746-5000 .. **Van Brocklin**, Gary L '75 -44 Fed Plz Central -Ste 204
-Youngstown 44503
VanBuren, Susan K '87 -(Address Unavailable)
(440) 708-1028 .. **VanBuskirk**, Margaret P '93 Vanbuskirk Legal Search LLC
-16445 Lucky Bell Ln -Chagrin Falls 44023
(216) 443-6985 .. **Vancavage**, Gerard '81 Cnty Ofc Emplymnt & Labor Relations
-1255 Euclid Av -Ste 310 -Cleveland 44115
(614) 336-3861 .. **Vance**, Catherine E '97 -1906 Slaton Ct -Columbus 43235
(513) 629-1882 .. **Vance**, James J '86 Wstrn & Sthrn Life Ins -400 Bway
-Cincinnati 45202
(330) 451-7897 .. **Vance**, Joseph E '99 Stark Cnty Pros -110 Central Plz -Ste 510
-Canton 44702
(954) 491-1120 .. **Vance**, Kevin E '98 %Greenspoon MHRR&B
-100 W Cypress Crk Rd -Ste 700 -Fort Lauderdale, FL 33309
Fx:771-9264
(513) 793-2353 .. **Vance**, Molly G '03 -10999 Reed Hartman Hwy -Ste 229
-Cincinnati 45242
(330) 836-9358 .. **Vance**, Patricia Ann '67 -544 White Pond Dr -Ste E -Akron 44320
(210) 221-2189 .. **Vance**, Randall J '86 US ARMY JAG -Hdqrts, 5th US Army
-Fort Sam Houston, TX 78234
(216) 444-9804 .. **Vance**, Victoria L '82 %Cleveland Clinic Fndtn/Gen Cnsl
-9500 Euclid Av -Cleveland 44195
(216) 348-1700 .. **Vance**, William '81 (Davis & Y) -101 Prospect Av W -Ste 1700
-Cleveland 44115 **Fx**:621-0602
(309) 671-7083 .. **Vance**, Willie J '77 NLRB -300 Hmltn Blvd -Ste 200
-Peoria, IL 61602
(740) 772-7467 .. **Van de Carr**, Charles R IV '76 Cnsl Ross Cnty Job/Fam Srvcs
-475 Wstrn Av -Ste B -Bx469 -Chillicothe 45601 **Fx**:772-7514
(216) 621-0200 .. **VanDeHey**, Margaret M '99 %Baker & H LLP -1900 E 9th
-Ste 3200 -Cleveland 44114 **Fx**:696-0740
(419) 255-6810 .. **Van Deilen**, James W '79 -1107 Adams -Toledo 43624
(419) 225-2015 .. **Vandemark**, Dale M '84 (Romey & V) -330 N Main -Bx1256
-Lima 45802
(614) 221-8317 .. **Van De Mark**, Julie A '82 -492 City Park Av -Columbus 43215
(419) 228-8403 .. **Vandemark**, William C '62 (Fisher V&F Co,LPA) -303 E High
-Lima 45801
(937) 333-4349 .. **Vanden Bosch**, Virginia C '85 Dayton Mun Ct -301 W 3rd
-% Ct Admin Rm 365 -Dayton 45402
(440) 930-5911 .. **VanDenBossche**, Achille C '01 -525 Avon Belden Rd
-Avon Lake 44012
(216) 642-3342 .. **Vanderburg**, Keith A '78 (Wegman H&V,LPA) -6055 Rockside
Wds Blvd -Ste 200 -Cleveland 44131 **Fx**:642-8826
(614) 866-9811 .. **Vanderhoff**, Anna M '99 -12161 Twincreek Dr -Pickerington 43147
(216) 621-0200 .. **VanderKaay**, Aaron M '01 %Baker & H LLP -1900 E 9th -Ste 3200
-Cleveland 44114 **Fx**:696-0740
(614) 645-8288 .. **VanDerKarr**, Scott D '82 Cnty Mun Ct Judge -375 S High
-Columbus 43215

(419) 448-4575 .. **Van der Klooster**, Susan C '89 %Behm & H -187 S Wshngtn
-Tiffin 44883 **Fx**:448-0543
(854) 943-6100 .. **VanderLaan**, Aaron A '98 %Arnzen & W -Bx472
-Covington, KY 41012
(513) 977-8200 .. **Vander Laan**, Mark A '73 (Dinsmore & S LLP) -255 E 5th
-Ste 1900 -Cincinnati 45202 **Fx**:977-8141
(216) 896-2156 .. **Vanderlip**, Nancy L '93 Parker Hannifin Corp -6035 Parkland Blvd
-Cleveland 44124 **Fx**:896-4027
(937) 298-0008 .. **VanderSchaaff**, Bertis J IV '96 %Scudder & E Co,LPA
-2912 Springboro W -Ste 105 -Dayton 45439
(734) 487-0076 .. **Van Der Velde**, Robert J '85 Eastern Mich Univ -202 Boone Hall
-Ypsilanti, MI 48197
(740) 653-0461 .. **Vandervoort**, Craig M '92 (Sitterley & V Ltd) -123 S Broad
-Ste 211 -Lancaster 43130
(740) 653-0461 .. **Vandervoort**, Jeffrey K '95 (Sitterley & V Ltd) -123 S Broad
-Ste 211 -Lancaster 43130
(614) 451-4224 .. **Van Dervoort**, John W '54 -5150 Reed Rd -Columbus 43220
(740) 653-0461 .. **Vandervoort**, Peter M '63 OfCnsl Sitterley & V Ltd -123 S Broad
-Ste 211 -Lancaster 43130
(740) 681-5023 .. **Vandervoort**, Terre L '90 Pros -Bx1008 -Lancaster 43130
(216) 621-0070 .. **Van Dervort**, Daina B '80 Friedman D&S Co,LPA -1370 Ontario
-Ste 600 -Cleveland 44113 **Fx**:621-4008
(304) 558-0526 .. **Van Dervort**,
Deborah Y '89 WV Pub Srvc Comm-Consumer Advocate
-723 Kanawha Blvd E -7th Fl Union Bldg -Charleston, WV 25301
Fx:558-3610
(216) 622-8200 .. **Vanderwist**, James C '83 (Calfee H&G LLP) -800 Superior Av
-Ste 1400 -Cleveland 44114 **Fx**:241-0816
(440) 498-5170 .. **Vanderwist**, Kathryn K '84 Pioneer-Standard Electronics Inc
-6065 Parkland Blvd -Mayfield Heights 44124
Vande Ryt, Richard C '02 -3390 Palmhill Ln -Cincinnati 45239
(614) 451-0480 .. **van Deusen**, Edwin H II '70 -1044 Parkleigh Rd -Columbus 43220
(216) 781-4000 .. **Van Deusen**, Roger W '68 (Van Deusen & W,LLC)
-1422 Euclid Av -Ste 1610 Hanna Bldg -Cleveland 44115
(440) 992-7101 .. **VanDevender**, Margaret A '85 -110 W 44th -Ashtabula 44004
(330) 535-6751 .. **VanDevere**, Christopher M '93 -265 S Main -Akron 44308
(614) 469-3286 .. **VandeWerken**, Jerry '74 (Thompson H LLP) -10 W Broad
-Ste 700 -Columbus 43215 **Fx**:469-3361
(888) 695-1100 .. **Vandiford**, Douglas A II '02 -4 W Main -Ste 908 -Springfield 45502
(216) 476-2125 .. **Vandrak**, Daniel J '65 -12300 Lorain Av -Cleveland 44111
(440) 239-9777 .. **Van Dress**, Dean W '99 -46 Front -Berea 44017
Fx:(775) 521-5756
(330) 672-2775 .. **van Dulmen-Krantz**, Jennifer J '04 Kent State Univ
-113 Bowman Hall -Dept of Justice Studies -Kent 44240
(216) 381-2441 .. **Van Dyke**, Anthony P '72 -4822 Monticello Blvd
-Richmond Heights 44143
(614) 462-5372 .. **Van Dyke**, Omia N '83 Franklin Cnty Dom Rltns Ct -373 S High
-5th Fl -Columbus 43215
(419) 634-5791 .. **VanDyne**, Charles P '54 -Huber Bldg -Ada 45810
(865) 545-7547 .. **VanDyne**, Janice K '94 St Marys Hlth Systm -900 E Oak Hill Av
-Knoxville, TN 37917
(614) 221-8668 .. **Van Dyne**, Jean E Jr. '72 -165 E Lvngstn Av -Columbus 43215
(419) 227-5858 .. **Van Dyne**, Mark A '90 (Baran PTF&T Co,LPA) -121 W High
-Ste 905 -Bx568 -Lima 45802 **Fx**:227-4569
(419) 866-0928 .. **Vaneck**, Alexandria R '80 (A Vaneck Co,LPA) -5620
Southwyck Blvd -Ste 103 -Toledo 43614
(216) 621-0070 .. **Vanek**, Stephen S '92 Friedman D&S Co,LPA -1370 Ontario
-Ste 600 -Cleveland 44113 **Fx**:621-4008
(614) 224-8187 .. **Van Eman**, Timothy L '81 (Lamkin VTB&D) -500 S Front -Ste 200
-Columbus 43215 **Fx**:224-4943
(216) 621-0200 .. **Van Euwen**, Peter W III '98 %Baker & H LLP -1900 E 9th
-Ste 3200 -Cleveland 44114 **Fx**:696-0740
(330) 494-1022 .. **Van Gaasbeek**, David A '77 -1303 W Maple -Ste 104
-North Canton 44720
(216) 696-9310 .. **VanGilder**, Donald N '98 %Cariglio & Assoc Co,LPA -75 Pub Sq
-Ste 920 -Cleveland 44113 **Fx**:696-0075
(419) 822-3324 .. **Van Gunten**, Amber L '99 OfCnsl GL Van Gunten -106 Main
-Delta 43515
(419) 843-6581 .. **Van Gunten**, Edward A '62 (E Van Gunten & Co,LPA)
-6545 W Central Av -Ste 209 -Toledo 43617
(419) 822-3324 .. **Van Gunten**, Gregory L '76 -106 Main -Delta 43515
(419) 213-4746 .. **van het Kaar**, Sally H '99 Lucas Cnty Cmn Pleas Ct -700 Adams
-Cnty Cthse Ste 110 -Toledo 43624
(614) 466-3180 .. **VanHeyde**, George J '76 Atty Gen -150 E Gay -Columbus 43215
Fx:466-9788
(614) 228-1541 .. **Van Heyde**, J Stephen '68 (Baker & H LLP) -65 E State -Ste 2100
-Columbus 43215 **Fx**:462-2616
(407) 841-1200 .. **Van Heyde**, Joseph J II '80 (Dean MEBC&B,PA)
-800 N Magnolia Av -Ste 1500 -Bx2346 -Orlando, FL 32802
Fx:423-1831
(330) 643-2785 .. **Van Ho**, Adam M '01 Summit Cnty Pros-Crim -53 Univ Av -7th Fl
-Akron 44308 **Fx**:643-8277
(630) 821-2062 .. **Van Hook**, Robert W Jr. '76 BP America Inc -4101 Winfld Rd
-2E Tax -Warrenville, IL 60555
(419) 423-8668 .. **Van Horn**, Andrew J '97 %SM Powell,LPA -108 E Main Cross
-Findlay 45840
(419) 893-6000 .. **Van Horn**, Darrell V Jr. '72 -2211 Rvr Rd -Ste 105 -Maumee 43537
(740) 452-8430 .. **Van Horn**, Kevin R '85 -715 Adair Av -Zanesville 43701
(614) 463-9444 .. **VanHorn**, Terry D '70 -Bx6408 -Columbus 43206
(419) 247-2500 .. **Van Horsten**, Craig J '76 (Fuller & H,Ltd) -One SeaGate -Ste 1700
-Bx2088 -Toledo 43603 **Fx**:247-2665
(513) 721-1504 .. **Van Houten**, Dennis W '76 Droder & M Co,LPA
-125 W Cntrl Pkwy -Cincinnati 45202 **Fx**:721-0310
(614) 469-3200 .. **Van Hoy**, Martha S '04 %Thompson H LLP -10 W Broad -Ste 700
-Columbus 43215 **Fx**:469-3361
(419) 243-3800 .. **Van Huysen**, Ian Scott '01 -1119 Adams -2nd Fl -Toledo 43624
Fx:243-4046
(216) 589-5622 .. **Van Iden**, Byron D '72 -55 Pub Sq -Ste 2200 -Cleveland 44113
(216) 241-2229 .. **Vanik**, John C '82 -1468 W 9th -Ste 750 -Cleveland 44113
(216) 928-7540 .. **Vanik**, Thomas C '75 (Vanik & B,LLP) -1406 W 6th -3rd Fl
-Cleveland 44113 **Fx**:928-7548
(614) 469-3939 .. **Van Kley**, Jack A '79 Cnsl Jones D -325 John H McConnell Blvd
-Ste 600 -Bx165017 -Columbus 43216 **Fx**:461-4198

(614) 485-1800 ..**Van Ligten**, Peter F '96 %Arnold T&W -2075 Marble Cliff Ofc Park
-Columbus 43215 **Fx**:485-1944
VanMeter, Stephanie L '04 -(Address Unavailable)

(614) 292-0611 ..**Vannatta**, Julie D '87 OSU/Legal Affrs -33 W 11th Av -Ste 209
-Columbus 43201

(614) 464-6400 ..**Vannatta**, Mark E '87 (Vorys SS&P LLP) -52 E Gay -Bx1008
-Columbus 43216 **Fx**:464-6350
Vannelli, Gail L '86 -Bx23363 -Chagrin Falls 44023

(440) 461-4433 ..**Van Ness**, Charles J '90 (Van Ness,LTD) -6181 Mayfld Rd
-Ste 104 -Mayfield Heights 44124

(330) 258-6462 ..**Van Ness**, Jean C '95 OfCnsl Buckingham D&B,LLP -50 S Main
-Bx1500 -Akron 44309 **Fx**:258-6559

(713) 335-4830 ..**Van Niel**, Jeffrey D '87 %Ware SF&J -2929 Allen Pkwy -42nd Fl
-Houston, TX 77019

(216) 621-0200 ..**VanNiel**, Michael A '01 %Baker & H LLP -1900 E 9th -Ste 3200
-Cleveland 44114 **Fx**:696-0740

(614) 644-0089 ..**VanNorman**, John S '00 Legis Srvc Commssn -77 S High
-Columbus 43215

(937) 222-7477 ..**VanNoy**, Anthony S '96 (Wright & V,LPA) -32 N Main -Ste 801
-Dayton 45402

(440) 777-6500 ..**Vannucci**, Dominic J '74 Burke V&G -22649 Lorain Rd
-Fairview Park 44126 **Fx**:777-0507

(513) 603-2316 ..**van Nuis**, Rosalie P '85 OH Casualty Ins Co -9450 Seward Rd
-Fairfield 45014

(419) 289-6888 ..**Vanosdall**, John A '78 (Harpster V&F) -60 W 2nd -Ashland 44805
Fx:281-2461

(513) 722-3800 ..**Van Pelt**, Jeanne A '97 -Bx773 -Milford 45150

(330) 376-5300 ..**VanRees**, Adam R '02 %Buckingham D&B,LLP -50 S Main
-Bx1500 -Akron 44309 **Fx**:258-6559

(440) 333-2572 ..**VanRooy**, Mark J '91 -20525 Ctr Ridge Rd -Ste 626
-Rocky River 44116

(614) 436-4154 ..**Van Runkle**, Peter E '82 OH Hlth Care Assn -55 Green Mdws Dr S
-Westerville 43081

(937) 225-5607 ..**Van Schaik**, Chris R '70 Montgomery Cnty Pros -301 W 3rd
-Bx972 -Dayton 45422 **Fx**:225-3410

(614) 846-6783 ..**Van Sickle**, John A '83 Amer One Title Agncy,Ltd -1000 N High
-Ste 6 -Worthington 43085

(419) 782-2253 ..**VanSickle**, Mary J '87 UAW Legal Srvcs -1500 Baltimore Rd
-Defiance 43512

(330) 683-5010 ..**VanSickle**, Timothy R '98 %Kropf WH&L, LLP -100 N Vine -Bx67
-Orrville 44667 **Fx**:683-5030

(614) 933-1200 ..**VanSlyck**, Steven B '86 The Stonehenge Co -41 N High
-New Albany 43054

(216) 622-0850 ..**Van Slyke**, David L '04 %McFadden & Assoc Co,LPA
-1370 Ontario -Ste 1700 -Cleveland 44113 **Fx**:622-0854

(614) 644-3037 ..**Vanterpool**, Donald L '87 EPA -122 S Front -Bx1049
-Columbus 43216

(419) 289-1199 ..**VanTilburg**, William D '62 (Troth & V) -245 Sandusky -Bx606
-Ashland 44805

(419) 625-4010 ..**Van Tine**, Linda R '92 (Van Tine Law Ofc) -1410 Central Av
-Sandusky 44870

(586) 979-6500 ..**VanTol**, Paul R '02 (Martin B&M) -44 1st -Bx2301
-Mount Clemens, MI 48046

(513) 272-3188 ..**Van Tuyl**, Jacquelyn D '03 -6155 Shadyglen Rd -Cincinnati 45243

(513) 241-0400 ..**Van Valkenburg**, Valerie L '86 %Aronoff R&H Co,LPA
-425 Walnut -Ste 2400 -Cincinnati 45202 **Fx**:241-2877

(440) 543-0486 ..**Van Valkenburgh**, Bruce G '82 -10130 Waterford Trl
-Chagrin Falls 44023

(216) 983-1014 ..**Van Valkenburgh**, Paul F '88 Univ of Hosp of Cleveland
-10524 Euclid Av -Cleveland 44106

(614) 227-2000 ..**Van Vlerah**, Darin L '03 %Porter WM&A LLP -41 S High
-Columbus 43215 **Fx**:227-2100

(330) 633-2069 ..**VanVorous**, Regina M '83 Haley Law Ofcs Co,LPA -867 Moe Dr
-Ste G -Akron 44310

(216) 931-6000 ..**Van Wagner**, Jeffrey W '79 (Ulmer & B LLP) -1300 E 9th
-Ste 900 Penton Media Bldg -Cleveland 44114 **Fx**:931-6001

(513) 698-1991 ..**VanWay**, Jeff '98 Kroger Co -1014 Vine -Cincinnati 45202
Fx:762-4935

(740) 345-3488 ..**Van Winkle**, Richard M '75 (Van Winkle & Assoc Co,LPA)
-8 Arcade Pl -Newark 43055

(419) 354-9339 ..**VanWinkle**, Tracy Frey '02 Wood Cnty Common Pleas Ct
-1 Cthse Sq -Bowling Green 43402

(216) 687-1900 ..**Vanyo**, Maialisa A '99 Legal Aid -1223 W 6th -Cleveland 44113
Fx:687-0779

(937) 393-1207 ..**Van Zant**, Gregory F '88 -110 N High -Hillsboro 45133
Vanzant, James B '00 -(Address Unavailable)

(330) 744-4495 ..**Vaporis**, John M '60 -302 Leg Arts Ctr -Youngstown 44503

(724) 465-5653 ..**Vaporis**, Michael N '79 -840 Phila -Ste 301 -Indiana, PA 15701

(216) 274-1601 ..**Vara**, Timothy J '82 Chase Manhattan Trust -250 W Huron Rd
-Ste 220 -Cleveland 44113

(614) 220-9440 ..**Varanese**, John R '90 -85 E Gay -Ste 1000 -Columbus 43215

(614) 469-3243 ..**Varchetti**, Anna V '99 %Thompson H LLP -10 W Broad -Ste 700
-Columbus 43215 **Fx**:469-3361

(330) 659-8900 ..**Varcho**, Raymond A '85 Natl Interstate Ins -3250 Intrstate Dr
-Richfield 44286

(440) 964-9444 ..**Varckette**, Francis A '53 -3602 Lk Av -Ashtabula 44004

(513) 381-5700 ..**Vardiman**, Edwin L Jr. '99 %Ritter & R,LLC -105 E 4th -Ste 1200
-Cincinnati 45202 **Fx**:381-0014

(216) 696-6000 ..**Vardzel**, Lisa A '03 %Dettelbach S&B,LPA -1801 E 9th
-1100 Ohio Svngs Plz -Cleveland 44114 **Fx**:696-3338

(440) 888-2770 ..**Varga**, Jane M '81 -5851 Pearl Rd -Ste 101 -Parma Heights 44130

(323) 653-8881 ..**Varga**, John '97 -468 N Camden Dr -#200 -Beverly Hills, CA 90210

(330) 618-0478 ..**Varga**, Michael J '95 -132 Ravenshollow Dr
-Cuyahoga Falls 44223 **Fx**:(775) 245-6812

(216) 226-7706 ..**Varga-Sinka**, Michael '82 -13749 Mad Av -Lakewood 44107

(216) 591-0727 ..**Vargas**, Edwin J '94 (Summers & V Co,LPA) -23240 Chagrin Blvd
-Ste 525 -Cleveland 44122 **Fx**:591-0740

(765) 477-3325 ..**Vargo**, Deborah J '83 Lafayette Life Ins Co -1905 Teal Rd -Bx7007
-Lafayette, IN 47903

(216) 621-0200 ..**Vargo**, Ernest E Jr. '85 (Baker & H LLP) -1900 E 9th -Ste 3200
-Cleveland 44114 **Fx**:696-0740

(440) 842-6717 ..**Vargo**, James A '83 -Bx30778 -Cleveland 44130

(614) 224-1222 ..**Vargo**, James G '97 %Maguire & S,LLP -250 Civic Ctr Dr -Ste 200
-Columbus 43215 **Fx**:224-1236

(614) 221-8004 ..**Vargo**, Thomas W '72 -299 E Lvngstn Av -Columbus 43215

(614) 645-7385 ..**Varhus**, Alan P '74 City Atty -90 W Broad -Columbus 43215

(214) 840-7481 ..**Vari**, Frank J '93 Deloitte & T LLP -2200 Ross Av -Ste 1600
-Dallas, TX 75201

(330) 434-4100 ..**Varian**, Donald S Jr. '70 -195 S Main -Ste 400 -Akron 44308

(860) 275-0637 ..**Varian**, Keith S '02 %Day B&H,LLP -City Plz I -Hartford, CT 06103

(330) 455-5195 ..**Variola**, Giancarlo '79 Caplea & V Co,LPA -306 Market Av N
-1024 Renkert Bldg -Canton 44702 **Fx**:455-2982
Varma, Sanjay K '89 -(Address Unavailable)

(614) 224-8374 ..**Varnado**, Leslie Jr. '74 Legal Aid -40 W Gay -Columbus 43215

(513) 281-0804 ..**Varnau**, Dennis J '89 Prohold Workholding -3316 Mntgmry Rd
-Cincinnati 45207

(614) 865-4724 ..**Varner**, Carrie M '97 OCSEA-AFSCME Local 11
-390 Worthngtn Rd -Ste A -Westerville 43082

(419) 724-0030 ..**Varner**, Julita '00 LAWO -520 Mad Av -Ste 640 -Toledo 43604
Fx:321-1582
Varner, Michal B '80 -(Address Unavailable)

(419) 698-2968 ..**Varner**, Philip W '92 Moore Business Forms -523 J
-Perrysburg 43551

(419) 242-8214 ..**Varnes-Richardson**, Jill M '96 Zaner & C -520 Mad Av -Ste 545
-Toledo 43604 **Fx**:242-8658

(614) 644-7739 ..**Varveris**, Nicholas M '91 Industrial Commssn of OH -30 W Spring
-9th Fl -Columbus 43215 **Fx**:752-8785

(614) 258-6000 ..**Varwig**, Audrey E '01 %Brenner BG&M Co,LPA -2109 Stella Ct
-Columbus 43215 **Fx**:258-6006

(216) 586-3939 ..**Vary**, Michael W '86 (Jones D) -901 Lakeside Av -Cleveland 44114
Fx:579-0212

(216) 252-7300 ..**Vas**, Rinda E '99 Amer Greetings Corp -1 Amer Rd
-Cleveland 44144

(614) 464-6400 ..**Vascura**, Chelsey M '03 %Vorys SS&P LLP -52 E Gay -Bx1008
-Columbus 43216 **Fx**:464-6350

(216) 696-3311 ..**Vaselaney**, Missia H '85 (Kahn K) -1301 E 9th -2600 Erievw Twr
-Cleveland 44114 **Fx**:623-4912

(386) 255-0911 ..**Vasilaros**, Steven T '78 (Vasilaros & P) -154 S Halifax Av
-Daytona Beach, FL 32118

(330) 253-1550 ..**Vasilatos**, Spiros Jr. '84 %Skidmore & Assoc -1 Cascade Plz
-12th Fl -Akron 44308

(330) 374-5540 ..**Vasko**, George B '63 Vasko R&E Co, LPA -137 S Main -Ste 206
-Akron 44308

(614) 834-9880 ..**Vasko**, Michael P '84 -19 N High -Canal Winchester 43110
Fx:837-4017

(419) 241-9770 ..**Vassar Dills Dawson & Bonfiglio,LLC** -420 Mad Av -Ste 1102
-Toledo 43604 **Fx**:241-9771

(419) 241-9770 ..**Vassar**, James M '68 (Vassar DD&B,LLC) -420 Mad Av -Ste 1102
-Toledo 43604 **Fx**:241-9771
Vassel, Barbara M '83 -918 Dan -Akron 44310

(330) 456-8341 ..**Vassiles**, Chrysanthe E '96 %Black MS&A,LPA -220 Market Av S
-Ste 1000 -Canton 44702 **Fx**:456-5756

(952) 820-0080 ..**Vasuta**, John M '93 August Tech Corp -4900 W 78th -Law Dept
-Bloomington, MN 55435

(216) 781-5245 ..**Vasvari**, Raymond V Jr. '91 %Berkman GM&D -55 Pub Sq
-2121 The Illuminating Bldg -Cleveland 44113 **Fx**:781-8207

(330) 376-3572 ..**Vasvari**, Thomas M '90 Eshelman Lgl Grp -263 Portage Trl Ext W
-Cuyahoga Falls 44223 **Fx**:376-0199

(740) 363-1259 ..**Vatsures**, Peter T '54 Vatsures & V -15 W Central Av
-Delaware 43015

(740) 363-1259 ..**Vatsures**, Stephen J '96 %Vatsures & V -15 W Central Av
-Delaware 43015

(740) 363-1259 ..**Vatsures**, Thomas P '89 Vatsures & V -15 W Central Av
-Delaware 43015

(419) 634-4664 ..**Vaubel**, Clarabelle V '71 -426 W Lima Av -Ada 45810

(419) 248-7848 ..**Vaughan**, Deon '90 Owens Corning -1 Owens Corning Pkwy
-Leg Dept -Toledo 43659

(419) 241-1969 ..**Vaughan**, Elizabeth A '83 -1709 Spielbusch Av -Ste 107
-Toledo 43624

(513) 684-3719 ..**Vaughan**, Engrid J '72 NLRB -550 Main -Ste 3003
-Cincinnati 45202

(330) 497-0700 ..**Vaughan**, Nathan D '04 %Krugliak WG&D Co,LPA
-4775 Munson NW -Bx36963 -Canton 44735 **Fx**:497-4020

(440) 250-4126 ..**Vaughn**, Aaron M '02 Amer Exprss Fncl Advsrs -2001 Crocker Rd
-Ste 300 -Westlake 44145 **Fx**:250-9318

(614) 865-4700 ..**Vaughn**, Allison J '97 OCSEA -390 Worthngtn Rd -Ste A
-Westerville 43082

(216) 561-3880 ..**Vaughn**, Ann S '02 Municipal Schl Dist -1380 E 6th
-Cleveland 44114

(614) 792-7916 ..**Vaughn**, Carol P '79 -6338 Emberwood Rd -Dublin 43017

(614) 277-1000 ..**Vaughn**, Corinna M '98 Atty Gen-OOCIC -Bx968
-Grove City 43123 **Fx**:277-1010

(330) 726-1654 ..**Vaughn**, Jack R '77 -120 Marwood Cir -Ste 201 -Bx3965
-Youngstown 44513

(216) 464-6776 ..**Vaughn**, Jane A '86 Allmerica Fin -23240 Chagrin Blvd -Ste 100
-Beachwood 44122 **Fx**:464-6996

(859) 371-3600 ..**Vaughn**, Jay R '02 Busald F&Z,PSC -226 Main -Bx6910
-Florence, KY 41022

(614) 464-6400 ..**Vaughn**, Jonathan R '82 (Vorys SS&P LLP) -52 E Gay -Bx1008
-Columbus 43216 **Fx**:464-6350

(301) 854-3200 ..**Vaughn**, Michael D '74 -13732 Lakeside Dr -Clarksville, MD 21029
Fx:854-3218

(937) 225-4652 ..**Vaughn**, Navay M '89 Montgomery Cnty Pub Def -117 S Main
-Ste 400 -Dayton 45422 **Fx**:225-3449

(937) 222-6635 ..**Vaughn**, Noel W '79 -131 N Ludlow -Ste 1205 -Dayton 45402

(614) 387-9530 ..**Vaughn**, Robert '98 Supreme Ct Case Mgmt Cnsl -65 S Front
-8th Fl -Columbus 43215 **Fx**:387-9539
Vaughn, Robert A '59 -1304 Rona Vllg Blvd -Fairborn 45324

(949) 851-3532 ..**Vaughn**, Steve C '97 Parker Hannifin Corp -14300 Alton Pkwy
-Irvine, CA 92618

(513) 569-6301 ..**Vaught**, Barbara A '03 TriHealth Inc -619 Oak -Cincinnati 45206
Vaughters-Johnson, Cecilie A '80 -(Address Unavailable)

(740) 695-4331 ..**Vavra**, John A '83 -132 W Main -Bx430 -Saint Clairsville 43950

(216) 252-7300 ..**Vavruska**, Jeffrey A '86 Amer Greetings Corp -1 Amer Rd
-Cleveland 44144

(216) 595-0949 .. **Vavruska,** Stasia M '86 Resource Intl,Inc -3681 S Green Rd
-Ste 410 -Cleveland 44122

(614) 466-2034 .. **Vawter,** Jana R '90 Legis Srvc Commssn -77 S High
-Columbus 43215

(330) 675-5646 .. **Vazmina-Koltnow,** Shelley C '89 Forum Hlth -1350 E Market
-Warren 44483

(440) 357-7199 .. **Vazzana,** James L '87 -2151 Kingsborough Dr -Ste 13
-Painesville 44077

(614) 846-2000 .. **Veatch,** Alan K '82 (Campbell HC&V,LLC) -7650 Rvrs Edge Dr
-Columbus 43235 **Fx:**846-2003

(317) 632-3232 .. **Veatch,** Karin L '94 Dann PN&K -1 Amer Sq -Ste 2300,Bx 82008
-Indianapolis, IN 46282

(216) 566-1424 .. **Vecchio,** Robert J '82 (R Vecchio Co,LPA) -526 Superior Av E
-720 Leader Bldg -Cleveland 44114

(216) 522-5396 .. **Vedouras,** Anna '89 Dfnse Fin & Accntng Srvc -1240 E 9th
-Cleveland 44199

(260) 407-6141 .. **Vegeler,** Robert O '97 (Bowers & V LLC) -110 W Berry -Ste 1200
-Fort Wayne, IN 46802 **Fx:**407-6160

(216) 696-5531 .. **Vegh,** Anthony J '88 -526 Superior Av E -Cleveland 44114

(330) 867-2444 .. **Vehar,** August R '78 ICWUC/UFCW Legal Dept -1655 W Market
-Akron 44313

(740) 385-9611 .. **Veidt,** Christopher E '68 -37 E Hunter -Logan 43138

(614) 552-0200 .. **Veigel,** Thomas L '69 -4800 Groves Rd -Columbus 43232

(330) 375-2730 .. **Veillette,** Jeremy A '98 Pros -217 S High -Ste 203 -Akron 44308

(713) 365-1801 .. **Veillette,** Michael R '81 Mitsubishi Caterpillar
-2121 W Sam Houston Pkwy N -Houston, TX 77043

(440) 414-5184 .. **Veillette,** Robert E '78 Nordson Corp -28601 Clemons Rd
-Westlake 44145

(513) 721-8210 .. **Veith,** Patrick R '02 %Spraul V&D -830 Main -Ste 200
-Cincinnati 45202

(513) 744-9600 .. **Veith,** Sarah A '02 %Javitch B&R -602 Main -Ste 500 -Cincinnati
45202 **Fx:**744-9602

(513) 721-8210 .. **Veith,** Terrence M '75 (Spraul V&D) -830 Main -Ste 200
-Cincinnati 45202

Velayudhan, Krishna K '02 -1871 Waterbrook Ln
-Columbus 43209

(561) 998-7808 .. **Veletean,** Kory A '00 %R Bagdasarian -1800 Corp Blvd NW
-Ste 302 -Boca Raton, FL 33431 **Fx:**241-3226

(740) 964-9271 .. **Veley,** Jonathan A '92 -325 W Broad -Bx154 -Pataskala 43062

(330) 666-7952 .. **Velie,** Garwin P '80 Hlth Mgmt Grp,Inc -395 Sprngside Dr
-Akron 44333

Velisek, James C '61 -(Address Unavailable)

(513) 381-2838 .. **Vella,** Theresa H '01 %Taft S&H LLP -425 Walnut -Ste 1800
-Cincinnati 45202 **Fx:**381-0205

(847) 402-2400 .. **Velotta,** Michael J '73 Allstate Life Ins Co -3100 Sanders Rd -J5B
-Northbrook, IL 60062

(937) 264-5116 .. **Velten,** Judy L '89 Industrial Commssn of OH -3401 Park Ctr Dr
-Ste 300 -Dayton 45414

(304) 691-8352 .. **Veltri,** Melissa A '04 %Huddleston BNP&C -611 3rd Av -Bx2185
-Huntington, WV 25722

Venable, Robert M '68 -133 Strathmore Av
-Fort Thomas, KY 41075

(614) 855-2292 .. **Venard,** Carl E '64 -11230 Johnstown Rd -Bx399
-New Albany 43054

(614) 677-2366 .. **Venard,** Catherine L '00 Nationwide Fin -One Nationwide Plz
-Columbus 43215

(440) 808-9750 .. **Venard,** Paul D '01 %S Gregor & Assoc Co,LPA -842 Corp Way
-Ste 850 -Cleveland 44145 **Fx:**808-9785

(859) 291-3533 .. **Venard,** Stephen M '94 -463 Cmmnwlth Av -Erlanger, KY 41018

(614) 466-3615 .. **Vendel,** Eric P '96 Legis Srvc Commssn -77 S High
-Columbus 43215

(330) 864-6060 .. **Venesy,** Barbara A '91 -2741 Foxwood Dr -Akron 44333
Fx:864-6060

(614) 365-2700 .. **Venesy,** Bryan J '88 (Squire S&D LLP) -41 S High
-1300 Huntngtn Ctr -Columbus 43215 **Fx:**365-2499

(513) 361-1200 .. **Venesy,** Bryan J '88 (Squire S&D LLP) -312 Walnut -Ste 3500
-Cincinnati 45202 **Fx:**361-1201

(330) 497-4501 .. **Venet,** Deborah L '00 -3205 Bretton NW -Ste 300 -Canton 44720

(216) 464-8420 .. **Veniziano,** Anne D '95 (AD Veneziano Co,LPA)
-24100 Chagrin Blvd -Ste 270 -Beachwood 44122 **Fx:**464-1210

(513) 723-2204 .. **Veneziano,** Frank J '85 (Weltman W&R Co,LPA) -525 Vine
-Ste 800 -Cincinnati 45202 **Fx:**723-2239

(330) 255-6000 .. **Vengrow,** Jeffrey S '74 Go-Jo Ind Inc -Bx991 -Akron 44309

Venizelos, Constantine P '04 -(Address Unavailable)

(440) 232-5100 .. **Venizelos,** James C '91 Transtar Ind,Inc -7350 Young Dr
-Cleveland 44146 **Fx:**232-7286

(513) 287-3023 .. **Vennemann,** Jerome A '79 Cinergy Corp -139 E 4th -25 Atrium II
-Bx960 -Cincinnati 45201

(330) 393-3426 .. **Vennitti,** Louis J '62 -280 N Park Av -Bx1294 -Warren 44482

(614) 752-0960 .. **Venters,** Ellen W '00 OH Dept Rehab & Correction
-1050 Fwy Dr N -Columbus 43229

(614) 462-3194 .. **Venters,** Yeura R '78 Franklin Cnty Pub Def -373 S High -12th Fl
-Columbus 43215

(513) 621-3394 .. **Venters-Wilson,** Lona J '00 Peck S&W,LLP -201 E 5th -Ste 900
-Cincinnati 45202 **Fx:**621-3813

(216) 289-8322 .. **Vento,** Phyllis L '93 Law Dept -585 E 222nd -Euclid 44123

Ventress, William W '59 -9525 Whitegate Ln -Cincinnati 45243

(937) 485-4241 .. **Ventura,** Douglas M '85 Reynolds & Reynolds Co -115 S Ludlow
-Dayton 45402

(513) 424-5000 .. **Venturella,** John J '82 (Clark Schaefer Hackett & Co)
-160 N Breiel Blvd -Middletown 45042

(973) 365-5858 .. **Venturelli,** Andrew '89 -1 Howe Av -1st Fl -Passaic, NJ 07055
Fx:365-4004

(740) 695-8987 .. **Verba,** Steven J '92 -227 E Main -Saint Clairsville 43950

(513) 977-8200 .. **Verchot,** Joan M '86 (Dinsmore & S LLP) -255 E 5th -Ste 1900
-Cincinnati 45202 **Fx:**977-8141

(614) 292-1575 .. **Verdun,** Vincene '90 OSU Moritz Cllg of Law -55 W 12th Av
-Columbus 43210 **Fx:**292-1383

(216) 875-6532 .. **Vereb,** Karen A '99 Parkwood Corp -2829 Euclid Av
-Cleveland 44115

(330) 746-1064 .. **Vereb,** Melodie E '02 Cnsl BJ Alan Co -555 Martin Luther
King Jr Blvd -Youngstown 44502

(859) 331-2838 .. **Vergamini,** Thomas P '80 %Taft S&H LLP -1717 Dixie Hwy
-Ste 340 -Covington, KY 41011 **Fx:**(513) 381-6613

(216) 622-8200 .. **Vergilii,** Jennifer L '01 %Calfee H&G LLP -800 Superior Av
-Ste 1400 -Cleveland 44114 **Fx:**241-0816

(216) 363-4500 .. **Verginis,** Theologos '02 %Benesch FC&A LLP -200 Pub Sq
-Ste 2300 -Cleveland 44114 **Fx:**363-4588

(330) 742-1574 .. **Vergon,** Charles B '72 Youngstown State Univ -1 Univ Plz
-Coll of Edu-Rm 4104 -Youngstown 44555

(216) 781-4994 .. **Vergon,** Frederick P Jr. '69 (Smith MW&V) -1965 E 6th
-500 Natl City-E 6th Bldg -Cleveland 44114 **Fx:**781-9448

(614) 466-3206 .. **Verich,** Michael G '84 SERB -65 E State -Ste 1200
-Columbus 43215 **Fx:**466-3074

Verity, Neal D '71 -1350 Aster Av -Akron 44301

(513) 651-4400 .. **Verkamp,** Jennifer M '96 Volkema TMBS&M,LPA -700 Walnut
-Ste 400 -Cincinnati 45202 **Fx:**651-4405

(614) 466-5610 .. **Verlaney,** Georgia L '99 Atty Gen -150 E Gay -Columbus 43215
Fx:752-2732

(216) 621-0200 .. **Verma,** Monica S '00 %Baker & H LLP -1900 E 9th -Ste 3200
-Cleveland 44114 **Fx:**696-0740

(419) 626-0055 .. **Vermeeren,** Barry W '75 (Tone GM&V) -1401 Cleveland Rd
-Sandusky 44870 **Fx:**626-0288

(440) 997-6175 .. **Vermilya,** Randy A '99 %Warren & Y,PLL -134 W 46th -Bx2300
-Ashtabula 44005 **Fx:**992-9114

(740) 345-9611 .. **Vernau,** Adam K '89 (Morrow G&B,Ltd) -33 W Main -Bx4190
-Newark 43058

(440) 716-2226 .. **Vernon,** Eileen B '92 Amer Arbitration Assn -25050 Cntry Clb Blvd
-#101 -North Olmsted 44070

(216) 621-8484 .. **Vernon,** Keith T '96 (Climaco LPW&G Co,LPA) -1228 Euclid Av
-Ste 900 Halle Bldg -Cleveland 44115 **Fx:**771-1632

(440) 483-4244 .. **Vernon,** Mary C '93 Marconi Medical Sys,Inc -595 Miner Rd
-Cleveland 44143

(614) 227-2000 .. **Verrett,** Kendall S '03 %Porter WM&A LLP -41 S High
-Columbus 43215 **Fx:**227-2100

(401) 331-2800 .. **Verri,** Richard G '77 (Verri & V) -95 Chestnut
-Providence, RI 02903

(401) 331-2800 .. **Verri,** Saundra B '74 (Verri & V) -95 Chestnut
-Providence, RI 02903

(614) 523-4094 .. **Verwohlt,** Jeffrey H '93 F & V Entrprses -2122 Farleigh Rd
-Columbus 43221

(404) 377-5700 .. **Vespa,** Adele M '84 Cnsl Huddle House,Inc -2969 E Pnc de
Leon Av -Decatur, GA 30030 **Fx:**687-0834

(859) 491-4222 .. **Vesper,** Paul J '73 -28 W 5th -Covington, KY 41011

(330) 384-5800 .. **Vespoli,** Leila Lee '84 FirstEnergy Corp -76 S Main -Akron 44308

(740) 373-5455 .. **Vessels,** Ethan T '03 %Theisen B,LPA -424 2nd -Bx739
-Marietta 45750 **Fx:**373-4409

(937) 339-7161 .. **Vest,** Margaret E '89 (Vest & L) -406 W Main -Troy 45373

(614) 752-8683 .. **Vest,** Pamela J '93 State Auditor -88 E Broad -Bx1140
-Columbus 43216

(440) 542-1330 .. **Vettel,** Louis M '86 Erico Intl,Corp -30575 Bainbrdg Rd -Ste 300
-Solon 44139

(419) 525-1611 .. **Vetter,** Adam Jr. '85 (Brown BM&M) -70 Park Av W
-Mansfield 44902 **Fx:**525-3810

Vexler, Laura B '98 -(Address Unavailable)

(412) 263-2000 .. **Vey,** Paul K '00 (Pietragallo B&G) -1 Oxford Ctr -38th Fl
-Pittsburgh, PA 15219

(330) 972-6410 .. **Viau,** William H '94 Univ of Akron -277 S Bway -Akron 44325

(419) 241-6168 .. **Vicente,** Brian D '94 -520 Mad Av -Ste 830 -Toledo 43604

(216) 443-7800 .. **Vick,** Gary A Jr. '99 %Cuyahoga Cnty Pros -1200 Ontario -8th Fl
-Cleveland 44113 **Fx:**698-2270

(740) 833-2690 .. **Vick,** Robert F '00 %Delaware Cnty Pros -140 N Sandusky -3rd Fl
-Delaware 43015

(216) 931-6000 .. **Vickers,** Frederick Thomas '83 (Ulmer & B LLP) -1300 E 9th
-Ste 900 Penton Media Bldg -Cleveland 44114 **Fx:**931-6001

(216) 861-5582 .. **Vickers,** Gregory S '97 (Fay SFM&M LLP) -1100 Superior Av
-7th Fl -Cleveland 44114 **Fx:**241-1666

(614) 466-5394 .. **Vickers,** Richard J '86 Pub Def -8 E Long -Columbus 43215

(216) 861-5582 .. **Vickers,** Robert V '61 (Fay SFM&M LLP) -1100 Superior Av -7th Fl
-Cleveland 44114 **Fx:**241-1666

(614) 224-8160 .. **Vickery,** Byron L '65 (Vickery R&A) -500 S Front -Ste 200
-Columbus 43215 **Fx:**224-4943

(614) 224-8160 .. **Vickery Riehl & Alter** -500 S Front -Ste 200 -Columbus 43215
Fx:224-4943

(513) 791-1539 .. **Victor,** Irving W '55 -3215 S Whitetree Cir -Cincinnati 45236

(216) 416-3280 .. **Victor,** Jennifer A '98 Forest City Entrprses,Inc -50 Pub Sq
-Ste 1160 -Cleveland 44113

(614) 543-1305 .. **Vidmar,** John M '03 (Vidmar & H,Ltd) -100 E Campus Vw Blvd
-Ste 250 -Columbus 43235 **Fx:**543-1306

(850) 245-2242 .. **Vielhauer,** Harold G '88 %DEP -3900 Cmmnwlth Blvd -MS 35
-Tallahassee, FL 32399 **Fx:**245-2303

(440) 461-5000 .. **Vierkorn,** Katherine A '92 Progressive Ins Co -300 N Cmmns Blvd
-box T62 -Mayfield Village 44143

(614) 888-0666 .. **Vierow,** Frederick A '60 -Bx1296 -Worthington 43085 **Fx:**888-0666

(614) 242-4242 .. **Viets,** James D '83 (Decker VSL&V Co LPA) -620 E Broad
-Columbus 43215 **Fx:**242-4243

(216) 771-3800 .. **Vieyra,** Katherine R '95 %DP Hochberg Co,LPA -1940 E 6th
-Baker Bldg 6th Fl -Cleveland 44113 **Fx:**771-3804

(615) 632-7317 .. **Viglucci,** Edward J '82 Tennessee Valley Auth
-400 W Summitt Hill Dr -Knoxville, TN 37902

(330) 297-3850 .. **Viglucci,** Victor V '77 Portage Cnty Pros -466 S Chestnut
-Ravenna 44266

(330) 394-5880 .. **Vigorito,** Philip M '89 -552 N Park Av -Warren 44481 **Fx:**393-9875

(740) 987-2521 .. **Vigue,** Ronald R '84 -Bx296 -Junction City 43748

Viland, Christopher P '04 -(Address Unavailable)

(419) 693-0610 .. **Vild,** Jeffrey T '85 -4117 Navarre Av -Oregon 43616

(216) 443-6350 .. **Vilfroy,** Ute L '91 8th Dist Ct of Appls -1 Lakeside Av -#202
-Cleveland 44113 **Fx:**443-2044

(216) 664-4827 .. **Villa,** Gina M '89 Prosecutor -1200 Ontario Av -8th Fl Justice Ctr
-Cleveland 44113 **Fx:**664-4399

(216) 622-3735 .. **Villa,** Herbert J '66 US Atty -801 W Superior -Ste 400
-Cleveland 44113 **Fx:**622-3370

(330) 740-2330 .. **Villani,** Michael T '96 Mahoning Cnty Pros -21 W Boardman
-6th Fl -Youngstown 44503 **Fx:**740-2008

(330) 565-5146 .. **Villano,** Mark A '00 (Villano & H Co,LPA) -1397 S Canfld-Niles Rd
-Austintown 44515 **Fx:**270-3696

(419) 223-1861 ..**Villarreal**, Teresa A '89 Ct of Appls 3rd Dist -Cthse -Bx1243
-Lima 45802

(614) 217-8849 ..**Villwock**, David S '97 %Banc One Invstmnt Mgmt Grp -340 S
Cleveland Av -Bldg 350 -Westerville 43081 **Fx:**244-6236

(412) 490-6955 ..**Viloski**, Benjamin J '93 Shopping Ctr Law Assoc,PC
-1000 Cliff Mine Rd -Ste 530 -Pittsburgh, PA 15275

(440) 352-4004 ..**Vilsack**, Robert D '87 (R Vilsack Co LPA) -8240 Tewksbury Ln
-Concord 44077

(440) 428-6044 ..**Vince**, George A Jr. '84 (Bates & V) -102 Main -Madison 44057

(513) 977-8200 ..**Vincent**, George H '82 (Dinsmore & S LLP) -255 E 5th -Ste 1900
-Cincinnati 45202 **Fx:**977-8141

(614) 221-2121 ..**Vincent**, John E Jr. '99 %Isaac BL&T,LLP -250 E Broad
-Ste 900 Mdlnd Bldg -Columbus 43215 **Fx:**365-9516

(216) 443-8605 ..**Vincent**, Leland G II '03 Cuyahoga Cnty Ct Cmmn Pleas
-1200 Ontario -Justice Ctr 11th Fl -Cleveland 44113

(216) 222-2379 ..**Vincent**, Musette T '81 Natl City Bank -1900 E 9th
-17th Fl Loc 01-2174 -Cleveland 44114

(614) 644-7250 ..**Vincent**, Rachelle Peloquin '00 Atty Gen -30 E Broad
-Columbus 43215 **Fx:**644-7634

(216) 621-5300 ..**Vincent**, Terry W '87 (Buckingham D&B,LLP) -1375 E 9th
-Ste 1700 -Cleveland 44114 **Fx:**621-5440

(202) 564-1256 ..**Vinch**, James J '93 US EPA -1200 Penn Av NW
-Washington, DC 20460

(419) 885-8300 ..**Vinciguerra**, Ralph D '76 Nrthrn OH Invstmnt Co -5700 Monroe
-Ste 300A -Sylvania 43560

(419) 843-2001 ..**Vindas**, Eva C '02 %Gallon & T Co,LPA -3516 Granite Cir
-Bx352018 -Toledo 43635 **Fx:**843-6665

(513) 732-8180 ..**Viney**, Lauri D '98 Clermont Cnty Pub Def -10 S 3rd
-Batavia 45103

(513) 651-6800 ..**Vineyard**, Joshua L '04 %Frost BT LLC -201 E 5th -2200 PNC Ctr
-Cincinnati 45202 **Fx:**651-6981

(330) 393-3058 ..**Vingle**, Joseph M '98 -252 Seneca Av -Warren 44481
Vining, Kymberlee R '04 -(Address Unavailable)

(330) 262-2510 ..**Vinion**, Lon R '79 -2206 Mechanicsburg Rd -Wooster 44691

(216) 623-0150 ..**Vinocur**, Jonathon H '03 %Roetzel & A,LPA -1375 E 9th
-One Cleve Ctr 9th Fl -Cleveland 44114 **Fx:**623-0134

(216) 839-7200 ..**Vinocur**, Peter A '79 Degussa Corp -23700 Chagrin Blvd
-Beachwood 44122

(937) 259-7348 ..**Vinolus**, Athan A '88 Dayton Power & Light Co -Bx8825
-Dayton 45401

(740) 455-9377 ..**Vinsel**, Jay F '83 -523 Cmbrdg Av -Zanesville 43701

(614) 327-8500 ..**Vinson**, Gary II '99 -7652 Sawmill Rd -MB #240 -Dublin 43016

(216) 781-1212 ..**Viola**, Anthony J '57 (Walter & H LLP) -1301 E 9th -Ste 3500
-Cleveland 44114 **Fx:**575-0911

(216) 241-2838 ..**Viola**, Matthew T '00 %Taft S&H LLP -200 Pub Sq -3500 BP Twr
-Cleveland 44114 **Fx:**241-3707

(440) 934-0474 ..**Violand**, James P '79 -3900 Stallion Ct -Avon 44011

(419) 241-8811 ..**Viren**, Jack F Jr. '78 -1018 Adams -Toledo 43624 **Fx:**241-7267

(614) 262-8283 ..**Virgil**, Albert E '88 -3620 N High -Suite B-9 -Columbus 43214

(330) 720-6012 ..**Virostek**, Janet E '82 -1330 Townsend Av -Youngstown 44505

(937) 778-0092 ..**Virzi**, Frank S '72 -316 N Downing -Piqua 45356

(216) 241-6602 ..**Visani**, Hernan N '86 (Weston HFP&H LLP) -50 Pub Sq
-2500 Trmnl Twr -Cleveland 44113 **Fx:**621-8369

(440) 937-4705 ..**Viscomi**, William A '69 -4251 Vilamoura Dr -Avon 44011

(216) 643-6659 ..**Visconsi**, Thomas A Jr. '75 SrCnsl Fedeli Grp,Inc -5005
Rockside Rd -Ste 500 -Bx318003 -Independence 44131
Fx:328-8081

(703) 588-5276 ..**Visger**, Mark A '96 US Army Legal Srvcs Agency -901 N Stuart
-JALS - GA -Arlington, VA 22203

(216) 987-4832 ..**Viskocil**, Timothy J '87 Cuyahoga Comm College
-700 Carnegie Av -Cleveland 44115

(216) 622-8200 ..**Visocan**, Karen A '93 %Calfee H&G LLP -800 Superior Av
-Ste 1400 -Cleveland 44114 **Fx:**241-0816

(650) 320-4923 ..**Viswanathan**, Aditi '97 %Wilson SG&R -650 Page Mill Rd
-Palo Alto, CA 94304

(614) 466-2766 ..**Vitale**, Dale T '78 %Atty Gen -30 E Broad -Columbus 43215
Fx:644-1926

(614) 486-0297 ..**Vitale**, Frank A '97 %S Jurus -1375 Dublin Rd -Columbus 43215
Fx:486-8580
Vitale, Jack G A '90 -(Address Unavailable)
Vitale, Joseph M '67 -46 LaSalle Ct SE -North Canton 44709

(330) 643-2765 ..**Vitale**, Lisa M '97 Summit Cnty Pros-CSEA -171 S Main
-Akron 44308 **Fx:**643-2822

(202) 764-2007 ..**Vitale**, Louise A '95 Navy Strategic Syst Prgrms -Bx5769
-Washington, DC 20016

(614) 481-6000 ..**Vitale**, Sheila P '97 Cooper & E LLC -2175 Riverside Dr
-Columbus 43221 **Fx:**481-6001

(440) 449-3333 ..**Vitantonio**, Dominic J '91 Argie D&V -6449 Wilson Mills Rd
-Mayfield Village 44143

(440) 746-1500 ..**Vitantonio**, Louis A Jr. '02 Grtr Cleveland Auto Dealers Assn
-10100 Brecksvll Rd -Brecksville 44141

(419) 499-4605 ..**Vitaz**, Heather M '97 (HM Vitaz Co,LPA) -16 W Church -Bx522
-Milan 44846
Vite, Barbara A '02 -1579 Crkside Rd -Amelia 45102

(513) 634-2648 ..**Vitenberg**, Vladimir '95 Procter & Gamble -1 PG Plz
-Cincinnati 45202

(330) 677-4549 ..**Vitone**, Patrick M '83 NE Educational TV of OH,Inc
-1750 Campus Ctr Dr -Bx5191 -Kent 44240

(419) 893-5555 ..**Vitou**, James F '79 (Boss & V Co,LPA) -111 W Dudley
-Maumee 43537 **Fx:**893-2797

(248) 646-5100 ..**Vitu**, Thomas L '98 (Moffett & D,PC) -255 E Brown
-Ste 340 Brown St Ctr -Birmingham, MI 48009 **Fx:**646-5332

(330) 270-9027 ..**Vitullo**, James A '82 -5232 Nashua Dr -Austintown 44515
Fx:270-9027

(216) 763-1004 ..**Vivarronda**, Steven J '00 %Siegel SJ&J Co,LPA
-25700 Science Park Dr -Ste 210 -Cleveland 44122 **Fx:**763-1016

(216) 479-8500 ..**Viviani**, Gregory J '84 (Squire S&D LLP) -127 Pub Sq
-4900 Key Twr -Cleveland 44114 **Fx:**479-8780

(330) 726-5518 ..**Vivo**, James S Jr. '00 -721 Boardman-Poland Rd -Ste 201
-Youngstown 44512

(614) 436-0539 ..**Vivyan**, Thomas F '71 (Baran PTF&T Co,LPA) -6877 N High
-Ste 105 -Columbus 43085 **Fx:**436-1713

(513) 946-3000 ..**Vizedom**, Anita '01 Hamilton Cnty Pros -230 E 9th
-Cincinnati 45202 **Fx:**946-3017
Vizy, Nicholas J '89 -12513 Burton Heights Blvd -Burton 44021

(814) 833-2743 ..**Vlahos**, Darlene M '85 -3305 Pittsburgh Av -Erie, PA 16508

(708) 688-4422 ..**Vlahos**, Georgia '85 US Navy -2601A Paul Jones -Ste 221
-Great Lakes, IL 60088

(216) 348-5400 ..**Vlasek**, Dale R '87 (McDonald H Co,LPA) -600 Superior Av E
-Ste 2100 -Cleveland 44114 **Fx:**348-5474

(216) 241-6602 ..**Vlasich**, Emily Allegretti '02 %Weston HFP&H LLP -50 Pub Sq
-2500 Trmnl Twr -Cleveland 44113 **Fx:**621-8369

(216) 739-5646 ..**Vlasuk**, Heather Baldwin '04 %Weltman W&R Co,LPA
-323 W Lakeside Av -Ste 200 -Cleveland 44113 **Fx:**363-4121

(330) 836-9971 ..**Vlosky**, Edward F '86 Cedarwood Co -1765 Merriman Rd
-Akron 44313

(216) 749-1150 ..**Vocaire-Tramposch**, Louis '86 JV Janitorial Srvcs
-1230 E Schaaf Rd -Brooklyn Heights 44131 **Fx:**749-1153

(859) 491-8595 ..**Vocke**, Robert K '91 -526 Greenup -Covington, KY 41011

(330) 385-3400 ..**Vodrey**, Jackman S '63 -517 Bway -3rd fl -East Liverpool 43920

(216) 664-3643 ..**Vodrey**, William F '92 Cleveland Municipal Ct -1200 Ontario
-12th Fl -Cleveland 44113

(614) 481-6500 ..**Voelker**, Dirken T '56 (Voelker & V) -1635 W 1st Av
-Columbus 43212 **Fx:**481-6505

(614) 481-6500 ..**Voelker**, Dow T '87 (Voelker & V) -1635 W 1st Av
-Columbus 43212 **Fx:**481-6505

(513) 421-4225 ..**Vogel**, Cedric W '72 OfCnsl Heis & W Co,LPA -817 Main -Ste 800
-Cincinnati 45202

(614) 744-0132 ..**Vogel**, John W '99 -Bx340873 -Columbus 43234

(216) 781-1168 ..**Vogel**, Philip Z '82 -1300 E 9th -14th floor -Cleveland 44114
Vogel, Walter J '60 -2264 W Bath Rd -Akron 44333

(216) 291-7393 ..**Vogele**, Allan W '75 Northrop Grumman -1900 Richmond Rd
-Cleveland 44124

(513) 946-3670 ..**Vogele**, James A '73 Hamilton Cnty Pub Def -230 E 9th -3rd Fl
-Cincinnati 45202 **Fx:**946-3707

(440) 247-9411 ..**Vogt**, Peter W '74 Multimedia Mgmt,Inc -23 Bell -Ste 2
-Chagrin Falls 44022

(937) 227-3700 ..**Voigt**, Eric P '03 %Faruki I&C PLL -10 N Ludlow
-500 Cthse Plz SW -Dayton 45402 **Fx:**227-3717

(310) 274-7111 ..**Voigtmann**, Fredrick W '94 %Inman & Assoc,PC
-9401 Wilshire Blvd -Beverly Hills, CA 90212

(330) 253-5060 ..**Voinovich**, George F '90 %Brennan M&D,LLC -75 E Market
-Akron 44308 **Fx:**253-1977

(513) 241-7111 ..**Vojtush**, Gayle P '89 %O'Connor A&L Co,LPA -1014 Vine -22nd Fl
-Cincinnati 45202 **Fx:**241-7197

(440) 237-7900 ..**Volcheck**, Mark J '94 Patrolmens Benevolent Assn
-10147 Royalton Rd -Ste J -Bx33803 -North Royalton 44133

(518) 271-7000 ..**Volk**, Catherine M '95 %Kaleel Jamison ConsultingGrp -279 River
-401 -Troy, NY 12180 **Fx:**270-9044

(330) 535-5711 ..**Volk**, Jay G '98 OfCnsl Brouse M -106 S Main -500 First Natl Twr
-Akron 44308 **Fx:**253-8601

(614) 221-4400 ..**Volkema**, Daniel R '79 Volkema TMBS&M,LPA -140 E Town
-Ste 1100 -Columbus 43215 **Fx:**221-6010

(614) 221-4400 ..**Volkema Thomas Miller Burkett Scott & Merry, LPA**
-140 E Town -Ste 1100 -Columbus 43215 **Fx:**221-6010

(513) 651-4400 ..**Volkema Thomas Miller Burkett Scott & Merry, LPA**
-700 Walnut -Ste 400 -Cincinnati 45202 **Fx:**651-4405

(419) 693-4433 ..**Voller**, Cindy M '92 -101 Main -2nd Fl -Bx8076 -Toledo 43605

(216) 479-8500 ..**Vollins**, James A '93 %Squire S&D LLP -127 Pub Sq
-4900 Key Twr -Cleveland 44114 **Fx:**479-8780

(513) 579-1707 ..**Vollman**, Carl W '51 OfCnsl Loeb V&F -1014 Vine
-2150 Kroger Bldg -Cincinnati 45202

(513) 421-4020 ..**Vollman**, Jeffrey S '98 %Cohen TK&S,LLC -250 E 5th -Ste 1200
-Cincinnati 45202 **Fx:**241-4490

(513) 651-6800 ..**Vollman**, Jill M '96 (Frost BT LLC) -201 E 5th -2200 PNC Ctr
-Cincinnati 45202 **Fx:**651-6981

(513) 579-1707 ..**Vollman**, Mark C '81 (Loeb V&F) -1014 Vine -2150 Kroger Bldg
-Cincinnati 45202

(513) 569-9999 ..**Vollman**, Paul J '95 %Triona & L,Ltd -2909 Vernon Pl
-Cincinnati 45219 **Fx:**569-9998

(330) 375-2030 ..**Vollman**, Sean W '99 %Law Dept -161 S High -Ste 202
-Akron 44308

(513) 421-4020 ..**Vollman**, Stanton H '66 (Cohen TK&S,LLC) -250 E 5th -Ste 1200
-Cincinnati 45202 **Fx:**241-4490

(937) 223-8171 ..**Vollmar**, Michelle S '95 (Rogers & G) -2160 Kettering Twr
-Dayton 45423 **Fx:**223-1649

(937) 222-2424 ..**Vollmar**, Thomas Andrew '94 (Freund F&A) -1 S Main -Ste 1800
-Dayton 45402 **Fx:**222-5369

(513) 762-7063 ..**Vollmer**, Hilary L '99 Kroger Co -1014 Vine -Cincinnati 45202

Vollmer, Michael W '99 -(Address Unavailable)

(614) 466-4314 ..**Vollmer**, Sara R '88 OH DYS -51 N High -Columbus 43215

(216) 687-1311 ..**Volpini**, Laura L '02 %Reminger & R -101 Prospect Av W
-1400 Mdlnd Bldg -Cleveland 44115 **Fx:**687-1841

(216) 781-5515 ..**Volsky**, Kerry S '80 (Hermann C&S,LLP) -1301 E 9th -Ste 500
-Cleveland 44114 **Fx:**781-1030

(216) 781-5515 ..**Volsky**, Mark R '81 -1301 E 9th -Ste 500 -Cleveland 44114

(614) 486-5392 ..**Voltolini**, Bruno E '57 (Mattis DV&V) -1350 W 5th Av
-Columbus 43212

(614) 486-5392 ..**Voltolini**, John P '86 (Mattis DV&V) -1350 W 5th Av
-Columbus 43212

(614) 486-5392 ..**Voltolini**, Mathew J '88 (Mattis DV&V) -1350 W 5th Av
-Columbus 43212

(330) 364-1112 ..**Von Allman**, Nanette D '84 (ND Von Allman Co LPA)
-134 2nd NW -New Philadelphia 44663

(614) 242-4242 ..**Vonau**, James M '81 (Decker VSL&V Co LPA) -620 E Broad
-Columbus 43215 **Fx:**242-4243

(713) 931-8902 ..**vonBerg**, Mary F '79 (Farnsworth & v,LLP) -333 N
Sam Houston Pkwy -Suite 300 -Houston, TX 77060 **Fx:**931-6032

(440) 605-6660 ..**von Boeselager**, Kurt J '78 (Hurtuk & D Co,LPA)
-6120 Parkland Blvd -Ste 100 -Cleveland 44124 **Fx:**605-6666

(216) 522-2248 ..**von Borcke**, Pamela J '83 USEEOC -1660 W 2nd -Ste 850
-Cleveland 44113

(419) 229-9800 ..**Von der Embse**, Marie A '83 (Jacobs & V) -558 W Spring
-Lima 45801

(937) 222-6926 .. **Vonderwell-Hull,** Marcy A '04 %PK Smith -120 W 2nd -1300 Lbrty Twr -Dayton 45402

(216) 363-5812 .. **Vondra,** Albert A '03 PricewaterhouseCoopers -200 Pub Twr -27th Fl -Cleveland 44114

(513) 825-6758 .. **Von Hagen,** Frank J '55 -767 Carlsbad Rd -Cincinnati 45240

(216) 479-8500 .. **von Mehren,** George M '77 (Squire S&D LLP) -127 Pub Sq -4900 Key Twr -Cleveland 44114 Fx:479-8780

(937) 224-3333 .. **Von Meister,** Peter F '72 (Green & G) -109 N Main -Ste 800 -Dayton 45402 Fx:224-4311

(513) 651-6800 .. **von Saucken,** Sylvius H '98 %Frost BT LLC -201 E 5th -2200 PNC Ctr -Cincinnati 45202 Fx:651-6981

(513) 579-7389 .. **Von Wahlde,** Stephen '82 Federated Dept Stores,Inc -7 W 7th -Cincinnati 45202

(216) 685-1050 .. **Voorhees,** Andrew C '04 %Weltman W&R Co,LPA -323 W Lakeside Av -Ste 200 -Cleveland 44113 Fx:363-4121

(513) 985-2500 .. **Voorhees,** Michael R '87 Phillips Law Firm,Inc -9521 Mntgmry Rd -Cincinnati 45242 Fx:985-2503

(614) 825-4029 .. **Vornbrock,** Kelley L '03 Ohio Bar Title Ins Co -8425 Pulsar Pl -Ste 210 -Columbus 43240

(614) 227-2394 .. **Vorys,** Anne Sferra '85 (Bricker & E LLP) -100 S 3rd -Columbus 43215 Fx:227-2390

(614) 313-2389 .. **Vorys,** George N '79 -215 Academy Woods Dr -Gahanna 43230

(614) 464-6400 .. **Vorys,** John C '80 (Vorys SS&P LLP) -52 E Gay -Bx1008 -Columbus 43216 Fx:464-6350

(614) 464-6400 .. **Vorys Sater Seymour & Pease LLP** -52 E Gay -Bx1008 -Columbus 43216 Fx:464-6350

(513) 723-4000 .. **Vorys Sater Seymour & Pease LLP** -221 E 4th -Ste 2000 Atrium Two -Bx0236 -Cincinnati 45201 Fx:723-4056

(216) 479-6100 .. **Vorys Sater Seymour & Pease LLP** -1375 E 9th -Ste 2100 One Cleve Ctr -Cleveland 44114 Fx:479-6060

(330) 208-1000 .. **Vorys Sater Seymour & Pease LLP** -106 S Main -First Natl Twr -Akron 44308

(614) 464-6400 .. **Vorys,** Webb I '85 (Vorys SS&P LLP) -52 E Gay -Bx1008 -Columbus 43216 Fx:464-6350

(614) 466-6092 .. **Vorys,** Yolanda V '81 OH Consumers' Cnsl -10 W Broad -Ste 1800 -Columbus 43215 Fx:466-9475

(937) 332-7000 .. **Votava,** Andrew R '94 Cnty Commissioners -201 W Main -Troy 45373

(904) 274-6200 .. **Votaw,** Ty M '87 Ladies Pro Golf Assoc -100 Intl Golf Dr -Daytona Beach, FL 32124

(937) 456-8156 .. **Votel,** Martin P '97 Preble Cnty Pros -100 E Main -Cthse 1st Fl -Eaton 45320 Fx:456-8199

(216) 241-1105 .. **Voth,** Robert F IV '74 -55 Pub Sq -Ste 1250 -Cleveland 44113 Fx:241-1756

(216) 592-5000 .. **Voudouris,** S Peter '92 Cnsl Tucker E&W LLP -925 Euclid Av -1150 Huntngtn Bldg -Cleveland 44115 Fx:592-5009

(305) 347-6834 .. **Voudris,** Stephan I '91 %Jorden B LLP -777 Brickell Av -Ste 500 -Miami, FL 33131 Fx:372-9928

(614) 487-5900 .. **Vourlis,** Simina '90 -1500 W 3rd Av -Ste 400 -Columbus 43212 Fx:481-7905

(330) 743-4116 .. **Vouros,** Joseph E '50 (Brennan FV&Y,Ltd) -29 E Front -2nd Fl -Youngstown 44503

(513) 677-2782 .. **Voyles,** David R '85 -6669 Quail Run Ct -Loveland 45140

(440) 582-6706 .. **Vozar,** Donna M '92 -Bx33724 -North Royalton 44133

(440) 746-0911 .. **Vozar Roberts & Matejczyk Co,LPA** -3505 E Royalton Rd -Ste 100 -Cleveland 44147

(440) 746-0911 .. **Vozar,** Thomas J '86 (Vozar R&M Co,LPA) -3505 E Royalton Rd -Ste 100 -Cleveland 44147

(216) 383-8413 .. **Vrabec,** Craig S '85 -111 E 199th -Euclid 44119

(330) 643-2929 .. **Vuillemin,** John E '76 Summit Cnty Juv Ct -650 Dan -Akron 44310

(330) 253-0785 .. **Vuillemin,** Lawrence W '73 (Gorman MP&V) -1 Cascade Plz -9th Fl -Akron 44308 Fx:253-7432

(740) 282-9746 .. **Vukelic,** David A '77 (Palumbo P&V) -502 Ohio Valley Twrs -Steubenville 43952

(919) 997-3280 .. **Vynalek,** John H '81 Nortel Ntwrks -Bx13828 -Research Triangle Park, NC 27709

Vysnionis, Linas Paul '93 -(Address Unavailable)

(216) 221-3100 .. **Waag,** Christian F Jr. '57 -14701 Detroit Av -Ste 540 -Lakewood 44107

(419) 936-3023 .. **Wachowiak,** Joseph W '83 Toledo Dept Pub Utilities -600 Collins Park Av -Toledo 43605

(513) 651-6800 .. **Wachs,** Jim S '58 (Frost BT LLC) -201 E 5th -2200 PNC Ctr -Cincinnati 45202 Fx:651-6981

(216) 526-2144 .. **Wachs,** William P '00 RWK Srvcs,Inc -5807 E Sprague Rd -Independence 44131

(614) 462-3194 .. **Wachsman,** Elizabeth E '03 Franklin Cnty Pub Def -373 S High -12th Fl -Columbus 43215

(937) 223-8177 .. **Wachstein,** Steven M '01 %Coolidge WW&L -33 W 1st -Ste 600 -Dayton 45402 Fx:223-6705

(216) 292-3300 .. **Wachter,** Mark I '77 Conway MWK&K Co,LPA -30195 Chagrin Blvd -Ste 300 -Cleveland 44124

Wachterman, Richard M '81 -10661 Gramercy Pl -Unit 303 -Columbia, MD 21044

(614) 431-1500 .. **Wachtman,** Andrew D '93 Perez & M LLC -8000 Ravines Edge Ct -Ste 300 -Columbus 43235 Fx:431-3885

(614) 415-7495 .. **Wachtman,** Kristen A '93 The Limited,Inc -3 Limited Pkwy -Columbus 43230

(614) 466-3998 .. **Wachunas,** Robert J '68 Unemploymnt Comp Commssn -145 S Front -Bx182299 -Columbus 43218

(330) 867-8422 .. **Wack,** Patrick J '73 -41 Merz Blvd -Akron 44333

(330) 253-1111 .. **Waddell,** David E '60 Calhoun W&H -159 S Main -Ste 707 -Akron 44308

(440) 259-0074 .. **Wadding,** Edward A '01 (Ponce de Leon & W LLC) -3537 N Ridge Rd -Perry 44081

(614) 463-9518 .. **Waddy,** John W Jr. '79 -111 Hmltn Pk -Columbus 43203

(614) 445-9300 .. **Wade,** E Roberta '91 Wade Law Ofc LLC -Bx6344 -Columbus 43206

(216) 502-0800 .. **Wade,** Edward S Jr. '75 -75 Pub Sq -Ste 333 -Cleveland 44113

(614) 462-2276 .. **Wade,** Felix C '77 (Schottenstein Z&D) -250 West -Bx165020 -Columbus 43216 Fx:462-5135

(614) 466-3998 .. **Wade,** Jared W '98 Unemploymnt Comp Commssn -145 S Front -Bx182299 -Columbus 43218

(937) 382-1494 .. **Wade,** Jeffrey C '94 %R&L Carriers -600 Gillam Rd -Bx271 -Wilmington 45177

(216) 941-3333 .. **Wade,** Jeffrey D '99 Western Management,Inc -14577 Lorain Av -Cleveland 44111

(614) 236-6549 .. **Wade,** Robert J Jr. '72 Capital Univ Law Sch -303 E Broad -Columbus 43215

(202) 622-3950 .. **Wade,** Roger E '92 IRS/Ofc Chief Cnsl -1111 Const Av NW -Washington, DC 20224

(513) 398-4891 .. **Wade,** Teresa R '94 %Peeler M&Z -423 Reading Rd -Mason 45040

(614) 228-1541 .. **Wadman,** Gary A '85 (Baker & H LLP) -65 E State -Ste 2100 -Columbus 43215 Fx:462-2616

(440) 526-6722 .. **Wadsworth,** Roger A '63 (Wadsworth & B) -8927 Brecksvll Rd -Brecksville 44141

(330) 796-4794 .. **Waechter,** Thomas C '67 Goodyear Tire & Rubber Co -1144 E Market -Akron 44316

(614) 525-5225 .. **Wafer,** Lisa A '01 %Ferron & Assoc,LPA -580 N 4th -Ste 450 -Columbus 43215 Fx:228-3255

(216) 586-3939 .. **Wagatsuma,** Wade R '99 %Jones D -901 Lakeside Av -Cleveland 44114 Fx:579-0212

(614) 424-7927 .. **Wagenbach,** Adam J '73 Battelle Memorial Inst -505 King Av -Columbus 43201

(614) 466-3016 .. **Wagenbrenner,** Diane L '00 PUCO -180 E Broad -Columbus 43266

(937) 225-5885 .. **Wagenfeld,** Steven L '90 Montgomery Cnty Pros/CSEA -14 W 4th -Ste 510 -Dayton 45402

(330) 848-8690 .. **Wagenknecht,** Carl R Jr. '89 -Bx22458 -Akron 44302

(419) 241-9000 .. **Wagenman,** Barton L '67 (Shumaker L&K,LLP) -1000 Jackson -Toledo 43604 Fx:241-6894

(419) 213-6749 .. **Waggoner,** Geoffrey M '80 Lucas Cnty Juv Ct -1801 Spielbusch Av -Toledo 43624 Fx:213-6898

(216) 520-0088 .. **Waggoner,** Glenn D '80 (Pepple & W LLP) -5005 Rockside Rd -Ste 260 -Cleveland 44131 Fx:520-0044

(937) 698-4112 .. **Wagner,** Allyn S '69 -102 S Miami -West Milton 45383

(513) 784-8616 .. **Wagner,** Barbara J '88 Chiquita Brands Intl -250 E 5th -Cincinnati 45202

(330) 755-1437 .. **Wagner,** Carol C '88 (Clements & W Co,LPA) -700 5th -Struthers 44471

(216) 241-7000 .. **Wagner,** Charles E '90 %Landskroner & Assoc -55 Pub Sq -Ste 1040 -Cleveland 44113

(216) 443-7800 .. **Wagner,** Christopher A '00 Cuyahoga Cnty Pros -1200 Ontario -8th Fl -Cleveland 44113 Fx:698-2270

(216) 586-3939 .. **Wagner,** Christopher J '03 %Jones D -901 Lakeside Av -Cleveland 44114 Fx:579-0212

(513) 621-8688 .. **Wagner,** David C '89 -1071 Celestial -Ste 904 -Cincinnati 45202

(330) 535-1555 .. **Wagner,** Dean R '87 %Teodosio M&W -One Cascade Plz -Ste 1000 -Akron 44308

(740) 385-2614 .. **Wagner,** Deborah A '87 Hocking Cnty Cmn Pleas Ct -1 E Main -Logan 43138

Wagner, Dora J '00 -(Address Unavailable)

(440) 888-2889 .. **Wagner,** Edwin J '67 -6360 Mnchstr Rd -Parma 44129

(440) 743-7561 .. **Wagner,** Erika Jordan '84 -5530 State Rd -Ste 9 -Cleveland 44134

(419) 797-4783 .. **Wagner,** Glen W '49 -3858 N Cliff Rd -Port Clinton 43452

Wagner, Heidi A '04 -(Address Unavailable)

(937) 294-2778 .. **Wagner,** Henry C '74 -424 Patterson Rd -Dayton 45419

(419) 526-3300 .. **Wagner,** James K '76 -3 N Main -808 Richland Bk Bldg -Mansfield 44902

(330) 864-3100 .. **Wagner,** James L '76 -529 White Pond Dr -Akron 44320

(440) 298-3760 .. **Wagner,** James L '75 -5626 Trask Rd -Madison 44057

(937) 204-1724 .. **Wagner,** Jared A '03 -9465 Sassafrass Rd -Lakeview 43331

(419) 468-1131 .. **Wagner,** Jay D '84 (Wagner Law Firm,PLL) -118 Hrdng Way W -Bx576 -Galion 44833

(317) 587-3351 .. **Wagner,** Jay H '92 SrCnsl Thomson Multimedia -10330 N Meridian -INH 340 -Bx1976 -Indianapolis, IN 46206

(513) 632-9526 .. **Wagner,** John J '71 -119 E Court -Cincinnati 45202

(419) 468-1131 .. **Wagner,** John L '55 (Wagner Law Firm,PLL) -118 Hrdng Way W -Bx576 -Galion 44833

(330) 753-3900 .. **Wagner,** Joy S '88 (Wagner & Assoc) -507 W Park Av -Barberton 44203

(513) 946-3431 .. **Wagner,** June E '96 1st Dist Ct of Appls -230 E 9th -12th Fl -Cincinnati 45202 Fx:946-3412

(216) 291-3811 .. **Wagner,** Laure A '82 City of Cleveland Hts -40 Severance Cir -Cleveland Heights 44118

(419) 524-3334 .. **Wagner,** Leslie K Jr. '67 -3 N Main -Ste 403 -Mansfield 44902

(330) 376-5300 .. **Wagner,** Louis F '84 (Buckingham D&B,LLP) -50 S Main -Bx1500 -Akron 44309 Fx:258-6559

(440) 473-5263 .. **Wagner,** Mark R '80 -1392 Som Center Rd -Mayfield Heights 44124

(937) 653-7174 .. **Wagner Maurice Davidson & Gilbert** -117 W Court -Urbana 43078

(419) 213-6951 .. **Wagner,** Melissa M '98 %Lucas Cnty Pros-Juv Div -1801 Spielbusch Av -Toledo 43624

(202) 418-2775 .. **Wagner,** Michael F '83 FCC -445 12th SW -Rm 2A523 -Washington, DC 20554

(330) 742-0500 .. **Wagner,** Michael J '81 Home Svngs & Loan Co -275 Fed Plz W -Bx1111 -Youngstown 44501

(419) 885-8920 .. **Wagner,** Michelle A '95 City Pros -6700 Monroe -Sylvania 43560

(513) 243-0818 .. **Wagner,** Nancy R '95 GE Transportation -1 Neuman Way -MD F17 -Cincinnati 45215

(216) 432-7200 .. **Wagner,** Nora B '00 Ctr for Families & Children -4500 Euclid Av -Cleveland 44103

Wagner, Patricia E '00 -(Address Unavailable)

(440) 333-2211 .. **Wagner,** Paul C Jr. '54 -21761 Gatehse Ln -Rocky River 44116

(937) 447-8111 .. **Wagner,** Paul E '97 -111 N Brdg -Gettysburg 45328

(419) 242-1400 .. **Wagner,** Peter Jan '72 -608 Mad Av -14th Fl -Toledo 43604

(330) 683-5010 .. **Wagner,** Richard S '58 (Kropf WH&L,LLP) -100 N Vine -Bx67 -Orrville 44667 Fx:683-5030

(614) 466-0281 .. **Wagner,** Steven A '96 OH Dept Hlth -246 N High -Bx118 -Columbus 43216

(216) 529-2870 .. **Wagner,** Steven B '94 (Paynter K&W) -11740 Clifton Blvd -Ste 202 -Lakewood 44107 Fx:529-2883

(216) 781-4000 .. **Wagner,** Thomas C '95 (Van Deusen & W,LLC) -1422 Euclid Av -Ste 1610 Hanna Bldg -Cleveland 44115

(216) 622-8200 .. **Wagner,** Thomas E '73 (Calfee H&G LLP) -800 Superior Av -Ste 1400 -Cleveland 44114 Fx:241-0816

Wagner, Thomas J '72 -1354 Westlake Av -Cleveland 44107
(859) 692-2100 .. **Wagner,** William J '81 Natl Underwriter Co -5081 Olympic Blvd -Erlanger, KY 41018
(440) 779-6632 .. **Wagoner,** Byron R '70 -24158 Woodmere Dr -North Olmsted 44070 **Fx:**779-2866
(330) 762-0700 .. **Wagoner,** Edmund Lee Jr. '87 %Slater Z&G -One Cascade Plz -Ste 2210 -Akron 44308 **Fx:**762-3923
(419) 246-5757 .. **Wagoner,** Gregory H '03 %Anspach M&N,LLP -300 Mad Av -Ste 1600 -Toledo 43604 **Fx:**321-6979
(614) 481-4480 .. **Wagoner,** Jacob D '01 Koffel & J -2130 Arlngtn Av -Columbus 43221
(419) 865-1251 .. **Wagoner,** John E '65 Wagoner & S,Ltd -7445 Airport Hwy -Holland 43528 **Fx:**866-8798
(419) 865-1251 .. **Wagoner,** Mark D '68 Wagoner & S,Ltd -7445 Airport Hwy -Holland 43528 **Fx:**866-8798
(419) 241-9000 .. **Wagoner,** Mark D Jr. '97 %Shumaker L&K,LLP -1000 Jackson -Toledo 43624 **Fx:**241-6894
(614) 242-4333 .. **Wagoner,** Robert J '98 F Todaro -471 E Broad -Ste 1303 -Columbus 43215
(419) 865-1251 .. **Wagoner & Steinberg,Ltd** -7445 Airport Hwy -Holland 43528 **Fx:**866-8798
(216) 983-1024 .. **Wahl,** Cheryl Forino '03 Univ Hosp Health Sys -10524 Euclid Av -Cleveland 44106
(614) 442-1953 .. **Wahl,** Eric M '01 %R Bracco & Assoc -1170 Old Henderson Rd -Ste 109 -Columbus 43220
(614) 224-8374 .. **Wahl,** Janice K '04 Legal Aid -40 W Gay -Columbus 43215
(216) 344-9007 .. **Wahl,** Jeffrey R '84 (JR Wahl Co,LPA) -323 W Lakeside Av -Ste 450 -Cleveland 44113
(614) 365-2700 .. **Wahl,** Jeffrey R '02 %Squire S&D LLP -41 S High -1300 Huntngtn Ctr -Columbus 43215 **Fx:**365-2499
(937) 227-3700 .. **Wahl,** Katrina L '03 %Faruki I&C PLL -10 N Ludlow -500 Cthse Plz SW -Dayton 45402 **Fx:**227-3717
(614) 464-6400 .. **Wahl,** Kyong W Nahm '00 %Vorys SS&P LLP -52 E Gay -Bx1008 -Columbus 43216 **Fx:**464-6350
(614) 464-6400 .. **Wahl,** Travis J '00 (Vorys SS&P LLP) -52 E Gay -Bx1008 -Columbus 43216 **Fx:**464-6350
(614) 621-1500 .. **Wahlers,** Kristopher L '91 (Calfee H&G LLP) -21 E State -1100 Fifth Third Ctr -Columbus 43215 **Fx:**621-0010
(412) 560-7011 .. **Wahlster,** Kristopher A '98 Morgan L&B,LLP -One Oxford Ctr -32nd Fl -Pittsburgh, PA 15219
(614) 222-8686 .. **Wahoff,** William J '82 (Scott S&W LLP) -50 W Broad -2500 LeVeque Twr -Columbus 43215 **Fx:**222-8688
(614) 227-3087 .. **Waid,** Elizabeth O '85 OH Education Assn -225 E Broad -Columbus 43215
(614) 761-1733 .. **Waid,** Phillip A '73 (Metcalf DMS&W,LLC) -655 Metro Pl S -Ste 210 -Dublin 43017
(440) 498-2126 .. **Wainblat,** Julia L '92 -7382 Hambleton Dr -Solon 44139
(216) 696-7600 .. **Wainblat,** Neal B '81 (Duvin C&H) -1301 E 9th -20th Fl Erievw Twr -Cleveland 44114 **Fx:**696-2038
(440) 838-8299 .. **Wainey,** Deborah A '91 -Bx41129 -Brecksville 44141
(859) 386-7329 .. **Wainio,** Amy E '98 Fidelity Invstmnts -100 Magellan Way -KWIC -Covington, KY 41015
Wainright, Amy M '97 -(Address Unavailable)
(513) 603-5255 .. **Wainscott,** Jason P '04 Cincinnati Ins Co -6200 S Gilmore -Fairfield 45014
(330) 451-7200 .. **Wainwright,** Marcus L '04 %Stark Cnty Pub Def -200 W Tuscarawas -Ste 200 -Canton 44702
(513) 763-7700 .. **Waite,** Charles J '81 (J Waite & Assoc Co,LPA) -830 Main -Ste 500 -Cincinnati 45202
(330) 762-6334 .. **Waite,** Eric R '97 (E Waite & Assoc) -520 S Main -Ste 2518 -Akron 44311
(513) 621-0267 .. **Waite Schneider Bayless & Chesley** -1 W 4th -1513 4th & Vine Twr -Cincinnati 45202
(937) 222-2424 .. **Waite,** Wayne E '82 (Freund F&A) -1 S Main -Ste 1800 -Dayton 45402 **Fx:**222-5369
(216) 241-6045 .. **Waiwood,** Michael F '71 Midland Title Sec,Inc -1111 Superior Av E -Ste 700 -Cleveland 44114
(937) 223-8177 .. **Wakefield,** Brian M '04 %Coolidge WW&L -33 W 1st -Ste 600 -Dayton 45402 **Fx:**223-6705
(740) 397-4040 .. **Wakefield,** Laura A '97 (Critchfield C&J Ltd) -10 S Gay -Mount Vernon 43050 **Fx:**397-6775
(216) 781-2600 .. **Wakefield,** Mark L '82 (Lowe EW&M Co,LPA) -1660 W 2nd -610 Skylight Ofc Twr -Cleveland 44113 **Fx:**781-2610
(301) 896-0600 .. **Wakeman,** Scott T '92 %Liniak BL&W -6550 Rock Spring Dr -Ste 240 -Bethesda, MD 20817
(330) 451-7204 .. **Wakser,** Barry T '92 Stark Cnty Pub Def -200 W Tuscarawas -Ste 200 -Canton 44702
(859) 255-6812 .. **Walasinski,** Kevin J '90 Consolidated Legal Ctr -3301 Leestown Rd -Lexington, KY 40511
(440) 826-3558 .. **Walczak,** Michael A '81 Baldwin-Wallace College -275 Eastland Rd -Berea 44017
(937) 434-9938 .. **Wald,** Kathryn S '80 -3033 Kettering Blvd -Ste 110 -Dayton 45439
(216) 443-5809 .. **Wald,** Sara L '01 Cuyahoga Cnty Pros -1910 Carnegie Av -Whitlatch Bldg -Cleveland 44115 **Fx:**443-5815
(216) 781-1212 .. **Waldeck,** John W Jr. '77 (Walter & H LLP) -1301 E 9th -Ste 3500 -Cleveland 44114 **Fx:**575-0911
(614) 523-3575 .. **Waldeck,** Tom R '90 Mills & M -1935 W Schrock Rd -Westerville 43081
(513) 333-0990 .. **Walden,** Charles C '84 (Martin & B) -120 E 4th -Ste 420 -Cincinnati 45202 **Fx:**333-0066
(614) 221-3155 .. **Walden,** Jon C '94 %Bailey C LLC -10 W Broad -Columbus 43215 **Fx:**221-0479
(440) 835-0600 .. **Waldheger Coyne, LPA** -1991 Crocker Rd -Ste 550 -Westlake 44145 **Fx:**835-1511
(440) 835-0600 .. **Waldheger,** Ronald J '76 (Waldheger C,LPA) -1991 Crocker Rd -Ste 550 -Westlake 44145 **Fx:**835-1511
(419) 695-9080 .. **Waldick,** Juergen A '85 (Shenk CW&C) -214 W 2nd -Bx304 -Delphos 45833
(412) 338-1000 .. **Waldman,** Harold K '01 (H Waldman & Assoc) -625 Lbrty Av -Ste 300 -Pittsburgh, PA 15222
(513) 943-7070 .. **Waldner,** Linda D '82 -2030 Laurel Oak Dr -Amelia 45102
(614) 619-9256 .. **Waldo,** David W '98 -Bx541 -New Albany 43054
(740) 532-4911 .. **Waldo,** James M '78 Waldo Law Ofc -413 Center -Ironton 45638
(740) 532-4911 .. **Waldo,** Kevin J '80 -413 Center -Ironton 45638

(304) 529-5261 .. **Waldo,** Rayetta W '82 US Army Corp of Engineers -502 8th -Huntington, WV 25701
(419) 627-0414 .. **Waldock,** Frederick D '54 Buckingham LM&Z Co,LPA -414 Wayne -Bx929 -Sandusky 44870 **Fx:**627-0009
Waldorf, David M '86 -(Address Unavailable)
(216) 687-7221 .. **Waldron,** Richard G '84 Medical Mutual of Ohio -2060 E 9th -Cleveland 44115
(330) 264-1164 .. **Waldron,** Suzanne M '89 -248 N Walnut -Wooster 44691
(419) 241-2300 .. **Walerius,** Timothy J '94 -316 N Mich -Ste 800 -Toledo 43624
(513) 381-2838 .. **Wales,** Ross E '74 (Taft S&H LLP) -425 Walnut -Ste 1800 -Cincinnati 45202 **Fx:**381-0205
(440) 886-2510 .. **Walick,** Joseph A '63 -5225 Thoreau Dr -Parma 44129
(419) 241-1200 .. **Walinski,** Richard S '69 (Cooper & W,LPA) -900 Adams -Toledo 43624 **Fx:**242-5675
Walis, Bruce J '79 -(Address Unavailable)
(216) 861-8734 .. **Walk,** Rochelle F '86 Cnsl Oglebay Norton Co -1001 Lakeside Av -Ste 1500 -Cleveland 44114
(513) 977-4220 .. **Walk,** Rodger N '74 -917 Main -Ste 400 -Cincinnati 45202 **Fx:**977-4218
(216) 861-5000 .. **Walk,** Steven M '82 Ernst & Young -925 Euclid Av -Ste 1300 -Cleveland 44115
(216) 586-3939 .. **Walker,** Andrew M '03 %Jones D -901 Lakeside Av -Cleveland 44114 **Fx:**579-0212
(859) 219-9833 .. **Walker,** Anne M '92 Westfield Grp -2525 Harrodsburg Rd -Ste 400 -Lexington, KY 40504
(513) 946-4323 .. **Walker,** Bernice L '93 Hamilton Cnty Dept Admin Srvcs -138 E Court -Rm 607 -Cincinnati 45202 **Fx:**946-4330
(614) 848-5888 .. **Walker,** Brian A '89 -6877 N High -Ste 300 -Worthington 43085
(740) 594-8228 .. **Walker,** Brian R '85 (Walker & W Co,LPA) -211 Columbus Rd -Bx2470 -Athens 45701
(614) 227-2339 .. **Walker,** Charles H '76 (Bricker & E LLP) -100 S 3rd -Columbus 43215 **Fx:**227-2390
(937) 226-9000 .. **Walker,** Christopher A '88 -137 N Main -Dayton 45402 **Fx:**226-9002
(216) 523-1920 .. **Walker,** Daniel G '00 (White & W Co,LPA) -75 Pub Sq -Ste 1310 -Cleveland 44113
(330) 384-4596 .. **Walker,** Debra Kay '95 FirstEnergy -76 S Main -Akron 44308
(330) 434-5118 .. **Walker,** Donald L '77 -265 S Main -Akron 44308
(703) 836-6400 .. **Walker,** Edward P '77 Oliff & B PLC -277 S Wshngtn -Ste 500 -Alexandria, VA 22314
(330) 448-1500 .. **Walker,** Elwood M '78 (Hoffman & W) -7553 Warren-Sharon Rd -Bx316 -Brookfield 44403
(614) 466-7447 .. **Walker,** Eric A '88 Atty Gen -150 E Gay -Columbus 43215
(513) 732-7893 .. **Walker,** Gayle A '83 Clermont Cnty CSEA -2400 Clermont Ctr Dr -Batavia 45103
(937) 208-2183 .. **Walker,** Geoffrey P '86 Miami Valley Hosp -1 Wyoming -Dayton 45409
(440) 357-6111 .. **Walker,** Gerald R '73 (Redmond W&M) -174 N St Clair -Painesville 44077
(513) 651-6800 .. **Walker,** H Lawson II '75 (Frost BT LLC) -201 E 5th -2200 PNC Ctr -Cincinnati 45202 **Fx:**651-6981
(740) 392-4151 .. **Walker,** Harlow H '94 -120½ E High -Mount Vernon 43050
(330) 887-0669 .. **Walker,** James M '81 Westfield Grp -1 Park Cir -Bx5001 -Westfield Center 44251 **Fx:**887-2588
(513) 621-0267 .. **Walker,** Jane H '84 Waite SB&C -1 W 4th -1513 4th & Vine Twr -Cincinnati 45202
(216) 431-4500 .. **Walker,** Janice '94 Cuyahoga Cnty Pros -3955 Euclid Av -Jane Edna Hunter Bldg -Cleveland 44115 **Fx:**431-4113
(513) 287-3970 .. **Walker,** Janice L '95 Cnsl Cinergy Corp -139 E 4th -25 Atrium II -Bx960 -Cincinnati 45201
(330) 721-0000 .. **Walker & Jocke,LPA** -231 S Bway -Medina 44256 **Fx:**722-6446
(937) 428-1665 .. **Walker,** John T '88 Nationwide Ins -6525 Centervll Business Pwky -Centerville 45459
(248) 728-7800 .. **Walker,** Joseph V '72 RL Polk & Co -26955 Nrthwstrn Hwy -Southfield, MI 48034
(937) 434-2885 .. **Walker,** Joseph W '78 J Walker Co,LPA -2233 Miamisburg-Centervll Rd -Dayton 45459
(330) 399-6434 .. **Walker,** Keith M '76 -280 N Park Av -Ste 220 -Bx1294 -Warren 44482
(336) 861-3500 .. **Walker,** Kenneth L '75 Sealy Inc -1 Ofc Pkwy -Bx2806 -Trinity, NC 27370
Walker, Kris H '00 -Bx21834 -Columbus 43221
(216) 241-2880 .. **Walker,** Kristin M '01 %Cowden HN&L -50 Pub Sq -Ste 1414 -Cleveland 44113 **Fx:**241-2881
(513) 732-5777 .. **Walker,** Lawrence '68 -60 N 4th -Batavia 45103
(614) 221-2838 .. **Walker,** Lawrence D '73 (Taft S&H LLP) -21 E State -12th Fl -Columbus 43215 **Fx:**221-2007
(216) 787-3030 .. **Walker,** Nancy Q '95 Atty Gen -615 W Superior Av -11th Fl -Cleveland 44115 **Fx:**787-3480
(330) 721-0000 .. **Walker,** Patricia A '81 (Walker & J,LPA) -231 S Bway -Medina 44256 **Fx:**722-6446
(614) 466-6901 .. **Walker,** Paul D '76 Industrial Commssn of OH -30 W Spring -9th Fl -Columbus 43215 **Fx:**752-8785
(614) 263-8750 .. **Walker,** Richard L '66 -162 Webster Park Av -Columbus 43214
(216) 586-3939 .. **Walker,** Robert S '82 (Jones D) -901 Lakeside Av -Cleveland 44114 **Fx:**579-0212
(281) 368-4201 .. **Walker,** Rondal A '99 Stone & Webster Engineering Corp -1430 Enclave Pkwy -Houston, TX 77077
(216) 443-3799 .. **Walker,** Sandra L '84 Cuyahoga Cnty Pros -1 Lakeside Av -Rm 49 -Cleveland 44115 **Fx:**443-3777
(614) 469-3939 .. **Walker,** Scott M '94 %Jones D -325 John H McConnell Blvd -Ste 600 -Bx165017 -Columbus 43216 **Fx:**461-4198
Walker, Sonia T '99 -(Address Unavailable)
(216) 360-9200 .. **Walker,** Stephen O '74 -23245 Fairmount -Beachwood 44122
(937) 225-4600 .. **Walker,** Steven M '76 Montgomery Cnty CSEA -Bx8744 -Dayton 45402
(614) 466-2872 .. **Walker,** Susan C '90 Atty Gen -30 E Broad -Columbus 43215 **Fx:**728-7592
(440) 526-4244 .. **Walker,** Wallace W Jr. '66 -7774 Oakhurst Cir -Bx470340 -Cleveland 44147
(216) 265-9463 .. **Walker,** William A '56 -27 Coventry Ct -Cleveland 44138
Walker, William E Jr. '87 -836 Savannah Av NE -Canton 44704

(740) 594-8228 .. **Walker,** William R '78 (Walker & W Co,LPA) -211 Columbus Rd -Bx2470 -Athens 45701

(330) 672-2982 .. **Walker,** Willis '81 Kent State Univ-Exec Ofcs -2nd Fl Library -Bx5190 -Kent 44242

(330) 825-2477 .. **Walkley Kennedy & Gutbrod Co,LPA** -4071 S Cleveland-Massillon Rd -Bx1080 -Norton 44203 **Fx:**825-2029

(330) 825-2477 .. **Walkley,** Thomas L '86 (Walkley K&G Co,LPA) -4071 S Cleveland-Massillon Rd -Bx1080 -Norton 44203 **Fx:**825-2029

(330) 253-5060 .. **Walko,** Lee S '93 (Brennan M&D,LLC) -75 E Market -Akron 44308 **Fx:**253-1977

(617) 228-4400 .. **Walko,** Matthew J '93 (Smith & D LLP) -Two Center Plz -Ste 620 -Boston, MA 02108 **Fx:**248-9320

(614) 435-6675 .. **Walkup,** Christine M '03 Nationwide -5100 Rings Rd -Dublin 43016

(614) 340-8820 .. **Wall,** Andrew J '93 -1700 Watermark Dr -Columbus 43215

(216) 621-0200 .. **Wall,** Brett A '98 %Baker & H LLP -1900 E 9th -Ste 3200 -Cleveland 44114 **Fx:**696-0740

(602) 528-4000 .. **Wall,** Donald A '71 (Squire S&D LLP) -40 N Central Av -Ste 2700 -Phoenix, AZ 85004 **Fx:**253-8129

(937) 228-2838 .. **Wall,** Hugh E III '72 (Taft S&H LLP) -110 N Main -Ste 900 -Dayton 45402 **Fx:**228-2816

(413) 394-2500 .. **Wall,** John G '03 (Burns W&H) -120 5th Av -Ste 2400 -Pittsburgh, PA 15222

(216) 523-4118 .. **Wall,** Katherine M '91 Eaton Corp -1111 Superior Av -Cleveland 44114

(614) 628-6880 .. **Wall,** Kirk M '93 (Dinsmore & S LLP) -175 S 3rd -10th Fl -Columbus 43215 **Fx:**628-6890

(419) 483-4543 .. **Wall,** Mary J '99 North Central Radiology -108 W Main -Bx305 -Bellevue 44811

(440) 331-1010 .. **Wall,** Philip J '56 -20800 Ctr Ridge Rd -Ste 222 -Rocky River 44116 **Fx:**331-8812

(513) 345-4539 .. **Wall,** Richard F '98 Grant Thornton LLP -625 Eden Park Dr -Ste 900 -Cincinnati 45202

(513) 352-1502 .. **Wall,** Stacy M '98 Law Dept -801 Plum -Rm 214 -Cincinnati 45202 **Fx:**352-1515

(419) 537-6700 .. **Wall,** Virginia M '89 -2920 W Central Av -Toledo 43606 **Fx:**537-0913

(803) 754-8786 .. **Wallace,** Braden E '79 Wallace Law Firm -Bx763 -Blythewood, SC 29016

(937) 444-2563 .. **Wallace,** Bruce S '83 (Kelly & W Co,LPA) -108 S High -Mount Orab 45154

(216) 443-6350 .. **Wallace,** Christine M '85 8th Dist Ct of Appls -1 Lakeside Av -#202 -Cleveland 44113 **Fx:**443-2044

(304) 723-7201 .. **Wallace,** Christopher J '95 %Hinerman & Assoc,PLLC -3203 Penn Av -Bx2465 -Weirton, WV 26062

(614) 365-4100 .. **Wallace,** David A '85 (Carpenter & L LLP) -280 N High -Ste 1300 280 Plz -Columbus 43215 **Fx:**365-9145

(216) 241-2838 .. **Wallace,** David H '86 (Taft S&H LLP) -200 Pub Sq -3500 BP Twr -Cleveland 44114 **Fx:**241-3707

(606) 331-6440 .. **Wallace,** Harry D '87 Cors & B LLC -1881 Dixie Hwy -Ste 350 -Fort Wright, KY 41011

(937) 225-4887 .. **Wallace,** Helen C '00 Montgomery Cnty Pros -303 W 2nd -Rm 113 -Dayton 45402

Wallace, Jacob M '03 -(Address Unavailable)

(740) 592-4463 .. **Wallace,** James A '81 -11 E Wshngtn -Bx337 -Athens 45701

(216) 901-0219 .. **Wallace,** Jodi M '98 -Bx31126 -Independence 44131

(570) 547-1990 .. **Wallace,** John E '92 FCI Allenwood -Bx1500 -White Deer, PA 17887

(740) 385-3880 .. **Wallace,** John T '86 -38½ N Market -Bx1122 -Logan 43138

Wallace, John W '95 -(Address Unavailable)

(216) 696-7600 .. **Wallace,** Lisa A '00 %Duvin C&H -1301 E 9th -20th Fl Erievw Twr -Cleveland 44114 **Fx:**696-2038

(330) 856-8879 .. **Wallace,** Lisa R '94 Avalon Holdings Corp -1 Amer Way -Warren 44484

(614) 221-3821 .. **Wallace,** Paul L '80 (Wallace & W Co,LPA) -171 E Lvngstn Av -Columbus 43215 **Fx:**221-6753

(216) 621-0200 .. **Wallace,** R Byron '74 (Baker & H LLP) -1900 E 9th -Ste 3200 -Cleveland 44114 **Fx:**696-0740

(937) 492-6191 .. **Wallace,** Richard H '75 (Elsass WES&Co) -100 S Main Av -Ste 102 -Bx499 -Sidney 45365 **Fx:**492-0876

(513) 241-9440 .. **Wallace,** Teri A '92 -1014 Vine -Ste 1919 Kroger Bldg -Cincinnati 45202

(513) 762-6200 .. **Wallace,** Traci L '00 %Ulmer & B LLP -600 Vine -Ste 2800 -Cincinnati 45202 **Fx:**762-6245

Wallace-Curry, Virginia M '88 -30799 Pinetree Rd -Ste 417 -Pepper Pike 44124

(216) 622-8200 .. **Wallach,** Mark I '74 (Calfee H&G LLP) -800 Superior Av -Ste 1400 -Cleveland 44114 **Fx:**241-0816

(740) 385-2250 .. **Wallar,** Richard M '81 Cnty Mun Ct Judge -Bx950 -Logan 43138

(740) 446-6921 .. **Wallen,** Barbara A '81 CSE Agncy -19½ Locust -Bx449 -Gallipolis 45631

(614) 228-2300 .. **Waller,** Barry A '74 (Fry W&M Co,LPA) -35 E Lvngstn Av -Columbus 43215 **Fx:**228-6680

(216) 755-5500 .. **Waller,** Michelle W '95 Developers Diversified Rlty Corp -3300 Enterprise Pkwy -Beachwood 44122

(203) 234-8638 .. **Waller,** Robert M Jr. '94 -68 Vllg -North Haven, CT 06473

(330) 364-5066 .. **Wallick,** Tina Galigher '86 -114 E High Av -New Philadelphia 44663 **Fx:**364-4337

(202) 565-6017 .. **Wallin,** Karissa L '98 Dept of Vets Affs/Appls -810 VT Av NW -Washington, DC 20420

(330) 744-3196 .. **Walling,** Michael I '65 Cmmnty Lgl Aid Srvcs,Inc -11 Fed Plz Central -7th Fl -Youngstown 44503 **Fx:**744-2503

(330) 656-1530 .. **Walling,** Richard R '55 -75 Atterbury Blvd -#301 -Hudson 44236

(419) 483-2621 .. **Wallingford,** David A '79 -117 W Main -Bx368 -Bellevue 44811

(330) 434-3461 .. **Walls,** Angela R '01 Legal Def -One Cascade Plz -Ste 1940 -Akron 44308

(703) 305-0933 .. **Walls,** Dionne A '96 USPTO -Crystal Plz 3 -Rm 2C02 -Washington, DC 20231

(513) 482-5039 .. **Walls,** Janetta S '01 Cognis Corp -5051 Estecreek Dr -Cincinnati 45232

(614) 221-2121 .. **Walls,** Jessica K '03 %Isaac BL&T,LLP -250 E Broad -Ste 900 Mdlnd Bldg -Columbus 43215 **Fx:**365-9516

(513) 378-8467 .. **Walls,** Melanie B '97 -Bx9883 -Cincinnati 45209

(330) 374-1110 .. **Walpole,** Daniel M '85 -120 E Mill -411 Quaker Sq -Akron 44308

(330) 872-0918 .. **Walrath,** Terry J '70 Cadle Co -100 N Center -Newton Falls 44444

(740) 246-4602 .. **Walser,** Thomas E '83 -39 Craig Dr -Bx510 -Thornville 43076

(330) 972-7751 .. **Walsh,** Charles M '91 %Univ of Akron/Sch of Law -150 Univ Av -Leg Clinic -Akron 44325

(614) 464-2392 .. **Walsh,** Christopher R '95 %Earl WA&D,LPA -136 W Mound -Columbus 43215 **Fx:**464-0754

Walsh, Debra L '90 -(Address Unavailable)

(513) 867-4823 .. **Walsh,** Dennis G '75 1st Natl Bk of SW OH -Bx476 -Hamilton 45012

(216) 443-7800 .. **Walsh,** Edward M '71 Cuyahoga Cnty Pros -1200 Ontario -8th Fl -Cleveland 44113 **Fx:**698-2270

(410) 962-3555 .. **Walsh,** Erin K '04 US Bankruptcy Ct -101 W Lombard -Baltimore, MD 21201

(614) 878-6553 .. **Walsh,** Eugene J '59 -3515 Rolling Hills Ln -Grove City 43123

(513) 868-1113 .. **Walsh,** Herbert V '72 (Condo & W) -301 S Front -Hamilton 45011

(216) 357-7000 .. **Walsh,** James F Jr. '98 US Dist Ct -801 W Superior Av -US Cthse -Cleveland 44113

(937) 222-1148 .. **Walsh,** James Joseph '63 -111 W 1st -Ste 1000 -Dayton 45402 **Fx:**222-3500

(440) 775-1751 .. **Walsh,** James L '81 City Solicitors Ofc -85 S Main -Oberlin 44074

(859) 331-6440 .. **Walsh,** James P '99 %Cors & B,LLC -1881 Dixie Hwy -Ste 350 -Fort Wright, KY 41011

(216) 755-5666 .. **Walsh,** Jane '85 Developers Diversified Rlty Corp -3300 Enterprise Pkwy -Beachwood 44122

(440) 356-5700 .. **Walsh,** Jonathan J '04 %Laubacher & G,LLP -20525 Ctr Ridge Rd -Ste 626 -Cleveland 44116

(419) 321-6444 .. **Walsh,** Joseph M '82 (JM Walsh Co,LPA) -300 Mad Av -Ste 1100 -Toledo 43604

(419) 627-7697 .. **Walsh,** Katherine H '76 Erie Cnty Pros -247 Columbus Av -Ste 319 -Sandusky 44870 **Fx:**627-7567

(216) 348-5400 .. **Walsh,** Kenneth J '75 (McDonald H Co,LPA) -600 Superior Av E -Ste 2100 -Cleveland 44114 **Fx:**348-5474

(609) 282-2140 .. **Walsh,** Kevin D '94 Merrill Lynch -800 Scudders Mill Rd -Human Resources -Plainsboro, NJ 08536

(513) 241-3100 .. **Walsh,** Kevin R '01 Lerner S&R -120 E 4th -8th Fl -Cincinnati 45202

(614) 719-8512 .. **Walsh,** Lyndsay M '03 Franklin Cnty Pub Def -373 S High -12th Fl -Columbus 43215 **Fx:**461-6470

(216) 621-5980 .. **Walsh,** Margaret M '86 Legal Aid -1223 W 6th -Cleveland 44113

(440) 333-3916 .. **Walsh,** Mary K '94 -19420 Lorain RD -#408E -Bx26013 -Fairview Park 44126

(216) 377-0615 .. **Walsh,** Mary V '76 -4403 St Clair -Cleveland 44103

(330) 702-2825 .. **Walsh,** Maureen A '85 Gillis & G -3660 Stutz Dr -Ste 100 -Canfield 44406

(440) 576-3699 .. **Walsh,** Patricia M '80 Ashtabula Cnty Cmn Pleas Ct -25 W Jffrsn -Jefferson 44047

(330) 650-0088 .. **Walsh,** Patrick M '03 %Bevan & Assoc LPA,Inc -10360 Nrthfld Rd -Northfield 44067 **Fx:**467-4493

(412) 258-2255 .. **Walsh,** Paul J III '04 (Walsh C&B) -707 Grant -Gulf Twr-Ste 2300 -Pittsburgh, PA 15219 **Fx:**263-5632

(216) 443-3360 .. **Walsh,** Richard F '71 Cuyahoga Cnty Cmn Pleas Ct -2163 E 22nd -Cleveland 44115

(202) 927-3057 .. **Walsh,** Sara L '96 Dept of Treasury -1125 15th NW -7th Fl -Washington, DC 20224

(330) 643-2800 .. **Walsh,** Sherri Bevan '85 (Summit Cnty Pros-Civil) -53 Univ Av -6th Fl -Akron 44308 **Fx:**643-2137

(216) 520-7177 .. **Walsh,** Terrence R '98 IRS -5990 Westcreek Rd -(Estate & Gift Tax) -Independence 44131

(330) 643-2765 .. **Walsh,** Timothy J '83 Summit Cnty Pros-CSEA -171 S Main -Akron 44308 **Fx:**643-2822

(419) 423-8055 .. **Walter,** Douglas M '84 %Whitman,LLC -101 W Sandusky -Findlay 45840 **Fx:**425-1508

(513) 263-4900 .. **Walter,** Edward L '87 IRS-Chief Cnsl Ofc -312 Elm -Ste 2300 -Cincinnati 45202

(216) 781-1212 .. **Walter & Haverfield LLP** -1301 E 9th -Ste 3500 -Cleveland 44114 **Fx:**575-0911

(419) 213-4700 .. **Walter,** James C '87 %Lucas Cnty Pros -Adams & Erie -Lucas Cnty Cthse -Toledo 43624

(419) 537-8679 .. **Walter,** James E '67 -2125 Hawthorne Rd -Toledo 43606

(513) 931-4910 .. **Walter,** Janis L '82 -684 Reynard Av -Cincinnati 45231

(330) 535-5711 .. **Walter,** Karen L '96 %Brouse M -106 S Main -500 First Natl Twr -Akron 44308 **Fx:**253-8601

(614) 461-5600 .. **Walter,** Robert J '72 (Buckley K,LPA) -10 W Broad -Ste 1300 -Columbus 43215

(216) 830-6830 .. **Walter,** Robert M '81 (Brouse M) -1001 Lakeside Av -Ste 1600 -Cleveland 44114 **Fx:**830-6807

(303) 564-0974 .. **Walter,** Ronald K '81 -8584 Pawnee Rd -Parker, CO 80134

(702) 433-3150 .. **Walter,** Thomas E '67 Dept Justice -3373 Pepper Ln -Las Vegas, NV 89120

(614) 464-3034 .. **Walter,** Todd A '04 %Vorys SS&P LLP -52 E Gay -Bx1008 -Columbus 43216 **Fx:**464-6350

(614) 565-1050 .. **Walters,** Ben R '88 -Bx10043 -Columbus 43201

(216) 566-5500 .. **Walters,** Gary L '99 %Thompson H LLP -127 Pub Sq -3900 Key Ctr -Cleveland 44114 **Fx:**566-5800

(440) 826-0084 .. **Walters,** James N III '73 -343 W Bagley Rd -Ste 101 -Bx297 -Berea 44017

(330) 668-6500 .. **Walters,** Jeffery A '84 C-Bus S&S -4040 Embssy Pkwy -Ste 100 -Akron 44333

(937) 335-0550 .. **Walters,** Jennifer J '96 Huffman L&W Co,LPA -80 S Plum -Troy 45373

(614) 628-6880 .. **Walters,** Marilena R '84 (Dinsmore & S LLP) -175 S 3rd -10th Fl -Columbus 43215 **Fx:**628-6890

(859) 431-6340 .. **Walters,** Michael A '98 -509 E 10th -Newport, KY 41071

(202) 782-5808 .. **Walters,** Michael L '82 US Army Labor Employment -Ofc of the Med Ctr -Washington, DC 20307

(513) 681-1800 .. **Walters,** Michele A '83 McAuley High Schl -6000 Oakwood Av -Cincinnati 45224

(614) 469-3939 .. **Walters,** Randall M '78 (Jones D) -325 John H McConnell Blvd -Ste 600 -Bx165017 -Columbus 43216 **Fx:**461-4198

(216) 447-1551 .. **Walters,** Richard E '86 (Ross B&S Co LPA) -6000 Freedom Square Dr -Ste 540 -Cleveland 44131 **Fx:**447-1554

(614) 469-3939 .. **Walters,** Ryan D '03 %Jones D -325 John H McConnell Blvd -Ste 600 -Bx165017 -Columbus 43216 **Fx:**461-4198

(614) 466-7447 ..**Walters**, Sally A '80 Atty Gen -150 E Gay -Columbus 43215
(216) 787-4486 ..**Walters**, Sally S '93 Workers Comp -615 W Superior
-Cleveland 44113 **Fx:**787-4487
(216) 687-1311 ..**Walters**, Stephen '83 (Reminger & R) -101 Prospect Av W
-1400 Mdlnd Bldg -Cleveland 44115 **Fx:**687-1841
(216) 241-6602 ..**Walters**, Stephen D '68 (Weston HFP&H LLP) -50 Pub Sq
-2500 Trmnl Twr -Cleveland 44113 **Fx:**621-8369
(419) 228-6365 ..**Walters**, Sumner E '74 Cory MWR&C,LPA -101 N Elizabeth
-Ste 607 -Bx1217 -Lima 45802 **Fx:**228-5319
Walters, Susan M '80 -112 Westwind Dr -Avon Lake 44012
(330) 630-2618 ..**Walters**, Thomas E '85 -101 Northeast Av -Tallmadge 44278
Fx:630-3735
(513) 983-8469 ..**Walther**, Christopher B '91 Procter & Gamble Co -1 Procter
& Gamble Plz -Leg Dept -Cincinnati 45202
(440) 960-2525 ..**Walther**, James T '87 J Walther Co,LPA -4461 Oberlin Av
-Ste 102 -Lorain 44053
(859) 225-4714 ..**Walther**, Jeff S '88 Walther RG&T PLC -167 E Main -Ste 300
-Bx1598 -Lexington, KY 40588
(330) 674-3055 ..**Waltman**, John R '70 (Critchfield C&J Ltd) -138 E Jackson -Ste A
-Millersburg 44654
(330) 683-1025 ..**Waltman**, Paul D '65 -144 N Main -Orrville 44667
(216) 621-1230 ..**Walton**, Gerald R '80 (G Walton & Assoc) -2800 Euclid Av
-Ste 320 -Cleveland 44115 **Fx:**621-3039
(330) 253-2729 ..**Walton**, Howard Jon '71 -120 E Mill -Ste 405 -Akron 44308
(614) 246-4054 ..**Walton**, Kelley K '01 Columbus Blue Jackets
-200 W Nationwide Blvd -Columbus 43215
(513) 946-5900 ..**Walton**, Michael L '73 Hamilton Cnty Ct Admin -410 Cnty Cthse
-Cincinnati 45202
(216) 283-6484 ..**Walton**, Robert G '81 -13111 Shaker Sq -304 -Cleveland 44120
(513) 723-4000 ..**Walton**, Victor A Jr. '91 (Vorys SS&P LLP) -221 E 4th
-Ste 2000 Atrium Two -Bx0236 -Cincinnati 45201 **Fx:**723-4056
(614) 462-3555 ..**Walton**, William R II '01 Franklin Cnty Pros -373 S High
-Columbus 43215
(440) 350-2624 ..**Waltonen**, Andrea L '87 Lake Cnty Probate Ct -47 N Park Pl
-Cnty Cthse -Painesville 44077
(740) 349-6195 ..**Waltz**, Brian T '00 Licking Cnty Pros -20 S 2nd -4th Fl
-Newark 43055
(216) 839-1111 ..**Waltz**, David T '93 (Waltz & Assoc Co,LPA) -22901 Millcreek Blvd
-Ste 395 -Cleveland 44122 **Fx:**839-1122
(440) 329-5297 ..**Waltz**, Lisa L '94 Cnsl Cnty Clerk of Cmn Pleas Ct -308 2nd
-Rm 300 -Elyria 44035 **Fx:**329-5400
(513) 651-6800 ..**Walulik**, David W '03 %Frost BT LLC -201 E 5th -2200 PNC Ctr
-Cincinnati 45202 **Fx:**651-6981
(216) 586-3939 ..**Walworth**, James W Jr. '01 %Jones D -901 Lakeside Av
-Cleveland 44114 **Fx:**579-0212
(513) 579-6400 ..**Walwyn**, Jennifer K '04 %Keating M&K PLL -1 E 4th
-1400 Provident Twr -Cincinnati 45202 **Fx:**579-6457
(419) 213-4700 ..**Walz**, Kenneth C '04 Lucas Cnty Pros -Adams & Erie
-Lucas Cnty Cthse -Toledo 43624
(614) 462-3580 ..**Wambaugh**, Carrie L '00 10th Dist Ct of Appeals -373 S High
-Columbus 43215
(937) 224-8100 ..**Wampler**, Earl J '65 -120 W 2nd -1515 Lbrty Twr -Dayton 45402
(614) 644-7250 ..**Wampler**, Elizabeth Cole '02 Atty Gen -30 E Broad
-Columbus 43215 **Fx:**644-7634
(614) 227-4889 ..**Wampler**, G Samuel '02 %Bricker & E LLP -100 S 3rd
-Columbus 43215 **Fx:**227-2390
(937) 252-0002 ..**Wampler**, Harold W III '83 -1343 Woodman Dr -Dayton 45432
(937) 224-8100 ..**Wampler**, Sherry L '77 -120 W 2nd -1515 Lbrty Twr
-Dayton 45402
(513) 977-8200 ..**Wamsley**, Andrew J '04 %Dinsmore & S LLP -255 E 5th -Ste 1900
-Cincinnati 45202 **Fx:**977-8141
(216) 586-3939 ..**Wamsley**, James L III '75 (Jones D) -901 Lakeside Av
-Cleveland 44114 **Fx:**579-0212
(740) 593-6400 ..**Wamsley**, Jay H '82 Pub Def -80 N Court -Athens 45701
Fx:591-2074
(614) 645-8815 ..**Wander**, Michael H '96 City Pros -375 S High -7th Fl
-Columbus 43215
(513) 793-7776 ..**Wang**, Charleston C '82 -6924 Plainfld Rd -Silverton 45236
(614) 466-6700 ..**Wang**, Thomas L '77 Tax Appeals -30 E Broad -Columbus 43215
Fx:644-5196
(216) 363-4500 ..**Wang**, Yanping '00 %Benesch FC&A LLP -200 Pub Sq -Ste 2300
-Cleveland 44114 **Fx:**363-4588
(419) 246-5757 ..**Wanick**, John R '70 OfCnsl Anspach M&N,LLP -300 Mad Av
-Ste 1600 -Toledo 43604 **Fx:**321-6979
(614) 466-0892 ..**Wanless**, Brock A '03 OH House of Rep -77 S High -14th Fl
-Columbus 43215
(937) 335-8760 ..**Wannemacher**, John A '66 Peoples Svngs Bank -14 S Weston Rd
-Troy 45373
(937) 773-8054 ..**Wannemacher**, John A Jr. '93 %Dungan & L Co,LPA -111 W Ash
-Bx1529 -Piqua 45356 **Fx:**773-3379
(216) 291-7726 ..**Wanner**, Kathleen A '78 Northrop Grumman -1900 Richmond Rd
-2N -Cleveland 44124
(330) 405-5061 ..**Wantz**, Joseph H '82 (Williams S&S Co,LPA) -2241 Pinnacle Pkwy
-Twinsburg 44087 **Fx:**405-5586
(440) 286-3260 ..**Wantz**, Robert N '63 -107 Water -Chardon 44024
(248) 258-7855 ..**Wapnick**, Eric R '85 Butzel L -100 Blmfld Hills Pkwy -Ste 200
-Bloomfield Hills, MI 48304
(216) 443-7800 ..**Warbel**, Michael S '01 Cuyahoga Cnty Pros -1200 Ontario -8th Fl
-Cleveland 44113 **Fx:**698-2270
(614) 464-2392 ..**Warburton**, Dick M Jr. '61 (Earl WA&D,LPA) -136 W Mound
-Columbus 43215 **Fx:**464-0754
(330) 650-4273 ..**Warburton**, Phillip L '70 -2680 Deer Hllw -Hudson 44236
(330) 535-1555 ..**Ward**, Barry M '84 (Teodosio M&W) -One Cascade Plz -Ste 1000
-Akron 44308
(419) 772-2255 ..**Ward**, Bryan H '93 ONU-Pettit Clg of Law -525 S Main -Ada 45810
(614) 621-1500 ..**Ward**, Christopher M '03 %Calfee H&G LLP -21 E State
-1100 Fifth Third Ctr -Columbus 43215 **Fx:**621-0010
(216) 515-1660 ..**Ward**, Daniel A '82 Frantz W LLP -127 Pub Sq -2500 Key Center
-Cleveland 44114 **Fx:**515-1650
(513) 455-5348 ..**Ward**, Dennis R '91 Andrew Jergens Co -2535 Spring Grove Av
-Cincinnati 45214
(419) 241-1200 ..**Ward**, George C '76 %Cooper & W,LPA -900 Adams
-Toledo 43624 **Fx:**242-5675

(330) 971-8190 ..**Ward**, Gregory M '00 Cuyahoga Falls Pros -2310 2nd
-Cuyahoga Falls 44221
(330) 424-7800 ..**Ward**, Jerry J '74 -115 N Beaver -Lisbon 44432
(330) 424-7800 ..**Ward**, John P '00 %J Ward -115 N Beaver -Lisbon 44432
(302) 774-8035 ..**Ward**, John W '79 El Du Pont de Nemours & Co -1007 Market
-Rm 2044A -Wilmington, DE 19898
(859) 647-9100 ..**Ward**, Julie Reinhardt '03 %Boggs & C -73 Cavalier Blvd -Ste 316
-Florence, KY 41042
(614) 224-9223 ..**Ward Kaps Bainbridge Maurer & Melvin** -199 S 5th
-Columbus 43215
(614) 466-1540 ..**Ward**, Leora A '83 Supreme Ct of OH -30 E Broad -2nd Fl
-Columbus 43215
(614) 466-4320 ..**Ward**, Lucas C '03 Atty Gen -150 E Gay -Columbus 43215
(419) 372-2378 ..**Ward**, Lynn M '70 Bowling Green State Univ -Dept of Leg Studies
-Bowling Green 43403
(513) 248-0317 ..**Ward**, Marcia A '78 -741 Milford Hills Dr -Milford 45150
(614) 224-9223 ..**Ward**, Paul F '39 Ward KBM&M -199 S 5th -Columbus 43215
(216) 687-1311 ..**Ward**, Paul Michael '75 (Reminger & R) -101 Prospect Av W
-1400 Mdlnd Bldg -Cleveland 44115 **Fx:**687-1841
(216) 621-6060 ..**Ward**, Rebecca E '04 Forest City Enterprises,Inc -50 Pub Sq
-1360 Trmnl Twr -Cleveland 44113
(513) 621-8210 ..**Ward**, Richard G '86 (Drew & W Co,LPA) -1 W 4th -Ste 2400
-Cincinnati 45202 **Fx:**621-5444
(513) 621-8210 ..**Ward**, Richard H '49 (Drew & W Co,LPA) -1 W 4th -Ste 2400
-Cincinnati 45202 **Fx:**621-5444
Ward, Robert E '75 -21010 Mastick Rd -Cleveland 44126
(937) 328-2574 ..**Ward**, Roger A '95 Clark Cnty Pros -50 E Columbia -Bx1608
-Springfield 45501
(937) 264-5116 ..**Ward**, Steven H '79 Industrial Commssn of OH -3401 Park Ctr Dr
-Ste 300 -Dayton 45414
(440) 329-5239 ..**Ward**, Susan L '92 Lorain Cnty Dom Rltns Ct -226 Middle Av
-5th Fl -Elyria 44035
(216) 830-6830 ..**Ward**, Theodore D '71 OfCnsl Brouse M -1001 Lakeside Av
-Ste 1600 -Cleveland 44114 **Fx:**830-6807
(614) 356-5000 ..**Ward**, Thomas A II '96 Cnsl Dominion Homes
-5000 Tuttle Xing Blvd -Bx5000 -Dublin 43016
(513) 381-2838 ..**Ward**, Tracy T '99 %Taft S&H LLP -425 Walnut -Ste 1800
-Cincinnati 45202 **Fx:**381-0205
(216) 696-5580 ..**Ward**, Vicki L '83 -815 Superior Bldg -Ste 1725 -Cleveland 44114
(937) 254-2600 ..**Warden & Driscoll LLP** -732 Watervliet Av -Dayton 45420
(937) 254-2600 ..**Warden**, Joseph K '89 (Warden & D LLP) -732 Watervliet Av
-Dayton 45420
(330) 490-4746 ..**Warder**, Gregory S '01 Diebold Inc -5995 Mayfair Rd
-North Canton 44720
(208) 344-6000 ..**Wardle**, Geoffrey M '96 %Howley TE&H LLP -877 Main -Ste 1000
-Bx1617 -Boise, ID 83702 **Fx:**342-3829
(513) 867-3514 ..**Ware**, Beth-Anne '93 OH Casualty Ins -Bx296 -Hamilton 45012
(414) 905-0111 ..**Ware**, Christopher E '95 Greater Milwaukee Comm
-301 W Wscnsn -Milwaukee, WI 53202
(614) 466-2752 ..**Ware**, John P '93 Brd of Proprietory Sch Reg -35 E Gay -Ste 403
-Columbus 43215
(937) 294-4100 ..**Ware**, Mark F '50 -451 Twrview Rd -Dayton 45429
(513) 541-0287 ..**Ware**, Nancy E '83 -1538 Cedar Av -Cincinnati 45224
(216) 621-0200 ..**Ware**, Nathan F '00 %Baker & H LLP -1900 E 9th -Ste 3200
-Cleveland 44114 **Fx:**696-0740
(216) 566-5783 ..**Ware**, Robert F Jr. '91 (Thompson H LLP) -127 Pub Sq
-3900 Key Ctr -Cleveland 44114 **Fx:**566-5800
Ware, Zachariah Vincent '03 -(Address Unavailable)
(216) 861-3086 ..**Wargo**, Andrew M '92 (Reid M&W) -55 Pub Sq -Ste 2010
-Cleveland 44113 **Fx:**861-4409
(440) 234-0662 ..**Wargo**, John J Jr. '75 (Wargo & W Co,LPA) -Bx332 -Berea 44017
Fx:234-4179
(216) 696-1422 ..**Wargo**, Leslie Erin '00 %McCarthy LC&L Co,LPA
-101 Prospect Av W -1800 Mdlnd Bldg -Cleveland 44115
Fx:696-1210
(419) 732-1041 ..**Wargo**, Louis P III '81 -122 N Adams -Port Clinton 43452
(614) 752-6417 ..**Warheit**, Melissa A '79 Atty Gen -30 E Broad -Columbus 43215
Fx:466-0013
(440) 930-4001 ..**Warhola**, Andrew J Sr. '51 OfCnsl Baumgartner & O
-5455 Detroit Rd (Rte 254) -Sheffield Village 44054 **Fx:**934-7205
(740) 439-7711 ..**Warhola**, Andrew J Jr. '79 -110 N 7th -Cambridge 43725
(330) 497-0700 ..**Warkall**, Michael A '94 (Krugliak WG&D Co,LPA)
-4775 Munson NW -Bx36963 -Canton 44735 **Fx:**497-4020
(937) 865-6800 ..**Warling**, Robin L '96 Lexis/Nexis -Bx933 -Dayton 45401
(440) 392-2737 ..**Warmeling**, Jonathan R '94 -Bx1011 -Fairport Harbor 44077
(513) 381-2838 ..**Warncke**, Daniel R '93 (Taft S&H LLP) -425 Walnut -Ste 1800
-Cincinnati 45202 **Fx:**381-0205
(419) 782-6055 ..**Warncke**, Marc F '89 (Clemens KL&W,Ltd) -419 5th -Ste 2000
-Bx787 -Defiance 43512
(216) 443-7223 ..**Warner**, Carlos '97 Cuyahoga Cnty Pub Def -1200 W 3rd NW
-100 Lakeside Pl -Cleveland 44113
(614) 227-2000 ..**Warner**, Charles C '70 (Porter WM&A LLP) -41 S High
-Columbus 43215 **Fx:**227-2100
(216) 822-3262 ..**Warner**, Cynthia A '01 SBC Inc -45 Erievw Plz -1405
-Cleveland 44114
(513) 579-9700 ..**Warner**, David L '98 Hunt Devlpmnt Corp -221 E 4th -Ste 2310
-Cincinnati 45202
(216) 371-2210 ..**Warner**, Deborah P '85 -2596 Fairmount Blvd -Cleveland 44106
(216) 931-6000 ..**Warner**, Jane F '02 %Ulmer & B LLP -1300 E 9th
-Ste 900 Penton Media Bldg -Cleveland 44114 **Fx:**931-6001
(740) 382-1121 ..**Warner**, Jason D '96 -284 S State -Bx531 -Marion 43301
(216) 486-2598 ..**Warner**, John L '59 -857 Leader Bldg -526 Superior Av E
-Cleveland 44114
(919) 821-6617 ..**Warner**, Kirk G '83 (Smith ABDM&J LLP) -Bx2611
-Raleigh, NC 27602
(740) 992-2186 ..**Warner**, Linda Rae '88 (Little S&W,LLP) -211-213 E 2nd -Bx686
-Pomeroy 45769 **Fx:**992-5168
(614) 229-3888 ..**Warner**, Matthew D '02 Cheek & Z,LLP -471 E Broad -18th Fl
-Bx15069 -Columbus 43215 **Fx:**241-5865
(614) 224-6000 ..**Warner**, Patrick G '95 DP Meyer Co,LPA -401 N Front -Ste 350
-Columbus 43215 **Fx:**224-6066
(216) 687-1311 ..**Warner**, Robert D '79 (Reminger & R) -101 Prospect Av W
-1400 Mdlnd Bldg -Cleveland 44115 **Fx:**687-1841

(614) 237-1221 .. **Warner**, Robert S '80 (R Warner & Co) -4389 Intl Gtwy -Ste 225 -Columbus 43219 Fx:235-5583

(614) 221-3821 .. **Warner**, Roger '81 (Wallace & W Co,LPA) -171 E Lvngstn Av -Columbus 43215 Fx:221-6753

(330) 674-3055 .. **Warner**, Sean M '02 %Critchfield C&J Ltd -138 E Jackson -Ste A -Millersburg 44654

(614) 221-5375 .. **Warner**, Sheryl D '96 Ohio Trucking Assoc -50 W Broad -Ste 1111 -Columbus 43215

(614) 466-5610 .. **Warner**, Stephanie L '00 Atty Gen -150 E Gay -Columbus 43215 Fx:752-2732

(216) 696-4700 .. **Warner**, Timothy G '93 (Spieth BM&N Co,LPA) -925 Euclid Av -2000 Huntngtn Bldg -Cleveland 44115 Fx:696-2706

(740) 363-3100 .. **Warnock**, Douglas W '78 (DW Warnock Co,LPA) -20 E Central Av -Delaware 43015

(513) 621-2825 .. **Warnock**, Frank E '88 (Brown & W) -1014 Vine -2550 Kroger Bldg -Cincinnati 45202

(216) 443-7800 .. **Warr**, Rufus L '72 Cuyahoga Cnty Pros -1200 Ontario -8th Fl -Cleveland 44113 Fx:698-2270

(419) 422-8713 .. **Warren**, Bradley S '95 (Oxley MHO&W,PLL) -301 E Main Cross -Bx1086 -Findlay 45840 Fx:422-6495

(740) 592-3206 .. **Warren**, Charles David '80 Athens Cnty Pros -Athens Cnty Cthse -Athens 45701 Fx:592-3291

(216) 621-0200 .. **Warren**, Daniel R '91 (Baker & H LLP) -1900 E 9th -Ste 3200 -Cleveland 44114 Fx:696-0740

(513) 621-6464 .. **Warren**, David S '89 (Graydon H&R LLP) -511 Walnut -1900 Fifth Third Ctr -Cincinnati 45202 Fx:651-3836

(440) 998-3039 .. **Warren**, E Terry '56 -Bx1420 -Ashtabula 44005

(440) 933-8282 .. **Warren**, James K '89 BIS Holdings -445 Avon Belden Rd -Ste B-1 -Avon Lake 44012

(937) 323-1131 .. **Warren**, James R '59 -4 W Main -934 BancOhio Bldg -Springfield 45502

(614) 766-1960 .. **Warren**, Jeffrey S '99 K Warren -5134 Blazer Pkwy -Dublin 43017

(614) 766-1960 .. **Warren**, Kenneth J '77 K Warren -5134 Blazer Pkwy -Dublin 43017

(405) 218-4735 .. **Warren**, Kimberly D '98 Cole & Reed PC -531 Couch Dr -Ste 200 -Oklahoma City, OK 73102

(845) 564-6700 .. **Warren**, Marvin Taylor '82 -Bx7009 -Newburgh, NY 12550

(513) 421-4428 .. **Warren**, Michael W '02 -602 Main -Ste 1010 -Cincinnati 45202

(216) 378-1579 .. **Warren**, Richard L Jr. '96 %J Henck & Assoc Co,LPA -23240 Chagrin Blvd -Ste 535 -Beachwood 44122

(216) 781-5515 .. **Warren**, Robert Jr. '74 (Hermann C&S,LLP) -1301 E 9th -Ste 500 -Cleveland 44114 Fx:781-1030

(216) 621-0200 .. **Warren**, Thomas D '04 (Baker & H LLP) -1900 E 9th -Ste 3200 -Cleveland 44114 Fx:696-0740

(216) 416-3275 .. **Warren**, William M '52 Forest City Enterprises,Inc -50 Pub Sq -Ste 1160 -Cleveland 44113

(440) 997-6175 .. **Warren & Young,PLL** -134 W 46th -Bx2300 -Ashtabula 44005 Fx:992-9114

(419) 824-0241 .. **Warrick**, Bert J '64 -Bx236 -Sylvania 43560

(614) 436-5880 .. **Warrick**, Glenn S '96 Allied Emplyr Rsrces -222 E Campus Vw Blvd -Columbus 43235

        Warrington, Mary G '88 -3433 Berry Av -Cincinnati 45208

(216) 368-0339 .. **Warshawsky**, Kittie D '95 Case Western Reserve -10900 Euclid Av -Schl of Medicine -Cleveland 44106

(216) 443-6350 .. **Warshawsky**, Laura K '96 8th Dist Ct of Appls -1 Lakeside Av -#202 -Cleveland 44113 Fx:443-2044

(330) 830-1718 .. **Warstler**, Keith A Jr. '00 Massillon Law Dept -2 James Duncan Plz -Massillon 44646 Fx:833-7144

(937) 223-8177 .. **Warwar**, Sam '81 (Coolidge WW&L) -33 W 1st -Ste 600 -Dayton 45402 Fx:223-6705

        Warwick, Chad C '72 -1701 Wexwood Ln -Cincinnati 45255

(513) 272-1200 .. **Wasco**, Heather H '01 %Doan K&B,LLC -5710 Wooster Pike -Ste 212 -Cincinnati 45227

(330) 453-8261 .. **Washam**, Scott A '87 Okey Law Firm,LPA -337 3rd NW -Canton 44702

(614) 461-4455 .. **Washburn**, Robert L Jr. '77 (Cloppert LS&W) -225 E Broad -Columbus 43215 Fx:461-0072

(614) 223-9300 .. **Washbush**, Thomas C '91 (Benesch FC&A LLP) -88 E Broad -Ste 900 -Columbus 43215 Fx:223-9330

(937) 222-2841 .. **Washington**, Cheryl R '87 (Jones & W Co,LPA) -118 W 1st -1308 Talbot Twr -Dayton 45402

(937) 496-1450 .. **Washington**, Dwight A '77 -4 S Main -1200 Wright Stop Plz -Dayton 45402 Fx:496-1453

(614) 221-2400 .. **Washington**, Gloria B '91 -233 S High -Ste 300 -Columbus 43215

        Washington, Joe '94 -(Address Unavailable)

(740) 942-2621 .. **Washington**, Michael B '01 Harrison Cnty Pros -111 W Warren -Bx248 -Cadiz 43907

(513) 946-9000 .. **Washington**, Scheherazade '91 Hamilton Cnty Juv Ct -800 Bway -Cincinnati 45202 Fx:946-9217

(216) 586-3939 .. **Washington**, Stephen L '98 %Jones D -901 Lakeside Av -Cleveland 44114 Fx:579-0212

        Washington, Tracy A '95 -(Address Unavailable)

(513) 723-4000 .. **Washington**, Ward B '03 %Vorys SS&P LLP -221 E 4th -Ste 2000 Atrium Two -Bx0236 -Cincinnati 45201 Fx:723-4056

(419) 243-6148 .. **Wasielewski**, Glenn E '82 Manahan PB&D -414 N Erie -Bx2328 -Toledo 43603

(216) 621-7499 .. **Wasil**, Jo Ann F '79 -75 Pub Square -Ste 1230 -Cleveland 44113

(440) 963-1165 .. **Wasilk**, Neil J '82 -643 Greenlawn -Amherst 44001

(937) 224-8763 .. **Waskowiak**, Amy M '99 %Hon J Froelich -41 N Perry -Cmmn Pleas Ct -Dayton 45422

(704) 444-1000 .. **Wasleff**, John A '88 Cnsl Alston & B,LLP -101 S Tryon -Ste 4000 -Charlotte, NC 28280

(973) 228-9900 .. **Wason**, Patricia M '83 %Post PGM&S,PA -425 Eagle Rck Av #200 -Roseland, NJ 07068 Fx:994-1705

(814) 459-2800 .. **Wassell**, Mark T '84 Knox MG&S -120 W 10th -Erie, PA 16501

(419) 243-1239 .. **Wasserman Bryan Landry & Honold,LLP** -405 N Huron -Ste 300 -Toledo 43604

(216) 367-7744 .. **Wasserman**, Eric '70 (Babcock & W Co,LPA) -55 Pub Sq -Ste 700 -Cleveland 44113

(419) 243-1239 .. **Wasserman**, John C '64 (Wasserman BL&H,LLP) -405 N Huron -Ste 300 -Toledo 43604

(513) 723-1600 .. **Wasserman**, Mark J '84 OfCnsl Mezibov & J -1726 Young -Cincinnati 45202

(216) 524-5700 .. **Wasserman**, Robert '76 Cnsl Old Republic Natl Title -6480 Rockside Wds Blvd S -Ste 290 -Independence 44131 Fx:524-2700

(216) 737-5000 .. **Wasserman**, Steven L '78 (Chernett WY&P) -1301 E 9th -Ste 3300 -Cleveland 44114 Fx:737-0011

(614) 237-0420 .. **Wasserman**, Susan S '77 -735 Euclaire Av -Bexley 43209

(513) 631-3724 .. **Wassermann**, Frank J '75 -6213 Robison Rd -Cincinnati 45213

(216) 831-8840 .. **Wasserstrom**, Sanford '51 -24200 Chagrin Blvd -Rm 237 -Beachwood 44122

(614) 789-5921 .. **Wasson**, Christopher E '97 CareWorks -5555 Glendon Ct -Bx182726 -Columbus 43218

(419) 243-4006 .. **Wasung**, John S '91 (Kitch DWD&V,PC) -405 Mad Av -Ste 1500 -Toledo 43604 Fx:243-7333

(937) 443-6812 .. **Wasylyna**, Victor J '03 %Thompson H LLP -2000 Cthse Plz NE -Bx8801 -Dayton 45401 Fx:443-6635

(330) 376-3300 .. **Waszak**, Ralph R Jr. '93 %Stark & K Co,LPA -76 S Main -Ste 1512 -Akron 44308 Fx:376-6237

(614) 228-8400 .. **Watchorn**, Christine E '03 %Ulmer & B LLP -88 E Broad -Ste 1600 -Columbus 43215 Fx:228-8561

(614) 462-5200 .. **Waterfield**, Melissa A '00 Franklin Cnty CSEA -80 E Fulton -Columbus 43215

(608) 265-2973 .. **Waterfield**, Steven C '97 Univ of Wisconsin -1440 Monroe -Madison, WI 53711

(216) 241-2838 .. **Waterhouse**, Bruce L Jr. '88 (Taft S&H LLP) -200 Pub Sq -3500 BP Twr -Cleveland 44114 Fx:241-3707

(614) 227-2378 .. **Waterman**, Charles H III '77 (Bricker & E LLP) -100 S 3rd -Columbus 43215 Fx:227-2390

(614) 224-5205 .. **Waterman**, Charles H IV '01 %Peck S&W,LLP -175 S 3rd -Ste 600 -Columbus 43215 Fx:224-0069

(419) 241-9000 .. **Waterman**, David F '79 (Shumaker L&K,LLP) -1000 Jackson -Toledo 43624 Fx:241-6894

(740) 947-7605 .. **Waterman**, Deborah A '81 Rhoads Law Ofc -305 N Market -Waverly 45690

(614) 466-6696 .. **Waterman**, Gerald H '74 Atty Gen -150 E Gay -Columbus 43215 Fx:752-2538

(614) 898-2696 .. **Waterman**, Joseph '59 (J Waterman,Inc) -Bx20425 -Columbus 43220

(614) 798-1321 .. **Waterman**, Ronald L '01 Champaign Natl Bank -5100 Parkcenter Av -Dublin 43017

(216) 861-5582 .. **Waters**, Joseph E '00 %Fay SFM&M LLP -1100 Superior Av -7th Fl -Cleveland 44114 Fx:241-1666

(513) 946-3000 .. **Waters**, Mark G '84 Hamilton Cnty Pros -230 E 9th -Cincinnati 45202 Fx:946-3017

(216) 443-7800 .. **Waters**, Matthew T '02 Cuyahoga Cnty Pros -1200 Ontario -8th Fl -Cleveland 44113 Fx:698-2270

(614) 523-7575 .. **Watkins**, Alison A '93 (Fusco MMS&W,LLP) -655 Cooper Rd -Westerville 43081 Fx:523-7580

(419) 241-2100 .. **Watkins Bates & Carey** -405 Mad Av -Ste 1900 -Toledo 43604 Fx:241-1960

(513) 932-2871 .. **Watkins**, Christopher A '83 %Gray & D -4 S Bway -Bx268 -Lebanon 45036

(614) 228-4546 .. **Watkins**, David '92 %Shuler P&B,LPA -145 E Rich -Ste 400 -Columbus 43215

(937) 593-6065 .. **Watkins**, David R '76 (Thompson DHMW&T) -1111 Rush Av -Bx68 -Bellefontaine 43311

(330) 262-3030 .. **Watkins**, Deborah C '02 Wayne Cnty Pros -115 W Lbrty -Wooster 44691 Fx:287-5412

(330) 675-2426 .. **Watkins**, Dennis '73 (Trumbull Cnty Pros) -160 High NW -Warren 44481

        Watkins, Elizabeth G '03 -(Address Unavailable)

(419) 673-9424 .. **Watkins**, Elizabeth M '87 Watkins Farm -9800 TR 179 -Kenton 43326

(513) 946-9000 .. **Watkins**, Katherine H '85 Hamilton Cnty Juv Ct -800 Bway -Cincinnati 45202 Fx:946-9217

(419) 241-4400 .. **Watkins**, Keith J '81 (Munger W Co,LPA) -626 Mad Av -Ste 400 -Toledo 43604

        Watkins, Linda K '90 -2303 Buckland Av -Fremont 43420

(330) 864-5550 .. **Watkins**, Mark A '88 (Hahn L&P LLP) -One GOJO Plz -Ste 300 -Akron 44311 Fx:864-7986

        Watkins, Richard D '94 -1549 Hibbard Dr -Stow 44224

(330) 686-8844 .. **Watkins**, Thomas W '92 -2515 Rvr Downs -Stow 44224

(440) 944-3660 .. **Watling**, Justin J '80 Justin J Watling Co -2778 SOM Center Rd -2nd Fl -Willoughby Hills 44094

(937) 223-6003 .. **Watring**, Stephen A '81 (Dunlevey M&F) -110 N Main -Ste 1000 -Dayton 45402 Fx:223-8550

(641) 787-8238 ..**Watson**, Bruce P '97 SrCnsl Maytag Corp -403 W 4th N -Bx39 -Newton, IA 50208 Fx:787-8170

(216) 991-4377 .. **Watson**, Caroline '03 -13610 Shaker Blvd -#703 -Cleveland 44120

(216) 522-7455 .. **Watson**, Charles L '73 EEOC -1660 W 2nd -Ste 850 -Cleveland 44113

(513) 651-6800 .. **Watson**, Clint C '04 %Frost BT LLC -201 E 5th -2200 PNC Ctr -Cincinnati 45202 Fx:651-6981

(216) 595-0944 .. **Watson**, Daniel J '03 -23220 Chagrin Blvd -#360 -Beachwood 44122 Fx:595-1350

(614) 444-3036 .. **Watson**, David C Jr. '85 Saia & P,PLL -713 S Front -Columbus 43206

(216) 348-5400 .. **Watson**, David D '94 (McDonald H Co,LPA) -600 Superior Av E -Ste 2100 -Cleveland 44114 Fx:348-5474

(312) 781-2000 .. **Watson**, David R '92 Commercial Law League of Amer -70 E Lake -Ste 630 -Chicago, IL 60601 Fx:781-2010

(440) 449-3555 .. **Watson**, David S '89 Watson Power Equip Co -6151 Wilson Mills Rd -Ste 304 -Highland Heights 44143

(412) 553-6300 .. **Watson**, Dennis A '94 (Grogan G,PC) -4 Gtwy Ctr -12th Fl -Pittsburgh, PA 15222

(330) 468-3990 .. **Watson**, James C '83 -61 W Aurora Rd -Northfield 44067

(614) 443-1221 .. **Watson**, James E '88 -1111 Parsons Av -Columbus 43206

(330) 672-2982 .. **Watson**, James R '83 Kent State Univ-Exec Ofcs -2nd Fl Library -Bx5190 -Kent 44242

(216) 241-2262 .. **Watson**, Jeffery S '91 %Yulish T & Assoc -1419 W 9th -Hilliard Bldg -Cleveland 44113

(419) 247-1687 .. **Watson**, Laurie A '02 %Eastman & S Ltd -1 Seagate -24th Fl -Bx10032 -Toledo 43699 Fx:247-1777

(740) 452-8484 .. **Watson**, Mark A '83 (Stubbins W&E Co LPA) -59 N 4th -Bx488 -Zanesville 43702

(216) 523-1100 ..**Watson**, Myron P '92 (Willis W&G) -113 St Clair Av -Ste 440
-Cleveland 44114

(330) 451-7897 ..**Watson**, Renee M '00 Stark Cnty Pros -110 Central Plz -Ste 510
-Canton 44702

(216) 696-4700 ..**Watson**, Richard T '60 (Spieth BM&N Co,LPA) -925 Euclid Av
-2000 Huntngtn Bldg -Cleveland 44115 **Fx:**696-2706

(740) 732-5685 ..**Watson**, Robert B '89 Noble Cnty Pros -409 Poplar -Ste A
-Caldwell 43724

(614) 486-8827 ..**Watson**, Robert T '87 Cmmrcl Prop Grp -1635 W 1st Av -Ste 130
-Columbus 43212

(216) 522-4070 ..**Watson**, Scott M '81 US DOJ/Antitrust Div -55 Erievw Plz -Ste 700
-Cleveland 44114

(614) 644-7233 ..**Watson**, Stephanie L '94 Atty Gen -150 E Gay -Columbus 43215
Fx:728-9327

(406) 523-1150 ..**Watson**, Stephen A III '83 Cnsl Envirocon,Inc -101 Intl Way
-Missoula, MT 59808 **Fx:**543-7987

(614) 461-4455 ..**Watson**, Sue A '97 %Cloppert L&W -225 E Broad
-Columbus 43215 **Fx:**461-0072

(614) 563-2343 ..**Watson**, Yvonne M '01 Watson & Assoc,LLC -Bx297
-Marysville 43040

(614) 464-6400 ..**Watt**, Kristin L '89 (Vorys SS&P LLP) -52 E Gay -Bx1008
-Columbus 43216 **Fx:**464-6350

Watt, Y Evette '98 -1908 Prospect Av -Norfolk, NE 68701

(614) 221-4000 ..**Watters**, Elizabeth J '91 (Chester W&S LLP) -65 E State -10th Fl
-Columbus 43215 **Fx:**221-4012

(513) 723-1121 ..**Watters**, Mark M '82 DuCharme McMillen & Assoc -312 Plum
-Ste 1100 -Cincinnati 45202

(216) 241-6700 ..**Watterson**, James G '65 OfCnsl Watts H Co,LPA
-1100 Superior Av E -Ste 1750 Diamond Bldg -Cleveland 44114
Fx:241-8151

(202) 942-2785 ..**Watterson**, Sean A '01 US SEC -450 5th NW
-Washington, DC 20009

(330) 456-2262 ..**Watterson**, Tim M '82 -111 2nd NW -Ste 300 -Canton 44702

(216) 579-2174 ..**Watts**, Andrew W '75 Fed Reserve Bk of Cleveland -1455 E 6th
-Bx6387 -Cleveland 44101

(513) 347-4407 ..**Watts**, Angela D '02 Joseph Transportation Inc -300 Pike
-Cincinnati 45202

(513) 556-6805 ..**Watts**, Barbara G '78 Univ of Cincinnati -2855 McFarlan Park Dr
-Cincinnati 45211

(216) 241-6700 ..**Watts Hoffmann Co, LPA** -1100 Superior Av E
-Ste 1750 Diamond Bldg -Cleveland 44114 **Fx:**241-8151

(415) 972-8395 ..**Watts**, Katherine L '81 Delta Dental Plan of CA -100 1st
-San Francisco, CA 94105

(216) 771-5511 ..**Watts**, Patrick M '02 (Reeve & W) -75 Pub Sq -Ste 1300
-Cleveland 44113

(937) 449-2800 ..**Watts**, Steven R '81 (Chernesky H&K PLL) -10 Cthse Plz SW
-Ste 1100 -Dayton 45402 **Fx:**449-2821

(513) 241-9400 ..**Watts**, Susan E '85 Legal Aid -215 E 9th -Ste 200
-Cincinnati 45202

(614) 464-6400 ..**Watts**, Tamara J '02 %Vorys SS&P LLP -52 E Gay -Bx1008
-Columbus 43216 **Fx:**464-6350

(419) 843-1333 ..**Waugh**, Bradley R '99 %Malone A&F -7654 W Bancroft
-Toledo 43617 **Fx:**843-3888

(419) 668-2067 ..**Waugh**, Frederick F '63 -13 E Main -Ste B -Norwalk 44857

(513) 627-7386 ..**Waugh**, Kevin L '01 Procter & Gamble -5299 Spring Grove Av
-Cincinnati 45217

(614) 464-6400 ..**Wautier**, Nathan J '03 %Vorys SS&P LLP -52 E Gay -Bx1008
-Columbus 43216 **Fx:**464-6350

(937) 229-2326 ..**Wawrose**, Susan C '95 Univ of Dayton Schl of Law -300 Cllg Park
-Dayton 45469

(419) 535-4200 ..**Wawrzyniak**, Jeffery J '93 Dana Corp -Bx1000 -Toledo 43697

(216) 514-9400 ..**Waxman**, David B '86 (Waxman B LLC) -29225 Chagrin Blvd
-Ste 350 -Cleveland 44122

(859) 344-9980 ..**Wayman**, Francine A '87 F Wayman PSC -2734 Chancellor Dr
-Ste 213 -Crestview Hills, KY 41017

(614) 764-1444 ..**Wayman**, Merl H '83 Mowery & Y -425 Metro Pl N -Ste 420
-Dublin 43017 **Fx:**760-8654

(937) 496-6616 ..**Waymire**, William D II '95 2nd Dist Ct of Appls -41 N Perry
-Rm 515 -Bx972 -Dayton 45422

(513) 621-2120 ..**Wayne**, Richard S '79 (Strauss & T,LPA) -150 E 4th -4th Fl
-Cincinnati 45202 **Fx:**241-8259

(216) 621-5300 ..**Wayne**, Ronald F '78 (Buckingham D&B,LLP) -1375 E 9th
-Ste 1700 -Cleveland 44114 **Fx:**621-5440

(937) 372-4436 ..**Wead Anderson Phipps & Aultman** -53 W Main -BxH
-Xenia 45385

(419) 562-6237 ..**Wead**, Edward R '66 -107 E Mansfld -Bucyrus 44820

(740) 335-8221 ..**Wead**, John H '76 -226 E Market -Bx606
-Washington Court House 43160

(937) 372-4436 ..**Wead**, Richard A '67 (Wead AP&A) -53 W Main -BxH
-Xenia 45385

(614) 462-3580 ..**Weakley**, Kyle D '03 10th Dist Ct of Appeals -373 S High -24th Fl
-Columbus 43215

(513) 381-9200 ..**Weakley**, Leonard A Jr. '77 (Rendigs FK&D,LLP) -One W 4th
-Ste 900 -Cincinnati 45202 **Fx:**381-9206

(937) 335-0550 ..**Weaks**, Gary L '70 Huffman L&W Co,LPA -80 S Plum -Troy 45373

(513) 425-6609 ..**Wean**, Sophie S '93 12th Dist Ct of Appls -1001 Reinartz Blvd
-Middletown 45042 **Fx:**425-8751

(419) 782-3010 ..**Weaner**, James K '96 %Weaner ZBY&H,Ltd -401 Wayne Av
-Defiance 43512 **Fx:**782-8426

(419) 782-3010 ..**Weaner**, John W '64 (Weaner ZBY&H,Ltd) -401 Wayne Av
-Defiance 43512 **Fx:**782-8426

(419) 782-3010 ..**Weaner Zimmerman Bacon Yoder & Hubbard,Ltd**
-401 Wayne Av -Defiance 43512 **Fx:**782-8426

(513) 829-0300 ..**Wear**, Maxwell N '67 -5145 Plsnt Av -Bx218 -Fairfield 45018

(330) 376-3300 ..**Wear**, Michael L '95 (Stark & K Co,LPA) -76 S Main -Ste 1512
-Akron 44308 **Fx:**376-6237

(216) 621-0200 ..**Wearsch**, Thomas M '04 %Baker & H LLP -1900 E 9th -Ste 3200
-Cleveland 44114 **Fx:**696-0740

(419) 423-5700 ..**Weasel**, Charles W '76 -2011 Old Mill Rd -Findlay 45840

Weaston, Daniel Q '80 -1814 Old Shay Ct -Columbus 43229

(216) 443-8430 ..**Weatherford**, Chris '97 Juvenile Court -2163 E 22nd
-Cleveland 44115

(216) 443-8859 ..**Weatherhead**, Ann '82 Cuyahoga Cnty Cmn Pleas Ct
-1 Lakeside Av -# 303 -Cleveland 44113

(216) 696-0900 ..**Weatherly**, Justin M '04 %Zukerman D&L,LPA -2000 E 9th
-Ste 700 -Cleveland 44115 **Fx:**696-8800

(614) 236-6531 ..**Weatherspoon**, Floyd D '85 Capital Univ -303 E Broad
-Columbus 43215

(330) 342-5515 ..**Weaver**, Benjamin Wayne '04 -6420 Wooded Vw Dr
-Hudson 44236

(937) 225-4652 ..**Weaver**, Brian D '69 Montgomery Cnty Pub Def -117 S Main
-Ste 400 -Dayton 45422 **Fx:**225-3449

(216) 575-1313 ..**Weaver**, Clark B '66 (CB Weaver Co,LPA) -55 Pub Square -#1310
-Cleveland 44113

(937) 324-5541 ..**Weaver**, David A '72 (Martin BH&H) -1 S Limestone -Ste 800
-Bx1488 -Springfield 45501 **Fx:**325-5432

(614) 466-4605 ..**Weaver**, Diane M '77 OH Dept Job & Fam Srvcs -30 E Broad
-32nd Fl -Columbus 43266

(419) 535-7221 ..**Weaver**, Donna M '82 -1022 Shadow Ln -Toledo 43615

(440) 942-6262 ..**Weaver**, Geoffrey W '91 (Wiles & R) -35350 Curtis Blvd -Ste 530
-Eastlake 44095 **Fx:**942-7211

(574) 329-1848 ..**Weaver**, Heath O '98 -1701 E Wayne -South Bend, IN 46615

(248) 901-4061 ..**Weaver**, Jeanna M '02 %Plunkett & C,PC -38505 Woodward Av
-Ste 2000 -Bloomfield Hills, MI 48304 **Fx:**901-4040

(440) 546-0778 ..**Weaver**, Jeannette M '88 -4320 E Sprague Rd
-Broadview Heights 44147

(919) 755-8163 ..**Weaver**, Kurt D '87 (Womble CS&R,PLLC) -150 Fayettevll St Mall
-Suite 2100 -Raleigh, NC 27602 **Fx:**755-2150

(614) 221-2121 ..**Weaver**, Mark R '95 OfCnsl Isaac BL&T,LLP -250 E Broad
-Ste 900 Mdlnd Bldg -Columbus 43215 **Fx:**365-9516

(216) 781-4994 ..**Weaver**, Philip J Jr. '74 (Smith MW&V) -1965 E 6th
-500 Natl City-E 6th Bldg -Cleveland 44114 **Fx:**781-9448

(216) 566-3940 ..**Weaver**, Richard M '82 Sherwin-Williams Co -101 Prospect Av NW
-Cleveland 44115

(216) 479-8500 ..**Weaver**, Robin G '74 (Squire S&D LLP) -127 Pub Sq
-4900 Key Twr -Cleveland 44114 **Fx:**479-8780

(614) 834-1750 ..**Weaver**, Roger L '88 -3 S High -Canal Winchester 43110

(513) 304-5410 ..**Weaver**, Rosiene H '89 -334 Ridgeway Rd -Cincinnati 45215

(614) 224-5811 ..**Weaver**, Ruthellen Q '85 -85 E Gay -Ste 612 -Columbus 43215

(419) 294-4977 ..**Weaver**, Stephanie A '92 Wyandot Cnty CSEA -120 E Johnson
-Upper Sandusky 43351

(216) 363-5220 ..**Weaver**, Susan M '80 (Lindner WC&B,LLP) -55 Pub Sq -Ste 1600
-Cleveland 44113

Webb, Audra L '01 -(Address Unavailable)

(513) 852-8565 ..**Webb**, Donald H '78 Hamilton Cnty Juv Ct -800 Bway
-Cincinnati 45202 **Fx:**946-9217

(513) 345-4160 ..**Webb**, Gail W '86 Pro Seniors,Inc -7162 Redding Rd -Ste 1150
-Cincinnati 45237

(513) 579-7920 ..**Webb**, Gary A '85 Federated Dept Stores,Inc -7 W 7th
-Cincinnati 45202

(740) 345-0417 ..**Webb**, Larry G Jr. '03 %K Burkett -21 W Church -Ste 201
-Newark 43055

(419) 882-5755 ..**Webb**, Linde Hurst '73 (Hetzer & W) -5800 Monroe -Bldg C
-Sylvania 43560

(419) 627-2087 ..**Webb**, Rush P '59 -215 E Shoreline Dr -Ste 802 -Sandusky 44870

(216) 443-3658 ..**Webb**, Therese M '93 Cuyahoga Cnty Pub Def -1200 W 3rd NW
-100 Lakeside Pl -Cleveland 44113

(419) 241-9000 ..**Webb**, Thomas I Jr. '73 (Shumaker L&K,LLP) -1000 Jackson
-Toledo 43624 **Fx:**241-6894

Webb, Valerie M '02 -3347 SR 752 -Ashville 43103

(440) 943-1200 ..**Webb**, William J '75 Lubrizol Corp -29400 Lakelnd Blvd
-Wickliffe 44092

(614) 464-6400 ..**Webb-Lawton**, Nina I '96 (Vorys SS&P LLP) -52 E Gay -Bx1008
-Columbus 43216 **Fx:**464-6350

(440) 246-1823 ..**Webber**, Barbara A '89 -761 Bway -Lorain 44052

(440) 246-1823 ..**Webber**, Henry T '62 -761 Bway -Lorain 44052

(440) 246-1823 ..**Webber**, Linda A '93 -761 Bway -Lorain 44052

(614) 224-4149 ..**Webber**, Marci L '97 C Briscoe -500 S Front -Ste 125
-Columbus 43215 **Fx:**224-0738

(216) 696-7600 ..**Webber**, Mark V '74 OfCnsl Duvin C&H -1301 E 9th
-20th Fl Erievw Twr -Cleveland 44114 **Fx:**696-2038

(216) 479-6100 ..**Webbs**, Jerome C '80 Vorys SS&P LLP -1375 E 9th
-Ste 2100 One Cleve Ctr -Cleveland 44114 **Fx:**479-6060

(513) 852-6000 ..**Weber**, Arthur D Jr. '73 (Wood & L LLP) -600 Vine -Ste 2500
-Cincinnati 45202 **Fx:**852-6087

(513) 721-5672 ..**Weber**, Bradford C '97 %Benjamin Y&H LLC -312 Elm -Ste 1850
-Cincinnati 45202 **Fx:**562-4388

(614) 462-5415 ..**Weber**, Christopher J '92 (Kegler BH&R) -65 E State -Ste 1800
-Columbus 43215 **Fx:**464-2634

(513) 621-2260 ..**Weber Dickey & Bellman** -813 Bway -1st Fl -Cincinnati 45202

(513) 621-2260 ..**Weber**, Donald L '61 (Weber D&B) -813 Bway -1st Fl
-Cincinnati 45202

(330) 761-4205 ..**Weber**, Douglas J '88 FirstEnergy Corp -76 S Main -18th Fl -Akron
44308

(330) 535-6185 ..**Weber**, Edward C '72 -159 S Main -Ste 1108 -Akron 44308

(513) 763-7124 ..**Weber**, Edward P III '98 Mitsui Marine Mgmt USA\GABMI
-49 E 4th -Ste 500 -Bx5435 -Cincinnati 45201

(330) 221-8157 ..**Weber**, Edward P Jr. '68 -656 Fairfld Ln -Bx555 -Aurora 44202
Fx:562-1737

(859) 341-1881 ..**Weber**, Elizabeth G '85 %Deters B&L,PSC -2701 Turkeyfoot Rd
-207 Thomas More Pkwy -Crestview Hills, KY 41017 **Fx:**341-1469

(419) 245-1895 ..**Weber**, Ford P '87 City of Toledo Public Utilities Authority
-420 Mad Av -#100 -Toledo 43604

(859) 344-8826 ..**Weber**, Gregory L '83 -663 Triple Lk Dr -Crescent Springs, KY
41017

(513) 721-2120 ..**Weber**, Harry P '74 Barrett & W -105 E 4th -Ste 500
-Cincinnati 45202

(216) 443-9000 ..**Weber**, Jeffrey J '93 %Porter WM&A LLP -925 Euclid Av -Ste 1700
-Cleveland 44115 **Fx:**443-9011

(937) 225-4863 ..**Weber**, Jennifer M '02 Montgomery Cnty Pros -303 W 2nd
-Rm 113 -Dayton 45402

(703) 428-1881 ..**Weber**, Jeremy S '96 US Air Force -6350 Walker Ln
-Alexandria, VA 22310

(513) 336-2545 ..**Weber**, Jody E '95 Cnsl Anthem BCBS -4361 Irwin Simpson Rd
-Mason 45040

Weber, John P '03 -7968 Hunters Knoll Ct -Cincinnati 45242

Weber, Joshua D '03 -161 Cameron Dr -Pataskala 43062

(513) 852-8200 .. **Weber**, Katharine C '89 Cors & B LLC -537 E Pete Rose Way
-Ste 400 -Cincinnati 45202

(330) 793-5488 .. **Weber**, Kirk D '82 OH Workers Comp -242 Fed Plz W -Ste 200
-Youngstown 44503 **Fx**:797-3225

(740) 622-3240 .. **Weber**, Linda H '95 -26700 Cnty Route 406 -Fresno 43824

(614) 227-2300 .. **Weber**, Maggie F '03 %Bricker & E LLP -100 S 3rd
-Columbus 43215 **Fx**:227-2390

(513) 579-6400 .. **Weber**, Mark J '80 (Keating M&K PLL) -1 E 4th
-1400 Provident Twr -Cincinnati 45202 **Fx**:579-6457

(330) 376-1242 .. **Weber**, Mark L '00 %Renner KGBT&W,LPA -106 S Main
-4th Fl First Natl Twr -Akron 44308 **Fx**:376-9646

(513) 684-3201 .. **Weber**, Mary H '76 IRS Chief Cnsl -312 Elm -Ste 2350
-Cincinnati 45202

(513) 621-2260 .. **Weber**, Michael L '89 Weber D&B -813 Bway -1st Fl -Cincinnati
45202

(440) 838-8800 .. **Weber**, Monica M '04 %Millisor & N Co,LPA -9150 S Hills Blvd
-Ste 300 -Cleveland 44147 **Fx**:838-8805

(614) 466-2091 .. **Weber**, Randall S '91 Industrial Commssn of OH -30 W Spring
-9th Fl -Columbus 43215 **Fx**:752-8785

(330) 376-1242 .. **Weber**, Ray L '72 Renner KGBT&W,LPA -106 S Main
-4th Fl First Natl Twr -Akron 44308 **Fx**:376-9646
Weber, Robert C '56 -(Address Unavailable)

(216) 586-3939 .. **Weber**, Robert C '76 (Jones D) -901 Lakeside Av
-Cleveland 44114 **Fx**:579-0212

(216) 771-1144 .. **Weber**, Robert M Jr. '03 %Behrens G&S Co,LPA -1360 W 9th
-Ste 400 -Cleveland 44113 **Fx**:736-7136

(513) 381-2838 .. **Weber**, Roger A '73 (Taft S&H LLP) -425 Walnut -Ste 1800
-Cincinnati 45202 **Fx**:381-0205

(740) 384-2111 .. **Weber**, Shannon S '01 %Oths H&M -16 E Bway -Bx309
-Wellston 45692

(419) 893-3360 .. **Weber & Sterling,LLC** -1721 Indn Wd Cir -Ste 1 -Maumee 43537
Fx:893-7146

(513) 946-3818 .. **Weber**, Terry A '81 Hamilton Cnty Pub Def -230 E 9th -3rd Fl
-Cincinnati 45202 **Fx**:946-3707

(614) 476-0350 .. **Weber**, Thomas L '69 -504 Havens Crnr Rd -Gahanna 43230

(614) 221-4000 .. **Weber**, Todd A '96 %Chester W&S LLP -65 E State -10th Fl
-Columbus 43215 **Fx**:221-4012

(216) 765-1800 .. **Weberman**, Philip '85 (P Weberman & Assoc,LLC)
-23611 Chagrin Blvd -Ste 227 -Beachwood 44122

(614) 464-6400 .. **Webner**, Robert N '85 (Vorys SS&P LLP) -52 E Gay -Bx1008
-Columbus 43216 **Fx**:464-6350

(216) 566-1144 .. **Webster**, Beth B '90 (Webster WK LLP) -1220 W 6th -Ste 600
-Cleveland 44113 **Fx**:566-1221

(216) 241-1400 .. **Webster**, Charles K '77 -55 Pub Sq -Ste 2200 -Cleveland 44113

(216) 566-1144 .. **Webster**, David B '91 (Webster WK LLP) -1220 W 6th -Ste 600
-Cleveland 44113 **Fx**:566-1221

(614) 461-1156 .. **Webster**, Geoffrey E '75 (Webster & Assoc) -2 Miranova Pl
-Ste 310 -Columbus 43215

(614) 464-6400 .. **Webster**, Norton R '52 OfCnsl Vorys SS&P LLP -52 E Gay
-Bx1008 -Columbus 43216 **Fx**:464-6350

(216) 781-4680 .. **Webster**, Stephen D '73 Van Aken W&W -629 Euclid Av
-1000 Natl City Bk Bldg -Cleveland 44114 **Fx**:241-1421

(740) 423-9548 .. **Webster**, Thomas P '75 (McCauley W&E) -1710 Wshngtn Blvd
-Bx196 -Belpre 45713

(330) 376-2700 .. **Webster**, Timothy J '87 (Roetzel & A,LPA) -222 S Main
-Akron 44308 **Fx**:376-4577

(614) 466-6750 .. **Webster**, Victoria G '77 OH Dept Taxation -30 E Broad -22nd Fl
-Columbus 43215

(216) 566-1144 .. **Webster Webster Kvale LLP** -1220 W 6th -Ste 600
-Cleveland 44113 **Fx**:566-1221

(419) 535-0075 .. **Webster**, William H '81 %Allotta F&W Co,LPA
-2222 Centennial Rd -Toledo 43617 **Fx**:535-1935

(740) 941-3287 .. **Weckbacher**, Joseph H '83 -5237 State Route 220 -Bx584
-Waverly 45690

(614) 224-9207 .. **Wecker**, Andrew P '96 Title First Agncy,Inc -555 S Front -Ste 400
-Columbus 43215

(216) 861-5088 .. **Wecksler**, Tina E '85 -75 Pub Square -Ste 1300 -Cleveland 44113

(937) 372-4411 .. **Weckstein**, Donald '62 Brandabur FJW&B -260 N Detroit
-Xenia 45385 **Fx**:372-4415

(330) 395-9500 .. **Weddell-Harwood**, Sandra S '91 Trumbull Cnty CSEA
-106 E Market -Ste 301 -Warren 44481

(419) 537-2268 .. **Wedding**, Donald K Sr. '67 Univ of Toledo Law Schl
-2801 W Bancroft -Toledo 43606

(440) 998-1110 .. **Weddleton**, Terry C '84 %Ashtabula Cnty CSEA -Bx1650
-Ashtabula 44005 **Fx**:998-1538

(216) 479-8500 .. **Wedel**, Jeffrey J '89 (Squire S&D LLP) -127 Pub Sq -4900 Key Twr
-Cleveland 44114 **Fx**:479-8780

(216) 241-5310 .. **Wedell**, Kristin L '00 %Gallagher SF&N -1501 Euclid Av -6th Fl
-Cleveland 44115 **Fx**:241-1608

(305) 856-0025 .. **Wedren**, Gerald E '60 Craig Capital Co -2655 S Bayshore Dr
-Miami, FL 33133

(740) 380-6346 .. **Weed**, Charles B '71 -6340 Monday Crk -TR 131
-New Straitsville 43766

(614) 464-1626 .. **Weeden**, Elizabeth S '89 L Smith & Assoc -929 Harrison Av
-Ste 300 -Columbus 43215

(614) 241-5550 .. **Weeden**, Eric L '87 OfCnsl Brunner Law Firm Co,LPA
-545 E Town -Columbus 43215 **Fx**:241-5551

(513) 867-3577 .. **Weeden**, Linda A '98 Pub Def -800 Bway -UB 1 -Cincinnati 45202

(216) 687-3543 .. **Weedon**, John A '61 CSU-Legal Affrs -2121 Euclid Av
-1212 Rhodes Twr -Cleveland 44115
Weeks, Amy S '01 -650 W Maple -Granville 43023

(513) 381-2838 .. **Weeks**, Steven W '77 (Taft S&H LLP) -425 Walnut -Ste 1800
-Cincinnati 45202 **Fx**:381-0205

(614) 221-7201 .. **Weeks**, Thomas W '75 OSLSA -555 Buttles Av -Columbus 43215

(614) 466-7264 .. **Weeks**, Winnifred N '87 OH Legal Rghts Srvc -8 E Long -5th Fl
-Columbus 43215

(304) 455-5033 .. **Weese**, Roger R '79 Weese Legal Srvcs -621 3rd
-New Martinsville, WV 26155

(405) 325-4311 .. **Wegemer**, Joel W '82 Univ of OK Law Schl -300 Timberdell Rd
-Norman, OK 73019

(614) 939-9822 .. **Wegener**, Oliver H '03 %JH Jordan -Bx30863 -Columbus 43230

(859) 635-4586 .. **Wegford**, Mark W '91 -8333 Alexandria Pike -Alexandria, KY
41001

(419) 213-4700 .. **Weglian**, John J '72 %Lucas Cnty Pros -Adams & Erie
-Lucas Cnty Cthse -Toledo 43624

(202) 616-0741 .. **Weglian**, Stephen M Jr. '70 US DOJ-Crim Div -6206 Bond Bldg
-Washington, DC 20530

(216) 642-3342 .. **Wegman Hessler & Vandenburg, LPA** -6055 Rockside Wds Blvd
-Ste 200 -Cleveland 44131 **Fx**:642-8826

(513) 791-4644 .. **Wegner**, Kenneth E '82 -9200 Mntgmry Rd -Bldg H, Ste 24A
-Cincinnati 45242

(859) 578-8544 .. **Wehby**, Joseph K '79 -215 E 8th -Newport, KY 41071

(330) 535-2151 .. **Wehener**, Ann L '94 %Guy L&T -106 S Main -Ste 2210
-Akron 44308 **Fx**:535-9048

(513) 621-3394 .. **Wehmer**, Brenda K '91 Peck S&W,LLP -201 E 5th -Ste 900
-Cincinnati 45202 **Fx**:621-3813

(937) 222-1800 .. **Wehner**, David K '76 -120 W 2nd -Ste 201 -Dayton 45402

(216) 221-8023 .. **Wehr**, Karen R '90 -13460 Lk Av -Lakewood 44107

(614) 365-2700 .. **Wehrer**, Greg R '97 %Squire S&D LLP -41 S High
-1300 Huntngtn Ctr -Columbus 43215 **Fx**:365-2499

(937) 274-3026 .. **Wehrle-Einhorn**, Robert J '85 -1554 Benson Dr -Dayton 45406

(740) 837-7146 .. **Wehrmann**, Kristin A '01 -8530 W Ohio State Ln -Lancaster 43130

(513) 626-1139 .. **Wei Berk**, Caroline '98 Procter & Gamble -11450 Grooms Rd
-Cincinnati 45242

(216) 696-3030 .. **Weibel**, David G '80 (Kadish H&W,LPA) -1717 E 9th -Ste 2112
-Cleveland 44114 **Fx**:696-3492

(614) 466-4605 .. **Weibl**, Mona L '85 OH Dept Job & Fam Srvcs -30 E Broad
-32nd Fl -Columbus 43266

(216) 621-0200 .. **Weible**, Robert A '78 (Baker & H LLP) -1900 E 9th -Ste 3200
-Cleveland 44114 **Fx**:696-0740

(330) 929-0507 .. **Weick**, David C '84 -234 Portage Trl -Cuyahoga Falls 44221

(954) 831-6955 .. **Weick**, James K Jr. '94 State Atty -201 SE 6th
-Fort Lauderdale, FL 33301 **Fx**:831-6171

(330) 929-0507 .. **Weick**, Paul A '54 -234 W Portage Trl -Cuyahoga Falls 44221

(216) 689-3908 .. **Weick**, Paul A II '79 KeyBank NA -127 Pub Sq -Cleveland 44114

(202) 565-6879 .. **Weida**, Krista M '00 Dept of Vets Affrs -111 VT Av NW
-Washington, DC 20011

(740) 345-6611 .. **Weidaw**, William W '73 Wilson Shannon & Snow Inc -10 W Locust
-Newark 43055

(614) 462-1057 .. **Weidenhamer**, Evan R '99 %Schottenstein Z&D -250 West
-Bx165020 -Columbus 43216 **Fx**:462-5135

(216) 321-2595 .. **Weidenthal**, Jeffrey L '88 -3219 Mdwbrk -201 -Cleveland Heights
44118

(614) 645-7385 .. **Weidman**, Nancy L '88 City Atty -90 W Broad -Columbus 43215

(216) 523-5000 .. **Weigand**, Kathleen A '88 Eaton Corp -1111 Superior Av
-Cleveland 44114

(216) 642-3342 .. **Weigand**, Lesley A '96 %Wegman H&V,LPA
-6055 Rockside Wds Blvd -Ste 200 -Cleveland 44131
Fx:642-8826

(513) 241-3111 .. **Weigand**, Maria L '88 ClarkSchaeferHackett & Co -105 E 4th -16th
Fl -Cincinnati 45202

(330) 848-6712 .. **Weigand**, Michael L '71 Mun Ct Judge -576 W Park Av
-Barberton 44203

(513) 723-4000 .. **Weigel**, W Breck '85 (Vorys SS&P LLP) -221 E 4th
-Ste 2000 Atrium Two -Bx0236 -Cincinnati 45201 **Fx**:723-4056

(937) 339-1180 .. **Weigl**, William '58 -1805 Conwood Dr -Troy 45373

(513) 241-3992 .. **Weigle**, Douglas S '76 (Bartlett & W Co,LPA) -432 Walnut
-Ste 1100 -Cincinnati 45202 **Fx**:241-1816

(513) 977-8200 .. **Weigle**, Gerald V Jr. '71 (Dinsmore & S LLP) -255 E 5th -Ste 1900
-Cincinnati 45202 **Fx**:977-8141

(419) 245-1946 .. **Weiher**, Roger R '56 Toledo Municipal Ct -555 N Erie -Housing Div
-Toledo 43624

(216) 575-3000 .. **Weihrauch**, Ronald L Jr. '02 Natl City Bank -1900 E 9th
-Loc#01-2224 -Cleveland 44114

(330) 420-0140 .. **Weikart**, Ryan P '03 %Columbiana Cnty Pros -105 S Market
-Lisbon 44432 **Fx**:424-0944

(615) 344-5994 .. **Weil**, David A II '93 HCA Inc -1 Park Plz -Nashville, TN 37203

(513) 721-1311 .. **Weil**, Rick L '98 %Reminger & R -7 W 7th -Ste 1990
-Cincinnati 45202 **Fx**:721-2553

(513) 621-2100 .. **Weil**, Sidney '50 (Beckman W&S LLC) -120 E 4th
-1200 Mercantile Ctr -Cincinnati 45202 **Fx**:621-0106

(614) 895-2000 .. **Weiland**, Kurt H '76 Century Surety Co -Bx163340
-Columbus 43216

(216) 241-2294 .. **Weilbacher**, David G '99 -1525 Leader Bldg -Cleveland 44114

(216) 363-4500 .. **Weiler**, Jeffry L '70 (Benesch FC&A LLP) -200 Pub Sq -Ste 2300
-Cleveland 44114 **Fx**:363-4588

(216) 475-4927 .. **Weiler**, Jennifer P '79 Mun Ct Judge -5555 Turney Rd
-Garfield Heights 44125 **Fx**:475-3087

(440) 526-0876 .. **Weiler**, Kevin P '79 (Weiler & Assoc) -8920 Brecksvll Rd
-Brecksville 44141

(513) 564-7350 .. **Weiler**, Kimberly M '94 6th Dist Ct of Appls -100 E 5th -Cthse
-Cincinnati 45202

(812) 934-0094 .. **Weiler**, Kristen R '96 -24 Red Maple Ct -Batesville, IN 47006

(216) 515-8337 .. **Weiler**, Richard L '91 Cuyahoga Cnty CSEA -1700 E 13th -#32
-Cleveland 44114

(614) 221-4286 .. **Weiler**, Robert J '83 (R Weiler Co) -41 S High -Ste 2200
-Columbus 43215

(419) 522-3398 .. **Weiler**, Samuel P '04 %Inscore RW&E,LPA -13 Park Av W
-Ste 400 -Mansfield 44902 **Fx**:522-5165

(330) 673-8047 .. **Weill**, Leo '72 -3853 Morley Dr -Kent 44240

(513) 684-6988 .. **Weill**, Neal J '78 US DOJ -36 E 7th -Ste 2030 -Cincinnati 45202

(216) 755-5647 .. **Weily**, Jennifer R '99 Developers Diversified Rlty Corp
-3300 Enterprise Pkwy -Beachwood 44122

(330) 364-5505 .. **Weimer**, Christine M '98 Pros -714 N Wooster Av -Dover 44622

(330) 896-4500 .. **Weimer**, David P '85 (Weimer & Co LLC) -1790 Town Park Blvd
-Ste B -Uniontown 44685

(614) 464-6400 .. **Weimer**, John B '89 (Vorys SS&P LLP) -52 E Gay -Bx1008
-Columbus 43216 **Fx**:464-6350

(330) 896-4500 .. **Weimer**, Paul E '50 OfCnsl Weimer & Co LLC
-1790 Town Park Blvd -Ste B -Uniontown 44685

(330) 746-1064 .. **Weimer**, William A '75 SrCnsl BJ Alan Co
-555 Martin Luther King Jr Blvd -Youngstown 44502 **Fx**:746-4410

(419) 354-1244 .. **Weinandy**, James R '89 -1180 N Main -Ste 4
-Bowling Green 43402 **Fx**:353-2733

(216) 685-1100 .. **Weinberg**, Alan H '74 (Weltman W&R Co,LPA)
-323 W Lakeside Av -Ste 200 -Cleveland 44113 **Fx**:363-4121

(513) 489-9200 .. **Weinberg**, Allen M '78 Chicago Title Ins Co -7890 E Kemper Rd -Ste 210 -Cincinnati 45249

(614) 645-7483 .. **Weinberg**, Denice '92 City Pros -375 S High -7th Fl -Columbus 43215

(216) 431-4500 .. **Weinberg**, Marilyn O '83 Cuyahoga Cnty Pros -3955 Euclid Av -Jane Edna Hunter Bldg -Cleveland 44115 **Fx:**431-4113

(419) 882-0533 .. **Weinberg**, Mark D '75 (Retske & W) -5414 Monroe -Toledo 43623

(216) 621-8234 .. **Weinberg**, Richard M '88 -1801 E 9th -Ste #920 -Cleveland 44114

(330) 929-0507 .. **Weinberger**, Mark S '84 -Bx535 -Cuyahoga Falls 44222

(330) 929-0507 .. **Weinberger**, Michael A '72 -234 W Portage Trl -Cuyahoga Falls 44221

(216) 696-3232 .. **Weinberger**, Peter H '75 (Spangenberg S&L,LLP) -1900 E 9th -2400 Natl City Ctr -Cleveland 44114 **Fx:**696-3924

(513) 984-6314 .. **Weiner**, Charles '57 -9750 Humphrey -Cincinnati 45242

(937) 461-6600 .. **Weiner**, Daniel D '63 -120 W 2nd -Ste 320 -Dayton 45402

(216) 479-8500 .. **Weiner**, David C '69 (Squire S&D LLP) -127 Pub Sq -4900 Key Twr -Cleveland 44114 **Fx:**479-8780

(216) 621-5036 .. **Weiner**, Douglas S '87 (Demer W&M,LLC) -2 Berea Cmmns -Ste 200 -Berea 44017 **Fx:**(440) 891-1684

(440) 543-8868 .. **Weiner**, Edwin S '56 (Weiner S&C) -17370 Hawksvw Ln -Chagrin Falls 44023

(614) 866-1640 .. **Weiner**, Jerry '52 Cnsl J Weiner & Assoc -1215 Park Plz Dr -Columbus 43213 **Fx:**866-1640

(216) 771-6500 .. **Weiner**, Keith D '82 (K Weiner & Assoc Co,LPA) -75 Pub Sq -4th Fl -Cleveland 44113 **Fx:**771-6540

(330) 670-8334 .. **Weiner**, Matthew C '02 Cooper Real Estate Mngmnt Co -300 N Cleveland-Massillon Rd -Akron 44333

Weiner, Paul L '82 -2081 Tembletvurst -South Euclid 44121

Weiner, Richard '77 -(Address Unavailable)

(713) 961-5222 .. **Weiner**, Ruben L '93 -1775 St James Pl -Ste 175 -Houston, TX 77056

(614) 443-6581 .. **Weiner**, Samuel B '73 -743 S Front -Columbus 43206

(513) 723-4000 .. **Weinewuth**, Elizabeth E W '04 %Vorys SS&P LLP -221 E 4th -Ste 2000 Atrium Two -Bx0236 -Cincinnati 45201 **Fx:**723-4056

(614) 466-0507 .. **Weinfeld**, Jennifer L '00 %Hon M O'Connor -30 E Broad -3rd Fl -Columbus 43215

(330) 723-9546 .. **Weingart**, Denise H '91 Medina Cnty Pros -72 Pub Sq -Medina 44256

(304) 340-3851 .. **Weingart**, Karin L '95 (Spilman T&B,PLLC) -300 Kanawha Blvd E -Bx273 -Charleston, WV 25321 **Fx:**340-3801

(216) 781-9000 .. **Weingart**, Lee C '91 LNE Group -2000 E 9th -Ste 420 -Cleveland 44115

(216) 222-2972 .. **Weingartner**, Lucile G '80 Natl City Bank -1900 E 9th -17th Fl Loc 01-2174 -Cleveland 44114

(216) 736-7242 .. **Weingrad**, Stephen C '73 OfCnsl Kohrman J&K PLL -1375 E 9th -One Cleve Ctr 20th Fl -Cleveland 44114 **Fx:**621-6536

(216) 524-1891 .. **Weinreich**, Thomas Wm '98 (TW Weinreich,Inc) -6000 Freedom Sq Dr -Ste 380 -Independence 44131 **Fx:**642-5813

(513) 423-8951 .. **Weinrich**, Lancer R Jr. '72 -2 N Main -Ste 304 -Middletown 45042

(330) 923-5315 .. **Weinschenk**, Barbara J '04 %MH Kreiner -2020 Front -Ste 200 -Cuyahoga Falls 44221

(419) 213-4755 .. **Weinstein**, Andrea C '92 %Hon PM Handwork -800 Jackson -Toledo 43624

(216) 621-0150 .. **Weinstein**, Edward A '86 (Hahn L&P LLP) -3300 BP Twr/200 Pub Sq -Ste 3300 -Cleveland 44114 **Fx:**241-2824

(216) 479-8500 .. **Weinstein**, Joseph C '83 (Squire S&D LLP) -127 Pub Sq -4900 Key Twr -Cleveland 44114 **Fx:**479-8780

(614) 462-5450 .. **Weinstein**, Melvin D '73 (Kegler BH&R) -65 E State -Ste 1800 -Columbus 43215 **Fx:**464-2634

(216) 381-5132 .. **Weinstein**, Norman H '52 -14176 Cedar Rd -#103 -Cleveland 44121

(561) 241-0414 .. **Weinstock**, Jeffrey D '96 %Buckingham D&B -2500 N Military Trl -Ste 480 -Boca Raton, FL 33431 **Fx:**241-9766

(216) 574-9090 .. **Weintraub**, Craig T '87 -23220 Chagrin Blvd -Ste 360 -Cleveland 44122

(216) 443-7800 .. **Weintraub**, Julianne L '96 Cuyahoga Cnty Pros -1200 Ontario -8th Fl -Cleveland 44113 **Fx:**698-2270

(419) 221-5227 .. **Weir**, Joseph H II '78 Lima Mun Ct -109 N Union -Bx1529 -Lima 45802

(740) 622-6464 .. **Weir**, Robert E '83 (Frase WB&M Co,LPA) -305 Main -4th Fl -Coshocton 43812 **Fx:**622-8107

(216) 443-9000 .. **Weir**, William R '84 (Porter WM&A LLP) -925 Euclid Av -Ste 1700 -Cleveland 44115 **Fx:**443-9011

(513) 634-1612 .. **Weirich**, David M '93 SrCnsl Procter & Gamble Co -6110 Ctr Hill Rd -Cincinnati 45224

(614) 228-4200 .. **Weis**, Amy Jo '96 Babbitt & W LLP -503 S Front -Ste 200 -Columbus 43215 **Fx:**228-4224

(614) 464-6400 .. **Weis**, Anthony D '99 %Vorys SS&P LLP -52 E Gay -Bx1008 -Columbus 43216 **Fx:**464-6350

(440) 232-5100 .. **Weis**, Geri L '99 Transtar Industries -7350 Young Dr -Cleveland 44146

(614) 228-1717 .. **Weis**, Karen D '01 %McLeod Law Ofc -471 E Broad -Ste 1900 -Columbus 43215

(419) 862-2415 .. **Weis**, Kenton P '75 -340 Rice -Bx47 -Elmore 43416

(419) 255-5111 .. **Weisberg**, Joseph D '67 -520 Mad Av -Ste 1030 -Toledo 43604 **Fx:**255-3231

(561) 994-0100 .. **Weisberg**, Leonard G W '81 OfCnsl Winter & S -2300 Corp Blvd NW -Boca Raton, FL 33431 **Fx:**241-1493

(216) 781-1212 .. **Weisberg**, Patricia Fromson '85 (Walter & H LLP) -1301 E 9th -Ste 3500 -Cleveland 44114 **Fx:**575-0911

(216) 932-5227 .. **Weisberger**, Donald D '60 -3391 Superior Park Dr -Cleveland Heights 44118

(216) 348-5400 .. **Weisblatt**, David E '94 %McDonald H Co,LPA -600 Superior Av E -Ste 2100 -Cleveland 44114 **Fx:**348-5474

(216) 591-9640 .. **Weisblatt**, Martin E '63 -25550 Chagrin Blvd -Ste 403 -Beachwood 44122

(937) 643-9999 .. **Weisbrod**, Alfred J '69 (Weisbrod & D) -580 Lincoln Park Blvd -Ste 222 -Dayton 45429 **Fx:**643-0777

(937) 643-9999 .. **Weisbrod & Dankof** -580 Lincoln Park Blvd -Ste 222 -Dayton 45429 **Fx:**643-0777

(513) 737-5100 .. **Weisbrod**, Michael P '85 -304 N 2nd -Hamilton 45011

(513) 352-3305 .. **Weise**, Robert L Jr. '97 Law Dept -801 Plum -Rm 214 -Cincinnati 45202 **Fx:**352-1515

(614) 487-4414 .. **Weisenberg**, William K '71 OH State Bar Assoc -1700 Lk Shr Dr -Pub Affairs/Gov Relations -Columbus 43204 **Fx:**487-1008

(513) 721-4450 .. **Weisenberger**, Andrew W '02 %Santen & H -312 Walnut -Ste 3100 -Cincinnati 45202

(330) 296-8000 .. **Weisenburger**, Dan J '81 -121 E Main -Ravenna 44266 **Fx:**296-7945

(419) 935-0171 .. **Weisenburger**, Eric R '90 (Thornton T&H) -111 Myrtle Av -Bx207 -Willard 44890

(419) 691-5745 .. **Weisenburger**, Margaret M '78 %VE Clark -617 Miami -Toledo 43605

(419) 321-6444 .. **Weisenburger**, Thomas E '62 (Cline C&W Co,LPA) -300 Mad Av -Ste 1100 -Toledo 43604 **Fx:**321-6430

(513) 381-9200 .. **Weisenfelder**, Wilson G Jr. '85 Rendigs FK&D,LLP -One W 4th -Ste 900 -Cincinnati 45202 **Fx:**381-9206

(513) 984-2040 .. **Weisensel**, Karen P '96 %Scheuer M&B LLC -11025 Reed Hartman Hwy -Cincinnati 45242 **Fx:**984-6590

(513) 241-7111 .. **Weisensel**, Michael D '97 %O'Connor A&L Co,LPA -1014 Vine -22nd Fl -Cincinnati 45202 **Fx:**241-7197

(330) 434-1000 .. **Weisensell**, John C '85 (Bernlohr W,LLP) -23 S Main -3rd Fl -Akron 44308 **Fx:**434-1001

(614) 265-7062 .. **Weiser**, Joan C '79 Dept Natural Resources -1930 Belcher Dr -D-3 -Columbus 43224

(216) 861-8888 .. **Weiser**, Larry A '71 (L Weiser Co,LPA) -1419 W 9th -Cleveland 44113

(440) 356-2828 .. **Weiser**, Rachel E '98 %Milano Law Ofc -2639 Wooster Rd -Rocky River 44116 **Fx:**356-2873

(440) 871-0394 .. **Weishar**, Fred A '55 -1814 Donna Dr -Westlake 44145

(614) 459-5600 .. **Weislogel**, George S '80 OSU Coll of Engineering -Bx20151 -Columbus 43220

(216) 696-3311 .. **Weisman**, Deborah A '94 %Kahn K -1301 E 9th -2600 Erievw Twr -Cleveland 44114 **Fx:**623-4912

(216) 781-1111 .. **Weisman**, Fred '51 Weisman G&W Co,LPA -101 Prospect Av -1600 Mdlnd Bldg -Cleveland 44115 **Fx:**781-6747

(216) 781-1111 .. **Weisman Goldberg & Weisman Co, LPA** -101 Prospect Av -1600 Mdlnd Bldg -Cleveland 44115 **Fx:**781-6747

(216) 781-1111 .. **Weisman**, Harry Jed '66 (Weisman G&W Co,LPA) -101 Prospect Av -1600 Mdlnd Bldg -Cleveland 44115 **Fx:**781-6747

(614) 462-3194 .. **Weisman**, J S '90 Franklin Cnty Pub Def -373 S High -12th Fl -Columbus 43215

(213) 356-6595 .. **Weisman**, James E '93 Pricewaterhouse Coopers -350 S Grand Av -Los Angeles, CA 90071

(614) 466-4425 .. **Weisman**, Lori J '84 %Hon FE Sweeney -30 E Broad -Columbus 43266

(330) 374-1144 .. **Weisman**, Mark B '87 Weisman & G -One Cascade Plz -Ste 1450 -Akron 44308

(330) 762-9621 .. **Weisman**, Mark S '85 Famous Entrprses -109 N Union -Bx1889 -Akron 44309

(216) 781-1111 .. **Weisman**, Mitchell A '83 Weisman G&W Co,LPA -101 Prospect Av -1600 Mdlnd Bldg -Cleveland 44115 **Fx:**781-6747

(614) 462-5139 .. **Weisman**, Robert D '75 (Schottenstein Z&D) -250 West -Bx165020 -Columbus 43216 **Fx:**462-5135

(260) 407-0040 .. **Weiss**, Andrew M '96 -126 W Columbia Av -Ste 300 -Fort Wayne, IN 46802

(202) 707-3964 .. **Weiss**, Bradley M '82 Library of Congress -101 Indpndnc Av SE -Madison Bldg -Washington, DC 20540

Weiss, Carol A '77 -6980 Carriage Hill Dr -Brecksville 44141

(614) 764-0681 .. **Weiss**, Carole D '86 %Blaugrund H&M,Inc -5455 Rings Rd -Ste 500 -Dublin 43017 **Fx:**764-0774

(419) 874-2261 .. **Weiss**, Dan M '96 (Weiss & Assoc) -330 Louisiana Av -Ste C -Perrysburg 43551

(216) 479-8500 .. **Weiss**, Dana B '03 %Squire S&D LLP -127 Pub Sq -4900 Key Twr -Cleveland 44114 **Fx:**479-8780

(614) 431-0781 .. **Weiss**, Daniel K '85 Hwy Patrol Rtrmnt Syst -6161 Busch Blvd -Ste 119 -Columbus 43229

(216) 755-1500 .. **Weiss**, David E '86 Developers Diversified Rlty Corp -3300 Enterprise Pkwy -Beachwood 44122

(305) 668-0084 .. **Weiss**, Elaine Florence '77 (Weiss & K,PA) -1550 Madruga Av -Ste 400 -Coral Gables, FL 33146 **Fx:**668-3799

(440) 838-7600 .. **Weiss**, Eric J '00 %Janik & D,LLP -9200 S Hills Blvd -Ste 300 -Cleveland 44147 **Fx:**838-7601

(614) 464-0381 .. **Weiss**, Eugene P '72 -536 S 3rd -Columbus 43215

(440) 350-7035 .. **Weiss**, Francis P '82 Lake Cnty Juv Ct -53 E Erie -Painesville 44077

(440) 247-0775 .. **Weiss & Freedman LLP** -35 River -Chagrin Falls 44022 **Fx:**893-9138

(216) 623-0150 .. **Weiss**, Gary A '90 OfCnsl Roetzel & A,LPA -1375 E 9th -One Cleve Ctr 9th Fl -Cleveland 44114 **Fx:**623-0134

(513) 579-6400 .. **Weiss**, Herbert B '65 (Keating M&K PLL) -1 E 4th -1400 Provident Twr -Cincinnati 45202 **Fx:**579-6457

(216) 589-9993 .. **Weiss**, Jerome F '72 -101 Prospect Av W -1600 Mdlnd Bldg -Cleveland 44115

(440) 729-7278 .. **Weiss**, Joseph H Jr. '70 -8228 Mayfld Rd -Ste 6B -Chesterland 44026 **Fx:**729-8132

(216) 787-3344 .. **Weiss**, Kathleen G '88 Ohio Lottery Commission -615 W Superior Av -Cleveland 44113

(216) 687-1311 .. **Weiss**, Leon A '66 (Reminger & R) -101 Prospect Av W -1400 Mdlnd Bldg -Cleveland 44115 **Fx:**687-1841

(330) 468-1056 .. **Weiss**, Leslie A '91 Halberg & Assoc Co,LPA -198 E Aurora Rd -Northfield 44067 **Fx:**468-1068

(216) 642-1105 .. **Weiss**, Linda A '79 WestWay Mgmt -3 Summit Park Dr -Ste 130 -Independence 44131

(216) 473-8783 .. **Weiss**, Lita L '78 -5025 Swetland Ct -Richmond Heights 44143

(513) 579-6400 .. **Weiss**, Mark A '92 (Keating M&K PLL) -1 E 4th -1400 Provident Twr -Cincinnati 45202 **Fx:**579-6457

(216) 621-7500 .. **Weiss**, Michael S '75 -602 Rckfllr Bldg -614 W Superior Av -Cleveland 44113

(216) 961-6840 .. **Weiss**, Michael S '81 A&C Auto Parts & Wrecking -3805 Ridge Rd -Cleveland 44144

Weiss, Rebekah Gelsey '04 -(Address Unavailable)

(216) 755-5500 .. **Weiss**, Renee B '95 Developers Diversified Rlty Corp -3300 Enterprise Pkwy -Beachwood 44122

(216) 771-4242 ..**Weiss**, Richard A '71 (RA Weiss Co,LPA) -1375 E 9th -Ste 1850 -Cleveland 44114

(440) 247-0775 ..**Weiss**, Roger J '66 (Weiss & F LLP) -35 River -Chagrin Falls 44022 **Fx:**893-9138

(216) 696-3366 ..**Weiss**, Ronald I '65 OfCnsl Goodman WM LLP -100 Erievw Plz -27th Fl -Cleveland 44114 **Fx:**363-5835

(248) 737-8000 ..**Weiss**, Ronald S '03 -7035 Orchrd Lk Rd -Ste 600 -West Bloomfield, MI 48322

(614) 228-6674 ..**Weiss**, Stephen M '68 -601 S High -Columbus 43215

(216) 348-1800 ..**Weiss**, Steven M '80 -55 Pub Sq -1250 -Cleveland 44113

(312) 362-8701 ..**Weissenberger**, Glen A '72 DePaul Univ Cllg of Law -25 E Jackson Blvd -Chicago, IL 60604

(513) 721-3236 ..**Weisser**, Mark B '83 (Weisser & W) -1014 Vine -Ste 1650 -Cincinnati 45202

(513) 721-3236 ..**Weisser & Wolf** -1014 Vine -Ste 1650 -Cincinnati 45202

(330) 253-2252 ..**Weissfeld**, Randall D '79 -614 E Market -Akron 44304

(440) 272-6640 ..**Weissinger**, Lee E '93 -32715 Wllwbrk Ln -North Ridgeville 44039

(216) 579-1818 ..**Weissman**, Esther S '61 (ES Weissman Co,LPA) -918 Rckfllr Bldg -Ste 918 -Cleveland 44113

(202) 387-8030 ..**Weissman**, Robert '96 Essential Info -Bx19405 -Washington, DC 20036

(614) 224-4155 ..**Weisz**, Michael J '82 -536 S Wall -Ste 300 -Columbus 43215 **Fx:**224-9258

(330) 434-3000 ..**Weitendorf**, Kurt R '80 (Roderick & L) -One Cascade Plz -Ste 1500 -Akron 44308 **Fx:**434-9220

(937) 653-3170 ..**Weithman**, Cathy J '78 -201 W Ct -Urbana 43078

(937) 653-3170 ..**Weithman**, Gil S '83 -201 W Ct -Urbana 43078

(202) 778-3000 ..**Weitsen**, Winifred M '00 %Porter WM&A LLP -1919 Penn Av NW -Ste 500 -Washington, DC 20006

(415) 924-7147 ..**Weixel**, James V Jr. '90 (Trevor & W,LLP) -300 Tamal Plz -Ste 180 -Corte Madera, CA 94925

Weizel, Hollace B '83 -230 3rd -Ste 100 -Elyria 44035

(937) 222-2500 ..**Welbaum**, Heather N '99 %Sebaly S&D -1900 Kettering Twr -Dayton 45423 **Fx:**222-6554

(212) 908-3914 ..**Welburn**, Stuart J '98 (Thompson H LLP) -1 Chase Manh Plz -58th Fl -New York, NY 10005 **Fx:**809-6890

(419) 422-8906 ..**Welch**, Allen L '81 (Snyder A&W,LPA) -233 S Main -Findlay 45840

(937) 225-4652 ..**Welch**, Carla E '97 Montgomery Cnty Pub Def -117 S Main -Ste 400 -Dayton 45422 **Fx:**225-3449

(614) 462-2800 ..**Welch**, Christopher S '92 %Unizan Bank -66 S 3rd -Columbus 43215

(614) 236-9066 ..**Welch**, Derek W '01 LandSel Title -2417 Plymouth Av -Columbus 43209

(614) 575-3530 ..**Welch**, Erin E '99 Chldrn Srvcs -1951 Gantz -Grove City 43123

(740) 374-6222 ..**Welch**, Janet D '80 -311 Scammel -Marietta 45750

(419) 523-5015 ..**Welch**, Jill S '99 Leopold W&S -321 E Main -Bx303 -Ottawa 45875

(937) 222-3322 ..**Welch**, John B '91 (Arnold T&W) -130 W 2nd -Ste 940 -Dayton 45402

(740) 922-4161 ..**Welch**, Kenneth R '79 (Connolly H&W) -201 N Main -Bx272 -Uhrichsville 44683

(614) 223-2431 ..**Welch**, Mark A '77 Amer Elec Power Inc -1 Riverside Plz -HR Srvcs -Columbus 43215

(614) 932-7000 ..**Welch**, Porter R '99 (Himmelrick & W,LLC) -7215 Sawmill Rd -Ste 215 -Dublin 43016

(740) 962-6478 ..**Welch**, Richard D '84 Morgan Cnty Pros -109 E Main -McConnelsville 43756

(513) 831-8511 ..**Welch**, Robert H III '04 %Crowe & W -1019 Main -Bx296 -Milford 45150

(513) 831-8511 ..**Welch**, Robert H Jr. '76 (Crowe & W) -1019 Main -Bx296 -Milford 45150

(513) 381-3525 ..**Welch**, Robert J Jr. '75 (Kircher R&W) -1014 Vine -Ste 2520 -Cincinnati 45202

(614) 462-3555 ..**Welch**, Ronald L '98 Franklin Cnty Pros -373 S High -Columbus 43215

(614) 783-2279 ..**Welch**, Rosemarie A '99 -Bx322 -Lewis Center 43035 **Fx:**(740) 657-1133

(419) 523-5015 ..**Welch**, Scott E '99 %Leopold W&S -321 E Main -Bx303 -Ottawa 45875

(614) 236-8000 ..**Welcome**, Kristen J '99 Zacks Law Grp LLC -33 S James Rd -3rd Fl -Columbus 43213

Weldele, Eric D '04 Capitol Cnsltng Grp -37 W Broad -Ste 750 -Columbus 43215

(419) 524-9811 ..**Weldon Huston & Keyser,LLP** -28 Park Av W -Bank One Bldg -Mansfield 44902 **Fx:**522-5758

(419) 241-0767 ..**Weldon**, Thomas P '94 US Atty -4 Seagate -Ste 308 -Toledo 43604 **Fx:**259-6360

(216) 778-5723 ..**Welfel**, Frederick M '92 Metro Health Systm -2500 Metro Health Dr -Cleveland 44109

(216) 696-4700 ..**Welfley**, Jennifer A '97 %Spieth BM&N Co,LPA -925 Euclid Av -2000 Huntngtn Bldg -Cleveland 44115 **Fx:**696-2706

(614) 469-3269 ..**Welin**, Peter D '88 (Thompson H LLP) -10 W Broad -Ste 700 -Columbus 43215 **Fx:**469-3361

(513) 946-3418 ..**Welker**, Paula L '88 1st Dist Ct of Appls -230 E 9th -12th Fl -Cincinnati 45202 **Fx:**946-3412

(614) 228-4200 ..**Wellbaum**, Gary S '85 (Babbitt & W LLP) -503 S Front -Ste 200 -Columbus 43215 **Fx:**228-4224

Wellemeyer, William D '91 -743 Uppr Merriman Dr -Akron 44303

(216) 736-7936 ..**Weller**, Charles D '73 -25 Prospect Av -1100 Republic Bldg -Cleveland 44115

(513) 579-6400 ..**Weller**, Jill A '85 (Keating M&K PLL) -1 E 4th -1400 Provident Twr -Cincinnati 45202 **Fx:**579-6457

(419) 244-7596 ..**Weller**, Lucinda J '99 -520 Mad Av -Ste 837 -Toledo 43604 **Fx:**255-5530

(216) 642-6653 ..**Weller**, Mark D '82 AGA Gas,Inc -6055 Rockside Wd Blvd -Bx94737 -Cleveland 44101

(614) 224-9223 ..**Weller**, Matthew A '93 Ward KBM&M -199 S 5th -Columbus 43215

(937) 435-4554 ..**Weller**, Michael G '86 %Gunnoe & Assoc -2525 Miamisburg Centervll Rd -Centerville 45459

(216) 371-1688 ..**Weller**, Robert R '72 (Weller & Assoc) -3171 Colerdg Rd -Cleveland Heights 44118

(419) 738-7025 ..**Weller**, Stanley M '79 -119 W Auglaize -Bx180 -Wapakoneta 45895

(216) 241-8300 ..**Welling**, David A '03 %TA Shimko & Assoc Co,LPA -925 Euclid Av -Ste 2010 -Cleveland 44115 **Fx:**241-2702

(513) 621-6464 ..**Wellington**, Kent '91 (Graydon H&R LLP) -511 Walnut -1900 Fifth Third Ctr -Cincinnati 45202 **Fx:**651-3836

(330) 792-2336 ..**Wellman Jeren Hackett & Skoufatos Co,LPA** -4990 Mahoning Av -Youngstown 44515 **Fx:**792-5403

(216) 479-8500 ..**Wellman**, Kristine M '95 %Squire S&D LLP -127 Pub Sq -4900 Key Twr -Cleveland 44114 **Fx:**479-8780

(614) 464-6400 ..**Wellner**, John P '79 (Vorys SS&P LLP) -52 E Gay -Bx1008 -Columbus 43215 **Fx:**464-6350

(608) 251-5000 ..**Wellnitz**, Jennifer S '94 %Quarles & B -Firstar Plz -Bx2113 -Madison, WI 53701

(859) 231-3000 ..**Wellons**, Kymberly T '93 (Stoll K&P,LLP) -300 W Vine -Ste 2100 -Lexington, KY 40507

(937) 432-9500 ..**Wells**, Amy L '04 %Burdge Law Ofc Co,LPA -2299 Miamisburg-Centervll Rd -Dayton 45459 **Fx:**432-9503

(513) 977-8200 ..**Wells**, Ben F '83 (Dinsmore & S LLP) -255 E 5th -Ste 1900 -Cincinnati 45202 **Fx:**977-8141

(614) 229-4746 ..**Wells**, Cheryl A '83 Deloitte & Touche LLP -155 E Broad -Columbus 43215

(937) 432-9500 ..**Wells**, Elizabeth A '04 %Burdge Law Ofc Co,LPA -2299 Miamisburg-Centervll Rd -Dayton 45459 **Fx:**432-9503

(801) 621-6183 ..**Wells**, Frank M '69 -2485 Grant Av -Ste 200 -Ogden, UT 84401

(513) 422-2001 ..**Wells**, James R '00 %Frost BT LLC -300 N Main -Ste 200 -Middletown 45042 **Fx:**422-3010

(330) 762-0275 ..**Wells**, Jason T '02 -441 Wolf Ledges Pkwy -Ste 400 -Bx0079 -Akron 44309

(740) 962-2262 ..**Wells**, John A '94 (Christie & W) -36 W Main -Bx419 -McConnelsville 43756

Wells, John N '94 Progressive Ins Co -5920 Landerbrook Dr -#PLG-OHL33 -Mayfield Heights 44124

(614) 279-9929 ..**Wells**, Joquetta S '81 -2365 Sullivant Av -Ste W -Bx272082 -Columbus 43227 **Fx:**272-2012

(614) 466-5610 ..**Wells**, Kimberley S '99 Atty Gen -150 E Gay -Columbus 43215 **Fx:**752-2732

(419) 877-5529 ..**Wells**, Michael H '87 -6532 Oakbrook Dr -Whitehouse 43571

(419) 772-2205 ..**Wells**, Mindi L '98 ONU-Pettit Clg of Law -525 S Main -Ada 45810

(440) 395-0246 ..**Wells**, R Mark '90 Progressive Ins Co -300 N Cmmns Blvd -OHF 11 -Mayfield Village 44143

(248) 258-7074 ..**Wells**, Steven W '99 (Schnelz WM&W, PC) -280 N Old Woodward Av -Ste 250 -Birmingham, MI 48009 **Fx:**258-7084

(513) 721-4450 ..**Wells**, Terese M '93 %Santen & H -312 Walnut -Ste 3100 -Cincinnati 45202

(248) 258-7074 ..**Wells**, Todd H '99 (Schnelz WM&W,PC) -280 N Old Woodward Av -Ste 250 -Birmingham, MI 48009 **Fx:**258-7084

(440) 248-7906 ..**Wells-Niklas**, Natasha A '96 %Mazanec R&R Co,LPA -34305 Solon Rd -Ste 100 -Cleveland 44139 **Fx:**248-8861

(330) 673-3444 ..**Welser**, Howard T Jr. '69 (Williams W&K) -11 S River -Bx396 -Kent 44240

Welsh, Coleen M '77 -(Address Unavailable)

Welsh, Elaine '90 -(Address Unavailable)

(614) 764-1900 ..**Welsh**, Gerald D '72 American Share Ins Corp -5656 Frantz Rd -Dublin 43017

(419) 522-2889 ..**Welsh**, Harry M '66 (Renwick W&B) -9 N Mulberry -Mansfield 44902

(614) 436-1197 ..**Welsh**, Jeannette M '89 -625 High -Worthington 43085

(330) 740-2104 ..**Welsh**, Kathi M '85 Mahoning Cnty Clerk of Cts -120 Market -Youngstown 44503

(216) 751-0181 ..**Welsh**, Martin J '60 -19015 Van Aken Blvd -Ste 205 -Shaker Heights 44122

(937) 333-4400 ..**Welsh**, Mary E '97 Dayton Pros -335 W 3rd -Ste 372 -Dayton 45402

(513) 946-3700 ..**Welsh**, Michael W '01 %Hamilton Cnty Pub Def -230 E 9th -3rd Fl -Cincinnati 45202 **Fx:**946-3707

Welsh, Patrick J '82 -(Address Unavailable)

(513) 723-4000 ..**Welsh**, Rosemary D '95 OfCnsl Vorys SS&P LLP -221 E 4th -Ste 2000 Atrium Two -Bx0236 -Cincinnati 45201 **Fx:**723-4056

(216) 622-8200 ..**Welsh**, Thomas M '03 %Calfee H&G LLP -800 Superior Av -Ste 1400 -Cleveland 44114 **Fx:**241-0816

(330) 480-5225 ..**Welsh**, Timothy G '86 Mahoning Cnty Common Pleas Ct -120 Market -Youngstown 44503

(513) 241-1989 ..**Welsh**, William M '92 -917 Main -2nd Fl -Cincinnati 45202

(513) 241-0607 ..**Welt**, David S '85 -1014 Vine -Ste 1919 -Cincinnati 45202

(614) 542-9358 ..**Welt**, Richard J '79 -673 Mohawk -Ste 203 -Columbus 43206

(330) 498-9820 ..**Weltman**, Jeffrey H '79 -4819 Munson NW -Canton 44718

(216) 685-1040 ..**Weltman**, Robert B '65 (Weltman W&R Co,LPA) -323 W Lakeside Av -Ste 200 -Cleveland 44113 **Fx:**363-4121

(216) 685-1032 ..**Weltman**, Scott S '90 (Weltman W&R Co,LPA) -323 W Lakeside Av -Ste 200 -Cleveland 44113 **Fx:**363-4121

(440) 237-7900 ..**Weltman**, Stephen Randall '85 Patrolmens Benevolent Assn -10147 Royalton Rd -Ste J -North Royalton 44133

(216) 685-1000 ..**Weltman Weinberg & Reis Co,LPA** -323 W Lakeside Av -Ste 200 -Cleveland 44113 **Fx:**363-4121

(614) 228-7272 ..**Weltman Weinberg & Reis Co,LPA** -175 S 3rd -Ste 900 -Columbus 43215 **Fx:**222-2193

(513) 723-2200 ..**Weltman Weinberg & Reis Co,LPA** -525 Vine -Ste 800 -Cincinnati 45202 **Fx:**723-2239

(937) 445-7679 ..**Weltner**, Robert B '81 NCR Corp -1700 S Patterson Blvd -WHQ-SE -Dayton 45479

(216) 222-2337 ..**Welton**, Copani M '01 Natl City Corp -1900 E 9th -Loc 01-2207 -Cleveland 44114

(216) 781-1212 ..**Welty**, David W '74 (Walter & H LLP) -1301 E 9th -Ste 3500 -Cleveland 44114 **Fx:**575-0911

(216) 781-2258 ..**Wendel**, Fred III '74 (Stewart & D Co,LPA) -1370 Ontario -Ste 1440 Standard Bldg -Cleveland 44113 **Fx:**781-8210

(614) 365-2700 ..**Wendel**, Lee A '87 (Squire S&D LLP) -41 S High -1300 Huntngtn Ctr -Columbus 43215 **Fx:**365-2499

(513) 241-8844 ..**Wendel**, Richard G II '92 -441 Vine -4400 Carew Twr -Cincinnati 45202

(614) 752-1765 ..**Wendell**, Christina M '99 OH Dept Rehab & Correction -1050 Fwy Dr N -Columbus 43229

(202) 879-5487 ..**Wendell**, Gitte J '00 %Jones DR&P -51 Louisiana Av NW -Washington, DC 20001 **Fx:**626-1700

(513) 352-6739 ..**Wendeln**, John H '84 (Thompson H LLP) -312 Walnut -14th Fl -Cincinnati 45202 **Fx:**241-4771

Wendling, Anne C '89 -1896 Alta West Rd -Mansfield 44903
(937) 224-7200 .. Wendling, Marcus N '02 %Horenstein N&B -124 E 3rd -5th Fl
-Dayton 45402 Fx:224-3353
(614) 444-3003 .. Wendt, Tracy Q '98 %E Battisti Jr -987 S High -Columbus 43206
(330) 744-1111 .. Wenger, Alan D '77 Harrington H&M,Ltd -26 Market -Ste 1200
-Youngstown 44503 Fx:744-2029
(740) 345-3431 .. Wenger, David W '79 (Reese PD&M,PLL) -36 N 2nd -Bx919
-Newark 44058 Fx:349-5116
(419) 243-8251 .. Wenk, Dawn M '97 Toledo-Lucas Cnty Port Auth
-One Maritime Plz -7th Fl -Toledo 43604
(513) 721-1997 .. Wenke, Stephen J '88 -917 Main -2nd Fl -Cincinnati 45202
(513) 791-1672 .. Wenker, Herman H '59 -8549 Mntmgry Rd -Cincinnati 45236
(513) 791-1672 .. Wenker, Michelle M '93 -8549 Mntgmry Rd -Cincinnati 45236
(513) 381-9200 .. Wenker, Paul F '67 (Rendigs FK&D,LLP) -One W 4th -Ste 900
-Cincinnati 45202 Fx:381-9206
(216) 443-8780 .. Wenneman, Ann F '82 Cuyahoga Cnty Probate Ct -1 Lakeside Av
-Cleveland 44113
(419) 423-5090 .. Wenner, Cheryl G '89 Charles Assoc,Inc -811 E Bigelow Av
-Bx1546 -Findlay 45839
(419) 241-7175 .. Wenner, William E '83 TolTest,Inc -1915 N 12th -Bx2186
-Toledo 43603
(419) 473-1350 .. Wenninger, Kenneth W '99 %Jasin S&M Co,LPA
-4303 Talmadge Rd -Ste 201 -Toledo 43623 Fx:473-1929
(419) 885-3597 .. Wensink, Karen J '02 %McHugh D&M,Ltd -5580 Monroe
-Sylvania 43560 Fx:885-3861
Wensink, Katherine E '02 -4510 Wood Rd -Monroeville 44847
(513) 421-4225 .. Wenstrup, Daniel J '76 (Heis & W Co,LPA) -817 Main -Ste 800
-Cincinnati 45202
(216) 586-3939 .. Wenstrup, Rose Mary '95 Cnsl Jones D -901 Lakeside Av
-Cleveland 44114 Fx:579-0212
(216) 579-1700 .. Wentsler, Stephen S '00 %Pearne & G LLP -1801 E 9th -Ste 1200
-Cleveland 44114 Fx:579-6073
(702) 385-3530 .. Wentworth, Andrew S '68 -302 Carson Av -Ste 902
-Las Vegas, NV 89101
(740) 349-7414 .. Wentworth, Karen H '94 (Christiansen & W) -172 Hudson Av
-Newark 43055
(740) 653-7825 .. Wentz, Gregory C '81 Coen W&W -323 E Main -Bx1028
-Lancaster 43130 Fx:653-3719
(614) 461-9212 .. Wentz, Jonathan C '97 Handelman & K -360 S Grant Av
-Columbus 43215
(859) 431-6100 .. Wentz, Richard E '76 (Arnzen & W,PSC) -600 Greenup -Bx472
-Covington, KY 41012 Fx:431-3778
(216) 685-9710 .. Wentz, Robert C '89 -1370 Ontario -Ste 1218 -Cleveland 44113
Fx:685-9714
(614) 466-0501 .. Wentzel, Jane E '96 Workers Comp -30 W Spring -Level 26
-Columbus 43215
(704) 331-3595 .. Wentzel, Suzanne '96 %Moore & V PLLC -100 N Tryon -Ste 4700
-Charlotte, NC 28202 Fx:331-1159
(937) 865-6800 .. Wenz, George L III '93 Lexis/Nexis -Bx933 -Dayton 45401
Wenzel, Lisa M '03 -29 Bon Jan Ln -Highland Heights, KY 41076
(937) 225-4652 .. Wenzke, James F '69 Montgomery Cnty Pub Def -117 S Main
-Ste 400 -Dayton 45422 Fx:225-3449
Wenzke, Margaret M '77 -1692 Woodman Dr -Dayton 45432
(937) 222-8885 .. Weprin, Ellen C '89 -130 W 2nd -Ste 450 -Dayton 45402
(937) 226-1776 .. Weprin, James I '67 (Froelich & W) -1812 Kettering Twr
-Dayton 45423 Fx:226-1945
(216) 687-2337 .. Werber, Stephen J '80 CSU-Marshall Cllg of Law -2121 Euclid Av
-LB138 -Cleveland 44115 Fx:687-6881
(859) 331-3900 .. Werden, George W '80 Apple Sauce,Inc -741 Centre Vw Blvd
-Crestview Hills, KY 41017
(212) 326-3939 .. Werder, Richard I Jr. '84 (Jones D) -222 E 41st -4th Fl
-New York, NY 10017 Fx:755-7306
(513) 583-9221 .. Werdmann, Timothy G '96 Clemans Nelson & Assoc
-411 W Loveland Av -Ste 101 -Loveland 45140
(330) 392-2533 .. Wern, Charles E III '99 %C Wern Jr,Ltd -210 Scott NE -Bx151
-Warren 44482 Fx:395-4304
(330) 392-2533 .. Wern, Charles E Jr. '59 C Wern Jr,Ltd -210 Scott NE -Bx151
-Warren 44482 Fx:395-4304
(216) 586-3939 .. Werner, Brooke D '04 %Jones D -901 Lakeside Av
-Cleveland 44114 Fx:579-0212
(216) 831-8838 .. Werner, Gary F '99 (Berns O&G,LLC) -3733 Park East Dr -Ste 200
-Beachwood 44122 Fx:464-4489
(419) 531-3887 .. Werner, Kim W '71 -3034 Barrington Dr -Toledo 43606
(419) 241-9000 .. Werner, Martin D '81 (Shumaker L&K,LLP) -1000 Jackson
-Toledo 43624 Fx:241-6894
(740) 587-0157 .. Wernet, William R '81 JCC -600 Newark Rd -Bx 381
-Granville 43023
(313) 871-3000 .. Wernette, Ronald C '99 (Bowman & B,LLP) -50 W Big Beaver Rd
-Ste 600 -Troy, MI 48084
(312) 540-7070 .. Wernick, Alan S '78 (Querrey & H) -175 Jackson Blvd -Ste 1600
-Chicago, IL 60604
(513) 381-2838 .. Wernicke, Vanessa A '04 %Taft S&H LLP -425 Walnut -Ste 1800
-Cincinnati 45202 Fx:381-0205
(330) 455-0173 .. Werren, John Curtis '92 (Day KRW&R,Ltd) -200 Market Av N
-Ste 300 -Bx24213 -Canton 44701 Fx:455-2633
(330) 453-2945 .. Werren, John E '91 Frank Gates Srvc Co -Bx8408 -Canton 44711
(330) 455-0173 .. Werren, John R '61 (Day KRW&R,Ltd) -200 Market Av N -Ste 300
-Bx24213 -Canton 44701 Fx:455-2633
(330) 761-9960 .. Werren, Nola R '89 State & Fed Comm,Inc -80 S Summit Ste 100
-Akron 44308 Fx:761-9965
(513) 721-4450 .. Wersching, James P '80 Santen & H -312 Walnut -Ste 3100
-Cincinnati 45202
(419) 522-2111 .. Werstiuk, Allen D '82 -600 Park Av W -Mansfield 44906
(614) 464-6400 .. Werth, Robert W '65 (Vorys SS&P LLP) -52 E Gay -Bx1008
-Columbus 43216 Fx:464-6350
(216) 378-9905 .. Wertheim, James S '85 OfCnsl McGlinchey S PLLC
-25550 Chagrin Blvd -Ste 406 -Cleveland 44122 Fx:378-9910
Wertheim, Walter R '63 -4866 Donald Av
-Richmond Heights 44143
(440) 720-0250 .. Wertheimer, Victor '48 -1897 Wnchstr Rd -Cleveland 44124
(412) 471-6554 .. Wertkin, Robin S '99 -2 Chatham Ctr -Ste 1450 -Pittsburgh,
PA 15219 Fx:261-3783

(330) 434-1000 .. Wertz, George R '79 (Bernlohr W,LLP) -23 S Main -3rd Fl
-Akron 44308 Fx:434-1001
(937) 865-6800 .. Wertz, Jeanne D '94 Lexis/Nexis -Bx933 -Dayton 45401
(419) 592-0010 .. Wesche, Michael J '73 -105 W Main -Napoleon 43545
(330) 376-5300 .. Weschler, Patrick J '81 (Buckingham D&B,LLP) -50 S Main
-Bx1500 -Akron 44309 Fx:258-6559
(740) 373-8151 .. Wesel, Marilyn S '93 Marietta Auto Warehouse,Inc -Tennis Ctr Dr
-Bx568 -Marietta 45750
(216) 458-1340 .. Wesel, Michael E '90 Mortgages & Money Mgmt -21139 Lorain Rd
-Cleveland 44126
(513) 721-0200 .. Weseli, Roger W '95 OfCnsl McKinney & N Co,LPA -15 E 8th
-Cincinnati 45202 Fx:632-5898
(513) 651-6800 .. Wesloh, Steven M '96 %Frost BT LLC -201 E 5th -2200 PNC Ctr
-Cincinnati 45202 Fx:651-6981
(614) 445-8218 .. Wesner, Arthur G '58 -999 S High -Columbus 43206
(513) 556-3483 .. Wesner, James E '92 Univ of Cincinnati -Bx210623
-Cincinnati 45221
(216) 621-2234 .. Wesorick, Richard S '95 (Tarolli SC&T) -526 Superior Av
-1111 Leader Bldg -Cleveland 44114 Fx:621-4072
(614) 228-5822 .. Wesp, Edward Joel '70 Rich C&D,LLC -300 E Broad -Ste 300
-Columbus 43215 Fx:228-2725
(513) 863-0083 .. Wessel & Froelke -6 S 2nd -315 Key Bldg -Hamilton 45011
(513) 863-0083 .. Wessel, Richard J '52 Wessel & F -6 S 2nd -315 Key Bldg
-Hamilton 45011
(513) 863-0083 .. Wessel, Robert F '51 Wessel & F -6 S 2nd -315 Key Bldg
-Hamilton 45011
Wesseler, Todd J '98 -(Address Unavailable)
(330) 375-3954 .. Wessell, Kelly M '94 Summa Hlth Syst -525 E Market -1st Fl
-Bx2090 -Akron 44309
Wesselman, Christy Lee '98 -Bx4 -Okeana 45053
(859) 344-1188 .. Wessels, Carlo R '91 (Hemmer SPD PLLC) -250 Grandvw Dr
-Ste 200 -Ft Mitchell, KY 41017
(937) 223-1130 .. Wessendarp, Richard J '80 Pickrel S&E -40 N Main
-2700 Kettering Twr -Dayton 45423 Fx:223-0339
(216) 464-8700 .. Wessman, Carol A '78 Wessman & Assoc -23230 Chagrin Blvd
-Ste 740 -Cleveland 44122 Fx:464-7990
(614) 445-2643 .. West, Charles E '74 Grange Mutual Cslty Co -650 S Front -Bx1218
-Columbus 43216
(513) 632-5328 .. West, Dave R '89 -117-121 E Court -Cincinnati 45202
(419) 421-4121 .. West, Elizabeth Ramsey '04 Marathon Ashland Petroleum,LLC
-539 S Main -Findlay 45840
(440) 323-7510 .. West, Harold A '54 -212 Middle Av -Elyria 44035
(216) 241-5310 .. West, Jennifer N '00 %Gallagher SF&N -1501 Euclid Av -6th Fl
-Cleveland 44115 Fx:241-1608
(859) 655-4200 .. West, John A '67 (Greenebaum D&M PLLC)
-50 E RiverCenter Blvd -Ste 1800 -Covington, KY 41011
Fx:655-4239
(770) 671-2199 .. West, John C '85 AIG Cnsltnts,Inc -1200 Abrnthy Rd NE
-Atlanta, GA 30328
(937) 593-3655 .. West, John D '61 -111 S Madriver -Bellefontaine 43311
(440) 884-4844 .. West, John H '82 (J West Co,LPA) -6650 Pearl Rd -Ste 202
-Parma Heights 44130
West, Kathleen L '79 -8957 Perkins Dr -Mentor 44060
(513) 946-5204 .. West, Melissa E '95 Hamilton Cnty Mun Ct -1000 Main
-Cincinnati 45202
(202) 305-0457 .. West, Pamela S '83 US DOJ -601 D NW -Rm 3118 -Bx663
-Washington, DC 20044
(937) 748-1749 .. West, Richard E '86 (R West & Assoc) -195 E Central Av -Bx938
-Springboro 45066
(216) 566-5500 .. West, Robert A Jr. '04 %Thompson H LLP -127 Pub Sq -3900
Key Ctr -Cleveland 44114 Fx:566-5800
(614) 466-7014 .. West, Sarah J '97 Pub Safety -1970 W Broad -Columbus 43223
Fx:752-6063
(614) 280-4141 .. West, Scott B '82 Pizzuti Co -2 Miranova Pl -Ste 800
-Columbus 43215
(937) 324-4171 .. West, William D '65 -200 N Fountain Av -Springfield 45504
(216) 778-5475 .. West, William G '74 Metro Health Systm -2500 Metro Health Dr
-South Pnt Ofc -Cleveland 44109
(419) 539-4092 .. West-Estell, Rebecca L '00 -2125 Parkdale -Toledo 43607
(740) 374-1581 .. Westbrock, Paul G '93 Marietta Health System-Legal Affrs
-401 Matthew -Marietta 45750 Fx:376-5581
(614) 268-0534 .. Westbrook, Gayle R '80 (Reves & W) -3207 N High
-Columbus 43202
(216) 736-6244 .. Westbrooks, Robert A '82 The East Ohio Gas Co -1717 E 9th
-Bx5759 -Cleveland 44101
(513) 852-6093 .. Westendorf, Douglas L '74 %Wood & L LLP -600 Vine -Ste 2500
-Cincinnati 45202 Fx:852-6087
(630) 682-0452 .. Westerbeck, Daniel J '72 -10 Union Cir -Wheaton, IL 60187
(513) 595-2325 .. Westerbeck, David F '72 Union Cntrl Life Ins Co
-1876 Waycross Rd -Bx40888 -Cincinnati 45240 Fx:595-2918
(513) 852-8200 .. Westerfield, Thomas J '81 OfCnsl Cors & B LLC
-537 E Pete Rose Way -Ste 400 -Cincinnati 45202
(440) 238-1011 .. Westerhaus, Michael F '74 -14255 Peppercreek Dr
-Strongsville 44136 Fx:572-1031
(614) 466-6511 .. Westerman, Matthew L '97 Dept Admin Srvcs -30 E Broad
-Columbus 43215
(614) 365-2700 .. Westerman, Philip R '98 %Squire S&D LLP -41 S High
-1300 Huntngtn Ctr -Columbus 43215 Fx:365-2499
Westermeyer, Jennifer T '95 -(Address Unavailable)
(614) 882-2339 .. Westervelt, Charles E Jr. '48 -18 W Cllg Av -Westerville 43081
(740) 593-6400 .. Westfall, James M '79 Pub Def -80 N Court -Athens 45701
Fx:591-2074
(216) 589-0600 .. Westfall, James W Jr. '77 (Eisen & W) -75 Pub Sq -Ste 1005
-Cleveland 44113
(614) 457-9731 .. Westfall, Lee W '96 %Harris & M -941 Chatham Ln -Ste 201
-Columbus 43221 Fx:457-3596
(419) 241-2300 .. Westfall, Sandra A '98 -316 N Mich -Ste 800 -Toledo 43624
(615) 726-3400 .. Westlake, Mark H '77 Westlake & M -Bx198888
-Nashville, TN 37219
(440) 930-5154 .. Westley, William K Jr. '69 -33782 Lk Rd -Avon Lake 44012
(859) 341-1881 .. Westling, Michael W '74 %Deters B&L,PSC -2701 Turkeyfoot Rd
-207 Thomas More Pkwy -Crestview Hills, KY 41017 Fx:341-1469

(330) 867-9998 .. **Westman**, Dean E '81 (Kastner W&W,LLC) -3480 W Market -Ste 300 -Akron 44333 Fx:867-3786

(419) 244-7041 .. **Westmeyer**, Joseph W III '99 %Westmeyer Law Ofc -421 N Mich -Ste C -Toledo 43624

(419) 244-7041 .. **Westmeyer**, Joseph W Jr. '66 -421 N Mich -Ste C -Toledo 43624

(614) 421-9200 .. **Weston**, Bruce J '80 -169 W Hubbard Av -Columbus 43215

(410) 727-6352 .. **Weston**, Gary J '92 Maryland Disability Law Ctr -1800 N Charles -Ste 400 -Baltimore, MD 21201

(419) 244-9500 .. **Weston**, Gretchen F Goranson '03 %Goranson P&B -405 Mad Av -Ste 2200 -Toledo 43604 Fx:(414) 244-9510

(513) 977-8200 .. **Weston**, Harris K '46 OfCnsl Dinsmore & S LLP -255 E 5th -Ste 1900 -Cincinnati 45202 Fx:977-8141

(216) 241-6602 .. **Weston Hurd Fallon Paisley & Howley LLP** -50 Pub Sq -2500 Trmnl Twr -Cleveland 44113 Fx:621-8369

(740) 397-5262 .. **Weston**, Robert B '71 (Zelkowitz B&C) -121 E High -Mount Vernon 43050

(440) 331-1142 .. **Weston**, William G Jr. '84 -20545 Ctr Ridge Rd -Ste 424 -Rocky River 44116

(480) 488-3860 .. **Westphal**, Marjorie L '79 -8545 E Double Eagle Rd -Carefree, AZ 85377

(513) 639-6519 .. **Westrich**, Whitney B '03 US Bank -205 W 4th -Cincinnati 45202

(216) 522-2657 .. **Westrick**, Timothy A '97 US DOJ -55 Erievw Plz -Ste 700 -Cleveland 44114 Fx:522-8332

(414) 276-1122 .. **Westrup**, David A '89 Von Briesen & R,SC -411 E Wscnsn Av -Ste 700 -Milwaukee, WI 53202

          Wetherald, Michele W '86 -(Address Unavailable)

(513) 528-0200 .. **Wetherall**, Gregory M '96 -4030 Mt Carmel-Tobasco Rd -Cincinnati 45255

(440) 576-3662 .. **Wetherholt**, Tamara A '98 Ashtabula Cnty Pros -25 W Jffrsn -Jefferson 44047

(419) 673-4176 .. **Wetherill Schwemer Markley & Schwemer** -109 E Franklin -Kenton 43326 Fx:673-8089

(419) 244-6788 .. **Wetli**, John F '69 (Bugbee & C) -405 Mad Av -Ste 1300 -Toledo 43604 Fx:244-7145

(419) 661-9500 .. **Wetmore**, Kenneth H '75 Glasstech,Inc -995 4th -Ampoint Indstrl Park -Perrysburg 43551

(614) 891-2222 .. **Wetterauer**, Damon E Jr. '74 -425 W Schrock Rd -Ste B1 -Westerville 43081

          Wetterer, Thomas R Jr. '83 -6090 Sandgate Rd -Columbus 43229

(513) 241-7244 .. **Wettstein**, Albert '41 -817 Main -Ste 200 -Cincinnati 45202

(614) 249-4727 .. **Wetzel**, Jonathan H '74 Nationwide Ins Co -Bx182166 -Columbus 43218

(216) 642-3342 .. **Wetzel**, Karl Robert '84 %Wegman H&V,LPA -6055 Rockside Wds Blvd -Ste 200 -Cleveland 44131 Fx:642-8826

(216) 443-8507 .. **Wetzel**, Rebecca B '90 Cuyahoga Cnty Crt Cmmn Pleas -1200 Ontario -4th Fl -Cleveland 44113

(614) 249-6910 .. **Wetzel**, Sandra M '77 Nationwide Ins Co -1 Nationwide Plz -Columbus 43215

          Wetzel, William C '59 -910 Mesquite Ln -Barberton 44203

(216) 622-8200 .. **Wexberg**, Marcia J '91 (Calfee H&G LLP) -800 Superior Av -Ste 1400 -Cleveland 44114 Fx:241-0816

(216) 566-5500 .. **Wexler**, Catherine Bassett '02 %Thompson H LLP -127 Pub Sq -3900 Key Ctr -Cleveland 44114 Fx:566-5800

(330) 792-6033 .. **Wexler**, Ilan '80 Anzellotti SP&S Co,LPA -21 N Wickliffe Cir -Youngstown 44515 Fx:793-3384

(703) 739-4900 .. **Weyer**, Stephen J '97 %Larson & T,PLC -1199 N Fairfax -Ste 900 -Alexandria, VA 22314

(330) 339-2288 .. **Weygandt**, Thomas J '95 Buckeye Career Ctr -545 Univ NE -New Philadelphia 44663

          Weyls, Donald R '01 -771 S 6th -Columbus 43206

(216) 896-5600 .. **Weyls**, Timothy J Jr. '98 %Levy & D -25200 Chagrin Blvd -Ste 310 -Beachwood 44122 Fx:896-5601

(330) 376-1112 .. **Whalen & Compton, LPA** -565 Wolf Ledges Pkwy -Bx2020 -Akron 44309 Fx:376-3200

(937) 544-6465 .. **Whalen**, Dana N '00 -216 N Market -West Union 45693 Fx:695-6137

(330) 376-1112 .. **Whalen**, Dennis M '66 Whalen & C,LPA -565 Wolf Ledges Pkwy -Bx2020 -Akron 44309 Fx:376-3200

(216) 781-0636 .. **Whalen**, Frank C '53 Whalen & F -526 Superior Av E -555 Leader Bldg -Cleveland 44114 Fx:781-0638

(513) 863-6700 .. **Whalen**, Jon P '97 (Millikin & F) -6 S 2nd -6th Fl -Bx598 -Hamilton 45012 Fx:863-0031

(615) 344-1984 .. **Whalen**, Kathleen M '89 HCA -1 Park Plz -Nashville, TN 37203

(513) 241-3100 .. **Whalen**, Melissa J '97 Lerner S&R -120 E 4th -8th Fl -Cincinnati 45202

(937) 255-7777 .. **Whalen**, Paul L '93 Air Force Inst of Tech -641 Twining Hall -2950 P -Wright Patterson AFB 45433

(606) 344-9038 .. **Whalen**, William P Jr. '68 -515 Kluemper Ct -Fort Wright, KY 41011

(513) 977-8200 .. **Whaley**, David A '03 %Dinsmore & S LLP -255 E 5th -Ste 1900 -Cincinnati 45202 Fx:977-8141

(614) 292-3814 .. **Whaley**, Douglas J '85 OSU Moritz Cllg of Law -55 W 12th Av -Columbus 43210 Fx:292-1383

(513) 983-7695 .. **Whaley**, Susan S '99 Procter & Gamble -1 Procter & Gamble Plz -Bx 9-Leg Dept -Cincinnati 45202

(216) 520-5600 .. **Whang**, Cynthia '93 West Grp -6111 Oak Tree Blvd -Bx318063 -Cleveland 44131

(614) 764-7440 .. **Whann**, Keith E '84 (Whann & Assoc) -6300 Frantz Rd -Dublin 43017

(513) 421-4646 .. **Wharton**, Bernard W '94 McCaslin I&M,LPA -632 Vine -Ste 900 -Cincinnati 45202 Fx:421-7929

(317) 226-6101 .. **Wharton**, Charles R '82 US Trustee -101 W Ohio -Ste 1000 -Indianapolis, IN 46204

(440) 285-2222 .. **Wharton**, Lawrence M '94 Geauga Cnty Pros -231 Main -Cthse Annx -Chardon 44024 Fx:286-4357

(513) 352-6853 .. **Wharton**, Lisa M '92 Thompson H LLP -312 Walnut -14th Fl -Cincinnati 45202 Fx:241-4771

(216) 348-1700 .. **Wharton**, Michele Y '93 %Davis & Y -101 Prospect Av W -Ste 1700 -Cleveland 44115 Fx:621-0602

(216) 781-1212 .. **Whatley**, Frederick W '81 (Walter & H LLP) -1301 E 9th -Ste 3500 -Cleveland 44114 Fx:575-0911

(202) 712-0000 .. **Wheat-Fortson**, Sandra J '88 US AID -Ronald Reagan Bldg -Washington, DC 20523 Fx:216-3524

(937) 445-5755 .. **Wheatley**, Bryan C '97 NCR Corp -1700 S Patterson Blvd -Dayton 45479

(513) 381-4700 .. **Wheatley**, Christine S '96 (Porter WM&A LLP) -250 E 5th -Ste 2200 -Cincinnati 45202 Fx:421-0991

(614) 224-3208 .. **Wheatley**, John C Jr. '52 -1 E Lvngstn Av -Ste B -Columbus 43215 Fx:365-9741

(440) 285-5731 .. **Wheatley**, Myron D '87 -151 Main -Bx71 -Chardon 44024

(216) 622-8200 .. **Wheatley**, Nathan A '00 %Calfee H&G LLP -800 Superior Av -Ste 1400 -Cleveland 44114 Fx:241-0816

(513) 381-2838 .. **Wheatley**, Susan E '86 (Taft S&H LLP) -425 Walnut -Ste 1800 -Cincinnati 45202 Fx:381-0205

          Wheaton, Carolyn W '89 -(Address Unavailable)

          Wheel-Carter, Karen D '88 -Bx450063 -Atlanta, GA 31145

          Wheeler, Anona K '04 -(Address Unavailable)

(330) 376-2668 .. **Wheeler**, Christine E '02 -209 S Main -8th Fl -Akron 44308 Fx:376-4828

(330) 796-6364 .. **Wheeler**, David E '84 Goodyear Tire & Rubber -144 E Market -Akron 44308

(513) 361-1200 .. **Wheeler**, David L '96 %Squire S&D LLP -312 Walnut -Ste 3500 -Cincinnati 45202 Fx:361-1201

(330) 848-9517 .. **Wheeler**, Evelyn M '89 -178 E Park Av -Barberton 44203

(614) 221-5216 .. **Wheeler**, James W '68 %Wiles BB&B Co,LPA -300 Spruce -1st Fl -Columbus 43215 Fx:221-5692

(216) 522-0800 .. **Wheeler**, John D '77 (Reed M&W,Ltd) -1801 E 9th -Cleveland 44114

(740) 922-1497 .. **Wheeler**, Joseph A '84 -113 E 3rd -Uhrichsville 44683

          Wheeler, Judith C '96 -(Address Unavailable)

(614) 451-6803 .. **Wheeler**, Pelton W '88 -Bx21170 -Columbus 43221

(330) 643-2250 .. **Wheeler**, Susan E '85 9th Dist Ct of Appeals -161 S High -5th Fl -Akron 44308 Fx:643-2091

(614) 221-0944 .. **Wheeler**, Terrence T '85 %Artz & D,LLP -560 E Town -Columbus 43215 Fx:221-2340

(740) 353-5044 .. **Wheeler**, Wayne B '82 -1248 Kinneys Ln -Portsmouth 45662

(419) 245-1080 .. **Wheelock**, Donald S '96 City of Toledo -1 Govt Ctr -Ste 2140 -Toledo 43604

(937) 449-2800 .. **Whelley**, Thomas P II '77 (Chernesky H&K PLL) -10 Cthse Plz SW -Ste 1100 -Dayton 45402 Fx:449-2821

(513) 977-8200 .. **Wherley**, James M Jr. '01 %Dinsmore & S LLP -255 E 5th -Ste 1900 -Cincinnati 45202 Fx:977-8141

(859) 341-1881 .. **Wherley**, Susanne R '01 Deters B&L,PSC -2701 Turkeyfoot Rd -207 Thomas More Pkwy -Crestview Hills, KY 41017 Fx:341-1469

(614) 487-2050 .. **Whetzel**, Eugene P '74 %OH State Bar Assoc -Bx16562 -Columbus 43216

(216) 443-5809 .. **Whinery**, Joanna A '92 Cuyahoga Cnty Pros -1910 Carnegie Av -Whitlatch Bldg -Cleveland 44115 Fx:443-5815

(216) 566-8200 .. **Whipple**, Douglas P '80 (Seeley S&E Co LPA) -600 Superior Av E -800 Bank One Ctr -Cleveland 44114 Fx:566-0213

          Whipple, Peggy A '85 -4706 Shale Oaks Av -Columbia, MO 65203

(614) 865-8415 .. **Whipple**, Robert C '02 Exel Inc -570 Polaris Pkwy -Westerville 43082

(614) 461-6006 .. **Whipps**, Edward F '61 (E Whipps & Assoc) -500 S Front -Ste 860 -Columbus 43215

(937) 225-5760 .. **Whisman**, Victor T '82 Montgomery Cnty Pros -301 W 3rd -Bx972 -Dayton 45422 Fx:225-3470

          Whitacre, Jason A '04 -(Address Unavailable)

(419) 627-6620 .. **Whitacre**, Jeffrey J '88 Erie Cnty Pub Def -220 Columbus Av -Ste 37 -Sandusky 44870 Fx:627-6633

(216) 771-6633 .. **Whitaker**, Andrea L '01 %Goldstein & O -526 Superior Av E -Ste 1040 Leader Bldg -Cleveland 44114 Fx:771-7559

(216) 226-1564 .. **Whitaker**, David W Jr. '82 -1782 E 65th -Cleveland 44103

(513) 723-4000 .. **Whitaker**, Glenn V '80 (Vorys SS&P LLP) -221 E 4th -Ste 2000 Atrium Two -Bx0236 -Cincinnati 45201 Fx:723-4056

(513) 398-1910 .. **Whitaker**, James A Jr. '72 -226 Reading Rd -Mason 45040

(513) 579-6400 .. **Whitaker**, James R '73 SrCnsl Keating M&K PLL -1 E 4th -1400 Provident Twr -Cincinnati 45202 Fx:579-6457

(614) 760-0500 .. **Whitaker**, Lowell D '86 -8798 Curran Pnt Ct -Powell 43065

(330) 821-4414 .. **Whitaker**, Mark A '79 -2031 Rdgwd Av -Alliance 44601

(614) 888-7686 .. **Whitaker**, Philip W '69 -333 Colonial Av -Worthington 43085

(614) 221-7663 .. **Whitaker**, Roger T '76 (Luper N&L,LPA) -50 W Broad -1200 LeVeque Twr -Columbus 43215 Fx:464-2425

(317) 226-7228 .. **Whitaker**, Tammy H '88 EEOC -101 W Ohio -Ste 1900 -Indianapolis, IN 46204

          Whitaker, William S '85 -10301 Barchester Dr -Concord 44077

(330) 762-0287 .. **Whitaker**, William T Jr. '72 (Whitaker & R Co,LPA) -190 N Union -Ste 301 -Akron 44304

(614) 228-1541 .. **Whitcomb**, David A '92 (Baker & H LLP) -65 E State -Ste 2100 -Columbus 43215 Fx:462-2616

(419) 241-4141 .. **Whitcomb**, Howard C III '91 -405 Mad Av -Ste 1440 -Toledo 43604

(216) 921-6900 .. **White**, Andrew D '96 OfficeMax,Inc -3605 Warrensvll Ctr Rd -Shaker Heights 44122

(740) 286-0071 .. **White**, Andrew T '01 %R Lewis -295 Pearl -Bx664 -Jackson 45640 Fx:286-2988

(614) 469-3235 .. **White**, Anthony C '93 (Thompson H LLP) -10 W Broad -Ste 700 -Columbus 43215 Fx:469-3361

(614) 485-9300 .. **White**, Arnold S '69 (White & F,LPA Inc) -1335 Dublin Rd -Ste 201C -Columbus 43215 Fx:485-9462

(419) 668-1886 .. **White**, Beverly M '60 (Lynch & W Co,LPA) -51 E Main -Ste B -Norwalk 44857 Fx:668-4172

(202) 293-7060 .. **White**, Brandon M '02 Sughrue Mion,PLLC -2100 Penn Av NW -Ste 800 -Washington, DC 20037

(304) 485-5372 .. **White**, Bruce M '02 (B White, LC) -720 Juliana -Parkersburg, WV 26101 Fx:485-6126

          White, Catherine M '01 -7036 Dean Farm Rd -New Albany 43054

(330) 869-5900 .. **White**, Craig M '87 -11 Mayfld Av -Akron 44313

(216) 621-0150 .. **White**, Craig O '83 (Hahn L&P LLP) -3300 BP Twr/200 Pub Sq -Ste 3300 -Cleveland 44114 Fx:241-2824

(614) 876-8240 .. **White**, Daniel J '80 -5999 Heritage Lks Dr -Hilliard 43026 Fx:876-8342

(216) 566-1600 .. **White**, Daniel S '90 (Schwarzwald & M) -1300 E 9th -Ste 616 -Cleveland 44114 Fx:566-1814

(216) 241-5310 .. **White**, Darlene E '00 %Gallagher SF&N -1501 Euclid Av -6th Fl -Cleveland 44115 Fx:241-1608

(908) 437-4136 ..**White**, David A '79 Harvard Industries,Inc -3 Werner Way -Ste 210 -Lebanon, NJ 08833

(937) 224-3926 ..**White**, David A '88 Montgomery Cnty Pub Def -117 S Main -Ste 400 -Dayton 45422 **Fx:**225-3449

(614) 249-7699 ..**White**, David Lin '81 Nationwide Ins Co -1 Nationwide Plz -Columbus 43215

(330) 533-2616 ..**White**, David R '68 -106 S Broad -Canfield 44406

(513) 732-1420 ..**White**, Donald W '73 (Nichols S&N) -237 Main -Batavia 45103

(678) 494-2367 ..**White**, Doris J '03 -4512 Inlet Rd -Marietta, GA 30066

(614) 466-5967 ..**White**, Duane M '76 Atty Gen -30 E Broad -Columbus 43215 **Fx:**466-8226

(415) 442-6679 ..**White**, Frederic P Jr. '73 Golden Gate Univ Schl of Law -536 Mission -San Francisco, CA 94105 **Fx:**442-6609

(216) 687-1900 ..**White**, Gail '81 Legal Aid -1223 W 6th -Cleveland 44113 **Fx:**687-0779

(419) 246-5757 ..**White**, Garrick O '98 %Anspach M&N,LLP -300 Mad Av -Ste 1600 -Toledo 43604 **Fx:**321-6979

(513) 723-4000 ..**White**, Geoffrey M '03 %Vorys SS&P LLP -221 E 4th -Ste 2000 Atrium Two -Bx0236 -Cincinnati 45201 **Fx:**723-4056

(330) 744-1148 ..**White**, George L IV '96 (Henderson CMN&T Co,LPA) -34 Fed Plz W -Ste 600 Wick Bldg -Youngstown 44503 **Fx:**744-3807

(216) 830-9000 ..**White**, George W Jr. '56 OfCnsl Berger & Z Co,LPA -614 W Superior Av -Ste 1425 Rckflr Bldg -Cleveland 44113 **Fx:**830-4200

(513) 241-3685 ..**White Getgey & Meyer Co,LPA** -1 W 4th -Ste 1700 -Cincinnati 45202 **Fx:**241-2399

(740) 345-9611 ..**White**, Glenn A '69 (Morrow G&B,Ltd) -33 W Main -Bx4190 -Newark 43058

(216) 622-3600 ..**White**, Gregory A '77 US Atty -801 W Superior -Ste 400 -Cleveland 44113 **Fx:**622-3370

(419) 241-9000 ..**White**, James F Jr. '65 OfCnsl Shumaker L&K,LLP -1000 Jackson -Toledo 43624 **Fx:**241-6894

(216) 692-3877 ..**White**, James J '56 -21601 Edgecliff Dr -Euclid 44123

(419) 479-3959 ..**White**, James W Jr. '80 -5749 Park Ctr Ct -Toledo 43615

                White, Janice G '78 -2467 Stafford Pl -Columbus 43209

                White, Jeanne M '87 -(Address Unavailable)

(937) 222-2424 ..**White**, Jennifer M '04 Freund F&A -1 S Main -Ste 1800 -Dayton 45402 **Fx:**222-5369

(330) 533-8885 ..**White**, Joanna B '04 R Ciotola Co,LPA -4590 Boardman Canfld Rd -Canfield 44406

(614) 464-6400 ..**White**, Julia Falenski '96 %Vorys SS&P LLP -52 E Gay -Bx1008 -Columbus 43216 **Fx:**464-6350

(419) 241-5522 ..**White**, Kenneth I Sr. '61 Amer First Title Agncy -241 N Superior -Ste 100 -Toledo 43604

(419) 254-4300 ..**White**, Kenneth J '74 Marshall & M,LLC -420 Mad Av -Ste 1100 -Toledo 43604

(513) 381-2838 ..**White**, Kristin N '03 %Taft S&H LLP -425 Walnut -Ste 1800 -Cincinnati 45202 **Fx:**381-0205

(937) 294-5800 ..**White**, Lawrence J '93 -2533 Far Hills Av -2nd Fl -Dayton 45419 **Fx:**298-1503

(614) 873-8740 ..**White**, Lisa A '03 -9745 New Calif Dr -Plain City 43064 **Fx:**873-8740

(440) 350-1909 ..**White**, Mark C '83 (White & W Co,LPA) -1475 Amberwood Ln -Painesville 44077

(330) 394-9692 ..**White**, Martin F '77 (M White Co,LPA) -156 Park Av NE -Bx1150 -Warren 44482 **Fx:**394-8589

(216) 621-1000 ..**White**, Mary E '03 %Moscarino & T,LLP -1422 Euclid Av -Hanna Bldg Ste 630 -Cleveland 44115 **Fx:**622-1556

(513) 241-7460 ..**White**, Maurice O '78 -7 W 7th -Ste 1850 -Cincinnati 45202

(513) 595-2333 ..**White**, Michael J '84 Union Ctrl Life Ins -1876 Waycross Rd -Bx40888 -Cincinnati 45240

(740) 852-3164 ..**White**, Monte C '70 -Bx887 -London 43140

(330) 758-0080 ..**White**, Richard N '76 (White & B) -755 Boardman-Canfld Rd -Bx9304 -Youngstown 44513 **Fx:**758-9533

(407) 423-7287 ..**White**, Robert A '72 (Bussey WM&F,PA) -105 E Robnsn -4th Fl -Bx531086 -Orlando, FL 32853 **Fx:**648-1376

(440) 322-5441 ..**White**, Robert C '91 (Lessing W&R Ltd) -374 Broad -Ste A -Elyria 44035

                White, Ryan O '00 -101 2nd Av SW #3N -Carmel, IN 46032

(440) 333-6202 ..**White**, Scott D '93 -21300 Lorain Rd -Fairview Park 44126

(304) 346-7000 ..**White**, Steven F '75 (Goodwin & G) -300 Summers -Ste 1500 -Charleston, WV 25301 **Fx:**344-9692

(304) 522-9100 ..**White**, Tamela J '94 (Farrell & F LC) -Bx6457 -Huntington, WV 25772

(419) 995-8386 ..**White**, Terry L '82 Lima Tech Cllg -4240 Campus Dr -Police Academy Cmmndr -Lima 45804

(937) 435-8780 ..**White**, Thomas A III '61 -7501 Paragon Rd -Dayton 45459

(513) 946-3819 ..**White**, Thomas C Jr. '00 Hamilton Cnty Pub Def -230 E 9th -3rd Fl -Cincinnati 45202 **Fx:**946-3707

                White, Timothy T '89 -(Address Unavailable)

(419) 227-6601 ..**White**, Walter L '48 (White W&W) -311 N Elizabeth -Lima 45801

(419) 227-6601 ..**White**, William H '70 (White W&W) -311 N Elizabeth -Lima 45801

(202) 822-6100 ..**White**, William R '67 (Russin & V) -815 Conn Av NW -Ste 650 -Washington, DC 20006

(216) 523-1920 ..**White**, William T '67 (White & W Co,LPA) -75 Pub Sq -Ste 1310 -Cleveland 44113

(216) 843-7550 ..**Whited**, James R '75 Summit Cnty Juv Ct -650 Dan -Akron 44310

(614) 438-2648 ..**Whitehead**, Daniel P '98 %CS Cobb -100 E Compus Vw Blvd -Ste 250 -Columbus 43235 **Fx:**438-2650

(440) 546-8611 ..**Whitehead**, David W '73 The Illuminating Co -6896 Miller Rd -Ste 210 -Brecksville 44141

(216) 831-5313 ..**Whitehead**, George W '53 -24819 Wimbledon Rd -Beachwood 44122

(216) 622-8200 ..**Whitehead**, Michael H '00 %Calfee H&G LLP -800 Superior Av -Ste 1400 -Cleveland 44114 **Fx:**241-0816

(614) 644-9110 ..**Whitehouse**, Richard A '87 Insp Gen -30 E Broad -Ste 1820 -Columbus 43215

(859) 341-1881 ..**Whitehouse**, Robert A II '02 %Deters B&L,PSC -2701 Turkeyfoot Rd -207 Thomas More Pkwy -Crestview Hills, KY 41017 **Fx:**341-1469

(513) 651-7232 ..**Whitehurst**, John R II '81 (Whitehurst Assoc) -4209 Carew Twr -Cincinnati 45202

(419) 422-2121 ..**Whiteleather**, Larry W '79 Marathon Ashland Petro LLC -539 S Main -Findlay 45840 **Fx:**421-8402

(513) 721-6151 ..**Whiteley**, Daniel E Jr. '75 -602 Main -Ste 1309 -Cincinnati 45202

(937) 652-1555 ..**Whitesell**, Jack W Jr. '89 Champaign Cnty Pros -200 N Main -Urbana 43078

(216) 592-5000 ..**Whitesell**, Jeffrey M '97 %Tucker E&W LLP -925 Euclid Av -1150 Huntngtn Bldg -Cleveland 44115 **Fx:**592-5009

(614) 236-2300 ..**Whiteside**, Alba L Jr. '54 (Whiteside & W) -2770 E Main -Ste 28 -Columbus 43209

                Whitfield, Vickie L Jackson '77 -Bx98 -Dania, FL 33004

(216) 622-8200 ..**Whitford**, Cornelius J '89 (Calfee H&G LLP) -800 Superior Av -Ste 1400 -Cleveland 44114 **Fx:**241-0816

(215) 221-8588 ..**Whitford**, Ronald O Jr. '95 Tasty Baking Co -2801 Hunting Park Av -Philadelphia, PA 19129

(216) 241-8333 ..**Whiting**, Timothy P '92 Ritzler C&S,Ltd -1001 Lakeside Av -1550 North Pnt Twr -Cleveland 44114 **Fx:**241-5890

(832) 239-3800 ..**Whiting**, Hugh R '74 (Jones DR&P) -600 Travis -Ste 6500 Chase Twr -Houston, TX 77002 **Fx:**239-3600

(937) 219-7726 ..**Whiting**, Kimberly M '03 Whiting Law Ofc -2312 Far Hills Av -#104 -Dayton 45419

(216) 321-7606 ..**Whiting**, Vanessa L '89 -2489 Coventry Rd -Cleveland Heights 44118

(419) 227-5531 ..**Whitlatch**, Robert E '82 SpclCnsl Allen Cnty Juvenile Ct -1000 Wardhill Av -Lima 45805 **Fx:**222-7403

(614) 888-7126 ..**Whitlock**, Scott N '67 -6081 Olentangy Rvr Rd -Worthington 43085

(513) 651-6800 ..**Whitlow**, Janice Baker '03 %Frost BT LLC -201 E 5th -2200 PNC Ctr -Cincinnati 45202 **Fx:**651-6981

(513) 852-8200 ..**Whitlow**, Matthew A '03 %Cors & B LLC -537 E Pete Rose Way -Ste 400 -Cincinnati 45202

(513) 421-3940 ..**Whitman**, Bruce B '80 -3536 Edwards Rd -Ste 100 -Cincinnati 45208

(216) 621-2234 ..**Whitman**, Daniel J '00 %Tarolli SC&T -526 Superior Av -1111 Leader Bldg -Cleveland 44114 **Fx:**621-4072

(202) 442-8167 ..**Whitman**, Elizabeth A '85 DC Ofc of Adjudication -941 N Cptl NE -Ste 9100 -Washington, DC 20002

(419) 423-8055 ..**Whitman**, Jeffrey J '77 -101 W Sandusky -Findlay 45840 **Fx:**425-1508

(419) 423-8055 ..**Whitman Law Office, LLC** -101 W Sandusky -Findlay 45840 **Fx:**425-1508

(513) 352-0401 ..**Whitman**, Virginia C '81 -1 W 4th -1700 4th & Vine Twr -Cincinnati 45202 **Fx:**241-2399

(330) 535-5711 ..**Whitmer**, Jerry F '60 (Brouse M) -106 S Main -500 First Natl Twr -Akron 44308 **Fx:**253-8601

(216) 479-6100 ..**Whitmer**, Mary K '75 OfCnsl Vorys SS&P LLP -1375 E 9th -Ste 2100 One Cleve Ctr -Cleveland 44114 **Fx:**479-6060

(330) 258-6252 ..**Whitmore**, Andreana R '00 Roadway Express, Inc -1077 Gorge Blvd -Bx471 -Akron 44309

(614) 688-4225 ..**Whitney**, Denton S '04 Ohio State Univ Medical Ctr -333 W 10th -Columbus 43210

(330) 253-7171 ..**Whitney**, Lawrence J '74 %Burdon & M -137 S Main -Ste 201 -Akron 44308 **Fx:**253-7174

(419) 522-3398 ..**Whitney**, M Loré '92 (Inscore RW&E,LPA) -13 Park Av W -Ste 400 -Mansfield 44902 **Fx:**522-5165

(419) 522-3398 ..**Whitney**, R Rolf '82 (Inscore RW&E,LPA) -13 Park Av W -Ste 400 -Mansfield 44902 **Fx:**522-5165

(216) 586-3939 ..**Whitney**, Richard B '73 (Jones D) -901 Lakeside Av -Cleveland 44114 **Fx:**579-0212

(330) 264-9454 ..**Whitney**, Richard K '87 Cmmnty Lgl Aid Srvcs,Inc -121 W North -Ste 100 -Wooster 44691

(419) 522-3398 ..**Whitney**, Robert H '62 (Inscore RW&E,LPA) -13 Park Av W -Ste 400 -Mansfield 44902 **Fx:**522-5165

(740) 657-7810 ..**Whitney**, Thomas R '73 Delaware Cnty Bank & Trust Co -110 Rvrbnd Av -Bx1001 -Lewis Center 43035

(216) 687-1900 ..**Whitsett**, Tonya D '94 Legal Aid -1223 W 6th -Cleveland 44113 **Fx:**687-0779

(412) 577-5200 ..**Whitson**, Keith E '96 Schnader HS&L LLP -120 5th Av -Pittsburgh, PA 15222

(937) 255-5270 ..**Whitt**, Gregory D '84 US Air Force -1864 4th -Rm 130A,AFMCLO/JAVP -Dayton 45433

(216) 621-6570 ..**Whitt**, Jennifer L '02 %Rademaker MM&G -55 Pub Sq -Ste 1775 -Cleveland 44113 **Fx:**621-1127

(216) 586-3939 ..**Whitt**, Mark A '97 %Jones D -901 Lakeside Av -Cleveland 44114 **Fx:**579-0212

(614) 221-7663 ..**Whittaker**, David M '79 (Luper N&L,LPA) -50 W Broad -1200 LeVeque Twr -Columbus 43215 **Fx:**464-2425

(513) 751-8300 ..**Whittaker**, James A '85 -432 Ray Norrish Dr -Cincinnati 45246 **Fx:**751-3230

(330) 535-5711 ..**Whitten**, Nora J '01 %Brouse M -106 S Main -500 First Natl Twr -Akron 44308 **Fx:**253-8601

(513) 243-5402 ..**Whittenburg**, Mark G '92 GE Aircraft Engines -1 Neumann Way -MD BBC7 -Cincinnati 45215

(614) 865-4709 ..**Whitter**, Herman S '90 OCSEA-AFSCME Local 11 -390 Worthngtn Rd -Ste A -Westerville 43082

(719) 333-9156 ..**Whittier**, Jennifer A '92 USAF HQUSAF/DFL -2354 Fairchild Dr -Ste IJ100 -U S A F Academy, CO 80840

(216) 771-7777 ..**Whittington**, Aaron Daniel '66 -55 Pub Sq -Ste 1550 -Cleveland 44113

(513) 423-1300 ..**Whittington**, John A '77 -2 N Main -6th Fl -Middletown 45042

(740) 349-6580 ..**Whittington**, John A '89 -65 E Main -Newark 43055

(216) 875-8206 ..**Whittington**, Nicholas M '00 KPMG,LLP -1375 E 9th -Ste 2600 -Cleveland 44114

(330) 384-8484 ..**Whittington**, Robert M Jr. '81 -159 S Main -Ste 1023 -Akron 44308

(513) 943-7200 ..**Whittle**, James T Jr. '82 Midland Co -7000 Mdlnd Blvd -Amelia 45102

(614) 644-7409 ..**Whitworth**, Jill A '94 Workers Comp -30 W Spring -Level 26 -Columbus 43215

(502) 895-2297 ..**Whonsetler**, Scott P '96 Whonsetler & Assoc,PSC -6100 Brownsboro Blvd -Ste E -Louisville, KY 40207

                Wiater, Justin J '03 -(Address Unavailable)

(614) 469-3297 ..**Wible**, Michael V '04 OfCnsl Thompson H LLP -10 W Broad -Ste 700 -Columbus 43215 **Fx:**469-3361

(614) 228-1128 ..**Wichman**, Jane C '89 -500 S Front -Ste 970 -Columbus 43215

(859) 342-5840 .. **Wichmann**, Frank A II '64 (FA Wichmann,PSC) -4132 Dixie Hwy -Bx18063 -Erlanger, KY 41018

(419) 213-4755 .. **Wichowski**, Judith E '87 %Hon ML Resnick -800 Jackson -Toledo 43624

(440) 899-9425 .. **Wick**, Bruce T '75 -24600 Ctr Ridge Rd -Ste 115 -Westlake 44145

(216) 621-0150 .. **Wick**, Christopher B '00 %Hahn L&P LLP -3300 BP Twr/200 Pub Sq -Ste 3300 -Cleveland 44114 **Fx:**241-2824

(419) 946-6367 .. **Wick**, Donald K '83 -23 E High -Bx15 -Mount Gilead 43338

(216) 535-0520 .. **Wick**, G Michael '89 US DHS,ICE -1240 E 9th -Rm 519 -Cleveland 44199

(216) 622-8823 .. **Wick**, Jennifer Buckey '01 %Calfee H&G LLP -800 Superior Av -Ste 1400 -Cleveland 44114 **Fx:**241-0816

Wick, Melissa S '04 -(Address Unavailable)

(440) 930-8000 .. **Wickens Herzer Panza Cook & Batista** -35765 Chester Rd -Avon 44011 **Fx:**937-4466

(937) 449-2800 .. **Wickham**, David R '83 (Chernesky H&K PLL) -10 Cthse Plz SW -Ste 1100 -Dayton 45402 **Fx:**449-2821

(614) 221-7663 .. **Wickham**, Henry F Jr. '79 (Luper N&L,LPA) -50 W Broad -1200 LeVeque Twr -Columbus 43215 **Fx:**464-2425

(614) 299-2859 .. **Wickliffe**, Marsha R '84 -912 Leona Av -Columbus 43201

(614) 462-2204 .. **Wickline**, Amanda L '03 %Schottenstein Z&D -250 West -Bx165020 -Columbus 43216 **Fx:**462-5135

(479) 204-1071 .. **Wickline**, Bruce E '92 Wal-Mart Stores,Inc -702 SW 8th -Bentonville, AR 72716

(937) 599-6242 .. **Wickline**, Gabriel D '04 Beck B&H -709 N Main -Bx549 -Bellefontaine 43311

(216) 896-2217 .. **Wickline**, Paul O '81 Parker-Hannifin Corp -6035 Parkland Blvd -Cleveland 44124

(419) 241-9000 .. **Wicklund**, David W '74 (Shumaker L&K,LLP) -1000 Jackson -Toledo 43624 **Fx:**241-6894

(216) 292-4504 .. **Wickter**, Lawrence D Jr. '02 -23220 Chagrin Blvd -Ste 300 -Cleveland 44122

(216) 283-8617 .. **Widder**, John M '64 (Widder & W) -18231 Sherrington Rd -Shaker Heights 44122

(330) 535-4191 .. **Widder**, Karen E '92 Cmmnty Lgl Aid Srvcs,Inc -265 S Main -3rd Fl -Akron 44308 **Fx:**535-0728

(216) 283-8617 .. **Widder**, Margaret M '86 (Widder & W) -18231 Sherrington Rd -Shaker Heights 44122

(513) 977-8200 .. **Widdowson**, Mary E '04 %Dinsmore & S LLP -255 E 5th -Ste 1900 -Cincinnati 45202 **Fx:**977-8141

(614) 224-8848 .. **Wideman**, Clark W '75 -4737 Nugent Dr -Columbus 43220 **Fx:**457-6387

(614) 221-9790 .. **Wideman**, Matthew B '02 %J Scott Co,LPA -35 E Lvngstn Av -Columbus 43215 **Fx:**228-6680

(614) 228-5711 .. **Wideman**, Stacey Lane '03 %Lucas PAG&N -600 S High -Columbus 43215 **Fx:**228-0982

(216) 931-6000 .. **Widen**, Frederick N '81 (Ulmer & B LLP) -1300 E 9th -Ste 900 Penton Media Bldg -Cleveland 44114 **Fx:**931-6001

(614) 466-4605 .. **Widener**, China L '92 OH Dept Job & Fam Srvcs -30 E Broad -32nd Fl -Columbus 43266

(614) 445-8801 .. **Widmaier**, James L '65 -901 S High -Columbus 43206

(216) 931-6000 .. **Widman**, Elizabeth M '04 %Ulmer & B LLP -1300 E 9th -Ste 900 Penton Media Bldg -Cleveland 44114 **Fx:**931-6001

(419) 874-7188 .. **Widman**, Marilyn L '97 (Allotta F&W Co,LPA) -27457 Holiday Ln -Ste W -Perrysburg 43551 **Fx:**874-7189

(614) 224-3344 .. **Widman**, Thomas G '92 Cnsl Midland Celtic Title -341 S 3rd -Columbus 43215 **Fx:**242-4054

(513) 618-6705 .. **Widmann**, Douglas J '02 Intelliseek Inc -1128 Main -4th Fl -Cincinnati 45202

(440) 934-3700 .. **Wieber**, Brett D '01 Fauver K-W&D -5333 Meadow Ln Ct -Elyria 44035 **Fx:**934-3708

Wieczorek, Katherine J '82 -(Address Unavailable)

(216) 622-8200 .. **Wiedemann**, John T '96 (Calfee H&G LLP) -800 Superior Av -Ste 1400 -Cleveland 44114 **Fx:**241-0816

(419) 668-8211 .. **Wiedemann**, Robert A '52 (Hiltz WA&K Co,LPA) -401 Ctzns Natl Bk Bldg -Bx640 -Norwalk 44857 **Fx:**668-2813

(216) 382-3666 .. **Wieder**, Michael D '69 -4625 Birchwold Rd -South Euclid 44121

(210) 652-5085 .. **Wiedie**, Charles E '95 USAF -550 D W -Ste 3 -Randolph AFB, TX 78150

(216) 289-2700 .. **Wiegand**, Richard A '78 Law Dept -585 E 222nd -Euclid 44123

(702) 407-6244 .. **Wiegand**, Scott E '93 Harrahs Entertainment,Inc -One Harrah Ct -Leg Dept -Las Vegas, NV 89119

Wieland, Susan T '03 -(Address Unavailable)

(970) 377-0223 .. **Wiemerslage**, Wayne L '01 -Bx271722 -Fort Collins, CO 80527 **Fx:**377-0223

(330) 535-5711 .. **Wiencek**, Thomas J '85 (Brouse M) -106 S Main -500 First Natl Twr -Akron 44308 **Fx:**253-8601

(937) 225-5705 .. **Wienekoski**, Victoria E '93 Montgomery Cnty Pros -301 W 3rd -Bx972 -Dayton 45422 **Fx:**225-3470

(419) 562-9782 .. **Wiener**, Michael J '01 Crawford Cnty Pros -112 E Mansfld -Ste 305 -Bucyrus 44820 **Fx:**562-9533

(216) 241-3880 .. **Wiener**, Stanley '53 -75 Pub Sq -Ste 1425 -Cleveland 44113

(740) 594-4043 .. **Wiens**, Keith M '98 -85 N Congress -Bx2628 -Athens 45701

(440) 930-8030 .. **Wiersma**, David C '76 Wickens HPC&B -35765 Chester Rd -Avon 44011 **Fx:**937-4466

(330) 342-8203 .. **Wiery**, Michael L '97 J Clunk Co LPA -5061 Hudson Dr -Ste 400 -Hudson 44236 **Fx:**342-8205

(216) 621-1312 .. **Wiery**, Suzanne F '98 %McMahon DH&L LLP -812 Huron Rd -Ste 650 The Caxton Bldg -Cleveland 44115 **Fx:**621-0577

(614) 559-1102 .. **Wiese**, John A '87 Chicago Title Ins Co -5150 Reed Rd -Columbus 43220

(330) 376-5300 .. **Wiese**, Philip R '96 %Buckingham D&B,LLP -50 S Main -Bx1500 -Akron 44309 **Fx:**258-6559

(419) 738-8165 .. **Wiesenmayer**, Robert C '65 -15 Willipie -Ste 300 -Bx299 -Wapakoneta 45895

(419) 738-8165 .. **Wiesenmayer**, Robert C II '93 %RC Wiesenmayer -15 Willipie -Ste 300 -Bx299 -Wapakoneta 45895

(216) 323-9116 .. **Wieser**, Molly B '98 Racial Fairness Report Project -2401 Superior Viaduct -Cleveland 44113

(614) 424-6589 .. **Wiesmann**, Klaus H '79 Battelle Memorial Inst -505 King Av -Columbus 43201

(614) 466-3801 **Wiest**, Christopher D '04 Atty Gen -150 E Gay -Columbus 43215

(330) 287-5574 .. **Wiest**, Karin C '89 Cnty CASA/GAL Prog -107 W Lbrty -Wooster 44691

(202) 514-4340 .. **Wietecha**, Annette M '90 DOJ-Tax Div -Bx502 -Washington, DC 20044

(513) 241-5551 .. **Wiethe**, Barbara R '79 -118 W 6th -Cincinnati 45202

(513) 684-3711 .. **Wiethe**, Donetta D '77 US Atty -221 E 4th -Ste 400 -Cincinnati 45202 **Fx:**684-6385

(513) 241-7332 .. **Wiethe**, Michael J '72 -7 W 7th -Ste 1800 -Cincinnati 45202

(513) 621-2666 .. **Wietholter**, Thomas A '87 %Statman HS&E LLC -255 E 5th -Ste 2900 Chemed Ctr -Cincinnati 45202 **Fx:**587-4477

(740) 452-7555 .. **Wietmarschen**, Donald A '81 (Gottlieb JB&D,PLL) -320 Main -Bx190 -Zanesville 43702 **Fx:**452-2257

Wiggers, Carol C '83 -(Address Unavailable)

(614) 203-4670 .. **Wiggin**, James W '85 OfCnsl Cohen & B LLP -22 E 4th Av -#3A -Columbus 43201

(614) 241-5550 .. **Wiggins**, Jennifer A '01 %Brunner Law Firm Co,LPA -545 E Town -Columbus 43215 **Fx:**241-5551

(937) 224-9291 .. **Wiggins**, Misty M '02 %Young & A Co,LPA -130 W 2nd -Ste 2000 -Dayton 45402 **Fx:**224-9679

(740) 349-8505 .. **Wigginton**, David Q '85 Schaller C&U -32 N Park Pl -Newark 43055

(330) 264-4444 .. **Wigham**, David J '92 (Critchfield C&J Ltd) -225 N Market -Bx599 -Wooster 44691 **Fx:**263-9278

(330) 262-4781 .. **Wigham**, John T '54 -1 Salter Pl -Wooster 44691

(614) 228-1541 .. **Wightman**, Alec '75 (Baker & H LLP) -65 E State -Ste 2100 -Columbus 43215 **Fx:**462-2616

(440) 933-3231 .. **Wightman**, Daniel G '76 %Smith & S Co,LPA -110 Moore Rd -Bx210 -Avon Lake 44012

(330) 434-6687 .. **Wigley**, Edmund A '55 -511 N Main -Akron 44310 **Fx:**762-3003

(614) 463-7241 .. **Wigton**, Charles E III '76 Natl City Bank -155 E Broad -Columbus 43251

(419) 625-6778 .. **Wilber**, Elizabeth F '02 EF Wilbur Law Ofc,LLC -224 E Water -Sandusky 44870

(419) 734-4060 .. **Wilber**, George C '77 (Wilber & W) -211 E 2nd -Port Clinton 43452

(937) 223-8177 .. **Wilberding**, Merle F '73 (Coolidge WW&L) -33 W 1st -Ste 600 -Dayton 45402 **Fx:**223-6705

Wilbur, Jonathan Z '00 -24998 Tunbrdg Ln -Beachwood 44122

(440) 845-1900 .. **Wilbur**, Thomas B '68 -6325 York Rd -Ste 305 -Parma Heights 44130

(740) 474-2780 .. **Wilburn**, Bernard P '84 Weldon & W -210 S Court -Bx418 -Circleville 43113

(740) 474-2780 .. **Wilburn**, Charles W '64 (Weldon & W) -210 S Court -Bx418 -Circleville 43113

(614) 466-8600 .. **Wilburn**, Melissa L '89 Atty Gen -30 E Broad -Columbus 43215 **Fx:**466-6090

(330) 864-5550 .. **Wilcox**, Amanda H '01 %Hahn L&P LLP -One GOJO Plz -Ste 300 -Akron 44311 **Fx:**864-7986

Wilcox, Darlene A '98 -1154 Linda -Rocky River 44116

(216) 621-0200 .. **Wilcox**, Deborah A '87 (Baker & H LLP) -1900 E 9th -Ste 3200 -Cleveland 44114 **Fx:**696-0740

(216) 621-8484 .. **Wilcox**, Dennis R '77 (Climaco LPW&G Co,LPA) -1228 Euclid Av -Ste 900 Halle Bldg -Cleveland 44115 **Fx:**771-1632

(216) 621-0200 .. **Wilcox**, Diane D '88 Baker & H LLP -1900 E 9th -Ste 3200 -Cleveland 44114 **Fx:**696-0740

(614) 875-1408 .. **Wilcox**, James L '64 Countrytyme Inc -1660 Gtwy Cir -Grove City 43123

Wilcox, James L '80 -871 Lyn Rd -Bowling Green 43402

(216) 861-0808 .. **Wilcox**, Jeffrey J '91 -614 W Superior Av -Ste 625 -Cleveland 44113

(614) 365-9900 .. **Wilcox**, Jonathan A '04 %Zeiger TL&L,LLP -41 S High -Ste 3500 Huntngtn Ctr -Columbus 43215 **Fx:**365-7900

(614) 466-8600 .. **Wilcox**, Kyle C '94 Atty Gen -30 E Broad -Columbus 43215 **Fx:**466-6090

(440) 602-5135 .. **Wilcox**, Richard K '85 -35350 Curtis Blvd -Ste 330 -Eastlake 44095

(614) 274-1107 .. **Wilcox**, Ronald L '61 -3303 Sullivant Av -Columbus 43204

(513) 352-6524 .. **Wilcoxon**, Kimberly D '01 %Thompson H LLP -312 Walnut -14th Fl -Cincinnati 45202 **Fx:**241-4771

(937) 496-7740 .. **Wilcoxson**, Clinton R II '93 Montgomery Cnty Juv Ct -303 W 2nd -Rm 1143 -Dayton 45422

(216) 363-4500 .. **Wild**, Jeffrey J '97 (Benesch FC&A LLP) -200 Pub Sq -Ste 2300 -Cleveland 44114 **Fx:**363-4588

(513) 221-8734 .. **Wild**, Jerry G '01 -345 Warren Av -Cincinnati 45220 **Fx:**221-8734

(419) 523-5015 .. **Wildenhaus**, William J '75 (Leopold W&S) -321 E Main -Bx303 -Ottawa 45875

(419) 421-2470 .. **Wilder**, J. Michael '01 Marathon Ashland Petro LLC -539 S Main -Findlay 45840 **Fx:**421-3124

(216) 696-8044 .. **Wilder**, John H '52 -1422 Euclid Av -Cleveland 44115

(937) 222-4529 .. **Wilder**, Lucas W '01 L Wilder,PC -120 W 2nd -Ste 400 -Dayton 45402

(513) 946-5744 .. **Wilder**, Mark A '99 Cnty Common Pleas Ct -1000 Main -Rm 540 -Cincinnati 45202

(937) 534-0500 .. **Wildermuth**, Brian L '96 (Subashi W&B) -2305 Far Hills Av -Oakwood Bldg -Dayton 45419 **Fx:**534-0505

(419) 774-5676 .. **Wildman**, Stephen M '89 Richland Cnty Pros -38 S Park -2nd Fl -Mansfield 44902 **Fx:**774-5589

(937) 865-7495 .. **Wildfeuer**, Steven R '96 Lexis/Nexis -Bx933 -Dayton 45401

(740) 852-8383 .. **Wildman**, Austin P '71 (Wildman S LLC) -26 E 4th -London 43140

(740) 852-8383 .. **Wildman Schooley LLC** -26 E 4th -London 43140

(937) 324-5541 .. **Wildman**, Walter A '68 (Martin BH&H) -1 S Limestone -Ste 800 -Bx1488 -Springfield 45501 **Fx:**325-5432

(614) 221-5216 .. **Wiles Boyle Burkholder & Bringardner Co,LPA** -300 Spruce -1st Fl -Columbus 43215 **Fx:**221-5692

(614) 221-5216 .. **Wiles**, Daniel G '66 (Wiles BB&B Co,LPA) -300 Spruce -1st Fl -Columbus 43215 **Fx:**221-5692

(614) 221-5216 .. **Wiles**, James M '70 (Wiles BB&B Co,LPA) -300 Spruce -1st Fl -Columbus 43215 **Fx:**221-5692

(440) 942-6262 .. **Wiles**, John W '59 (Wiles & R) -35350 Curtis Blvd -Ste 530 -Eastlake 44095 **Fx:**942-7211

(330) 262-3030 .. **Wiles**, Latecia E '04 Wayne Cnty Pros -115 W Lbrty -Wooster 44691 **Fx:**287-5412

(937) 228-2838 .. **Wiles**, Matthew J '02 %Taft S&H LLP -110 N Main -Ste 900 -Dayton 45402 **Fx:**228-2816

(440) 942-6262 .. **Wiles & Richards** -35350 Curtis Blvd -Ste 530 -Eastlake 44095
Fx:942-7211

(419) 691-4232 .. **Wiley**, David F '63 -624 Main -Toledo 43605 Fx:691-4482

(513) 677-0999 .. **Wiley**, Donald L '71 -11935 Mason Mntgmry Rd -Ste 130
-Cincinnati 45249

(330) 499-6000 .. **Wiley**, Donald P '84 (Baker DBW&M) -400 S Main -Canton 44720
Fx:449-6423

(513) 246-0036 .. **Wiley**, Julia H '82 US DOE-Chf Cnsl Ofc -175 Tri Cnty Pkwy
-Cincinnati 45246

(419) 249-7900 .. **Wiley**, Julia S '84 (Robison C&O) -Four SeaGate -9th Fl
-Toledo 43604 Fx:249-7911

(614) 621-1500 .. **Wiley**, Stephen C '97 %Calfee H&G LLP -21 E State -1100 Fifth
Third Ctr -Columbus 43215 Fx:621-0010

(614) 447-0100 .. **Wilford**, Barry W '77 (Kura & W Co LPA) -26 W Henderson Rd
-Columbus 43214 Fx:447-0152

(216) 621-0200 .. **Wilharm**, John H Jr. '60 (Baker & H LLP) -1900 E 9th -Ste 3200
-Cleveland 44114 Fx:696-0740

(513) 530-1634 .. **Wilheim**, Ronald S '96 Communicare Hlth Srvcs
-4700 Ashwood Dr -Ste 200 -Cincinnati 45241

(614) 890-3724 .. **Wilhelm**, Anne M '84 A&W Assn Srvcs -421 Bellfrey Dr
-Westerville 43081

(614) 488-2515 .. **Wilhelm**, James E Jr. '64 (J Wilhelm,Jr,Co,LPA) -1390 Dublin Rd
-Columbus 43215

(937) 496-3161 .. **Wilhelm**, Jenifer L '90 Montgomery Cnty Juv Ct -14 W 4th -8th Fl
-Dayton 45402

(614) 466-5394 .. **Wilhelm**, Joseph E '91 Pub Def -8 E Long -Columbus 43215

(765) 647-4161 .. **Wilhelm**, Melvin F '77 -424 Court -BxB -Brookville, IN 47012

(859) 655-4200 .. **Wilhelm**, Paul A '02 %Greenebaum D&M PLLC
-50 E RiverCenter Blvd -Ste 1800 -Covington, KY 41011
Fx:655-4239

(419) 244-6788 .. **Wilhelms**, Andrew Jon '96 %Bugbee & C -405 Mad Av -Ste 1300
-Toledo 43604 Fx:244-7145

(419) 244-6788 .. **Wilhelms**, Tybo A '76 (Bugbee & C) -405 Mad Av -Ste 1300
-Toledo 43604 Fx:244-7145

(513) 977-8200 .. **Wilhelmy**, Alicia L '01 %Dinsmore & S LLP -255 E 5th -Ste 1900
-Cincinnati 45202 Fx:977-8141

(419) 259-6420 .. **Wilhelmy**, Kristi Kress '04 US Dstrct Ct - Nrthn Dstrct
-1716 Spielbusch Av -#203 -Toledo 43624

(937) 298-0008 .. **Wilhite**, Stacy E '98 %Scudder & E Co,LPA -2912 Springboro W
-Ste 105 -Dayton 45439

(216) 781-5470 .. **Wilk**, Lisa J '01 %Ziegler M&M LLP -925 Euclid Av
-2020 Huntngtn Bldg -Cleveland 44115 Fx:781-0714

(513) 946-3580 .. **Wilke**, Wayne F '60 Hamilton Cnty Probate Ct -230 E 9th -10th Fl
-Cincinnati 45202 Fx:946-3581

(513) 333-0700 .. **Wilken**, Steven J '84 Neace/Lukens -419 Plum -Cincinnati 45202

(419) 865-1837 .. **Wilkerson**, Carolyn S '74 OH Education Assn -6135 Trust Dr
-Ste 218 -Holland 43528

(216) 696-0808 .. **Wilkerson**, Ernest L Jr. '86 (Wilkerson & Assoc Co,LPA)
-1422 Euclid Av -Ste 248 -Cleveland 44115 Fx:696-4970

(614) 628-0790 .. **Wilkerson**, John P Jr. '81 (Carlile P&M LLP) -366 E Broad
-Columbus 43215 Fx:221-0216

(513) 887-3318 .. **Wilkerson**, Patricia A '93 Butler Cnty Juv Ct -280 N Fair Av
-Hamilton 45011

(330) 743-1717 .. **Wilkes**, Larry D '84 (Davis & Y) -201 E Commerce -Ste 100
-Youngstown 44503 Fx:743-6347

(216) 586-3939 .. **Wilkes**, Meredith M '00 %Jones D -901 Lakeside Av
-Cleveland 44114 Fx:579-0212

(614) 462-5417 .. **Wilkes**, Nicholas E '95 %Kegler BH&R -65 E State -Ste 1800
-Columbus 43215 Fx:464-2634

(419) 246-3777 .. **Wilkins**, Douglas A '82 -1931 Scottwood -Ste 700 -Bx4967
-Toledo 43610

(330) 497-0700 .. **Wilkins**, F Stuart S Jr. '52 (Krugliak WG&D Co,LPA)
-4775 Munson NW -Bx36963 -Canton 44735 Fx:497-4020

(330) 867-9998 .. **Wilkins**, James P '83 (Kastner W&W,LLC) -3480 W Market
-Ste 300 -Akron 44333 Fx:867-3786

(937) 228-9000 .. **Wilkins**, Lawrence A '96 (Thorson SW&S,LLP) -130 W 2nd
-Ste 1508 -Dayton 45402 Fx:228-3550

(614) 447-7050 .. **Wilkins**, Linda A '96 -2680 Southrdg Dr -Columbus 43224

(330) 867-9998 .. **Wilkins**, Linda L '83 %Kastner W&W,LLC -3480 W Market
-Ste 300 -Akron 44333 Fx:867-3786

Wilkins, Mary E '04 -(Address Unavailable)

(513) 793-7200 .. **Wilkins**, Nancy E '95 -4866 Cooper Rd -Ste 103 -Cincinnati 45242
Fx:793-7020

(614) 221-9800 .. **Wilkins**, Paul G '02 Equal Justice Fndtn -88 E Broad -Ste 1590
-Columbus 43215 Fx:221-9810

(513) 793-4911 .. **Wilkinson**, Carl E '58 -29 Carpenters Ridge -Cincinnati 45241

(513) 977-8200 .. **Wilkinson**, George B '82 (Dinsmore & S LLP) -255 E 5th
-Ste 1900 -Cincinnati 45202 Fx:977-8141

(419) 893-1444 .. **Wilkinson**, Grant W '87 (Farrar N&W,Ltd) -1605 Indn Wd Cir
-Ste 200 -Maumee 43537

(513) 424-2401 .. **Wilkinson**, Rebecca L '83 (Casper & C) -1 N Main -Bx510
-Middletown 45042 Fx:424-0622

(614) 469-3266 .. **Wilkinson**, William C '76 (Thompson H LLP) -10 W Broad
-Ste 700 -Columbus 43215 Fx:469-3361

(330) 453-6344 .. **Wilkof**, Jeffrey S '80 -124 15th NW -Canton 44703

(216) 592-5000 .. **Wilkov**, Scott J '04 %Tucker E&W LLP -925 Euclid Av
-1150 Huntngtn Bldg -Cleveland 44115 Fx:592-5009

(513) 579-6400 .. **Wilkowski**, E Todd '98 %Keating M&K PLL -1 E 4th
-1400 Provident Twr -Cincinnati 45202 Fx:579-6457

(513) 946-3279 .. **Wilkowski**, Heather A '98 %Hamilton Cnty Pros -230 E 9th
-Cincinnati 45202 Fx:946-3017

(419) 241-9770 .. **Wilkowski**, Keith A '82 OfCnsl Vassar DD&B,LLC -420 Mad Av
-Ste 1102 -Toledo 43604 Fx:241-9771

(614) 621-1500 .. **Will**, Anne E '03 Calfee H&G LLP -21 E State -1100 Fifth Third Ctr
-Columbus 43215 Fx:621-0010

(440) 329-5389 .. **Will**, Dennis P '87 Lorain Cnty Pros -225 Court -3rd Fl
-Elyria 44035

(412) 281-5110 .. **Will**, Thomas A '94 Cnsl TA Will & Assoc -603 Stanwix
-Ste 300 Two Gtwy Ctr -Pittsburgh, PA 15222 Fx:201-9124

(513) 241-9400 .. **Willacker**, Terence M '76 Legal Aid -215 E 9th -Ste 200
-Cincinnati 45202

(216) 241-7740 .. **Willacy**, Aubrey B '70 (Willacy L&M) -1468 W 9th
-700 Wstrn Reserve Bldg -Cleveland 44113

(216) 566-2600 .. **Willacy**, Hazel M '76 Sherwin Williams Co -101 Prospect Av
-12th Fl -Cleveland 44115

(216) 241-7740 .. **Willacy Lopresti & Marcovy** -1468 W 9th
-700 Wstrn Reserve Bldg -Cleveland 44113

(419) 228-8335 .. **Willamowski**, John R '85 (Willamowski & W) -730 W North
-Lima 45801

(419) 228-8335 .. **Willamowski**, Mona L '87 (Willamowski & W) -730 W North
-Lima 45801

(513) 844-8181 .. **Willard**, John T '66 -6 S 2nd -Ste 206 -Hamilton 45011

(614) 466-3615 .. **Willard**, Kirsten J '98 Legis Srvc Commssn -77 S High
-Columbus 43215

(740) 373-4500 .. **Willard**, Michele H '84 -100 Front -Ste 302 -Marietta 45750

(614) 457-9731 .. **Willard**, Robert H '80 (Harris & M) -941 Chatham Ln -Ste 201
-Columbus 43221 Fx:457-3596

(740) 353-1157 .. **Willard**, Steven M '87 %Bannon H&D -325 Masonic Bldg -Bx1384
-Portsmouth 45662

(513) 352-6700 .. **Willbrand**, David J '96 %Thompson H LLP -312 Walnut -14th Fl
-Cincinnati 45202 Fx:241-4771

(865) 376-2145 .. **Willcox**, Edith S '91 Dist Atty Gen - 9th Jud Dist
-1008 Bradford Way -Ste 100 -Bx703 -Kingston, TN 37763

(614) 221-4000 .. **Willcox**, Roderick H '58 (Chester W&S LLP) -65 E State -10th Fl
-Columbus 43215 Fx:221-4012

(614) 728-7055 .. **Wille**, Charles L '79 Atty Gen -30 E Broad -Columbus 43215
Fx:728-8600

(908) 231-5721 .. **Wille**, Louis J '90 Aventis Pharm,Inc -Rte 202-206 -Patent Dept
-Bx6800 -Bridgewater, NJ 08807

(513) 744-7754 .. **Willen**, Diana J '78 Fifth 3rd Bank -38 Fountain Sq Plz
-MD 1090F4 -Cincinnati 45263

(330) 868-7747 .. **Willen**, Gary L '78 (G Willen Co,LPA) -200 N Main -Minerva 44657

(859) 581-5177 .. **Willenborg**, Thomas R '74 -130 Park Pl -Covington, KY 41011

(513) 558-5696 .. **Willenbrink**, Matthew '03 Univ of Cincinnati -3223 Eden Av
-Wherry Hall G-07 -Cincinnati 45267

Willer, Glenn P '98 -7610 Slate Ridge Rd -Reynoldsburg 43068

(614) 757-3428 .. **Willet**, Debra A '89 Cardinal Hlth -7000 Cardinal Pl -Dublin 43017

(614) 863-9372 .. **Willette**, Philip B '76 (P Willette Co,LPA) -9095 Cotswold Dr NW
-Pickerington 43147

(419) 241-3310 .. **Willey**, David S '02 -520 Mad Av -366 Spitzer Bldg -Toledo 43604

(419) 241-6000 .. **Willey**, John D Jr. '79 (Eastman & S Ltd) -1 Seagate -24th Fl
-Bx10032 -Toledo 43699 Fx:247-1777

(419) 242-1515 .. **Willey**, Loretta J '99 Roose & R PA -Four SeaGate -Ste 600
-Toledo 43604

(202) 514-2807 .. **Willey**, Steven J '79 US DOJ -10th & Penn Av NW
-Washington, DC 20530

(614) 888-7090 .. **Willi**, Kaye P '83 -445 Hutchnsn Av -Ste 800 -Columbus 43235

(330) 454-7777 .. **Williams**, Agatha Martin '91 (AM Williams Co,LPA)
-116 Cleveland Av NW -Ste 318 -Canton 44702

(330) 375-2007 .. **Williams**, Annalisa S '84 Municipal Ct Judge -217 S High
-Akron 44308

Williams, Anne E '99 -(Address Unavailable)

(419) 291-2034 .. **Williams**, Anne K '94 ProMedica Hlth Syst -2121 Hughes Dr
-Toledo 43606

(859) 219-8901 .. **Williams**, April M '94 -576 Newbury Way -Lexington, KY 40514

(614) 466-3947 .. **Williams**, Ayn Phalyn '93 OH Brd of Nursing -17 S High -Ste 400
-Columbus 43215

(419) 853-4603 .. **Williams**, Barbara L '79 -Bx261 -West Salem 44287

(330) 725-6666 .. **Williams & Batchelder, LLP** -105 W Lbrty -Bx394 -Medina 44258

(330) 762-0080 .. **Williams**, Brian J '79 (B Williams Co,LPA) -611 W Market -Ste C
-Akron 44303

(419) 243-6610 .. **Williams**, Brian Ray '78 (Williams & R) -420 Mad Av
-Toledo 43604

(216) 263-3414 .. **Williams**, Brinley H Jr. '71 FTC -1111 Superior Av E -Ste 200
-Cleveland 44114

(330) 784-1271 .. **Williams**, Caroline '77 Edwin Shaw Hsptl -1621 Flickinger Rd
-Akron 44312

(216) 586-3939 .. **Williams**, Caroline M '04 %Jones D -901 Lakeside Av
-Cleveland 44114 Fx:579-0212

(330) 337-3253 .. **Williams**, Charles B '83 (Williams & A Co LPA) -1376 E State
-Salem 44460 Fx:337-0424

(614) 228-0207 .. **Williams**, Charles T '74 -555 S Front -Ste 320 -Columbus 43215
Fx:228-3102

(216) 520-0088 .. **Williams**, Christian M '94 Pepple & W Ltd -5005 Rockside Rd
-Ste 260 -Cleveland 44131 Fx:520-0044

(330) 683-5285 .. **Williams**, Christine C '96 Wayne Cnty -538 N Market
-Wooster 44691

(216) 622-8200 .. **Williams**, Christopher S '00 (Calfee H&G LLP) -800 Superior Av
-Ste 1400 -Cleveland 44114 Fx:241-0816

Williams, Clarence D III '83 -1508 Dixmont Av -Cincinnati 45207

(216) 696-4700 .. **Williams**, Clyde E Jr. '45 (Spieth BM&N Co,LPA) -925 Euclid Av
-2000 Huntngtn Bldg -Cleveland 44115 Fx:696-2706

(937) 393-2422 .. **Williams**, Cynthia Ann '91 Highland Cnty Cmn Pleas Ct
-105 N High -Hillsboro 45133

(614) 469-5715 .. **Williams**, Dale E Jr. '79 US Atty -303 Marconi Blvd -Ste 200
-Columbus 43215

(216) 241-1177 .. **Williams**, Danny R '78 Amer Cancer Soc-OH Div Inc
-10501 Euclid Av -Ste 514 -Cleveland 44106

(330) 673-3444 .. **Williams**, David E '76 (Williams W&K) -11 S River -Bx396
-Kent 44240

(419) 784-1072 .. **Williams**, David H '76 Law Dept -324 Perry -City Bldg
-Defiance 43512 Fx:784-0492

Williams, David L '04 -(Address Unavailable)

(216) 291-7702 .. **Williams**, David R '66 Northrop Grumman -1900 Richmond Rd
-Cleveland 44124

(419) 893-3360 .. **Williams**, Dennis P '90 (Weber & S,LLC) -1721 Indn Wd Cir -Ste 1
-Maumee 43537 Fx:893-7146

(859) 394-6200 .. **Williams**, Dennis R '90 (Adams SW&D) -40 W Pike -Bx861
-Covington, KY 41012 Fx:291-7902

(440) 338-5051 .. **Williams**, Donald '53 -Bx536 -Novelty 44072 Fx:338-3419

(216) 696-4345 .. **Williams**, Donald C '73 (DC Williams Co,LPA) -1370 Ontario
-Ste 1328 Standard Bldg -Cleveland 44113

(614) 415-1652 .. **Williams**, Douglas L '80 The Limited,Inc -3 Limited Pkwy
-Bx16000 -Columbus 43216

(216) 348-5056 .. **Williams**, Earl Jr. '80 Cuyahoga Metro Housing Auth -1441 W 25th
-Cleveland 44113

(330) 305-6400 ..**Williams,** Eric J '00 %Pelini & F,Ltd -8040 Cleveland Av NW
-Ste 400 -North Canton 44720 **Fx:**305-0042

(614) 221-0240 ..**Williams,** Erica K '96 (Hahn L&P LLP) -65 E State -Ste 1400
-Columbus 43215 **Fx:**221-5909

(614) 227-2374 ..**Williams,** Faith M '96 (Bricker & E LLP) -100 S 3rd
-Columbus 43215 **Fx:**227-2390

(937) 226-2069 ..**Williams,** Frank B III '77 Natl City Bank/Trust Dept -6 N Main
-Dayton 45412

Williams, Gary D '02 DHHS - Ctr for Medicare & Medicaid Srvcs
-7500 Security Blvd -Baltimore, MD 21244

(216) 687-2297 ..**Williams,** Gary R '84 CSU-Marshall Cllg of Law -2121 Euclid Av
-LB138 -Cleveland 44115 **Fx:**687-6881

(216) 443-7800 ..**Williams,** Gayle F '01 Cuyahoga Cnty Pros -1200 Ontario -8th Fl
-Cleveland 44113 **Fx:**698-2270

(330) 923-0040 ..**Williams,** Glen A '61 -1031 Curtis Av -Cuyahoga Falls 44221
Fx:945-4225

(419) 241-3213 ..**Williams,** Gregory A '87 Ritter RM&J -405 Mad Av -Ste 1850
-Toledo 43604 **Fx:**241-4925

(216) 687-1900 ..**Williams,** Harold L '76 Legal Aid -1223 W 6th -Cleveland 44113
Fx:687-0779

(216) 595-0071 ..**Williams,** Jackson Ryan '03 %Roth B LLP -5196 Richmond Rd
-Bedford Heights 44146 **Fx:**595-0073

(937) 382-3831 ..**Williams,** James H '79 (Dennis & W Co,LPA) -245 N South
-Wilmington 45177

(513) 721-1078 ..**Williams,** James R '75 -1014 Vine -Ste 2400 -Cincinnati 45202

Williams, Jeanette B '95 -28 Towanda Dr
-Highland Heights, KY 41076

(216) 765-0123 ..**Williams,** Jeffery D '02 Budish & S Ltd -23240 Chagrin Blvd
-Ste 450 Commerce Park 4 -Beachwood 44122 **Fx:**595-2787

(740) 393-6796 ..**Williams,** Jeffrey C '87 Knox Cnty Prob/Juv Ct -111 E High
-Mount Vernon 43050

(419) 993-2930 ..**Williams,** Jeffrey G '83 -2244 Baton Rouge -Bx5044 -Lima 45802
Fx:993-2933

(614) 228-1541 ..**Williams,** Jeffrey T '88 (Baker & H LLP) -65 E State -Ste 2100
-Columbus 43215 **Fx:**462-2616

(304) 485-3851 ..**Williams,** Jennifer '03 %Golden & A,PLLC -543 5th
-Parkersburg, WV 26101

(419) 241-2122 ..**Williams Jilek Lafferty Gallagher & Scott Co,LPA** -416 N Erie
-Ste 500 -Toledo 43624 **Fx:**245-3849

(513) 651-3456 ..**Williams,** John J '89 (Gonzalez S&H LLP) -441 Vine -Ste 3615
-Cincinnati 45202 **Fx:**651-3446

(330) 262-3030 ..**Williams,** John M '85 Wayne Cnty Pros -115 W Lbrty
-Wooster 44691 **Fx:**287-5412

(513) 946-3000 ..**Williams,** John M '93 Hamilton Cnty Pros -230 E 9th
-Cincinnati 45202 **Fx:**946-3017

(206) 324-8969 ..**Williams,** John M '94 Teller & Assoc -1139 34th Av -Ste A
-Seattle, WA 98122

(513) 621-0930 ..**Williams,** John M '94 (Delev & W,LLC) -432 Walnut
-800 Tri State Bldg -Cincinnati 45202 **Fx:**562-8822

(513) 579-3100 ..**Williams,** John P Jr. '66 Grtr Cincinnati Chamber of Commmerce
-441 Vine -Ste 300 -Cincinnati 45202

(614) 466-2980 ..**Williams,** John T '78 Atty Gen -30 E Broad -Columbus 43215
Fx:728-9470

(614) 466-4801 ..**Williams,** Julia K '95 Industrial Commssn of OH -30 W Spring
-9th Fl -Columbus 43215 **Fx:**752-8785

(937) 866-0352 ..**Williams,** Karen S '78 -133 Lk Forest Dr -Dayton 45449

(216) 771-6303 ..**Williams,** Kathryn A '98 (Torres W Co,LPA) -75 Pub Sq -Ste 800
-Cleveland 44113 **Fx:**771-6993

(330) 796-4995 ..**Williams,** Kenneth C '75 Goodyear Tire & Rubber Co
-1144 E Market -Akron 44321

(614) 220-5611 ..**Williams,** Kevin L '93 %Manley D&K,LLC -495 S High -Ste 300
-Columbus 43215 **Fx:**220-5613

(216) 443-5009 ..**Williams,** Laura Ann '83 Cuyahoga Cnty Cmn Pleas Ct
-2163 E 22nd -Cleveland 44115

(937) 277-2950 ..**Williams,** Lawrence R Jr. '89 -Bx60608 -Dayton 45406

(614) 224-7291 ..**Williams,** Lewis E Jr. '74 (L Williams Co,LPA) -330 S High
-Columbus 43215

(304) 353-8178 ..**Williams,** Louis F Jr. '82 (Steptoe & J) -Bx1588
-Charleston, WV 25326

Williams, Mark F '88 -(Address Unavailable)

Williams, Mark R '70 -1700 SE 15th -#301
-Fort Lauderdale, FL 33316

(419) 241-2122 ..**Williams,** Martin W '69 (Williams JLG&S Co,LPA) -416 N Erie
-Ste 500 -Toledo 43624 **Fx:**245-3849

(614) 221-8640 ..**Williams,** McCullough A III '78 Greentree Brokerage Srvcs
-411 E Town -Columbus 43215

(614) 462-3988 ..**Williams,** Megan J '92 Franklin Cnty Ct of Appls -373 S High
-24th Fl -Columbus 43215

(937) 783-2476 ..**Williams,** Michael B '02 CCPI Inc -838 Cherry -Blanchester 45107

(614) 221-8448 ..**Williams,** Michael L '92 (Buckingham D&B,LLP)
-191 W Nationwide Blvd -Ste 300 -Bx151120 -Columbus 43215
Fx:221-8590

(216) 241-5300 ..**Williams,** Michael T '92 %D Dreyfuss Co,LPA -1801 E 9th
-Ste 740 -Cleveland 44114

(614) 462-3194 ..**Williams,** Mitchell A '97 Franklin Cnty Pub Def -373 S High
-12th Fl -Columbus 43215

(216) 524-4855 ..**Williams,** Monica B '84 -6866 Grandvw Dr -Independence 44131

(330) 376-2668 ..**Williams,** Orlando J '86 -209 S Main -8th Fl -Akron 44308

(330) 602-9666 ..**Williams,** Patrick J '92 -204 2nd NE -New Philadelphia 44663

(216) 752-9868 ..**Williams,** Paul A '86 National City Bk -1900 E 19th -Cleveland
44114

(614) 757-7768 ..**Williams,** Paul S '87 Cardinal Hlth -7000 Cardinal Pl
-Dublin 43017

(216) 443-8970 ..**Williams,** Perdexter H '92 Cuyahoga Cnty Probate Ct
-1 Lakeside Av -Cleveland 44113

(614) 224-0531 ..**Williams & Petro Co,LLC** -338 S High -2nd Fl -Columbus 43215
Fx:224-0553

(937) 864-3000 ..**Williams,** Ralph B '77 Speedway SuperAmer LLC -Bx1500
-Springfield 45501

(216) 687-1902 ..**Williams,** Reginald D '03 %S Haygood & Assoc -1422 Euclid Av
-Ste 1510 -Cleveland 44115 **Fx:**687-1906

(614) 224-0531 ..**Williams,** Richard A '82 (Williams & P Co,LLC) -338 S High
-2nd Fl -Columbus 43215 **Fx:**224-0553

(330) 328-4736 ..**Williams,** Richard J '03 -Bx80042 -Akron 44308

(847) 384-6127 ..**Williams,** Robert A '91 Kanabay Inc -6400 Shafer Ct -Ste 100
-Rosemont, IL 60018

(419) 213-4061 ..**Williams,** Robert B '67 %Lucas Cnty Pros-Foreclosure
-One Govt Ctr -Ste 500 -Toledo 43604

(614) 716-0500 ..**Williams,** Robert E '93 %Onda L&R Co,LPA -266 N 4th -Ste 100
-Columbus 43215 **Fx:**716-0511

(440) 333-3100 ..**Williams,** Robert H '80 -21430 Lorain Rd -Fairview Park 44126

(330) 405-5061 ..**Williams,** Roger H '79 (Williams S&S Co,LPA)
-2241 Pinnacle Pkwy -Twinsburg 44087 **Fx:**405-5586

(216) 579-4114 ..**Williams,** Saber Rathbun '02 %McIntyre K&K Co LPA -1301 E 9th
-Ste 1200 -Cleveland 44114

(614) 716-2037 ..**Williams,** Sandra K '83 Amer Elec Pwr Co -1 Riverside Plz
-Columbus 43215

(440) 891-8850 ..**Williams,** Scott A '91 (SA Williams & Assoc,LPA)
-398 W Bagley Rd -Ste 14 -Berea 44017

(614) 228-6061 ..**Williams,** Scott E '92 Hammond & S -556 E Town
-Columbus 43215

(330) 405-5061 ..**Williams Sennett & Scully Co, LPA** -2241 Pinnacle Pkwy
-Twinsburg 44087 **Fx:**405-5586

(216) 621-2110 ..**Williams Sennett & Scully Co, LPA** -55 Pub Sq -Ste 1850
-Cleveland 44113 **Fx:**621-2164

(770) 859-6000 ..**Williams,** Shawnell '91 GE Power Systems -4200 Wildwood Pkwy
-Atlanta, GA 30339

(513) 233-0756 ..**Williams,** Stacey R '00 Lexis Nexis -6006 Stan Hill Ct
-Cincinnati 45230

(216) 902-8540 ..**Williams,** Stanley A '61 Capstone Rlty LLC -1120 Chester Av
-Ste 300 -Cleveland 44114 **Fx:**902-8501

(440) 576-3027 ..**Williams,** Susan J '93 Ashtabula Cnty Cmn Pleas Ct -25 W Jffrsn
-Jefferson 44047

(513) 651-6800 ..**Williams,** Tamra G '04 %Frost BT LLC -201 E 5th -2200 PNC Ctr
-Cincinnati 45202 **Fx:**651-6981

(216) 931-6000 ..**Williams,** Tanya L '04 %Ulmer & B LLP -1300 E 9th
-Ste 900 Penton Media Bldg -Cleveland 44114 **Fx:**931-6001

(614) 854-4841 ..**Williams,** Thomas A '92 Farmland Ins -5525 ParkCenter Cir
-Dublin 43017

(614) 464-1211 ..**Williams,** Thomas V '77 (Frost BT LLC) -10 W Broad -Ste 1000
-Columbus 43215 **Fx:**464-1737

(202) 693-5686 ..**Williams,** Timothy S '91 Dept of Labor -200 Const Av -N-2117
-Washington, DC 20210

(513) 612-2300 ..**Williams,** Tina M '03 Cincom Systems,Inc -55 Merchant
-Cincinnati 45246

(419) 843-2001 ..**Williams,** Vernos J '76 (Gallon & T Co,LPA) -3516 Granite Cir
-Bx352018 -Toledo 43635 **Fx:**843-6665

(419) 882-0601 ..**Williams,** Vesper C II '73 -4643 Sylvania Av W -Toledo 43623

(440) 356-0180 ..**Williams,** Warren J Jr. '71 -22255 Ctr Ridge -Ste 200
-Cleveland 44116

(216) 787-3030 ..**Williams,** Wayne D '88 Atty Gen -615 W Superior Av -11th Fl
-Cleveland 44113 **Fx:**787-3480

(330) 673-3444 ..**Williams Welser & Kratcowski** -11 S River -Bx396 -Kent 44240

(330) 497-0700 ..**Williams,** William G '75 (Krugliak WG&D Co,LPA)
-4775 Munson NW -Bx36963 -Canton 44735 **Fx:**497-4020

(216) 522-7454 ..**Williams-Alexander,** Donna L '87 -1660 W 2nd -Ste 850
-Cleveland 44113

(419) 242-1555 ..**Williams-Young,** Marc G '82 (Spitler & W-Y Co,LPA)
-1000 Adams -Ste 200 -Toledo 43624

Williamson, Brenda M '04 -(Address Unavailable)

(740) 382-1027 ..**Williamson,** David E '72 (Williamson & W) -196½ W Center
-Marion 43302 **Fx:**382-0132

(513) 421-6630 ..**Williamson,** David E '99 %Lindhorst & D Co,LPA -312 Walnut
-Ste 2300 -Cincinnati 45202

(937) 223-3277 ..**Williamson,** David P '78 (Bieser G&L LLP) -6 N Main
-400 Natl City Ctr -Dayton 45402 **Fx:**223-6339

(304) 327-0573 ..**Williamson,** Janet C '80 (Shott G&W) -Bx490
-Bluefield, WV 24701

(740) 382-8892 ..**Williamson,** Jonathan '76 -355 E Center -Ste 101 -Marion 43302

(419) 213-3203 ..**Williamson,** Julie T '89 Lucas Cnty CSEA -701 Adams
-Toledo 43624

(513) 621-8688 ..**Williamson,** Karl E '90 -1071 Celestial -Ste 904 -Cincinnati 45202

(419) 247-1808 ..**Williamson,** Lane D '89 (Eastman & S Ltd) -1 Seagate -24th Fl
-Bx10032 -Toledo 43699 **Fx:**247-1777

(513) 733-3332 ..**Williamson,** Leonard A '75 -10339 Giverny Blvd -Ste 1
-Cincinnati 45241

(216) 443-7800 ..**Williamson,** Lisa R '89 Cuyahoga Cnty Pros -1200 Ontario -8th Fl
-Cleveland 44113 **Fx:**698-2270

(513) 621-2120 ..**Williamson,** William O '04 %Strauss & T,LPA -150 E 4th -4th Fl
-Cincinnati 45202 **Fx:**381-8259

(330) 633-7373 ..**Williger,** Marta J '85 (Williger & P) -323C S Main -Bx368
-Munroe Falls 44262 **Fx:**633-6353

(330) 848-9393 ..**Williger,** Richard Lee '82 (R Williger Co,LPA) -2070 E Av
-Akron 44314

(216) 566-5655 ..**Williger,** Stephen D '82 (Thompson H LLP) -127 Pub Sq
-3900 Key Ctr -Cleveland 44114 **Fx:**566-5800

Willingham, Layla K '02 -322 Grove Rd -Woodlawn 45215

(614) 529-8988 ..**Willis,** C Stanley II '91 (Willis S&W Co LPA) -5017 Cemetary Rd
-Hilliard 43026 **Fx:**334-8989

(216) 789-4625 ..**Willis,** Craig E '83 -2984 Becket Rd -Cleveland 44120

(513) 784-7132 ..**Willis,** Craig R '04 Deloitte & Touch,LLP -250 E 5th -Ste 1900
-Cincinnati 45202

(216) 523-1100 ..**Willis,** James R '53 (Willis W&G) -113 St Clair Av -Ste 440
-Cleveland 44114

(740) 352-1646 ..**Willis,** Jay S '95 Scioto Cnty Cmn Pleas Ct -602 7th
-Portsmouth 45662

(513) 977-8200 ..**Willis,** Jeffrey A '02 %Dinsmore & S LLP -255 E 5th -Ste 1900
-Cincinnati 45202 **Fx:**977-8141

Willis, John M '89 -143 Durling Dr -#B-11 -Wadsworth 44281

(616) 957-2714 ..**Willis,** Joseph H '74 %Chicago Title Ins -5311 36th SE
-Grand Rapids, MI 49512

(614) 529-8988 ..**Willis,** Kelly A '92 (Willis S&W Co LPA) -5017 Cemetary Rd
-Hilliard 43026 **Fx:**334-8989

(513) 381-9200 ..**Willis,** Marisa A '03 %Rendigs FK&D,LLP -One W 4th -Ste 900
-Cincinnati 45202 **Fx:**381-9206

(330) 434-5297 ..**Willis,** Mark C '87 Willis & W -670 W Market -Akron 44303

(413) 253-1515 ..**Willis,** Mary A '87 Natl Religious Prtnrshp for the Environment
-49 S Plsnt -Amherst, MA 01002

(513) 248-0121 ..**Willis,** Nancy A '74 -721 Indn Hill Rd -Terrace Park 45174

(216) 381-3400 ..**Willis,** Robert J '94 (Petronzio S Co,LPA) -5001 Mayfld Rd -Ste 201 -Cleveland 44124

(513) 381-2838 ..**Willis,** Ryan L '01 %Taft S&H LLP -425 Walnut -Ste 1800 -Cincinnati 45202 **Fx:**381-0205

(614) 529-8988 ..**Willis Shufeldt & Willis Co LPA** -5017 Cemetary Rd -Hilliard 43026 **Fx:**334-8989

(330) 434-5297 ..**Willis,** Todd L '98 Willis & W -670 W Market -Akron 44303

(216) 523-1100 ..**Willis Watson & Gooden** -113 St Clair Av -Ste 440 -Cleveland 44114

(440) 988-2858 ..**Willis,** William J Jr. '89 -248 Park Av -Amherst 44001

(614) 228-6888 ..**Willis,** William L Jr. '87 (Havens W LLC) -141 E Town -Ste 200 -Columbus 43215 **Fx:**228-6878

(614) 221-3938 ..**Willison,** Eric E '96 G Lewis -625 City Park Av -Columbus 43206 **Fx:**221-3713

(513) 381-9200 ..**Willits,** Chad E '96 Rendigs FK&D,LLP -One W 4th -Ste 900 -Cincinnati 45202 **Fx:**381-9206

(419) 448-4444 ..**Willman,** Angela M '21 Seneca Cnty Pros -71 S Wshngtn -Ste E -Bx667 -Tiffin 44883 **Fx:**448-7911

(513) 985-2500 ..**Willmann,** Neal O '93 OfCnsl Phillips Law Firm,Inc -9521 Mntgmry Rd -Cincinnati 45242 **Fx:**985-2503

(440) 398-7522 ..**Willmann,** Wendel E '69 -2118 Oaklawn Dr -Parma 44134

(330) 670-3007 ..**Willoughby,** John A '73 Republic Tech Intl LLC -3770 Embssy Pkwy -Akron 44333

(440) 838-7600 ..**Wills,** Nathan J '04 %Janik & D,LLP -9200 S Hills Blvd -Ste 300 -Cleveland 44147 **Fx:**838-7601

                 Wills, Roger E Jr. '69 -(Address Unavailable)

(513) 721-5707 ..**Wills,** Teddy L '92 -414 Walnut -Ste 707 -Cincinnati 45202

(440) 610-4443 ..**Wills,** Wendy I '83 Wills Law Ofc -20088 Center-Ridge Rd -Ste 205 -Rocky River 44116

(937) 278-0652 ..**Wilmes,** John A '76 -4428 N Dixie Dr -Dayton 45414

(330) 375-2730 ..**Wilms,** Gertrude E '01 Pros -217 S High -Ste 203 -Akron 44308

(614) 469-7446 ..**Wilsbacher,** MaryAnne B '91 US Trustee -170 N High -Ste 200 -Columbus 43215

(216) 589-9600 ..**Wilsman,** James M '64 (Wilsman & S,LLC) -1301 E 9th -Ste 1420 -Cleveland 44114

(216) 589-9600 ..**Wilsman & Schoonover,LLC** -1301 E 9th -Ste 1420 -Cleveland 44114

                 Wilson, Amy J '04 -2325 Clay Pike -Zanesville 43701

(419) 289-6500 ..**Wilson & Anderson** -46 W Main -Bx650 -Ashland 44805 **Fx:**281-8492

(216) 898-2345 ..**Wilson,** Andrea Sinclair '97 Electrolux -18013 Cleve Pkwy -Ste 100 -Cleveland 44135

(419) 241-1200 ..**Wilson,** Beth Ann '97 Cooper & W,LPA -900 Adams -Toledo 43624 **Fx:**242-5675

(330) 453-8261 ..**Wilson,** Brian R '87 (Okey Law Firm,LPA) -337 3rd NW -Canton 44702

(330) 253-8300 ..**Wilson,** Bruce H '64 -789 W Market -Akron 44303

(419) 882-7100 ..**Wilson,** Cecil G '77 Lydy & M,Ltd -4930 Holland Sylvania Rd -Sylvania 43560 **Fx:**882-1120

(614) 292-3079 ..**Wilson,** Charles E '86 OSU Moritz Cllg of Law -55 W 12th Av -Columbus 43210 **Fx:**292-1383

(937) 544-2301 ..**Wilson,** Charles H Jr. '59 -108 E Mulberry -West Union 45693

(513) 489-7484 ..**Wilson,** Charles R '70 -4729 Cornell Rd -Cincinnati 45241

(304) 845-9750 ..**Wilson,** Charles R '97 (Gold K&T,LC) -510 Tomlinson Av -Moundsville, WV 26041

                 Wilson, Charlotte M '00 -875 Zan Ct -Cincinnati 45226

(740) 501-1332 ..**Wilson,** Christina Ritchey '93 -Bx722 -Newark 43058 **Fx:**763-4090

(513) 397-6351 ..**Wilson,** Christopher J '91 Cincinnati Bell -201 E 4th -Ste 102-620 -Cincinnati 45202

(614) 462-4554 ..**Wilson,** Courtney '97 Franklin Cnty CSEA -80 E Fulton -Columbus 43215

(330) 762-2600 ..**Wilson,** Dale V '83 %Joondeph & B,LLP -50 S Main -Ste 700 -Akron 44308 **Fx:**762-2604

                 Wilson, Danielle M '04 -(Address Unavailable)

(937) 328-2574 ..**Wilson,** David A '01 Clark Cnty Pros -50 E Columbia -Bx1608 -Springfield 45501

(513) 721-7010 ..**Wilson,** David E '82 Eagle Picher Indstrs,Inc -250 E 5th -Bx779 -Cincinnati 45201

(740) 342-3156 ..**Wilson,** Dean L '83 Cnty Ct Judge -105 N Main -Bx207 -New Lexington 43764

                 Wilson, Douglas A '75 CFO Business Partners -2635 Spreading Oaks Ln -Jacksonville, FL 32223

(419) 394-2323 ..**Wilson,** Eric J '93 Wilson Law Ofc -101 N Front -Bx69 -Saint Marys 45885

(860) 565-7364 ..**Wilson,** Fred S '81 United Tech/Pratt & Whitney -400 Main -MS 133-54 -East Hartford, CT 06108

(513) 961-6200 ..**Wilson,** George R '81 (Markesbery & R Co,LPA) -2368 Victory Pkwy -Ste 200 -Bx6491 -Cincinnati 45206

(216) 696-1422 ..**Wilson,** Glenn R '90 (McCarthy LC&L Co,LPA) -101 Prospect Av W -1800 Mdlnd Bldg -Cleveland 44115 **Fx:**696-1210

(419) 394-2323 ..**Wilson,** Gregory D '69 Wilson Law Ofc -101 N Front -Bx69 -Saint Marys 45885

(513) 352-5858 ..**Wilson,** Gregory R '78 -1411 Sycamore -Cincinnati 45202

(513) 561-1470 ..**Wilson,** Harold G '89 -9225 Old Indn Hill Rd -Indian Hill 45243

(440) 826-2220 ..**Wilson,** Hilary B '86 Baldwin-Wallace College -275 Eastland Rd -Berea 44017

(860) 297-5862 ..**Wilson,** Holly A '81 CT Dept of Rev Srvc -25 Sigourney -Hartford, CT 06106

(216) 687-1311 ..**Wilson,** Holly M '01 %Reminger & R -101 Prospect Av W -1400 Mdlnd Bldg -Cleveland 44115 **Fx:**687-1841

(614) 464-6400 ..**Wilson,** James A Jr. '85 (Vorys SS&P LLP) -52 E Gay -Bx1008 -Columbus 43216 **Fx:**464-6350

(614) 469-5715 ..**Wilson,** James C '03 US Atty -303 Marconi Blvd -Ste 200 -Columbus 43215

(216) 861-6393 ..**Wilson,** James D '89 -75 Pub Sq -Ste 1100 -Cleveland 44113 **Fx:**861-6394

(216) 687-2269 ..**Wilson,** James G '81 CSU-Marshall Cllg of Law -2121 Euclid Av -LB138 -Cleveland 44115 **Fx:**687-6881

(440) 871-7646 ..**Wilson,** James M '91 -29309 Osborn Rd -Bay Village 44140

(440) 256-6828 ..**Wilson,** Jane P '84 (JP Wilson & Assoc Co,LPA) -8580 Eagle Rd -Kirtland 44094

                 Wilson, Jeffrey J '01 -7453 Finchwood Ln -Toledo 43617

                 Wilson, Jennifer L '04 -(Address Unavailable)

(216) 263-4591 ..**Wilson,** Jesslyn C '82 Cleveland Municipal Ct -1200 Ontario -11th Fl -Cleveland 44113

(513) 522-1255 ..**Wilson,** Joanne A '84 Wilson & W Co,LPA -8228 Winton Rd -Ste 300C -Cincinnati 45231

(859) 240-0653 ..**Wilson,** John D '83 The Ellison Grp -9062 Symmes Vw Ct -Loveland 45140

(419) 693-7717 ..**Wilson,** John M '82 NW OH Building Trades -909 Front -Toledo 43605

(860) 229-1996 ..**Wilson,** John R '04 -205 Hartford Rd -#D14 -New Britain, CT 06053

(419) 259-6376 ..**Wilson,** Joseph R '81 US Atty -4 Seagate -Ste 308 -Toledo 43604 **Fx:**259-6360

(513) 475-4902 ..**Wilson,** Julie K '83 Cincinnati Pub Sch -2651 Burnet Av -Bx5381 -Cincinnati 45201

(330) 670-0101 ..**Wilson,** Katherine A '01 %Nurses In Aids Care -3538 Rdgwd Rd -Akron 44333

(251) 441-5441 ..**Wilson,** Kenneth '94 SSA/Ofc of Hearings -550 Govt -Ste 200 -Mobile, AL 36602

(513) 381-2838 ..**Wilson,** LaQuita S '03 %Taft S&H LLP -425 Walnut -Ste 1800 -Cincinnati 45202 **Fx:**381-0205

(313) 943-5300 ..**Wilson,** LaTanya R '95 UAW-GM Lgl Srvcs Plan -5220 Oakman Blvd -Dearborn, MI 48126

(937) 496-6917 ..**Wilson,** Laura L '97 Montgomery Cnty Pros -301 W 3rd -Bx972 -Dayton 45422 **Fx:**225-3470

(216) 781-2258 ..**Wilson,** Lawrence J Jr. '03 Stewart & D Co,LPA -1370 Ontario -Ste 1440 Standard Bldg -Cleveland 44113 **Fx:**781-8210

(614) 228-1541 ..**Wilson,** Leigh Ann '99 %Baker & H LLP -65 E State -Ste 2100 -Columbus 43215 **Fx:**462-2616

(216) 271-5482 ..**Wilson,** Marianne E '86 -17463 Woodford Av -Lakewood 44107

(727) 938-6850 ..**Wilson,** Mark L '90 MGM Real Estate Srvcs,Inc -4337 Ellinwood Blvd -Palm Harbor, FL 34685

(614) 224-6969 ..**Wilson,** Mark R '82 (Blue W+B LLC) -471 E Broad -Columbus 43215 **Fx:**224-6999

(419) 843-2001 ..**Wilson,** Martha J '97 %Gallon & T Co,LPA -3516 Granite Cir -Bx352018 -Toledo 43635 **Fx:**843-6665

(216) 696-0022 ..**Wilson,** Marvin Scott '84 (Collins & S LLP) -50 Pub Sq -3300 Trmnl Twr -Cleveland 44113 **Fx:**696-1166

(216) 621-0200 ..**Wilson,** Mary A '83 OfCnsl Baker & H LLP -1900 E 9th -Ste 3200 -Cleveland 44114 **Fx:**696-0740

(415) 552-6047 ..**Wilson,** Matthew H '84 -17 Bird -San Francisco, CA 94110

(614) 469-3939 ..**Wilson,** Matthew R '00 %Jones D -325 John H McConnell Blvd -Ste 600 -Bx165017 -Columbus 43216 **Fx:**461-4198

(937) 432-9300 ..**Wilson,** Melinda M '01 (Wilson & M) -4625 Far Hills Av -Dayton 45429 **Fx:**432-9311

(740) 432-7844 ..**Wilson,** Melissa M '03 %FA McClure,LPA -213 N 8th -Cambridge 43725 **Fx:**439-4950

(440) 358-1100 ..**Wilson,** Neil R '73 (N Wilson Co, LPA) -56 Lbrty -Ste 205 -Painesville 44077

                 Wilson, Nicholas B '74 -2054 Wickford -Columbus 43221

(216) 566-5623 ..**Wilson,** Nicole C '01 %Thompson H LLP -127 Pub Sq -3900 Key Ctr -Cleveland 44114 **Fx:**566-5800

(770) 587-7214 ..**Wilson,** Patrick C '81 Kimberly Clark Corp -1400 Holcomb Brdg Rd -Bldg 200/1 -Roswell, GA 30076

(330) 392-1541 ..**Wilson,** Patrick K '88 Harrington H&M,Ltd -108 Main Av SW -Ste 500 -Bx1510 -Warren 44482 **Fx:**394-6890

(216) 586-3939 ..**Wilson,** Paula Batt '95 (Jones D) -901 Lakeside Av -Cleveland 44114 **Fx:**579-0212

(216) 685-9940 ..**Wilson,** Rachel C '97 (Pagano WT&G) -1370 Ontario -Ste 1240 -Cleveland 44113 **Fx:**685-9942

(330) 477-6781 ..**Wilson,** Randy K '76 Stark Cnty Engineer -5165 Southway SW -Canton 44706

(330) 678-2850 ..**Wilson,** Richard A '74 -1221 S Water -Kent 44240

(440) 708-0445 ..**Wilson,** Robert D '84 (RD Wilson Co,LPA) -16716 Chilicothe Rd -Ste 100 -Chagrin Falls 44023 **Fx:**708-0511

(740) 387-0970 ..**Wilson,** Robert E '68 (Wilson & K Co,LPA) -132 S Main -Marion 43302

                 Wilson, Robert M '77 -1 Burton Hills Blvd -Ste 375 -Nashville, TN 37215

(248) 258-1616 ..**Wilson,** Robert T '94 %Butzel L,PC -100 Blmfld Hills Pkwy -Ste 200 -Bloomfield Hills, MI 48304 **Fx:**258-1439

(412) 355-2600 ..**Wilson,** Roberta R '84 DKW Law Grp,PC -600 Grant -58th Fl -Pittsburgh, PA 15219

(216) 566-5572 ..**Wilson,** Robin M '96 %Thompson H LLP -127 Pub Sq -3900 Key Ctr -Cleveland 44114 **Fx:**566-5800

(513) 765-6000 ..**Wilson,** Robin R '93 LensCrafters,Inc -4000 Luxottica Pl -Mason 45040

(303) 721-7406 ..**Wilson,** Rodger L '75 (Wilson & F LLC) -6400 S Fiddlers Green Cir -Ste 750 -Englewood, CO 80111 **Fx:**721-9117

(216) 622-8200 ..**Wilson,** Scott R '77 (Calfee H&G LLP) -800 Superior Av -Ste 1400 -Cleveland 44114 **Fx:**241-0816

                 Wilson, Shawna J '02 US AID -7030 Almaty Pl -Dulles, VA 20189

(216) 687-3543 ..**Wilson,** Sonali B '86 CSU-Legal Affrs -2121 Euclid Av -1212 Rhodes Twr -Cleveland 44115

(740) 345-4550 ..**Wilson,** Stephen B '88 -35 S Park Pl -Ste 201 -Newark 43055

(330) 296-9642 ..**Wilson,** Stephen M '79 (Wilson & M) -250 S Prospect -Ravenna 44266 **Fx:**296-9644

(216) 522-3715 ..**Wilson,** Steven D '80 NLRB -1240 E 9th -1695 Celebrezze Bldg -Cleveland 44199 **Fx:**522-2418

(440) 243-2800 ..**Wilson,** Stewart S '79 %Phillips M&C Co,LPA -7530 Lucerne Dr -Ste 200 -Middleburg Heights 44130 **Fx:**243-2852

(614) 224-5205 ..**Wilson,** Thomas A '90 (Peck S&W,LLP) -175 S 3rd -Ste 600 -Columbus 43215 **Fx:**224-0069

(216) 586-3939 ..**Wilson,** Thomas A '03 %Jones D -901 Lakeside Av -Cleveland 44114 **Fx:**579-0212

(330) 746-5643 ..**Wilson,** Thomas J '76 (Comstock S&W Co,LPA) -100 Fed Plz E -Ste 926 -Youngstown 44503 **Fx:**746-4925

(216) 575-0777 ..**Wilson,** Thomas M '87 (Kelley & F,LLP) -1300 E 9th -Ste 1901 -Cleveland 44114 **Fx:**575-0799

(513) 891-6600 ..**Wilson,** Thomas P '88 Wilson Advisory Grp LLC -8040 Hosbrook Rd -Ste 107 -Cincinnati 45236

(740) 264-4024 ..**Wilson,** Thomas S '76 -4017-A Sunset Blvd -Steubenville 43952 **Fx:**266-2998

(937) 324-5870 ..**Wilson,** Thomas W '79 -466 N Plum -Springfield 45504

Wilson, Timothy A '77 -(Address Unavailable)

(937) 866-2103 .. **Wilson**, Vernon '52 -443 E Central Av -Miamisburg 45342

(513) 651-6800 .. **Wilson**, W Russell '83 (Frost BT LLC) -201 E 5th -2200 PNC Ctr
-Cincinnati 45202 Fx:651-6981

(740) 535-1643 .. **Wilson**, William E '75 -621 Wstrn Av -Mingo Junction 43938

(614) 644-3037 .. **Wilson**, William S '82 EPA -122 S Front -Bx1049
-Columbus 43216

(937) 878-8649 .. **Wilson**, Yvonne N '03 %Martin MW&R -26 N Wright Av
-Fairborn 45324 Fx:878-8479

(440) 942-8886 .. **Wilt**, Daniel D '70 -35000 Chardon Rd -#125 -Willoughby 44094

(216) 621-5300 .. **Wilt**, Ronald M '92 (Buckingham D&B,LLP) -1375 E 9th -Ste 1700
-Cleveland 44114 Fx:621-5440

(937) 325-1588 .. **Wilt**, Valerie J '88 (Juergens W&S) -200 N Fountain Av
-Springfield 45504

(216) 664-2687 .. **Wiltshire**, Cheryl M '04 -1200 Ontario -Housing Ct -13th Fl
-Cleveland 44113

(440) 914-2000 .. **Wimbiscus**, Denise M '96 Cambridge Intgrtd Srvcs -31500
Solon Rd -Solon 44139

(216) 525-7939 .. **Winans**, Jill M '90 GMAC Ins Co -7100 E Plsnt Vlly Rd -Ste 270
-Independence 44131

(740) 587-2209 .. **Wince**, Philip D '76 -2350 Bway W -Granville 43023

(216) 621-8700 .. **Wincek**, Christopher G '86 %Wincek & D Co,LPA -1370 Ontario
-1500 Standard Bldg -Cleveland 44113

(216) 621-8700 .. **Wincek & De Rosa Co, LPA** -1370 Ontario -1500 Standard Bldg
-Cleveland 44113

(505) 843-4272 .. **Winchell**, Bruce M '74 Sandia Natl Labs -MS-0103 -Bx5800
-Albuquerque, NM 87185 Fx:246-2891

(330) 753-8968 .. **Winchell**, Dennis R '76 -384 Newell -Barberton 44203

(330) 927-3120 .. **Winchell**, V Lee '77 -34 S Main -Rittman 44270 Fx:927-0007

(216) 621-9870 .. **Winchester**, Brian T '98 (McNeal SA&B Co,LPA)
-123 W Prospect Av -Ste 250 Van Sweringen Arcade
-Cleveland 44115 Fx:522-1112

(614) 469-3939 .. **Winchester**, Jeffrey D '97 %Jones D -325 John H McConnell Blvd
-Ste 600 -Bx165017 -Columbus 43216 Fx:461-4198

(419) 690-8022 .. **Winckowski**, Scott A '89 (Breier & W,Ltd) -2741 Navarre Av
-Ste 402 -Oregon 43616

(216) 443-7583 .. **Windham**, Patricia K '91 Cuyahoga Cnty Pub Def
-1200 W 3rd NW -100 Lakeside Pl -Cleveland 44113

(202) 842-3900 .. **Windley**, Jacqueline T '89 Natl Bar Assoc -1225 11th NW
-Washington, DC 20001

(330) 376-0000 .. **Windon**, Jeffrey D '74 Lawyers Title Ins Corp -195 S Main
-Ste 202 -Akron 44308 Fx:702-2349

(937) 325-7058 .. **Wineberg**, Robert A '80 (Gorman VH&W) -4 W Main -Ste 723
-Springfield 45502 Fx:325-9914

(804) 783-7270 .. **Winegardner**, Douglas A '94 %Sands AM&M,PC -801 E Main
-Bx1998 -Richmond, VA 23218

Winegardner, Jennifer A '94 Supreme Ct -500 S Duval
-Tallahassee, FL 32399

(419) 486-9999 .. **Wineland**, Erik J '00 (Wineland Lgl Srvcs Corp) -520 Mad Av
-Ste 915 -Toledo 43604 Fx:486-8939

(419) 668-6840 .. **Wineman**, Reese M '76 -6 W Main -Norwalk 44857 Fx:668-7720

(440) 563-4444 .. **Winer**, Jonathan W '87 -5276 Rome Rock Crk Rd -Rome 44085

(740) 593-3357 .. **Wines**, Larry D '97 %Mollica GS&S Co,LPA -35 N Cllg -Drwr958
-Athens 45701

(216) 289-5297 .. **Winfield**, Patricia L '84 -22034 Lakeshr Blvd -Euclid 44123

(614) 222-5853 .. **Winfree**, James R '75 SERS -300 E Broad -Ste 100
-Columbus 43215

(419) 334-9501 .. **Wingard**, William A '73 -410 Croghan -Fremont 43420

(419) 243-3800 .. **Wingate**, Ronnie L '79 -1119 Adams -2nd Fl -Toledo 43624

(216) 222-9427 .. **Wingenfeld**, Paul F '92 Natl City Corp -1900 E 9th
-Law Dept Loc 01-2174 -Cleveland 44114

(216) 581-1644 .. **Winger**, Lora A '96 Trinity High Schl -12425 Granger Rd
-Garfield Heights 44125

(937) 845-8776 .. **Wingert**, Howard E '85 Concrete Sealants,Inc -Bx176
-New Carlisle 45344

(513) 243-0792 .. **Winget**, James L '95 GE Aircraft Engines -1 Neumann Way
-MD J165 -Cincinnati 45215

(330) 867-3247 .. **Winick**, Bernard S '64 -1653 Merriman Rd -Ste 109 -Akron 44313
Fx:867-3247

(440) 349-5955 .. **Winik**, Jane L '96 Swagelok Co -31500 Aurora Rd -Solon 44139

(419) 422-9875 .. **Winkeljohn**, John T '72 OH Automotive Supply
-310 Church Hill Dr -Findlay 45840

(740) 592-6399 .. **Winkelmann**, David J '94 (Biddlestone & W Co,LPA) -8 N Court
-Ste 308 -Athens 45701 Fx:573-6341

(330) 433-6800 .. **Winkhart**, Thomas W '89 Cornerstone RE Title -801 S Main
-Canton 44720

(614) 222-0535 .. **Winkle**, Dawn M '04 %Sabath & J Co,LPA -338 S High
-Columbus 43215

(800) 243-0210 .. **Winkler**, Daniel A '94 Westfield Grp -1 Park Cir -Bx5001
-Westfield Center 44251 Fx:(330) 887-2588

(513) 621-5500 .. **Winkler**, Diane E '91 -817 Main -Ste 500 -Cincinnati 45202
Fx:621-5646

(614) 466-9567 .. **Winkler**, Dirken D '97 OH Consumers' Cnsl -10 W Broad
-Ste 1800 -Columbus 43215 Fx:466-9475

(614) 559-3839 .. **Winkler**, John F '83 (Robol & W,LLC) -555 City Park Av
-Columbus 43215

(859) 292-7537 .. **Winkler**, John F II '90 Huntington Natl Bank -540 Mad Av -4th Fl
-Covington, KY 41011

(404) 659-6700 .. **Winkler**, Kenneth N '93 Elarbee T&T, LLP -229 Pchtree NE
-Ste 800 -Atlanta, GA 30303

(513) 946-5175 .. **Winkler**, Ralph E '87 Cnty Mun Ct Judge -1000 Main -Rm 178
-Cincinnati 45202

(513) 946-5143 .. **Winkler**, Robert C '87 Cnty Mun Ct Judge -1000 Main
-Cincinnati 45202

(937) 325-7365 .. **Winks**, Paul W '71 (Emerich W&P) -20 S Limestone -Ste 300
-Bx1087 -Springfield 45501

(740) 450-1559 .. **Winnefeld**, Sheila M A '03 -507 Main -Ste 200 -Zanesville 43701

(614) 221-8868 .. **Winner**, Joseph C '76 (McFadden W&S) -175 S 3rd -Ste 210
-Columbus 43215 Fx:221-3985

(216) 368-4495 .. **Winner**, Sonia M '91 CWRU Law Schl -11075 East Blvd
-Cleveland 44106

(937) 512-1531 .. **Winquist**, Stephanie L '02 US Dist Ct -200 W 2nd -9th Fl
-Dayton 45402

(610) 270-7513 .. **Winslow**, Andrea L '01 Cnsl Glaxo Smith Kline
-709 Swedeland Rd -UW2220 -Bx1539
-King Of Prussia, PA 19406 Fx:270-5090

(440) 248-7906 .. **Winslow**, Patrick W '77 (Mazanec R&R Co,LPA) -34305 Solon Rd
-Ste 100 -Cleveland 44139 Fx:248-8861

(614) 728-8400 .. **Winslow**, Timothy C '99 Atty Gen/Fincl Inst -77 S High -21st Fl
-Columbus 43215

(513) 579-6400 .. **Winstead**, John N '98 %Keating M&K PLL -1 E 4th
-1400 Provident Twr -Cincinnati 45202 Fx:579-6457

(216) 621-0200 .. **Winston**, David S '96 %Baker & H LLP -1900 E 9th -Ste 3200
-Cleveland 44114 Fx:696-0740

(216) 830-9000 .. **Winston**, Douglas L '86 %Berger & Z Co,LPA -614 W Superior Av
-Ste 1425 Rckfllr Bldg -Cleveland 44113 Fx:830-4200

(614) 592-1911 .. **Winston**, Michael D '02 -3055 Cleveland Av -Columbus 43224
Fx:447-8672

(216) 771-3314 .. **Winston**, Robert M '77 -1370 Ontario -Ste 330 -Cleveland 44113

(440) 838-7600 .. **Winter**, Jason D '03 %Janik & D,LLP -9200 S Hills Blvd -Ste 300
-Cleveland 44147 Fx:838-7601

(859) 344-1188 .. **Winter**, Robert A Jr. '87 Hemmer SPD&K -250 Grandvw Dr
-Ste 200 -Ft Mitchell, KY 41017

(614) 624-5686 .. **Winter**, William J '91 Ross Products-Abbott Labs
-625 Cleveland Av -Columbus 43215

(419) 241-9770 .. **Winterhalter**, Keith J '87 Vassar DD&B,LLC -420 Mad Av
-Ste 1102 -Toledo 43604 Fx:241-9771

(937) 223-1130 .. **Winterhalter**, Paul J '66 Pickrel S&E -40 N Main
-2700 Kettering Twr -Dayton 45423 Fx:223-0339

(216) 696-0606 .. **Wintering**, Mark J '77 RE Sweeney Co,LPA -55 Pub Sq -Ste 1500
-Cleveland 44113 Fx:696-0679

(614) 888-8611 .. **Wintering**, Michael R '78 -1103 Schrock Rd -Ste 209
-Columbus 43229

(419) 734-6755 .. **Winters**, Bruce A '88 Ottawa Cnty Ct of Common Pleas
-315 Madison -Port Clinton 43452 Fx:734-6875

(614) 221-3388 .. **Winters**, Charles W '53 -600 S High -Columbus 43215

(216) 781-2822 .. **Winters**, Christopher S '82 (Winters & M Co,LPA) -820 W Superior
Av -Ste 600 -Cleveland 44113 Fx:344-2720

(614) 228-0068 .. **Winters**, David C '75 (Winters & M) -500 S Front -Ste 900
-Columbus 43215 Fx:228-1660

(614) 365-2700 .. **Winters**, Karen A '81 (Squire S&D LLP) -41 S High
-1300 Huntngtn Ctr -Columbus 43215 Fx:365-2499

(614) 491-1401 .. **Winters**, Leslie A '80 Rickenbacker Port Auth -7400 Alum Crk Dr
-Columbus 43217

(513) 421-4646 .. **Winters**, Ralph G '76 McCaslin I&M,LPA -632 Vine -Ste 900
-Cincinnati 45202 Fx:421-7929

(419) 321-6444 .. **Winters**, Steven B '96 %Cline C&W Co,LPA -300 Mad Av
-Ste 1100 -Toledo 43604 Fx:321-6430

(614) 267-6401 .. **Winters**, Susan J '82 -333 Arden Rd -Columbus 43214

(614) 464-6400 .. **Winters**, Thomas R '84 (Vorys SS&P LLP) -52 E Gay -Bx1008
-Columbus 43216 Fx:464-6350

(202) 756-8061 .. **Winterscheid**, Joseph F '78 (McDermott W&E) -600 13th NW
-Washington, DC 20005 Fx:756-8087

(859) 647-2867 .. **Wintersheimer**, Mark D '88 -71 Cavalier Blvd -Ste 131
-Florence, KY 41042

(216) 763-5467 .. **Wintner**, Alix A '85 -3659 Green Rd -Ste 100 -Beachwood 44122

(216) 932-4443 .. **Wintner**, Jennifer E '84 -2733 Scarborough Rd
-Cleveland Heights 44115

(216) 475-8100 .. **Winton**, Jeffrey D '79 Garfield Hghts Schls -5640 Briarcliff Dr
-Garfield Heights 44125

(513) 887-3844 .. **Winton**, Joel F '04 %Butler Cnty Pros -315 High -11th Fl -Bx515
-Hamilton 45012

(937) 294-6000 .. **Winwood Crossman & Associates** -3077 Kettering Blvd
-Ste 210 -Dayton 45439

(937) 294-6000 .. **Winwood**, Jeffrey A '72 (Winwood C & Assoc)
-3077 Kettering Blvd -Ste 210 -Dayton 45439

(419) 445-4511 .. **Winzeler**, Brent L '79 (Gooding & W,Ltd) -201 Vine -Archbold
43502 Fx:445-2353

(216) 774-8104 .. **Winzig**, Virginia V '84 The Doctors Co -1301 E 9th -Ste 1130
-Cleveland 44114

(330) 287-5490 .. **Wire**, Beverly J '85 Pub Def -113 W Lbrty -Wooster 44691

(513) 398-8900 .. **Wireman**, Daniel R '95 Cleveland Cnstrctn Inc -5390 Coursevw Dr
-Mason 45040

(614) 791-5730 .. **Wires**, Eileen M '86 Sterling Commerce -4600 Lakehurst Ct
-Dublin 43016

(330) 493-0787 .. **Wirsching**, David B Jr. '65 -7110 Whipple Av NW -Ste C101
-Canton 44720

Wirt, Laurie B '95 -7752 Northwind Ct -Columbus 43235

(614) 443-4866 .. **Wirth**, David S '01 %J Nemeth & Assoc -21 E Frankfort
-Columbus 43206 Fx:443-4860

(937) 866-8454 .. **Wirth**, Gerald R '73 -110 E Central Av -Miamisburg 45342

(513) 579-2980 .. **Wirthlin**, John R '85 Provident Bank -1 E 4th -860 A
-Cincinnati 45202

(513) 221-1745 .. **Wirthlin**, John S Jr. '79 (Beirne & W Co,LPA) -1745 Madison Rd
-Bx6111 -Cincinnati 45206 Fx:221-6666

(513) 221-1745 .. **Wirthlin**, Michael F '82 Beirne & W Co,LPA -1745 Madison Rd
-Bx6111 -Cincinnati 45206 Fx:221-6666

(740) 662-5297 .. **Wirtshafter**, Don E '85 -7002 State Route 329 -Guysville 45735

(216) 348-5400 .. **Wirtshafter**, John M '84 (McDonald H Co,LPA) -600 Superior Av E
-Ste 2100 -Cleveland 44114 Fx:348-5474

(216) 363-1313 .. **Wirtz**, Amy Y '92 %Skirbunt & S Co,LPA -55 Pub Sq -Ste 1310
-Cleveland 44113

(330) 454-2444 .. **Wirtz**, John B '73 -220 Market Av S -#300 -Canton 44702

(210) 351-3736 .. **Wirtz**, Wayne A '80 SBC Comm,Inc -175 E Houston -12th Fl
-San Antonio, TX 78205

(513) 943-1222 .. **Wischer**, William P '03 ADC Auto Distribution Ctr
-4101 Founders Blvd -Batavia 45103 Fx:943-8580

Wisdom, David L '03 -(Address Unavailable)

(513) 381-2838 .. **Wise**, Bryan E '03 %Taft S&H LLP -425 Walnut -Ste 1800
-Cincinnati 45202 Fx:381-0205

(614) 221-1166 .. **Wise**, C Michael '88 %Plymale & Assoc -495 S High -Ste 400
-Columbus 43215 Fx:221-6633

(419) 252-6228 .. **Wise**, David G '67 (Spengler N PLL) -608 Mad Av -Ste 1000
-Toledo 43604 Fx:241-8599

(216) 351-6560 .. **Wise**, David M '87 -4499 Broadvw Rd -Cleveland 44109

(419) 327-4303 ..**Wise & Dorner,Ltd** -151 N Mich -Ste 333 -Toledo 43624
    Fx:327-4302

(330) 451-7897 ..**Wise,** Earle E Jr. '97 Stark Cnty Pros -110 Central Plz -Ste 510
    -Canton 44702

(614) 237-5414 ..**Wise,** Janice W '81 OH Nurses Assn -4000 E Main
    -Columbus 43213

(614) 247-5853 ..**Wise,** Katherine J '97 OSU Stdnt Housing Leg Clnc -1739 N High
    -Columbus 43210

(412) 434-5415 ..**Wise,** Meghan F '02 %Zimmer K,PLLC -600 Grant
    -3300 US Steel Twr -Pittsburgh, PA 15219

(614) 466-8600 ..**Wise,** Michael A '02 Atty Gen -30 E Broad -Columbus 43215
    Fx:466-6090

(216) 348-5400 ..**Wise,** Michael W '90 (McDonald H Co,LPA) -600 Superior Av E
    -Ste 2100 -Cleveland 44114 **Fx:**348-5474

(419) 327-4300 ..**Wise,** Patricia A '85 (Wise & D,Ltd) -151 N Mich -Ste 333
    -Toledo 43624 **Fx:**327-4302

(419) 238-5307 ..**Wise,** Perry G '50 Wise & Assoc Co, LPA -229 N Wshngtn
    -Van Wert 45891

(419) 627-0414 ..**Wisehart,** Troy D '91 Buckingham LM&Z Co,LPA -414 Wayne
    -Bx929 -Sandusky 44870 **Fx:**627-0009

(440) 338-3392 ..**Wiseley,** Paul J '50 -13645 Fox Den E -Novelty 44072

(937) 223-8177 ..**Wiseman,** Lisa K '01 %Coolidge WW&L -33 W 1st -Ste 600
    -Dayton 45402 **Fx:**223-6705

(216) 391-5444 ..**Wiseman,** Mark N '92 Housing Advocates Inc -3655 Prospect Av E
    -Cleveland 44115 **Fx:**391-5404

(937) 227-3700 ..**Wiseman,** Mary L '91 (Faruki I&C PLL) -10 N Ludlow
    -500 Cthse Plz SW -Dayton 45402 **Fx:**227-3717

(614) 227-2310 ..**Wiseman,** Randolph C '74 (Bricker & E LLP) -100 S 3rd
    -Columbus 43215 **Fx:**227-2390

(330) 747-1471 ..**Wiseman,** Robert L Jr. '78 Vindicator Printing Co
    -107 Vindicator Sq -Youngstown 44503

(440) 230-0800 ..**Wishnosky,** David M '89 -11210 Falmouth Cir -North Royalton
    44133

(614) 891-3512 ..**Wisner,** Edwin A '66 Republic-Franklin Ins Co
    -2600 Corp Exchange Dr -Bx29906 -Columbus 43229

(419) 291-2034 ..**Wisniewski,** Jeffrey T '00 Cnsl ProMedica Hlth Syst,Inc
    -2121 Hughes Dr -Ff E -Toledo 43606 **Fx:**479-6918

(419) 874-3177 ..**Wisniewski,** Marshall D '81 (Pheils & W) -410 Louisiana Av
    -Perrysburg 43551 **Fx:**874-0180

(419) 241-5175 ..**Wisniewski,** Samara L '04 %Maloney M&K -520 Mad Av -Ste 330
    -Toledo 43604

(513) 684-3225 ..**Wissman,** Brian M '00 ATF -550 Main -Rm 1516 -Cincinnati 45202

(937) 667-8458 ..**Wist,** Edmund J '68 (Moorman & W Co LPA) -8 S 3rd -Tipp
    City 45371

(614) 461-6006 ..**Wistner,** Robert N '62 OfCnsl E Whipps & Assoc -500 S Front
    -Ste 860 -Columbus 43215

(614) 469-3939 ..**Witalec,** Joseph M '94 Cnsl Jones D -325 John H McConnell Blvd
    -Ste 600 -Bx165017 -Columbus 43216 **Fx:**461-4198

(419) 243-9873 ..**Witcher,** Jenelda E '95 -1900 Monroe #111 -Ste 111
    -Toledo 43624 **Fx:**243-9917

(614) 462-2202 ..**Withee,** Stephen P '98 %Schottenstein Z&D -250 West -Bx165020
    -Columbus 43216 **Fx:**462-5135

(419) 241-9000 ..**Witherell,** Dennis P '77 (Shumaker L&K,LLP) -1000 Jackson
    -Toledo 43624 **Fx:**241-6894

(216) 781-4680 ..**Withers,** Carl R '54 (Van Aken W&W) -629 Euclid Av -1000
    Natl City Bk Bldg -Cleveland 44115 **Fx:**241-1421

(937) 222-2424 ..**Witherspoon,** John G Jr. '83 %Freund F&A -1 S Main -Ste 1800
    -Dayton 45402 **Fx:**222-5369

(614) 757-5000 ..**Withrow,** Brent M '03 Cardinal Hlth -7000 Cardinal Pl
    -Dublin 43017

(216) 861-5582 ..**Withrow,** Jonathan A '02 %Fay SFM&M LLP -1100 Superior Av
    -7th Fl -Cleveland 44114 **Fx:**241-1666

(859) 655-4200 ..**Withrow,** Michael V '73 (Greenebaum D&M PLLC)
    -50 E RiverCenter Blvd -Ste 1800 -Covington, KY 41011
    Fx:655-4239

(775) 887-2072 ..**Witker,** Melissa M '02 Dist Atty Ofc -885 E Musser
    -Carson City, NV 89701

(419) 213-3000 ..**Witko,** Michael G '83 Lucas Cnty CSEA -701 Adams
    -Toledo 43624

(216) 621-7227 ..**Witkowski,** Richard G '85 (Nicola G&C,LLC) -25 W Prospect Av
    -Republic Bldg Ste 1400 -Cleveland 44115 **Fx:**621-3999

(216) 586-3939 ..**Witmer-Rich,** Jonathan P '01 %Jones D -901 Lakeside Av
    -Cleveland 44114 **Fx:**579-0212

(330) 882-4061 ..**Witner,** David A '94 -6456 Southvw Dr -Clinton 44216

(330) 451-7918 ..**Witner,** Kristine S '94 Hon JF Boggins -110 Central Plz S -Ste 320
    -Canton 44702

(614) 487-5100 ..**Witney,** William P '90 Uppr Arlington City Schls -1850 Hastings Ln
    -Hastings Middle Schl -Columbus 43220

(330) 665-5117 ..**Witschey,** Frank J '92 (Witschey & W Co,LPA)
    -300 N Cleveland-Massillon Rd -Ste 104 -Akron 44333

(330) 665-5117 ..**Witschey,** Jeffrey T '92 (Witschey & W Co,LPA)
    -300 N Cleveland-Massillon Rd -Ste 104 -Akron 44333

.. **Witt,** Clyde David '73 -9962 Gatewood Dr -Brecksville 44141

(313) 270-1216 ..**Witt,** Francis J III '78 A&P,Inc -18718 Borman Av -Labor Relations
    -Detroit, MI 48228

(513) 421-5297 ..**Witt,** Jeffrey A '96 -214 E 9th -Cincinnati 45202

(440) 734-6158 ..**Witt,** Mark S '83 -6209 Barton Rd -North Olmsted 44070

(419) 241-3251 ..**Witt,** Robert E '66 -316 N Mich -Ste 312 -Toledo 43624

(303) 272-8064 ..**Witte,** Eric P '88 Sun Microsystems,Inc -500 Eldorado Blvd
    -MS-UBRM-01-200 -Broomfield, CO 80021

(216) 861-5000 ..**Witte,** Michael C '96 Ernst & Young -1300 Huntngtn Bldg
    -925 Euclid Av -Cleveland 44115

(513) 794-0934 ..**Witte,** Monte D '74 -3578 Tiffany Ridge Ln -Cincinnati 45241

.. **Witte,** Richard C '57 -596 Abilene Trl -Cincinnati 45215

(330) 821-2627 ..**Witte,** Wylan W '73 -950 S Sawburg Av -Alliance 44601

(304) 346-0321 ..**Wittemeier,** Susan C '81 Goodwin & G -300 Summers -Ste 1500
    -Charleston, WV 25301 **Fx:**344-9692

(614) 466-4328 ..**Witten,** Amy C '69 Atty Gen -150 E Gay -Columbus 43215
    Fx:995-0266

(330) 544-0424 ..**Witten,** Debora Kay '80 (Witten & D) -465 Robbins Av
    -Niles 44446

(202) 879-5451 ..**Witten,** Jesse A '91 (Jones D) -51 Louisiana Av NW
    -Washington, DC 20001 **Fx:**626-1700

(614) 246-2500 ..**Witten,** John P '77 Stonehenge Captl Corp
    -191 W Nationwide Blvd -Ste 600 -Columbus 43215

(513) 721-1975 ..**Wittenauer,** Ann K '02 %Freking & B -215 E 9th -5th Fl
    -Cincinnati 45202 **Fx:**651-2570

(704) 583-8710 ..**Wittenauer,** Kenneth L '82 SrCnsl Continental Tire NA Inc
    -1800 Continental Blvd -Charlotte, NC 28273

(614) 258-1983 ..**Wittenberg,** Eric J '87 (E Wittenberg Co,LPA) -923 E Broad
    -Columbus 43205

(419) 535-7444 ..**Wittenberg,** Joseph L '72 (J Wittenberg LPA)
    -2727 N Holland Sylvania Rd -Ste G -Toledo 43615

(419) 255-6070 ..**Wittenberg Phillips Levy & Nusbaum** -520 Mad Av -Ste 840
    -Toledo 43604

(419) 255-6070 ..**Wittenberg,** Sheldon S '69 (Wittenberg PL&N) -520 Mad Av
    -Ste 840 -Toledo 43604

(216) 739-5645 ..**Wittenberg,** Stacie H '00 %Weltman W&R Co,LPA
    -323 W Lakeside Av -Ste 200 -Cleveland 44113 **Fx:**363-4121

(216) 444-1275 ..**Wittenmyer,** Nelson J Jr. '90 Cleveland Clinic Fndtn
    -9500 Euclid Av -Cleveland 44195

(419) 228-6365 ..**Witter,** Donald J '62 (Cory MWR&C,LPA) -101 N Elizabeth
    -Ste 607 -Bx1271 -Lima 45802 **Fx:**228-5319

(330) 796-3614 ..**Wittkamper,** Gerry Van '72 Goodyear Tire & Rubber Co
    -1144 E Market -Akron 44313

(513) 896-7767 ..**Wittman,** Dennis L '71 -Bx117 -Hamilton 45012

(330) 744-5321 ..**Wittman,** Donald B '00 MS Cnsltnts,Inc -333 E Fed -Youngstown
    44503

.. **Witzman,** Joseph D K '01 -(Address Unavailable)

(937) 434-2167 ..**Wiviott,** Melvin '70 -1599 Ambrdg Rd -Centerville 45459

(330) 729-9000 ..**Wloch,** Vincent J '74 -412 Boardman-Canfld Rd
    -Youngstown 44512

(614) 227-2000 ..**Wobst,** Franck G '83 (Porter WM&A LLP) -41 S High
    -Columbus 43215 **Fx:**227-2100

(216) 443-3439 ..**Wochna,** Charles F '85 Cuyahoga Cnty Cmn Pleas Ct
    -2163 E 22nd -Cleveland 44115

(330) 556-3750 ..**Wochna,** Donald A '83 -1585 King Rd -Hinckley 44233

(216) 321-3230 ..**Woda,** Elizabeth M '78 -3008 Monticello Blvd -#225
    -Cleveland Heights 44118 **Fx:**321-1714

(614) 462-3555 ..**Wodarcyk,** Mark J '90 Franklin Cnty Pros -373 S High
    -Columbus 43215

(513) 241-4722 ..**Woeber,** Linda L '87 (Montgomery R&J,LPA) -36 E 7th -Ste 2100
    -Cincinnati 45202 **Fx:**241-8175

(513) 852-6044 ..**Woebkenberg,** Thomas M '86 (Wood & L LLP) -600 Vine
    -Ste 2500 -Cincinnati 45202 **Fx:**852-6087

(614) 279-8188 ..**Woelfel,** Bradford B '83 -3356 Lindstrom Dr -Columbus 43228

(606) 635-1662 ..**Woeste,** Richard A '82 (Bathalter & W) -Bx92
    -Alexandria, KY 41001

(614) 469-3939 ..**Wofford,** Isaac S '02 %Jones D -325 John H McConnell Blvd
    -Ste 600 -Bx165017 -Columbus 43216 **Fx:**461-4198

(614) 228-4201 ..**Woggon,** Linda S '92 OH Chamber of Cmmrce -230 E Town
    -Columbus 43215

(419) 242-6505 ..**Wohl,** Doris K '73 (Wohl & Assoc) -520 Mad Av -563 Spitzer Bldg
    -Toledo 43604

(216) 831-0200 ..**Wohl,** William M '67 -23230 Chagrin Blvd -Ste 800
    -Beachwood 44122 **Fx:**831-5064

(440) 526-0414 ..**Wojciak,** David J '95 -3846 Bxelder Dr -Brecksville 44141

(216) 241-2628 ..**Wojcik,** Waldemar J '80 -526 Superior Av -Ste 1030
    -Cleveland 44114

(440) 442-4681 ..**Wojnar,** Christopher F '92 -5171 Lynd Av -Lyndhurst 44124

(216) 771-1111 ..**Wojnar,** Nicoleta D '97 (Wojnar & Assoc) -1370 Ontario -Ste 1100
    Standard Bldg -Cleveland 44113

(419) 930-3030 ..**Wojtas,** Yvonne A '04 %SJ Groth & Assoc -4032 Secor Rd -Ste A
    -Toledo 43623

(440) 356-2631 ..**Wojton-Grisanti,** Francine J '94 -3640 Bradfords Gate
    -Rocky River 44116

(216) 348-0707 ..**Wolanin,** John S '91 -127 Pub Sq -Ste 4110 -Cleveland 44114

(800) 457-7703 ..**Wolery,** Alan K '99 Dimension -400 Metro Pl N -Ste 3017
    -Dublin 43017

(614) 262-3336 ..**Wolery,** Don E '79 -3620 N High -Ste 300 -Columbus 43214

(216) 623-9999 ..**Wolf & Akers,LPA** -1717 E 9th -Ste 1515 -Cleveland 44114
    Fx:623-0629

(740) 833-2554 ..**Wolf,** Alicia F '99 Delaware Cnty Common Pleas Ct
    -91 N Sandusky -3rd Fl -Delaware 43015

.. **Wolf,** Barbara A '80 -3443 Hammond Blvd -Akron 44321

(513) 772-6887 ..**Wolf,** Barbara W '93 Talbot Wolf Ahearn -102 Hetherington Ln
    -Cincinnati 45246

.. **Wolf,** Daniel B '75 -5227 Dogwood Trl -Cleveland 44124

(513) 984-3030 ..**Wolf,** David A '66 Comm Mgmt Corp -10925 Reed Hartman Hwy
    -200 -Cincinnati 45242

(937) 599-7272 ..**Wolf,** Deborah K '83 Logan Cnty Pros -117 E Columbus Av
    -Ste 200 -Bellefontaine 43311 **Fx:**599-7271

(330) 674-7015 ..**Wolf,** Donald D '77 Wayne-Dalton Corp -Bx67 -Mount Hope 44660

(216) 983-1052 ..**Wolf,** Elizabeth M '92 Cnsl University Hosp of Clvlnd
    -10524 Euclid Av -Ste 1100 -Cleveland 44106 **Fx:**983-1057

(513) 946-5174 ..**Wolf,** Ellen T '78 Municipal Ct -1000 Main -Rm 205
    -Cincinnati 45202

(330) 762-6334 ..**Wolf,** Erin L '04 %E Waite & Assoc -520 S Main -Ste 2518 -Akron
    44311

(614) 220-5611 ..**Wolf,** Holly N '97 %Manley D&K,LLC -495 S High -Ste 300
    -Columbus 43215 **Fx:**220-5613

(513) 731-3800 ..**Wolf,** James G '86 -5102 Carthage Av -Norwood 45212

(920) 684-7071 ..**Wolf,** Laura J '81 FSCC Hlth Care Ministry,Inc -1415 S Rapids Rd
    -Manitowoc, WI 54220

(513) 621-2120 ..**Wolf,** Leon L '50 OfCnsl Strauss & T,LPA -150 E 4th -4th Fl
    -Cincinnati 45202 **Fx:**241-8259

(419) 524-5297 ..**Wolf,** Marcus A '80 M Wolf Co,LPA -13 Park Av W -Ste 300
    -Mansfield 44902

(216) 623-9999 ..**Wolf,** Marshall J '67 (Wolf & A,LPA) -1717 E 9th -Ste 1515
    -Cleveland 44114 **Fx:**623-0629

(513) 731-7798 ..**Wolf,** Martin H '75 -6750 Glen Acres Dr -Cincinnati 45237

.. **Wolf,** Mary L '02 -(Address Unavailable)

(513) 863-0664 ..**Wolf,** Myron A '75 M Wolf -120 N 2nd -Bx741 -Hamilton 45012

(513) 863-0664 ..**Wolf,** Myron D III '80 -120 N 2nd -Hamilton 45012 **Fx:**868-1800

(216) 241-0300 ..**Wolf,** Paul V '87 -50 Pub Sq -Ste 920 -Cleveland 44113

(419) 259-8158 ..**Wolf,** Philip H '78 KeyBank,NA -Bx10099 -Toledo 43699

(937) 496-3212 .. **Wolf**, Rebecca J '83 Montgomery Cnty Juv Ct -14 W 4th
    -Reibold Bldg 8th Fl -Dayton 45422
(513) 852-8230 .. **Wolf**, Sara S '96 Cors & B LLC -537 E Pete Rose Way -Ste 400
    -Cincinnati 45202
(513) 721-3236 .. **Wolf**, Scott A '84 (Weisser & W) -1014 Vine -Ste 1650
    -Cincinnati 45202
(740) 363-1213 .. **Wolf**, Scott A '97 (Firestone BHNW&Y,LLP) -15 W Winter
    -Delaware 43015 **Fx:**369-0875
(440) 329-9380 .. **Wolf**, Scott A '00 Bendix Cmmrcl Vehicle Systms LLC
    -901 Cleveland -Elyria 44035 **Fx:**329-9265
(216) 983-1289 .. **Wolf**, Seth M '94 Univ Hosp of Cleveland -10524 Euclid Av
    -Ste 1100 -Cleveland 44106
(513) 421-4248 .. **Wolf**, Stephen G '78 Amer Lgl Pub Corp -432 Walnut -Ste 1200
    -Cincinnati 45202 **Fx:**763-3562
(216) 687-1311 .. **Wolf**, Thomas R '94 (Reminger & R) -101 Prospect Av W
    -1400 Mdlnd Bldg -Cleveland 44115 **Fx:**687-1841
(330) 729-9835 .. **Wolfcale**, Arthur D Jr. '54 NID Corp -100 DeBartolo Pl -Bx9430
    -Youngstown 44513
(740) 532-7000 .. **Wolfe & Bentley** -425 Center -Ironton 45638 **Fx:**532-7722
(614) 224-3080 .. **Wolfe**, Carrie D '02 K O'Brien & Assoc Co,LPA -995 S High
    -Columbus 43206
(330) 965-9910 .. **Wolfe**, David J Jr. '93 Am Archtctrl Prdcts
    -860 Boardman Canfld Rd -Ste 107 -Boardman 44512
(614) 263-5297 .. **Wolfe**, George M '94 (Wolfe Legal Srvcs) -3212 N High -2nd Fl
    -Columbus 43202
(614) 221-2330 .. **Wolfe**, Grant A '81 -254 S 4th -Bx1505 -Columbus 43216
(740) 453-9600 .. **Wolfe**, James B '96 -37 S 7th -Zanesville 43701
(513) 984-2699 .. **Wolfe**, Jennifer C '99 -9724 Sycamore Trace -Cincinnati 45242
(740) 532-7000 .. **Wolfe**, John H '69 (Wolfe & B) -425 Center -Ironton 45638
    Fx:532-7722
(330) 535-2441 .. **Wolfe**, John L '53 -1 Cascade Plz -Ste 740 -Akron 44308
    Fx:535-9564
(216) 781-1212 .. **Wolfe**, Leslie Green '00 %Walter & H LLP -1301 E 9th -Ste 3500
    -Cleveland 44114 **Fx:**575-0911
    Wolfe, Marc D '95 -2976 E Derbyshire Rd -#1 -Cleveland 44118
(216) 436-2198 .. **Wolfe**, Mary S '90 United Way Srvcs -1331 Euclid Av
    -Cleveland 44115
(419) 289-3777 .. **Wolfe**, Richard P II '73 City of Ashland -1213 E Main
    -Ashland 44805
    Wolfe, Ruth Anne G '94 -3112 Gloss Av -Cincinnati 45213
(330) 773-3351 .. **Wolfe**, Terry W '73 -1826 S Main -Akron 44301
(740) 455-7142 .. **Wolfe**, William Allen '71 Muskingam Cnty Common Pleas Ct
    -401 Main -Zanesville 43701
(260) 422-9454 .. **Wolfer**, Cindy A '91 Rothberg L&W,LLP -110 W Berry -Ste 2100
    -Fort Wayne, IN 46802 **Fx:**422-1622
(216) 621-7227 .. **Wolff**, Brenda C '94 %Nicola G&C,LLC -25 W Prospect Av
    -Republic Bldg Ste 1400 -Cleveland 44115 **Fx:**621-3999
(419) 252-6238 .. **Wolff**, Cheryl F '79 (Spengler N PLL) -608 Mad Av -Ste 1000
    -Toledo 43604 **Fx:**241-8599
(202) 324-2500 .. **Wolff**, Daniel W '01 %Crowell & M LLP -1001 Penn Av NW
    -Washington, DC 20004 **Fx:**328-5116
(937) 253-7171 .. **Wolff**, David G '94 Tomkins Ind,Inc -4801 Sprngfld -Dayton 45431
(330) 746-6301 .. **Wolff**, Heidi A '02 -219 W Boardman -Youngstown 44503
(419) 936-5120 .. **Wolff**, Jill E '95 -411 N Mich -Toledo 43624
    Wolff, Karen P '97 -(Address Unavailable)
(859) 581-4200 .. **Wolff**, Otto D IV '77 -405 Garrard -Covington, KY 41011
(419) 252-6253 .. **Wolff**, Richard P '80 (Spengler N PLL) -608 Mad Av -Ste 1000
    -Toledo 43604 **Fx:**241-8599
(216) 696-7600 .. **Wolff**, Robert M '80 (Duvin C&H) -1301 E 9th -20th Fl Erievw Twr
    -Cleveland 44114 **Fx:**696-2038
(513) 868-2731 .. **Wolfgang**, Rex A '88 -246 High -Hamilton 45011 **Fx:**868-1190
(317) 237-0300 .. **Wolfla**, Paul A '98 %Baker & D -300 N Meridian -Ste 2700
    -Indianapolis, IN 46204 **Fx:**237-1000
(740) 474-6066 .. **Wolford**, Judy C '93 Pros -Bx910 -Circleville 43113
(614) 445-2644 .. **Wolfram**, Jill A '96 Grange Ins -650 S Front -Bx1218
    -Columbus 43216
    Wolfrum, Todd D '02 -327 N Wshngtn -Van Wert 45891
(330) 945-8322 .. **Wolfson**, Daniel E '87 -1087 Drummond Ct -Stow 44224
(330) 678-5508 .. **Wolfson**, Michael D '77 -424-107 Lk -Kent 44240
(330) 278-2001 .. **Wolgamuth**, Keith R '82 McCormack & W Co,LPA
    -1450 Hinckley Hills Rd -Hinckley 44233
(614) 228-1541 .. **Wolinetz**, Barry H '71 (Baker & H LLP) -65 E State -Ste 2100
    -Columbus 43215 **Fx:**462-2616
(513) 732-1632 .. **Woliver**, John D '75 -204 North -Batavia 45103
(440) 498-9655 .. **Wolk**, Alan M '55 -Bx39576 -Solon 44139
    Wolk, Reuben '57 -3997 Cloud Park Dr #A-6 -Dayton 45424
(440) 746-2128 .. **Wolk**, Terry J '82 Dept of Vets Affrs -10000 Brecksvll Rd
    -Brecksville 44141
(408) 567-0340 .. **Wolken**, George I Jr. '81 OfCnsl Michaelson & Assoc -Bx640031
    -San Jose, CA 95164 **Fx:**567-0341
(216) 861-0808 .. **Wolkin**, Steven E '77 -614 W Superior Av -625 Rckfllr Bldg
    -Cleveland 44113
(330) 995-5005 .. **Wolkov**, Leonard A '67 -237 Chelsea Ct -Aurora 44202
(464) 466-4863 .. **Wollam**, Shawn M '04 %Atty Gen -150 E Gay -Columbus 43215
(888) 622-0800 .. **Wollett**, Ronald L '69 -2855 PGA Blvd
    -Palm Beach Gardens, FL 33410
(614) 229-4755 .. **Wollett**, Ronald S '94 Deloitte & Touche -155 E Broad
    -Columbus 43215
(614) 280-1000 .. **Wolman**, Benson A '88 (Wolman & Assoc) -341 S 3rd -Ste 301
    -Columbus 43215 **Fx:**280-9000
(614) 885-7577 .. **Wolock**, Margaret M '90 Heartbeat Intl,Inc
    -665 E Dublin-Granvll Rd -Ste 440 -Columbus 43229
(614) 221-4000 .. **Wolper**, Beatrice E '78 (Chester W&S LLP) -65 E State -10th Fl
    -Columbus 43215 **Fx:**221-4012
(216) 391-7111 .. **Wolpert**, Michael L '86 %Silver & Assoc -3421 Prospect Av
    -Cleveland 44115
(419) 435-1039 .. **Wolph**, Alexandra K '87 -123 S Main -Fostoria 44830
(614) 221-6969 .. **Wolske & Barclay,LPA** -580 S High -Ste 300 -Columbus 43215
(614) 221-6969 .. **Wolske**, Walter J Jr. '56 (Wolske & B,LPA) -580 S High -Ste 300
    -Columbus 43215
(614) 221-6969 .. **Wolske-Donaldson**, Sarah J '01 %Wolske & B,LPA -580 S High
    -Ste 300 -Columbus 43215

(513) 829-6700 .. **Wolterman**, Stephen J '94 (Millikin & F) -530 Wessel Dr -Ste 2A
    -Fairfield 45014 **Fx:**829-0258
(859) 394-6200 .. **Woltermann**, James G '96 (Adams SW&D) -40 W Pike -Bx861
    -Covington, KY 41012 **Fx:**291-7902
(216) 623-0000 .. **Wolters**, Daniel C '03 %Javitch B&R -1300 E 9th -14th Fl
    -Cleveland 44114 **Fx:**623-0190
(513) 754-3640 .. **Womack**, Michael A '93 Cintas Corp -6800 Cintas Blvd -MD 119
    -Cincinnati 45262 **Fx:**701-1940
(937) 562-5250 .. **Womack**, Tamela A '98 Greene Cnty Pros -61 Greene
    -Xenia 45385
(216) 241-8376 .. **Womer**, George S '51 -30799 Pinetree Rd PMB 304
    -Pepper Pike 44124
(513) 421-2730 .. **Wong**, Bernard F '89 -830 Main -Ste 804 -Cincinnati 45202
(513) 541-0100 .. **Wong**, Dan Y '78 -1538 Cedar Av -Cincinnati 45224
(216) 566-9908 .. **Wong**, Margaret Wai '77 M Wong & Assoc Co,LPA
    -3150 Chester Av -Ste 200 -Cleveland 44114 **Fx:**566-1125
(614) 224-7291 .. **Wonnell**, Nancy K '87 Wonnell & W -330 S High -Columbus 43215
    Fx:224-7268
(937) 865-2057 .. **Woo-Haltresht**, Roseanne M '96 Paxar Corp -170 Monarch Ln
    -Miamisburg 45342
(614) 644-3037 .. **Wood**, Ann M '95 EPA -122 S Front -Bx1049 -Columbus 43216
(614) 857-4332 .. **Wood**, Brian D '02 %Weltman W&R Co,LPA -175 S 3rd -Ste 900
    -Columbus 43215 **Fx:**222-2193
    Wood, Carol S '88 -3016 Lischer Av -Cincinnati 45211
(513) 621-8688 .. **Wood**, Daniel J '86 -1071 Celestial -Ste 904 -Cincinnati 45202
(248) 813-1202 .. **Wood**, David P '96 Delphi -5828 Delphi Dr -MC 480-410-202
    -Troy, MI 48098
(513) 946-3000 .. **Wood**, David R '87 Hamilton Cnty Pros -230 E 9th
    -Cincinnati 45202 **Fx:**946-3017
(614) 505-0808 .. **Wood**, David W '86 (Ellis & V) -8824 Commerce Loop Dr
    -Columbus 43240 **Fx:**985-6698
(419) 626-2939 .. **Wood**, Deborah L '88 -330 E Madison -Bx371 -Sandusky 44871
(614) 235-6406 .. **Wood**, Donald E '98 -4437 Wright Av -Whitehall 43213
(513) 765-6906 .. **Wood**, Elizabeth H '89 LensCrafters Inc -4000 Luxottica Pl
    -Mason 45040
(513) 936-5663 .. **Wood**, Frank G II '76 (Wood & M) -1101 St Gregory -Ste 345
    -Cincinnati 45202
    Wood, Gregory J '83 -(Address Unavailable)
(304) 723-4400 .. **Wood**, Heather A '02 %Frankovitch AC&S -337 Penco Rd
    -Weirton, WV 26062
(513) 241-2324 .. **Wood Herron & Evans LLP** -441 Vine -Ste 2700
    -Cincinnati 45202 **Fx:**421-7269
(216) 573-6000 .. **Wood**, Jeremiah J '02 %Licata & Assoc Co,LPA
    -6480 Rockside Wds Blvd S -Ste 390 -Independence 44131
    Fx:573-6333
(330) 422-1978 .. **Wood**, Jodi L '85 -9294 State Route 43 -Streetsboro 44241
    Wood, John Y '92 -12614 Britton Dr -Cleveland 44120
(419) 245-1862 .. **Wood**, Karen E '89 Toledo Mun Ct -555 N Erie -Toledo 43624
    Wood, Kathleen E '96 -(Address Unavailable)
(330) 467-5030 .. **Wood**, Kenneth '74 UAW Legal Srvc Plan -8536 Crow Dr -Ste 110
    -Macedonia 44056
(513) 852-6000 .. **Wood & Lamping LLP** -600 Vine -Ste 2500 -Cincinnati 45202
    Fx:852-6087
(614) 228-4422 .. **Wood**, Lee M '86 (Chappano W PLL) -8 E Long -9th Fl
    -Columbus 43215 **Fx:**228-4423
(216) 368-3600 .. **Wood**, Lisa M '88 CWRU Law Schl -11075 East Blvd
    -Cleveland 44106
(614) 645-4530 .. **Wood**, Melanie '98 City Atty -120 Marconi Blvd -Columbus 43215
(330) 626-1212 .. **Wood**, Rick B '83 -9294 State Route 43 -Streetsboro 44241
(513) 922-4916 .. **Wood**, Robert A '49 -1859 Forestvw Ln -Cincinnati 45233
(216) 241-6045 .. **Wood**, Robert A '69 First Am Title Ins Co -1111 Superior Av
    -Ste 700 -Cleveland 44114 **Fx:**241-4183
    Wood, Robert C '00 -6756 Annelise Ln -Westerville 43081
(740) 653-6464 .. **Wood**, Scott P '94 (Dagger JMO&H) -144 E Main -Bx667
    -Lancaster 43130 **Fx:**653-8522
(614) 337-2427 .. **Wood**, Thomas C Jr. '74 -501 Morrison Rd -Ste 203
    -Columbus 43230
    Wood, Thomas F '75 -3060 Eggers Av -Cleveland 44105
(216) 830-6830 .. **Wood**, Timothy D '72 (Brouse M) -1001 Lakeside Av -Ste 1600
    -Cleveland 44114 **Fx:**830-6807
(937) 225-4063 .. **Wood**, Timothy D '84 Montgomery Cnty Dom Rltns Ct -301 W 3rd
    -Rm 204 -Bx972 -Dayton 45422
(513) 487-5984 .. **Wood**, Walter S '84 Milacron Inc -2090 Florence Av
    -Cincinnati 45206
    Wood, Wendy A '81 -4354 E Cliff Rd -Port Clinton 43452
(740) 594-5000 .. **Wood**, Wheaton B '02 -Bx1050 -Athens 45701
(330) 334-4053 .. **Woodall**, Forrest W '58 -Bx38 -Sharon Center 44274
(330) 535-7510 .. **Woodall**, Jefferson Jr. '78 -1006 Ironwood Cir -Akron 44312
(330) 535-7510 .. **Woodall**, Shelby L '94 -1006 Ironwood Cir -Akron 44312
(330) 373-1035 .. **Woodall**, William D '67 Letson GWL&R -155 S Park Av -Ste 250
    -Bx151 -Warren 44482 **Fx:**392-5419
(410) 205-0500 .. **Woodard**, Jeffrey S '00 The St Paul Co -5801 Smith Av
    -Baltimore, MD 21209
(330) 343-8848 .. **Woodard**, John L '40 Woodard & B -121 W 3rd -Dover 44622
    Fx:343-3496
(513) 744-8782 .. **Woodard**, Kevin S '91 Fifth 3rd Bank -38 Fountain Sq Plz
    -MD 10AT68 -Cincinnati 45263
(307) 634-2731 .. **Woodard**, Rhonda S '79 (Woodard & W,PC) -1720 Carey Av
    -Ste 600 -Bx329 -Cheyenne, WY 82003 **Fx:**635-4040
(614) 466-4341 .. **Woodbeck**, Charles A '91 State Med Brd -77 S High -17th Fl
    -Columbus 43215
(330) 258-6506 .. **Woodburn**, David W '97 %Buckingham D&B,LLP -50 S Main
    -Bx1500 -Akron 44309 **Fx:**258-6559
(216) 781-1212 .. **Woodhall**, Amy L '96 (Walter & H LLP) -1301 E 9th -Ste 3500
    -Cleveland 44114 **Fx:**575-0911
(419) 255-3948 .. **Woodley**, Robert A '77 -1900 Monroe -Toledo 43624
(703) 695-4384 .. **Woodling**, Dale N '78 US Army JAG Ofc -Dept of Army Hdqrtrs
    -Washington, DC 20310
(216) 831-8139 .. **Woodling**, George V Jr. '66 -22250 McCauley
    -Shaker Heights 44122
(440) 256-4150 .. **Woodling Krost & Rust** -9213 Chillicothe Rd -Kirtland 44094
    Woodman, Dawn S '99 -(Address Unavailable)

(614) 461-1551 .. **Woodrow,** Paul F '93 Barkan & B Co LPA -81 S 4th -Ste 300 -Columbus 43215

(937) 866-1629 .. **Woodruff,** Edward L '01 %Ruschau & L -443 E Central Av -Miamisburg 45342

(330) 762-5627 .. **Woodruff,** Gigi A '83 Info Line Inc -474 Grant -Akron 44311

(614) 728-6487 .. **Woodruff,** P Thomas '98 Workers Comp -30 W Spring -Level 26 -Columbus 43215

(419) 668-8215 .. **Woodruff,** Richard R '80 Huron Cnty Pros -12 E Main -Norwalk 44857

(216) 382-3080 .. **Woodrum,** Amy N '92 -1180 Winston Rd -Cleveland 44121

(614) 365-2700 .. **Woods,** C Craig '81 (Squire S&D LLP) -41 S High -1300 Huntngtn Ctr -Columbus 43215 **Fx:**365-2499
       Woods, Clay L '04 -(Address Unavailable)

(740) 852-1073 .. **Woods,** Corey R '00 Woods Law Ofc -66 W High -London 43140

(419) 772-2075 .. **Woods,** Dexter R Jr. '82 College of Business Admin -Ohio Nrthrn Univ -Ada 45810 **Fx:**772-3125

(216) 485-8400 .. **Woods,** Jennifer A '03 Asset Acceptance LLC -600 W Resource Dr -Independence 44131

(419) 249-6685 .. **Woods,** Joyce Ann '80 Lucus Cnty Juv Ct -429 Mich -Toledo 43624

(407) 628-3295 .. **Woods,** Linda L '79 IRS -850 Trafalgar Ct -2nd fl -Maitland, FL 32751
       Woods, Lisa A '02 -223 Purple Finch Loop -Pataskala 43062

(937) 223-8177 .. **Woods,** Lowell T Jr. '97 %Coolidge WW&L -33 W 1st -Ste 600 -Dayton 45402 **Fx:**223-6705

(614) 431-1500 .. **Woods,** Michelle Gehring '98 Perez & M LLC -8000 Ravines Edge Ct -Ste 300 -Columbus 43235 **Fx:**431-3885

(216) 443-7800 .. **Woods,** Nicole J '02 Cuyahoga Cnty Pros -1200 Ontario -8th Fl -Cleveland 44113 **Fx:**698-2270

(740) 852-1073 .. **Woods,** Robert D '69 Woods Law Ofc -66 W High -London 43140

(972) 831-3559 .. **Woods,** Teresa A '99 EMC Mortgage Corp -909 Hidden Ridge Dr -Ste 200 -Irving, TX 75038

(937) 222-1090 .. **Woods,** Tina F '97 %Statman HS&E LLC -110 N Main -Ste 1520 -Dayton 45402 **Fx:**222-1046

(614) 228-6131 .. **Woods,** William H '73 (McNamara & M,LLP) -88 E Broad -Ste 1250 -Columbus 43215 **Fx:**228-6126

(513) 977-8200 .. **Woodside,** Frank C III '69 (Dinsmore & S LLP) -255 E 5th -Ste 1900 -Cincinnati 45202 **Fx:**977-8141

(330) 753-1724 .. **Woodside,** Robert N '72 -682 W Tuscarawas Av -Barberton 44203

(419) 289-8141 .. **Woodside,** William J '99 Ashland Cnty DOJFS -15 W 4th -Ashland 44805

(419) 797-7311 .. **Woodson,** Riley D '84 Desert Thoracic & Cardio Srgry -4445 E Marin Pines -Port Clinton 43452

(330) 399-1381 .. **Woodward,** Calvin J Jr. '68 -366 Mahoning Av NW -Warren 44483

(419) 774-5575 .. **Woodward,** Deborah E '89 Richland Cnty Cmn Pleas Ct -50 Park Av E -Mansfield 44902

(419) 241-9000 .. **Woodward,** Kathryn J '87 (Shumaker L&K,LLP) -1000 Jackson -Toledo 43624 **Fx:**241-6894

(614) 719-3312 .. **Woodward,** Lisa M '99 %Hon JD Holschuh -85 Marconi Blvd -Columbus 43215

(513) 398-6891 .. **Woodward,** Richard H Jr. '77 -3269 Chestnut Landing Dr -Maineville 45039

(330) 456-8341 .. **Woolbert,** Gordon D II '97 (Black MS&A,LPA) -220 Market Av S -Ste 1000 -Canton 44702 **Fx:**456-5756

(614) 221-1662 .. **Wooldridge,** Gregory D '88 (Frank & W Co LPA) -600 S Pearl -Columbus 43206

(216) 621-0200 .. **Wooley,** James R '86 (Baker & H LLP) -1900 E 9th -Ste 3200 -Cleveland 44114 **Fx:**696-0740

(614) 462-4771 .. **Woolley,** Julie M '03 %Baker & H LLP -65 E State -Ste 2100 -Columbus 43215 **Fx:**462-2616

(513) 489-4157 .. **Woolsey,** Monica K '04 Kennedy & K Co,LPA -10723 Mntgmry Rd -Ste 1 -Cincinnati 45242

(614) 460-6954 .. **Woosley,** Stephen E '98 Columbia Gas Distro Co -200 Civic Ctr Dr -Columbus 43215

(513) 983-1493 .. **Wooten,** Kelli L '01 Procter & Gamble Co-Legal -1 Procter & Gamble Plz -Cincinnati 45202

(330) 225-6546 .. **Wootton,** Arthur W '68 Prof Mrtg Corp -5843 Myrtle Hill Rd -Valley City 44280

(216) 621-1113 .. **Worgull,** Jason A '99 %Renner OB&S,LLP -1621 Euclid Av -19th Fl -Cleveland 44115 **Fx:**621-6165

(330) 650-6000 .. **Worhatch,** S David '81 -4920 Darrow Rd -Stow 44224 **Fx:**650-2390

(330) 438-0638 .. **Workman,** Billie J '88 Workers Comp -400 3rd SE -Canton 44702 **Fx:**438-0596

(330) 740-2330 .. **Workman,** James E Jr. '78 Mahoning Cnty Pros -21 W Boardman -6th Fl -Youngstown 44503 **Fx:**740-2008

(614) 486-0297 .. **Workman,** John R '74 -1375 Dublin Rd -Columbus 43215 **Fx:**486-8580

(386) 851-7950 .. **Workman,** Mark A '92 BDR Title Corp -775 Harley Strickland Blvd -Ste 106 -Orange City, FL 32763

(419) 222-7861 .. **Workman,** Rickard A '84 Mun Ct Judge -109 N Union -Bx1529 -Lima 45802

(212) 986-6181 .. **Workman,** Thomas E '69 %Life Ins Cncl of NY -551 5th Av -29th Fl -New York, NY 10176 **Fx:**986-6549

(216) 623-1155 .. **Workum,** Denise B '96 Nationwide Ins -323 Lakeside Av W -Ste 410 Lakeside Pl -Cleveland 44113

(859) 581-8787 .. **Worland,** Francis E Jr. '78 (F Worland, Jr PSC) -1005 Mad Av -Bx2420 -Covington, KY 41012

(614) 644-8716 .. **Worley,** Glenn T '83 SERB -65 E State -Ste 1200 -Columbus 43215 **Fx:**466-3074

(937) 378-4121 .. **Worley,** Joseph M '83 -932 Mt Orab Pike -Georgetown 45121

(419) 243-6281 .. **Worline,** Daniel A '74 Shindler NH&S,LLP -300 Mad Av -Ste 1200 -Toledo 43604 **Fx:**243-0129

(419) 248-2419 .. **Worline,** Robin A '01 %G Gusses Co,LPA -33 S Huron -Toledo 43604 **Fx:**321-6379

(740) 363-9192 .. **Worly,** Donald G '89 Worly Steel & Supply Co,Inc -65 London Rd -Delaware 43015

(614) 644-7250 .. **Worly,** Mindy A '86 Atty Gen -30 E Broad -Columbus 43215 **Fx:**644-7634

(740) 387-1120 .. **Worobiec,** Michele S '96 %Kegler BH&R -250 Exec Dr -Ste B -Marion 43302 **Fx:**387-3630

(513) 621-6464 .. **Worrell,** A Christian III '85 (Graydon H&R LLP) -511 Walnut -1900 Fifth Third Ctr -Cincinnati 45202 **Fx:**651-3836

(330) 365-3266 .. **Worth,** David W '77 Tuscarawas Cnty Prob/Juv Ct -101 E High Av -Rm 103 -New Philadelphia 44663

(614) 890-4543 .. **Worth,** Randall T '78 (Griffith & W) -575 Copeland Mill Rd -Ste 2C -Westerville 43081

(513) 489-2656 .. **Worth,** Robert W '60 -8064 Silkyrider Ct -Sycamore 45249

(440) 239-8881 .. **Worthing,** Donald E '77 Safeco P&C Ins -18151 Jffrsn Park Rd -Ste 104 -Middleburg Heights 44130 **Fx:**239-8882
       Worthington, Dean P '03 -(Address Unavailable)

(614) 851-2631 .. **Worthington,** Dianne '84 -Bx425 -Galloway 43119

(937) 456-8156 .. **Worthington,** Kathryn M '01 Preble Cnty Pros -100 E Main -Cthse 1st Fl -Eaton 45320 **Fx:**456-8199

(419) 424-7090 .. **Wortman,** Drew A '00 Hancock Cnty Pros -222 Bway -#104 -Findlay 45840 **Fx:**424-7889

(614) 837-1546 .. **Wortman,** Mary A '82 -20 S High -Canal Winchester 43110 **Fx:**837-0206

(216) 464-0001 .. **Wortzman,** William A '74 The Wortzman Co -3550 Lander Rd -Ste #310 -Pepper Pike 44124

(937) 254-7325 .. **Woryk,** Mildred P '84 Tomkins Indust,Inc -6450 Poe Av -Ste 109 -Dayton 45414

(216) 479-6100 .. **Woyt,** Elia O '01 %Vorys SS&P LLP -1375 E 9th -Ste 2100 One Cleve Ctr -Cleveland 44114 **Fx:**479-6060
       Wozniak, Gregory '75 -9A Carroll Rd -North Grafton, MA 01536

(217) 351-7479 .. **Wozniak,** Michael A '01 %Livingston BB&S -2506 Galen Dr -Ste 108 -Champaign, IL 61821 **Fx:**351-6870

(216) 687-1902 .. **Wozniak,** Peter M '91 OfCnsl S Haygood & Assoc -1422 Euclid Av -Ste 1510 -Cleveland 44115 **Fx:**687-1906

(614) 299-6000 .. **Wrachford,** Jason S '97 Columbus Discovery America Grp -433 W 6th Av -Columbus 43201

(740) 820-4131 .. **Wrage,** Eric A '99 -564 Bull Run Rd -Minford 45653 **Fx:**820-4138

(330) 675-2426 .. **Wrenn,** Thomas C '91 Trumbull Cnty Pros -160 High NW -Warren 44481

(330) 425-4201 .. **Wrentmore,** James C '90 Reimer L&A Co,LPA -2450 Edison Blvd -Bx968 -Twinsburg 44087 **Fx:**487-0923

(216) 443-9000 .. **Wright,** Alan D '59 (Porter WM&A LLP) -925 Euclid Av -Ste 1700 -Cleveland 44115 **Fx:**443-9011

(330) 376-2700 .. **Wright,** Alisa L '93 (Roetzel & A,LPA) -222 S Main -Akron 44308 **Fx:**376-4577

(937) 225-4063 .. **Wright,** Annette M '87 Montgomery Cnty Dom Rltns Ct -301 W 3rd -Rm 204 -Bx972 -Dayton 45422

(330) 714-0105 .. **Wright,** Barbara E '87 -5675 Arlynne Ln -Medina 44256

(410) 786-4292 .. **Wright,** Barbara J '82 DHHS/Medicare-Medicaid Srvcs -7500 Security Blvd -Mailstop C3-14-00 -Baltimore, MD 21244

(513) 932-1414 .. **Wright,** Bernard H Jr. '75 Lebanon Citizens Natl Bank -2 N Bway -Bx59 -Lebanon 45036 **Fx:**932-1492

(614) 348-3847 .. **Wright,** Beth A '95 -Bx21299 -Columbus 43221

(330) 376-2700 .. **Wright,** Bradley A '90 (Roetzel & A,LPA) -222 S Main -Akron 44308 **Fx:**376-4577

(937) 227-3700 .. **Wright,** Brian D '02 %Faruki I&C PLL -10 N Ludlow -500 Cthse Plz SW -Dayton 45402 **Fx:**227-3717

(614) 224-2999 .. **Wright,** Carol A '85 -318 Berger Alley -Columbus 43206

(216) 241-2838 .. **Wright,** Daniel K II '79 (Taft S&H LLP) -200 Pub Sq -3500 BP Twr -Cleveland 44114 **Fx:**241-3707

(513) 241-3992 .. **Wright,** Darrell S '86 %Bartlett & W Co,LPA -432 Walnut -Ste 1100 -Cincinnati 45202 **Fx:**241-1816

(812) 377-3269 .. **Wright,** David C '76 Cummins Engine Co,Inc -500 Jackson -MC 60701 -Bx3005 -Columbus, IN 47202

(330) 339-7272 .. **Wright,** Edd K '68 -Bx711 -New Philadelphia 44663

(216) 566-5716 .. **Wright,** Elizabeth B '84 (Thompson H LLP) -127 Pub Sq -3900 Key Ctr -Cleveland 44114 **Fx:**566-5800

(330) 264-4444 .. **Wright,** Elizabeth L '01 %Critchfield C&J Ltd -225 N Market -Bx599 -Wooster 44691 **Fx:**263-9278

(513) 946-6404 .. **Wright,** Gail A '96 Cnty Sheriffs Ofc -1000 Sycamore -Rm 110 -Cincinnati 45202

(614) 227-8874 .. **Wright,** Harry IV '90 (Bricker & E LLP) -100 S 3rd -Columbus 43215 **Fx:**227-2390

(614) 764-3323 .. **Wright,** Herman L II '86 Wendys Intl -4288 W Dublin-Granvll Rd -Bx256 -Dublin 43017

(304) 231-0443 .. **Wright,** James C '94 %Steptoe & J -14th & Chapline -Bx150 -Wheeling, WV 26003

(330) 482-3825 .. **Wright,** James R '60 -11 S Main -Columbiana 44408

(614) 221-6969 .. **Wright,** Jason K '01 Wolske & B,LPA -580 S High -Ste 300 -Columbus 43215

(937) 382-0946 .. **Wright,** Jeffrey L '74 (Buckley M&W) -145 N South -Wilmington 45177

(216) 883-5390 .. **Wright,** John J '69 Catholic Cemeteries Assoc -10000 Miles Av -Bx605310 -Cleveland 44105

(859) 341-1881 .. **Wright,** Kimberly D '99 %Deters B&L,PSC -2701 Turkeyfoot Rd -207 Thomas More Pkwy -Crestview Hills, KY 41017 **Fx:**341-1469

(513) 771-7266 .. **Wright,** LaTonia Denise '97 LD Wright,LLC -Bx15756 -Cincinnati 45215 **Fx:**771-0673

(216) 523-5161 .. **Wright,** Lizbeth '94 Eaton Corp -1111 Superior Av -Cleveland 44114

(614) 692-3284 .. **Wright,** Marsha M '84 US Dfnse Lgstcs Agncy -Bx3990 -Columbus 43218

(614) 644-9618 .. **Wright,** Melissa G '04 %Atty Gen -30 E Broad -Columbus 43215 **Fx:**728-7582

(330) 376-8855 .. **Wright,** Michael J '02 %E Gilbert Co,LPA -1 Cascade Plz -Ste 825 -Akron 44308

(937) 222-7477 .. **Wright,** Michael L '97 (Wright & V,LPA) -32 N Main -Ste 801 -Dayton 45402

(614) 791-9112 .. **Wright,** Paul Leo '78 Wright Law Co,LPA -4266 Tuller Rd -Ste 101 -Dublin 43017 **Fx:**791-9116

(614) 224-1222 .. **Wright,** Phillip L Jr. '00 %Maguire & S,LLP -250 Civic Ctr Dr -Ste 200 -Columbus 43215 **Fx:**224-1236

(740) 345-6667 .. **Wright,** Richard P '87 -21 W Church -Ste 208 -Newark 43055
       Wright, Rosa P '91 -3213 Burnette Dr NE -Roswell, GA 30075

(513) 723-3467 .. **Wright,** Ross A '94 Convergys Corp -201 E 4th -Cincinnati 45202

(614) 228-2678 .. **Wright,** Scott E '89 (Matan G&W) -261 S Front -Columbus 43215

(330) 376-7245 .. **Wright,** Stephan R '03 %Curtin & Assoc -159 S Main -920 Key Bldg -Akron 44305 **Fx:**376-8128

(305) 743-8118 .. **Wright,** Thomas D '75 -10095 Overseas Hwy -10 -Bx500309 -Marathon, FL 33050 **Fx:**743-8198

(330) 744-8695 ..**Wright,** Thomas R '91 Rossi & R -26 Market -Ste 802 -Youngstown 44501 **Fx:**744-0334

(216) 348-1700 ..**Wright,** Thomas W '84 (Davis & Y) -101 Prospect Av W -Ste 1700 -Cleveland 44115 **Fx:**621-0602

(937) 222-7477 ..**Wright & VanNoy,LPA** -32 N Main -Ste 801 -Dayton 45402

(614) 466-4395 ..**Wright,** William L '84 Atty Gen -150 E Gay -Columbus 43215 **Fx:**644-8764

(606) 824-0200 ..**Wright-Hatfield,** Jennifer K '93 %Knight HL&A,PSC -26 Bway -Bx17 -Dry Ridge, KY 41035

(614) 255-3388 ..**Wrightsel,** Bradley B '93 (Wrightsel & W) -3300 Riverside Dr -Ste 100 -Columbus 43221 **Fx:**255-3389

(614) 255-3388 ..**Wrightsel,** Richard D '65 (Wrightsel & W) -3300 Riverside Dr -Ste 100 -Columbus 43221 **Fx:**255-3389

(816) 374-3200 ..**Writz,** Cassandra L '96 %Bryan C LLP -1200 Main -3500 One Kansas Cty Pl -Kansas City, MO 64105

(419) 843-9960 ..**Wroblewski,** Dennis E '79 -2639 Wimbledon Park Blvd -Toledo 43617

(330) 744-3196 ..**Wrona,** Michelle A '99 Cmmnty Lgl Aid Srvcs,Inc -11 Fed Plz Central -7th Fl -Youngstown 44503 **Fx:**744-2503

(800) 837-8908 ..**Wu,** Karen P '04 LAWO -121 N Arch -Fremont 43420 **Fx:**(419) 334-9148

(937) 223-5200 ..**Wuebben,** Kristi A '00 Flanagan LH&S -318 W 4th -Dayton 45402 **Fx:**223-3335

(513) 629-1469 ..**Wuebbling,** Donald J '74 Wstrn & Sthrn Life Ins Co -400 Bway -Cincinnati 45202

(614) 228-6885 ..**Wuerth,** Richard O '73 (Lane A&H LLC) -175 S 3rd -Ste 700 -Columbus 43215 **Fx:**228-0146

(440) 838-8800 ..**Wuertz,** Maribeth G '84 Millisor & N Co,LPA -9150 S Hills Blvd -Ste 300 -Cleveland 44147 **Fx:**838-8805

(440) 331-7206 ..**Wukovich,** George N '85 -20312 Lorain Rd -Ste 309 -Fairview Park 44126

(614) 757-7765 ..**Wulf,** James V '91 Cardinal Hlth -7000 Cardinal Pl -Dublin 43017

(216) 781-7777 ..**Wuliger Fadel & Beyer** -1340 Sumner Ct -Brownell Bldg -Cleveland 44115 **Fx:**781-0621

(216) 781-7777 ..**Wuliger,** William T '69 OfCnsl Wuliger F&B -1340 Sumner Ct -Brownell Bldg -Cleveland 44115 **Fx:**781-0621

(513) 983-4370 ..**Wunsch,** Eric J '97 Cnsl Procter & Gamble Co -1 Procter & Gamble Plz -Cincinnati 45202

(513) 352-6700 ..**Wuorinen,** Susan E '89 %Thompson H LLP -312 Walnut -14th Fl -Cincinnati 45202 **Fx:**241-4717

(614) 744-3418 ..**Wurgler,** Barry A '93 Casto Communities -191 W Nationwide Blvd -Ste 200 -Columbus 43215

(614) 292-1056 ..**Wurster,** Lee E '71 OSU -1800 Cannon Dr -Lincoln Twr, Rm 250 -Columbus 43210

(419) 535-4675 ..**Wurster,** Lisa A '85 Dana Corp -4500 Dorr -Bx1000 -Toledo 43697

(419) 843-5355 ..**Wurster,** Phillip D '84 (Goldberg W&H) -6800 W Central Av -Toledo 43617

(513) 583-0600 ..**Wurster,** Walter C II '74 -8044 Mntgmry Rd -Ste 120 -Cincinnati 45236

(202) 737-6770 ..**Wyand,** Jeffrey A '80 Leydig V&M -700 13th NW -3rd Fl -Washington, DC 20005

(740) 374-0664 ..**Wyant,** Daniel M '95 Camco Title Ins Agncy,Inc -226 3rd -Marietta 45750

(309) 999-4635 ..**Wyant,** John M '94 Illinois Central College -One Cllg Dr -Peoria, IL 61635

(440) 349-5757 ..**Wyatt,** Jack D '74 SrCnsl Nestle USA -30003 Bainbrdg Rd -Solon 44139 **Fx:**248-1617

(909) 869-2407 ..**Wyatt,** John B III '78 CA State Polytech Univ -3801 W Temple Av -Dept FRL,Bldg 66,Rm 222 -Pomona, CA 91768

(317) 488-6264 ..**Wyatt,** Michael C '84 Anthem,Inc -120 Monument Cir -Indianapolis, IN 46204

(614) 785-6600 ..**Wyatt,** Thomas D '03 -951B High -Columbus 43085

(216) 447-1551 ..**Wyatt,** Thomas R '86 %Ross B&S Co LPA -6000 Freedom Sq Dr -Ste 540 -Cleveland 44131 **Fx:**447-1554

(614) 464-8354 ..**Wyckoff,** Robin Grant '04 %Vorys SS&P LLP -52 E Gay -Bx1008 -Columbus 43216 **Fx:**719-4617

(412) 281-3233 ..**Wyckoff,** Steven H '94 (Wyckoff & N) -428 Forbes Av -Ste 220 -Pittsburgh, PA 15219

(419) 425-2769 ..**Wykes,** Stephanie M '03 %Crow,Ltd -124 W Front -Ste 201 -Findlay 45840 **Fx:**427-4673

(513) 621-7600 ..**Wykoff,** John R '79 (Eagen W&H Co,LPA) -2337 Victory Pkwy -Cincinnati 45206 **Fx:**455-8246

Wykoff, Peter C '61 -2922 Scarborough Rd -Cleveland 44118

(330) 455-0173 ..**Wyler,** Alicia M '78 (Day KRW&R,Ltd) -200 Market Av N -Ste 300 -Bx24213 -Canton 44701 **Fx:**455-2633

(513) 352-3337 ..**Wyler,** Deborah H '01 Law Dept -801 Plum -Rm 214 -Cincinnati 45202 **Fx:**352-1515

(513) 579-1414 ..**Wyler,** William S '72 (Schwartz M&R) -441 Vine -Ste 2900 -Cincinnati 45202 **Fx:**579-1418

(216) 522-7800 ..**Wyman,** Dean P '82 US Trustees Ofc -200 Pub Sq -Ste 3300 -Cleveland 44114 **Fx:**522-4988

(216) 398-1023 ..**Wyman,** James G '72 -509 South -Brooklyn Heights 44131

(216) 621-0200 ..**Wymer,** Martin T '84 (Baker & H LLP) -1900 E 9th -Ste 3200 -Cleveland 44114 **Fx:**696-0740

(216) 831-1551 ..**Wymor,** Larry L '61 -3162 Lander Rd -Pepper Pike 44124

(216) 292-3300 ..**Wyner,** Jeffrey G '71 (Conway MWK&K Co,LPA) -30195 Chagrin Blvd -Ste 300 -Cleveland 44124

(412) 433-4865 ..**Wynkoop,** Randall L '83 US Steel Corp -600 Grant -Rm 2687 -Pittsburgh, PA 15219

Wynn, John A '72 -914 Marble Dr -Naples, FL 34104

(440) 576-9003 ..**Wynn,** Robert S '73 -7 Lawyers Row -Bx121 -Jefferson 44047

(513) 241-3111 ..**Wynn,** Suzanne L '91 ClarkSchaeferHackett & Co -105 E 4th -16th Fl -Cincinnati 45202

(216) 861-4533 ..**Wynne,** Thomas More '94 (Ray RC&D PLL) -1717 E 9th -Cleveland 44114 **Fx:**861-4568

(212) 526-7000 ..**Wynocker,** Mason L '99 %Lehman Bros -745 7th Av -2nd Fl -New York, NY 10019

(614) 466-4961 ..**Wynsen,** Pamela G '83 %Sup Crt of OH -30 E Broad -2nd Fl -Columbus 43215

(216) 861-7100 ..**Wypasek,** Michael A '83 Chicago Title Ins Co -1360 E 9th -Ste 500 -Cleveland 44114

Wyrobnik, Leonard E '76 -(Address Unavailable)

Wysin, Gregory J '02 -Bx3 -Akron 44309

(330) 376-2700 ..**Wyss,** Jerome G '01 %Roetzel & A,LPA -222 S Main -Akron 44308 **Fx:**376-4577

(330) 499-6000 ..**Wyss,** Kimberly K '93 (Baker DBW&M) -400 S Main -Canton 44720 **Fx:**449-6423

(513) 721-2424 ..**Xanders,** George L III '80 (Xanders & X Co,LPA) -808 Elm -Ste 200 -Cincinnati 45202

(216) 443-7800 ..**Xavier,** Chipper F '01 Cuyahoga Cnty Pros -1200 Ontario -8th Fl -Cleveland 44113 **Fx:**698-2270

(614) 229-5052 ..**Xavier,** Ronald E '98 Ernst & Young,LLP -41 S High -Ste 1100 -Columbus 43215

(804) 783-6613 ..**Yacano,** Mark S '88 (Wright RO&T) -411 E Franklin -Ste 400 -Richmond, VA 23219

(859) 341-5090 ..**Yacks,** Collin Timothy '00 Cnsl Title 1st Agency,Inc -541 Buttermilk Pike -Ste 100 -Crescent Springs, KY 41017 **Fx:**341-5916

(330) 455-0173 ..**Yackshaw,** Matthew '79 (Day KRW&R,Ltd) -200 Market Av N -Ste 300 -Bx24213 -Canton 44701 **Fx:**455-2633

(614) 228-6453 ..**Yacobozzi,** Dennis V II '03 %Colley S&A Co,LPA -536 S High -Columbus 43215 **Fx:**228-7122

(513) 648-7061 ..**Yaeger,** Daniel A '81 Fluor Fernald Inc -Bx398704 -Cincinnati 45239

(614) 224-8187 ..**Yaeger,** Keri N '01 %Lamkin VTB&D -500 S Front -Ste 200 -Columbus 43215 **Fx:**224-4943

(614) 221-1578 ..**Yaeger,** Nicholas W '04 P Scott Co,LPA -536 S High -Columbus 43215

Yager, Brent W '83 -Bx499 -Caledonia 43314

(513) 721-5151 ..**Yager,** Christina S '99 Katz G&N,LLP -105 E 4th -4th Fl -Cincinnati 45202 **Fx:**621-9285

(614) 443-1333 ..**Yagoda,** Andrea R '77 -897 S Front -Columbus 43206

(330) 386-3640 ..**Yajko,** Mark A '83 Hoppel & Y Co,LPA -48938 Calcutta-Smith Ferry Rd -East Liverpool 43920

(614) 241-2156 ..**Yaklevich,** John A '79 (Moore Y&M) -326 S High -Columbus 43215

(216) 378-9905 ..**Yaksic,** Barbara F '81 (McGlinchey S PLLC) -25550 Chagrin Blvd -Ste 406 -Cleveland 44122 **Fx:**378-9910

(440) 564-9111 ..**Yaksic,** Michael '81 Kinetico Inc -10845 Kinsman Rd -Newbury 44065

(330) 392-8200 ..**Yakubek,** Nancy E '83 -524 N Park Av -Warren 44481

(216) 696-1275 ..**Yakunovich,** Joanie L '02 Chicago Title Ins Co -1360 E 9th -Ste 500 -Cleveland 44114 **Fx:**696-8107

(614) 487-2050 ..**Yalamanchili,** Kalpana '84 %OH State Bar Assn -1700 Lk Shr Dr -Columbus 43204

(419) 568-5751 ..**Yale,** Benjamin F '80 (BF Yale & Assoc,LPA) -102 W Wapakoneta -Bx100 -Waynesfield 45896

(216) 687-1311 ..**Yallech,** Robert S '02 %Reminger & R -101 Prospect Av W -1400 Mdlnd Bldg -Cleveland 44115 **Fx:**687-1841

(212) 813-8800 ..**Yanchar,** Georgia K E '99 %Goodwin P LLP -599 Lex Av -40th Fl -New York, NY 10022 **Fx:**355-3333

(614) 248-6207 ..**Yang,** Carrie A '01 Bank One Corp -1111 Polaris Pkwy -Ste 4P -Columbus 43271

(614) 228-1541 ..**Yang,** Rosanne T '99 %Baker & H LLP -65 E State -Ste 2100 -Columbus 43215 **Fx:**462-2616

Yanick, Michael E '82 -2105 W 13th -Lorain 44052

(740) 593-3385 ..**Yanity,** Joseph B Jr. '53 -18 W State -Drwr748 -Athens 45701

(304) 232-6322 ..**Yannerella,** Don A '84 -403 Board of Trade Bldg -Wheeling, WV 26003

(614) 847-1688 ..**Yannon,** Albert A '57 -3380 Rdgwd Dr -Hilliard 43026

(330) 375-5716 ..**Yannucci,** Samuel A '79 US Atty -2 S Main -Ste 208 -Akron 44308

(614) 464-6400 ..**Yano,** James A '77 (Vorys SS&P LLP) -52 E Gay -Bx1008 -Columbus 43216 **Fx:**464-6350

(440) 835-1200 ..**Yanok,** Michelle A '01 %Kolick & K -24500 Ctr Ridge Rd -Ste 175 -Westlake 44145

(216) 765-7430 ..**Yanowitz,** Alan E '85 Cleveland Fin Grp -28601 Chagrin Blvd -Ste 300 -Cleveland 44122

(216) 696-3311 ..**Yanowitz,** Bennett '49 SrCnsl Kahn K -1301 E 9th -2600 Erievw Twr -Cleveland 44114 **Fx:**623-4912

(216) 622-5292 ..**Yantek,** Kenneth R '86 Colliers Intl -1100 Superior Av NE -Ste 800 -Cleveland 44114

(216) 522-4970 ..**Yarab,** Donald S '90 US Dept of Edu/Civ Rghts -600 Superior Av -#750 -Cleveland 44114

(614) 249-7150 ..**Yarbrough,** Heather Ann '96 Cnsl Nationwide Ins Co -One Nationwide Plz -1-9-V6 -Columbus 43215

(614) 464-1211 ..**Yarbrough,** Michael K '76 (Frost BT LLC) -10 W Broad -Ste 1000 -Columbus 43215 **Fx:**464-1737

(419) 824-8389 ..**Yarbrough,** Stephen A '74 -7818 Westcroft Dr -Sylvania 43560

(330) 379-3838 ..**Yarcusko,** Alan C '93 Bridgestone/Firestone -1200 Firestone Pkwy -Akron 44317

(937) 436-9870 ..**Yarema-Dubel,** Julia B '86 Miami Vlly Cytology Assoc Inc -6818 Loop Rd -Centerville 45459

(419) 238-1166 ..**Yarger,** Eva J '89 (Young T&Y) -120 W Main -Bx525 -Van Wert 45891

(216) 737-5000 ..**Yarger,** Jonathon M '90 (Chernett WY&P) -1301 E 9th -Ste 3300 -Cleveland 44114 **Fx:**737-0011

(216) 566-2501 ..**Yaro,** John M '87 Sherwin-Williams Co -101 Prospect Av NW -Cleveland 44115

(859) 431-8200 ..**Yaros,** Alma P '77 Legal Aid -302 Greenup -Covington, KY 41011

(614) 227-2180 ..**Yaross,** Todd D '04 %Porter WM&A LLP -41 S High -Columbus 43215 **Fx:**227-2100

(330) 743-4116 ..**Yarwood,** Ronald D '97 (Brennan FV&Y,Ltd) -29 E Front -2nd Fl -Youngstown 44503

(614) 223-9300 ..**Yashko,** Gary G '97 %Benesch FC&A LLP -88 E Broad -Ste 900 -Columbus 43215 **Fx:**223-9330

(239) 337-3850 ..**Yashko,** Michael S '87 (Roetzel & A) -2320 First -Ste 1000 -Fort Myers, FL 33901 **Fx:**337-0970

(330) 867-1500 ..**Yashnik,** Steven L '85 -3250 W Market -Ste 14 -Fairlawn 44333

(614) 469-5715 ..**Yates,** Christopher R '95 US Atty -303 Marconi Blvd -Ste 200 -Columbus 43215

(513) 983-1477 ..**Yates,** Irene W '96 Proctor & Gamble -Bx599 -Cincinnati 45201

(419) 247-2500 ..**Yates,** James B '90 (Fuller & H,Ltd) -One SeaGate -Ste 1700 -Bx2088 -Toledo 43603 **Fx:**247-2665

(513) 564-7072 ..**Yates,** Janice E '82 6th Circuit Ct of Appls -524 Potter Stewart US POCH -Cincinnati 45202

(937) 222-2500 ..**Yates,** Nita S '83 (Sebaly S&D) -1900 Kettering Twr -Dayton 45423 **Fx:**222-6554

(216) 771-5300 .. **Yates,** Paul W '73 (P Yates Co,LPA) -1370 Ontario
-800 Standard Bldg -Cleveland 44113 **Fx:**621-0575

(513) 281-5474 .. **Yates,** Tyrone K '83 -2200 Victory Pkwy -Ste 707 -Cincinnati 45206

(513) 988-6169 .. **Yauch,** Elizabeth A '88 Hedges & Y -240 E State -Trenton 45067

(304) 344-5800 .. **Yaussy,** David L '85 (Robinson & M PLLC) -500 VA E
-600 United Ctr -Bx1791 -Charleston, WV 25326 **Fx:**344-9566

(614) 224-1979 .. **Yavitch,** Bernard Z '71 -592 S 3rd -Columbus 43215 **Fx:**224-1984

(614) 224-6142 .. **Yavitch,** Eric J '95 (Yavitch & P Co,LPA) -511 S High
-Columbus 43215 **Fx:**228-6078

(216) 771-4444 .. **Yavitch,** Hallie I '03 Playhouse Sq Fndtn -1501 Eculid Av -Ste 200
-Cleveland 44107

(419) 243-7243 .. **Yavorcik,** James E '79 Cubbon & Assoc Co,LPA -405 N Huron
-Ste 500 -Toledo 43604

Yavorcik, Martin E '99 -3737 South Av -Youngstown 44502

Yballe, Raechelle C '03 -(Address Unavailable)

(614) 221-0240 .. **Yeager,** Jeffrey A '97 %Hahn L&P LLP -65 E State -Ste 1400
-Columbus 43215 **Fx:**221-5909

(513) 721-4500 .. **Yeager,** Stephen M '81 (Patsfall Y&P LLC) -1 W 4th -Ste 1800
-Cincinnati 45202 **Fx:**639-7554

(216) 931-6000 .. **Yeagley,** David D '89 (Ulmer & B LLP) -1300 E 9th -Ste
900 Penton Media Bldg -Cleveland 44114 **Fx:**931-6001

(330) 337-9515 .. **Yeagley Kirkland & Bartlett** -585 E State -Salem 44460

(330) 784-8800 .. **Yeargin,** Rocco P '96 %Young & M -507 Canton Rd -Bx6210
-Akron 44312

(330) 784-8800 .. **Yeargin,** Stephen J '04 Young & M -507 Canton Rd -Bx6210
-Akron 44312

(614) 457-6991 .. **Yearling,** Joseph H '56 -1310 Fountaine Dr -Columbus 43221
Fx:451-8103

(304) 720-7154 .. **Yeary,** Jo Ellen '80 Triana Energy LLC -Bx6070
-Charleston, WV 25362

(614) 228-7005 .. **Yeazel,** Keith A '89 -65 S 5th -Columbus 43215

Yee, Julianna Herrick '03 -312 Northrdg Oval -Brooklyn 44144

(216) 292-3300 .. **Yeh,** Michele R '97 %Conway MWK&K Co,LPA
-30195 Chagrin Blvd -Ste 300 -Cleveland 44124

(216) 831-0042 .. **Yelsky,** Debra A '93 OfCnsl Meyers RF&L LPA
-28601 Chagrin Blvd -Ste 500 -Cleveland 44122 **Fx:**831-0542

(216) 514-1899 .. **Yelsky,** Jeffrey M '91 -75 Pub Sq -Ste 800 -Cleveland 44113

(216) 781-2550 .. **Yelsky,** Lauryn M '94 %Yelsky & L Co,LPA -75 Pub Sq -Ste 800
-Cleveland 44113 **Fx:**781-6688

(216) 781-2550 .. **Yelsky,** Leonard W '59 (Yelsky & L Co,LPA) -75 Pub Sq -Ste 800
-Cleveland 44113 **Fx:**781-6688

(216) 781-2550 .. **Yelsky & Lonardo Co, LPA** -75 Pub Sq -Ste 800
-Cleveland 44113 **Fx:**781-6688

(216) 781-2550 .. **Yelsky,** Mitchell J '87 %Yelsky & L Co,LPA -75 Pub Sq -Ste 800
-Cleveland 44113 **Fx:**781-6688

(513) 621-9000 .. **Yelton,** Donald G '94 New Englnd Fin -625 Eden Park Dr #1150
-Cincinnati 45202

(513) 734-2283 .. **Yelton,** Paul R '56 (West W&Y) -Bx67 -Bethel 45106

(614) 228-2699 .. **Yemc,** Dominic J Jr. '95 -600 S High -Ste 204 -Columbus 43215

Yen, Dominic F '81 -2757 Landon Rd -Shaker Heights 44122

(614) 464-6400 .. **Yeoman,** Kelly J '04 %Vorys SS&P LLP -52 E Gay -Bx1008
-Columbus 43216 **Fx:**464-6350

(216) 443-3439 .. **Yeomans,** Patricia M '84 Cuyahoga Cnty Cmn Pleas Ct
-2163 E 22nd -Cleveland 44115

(614) 469-7404 .. **Yerian,** Paul E '82 SSA-OHA, Columbus -280 N High -3rd Fl
-Columbus 43215

(859) 386-4005 .. **Yerke,** Gary L '87 Fidelity Inst Rtrmnt Srvcs -200 Magellan Way
-KS2B -Covington, KY 41015

(317) 684-5441 .. **Yerkeson,** Douglas A '94 Bose M&E -135 N Penn
-2700 1st Indna Plz -Indianapolis, IN 46204

(419) 249-6745 .. **Yerman,** John W Jr. '77 Lucas Cnty Juv Ct -1801 Speilbusch Av
-Toledo 43624

(216) 622-8200 .. **Yerrace,** Lisa Marie '03 %Calfee H&G LLP -800 Superior Av
-Ste 1400 -Cleveland 44114 **Fx:**241-0816

(248) 646-9730 .. **Yert,** Jason '03 %E Simon & Assoc -355 S Old Woodward Av
-Birmingham, MI 48009

Yetter, Jerry J '73 -6174 Seiler Dr -Cincinnati 45239

(937) 258-3668 .. **Yiambilis,** Paulette '97 %Fox & Assoc Co,LPA
-1344 Woodman Dr -Ste F -Dayton 45432 **Fx:**258-3098

(614) 351-8010 .. **Yiangou,** Andrew '91 (Bergman & Y) -3099 Sullivant Av
-Columbus 43204

(937) 223-8888 .. **Yim,** Edward C '96 Dyer GM&S -131 N Ludlow -Ste 1400
-Dayton 45402 **Fx:**223-0127

(216) 621-7227 .. **Yingling,** Ronald Christopher '96 %Nicola G&C,LLC
-25 W Prospect Av -Republic Bldg Ste 1400 -Cleveland 44115
Fx:621-3999

(216) 443-8604 .. **Yingst,** Rebecca A '03 Cuyahoga Cnty Ct Cmmn Pleas
-1200 Ontario -Justice Ctr 11th Fl -Cleveland 44113

(216) 241-6700 .. **Yirga,** John A '03 %Watts H Co,LPA -1100 Superior Av E
-Ste 1750 Diamond Bldg -Cleveland 44114 **Fx:**241-8151

(216) 621-5300 .. **Yoakum,** Grant M '94 %Buckingham D&B,LLP -1375 E 9th
-Ste 1700 -Cleveland 44114 **Fx:**621-5440

(614) 728-3053 .. **Yoakum,** Kerry R '99 BWC -30 W Spring -Columbus 43215

Yobe-Scott, Jennifer '03 -(Address Unavailable)

(614) 552-1696 .. **Yockey,** Albert M III '94 Amer Elctrc Power -700 Morrison Rd
-Gahanna 43230

(513) 721-5672 .. **Yocum,** Thomas R '79 (Benjamin Y&H LLC) -312 Elm -Ste 1850
-Cincinnati 45202 **Fx:**562-4388

(419) 784-3700 .. **Yoder,** Jayne Z '79 Defiance Cnty Pros -607 W 3rd
-Defiance 43512 **Fx:**782-0594

(330) 375-2730 .. **Yoder,** Jonathan R '03 Pros -217 S High -Ste 203 -Akron 44308

(440) 686-9000 .. **Yoder,** Kimberly K '95 OfCnsl Goodwin & B LLP -22050
Mastick Rd -Fairview Park 44126 **Fx:**686-9001

(330) 725-0612 .. **Yoder,** Lois J '80 -5201 Park Dr -Bx1293 -Medina 44258

(419) 782-3010 .. **Yoder,** Stanley J '80 (Weaner ZBY&H,Ltd) -401 Wayne Av
-Defiance 43512 **Fx:**782-8426

(419) 865-5515 .. **Yoder,** Thomas A '77 -7945 Airport Hwy -Bx818 -Holland 43528

(330) 893-2600 .. **Yoder,** Thomas C '95 Hummel Ins Agncy -4585 State Route 39
-Bx250 -Berlin 44610 **Fx:**893-3339

(330) 887-0542 .. **Yogmour,** Gus Jr. '85 Westfield Grp -1 Park Cir -Bx5001
-Westfield Center 44251 **Fx:**887-2588

(440) 350-2167 .. **Yohe,** Lynne A '85 Lake Cnty Domestic Relatns Ct -Bx490
-Painesville 44077

(440) 205-8525 .. **Yohman,** Kathy A '94 OHIC Ins Co -155 E Broad St
-Columbus 43215

(440) 603-7616 .. **Yokaitis-Skutnik,** Judith A '86 Progressive Ins Co
-5920 Landerbrook Dr -#PLG-OHL33 -Mayfield Heights 44124

(304) 697-4700 .. **Yon,** Daniel T '99 (Bailes C&Y) -401 10th -Ste 500 -Bx1926
-Huntington, WV 25720

(937) 865-6800 .. **Yonak,** Christopher R '00 Lexis/Nexis -Bx933 -Dayton 45401

(740) 695-4412 .. **Yonak,** Helen '95 Belmont Cnty Pros -147-A W Main
-Saint Clairsville 43950

(513) 863-9100 .. **Yonas,** John J '00 (Yonas & R LLC) -9100 Centre Pnte Dr -Ste 250
-West Chester 45069 **Fx:**863-9110

Yonchak, Robert F '88 -30035 Jffrsn Way -Cleveland 44145

(216) 515-1660 .. **Yoo,** Steven R '94 %Frantz W LLP -127 Pub Sq -2500 Key Center
-Cleveland 44114 **Fx:**515-1650

(419) 352-2535 .. **Yoon,** Mimi S '92 Spitler HY&N,LLP -131 E Court
-Bowling Green 43402 **Fx:**353-8728

(419) 243-6281 .. **Yoppolo,** Louis J '80 (Shindler NH&S,LLP) -300 Mad Av -Ste 1200
-Toledo 43604 **Fx:**243-0129

(502) 582-6446 .. **York,** Gloria B '83 SSA-OHA -601 W Bway -3rd Fl
-Louisville, KY 40202

(330) 375-2030 .. **York,** John R '95 Law Dept -161 S High -Ste 202 -Akron 44308

York, Michele N '04 -(Address Unavailable)

(216) 592-5000 .. **York,** Nicholas C '93 %Tucker E&W LLP -925 Euclid Av
-1150 Huntngtn Bldg -Cleveland 44115 **Fx:**592-5009

(330) 253-5678 .. **York,** Olen L III '02 %Patent Cpyrt & Trdmrk Law Grp,LLC
-137 S Main -Ste 202 -Akron 44308 **Fx:**762-5063

(330) 399-1481 .. **York,** Robert L '67 -138 E Market -Warren 44481

(330) 375-2030 .. **York,** Stephanie H '95 Law Dept -161 S High -Ste 202
-Akron 44308

(513) 871-8219 .. **York Schiff,** Elizabeth '90 -2 Forest Hll Dr -Cincinnati 45208

(216) 928-3474 .. **Yormick,** Jon P '90 (Yormick & Assoc Co,LPA) -127 Pub Sq
-Ste 5200 -Cleveland 44114 **Fx:**566-0857

(419) 636-3166 .. **Yosick,** Kirk A '98 (Gallagher S&Y,Ltd) -216 S Lynn -Bryan 43506
Fx:636-5743

(614) 462-3555 .. **Yosowitz,** Andrew N '02 %Franklin Cnty Pros -373 S High
-Columbus 43215

Yosowitz, Sanford '64 -2585 Larchmont Dr -Beachwood 44122

(740) 472-0707 .. **Yoss,** Richard A '68 -122 N Main -Woodsfield 43793

(216) 515-1300 .. **Yost,** Agnes J '94 ProAssurnace,Inc -113 St Clair Av NE -Ste 300
-Cleveland 44114

(901) 434-8489 .. **Yost,** Christopher J '97 FedEx -3620 Hacks Cross Rd
-Bldg B 2nd Fl -Memphis, TN 38125

(614) 466-7264 .. **Yost,** Cynthia A '89 OH Legal Rghts Srvc -8 E Long -5th Fl
-Columbus 43215

(740) 833-2690 .. **Yost,** David A '91 Delaware Cnty Pros -140 N Sandusky -3rd Fl
-Delaware 43015

Yost, Gerard T '91 -215 Selby -Alliance 44601

(614) 466-7266 .. **Yost,** Melissa R '99 Atty Gen -30 E Broad -Columbus 43215
Fx:644-1926

(612) 766-7760 .. **Yost,** Peter A '94 %Faegre & B LLP -90 S 7th
-2200 Wells Fargo Ctr -Minneapolis, MN 55402 **Fx:**766-1600

(614) 764-1444 .. **Youell,** Spencer M '74 (Mowery & Y) -425 Metro Pl N -Ste 420
-Dublin 43017 **Fx:**760-8654

(513) 421-8100 .. **Youkilis,** John C '87 VY Inc -37 W 7th -Cincinnati 45202

(215) 580-2714 .. **Younce,** Patricia A '79 Cnsl US SBA -900 Market -5th Fl
-Philadelphia, PA 19107 **Fx:**580-2758

(937) 224-9291 .. **Young & Alexander Co,LPA** -130 W 2nd -Ste 2000
-Dayton 45402 **Fx:**224-9679

(513) 326-5555 .. **Young & Caldwell Co,LPA** -110 Boggs Ln -Ste 350
-Cincinnati 45246

(216) 621-2300 .. **Young,** Andrew R '99 Nurenberg PH&M LPA -1370 Ontario
-Ste 100 -Cleveland 44113 **Fx:**771-2242

(614) 341-6367 .. **Young,** Betty K '00 Franklin Univ -201 S Grant -Columbus 43215
Fx:228-8478

(239) 821-6624 .. **Young,** Blaine R '03 -4280 Tamiami Trl E -Ste 302
-Naples, FL 34112 **Fx:**774-5526

(330) 764-6026 .. **Young,** Brian R '04 6th Circuit Ct of Appeals -143 W Lbrty
-Medina 44256

(937) 544-5095 .. **Young & Caldwell** -225 N Cross -West Union 45693

(614) 466-6700 .. **Young,** Carrie C '86 Tax Appeals -30 E Broad -Columbus 43215
Fx:644-5196

(216) 623-1123 .. **Young,** Charles M '74 (Sindell YG&S,PLL) -55 Pub Sq -Ste 1020
-Cleveland 44113 **Fx:**623-1124

(614) 466-7046 .. **Young,** Christopher R '89 Personnel Brd of Review -65 E State
-12th Fl -Columbus 43215

(860) 547-4163 .. **Young,** Cynthia H '91 The Hartford Ins Co -690 Asylum Av
-Hartford Plz -Hartford, CT 06105

(216) 566-5738 .. **Young,** Daniel T '90 (Thompson H LLP) -127 Pub Sq -3900 Key
Ctr -Cleveland 44114 **Fx:**566-5800

(330) 298-4444 .. **Young,** David A '05 -209 S Chestnut -Ste 205 -Ravenna 44266

(614) 228-1200 .. **Young,** David C '86 (Sunbury & Y) -495 S High -Columbus 43215

(614) 365-2700 .. **Young,** David J '55 SrCnsl Squire S&D LLP -41 S High
-1300 Huntngtn Ctr -Columbus 43215 **Fx:**365-2499

(330) 784-8800 .. **Young,** Dean A '77 (Young & M) -507 Canton Rd -Bx6210
-Akron 44312

(216) 861-4891 .. **Young,** Derek W '87 Pat Young Service -1550 W 25th
-Cleveland 44113

(740) 363-1213 .. **Young,** Don J III '00 (Firestone BHNW&Y,LLP) -15 W Winter
-Delaware 43015 **Fx:**369-0875

(216) 830-6830 .. **Young,** E Mark '00 %Brouse M -1001 Lakeside Av -Ste 1600
-Cleveland 44114 **Fx:**830-6807

(216) 931-6000 .. **Young,** Elin B '98 %Ulmer & B LLP -1300 E 9th -Ste 900 Penton
Media Bldg -Cleveland 44114 **Fx:**931-6001

(859) 572-6031 .. **Young,** Eric W '03 N Kentucky Univ -Sl Chase Coll of Law
-Nunn Hall #116 -Highland Heights, KY 41099

(937) 335-2622 .. **Young,** Fredric L '92 Utrecht & Y -12 S Plum -Troy 45373

(513) 243-0083 .. **Young,** Gregory E '78 GE Aircraft Engines -1 Neumann Way
-MD J104 -Cincinnati 45215

(513) 721-1077 .. **Young,** Gregory S '86 (G Young Co,LPA) -632 Vine -Ste 500
-Cincinnati 45202 **Fx:**721-1919

(330) 796-2956 .. **Young,** Henry C Jr. '63 Goodyear Tire & Rubber Co
-1144 E Market -Akron 44316

(419) 668-9830 .. **Young,** Henry E '49 -115 W Main -Norwalk 44857

(248) 258-2700 .. **Young,** Howard B '72 (Weisman YS&R,PC) -30100 Telegraph Rd
-Suite 428 -Bingham Farms, MI 48025

(740) 354-3643 .. **Young,** Jack D '61 -812 6th -Portsmouth 45662

(216) 586-3939 .. **Young,** James E '72 (Jones D) -901 Lakeside Av -Cleveland
44114 **Fx:**579-0212

(440) 984-3551 .. **Young,** James H '87 -860 Tarry Ln -Amherst 44001

(419) 243-3261 .. **Young,** Jeremy G '01 -520 Mad Av -864 Spitzer Bldg
-Toledo 43604

(803) 643-1037 .. **Young,** Joan E '85 CBS Brdcstng Inc -1515 Bway
-New York, NY 10036

(803) 252-3663 .. **Young,** John M '71 (Young & S, LLP) -917 Calhoun
-Columbia, SC 29201

(216) 623-3688 .. **Young,** John Talbot Jr. '75 (Young & D) -1801 E 9th
-1425 Ohio Svngs Plz -Cleveland 44114 **Fx:**623-3692

(614) 442-1375 .. **Young,** John Timothy '77 -5010 Riverside Dr -Columbus 43220

(216) 431-4500 .. **Young,** Joseph C '91 Cuyahoga Cnty Pros -3955 Euclid Av
-Jane Edna Hunter Bldg -Cleveland 44115 **Fx:**431-4113

(330) 743-1171 .. **Young,** Joseph R Jr. '82 (Manchester BP&U) -201 E Commerce
-Atrium Level 2 Commerce Bldg -Youngstown 44503
Fx:743-1190

(419) 294-2232 .. **Young,** Kenneth L '93 (Roth BY) -50 Court
-Upper Sandusky 43351 **Fx:**294-2488

(216) 664-6900 .. **Young,** Kevin M '85 (Brzytwa Q&M LLC) -1660 W 2nd
-900 Skylight Ofc Twr -Cleveland 44113 **Fx:**664-6901

(419) 244-7885 .. **Young,** Kurt M '93 -709 Mad Av -Ste 307 -Toledo 43624
Fx:244-7886

(216) 321-6323 .. **Young,** Laura A '96 Lexis-Nexis -3550 Radcliffe Rd
-Cleveland 44121

               Young, Leigh Anne '04 -(Address Unavailable)

(216) 931-6000 .. **Young,** Leonard D '75 (Ulmer & B LLP) -1300 E 9th
-Ste 900 Penton Media Bldg -Cleveland 44114 **Fx:**931-6001

(740) 732-2309 .. **Young,** Lucien C Jr. '59 -508 North -Caldwell 43724

(740) 732-8441 .. **Young,** Lucien C III '83 -302 East -Caldwell 43724

(513) 352-6617 .. **Young,** Malcolm Scott '93 %Thompson H LLP -312 Walnut
-14th Fl -Cincinnati 45202 **Fx:**241-4771

(937) 461-4646 .. **Young,** Margaret R '87 -131 N Ludlow -1311 Talbott Twr
-Dayton 45402

(513) 721-1200 .. **Young,** Martin M '59 (Young R&M Co,LPA) -1014 Vine -Ste 2400
-Cincinnati 45202 **Fx:**721-7116

               Young, Marvin E '40 -484 Crkside Dr -Lebanon 45036

(614) 469-3939 .. **Young,** Mary Beth Brookshire '01 %Jones D
-325 John H McConnell Blvd -Ste 600 -Bx165017
-Columbus 43216 **Fx:**461-4198

(216) 685-1000 .. **Young,** Matthew M '02 %Weltman W&R Co,LPA
-323 W Lakeside Av -Ste 200 -Cleveland 44113 **Fx:**363-4121

(330) 784-8800 .. **Young & McDowall** -507 Canton Rd -Bx6210 -Akron 44312

(513) 825-7600 .. **Young,** Michael T '83 Springdale Title Agncy,LLC
-415 Glensprings Dr -Ste 205 -Cincinnati 45246

(513) 721-1077 .. **Young,** Michele L '93 %G Young Co,LPA -632 Vine -Ste 500
-Cincinnati 45202 **Fx:**721-1919

(614) 227-2000 .. **Young,** Nancy B '77 (Porter WM&A LLP) -41 S High -Columbus
43215 **Fx:**227-2100

(330) 253-9118 .. **Young,** Peter F '62 -7679 Sugarbush Trl -Hudson 44236

(937) 224-1981 .. **Young Pryor Lynn & Jerardi** -130 W 2nd -Ste 800
-Dayton 45402

(513) 721-1200 .. **Young Reverman & Mazzei Co,LPA** -1014 Vine -Ste 2400
-Cincinnati 45202 **Fx:**721-7116

(740) 549-6073 .. **Young,** Robert A '90 Greif Bros Corp -425 Winter Rd
-Delaware 43015

(419) 238-1166 .. **Young,** Robert C '64 (Young T&Y) -120 W Main -Bx525
-Van Wert 45891

(419) 259-6376 .. **Young,** Robert G '71 US Atty -4 Seagate -Ste 308 -Toledo 43604
Fx:259-6360

(440) 886-5667 .. **Young,** Robert H '86 -6234 Pearl Rd -Parma Heights 44130

(614) 466-2590 .. **Young,** Robert J '94 State Hwy Patrol -1970 W Broad
-Columbus 43223

(937) 222-2424 .. **Young,** Robert W '95 (Freund F&A) -1 S Main -Ste 1800
-Dayton 45402 **Fx:**222-5369

(513) 352-6700 .. **Young,** Rodney M '95 (Thompson H LLP) -312 Walnut -14th Fl
-Cincinnati 45202 **Fx:**241-4771

(614) 336-7072 .. **Young,** Ronald G '96 OH Adjutant Genl Dept
-2825 W Dublin Granvll Rd -Columbus 43235

(513) 621-2120 .. **Young,** Shawn M '87 (Strauss & T,LPA) -150 E 4th -4th Fl
-Cincinnati 45202 **Fx:**241-8259

(216) 781-1212 .. **Young,** Sheldon M '51 OfCnsl Walter & H LLP -1301 E 9th
-Ste 3500 -Cleveland 44114 **Fx:**575-0911

(419) 772-2206 .. **Young,** Sherry Ann '84 ONU-Pettit Clg of Law -525 S Main
-Ada 45810

(614) 752-1784 .. **Young,** Stephen A '84 OH Dept Rehab & Correction
-1050 Fwy Dr N -Columbus 43229

(419) 238-1166 .. **Young Taylor & Yarger** -120 W Main -Bx525 -Van Wert 45891

(614) 227-2000 .. **Young,** Thomas A '73 (Porter WM&A LLP) -41 S High
-Columbus 43215 **Fx:**227-2100

(216) 861-5582 .. **Young,** Thomas E '75 OfCnsl Fay SFM&M LLP -1100 Superior Av
-7th Fl -Cleveland 44114 **Fx:**241-1666

(419) 247-1114 .. **Young,** Thomas Lee '72 Owens-Illinois,Inc -One SeaGate
-Toledo 43666

               Young, Thomas V '89 -165 Tamarack Dr -Berea 44017

(216) 664-4842 .. **Young,** Tiffeny U '03 Prosecutor -1200 Ontario Av
-8th Fl Justice Ctr -Cleveland 44113 **Fx:**664-4399

(937) 496-7478 .. **Young,** Timothy '92 Montgomery Cnty Pub Def -117 S Main
-Ste 400 -Dayton 45422 **Fx:**225-3449

(440) 234-6693 .. **Young,** Vincent E '58 -165 Tamarack Dr -Berea 44017

(513) 793-5150 .. **Young,** Wallace H '00 -10426 Briarcove Ln -Cincinnati 45242

(330) 725-6666 .. **Young,** William B '78 (Williams & B,LLP) -105 W Lbrty -Bx394
-Medina 44258

(216) 592-5000 .. **Youngblood-Jalics,** Courtenay '04 %Tucker E&W LLP
-925 Euclid Av -1150 Huntngtn Bldg -Cleveland 44115
Fx:592-5009

(614) 462-3194 .. **Younger,** Mary A '84 Franklin Cnty Pub Def -373 S High -12th Fl
-Columbus 43215

(419) 878-9988 .. **Youngston,** Diane L '90 -1225 Bernath -Toledo 43615

(216) 566-5670 .. **Youngstrom,** Karen D '76 (Thompson H LLP) -127 Pub Sq
-3900 Key Ctr -Cleveland 44114 **Fx:**566-5800

               Younkin, Brett E '03 -(Address Unavailable)

(614) 464-4100 .. **Younkin,** Tracy A '94 (AuCoin DH&Y LLC) -495 S High -Ste 250
-Columbus 43215

(419) 224-1353 .. **Younkman,** Derek A '93 %King & B -212 N Elizabeth -Lima 45801
Fx:224-5305

(614) 227-2336 .. **Yount,** Sue W '86 (Bricker & E LLP) -100 S 3rd -Columbus 43215
Fx:227-2390

(330) 747-2661 .. **Yourstowsky,** Ronald J '91 Cafaro Co -2445 Belmont Av -Bx2186
-Youngstown 44504

(614) 463-9770 .. **Youssef,** Leslie Howard '04 %Roetzel & A,LPA -155 E Broad
-Natl City Ctr 12th Fl -Columbus 43215 **Fx:**463-9792

(419) 885-3000 .. **Youssef-Coyle,** Lami H '84 (Brady C&S LLP)
-4052 Holland-Sylvania Rd -Toledo 43623 **Fx:**885-1120

(513) 352-6796 .. **Youtsey,** Deborah A '88 (Thompson H LLP) -312 Walnut -14th Fl
-Cincinnati 45202 **Fx:**241-4771

(904) 359-1244 .. **Yovanovic,** Nicholas S '76 CSX Trans -500 Water
-Jacksonville, FL 32202

(513) 977-8200 .. **Yu,** Tracy R '99 %Dinsmore & S LLP -255 E 5th -Ste 1900
-Cincinnati 45202 **Fx:**977-8141

(216) 241-5310 .. **Yue,** Deborah W '94 %Gallagher SF&N -1501 Euclid Av -6th Fl
-Cleveland 44115 **Fx:**241-1608

(614) 223-3448 .. **Yuhas,** James E '95 United Illuminating Co -157 Church -Bx1564
-New Haven, CT 06506

(937) 223-5200 .. **Yuhas,** Steven E '86 %Flanagan LH&S -318 W 4th -Dayton 45402
Fx:223-3335

(330) 376-7245 .. **Yukish,** Kristen M '04 Curtin & Assoc -159 S Main -920 Key Bldg
-Akron 44305 **Fx:**376-8128

(216) 241-2262 .. **Yulish Twohig & Associates** -1419 W 9th -Hilliard Bldg
-Cleveland 44113

(513) 651-6800 .. **Yund,** George E '77 (Frost BT LLC) -201 E 5th -2200 PNC Ctr
-Cincinnati 45202 **Fx:**651-6981

(937) 299-1506 .. **Yung,** Gerald E '75 -1574 Big Hill Rd -Kettering 45429

(937) 642-4070 .. **Yurasek,** Stephen J '79 (Allen Y&M) -233 W 5th -Bx391
-Marysville 43040

(513) 723-4000 .. **Yurchuck,** Roger A '62 OfCnsl Vorys SS&P LLP -221 E 4th
-Ste 2000 Atrium Two -Bx0236 -Cincinnati 45201 **Fx:**723-4056

(513) 932-3060 .. **Yurick,** Mark S '87 Lebanon -50 S Bway -Lebanon 45036

(614) 228-6885 .. **Yurik,** Stephen B '96 %Lane A&H LLC -175 S 3rd -Ste 700
-Columbus 43215 **Fx:**228-0146

(614) 464-6400 .. **Yurkiw,** Heidi L '99 %Vorys SS&P LLP -52 E Gay -Bx1008
-Columbus 43216 **Fx:**464-6350

(614) 227-2000 .. **Yurkiw,** Jay A '97 %Porter WM&A LLP -41 S High
-Columbus 43215 **Fx:**227-2100

(614) 224-8326 .. **Yurovich,** Dale R '84 -5 E Long -Ste 100 -Columbus 43215

(630) 821-2450 .. **Yusko,** David P '82 BP America Inc-Law Dept -4101 Winfld Rd
-Warrenville, IL 60555

(216) 831-8111 .. **Zabell,** Cary J '76 (CJ Zabell Co,LPA) -25700 Science Park Dr
-Ste 250 -Beachwood 44122

(216) 687-1311 .. **Zaber,** Brian M '02 %Reminger & R -101 Prospect Av W
-1400 Mdlnd Bldg -Cleveland 44115 **Fx:**687-1841

(614) 818-1100 .. **Zabkar,** William J '76 Stewart Title Grnty -259 W Schrock Rd
-Westerville 43081

(614) 729-4909 .. **Zablocki-Gage,** Kathy L '99 Alliance Data Syst Inc
-800 Techcenter Dr -Gahanna 43230

(740) 852-1576 .. **Zabloudil,** Renae E '01 Tanner M&H -2 S Main -London 43140

(216) 566-0064 .. **Zaccagnini,** Bruce A '86 (Armstrong MD&Z) -101 Prospect Av W
-1725 The Mdlnd Bldg -Cleveland 44115 **Fx:**566-0224

(248) 433-1414 .. **Zacharski,** Dennis E '93 %Lacey & J -600 S Adams
-Birmingham, MI 48009

(330) 376-1112 .. **Zacharyasz,** Mari A '00 Whalen & C,LPA -565 Wolf Ledges Pkwy
-Bx2020 -Akron 44309 **Fx:**376-3200

(330) 764-7252 .. **Zachman,** Janis H '95 Firstmerit Bank -39 Pub Sq -Medina 44256
               Zachman, Thomas F '80 -16304 W Escondido Ct
-Surprise, AZ 85374

(937) 372-7605 .. **Zachritz,** James D '65 -67 W Main -Xenia 45385

(330) 966-0095 .. **Zackaroff,** Peter T '80 Maximus Just Sltns Div -5399 Lauby Rd
-Ste 200 -North Canton 44720

(513) 651-6800 .. **Zackerman,** Jeffrey L '97 %Frost BT LLC -201 E 5th
-2200 PNC Ctr -Cincinnati 45202 **Fx:**651-6981

(614) 236-8000 .. **Zacks,** Benjamin S '88 Zacks Law Grp LLC -33 S James Rd
-3rd Fl -Columbus 43213

(330) 264-5141 .. **Zacour,** Wayne A '79 Taggart Law Firm -142 W Lbrty -Bx218
-Wooster 44691 **Fx:**262-1046

(614) 488-7847 .. **Zadnik,** Rudolph S '51 -2301 Brixton Rd -Columbus 43221

(330) 643-8200 .. **Zaehringer,** Brittany G '99 Summit Cnty Human Resources Dept
-47 N Main -Bldg 1 -Akron 44308

(440) 329-5359 .. **Zafarana,** Renee '86 Lorain Cnty Dom Rltns Ct -226 Middle Av
-Elyria 44035

(440) 461-1810 .. **Zaffiro,** Carl J '66 -5555 Mayfld Rd -Lyndhurst 44124

(216) 520-1464 .. **Zaffiro,** James A '97 -4200 Rockside R -101 -Independence 44131

(216) 382-0444 .. **Zaffiro,** Thomas J '91 -4577 Mayfld Rd -Cleveland 44121

(440) 449-8811 .. **Zaffiro,** William T '73 -5555 Mayfld Rd -Lyndhurst 44124

(440) 449-8811 .. **Zaffiro,** William T Jr. '04 -5555 Mayfld Rd -Lyndhurst 44124

(614) 719-3330 .. **Zafris,** James L '89 US Ct of Appls -85 Marconi Blvd
-Columbus 43215

               Zagara, Charles '85 -(Address Unavailable)

(216) 479-8500 .. **Zagore,** David A (Squire S&D LLP) -127 Pub Sq -4900 Key
Twr -Cleveland 44114 **Fx:**479-8780

(440) 934-7000 .. **Zagrans,** Eric H '77 -5338 Meadow Lane Ct -Elyria 44035

(330) 729-9823 .. **Zahar,** Deborah A '92 NID Corp -100 DeBartolo Pl -Ste 300
-Bx9430 -Youngstown 44513

(937) 372-9236 .. **Zaharieff,** Anthony J '70 (Silverberg Z&O Co,LPA) -100 E Market
-Bx40 -Xenia 45385

(330) 753-4511 .. **Zahirsky,** Linda A '85 -91 Stirling Av -Bx271 -Barberton 44203

(216) 861-5582 .. **Zahn,** Jeffrey N '04 %Fay SFM&M LLP -1100 Superior Av -7th Fl
-Cleveland 44114 **Fx:**241-1666

(513) 665-3500 .. **Zahniser,** David W '04 %Freund F&A -105 E 4th -Ste 1400
-Cincinnati 45202 **Fx:**665-3503

(513) 381-2838 .. **Zahniser,** Rachel Sublett '03 %Taft S&H LLP -425 Walnut
-Ste 1800 -Cincinnati 45202 **Fx:**381-0205

(614) 799-2800 ..Zaino & Humphrey LPA -5775 Perimeter Dr -Ste 275
-Dublin 43017 Fx:799-1500

(614) 799-2800 ..Zaino, Michael J '83 (Zaino & H LPA) -5775 Perimeter Dr -Ste 275
-Dublin 43017 Fx:799-1500

(614) 458-0025 ..Zaino, Thomas M '89 (McDonald H Co,LPA) -41 S High -Ste 3650
-Columbus 43215 Fx:458-0028

(216) 664-3528 ..Zajaczkowski, Scott D '01 City Dept Consumer Affrs -1301 E 6th
-Cleveland Convntn Ctr -Cleveland 44114

(330) 365-3272 ..Zajkowski, Karen B '93 Tuscarawas Cnty Cmn Pleas Ct
-101 E High Av -Ste 205 -New Philadelphia 44663 Fx:602-8811

(614) 466-2765 ..Zalenski, Scott T '90 Industrial Commssn of OH -30 W Spring
-9th Fl -Columbus 43215 Fx:752-8785

(740) 322-5341 ..Zaleski, Aimee A '98 Longaberger Co -1500 E Main
-Newark 43055

(440) 282-9109 ..Zaleski, Donald M '84 -4463 Oberlin Av -Lorain 44053

(216) 861-5582 ..Zalevsky, Marina V '04 %Fay SFM&M LLP -1100 Superior Av
-7th Fl -Cleveland 44114 Fx:241-1666

(419) 252-5859 ..Zalewski, Cynthia M '94 HCR ManorCare -Bx10086
-Toledo 43699

(440) 826-3333 ..Zalic, John D '91 -7550 Lucerne Dr -Ste 302
-Middleburg Heights 44130

(614) 221-3151 ..Zalimeni, Gail M '90 %Butler C&D -50 W Broad -Ste 700
-Columbus 43215

(859) 431-2228 ..Zalla, Daniel J '03 -51 W Lakeside Av -Lakeside Park, KY 41017

(216) 363-4500 ..Zalud, Eric L '87 (Benesch FC&A LLP) -200 Pub Sq -Ste 2300
-Cleveland 44114 Fx:363-4588

(330) 726-1654 ..Zamary, Gary M '83 -120 Marwood Cir -Bx3965
-Youngstown 44513

(513) 381-9200 ..Zamary, George J '99 Rendigs FK&D,LLP -One W 4th -Ste 900
-Cincinnati 45202 Fx:381-9206

(513) 381-0656 ..Zamary, Kimberly A '00 %Kohnen & P LLP -201 E 5th -Ste 800
-Cincinnati 45202 Fx:381-5823

(614) 221-1300 ..Zamora, Charles '91 -85 E Gay -Ste 802 -Columbus 43215

(216) 752-4200 ..Zamore, Joseph D '71 (Zamore & S) -20600 Chagrin Blvd
-Shaker Heights 44122 Fx:752-0042

(216) 752-4200 ..Zamore & Sprague -20600 Chagrin Blvd -Shaker Heights 44122
Fx:752-0042

(440) 885-8132 ..Zampedro, Anthony J '91 Law Dept -6611 Ridge Rd
-Parma 44129

(419) 843-2001 ..Zan, Kelley A '02 %Gallon & T Co,LPA -3516 Granite Cir
-Bx352018 -Toledo 43635 Fx:843-6665

(330) 721-5092 ..Zanath, Debra A '91 Medina Gen Hosp -1000 E Wshngtn
-Medina 44256 Fx:721-4906

(614) 365-2700 ..Zancourides, Lori Maiorca '03 %Squire S&D LLP -41 S High
-1300 Huntngtn Ctr -Columbus 43215 Fx:365-2499

(419) 242-8214 ..Zaner & Cimerman -520 Mad Av -Ste 545 -Toledo 43604
Fx:242-8658

(419) 242-8214 ..Zaner, Lorin Jay '76 (Zaner & C) -520 Mad Av -Ste 545
-Toledo 43604 Fx:242-8658

(216) 861-7463 ..Zangerle, John A '67 -1900 E 9th -Ste 3200 -Cleveland 44114
Fx:696-0740

(440) 392-7108 ..Zangerle, John A III '91 Steris Corp -5960 Heisley Rd
-Mentor 44060

(216) 861-5582 ..Zanghi, John S Jr. '95 %Fay SFM&M LLP -1100 Superior Av
-7th Fl -Cleveland 44114 Fx:241-1666

(740) 397-7420 ..Zanghi, Mark A '04 %McDevitt M&M,LPA -1 Pub Sq
-Mount Vernon 43050 Fx:397-6611

(740) 283-4781 ..Zani, Thomas E '99 SE OH Lgl Srvcs -100 N 3rd
-Steubenville 43952

(216) 739-2600 ..Zanney, Raymond C '93 -9701 Brookpark Rd -Ste 241
-Cleveland 44129 Fx:661-9292

(419) 663-0934 ..Zannieri, Joseph A '86 -70 W Chestnut -Norwalk 44857
Zap, Jennifer L '04 -(Address Unavailable)

(440) 356-4980 ..Zapis, Donna M '88 -22900 Ctr Ridge Rd -Rocky River 44116

(216) 623-0900 ..Zapka, Dennis P '75 (McLaughlin & M,LLP) -1111 Superior Av E
-Ste 1350 Eaton Ctr -Cleveland 44114 Fx:623-0935

(614) 466-8444 ..Zapp, William A '72 Supreme Ct of OH -30 E Broad -35th Fl
-Columbus 43266

(216) 241-8158 ..Zaransky, Stephen P '80 S Zaransky Co,LPA -614 Superior
Av NW -Ste 750 -Cleveland 44113

(920) 235-2415 ..Zarbano, John S '97 -1806 Doemel -Oshkosh, WI 54901

(330) 208-1000 ..Zaremba, Amanda J '04 %Vorys SS&P LLP -106 S Main
-First Natl Twr -Akron 44308

(419) 254-5246 ..Zaremba, Thomas S '77 (Roetzel & A,LPA) -One SeaGate -9th Fl
-Toledo 43604 Fx:242-0316

(614) 229-4445 ..Zaremski, Laura M '00 %Luper N&L,LPA -50 W Broad
-1200 LeVeque Twr -Columbus 43215 Fx:464-2425

(216) 831-5488 ..Zaremsky, Michael L '78 -3659 Green Rd -Ste 208
-Beachwood 44122

(216) 696-4009 ..Zaretsky, Erwin V '63 -614 Superior Av W -Ste 911 Rckfllr Bldg
-Cleveland 44113

(216) 566-5647 ..Zarlenga, Audra J '96 %Thompson H LLP -127 Pub Sq
-3900 Key Ctr -Cleveland 44114 Fx:566-5800

(202) 383-7046 ..Zarlenga, Carmine R III '84 (Howrey & S) -1299 Penn Av NW
-Washington, DC 20004

(216) 566-7994 ..Zarlingo, Pamela '89 Thompson H LLP -127 Pub Sq -3900 Key
Ctr -Cleveland 44114 Fx:566-5800

(330) 427-1823 ..Zarnick, Jacklynn M '89 Lexis-Nexis,Reed Elsevier -446
Sleepy Hllw Dr -Leetonia 44431 Fx:427-1823

(419) 321-1460 ..Zarou, Mechelle '00 %Shumaker L&K,LLP -1000 Jackson
-Toledo 43624 Fx:241-6894

(216) 766-5828 ..Zartman, Michael B '84 Genesis Prof Liab Underwriters
-25550 Chagrin Blvd -#300 -Beachwood 44122

(216) 443-7800 ..Zarzycki, Scott C '00 Cuyahoga Cnty Pros -1200 Ontario -8th Fl
-Cleveland 44113 Fx:698-2270

(216) 696-4441 ..Zashin, Andrew A '93 (Zashin & R Co,LPA) -55 Pub Sq -Ste 1490
-Cleveland 44113 Fx:696-1618

(216) 696-4441 ..Zashin & Rich Co, LPA -55 Pub Sq -Ste 1490 -Cleveland 44113
Fx:696-1618

(614) 224-4411 ..Zashin & Rich Co, LPA -21 E State -Ste 1900 -Columbus 43215
Fx:224-4433

(216) 696-4441 ..Zashin, Robert I '68 (Zashin & R Co,LPA) -55 Pub Sq -Ste 1490
-Cleveland 44113 Fx:696-1618

(216) 696-4441 ..Zashin, Stephen S '95 %Zashin & R Co,LPA -55 Pub Sq
-Ste 1490 -Cleveland 44113 Fx:696-1618

(614) 462-5497 ..Zatezalo, Michael E '75 (Kegler BH&R) -65 E State -Ste 1800
-Columbus 43215 Fx:464-2634

(440) 951-6245 ..Zatyko, Donald R '75 -38041 Lk Shr Blvd -Willoughby 44094

(330) 539-1052 ..Zauderer, Philip Q '64 -6345 Sodom Hutchings Rd -Girard 44420

(313) 854-3881 ..Zaums, Peter M '73 -8113 Secor Rd -Bx183
-Lambertville, MI 48144

(513) 977-8200 ..Zaunbrecher, Susan B '90 (Dinsmore & S LLP) -255 E 5th
-Ste 1900 -Cincinnati 45202 Fx:977-8141

(314) 721-6040 ..Zavac, Matthew J '89 -8008 Carondelet -Ste 301
-Clayton, MO 63105

(937) 438-2000 ..Zavakos, Christ L '62 Sterling Lnd Title Agncy,Inc -7016 Corp Way
-Dayton 45459

(216) 831-8678 ..Zavarella, Gino P '95 -4701 Richmond Rd -Ste 220
-Warrensville Heights 44128

(330) 762-9700 ..Zavarello, A William '64 Cnsl AW Zavarello Co,LPA -313 S High
-Akron 44308 Fx:762-1680

(513) 579-7877 ..Zavatsky, Kathleen H '79 Federated Dept Stores,Inc -7 W 7th
-Cincinnati 45202

(513) 381-2838 ..Zavatsky, Michael J '80 (Taft S&H LLP) -425 Walnut -Ste 1800
-Cincinnati 45202 Fx:381-0205

Zavelson, Andrew P '02 -3296 Ingleside Rd -Shaker Heights
44122

Zavelson, Nancy F '91 -3296 Ingleside Rd -Shaker Heights 44122

(216) 363-4500 ..Zaverton, Michael D '87 %Benesch FC&A LLP -200 Pub Sq
-Ste 2300 -Cleveland 44114 Fx:363-4588

(216) 830-9000 ..Zavesky, Robert J '83 (Berger & Z Co,LPA) -614 W Superior Av
-Ste 1425 Rckfllr Bldg -Cleveland 44113 Fx:830-4200

(330) 296-8133 ..Zavinski, Dennis M '74 -409 S Prospect -Bx268 -Ravenna 44266

(330) 297-2307 ..Zawadski, Thaddeus F '75 Robinson Meml Hsptl
-6847 N Chestnut -Bx1204 -Ravenna 44266

(614) 889-9282 ..Zawaly, Peter P II '73 -6238 Inverurie Dr W -Dublin 43017

(513) 621-4224 ..Zayas-Davis, Marilyn '99 -323 W 5th -Cincinnati 45202

(419) 241-1200 ..Zazycki, Suzanne '03 %Cooper & W,LPA -900 Adams
-Toledo 43624 Fx:242-5675

(330) 375-5834 ..Zbiegien, Michael J Jr. '04 US Dist Ct - Nthrn Dst -2 S Main
-Akron 44308

(513) 622-3952 ..Zea, Betty J '91 SrCnsl Procter & Gamble Co
-8700 Mason-Mntgmry Rd -Mason 45040

(513) 362-8700 ..Zealey, Sharon J '84 (Blank R) -201 E 5th -Ste 1700
-Cincinnati 45202 Fx:362-8773

(330) 452-2266 ..Zedell, Albert L '76 -1128 18th NW -Zedell Bldg -Canton 44703
Fx:452-2266

(330) 453-8786 ..Zedell, Robert A '82 -1516 18th NW -Canton 44703 Fx:453-8790

(330) 725-8861 ..Zee, Sharlene A '88 Medina City Pros -132 N Elmwood
-Medina 44256

(614) 229-3888 ..Zeehandelar, Steven J '82 (Cheek & Z,LLP) -471 E Broad -18th Fl
-Bx15069 -Columbus 43215 Fx:341-5865

(513) 651-4226 ..Zegarski, Daniel S '95 (Zegarski & I Co,LPA) -917 Main -Ste 200
-Cincinnati 45202

(330) 494-6611 ..Zeglen, Joseph M '85 (Robertson Z&P) -4690 Munson NW -Ste C
-Canton 44718

(315) 426-9745 ..Zehe, Theresa M '97 %MA Bjork -300 S State -1 Park Pl
-Syracuse, NY 13202 Fx:426-0700

(440) 942-6267 ..Zeid, Gary D '75 (Sternberg & Z Co,LPA) -7547 Mentor Av
-Mentor 44060 Fx:942-6504

(614) 224-9221 ..Zeidan, Georges S '02 Bloomfield & K -199 S 5th
-Columbus 43215

(614) 783-6479 ..Zeidan, Tariq H '04 Zeidan Lgl Srvcs LLC -2649 N High -Ste A
-Columbus 43202

Zeiger, Eric N '91 -(Address Unavailable)

(614) 365-9900 ..Zeiger, John W '72 (Zeiger TL&L,LLP) -41 S High -Ste
3500 Huntngtn Ctr -Columbus 43215 Fx:365-7900

(614) 365-9900 ..Zeiger, Matthew S '02 %Zeiger TL&L,LLP -41 S High -Ste 3500
Huntngtn Ctr -Columbus 43215 Fx:365-7900

(216) 689-4126 ..Zeiger, Richard G '82 KeyBank NA -127 Pub Sq -2nd Fl
-Cleveland 44114

(614) 365-9900 ..Zeiger Tigges Little & Lindsmith, LLP -41 S High
-Ste 3500 Huntngtn Ctr -Columbus 43215 Fx:365-7900

(740) 387-0900 ..Zeigler, Fredrick S '69 (Spohn S&Z) -144 E Center -Marion 43302

(419) 627-0414 ..Zeiher, Kevin J '77 Buckingham LM&Z Co,LPA -414 Wayne
-Bx929 -Sandusky 44870 Fx:627-0009

(513) 794-6515 ..Zeinner, Lawrence A '99 Ohio Natl Financial Srvcs -One Fncl Way
-Cincinnati 45242

(440) 449-9311 ..Zeiser, Daniel G '84 (D Zeiser Co,LPA) -Bx43280
-Cleveland 44143 Fx:449-9311

(419) 468-7766 ..Zeisler, Jeffrey D '93 (Keller Z&M) -659 Hrdng Way W
-Galion 44833

(216) 771-4050 ..Zelasko, Bradford D '78 %Jeffries KF&M Co,LPA
-101 W Prospect Av -1650 Mdlnd Bldg -Cleveland 44115
Fx:771-0732

(614) 464-6400 ..Zelasko, Gregory J '81 Vorys SS&P LLP -52 E Gay -Bx1008
-Columbus 43215 Fx:464-6350

Zeldin, Laura Sue '94 -7558 King Goerge Dr -New Albany 43054

(440) 602-5120 ..Zele, Ronald J '71 (Zele & Z Co,LPA) -35350 Curtis Blvd -#330
-Eastlake 44095 Fx:602-5124

(440) 602-5120 ..Zele, Scott J '98 (Zele & Z Co,LPA) -35350 Curtis Blvd -#330
-Eastlake 44095 Fx:602-5124

(440) 602-5120 ..Zele, Zachary F '03 (Zele & Z Co,LPA) -35350 Curtis Blvd -#330
-Eastlake 44095 Fx:602-5124

Zelizer, Carol A '77 -2374 Bexley Park Rd -Bexley 43209

(740) 397-5262 ..Zelkowitz Barry & Cullers -121 E High -Mount Vernon 43050
Zell, Jonathan R '86 -(Address Unavailable)

(740) 452-8439 ..Zellar, Crystal I '87 (Zellar & Z Inc) -720 Market -Bx2172
-Zanesville 43702

(614) 462-3555 ..Zeller, Jeanne M '03 Franklin Cnty Pros -373 S High
-Columbus 43215

(216) 621-2300 ..Zeller, Robert S '85 Nurenberg PH&M LPA -1370 Ontario -Ste 100
-Cleveland 44113 Fx:771-2242

(330) 337-4820 ..Zellers, Christopher B '93 (Zellers Law Ofcs) -585 E State
-Salem 44460

(213) 430-3400 ..**Zellers**, Michael C '80 (Tucker E&W LLP) -725 S Figueroa
-Ste 3400 -Los Angeles, CA 90017

(330) 702-0780 ..**Zellers**, Richard G '74 (Luckhart MZ&R) -3810 Starrs Centre Dr
-Canfield 44406

(216) 444-2340 ..**Zellmer**, Ann E '79 Cleveland Clinic Fndtn -9500 Euclid Av
-Cleveland 44195

(216) 348-5400 ..**Zellmer**, Charles B '72 (McDonald H Co,LPA) -600 Superior Av E
-Ste 2100 -Cleveland 44114 **Fx:**348-5474

(216) 621-0150 ..**Zellner**, Richard A '67 Cnsl Hahn L&P LLP
-3300 BP Twr/200 Pub Sq -Ste 3300 -Cleveland 44114
Fx:241-2824

(212) 857-8802 ..**Zelnar-Kelly**, Melissa L '04 US Ct of Appeals-2nd Cir -40 Foley Sq
-New York, NY 10007

(419) 625-6955 ..**Zelvy**, Robert '69 (R Zelvy & Assoc) -158 E Market -Ste 606
-Sandusky 44870 **Fx:**625-7334

Zemanek, Matthew L '04 -(Address Unavailable)

(216) 787-3030 ..**Zemba**, Mark J '86 Atty Gen -615 W Superior Av -11th Fl
-Cleveland 44113 **Fx:**787-3480

(615) 284-2653 ..**Zembar**, Stephanie A '84 Baptist Healing Hosp Trust
-1919 Charlotte Av -Ste 320 -Nashville, TN 37203 **Fx:**284-2683

(412) 281-4541 ..**Zemel**, Mitchel B '03 %Weber GSSR -2 Gtwy Ctr -14th Fl
-Pittsburgh, PA 15222

(330) 364-6553 ..**Zemis**, Kristin R '93 %Black MHD&B -130 W 3rd -Bx2330
-Dover 44622 **Fx:**364-2739

(419) 242-7415 ..**Zemmelman**, Connie F '82 (Britz & Z) -416 N Erie -Ste 100
-Toledo 43624 **Fx:**241-7818

(330) 629-9030 ..**Zena**, Thomas E '72 -1032 Boardman-Canfld Rd
-Youngstown 44512 **Fx:**629-9036

(216) 623-0150 ..**Zenkewicz**, Kristine R '02 %Roetzel & A,LPA -1375 E 9th
-One Cleve Ctr 9th Fl -Cleveland 44114 **Fx:**623-0134

(216) 443-9000 ..**Zepp**, Charles W '97 %Porter WM&A LLP -925 Euclid Av
-Ste 1700 -Cleveland 44115 **Fx:**443-9011

(440) 323-3334 ..**Zerbini**, Elio P '65 -315 Middle Av -Elyria 44035

(513) 651-6800 ..**Zerbst**, Hilla M '78 (Frost BT LLC) -201 E 5th -2200 PNC Ctr
-Cincinnati 45202 **Fx:**651-6981

(513) 627-2885 ..**Zerby**, Kim W '84 Procter & Gamble Co -11810 E Miami Rvr Rd
-Bx538707 -Cincinnati 45253

(419) 673-8188 ..**Zerby**, Ryan A '97 -28 N Main -Kenton 43326

(330) 762-0280 ..**Zerebniak**, Harry M '83 -7 W Bowery -10th Fl -Akron 44308

Zerefos, James N '85 -395 Powderhorn Dr -Monument, CO 80132

(330) 836-5500 ..**Zerrusen**, Kenneth M '99 Aronson & Assoc -3085 W Market
-Ste 130 -Akron 44333

(614) 723-2017 ..**Zervas**, John A '89 (Roetzel & A,LPA) -155 E Broad -Natl City Ctr
12th Fl -Columbus 43215 **Fx:**463-9792

(412) 394-2565 ..**Zeszutek**, C James '96 (Thorp R&A,LLP) -301 Grant -14th Fl
-Pittsburgh, PA 15219 **Fx:**394-2555

(614) 462-2244 ..**Zets**, Brian M '96 %Schottenstein Z&D -250 West -Bx165020
-Columbus 43215 **Fx:**462-5135

(513) 868-3740 ..**Zettler**, Jack A '77 -15 N 3rd -Hamilton 45011

(614) 276-5263 ..**Zettler**, Lois A '85 Bishop Ready High Sch -707 Salisbury
-Columbus 43204

(216) 771-0270 ..**Zetzer**, Paul M '83 -614 W Superior Av -Ste 804 Rckfllr Bldg
-Cleveland 44113

(859) 371-3600 ..**Zevely**, Wilbur M '72 Busald FZ -226 Main -Bx6910
-Florence, KY 41022

(614) 462-3555 ..**Zeyen**, David F '97 Franklin Cnty Pros -373 S High
-Columbus 43215

(419) 865-1251 ..**Zhang**, Fan '99 Wagoner & S,Ltd -7445 Airport Hwy
-Holland 43528 **Fx:**866-8798

(954) 983-6176 ..**Zhou**, Linfeng '92 (L Zhou,PA) -3107 Stirling Rd -Ste 106
-Fort Lauderdale, FL 33312 **Fx:**983-7198

(330) 665-5117 ..**Ziance**, Christopher E '02 %Witschey & W Co,LPA
-300 N Cleveland-Missillon Rd -Ste 104 -Akron 44333

(614) 464-6400 ..**Ziance**, Scott J '97 (Vorys SS&P LLP) -52 E Gay -Bx1008
-Columbus 43216 **Fx:**464-6350

(330) 499-6000 ..**Ziarko**, Andrea K '01 %Baker DBW&M -400 S Main
-Canton 44720 **Fx:**449-6423

(212) 953-6633 ..**Zibas**, Jura C '91 OfCnsl Cox PS&S LLP -630 3rd Av -19th Fl
-New York, NY 10017 **Fx:**949-6943

(614) 221-9100 ..**Zibners**, Amanda K '01 %Stein C & Assoc LLC -32 W Hoster
-Ste 200 -Columbus 43215 **Fx:**221-9272

(614) 221-9100 ..**Zibners**, Harry '03 OfCnsl Stein C & Assoc LLC -32 W Hoster
-Ste 200 -Columbus 43215 **Fx:**221-9272

(216) 664-2577 ..**Ziccardi**, Robert P '81 Cleveland Mun Ct -1200 Ontario
-Cleveland 44113

(440) 225-0500 ..**Ziccarelli**, Mark A '79 (Gibson BZ&M) -8353 Mentor Av
-Mentor 44060 **Fx:**225-8426

(216) 787-3030 ..**Zidar**, Michael J '88 Atty Gen -615 W Superior Av -11th Fl
-Cleveland 44113 **Fx:**787-3480

(440) 930-8096 ..**Zidar**, Rachelle K '96 Wickens HPC&B -35765 Chester Rd
-Avon 44011 **Fx:**937-4466

(216) 781-1212 ..**Zidek**, Susan M '92 %Walter & H LLP -1301 E 9th -Ste 3500
-Cleveland 44114 **Fx:**575-0911

(216) 621-0150 ..**Ziegler**, Ann C '03 %Hahn L&P LLP -3300 BP Twr/200 Pub Sq
-Ste 3300 -Cleveland 44114 **Fx:**241-2824

(330) 872-7776 ..**Ziegler**, Charles A '80 -127 N Canal -Unit B -Newton Falls 44444

(330) 376-5756 ..**Ziegler**, Deborah A '85 Emershaw M&S -120 E Mill -#437 -Akron
44308 **Fx:**762-5980

(614) 481-9325 ..**Ziegler**, Edward J '02 Card Fact,Ltd -2396 Andvr Rd
-Columbus 43221 **Fx:**481-9326

(614) 228-9550 ..**Ziegler**, Elaine K '01 %Javitch B&R -33 N 3rd -Ste 300
-Columbus 43215 **Fx:**228-2818

(740) 779-6662 ..**Ziegler**, Lisa E '02 4th Dist Ct of Appeals -14 S Paint -Ste 38
-Chillicothe 45601

(216) 781-5470 ..**Ziegler Metzger & Miller LLP** -925 Euclid Av
-2020 Huntngtn Bldg -Cleveland 44115 **Fx:**781-0714

(440) 352-3003 ..**Ziegler Metzger & Miller LLP** -152 Main -Painesville 44077
Fx:354-3299

(216) 360-9000 ..**Ziegler Metzger & Miller LLP** -30100 Chagrin Blvd -Ste 301
-Pepper Pike 44122 **Fx:**360-0303

(614) 466-1305 ..**Ziegler**, Michael S '89 Atty Gen -30 E Broad -Columbus 43215
Fx:466-8898

(216) 621-9870 ..**Ziegler**, Paul W '71 (McNeal SA&B Co,LPA) -123 W Prospect Av
-Ste 250 Van Sweringen Arcade -Cleveland 44115 **Fx:**522-1112

(440) 543-5313 ..**Ziegler**, Richard P '75 -17800 Chillicothe Rd -Bainbrdg Cmmns
Ste 270 -Chagrin Falls 44023

(513) 271-0053 ..**Ziegler**, Thomas F '95 -6506 Kenwood Rd -Cincinnati 45243

(859) 426-1300 ..**Ziegler**, Wilbert L '56 (Ziegler & S,PSC) -541 Buttermilk Pike
-Ste 500 -Bx175710 -Covington, KY 41017

(216) 348-1700 ..**Ziehm**, Ronald J '91 %Davis & Y -101 Prospect Av W -Ste 1700
-Cleveland 44115 **Fx:**621-0602

(440) 395-0246 ..**Zielaskiewicz**, Joshua M '03 Progressive Ins Co -300 N Cmmns
Blvd -OHF 11 -Mayfield Village 44143

(216) 363-1400 ..**Zielinski**, Deborah D '00 %Buckley K,LPA -600 E Superior Av
-Ste 1400 -Cleveland 44114 **Fx:**363-1401

(330) 468-0700 ..**Zielinski**, Richard J '95 Patio Enclosures Inc -750 E Highland Rd
-Macedonia 44056

(216) 676-9185 ..**Zielinski**, Vernon J '83 -6068 Middlebrook Blvd -Brook Park 44142

(330) 533-6821 ..**Zielke**, Larry A '79 -73 N Broad -Canfield 44406

(616) 787-1303 ..**Ziemke**, William H '89 Alticor,Inc -7575 Fulton -Ada, MI 49355

(740) 383-4795 ..**Ziercher**, Mark C '96 -317 S Main -Marion 43302

(513) 579-7900 ..**Ziermaier**, Klaus M '70 Federated Dept Stores,Inc -7 W 7th
-Cincinnati 45202

(616) 392-1821 ..**Zietlow**, Mark H '79 (Cunningham D,PC) -321 Sttlrs Rd -Bx1767
-Holland 49422

(330) 733-6291 ..**Ziga**, Timothy P '83 ASW Srvcs Inc -3375 Gilchrist Rd
-Mogadore 44260

(216) 664-2814 ..**Zigli**, William T '85 Dept of Law -601 Lakeside Av
-Rm 106 City Hall -Cleveland 44114 **Fx:**664-2663

(513) 241-9400 ..**Zigman**, Andrea K '95 Legal Aid -215 E 9th -Ste 200
-Cincinnati 45202

(419) 244-3006 ..**Zigray**, Daniel F '91 (Kolb & Z) -405 Mad Av -Ste 2000
-Toledo 43604 **Fx:**246-4754

(614) 241-5550 ..**Zikas**, J Michael II '83 OfCnsl Brunner Law Firm Co,LPA
-545 E Town -Columbus 43215 **Fx:**241-5551

(419) 255-1515 ..**Zilba**, Jeffrey C '87 (Zilba & Assoc) -5 Canton Sq -Toledo 43624

(440) 248-4200 ..**Zilich**, George J '04 BPI Incustries,Inc -30775 Bainbrdg Rd
-Ste 280 -Solon 44139

(614) 224-1979 ..**Zilka**, Heather R '99 -592 S 3rd -Columbus 43215

(614) 644-3037 ..**Zima**, Bryan F '86 EPA -122 S Front -Bx1049 -Columbus 43216

(419) 841-1411 ..**Zima**, John P '87 -7014 Mourning Dove Ct -Toledo 43617
Fx:843-7176

(513) 721-1513 ..**Zimmer**, Barry H '79 Zimmer Law Firm,LLC -4540 Cooper Rd
-Ste 300 -Cincinnati 45242 **Fx:**287-8623

(513) 352-3321 ..**Zimmer**, Christine M '84 Law Dept -801 Plum -Rm 214
-Cincinnati 45202 **Fx:**352-1515

(614) 466-0750 ..**Zimmer**, Dale A '78 SERB -65 E State -Ste 1200
-Columbus 43215 **Fx:**466-3074

(216) 586-3939 ..**Zimmer**, David O '99 Jones D -901 Lakeside Av -Cleveland 44114
Fx:579-0212

Zimmer, Fred P '58 -6072 Star Mesa Dr -Frisco, TX 75034

Zimmer, Frederick C '59 -306 Tournament Trl -Cortland 44410

(513) 852-8200 ..**Zimmer**, Hans M '84 Cors & B LLC -537 E Pete Rose Way
-Ste 400 -Cincinnati 45202

(614) 462-3194 ..**Zimmer**, Osias D '88 Franklin Cnty Pub Def -373 S High -12th Fl
-Columbus 43215

(937) 512-1550 ..**Zimmer**, Patricia A '84 US Cts/SD OH -200 W 2nd -902 Fed Bldg
-Dayton 45402

(937) 223-1130 ..**Zimmer**, Paul E '73 Pickrel S&E -40 N Main -2700 Kettering Twr
-Dayton 45423 **Fx:**223-0339

(937) 255-5270 ..**Zimmerle**, Sandra G '84 AFMCLO/JAN -1864 4th -Rm 130A
-Wright Patterson AFB 45433

(330) 454-8056 ..**Zimmerman**, Brian L '89 -236 3rd SW -Canton 44702

(216) 291-2400 ..**Zimmerman Caticchio Eisenberg & Modica** -5001 Mayfld Rd
-Ste 105 -Cleveland 44124

(937) 322-1921 ..**Zimmerman**, Charles B Jr. '58 -10 S Spring -Springfield 45502

(216) 443-7800 ..**Zimmerman**, David M '87 Cuyahoga Cnty Pros -1200 Ontario
-8th Fl -Cleveland 44113 **Fx:**698-2270

Zimmerman, Deborah J '04 -(Address Unavailable)

(330) 364-1614 ..**Zimmerman**, Donald B '78 Fitzpatrick Z&R Co LPA
-140 Fair NW -Bx1014 -New Philadelphia 44663 **Fx:**343-3077

(513) 232-0846 ..**Zimmerman**, Donald J '61 Zimmerman Consulting -5616 Shady
Hllw Ln -Cincinnati 45230

(330) 364-1614 ..**Zimmerman**, Donald W '51 Fitzpatrick Z&R Co LPA
-140 Fair NW -Bx1014 -New Philadelphia 44663 **Fx:**343-3077

(513) 831-3373 ..**Zimmerman**, Elizabeth W '92 (Thomson & Z Co,LPA)
-400 TechneCenter Dr -Ste 400 -Milford 45150 **Fx:**831-3402

(937) 294-9684 ..**Zimmerman**, George E '55 -736 W Stroop Rd -Kettering 45429

(513) 381-2838 ..**Zimmerman**, James M '99 %Taft S&H LLP -425 Walnut -Ste 1800
-Cincinnati 45202 **Fx:**381-0205

(216) 696-3525 ..**Zimmerman**, Katherine Ann '92 Cleveland Bar Assn -1301 E 9th
-Ste BU620 -Cleveland 44114 **Fx:**696-2413

(614) 839-5700 ..**Zimmerman**, Kevin J '99 %E Hollern Co,LPA -51 Drchster Ln
-Westerville 43081 **Fx:**839-4200

(216) 696-3311 ..**Zimmerman**, Robert A '91 (Kahn K) -1301 E 9th -2600 Erievw Twr
-Cleveland 44114 **Fx:**623-4912

(419) 531-4544 ..**Zimmerman**, Roger K '79 -2735 N Holland Sylvania Rd -Ste A-2
-Toledo 43615

(330) 762-7477 ..**Zimmerman**, Terry D '75 (Hardesty K&Z) -520 S Main -Ste 500
-Akron 44311 **Fx:**762-8059

(419) 248-2600 ..**Zimmerman**, Todd M '97 (Rohrbachers LC&T Co,LPA)
-405 Mad Av -8th Fl -Toledo 43604 **Fx:**248-2614

(937) 492-1969 ..**Zimmerman**, William R '79 Shelby Cnty Pub Def -108 E Poplar
-Sidney 45365

(614) 241-2227 ..**Zimmers**, Neal F Jr. '67 -37 W Broad -Columbus 43215

(216) 363-4500 ..**Zimon**, Jeffrey D '92 (Benesch FC&A LLP) -200 Pub Sq -Ste 2300
-Cleveland 44114 **Fx:**363-4588

Zimon, Jill M '92 -(Address Unavailable)

(740) 653-8866 ..**Zimpfer**, George F '41 -109 E Main -Lancaster 43130

(330) 864-4093 ..**Zindle**, Charles W '70 -4947 Coleman Dr -Akron 44319

(216) 696-7170 ..**Zingale**, Salvatore A '66 -700 Rckfllr Bldg -614 Superior Av NW
-Cleveland 44113

(770) 521-2627 ..**Zingales**, Anthony M '91 Ryder Trnsprtn -6000 Windward Pkwy
-Alpharetta, GA 30005

(440) 232-3420 ..**Zingales**, Joseph A '52 Bedford Mun Ct -65 Columbus Rd -Bedford 44146

(440) 461-3600 ..**Zingales**, Joseph D '76 -6009 Landerhaven Dr -#C-1 -Cleveland 44124 **Fx:**461-4525

(937) 227-3700 ..**Zink**, Julie E '99 %Faruki I&C PLL -10 N Ludlow -500 Cthse Plz SW -Dayton 45402 **Fx:**227-3717

(330) 492-2225 ..**Zink**, Larry A '75 (Zink Z&Z Co,LPA) -3711 Whipple Av NW -Canton 44718 **Fx:**492-3956

(216) 621-1113 ..**Zink**, Marisa J '01 %Renner OB&S,LLP -1621 Euclid Av -19th Fl -Cleveland 44115 **Fx:**621-6165

(419) 332-5579 ..**Zinkand**, John L '69 -211 S Park Av -Fremont 43420

(419) 241-1200 ..**Zinz**, Marguerite A '01 %Cooper & W,LPA -900 Adams -Toledo 43624 **Fx:**242-5675

(213) 250-1800 ..**Zipkin**, Judith A '98 (Lewis BB&S LLP) -221 N Figueroa -Ste 1200 -Los Angeles, CA 90012

(216) 514-6400 ..**Zipkin**, Lewis A '64 (Zipkin W Co LPA) -3637 S Green Rd -Zipkin Whiting Bldg -Cleveland 44122 **Fx:**514-6406

(216) 514-6400 ..**Zipkin Whiting Co LPA** -3637 S Green Rd -Zipkin Whiting Bldg -Cleveland 44122 **Fx:**514-6406

(937) 228-2666 ..**Zipperstein**, Irvin J '49 IJ Zipperstein Co,LPA -118 W 1st -Ste 650 -Dayton 45402 **Fx:**228-0508

(216) 689-7370 ..**Zirke**, Christopher J '02 Key Bank -2025 Ontario Av -MC OH 01 00 0705 -Cleveland 44115

(216) 664-4820 ..**Zirke**, Heather M '02 Prosecutor -1200 Ontario Av -8th Fl Justice Ctr -Cleveland 44113 **Fx:**664-4399

(216) 781-1212 ..**Zirm**, Kenneth A '84 (Walter & H LLP) -1301 E 9th -Ste 3500 -Cleveland 44114 **Fx:**575-0911

(330) 456-8389 ..**Zirpolo**, Michael P Jr. '75 -1101 Bk One Twr -Canton 44702

(614) 249-9344 ..**Zisser**, Steven L '83 Cnsl Nationwide Ins Co -1 Nationwide Plz -Columbus 43215

(614) 799-9494 ..**Zitesman**, James A '93 -5701 Springburn Dr -Dublin 43017

(216) 961-3521 ..**Zitiello**, Rose A '93 Cleveland Dept of Comm Dvlpmnt -1255 W 69th -Cleveland 44102

(312) 427-2737 ..**Zito**, Anthony S Jr. '67 John Marshall Law Schl -315 S Plymouth Ct -Chicago, IL 60604

(440) 816-1877 ..**Zito**, Maureen F '86 -7530 Lucerne Dr -#200 -Middleburg Heights 44130 **Fx:**

(313) 965-7905 ..**Zitterman**, Susan H '91 %Kitch DWD&V -1 Woodward Av -10th Fl -Detroit, MI 48226

(216) 241-2838 ..**Zix**, Timothy L '91 (Taft S&H LLP) -200 Pub Sq -3500 BP Twr -Cleveland 44114 **Fx:**241-3707

(216) 787-5180 ..**Zlojutro**, Milutin '88 Industrial Commssn of OH -615 Superior Av NW -Cleveland 44113 **Fx:**787-3483

(702) 388-6336 ..**Zlotnick**, Howard J '78 US Atty -333 Las Veg Blvd S -Ste 5000 -Las Vegas, NV 89101

(440) 285-2242 ..**Znidarsic**, Joseph R '76 Thrasher D&D,LPA -100 7th Av -Ste 150 -Chardon 44024 **Fx:**285-9423

(216) 781-0004 ..**Zobec**, Frankee T '81 -1616 Standard Bldg -Cleveland 44113

..**Zochowski**, Myra M '02 -9570 Refugee Rd SW -Pataskala 43062

(216) 621-6138 ..**Zocolo**, Lori Ann '98 %Abel & Z,LPA -815 Superior Av -The Superior Bldg Ste 1915 -Cleveland 44114 **Fx:**241-5620

(440) 746-1177 ..**Zoeckler**, John P '99 %Baran PTF&T Co,LPA -8748 Brecksvll Rd -Ste 200 -Cleveland 44141 **Fx:**746-9637

(216) 222-2978 ..**Zoeller**, David L '82 Natl City Corp -1900 E 9th -Law Dept Loc 01-2174 -Bx5756 -Cleveland 44101

(202) 783-0800 ..**Zogg**, Sara P '04 %Howrey SA&W,LLP -1299 Penn Av NW -Washington, DC 20004 **Fx:**383-6610

(419) 352-8844 ..**Zografides**, Christopher A '00 %TA Pomeroy -113 N Main -Bowling Green 43402 **Fx:**352-8833

(734) 741-8750 ..**Zohar**, Wendy J '96 -2760 Gladstone Av -Ann Arbor, MI 48104

(216) 991-6914 ..**Zohn**, Patrick M '78 -3144 Huntngtn Rd -Shaker Heights 44120

(614) 227-2000 ..**Zola**, George E '85 OfCnsl Porter WM&A LLP -41 S High -Columbus 43215 **Fx:**227-2100

(216) 921-8627 ..**Zolich**, Jason '70 -3188 Chadbourne Rd -Shaker Heights 44120

(419) 841-9623 ..**Zoll**, David W '77 (Zoll & K) -6620 W Central Av -Ste 200 -Toledo 43617

(419) 841-9623 ..**Zoll & Kranz** -6620 W Central Av -Ste 200 -Toledo 43617

(216) 696-3311 ..**Zoller**, Elizabeth M '01 %Kahn K -1301 E 9th -2600 Erievw Twr -Cleveland 44114 **Fx:**623-4912

(216) 241-2200 ..**Zoller**, John D '86 (Zoller & S) -812 Huron Rd -Caxton Bldg, Ste 490 -Cleveland 44115

(216) 621-3251 ..**Zoller**, Nancy A '87 %Gurney M&M -75 Pub Sq -Ste 525 -Cleveland 44113 **Fx:**621-1332

(404) 335-6535 ..**Zoller**, Norman E '75 US Ct of Appeals/11th Circ -56 Forsyth -Atlanta, GA 30303

(216) 241-2200 ..**Zoller & Scholl** -812 Huron Rd -Caxton Bldg, Ste 490 -Cleveland 44115

(330) 497-2886 ..**Zollinger D'Atri Gruber Thomas & Co** -6370 Mt Plsnt NW -Bx2985 -Canton 44720

(330) 526-0104 ..**Zollinger**, Frederick H III '94 (Zollinger & B Ltd) -Bx2368 -Canton 44720 **Fx:**(866) 311-9964

(330) 497-2886 ..**Zollinger**, Frederick H Jr. '73 (Zollinger DGT & Co) -6370 Mt Plsnt NW -Bx2985 -Canton 44720

(330) 455-0173 ..**Zollinger**, Richard C Jr. '99 %Day KRW&R,Ltd -200 Market Av N -Ste 300 -Bx24213 -Canton 44701 **Fx:**455-2633

(614) 466-0212 ..**Zollinger**, Sue A '04 %Atty Gen -150 E Gay -Columbus 43215

..**Zolman**, Courtney L '99 -294 Twp Rd 1076 -South Point 45680

(419) 872-6070 ..**Zoltanski**, Edward F '58 -Bx84 -Monclova 43542

(330) 744-5211 ..**Zomoida**, John N Jr. '00 %Roth BRS&L,LPA -100 Fed Plz E -Ste 600 -Youngstown 44503 **Fx:**744-3184

(440) 888-9933 ..**Zomparelli**, Gino '89 -7900 Pearl Rd -Middleburg Heights 44130

(330) 836-4181 ..**Zona-Peters**, Anita '93 -Bx5924 -Akron 44372

..**Zonak**, Irene S '83 -1425 Kingsgate Rd -Columbus 43221

(330) 499-1016 ..**Zondorak**, Lynn A '03 OfCnsl Herbert & B -4571 Stephen Cir NW -Canton 44718 **Fx:**499-0790

(216) 736-6242 ..**Zontini**, John M '84 The East OH Gas Co -1717 E 9th -Cleveland 44114

..**Zore**, Ernest F '78 -645 McKee Trl -Hinckley 44233

(614) 462-3221 ..**Zorn**, James E Sr. '88 Franklin Cnty Children Srvcs -855 W Mound -Columbus 43223 **Fx:**275-2589

(513) 946-9000 ..**Zorn**, Philip L Jr. '73 Hamilton Cnty Dom Rltns Ct -800 Bway -2nd Fl -Cincinnati 45202

(513) 737-9770 ..**Zornow**, Harry B '84 -860 NW Wshngtn Blvd -Ste J -Hamilton 45013

(412) 281-8000 ..**Zotter**, John W '88 Zimmer K,PLLC -600 Grant -Pittsburgh, PA 15219

(419) 247-2500 ..**Zouhary**, Jack '76 OfCnsl Fuller & H,Ltd -One SeaGate -Ste 1700 -Bx2088 -Toledo 43603 **Fx:**247-2665

(419) 893-5908 ..**Zouhary**, Kathleen M '76 St Lukes Hosp -5901 Monclova -Maumee 43537

(614) 462-2216 ..**Zox**, Benjamin L '62 OfCnsl Schottenstein Z&D -250 West -Bx165020 -Columbus 43216 **Fx:**462-5135

(614) 462-2241 ..**Zox**, Melissa L '90 OfCnsl Schottenstein Z&D -250 West -Bx165020 -Columbus 43216 **Fx:**462-5135

(614) 255-3333 ..**Zox**, William P '92 Diamond Hill Cap Mngmnt -375 N Front -Ste 300 -Columbus 43215

(419) 882-4546 ..**Zraik**, Thomas G '64 -5558 Bent Oak Rd -Sylvania 43560

(419) 882-2559 ..**Zraik**, Thomas J '77 Zraik & Assoc -5579 Monroe -Sylvania 43560

..**Zrenda**, Anne Phillips '04 -(Address Unavailable)

(614) 263-4299 ..**Zuber**, Joan E '57 -4710 Scenic Dr -Columbus 43214

(614) 486-8052 ..**Zuber**, Thomas J '58 -1487 W 5th Av PMB 118 -Columbus 43212

..**Zubricky**, Douglas J '03 -5702 Westlake Av -Parma 44129

(216) 241-2500 ..**Zucco**, George C '64 (Monroe & Z) -526 Superior Av -Ste 1525 -Cleveland 44114

(216) 566-8711 ..**Zucco**, Jeff T '71 -1370 Ontario Av -Ste 1200 -Cleveland 44113

(440) 255-2421 ..**Zuch**, Frederic L '72 Mentor Hts Nursery Ltd -7343 Chillicothe Rd -Mentor 44060

(440) 247-5665 ..**Zucker**, Dale P '74 D Zucker Co,LPA -512 E Wshngtn -Chagrin Falls 44022

(513) 241-7111 ..**Zucker**, Elizabeth M '92 O'Connor A&L Co,LPA -1014 Vine -22nd Fl -Cincinnati 45202 **Fx:**241-7197

..**Zuckerman**, Laura U '78 -(Address Unavailable)

(440) 646-9218 ..**Zuckerman**, Richard '71 R Zuckerman Co,LPA -5317 Golfway Ln -Lyndhurst 44124

(330) 726-6404 ..**Zuckerman**, Zvi A '91 Cnsl Zuckerman Properties -7880 Market -Bx3106 -Boardman 44513

(662) 342-1333 ..**Zuefle**, Howard M Jr. '77 (Holland & Z) -3040 Goodman Rd W -Horn Lake, MS 38637

(419) 841-6786 ..**Zugay**, Anthony A Jr. '70 -Bx23232 -Toledo 43623

(937) 890-1739 ..**Zugelder**, Mark A '82 -7825 N Dixie Dr -Ste A -Dayton 45414

(513) 752-2338 ..**Zugelter**, Carl W '75 -1285 W Ohio Pike -Amelia 45102

(818) 769-3411 ..**Zugelter**, Frank L '58 -10109 Toluca Lk Av -North Hollywood, CA 91602 **Fx:**769-3411

(330) 666-6900 ..**Zugrave**, George V Jr. '87 -310 N Cleveland-Massillon Rd -Akron 44333

(937) 332-7084 ..**Zuhl**, Gary E '76 Miami Cnty Mun Ct -201 W Main -Troy 45373

(216) 931-6000 ..**Zujkowski**, Melissa L '04 %Ulmer & B LLP -1300 E 9th -Ste 900 Penton Media Bldg -Cleveland 44114 **Fx:**931-6001

(614) 228-5781 ..**Zuk**, Nicholas W '78 White Castle Mngmnt Co -Bx1498 -Columbus 43216

(513) 752-1300 ..**Zuk**, Walter K '72 WK Zuk Co,LPA -325 W Ohio Pike -Amelia 45102

(216) 696-0900 ..**Zukerman Daiker & Lear, LPA** -2000 E 9th -Ste 700 -Cleveland 44115 **Fx:**696-8800

(216) 696-0900 ..**Zukerman**, Larry W '85 (Zukerman D&L,LPA) -2000 E 9th -Ste 700 -Cleveland 44115 **Fx:**696-8800

(937) 449-2800 ..**Zukowsky**, Philip A '85 (Chernesky H&K PLL) -10 Cthse Plz SW -Ste 1100 -Dayton 45402 **Fx:**449-2821

(216) 931-6000 ..**Zulandt**, Robert E III '99 %Ulmer & B LLP -1300 E 9th -Ste 900 Penton Media Bldg -Cleveland 44114 **Fx:**931-6001

(440) 286-6177 ..**Zulandt**, Robert E Jr. '73 (Zulandt & S) -114 E Park -Chardon 44024 **Fx:**286-6158

(440) 286-6177 ..**Zulandt & Smalheer** -114 E Park -Chardon 44024 **Fx:**286-6158

(216) 771-1111 ..**Zullig**, Olga Y '99 %Wojnar & Assoc -1370 Ontario -Ste 1100 Standard Bldg -Cleveland 44113

(330) 821-2516 ..**Zumbar**, Andrew L '92 (Lundgren G&Z) -526 E Main -Bx2595 -Alliance 44601

(330) 376-2700 ..**Zumkehr**, Charles E '64 OfCnsl Roetzel & A,LPA -222 S Main -Akron 44308 **Fx:**376-4577

(513) 381-0656 ..**Zummo**, Mark J '80 (Kohnen & P LLP) -201 E 5th -Ste 800 -Cincinnati 45202 **Fx:**381-5823

(513) 946-6065 ..**Zummo**, Valerie B '82 Hamilton Cnty Domstc Relatns Ct -800 Bway -Rm 3-001 -Cincinnati 45202

(614) 224-8511 ..**Zunshine**, Zach '91 -35 E Lvngstn Av -Columbus 43215

(216) 443-8650 ..**Zunt**, Monica C '92 -1200 Ontario -11th Flr-Staff Attys -Cleveland 44113

(216) 813-6847 ..**Zupan**, John F '92 KeyCorp -4900 Teideman Rd -OH-01-49-0229 -Brooklyn 44144

(330) 425-1477 ..**Zupon**, Janice E '92 Heartland Insulation -8272 Bavaria Rd -Macedonia 44056

(330) 497-0700 ..**Zurakowski**, Scott M '98 %Krugliak WG&D Co,LPA -4775 Munson NW -Bx36963 -Canton 44735 **Fx:**497-4020

(614) 866-3411 ..**Zuravsky**, Marvin A '91 -1255 Hill Rd N -Ste #102 -Pickerington 43147

..**Zurbrugg**, Aaron J '04 -(Address Unavailable)

(614) 229-3888 ..**Zury**, James C '95 Cheek & Z,LLP -471 E Broad -18th Fl -Bx15069 -Columbus 43215 **Fx:**241-5865

(330) 253-3337 ..**Zurz**, Richard V '53 Blakemore M&B Co,LPA -19 N High -Akron 44308 **Fx:**253-4131

(330) 762-0700 ..**Zurz**, Richard V Jr. '82 (Slater Z&G) -One Cascade Plz -Ste 2210 -Akron 44308 **Fx:**762-3923

(330) 652-1609 ..**Zuzolo**, Christopher P '93 (Zuzolo Z&Z) -700 Youngstown-Warren Rd -Niles 44446 **Fx:**652-9421

(330) 652-1609 ..**Zuzolo**, Ralph A '68 (Zuzolo Z&Z) -700 Youngstown-Warren Rd -Niles 44446 **Fx:**652-9421

(330) 652-1609 ..**Zuzolo**, Ralph A Jr. '95 (Zuzolo Z&Z) -700 Youngstown-Warren Rd -Niles 44446 **Fx:**652-9421

(216) 443-8577 ..**Zvomuya**, Katherine Sommers '03 Cuyahoga Cnty Ct Cmmn Pleas -1200 Ontario -Justice Ctr 11th Fl -Cleveland 44113

(330) 375-2730 ..**Zwaig**, Brian J '92 Pros -217 S High -Ste 203 -Akron 44308

..**Zweig**, Bertram R '62 -10345 Olympic Blvd -3rd Fl -Los Angeles, CA 90064

(859) 564-4012 ..**Zweigart**, Robert G '70 (Royse ZK&B) -215 Ct -Maysville, KY 41056

(937) 335-5658 .. **Zweizig,** Jonathan S '98 %Lopez S&P Co,LPA -18 E Water
-Troy 45373 **Fx:**339-6446

Zwick, Coleman D '64 -1792 Beaconwood Av -South Euclid 44121

(216) 781-1212 .. **Zwick,** Gary A '80 (Walter & H LLP) -1301 E 9th -Ste 3500
-Cleveland 44114 **Fx:**575-0911

(330) 452-5781 .. **Zwick,** Leander P III '75 Zwick Law Ofcs -1500 Market Av N
-Bx8409 -Canton 44711

Zwolinski, Rachel L '03 -(Address Unavailable)

(614) 466-5205 .. **Zwyer,** David A '77 OH DD Cncl -8 E Long -12th Fl
-Columbus 43215

(216) 566-5605 .. **Zych,** Thomas F '83 (Thompson H LLP) -127 Pub Sq
-3900 Key Ctr -Cleveland 44114 **Fx:**566-5800

(419) 842-1166 .. **Zychowicz,** Michael J '85 (Borgstahl & Z) -6591 W Central Av
-Ste 201 -Toledo 43617

(419) 213-4700 .. **Zychowicz,** Ralph C '79 %Lucas Cnty Pros -Adams & Erie
-Lucas Cnty Cthse -Toledo 43624

Zydor, Ava A '78 -660 Colonial Av -Pelham Manor, NY 10803

Zygela, Frank I '90 -8408 Brdgnd Ct -Plano, TX 75024

(419) 243-1144 .. **Zyndorf,** Sol '74 (Zyndorf & S) -320 N Mich -2nd Fl -Toledo 43624

(517) 496-6126 .. **Zyskowski,** James C '82 SrCnsl Dow Corning Corp -Bx994
-Midland, MI 48686

This Ohio Bar Directory
is kept up to date all year long.

If changes occur in your listing during the year,
please do not wait until the end of the year to notify us.

Write as soon as you know about a change in your listing.

The Ohio Legal Pages®
Attn: Mary Lurie
P.O. Box 1214
Newark, New Jersey 07101-1214
(800) 444-4041, Ext. 131
Fax (973) 621-9027
Email: mlurie@lawdiary.com
Internet: www.lawdiary.com

2005
OHIO BAR DIRECTORY
CLASSIFIED ACCORDING TO CITIES

Explanatory Note: The date immediately following individual names denotes the year of admission to the Ohio Bar. For further information about these listings please refer to the alphabetical green pages of this volume.

Every effort has been made to obtain accuracy in the listings but the publishers do not guarantee its accuracy. Difficulty is sometimes experienced in securing information as to changes of addresses. In instances where communications requesting address and firm data have elicited no response, the old addresses have been retained without comment.

ABERDEEN
Brown County
(937) 795-0036 **Shaw** Gerald W '69

ADA
Hardin County
(419) 772-2205 **Christoff** John P '77
(419) 772-2205 **Crago** David C '77
(419) 772-1870 **Crider** Cecily A '93
(419) 772-2208 **Evans** William L '71
(419) 634-0481 **Failor** Kenneth G '66
(419) 772-2216 **French** Bruce C '85
(419) 634-0794 **Goodin** David K '03
(419) 634-6646 **Grimslid** Gregory A '81
(419) 634-6646 **Hood** James M '81
Johnson Scott B '04
(419) 634-5791 **McNeal** Jan C '66
(419) 772-1933 **Mittendorf** Allison A '99
(419) 634-6646 **Neville** John B '74
(419) 634-9400 **Previte** Peter A '78
(419) 772-2218 **Sabol** Nancy P '87
(419) 634-3666 **Schulman** Jeffrey M '78
(419) 634-5791 **VanDyne** Charles P '54
(419) 634-4664 **Vaubel** Clarabelle V '71
(419) 772-2225 **Ward** Bryan H '93
(419) 772-2205 **Wells** Mindi L '98
(419) 772-2075 **Woods** Dexter R Jr. '82
(419) 772-2206 **Young** Sherry Ann '84

AKRON
Summit County
Abdoulkarim Abdoul R '74
(330) 865-7722 **Aberth** Joel R '71
(330) 867-0363 **Adair** Delilah A '84
(330) 869-9849 **Adams** Jason T '89
(330) 761-2333 **Adams** Tanzie D '85
(330) 253-7171 **Adamson** Paul F '82
(330) 535-8771 **Adgate** Thomas L '87
(330) 643-7786 **Adkins** Yamini K '93
(330) 666-3833 **Alberti** John Curtis '79
(330) 375-2285 **Albrecht** Sophie E '78
(330) 384-5793 **Alexander** Anthony J '76
(330) 785-3337 **Alexander** John P '01
(330) 376-5300 **Allan** Ronald C '66
(330) 761-4306 **Allison** Paul W '79
(330) 836-2636 **Altier** Mary W '79
(330) 867-6600 **Altwies** Charles J '76
(330) 375-2030 **Ambrose** Patricia C '77
(330) 762-2411 **Amer Cunningham Co,LPA**
(330) 535-6650 **Amourgis** Julius P '98
(330) 375-8349 **Amundsen** Richard S '74
(330) 535-4000 **Anderson** Dreama '90
(330) 535-4000 **Anderson Miller & Lowry**
(330) 253-5060 **Andreeff** Nickolas P '60
(330) 535-1555 **Antoniotti** Erica L '99
Antonuk Theodore E '86
(330) 434-2113 **Armbruster Kelley Kot Honeck & Baker**
(330) 434-2113 **Armbruster** Robert '78
(330) 643-2900 **Armstrong** James W '91
(800) 998-9454 **Arnold** Alanna S '01
(330) 375-8648 **Arnold** Suzanne E '98
(330) 643-2788 **Aronson** Beth E '99
(330) 836-5506 **Aronson** Stanley P '72
(330) 867-2808 **Ashley** Richard W '74
(330) 836-9300 **Askin** William P '98
(330) 864-5916 **Assaf** Timothy P '83
(330) 375-1311 **Atwell** D Cheryl '80
(330) 762-8111 **Axner** Edward A '62
(330) 643-2250 **Aynes** Kathleen S '77
(330) 972-7331 **Aynes** Richard Lee '75
(330) 344-6005 **Babbitt** Craig M '97
(330) 434-3000 **Bach** Lawrence R '84
(330) 535-5711 **Bagga** Rajesh '97
(330) 434-2113 **Baker** Robert C '77
(330) 643-2943 **Ballard** Charmine T '02
(330) 208-1000 **Balmert** F Daniel '76
(330) 643-2788 **Banbury** Michelle L '98
(330) 376-2700 **Bare** Betsy L '04
(330) 535-5711 **Barnes** Heather M '99
(330) 762-6281 **Barrett & Davis**
(330) 687-9605 **Barrett** Gene C '04
(330) 784-8580 **Bartek** Dennis J '71
(330) 535-2151 **Bartilson** Thomas R '04
(330) 643-3550 **Bartko** James J '92
(330) 643-3330 **Bash** Gary M '81
(330) 972-7869 **Bates** Christine R '02
(330) 535-5711 **Battagline** Richard F '70
(330) 849-6500 **Bauer** Roland H '80
(330) 375-5716 **Bauer** Thomas M '72
(330) 253-7171 **Bauer** Thomas M Jr. '01
(330) 376-2700 **Bayer** Cynthia P '04
(330) 384-7305 **Bean** Gregory R '77
(330) 376-2700 **Becker** John W '95
(330) 375-5716 **Becker** Robert J '82
(330) 865-9635 **Bednarski** Holly '03
(330) 434-3000 **Beidler** Craig W '86
(330) 376-5300 **Beistel** Peggy Sue '99
(330) 384-5795 **Beiting** Michael R '85
(330) 535-0505 **Belfance** Eve V '90
(330) 535-0505 **Belfance** Kathryn A '77
(330) 796-9731 **Belfiglio** Ralph A Jr. '84
(330) 796-1818 **Bell** Bertram '76
(330) 535-5711 **Bell** Daniel L '90
(330) 384-3864 **Bell** Mary E '97
(330) 644-5404 **Bell** Robin L '84
(330) 643-2985 **Bennett** Linda M '00
(330) 865-9369 **Bennett** Richard J '84
(330) 535-5711 **Bennett** Timothy D '02
(330) 762-4757 **Benson** Walter J '94
(330) 384-5802 **Benz** Gary D '84
(330) 745-1000 **Berg** Sharon '76
(330) 253-2195 **Berger** Gerald W '75
(330) 376-5300 **Berger** Joshua S '97
(330) 668-7777 **Berk** Robert C '84
(330) 208-1000 **Berke** Aaron S '00
(330) 376-2700 **Bernard** Aretta K '87
(330) 434-1000 **Bernlohr** Mark W '87
(330) 434-1000 **Bernlohr Wertz, LLP**
(330) 376-0000 **Berry** James F '78
(330) 953-7588 **Bertolo** Peter F '86
(330) 376-5300 **Bertsch** David P '78
(330) 643-2946 **Bertsch** Eva K '85
(330) 665-1855 **Best** David M '75
(330) 668-9479 **Bhakuni** Pravin S '04
(330) 375-5716 **Bickett** James L '74
(330) 643-2765 **Bickett** William W II '72
(330) 643-2788 **Biglow** Michael K '02
(330) 972-7302 **Billow** Patricia M '81
(330) 753-6874 **Bishop** Christy B '03
(330) 762-2600 **Bittel** Timothy M '71
(330) 253-3337 **Blakemore Meeker & Bowler Co,LPA**
(330) 384-5431 **Blank** David M '78
(330) 376-1242 **Bobak** Donald J '73
(330) 643-2791 **Bogdanoff** Philip D '81
(330) 384-7306 **Bonchack** Robert M '75
(330) 376-9691 **Bonetti** Albert E Jr. '87
(330) 666-3591 **Bonsky** Jack A '64
(330) 796-6738 **Bordenkircher** Steven C '98
(330) 670-7300 **Borla** Robert B '04
(330) 643-2765 **Boughton** Lisa A '98
(330) 376-5756 **Bower** Terry L '71
(330) 253-3337 **Bowler** Michael B '73
(330) 643-8301 **Bown** Thomas D '04
(330) 376-2700 **Box** Susan S '85
(330) 375-2030 **Bozeka** George A '81
(330) 375-8471 **Bozzelli** Karen A '87
(330) 535-5711 **Bradley** Kate M '01
(330) 434-3000 **Bradshaw** Duard D '73
(330) 670-8400 **Breaux** Alison M '01
(330) 374-9444 **Breen** Kevin J '86
(330) 434-2300 **Breiding** Leonard J II '90
(330) 253-5060 **Brennan** David L '57
(330) 253-5060 **Brennan Manna & Diamond, LLC**
(330) 643-2943 **Brevetta** Nicholas A '02
(330) 643-2519 **Briggs** Kasie L '98
(330) 644-7922 **Briggs** Randy D '83
(330) 376-5300 **Briggs** Robert W '66
(330) 374-0300 **Brightbill** James E '87
(330) 865-9980 **Brosnan** Margaret A '73
(330) 535-5711 **Brouse McDowell**
(330) 762-0700 **Brown** James E '83
(330) 376-3000 **Brown** Robert H '65
(330) 761-9960 **Browne** Susan E '88
(330) 376-2700 **Bruggeman** Amie L '82
(330) 376-5300 **Buckingham Doolittle & Burroughs, LLP**
(330) 643-2250 **Buckles** Tammy R '01
(330) 376-5300 **Buehrle** Edward V '93
(330) 375-5716 **Bulford** Robert E Jr. '76
(330) 253-7171 **Burdon** James L '67
(330) 253-7171 **Burdon & Merlitti**
(330) 384-5225 **Burgess** Thomas C '86
(330) 384-5861 **Burk** James W '91
(330) 253-5060 **Burke** Richard W '83
(330) 643-2242 **Burnett** Crystal D '03
(330) 867-9717 **Burns** Mary Lou '99
(330) 670-7300 **Butler** Brian J '01
(330) 253-5060 **Butterworth** Jason A '00
(330) 376-8019 **Buzzelli** Laurence F '73
(330) 376-5297 **Buzzi** Paul F '68
(330) 643-2365 **Cable** Ronald L Jr. '01
(330) 376-5300 **Cahoon** Peter T '77
(330) 434-6685 **Calderone** Andrew J '73
(330) 670-7300 **Calderone** Kenneth A '90
(330) 253-1111 **Calhoun** Howard L '51
(330) 253-1111 **Calhoun Waddell & Hunt**
(330) 376-9260 **Callahan Greven Rilley & Sinn LLC**
(330) 376-9260 **Callahan** Michael T '82
(330) 434-3461 **Camp** Miles A '94
(330) 922-2123 **Campbell** David A Jr. '74
(330) 645-0431 **Campbell** James M '84
(330) 253-6121 **Campbell** Robert P '80
(330) 670-7300 **Campbell** Timothy C '82
(330) 643-2943 **Capes** Robert C '02
(330) 376-5300 **Caplan** William L '80
(330) 535-5711 **Capotosto** Nicholas P '03
(330) 376-7500 **Capriolo** Ralph A '74
(330) 762-2411 **Carano** Sergio A '89
(330) 375-1311 **Cargle** Amy Elizabeth '98
(330) 376-4444 **Carlozzi** Joyce E '87
(330) 715-3573 **Carr** Melissa B '04
(330) 972-7751 **Carro** J D '78
(330) 376-1112 **Carroll** Helen S '92
(330) 643-2788 **Carroll** Michael E '72
(330) 643-7955 **Carter** Allen G Sr. '86
(330) 761-9960 **Carter** Cornell P '94
(330) 376-5756 **Carter** Trina M '98
(330) 867-8422 **Casalinova** Gregory Jerry '54
(330) 376-1350 **Casalinuovo** John A '84
(330) 535-0177 **Casey** James D '88
(330) 255-0037 **Casolari** Samuel Guy Jr. '86
(330) 864-6611 **Cassetty** Michael T '93
(330) 376-2700 **Casto** Jeffrey J '81
Catanzarite Jeffrey A '79
(330) 864-7155 **Cavanaugh** Mark C '75
(330) 434-1000 **Cavanaugh** Sarah B '04
(330) 253-5678 **Cek** Derek '00
(330) 865-7722 **Champion** Timothy H '88
(330) 644-4508 **Chaplin** Mardis R '97
(330) 945-8110 **Chapman** James B '66
(330) 376-5300 **Chenoweth** Richard A '48
(330) 255-5016 **Cherkala** Brian L '78
(330) 645-4907 **Cherpas** Christopher T '52
(330) 253-5678 **Chester** David M '95
(330) 376-8336 **Chicatelli** Joy L '00
(330) 375-6696 **Childers** William E '88
(330) 643-8003 **Childress** Marilyn R '90
(330) 253-5060 **Childs** John N '74
(330) 376-9260 **Chin** Maria E '02
(330) 670-7300 **Chlysta** John R '92
(330) 865-4949 **Choken** Charles Vincent '99
(330) 434-3000 **Chris** William G '85
(330) 375-2030 **Christensen** Bruce H Jr. '86
(330) 376-7334 **Christie** Michael G '88
(330) 643-2921 **Christman** Bradford J '86
(330) 835-0500 **Chuparkoff** Michael A '96
(330) 835-0500 **Chuparkoff** Theodore '62
(330) 255-6348 **Ciavarella** Nick E '97
(330) 753-1051 **Ciccolini** Eliodoro '53
(330) 753-1051 **Ciccolini** Michael E '84
(330) 753-1051 **Ciccolini** Thomas A '73
(330) 796-4565 **Ciccolini** Vincent N '91
(330) 864-7285 **Ciotola** Janet M '89
(330) 643-3100 **Citrino** Diane E '94
(330) 668-2464 **Clark** George A '66
(330) 376-6191 **Clark** Lynn M '90
(330) 864-5550 **Clark** Robert J '96
(330) 374-0207 **Clum** Ronald '03
(330) 535-4191 **Codrea** John Eli '75
(330) 376-6766 **Cody** Daniel S '90
(330) 796-7095 **Cody** Nancy C '81
(330) 253-8877 **Coffee** Thomas P '87
(330) 972-7960 **Cole** Dana K '86
(330) 376-6339 **Cole** Gary M '91
(330) 761-4074 **Cole** James L '94
(330) 643-2788 **Cole** Jay A '92
(330) 666-5550 **Cole** Leland D '69
(330) 376-1717 **Collins** Gregory H '88
(330) 374-6906 **Collins** John C '82
(330) 643-2083 **Collins** Stephan B '98
(330) 762-8638 **Collins-Berger** Susan M '87
(330) 376-1350 **Colopy** Daniel M '81
(330) 643-1028 **Comanor** Lawrence B '73
(330) 376-1112 **Compton** George F Jr. '73
(330) 253-3337 **Congeni** Christopher B '04
(330) 643-2247 **Connell** Todd M '02
(330) 923-2451 **Conner** James W '67
(330) 253-7171 **Conrad** Bruce R '79
(330) 745-2175 **Conway** Thomas P '91
(330) 535-5711 **Cook** Deron A '00
(330) 867-5105 **Cook** Katarina V '90
(330) 836-3385 **Cook** Lawrence J '77
(330) 972-5787 **Cook** Maria C '87
(330) 972-2358 **Cook** Stephen R '96
(330) 644-5208 **Coombs** William D '66
(330) 376-5600 **Cooper** Angela T '79
(330) 666-3777 **Cooper** Gary G '78
(330) 761-4208 **Cooper** Jacqueline Sue '97
(330) 668-4080 **Cooperman** Jonathan M '94
(330) 753-6874 **Corgan** Jacquenette G '00
(330) 376-5756 **Corgan** William H III '01
(330) 434-3000 **Corns** Frederick S '67
(330) 443-5772 **Corrigan** Michael J '96
(330) 670-0770 **Corzin** Christine K '00
(330) 670-0770 **Corzin** Harold A '75
(330) 670-0770 **Corzin Sanislo Ufholz & Freedman**
(330) 644-0076 **Costello** Anthony J '82
(330) 384-7146 **Couchman** David M '88
(330) 796-3079 **Coven** Christine L '74
(330) 376-2700 **Cox** Jerome '99
(330) 376-2700 **Cox** Steven S '94
(330) 376-2700 **Coyne** John M III '95
(330) 643-2765 **Craft** James D '90
(330) 796-9435 **Crane** Robyn L '77
(330) 836-0409 **Crawford** Joseph A '87
(330) 865-4434 **Creveling** Michael A '94
(330) 865-4434 **Creveling** Wendy S '95
(330) 643-2112 **Croce** Christine L '94
(330) 643-2902 **Crocker** Robin G '96
(330) 208-1000 **Crookes** Thomas R '87
(330) 864-5550 **Crooks** Walter E '02
(330) 753-1151 **Culbertson** David E '65
(330) 762-9933 **Culver** Kathryn F '82
(330) 864-5550 **Cunniff** John J '99
(330) 375-2030 **Cunningham** Cheri B '82
(330) 344-7626 **Cunningham** Daniel P '78
(330) 535-5711 **Cunningham** Richard T '53
(330) 253-5060 **Curran** Colleen C '97
(330) 376-7245 **Curtin** Cynthia K '89
(330) 376-7245 **Curtin** G Michael '83
(800) 646-0400 **Dacoros** Carol L '97
(330) 762-9191 **Daily & Haskins**
(330) 762-9191 **Daily** John A '63
(330) 315-1060 **Dalayanis** Antoni '97
(330) 255-5910 **Daly** Brendan J '00
(330) 376-5050 **D'Andrea** Patrick J '81
(330) 972-5965 **Daniels** Isiah III '76
(330) 535-8116 **D'Aurelio** Gina M '99
(330) 375-2030 **Davidson** Elaine B '78
(330) 376-9691 **Davidson** Roger K '77
(330) 867-9998 **Davies** Richard '80
(330) 643-2800 **Davis** Anita L '83
Davis Clifford L '62
(330) 762-0700 **Davis** Donald W Jr. '85
(330) 376-2700 **Davis** Elizabeth N '84
(330) 434-3000 **Davis** James E '61
(330) 434-6600 **Davis** Kevin G '79
(330) 762-9700 **Davis** Rhonda G '94
(330) 762-6281 **Davis** Thomas E '80
(330) 376-1717 **Davis & Young**
(330) 867-0215 **Davison** Edward Larry '77
(330) 379-1840 **Dawson** Chester C Jr. '70
(330) 867-9242 **DeCamp** Clifford Lee '85
(330) 867-9242 **DeCamp Roth & Devany**
(330) 434-3000 **DeCarlo** Michael '86
(330) 375-2030 **Defibaugh** Michael J '00
(330) 434-1000 **Delgros** Melissa R '99
(330) 535-5711 **DelGrosso** Lisa S '95
(330) 535-9330 **Delino** Lawrence L Jr. '84
(330) 376-4558 **DelMedico** Michael J '80
(330) 252-1266 **DeLoach** Jana B '99
(330) 796-8757 **DeLong** John D '00
(330) 376-1600 **DeMarco** Louis M '79
(330) 920-2620 **Dengg** Edwin L '99
(330) 434-1995 **Dennis** Mark R '03
(330) 643-2372 **Dennis** Sharon '87
(330) 375-5834 **Derivan** Sharon K '87
(330) 376-4444 **DeSantis** Vicki L '02
(330) 575-5934 **De Sario** Nicole J '03
(330) 762-7377 **DeSaussure** Hamilton Jr. '83
(330) 434-3000 **Detweiler** William J '87
(330) 867-9242 **Devany** David M '85
(330) 761-2912 **DeVita** Stephen L '83
(330) 867-4891 **DeYoung** Bruce R '85
(330) 535-2151 **Dhinojwala** Duriya A '02
(330) 253-5060 **Diamond** John T '83
(330) 375-2730 **DiCaudo** Thomas M '88
(330) 535-5711 **Dickinson** Clair E '77
(330) 643-8301 **Dickinson** Matthew A '03
(330) 376-2700 **Dietrich** George A '68
(330) 535-6644 **DiFiore** David V '96
(330) 535-6644 **DiFiore** Sandy A '70
(330) 643-2765 **DiMartino** Heaven R '01
(330) 376-5300 **Dimengo** Steven A '86
(330) 255-6419 **DiPaola** Peggy R '82
(330) 643-2230 **Dirksen** Teresa L '02
(330) 258-6456 **Divine** Phylip J '00
Dixon Harold V Jr. '77
(330) 376-6766 **Djordjevic** Michael M '77
(330) 666-6400 **Dobbins** Elizabeth A '03
(330) 666-6400 **Dobbins & Henshaw**
(330) 666-6400 **Dobbins** Richard E '77
(330) 864-6611 **Dodson** Jason D '04
(330) 643-2788 **Doherty** Rebecca L '92
(330) 376-6300 **Dohner** John M '86
(330) 643-8052 **Doty** Karen M '81
Dougherty Diane L '88
(330) 762-7377 **Dowling** William D Jr. '80
(330) 668-6500 **Drago** Michelle M '99
(330) 535-0124 **Drahovsky** Timothy J '00
(330) 972-7972 **Dratler** Jay Jr. '01
(330) 376-1242 **Drenski** Tama L '03
(330) 762-0080 **Drew** David P '91
(330) 762-2411 **Duff** Andrew R '79
(330) 379-6582 **Dumas** David M '91
(330) 376-5300 **Duncan** Matthew R '03
(330) 733-7369 **Dunlap** Jeffrey D '75
(330) 376-3304 **Dunseath** Frances N '94
(330) 375-2730 **Durian** Chad M '04
(330) 643-2248 **Dutt** Janet L '92
(330) 643-2788 **Easter** Felicia '01
(330) 745-2175 **Eastman** David R '88
(330) 745-2175 **Eastman** Fred E '54
(330) 785-9155 **Eckberg** Barbara S '90
(330) 384-5289 **Eckert** Phillip W '82
Edminister Joseph A '74
(330) 376-4444 **Edminister** Michael E '87
(330) 535-0124 **Eicher** Geoffrey L '89
(330) 376-1440 **Elliott** Michael J '98
(330) 434-7733 **Elliott** Steven S '03
(330) 376-5756 **Emershaw** George J '68
(330) 376-5756 **Emershaw Mushkat & Schneier**
(330) 535-5711 **Emerson** Roger D '87
(330) 384-7309 **Enright** Timothy J '73
(800) 998-9454 **Enriquez** Rick '87
(330) 434-7733 **Eoff** Craig M '99
(330) 376-2700 **Ephlin** Laura A '91
(330) 644-2060 **Esber** David M '75
(330) 376-5300 **Esker** Christopher C '88
(330) 208-4520 **Evanchan** Nicholas L Jr. '79

(330) 208-4520 **Evanchan & Palmisano**
(330) 643-2617 **Evans** Marvin D '91
(330) 643-3104 **Evans** Todd W '93
(330) 434-4050 **Evans** William D II '92
(330) 535-5711 **Everett** Stanley E '81
(330) 668-9747 **Eversman** Erica L '93
(330) 867-9998 **Fahey** Bruce H '80
(330) 535-5711 **Fairweather** John C '77
Falcone Juliet K '03
(330) 375-2030 **Fallis** Stephen A '74
(330) 379-7000 **Farkas** Toni Q '96
(330) 376-2700 **Farolino** Shane A '88
(330) 253-3444 **Farris** George L '81
(330) 376-2700 **Faust** Laura M '92
(330) 253-8877 **Favalon** Paul J '70
(216) 403-3388 **Fedor** Victoria L '92
(330) 896-2889 **Feinberg** Kenneth S '87
(330) 761-4207 **Feld** Stephen L '99
(330) 873-9251 **Feldman** James K '74
(330) 384-5778 **Feltner** David Lee '76
(330) 762-9933 **Ferguson** David H '70
(330) 762-9933 **Ferguson & Hanlon**
(330) 535-5711 **Fickes** John C '85
(330) 762-2411 **Fike** Lisa A '94
(330) 375-8729 **Finley** Michael J '81
(330) 376-2700 **Finn** Terrence S '87
(330) 376-2600 **Finney** Christopher N '03
(330) 899-9335 **Fiocca** Carl J '76
(330) 376-2700 **Firca** Donald J Jr. '01
(330) 665-5117 **Firestine** David L '00
(330) 920-9920 **Fischer** Cheryl A '93
(330) 376-5300 **Fisher** James L III '71
(330) 535-4191 **Fitch** Susan M '87
(330) 255-5012 **Flaherty** Mary K '02
(330) 761-4206 **Flannery** Harry A '00
(330) 762-2961 **Flannery** Theresa '03
(330) 645-4500 **Flasck** Estelle D '88
(330) 253-7171 **Flower** Nancy J '92
(330) 535-5711 **Ford** Brandon L '04
(330) 375-2030 **Forfia** Deborah M '86
(330) 665-5445 **Fortney & Klingshirn**
(330) 665-5445 **Fortney** Michael L '86
(330) 864-1335 **Foster** Greta L '79
(330) 972-6102 **Foster** Sidney C Jr. '74
(330) 253-2227 **Fox** Robert Roe '89
(330) 668-5334 **Frankovich** George S '80
(330) 670-0770 **Freedman** Bruce R '81
(330) 666-3973 **Freeman** Gregory J '01
Frentz John C '50
(330) 670-7300 **Fricke** Lori A '92
(330) 762-7477 **Friedman** David '58
(330) 376-2700 **Frisina** Dominic A '04
(330) 379-5511 **Frye** Michael T '02
(330) 376-2700 **Fuchs** Michael J '03
(330) 576-1234 **Fuhry** Gigi H '99
(330) 376-2700 **Funk** Stephen W '92
(330) 836-9302 **Furey-Ligan** Amy J '04
(330) 645-4866 **Gaffney** Corina S '91
(330) 670-7300 **Gall** Juliana S '89
(330) 867-4013 **Gallucci** Michael Jr. '80
(330) 643-2765 **Galonski** John F '93
(330) 643-7528 **Galonski** Tavia D '95
(330) 384-9000 **Gamache** Elisa A '94
(330) 535-5757 **Gardner** James E '91
(330) 762-9191 **Garretson** Mark F '95
(330) 384-1717 **Gasparovic** John J '82
Gatskie James M '74
(330) 762-1309 **Gatts** Ronald T '98
(330) 376-2700 **Gaum** Karen D '01
(330) 864-5550 **Gaum** R Eric '96
(330) 376-4558 **Gearinger** Bradford M '69
(330) 761-7709 **Gegick** Erik P '99
(330) 972-6939 **Genetin** Bernadette B '88
(330) 376-1242 **Gentilcore** Laura J '86
(330) 666-2226 **George** Joyce J '66
(330) 535-9655 **George** Michael E '91
(330) 376-3300 **George** Michael E '95
(330) 376-5300 **George** Nicholas T '70
(330) 375-7515 **Gerberry** Robert A '97
(330) 753-1051 **Germano** Jacqueline J '82
(330) 753-1051 **Germano Rondy & Ciccolini Co,LPA**
(330) 762-7377 **Gerney** Blake R '95
(330) 376-8336 **Gertz** Marc P '77
(330) 643-2788 **Gessner** Brad L '86
(330) 867-8443 **Giancarli** Mark A '85
(330) 384-5893 **Giannantonio** Rickey C '85
(330) 864-5270 **Gibson** Ruth Ann '83
(330) 864-4419 **Gibson** Thomas H III '96
(330) 762-0700 **Gigliotti** Louis J Jr. '91
(330) 762-0700 **Gilbert** Edward L '80
(330) 836-5373 **Gill** James J '54
(330) 796-8299 **Gingo** Joseph M '71
(330) 253-7100 **Gingrich** Mitchell L '88
(330) 253-0785 **Giordano** Deena M '01
(330) 255-0716 **Gippin** Robert M '73
(330) 535-1660 **Glassman** Ronald R '79
(330) 344-6005 **Glessner** Daniel K '93
(330) 644-0076 **Glick** Sidney '91
(330) 867-8422 **Glick** Sol Mark '57
(330) 867-6600 **Glinsek** Gerald J '67
(330) 867-6600 **Glinsek & Hingham**
(330) 376-5300 **Godshall** Cathy C '76
(330) 670-7300 **Godshall** Douglas N '76
(330) 376-8336 **Goldman & Rosen,Ltd**
(330) 434-3880 **Goldsmith** Richard L Jr. '69
Goodlet Charles William Jr. '75
(330) 376-2700 **Gordon** Amanda E '90
(330) 253-0785 **Gorman** Joseph F '94
(330) 253-0785 **Gorman Malarcik Pierce & Vuillemin**
(330) 384-7035 **Gow** Robert M '92
(330) 535-5711 **Gradert** Lisa Novosat '88
(330) 762-2411 **Gradisher** Suzanne M '04
(330) 996-4099 **Graham-Hurd** Melissa A '84
(330) 762-0765 **Grant** Paul M '95
(330) 253-4424 **Grant** Priscilla A '97
(330) 374-6906 **Graske** Leslie S '83
(330) 375-0126 **Green** Richard A '80
(330) 867-9998 **Green** Thomas E '02
(330) 867-0215 **Greene** Charles L '77
(330) 376-1242 **Greive** Edward G '67
(330) 376-9260 **Greven** John W '94
(330) 643-8124 **Griffin** Alpha T '02
(330) 535-8171 **Grisi** Charles E '70
(330) 666-7765 **Groner** Betty '85
(330) 253-5678 **Gugliotta** John D '94
(330) 643-2374 **Gui** Janice M '78
(330) 630-7908 **Guran** John M '83
Guran Linda Sue '87
(330) 668-6501 **Gustafson** Davin R '86
(330) 384-5228 **Guster** Christine M '84
(330) 255-6205 **Guten** Sharon M '84
(330) 535-2151 **Guy** John J '70
(330) 535-2151 **Guy Lammert & Towne**
(330) 374-1144 **Guzzo** Diane R '89
(330) 643-2040 **Haas** Paula D '97
(330) 376-8336 **Hackenberg** Stacey T '96
(330) 761-4312 **Hadick** Stephen N '94
(330) 864-5550 **Hahn Loeser & Parks LLP**
(330) 867-1490 **Hail** Gregory Lee '92
(330) 633-2069 **Haley** Robert S '82
(330) 384-7098 **Hall** James A '76
(330) 376-1600 **Hamer** Kate M '03
(330) 376-5300 **Hammersmith** Stephen M '81
(330) 867-9998 **Haneline** Kenneth M '86
(330) 762-9933 **Hanlon** Deidre A '79
(330) 670-7300 **Hanna Campbell & Powell, LLP**
(330) 670-7300 **Hanna** David J '79
(330) 745-2175 **Hanna** Joseph E '78
(330) 253-2227 **Hanna** Timothy H '85
Hansen Bowanne S '92
(330) 643-2724 **Hanshaw** Regina S '04
(330) 379-2066 **Hanson-Estep** Laurie B '92
(330) 375-2730 **Hanus** Craig J '01
(330) 867-4050 **Hanzel** Donald C '77
(330) 643-7098 **Harbin** Martha R '90
(330) 762-7477 **Hardesty Kaffen & Zimmerman**
(330) 762-7477 **Hardesty** Stephen D '73
(330) 376-4558 **Hardman** Kevin P '85
Hardway Angela M '04
(330) 869-9101 **Haridakis** Paul M '84
(330) 645-6282 **Harkins** Lewis James '53
(330) 434-3000 **Harnak** Brian K '94
(330) 376-2700 **Harpst** Todd A '96
(330) 375-2037 **Harrill** James F '84
(330) 645-4455 **Harris** George B '48
(330) 873-9931 **Harris** Jo Ann '86
(330) 535-5711 **Harris** Richard H III '80
(330) 666-6900 **Harrison** Joseph R '75
(330) 376-4558 **Hart** Patrick J '75
(330) 535-5711 **Harvey** Frank H Jr. '55
(330) 376-2272 **Harvey-Williams** Lynda E '89
(330) 762-9191 **Haskins** Thomas F Jr. '76
(330) 253-2227 **Hayes** Andrew T '02
(330) 761-4306 **Hayes** Timothy A '87
(330) 643-2788 **Hazelett** Leonard W '87
(330) 762-7377 **Hebert** Halle M '00
(330) 762-6001 **Heimbaugh** Rebecca DiDonato '90
(330) 253-5060 **Heinle** Matthew A '95
(330) 535-5711 **Heintz** Jeffrey T '75
Heinzerling Barbara M '79
(330) 836-4141 **Heiser** Edward N Jr. '55
(330) 376-8336 **Hendler** Michael B '63
(330) 796-3151 **Hendricks** Bruce J '81
(330) 762-1935 **Henges** John J '94
(330) 376-7800 **Henretta** J T '75
(330) 666-6400 **Henshaw** James M '81
(330) 864-8866 **Henshaw** Jean M '86
Herbaugh Phillip L '95
(330) 535-2174 **Herman** John F '68
(330) 864-3840 **Herrington** Linda M '75
(330) 972-6462 **Herrnstein** Becky H '85
(330) 836-8523 **Hesske** Constance A '93
(330) 666-6400 **Hete** Emily M '97
(330) 434-3000 **Hickman** Jason E '95
(330) 376-5756 **Hicks** Donald R '83
(330) 867-6600 **Higham** Robert C '04
(330) 867-6600 **Higham** Robert W '69
(330) 376-5300 **Hilkert** David W '74
(330) 535-5122 **Hilkert** Jennifer R '91
(330) 376-4558 **Hilkert** Mark '76
(330) 643-3347 **Hill** Christine S '02
(330) 375-2730 **Hill** Elisa B '98
(330) 376-4558 **Hill** John F '88
(330) 535-4191 **Hill** Patricia A '80
(330) 384-4803 **Hilston** Thomas A '77
(330) 374-1030 **Himmel** Gary L '80
(330) 643-2925 **Hinton** Belinda J '81
(330) 666-8140 **Hinton** James R '56
(330) 865-0153 **Hiscock** Matthew G '97
(330) 253-2227 **Hobson** Steven R II '98
(330) 376-1242 **Hodgkiss** Timothy A '03
(330) 745-2175 **Hofer** Keith R '89
(330) 264-6464 **Hoff** George L '85
(330) 376-1600 **Hogan** Thomas C '01
(330) 375-2052 **Holcomb** John E '74
(330) 762-0765 **Holda** Sheri L '01
(330) 535-5711 **Holden** Joseph M '52
(330) 964-1001 **Holder** William P Jr. '66
(330) 666-5550 **Holford** Andrew M '01
(330) 867-1490 **Holland & Muirden**
(330) 535-1202 **Holland Myers & Myers**
(330) 376-2700 **Hollinger** Brandie N '03
(330) 867-6147 **Holloway** Donald P '55
(330) 796-7516 **Holmes** Karen M '85
(330) 762-8638 **Holub** Jerome L '51
(330) 376-2272 **Hom** Martha L '98
(330) 434-2113 **Honeck** Richard D '79
(330) 665-5117 **Horbus** Craig S '04
(330) 379-4605 **Hornickel** John H '78
(330) 670-7300 **Horton** Harland B Jr. '72
(330) 865-0021 **Horvath** Michael L '85
(330) 535-8771 **Houlihan** Susan F '98
(330) 762-2411 **Houlihan** Thomas R '98
(330) 376-3607 **Howard** William E Jr. '68
(330) 643-0212 **Hrina** David J '00
(330) 864-5550 **Hrivnak** Bret A '04
(330) 376-2700 **Hudak** Michael J '87
(330) 375-5412 **Huebert** Jacob H '04
(330) 972-7331 **Huhn** Wilson Ray '77
(330) 762-6767 **Hull** Alexandra '89
(330) 643-2234 **Humphrys** Dawn A '98
(330) 208-1000 **Hunsicker** J Bruce '80
(330) 535-5711 **Hunsicker** Oscar A Jr. '48
(330) 253-1111 **Hunt** Robert C '76
(330) 535-5711 **Hunter** David M '75
(330) 376-8888 **Huston** Charles M '70
(330) 753-1051 **Incorvati** Robert A '90
(330) 376-2700 **Isham** Duane L '53
(330) 796-3084 **Ito** Takashi '63
(330) 376-2700 **Ivey** Timothy C '87
(330) 762-2448 **Jaballas** Roderick R '93
(330) 972-7074 **Jackson** Candace Campbell '95
(330) 379-2041 **Jackson** Montrella S '99
(330) 376-2700 **Jackson** Paul L '88
(330) 434-1000 **Jacquemain** Jennifer J '98
(330) 643-8124 **James** Amy Casner '03
(330) 836-0374 **James** Frances White '81
(330) 535-9655 **James** Jeffrey N '91
(330) 375-1311 **Jamison** Andrew D '98
(330) 253-5454 **Janos** Peter P '92
(330) 375-7331 **Jenkins** Donald M '64
(330) 633-1933 **John** Michael L '83
(330) 928-0307 **Johnson** Allan Jr. '49
(330) 665-4547 **Johnson** Edward A '50
(330) 929-2838 **Johnson** Mary D '91
(330) 434-7988 **Jones** Crystal L '89
(330) 376-7500 **Jones** Erik M '00
(330) 643-2250 **Jones** Julie A '91
(330) 535-8116 **Jones** Mary H '88
(330) 643-3550 **Jones** Michael A '87
(330) 376-2700 **Jones** Wayne M '89
(330) 762-2600 **Joondeph & Bittel,LLP**
(330) 762-2600 **Joondeph** Jerome J '68
(330) 668-7755 **Julius** John C '01
(330) 796-3024 **Junod** Scott K '02
(330) 375-5630 **Kacarab** Peter J '93
(330) 762-7477 **Kaffen** Ronald O '74
(330) 253-0719 **Kaforey** Ellen C '89
(330) 867-9998 **Kainec** Lisa A '93
(330) 643-2788 **Kanellis** Margaret A '94
(330) 666-7922 **Kaplan** Michael J '76
(330) 643-2788 **Kaplan-Quinn** Kimberly A '93
(330) 643-2788 **Kasay** Richard S '77
(330) 867-9998 **Kastner** Harley M '73
(330) 867-9998 **Kastner Westman & Wilkins,LLC**
(330) 375-2030 **Kaszowski** Tammy L '00
(330) 375-5412 **Katz** Jason M '03
(330) 762-7655 **Kaufmann** Philip S '71
(330) 867-9998 **Kazaglis** Ted N '88
Kearns David B '02
(330) 376-5300 **Keating** Patrick J '83
(330) 644-9930 **Keith** David A '80
(330) 376-5300 **Keller** Clay K '00
(330) 375-5900 **Keller** Kerri L '02
(330) 434-2113 **Kelley** Thomas '78
(330) 253-2227 **Kelling** Gilbert V Jr. '67
(330) 376-5756 **Kelly** Timothy M '83
(330) 996-3190 **Kemp** Edward G '68
(330) 376-2700 **Kennedy** Ryan P '04
(330) 434-3461 **Kennedy** Traci F '84
(330) 376-1242 **Kenner** Phillip L '65
(330) 864-3323 **Kepple** Donald P '75
(330) 376-5300 **Kern** David '90
(330) 535-3882 **Kernan** Joseph M '93
(330) 376-7446 **Kerper** Robert E Jr. '78
(330) 535-5711 **Kersker** Linda B '72
(330) 310-3802 **Kidd** Michael Scott '02
(330) 643-3540 **Kiggans** Jeffrey M '03
(330) 375-2070 **Killian** Laura A '90
(330) 644-6746 **Killian** Timothy J '76
(330) 724-4442 **Killinger** Rebecca '82
(330) 434-2000 **Kim** John Y '96
(330) 376-9260 **Kim-Knox** Candace A '03
(330) 253-8877 **Kimbler** Joyce V '82
(330) 535-8771 **Kinder** Richard A '93
(330) 972-8475 **King** Dawn M '04
(330) 379-6851 **Kingsbury** Thomas R '97
Kisling Gary W '77
(330) 375-5780 **Kitchell** Marjorie H '90
(330) 643-5458 **Kleckner** Janet Lee '84
(330) 665-5445 **Klingshirn** Neil E '86
(330) 376-3300 **Knoll** Jeffrey T '91
(330) 376-3300 **Knoll** Thomas G '65
(330) 253-5060 **Kobzowicz** Leigh A '03
(330) 253-2729 **Koch** Matthew J '67
(330) 762-6474 **Kodish** Joseph S '69
(330) 644-3572 **Koehler** Ronald J '86
(330) 643-2943 **Kohrs** Brendon J '04
(330) 434-2713 **Kohut** Eric T '02
(330) 668-1050 **Kolarik** Todd M '96
(330) 384-4580 **Kolich** Kathy J '87
(330) 374-1040 **Kolk** Joseph M '86
(330) 338-1609 **Kondoleon** Nicholas L '01
(330) 253-2195 **Konstand** Dean '79
(330) 253-2195 **Konstand** Robert G '77
(330) 972-6793 **Koosed** Margery B '74
(330) 376-2700 **Kopp** Ronald S '79
(330) 384-5849 **Korkosz** Arthur E '80
(330) 745-9927 **Kormanec** Stephanie Rae '00
(330) 535-5711 **Kosiewicz** Joy D '98
(330) 643-2935 **Kostoff** Maria V '95
(330) 376-2700 **Kostoff** Peter M '82
(330) 434-2113 **Kot** Thomas P '79
(330) 535-6650 **Kotler** Todd B '99
(330) 668-2580 **Kovach** John J '87
(330) 643-2788 **Kovach** Mary Ann '75
(330) 972-6794 **Kovach** Richard J '74
(330) 535-4191 **Kozlowski** Timothy E Jr. '91
(330) 376-3300 **Krajewski** John K '85
(330) 762-7655 **Krall** Roy A '89
(330) 762-7377 **Kramer** Reginald S '80
(330) 376-5300 **Kraus** James D '83
Kreek Louis F Jr. '55
(330) 375-1311 **Kremer** Stephan C '93
(330) 535-6868 **Krohn** Mark E '96
(330) 796-3204 **Kruger** Gary I '77
(330) 376-2700 **Kurek** James D '81
(330) 375-1311 **Kuri** Phillip A '93
(330) 762-1134 **Kutuchief** Richard P '78
(330) 762-7477 **Laatsch** Morris H III '75
(330) 535-5711 **Lacher** Frederick K '50
(330) 434-5444 **Lambert** John D '79
(330) 535-2151 **Lammert** Thomas E '76
(330) 375-2730 **Larson** Gerald K '91
(330) 972-6479 **LaSalvia** Anthony J '72
(330) 745-1500 **Lax** Susan J '96
(330) 434-3880 **Laybourne** Robert B '73
(330) 666-6900 **Lazar** John P '83
(330) 670-8588 **Leary** Jeffrey N '00
(330) 376-7800 **Leb** Gerald P '82
(330) 762-9191 **LeBoeuf** Bradley S '99
(330) 644-6161 **Lee** Robert E '74
(330) 376-2700 **Lee** Ronald B '78
(330) 535-5711 **Leffler** Amanda M '02
(330) 253-5996 **Leffler** Daniel J '03
(330) 376-2700 **Leffler** Frederick W '90
(330) 996-3185 **Lefton** Karen C '84
(330) 253-2227 **Leiby** Stephen P '73
(330) 434-3000 **Lembright** Ronald K '73
(330) 972-6357 **Lenart** Lynn M '00
(330) 376-2700 **Leonard** Jeffrey W '83
(330) 643-7758 **Leong** Joann M '99
(330) 643-7952 **Lepidi-Carino** Madeline J '03
(330) 376-3300 **Lepp** Aaron G '95
(330) 376-3575 **Leslie** Mary Ellen '01
(330) 253-5060 **Lettieri** Frank A '74
(330) 836-5297 **Levin** Richard V '67
(330) 643-2788 **Lewandowski** Connie J '91
(330) 376-5300 **Lewis** David J '87
(330) 643-2765 **Lewis** Susana B '91
(330) 972-6229 **Lieberman** Alvin H '64
(330) 867-6600 **Liggins** Jasper '75
(330) 873-2518 **Lindenberger** Jeffrey K '82
(330) 865-9635 **Lindow** Michael B '04
(330) 761-9960 **Lindsay** Shawn P '04
(330) 376-2700 **Link** Terrence H II '99
(330) 258-8000 **Linnen** Jerome T Jr. '87
(330) 434-3000 **Linton** Robert F '60
(330) 643-3554 **Lischner** Anna E '90
(330) 643-2250 **Little** Jonathan D '04
(330) 836-9111 **Livick** Anthony '80
(330) 208-1000 **Lloyd** Philip A '72
(330) 253-1101 **LoCascio** Thomas J '88
(330) 869-8149 **Lockhart** John D '01
(330) 376-3300 **Lockshin** Mary Jo '81
(330) 643-2765 **Lohr** Mary A '99
(330) 643-3110 **Lohr** Richard A Jr. '99
(330) 535-9655 **Lombardi** David G '89
(330) 745-2175 **Lombardi** Donald E '68
(330) 376-5300 **Lombardi** Frederick M '62
(330) 535-9655 **Lombardi George & James, Ltd**
(330) 745-2175 **Lombardi Hofer Hanna Conway & Eastman**
(330) 785-3337 **Looney** David A '74
(330) 644-0607 **Love** William E II '76
(330) 867-2444 **Lowrey** Robert W '74
(330) 376-2004 **Lowry** David M '82
(330) 376-4558 **Lucht** Gregory J '02
(330) 666-5550 **Ludwig** Mark H '74
(330) 761-4207 **Luecken** John J Jr. '90
(330) 535-5711 **Lux** Sallie C '81
(330) 762-2600 **Lyden** Kevin T '87
(330) 535-5711 **Lyden** Shawn M '95
(330) 374-0066 **Lynch** Margaret T '90
(330) 434-3000 **Lynett** John J '61
(330) 762-0700 **Lynett** John J Jr. '93
(330) 375-2285 **Lynett** Thomas F Jr. '57
(330) 670-7300 **Lyons** James M Jr. '82
(330) 434-5444 **MacDonald** Ida Lyn '83
(330) 762-2411 **Mackey** James F '98
(330) 996-8585 **Macro** Judith A '93
(330) 376-2272 **Madison** Walter T '99
(330) 796-1755 **Maffei** Rocco J '77
(330) 762-8691 **Maher** Douglas B '77
(330) 643-2250 **Mahlay** Natalia B '03
(330) 253-0785 **Malarcik** Donald J Jr. '93
(330) 374-5540 **Malek** Linda M '01
(330) 644-6161 **Mallo** George D '74
(330) 972-7945 **Mallo** Ted A '72
(330) 376-5300 **Malone** Robert W '76
(330) 796-4908 **Manella** Michael J '97
(330) 762-1199 **Manes** Gregg A '84
(330) 208-1000 **Manfull** Ashley M '99
(330) 668-9696 **Mangon** Brett J '01
(330) 379-1796 **Mangon** Elizabeth R '01
(330) 643-2800 **Manley** John F '88
(330) 253-5060 **Manna** Anthony S '86
(330) 745-4477 **Manos** Chris G '85
(330) 535-1555 **Manos** George T '54
(330) 384-5272 **Marconi** John R '94
(330) 375-1390 **Marczely** David W '91
Marino Nicholas J '81
(330) 670-0005 **Markling** Matthew J '97
(330) 384-1623 **Markovich** Edward P '97
(330) 633-1933 **Marks** Donald L '53
(330) 376-5300 **Marshall** Craig S '86
(330) 255-0037 **Marshall Dennehey Warner Coleman & Goggin**
(330) 253-5060 **Martin** John F '84
(330) 923-8297 **Martin** Ronald M '69
(330) 670-7300 **Martin** Margaret L '92
(330) 643-2788 **Mascolo** John A '93
(330) 434-4399 **Mason** Cynthia Ann '93
(330) 643-2943 **Mastran** Christine E '96
(330) 434-3000 **Mastrantonio** Steven W '93
(330) 376-5300 **Matasich** Michael J '04
(330) 972-8243 **Matejkovic** John E '79
(330) 375-5934 **Mather** Jason N '00
(330) 643-7954 **Matz** Deborah Sue '92
(330) 666-5555 **Maurer** Steven A '88
(330) 643-2930 **Maxwell** Kristin Wardell '92
(330) 374-1334 **Maxwell** MaryBeth G '82
(330) 376-5300 **Mayer** Christine A '96
(330) 643-2788 **Mayer** Kevin A '93
(330) 762-8885 **Mazak** Edward P Jr. '81
(330) 670-7300 **Mazgaj** Frank G '87
(330) 666-5555 **Mazur** Louise M '82
(330) 384-5570 **Mazurek** Michelle Ann '85
(330) 434-3000 **Mazzola** Todd A '93
(330) 375-2611 **McCarty** Alison E '87
(330) 864-6611 **McCarty** Justin D '82
(330) 864-6611 **McCarty & Pry**
(330) 643-2900 **McCarty** Robert A '88
(330) 873-1199 **McCarty** Thomas M '82
(330) 535-4450 **McClain** Andrew B '97
(330) 376-1242 **McCue** Shannon V '98
(330) 784-8800 **McDowall** Laura K '87
(330) 796-3917 **McElroy** James Jr. '97
(330) 535-4191 **McGarrity** Steven J '96
(330) 864-2236 **McGowan** Michael L '60

(330) 929-4155 **McGowan** Raymond J II '78
(330) 670-0005 **McGown** Susan S '88
(330) 643-5328 **McGuckin** Denise M '86
(330) 836-9200 **McGuckin** Richard B '65
McIntyre Patricia Ann '85
(330) 376-6400 **McKenney** Todd M '89
(330) 867-9998 **McKenzie** John W '92
(330) 864-3100 **McKinzie** Timothy D '93
(330) 376-9691 **McLaughlin** Kelly Lyn '87
(330) 376-5300 **McLean** Hillary B '04
(330) 375-0126 **McMahon DeGulis Hoffmann & Lombardi LLP**
(330) 466-6103 **McNeil** Keith P '81
(330) 376-2700 **McQueen** Aaron E '97
(330) 867-5310 **Meador** Carl E '66
(330) 253-3337 **Meeker** Robert C '69
(330) 376-1242 **Meinerding** Wesley C '02
(330) 535-9160 **Mendenhall** Warner D III '98
(330) 762-1309 **Menicos** Patrick L '76
(330) 376-7500 **Mentzer** Howard E '69
(330) 376-7500 **Mentzer** Linda B '83
(330) 376-7500 **Mentzer & Mygrant, Ltd**
(330) 643-2788 **Mercurio** Nancy L '96
(330) 643-3550 **Meriweather** Lavonne A '78
(330) 535-5711 **Merklin** Marc B '84
(330) 253-7171 **Merlitti** James A '74
(330) 375-2730 **Merryweather** Elizabeth A '97
(800) 998-9454 **Meyer** Elin S '88
(330) 253-7800 **Michael** Kathryn Ann '86
Michalec Mitchell J '03
(330) 762-6474 **Migdal** Kirk A '91
(330) 867-5964 **Migdal** Stanley B '56
(330) 922-8060 **Mihiylov** Robert L '75
(330) 434-1211 **Mikesell** William F '84
(330) 665-8519 **Milane** Robert M '79
(330) 796-7975 **Miller** Anthony E '77
(800) 998-9454 **Miller** David F Jr. '89
(330) 535-4000 **Miller** Harvey F '94
(330) 873-1001 **Miller** John R '76
(330) 643-2943 **Miller** Lucy R '02
(330) 896-2889 **Miller** Paul L '91
(330) 643-2158 **Miller-Leonard** Allyson '92
(330) 864-3100 **Milligan** Kerry G '93
(330) 329-3170 **Mills** Lori Ann '93
(330) 668-8243 **Minc** David C '74
(330) 666-0000 **Minichiello** Alfred C '55
(330) 864-5550 **Minns** Michael H '85
(330) 762-0700 **Mitchell** John A '98
(330) 620-2642 **Mitchell** Mary Gibbs '86
(330) 670-8400 **Mitsopoulos** Sophia '97
Modugno Vincent R '78
(330) 864-5132 **Mohler** Robert E '47
(330) 665-5117 **Molnar** Kelly A '00
(330) 643-8387 **Monaco** Deborah J '97
(330) 869-4031 **Moncrief** Cynthia Ann '88
(330) 535-5925 **Montgomery** Jerry F '54
(330) 701-2362 **Moody** LoVeen Joy '03
(330) 376-2700 **Moore** Brian J '84
(330) 375-2053 **Moore** Carla D '77
(330) 666-5555 **Moore** Gregory J '03
(330) 376-2700 **Moore** Randall J '84
Morgan Richard G '74
(330) 253-5060 **Morley** Michael P '89
(330) 376-5300 **Morris** Duane '53
(330) 835-2323 **Morris** Joseph R '96
(330) 253-7100 **Morris** Michele '84
(330) 762-2411 **Morrison** Jack Jr. '81
(330) 376-1242 **Morton** Andrew B '93
(330) 384-7314 **Mosley** Mark A '87
(330) 384-7060 **Moss** A E '83
(330) 670-7300 **Moss** David T '82
(330) 643-6981 **Motter** Allen H '93
(330) 376-2700 **Mowery** Chad L '00
(330) 376-2700 **Moxon** George W II '75
(330) 535-5711 **Moxon** Joy A '99
(330) 762-7377 **Mueller** Raymond C '88
(330) 972-5315 **Mumper** John E '82
(330) 434-3461 **Muntean** Christopher P '04
(330) 375-2030 **Muntean** David A '87
(330) 643-7794 **Murphy** Linda M '91
(330) 253-2729 **Murray** Philip W '64
(330) 645-9399 **Musarra** Thomas M '84
(330) 864-6611 **Muse** Edward S '89
(330) 376-5756 **Mushkat** Barbara S '70
(330) 535-5535 **Musitano** Dominic A Jr. '60
(330) 869-0744 **Mussig** Linda Mae '89
(330) 668-9696 **Mussig** Mark L '87
(330) 762-7655 **Mutersbaugh** Steven P '02
(330) 535-1202 **Myers** John F '85
(330) 535-1202 **Myers** Nancy H '86
(330) 376-7500 **Mygrant** John W '77
(330) 867-9242 **Nace** R Bryan '85
(800) 998-9454 **Nanni** Thomas J '93
(330) 208-4520 **Nass** Terri L '89
(330) 873-1776 **Neiman** Maurice P '53
(330) 643-2628 **Neiman** Michelle L '96
(330) 665-3186 **Nelson** Kimberly B '88
(330) 762-6474 **Newman** Dianne M '79
(330) 535-7027 **Newman** Herbert '65
(330) 434-3000 **Nichol** David S '00
(330) 434-1000 **Niekamp** Christopher J '90
(330) 535-5711 **Nilges** Hans A '03
(330) 384-5624 **Nilsson** Nils E '86
(330) 643-3550 **Nitzsche** Deborah A '90
(330) 253-5454 **Nolan** Chris T '73
(330) 644-0706 **Norris** Andrea L '85
(330) 644-0706 **Norris** Randolph C Jr. '53
(330) 643-8550 **Nott** David L '92
(330) 379-2727 **Nukes** Sotir S '57
(330) 644-0325 **Nye** William B '60
(330) 376-1717 **O'Brien** Ann M '91
(330) 762-5500 **O'Brien** Kerry M '75
(330) 434-3000 **O'Brien** Tamara A '92
(330) 762-7377 **Oby** Matthew W '87
(330) 208-1000 **Ochmann** Patricia M '01
(330) 376-2700 **Ochsenhirt** Timothy J '71
(330) 670-7300 **Ockerman** Michael '91
(330) 643-2227 **O'Connor** Kandi Sue '97
(330) 796-4827 **Okey** Deborah A '87
Olah Michael J '85
(330) 376-4558 **Oldfield** Joy D '00
(330) 762-7377 **Oldham & Dowling**
(330) 762-7377 **Oldham** Jon A '02
(330) 762-7377 **Oldham** Joseph K '95
(330) 434-2113 **Oldham** Peter D '72
(330) 864-5550 **Oldham** Scott M '91
(330) 762-7377 **Oldham** William M '67
(330) 253-6121 **Olesh** Kristen E '01
(330) 869-9944 **Oliver** Joseph E '83
(800) 998-9454 **Oliver** Kimberly L '03
Olminsky Charles W Jr. '00
(330) 434-6687 **O'Neil** Augustin F '82
(330) 761-6369 **O'Neil** Kevin C '81
(330) 384-5224 **O'Reilly** Mary E '84
(330) 644-9917 **Owens** Robert E '78
(330) 376-5300 **Pacenta** Patricia A '81
(330) 666-3777 **Pachell** James T '84
(330) 379-6543 **Palmer** Meredith E '01
(330) 208-4520 **Palmisano** Ralph J '73
(330) 376-6766 **Pantages** Pamela E '90
(330) 643-2943 **Papanicolaou** Vayia '03
(330) 379-2083 **Papas** Katerina C '89
(330) 643-3550 **Pappas** Carol L '85
(330) 535-6185 **Pappas** George C '86
(330) 867-6221 **Parker** Harold G '69
(330) 253-2227 **Parker Leiby Hanna & Rasnick,LLC**
(330) 253-2227 **Parker** Thomas M '79
(330) 376-6136 **Parms** Edwin L '65
(330) 665-4547 **Parrish** Thomas E '77
(330) 376-6611 **Parsons** Joseph D '87
Pastis Alix G '85
(330) 434-5118 **Patrino** Anthony V '50
(330) 670-8989 **Patterson** Barbara J '85
(330) 384-7033 **Patton** Terry E '75
(330) 253-1131 **Pavick** Dean G '80
(330) 253-1131 **Pavick** Michael J '50
(330) 376-5300 **Pavlidis** Marietta M '97
(330) 896-6300 **Paxton** William A '89
(330) 375-2030 **Payne** James E '79
(330) 535-4191 **Payne** Paul D II '77
(330) 796-4503 **Payntor** Carl S '82
(330) 643-2788 **Peacock** Gregory W '93
(330) 258-6565 **Peak** Jack E '96
(330) 253-5454 **Perantinides & Nolan Co,LPA**
(330) 253-5454 **Perantinides** Paul G '69
(330) 796-7082 **Perez** Edward R '87
(330) 253-2195 **Perris** Alexander C '94
(330) 668-3994 **Peters** Suzanne '82
(330) 869-2177 **Petersen** James Lee '81
(330) 376-1600 **Peterson** Mary J '87
(330) 796-4141 **Peterson** Michael R '93
(330) 376-1242 **Petrosky** Sylvia A '87
(330) 762-0700 **Petti** Gary M '95
(330) 376-1600 **Pfeister** Alison J '85
(330) 384-6386 **Pfister** Eugene W '95
(330) 643-2943 **Pience** Jamie L '02
Piepho Scott R '94
(330) 253-0785 **Pierce** Brian M '94
Pierce Edwin C '64
(330) 836-8159 **Pierson** John C '82
(330) 376-2700 **Pietrowski** Moira H '98
(330) 376-5756 **Pignatelli** Francis M '88
(330) 753-7080 **Piotrowski** Michael W '94
(330) 666-5550 **Pirozzi** Mark C '77
(330) 376-2700 **Pitchford** Marshal M '99
(330) 762-0280 **Pitts** Thomas R '79
(330) 865-0100 **Pizzino** Elisa P '89
(330) 923-8297 **Plesich** Gregory T '73
(330) 643-2765 **Plesich** Matthew J '03
(330) 253-2227 **Plum** Donald S '88
(330) 253-9747 **Pond** Donald K Jr. '97
(330) 208-1000 **Porter** Jay P '78
(330) 535-6185 **Portman** Irving Abe '55
(330) 670-7300 **Potenza** Rocco D Jr. '92
(330) 643-2943 **Poth-Wypasek** Angela K '01
(330) 643-2336 **Poulos** Larry G '73
(330) 375-3954 **Powel** William A III '92
(330) 670-7300 **Powell** Donald A '65
(330) 253-3900 **Powell** Georgene S '79
(330) 253-3900 **Powell** Joseph A '78
(330) 836-5110 **Powers** Annette L '81
(330) 375-2730 **Powley** Douglas J '79
(330) 666-3889 **Prentice** Sally A '82
(330) 974-8254 **Preston** Kenneth G Jr. '65
(330) 376-7245 **Price** William J '99
(330) 375-1311 **Prislipsky** Thomas A '97
(330) 762-6474 **Pritchard** Sheree T '97
(330) 376-2600 **Pritchard** Susan K '80
(330) 434-3000 **Pruneski** Stephen J '85
(330) 864-6611 **Pry** Russell M '84
(330) 867-9998 **Pryatel** Keith L '86
(330) 762-0700 **Pullekins** Edward C '75
Quinn Charles R '79
(330) 535-5711 **Quirk** Frank E '59
(330) 376-2700 **Ragon** Stacy A '96
(330) 643-2788 **Ragsdale** Susan L '91
(330) 463-3802 **Rakowsky** Boris '68
(330) 434-5070 **Ramos** George L '92
(330) 253-7171 **Ranftl** James R '76
(330) 643-2617 **Rankins** Milton C '91
(330) 253-2227 **Rasnick** John F '82
(330) 864-1183 **Rawlings** Thomas E '77
(330) 253-7171 **Ray** Nathan A '89
(330) 643-2788 **Raynes** Kristina D '00
(330) 535-5711 **Raynor** David F '76
(330) 972-6329 **Redle** David A '80
(330) 255-0037 **Reece** John C '89
(330) 643-2250 **Reece** John W '61
(330) 865-9635 **Reece** Richard A Jr. '03
(330) 745-2175 **Reed** Carl L '66
(330) 375-2285 **Reed** James K '88
(330) 762-2060 **Reed** Joel D '96
(330) 376-5300 **Reed** Orville L '73
(330) 643-2942 **Rees** Christine '00
(330) 643-2788 **Reese** Holly E '99
(330) 535-5711 **Reffner** Robert P '77
(330) 253-2729 **Regal** Edwin M '70
(330) 376-2700 **Regallis** Caroline '02
(330) 376-1242 **Reginelli** Arthur M '95
(330) 375-2084 **Reid** Margaret K '92
(330) 972-6197 **Reilly** Elizabeth A '78
(330) 864-7030 **Reitzes** Jeffrey H '69
(330) 375-1311 **Reminger & Reminger**
(330) 376-3300 **Rench** James L '74
(330) 376-1242 **Renner Kenner Greive Bobak Taylor & Weber, LPA**
(330) 376-5300 **Reyes** John L '78
(330) 376-5300 **Reymann** Patrick H '72
(330) 643-2944 **Richards** Beverly J '98
(330) 864-1459 **Richards** Donald '55
(330) 384-5272 **Richardson** Tammy S '96
(330) 972-7447 **Richert** Paul '77
(330) 972-7189 **Rickett** William G '86
(330) 796-3328 **Rickey** June E '97
(330) 796-6635 **Rickman** Michael R '87
(330) 535-8171 **Riegler** Edward J '74
(330) 434-3000 **Riemenschneider** John K '69
(330) 376-9260 **Rilley** Scott A '93
(330) 376-2700 **Rimmel** Brad A '99
(330) 867-1490 **Roach** Jason R '96
(330) 374-5540 **Roberto** Carmen V '73
(330) 376-2272 **Robinson** Kandee S '04
(330) 665-1117 **Robinson** Michael L '77
(330) 869-6121 **Robinson** Saundra W '77
(330) 376-9225 **Robinson** Virginia R '86
(330) 535-8116 **Rochford** Bernard A '90
(330) 643-2963 **Rochford** Rita M '85
(330) 434-3000 **Roderick & Linton**
(330) 376-2700 **Roetzel & Andress,LPA**
(330) 643-3550 **Rogers** Clement H III '84
(330) 376-5300 **Rohrich** Richard P '73
(330) 253-8877 **Roman** Kirk E '85
(330) 762-0765 **Romanoski** Janice Crossland '81
(330) 761-2912 **Romans** Clifford S '85
(330) 376-2700 **Ropchock** Mark A '85
(330) 374-1144 **Rose** Beverly J '74
(330) 535-5711 **Rose** Paul A '82
(330) 376-8336 **Rosen** Gary M '78
(330) 376-5300 **Rosin** George H '76
(330) 796-6354 **Rosner** Michael J '86
(330) 643-2617 **Ross** Christopher C '01
(330) 643-2250 **Ross** Karen E '01
(330) 643-2800 **Ross** Susan Baker '91
(330) 670-7300 **Rossi** Gregory T '90
(330) 379-3957 **Roth** Kathleen E '97
(330) 867-9242 **Roth** William J Jr. '83
(330) 375-2030 **Rothal** Max '57
(330) 253-2195 **Roubenes** Jerry G '65
(330) 376-3300 **Roush** Carrie M '99
(330) 762-0287 **Rowlands** Mary M '89
(330) 376-4558 **Royer** Robert A '84
Rozmajzl Michael F '01
(330) 643-2800 **Rubino** Sandy J '78
(330) 376-5050 **Ruby** Deborah L '99
(330) 762-6335 **Rucinski** Keith Lee '94
(330) 643-2617 **Rudgers** James A '73
(330) 670-0005 **Ruffin** Sean P '98
(330) 535-7174 **Ruffner** Keith C II '88
(330) 864-5369 **Rumel** John E '75
(330) 666-5555 **Rupert** Scott H '74
(330) 535-4191 **Ryan** Anne J '97
(330) 535-4191 **Sahl** Joann M '86
(330) 972-6753 **Sahl** John P '92
(330) 535-4191 **Sain** Gregory R '76
(330) 376-1717 **Salamone** James P '00
(330) 643-2788 **Sallerson** Daniel F '95
(330) 972-7898 **Samuels** Jeffrey M '99
(330) 434-3000 **Sanders** Rodd A '94
(330) 670-0770 **Sanislo** Kevin R '79
(330) 376-2700 **Sarkis** George R '80
(330) 865-1937 **Savalan** Thomas L '61
Savula Marta L '91
(330) 253-3444 **Sawan** Edmund M '76
(330) 643-2943 **Sawyers** Paula M '93
(330) 762-2411 **Saxer** Thomas M '91
(330) 376-4558 **Scanlon & Gearinger Co, LPA**
(330) 376-4558 **Scanlon** John T '94
(330) 376-1440 **Scanlon** Lawrence J '78
(330) 376-4558 **Scanlon** Maura E '88
(330) 535-2174 **Scanlon** Michael C '66
(330) 836-9441 **Scanlon** Terence E '76
(330) 376-4558 **Scanlon** Timothy F '62
(330) 762-7377 **Scarpitti** Mark J '02
(330) 864-2003 **Schafer** Julie A '02
(330) 899-9335 **Schafer** Victoria E '83
(330) 376-2700 **Scheatzle** Kyle S '02
(330) 643-2250 **Scheffler** Bethany R '02
(330) 762-0080 **Schiller** Glenn M '98
(330) 376-2700 **Schlue** Daniel J '01
(330) 535-4000 **Schmid** Mora Lowry '99
(330) 643-5456 **Schneider** Edward M '95
(330) 836-8777 **Schneiderman** Stanley B '54
(330) 376-5756 **Schneier** Bernard '62
(330) 670-7300 **Schobert** Jeffrey E '85
(330) 643-8800 **Schoenewald** Michael A '88
(330) 253-5060 **Schomer** John B '91
(330) 835-4523 **Schott** Lyn M '79
(330) 762-0765 **Schrader** Alfred E '78
(330) 376-2700 **Schrader** Bruce R II '87
(330) 665-5178 **Schwab** Harry W '54
(330) 535-5711 **Schwemler** John A '54
(800) 998-9454 **Scott** David A '88
(330) 836-5500 **Scribner** Theodore '03
(330) 434-1166 **Segedy** Alan G '72
(330) 645-0431 **Sell** Linda G '94
(330) 535-0124 **Semple & Eicher**
(330) 535-0124 **Semple** Neil M '02
(330) 535-0124 **Semple** Thomas P '88
(330) 972-6018 **Sermersheim** Michael D '73
(330) 376-6766 **Sethna** Farhad B '91
(330) 668-1893 **Shaffer** David H '73
(330) 762-6224 **Shama** Cynthia Lou '89
(330) 375-2007 **Shapiro** Marvin A '65
Sheard Elizabeth K '02
(330) 784-2292 **Shenise** Larry D '97
(330) 253-3128 **Sheppard** Raymond C '55
(330) 376-1717 **Sherrod** John P '04
(330) 762-6474 **Shifrin** Debra Sue '81
(330) 253-5060 **Shoaff** Joseph A '99
(330) 643-2397 **Shoemaker** John H '71
(330) 643-2788 **Shuki** Jennie R '98
(330) 869-0522 **Siff** Alan L '63
(330) 867-3545 **Silas-Butler** Jacqueline A '84
(330) 762-2411 **Silfani** Daniel L '99
(330) 972-6979 **Simmons** Franklin B III '87
(330) 384-7863 **Simpson** Helen Mae '89
(330) 643-2788 **Sims** Colleen M '98
(330) 376-8019 **Sims** David L '97
(800) 998-9454 **Sin** Nancy P '96
(330) 644-9917 **Singer** Paul Jay '71
(330) 670-7300 **Singletary** Gary S '86
(330) 376-5300 **Sinn** Deanna N '98
(330) 376-9260 **Sinn** Jonathan T '94
(330) 869-5297 **Sinopoli** Debra L '92
(330) 869-5297 **Sinopoli** Vito F '92
(330) 255-0041 **Sitler** Martin H '04
(330) 376-5300 **Skakun** Mark J III '74
(330) 434-4000 **Skelton** James R '97
(330) 535-5711 **Skeriotis** John M '98
(330) 253-1550 **Skidmore** Archie W '55
(330) 253-1550 **Skidmore** Brian K '84
(330) 253-1550 **Skidmore** Eric E '89
(330) 379-2745 **Skidmore** Thomas A '88
(330) 762-7377 **Skinner** Colin G '95
(330) 376-1242 **Skoglund** Rodney L '91
(330) 762-0700 **Slater** James W '70
(330) 762-0700 **Slater Zurz & Gilbert**
(330) 643-2663 **Sloan** Jerry Kay '71
(330) 376-2700 **Small** Janis L '83
(330) 434-7167 **Smith** A Russell '61
(330) 671-5226 **Smith** Anne E '00
(330) 643-2250 **Smith** Christina I '03
(330) 762-8885 **Smith** Dean E '72
(330) 253-2729 **Smith** Deborah L '96
(330) 376-2272 **Smith** Edward T '92
Smith Katherine C '88
(330) 376-9121 **Smith** Lawrence R '72
(330) 376-4558 **Smith** Melinda E '99
(330) 762-6474 **Smith** Scott F '98
(330) 376-5300 **Smithern** Michelle A '86
(330) 376-3300 **Snitchler** Todd '02
(330) 643-2326 **Snyder** Ann L '83
(330) 762-7488 **Snyder** Christopher R '02
(330) 643-2800 **Sokolowski-Craft** Arlene '01
(330) 208-1000 **Solomon** John W '73
(330) 996-1087 **Sommerfeld** Barbara I '99
(330) 253-5060 **Sossi** Frank T '78
(330) 376-2700 **Souza** Jennifer L '98
(330) 643-2341 **Spahr** Kenneth G Jr. '74
(330) 253-8877 **Spetrino** Michael J '80
(330) 836-9971 **Sponseller** Alan W '80
(330) 434-2713 **Spragin** Lydia E '94
(330) 376-2700 **Spring** Gary W '79
(330) 882-2920 **Squires** Thomas B '90
(330) 972-1923 **Srail** Roger A '69
(330) 644-0061 **Sremack** William M '75
(330) 643-2371 **Stabler** Rhonda L '87
(330) 253-0719 **Stacey** Kelly M '95
(330) 644-2940 **Stachowiak** Robert W '69
(330) 762-7377 **Staley** Cara L '04
(330) 664-6524 **Staples** Elizabeth A '85
(330) 376-3300 **Stark & Knoll Co,LPA**
(330) 376-3300 **Stark** Michael L '67
(330) 761-4207 **Stark** Wendy E '97
(330) 376-3300 **Starkey** Ronald K '92
(330) 762-2411 **Stasitis** Mark G '01
(330) 996-2037 **Stauffenger** Leonard W '83
(330) 253-5060 **Stecz** Eric J '96
(330) 376-8336 **Steel** Frank E Jr. '63
(330) 376-8336 **Steel** Michael A '00
Steen Daniel V '72
(330) 253-7070 **Stein** Ernest R '51
(330) 384-7287 **Steiner** Judith A '87
(330) 535-1010 **Steinhauer** John S '69
(330) 643-8457 **Steinhauer** Susan K '98
(330) 375-2285 **Stephens** Suzanne L '88
(330) 762-6474 **Sternberg Newman Shifrin & Associates**
(330) 762-6474 **Sternberg** Richard '52
(330) 643-3550 **Sterner** Steven L '85
(330) 761-9960 **Stetson** Scott V '03
(330) 643-2326 **Stevenson** Diana M '92
(330) 376-2700 **Stevenson** Roger J '81
(330) 762-0765 **Stevenson** Scot A '92
(330) 864-0117 **Stich** Janet I '86
(330) 252-0300 **Stimler** James T '77
(330) 252-0300 **Stimler** Kathleen E '80
(330) 643-2850 **Stith** Michael R '79
(330) 255-5854 **Stocker** Wendall W '85
(330) 643-2082 **Stoner** Tracy D '91
(330) 535-4191 **Strattan** Sara E '76
(330) 376-2700 **Strong** Richard R '80
(330) 376-8336 **Sugerman** Irving B '82
(330) 867-6600 **Summers** Patrick M '88
(330) 376-3300 **Susany** John P '87
(330) 376-3607 **Sutton** Charlotte A '04
(330) 375-5465 **Swanson** Michael P '80
(330) 535-5711 **Swearingen-Hilker** NiCole A '03
(330) 535-5711 **Sweeney** Michael A '76
(330) 762-7655 **Swett** Loma L '80
(330) 535-5711 **Swing** Christopher F '91
(330) 666-6400 **Swyrydenko** Nicholas '89
(330) 762-2411 **Tarchinski** Theresa A '89
(330) 535-2151 **Taylor** E Jane '81
(330) 376-1112 **Taylor** Elizabeth G '91
(330) 643-2365 **Teleis** Kenneth R '93
(330) 535-1555 **Teodosio Manos & Ward**
(330) 535-1555 **Teodosio** Thomas A '82
(330) 665-5117 **Teresczuk** Timothy G '94
(330) 670-8588 **Terjesen** Barry E '73
(330) 208-1000 **Tersigni** Vincent J '88
(330) 376-2700 **Terzola** Mark C '96
(330) 376-8019 **Thomas** Bradley J '97
(330) 255-4200 **Thomas** David A '64
(330) 535-0505 **Thomas** Robert S II '97
(330) 643-7638 **Thomason** Jacqueline '89
(330) 762-6223 **Thomasson** James S '69
(330) 753-6874 **Thompson** Dennis Ray '85
(330) 535-5711 **Thomson** Daniel A '99
(330) 665-0916 **Thrasher** Michael L '96
(330) 670-8400 **Tipping** Christopher A '95
(330) 670-8400 **Tipping** Harry A '71
(330) 668-6500 **Tobin** Alan J '81
(330) 535-5149 **Tobin** Alfred S '82
(330) 869-9421 **Todd** Tamara J '03
(330) 643-2765 **Tomer** Michele A '92
(330) 253-5060 **Toney** Darrin R '95
(330) 796-4456 **Toppen** Timothy R '92
(330) 535-5711 **Towell** Jennifer D '03

(330) 535-2151 **Towne** Ronald N '69
(330) 535-3103 **Tramonte** Michael A '76
(330) 535-0505 **Trattner** Robert B '93
(330) 376-2700 **Treadon** Thomas A '75
(330) 208-1000 **Treier** J Bret '85
(330) 796-5019 **Tritt** William C '88
(330) 376-5300 **Trotter** Thomas R '75
(330) 434-3000 **Truby** Timothy J '72
(330) 376-8336 **Tsarnas** George P '63
(330) 376-8336 **Tsarnas** Peter G '03
(330) 253-5454 **Tsarouhas** Antonios P '94
Tschantz Mary Myers '78
(330) 376-5300 **Tschugunov** Eleanor J '79
(330) 253-1900 **Tuccillo** Anthony '59
(330) 379-2002 **Tucker** Catherine P '93
(330) 253-7100 **Tucker** John A '91
(330) 762-9191 **Tucker** Jon D '97
(330) 670-7300 **Tucker** Robert L '84
(330) 836-2292 **Turowski** Kenneth Lee '83
(330) 670-0770 **Ufholz** Louis T '74
(330) 376-2700 **Uhlmann** David C '00
(330) 762-2411 **Urban** Michael S '87
(330) 376-1717 **Utley** David G '87
(330) 670-7300 **Vadas** Kathryn A '99
(330) 643-2765 **Valenti** Kimberly A '02
(330) 836-9358 **Vance** Patricia Ann '67
(330) 535-6751 **VanDevere** Christopher M '93
(330) 643-2785 **Van Ho** Adam M '01
(330) 258-6462 **Van Ness** Jean C '95
(330) 376-5300 **VanRees** Adam R '02
(330) 633-2069 **VanVorous** Regina M '83
(330) 434-4100 **Varian** Donald S Jr. '70
(330) 253-1550 **Vasilatos** Spiros Jr. '84
(330) 374-5540 **Vasko** George B '63
Vassel Barbara M '83
(330) 867-2444 **Vehar** August R '78
(330) 375-2730 **Veillette** Jeremy A '98
(330) 666-7952 **Velie** Garwin P '80
(330) 864-6060 **Venesy** Barbara A '91
(330) 255-6000 **Vengrow** Jeffrey S '74
Verity Neal D '71
(330) 384-5800 **Vespoli** Leila Lee '84
(330) 972-6410 **Viau** William H '94
(330) 643-2765 **Vitale** Lisa M '97
(330) 836-9971 **Vlosky** Edward F '86
Vogel Walter J '60
(330) 253-5060 **Voinovich** George F '90
(330) 535-5711 **Volk** Jay G '98
(330) 375-2030 **Vollman** Sean W '99
(330) 208-1000 **Vorys Sater Seymour & Pease LLP**
(330) 643-2929 **Vuillemin** John E '76
(330) 253-0785 **Vuillemin** Lawrence W '73
(330) 867-8422 **Wack** Patrick J '73
(330) 253-1111 **Waddell** David E '60
(330) 796-4794 **Waechter** Thomas C '67
(330) 848-8690 **Wagenknecht** Carl R Jr. '89
(330) 535-1555 **Wagner** Dean R '87
(330) 864-3100 **Wagner** James L '76
(330) 376-5300 **Wagner** Louis F '84
(330) 762-0700 **Wagoner** Edmund Lee Jr. '87
(330) 762-6334 **Waite** Eric R '97
(330) 384-4596 **Walker** Debra Kay '95
(330) 434-5118 **Walker** Donald L '77
(330) 253-5060 **Walko** Lee S '93
(330) 434-3461 **Walls** Angela R '01
(330) 374-1110 **Walpole** Daniel M '85
(330) 972-7751 **Walsh** Charles M '91
(330) 643-2800 **Walsh** Sherri Bevan '85
(330) 643-2765 **Walsh** Timothy J '83
(330) 535-5711 **Walter** Karen L '96
(330) 668-6500 **Walters** Jeffery A '84
(330) 253-2729 **Walton** Howard Jon '71
(330) 535-1555 **Ward** Barry M '84
(330) 376-3300 **Waszak** Ralph R Jr. '93
(330) 864-5550 **Watkins** Mark A '88
(330) 376-3300 **Wear** Michael L '95
(330) 761-4205 **Weber** Douglas J '88
(330) 535-6185 **Weber** Edward C '72
(330) 376-1242 **Weber** Mark L '00
(330) 376-1242 **Weber** Ray L '72
(330) 376-2700 **Webster** Timothy J '87
(330) 535-2151 **Wehener** Ann L '94
(330) 670-8334 **Weiner** Matthew C '02
(330) 434-1000 **Weisensell** John C '85
(330) 374-1144 **Weisman** Mark B '87
(330) 762-9621 **Weisman** Mark S '85
(330) 253-2252 **Weissfeld** Randall D '79
(330) 434-3000 **Weitendorf** Kurt R '80
Wellemeyer William D '91
(330) 762-0275 **Wells** Jason T '02
(330) 761-9960 **Werren** Nola R '89
(330) 434-1000 **Wertz** George R '79
(330) 376-5300 **Weschler** Patrick J '81
(330) 375-3954 **Wessell** Kelly M '94
(330) 867-9998 **Westman** Dean E '81
(330) 376-1112 **Whalen & Compton, LPA**
(330) 376-1112 **Whalen** Dennis M '66
(330) 376-2668 **Wheeler** Christine E '02
(330) 796-6364 **Wheeler** David E '84
(330) 643-2250 **Wheeler** Susan E '85
(330) 762-0287 **Whitaker** William T Jr. '72
(330) 869-5900 **White** Craig M '87
(330) 643-7550 **Whited** James R '75
(330) 535-5711 **Whitmer** Jerry F '60
(330) 258-6252 **Whitmore** Andreana R '00
(330) 253-7171 **Whitney** Lawrence J '74
(330) 535-5711 **Whitten** Nora J '01
(330) 384-8484 **Whittington** Robert M Jr. '81
(330) 535-4191 **Widder** Karen E '92
(330) 535-5711 **Wiencek** Thomas J '85
(330) 376-5300 **Wiese** Philip R '96
(330) 434-6687 **Wigley** Edmund A '55
(330) 864-5550 **Wilcox** Amanda H '01
(330) 867-9998 **Wilkins** James P '83
(330) 867-9998 **Wilkins** Linda L '83
(330) 375-2007 **Williams** Annalisa S '84
(330) 762-0080 **Williams** Brian J '79
(330) 784-1271 **Williams** Caroline '77
(330) 796-4995 **Williams** Kenneth C '75
(330) 376-2668 **Williams** Orlando J '86
(330) 328-4736 **Williams** Richard J '03
(330) 848-9393 **Williger** Richard Lee '82
(330) 434-5297 **Willis** Mark C '87
(330) 434-5297 **Willis** Todd L '98
(330) 670-3007 **Willoughby** John A '73
(330) 375-2730 **Wilms** Gertrude E '01
(330) 253-8300 **Wilson** Bruce H '64
(330) 762-2600 **Wilson** Dale V '83
(330) 670-0101 **Wilson** Katherine A '01
(330) 376-0000 **Windon** Jeffrey D '74
(330) 867-3247 **Winick** Bernard S '64
(330) 665-5117 **Witschey** Frank J '92
(330) 665-5117 **Witschey** Jeffrey T '92
(330) 796-3614 **Wittkamper** Gerry Van '72
Wolf Barbara A '80
(330) 762-6334 **Wolf** Erin L '04
(330) 535-2441 **Wolfe** John L '53
(330) 773-3351 **Wolfe** Terry W '73
(330) 535-7510 **Woodall** Jefferson Jr. '78
(330) 535-7510 **Woodall** Shelby L '94
(330) 258-6506 **Woodburn** David W '97
(330) 762-5627 **Woodruff** Gigi A '83
(330) 376-2700 **Wright** Alisa L '93
(330) 376-2700 **Wright** Bradley A '90
(330) 376-8855 **Wright** Michael J '02
(330) 376-7245 **Wright** Stephan R '03
Wysin Gregory J '02
(330) 376-2700 **Wyss** Jerome G '01
(330) 375-5716 **Yannucci** Samuel A '79
(330) 379-3838 **Yarcusko** Alan C '93
(330) 784-8800 **Yeargin** Rocco P '96
(330) 784-8800 **Yeargin** Stephen J '04
(330) 375-2730 **Yoder** Jonathan R '03
(330) 375-2030 **York** John R '95
(330) 253-5678 **York** Olen L III '02
(330) 375-2030 **York** Stephanie H '95
(330) 784-8800 **Young** Dean A '77
(330) 796-2956 **Young** Henry C Jr. '63
(330) 784-8800 **Young & McDowall**
(330) 376-7245 **Yukish** Kristen M '04
(330) 376-1112 **Zacharyasz** Mari A '00
(330) 643-8200 **Zaehringer** Brittany G '99
(330) 208-1000 **Zaremba** Amanda J '04
(330) 762-9700 **Zavarello** A William '64
(330) 375-5834 **Zbiegien** Michael J Jr. '04
(330) 762-0280 **Zerebniak** Harry M '83
(330) 836-5500 **Zerrusen** Kenneth M '99
(330) 665-5117 **Ziance** Christopher E '02
(330) 376-5756 **Ziegler** Deborah A '85
(330) 762-7477 **Zimmerman** Terry D '75
(330) 864-4093 **Zindle** Charles W '70
(330) 836-4181 **Zona-Peters** Anita '93
(330) 666-6900 **Zugrave** George V Jr. '87
(330) 376-2700 **Zumkehr** Charles E '64
(330) 253-3337 **Zurz** Richard V '53
(330) 762-0700 **Zurz** Richard V Jr. '82
(330) 375-2730 **Zwaig** Brian J '92

ALEXANDRIA
Licking County

(740) 587-0733 **Reed** Troy A '93
Trimble Kathy M '01

ALLIANCE
Stark County

(330) 821-1430 **Amsden-Michel** Alissa A '01
(330) 829-0150 **Boyce** Richard M '85
(330) 821-6411 **Burnquist** John A '84
(330) 821-0701 **Casale** Joseph A '59
(330) 821-0701 **Casale** Ned J '84
(330) 823-9142 **Clunk** Dennis R '82
(330) 821-3293 **Coco** Anthony J '56
(330) 823-1190 **England** Daniel L '80
(330) 829-3219 **Francis** Philip Lee '83
(330) 821-1430 **Geiger Teeple Smith & Hahn**
(330) 821-2516 **Goldthorpe** Christopher J '72
(330) 821-1430 **Hahn** Brian Scott '80
(330) 823-7411 **Haupt** John E Jr. '83
(330) 823-1220 **Hunter** Robert R '50
(330) 823-1220 **Hunter** Robert R Jr. '75
(330) 823-9757 **Jakmides** Jeffrey Ray '81
(330) 823-5100 **James** Robert N '67
Krash Allan L '61
(330) 823-9262 **Krugliak Wilkins Griffiths & Dougherty Co,LPA**
(330) 823-9080 **Lamb** Joyce A '90
(330) 821-2516 **Lundgren** David J '76
(330) 821-2516 **Lundgren Goldthorpe & Zumbar**
(330) 821-9997 **Luther** Brant A '02
(330) 821-2130 **McAlister** David C '82
(330) 935-2359 **McAlister** Don E '64
(330) 823-4111 **Morris** Evan W '65
(330) 823-9080 **Morris** John D '75
(330) 823-3575 **Morris** William F '71
(330) 821-1430 **Moushey** Thomas P '77
(330) 829-7496 **Murray** Michael F '69
(330) 829-6560 **Newbold** Pamela H '88
(330) 821-6648 **Norton** Amy J '00
(330) 821-1430 **Ogline** Michael A '78
(330) 823-1970 **Puckett** James P '69
(330) 821-1430 **Randall** Thomas K '68
(330) 823-1140 **Robertson** Alex J '55
(330) 823-1140 **Robertson** Alex J '91
(330) 823-1140 **Robertson** Erin K '02
(330) 823-1140 **Robertson** Shawn O '93
(330) 823-2226 **Shetler** William B '73
(330) 821-1430 **Smith** Bruce E '75
(330) 823-2226 **Spalding** David B '80
(330) 823-0696 **Stone** Donald S Jr. '73
(330) 823-0740 **Stone** Robert H Jr. '91
(330) 821-5330 **Tangi** Thomas J '86
(330) 821-4414 **Whitaker** Mark A '79
(330) 821-2627 **Witte** Wylan W '73
Yost Gerard T '91
(330) 821-2516 **Zumbar** Andrew L '92

ALPHA
Greene County

(937) 372-8888 **Buerger** Robert E '00

AMANDA
Fairfield County

Lunn John P '78

AMELIA
Clermont County

(513) 753-4303 **Baker** Scott W '93
(513) 943-7100 **Bevington** Maria D '98
(513) 947-9490 **Blomer** Philip J '77
(513) 943-7100 **Brizzolara** Paul T '82
(513) 753-7277 **Dietrich** Clifford A '03
(513) 943-7200 **Dinnen** Jeffrey A '98
(513) 943-7500 **Gill** Nancy Jo '79
(513) 943-7100 **Griffith** Charles S III '97
Hartman Curt C '94
(513) 943-7100 **Kiessling** Kurt M '92
(513) 752-1300 **Koligian** Helene '97
(513) 943-7100 **Mason** Natalie Ann '01
(513) 753-7277 **Rapp** William J '87
(513) 943-7100 **Reed** Kate E '99
Vite Barbara A '02
(513) 943-7070 **Waldner** Linda D '82
(513) 943-7200 **Whittle** James T Jr. '82
(513) 752-2338 **Zugelter** Carl W '75
(513) 752-1300 **Zuk** Walter K '72

AMHERST
Lorain County

(440) 988-7918 **Anderson** Alan W '72
Bracy Michele L '02
(440) 989-4100 **Bradley** Sam R '87
(440) 989-5700 **Budway** R J '93
(440) 988-0340 **Chadwick** Geneva C '83
(440) 988-4537 **Conry** Martin J '74
Dietrich Ellen E '91
(440) 988-8786 **Gray** Russell W '87
(440) 988-4172 **Janik** Frank J III '90
(440) 989-4100 **Nicol** Wayne R '04
(813) 843-2263 **Pearsall** Wayne G '03
(440) 988-8455 **Riske** Michelle L '92
(440) 984-3782 **Torma** Mary D '92
(440) 963-1165 **Wasilk** Neil J '82
(440) 988-2858 **Willis** William J Jr. '89
(440) 984-3551 **Young** James H '87

ANDOVER
Ashtabula County

(440) 293-6346 **Kotila** Richard B '80
(440) 293-6346 **McCombs** David L '74

ANTWERP
Paulding County

(419) 258-2191 **Ramsier** Floyd A '72
(419) 258-1550 **Rister** Suzanne S '00

ARCADIA
Hancock County

(419) 894-6842 **Riddle** Loretta A '02

ARCANUM
Darke County

(937) 692-5278 **Blinn** Caroline R '01
(937) 548-4699 **Cox** Robert J '51
(937) 692-5712 **Dynes** Craig A '79
(937) 692-5278 **Garbig & Blinn,LLC**
(937) 692-5278 **Garbig** Phillip R '85

ARCHBOLD
Fulton County

(419) 445-4511 **Gooding** Jack D '69
(419) 445-8815 **Hagans** Mark D '94
(419) 445-8815 **Hensal** James E '71
(419) 445-3015 **Lammy** James E '78
(419) 445-8815 **Plassman** Harold H '59
(419) 445-8815 **Plassman Rupp Hensal Short & Hagans**
(419) 445-8815 **Rupp** David P Jr. '65
(419) 445-8815 **Short** Peter D '78
(419) 445-4511 **Winzeler** Brent L '79

ASHLAND
Ashland County

(419) 289-2183 **Akers** Eric J '73
(419) 289-6500 **Anderson** Charles D '59
(419) 289-2220 **Budd** Thomas J II '78
(419) 281-3561 **Cahill** Erin N '99
(419) 496-3680 **Caley** Beverly A '92
(419) 289-1710 **DeSanto** Robert P '77
(419) 289-6888 **Findley** Daniel G '97
(419) 282-4290 **Forsthoefel** Ronald P '83
(419) 289-2555 **Ginty** James R '50
(419) 281-2556 **Glick** Howard W '80
(419) 207-0553 **Good** John L '91
(419) 289-2555 **Halligan** Brian J '83
(419) 289-6888 **Harpster** Russell L '58
(419) 289-6888 **Harpster Vanosdall & Findley**
(419) 281-3409 **Honaker** Jeffrey C '02
(419) 289-1600 **Kearns** Joseph P Jr. '94
(419) 289-8857 **Kellogg** Karen L '00
(419) 289-1234 **Lett** Robert W '38
(419) 289-1234 **Lett** Sam J '77
(419) 281-0171 **Locke** Gregory F '78
(419) 281-0171 **Locke** Nancy N '77
(419) 289-1600 **Mason** Josiah L '60
(419) 289-1600 **Mason Mason & Kearns**
(419) 289-1600 **Mason** Thomas L '89
McGinnis Lori A '89
(419) 289-3777 **Montague** Walter D '78
(419) 289-8857 **Moroney** Melissa P '97
(419) 289-3800 **Murray** Oliver J '62
Nelson James E '53
(419) 281-0171 **Nordstrom** Kenneth J '46
(419) 281-0171 **Nordstrom & Locke**
(419) 289-8857 **O'Reilly** Paul E '84
(419) 281-3561 **Oxley** Fred M '73
(419) 289-6888 **Potts** Timothy E '97
(419) 289-8857 **Rogers** Ramona J '82
(419) 289-0509 **Samsel** David A '72
Schaefer Gerald J '03
(419) 289-3800 **Shafer** Philip H '65
(419) 289-3800 **Sullivan** Michael P '87
(419) 289-8857 **Tunnell** Christopher R '00
(419) 289-6888 **Vanosdall** John A '78
(419) 289-1199 **VanTilburg** William D '62
(419) 289-6500 **Wilson & Anderson**
(419) 289-3777 **Wolfe** Richard P II '73
(419) 289-8141 **Woodside** William J '99

ASHTABULA
Ashtabula County

(440) 964-2700 **Altier** Christopher T '89
(440) 964-3311 **Altier** Samuel L Jr. '82
(440) 998-6835 **Andrews** Mark W '76
(440) 998-6835 **Andrews & Pontius LLC**
(440) 998-2628 **Bayer** Leigh A '02
(440) 998-2628 **Bell** Kimberly E '02
(440) 998-4214 **Bobulsky** William P '72
(440) 992-7196 **Camplese** Albert S '85
(440) 964-5125 **Cantagallo** Anthony J Jr. '64
(440) 992-6067 **Cimorell** Bret J '85
(440) 997-6175 **Cordell** Stuart W '81
(440) 998-6835 **Cordova** Philip E '01
(440) 997-6175 **Coxon** Jeffrey L '92
(440) 998-1811 **DiGiacomo** Laura M '94
(440) 992-5891 **Douglas** Malcolm S '89
(440) 998-6835 **Dubsky** Duane J '73
(440) 998-1202 **Dunne** Robert W Jr. '82
(440) 992-5522 **Field** Jon T '81
(440) 998-6835 **Ford** Jeffry A '82
(440) 998-0770 **Franklin** Michael '81
(440) 964-0236 **Hamilton** Terry L '85
(440) 992-0647 **Hawn-Jackson** Jane A '83
(440) 998-2628 **Heasley** Phillip L '90
(440) 998-0611 **Hitchcock** Thomas '77
(440) 994-6000 **Hough** Edith M '91
(440) 998-6835 **Houston** Pamela D '99
(440) 998-2628 **Humpolick** Joseph A '79
(440) 997-9222 **Kobelak** William A '80
(440) 997-8130 **Lambros** Thomas D '52
(440) 998-2628 **Lane** Dorothy M '91
(440) 992-3120 **Larson** Bernadette T '77
(440) 992-2499 **Lesko** Jane L '96
(440) 998-1110 **McMillan** Debra S '85
(440) 964-2700 **Meaney** Michael P '87
(440) 998-5337 **Mikolay** Joseph C '91
(440) 997-6175 **Muller** Carl F '72
O'Day Edwin R '54
(440) 992-5561 **Pertz** Julianne P '84
(440) 998-6835 **Pontius** David E '79
(440) 998-2628 **Reid** Dennis M '73
(440) 997-6175 **Riedel** Katherine S '00
(440) 997-6175 **Riedel** William E '69
(440) 998-5337 **Rosenthal** Scott A '89
(440) 992-8322 **Sartini** James J '91
(440) 997-6175 **Sernik** Craig F '97
(440) 998-6923 **Sheldon** David C '73
(440) 992-8211 **Shiflet** Hobart M '82
(440) 964-2200 **Simon** Thomas J '81
(440) 964-6466 **Spotts** David M '75
(440) 998-1110 **Thomas** Nicholas K '89
(440) 992-5891 **Topalof** Dean F '96
(440) 992-7101 **VanDevender** Margaret A '85
(440) 964-9444 **Varckette** Francis A '53
(440) 997-6175 **Vermilya** Randy A '99
(440) 998-3039 **Warren** E Terry '56
(440) 997-6175 **Warren & Young,PLL**
(440) 998-1110 **Weddleton** Terry C '84

ASHVILLE
Pickaway County

(740) 983-4074 **Brown** Charles D '90
(740) 983-2557 **Gussler** Stephen S '66
(740) 983-2557 **Hall** Leo J '65
(740) 983-2557 **Hosterman** John W '74
(740) 983-2557 **Margulis Gussler Hall & Hosterman**
(740) 983-3336 **Sedlak** Alan F '75
(740) 983-0155 **Sherman** Richard B '03
Webb Valerie M '02

ATHENS
Athens County

(740) 594-8093 **Baer** David G '80
(740) 592-9043 **Baker** Adam J '92
(740) 597-1819 **Bell** Kelli L '99
(740) 592-3328 **Bennett** Douglas J '75
(740) 592-6399 **Biddlestone** William R Jr. '84
(740) 593-5828 **Bradford** Melinda K '97
(740) 593-2626 **Burns** John F '69
(740) 594-8388 **Carson** Herman A '80
(740) 592-3332 **Charriez** Gilberto J '04
(740) 593-2631 **Conrad** Robert F '93
(740) 594-2788 **Cornn** Thomas L '73
(740) 594-3558 **Crates** Katrina O '04
(740) 797-7909 **Cunningham** Matthew A '98
(740) 593-2626 **Dioguardi** Nicolette '84
(740) 592-3061 **Driscoll** Robert P '93
(740) 592-3332 **Eliason** Lisa A '87
(740) 593-6410 **Eslocker** Thomas E '76
(740) 594-3401 **Fenstermaker** Eric B '75
(740) 594-8388 **Ferrier** Lisbeth B '85
(740) 592-3208 **Flanagan** Colleen Sue '95
(740) 593-6909 **Foran** Timothy J '76
Frey C David '70
(740) 593-3357 **Gall** Cherie H '83
(740) 593-3357 **Gall** Robert J '87
(740) 592-3247 **Garrison** Gary L '87
(740) 593-3800 **Gerig** Christian S '96
(740) 593-3800 **Gerig** Paul J '68
(740) 592-5839 **Grace** Todd L '01
(740) 594-2241 **Grim** William A '74
(740) 594-8686 **Gwinn** Susan L '79
(740) 592-3240 **Harvey** Karen M '89
(740) 594-8388 **Hazelbaker** Joseph A '00
(740) 592-2435 **Hedges** Richard H '95
(740) 592-3208 **Huff** Michael R '83
(740) 592-5580 **Hunter** Garry E '74
(740) 593-6400 **Jamison** Patricia A '81
(740) 593-6400 **Jones** Glenn T '97
(740) 593-9323 **Keifer** John L '71
(740) 593-2069 **Keifer** Mary C '71
(740) 593-9418 **Landen** Frank Gifford '78
(740) 707-4740 **Lang** Patrick J '03
(740) 593-3347 **Lavelle** Francis A '82
(740) 593-3348 **Lavelle** John P '82
(740) 594-9625 **Lavelle** William A '52
(740) 593-1643 **Lonsinger** Linda Lee '87
(740) 592-3247 **Malloy** Susan E '97
(740) 693-2063 **Marinelli** Arthur J Jr. '67
(740) 592-3332 **McCarthy** George P '90

(740) 592-5839 **McGee** Patrick C '79
(740) 592-3332 **Miller** Michael D '02
(740) 593-3357 **Mollica** Andrew J '89
(740) 797-4386 **Mollica** Anthony C '83
(740) 593-3357 **Mollica Gall Sloan & Sillery Co,LPA**
(740) 593-3357 **Mollica** Gerald A '63
(740) 589-7135 **Morman** Todd A '03
(740) 594-8178 **Myers** Laura L '94
(740) 593-9844 **Nalazek** Barbara U '99
(740) 593-6410 **Oremus** Frederick L '73
(740) 592-3236 **Perrin** Jonathan M '92
(740) 593-3348 **Pettey** Sky '00
(740) 594-8388 **Rambo** Madeline A '91
(740) 592-3208 **Reitmeier** George J '95
(740) 593-2013 **Roach** Bonnie L '03
(740) 593-5576 **Robe** Scott M '91
(740) 593-2066 **Roberson** Jessie C Jr. '80
(740) 592-3208 **Ross** Richard L '76
(740) 594-3558 **Rubin** Anne S '81
(740) 592-5025 **Safranek** William H III '72
(740) 594-8093 **Sallah** Margaret A '03
(740) 593-5828 **Shostak** Robert J '90
(740) 593-3357 **Sillery** James D '73
(740) 593-3357 **Sloan** Steven T '73
(740) 594-8388 **Sowash Carson & Ferrier**
(740) 594-8388 **Sowash** Jonathan B '80
(740) 594-3558 **Strader** Rekha S '04
(740) 593-3187 **Toy** Kerry R '77
(740) 594-8228 **Walker** Brian R '85
(740) 594-8228 **Walker** William R '78
(740) 592-4463 **Wallace** James A '81
(740) 593-6400 **Wamsley** Jay H '82
(740) 592-3208 **Warren** Charles David '80
(740) 593-6400 **Westfall** James M '79
(740) 594-4043 **Wiens** Keith M '98
(740) 593-3357 **Wines** Larry D '97
(740) 592-6399 **Winkelmann** David J '94
(740) 594-5000 **Wood** Wheaton B '02
(740) 593-3385 **Yanity** Joseph B Jr. '53

AURORA
Portage County

(330) 562-4623 **Baker** Douglas R '79
(330) 562-6800 **Benjamin** David M '77
(330) 995-7702 **Brodsky** Jerry '87
(330) 562-6538 **Buonpane** Susan K '85
(330) 995-0971 **Carpenter** Paul E '82
(330) 562-3156 **Christley Herington & Pierce**
(330) 562-3156 **Christley** Norman L '68
(330) 562-4862 **Cindric** Michael J '97
(330) 562-9588 **Disantis** John P '75
(330) 562-6800 **Dismuke** Daniel K '01
Dunbar Brian D '91
(330) 562-2424 **Fromhercz** Stephen P '82
(330) 562-3156 **Habowski** Ronald J '85
Harris Brad '03
(330) 562-3156 **Herington** Leigh E '76
(330) 562-3156 **Hirt** David S '94
(330) 995-0051 **Kimmel** Roger A Jr. '72
(330) 562-3156 **Marsilio** Tommie Jo '98
Miller Deena C '93
(330) 562-2793 **Minton** Andrea J '74
(330) 562-1339 **Moroney** Carole J '64
(330) 562-4404 **Moss** Frank '57
(330) 543-4732 **O'Connell-Burton** Kathleen M '80
O'Driscoll Janet I '85
(330) 562-4076 **Oswick** Barbara R '92
(330) 562-3156 **Paul** Douglas K '95
(330) 562-2930 **Purcell** Carl W '67
(330) 562-3156 **Reitz** Thomas R '88
(330) 562-3156 **Shorr** Alan I '70
(330) 562-3156 **Silver** James R '80
(330) 562-7277 **Tomasko** Elizabeth S '91
(330) 995-8663 **Turell** Russell B '70
(330) 221-8157 **Weber** Edward P Jr. '68
(330) 995-5005 **Wolkov** Leonard A '67

AUSTINBURG
Ashtabula County

(440) 275-1333 **Cooper** Hal D '63

AUSTINTOWN
Mahoning County

(330) 792-7061 **Dunn** Francis L Jr. '00
(330) 797-0086 **Goske** Stephen Paul '81
(330) 797-0086 **Green Haines & Sgambati, Co LPA**
(330) 565-5147 **Hrina** Pamela S '01
(330) 799-0129 **Kinnick** Paul G '92
(330) 793-4610 **Lefoer** Dominic S '65
(330) 793-2698 **Regginello** John A '99
(330) 797-0086 **Slipski** Ronald Edward '79
(330) 270-7041 **Smith** Shirley J '97
(330) 270-9016 **Steen** Jon R '82
(330) 565-5146 **Villano** Mark A '00
(330) 270-9027 **Vitullo** James A '82

AVON
Lorain County

(440) 930-8072 **Altieri** Mark P '80
Amendola Mark A '89
(440) 930-8052 **Ashar** Linda C '85
Balunek Adelbert A '66
(440) 353-9462 **Barker** James E '85
(440) 930-8066 **Batista** Daniel P '59
(440) 934-2199 **Belardo** Lee E '95
(440) 930-8083 **Collett** Marsha L '80
(440) 930-8045 **Cook** Daniel A '68
(440) 930-8085 **Ellis** Robert P Jr. '75
(440) 934-7676 **Gasior** John A '84
(440) 930-8065 **Herzer** David L '70
(440) 934-6164 **Holcomb** Craig A '83
(440) 930-8048 **Kolis** William F Jr. '80
(440) 934-3441 **Marta** Wayne P '77
(440) 937-5911 **Mast** David L '88
(440) 934-7676 **McDermott** Kevin E '84
(440) 930-8068 **Moennich** James W '77
(440) 930-8074 **Naegele** Richard A '79
(440) 930-8051 **Nakon** Matthew W '88
(440) 930-8042 **Niederbaumer** Michael R '00
(440) 937-4019 **Opsitnick** Timothy M '85
(440) 930-8055 **Panza** Richard D '73
(440) 930-8041 **Pawlukiewicz** Charles J '83
(440) 930-8069 **Peters** James E '97
(440) 937-5545 **Phillips** Gerald W '77
(440) 930-8035 **Pillari** Thomas '73
(440) 930-8067 **Prescott** William P '89
(440) 930-8079 **Rothman** Jason A '03
(440) 930-8031 **Rutman** Rennie C '01
(440) 930-8044 **Ryan** Spencer A '01
(440) 930-8075 **Rybarczyk** John D '87
(440) 930-8081 **Schrader** Todd A '96
(440) 937-6266 **Stamatis** John N '85
(440) 930-8056 **Stefanik** Thomas J Jr. '96
(440) 934-7676 **Stringer** Anthony R '67
(440) 934-7676 **Stringer** Daniel P '63
(440) 934-7676 **Stringer Stringer & Gasior**
(440) 934-7676 **Stringer** Thomas C '03
(440) 871-8048 **Timm** Richard M Jr. '95
(440) 934-1425 **Tomassi** John A '90
(440) 930-8082 **Urban** Daniel C '96
(440) 934-0474 **Violand** James P '79
(440) 937-4705 **Viscomi** William A '69
(440) 930-8000 **Wickens Herzer Panza Cook & Batista**
(440) 930-8030 **Wiersma** David C '76
(440) 930-8096 **Zidar** Rachelle K '96

AVON LAKE
Lorain County

(440) 930-3825 **Ban** Woodrow W '81
(440) 933-4469 **Bonds** William T '64
(440) 933-2029 **Branch** David A '96
(440) 933-6718 **Bretnall** Dorothy H '81
(440) 930-2600 **Brusnahan** Kreig J '81
(440) 933-5442 **Butler** Barbara A '00
(440) 933-3231 **DeGeeter** Pamela A '97
(440) 933-4288 **Everson** Anne M '86
(440) 933-6188 **Everson** John H '86
(440) 933-3231 **Frankel** Kenneth P '75
(440) 933-3231 **Gentile** Leslie A '96
(440) 930-1361 **Hahn** Richard E '71
(440) 933-3231 **Hallett** Matthew H '98
(440) 933-9884 **Hurst** Bonita M '95
(440) 930-7665 **Hyland** John P '71
(440) 933-6278 **Kerner** James B '94
(440) 933-6461 **Kerner** William J Sr. '71
(800) 346-4497 **Kuebler** Christopher D '82
(440) 933-8938 **Lang** William P '79
(440) 930-3827 **Larson** Lee E '72
(440) 930-5678 **Lenahan** Christopher R '00
(440) 930-4103 **Mackin** John F '61
(440) 933-3177 **Mackin** Patrick C '87
(440) 933-5442 **Marcie** Jay C '92
(440) 933-3231 **McClure** Richard D '72
(216) 272-8518 **Nelson** Kenneth A II '03
(440) 933-0674 **Pincura** John D III '65
(440) 930-3317 **Powell** Joe A '75
(440) 930-2600 **Prudhoe** Jeffrey R '98
(440) 933-8938 **Reddy** James P Jr. '82
(440) 933-6377 **Russell** Anson H '56
Sarady Alexander V '02
(440) 933-3231 **Smith** Gerald M '61
(440) 933-3231 **Smith** James J '88
(440) 933-3231 **Smith** Timothy T '69
(440) 930-2600 **Stuart** Richard P '90
Tammisaar Eric J '77
(440) 930-7529 **Taylor** Tyra L '94
Thieken Andrew J '97
(440) 930-1318 **Titas** Francis G '73
(440) 930-5911 **VanDenBossche** Achille C '01
Walters Susan M '80
(440) 933-8282 **Warren** James K '89
(440) 930-5154 **Westley** William K Jr. '69
(440) 933-3231 **Wightman** Daniel G '76

BALTIMORE
Fairfield County

(740) 862-4191 **Dern** Robert O '03
(740) 862-4191 **Jackson Keller Shook & Dern**
(740) 862-4191 **Keller** James L '75
(740) 862-4191 **Shook** Stephanie K '00
Stoner Andrea H '92

BARBERTON
Summit County

(330) 860-6762 **Ahonen** Robert M '87
(330) 745-5061 **Alfera** Vincent J '75
(330) 753-6416 **Benedict** Robert L '77
(330) 753-7777 **Boley** Thomas R '74
Cich Frank A '74
(330) 825-9858 **Daly** James E '71
(330) 745-0006 **Deibel** John W '63
(330) 745-0016 **Deuber** Frederick J '61
(330) 860-2086 **Dool** Carl D '71
(330) 860-6205 **Dziewisz** John J '92
(330) 848-6728 **Fish** David E '84
(330) 745-1611 **Gayetsky-Ghadiri** Marie T '91
(330) 860-1522 **Gingo** Michael J '81
(330) 825-9991 **Gipson** Thomas B '80
(330) 860-1471 **Grady** Michael J '86
(330) 745-5995 **Harnden** Thomas L '76
(330) 860-6108 **Hennis** Steven E '92
(330) 860-1634 **Howdyshell** Donald E '86
(330) 860-2702 **Hurt** John P '79
(330) 564-4000 **Lynch** Joseph M Jr. '80
Lysenko John '99
(330) 848-6715 **Macko** Gregory '93
(330) 860-6606 **Marich** Eric '85
(330) 745-9027 **May** Bruce J '85
(330) 753-2261 **McNulty** Michael J '74
(330) 848-6710 **Miller** Lisa O '91
(330) 753-6664 **Naumoff** Mitchell A '76
(330) 753-3900 **Peck** Andrew F '85
(330) 745-0006 **Puglisi** Salvatore P '75
Radanof Richard G '69
(330) 861-7193 **Reilly** Susan K '03
(330) 860-1477 **Seymour** Michael J '04
(330) 753-3900 **Wagner** Joy S '88
(330) 848-6712 **Weigand** Michael L '71
Wetzel William C '59
(330) 848-9517 **Wheeler** Evelyn M '89
(330) 753-8968 **Winchell** Dennis R '76
(330) 753-1724 **Woodside** Robert N '72
(330) 753-4511 **Zahirsky** Linda A '85

BARNESVILLE
Belmont County

(740) 425-1211 **Chaney** William E '53
(740) 425-4020 **Hampton** Thomas A '84
(740) 425-2372 **Hoffman** Grace L '91
(740) 425-1023 **Jefferis** Paul B '80

BATAVIA
Clermont County

(513) 732-2214 **Adams** Catherine '83
(513) 735-9100 **Anderson** William H '69
(513) 732-7683 **Arbaugh** Anne M '91
(513) 797-0802 **Backscheider** Clifford R '79
(513) 732-5900 **Ball** Douglas A '90
(513) 732-2800 **Bastin** Dexter K '71
(513) 753-9114 **Bechmann** Anita M '92
(513) 732-7385 **Bedinghaus** Kate E '00
(513) 732-7313 **Birck** Mary L '94
(513) 732-9191 **Blust** Thomas L '73
(513) 732-1141 **Bradford** Douglas J '74
(513) 732-7313 **Breyer** Daniel J '77
(513) 732-7313 **Brock** Anthony W '93
(513) 732-1141 **Burreson Bradford & Hill**
(513) 732-7243 **Carlier** Lawrence W '59
(513) 732-8100 **Carroll** Rebecca R '90
(513) 732-1420 **Carter** David E '91
(513) 732-7313 **Chapman** Gregory A '78
(513) 732-8121 **Colyer** Jason M '04
(513) 732-3200 **Dean** John R '79
(513) 732-0442 **Decatur** Caitlin L '87
(513) 732-2212 **Durkee & Uhle**
(513) 732-6033 **Eberwein** Thomas C '73
(513) 732-7313 **Edwards** Allan Lee '87
(513) 732-7429 **Ellison** Theresa B '92
(513) 732-2140 **Ely & True**
(513) 732-2332 **Erhardt** Chris '62
(513) 732-2332 **Erhardt** Christian IV '94
(513) 732-1104 **Erhardt** John D '52
(513) 732-6871 **Faris** Corinne M '80
(513) 732-1141 **Faris** Dwight V '80
(513) 732-2140 **Ferenc** Richard P '77
(513) 732-7327 **Finney** Michael J '79
(513) 732-3040 **Fisse** Lawrence R '78
(513) 732-1420 **Flessa** Thomas H '82
(513) 732-1420 **Frey** David J '75
(513) 732-7327 **Gates** Penny Ann '84
Goodwin Jonathon T '84
(513) 732-5888 **Greer** Gary R '78
(513) 732-7929 **Haddad** Victor M '89
(513) 732-2214 **Hannon** Richard D '77
(513) 732-3200 **Hauck** Stephen L '77
(513) 732-7313 **Hawkins** Darrell C '89
(513) 735-0300 **Haynes** Willard S '83
(513) 732-7810 **Heimlich** Rebecca S '94
(513) 732-2140 **Henderson** James C '76
(513) 732-7313 **Hoffmann** David H '84
Hondorf Sherrill P '87
(513) 732-0770 **Hunt** James A '74
(513) 732-7327 **Johnson** Winslow W '80
(513) 732-2040 **Kennedy** Michael A '78
(513) 732-3415 **Knepp** Gary L '94
(513) 732-1141 **Korfhagen** John C '82
(513) 732-0443 **Lee** Joan C '85
(513) 732-7385 **Linneman** Daniel E '04
(513) 732-7220 **Malott** Frank W '77
(513) 732-7313 **Mason** Helen E '91
(513) 732-7313 **Mather** James M '96
(513) 724-6111 **Meurer** Gregory J '74
(513) 732-7313 **Miles** Kevin T '99
(513) 732-8145 **Miller** Darren Dee '97
(513) 735-0800 **Mineer** Susan '97
(513) 732-2900 **Montgomery** George P '90
(513) 732-7313 **Nagel** Jason E '99
(513) 732-5311 **Neal** Catherine S '98
(513) 732-1420 **Nichols** James G '68
(513) 732-1420 **Nichols Speidel & Nichols**
(513) 732-2254 **O'Donnell** Priscilla S '77
(513) 732-2140 **Ostendarp** Gary D '71
(513) 732-3800 **Pattison** George E '72
(513) 732-2040 **Rodenberg** Kathleen M '83
Rogus Claire V '95
(513) 732-0300 **Rosenhoffer** Gary A '79
(513) 732-7313 **Rowe** Carol A '01
(513) 732-7573 **Sales** Arrianna '03
(513) 752-1350 **Schaeffer** Earl R '72
(513) 553-4049 **Schuler** Richard P '69
(513) 732-7313 **Scovanner** Thomas W '86
(513) 732-7327 **Shoemaker** Gitte K '94
(513) 732-7360 **Smith** Scott C '02
(513) 735-0300 **Snyder** Terrell B '83
(513) 732-1691 **Stearns** William A '71
(513) 732-1420 **Stoffel** Todd S '89
(513) 732-6740 **Stoner-Barone** Denise '92
(513) 723-2889 **Strasser** Peter J '74
(513) 732-7302 **Thaler** Andrew R '03
(513) 732-2140 **True** James R '63
(513) 732-2212 **Uhle** D'Anne D '83
(513) 732-2212 **Uhle** Richard B Jr. '83
(513) 732-8180 **Viney** Lauri D '98
(513) 732-7893 **Walker** Gayle A '83
(513) 732-5777 **Walker** Lawrence '68
(513) 732-1420 **White** Donald W '73
(513) 943-1222 **Wischer** William P '03
(513) 732-1632 **Woliver** John D '75

BATH
Summit County

(216) 408-3800 **Horwitz** Stuart M '85
(330) 666-4247 **Mertens** Ernest A '86
(330) 869-6701 **Meyer** Paul E '74

BAY VILLAGE
Cuyahoga County

Audi-DeGidio Annette R '92
(440) 835-5396 **Biesterfeldt** John P '99
(440) 871-5899 **Daffner-Gulla** Laura A '91
Finan Nancy C '89
(440) 892-3670 **Hobar** Susan G '92
Honicky David A '94
(440) 835-2463 **Hook** Kenneth A '72
Humphrey Laurie F '01
Hurley William H '01
(216) 870-7500 **Kapp** C Terrence '71
(440) 835-5620 **Mahall** Stephen K '94
(440) 871-0310 **Marcis** Robert A '69
(440) 871-0109 **McClain** Bruce W '82
(440) 899-8990 **McDowell** Sharon L '86
(440) 892-1355 **Reynolds** Corrine '79
Toepfer Robert A '43
(440) 871-7646 **Wilson** James M '91

BEACH CITY
Stark County

(330) 767-3143 **Cunningham** Priscilla J '95

BEACHWOOD
Cuyahoga County

(216) 292-8500 **Abbuhl** David W '81
(216) 751-8183 **Adair** James G '75
(216) 755-5500 **Allgood** Joan U '77
(216) 765-5013 **Allport** William W '69
(216) 514-4981 **Amirault** Donald P '01
(216) 360-3737 **Arnoff** Fred J '75
(216) 292-4666 **August** Steven L '92
(216) 514-9500 **Barrett** Lisa M '92
(216) 765-0550 **Bassett** Stephen J '65
(216) 464-8181 **Becker** Amy A '84
(216) 283-8970 **Belkin** Keith E '76
(216) 831-6100 **Bell** Eric E '92
(216) 464-6666 **Bendau** James M '72
(216) 514-1566 **Bennett** Stanley '60
(216) 514-9879 **Berenholz** Jeffrey S '98
(216) 691-4692 **Berger** Steven B '93
(216) 831-8838 **Berns** Jordan B '90
(216) 831-8838 **Berns Ockner & Greenberger, LLC**
(216) 831-8838 **Berns** Sheldon I '60
(216) 831-8900 **Bilsky** Jeremy L '01
(216) 292-4900 **Birne** Kenneth A '81
(216) 514-4981 **Blakely** Jonathan P '89
(216) 464-2400 **Bohm** Lori B '85
(216) 831-0284 **Bohm** Marvin W '77
(216) 896-1410 **Bonaguro** Mark N '90
(216) 896-5600 **Brokaw** Kevin M '00
(216) 591-1610 **Brooks** Jeffrey M '69
(216) 292-5807 **Brown** Troy R '72
(216) 464-6700 **Bruce** Gordon S '76
(216) 765-0123 **Budish** Armond D '79
(216) 765-0123 **Budish & Solomon Ltd**
Burland Bradley D '80
(216) 292-5807 **Burns** John J '98
(216) 766-5712 **Busch** Lawrence J '79
(216) 831-1400 **Carmen** Fred N '81
(216) 831-8331 **Carter** Van P '80
(216) 896-5600 **Chyun** Edward H '03
(216) 765-8080 **Cole** David G '93
(216) 464-1610 **Comet-Epstein** Sharon J '92
(216) 831-1434 **Cook** Denise M '00
(216) 378-6220 **Costello** William L '88
(216) 755-5660 **Cotton** Eric C '79
(216) 292-5807 **Cullen** Jean M '91
(216) 755-5500 **Cyncynatus** Jerry M '83
(216) 464-6776 **Damelio** Anthony J Jr. '78
Deckman Adrienne L '78
(216) 292-5807 **Desberg** Gary S '85
(216) 831-3212 **Dettelbach** Thomas L '66
(440) 821-6289 **Dickerson** Susanne E '98
(216) 573-6174 **Dubin** Lawrence D '91
(216) 896-5600 **Dubyak** Robert J '92
(216) 861-4020 **Duda** John E '61
(216) 514-3127 **Dyer** John J III '93
(216) 766-5449 **Eastman** Richard M '88
(216) 514-4981 **Edelstein** Robert '83
(216) 292-8116 **Elconin** Eugene '66
(216) 464-6626 **Eli** David A Jr. '79
(216) 464-1610 **Epstein** Robert E '76
(216) 591-1455 **Fine** Philip R '69
(216) 464-3570 **Finkelstein** Tracy K '92
(216) 464-2000 **Fisher** Dennis J '93
(216) 765-0123 **Fisher** Stanley M '53
(216) 831-3511 **Flinker** Jon C '72
(216) 514-9500 **Forbes** Steven Jay '89
(216) 752-4600 **Francis-Sable** Kenneth J '04
(216) 766-5722 **Fuerst** Harrison M '50
(216) 464-2568 **Gatto** Gregory D '95
(216) 766-5093 **Gibson** Richard M '93
(216) 464-6776 **Glassman** Linda S '84
(216) 831-6100 **Goldberg** Jordan A '97
(216) 514-9500 **Golding** Michael L '93
(216) 360-3737 **Goldstein** Jerrold L '67
(216) 295-2114 **Goldstein** Michael S '74
(216) 831-6767 **Goloboff** Barry D '63
(216) 292-5807 **Gorski** Jeffrey A '94
(216) 292-4261 **Goulder** Herbert I '63
(216) 831-5100 **Green** Brian J '94
(216) 491-1684 **Green-Howard** Betty J '83
(216) 831-8838 **Greenberger** Paul M '75
(216) 831-5100 **Greller** Renee Zaidenras '02
(216) 272-3918 **Grunberger** Armand '77
(216) 946-5700 **Halpert** Sanford A '57
(216) 831-2959 **Handelman** James M '78
(216) 765-0123 **Hawkins** Paula L '90
(216) 752-6811 **Hazelton** Cynthia L '84
(216) 464-6153 **Heintel** Robert C '96
(216) 378-1579 **Henck** John C '96
(216) 682-0141 **Herrick** John F '63
(216) 292-1880 **Hersch** Marvin H '54
(216) 292-4900 **Hess** Timothy A '02
(216) 755-5500 **Hewitt** Erin C '04
(216) 378-2915 **Hogan** Doris A '81
(216) 381-1902 **Holt** Donald H '77
(216) 831-0690 **Horwitz** Martin S '79
Huff Leslye M '99
(216) 595-1040 **Hughes** Michael M Jr. '89
(216) 595-1003 **Hyams** Douglas K '90
(216) 514-7865 **Hyde** William J '74
(216) 464-3570 **Isaacson** Arnold M '87
(216) 514-9500 **Jackson** Iverson M '03
(216) 464-0504 **Jacobs** Thomas L '61
(216) 831-1916 **Jacobson** Aaron '59
(216) 360-3737 **Jaffe** Donald N '61
(216) 464-3570 **Johnson** Melissa S '96
(216) 382-0789 **Jones** Steven D '80
(216) 595-8222 **Kabat** Gary B '65
(216) 595-8222 **Kabat Mielziner & Sobel**
(216) 292-2970 **Kahn** Lawrence M '66

(216) 292-5807 **Kauntz** Edmund G '87
(216) 514-1413 **Kent** Stanley B '50
(216) 755-5649 **Kessinger** Kevin J '97
(216) 360-0070 **King** David M '72
(216) 292-6450 **Kobyljanec** William '81
(216) 464-9967 **Kosmin** Martin A '70
(216) 766-5416 **Kowalski** Alexandra M '98
(216) 765-0123 **Krasovec** Frank C Jr. '83
(216) 556-1457 **Kraus** David P '88
(216) 896-5600 **Kushkin** Lauren M '98
(216) 831-5010 **Kwait** Todd M '84
(216) 766-5416 **Lafferty** Michelle A '89
(216) 595-9828 **Lander** Steven E '85
(216) 839-0012 **Lange** Frederick J Jr. '75
Lash David L '77
(216) 464-3570 **Leiken** Robert S '71
(216) 896-5600 **Leskovec** Mark E '86
(216) 896-5600 **Levy & Dubyak**
(216) 896-5600 **Levy** Gregg S '91
(216) 591-1599 **Linick** David I '75
(216) 514-1919 **Longo** Charles V '85
(216) 896-0707 **Luft** Julie R '88
(216) 283-8970 **Luria** Robert A '65
(216) 292-4666 **Madorsky** Larry I '67
Madow Paul B '80
(216) 755-5667 **Manley-Dutton** Maria C '00
(216) 292-2600 **Marks** Seth B '71
(216) 291-2807 **Marocco** William '69
(216) 755-5500 **Mathoslah** Rachel K '04
(216) 292-7355 **McCamley** Janet S '81
(216) 292-5015 **McGraw** Shawn M '94
(216) 595-8222 **McMillan** Kevin R '98
(216) 292-5807 **Melsher** Gary W '64
(216) 831-5100 **Michel** David S '84
(216) 595-8222 **Mielziner** Bruce L '66
(216) 241-0000 **Miller** Robert L '71
(216) 292-5807 **Mills** William M '75
(216) 292-8117 **Morton** John A '75
(216) 751-8271 **Neff** James A '86
(216) 514-9500 **Norchi** Kevin M '86
(216) 241-0000 **Nusbaum** Alan H '71
(216) 464-7656 **Occhionero** Michael J '74
(216) 831-8838 **Ockner** Benjamin J '86
(216) 360-3737 **O'Daire** Lacie L '03
(216) 765-8888 **Ostrovsky** Mark L '76
(216) 765-0123 **Peck** Jennifer E '93
(216) 292-8500 **Peckinpaugh** Roger T '70
(216) 292-4900 **Peltz & Birne**
(216) 292-4900 **Peltz** Richard B '68
(216) 360-3737 **Persky Shapiro & Arnoff Co,LPA**
(216) 591-0927 **Peto** Terri M '88
(216) 839-4000 **Pfundstein** Joseph A '91
(216) 766-5416 **Pizarro** Robert T '97
(216) 360-3737 **Posner** Jeffrey P '76
(216) 464-2125 **Rader** Elizabeth A '87
(216) 861-4020 **Raso** Frank A '98
(216) 514-4981 **Relman** Craig W '90
(216) 831-1434 **Rickel** Alice '77
(216) 766-5486 **Riley** Patrick G '98
(216) 360-3737 **Ritzert** Patricia M '77
(216) 360-3737 **Roll** Stewart D '87
(216) 292-7355 **Rosenbaum** Robert F '72
(216) 360-3737 **Rosenberger** Paul R '98
(216) 831-7300 **Rosman** Barbara Goldberg '88
(216) 691-0112 **Ross** Kenneth R '89
(216) 591-9150 **Ryan** John S '04
(216) 360-0001 **Sabroff** Brett M '77
(216) 292-5807 **Sayoc** Jeffrey A '00
(216) 514-1919 **Scalise** Justin T '03
(216) 381-0454 **Schamovic** Arthur '89
(216) 360-3737 **Schleimer** Mary A '02
Schreckinger Linda I '77
(216) 831-1434 **Schuster** Linda B '93
(216) 896-5600 **Sexton** Aileen S '99
(216) 831-5100 **Shapero & Green LLC**
(216) 831-5100 **Shapero** Michael I '71
(216) 360-3737 **Shapiro** Michael J '94
(216) 360-3737 **Shapiro** Paul Y '63
(216) 766-5416 **Shaver** Elizabeth A '92
(216) 831-3366 **Shifrin** David B '87
(216) 464-7000 **Shore** Michael A '59
(216) 595-1631 **Sidaway** Linda D '93
(216) 595-0944 **Siegel** Neil W '91
(216) 360-9312 **Singerman** Egon P '88
(216) 292-5807 **Singerman Mills Desberg & Kauntz**
(216) 292-5807 **Singerman** Paul J '83
(216) 360-4247 **Slomak** Michael J '76
(216) 292-3430 **Smith** Michael L '76
(216) 595-8222 **Sobel** Jonathan F '79
(216) 464-5990 **Soclof** Richard L '98
(216) 378-7570 **Socrates** Christine S '93
(216) 765-0123 **Solomon** Michael L '76
(216) 514-9665 **Sorin** Marvin '59
(216) 755-5500 **Spencer** William W '86
(216) 292-5048 **Sprenger** Michael T '98
(216) 292-5807 **Stavnicky** Michael R '94
(216) 831-8828 **Stein** Paul N '73
(216) 360-7500 **Stein-Sapir** Leonard Roy '63
(216) 765-0123 **Steiner** Laurie G '89
(216) 831-1125 **Stewart** Cheryl R '99
(216) 765-1130 **Stone** Richard E '75
(216) 292-4742 **Summers** Richard M '80
Sustin Kenneth S '71
(216) 464-6776 **Sutherland** Robert B '94
(216) 831-0200 **Swirsky** Judith R '91
(216) 360-9485 **Thomas** Andrew R '02
Thompson Oliver A '52
(216) 292-8500 **Thornton** Arthur C Jr. '69
(216) 292-5156 **Tierney** James L II '93
(216) 755-5665 **Titterington** Camilla '00
(216) 831-3140 **Tucker** Peter C '93
(216) 464-6776 **Vaughn** James R '86
(216) 464-8420 **Veneziano** Anne D '95
(216) 839-7200 **Vinocur** Peter A '79
(216) 360-9200 **Walker** Stephen O '74
(216) 755-5500 **Waller** Michelle W '95
(216) 755-5666 **Walsh** Jane '85
(216) 378-1579 **Warren** Richard L Jr. '96
(216) 831-8840 **Wasserstrom** Sanford '51
(216) 595-0944 **Watson** Daniel J '03
(216) 765-1800 **Weberman** Philip '85
(216) 755-5647 **Weily** Jennifer R '99
(216) 591-9640 **Weisblatt** Martin E '63
(216) 755-1500 **Weiss** David E '86
(216) 755-5500 **Weiss** Renee B '95
(216) 831-8838 **Werner** Gary F '99
(216) 896-5600 **Weyls** Timothy J Jr. '98
(216) 831-5313 **Whitehead** George W '53
Wilbur Jonathan Z '00
(216) 765-0123 **Williams** Jeffery D '02
(216) 763-5467 **Wintner** Alix A '85
(216) 831-0200 **Wohl** William M '67
Yosowitz Sanford '64
(216) 831-8111 **Zabell** Cary J '76
(216) 831-5488 **Zaremsky** Michael L '78
(216) 766-5828 **Zartman** Michael B '84

BEAVER
Pike County
(740) 226-2113 **Chandler** James A '82
(740) 820-3145 **Salisbury** Mark A '85

BEAVERCREEK
Montgomery County
(937) 427-9450 **Brenner** Robert A '97
(937) 427-3567 **Chachula** Bernard M '01
(937) 426-3230 **Cloud** Darrel G '88
(937) 426-3310 **Hammond** Richard H '68
(937) 426-3310 **Hammond Stier & Stadnicar**
(937) 429-3841 **Hart** Tracy L '94
(937) 427-4360 **Hess** Loren H '92
(937) 426-9564 **Hidy** Joseph D '03
(937) 427-2000 **Hill** James M '85
(937) 429-0577 **Huber** John B '67
(937) 427-1367 **Kieffaber** Megan A '01
(937) 427-1367 **McNamee** Cynthia P '91
(937) 427-9650 **McNamee** David M '97
(937) 427-1367 **McNamee** Michael P '90
(937) 427-1367 **O'Connor** Gregory B '04
(937) 293-0810 **Perkins** David C '93
(937) 426-0845 **Petty** Timothy L '81
(937) 426-5962 **Reid** Marilyn J '66
(937) 427-2000 **Reynolds** George B '99
(937) 426-7010 **Shira** William A III '67
(937) 431-3170 **Simms** Thomas W '72
(937) 426-3310 **Stadnicar** Joseph W '90
(937) 426-3310 **Stier** Charles H Jr. '77
(937) 426-5497 **Stokely** Elizabeth S '93
(937) 427-9650 **Stone** Mark E '82
(937) 427-1367 **Suich** David P '97

BEDFORD
Cuyahoga County
(440) 232-6288 **Acosta** Lori A '89
(440) 786-1910 **Barnabee** Randi A '04
(440) 232-9303 **Bettasso** Katharine Lang '79
(440) 439-5959 **Carson** Robert Otto '73
(440) 292-7060 **Fenton** Gary H '80
(440) 232-2701 **Harding** James N '73
(440) 232-6288 **Laffin** Keith A '88
(440) 232-2223 **Lecso** Madeleine L '89
Maroun Anita S '97
(440) 232-2701 **Melling** Blair N '80
(440) 232-3420 **Melling** Brian J '74
(440) 232-2701 **Melling Harding & Montello,LPA**
(440) 232-2701 **Montello** John J '87
(440) 439-4777 **Motsco** Martha A '88
(440) 232-1900 **Pidala** Sherry A '85
(440) 786-1910 **Smith** Deborah A '88
(440) 439-4240 **Stewart** Charles C '66
(440) 232-3420 **Zingales** Joseph A '52

BEDFORD HEIGHTS
Cuyahoga County
(216) 595-0071 **Bierman** Victor J III '99
(440) 439-3400 **Chapman** Howard S '71
(216) 595-0071 **Diaz-Rex** Julia '00
(216) 595-0071 **Fisher** Vincent E '99
(440) 735-1010 **Koreness** Gregory B '99
(216) 595-0071 **L'Hommedieu** Mary Louisa '96
(216) 662-7711 **Mallin** Christopher J '74
(440) 439-1616 **Medford** Cecil L '86
(440) 786-3229 **Merchant** Charles E '62
(216) 591-0707 **Morad** Rick J '95
(216) 902-8000 **Nici** Anthony T '97
(440) 232-5980 **Peace** Christine M '93
(216) 595-0071 **Rosenbaum** Beth Stoller '89
(216) 595-0071 **Roth Bierman LLP**
(216) 595-0071 **Roth** Dennis A '67
(216) 595-0071 **Williams** Jackson Ryan '03

BELLAIRE
Belmont County
(740) 676-2111 **Banker** Floyd A '57
(740) 676-2111 **Banker** Megan '94
(740) 676-3473 **Bonfini** Emilio M '50
(740) 676-2743 **Frizzi** Daniel L Jr. '77
(740) 676-2034 **Lancione & Lloyd,LPA**
(740) 676-2034 **Lancione** Richard L '66
(740) 676-2034 **Lloyd** Scott A '93
(740) 676-2034 **Lloyd** Tracey L '90

BELLBROOK
Greene County
(937) 848-6711 **Boland** Amy S '81
(937) 848-9042 **Freudenberger** Richard A '86
(937) 848-3461 **Hieber** Raymond C '57
(937) 427-1747 **Hill** Cynthia M '90
(937) 848-7446 **Johnson** DeAnna D '94
(937) 848-8400 **Martin** Cynthia G '92

BELLE CENTER
Logan County
(937) 464-5861 **Reed** Robert G Jr. '60

BELLEFONTAINE
Logan County
(937) 599-6242 **Beck** Ann E '86
(937) 593-3655 **Bennett** Daniel L '00
(937) 599-7260 **Billiar** Amy J '93
(937) 593-8510 **Braig** Kevin P '93
(937) 593-3655 **Chamberlain** Charles D '69
(937) 593-3655 **Chamberlain** Matthew R '03
(937) 593-1020 **DeSomma** Peter K '94
(937) 599-5834 **Dougherty** Edwin '91
(937) 593-6065 **Dunlap** Robert E '57
(937) 593-8075 **Goslee** William T '89
(937) 593-6065 **Hanna** Dane M '91
(937) 592-8603 **Haushalter** Barbara J '89
(937) 599-6242 **Hawkins** Bridget D '91
(937) 599-7272 **Heaton** Gerald L '77
(937) 592-9559 **Hemphill** Richard A '85
(937) 593-6065 **Heydinger** Thomas A '58
(937) 593-9015 **Hilliker** Donald J '74
(937) 599-7272 **Kellogg-Martin** Kimberly J '84
(937) 592-2776 **Kelly** John B '51
(937) 593-6591 **LaRoche** Daniel J '98
(937) 592-2831 **Lawrence** John T '67
Lile Levi W '72
(937) 593-6065 **MacDonald** Robert B Jr. '75
(937) 593-8725 **MacGillivray** Douglas D '65
(937) 599-7260 **Minahan** Wade T '88
(937) 592-2004 **Minnich** Sheila E '87
(937) 593-8510 **Montgomery** William R '68
(937) 599-7232 **Rhea** Mark L '99
(937) 593-6065 **Ross** Chad A '96
(937) 599-6127 **Ross** John L '74
(937) 593-8510 **Smith** Douglas M '92
(937) 593-8510 **Smith** John M '66
(937) 593-8510 **Smith Smith & Montgomery**
(937) 592-2827 **Snapp** Jeffrey C '90
(937) 599-7272 **Stewart** Eric C '99
(937) 593-6065 **Stolly** Terrence G '01
(937) 593-8725 **Stoner** Linda C '89
(937) 593-6065 **Thompson Dunlap Heydinger MacDonald Watkins & Trau**
(937) 593-6065 **Traul** Howard A II '76
(937) 593-6591 **Triplett** Marc S '77
(937) 593-6065 **Watkins** David R '76
(937) 593-3655 **West** John D '61
(937) 599-6242 **Wickline** Gabriel D '04
(937) 599-7272 **Wolf** Deborah K '83

BELLEVUE
Huron County
(419) 483-2141 **Aigler & Paul**
(419) 483-2141 **Aigler** Thomas L '83
(419) 483-2141 **Aigler** William F '43
Alkire Laura '04
(419) 483-7119 **Bova** Barry W '88
(419) 483-3739 **Fox** Kenneth P '67
(419) 483-6748 **Meyers** John E '69
(419) 483-2141 **Paul** Roger D '72
(419) 465-2534 **Rathbun** Timothy J '89
(419) 483-5744 **Ray** Jeremiah S '02
(419) 483-7724 **Smith** Ronald R '74
(419) 483-4543 **Wall** Mary J '99
(419) 483-2621 **Wallingford** David A '79

BELPRE
Washington County
(740) 423-9548 **Emrick** Gregg M '77
(740) 423-7569 **Fox** Jim D '73
(740) 423-9548 **McCauley** James H '70
(740) 423-9548 **McCauley Webster & Emrick**
(740) 423-9548 **Webster** Thomas P '75

BENTLEYVILLE
Cuyahoga County
(440) 247-1227 **Thomas** Anne B '94

BEREA
Cuyahoga County
(440) 816-0600 **Berry** Ralph A Jr. '73
(440) 234-1314 **Bobinsky** Sylvester F '49
(440) 243-8330 **Calabrase** Mark '86
Colabianchi James Jr. '99
(440) 243-5668 **Coury** John M '90
(216) 621-5036 **Demer** John A '71
(216) 621-5036 **Demer Weiner & Marniella,LLC**
(440) 239-7767 **Forstner** Gerald C Jr. '67
(440) 826-1616 **French** Richard H Jr. '84
(440) 239-3127 **Frost** Robert R '70
(440) 234-0662 **Fusco** Mark S '88
(440) 846-6789 **Glaze** Ryan A '96
(440) 243-2955 **Groh-Wargo** Francis J '80
(440) 239-9777 **Hanson** Mary Jo '04
(440) 234-2081 **Isaac** Sharon D '84
(440) 816-0600 **Jamison** Neal M '83
(440) 238-2601 **Jeske** Kendra J '97
(440) 234-8745 **Jones** Barbara L '89
(440) 891-8320 **Karl** Margaret T '03
(440) 816-0600 **Kraus** Thomas J '84
(440) 816-0600 **Lambros** David A '85
(440) 816-0600 **Largent Berry Preston & Jamison Co,LPA**
Leone Denio A '84
(440) 891-5019 **MacCracken** Alan L III '00
(440) 826-5803 **Madzy** Matthew J '99
(440) 234-0662 **Mahoney** William F '75
(216) 621-5036 **Marniella** James A '01
(440) 826-5860 **Marniella** Marisa Ann '95
(440) 238-5362 **Miesse** Timothy S '79
(440) 891-5000 **Novick** Lorne J '00
(440) 243-2955 **Opsincs** Katherine H '04
(440) 243-2955 **Powers** Donald H '64
(440) 243-2955 **Powers** Donna J '83
(440) 243-2955 **Powers & Groh-Wargo**
(440) 816-0600 **Preston** Kenneth G '60
(440) 816-0600 **Preston** Kevin M '81
(440) 234-0662 **Rady** Marie M '90
(440) 243-1222 **Riemenschneider** Walter E Jr. '59
(440) 891-8320 **Rooney** John J '84
(440) 243-2955 **Ruschak** Melinda L '86
(440) 816-0600 **Selby** Matthew J '03
(440) 891-8320 **Smith** Anthony J '84
Spangler Craig D '79
(440) 826-4114 **Sponseller** Gregory M '82
(440) 234-2081 **Steiner** James T '83
(440) 234-2081 **Tsevdos** Noelle T '89
(440) 239-9777 **Van Dress** Dean W '99
(440) 826-3558 **Walczak** Michael A '81
(440) 826-0084 **Walters** James N III '73
(440) 234-0662 **Wargo** John J Jr. '75
(216) 621-5036 **Weiner** Douglas S '87
(440) 891-8850 **Williams** Scott A '91
(440) 826-2220 **Wilson** Hilary B '86
Young Thomas V '89
(440) 234-6693 **Young** Vincent E '58

BERLIN
Holmes County
(330) 893-2600 **Miller** Ellis Y '98
(330) 893-2600 **Yoder** Thomas C '95

BERLIN CENTER
Mahoning County
(330) 547-3722 **Orr** Thomas T '81

BETHEL
Clermont County
(513) 734-2283 **Ferguson** Jeffry D '85
(513) 734-7470 **Gossett** Tresa '89
(513) 734-0950 **Gregory** Patrick L '79
(513) 734-4848 **Leicht** George P '72
(513) 734-2283 **Yelton** Paul R '56

BEVERLY
Washington County
(740) 558-9997 **Landaker** Shawna M '02

BEXLEY
Franklin County
Ashton Robert E '84
(614) 266-2961 **Bell** John A '84
Berger Lisa J '98
(614) 236-2222 **Bolon** Thomas M Jr. '91
(614) 258-6063 **Bonfield** Lauren B '03
Center April H '86
(614) 237-7440 **Cleary** Michael P '77
(614) 231-9162 **Hart** Douglas J '82
(614) 252-7221 **Kamin-Meyer** Tamar '91
Pierce Walter R '74
Rolf Matthew W '02
(614) 252-7906 **Schwartz** Robert S '86
(614) 470-2664 **Shanahan** Thomas G '82
(614) 237-0420 **Wasserman** Susan S '77
Zelizer Carol A '77

BLACKLICK
Franklin County
Anderson Scott A '93
(614) 939-1510 **Blackmore** Josiah H II '62
(614) 322-9500 **Chiu** Alicia M '04
(614) 860-9670 **Flowers** Janice M '01
(614) 864-9971 **Hansen** Jennifer B '94
(614) 855-3220 **Harmon** Vanessa R '98
(614) 860-9249 **Hill** Steven A '84
Rogers Barbara A '97

BLANCHESTER
Clinton County
(937) 783-2401 **Dunlap** Brenda N '79
(937) 783-2454 **Goettke** Richard L '76
(937) 783-2401 **Lyons McHenry & Dunlap**
(937) 783-2401 **McHenry** Ronald J '72
(937) 783-2476 **Williams** Michael B '02

BLOOMINGBURG
Fayette County
(740) 437-7142 **Pontious** Carole G '99

BLOOMINGDALE
Jefferson County
(740) 944-1925 **Scarnecchia** Dan B '91

BLUE ASH
Hamilton County
(513) 891-5630 **Bender** Eric D '91
(513) 891-5666 **Candito** Joseph '86
(513) 791-8916 **McKenna** Matthew C '93

BLUFFTON
Allen County
(419) 358-2464 **Anderson** David L '79
(419) 358-5606 **Diller** Samuel W '60
(419) 358-5606 **Kingsley** Mitchell L '93
(419) 358-5606 **Staley-Burley** Gina C '92

BOARDMAN
Mahoning County
(330) 675-2426 **Arnaut** Gina B '02
(330) 746-7575 **Boano** Michael L '80
(330) 729-9124 **Burdette** Kevin S '92
(330) 629-8882 **Chermely** Diane L '89
(330) 729-9240 **Ciambotti** Anna M '87
(330) 726-2441 **Czopur** Edward C '73
(330) 965-8000 **DeLaurentis** Dominic J Jr. '88
(330) 758-7313 **DiMartino** Dennis A '87
(330) 729-9777 **Engler** David L '85
(330) 782-7000 **Epstein** Bruce R '77
(330) 758-4900 **Fekete** Matthew T '83
(330) 726-3736 **Gemma** William A '46
(330) 726-3711 **Gerchak** David J '98
(330) 965-8000 **Gongaware** Aaron P '03
(330) 788-9174 **Green** William Jr. '54
(330) 758-9482 **Harper** Paul R '92
(330) 758-2308 **Ingram** John Gerald Jr. '78
(330) 758-2308 **Juhasz** John B Jr. '83
(330) 729-9777 **Kalfas** Plato J '87
(614) 595-7500 **Ludwig** William C '73
(330) 726-8300 **Mastriana** Richard J '79
(330) 758-7992 **Nunziato** Carl A '71
(330) 965-8000 **Osborne Delaurentis & Sontich Co LPA**
(330) 965-8000 **Osborne** Glenn R '87
(330) 726-6999 **Petrella** Shelli E '99
(330) 965-7501 **Piccirillo** Michael R '91
(330) 965-8000 **Rafidi** Mark A '98
(330) 758-2200 **Rich** Michael J '95
(330) 729-9777 **Robbins** Jennifer R '03
(330) 965-9190 **Rodfong** G Thomas '88
(330) 726-8669 **Romano** Karen M '00
(330) 783-1488 **Sakmar** Michael A '93
(330) 729-9777 **Sciortino** Michael '03
(330) 782-3000 **Shultz** John F '76

(330) 965-8000 **Sontich** Joseph P Jr. '86
(330) 965-8000 **Sontich** Joseph P Sr. '49
(330) 758-2308 **Stephens** Mary Jane '83
(330) 726-1654 **Sweeney** Maureen A '93
(330) 726-1654 **Tarasuck** Raymond M Jr. '95
(330) 783-1488 **Tareshawty** Brian J '90
(330) 965-7507 **Thompson** Kathleen '03
(330) 629-8882 **Tusek** Tim '83
(330) 965-9910 **Wolfe** David J Jr. '93
(330) 726-6404 **Zuckerman** Zvi A '91

BOWLING GREEN
Wood County

(419) 354-9278 **Atkins** Timothy C '93
(419) 353-5615 **Bachman** Evelyn J '62
(419) 354-9250 **Baker** Heather M '04
(419) 352-4621 **Bakies** Gregory E '85
(419) 352-8100 **Bamburowski** Thomas J '75
(419) 354-9244 **Barone** Mary S '88
(419) 352-8095 **Bevelhymer** Darlene P '87
(419) 354-9250 **Bishop** Gary D '87
(419) 352-1581 **Burton** Julie A '95
(419) 354-4632 **Calderon** Reina A '92
(419) 354-1244 **Callejas** Esteban R '89
(419) 352-3554 **Campbell** Craig W '90
(419) 354-9238 **Cavitt** Valencia G '96
(419) 352-4659 **Cheetwood** John S '69
(419) 352-4621 **Cody** David A '81
(419) 352-2614 **Coggin** Betty F '86
(419) 354-4442 **Coon** Scott T '84
(419) 354-9244 **Daler** Justin E '01
(419) 372-2030 **Daly** Lawrence J '87
(419) 354-9217 **de la Serna** Arlen B '96
(419) 354-9250 **Dobson** Paul A '94
(419) 352-8222 **Dunipace** John M '75
(419) 353-2108 **Durney** Ronda L '01
(419) 354-9250 **Fischer** Raymond C '82
(419) 372-2951 **Fleming** Rodney A '91
(419) 353-1062 **Foraker** M Angela '00
(419) 352-5164 **Geer** Norman J '71
(419) 343-6952 **Green** Michelle S '98
(419) 352-5164 **Halleck** Michael J '71
(419) 353-8491 **Halleck** Peter T '73
(419) 354-9244 **Hamm** Kathleen M '83
(419) 352-1581 **Hammer** James A '86
(419) 354-9600 **Hanes** Duncan L '03
(419) 352-6501 **Hanna** Drew A '72
(419) 352-6501 **Hanna** Harold M '71
(419) 353-3075 **Harlett** William A '69
(419) 353-1062 **Harms** Robert G '77
(419) 354-9244 **Hart** Andrew P '02
(419) 215-5982 **Heisler** Dwight Daniel '81
(419) 353-3886 **Heringhaus** Pamela A '81
(419) 352-5164 **Hess** Renee E '92
(419) 354-9244 **Hicks** James S '82
(419) 352-5458 **Hock** Jerome H '58
(419) 354-9250 **Holmes** Linda L '83
(419) 354-9250 **Howe-Gebers** Gwendolyn K '89
(419) 352-2535 **Huffman** Diane R '82
(419) 352-2535 **Huffman** Rex H '79
(419) 352-7537 **Jones** James E '79
(419) 354-1899 **Jones** Wendell R '86
(419) 353-5073 **Kuzoff** George D '62
(419) 353-2365 **Ladd** Elisabeth S '91
(419) 352-8627 **Latta** Delbert L '44
(419) 353-0311 **Lee** Jerry W '78
(419) 354-9250 **Mack** Mary L '90
(419) 352-8222 **Marcin** Chester H '69
(419) 352-2518 **Marsh** Michael J '79
(419) 354-4442 **Matthews** Frederic E '80
(419) 352-4621 **Maurer Newlove & Bakies**
(419) 352-4621 **Maurer** Robert W '68
(419) 352-5263 **McDermott** Thomas J '93
(419) 354-9250 **Meneses** Walter M '96
(419) 354-9244 **Mertz** Elizabeth A '97
(419) 352-7522 **Middleton Roebke & Nelson**
(419) 352-7522 **Middleton** Staten T '93
(419) 352-7522 **Middleton** Thomas S '63
(419) 352-1581 **Mitchell Stearns & Hammer**
(419) 354-2727 **Moenich** Terrence R '88
(419) 372-8364 **Mota** Sue Ann '84
(419) 352-7522 **Nelson** Jeffrey A '79
(419) 352-4621 **Newlove** John F '84
(419) 352-2535 **Newlove** Megan E '95
(419) 354-9250 **Ohanian** Aram M '94
(419) 372-7377 **Pauken** Patrick D '94
(419) 352-8844 **Pomeroy** Todd A '98
(419) 353-7547 **Potter** Albert L II '82
(419) 354-4442 **Rayle Mathews & Coon**
(419) 354-4442 **Rayle** Max E '76
(419) 354-6285 **Reger** Matthew L '93
(419) 327-6313 **Reisner** John R '81
(419) 352-7522 **Roebke** Harry G '42
(419) 354-9244 **Schemrich** LeAnn R '03
(419) 353-0152 **Schmidt** Richard A '86
(419) 354-9250 **Schuman** Andrew R '00
(419) 353-1062 **Sharp** James M '83
(419) 354-9250 **Shultz** Jacqueline M '97
(419) 372-2951 **Skulina** Michael S '92
(419) 327-6304 **Souder** William G Jr. '86
(419) 352-2535 **Spitler** Daniel T '65
(419) 352-2535 **Spitler Huffman Yoon & Newlove,LLP**
(419) 352-2535 **Spitler** Robert E '74
(419) 352-2535 **Spitler** Steven L '96
(419) 352-1581 **Stearns** Jodie L '84
(419) 354-9244 **Stephenson** William V '87
(419) 352-7522 **Stevens** Bruce B '99
(419) 354-8787 **Teet** Thomas E '88
(419) 353-1062 **Ten Brink** Victor N '83
Thompson Maurice A '04
(419) 354-9270 **Tiell** Gene V '88
(419) 352-1776 **Tolles** Mark D '81
(419) 353-1062 **Twyman TenBrink Harms & Sharp**
(419) 354-9339 **VanWinkle** Tracy Frey '02
(419) 372-2378 **Ward** Lynn M '70
(419) 354-1244 **Weinandy** James R '89
Wilcox James L '80
(419) 352-2535 **Yoon** Mimi S '92
(419) 352-8844 **Zografides** Christopher A '00

BRATENAHL
Cuyahoga County

(216) 451-2323 **Coghill** George J '75
(216) 681-1553 **Srail** Donald J '79
(216) 681-1551 **Tyler** Thomas S '88

BRECKSVILLE
Cuyahoga County

(440) 746-1500 **Adams** Gary S '83
(440) 526-6722 **Balzano** Laura A '80
(440) 546-0483 **Bates** James C '97
Beach Victoria M '78
(440) 546-1404 **Beck** Janet R '77
(440) 746-2118 **Bedell** Michael L '73
Brennan Kevin J '02
(440) 526-9440 **Carson** Gayle J '76
(440) 717-9595 **Castro** Michael M '80
(440) 526-1021 **Childs** Carol A '91
(216) 447-6412 **Clegg** Christopher R '88
(440) 717-1517 **Cohn** Wendy J '88
(440) 526-0610 **Collins** Forrest L '73
(440) 838-5104 **Creager** Michael J '78
(440) 526-5875 **Dacek** James S '76
(216) 241-9999 **Day** William J '79
(440) 546-9200 **Di Geronimo** Sergio I '89
(419) 262-1429 **Di Piero** Frank A '82
(216) 351-3207 **Donaldson** Michael R '85
(440) 526-4500 **Fischer** Kathleen L '82
(440) 717-9850 **French-Scaggs** Susan K '96
(440) 746-1500 **Harrington** Patrick J '91
(216) 447-5000 **Harvey** Gregory S '95
(440) 546-8614 **Hogan** Douglas J '88
(440) 746-9550 **Holtz** Theodore S '52
(440) 526-6722 **Hronek** Christina M '02
(440) 546-1294 **Ivchenko** Andrew '89
(440) 526-5001 **Kovacs** Julius E '67
(440) 546-9200 **Kroll** Thomas J II '04
(440) 526-2014 **Laurie** Charles R Jr. '74
(440) 526-3759 **McBride** Judith B '86
(440) 746-9740 **McCabe** Daniel M '85
(440) 503-6099 **McCreery** Robert D Jr. '86
(216) 459-9040 **McGrath** James J IV '89
(440) 526-1581 **Motiska** Robert J '69
(440) 526-6400 **Nemer** Charles A '83
(440) 526-0430 **Oker** Michael R '71
Onders Kathleen D '94
(440) 526-4500 **Papp** James E '72
(440) 746-1600 **Poklar** Robert A '73
(330) 722-2222 **Ratajczak** Michael P '93
(440) 262-1423 **Ronyak** David M '75
Ross Anne H '93
(440) 746-1600 **Ross** Heather '99
(216) 447-5436 **Rudolph** Richard Jay '92
(216) 791-3800 **Saba** Ruth H '80
Sakai Michael H '78
(440) 546-0483 **Seink** Daniel P '92
(440) 746-2116 **Shurell** Carolyn J '80
(440) 526-2067 **Simmons** Adele O '89
Skaljac Stella K '00
Stanley Devon A '02
(440) 717-1010 **Steely** Robert L '71
(440) 717-1517 **Termini** Mark M '84
(440) 526-4500 **Tuma** Brian G '91
(440) 526-4500 **Tuma** Jeffrey A '01
(440) 526-4500 **Tuma** Robert L '64
(440) 526-4500 **Tuma** Scott M '99
(440) 717-9925 **Tyner** Michaele '76
(440) 746-1500 **Vitantonio** Louis A Jr. '02
(440) 526-6722 **Wadsworth** Roger A '63
(440) 838-8299 **Wainey** Deborah A '91
(440) 526-0876 **Weiler** Kevin P '79
Weiss Carol A '77
(440) 546-8611 **Whitehead** David W '73
Witt Clyde David '73
(440) 526-0414 **Wojciak** David J '95
(440) 746-2128 **Wolk** Terry J '82

BREWSTER
Stark County

(330) 767-3401 **Severtis** Sarah A '03

BRIDGEPORT
Belmont County

(740) 635-6259 **Bench** Kevin W '01
(740) 635-0162 **Davies** Albert E III '93
(740) 635-1217 **Davis** David William '73
(740) 635-0162 **Fregiato** Francis A '77
(740) 635-0162 **Gagin** Christopher J '94
(740) 635-0162 **Myser** Richard A '78
(740) 635-0347 **Sustersic** Edward G '69
(740) 635-0162 **Thomas Fregiato Myser Hanson & Davies**

BROADVIEW HEIGHTS
Cuyahoga County

(440) 746-0707 **Burke** James F '77
(440) 526-8888 **Cameratta** Karen Jo '93
(440) 526-9301 **Conlon** James E '86
(440) 922-5200 **Grendell** Henry G '94
(440) 746-9600 **Grendell & Simon Co,LPA**
(440) 746-9600 **Grendell** Timothy J '78
(440) 746-0707 **Horrigan** John J '75
(440) 546-0100 **Jackson** Dennis C '82
(440) 526-8018 **Jakubaitis** Janis M '75
(440) 546-0100 **Kennedy** James D '91
(440) 526-7200 **Kozelka** Kay J '78
(440) 526-2428 **Kucha** Helen A '77
(440) 746-3600 **Landoll** Richard W '95
(440) 223-4260 **Leneghan** David M '93
(440) 746-3700 **Major** James L Jr. '89
(440) 746-1000 **Motylinski** Michael '03
(440) 526-8018 **Nosan** Bernard J '73
(440) 746-1000 **Oakar** Ann C '01
(440) 746-1000 **Oakar** James L '62
(440) 746-1000 **Oakar & Ruffa**
O'Connor Debra L '95
Raslan Lila D '01
(440) 746-9602 **Rausch** Edward W Jr. '74
(440) 746-1000 **Ruffa** Vincenzo '96
(440) 838-1222 **Salisbury** Joyce A '93
(440) 838-1222 **Salisbury** Richard L '79
Scudder Michael Y Jr. '01
(440) 717-1580 **Shearer** Mark S '96
(440) 526-8818 **Simon** Andrew J '86
(440) 746-9600 **Simon** George T '99
(440) 230-9643 **Smith** Csilla E '88
(440) 717-9370 **Suh** Luke K '96
(440) 546-0778 **Weaver** Jeannette M '88

BROOKFIELD
Trumbull County

(330) 448-1500 **Hoffman** James E III '76
(330) 448-1133 **Kokor** Robert C '93
(330) 448-6818 **O'Brien** James A '65
(330) 534-3103 **Paroz** Roger C '80
(330) 448-1500 **Walker** Elwood M '78

BROOKLYN
Cuyahoga County

(216) 459-1405 **Boigner** David P '77
(216) 813-0167 **DiBaggio** Julie A '04
(216) 281-2400 **Gicei** Leslie L '85
(216) 635-4275 **Goldberg** Hillary Z '96
(216) 961-3500 **Graf** Frederick L '79
(440) 886-7901 **Graves** Marco E '92
Runco Laryn D '02
Yee Julianna Herrick '03
(216) 813-6847 **Zupan** John F '92

BROOKLYN HEIGHTS
Cuyahoga County

(216) 741-2365 **Brooks** Sylvester Jr. '75
(216) 635-4340 **DeGross** Charles M '94
(216) 741-2365 **Del Monte** Jordan S '72
Dobbins Mark E '82
(216) 741-2365 **Holder** Timothy D '77
(216) 741-2365 **Hoover** Gregory E '81
(216) 741-2365 **Paradise** Ramona E '79
(216) 741-2365 **Robusto** Michael A '79
(216) 741-2365 **Schoen** James S '79
(216) 741-2365 **Swisher** Helane J '77
(216) 749-1150 **Vocaire-Tramposch** Louis '86
(216) 398-1023 **Wyman** James G '72

BROOK PARK
Cuyahoga County

(216) 676-4600 **Armanini** Todd T '87
(216) 433-1300 **Cardaman** Victoria L '95
(216) 676-7590 **Gerbino** Perry L '76
(216) 676-6800 **Goulder** Richard A '60
(216) 676-3897 **Krantz** Timothy J '81
(216) 267-1144 **Palmer** John A '76
(216) 676-3898 **Ramos** Anita M '91
Reber Susan G '91
(216) 676-9185 **Zielinski** Vernon J '83

BROOKVILLE
Montgomery County

(937) 833-5659 **Gilbert** B. Eugene '92
(937) 833-2772 **Guenther** Vanessa L '84
(937) 833-6326 **Stephan** Rodney L '83

BRUNSWICK
Medina County

(330) 273-3208 **Abood** Mark S '98
(330) 220-8383 **Baumgartner** Matthew J '95
(330) 225-1288 **Bonda** Thomas J '92
(330) 220-9170 **Clark** Amy L '92
Conrad Kelly R '02
(330) 220-7660 **Conway** Michael T '92
(330) 225-7220 **Deliman** Scott M '98
(330) 225-2508 **Edmunds** James Timothy '82
(330) 225-1491 **Gaeckle** Matthew P '04
(330) 225-7177 **Goldsmith** Harvey S '66
Hay Walter H '59
Kerek Wayne L '83
(330) 225-1491 **Kray** Paul J '91
(330) 225-1491 **Laribee Hertrick & Kray**
(330) 273-9710 **McKinney** Karin H '86
(330) 225-7646 **Porter** John N '75
(330) 225-5025 **Relic** Grant D '78
(330) 273-3450 **Riehl** David S '74
(440) 572-1151 **Roberts** Jacqueline I K '03
(440) 572-1151 **Steiger** William E II '03
(330) 220-5200 **Theiss** Raymond E '85
(330) 225-7220 **Tinl** Robert T '75

BRYAN
Williams County

(419) 636-5666 **Bish Butler & Thompson,Ltd**
(419) 636-5666 **Bish** William A '69
(419) 636-3166 **Bok** Kelli S '03
(419) 636-3196 **Breininger** Ryan S '99
(419) 636-5666 **Butler** Charles C '92
(419) 636-2999 **Duggan** Paul H '93
(419) 636-2596 **Fisher** Rhonda L '91
(419) 636-3166 **Gallagher** Karen K '86
(419) 636-3166 **Gallagher** Ralph W '70
(419) 636-3166 **Gallagher Stelzer & Yosick,Ltd**
Grocki Dale M '91
(419) 636-2644 **Harvey** Mary Ann '92
(419) 636-6725 **Hollin** Kimberly J '89
(419) 636-5951 **Kiacz** Joseph R '73
(419) 636-3196 **Newcomer** David C '72
(419) 636-3196 **Newcomer Shaffer & Spangler**
(419) 636-4411 **Roth** Craig L '76
(419) 636-3196 **Shaffer** John S '81
(419) 636-3196 **Shaffer** Michael A '90
(419) 636-3196 **Shaffer** Wayne E '49
(419) 636-3196 **Spangler** Michael W '86
(419) 636-3166 **Stelzer** John T '81
(419) 636-5666 **Thompson** Ryan S '04
(419) 636-5666 **Thompson** Thomas A '97
(419) 636-3166 **Yosick** Kirk E '98

BUCHTEL
Athens County

(740) 753-3232 **Oakley** Jack V '73

BUCKEYE LAKE
Licking County

Thomas Corrie D '00

BUCYRUS
Crawford County

(419) 562-7762 **Cory** David R '82
(419) 562-7762 **Cory** Richard L '51
(419) 562-9782 **Felgenhauer** Jack L '00
(419) 562-5928 **Flegm** Stanley E '73
(419) 562-4075 **Gernert** Terry L '79
(419) 562-9856 **Griebling** Eric H '79
(419) 562-4075 **Hoeffel** Paul E '73
(419) 562-5771 **Holm** Mary E '77
(419) 562-2731 **Hoover** James L '69
(419) 562-4986 **Jones** Regis R '59
(419) 562-7958 **Kennedy** Michael A '66
(419) 562-4075 **Kennedy Purdy Hoeffel & Gernert**
(419) 562-1896 **Kurek** Edward L '94
(419) 562-5560 **Leuthold** Sean E '95
(419) 562-5560 **Leuthold** Shane M '98
(419) 562-9856 **McBride** Gordon S '86
(419) 562-3007 **Motter** John A '82
(419) 562-4989 **Murphy** Patrick T '80
(419) 562-1951 **Neff** Robert C Jr. '83
(419) 562-8998 **Nicholson** Thomas G '88
(419) 562-9856 **Pry** James W II '71
(419) 562-9856 **Sears** John D Jr. '50
(419) 562-6624 **Spiegel** John L '75
(419) 562-9856 **Spurlock Sears Pry Griebling & McBride,PLL**
(419) 562-4529 **Starkey** Bradley S '87
(419) 562-4529 **Stoll** Geoffrey L '87
(419) 562-6237 **Wead** Edward R '66
(419) 562-9782 **Wiener** Michael J '01

BURTON
Geauga County

(440) 834-4492 **Fuhry** David L '77
(440) 834-4492 **Fuhry** Kenneth A '78
(440) 548-2312 **Gazley** Lucinda '87
(440) 834-5000 **Snyder** Timothy H '96
Vizy Nicholas J '89

BYESVILLE
Guernsey County

(740) 685-7611 **Keith** Mary B '01

CADIZ
Harrison County

(740) 942-8282 **Beetham** Rupert N '72
(740) 942-2356 **Beetham** Thomas Mark '75
(740) 942-2621 **Greenwood** Rhonda L '95
(740) 942-2621 **Hervey** Thomas S '97
(740) 942-2936 **Hutyera** Andrew '69
(740) 942-2127 **Mosser** Geoffrey B '71
(740) 942-2080 **Pincola** Charles A '89
(740) 942-8181 **Spiker** William E '60
(740) 942-3130 **Tabacchi** John O '76
(740) 942-2621 **Washington** Michael B '01

CALDWELL
Noble County

(740) 732-7559 **Blakeslee** Jack A '76
(740) 732-2222 **Fox** Fred F '50
(740) 732-5685 **Sickler** Clifford N '77
(740) 732-7667 **Tanner** Sharon L '83
(740) 732-5685 **Watson** Robert B '89
(740) 732-2309 **Young** Lucien C Jr. '59
(740) 732-8441 **Young** Lucien C III '83

CAMBRIDGE
Guernsey County

(740) 432-6397 **Baker** Richard A '67
(740) 439-2719 **Bennett** David B '85
(740) 439-2719 **Bennett** William M '77
(740) 432-6322 **Biegler** Kent D '82
(740) 432-3281 **Booth** Russell H Jr. '57
(740) 439-1499 **Brockwell** Jeremy W '84
(740) 432-5638 **Brown** Donald D '76
(740) 432-6397 **DeSelm & Baker**
(740) 432-6397 **DeSelm** David H '65
(740) 432-7773 **Eyen** Stephen P '80
(740) 432-4502 **Ferguson** William H '85
(740) 432-2389 **Granitsas** G '53
Hayes Josephine E '93
(740) 432-4502 **Heine** Stephen C '74
(740) 432-6990 **Howard** Patrick J '89
(740) 432-4030 **Jones** Gerald L '76
(740) 439-2719 **Knowlton & Bennett**
(740) 432-7414 **Lloyd** Thomas R '47
(740) 432-7844 **McClure** Frank A '75
(740) 439-5900 **McKnight** Charles E '89
(740) 432-6322 **Mitchell** Stephanie L '01
(740) 432-9252 **Moll** Jeanette M '96
(740) 432-4030 **Morris** Roy L '54
(740) 439-1430 **Nicholson** John M '83
(740) 439-3077 **Nicholson** William T '85
(740) 432-5648 **Nicolozakes** William A '95
(740) 432-6322 **Padden** Daniel G '87
(740) 432-6322 **Plummer** Charles K '81
(740) 432-2389 **Raptis** Stamatios L '77
(740) 432-6322 **Scott** James R '62
(740) 439-2842 **Tostenson** Neal S '58
(740) 432-6322 **Tribbie Scott Plummer & Padden**
(740) 432-6322 **Tribbie** Thomas L '52
(740) 439-7711 **Warhola** Andrew J Jr. '79
(740) 432-7844 **Wilson** Melissa M '03

CAMDEN
Preble County

(937) 452-7214 **Hickey** Firmin A Jr. '01

CAMPBELL
Mahoning County

(330) 755-2165 **Almasy** John P '55
Billec Brett R '02
(330) 750-9251 **Miles** Sherman J Jr. '91
(330) 750-1333 **Shultz** Michael W '95

CANAL FULTON
Stark County

(330) 854-3881 **Hoover** Catherine J '92

CANAL WINCHESTER
Fairfield County

(614) 837-5030 **Dean** Martha F '84
(614) 833-5700 **Gerth** Philip W '98
(614) 837-0750 **Harman** Kenneth C '69
(614) 837-4238 **Hatton** Jerry R '74
(614) 837-6151 **Herzberger** Brian L '82
(614) 837-0793 **Hofmeister** Raymond E '72
(614) 834-7777 **Kantner** John M '87
Kiesling C Mark '80
(614) 920-2261 **Leininger** Robert E '00
(614) 837-2308 **McNemar** Joseph G '78
Miller Daniel J '02
(614) 836-3611 **Moreland** Jay M '96
(614) 833-3804 **Peters** Megan J '80
(614) 837-1750 **Pettorini** John H '73
(614) 920-3941 **Shepard** Gene A '78
(614) 837-2486 **Stevenson** William W '56
(614) 834-9880 **Vasko** Michael P '84
(614) 834-1750 **Weaver** Roger L '88
(614) 837-1546 **Wortman** Mary A '82

CANFIELD
Mahoning County

Bagnola William E '01
(330) 533-2601 **Beck** James H '59
(330) 746-8484 **Betras** David J '85
(330) 746-8484 **Betras Maruca & Kopp LLC**
(330) 702-2830 **Blair** Harry G '95
Bordner Kellie D '93
(330) 533-1700 **Brannigan** Mary E '90
(330) 702-0780 **Bresko** Andrew G '75
(330) 533-8323 **Brott** Gary N '83
(330) 533-8885 **Ciotola** Robert A '77
(330) 533-8980 **Coniglio** Shirley J '89
(330) 533-4373 **Davis** Henry W '55
(330) 533-4373 **Davis** James H '79
(330) 533-0916 **DeFazio** John T '73
(330) 702-1960 **DeVicchio** Mark A '91
(330) 702-1747 **DeVicchio** Matthew L '99
(330) 702-0033 **Dunlap** Charles E '77
(330) 702-1800 **Elliott** Rush E '68
(330) 533-0916 **Ferrante** Joseph A '88
(330) 533-0052 **Ferris** Dean F '51
(330) 533-4823 **Fowler** Pamela P '85
(330) 533-1118 **Gardner** Joseph W '77
(330) 702-0780 **Gazda** Melody D '90
(330) 533-6565 **Gervelis** Mark S '76
(330) 503-5032 **Hendryx** Bruce D '87
(330) 533-1828 **Hill** Thomas A '84
(330) 533-6119 **Hunter** Scott D '88
(330) 758-6422 **Jakubek** John T '57
(330) 533-1921 **Johnson** Eric C '83
(330) 533-1921 **Johnson & Johnson**
(330) 533-1921 **Johnson** Nils P Jr. '76
(330) 404-1901 **Joseph** Jeffrey A '98
(330) 533-2617 **Kalasky** William G '78
(330) 533-4373 **Kay** Charles J '93
(330) 746-8484 **Kish** Brian P '01
(330) 533-6821 **Kish** William J '70
(330) 746-8484 **Kopp** Brian P '95
(330) 533-5447 **Lane** Joseph D '84
(330) 702-0780 **Luckhart Mumaw Zellers & Robinson**
(330) 702-0033 **Machuga** Richard W '87
(330) 746-8484 **Maruca** Christopher A '98
(330) 746-8484 **Maruca** Susan Gaetano '95
(330) 533-8315 **Mercer** Jeralyn G '93
(330) 533-6821 **Montgomery** Richard K '76
Moore Robert S '86
(330) 702-0230 **Morgione** Vincent J '89
(330) 533-9660 **Morris** Patricia A '89
(330) 533-1700 **Moses** Norman A Jr. '97
(330) 702-8800 **Motosko** Linda A '80
(330) 533-8304 **Ortenzio** Albert J '51
(330) 533-0916 **Prassinos** Constant A '72
(330) 702-0780 **Price** Robert W '01
(330) 533-6869 **Rheuban** Norman A '48
(330) 533-1990 **Rimmel** James E '83
(330) 702-0780 **Robinson** Henry C '49
(330) 533-3341 **Rosati** Gary J '84
(330) 702-1436 **Ruse** Linda S '85
(330) 533-5447 **Rusu** Robert N Jr. '93
(330) 702-0033 **Shugart** Ursula P '03
(330) 533-6119 **Stevens** Robert L '74
(330) 533-9810 **Toot** Douglas M '73
(330) 533-1700 **Travers** Thomas J Jr. '76
(330) 533-0916 **Tsarnas** Nomiki P '03
(330) 702-2825 **Walsh** Maureen A '85
(330) 533-2616 **White** David R '68
(330) 533-8885 **White** Joanna B '04
(330) 702-0780 **Zellers** Richard G '74
(330) 533-6821 **Zielke** Larry A '79

CANTON
Stark County

Abel Michael A '95
(330) 456-8376 **Adlon** James P '81
(330) 456-8376 **Ake** David S '72
(330) 456-0050 **Albu** Thomas P '75
(330) 456-8389 **Aman** George J '54
(330) 492-8717 **Amiet** Ralph D '67
(330) 471-4044 **Amrhein** Christine B '87
(330) 499-0900 **Andrews** Timothy G '73
(330) 492-5151 **Anthony** John F II '77
(330) 455-0173 **Archer** John P '01
(330) 437-0025 **Arkow** Seth W '98
(330) 491-5216 **Armatas** Steven A '84
(330) 499-8648 **Armstrong** John A '98
(330) 456-7702 **Arnold** Jennifer L '99
(330) 455-0173 **Arnold** Richard W '94
(330) 492-2323 **Ayers** Charles Stephen '87
(330) 451-7884 **Aylward** Kristen B '85
(330) 493-1570 **Baasten** Cornelius J '73
(330) 458-2411 **Baca** Rodney A '99
(330) 455-0173 **Badger** William B '61
(330) 499-6000 **Baker Dublikar Beck Wiley & Mathews**
(330) 492-1001 **Baker** Gerald L '68
(330) 499-6000 **Baker** Jack R '69
(330) 492-8717 **Banas** Gary A '57
(330) 456-8341 **Barnhart** Gene '53
(330) 489-5065 **Barone** Anthony N '91
(330) 451-7897 **Barr** Dennis E '84
Barr Lisa J '97
(330) 471-7362 **Basinski** David A Jr. '89
(330) 499-0900 **Batista** Roy H '65
(330) 451-7897 **Baumoel** Jonathan S '92
(330) 456-8361 **Baumoel** Lynn R '90
(330) 451-7765 **Beard** Kristine W '89
(330) 499-6000 **Beck** Gregory A '81
(330) 489-3214 **Belden** Stephen F '79
(330) 430-6109 **Bell** Catherine M '99
(330) 492-8717 **Bell** Lee J '73
(330) 489-1001 **Bennington** Ronald K '61
(330) 499-1016 **Benson** Don M '65
(330) 244-1174 **Beoglos** Laura L '92
(330) 456-1112 **Bergert** Jennifer L '01
(330) 454-1967 **Bergert** Todd A '90
(330) 492-2900 **Bernabei** Thomas M '75
(330) 451-7200 **Bible** April R '92
Bickis Michael S '02
(330) 492-8865 **Bing** Jason N '00
(330) 452-1343 **Bing** Richard George '56
(330) 456-8341 **Black McCuskey Souers & Arbaugh, LPA**
Black Sharon L '02
(330) 455-0173 **Black** Sheila Markley '72
(330) 499-1016 **Blair** William P III '71
(330) 451-7200 **Blake** Allyson J '99
(330) 455-0173 **Blake** James R '73
(330) 451-7456 **Blank** Norma H '84
(330) 455-0173 **Boettler** Louis A '55
(330) 497-0700 **Bogdan** Michael J '04
(330) 452-3003 **Boggins** John V '86
(330) 497-0700 **Bogniard** John J '72
(330) 492-4717 **Bond** Douglas C '89
(330) 456-8361 **Bonta** Darlene B '94
(330) 499-2396 **Borcoman** Tom A '74
(330) 455-6400 **Boske** Michael A '95
(330) 451-8892 **Boyle** Alicia L '99
(330) 455-0173 **Brannen** John H '75
(330) 491-5222 **Braun** Dianne Blocker '76
(330) 494-2121 **Brian** Richard F '82
(330) 494-2121 **Brian** Steven J '88
(330) 451-7897 **Bridenstine** David M '80
Briner Merlin G '66
(330) 455-0173 **Brooker** James K '62
(330) 499-6000 **Brown** Anthony E '98
(330) 455-0173 **Brown** Larry R '60
(330) 497-3681 **Brunn** Richard C '59
(330) 492-8717 **Buckingham Doolittle & Burroughs, LLP**
(330) 451-7768 **Buehler** Trevor K '73
(330) 455-0173 **Bules** Raymond T '81
(330) 471-3949 **Bump** Mark W '83
(330) 456-8341 **Bundy** Todd S '80
(330) 456-3200 **Burick** Elizabeth A '84
(330) 526-0104 **Burleson** David G '92
(330) 454-2136 **Burns** Thomas A '75
(330) 451-7770 **Burton** Diane C '91
(330) 438-0976 **Butera** Constance D '82
(330) 491-5217 **Butera** Karen D '99
(330) 497-0700 **Butz** David E '87
(330) 499-8387 **Calabretta** Joseph W '71
(330) 497-0700 **Caldwell** Jacqueline B '85
(330) 451-7897 **Caldwell** Ronald M '85
(330) 456-8341 **Callas** Gust '78
(330) 455-4555 **Caplea** Don E '72
(330) 471-9522 **Carter** Ross A '90
(330) 451-7900 **Carver** Aletha M '92
(330) 456-8341 **Centrone** Francis G '68
(330) 456-4590 **Cespedes** Anthony J '78
(330) 451-8970 **Chaney-Hopwood** Kimberly R '90
(330) 451-7897 **Chawla** Kathi W '98
(330) 489-3251 **Chessler** Craig E '83
(330) 489-5243 **Christ** Roger A '87
(330) 497-0700 **Clark** John D '97
(330) 499-8899 **Cleaver** Sandra W '88
(330) 455-0173 **Cline** William S '78
(330) 477-2539 **Cochrane** William Jr. '50
(330) 492-8717 **Coey** G Brenda '03
(330) 451-8796 **Coleman** Jerry A '99
(330) 499-1016 **Collum** James J '99
(330) 451-8796 **Compton** Quay D '99
(330) 453-1900 **Conley** Craig T '83
(330) 456-8341 **Connors** Thomas W '78
(330) 497-0700 **Contini** James F II '92
(330) 455-0173 **Cooper** Jack B '98
(330) 451-7240 **Cooper** Melinda S '93
(330) 966-2869 **Cope** Leland H '53
(330) 451-7897 **Cordova** Michelle L '96
(330) 455-6112 **Corroto** Gary A '91
(330) 454-2136 **Coury** John S '77
(330) 456-0061 **Craig** Steven L '84
(330) 454-5612 **Cranston** Thomas K '76
(330) 452-6773 **Crawford** George Ian '84
(330) 477-8535 **Cross & Rose Co,LPA**
(330) 493-4443 **Curati** Jennifer E '00
(330) 456-7922 **Cusma** Patrick L '96
(330) 493-9611 **Cutler** Jay L '83
(330) 471-3530 **Cyperski** Nancy L '84
(330) 492-6659 **Cyperski** Robert H '84
(330) 494-6666 **Daane** Robert B '75
(330) 451-7716 **Dahl** Milton Dean '96
(330) 451-7241 **Dahler** Fred W '92
(330) 497-2886 **D'Atri** Edward L '63
(330) 451-7855 **Dave** Jennifer L '94
Davies Steven W '02
(330) 455-0173 **Davis** David D L '03
(330) 494-5504 **Davis** Jane M '96
(330) 497-0700 **Davis** Richard E II '76
(330) 438-0865 **Dawson** Deborah A '81
(330) 455-0173 **Day Ketterer Raley Wright & Rybolt, Ltd**
(330) 489-3395 **Day** Melissa '99
(330) 456-8341 **Dayton** Joel K '77
(330) 494-2121 **Debski** Dana M '96
(330) 497-0700 **de Forest** Benjamin B II '84
(330) 588-9700 **DeGirolamo** Anthony J '92
(330) 478-4711 **DeHoff** Harold E '50
(330) 454-2136 **Demchak** Michael D '77
(330) 492-2511 **DePasquale** David F '88
(330) 492-2511 **DePasquale** Lauren E '83
(330) 452-1144 **Dickes** Don D '64
(330) 477-9675 **Dickson** William H '72
(330) 499-6000 **DiCola** Renee N '03
(330) 455-6112 **Dingwell** David L '92
(330) 493-1570 **DioGuardi** Anthony M II '86
(330) 491-0900 **Dionisio** Christopher '00
(330) 451-7785 **Dobbs** Shaunna L '01
(330) 456-8341 **Dodez** Richard D '69
(330) 477-8535 **Dodson** Irene Elizabeth '04
(330) 477-8535 **Dodson** Richard S Jr. '77
(330) 451-7709 **Dossi** Jacquelyn M '98
(330) 489-5057 **Dougherty** Richard L '77
(330) 497-0700 **Dougherty** Ronald W '60
(330) 489-5410 **Dressler** Donald J '73
(330) 499-6000 **Dublikar** Justin A '04
(330) 499-6000 **Dublikar** Ralph F '74
(330) 430-3804 **Duffrin** Vivianne W '93
(330) 491-5230 **Dukat** James C '69
(330) 489-5096 **Dukes** Patrick M '91
(330) 489-4430 **Durben** Annette M '99
(330) 491-5289 **Dureska** David P '87
(330) 456-8341 **Dylewski** Faith R '02
(330) 493-4877 **Eckinger** Robert W '95
(330) 456-8341 **Efremoff** Anthony E '63
(330) 451-7453 **Efremoff** Sarah A '63
(330) 491-5240 **Emley** William W Sr. '71
(330) 762-2255 **Englert** Holly J '97
(330) 451-8964 **Eoff** Cristina G '99
(330) 453-0185 **Ergazos** John W '52
Espenschied Diana L '86
(330) 455-0173 **Evans** Merle D III '83
Ewashinka Heather E '95
(330) 493-1570 **Falletta** Salvatore J '67
(330) 493-4443 **Fallon** Martin J '89
(330) 489-3216 **Falvey** Mary Ann '79
(330) 451-7910 **Farmer** Kristin G '01
(330) 471-4162 **Feielin** Robert M '99
(330) 451-7637 **Feisthamel** Toni B '00
(330) 492-8717 **Feltes** Joseph J '78
(330) 452-7531 **Ferrell** David B '78
(330) 452-6400 **Ferruccio** Samuel J Jr. '79
(330) 497-0700 **Fickes** Jeffrey A '01
(330) 456-6200 **Fidler** James G '95
(330) 493-0040 **Figler** Ronald G '71
(330) 497-2000 **Finnucan** John C '93
(330) 452-3762 **Firestone** Eric A '78
(330) 438-6360 **Fisher** Jeanine M '99
(330) 493-0460 **Fladen** Sharon V '78
(330) 489-5258 **Flanagan** Rosemary M '79
(330) 451-7721 **Flowers** Lori Ann '01
(330) 451-7200 **Flynn** Beth A '04
(330) 456-9656 **Foltz** Jeremy J '99
(330) 489-3395 **Forchione** Francis G '86
(330) 489-3395 **Forte** Jennifer L '00
(330) 478-3833 **Fowler** Douglas T '95
(330) 493-0040 **Fox** Dennis J '71
(330) 438-0611 **Frame** Gary J '93
(330) 451-7200 **Frame** Kenneth W '96
(330) 266-1931 **Framer** Lee W '77
(330) 493-6515 **Frank** John R '91
(330) 493-4443 **Frank** Michael '90
(330) 492-8717 **Frasure** Mark D '74
(330) 497-2886 **Freeman** Christopher J '91
(330) 456-8341 **Friedman** Robert I '64
Fuchs Lorrie E '86
(330) 499-6000 **Funk** Daniel J '94
(330) 456-4646 **Gaitanos** Mario '84
(330) 492-8717 **Gary** Denise A '98
(330) 451-8175 **Genetin** Judee L '79
(330) 456-8171 **Georges** William H '69
(330) 447-4511 **Gilbertson** Glen G '79
(330) 498-4411 **Gill** Lance D '89
(330) 492-4249 **Ginella** Andrea A '95
(330) 492-3636 **Ginella** Stephen A Jr. '87
(330) 452-6400 **Giua** John R '77
(330) 492-1800 **Glantz** Arnold F '86
(330) 452-8755 **Golub** Gerald B '73
(330) 493-1570 **Gore** William B '64
Goulet Kathryn H '01
(330) 494-1015 **Goutras** Gust '85
(330) 494-1015 **Goutras** Lora L '89
(330) 499-1016 **Graham** Wayne E Jr. '85
(330) 456-1112 **Green** Lemuel R '72
(330) 497-0700 **Greene** Stephanie M '99
(330) 492-8717 **Greenfelder** Justin S '04
(330) 499-0900 **Gregg** James R '64
(330) 491-5262 **Griffin** Stephen P '88
(330) 456-8341 **Griffith** Daniel R '02
(330) 497-0700 **Griffiths** Raymond E '57
(330) 493-1570 **Groff** Shawn C '92
(330) 497-2886 **Gruber** Michael S '77
(330) 489-3395 **Guardado** Kristen D '95
(330) 489-3374 **Guarnieri** Lewis D '99
(330) 244-4200 **Guiley** Richard R '85
(330) 244-4200 **Guiley** Rodney R '75
(330) 477-6781 **Gutierrez** Roy '61
(330) 649-9102 **Haag** Charles A '80
(330) 493-0272 **Hale** Kathleen M '81
(330) 453-2336 **Hall** Charles D III '83
(330) 453-2336 **Hall** Rosemarie A '92
(330) 491-5221 **Halm** Jeffrey A '73
(330) 433-5349 **Hammond** Elizabeth E '83
(330) 484-3239 **Hanner** Willard K Jr. '80
(330) 499-6000 **Hanratty** James P '89
(330) 489-6407 **Hardesty** Lee P '98
(330) 438-0889 **Hardy** Charlene S '96
(330) 492-8717 **Harless** Kristina M '99
(330) 451-7897 **Harris** Jamila M '04
(330) 453-1906 **Harrison** Stephen J '80
(330) 438-0897 **Hartnett** Chryssa N '95
(330) 455-0173 **Hartnett** Thomas E '93
(330) 454-3479 **Hauch** Michael T '76
(330) 497-0700 **Haupt** Fred J '67
(330) 497-0700 **Haupt** Jason F '02
(330) 492-3957 **Haupt** Jeffrey D '85
(330) 489-3395 **Hauritz** Tyrone D '90
(330) 494-6115 **Haut** Annette R Ciavarella '03
(330) 456-7737 **Heath Cholley** Taryn '82
(330) 456-0061 **Heichel Craig & Prelac Co, LPA**
(330) 453-0458 **Heinbach** Charles C Jr. '83
(330) 451-7152 **Hemphill** Dwaine R '88
(330) 479-9825 **Henning** Richard L '76
(330) 479-9825 **Henning** Sally D '78
(330) 499-1016 **Herbert & Benson**
(330) 499-1016 **Herbert** David L '74
(330) 437-0026 **Hervey** Paul B '94
(330) 833-3192 **Hilterbrand** Charles M Jr. '94
(330) 492-8717 **Himmelspach** Thomas R '87
(330) 497-7815 **Hinkel** Walter W '73
(330) 493-6966 **Holland** Darrell W Jr. '82
(330) 456-0091 **Hollingsworth** Jon M '76
(330) 489-5003 **Hopwood** Arthur H Jr. '91
(330) 456-0091 **Hornbrook** John H '82
(330) 456-7901 **Hossler** Jerome H '49
(330) 455-6112 **Houston** Denise M '95
(330) 451-7455 **Howard** Michael L '79
(330) 492-8717 **Howes** Philip E '60
(330) 492-8717 **Humphrey** Christopher S '93
(330) 489-3395 **Hunt** Bernard L '84
(330) 497-0700 **Hunt** Randall C '78
(330) 438-8659 **Huntley** Jacquelyn M '89
(330) 455-6112 **Huryn** Christopher M '93
(330) 452-6400 **Iams** Bradley R '81
(330) 454-6555 **Inboden** Marc B '73
(330) 489-3395 **Infantino** Vernon M '03
(330) 456-2300 **Ionno** John M '72
Jay David E '79
(330) 456-0061 **Jeffries** Timothy J '00
(330) 493-6966 **Johnson** Christine A '99
(330) 451-7200 **Johnson** Tammi R '85
(330) 456-8341 **Jonas** Daniel M '68
(330) 477-5570 **Jones** Douglas D '80
(330) 456-8341 **Juergensen** John L '99
(330) 499-5104 **Kahn** Bernard L '51
(330) 456-8341 **Kamerer** James P '74
(330) 455-0173 **Kaminski** John S '03
(330) 456-8376 **Kandel** James R '72
(330) 454-9960 **Kaplanis** Anthony T '89
(330) 456-2853 **Kaschak** Bryan C '04
(330) 456-2853 **Kaschak** Wayne R '72
(330) 493-9149 **Kattman** Jeffrey C '81
(330) 455-0173 **Keenan** J Sean '67
(330) 451-7911 **Kellar** Cynthia A '86
(330) 497-0389 **Kennedy** Christopher P '02
(330) 492-8717 **Kennedy** Edward T '00
(330) 456-8341 **Kessler** Terrence P '75
(330) 479-4371 **Kettler** John Scott '76
(330) 494-1120 **Killian** Robert R '77
Kinnear Kevin R '94
(330) 452-5781 **Klapp** Victoria Z '75
(330) 494-4748 **Klingensmith** Robert D '79
(330) 492-8717 **Knapic** Barbara A '86
(330) 471-4101 **Knudsen** Nancy S '82
(330) 451-7897 **Konovsky** Hope S '98
(330) 493-0040 **Kotnik** Donald P '90
(330) 458-2411 **Koukoutas** Anthony '96
(330) 471-1105 **Kovach** Linda K '91
(330) 456-8361 **Krocker** Michelle L '02
(330) 497-0700 **Krugliak Wilkins Griffiths & Dougherty Co,LPA**
(330) 489-3210 **Kubilus** Richard J '78
(330) 452-6400 **Kuhn** John S '77
(330) 452-7334 **Kuhn** Richard R '80
(330) 497-0700 **Kuntz** Leslie I '86
(330) 455-0173 **Kyhos** Wayne C '69
(330) 966-1866 **Lacki** Ralph S '77
(330) 499-5474 **Lally** Thomas W '73
(330) 454-1674 **Lancaster** Judith E '94
(330) 477-8535 **Lancianese** Frank W '84
(330) 456-4571 **Lattavo** Philip E '67
(330) 497-2886 **Layman** Brian C '00
(330) 492-8717 **Leb** Arthur S '55
(330) 455-6112 **Lee** Cheryl S '00
(330) 493-0040 **Lesh Casner & Miller**
(330) 430-1998 **Leuchtag** Holly A '83
(330) 489-3251 **L'Hommedieu** Kevin R '96
(330) 451-7705 **Lile** Jennifer L '00
(330) 499-6000 **Lindamood** John B '66
(330) 453-3999 **Lindsey** James B Jr. '77
(330) 456-4576 **Little** Donald R '66
(330) 454-9960 **Lo Dico** Steven L '89
(330) 492-8717 **Lolli** Richard J '76
(330) 454-9041 **Lombardi** Robert M '55
(330) 493-0040 **Lombardi** Thomas J '66
(330) 493-9901 **Lonas McGonegal & Tsangeos**
(330) 493-9901 **Lonas** Webster M Jr. '65
(330) 438-0767 **Longbrake** Suzanne Trocki '95
(330) 456-4308 **Love** Kenyon D '52
(330) 451-7213 **Lowman** Catherine S '01
Lowry Derek J '98
(330) 451-8659 **Lowry** Jennifer T '99
(330) 451-7214 **Lunich** Dana L '85
(330) 499-6000 **Lute** Melvin L Jr. '90
(330) 499-0049 **Maasz** Philip Steven '91
(330) 493-1570 **Macala Baasten McKinley & Gore,LLC**
(330) 493-1570 **Macala** Ronald G '74
(330) 478-2595 **Machan** Mitchell A '81
(330) 452-6567 **Mackey** John N '71
(330) 451-7200 **Madden** Jean A '90
(330) 477-1510 **Majors** Shirley F '78
(330) 497-0700 **Malesick** Paul H II '81
(330) 455-2222 **Malone** Brian J '97
(330) 451-7203 **Manello** James S '85
(330) 455-6112 **Mannos** James G '77
(330) 492-7107 **Markijohn** Darrell N '85
Markijohn Jayne L '89
(330) 456-8105 **Marsh** Bobbie L '89
(330) 456-8341 **Marsh** Victor R Jr. '66
(330) 471-0187 **Marshall** Donald D '78
(330) 471-6831 **Martin** Byron D '94
(330) 453-8279 **Martin** Sherri L '84
(330) 489-3251 **Martuccio** Joseph '81
(330) 451-7881 **Mastriacovo** Paul A '78
(330) 455-0173 **Matasich** Stephen E '96
(330) 499-6000 **Mathews** James F '88
(330) 489-5434 **Mayle** Kimberly A '90
(330) 455-0173 **McBride** Robert J '95
(330) 493-0040 **McCall** John S Jr. '74
(330) 453-9999 **McCallin** Alfred D '82
(330) 356-0314 **McClowry** Derek C '04
McDaniels Jeaneen J '84
(330) 453-5302 **McFarren** Randy '74
(330) 458-0484 **McGinnis** William F '91
(330) 493-9901 **McGonegal** Terrance J '77
(330) 455-6112 **McHugh** James M '90
(330) 493-1570 **McKinley** Kathleen K '90
(330) 455-0173 **McQueen** Jill C '86

(330) 497-0700 **McQueen** Karen S '84
(330) 471-2097 **Mehosky** Brian L '86
(330) 451-7979 **Melia** Patricia C '97
(330) 458-2411 **Merrill** Sandra L '86
(330) 456-8341 **Mertes** Brian R '95
(330) 489-5411 **Messerly** Edwin C '74
(330) 489-3251 **Mestel** Mariella '77
(330) 492-8717 **Meyer** Robert C '78
(330) 492-8888 **Mihalik** Kathleen A '01
(330) 456-9911 **Miller** Donald M '74
(330) 493-0040 **Miller** Rex W '70
(330) 497-0700 **Miller** Scott R '97
(330) 438-0870 **Miller** Sharon D '95
(330) 492-8717 **Milligan** Richard S '80
(330) 493-8525 **Millisor & Nobil Co,LPA**
(330) 456-0506 **Mills** Daniel M '86
(330) 456-0506 **Mills** Laura L '94
(330) 456-0506 **Mills Mills Fiely & Lucas**
(330) 455-0173 **Minkler** Daniel A '79
(330) 452-4751 **Mittas** William G '91
(330) 451-7897 **Mlinar** Kristen L '96
(330) 491-2222 **Moore** Edgar M Jr. '77
(330) 456-8361 **Moore** Laureen M '84
(330) 497-0700 **Moore** Terry A '80
(330) 454-9960 **Morello** Herbert J '94
(330) 451-7200 **Morgan** Carl A '02
(330) 453-0008 **Morris** Jonathan E '94
(330) 497-0700 **Morrison** Jessica A '04
(330) 492-8717 **Morrow** Tod T '89
(330) 493-2685 **Motz** Frank J '78
(330) 494-6688 **Muckley** Timothy R '97
(330) 497-0700 **Mullen** Matthew P '94
(330) 489-4414 **Mullen** Robert K '97
(330) 455-0173 **Murphy** John A Jr. '81
(330) 456-8341 **Murphy** Robert J '04
(330) 497-0700 **Murray** Edward D '91
Murray Kelly S '03
(330) 438-8811 **Muth** Randall B '94
(330) 438-0422 **Myers** John E '91
(330) 491-5238 **Nalawadi** Sushila J '01
(330) 453-3709 **Neal** Marianna D '77
Newell Janel M '94
(330) 454-3508 **Newell** William T '97
(330) 452-6400 **Newlon** Christopher A '94
(330) 455-0935 **Niarchos** Gust P II '67
(330) 453-7045 **Nicodemo** John L '72
(330) 453-8261 **Nicodemo** Richard A '84
(330) 451-7305 **Nist** David R '92
(330) 471-4363 **Nolin** David B '91
(330) 453-7874 **Oberholtzer** Mattheuw W '89
(330) 471-3937 **Oberster** Alan C '93
(330) 489-3395 **O'Byrne** Eugene D IV '98
(330) 453-8261 **Okey** Mark D '76
(330) 453-8261 **Okey** Steven P '87
(330) 491-9880 **Oleksy** Lisa A '96
(330) 489-3395 **Osler** Tammie M '01
(330) 492-0010 **Pac-Urar** Mary L '89
(330) 451-7716 **Park** Dixilene T '92
(330) 497-2886 **Pastore** Catherine A '87
(330) 455-0173 **Paulino** Joanne G '96
(330) 497-4604 **Perlman** Marjorie R '77
Peshek Linda M '86
(330) 265-8278 **Petit** Matthew A '01
(330) 493-9080 **Pfendler** Christopher C '79
(330) 471-6361 **Phillips** James P A '02
(330) 494-6611 **Pidcock** William S '82
(330) 452-7921 **Pinhard** Richard B '85
(330) 458-2411 **Pitinii** Fredrick M '96
(330) 458-2411 **Pitinii** Melissa Voros '03
(330) 455-6112 **Plakas** Leonidas E '76
(330) 456-8361 **Poh** Jaime-Lyn '03
(330) 489-3288 **Poulos** John A '81
(330) 455-0173 **Powell** Tim A '76
(330) 451-7217 **Powers-Griffiths** Kristina R '97
(330) 456-0061 **Prelac** John M '84
(330) 456-8341 **Preston** Robert B III '04
(330) 455-0173 **Princic** Richard A '76
(330) 492-5151 **Procario** Gary J '69
(330) 452-5781 **Proctor** James P '80
(330) 491-9880 **Proctor-Donald** Beverly P '98
(330) 497-1300 **Pucci-Sutton** Susan '94
(330) 492-8717 **Pusateri** Paul J '97
(330) 458-0484 **Puterbaugh** Michael R '89
(330) 498-9485 **Putman** Timothy J '85
(330) 497-1300 **Quinlan** Karen Ross '92
(330) 451-7200 **Ragner** John C '02
(330) 455-6112 **Raies** Elizabeth A '86
(330) 478-0755 **Raines** Kimberly A '99
(330) 456-8341 **Rambacher** John J '86
(330) 499-3878 **Ramsey** James Kevin '63
(330) 456-8341 **Randall** Mary E '83
(330) 497-0700 **Rarric** Owen J '02
(330) 451-7765 **Reader** Willard Donald Jr. '58
(330) 492-3957 **Recupero** James R '86
(330) 453-0008 **Redinger** Ivan L Jr. '85
(330) 489-3395 **Reese** Jason P '97
(330) 491-9999 **Reese** Robert G '93
(330) 649-9102 **Regas & Haag, Ltd**
(330) 649-9102 **Regas** John S '93
(330) 649-9102 **Regas** Sharon S '93
(330) 451-2040 **Reiners** Paul R '78
(330) 451-7200 **Reisch** Steven A '97
(330) 244-4200 **Reolfi** Michael L '92
(330) 451-7863 **Rhodes** Ross A '00
(330) 492-7107 **Richards** Homer R '77
(330) 497-0700 **Ringer** Charles E '89
(330) 455-3488 **Rinier** Alton L '48
(330) 438-1180 **Roberts** Jeffrey D '90
(330) 494-6611 **Robertson** James T '74
(330) 494-6611 **Robertson Zeglen & Pidlock**
(330) 497-4546 **Rockenfelder** Wendy J '79
(330) 497-0700 **Rodgers** Susan C '91
(330) 456-8341 **Rohrer** Amanda K '03
(330) 451-7898 **Roland** Deborah N '89
(330) 455-0173 **Roland** Robert E '85
(330) 363-7463 **Rose** Mark N '92
(330) 492-8717 **Ross** John C '82
(330) 456-4400 **Roth** Stacie L '99
(330) 493-1144 **Rothermel** Nancy J '86
(330) 456-0083 **Rubin** Robert G '68
(330) 453-7104 **Rubin** Rosemary G '74
(330) 455-5206 **Rubin** Stanley R '76
(330) 438-0838 **Rufo** Alice F '87
(330) 456-8389 **Rufo** Gregory J '83
(330) 497-0389 **Russell** Michael S '77
(330) 580-2568 **Rutledge** James H '79
Sales Gary N '80
(330) 438-0611 **Sampson** Karen P '84
(330) 244-1174 **Sand** Michael '69
(330) 244-1174 **Sand & Sebolt**
(330) 456-8341 **Sandrock** Scott P '78
(330) 471-5755 **Saylor** Caroline A '00
(330) 456-4400 **Saylor** Timothy B '89
(330) 451-7200 **Scavelli** John A '04
(330) 456-1112 **Schandel** Phillip D '67
(330) 499-9200 **Schenck** Brett A '04
(330) 471-4226 **Scherff** Scott A '79
(330) 497-4501 **Schnars** Richard T '93
(330) 214-4202 **Schneiderman-Welch** Ellen L '88
(330) 456-4400 **Schulman** Allen Jr. '75
(330) 452-2889 **Schwartz** Steven '86
(330) 452-9255 **Scott** Frederic R '92
(330) 244-1174 **Sebolt** Joseph A '92
(330) 456-8341 **Seeberger** Terrence L '79
(330) 452-4005 **Sekula** Mary Lou '96
(330) 453-7104 **Selby** Joan P '78
(330) 453-7377 **Selegean-Dostal** Sue E '96
(330) 452-6400 **Serra** Jeffry V '03
(330) 455-0173 **Shandor** Steven D '04
(330) 455-5379 **Sheehan** Earl C '52
(330) 456-8341 **Shifman** Arnold R '64
(330) 456-0900 **Silagy** Anne Piero '85
(330) 497-0700 **Simiele** David L '63
(330) 497-0700 **Simmerman** Sam O '79
(330) 499-8899 **Simmons & Cleaver**
(330) 499-8899 **Simmons** David J '82
(330) 478-1947 **Sirak** Norman L '72
(330) 493-8525 **Slater** John R '81
(330) 497-9644 **Slesnick** Elizabeth M '92
(330) 492-8136 **Slick** Mary J '84
Slowey Suzanne L '01
(330) 453-8788 **Smith** Corey L '01
(330) 456-4793 **Smith** David L '97
(330) 492-0101 **Smith** Roger Louis '75
(330) 456-8341 **Snow** Randolph L '71
(330) 456-8341 **Soares** Bruce M '80
(330) 477-4515 **Soehnlen** Emil A '96
(330) 499-8899 **Sokolowski** Sue A '01
Solomon Aurel '52
(330) 455-0345 **Souers** Loren E Jr. '74
(330) 493-7211 **Sparks** William R '77
(330) 493-1144 **Sponseller** John N '65
(330) 456-0663 **Staudt** Elmer Roman III '74
(330) 452-8640 **Stocker** Steven E '76
(330) 492-3957 **Stone** Angela D '96
(330) 456-8341 **Strawn** James R '76
(330) 499-6000 **Streb** Jude B '99
(330) 493-9901 **Struhar** Steven A '84
(330) 438-1223 **Sweeney** Robert M '67
(330) 497-0700 **Swope** Gregory D '95
(330) 492-7505 **Tarian** Romain Joseph '77
(330) 456-4503 **Tarr** David T '66
(330) 456-7780 **Tatarsky** Kathleen M '79
(330) 497-2886 **Thomas** David M '88
(330) 497-0700 **Thompson** Michael A '74
(330) 471-4094 **Thouvenin** Scott G '96
(330) 451-7931 **Timken** Jane M '94
(330) 497-2886 **Tolbert** Valerie L '97
(330) 456-6000 **Trifelos** George H '54
(330) 493-9901 **Tsangeos** Angelo J '85
(330) 456-4576 **Tscholl** John A '74
(330) 456-7702 **Tscholl** Robert J '76
(330) 497-0700 **Tucker** John M '96
(330) 456-8341 **Tyburski** Charles J '64
(330) 455-6112 **Tzangas** George J '57
(330) 455-6112 **Tzangas Plakas Mannos & Raies**
(330) 437-0101 **Urban** George '94
(330) 451-8796 **Vaccaro** Michael B '95
(330) 456-4122 **Vagotis** Angela T '90
(330) 491-5235 **Van Abel** John P '59
(330) 451-7897 **Vance** Joseph E '99
(330) 455-5195 **Variola** Giancarlo '79
(330) 456-8341 **Vassiles** Chrysanthe E '96
(330) 497-0700 **Vaughan** Nathan D '04
(330) 497-4501 **Venet** Deborah L '00
(330) 451-7200 **Wainwright** Marcus L '04
(330) 451-7204 **Wakser** Barry T '92
Walker William E Jr. '87
(330) 497-0700 **Warkall** Michael A '94
(330) 453-8261 **Washam** Scott A '87
(330) 451-7897 **Watson** Renee M '00
(330) 456-2262 **Watterson** Tim M '82
(330) 498-9820 **Weltman** Jeffrey H '79
(330) 455-0173 **Werren** John Curtis '92
(330) 453-2945 **Werren** John E '91
(330) 455-0173 **Werren** John R '61
(330) 499-6000 **Wiley** Donald P '84
(330) 497-0700 **Wilkins** F Stuart S Jr. '52
(330) 453-6344 **Wilkof** Jeffrey S '80
(330) 454-7777 **Williams** Agatha Martin '91
(330) 497-0700 **Williams** William G '75
(330) 453-8261 **Wilson** Brian R '87
(330) 477-6781 **Wilson** Randy K '76
(330) 433-6800 **Winkhart** Thomas W '89
(330) 493-0787 **Wirsching** David B Jr. '65
(330) 454-2444 **Wirtz** John B '73
(330) 451-7897 **Wise** Earle E Jr. '97
(330) 451-7918 **Witner** Kristine S '94
(330) 456-8341 **Woolbert** Gordon D II '97
(330) 438-0638 **Workman** Billie J '88
(330) 455-0173 **Wyler** Alicia M '78
(330) 499-6000 **Wyss** Kimberly K '93
(330) 455-0173 **Yackshaw** Matthew '79
(330) 452-2266 **Zedell** Albert L '76
(330) 453-8786 **Zedell** Robert A '82
(330) 494-6611 **Zeglen** Joseph M '85
(330) 499-6000 **Ziarko** Andrea K '01
(330) 454-8056 **Zimmerman** Brian L '89
(330) 492-2225 **Zink** Larry A '75
(330) 456-8389 **Zirpolo** Michael P Jr. '75
(330) 497-2886 **Zollinger D'Atri Gruber Thomas & Co**
(330) 526-0104 **Zollinger** Frederick H III '94
(330) 497-2886 **Zollinger** Frederick H Jr. '73
(330) 455-0173 **Zollinger** Richard C Jr. '99
(330) 499-1016 **Zondorak** Lynn A '03
(330) 497-0700 **Zurakowski** Scott M '98
(330) 452-5781 **Zwick** Leander P III '75

CARDINGTON
Morrow County
(419) 864-6016 **Ray** Thomas E '57

CAREY
Wyandot County
(419) 396-6190 **Beck** Linden J '73
(419) 396-6662 **Beeler** Robert L '83
(419) 396-6190 **Burson** Paul A '49
(419) 396-7691 **Maison** Robert T '73

CARROLL
Fairfield County
(614) 837-1029 **Clapham** Edward Geoffrey '63

CARROLLTON
Carroll County
(330) 627-4555 **Asper** Edward S '95
(330) 627-5577 **Barnett** Steven D '04
(330) 627-5314 **Benson** Paul F '50
(330) 627-4555 **Burns** Donald R Jr. '88
(330) 627-5577 **Campbell** John S '77
(330) 627-4770 **Childers** John C '78
(330) 627-2191 **Hannon** Richard C Jr. '79
(330) 627-2918 **Rumbaugh** Richard Lee '72
(330) 627-4770 **Smith** Sean R H '81
(330) 627-6642 **Stoneman** Kathleen A '82

CEDARVILLE
Greene County
(937) 766-4861 **Bogenschutz** Stephen A '73
(937) 766-2020 **Gentry** Daniel J '95

CELINA
Mercer County
(419) 586-1072 **Boley** Leisa R '94
(419) 584-1004 **Chapel** Matthew W '95
(419) 586-5181 **Dean** Rebecca L '98
(419) 586-6886 **Faber** Keith L '91
(419) 586-1334 **Finke** Ross J '03
(419) 586-8677 **Fox** Matthew K '91
(419) 586-8120 **Gilmore** Matthew L '94
(419) 586-8677 **Hinders** Andrew J '81
(419) 586-7171 **Hogan** James P '72
(419) 586-8677 **Ikerd** Amy B '96
(419) 586-6444 **Knapke** Henry J Jr. '72
(419) 586-6444 **Knapke** Jeffrey P '93
(419) 586-6442 **Lammers** Thomas D '77
(419) 586-6481 **Luth** Thomas E '77
(419) 586-7328 **McKirnan** Kevin M '76
(419) 586-6481 **Meikle Tesno & Luth**
(419) 586-6481 **Meikle** William M '59
(419) 586-2323 **Mielke** Steven P '95
(419) 586-2396 **Myers** Daniel '76
(419) 586-2024 **Nolan** Gary L '80
(419) 586-2915 **Post** Donna M '86
(419) 586-6442 **Purdy Lammers & Schiavone**
(419) 586-5669 **Sacher** John W '68
(419) 586-5669 **Sacher** Michael S '78
(419) 586-6886 **Schemenaur** Wesley A '04
(419) 586-6442 **Schiavone** Louis J '84
(419) 586-6481 **Tesno** James A '75
(419) 586-8120 **Van Arsdel** Peter R '82

CENTERBURG
Knox County
(740) 625-5215 **Cooper** Thom L '83
(740) 625-5215 **Lavin** Christopher '98

CENTERVILLE
Montgomery County
(937) 436-0699 **Copley** Charles Douglas '96
(937) 435-2530 **Dearbaugh** William C '84
(937) 438-3122 **Dundon** Jeffrey R '85
(937) 438-2828 **Friedman** Mark J '79
(937) 885-7272 **Gerbs** Barbara L '85
(937) 435-4554 **Gunnoe** Gerald E '73
(937) 291-3400 **Knapp** William G III '81
(937) 885-3612 **Lehman** Barbara L '93
(937) 435-4554 **Liptock** Thomas P '86
(937) 291-3400 **Manning** Thomas J '92
(937) 438-3122 **Markowski** Joseph H '99
(937) 433-5513 **Martinson** Charles L '76
(937) 434-9393 **Matthews** Craig T '78
(937) 291-3400 **Maurer** Ronald J '94
(937) 885-0871 **McGuire** James C '80
(937) 212-3158 **Neville** Jeffrey A '99
(937) 436-2606 **Novick** Wayne P '81
(937) 433-7371 **Randolph** William F '77
(937) 435-3393 **Rawers** Thomas G '69
(937) 438-1001 **Soltau** Hans H '73
(937) 255-4915 **Swanton** Sandra L '86
(937) 428-1665 **Walker** John T '88
(937) 435-4554 **Weller** Michael G '86
(937) 434-2167 **Wiviott** Melvin '70
(937) 436-9870 **Yarema-Dubel** Julia B '86

CHAGRIN FALLS
Cuyahoga County
(440) 247-0003 **Adelman** Kelly G '96
(440) 247-4420 **Arnold** Carol '79
(440) 247-0775 **Bagley** Donald B III '93
(440) 247-7083 **Bartunek** Clarence J '67
(440) 247-2722 **Belkin-Laureno** Lisa '88
(440) 247-7800 **Bell** Denise D '86
(440) 247-5555 **Brenner** Robert C '79
(440) 247-9100 **Brown** Don P '61
(440) 247-9100 **Brown** Richard H '68
Burroughs Nancy H '82
(440) 338-4650 **Caimi** Paul A '86
(440) 247-4765 **Canonico** Jesse W '03
Chesler Lisa M '91
(440) 247-6960 **Corcoran** Daniel R '52
Cull William J '72
(440) 729-7450 **D'Aurelio** Michael J '96
Debernardi Linda M '96
Dennis Shari E '87
(440) 247-2104 **Dolan** Eva H '84
(440) 247-7800 **Drake** Therese Sweeney '84
Edwards-Smith Karen L '81
Estafanous Katherine E '99
(440) 893-2327 **Ferguson** Mark A '86
(440) 708-0720 **Firehammer** Richard A Jr. '94
(440) 543-2664 **Fisher** Jeffrey M '84
(440) 247-9200 **Fitzpatrick** Jon D '77
(440) 247-2800 **Fixler** Michael A '97
(440) 247-0775 **Freedman** Howard J '70
(440) 247-4765 **Fried** Lorna J '92
(440) 247-0003 **Geisse** Timothy F '84
(216) 292-8108 **Glick** Gregory R '73
(440) 247-4765 **Gold** John W '04
(440) 247-5585 **Gorretta** Laura J '86
(216) 831-8664 **Gray** Thomas J '41
(440) 247-5585 **Griffiths** David E '57
(440) 893-9686 **Gruber** James P '89
(440) 914-9624 **Hall** Charles M '79
(440) 338-7141 **Hardacre** Lynn L '93
Harvey Thomas F '64
Hayman Edward D '80
(440) 247-6060 **Herrick** Craig W '91
Hopkins Gregory L '89
(440) 543-5001 **Irwin** John R '76
(440) 247-5555 **Kaprosy** David V '73
(440) 247-4470 **King** Douglas A Sr. '78
(216) 544-8888 **King** Julie Mitrovich '94
(440) 543-3879 **Klammer** Martin A '85
(440) 247-2562 **Krahe** Mitchell W '96
(440) 247-6167 **Kramer** Nancy W '79
(440) 708-0115 **Lamanna** Michael A '91
(440) 247-7800 **Lee** Karen E '82
(440) 247-7876 **Leech** John D '64
(440) 247-1990 **Lencewicz** Christopher A '95
(440) 247-8701 **Lentz** Mary A '73
(440) 247-5078 **Liber** John R II '92
(440) 893-7700 **Lieberman** Gary L '81
(440) 543-6509 **Linton** Thomas A '73
(440) 708-2000 **Lybarger** Leonard F '63
(440) 543-6790 **Lynch** Matthew J '80
(440) 338-8935 **Lynch** Stephen T '98
(440) 247-5740 **Mac Iver** Michael A '82
(440) 338-6338 **Magyaros** Anne S '90
(440) 247-6862 **Maistros** David M '90
(440) 543-6498 **Martin** Dallan W '74
(440) 543-2979 **Martorana** Kim Gerette '92
Massa Vincent J '69
(440) 835-1531 **Mathews** Eileen T '96
(440) 543-8511 **McCarthy** Patrick J '93
McCormack Thomas A '79
McCrystal Thomas W '80
(440) 247-7800 **McSherry** James C '87
(440) 543-8445 **Menefee** Donald R '01
(440) 543-8418 **Miller** Barbara L '90
Miller Cherrie N '78
Morrison Donald W '74
Musallam-Martin Yasmina T '01
O'Neil Kelly R '99
(440) 247-7800 **Papesh** Amy L '00
(440) 247-7800 **Patton** Steven E '84
(440) 247-7800 **Paulett-Toumert** Mary J '87
Rabb Sheldon E '62
(440) 893-0338 **Redmond** William K '83
(440) 247-3666 **Resnick** Ramie A '84
(440) 247-1452 **Rogoff** Nancy H '85
(440) 247-8601 **Ruiter** Paul J '98
Rule Hilary W '88
(440) 247-4765 **Samad** Debra J '78
(440) 708-2626 **Sass** Lorrie A '90
Scharfeld Leonard B '51
(440) 543-8059 **Schiller** Mary Sharon '77
(440) 247-8200 **Searby** Edmund W '97
Shaper Thomas O '82
(440) 247-0606 **Simon** Lynn B '80
(440) 247-6100 **String** Kevin L '91
(440) 543-8868 **Suit** Edward K '67
(440) 247-4765 **Thomas** Stephen G '77
(440) 338-1169 **Todd** Walker F '95
Trivelli Annette C '89
(440) 247-0003 **Turner** Thomas M '73
(440) 708-1028 **VanBuskirk** Margaret P '93
Vannelli Gail L '86
(440) 543-0486 **Van Valkenburgh** Bruce G '82
(440) 247-9411 **Vogt** Peter W '74
(440) 543-8868 **Weiner** Edwin S '56
(440) 247-0775 **Weiss & Freedman LLP**
(440) 247-0775 **Weiss** Roger J '66
(440) 708-0445 **Wilson** Robert D '84
(440) 543-5313 **Ziegler** Richard P '75
(440) 247-5665 **Zucker** Dale P '74

CHARDON
Geauga County
(440) 285-2401 **Badovick** George L '83
(440) 285-2222 **Bell** Janette M '90
(440) 285-4332 **Bender** Mary K '81
(440) 285-4040 **Bhatia** Megan H '94
(440) 285-3123 **Bond** Daniel E '75
(440) 286-7460 **Brady** Joanne C '82
(440) 286-9549 **Brice** Edward T '74
(440) 285-3511 **Brooks** Keith K '69
(440) 564-7987 **Brown** Douglas B '85
(440) 286-9571 **Carey** Lisa J '93
(440) 286-9571 **Carrabine** James P '84
(440) 285-7065 **Carse** William O '73
(440) 942-1034 **Cisan** Heidi M '89
(440) 285-7536 **Cooper** Patricia A '96
(440) 285-8190 **Dauscher** Raymond G '58
(440) 285-3511 **Day** Carol L '93
(440) 285-2242 **Dolan** Matthew J '90
(440) 286-1907 **Eardley** David J '57
(440) 286-9571 **Flaiz** James R '02
(440) 285-2242 **Flynn** John J '03
(440) 285-2222 **Gargiulo** Dawn M '92
(440) 286-7195 **Gillette** James M '74

(440) 286-4770 **Green** Frederick H '75
(440) 285-3501 **Hanus** Ronald B '74
(440) 285-7750 **Heffter** Sarah L '95
(440) 285-2242 **Hicks** Todd C '94
(440) 285-2247 **Hofstetter** William C '75
(440) 285-2222 **Hollins** Marcia A '92
(440) 285-3511 **Ibold** Dennis J '73
(440) 285-3511 **Ibold** Michael G '80
(440) 286-8887 **Irvin** James D '74
(440) 286-9549 **Jevnikar** David W '81
(440) 285-2222 **Joyce** David P '82
Kelleher Vincent F '49
(440) 269-6246 **Klock** Sally J '87
(440) 285-2222 **LaChapelle** Laura Ann '96
(440) 285-5041 **Leary** Arthur Pearch III '74
(440) 285-2222 **Lee** Dorothy H '94
(440) 285-0300 **Lloyd** Scott A '90
(440) 285-2242 **Lowe** David E '70
(440) 285-2222 **Lubecky** David '87
(440) 285-2242 **Markowitz** Dale H '75
(440) 286-9571 **McGee** David A '82
(440) 285-4771 **McGregor** Emanuel H '48
(440) 286-5228 **Mooney** Paul J '88
(440) 285-3986 **Moser** Lewis G '82
(440) 286-9726 **Mullen** Thomas J '66
(440) 285-8311 **Navatsyk** Donald A '80
(440) 286-9549 **Newman & Brice**
(440) 286-9549 **Newman** Paul A '77
(440) 285-3511 **O'Brien** Casey P '00
(440) 285-2242 **Ondrey** David M '80
(440) 286-9405 **O'Reilly** David Kevin '68
(440) 285-1710 **Orndorff** Jeffrey T '77
Peck Michael N '03
(440) 564-8282 **Perotti** Thomas I '95
(440) 285-3511 **Petersen & Ibold**
(440) 285-3511 **Petersen** Jerry A '66
(440) 285-3511 **Petersen** Todd E '96
(440) 286-4215 **Pfeiffer** Donald E '74
(440) 286-9571 **Reardon** James W '92
(440) 285-2222 **Reid** Stacey '02
(440) 285-2222 **Richter** Brian M '88
Roussey Vera G '00
(440) 285-2222 **Salem** Sheila M '97
(440) 285-2222 **Schlag** Rebecca F '93
(440) 285-3123 **Simon-Seymour** Christine M '90
(440) 285-0337 **Skrabec** David J '75
(440) 285-2242 **Slattery** Kelly A '02
(440) 286-6177 **Smalheer** Bruce C '90
(440) 285-2222 **Staley** Anita C '93
(440) 285-3511 **Stanley** Robin L '03
(440) 286-9571 **Svete** Joseph T '64
(440) 286-9571 **Svete McGee & Carrabine Co,LPA**
(440) 285-2242 **Thrasher Dinsmore & Dolan,LPA**
(440) 285-2222 **Tremsyn** John P '76
Umholtz Raymond Robert '84
(440) 286-3260 **Wantz** Robert R '63
(440) 285-2222 **Wharton** Lawrence M '94
(440) 285-5731 **Wheatley** Myron D '87
(440) 285-2242 **Znidarsic** Joseph R '76
(440) 286-6177 **Zulandt** Robert E Jr. '73
(440) 286-6177 **Zulandt & Smalheer**

CHESAPEAKE

Lawrence County

(740) 867-3159 **Kaiser** James Stewart '64
(740) 867-3166 **Meyers** Richard B '67
(740) 867-3217 **Neville** Brenda K '93

CHESTERLAND

Geauga County

(440) 729-7996 **Blageff** Lillian V '91
(440) 729-7336 **Bloom** Robert M '73
(440) 729-7996 **Chaloupka** Robert S '01
(440) 729-7551 **Chubb** Kathryn A '91
(440) 729-2959 **Doles** Edward A '84
(440) 729-7181 **Durn** Raymond J '53
(440) 729-2258 **Fant** John F Jr. '56
(440) 729-0296 **Gardner** Robert E '65
(440) 729-7278 **Gibson** Tammy G '96
(440) 729-7996 **Griffith** Thomas J '90
(440) 423-1259 **Hanover** Stanley I '78
(440) 729-2340 **Havens** Patrick J '91
(440) 729-7996 **Holland** Mara J '98
(440) 729-7278 **Jimison** Mark S '96
(440) 729-7279 **Judy** Michael T '95
(440) 729-5601 **Korosec** Jason A '97
(440) 729-1414 **Korosec** Kenneth D '67
(440) 729-3770 **Larrick** Scott A '96
(440) 729-7278 **Makowski** Pamela A '81
(440) 729-8260 **Malik** David B '80
(440) 729-8100 **Norton** John F '59
(440) 729-3930 **Patete** Nancy Fioritto '86
(440) 729-7996 **Payton** Janet G '88
(440) 729-2378 **Purdy** Dorrit W '78
(440) 729-3488 **Robertson** John B '61
(440) 729-1848 **Rushworth** Kim R '76
(440) 729-9677 **Sexton** Sheila M '97
Snyder Philip M '99
(440) 729-1252 **Sos** Emil F Jr. '70
(440) 729-7278 **Weiss** Joseph H Jr. '70

CHEVIOT

Hamilton County

(513) 481-8444 **Laumann** John M '77
(513) 481-8444 **Nolan** Gregory M '78

CHILLICOTHE

Ross County

(740) 779-7593 **Arrowsmith** Monica S '94
(740) 775-1700 **Ater** Jennifer L '95
(740) 702-3100 **Ater** Michael M '94
(740) 773-0012 **Babcox** Josephine M '04
(740) 773-5941 **Baerkircher** Alfred E '73
(740) 779-6662 **Banfield** Amanda L '04
(740) 772-5000 **Barrington** Deborah Douglas '77
(740) 774-2121 **Barrington** James E '74
(740) 773-3600 **Benson** J Jeffrey '82
Black Sher A '98
(740) 775-1700 **Blair & Ater LLP**
(740) 775-1700 **Blair** John G '59
(740) 775-5312 **Boulger** James T '79
(740) 773-1666 **Boulger** William C '51
(740) 773-3952 **Brown** Edward J '74
(740) 702-3115 **Brown** Judith H '89
(740) 773-0012 **Buchanan** Robert J Jr. '85
(740) 775-3300 **Bugg** Clifford N '92
(740) 774-4710 **Bunch** Thomas E '80
(740) 775-5600 **Bunstine** Edward R '81
(740) 779-7500 **Cole** Denise Lanier '04
(740) 773-0012 **Cook** Linda I '87
(740) 775-1700 **Cook** Rebecca E '02
(740) 772-5595 **Cutright** James K '84
(740) 772-5595 **Cutright** James M '50
(740) 772-7466 **DeMers** Karen D '96
(740) 702-3035 **DiCesare** John C '86
(740) 773-9000 **Drake** Claire F '99
(740) 702-3100 **Drotleff** Steven E '94
Eddy Toni L '00
(740) 773-2651 **Evans** Gary L '93
(740) 773-9982 **Fleshman** Gary A '94
(740) 775-2066 **Fuchsman** Rita S '77
(740) 773-1875 **Fuller** Don E '55
(740) 774-1174 **Hannan** Christine B '80
(740) 774-6152 **Hess** Robert C '74
(740) 773-8119 **Hill Motes** Laura J '00
(740) 772-6400 **Hine** Katherine '77
(740) 773-3660 **Hirsch** Carl P Jr. '76
(740) 773-3800 **King** Nancy L '79
(740) 772-7472 **Lamphear** Patricia J '89
(740) 779-6662 **Maerten-Moore** Sharon A '98
(740) 775-2222 **Mann** James L '68
(740) 775-5321 **Martin** Jane Spring '78
(740) 779-6662 **McHenry** Aaron M '99
(740) 774-2142 **McMahon** Paige J '88
(740) 773-0012 **Missler** Betsie L '98
(740) 774-9421 **Motes** Joseph E '96
(740) 773-2105 **Newman** Steven C '94
(740) 702-3100 **Nusbaum Ater & Wissler**
(740) 702-3100 **Nusbaum** Scott W '78
(740) 775-3300 **Phillips** David M '52
(740) 775-3300 **Phillips & Street**
(740) 775-2222 **Preston** Mark A '80
(740) 774-2142 **Radcliffe** Gerald E '50
(740) 772-4772 **Rainsberger** Ben A '81
(740) 772-4772 **Rankin** Lori Jo '95
(740) 775-6254 **Rout** Michele R '94
(740) 775-7434 **Rutherford** Sherri K '98
(740) 772-4772 **Scherff** John M '89
(740) 702-3100 **Schmidt** Matthew S '02
(740) 773-1141 **Shively** Arlene T '98
(740) 772-4772 **Silcott** Daniel L '84
(740) 774-3300 **Sladoje** Douglas S '88
(740) 774-2142 **Spetnagel & McMahon**
(740) 774-2142 **Spetnagel** Thomas M '75
(740) 773-3660 **Stout** Cherita E '94
(740) 775-3300 **Street** John S Jr. '54
(740) 774-6320 **Sulzer** Joseph P '82
(740) 772-7467 **Van de Carr** Charles R IV '76
(740) 779-6662 **Ziegler** Lisa E '02

CINCINNATI

Hamilton County

(513) 852-5600 **Abaray** Janet G '82
(513) 723-4000 **Abare** Terri Reyering '83
(513) 243-2245 **Abbott** David L '84
(513) 621-1045 **Abel** Frederick Bruce '64
(513) 621-2120 **Abernethy** William S Jr. '67
(513) 977-8200 **Abes** Alan H '93
(513) 721-4876 **Abrams** Laura A '91
(513) 983-7854 **Abrams** Sharon E '85
(513) 977-8200 **Abreu** Steven A '04
(513) 241-7111 **Acciani** Henry D '79
(513) 651-6800 **Acheson** Edwin R Jr. '89
(513) 651-6800 **Adams** Deborah S '82
(513) 381-9200 **Adams** Donald C '82
(513) 651-6800 **Adams** Edmund J '63
(513) 241-5670 **Adams** Gregory L '77
(513) 977-8200 **Adams** Gregory P '91
(513) 651-6800 **Adams** James R '63
(513) 542-7111 **Adams** Jeffrey L '92
(513) 946-3000 **Adams** Paula E '98
(513) 929-9333 **Adams** Steven R '91
(513) 626-1602 **Addington** Eric T '03
(513) 554-1110 **Addy** Robert Mark '87
(513) 771-4800 **Adee** Jonathan D '98
(513) 684-6023 **Adkins** Douglas D '03
(513) 241-5670 **Agar** Elizabeth E '80
(513) 681-8616 **Ahlers** Donald B '53
(513) 621-1652 **Ahlers** Edward C '82
(513) 533-8347 **Ahlers** Heinz W '76
(513) 751-4420 **Ahlers** Laurie K '95
(513) 251-1247 **Ahlrichs & Ahlrichs**
(513) 251-1247 **Ahlrichs** James W '56
(513) 251-1247 **Ahlrichs** Susan M '85
(513) 579-1100 **Ahrens** Gerard J '77
(513) 241-2324 **Ahrens** Gregory F '87
(513) 583-4200 **Ahrens** Megan Cochran '03
(513) 381-2838 **Akin** Edward P '01
(513) 651-6800 **Albainy-Jenei** Stephen R '95
(513) 946-6611 **Albanese** Francis D '65
(513) 946-3000 **Albert** John E '78
(513) 732-5950 **Albi** Joy M '95
(513) 475-8027 **Albrinck** Daniel E '96
(513) 612-3095 **Albrinck** John Jeffrey '87
(513) 587-2884 **Alexander** Christopher M '01
(513) 621-6464 **Alexander** Henry G '75
(513) 241-3100 **Alexander** Tony M '00
(513) 533-2996 **Algenio** Rebecca N '01
(513) 723-2212 **Algie** Glenn E '89
(513) 241-3685 **Alig** Wesly A '02
(513) 352-6743 **Alkire** Erin M '01
(513) 352-6658 **Allaer** Paul A '86
(513) 621-2120 **Allen** Claudia G '88
(513) 241-7111 **Allen** Eric P '89
(513) 946-5203 **Allen** Lisa C '84
(513) 946-3210 **Allen** Michael K '84
(513) 946-5154 **Allen** Nadine L '77
(513) 621-2120 **Allen** Samuel M '57
(513) 241-2324 **Allen** William R '00
(513) 729-3198 **Allf** Rebecca J '86
(513) 977-8200 **Allison** Jonathan B '01
(513) 352-6713 **Allman** Bruce M '74
(513) 684-8000 **Almaguer** Alejandro E '98
(513) 271-8242 **Alsfelder** Deborah T '91
(513) 271-8242 **Alsfelder** Robert F Jr. '81
(513) 629-1702 **Altenau** Michael J '88
(513) 621-6699 **Altimari** Rita M '88
(513) 721-2180 **Altman** Dennis D '74
(513) 381-9200 **Aluotto** Christopher J '92
(513) 287-2649 **Alvaro** Jay R '95
(513) 533-2996 **Amlung** Pamela K '91
(513) 241-4722 **Ammer** Timothy C '98
(513) 634-1873 **Ammons** Bridget D '01
(513) 651-6800 **Amrine** Kimberly S '00
(513) 731-8080 **Anaya** George Antonio '97
(513) 721-1997 **Ancona** Perry L '72
Andersen Wendy L '98
(513) 636-4000 **Anderson** James M '67
Anderson Shirley L '04
(513) 263-4687 **Anderson** William H II '94
(513) 946-3000 **Anderson** William H Jr. '87
(513) 243-5955 **Andes** William S '92
(513) 381-2838 **Andrew** Marcia V '88
(513) 421-1313 **Anness** Harold L '78
(513) 621-2100 **Anstaett** Jennifer G '01
(513) 721-1311 **Antaki** Vincent P '00
(513) 241-6748 **Anten** Brian J '79
(513) 946-9200 **Anthony** Brenda A '99
(513) 852-3497 **Anthony** Lori A '97
(513) 651-6800 **Anthony** Thomas D '77
(513) 791-8600 **Apocotos** Thomas G '92
(513) 651-6800 **Appel** John H '74
(513) 651-6800 **Applegarth** Barbara C '79
(513) 528-1414 **Applegate** James E '54
(513) 929-3400 **Appleton** William '78
(513) 651-5666 **Arenstein** Hal R '79
(513) 579-6980 **Argo** Susan M '96
(513) 977-8200 **Armstrong** Jody H '92
(513) 458-2320 **Armstrong** John B '73
(513) 665-3500 **Armstrong** Kelly A '03
(513) 287-3024 **Arnett** Bradley C '95
(513) 351-1174 **Arnold** Jason D '96
(513) 946-3044 **Arnold** John J '78
(513) 556-0072 **Arnzen** Melissa L '02
(513) 241-0400 **Aronoff Rosen & Hunt Co,LPA**
(513) 241-0400 **Aronoff** Stanley J '58
Arostegui Julie L '99
(513) 569-1500 **Asante** Lori S '95
(513) 241-9400 **Asbury** Mary '80
(513) 977-8200 **Ash** Linda A '91
(513) 762-4423 **Ash** Patricia T '79
(513) 762-6200 **Ash** Reuel D '91
(513) 936-8062 **Ashby** Todd P '96
(513) 621-2120 **Ashdown** Charles C '86
(513) 621-2120 **Ashdown** Philomena S '86
(513) 381-2838 **Ashton** Amy C '00
(513) 985-0515 **Asquith** Susan S '98
(513) 621-2120 **Atkins** Charles G '62
(513) 977-8200 **Atkins** Katrina R '03
(513) 784-0600 **Attenborough** Bruce W '84
(513) 772-8588 **Attix** Harold B '71
(513) 522-5800 **Atwood** Daniel C '89
(513) 421-7500 **Aubin** Arthur N '83
(513) 579-7881 **Auerbach** Boris '54
(513) 721-4532 **Auttonberry** Sheri E '99
(513) 684-3211 **Averbeck** Linda R '98
(513) 651-6800 **Ayers** G Randall '88
(513) 521-2929 **Baas** Patricia A '83
(513) 579-6400 **Babb** Brian M '86
(513) 579-6400 **Babinec** Gehl P '67
(513) 721-8831 **Bacevich** Michael P '96
(513) 489-7522 **Bach** Michael B '87
(513) 946-3700 **Bachman** Laura A '99
(513) 946-3000 **Bachman** Michael L '84
(513) 731-9571 **Back** David A '96
(513) 421-0045 **Backsman** Mary Goeke '58
(513) 772-6508 **Bacon** Todd D '92
(513) 948-5061 **Baechle** Lisa G '98
(513) 621-6464 **Baechtold** William J '72
(513) 241-7111 **Bagliore** Jayma C '80
(513) 983-4154 **Bailey** Ann K '76
(513) 745-0400 **Bailey** Donyetta D '00
(513) 946-3000 **Bailey** Kathleen H '92
(513) 852-5600 **Bailey** Melanie S '03
(513) 631-0022 **Bailey** Michael S '91
(513) 333-0990 **Bailey** Stephen A '71
(513) 455-7600 **Bailey** Todd H '76
(513) 977-5690 **Bailey-Newell** Susan M '94
(513) 347-7800 **Bajwa** Loveleen K '02
(513) 929-3400 **Baker & Hostetler LLP**
(513) 241-7600 **Baker** Joseph R '96
(513) 977-8200 **Baker** Neal D '84
(513) 381-2221 **Bakst** Jeffrey S '83
(513) 421-4225 **Balash** Paul E '76
(513) 651-6800 **Baldwin** Gerald L '69
(513) 872-5162 **Baldwin** Thomas A '75
(513) 723-4000 **Baldwin** William D '97
(513) 723-9222 **Ballard-Salyer** Susan M '96
(513) 983-1100 **Bamber** Jeffrey V '84
(513) 946-3435 **Banker** Marcia A '84
(513) 221-5510 **Banner** John G '80
(513) 241-0400 **Barbanel** Roberta J '02
(513) 721-2157 **Barbeau** Jeannine C '93
(513) 922-5200 **Barber** Raymond P '73
(513) 583-4200 **Barbiere** Lawrence E '77
(513) 421-3940 **Bardach** Richard B '95
(513) 621-2666 **Bardach** Robert A '89
(513) 946-3865 **Barden** Barbara K '74
(513) 381-0656 **Barker** Peggy M '95
(513) 621-2120 **Barlow** Anthony M '90
(513) 684-3711 **Barnes** Christopher K '75
(513) 977-8200 **Barnes** John E '83
(513) 636-3100 **Barnes** Michael D '96
(513) 629-1473 **Barnett** Michael N '90
(513) 455-2301 **Barnhart** Thomas M II '90
(513) 946-3003 **Baron** Lawrence C '84
(513) 361-1200 **Barresi** James J '91
(513) 721-2120 **Barrett** Charles F '71
(513) 721-2120 **Barrett** Michael R '77
(513) 618-8700 **Barrett** Tina Jo '04
(513) 721-2120 **Barrett & Weber**
(513) 721-1975 **Barron** Carrie A '95
(513) 651-6800 **Barron** Dennis J '56
(513) 871-2369 **Barron** Dennis P '85
(513) 721-1350 **Barron** Michael S '93
(513) 721-1350 **Barron** Norman I '60
(513) 721-1350 **Barron Peck Bennie & Schlemmer**
(513) 621-4006 **Barsman** Marvin J '50
(513) 852-8228 **Barth** David L '78
(513) 977-4212 **Bartlett** Charles H Jr. '79
(513) 241-3992 **Bartlett & Weigle Co,LPA**
(513) 241-3992 **Bartlett** William T '74
(513) 871-2720 **Barton** James R '61
(513) 533-1885 **Barton** Jery E '72
(513) 381-2838 **Barty** Lawrence J '73
(513) 381-9605 **Basil** Beth L '91
(513) 793-6650 **Basil** Mark A '83
(513) 651-6800 **Baskett** William D III '64
(513) 451-1443 **Basler** Susan M '93
(513) 579-1414 **Bass** Herbert '49
(513) 852-8200 **Bassett** Kenneth B '56
(513) 684-3201 **Bassin** Jeffrey L '85
(513) 651-6800 **Bastian** Eliot G '99
(513) 922-7505 **Bauer** John C '72
(513) 621-6621 **Bavely** Ernest Hanlin '64
(513) 352-4705 **Baylen** Kenneth B '74
(513) 369-0200 **Bazeley & LaDue**
(513) 369-0200 **Bazeley** Terrence D '80
(513) 287-2215 **Beach** Richard G '99
(513) 533-1551 **Beacock** Kathy A '79
(513) 977-8200 **Beatty** John W '65
(513) 352-6790 **Bechhold** Christopher M '80
(513) 315-5541 **Beck** Suzanne H '00
(513) 721-7522 **Becker** Dennis A '77
(513) 977-8200 **Becker** Gary E '84
(513) 241-6748 **Becker** Raymond '89
(513) 621-2100 **Beckman Weil & Shepardson LLC**
(513) 345-4160 **Bedall** Thomas G '78
(513) 621-8770 **Bedell** Christopher J '95
(513) 723-4000 **Bedree** Melvin A '84
(513) 381-2838 **Bee** Gregory W '02
(513) 381-0656 **Beech** Joseph III '73
(513) 419-3249 **Beerck** Daniel R '94
(513) 618-8700 **Beers** Janet E '04
(513) 684-3711 **Behlen** Robert A Jr. '80
(513) 946-6464 **Beiderbeck** Janice H '02
(513) 651-4130 **Beirne** Patrick J '96
(513) 221-1745 **Beirne & Wirthlin Co,LPA**
(513) 271-6554 **Bell** James R '84
(513) 721-2120 **Bell** Janet L '84
(513) 946-3700 **Bell** Nathan C '03
(513) 361-1200 **Bell** Ronald A '94
(513) 852-8200 **Bell** Susan R '98
(513) 241-2355 **Bell** William D '77
(513) 241-7111 **Bella** Ronald T '79
(513) 455-7600 **Bellamy** Glenn D '99
(513) 621-2260 **Bellman** Gregory W Sr. '97
(513) 651-6800 **Bence** David S '90
(513) 852-6002 **Bender** Edward D '95
(513) 946-3000 **Bender** Gwendolyn M '91
(513) 794-6316 **Benedict** Ronald L '68
(513) 977-8200 **Benintendi** Christopher A '90
(513) 870-2000 **Benintendi** John K '94
(513) 241-2324 **Benintendi** Steven W '03
(513) 721-5672 **Benjamin** Jack A '40
(513) 352-1565 **Benjamin** Marva K '96
(513) 721-5672 **Benjamin Yocum & Heather LLC**
(513) 977-8200 **Bennett** Clyde II '92
(513) 793-4400 **Bennett** Lawrence T '79
(513) 721-1350 **Bennie** Daniel M '73
(513) 241-3992 **Benson** Matthew L '03
(513) 412-4925 **Beraha** Stephen C '97
(513) 621-2666 **Berberich** Gregory J '89
(513) 946-3000 **Berding** Anita P '96
(513) 793-8282 **Berg** John L '76
(513) 721-4532 **Berger** Andrew R '78
(513) 361-1200 **Bergeron** Pierre H '99
(513) 946-3000 **Berghausen** Andrew A '93
(513) 621-2666 **Bergman** Thomas H '78
(513) 385-5574 **Bergmann** Michael J '82
(513) 352-3618 **Beridon** Thomas O '99
(513) 621-2120 **Berliant** Mark H '57
(513) 821-5536 **Berlon** Henry G Jr. '65
(513) 674-1111 **Berman** Ira M '75
(513) 651-1111 **Bernard** Kathryn S '79
(513) 946-5820 **Bernat** Richard A '75
(513) 421-4646 **Bernat** Stephen M '98
(513) 636-4070 **Berner** Melissa A '90
(513) 753-2800 **Berner** Milton T '74
(513) 946-3000 **Bernhard** Dale H '77
(513) 852-3497 **Berning** Randal C '78
(513) 852-6088 **Berninger** Paul R '71
(513) 671-1744 **Berry** Theodore N '89
(513) 241-6848 **Best** Scott A '02
(513) 563-1400 **Betagole** Marty '94
(513) 556-0958 **Bettman** Marianna B '77
Betts Carolyn A '84
(513) 487-5985 **Bevan** Patricia M '90
(513) 618-7800 **Bever** Mark S '84
(513) 745-0400 **Bhakta** Suraj J '03
(513) 662-0300 **Bibus** Thomas W '76
(513) 241-8313 **Bieber** Alan E '86
(513) 651-3505 **Bieler** Cole A '78
(513) 929-3400 **Bigler** Michael F '84
(513) 381-2838 **Bilott** Robert A '90
(513) 241-2025 **Bishop** Alvertis W Jr. '84
(513) 352-4708 **Bishop** Jennifer I '84
(513) 721-4532 **Bishop** Jerome C '02
(513) 723-4084 **Bissinger** Charles C Jr. '79
(513) 352-3346 **Bissinger** Julie F '84
(513) 977-8200 **Bissinger** Mark C '83
(513) 721-5672 **Bitter** Lisa M '91
(513) 352-6536 **Blachman** Gary D '95
(513) 977-8200 **Black** David D '94
(513) 474-6532 **Black** Kevin M '97
(513) 621-6464 **Black** Stephen L '74
(513) 946-5138 **Black** Timothy S '83
(513) 621-3550 **Blackburn** Katherine B '89
(513) 983-7676 **Blackburn** Kenneth L '03
(513) 621-3550 **Blackburn** Troy A '92
(513) 651-6800 **Blade** Bryan S '95
(513) 469-6908 **Blair** Linda A '86
(513) 551-1988 **Blaker** Joseph A '01
(513) 381-0656 **Blandford** Colleen M '93
(513) 362-8700 **Blank Rome**
(513) 721-3330 **Blankenship** Randy J '86
(513) 852-6003 **Blaske** Nathan H '03

(513) 745-9019 **Blatt** Henry J '97
(513) 241-2324 **Blatt** Paul A '98
(513) 564-0088 **Bleile** Adam B '99
Bleser Donald L '82
(513) 621-9191 **Blessing** David S '04
(513) 385-1234 **Blessing** Louis W Jr. '76
(513) 621-9191 **Blessing** William H '76
(513) 651-6800 **Blickensderfer** Matthew C '00
(513) 751-4420 **Bloch** Randal S '73
(513) 621-3394 **Blocher** Mark D '79
(513) 241-3100 **Block** Patricia K '98
(513) 721-1504 **Block** Robert G '75
(513) 651-6800 **Blomeke** Stacy C '00
(513) 946-3582 **Bloniarz** Mindy M '03
(513) 742-6163 **Bloomhuff** Amy B '91
(513) 421-3514 **BoBo** Kevin T '96
(513) 421-7300 **Bodnar** Julie M '84
(513) 421-2255 **Boehm** David F '72
(513) 421-2255 **Boehm** Kurt J '03
(513) 421-2255 **Boehm Kurtz & Lowry**
Boesch James D '75
(513) 503-7251 **Bogen** James F '02
(513) 751-0115 **Boggs** Duane A '84
(513) 241-3447 **Bogner** Eugene P '88
(513) 621-6556 **Bohlen** Monica R '74
(513) 627-7533 **Bolam** Brian M '93
(513) 946-6611 **Boldt** Edwin H Jr. '68
(513) 421-2500 **Bolin** Linda S '85
(513) 241-3100 **Boll** Edward J III '00
(513) 946-9000 **Boller-Koch** Kathryn M '89
(513) 421-4248 **Bollhauer** Raymond G '90
(513) 721-1200 **Bolotin** Jay A '96
(513) 621-7878 **Bolsinger** Gregg D '86
(513) 852-3497 **Bond** Dianna K '90
(513) 651-6800 **Bond** Kasey L '04
(513) 861-9978 **Bonhaus** Laurence A '76
Booher Mark S '90
(513) 946-3000 **Books** Diane E '82
(513) 651-6800 **Boord** L Roger '03
(513) 556-6361 **Borger** Patricia A '93
(513) 744-9600 **Borgmann** Barbara A '00
(513) 721-5151 **Borland** Cheryl L '95
(513) 768-4626 **Borne** Troy A '95
(513) 381-8696 **Bortz** Christopher N '03
(513) 772-7844 **Bortz** Lee '50
(513) 397-7730 **Bosse** Thomas W '95
(513) 421-4420 **Bossin** Phyllis G '77
(513) 762-6200 **Boster** B Scott '85
Botschner Andrew T '88
(513) 326-5555 **Bottoms** James M '01
(513) 946-9200 **Bouchard** Bernard A '95
Bouchard Roger P '02
(513) 579-6400 **Bouffard** Alison J '04
(513) 632-4506 **Bowie** Karen L '95
(513) 721-2120 **Bowman** Stephanie K '00
(513) 946-3158 **Boychan** Thomas J Jr. '88
(513) 241-2382 **Boyd** David J '64
(513) 455-7600 **Boydston** Richard M Jr. '77
(513) 421-4020 **Boylan** Michael J '76
(513) 361-0250 **Boylan** Peter J '82
(513) 629-2443 **Boyle** Mark S '84
(513) 352-6700 **Boyle** Tanya L '03
(513) 723-1600 **Brabenec-Page** Susan '02
Brady Robert M Jr. '74
(513) 762-6200 **Brammer** Matthew V '93
(513) 621-9100 **Branch** Jennifer L '87
(513) 531-3428 **Brand** Jack I '86
(513) 752-5350 **Brandenburg** George P '78
(513) 381-8033 **Brandt** Jeffrey M '95
(513) 946-3000 **Branson** Dorothy K '98
(513) 721-4532 **Brant** Joel S '97
(513) 721-4532 **Brant** Joseph A '61
(513) 721-4532 **Brant** Robert E '74
(513) 621-2120 **Braun** Joseph J '98
(513) 521-8499 **Braverman** Tobie A '79
(513) 381-2838 **Braxton** Patricia D '90
(513) 852-6076 **Breed** Thomas J '74
(513) 784-5701 **Breen** Timothy P '86
(513) 556-6530 **Brehm** Marianne Jones '02
(513) 721-2120 **Breidenstein** Thomas W '94
(513) 621-6464 **Breitenbach** Thomas A '90
(513) 984-0074 **Breitholle** Howard F '50
(513) 381-2838 **Breitkreutz** Brenda M '98
(513) 247-0077 **Brendamour** Douglas P '82
(513) 241-3685 **Brendamour** Reeta H '96
(513) 556-6814 **Brennan** Kellie L '04
(513) 621-6464 **Brennan** Thomas A '66
(513) 352-6638 **Brenneman** Deborah S '93
(513) 530-9595 **Bretz** Charles G Jr. '71
(513) 929-3430 **Brewer** Bryant L '00
(513) 721-5151 **Brewer** Kevin R '97
(513) 412-5400 **Brewer** Stephen J '77
(513) 684-3711 **Brichler** Robert C '74
(513) 421-4248 **Brickner** Lisa M '92
(513) 455-7600 **Bride** Nancy J '97
(513) 579-6400 **Briggs** Laurie A '89
(513) 621-2244 **Brigham** Charles A III '85
(513) 665-4888 **Brinker** John R '87
(513) 922-3200 **Brinker** Stephen G '77
(513) 241-2324 **Brinkman** David H '94
(513) 632-5310 **Brinkman** Karen R '84
Brinkman Kathleen M '75
(513) 241-3100 **Brinkman** Michael R '88
(513) 621-2120 **Brinn** Stuart C '76
(513) 564-9222 **Bristol** William M '01
(513) 794-4020 **Britt** Curtis D '99
(513) 723-4000 **Britt** Kent A '97
(513) 977-8200 **Brittingham** J David '93
(513) 977-8200 **Brock** Louise S '96
(513) 946-3032 **Brocker** Nanci H '98
(513) 243-2264 **Brockman** Cynthia K '82
(513) 421-6630 **Brockman** James F '81
(513) 579-7560 **Broderick** Dennis J '76
(513) 272-1200 **Brokamp** Larry J '97
(513) 977-8200 **Bromberg** Barbara S '73
(513) 651-0100 **Bromberg** Robert S '72
(513) 723-4000 **Bronson** Michael J '01
(513) 241-9400 **Bronson** Mya E '99
(513) 721-1350 **Brooks** Kyle C '88
(513) 381-0656 **Bross** David J '04
(513) 621-2825 **Brown** Albert T Jr. '66
(513) 851-4646 **Brown** Barbara M '80
(513) 475-0200 **Brown** Caleb Jr. '74
(513) 977-8200 **Brown** Charles H III '87
(513) 861-9830 **Brown** Darrell '79
(513) 742-8811 **Brown** Donté P '03
(513) 763-5514 **Brown** Leon F '96
(513) 241-1950 **Brown Lippett Heile & Evans**
(513) 221-2510 **Brown** Michael A '97
(513) 455-7600 **Brown** Michael H '82
(513) 241-6466 **Brown** Phyllis E '86
(513) 381-9200 **Brown** Robert F '88
(513) 381-2121 **Brown** Robert S '67
(513) 487-5584 **Brown** Ronald D '78
(513) 651-6800 **Brown** Scott R '95
(513) 352-6800 **Brown** Timothy R '87
(513) 361-0300 **Brownfield** Matthew '84
(513) 977-8200 **Bruch** Charles A '03
(513) 361-0200 **Bruestle** Eric G '77
(513) 579-6400 **Brun** James H '76
(513) 381-2838 **Bruns** Jeanne M '99
(513) 651-6800 **Bruns** Julie M '99
(513) 621-3394 **Bruns** Robert T '75
(513) 665-3500 **Bruns** Thomas B '90
(513) 674-5259 **Brunsman** Theresa M '84
(513) 421-1108 **Brush** Thomas B '64
(513) 564-7656 **Bryan-Caron** Mary C '92
(513) 651-6800 **Bryson** Craig M '03
(513) 595-2341 **Bryson** Gary A '78
(513) 891-5580 **Bucciere** Robert L '97
(513) 651-6800 **Buchanan** Beth A '97
(513) 946-3800 **Buchert** Christopher B '98
(513) 579-6400 **Buck** Matthew K '96
(513) 723-4000 **Buckley** Daniel J '74
(513) 412-5400 **Buckley King,LPA**
(513) 684-3211 **Budde** John E '88
(513) 421-9222 **Budinger** Carrie L '88
(513) 684-3093 **Budzynski** Kristin E '92
(513) 579-1500 **Buechner Haffer O'Connell Meyers & Healey Co,LPA**
(513) 579-1500 **Buechner** Robert W '74
(513) 621-2666 **Buerger** Kathryn E '97
(513) 684-2572 **Buffington** Carolyn B '85
(513) 977-8200 **Buford** Calvin D '85
(513) 634-1948 **Bullock** Roddy M '97
(513) 241-3685 **Bunch** Nicholas E '80
Bunyan George W Jr. '52
(513) 793-9950 **Burd** Jeffrey A '96
(513) 671-3201 **Burger** John J '99
(513) 241-2324 **Burger** Thomas J '86
(513) 891-3270 **Burgin** Lester J '82
(513) 621-6464 **Burke** Daniel E '88
(513) 708-1096 **Burke** Daniel F Jr. '77
(513) 421-4225 **Burke Fitzgerald Burns & Balash,LLP**
(513) 579-6400 **Burke** James E '78
(513) 381-2838 **Burke** Kim K '81
(513) 381-4700 **Burke** Rachel '96
(513) 723-4000 **Burke** Tara K '00
(513) 721-5525 **Burke** Timothy M '73
(513) 621-4496 **Burks** Margaret A '85
(513) 241-4110 **Burleigh** David W '95
(513) 946-5122 **Burlew** John H '75
(513) 241-4722 **Burnham** Ralph E '97
(513) 891-3270 **Burns** Andrea L '97
(513) 852-8200 **Burns** Joseph S '02
(513) 618-7800 **Burns** Nancy J '95
(513) 421-4225 **Burns** Robert W '74
(513) 412-0068 **Burr** Heather M '01
(513) 721-1350 **Burr** Peter A '88
(513) 852-6000 **Burrell** Peter M '90
(513) 946-3000 **Burroughs** Katie M '97
(513) 352-4719 **Burtch** Karla J '83
(513) 977-8200 **Burton** Shawn P '04
(513) 352-6700 **Busacker** Bret F '00
(513) 983-1479 **Buse** Jennifer D '92
(513) 421-4499 **Busemeyer** William A '65
(513) 621-1414 **Butkovich** Joseph A '93
(513) 621-1414 **Butkovich Schimpf Schimpf & Ginocchio Co,LPA**
(513) 946-3000 **Butler** James E '75
(513) 621-2120 **Butler** Martin C '77
(513) 891-7087 **Butler** Robert T '90
(513) 352-6587 **Butler** Stephen J '77
(513) 946-3000 **Butler** Yvette S '97
(513) 621-6464 **Buttress** Christine A '79
(513) 612-2300 **Byrne** Kenneth L '71
(513) 381-6600 **Byrne** Mark J '83
(513) 721-7522 **Cade** Howard D III '88
(513) 985-0550 **Cain** Charles C '80
(513) 946-3000 **Calambas** Linda '02
(513) 598-5000 **Calardo** Stephen P '81
(513) 351-9400 **Calaway** Wendy R '98
(513) 977-8200 **Calder** Thomas S '57
(513) 721-2506 **Caldwell** Sean M '91
(513) 621-2120 **Calico** Paul B '80
(513) 977-8200 **Callan** Sean P '93
(513) 852-6012 **Callow** Amy G '94
(513) 579-6400 **Callow** Joseph M Jr. '93
(513) 721-1975 **Calloway-Campbell** Marsha G '85
(513) 946-3800 **Cambron** Robyn W '00
(513) 977-8200 **Camden** Bonnie G '89
(513) 946-3700 **Cameron** Kendra M '02
(513) 241-8844 **Cameron** Phillip F '71
(513) 626-3371 **Camp** Jason J '98
(513) 762-5126 **Campbell** Hugh K '84
(513) 421-4020 **Campbell** Janet B '79
(513) 381-0656 **Campbell** John L '77
(513) 621-2666 **Campbell** Maura Moran '96
(513) 241-9400 **Campbell** Regina R '96
(513) 241-8600 **Caneris** Adonis A '93
(513) 762-7700 **Cantleberry** Jill C '84
(513) 381-2838 **Canton** Doreen '88
(513) 946-9064 **Caplinger** Candace C '82
(513) 621-6464 **Cappel** Harry W '96
(513) 231-0262 **Carey** Robert P '80
(513) 579-7573 **Cariappa** Padma T '82
(513) 352-1575 **Carman** Dorothy N '80
(513) 352-4703 **Carney** Julia B '04
(513) 528-5788 **Carpenter** James W '66
(513) 977-8200 **Carpenter** Robert A '95
(513) 651-5651 **Carr** Joseph G '69
(513) 295-3067 **Carr** Michael G '01
(513) 651-5651 **Carr & Shiverdecker**
(513) 852-8205 **Carroll** James J '78
(513) 852-3489 **Carroll** James M '76
(513) 381-0656 **Carroll** Karen A '87
(513) 241-6748 **Carroll** Patrick F '84
(513) 723-4000 **Carroll** Scott A '93
(513) 368-5221 **Carson** Cheryl L '90
(513) 651-6800 **Carter** Janda' M '02
(513) 671-1744 **Carter** Karen E '94
Carter Kathleen Yates '02
(513) 381-0656 **Caruso** Anthony J '88
(513) 381-9200 **Carville** Christopher R '97
(513) 946-3000 **Casey** Deborah A '94
(513) 621-2602 **Cash** Albert D Jr. '59
(513) 243-2000 **Cash** Joshua N '97
(513) 621-2602 **Cash** Robert B '64
(513) 651-6800 **Casper** Paul W Jr. '81
(513) 621-2100 **Cassady** Peter L '83
(513) 721-1311 **Cassinelli** Tracy A '95
(513) 852-6058 **Castaneda** Janet Y '96
(513) 621-2345 **Castelli** Anthony D '81
(513) 871-1083 **Castellini** Richard A '64
(513) 621-9100 **Caster** Donald R '04
(513) 762-6200 **Cathey** Christopher D '99
(513) 634-1368 **Caudill** Rhonda L '94
(513) 381-2838 **Cavanaugh** Natasha M '02
(513) 665-3500 **Cawood** James M '04
(513) 731-3188 **Cettel** Robert W '74
(513) 352-6550 **Chaiken** Frank D '94
(513) 684-7376 **Chain** Donald J '80
(513) 381-8616 **Chalfie** James J '66
(513) 241-2324 **Chambers** J R '74
(513) 232-1800 **Chang** Nadya '88
(513) 723-2202 **Chapman** Brian E '88
(513) 744-9600 **Chapman** Michael J '03
(513) 627-4229 **Charles** Mark A '04
(513) 661-1332 **Charls** Joseph E '71
(513) 621-2120 **Chasar** Matthew R '02
(513) 621-5428 **Chatfield & Marshall**
(513) 621-5428 **Chatfield** Melancthon W '85
(513) 621-5428 **Chatfield** William H '72
(513) 534-4847 **Chattoraj** Tarun K '00
(513) 632-4085 **Cheng** Lan-Lan J '00
(513) 621-0267 **Chesley** Stanley M '60
(513) 287-7019 **Chester** Victoria L '92
(513) 381-9200 **Chiaro** Cynthia M '96
(513) 352-6700 **Childs** Erin Cunniff '02
(513) 946-3000 **Chin** Nee F '87
(513) 381-2838 **Christian** Ronald C '87
(513) 977-8200 **Christopher** John E Jr. '95
(513) 651-6800 **Christy** Diana R '01
(513) 627-5145 **Chuey** Steven R '94
(513) 579-6400 **Chumley** Mark J '96
(513) 661-1888 **Church** William B III '73
(513) 579-7371 **Ciclet** Donna R '93
(513) 362-8700 **Cioffi** Michael A '03
(513) 362-8700 **Cioffi** Michael L '79
(513) 946-3580 **Cissell** James C '66
(513) 232-1800 **Clancey** Michael E '88
(513) 381-2011 **Clark** Craig S '63
(513) 352-6700 **Clark** Eric S '99
(513) 574-9713 **Clark** George W '71
(513) 622-3949 **Clark** Karen F '87
(513) 721-3236 **Clark** Lisa M '97
(513) 721-1975 **Clark** Megan E '95
(513) 587-2887 **Clark** Ravert J '89
(513) 241-6998 **Clark** Thomas H '49
(513) 762-6200 **Clark** Tiffany Reece '02
(513) 651-6800 **Clarke** Deanne E '00
(513) 352-6534 **Clarke** Jeffrey M '99
(513) 684-3650 **Clarke** Naima R '95
(513) 474-1508 **Clary** Daniel K '84
(513) 723-2208 **Clausen** Cynthia R '02
(513) 626-0575 **Clay** Cynthia L '02
(513) 771-8500 **Claybon** Stanley L '71
(513) 381-3525 **Claycomb** Gregory J '89
(513) 421-5999 **Claymon** Allan W '64
(513) 684-8042 **Claytor** William G '76
Clear Rory T '78
(513) 721-6500 **Clements Mahin & Cohen**
(513) 721-6500 **Clements** William E '79
(513) 421-6630 **Clemons** Michelle L '97
(513) 531-1777 **Cleves** Cynthia M '85
(513) 333-4054 **Cliffe** David W '92
(513) 723-3463 **Cline** Claudia L '87
(513) 621-5252 **Clodfelter** David C '92
(513) 621-5252 **Clodfelter & Gutzwiller**
(513) 984-2640 **Clore** W Edward '96
(513) 421-4020 **Cobey** John G '69
(513) 852-8084 **Coes** Kendal M '94
(513) 741-9800 **Coffaro** Joseph M '69
(513) 569-6331 **Coffaro** Katrina L '95
(513) 579-6400 **Coffaro** Steve C '95
(513) 621-8333 **Coffey** Shirley A '92
(513) 460-3365 **Cogen** Richard M '98
(513) 421-4020 **Cohen** Alfred M '53
(513) 721-6500 **Cohen** Edward '82
(513) 621-9016 **Cohen** Gregory A '93
(513) 977-8200 **Cohen** Harvey Jay '87
(513) 579-6400 **Cohen** Jason M '03
(513) 721-6500 **Cohen** Lane N '88
(513) 931-1890 **Cohen** Stephen '60
(513) 421-4020 **Cohen Todd Kite & Stanford,LLC**
(513) 621-6464 **Colbert** John P '96
(513) 474-1712 **Coldiron** James F '75
(513) 946-3700 **Coleman** John K '99
(513) 579-6400 **Coletti** Robert E '82
(513) 621-5959 **Collett** Thomas E '75
(513) 361-8390 **Collier** Julia A '87
(513) 721-1504 **Collins** Edward J '77
(513) 579-1177 **Collins** James M III '69
(513) 794-6230 **Collins** Marcus L '97
(513) 946-3000 **Collins** Rebecca L '01
(513) 632-5342 **Collins** Regina A '97
(513) 744-9600 **Collister** Scott E '99
(513) 721-4532 **Colvin** Adam D '03
(513) 977-8200 **Colvin** Sterling W '98
(513) 381-0656 **Combs** Ann R '77
(513) 981-6342 **Combs** Claire G '88
(513) 381-2838 **Combs** Eric K '96
(513) 946-3500 **Combs** Mark E '77
(513) 232-4449 **Comey** Margaret W '77
(513) 977-8200 **Comodeca** James A '87
(513) 421-4646 **Concannon** John P '76
(513) 985-9333 **Condit** James J '62
(513) 651-3456 **Conkin** Elizabeth '95
(513) 290-5646 **Connelly** John C '96
(513) 381-5700 **Conner** Mia L '04
(513) 751-7056 **Conners** Thomas J '50
(513) 579-1414 **Conrad** Ralph J '87
(513) 369-5747 **Consalvi** Genina '80
(513) 762-6200 **Conte** Jason P '99
(513) 362-8700 **Conte** Jonathan A '93
(513) 621-2044 **Conway** Patrick J '82
(513) 381-6810 **Conyers** Sallie A '02
(513) 621-8210 **Coogan** James H '61
(513) 977-4213 **Cook** Barbara J '77
(513) 241-4029 **Cook** Cathy R '82
(513) 627-0032 **Cook** Christopher B '93
(513) 721-7500 **Cook** David M '78
(513) 381-2221 **Cook** Michael A '92
(513) 281-2000 **Cook** Tracy B '90
(513) 684-3711 **Coombe** James M '84
(513) 977-8200 **Cooney** J Michael '75
(513) 651-6800 **Cooney** Kevin L '98
(513) 412-1001 **Cooper** Jeffrey R '87
(513) 621-3394 **Cooper** Todd L '81
(513) 574-5598 **Copeland** William M '78
(513) 684-6022 **Copenhaver** David T '00
(513) 352-6696 **Copetas** Theodore C '97
(513) 352-6666 **Cordes** William H '73
(513) 227-5765 **Cordrey** Aimee N '99
(513) 984-2040 **Corker** Robert S '82
(513) 771-2444 **Cornetet** John B '87
(513) 852-8226 **Cornett** Curtis L '93
(513) 561-7755 **Corr** Elizabeth D '77
(513) 852-8200 **Cors & Bassett LLC**
(513) 852-8200 **Cors** L B '61
(513) 626-4756 **Corstanje** Brahm J '89
(513) 621-0267 **Corwin** Melanie S '90
(513) 946-3055 **Cosgrove** Jonathan B '01
(513) 762-6200 **Cosgrove** Paul J '01
(513) 352-4701 **Cosgrove** Terrence R '76
(513) 651-3505 **Counts** Paul W '77
(513) 621-8210 **Covatta** Anthony G Jr. '79
(513) 381-2838 **Cover** Melissa Kurzhals '00
(513) 651-6800 **Cowan** Grant S '85
(513) 381-6810 **Cox** Daniel A '03
(513) 333-0990 **Cox** James S '91
(513) 528-6000 **Cox** Lance S '70
(513) 412-1463 **Coy** Rhonda S '85
(513) 361-1200 **Coyle** Timothy L '87
(513) 922-3200 **Coyne** Kenneth P '98
(513) 244-6648 **Coz** Thomas A '79
(800) 890-5001 **Crafton** Constance J '95
(513) 381-2838 **Craig** L Clifford '64
(513) 241-9400 **Cramer** David C '73
(513) 703-5127 **Cramerding** Jeffrey M '01
Cranley John J IV '00
(513) 977-8200 **Crase** Charles S '04
Crawford Lisa K '91
(513) 412-2311 **Crawford** Shawn J '94
(513) 361-1200 **Craycraft** Kenneth R Jr. '01
(513) 381-9200 **Crehan** Kenneth J '02
(513) 579-6400 **Creighton** Richard L Jr. '73
(513) 793-9170 **Crilley** Patrick R '77
(513) 977-8200 **Crisler** Scott A '01
(513) 381-4700 **Croall** David T '81
(513) 721-8210 **Cronin** Patrick J '77
(513) 241-6166 **Croog** Charles F '94
(513) 287-2209 **Cropper** Leanne Rauh '92
(513) 397-1463 **Cross** Anita S '91
(513) 861-7100 **Cross** Wende C '93
(513) 621-1414 **Crosthwaite** Daryl A '89
(513) 241-5670 **Croswell & Adams Co,LPA**
(513) 241-5670 **Croswell** Robert S III '74
(513) 721-4876 **Crouse** Candace C '00
(513) 225-6666 **Croushore** Paul G '91
(513) 721-7002 **Crout** Daniel W '76
(513) 352-6641 **Crowe** James J '66
(513) 621-1652 **Crowley Ahlers & Roth Co,LPA**
(513) 621-1652 **Crowley** James C IV '76
(513) 751-2148 **Crutcher** John T '75
(513) 574-9600 **Cruze** John J '70
(513) 619-1549 **Cullen** Blake W '02
(513) 762-7620 **Cummings** John C '94
(513) 946-3000 **Cummings** Philip R '89
(513) 634-1906 **Cummings** Theodore P '03
(513) 621-0267 **Cummins** James R '67
(513) 683-9000 **Cummins** John R '86
(513) 771-6768 **Cuni Ferguson & LeVay Co,LPA**
(513) 771-6768 **Cuni** Thomas L Jr. '75
(513) 871-0447 **Cunningham** James J '73
(513) 241-4110 **Cunningham** Pierce E '60
(513) 793-4400 **Cunningham** William D '75
(513) 352-6647 **Curran** Matthew C '03
(513) 421-4646 **Cussen** Michael P '95
(513) 421-6630 **Cussen** William M '69
(513) 684-7376 **Custis** Douglass L '67
(513) 381-1234 **Cutcher** Timothy R '74
(513) 946-3820 **Cutler** Nancy J '93
(513) 579-6400 **D'Addesa** Danielle M '03
(513) 381-4888 **Dady** James P '94
(513) 232-1700 **Daggett** John K '82
(513) 679-1853 **Dahl** Elisabeth A '95
(513) 977-8200 **Dailey** Michael G '99
(513) 381-2011 **Dalal** Amy R '04
(513) 762-6946 **Dallob** Naomi C '79
(513) 241-9400 **Daly** Hugh F '87
(513) 587-2882 **Dameron** Jonathan P '91
(513) 241-6650 **Dameron** Nancy J '93
Damon Geoffrey P '84
(513) 232-4165 **Danehy** James S '85
(513) 745-0400 **Dannenfelser** Jeanette N '98
(513) 977-8200 **Darrow** Helana A '98
(513) 528-6444 **Daugherty** Kendra L '82
(513) 579-5678 **Dauterman** Steven L '78
(513) 352-3333 **Davidson** Allison A '99
(513) 891-2100 **Davidson** James P '86
(513) 241-2324 **Davidson** Kristi L '97
(513) 793-5297 **Davidson** Laurence J '93
(513) 362-8700 **Davidson** Patricia A '85
(513) 579-6400 **D'Avignon** David A '73

(513) 721-4500 **Davis** Charles J '77
(513) 721-7295 **Davis** Francis G '42
(513) 852-6085 **Davis** Gary Jon '79
(513) 632-8701 **Davis** James F '75
(513) 241-2324 **Davis** John P '01
(513) 621-3366 **Davis** Michael W '73
(513) 241-9773 **Davis** Myron Y Jr. '69
(513) 751-8495 **Davis** Norma H '82
(513) 241-1991 **Davis** Perry Jr. '87
(513) 241-3500 **Davis** Robert L '58
(513) 761-4415 **Davis** Sherry L '85
(513) 721-1350 **Davis** Steven C '96
(513) 731-5980 **Davis** William B '95
(513) 929-3312 **Dawson** Phyllis I '94
(513) 723-2206 **Day** John L Jr. '81
(513) 621-5631 **Day** Stephanie M '00
(513) 361-1200 **Deabler** Christopher A '04
(513) 522-2100 **Dean** Sheila C '83
(513) 946-3700 **Deardorff** Julie A '87
(513) 872-7900 **Deardorff** Timothy J '79
(513) 559-1300 **Deardurff** Dayle D '79
(513) 421-4428 **Dearfield** George T '88
(513) 621-6464 **Debbeler** J Michael '80
(513) 241-3100 **DeBlasis** Rick D '80
(513) 721-4450 **DeCenso** William A '79
(513) 931-1837 **Decile** Jeffrey M '77
(513) 412-4324 **Dedischew** Carol L '84
(513) 981-6282 **Deen** Jana B '91
(513) 946-3000 **Deering** Jennifer K '96
(513) 771-2676 **DeGraffenreid** Stacey L '00
(513) 241-0400 **DeGregorio** Edmonde P '77
(513) 721-3330 **DeHaan** Elizabeth S '76
(513) 489-7522 **DeHaan** Peter R '74
(513) 381-2838 **Dehan** Paula J '03
(513) 651-6800 **Dehner** Joseph J '73
(513) 621-0930 **Delev** Gregory D '91
(513) 621-0930 **Delev & Williams,LLC**
(513) 977-8200 **DeLong** Deborah '75
(513) 651-6800 **DeLuca** Christopher '92
(513) 621-0267 **De Marco** Paul M '89
(513) 621-2120 **Demmerle** Daniel H II '73
(513) 946-9338 **DeMott** Paul D Sr. '85
(513) 794-5040 **Dempsey** Joel L '00
(513) 621-9660 **Denicola** Ronald J '67
(513) 621-3440 **Denlinger Rosenthal & Greenberg Co, LPA**
(513) 852-6000 **Denney** Mark A '95
(513) 671-0994 **Dennie** Daryl T '97
(513) 651-6800 **Dennis** Douglas R '95
(513) 579-6400 **Denton** David B '00
(513) 621-2100 **Dershaw** Brian G '00
(513) 721-4450 **Desai** Deepak K '93
(513) 632-7600 **Desmond** William J '78
(513) 639-2834 **DeStigter** Mitchell Lee '00
(513) 241-4110 **Deters Benzinger & Lavelle,PSC**
(513) 946-3000 **Deters** Joseph T '82
(513) 421-2540 **Deters** William M II '95
(513) 793-5505 **Deutch** Joel G '93
(513) 632-5332 **DeVita** David W '78
(513) 558-5651 **DeWalt** Marquel A '98
(513) 983-1549 **Dewan** Margaret W '78
(513) 579-6400 **DeWine** Richard P '95
(513) 946-3000 **Deye** Thomas E '79
(513) 929-1108 **Diamond** Barbara M '00
(513) 651-6800 **Dias** Monica L '01
(513) 621-4488 **DiCesare** Francis J '87
(513) 361-1200 **Dickerson** James M Jr. '03
(513) 621-2260 **Dickey** Patricia L '89
(513) 871-1545 **Diedrichs** Francis M '76
(513) 621-2250 **Dieffenbach** Roxann H '78
(513) 241-3100 **Dierks** Mark N '88
(513) 721-4256 **Diersing** George A Jr. '76
(513) 946-3432 **Dietz** Christopher P '79
(513) 621-2120 **Dill** Stephanie A '99
(513) 381-2838 **Diller** Edward D '76
(513) 381-0656 **Dilts** Joseph L '81
(513) 333-4076 **Dimasi** Vincent A '91
(513) 579-6400 **DiMauro** Caroline M '99
(513) 241-3100 **Dimitt** Jill L '00
(513) 651-6800 **Dimling** Robert A '66
(513) 621-2888 **DiMuzio** David C '77
(513) 241-9400 **DiNardo** Nicholas J '98
(513) 241-4722 **Dine** Jennifer Dunlap '03
(513) 977-8200 **Dinsmore & Shohl LLP**
(513) 241-3100 **Dix** Robert C '01
(513) 352-4715 **Dixon** Gertrude P '97
(513) 336-2539 **Dizenhuz** Robert S '91
(513) 272-1200 **Doan** Burgess L '65
(513) 576-9579 **Doan** Charles H '72
(513) 272-1200 **Doan Keith & Brokamp,LLC**
(513) 241-6116 **Doggett** Robert I '58
(513) 381-2838 **Dolive** Devin C '02
(513) 621-4849 **Dolle** Robert H '73
(513) 621-4849 **Dolle Rueger & Mathews Co,LPA**
(513) 632-5311 **Donenfeld** Jack A '76
(513) 474-1919 **Donithan** Dayle E '88
(513) 579-6400 **Donnellon** Daniel J '86
(513) 891-7087 **Donnellon Donnellon & Miller**
(513) 891-7087 **Donnellon** Terrence M '79
(513) 891-7087 **Donnellon** Thomas E '76
(513) 721-4500 **Donnelly** Matthew J '01
(513) 221-7722 **Donnelly** Thomas C '85
(513) 241-0400 **Donnelly** Tina M '00
(513) 455-4366 **Donnelly** William R '92
(513) 421-4000 **Donnett** David D '80
(513) 723-4000 **Donovan** Corey A '02
(513) 352-4706 **Donovan** Kevin O '85
(513) 651-5900 **Donovan** Mary Jill '01
(513) 533-2996 **Donovan** Sean P '98
(513) 381-2838 **Donson** G Jack Jr. '71
(513) 684-9975 **Doppes** Michael J '83
(513) 579-6400 **Dorger** Paul D '92
(513) 381-2838 **Dornette** W Stuart '75
(513) 741-3939 **Dorr** James W '55
(513) 421-6630 **Dorsey** Edward S '87
(513) 241-2324 **Dorton** David W '01
(513) 621-2120 **Dosker** Marshall K '91
(513) 542-8940 **Dourson** Martha C '83
(513) 946-3015 **Dowling** Kerry B '91
(513) 632-3170 **Doyle** James R Jr. '72
(513) 946-3000 **Doyle** Michael T '83
(513) 977-8200 **Drasnin** Lori '01
(513) 852-8200 **Draugelis** Peter A '00
(513) 634-1452 **Dressel** Sarah Ann '04
(513) 931-6800 **Dressing** John W '70
(513) 946-3000 **Dressing** Patrick X '94
(513) 627-4132 **Dressman** Marianne '99
(513) 621-8210 **Drew** George R '50
(513) 621-8210 **Drew & Ward Co,LPA**
(513) 469-1472 **Dreyer** Kevin T '87
(513) 558-5277 **Driscoll** Kathleen M '82
(513) 651-6800 **Droder** Eugene J III '04
(513) 721-1504 **Droder & Miller Co,LPA**
(513) 241-2124 **Duesing** Jerome A '62
(513) 684-3646 **Duffey** Jonathan D '98
(513) 946-9222 **Dugan** Leah A '78
(513) 784-7209 **Dugan** Matthew J '97
(513) 361-0200 **Dulaney** William H III '87
(513) 946-3176 **Dulemba** Gerard A '89
(513) 474-3495 **Dumbacher** David A Jr. '67
Duncan Julie L '97
(513) 412-1460 **Dunn** Carol E '85
(513) 621-0397 **Dunn** Dolores A '75
(513) 352-0500 **Dunn** Elizabeth S '04
(513) 721-1311 **Dunn** John M '04
(513) 929-3400 **Dunn** Martiné R '85
(513) 381-9200 **Dupuis** Charles T '68
(513) 352-3334 **Dupuis** Mary F '69
(513) 381-2838 **Duran** Samuel M '84
(513) 632-5318 **Durham** Leona L '83
(513) 651-4900 **Durham** Mark Freeman '83
(513) 929-3400 **Dusing** Benjamin G '04
(513) 791-6500 **Dusterberg** Richard B '66
(513) 579-6400 **Dutro** Daniel G Jr. '94
(513) 946-3700 **Dutta** Soumyajit '03
(513) 421-2700 **Duwel** David M '73
(513) 287-2643 **Dwight** George II '98
(513) 946-3000 **Dziech** Robert W '96
(513) 977-8200 **Eagen** Michael D '74
(513) 621-7600 **Eagen** Thomas L Jr. '70
(513) 621-7600 **Eagen Wykoff & Healy Co,LPA**
(513) 369-0222 **Earls** William T Jr. '71
(513) 352-3794 **Eatmon** Kristen A '01
(513) 977-8200 **Eaton** Shana N '04
(513) 946-3800 **Eaves** Kacy C '97
(513) 533-9898 **Eberly** David A '96
(513) 533-9898 **Eberly McMahon Hochscheid,LLC**
(513) 723-4000 **Eberly** Stephen S '73
(513) 455-7600 **Ebling** Gretchen R '87
(513) 455-7600 **Ebling** Louis K '95
(513) 621-2888 **Ebner** Drake W '73
(513) 241-2324 **Eby** Clyde R II '68
(513) 721-5525 **Eby** Gary M '76
(513) 651-6800 **Ecker** Karen M '92
(513) 662-1818 **Eckert** Charles A '55
(513) 662-1818 **Eckert** John C '92
(513) 421-4420 **Eckner** Shannon F '03
(513) 528-2850 **Eddy** Marilyn M '88
(513) 851-3337 **Eder** Robert F '93
(513) 852-6025 **Eder** William H Jr. '63
(513) 632-5321 **Edmiston** James P '75
(513) 721-5151 **Edmiston** Robert G '82
(513) 556-1590 **Edwards** Ruth M '74
(513) 381-2838 **Edwards** Ryan C '02
(513) 721-5151 **Edwards** Tawanda J '00
Egbers Mary E '94
(513) 474-0028 **Eifrig** Eric W '03
Eiler Janis E '97
(513) 852-6079 **Eilers** John W '67
(513) 946-3000 **Elfers** Kathleen M '82
(513) 721-2120 **Eling** Kenneth J '93
(513) 977-8200 **Elleman** Lawrence R '66
(513) 381-2838 **Ellerman** Paige L '99
(513) 753-2300 **Elliff** Brian E '95
(513) 852-6026 **Ellington** Sarah B '03
(513) 651-6946 **Elliott** Lisa A '00
(513) 721-5151 **Ellis** Lisa M '91
(513) 852-6067 **Ellis** William R '85
(513) 721-7522 **Ellison** Richard G '76
(513) 559-0553 **Ellsworth** Wilkes R '97
(513) 381-4700 **Elsener** Mark E '80
(513) 852-8200 **Emmert** Andrew C '88
(513) 871-2459 **Emmert** Marianne S '84
(513) 946-3700 **Emmrich** Joseph L '72
(513) 241-7332 **Engle** John H '68
(513) 271-9026 **Englehart** Andrew T '94
(513) 381-9200 **Englert** James J Jr. '90
(513) 421-2540 **Ennis Roberts & Fischer**
(513) 421-2540 **Ennis** William J '66
(513) 624-6204 **Epling** John A '57
(513) 631-1501 **Eppstein** Steven D '74
(513) 579-6400 **Erhart** Sue A '96
(513) 651-6800 **Erickson** Richard J '71
(513) 579-5324 **Erickson** Robert M '74
Ericsson John M '94
(513) 287-2087 **Erisen** Candace S '99
(513) 579-9500 **Ernst** Matthew T '96
(513) 946-9200 **Ernst** Tina I '91
(513) 977-8200 **Erny** Frederick M '87
(513) 326-5555 **Erven** Thomas P '83
(513) 946-5200 **Erwin** Anne B '81
(513) 474-3700 **Espohl** Frank E '96
(513) 721-5151 **Essig** Ellen '86
(513) 629-2529 **Evans** David N '79
(513) 621-6033 **Evans** Franklin R '99
(513) 579-2536 **Evans** James E '71
(513) 936-2012 **Evans** Lisa M '94
(513) 241-1950 **Evans** Marquette D '77
(513) 721-5151 **Evans** Ross M '86
(513) 381-9200 **Evans** Thomas M '86
(513) 977-8200 **Everett** Denise Mullen '02
Eynon Ernest A II '69
(513) 621-2666 **Eyrich** David J '73
(513) 977-4223 **Ezenagu** Samuel O '98
(513) 721-5525 **Fabe** George '81
(513) 421-6630 **Fagel** Barry F '92
(513) 352-6214 **Fagel** Stephen J '80
(513) 621-6464 **Fairweather** Neil '00
(513) 723-4000 **Fairweather** Sarah Buzzee '02
(513) 241-3111 **Fales** Roy D '91
(513) 946-3700 **Fallat** Kathryn A '00
(513) 579-1266 **Faller** Raymond T '76
(513) 651-6800 **Faller** Susan G '75
(513) 946-9200 **Falter** Karen K '96
(513) 542-3469 **Farina** Ciro P '82
(513) 561-4602 **Farley** Bobbie K W '80
(513) 381-8616 **Farley** Katrina Z '92
(513) 762-6200 **Farrell** E Beth '90
(513) 721-1200 **Farrell** Thomas M Jr. '92
(513) 621-9921 **Farrell** William I III '89
(513) 784-7319 **Farris** Michael J '03
(513) 621-8700 **Farrish** Kelly Jr. '79
(513) 723-2210 **Faulkner** Laura R '99
(513) 421-7500 **Faulkner & Tepe,LLP**
(513) 381-2838 **Fausz** Daniel E '94
(513) 871-8076 **Favret** Bruce A '77
(513) 626-2408 **Fayette** Thibault '00
(513) 946-3000 **Fazio** Cynthia A '88
(513) 852-8200 **Feazell** Kevin R '92
(513) 621-2666 **Fecher** William B '87
(513) 977-8200 **Feichtner** Douglas J '02
(513) 621-1660 **Feil** Richard D III '92
(513) 621-2100 **Feldhaus** Joseph H '82
(513) 421-3323 **Feldkamp** Joseph F Jr. '66
(513) 985-3200 **Feldmann** Donald J '75
(513) 721-4876 **Feldmeier** John P '91
(513) 287-3331 **Feldmeier** Melissa M '97
(513) 922-7700 **Felix** Jeffrey A '91
(513) 721-5525 **Fellerhoff** Matthew W '94
(513) 381-2838 **Felson** Cynthia C '93
(513) 721-2500 **Felson** Edward J '89
(513) 721-4900 **Felson** Stephen R '66
(513) 651-7222 **Ferestad** Mark A '92
(513) 771-6768 **Ferguson** Amy S '92
(513) 751-6119 **Fernandez** Justin E '94
(513) 381-2838 **Ferrell** Richard L III '94
(513) 231-1100 **Ferris** James K '85
(513) 579-6400 **Fershtman** Alan S '94
(513) 241-3630 **Fettner** Saul A '85
(513) 961-1672 **Fichter** Tawn A '79
(513) 287-2660 **Ficke** Gregory C '90
(513) 579-7968 **Fiddes** Richard C '80
(513) 621-5088 **Fidler** Edward '37
(513) 241-7600 **Fidler** Mark W '84
(513) 684-9000 **Field** Eileen K '82
(513) 784-7338 **Fielman** Tracey A '93
(513) 352-6659 **Filiatraut** Renee S '88
(513) 684-3677 **Finch** Linda B '80
(513) 761-9300 **Finesman** Theodore H '69
(513) 936-9300 **Fingerman** Debra M '80
(513) 241-9400 **Fink** Elaine E '85
(513) 381-2838 **Fink** Jerold A '66
(513) 621-6464 **Finke** Harry J IV '82
(513) 333-7528 **Finke** Nicholas D '80
(513) 621-9921 **Finkelmeier** Louis J Jr. '68
(513) 533-2996 **Finney** Christopher P '87
(513) 533-2996 **Finney Stagnaro Saba & Klusmeier Co,LPA**
(513) 287-3601 **Finnigan** John J Jr. '79
(513) 983-7190 **Finocharo** John J '84
(513) 381-6810 **Finucane** Michael E '88
(513) 745-2050 **Fiorelli** Paul E '81
Fiorenza Robert O '98
(513) 632-8338 **Firm** Christopher E '99
(513) 421-2540 **Fischer** John M '70
(513) 621-3440 **Fischer** John W II '81
(513) 621-3394 **Fischer** John W III '68
(513) 794-6442 **Fischer** Joseph M '80
(513) 579-6400 **Fischer** Patrick F '88
(513) 533-0233 **Fischer** Timothy A '71
(513) 771-8500 **Fischoff** Alan H '73
(513) 632-9595 **Fish** Baruch D '73
(513) 579-5479 **Fisher** Francis J Jr. '75
(513) 325-9660 **Fisher** Paul H '89
(513) 731-8460 **Fitch** Mark R '87
(513) 362-8217 **Fitton** Jay S '97
(513) 629-1467 **FitzGerald** Alice M '79
FitzGerald Benjamin J '89
(513) 421-4225 **Fitzgerald** William F '62
(513) 634-4287 **Fitzpatrick** Matthew P '96
(513) 977-8200 **Fitzsimmons** Becky B '00
(513) 852-3497 **Fixler** Steven P '81
(513) 271-2482 **Fjord** Hilliard J '54
(513) 381-9200 **Flacks** Kenneth B '73
(513) 745-0400 **Flagel** Todd J '96
(513) 381-2838 **Flamm** Justin D '99
(513) 946-3117 **Flanagan** Anne S '83
(513) 621-6464 **Flanagan** John A '77
(513) 471-5008 **Flax** James A '04
(513) 381-6223 **Flax** William E '59
(513) 352-5858 **Fledderman** Anne M '86
(513) 421-3494 **Flege** John B Jr. '93
(513) 977-4209 **Fleischer** Neil I '00
(513) 977-4209 **Fleischer** Richard I '71
(513) 621-2666 **Flemer** Lawrence A '80
(513) 721-2120 **Fleming** Mary M '79
(513) 745-3648 **Fleming** Rose Ann '89
(513) 381-1234 **Flessa** John H '82
(513) 421-1313 **Fletcher** Michael C '69
(513) 243-1645 **Fletcher** Robert S '96
(513) 977-4777 **Florez** Michael G '82
(513) 946-5470 **Florez** Rosalind C '89
(513) 684-3638 **Floth** Kathleen A '01
(513) 751-4420 **Flottman** Anne B '01
(513) 768-7416 **Flowers** Laura J '02
(513) 762-4303 **Flynn** John M '68
(513) 421-1313 **Flynn** Kevin R '87
(513) 946-9200 **Flynn** Thomas J '76
(513) 241-2324 **Flynn** Thomas W '69
(513) 621-2120 **Flynn** William K '85
(513) 241-3100 **Fogelman** Adam R '01
(513) 785-4561 **Foley** John P III '76
(513) 381-9200 **Foley** Michael P '93
(513) 221-2345 **Foote** Carl F '75
(513) 946-3000 **Foote** Philip E '01
(513) 852-6092 **Forbes** Jeffrey D '01
(513) 784-5561 **Ford** William W III '85
(513) 352-3340 **Forman** Keith C '01
(513) 421-2881 **Forney** Ferdinand A '54
(513) 977-8200 **Fornshell** David P '99
(513) 579-5140 **Foster** Philip A '80
Foster Robin W '00
(513) 241-3430 **Foster** Thomas C '60
(513) 421-4855 **Foster** Ty L '81
(513) 983-3585 **Foureman** William C '84
(513) 579-7902 **Fowler** Byron T '96
(513) 961-6644 **Fox** Bernard C '50
(513) 961-6644 **Fox** Bernard C Jr. '78
(513) 564-0088 **Fox** Bradley W '03
(513) 357-9767 **Fox** Elizabeth '92
(513) 961-6644 **Fox & Fox Co,LPA**
(513) 381-3525 **Fox** Peter M '85
(513) 852-6000 **Frank** Kevin K '04
(513) 598-4276 **Frank** William N '78
(513) 871-8855 **Franke** Carolyn Mussio '83
(513) 564-9222 **Franke** Gary F '85
(513) 941-1850 **Franke** Hal F '53
(513) 564-9222 **Franke** Hal L '83
(513) 761-9255 **Frankel** Edward M '77
(513) 852-6045 **Frankel** Jan M '78
(513) 621-1505 **Frankel** Renee S '84
(513) 651-6800 **Franklin** David E '95
(513) 983-6064 **Franz** Paul A '82
(513) 977-8200 **Freedman** William M '73
(513) 977-8200 **Freeman** Harold S '60
(513) 381-8115 **Freeman** Herbert E '73
(513) 684-3211 **Freeman** John A '74
(513) 241-2324 **Frei** Donald F '65
(513) 721-1975 **Freking & Betz**
(513) 721-1975 **Freking** Randolph H '82
(513) 287-2136 **French** Eric S '99
(513) 641-4692 **French** Gregory S '85
(513) 665-3500 **Freund Freeze & Arnold**
(513) 385-1505 **Friedhoff** Gary E '86
(513) 772-0740 **Friedman** Benjamin S '01
(513) 421-9090 **Friedman** Penny '77
(513) 721-4532 **Friedman** Tedd H '92
(513) 579-1707 **Friedmann** Roger E '76
(513) 626-2721 **Frieko** Laura L '04
(513) 983-4187 **Friel** Carol S '80
(513) 763-4315 **Fries** Joseph C '91
(513) 977-8200 **Frink** Neal A '99
(513) 487-5979 **Friskney** Stephen H '80
(513) 241-5670 **Froncek** Theodore J Jr. '80
(513) 579-6400 **Fronduti** John S '03
(513) 421-6630 **Frooman** James C '90
(513) 754-3584 **Frooman** Thomas E '94
(513) 651-6800 **Frost Brown Todd LLC**
(513) 347-0861 **Frost** Hugh O II '68
(513) 977-8200 **Fruechtemeyer** A Scott '95
(513) 684-3769 **Fry** Patricia R '80
(513) 421-6000 **Fry** Sallee M '89
(513) 381-9200 **Fry** William R '66
(513) 352-6741 **Fuchs** Jack F '82
(513) 723-7043 **Fuchs** Jill N '83
(513) 946-3000 **Fullen** Kirstin T '02
(513) 579-7762 **Furlong** Kathleen A '80
(513) 745-0400 **Furnier** Robert R '83
(513) 745-0400 **Furnier Thomas,LLP**
(513) 348-4813 **Gabelman** Richard P '02
(513) 723-4000 **Gabelman** Thomas L '84
(513) 721-3330 **Gaier** Thomas M '75
(513) 287-2633 **Gainer** James B '86
(513) 475-0200 **Gaines** Deborah K Brown '72
(513) 961-9900 **Gaines** Leslie I '72
(513) 271-0254 **Gaines** Terry D '69
(513) 721-3330 **Galasso** Michael A '00
(513) 721-1200 **Gall** Kenneth Z '97
(513) 651-6800 **Gallagher** William E '01
(513) 651-5666 **Gallagher** William R '95
(513) 287-2641 **Gambill** Barbara F '97
(513) 946-3800 **Gandert** William T '98
(513) 723-4000 **Gann** Erica D '04
(513) 721-2220 **Ganson** Michael B '78
(513) 651-6800 **Ganulin** Neil '73
(513) 352-3329 **Ganulin** Richard '77
(513) 579-5472 **Garber** David W '75
(513) 922-3200 **Garber** Deanna R '90
Garber Valerie L '75
(513) 579-6400 **Gardner** Don R '60
(513) 579-6400 **Gardner** J Neal '71
(513) 503-4998 **Gardner** Matthew A '03
(513) 352-6530 **Garfinkel** Jane E '80
(513) 337-8559 **Garner** Dean L '91
(513) 870-2000 **Garner** Kimberly V '95
(513) 871-8900 **Garretson** Matthew L '98
(513) 421-8888 **Garrett** Edward J Jr. '83
(513) 241-7406 **Garrigan** Terrence M '87
(513) 791-1672 **Garrison** Harold K '93
(513) 946-3000 **Garry** Bruce S '71
(513) 684-0339 **Garry** Patrick J '91
(513) 579-6400 **Garry** Timothy A '61
(513) 852-6035 **Garry** Timothy A Jr. '86
(513) 852-3497 **Garry** Victoria D '86
(513) 665-3500 **Garvey** John J III '92
(513) 241-1950 **Garvin** James R '95
(513) 241-2540 **Gast** David M '98
(513) 621-1414 **Gast** Stephen P '86
(513) 984-3587 **Gatch** Lewis G '61
(513) 352-6676 **Gates** Joan M '00
(513) 247-0082 **Gaugh** Thomas B '02
(513) 521-5344 **Gaulding** Jerry M '88
(513) 579-6400 **Gaunt** Karen E '97
(513) 629-1470 **Gavin** Kevin K '95
(513) 852-8203 **Gay** Michael L '77
(513) 287-6900 **Gay** Steven F '82
(513) 412-2852 **Gaynor** William T Jr. '99
(513) 977-5682 **Gazaway** Joy E '95
(513) 381-2838 **Gearding** Monica L '98
(513) 221-1900 **Gebhart** David E '61
(513) 489-8787 **Gee** John M '75
(513) 241-6748 **Gee** Rebecca C '03
(513) 946-3000 **Geers** Ronald M '97
(513) 421-9010 **Gehrig** Michael F '74
(513) 621-6464 **Geiger** Lee P '00
(513) 352-3338 **Geiler** Geri H '89
(513) 946-3000 **Geiser** Edward J '89
(513) 870-2206 **Gelfand** Eugene M '71
(513) 621-3440 **Gelhaus** Emily J '03
(513) 762-4426 **Gellenbeck** Lynne '77
(513) 381-9200 **Gelwicks** Joseph W '76
(513) 421-6688 **Gelwicks** Thomas A '82
(513) 621-0267 **Geoppinger** Jean M '90
(513) 762-6200 **Geoppinger** Jeffrey D '01
(513) 762-4538 **George** Denis E '85
(513) 977-8200 **Georgiton** Peter J '02
(513) 595-2200 **Gephart** John F '79
(513) 929-3400 **Geppert** Eric J '98
(513) 621-9100 **Gerhardstein** Alphonse A '76
(513) 579-6948 **Gerhardt** Charles H III '86
(513) 891-8940 **Gerla** Barbara Ullman '80
(513) 977-8200 **Gerlach** Benjamin J '04
(513) 352-6527 **Germain** Kenneth B '89
(513) 241-7722 **Gerner** David E '83
(513) 621-2120 **Gerwin** Ann W '79
Gettler Benjamin '49
(513) 791-1673 **Geygan & Geygan Ltd**
(513) 791-1673 **Geygan** Thomas J '63

(513) 791-1673 **Geygan** Thomas J Jr. '98
(513) 455-7600 **Ghassomian** Kevin R '02
(513) 721-1975 **Ghiz** Leslie E '94
(513) 983-1100 **Ghuman** Shiv P '01
(513) 762-6200 **Giannella** Andrew R '96
(513) 721-4532 **Gibson** Cynthia L '89
(513) 946-3000 **Gibson** Richard G '83
(513) 723-4823 **Gibson** Whitney C '04
(513) 784-9111 **Gick** Kathleen M '91
(513) 721-4532 **Gierl** John R '83
(513) 563-2992 **Giffin** Patricia K '85
(513) 352-3339 **Giglio** Augustine '70
(513) 241-7722 **Gilbert** Scott T '03
(513) 651-4130 **Gilday** Anne L '03
(513) 621-5631 **Gilday** Michael D '77
(513) 621-2666 **Giles** Brian T '00
(513) 923-5232 **Gilkey** Sue E '00
(513) 745-7003 **Gill** David L '82
(513) 684-3655 **Gill** Eric J '94
(513) 241-9400 **Gillam** Marcheta L '82
(513) 396-8787 **Gillan** Brian P '85
(513) 455-7600 **Gillen** Stephen E '80
(513) 870-2811 **Gilliam** Scott A '86
(513) 579-6400 **Gilligan** Louis F '68
(513) 621-2666 **Gilligan** T Scott '82
(513) 241-3100 **Gillum** Amy L '03
(513) 564-7330 **Ginocchio** Deborah N '79
(513) 872-7900 **Ginocchio** James S '79
(513) 977-5578 **Ginocchio** Ralph P '77
(513) 762-6200 **Ginsburg** Pamela K '00
(513) 421-9222 **Giuliano** Jeffrey P '83
(513) 672-8811 **Glaser** Hermina M '84
(513) 352-6765 **Glass** Gary M '89
(513) 651-6800 **Glass** Joanne W '94
(513) 621-2120 **Glass** Thomas P '93
(513) 361-1200 **Glassman** Benjamin C '04
(513) 977-8200 **Glassman** Michael S '76
(513) 564-7630 **Glassman** Michelle C '03
(513) 579-0080 **Glassman** Thomas F '93
(513) 271-0075 **Glassmann** Lawrence A '86
(513) 634-3244 **Glazer** Julia A '96
(513) 489-7200 **Glazer** Richard H '70
Gleich Caryn F '99
(513) 381-8430 **Glennon** Thomas M '00
(513) 579-7339 **Glueck** Neal J '80
(513) 651-6800 **Godar** Mary M '02
(513) 241-6650 **Godbey** Mark E '89
(513) 381-5700 **Godby** Marissa L '94
(513) 352-6760 **Goderre** Diane M '98
(513) 556-0107 **Godsey** Mark A '01
(513) 621-8210 **Goeddel** Frederic L '73
(513) 651-6800 **Goehler** Richard M '82
(513) 621-0912 **Goering** Eric W '93
(513) 621-0912 **Goering & Goering**
(513) 621-0912 **Goering** Robert A '62
(513) 621-0912 **Goering** Robert A '86
(513) 621-0912 **Goering** Ruth F '59
(513) 651-6800 **Gold** Ronald E '93
(513) 721-3111 **Goldberg** Brian M '85
(513) 946-6464 **Goldberg** Brian T '04
(513) 421-6630 **Goldberg** John A '73
(513) 321-2662 **Goldberg** Richard J '75
(513) 624-3100 **Goldcamp** Robert T '79
(513) 541-3900 **Golden** Jason A '03
(513) 345-8291 **Goldenberg** Jeffrey S '94
(513) 651-8437 **Goldman** Alan L '90
(513) 381-9200 **Goldman** Edward R '73
(513) 621-2666 **Goldman** Fern E '81
(513) 723-0400 **Goldman** Gary S '94
Goldman Jacqueline Meyer '02
(513) 794-6849 **Goldsmith** Katherine D '96
(513) 651-6800 **Goldstein** Steven J '75
(513) 721-1311 **Goldwasser** Brian D '93
(513) 419-6982 **Gollomp** Jeffrey A '01
(513) 651-3456 **Gonzalez Saggio & Harlan LLP**
(513) 621-5252 **Good** Martha H '85
(513) 946-3000 **Goodin** Steven P '99
(513) 561-9800 **Goodman** Barry A '67
(513) 621-1505 **Goodman** Jeffrey S '93
(513) 533-0528 **Goodman** Richard Lanahan '74
(513) 621-1505 **Goodman** Ronald J '62
(513) 621-1505 **Goodman** Stanley '55
(513) 621-0267 **Goodman** Terrence L '84
(513) 621-5631 **Goodson** Brett C '76
(513) 621-5631 **Goodson & Mullins,Ltd**
(513) 579-6400 **Goodson** Stephen M '80
(513) 946-3000 **Goolsby** Henrietta L '94
(513) 381-9200 **Gora** Felix J '80
(513) 751-2145 **Gordon** Abram S '87
(513) 381-0656 **Gores** Henrietta D '01
(513) 721-4532 **Goret** Ronald J '64
(513) 946-5760 **Gorrasi-Dwenger** Lisa M '03
(513) 321-4238 **Gortsas** Alex '58
(513) 639-5421 **Gossett** Deanna C '98
(513) 762-1384 **Gothard** Jennifer K '92
(513) 651-2121 **Gottesman** Zachary '92
(513) 241-2324 **Graber** Sarah Otte '97
(513) 651-6800 **Gracey** Stephen M '03
(513) 961-6200 **Gradwohl** Samuel A '99
(513) 721-3323 **Graeter** Richard A II '89
(513) 421-1313 **Graf** Andrew D '97
(513) 618-7800 **Graf Stiebel & Moyers, LPA**
(513) 618-7800 **Graf** William R Jr. '76
(513) 579-2540 **Grafe** Karl J '85
(513) 474-0648 **Graham** Richard K '92
(513) 221-1745 **Grant** James A '85
(513) 946-3700 **Grant** Joan L '78
(513) 684-3211 **Grant** Joseph P '87
(513) 471-9405 **Grant** Marvin F '55
(513) 723-1121 **Grau** Kenneth M '88
(513) 762-4252 **Graves** Joan H '94
Gray Edell R '96
(513) 946-9200 **Gray** Robin D '93
(513) 232-1700 **Gray** Victoria M '93
(513) 621-6464 **Graydon Head & Ritchey LLP**
(513) 345-4700 **Grayson** Deborah R '94
(513) 651-6800 **Green** Chelsea C '00
(513) 769-0840 **Green** F Harrison '72
(513) 977-8200 **Green** K C '84
(513) 651-6800 **Green** Melissa D '04
(513) 946-3000 **Greenberg** Bradley J '91
(513) 621-3440 **Greenberg** Gary L '78
(513) 381-2838 **Greenberg** Gerald S '88
Greenberg Marc L '78
(513) 946-3695 **Greenberg** Matthew L '00
(513) 721-5151 **Greenberger** Jeffrey J '92
(513) 489-1633 **Greenberger** Karen K '92
(513) 721-5151 **Greenberger** Mark A '66
(513) 621-6464 **Greene** Everett L '04
(513) 362-2847 **Greene** Gerald H Jr. '02
(513) 381-9200 **Greene** Gordon C '60
(513) 455-7600 **Greenebaum Doll & McDonald PLLC**
(513) 943-4200 **Greenwood** Scott T '89
(513) 487-5980 **Gregg** John W '79
(513) 243-3329 **Greiner** Carey A '00
(513) 621-6464 **Greiner** John C '83
(513) 665-9600 **Greiner** Scott A '92
(513) 977-4774 **Greiwe** Nancy S '83
(513) 337-3535 **Gressel** Gerard S '92
(513) 648-7067 **Greulich** John E '69
(513) 632-8445 **Grey** Billie J '97
(513) 891-2100 **Gribbell** Frederick H '90
(513) 287-3017 **Gribler** Michael A '75
(513) 651-6800 **Griess** Murray W '95
(513) 551-1985 **Griest** Shane E '00
(513) 621-6464 **Griffin** Christopher A '03
(513) 530-0152 **Griffin** Daniel W '87
(513) 421-1313 **Griffin-Fletcher,LLP**
(513) 396-6117 **Griffith** John B '71
(513) 381-2838 **Griffith** Stephen M Jr. '81
(513) 263-4071 **Grigsby** Donald E '69
(513) 977-8200 **Groemminger** Brian K '04
(513) 723-4000 **Groenke** David A '81
Grogan Jerome J '03
(513) 345-8291 **Groh** Theresa L '85
(513) 946-3000 **Groneman** Raymond C '73
(513) 632-9595 **Groner** Simon '75
(513) 762-6200 **Gronotte** Sharon E '99
(513) 985-3200 **Groshoff** David A '96
(513) 357-9778 **Grosse** Lisa L '77
(513) 381-4700 **Grosser** Theodore D '77
(513) 621-0550 **Grossheim** Elmer R '60
(513) 247-9094 **Grossman** Joanne B '83
(513) 241-2324 **Grossman** Kurt L '83
(513) 946-9000 **Grossmann** David E '52
(513) 381-2838 **Grossmann** Thomas E '82
(513) 241-3993 **Grote** Jane M '76
(513) 554-3000 **Grote** Leo F '84
(513) 721-7906 **Grubbs** Gerald R '89
(513) 651-6800 **Grubbs** Kyle R '01
(513) 412-1462 **Gruber** John P '89
(513) 421-4646 **Gruber** Joseph C '86
(513) 421-4646 **Gruber** Thomas J '79
(513) 791-3558 **Gruenschlaeger** Jeanne E '76
(513) 627-0079 **Grunzinger** Laura R '01
(513) 946-5238 **Guckenberger** Guy C '69
(513) 946-9200 **Guenthner** Carla A '90
(513) 533-2996 **Gugino** Julie M '01
(513) 946-3000 **Guinan** Richard D '96
(513) 631-0022 **Gunderson** Eric J '92
(513) 579-4328 **Gunter** Stephanie A '99
(513) 651-6800 **Gurney** D Scott '86
(513) 241-7880 **Gustafson** Derek W '84
(513) 651-4130 **Gustafson** Jill '90
(513) 621-4477 **Gustavson** William M '78
(513) 621-8200 **Gustin** James W '55
(513) 621-5252 **Gutzwiller** Robert H '78
(513) 721-4532 **Haas** Bradley G '86
(513) 651-6800 **Haas** Colleen M '97
(513) 721-1126 **Haas** Herbert J '81
(513) 651-5651 **Haas** Michael R '04
(513) 651-6800 **Habel** Christopher S '95
(513) 333-0050 **Hackett** Paul L III '88
(513) 281-1040 **Hadden** Richard Ray '76
(513) 852-3497 **Haders** William D '75
(513) 579-1500 **Haffer** Gloria S '77
(513) 721-2120 **Haffner** Karri K '94
(513) 369-5947 **Haffner** Paul F '94
(513) 762-6200 **Hageman** Jennifer J '96
(513) 774-0440 **Hagerstrand** Eric C '74
(513) 651-6800 **Haggerty** Walter E Jr. '78
(513) 983-4282 **Hagopian** Gary '76
(513) 381-0656 **Haines** Richard M '76
(513) 352-0500 **Hale** Jeffrey S '04
(513) 651-6800 **Halenkamp** Erin Rieger '02
(513) 651-6800 **Hall** Adam P '89
(513) 241-0400 **Hall** Gary L '79
(513) 534-4772 **Hall** Kari K '03
(513) 665-9333 **Hall** Michael S '84
(513) 762-6200 **Hallenbeck** Prentiss W Jr. '98
(513) 921-8433 **Haller** Brad E '00
(513) 852-8200 **Halloran** James W '60
(513) 793-4400 **Halper** Steven D '75
(513) 977-8200 **Halpert** Douglas J '94
(513) 241-3447 **Halpin** John '04
(513) 852-8210 **Halpin** Victor C II '97
(513) 956-6136 **Hamagami** Monica Y '93
(513) 345-4160 **Hambley** William C '87
Hamilton Brian K '98
(513) 558-4768 **Hamilton** Frederick N '92
(513) 721-5672 **Hamilton** Richard O Jr. '00
(513) 721-3242 **Hammelrath** W S '65
(513) 263-3906 **Hammer** Vickie L '80
(513) 381-2011 **Hammond** Michael F '89
(513) 561-6562 **Hancock** John W '68
(513) 977-8200 **Handler** Allyson B '03
(513) 762-6200 **Hands** John M '88
(513) 232-8000 **Hanessian** Edward J '77
(513) 651-6800 **Haney** Maureen P '99
Hanselman John L Jr. '73
(513) 381-5552 **Hara** Colin '98
(513) 721-7300 **Hardin** David E '96
(513) 721-7300 **Hardin** Donald E '63
(513) 241-1334 **Hardin** Jim L '91
(513) 721-7300 **Hardin Lefton Lazarus & Marks LLC**
(513) 241-3685 **Hardin** Leona B '01
(513) 352-1570 **Hardin** Roshani D '90
(513) 946-3000 **Hardman** Kevin M '96
(513) 621-4220 **Hardy** William R '63
(513) 762-6200 **Hargreaves** Jeanette '95
(513) 977-8200 **Harmeyer** John V '96
(513) 241-1991 **Harmon** Arthur W Jr. '81
(513) 852-8200 **Harmon** Jeffrey J '81
(513) 579-1500 **Harmon** Laurie M '92
(513) 352-2452 **Harmon** Michael J '74
(513) 946-3000 **Harper** James W '74
(513) 579-1414 **Harper** Tessea M '01
(513) 558-7748 **Harpster** Linda M '80
(513) 564-7051 **Harrell** Dennis Ora '75
(513) 561-5366 **Harrington** John P '53
(513) 891-3270 **Harris & Burgin**
(513) 861-3100 **Harris** Demetrious A '98
(513) 558-5042 **Harris** Gary R '84
(513) 621-3333 **Harris** Irving '51
(513) 621-2666 **Harris** Jeffrey P '76
(513) 891-3270 **Harris** Jeffrey W '03
(513) 891-3270 **Harris** Jerald D '72
Harris Rodney J '97
(513) 741-7888 **Harris** Ronald C '78
(513) 977-8200 **Harrison** Gregory A '85
(513) 651-6800 **Harrison** Jack B '93
(513) 852-6047 **Harrison** James B '83
(513) 561-9229 **Harrison** William K Jr. '59
(513) 651-6800 **Hart** Douglas E '82
(513) 946-3000 **Hart** Lashawn C '01
(513) 381-0380 **Hart** Robert R Jr. '85
(513) 977-4210 **Hartke** James R '73
(513) 241-4110 **Hartman** Alan J '84
(513) 381-4395 **Hartmann** Dennis P '73
(513) 946-3000 **Hartmann** Gregory P '99
(513) 929-3400 **Harvey** Robin E '83
(513) 684-3211 **Hassebrock** Richard J '98
(513) 721-7500 **Hastings** Deborah C '94
(513) 381-2838 **Hastings** Kerry P '96
(513) 721-7500 **Hastings** Robert R Jr. '73
(513) 946-3263 **Hatcher** John R '98
(513) 621-2100 **Hathaway** David E '80
(513) 621-0800 **Hauck** John W '78
(513) 651-6800 **Haughey** Stephen N '84
(513) 241-2324 **Haupt** Keith R '92
(513) 621-6787 **Haussler** Jakki L '89
(513) 922-3200 **Haverkamp Brinker Rebold & Riehl Co,LPA**
(513) 922-3200 **Haverkamp** Gary J '63
(513) 794-6473 **Haverkamp** Michael F '74
(513) 684-6988 **Hawkins** Douglas N '87
(513) 352-6700 **Hawkins** Heather MacGregor '04
(513) 556-7040 **Hawkins** Ilse Sue '77
(513) 984-4554 **Hawkins** Lawrence C Jr. '75
(513) 621-3394 **Hawkins** Melissa N '03
(513) 977-8200 **Hawkins** Michael W '72
(513) 684-6018 **Hawkins** Robert B '04
(513) 621-2666 **Hawkins** Tracy L '00
(513) 723-7049 **Hawkins** William H II '78
(513) 721-4505 **Hawley** Kenneth G '79
(513) 929-3400 **Hayden** Angela M '99
(513) 621-2120 **Hayden** Jeremy A '02
(513) 455-7600 **Hayden** Mark T '96
(513) 721-4532 **Hayden** William T '79
Hayes Kathleen E '82
(513) 639-3876 **Hayes** Thomas A '68
(513) 723-4000 **Hayes** William D '86
(513) 241-2025 **Hayhow** Stephen F '70
(513) 421-8422 **Hazen** Glen E Jr. '86
(513) 579-1500 **Healey** Roger W '76
(513) 621-7600 **Healy** Jack S '73
(513) 977-8200 **Healy** Mary J '78
(513) 326-1500 **Hearn** Robert L '74
(513) 632-5132 **Heater** Deborah Ann '94
(513) 721-5672 **Heather** Timothy P '80
(513) 651-6800 **Heekin** Albert E III '65
(513) 421-3399 **Heekin** Christopher R '89
(513) 381-2838 **Heekin** Thomas D '62
(513) 421-3399 **Heekin** Thomas D Jr. '88
(513) 241-7644 **Heekin** William C '84
(513) 946-3227 **Heenan** Scott M '02
(513) 530-4230 **Heidrich** William A III '79
(513) 421-3940 **Heilbrun** John L '77
(513) 241-1950 **Heile** Charles D '62
(513) 946-3000 **Heile** Jeffrey M '03
(513) 946-3249 **Heile** William P '70
(513) 761-0011 **Heinichen** Jeffrey K '78
(513) 579-0080 **Heinkel** John C '81
(513) 651-6800 **Heinlen** Ronald E '62
(513) 381-9200 **Heintz** Isaac T '01
(513) 421-4225 **Heis** Forest S '69
(513) 762-6200 **Heis** Jennifer Snyder '03
(513) 421-4225 **Heis & Wenstrup Co,LPA**
(513) 345-1532 **Heiser** Stacey M '94
(513) 651-6800 **Heitchue** Catherine A '03
(513) 946-5791 **Hekler** Krista A '02
(513) 923-9740 **Helbling** John J '90
(513) 621-2120 **Heldman** James G '81
(513) 762-4421 **Heldman** Paul W '77
(513) 946-3875 **Helfrich** Kimberly Ann '97
(513) 632-5317 **Helfrich** Loretta Marie '89
(513) 421-2400 **Helmer** James B Jr. '75
(513) 421-2400 **Helmer Martins Rice & Popham Co,LPA**
(513) 793-5297 **Helmes** Andrew J '97
(513) 651-9666 **Helmick** Bertha G '95
(513) 563-2194 **Helmling** Margaret R '59
(513) 761-9393 **Helwig** Nancy Coe '80
(513) 489-5495 **Hemingway** Ronald Lee '68
(513) 634-2084 **Hemm** Erich D '00
(513) 241-3100 **Henderson** Thomas L '88
(513) 621-6464 **Hendricks** Jeffrey M '96
(513) 351-7599 **Hendricks** Robert S '93
(513) 771-7449 **Hendrickson** Nora C '86
(513) 651-6800 **Hendy** Daniel J '04
(513) 381-9200 **Hengehold** Steven D '85
(513) 721-7295 **Hengelbrok** James W '48
(513) 723-4000 **Henkel** Mary C '88
Henley Walter G '90
(513) 243-6065 **Hensley** Douglas L '93
(513) 684-3201 **Herbert** Nancy B '78
(513) 946-5840 **Herberth** Gretta M '03
Hermanies John H '48
(513) 421-1313 **Herndon** Richard D '86
(513) 684-3211 **Herrell** Robin L '84
(513) 768-7403 **Herrmann** Julie R '93
(513) 534-4900 **Herron** David L '96
(513) 333-4020 **Hersh** Gail C Jr. '92
(513) 627-0633 **Hersko** Bart S '86
(513) 977-8200 **Hertlein** Charles F Jr. '80
(513) 241-3685 **Hertzman** Glenda M '79
(513) 533-0888 **Hery** Mary J '79
(513) 731-6601 **Hesch** William E '80
(513) 455-7600 **Hess** W Ashley '03
(513) 721-2220 **Heuck** Kenneth Jr. '70
(513) 621-0267 **Heuck** Robert II '91
(513) 731-4247 **Hewitt** Harry L '00
(513) 684-9700 **Hext** Stephen R '72
(513) 621-6464 **Heyd** Daniel C '86
(513) 243-6678 **Heyd** Joseph D '95
(513) 946-3142 **Hickenlooper** Smith D '00
(513) 651-6800 **Hickey** Nicole Vickroy '95
(513) 721-1904 **Hickey** Timothy A '71
(513) 634-5395 **Hickman** Ingrid N '02
(513) 579-6400 **Hicks** Drew M '03
(513) 984-1899 **Hicks** Steven R '90
(513) 352-3613 **Hicks** William C '97
(513) 946-3000 **Hidy** Kathleen M '92
(513) 632-4132 **Hidy** Richard J '88
(513) 984-0061 **Hieatt** Jennifer F '96
(513) 243-1025 **Hieatt** Steven W '96
(513) 564-7200 **Higgins** James A '69
(513) 651-6800 **Higgins** John S Jr. '97
(513) 852-6024 **Higgins** Karen A '98
(513) 946-3000 **Hild** Allison E '99
(513) 721-4532 **Hild** Guy M '62
(513) 852-3497 **Hildebrandt** Dolores M '73
(513) 684-9000 **Hill** Christine B '88
(513) 984-2640 **Hill** Constance A '79
(513) 684-3211 **Hill** Louis H '88
Hill Shauna M '02
(513) 381-2838 **Hill** Thomas C '73
(513) 583-4200 **Hiller** Robert S '77
(513) 381-9200 **Hillerich** Laura I '02
(513) 977-8200 **Hils** M Gabrielle '84
(513) 579-2203 **Hils** Mary E '80
(513) 651-6800 **Hiltz** Allison L '03
(513) 621-2100 **Hilvert** Margaret A '89
(513) 977-8200 **Hinebaugh** Jeffrey P '92
(513) 665-3500 **Hinegardner** Charles L '95
(513) 721-4532 **Hinegardner** Laura A '97
(513) 721-2525 **Hines** Glenn R '75
(513) 381-0656 **Hines** Jeffrey M '99
(513) 556-4835 **Hinkel** Rebecca A '04
(513) 721-3330 **Hinners** Jason R '03
(513) 534-3165 **Hinshaw** Steven A '77
Hirsch William C '46
(513) 621-6464 **Hirschfeld** Michael A '77
(513) 287-1238 **Hobbs** Jacqueline Schuster '97
(513) 381-2838 **Hoberg** Timothy E '70
(513) 721-2744 **Hobson** Anthony W '82
(513) 321-8100 **Hobson** Mary G '84
Hochbein Joseph J '80
(513) 533-9898 **Hochscheid** Tabitha M '95
(513) 752-8855 **Hock** Thomas P '73
(513) 564-7053 **Hodesh** Janine '82
(513) 579-6400 **Hodge** Pamela M '89
(513) 489-7800 **Hodgeman** Ronald L '98
(513) 723-4000 **Hodges** Jason L '00
(513) 241-2540 **Hoefle** Henry F '65
(513) 574-4464 **Hoehne** Jeffry M '70
(513) 621-1414 **Hof** Robert E '92
(513) 241-0466 **Hoff** Louis A '61
(513) 381-2838 **Hoffheimer** Daniel J '76
(513) 421-7666 **Hoffheimer** Jon '65
(513) 381-2838 **Hoffman** Bridget C '02
(513) 621-6464 **Hoffman** Bruce A '75
(513) 677-0999 **Hoffmann** Gary R '73
(513) 684-2572 **Hoffmann** Timothy W '03
(513) 241-4722 **Hoffpauir** Gregory T '95
(513) 579-1500 **Hoffsis** Stephen B '86
(513) 388-2919 **Hoft** Thomas W '89
(513) 381-0656 **Hogan** Andrew J '87
(513) 579-6400 **Hogan** Patricia B '89
Hogan Robert B '72
(513) 744-9600 **Hogan** Robert K '82
(513) 983-4374 **Hogan** Tara C '01
(513) 721-1311 **Hojnoski** Robert W '98
(513) 721-4505 **Holbrook** Lanny R '71
(513) 929-3400 **Holcombe** David G '81
(513) 579-3153 **Holifield** Johnathan M '96
(513) 852-8200 **Hollingsworth** Robert J '73
(513) 721-5672 **Hollis** Charles F III '97
(513) 534-6030 **Holmes** Richard W Jr. '00
(513) 241-6650 **Holmes** Robert F '01
(513) 852-8200 **Holmes** Stephen S '82
(513) 721-4450 **Holschuh** John D Jr. '80
(513) 946-9000 **Holtmeier** Denis G '75
(513) 684-3711 **Holtzman** Jan M '72
(513) 852-6041 **Holzapfel** Eric C '72
(513) 761-6161 **Holzman** Robert S '64
(513) 761-6161 **Holzman** Wallace R Jr. '65
(513) 931-2200 **Honerlaw** Joseph S '80
(513) 931-2200 **Honerlaw** Michael J '86
(513) 621-2120 **Hood** Gordon H '53
(513) 977-8200 **Hoops** Michael W '03
(513) 563-3266 **Hopewell** Craig S '80
(513) 421-1313 **Hopkins** Bruce G '90
(513) 533-3850 **Hopkins** Rick A '84
(513) 232-7578 **Hopper** Kevin J '78
(513) 621-2100 **Hopple** Richard M '73
(513) 579-1414 **Hordes** Donald B '82
(513) 574-5100 **Horn** David A '84
(513) 984-2040 **Horn** Stephanie D '92
(513) 369-5009 **Horrell** Karen H '77
(513) 451-0168 **Horsley** William T '00
(513) 852-8207 **Horwitz** Elizabeth A '85
(513) 362-8228 **Hosking** Tina D '95
(513) 977-8200 **Hoskins** Robert H '97
(513) 931-7755 **Houston** Daniel Ray '66
(513) 352-6700 **Houston** James D '00
(513) 852-8200 **Houston** Janet L '89
(513) 421-7300 **Howard** Barbara J '79
(513) 421-7300 **Howard & Bodnar Co,LPA**
(513) 381-2838 **Howard** Catherine E '03
(513) 534-3167 **Howard** Jerry R '01
(513) 632-5332 **Howe** William D '77
(513) 534-0680 **Hubanks** Tanya A '98
(513) 744-6765 **Hubbard** James R '91
(513) 481-1999 **Huber** Giselle K '86
(513) 744-8780 **Huber** John C '94
(513) 574-8900 **Huddleson** William A '74
(513) 241-3100 **Hudec** Pamela A '96
(513) 929-4834 **Hudson** Calvin R '93
(513) 421-4020 **Hughes** Angela M '04
(513) 243-1412 **Hughes** Matthew W '85

(513) 983-0925 **Hughes** Richard A '88
(513) 852-8200 **Hughes** Richard Scott '99
(513) 870-2287 **Huller** Mark J '82
(513) 768-4344 **Humbert** Mark A '90
(513) 241-2324 **Humphrey** Thomas W '93
(513) 381-7399 **Hunt** Marshall C Jr. '67
(513) 241-0400 **Hunt** Stephen R '80
(513) 684-3711 **Hunt** William E '72
(513) 721-4532 **Hunter** Bruce A '84
(513) 763-3585 **Huprich** David L '58
(513) 421-4646 **Hurd** John K '74
(513) 421-6630 **Hurlbutt** Christopher H '00
(513) 381-2838 **Hurley** Timothy J '76
(513) 362-8700 **Huse** William M '03
(513) 421-7700 **Hust** Bruce K '86
(513) 583-4200 **Hust** John W '75
(513) 753-2800 **Husvar** Amy G '95
(513) 381-9200 **Hutcherson** William H Jr. '54
(513) 891-1530 **Hutchins** Johanna B '98
(513) 421-4020 **Hutson** Joseph M '98
(513) 381-5700 **Hyland** Robert G '72
(513) 381-2838 **Hylander** Brian R '03
(513) 977-8200 **Hylander** Jessica S '03
(513) 481-9800 **Hyle** Francis M '74
(513) 481-9800 **Hyle & Mecklenborg Co,LPA**
(513) 421-9500 **Hylton** Sheri L '96
(513) 721-5672 **Iaciofano** Anthony J '85
(513) 651-4226 **Ice** Andrew G '96
(513) 961-1114 **Idinopulos** Lea S '83
(513) 977-8200 **Iery** Clare M '01
(513) 534-8705 **Igel** Nancy Hils '03
(513) 946-9000 **Igoe** Elizabeth S '93
(513) 762-6200 **Imbus** Karen L '96
(513) 721-5151 **Imm** Stephen E '87
(513) 381-8430 **Immerman & Tobin Co,LPA**
(513) 708-1011 **Imwalle** Mark A '02
(513) 621-0267 **Infante** Renee A '91
(513) 793-0333 **Ingles** Roxanne L '03
(513) 608-1247 **Inskeep** Nancy Ann '93
(513) 946-9472 **Ionna** Massimino M '00
(513) 721-1350 **Irey** Kurt M '04
(513) 579-6400 **Irwin** Kevin E '77
(513) 721-7522 **Isaly** Charles W '77
(513) 421-3772 **Issenmann** Jack K '67
(513) 241-0400 **Ivy** Christine J '86
(513) 579-6400 **Izenson** Daniel E '90
(513) 721-1350 **Jaap** Joseph B '89
(513) 564-7365 **Jackson** Arthur L '91
(513) 241-3100 **Jackson** Brian S '97
(513) 929-3400 **Jackson** Kory A '00
(513) 352-2417 **Jackson** Lisa M '91
(513) 241-2324 **Jackson** Randall S Jr. '98
(513) 489-9191 **Jackson** Thomas A '82
(513) 921-1400 **Jacob** Nancy V '87
(513) 621-4556 **Jacobs Jensen & Napolitano, LLC**
(513) 721-7430 **Jacobs** Jon H '62
(513) 381-6600 **Jacobs Kleinman Seibel & McNally**
(513) 381-5700 **Jacobs** Mary Ann '82
(513) 793-4684 **Jacobs** Neal D '01
(513) 621-4556 **Jacobs** Thomas W '89
(513) 241-2324 **Jacobs** Wayne L '90
(513) 621-2120 **Jacobs** William R '73
(513) 723-4000 **Jacobson** Barbara Bison '75
(513) 721-4532 **Jahnke** Mark J '79
(513) 361-8400 **Jakab** Jill E '77
(513) 352-3343 **Jake** Charles E IV '01
(513) 891-8900 **James** Thomas C Jr. '01
(513) 621-1935 **Jameson** Kenneth D '79
(513) 852-2584 **Jamison** Tracy B '96
(513) 984-8989 **Janning** Nancy M '96
(513) 579-6400 **Jansing** James M '82
(513) 287-3025 **Janson** Julia S '88
(513) 621-2120 **Janszen** August T '93
(513) 631-6666 **Jarvis** Robin Ann '98
(513) 481-9800 **Jarvis** Timothy P '03
(513) 744-9600 **Javitch Block & Rathbone**
(513) 241-2324 **Jefferies** David E '98
(513) 556-0075 **Jefferson** Mina J '90
(513) 381-2838 **Jeffries** Lori E '97
(513) 983-6388 **Jemison** Steven W '75
(513) 241-9119 **Jenike** David L '74
(513) 723-1600 **Jenkins** Christian A '99
(513) 579-6400 **Jennings** Robert W Jr. '82
(513) 984-8080 **Jennings** Thomas M '86
(513) 241-3100 **Jensen** Joel K '82
(513) 621-4556 **Jensen** Robert M '04
(513) 977-8200 **Jevicky** John E '81
(513) 977-8200 **Johns** Michael D '97
(513) 241-3100 **Johnson** David E '99
(513) 533-8508 **Johnson** Eileen A '79
(513) 983-2069 **Johnson** James Jay '74
(513) 352-6990 **Johnson** James L '80
(513) 651-8437 **Johnson** Keith K '77
(513) 636-1259 **Johnson** Keith W '91
(513) 634-3849 **Johnson** Kevin C '90
(513) 946-3446 **Johnson** Linda F '88
(513) 579-4277 **Johnson** Margaret S '95
(513) 761-7585 **Johnson** Maynard R '81
(513) 381-2838 **Johnson** Patrick G '03
(513) 984-6672 **Johnson** Richard H '68
(513) 352-6769 **Johnson** Robert P '88
(513) 946-3700 **Johnson** Stephen D '84
(513) 241-3100 **Johnson** Tracey M '97
(513) 588-3055 **Johnson** William E III '83
(513) 929-4834 **Johnson** Winston K '86
(513) 723-4000 **Johnston** Bradley K '98
(513) 793-2992 **Johnston** Robert A '60
(513) 946-3040 **Johnstone** Robert H Jr. '71
(513) 721-1311 **Jones** B Scott '98
(513) 587-2897 **Jones** Christine Y '91
(513) 977-8200 **Jones** Daniel L Jr. '99
(513) 241-5550 **Jones** Donald T '80
(513) 241-3100 **Jones** Jeniece D '02
(513) 626-2127 **Jones** Juliet A '04
(513) 762-6200 **Jones** Karen E '04
(513) 651-0505 **Jones** Kevin P '74
(513) 634-6944 **Jones** Melody A '98
(513) 621-6464 **Jones** Michael S '94
(513) 362-8700 **Jones** Nathaniel R '57
(513) 684-2572 **Jones** Richard B '96
(513) 241-7111 **Jones** Robert R '85
(513) 769-0007 **Jones** Stephen R '00
(513) 241-3100 **Jones** Wendy J '98
(513) 241-4722 **Jonson** George D '83
(513) 241-2324 **Jordan** Joseph R '68
(513) 721-4450 **Jordan** Mark W '80
(513) 381-5500 **Jorling** Jeffrey D '93
(513) 721-3000 **Joseph** Gregory G '87
(513) 721-3000 **Joseph** Richard S '91
(513) 721-3000 **Joseph** Robert G '67
(513) 721-3000 **Joseph** Ronald G '61
(513) 241-2324 **Josephic** David J '66
(513) 721-4532 **Jreisat** Wijdan '94
(513) 241-9400 **Juenke** Timothy R '93
(513) 579-7337 **Julian** Frank G '82
(513) 381-9200 **Jurs** Peter B '97
(513) 791-8800 **Jutze** Robert G '92
(513) 651-6800 **Kaake** Andrew R '00
(513) 762-6200 **Kadish** Scott P '85
(513) 946-3000 **Kadon** Karl P III '84
(513) 684-3211 **Kagy** James E '81
(513) 929-3400 **Kahle** Thomas W '75
(513) 241-3100 **Kahmann** Kathleen E '02
(513) 541-5410 **Kahn** Marla J '01
(513) 684-3211 **Kaiser** Robert D '74
(513) 474-5469 **Kaiser** Robert S '87
(513) 357-9750 **Kalafut** Christopher M '87
(513) 961-6200 **Kaleda** Jeffery A '98
(513) 723-4000 **Kallas** Hani R '94
(513) 761-5221 **Kaltman** Sandra P '85
(513) 721-6151 **Kamine** Charles S '76
(513) 721-6151 **Kamine** Darlene M '76
(513) 684-3711 **Kaminski** Gerald F '70
(513) 241-8137 **Kammer** David D '93
(513) 241-0738 **Kammer** Joseph C '55
(513) 241-3685 **Kamp** David P '81
(513) 621-6464 **Kane** Joseph E '70
(513) 361-1200 **Kane** Scott A '97
(513) 469-6580 **Kanter** Mark S '83
(513) 723-4000 **Kaplan** Andrew M '83
(513) 381-5552 **Kaplan** Bradley D '88
(513) 721-2820 **Kapor** David W '81
(513) 852-8208 **Kappers** Stephen A '79
(513) 241-3447 **Kapsal** Christopher P '01
(513) 852-8635 **Karam** Ernest H '47
Karam Gregory L '82
(513) 632-5310 **Karl** Kristie A '99
(513) 721-1200 **Karl** Robert D '92
(513) 929-0254 **Kasson** Henry C '69
(513) 243-7410 **Kastner** Richard G '82
(513) 243-4475 **Kates** Darryl M '91
(513) 665-3500 **Katrus** Ilona '03
(513) 651-6800 **Katsanis** James A '58
(513) 731-6601 **Katt** Angela G '99
(513) 721-5151 **Katz Greenberger & Norton,LLP**
(513) 721-5151 **Katz** Louis H '73
(513) 241-3447 **Katz** Raymond L '01
(513) 721-4532 **Katz** Reuven J '50
(513) 721-3111 **Katz** Richard L '74
(513) 721-4532 **Katz Teller Brant & Hild**
(513) 793-4400 **Katzman** Amy S '77
(513) 793-4400 **Katzman** Irwin '49
(513) 793-4400 **Katzman Logan Halper & Bennett**
(513) 621-4899 **Kaufman** Jacob M '93
(513) 487-2008 **Kavouras** Maria S '91
(513) 784-1532 **Kaye** Rebecca Kay '78
(513) 328-4100 **Kearney** Eric H '89
(513) 961-3331 **Kearney** Jan-Michele L '91
(513) 977-8200 **Kearns** Jerome H '66
(513) 561-0900 **Kearns** Michael A '94
(513) 241-7722 **Kearns** Michael S '93
(513) 397-1480 **Keating** Brian G '80
(513) 579-4118 **Keating** Michael K '80
(513) 579-6400 **Keating Muething & Klekamp PLL**
(513) 891-1530 **Keating Ritchie & Swick**
(513) 891-1530 **Keating** Thomas T '74
(513) 321-5357 **Keating** William J '50
(513) 579-6400 **Keating** William J Jr. '79
(513) 651-6800 **Keck** Linda M '96
(513) 369-5057 **Keefe** Daniel M '78
(513) 556-6932 **Keefe** Thomas W '75
(513) 651-9222 **Keegan** John M '92
(513) 752-3900 **Keegan** Walter C '88
(513) 946-3000 **Keeling** James M '97
(513) 361-8310 **Keeling** Julianne M '97
(513) 946-3443 **Keeney** Kathleen B '83
(513) 389-3700 **Keer** Gregory A '81
(513) 977-5579 **Kehres** Julie Schimpf '92
(513) 272-1200 **Keith** Robert F '97
(513) 381-2838 **Keller** Aimee L '93
(513) 385-9080 **Keller** Edward O '75
(513) 651-2121 **Keller** James F '92
(513) 579-1414 **Keller** James K '94
(513) 872-5166 **Keller** John T '75
(513) 522-2000 **Keller** Larry W '81
(513) 946-9000 **Kelley** Catherine M '88
(513) 946-3000 **Kelley** David J '89
(513) 321-4454 **Kelley** John J Jr. '50
(513) 381-0656 **Kelley** John J Jr. '60
(513) 651-2100 **Kelley** Rebecca '97
(513) 421-4225 **Kelley** Terrence E '02
(513) 381-9200 **Kellogg** Paul J '93
(513) 421-6630 **Kelly** Charles J '65
(513) 721-3330 **Kelly** James M '76
(513) 396-6339 **Kelly** Jeffrey B '78
(513) 733-5683 **Kelly-Schilling** Sandra '79
(513) 977-8200 **Kemphaus** Nicholas J '04
(513) 627-0081 **Kendall** Dara M '97
(513) 946-3877 **Kendrick** Helen M '79
(513) 579-2538 **Kennedy** James C '76
(513) 489-4157 **Kennedy** John T '79
(513) 489-4157 **Kennedy** Sherri M '79
(513) 721-1504 **Kenney** Jeffrey T '91
(513) 381-0656 **Kern** David G '00
(513) 721-4500 **Kern** David O '97
(513) 651-6800 **Kern** Melissa A '01
(513) 381-5700 **Kerr** David L '73
(513) 241-7111 **Kerr** Maggie '00
(513) 361-0200 **Kessler** Gregory S '96
(513) 853-4841 **Keyes** Royal M '72
(513) 684-3935 **Kieffer-Dunn** Aisa M '03
(513) 232-4449 **Kiel** Frederick O '66
(513) 421-4020 **Kilcoyne** John W '34
(513) 421-4020 **Kilcoyne** Thomas C '84
(513) 769-4040 **Kiley** Robin O '89
(513) 946-3000 **Kim** Donna L '99
(513) 651-6800 **Kindel** Frederick W '80
(513) 564-7054 **Kindel** Patricia A '80
(513) 852-2594 **Kinder** Kenneth H II '00
(513) 421-4020 **Kindt** Monica V '00
(513) 728-3700 **King** Brad A '79
(513) 231-2699 **King** Douglas E '73
(513) 948-5072 **King** Frederick G '91
(513) 579-6400 **King** Gail T '90
(513) 852-8635 **King** Kathleen C '75
(513) 352-3336 **King** Patricia M '93
(513) 352-6746 **King** Stephen M '85
(513) 793-2353 **King** Stephen R '96
(513) 559-5299 **King** William G '62
(513) 352-6783 **Kinnen** Jennifer L '02
(513) 347-7260 **Kinney** Ann J '01
(513) 721-4876 **Kinsley** Jennifer M '99
(513) 636-2725 **Kinsman** Anne Marie '04
(513) 651-6800 **Kipling** James M '72
(513) 381-3525 **Kircher Robinson & Welch**
(513) 381-3525 **Kircher** Thomas J '70
(513) 272-1100 **Kirk** Roger W '82
(513) 421-6630 **Kirkham** William N '75
(513) 665-3500 **Kirkpatrick** Jennifer L '96
(513) 352-6728 **Kirkwood** Thomas J '74
(513) 241-3630 **Kirschner** Leonard '50
(513) 721-1350 **Kirzner** Ryan D '00
(513) 721-4532 **Kisling** Stephen C '76
(513) 242-0600 **Kissel** Larry E '69
(513) 381-9200 **Kissinger** Curtis E '90
(513) 421-4020 **Kite** Matthew M '95
(513) 621-2120 **Klaine** Franklin A Jr. '67
(513) 721-4532 **Klee** Tara A '98
(513) 762-6200 **Klein** Joseph C '03
(513) 721-8358 **Kleinhaus** Ferdinand H Jr. '75
(513) 489-9220 **Kleinman** Marvin '53
(513) 579-6400 **Klekamp** Donald P '57
(513) 579-6400 **Klekamp** Jody T '92
(513) 481-9800 **Klett** Jerome R '85
(513) 333-4075 **Klineman** Susan B '01
(513) 665-9500 **Klingler** Robert A '85
(513) 923-2120 **Klocke** Dale W '73
(513) 352-6700 **Kloos** Brenda M '82
(513) 533-2996 **Klusmeier** Mark H '83
(513) 621-1767 **Knabe** Arthur T '58
(513) 621-1767 **Knabe** Bruce D '94
(513) 936-0001 **Knapp** William C '79
(513) 946-3800 **Kneflin** Mark C '00
(513) 534-1964 **Knight** M Michelle '93
(513) 241-3800 **Knox** Scott E '85
(513) 381-2838 **Kobasuk** Mark G '90
(513) 983-2630 **Koch** Elizabeth M '97
(513) 241-8844 **Koenig** Kenneth J '77
(513) 579-1500 **Koenig** Peter E '81
(513) 852-8200 **Kohlhepp** William G '69
(513) 631-6159 **Kohn** Michael G '78
(513) 621-6464 **Kohnen** Monica Donath '85
(513) 381-0656 **Kohnen & Patton LLP**
(513) 684-3711 **Kohnen** Ralph W '86
(513) 352-6545 **Kolesar** Andrew L '97
(513) 821-1000 **Kolodny** Victor M '62
(513) 852-6082 **Korbee** Harold G '65
(513) 651-4130 **Korbee** Thomas C '77
(513) 977-8200 **Korfhage** Melissa L '00
(513) 651-1010 **Kotian** Manisha B '93
Kotlarsic Liza Ann '89
(513) 621-3616 **Koustmer** Thomas R '81
(513) 977-8200 **Kozlowski** Holly D '96
(513) 455-7600 **Krafte** Lori E '98
(513) 629-2417 **Krall** David G '86
(513) 983-3063 **Krass** Marc S '81
(513) 515-5210 **Kraus** Christopher Eli '96
(513) 241-8137 **Kraus** Marvin H '54
(513) 621-5252 **Krause** Joseph M '04
(513) 636-8074 **Kravetsky** Lorie J '90
(513) 936-0800 **Kravetz** Scott H '93
(513) 626-4856 **Krebs** Jay A '95
(513) 579-6400 **Kreider** Gary P '64
(513) 579-6400 **Kreider** Kenneth P '89
(513) 621-6464 **Kreidler** Robert L '62
(937) 604-0488 **Kress** Timothy S '03
(513) 241-1234 **Krone** Bruce A '82
(513) 984-2640 **Kronke** Suzanne M '99
(513) 621-6464 **Kropp** John J '72
(513) 651-6800 **Krug** John C '89
(513) 241-4480 **Krumbein** Mark S '83
(513) 946-3124 **Krumpelbeck** Gerald W '77
(513) 241-3676 **Kruse** Daniel A '70
Kruse Daniel A Jr. '02
(513) 361-6955 **Kruse** John A Jr. '78
(513) 421-6630 **Kubicki** Margaret G '93
(513) 977-8200 **Kuhnell** Clayton L '01
(513) 985-1524 **Kulick** Susan G '92
(513) 946-3103 **Kunkel** Jerome A '88
(513) 977-8200 **Kunst** John M Jr. '66
(513) 977-3835 **Kuprionis** Mary D '95
(513) 946-3700 **Kurlansky** Amy L '98
(513) 421-2255 **Kurtz** Michael L '86
(513) 232-2600 **Kurtzer** Jamey L '94
(513) 977-8680 **Kwiatkowski** Andrew R '02
(513) 651-6800 **Kyte** Lawrence H Jr. '66
(513) 721-7500 **Laber** Christopher T '79
(513) 595-2470 **Labmeier** John F '75
(513) 369-0200 **LaDue** Edna G '89
(513) 381-2838 **Laing** Michael A '04
(513) 241-1950 **Laite** David A '90
(513) 684-3641 **Laite** Theresa L '93
(513) 621-6464 **LaJeunesse** Richard T '80
(513) 621-6464 **Lake** Matthew B '99
(513) 621-2100 **Lamb** Laurie A '03
(513) 421-2400 **Lambert** Jennifer L '02
(513) 721-1350 **Lameier** Richard D '68
(513) 421-2540 **Lampe** David J '00
(513) 922-5200 **Lampe** Gerald A '71
(513) 534-0681 **Lampe** Molly Kay '00
(513) 723-4000 **Lampley** Nathaniel Jr. '89
(513) 984-3030 **Land** Gregory E '84
(513) 455-7600 **Land** Suzanne P '90
(513) 421-8173 **Landen** Everett E '73
(513) 621-6464 **Landen** J Jeffrey '82
(513) 381-2838 **Landers** Dawn R '00
(513) 621-2888 **Landis** Richard M '69
(513) 946-3557 **Landon** Thomas W '97
(513) 651-6800 **Landrum** Lori A '93
(513) 762-4231 **Landrum** Ricky J '93
(513) 946-3000 **Landthorn** Tricia L '95
(513) 922-7700 **Lane** David C '82
(513) 721-1504 **Lane** Donald A '87
(513) 922-7700 **Lane Felix & Raisbeck Co,LPA**
(513) 634-3617 **Lane** Patrick D '80
(513) 983-5302 **Lane** Sandra T '93
(513) 621-0267 **Lang** Melissa M '04
(513) 577-7380 **Langdon** David R '96
(513) 421-6630 **Langenbahn** Jay R '76
(513) 651-6800 **Langenkamp** Max V '02
(513) 946-3415 **Langlois** Thomas W '91
(513) 528-9350 **Langner** Kevan K '75
(513) 381-0656 **Langston** Malinda L '97
(513) 263-3589 **Lanman** Diana S '01
(513) 921-1555 **Lanzillotta** Michael A '84
(513) 741-9738 **Lape** Lynn Ann '97
(513) 946-3000 **Lapp** Judith A '83
(513) 244-6953 **Larimer** John T '66
(513) 721-4555 **Larsen** Beatrice V '69
(513) 241-2540 **Larson** Robert K Jr. '89
(513) 922-8100 **LaScalea** Nicholas J '73
(513) 621-6464 **Lasher** Katherine M '99
(513) 556-0096 **Lassiter** Harvey C '97
(513) 421-8500 **Latter** Bruce E '75
(513) 651-6800 **Laub** Patricia D '83
(513) 721-3330 **Lauer** Richard T '94
(513) 621-9100 **Laufman & Gerhardstein**
(513) 621-9100 **Laufman** Paul M '96
(513) 621-9100 **Laufman** Robert F '61
(513) 632-5350 **Laurens** Jesse S '01
(513) 771-5455 **Lausche** Louis F '65
(513) 723-4000 **Lautzenhiser** Roger E Jr. '79
(513) 579-1414 **Laux** Colleen B '94
(513) 579-0080 **Lavender-Che** Joyce C '89
(513) 651-6800 **Lawrence** James K '65
(513) 651-4130 **Lawrence** Jennifer L '96
Lawrence Joy '85
(513) 651-4130 **Lawrence** Richard D '71
(513) 721-4466 **Lawson** Jerry H '68
(513) 345-5000 **Lawson** Kenneth L '89
(513) 381-2838 **Lawson** Margaret A '82
(513) 241-9400 **Lawson** Mark B '98
(513) 977-8200 **Lawson** Nancy A '75
(513) 241-7460 **Lazarus** David '82
(513) 721-7300 **Lazarus** Stephen S '89
(513) 381-2011 **Le** Peter L '03
(513) 241-3100 **Leach** Lori R '98
(513) 751-6860 **Leahr** David W '95
(513) 626-1597 **Leal** George H '03
(513) 621-3394 **Learmonth** Doloris F '78
(513) 721-5672 **Lee** Brian A '00
(513) 946-3000 **Lee** Ernest W Jr. '01
(513) 983-9529 **Lee** Tanya M '01
(513) 381-0656 **Leeper** Andrew R '85
(513) 721-7300 **Lefton** David H '87
(513) 721-1350 **Lefton** Jimmy J '94
Lefton Stacy B '02
(513) 241-3100 **Legel** Tracy M '03
(513) 579-0080 **Lehman** Linda L '92
(513) 852-6013 **Lehner** Lisa d '01
(513) 946-6400 **Leis** Simon L Jr. '66
(513) 931-8564 **Leist** Nelson R '81
(513) 665-9400 **Leksan** Thomas J '82
(513) 651-6800 **Lemasters** P R '72
(513) 665-3500 **Lemasters** Poul H '04
(513) 381-2838 **Lembke** Raymond W '84
(513) 522-8111 **Lemmink** Robert D '91
(513) 977-8200 **Lenhart** Amanda L '00
(513) 651-6800 **Lenhart** Elizabeth A '04
(513) 352-6675 **Lenox** Bryce A '98
(513) 946-3000 **Leon** Gus A '85
(513) 721-2180 **Leonard** Amy J '88
(513) 946-3489 **Leonard** Margaret M '88
(513) 321-2250 **Leonard** William L Jr. '50
(513) 771-0771 **Lerman** Murray '89
(513) 241-3100 **Lerner** Donald M '60
(513) 241-3100 **Lerner Sampson & Rothfuss**
(513) 361-1200 **Lerner** Stephen D '91
(513) 621-9660 **Lesser** Richard F '82
(513) 946-3000 **Leurck** Brian F '97
(513) 771-6768 **LeVay** Helen F '85
(513) 618-7800 **Levin** Debbe A '79
(513) 241-6748 **Levine** Arnold S '67
(513) 369-3715 **Levine** David S '78
(513) 621-2666 **Levison** Jill S '01
(513) 241-7111 **Levy** Barry D '76
(513) 241-2540 **Levy** Barry R '89
(513) 985-2500 **Levy** Howard S '89
(513) 621-2120 **Levy** John M '04
(513) 946-9200 **Levy** Judith Ann '89
(513) 684-3954 **Lewin** Gail S '80
(513) 977-8200 **Lewis** Colleen P '89
(513) 531-0909 **Lewis** Cornelius "Carl" '91
(513) 723-4000 **Lewis** Donald B '77
(513) 665-9222 **Lewis** Gary R '78
(513) 870-2118 **Lewis** George G '79
(513) 232-6959 **Lewis** Jeffrey Roy '79
(513) 412-4842 **Lewis** Kevin C '95
(513) 977-8200 **Lewis** Kim Martin '89
(513) 651-4130 **Lewis** Robert D Jr. '97
(513) 977-8200 **Lewis** Sarah V '03
(513) 241-3100 **Li** YanFang M '01
(513) 579-4203 **Liddy** J Patrick '76
(513) 721-5700 **Lieberman** Bernard '52
(513) 241-3100 **Lieberman** Jon J '92
(513) 674-1111 **Lieberman Lipez & Berman**
(513) 674-1111 **Lieberman** Sidney C '68
(513) 721-1904 **Liebman** Robert L '73
(513) 241-3100 **Liepold** Christina M '98
(513) 530-9595 **Liggett** Dennis A '64
(513) 534-3719 **Lind** Harry S '94
(513) 381-2838 **Lindberg** Charles D '54
(513) 361-8033 **Lindeman-Lorenz** Laura '91
(513) 721-1129 **Lindgren** Lawrence F '95
(513) 421-6630 **Lindhorst & Dreidame Co,LPA**
(513) 489-1040 **Lineback** Charles S '78
(513) 381-8430 **Linn** Cliff G '85
(513) 721-4450 **Linneman** Jerome Robert '01
(513) 607-4002 **Linnenberg** John W '69

(513) 674-1111 **Lipez** Ronald A '70
(513) 621-6464 **Lippert** Amy E '01
(513) 563-6161 **Lippert** Gary M '70
(513) 241-1950 **Lippert** James W '69
(513) 241-1950 **Lippert** Richard H '65
(513) 381-2838 **Lips** J Alan '68
(513) 421-6630 **Liss** William Jay '97
(513) 871-8900 **Little Meyers Garretson & Associates**
(513) 946-3000 **Littner** Jay G '86
(513) 357-9776 **Litts** Norman W Jr. '91
Litwin Amy L '92
(513) 721-8880 **Litz** Stanley J '77
(513) 871-8812 **Litzinger** Jerrold J '77
(513) 961-6200 **Lively** Michael E '96
(513) 569-9999 **Lockemeyer** David S '92
(513) 556-0093 **Lockwood** Bert B Jr. '81
(513) 853-2850 **Lockwood** Thomas M '92
(513) 579-1707 **Loeb Vollman & Friedmann**
(513) 381-2838 **Loftus** Matthew C '02
(513) 793-4400 **Logan** Philip A '72
(513) 333-0050 **Long** Edward III '95
(513) 946-3000 **Longano** Bernadette M '97
(513) 946-3000 **Longano** Thomas P '74
(513) 455-7600 **Longenecker** Mark H Jr. '79
(513) 381-9200 **Longtin** Lynne M '99
(513) 853-5906 **Looney** Kimberly G '99
(513) 852-5600 **Lopez Hodes Restaino Milman & Skikos**
(513) 585-7155 **Lopez** Mary J '01
(513) 634-2084 **Lorentz** Bryn M Taylor '03
(513) 977-8200 **Lorentz** Joshua A '01
(513) 721-1975 **Loring** Elizabeth S '03
(513) 985-0110 **Loudermilk** Timothy D '91
(513) 345-5000 **Love** Ayanna '01
(513) 534-4529 **Love** David C '04
(513) 621-3498 **Love** Ellsworth '74
(513) 870-2288 **Love** Lisa A '91
(513) 243-8993 **Lowe** Cynthia Kay '00
(513) 793-7737 **Lowery** Robert R '63
(513) 421-2255 **Lowry** John P '86
(513) 381-2838 **Lowry** Patricia O '85
(513) 977-8200 **Lucas** Robert A '01
(513) 891-2084 **Lucas** Ronna S '94
(513) 621-6674 **Ludwig** James D '95
(513) 984-4554 **Ludwig** Mina K '93
(513) 961-6644 **Luebbers** Jody M '91
(513) 621-3394 **Luebbers** Thomas A '66
(513) 784-1280 **Lugbill** Ann '80
(513) 967-1857 **Luke** Gregory C '90
(513) 352-3250 **Luken** Charles J '76
(513) 241-2324 **Luken** Clement H Jr. '86
(513) 977-8200 **Luken** John D '81
(513) 984-2640 **Luken** Joseph M '88
(513) 684-3686 **Luken** Kevin P '98
(513) 977-8380 **Luken** Susan M '02
(513) 352-3346 **Luken** Thomas A '50
(513) 591-2000 **Lukey** Paul E '75
(513) 621-2120 **Lundrigan** Nicole M '02
(513) 721-5525 **Lundrigan** William K '92
(513) 241-2324 **Lunn** Gregory J '79
(513) 674-4827 **Luther** Dana R '04
(513) 321-7728 **Luttenegger** Jerry F '71
(513) 771-2444 **Lutz Cornetet Meyer & Rush Co,LPA**
(513) 651-6800 **Lutz** Douglas L '95
(513) 771-2444 **Lutz** James G '60
(513) 621-3440 **Lutz** Mark E '81
(513) 977-8200 **Lydon** Deborah R '81
(513) 241-3100 **Lykins** Susana E '02
(513) 241-2324 **Lyman** Beverly A '96
(513) 946-3163 **Lynch** Teresa P '91
(513) 852-5600 **Lyon** Joseph M '03
(513) 421-6630 **Lyon** Michael F '75
(513) 621-6673 **Lyons & Fries Co,LPA**
(513) 621-6673 **Lyons** James L '50
(513) 621-6673 **Lyons** James W '75
(513) 621-2120 **Maag** Marilyn J '86
(513) 321-2334 **MacConnell** Stephen T '72
(513) 665-3500 **MacDonald** Mark A '80
(513) 621-2044 **Macey & Chern**
(513) 946-3000 **Machol** Melynda J '88
(513) 931-1086 **Mack** Thomas A '79
MacKay Walter S '58
(513) 751-3600 **MacLeid** Matthew T '63
(513) 852-3497 **MacQueeney** Vincent P '89
(513) 621-8700 **Madden** Stephan D '80
(513) 241-3100 **Maddix** Anita L '02
(513) 579-0080 **Magas** Steven M '82
(513) 621-9660 **Magee** James V Jr. '74
Magee Linda L '73
(513) 579-2861 **Magee** Mark E '75
(513) 241-7111 **Magenheim** Alissa J '04
(513) 977-8306 **Maggio** Margaret M '02
(513) 621-8280 **Magner** George E Jr. '85
(513) 721-0200 **Magnus** Michele L '03
(513) 731-2889 **Magnus** Richard A '82
(513) 721-6500 **Mahin** John E '77
(513) 784-7127 **Mahon** Scott J '89
(513) 361-1200 **Mahon** Stephen C '93
(513) 241-7711 **Mahoney** Dennis C '90
(513) 762-6200 **Maichl** Linda E '89
(513) 352-6747 **Maiman** Earle J '81
(513) 631-8292 **Main** David K '74
(513) 562-2971 **Maio** Michael L '83
(513) 721-5555 **Maislin** Blake R '97
(513) 946-3500 **Majba** Michael P '03
(513) 621-2349 **Major** Ronald D '74
(513) 639-2832 **Makos** Susan S '79
(513) 579-6400 **Malas** Mary Ellen '91
(513) 321-5816 **Malblanc** Craig J '96
(513) 984-6100 **Male** Gregory R '85
(513) 721-7500 **Maley** George S '81
(513) 977-8200 **Mallory** Donald W '99
(513) 352-4712 **Mallory** Dwane K '00
(513) 946-5112 **Mallory** William L Jr. '86
(513) 622-5419 **Malloy** Matthew M '95
(513) 852-6043 **Malloy** Robert P '74
(513) 651-6800 **Malof** Kevin K '00
(513) 241-9400 **Malone** Kathleen A '87
(513) 381-2838 **Mancino** David A '94
Mandell-Brown Marianne '88
(513) 579-1414 **Manes** Dennis L '73
(513) 977-4214 **Manes** Marlene P '70
(513) 618-7800 **Mangan** Sean K '04
(513) 419-6933 **Mangan** Timothy S '98
(513) 469-0470 **Mangels** Alfred J '64
(513) 721-5525 **Manley Burke**
(513) 721-5525 **Manley** Robert E '60
(513) 621-2888 **Mann** David S '68
(513) 621-2888 **Mann** Michael T '01
(513) 923-4647 **Mansoor** Raeshon M '04
(513) 977-8200 **Manzler** Michael A '92
(513) 381-4888 **Mapother & Mapother, PSC**
(513) 762-7674 **Mara** Timothy G '78
(513) 661-7790 **Maraan** Benjamin M II '91
(513) 629-2149 **Marchese** Michael III '90
(513) 684-9393 **Marinakis** George S '91
(513) 684-9393 **Marinakis** Marina '91
(513) 961-6200 **Markesbery** Glenn A '88
(513) 853-5642 **Markesbery** Maria A '86
(513) 961-6200 **Markesbery & Richardson Co,LPA**
(513) 977-4774 **Markovits** Wilbert B '83
(513) 421-4400 **Marks** Edward G '67
(513) 361-1200 **Marks** Jeffrey A '81
(513) 287-6900 **Marlow** James R '67
(513) 76-4441 **Marmer** Lynn '86
(513) 579-1500 **Marnell** Francis X '82
(513) 762-6200 **Marrero** Michael A '77
(513) 621-5428 **Marshall** Courtland E '49
(513) 241-4722 **Marshall** Pamela '04
(513) 421-6464 **Marsick** Philip J Jr. '72
(513) 333-0990 **Martin & Bailey**
(513) 984-3940 **Martin** Carol Ann '82
(513) 281-1544 **Martin** Gary P '96
(513) 558-0057 **Martin** Joyce M '03
(513) 333-0990 **Martin** Robert C '53
(513) 621-2666 **Martin** S Scott '99
(513) 929-3400 **Martin** Ted T '82
(513) 421-6630 **Martin** Thomas E '79
(513) 352-6764 **Martin** William L Jr. '71
(513) 563-4700 **Martin** William P II '95
(513) 852-3497 **Martinez** Jose A '93
(513) 595-2200 **Martini** Elizabeth F '84
(513) 241-6600 **Martini** James C '85
(513) 421-2400 **Martins** Paul B '79
(513) 977-8200 **Marx** James A '97
(513) 489-0829 **Mason** Jeremy R '00
(513) 489-0829 **Mason** Jonathan A '79
(513) 984-4172 **Mason** Michael G '68
(513) 489-0829 **Mason** Rachel J '03
(513) 489-0829 **Mason Schilling & Mason Co,LPA**
(513) 528-2850 **Massa** William G '92
(513) 528-1414 **Masters** Robert L '71
(513) 421-6464 **Mastruserio** Dominic J '73
(513) 421-1313 **Mastruserio** Karen L '86
(513) 381-5552 **Masuda Funai Eifert & Mitchell,Ltd**
(513) 351-1525 **Mathews** Stanley A '68
(513) 351-1525 **Mathews** Stanley M '99
(513) 621-4849 **Mathews** William S II '77
(513) 671-6333 **Matre** James A '75
(513) 671-6333 **Matre** Kerrie K '98
(513) 634-7419 **Mattheis** David K '01
(513) 626-0673 **Matthews** Armina E '98
(513) 579-6400 **Matthews** James R '90
(513) 243-8406 **Matthews** Kevin G '95
(513) 579-6400 **Matthews** Timothy B '82
(513) 632-8618 **Mattingly** Elizabeth B '75
(513) 977-8200 **Mattingly** Paul R '75
(513) 651-6800 **Mauer** Kimberly K '87
(513) 651-6800 **Mauer** Vincent E '87
(513) 583-4200 **Maundrell** Michael E '74
(859) 781-6620 **Maxey** Jeannette E '02
(513) 579-6400 **Maxwell** Robert W II '68
(513) 333-0990 **May** Douglas J '89
(513) 588-3050 **May** Jeffrey M '90
(513) 381-2838 **Mayer** James J '69
(513) 381-0656 **Mayer** Kimberly A '96
(513) 721-1200 **Mazzei** Stephen S '80
(513) 352-3332 **McAdams** Ernest F Jr. '79
(513) 946-3822 **McBeth** Steven J '94
(513) 634-1402 **McBride** James F '92
(513) 931-2100 **McBride** Maria L '88
(513) 931-2100 **McBride** Michael L '87
(513) 977-8200 **McBroom** Christine L '81
(513) 772-3962 **McCabe** Penelope '79
(513) 651-5900 **McCafferty** Michael P '04
(513) 721-5525 **McCarthy** Daniel J '04
(513) 721-4532 **McCarthy** James F III '77
(937) 367-8697 **McCarthy** Steven D '87
(513) 381-9200 **McCartney** Paul W '88
(513) 421-4646 **McCaslin Imbus & McCaslin,LPA**
(513) 369-3070 **McClain** Elizabeth N '84
(513) 745-0400 **McCloskey** Hugh P Jr. '00
(513) 621-8280 **McClure** John D '72
(513) 421-6630 **McCluskey** Laurie A '02
(513) 421-2540 **McCord** Charles B III '97
(513) 241-4722 **McCord** Elizabeth A '82
(513) 487-2047 **McCormick** Charles D Jr. '83
McCort Melanie J '97
(513) 381-2838 **McCoy** John J '77
(513) 556-3483 **McCrate** Mitchell D '90
(513) 752-2611 **McCue** Richard G '68
(513) 241-3685 **McCullough** C. J '98
(513) 629-2407 **McCune** Francis P '83
(513) 684-0808 **McDaniel** James F '78
(513) 744-8944 **McDaniel** John Lee Jr. '92
(513) 936-5663 **McDaniel** Sarah L '95
(513) 241-2225 **McDaniel** Vernon W '41
(513) 977-8200 **McDonald** Angelina N '04
McDonald Ryan P '02
(513) 352-3334 **McDonnell** Ursula M '95
(513) 946-6464 **McDonough** Amy S '92
(513) 421-4020 **McDonough** Kevin C '89
(513) 794-6428 **McDonough** Therese S '88
(513) 634-0102 **McDow-Dunham** Kelly L '97
(513) 977-8200 **McDowell** Christopher R '00
(513) 977-8200 **McDowell** John E '52
(513) 984-1811 **McElwee** John L '77
(513) 369-0360 **McEvilley** Chris '85
(513) 369-0360 **McEvilley** Robert Michael '74
(513) 791-2122 **McFall** Tanner B '04
(513) 241-6748 **McFarland** Andrew D '00
McGary Ryan C '01
(513) 651-6800 **McGavran** Frederick J '72
(513) 948-1080 **McGehee** John H '80
(513) 287-2781 **McGehee** Julie Ann '92
(513) 287-8768 **McGhghy** Julie A '03
(513) 721-1975 **McGinnis** Charles T III '78
(513) 977-8200 **McGrath** Jennifer L '02
(513) 852-6066 **McGrath** V Brandon '00
(513) 651-6800 **McGraw** Bridget Gannon '03
(513) 579-6400 **McGraw** James J Jr. '74
(513) 651-6800 **McGuire** Joel F '01
(513) 922-3200 **McHenry** Martin '83
(513) 977-8200 **McHenry** Powell '51
(513) 852-3253 **McIlwain** Carol N '77
(513) 721-7906 **McIlwain** Harry H Jr. '76
(513) 929-4040 **McIntosh** Anthony B '96
(513) 929-4040 **McIntosh** Bruce B '60
(513) 762-4425 **McIntosh** Jill V '97
(513) 929-4040 **McIntosh** Michael T '93
(513) 762-6200 **McIntosh** Thomas G '03
(513) 381-2838 **McInturf** Lora N '03
(513) 579-6400 **McIntyre** M Scott '02
(513) 651-6800 **McKay** Bernard L '94
(513) 621-1767 **McKay** Timothy E '88
(800) 456-2375 **McKellar** Amy C '99
(513) 241-9400 **McKenna** Melissa A '03
(513) 946-3000 **McKenna** Timothy J '02
(513) 721-0200 **McKinney** Daniel H III '59
(513) 721-0200 **McKinney & Namei Co,LPA**
(513) 381-9200 **McLaughlin** John F '91
(513) 651-6800 **McLaughlin** Karen M '81
(513) 752-2111 **McLaughlin** Robert C '97
(513) 381-9200 **McLean** James E Jr. '90
(513) 870-2000 **McMackin** Thomas K '80
(513) 533-9898 **McMahon** Robert A '95
(513) 241-3685 **McManus** Barbara J '82
(513) 946-9460 **McManus** John F '80
(513) 721-1311 **McMillan** Shelby M '97
(513) 946-9200 **McMullen** Martin E '67
(513) 651-6800 **McMurray** Kevin N '89
(513) 977-8200 **McNabb** Suzanne C '00
(513) 381-0656 **McNair** Brian E '86
(513) 381-6600 **McNally** John W Jr. '74
(513) 752-5466 **McNally** Robert A '66
(513) 352-3334 **McNeil** Julia Rita '89
(513) 621-8210 **McNeil** Michael D '91
(513) 421-6630 **McPeek** Bradley D '99
(513) 651-6800 **McPeek** Monica Hart '99
(513) 651-6800 **McPherson** David J '86
(513) 232-0903 **McQuade** Shannon L '96
(513) 852-6087 **McSherry** Jeffrey P '91
(513) 621-8700 **McTigue** Edward J '79
(513) 281-2339 **Meadows** Mary T '92
(513) 943-9278 **Meadows** Perry '01
(513) 381-9200 **Meagher** James K '60
(513) 721-3114 **Mebs** Frederick W '52
(513) 353-1773 **Mechley** Albert Jr. '65
(513) 475-9883 **Mechley** Braden A '61
(513) 481-9800 **Mecklenborg** Robert P '78
(513) 721-8808 **Meckstroth** James J '94
(513) 721-8808 **Meckstroth** John R Jr. '81
(513) 891-3270 **Medven** Ann-Dana '99
(513) 621-5252 **Meek** Patricia S '98
(513) 639-7000 **Meeks** Lisa T '93
(513) 871-7562 **Mehas** Andrew G '41
(513) 684-3678 **Mehas** Mark G '84
(513) 467-9903 **Meier** Aimee D '97
(513) 467-9903 **Meier** Robert C '97
(513) 762-8022 **Meisenhelder** Jamie L '00
(513) 579-6400 **Meisenhelder** John F '91
(513) 921-5297 **Meiser** Stephen M '86
(513) 381-2838 **Meister** Julia B '95
(513) 345-4700 **Meizlish** Bruce H '77
(513) 579-6400 **Mellen** Joseph P '77
(513) 621-2666 **Mellott** John Thomas '89
(513) 621-2120 **Melville** Charles H '62
(513) 946-9000 **Melvin** William H '83
(513) 352-6546 **Mendelsohn** Donald S '75
(513) 793-0800 **Mendelsohn** Robert N '93
(513) 629-1471 **Menke** David J '81
(513) 852-6033 **Menninger** Henry E Jr. '77
(513) 563-3271 **Mentrup** Clifford C '01
(513) 326-4675 **Meranus** David '91
(513) 621-3394 **Merchant** John C '92
(513) 977-8200 **Merchant** Toby D '04
(513) 258-7675 **Mercurio** Michael T '00
(513) 564-7362 **Merling** Joseph C '77
(513) 221-8800 **Mesh** Gene I '64
(513) 983-1552 **Mess** Thomas J '79
(513) 381-2838 **Messer** Earl K '91
(513) 381-4700 **Metz** Jerome J Jr. '80
(513) 241-8844 **Metz** John H '77
(513) 870-2207 **Meyer** Barry A '76
(513) 721-4450 **Meyer** Charles M '78
(513) 579-6400 **Meyer** David A '96
(513) 357-9764 **Meyer** Joseph W '93
(513) 771-2444 **Meyer** Karen P '92
(513) 381-0656 **Meyer** Keith D '80
(513) 624-7300 **Meyer** Marsha Rea '96
(513) 521-2527 **Meyer** Richard E '66
(513) 241-3685 **Meyer** Ronald A '69
Meyer Scott A '89
(513) 272-1940 **Meyer** Stanley P '67
(513) 561-4065 **Meyer** William F '70
(513) 723-4000 **Meyers** Eliot N '94
(513) 871-8900 **Meyers** Karen D '78
(513) 946-9200 **Meyers** Paul W '78
(513) 579-1500 **Meyers** Robert J '75
(513) 221-7831 **Meyn** Malcolm A Jr. '89
(513) 474-3700 **Mezher** Kathleen D '84
(513) 723-1600 **Mezibov & Jenkins**
(513) 723-1600 **Mezibov** Marc D '74
(513) 381-2838 **Miano** Tamara A '01
(513) 579-6400 **Michel** Lisa Wintersheimer '88
(513) 922-3200 **Michel** Timothy A '88
(513) 977-8200 **Middelhoff** Mary-Jo '91
(513) 784-0182 **Might** Daniel P '96
(513) 793-5297 **Mikita** William H '83
(513) 852-8946 **Milazzo** Charles C '82
(513) 852-8560 **Miller** Allen R '72
(513) 621-2666 **Miller** Ann B '84
(513) 721-1504 **Miller** Arthur D '73
(513) 579-8900 **Miller** Charles M '89
(513) 977-8200 **Miller** G Franklin '63
(513) 721-1504 **Miller** Geoffrey M '02
(513) 554-1110 **Miller** Kristi A '99
(513) 945-5413 **Miller** Lynne M '91
(513) 977-8200 **Miller** Martin J '91
(513) 241-3430 **Miller** Marvin A '66
(513) 621-6464 **Miller** Michael R '83
(513) 241-3430 **Miller** Orville J '70
(513) 382-2059 **Miller** Peter J '88
(513) 891-7087 **Miller** Richard D '81
(513) 983-1100 **Miller** Robert J '77
(513) 361-0250 **Miller** Sarah J '75
(513) 723-4000 **Miller** Steven R '94
(513) 634-6332 **Miller** Steven W '84
(513) 381-2838 **Miller** W Timothy '92
(513) 621-3440 **Mills** James A '80
(513) 732-9999 **Mills** Tina R '99
(513) 241-9400 **Minch** Christina L '03
Miner Deborah Ann '82
Minnillo Mary T '95
(513) 752-3900 **Minnillo** Paul J '95
(513) 595-8800 **Minutolo** James P '83
(513) 421-4020 **Mire** Terrence A '73
(513) 421-4855 **Mire** William N '49
(513) 574-0606 **Mitchell** Charles E '78
(513) 243-9926 **Mitchell** Darryl '93
(513) 977-8200 **Mitchell** Jennifer O '98
(513) 381-2838 **Mitchell** Patrick J '86
(513) 381-9200 **Mitchell** Ralph F '51
(513) 721-5525 **Mitchell** Robert H '86
(513) 677-0999 **Mitchell** William J '97
(513) 381-2838 **Mitroussia** Antonia '91
(513) 624-9276 **Mittendorf** Richard K '50
(513) 563-6161 **Mock** Russell J '96
(513) 579-6400 **Moeddel** Michael J '02
(513) 721-5525 **Moeller** George F '85
(513) 487-5610 **Mohan** Patrick M '99
(513) 241-0400 **Mohar** Gregory '82
(513) 721-3330 **Mohler** Jarrod M '00
(513) 381-2838 **Molinsky** George D '94
(513) 721-5555 **Mollaun** Terrance T '00
(513) 793-5297 **Monnie & O'Connor Co,LPA**
(513) 793-5297 **Monnie** Terrance R '74
(513) 563-3031 **Monroe** Dain T '92
Montfort Donald G '51
(513) 345-3832 **Montgomery** David '79
(513) 579-6400 **Montgomery** David K '88
(513) 241-4722 **Montgomery** James J '76
(513) 574-1999 **Montgomery** Kenneth A Jr. '99
(513) 721-1975 **Montgomery** Leanne R '01
(513) 574-8900 **Montgomery** Matthew A '98
(513) 651-6800 **Montgomery** Mekesha H '01
(513) 241-4722 **Montgomery Rennie & Jonson,LPA**
(513) 762-6200 **Mooney** Donald J Jr. '75
(513) 651-6800 **Mooney** Martin E '78
(513) 977-4213 **Mooney** Michael J '72
(513) 583-4200 **Moore** Christopher L '93
(513) 752-2111 **Moore** Daniel '03
(513) 752-2111 **Moore** Donald C Jr. '80
(513) 333-0050 **Moore** Gregory A '93
(513) 421-6630 **Moore** James M '72
(513) 626-2238 **Moore** Jeffrey R '00
(513) 924-0571 **Moore** Keith D '93
(513) 241-6748 **Moore** Kellye N '03
(513) 345-4160 **Moore** Rhonda Y '87
(513) 723-4000 **Moore** Richard L '93
(513) 651-6800 **Moore** Rodger W '01
(513) 381-0656 **Moore** Terry E '86
(513) 852-8200 **Moran** Paul R '59
(513) 241-4110 **Moran** William J Jr. '92
(513) 629-1479 **Morand** Robert F '75
(513) 983-0004 **Mordan** William R '97
(513) 421-7500 **Mordino** Joseph T '95
(513) 922-3200 **Morehart** Douglas M '87
(513) 651-6800 **Moreno** Victor C '95
(513) 621-3418 **Morgan** Amy T '99
(513) 721-7500 **Morgan** Ann M '80
(513) 651-4400 **Morgan** Frederick M Jr. '83
(513) 651-6800 **Morgan** Katherine C '97
(513) 621-3418 **Morgan** Michael D '99
(513) 241-9400 **Morgan** Noel M '96
(513) 721-1040 **Morgeson** Junior A '69
(513) 721-1040 **Morgeson** Philip J '00
(513) 421-9500 **Moriarty** Kate E '96
(513) 744-7432 **Morris** Gwen M '98
(513) 621-1505 **Morrisroe** Donald P '79
(513) 946-3000 **Morthorst** Michael E '77
(513) 983-2558 **Morton** William S '74
(513) 929-3400 **Morwood** Robert F '04
(513) 665-3500 **Mosbaugh** Jason A '04
(513) 771-2444 **Moschandreas** John '03
(513) 977-8200 **Moser** Emerson C '02
(513) 721-3111 **Moskowitz** James H '94
(513) 721-3111 **Moskowitz** Joel S '65
(513) 721-3111 **Moskowitz** Michael A '89
(513) 721-3111 **Moskowitz & Moskowitz**
(513) 381-2838 **Mottley** J Donald '91
(513) 983-3859 **Moyer** David M '80
(513) 618-7800 **Moyers** Michael K '98
(513) 772-3962 **Muehleisen** Robert A Jr. '93
(513) 621-3636 **Mueller** John J '79
(513) 381-2838 **Mueller** John M '97
(513) 579-6400 **Muething** Brian P '03
(513) 579-6400 **Muething** John L '48
(513) 333-5515 **Muething** Mark F '84
(513) 579-6400 **Muething** Paul V '77
(513) 471-4700 **Muething** Thaddeus A '80
(513) 241-9400 **Mulcahy** Elizabeth A '02
(513) 852-8200 **Mullee** Michelle A '85
(513) 946-3000 **Mullen** Judith A '83
(513) 684-6023 **Mullen** M Holly '01
(513) 232-4200 **Mullenix** Charles D '73
(513) 621-6674 **Muller** Bradley K '78
(513) 621-8210 **Mullin** Sybil B '95
(513) 621-5631 **Mullins** Jeffrey S '87
(513) 721-5672 **Mulvaney** Christopher J '97
(513) 721-0001 **Mulvey** John J '94
(513) 621-6674 **Mulvey & Muller LLC**
(513) 621-6674 **Mulvey** William J Jr. '75
(513) 983-1042 **Muncy** Jason P '00

(513) 489-4988 **Mundy** Ralph B '94
(513) 946-9000 **Murdock** Constance C '92
(513) 345-8291 **Murdock Goldenberg Schneider & Groh**
(513) 241-4042 **Murdock** Jack A '57
(513) 345-8291 **Murdock** John C '94
(513) 345-8291 **Murdock** Norman A '68
(513) 946-5138 **Murphy** Carolyn S '87
(513) 281-0346 **Murphy** John J '76
(513) 977-5576 **Murphy** Laura Irving '86
Murphy Ross A '90
(513) 634-4268 **Murphy** Stephen T '02
(513) 723-7314 **Murphy** Thomas J '98
(513) 946-9200 **Murphy** William Leo '82
(513) 721-4450 **Murray** Elizabeth R '90
(513) 946-3427 **Murray** Katherine K '93
(513) 241-2200 **Murray** Michael C '89
(513) 381-2011 **Musillo** Christopher T '98
(513) 242-1541 **Muth** Alison H '91
(513) 455-7600 **Muth** Carl C '80
(513) 388-2914 **Muto** Anthony J '78
(513) 721-5808 **Muzzo** Albert L '70
(513) 977-8200 **Muzzo** Christopher L '97
(513) 946-5102 **Myers** Beth A '82
(513) 977-8200 **Myers** David J '04
(513) 891-9544 **Myers** James Y '95
(513) 721-1975 **Myers** Kelly M '95
(513) 621-2100 **Myers** Kristen M '04
(513) 792-0792 **Myers** Marcia J '85
(513) 723-2205 **Myers** Thomas R '88
(513) 621-1652 **Naegel** Mark R '74
(513) 361-0250 **Nagel** Ellen L '87
(513) 579-6400 **Nageleisen** Christy M '03
(513) 556-0113 **Nagy** Donna M '00
(513) 381-2838 **Nakao** Toshio '92
(513) 381-2838 **Nalbandian** John B '00
(513) 871-8755 **Nalepka** Paul M '88
(513) 621-6556 **Namanworth** Elias '76
(513) 721-0200 **Namei** Firooz T '82
(513) 721-1975 **Napier** Mark W '78
(513) 621-4556 **Napolitano** Gregory A '97
(513) 636-0800 **Nauman** Stephen R '93
(513) 651-6800 **Naylor** Beth S '89
(513) 345-8291 **Naylor** Todd B '97
(513) 272-0336 **Neagle** Carolyn C '92
(513) 381-2011 **Neal** Sherry L '94
(513) 381-2838 **Nechemias** Stephen M '69
(513) 361-8013 **Neff** Roger Lee IV '01
(513) 556-3483 **Neiger** Jan A '90
(513) 579-1500 **Neiheisel** Michael E '69
(513) 791-8600 **Neiswonger** Garret S '98
(513) 621-1771 **Nelson** Jason M '99
(513) 421-4020 **Nelson** Richard D '74
(513) 946-3149 **Nelson** Ryan L '97
(513) 961-3111 **Nelson** Steven A '77
(513) 352-3327 **Nestor** Terrance A '95
(513) 621-2120 **Neuman** Larry A '70
(513) 352-6772 **Neumark** Michael H '70
(513) 651-6800 **Neusch** Raymond D '78
(513) 362-8248 **Newbauer** Frank L '88
(513) 541-0100 **Newberry** Jeffrey S '82
(513) 421-4225 **Newberry** Peter C '88
(513) 721-1311 **Newman** Danny M Jr. '02
(513) 731-9888 **Newman** James O '66
(513) 241-7111 **Newman** Mark L '89
(513) 977-8200 **Newman** Michael J '89
(513) 455-7600 **Newman** Peter K '80
(513) 639-7000 **Newman** Robert B '73
(513) 983-1100 **Newton** Robert A '02
(513) 983-4517 **Ney** Carol J '87
(513) 381-9200 **Ney** Peter L '87
(513) 946-3700 **Nicholas** James A '80
(513) 983-3817 **Nichols** Vanessa M '98
(513) 564-7670 **Nicholson** Laurie J '92
(513) 821-0029 **Nidich** Paul A '74
(513) 241-2226 **Nieberding** James L '87
(513) 241-2226 **Nieberding** James R '63
(513) 352-6700 **Nieberding** Michael J '94
(513) 421-5999 **Niehaus** Barron M '76
(513) 251-4900 **Niehaus** Francis J '78
(513) 421-5999 **Niehaus** Maurice A '41
(513) 852-6062 **Niehaus** Roccina S '81
(513) 621-3394 **Niehoff** Harry C '73
(513) 684-3225 **Niekamp** Thomas J '87
(513) 665-4888 **Nielsen** Jessica A '04
(513) 662-1818 **Nieman** Joseph D '57
(513) 629-1472 **Niemeyer** Jonathan D '98
(513) 569-6062 **Nienaber** Donna S '82
(513) 558-5653 **Nienaber** Douglas J '02
(513) 772-7245 **Nippert** Alfred K Jr. '76
(513) 772-7245 **Nippert & Nippert**
(513) 455-7600 **Nishizu** Mikio '00
(513) 665-3500 **Nobbe** Michelle L '01
(513) 381-7333 **Noe** Charles E '77
(513) 579-6400 **Noel** W Keith '88
(513) 243-1457 **Nogueira** Mark W '98
(513) 579-0080 **Nolan** James P II '91
(513) 272-3000 **Nolan** John J '56
(513) 421-6630 **Nolan** Joshua J '04
Nolan Timothy P '84
(513) 948-2782 **Nolen** Kay C '82
(513) 585-6453 **Nordlund** Christa F '91
(513) 723-4000 **Norman** Mark A '83
(513) 665-4040 **Norris** Daniel W '87
(513) 946-9140 **Norton** Barbara L '78
(513) 721-3330 **Norton** Esther M '00
(513) 721-5151 **Norton** Richard L '64
(513) 381-8213 **Norwine** John C Jr. '76
(513) 381-2838 **Noser** Patrick E '02
(513) 241-6748 **Nuckols** Gerald L '79
(513) 241-3100 **Nunley** Kerri L '01
(513) 651-6800 **Nunn** Sandra L '95
(513) 721-3330 **Nurre** Lawrence R '50
(513) 621-6674 **Nye** Darrin E '02
(513) 684-3711 **Nyktas** Anthony W '71
(513) 684-3711 **Oakley** Timothy D '88
(513) 946-3872 **Oakley-Everson** Karen '00
(513) 977-8200 **Oberhaus** Geoffrey L '98
(513) 381-2838 **Oberklein** Daniel F '00
(513) 651-6800 **Oberschmidt** E Richard '78
O'Brien Thomas P Jr. '74
(513) 891-1066 **O'Brien** William F '80
(513) 977-8200 **O'Connell** Brian J '92
(513) 579-1500 **O'Connell** Edward M Jr. '73
(513) 621-6464 **O'Connell** Gerald F Jr. '84
(513) 421-6630 **O'Connell** James L '58
(513) 241-7111 **O'Connor Acciani & Levy Co, LPA**
(513) 621-2000 **O'Connor** Kathleen A '03
(513) 793-5297 **O'Connor** Michael J '89
(513) 241-7111 **O'Connor** Michael P '79
O'Connor Michael R '78
(513) 977-8200 **Odmark** Gwendolyn M '00
(513) 487-5982 **O'Donnell** Hugh C '77
(513) 241-0391 **O'Dowd** Jerome L '70
(513) 352-6631 **Oestreicher** Michael R '78
(513) 983-1648 **O'Grady** Erin E '93
(513) 651-6800 **O'Grady** Michael J '95
(513) 651-6800 **O'Guinn** Jennifer A '03
(513) 977-8200 **O'Guinn** M Dave III '01
(513) 621-6464 **Okerson** Eric C '80
(513) 961-5311 **Okrzynski** Sarah A '03
(513) 241-9400 **Olden** Stephen H '77
(513) 621-6464 **Oliver** Christine E '99
(513) 684-3642 **Oliver** Eric V '83
(513) 556-4361 **Oliver** Nancy A '90
(513) 419-5770 **Olmstead** Dina M '97
(513) 621-3394 **Olson** Carol D '90
(513) 651-6800 **Olson** David C '78
(513) 784-8804 **Olson** Robert W '91
(513) 946-3243 **O'Neill** Michael D '02
(513) 241-0400 **O'Neill** Patrick M '93
(513) 626-3047 **Oney** Jack Lee Jr. '01
(513) 556-0062 **O'Reilly** James T '74
(513) 381-8213 **Orlet** Dimity V '97
(513) 772-1140 **Orner** Danny R '78
(513) 677-1008 **Ororokuma** Inyeai E '84
(513) 621-4612 **Osborn** Marilyn J '77
(513) 369-0200 **Osborne** Frank E '72
(513) 977-8200 **Ose** Paul A '77
(513) 287-2062 **O'Shea** Jill T '86
(513) 421-4020 **O'Shea** John L '89
(513) 595-2200 **Osmond** Charles D '84
(513) 852-6071 **Oster** E Wednesday '04
(513) 723-4000 **Osterlund** Anthony L '99
(513) 243-5617 **O'Sullivan** Daniel F '93
(513) 946-5200 **Outcalt** Peter L '78
(513) 983-4463 **Overbey** Terry L '75
(513) 946-3700 **Owens** Robert E '74
(513) 241-9400 **Owens** Ross C III '85
(513) 852-5600 **Pace** Beverly H '86
(513) 977-8200 **Pacheco** Bryan E '97
(513) 579-6400 **Packard** Dwight A II '96
(513) 721-5555 **Padro** Diego J III '99
(513) 287-3075 **Pahutski** Michael J '99
(513) 739-4013 **Painter** John W '91
(513) 762-9800 **Palermo** Julia B '01
(513) 381-8213 **Palermo** Maria C '91
(513) 651-6800 **Paliobeis** Bill J '96
(513) 241-5400 **Pandilidis** Peter '65
(513) 684-3711 **Pantel** Nicholas J '72
(513) 241-0400 **Paolo** Richard A '82
(513) 946-3000 **Paolucci** Krista R '91
(513) 651-1219 **Paolucci** Michael A '91
(513) 541-0061 **Papakirk** Maria J '97
(513) 232-1111 **Papner** Donald F '60
(513) 977-4208 **Park** Robert G '77
(513) 381-2838 **Parker** R Joseph '69
(513) 345-5000 **Parker** Tamara R '04
(513) 621-2120 **Parnell** John G Jr. '71
(513) 241-9400 **Parrish** Donita S '01
(513) 455-5324 **Parrish** Matthew S '94
(513) 621-6464 **Parsley** Sharon S '04
(513) 946-3700 **Patel** Christine A '91
(513) 489-6678 **Patel** Ken K '90
(513) 977-8200 **Patel** Polly E '02
(513) 721-4500 **Patsfall** Stephen J '81
(513) 721-4500 **Patsfall Yeager & Pflum LLC**
(513) 381-8213 **Patterson** Edwin W III '79
(513) 272-3000 **Patterson** George F Jr. '48
(513) 684-6022 **Patterson** Karen A M '02
(513) 721-3330 **Patterson** Mark C '79
(513) 241-3100 **Patterson** Steven H '01
(513) 533-2996 **Patterson** William J '00
(513) 221-2345 **Patton** James W '72
(513) 583-4200 **Patton** Jay D '97
(513) 744-7146 **Patton** Mona L '98
(513) 412-1467 **Patton** Nancy S '87
(513) 381-0656 **Patton** William A '68
(513) 744-7077 **Paul** Therese M '96
(513) 421-7300 **Payne** April M '98
(513) 475-0200 **Payne** Darrell D '91
(513) 621-6464 **Pearson** Jennifer S '03
(513) 381-2838 **Peck** David Hamilton '92
(513) 381-9200 **Peck** David W '66
(513) 721-1350 **Peck** David W '70
(513) 762-6207 **Peck** Jeffrey F '82
(513) 621-3394 **Peck** John Weld '69
(513) 621-3394 **Peck Shaffer & Williams,LLP**
(513) 621-2100 **Pecquet** Janet E '81
(513) 626-2404 **Peebles** Brent M '94
(513) 621-0777 **Peller** Kenneth E '76
(513) 352-2732 **Penix** Leonard N '85
(513) 369-5059 **Pennekamp** Lisa A '84
(513) 744-9600 **Penney** Robert J '03
(513) 984-2040 **Penney** Todd D '92
(513) 361-1200 **Pepper** David A '99
(513) 752-2111 **Pera** Marc G '98
(513) 369-5611 **Peraino** Vito C '81
(513) 852-8200 **Perez** John X '04
(513) 621-8256 **Perez** Robert A Sr. '83
(513) 793-2222 **Perin** Martha H '49
(513) 632-5335 **Perkins** Bryan R '93
(513) 723-2211 **Perr** Karolina F '96
(513) 852-8634 **Perrino** Dominic F '62
(513) 421-4855 **Perrino** Nicholas A '69
(513) 977-8200 **Perry** Brian P '93
(513) 852-3311 **Perry** David A '87
(513) 621-0442 **Perry** Edward C '91
(513) 621-0442 **Perry** James N '62
(513) 977-8200 **Persiani** John B '03
(513) 946-9200 **Persley** Elisa M '94
(513) 241-3100 **Petas** Pamela S '92
(513) 241-3100 **Petersmann** Sara M '91
(513) 621-6464 **Petrie** Bruce I Jr. '80
(513) 579-2210 **Petrie** Laura S '89
(513) 684-8740 **Petrucci** Michael L '95
(513) 946-4209 **Pettit** Kenton K '00
(513) 946-5800 **Petty** Kimberly A '02
(513) 241-6748 **Pflanz** David E '86
(513) 721-4500 **Pflum** Joseph F '89
(513) 684-6002 **Phalen** Thomas F Jr. '67
(513) 381-9200 **Phelps** Arthur E Jr. '85
(513) 941-6711 **Phillipps** James E '66
(513) 985-2500 **Phillips** John H '90
(513) 923-5232 **Phillips** Mary K '99
(513) 651-6800 **Phillips** Scott D '89
(513) 651-6800 **Phillips** T Stephen '66
(513) 241-9400 **Pieples** Gary J '96
(513) 242-7591 **Piepmeier** Mark E '81
(513) 522-7700 **Pierce** James R '81
(513) 474-9437 **Pierce** Mary E '91
(513) 626-4055 **Pierre** Kenya T '01
Pietrandrea Beth L '85
(513) 852-6000 **Pikna** Raymond J Jr. '79
(513) 621-5252 **Pillich** Constance M '98
(513) 721-4876 **Pinales** Martin S '68
(513) 621-6464 **Pinney** John B '74
(513) 721-4532 **Pitcairn** Robert A Jr. '73
(513) 871-8812 **Pitocco** Joseph A '77
(513) 771-6768 **Pitstick** Joseph V '93
(513) 587-2888 **Pittman** Geoffrey W '91
(513) 263-3634 **Pitula** Julie M '97
(513) 621-4477 **Pitzer** Philip E '71
(513) 794-6278 **Plante** Kimberly A '99
(513) 985-2500 **Plotnick** Harry B '77
(513) 621-0005 **Poe** Harold F '72
(513) 241-2324 **Poffenberger** John D '61
(513) 241-2324 **Poffenberger** John D Jr. '94
(513) 871-1300 **Polanco** Hector A '00
(513) 793-5999 **Polaniecki** Elliott '76
(513) 238-5244 **Politsky** Aleshia J '03
(513) 762-4503 **Pontius** Erica S '98
(513) 763-1978 **Pontius** Jarrod B '98
(513) 352-5394 **Poole** Jadene P '01
(513) 421-2400 **Popham** Julie W '92
(513) 977-8200 **Porotsky** Richard D Jr. '96
(513) 621-3993 **Porter** Robert C III '79
(513) 621-3993 **Porter** Robert C Jr. '52
(513) 381-4700 **Porter Wright Morris & Arthur LLP**
(513) 579-6400 **Posey** William A '79
(513) 482-3157 **Post** Sharon L '85
(513) 621-2120 **Postow** Charles J '77
(513) 381-2838 **Potter** John R '03
(513) 241-9400 **Potthast** Elizabeth Shinkle '04
(513) 721-1504 **Powell** Bradley A '86
(513) 721-5525 **Powell** Gary E '84
(513) 241-9400 **Powell** Jessica L '01
(513) 871-8915 **Power** Wallace M '48
(513) 271-0419 **Powers** John A '92
(513) 421-6100 **Powers** Melissa A '91
(513) 583-4200 **Powers** Todd M '84
(513) 721-5525 **Prager** Gerald D '00
(513) 569-7037 **Prahalad** Punam K '03
(513) 946-3700 **Pratt** Charles A '66
(513) 381-1234 **Prem** David L '87
(513) 561-5900 **Prescott** Karen C '83
(513) 861-3200 **Pressler** Frederick '03
(513) 852-3497 **Pressman** Marianne '92
(513) 621-6464 **Prewitt** Thomas A '93
(513) 852-3416 **Price** Benjamin L '03
(513) 661-3223 **Price** Edwin C Jr. '57
(513) 794-6078 **Price** William C '90
(513) 946-3000 **Pridemore** Katherine E '98
(513) 340-7105 **Principe** Julia K '04
(513) 241-2324 **Pritchard** David E '93
(513) 241-3100 **Proctor** Michael R '03
(513) 381-5552 **Proctor** Stephen M '98
(513) 948-5402 **Proietti** Louis D '91
(513) 946-3700 **Prouty** Frank H Jr. '73
(513) 381-2838 **Pryor** Patricia A '98
(513) 579-6400 **Pryse** Gail Glassmeyer '88
(513) 530-5357 **Przywara** Kathryn K '90
(513) 564-9999 **Pundzak** Lynn D '86
(513) 851-3700 **Purdy** Eugene K '53
(513) 241-3100 **Purtell** William L '02
(513) 381-2838 **Puthoff** Tracey A '95
Qualls John R '77
(513) 381-2838 **Quinn** Timothy J '75
(513) 946-3132 **Rabanus** Lisa '98
(513) 381-9697 **Rabenold** Keith M '89
(513) 287-7428 **Rabkin** Morton '61
(513) 621-0267 **Rabourn** Dexter A '79
(513) 287-2089 **Raby** Vivian M '86
(513) 632-9521 **Rader** James A '79
(513) 421-4020 **Rafferty** Donald J '89
(513) 247-0082 **Ragiel** Ronan C '02
(513) 528-9400 **Ragonesi** Christopher '90
(513) 421-4420 **Raimey** Kyra M '00
(513) 922-7700 **Raisbeck** Thomas E '92
(513) 243-2256 **Ramaswamy** Vadakanchery G '98
(513) 768-8903 **Rambo** Deborah P '87
(513) 768-8901 **Rambo** William C '82
(513) 241-3100 **Ramirez** Carlos S '97
(513) 922-5836 **Rammelsberg** Sharri U '92
(513) 852-6051 **Rammes** Lisa M '96
(513) 221-8383 **Ramos** Gabriel E Jr. '77
(513) 531-8725 **Ramsey** Ann G '87
(513) 579-6400 **Ramsey** Jamie M '99
(513) 287-3020 **Ramundo** Frank A II '95
(513) 352-6656 **Ramundo** Kimberly E '96
(513) 684-2496 **Ran** Ronald S '69
(513) 721-3290 **Randman** Debra J '93
(513) 381-5700 **Randolph** Daniel P '77
(513) 381-5700 **Randolph** Marc A '98
(513) 241-8776 **Randolph** Peter J '59
(513) 651-5900 **Ranz** David A '01
(513) 621-8688 **Ranz** Robert J '80
(513) 381-2838 **Rapien** Gerald J '68
(513) 469-7444 **Ratliff** Robert A '97
(513) 946-3534 **Rattermann** Paul D '85
(513) 271-0800 **Rauchman** Judith L '83
(513) 397-5420 **Ray** Mary F '90
(513) 977-8200 **Ray** Steven H '88
(513) 721-0200 **Rebel** John A '72
(513) 922-3200 **Rebold** Peter M '68
(513) 852-6054 **Reckman** Mark S '79
(513) 852-6019 **Reckman** Robert F '48
(513) 784-0357 **Rector** Daniel G '84
(513) 621-2100 **Redden** Brian R '99
(513) 946-9471 **Reed** Kevin A '94
(513) 946-9200 **Reed** Mark H '91
(513) 618-6732 **Reed** Mark W '99
(513) 381-4700 **Reed** Michael G '81
(513) 721-7522 **Reed** Robert F '64
(513) 852-3497 **Reese** Mary Anne '90
(513) 919-9429 **Reeve** Kevin S '97
(513) 241-3100 **Regan** Robyn M '02
(513) 263-4823 **Regberg** Neil S '76
(513) 569-6805 **Rehbock** Betty J '80
(513) 621-0267 **Rehme** Thomas F '54
(513) 762-8215 **Reiber** Kurt L '84
(513) 381-4700 **Reichert** David '54
(513) 241-2248 **Reichert** James A '73
(513) 977-8200 **Reid** Robert J '93
(513) 381-2838 **Reilly** Timothy P '78
(513) 241-0400 **Reis** Mark W '83
(513) 381-6810 **Reisenfeld** Bradley A '90
(513) 381-6810 **Reisenfeld** Sylvan P '60
(513) 352-4716 **Reising** Melanie J '86
(513) 579-5688 **Reiss** Anthony E '94
(513) 621-6464 **Reitz** Daniel E '01
(513) 946-9000 **Rellahan** Jacqueline J '90
(513) 241-2324 **Remaklus** Theodore R '93
(513) 723-4030 **Remesnitsky** Jackie R '04
(513) 721-1311 **Reminger & Reminger**
(513) 241-4722 **Rennie** Douglas W '78
(513) 946-3000 **Rentz** Margaret B '87
(513) 621-6464 **Renz** Karen J '97
(513) 946-3167 **Resler** Mark L '82
(513) 243-0506 **Resnick** Kenneth S '81
(513) 721-1975 **Reul** George M Jr. '98
(513) 579-6400 **Reuter** F Mark '96
(513) 521-8400 **Reuter** James E '78
(513) 791-6000 **Reutter** Mary J '99
(513) 721-1200 **Reverman** Richard E '80
(513) 721-4450 **Reynolds** Charles E '81
(513) 579-4370 **Reynolds** Paul L '86
(513) 351-8828 **Rhiney** Sean L '95
(513) 534-5958 **Riccardi** John R '03
(513) 871-1545 **Rice & Diedrichs LLP**
(513) 871-1545 **Rice** James K '67
(513) 530-6563 **Rice** John D '73
(513) 243-2632 **Rice** Kenneth C '94
(513) 768-5701 **Rice** Michael D '86
(513) 421-2400 **Rice** Robert M '93
(513) 723-4000 **Rich** Michael L '04
(513) 241-3430 **Rich Pott Wetherell Foster & Miller**
(513) 381-2838 **Rich** Robert E '70
(513) 551-4357 **Richard** Arthur M III '93
(513) 621-1991 **Richards** Gates T '69
(513) 241-3447 **Richards** Stuart L '62
(513) 871-8755 **Richards** Thomas D '84
(513) 961-6200 **Richardson** David G '93
(513) 723-4000 **Richardson** Eric W '96
(513) 651-6800 **Richardson** Scott M '02
(513) 352-6768 **Richey** Stephen L '93
(513) 621-6033 **Richman** Harvey A '95
(513) 621-2666 **Richshafer** Howard L '75
(513) 721-7500 **Rickey** Robert E '02
(513) 579-6400 **Riddell** Brian A '04
(513) 922-3200 **Riehl** Keith S '81
(513) 977-8200 **Riggs** Harry L Jr. '57
(513) 621-2888 **Riker** Jan T '77
(513) 241-4722 **Riley** Kimberly V '97
(513) 621-3394 **Riley** R Patrick '69
(513) 255-2345 **Rimedio** James R '65
(513) 721-1504 **Rinear** Richard J '84
(513) 244-5655 **Rinear** Robert L '65
(513) 352-6700 **Rines** David A '04
(513) 381-2838 **Ringenbach** Laura A '83
(513) 621-2120 **Rink** Thomas C '70
(513) 287-2929 **Rios** Martin Jr. '99
(513) 421-4225 **Risch** Dennis S '80
(513) 891-1530 **Ritchie** Warren J '74
(513) 361-0250 **Rittenhouse** Roger P '75
(513) 763-1932 **Ritter** Paul F '88
(513) 381-5700 **Ritter & Randolph,LLC**
(513) 579-6400 **Roach** Adrienne J '96
(513) 984-2040 **Roach** Megan K '01
(513) 977-8200 **Robbins** Eric M '01
(513) 721-3330 **Robbins** Fredric J '74
(513) 721-3330 **Robbins Kelly Patterson & Tucker**
(513) 558-7380 **Robbins** Mary K '80
(513) 579-6400 **Robenson** Todd E '04
(513) 621-6464 **Roberts** Douglas D '93
(513) 421-6630 **Roberts** Edward '95
(513) 421-2540 **Roberts** George E III '69
(513) 233-3666 **Roberts** Kevin P '88
(513) 621-6464 **Roberts** Michael A '90
(513) 946-3391 **Roberts** Norton B '93
(513) 474-7900 **Roberts** Richard S '70
(513) 563-6161 **Robertson** David F Jr. '01
(513) 396-5821 **Robinette** Joseph A '87
(513) 762-6200 **Robins** Teri E '02
(513) 651-6800 **Robinson** Ann G '94
(513) 351-9112 **Robinson** Gerald J '59
(513) 626-3356 **Robinson** Ian S '03
(513) 381-3525 **Robinson** James B '75
(513) 455-7600 **Robinson** William T III '71
(513) 412-3483 **Robison** Stephen L '86
(513) 852-3497 **Robson-Higgins** Yanna M '98
(513) 352-4713 **Rodell** Maria L '96
(513) 721-1200 **Rodenbeck** Stephen P '82
(513) 574-9264 **Rodgers** Lori B '99
(513) 744-8537 **Rodgers** Timothy A '99
(513) 977-8200 **Roe** Clifford A Jr. '67
(513) 731-6601 **Roell** Steven R '01
(513) 621-1935 **Roelker** Robert K '62
(513) 977-8200 **Roesch** Charles M '84
(513) 977-8200 **Roesch** Lynda E '79
(513) 361-0200 **Roetzel & Andress,LPA**
(513) 381-2838 **Rogers** Brie S '02
(513) 381-2838 **Rogers** Gregory Parker '89
(513) 564-7000 **Rogers** Susan S '78
(513) 412-5400 **Rogus** Timothy E '94
(513) 723-2216 **Rohner** Nicholas K '01
(513) 621-6464 **Rohr** Jeffrey L '85
(513) 519-0766 **Rolcik** Karen A '86
(513) 579-0080 **Rolfes** Jerome F '89
(513) 721-4185 **Rolfes** Thomas A '95
(513) 579-0080 **Roller** Pamela A '01
(513) 852-6057 **Rollman** Jeffrey M '74
(513) 634-5209 **Roof** Carl J '92

(513) 241-2324 **Rooney** Kevin G '92
(513) 381-2838 **Rorer** Sara S '88
(513) 482-5081 **Rosado** Raul Jr. '89
(513) 531-1197 **Rose** Janet T '78
(513) 621-7902 **Rose** John W '81
(513) 241-3100 **Roselle** Cynthia M '01
(513) 621-0267 **Roselle** Louise M '72
(513) 241-0400 **Rosen** Irving H '57
(513) 923-5232 **Rosenacker** Frank B '83
(513) 564-7654 **Rosenberg** Hilda '90
(513) 579-6400 **Rosenberg** J David '74
(513) 792-6729 **Rosenberg** Jay A '66
(513) 651-6800 **Rosenstiel** Jeffrey S '96
(513) 621-3440 **Rosenthal** Daniel G '77
(513) 621-2257 **Rosenwald** Peter '73
(513) 681-5617 **Roser** Christopher P '90
(513) 983-1100 **Rosnell** Tara M '91
(513) 984-9098 **Rosner** Lisa Miner '83
(513) 621-7900 **Ross** Kenneth L '74
(513) 621-2120 **Ross** Lori A '00
(513) 621-1652 **Roth** Neil J '84
(513) 579-8900 **Rothchild** Barry A '90
(513) 579-8900 **Rothchild** Eugene M '56
(513) 241-3100 **Rothfuss** Richard M '77
(513) 721-5151 **Rothstein** Steven M '77
(513) 946-3500 **Rottinghaus** Thomas J '73
(513) 621-8210 **Rounding** Ruth I '79
(513) 579-6400 **Rouse** Joseph P '70
(513) 706-5025 **Routh** Jeffrey S '89
(513) 579-6400 **Rowe** Rachael A '96
(513) 723-8266 **Rowland** Michelle L '01
(513) 763-7700 **Rozic** James P '92
(513) 352-4702 **Rubenstein** Charles A '81
(513) 241-7460 **Rubenstein** Jack C '67
(513) 241-7460 **Rubenstein** Louis '78
(513) 241-7460 **Rubenstein** Scott A '99
(513) 241-7460 **Rubenstein & Thurman**
(513) 421-4020 **Rubin** Marc W '74
(513) 421-4020 **Rubin** Robert S '79
(513) 351-9700 **Rubin** Walter I '66
(513) 579-1414 **Ruby** Stanley L '71
(513) 721-4450 **Rucker** Fanon A '96
(513) 961-6200 **Rudell** Barry A '00
(513) 388-2830 **Rudolph** Glenn P '89
(513) 621-8210 **Ruebel** Richard J '73
(513) 621-4849 **Rueger** James M '77
(513) 381-4888 **Ruehle** Ryan J '99
(513) 723-4000 **Ruehlmann** Eugene P '50
(513) 361-1200 **Ruehlmann** Gregory A '81
(513) 361-1200 **Ruehlmann** Mark J '87
(513) 621-2120 **Ruh** Michael A Jr. '96
(513) 786-1518 **Ruiz** Fernando A '96
(513) 579-1414 **Rumberg** Orly R '93
(513) 534-0803 **Rummer** Keith A '01
(513) 552-4377 **Rumpf** John M '89
(513) 825-2492 **Rupp** Susan C '80
(513) 242-7591 **Rusche** Joseph F '49
(513) 771-2444 **Rush** D Todd '97
(513) 651-6800 **Rush** Jeffery R '75
(513) 381-2838 **Russell** Allison S '99
Russell William S '04
(513) 721-4532 **Russo** William F '79
(513) 421-6555 **Rust** Mary E '83
(513) 381-2838 **Rust** Mary L '87
(513) 977-5681 **Rust** Richard S IV '74
(513) 983-2513 **Rutherford** Elizabeth M '92
(513) 636-4707 **Rutherford** Melvin L Jr. '76
(513) 721-8822 **Ruttle** Timothy M '80
(513) 621-3394 **Ruwe** Bradley N '97
(513) 489-0829 **Ruwe** Joseph M '98
(513) 381-2838 **Ruwe** Katherine A '02
(513) 271-0808 **Ruwe** Thomas J '83
(513) 361-1200 **Ryan** Carrie W '00
(513) 381-2838 **Ryan** James J '54
(513) 861-1544 **Ryan** James J '58
(513) 723-8261 **Ryan** Laura A '92
(513) 946-3000 **Ryan** Rae M '85
(513) 381-6810 **Ryan** Shawn R '89
(513) 871-7090 **Ryder** Ely M T '71
(513) 397-1333 **Saba** Delia R '98
(513) 533-2996 **Saba** Paul T '94
(513) 533-2996 **Saba** Peter A '91
(513) 946-3000 **Sack** Tamara S '99
(513) 977-8200 **Sackenheim** Alison N '03
(513) 241-3100 **Sacks** Steven L '03
(513) 762-6200 **Saelinger** Gina M '93
(513) 621-6464 **Saelinger** Robert R '88
(513) 381-2838 **Safier** Kristen L '01
(513) 721-3330 **Sager** Stephen M '97
(513) 385-0030 **Saksefski** Louis M '76
(513) 552-1400 **Salinas** Vincent A '74
(513) 946-9000 **Salinger** Ann J '82
(513) 977-8200 **Sallee** Jerry S '80
(513) 977-8200 **Sallee** Joseph L Jr. '85
(513) 762-7648 **Salmen** Gerald G '76
(513) 762-6200 **Salmon** James L '00
(513) 721-4500 **Salyer** Susan M '03
(513) 626-2269 **Sambrook** Michael J '03
(513) 946-3000 **Sampang** Jocelyn M '94
(513) 241-3100 **Sampson** Kirk '75

(513) 891-8900 **Sanders** Michael B '88
(513) 352-5255 **Sanders** Nicole '03
(513) 579-6400 **Sanker** Robert G '87
(513) 421-7700 **Sanks** Julius F '82
(513) 559-1160 **Sansalone** Anthony M '87
(513) 871-8755 **Santangelo** Scott M '86
(513) 241-9400 **Santen** Edward E '88
(513) 721-4450 **Santen** Harry H '57
(513) 721-4450 **Santen & Hughes**
(513) 721-4450 **Santen** William E '55
(513) 721-4450 **Santen** William E Jr. '84
(513) 621-2666 **Sapinsley** Thomas S '82
(513) 241-7111 **Sarapata** Michael A '04
(513) 579-0080 **Sarge** Carmen C '00
(513) 762-4592 **Sarra** Martha C '88
(513) 353-3287 **Satterfield** Clarence R '74
(513) 946-3172 **Sauers** Mark E '79
(513) 744-9600 **Saunders** Karen A '04
(513) 946-3447 **Sauter** Harold K '91
(513) 665-9500 **Sauter** Susan M '91
(513) 381-9200 **Saxton** Jonathan P '89
(513) 556-4200 **Sayers** Steven E '89
(513) 381-2838 **Sayre** Russell S '90
(513) 241-7600 **Scacchetti** David J '82
(513) 421-3033 **Scacchetti** Marcia E '83
(513) 241-3430 **Scahill** John P '52
(513) 241-4722 **Scandy** Kelly C '86
(513) 595-2811 **Schaaf** Mary E '97
(513) 241-2880 **Schaefer** Barbara B '97
(513) 946-3000 **Schaefer** Christian J '76
(513) 946-3000 **Schaefer** James J '89
(513) 621-8210 **Schaefer** James R '92
(513) 381-5700 **Schaefer** Jeffrey R '93
(513) 723-4000 **Schaefer** Kimberly J '98
(513) 619-5041 **Schaefer** Lesley N '03
(513) 946-3416 **Schaen** Susan D '99
(513) 651-6800 **Schalnat** Eleanor Maria F '99
(513) 381-4700 **Scharff** Daniel W '91
(513) 241-2324 **Schatz** Brett A '00
(513) 579-6400 **Scheier** Michael L '91
(513) 241-3100 **Scheimann** Mary M '04
(513) 284-8361 **Schenck** Donald A '62
(513) 651-6800 **Schenk** Mary Ann '76
(513) 665-3500 **Schenkel** Timothy B '93
(513) 621-8333 **Scheper** James H '68
(513) 552-1400 **Scheper** Norbert J '74
(513) 984-2040 **Scheuer** Edna V '80
(513) 984-2040 **Scheuer Mackin & Breslin LLC**
(513) 946-3049 **Scheve** Thomas J '78
(513) 287-3427 **Schick** William W Jr. '86
Schiff Jonathan E '81
(513) 421-4000 **Schiff** Phyllis B '92
(513) 489-0829 **Schilling** Richard D '77
(513) 721-6151 **Schilling** Ronald D '77
(513) 241-7715 **Schimanski** James R '91
(513) 474-3309 **Schimpf** Jerome L '66
(513) 977-5585 **Schimpf** Joseph M '01
(513) 977-5577 **Schimpf** Richard J '67
(513) 977-8200 **Schisler** H Toby II '97
(513) 381-9200 **Schisler** Heather M '03
(513) 721-1350 **Schlemmer** Arthur H '76
(513) 381-2838 **Schloemer** Jeffrey S '83
(513) 762-6200 **Schloss** Stuart A Jr. '72
(513) 381-4700 **Schlosser** R Jeffrey '84
(513) 872-7505 **Schlotman** James T '78
(513) 591-6501 **Schlueter** Daniel J '74
(513) 352-0500 **Schmalz** Anna '04
(513) 621-6464 **Schmalzl** Richard G '87
(513) 922-3861 **Schmerber** Donald E '74
(513) 241-4110 **Schmid** Peter A '04
(513) 852-6052 **Schmidt** Carl J III '83
(513) 721-4450 **Schmidt** Charles Gregory '80
(513) 621-8688 **Schmidt** Dale G '65
(513) 595-2879 **Schmidt** Jerome C '73
(513) 977-8200 **Schmidt** John J '92
(513) 533-2996 **Schmidt** Michael C '01
(513) 421-4020 **Schmidt** Michael R '81
(513) 621-8688 **Schmidt** Richard L '83
(513) 521-0651 **Schmidt** Timothy J '92
(513) 651-6800 **Schmit** David E '75
(513) 852-8200 **Schmitt** David J '91
(513) 651-6800 **Schnapp** Karlyn A '00
(513) 421-7500 **Schneider** Ann E '99
(513) 579-6400 **Schneider** Benjamin A '00
(513) 333-0013 **Schneider** Donald E '75
(513) 579-1414 **Schneider** Hallie L '03
(513) 984-0300 **Schneider** Harry R '80
(513) 852-6021 **Schneider** Kenneth J '66
(513) 381-0656 **Schneider** Louis C '03
(513) 946-3164 **Schneider** Richard J '77
(513) 345-8291 **Schneider** Theodore J '92
(513) 621-2120 **Schneiderman** Diane T '89
(513) 946-9000 **Schnieders** Joseph A '82
(513) 651-8486 **Schoenberger** Jeanne L '91
(513) 421-2540 **Schoenfeld** Emily A '03

(513) 241-5005 **Schoenfeld** Thomas R '80
(513) 381-0656 **Schoeni** Kenneth R '83
(513) 651-6800 **Schoeny** James D '03
(513) 946-9000 **Schoettmer** Sara Ann '82
(513) 241-2324 **Scholer** Douglas A '00
(513) 729-3198 **Scholles** James R '77
(513) 729-3198 **Scholles** Jeffrey J '86
(513) 579-0080 **Schomaker** John P '03
(513) 621-6464 **Schooley** Ann K '99
Schott Donald L '67
(513) 792-0792 **Schottenstein Zox & Dunn**
(513) 977-8200 **Schreiber** Steven H '81
(513) 977-8200 **Schreiner** Joanne M '80
(513) 241-9400 **Schrider** John E Jr. '74
(513) 621-2044 **Schroeck** Rebecca L '00
(513) 583-4200 **Schroeder Maundrell Barbiere & Powers**
(513) 583-4200 **Schroeder** William P '68
(513) 651-6800 **Schroer** Charles E '79
(513) 744-7260 **Schroer** Dianna L '97
(513) 232-0922 **Schuch** Paul W '53
(513) 381-2838 **Schuck** Thomas R '76
(513) 321-2662 **Schuh & Goldberg,LLP**
(513) 321-2662 **Schuh** John A '77
(513) 321-2662 **Schuh** Stephen J '78
(513) 946-9000 **Schulcz** Mary C '87
(513) 521-7430 **Schulman** Alan A '72
(513) 561-3907 **Schultz** Susan E '99
(513) 981-6280 **Schuster** Richard L '88
(513) 221-1745 **Schutte** Michael J '94
(513) 584-5042 **Schwallie** David F '84
(513) 721-4876 **Schwartz** Howard M '75
(513) 579-1414 **Schwartz Manes & Ruby**
(513) 579-1414 **Schwartz** Michael G '92
(513) 241-3447 **Schwartz** Michael S '71
(513) 579-1414 **Schwartz** Richard M '68
(513) 361-0250 **Schwartz** Robert H '93
(513) 241-3447 **Schwartz** Robert L '64
(513) 792-0606 **Schwartz** Ronald E '91
(513) 771-2444 **Schwartz** Steven L '97
(513) 533-3495 **Schwarz** Douglas A '98
(513) 632-4292 **Schwarz** Paul E '92
(513) 412-8260 **Schwegman** Jennifer L '01
(513) 489-0881 **Schweiger** Scott M '83
(513) 977-8200 **Schweller** Stephen G '84
(513) 381-5700 **Schwierling** John T '57
(513) 455-7600 **Schworer** Philip J '86
(513) 651-6800 **Scoggins** Samuel M '75
(513) 851-0600 **Scott** Alexis Z '86
(513) 564-0088 **Scott** James R '99
(513) 621-6464 **Scott** Jamie D '87
(513) 421-7500 **Scott** John C '85
(513) 583-4200 **Scranton** Derek W '02
(513) 584-5042 **Scrivens** Kathleen M '88
(513) 621-4886 **Scrofano** Salvatore G '74
(513) 771-7070 **Scroggins** Robert C '96
(513) 241-5670 **Sears** Julia A '86
(513) 946-3082 **Sears** Pamela J '84
(513) 361-1200 **Seaton** Kim D '97
(513) 579-6400 **Sebastian** Steven W '00
(513) 419-3248 **Secrest** Thomas A '94
(513) 564-9222 **Segal** Andrew L '98
(513) 946-3000 **Seibel** Adam F '00
(513) 381-6600 **Seibel** Kenneth F '69
(513) 381-6600 **Seibel** Paul K '04
(513) 721-1975 **Seibel** Ronald E '04
(513) 381-6600 **Seibel** Scott K '98
(513) 961-1672 **Seiler** Lewis H '79
(513) 381-2838 **Seitz** William J III '78
(513) 352-6663 **Selak** Robert A '79
(513) 421-4020 **Selden** Heidi A '96
(513) 241-4722 **Self** Janet A '88
(513) 946-4280 **Sellers** David L '83
(513) 946-3417 **Sellers** John P III '82
(513) 721-1504 **Sellins** Warren John '76
(513) 684-3211 **Serena** Terry '78
(513) 793-0710 **Sestito** John P '83
(513) 946-3000 **Seta** Emma L '00
(513) 733-1759 **Setterberg** Richard A '86
(513) 381-2838 **Settles** Brian S '04
(513) 345-4160 **Sewall** Grace C '86
(513) 762-6200 **Shadley** Frederic X '81
(513) 723-4000 **Shafer** Cynthia A '86
(513) 577-7380 **Shafer** Jeffrey A '97
(513) 455-7600 **Shaffer** Elizabeth Monroe '03
(513) 723-4000 **Shaffer** Robert M '96
(513) 985-3200 **Shanahan** James P Jr. '84
(513) 946-3000 **Shanahan** Megan E '00
Shank Diane S '89
(513) 651-6800 **Shank** Robert D '98
(513) 381-2838 **Shanley** Sharon I '99
(513) 946-9006 **Shannon** Raymond E '48
(513) 381-2838 **Shapiro** Joshua A '99
(513) 561-3347 **Sharp** Timothy H '97
(513) 621-2888 **Shartzer** Sharon M '04
(513) 763-4329 **Shaut** Michael H '80
(513) 651-2121 **Shaw** Stephen K '79
(513) 651-6800 **Shea** Jane H '79
(513) 621-8333 **Shea** Joseph W III '74

(513) 579-2010 **Shea** Kevin M '79
(513) 771-4557 **Shear** Donald '53
(513) 665-3500 **Shearer** David A Jr. '99
(513) 731-8014 **Sheeran** Thomas M '51
(513) 721-5100 **Sheldon** Henry E III '03
(513) 421-8338 **Sheline** Miriam H '84
(513) 634-1148 **Shelton** Kristy L '01
(513) 621-2100 **Shepardson** Warren P Jr. '71
(513) 665-3500 **Sheriff-MacDonald** Dee C '84
(513) 381-7971 **Sherman** Terrie A '91
(513) 977-8200 **Sherman** Thomas J '69
(513) 977-8200 **Sherman** William A '87
(513) 721-3330 **Sherman** William D '94
(513) 241-4722 **Sherwood** Elizabeth Poe '87
(513) 595-2823 **Shick** Daniel S '83
Shields William S '78
(513) 531-4088 **Shifman** Julie C '87
(513) 946-3171 **Shilling** Karen R '91
(513) 381-0656 **Shipp** Jeffrey C '87
(513) 651-5651 **Shiverdecker** Merlyn D '72
(513) 552-5838 **Shoemaker** Kent A '94
(513) 983-4225 **Shook** Susan M '97
(513) 361-0200 **Shoskin** Jeffrey S '83
(513) 621-2120 **Shott** Andrew M '81
(513) 381-2838 **Shotten** Melvin S '68
(513) 684-3211 **Shuler** Gary R Jr. '98
(513) 977-8200 **Shuler** Matthew D '98
(513) 723-4000 **Shuller** Donald J '76
(513) 241-3100 **Siegel** Christopher J '98
(513) 579-6400 **Siegel** Richard D '71
(513) 621-2666 **Siegel** Robert H '75
(513) 977-8200 **Siegel** Steve N '97
(513) 361-1200 **Siehl** Jeffrey D '98
(513) 731-1402 **Sigalov** Vlad '99
(513) 352-4707 **Sigman** Gloria J '95
(513) 977-8200 **Silbersack** Mark L '71
(513) 946-4046 **Silver** Susan '81
(513) 241-9844 **Silverman** Beth I '84
(513) 624-6720 **Silvers** Jane E '86
(513) 745-0400 **Simmonds** Rasheed A '97
(513) 352-6782 **Simmons** Gerald W '67
(513) 579-2542 **Simon** Samuel J '82
(513) 721-7500 **Simon** Stephen A '97
(513) 684-9922 **Simons** Thomas A Jr. '71
(513) 852-6512 **Simpson** Yvette R '04
(513) 977-8200 **Sims** Jason B '94
(513) 651-6800 **Sims** Jud B '99
(513) 621-6464 **Sims** Mark E '81
(513) 651-2009 **Sims** Victor D '89
(513) 621-3200 **Sinclair** Jonathan R '96
(513) 977-8200 **Singer** Peter S '03
(513) 721-0778 **Singer** William B '67
(513) 421-1108 **Singleton** David A '02
(513) 821-1510 **Sirkin** Alan L '70
(513) 721-4876 **Sirkin** H Louis '65
(513) 721-4876 **Sirkin Pinales & Schwartz LLP**
(513) 563-4131 **Sizemore** Gregory L '92
(513) 579-0080 **Skavdahl** Duane R '93
(513) 621-0267 **Skeens** Troy W Jr. '81
(513) 421-6630 **Skidmore** Charles G '92
(513) 651-6800 **Skidmore** David A Jr. '91
(513) 381-2121 **Skilken** Lynne E '75
(513) 651-6800 **Skinkiss** Ralph J '73
(513) 721-5494 **Skirvin** Rae '60
(513) 792-2942 **Skoog** Norma '83
(513) 579-6400 **Skufca** Christopher J '94
(513) 621-6464 **Slater** Peter M '93
(513) 946-3700 **Slattery** James J Jr. '71
(513) 632-5315 **Slauson** John G '66
(513) 861-5065 **Sloan** Ayana L '91
(513) 946-3000 **Slocum** Lee R '78
(513) 683-9000 **Slovin** Randy T '83
(513) 579-1414 **Slovin** Scott M '77
(513) 241-9844 **Slovin** Sherri G '79
(513) 793-5560 **Slutsky** June C '91
(513) 793-5560 **Slutsky** Norman L '70
(513) 333-4012 **Smith** Anne M '89
(513) 651-6800 **Smith** Brett A '04
(513) 621-8688 **Smith** Darlene S M '03
(513) 621-0442 **Smith** David S '71
(513) 361-0250 **Smith** Deborah '82
(513) 762-6200 **Smith** Denise M '97
(513) 361-1200 **Smith** Elliot M '04
(513) 946-3700 **Smith** Gerald A '74
(513) 861-7100 **Smith** Gloria L '93
(513) 241-4722 **Smith** Hope A '02
(513) 421-4646 **Smith** Ian R '97
(513) 421-6630 **Smith** James H III '75
(513) 621-6556 **Smith** Jenny N '92
(513) 541-0207 **Smith** Jonathan K '97
(513) 984-3320 **Smith** Joseph A '70
(513) 241-2324 **Smith** Kathryn E '96
(513) 651-8317 **Smith** Kimberly A '90
(513) 381-2838 **Smith** Marcella Kay '04
(513) 287-7447 **Smith** Mark B '84
(513) 752-5350 **Smith** Mark F '85
(513) 579-0080 **Smith** Matthew J '84
(513) 564-7616 **Smith** Patrick F '97

(513) 621-2120 **Smith** Pete A '94
(513) 723-4000 **Smith** Phillip J '94
(513) 556-6805 **Smith** Rachel Jay '00
(513) 579-0080 **Smith Rolfes & Skavdahl Co,LPA**
(513) 762-6200 **Smith** Ronald G '98
(513) 721-1975 **Smith** Sheila M '95
(513) 684-0336 **Smith** Steven L '92
(513) 455-7600 **Smith** Steven R '84
(513) 977-8200 **Smith** Susan A '03
(513) 922-3200 **Smith** Thomas R '57
(513) 632-5333 **Smith** Timothy A '77
(513) 929-4834 **Smith-Monahan** Richard '95
(513) 352-6731 **Smitson** Patricia M '77
(513) 621-8210 **Smyth** Robert M '94
(513) 852-3344 **Snelling** Angela '99
(513) 891-1373 **Snouffer** Gary H '75
(513) 241-7460 **Snyder** Richard '64
(513) 281-1544 **Snyder** William D '76
(513) 745-0400 **Sobecki** Judi L '96
(513) 533-2723 **Sobers** Sharon J '85
(513) 352-6784 **Solimine** Louis F '76
(513) 556-0102 **Solimine** Michael E '81
(513) 421-3494 **Sollmann** William J '74
Solomon Paul F '86
(513) 241-6748 **Somers** Blake P '04
(513) 563-3003 **Sommer** Rick J '99
(513) 241-3100 **Sorg** Steven V '92
(513) 241-6748 **Southard** Mark M '88
(513) 421-8686 **Southard** Terence J '83
Sova Gregory '76
(513) 977-8200 **Sowder** Trenna K '03
(513) 721-3330 **Spaeth** Barry A '94
(513) 731-3927 **Spaite** Paul W '64
Spanja Stephanie G '04
(513) 421-0300 **Spaulding** Frederick D '91
(513) 731-8460 **Spegal** Karen L '93
(513) 761-9255 **Spiegel** Walter E '02
(513) 381-1500 **Spiering** Kevin J '94
(513) 287-2094 **Spiller** Amy B '90
(513) 352-6722 **Spiller** Keith P '89
(513) 631-7455 **Spitz** Gregory G '72
(513) 587-3403 **Splain** John F '85
(513) 579-6400 **Spoor** Richard D '72
(513) 852-8200 **Spraetz** Deborah L '88
(513) 721-8210 **Spraul** Daniel G '82
(513) 721-8210 **Spraul** Holly Doan '88
(513) 721-8210 **Spraul Veith & Doan**
(513) 651-6800 **Sprecher** Christina M '96
(513) 651-6800 **Sprecher** Kevin S '95
(513) 345-4160 **Spring** Jean M '98
(513) 684-3711 **Springer** Anthony '97
(513) 946-3000 **Springman** Ronald W Jr. '89
(513) 721-5525 **Sprong** Nathan W '04
(513) 719-1100 **Squeri** Donna M '84
(513) 361-1200 **Squire Sanders & Dempsey LLP**
(513) 381-2838 **Stachler** Robert G '57
(513) 621-2120 **Stachler** Thomas L '89
(513) 352-3350 **Stackpole** Peter J '00
(513) 621-8755 **Stagnaro** Eugene J Jr. '63
(513) 241-0662 **Stagnaro** Gene A '86
(513) 533-2996 **Stagnaro** Jeffrey G '89
(513) 241-3447 **Stagnaro** Michaela M '92
(513) 621-6464 **Stainton** Jeffrey L '97
(513) 574-8899 **Staley** Jeffrey J '77
(513) 412-5400 **Stalf** Dale A '83
(513) 241-2324 **Stallard** David S '71
(513) 977-8200 **Stamp** Vincent B '69
(513) 421-4020 **Stanford** Stanley L '58
(513) 961-8464 **Stansel** Teresa L '88
(513) 946-3571 **Stargel** Rogena D '82
(513) 977-8200 **Starkey** Denise M '04
(513) 352-6737 **Starkey** James Shane '96
(513) 721-7430 **Startsman** Daniel B Jr. '73
(513) 621-2666 **Statman** Alan J '83
(513) 621-2666 **Statman Harris Siegel & Eyrich LLC**
(513) 636-4069 **Stautberg** Elizabeth Ann '92
(513) 632-7077 **Stautberg** Julia A '95
(513) 977-8200 **Stautberg** Lee A '93
(513) 579-6400 **Stautberg** Peter J '93
(513) 621-7600 **Steele** Christine C '91
(513) 533-2996 **Steele** Matthew C '03
(513) 381-5700 **Steffen** Carey K '00
(513) 983-7738 **Stegbauer** Joseph A '96
(513) 762-7800 **Stegman** Michael J '83
(513) 381-5700 **Stegman** Mollie T '01
(513) 684-9900 **Steiden** Eric A '94
(513) 946-5133 **Stein-Russell** Heather E '83
(513) 621-0267 **Steinberg** Robert A '67
(513) 579-6400 **Steiner** Edward E '83
(513) 579-7872 **Steines** Ann M '90
(513) 983-4349 **Steinmanis** Karl S '73
(513) 791-2945 **Steltenpohl** Robert H '76
(513) 381-2838 **Stepaniak** Mark J '80
(513) 381-2838 **Stephan** Charles Michael '79

(513) 556-0130 **Stephani** Andrew J '00
(513) 762-6968 **Stephens** Mark W '82
(513) 946-3419 **Stephens** Philip W '00
(513) 977-8200 **Stern** Noah J '99
(513) 936-2011 **Stern** Steven D '04
(513) 421-2700 **Stethem & Duwel**
(513) 233-2525 **Stevens** Annette K '90
(513) 946-3120 **Stevenson** David T '81
(513) 381-2838 **Stewart** Frank H '59
(513) 671-6333 **Stewart** Jay T '02
(513) 362-8700 **Stewart** Thomas H '92
(513) 241-3685 **Stich** Carl J Jr. '80
(513) 618-7800 **Stiebel** Mark A '80
(513) 421-2400 **Stiens** Donald G Jr. '03
(513) 946-3425 **Stier** Mary A '94
(513) 561-5444 **Stigler** Margaret M '83
(513) 936-0800 **Stillpass** John E '81
(513) 621-0267 **Stilz** Fay E '78
(513) 241-2324 **Stinebruner** Scott A '98
(513) 533-0020 **Stineman** Jerome P '91
(513) 381-4700 **Stith** John S '64
(513) 579-6400 **Stitt** Jason V '04
(513) 946-5160 **Stockdale** David C '76
(513) 381-7333 **Stocker** David E '79
(513) 243-7384 **Stockton** Susan M '91
(513) 621-7474 **Stoller** Harry '58
(513) 651-6800 **Stolper** Rita Mannheimer '91
(513) 421-4020 **Stone** Richard M '77
(513) 621-2120 **Stoner** Michael B '97
Story Garlinn H '80
(513) 791-1673 **Stout** Gregory A '02
Stout William A Jr. '81
(513) 621-2889 **Strain** Charles E '81
(513) 651-6800 **Strangfeld** William C '84
(513) 352-6725 **Strasser** JoAnn M '94
(513) 929-3400 **Stratigeas** Eleni V '01
(513) 852-3497 **Straus** Thomas J '78
(513) 946-3511 **Strauss** Gordon M '75
(513) 768-8900 **Strauss** Stephen D '66
(513) 621-2120 **Strauss & Troy, LPA**
(513) 621-2120 **Strauss** William V Jr. '67
(513) 745-0713 **Stretcher** Brian N '98
(513) 946-3000 **Stricker** George Jr. '73
(513) 977-4211 **Stridsberg** Roger C '49
(513) 946-3700 **Strigari** Louis F '73
(513) 241-2090 **Strong** Michael H '92
(513) 621-4775 **Strubbe** William B '79
(513) 241-4722 **Stubbs** Matthew E '96
(513) 807-7510 **Stuhlbarg** Steven F '92
(513) 983-4194 **Suarez** Joseph P '82
(513) 412-5400 **Subit** Melissa C '99
(513) 639-3924 **Suder** Sean S '04
(513) 579-1414 **Sudman** Harry S '72
(513) 762-6200 **Suffern** Michael J '93
(513) 333-0014 **Suhre** Joseph B IV '99
(513) 621-8210 **Sulau** William C '81
(513) 977-8200 **Sullivan** Brian S '88
(513) 977-8200 **Sullivan** David S '00
(513) 522-5575 **Sullivan** James P '77
(513) 522-5575 **Sullivan** John J '51
(513) 983-9787 **Sullivan** Lisa A '93
(513) 621-3394 **Sullivan** Mary W '80
(513) 381-2838 **Sullivan** Timothy C '85
(513) 474-5020 **Sullivan** Wendall '50
(513) 241-2324 **Summe** Kurt A '91
(513) 522-7700 **Summers** Cynthia L '81
(513) 794-6287 **Summers** Stuart G '68
(513) 583-6921 **Sunderman** Robert E '80
(513) 946-3000 **Sundermann** Elizabeth A '03
(513) 232-1004 **Sunyak** Nicholas E III '91
(513) 721-5525 **Supinger** Emily T '01
(513) 723-4000 **Suprock** Mary E '04
(513) 489-0404 **Surkamp** Richard E Jr. '89
(513) 621-6464 **Surrey** Michael C '98
(513) 762-6200 **Susskind** Stuart R '69
(513) 977-8200 **Sutton** James T '04
(513) 381-2838 **Suwanski** Jillian M '02
Swartz Donald K '97
(513) 977-8200 **Swartz** Jennifer K '00
(513) 872-2290 **Swehla** Marcia A '93
(513) 891-1530 **Swehla** Nathaniel L '02
Swenty Peter W '55
(513) 891-1530 **Swick** Kevin L '81
(513) 381-2838 **Swigert** J Mack '37
(513) 721-1125 **Swillinger** Bradley M '01
(513) 721-1125 **Swillinger** Steven R '74
(513) 531-2900 **Swisher** Sarah E '93
(800) 592-8422 **Swob** Jay D '81
(513) 794-6389 **Szeremet** David M '97
(513) 784-6402 **Szucsik** Barbara R '93
(513) 381-0656 **Tafaro** John P '83
(513) 627-1888 **Taffy** Frank '01
(513) 621-2120 **Taft** Richard Guy '76
(513) 381-2838 **Taft Stettinius & Hollister LLP**
(513) 381-9200 **Taggart** Carolyn A '78
(513) 381-5700 **Taggart** Georgana '81
(513) 721-8822 **Tailer** Christine D '84
Taliaferro George W Jr. '93
(513) 381-6555 **Tamarkin** Ivan L '67
(513) 533-4416 **Tami** Molly T '93
(513) 721-4450 **Tankersley** Sarah B '97
(513) 381-2838 **Tarvin** Julia E '02
(513) 533-0633 **Tassone** Gregory J '88
(513) 333-4065 **Tate** Charles L '00
(513) 784-6306 **Tate** John M '72
(513) 762-6200 **Tate** Mary L '02
(513) 621-3440 **Tauber** Jill Stanforth '01
(513) 891-8900 **Taulbee** Matthew A '04
(513) 946-3700 **Taunton** Leigh Kimbrough '02
(513) 721-6500 **Taylor** Catharin R '92
(513) 287-2929 **Taylor** Douglas C '86
(513) 684-3660 **Taylor** Eric A '93
(513) 636-1288 **Taylor** Lisa A '00
(513) 791-8600 **Taylor** Sharon G '80
(513) 487-5977 **Taylor** Wayne F '70
(513) 352-4710 **Teass** Lura I '91
(513) 651-6800 **Teeters** Jeffrey R '93
(513) 752-0001 **Tekulve** Charles J '58
(513) 752-0001 **Tekulve** Mark J '87
(513) 721-4532 **Teller** Jerome S '53
(513) 361-0250 **Temin** Larry A '80
(513) 721-3330 **Temming** Daniel J '79
(513) 561-0883 **Tent** Brian A '03
(513) 721-7500 **Tepe** Thomas M '72
(513) 579-6400 **Tepe** Thomas M Jr. '99
(513) 977-8200 **Tepe** Timothy A '87
(513) 381-2838 **Terp** Thomas T '73
(513) 321-6988 **Tewksbury** Linn A '87
(513) 946-3000 **Tharp** Clay '03
(513) 741-2651 **Thaxton** James E '88
(513) 621-3394 **Thayer** Abbot A II '80
(513) 946-9200 **Theile** Gregory R '79
(513) 621-2120 **Theissen** Timothy B '87
(513) 236-0166 **Theobald** Jason M '04
(513) 629-1939 **Theurich** David E '91
(513) 235-3902 **Thole** Lori D '93
(513) 231-4900 **Thole** Thomas J '74
(513) 621-6464 **Thomas** Brian C '01
(513) 381-2838 **Thomas** Cindy-Ann L '99
(513) 241-3100 **Thomas** Craig A '86
(513) 961-5311 **Thomas** Ernest V III '82
(513) 961-5311 **Thomas** Ernest V Jr. '68
(513) 961-5311 **Thomas** Evan D '00
(513) 762-6200 **Thomas** Joseph P '88
(513) 221-0007 **Thomas** Leslie F '95
(513) 241-1950 **Thomas** Michael E '97
(513) 745-0400 **Thomas** Scott R '93
(513) 961-5311 **Thomas & Thomas**
(513) 961-5311 **Thomas** Vincent E '87
(513) 241-3111 **Thompson** Allan R II '80
(513) 946-3700 **Thompson** Bruce F '72
(513) 961-6200 **Thompson** Cory D '04
(513) 352-6700 **Thompson Hine LLP**
(513) 232-7576 **Thompson** James W '68
(513) 891-1867 **Thompson** Molly M '95
(513) 632-5330 **Thompson** Stephen G '83
(513) 721-1975 **Thompson** Tod J '03
(513) 651-6800 **Thomson** Douglas D '86
Thomson Stephanie Schrimpf '87
(513) 489-1955 **Thornton** Charles W Jr. '72
(513) 891-1222 **Thornton** Jack F '69
(513) 381-9200 **Thumann** Robert J '02
(513) 241-7460 **Thurman** Milton Jr. '61
(513) 721-1200 **Thye** Kelly W '01
(513) 946-3125 **Tieger** Seth S '78
(513) 946-3000 **Tierney** Kevin M '00
(513) 946-3000 **Tierney** Mark R '95
(513) 629-1470 **Tierney** Selena M '99
(513) 761-2958 **Tillar** Mark T '85
(513) 631-3481 **Tillery** Dwight '73
(513) 721-7522 **Tilton** Fredric F '73
(513) 870-2116 **Timmel** Timothy L '76
(513) 631-2112 **Tincher** James R '04
(513) 983-4661 **Ting** Jennifer J '00
(513) 621-6464 **Tinkler** Hans M '02
(513) 241-2324 **Tittel** Bruce '64
(513) 241-8137 **Tobias Kraus & Torchia**
(513) 241-8137 **Tobias** Paul H '62
(513) 381-8430 **Tobin** Stuart '69
(513) 421-4020 **Todd** David H '63
(513) 946-3000 **Tolbert** Steven M '78
(513) 651-6800 **Tomain** Joseph A '03
(513) 621-2120 **Tonne** Jason D '03
(513) 241-3100 **Top** Andrew M '98
(513) 241-8137 **Torchia** David G '84
(513) 569-9999 **Torok** Ruth M '85
(513) 412-8336 **Toron** Moses J '99
(513) 381-2838 **Townsend** Robert J '64
(513) 745-3129 **Tracey** Ann M '75
(513) 595-2328 **Trammell** Dennis L '77
(513) 983-1100 **Tramonte** Tracy M '01
(513) 946-3000 **Tranter** Amy L '00
(513) 621-9204 **Tranter** Michael L '02
(513) 977-8200 **Tranter** Richard B '85
(513) 621-9204 **Tranter** Terence M '69
(513) 621-9204 **Tranter** Terry W '99
(513) 665-9500 **Trapp** Michael J '97
(513) 579-6400 **Trauth** Joseph L Jr. '73
(513) 421-7500 **Trautmann** Richard S '74
(513) 531-2889 **Travis** Philip C '72
(513) 852-5600 **Tregre** Calvin S Jr. '01
(513) 489-9200 **Treinen** Arthur R '92
(513) 621-1767 **Trenz** Alan R '81
(513) 621-1767 **Trenz McKay & Knabe Co,LPA**
(513) 946-5180 **Triggs** Alan C '96
Trimboli Jon A '89
(513) 569-9999 **Triona** James P '78
(513) 569-9999 **Triona & Lockemeyer,Ltd**
(513) 723-4000 **Tripp** Douglas S '92
(513) 579-0080 **Trombetta** Patricia J '82
(513) 684-2572 **Troutman** Jane M '97
(513) 794-6443 **Trumbo** Steven R '88
(513) 721-0060 **Tuch** Gayle G '89
(513) 721-3330 **Tucker** Jack L '83
(513) 946-3451 **Tucker** Stacy L '00
(513) 984-8700 **Turner** Richard P '98
(513) 352-4718 **Tye** Elizabeth A '03
(513) 585-0647 **Tyler** June S '86
(513) 561-3313 **Uhl** Jay J '74
(513) 665-3500 **Uhl** Judd R '99
(513) 345-6772 **Uhrig** Robert F '92
(513) 388-9222 **Ulbrich** Channing L '00
(513) 388-9222 **Ulbrich** Peter '72
(513) 388-9222 **Ulbrich** Wayne E '00
(513) 241-3100 **Ullman** Alan J '83
(513) 489-0881 **Ullner** Jonathan M '81
(513) 651-6800 **Ulmer** Andrew B '03
(513) 762-6200 **Ulmer & Berne LLP**
(513) 922-8836 **Ultsch** William F '50
(513) 721-8822 **Urling** James P '99
(513) 563-4555 **Utaski** Thomas J '87
(513) 721-4532 **Utt** Daniel P '86
(513) 579-6400 **Utter** Gregory M '81
Utz Eugene J '53
(513) 852-8200 **Vahlsing** Joseph H '72
(513) 984-8700 **Valencia** Louis E '04
(513) 852-8200 **Valleau** Richard J '62
(513) 579-1500 **Valz** David R '94
(513) 629-1882 **Vance** James J '86
(513) 793-2353 **Vance** Molly G '03
(513) 977-8200 **Vander Laan** Mark A '73
Vande Ryt Richard C '02
(513) 721-1504 **Van Houten** Dennis W '76
(513) 272-3188 **Van Tuyl** Jacquelyn D '03
(513) 241-0400 **Van Valkenburg** Valerie L '86
(513) 698-1991 **VanWay** Jeff '98
(513) 381-5700 **Vardiman** Edwin L Jr. '99
(513) 281-0804 **Varnau** Dennis J '89
(513) 684-3719 **Vaughan** Engrid J '72
(513) 569-6301 **Vaught** Barbara A '03
(513) 721-8210 **Veith** Patrick R '02
(513) 744-9600 **Veith** Sarah A '02
(513) 721-8210 **Veith** Terrence M '75
(513) 381-2838 **Vella** Theresa H '01
(513) 361-1200 **Venesy** Bryan J '88
(513) 723-2204 **Veneziano** Frank J '85
(513) 287-3023 **Vennemann** Jerome A '79
(513) 621-3394 **Venters-Wilson** Lona J '00
Ventress William W '59
(513) 977-8200 **Verchot** Joan M '86
(513) 651-4400 **Verkamp** Jennifer M '96
(513) 791-1539 **Victor** Irving W '55
(513) 977-8200 **Vincent** George H '82
(513) 651-6800 **Vineyard** Joshua L '04
(513) 634-2648 **Vitenberg** Vladimir '95
(513) 946-3000 **Vizedom** Anita '01
(513) 421-4225 **Vogel** Cedric W '72
(513) 946-3670 **Vogele** James A '73
(513) 241-7111 **Vojtush** Gayle P '89
(513) 651-4400 **Volkema Thomas Miller Burkett Scott & Merry, LPA**
(513) 579-1707 **Vollman** Carl W '51
(513) 421-4020 **Vollman** Jeffrey S '98
(513) 651-6800 **Vollman** Jill M '96
(513) 579-1707 **Vollman** Mark C '81
(513) 569-9999 **Vollman** Paul J '95
(513) 421-4020 **Vollman** Stanton H '66
(513) 762-7063 **Vollmer** Hilary L '99
(513) 825-6758 **Von Hagen** Frank J '55
(513) 651-6800 **von Saucken** Sylvius H '98
(513) 579-7389 **Von Wahlde** Stephen '82
(513) 985-2500 **Voorhees** Michael R '87
(513) 723-4000 **Vorys Sater Seymour & Pease LLP**
(513) 651-6800 **Wachs** Jim S '58
(513) 784-8616 **Wagner** Barbara J '88
(513) 621-8688 **Wagner** David C '89
(513) 632-9526 **Wagner** John J '71
(513) 946-3431 **Wagner** June E '96
(513) 243-0818 **Wagner** Nancy R '95
(513) 763-7700 **Waite** Charles J '81
(513) 621-0267 **Waite Schneider Bayless & Chesley**
(513) 333-0990 **Walden** Charles C '84
(513) 381-2838 **Wales** Ross E '74
(513) 977-4220 **Walk** Rodger N '74
(513) 946-4323 **Walker** Bernice L '93
(513) 651-6800 **Walker** H Lawson II '75
(513) 621-0267 **Walker** Jane H '84
(513) 287-3970 **Walker** Janice L '95
(513) 345-4539 **Wall** Richard F '98
(513) 352-1502 **Wall** Stacy M '98
(513) 241-9440 **Wallace** Teri A '92
(513) 762-6200 **Wallace** Traci L '00
(513) 482-5039 **Walls** Janetta S '01
(513) 378-8467 **Walls** Melanie B '97
(513) 241-3100 **Walsh** Kevin R '01
(513) 263-4900 **Walter** Edward L '87
(513) 931-4910 **Walter** Janis L '82
(513) 681-1800 **Walters** Michele A '83
(513) 983-8469 **Walther** Christopher B '91
(513) 946-5900 **Walton** Michael L '73
(513) 723-4000 **Walton** Victor A Jr. '91
(513) 651-6800 **Walulik** David W '03
(513) 579-6400 **Walwyn** Jennifer K '04
(513) 977-8200 **Wamsley** Andrew J '04
(513) 455-5348 **Ward** Dennis R '91
(513) 621-8210 **Ward** Richard G '86
(513) 621-8210 **Ward** Richard H '49
(513) 381-2838 **Ward** Tracy T '99
(513) 541-0287 **Ware** Nancy E '83
(513) 381-2838 **Warncke** Daniel R '93
(513) 579-9700 **Warner** David L '98
(513) 621-2825 **Warnock** Frank E '88
(513) 621-6464 **Warren** David S '89
(513) 421-4428 **Warren** Michael W '02
Warrington Mary G '88
Warwick Chad C '72
(513) 272-1200 **Wasco** Heather H '01
(513) 946-9000 **Washington** Scheherazade '91
(513) 723-4000 **Washington** Ward B '03
(513) 723-1600 **Wasserman** Mark J '84
(513) 631-3724 **Wassermann** Frank J '75
(513) 946-3000 **Waters** Mark G '84
(513) 946-9000 **Watkins** Katherine H '85
(513) 651-6800 **Watson** Clint C '04
(513) 723-1121 **Watters** Mark M '82
(513) 347-4407 **Watts** Angela D '02
(513) 556-6805 **Watts** Barbara G '78
(513) 241-9400 **Watts** Susan E '85
(513) 627-7386 **Waugh** Kevin L '01
(513) 621-2120 **Wayne** Richard S '79
(513) 381-9200 **Weakley** Leonard A Jr. '77
(513) 304-5410 **Weaver** Rosiene H '89
(513) 852-8565 **Webb** Donald H '78
(513) 345-4160 **Webb** Gail W '86
(513) 579-7920 **Webb** Gary A '85
(513) 852-6000 **Weber** Arthur D Jr. '73
(513) 721-5672 **Weber** Bradford C '97
(513) 621-2260 **Weber Dickey & Bellman**
(513) 621-2260 **Weber** Donald L '61
(513) 763-7124 **Weber** Edward P III '98
(513) 721-2120 **Weber** Harry P '74
Weber John P '03
(513) 852-8200 **Weber** Katharine C '89
(513) 579-6400 **Weber** Mark J '80
(513) 684-3201 **Weber** Mary H '76
(513) 621-2260 **Weber** Michael L '89
(513) 381-2838 **Weber** Roger A '73
(513) 946-3818 **Weber** Terry A '81
(513) 867-3577 **Weeden** Linda A '98
(513) 381-2838 **Weeks** Steven W '77
(513) 791-4644 **Wegner** Kenneth E '82
(513) 621-3394 **Wehmer** Brenda K '91
(513) 626-1139 **Wei Berk** Caroline '98
(513) 241-3111 **Weigand** Maria L '88
(513) 723-4000 **Weigel** W Breck '85
(513) 241-3992 **Weigle** Douglas S '76
(513) 977-8200 **Weigle** Gerald V Jr. '71
(513) 721-1311 **Weil** Rick L '98
(513) 621-2100 **Weil** Sidney '50
(513) 564-7350 **Weiler** Kimberly M '94
(513) 684-6988 **Weill** Neal J '78
(513) 489-9200 **Weinberg** Allen M '78
(513) 984-6314 **Weiner** Charles '57
(513) 723-4000 **Weinewuth** Elizabeth E W '04
(513) 634-1612 **Weirich** David M '93
(513) 352-3305 **Weise** Robert L Jr. '97
(513) 721-4450 **Weisenberger** Andrew W '02
(513) 381-9200 **Weisenfelder** Wilson G Jr. '85
(513) 984-2040 **Weisensel** Karen P '96
(513) 241-7111 **Weisensel** Michael D '97
(513) 579-6400 **Weiss** Herbert B '65
(513) 579-6400 **Weiss** Mark A '92
(513) 721-3236 **Weisser** Mark B '83
(513) 721-3236 **Weisser & Wolf**
(513) 381-3525 **Welch** Robert J Jr. '75
(513) 946-3418 **Welker** Paula L '88
(513) 579-6400 **Weller** Jill A '85
(513) 621-6464 **Wellington** Kent '91
(513) 977-8200 **Wells** Ben F '83
(513) 721-4450 **Wells** Terese M '93
(513) 946-3700 **Welsh** Michael W '01
(513) 723-4000 **Welsh** Rosemary D '95
(513) 241-1989 **Welsh** William M '92
(513) 241-0607 **Welt** David S '85
(513) 723-2200 **Weltman Weinberg & Reis Co,LPA**
(513) 241-8844 **Wendel** Richard G II '92
(513) 352-6739 **Wendeln** John H '84
(513) 721-1997 **Wenke** Stephen J '88
(513) 791-1672 **Wenker** Herman H '59
(513) 791-1672 **Wenker** Michelle M '93
(513) 381-9200 **Wenker** Paul F '67
(513) 421-4225 **Wenstrup** Daniel J '76
(513) 381-2838 **Wernicke** Vanessa A '04
(513) 721-4450 **Wersching** James P '80
(513) 721-0200 **Weseli** Roger W '95
(513) 651-6800 **Wesloh** Steven M '96
(513) 556-3483 **Wesner** James E '92
(513) 632-5328 **West** Dave R '89
(513) 946-5204 **West** Melissa E '95
(513) 852-6093 **Westendorf** Douglas L '74
(513) 595-2325 **Westerbeck** David F '72
(513) 852-8200 **Westerfield** Thomas J '81
(513) 977-8200 **Weston** Harris K '46
(513) 639-6519 **Westrich** Whitney B '03
(513) 528-0200 **Wetherall** Gregory M '96
(513) 241-7244 **Wettstein** Albert '41
(513) 241-3100 **Whalen** Melissa J '97
(513) 977-8200 **Whaley** David A '03
(513) 983-7695 **Whaley** Susan S '99
(513) 421-4646 **Wharton** Bernard W '94
(513) 352-6853 **Wharton** Lisa M '92
(513) 381-4700 **Wheatley** Christine S '96
(513) 381-2838 **Wheatley** Susan E '86
(513) 361-1200 **Wheeler** David L '96
(513) 977-8200 **Wherley** James M Jr. '01
(513) 723-4000 **Whitaker** Glenn V '80
(513) 579-6400 **Whitaker** James R '73
(513) 723-4000 **White** Geoffrey M '03
(513) 241-3685 **White Getgey & Meyer Co,LPA**
(513) 381-2838 **White** Kristin N '03
(513) 241-7460 **White** Maurice O '78
(513) 595-2333 **White** Michael J '84
(513) 946-3819 **White** Thomas C Jr. '00
(513) 651-7232 **Whitehurst** John R II '81
(513) 721-6151 **Whiteley** Daniel E Jr. '75
(513) 651-6800 **Whitlow** Janice Baker '03
(513) 852-8200 **Whitlow** Matthew A '03
(513) 421-3940 **Whitman** Bruce B '80
(513) 352-0401 **Whitman** Virginia C '81
(513) 751-8300 **Whittaker** James A '85
(513) 243-5402 **Whittenburg** Mark G '92
(513) 977-8200 **Widdowson** Mary E '04
(513) 618-6705 **Widmann** Douglas J '02
(513) 241-5551 **Wiethe** Barbara R '79
(513) 684-3711 **Wiethe** Donetta D '77
(513) 241-7332 **Wiethe** Michael J '72
(513) 621-2666 **Wietholter** Thomas A '87
(513) 352-6524 **Wilcoxon** Kimberly D '01
(513) 221-8734 **Wild** Jerry G '01
(513) 946-5744 **Wilder** Mark A '99
(513) 677-0999 **Wiley** Donald L '71
(513) 246-0036 **Wiley** Julia H '82
(513) 530-1634 **Wilheim** Ronald S '96
(513) 977-8200 **Wilhelmy** Alicia L '01
(513) 946-3580 **Wilke** Wayne F '60
(513) 333-0700 **Wilken** Steven J '84
(513) 793-7200 **Wilkins** Nancy E '95
(513) 793-4911 **Wilkinson** Carl E '58
(513) 977-8200 **Wilkinson** George B '82
(513) 579-6400 **Wilkowski** E Todd '98
(513) 946-3279 **Wilkowski** Heather A '98
(513) 241-9400 **Willacker** Terence M '76
(513) 352-6700 **Willbrand** David J '96
(513) 744-7754 **Willen** Diana J '78
(513) 558-5696 **Willenbrink** Matthew '03
Williams Clarence D III '83
(513) 721-1078 **Williams** James R '75
(513) 651-3456 **Williams** John J '89
(513) 946-3000 **Williams** John M '93
(513) 621-0930 **Williams** John M '94
(513) 579-3100 **Williams** John P Jr. '66
(513) 233-0756 **Williams** Stacey R '00
(513) 651-6800 **Williams** Tamra G '04
(513) 612-2300 **Williams** Tina M '03
(513) 421-6630 **Williamson** David E '99
(513) 621-8688 **Williamson** Karl E '90
(513) 733-3332 **Williamson** Leonard A '75
(513) 621-2120 **Williamson** William O '04
(513) 784-7132 **Willis** Craig R '04
(513) 977-8200 **Willis** Jeffrey A '02
(513) 381-9200 **Willis** Marisa A '03
(513) 381-2838 **Willis** Ryan L '01
(513) 381-9200 **Willis** Chad E '96
(513) 985-2500 **Willmann** Neal O '93
(513) 721-5707 **Wills** Teddy L '92
(513) 489-7484 **Wilson** Charles R '70
Wilson Charlotte M '00
(513) 397-6351 **Wilson** Christopher J '91
(513) 721-7010 **Wilson** David E '82
(513) 961-6200 **Wilson** George R '81
(513) 352-5858 **Wilson** Gregory R '78
(513) 522-1255 **Wilson** Joanne A '84
(513) 475-4902 **Wilson** Julie K '83
(513) 381-2838 **Wilson** LaQuita S '03

(513) 891-6600 **Wilson** Thomas P '88
(513) 651-6800 **Wilson** W Russell '83
(513) 243-0792 **Winget** James L '95
(513) 621-5500 **Winkler** Diane E '91
(513) 946-5175 **Winkler** Ralph E '87
(513) 946-5143 **Winkler** Robert C '87
(513) 579-6400 **Winstead** John N '98
(513) 421-4646 **Winters** Ralph G '76
(513) 579-2980 **Wirthlin** John R '85
(513) 221-1745 **Wirthlin** John S Jr. '79
(513) 221-1745 **Wirthlin** Michael F '82
(513) 381-2838 **Wise** Bryan E '03
(513) 684-3225 **Wissman** Brian M '00
(513) 421-5297 **Witt** Jeffrey A '96
(513) 794-0934 **Witte** Monte D '74
Witte Richard C '57
(513) 721-1975 **Wittenauer** Ann K '02
(513) 241-4722 **Woeber** Linda L '87
(513) 852-6044 **Woebkenberg** Thomas M '86
(513) 772-6887 **Wolf** Barbara W '93
(513) 984-3030 **Wolf** David A '66
(513) 946-5174 **Wolf** Ellen T '78
(513) 621-2120 **Wolf** Leon L '50
(513) 731-7798 **Wolf** Martin H '75
(513) 852-8230 **Wolf** Sara S '76
(513) 721-3236 **Wolf** Scott A '84
(513) 421-4248 **Wolf** Stephen G '78
(513) 984-2699 **Wolfe** Jennifer C '99
Wolfe Ruth Anne G '94
(513) 754-3640 **Womack** Michael A '93
(513) 421-2730 **Wong** Bernard F '89
(513) 541-0100 **Wong** Dan Y '78
Wood Carol S '88
(513) 621-8688 **Wood** Daniel J '86
(513) 946-3000 **Wood** David R '87
(513) 936-5663 **Wood** Frank G II '76
(513) 241-2324 **Wood Herron & Evans LLP**
(513) 852-6000 **Wood & Lamping LLP**
(513) 922-4916 **Wood** Robert A '49
(513) 487-5984 **Wood** Walter S '84
(513) 744-8782 **Woodard** Kevin S '91
(513) 977-8200 **Woodside** Frank C III '69
(513) 489-4157 **Woolsey** Monica K '04
(513) 983-1493 **Wooten** Kelli L '01
(513) 621-6464 **Worrell** A Christian III '85
(513) 241-3992 **Wright** Darrell S '86
(513) 946-6404 **Wright** Gail A '96
(513) 771-7266 **Wright** LaTonia Denise '97
(513) 723-3467 **Wright** Ross A '94
(513) 629-1469 **Wuebbling** Donald J '74
(513) 983-4370 **Wunsch** Eric J '97
(513) 352-6700 **Wuorinen** Susan E '89
(513) 583-0600 **Wurster** Walter C II '74
(513) 621-7600 **Wykoff** John R '79
(513) 352-3337 **Wyler** Deborah H '01
(513) 579-1414 **Wyler** William S '72
(513) 241-3111 **Wynn** Suzanne L '91
(513) 721-2424 **Xanders** George L III '80
(513) 648-7061 **Yaeger** Daniel A '81
(513) 721-5151 **Yager** Christina S '99
(513) 983-1477 **Yates** Irene W '96
(513) 564-7072 **Yates** Janice E '82
(513) 281-5474 **Yates** Tyrone K '83
(513) 721-4500 **Yeager** Stephen M '81
(513) 621-9000 **Yelton** Donald G '94
Yetter Jerry J '73
(513) 721-5672 **Yocum** Thomas R '79
(513) 871-8219 **York Schiff** Elizabeth '90
(513) 421-8100 **Youkilis** John C '87
(513) 326-5555 **Young & Alexander Co,LPA**
(513) 243-0083 **Young** Gregory E '78
(513) 721-1077 **Young** Gregory S '86
(513) 352-6617 **Young** Malcolm Scott '93
(513) 721-1200 **Young** Martin M '59
(513) 825-7600 **Young** Michael T '83
(513) 721-1077 **Young** Michele L '93
(513) 721-1200 **Young Reverman & Mazzei Co,LPA**
(513) 352-6700 **Young** Rodney M '95
(513) 621-2120 **Young** Shawn M '87
(513) 793-5150 **Young** Wallace H '00
(513) 352-6796 **Youtsey** Deborah A '88
(513) 977-8200 **Yu** Tracy R '99
(513) 651-6800 **Yund** George E '77
(513) 723-4000 **Yurchuck** Roger A '62
(513) 651-6800 **Zackerman** Jeffrey L '97
(513) 665-3500 **Zahniser** David W '04
(513) 381-2838 **Zahniser** Rachel Sublett '03
(513) 381-9200 **Zamary** George J '99
(513) 381-0656 **Zamary** Kimberly A '00
(513) 977-8200 **Zaunbrecher** Susan B '90
(513) 579-7877 **Zavatsky** Kathleen H '79
(513) 381-2838 **Zavatsky** Michael J '80
(513) 621-4224 **Zayas-Davis** Marilyn '99
(513) 362-8700 **Zealey** Sharon J '84
(513) 651-4226 **Zegarski** Daniel S '95
(513) 794-6515 **Zeinner** Lawrence A '99
(513) 651-6800 **Zerbst** Hilla M '78
(513) 627-2885 **Zerby** Kim W '84
(513) 271-0053 **Ziegler** Thomas F '95
(513) 579-7900 **Ziermaier** Klaus M '70
(513) 241-9400 **Zigman** Andrea K '95
(513) 721-1513 **Zimmer** Barry H '79
(513) 352-3321 **Zimmer** Christine M '84
(513) 852-8200 **Zimmer** Hans M '84
(513) 232-0846 **Zimmerman** Donald J '61
(513) 381-2838 **Zimmerman** James M '99
(513) 946-9000 **Zorn** Philip L Jr. '73
(513) 241-7111 **Zucker** Elizabeth M '92
(513) 381-0656 **Zummo** Mark J '80
(513) 946-6065 **Zummo** Valerie B '82

CIRCLEVILLE
Pickaway County

(740) 474-2000 **Agin** Kevin T '91
(740) 477-8887 **Archer** William L Jr. '88
(740) 474-7561 **Bennington** Kevin G '99
(740) 474-7561 **Bennington** Roger E '64
(740) 474-6900 **Berger** Allan '59
Bickel Leif P '03
(740) 474-7231 **Blasko** Stacey L '96
(740) 477-1361 **Bowers** John E '79
(740) 474-6026 **Branham** Elisa M '93
(740) 474-6900 **Brown** Jennifer Lyn '89
(740) 477-2173 **Clark** Lori D '94
(740) 474-2179 **Crowder-Dorsey** Kathy Jo '89
(740) 474-7841 **Dawson** Laura W '97
(740) 474-7841 **DePaul** Sara C '04
(740) 474-6021 **Dumm** Gary R '77
(740) 474-5237 **Eyerman** Susan E '84
(740) 474-3103 **Farthing** John H '73
(740) 474-7575 **Gerhardt** Richard L '66
(740) 477-6044 **Greene** Patrick K '84
(740) 474-6066 **Harsha** Shelly R '86
(740) 477-2173 **Hill** James K '72
(740) 474-2179 **Huffer & Huffer Co,LPA**
(740) 474-2179 **Huffer** Robert H '56
(740) 474-2179 **Huffer** Roy H Jr. '64
(740) 477-2536 **Kenworthy** Gary D '80
(740) 477-2546 **Kingsley** James R '72
(740) 474-6043 **Kitchen** James D '70
(740) 477-1605 **Long** Paul E II '74
(740) 474-7500 **Lucks** Barbara J '76
(740) 474-7642 **Marting** Rodger A '74
(740) 474-5437 **Noble** Ricky D '93
(740) 474-5407 **Penn** Richard W '50
(740) 474-5437 **Reed** Kristen S '89
(740) 420-8286 **Rudawsky** Sandra E '00
(740) 477-2502 **Steely** Melody L '78
(740) 474-7588 **Tonn** Jason W '01
(740) 474-6021 **Tootle** Thomas F '73
(740) 474-2780 **Wilburn** Bernard P '84
(740) 474-2780 **Wilburn** Charles W '64
(740) 474-6066 **Wolford** Judy C '93

CLEVELAND
Cuyahoga County

(216) 522-1555 **Abakumov** Georg '77
(216) 687-1311 **Abbarno** Kenneth P '92
(216) 583-1160 **Abbass** Rolla Z '99
(216) 621-6138 **Abel** Jack W '74
(216) 443-8602 **Abens** Matthew B '02
(216) 691-2405 **Abramoff** Howard B '77
(216) 575-0777 **Acton** Shawn M '00
(440) 888-6660 **Adamczyk** Beverly A '90
(216) 586-3939 **Adamo** Kenneth R '84
(216) 621-0200 **Adams** Albert T '77
(216) 664-6900 **Adams** Beth M '02
(216) 443-8589 **Adams** Beverly A '02
(216) 502-0600 **Adams** Gregory J '98
(216) 931-6000 **Adams** Jennifer Lawry '96
(216) 443-7223 **Adams** John F '76
(216) 787-3407 **Adams** Margaret E '92
Adams Michael W '01
(216) 621-1113 **Adams** Thomas W '92
(216) 696-3332 **Adamson** Charles Z '78
(216) 983-1053 **Adelman** Harlin G '90
(216) 781-0755 **Adelstein** Carol B '88
(216) 883-0509 **Adelstein** Louis S '86
(216) 277-0702 **Adkins** Ilah M '03
(216) 623-0150 **Adkins** Lewis W Jr. '93
(216) 696-4200 **Adler** Charles F III '83
(216) 586-3939 **Adler** David F '87
(216) 566-5086 **Adorno** Juan E '79
(216) 241-0286 **Adrine** Ethel M '93
(216) 664-4974 **Adrine** Ronald B '73
(216) 479-8500 **Agati** Andrew '95
(216) 291-1300 **Agins** Kerry M '00
(216) 696-1550 **Agopian** Richard V '75
(216) 586-3939 **Agozzino** Leozino '85
(216) 575-1002 **Ahern** Ann-Marie R '98
Ainley Gary L '86
(216) 241-5310 **Aitken** Janice P '96
(216) 623-9999 **Akers-Parry** Deborah '76
(216) 931-6000 **Al-Shidhani** Lynnette L '03
(216) 586-3939 **Alavi** Atossa M '03
(440) 826-0125 **Albanese** Michael A '97
(216) 368-6353 **Alber** Alyson S '98
(216) 479-6100 **Albers** Matthew E '02
(216) 931-6000 **Albert** Steven W '71
(216) 241-8172 **Albin** Jason T '04
(216) 587-6500 **Albright** Mylayna S '00
(216) 398-0591 **Albu** John F '92
(216) 575-1560 **Alcox** Patrick J '76
(216) 586-3939 **Alden** David B '83
(216) 252-7300 **Alden** Phyllis C '89
(216) 566-5749 **Aldrich** Thomas A '82
(216) 430-1200 **Alexander** Andrew C '89
(216) 928-1010 **Alexander** Joseph P '81
(216) 621-1530 **Alexander** Louis P Jr. '03
(216) 241-5310 **Alexandersen** Kevin C '86
(216) 443-6350 **Aliberti** Louis S '99
(216) 348-5400 **Alikhan** Mariam '04
(216) 377-0598 **Allan** Sean P '89
(216) 523-5000 **Allbery** Scott E '87
(216) 433-2317 **Allen** Carolyn W '72
(216) 241-2838 **Allen** David V '87
(216) 771-4000 **Allen** Thomas F '68
(216) 689-5775 **Allen** Thomas S '79
(216) 297-7000 **Allison** Thomas H '87
(216) 621-0200 **Allotta** John J '01
(216) 443-7800 **Almaro** Isadora A '00
(216) 464-7015 **Alperin** Mitchell L '77
(216) 696-7600 **Alten** Heidi L '97
(216) 931-6000 **Alten** John M '99
(216) 696-6776 **Althouse** Philip D '91
(216) 383-2708 **Altieri** Bruce E '85
(216) 861-5070 **Altmeyer** Susan M '91
(216) 687-1311 **Alusheff** Charles P '85
(216) 274-0800 **Amaddio** Mark D '89
(216) 443-7295 **Amata** Salvatore '81
(216) 651-5000 **Amata** Theodore A '95
Amato Anthony J '92
(216) 431-8405 **Amato** Darlene D '91
(216) 696-1400 **Amato** Marion B '62
(216) 621-0200 **Ambriola-Anastos** Lori M '97
(216) 586-3939 **Amer** Kathleen M '04
(216) 581-8200 **Amer** Margaret E '94
(216) 589-0640 **Amigoni** Albert R '75
(216) 696-8730 **Amin** Himanshu S '95
(216) 696-8730 **Amin & Turocy LLP**
(216) 932-5100 **Amini** Saeid Baradaran '99
(216) 687-2300 **Ammons** Linda L '87
(216) 781-1212 **Ammons** Randal G '92
(216) 928-2200 **Amos** Marc D '04
(216) 664-4407 **Amponsah** Kim D '85
(216) 575-3283 **Amstadt** Nancy Rae '99
(216) 741-8552 **Anastos** James M '92
(216) 664-2737 **Anastos** Thomas Leo '89
(216) 368-3600 **Andelman** Barbara F '86
(216) 443-9000 **Anderle** Robert D '95
(216) 861-2388 **Andersen** Todd J '87
(216) 781-1111 **Anderson** Benjamin H '97
(216) 586-3939 **Anderson** Laura R '97
(216) 696-7600 **Anderson** Timothy S '99
(216) 592-5000 **Anderton** A Michael '93
(216) 621-0200 **Andorka** Frank H '75
(216) 621-0200 **Andrassy** Dana R '94
(216) 586-3939 **Andreini** Mark J '94
(216) 520-0088 **Andrew** Donna M '96
(216) 621-0200 **Andrews** Barry W '95
(216) 621-0150 **Andrews** Catherine V '00
(216) 447-1551 **Andrews** David T '93
(216) 771-1430 **Andrews** Douglas A '84
(216) 621-0200 **Andrews** Oakley V '65
(216) 687-1311 **Anenson** T Leigh '94
(216) 789-5536 **Angelo** Michael J '84
(216) 443-5710 **Angelotta** John L '52
(216) 443-8579 **Angley** Sonia R '98
(216) 363-4500 **Angney** Jessica L '01
(216) 931-2346 **Anhold** Gordon A '71
(216) 241-8333 **Ankuda** Christopher J '01
(216) 360-7200 **Annos** George J '92
(216) 621-0150 **Ansberry** Sean M '99
(216) 485-1040 **Anselmo** Christopher A '89
(216) 621-0200 **Anselmo** Michelle B '04
(216) 566-0064 **Anselmo** Victor V '88
(216) 241-3400 **Anthony** Hilary J '00
(216) 861-2222 **Antonelli** Dominic M '87
Antonelli Mariellen M '02
(216) 479-8279 **Anway** Stephen P '02
(216) 771-6597 **Apelt** Ronald A '90
(216) 696-3550 **Apicella** Felix M '54
(216) 566-5548 **Appelbaum** Jeffrey R '77
(216) 514-4125 **Apple** Sheldon A '63
(216) 621-4636 **Arabian** Anjanette C '01
(216) 622-3600 **Arbeznik** Gary D '76
(216) 443-3674 **Arbie-McClelland** Valerie R '93
(216) 787-3638 **Arcangelini** F. M '93
(216) 621-9870 **Archibald** Robert D '56
Arciaga Arthur A '81
(216) 931-6000 **Arendt** Michelle R '98
(216) 623-0150 **Arfons** Walter Chad II '97
(216) 443-7295 **Arinze** Francis M '98
(216) 515-1660 **Arison** Barbara J '75
(216) 363-1400 **Armstrong** Barbara L '87
Armstrong Heidi A '93
(216) 696-3311 **Armstrong** Lester W '86
(216) 566-0064 **Armstrong Mitchell Damiani & Zaccagnini**
(216) 566-0064 **Armstrong** Timothy J '72
(216) 348-0041 **Armstrong** William E '67
(216) 664-3584 **Armstrong** William H Jr. '92
(216) 241-6602 **Arnold** David G '66
(216) 664-2693 **Arnold** Jack M '78
(216) 642-7878 **Arnold** Kemper D '80
(216) 761-7601 **Arnold** Wanda R '80
(216) 621-0200 **Arnold** William L '77
(216) 363-4500 **Aronoff** George N '58
(216) 566-5504 **Aronoff** James B '84
(216) 787-3030 **Aronoff** Steven K '86
(216) 621-0040 **Arrighi** Amy L '98
(216) 443-8868 **Arrington** Joan K '93
(216) 523-1500 **Arvin** Ashley M '04
(216) 443-7800 **Asad** Faris Y '98
(216) 696-5580 **Asale** Shirley M '94
(216) 586-3939 **Asam** Michael R '01
(216) 522-5560 **Asher** Kenneth D '91
(216) 522-3870 **Ashley** Elizabeth R '90
(216) 515-1660 **Ashmus** Keith A '74
(216) 443-6350 **Ashwill** Ellen L '86
(216) 664-2716 **Assad** Awatef '95
(216) 443-8550 **Asseff** Michael C '97
(216) 781-7455 **Astrab** Michael K '97
(216) 687-1311 **Atkinson** Kathleen A '02
(216) 623-1901 **Attali** Michael D '02
(216) 443-7223 **Atzberger** Jennifer N '00
(216) 241-5310 **Auciello** Ernest W Jr. '85
(216) 443-6350 **Audey** Susan M '94
(216) 698-6410 **Audi** Frederick R '88
(216) 787-3633 **Augusta** James M '96
(216) 787-3649 **Augusta** Lori A '99
(216) 429-5251 **Augustine** Katherine A '95
(216) 443-8505 **Augustyn** Kevin C '92
(216) 443-7800 **Ault** Micah R '04
(216) 382-7114 **Aurslanian** Richard N '68
(216) 736-4540 **Ausprunk** Kenneth S '85
(216) 830-6830 **Aussem** James S '75
(216) 771-4445 **Austin** Gregg A '81
(216) 566-5927 **Austin** Heather A '93
(216) 241-4100 **Austin** Jeffrey L '98
(216) 381-3400 **Austin** Nicholas A '98
(216) 621-1000 **Austria** Robert L '98
Autero Brian K '04
(216) 363-4500 **Auvil** Steven M '94
(440) 684-1600 **Aveni** James V '93
(216) 363-4500 **Avsec** Mark E '95
Awadallah Mahmoud S '03
(216) 443-7800 **Awadallah** Saleh S '94
(216) 689-4959 **Axel** Michael A '83
(216) 781-1710 **Axner** Gary R '71
(216) 621-0200 **Azoff** Elliot S '73
(216) 622-8306 **Babbit** Harold W '67
(216) 363-4500 **Babbitt** Lindsay C '04
(216) 328-8700 **Babbitt** Michael R '75
(216) 621-0150 **Babbitt** Ross M '00
(216) 367-7744 **Babcock** Clifford G '90
(216) 367-7744 **Babcock & Wasserman Co,LPA**
Babington Margaret M '84
(216) 443-6373 **Babinski** Michael T '98
(216) 443-7800 **Bacchus** Renee A '94
(216) 830-8800 **Bacevice** John P '84
(216) 696-9100 **Backus** Russell P '95
(216) 515-1660 **Bacon** Brett K '72
(216) 381-9878 **Baczewski** Barbara A '89
(216) 621-0200 **Baddeley** Jeffrey A '83
(216) 357-7098 **Badertscher** Sharon J '92
(216) 523-4101 **Baechle** Thomas J '72
(216) 566-5500 **Baek** Annie Jinyun '04
(216) 443-8505 **Bagnato** Elizabeth R '82
(216) 928-0600 **Bailey** Erika D '02
(216) 222-2974 **Bailey** William J Jr. '94
(216) 363-1400 **Bain** Richard M '79
(216) 622-8200 **Baisden** W Eric '91
(216) 222-9139 **Bajus** Susan M '90
(216) 622-3600 **Bakeman** Ronald B '73
(216) 771-3966 **Baker** Adam S '98
(216) 566-8200 **Baker** Eric D '98
(216) 664-6079 **Baker** Gail D '95
(216) 621-0200 **Baker & Hostetler LLP**
(216) 896-2138 **Baker** James A '70
(216) 771-3966 **Baker** Jason T '99
(216) 623-0000 **Baker** Kenneth B '76
(216) 696-1158 **Baker** Lawrence M '61
(216) 443-2054 **Baker** Linda Lou '88
(216) 771-3966 **Baker** Martin '71
(216) 241-0673 **Baker** Michael D '94
(216) 875-3167 **Baker** Michael R '88
(216) 687-1311 **Baker** Stacie L '99
(216) 928-2200 **Baker** Stuart D '04
(216) 592-5000 **Baker** Thomas W '99
(216) 781-7777 **Baker** William Joseph '00
(216) 696-1422 **Balantzow** Robert S '65
(216) 566-9700 **Balazs** James A '99
(216) 241-2838 **Balazs** Mary G '80
(216) 241-4482 **Balbier** Ronald C '73
(216) 781-5470 **Bales** Stephen M '83
(216) 451-1133 **Ball** Fred J '45
(216) 622-8269 **Ballard** Brent D '85
(216) 621-5300 **Ballard** John F Jr. '78
(216) 328-8700 **Ballard** Lynn A '91
(216) 696-1275 **Ballard-Eisman** Mary B '78
(216) 479-8500 **Ballin** Stacy D '83
(216) 469-9337 **Ballou** Emily A '92
(216) 776-9000 **Ballou** Scott H '80
(216) 479-6100 **Balmert** F Daniel '76
(216) 351-3935 **Baloga** David M '94
(216) 348-7741 **Balogh** Virginia E '92
(216) 621-0200 **Bamberger** Richard H '72
(216) 622-3881 **Bamberger** Roger S '72
(216) 566-7666 **Banchek** Melvin H '73
(216) 443-7223 **Bancroft** Michael R '83
(216) 781-0111 **Bancsi** Joseph '72
(216) 861-5582 **Bandy** Mark E '91
(216) 522-4870 **Bang** Jun S '01
(216) 566-5555 **Bank** Malvin E '57
(216) 566-5100 **Banks** Kenneth E '73
(216) 443-8580 **Banks** Marie C '01
(216) 566-0770 **Banta** Michael E '73
(440) 746-1177 **Baran Piper Tarkowsky Fitzgerald & Theis CO,LPA**
(216) 348-5400 **Baraona** Robert C '98
(216) 771-4050 **Barbour** Mark E '88
(216) 586-3939 **Baringer** Jennifer H '02
(216) 586-3939 **Baringer** Randal S '90
(216) 348-1700 **Barker** Pamela A '82
(216) 623-0150 **Barlow** J C Jeffrey '02
(216) 687-1311 **Barmen** Bradley J '03
(216) 341-2022 **Barnak** Andrew M '73
(216) 931-6000 **Barnard** Thomas H Jr. '64
(216) 687-1902 **Barnes** Austin B III '91
(216) 479-8500 **Barnes** Geoffrey K '73
(216) 696-3311 **Barnes** Kevin D '79
(216) 566-5578 **Barnes** Nancy M '02
(216) 443-7800 **Barnett** Kelley J '99
(216) 698-3204 **Barnett** Kimberly G '01
(216) 524-0710 **Barnett** Michelle L '04
(216) 861-7114 **Barnett** William A '81
(216) 687-2315 **Barnhizer** David R '73
(216) 443-3662 **Barnhizer** Joshua R '01
(440) 446-1100 **Barni** Thomas A '95
(216) 443-7800 **Baron** Nicole '00
(216) 781-3858 **Baron** Russell Z '55
(216) 651-3400 **Barr** Anthony S '02
(216) 363-1400 **Barr** Douglas N '72
(216) 931-6000 **Barr** Lewis T '67
(216) 696-6000 **Barr** Robert D '96
(216) 586-3939 **Barragate** Brett P '96
(216) 263-3402 **Barragate** Dana C '95
(216) 621-1530 **Barragate** Phillip C '94
(216) 696-1545 **Barrett** Joyce E '71
(216) 566-1600 **Barrows** Melissa E '03
(216) 479-8500 **Barry** George R '64
(216) 687-1311 **Barsoum** Marianne K '99
(216) 861-6000 **Bartel** Willard E '74
(216) 771-1900 **Bartell** Jonathan A '00
(216) 621-1180 **Bartell** Laurence A '72
(216) 771-1760 **Bartimole** Todd W '93
(216) 696-3311 **Bartman** Douglas V '00
(216) 928-2200 **Barto** Victoria D '99
(216) 351-6300 **Barz** Patricia '85
(216) 664-4397 **Bascone** Joan M '00
(216) 621-0200 **Bash** Brian A '75
(216) 771-3239 **Bashein & Bashein Co, LPA**
(216) 771-3239 **Bashein** Richard W '89
(216) 771-3239 **Bashein** William Craig '86
(216) 443-7295 **Basil** Autumn '95
(216) 689-0512 **Basil** David A '80
(216) 685-9500 **Basinger** Matthew R '03
(216) 621-3346 **Baskin** Sheldon E '62
(216) 464-4340 **Bass** Debra D '79
(216) 443-7725 **Bassett** Benton '64
(216) 357-5900 **Basta** Samuel W '95
(216) 479-6100 **Batista** Bruce P '94
(216) 621-0200 **Bator** Chris '87
(216) 622-8225 **Batt** John P '78
(216) 274-4536 **Battaglia** Lisa R '90
(216) 502-0350 **Baucco** Anthony A '03
(216) 241-1010 **Bauders** Robert S '70
(216) 426-4753 **Bauer** Fred D '90
(440) 746-2117 **Bauer** George J '75
(216) 586-3939 **Bauer** Gregory A '97
(216) 621-7227 **Bauer** James P '93
(216) 566-8500 **Bauernschmidt** Charles J '74
(216) 566-8500 **Bauernschmidt** Karen H '76
(216) 687-1244 **Baughman** R Patrick '63
(216) 781-5245 **Baumgardner** Lorraine R '80
(216) 696-6000 **Baumgart** Richard A '78
(216) 621-0200 **Baumgartner** Bruce O '67
(216) 696-3311 **Bautista** Philip R '01
(216) 875-6122 **Bays** James C '74
(216) 771-1760 **Beal** David A '82
(216) 664-2680 **Beasley** Teresa M '93
(216) 241-5310 **Beaudry** Stephen M '03

Beck Nancy F '86
(216) 241-2600 **Becker & Mishkind Co,LPA**
(216) 687-2323 **Becker** Susan J '84
(216) 344-1040 **Beckor** Colin '03
(216) 622-8501 **Beckstrom** Sean C '95
(216) 586-3939 **Bedell** Richard J Jr. '87
(216) 664-6924 **Bednar** Michael A '83
(216) 579-4214 **Beebe** Richard A '73
(216) 622-8639 **Beg** Murad A '01
(216) 687-3948 **Beggs** Gordon J '74
(216) 281-3838 **Begin** Robert T '77
(216) 771-1144 **Behrens Gioffre & Schroeder Co, LPA**
(216) 771-1144 **Behrens** James E '78
(216) 592-5000 **Bekeny** Karl A '02
(216) 586-3939 **Belasic** Mark A '86
(216) 664-4959 **Belcher** Gayle A '81
(216) 696-5887 **Belcher** Michael L '77
(216) 431-4500 **Belcher** Robin Donnell '02
(216) 621-7860 **Belden** Thomas G '71
(216) 583-3156 **Belenkaya** Tatiana '02
(216) 696-7600 **Belkin** Jeffrey A '65
(216) 622-8200 **Bell** Alyssa J '02
(216) 861-1148 **Bell** Edward J '83
(216) 295-8491 **Bell** Everett A '76
(216) 363-4500 **Bell** Lawrence M '61
(216) 443-7800 **Bell** Richard A '89
(216) 575-1002 **Bell** Steven D '79
(216) 566-5547 **Belman** Susan L '77
(440) 238-4622 **Belock** Wayne J '82
(440) 248-7906 **Belzer** Geoffrey A '00
(216) 579-1700 **Bembenick** Brian G '98
(216) 566-8200 **Bemer** Andrew D Jr. '73
(216) 241-0715 **Bencivenni** Michael R '88
(216) 928-1010 **Bender** John Timothy '78
(216) 579-9782 **Bender** Kyle R '98
(216) 778-4991 **Benedict** James J Jr. '96
(216) 363-4500 **Benesch Friedlander Coplan & Aronoff LLP**
(216) 781-4522 **Benford** Sheryl King '80
(216) 831-8234 **Benjamin** Lawrence S '74
(216) 622-8200 **Benjamin** Virginia D '76
(216) 861-1365 **Benko** Kerilyn '98
(216) 241-7000 **Bennett** Charles W '99
(216) 522-4914 **Bennett** Donald E '76
(216) 447-1551 **Bennett** Jennifer A '94
(216) 241-6602 **Bennett** Mark S '98
(216) 515-1660 **Bennett** Rebecca J '98
(216) 787-3030 **Bennett** Thomas D '03
(216) 535-0446 **Benos** Wayne F '80
(216) 241-6650 **Bensing** Russell S '75
(216) 583-1234 **Bensinger** Valerie J '99
(216) 241-2510 **Benson** David M '93
(216) 861-1234 **Bentoff & Duber Co,LPA**
(216) 363-1323 **Bentoff** Freddie J '61
(216) 861-9899 **Bentoff** Jerome L '54
(216) 241-0520 **Benza** Michael J '93
(216) 479-8500 **Beredo** Cipriano S III '99
(216) 621-0200 **Beredo** Gina A '99
(216) 621-0200 **Beredo** Mathew B '98
(216) 937-4000 **Berenger** Lori A '93
(216) 787-3030 **Beres** Susan Ann '81
(216) 586-3939 **Beresh-Taylor** Laura '00
(216) 696-6500 **Berg** Aaron P '01
(216) 781-5470 **Berg** Megan S '00
(216) 443-7800 **Berger** Gayl M '00
(216) 830-9000 **Berger** Isreal Joseph '50
Berger Sanford J '52
(216) 830-9000 **Berger & Zavesky Co, LPA**
(216) 479-8500 **Berick** Daniel G '92
(216) 771-8121 **Berk** Gerald A '70
(216) 241-3880 **Berk** Robert J '69
(216) 781-5245 **Berkman Gordon Murray & DeVan**
(216) 781-5515 **Berkson** Hugh D '94
(216) 479-0400 **Berlin** Jennifer W '97
(216) 696-3311 **Berliner** Irving H '79
(216) 622-8200 **Berliner** Stacy '03
(216) 621-5980 **Berman** Keevin J '77
(216) 291-3600 **Bernard & Haffey Co,LPA**
(440) 808-4242 **Berney** Sean F '92
(216) 781-7111 **Berris** Richard J '80
(216) 520-5546 **Berry** Melissa D '93
(216) 348-5400 **Berry** Patrick J '89
(216) 736-7219 **Bersticker** Steven C '86
(216) 664-3312 **Bertovich** Richard '92
(216) 265-2658 **Bertram** Ricky L '84
(216) 621-1000 **Bertsch** Michael J '82
(216) 382-2500 **Besser** Barbara Kaye '73
(216) 522-7675 **Besser** Howard R '66
(216) 664-2806 **Best** Christel '92
(216) 822-4723 **Bettendorf** Edward L '81
(216) 781-1212 **Betts** James E '76
(216) 241-5310 **Betz** Thomas E '68
(216) 622-3600 **Betzer** Linda M '76
(216) 622-8200 **Beus** Karl S '92
(216) 781-7777 **Beyer** William D '69
(216) 574-9128 **Bialer** Bruce A '75
(216) 664-2070 **Bickerstaff** Linda L '91
(216) 443-7800 **Bickerstaff** Valerie D '95
(216) 621-7860 **Bidar** Mohammed J '84
(216) 586-3939 **Biernacki** John V '01
(216) 586-3939 **Bigler** Laura A '01
(216) 363-4500 **Bilchik** Gary B '71
(216) 696-5297 **Bilfield** Murray D '74
(216) 696-5297 **Bilfield & Sandel Co, LPA**
(216) 696-7600 **Billick** John T '73
(216) 592-5000 **Billingsley** Henry E II '78
(216) 431-4500 **Billingsley** Yvonne C '84
(216) 522-4083 **Binder** Paul L '72
(216) 363-4500 **Binford** Gregory G '73
(216) 344-8398 **Binns** Cynthia A '95
(216) 566-7995 **Binzley** Richard C '66
(216) 443-8780 **Birch** Wanda J '91
(216) 445-6653 **Bishop** Sherri L '91
(216) 621-0200 **Bittence** Mary M '82
(216) 586-3939 **Bittence** Stephen L '04
(216) 739-5125 **Bitterman** Eileen M '97
(216) 931-6000 **Bixenstine** Barton A '81
(216) 983-1911 **Bixenstine** Kim F '82
(440) 526-1202 **Bjelovuk** Gordana L '92
(216) 586-3939 **Black** Carl E '98
(216) 334-2904 **Black** Lisa G '92
(216) 241-6602 **Blackford** Jason C '64
(216) 623-0150 **Blackham** Robert E '87
(216) 291-7359 **Blackhurst** Scott D '90
(440) 838-8800 **Blackie** William E III '79
(216) 687-2538 **Blair** Beverly J '85
(216) 622-8361 **Blair** Mitchell G '82
(216) 781-5245 **Blair** Nancy P '03
(216) 574-9474 **Blair** Rebecca S '86
(216) 621-0150 **Blake** Christopher S '99
(216) 464-7600 **Blake** Martin C '57
(216) 689-4129 **Blake** William J '81
(216) 928-2200 **Blakemore** Edward H '00
(440) 247-5995 **Blattner** Robert A '59
(216) 696-7600 **Bloch** Marc J '69
(216) 623-0000 **Block** Brian C '03
(216) 623-0000 **Block** Bruce A '76
(216) 696-1422 **Blocker** David S '02
(216) 771-6500 **Blomgren** Gilbert E '95
(216) 781-4110 **Bloom** Douglas E '01
(216) 522-3380 **Bloom** Richard S '77
(216) 575-9100 **Bloom** Stephen E '85
(216) 292-1144 **Blum** Kevin R '93
(216) 514-9400 **Blumenthal** Michael R '89
(216) 830-6823 **Bluso** Linda L '82
(216) 360-7200 **Blythe-Glaze** Amy M '99
(440) 838-7600 **Boatwright** Joseph W IV '04
(216) 771-6500 **Bobka** Todd A '99
(216) 696-3311 **Bobrow** Howard J '96
(216) 241-6045 **Boccardi** Maria '94
(216) 642-0323 **Bocciarelli** Kathryn I '03
(216) 928-2200 **Bocciarelli** Marco G '03
(216) 222-2991 **Boddy** Carla D '96
(216) 687-1311 **Bode** Hugh J '78
(216) 579-1700 **Bodi** Robert F '00
(216) 692-1222 **Bodnar** Brenda T '84
(440) 460-3600 **Bodnar** Rebecca J '99
(216) 621-1113 **Boehlefeld** Heidi A '90
(216) 623-0900 **Boehm** David H '00
(216) 443-4698 **Bogart** Bruce P '75
(216) 583-1038 **Bogdanski** Tammy L '99
(216) 861-8888 **Bohac** Edward T '97
(888) 901-4647 **Boikova** Nataliya A '03
(216) 566-5785 **Boise** April V '00
(216) 368-8849 **Boise** Craig M '00
(216) 621-1113 **Boisselle** Armand P Sr. '65
(216) 749-0808 **Bokor** David B '93
(216) 635-0636 **Boland** Dean M '95
(216) 623-1123 **Bolek** Cathleen M '92
(216) 831-0004 **Bolek** Joseph E Jr. '67
(216) 621-2234 **Bolinger** Brian W '02
(216) 566-5786 **Bollin** Kip T '95
(216) 781-7990 **Bolmeyer** Franklin G Jr. '81
(216) 861-4357 **Bolotin** Fredric N '90
(216) 443-7800 **Bolton** Pamela A '99
(216) 479-8500 **Bomberger** Jeffrey A '86
(216) 443-7800 **Bombik** Richard J '78
(216) 621-2034 **Bompiedi** Michelle T '04
(216) 664-4844 **Bonacci** Louis M '73
(216) 595-4903 **Bonder** Daniel L '84
(216) 381-8470 **Bondra** Anthony J '86
(216) 875-2767 **Bonezzi Switzer Murphy & Polito Co LPA**
(216) 875-2767 **Bonezzi** William D '73
(216) 522-3530 **Bongiovanni** Franklin V '84
(216) 621-8484 **Bonk** Colleen M '96
(216) 622-8200 **Bonko** Robert J '93
(216) 622-8200 **Bonner** Chet J '02
(216) 514-1100 **Bonsall** Eric J '03
(216) 687-1900 **Bonthius** Robert H Jr. '76
(216) 787-5224 **Booker** Lisa '92
(216) 241-5310 **Boop** Gregory K '97
(216) 687-1311 **Borchelt** Joseph W '02
(216) 344-9220 **Borchert** Kimberly L '02
(216) 263-6200 **Borders** Keith L '00
(216) 566-5527 **Bork** Derek D '96
(216) 522-4914 **Borling** David C '74
(216) 222-9038 **Bornhorst** Nicole K '95
(216) 689-3918 **Boron** Martin C '82
(440) 843-8089 **Borosh** Lawrence P '70
(216) 696-8730 **Bortnick** Daniel B '00
(216) 664-2689 **Bosu** Linda M '99
(216) 621-1424 **Boukalik** William T '68
(216) 696-1076 **Boukis** Christ '65
(216) 696-1076 **Boukis** Kenneth '66
(216) 241-2838 **Bowers** Charles A '94
(216) 431-4500 **Bowers** Cynthia '81
(216) 689-5089 **Bowes** Robert C '78
(216) 479-8500 **Bowling** Chandra S '93
(216) 586-3939 **Bownas** Pearson N '97
(216) 931-6000 **Boxer** Yelena B '99
(216) 586-3939 **Boyce** Jennifer Hanley '96
(216) 586-3939 **Boyce** Kevin D '96
(216) 222-3330 **Boyd** John W '85
(216) 696-0800 **Boyd** Robert A '80
(216) 622-8270 **Boyd** William A '74
(216) 987-5037 **Boyko** Michael E '84
(216) 623-1123 **Boyle** James P '91
Bozell Catherine L '02
(216) 689-0346 **Bradbury** Petra J '88
(216) 566-5500 **Bradford** Matthew '01
(216) 522-7546 **Bradley** Mary L '00
(216) 781-0722 **Bradley** Steven L '90
(440) 808-4242 **Brady** David T '00
(216) 523-5000 **Brady** Matthew T '85
(216) 861-3810 **Bragg** Caprice H '89
(216) 696-4659 **Bragg** Charles H '84
(216) 443-8290 **Brandenburg** Valerie '85
(216) 621-1610 **Brandt** Jean M '89
(216) 586-3939 **Brandt** Tamara S '00
(216) 222-3331 **Brantley** Sandra J '80
(216) 522-1400 **Brantley** William S Jr. '80
(216) 566-9908 **Bratton** Scott E '97
(216) 621-0150 **Brauer** Jeffrey A '98
(216) 621-6684 **Braun** Katherine M '93
(216) 781-1212 **Braverman** Herbert L '72
(216) 689-5369 **Braverman** Jeffrey L '92
(216) 621-3346 **Braverman** Sheldon L '65
(216) 931-6000 **Bravo** Kenneth A '67
(216) 696-0800 **Brelo** Clayton E '67
(216) 621-0200 **Brennan** Bridget M '00
(216) 696-1422 **Brennan** Kimberly A '93
(216) 621-0200 **Brennan** Maureen A '89
(216) 781-5515 **Brennan** Michael D '96
(216) 621-0200 **Brennan** Terry M '95
(216) 689-8064 **Brenner** Paul M '86
(216) 621-4268 **Brett** Maureen '98
(216) 642-8234 **Brewer** Blake O '84
(216) 241-5310 **Brick** Timothy T '88
(216) 523-5405 **Bricker & Eckler LLP**
(216) 522-7690 **Brickner** Paul '66
(216) 781-7990 **Briggs** David J '81
(216) 586-3939 **Briggs** Thomas A '94
(216) 696-4700 **Bright** James R '76
(216) 983-1058 **Bright** Mary C '76
(216) 443-6381 **Brighton** Anthony R '98
(216) 830-6830 **Brink** Michael C '03
(440) 838-8800 **Briskin** Seth P '95
(216) 781-7956 **Bristol** Jason R '00
(216) 447-1551 **Brittain** Brian K '81
(216) 622-8200 **Brittain** Michael E '79
(216) 642-0323 **Britton** John E '81
(216) 642-0323 **Britton Smith Peters & Kalail Co, LPA**
(216) 896-2584 **Brobst** Claudia Mae '81
(216) 696-3232 **Brodhead** Peter J '79
(216) 443-7800 **Brodnik** Louis J '83
(216) 781-5550 **Brodsky** Philip R '52
(216) 875-9843 **Broering-Jacobs** Carolyn '94
(216) 621-1511 **Brogley** Joycelyn '91
(216) 363-5220 **Brondou** Derek M '00
(216) 241-6045 **Brooks** Christopher F '94
(216) 479-8500 **Brooks** Patrick J '98
(216) 621-2929 **Brooks** Phyllis E '81
(216) 522-1920 **Brooks** Robert C II '88
(216) 694-4307 **Brooks** William H '79
(216) 928-1010 **Broome** Jeffrey Scott '89
(216) 737-5000 **Broski** Todd A '00
(216) 831-0042 **Brosse** Peter D '84
(216) 861-4533 **Brouhard** Julia R '89
(216) 830-6830 **Brouse McDowell**
(216) 363-6036 **Browarek** Matthew F '88
Brown Anne M '00
(216) 830-2312 **Brown** Catherine M '96
(216) 443-8970 **Brown** Charles T '85
(216) 696-7600 **Brown** Craig M '79
(440) 838-7600 **Brown** David H '02
(216) 363-4500 **Brown** Harry M '72
Brown Hugh D '79
(216) 622-8200 **Brown** Jaron R '02
(216) 851-3304 **Brown** Joanne '77
(216) 241-2838 **Brown** John D '69
(216) 481-8100 **Brown** Leslie S '96
(216) 241-5310 **Brown** Lori E '99
(216) 464-6700 **Brown** Michael C '88
(216) 363-1031 **Brown** Neil A '81
(216) 861-4414 **Brown** Robert L '92
(216) 664-3765 **Brown** Russell R III '91
(216) 228-7200 **Brown & Szaller**
(216) 443-7791 **Brown** Thomas C '74
(216) 781-1212 **Brown** Timothy Christopher '97
(216) 443-8812 **Brown** Timothy R '88
(216) 851-3304 **Brown** Virgil E Jr. '74
(216) 771-8121 **Brown** William D '91
(216) 696-0808 **Brown-Williams** Tabitha L '99
(216) 774-0000 **Browner** Jeremy T '03
(216) 586-3939 **Browning** Marc D '98
(216) 523-5405 **Brozovic** Maura L '00
(216) 363-4500 **Brule** Thomas R '93
(216) 566-9477 **Bruner** Harvey B '74
(216) 566-9477 **Bruner & Jordan Co LPA**
(216) 623-7300 **Brunn** Thomas L Sr. '67
(216) 623-7300 **Brunn** Thomas L Jr. '89
(216) 621-0200 **Brunner** Kimberly C '02
(216) 265-1630 **Brunst** Christa D '85
(216) 522-4856 **Bryan** Edward G '91
(216) 382-3559 **Bryant** Juanita '86
(216) 522-2084 **Bryce** Rita M '90
(216) 621-0200 **Bryenton** Gary L '65
(216) 664-6900 **Brzytwa** Edward John Jr. '68
(216) 664-6900 **Brzytwa Quick & McCrystal LLC**
(216) 621-8700 **Bucalo** John C '94
(216) 443-8505 **Bucha** Stephen M III '95
(216) 363-0982 **Buchanan Ingersoll PC**
(216) 696-7600 **Buck** Frank W '80
(216) 622-3712 **Buck** Lynne H '84
(216) 363-4500 **Buck** Maynard A III '83
(216) 621-5300 **Buckingham Doolittle & Burroughs, LLP**
(216) 252-8436 **Buckles** Howard E '76
(216) 363-1400 **Buckley** Brent M '82
(216) 443-7223 **Buckley** Joseph D '89
(216) 363-1400 **Buckley King,LPA**
(216) 241-6602 **Buckman** Herbert Jr. '40
(216) 875-2767 **Buckner** Andrew P '67
(216) 696-5222 **Budzik** James A '85
(216) 664-4823 **Buelow** Edward T '82
(216) 566-5657 **Buescher** Stephen L '69
(216) 621-6101 **Bufe** Eric T '96
(216) 241-3222 **Buford** Thomas C '77
(216) 348-5056 **Bugaj** Dale S '89
(216) 579-3108 **Bugaj** Rebecca '99
(216) 479-8500 **Buller** Carolyn J '81
(216) 621-1000 **Bulloch** John T '91
(216) 689-5109 **Bulloch** Steven N '74
(216) 696-3030 **Bulloff** Aaron H '81
(216) 621-1113 **Bulson** Don W '76
(216) 515-1660 **Bumpass** Thomas Merritt Jr. '72
(216) 787-3030 **Bundy** Charlett A '91
(216) 781-1720 **Bundy** Roger M Jr. '02
(216) 664-3584 **Bungard** Susan M '92
(216) 263-3403 **Bungo** Larissa L '96
(216) 479-8500 **Burchmore** David W '86
(216) 621-2424 **Burdell-Ware** Andrea L '03
(216) 443-8610 **Burg** Matthew G '00
(216) 621-0200 **Burgan** Kelly S '01
(216) 921-8900 **Burge** David A '71
(216) 566-5790 **Burger** Robert W '97
(216) 696-8700 **Burger** Todd M '02
(216) 222-2963 **Burgess** Julia E '80
(216) 348-5400 **Burgess** M John '02
(216) 566-5500 **Burgess** Patricia A '02
(216) 241-2838 **Burke** David E '64
(216) 586-3939 **Burke** James P '01
(216) 267-0445 **Burke** Jerome L '71
(216) 523-1500 **Burke** John F III '92
(216) 586-3939 **Burke** Kathleen B '73
(216) 696-6525 **Burke** Kevin T '96
(216) 622-8200 **Burke** Matthew E '95
(216) 479-8500 **Burke** Patrick J '03
(216) 642-3342 **Burkhardt** Amy M '95
(216) 787-3145 **Burkhart** Elizabeth L '84
(216) 479-8500 **Burlingame** Alexander G '98
(216) 443-7223 **Burnett** Rochelle A '81
(216) 621-1200 **Burns** James L '90
(216) 621-4636 **Burns** Kenneth B '62
(216) 689-4970 **Burns** Robert J '80
(216) 583-2539 **Burridge-Olah** Christee S '84
(216) 787-3297 **Burton** Andre L '95
(216) 574-7184 **Burtzlaff** Kevin J '88
(216) 830-2106 **Busby** Mary S '88
(216) 431-9900 **Busby** William C '99
(216) 621-9800 **Bush** Theodore J '94
(216) 241-6220 **Bustamante** Michael T '88
(216) 363-4500 **Butch** Mariann E '96
(216) 781-2258 **Butcher** Samuel V '84
(216) 523-4625 **Butensky Brehm** Ilene '86
(216) 622-3718 **Butler** Annette G '73
(216) 691-9404 **Butler** Charles S '67
(216) 621-3870 **Butler** Dennis F '70
(216) 621-7260 **Butler** Donald '82
(216) 621-0200 **Butler** Geraldine J '00
(216) 241-9990 **Butler** Kevin M '01
(216) 241-7255 **Butler** Michael P '83
(216) 928-7540 **Butscher** Alisa C '96
(216) 642-3342 **Button** David R '92
(216) 575-2284 **Buxton** Mark W '93
(216) 861-0360 **Buzney** Sandra J '99
(216) 479-8500 **Byrd** Nailah K '02
(216) 621-1312 **Byrne** James A '90
(216) 771-6650 **Byroads** Shaun D '04
(216) 241-5310 **Cabral** Thomas J '86
(216) 241-0715 **Cada** Gregory A '78
(216) 479-8500 **Cadle** Amy L '02
(216) 363-6014 **Cafferkey** Kevin M '85
(216) 522-3872 **Cafferkey** Maureen M '85
(216) 664-6900 **Cahill** Robert E '00
(216) 443-7800 **Cahill** Thomas M '94
(216) 781-5515 **Cahn** James S '73
(216) 696-7600 **Cahn** Stephen J '61
(216) 281-6122 **Cain** Elizabeth A '82
(216) 622-3600 **Cain** James M '72
(440) 248-2482 **Caine** Steven R '92
(216) 443-7808 **Caine** William R '79
(216) 696-4700 **Cairns** J Donald '58
(216) 479-6100 **Calabrese** Anthony O III '97
(216) 479-8500 **Calabrese** J Philip '00
(440) 746-1177 **Calandra** John P '64
(216) 621-0150 **Calderas** Erica L '94
(216) 479-6100 **Caldwell** Carrie M '02
(216) 622-8200 **Calfee Halter & Griswold LLP**
(216) 696-4700 **Calkins** Benjamin '83
(216) 397-9749 **Calkins** Hugh '51
(216) 464-5255 **Callaghan** Gregory J '69
(216) 781-4868 **Callaghan** Thomas M '53
(216) 443-7900 **Callahan** Michael F '85
(216) 291-1718 **Callahan** Michael W '91
(216) 566-5612 **Callahan** Thomas J '85
(216) 621-0200 **Callesen** Phillip M '87
(216) 696-2286 **Callsen** Julie A '93
(216) 443-7800 **Cameron** Denise R '79
(216) 292-3300 **Cameron** Sondra R '76
(216) 622-8200 **Cameron** Stacy '03
(216) 241-1907 **Camino** Carmine '80
(216) 685-1360 **Camino** Paula E '91
(216) 443-8355 **Camino** Walter '79
(216) 241-5310 **Campagna** Maria A '93
(216) 566-5500 **Campana** Jeremy M '02
(216) 621-0200 **Campanella** Thomas S '77
(216) 479-6100 **Campbell** David A III '96
(216) 651-2061 **Campbell** Edward J '79
(216) 621-9338 **Campbell** Eloise A '94
(216) 621-1113 **Campbell** Jay R '89
(216) 651-2061 **Campbell** Joseph P '83
(216) 443-8589 **Campbell** Kathrin D '97
(216) 621-7743 **Campbell** William P '93
(216) 586-3939 **Canala** Robert L '86
(216) 241-0033 **Canaris** James E '56
(216) 696-6500 **Canda** Ronald J '86
(216) 443-6530 **Canfil** Ellen J '83
(216) 363-6033 **Canfil** Steve W '77
(216) 241-2838 **Cannon** Margaret A '73
(216) 881-5411 **Capers** Jean M '45
(216) 431-7700 **Capka** Paul V '96
(216) 621-9870 **Cappara** Janeane R '00
(216) 241-6602 **Cappel** Carolyn M '77
(216) 586-3939 **Cappellazzo** Ronald L '89
(216) 696-6500 **Caravona & Czack, PLL**
(216) 696-6500 **Caravona** Donald E '73
(216) 861-3000 **Carbone** Joseph A Jr. '75
(216) 623-0150 **Cardenas** Ricardo J '96
(216) 443-9000 **Caresani** Ann M '94
(216) 357-7160 **Carey** Amy H '00
(216) 622-8200 **Carfagna** Peter A '79
(216) 443-6350 **Cargill** Newton S '01
(216) 696-9310 **Cariglio** Terrence Lee '81
(216) 266-2545 **Carino** Philip J '90
(216) 522-3718 **Carissimi** Mark M '76
(216) 586-3939 **Carkhuff** Denise A '95
(216) 426-9708 **Carl** Terrence P '99
(216) 861-4533 **Carle** William D III '55
(216) 241-6602 **Carlin** Angela G '55
(216) 622-0700 **Carlin** John H '73
(216) 781-4680 **Carlini** Lawrence J '73
(216) 360-7200 **Carlisle** Gerald K '60
(216) 360-7200 **Carlisle McNellie Rini Kramer & Ulrich Co,LPA**
(216) 622-8200 **Carlisle** Zoe K '04
(216) 241-6277 **Carlozzi** Louis J '94
(216) 621-0150 **Carlson** Douglas C '75
(216) 566-5556 **Carlson** James R '75
(216) 222-2894 **Carnahan** Anne S '79
(216) 520-5540 **Carnahan** James R Jr. '87
(216) 581-2600 **Carnahan** John A '55
(216) 621-7227 **Carnahan** Timothy D '79
(216) 830-6830 **Carney** Christopher J '86
(216) 861-0111 **Carney** Christopher J '93
(216) 368-3301 **Carney** David J '89
(440) 892-4900 **Carney** James A '73
(440) 892-4900 **Carney** John J '69
(216) 736-7223 **Carr** Connie S '94
(216) 241-5310 **Carr** George H '98

(216) 621-0200 **Carr** Lidia V '01
(216) 515-1660 **Carr** Lindsey A '01
(216) 443-7800 **Carr** Pinkey S '93
(216) 696-3366 **Carson** Drew A '86
(216) 515-1660 **Carson** Jay R '97
(216) 771-3303 **Carson** John H Jr. '64
(216) 479-8500 **Carson** Van '66
(216) 363-1400 **Carter** Daniel P '02
(216) 623-0150 **Carulas** Anna Moore '86
(216) 522-4914 **Cary** Judith D '96
(216) 592-5000 **Caryl** Christopher J '98
(216) 623-0150 **Casarona** Robert B '86
(216) 781-1212 **Cascarilla** Ralph E '76
(216) 241-5310 **Cass** Edward J '62
(216) 696-4442 **Cassaro** Bessie J '67
(216) 696-4442 **Cassaro** Charles T '70
(216) 443-7800 **Cassidy** Marilyn B '83
(216) 241-7255 **Castele** John T '92
(216) 583-3373 **Castelluccio** Tracy W '94
(216) 664-4855 **Castro** Pablo A '02
(216) 931-6000 **Castrodale** Joseph A '83
(216) 522-3530 **Catanzarite** Marc T '99
(216) 523-1500 **Cathcart** David B '75
(440) 248-7906 **Cathcart** Robert F IV '99
(216) 291-2400 **Caticchio** Michael J '82
(216) 297-0910 **Caticchio** Pasquale '64
(216) 443-7295 **Cavallo** Francis J '01
(216) 433-0542 **Cavanaugh** Mary A '93
(216) 687-1311 **Cavasinni** Joseph E '95
(216) 621-7860 **Cavitch Familo Durkin & Frutkin**
(216) 696-7600 **Cawley** Michael Terence '90
(216) 621-7860 **Cawley** Thomas M '82
(216) 664-4942 **Celebrezze** Leslie A '99
(216) 692-0020 **Centa** Emil J '54
(216) 692-0020 **Centa** Ernest R '55
(216) 696-0250 **Cerio** Arthur R '55
(216) 586-3939 **Cernansky** Justin M '04
(216) 622-8200 **Cernelich** John R '86
(216) 586-3939 **Chaffee** Eric C '02
(216) 486-1777 **Chalko** Paul P '52
(216) 781-1111 **Chamberlain** Henry W '90
(216) 443-3436 **Chandler** Johnny Mac '82
(216) 522-2677 **Chandra** Meenakshi M '93
(216) 443-8868 **Chaney** Cathleen J '93
(216) 861-0660 **Chaplin** Daniel S '83
(216) 621-0200 **Chapman** Diane P '78
(216) 696-1133 **Chapman** Frank H II '96
(216) 241-8172 **Chapman** John S '84
(216) 931-6000 **Chappell** Inajo D '88
(216) 689-5258 **Charlton** Melody K '97
(216) 781-4900 **Charms** Stephen J '81
(216) 522-5020 **Chatfield** Hedy S '92
(216) 621-5300 **Chattman** Gerald B '67
(216) 698-2698 **Chavers** Dana C '82
(216) 588-5945 **Cheatham** Stephen V '77
(216) 592-5000 **Chema** Thomas V '71
(216) 621-8742 **Chenette** Frank A '76
(216) 222-2979 **Chenin** Avery M '89
(216) 588-5193 **Cherchiglia** Dean K '84
(216) 737-5000 **Chernett** Robert I '73
(216) 737-5000 **Chernett Wasserman Yarger & Pasternak**
(216) 621-6101 **Chernosky** David J '90
(216) 928-3082 **Cheselka** Michael J Jr. '03
Chesler Steven B '84
(216) 515-1660 **Chesney** Michael N '92
(216) 696-5580 **Chestang-Fossett** Renee S '85
(216) 241-5310 **Cheung** Jeremy G '04
(216) 689-0509 **Cheverine** Carolyn E '96
(216) 443-8427 **Chimo** Elaine J '62
(216) 479-8500 **Chin** Elleanor H '99
(216) 241-0646 **Chin** James W '76
(216) 522-3881 **Chinni** Benjamin T '70
(216) 368-2655 **Chisolm** Laura B '81
(216) 696-8700 **Chlarson** Kevin L '03
(216) 621-8484 **Chmielewski** Dawn M '04
(216) 522-3715 **Choe** Iva Y '95
(216) 621-0200 **Chotlos** Elaine A '83
(216) 522-3715 **Choudhury** Rudra '99
(216) 291-7380 **Christ** Paula B '91
(216) 222-3668 **Christhilf** George H '96
(216) 535-0520 **Christian** Victoria A '80
(216) 579-1602 **Christie** John R '97
(216) 241-5019 **Christman** Leif B '98
(216) 622-8200 **Christopher** S Paige '96
(216) 514-6400 **Christy** Chastity L '03
(216) 443-7800 **Christyson** Robert J Jr. '85
(216) 621-7227 **Chriszt** James R '87
(216) 586-3939 **Chu** Howard W '04
(216) 931-6000 **Chudakoff** Robert E '87
(216) 671-3364 **Chudner** Richard '98
(216) 523-1900 **Chudyk** Peter J '80
(216) 586-3939 **Chunyo** Jennifer J '96
(216) 781-5515 **Chylla** Heidi P '99
(216) 687-1311 **Ciano** Mario C '68
(216) 658-9900 **Ciano** Phillip A '96
(216) 344-9220 **Cibella** Mary L '84
(216) 622-8200 **Cicarella** Thomas A '74
(216) 621-7227 **Cicero** Michael E '92
(440) 449-2662 **Cimperman** Marilyn L '96
(216) 222-8441 **Cipiti** Anthony Jr. '01
(216) 622-8200 **Cipolla** John S '89
(216) 931-6000 **Citeroni** Maria A '01
(440) 884-2036 **Ciulla** Joseph F '65
(216) 363-4500 **Clady** Susan E '96
(440) 483-2373 **Clair** Eugene E III '94
(216) 368-6280 **Clancy** Daniel T '62
(216) 443-7800 **Clancy** Maureen E '91
(216) 861-1400 **Clapp** Jane E '91
(216) 861-1400 **Clapp** Robert Jack '90
(216) 689-4118 **Clark** Janet C '94
(216) 566-9700 **Clark** Kenneth A '86
(216) 522-0183 **Clark** Pinkie L '92
(216) 622-8200 **Clark** Wade D '80
(216) 479-8500 **Clarke** Charles F '46
(216) 443-7800 **Claussen** Scott D '01
Clawson Sandra A '86
(216) 781-1212 **Clay** Darrell A '97
(216) 443-5809 **Clay** Pamela S '96
(216) 642-0323 **Clayborne** Sherrie D '96
(216) 522-4856 **Cleary** Amy B '97
(216) 443-7800 **Cleary** Daniel A '02
(216) 642-7878 **Cleary** Michael F '84
(216) 222-9963 **Cleary** Vicki M '86
(216) 621-7227 **Clements** Arthur L III '87
(216) 443-7875 **Cleveland** Phyllis E '89
(216) 664-4955 **Clifford** Gregory F '81
(216) 241-0022 **Clifford** Lisa A '01
(216) 621-8484 **Climaco** John R '67
(216) 621-8484 **Climaco Lefkowitz Peca Wilcox & Garofoli Co, LPA**
(440) 248-7906 **Climer** James A '80
(216) 481-8100 **Cline** Guy G Jr. '78
(216) 447-1551 **Cline** Jerry P '02
(216) 348-5400 **Cline** Richard W '97
(216) 689-4117 **Cloonan** William P '92
(216) 443-7800 **Clough** John A III '77
(216) 687-1311 **Coakley** George S '75
(216) 444-2200 **Coate** Brian R '95
(216) 621-5300 **Coaxum** Edward C Jr. '71
(216) 621-0150 **Cobb** Arthur L '77
(216) 689-5436 **Coburn** Howard E '84
(216) 586-3939 **Cochran** David B '96
(216) 443-7800 **Cochran** James C '78
(216) 381-8800 **Cocirteu** Cosmin '03
(216) 687-9318 **Codinach** Maria J '76
(216) 368-2282 **Coffey** Ronald J '61
(216) 592-5000 **Coffey** Thomas W '90
(216) 621-7860 **Cohan** Michael C '77
(216) 621-0200 **Cohen** Avery S '61
(216) 442-9295 **Cohen** Hyman '69
(216) 781-7956 **Cohen** Joshua R '84
Cohen Mitchell I '94
(216) 781-7956 **Cohen Rosenthal & Kramer LLP**
(216) 696-4009 **Cohen** Ryan W '04
(216) 752-0955 **Cohn** Howard M '92
(216) 696-1422 **Cohn** Mark B '74
(216) 883-5451 **Colabianchi** Nicholas A '86
(216) 586-3939 **Colacarro** Robert J '02
(216) 696-5222 **Colaluca** Thomas L '78
(216) 566-2000 **Cole** Allison E '00
(216) 623-5012 **Cole** John M '00
(216) 579-2848 **Cole** Kevin P '80
(216) 566-7100 **Cole** Michael L '00
(216) 586-3939 **Cole** Randall A '73
(216) 621-0150 **Coleman** Deborah A '76
(216) 771-8121 **Coleman** L Christopher '02
(216) 622-2727 **Coletta** Dominic J '04
(216) 765-1199 **Collier** Brandon S '02
(216) 765-1199 **Collier** Richard A '70
(216) 765-1199 **Collier Sarner & Assoc Inc**
(216) 621-0200 **Collier** Wan C '02
(216) 621-9190 **Collier-Williams** Cassandra '91
(216) 902-6062 **Collin** James M '95
(216) 566-5509 **Collin** Thomas J '75
(216) 671-6542 **Collins** Daisy G '70
(216) 696-5400 **Collins** Patrick S '84
(216) 696-0022 **Collins & Scanlon LLP**
(216) 696-0022 **Collins** Tim L '86
(216) 787-3030 **Collyer** Michael L '93
(216) 621-0200 **Colombo** Louis A '73
(216) 621-5500 **Colovas** Dean A '86
(216) 932-5659 **Comella** Ignatius A '51
(216) 664-3559 **Comer** Michele R '93
(216) 622-8830 **Comodeca** Peter J '91
(216) 481-6700 **Compoli** Joseph R Jr. '82
(216) 623-0150 **Conde** Stephenie L '94
(216) 771-1760 **Condeni** Joseph A '82
(216) 222-2542 **Condon** Maurice J Jr. '83
(216) 443-7223 **Condosta** Thomas J '86
(216) 861-4533 **Coniam** Robert T '86
(216) 586-3939 **Conley** Colleen A '01
(216) 664-4972 **Connally** Cecelia E '71
(216) 696-7600 **Connell** Daniel M '04
(216) 479-8500 **Connell** Michele L Ondako '03
(216) 515-1660 **Conner** Larry W II '97
(216) 479-8500 **Conner** William H '67
(216) 367-1150 **Connick** Michael J '90
(216) 348-1700 **Connick** Thomas J '90
(216) 622-8200 **Connors** Timothy J '89
(440) 248-7906 **Conomy** Christopher P '00
(216) 771-3336 **Cononico** Vincent E '94
(216) 621-0200 **Conrad** Deanna M '04
(216) 781-5515 **Conrad** Jane K '00
(216) 781-1212 **Conroy** James P '74
(216) 622-8200 **Conroy** Suzanne M '95
(216) 566-7744 **Consiglio** Charles J '61
(216) 696-5400 **Consolo** Frank '89
(216) 348-5400 **Consolo** Jeffrey P '79
(216) 696-7600 **Conti** Patricia S '95
(216) 292-3300 **Conway** James J '55
(216) 368-5845 **Conway** James P '61
(216) 861-1365 **Conway** Kara A '02
(216) 292-3300 **Conway Marken Wyner Kurant & Kern Co,LPA**
(216) 574-9550 **Conwell** Jocelyn '89
(216) 687-3613 **Cook** Brian S '85
(216) 252-0372 **Cook** Craig D '91
(216) 348-5400 **Cook** Jerome W '86
(216) 586-3939 **Coolbaugh** Stephen P '01
(216) 696-6570 **Cooley** Sheila P '76
(216) 443-6350 **Cooney** John G '79
(216) 771-9750 **Cooney** Patrick J III '91
(216) 696-3844 **Cooper** Gerald F '57
(216) 592-5000 **Cooper** Jonathan R '86
(216) 586-3939 **Cooper** Lorri W '02
(216) 621-6101 **Cooper** Margaret E '00
(216) 621-7227 **Cooper** Richard A '77
(216) 348-5400 **Cooper** Richard S '81
(216) 696-3844 **Cooper Spector & Weil Co, LPA**
(216) 502-0600 **Cooper** William J '98
(216) 696-9077 **Copeland** Terence E '74
(216) 586-3939 **Coquillette** William H '75
(216) 781-8543 **Corchado** Carlos Jr. '98
(216) 397-0777 **Corcoran** James I '66
(216) 621-0200 **Corcoran** Melanie S '91
(216) 357-5900 **Corder** Bradley S '90
(216) 861-3086 **Coreno** Terese M '99
(216) 241-5210 **Corman** Lawrence W '69
(440) 248-7906 **Cormany** Carl E '80
(216) 348-1700 **Cormier** Shawn A '98
(216) 861-5582 **Cornely** John P '95
(216) 664-2775 **Cornely** Mary Z '96
(216) 241-2838 **Cornett** Adam D '04
(216) 592-5000 **Cornett** Harry D Jr. '71
(216) 514-9999 **Cornrich** Neil M '83
(216) 514-9999 **Cornrich** Sidney M '51
(216) 622-8200 **Corpora** Corine R '92
(216) 642-3342 **Corpus** Christopher A '00
(216) 696-8730 **Corpus** Deborah Liu '00
(216) 696-0222 **Corrado** David A '91
(216) 781-2895 **Corrado** Paul J '86
(216) 928-2200 **Corrigall** Amy K '01
(216) 348-5400 **Corrigan** Anne T '92
(216) 696-0606 **Corrigan** Brian T '94
(216) 696-7445 **Corrigan** Christopher M '99
(216) 443-7223 **Corrigan** Daniel P '87
(216) 443-7800 **Corrigan** Edward J '89
(216) 622-8200 **Corrigan** Heather C '01
(216) 861-1177 **Corrigan** James G '81
(216) 621-8484 **Corrigan** John F '86
(216) 586-3939 **Corrigan** Karen J '93
(216) 696-6454 **Corrigan** Patrick S '90
(216) 443-7800 **Corrigan** Peter J '96
(216) 771-0875 **Corrigan** William H '52
(216) 241-7660 **Corsi** Mary J '93
(216) 241-7660 **Corsi** Megan J '97
(216) 241-2200 **Corso** Heather L '99
(216) 642-3342 **Corso** Jennifer A '94
(216) 579-1700 **Corso** Joseph J '69
(216) 622-3600 **Corts** Robert F '89
(216) 566-5769 **Coscarelli** Dianne S '78
(216) 348-5400 **Cosentino** Leonard M '87
(216) 664-3574 **Cosgrove** Michael F '00
(216) 479-8500 **Cosgrove** Timothy J '87
(216) 443-8933 **Cosiano** Ralph V '59
(216) 479-8500 **Cossler** Christine T '02
(216) 861-6622 **Coticchia** Joseph L '75
(216) 687-1311 **Coticchia** Lori A '88
(216) 426-4511 **Coticchia** Michael L '88
(216) 621-0200 **Cotronakis** Emanuel J '98
(216) 781-2787 **Cottle** Cullen J '00
(216) 241-8333 **Coughlin** Thomas M Jr. '91
(216) 566-5523 **Coughlin** Timothy J '84
(216) 622-8334 **Coughlin** William E '83
(216) 586-3939 **Couhig** Stephanie S '02
(216) 696-0600 **Courtney** Michael M '75
(216) 696-4441 **Courtright** Joy Zeiler '00
(216) 443-7800 **Coury** Donna M '00
(216) 443-7800 **Coury** Robert F '86
(216) 241-3366 **Couture** Bernard P '91
(216) 621-2234 **Covell** Calvin G '68
(216) 696-7600 **Covey** Christine C '80
(216) 241-2880 **Cowden** Gerald W '75
(216) 241-2880 **Cowden Humphrey Nagorney & Lovett**
(216) 566-5747 **Cox** Andrew H '99
(216) 621-6684 **Cox** Duane E '79
(216) 522-4300 **Cox** Earl G '70
(216) 426-4000 **Coy** Betsy H '00
(216) 523-1500 **Coyne** Anthony J '88
(216) 781-9162 **Coyne** Dennis M '85
(216) 687-1311 **Coyne** John C '01
(216) 781-1980 **Coyne** John P '56
(440) 891-8388 **Coyne** Loretta A '70
(216) 664-4850 **Coyne** Lorraine '96
Coyne Michael F '90
(216) 642-3342 **Coyne** Richard T '89
(216) 566-5781 **Coyne** Thomas J '85
(216) 348-9878 **Cozart** Stacy E '99
(216) 443-7800 **Craig** Kathleen S '84
(216) 615-7302 **Craig** Mark F '02
(216) 622-3600 **Cramer** Marily A '77
(216) 622-8200 **Crandall** David J '91
(216) 622-8200 **Crandall** Tracy D '97
(216) 931-6000 **Crane** James M '04
(216) 443-2791 **Crane** Jonathan O '81
(216) 861-1400 **Crane** Kyle L '95
(216) 621-0200 **Crane** Matthew B '02
(216) 363-5220 **Crane** Robert P '94
(216) 692-7197 **Crawford** Matthew V '94
(216) 522-2918 **Crawford** Richard D '90
(216) 479-8500 **Crawford** Stephen J '97
(216) 348-1700 **Creagan** John M '85
(216) 443-8591 **Creed** Laura W '93
(216) 252-7300 **Creger** Michelle B '81
(216) 931-6000 **Crehore** Charles A '76
(216) 522-4914 **Crespy** Gregory P '87
(216) 523-7240 **Cribbs** Nancy J '72
(216) 663-1650 **Crimaldi** Lisa M '98
(216) 574-2550 **Crisafi** David A '92
(216) 592-5000 **Crisafi** Marilyn M '92
(216) 931-6000 **Crisci** George S '83
(216) 363-4500 **Crist** Thomas O '95
(440) 248-7906 **Cristallo** Paul J '93
(216) 363-6056 **Crites** Andrew J '89
(216) 696-5400 **Crosby** Elizabeth A '89
(216) 696-5959 **Crosby** Fred C '88
(216) 696-5400 **Crosby O'Brien & Associates Co, LPA**
(216) 771-4648 **Crosby** William M '82
(216) 363-4500 **Cross** Robert C '87
(216) 861-3086 **Crossman** Darryl H '93
(216) 363-4500 **Crossman** Jeffrey A '01
(216) 241-8111 **Crowe** Frances N '04
(216) 761-4203 **Crowther** Denise C '96
(216) 642-3342 **Crowther** Lawrence S '84
(216) 781-1212 **Crump** Robert J '68
(216) 696-1422 **Crystal** Larry '65
(216) 592-5000 **Csikos** Debra '94
(216) 621-0200 **Csomos** Andrea L '01
(216) 621-9870 **Cubar** John C '78
(216) 523-4077 **Cudak** Gail L '77
(440) 995-3008 **Cuellar** Michael M '92
(216) 771-6500 **Cuilli** Leonard A '97
(216) 931-6000 **Culbertson** Mary M '95
(216) 621-0200 **Culbertson** William J '95
(216) 621-2090 **Cullen** John L '93
(216) 621-0150 **Culler** M Patricia '85
(216) 479-8500 **Cullers** Michael A '95
(216) 875-7500 **Cullers** Romney B '91
(216) 566-2381 **Cummins** Michael T '83
Cunliffe Erika B '01
(216) 348-5400 **Cupar** David B '99
(216) 621-8484 **Cuppage** David M '90
(216) 687-1900 **Curran** Mallory C '02
(216) 589-8399 **Currie** Douglas F '88
(216) 586-3939 **Currivan** John D '78
(216) 771-6500 **Curry** Matthew P '04
(216) 586-3939 **Curtin** John D '03
(216) 696-1076 **Curtis** Jack S '85
(216) 443-7800 **Curtis-Patrick** Saundra J '80
(216) 622-8200 **Cushwa** Mara E '90
(216) 479-8500 **Cusick** Mark A '75
(216) 771-1760 **Cusimano** Jennifer B '93
(216) 696-0650 **Cusimano** Joseph J III '92
(216) 443-8590 **Cuthbert** Amy R '02
(216) 515-1635 **Cuthbertson** Jennifer L '04
(216) 621-1000 **Cuthbertson** Patricia R '90
(216) 696-4200 **Cvetkovic** Adrienne N '04
(216) 781-2600 **Cybulski** Donald F '75
(216) 781-1212 **Cyphert** Michael A '73
(216) 696-6500 **Czack** Michael W '84
Czupik Nancy M '84
(216) 621-0200 **Dabb** Wayne C Jr. '71
(216) 574-2600 **Daddona** David S '83
(216) 443-7800 **Daher** Paul A '01
(216) 348-5400 **Dahl** Sherri L '01
(216) 592-5000 **Daiker** Matthew M '04
(216) 696-0900 **Daiker** Paul B '93
(216) 687-6878 **Daiker-Middaugh** Pamela A '89
(216) 479-8500 **Dakin** Carol F '69
(216) 443-7800 **Daley** Paul J '83
(216) 566-5818 **Daloia** Andrea B '01
(216) 623-1155 **Damelio** Marillyn F '78
(216) 566-0064 **Damiani** Louis C '79
(216) 291-2400 **D'Amico** Ann M '88
(216) 622-8200 **D'Amico** Cheryl A '96
(216) 522-4856 **Dane** Michael G '71
(216) 623-7311 **D'Angelo** Patrick A '77
(216) 696-5400 **Daniel** Eric S '04
(216) 622-8200 **Daniels** Anthea R '89
(216) 861-5582 **Daniels** Edward Kent Jr. '71
(216) 621-1312 **Daniels** Stephen H '78
(216) 586-3939 **Daniels** Thomas C '86
(216) 443-8560 **Danko** William L '73
(216) 566-2482 **Danzig** Allen J '91
(216) 479-6807 **Danzinger** Robert K '92
(216) 781-2227 **D'Arcy** Charles J '78
(216) 781-5470 **Darlington** Stephen M '67
(440) 605-6660 **Daroff** Charles II '88
(216) 861-7572 **DasVarma** Jay R '96
(216) 830-6830 **Dattilo** Joseph T '73
(216) 621-0200 **Davet** Anne M '04
(216) 696-5959 **Davey** James A '04
(216) 241-6602 **Davey** Karen A '80
(216) 696-5510 **Davidoff** Jason A '99
(216) 771-5300 **Davidson** Gerry '72
(216) 861-4533 **Davies** David G '62
(216) 348-5056 **Davis** Audrey H '77
(216) 241-5310 **Davis** Catherine A '98
(216) 241-1430 **Davis** Jillian S '96
(216) 363-6000 **Davis** Leonard '66
(216) 523-1300 **Davis** Marilyn T '82
(216) 621-0995 **Davis** Mark R '82
(216) 297-7000 **Davis** Marleina Thomas '00
(216) 566-8200 **Davis** Mary '88
(216) 566-5782 **Davis** Renee L '03
(216) 696-0606 **Davis** Robert E '77
(216) 664-2677 **Davis** Scott J '02
(216) 781-3311 **Davis** Steven S '75
(216) 464-4105 **Davis** Todd S '89
(216) 348-1700 **Davis & Young**
(216) 987-8834 **Davis-Momon** Andrea Y '95
(216) 241-2838 **Davison** Lawrence C '91
(216) 687-1900 **Dawson** David B '73
(216) 622-8200 **Dawson** Philip M '72
(216) 621-0200 **Dawson** Todd A '98
(216) 766-5777 **Dawson** William L '00
(216) 348-0041 **Deacon** Robert F '79
(216) 443-0450 **Dean** Jeffrey L '80
(216) 592-5000 **Dean** Richard A '73
(216) 579-4114 **Dean** Scott J '98
(216) 696-6373 **DeBaggis** Henry F II '81
(216) 621-2034 **De Baltzo** Michelle L '97
(216) 522-3879 **DeBaltzo** Michelle M '97
(216) 696-5222 **DeBaltzo** Nicholas J Jr. '99
(216) 696-3232 **Debevec** Rhonda Baker '97
(216) 621-0150 **Debitetto** Rocco I '01
(216) 586-3939 **DeBord** David L '03
(216) 363-1400 **Debose** Lorraine '03
(216) 447-1551 **Debski** Christopher R '97
(216) 721-7700 **de Caris** Gian M '89
(216) 937-2000 **de Caris** Mario D '83
(216) 621-7860 **DeCaro** Sara E '00
(216) 687-7190 **Decensi** Patricia B '87
(216) 781-2258 **DeChant** Thomas H '58
(216) 443-7800 **Deckert** Brian S '99
(216) 771-2300 **DeCosky** Richard L '81
(216) 622-8466 **Dedmon** Shelly Gay '88
(216) 566-0500 **Deegan** F Timothy '73
(216) 443-6388 **Deegan** Hallie M '02
(216) 621-5300 **deFilippis** Lisa M '86
(216) 931-6000 **DeFlaun** Claudia Rose '01
(216) 771-1330 **DeFoy** Ernest D '88
(216) 696-4600 **DeFranco** Ralph T '73
(216) 696-4600 **DeFranco** Thomas G '99
(216) 664-2858 **DeGennaro** Susanne M '04
(216) 523-1900 **Degrandis** Ronald L '73
(216) 621-1312 **DeGulis** Gregory J '90
(216) 360-7200 **Deighton** Eric T '99
(216) 579-1700 **Deioma** David B '65
(216) 696-1448 **DeJohn** John E '90
DeJohn Michael '03
(216) 861-6282 **DeJohn** Michael C '04
(216) 241-2414 **DeJohn** Stephen E '72
(216) 861-2500 **Delaney** John C '77
(216) 566-8500 **Delaney** Kelly C '03
(216) 861-2500 **Delaney** Timothy J '76
(216) 574-2593 **Delatte** Margaret L '04
(216) 241-5310 **Del Balso** Colleen R '02
(216) 443-7800 **DelBalso** Dominic J '72
(216) 479-8500 **Delchin** Steven A '97
(216) 621-1113 **Del Col** John J '98
(216) 443-5143 **DeLeon** Jose E '93
(216) 502-0588 **Delguyd** Joseph A '85

(216) 781-8700 **Deliberato** Matthew D '99
(216) 621-0200 **Dellinger** Elizabeth A '87
(216) 931-6000 **Del Monaco** Maria A '97
(216) 367-7744 **Delon** Evana C '04
(216) 443-8575 **DeLong** Hallryn S '00
(216) 443-6350 **Deltorto** Darci L '04
(216) 443-9000 **DeLuca** Amy L '03
(216) 479-8500 **Demanelis** Ernie K '81
(216) 621-0150 **DeMarco** Daniel A '87
(216) 736-6334 **Demarr** Jean A '83
(216) 274-1608 **Demaske** Susan J '84
(216) 771-1525 **DeMelto** Vincent K '71
(440) 826-1560 **Demer** Adrian J '74
(216) 621-5980 **DeMetz** Kathleen S '77
(216) 642-3342 **Demian** Simon P '92
(216) 621-0200 **DeMinico** Michael P '03
(216) 520-5527 **Demis-Young** Elisa C '88
(216) 586-3939 **Demitrack** Thomas '79
(216) 443-7800 **Demosthenes** Suzie '95
(216) 687-2300 **Dempsey** Louise P '82
(216) 621-2300 **Demsey** Richard L '82
(216) 566-5574 **Denkewalter** Jack Kurt '90
(216) 861-4533 **Denny** Douglas R '74
(216) 696-4700 **Dent** Rebecca Holloway '91
(216) 586-3939 **DeNuzzo** Noreen '86
(216) 575-0777 **DePerro** Dayna M '04
(216) 696-8860 **DePiero** Daniel R '94
(216) 363-4500 **Derenthal** Jacob B '04
(216) 931-6000 **DeRienzo** Elizabeth M '04
(216) 771-3336 **Derkin** William S '73
(800) 397-8529 **DeRoberts** David N '95
(216) 987-3257 **DeRosa** James D '95
(216) 621-8700 **De Rosa** Joseph C '79
(216) 621-1742 **DeRose** Carole A '63
(216) 621-7227 **Dertouzos** Nicholas J '99
(216) 861-5142 **Dertouzos** Nicole B '99
(216) 787-5299 **DeSantis** Fedele '84
(216) 566-5514 **DeSantis** Frank R '83
(216) 898-1800 **DeSantis** Lynette S '84
(216) 781-1212 **Deseran** Sophia M '92
(216) 642-3342 **DeShon** A. M '96
(440) 356-0408 **Despins** Martin P '72
(216) 861-6000 **Dettelbach** Sally Marcia '83
(216) 696-6000 **Dettelbach Sicherman & Baumgart, LPA**
(216) 622-3600 **Dettelbach** Steven M '91
(216) 781-5245 **DeVan** Mark R '74
(216) 443-7800 **Dever** Andrew Steven '85
(216) 861-1365 **Devine** Sara C Clicquennoi '02
(216) 687-1212 **DeVito** Christopher M '90
(216) 861-4414 **DeVito** Maureen M '98
(216) 348-5400 **DeVore** Tara C '02
(440) 838-8800 **Dezort** Robert E Jr. '92
(216) 696-3311 **Diamant** Michael H '71
(216) 902-6010 **Diamond** Clayton L '00
(216) 621-0150 **Diaz** Derek E '98
(216) 621-0150 **Diaz** Robert J '04
(216) 621-0200 **DiBaggio** Joseph E '02
(216) 696-3232 **DiCello** Nicholas A '02
(216) 928-2200 **Dickerson** Denise A '95
(216) 696-5444 **Dickerson** Emmanuel E '52
(216) 621-7860 **Dickinson** James G '73
(216) 621-7743 **Dickson** Blake A '92
(216) 328-8700 **Diemer** Dennis J '82
(216) 623-3688 **Dietsch** Gary J '77
(216) 592-5000 **DiFranco** Sandra M '03
(216) 566-9700 **Digges** Randolph E III '92
(216) 621-5300 **DiGirolamo** Alan P '89
(216) 696-7600 **Dileno** Jon M '88
(216) 623-1155 **Di Lisi** Richard A '89
(216) 368-5136 **Dillman** Jeffrey D '00
(216) 241-6602 **DiMarco** Victor T '00
(216) 621-0150 **DiMassa** Pasquale Jr. '01
(216) 348-5400 **Dimitrijevs** James A '94
(216) 241-1909 **Dimond** Douglas A '80
(440) 446-1100 **Dinn Hochman & Potter,LLC**
(440) 446-1100 **Dinn** Irwin J '64
(216) 592-5000 **Dinner** Gary L '73
(216) 685-9188 **Dintaman** Robert E Jr. '98
(216) 621-7860 **DiPalma** Douglas A '85
(216) 378-9905 **DiPalma** Joy A '00
(216) 696-4441 **DiPetta** Deanna L '87
(216) 696-3311 **DiPuccio** Dominic A '90
(216) 363-1400 **Disantis** Richard J '66
(216) 771-2533 **Disbro** Terry R '93
(216) 687-1311 **DiSilvio** Marilena '95
Ditchey Matthew J '97
(216) 348-6384 **Ditchey** Timothy J '00
(216) 621-6138 **Ditko-Bevione** Sharon R '04
(216) 348-5400 **DiVenere** Anthony J '67
(216) 515-1660 **Dixon** James T '04
(216) 432-1992 **Dixon** Robert A '81
(216) 689-3621 **Djulvezan** Florentina G '95
(216) 875-4800 **DKW Law Group**
(216) 696-5400 **Dlott** Steven P '85
(216) 523-4109 **Doan** James N '71
(216) 443-6344 **Dobeck** Rochelle L '88
(216) 687-1900 **Dobos** Dennis A '92
(216) 622-8200 **Dobrea** Diane L '94
(216) 787-3083 **Dobronos** Michael G '91
(216) 443-7295 **Dobroshi** Anduena '99
(216) 622-8416 **Docherty** Pamela Ann '94
(216) 292-3300 **Dodd** Stephen D '00
(216) 443-7800 **Dodrill** Joyce M '84
(216) 566-8816 **Doerner** Maureen A '92
(216) 522-4373 **Doganiero** Mara D '80
(216) 592-5000 **Doheny** John T '74
(216) 579-4114 **Dolan** Michael A '91
(216) 241-1278 **Doman** Paul M '95
(216) 529-8400 **Domanovic** Dieter '81
(216) 621-0070 **Domiano** Joseph C '57
(216) 566-5771 **Dominguez** Kathryn I '00
(216) 523-1500 **Donahue** Mary E '94
(216) 896-3295 **Donchess** James M '89
(216) 241-9628 **Donnelly** Kathleen '89
(216) 621-8484 **Donnelly** Michael P '92
(216) 685-1039 **Donnersbach** Sara M '98
(216) 592-5000 **Donovan** Larry B '99
(216) 348-1700 **Donze** Shannon M '04
(216) 685-4289 **Doran** James M '98
(216) 479-8500 **Doris** Alan S '72
(440) 838-7600 **Dorman** Andrew J '94
(216) 687-6264 **Dorrell** John S '75
(216) 522-4373 **Dorsey** Joseph D '03
(216) 443-8549 **Dorton** Jennifer M '01
(216) 263-3405 **Doubrava** Brenda W '78
(216) 861-6833 **Doucette** Stephen B '93
(216) 267-5600 **Dougher** Kevin A '87
(216) 586-3939 **Dougherty** James P '05
(216) 687-2348 **Dougherty** Veronica M '87
(216) 361-1112 **Doughten** David L '81
(216) 696-7600 **Douglas** Sue M '84
(440) 808-4242 **Douglass** David M '79
(216) 771-1330 **Douglass** James R '80
(216) 523-5465 **Douthett** Breaden M '91
(216) 241-5310 **Dover** Thomas E '80
(216) 849-8296 **Dow** Tijuan M '03
(216) 664-4946 **Dowling** Joseph P '80
(216) 696-6700 **Downey** Brian P '89
(216) 861-9111 **Downing** Michael J '83
(216) 931-6000 **Downing** Timothy J '89
(216) 623-1155 **Downs** Thomas J '82
(216) 363-6048 **Doyle** William T Jr. '72
(216) 592-5000 **Drago** Christian R '01
(216) 621-3000 **Drain** John Michael Jr. '70
(216) 861-8736 **Drake-Kinnear** Alison L '94
(216) 443-7223 **Draper** James A '75
(216) 357-7000 **Drasner** Lawrence S '92
(216) 479-8500 **Draucker** Carl A '77
(216) 621-5300 **Drechsler** David L '89
(216) 861-5582 **Dreher** Joseph D '91
(216) 583-3692 **Dreis** Michael E '97
(216) 642-3342 **Dresp** Donna M '95
(216) 241-5300 **Dreyfuss** Daniel W '78
(216) 241-5310 **Drinko** Donald G '93
(216) 621-0200 **Drinko** John D '45
(216) 443-7800 **Driscoll** Jennifer A '01
(216) 363-4500 **Drockton** Leslie A '86
(216) 621-0150 **Drozdowski** James M '95
(216) 861-5777 **Drucker** David H '84
(216) 771-5356 **Drucker** Marvin '56
(216) 771-1900 **Drucker** Richard H '81
(440) 546-7616 **Drushel** Kelly E '90
(216) 241-5310 **Dub** Stanley M '75
(216) 787-3030 **Duber** Jeffrey B '84
(216) 861-1234 **Duber** Michael J '73
(216) 241-6055 **Dubin** Gary W '65
(216) 623-0000 **Dubin** Jeffrey E '97
(216) 241-6055 **Dubin Joseph & Shagrin**
(216) 241-0300 **Dubyak** Joseph A '69
(216) 586-3939 **Ducatman** Robert P '80
(216) 621-1113 **DuChez** Neil A '72
(216) 443-7800 **Ducoff** Ronni E '88
(216) 931-6000 **Duddy** Suzanne E '00
(216) 443-3178 **Dudley** Vincent B '97
(216) 241-2838 **Duff** Timothy J '90
(216) 522-4169 **Duffy** James M '82
(216) 222-8013 **Duffy** Kevin T '76
(216) 696-3030 **Duffy** Mary Beth '89
(216) 583-1455 **Dugan** Joan E '93
(216) 861-5582 **Dugan** Matthew P '00
(216) 689-5882 **Dugovics** Jill T '84
(216) 479-6100 **Duhamel** Marcel C '93
(216) 586-3939 **Dulabon** David W '01
(216) 696-3833 **Dumas** Wesley A '80
(216) 592-5000 **Duncan** Ed E '74
(216) 696-3030 **Duncan** William A '87
(216) 566-5500 **Dunford** Oliver J '01
(216) 931-6000 **Dunlap** Jeffrey S '97
(216) 479-6100 **Dunn** Carrie M '03
(216) 241-2838 **Dunn** George J '60
(216) 443-5834 **Dunn** Howard A '78
(216) 241-7255 **Dunn** James J '84
(216) 586-3939 **Dunn** John P '74
(216) 252-3542 **Dunn** Robert D '92
(216) 634-7777 **Dunn** Robert M '81
(216) 363-1400 **Dunn** Theodore M Jr. '82
(216) 515-1660 **Dunn** William P '03
(216) 621-7860 **Durkin** George J '62
(216) 696-3525 **Duvall** Wendy E '03
(216) 696-7600 **Duvin Cahn & Hutton**
(216) 696-7600 **Duvin** Robert P '63
(216) 736-7224 **Dvorin** David M '97
(216) 623-0150 **Dyczek** Carl J '80
(216) 443-8612 **Dyke** John T '01
(216) 443-7295 **Dyke** Lorianne E '98
(216) 583-4884 **Dysert** David C '90
(216) 621-5300 **Dzenitis** Paul A '03
(216) 694-4356 **Dzik** Robert B '73
(216) 443-7800 **Earley** Michelle D '99
(216) 348-5400 **Earp** Robert H III '96
(216) 566-8200 **Ebert** Gary A '78
(216) 443-8868 **Echols** Sharon A '91
(216) 621-0200 **Eckart** Dennis E '74
(216) 621-3346 **Eckstein** Georgia L '89
(216) 621-1500 **Eddington** Isaac J '00
(216) 241-5310 **Eddy** Robert H III '79
(216) 378-9905 **Edelman** Mark S '86
(216) 522-4914 **Edelstein** Joseph '84
(216) 689-3894 **Edgehouse** Gregory J '79
(216) 523-5606 **Edmister** Richard R '67
(216) 443-6350 **Edwards** Amanda B '01
(216) 443-8868 **Edwards** Michelle C '92
(216) 348-5400 **Edwards** Paul N '79
(216) 931-6000 **Edwards** William A '62
(216) 931-6000 **Edwards** William D '94
(216) 622-3651 **Edwards** William J '69
(216) 621-0200 **Egan** Patrick J '01
(216) 447-6297 **Ehlers** Kristin M '94
(216) 443-3653 **Ehrbar** Jeffrey J '97
Ehrbar Kurt F '95
(216) 861-1070 **Ehrenreich** Leonard '73
(216) 443-9000 **Ehrman** James W '74
(216) 830-6830 **Eiber** Keven D '90
(216) 687-1900 **Eidenmiller** David K '00
(216) 479-8500 **Eidnier** Robert J '82
(216) 566-5593 **Eilers** S Stuart '63
(216) 696-3311 **Einhorn** Theodore '97
(216) 687-0900 **Eisen** Brian N '92
(216) 589-0600 **Eisen** Hermine G '81
(216) 522-7800 **Eisen** Saul '60
(216) 363-4500 **Eisenberg** Gregg A '97
(216) 291-2400 **Eisenberg** Richard D '63
(216) 621-0200 **Eisenberg** Steven A '95
(216) 566-0356 **Eisenhardt** Howard A '82
(216) 687-1900 **Eisenstat** Carol S '96
(216) 781-3533 **Eisner** Gary W '73
(216) 621-0070 **Eisner** Michael L '95
(216) 781-2600 **Eklund** Claudia Rieth '79
(216) 622-8200 **Eklund** John J '80
(216) 348-1700 **Eklund** Paul D '78
(440) 248-7906 **Elbert** Kevin P '97
(216) 382-2500 **Elfvin & Besser**
(216) 382-2500 **Elfvin** Bruce B '72
(216) 621-2034 **Elhamshari** Muhammad K '01
(216) 522-1555 **El-Kamhawy** Abdel H '00
(216) 696-4422 **Ellerin** Jerome M '56
(216) 861-3099 **Elliott** Daniel R Jr. '70
(216) 622-8200 **Elliott** Linda U '91
(216) 592-5000 **Elliott** Michael E '80
(216) 363-4500 **Elliott** Pete C '84
(216) 444-9234 **Ellis** James D '98
(216) 443-9000 **Ellis** Michael A '77
(216) 592-5000 **Ellis** Stephen C '72
(216) 635-3243 **Ellsworth** Gary L '91
(216) 566-0415 **Elson** Martin W '83
(216) 861-6645 **Elwell** James N '83
(216) 861-0804 **Elzeer** Bradley E II '91
(216) 861-6191 **Elzeer** Jeffrey M '91
(216) 861-3086 **Elzeer** Kimrey D '96
(216) 523-1500 **Embleton** Jeffrey M '75
(216) 664-3671 **Embry** Myra T '94
(216) 739-5647 **Emery** Steven H '02
(216) 781-3434 **Emoff** Jerome M '74
(216) 348-1666 **Emrick** Charles R Jr. '58
(216) 363-1400 **Engle** David C '81
(216) 696-7600 **Englehart** Fredrick W '97
(216) 781-9917 **English** Brent L '80
(216) 881-6600 **English** Lawrence K '89
(216) 479-6100 **English** Matthew D '99
(216) 661-4164 **Englund** Joan M '88
(216) 642-3342 **Ennis** Charles Roe '73
(216) 830-6830 **Ensign** Cathryn R '86
(216) 362-3818 **Ensign** Gregory M '75
(216) 861-0026 **Epp** Henry C '72
(216) 443-9000 **Erb** L William '00
(216) 241-2838 **Erenburg** Kristin R '04
(216) 443-4939 **Ergun** Serpil '84
(216) 222-2227 **Erkkila** Linda K '99
(216) 575-7575 **Ernewein** Michael E '73
(216) 566-5831 **Erney** Jeffry J '88
(216) 241-6602 **Ernst** Christopher M '91
(216) 445-7076 **Ertle** Patrick Jay '90
(216) 348-5400 **Esborn** Theodore J '79
(216) 586-3939 **Eschbach-Hall** Patricia L '99
(216) 621-0200 **Eschedor** Jennifer L '93
(216) 502-0600 **Eschweiler** Thomas G '97
(216) 771-8121 **Escovar** Thomas J '69
(216) 787-4381 **Evanick** Barbara A '95
(216) 696-1448 **Evans** Charles E III '68
(216) 781-6166 **Evans** Cheryl N '01
(216) 621-0150 **Evans** Christina D '91
(216) 664-4839 **Evans** James D Jr. '04
(216) 443-7800 **Evans** Jennifer '95
(216) 621-0150 **Evans** Neil K '64
(216) 443-8299 **Evans** Ronald M '99
(216) 241-5735 **Evans** Susan M '93
(216) 479-6100 **Everett** Margaret Dodane '85
(216) 522-2671 **Ext** Traci L '98
(216) 621-0200 **Eyre** Paul P '82
(216) 566-5736 **Fabens** Andrew L III '67
(216) 621-0200 **Fabian** Bethany L '02
(216) 586-3939 **Fabian** John D '02
(216) 781-7777 **Fadel** William I '69
(216) 696-3366 **Faeges** Jay R '91
(216) 621-1113 **Fafrak** Kenneth W Jr. '03
(216) 861-5582 **Fagan** Christopher B '65
(440) 260-6616 **Fagan** Christopher P '03
(216) 348-1700 **Fagnilli** David J '86
(216) 241-8004 **Failor** Gary L '75
(216) 621-1000 **Falin** William H '87
(216) 348-5400 **Falk** Bryan H '97
(216) 622-8200 **Falk** Ryan W '03
(216) 348-5400 **Falkowski** Lynnette M '98
(216) 241-1200 **Fallon** Brian G '96
(216) 621-0177 **Fallon** Brian M '80
(216) 241-1200 **Fallon** Dominic J '59
(216) 566-2000 **Fallon** James C '94
(216) 771-1760 **Fallsgraff** Gary F '87
(216) 479-6820 **Fanger** Jeffrey J '92
(216) 689-4114 **Fanos** William R '80
(216) 621-0200 **Fanter** Guenther K '02
(216) 443-7800 **Faraglia** Anna M '96
(216) 928-2200 **Farchione** Joseph A Jr. '87
(216) 479-6100 **Farkas** Bryan J '00
(216) 447-1551 **Farkas** David S '03
(216) 515-1660 **Farkas** Gregory R '98
(216) 621-1922 **Farley** Betty C '88
(216) 241-7255 **Farley** Donald W '57
(216) 357-3301 **Farling** Harold E '91
(216) 696-4200 **Farmer** James P Jr. '81
(216) 931-6000 **Farnan** Brian P '02
(216) 241-6602 **Farnan** John G '87
(216) 687-1311 **Farrall** William P '72
(216) 621-2838 **Farrell** Michael F '76
(216) 621-0200 **Farrell** Michael K '88
(216) 696-5297 **Farren** Anthony S '96
(216) 586-3939 **Farroni** Mark B '83
(216) 696-2348 **Fatica** John A '91
(216) 781-3600 **Faulkner** David G '86
(216) 781-3600 **Faulkner** George H '60
(216) 781-3600 **Faulkner Muskovitz & Phillips, LLP**
(216) 861-1365 **Faust** Daniel M '02
(216) 479-6100 **Fauvie** Lori L '03
(216) 586-3939 **Faxon** Robert S '92
(216) 586-3939 **Fay** Regan J '74
(216) 861-5582 **Fay Sharpe Fagan Minnich & McKee LLP**
(216) 241-5310 **Fazio** Catherine '04
(216) 381-4424 **Fazio** John C '65
(216) 802-0077 **Fazio** Mario J '89
(216) 381-6400 **Fazio** Ruth Morton '02
(216) 479-8500 **Fazio** Stephen M '03
(216) 589-5622 **Fazio** Tyrone C '79
(216) 937-2222 **Feagan** Glenn D '89
(216) 781-0808 **Federman** Jerry I '76
(216) 586-3939 **Feeling** F Drexel '95
(216) 621-8484 **Fegen** Joseph P '95
(216) 566-5532 **Feher** Thomas L '87
(216) 664-4984 **Feighan** Ann M '92
(216) 651-9566 **Feighan** Joseph E III '96
(216) 631-4740 **Feighan** Joseph E Jr. '60
(216) 621-0200 **Feigi** Diane L '98
(216) 931-6000 **Fein** Robert A '70
(216) 875-2622 **Fein** Robert U '88
(216) 522-3715 **Feinberg** Melvin E '69
(216) 621-0200 **Feinberg** Paul H '79
(216) 861-4000 **Feinleib** Rachel C '93
(216) 363-3900 **Felber** Mark B '84
(216) 363-4500 **Feldman** Irwin M '64
(216) 931-6000 **Feldman** Marc H '02
(216) 781-6100 **Feldman** Marvin J '55
(216) 523-1525 **Feldman** Michael J '76
(216) 902-8531 **Feldman** Steven M '95
(216) 621-0200 **Feliciano** Jose C '75
(440) 605-6660 **Felker** Nathan A '02
(216) 449-8023 **Fell** Gary R '85
(216) 787-3030 **Fellenbaum** Mark '78
(216) 621-1530 **Felty** Kriss D '83
(440) 473-1025 **Feneli** Dale C '75
(440) 248-7906 **Fenn** David R '98
(216) 689-5106 **Fenner** Kathleen B '81
(216) 861-5000 **Fenske** Audrey A '89
(216) 622-3709 **Feran** Edward F '87
(216) 443-7800 **Ferguson** Anna B '01
(216) 641-8580 **Ferguson** Rhonda S '94
(216) 522-8191 **Fernandez** Susan E '87
(216) 579-1700 **Fernengel** Gregory D '03
(216) 928-2200 **Ferrante** Jason P '04
(216) 586-3939 **Ferraro** Adrienne M '03
(216) 575-0777 **Ferraro** James L '03
(216) 416-3730 **Ferstman** Jerome M '70
(216) 696-4441 **Fertel** Robert M '72
(216) 241-9990 **Fesler** Michael B '96
(216) 621-7227 **Feudo** Vincent A '65
(216) 360-7200 **Feuerman** Richard J '99
(216) 696-4200 **Fidler** John Paul '96
(216) 696-7170 **Fields** Darrell A '83
(216) 623-1220 **Fifner** Greta E '86
(216) 696-7600 **Fiftal** Emily C '04
(216) 514-1100 **Fiktus** Richard D '78
(216) 241-4554 **Filak** John J Jr. '84
(216) 443-7800 **Filiatraut** Kevin R '02
(216) 241-6602 **Fincun** Jeffrey D '73
(216) 514-6400 **Fine** Michael L '03
(216) 696-7525 **Fine** Michael W '81
(216) 621-2222 **Finelli** Daniel M '93
(216) 241-3400 **Fini** Rosalina M '94
(216) 889-5530 **Fink** Franklin E '04
(216) 586-3939 **Fink** Kevin H '04
(216) 781-8700 **Fink** Scott D '98
(216) 241-0044 **Finkenthal** Robert J '85
(216) 781-1212 **Finley** Bonnie S '95
(216) 574-4814 **Finley** David G '84
(216) 941-0101 **Finley** Kenneth W '81
(216) 642-9200 **Finnerty** Audrine P '92
(216) 621-0150 **Fiore** Rose Marie L '95
(216) 586-3939 **Fiorella** Andrew G '03
(216) 621-0200 **Firestone** Julie E '96
(216) 932-2466 **Fischbein-Cohen** Ruth R '89
(216) 731-3535 **Fischer** Henry B '64
(216) 586-3939 **Fischer** Lynne C '96
(216) 586-3939 **Fischer** Michelle K '89
(216) 443-9000 **Fischer** Rebecca K '99
(216) 241-2838 **Fischer** Robert H Jr. '99
(216) 731-3535 **Fischer-Doyle** Julie Anne '99
(216) 441-7688 **Fisco** Ernest B '78
(216) 522-3380 **Fisher** Christopher A '84
(216) 931-6000 **Fisher** Christopher P '97
(216) 566-5502 **Fisher** Damaris G '01
(216) 443-9000 **Fisher** Donald J '76
(216) 586-3939 **Fisher** Jo Ann '79
(216) 696-7661 **Fisher** Kenneth J '76
(216) 432-7200 **Fisher** Lee I '76
(440) 617-1528 **Fisher** Michael T '94
(216) 373-7400 **Fisher** Norman R Jr. '72
(216) 621-7905 **Fisher** Ryan H '89
(216) 787-3030 **Fisher** Virginia E '82
(216) 579-1700 **Fishman** Aaron A '99
(216) 621-9181 **Fishman** Gary S '82
(216) 621-6060 **Fishman** Lawrence R '69
(216) 781-4800 **Fishman** Mark S '81
(216) 621-1113 **Fistek** Thomas G '04
(216) 241-5310 **Fister** Anna S '03
(216) 687-1902 **FitzGerald** Claudia P '80
(216) 443-7800 **FitzGerald** Michael P '00
(216) 689-3292 **Fitzgerald** Patricia E '82
(216) 241-5310 **Fitzgerald** Timothy J '89
(216) 261-0200 **Fitzmaurice** John P '91
(216) 696-6454 **Fitzpatrick** Michael D '87
(216) 621-7227 **Fitzsimmons** Matthew T '80
(216) 622-8200 **FitzSimmons** Thomas A '00
(216) 592-5000 **FitzSimons** Brian W '74
(216) 363-6031 **Flament** Michael J '77
(216) 241-2838 **Flammang** Donna M '75
(216) 566-5500 **Flannery** Sarah C '02
(216) 687-1311 **Fleck** Robert E '58
Fleischmann-Fellowes Dagmar '93
(216) 522-4856 **Fleming** Charles E '90
(216) 566-5840 **Fleming** Jennifer Lesny '93
(216) 621-0200 **Fleming** Kyle B '95
(216) 651-8484 **Fleming** Nancy J '89
(216) 623-4143 **Flowers** Michael J '04
(216) 344-9393 **Flowers** Paul W '90
(216) 689-2707 **Floyd** Lawrence R '91
(216) 566-5836 **Floyd** Mark S '83
(216) 861-5582 **Floyd** Patrick D '93
(216) 222-8014 **Flynn** Patrick J '92
(216) 687-7625 **Fogarty** David H '95
(216) 348-1700 **Fogarty** Dennis R '91
(216) 621-0150 **Fogarty** Robert J '77
(440) 423-0154 **Foley** Margaret R '85
(216) 251-9755 **Foley** Michael P '95
(216) 696-0606 **Foley** Stephen C '82
(216) 522-3840 **Folkman** Debra L '91
(216) 566-5813 **Folland** Robert C '95
(216) 621-3247 **Fonda** Charles W '81
(216) 781-8700 **Foos** James R Jr. '80
(216) 696-7170 **Forbes Fields & Associates Co, LPA**
(216) 696-7170 **Forbes** George L '62
(216) 696-7170 **Forbes** Helen M '85
(216) 479-6100 **Forbes** Lisa Babish '92
(216) 696-7170 **Forbes** Mildred O '98
(216) 586-3939 **Ford** Anne Owings '89
(216) 830-2770 **Ford** Frank I '81
(216) 787-3200 **Ford** Jeffrey S '90
(216) 589-9030 **Ford** Joan A '83

(216) 622-3600 **Ford** Laura M '02
(216) 566-5603 **Ford** Robert B '68
(216) 696-7600 **Forman** Jonathan S '94
(216) 410-1456 **Forman** Thomas M '82
(216) 736-7226 **Fornshell** Matthew L '93
(216) 579-0800 **Forrest** Audrey P '78
(216) 844-3777 **Forrest** Carl L '04
(216) 771-4050 **Forrest** David A '79
(216) 687-2342 **Forte** David F '86
(216) 664-4825 **Fortunato** Christopher R '87
(216) 685-1105 **Fortunato** Theresa A '92
(216) 579-2861 **Fosnight** William D '84
(216) 444-3619 **Foss** Carolyn M '04
(216) 689-0773 **Fourmas** Thomas A '98
(216) 621-9870 **Fout** Karen Burke '04
(216) 622-8200 **Fowkes** Joshua A '02
(216) 902-6010 **Fowles** Ted R '00
(216) 357-5123 **Fox** Angela '92
(216) 241-5310 **Foy** Patrick M '87
(216) 583-4948 **Frabotta** Craig M '96
(216) 586-3939 **Fraelich** Timothy P '93
(216) 621-3000 **Franceschini** Antonio S '99
(216) 771-0157 **Franey** Martin F '48
(216) 579-1602 **Franey** Martin T '78
(216) 515-1660 **Frank** Ian H '96
(440) 446-1100 **Frank** Irwin M '72
(216) 623-0000 **Frank** John J '98
(216) 241-7226 **Frank** Mark S '81
(216) 363-1400 **Frankel** Dov Y '04
(216) 523-4103 **Franklin** Earl R '68
(216) 476-7002 **Franklin** Marlene L '91
(216) 621-1530 **Franks** Jennifer R '02
(216) 515-1660 **Frantz** Michael J '76
(216) 515-1660 **Frantz Ward LLP**
(216) 586-3939 **Franz** Paul E '02
(216) 443-3429 **Fraunfelder** William A Jr. '68
(216) 391-7700 **Frazier** Linda M '96
(440) 461-3600 **Freda** Joy C '79
(216) 781-3434 **Frederick** Ronald I '94
(216) 622-0850 **Freeburg** David A '99
(216) 249-3199 **Freedman** Steven A '76
(216) 696-7600 **Freeman** Barry Y '93
(216) 621-7743 **Freeman** Bryan S '99
(216) 771-9980 **Freeman** Kenneth J '81
(216) 689-3851 **Freeman** Mark T '97
(216) 566-2410 **Freeman** Michelle M '99
(216) 685-1107 **Freeman** Thomas J '82
(216) 222-2272 **Frei** Susan E '89
(216) 479-8500 **Freimuth** Marc W '71
(216) 621-0200 **French** Charles J III '78
(216) 621-4260 **French** James H '74
(216) 621-5090 **French** Jo A '88
(216) 696-4200 **French** Michael K '01
(216) 622-3687 **French** Richard J '73
(216) 781-0636 **Frenden** John A '64
(216) 781-0636 **Frenden** John B '03
(216) 928-7700 **Frey** Ronald L II '04
(216) 696-4700 **Fricke** Wade M '89
(216) 687-1311 **Fried** Adam M '95
(216) 831-0042 **Friedberg** Ronald P '91
(216) 781-1212 **Friedell** Katherine A '92
(216) 696-0600 **Friedland** Dale R '76
(216) 222-9473 **Friedlander** Daniel A '83
(216) 631-0280 **Friedlander** Jody E '01
(216) 615-7358 **Friedlander** Lawrence H '65
(216) 621-9282 **Friedman** Avery S '73
(216) 787-3030 **Friedman** Betsey N '82
(216) 621-0070 **Friedman Domiano & Smith Co,LPA**
(216) 241-1430 **Friedman & Gilbert**
(216) 241-1430 **Friedman** Gordon S '68
(216) 931-6000 **Friedman** Harold E '59
(216) 928-7700 **Friedman** Ian N '97
(216) 363-4500 **Friedman** James M '66
(216) 621-0070 **Friedman** Jeffrey H '73
(216) 781-5232 **Friedman** Laurence A '93
(216) 621-0580 **Friedman** Lisa S '94
(216) 651-6800 **Friedman** Mitchell J '01
(216) 241-1007 **Friedman** Paul M '77
(216) 781-8823 **Friedman** Richard L '82
(216) 514-1180 **Friedman** Robert G '94
(216) 479-8500 **Friedman** Steven A '92
(216) 292-1148 **Friedman** Zeev '78
(216) 520-5516 **Friedmann** Richard V '98
(216) 781-1452 **Friel** Thomas J '49
(216) 621-0200 **Frient** Megan P '98
(216) 523-1500 **Friesen** Brendon P '03
(216) 664-4822 **Fritz** Bryan J '78
(216) 771-1525 **Froberg** Steven C '75
(216) 586-3939 **Frodyma** Scott F '98
(216) 595-8222 **Fromet** Avery H '72
(216) 595-1300 **Fromson** A Scott '87
(216) 861-6833 **Fromson** Richard A '55
(216) 575-0777 **Frost** Corey W '87
(216) 622-8895 **Frost** Kristin J '01
(216) 566-8200 **Frutig** Patricia R '84
(216) 621-7860 **Frutkin** Harvey L '72
(216) 861-5582 **Fry** Jude A '91
(216) 689-4663 **Fry** Sherry L '97
(216) 357-7270 **Fuchs** Siegmund F '04
(216) 522-1200 **Fuente** Alan D '93
(216) 443-7950 **Fuerst** Gerald E '59
(216) 696-3311 **Fuerst** Robert A '79
(216) 566-2961 **Fuhrer** Eryn Ace '00
(216) 566-5665 **Fuller** Adam D '03
(216) 621-1111 **Fullmer** Jerry A '69
(216) 348-5400 **Fullmer** William A '84
(216) 931-6000 **Fulton** Arlishea L '99
(216) 241-5310 **Fulton** Burt J '52
(216) 241-0707 **Fulton** William H '73
(216) 566-8200 **Fumich** William M Jr. '76
(216) 689-1290 **Fung** Mia M '96
(216) 566-1600 **Fusco** David M '84
(216) 443-4940 **Fuss** Gregory C '78
(216) 368-3288 **Gabinet** Leon '70
(216) 736-7206 **Gabinet** Sarah J '82
(216) 479-8500 **Gabriel** D Bruce '80
(216) 443-5809 **Gabriel** Gary V '84
(216) 931-6000 **Gagliano** Bill J '80
(216) 579-1700 **Gagnon** Suzanne B '00
(216) 566-5722 **Gaillard** Clevonne M '02
(216) 566-5931 **Gaj** Brian L '85
(216) 830-6830 **Gajda** Patricia A '90
(216) 771-8038 **Galaska** Edward J '82
(216) 363-4500 **Gale** Gregory K '03
(216) 621-1113 **Galin** Morris David '96
(216) 443-7800 **Gall** Steven E '91
(216) 781-9440 **Gall** Timothy L '79
(216) 241-8193 **Gallagher** Candace M '75
(216) 443-8509 **Gallagher** Eileen T '96
(216) 241-8193 **Gallagher** Francis P '75
(216) 443-7800 **Gallagher** Hollie L '95
(216) 443-7583 **Gallagher** Jean M '86
(216) 443-7800 **Gallagher** John J '86
(216) 622-3600 **Gallagher** Kathleen M '93
(216) 689-0324 **Gallagher** Kimberly A '94
(216) 241-5310 **Gallagher** Michael R '49
(216) 377-0598 **Gallagher** Patrick J '89
(216) 443-6350 **Gallagher** Shannon M '04
(216) 241-5310 **Gallagher Sharp Fulton & Norman**
(216) 566-1600 **Gallagher** Timothy J '92
(216) 771-1081 **Gallo** Charles J '55
(216) 771-1081 **Gallo** Charles J Jr. '89
(216) 771-1081 **Gallo** Lori M '83
(216) 621-0200 **Galloway** Robert R '88
(216) 575-0777 **Gallucci** Anthony '96
(216) 861-0804 **Gallucci** Frank L III '00
(216) 621-4636 **Gallup Burns & Associates**
(216) 621-4636 **Gallup** David B '79
(216) 621-7860 **Gallup** Jeffrey W '03
(216) 622-3600 **Galvin** Kelly L '93
(216) 687-1311 **Galvin** Martin T '94
(216) 592-5000 **Gambaccini** Janice R '03
(216) 363-4500 **Gambaccini** John S '00
(216) 289-3366 **Gamiere** Dorothy S '75
(216) 357-7243 **Gamiere** Jess E '02
(216) 689-3241 **Gamin** Dean D '87
(216) 586-3939 **Gammie** Sandra E '86
(216) 472-2216 **Gamso** Jeffrey M '90
(216) 687-1311 **Gannon** Brian T '04
(216) 696-6454 **Gannon** John F '72
(216) 586-3939 **Ganske** Lyle G '84
(216) 592-5000 **Gantous** Anthony M '03
(216) 861-5000 **Garanich** James G '84
(216) 687-2263 **Gard** Stephen W '80
(216) 241-5310 **Gardner** Abigail J '98
(216) 687-1311 **Gardner** Francis X '79
(216) 931-6000 **Gardner** Gary T '97
(216) 348-5400 **Gardner** George Andrew '96
(216) 696-9800 **Gardner** Mark J '93
(216) 348-5400 **Gardner** Steven L '76
(216) 664-4419 **Gareau** William E Jr. '97
(216) 574-2600 **Garfield** Robert E '63
(216) 621-0150 **Gariepy** Stephen H '77
(216) 348-1700 **Garner** Richard M '93
(216) 592-5000 **Garred** John X '84
(216) 781-5470 **Garrett** Glen H '95
(216) 696-8730 **Garritano** Carlos P '04
(216) 592-5000 **Garritano** Frank O '04
(216) 432-1800 **Garson** Brent D '83
(216) 696-9330 **Garson** Stuart I '76
(216) 391-1112 **Garver** Jonathan N '74
(216) 522-3873 **Garvey** Mary A '80
(216) 579-1700 **Garvey** Michael W '91
(216) 621-0150 **Garvin** Michael J '84
(216) 443-6376 **Gary** Christina M '01
(216) 771-1900 **Gasper** Frank C '68
(216) 586-3939 **Gates** Lisa B '88
(216) 348-5400 **Gates** Martin S '88
(216) 622-8200 **Gattozzi** Lynn M '87
(216) 830-6830 **Gattozzi** Thomas A '94
(216) 771-4444 **Gaul** Patricia A '93
(216) 443-8560 **Gauntner** Timothy M '04
(216) 523-1500 **Gavin** Michael T '55
(216) 566-5908 **Gawlik** Gregory J '00
(216) 429-9493 **Gay** James A '79
(216) 696-3311 **Gaynor** Bruce E '72
(440) 442-9630 **Gaynor** Donald A '50
(216) 443-8979 **Gedeon** Richard L '85
(216) 861-1424 **Gedos** Anthony A '73
(216) 621-1000 **Gee** Kathleen E '02
(216) 566-5666 **Geffert** Alexandra J '03
(216) 525-1998 **Geffert** John J '01
(216) 241-2838 **Gehring** Ronn J '03
(216) 592-5000 **Geib** Richard P '95
(216) 586-3939 **Geiger** Richard S '99
(216) 586-3939 **Geise** Steven N '96
(216) 781-9499 **Gelbman** Alan G '64
(216) 831-0042 **Geneva** Fount S '00
(216) 687-2346 **Geneva** Louis B '73
Gentile Anthony M Jr. '80
(216) 875-3050 **Gentile** Matthew D '04
(216) 221-0400 **Gentry** Eldred A Jr. '59
(216) 221-0400 **Gentry** James E '78
(216) 361-2273 **George** Allen '73
(216) 861-4533 **George** Gene B '74
(216) 443-7800 **George** George M '87
(216) 524-7100 **George** Mark M '88
(216) 348-5400 **George** Susan Fenwick '04
(216) 241-4100 **George** Warren S '89
(216) 575-7575 **Georgeadis** Philip N '70
(216) 771-2680 **Geraci & LaPerna Co, LPA**
(216) 771-2680 **Geraci** Rudolph J '62
(216) 623-0150 **Geraci** Victor T '88
(216) 479-6100 **Gerak** John '02
(216) 586-3939 **Gerber** Susan M '99
(216) 586-3939 **Gerbick** Amy E '02
(216) 586-0964 **Gerfen** Chance N '02
(216) 443-2059 **Gerity** Eileen T '89
(216) 523-1500 **Gerlack** Julius R '62
(216) 241-4100 **Gerlack-George** Lisa M '89
(440) 461-9661 **Gerred** Michelle M '01
(216) 622-8200 **Gertsburg** Alexander E '01
(216) 586-3939 **Gest** Kristen Lau '03
(216) 622-3840 **Getz** Thomas E '88
(216) 696-7777 **Ghaster** Earl F Jr. '80
(216) 621-0200 **Gherlein** John M '80
(216) 658-4729 **GiaMaria** Melanie R '03
(216) 368-2098 **Giannelli** Paul C '87
(216) 522-7800 **Giannirakis** Maria D '87
(216) 781-1212 **Gibbon** Christopher L '77
(216) 781-1212 **Gibbon** John H '72
(216) 621-2090 **Gibbons & Cullen LLP**
(216) 622-3645 **Gibbons** Gregory R '78
(216) 961-3500 **Gibbons** Jason M '91
(216) 363-6048 **Gibbons** John B '75
(216) 344-9220 **Gibbons** Joseph P '79
(216) 443-5595 **Gibbons** Katherine H '02
(216) 664-2809 **Gibbons** Kevin J '92
(216) 394-5063 **Gibbons** M Colette '76
(216) 621-2090 **Gibbons** Mark T '93
(216) 623-8000 **Gibbons** William P '73
(216) 621-0150 **Gibbs** Arthur E III '96
(216) 696-8070 **Gibel** George R '96
(216) 586-3939 **Giblin** Stephen Q '80
(216) 696-0800 **Gibson Brelo Ziccarelli & Martello**
(216) 696-0800 **Gibson** Joseph '72
(216) 479-8500 **Gibson** L Todd '04
(216) 621-0200 **Gibson** Wendy J '79
(216) 241-5310 **Gibson** William F '73
(216) 642-3342 **Gideon** Antoinette F '87
(216) 443-7800 **Giegerich** Laurence D '00
(216) 621-5161 **Giffen & Kaminski, LLC**
(216) 621-5161 **Giffen** Karen L '89
(216) 241-1430 **Gilbert** Terry H '73
(216) 687-1311 **Gilbride** Michael P '93
(216) 575-9272 **Gilchrist** Thomas C '91
(216) 522-3380 **Gill** Anita A '90
(216) 771-2680 **Gill** John J '62
(216) 861-8000 **Gill** Steven R '91
(216) 241-7255 **Gill** Thomas P '73
(216) 451-8540 **Gillespie-Mobley** Ricky L '89
(216) 687-9413 **Gillombardo** Carl F Jr. '67
(216) 363-4500 **Gilman** Jeremy '83
(216) 896-0606 **Gilmore** Alvin I '63
(216) 736-7240 **Gilmore** Robert S '86
(216) 241-6602 **Gimbel** Adam H '01
(216) 443-7223 **Ginsberg** Amy Jo '94
(216) 621-0200 **Ginsburg** Edward S '75
(216) 771-1144 **Gioffre** Joseph R '85
(216) 522-4914 **Giuffre** Susan G '83
(216) 241-0520 **Giuliani** Albert '83
(216) 348-9800 **Giusto** Blaise C '73
(216) 515-1660 **Gladstone** Stephen F '81
(216) 696-2938 **Glaser** Robert E '60
(216) 579-7150 **Glavinos** George Jr. '71
(216) 586-3939 **Gleason** Michael J '01
(216) 622-8200 **Gleespen** Melissa M '03
(216) 447-9000 **Gleespen** Michael W '84
(216) 522-3715 **Gleine** Gregory M '00
(216) 664-3567 **Glenn** Cordelia A '83
(216) 431-8060 **Glenn** Douglas H '71
(216) 416-3259 **Glenn-Katzakis** Joan C '93
(216) 241-6882 **Glesius** Amy S '96
(216) 361-4400 **Glick** Nancy J '87
(216) 931-6000 **Glickman** Albert B '62
(216) 696-1422 **Glickman** Robert T '92
(216) 861-3086 **Glover** James T '89
(216) 696-7445 **Glowacki** James L '80
(216) 241-4300 **Gluck** Jerry '79
(216) 515-1660 **Gluek** Carl H '85
(216) 696-4700 **Gluntz** Kevin P '95
(216) 696-2719 **Goddard** Lisa M '90
(216) 622-8200 **Goddard** Richard P '79
(216) 563-2009 **Goering** Shelly A '87
(216) 621-7860 **Goetsch** Alexander E '95
(216) 781-1111 **Goetz** Daniel P '95
(216) 241-6602 **Goff** Robert E Jr. '98
(216) 514-1100 **Goffman** Ira S '81
(216) 931-6000 **Goggins** Bari E '80
(216) 931-6000 **Goheen** John C '83
(216) 931-6000 **Goins** Frances Floriano '77
(216) 687-1311 **Gold** Erin R '99
(216) 696-6122 **Gold** Gerald S '54
(216) 731-1529 **Gold** Laura A '95
(216) 696-6122 **Gold & Pyle Co, LPA**
(216) 479-8500 **Gold** Roger M '91
(216) 593-0001 **Gold** Rosemary G '82
(216) 391-5444 **Gold-Scott** Lisa L '94
(216) 443-7800 **Goldberg** Francine B '91
(216) 781-1111 **Goldberg** James R '64
(216) 696-4514 **Goldberg** Michael J '88
(216) 241-0011 **Goldberg & O'Shea**
(216) 351-7212 **Goldberg** Scott E '85
(216) 881-5300 **Goldblatt** Jay A '83
(216) 621-0150 **Goldenberg** Warren '81
(216) 241-0300 **Goldense** David W '77
(216) 696-0606 **Goldfarb** Bernard S '40
(216) 579-1117 **Goldfarb** Gary M '72
(216) 291-1155 **Goldfarb** Joanne D '75
(216) 621-0150 **Goldfarb** Steven A '85
(216) 696-1122 **Goldman** Donald L '60
(216) 621-0200 **Goldman** Matthew R '82
(216) 363-4500 **Goldner** Allan '73
(216) 931-6000 **Goldsmith** James A '80
(216) 566-5559 **Goldstein** Heidi B '95
(216) 341-7800 **Goldstein** Joshua D '97
(216) 771-6633 **Goldstein** Joyce '84
(216) 241-6677 **Goldstein** Michael D '02
(216) 771-6633 **Goldstein & O'Connor**
(216) 241-6677 **Goldstein** William M '69
(216) 658-9900 **Goldwasser** Andrew S '97
(216) 687-1311 **Goldwasser** Gary H '67
(216) 592-5000 **Goldwood** Jon J '98
(216) 696-3366 **Goler** Michael D '77
(216) 443-7800 **Golish** Matthew D '99
(216) 687-2737 **Golovan** Kathleen R '94
(216) 622-8200 **Golrick** Mary E '85
(216) 341-0940 **Golubski** Robert J '81
(216) 696-0440 **Gonda** Diane M '92
(216) 781-1212 **Gonyer** Todd E '02
(216) 664-2894 **Gonzalez** Jose M '84
(216) 621-5980 **Gonzalez** Linda V '98
(216) 443-8556 **Gonzalez** Tracey S '03
(216) 651-1919 **Gonzalez** Vincent F '74
(216) 522-7800 **Good** Amy L '91
(216) 241-1200 **Good** Christine F '91
(216) 696-0650 **Good** Darcy M '97
(216) 566-5500 **Good** Jonathan A '95
(216) 523-1100 **Gooden** Deborah M '94
(216) 781-3434 **Goodman** Alan I '69
(216) 523-1525 **Goodman** Alan M '75
(216) 363-4500 **Goodman** Bernard D '60
(216) 479-8500 **Goodman** David S '77
(216) 586-3939 **Goodman** Eric R '03
(216) 928-9990 **Goodman** Grant A '95
(216) 216-0606 **Goodman** John L '70
(216) 781-1212 **Goodman** Jonathan H '99
(216) 696-3366 **Goodman** Robert A '60
(216) 696-3366 **Goodman Weiss Miller LLP**
(216) 621-1541 **Goodrich** Paula J '80
(216) 575-7666 **Goodwin** David J '82
(216) 241-3646 **Goodwin** Paula R '77
(216) 696-2719 **Goodwin** Sally A '93
(216) 586-3939 **Goots** Thomas R '96
(216) 687-0404 **Gorczyca** Francis A '81
(440) 846-5700 **Gordillo** Gregory A '94
(216) 443-7800 **Gordillo** Michael J '00
(216) 579-1700 **Gordon** Charles B '52
(216) 621-6060 **Gordon** David J '78
(216) 621-2300 **Gordon** Harlan M '68
(216) 641-4701 **Gordon** Heather A '94
(216) 523-4134 **Gordon** Howard D '71
(216) 781-5245 **Gordon** Larry S '56
(216) 861-5175 **Gordon** Loren M '93
(216) 479-6100 **Gordon** Michael Scot '99
(216) 566-5629 **Gordon** Sean A '01
(216) 592-5000 **Gore** George F III '64
(216) 592-5000 **Gore** Janet S '86
(216) 575-2253 **Gorensek** Thomas F '85
(216) 357-7120 **Goretzke** Cullen '04
(216) 566-1778 **Gorjanc** Laura T '04
(216) 931-7509 **Gorman** Jennifer H '89
(216) 623-0000 **Gormley** Darryl E '97
(216) 621-0150 **Gorom** Stanley R III '93
(216) 687-2325 **Goshien** David B '76
(216) 861-5582 **Goss** Colleen Flynn '80
(440) 717-1680 **Gossick** Lucius C '63
(216) 696-7525 **Gottehrer** Blaine L '80
(216) 348-2800 **Gottfried** R. Mark Jr. '87
(216) 443-9000 **Gourash** Daniel F '83
(216) 241-5310 **Gowan** James G '65
(216) 621-8744 **Gozdanovic** Amy E '97
(216) 621-0200 **Graban** Matthew D '97
(216) 241-5310 **Grable** Jason P '03
(216) 479-6100 **Grabow** Rachel J '97
(216) 222-2000 **Grady** Kathleen S '81
(216) 928-1010 **Gragel** Susan L '80
(216) 622-8200 **Graham** James D '95
(216) 263-6200 **Graham** Maurice E '00
(216) 443-3584 **Graham** Richard T '74
(216) 514-1180 **Graham** Sarah S '99
Graham Sulaiman Roy '99
(216) 443-7800 **Grano** Robert H Jr. '84
(216) 241-6868 **Grant** David L '76
(216) 771-1760 **Grant** David R '95
(216) 443-8826 **Grant** Garlandine J '86
(216) 721-3606 **Grant** Joseph K '99
(216) 476-1299 **Granzier** Paul A '59
(216) 348-5400 **Grassi** Carl J '84
(216) 328-2600 **Grasso** James A '83
(216) 579-1602 **Gravens** Terrance P '77
(440) 356-5700 **Graves** David M '98
(216) 696-2022 **Graves** Donet D '79
(216) 696-2022 **Graves & Horton, LLC**
(216) 831-2255 **Gray** Brenda J '93
(216) 622-8200 **Gray** David E II '99
(216) 479-8500 **Gray** James D '91
(216) 781-5832 **Gray** Louis '42
(216) 579-0800 **Gray** Roland B '83
(216) 928-2200 **Gray** Todd A '99
(216) 522-0171 **Grays** Winston '83
(216) 241-5310 **Greathouse** Larry C '83
(216) 433-2650 **Greco** Frank J '86
(216) 696-8700 **Greco** Karen L '82
(216) 861-5000 **Greco** Richard A Jr. '82
(216) 696-1275 **Green** Linda M '82
(216) 685-1154 **Green** Stanley '69
(216) 621-5112 **Greenberg** Barbara C '94
(216) 781-1212 **Greenberg** Jonathan D '83
(216) 696-7533 **Greenberg** Sheldon J '64
(216) 566-9706 **Greenblatt** Ronald H '74
(216) 575-5200 **Greene** Bradley L '89
(216) 687-0900 **Greene & Eisen Co, LPA**
(216) 573-7853 **Greene** Joan E '94
(216) 443-7223 **Greene** John F '85
(216) 921-2011 **Greene** Thornton R '52
(216) 687-0900 **Greene** William M '72
(216) 363-1400 **Greenfield** Harry W '70
(216) 931-6000 **Greenlee** Gary S '97
(216) 579-2163 **Greenlee** Mark B '97
(216) 861-2588 **Greenspan** Ronald B '74
(216) 621-4411 **Greenwald** Leonard S '68
(216) 241-5310 **Greer** Mark A '86
(216) 589-8399 **Greggo** Robert M '84
(440) 808-9750 **Gregor** Sean S '98
(216) 586-3939 **Gregory** Earnest B '04
(216) 687-1900 **Gregory** Herman E III '87
(440) 753-1490 **Grenell** David J '87
(216) 592-5000 **Gretter** Craig T '02
(216) 861-3366 **Greulich** David P Jr. '96
(216) 621-6570 **Greve** Thomas F '81
(216) 522-9000 **Grieco** Paul '95
(216) 689-0509 **Griffin** Cathryn D '94
(216) 268-1126 **Griffin** Willie L '87
(216) 586-3939 **Griffith** Calvin P '88
(216) 348-5400 **Griffith** James A '58
(216) 231-7300 **Griffith** Nancy L '90
(216) 696-8730 **Grillo** David W '03
(216) 479-8500 **Grinham** Jill A '02
(216) 447-9000 **Grisko** Jerome P Jr. '87
(216) 621-0200 **Griswold** James B '74
(216) 771-5717 **Griveas** Thomas '80
(216) 931-6000 **Groedel** Howard M '92
(216) 687-1311 **Groedel** Marc W '79
(216) 566-9200 **Gross** Alan D '74
(216) 621-0150 **Gross** Joan M '76
(216) 363-4500 **Gross** Joseph N '91
(216) 623-0150 **Gross** Lynn A '00
(216) 931-6000 **Gross** Michael A '00
(216) 839-1111 **Gross** Robert L '93
(216) 839-1111 **Gross** Sanford '66
(216) 586-3939 **Grossman** Theodore M '87
(216) 696-2404 **Groth** Mary C '83
(216) 621-7227 **Grove** James H '88
(216) 664-4984 **Groves** Emanuella D '81
(216) 781-5515 **Grubb** Natalie F '93
(216) 586-3939 **Grube** Brian K '97
(216) 595-6300 **Gruenspan** Charles '82
(216) 861-5555 **Gruhin** Gloria S '93
(216) 861-5555 **Gruhin** Michael H '76
(216) 621-4244 **Grumbine** Kylie L '03
(216) 689-4960 **Grunick** Rebecca J '85
(216) 771-6464 **Guarnieri** William T '62
(216) 621-7227 **Gudbranson** Margaret A '83
(216) 621-7227 **Gudbranson** Robert N '61
(216) 687-1311 **Guice** Gregory G '03

(216) 623-1123 **Guidubaldi** David J '72
(216) 622-8200 **Guinn** Guy F '81
(440) 695-6500 **Gullia** Theodore A Jr. '66
(440) 842-1313 **Gulyassy** Victor J '50
(216) 861-1070 **Gundy** John M Jr. '92
(216) 623-0150 **Gunning** David H II '94
(216) 586-3939 **Gunning** Gina K '95
(216) 623-0000 **Gupta** Manju '03
(216) 479-8500 **Gurbst** Richard S '71
(440) 460-3705 **Gurin** Timothy B '87
(216) 621-3251 **Gurney Miller & Mamone**
(216) 931-6000 **Gurney** Neil W '78
(440) 888-1177 **Gusley** Mark R '91
(216) 443-7800 **Gutierrez** James A '85
(216) 739-2901 **Gutin** Robert D '68
(216) 621-1530 **Gutkoski** Brian R '03
(216) 363-4500 **Gutmacher** Norman W '71
(216) 696-4006 **Guttman** Rubin '77
(216) 522-4914 **Guzzo** Fred J '73
(216) 363-4500 **Haas** Douglas E '77
(216) 472-1500 **Haas** Gary C '69
(216) 623-0150 **Haas** Michael J '94
(216) 348-5400 **Haas** Patricia J '99
(216) 689-4169 **Haas** Robert M '75
(216) 861-5582 **Haas** Steven M '94
(216) 687-1311 **Haber** Richard C '90
(216) 241-8282 **Hackerd** Richard E '91
(216) 623-0000 **Hacking** Timothy J '01
(216) 586-3939 **Hackwelder** Scott W '04
(216) 281-5210 **Haddad** Tina R '89
(216) 241-5310 **Haemmerle** Todd M '93
(216) 291-3600 **Haffey** James R Jr. '64
(216) 291-3600 **Haffey** Timothy P '89
(216) 622-8200 **Hagedorn** Gina K '04
(216) 586-3939 **Hagen** Daniel C '80
(440) 808-4242 **Hager** Jason P '03
(216) 621-5300 **Hager** Robert A '88
(216) 931-6000 **Haggerty** John J '03
(216) 515-1660 **Haggerty** Patrick F '85
(216) 391-5110 **Haggins** Edward T '66
(216) 432-9222 **Hahn** Lisa A '94
(216) 621-0150 **Hahn Loeser & Parks LLP**
(216) 861-6160 **Hahn** Victor H '50
(216) 696-1422 **Haiman** Irwin S '41
(216) 875-6226 **Haimes** Rand S '84
(216) 622-8200 **Haines** Warren M II '00
(216) 861-2222 **Hairston** Craig A '99
(216) 664-2685 **Hajjar** Joseph G '98
(216) 348-5400 **Hales** David K '96
(216) 586-3939 **Halfon** Ellen E '88
(216) 928-3474 **Halim** Henny N '03
(216) 622-8200 **Hall** Arthur C III '95
(216) 443-8800 **Hall** Barbara S '79
(216) 696-1616 **Hall** Edison H Jr. '79
(216) 781-1212 **Hall** Eric J '01
(216) 520-5554 **Hall** Kenneth P '92
(216) 623-0000 **Hall** Lindsey I '02
(216) 696-1616 **Hall** Mary E '91
(216) 931-6000 **Hall** Michael J '04
(216) 443-5809 **Hall** Stephanie N '01
(216) 363-1400 **Hallbauer** John A '66
(216) 443-7295 **Haller** Jason G '00
(216) 623-2035 **Hallick** Patricia J '79
(216) 771-5588 **Halliday** Brian J '01
Hallquist Kevin P '86
(216) 696-7550 **Halpern** Marvin N '61
(216) 696-6700 **Hamed** Michael R '98
(216) 621-0200 **Hamilton** J Richard '56
(216) 522-4107 **Hamilton** Richard T Jr. '89
(216) 586-3939 **Hamilton** Thomas A '93
(216) 574-8321 **Hamm** George E Jr. '92
(216) 635-1705 **Hammer** Lisa A '98
(216) 771-6500 **Hammond** Kim M '93
(216) 664-2816 **Hammons-Brown** Terri M '93
(216) 566-5257 **Hampton** Bruce E '82
(216) 844-3372 **Hancock** Kathleen L '95
(216) 344-8401 **Hanna** John T '90
(216) 514-7480 **Hanna** Marcy J '04
(216) 664-3739 **Hanna** Mary N '03
(216) 592-5000 **Hanna** Robert J '86
(216) 830-6830 **Hanna** Valerie M '91
(216) 479-8500 **Hanna** W Michael '80
(216) 781-1212 **Hanna** William R '97
(216) 443-7800 **Hannan** Charles E Jr. '86
(216) 566-5723 **Hannan** Tracy A '03
(216) 479-8500 **Hanover** Pamela I '80
(216) 664-4504 **Hansbrough** Keith '00
(216) 621-0200 **Hanselman** Suzanne K '91
(216) 348-5400 **Hansen** Beth E '01
(216) 241-2880 **Hansen** Glenn S '86
(216) 241-6602 **Hanson** Jay S '85
Happeny Stephen R '03
(216) 566-5634 **Hara** Halle B '98
(216) 514-1100 **Haran** Craig T '00
(216) 623-0150 **Harbarger** David R '75
(216) 689-4967 **Harbottle** Scott A '89
(216) 443-5809 **Hardaway** Ayesha Bell '04
(216) 431-5000 **Harden** Regina '01
(216) 363-4500 **Harders** Walter Scott '99
(216) 502-0800 **Hardiman** James L '68
(216) 586-3939 **Hardin** Charles W Jr. '87
(216) 621-9767 **Hardin-Levine** Peter S '84
(216) 687-1900 **Harding** Sandra G '93
(216) 566-5804 **Hardy** Michael L '72
(216) 931-6000 **Hardy** Richard G '78
Hargate Edwin V III '83
(216) 589-9615 **Harlow** Kathryn '91
(216) 844-1686 **Harmon** Heather M '00
Harp Malinda D '89
(216) 991-9122 **Harper** Sara J '52
(216) 622-8200 **Harper** Walter G '74
(216) 623-4900 **Harris** Alan B '74
(216) 241-6602 **Harris** Beverly A '78
(216) 621-2234 **Harris** Christopher P '97
(216) 696-5444 **Harris** Eugenya Yvonne '92
(216) 622-8200 **Harris** Julie A '95
(216) 861-5542 **Harris** Leodis '63
(216) 432-7200 **Harris** Marsha E '95
(216) 592-5000 **Harris** Michael F '77
(216) 696-1545 **Harris** Pamala S '02
(216) 689-0350 **Harris** Paul N '83
(216) 443-8746 **Harrison** Gladys E '84
(216) 696-7600 **Harrold** Linda Hauserman '79
(216) 621-0150 **Hart** Randy J '90
(216) 787-3030 **Hartke** Gregory T '84
(216) 781-5515 **Hartman** Anthony J '68
(216) 291-1554 **Hartman** Dale M '87
(216) 443-7295 **Hartman** Margaret A '04
(216) 771-3336 **Hartman** Richard J '73
(216) 696-4441 **Hartman** Robert W '04
(216) 689-5090 **Hartman** Sheldon R '71
(216) 443-8831 **Hartmann** Marie M '86
(216) 566-5500 **Hartwig** Jeffrey R '04
(216) 696-1080 **Hartzell** Angelique M '99
(216) 931-6000 **Harvey** Elizabeth A '96
(440) 838-8800 **Harvey** Robert Scot '90
(216) 368-6280 **Harvey** Sara D '01
(216) 348-0041 **Harwood** Peter R '65
(216) 586-3939 **Hassell** Charles D '73
(216) 771-1760 **Hassett** Brian R '94
(216) 787-3030 **Hastings** Jeffrey P '91
(216) 621-0150 **Hastings** Kim M '86
(216) 664-2665 **Hastings** L Stewart Jr. '80
(216) 522-3877 **Hastings** Linda M '94
(216) 479-8500 **Hastings** Susan C '85
(216) 771-6960 **Hatch** Lawrence H '87
(216) 586-3939 **Hatina** Joseph D '99
(216) 861-5582 **Hauber** Karl W '01
(216) 687-1311 **Haude** Daniel R '97
(216) 348-1700 **Haude** Kristi L '02
(216) 622-8200 **Hauer** Richard J Jr. '75
(216) 692-3198 **Haumann** Theresa R '88
(216) 787-5329 **Haun** Sharla R '99
(216) 781-4110 **Hauptman** Nadine '99
(216) 875-8221 **Haus** Andrew M '92
(216) 479-8500 **Hauser** Karen A '97
(216) 566-5660 **Hauser** Laura A '89
(216) 368-1797 **Hausman** Thomas I '73
(216) 696-4700 **Havach** James M '74
(216) 621-0150 **Havener** Kathleen B '98
(216) 479-8500 **Havener** Thomas G '87
(216) 781-5515 **Havens** Hunter S '84
(216) 479-8500 **Haverstick** Rebecca Wistner '96
(216) 696-3232 **Hawal** William '80
(216) 383-2061 **Hawk** George W Jr. '87
(216) 781-1212 **Hawk** Morris M '95
(216) 443-5809 **Hawk** Sharon L '81
(216) 861-1365 **Hawkins** Ann M '80
(216) 861-1365 **Hawkins** John T '87
(440) 484-2000 **Hawkins** Pamela A '04
(216) 479-8500 **Hawley** Barbara L '77
(216) 689-4111 **Hawrylak** Richard S '88
(216) 514-3336 **Hawthorne** Nathaniel '69
(216) 566-2660 **Hayes** Madeline M '81
(216) 687-1902 **Haygood** Sebraien M '90
(216) 621-0200 **Haylor** Jane T '86
(216) 566-5896 **Haymond** Daniel M '93
(216) 621-0150 **Haynes** Dawn T '01
(216) 875-6041 **Haynes** Ernest M Jr. '97
(216) 861-4355 **Hazelwood** James Michael '83
(216) 739-5006 **Head** David A '02
(216) 394-5064 **Headen** Raymond C '87
(216) 592-5000 **Healy** Jeffrey A '92
(216) 561-6811 **Heard** Arthur B '63
(216) 696-4700 **Hearey** Bruce G '82
(216) 696-4700 **Hearey** Dianne Foley '85
(216) 622-3785 **Hearey** Virginia D '84
(216) 431-5297 **Heben** Edward J Jr. '75
(216) 787-3934 **Heddesheimer** Don J '74
(216) 696-3030 **Hedman** Kent S '97
(216) 781-1212 **Heer** John A II '91
(216) 241-0040 **Heffernan** Edward A '78
(216) 621-0200 **Heffernan** John M '96
(216) 875-2767 **Heffernan** Michael V '02
(216) 449-3266 **Hehr** Albert G Jr. '74
(216) 586-3939 **Heidorf** Travis M '03
(216) 586-3939 **Heiman** David G '71
(216) 621-4100 **Heindel** Edward M '90
(216) 787-3663 **Heine** William J '81
(216) 664-4224 **Heinert O'Leary** Jennifer C '97
(216) 579-1700 **Heinke** Lowell L '60
(216) 931-6000 **Heiser** Donald E '63
(216) 523-5467 **Heiser** Joel S '94
(216) 781-1164 **Helbling** Lauren Y '87
(216) 241-2838 **Helfman** Jill Friedman '87
(216) 381-3400 **Heller** Nancy J '96
(216) 771-0811 **Heller** Roger D '75
(216) 696-3311 **Hellner-Cord** Leigh A '04
(216) 241-2880 **Helon** Phillip A '04
(216) 241-7430 **Hemmons** Willa M '77
(216) 443-7295 **Hencke** Tiffany L '00
(216) 774-0000 **Henderson** Brandon J '02
(216) 566-5779 **Henderson** Harold W '76
(216) 241-2132 **Henderson** Ivan L '98
(216) 696-6555 **Henderson** Louis G '82
(216) 861-4416 **Henderson** Ronald E '80
(440) 729-7374 **Henderson** Susan S '84
(216) 991-3574 **Henes** Samuel E '62
(216) 566-5806 **Henkel** Oliver C Jr. '64
(216) 781-8288 **Henkin** Howard A '71
(216) 771-8288 **Henkin** Merrill H '78
(440) 544-2000 **Hennenberg** Michael C '74
(216) 523-4107 **Hennessey** Joseph M '70
(216) 222-2987 **Hennig** Janet L '86
(216) 621-6570 **Henrikson** Kirk R '91
(216) 382-1496 **Henry** Alice K '65
(216) 241-6602 **Henry** Deirdre G '77
(216) 433-2313 **Henry** Laura A '83
(216) 830-2770 **Henry** Lynn M '84
(216) 348-1700 **Hentemann** Henry A '63
(216) 623-0150 **Herbert** Joseph E '92
(216) 696-6170 **Herman** Richard T '93
(216) 781-5515 **Hermann Cahn & Schneider, LLP**
(216) 781-5515 **Hermann** Gary D '71
(216) 443-7295 **Hernandez** Juan C '87
(216) 642-3342 **Herrington** David W '86
(216) 586-3939 **Herrmann** Mark '90
(216) 621-9721 **Herron** Mark P '91
(216) 689-8328 **Herubin** John F '87
(216) 621-0200 **Hervey** Michelle M '00
(216) 586-3939 **Herzberger** William A '87
(216) 522-3878 **Heslop** Bruce C '72
(216) 687-1311 **Hess** Erin S '01
(216) 642-3342 **Hessler** David J '68
(216) 368-2769 **Hessler** Katherine M '96
(216) 642-3342 **Hessler** Nathan E '95
(216) 642-3342 **Hessler** Peter A '78
(216) 443-8262 **Hessler** Stephanie E '03
(216) 241-1000 **Heutsche** John V '73
(216) 586-3939 **Hewitt** Christopher J '98
(216) 241-5700 **Hewitt** James H III '80
(216) 687-5508 **Heyward** Carole O '93
(216) 222-1087 **Hibbs** Lisa A '98
(216) 241-1872 **Hickey** Christopher J '95
(216) 443-7800 **Hickey** Elizabeth A '81
(216) 861-6000 **Hickey** Geoffrey S '01
(216) 749-6556 **Hickey** John W '63
(216) 749-6556 **Hickey** Theresa A '86
(216) 861-0360 **Hickman** Franklin J '73
(216) 861-0360 **Hickman & Lowder Co, LPA**
(216) 685-1108 **Hicks** George R Jr. '88
(216) 928-2200 **Hidek** Christina T '00
(216) 515-1660 **Higgins** Ralph P Jr. '80
(216) 861-5582 **Highman** Eric M '97
(216) 586-3939 **Hilbert** Peter G '03
(216) 621-1006 **Hildebrandt** David W '87
(216) 222-9694 **Hildebrandt** Thomas J '81
(216) 368-0553 **Hill** Beatrice Jessie '02
(216) 623-1400 **Hill** David G '61
(216) 522-7792 **Hill** James A '76
(216) 363-4500 **Hill** James M '88
(216) 566-9700 **Hill** Stephen A '74
(216) 622-8200 **Hillman** Jean M '94
(216) 622-8200 **Hillyer** Shelly K '02
(216) 443-7800 **Hilow** Eleanore E '91
(216) 344-9220 **Hilow** Henry J '81
(216) 443-8989 **Hilow** Roseanne '84
(216) 694-5671 **Hindel** Joanne E '84
(216) 357-7100 **Hink** Ralph M '85
(216) 696-3030 **Hinkel** Kevin M '80
(216) 689-0333 **Hinkle** Steven D '84
(216) 241-6700 **Hinton** Jennifer N '98
(216) 771-5800 **Hirshman** Ellen H '82
(216) 771-5800 **Hirshman** Tobias J '78
(216) 831-0042 **Hirth** Alan N '73
(216) 586-3939 **Hiser** Ted S '85
(216) 443-7800 **Hixson** Traci M '90
(216) 515-1660 **Hlavaty** Joel R '83
(216) 241-6700 **Hlavka** John R '76
(216) 520-5638 **Hlucky** Lori '95
(216) 481-4815 **Hoag** Joan '77
(216) 622-8200 **Hoban** Thomas M '99
(216) 771-4949 **Hobt** Stephen D '78
(216) 771-3800 **Hochberg** David Peter '76
(216) 739-5649 **Hochheiser** Alan C '89
(440) 446-1100 **Hochman** David B '74
(216) 586-3939 **Hochman** Kenneth G '73
(216) 355-5336 **Hodge** Bruce E '95
(216) 685-1164 **Hoen** Benjamin N '04
(216) 956-3044 **Hoenigman** Richard A '70
(216) 776-1000 **Hofelich** James A '69
(216) 443-7800 **Hofelich** James J '00
(216) 515-4546 **Hoffer** Christine S '87
(216) 831-2552 **Hoffman** Gary H '76
(216) 781-3600 **Hoffman** Joseph C Jr. '91
(216) 621-0200 **Hoffman** L Dennis '97
(216) 222-3495 **Hoffman** Mark A '80
(216) 292-5200 **Hoffman** William A III '79
(216) 621-1312 **Hoffmann** David S '85
(216) 479-6100 **Hogan** James A '99
(216) 696-0606 **Hogan** Michael W '85
(216) 241-2880 **Hogg** James S '85
(216) 523-4112 **Hogsett** William F '73
(216) 241-5310 **Hohenberger** Leah M '02
(216) 586-3939 **Hohler** Kathleen '80
(216) 696-1076 **Hohmann Boukis & Curtis Co, LPA**
(216) 696-1076 **Hohmann** William T '65
(216) 696-6525 **Hokky** Naomi '89
(216) 685-1141 **Holbrook** Amy Clum '02
(216) 621-0200 **Holbrook** Scott C '00
(216) 363-4500 **Holderman** Gretchen A '92
(216) 875-2767 **Holdsworth** Peter A '02
(216) 642-3342 **Holecek** Christopher A '88
(216) 642-3342 **Holecek** Tanja M '89
(216) 696-4009 **Holland** David R '97
(216) 931-6000 **Hollander** Jason S '99
(216) 881-6600 **Hollander** Lisa E '84
(216) 479-8500 **Hollern** Pamela Ellinger '03
(216) 781-2626 **Hollingsworth** Leigh A '88
(216) 621-0200 **Hollington** Richard R Jr. '57
(330) 558-7107 **Hollister** Terry R '74
(216) 621-7860 **Holman** Ronald D II '86
(216) 991-0049 **Holmes** Clarence H '53
(216) 520-0088 **Holmes** Thomas C '01
(216) 586-3939 **Holmgren** Cedar R '03
(216) 621-6570 **Holt** Nicole M '02
Holt-Hudson Christine J '02
(216) 623-9274 **Holtz** Gregory T '77
(216) 586-3939 **Holzer** Walter S '95
(216) 523-1900 **Holzheimer** Edward T '69
(216) 443-8830 **Homolak** John R '80
(216) 586-7055 **Hong** Karen G '04
(216) 479-8500 **Hong** Laura K '86
(216) 222-3345 **Honohan** Kathleen R '91
(216) 566-5621 **Hooker** David J '75
(216) 363-4500 **Hooper** Ryan P '01
(216) 661-4668 **Hoover** Garin C '93
(216) 736-7232 **Hoover** Valoria C '92
(216) 416-3419 **Hopps** Lisa R '93
(216) 781-1212 **Horbaly** Robert S '70
(216) 696-1275 **Horejs** Edward R Jr. '76
(216) 475-8497 **Horhn** Ma'Rion D '99
(216) 566-7992 **Horn** Byron J '89
(216) 431-1636 **Horn** Christopher H '76
(216) 831-0042 **Horn** Debra J '86
(216) 586-3939 **Horn** Melissa E '03
(216) 443-7800 **Horn** Michael D '77
(216) 241-2262 **Horning** Gerald R '84
(216) 787-3030 **Horrigan** Bruce D '90
(216) 861-5550 **Horrigan** Suzanne K '75
(216) 523-4122 **Horst** John R '68
(216) 443-8586 **Horst** Rebecca Mathewson '03
(216) 696-2022 **Horton** Brett E '94
(216) 623-0150 **Horton** Cathy B '86
(216) 696-4345 **Horton** Debbie K '86
(216) 696-2022 **Horton** Earle C '69
(216) 664-2808 **Horvath** Richard F '77
(216) 586-3939 **Horvitz** Michael J '75
(216) 664-4165 **Horwatt** Robert F Jr. '00
(216) 443-6350 **Horwitz** Mary P '92
(216) 622-8200 **Horwitz** Susan R '98
(216) 579-4114 **Horwitz** Thomas M '93
(216) 622-8200 **Hoskins** George R '98
(216) 443-8560 **Hostovich** Julianne V '00
(216) 621-0150 **Hotchkiss** Herbert G '96
(216) 266-8216 **House** Robert N '80
(216) 363-6038 **Housel** Robert V Jr. '73
(216) 241-6689 **Hovinen** Jeffrey R '95
Howard Donald E '77
(216) 348-5400 **Howard** Kristin K '99
(216) 475-4600 **Howard** Randolph '95
(216) 443-5809 **Howard** Shataia G '01
(216) 621-4244 **Howard** Timothy J '68
(216) 443-5829 **Howe** Elizabeth '97
Howery Katrice M '02
(216) 736-7279 **Hoza** Michele L '01
(216) 566-5562 **Hubbard** Kenneth W '96
(216) 566-5644 **Hubbard** William J '03
(216) 736-7215 **Hubbert** Christopher J '91
(216) 586-3939 **Huber** Mary Elizabeth '96
(216) 928-2200 **Hudak** David J '99
(216) 292-3900 **Hudak** James A '74
(216) 241-0011 **Hudson** Matthew C '04
(216) 586-3939 **Hudson** Timothy M '04
(216) 861-5582 **Hudzinski** Michael E '89
(216) 771-1330 **Huettner** John A '87
(216) 241-2838 **Huff** Kimberlie L '00
(216) 381-8800 **Hufford** Allen C '02
(216) 566-5500 **Huggins** Emily S '04
(216) 522-4856 **Hughes** Debra M '87
(216) 574-8210 **Hughes** Kathleen M '95
(216) 622-8200 **Hughes** Maura L '93
(216) 515-1660 **Hughes** Michael M '62
(216) 622-8200 **Hull** Mark R '04
(216) 687-1311 **Hulme** Roy A '79
(216) 696-1422 **Hultin** Pamela N '89
(216) 583-4629 **Humbarger** Michael L '96
(216) 222-2967 **Hummel** Jaqueline M '02
(216) 241-2880 **Humphrey** Robert M '82
(216) 398-4100 **Hungerford** James M '80
(216) 861-4104 **Hunt** Judith S '84
(216) 781-1212 **Hunt** Robert Todd '84
(216) 696-9555 **Hunt** Thomas J '96
(216) 896-2461 **Hunter** Christopher H '89
(216) 292-5200 **Hunter** Douglas S '00
(216) 522-1900 **Hunter** Sandra K '77
(216) 348-5400 **Huntsberger** Jeffrey R '80
(216) 861-6556 **Hupertz** Lawrence R '83
(216) 566-2504 **Hupp** Diane H '89
(216) 875-2767 **Hupp** Steven J '88
(216) 241-1000 **Hurd** Gail A '85
(216) 566-2486 **Hurlbut** Chris L '88
(216) 241-2838 **Hurley** Nora L '89
(216) 621-5980 **Hurley** Scott R '94
(216) 514-9999 **Hurst** Jonathan R '01
(216) 696-5297 **Hurst** Tricia L '04
(216) 321-2775 **Hurt** Marcia E '81
(440) 605-6660 **Hurtuk & Daroff Co,LPA**
(440) 605-6660 **Hurtuk** Edward A '79
(216) 443-8603 **Hutchins** Sara E '03
(216) 830-6830 **Hutchinson** Joseph F Jr. '74
(216) 696-7600 **Hutton** Lee J '75
(216) 443-7295 **Hyland** John P '86
(216) 687-1311 **Hyman** Jonathan T '97
(216) 664-2687 **Hyun** Cecilia J '04
(216) 771-1760 **Icove** Edward A '77
(216) 781-1212 **Iddings** Sarah L '03
(216) 692-0888 **Idzelis** Augustine '90
(216) 696-3311 **Igel** Peter A '86
(216) 443-7800 **Ikuma** Kaya A '99
(216) 696-5700 **Iler** Don C '60
(216) 696-5700 **Iler** Nancy C '87
(216) 664-4838 **Imbacuan** Bruce D '00
(216) 696-7445 **Imbrigiotta** James J '88
(216) 566-8099 **Immormino** Mark '80
(216) 787-4119 **Incorvati** Nancy C '90
(216) 363-6030 **Ingalls** James D '91
(216) 579-4111 **Ingersoll** John D '85
(216) 443-7583 **Ingersoll** Robert M '81
(216) 861-4000 **Inglis** David S '82
(216) 566-0371 **Ipavec** Charles F '51
(216) 696-5530 **Ireland-Phillips** Karen S '96
(216) 621-0200 **Irwin** Scott D '92
(216) 252-1700 **Isabella** Joseph N '93
(216) 357-5123 **Isakoff** Andrew H '86
(216) 515-1660 **Isakoff** Janice A '86
(216) 687-1900 **Iskin** Peter M '73
(216) 443-7295 **Isquick** Margaret O '85
(216) 696-6700 **Israel** Rachael L '00
(216) 931-6000 **Isroff** Ronald H '67
(216) 861-1400 **Ita** Timothy A '85
(216) 444-2385 **Ivancic** Robert J '75
(216) 586-3939 **Izanec** Peter E '04
(216) 687-1311 **Jackett** Todd M '03
(216) 479-8500 **Jackson** Denise A '94
(216) 664-2309 **Jackson** Frank G '86
(216) 928-2200 **Jackson** John V II '72
(216) 707-2585 **Jackson** Karen L '91
(216) 566-1600 **Jackson** Michael E '76
(216) 696-8700 **Jackson** Robert H '61
(216) 502-0800 **Jackson** Stanley Jr. '03
(216) 687-1910 **Jackson** Stephanie M '87
(216) 622-3600 **Jackson** Steven L '94
(216) 241-6602 **Jackson** Todd G '85
(216) 515-1660 **Jackson** Travis F '99
(216) 241-3400 **Jackson-Winston** Judy A '99
(216) 621-1113 **Jacobs** Christopher B '95
(216) 383-8055 **Jacobs** Jacqueline A '91
(216) 831-5083 **Jacobs** James K '80
(216) 566-5675 **Jacobs** Leslie W '68
(216) 696-3311 **Jacobs** Mark R '99
(216) 898-2343 **Jacobs** William G '69
(216) 566-5533 **Jacobs** William W '76
(216) 621-2300 **Jacobson** William S '84
(216) 586-3939 **Jacono** Anthony T '00
(440) 460-3661 **Jacovetty** Cynthia S '88
(216) 736-7209 **Jaffe** Ari H '87
(216) 479-8500 **Jaffe** Daniel A '89
(216) 581-1481 **Jahn** Frederick J '92
(216) 363-4500 **Jaketic** Bryan J '04
(216) 621-0200 **Jakiel** Kristin J '98

(216) 523-5479 **Jakubaitis** Jayne L '92
(216) 696-4441 **Jakubs** Michele L '99
(216) 689-1761 **Jakyma** Christopher P '94
(216) 621-0200 **Jambe** Suzanne M '93
(216) 241-6988 **Jamieson** Daniel J '80
(216) 931-6000 **Jamieson** Sally A '00
(216) 621-8484 **Janice** Christina M '91
(440) 838-7600 **Janik & Dorman,LLP**
(440) 838-7600 **Janik** Steven G '76
(216) 566-5061 **Janis** Paul A '86
(216) 586-3939 **Janke** Ronald R '74
(216) 687-1311 **Janovitz** Barbara B '83
(216) 241-6602 **Janusz** John M '98
(216) 241-3114 **Jaquay** Robert B '81
(216) 781-1771 **Jarabek** Timothy J '98
(216) 664-4978 **Jasper** Mabel M '77
(216) 623-0000 **Javitch Block & Rathbone**
(216) 623-0000 **Javitch** Victor M '62
(216) 241-6602 **Jeffers** John W '64
(216) 883-2671 **Jefferson** Milton D '90
(216) 771-4050 **Jeffries Kube Forrest & Monteleone Co, LPA**
(216) 681-1554 **Jencson** Gary E '78
(216) 443-7800 **Jenkins** George A Jr. '96
(216) 363-6003 **Jenkins** James A '85
(216) 622-8200 **Jenkins** John J '86
(216) 586-3939 **Jenkins** Lindsay C '02
(216) 586-3939 **Jenks** Carl M '82
(216) 479-8500 **Jennings** Colin R '97
(216) 763-1004 **Jennings** James Kieran III '95
(216) 771-2680 **Jennrich** Terry R '83
(216) 687-1311 **Jenny** Leslie M '96
(216) 931-6000 **Jerdonek** Elizabeth A '97
(216) 348-5400 **Jereb** Brian J '83
(216) 664-4824 **Jerlstrom** Stephanie L '95
(216) 241-9990 **Jerome** Joseph B '75
(216) 621-1000 **Jerse** Edward S '83
(216) 430-8223 **Jerse** Shannon F '88
(216) 344-3838 **Jesse** David A '82
(216) 241-2838 **Jett** Stephen H '90
(440) 442-7500 **Jiannetti** Michael A '82
(216) 471-6865 **Jobe** Lisa A '01
Johnson Andrew L Jr. '60
(216) 621-2300 **Johnson** Brenda M '93
(216) 566-5911 **Johnson** Christopher R '00
(216) 295-0826 **Johnson** Clarence '60
(216) 696-5222 **Johnson & Colaluca,LLC**
(216) 861-5000 **Johnson** David G '83
(216) 479-8500 **Johnson** Eric J '00
(216) 696-5222 **Johnson** Gary C '80
(216) 241-6602 **Johnson** Gary W '79
(216) 522-4856 **Johnson** Jacqueline A '84
(216) 523-6354 **Johnson** James M '84
(216) 696-9330 **Johnson** Jeffrey D '04
(216) 267-1985 **Johnson** Kevin C '79
(216) 731-1080 **Johnson** Lance B '69
(216) 523-1500 **Johnson** Linda L '96
(216) 622-3600 **Johnson** Lisa H '93
(216) 622-3600 **Johnson** Marcia W '76
(216) 621-1113 **Johnson** Mark C '00
(216) 622-3689 **Johnson** Michael Anne '78
(216) 861-4076 **Johnson** Nelli I '84
(216) 566-2645 **Johnson** Pamela M '91
(216) 696-1000 **Johnson** Richard G '90
(216) 622-2700 **Johnson** Rita R '96
(216) 787-3030 **Johnson** Scott W '91
(216) 241-6602 **Johnson** Timothy D '74
(216) 556-0858 **Johnson** Tonya R '99
(216) 622-8200 **Johnson** Tracy Scott '95
(216) 621-0200 **Johnson** Victoria L '91
(216) 523-4132 **Johnston** Roger A '68
(216) 622-8200 **Johnston** William A '99
(216) 479-8500 **Jones** Bruce P '73
(216) 621-0150 **Jones** Candace M '92
(216) 687-1900 **Jones** Carl Lyonel '63
(216) 586-3939 **Jones Day**
(216) 736-7231 **Jones** Gary L '97
(216) 523-7200 **Jones** Gretchen C '82
(216) 363-4500 **Jones** Jeffrey P '01
(216) 664-4996 **Jones** Larry A '78
(216) 566-5500 **Jones** Larry J '02
(216) 241-2838 **Jones** Lessie Milton '85
(216) 515-1437 **Jones** Melissa A '02
(216) 623-0150 **Jones** Peter Lawson '80
(216) 623-0150 **Jones** Richard Mark '83
(216) 443-7800 **Jones** Sean C '97
(216) 861-7585 **Jones** Theodore W '51
(216) 696-4700 **Jontz** Jennifer Cook '94
(216) 861-5000 **Joranko** David B '85
(216) 664-2775 **Jordan** Anthony D '96
(216) 566-9477 **Jordan** Bret '92
(216) 781-1212 **Jordan** Michael J '79
(216) 432-7200 **Jordan** Sharon Sobol '84
(216) 621-1500 **Jorgensen** Matthew W '96
(216) 622-8200 **Jorgensen** Thomas A '68
(216) 696-8730 **Jorgenson** Eric D '02
(216) 479-8500 **Jorgenson** Mary Ann '75
(216) 621-2505 **Joseph** Edward L '82
(216) 522-3380 **Joseph** James A '78
(216) 241-6055 **Joseph** James G '73
(216) 522-1600 **Joseph** Joseph T Jr. '99
(216) 621-1530 **Joseph** Samantha S '99
(216) 241-6602 **Joseph** William R '72
(216) 696-8070 **Josselson** Stanley L '66
(216) 391-0749 **Jovanovic** Alex '84
(216) 687-1244 **Joyce** Eileen M '98
(216) 241-6602 **Joyce** Therese P '99
(216) 241-7000 **Judge** Beth A '04
(216) 241-5310 **Juergens** Julie L '96
(216) 621-5259 **Julian** Christine M '93
(216) 621-5259 **Julian** Linda M '91
(216) 621-7227 **Juliano** Louis J Jr. '77
(216) 586-3939 **Junge** A Gregory '04
(216) 622-8200 **Jupin** Seth M '96
(440) 871-1721 **Jurca** Irene S '00
(216) 771-4650 **Jurczenko** Alexander '73
(216) 622-8200 **Juster** Joseph K '89
(216) 687-1311 **Kabat** Andrew A '94
(216) 844-1252 **Kabb** Marilyn S '91
(216) 291-9126 **Kabb-Effron** Rachel A '98
(216) 444-3695 **Kaber** Steven C '84
(216) 398-9870 **Kacenjar** Allen A '74
(216) 479-8500 **Kacenjar** Allen A '99
(216) 579-1700 **Kachmarik** Ronald M '94
(216) 348-5400 **Kacmar** Donald E '97
(216) 348-5400 **Kaczka** Michael J '03
(216) 586-3939 **Kaczynski** Stephen J '86
(216) 696-3030 **Kadish Hinkel & Weibel, LPA**
(216) 696-3030 **Kadish** Matthew F '87
(216) 696-3030 **Kadish** Stephen L '65
(216) 875-2767 **Kadlec** Kevin O '87
(330) 225-2600 **Kaesgen** Derek '93
(216) 241-5310 **Kagels** Edward G '63
Kahan David D '64
(216) 696-5757 **Kahan** Julian '59
(216) 621-6101 **Kahn** Craig A '94
(216) 696-3311 **Kahn Kleinman**
(216) 931-6000 **Kahn** Ronald L '73
(216) 579-4114 **Kahn** Scott H '82
(216) 586-3939 **Kahrl** Robert C '75
(216) 295-8378 **Kaigler** Lawrence M '77
(216) 574-9500 **Kainski** Dale F '75
(216) 479-8500 **Kaiser** Gordon S Jr. '73
(216) 664-2852 **Kaiser** Thomas J '82
(216) 642-0323 **Kalail** Karrie M '88
(216) 741-6334 **Kalbrunner** Roger J '73
(216) 592-5000 **Kaleps** Krista L '04
(216) 881-5300 **Kalette** Stephen R '74
(216) 502-0570 **Kalish** Daniel Scott '94
(216) 523-4131 **Kalka** Daniel S '86
(216) 348-5400 **Kall** David M '93
(216) 586-3939 **Kallergis** Gus '99
(216) 348-5400 **Kalnay** John T '98
(216) 348-9878 **Kalnoki** Aniko T '91
(216) 696-0650 **Kaman & Cusimano**
(216) 696-0650 **Kaman** David W '80
(216) 522-6103 **Kamat** Deborah L '82
(216) 685-4290 **Kamensky** Fedor F '03
(216) 621-5161 **Kaminski** Kerin Lyn '85
(216) 696-5211 **Kammer** Karl D '53
(216) 621-0200 **Kammer** Sean M '04
(216) 251-8023 **Kampani** Dharminder L '75
(216) 781-4110 **Kampinski** Charles I '74
(216) 781-5470 **Kampman** Joseph W '80
(216) 363-4500 **Kancler** Edward '64
(216) 736-2653 **Kane** Gail R '83
(216) 520-0088 **Kapitan** Robert B '01
(216) 363-4500 **Kaplan** Ira C '79
(216) 861-8888 **Kaplan** Morton L '67
(216) 781-8823 **Kaplow** Richard J '73
(216) 586-3939 **Kapur** Sanjiv K '92
(216) 781-5515 **Kapusta-Dorogi** Jonetta '92
Karakoudas Smaragda E '96
(216) 241-6602 **Karakul** Kurt '79
(216) 696-1422 **Karas** Kimon P '78
(216) 292-3300 **Karberg** Bruce K '75
(216) 696-3344 **Karlovec** Lucien B Jr. '62
(216) 575-2383 **Karnatz** William E Jr. '92
(216) 566-5748 **Karnatz** William E Sr. '62
(216) 941-7760 **Karnes** William M '71
(216) 622-1851 **Karon** Daniel R '98
(216) 685-1360 **Karp & Camino, Ltd**
(216) 685-1360 **Karp** Harlan D '89
(216) 931-6000 **Karp** Marvin L '58
(216) 696-3515 **Karp** Sheldon '67
(216) 348-5400 **Karr** Bernard L '73
(216) 621-3346 **Karson** Jeffrey A '89
(216) 586-3939 **Karzmer** Erin E '01
(216) 622-8526 **Karzmer** Steven C '01
(216) 443-7800 **Kasaris** Daniel M '89
(216) 621-7860 **Kasdan** Howard P '69
(216) 574-2600 **Kaselak** Dennis J '74
(216) 348-0652 **Kasicki** Nancy M '95
(216) 861-4355 **Kasle** Andrew R '89
(216) 523-4138 **Kasper** Leslie J '73
(216) 523-4136 **Kastelic** John A '90
(216) 622-8200 **Kastelic** Tara A '91
(216) 586-7307 **Kastelic** Thomas J '82
(216) 621-8550 **Katz** Burton A '74
(216) 696-5250 **Katz** Daniel M '96
(216) 696-5250 **Katz** David A '65
(216) 831-6721 **Katz** Herbert R '69
(216) 368-3287 **Katz** Lewis R '73
(216) 931-6000 **Katz** Mark D '74
(216) 464-5130 **Katz** Roger A '74
(216) 595-3200 **Katzenmeyer** Dale L '87
(216) 621-0150 **Kaufman** Arthur M '83
(216) 363-1400 **Kaufman** Elliot M '64
(216) 696-8200 **Kaufman** Paul M '74
(216) 861-5542 **Kaufman** Roy M '71
(216) 566-5528 **Kaufman** Steven S '75
(216) 443-4953 **Kavalec** Marita L '89
(216) 479-8500 **Kavuru** Joan A '92
(216) 579-6252 **Kay** Abraham F '79
(440) 248-7906 **Kay** Jeffrey T '98
(216) 522-3530 **Kayton** Jodee C '01
(216) 621-1375 **Kazdin** Gary A '62
(216) 515-4338 **Kazimir** James '95
(216) 621-9870 **Kealy** John C '70
(216) 443-7800 **Keane** Martin J '02
(216) 583-8236 **Keco** Laurie A '96
(216) 642-3342 **Kedzior** John D '81
(216) 479-8500 **Keefe** F Barry '73
(216) 771-5800 **Keefe** Stephen T Jr. '96
(216) 721-7700 **Keenan** Martin J '77
(216) 875-4800 **Keevican** Leo A Jr. '01
(216) 621-1500 **Kehoe** Robert D '82
(216) 515-1660 **Keim** Christopher G '96
(216) 642-0323 **Keim** Krista K '96
(216) 348-5400 **Keiper** Jeffrey B '94
(216) 241-4100 **Keis / George LLP**
(216) 241-4100 **Keis** William H Jr. '82
(216) 771-1760 **Keith** Michele A '88
(216) 241-0520 **Kelleher** Jeffry F '75
(216) 931-6000 **Keller** C Reynolds Jr. '63
(216) 781-3366 **Keller** Cleveland R '88
(216) 771-4830 **Keller** Ellen H '79
(216) 566-7100 **Keller** Stanley S '58
(216) 443-8583 **Kelley** Brendan P '04
(216) 523-1113 **Kelley** Elizabeth '94
(216) 575-0777 **Kelley & Ferraro,LLP**
(216) 902-4444 **Kelley Jasons McGuire & Spinelli LLP**
(216) 937-1380 **Kelley** Kevin E '77
(216) 443-9000 **Kelley** Kevin J '04
(216) 941-1795 **Kelley** Lawrence P '54
(216) 575-0777 **Kelley** Lynn A '85
(216) 575-0777 **Kelley** Michael V '82
(216) 622-3600 **Kelley** Nancy L '79
(216) 522-3530 **Kelley** Shannon M '01
(216) 241-5040 **Kelley** Thomas G '72
(216) 621-0200 **Kellogg** Amy E '86
(216) 443-7223 **Kellon** Anthony J '89
(216) 687-6051 **Kelly** Amy C '94
(216) 515-1660 **Kelly** Brian J '94
(216) 586-3939 **Kelly** Christopher M '01
(216) 586-3939 **Kelly** Dennis M '68
(216) 696-5444 **Kelly** Edwin '86
(216) 671-2888 **Kelly** Mary W '87
(216) 664-2887 **Kelly** Nancy A '85
(216) 443-7800 **Kelly** Patrick R '92
(216) 502-0791 **Kelly** R Patrick '73
(216) 861-4533 **Kelly** Sandra Maurer '86
(216) 592-5000 **Kelly** Scott J '98
(216) 696-0606 **Kelly** Sean S '02
(216) 622-8200 **Kelly** Sheryl K '80
(216) 443-7223 **Kelly** William B '84
(216) 566-5768 **Kelly Grasso** Karen '94
(216) 622-8200 **Kendall** Laura K '04
(216) 621-3346 **Kendis** James D '66
(216) 621-3346 **Kendis** Robert D '69
(216) 586-3939 **Kennedy** Charles M '80
(216) 875-3568 **Kennedy** Kathleen M '96
(216) 363-4500 **Kennedy** Margaret A '76
(216) 781-1111 **Kennedy** Robert Eric '80
(216) 931-6000 **Kennedy** Stephanie E '98
(216) 583-1504 **Kennedy** Terence M '90
(216) 433-2314 **Kennemuth** Jerald J '78
(216) 621-1500 **Kenney** James Brian '01
(216) 241-5300 **Kenney** Mary A '87
(216) 622-0410 **Kenney** Richard C Jr. '79
(216) 368-2766 **Kenny** Maureen Sheridan '98
(216) 443-7800 **Kenny** Michael A Jr. '98
(216) 363-1400 **Keogh** Kevin R '83
(216) 664-4990 **Keough** Kathleen Ann '88
(216) 621-0200 **Kepple** Brandon E '03
(216) 687-2284 **Kerber** Sandra J '82
(216) 861-6191 **Kerka** Kathryn A '85
(216) 771-1430 **Kern** Anna M '98
(216) 348-5400 **Kern** Heather M '04
(216) 344-1033 **Kern** Keith W '75
(216) 622-3600 **Kern** Robert W '82
(216) 781-5515 **Kerr** Henry V '74
(216) 241-3470 **Kersey** James M '73
(216) 621-0200 **Kestner** R Steven '79
(216) 479-8500 **Ketler** Suzanne K '01
(216) 241-4525 **Keyes** Robert L '54
(216) 592-5000 **Keyse-Walker** Irene C '82
(216) 520-0088 **Khoury** Lisa N '01
(216) 592-5000 **Kidder** Richelle '03
(216) 586-3939 **Kiedrowski** Carrie L '03
(216) 771-6650 **Kiefer** Daran P '94
(216) 621-9870 **Kieltsch-Packard** Kristina M '00
(216) 348-5400 **Kiffner** Kent C '04
(216) 252-7300 **Kilbane** Catherine M '87
(216) 687-1311 **Kilbane** Thomas B '96
(216) 479-8500 **Kilbane** Thomas S '66
(216) 592-5000 **Killeen** Eugene M '88
(216) 566-5948 **Kim** Eduardo '00
(216) 363-4500 **Kimmel** Lisa C '86
(216) 664-4845 **Kinast** Aric H '98
(216) 623-0150 **Kinast** Hugh S '04
(216) 621-1113 **Kinder** Gordon D II '77
(216) 771-9745 **King** Alison M '95
(216) 443-3087 **King** Barry '82
(216) 479-8500 **King** Chaundra C '04
(216) 443-7223 **King** David M '91
(216) 479-8500 **King** Henry T Jr. '63
(216) 664-6924 **King** Joan M '83
(216) 426-4304 **King** Joseph D '96
(216) 621-0200 **King** Kelly M '03
(216) 443-7800 **King** Matthew J '96
(216) 621-0200 **King** Tom A Jr. '90
(216) 363-1400 **King** Woods III '83
(216) 622-8200 **King** Zachary W '04
(216) 446-0300 **Kinkaid** Amy I '92
(440) 842-1313 **Kinkela** Gabrielle G '69
(440) 842-1313 **Kinkela & Kinkela**
(440) 842-1313 **Kinkela** Robert V '69
(216) 621-6570 **Kinkopf** Charles W '94
(216) 623-0150 **Kinkopf** Lauren K '92
(216) 623-0150 **Kinkopf-Zajac** Ingrid A '96
(216) 520-5584 **Kipfstuhl** Denise L '92
(216) 696-8860 **Kipp** Therese R '94
(216) 621-0200 **Kirchick** Calvin B '72
(216) 363-4500 **Kirchick** Ross J '00
(216) 787-3344 **Kirk** Quan T '98
(216) 621-0200 **Kirkpatrick** Andrew W '03
(216) 363-4500 **Kirsanow** Peter N '79
(216) 621-0890 **Kirschenbaum** Dan G '84
(216) 664-4826 **Kirvel** Brent C '01
(216) 875-2767 **Kiss** Lynette E '00
(216) 621-0200 **Kitchen** David E '04
(216) 622-8200 **Klaben** Matthew J '95
(216) 687-1900 **Klaric** Betty '84
(216) 241-5300 **Klein** Ann M Fitzpatrick '94
(216) 861-0111 **Klein** Larry S '80
(216) 696-5157 **Klein** Richard C '64
(216) 861-5582 **Klein** Richard M '85
(216) 566-5500 **Klein** Shana F '01
(216) 363-4500 **Kleinman** Allan D '52
(216) 736-7239 **Kleinman** Kenneth W '74
(216) 522-7800 **Kleinman** Lenore '86
(216) 348-5400 **Kleinman** Roger L '84
(216) 931-6000 **Klepach** Anne M '03
(216) 348-5400 **Klimek** Mark D '93
(216) 931-6000 **Kline** James N '84
(216) 621-0200 **Kline** Melinda M '04
(216) 363-4500 **Kline** Rita E '00
(216) 781-1212 **Klink** Bradley J '04
(216) 241-0666 **Klonowski** Daniel J '78
(216) 771-4304 **Klopp** Ralph M Jr. '75
(216) 515-6532 **Klucher** Gregory W '86
(216) 781-5470 **Klug** Paul S '75
(216) 402-9515 **Kluge** Graig E '97
(216) 241-6602 **Kluznik** Jack S '77
(216) 621-6570 **Klym** Christopher J '93
(216) 861-5000 **Kmetich** Victor G '84
(216) 241-2838 **Kmetz** Kristi J '03
(216) 696-0650 **Kmiecik** Robert E '84
(216) 228-7200 **Knabe** Kenneth J '79
(216) 621-4882 **Knecht** Denise J '81
(216) 621-0150 **Knerly** Stephen J Jr. '76
(216) 348-0333 **Knevel** Mark H '77
(216) 241-5310 **Knisely** Joseph Colin '97
(216) 928-7518 **Knopf** Christopher D '89
(216) 523-5484 **Knoth** Richard M '89
(216) 502-0350 **Knott** Paul S '92
(216) 642-3342 **Knowles** David R '74
(216) 241-4100 **Knowles** Scott T '03
(216) 201-3504 **Knull** Ralph E '92
(216) 363-4500 **Knuth** Ann E '93
(216) 241-2500 **Koach** Jules N '66
(216) 781-2258 **Kobal** Cindy L '00
(216) 566-5833 **Kobasic** Dena M '89
(216) 781-5470 **Koberg** Jeffrey L '90
(216) 861-6833 **Koberna** Mark R '87
(216) 621-3012 **Koblentz & Koblentz**
(216) 621-3012 **Koblentz** Richard S '75
(216) 292-7230 **Koblentz** Steven B '81
(216) 621-0150 **Koblenz** N Herschel '60
(216) 621-4244 **Kobylski** Kimberly J '04
(216) 781-5245 **Kocab** Brooke F '85
(216) 443-9000 **Koch** Suzana Krstevski '01
(216) 363-6050 **Kochis** Joseph A '78
(216) 781-9090 **Kochis** Rob M '90
(216) 443-7800 **Kocian** Jeffrey V '03
(216) 861-5582 **Kocovsky** Thomas E Jr. '78
(216) 977-0492 **Kodger** Donald O '98
(216) 566-0580 **Kodish** Joan A '79
(216) 515-1660 **Koehler** Christopher C '92
(216) 241-5310 **Koehler** James F '73
(216) 443-8970 **Koenig** Heidi M '86
(216) 566-5503 **Koenig** James C '87
(216) 522-6812 **Koenig** John P '82
(216) 861-5582 **Koenig** Sandra M '87
(216) 566-6600 **Koenig** William M '95
(216) 621-0200 **Koerwitz** Deborah L '99
(216) 443-9000 **Koesel** Margaret M '89
(216) 696-1433 **Koeth Rice & Leo Co, LPA**
(216) 696-1433 **Koeth** Robert J '82
(216) 586-3939 **Koethe** Paul D '86
(216) 694-4337 **Kohn** Andrew '74
(216) 696-8700 **Kohrman Jackson & Krantz PLL**
(216) 696-8700 **Kohrman** Soloman Lee '53
(216) 443-7800 **Kolasinski** Ralph A '83
(216) 575-7575 **Kolick** David '74
(216) 575-7575 **Kolick Georgeadis & Ernewein Co,LPA**
(216) 522-3715 **Kollar** John '56
(216) 441-5100 **Kollin** Clement '75
(216) 443-7800 **Kollin** Timothy J '85
(216) 363-4500 **Kolocouris** Gregory S '02
(216) 341-5666 **Komorowski** James J '71
(216) 622-8200 **Kondas** Brian E '95
(216) 622-3600 **Konen** Betty J '89
(216) 579-9740 **Konet** Thomas J '72
(216) 575-2154 **Konfala** John A '85
(216) 348-5400 **Konkoly** Anthony D '86
(216) 623-0000 **Konstantinopoulos** Theodore A '95
(216) 696-2040 **Koosed** Lee A '74
(216) 621-0150 **Kopit** Alan S '77
(216) 241-5735 **Kopkas** Andrew J '59
(216) 696-5211 **Koplow** James B '56
(216) 696-5400 **Kopp** Rebecca A '04
(216) 622-3600 **Kopp** William J '80
(216) 861-8888 **Koral** Timothy J '67
(216) 592-5000 **Kordas** Anne M '95
(216) 696-7600 **Kordeleski** Kathleen M '86
(216) 621-6684 **Kordic** Gregory L '83
(216) 771-7030 **Korey** Philip J '80
(216) 363-4500 **Korland** Lee M '03
(216) 363-4500 **Korman** Jean Kerr '90
(216) 839-8500 **Kornblut** Gerri L '88
(216) 696-0022 **Kornblut** Russell D '86
(216) 368-3283 **Korngold** Gerald '95
(216) 586-3939 **Korpics** J Joseph '91
(216) 643-9331 **Kortan** Katherine M '93
(216) 642-0323 **Kosakowski** Lori A '03
(216) 621-0200 **Kosanovich** Laurie G '97
(216) 522-3380 **Kosar** Katherine L '87
(216) 830-6830 **Koschik** Alan M '96
(216) 566-5732 **Kosek** Kelly A '02
(216) 443-7800 **Kosko** John R '81
(216) 515-1660 **Kostelnik** John F III '81
(216) 696-3366 **Kostura** Sarah Hauser '04
(216) 983-1262 **Kostyack** Paul T '01
(216) 696-7445 **Kotar** William H III '01
(216) 965-5400 **Koury** Laurice M '74
(216) 771-5525 **Kovac** James E '77
(216) 621-1530 **Kovach** Christopher M '95
(216) 357-3301 **Kovach & Farling Co,LPA**
(216) 696-7600 **Kovach** Lynda L '02
(216) 357-3301 **Kovach** Thomas G '90
(216) 348-7550 **Kovach** William M '80
Kovacs George C '77
(216) 696-5222 **Koval** Joseph S '04
(216) 621-2388 **Kovanda** Ralph D '50
(216) 621-6570 **Kovass** David A '02
(216) 687-4825 **Kowalski** Kenneth J '81
(216) 579-4114 **Kracht** Robert Roy '83
(216) 464-2777 **Kraemer** Lisa R '79
(216) 348-5400 **Kraguljac** Peter '94
(216) 861-6833 **Krahe** Shawn Marie '96
(216) 696-6525 **Kraig** Barbara A '03
(216) 696-4009 **Kraig** Brian S '88
(216) 861-4357 **Krainess** Jonathan I '00
(216) 583-1273 **Krajcer** Michael A '01
(216) 443-7295 **Krajenke** Francis R Jr. '96
(216) 363-1400 **Krajewski** Eric D '04
(216) 522-2123 **Kramer** Barbara L '91
(216) 431-5300 **Kramer** Edward G '75
(216) 781-7956 **Kramer** Ellen M '91
(216) 621-7974 **Kramer** Eugene L '64
(216) 621-9870 **Kramer** Fredric E '62
(216) 360-7200 **Kramer** Herbert J '84
(440) 461-3461 **Kramer** Ivan '79
(216) 566-1208 **Kramer** John F '90
(216) 241-5358 **Kramer** Roger S '77
(216) 522-3876 **Kramer** Sandra B '80
(216) 696-8700 **Krantz** Brett S '98
(216) 736-7210 **Krantz** Byron S '62
(216) 514-1180 **Krantz** Howard J '86
(216) 736-7204 **Krantz** Marc C '93

(216) 514-1180 **Krantz Powers & Friedman,PLL**
(216) 514-1180 **Krantz** Stuart W '93
(216) 394-5074 **Krasovec** Jay E '98
(216) 523-5469 **Krassen** Glenn S '80
(216) 696-4700 **Kratus** Eugene A '76
(216) 831-8771 **Kraus** Alan H '81
(216) 623-0000 **Kraus** Edward H '86
(216) 642-3342 **Krause** Christopher W '93
(216) 687-1311 **Krause** David H '99
(440) 808-6322 **Krause** Douglas R '93
(216) 621-0890 **Krause** Edward A '67
(216) 357-7268 **Kravetz** Cheryl L '02
(216) 749-0808 **Kravitz** Lee R '80
(216) 685-9188 **Krawczak** Kenneth F '77
(216) 623-6614 **Kray** Richard A '83
(216) 771-2243 **Krebs** Martha H '79
(216) 241-2838 **Krebs** Patrick J '00
(440) 460-5000 **Kreiner** Frederick J '96
(216) 771-6650 **Kreiner & Peters Co,LPA**
(216) 875-7500 **Krembs** Andrew P '76
(216) 781-5515 **Krembs** Peter J '73
(440) 838-7600 **Kremser** Mark E '96
(216) 778-5174 **Krenek** Robert F '84
(216) 622-8200 **Kresnye** Stephen P '77
Krevis Noreen M '89
(216) 241-2838 **Krewson** Patricia Fleming '03
(216) 861-7994 **Kriedman** Cynthia B '85
(216) 831-0042 **Kriessler** Lynn A '91
(216) 696-7600 **Kristan** Bonita L '01
(216) 902-4444 **Kristan** John A Jr. '01
(216) 586-3939 **Krivinskas** Dainius A '03
(216) 787-3030 **Kriynovich** Wayne S '88
(216) 566-7100 **Krohngold** Walter H '83
Krol Kenneth H '81
(216) 566-9399 **Kroll** Catherine A '96
(216) 426-2970 **Kronenberg** Jacob A '76
(216) 566-7010 **Krosin** Donald N '58
(216) 781-4680 **Krotinger** Myron N '39
(216) 642-3342 **Krueger** Jeffrey W '85
(216) 491-3628 **Krueger** William J '93
(216) 479-8500 **Kruppa** Andrew R '00
(216) 579-4114 **Kruse** Mark F '85
(216) 479-8500 **Kryshtalowych** Helen Z '80
(216) 566-5642 **Kryszak** Michele T '03
(216) 696-9800 **Kucharski** Timothy J '93
(216) 363-4500 **Kucharson** Michael C '04
(216) 263-6593 **Kuderna** Dawn M '97
(216) 241-0040 **Kuenzi** Hans C '83
(216) 348-7550 **Kuepper** Richard R '80
(216) 241-6770 **Kugelman** Harvey '84
(216) 592-5000 **Kuhar** Deviani M '94
(216) 696-5222 **Kuhlman** Gina A '96
(216) 771-6500 **Kukovec-Krasnicki** Suzana '01
(216) 241-2600 **Kulwicki** David A '88
(216) 586-3939 **Kunkle** Lisa K '94
(216) 696-3366 **Kunselman** David A '01
(216) 566-9477 **Kuntz** Christine M '04
(216) 292-3300 **Kurant** Jack '72
(216) 664-4190 **Kurdila** Julianne '89
(216) 696-3311 **Kurit** Neil B '64
(216) 541-3311 **Kurland** Gerald '68
(216) 363-4500 **Kursh** Deanna C '74
(216) 382-2249 **Kurtz** John C '68
(216) 443-8422 **Kurtz** William A '72
(216) 696-6700 **Kushner** Philip S '90
(216) 696-6700 **Kushner & Rendon Co, LPA**
(216) 937-4000 **Kusner** Andrew T '94
(216) 586-3939 **Kutik** David A '80
(216) 443-7223 **Kuzmins** Paul A '01
(216) 566-1144 **Kvale** Craig P '91
(216) 737-0000 **Kwarciak** Richard F '94
(216) 241-4664 **Kwiatkowski** Peter S '91
(216) 479-8500 **Labes** Robert D '88
(216) 696-0022 **Labovitz** Harvey '69
(216) 622-8200 **LaCerva** Anthony J '86
(216) 622-4363 **Lachman** Roy E '80
(216) 621-1530 **LaCivita** Richard J '00
(216) 621-1530 **LaCivita** Robert J '02
(216) 831-2345 **Ladanyi** Albert L II '83
(216) 520-5512 **Ladegaard** Brenda Lee '94
(216) 664-2569 **Lady** Julie A '02
(216) 522-1200 **Lafave** Arthur J Jr. '60
(216) 522-6104 **Lafferty** Scott W '80
(216) 696-4200 **LaFond** Thomas J '66
(216) 641-7575 **Lah** Andrej N '89
(216) 664-3316 **Laine** Robin L '77
(216) 696-4200 **Laino** Kenneth J '81
(216) 622-3911 **Laisure** Lori E '92
(216) 225-7572 **Lake** Robert A '99
(216) 586-7514 **Lalchandani** Kabir A '04
(216) 523-1525 **Lallo** Ernest A '79
(216) 348-4809 **Lally** Charles J '81
(216) 579-4114 **Lally** Robert J '92
(216) 479-8500 **Lally Spicer** Meegan '93
(216) 566-5590 **Lamb** Brian J '91
(216) 520-6400 **Lamb** Jason C '02
(216) 443-5869 **Lambert** David G '85
(216) 621-8484 **Lambert** Phillip Wesley '03
(440) 838-7600 **Lambros** Thomas D '52
(216) 368-2696 **Lamis** Alexander P '97
(216) 447-4477 **Lammert** Cynthia A '91
(216) 621-4268 **Lamos** Philip D '96
(216) 622-8200 **Lampert** Donald E '86
(216) 881-9191 **Lanci** Wallace J '02
(216) 623-4949 **Lancione** John A '88
(216) 623-4949 **Lancione** John G '59
Landefeld Anne M '52
(216) 687-2331 **Landever** Arthur R '81
(216) 781-1111 **Landever** David C '95
(216) 522-9000 **Landskroner** Jack '92
(216) 241-7000 **Landskroner** Lawrence '51
(216) 781-1212 **Lane** Aimee W '99
(216) 431-4500 **Lane** Cheryl R '97
(216) 781-5515 **Lane** James L '99
(216) 622-8200 **Lang** James F '92
(216) 241-6602 **Lang** Jeffrey R '02
(216) 514-1100 **Lang** Paul A II '92
(216) 687-1900 **Lange** Jill J '87
(216) 222-3339 **Langer** Carlton E '79
(216) 443-9000 **Langer** Philip E '73
(216) 664-2893 **Langhenry** Barbara A '87
(216) 491-8170 **Lanham** Verna J '84
(216) 696-3232 **Lansdowne** Dennis R '81
(216) 771-2680 **LaPerna** Anthony A '62
(216) 623-0150 **Lapine** Kenneth M '67
(216) 622-8200 **LaPorte** Dale C '66
(440) 838-8800 **Lardakis** Terry E '77
(216) 443-8868 **Laribee** Shirley S '96
(216) 515-1660 **Larsen** Hans L '92
(216) 619-0072 **Larsen** Lynn R '91
(216) 696-3311 **Larsen** Stuart L '93
(216) 479-8500 **Larson** John S '77
(216) 696-3510 **Larson** Paul E '98
(216) 696-8995 **LaRue** Edward R '92
(216) 621-0070 **LaSalvia** Christine M '03
(216) 241-2880 **Lasch** Debora S '88
(216) 621-9646 **Lasko** John J Jr. '77
(216) 574-2600 **Lasko & Lind Co,LPA**
(216) 222-8056 **Lasky** Rebecca L '95
(216) 787-4183 **Laszcz** Joseph S '81
(216) 586-3939 **Lathrop** Lisa S '01
(440) 356-5700 **Laubacher** Eric R '99
(216) 363-1400 **Laube-Haughton** Emily '04
(216) 622-8200 **Lauderdale** Jeffrey J '02
(216) 579-1700 **Lauricia** Una L '02
(216) 781-2787 **Lavelle** Neal P '60
(216) 443-7800 **Lavelle** Patrick J Jr. '93
(216) 621-9870 **Lavelle** Patrick S '93
(216) 931-6000 **Laven** Stuart A '70
(216) 363-4500 **Laven** Stuart A Jr. '99
(216) 479-8500 **Lavey** David B '87
(216) 479-8500 **Lavey** Wendlene M '89
(216) 443-8603 **Lavin** Sean T '01
Lavrisha Anton M '79
(216) 252-6555 **Lawko** Susan M '84
(216) 252-6555 **Lawko** William A '50
(216) 622-8200 **Lawniczak** James M '89
(216) 689-3692 **Lawrence** Kimberly A '95
(216) 858-6451 **Lawrence** Michael J '91
(216) 621-9800 **Lawrence-Auten** Deborah J '94
(216) 443-8587 **Laws** Meghan Graves '02
(216) 881-3928 **Lawson** John H '76
(440) 409-0135 **Lawson** Scott E '94
(216) 621-0794 **Lawther** Jennifer Lee '96
(216) 586-3939 **Layman** Richard P '80
(216) 443-3377 **Layne** Judith L '91
(216) 586-3939 **Lazar** Kathy P '82
(216) 687-2347 **Lazarus** Stephen R '74
(216) 931-6000 **Lazich** Patricia D '91
(216) 515-1660 **Lazzaro** Anthony J '04
(216) 831-8771 **Lazzaro** Michele M '81
(216) 522-4916 **Lazzaro** Patrick G '57
(216) 928-2200 **Leach** John C '02
(216) 515-1660 **Leader** Edward J '99
(216) 621-5300 **Leahy** William B '68
(216) 623-0150 **Leak** Douglas G '89
(216) 696-0900 **Lear** Scott Michael '89
(216) 443-7800 **Leary** Patrick S '00
(216) 621-0200 **Lease** Robert K '76
(216) 368-3585 **Leatherberry** Wilbur C '68
(216) 586-3939 **Leavitt** Jeffrey S '73
(216) 566-2439 **Lebold** John W '82
(216) 621-2300 **Lebovitz** Jamie R '82
(216) 621-0200 **Lebowitz** Todd H '97
(216) 274-2354 **Lechowick** Sonja M '01
(216) 586-3939 **Leddy** Patrick J '90
(216) 445-6231 **Leduc** Marie-Jeanne S '03
(216) 520-5559 **Lee** Lori Ann '95
(216) 752-8027 **Lee** Martha C '76
Lee Robert E '61
(216) 271-8947 **Lee** Stephen C '96
(216) 241-2838 **Lee** Thomas J '77
(216) 631-4301 **Leece** Wilson A II '69
(440) 892-3315 **Leeders** Lawrence D '80
(216) 623-0150 **Lees** Tammi J '04
(440) 838-8800 **Lefelar** Scott A '99
(216) 928-2200 **Lefferts** Susan H '86
(216) 621-8484 **Lefkowitz** Paul S '74
(216) 566-2478 **Legenza** Richard A '84
(216) 778-5776 **Legerski** Mary L '94
(440) 838-8585 **Legerski** Steven A '94
(216) 431-3406 **Lehman** Jeffrey T '89
(216) 621-0200 **Leiken** Earl M '67
(216) 479-8500 **Leiken** Jonathan B '97
(216) 621-2300 **Leikin** Jeffrey A '85
(440) 779-6922 **Leitch** David B '94
(216) 861-3550 **Leizman** William S '51
(216) 443-7800 **Leland** William G '03
(216) 621-1530 **Lembright** Mark R '89
(216) 781-3600 **Lemmerbrock** Ryan J '03
(216) 861-7200 **Lenahan** Brian J '92
(216) 651-4600 **Leneghan** Christine T '91
(216) 651-4600 **Leneghan** Patrick P '89
(216) 694-5470 **Lenhard** John E '66
(216) 583-3371 **Lenhard** Kevin J '93
(216) 241-2880 **Lenhard** Matthew J '99
(216) 861-8888 **Lenhardt** Fred P '94
(216) 881-6600 **Lenhart** Thomas E '88
(216) 586-3939 **Lennox** Heather '92
(216) 621-0070 **Lenson** Kevin Lee '96
(216) 931-6000 **Lenson** Murray K '68
(216) 443-7800 **Lentz** Edward G '93
(216) 689-4389 **Lentz** James F '01
(216) 696-1433 **Leo** Ann E '79
(216) 523-4488 **Leo** Victor J '79
(216) 586-3939 **Leonard** Irvin A '70
(216) 621-0200 **Leonard** Melissa A '95
(216) 752-1000 **Leonetti** Albert F '66
(216) 443-3454 **Leonetti** Ellen M '86
(216) 752-1000 **Leonetti** Frank Jr. '56
(216) 687-1311 **Leonetti** Frank III '82
(216) 592-5000 **Leonti** Joseph R '00
(216) 696-4676 **Leopold** David W '85
(216) 566-5520 **Lepene** Alan R '71
(216) 443-9000 **Lepene** Scott B '03
(216) 889-5478 **Lerner** Rachel D '96
(216) 420-9000 **Lesco** Richard A '61
(216) 931-6000 **Lester** David L '83
(216) 623-1155 **Letts** Laurel E '91
(216) 586-3939 **Leukart** Barbara J '75
(216) 621-0200 **Leukart** Richard H II '67
(216) 566-5656 **Leung** Diane S '92
(216) 274-2346 **Levasseur** Eric B '02
(216) 696-1111 **Levey** Harold L '68
(216) 241-3333 **Levey** Scott I '78
(216) 621-1543 **Levin** Ann R '80
(216) 781-5233 **Levin** Daniel J '91
(216) 831-3939 **Levin** Dennis P '78
(216) 281-3535 **Levin** James A '79
(216) 928-0600 **Levin** Joel L '84
(216) 781-5236 **Levin** Morris '52
(216) 771-2175 **Levin** Morton Q '66
(216) 696-1233 **Levine** Alan S '79
(216) 321-4477 **Levine** Barbara H '04
(216) 696-1233 **Levine** David L '53
(216) 363-4500 **Levine** David M '94
(216) 623-2110 **Levine** Gary H '76
(216) 522-1200 **Levine** Lisa K '96
(216) 363-4500 **Levine** Mary Beth '87
(216) 241-0050 **Levy** Donald M '65
(216) 363-4500 **Levy** Howard A '73
(216) 241-6336 **Lewandowski** Joseph A Jr. '80
(216) 241-2838 **Lewanski** Christine A '96
(216) 522-3715 **Lewis** Bert II '69
(216) 443-9000 **Lewis** David M '00
(216) 222-2227 **Lewis** David P '87
(216) 586-3939 **Lewis** Jennifer C '95
(216) 621-0200 **Lewis** John B '80
(216) 479-8500 **Lewis** John F '58
(216) 586-3939 **Lewis** John Q '96
(216) 436-3237 **Lewis** Julie E '96
(216) 241-1074 **Lewis** Kenneth J '00
(216) 622-8200 **Lewis** Leonard L III '84
(216) 592-5000 **Lewis** Martin H '79
(216) 586-7078 **Lewis** Nathan Thomas '04
(216) 592-5000 **Lewis** Nicole E '01
(216) 696-7600 **Lewis** Patrick H '85
(216) 443-9000 **Lewis** Patrick T '04
(216) 621-5980 **Lewis** Robert L '73
(216) 566-5500 **Lewis** Robert S '02
(216) 664-2270 **Lewis** Sandra R '91
(216) 831-0042 **Lewis** Scott M '84
(216) 443-7800 **Lewis-Bevel** Ellainna J '92
(216) 696-3232 **Liber** John D '63
(216) 583-8266 **Licastro** Gabriel M '83
(216) 928-1503 **Lichko** Gregory M '75
(216) 902-4444 **Lichtig** Steven M '92
(216) 522-0562 **Lichtman** Jeffrey E '71
(216) 586-3939 **Licygiewicz** Arthur P '97
(216) 861-0360 **Lidrbauch** Elena A '99
(216) 566-5653 **Liebson** Matthew E '99
(216) 291-3600 **Liederbach** Kirk W '92
(216) 987-4648 **Lietzke** Jeffrey S '96
(216) 696-1422 **Liffman** Kenneth B '79
(216) 515-4361 **Light** Jeffrey H '86
(216) 621-8484 **Lightner** Terri A '04
(216) 781-1700 **Lill** Abby K '04
(216) 363-4500 **Lillie** Richard G '79
(216) 781-8435 **Lilly** John C '77
(440) 838-7600 **Lilly** Stacy N '00
(216) 381-3400 **Lim** Gene M '92
(216) 574-2600 **Lind** John K Jr. '91
(216) 687-5506 **Lind** Kermit J '85
(216) 586-3939 **Lindahl** Burkhart R '00
(216) 621-0200 **Lindberg** Lawrence V '73
(216) 621-0590 **Linden** Michael J '75
(216) 363-5220 **Lindner** Daniel F '94
(216) 621-5300 **Lindner** David J '01
(216) 363-5220 **Lindner Weaver Crane & Brondou,LLP**
(216) 566-5500 **Lindquist** David C '04
(216) 344-3944 **Lineberger** Martha E '94
(216) 348-5400 **Linehan** Paul W '98
(216) 621-0150 **Linetsky** Yuri R '00
(216) 621-1113 **Ling** Daniel R '03
(216) 696-8730 **Ling** John M '02
(216) 443-6350 **Ling** Wendy A '93
(216) 621-0150 **Link** Bradley C '04
(216) 263-8548 **Linn** Martin P '82
(216) 623-0000 **Linn** Michael D '86
(216) 491-5000 **Linn** Michael S '69
(216) 771-5800 **Linton & Hirshman**
(216) 771-5800 **Linton** Robert F Jr. '84
(216) 566-5596 **Linville** Timothy H '03
(216) 621-2234 **Lipcsik** Robert N '96
(216) 696-7666 **Lippe** Stuart H '75
(216) 861-5000 **Lipski** Christopher '89
(216) 241-7226 **Lipson** Ronald M '58
(216) 368-3318 **Lipton** Judith P '80
(216) 241-0220 **Lisboa** Kimberly A '93
(216) 787-3030 **Lisowski** Sandra J '87
(216) 696-7600 **List** Martin S '81
(216) 363-4500 **Listati** Ezio A '90
(216) 586-3939 **Litt** Shoshana E '03
(216) 621-3344 **Litzow** Joan M '84
(216) 241-2838 **Livingstone** Fred J '50
(216) 831-0042 **Lloyd** Thomas J '99
(216) 664-4287 **Loar** Estella L '80
(216) 861-6820 **Lobe** Thomas G '79
(216) 566-1661 **Lobo** Alfred D '64
(216) 696-7600 **Lobritz** Meredith A '03
(216) 520-0088 **Locke** Kevin J '90
(216) 689-3907 **Locke** Susan S '78
(216) 696-7170 **LoConti** Dennis N '82
LoConti Joseph E '77
(216) 621-0200 **Loeb** James A '88
(216) 621-0200 **Loesch** Robert M '92
(216) 241-6602 **Loesel** Pamela E '95
(216) 592-5000 **Logan Melick** Heather '97
(216) 622-8200 **Lohiser** Kenneth L '88
(216) 241-4100 **Lohr** Carole A '00
(216) 830-9000 **Lojewski** Jeffrey D '82
(216) 520-5642 **Lokiec** Benjamin K '01
(216) 621-1312 **Lombardi** Maria T '92
(216) 241-9990 **Lombardi** John J '71
(216) 621-0400 **Lombardo** Vincent J '82
(216) 787-3030 **Lombardo** Vincent T '81
(216) 771-6500 **Lombardy** Matthew P '01
(216) 781-2550 **Lonardo** Angelo F '79
(216) 621-5980 **London** James D '67
(216) 692-5934 **Loney** David '77
(216) 696-4441 **Long** Ryan L '04
(216) 622-3600 **Long** Sharon L '78
(216) 771-3737 **Longauer** Nicholas E '76
(216) 231-7936 **Longino** Nicole C '83
(216) 861-3444 **Lonjak** George F '82
(216) 622-8200 **LoPresti** Charles A '96
(216) 348-5400 **LoPresti** Joseph J Jr. '73
(216) 443-4945 **LoPresti** Mary C '85
(216) 241-7740 **LoPresti** Salvatore J '73
(216) 928-2200 **LoPrinzi** Brian V '96
(216) 696-5673 **Lord** Frank H '56
(216) 696-5673 **Lord** Kimberly M '85
(216) 689-4969 **Lorentzen** Lee Ann '79
(216) 367-6260 **Loreta** Daniel R '89
(216) 443-7800 **Loritts** Lynn D '91
(216) 696-7600 **Louard** Janette A '96
(216) 834-0400 **Loucas** Cathryn N '01
(216) 834-0400 **Loucas** George E '85
(216) 834-0400 **Loucas** Penny E '87
(216) 778-8475 **Loue** Sana '96
(216) 241-5310 **Lougovskaia** Elena N '00
(216) 525-1939 **Louttit** Kathryn H '04
(216) 621-0200 **Loux** Lloyd F Jr. '53
(216) 586-3939 **Love** Julia Ann '95
(216) 586-3939 **Love** Sheryl H '95
(216) 928-3474 **Lovequist** Sarah E '01
(216) 241-2880 **Lovett** Mary F '85
(216) 622-8200 **Lovett** Ruth L '85
(216) 621-7045 **Lovinger** Daniel L '67
(216) 861-0360 **Lowder** Janet L '92
(216) 241-2838 **Lowe** Bruce J '79
(216) 781-2600 **Lowe Eklund Wakefield & Mulvihill Co, LPA**
(216) 781-2600 **Lowe** James A '72
(216) 787-3668 **Lowes** Lawrence J '78
(216) 274-0520 **Lowry** Van M '83
(216) 592-5000 **Lu** David S '96
(216) 622-8200 **Luarde** Sharon A '99
(216) 696-7777 **Lucarelli** Robert R '86
(216) 241-5735 **Lucas** Matthew H '91
(216) 443-6654 **Lucas** Paul H '97
(216) 696-4200 **Lucas** Sandra C '00
(216) 621-5300 **Lucas** Walter A '97
(216) 771-8340 **Lucas** William J '75
(216) 621-0200 **Lucchesi** Thomas R '84
(216) 586-3939 **Lucci** John Paul '03
(216) 621-0590 **Lucey** James B '88
(216) 844-4477 **Ludgin** John R '87
(216) 520-5600 **Luedeke** Theresa '87
(216) 531-5390 **Luikart** Loyal E Jr. '54
(216) 575-0777 **Luka** Lori Ann '00
(216) 621-4244 **Lukacs** Cheryl A '92
Lukas Henry F Jr. '60
(216) 522-4180 **Lukich** Richard A '82
(216) 830-6830 **Lum** David A '94
(216) 522-8179 **Lund** Paul C '73
(216) 621-0200 **Lundberg** Arthur H '94
(440) 483-4281 **Lundin** Thomas M '98
(216) 514-6400 **Lurie** Jeffrey K '89
(216) 623-0000 **Lurie** Robert N '94
(216) 443-7223 **Lurie-Licata** Rochelle M '85
(216) 781-2126 **Luskin** John P '88
(216) 443-8423 **Lusnia** Kenneth J '74
(216) 443-7800 **Lusnia** Kristen L '99
(216) 241-5735 **Lustig** Arthur F '60
(216) 241-5735 **Lustig Evans & Lucas Co,LPA**
(216) 241-5735 **Lustig** Robert M '60
(216) 348-1700 **Lutjen** George W '64
(216) 586-3939 **Lutz** Nathan L '02
(216) 621-0200 **Lutzko** Rebecca C '98
(216) 787-3635 **Lynch** Debra P '83
(216) 622-3600 **Lynch** James C '68
(216) 771-2545 **Lynch** John Kennedy '57
(216) 664-3579 **Lynch** Robert P Jr. '00
(216) 621-4636 **Lynch** Tiaon M '98
(216) 443-4292 **Lynch-King** Joan M '95
(216) 622-8200 **Lyon** Charles B '71
(888) 955-2947 **Lytle** Alicia M '98
(216) 664-4333 **Ma** Catherine '98
(216) 621-4244 **MacAdams** Pamela J '84
(216) 523-1400 **Macdonald** George W '79
(216) 443-9000 **MacDougall** Irene M '83
(216) 443-5809 **Mace** Birgit '90
(216) 479-8500 **Mace** Damond R '84
(216) 360-9919 **Macedonio** Rosemary A '80
(216) 360-9919 **Macedonio Toerek & Box,PLL**
(216) 515-1660 **Maciak** Brian A '00
(216) 861-1700 **Mack** David E '75
Mack Fernando O '94
(216) 566-7800 **Mack** Jimmie Jr. '79
(216) 520-5502 **Mack** Khara M Singer '02
(216) 881-6600 **Mack** Lisa A '86
(216) 575-2708 **Mack** Richard W '78
(216) 520-5508 **Mack** Stephanie M '00
(440) 886-4500 **Mackay** Michael '77
(216) 696-7177 **Mackey** Cheryl A '95
(216) 781-1212 **Mackey** James M '74
(216) 443-7800 **Mackin** Brendan J '96
(216) 522-4914 **Mackin** Maura C '89
(216) 522-9000 **Madden** Justin F '93
(216) 696-1080 **Madden** Michael I '85
(216) 698-4785 **Madigan** Holley M '97
(216) 522-5396 **Madigan** Joseph P '76
(216) 781-5470 **Madigan** Kathleen A '04
Madorsky Harold A '81
(216) 586-3939 **Maersch** Karl M '02
(216) 241-6602 **Maestle** Shawn W '94
(216) 443-7223 **Magee** David T '95
(216) 771-5588 **Magner** Caitlin E '02
(800) 600-1222 **Maguire & Schneider, LLP**
(216) 443-7800 **Mahaney** Kimberly A '92
(216) 443-7295 **Maher** Christopher S '91
(216) 696-4161 **Maher** Edward J '64
(216) 443-7800 **Mahnic** Lisa M '95
(216) 621-1424 **Mahoney** Lisa M '02
(216) 443-7800 **Mahoney** Mark J '89
(216) 687-1480 **Mahoney** Michael J '79
(216) 443-8611 **Mahoney** Molly C '98
(216) 361-0002 **Maier** John P '01
(216) 592-5000 **Maimbourg** Rita A '81
(216) 520-0088 **Maimona** Cheryl L '75
(216) 586-3939 **Maiorana** David M '99
(216) 479-8500 **Maiwurm** James J '74
(216) 443-3789 **Majer** Mark R '92
(216) 394-5072 **Majernik** Meghan D '02
(216) 443-7800 **Majeski** Colleen A '97
(216) 443-6393 **Majka** Susan L '95
(216) 522-4086 **Majkrzak** Theresa M '80
(216) 348-5400 **Makee** Dan L '85
(216) 241-2838 **Makee** Joel A '69
(216) 241-2838 **Makhlouf** Majeed G '01
(216) 348-5400 **Makofsky** Michael D '99
(216) 787-3030 **Makowski** Richard J '77
(216) 579-9938 **Malaker** Albert D '85
(216) 541-8200 **Malbasa** Stephanie H '79
(216) 987-4418 **Maleckar** Rebecca J '91
(216) 443-0450 **Malek** Nader N '96

(216) 687-1311 **Malemud** Franklin C '97
(216) 241-2863 **Malensek** Jennifer L '98
(216) 802-3664 **Malick** Keith G '00
(216) 781-3434 **Malicki** Jack A '04
(216) 771-6500 **Malkin** Jack S '81
(216) 222-3443 **Malkin** Jennifer R '86
(216) 621-2090 **Mallamad** Shawn M '84
(216) 348-5400 **Malloy** Sean D '00
(216) 563-2146 **Malloy** Timothy P '85
(216) 687-1311 **Malnar** PattiJo '92
(216) 687-1311 **Malone** James L '70
(216) 861-5511 **Malone** John P Jr. '71
(216) 621-0200 **Malone** Raymond M '82
Malone Robert B '96
(216) 522-4856 **Malone** Vanessa F '96
(216) 586-3939 **Maloney** Mary D '87
(216) 523-1900 **Maloney** Matthew J '91
(216) 621-0200 **Maloney** Ruth Ann '90
(440) 234-8888 **Maloof** George M '78
(216) 357-7000 **Malumphy** Christopher R '88
(216) 360-7200 **Malvasi** Maurus G '94
(216) 621-5161 **Malynn** Steven R '96
(216) 787-3030 **MaMana** Frank J Jr. '78
(216) 514-6400 **Mamich** Samuel J '73
(216) 621-3251 **Mamone** Edward J '87
(216) 621-3251 **Mamone** Joseph A '61
(216) 696-5222 **Mancino** Brett M '99
(216) 575-0777 **Mancino** Jennifer L '04
(216) 621-1742 **Mancino** Paul A Jr. '63
(216) 687-2675 **Mancino** Paul III '92
(216) 391-6680 **Mandel** Bernard '68
(216) 931-6000 **Mandel** Bruce P '76
(216) 771-7080 **Mandell** Ellen S '78
(216) 771-1430 **Mangano** Basil W '96
(216) 586-3939 **Manghillis** Jeffrey R '00
(216) 696-8700 **Manghillis** Katherine G '04
(216) 241-5094 **Maniker** Howard B '68
(216) 687-1900 **Manly** Cornelius A '73
(216) 583-1258 **Manly** Michael N '96
(216) 241-5310 **Mann** Eric H '80
(216) 566-5546 **Mann** Kent L '76
(216) 696-7600 **Mann** Lisa F '80
(216) 621-6147 **Mann** Theodore M Jr. '76
(216) 241-5310 **Manning** Jamie '80
(216) 641-7500 **Manning** Janice G '90
(216) 621-1113 **Manning** Timothy E '98
(216) 928-2200 **Mannion** Thomas P '93
(216) 479-8500 **Manoloff** Richard D '92
(216) 523-1500 **Manos** Eli '58
(216) 681-1818 **Manos** John M '84
(216) 983-1288 **Manson** Marcie A '89
(216) 523-1500 **Mansour** Ernest P '55
(216) 523-1500 **Mansour Gavin Gerlack & Manos Co,LPA**
(216) 696-7661 **Mansour** Robert G '86
(216) 479-8500 **Mantione** Lianne R '03
(216) 241-6277 **Mantz** Allison M '04
(216) 443-7838 **Marburger** Barbara R '84
(216) 621-0200 **Marburger** David L '84
(216) 363-4500 **Marchant** Robert A '01
(216) 692-1222 **Marcinkevicius** Egidijus K '77
(216) 575-0777 **Marcis** Robert A II '98
(216) 241-7740 **Marcovy** Timothy A '77
(216) 464-6555 **Marcus** Terry H '85
(216) 566-5560 **Marcuz** Denise L '01
(216) 687-4614 **Marczely** Bernadette A '95
(216) 781-0722 **Marein & Bradley**
(216) 781-0722 **Marein** Mark B '82
(216) 241-0011 **Margolis** Daniel M '96
(216) 368-5160 **Margolis** Kenneth R '78
(216) 363-4500 **Margolis** Kevin D '89
(216) 641-1071 **Margolis** Loren J '83
(216) 363-4500 **Margolis** Richard D '63
(216) 621-2222 **Margolis** Ronald A '83
(216) 621-2034 **Margolius** Andrew L '83
(216) 621-2034 **Margolius** Marcia W '83
(216) 621-2034 **Margolius Margolius & Associates, LPA**
(216) 479-8500 **Margulies** Jeffrey J '73
(216) 622-8200 **Marhofer** Michael F '91
(216) 443-7800 **Marino** Carmen M '71
(216) 619-5223 **Mariotti** Mark '97
(216) 292-3300 **Marken** Howard A '50
(216) 443-8610 **Markey** Daniel J '03
(216) 621-0200 **Markey** Robert G '64
(216) 586-3939 **Markovic** Sasha '04
(440) 759-1420 **Markovich** Anna '03
(216) 861-3086 **Markowski** Anne M '98
(216) 479-8500 **Marks** Erin E '04
(216) 664-2715 **Marks** Jeffrey B '69
(216) 523-5405 **Marks** Joshua M '96
(216) 651-6100 **Marksz** John A '65
(216) 531-5898 **Markulin** Katica K '89
(216) 621-0150 **Markus** Robert D '67
(216) 931-6000 **Markus** Stephen A '79
(216) 523-1500 **Markworth** Dale E '73
(216) 781-4900 **Marmaros** Peter W '83
(216) 696-0990 **Marnecheck** Philip A '81
(216) 781-8286 **Marolt** Evelyn R '87
Marosan Joseph E '84
(216) 241-7740 **Marotta** Thomas P '81
(216) 623-0880 **Marra** Joni L '91
(216) 241-2838 **Marrer** Steven A '83
(216) 861-3086 **Marshall** Bernadette '85
(216) 928-2200 **Marshall** Christina J '98
Marshall Giles T '78
(216) 443-7800 **Marshall** Mark R '91
(216) 781-4994 **Marshall** Wentworth J Jr. '56
(216) 523-5000 **Marsteller** Marcia E '95
(216) 566-5699 **Martahus** Craig R '79
(216) 696-0800 **Martello** James P '74
(216) 523-1500 **Martillotta** Samuel R '80
(216) 928-2200 **Martin** Adam W '04
(216) 514-1100 **Martin** Aric D '95
(216) 443-7583 **Martin** John T '84
(216) 771-3033 **Martin** John W '69
(216) 443-7800 **Martin** Kathleen A '81
(216) 889-5530 **Martin** Tammy L '92
(216) 664-4503 **Martinek** Steven '75
(216) 875-5555 **Martinez** Hector G Jr. '97
(216) 586-3939 **Marting** Michael G '74
(216) 479-6100 **Martinsek** Amanda J '92
(216) 222-3495 **Martis** Charles G '55
(216) 586-3939 **Martis** Michael S '85
(216) 861-4700 **Martyn** Hartley B '86
(216) 476-4002 **Marvar** Raymond J '79
(216) 931-6000 **Marvinney** Craig A '82
(216) 443-9000 **Marvinney** Michelle Powe '84
(216) 687-1311 **Masch** Clifford C '83
(216) 621-0200 **Mason** Lance T '96
(216) 443-7800 **Mason** William D '86
(216) 621-4859 **Massaro** Peter T '91
(216) 771-3336 **Massetti** Regina M '81
(216) 586-3939 **Mast** Bernadette Mihalic '88
(216) 771-1430 **Masters** John M '85
(216) 781-2822 **Masters** William N '83
(216) 432-1992 **Masterson** Nora M '02
(216) 787-3030 **Mastrangelo** Mark E '82
(216) 622-8200 **Matasar** Scott C '00
(216) 241-6602 **Matchinga** Walter R '73
(216) 589-9939 **Mate** James T '77
(440) 746-0911 **Matejczyk** David M '89
(216) 664-2678 **Matejka** Dennis A '83
(440) 838-8800 **Matejkovic** Margaret Andreeff '92
(216) 443-6371 **Matheney** Bridey '99
(216) 515-1660 **Matheney** Matthew H '98
(216) 689-4725 **Mather** Laura M '93
(216) 348-5400 **Mathews** Tyler L '94
(216) 621-1000 **Matile** Michael W '00
(216) 443-7800 **Mattes** Jay L '90
(216) 781-4110 **Matthews** Laurel Ann '94
(216) 875-4008 **Matts** Joseph J '92
(216) 621-6570 **Matty** David J '79
(216) 685-1037 **Mausar** Donald A '95
(216) 787-4901 **Mausser** Cynthia B '91
(216) 621-7860 **Maxfield** Harold O Jr. '86
(216) 696-5444 **Maxton** Reginald N '93
(216) 696-5750 **Maxwell** Gary J '88
(216) 363-1400 **Maxwell** Lindsay '93
(216) 875-9842 **May** Claire C '96
(216) 431-4500 **May** James D '01
(216) 621-0150 **May** James W '04
(216) 241-2880 **May** Karl E '74
(216) 348-5400 **May** Katayoon Sadre '04
(216) 937-1390 **Maybee** Matthew E '04
(216) 592-5000 **Mayer** Kristen L '91
(216) 621-7743 **Mayle** Andrew R '02
(216) 363-4500 **Mayo** David R '76
(216) 292-3300 **Mays** Alfred R '56
(216) 522-4796 **Mays** Lawrence '75
(216) 696-4421 **Mays** Thomas C '86
(216) 479-8500 **Mazanec** Daniel C '04
(216) 621-0200 **Mazanec** Mark R '88
(440) 248-7906 **Mazanec Raskin & Ryder Co,LPA**
(216) 522-0800 **Mazanec** Richard O '76
(440) 248-7906 **Mazanec** Thomas S '76
(216) 586-3939 **Mazey** John E '98
(216) 787-3030 **Mazorow** Laurel D '82
(216) 579-9800 **Mazurkiewcz** Janice L '79
(216) 443-3432 **Mazza** Margaret M '63
(216) 623-0880 **Mazzella** Michael J '99
(216) 781-5515 **Mazzi** Alicia L '02
(216) 781-1180 **Mazzone** Frank B '76
McAllister Ralph A '56
(216) 589-9600 **McAndrew** Moira A '00
(216) 363-4500 **McAndrews** James P '74
(216) 861-3448 **McBride** Brian A '85
(216) 765-1199 **McBride** Danielle L '99
(216) 529-6242 **McBride** Robert D '73
(216) 781-7011 **McCabe** Peter J '88
(216) 861-6116 **McCafferty** Joseph P '86
(216) 771-0270 **McCafferty** Owen J '55
(216) 623-0900 **McCaffrey** John F '87
(216) 241-5310 **McCain** Kenneth W '98
(216) 696-4700 **McCallum** Allison '99
(216) 861-6655 **McCarroll** John J '89
(216) 586-3939 **McCartan** Patrick F '60
(216) 566-5500 **McCarthy** Brendan J '04
(216) 696-1422 **McCarthy** Daniel R '54
(216) 621-2300 **McCarthy** Ellen M '90
(216) 696-1422 **McCarthy Lebit Crystal & Liffman Co, LPA**
(216) 592-5000 **McCarthy** Mark F '76
(216) 363-4500 **McCarthy** Thomas Cormac '99
(216) 696-4009 **McCarty** John M '04
(216) 586-3939 **McCarty** Philip W '03
(216) 228-9400 **McCarty** Robert L '69
(216) 861-6833 **McCauley** Ann M '00
(216) 622-8200 **McCauley** Stephen L '93
(216) 523-1500 **McClatchey** Christopher J '97
(216) 621-6570 **McClelland** Robert C '80
(216) 443-7223 **McClelland** Warren L Jr. '81
(216) 689-4690 **McClintic** Janine M '02
(216) 566-9700 **McClintic** Shawn A '02
(216) 861-5582 **McCollister** Scott A '89
(216) 443-3344 **McCollough** Heather C '03
(216) 696-5400 **McComas** Sherri N '86
(216) 566-3741 **McConnell** Donald J '90
(216) 664-6791 **McCorkle** Martha R '90
(216) 443-7181 **McCormack** John T '72
(216) 241-8333 **McCormick** Courtney M '04
(216) 622-8200 **McCoy** Darlene E '79
(216) 931-6000 **McCracken** Christopher C '77
(216) 575-1002 **McCracken** Matthew J '04
(216) 443-7800 **McCreary** Sherry M '78
(216) 586-3939 **McCrum** Ryan B '99
(216) 664-6900 **McCrystal** James L Jr. '73
(216) 851-3304 **McCully** Joanne '77
(216) 522-7807 **McDermott** Daniel M '78
(216) 348-1700 **McDonald** Charles R '73
(216) 348-5400 **McDonald Hopkins Co, LPA**
(216) 566-2432 **McDonald** Robert E '79
(216) 781-2125 **McDonnell** Daniel P '52
(216) 781-2125 **McDonnell** James J '82
(216) 689-5707 **McDowell** Robert F Jr. '99
(216) 721-8903 **McDuffie** Kenard '74
(216) 621-7860 **McEaneney** Shannon L '98
(440) 838-7600 **McElroy** Brian T '01
McElroy Kenneth K '99
(216) 622-0850 **McFadden** Donald P '73
McFarland Anne S '74
(216) 586-9537 **McFaul** Kevin T '86
(216) 481-4495 **McGaffick** Jeffrey M '86
(216) 622-8200 **McGann** Amy B '01
(216) 696-7883 **McGann** Regis E Jr. '75
(216) 566-0500 **McGarry** James J Jr. '63
(216) 621-7227 **McGarry** Timothy L '91
(216) 348-5400 **McGaughey** George L Jr. '75
(216) 241-8333 **McGill** Danielle M '03
(216) 241-5224 **McGinness** Joseph T '69
(216) 696-8440 **McGinness** Neil M '69
(216) 344-9220 **McGinty Gibbons Hilow & Spellacy Co,LPA**
(216) 344-9220 **McGinty** William T '80
(216) 378-9905 **McGlinchey Stafford PLLC**
(216) 621-0200 **McGowan** John J Jr. '84
(440) 333-6300 **McGowan** Thomas B III '69
(440) 333-6300 **McGowan** Thomas B IV '96
(216) 787-3030 **McGrail** Timothy X '81
(216) 443-7800 **McGrath** Mary H '89
(216) 443-3997 **McGrath** Michele A '96
(216) 574-2516 **McGraw** Brian R '86
(216) 265-6009 **McGraw** Candace S '88
(216) 566-3009 **McGraw** Joseph E '88
(216) 566-8780 **McGraw** Mark D '77
(216) 574-2516 **McGraw** Mary H '84
(216) 787-3175 **McGraw** Patrick A '66
(216) 696-4700 **McGregor** Erica E '98
(216) 931-6000 **McGrew** Steven D '01
(216) 623-0150 **McGrievy** Mark P '93
(216) 222-9708 **McGuire** Daniel J '88
(216) 622-8200 **McGuire** John J '98
(216) 348-5056 **McGuire** Michael P '93
(216) 787-3030 **McGuire** Thomas D '83
(216) 472-1500 **McHale** Katharine N '84
(216) 522-2675 **McHargh** Kelly-Marie '98
(216) 566-5261 **McIntyre** John F III '96
(216) 579-4114 **McIntyre Kahn & Kruse Co LPA**
(216) 830-6830 **McIntyre** Patrick J '89
(216) 579-4114 **McIntyre** Robert W '75
(216) 586-1292 **McIntyre** Sharon R '82
(216) 443-9000 **McKay** Hugh E '82
(216) 861-5582 **McKee** James W '69
(216) 861-0360 **McKee** Mary B '97
(216) 622-8200 **McKee** Thomas F '75
(216) 241-5310 **McKeegan** Jennifer L '97
(216) 875-3122 **McKeever** Kelly L '98
(216) 586-7042 **McKenna** Mary P '96
(216) 241-5310 **McKeon** Sheila A '84
(216) 523-8165 **McKew** Walter M '72
(216) 931-6000 **McKinley** Stacey L '97
(216) 368-6360 **McKinney** Louise E '78
(216) 622-8200 **McKnight** Douglas B '00
(440) 248-7906 **McLandrich** John T '83
(216) 241-8230 **McLaughlin** John B '72
(216) 623-0900 **McLaughlin & McCaffrey, LLP**
(216) 623-0900 **McLaughlin** Patrick M '76
(216) 622-8660 **McMahon** Brian A '94
(216) 241-8040 **McMahon** Carl G '75
(216) 621-1312 **McMahon DeGulis Hoffmann & Lombardi LLP**
(216) 566-5639 **McMahon** Louis L '96
(216) 621-1312 **McMahon** Michael S '81
(216) 621-1000 **McMahon** Seamus J '03
(216) 241-2838 **McManus** Robert P '78
(216) 781-1212 **McMenamin** Michael T '68
(216) 622-8200 **McMillan** Ronald M '00
(216) 522-7453 **McMillan** Solvita A '78
(216) 443-8400 **McMillen** Nancy G '82
(216) 443-7800 **McMonagle** Christopher N '97
(216) 479-6100 **McMonagle** James J '70
(216) 575-0777 **McMonagle** Matthew A '04
(216) 622-8200 **McMullen** Daniel J '83
(216) 566-1600 **McNair** Eben O IV '83
(216) 861-5225 **McNally** Kimberly D '98
(216) 515-1660 **McNamara** Marislynn J '93
(216) 621-0200 **McNamara** Michael P Jr. '96
(216) 731-1400 **McNamara** Thomas R '79
(216) 621-9870 **McNeal Schick Archibald & Biro Co, LPA**
(216) 360-7200 **McNellie** Richard L '75
(216) 592-5000 **McQuade** Rachel M '95
(216) 479-8500 **McWilliams** Douglas A '94
(216) 696-3327 **Meade** Karen K '83
(216) 787-3094 **Meador** Eugene B '82
(440) 461-9010 **Meador** Garnett R '86
(216) 687-1311 **Meadows** William A '86
(216) 291-3441 **Meaker** Mary A '84
(216) 348-5400 **Meaney** Michael J '77
(216) 687-2344 **Mearns** Geoffrey S '99
(216) 621-0200 **Mearns** Geoffrey S '99
(216) 696-8730 **Medley** Michael J '04
(216) 479-8500 **Meehan** Ellen K '92
(216) 444-2340 **Meehan** Michael Jan '82
Meehan Michael P '92
(216) 687-1311 **Meeker** Brian A '94
(216) 781-2770 **Meers** Elizabeth A '84
(216) 363-4500 **Mehalko** Megan L '90
(440) 838-7600 **Mehendale** Ellyn B '94
(216) 368-3983 **Mehlman** Maxwell J '88
(216) 696-4676 **Mehta** Khorzad A '04
(216) 696-3300 **Meimaris** James G '87
(216) 687-1900 **Meissner** Joseph P '66
(216) 479-8500 **Meissner** Michael G '79
(216) 241-5310 **Meko** Margaret M '84
(216) 623-0000 **Melamed** Marc A '77
(216) 443-7757 **Melena** Timothy J '91
(216) 621-8348 **Mellino** Christopher M '84
(216) 771-3800 **Mellino** Sean F '02
(216) 363-4500 **Mellott** David W '78
(216) 621-0150 **Mellyn** John E Jr. '73
(216) 642-6600 **Melnick** Mark G '00
(216) 664-4304 **Melnyk** Stephanie K '99
(216) 685-9188 **Meloy** Thomas C '70
(216) 566-5856 **Mendelsohn** Clifford S '01
Mendenhall Audrey '83
(216) 765-7400 **Mendes** Scott M '92
(216) 622-8200 **Mendoza** Matthew M '97
(216) 861-4414 **Menefee** M Terrell '99
(216) 241-3272 **Mentrek** Joseph M '85
(216) 928-2200 **Menuez** Jonathan M '95
(216) 664-4285 **Menzalora** William M '93
(216) 443-5830 **Menzies** John W Jr. '75
(216) 687-1311 **Meraglio** Russell J Jr. '83
(216) 621-0150 **Mercer** Harry D '67
(216) 368-2173 **Mercer** Kathryn L '83
(216) 491-3850 **Meredith** Colleen M '87
(216) 222-9723 **Mericle** Denise A '96
(216) 621-0580 **Meros** John C '80
(216) 931-6000 **Merriam** Stephen C '85
(216) 771-8121 **Merrick** Patrick P '04
(216) 621-0200 **Mersol** Gregory V '85
(440) 878-2953 **Mesel** Kathleen L '97
(216) 574-9990 **Messerman** Gale S '71
(216) 574-9990 **Messerman** Gerald A '62
(216) 861-8890 **Messerman** Richard D '71
(216) 566-5571 **Messinger** Donald H '68
(440) 605-1543 **Messinger-Rapport** Kenneth H '84
(216) 621-2300 **Mester** Jonathan D '98
(216) 621-2300 **Mester** Thomas '69
(216) 479-8500 **Metcalf** J Seth '04
(440) 243-8636 **Mettler** Michelle D '96
(216) 241-6602 **Metz** Carol K '00
(216) 781-5470 **Metzger** Robert L '62
(216) 621-8484 **Metzinger** Margaret M '95
(216) 696-7600 **Meyer** Andrew C '76
(216) 444-2340 **Meyer** Donna J '95
(216) 479-8500 **Meyer** G Christopher '73
(216) 689-4633 **Meyer** Lisa A '94
(216) 443-7800 **Meyer** Matthew E '02
(216) 896-2809 **Meyer** Thomas Lee '79
(216) 831-0042 **Meyers** Anne L '77
(216) 831-0042 **Meyers Roman Friedberg & Lewis LPA**
(216) 696-9330 **Meyerson** David L '84
(216) 241-3377 **Mezacapa** Victor A III '91
(216) 961-2313 **Michaels** Thomas N '97
(216) 241-5310 **Michalec** Daniel J '89
(216) 622-8200 **Michals** Thomas I '88
(216) 621-0150 **Michalski** David J '94
(216) 689-5901 **Michel** Lisa H '84
(216) 623-1155 **Micheli** Mark V '84
(216) 696-3366 **Michelson** Deborah J '92
(216) 348-0700 **Michelson** Michael B '79
(216) 566-8000 **Middleton** Frederick D '73
(216) 622-3600 **Midian** Kathleen L '82
(216) 588-5051 **Miehls** Donald E '84
(216) 621-0200 **Mierau** Michael D Jr. '98
(216) 522-4856 **Migdal** Debra K '92
(440) 746-1177 **Miggins** Janet L '81
(216) 621-2030 **Miguel** Melanie V '95
(216) 566-5752 **Mihet** Horatio G '02
(216) 687-5278 **Mika** Karin '90
(216) 781-6166 **Mikhail** Bishoy M '03
(216) 696-7600 **Mikhail** Sherrie '01
(216) 575-8016 **Mikol** Lisa M '04
(216) 443-6350 **Mileti** Charlene R '91
(216) 696-0808 **Miley** Kathryn M '96
(216) 263-3419 **Milgrom** Michael '83
(216) 363-1400 **Milicic** Heidi J '96
(216) 431-4500 **Milkes** Robert A '88
(216) 431-4500 **Millas** Gregory S '96
(216) 363-4500 **Miller** Barry J '83
(216) 875-2767 **Miller** Brett A '01
(216) 889-5062 **Miller** Carol J '97
(216) 566-5635 **Miller** Catherine L '01
(216) 228-9400 **Miller** Clinton J III '75
(216) 931-6000 **Miller** Craig S '97
(216) 875-8217 **Miller** Dana C '97
(216) 622-8200 **Miller** Ebony L '03
(216) 586-3939 **Miller** Heather Varley '03
(216) 363-1400 **Miller** James L '96
(216) 844-3817 **Miller** Janet L '79
(216) 696-5222 **Miller** Jeffrey C '97
(216) 443-5809 **Miller** Jennifer L '97
(216) 622-8200 **Miller** John E '97
(216) 241-6700 **Miller** Michael A '02
(216) 586-3939 **Miller** Nicholas M '98
(216) 621-3251 **Miller** Ralph A '48
(216) 622-8200 **Miller** Robert A '82
(216) 621-0040 **Miller** Robert G '73
(216) 621-1530 **Miller** Ross P '01
(216) 689-3691 **Miller** Scott D '79
(216) 623-5646 **Miller** Scott M '95
(216) 241-0622 **Miller** Scott R '93
(216) 696-3366 **Miller** Steven J '81
(216) 861-6000 **Miller Stillman & Bartel**
(216) 621-0200 **Miller** Tanya F '99
(216) 443-7800 **Miller** Timothy B '87
(216) 765-7431 **Millet** David G '98
(216) 765-1188 **Millet** Paul L '77
(216) 621-0200 **Millette** Ann G '98
(216) 241-6602 **Millican** James T II '67
(216) 928-7700 **Milligan** Patrick J '04
(440) 838-8800 **Millisor** Kenneth R '61
(440) 838-8800 **Millisor & Nobil Co,LPA**
(440) 838-8800 **Millisor** Richard A '94
(216) 586-3939 **Mills** David E '02
(216) 621-0200 **Mills** Jennifer A '96
(216) 479-8500 **Mills** Osborne Jr. '75
(216) 479-8500 **Millstone** David J '71
(216) 987-4856 **Miltner** Lawrence J '78
(216) 706-9250 **Minahan** Kathleen M '95
(216) 622-8200 **Minchak** JoEllen M '85
(216) 357-5349 **Mindes** Paula '97
(216) 621-2030 **Mindlin** Lewis B '75
(216) 694-3930 **Mineff** George Jr. '84
(216) 687-1311 **Mingus** Ronald A '90
(216) 520-0088 **Minney** Ronzel B '78
(216) 861-5582 **Minnich** Richard J '65
(216) 622-8200 **Mino** John M '84
(216) 357-5900 **Minshall** Kent R Jr. '79
(216) 351-0311 **Mintz** Gary L '79
(216) 696-1422 **Mintz** Stuart A '78
(216) 566-5508 **Miraldi** Leslee W '78
(216) 696-7777 **Miralia** Benedict P Sr. '68
(216) 696-7777 **Miralia** Benedict P Jr. '88
(216) 443-7800 **Miranda de Ahrendt** Myriam A '95
(216) 931-6000 **Mischka** Cash H '91
(216) 241-2600 **Mishkind** Howard D '80
(216) 241-5310 **Mitchell** Ann R '95
(216) 566-5500 **Mitchell** John R '96
(216) 586-3939 **Mitchell** Kimberley P '04
(216) 486-0024 **Mitchell** LuAnn '83

(216) 443-8586 **Mitchell** Mamie J '96
(216) 381-2183 **Mitchell** Richard N '60
(216) 623-0150 **Mitchell** Richard S '84
(440) 483-4245 **Mitchell** Sheila N '92
(216) 621-0200 **Mitchell** Wade A '85
(216) 566-0064 **Mitchell** William Jr. '78
(216) 431-4500 **Mitchell** Willie L '95
(216) 586-3939 **Mixter** Stephen C '86
(216) 592-5000 **Mizer** Susan L '93
(440) 842-1138 **Mizisin** John '52
(216) 363-4500 **Mlakar** Ginger Fuller '92
(216) 687-1900 **Mlakar** Thomas '92
(216) 522-3715 **Modic** Catherine A '87
(216) 291-2400 **Modica** Donald A '70
(216) 566-0835 **Modney** Robert T '75
(216) 781-5515 **Moeller** Jeffrey S '02
Moffet Beverly Lou '75
(216) 479-8500 **Mog** Cynthia C '93
(216) 861-5582 **Moldovanyi** Jay F '84
(216) 241-0300 **Molnar** Edward S '64
(216) 443-8588 **Molnar** Elizabeth A '03
(216) 586-3939 **Molnar** Isaac A '03
(216) 896-2212 **Molnar** John A '92
(216) 621-7860 **Molyneaux** Rebecca S '02
(216) 348-5400 **Monachino** Grant A '03
(216) 348-5400 **Monachino** Nicole M '03
(216) 574-9400 **Monastra** Carl C '81
(216) 443-9000 **Mondalek** Allyson J '04
(216) 664-4507 **Monegan** Theodora M '87
(216) 443-9000 **Monica** John C Jr. '03
(216) 696-4700 **Monihan** M Elizabeth '84
(216) 566-5607 **Monnin** Robert D '68
(216) 622-8200 **Monroe** Gerald A '92
(216) 781-1212 **Monroe** John W '93
(216) 861-1365 **Monroe** Robert W '85
(216) 241-2500 **Monroe** Thomas W '91
(216) 241-2500 **Monroe** William T '53
(216) 241-2500 **Monroe & Zucco**
(216) 566-1600 **Montana** Amy M '01
(216) 771-4050 **Monteleone** Joseph Michael '74
(216) 523-5482 **Montgomery** Michael J '99
(216) 566-5500 **Montville** Julianne '02
(216) 685-1136 **Monty** Jennifer M '03
(440) 248-7906 **Moody** Steven J '02
(216) 443-7800 **Mooney** Brian P '96
(216) 689-6176 **Mooney** Kevin M '00
(216) 830-9000 **Mooney** Laura J '79
(216) 586-3939 **Moore** Anthony R '75
(216) 363-4500 **Moore** Craig L '94
(216) 622-8200 **Moore** Edward W '82
(216) 579-1700 **Moore** James M '88
(216) 443-7223 **Moore** Kathy L '79
(216) 479-8500 **Moore** Kenneth C '73
(216) 696-7170 **Moore** Leslie N '00
(216) 241-5310 **Moore** Lynn L '84
(216) 241-3400 **Moore** Mary B '00
(216) 771-9745 **Moore** Sarah J '95
(216) 771-6776 **Moore** William D '60
(216) 522-4914 **Moore** Zoe Ann '86
(216) 344-3800 **Moorhead** Russell A '85
(216) 622-8200 **Moorhead** Sean T '93
(216) 622-8200 **Moorman** Pauline L '89
(216) 443-6984 **Morales** Egdilio J '94
(216) 348-1700 **Moran** R Emmett '77
(440) 617-1528 **Moran** Susan J '96
(216) 348-1100 **Morell** Karen M '88
(216) 931-6000 **Morelli** Matthew J '94
(216) 416-3114 **Morelli** Theresa E '89
(216) 622-3600 **Morford** James L '84
(216) 592-5000 **Morford** Joseph J '96
(216) 721-7700 **Morgan** Charles M Jr. '86
(216) 663-8820 **Morgan** Gerard R '02
(216) 566-0064 **Morgan** Hugh J '78
(216) 588-3788 **Morgan** Jeffrey L '92
(216) 621-4244 **Morganstern MacAdams & DeVito Co, LPA**
(216) 621-4244 **Morganstern** Stanley '67
(216) 241-2800 **Morgenstern** Conrad J '49
(216) 696-3311 **Morgenstern** Marc H '75
(216) 687-1900 **Morgenstern** Susan E '86
(216) 592-5000 **Moriarty** Matthew P '81
(216) 566-8228 **Moriarty** Robert B '94
(216) 621-3012 **Morice** Craig J '95
(216) 621-5300 **Morley** Ryan J '04
(216) 622-3600 **Moroney** James V '82
(216) 687-1200 **Moroscak** John M '96
(216) 951-8500 **Moroscak** Richard J '70
(216) 592-5000 **Morrical** Glenn E '77
(216) 961-8116 **Morris** Daniel G '88
(216) 529-0963 **Morris** Edward L '90
(216) 623-0000 **Morris** Melissa A '00
(216) 696-5400 **Morris** William B '94
(216) 687-0343 **Morrison** Harvey S '62
(216) 696-6900 **Morrison** Jennifer L '89
(440) 838-8800 **Morrison** Paul C '64
(216) 941-5566 **Morscher** Roy C '92
(216) 861-2400 **Morse** Andrew R '78
(216) 241-0520 **Morse** Joseph P '01
(216) 939-2065 **Morse** Stephen S '75
(216) 479-8500 **Morsek** Leslie A '01
(216) 586-3939 **Moscarino** George J '58
(216) 621-1000 **Moscarino** George M '83
(216) 621-1000 **Moscarino & Treu, LLP**
(216) 586-3939 **Moscioni** Anna L '00
(216) 502-2002 **Moser** Barbara J '82
(216) 621-0200 **Moser** Christina J '02
(216) 622-8200 **Moses** Kimberly '85
(216) 522-1424 **Mosher** Louise H '74
(216) 586-3939 **Mosier** Eric H '97
(216) 621-1000 **Moskowitz** Carol J '02
(216) 749-6300 **Moskowitz** Jan S '68
(216) 931-6000 **Moskowitz** Suzann R '04
(216) 443-7800 **Moss** James E '93
(216) 263-1715 **Moss** Jerald L '83
(216) 771-5588 **Moss** Karen Gabriel '89
(216) 696-3311 **Moss** Steven M '91
(216) 443-7800 **Motley** Bianca A '03
(216) 586-3939 **Mott** Cassandra G '99
(216) 443-7800 **Moulin** Darcy A '91
(440) 886-7878 **Moultrie** Stuart C '91
(216) 241-5310 **Mountcastle** Colleen A '98
(216) 566-5874 **Mountcastle** Jennifer M '00
(216) 781-1212 **Mounts** Mia M '98
(216) 348-5400 **Movius** David T '98
(216) 861-5582 **Moy** Philip J Jr. '89
(216) 266-2487 **Mueller** Wally M '90
(216) 443-9000 **Mugnano** John A '01
(216) 896-2458 **Mulac** Carol A '86
(216) 622-8200 **Mulcahy** Michael T '76
(216) 523-1400 **Mull** Donald P '52
(216) 348-5400 **Mulligan** John T '74
(216) 241-7700 **Mullin** Edward M '88
(216) 443-7223 **Mullin** Gregory K '86
(216) 781-2600 **Mulvihill** Dennis P '94
(216) 621-0200 **Mumford** Michael E '01
(216) 523-1500 **Muniak** William J '92
(216) 586-3939 **Munson** Adam D '01
(216) 889-5190 **Murdoch** Robert B '94
(216) 515-1660 **Murnane** Colleen C '95
(440) 838-7600 **Murner** Barry R '98
(216) 241-0011 **Murner** Brett F '01
Murphy Ann Marie '03
(216) 621-1113 **Murphy** Cynthia S '88
(216) 586-3939 **Murphy** Dennis L '94
(216) 883-9220 **Murphy** Donald R '72
(216) 479-8500 **Murphy** James P '69
(216) 802-7571 **Murphy** Jane C '96
(216) 575-0777 **Murphy** John M '96
(216) 241-5310 **Murphy** John T '90
(440) 605-6660 **Murphy** Kevin P '03
(216) 348-1700 **Murphy** Martin J '63
(216) 875-2767 **Murphy** Patrick J '74
(440) 243-4600 **Murphy** Rebecca Stubbs '82
(440) 888-0165 **Murphy** William L '73
(216) 583-2896 **Murphy** William P '95
(216) 621-0200 **Murray** Andrew J '04
(216) 622-8200 **Murray** Brian M '99
(216) 479-8500 **Murray** Jan E '78
(216) 781-5245 **Murray** John Michael '76
(216) 664-4329 **Murray** Lynn A '89
(216) 522-1200 **Murray** Margaret A '96
(216) 443-3431 **Murray** Peter A '84
(216) 521-5555 **Murtaugh** Francis D Jr. '71
(216) 579-1700 **Murtaugh** John P '81
(216) 241-2838 **Murway** Carl A '83
(216) 566-5943 **Musallam** Samer M '04
(216) 696-7777 **Musca & Miralia**
(216) 898-2351 **Muscarella** Lawrence G '83
(216) 623-0150 **Musick** Douglas S '92
(216) 781-3600 **Muskovitz** Susannah '84
(216) 623-0150 **Musnuff** Basil J '89
(216) 566-5869 **Myer** John D '01
(216) 623-0150 **Myers** James P '02
(216) 621-5300 **Myers** Jennifer L '02
(216) 696-0606 **Myers** John C '87
(216) 241-3900 **Myers** Kenneth D '91
(216) 431-4500 **Myers** Michelle A '94
(216) 362-9212 **Myers** O Lee '03
(216) 687-1900 **Myerson** Anita L '81
(216) 443-7800 **Myles** Paul J '85
(216) 592-5000 **Naeem** Tariq M '00
Naegele Joseph J '64
(216) 443-8838 **Naegele** Sherry A '00
(216) 566-5625 **Naftzinger** David J '73
(216) 621-5300 **Nagel** Beth A '97
(216) 241-0715 **Nager** David E '90
(216) 241-2880 **Nagorney** Frank P '75
(216) 222-2000 **Nagy** Matthew E '99
(216) 443-7800 **Naiman** Deborah R '88
(216) 621-5300 **Nam** Brian K '04
(216) 522-0183 **Nance** Donald S '79
(216) 479-8500 **Nance** Frederick R Jr. '78
(216) 586-3939 **Nandi** Melissa J '98
(216) 664-3774 **Nandi** Neal R '99
(216) 621-0200 **Napoli** James R '95
(216) 291-1246 **Nash** Carl '60
(216) 566-5774 **Nash** David E '81
(216) 291-1246 **Nash** Jean K '77
(216) 691-3000 **Nash** Joel A '93
(216) 443-2688 **Nash** Kelly R '98
(216) 787-4186 **Nash** Robin A '82
(216) 443-7800 **Naso** Carmen '78
(216) 515-1660 **Natale** Andrew J '89
(216) 241-5310 **Naughton** Thomas F '00
(216) 861-5582 **Nauman** Timothy E '83
(216) 566-5500 **Nazette** Adam R '03
(216) 241-5310 **Neal** John N '02
(216) 515-1660 **Nealis** Melanie Meyer '01
(216) 479-6418 **Nealis** Peter S '00
(216) 622-8200 **Neary** Douglas A '85
(216) 696-2719 **Nebel** Deborah J '88
(440) 838-7600 **Nee** Matthew M '00
(216) 621-8484 **Neel** David W '86
(216) 443-7800 **Neff** Richard A Jr. '88
(216) 741-2250 **Negrelli** William E '66
(216) 622-8200 **Neill** Ronald H '69
(216) 522-7963 **Neilsen** Karen N '95
(216) 861-5000 **Nejedlik** David B '86
(216) 696-4700 **Nelson** Douglas M II '96
(216) 472-0273 **Nelson** Michael L '90
(216) 621-7860 **Nelson** Robert M '71
(216) 621-1230 **Nemec** Andrew '99
(216) 566-5552 **Nemer** Laura Bancroft '99
(216) 479-8500 **Nemeth** Laura D '89
(216) 502-1300 **Nemeth** Richard H '84
(216) 621-3801 **Nerren** Guy V '71
(216) 368-3297 **Neth** Spencer '64
(216) 522-3715 **Neubecker** Mark F '78
(216) 696-7660 **Neuger** Charles J '54
(216) 363-4500 **Neumann** David M '97
(216) 696-7661 **Nevar** Denis A '04
(216) 687-1311 **Neville** John A '68
(216) 621-0200 **Newborn** Karen B '76
(216) 696-4700 **Newell** Sterling Jr. '49
(216) 621-2034 **Newendorp** Paul W '82
(216) 443-8824 **Newman** Daniel M '01
(216) 621-1541 **Newman** Joel I '72
(216) 586-3939 **Newman** John M Jr. '76
(216) 443-7800 **Nichol** Andrew J '00
(440) 248-7906 **Nicholas** Joseph F Jr. '87
(216) 241-5310 **Nicholson** Gary L '84
(216) 621-7227 **Nicola Gudbranson & Cooper, LLC**
(216) 479-8500 **Nicols** Howard J C '81
(440) 838-7600 **Nicosia** Crystal L '04
(216) 515-1660 **Niehaus** Bernard H Jr. '55
(216) 515-1660 **Niehaus** James B '83
(216) 479-8500 **Niehaus** Stephanie E '02
(216) 621-9870 **Nigro** Suzanne M '83
(216) 621-1530 **Niklas** Christian E '96
(216) 787-3030 **Nimrick** Sandra L '89
(216) 231-6121 **Nimrod** Alfred F '57
(216) 363-4500 **Ninneman** Sheila M '89
(216) 623-0150 **Nintcheff** Peter C '99
(440) 247-6800 **Nischwitz** Jeffrey L '84
(440) 838-7600 **Nitschke** Kathleen A '01
Nixon James C '85
(216) 781-1212 **Noall** Nancy A '81
(440) 838-8800 **Nobil** Steven M '72
(216) 781-1212 **Noble** David D '68
(216) 586-3939 **Noble** Josephine S '04
(216) 451-8655 **Noble** Scott A '88
(216) 583-3688 **Nolan** William G '96
(216) 621-0150 **Nolfi** Gregory M '77
(216) 781-5470 **Norcross** Scott A '01
(216) 479-8500 **Norfus** Natalie E '04
(216) 631-7774 **Norman** Dennis O '69
(216) 241-5310 **Norman** Forrest A III '92
(216) 241-5310 **Norman** Forrest A Jr. '54
(216) 443-7800 **Norman** Matthew T '99
(216) 566-2415 **Normington** Dale A '69
(216) 696-1133 **Norton** Eric E '99
(216) 566-8200 **Norton** John P '91
(216) 398-4100 **Norton** Margaret M '83
(216) 566-0064 **Norton** Maura '91
(216) 621-7292 **Norton** Michele L '02
(216) 586-3939 **Norton** Patrick J '98
(216) 664-3513 **Norton** Susan L '00
(216) 621-8447 **Nosse** Elizabeth A '88
(216) 443-5842 **Novak** David M '76
(216) 515-1660 **Novak** Jenifer E '99
(216) 664-4303 **Novak** Katarina K '98
(216) 781-8700 **Novak Robenalt Pavlik & Scharf, LLP**
(216) 781-8700 **Novak** William J '73
(216) 241-6045 **Novinc** Raymond C '76
(216) 348-0800 **Novotney** George C Jr. '81
(216) 615-7319 **Nowak** Dale A '80
(216) 831-0042 **Nowak** Stephen M '04
(216) 771-4504 **Nuccio** Anthony J '56
(216) 687-7874 **Nudelman** Marc S '90
(216) 621-0150 **Nudelman** Sidney '63
(216) 222-3638 **Nukes** Elizabeth L '96
(216) 502-2000 **Nurczyk** Jean A '01
(216) 621-2300 **Nurenberg Plevin Heller & McCarthy LPA**
(216) 586-3939 **Nurgaliyeva** Aidana K '04
(216) 241-4100 **Nussle** Herbert L '94
Nwabara Chisara S '85
(216) 443-6350 **Nykulak** Nick A '03
(216) 431-5300 **Oakley** David G '97
(216) 431-4500 **Obed** Debra A '88
(216) 622-8200 **Oberdorff** Marc L '80
(216) 586-3939 **Oblander** R Jason '00
(216) 696-4421 **Obral** Mark J '84
(216) 443-6350 **O'Brien** Bridget M '01
(216) 241-3377 **O'Brien** Cheryl A '89
(440) 838-8800 **O'Brien** Daniel P '84
(216) 241-6602 **O'Brien** Gregory E '86
(216) 241-2838 **O'Brien** Gregory J '94
(216) 696-8700 **O'Brien** Mark S '00
(216) 472-1500 **O'Brien** Michael J '83
(216) 696-5400 **O'Brien** Terence K '88
(216) 696-1400 **O'Brien** Timothy F '69
(440) 248-7906 **Obringer** Timothy R '91
(216) 566-5686 **O'Bryan** Keely J '99
(216) 241-2838 **O'Bryan** Stephen M '69
(216) 830-2229 **Ochs** Robert C '89
(216) 252-2936 **Ockuly** Jane C '89
(216) 928-2200 **O'Connell** Matthew C '83
(216) 771-6633 **O'Connor** Bryan P '96
(216) 241-0033 **O'Connor** Donald J '60
(216) 687-1311 **O'Connor** James Jr. '94
(216) 736-7213 **O'Connor** Kevin T '77
(216) 514-7480 **Oddi** Joseph S '00
(216) 520-5552 **O'Dell** Kathy G '88
(216) 830-6830 **O'Donnell** Michael P '04
(216) 621-0200 **O'Donnell** Patricia J '82
(216) 283-4225 **O'Donnell** Thomas P '84
(216) 622-8200 **O'Donnell** Thomas R '96
(216) 443-7800 **Oebker** Jon W '94
(216) 523-4117 **O'Flaherty** Sharon L '82
(216) 623-0000 **Oh** James W '99
(216) 586-3939 **O'Hearn** Timothy J '84
(216) 621-0200 **Okada** Ronald S '85
(216) 621-0150 **O'Keefe** F Ronald '77
(216) 479-8500 **Okun** Jill G '86
(216) 241-5310 **Olarczuk-Smith** Holly M '01
(216) 664-3572 **O'Leary** Ronald J '97
(216) 621-0040 **Olender** Robert J '76
(216) 479-8500 **Oliss** Philip M '96
(216) 479-8500 **Oliver** James P '69
(216) 621-0150 **Oliver** Nancy A '99
(216) 621-0200 **Ollinger** W James II '68
(216) 479-8500 **O'Loughlin** Daniel J '51
(216) 523-4111 **O'Loughlin** David M '74
(440) 838-7600 **Olsavsky** Charles R Jr. '87
(216) 771-4055 **Olson** Nancy L '80
(216) 566-2587 **Olson** Robert K '96
(216) 685-1000 **Olsztyn** Christopher E '04
(216) 479-6100 **O'Malley** Anthony J '84
(216) 689-7638 **O'Malley** Catherine M '98
(216) 443-7800 **O'Malley** Erin R '00
(216) 241-7255 **O'Malley** Joseph P '92
(216) 241-6868 **O'Malley** Michael P '80
(216) 696-0606 **O'Malley** Patrick J '92
(216) 241-4100 **O'Malley** Patrick J '95
(216) 241-7255 **O'Malley** Thomas F '57
(216) 241-7255 **O'Malley** Thomas F Jr. '86
(216) 515-1300 **O'Malley** William D '83
(216) 341-7261 **O'Meara** James E III '66
(216) 479-8500 **Omerza** Raphael J '95
(440) 605-6660 **Ondak** Robert C Jr. '98
(216) 622-8200 **O'Neil** Colleen M '96
(216) 687-1311 **O'Neil** John P '97
(216) 861-4700 **O'Neil** Michael W '94
(216) 902-8803 **ONeill** Brian M '87
(216) 241-2022 **O'Neill** James P '79
(216) 241-2022 **O'Neill** Keelin G '82
(216) 687-5282 **O'Neill** Kevin F '85
(216) 566-1144 **O'Neill** Laura E '00
(216) 241-6602 **O'Neill** Mark P '52
(216) 348-5400 **O'Neill** William J '85
(216) 522-1200 **Oney** John S '77
(216) 479-6100 **Onusko** Thomas J '77
(216) 566-5256 **Opett** Edward J '75
(216) 348-5400 **Opincar** Scott N '94
(216) 787-3030 **Oppenheimer** David A '94
(216) 443-7800 **Oradini** Reno J Jr. '88
(216) 987-5214 **O'Rear-Lassen** Lisa E '85
(216) 896-0935 **Oreh** John P '85
(216) 664-2916 **Oren** Cortney R '03
(216) 696-8730 **Orlando** Gerardo C '90
(216) 696-7600 **Orlando** Lisa A '02
(216) 522-1200 **Orloff** Jeffrey K '89
(216) 267-1200 **Ornstein** Warren K '52
(216) 696-4441 **Oroz** Helen '02
(216) 429-5047 **Orr** Michelle F '91
(216) 771-5588 **Ortman** Bradley L '96
(216) 592-5000 **Osborne** Frank R '73
(216) 621-0150 **Oscar** Lawrence E '81
(216) 348-5400 **O'Shaughnessy** Lucy K '99
(216) 241-0011 **O'Shea** Michael J '87
(216) 621-0040 **O'Stafy** Stacey A '99
(216) 931-6000 **Ostrowski** Thomas W '93
(216) 696-7600 **Oswald** Suellen '90
(216) 592-5000 **O'Toole** Charles J '64
O'Toole Colleen M '91
(216) 443-6350 **O'Toole** Erin M '97
(216) 685-9940 **O'Toole** John K '67
(216) 241-7255 **O'Toole** Thomas E '78
(216) 771-2600 **Ott** Steven M '80
(216) 621-1113 **Otto** Donald L '64
(216) 664-4969 **Ousley** Bobette S '75
(216) 861-5582 **Overberger** Erik J '00
(216) 621-5045 **Oviatt** Richard A '67
(216) 241-2838 **Owen** Robert B '00
(216) 586-3939 **Owendoff** Michael S '96
(216) 621-0150 **Owendoff** Stephen P '69
(216) 696-3311 **Owens** Mark E '97
(216) 592-5000 **Owens** Susan E '04
(216) 574-8690 **Pace** Gerald J '02
(216) 696-4700 **Pace** Stanley Dan '75
(216) 622-3600 **Paffilas** Steven J '86
(216) 685-9940 **Pagano** Joseph V '01
(216) 685-9940 **Pagano Wilson Thomarios & Gillissie**
(216) 382-0444 **Paghis** Stacy D '91
(216) 241-8333 **Paglia** Michael A '99
(216) 687-1900 **Painter** Kevin R '94
(216) 241-2606 **Palda** George W '76
(216) 621-1312 **Palik** Evan J '85
Palinkas Laura T '88
(216) 771-3777 **Palkovitz** Herbert '69
(216) 383-6836 **Pallam** John J '65
(216) 928-1211 **Palm** Edward O '98
(216) 241-7000 **Palmer** Brian W '92
(216) 241-6602 **Palmer** Jeffrey G '99
(216) 566-5500 **Palmer** Stacey A '04
(216) 622-8200 **Palmer** Todd F '90
(216) 696-1400 **Palmieri** Anthony G Jr. '75
(216) 696-0990 **Palnik** Matthew A '97
(216) 623-1123 **Palombo** Antonio N '95
(216) 443-8800 **Palos** Diane M '84
(216) 696-9555 **Paluf** Timothy G '78
(216) 592-5000 **Palumbo** John P '70
(216) 241-5310 **Pangrace** Martin J '01
Paolano Mary J '74
(216) 479-8500 **Papajcik** Dale E '86
(216) 621-8600 **Papandreas** John G '54
(216) 621-0200 **Papp** Edward D '97
(216) 241-5310 **Pappalardo** Joseph W '80
(216) 621-0200 **Paravano** Jeffrey H '91
(216) 443-6350 **Parchem** David F '80
(216) 520-5600 **Paredes** Marie-Joy L '01
(216) 621-2300 **Paris** David M '78
(216) 575-7500 **Paris** E T '87
(216) 575-7500 **Paris** John T '85
(216) 664-4955 **Paris** Michelle L '84
(216) 687-1902 **Paris** Scott W '03
(216) 575-7500 **Paris** Thomas '53
(216) 586-3939 **Paris** Zachary T '73
(216) 443-8618 **Park** Eliza J '02
(216) 687-1311 **Parker** Alan B '88
(216) 928-7700 **Parker** Anthony T '97
(216) 621-5300 **Parker** Christopher L '91
(216) 479-8500 **Parker** Elton L '99
(216) 635-1705 **Parker** Jennifer E '97
(216) 586-3939 **Parker** Johanna Fabrizio '99
(216) 621-0200 **Parker** John D '83
(216) 881-0900 **Parker** John P '89
(216) 831-0042 **Parkins** Matthew E '00
(216) 479-6100 **Parobek** Drew T '84
(216) 586-3939 **Parsons** Theodore C '98
(216) 621-4244 **Partlow** Michael A '86
Pasalis Thano G '71
(216) 664-2692 **Paspek** Andrea M '89
(216) 696-0040 **Passalacqua** Edele '90
(216) 621-7905 **Passov** Robert S '70
(216) 737-5000 **Pasternak** Michael B '92
(216) 348-1100 **Patel** Ami J '04
(216) 658-3999 **Patel** Ketan K '95
(216) 261-3500 **Patel** Nirav A '03
(216) 586-3939 **Patel** Vipul B '03
(216) 696-9330 **Patno** Christian R '90
(216) 523-1500 **Patrick** Bradford J '99
(216) 687-1311 **Patrick** John '93
(216) 228-9400 **Patsouras** Peter L '75
(216) 241-6602 **Patterson** Jill S '98
(216) 592-5000 **Patterson** John P '03
(440) 746-1177 **Patti** Rose A '91
(216) 231-9963 **Patton** Charles L Jr. '83
(216) 523-1500 **Patton** Edward O '89
(440) 734-9494 **Patton** Richard F '54
(216) 696-7600 **Patton** Shannon K '98
(216) 241-7740 **Pauken** Margaret M '90
(216) 621-0200 **Pauken** Patrick J '78
(216) 928-0600 **Paul** Aparesh '03
(216) 621-5300 **Paul** Douglas J '74
(216) 797-1796 **Paulett** Harold K '82
(216) 781-8700 **Pavlik** Thomas C '66
(216) 623-0000 **Pavlovic** Nevenka '00
(216) 357-7182 **Pawlik** James D '90
(216) 736-8907 **Paxton** Jeffrey C '90
(216) 664-2868 **Payne** Jerome A Jr. '97
(216) 642-3342 **Peacock** Bruce E '88
(216) 479-8500 **Pearlman** Samuel S '67
(216) 579-1700 **Pearne & Gordon LLP**
(216) 622-3600 **Pearson** Benita Y '95
(216) 623-1155 **Pearson** Shawn R '90
(216) 621-8484 **Peca** John A Jr. '77
(216) 348-2800 **Pecchio** Jennifer M '99

(216) 685-1104 **Pecenka Cullen** Danielle L '98
(216) 348-3840 **Pedace** Theresa A '84
(216) 861-6000 **Peebles** David C '92
(216) 443-7800 **Peebles** Tracy M '98
(216) 479-8500 **Peer** Christina Henagen '99
(216) 621-0150 **Peer** Christopher W '03
(216) 622-8835 **Pejic** Nenad '96
(216) 443-8856 **Pellegrin** Joan K '80
(216) 621-0200 **Pelliccioni** Christopher D '03
(216) 622-3600 **Penhallurick** Kent W '76
(216) 222-2189 **Penko** Joseph C '87
(216) 586-3939 **Penrod** Stephen R '00
(216) 983-1051 **Penttila** Jane E '92
(216) 737-5000 **Pentz** Joel R '99
(216) 621-3012 **Penvose** Bryan L '01
(216) 479-8500 **Peppard** Sean T '01
(216) 520-0088 **Pepple & Waggoner Ltd**
(216) 520-0088 **Pepple** William C '82
(216) 621-0200 **Perdion** Jason P '98
(216) 664-2801 **Perez** Victor R '01
(216) 566-2543 **Perisutti** Stephen J '88
(216) 664-4982 **Perk** Ralph J Jr. '83
(216) 781-6550 **Perl** Warren R '78
(216) 621-6501 **Perlmuter** Jeffrey A '75
(216) 696-4009 **Perlmutter** Joel A '87
(216) 222-8057 **Perrette** John E '76
(216) 928-2200 **Perrico** Daniel E '99
(216) 884-4436 **Perrin** Ronald J '54
(216) 479-8500 **Perris** Terrence G '72
Perrucci Christopher R '85
(216) 348-5400 **Perry** Andrew S '00
(216) 875-2767 **Perry** Bret C '01
(216) 472-3300 **Perry** Dominic V '80
(216) 687-1900 **Perry** Karla L '93
(216) 241-5310 **Persia** Stephen T '04
(216) 689-5159 **Persing** Brenda L '98
(216) 344-7908 **Pesuit** Jo Ann Durk '95
(216) 579-9782 **Peters** Deborah L '94
(216) 664-4331 **Peters** George E IV '93
(440) 838-7600 **Peters** Jeffrey Tim '99
(216) 263-6200 **Peters** Melissa L '00
(216) 642-0323 **Peters** Scott C '92
(216) 696-3232 **Petersen** Susan E '98
(216) 771-1900 **Peterson** Michael H '70
(216) 664-2807 **Peterson** Natalie L '97
(216) 265-2570 **Peterson** Robert J '82
(216) 931-6000 **Peto** John G '78
(216) 621-8484 **Petralia** Shelly R '04
(216) 621-0200 **Petras** Stephen J Jr. '79
(216) 928-2200 **Petrello** Colleen H '89
(216) 479-8500 **Petrey** Katherine G '74
(216) 781-3600 **Petroff** Dimitre James '89
(216) 696-5222 **Petronelli** Jack L '80
(216) 381-3400 **Petronzio** Anna M '93
(216) 381-3400 **Petronzio Schneier Co,LPA**
(216) 241-5310 **Petrov** Alan M '74
(216) 622-8200 **Petrov** Daniel P '01
(216) 689-3887 **Petrulis** Richard D '77
(216) 621-0200 **Petrulis** Robert C '88
(216) 623-0900 **Petruzzi** Anthony R '98
(216) 523-4105 **Petry** Samuel R II '67
(216) 664-6900 **Petticord** Daniel F '92
(216) 781-7777 **Pettinelli** Joan E '90
(216) 348-0900 **Peyton** Jennifer I '98
(216) 621-0112 **Pfaff** Robert E '86
(216) 586-3939 **Pfleiderer** Shane T '03
(440) 838-7600 **Philipp** Jonathan W '89
(216) 523-1500 **Phillips** Amy L '98
(216) 523-1286 **Phillips** David G '90
(216) 622-8200 **Phillips** Gregory J '04
(216) 687-8100 **Phillips** James E '81
(216) 363-4500 **Phillips** Mark A '90
(216) 622-8200 **Phillips** Michael D '77
(216) 939-3000 **Phillips** Paul R '89
(216) 781-3600 **Phillips** Robert M '71
(216) 522-7451 **Phillips** Ronald L '98
(216) 861-5582 **Phillips** Sue Ellen '85
(216) 622-8200 **Phillips** William M '83
(216) 664-4989 **Pianka** Raymond Lee '78
(216) 621-0200 **Piatak** Thomas J '89
(216) 696-6993 **Piazza** Anthony M '77
(440) 446-1100 **Pienta** Renee S '01
(216) 621-0200 **Pierce** Raymond C '89
(216) 479-8500 **Pierpont** Christine Murphy '91
(216) 898-2350 **Pietch** Richard S '80
(216) 622-8200 **Pietrafese** Brent M '03
(216) 515-1660 **Pietrzen** Julie L '04
(216) 377-2604 **Pietz** Lynne P '91
(216) 621-7860 **Pigott** Stephen E '80
(216) 241-5310 **Pike** Michael J '01
(216) 579-4114 **Pilat** George V '87
(216) 579-1602 **Pilawa** Dennis M '78
(216) 241-6700 **Pinchak** George L Jr. '91
(216) 348-5400 **Pine Wood** Jane '88
(216) 696-8730 **Pingor** James J '99
(216) 622-3600 **Pinjuh** Joseph M '99
(216) 566-9908 **Pinjuh** Lori A '99
(216) 861-4416 **Pinkney** Betty K '77
(216) 696-8700 **Pinney** Jon J '00
(216) 696-2900 **Pinto** Libert '80
(216) 896-3000 **Piraino** Thomas A Jr. '74
(216) 241-8300 **Piscitelli** Frank E Jr. '93
(216) 416-3268 **Pitcock** Charles L '67
(216) 291-1005 **Pittman** Darryl E '73
(216) 566-5500 **Pittman** Lori A '04
(216) 621-2234 **Pitzer** Gary J '99
(216) 586-3939 **Pivonka** Robert C II '96
(216) 522-1555 **Pla** Jorge L '00
(216) 222-2112 **Plant** Thomas A '74
(216) 696-3525 **Platfoot Lacey** Denise L '01
(216) 696-3030 **Platko** Jeffrey J '97
(216) 621-1113 **Platt** Jonathan A '97
(216) 621-8348 **Platten** Paige H '04
(216) 881-1950 **Plavac** George N '54
(216) 586-3939 **Plesec** William T '71
Plevin Leon M '57
(216) 623-0150 **Plewacki** Richard A '80
(216) 696-4644 **Plotkin** Patricia H '77
(216) 861-7101 **Podboy** Alvin M Jr. '72
(216) 687-4449 **Pofok** Teresa R '94
(216) 586-7300 **Pogue** Richard W '57
(216) 443-8820 **Pokorny** Frank J '73
(216) 360-7200 **Poland** Mark A '00
(216) 928-2200 **Poling** Brant E '94
(216) 621-1530 **Polinko** John A '01
(216) 443-8979 **Polito** John A '73
(216) 875-2767 **Polito** John S '77
Polito LuAnn A '91
(216) 687-1311 **Polk** Shannon J '00
(216) 289-8304 **Polke** Dennis J '81
(216) 586-3939 **Pollack** Joseph D '84
(216) 931-6000 **Pollack** Lawrence D '89
(216) 514-1100 **Pollack** Matthew I '03
(216) 875-8343 **Pollard** Karen R '97
(216) 589-1354 **Pollina** Daniel T '94
(216) 621-0150 **Pollis** Andrew S '90
(216) 861-6160 **Pollock** Candace M '87
(216) 348-5400 **Pollock** Robert Jeffrey '76
(216) 471-3420 **Pollock** Ross H '88
(216) 861-4700 **Polly** Steven C '99
(216) 696-5959 **Pomerantz** David I '85
(216) 443-9000 **Pompeani** Fred J '82
(216) 739-5001 **Pona** Charles G '87
(216) 522-3380 **Poole** Donza M '87
(216) 696-5444 **Poole** Marcus L '78
(216) 621-0200 **Poole** Patricia A '91
(216) 689-5105 **Poore** Gregory R '72
(216) 291-7680 **Pope** Paul T '88
(216) 664-4918 **Pope** Ruben E III '78
(216) 896-2504 **Pophal** Joseph J '93
(440) 603-7525 **Popovich** Elizabeth '97
(216) 443-8635 **Popovich** Gregory M '89
(216) 928-2200 **Popson** James M '00
(216) 687-1900 **Porath** Ann M '82
(216) 566-1600 **Porcaro** James G '99
(216) 622-8200 **Port** Cynthia Krips '02
(216) 621-0150 **Port** Robert B '04
(216) 586-3939 **Porter** David P '81
(216) 522-7425 **Porter** Elliott V '76
(440) 838-8883 **Porter** Gerald M '63
(216) 739-5003 **Porter** John B C '02
(216) 227-2727 **Porter** Leah B '01
(216) 348-5400 **Porter** Mark E '00
(216) 696-7600 **Porter** Richard D '02
(216) 566-9700 **Porter** Wayne D Jr. '77
(216) 443-9000 **Porter Wright Morris & Arthur LLP**
(216) 241-2400 **Porterfield** Michael C '76
(216) 621-0200 **Posner** David A '89
(216) 696-2118 **Post** Rexford W '83
(216) 736-7218 **Posteraro** David R '81
(216) 771-8400 **Potash** Lester S '75
(440) 446-1100 **Potter** Steven B '81
(216) 751-9131 **Pottinger** Albert A Jr. '60
(216) 348-0800 **Potts** Timothy J '67
(216) 479-2500 **Poulos** Maria A '95
(216) 241-2838 **Poulos** Peter M '90
(216) 621-0150 **Powar** Lee D '63
(216) 696-1422 **Powell** Eric C '01
(216) 443-7223 **Powell** Noelle A '03
(216) 664-4800 **Powell** Verlinda L '01
(216) 781-3456 **Powers** Dale D '60
(216) 928-7700 **Powers** John A '01
(216) 514-1180 **Powers** Laurence J '87
(216) 566-7100 **Powers** Martin T '91
(216) 241-4244 **Pozzuto** Bridgette D '94
(216) 621-0150 **Prasse** Richard T '81
(216) 623-0000 **Prehn** Diana J '02
(216) 566-2370 **Prekop** Joseph E '83
(216) 267-1200 **Presti** Geralyn M '89
(216) 479-6100 **Prewitt** Jocelyn N '03
(216) 696-3311 **Pribisko** Patricia W '79
(216) 687-1900 **Price** Andrea K '83
(216) 830-6830 **Price** Charles D '95
(216) 861-6000 **Price** Donald C '58
(216) 431-4500 **Price** James M Jr. '01
(216) 830-6830 **Price** Jessica E '97
(216) 685-9710 **Price** John T '73
(216) 363-4500 **Price** Julie M '99
(216) 522-6104 **Priest** Charlie W Jr. '96
(216) 622-3600 **Primes** Marlon A '90
(216) 363-4500 **Primrose** Michael A '89
(216) 531-4116 **Prince** John J '55
(216) 649-0399 **Prince** Troy S '04
(216) 642-3342 **Privitera** Angela M '98
(440) 248-7906 **Proctor** Edward A '98
(216) 265-6000 **Prugh** Leigh S '00
(216) 696-8730 **Prulhiere** Jeffrey N '84
(216) 928-3474 **Prusinski** Cathy C '03
(216) 642-3342 **Pryatel** Steven E '86
(216) 586-3939 **Przybysz** Christine M '04
(216) 363-4500 **Psaropoulos** Robert C '96
(216) 928-3082 **P'Simer** Irina '04
(216) 363-1400 **Psota** Paul P '89
(216) 621-0200 **Ptaszek** Edward G Jr. '78
(216) 522-3818 **Pubal** Daniel J '03
(216) 486-6500 **Puckett** Kathryn '77
(216) 736-8907 **Pudner** F Joseph '01
(216) 586-3939 **Pugh** Charles W '04
(216) 479-5085 **Pullen** Cassandra '00
(216) 479-6100 **Purcell** Mary Eileen '94
(216) 781-1212 **Purtiman** Teresa E '01
(216) 586-3939 **Pustulka** Kimberly J '00
(216) 443-7223 **Puzin** Gary W '75
(216) 696-6122 **Pyle** John S '74
(216) 875-2767 **Quallich** Patrick J '99
Quartell Robert J '98
(216) 443-9000 **Quathamer** Nicole J '99
(216) 664-6900 **Quick** Harry T '65
(216) 523-1500 **Quinlan** Michael P '96
(216) 696-3622 **Quintrell** Thomas A '48
(216) 589-8399 **Quirk** Jamie Joy '93
(216) 696-1422 **Rabb** Richard A '90
(216) 771-8084 **Rabin** Julie E '81
(216) 771-8084 **Rabin** Mary Ann '78
(216) 592-5000 **Racey** Susan L '89
(216) 586-3939 **Radefeld** Mark B '03
(216) 737-5000 **Radel** Victor D '02
(216) 621-6570 **Rademaker** Dennis A '77
(216) 621-6570 **Rademaker Matty McClelland & Greve**
(216) 222-2965 **Radonjich** Rajko '86
(216) 687-3558 **Radzyminski** Sharon G '03
(216) 443-4010 **Rae** Michael T '84
(216) 443-7800 **Rafalski** Lawrence '80
(216) 685-1360 **Rahija** Michelle A '92
(216) 515-1660 **Rains** Merritt Neal '68
(216) 592-5000 **Raker** Keith H '92
(216) 931-6000 **Ramm** Brian N '87
(216) 623-7300 **Ramsey** Alison D '04
(216) 696-1500 **Ramsey** Wendle Scott '99
(440) 684-1600 **Ranallo** Robert A '80
(216) 522-8188 **Randazzo** Thomas M '88
(216) 241-6700 **Raney** Linn J '68
(216) 575-7660 **Ranke** Carolyn K '89
(216) 787-3030 **Ranke** Daniel R '90
(216) 566-9700 **Rankin** Carl A '62
(216) 566-9700 **Rankin Hill Porter & Clark,LLP**
(216) 696-4200 **Ranney** Phillip Allyn '61
(216) 589-3932 **Rapacz** Walter S '95
(216) 696-0600 **Rapoport** Alan J '75
(216) 696-0600 **Rapoport Spitz Friedland & Courtney**
(216) 931-6000 **Rapp** Adrienne L '04
(216) 622-8200 **Rapp** Robert N '72
(216) 685-1060 **Rasbach Yurechko** Amanda '00
(216) 363-4500 **Raske** Anna K '96
(440) 248-7906 **Raskin** Todd M '80
(216) 696-9100 **Rasmussen** Jennifer A '00
(216) 566-5500 **Rassi** Christopher M '03
(216) 443-8872 **Rath** Janet M '91
(216) 623-0000 **Rathbone** Joel H '79
(216) 623-0000 **Rathbone** Kimberly L '01
(216) 479-8500 **Rathke** Sarah K '01
(216) 479-6100 **Ratliff** Elizabeth A '02
(216) 575-3105 **Rauch** Je'anne M '98
(216) 443-9000 **Rauf** Natalie H '01
(216) 263-6200 **Rauser** Victor P '93
(216) 736-7221 **Rauss** Alan M '72
(216) 363-1400 **Rauzi** Harold R '89
(216) 781-2600 **Ravas** Sara S '03
(216) 586-3939 **Rawlin** Dustin B '00
(216) 579-1602 **Rawlin** Ronald V '72
(216) 579-1602 **Rawlins Gravens & Franey Co,LPA**
(216) 586-3939 **Rawson** Rachel L '95
(216) 586-3939 **Rawson** Robert H Jr. '71
(216) 586-3939 **Ray** Brian E '01
Ray Jeremy J '00
(216) 861-4533 **Ray Robinson Carle & Davies PLL**
(216) 664-4348 **Rea** Raymond '97
(216) 566-5778 **Read** Deborah Z '87
(216) 479-6100 **Read** John Winship '85
(216) 931-6000 **Reader** Harold H III '74
(216) 241-1000 **Ready** John J '88
(216) 687-1311 **Reagan** John J '96
(216) 443-7800 **Reali** Colleen A '00
(216) 566-5500 **Reblin** Kelly L '97
(216) 348-5400 **Rechner** Matthew R '01
(216) 522-3715 **Recko** Nancy '78
(216) 781-5470 **Redeker** John E '74
(216) 621-5300 **Reder** Henry I '79
(216) 522-4970 **Redmond** Brenda '96
(216) 566-5820 **Redmond** Hope E '01
(216) 443-8581 **Redmond** Ian M '02
(216) 621-0200 **Reece** Lora M '02
(216) 566-8200 **Reed** David T '74
(216) 928-2200 **Reed** James E '01
(216) 522-0800 **Reed Mazanec & Wheeler,Ltd**
(216) 522-0800 **Reed** Robert C Jr. '75
(216) 231-7936 **Reed** Tyrone E '76
(216) 363-6033 **Reeder** Harold C Jr. '82
(216) 737-0000 **Reese** Olan R '84
(216) 689-3507 **Reese** Veronica T '84
(216) 953-2856 **Reeve** Mary E '82
(216) 771-5511 **Reeve & Watts**
(216) 621-2034 **Regas** Jennifer H '92
(216) 443-7800 **Regas** Tracy Allan '96
(216) 586-3939 **Rego** John A '88
(216) 696-6454 **Rehor** Dennis G '94
(216) 831-0042 **Reichard** Jenifere M '03
(216) 241-6930 **Reichek** Edward R '57
(216) 431-4500 **Reichenbach** Dorothy F '75
(216) 687-1311 **Reid** Christine S '93
(216) 443-9000 **Reid** Lisa A '88
(216) 861-3086 **Reid Marshall & Wargo**
(216) 787-3666 **Reid** Sandra B '77
(216) 861-3086 **Reid** Timothy T '71
(216) 781-5470 **Reidy** John J Jr. '57
(440) 838-8800 **Reidy** Michael J '78
(216) 781-5245 **Reiffer** Erin L '04
(216) 622-8200 **Reil** Mary M '82
(216) 368-4286 **Reilly** John J '89
(216) 687-0400 **Rein** Thomas A '89
(216) 522-5404 **Reinhart** Lulita '97
(216) 771-2533 **Reinker** Robb F '77
(216) 875-2767 **Reinker** Susan M '79
(216) 830-9000 **Reinshagen** Amy L '04
(216) 664-4918 **Reitzloff** Barbara A '86
(216) 479-8500 **Rekstis** W Jack III '72
(216) 687-1311 **Reminger & Reminger**
(216) 687-1311 **Reminger** Richard T '57
(216) 621-0150 **Remington** Royce R '88
(216) 834-0400 **Remmert** Danae K '03
(216) 696-6700 **Rendon** Carole O '99
(216) 371-7632 **Renkert** Richard C '50
(216) 621-1113 **Renner** John W '54
(216) 621-1113 **Renner Otto Boisselle & Sklar, LLP**
(216) 523-1313 **Rennillo** Irene A '83
(216) 696-3232 **Rennillo** Jennifer W '99
(216) 664-2670 **Renwald Marquit** Amy E '01
(216) 502-0350 **Repicky** Thomas G '79
(216) 586-3939 **Reppert** Richard L '74
(216) 241-6868 **Resnick** Elliott I '77
(216) 696-4994 **Ressler** George E '74
(216) 363-4500 **Reuscher** Christopher P '02
(216) 621-5980 **Rexford** Kenneth J '95
(216) 621-0200 **Reynolds** Melinda L '97
(216) 241-5310 **Rezie** Richard C '99
(216) 781-0383 **Reznick** Morris M '51
(216) 443-6350 **Rhodes** Tina Y '86
(216) 861-1100 **Rhyner** Cynthia J '96
(216) 664-3827 **Riccardi** Richard M '85
(216) 696-1433 **Rice** Clark D '80
(216) 664-4865 **Rice** Donald '97
(216) 241-5310 **Rice** Jay C '79
(216) 621-0150 **Rice** Sonja C '01
(216) 479-6100 **Rice** Weldon H '03
(216) 931-6000 **Rich** Jodi B '00
(216) 696-4441 **Rich** Jonathan A '93
(216) 696-4441 **Rich** Lawrence J '67
(216) 479-8500 **Richard** Renee Tramble '88
(216) 241-6602 **Richards** Daniel A '92
Richards Dorothy Regas '94
(216) 861-5000 **Richards** Joseph V Jr. '76
(216) 621-0200 **Richards** Timothy J '04
(216) 931-6000 **Richardson** Donald J '97
(216) 861-1234 **Richardson** Glen S '81
(216) 619-9002 **Richardson** Jeffrey S '93
(216) 931-6000 **Richardson** Nita Kay '94
(216) 592-5000 **Richardson** Scott A '96
(216) 696-5250 **Richelson** Murray '80
(216) 623-1990 **Richman** Brian H '69
(216) 472-1500 **Richman** Ellen J '90
(216) 556-0226 **Richman** Stephen D '86
(216) 881-0502 **Richmond** Toni M '03
(216) 241-5310 **Richthammer** Theresa A '97
(216) 586-3939 **Rickert** Jeanne M '80
(216) 241-0715 **Ricotta** John J '80
(440) 842-4080 **Riczo** John J Jr. '75
(216) 664-4807 **Ridenour** Marlene J '94
(216) 696-0800 **Rider** William H Jr. '74
(216) 685-5000 **Riebe** Radd L '78
(216) 781-1212 **Riehl** Charles T '71
(216) 696-4240 **Riek** F Benjamin III '78
(216) 839-1111 **Rieke** Michael K '00
(216) 621-5300 **Riemenschneider** Dirk E '91
(216) 696-0990 **Riemer** Donald G '84
(216) 241-6602 **Riester** Jennifer A '99
(216) 861-2222 **Rieth & Antonelli**
(216) 696-4200 **Rieth** Janice Edgehouse '78
(216) 861-2222 **Rieth** Richard C '79
(216) 464-8300 **Rieth** Robert G '84
(216) 861-6833 **Riffe** George B '01
(440) 838-8883 **Rifici** Anthony M '97
(216) 357-7000 **Riga** Lori B '96
(216) 241-6602 **Riley** Brian P '00
(216) 348-5400 **Riley** Michael G '87
(216) 348-5400 **Riley** Shawn M '86
(216) 621-2771 **Riley** Timothy J '89
(216) 515-1040 **Rinaldi** Anthony '02
(216) 362-6081 **Rini** Denise N '03
(216) 687-1910 **Rini** Gusty A '71
(216) 787-3030 **Rini** Mary Ann '79
(216) 360-7200 **Rini** William T '75
(216) 363-0982 **Rinicella** Randy D '86
(216) 622-8200 **Rink** Robert P '86
(216) 523-1500 **Rinker** Bruce G '77
(216) 687-1311 **Rinkes** Jennifer K '04
(216) 443-6350 **Riordan** Timothy P '87
(216) 522-7800 **Rippy** Derrick V '90
(216) 241-6602 **Rispo** Ronald A '67
(216) 241-6602 **Ristau** Timothy P '66
(216) 222-8016 **Ritchey** John J '73
(216) 472-4000 **Ritchie** Alan S '94
(216) 771-5588 **Ritter** Marin K '96
(216) 586-3939 **Ritts** Geoffrey J '93
(216) 432-3384 **Ritz** Steven W '88
(216) 696-3252 **Ritzenberg** Marvin '52
(216) 241-8333 **Ritzler Coughlin & Swansinger, Ltd**
(216) 241-8333 **Ritzler** Joseph G '91
(440) 446-1100 **Rivchun** Ryan L '02
(216) 586-3939 **Rivera** Robert F '03
(216) 696-3311 **Rivitz** Richard S '67
(216) 566-5885 **Roach** Jennifer S '01
(216) 696-4009 **Roach** Lawrence J '01
(216) 566-5755 **Robenalt** James D '81
(216) 781-8700 **Robenalt** Thomas D '91
(216) 443-7223 **Roberson** Christopher W '92
(216) 431-5300 **Roberts** David D '92
(216) 698-2820 **Roberts** Dennis L '99
(440) 746-0911 **Roberts** Glenna M '87
(216) 781-6166 **Roberts** Kevin T '86
(216) 931-6000 **Roberts** Megan K '02
(216) 361-2500 **Roberts** Tommy Jr. '84
(216) 586-3939 **Roberts-Mamone** Lisa A '88
(216) 881-6600 **Robertson** Darnella T '96
(216) 241-7255 **Robertson** Deanna '91
(216) 687-9264 **Robertson** Heidi Gorovitz '97
(216) 348-5400 **Robertson** Jean R '98
(216) 621-0200 **Robertson** Kevin G '84
(216) 581-8200 **Robey** Gregory S '91
(216) 687-1976 **Robie** Julie E '04
(216) 696-3510 **Robinette** Burl C '87
(216) 520-5518 **Robinson** Craig A '92
(216) 688-3737 **Robinson** Kenneth F '86
(216) 781-3600 **Robinson** Loreen M '88
(216) 479-6100 **Robinson** Marquettes D '01
(216) 621-3839 **Robinson** Ronald '85
(216) 696-0808 **Robinson** Scott J '01
Roche Michael J '02
(216) 348-1700 **Roche** Patrick F '76
(216) 348-1700 **Roche** Patrick M '99
(216) 861-5582 **Roche** Patrick R '78
(216) 671-0599 **Roche** Peter M '03
(216) 443-8195 **Roche** Thomas J '84
(216) 443-6350 **Rodak** Andrew N '83
(216) 696-1122 **Rode** Michael K '80
(216) 621-1530 **Rodgers** Jeffrey A '96
(216) 479-8500 **Rodgers** Joseph P '98
(216) 861-6191 **Rodgers** Walter A '70
(216) 515-1660 **Rodio** Mark L '95
(216) 664-4802 **Rodriguez** Angela L '01
(216) 443-7800 **Rodriguez** Oscar E '01
(216) 621-0040 **Roessler** Kirk W '93
(216) 623-0150 **Roetzel & Andress,LPA**
(216) 622-8200 **Rogers** Karla M '97
(216) 267-7100 **Rogers** Niles P '86
(216) 622-8410 **Rogge** Gretchen H '97
(216) 443-8578 **Rogo** Patricia A '79
(216) 523-4515 **Rogozinski** Lynn R '95
(216) 263-6200 **Rohr** Nicole L '04
(216) 615-9100 **Rohrs** Jeffrey K '94
(216) 622-3673 **Rokakis** Alexander A '82
(216) 443-7400 **Rokakis** James '84
(216) 514-1100 **Rolf** Carol '76
(216) 514-1100 **Rolf & Goffman Co,LPA**
(216) 622-8200 **Rolitsky** Sandra G '82
(216) 348-1700 **Roller** Jan L '83
(216) 781-1700 **Roloff** David E '78
(216) 241-0715 **Romaine** Daniel A '96

(216) 831-0042 **Roman** Barbara Sue K '77
(216) 479-8500 **Romancher** Catherine Ziroli '03
(216) 592-5000 **Romano** Matthew '03
(216) 522-4914 **Romanowski** Esther B '79
(216) 931-6000 **Rome** Peter A '84
(216) 641-2400 **Romer** James D '98
(216) 515-1660 **Roof** Brian E '99
(216) 696-3030 **Rooney** Dean M '83
(216) 763-1004 **Rooney** Erin K '01
(216) 623-0150 **Rooney** George W Jr. '74
(440) 838-8800 **Rooney** Thomas D '72
(216) 635-0636 **Roosa** James K '87
(216) 586-3939 **Rorimer** Louis '75
(216) 522-4914 **Roscoe** George D '81
(216) 241-6602 **Rose** Dana A '84
(216) 861-8737 **Rose** Daniel C '90
(216) 642-0323 **Rose** David A '01
(216) 621-0150 **Rose** Dennis R '87
(216) 241-7255 **Rose** Jeri-ellen '93
(216) 771-1777 **Rose** Joseph B III '71
(216) 443-7800 **Rose** Susan E '96
(216) 771-8420 **Rose** Timothy F '82
(216) 621-7227 **Roseman** James D '72
(216) 781-3055 **Rosen** Allard J '51
(216) 579-4114 **Rosen** Jonathan D '00
(216) 592-5000 **Rosenbaum** Jacob I '52
(216) 781-5245 **Rosenbaum** Jeremy A '85
(216) 586-3939 **Rosenberg** Martin Joseph '99
(216) 696-9300 **Rosenfield** Ronald L '70
(216) 662-1880 **Rosenthal** Barbara S '87
(216) 781-7956 **Rosenthal** James B '94
(216) 696-9936 **Rosenthal** Sandra J '88
(216) 589-9600 **Rosenthal** Scott S '98
(216) 696-1422 **Rosenzweig** David L '68
(216) 664-2788 **Rosman** Debra Dee '82
(216) 241-6602 **Rosman** Warren M '76
(216) 696-3311 **Rosner** Richard A '64
(216) 771-5588 **Rosner** William R '83
(216) 566-5861 **Rospert** Anthony J '03
(216) 447-1551 **Ross** Alan G '75
(216) 523-5405 **Ross** Alan J '75
(216) 447-1551 **Ross Brittain & Schonberg Co LPA**
(216) 348-1000 **Ross** Daryl B '93
(216) 687-1311 **Ross** David '76
(216) 861-1313 **Ross** Harold A '56
(216) 781-7777 **Ross** Richard G '83
(216) 622-8200 **Ross** Robert A '85
(216) 622-8200 **Ross** William L '82
(440) 684-0070 **Rossen** Howard M '64
(216) 522-5396 **Rossen** Joel M '73
(440) 684-0070 **Rossen** Marc D '94
(800) 888-8424 **Rossi** Assunta '89
(216) 231-5000 **Rossi** David J '88
(216) 931-6000 **Rossiter** Britt J '98
(216) 241-3658 **Rossman** Alan C '81
(216) 378-9905 **Rotatori** Arthur J '81
(216) 928-1010 **Rotatori Bender Gragel Stoper & Alexander Co LPA**
(216) 928-1010 **Rotatori** Robert J '62
(216) 623-9000 **Roth** Daniel M '72
Roth Henry A '66
(216) 622-8200 **Roth** Jennifer Lawless '02
(216) 241-5310 **Roth** Timothy P '94
(216) 685-1135 **Rothenberg** Larry R '78
(216) 394-5075 **Rothenbuecher** H Alan '89
(216) 831-3171 **Rothschild** Edmund W '58
(216) 241-5152 **Rotman** Dennis A '76
(216) 781-9090 **Roulston** Laurie L '82
(216) 522-4914 **Round** Edmund B '75
(216) 586-3939 **Roush** Jeffrey D '02
(216) 586-3939 **Routh** Ryan T '00
(216) 479-8500 **Rowan** David W '78
(216) 685-1033 **Rowan** Maria A '03
(216) 522-4856 **Rowan** Sonja C '91
(216) 861-3810 **Rowan** Stephen '83
(216) 622-3847 **Rowland** Ann C '76
(216) 348-1100 **Rowles** Kami D '99
(216) 696-3030 **Rownd** James H '93
(216) 781-2787 **Rowthorn** David L '76
(216) 381-2880 **Roy** Debra E '85
(216) 696-1422 **Royer** Charles P '86
(216) 771-4050 **Rua** Mary Jane '86
(216) 687-2310 **Ruben** Alan M '72
(216) 464-4060 **Ruben** Susan Grody '95
(216) 566-5815 **Rubin** Karen E '85
(216) 514-6400 **Rubin** Neil S '98
(216) 928-2200 **Rubin** Ryan K '04
(216) 931-6000 **Rubinstein** Richard E '64
(440) 239-1790 **Ruck** Theresa Nelson '00
(216) 574-8232 **Ruda** Lisa M '94
(216) 687-1900 **Ruden** Alexandria M '80
(216) 931-6000 **Rudnick** Elizabeth S '99
(216) 721-7700 **Rudy** Mark T '90
(216) 687-1999 **Ruf** Mark W '90
(216) 861-1940 **Ruggeri** Robert A '68
(216) 622-8200 **Ruiz** David A '02
(216) 685-1182 **Ruiz-Bueno** J Charles '90
(216) 443-7800 **Rukovena** George '72
(216) 696-1080 **Rumizen** Scott A '92
(216) 622-8200 **Rundelli** Raymond '85
(216) 621-0200 **Rupert** Aaron '02
(216) 363-1400 **Ruple** Jeffrey W '97
(216) 689-3937 **Ruppert** Rebecca S '93
(216) 621-3370 **Ruschel** Brian G '90
(216) 443-6022 **Russ** Christopher J '83
(216) 592-5000 **Russell** Carolyn C '01
(216) 252-1100 **Russell** James F '66
(216) 479-8500 **Russell** Shawn R '86
(216) 642-1425 **Russin** Rodion J '60
(216) 583-4538 **Russo** Andrea '99
(216) 623-0150 **Russo** Rachael L '99
(216) 621-0058 **Rutherford** Guy D '96
(216) 479-6100 **Rutigliano** Barbara A '83
(216) 739-5004 **Rutkowski** Robert W '91
(216) 381-3400 **Rutsky** Bruce S '83
(216) 642-1425 **Rutter** Robert P '79
(216) 586-3939 **Ruxin** Paul T '77
(216) 363-6048 **Ryan** Daniel J '73
(216) 931-6000 **Ryan** Kate E '97
(216) 664-4729 **Ryan** Michael J '96
(216) 363-1700 **Ryan** Terrance Lee '76
(216) 641-8265 **Rybka** Edward W '81
(216) 641-1509 **Rybka** Robert S '84
(440) 248-7906 **Ryder** Edward M Jr. '77
(216) 586-3939 **Rydzel** James A '72
(216) 241-5310 **Ryhal** James L Jr. '52
(216) 586-3939 **Ryland** Joshua M '99
(216) 687-1311 **Rymond** Richard J '82
(216) 586-3939 **Saada** John M Jr. '93
(216) 416-3251 **Sabatine** Jeffrey P '87
(216) 228-7200 **Saccany** John C '83
(216) 443-8866 **Sacco** Joel F '83
(216) 566-5761 **Saccogna** Patrick J '90
(216) 781-7095 **Sackett** Peter A '81
(216) 321-2249 **Sadd** George J '67
(216) 696-8730 **Sadlowski** Jeffrey R '90
(216) 787-3030 **Saferin** Stuart A '74
(216) 622-2700 **Saffold** Jeffrey P '96
(216) 622-2700 **Saffold & Johnson**
(216) 479-6100 **Saganich** John M '98
(216) 523-5405 **Saganich** Suzanne Kleinsmith '98
(216) 898-1800 **Saine** Christian D '97
(216) 861-3086 **St George** Jason M '01
(216) 443-5100 **St John** Janice L '95
(216) 621-2300 **St John** Kathleen J '82
St Onge Susan P '92
(216) 586-3939 **Saks** Jeffrey '99
(216) 291-7392 **Salada** Maurice R '82
(216) 781-5515 **Salamon** Jay H '80
(216) 348-5400 **Salata** Robert Christopher '01
(216) 241-1074 **Saleh** Abeer T '03
(216) 781-8700 **Salerno** Denise J '03
(216) 348-5400 **Salerno** Matthew A '99
(216) 566-5507 **Salisbury** David W '84
(216) 689-5736 **Salisbury** Elizabeth W '84
(216) 522-3240 **Sallee** Brian C '97
(216) 514-1100 **Salsbury** Scott E '87
(216) 696-1080 **Saltzer** Michael A '88
(216) 696-9290 **Saltzman** Barbara E '77
(216) 861-0360 **Saltzman** Judith C '98
(216) 529-9377 **Saltzman** Michael J '70
(216) 623-0150 **Salvatore** Albert N '82
(216) 781-7990 **Sammon** Albert C '85
(216) 781-7990 **Sammon & Bolmeyer Co, LPA**
(216) 781-8700 **Sammon** Colin P '03
(216) 622-3600 **Sammon** John D '86
(216) 443-7800 **Sammon** Thomas J '70
(216) 443-8587 **Samson** Shana A '00
(216) 453-3033 **Samuels** James A '76
(216) 479-8500 **Sanborn** Elizabeth M '81
(216) 431-4131 **Sanchez** Alexander M '93
(216) 515-1660 **Sanchez** Marc A '94
(216) 623-0150 **Sandacz** Beverly A '94
(216) 696-5297 **Sandel** Martin L '73
(216) 651-4422 **Sander** Richard W '75
(800) 600-1222 **Sandhu** Manbir S '02
(216) 781-2258 **Sanislo** Paul S '61
(216) 241-5310 **Sansalone** Monica A '95
(216) 861-4100 **Sanson** Michael A '74
(216) 621-4268 **Santa** Kevin J '86
(216) 241-0033 **Santoli** David M '88
(216) 671-6975 **Santon** Roger A '93
(216) 241-5310 **Santoro** Joseph J '97
(216) 443-6389 **Santosuosso** Cara L '98
(216) 592-5000 **Saponaro** Joseph M '99
(216) 621-1113 **Saralino** Mark D '90
(216) 348-1700 **Sardina** Jennifer '00
(216) 522-7438 **Sargent** John D '71
(216) 831-0042 **Sarkar** Neil S '97
(216) 931-6000 **Sarkar** Richik '98
(216) 574-4421 **Sarkisian** Susan A '82
(216) 623-0150 **Sarlson** Mark L '86
(216) 861-5070 **Sasala** Kathleen M '87
(216) 360-7200 **Sassano** James L '93
(216) 592-5000 **Sassé** Benjamin C '00
(216) 622-3600 **Sasse** Gregory C '76
(216) 479-8500 **Satola** James W '89
(216) 687-1311 **Satullo** Nick '85
(216) 586-3939 **Sauer** Joseph M '02
(216) 621-0200 **Sauer** McKinley H III '87
(216) 464-0008 **Sauvain** Timothy W '70
(216) 566-5721 **Savage** Jennifer A '90
(216) 479-8500 **Savage** Mark J '98
(216) 566-8200 **Savidge** Keith A '72
(216) 771-6597 **Savren** Joy B '82
(216) 241-6655 **Sawyer** Robert J '61
(216) 586-3939 **Sayler** Richard H '85
(216) 621-7227 **Sayre** John D '77
(216) 696-7600 **Scadden** Kathy J '03
(216) 216-2840 **Scalish** Rachel N '90
(216) 586-3939 **Scanlon** Stephen D '85
(216) 696-0022 **Scanlon** Thomas J '63
(216) 861-5582 **Scarbrough** James E '97
(216) 687-0290 **Scarcella** Nancy '91
(216) 621-1530 **Scarlato** Antonio J '01
(216) 363-4500 **Schabes** Alan E '81
(216) 781-1212 **Schaefer** Charles R '69
(216) 696-1422 **Schaefer** David A '74
(216) 822-3973 **Schafer** Cynthia C '86
(216) 664-6436 **Schaltenbrand** Rebecca K '95
(216) 781-8700 **Scharf** Scott H '90
(216) 252-7300 **Scharf** Stephen L '99
Scharff Marisa M '00
(216) 621-6101 **Scharville** James D '99
(216) 881-6600 **Schatz** William B '73
(216) 928-1503 **Schechter** Roy J '86
(216) 781-4994 **Schedlbauer** Kara M '03
(216) 441-5100 **Scheid** Katherine A '87
(216) 621-7227 **Scheiman** Becky M '00
(216) 696-4400 **Schellenberger** Anna Marie '91
(216) 739-5644 **Schenz** Beth A '01
(216) 623-0150 **Scherzer** Donald S '75
(216) 931-6000 **Scheufler** Alan W '83
(216) 861-5338 **Schiau** Daniel L '91
(216) 491-3850 **Schickler** Ronald S '91
(216) 687-1902 **Schieman** Nancy E '91
(216) 621-7743 **Schiff & Dickson, LLC**
(216) 621-7743 **Schiff** Marvin H '84
(216) 696-8700 **Schildhouse** Mark B '80
(216) 781-1212 **Schiller** John E '84
(216) 579-1700 **Schiller** Thomas P '60
(216) 583-3128 **Schindler** Michael D '03
(216) 265-0856 **Schiopota** Eugene '64
(216) 781-3434 **Schlachet** Jaye M '79
(216) 696-5222 **Schlachet** Mark '69
(216) 621-0200 **Schlegelmilch** Stephan J '00
(216) 579-1554 **Schleifer** Karin F '87
(216) 696-1433 **Schlesinger** Shawn W '98
(216) 696-1422 **Schloss** Richard A '02
(216) 566-8703 **Schloz** Jo A '85
(216) 283-2376 **Schmedlen** George W '93
(216) 781-3400 **Schmelzer Caterino & Helfgott**
(216) 781-3400 **Schmelzer** Thomas '77
(216) 378-9905 **Schmidley** Eugenia M '85
(216) 621-6752 **Schmidt** David G '71
(216) 523-1525 **Schmidt** Jesse M '04
(216) 619-5925 **Schmidt** Robert N '81
(216) 622-3758 **Schmitz** Joseph P '79
(216) 443-8615 **Schmitz** Michael F '95
(216) 696-5222 **Schmitz** William F '85
(216) 348-5400 **Schnee** Douglas B '94
(216) 241-4740 **Schneiberg** Jerald A '93
(216) 591-0727 **Schneider** Albert E III '69
(216) 671-9840 **Schneider** James J '56
(216) 621-1230 **Schneider** John J '01
(216) 258-0996 **Schneider** Joseph G '57
(216) 781-5515 **Schneider** Kent B '78
(216) 443-7800 **Schneider** Mark A '00
(216) 241-5310 **Schneider** Paul Kohl '92
(216) 696-4200 **Schneider Smeltz Ranney & LaFond PLL**
Schneiderman Karen R '84
(216) 381-3400 **Schneier** Jamie B '93
(216) 586-3939 **Schnopp** Stefan K '97
(216) 621-0200 **Schoenfield** Nichol M '96
(216) 241-2200 **Scholl** Mary J '90
(216) 621-0200 **Scholz** Karin M '03
(216) 447-1551 **Schonberg** Evelyn P '81
(216) 363-4500 **Schonberg** William E '79
(216) 621-5680 **Schonfeld** Jay M '70
(216) 696-7170 **Schooler** Scott H '84
(216) 589-9600 **Schoonover** John E '84
(216) 514-7480 **Schorr** Brian D '86
(216) 621-6501 **Schottenstein Zox & Dunn**
(216) 781-1212 **Schrader** Thomas C '68
(216) 621-7292 **Schreiber** Svetlana J '82
(216) 687-0900 **Schreibman** Eric M '97
(440) 838-8800 **Schreiner** David E '73
(440) 838-8800 **Schreiner** Melanie Webber '99
(216) 583-8340 **Schreiner** Thomas E '82
(216) 241-5310 **Schremp** Pamela S '98
(216) 623-0150 **Schriner** John J '99
Schroeder Michael A '91
(216) 771-1144 **Schroeder** Michael S '95
(216) 486-2100 **Schron** Jack H Jr. '75
(216) 621-0580 **Schulman** Howard A '78
(216) 621-0580 **Schulman** Jack M '67
(216) 621-0580 **Schulman Schulman & Meros, LPA**
(216) 622-8200 **Schultz** Lawrence N '79
(216) 520-5600 **Schultz** Richard F '91
(216) 241-6700 **Schultz** Stephen J '78
(216) 931-6000 **Schulz** Isaac '71
(216) 696-9696 **Schulz** James H Jr. '83
(216) 222-2536 **Schulz** Martin C '92
(216) 771-1760 **Schulz** William J '83
(216) 514-6400 **Schumacher** James T '90
(216) 241-5310 **Schumacher** Paul J Jr. '83
(216) 348-1100 **Schuster** Nancy C '68
(216) 348-1100 **Schuster & Simmons Co,LPA**
(216) 222-2984 **Schwab** Richard B '76
(216) 622-8200 **Schwartz** Bryan A '04
(216) 277-0283 **Schwartz** Craig H '95
(216) 664-4958 **Schwartz** Diane S '79
(216) 696-6700 **Schwartz Downey & Co, LPA**
(216) 363-4500 **Schwartz** H Jeffrey '80
(216) 696-6700 **Schwartz** Jennifer E '91
(216) 696-7600 **Schwartz** Kenneth D '99
(216) 360-0440 **Schwartz** Mark B '67
(216) 696-6700 **Schwartz** Niki Z '64
(216) 696-1422 **Schwartz** Robert Dov '97
(216) 787-3030 **Schwartz** Ying-yu Janice '00
(216) 623-0000 **Schwarz** Harold M III '04
(216) 566-1600 **Schwarzwald & McNair**
(216) 566-1600 **Schwarzwald** Melvin S '62
(216) 522-4058 **Schwegler** Mary B '80
(216) 761-7387 **Schweighoefer** David E '04
(216) 241-2880 **Schwieg** Frederic P '85
(216) 443-8579 **Schwotzer** Tracy R '02
(440) 248-7906 **Scialdone** Frank H '02
(216) 321-3562 **Scola** Ralph J '69
(216) 781-2600 **Scott** Gregory S '96
(216) 623-0150 **Scott** James C '91
(216) 687-1311 **Scott** John R '86
(216) 664-3727 **Scott** Joseph F '85
(216) 781-0083 **Scott** Michael J '78
(216) 696-3232 **Scott** Stuart E '95
(216) 664-4828 **Scott** W Mona '03
(216) 623-0150 **Screen** Donald P '90
(216) 443-9000 **Screen** Patricia A '85
(216) 781-5661 **Scrivens** Scott L '81
(216) 621-2110 **Scully** William F Jr. '75
(216) 687-1311 **Seacrist** Susan M '92
(216) 696-1080 **Seaman** Dennis M '67
(216) 579-1535 **Sears** Ronald A '75
(216) 621-0150 **Seasly** Steven E '99
(216) 875-2767 **Sebaugh** Beth A '80
(216) 586-3939 **Sebold** Edward J '94
(216) 444-3126 **Secrist** Robert V Jr. '72
(216) 642-0323 **Seed** David H '96
(216) 566-8200 **Seeley** Glenn J '55
(216) 566-8200 **Seeley** Gregory D '72
(216) 566-8200 **Seeley** Matthew K '97
(216) 566-8200 **Seeley Savidge & Ebert Co LPA**
(216) 696-7600 **Seeley** Stephanie L '01
(216) 583-2791 **Seeley** William B '04
(216) 416-3281 **Seewald** Amanda M '95
(216) 781-8288 **Seewald** Jerome Gary '71
(216) 621-0200 **Seger** Paula Friedman '79
(216) 621-0200 **Seger** Thomas M '72
(216) 696-3311 **Segulin** Mary R '04
(216) 696-4700 **Seibert** Henry E IV '68
(216) 822-3504 **Seibert** Mark E '97
(216) 696-1422 **Seich** John S '82
(216) 222-3584 **Seifert** Jason L '99
(216) 431-4500 **Seifert** Patricia L '99
(216) 781-0150 **Seitz** Brian J '03
(216) 514-9999 **Seitz** Charles R '92
(216) 931-6000 **Seleman** Fred N '97
(440) 248-7906 **Selker** Eugene I '53
(216) 696-9100 **Selzer** Lynn K '92
Seman Lawrence A '90
(216) 431-4500 **Semanco** Tammy L '00
(216) 344-3838 **Seminatore** Kenneth F '71
(216) 623-0880 **Semmelroth** Cindy A '01
(216) 661-6468 **Senich** Kevin J '84
(216) 621-7860 **Senra** Matthew E '00
(216) 479-8500 **Senturia** Harris A '93
(216) 896-2430 **Serbin** Daniel S '89
(216) 579-1700 **Serbinowski** Paul A '95
(216) 586-3939 **Serevitch** Katherine M '04
(216) 621-0200 **Sergent** Douglas R '99
(216) 444-8657 **Serkey** Janet M '94
(216) 696-8730 **Serra** Wayne M '02
(216) 622-3873 **Serrano** Blas E Jr. '76
(216) 696-2150 **Serrat** Jaime P '83
(216) 621-5300 **Sesek** Deborah '76
(216) 931-6000 **Sesnowitz** Douglas K '94
Sestak James Christopher '92
(216) 523-4909 **Severs** Deborah R '81
(216) 621-0500 **Sexton** William J '58
(216) 696-7600 **Seymour** Carolyn K '85
(216) 696-7600 **Sferra** Stephen J '86
(216) 566-2642 **Sgambellone** James J '83
(216) 696-1545 **Shafran** John '60
(216) 781-5245 **Shafron** Steven D '87
(216) 241-6055 **Shagrin** Michael B '64
(216) 621-2234 **Shaheen** Matthew M '97
(216) 861-5217 **Shakarian** Melanie A '03
(216) 586-7799 **Shakelton** Paula G '04
(216) 391-7111 **Shamberg** Stefen K '00
(216) 621-0200 **Shamsi** Azfar Bin '03
(216) 357-5123 **Shanabruch** Michael R '94
(216) 687-7492 **Shanahan** Brien W '79
(216) 363-1700 **Shanahan** J K '72
(216) 297-7000 **Shanahan** Karen F '72
(216) 368-3292 **Shanker** Morris G '52
(216) 443-8995 **Shankman** Alan D '79
(216) 241-5040 **Shannon** James F '74
(216) 781-1700 **Shapero** Neal E '84
(216) 781-1700 **Shapero & Roloff Co, LPA**
(216) 621-1530 **Shapiro & Felty, LLP**
(216) 685-1106 **Shapiro** Jeffrey A '93
(216) 522-3380 **Shapiro** Marc A '87
(216) 696-0990 **Shapiro Marnecheck & Riemer**
(216) 241-7442 **Shapiro** Shia N '64
(216) 479-8500 **Sharb** Michael L '97
(216) 696-1076 **Sharma** Jandhyala L '83
(216) 348-9878 **Sharon & Kalnoki LLC**
(216) 348-9878 **Sharon** Michael H '82
(216) 696-7600 **Sharp** Jeremy J '99
(216) 579-1700 **Sharpe** Richard A '92
(216) 721-7700 **Shaughnessy** Thomas E '90
(216) 228-1888 **Shaw** Christopher J '85
(216) 621-0200 **Shaw** Hewitt B Jr. '80
(216) 689-5104 **Shaw** Laura J '97
(216) 291-7286 **Shaw** Nancy A '80
(216) 781-1212 **Shaw** Russell C '65
(216) 479-8500 **Shea** Christopher R '93
(216) 586-3939 **Sheaffer** Jenny L '98
(216) 443-7800 **Sheehan** Brendan J '94
(216) 696-8860 **Sheehan** John J Jr. '67
(216) 687-1311 **Sheehan** Michelle J '93
(216) 696-8860 **Sheehan** Thomas F '72
(216) 771-3239 **Sheehan** Thomas J '98
(216) 622-0850 **Sheehan** William J '99
(216) 522-7840 **Sheehe** Barbara W '80
(216) 479-8500 **Sheeran** Timothy J '75
(216) 241-3646 **Sheerer** Benjamin B '65
Shelby James D '73
(216) 479-8500 **Shelley** John F '68
(216) 623-0000 **Shelley** John S '03
(216) 802-3601 **Shellhaas** Samuel D '92
(216) 363-4500 **Shelton** Peter K '93
(216) 523-1300 **Shelton** William R '86
(216) 689-3851 **Shemisa** Jenann O '99
(216) 522-1555 **Shenyey** Peter F '76
(216) 426-2276 **Shepard** Robert '80
(216) 961-4530 **Sherban** Diane L '79
(216) 589-0088 **Sheridan** James P '99
(216) 696-7600 **Sherman** Bradley A '94
(216) 479-8500 **Sherman** Charna E '90
(216) 831-3181 **Sherman** Dennis H '66
(216) 566-5616 **Sheth** Mili K '03
(216) 351-5300 **Shiffra** Robert '66
(216) 781-0070 **Shillman** David B '61
(216) 241-8300 **Shimko** Timothy A '76
(216) 579-1700 **Shimola** Howard G '70
(216) 363-4500 **Shin** William J '02
(216) 443-6350 **Shively** David A '90
(216) 931-6000 **Shlonsky** Patricia A '84
(216) 363-4500 **Shofar** Nick D '87
(216) 661-6468 **Shonk** Paul W '03
(216) 621-4268 **Shopneck** Craig H '84
(216) 906-1300 **Shorey** James D '96
(216) 631-1221 **Shorr** Randall B '86
(216) 771-1760 **Short** Jeffrey R '91
(216) 687-1311 **Shroge** Michael D '00
(216) 241-2500 **Shucofsky** Joseph F '86
(216) 931-6000 **Shultz** David E '02
(216) 664-4820 **Shultz** Jaclyn R '03
(216) 348-5400 **Shumaker** Roger L '76
(216) 228-2900 **Shumay** Robert G '89
(216) 621-0200 **Shunk** Thomas H '79
(216) 621-0150 **Shuster** Michael P '95
(216) 696-6000 **Sicherman** Marvin A '60
(216) 771-1760 **Siciliano** Dennis J '89
(216) 357-3305 **Sidoti** Marcus S '04
(216) 357-3305 **Sidoti** Nicholas R II '03
(216) 861-5582 **Sidoti** Robert A '98
(216) 357-7214 **Siebenschuh** Ellen A '95
(216) 763-1004 **Siegel** Daniel S '93
(216) 763-1004 **Siegel** Fred '55
(216) 763-1004 **Siegel** Jay P '97

(216) 291-1300 **Siegel** Nessa G '86
(216) 763-1004 **Siegel Siegel Johnson & Jennings Co, LPA**
(216) 931-6000 **Siegfried** Kurt S '94
(216) 622-3754 **Sierleja** David A '82
(216) 586-3939 **Sigalow** Steven E '75
(216) 241-6602 **Sigmier** Harry T '80
(216) 433-2318 **Sikora** John W '76
(216) 443-8582 **Sikorski** Paul A '03
(216) 241-3033 **Silberman** Marc N '80
(216) 696-6500 **Silk** Thomas J '85
(216) 241-5250 **Silliman** Kenneth G '88
(216) 687-1311 **Silverman** Brent S '94
(216) 898-2344 **Silveroli** Genevieve A '97
(216) 586-3939 **Silverstein** Marc A '89
(216) 586-3939 **Silversten** Matthew P '02
(216) 443-6654 **Simek** Douglas R '03
(216) 443-7295 **Simmons** Jennifer L '03
(216) 694-4888 **Simmons** Kenneth D '74
(216) 689-5834 **Simmons** Michael A '00
(216) 592-5000 **Simmons** Thomas R '93
(330) 425-2825 **Simms** Andrew E '01
(216) 931-6000 **Simms** Edward P '98
(216) 931-6000 **Simms** Joseph S '96
(216) 583-2952 **Simon** Christie L '01
(216) 621-6201 **Simon** David O '75
(216) 664-9800 **Simon** Debra P '89
(216) 575-1002 **Simon** Ellen S '81
(216) 696-3311 **Simon** Eric M '87
(216) 241-5310 **Simon** John A '90
(216) 241-0040 **Simon** Sunny M '88
(216) 520-5572 **Simonetta** Paulette '89
(216) 523-4525 **Simonetti** John A '76
(216) 621-8484 **Simpkins** Scott D '96
(216) 522-1200 **Simpson** Jacqueline '77
(216) 931-6000 **Sims** Alan S '58
(216) 502-0800 **Sims** Rufus '88
(216) 586-3939 **Sinatra** John L Jr. '98
(216) 623-1123 **Sindell** Steven A '68
(216) 623-1123 **Sindell Young Guidubaldi & Sucher, PLL**
(216) 621-9870 **Singer** Marilyn J '79
(216) 291-7949 **Singer** Scott M '96
(440) 446-1529 **Sintsirmas** George '84
(440) 248-7906 **Sipusic** David J '01
(216) 692-1222 **Sirvaitis** Algis '66
(216) 502-0591 **Siskovic** Carole N '83
(216) 575-0777 **Sivinski** John A '86
(216) 522-3713 **Sizemore** Cheryl A '01
(216) 928-2200 **Skall** David W '97
(216) 241-8333 **Skaryd** Drue Marie '99
(216) 861-5582 **Skerry** Ann M '97
(216) 861-3327 **Skingle** Ronald A '94
(216) 363-1313 **Skirbunt** James R '74
(216) 363-1313 **Skirbunt** Sharon A '86
(216) 621-1113 **Sklar** Warren A '73
(216) 642-3342 **Skoczen** Danielle A '99
(216) 443-7326 **Skoczen** Stacey L '02
(216) 685-9991 **Skolnick** Howard E '93
(216) 623-0150 **Skove** Thomas M Jr. '77
(216) 443-7800 **Skutnik** Carol M '92
(216) 383-1637 **Slabaugh** Susan K '88
(216) 861-5582 **Slaby** Scott M '03
(216) 363-4500 **Sladek** Todd L '04
(216) 521-7922 **Slaga** John M '82
(216) 621-5300 **Slagter** John P '91
(216) 621-0200 **Slater** James A Jr. '02
(216) 589-0669 **Slavin** Jeffrey F '74
(216) 771-8990 **Sleggs** Todd W '88
(216) 381-8800 **Sleibi** Jalal T '03
(216) 696-4200 **Slifko** Jessica Flickinger '98
(216) 566-1111 **Slive** Harriet W '84
(216) 566-1111 **Slive** Steven H '76
(216) 696-4700 **Slivka** John M '81
(216) 641-9191 **Sliwinski** Teddy '76
(216) 586-3939 **Sloan** David W '74
(216) 623-0000 **Slodov** Michael D '91
(216) 241-3400 **Slone-Young** Tava D '99
(216) 685-9500 **Smaili** Jihad M '98
(216) 861-3086 **Smakula** Michael J '76
(216) 664-2767 **Smayda** Emily A '01
(216) 781-4994 **Smearman** Ralph Eric '93
(216) 696-4200 **Smeltz** John E '48
(216) 443-7800 **Smerillo** John J '88
Smialek Arthur D '77
(216) 363-4500 **Smidansky** Kurt J '84
(216) 443-7800 **Smilanick** Diane M '83
(216) 931-6000 **Smith** Aliceia J '04
(216) 274-4556 **Smith** Ann K '86
(216) 394-5067 **Smith** Barbara J '77
(216) 622-3600 **Smith** Bernard A '82
(216) 592-5000 **Smith** Bernard J '85
(216) 875-6512 **Smith** Bradley S '91
(216) 771-1760 **Smith & Condeni LLP**
(216) 752-0612 **Smith** Craig I '75
(216) 791-1900 **Smith** Cynthia D '83
(216) 642-0323 **Smith** David Kane '84
(216) 443-7800 **Smith** Drew A '98
(216) 621-1312 **Smith** Erick C '88
(216) 357-7000 **Smith** Geri M '81
(216) 523-4081 **Smith** Gregory A '87
(216) 696-7600 **Smith** James P '01
(440) 838-8800 **Smith** Jeffrey D '04
(216) 696-6525 **Smith** Joseph H '89
(216) 696-1133 **Smith** Justin M '00
(216) 622-8200 **Smith** Kenneth J '00
(216) 443-7800 **Smith** Kestra J '90
(216) 357-7130 **Smith** Kevin M '04
(216) 378-9905 **Smith** Kimberly Y '96
(216) 687-1900 **Smith** Maria A '84
(216) 566-5915 **Smith** Mark A '00
(216) 781-4994 **Smith Marshall Weaver & Vergon**
(216) 621-0070 **Smith** Maurice D '70
(216) 515-1660 **Smith** Michael E '89
(216) 771-1760 **Smith** Ned Lindsey '76
(216) 752-6401 **Smith** Orlando E '91
(216) 443-7223 **Smith** Paul '91
(216) 685-9940 **Smith** Rebecca R '01
(216) 574-6300 **Smith** Rene' D '93
(440) 333-2551 **Smith** Richard F Jr. '85
(216) 502-0800 **Smith** Robert III '84
(216) 225-7972 **Smith** Samuel R II '03
(216) 241-6602 **Smith** Scott C '88
(216) 520-5600 **Smith** Steven S '82
(216) 344-9339 **Smith** Stourton S '95
(216) 382-3447 **Smith** Thomas E '72
(216) 566-1600 **Smith** Todd M '91
(216) 621-0058 **Smith** William H '77
(216) 931-6000 **Smith** William K '81
(216) 479-8500 **Smits** Anthony M '99
(216) 348-5400 **Smolin** Michele A '92
(216) 771-7322 **Smrdel** Patricia A '91
(216) 566-5830 **Smyers** Robyn Minter '01
(216) 241-6868 **Smythe** Marie T '93
(216) 861-3086 **Sneiderman** Lisa N '94
(216) 621-0150 **Sneiderman** Steven H '91
(216) 751-2877 **Snipes** Alonzo Jr. '68
(216) 771-1760 **Snodgrass** Cristin R '03
(216) 621-4666 **Snow** David A '73
(216) 443-7800 **Snow** Renee L '97
(216) 586-3939 **Snyder** Amanda M '03
(216) 621-0200 **Snyder** Kenneth F '66
(216) 787-4740 **Snyder** Laurence R '86
(216) 687-3889 **Snyder** Lloyd B '70
(216) 348-5400 **Snyder** Michael L '88
(216) 361-0102 **Snyder** Patricia A '80
(216) 621-9767 **Sobel** Ryan A '04
(216) 583-3819 **Sobieski** Jeffrey S '98
(216) 443-8768 **Sobieski** Ralph P '81
(216) 426-4976 **Sobnosky** Mary T '84
(216) 586-3939 **Sobolewski** Brad A '00
(216) 696-1422 **Sogg** Wilton S '60
(216) 586-3939 **Solecki** Michael J '01
(216) 622-4364 **Solganik** Vivian L '70
(216) 416-3273 **Solomon** Douglas H '83
(216) 861-3366 **Solomon** Lanny M '76
(216) 621-0200 **Solomon** Randall L '73
(216) 579-1700 **Solomon** Steven J '03
(216) 431-4500 **Solyn** Melissa L '00
(216) 575-0777 **Sommers** Sandra Becher '85
(216) 241-0040 **Somogyi** Robert E '93
Somrak Noreen H '82
(216) 861-8844 **Sondik** Kenneth I '90
(216) 861-6833 **Sonkin** Jeffrey M '92
(216) 861-6833 **Sonkin & Koberna Co, LPA**
(216) 861-6833 **Sonkin** Rick D '87
(216) 861-6833 **Sonkin** Shale S '53
(216) 861-6833 **Sonkin** Yvette B '90
(216) 579-1700 **Sopko** Jeffrey J '75
(216) 566-5500 **Sosin** Jeremy S '04
(216) 696-0022 **Sosnowski** Kristie M '01
Sotera Mary C '86
(216) 623-0000 **Soucie** Michele P '82
(216) 443-7800 **Soucie** Paul M '82
(216) 781-5470 **Soukup** Christopher E '75
(216) 348-5400 **Southworth** Glenn D '93
(216) 861-1100 **Southworth** John D '98
(216) 586-3939 **Sozio** Stephen G '83
(216) 443-5809 **Spackman** Timothy G '90
(216) 443-7223 **Spadaro** Mark A '92
(440) 838-7600 **Spagnoli** Charles C '02
(216) 222-2976 **Spain** Charles H Jr. '82
(216) 621-0200 **Spallino** James Jr. '93
(216) 621-1530 **Spaner** Martha R '02
(216) 696-3232 **Spangenberg Shibley & Liber, LLP**
(216) 522-7548 **Spanos** Paul G '98
(216) 241-6689 **Sparacia** Andrew J '92
(216) 566-9700 **Spaw** David E '91
(216) 332-9280 **Spector** Robert S '73
(216) 241-0520 **Spellacy** John J '95
(216) 344-9220 **Spellacy** Kevin M '89
(216) 443-2025 **Spellacy** Leo M '59
(216) 443-9000 **Spellacy** Leo M Jr. '96
(216) 696-9300 **Spero** Keith E '56
(216) 861-9899 **Spero** Scott A '89
(216) 383-1500 **Speros** John W '84
(216) 583-3269 **Speyer** Paul H '87
(216) 592-5000 **Spielman** Michael A '02
(216) 696-4700 **Spieth Bell McCurdy & Newell Co, LPA**
(440) 842-0770 **Spinks** Thomas F '74
(216) 363-4500 **Spira** Robert M '72
(216) 781-4680 **Spirgen** Dennis R '96
(216) 621-1530 **Spirko** Daniel M '00
(216) 443-6350 **Spirko** Nicole M '99
(216) 621-5300 **Spirko** Timothy A '99
(216) 363-1400 **Spisak** Michael J '94
(440) 838-7600 **Spitz** Brian D '97
(216) 696-0600 **Spitz** James E '69
(216) 574-2600 **Spoonster** Joseph R III '99
(216) 443-6396 **Spotts** Mercedes H '81
(216) 781-5470 **Spotz** Richard T Jr. '73
(216) 443-3425 **Sprague** Charles E '82
(216) 241-4100 **Sprague** Timothy L '99
(216) 781-5470 **Spring** William L '67
(216) 566-5894 **Springfield** Delisa Y '01
(216) 586-3939 **Squeri** Stephen J '79
(216) 479-8500 **Squire Sanders & Dempsey LLP**
(216) 771-2600 **Srinivasan** Latha M '98
(216) 522-2526 **Stack** Brian J '98
(216) 241-8333 **Stadler** David P III '01
(216) 241-1074 **Stafford** Joseph G '85
(216) 241-1074 **Stafford** Vincent A '92
(216) 621-0150 **Staib** Mark E '73
(216) 241-5310 **Stakes** Jennifer N '02
(216) 687-1311 **Stalzer** John B '01
(216) 241-7660 **Stanard & Corsi Co,LPA**
(216) 443-7223 **Stanard** John P '87
(216) 241-7660 **Stanard** Margaret E '81
Stanceu James T '79
(216) 621-3346 **Stanek** Carl J '80
(216) 586-3939 **Stanger** Nicole D '98
(216) 689-4107 **Stanley** Forrest F '78
(216) 592-5000 **Stanley** Hugh M Jr. '69
(216) 623-0150 **Stanley** Mitchell A '92
(440) 888-6448 **Stano** Paul J '81
Stano Susan L '96
(216) 622-8200 **Stansbury** Ronald C '74
(216) 479-8500 **Stanton** R Thomas '69
(440) 838-7600 **Stanuszek** Michael J '04
(216) 426-8400 **Stark** J Norman '73
(216) 696-4200 **Stark** Jonathan L '91
(216) 696-7600 **Stark** Kenneth B '79
(216) 464-6666 **Starke** Sheldon P '71
(216) 622-8200 **Starkoff** Jack R '94
(216) 368-8523 **Starr** Mark R '04
(216) 241-2200 **Starrett** Kevin L '84
(216) 687-1900 **Stauffer** Susan P '70
(440) 886-0001 **Stavole** C Anthony '61
(216) 241-2838 **Stavole** William J '88
(216) 651-9500 **Stealey** Patricia A '80
(216) 875-6529 **Steeb** Cynthia L '01
(216) 241-2880 **Steel** Terrence J '71
(216) 443-7223 **Stefan** Mark A '93
(216) 394-5068 **Stefancin** Robert M '90
(216) 696-6170 **Stefanova** Vania T '96
(216) 348-0700 **Stege** Edward Richard Jr. '68
(216) 348-0700 **Stege & Michelson Co, LPA**
(216) 696-6454 **Steiber Harbaugh** Molly '83
(216) 696-3515 **Steiger** David J '92
(216) 771-8104 **Steiger** Sheldon G '72
(216) 445-4009 **Stein** David J '02
(440) 461-6767 **Stein** Elizabeth A '94
(216) 621-4244 **Stein** Laurel G '00
(216) 781-8040 **Stein** Robert N '86
(216) 696-7449 **Stein** Sheldon '76
(216) 621-2424 **Stein** Stanley E '62
(216) 696-9900 **Steinberg** Gerald L '76
(216) 363-4500 **Steindler** Howard A '67
(216) 751-4918 **Steiner** Carolyn L '91
(216) 771-1310 **Steiner** William F '51
(216) 586-3939 **Steines** Charles M '77
(216) 687-2300 **Steinglass** Steven H '81
(216) 781-1212 **Steinmetz** Arthur P '51
(216) 566-2648 **Steltenkamp** Gerald L '73
(216) 692-1222 **Stempuzis** Almis J '00
(216) 687-1311 **Stepan** Linda L '91
(216) 621-0200 **Stepanovic** Ronald A '88
(216) 685-9195 **Stephanoff** Susan M '83
(216) 241-5310 **Stephens** Alton L Jr. '75
(216) 479-8500 **Stephenson** Dale E '82
(216) 861-3086 **Stephenson** James E '01
(216) 291-1050 **Sterkel** Timothy R '94
(216) 586-3939 **Sterling** John L '68
(216) 781-1700 **Stern** Harold S '52
(216) 771-1310 **Stern** Howard S '56
(216) 522-7458 **Stern** Jeffrey A '77
(216) 861-0006 **Stern** Mitchell A '77
(216) 360-7200 **Sternberg** Sandor W '84
(216) 781-0005 **Steuer** Arlene B '52
(216) 771-8121 **Steuer Escovar Berk & Brown Co, LPA**
(216) 522-0564 **Stevens** Anne M '00
(216) 696-4700 **Stevens** Eugene '58
(216) 861-1700 **Stevens** Fred A '73
(216) 689-3196 **Stevens** Thomas C '74
Stevenson Anthony M '96
(216) 781-2258 **Stewart & DeChant Co, LPA**
(216) 696-1422 **Stewart** Enos Roger '98
(216) 881-2690 **Stewart** Kirk '76
(216) 781-2258 **Stewart** Lawrence E '50
(216) 687-4692 **Stewart** Melody J '89
(216) 781-2258 **Stewart** Scott E '76
(216) 566-5580 **Stewart** William R '68
(216) 398-2000 **Stibich** Paul R Sr. '78
(216) 581-2600 **Stibley** Michael R '04
(216) 622-3600 **Stickan** Christian H '75
(216) 241-0140 **Stickney** John M '51
(216) 241-0140 **Stickney** Melissa Wiley '03
(216) 241-0140 **Stickney** Thomas Moore '95
(216) 348-5400 **Stief** James E '97
(216) 241-6602 **Stienecker** C Andrew '00
(216) 696-6122 **Stifel** Orville E II '88
(216) 416-3771 **Stile** David M '94
(216) 771-1760 **Stiller** Robin R '00
(216) 642-0323 **Stinn** Michael E '84
(216) 589-0302 **Stocker** Suzanne '86
(216) 736-3333 **Stockman** Mark J '96
(216) 696-4006 **Stockmaster** Ann Marie '96
(216) 621-6501 **Stockslager** Matthew J '92
(216) 664-4986 **Stokes** Angela R '84
(216) 479-8500 **Stokes** Louis '53
(216) 694-3987 **Stolarsky** Lon D '84
(216) 363-4500 **Stoll** Edward J Jr. '94
(216) 694-3846 **Stoll** Myron S '60
(216) 687-1900 **Stoller** Jennifer R '00
(216) 348-5400 **Stone** James M '86
(216) 433-8855 **Stone** Kent N '77
(216) 928-1010 **Stoper** Richard L Jr. '84
(216) 771-5588 **Storie** Lloyd F Jr. '73
(216) 696-2040 **Stotter** Robert H '73
Stottner Joseph L '03
(216) 902-8880 **Stouffer** Christine M '00
(216) 931-6000 **Stovsky** Michael D '91
(216) 875-3000 **Stovsky** Richard P '83
(216) 621-0040 **Strachan Miller Olender & Roessler Co LPA**
(216) 621-0040 **Strachan** William R '72
(216) 443-9000 **Strain** Howard G '98
(216) 941-5566 **Straka** Joseph J '92
(216) 524-7499 **Stralka** Gregory T '87
(216) 592-5000 **Strang** Carter E '84
(216) 692-1172 **Stranke** Terry L '78
(216) 297-7000 **Strassfeld** Anne F '91
(440) 838-8800 **Strassman** Carol D '80
(216) 586-3939 **Stratford** Tracy K '98
(216) 937-1367 **Stratton** Robert B '92
(216) 586-3939 **Strauch** John L '64
(216) 621-0200 **Strauss** David J '67
(216) 736-7234 **Strauss** Marc I '86
(216) 622-8200 **Streicher** James F '66
(216) 443-9000 **Streza** Ralph '82
(216) 566-5733 **Striefsky** Linda A '77
(216) 621-0200 **Strimbu** Victor Jr. '60
(216) 622-8214 **Stringer** Anthony F '99
(216) 443-6632 **Stroh** Gary E '92
(216) 433-6679 **Strohbehn** Karl '00
(216) 622-8200 **Strom** Susan '90
(216) 621-0200 **Stronczer** Michelle P '96
(216) 771-5777 **Struger** Marlene S '80
(216) 348-4487 **Strunk** Wayne E '80
(216) 623-2004 **Studly** Paul A '70
(216) 583-2363 **Studnicha** Cynthia H '92
(216) 383-2890 **Stueber** Frederick G '82
(216) 621-8484 **Stueber** Jennifer L '96
(216) 269-0803 **Stuehr** Eric W '03
(216) 586-3939 **Stuhan** Richard G '86
(216) 241-5310 **Stuhldreher** George W '51
(216) 479-6100 **Stump** Kenneth A '94
(440) 729-3040 **Stupica** Terri L '88
(216) 623-1123 **Sucher** Daniel M '91
(216) 241-7255 **Sudilovsky** Ariel '93
Sukenik Rosalyn K '79
(216) 687-1311 **Sullivan** Brian D '94
(216) 621-0200 **Sullivan** John E '84
(216) 241-8111 **Sullivan** John E III '86
(216) 241-8111 **Sullivan** Julia R '86
(216) 622-8200 **Sullivan** K James '01
(216) 566-9909 **Sullivan** Mark E '82
(216) 479-8500 **Sullivan** Martha S '94
(216) 522-3530 **Sullivan** Mary C '89
(216) 443-7800 **Sullivan** Michael A '95
(216) 875-6530 **Sullivan** Patrick F '87
(216) 443-4022 **Sullivan** Terrence C '89
(216) 781-1452 **Sullivan** Terrence P '86
(216) 479-8500 **Summers** Kelly L '02
(216) 931-6000 **Summers** Linda DelaCourt '96
(216) 696-9300 **Summers** Lisa D '87
(216) 436-3449 **Summers** Lorraine A '92
(216) 348-5400 **Summers** Richard D '98
(216) 791-3137 **Summers** Sylvester Jr. '89
(216) 591-0727 **Summers & Vargas Co,LPA**
(216) 591-0727 **Summers** William L '69
(216) 621-2234 **Sundheim** Robert B '64
(216) 664-2444 **Sundheimer** Marlene '79
(216) 621-0200 **Suri** Sunil '04
(216) 520-5677 **Surovy** Thomas J '02
(216) 621-0150 **Sussman** Cathryn A '98
(216) 621-2234 **Sutkus** Richard A '99
(216) 771-2600 **Sutter** Kimberly M '03
(216) 928-2200 **Sutter** Lawrence A III '89
(216) 928-2200 **Sutter O'Connell Mannion & Farchione**
(216) 579-2164 **Sutter-Hodgins** Grace A '91
(216) 781-3600 **Sutton** Betty S '91
(216) 523-4358 **Sutton** Lisa D '94
(216) 621-0200 **Sutton** Stephen C '91
(216) 328-1531 **Sutula** Mark C '90
(216) 861-5582 **Svat** Mark S '89
(216) 696-4441 **Svec** Jennifer S '99
(216) 589-5435 **Swain** Maureen R '96
(216) 752-9978 **Swain** William L '84
(216) 447-1551 **Swanda** Danielle D '02
(216) 241-8333 **Swansinger** John '89
Swanson Charles A '75
(216) 685-9188 **Swartz Campbell LLC**
(216) 479-8500 **Swartz** Catherine M '02
(216) 241-6602 **Swartz** Joseph B '70
(216) 588-4365 **Swartz** Steven S '82
(216) 586-3939 **Swartzbaugh** Marc L '61
(216) 621-0150 **Swary** Mark F '73
(216) 363-4500 **Swearengen** Michael K '89
(216) 931-6000 **Sweebe** Richard D '79
(216) 622-3600 **Sweeney** Emily M '81
(216) 928-9288 **Sweeney** Francis E Jr. '92
(216) 241-5310 **Sweeney** James F '59
(216) 348-7550 **Sweeney** Kathleen M '85
(216) 787-3030 **Sweeney** Kelley A '97
(216) 443-7295 **Sweeney** Kristin W '95
(216) 696-0606 **Sweeney** Mary B '89
(216) 566-5793 **Sweeney** Patrick J '86
(216) 696-0606 **Sweeney** Robert E '51
(216) 696-0606 **Sweeney** Robert P '76
(216) 363-1400 **Sweeney** Rosemary '87
(216) 621-1000 **Sweeney** Sean M '99
(216) 443-7223 **Sweeney** Suzan M '91
(216) 619-0071 **Sweeney** Timothy F '87
(216) 875-2767 **Sweeney** Timothy G '84
(216) 664-2853 **Sweeney** William A '89
Sweet Joy A '83
(216) 621-6400 **Swencki** Ronald C '69
(216) 222-9892 **Swetlin** Seema H '94
(216) 621-0200 **Swift** Christopher J '80
(800) 362-4500 **Swisher** Danielle M '99
(216) 875-2767 **Switzer** Donald H '78
(216) 586-3939 **Switzer** H Duane '64
(216) 831-0042 **Switzer** Kennee '88
(216) 444-2340 **Switzer** Stephanie N '94
(216) 432-0306 **Sylvester** Edward T '01
(216) 622-2727 **Synenberg** Roger M '77
(216) 696-0650 **Sysack** Russell '01
(216) 446-0300 **Szabo** Gabriel S Jr. '53
(440) 446-0300 **Szabo** John Z '69
(216) 622-8200 **Szabo** Magda B '77
(216) 622-8200 **Szabo** Paul E '79
(216) 228-7200 **Szaller** James F '75
(216) 522-3380 **Szczepanik** Carol A '81
(216) 621-0200 **Szilvas** Alexander J '87
(216) 443-7229 **Szorady** Ernest A '82
(216) 623-2008 **Szpalik** Peter R '91
(216) 696-9330 **Szubski** Grace A '82
(216) 861-0503 **Szuter** Gregory P '73
(216) 592-5000 **Taber** Edward E '96
(216) 382-4848 **Taddeo** Joseph H '69
(216) 363-4500 **Taft** Clare R '03
(216) 696-4700 **Taft** Frederick I '72
(216) 241-2838 **Taft Stettinius & Hollister LLP**
(216) 685-1103 **Taft-Milby** Rosemary '91
(216) 781-0070 **Taich** Harry H '73
(216) 622-8200 **Tait** Christina '96
(216) 685-1137 **Talaganis** Dean S '89
(216) 621-0200 **Talbot** Kevin R '01
(216) 875-4800 **Talcott** Thomas J '76
(216) 443-7800 **Talley** Debra L '93
(216) 443-5809 **Tamas** Barbara A '00
(216) 664-4506 **Tamayo-Sarver** Maritza '02
(216) 566-2360 **Tamburrino** Ronnie M '83
(216) 664-2220 **Tame** Craig A '91
(216) 241-5080 **Tancredi** Dara A '92
(216) 443-8800 **Tanner** James R Jr. '92
(216) 889-3658 **Tansler** Vicki S '96
(216) 348-5056 **Taoras** Bronius K '74
(440) 720-7610 **Taormina** Robert A '89
(216) 621-8484 **Tarantino** Thomas J '90
(216) 621-7500 **Taricska** Richard C '77
(440) 838-7600 **Tark** Lori Ross '03
(216) 787-3030 **Tarka** Dawn M '92
(216) 443-8609 **Tarnow** Sara E '00
(216) 621-2234 **Tarolli** James L '91
(216) 621-2234 **Tarolli Sundheim Covell & Tummino**
(216) 621-2234 **Tarolli** Thomas L '61
(216) 664-6900 **Tasse** Jeffrey L '81
(216) 621-9091 **Tassi** Arthur J '79
(216) 787-3030 **Tassie** Sharon D '85
(216) 566-5602 **Tatter** Rachel J '01

(216) 621-0794 **Taubman** Bruce D '76
(216) 363-6020 **Tavens** James E '87
(216) 696-3311 **Tavolier** David R '86
(216) 787-3298 **Tayek** Richard W '82
(216) 696-0800 **Tayfel** Eric W '97
(216) 241-1400 **Taylor** Daniel W '79
(216) 664-6271 **Taylor** Heather Ann '00
(216) 241-6602 **Taylor** Hilary S '77
(216) 575-0777 **Taylor** Jaeson L '01
(216) 241-5700 **Taylor** Matthew W '03
(216) 241-6602 **Taylor** Randy L '98
(216) 621-0070 **Taylor-Kolis** Donna J '84
(216) 696-7177 **Teamor** Ricardo B '77
(216) 363-4500 **Tegreene** Joseph G '84
(216) 595-3234 **Teitelbaum** Michael J '87
(216) 443-5837 **Telep** Michael B '89
(216) 692-2010 **Telich** Leslie A '84
(216) 531-4470 **Telich** Mark S '82
(216) 351-8244 **Temas** Jeffery D '88
(216) 621-0200 **Tenerowicz** Matthew A '98
(216) 363-4500 **Teplitzky** Ronald J '87
(216) 522-4856 **Terez** Dennis G '85
(216) 621-0200 **Terrion** Halle F '93
(216) 687-1910 **Terry** Margaret L '72
(216) 928-2200 **Terry** Thomas H III '79
(216) 566-7744 **Tessler** Harvey E '71
(216) 575-0777 **Testa** Catherine J '04
(216) 689-7112 **Thacker** Michael J '84
(216) 445-7176 **Theofrastous** Theodore C '99
(216) 623-0150 **Thimmig** Diana M '83
(216) 685-9940 **Thomarios** Elizabeth A '99
(216) 443-8560 **Thomas** Angela T '00
(216) 443-7800 **Thomas** Blaise D '85
(216) 929-0700 **Thomas** Clyde E '56
(216) 621-9110 **Thomas** David P '93
(216) 479-8500 **Thomas** Dynda A '86
(216) 696-1500 **Thomas** Gregory S '93
(216) 479-8500 **Thomas** James D '87
(216) 929-0700 **Thomas** John E '89
(216) 443-8355 **Thomas** Kathryn A '84
(216) 696-6454 **Thomas** Keith D '87
(216) 875-2767 **Thomas** Kimberly A '04
(216) 931-6000 **Thomas** Max W '03
(440) 356-6900 **Thomas** Michael A '75
(216) 698-6410 **Thomas** Patrick J '02
(216) 830-9000 **Thomas** Sam III '97
(216) 479-8500 **Thomas** Terence L '94
(216) 241-3033 **Thomas & Thomas**
(216) 222-3164 **Thomay** Mark L '83
(216) 292-3300 **Thomey** H Charles '03
(216) 574-8279 **Thompson** Adrian D '86
(216) 348-0700 **Thompson** Andrew J '99
(216) 732-2854 **Thompson** Barbara A '54
(216) 443-7583 **Thompson** Darin G '96
(216) 378-9905 **Thompson** David W '98
(216) 771-6650 **Thompson** Helen A '96
(216) 566-5500 **Thompson Hine LLP**
(216) 522-3875 **Thompson** Janice L '85
(216) 522-3870 **Thompson** Marcella L '79
(216) 479-8500 **Thompson** Mitchell S '94
(440) 243-2500 **Thompson** Stephen F '00
(216) 261-5680 **Thompson** William J '62
(216) 443-7223 **Thompson** William W IV '80
(216) 621-9767 **Thorman** Christopher P '91
(216) 732-2854 **Thornton** Kevin W '74
(216) 357-7000 **Throckmorton** Keith A '93
(216) 771-3777 **Thurman** Adam J '97
(216) 443-7800 **Tiburzio** Terese M '92
(216) 781-3858 **Ticktin Baron Co, LPA**
(216) 781-3858 **Ticktin** Daniel S '85
(216) 781-3858 **Ticktin** Harold '53
(216) 771-6633 **Tidball** Emily A '02
(216) 267-3044 **Tighe** Robert F '73
(216) 566-2575 **Timmons** Joseph F '87
(216) 781-0722 **Tipping** Mary Jo '91
(216) 357-5123 **Tira** Joseph R '77
(216) 566-2000 **Tirey** Arthi K '00
(216) 696-1422 **Titlebaum** Ellen R '98
(216) 522-3380 **Tkacik** John M Jr. '93
(216) 881-8030 **Tobik** Robert L '70
(216) 787-3030 **Tobocman** Marilyn '83
(216) 566-2492 **Tocci** Dennis M '85
(216) 479-6100 **Tocco** David J '86
(216) 621-0890 **Todt** Robert W '86
(216) 360-9919 **Toerek** Sharon L '91
Toler Lynn C '84
(216) 231-8440 **Tolliver** Stanley E Sr. '53
(216) 251-6655 **Tolt** Lester T '63
(216) 261-0200 **Toma** Timothy N '87
(216) 622-0850 **Toman** Bradley P '89
(216) 592-5000 **Tomaro** Robert B '74
(216) 664-3776 **Tomasello** Shirley A '92
(216) 749-7466 **Tomon** Bert R '72
(216) 479-8500 **Tompkins** Catherine C '95
(216) 241-2838 **Tomsick** Richard D '84
(216) 241-2838 **Tonsing** Heather L '98
(216) 586-3939 **Toohey** Brian F '80
(216) 586-3939 **Toohey** Meagan E '03
(216) 861-6282 **Toohig** Kevin T '96
(216) 363-1400 **Toole** Jeffrey C '95
(216) 621-0200 **Toomajian** William M '78
(216) 689-5086 **Torch** Glenn F '74
(216) 241-6602 **Torgerson** Kenneth A '66
(216) 361-0002 **Torok** Rosemary '86
(216) 781-6450 **Torres-Lugo** Jazmin G '94
(216) 771-6303 **Torres-Ramirez** José A '94
(216) 961-2100 **Torres-Waldo** Rosa '96
(216) 514-1100 **Tost** Christopher M '99
(216) 241-2600 **Tosti** Jeanne M '92
(216) 363-4500 **Tracanna** Richard F '87
(216) 861-2424 **Traeger** Kenneth '73
(216) 363-4500 **Trainer** Mark D '02
(216) 765-8110 **Tramer** Neil M '83
(216) 696-3550 **Trapp** Mary Jane '81
(216) 771-4700 **Trattner** Barry A '68
(216) 771-4700 **Trattner** Mary Lou '74
(216) 771-6650 **Traut** Ted M '00
(216) 443-7800 **Travaglini** Kristine R '97
(216) 241-5310 **Travis** D John '76
(216) 664-2673 **Travis** Gary N '82
(216) 443-7800 **Travis** Linda R '79
(216) 566-7022 **Treinish** Alan J '74
(216) 861-3000 **Treister** William R '76
(216) 443-6350 **Trejbal** Amy '98
(216) 368-4286 **Treml** Colleen G '91
(216) 621-0200 **Trent** Niesa R '03
(216) 241-5310 **Trenta** Melinda B '99
(216) 481-4960 **Trentes** John H '87
(216) 241-2600 **Tresl** Jacqueline D '03
(216) 621-1000 **Treu** Kris H '83
(216) 861-6677 **Tricarichi** Carla M '83
(216) 621-5980 **Tricarichi** Tina L '96
(216) 586-3939 **Trilling** Jessica E '03
(216) 621-0200 **Trim** Roger G '03
(216) 664-4992 **Triozzi** Robert J '82
(216) 881-4243 **Tripi** Joseph M '03
(216) 622-3600 **Tripi** Phillip J Jr. '78
(216) 696-5444 **Trivers** Oscar '60
(216) 621-7227 **Troia** Anthony R '66
(440) 248-7906 **Trombetto** Julius E '02
(216) 479-8500 **Troxell** James D '76
(216) 781-4454 **Troyan** Gregory M '91
(216) 566-5654 **Troyer** Brian A '92
(216) 621-7860 **Trubiano** Mark A '88
(216) 931-6000 **Trudeau** Stephanie E '82
(216) 991-9122 **Trumbo** George W '53
(216) 443-9000 **Tryon** David C '85
(216) 566-2487 **Tsang** Vivien Y '96
(216) 479-8500 **Tsilimos** Jonathan S '02
(216) 696-3311 **Tucci** Michael R '99
(216) 592-5000 **Tucker Ellis & West LLP**
(216) 931-6000 **Tucker** Michael S '86
(216) 592-5000 **Tucker** Robert C '76
(216) 621-1113 **Tucker** Todd R '95
(216) 321-8789 **Tuckerman** John L '54
(216) 566-5500 **Tuggle** Curtis L '04
(216) 931-6000 **Tulley** Patrick J '94
(216) 687-3595 **Tumeo** Mark A '02
(216) 621-2234 **Tummino** Barry L '80
(216) 881-7939 **Turbow** Laurence A '76
(216) 687-1311 **Turek** James J '82
(216) 391-4000 **Turk** Edmund J '55
(216) 443-9000 **Turnbull** Tracey L '96
(216) 566-5604 **Turnell** Roy L '74
(216) 664-4942 **Turner** Franzetta D '87
(216) 586-3939 **Turner** Henry E '03
(216) 621-0200 **Turner** Jack '02
(216) 241-5310 **Turner** Mark M '02
(216) 292-3300 **Turner** Peter '81
(216) 378-9905 **Turner-Bautista** Brooke D '00
(216) 696-8730 **Turocy** Gregory '91
(216) 561-8000 **Turoff** Daniel C '63
(216) 781-0150 **Turoff** Jack N '60
(216) 781-0150 **Turoff** Robert S '63
(216) 621-5161 **Turoff** Tracy A '02
(216) 566-5617 **Turscak** Andrew L Jr. '01
(216) 861-5582 **Turung** Brian E '91
(216) 771-4600 **Tushman** Sol '53
(216) 241-2262 **Twohig** Catherine B '96
(216) 241-2262 **Twohig** Mark M III '73
(216) 324-7893 **Tye** Russell W '96
(216) 443-7223 **Tylee** Mary C '85
(216) 687-5166 **Tyler** Barbara J '89
(216) 621-0200 **Tyler** Corinne M '98
(216) 241-5310 **Tyminski** James T Jr. '99
(216) 241-8333 **Tyminski** Michael J '01
(216) 621-1113 **Tyrpak** Michele M '96
(216) 830-6830 **Ubbing** Thomas J '85
(216) 586-3939 **Ubersax** Jeffery D '88
(216) 696-4700 **Ubersax** Kristin L '87
(216) 447-1551 **Ullman** Meredith L '02
(216) 931-6000 **Ulmer & Berne LLP**
(216) 360-7200 **Ulrich** Phyllis A '91
(216) 931-6000 **Ungar** Michael N '84
(216) 523-4126 **Union** Marvin L '69
(216) 241-4244 **Urban** Brian M '79
(216) 222-2934 **Urban** Margaret N '83
(216) 486-8200 **Urbancic** Brano '56
(216) 687-1900 **Urbanek** Jerry R '04
(216) 498-5397 **Urbank** Donna E '95
(216) 781-3700 **Urse** Michael F '84
(216) 522-2683 **Ussery** Karla K '97
(216) 575-0777 **Uzl** William E '90
(216) 685-1157 **Vaccarelli** Julie A '03
(216) 664-4971 **Vagi** Jolan B '82
(216) 696-4200 **Vail** James D '79
(216) 896-2734 **Vail** Julia B '84
(216) 241-5310 **Valenti** John A '80
(216) 241-8471 **Valentine** James E '86
(216) 621-0150 **Valentine** Nancy A '98
(216) 363-6489 **Valentino** Nicholas '77
(216) 696-3311 **Valerian** Robert J '76
(216) 696-1400 **Valli** Richard A '85
(216) 689-4467 **Vallorz** Ernest L Jr. '84
(216) 271-8983 **Vallorz** Sonia C '84
(216) 443-7800 **Valore** Dean M '00
(216) 241-2838 **Valponi** Mark J '77
(216) 566-5348 **Vana** Robert J '77
(216) 781-4680 **Van Aken Withers & Webster**
(440) 838-7600 **Van Blargan** Christopher J '96
(216) 443-6985 **Vancavage** Gerard '81
(216) 444-9804 **Vance** Victoria L '82
(216) 348-1700 **Vance** William '81
(216) 621-0200 **VanDeHey** Margaret M '99
(216) 642-3342 **Vanderburg** Keith A '78
(216) 621-0200 **VanderKaay** Aaron M '01
(216) 896-2156 **Vanderlip** Nancy L '93
(216) 621-0070 **Van Dervort** Daina B '80
(216) 622-8200 **Vanderwist** James C '83
(216) 781-4000 **Van Deusen** Roger W '68
(216) 476-2125 **Vandrak** Daniel J '65
(216) 621-0070 **Vanek** Stephen S '92
(216) 621-0200 **Van Euwen** Peter W III '98
(216) 696-9310 **VanGilder** Donald N '98
(216) 589-5622 **Van Iden** Byron D '72
(216) 241-2229 **Vanik** John C '82
(216) 928-7540 **Vanik** Thomas C '75
(216) 621-0200 **VanNiel** Michael A '01
(216) 622-0850 **Van Slyke** David L '04
(216) 983-1014 **Van Valkenburgh** Paul F '88
(216) 931-6000 **Van Wagner** Jeffrey W '79
(216) 687-1900 **Vanyo** Maialisa A '99
(216) 274-1601 **Vara** Timothy J '82
(216) 696-6000 **Vardzel** Lisa A '03
(216) 591-0727 **Vargas** Edwin J '94
(216) 621-0200 **Vargo** Ernest E Jr. '85
(440) 842-6717 **Vargo** James A '83
(216) 586-3939 **Vary** Michael W '86
(216) 252-7300 **Vas** Rinda E '99
(216) 696-3311 **Vaselaney** Missia H '85
(216) 781-5245 **Vasvari** Raymond V Jr. '91
(216) 561-3880 **Vaughn** Ann S '02
(216) 252-7300 **Vavruska** Jeffrey A '86
(216) 595-0949 **Vavruska** Stasia M '86
(216) 566-1424 **Vecchio** Robert J '82
(216) 522-5396 **Vedouras** Anna '89
(216) 696-5531 **Vegh** Anthony J '88
(440) 808-9750 **Venard** Paul D '01
(440) 232-5100 **Venizelos** James C '91
(216) 875-6532 **Vereb** Karen A '99
(216) 622-8200 **Vergilii** Jennifer L '01
(216) 363-4500 **Verginis** Theologos '02
(216) 781-4994 **Vergon** Frederick P Jr. '69
(216) 621-0200 **Verma** Monica S '00
(216) 621-8484 **Vernon** Keith T '96
(440) 483-4244 **Vernon** Mary C '93
(216) 443-7800 **Vick** Gary A Jr. '99
(216) 931-6000 **Vickers** Frederick Thomas '83
(216) 861-5582 **Vickers** Gregory S '97
(216) 861-5582 **Vickers** Robert V '61
(216) 416-3280 **Victor** Jennifer A '98
(216) 771-3800 **Vieyra** Katherine R '95
(216) 443-6350 **Vilfroy** Ute L '91
(216) 664-4827 **Villa** Gina M '89
(216) 622-3735 **Villa** Herbert J '66
(216) 443-8605 **Vincent** Leland G II '03
(216) 222-2379 **Vincent** Musette T '81
(216) 621-5300 **Vincent** Terry W '87
(216) 623-0150 **Vinocur** Jonathon H '03
(216) 781-1212 **Viola** Anthony J '57
(216) 241-2838 **Viola** Matthew T '00
(216) 241-6602 **Visani** Hernan N '86
(216) 987-4832 **Viskocil** Timothy J '87
(216) 622-8200 **Visocan** Karen A '93
(216) 763-1004 **Vivarronda** Steven J '00
(216) 479-8500 **Viviani** Gregory J '84
(216) 348-5400 **Vlasek** Dale R '87
(216) 241-6602 **Vlasich** Emily Allegretti '02
(216) 739-5646 **Vlasuk** Heather Baldwin '04
(216) 664-3643 **Vodrey** William F '92
(216) 781-1168 **Vogel** Philip Z '82
(216) 291-7393 **Vogele** Allan W '75
(216) 479-8500 **Vollins** James A '93
(216) 687-1311 **Volpini** Laura L '02
(216) 781-5515 **Volsky** Kerry S '80
(216) 781-5515 **Volsky** Mark R '81
(440) 605-6660 **von Boeselager** Kurt J '78
(216) 522-2248 **von Borcke** Pamela J '83
(216) 363-5812 **Vondra** Albert A '03
(216) 479-8500 **von Mehren** George M '77
(216) 685-1050 **Voorhees** Andrew C '04
(216) 479-6100 **Vorys Sater Seymour & Pease LLP**
(216) 241-1105 **Voth** Robert F IV '74
(216) 592-5000 **Voudouris** S Peter '92
(440) 746-0911 **Vozar Roberts & Matejczyk Co,LPA**
(440) 746-0911 **Vozar** Thomas J '86
(216) 292-3300 **Wachter** Mark I '77
(216) 502-0800 **Wade** Edward S Jr. '75
(216) 941-3333 **Wade** Jeffrey D '99
(216) 586-3939 **Wagatsuma** Wade R '99
(216) 520-0088 **Waggoner** Glenn D '80
(216) 241-7000 **Wagner** Charles E '90
(216) 443-7800 **Wagner** Christopher A '00
(216) 586-3939 **Wagner** Christopher J '03
(440) 743-7561 **Wagner** Erika Jordan '84
(216) 432-7200 **Wagner** Nora B '00
(216) 781-4000 **Wagner** Thomas C '85
(216) 622-8200 **Wagner** Thomas E '73
Wagner Thomas J '72
(216) 983-1024 **Wahl** Cheryl Forino '03
(216) 344-9007 **Wahl** Jeffrey R '84
(216) 696-7600 **Wainblat** Neal B '81
(216) 241-6045 **Waiwood** Michael F '71
(216) 781-2600 **Wakefield** Mark L '82
(216) 443-5809 **Wald** Sara L '01
(216) 781-1212 **Waldeck** John W Jr. '77
(216) 687-7221 **Waldron** Richard G '84
(216) 861-8734 **Walk** Rochelle F '86
(216) 861-5000 **Walk** Steven M '82
(216) 586-3939 **Walker** Andrew M '03
(216) 523-1920 **Walker** Daniel G '00
(216) 431-4500 **Walker** Janice '94
(216) 241-2880 **Walker** Kristin M '01
(216) 787-3030 **Walker** Nancy Q '95
(216) 586-3939 **Walker** Robert S '82
(216) 443-3799 **Walker** Sandra L '84
(440) 526-4244 **Walker** Wallace W Jr. '66
(216) 265-9463 **Walker** William A '56
(216) 621-0200 **Wall** Brett A '98
(216) 523-4118 **Wall** Katherine M '91
(216) 443-6350 **Wallace** Christine M '85
(216) 241-2838 **Wallace** David H '86
(216) 696-7600 **Wallace** Lisa A '00
(216) 621-0200 **Wallace** R Byron '74
(216) 622-8200 **Wallach** Mark I '74
(216) 443-7800 **Walsh** Edward M '71
(216) 357-7000 **Walsh** James F Jr. '98
(440) 356-5700 **Walsh** Jonathan J '04
(216) 348-5400 **Walsh** Kenneth J '75
(216) 621-5980 **Walsh** Margaret M '86
(216) 377-0615 **Walsh** Mary V '76
(216) 443-3360 **Walsh** Richard F '71
(216) 781-1212 **Walter & Haverfield LLP**
(216) 830-6830 **Walter** Robert M '81
(216) 566-5500 **Walters** Gary L '99
(216) 447-1551 **Walters** Richard E '86
(216) 787-4486 **Walters** Sally S '93
(216) 687-1311 **Walters** Stephen '83
(216) 241-6602 **Walters** Stephen D '68
(216) 621-1230 **Walton** Gerald R '80
(216) 283-6484 **Walton** Robert G '81
(216) 839-1111 **Waltz** David T '93
(216) 586-3939 **Walworth** James W Jr. '01
(216) 586-3939 **Wamsley** James L III '75
(216) 363-4500 **Wang** Yanping '00
(216) 291-7726 **Wanner** Kathleen A '78
(216) 443-7800 **Warbel** Michael S '01
(216) 515-1660 **Ward** Daniel A '82
(216) 687-1311 **Ward** Paul Michael '75
(216) 621-6060 **Ward** Rebecca E '04
Ward Robert E '75
(216) 830-6830 **Ward** Theodore D '71
(216) 696-5580 **Ward** Vicki L '83
(216) 621-0200 **Ware** Nathan F '00
(216) 566-5783 **Ware** Robert F Jr. '91
(216) 861-3086 **Wargo** Andrew M '92
(216) 696-1422 **Wargo** Leslie Erin '00
(216) 443-7223 **Warner** Carlos '97
(216) 822-3262 **Warner** Cynthia A '01
(216) 371-2210 **Warner** Deborah P '85
(216) 931-6000 **Warner** Jane F '02
(216) 486-2598 **Warner** John L '59
(216) 687-1311 **Warner** Robert D '79
(216) 696-4700 **Warner** Timothy G '93
(216) 443-7800 **Warr** Rufus L '72
(216) 621-0200 **Warren** Daniel R '91
(216) 781-5515 **Warren** Robert Jr. '74
(216) 621-0200 **Warren** Thomas D '04
(216) 416-3275 **Warren** William M '52
(216) 368-0339 **Warshawsky** Kittie D '95
(216) 443-6350 **Warshawsky** Laura K '96
(216) 586-3939 **Washington** Stephen L '98
(216) 621-7499 **Wasil** Jo Ann F '79
(216) 367-7744 **Wasserman** Eric '70
(216) 737-5000 **Wasserman** Steven L '78
(216) 241-2838 **Waterhouse** Bruce L Jr. '88
(216) 861-5582 **Waters** Joseph E '00
(216) 443-7800 **Waters** Matthew T '02
(216) 991-4377 **Watson** Caroline '03
(216) 522-7455 **Watson** Charles L '73
(216) 348-5400 **Watson** David D '94
(216) 241-2262 **Watson** Jeffery S '91
(216) 523-1100 **Watson** Myron P '92
(216) 696-4700 **Watson** Richard T '60
(216) 522-4070 **Watson** Scott M '81
(216) 241-6700 **Watterson** James G '65
(216) 579-2174 **Watts** Andrew W '75
(216) 241-6700 **Watts Hoffmann Co, LPA**
(216) 771-5511 **Watts** Patrick M '02
(216) 514-9400 **Waxman** David B '86
(216) 621-5300 **Wayne** Ronald F '78
(216) 621-0200 **Wearsch** Thomas M '04
(216) 443-8430 **Weatherford** Chris '97
(216) 443-8859 **Weatherhead** Ann '82
(216) 696-0900 **Weatherly** Justin M '04
(216) 575-1313 **Weaver** Clark B '66
(216) 781-4994 **Weaver** Philip J Jr. '74
(216) 566-3940 **Weaver** Richard M '82
(216) 479-8500 **Weaver** Robin G '74
(216) 363-5220 **Weaver** Susan M '80
(216) 443-3658 **Webb** Therese M '93
(216) 696-7600 **Webber** Mark V '74
(216) 479-6100 **Webbs** Jerome C '80
(216) 443-9000 **Weber** Jeffrey J '93
(440) 838-8800 **Weber** Monica M '04
(216) 586-3939 **Weber** Robert C '76
(216) 771-1144 **Weber** Robert M Jr. '03
(216) 566-1144 **Webster** Beth B '90
(216) 241-1400 **Webster** Charles K '77
(216) 566-1144 **Webster** David B '91
(216) 781-4680 **Webster** Stephen D '73
(216) 566-1144 **Webster Webster Kvale LLP**
(216) 861-5088 **Wecksler** Tina E '85
(216) 479-8500 **Wedel** Jeffrey J '89
(216) 241-5310 **Wedell** Kristin L '00
(216) 687-3543 **Weedon** John A '61
(216) 642-3342 **Wegman Hessler & Vandenburg, LPA**
(216) 696-3030 **Weibel** David G '80
(216) 621-0200 **Weible** Robert A '78
(216) 689-3908 **Weick** Paul A II '79
(216) 523-5000 **Weigand** Kathleen A '88
(216) 642-3342 **Weigand** Lesley A '96
(216) 575-3000 **Weihrauch** Ronald L Jr. '02
(216) 241-2294 **Weilbacher** David G '99
(216) 363-4500 **Weiler** Jeffry L '70
(216) 515-8337 **Weiler** Richard L '91
(216) 685-1100 **Weinberg** Alan H '74
(216) 431-4500 **Weinberg** Marilyn O '83
(216) 621-8234 **Weinberg** Richard M '88
(216) 696-3232 **Weinberger** Peter H '75
(216) 479-8500 **Weiner** David C '69
(216) 771-6500 **Weiner** Keith D '82
(216) 781-9000 **Weingart** Lee C '91
(216) 222-2972 **Weingartner** Lucile G '80
(216) 736-7242 **Weingrad** Stephen C '73
(216) 621-0150 **Weinstein** Edward A '86
(216) 479-8500 **Weinstein** Joseph C '83
(216) 381-5132 **Weinstein** Norman H '52
(216) 574-9090 **Weintraub** Craig T '87
(216) 443-7800 **Weintraub** Julianne L '96
(216) 443-9000 **Weir** William R '84
(440) 232-5100 **Weis** Geri L '99
(216) 781-1212 **Weisberg** Patricia Fromson '85
(216) 348-5400 **Weisblatt** David E '94
(216) 861-8888 **Weiser** Larry A '71
(216) 696-3311 **Weisman** Deborah A '94
(216) 781-1111 **Weisman** Fred '51
(216) 781-1111 **Weisman Goldberg & Weisman Co, LPA**
(216) 781-1111 **Weisman** Harry Jed '66
(216) 781-1111 **Weisman** Mitchell A '83
(216) 479-8500 **Weiss** Dana B '03
(440) 838-7600 **Weiss** Eric J '00
(216) 623-0150 **Weiss** Gary A '90
(216) 589-9993 **Weiss** Jerome F '72
(216) 787-3344 **Weiss** Kathleen G '88
(216) 687-1311 **Weiss** Leon A '66
(216) 621-7500 **Weiss** Michael S '75
(216) 961-6840 **Weiss** Michael S '81
(216) 771-4242 **Weiss** Richard A '71
(216) 696-3366 **Weiss** Ronald I '65
(216) 348-1800 **Weiss** Steven M '80
(216) 579-1818 **Weissman** Esther S '61
(216) 778-5723 **Welfel** Frederick M '92
(216) 696-4700 **Welfley** Jennifer A '97
(216) 736-7936 **Weller** Charles D '73
(216) 642-6653 **Weller** Mark D '82
(216) 241-8300 **Welling** David A '03
(216) 479-8500 **Wellman** Kristine M '95

(440) 248-7906 **Wells-Niklas** Natasha A '96
(216) 622-8200 **Welsh** Thomas M '03
(216) 685-1040 **Weltman** Robert B '65
(216) 685-1032 **Weltman** Scott S '90
(216) 685-1000 **Weltman Weinberg & Reis Co,LPA**
(216) 222-2337 **Welton** Copani M '01
(216) 781-1212 **Welty** David W '74
(216) 781-2258 **Wendel** Fred III '74
(216) 443-8780 **Wenneman** Ann F '82
(216) 586-3939 **Wenstrup** Rose Mary '95
(216) 579-1700 **Wentsler** Stephen S '00
(216) 685-9710 **Wentz** Robert C '89
(216) 687-2337 **Werber** Stephen J '80
(216) 586-3939 **Werner** Brooke D '04
(216) 378-9905 **Wertheim** James S '85
(440) 720-0250 **Wertheimer** Victor '48
(216) 458-1340 **Wesel** Michael E '90
(216) 621-2234 **Wesorick** Richard S '95
(216) 464-8700 **Wessman** Carol A '78
(216) 241-5310 **West** Jennifer N '00
(216) 566-5500 **West** Robert A Jr. '04
(216) 778-5475 **West** William G '74
(216) 736-6244 **Westbrooks** Robert A '82
(216) 589-0600 **Westfall** James W Jr. '77
(216) 241-6602 **Weston Hurd Fallon Paisley & Howley LLP**
(216) 522-2657 **Westrick** Timothy A '97
(216) 642-3342 **Wetzel** Karl Robert '84
(216) 443-8507 **Wetzel** Rebecca B '90
(216) 622-8200 **Wexberg** Marcia J '91
(216) 566-5500 **Wexler** Catherine Bassett '02
(216) 781-0636 **Whalen** Frank C '53
(216) 520-5600 **Whang** Cynthia '93
(216) 348-1700 **Wharton** Michele Y '93
(216) 781-1212 **Whatley** Frederick W '81
(216) 622-8200 **Wheatley** Nathan A '00
(216) 522-0800 **Wheeler** John D '77
(216) 443-5809 **Whinery** Joanna A '92
(216) 566-8200 **Whipple** Douglas P '80
(216) 771-6633 **Whitaker** Andrea L '01
(216) 226-1564 **Whitaker** David W Jr. '82
(216) 621-0150 **White** Craig O '83
(216) 566-1600 **White** Daniel S '90
(216) 241-5310 **White** Darlene E '00
(216) 687-1900 **White** Gail '81
(216) 830-9000 **White** George W Jr. '56
(216) 622-3600 **White** Gregory A '77
(216) 621-1000 **White** Mary E '03
(216) 523-1920 **White** William T '67
(216) 622-8200 **Whitehead** Michael H '00
(216) 592-5000 **Whitesell** Jeffrey M '97
(216) 622-8200 **Whitford** Cornelius J '89
(216) 241-8333 **Whitford** Timothy P '92
(216) 621-2234 **Whitman** Daniel J '00
(216) 479-6100 **Whitmer** Mary K '75
(216) 586-3939 **Whitney** Richard B '73
(216) 687-1900 **Whitsett** Tonya D '94
(216) 621-6570 **Whitt** Jennifer L '02
(216) 586-3939 **Whitt** Mark A '97
(216) 771-7777 **Whittington** Aaron Daniel '66
(216) 875-8206 **Whittington** Nicholas M '00
(216) 621-0150 **Wick** Christopher B '00
(216) 535-0520 **Wick** G Michael '89
(216) 622-8823 **Wick** Jennifer Buckey '01
(216) 896-2217 **Wickline** Paul O '81
(216) 292-4504 **Wickter** Lawrence D Jr. '02
(216) 931-6000 **Widen** Frederick N '81
(216) 931-6000 **Widman** Elizabeth M '04
(216) 622-8200 **Wiedemann** John T '96
(216) 241-3880 **Wiener** Stanley '53
(216) 621-1312 **Wiery** Suzanne F '98
(216) 323-9116 **Wieser** Molly B '98
(216) 621-0200 **Wilcox** Deborah A '87
(216) 621-8484 **Wilcox** Dennis R '77
(216) 621-0200 **Wilcox** Diane D '88
(216) 861-0808 **Wilcox** Jeffrey J '91
(216) 363-4500 **Wild** Jeffrey J '97
(216) 696-8044 **Wilder** John H '52
(216) 621-0200 **Wilharm** John H Jr. '60
(216) 781-5470 **Wilk** Lisa J '01
(216) 696-0808 **Wilkerson** Ernest L Jr. '86
(216) 586-3939 **Wilkes** Meredith M '00
(216) 592-5000 **Wilkov** Scott J '04
(216) 241-7740 **Willacy** Aubrey B '70
(216) 566-2600 **Willacy** Hazel M '76
(216) 241-7740 **Willacy Lopresti & Marcovy**
(216) 263-3414 **Williams** Brinley H Jr. '71
(216) 586-3939 **Williams** Caroline M '04
(216) 520-0088 **Williams** Christian M '94
(216) 622-8200 **Williams** Christopher S '90
(216) 696-4700 **Williams** Clyde E Jr. '45
(216) 241-1177 **Williams** Danny R '78
(216) 291-7702 **Williams** David R '66
(216) 696-4345 **Williams** Donald C '73
(216) 348-5056 **Williams** Earl Jr. '80
(216) 687-2297 **Williams** Gary R '84
(216) 443-7800 **Williams** Gayle F '01
(216) 687-1900 **Williams** Harold L '76
(216) 771-6303 **Williams** Kathryn A '98
(216) 443-5009 **Williams** Laura Ann '83
(216) 241-5300 **Williams** Michael T '92
(216) 752-9868 **Williams** Paul A '86
(216) 443-8970 **Williams** Perdexter H '92
(216) 687-1902 **Williams** Reginald D '03
(216) 579-4114 **Williams** Saber Rathbun '02
(216) 621-2110 **Williams Sennett & Scully Co, LPA**
(216) 902-8540 **Williams** Stanley A '61
(216) 931-6000 **Williams** Tanya L '04
(440) 356-0180 **Williams** Warren J Jr. '71
(216) 787-3030 **Williams** Wayne D '88
(216) 522-7454 **Williams-Alexander** Donna L '87
(216) 443-7800 **Williamson** Lisa R '89
(216) 566-5655 **Williger** Stephen D '82
(216) 789-4625 **Willis** Craig E '83
(216) 523-1100 **Willis** James R '53
(216) 381-3400 **Willis** Robert J '94
(216) 523-1100 **Willis Watson & Gooden**
(440) 838-7600 **Wills** Nathan J '04
(216) 589-9600 **Wilsman** James M '64
(216) 589-9600 **Wilsman & Schoonover,LLC**
(216) 898-2345 **Wilson** Andrea Sinclair '97
(216) 696-1422 **Wilson** Glenn R '90
(216) 687-1311 **Wilson** Holly M '01
(216) 861-6393 **Wilson** James D '89
(216) 687-2269 **Wilson** James G '81
(216) 263-4591 **Wilson** Jesslyn C '82
(216) 781-2258 **Wilson** Lawrence D Jr. '03
(216) 696-0022 **Wilson** Marvin Scott '84
(216) 621-0200 **Wilson** Mary A '83
(216) 566-5623 **Wilson** Nicole K '01
(216) 586-3939 **Wilson** Paula Batt '95
(216) 685-9940 **Wilson** Rachel C '97
(216) 566-5572 **Wilson** Robin M '96
(216) 622-8200 **Wilson** Scott R '77
(216) 687-3543 **Wilson** Sonali B '86
(216) 522-3715 **Wilson** Steven D '80
(216) 586-3939 **Wilson** Thomas A '03
(216) 575-0777 **Wilson** Thomas M '87
(216) 621-5300 **Wilt** Ronald M '92
(216) 664-2687 **Wiltshire** Cheryl M '04
(216) 621-8700 **Wincek** Christopher G '86
(216) 621-8700 **Wincek & De Rosa Co, LPA**
(216) 621-9870 **Winchester** Brian T '98
(216) 443-7583 **Windham** Patricia K '91
(216) 222-9427 **Wingenfeld** Paul F '92
(216) 368-4495 **Winner** Sonia M '91
(440) 248-7906 **Winslow** Patrick W '77
(216) 621-0200 **Winston** David S '96
(216) 830-9000 **Winston** Douglas L '86
(216) 771-3314 **Winston** Robert M '77
(440) 838-7600 **Winter** Jason D '03
(216) 696-0606 **Wintering** Mark J '77
(216) 781-2822 **Winters** Christopher S '82
(216) 774-8104 **Winzig** Virginia V '84
(216) 348-5400 **Wirtshafter** John M '84
(216) 363-1313 **Wirtz** Amy Y '92
(216) 351-6560 **Wise** David M '87
(216) 348-5400 **Wise** Michael W '90
(216) 391-5444 **Wiseman** Mark N '92
(216) 781-4680 **Withers** Carl R '54
(216) 861-5582 **Withrow** Jonathan A '02
(216) 621-7227 **Witkowski** Richard G '85
(216) 586-3939 **Witmer-Rich** Jonathan P '01
(216) 861-5000 **Witte** Michael C '96
(216) 739-5645 **Wittenberg** Stacie H '00
(216) 444-1275 **Wittenmyer** Nelson J Jr. '90
(216) 443-3439 **Wochna** Charles F '85
(216) 241-2628 **Wojcik** Waldemar J '80
(216) 771-1111 **Wojnar** Nicoleta D '97
(216) 348-0707 **Wolanin** John S '91
(216) 623-9999 **Wolf & Akers,LPA**
Wolf Daniel B '75
(216) 983-1052 **Wolf** Elizabeth M '92
(216) 623-9999 **Wolf** Marshall J '67
(216) 241-0300 **Wolf** Paul V '87
(216) 983-1289 **Wolf** Seth M '94
(216) 687-1311 **Wolf** Thomas R '94
(216) 781-1212 **Wolfe** Leslie Green '00
Wolfe Marc D '95
(216) 436-2198 **Wolfe** Mary S '90
(216) 621-7227 **Wolff** Brenda C '94
(216) 696-7600 **Wolff** Robert M '80
(216) 861-0808 **Wolkin** Steven E '77
(216) 391-7111 **Wolpert** Michael L '86
(216) 623-0000 **Wolters** Daniel C '03
(216) 566-9908 **Wong** Margaret Wai '77
Wood John Y '92
(216) 368-3600 **Wood** Lisa M '88
(216) 241-6045 **Wood** Robert A '69
Wood Thomas F '75
(216) 830-6830 **Wood** Timothy D '72
(216) 781-1212 **Woodhall** Amy L '96
(216) 382-3080 **Woodrum** Amy N '92
(216) 443-7800 **Woods** Nicole J '02
(216) 621-0200 **Wooley** James R '86
(216) 621-1113 **Worgull** Jason A '99
(216) 623-1155 **Workum** Denise B '96
(216) 479-6100 **Woyt** Elia O '01
(216) 687-1902 **Wozniak** Peter M '91
(216) 443-9000 **Wright** Alan D '59
(216) 241-2838 **Wright** Daniel K II '79
(216) 566-5716 **Wright** Elizabeth B '84
(216) 883-5390 **Wright** John J '69
(216) 523-5161 **Wright** Lizbeth '94
(216) 348-1700 **Wright** Thomas W '84
(440) 838-8800 **Wuertz** Maribeth G '84
(216) 781-7777 **Wuliger Fadel & Beyer**
(216) 781-7777 **Wuliger** William T '69
(216) 447-1551 **Wyatt** Thomas R '86
Wykoff Peter C '61
(216) 522-7800 **Wyman** Dean P '82
(216) 621-0200 **Wymer** Martin T '84
(216) 292-3300 **Wyner** Jeffrey G '71
(216) 861-4533 **Wynne** Thomas More '94
(216) 861-7100 **Wypasek** Michael A '83
(216) 443-7800 **Xavier** Chipper F '01
(216) 378-9905 **Yaksic** Barbara F '81
(216) 696-1275 **Yakunovich** Joanie L '02
(216) 687-1311 **Yallech** Robert S '02
(216) 765-7430 **Yanowitz** Alan E '85
(216) 696-3311 **Yanowitz** Bennett '49
(216) 622-5292 **Yantek** Kenneth R '86
(216) 522-4970 **Yarab** Donald S '90
(216) 737-5000 **Yarger** Jonathon M '90
(216) 566-2501 **Yaro** John M '87
(216) 771-5300 **Yates** Paul W '73
(216) 771-4444 **Yavitch** Hallie I '03
(216) 931-6000 **Yeagley** David D '89
(216) 292-3300 **Yeh** Michele R '97
(216) 831-0042 **Yelsky** Debra A '93
(216) 514-1899 **Yelsky** Jeffrey M '91
(216) 781-2550 **Yelsky** Lauryn M '94
(216) 781-2550 **Yelsky** Leonard W '59
(216) 781-2550 **Yelsky & Lonardo Co, LPA**
(216) 781-2550 **Yelsky** Mitchell J '87
(216) 443-3439 **Yeomans** Patricia M '84
(216) 622-8200 **Yerrace** Lisa Marie '03
(216) 621-7227 **Yingling** Ronald Christopher '96
(216) 443-8604 **Yingst** Rebecca A '03
(216) 241-6700 **Yirga** John A '03
(216) 621-5300 **Yoakum** Grant M '94
Yonchak Robert F '88
(216) 515-1660 **Yoo** Steven R '90
(216) 592-5000 **York** Nicholas C '93
(216) 928-3474 **Yormick** Jon P '90
(216) 515-1300 **Yost** Agnes J '94
(216) 621-2300 **Young** Andrew R '99
(216) 623-1123 **Young** Charles M '74
(216) 566-5738 **Young** Daniel T '92
(216) 861-4891 **Young** Derek W '87
(216) 830-6830 **Young** E Mark '01
(216) 931-6000 **Young** Elin B '98
(216) 586-3939 **Young** James E '72
(216) 623-3688 **Young** John Talbot Jr. '75
(216) 431-4500 **Young** Joseph C '91
(216) 664-6900 **Young** Kevin M '85
(216) 321-6323 **Young** Laura A '96
(216) 931-6000 **Young** Leonard D '75
(216) 685-1000 **Young** Matthew M '02
(216) 781-1212 **Young** Sheldon M '51
(216) 861-5582 **Young** Thomas E '75
(216) 664-4842 **Young** Tiffeny U '03
(216) 592-5000 **Youngblood-Jalics** Courtenay '04
(216) 566-5670 **Youngstrom** Karen D '76
(216) 241-5310 **Yue** Deborah W '94
(216) 241-2262 **Yulish Twohig & Associates**
(216) 687-1311 **Zaber** Brian M '02
(216) 566-0064 **Zaccagnini** Bruce A '86
(216) 382-0444 **Zaffiro** Thomas J '91
(216) 479-8500 **Zagore** David A '88
(216) 861-5582 **Zahn** Jeffrey N '04
(216) 664-3528 **Zajaczkowski** Scott D '01
(216) 861-5582 **Zalevsky** Marina V '04
(216) 363-4500 **Zalud** Eric L '87
(216) 861-7463 **Zangerle** John A '67
(216) 861-5582 **Zanghi** John S Jr. '95
(216) 739-2600 **Zanney** Raymond C '93
(216) 623-0900 **Zapka** Dennis P '75
(216) 241-8158 **Zaransky** Stephen P '80
(216) 696-4009 **Zaretsky** Erwin V '63
(216) 566-5647 **Zarlenga** Audra J '96
(216) 566-7994 **Zarlingo** Pamela '89
(216) 443-7800 **Zarzycki** Scott C '00
(216) 696-4441 **Zashin** Andrew A '93
(216) 696-4441 **Zashin & Rich Co, LPA**
(216) 696-4441 **Zashin** Robert I '68
(216) 696-4441 **Zashin** Stephen S '95
(216) 363-4500 **Zaverton** Michael D '87
(216) 830-9000 **Zavesky** Robert J '83
(216) 689-4126 **Zeiger** Richard G '82
(440) 449-9311 **Zeiser** Daniel G '84
(216) 771-4050 **Zelasko** Bradford D '78
(216) 621-2300 **Zeller** Robert S '85
(216) 444-2340 **Zellmer** Ann E '79
(216) 348-5400 **Zellmer** Charles B '72
(216) 621-0150 **Zellner** Richard A '67
(216) 787-3030 **Zemba** Mark J '86
(216) 623-0150 **Zenkewicz** Kristine R '02
(216) 443-9000 **Zepp** Charles W '97
(216) 771-0270 **Zetzer** Paul M '83
(216) 664-2577 **Ziccardi** Robert P '81
(216) 787-3030 **Zidar** Michael J '88
(216) 781-1212 **Zidek** Susan M '92
(216) 621-0150 **Ziegler** Ann C '03
(216) 781-5470 **Ziegler Metzger & Miller LLP**
(216) 621-9870 **Ziegler** Paul W '71
(216) 348-1700 **Ziehm** Ronald J '91
(216) 363-1400 **Zielinski** Deborah D '00
(216) 664-2814 **Zigli** William T '85
(216) 586-3939 **Zimmer** David O '99
(216) 291-2400 **Zimmerman Caticchio Eisenberg & Modica**
(216) 443-7800 **Zimmerman** David M '87
(216) 696-3525 **Zimmerman** Katherine Ann '92
(216) 696-3311 **Zimmerman** Robert A '91
(216) 363-4500 **Zimon** Jeffrey D '92
(216) 696-7170 **Zingale** Salvatore A '66
(440) 461-3600 **Zingales** Joseph D '76
(216) 621-1113 **Zink** Marisa J '01
(216) 514-6400 **Zipkin** Lewis A '64
(216) 514-6400 **Zipkin Whiting Co LPA**
(216) 689-7370 **Zirke** Christopher J '02
(216) 664-4820 **Zirke** Heather M '02
(216) 781-1212 **Zirm** Kenneth A '84
(216) 961-3521 **Zitiello** Rose A '93
(216) 241-2838 **Zix** Timothy L '91
(216) 787-5180 **Zlojutro** Milutin '88
(216) 781-0004 **Zobec** Frankee T '81
(216) 621-6138 **Zocolo** Lori Ann '98
(440) 746-1177 **Zoeckler** John P '99
(216) 222-2978 **Zoeller** David L '92
(216) 696-3311 **Zoller** Elizabeth M '01
(216) 241-2200 **Zoller** John D '86
(216) 621-3251 **Zoller** Nancy A '87
(216) 241-2200 **Zoller & Scholl**
(216) 736-6242 **Zontini** John M '84
(216) 241-2500 **Zucco** George C '64
(216) 566-8711 **Zucco** Jeff T '71
(216) 931-6000 **Zujkowski** Melissa L '04
(216) 696-0900 **Zukerman Daiker & Lear, LPA**
(216) 696-0900 **Zukerman** Larry W '85
(216) 931-6000 **Zulandt** Robert E III '99
(216) 771-1111 **Zullig** Olga Y '99
(216) 443-8650 **Zunt** Monica C '92
(216) 443-8577 **Zvomuya** Katherine Sommers '03
(216) 781-1212 **Zwick** Gary A '80
(216) 566-5605 **Zych** Thomas F '83

CLEVELAND HEIGHTS

Cuyahoga County

Adelman Robert E '98
(216) 321-5068 **Agle** Katherine S '98
(216) 382-8586 **Alexander** James Jr. '71
Bailey Jonathan A '97
(216) 371-5220 **Bakst** Gary N '82
Bargmeyer Brian A '01
(216) 321-1234 **Barnard** Geoffrey W '93
(216) 932-6045 **Berkeley** Jerome S '60
(216) 371-5551 **Billington** Glenn E '70
(216) 321-0388 **Boncella** Elizabeth W '77
(216) 246-9033 **Brockler** Aaron J '04
(216) 932-0762 **Brown-Daniels** Barbara C '91
(216) 291-3184 **Buchanan** Alan Deane '73
(216) 381-8747 **Burke** Delia A '81
(216) 397-1270 **Buss** William D II '70
(216) 795-4117 **Chilcote** Lee A '72
(216) 371-2438 **Cushing** Mary T '81
David Audrey D '79
(216) 932-4680 **DeVito** Ronald A '75
(216) 932-4978 **Domb** Brian '93
Earl Lillian B '92
(216) 382-1500 **Eloff** Kathryn G '81
(216) 320-0976 **Fahey** Melanie S '93
(216) 397-9180 **Gamble** Ranelle A '72
Gardner Lauren A '93
(216) 372-7104 **Goodluck** James R '89
(216) 932-5226 **Goshien** Deborah P '70
(216) 932-1006 **Guarnieri** Christine '80
(216) 932-8109 **Guerra** John B '57
(216) 381-1881 **Haines** Jacque M '58
(216) 291-1117 **Haka** Katherine M '90
Hart April N '97
(216) 932-3976 **Hartman** Franklin L '66
Hartup Bret R '04
(216) 932-7331 **Hurd** Calvin F Jr. '61
(216) 795-4117 **Jenner** Simon '03
(216) 321-3514 **Kramer** Lawrence J Jr. '03
(216) 721-6650 **Lally** Marlene N '89
(216) 291-3806 **Lefferts** Dale E '85
(216) 291-4983 **Lentz** Martin G '68
(216) 321-5606 **Luria** Neil F '92
(216) 771-0999 **Lynch** Robert T '75
(216) 932-0663 **Mastandrea** Joseph M '87
(440) 743-4749 **Mastroianni** Anthony '83
(216) 382-3835 **McElrath** Lenza Jr. '85
(216) 397-8800 **Meckler** Theodore E '75
(216) 321-3897 **Millett** Diane E '87
(216) 320-5800 **Montlack** Kenneth R '67
(216) 371-0607 **Morgan** Cynthia M '92
(216) 397-0420 **Nave** Michele Garrick '82
(216) 371-7767 **Newell** Evelyn B '84
Parkes Wright C '83
(216) 932-3077 **Pederson** Jeffrey W '80
(216) 371-9644 **Petrey** Kenneth D '74
Prugh David C '49
(216) 791-0986 **Ratnoff** Marian F '67
Rich Aviva R '02
(216) 932-4255 **Rodney** David E '83
(216) 397-9999 **Rose** Bruce R '75
(216) 371-7121 **Sack** Mark J '97
(216) 321-7335 **Saks** William M '91
(216) 321-9144 **Schade** Nancy V '87
(216) 291-3783 **Schmidt** Georgeann R '78
(216) 932-8344 **Schreck** Richard A '53
(216) 932-4724 **Scully** Daniel G '94
(216) 291-5775 **Segebarth** Kim T '73
(216) 371-5220 **Silver** Paul Jay '87
(216) 451-1437 **Small** Robert E '61
Sollitto Sharmon '77
(216) 321-9494 **Sonkin** Loren M '89
(216) 397-7820 **Spurgeon** Roberta Kaye '77
(216) 321-4608 **Trattner** Douglas L '93
(216) 291-3811 **Wagner** Laure A '82
(216) 321-2595 **Weidenthal** Jeffrey L '88
(216) 932-5227 **Weisberger** Donald D '60
(216) 371-1688 **Weller** Robert R '72
(216) 321-7606 **Whiting** Vanessa L '89
(216) 932-4443 **Wintner** Jennifer E '84
(216) 321-3230 **Woda** Elizabeth M '78

CLEVES

Hamilton County

(859) 371-7581 **Jennings** Thomas P '94
(513) 353-3439 **Neyer** James P '95

CLIFTON

Hamilton County

Braun Fredrick H '57

CLINTON

Summit County

(330) 825-8670 **Hite** Roger M '72
(330) 854-5177 **Ross** William J '74
(330) 882-4061 **Witner** David A '94

CLYDE

Sandusky County

(419) 547-9471 **Bales** Beth A '04
(419) 547-9585 **Bennett** Frank H '56
(419) 547-9471 **Dewey** John P '72
(419) 547-9471 **Dewey** Thomas F Jr. '70
(419) 547-7770 **Fiser** Mary E '86
(419) 547-9515 **Knight** Christopher J '78
(419) 547-0553 **Pearce** William D '72

COLDWATER

Mercer County

(419) 678-4317 **Bruns** David W '75
(419) 678-7111 **Howell** Paul E '85
(419) 678-2378 **Koesters** Judy A '86
Nickell Angela R '94
(419) 678-2378 **Speelman** Kathryn W '98

COLUMBIANA

Columbiana County

(330) 482-4040 **Fox** C Richard '52
(330) 482-1222 **Hum** Robert W II '86
(330) 482-3356 **Hutson** Mark A '83
(330) 482-3356 **Powers** David P '84
(330) 482-3825 **Roth Blair Roberts Strasfeld & Lodge,LPA**
(330) 482-3356 **Stacey Hutson Stacey & Powers LPA**
(330) 482-3356 **Stacey** Lawrence W '59
(330) 482-3356 **Stacey** Lawrence W II '91
(330) 482-3825 **Wright** James R '60

COLUMBIA STATION

Lorain County

(440) 236-8412 **Fetchet** Frank '54
(440) 236-5015 **Gurnick** Raymond L '90
Tallos Edmund G '01

COLUMBUS

Franklin County

(614) 228-6453 **Abraham** Daniel N '83
(614) 221-5474 **Abraham** Joseph R '97
(614) 221-5474 **Abraham** Rick J '87

(614) 225-8528 **Abrahamsen** Erik E '86
(614) 221-4000 **Abrams** James D '03
(614) 466-1943 **Abrams** Kevin R '82
(614) 461-6066 **Abramson** Lawrence D '78
(614) 221-8448 **Abromowitz** David M '91
(614) 443-7000 **Abroms** Hillard M '72
(614) 220-8877 **Acker** Alan S '90
(614) 462-3960 **Adair** Allen V '72
(614) 451-6050 **Adair** James W III '74
(614) 464-2392 **Adams** Andrew S '75
(614) 221-8448 **Adams** Bret A '84
Adams John M '54
(614) 475-9511 **Adams** Mark A '78
(614) 415-7078 **Adams** Theodore L '91
(614) 221-3155 **Adams** William A '85
(614) 221-0944 **Addesa** Thomas J '85
(614) 464-6400 **Addison** Colborn M '60
(614) 462-3194 **Adel** Mitchell J '01
(614) 464-3563 **Adkins** Jonathan E '04
(614) 469-1882 **Adkinson** Christopher D '01
(614) 464-3332 **Affeldt** Kelly I '93
(614) 469-5715 **Affeldt** Kenneth F '91
(614) 221-3318 **Agee Clymer Mitchell & Laret**
(614) 466-3191 **Agler** Alfred P '74
(614) 466-0108 **Agranoff** Jay S '88
(614) 464-6400 **Airey** Wilfred Jonathan '73
(614) 443-4063 **Akamine** Nathan Sei '95
(614) 365-2700 **Akers** Laing P '00
(614) 644-6896 **Akers** Leslie A '86
(614) 466-6696 **Alatis** Andrew J '89
(614) 464-4414 **Albers** James B '50
(614) 464-4414 **Albers** James S '77
(614) 464-4414 **Albers** John B II '82
(614) 466-8600 **Albers** Rebecca Jo '92
(614) 221-1216 **Albrecht** Benjamin S '00
(614) 752-6889 **Albrecht** Cynthia L '92
(614) 445-8811 **Albrecht** Geoffrey E '75
(800) 783-9655 **Albrecht** Mark A '92
(614) 228-5711 **Albright** Robert E '50
(614) 469-5577 **Albu** George M '93
(614) 410-6726 **Alden** Erick R '72
(614) 221-1306 **Alden** John L '72
(614) 410-6726 **Alden** Matthew L '95
(614) 846-2000 **Aldrich** Misty H '85
(614) 559-2501 **Alexander** Arlene K '87
(614) 365-2700 **Alexander** David W '82
(614) 466-4605 **Alexander** Linette M '94
(614) 221-5627 **Alexander** Suzanne K '03
(614) 248-7973 **Alexsy** Steven F '89
(614) 227-2000 **Ali** Karim A '03
(614) 645-8500 **Allbritain** Michael C '02
(614) 436-6690 **Alleman** Brenda B '81
(614) 228-1174 **Allen** Daniel J '89
(614) 462-3555 **Allen** Jeffrey R '72
(614) 227-8834 **Allen** Jerry O '84
(614) 224-4114 **Allen** John R '73
(614) 221-8500 **Allen Kuehnle & Stovall LLP**
(614) 466-2980 **Allen** Michael D '80
(614) 222-0521 **Allen** Philip Lon '86
(614) 221-8500 **Allen** Thomas R '81
(614) 462-3555 **Allen** Thomas W '98
(614) 462-7312 **Allendorf** Thea L '99
(614) 444-5700 **Allerding** Michael P '75
(614) 466-5638 **Allison** Adrian E '98
(614) 848-6500 **Allison** James H '68
(614) 221-8668 **Allison** John J II '80
(614) 644-0986 **Allison** Jonathan A '94
(614) 462-7450 **Allison** Linda K '00
(614) 337-5140 **Allison** Michael R '82
Alluis Louise J '82
(614) 224-2428 **Alo** Mohammed N '04
(614) 224-8160 **Alter** Mitchell J '81
(614) 475-3178 **Althauser** Martha G '80
(614) 462-3194 **Altman** Marylou G '91
(614) 221-6751 **Alton** John M '77
(614) 461-4444 **Ambro** George R '76
(614) 221-6755 **Ambrosio** Lawrence J '76
(614) 644-2640 **Amerine** Amy C '81
(614) 792-3409 **Amerine** Hal D '86
(614) 464-6400 **Amerine** Marjorie Frazier '04
(614) 421-5605 **Ames** Kristen M '00
(614) 577-9970 **Ames** Stephen P '85
(614) 583-0200 **Amid** Jeanine A '85
(614) 462-3555 **Amlin** Renee L '98
(614) 462-5013 **Anderson** Daniel M '96
(614) 719-1579 **Anderson** Douglas L '91
(614) 529-7099 **Anderson** Douglas R '93
(614) 227-2000 **Anderson** Jon M '61
(614) 644-7342 **Anderson** Kimberly C '93
(614) 692-3284 **Anderson** Kyle B '03
(614) 466-3132 **Anderson** Mark S '70
(614) 464-1877 **Anderson** Marty '77
(614) 644-1414 **Anderson** McDonald E '82
(614) 462-3194 **Anderson** Melani C '87
(614) 462-3194 **Anderson** Norman Q '77
(614) 464-6400 **Anderson** Raymond D '79
(614) 460-4645 **Anderson** Rodney W '85
(614) 464-6400 **Anderson** Sandra Jo '76
(614) 387-9305 **Anderson** Scott A '91
(614) 221-2121 **Anderson** Scyld D '95
(614) 644-2840 **Anderson** Todd A '91
(614) 224-1222 **Andorka** Gary D '86
(614) 464-1999 **Andrew** Craig D '80
(614) 228-8400 **Andrews** Alexander M '81
(614) 248-6035 **Andrews** Charles F '74
(614) 224-1222 **Andrews** Donald S '98
(614) 228-5931 **Andrews** Scott R '02
(614) 221-2700 **Andrioff** James J '85
(614) 228-5931 **Anelli** Dianna M '94
(614) 462-4283 **Angel** Michael W '78
(614) 466-2766 **Angell** Lauren C '89
(614) 466-6750 **Angus** George P '78
(614) 466-1158 **Aninao** Joseph G '84
(614) 297-4483 **Anker** Ruth L '02
(614) 466-1938 **Annarino** John A '85
(614) 221-2121 **Anspaugh** Donald Lee '80
(614) 628-8000 **Anstaett** Elizabeth L '91
(614) 827-7300 **Anthony** Carl A '91
(614) 227-2366 **Anthony** Laura G '95
(614) 771-1010 **Anthony** Marcell R '72
(614) 340-0011 **Anthony** Michael J '96
(614) 621-1500 **Antipova** Yelena Y '03
(614) 442-3355 **Antolino** Ralph Jr. '80
(614) 221-8448 **Antrim** Donald A '74
(614) 645-7483 **Anzelmo** James A '97
(614) 728-7055 **Appel** Henry G '97
(614) 239-4822 **Applegate** Amanda M '98
(614) 644-7467 **Arata** Jane S '87
(614) 466-6511 **Archie** Deborah '85
(614) 466-6928 **Arkenberg** Tina M '96
(614) 237-6718 **Armstrong** Daniel G '01
(614) 326-0919 **Armstrong** Leslie '89
(614) 227-8821 **Armstrong** Maria J '87
(614) 462-2235 **Arndt** Randall S '81
(614) 481-8416 **Arnebeck** Clifford O Jr. '70
(614) 224-7771 **Arnett** Henry A '76
(614) 466-6700 **Arnold** Bradford P '88
(614) 752-7204 **Arnold** Daren G '00
(614) 485-1800 **Arnold** Gayle E '80
(614) 487-1335 **Arnold** George J '70
(614) 469-1400 **Arnold** James E '87
(614) 462-3555 **Arnold** Stephen W '03
(614) 485-1800 **Arnold Todaro & Welch**
(614) 462-3555 **Arsenault** Laurie A '00
(614) 221-4000 **Art** Andrew J '90
(614) 228-0326 **Arthur** Geoffrey W '91
Arthur James E '82
(614) 227-2000 **Arthur** William E '53
(614) 221-0944 **Artz** Brian S '80
(614) 221-0944 **Artz & Dewhirst,LLP**
(614) 462-2700 **Arville** Alan J '03
(614) 459-3868 **Ary** Richard E '87
(614) 275-5935 **Asbury** Damon A '93
(614) 365-2700 **Aschenbrand** Tara A '02
(614) 228-1541 **Asensio** Manuel J III '85
(614) 466-6935 **Ashanin** Janine S '00
(614) 645-7385 **Ashbrook** Susan E '87
(614) 478-6000 **Ashton** Rick L '04
(614) 227-2000 **Atchison** Julie L '98
(614) 854-8672 **Atkins** Lisa Ann '96
(614) 365-2700 **Atriano** Vincent '88
(614) 224-8178 **Aubrey** Joanne E '81
(614) 464-4100 **AuCoin DuPont Hetterscheidt & Younkin LLC**
(614) 464-4100 **AuCoin** Paul M '76
(614) 464-6400 **Auge** Craig R '97
(614) 995-4868 **Augsburger** Mary Amos '02
(614) 559-1188 **Auker** Jeffrey A '83
(614) 336-7022 **Aukland** Duncan D '82
(614) 421-5609 **Austin** Linda M '00
(614) 424-5400 **Austin** Russell P '86
(614) 221-7711 **Auten** Anthony R '72
(614) 237-8050 **Avellano** Andrew P '94
(614) 227-2000 **Aveni** Carl A II '99
(614) 464-6400 **Axelrod** David F '78
(614) 644-6530 **Axtell** Amanda M '99
(614) 221-0770 **Ayers** James C '77
(614) 249-1002 **Ayers** Stephen F '04
(614) 734-0991 **Baba** Martin N '91
(614) 228-4200 **Babbitt** Gerald J '79
(614) 228-4200 **Babbitt & Wellbaum LLP**
(614) 716-1615 **Bacha** James R '79
(614) 249-9092 **Bachmann** Gregg H '87
(614) 249-7452 **Bacon** Brian M '84
(614) 799-3207 **Bacon** Kevin R '98
(614) 387-2243 **Badurina** Elizabeth M '86
(614) 221-4911 **Bahgat** Abe '87
(614) 424-7360 **Bahlmann** Jerome R '67
(614) 583-0088 **Bahnsen** Deborah Nay '84
(614) 221-3155 **Bailey Cavalieri LLC**
(614) 221-3155 **Bailey** Daniel A '78
(614) 885-8272 **Bailey** Richard W '57
(614) 885-8272 **Bailey & Slavin**
(614) 224-9223 **Bainbridge** Andrew J '96
(614) 224-9223 **Bainbridge** Thomas H Jr. '67
(614) 224-4114 **Bainter** David T '69
(614) 466-3016 **Bair** Jodi J '94
(614) 227-2300 **Baird-Veley** Catherine J '04
(614) 895-3007 **Baisden** Larry J '76
(614) 221-2253 **Baker** Blaise G '83
(614) 227-2000 **Baker** Bradley K '91
(614) 227-2364 **Baker** David G '72
(614) 444-2200 **Baker** Elizabeth J '85
(614) 227-2487 **Baker** Frederick L '82
(614) 224-3504 **Baker** Geoffrey L '95
(614) 462-2344 **Baker** Gregory S '98
(614) 228-1541 **Baker & Hostetler LLP**
(614) 645-7483 **Baker** Lara N '94
(614) 752-1200 **Baker** Richard L '93
(614) 236-8036 **Baker** Samuel M '72
(614) 466-7919 **Baker** Shelagh F '79
(614) 488-2202 **Baker** Thomas S Jr. '68
(614) 716-0500 **Balaloski** Daniel K '97
(614) 538-1840 **Balcerzak** Thomas J '89
(614) 224-2329 **Balch** Jacintha M '79
(614) 224-2329 **Balch** John R '84
(614) 228-9550 **Baldree** Cheri M '04
(614) 273-0171 **Baldwin** Melissa W '96
(614) 466-8944 **Baldwin** Shannon Freed '02
(614) 228-1357 **Ball** Claire M Jr. '67
(614) 464-6400 **Ball** James M '74
(614) 488-6166 **Ball** Karen L '87
(614) 624-5017 **Ball** Michael D '94
(614) 447-8550 **Ball** Steven L '74
(614) 224-8374 **Ballam** William F '80
(614) 227-8806 **Ballard** Catherine M '85
(614) 466-3636 **Ballard** Steven '83
(614) 888-3185 **Ballenger** Kathleen A '79
(614) 466-4100 **Ballenger** Mark J '89
(614) 469-3226 **Balthaser** James H '78
(614) 445-8287 **Bamberger** Kathryn A '91
(614) 236-2483 **Bametzrieder** Lori A '03
(614) 462-2274 **Banchefsky** Mitchell H '83
(614) 848-5975 **Bandman** Marc B '87
(614) 236-6245 **Bank** Danny W '90
(614) 227-8836 **Bank** H Randy '84
(614) 469-3939 **Bankovich** Candace A '02
(614) 294-5040 **Bannerman** Robert C '97
(614) 365-9900 **Banvard** Kris '03
(614) 436-0539 **Baran Piper Tarkowsky Fitzgerald & Theis Co,LPA**
(614) 227-2000 **Baranowski** Edwin M '82
(614) 462-2311 **Barath** William J '89
(614) 466-5967 **Barber** Barbara L '97
(614) 995-4934 **Barbosky** Pamella A '92
(614) 231-0003 **Barch** Bryan C '03
(614) 221-6969 **Barclay** Craig D '73
(614) 310-0200 **Bardash** James T '97
(614) 445-6757 **Bardwell** Robert E Jr. '88
(614) 227-2000 **Bares** Bryce A '04
(614) 469-7417 **Barkan** Alexander G '71
(614) 461-1551 **Barkan** Irving '57
(614) 461-1551 **Barkan** Neal J '78
(614) 221-4221 **Barkan + Neff**
(614) 888-9611 **Barker** Larry D '74
(614) 644-6905 **Barley** Christopher E '93
(614) 228-6885 **Barley-McBride** Mary '86
(614) 228-6885 **Barnes** Belinda S '87
(614) 466-6696 **Barnes** James A '85
(614) 716-1925 **Barnes** Jenny C '94
(614) 249-8169 **Barnes** Thomas E '78
(614) 728-1922 **Barnes** Yolanda L '87
(614) 228-1541 **Barnett** Eric R '04
(614) 462-2315 **Barnett** Valerie T '04
(614) 224-3838 **Barnhart** David B '81
(614) 462-2246 **Barnhart** Richard A '79
(614) 228-6885 **Barno** John C '94
Barnum Carol L '77
(614) 466-8600 **Barone** Juliane E '01
(614) 462-3310 **Barrett** Mark J '82
(614) 227-2000 **Barrett** Phillip H '68
(614) 227-2000 **Barrick** Penny L '01
(614) 644-0876 **Barron** John W '01
(614) 462-5458 **Barsotti** Stephen C '02
(614) 338-1800 **Barstow** Todd W '91
(614) 693-6842 **Barta** Mark B '91
(614) 227-2379 **Bartemes** Amy S '93
(614) 228-1541 **Bartholomew** Kirsten L '04
(614) 466-2926 **Bartleson** David T '92
(614) 466-1551 **Bartlett** Keith T '81
(614) 249-2300 **Bartlett** Philip B '85
(614) 466-2766 **Bartley** John P '87
(614) 480-5423 **Barton** L Scott '97
(614) 469-0400 **Basil** Brian A '95
(614) 462-3194 **Basnett** Jeffrey M '91
(614) 431-2277 **Bass** Leon D '98
(614) 224-9207 **Basta** Angie W '93
(614) 221-3630 **Bates** John H '93
(614) 224-0531 **Bates** Lorri J '97
(614) 221-8448 **Bathija** Priya J '04
(614) 221-3155 **Batke** Gary S '85
(614) 262-9600 **Batross** Martin E '77
(614) 444-3003 **Battisti** Eugene F Jr. '87
(614) 469-7411 **Battisti** Linda M '79
(614) 227-2000 **Baughman** Scott E '92
(614) 466-2966 **Baumann** M Elizabeth '99
(614) 466-8288 **Baumgarten** Marc T '86
(614) 221-6088 **Baumwell** Howard E '85
(614) 227-2314 **Baxter** Martha P '82
(614) 466-5394 **Bay** John A '80
(614) 466-6192 **Beachler** Jayne S '76
(614) 252-5116 **Beachler** Jinx S '79
(614) 444-3900 **Beal** Thomas D '75
(614) 227-2000 **Beale** Jennifer E '01
(614) 387-1935 **Beale** Victoria F '04
(614) 224-8187 **Beals** David A '87
(614) 464-6400 **Beard** Douglas M '01
(614) 294-7067 **Beatley** Jack K '79
(614) 464-6400 **Beatley** James R Jr. '65
(614) 263-7000 **Beattey** Robert A Jr. '03
(614) 221-2400 **Beatty** Laurel A '99
(614) 228-1541 **Beatty** Otto III '94
(614) 221-2400 **Beatty** Otto Jr. '66
(614) 466-4605 **Beatty** Patrick W '92
(614) 224-0919 **Beauchamp** Sarah H '86
(614) 224-8166 **Beausay** Thomas J '87
(614) 222-4734 **Beaver** Michael P '04
(614) 227-2361 **Beavers** John P '72
(614) 464-6400 **Bechtold** Timothy J '78
(614) 221-7201 **Beck** Amanda M '00
(614) 340-2329 **Beck** Bethany A '77
(614) 469-3939 **Beck** David A '00
Beck David F '72
(614) 273-3300 **Beck** Donald P '01
(614) 464-6400 **Beck** Jonathan P '81
(614) 462-3194 **Beck** Robert J Jr. '98
(614) 228-2531 **Beck** Stacey L '00
(614) 457-7863 **Becker** James C '80
(614) 464-6400 **Becker** Jeffrey R '02
(614) 387-2635 **Becker** Julie E '94
(614) 469-4778 **Becker** Michael R '76
(614) 466-7447 **Becker** William C Jr. '81
(614) 227-2000 **Beckett** Donald L '57
(614) 415-7468 **Beckman** Michelle F '96
(614) 461-0256 **Beckman** Stacy S '94
Beebe David K '75
(614) 365-4100 **Beekhuizen** Michael N '95
(614) 227-2000 **Beeler** John C '76
(614) 466-4396 **Beeler** Steven Logan '04
(614) 466-5394 **Beeler-Andrews** Jill E '98
(614) 228-8575 **Beery** Eric W '96
(614) 538-1277 **Beggs** Robert J '82
(614) 464-2025 **Behal** Robert J '77
(614) 466-2766 **Behlen** Thomas P '89
(614) 466-6696 **Behm** Dennis H '94
(614) 668-4517 **Behrens** Shanda M '02
(614) 249-7111 **Beldy** Michael D '97
(614) 466-4882 **Belenker** Rachel L '81
(614) 464-0400 **Belinky** David A '77
(614) 466-8288 **Belinky** Debra M '78
(614) 278-6762 **Bell** Albert J '85
(614) 464-6400 **Bell** Anker M '82
(614) 586-1310 **Bell** Jessica Rodriguez '02
(614) 228-0704 **Bell** Langdon D '63
(614) 464-6400 **Bell** Robert A Jr. '00
(614) 228-0704 **Bell Royer & Sanders Co,LPA**
(614) 239-5032 **Bell** Suzanne P '97
(614) 645-8906 **Bell** Tannisha D '03
(614) 621-1500 **Belleville** Mark L '95
(614) 444-6556 **Belli** Dennis C '79
(614) 227-8885 **Belo** Vladimir P '99
(614) 457-2034 **Belton** John T '77
(614) 716-1647 **Belville** Barbara A '80
(614) 644-7250 **Belville** Dan E '88
(614) 466-7190 **Belz** Robert B '74
(614) 878-7251 **Bendig** Charles H III '78
(614) 274-0033 **Bendycki** Mary L '84
(614) 228-7775 **Benedict** Spencer R '76
(614) 223-9300 **Benesch Friedlander Coplan & Aronoff LLP**
(614) 463-1551 **Benis** Stuart A '71
(614) 719-1589 **Benjamin** Ann Womer '78
(614) 464-3900 **Bennett** Adam J '04
(614) 488-1161 **Bennett** Bradley E '03
(614) 462-4450 **Bennett** John Ira '73
(614) 645-8988 **Bennett** Sue A '83
(614) 645-7483 **Bennington** Jeffrey R '00
(614) 827-1625 **Benson** Pamela C '90
(614) 221-5216 **Benson** William B '90
(614) 221-4000 **Bentine** John W '75
(614) 445-3962 **Benton** Frederick D Jr. '80
(614) 258-6000 **Benton** Shannon K '00
(614) 752-6417 **Benyo** Steven J '89
(614) 469-7404 **Beran** Barbara L '82
(614) 227-8870 **Berendsen** James R '71
(614) 445-2348 **Berg** John R '92
(614) 461-0256 **Berger** Robert R '95
(614) 227-2000 **Bergman** Andrew S '91
(614) 279-7058 **Bergman** Robert D '76
(614) 466-9559 **Bergmann** David C '76
(614) 233-5603 **Bering** Adam D '97
(614) 274-6700 **Berkemer** Frederick L '77
(614) 716-1648 **Berkemeyer** Thomas G '86
(614) 469-3268 **Berliner** Alan F '76
(614) 462-3194 **Bernard** Robert M '79
(614) 225-4382 **Berndt** Ellen G '84
(614) 280-9300 **Berndt** Jeffrey A '83
(614) 464-6400 **Berner** Michael G '03
(614) 228-1541 **Bernert** Edward J '77
(614) 249-0878 **Berridge** Thomas E '72
(614) 728-7055 **Berrien** Tara L '01
(614) 221-1215 **Berry** Robert L '75
(614) 221-0725 **Bertram** Pamela J '82
(614) 436-8100 **Bertram** William C '82
(614) 268-8410 **Beshears** Ruth E '91
(614) 206-4945 **Besser** Kenneth R '97
(614) 464-2200 **Bethel** Blythe M '84
(614) 463-4201 **Bettendorf** Margaret C '97
(614) 222-4900 **Bhatt** Sanjay K '94
(614) 466-3280 **Bialczak** Stanley T '84
(614) 866-9143 **Biancamano** John J '76
(614) 241-2154 **Bibbo** Jeffrey R '91
(614) 236-6496 **Biddle** James H '75
(614) 252-5116 **Bidwell** David M '80
(614) 221-3155 **Biehl** Adam J '95
(614) 463-6661 **Bielby** Jeanine L '87
(614) 716-2759 **Bilenko** David '03
(614) 236-8000 **Billings** James R '93
(614) 228-6885 **Bills** Joshua R '99
(614) 464-2572 **Binau** Dan J '76
(614) 228-6888 **Binder** Maura E '04
(614) 752-5081 **Binkovitz** David J '78
(614) 224-1979 **Binning** John B '76
(614) 224-1982 **Binning** Peter J T '04
(614) 227-2325 **Birath** John F Jr. '71
(614) 461-1100 **Birrer** Scott B '94
(614) 223-9300 **Bisesi** Phillip P '98
(614) 657-6944 **Biswas** Naren '59
(614) 462-2228 **Bittner** Paul L '93
(614) 716-3068 **Bivens** Gina S '99
(614) 253-4744 **Bivens** Michael T '03
(614) 228-1541 **Bjerke** Jack A '70
(614) 761-8113 **Black** Christopher G '97
(614) 241-2174 **Black** David R '01
(614) 224-6257 **Black** Lori A '90
(614) 752-4219 **Black** Rachael T '92
(614) 225-0760 **Blackburn** John D '74
(614) 461-5600 **Blackburn** Thomas I '79
(614) 466-3957 **Blackford** Megan Davis '04
(614) 272-6951 **Blackman** Gordon A '75
(614) 464-0082 **Blackmer** Mark R '82
(614) 221-1341 **Blackmore** Margaret L '81
(614) 466-0722 **Blair** Adrianne M '90
(614) 481-4480 **Blake** Curtis R '89
(614) 462-3555 **Blake** Jeffrey A '88
(614) 752-4153 **Blake** Richard E '85
(614) 424-7352 **Blanda** John J '70
(614) 249-0295 **Blankenship** Alice K '83
(614) 572-0046 **Blankenship** Arnold D II '93
(614) 274-2889 **Blankenship** Jeffrey A '83
(614) 224-5205 **Blaser** Jennifer R '99
(614) 324-5969 **Blasko** Joseph C '97
(614) 728-5100 **Bledsoe** Tony W Jr. '99
(614) 629-5357 **Bloch** Daniel D '02
(614) 236-6560 **Blocher** Janet G '90
(614) 236-8020 **Bloom** Theodore S '80
(614) 224-9221 **Bloomfield** David S '69
(614) 227-2000 **Bloomfield** David S Jr. '97
(614) 224-9221 **Bloomfield & Kempf**
(614) 227-2368 **Bloomfield** Sally W '69
(614) 224-3080 **Blosser** Jeffery M '98
(614) 466-6696 **Blosser** Keith D '90
Blower George H '02
(614) 223-9300 **Blubaugh** Marc S '97
(614) 224-6969 **Blue** Douglas J '92
(614) 224-6969 **Blue** Jason A '64
(614) 224-6969 **Blue Wilson + Blue LLC**
(614) 445-8416 **Blum** Charles J '66
(614) 445-8416 **Blum** Jason C '00
(614) 475-9511 **Blumenstiel** Braden A '04
(614) 475-9511 **Blumenstiel Huhn Adams & Evans,LLC**
(614) 475-9511 **Blumenstiel** James B '67
(614) 475-9511 **Blumenstiel** Laura C '97
(614) 220-9200 **Blumenthal** Kenneth S '83
(614) 236-6124 **Bluth** William H '70
(614) 221-2121 **Boatright** Douglas C '89
(614) 462-3194 **Bobbitt** Geoffrey C '82
(614) 889-2531 **Bobbitt** Lawrence C '93
(614) 466-8600 **Bockbrader** Katherine J '96
(614) 224-4114 **Boda** Daniel K '75
(614) 466-5394 **Bodiker** David H '63
(614) 644-7233 **Bodine** John J Jr. '89
(614) 464-1211 **Bodoh** William T '64
(614) 228-1541 **Boeckman** Joseph P '87
(614) 415-7100 **Bogart** Amy '95
(614) 464-6400 **Boggs** Kelly A '98

(614) 451-9646 **Boggs** Kenneth R '80
(614) 228-4546 **Boggs** Patrick H '85
(614) 464-6400 **Boggs** Theodore A '86
(614) 861-1350 **Bohan** Michelle L '00
Bohm Anneliese A '99
(614) 466-8911 **Boiarsky** Megan H '04
(614) 252-8066 **Boiston** Bernard G '69
(614) 227-2000 **Bojko** Andrew M '98
(614) 466-7967 **Bojko** Kimberly W '98
(614) 462-3555 **Bokelman** Christopher '99
(614) 466-3339 **Boller** Jack A '81
(614) 338-8485 **Bolon** David D '92
(614) 693-6841 **Bolon** William T '88
(614) 365-2700 **Bolyard** Beth C '01
(614) 461-1100 **Bonasera** Michael D '03
(614) 469-3259 **Bonasera** Thomas J '75
(614) 466-2766 **Bonaventura** Mark G '79
(614) 462-2500 **Bond** Anthony R '93
(614) 462-3555 **Bond** Kimberly MacVicar '03
(614) 222-8686 **Bondy** Melissa Martinez '96
(614) 228-0200 **Boone** Timothy J '76
(614) 692-3284 **Booth** Gail L '90
(614) 784-9451 **Booth** Sandra E '79
(614) 466-8838 **Borchert** Daniel R '78
(614) 239-4014 **Borden** Rod C '81
(614) 463-9441 **Born** Michael E '88
Bornstein Michael D '89
(614) 227-2000 **Borowicz** Stacey A '03
(614) 840-3697 **Bosko** Marybeth '93
(614) 469-5715 **Bosley** David J '78
(614) 464-2572 **Bossart** Emily J '04
(614) 481-6999 **Bosworth** Angela L '91
(614) 221-4000 **Bott** April R '96
(614) 227-2000 **Botti** James P '82
(614) 466-4320 **Bowe** Carolyn S '02
(614) 629-3000 **Bower** Amelia A '84
(614) 621-4060 **Bower** Eileen R '95
(614) 728-7244 **Bowers** Andrew D '99
(614) 464-6400 **Bowers** Brenda K '90
(614) 443-6548 **Bowers** John S '58
(614) 221-1166 **Bowman** John S '98
(614) 466-3180 **Bowman** Jonathan M '94
(614) 221-3155 **Bowman** Katharine B '83
(614) 221-0922 **Bownas** James H '71
(614) 466-3998 **Bowshier** Denis J '90
(614) 280-8718 **Boyd** Alan B '74
(614) 466-3615 **Boyd** Bethany R '90
(614) 224-8374 **Boyd** Eric R '86
(614) 891-6584 **Boyd** James W Sr. '73
(614) 229-3888 **Boyd** Robert E '97
(614) 716-0500 **Boyd** Robert E III '79
(614) 451-5000 **Boyd** Roy F '76
(614) 462-4492 **Boyd** Sally W '81
(614) 462-3555 **Boyd** Tracie M '98
(614) 645-6763 **Boyer** Betsy A '03
(614) 464-6400 **Boyer** John N '00
(614) 224-8446 **Boyer** Kelly S '03
Boyer Patricia A '01
(614) 461-6973 **Boylan** Richard L '68
(614) 221-5216 **Boyle** Kerry T '00
(614) 457-7219 **Boyle** Sean O '88
(614) 221-5216 **Boyle** Thomas E '72
(614) 443-8731 **Boyuk** Walter C '68
(614) 442-1953 **Bracco** Robert A '82
(614) 416-5120 **Bradigan** Brian J '81
(614) 716-2934 **Bradley** Elizabeth M '03
(614) 239-1389 **Bradley** Philip Raymond '50
(614) 227-2000 **Brady** John E '70
(614) 228-4546 **Brahm** Richard C '70
Braithwaite Melanie J '81
(614) 464-6400 **Brandt** Adam K '96
(614) 645-8296 **Brandt** Michael T '68
(614) 431-1500 **Brankamp** Joshua W '04
(614) 326-5544 **Brannock** Keith W '57
(614) 221-2121 **Brant** Charles E '59
(614) 460-4658 **Brant** Marjorie H '83
(614) 459-5200 **Brantner** Jeffrey W '74
(614) 644-3037 **Brault** Eva M '98
(614) 463-9770 **Braun** Jeffrey S '02
(614) 410-6500 **Braun** JoAnna Christie '92
(614) 469-3939 **Braun** Tonya Blosser '02
(614) 292-2342 **Braunstein** Michael '93
(614) 365-5673 **Braverman** Loren L '77
(614) 463-9770 **Bravo** Eric S '90
(614) 486-7716 **Breen** John E '82
(614) 351-8570 **Brehmer** Marcia L '76
(614) 464-4201 **Breitfeller** Ralph E '78
(614) 249-4572 **Breitstadt** Charles P '74
(614) 751-1000 **Brennan** Kevin J '89
(614) 258-6000 **Brenner Brown Golian & McCaffrey Co,LPA**
(614) 258-6000 **Brenner** Todd A '91
(614) 462-5472 **Brenning** Mary F '96
(614) 716-2147 **Breseman** Ross E '93
(614) 466-3576 **Bressler** Marla K '92
(614) 538-1116 **Bressman** David A '90
(614) 466-6750 **Brewer** Margaret A '85
(614) 466-8980 **Brey** Diane R '88
(614) 221-4000 **Brey** Donald C '81
(614) 227-2312 **Bricker** Christine A '95
(614) 488-1161 **Bricker** Derek F '01
(614) 269-4900 **Bricker** Douglas M '69
(614) 227-2300 **Bricker & Eckler LLP**
(614) 269-4900 **Bricker & Maxfield,LLC**
(614) 365-4100 **Bricker** Timothy R '93
(614) 228-1541 **Bridges** Michael D '93
(614) 464-6400 **Bridgman** G Ross Jr. '73
(614) 221-7777 **Brightwell** Julie M '93
(614) 221-0240 **Brigner** Julie E '96
(614) 462-5015 **Brigner** Nancy A '92
(614) 221-5216 **Brill** Lauren S '03
(614) 466-3269 **Brill** William L '80
(614) 221-5216 **Bringardner** Daniel E '78
(614) 221-5216 **Bringardner** Richard D '78
(614) 481-4480 **Brininger** Tod A '98
(614) 438-3001 **Brinkman** Dale T '77
(614) 224-4149 **Briscoe** Colleen H '77
(614) 466-3998 **Briscoe** Emily K '96
(614) 445-8461 **Brisk** Marlene B '89
(614) 228-4526 **Bristol** Rachelle E '98
(614) 224-8339 **Britt Campbell Nagel & Sproat**
(614) 224-8339 **Britt** James C Jr. '73
(614) 251-4000 **Britton** John B '98
(614) 620-2196 **Brock** Thomas J '96
(614) 225-7020 **Brockman** Vincent C '88
(614) 228-8400 **Brodnik** Martyn T '80
(614) 462-5456 **Brody** John P '79
(614) 848-4300 **Brookes** Mark C '83
(614) 224-9900 **Brooks** Keith H '75
(614) 457-1010 **Brooks & Logan Co,LPA**
(614) 457-1010 **Brooks** Paula L '83
(614) 221-3155 **Brooks** Richard D Jr. '72
(614) 462-3996 **Brooks** Stephanie L '86
(614) 464-3563 **Brosius** Donald F '80
(614) 491-1080 **Browell** Douglas K '78
(614) 227-2344 **Brown** Alexander M '99
(614) 337-8366 **Brown** Amanda B '02
(614) 221-6800 **Brown** Angela F '88
(614) 466-3998 **Brown** Blaine W '95
(614) 469-5715 **Brown** Daniel A '73
(614) 481-6000 **Brown** David A '92
(614) 464-6400 **Brown** Donald A '77
(614) 466-9546 **Brown** Emily M '99
(614) 258-9595 **Brown** Eric L '91
(614) 462-6288 **Brown** Eric S '79
(614) 488-3159 **Brown** Gary E '73
(614) 221-4225 **Brown** Herbert R '56
(614) 445-2647 **Brown** James D '91
(614) 224-4114 **Brown** James W '82
(614) 224-4114 **Brown** Jeffrey A '78
(614) 221-4255 **Brown** Jeffrey L '79
(614) 487-4426 **Brown** Kenneth A '84
(614) 331-9554 **Brown** Kerry T '93
(614) 237-2595 **Brown** Kevin W '82
(614) 227-8894 **Brown** Kimberly J '95
(614) 365-2700 **Brown** Kristen J '90
(614) 461-0256 **Brown** Lori J '88
(614) 223-9300 **Brown** Lyle B '98
(614) 225-4358 **Brown** Nancy G '74
(614) 252-2026 **Brown** Paul R '75
(614) 464-2000 **Brown** Paula M '97
(614) 464-6400 **Brown** Philip A '74
(614) 258-6000 **Brown** Philip F '85
(614) 451-2555 **Brown** Ray G '61
(614) 461-5600 **Brown** Richard D '81
(614) 488-1169 **Brown** Stephen W '75
(614) 241-5550 **Brown** Steven M '84
(614) 464-6400 **Brown** Susan E '71
(614) 460-4203 **Brown** Thomas J Jr. '75
(614) 462-5064 **Brown** Tonia R '03
(614) 445-8287 **Brown** Wayne A '73
(614) 890-9099 **Brown** William W '60
(614) 722-4044 **Brown** Yvette M '85
(614) 488-6005 **Brown-Schwart** Mary A '92
(614) 464-2201 **Brownfield** C William '71
(614) 464-3900 **Browning & Cook**
(614) 464-3900 **Browning** Jon M '86
(614) 471-0085 **Browning & Meyer Co,LPA**
(614) 462-3117 **Browning** Pamela B '83
(614) 464-6400 **Browning** Stephen D '93
(614) 471-0085 **Browning** William J '83
(614) 227-2301 **Brownlee** Thomas R Jr. '89
(614) 464-6400 **Broz** Alycia N '98
(614) 227-2000 **Brubaker** Robert L '72
(614) 292-0795 **Brudney** James J '95
(614) 461-1311 **Brudny** James J Jr. '83
(614) 464-6400 **Brunetto** Joseph A '80
(614) 241-5550 **Brunner** Rick L '80
(614) 461-1311 **Brunton** Gregory D '93
(614) 228-6131 **Bryan** Jonathan M '95
Bryant Kevin L '01
(614) 228-1541 **Bryant** Letitia S '04
(614) 466-4605 **Bubutiev** Jim K '94
(614) 575-3530 **Bucci** Tammie S '01
(614) 464-6400 **Buchenroth** Stephen R '74
(614) 480-3110 **Buchholz** Thomas M '90
(614) 462-3555 **Buchman** David M '77
(614) 221-8448 **Buckingham Doolittle & Burroughs, LLP**
(614) 461-5600 **Buckley King,LPA**
(614) 460-4664 **Buckley** Shalu T '96
(614) 221-3456 **Buda** David M '74
(614) 298-8150 **Buergenthal** Alan E '96
(614) 645-4980 **Bui** Hoang Diem '04
(614) 466-0118 **Bulgrin** Richard M '87
(614) 487-1106 **Bull** John A '84
(614) 688-5699 **Bull** Joseph O '86
(614) 466-8950 **Bull** Julianna F '84
(614) 249-6276 **Bull** Mary M '95
(614) 677-8224 **Bullock** Elizabeth S '80
(614) 387-9571 **Bumbico** James F '99
(614) 294-1900 **Bumgarner** Christopher D '04
(614) 486-0297 **Bumgarner** Robert B '95
(614) 252-1131 **Burchfield** James R '78
(614) 228-5800 **Burchinal** Christopher J '99
(614) 224-2590 **Burden** Eric J '81
Burdge Matthew D '02
(614) 481-0332 **Burgoon** Joseph J Jr. '59
(614) 436-0600 **Burke** Diane E '98
(614) 464-6400 **Burke** Jennifer M '01
(614) 249-6716 **Burke** Joseph E '03
(614) 221-4400 **Burkett** Elizabeth S '86
(614) 221-3155 **Burkhart** Matthew J '97
(614) 221-5216 **Burkholder** Bruce H '80
(614) 464-1877 **Burleigh** Barbra A '03
(614) 466-3615 **Burley** James W '80
(614) 857-3102 **Burley** John D '84
(614) 221-8900 **Burman** Robert N '73
(614) 221-8900 **Burman & Robinson**
(614) 469-3939 **Burnell** Brigette A '02
(614) 227-8804 **Burnes** James P '78
(614) 438-1217 **Burns** Darla J '85
(614) 444-1190 **Burns** John A '73
(614) 469-5715 **Burns** Michael J '79
(614) 292-9307 **Burns** Robert E '78
(614) 466-7853 **Burns** William M '76
(614) 387-9024 **Burpee** Robert L '96
(614) 224-8824 **Burrier** Brian C '92
(614) 466-7424 **Burrow** Marcie P '98
(614) 876-3862 **Burt** LoAnn Q '96
(614) 466-4882 **Burtch** James M III '75
(614) 228-1541 **Burtch** John H '74
(614) 888-6067 **Burton** Martin D '95
(614) 387-2065 **Burwell** David W '76
(614) 258-1983 **Busam** David R '91
(614) 421-1980 **Buscemi** Anthony W '93
(614) 280-1100 **Bush** Kevin R '85
(614) 466-3998 **Bush** Robert S '90
(614) 445-6265 **Butauski** Joseph A '87
(614) 221-3151 **Butler Cincione & DiCuccio**
(614) 221-4000 **Butler** David J '97
(614) 221-3882 **Butler** Eugene R '86
(614) 461-1100 **Butler** John C '72
(614) 486-3585 **Butzer** Dane C '00
(614) 227-2000 **Buzby** Brian L '74
(614) 442-5626 **Byard** Robert R '89
(614) 462-3580 **Byers** Brad R '89
(614) 228-6283 **Byers** Kevin P '88
(614) 221-2838 **Byers** Michael A '78
(614) 752-7811 **Byers** Renee L '99
(614) 466-4510 **Byrne** Robert J '88
(614) 469-3939 **Byrne** Sean P '04
(614) 466-3615 **Byrnett** Megan E '04
(614) 224-8374 **Byrom** Robert G '77
(614) 645-8815 **Byron** Linda '98
(614) 462-3555 **Cable** Daniel J '92
(614) 445-6265 **Caborn** David A '86
Caborn Leslie Thorpe '89
(614) 461-8103 **Cabot** Jeffery A '87
(614) 464-1211 **Cadwallader** John I '78
(614) 249-9001 **Cahill** John C '83
(614) 644-8381 **Cain** Kenneth R Jr. '96
(614) 222-8686 **Cain** Lacey L '00
(614) 464-2000 **Cairns** Jacob A '03
(614) 469-3200 **Calcaterra** Craig A '98
(614) 621-1500 **Calfee Halter & Griswold LLP**
(614) 644-9632 **Calhoun** Jason H '82
(614) 252-2300 **Calig & Handelman,LPA**
(614) 252-2300 **Calig** Samuel L '74
(614) 461-0256 **Caligiuri** Joseph M '02
(614) 461-4455 **Callahan** Rory P '00
(614) 466-5394 **Callais** Melissa J '04
(614) 728-8537 **Callender** Cynthia N '96
(614) 224-5700 **Callender** Gwen E '91
(614) 645-7385 **Calloway** George H '83
(614) 487-3202 **Cameron** Bruce L '69
(614) 221-3318 **Cameron** Eric B '04
(614) 387-0605 **Cameron** Julie A '03
(614) 469-3939 **Camillus** John C '04
(614) 340-2053 **Campbell** Bruce A '65
(614) 227-2319 **Campbell** Drew H '90
(614) 846-2000 **Campbell** Fred M '54
(614) 846-2000 **Campbell Hornbeck Chilcoat & Veatch,LLC**
(614) 224-8339 **Campbell** Joel R '72
(614) 469-3311 **Campbell** Scott A '95
(614) 644-7233 **Campbell** Scott M '99
(614) 449-0926 **Canale** David M '85
(614) 644-1583 **Canan** Crystal A '86
(614) 462-3555 **Canepa** Angela R '91
(614) 466-4638 **Canepa** James V '89
(614) 221-3318 **Canestraro** Carl R '93
(614) 722-3940 **Canowitz** Robin L '92
(614) 464-6400 **Canter** Michael J '72
(614) 252-2026 **Caplan** Robert L '94
(614) 785-4676 **Carducci** Daniel G '81
(614) 224-5205 **Cardwell** Richard D '91
(614) 227-4891 **Carey** Kimball H '79
(614) 228-9707 **Carey** Laura M '98
(614) 278-6800 **Carey** Rick V '03
(614) 276-4000 **Carleton** Betsy A '94
(614) 280-1100 **Carlino** Steven G '01
(614) 728-5693 **Carlson** Christopher T '91
(614) 227-2000 **Carlson** Craig R '91
(614) 231-8900 **Carlson** Leonard A '78
(614) 462-3888 **Carlson** Melinda S '88
(614) 464-6400 **Carman** Corrine S '92
(614) 445-6499 **Carnahan** John A '55
(614) 442-5626 **Carnahan** Russell E '84
(614) 227-2000 **Carney** John P '01
(614) 466-8980 **Carney** Stephen P '94
(614) 228-6885 **Carpenter** James C '75
(614) 444-6467 **Carpenter** Kendra L '01
(614) 365-4100 **Carpenter & Lipps LLP**
(614) 365-4100 **Carpenter** Michael H '77
(614) 466-8911 **Carr** James A '80
(614) 846-7160 **Carr** Steven C '80
(614) 547-0350 **Carroll** David W '76
(614) 221-3155 **Carroll** Donald D '90
(614) 644-7250 **Carroll** Roger F '79
(614) 547-0350 **Carroll Ucker & Hemmer,LLC**
(614) 481-9655 **Carruthers** David F '79
(614) 716-3849 **Carson** Cynthia Butler '96
(614) 223-9300 **Carsonie** Frank W '92
(614) 221-2121 **Carter** Danielle M '99
(614) 645-5817 **Carter** Melinda D '89
(614) 645-8300 **Carter** Theresa L '85
(614) 459-4140 **Carter** Wanda L '82
(614) 645-7483 **Carty** Bridget E '00
(614) 464-6400 **Cary** Nelson D '01
(614) 224-1222 **Casanova** Janice E '02
(614) 480-4891 **Case** Larry D '82
(614) 469-3208 **Case** William R '73
(614) 564-2666 **Casey** John F '65
(614) 462-7492 **Casey** Karen S '91
(614) 227-2300 **Casey** Peter R IV '01
(614) 228-6888 **Cassone** Michael J '04
(614) 645-7385 **Castle** Kelly M '86
(614) 228-5331 **Casto** Don M III '72
(614) 249-8782 **Casto** Jamie R '96
(614) 224-4114 **Catalano** William A Jr. '74
(614) 481-4480 **Caudill** Christal L '97
(614) 221-4255 **Cavalaris** Nicholas C '93
(614) 221-3155 **Cavalieri** Nick V '73
(614) 224-5205 **Cavezza** Edward '82
(614) 466-2766 **Cayton** John F '00
(614) 529-8000 **Cecil** Andrew W '86
(614) 221-0888 **Cennamo** Louis W '77
(614) 466-6700 **Chafin** Matthew H '93
(614) 849-0134 **Chaiten** Louis A '00
(614) 457-7989 **Chakeres** David J '77
(614) 459-7109 **Chambers** Yvonne F '82
(614) 228-6135 **Champ** Stephanie D '02
(614) 462-7237 **Chance** Sharlene I '99
(614) 221-9100 **Chapin** Lance A '98
(614) 466-6594 **Chapman** Joseph "Ted" '00
(614) 466-4656 **Chapman** Shirley E '93
(614) 228-4422 **Chappano** Perry M '86
(614) 228-4422 **Chappano Wood PLL**
(614) 221-0240 **Chappelear** Stephen E '77
(614) 462-3194 **Charlesworth** Thomas F '89
(614) 752-6890 **Charney** Deborah J '92
(614) 644-7342 **Charvat** Marie '78
(614) 249-5276 **Chatterton** Lisa A '94
Chavanne Michelle L '01
(614) 462-3194 **Chavers** Dane C '81
(614) 469-5576 **Chavers** Darlene E '87
(614) 224-3827 **Chavez** Margaret L '00
(614) 262-2539 **Cheadle** Michele M '74
(614) 480-4647 **Cheap** Richard A '80
(614) 229-3888 **Cheek** Emerson III '70
(614) 229-3888 **Cheek & Zeehandelar,LLP**
(614) 644-5470 **Chesley-Lahm** Diane M '77
(614) 447-3812 **Chester** Casey E '92
(614) 221-4000 **Chester** James J '87
(614) 221-4000 **Chester** John J '48
(614) 221-4000 **Chester** John J Jr. '89
(614) 221-4000 **Chester Willcox & Saxbe LLP**
(614) 466-2766 **Cheugh** Robert W II '79
(614) 293-7802 **Chicoine** Julie E '03
(614) 466-8600 **Chieffo** Dominic J '66
(614) 846-2000 **Chilcoat** David L '84
(614) 846-2000 **Chilcoat** Jeffrey R '98
(614) 462-3194 **Chimbidis** Peter E '96
(614) 462-3555 **Chiu** Vincent S '04
(614) 338-0700 **Chodosh** Louis J '77
(614) 338-0700 **Chodosh** Sheila R '86
(614) 247-5853 **Choe** Susan A '96
(614) 466-4314 **Cholar** Richard T Jr. '92
(614) 469-1301 **Chorpenning** Brian E '83
(614) 469-1301 **Chorpenning Good & Pandora Co,LPA**
(614) 229-5124 **Chou** Chun-Yi K '02
(614) 464-1211 **Chouinard** Erika J '04
(614) 227-5835 **Chretien** Alfred M '92
(614) 249-7875 **Chrisley** Gail D '99
(614) 221-1830 **Christensen Christensen & DeVillers**
(614) 221-1830 **Christensen** Jon A '81
(614) 275-3444 **Christensen** Lisa M '04
(614) 221-1830 **Christensen** Mary W '83
(614) 275-3444 **Christensen** Michael D '99
(614) 443-4606 **Christensen** William J '68
(614) 645-6323 **Christie** Chester C '83
(614) 644-9326 **Christoff** Susan B '88
(614) 466-6227 **Christopher** Jack L '98
(614) 221-4747 **Christopher** Judith E '75
(614) 466-2166 **Chung** Eun Sook '02
(614) 464-2392 **Chuparkoff** Mark A '00
(614) 462-3194 **Churchill** Philip T '80
(614) 487-4439 **Cianca** Stephen P '93
(614) 466-4605 **Cicatiello** Judith L '92
(614) 228-2600 **Cicero** Christopher T '88
(614) 387-9040 **Ciecka** Emily H '04
(614) 267-7966 **Cimperman** Anthony J '89
(614) 221-3151 **Cincione** Alphonse P '61
(614) 464-6400 **Cincione** Karen A '89
(614) 221-3151 **Cincione** Matthew P '85
(614) 464-6400 **Ciriaco** Anthony C '83
(614) 469-2999 **Clark** Alison M '99
(614) 224-3838 **Clark** Allison A '04
(614) 365-2700 **Clark** D Lewis Jr. '90
(614) 464-6400 **Clark** Daniel J '02
(614) 644-0729 **Clark** Jeffery W '81
(614) 469-1400 **Clark Perdue Roberts & Scott Co,LPA**
(614) 466-5988 **Clark** Ralph D '89
(614) 538-5381 **Clark** Richard M '92
(614) 340-3895 **Clark** Sheila A '80
(614) 221-2838 **Clark** Shelli T '00
(614) 224-2125 **Clark** Toki M '89
(614) 228-1144 **Clark** Trevor M '02
(614) 221-3911 **Clark** William A '81
(614) 459-1012 **Clark** William L '60
(614) 236-6685 **Clary** Lori A '96
(614) 227-2000 **Clary** Mary Beth M '83
(614) 463-4201 **Clary** Wendy K '04
(614) 475-4598 **Cleamons** Geneva G '78
(614) 487-8210 **Cleary** Lora H '91
(614) 466-4605 **Clevenger** Bonnie L '81
(614) 222-3152 **Cliffel** Albert P III '90
(614) 224-0933 **Clifford** Damion M '04
(614) 644-7250 **Clifford** Mary-Kathleen '99
(614) 752-4650 **Cline** Jo E '94
(614) 464-6400 **Cline** Michael A '79
(614) 224-4114 **Cline** Richard A '81
(614) 752-9271 **Clodfelder** Wiley H '83
(614) 461-4455 **Cloppert** Frederick G Jr. '72
(614) 461-4455 **Cloppert Latanick Sauter & Washburn**
(614) 221-5216 **Close** Michael L '75
(614) 529-2900 **Close** Stephen P '79
(614) 436-3211 **Cloud** Clifford R '61
(614) 436-3211 **Cloud & Owen**
(614) 464-1877 **Clouse** Gerard J '84
(614) 485-1800 **Clouse** Karen L '86
(614) 292-7745 **Clovis** Albert Lee '62
(614) 466-5394 **Clovis** Charles B '00
(614) 752-8919 **Clyde** Robert M Jr. '72
(614) 221-3318 **Clymer** James G '74
(614) 374-4997 **Clymer** Tony A '91
(614) 253-8723 **Coady** Michael F '82
(614) 227-2000 **Coady** Thomas C '64
(614) 228-6888 **Coates** Kristen C '04
(614) 221-2993 **Coatney** Jennifer A '02
(614) 438-2648 **Cobb** Craig S '82
(614) 464-6400 **Cobb** Tiffany Strelow '97
(614) 863-0045 **Cochran** Michael H '71
(614) 469-3292 **Cochran** Philip B '81
(614) 462-2248 **Cochran** Robert J '91
Cockerill Curtis A '93
(614) 221-7025 **Cockrum** William G '75
(614) 464-2572 **Coco** Mark S '77
(614) 221-8448 **Cocroft** Kimberly '00
(614) 466-8669 **Cody** Robert M '82
(614) 224-1884 **Cogan** Anne M '94
(614) 469-3939 **Cogan** J Kevin '78
(614) 466-2872 **Coglianese** Richard N '96
(614) 523-1927 **Cohan** Sanford J '74
(614) 224-8176 **Cohen** Bernard '52
(614) 583-7606 **Cohen** David M '72
(614) 444-4211 **Cohen** Lloyd D '79
(614) 294-5040 **Cohen** Marshall D '90

(614) 462-5400 **Cohen** Robert G '89
(614) 227-2000 **Cohen** Robert H '76
(614) 464-6400 **Cohen** Susan A '87
(614) 223-1000 **Cohn** Robert G '91
(614) 224-1222 **Colantonio** Lawrence J '04
(614) 451-7711 **Colasurd** Christopher P '86
(614) 221-8401 **Colasurd** Michael D '84
(614) 888-0040 **Colasurdo** Kelly M '97
(614) 466-7502 **Colbert** Paul A '92
(614) 430-8175 **Colburn** Joseph L Jr. '78
(614) 461-1516 **Colby** Richard D '74
(614) 466-8980 **Cole** Douglas R '99
(614) 221-1827 **Cole** Eric R '02
(614) 466-1385 **Cole** Kimber L '93
(614) 442-6601 **Cole** Linda J '93
(614) 224-8500 **Cole** Philip E '82
(614) 644-7233 **Cole** Stuart A '77
(614) 466-2980 **Cole** William J '97
(614) 252-7853 **Coleman** Alicia R '94
(614) 462-3655 **Coleman** Cindy A '89
(614) 445-2649 **Coleman** LaVawn D '89
(614) 464-2572 **Coleman** Michael A '86
(614) 235-3653 **Coleman** Paul H '68
(614) 487-8887 **Colley** David A '78
(614) 228-6453 **Colley** Michael F '61
(614) 228-6453 **Colley Shroyer & Abraham Co,LPA**
(614) 223-9300 **Collier** Orla E III '75
Collins Amy B '92
(614) 466-2765 **Collins** Donald M '87
(614) 443-3100 **Collins** Mark C '93
(614) 443-4866 **Collins** Michael J '94
(614) 228-1144 **Collins** Philip M '73
(614) 486-3909 **Collis** Elizabeth Y '93
(614) 486-3909 **Collis** Todd W '91
(614) 228-6040 **Colner** James D '79
(614) 462-2232 **Colombo** J Corey '00
(614) 466-7900 **Colvin** Terra L '99
(614) 213-1828 **Comeaux** James F '97
(614) 457-6662 **Comeras** Leonard A '75
(614) 228-3372 **Comisford** Tracy S '91
(614) 752-8805 **Compson** Christopher C '80
(614) 227-2351 **Conard** William T '83
(614) 275-2783 **Congrove** Kathryn P '94
(614) 677-5932 **Conkle** Thomas J '89
(614) 464-8241 **Conley** Robert W '04
(614) 464-6400 **Connelly** Christopher L '04
(614) 438-1214 **Connelly** John M II '80
(614) 464-6400 **Conners** Kevin R '89
(614) 464-2025 **Connor Behal LLP**
(614) 464-2025 **Connor** Daniel D '68
(614) 461-8000 **Connor** David A '82
(614) 341-1900 **Connor** Roger L Jr. '76
(614) 466-8189 **Connor** Thomas S '91
(614) 221-6868 **Connors** James P '86
(614) 466-3664 **Conomy** Lisa J '91
(614) 227-2304 **Conrad** David K '80
(614) 326-3353 **Conroy** John T '62
(614) 227-2000 **Conway** Daniel R '80
(614) 462-3555 **Cook** Aldous B '03
(614) 466-3180 **Cook** Brian C '87
Cook Bryn A '94
(614) 221-5216 **Cook** Dale D '82
(614) 464-6400 **Cook** David W '88
(614) 645-7385 **Cook** Frank H '96
(614) 854-3280 **Cook** Gwendolyn A '83
(614) 464-0082 **Cook** John W '77
(614) 227-2383 **Cook** John W III '78
(614) 248-5703 **Cook** Joseph R '71
(614) 228-6061 **Cook** Laura F '99
(614) 227-2000 **Cook** S Ronald Jr. '70
(614) 228-5151 **Cook** Sonya L '04
(614) 629-3000 **Cook** Todd A '91
(614) 464-3900 **Cooke** Andrew P '88
(614) 688-3069 **Cooke** Elizabeth I '94
(614) 222-0531 **Cooke** Reginald A '84
(614) 248-5700 **Cookson** Eloise G '76
(614) 462-5400 **Cookson** Kenneth Ray '77
(614) 481-6000 **Cooper** Charles H Jr. '86
(614) 252-2352 **Cooper** Christopher M '84
(614) 223-2417 **Cooper** Curt D '86
(614) 481-6000 **Cooper & Elliott LLC**
(614) 228-9723 **Cooper** Kitt C Sr. '87
Cooper Kymberly R '01
(614) 644-3037 **Cooper** Martha J '83
(614) 459-4300 **Cope** Jon M '68
(614) 459-4300 **Cope** Jonathan M '97
(614) 857-4320 **Cope** Monette W '97
(614) 221-8448 **Copley** Michael F '86
(614) 276-8959 **Copp** Matthew R '94
(614) 464-6400 **Corbin** Trisha M '01
(614) 469-3939 **Corcoran** Matthew C '04
(614) 466-4656 **Cordero** Leandro Martin '95
(614) 464-6400 **Corey** George N '73
(614) 857-4393 **Coriell** Angela K '03
(614) 462-3555 **Coriell** Jennifer L '00
(614) 466-2434 **Corletzi** Carl J '77
(614) 644-2640 **Corley** Edward C '83
(614) 466-7447 **Corn** Peggy W '89
(614) 480-3869 **Corn** Ronald J '74
(614) 466-5610 **Cornelius** Melanie '85
(614) 365-2700 **Cornelius** Patrick D '97
(614) 228-5711 **Cornely** John R '00
(614) 466-7264 **Corner** Barbara S '95
(614) 294-0313 **Corner** Beverly J '89
(614) 225-9316 **Cornwell** Virginia C '99
(614) 752-6888 **Corrigan** Hugh A Jr. '95
(614) 719-3390 **Corwin** Jonathan P '02
(614) 461-0256 **Costa** Carol A '90
Costello Catherine C '81
(614) 227-2000 **Costello** Daniel W '80
(614) 523-3575 **Cottone** Carl N '03
(614) 213-4505 **Couch** James E '83
(614) 461-0256 **Coughlan** Jonathan E '78
(614) 224-0531 **Coulter** Lisa Weekley '88
(614) 227-7867 **Counts** Thomas S '85
(614) 462-3194 **Courtney** Amy Sue '00
(614) 462-3664 **Courtney** Michael J '01
(614) 461-1311 **Courtwright** Angela M '04
(614) 464-6400 **Coval** Paul J '79
(614) 462-4553 **Coverdale** Tracie A '91
(614) 222-8686 **Cowans** Timothy E '88
(614) 228-6885 **Cox** David G '89
(614) 224-4357 **Cox** Edward J Jr. '72
(614) 464-2572 **Cox** Garth G '81
(614) 645-7385 **Cox** Joshua T '85
(614) 267-2871 **Cox** Michael A '02
(614) 645-7483 **Cox** Michelle L '03
(614) 621-2313 **Cox** Paul L III '75
(614) 221-3155 **Cox** Yvette A '79
(614) 227-2000 **Crabtree** Molly S '01
(614) 249-7683 **Craig** Roger A '89
(614) 224-7193 **Craine** Kevin A '82
(614) 466-8911 **Crawford** Franklin E '03
(614) 466-1154 **Crawford** Linda S '84
(614) 249-3398 **Crawford** Timothy D '97
(614) 462-3555 **Creedon** William R '95
(614) 244-5700 **Cremeans** Kay E '88
(614) 464-1626 **Crider** Benjamin W '01
(614) 752-8984 **Crim** Connie A '89
(614) 644-7233 **Criss** Michael Scott '97
Crissman Charlette M '00
(614) 462-2243 **Crist** Tyson A '99
(614) 221-1166 **Critchett** Eugene R '01
(614) 228-5822 **Crites** Don Michael '78
(614) 462-2281 **Crognale** Corey V '80
(614) 466-8457 **Cromley** Robert E Jr. '82
(614) 466-7264 **Cronheim** George K '98
(614) 716-1580 **Cross** Jeffrey D '82
(614) 677-2406 **Crossett** Kevin S '02
(614) 224-8374 **Crotte** Alberto D '94
(614) 463-9770 **Crow** Scot C '97
(614) 466-3947 **Crowe** Jodi F '93
(614) 462-3555 **Crowell** Adam E '02
(614) 846-3870 **Crowley** Charles E '63
(614) 466-3703 **Cuckler** Steven R '02
(614) 252-2026 **Culbreath** Stanlee E '75
(614) 292-0582 **Culley** Christopher M '82
(614) 287-2592 **Cullison** Daryl L '82
(614) 466-5394 **Culshaw** Kelly L '96
(614) 693-8134 **Cummings** Cynthia C '78
(614) 228-5125 **Cummiskey** Thomas M '97
(614) 228-4546 **Cunningham** Catherine A '83
(614) 424-4566 **Cunningham** Guy H '98
(614) 464-6400 **Cupps** David S '72
(614) 280-1100 **Curley** William C '78
(614) 221-2838 **Curp** John P '95
(614) 227-2000 **Curphey** James D '83
(614) 227-2000 **Currence** Kysha L '02
(614) 469-3241 **Currie** Michael W '83
(614) 227-2000 **Currin** Joseph H '99
(614) 430-8885 **Curry** Bruce A '91
(614) 430-8885 **Curry Roby Schoenling & Mulvey Co,LLC**
(614) 221-2702 **Curtin** James B '85
(614) 523-2251 **Curtin** Richard A '76
(614) 442-9300 **Curtis** Douglas E '87
(614) 469-5737 **Cusack** William W '85
(614) 221-1400 **Cutter** James M '77
(614) 221-3155 **Cvetanovich** Danny L '77
(614) 464-6400 **Czerwonka** Kevin M '90
(614) 236-1950 **Dachner** David A '72
(614) 228-4200 **Dahlberg** Carl G '01
(614) 857-4330 **Dahmer** Douglas M '93
(614) 677-2989 **Dailey** Gerald E '82
(614) 469-5715 **D'Alessandro** Mark T '79
(614) 280-4000 **Daley** Richard C Jr. '78
(614) 466-2980 **Damaser** Hilary R '92
(614) 995-1629 **Damschroder** William R '88
(614) 222-6465 **Damsel** William R II '86
(614) 253-1010 **Dana & Pariser Co,LPA**
(614) 221-6424 **Danchak** Michael G '78
(614) 365-2700 **Dane** Philomena M '90
(614) 387-9370 **Dangel** Ruth B '87
(614) 486-5392 **Daniell** Ric '78
(614) 365-2700 **Daniels** Gregory R '01
(614) 221-7201 **Daniels** James M '78
(614) 249-3281 **Dankovic** Rae Ann '98
(614) 227-2000 **Dansa** Jaime A '02
(614) 225-8749 **Dardinger** Debora C '96
(614) 236-6517 **Darling** Stanton G II '84
(614) 462-2237 **Darr** Elaine M '01
(614) 221-1111 **Darvishi** Michelle R '99
(614) 224-6969 **D'Ascenzo** Rocco O '04
(614) 227-2000 **Daugherty** Greg M '04
(614) 224-1884 **Daulton** Stephen W '74
(614) 752-6864 **Daum** Rebecca L '90
(614) 221-7663 **D'Aurora** Jack '91
(614) 463-8989 **Davidson** Alan J '81
(614) 462-2286 **Davidson** James E '80
(614) 221-3155 **Davies** Donald A '62
(614) 462-3555 **Davies** William J '99
(614) 249-2019 **Davin** Elizabeth A '89
(614) 728-0276 **Davis** Cynthia D '91
(614) 466-7788 **Davis** Delores L '97
(614) 464-6400 **Davis** Gary E '76
(614) 462-3555 **Davis** Jeffrey R '94
(614) 485-1800 **Davis** Jeffrey T '92
(614) 242-4242 **Davis** Jennifer M '01
(614) 463-9770 **Davis** Jessica L '02
(614) 229-5025 **Davis** John R '86
(614) 478-3424 **Davis** Julia A '85
(614) 222-8686 **Davis** Kathleen Vivian '03
(614) 462-3987 **Davis** Martin L '92
(614) 461-1922 **Davis** McKenzie K '02
(614) 237-3525 **Davis** Murray A '91
(614) 752-1200 **Davis** Peter '75
(614) 228-2945 **Davis** Ronald E '62
(614) 227-2300 **Davis** Scott W '04
(614) 444-0566 **Davis** Thomas E '94
(614) 464-2392 **Davis** Thomas L '82
(614) 883-1072 **Davis** Thomas R '73
(614) 221-3151 **Davis** William A '74
(614) 866-5455 **Davis** Yvette Carmon '85
(614) 462-5400 **Davisson** E Rod '02
(614) 854-0615 **Dawicke** Jason E '01
(614) 462-2290 **Dawley** Kris M '85
(614) 404-2691 **Dawsey** David J '02
(614) 488-9668 **Dawson** Clyde W Jr. '64
(614) 246-1000 **Dawson** Cynthia L '98
(614) 269-4900 **Dawson** Shane M '96
(614) 221-2993 **Day** David L '67
(614) 224-7291 **Day** Dennis G '82
(614) 752-8496 **Day** Jennifer E '91
(614) 462-3555 **Day** Susan E '78
(614) 882-3213 **Ddumba** James '03
(614) 340-9823 **Deal** John C '74
(614) 291-6096 **Deal** Roger F '88
(614) 464-2235 **Dean** Nannette B '95
(614) 621-1500 **DeAngelo** Peter M '69
(614) 220-5611 **Deas** Brian T '93
(614) 221-2121 **Deavers** Maribeth M '91
(614) 444-3900 **DeBacco** Thomas J '79
(614) 457-1911 **DeBeneditto** Umberto A '94
(614) 466-2766 **DeBoe** Todd K '00
(614) 466-3145 **Debolt** Sallie J '87
(614) 644-7257 **Decker** Jack W '78
(614) 242-4242 **Decker** Mark '73
(614) 242-4242 **Decker Vonau Seguin Lackey & Viets Co LPA**
(614) 231-9478 **Deeds** Gary W '77
(614) 466-2766 **Deeds** Holly N '03
(614) 466-0637 **Deemer** Michael W '02
(614) 469-3939 **Deep** Colleen A '93
(614) 224-2319 **Deeter** Leann R '83
(614) 224-8166 **Defossez** Mark E '91
(614) 466-2980 **DeFrank** Stephen E Jr. '90
(614) 785-6495 **DeGennaro** Nicholas C '00
(614) 752-8683 **DeGenova** Jacqueline F '92
(614) 462-3194 **Dehnart** Stephen D '87
(614) 898-9305 **Deis** Michelle D '85
(614) 487-7506 **Deisner** Vicki L '92
(614) 464-6400 **Dejelo** P Jason '03
(614) 645-6933 **Delaney** Patricia A '90
(614) 221-5439 **deLanglade-Spriggs** Elise M '97
(614) 693-6838 **DelaRosa** Regina M '88
DeLeone James F '51
(614) 224-5294 **deLevie** Raymond M '92
(614) 249-8510 **Deley-Shimer** Julie A '91
(614) 457-5901 **De Libera** John S '63
(614) 457-5901 **De Libera Lyons & Bibbo**
(614) 228-1313 **De Libera Lyons & Bibbo**
(614) 457-6101 **De Libera** Malissa M '97
(614) 221-2580 **Delligatti** Michael J '88
(614) 466-5394 **Delos Santos** Luis D '00
(614) 890-3300 **DeLuca** Gaither B '93
(614) 466-7447 **DeMarco** Peter E '84
(614) 466-1305 **Dembinski** David M '84
(614) 628-6880 **Demers** Andrew B '02
(614) 466-7900 **Demers** Stephanie Bostos '93
(614) 228-9550 **Demian** Mark J '94
(614) 365-2700 **DeMonte** Jessica E '00
(614) 262-5737 **Denbow-Hubbard** Stefania A '84
(614) 224-0531 **Dendis** Lorree L '00
(614) 464-6400 **Dengler** A Brian '85
(614) 228-5271 **Denmead** Craig '72
(614) 228-5271 **Denmead & Maloney**
(614) 457-8260 **Denney** Patti L '85
(614) 471-2900 **Dennis** Keith A '84
(614) 447-3613 **Dennis** Michael W '95
(614) 228-3413 **Dennison** Sallynda P '97
(614) 224-2428 **Dentinger** David P '97
(614) 298-8200 **DePascale** Diane M '81
(614) 224-9207 **DePascale** Paul A '87
(614) 298-8200 **DePascale** Vincent N '67
(614) 227-2000 **DePew** Lloyd G Jr. '81
(614) 221-4221 **DeRose** Robert E II '91
(614) 464-6400 **DeRousie** Charles S '73
(614) 444-8777 **DeSanto** Debra J '83
(614) 444-8777 **DeSanto & McNichols**
(614) 466-4705 **DeTemple** Matthew J '82
(614) 246-1000 **Detrick** Joanne F '89
(614) 299-1008 **Deutsch** Adam J '99
(614) 466-2872 **DeVictor** Audra O '96
(614) 469-5715 **DeVillers** David M '92
(614) 221-1830 **DeVillers** Sean P '96
(614) 228-1541 **Devine** Joseph C '95
(614) 462-2238 **Devine** Patrick A '80
(614) 228-1541 **deVyver** K Issac '00
(614) 848-6500 **DeWeese** Stephen S '90
(614) 221-0944 **Dewhirst** Scot E '78
(614) 469-1301 **DeWitt** Michael W '96
(614) 224-1222 **DeYoung** Kathleen A '99
(614) 224-8271 **DiCeglio** Gary M '92
(614) 224-6488 **Dicker** Gary H '87
(614) 224-1222 **Dickerson** Brian E '98
(614) 466-4683 **Dickhaut** Ellen A '79
Dickie Erin A '94
(614) 540-4000 **Dickinson** Richard J '70
Dickinson Sandra J '97
(614) 221-3151 **DiCuccio** Nicholas G '66
(614) 221-3151 **DiCuccio** Nicole '99
(614) 645-7483 **Diederick** Melissa E '01
(614) 466-1288 **Diehm** Paul C '69
(614) 273-0580 **Dieker** Jeannie K '94
(614) 486-1428 **Dieker** Lawrence L '72
(614) 273-0580 **Dieker** Lawrence Leo Jr. '93
(614) 469-6638 **Diem** Lisa M '98
(614) 442-5539 **Dieterich** Eric R '82
(614) 249-7638 **Dietrich** Thomas W '76
(614) 224-9221 **DiFranco** Brian C '03
(614) 752-2761 **Dile** Madelyn M '84
(614) 221-3155 **Dilenschneider** John J '59
(614) 464-2572 **Dill** Ralph E '75
(614) 466-3934 **Dilling** Thomas A '87
(614) 469-3200 **Dillman** Jennifer L '00
(614) 249-3077 **Dillon** Cynthia L '89
(614) 461-1551 **Dillon** Julia B '04
(614) 463-9770 **Dillon** Thomas A '74
(614) 459-0047 **DiLorenzo** John F Jr. '81
(614) 365-2700 **DiMickele** Susan M '95
(614) 228-4494 **Dimond** Richard L '57
(614) 462-2214 **Dingledy** Jay R '72
(614) 542-0220 **Dingus** Michael S '98
(614) 462-5200 **Dinsmore** Beth A '91
(614) 466-7447 **Dinsmore** James P '91
(614) 628-6880 **Dinsmore & Shohl LLP**
(614) 262-1704 **DiPasquale** Anita A '88
(614) 466-2166 **Dirina** John G '95
(614) 466-9305 **Diroll** David J '77
(614) 461-1156 **Disantis** Paul V '96
(614) 575-3519 **Disantis** Sandra M '91
(614) 236-6553 **Distelhorst** Michael '76
(614) 228-5822 **Dittmer** Jeffrey A '89
(614) 238-2828 **Ditullio** Jessica K '87
(614) 461-1516 **Ditullio** Mark A '85
(614) 221-7663 **Dixon** Matthew R '02
(614) 870-3000 **Dobbs** James B '70
(614) 224-3838 **Dobres** Jacob '99
(614) 621-1500 **Dobrowski** Stanley J '76
(614) 464-6400 **Dobyns** Timothy J '96
(614) 464-2572 **Dodd** Stephen H '85
(614) 443-2494 **Dodgion** Jeremy M '97
(614) 462-3194 **Dolchin** Marla R '89
(614) 236-1545 **Dolin** Jason M '89
(614) 469-5715 **Dominguez** Salvador A '91
(614) 644-1989 **Dominic** Elizabeth Tsvetkoff '04
(614) 462-3555 **Domis** Christian B '98
(614) 224-8166 **Donahey** Richard S Jr. '68
(614) 224-1222 **Donahue** William C '70
(614) 228-6611 **Donchatz** Kenneth R '93
(614) 840-3698 **Doney** Timothy J '85
(614) 224-8374 **Donofrio** Susan S '79
(614) 985-3651 **Donovan** Richard J '93
Donovan Zachary T '88
(614) 485-2010 **Donovsky** Nicole M '00
(614) 464-6305 **Doran** Perry W II '00
(614) 464-6400 **Doran** Scott M '86
(614) 462-2700 **Dorgan** Brandi L '03
(614) 466-7250 **Dorgan** James Q III '03
(614) 461-1234 **Dorner** Nancy L '93
(614) 644-7233 **Dorris** Tomi L '89
(614) 228-1541 **Dortch** Michael D '90
(614) 466-5394 **Dotson** Wendi L '99
(614) 444-5700 **Doucet** Elizabeth H '86
(614) 280-1100 **Doucher** Paul M '80
(614) 798-1933 **Dougherty** Douglas B '80
(614) 461-6300 **Dougherty** Gina M '82
(614) 224-8187 **Dougherty** Kathy A '92
(614) 365-2700 **Doughty** H Cort Jr. '66
(614) 462-4679 **Doughty** Tara L '01
(614) 221-7663 **Douglas** Danyelle E '04
(614) 221-0446 **Douglas** David W '78
(614) 466-4929 **Dove** Richard A '83
(614) 466-1055 **Dowling-Fitzpatrick** Carla R '89
(614) 221-1216 **Downes Hurst & Fishel**
(614) 221-1216 **Downes** Jonathan J '79
(614) 469-3939 **Downey** Brian J '98
(614) 221-2121 **Downey** Daniel T '94
(614) 464-6400 **Downey** Philip F '88
(614) 292-3159 **Doyle** Anne M '93
(614) 462-4023 **Doyle** David A '86
(614) 229-3888 **Doyle** Jon S '03
(614) 469-3939 **Doyle** Meghan E '01
(614) 249-4726 **Doyle** Michael F '00
(614) 228-1541 **Doyle** R Christopher '79
(614) 224-1222 **Dozer** Jodi L '97
(614) 890-4770 **Drabick** Thomas C Jr. '94
(614) 249-6583 **Dracopoulos** James J '80
(614) 228-6453 **Drakatos** Eleni A '03
(614) 466-3206 **Drake** Carol Nolan '85
(614) 645-7385 **Drake** Daniel W '70
(614) 267-9367 **Dranichak** Michelle L '91
(614) 443-6839 **Dray** Michael G '99
(614) 628-1601 **Dreher** Darrell L '74
(614) 628-8000 **Dreher Langer & Tomkies LLP**
(614) 481-8943 **Dreifke** Stuart L '75
(614) 469-3939 **Dreitler** Joseph R '79
(614) 621-1500 **Drew** Joan N '01
(614) 221-0922 **Drexel** Ray P '74
(614) 461-4177 **Driscoll** William P '76
(614) 464-4644 **Dritz** Stanley B '73
(614) 444-7655 **Druen** W Sidney '70
Drummond Bonnie R '91
(614) 227-2000 **Dryer** Aaron A '98
(614) 462-3194 **Drzewiecki** Stanley L '93
(614) 466-0570 **Duco** Michael P '92
(614) 221-6563 **Duffey** David L '80
(614) 224-5205 **Duffey** Mary S '87
(614) 227-4885 **Duffy** Alan D '02
(614) 728-2845 **Duffy** Drew M '86
(614) 716-1617 **Duffy** Kevin F '72
(614) 466-0122 **Duffy** Paul J '74
(614) 365-2700 **Dugan** Patrick J '82
Dugan Thomas P '02
(614) 445-6161 **Dugan** Vincent A Jr. '83
(614) 249-1432 **Dugasz** Erwin J '91
(614) 221-4255 **Dugger** Glen A '84
(614) 466-7900 **Dull** Patrick M '95
(614) 995-9566 **Dunbar** Frank C III '64
(614) 231-9086 **Duncan** Robert M '52
(614) 253-2740 **Dunlap** B William '66
Dunlap William E III '68
(614) 462-2236 **Dunlay** Catherine T '84
(614) 228-5151 **Dunn** Danielle R '02
(614) 462-2339 **Dunn** Gregory J '78
(614) 462-2212 **Dunn** Harvey '66
(614) 722-3940 **Dunn** Kathleen M '94
(614) 236-8000 **Dunn** Marcus D '94
(614) 221-3155 **Dunn** Robert R '91
(614) 464-4100 **DuPont** Gregory S '92
(614) 224-1222 **Duran** Ysidro E '86
(614) 481-3210 **Durban** Lee E '78
(614) 466-7788 **Durfey** Miles C '70
(614) 228-5822 **Durham** Joseph R '91
Durham Susan C '81
(614) 891-8422 **Durkin** Kevin P '80
(614) 846-1081 **Durst** Alan T '65
(614) 846-1126 **Durst** Nathan A '88
(614) 583-7602 **Dutton** F Mitchell '82
(614) 462-3555 **Dutton** Jennifer D '97
(614) 469-3939 **Dutton** Thomas E '83
(614) 889-2531 **Duvall** James '63
(614) 462-3555 **Duvall** Jennifer L '95
(614) 462-5400 **Dyas** Charles R Jr. '86
(614) 461-1100 **Dye** David A '85
(614) 224-7298 **Dye** Lewis T '04
(614) 224-7298 **Dye** Lewis W '72
(614) 464-6400 **Dykes** Robert G '81
(614) 365-5575 **Dysert** Jonita W '95
(614) 565-2609 **Eagleson** Freeman T III '91
(614) 228-6148 **Eakins** Alan D '86
(614) 464-2392 **Earl** Ted L '60
(614) 464-2392 **Earl Warburton Adams & Davis,LPA**
(614) 577-9970 **Eastep** Kipley M '92
(614) 365-2700 **Eastham** Ryan G '97
(614) 752-1300 **Eastman** Brian J '89
(614) 462-3973 **Eaton** Douglas W '92
(614) 581-0541 **Eaton** Michael D '96
(614) 464-0082 **Eberhart** Robert L '64
(614) 221-3155 **Eblin** Robert L '91
(614) 224-6011 **Ebner** Cynthia L '93
(614) 462-5875 **Eby** James E '83
(614) 221-6766 **Eck** Alice E '77

(614) 228-4546 **Eck** Franklin E Jr. '89
(614) 228-1541 **Eckelberry** Rodger L '99
(614) 221-7663 **Ecker** Deborah P '80
(614) 248-5700 **Eckhart** Anne E '93
(614) 461-0984 **Eckhart** Henry W '58
(614) 227-2000 **Edelman** Joyce D '83
(614) 227-2000 **Edmund** Robert W '98
(614) 469-3223 **Edwards** Daniel F '92
(614) 785-9958 **Edwards** Delena '87
(614) 466-4328 **Edwards** Jennifer L '00
(614) 466-3379 **Edwards** Judith T '97
(614) 221-1306 **Edwards** Robert D '00
(614) 462-3555 **Edwards** Warren T '01
(614) 224-8166 **Edwards** William J '85
(614) 462-3194 **Efta** Thomas J '87
(614) 227-2000 **Eftimoff** Katerina M '94
(614) 262-3800 **Egan** Daniel S '87
(614) 241-5550 **Egelhoff** Rebecca L '03
(614) 221-5216 **Eggspuehler** Jay B '90
(614) 464-6400 **Ehler** Anthony L '87
(614) 257-3892 **Ehrie** Dennis B Jr. '76
(614) 728-6724 **Ehrle** Kathryn C '93
(614) 436-4200 **Eichner** Kevin F '89
(614) 228-8400 **Eidelberg** David L '88
(614) 222-0540 **Eisenman** Susan G '74
(614) 486-8601 **Eisnaugle** Ralph W '60
(614) 255-9256 **Elam** John W '82
(614) 227-2000 **El-Amin** Taheerah K '02
(614) 213-0216 **Eldridge** Brenda L '93
(614) 221-2400 **Eldridge** Matthew A '84
(614) 825-3539 **Eley** James R '90
(614) 464-2200 **Eliot** Adam S '94
(614) 868-8718 **Elkin** Joel K '85
(614) 238-6738 **Ellard** Steven M '04
(614) 464-1211 **Ellcessor** Steven J '77
(614) 272-1112 **Elleman** James R '66
(614) 728-7055 **Ellensohn** Carol A '02
(614) 486-6446 **Ellerbrock** Donn G '75
(614) 462-5452 **Ellinger** Eve M '01
(614) 210-9255 **Elliott** Cynthia L '95
(614) 227-2000 **Elliott** Joseph F '82
(614) 481-6000 **Elliott** Rex H '91
(614) 221-5216 **Elliott** Steven P '79
(614) 481-9173 **Elliott** Wiley J '93
(614) 225-9707 **Ellis** Madry L '97
(614) 505-0808 **Ellis** Robert L '84
(614) 505-0808 **Ellis & Venable**
(614) 466-3445 **Elsass-Locker** Jodi M '92
(614) 464-6400 **Elvers** Jason C '00
(614) 752-8983 **Elwing** Alicia F '98
(614) 459-5200 **Ely** Donald E '68
(614) 221-1314 **Embrey** Elizabeth A '04
(614) 221-4000 **Emens** John R II '64
(614) 227-2000 **Emerson** Andrew C '00
(614) 461-1311 **Enders** Warren M '76
(614) 227-2327 **Engel** Mark A '79
(614) 249-6096 **English** John A '94
(614) 566-5151 **English** Katrina M '90
(614) 292-9592 **Enns** Terri L '96
(614) 227-2300 **Ensign** John A '03
(614) 297-6409 **Eppich** Robert J '94
(614) 469-7404 **Eppler** Rita S '81
(614) 457-6233 **Epps** Richard M '76
(614) 481-6000 **Epstein** Aaron D '94
(614) 221-3966 **Epstein** Barry W '77
(614) 464-9112 **Erdy** Pamela S '91
(614) 469-1858 **Erfurt** Edward W III '77
(614) 228-1346 **Erkman** Annemarie M '96
(614) 224-1222 **Erlenbach** Thomas S '60
(614) 466-2766 **Erlewine** Kristina L '99
(614) 221-1111 **Ernest** John T '99
(614) 258-6100 **Erney** Robert D '84
(614) 716-0500 **Ernsberger** Todd A '04
(614) 228-6885 **Ervin** Amy J '96
(614) 438-2648 **Erwin** Joseph V '91
(614) 466-7447 **Eschbacher** Lisa M '98
(614) 278-4795 **Eschbacher** Timothy J '98
(614) 227-2000 **Eschleman** Lisa L '87
(614) 228-6647 **Eshman** Patricia S '85
(614) 466-3180 **Espinoza** David J '83
Esposito Michael A '80
(614) 228-2722 **Espy** Bennie E '69
(614) 462-3194 **Essex** Robert D '93
(614) 486-9366 **Essey** Norman A '86
(614) 466-7964 **Etter** Terry L '97
(614) 224-8374 **Eubanks** Renee F '01
(614) 466-2766 **Eubanks** Robert A '01
(614) 464-2025 **Evans** Dennis P '85
(614) 462-6285 **Evans** Gale A '99
(614) 224-8166 **Evans** Gordon D II '01
(614) 475-9511 **Evans** James M '67
(614) 466-2980 **Evans** James M '81
(614) 227-4892 **Evans** Mark E '01
(614) 227-2000 **Evans** Mason IV '77
(614) 890-4770 **Evans** Michelle R '02
(614) 227-2000 **Evans** R Leland '83
(614) 249-2983 **Evans** Ronda L '89
(614) 444-0016 **Everett** John K '71
Everetts Jason A '00
(614) 249-0286 **Everson** Deborah S '77
(614) 292-1882 **Eyerly** Gloria A '76
(614) 885-0123 **Eysser** Dieter W '00
(614) 227-0306 **Ezell** Larry A '98
(614) 221-8448 **Ezzie** Joseph E '02
(614) 961-4848 **Faehnle** Matthew C '00
(614) 237-7634 **Fagin** Marc K '85
(614) 464-6400 **Fahey** Richard P '73
(614) 228-2605 **Fahnenbruck** K Clarke '78
(614) 447-3600 **Faine** Chris W '80
(614) 464-6400 **Fairfield** Mary Ellen '73
(614) 645-7655 **Fais** James J '70
(614) 561-6775 **Fais** Robert G '74
(614) 227-2000 **Faller** Bryan R '00
(614) 326-1009 **Falleur** Michael D '77
(614) 475-9511 **Falvo** Aaron R '03
(614) 462-3555 **Farbacher** Marla H '93
(614) 221-5200 **Farber** Robert H Jr. '62
(614) 462-5290 **Fardal** Patrick M '92
(614) 242-4333 **Fargo** John Z '64
(614) 232-3088 **Faris** Juliana M '89
(614) 222-2356 **Farkas** Jeffrey W '93
(614) 466-8057 **Farkas** Scott E '86
(614) 759-0123 **Farmer** Derek A '99
(614) 221-2838 **Farmer** James B '76
(614) 466-5394 **Farnbacher** Barbara A '86
(614) 248-6047 **Farquhar** Christine M '81
(614) 464-6400 **Farrar** Elizabeth T '82
(614) 221-1827 **Farrell** Clifford M '82
(614) 466-5967 **Farrin** Richard C '72
(614) 469-3939 **Fate** Jennifer L '97
(614) 466-3596 **Fate** Lisa Wu '93
(614) 228-6148 **Fauber** Sue A '82
(614) 228-1541 **Faulkner** Sandra Parks '93
(614) 227-2000 **Faure** David C '96
(614) 478-3918 **Favor** Hugh M Jr. '93
(614) 221-5151 **Fawley** Darrell E Jr. '79
(614) 464-1211 **Fay** Terrence M '78
(614) 677-5932 **Featherstone** James E '96
(614) 466-2980 **Febus** Charles E '94
(614) 224-8187 **Federico** John A '97
(614) 292-9177 **Federle** Katherine H '98
(614) 462-5432 **Feheley** Lawrence F '73
(614) 223-9324 **Feibel** James B '59
(614) 469-3273 **Fein** William S '71
(614) 463-9770 **Feinstein** Donald L '70
(614) 229-4768 **Feldbauer** Steven T '01
(614) 223-9300 **Feldkamp** Janet K '90
(614) 222-5924 **Feldman** Toba J '77
(614) 466-6750 **Feldman** William B '73
(614) 644-3037 **Feldmann** Stephen R '87
(614) 222-3957 **Fenker** Kristen K '94
(614) 466-5394 **Fenlon** John M '89
(614) 223-3302 **Fenlon** Mary R '88
(614) 463-4201 **Ferber** James M '74
(614) 431-6006 **Fergus** John C II '78
(614) 451-7517 **Fergus** Kevin B '61
(614) 644-8213 **Fergus** Ronda H '80
(614) 464-6400 **Ferguson** Gerald P '79
(614) 466-3664 **Ferguson** Kathy A '91
(614) 481-4030 **Ferguson** Melissa E '93
(614) 228-6885 **Ferguson** Melissa M '98
(614) 692-3284 **Ferguson** Richard D '88
(614) 464-6400 **Ferguson** Victor J '98
(614) 466-3947 **Ferguson-Ramos** Lisa A '94
(614) 341-2645 **Fernald** Willard T '93
(614) 365-9900 **Ferrell** Bradley T '99
(614) 466-5394 **Ferrell** Stephen A '93
(614) 228-1541 **Ferrell** Tara M '03
(614) 275-2672 **Ferriman** David B '84
(614) 228-1541 **Ferris** Andrew M '95
(614) 889-4777 **Ferris** Boyd B '67
(614) 889-4777 **Ferris** David A '92
(614) 645-5849 **Ferris** Jacqueline A '04
(614) 228-5225 **Ferron** John W '85
(614) 228-3822 **Fesenmyer** Thomas M '01
(614) 462-2264 **Fewell** Jennifer L '03
(614) 232-9100 **Fey** Carol A '85
Feyko James '90
(614) 228-1541 **Fidler** Christopher D '92
(614) 462-3555 **Fields** Adria P '95
Fields Matthew H '99
(614) 248-6308 **Figetakis** Frances L '87
(614) 621-1500 **Finan** Richard H '59
(614) 827-7300 **Findley** Stephen C '80
(614) 466-0722 **Finegold** Jordan '86
(614) 466-2766 **Finfrock** Teri Jo '87
(614) 228-0234 **Fink** Andrew B '01
(614) 227-2000 **Fink** Howard P '70
(614) 249-6258 **Finley** Cathy M '80
(614) 485-6207 **Finley** Kim M '00
(614) 227-8897 **Finley** Price D '90
(614) 644-7741 **Finnegan** Matthew L '86
(614) 227-2000 **Finneran** Mary Theresa '89
(614) 846-1440 **Finneran** Russell D '54
(614) 457-6147 **Finneran** Thomas J '54
(614) 464-0776 **Finneran** Todd G '81
(614) 466-4328 **Finnerty** Beth A '91
(614) 221-4734 **Finnerty** Gregory N '87
(614) 759-0123 **Finucane** Sandra J '96
(614) 469-7130 **Fiocca** John A Jr. '75
(614) 228-4201 **Fiore** Anthonio C '04
(614) 645-8946 **Firestone** Lesley A '97
(614) 228-6345 **Firstenberger** Aaron C '00
(614) 644-3037 **Fischbein** William T '94
(614) 221-8699 **Fischberg** Jenna S '97
(614) 466-8600 **Fischer** Holly R '91
(614) 645-4650 **Fischer** Thomas M '89
(614) 485-9300 **Fish** Jeffrey D '91
(614) 865-2908 **Fish** Stanley R '81
(614) 466-2766 **Fishel** Joan I '87
(614) 221-1216 **Fishel** Marc A '87
(614) 469-1882 **Fisher** David W '81
(614) 469-2455 **Fisher** Donald P '96
(614) 221-0446 **Fisher & Douglas**
(614) 462-2277 **Fisher** Fredrick L '76
(614) 445-0372 **Fisher** Gary E '85
(614) 233-6950 **Fisher** George V '53
(614) 221-8500 **Fisher** J Matthew '96
(614) 248-6479 **Fisher** Judith M '86
(614) 221-8448 **Fisher** Kenneth A Jr. '95
(614) 645-5150 **Fisher** Lawrence L '67
(614) 227-2000 **Fisher** Lloyd E Jr. '50
(614) 221-0446 **Fisher** Mark R '80
(614) 487-8210 **Fisher** Mary B '89
(614) 365-2700 **Fisher** Roberta Lee '76
(614) 233-6950 **Fisher & Skrobot LLC**
(614) 227-2000 **Fisher** Theodore G '69
(614) 262-1605 **Fisher** Windell F '61
(614) 227-2640 **Fitch** David A '82
(614) 445-2661 **Fitch** Glori E '89
(614) 221-6969 **Fitch** John K '79
(614) 221-4000 **Fitch** Stephen C '73
(614) 287-2482 **Fitrakis** Robert J '03
(614) 644-1768 **Fitzgerald** Scott M '95
(614) 469-3294 **Flahive** Carolyn S '00
(614) 464-6400 **Flahive** Shawn M '84
(614) 469-7404 **Flanagan** Francis P '80
(614) 462-3194 **Flanigan** Tanya D '03
(614) 851-9464 **Flecha** Crucita '95
(614) 224-0919 **Fleck** William J Jr. '75
(614) 227-2000 **Fleischauer** Marc L '95
(614) 466-4605 **Fleischman** David A '93
Fleishman Jill T '80
(614) 462-3194 **Fleming** Tyson L '00
(614) 443-4814 **Fletcher** Daniel J '85
Fletcher Jackalynne A '95
(614) 228-6675 **Fletcher** Robert E '76
(614) 944-5055 **Flickinger** Russell N Jr. '82
(614) 461-1234 **Flint** Christopher A '95
(614) 227-2300 **Flint** Jennifer A '92
(614) 449-2376 **Floetker** Bernard M '78
(614) 227-2340 **Flowers** Michael E '79
(614) 227-8855 **Flynn** James F '90
(614) 228-1541 **Flynn** Sean P '01
(614) 529-9085 **Fogle** Shawn C '90
(614) 229-4808 **Foisset** Chad A '02
(614) 292-4288 **Foley** Edward B '99
(614) 464-6400 **Foley** F James '77
(614) 466-5394 **Foley** James R '98
(614) 469-7404 **Foley** Kenneth M '64
(614) 461-1311 **Foley** Kevin P '92
(614) 461-1234 **Foley** Mark A '69
(614) 752-8683 **Foley** Mary B '93
(614) 227-2000 **Foliano** Gregory B '90
(614) 466-7447 **Folkert** Douglas R '82
(614) 227-2000 **Folkerth** Andrew A '87
(614) 228-2945 **Folkerth Haddow & Davis**
(614) 228-2945 **Folkerth Haddow & Davis**
(614) 466-7264 **Folkerth** Jeffrey T '72
(614) 444-3036 **Forbes** Brian C '99
(614) 464-6400 **Ford** Gail C '86
(614) 464-6400 **Ford** Jacklyn J '91
(614) 464-6400 **Foreman** Ivery D '78
(614) 825-3539 **Forhan** Michael A '99
(614) 463-9790 **Forman** Edward R '03
(614) 461-1551 **Forman** Richard J '77
(614) 224-1500 **Fornia Luftman & Heck,LLP**
(614) 224-1500 **Fornia** William J '03
(614) 644-6338 **Forrester** Mary E '81
(614) 462-2254 **Forry** Steven '02
(614) 228-2345 **Forsythe** Frank E '65
(614) 466-5337 **Fortkamp** Jeffrey D '02
(614) 752-6417 **Fortman** Judith W '72
(614) 644-7233 **Fosnaught** Jerri L '04
(614) 466-5640 **Foster** Kelly L '99
Foster Robert H '73
(614) 833-0750 **Foster-Littlefield** Deborah E '92
(614) 228-5151 **Founds** Mark J '98
(614) 227-3333 **Foust** Hollie K '00
(614) 447-3600 **Foust** Jennifer A '00
(614) 466-6750 **Fox** Carolyn M '88
(614) 224-5209 **Fox** Clenzo B '53
(614) 466-1073 **Fox** Daniel W '86
(614) 466-3615 **Fox** Diana C '01
(614) 463-8826 **Fox** Karol C '89
(614) 493-9730 **Fox** Kelly J '95
(614) 462-3194 **Fox** Steven T '99
(614) 228-8400 **Fox** Timothy M '87
(614) 228-5331 **Fraas** Henry C Jr. '94
(614) 337-8366 **Fraley** Joseph A '91
(614) 752-4267 **Francis** Caryn A '93
(614) 228-5931 **Frank** David K '74
(614) 469-3939 **Frank** Marlene P '82
(614) 645-7477 **Frank** Melinda J '99
(614) 221-1662 **Frank & Wooldridge Co LPA**
(614) 293-6500 **Frank-Scott** Christine '03
(614) 466-4605 **Frankart** Robert J '78
(614) 466-8288 **Franke** Janice R '83
(614) 487-1488 **Franklin** Charles E '77
(614) 365-2700 **Franzmann** Christopher J '98
(614) 326-5544 **Frasch** Joseph F Jr. '74
(614) 227-2000 **Frasier** Ralph K '76
(614) 221-9400 **Frazier** Jean M '87
(614) 466-2766 **Frazzini** Cynthia K '96
(614) 228-3372 **Frederick** Michael A '00
(614) 442-4628 **Freed** Robert P '03
(614) 235-6117 **Freed** Ruth P '58
(614) 466-7090 **Freel** David E '77
(614) 221-2848 **Freeman** Chester T '57
(614) 469-3280 **Freiburger** Charles F IV '70
(614) 644-0876 **French** Judith L '88
(614) 461-1311 **Fresco** Ronald A '92
(614) 827-7300 **Freund Freeze & Arnold**
(614) 480-5181 **Freye** Deborah L '00
(614) 365-9900 **Freytag** Daniel R '75
(614) 297-1000 **Frick** Bradley N '78
(614) 228-2678 **Frick** James B '53
(614) 415-7199 **Fried** Samuel '92
(614) 292-3856 **Friedman** Jerome E '77
(800) 977-7711 **Friedman** Marc R '74
(614) 221-0090 **Friedman & Mirman Co,LPA**
(614) 221-0090 **Friedman** Scott N '98
(614) 224-3814 **Friedman** Thomas E '74
(614) 221-9200 **Friedman** Tod H '89
(614) 221-0090 **Friedman** William S '66
(614) 221-3355 **Friend** Daniel K '73
(614) 228-8111 **Friscoe** Louis A '72
(614) 719-2850 **Froehle** Thomas L '93
(614) 645-8849 **Froehlich** Mark S '80
(614) 464-6400 **Froling** David A '95
(614) 464-6400 **Froling** Lynne M '03
(614) 466-0570 **Froment** Jillian E '99
(614) 324-5955 **Fromm** Barry H '80
(614) 463-9770 **Fromson** Jeffrey E '69
(614) 464-1211 **Frost Brown Todd LLC**
Frost Earl L '98
(614) 221-6424 **Frost** Earle R Jr. '69
(614) 228-1541 **Frost** John J '03
(614) 752-9496 **Frost** Kristina D '84
(614) 224-0933 **Frost & Maddox Co,LPA**
(614) 224-0933 **Frost** Robert E '64
(614) 228-2300 **Fry** Carl B '74
(614) 228-2300 **Fry Waller & McCann Co,LPA**
(614) 462-5474 **Fuhrer** Loriann E '97
(614) 752-2646 **Fulcher** Laura P '91
(614) 728-7055 **Fulkerson** Jonathan R '97
(614) 469-3939 **Fulkert** Marc A '03
(614) 224-6485 **Fullem** Brett E '00
Fullen Craig M '92
(614) 228-6611 **Fuller & Henry,Ltd**
(614) 799-0898 **Fullerton** Jacqueline D '93
(614) 221-6755 **Fullerton** William D '86
(614) 466-0457 **Fullin** Daniel E '82
(614) 923-5800 **Fullin** Francis X '85
(614) 221-5627 **Fulton** Christopher L '74
(614) 224-3838 **Fulton** Philip J '80
(614) 228-9550 **Funk** Audra T '01
(614) 228-1541 **Funk** David R '98
(614) 443-5404 **Funkhouser** Douglas A '95
(614) 645-7385 **Furbee** Jeffrey S '94
(614) 416-5611 **Furman** Sandra M '79
(614) 227-8919 **Furniss** John F III '00
(614) 464-2025 **Fusco** Daniel J '99
(614) 464-6400 **Fusonie** Thomas H '01
(614) 586-1586 **Gaba** Elizabeth N '94
(614) 249-7609 **Gainey** Scott A '99
(614) 224-0761 **Gairing** Ann F '86
(614) 469-3939 **Gale** Erick D '02
(614) 628-8000 **Gall** Charles V '99
(614) 365-2700 **Gall** John R '71
(614) 469-3939 **Gall** Maryann B '70
(614) 228-5151 **Gallagher Gams Pryor Tallan & Littrell LLP**
(614) 228-5151 **Gallagher** James R '81
(614) 221-3536 **Gallagher & Kavinsky,LPA**
(614) 221-7614 **Gallagher** Mary L '92
(614) 397-8909 **Gallagher** Michael J '01
(614) 221-3536 **Gallagher** Terence L '83
(614) 227-2384 **Gallagher** Theodore J '91
(614) 224-1222 **Gallagher** Thomas J '85
(614) 227-2000 **Gallon** Eric Benjamin '99
(614) 228-5271 **Gamble** Amanda D '01
(614) 221-0922 **Gamble** Eric B '02
(614) 221-0922 **Gamble Hartshorn Johnson Co,LPA**
(614) 221-0922 **Gamble** Kenneth A '72
(614) 645-7385 **Gams** Jennifer S '94
(614) 228-5151 **Gams** Mark H '84
(614) 228-6885 **Gantz** Curtis F '68
(614) 469-1990 **Garabis** Francisco A '77
(614) 249-6816 **Garber** Joseph F '91
(614) 292-1315 **Garber** Kathleen M '95
(614) 274-1107 **Garber** Kenneth E '67
(614) 464-6400 **Garceau** Mary L '97
(614) 464-6400 **Garcia** Daren S '03
(614) 228-6453 **Garcia** Roger '96
(614) 459-1466 **Gardiner** Donald B '67
(614) 221-0749 **Gardner** Robert F '58
(614) 252-4010 **Gardner** William A '79
(614) 221-3155 **Garel** Jules L '56
(614) 228-6675 **Garland** Lorie D '84
(614) 228-1541 **Garling** Ellen J '89
(614) 228-5151 **Garner** Robika L '04
(614) 248-5700 **Garrett** William A '87
(614) 221-4000 **Garrison** W Travis '03
(614) 327-2068 **Garrity** Colleen M '04
(614) 442-6601 **Gartland** Frank A '89
(614) 464-6400 **Gartland** Sheila Nolan '86
(614) 225-9000 **Garvin & Hickey,LLC**
(614) 225-9000 **Garvin** Preston J '74
(614) 228-6885 **Garvine** Brian M '97
(614) 227-2300 **Gaschen** Dane A '94
(614) 586-1586 **Gasior** Charles V '03
(614) 470-8000 **Gasior** Joel C '92
(614) 225-8593 **Gaskill** Charles R II '76
(614) 462-4017 **Gass** Dorothy T '95
(614) 462-3118 **Gast** Melissa Moriarty '03
(614) 466-2118 **Gates** Timothy L '97
(614) 224-9241 **Gatterdam** Katherine N '92
(614) 464-2000 **Gatterdam** Kort W '88
(614) 224-0220 **Gauer** Philip J '91
(614) 462-3555 **Gaugler** Scott J '04
(614) 232-3224 **Gavin** Robert P '99
(614) 560-6279 **Gayton** Charles W '72
(614) 249-2400 **Gearhardt** Larry R '79
(614) 221-5151 **Gearhiser** Kurt O '83
(614) 692-1084 **Geary** Matthew O '91
(614) 227-2330 **Geary** Susan E '89
(614) 228-1968 **Geary** William L '79
(614) 228-2678 **Geer** Christopher J '78
(614) 424-4293 **Gegenheimer** Charles M Jr. '85
(614) 841-1000 **Geiger** Franz A '91
(614) 716-3305 **Geiger** Heather L '93
(614) 221-1166 **Geiser** Michael K '91
Gengler Brenda J '02
(614) 228-6345 **Genshaft** Nelson E '73
(614) 462-7648 **Genshock** Lauren R '03
(614) 431-1500 **Gentile** Elisabeth D '96
(614) 466-4328 **Gentile** Mitchell L '81
(614) 337-9000 **George** Gary J Jr. '95
(614) 224-5205 **George** Jason L '98
(614) 466-7014 **George** Lewis C '89
(614) 337-2785 **Georgeff** George C '82
(614) 462-3555 **Geraghty** Elizabeth A '00
(614) 221-5216 **Gerber** Richard S '84
(614) 461-4455 **Gerhardstein** Walter J Jr. '73
(614) 570-9949 **Gerhardt** Richard L II '97
(614) 228-6885 **Gerling** Joseph A '77
(614) 224-8824 **Gerrity** Timothy D '70
(614) 464-6400 **Gertmenian** Russell M '72
(614) 463-9393 **Gertner** Michael H '66
(614) 466-5394 **Gerus** Wendie A '84
(614) 462-5038 **Geswein** Mary Frances '94
(614) 445-2923 **Getty** Kathryn E '03
(614) 464-4201 **Geyer** Catherine C '90
(614) 221-3155 **Geyer** Thomas E '90
(614) 488-4424 **Ghidotti** Paul G '90
(614) 248-5700 **Giampapa** Joseph A '83
(614) 224-9985 **Gianangeli** Brian M '00
(614) 224-2366 **Gibbs** Jack G Jr. '82
(614) 221-3155 **Gibbs** Rollyn C '59
(614) 228-5000 **Gibson** Janet D '81
(614) 445-5858 **Gibson** Joseph Miles '78
(614) 221-7381 **Gibson** Peter J '92
(614) 469-3939 **Gibson** Rick J '96
(614) 228-3566 **Gibson** Stephanie L '97
(614) 430-3377 **Gideon** John J '78
(614) 326-1222 **Giffin** Robert E '73
(614) 469-3939 **Gifford** Brian L '97
(614) 466-3934 **Gilbert** Lori S '93
(614) 866-2510 **Gilbert** Roland T '58
(614) 462-3555 **Gilbert** Seth L '00
(614) 466-4605 **Gilbride** Thomas F '79
(614) 464-1919 **Gilchrist** John '72
(614) 462-1055 **Gilcrest** Roger A '85
(614) 469-3274 **Gildee** Eva C '00
(614) 227-2000 **Gildehaus** Ralph F III '90
(614) 228-1541 **Gill** M Elizabeth '88
(614) 397-7298 **Gill** Sterling E II '78
(614) 857-2337 **Gillespie** John D '94
(614) 461-5600 **Gillett** Gary A '85
(614) 462-2221 **Gilligan** John P '81

(614) 469-7404 **Gillingham** John C '75
(614) 228-5822 **Gillis** Mark H '96
(614) 227-2353 **Gillis** Sylvia L '89
(614) 469-3295 **Giorgianni** Paul '95
(614) 462-3896 **Giorgione** Edmund E '83
(614) 457-8608 **Giovanetti** Richard J '62
(614) 227-2318 **Gire** Michael K '77
(614) 221-4000 **Gitlitz** Gary B '76
(614) 222-4735 **Gittes** Frederick M '75
(614) 222-4735 **Gittes & Schulte**
(614) 464-6400 **Giuliani** Anthony J '88
(614) 227-8825 **Giumenti** Katherine S '89
(614) 462-3194 **Gjostein** Thomas A '88
(614) 469-3939 **Gladman** Michael R '92
(614) 645-8214 **Glaeden** Carrie E '89
(614) 469-3939 **Glaros** Christopher M '03
(614) 225-1620 **Glasgow** Aaron M '02
(614) 462-3555 **Glasgow** Jeffrey L '75
(614) 466-2434 **Glass** Greg C '78
(614) 223-9300 **Gleason** John A '87
(614) 222-4798 **Gleaves** Mark M '78
(614) 462-3194 **Glisson** David L '91
(614) 466-6298 **Gnann** Deborah G '84
(614) 292-5899 **Gobey** Nancilynn B '88
(614) 462-2700 **Godby** Herbert R '73
(614) 228-8833 **Goddard** Gabriel Lee '98
(614) 227-4090 **Goff** Tyler W '02
(614) 224-6000 **Goings** Hope M '98
(614) 466-3615 **Gold** David M '78
(614) 644-9293 **Gold** Yitzchak E '74
(614) 466-2927 **Goldbaum** Donald M '75
(614) 228-6345 **Goldberg** Kenneth R '92
(614) 222-8686 **Goldberg** Richard '83
(614) 292-1536 **Goldberger** David A '81
(614) 258-1983 **Golden** Keith E '84
(614) 418-3100 **Goldhand** Joanne I '96
(614) 224-5811 **Goldin** Larry M '79
(614) 228-2325 **Goldman** Dennis J '70
(614) 864-4359 **Goldman** Jerome S '73
(614) 365-2700 **Goldman** Jessica '03
(614) 227-2300 **Goldsand** Corey A '04
(614) 297-1000 **Goldson** Jennifer C '96
Goldstein Amy R '82
(614) 839-5700 **Goldstein** David A '95
(614) 221-9800 **Goldstein** Judith B '98
(614) 274-0033 **Goldstein** Robert R '92
(614) 258-6000 **Golian** Joseph J '85
(614) 464-6400 **Golonka** Kenneth A Jr. '86
(614) 466-1305 **Gonidakis** Michael L '99
(614) 224-7291 **Gooch** Rebecca A '93
(614) 469-1301 **Good** Elliott R '81
(614) 463-4201 **Goodburn** Paul R Jr. '98
(614) 462-7242 **Goodburn** Shannon E '98
(614) 466-0114 **Gooden** Robert R '78
(614) 221-4221 **Goodin** Eileen S '80
(614) 466-8064 **Goodman** J David '92
(614) 223-9300 **Goodman** Norton Victor '61
(614) 462-5295 **Goodrich** Mary W '92
(614) 299-4513 **Gordon** Clarence T II '75
(614) 228-0888 **Gordon** James H '74
(614) 228-0888 **Gordon** James H Jr. '97
(614) 846-1767 **Gordon** John P '78
(614) 621-4135 **Gordon** Nathan '72
(614) 645-7385 **Gordon** Pamela J '85
(614) 487-8887 **Gordon** Thomas S '00
(614) 387-9560 **Gormley** David M '90
(614) 566-5151 **Gorno** Lorri A '91
(614) 469-3939 **Gorospe** Gregory A '93
(614) 445-8416 **Gorrell** Debra L '94
(614) 228-5822 **Gorry** James R Jr. '72
(614) 466-3615 **Goshay** Pamela M '00
(614) 221-4000 **Gosnell** Gerhardt A II '95
(614) 228-6438 **Goss** Dianne '82
(614) 728-7055 **Gosselin** Heather L '00
(614) 221-4349 **Gotherman** John E '61
(614) 297-1211 **Gottfried** Gary J '73
(614) 464-6400 **Gottschall** Matthew D '97
(614) 461-1100 **Gouhin** Sean M '94
(614) 466-4982 **Govern** Jodi A '89
(614) 274-8100 **Grabovac** Greg R '94
(614) 462-3555 **Graceffo** John P '96
(614) 228-5225 **Graden** Leslie B '91
(614) 849-0378 **Grady** Terrence A '82
(614) 227-2000 **Grady** Timothy E '79
(614) 716-1649 **Graf** Ann B '84
(614) 252-7108 **Graf** Brenda J '96
(614) 481-2020 **Graf** Jack R Jr. '73
(614) 447-0314 **Graf-Caswell** Mary L '96
(614) 228-5800 **Graff** Douglas E '85
(614) 462-5455 **Graham** David T '98
(614) 228-2300 **Graham** Derek L '04
(614) 645-8730 **Graham** Kathleen E '82
(614) 221-0922 **Graham** Richard C '68
(614) 469-3939 **Gramann** Margaret L '85
(614) 464-6400 **Grande** Monica E '04
(614) 644-5312 **Grandon** Jon D '87
(614) 728-8400 **Grandon** Pamela Jo '81
(614) 461-7799 **Graney** Michael P '68
(614) 462-2312 **Granger** Aaron L '97
(614) 854-0615 **Granger** Mark S '97
(614) 221-3155 **Grant** Dennis D '65
(614) 224-5205 **Grassbaugh** Stephen P '84
(614) 221-0240 **Grauel** Dawn-Rae '01
(614) 365-2700 **Grauer** David W '85
(614) 236-6681 **Grauer** Myron C '85
(614) 442-7903 **Graves** Arthur C '64
(614) 224-1222 **Gray** Deborah B '91
(614) 227-4834 **Gray** James S '00
(614) 227-2329 **Gray** Stephen C '97
(614) 462-2700 **Grayem** Jeremy M '00
(614) 463-9770 **Graziano** Robert B '91
(614) 227-2000 **Greaney** Constance M '92
Greco Anthony W '93
(614) 351-9827 **Green** George M '94
(614) 462-4677 **Green** Kelly A '02
(614) 462-1058 **Green** Matthew T '02
(614) 293-8446 **Green** Sue Z '99
(614) 227-8848 **Greenberger** Susan B '83
(614) 221-9200 **Greenfield** Gerald '94
(614) 854-9150 **Greenlee** David A '97
Greentree Hugh A '85
(614) 221-1111 **Greenwald** Gary D '71
(614) 431-6358 **Greer** David K '89
(614) 469-3221 **Gregg** Heather D '01
(614) 264-0304 **Gregori** Terri B '93
(614) 462-5416 **Gregory** Donald W '82
(614) 457-5990 **Gregory** Janet K '82
(614) 644-0855 **Greim** David M '88
(614) 461-0734 **Gresham** Cyane W '03
(614) 469-3939 **Gresko** Janice L '96
(614) 462-3555 **Gretz** Jennifer A '98
(614) 466-7447 **Greuel** Tracy M '01
(614) 466-0278 **Gridley** Wendy H '84
(614) 846-3378 **Grier** Jerry '68
(614) 677-5410 **Grier** Jill S '93
(614) 475-9511 **Grieser** Charles R '49
(614) 469-7404 **Griesheimer** Jeffrey A '81
(614) 469-3939 **Griesmer** Kelley M '93
(614) 464-6400 **Griffaton** Michael C '93
(614) 228-1541 **Griffin** Jeanne A '91
(614) 462-2720 **Griffin** Kerri J '98
(614) 224-1222 **Griffin** Robert H Jr. '85
(614) 462-6087 **Griffin** Vanessa M '98
(614) 488-7878 **Griffith** Jeffrey A '99
(614) 227-2000 **Griffith** Kevin E '86
(614) 841-9258 **Griffiths** George K '78
(614) 228-1541 **Grillo** Mary Catherine P '94
(614) 462-3555 **Gripshover** John P '90
(614) 466-2520 **Grodhaus** D Michael '84
(614) 227-2332 **Grody** Warren I '93
(614) 848-3400 **Groeber** Anthony A '72
(614) 486-6416 **Grogan** Robert J Jr. '93
(614) 486-2618 **Grohoske** Donald E '00
(614) 221-3155 **Groner** James M '91
(614) 464-6400 **Gross** James H '66
(614) 466-6750 **Gross** William F '81
(614) 225-8505 **Gross** William J '01
(614) 221-7711 **Grossman** Andrew S '96
(614) 221-7711 **Grossman** Jeffrey A '72
(614) 466-4314 **Grossman** Lillian Y '84
(614) 443-1800 **Grove** Raymond F '71
(614) 645-8207 **Grubb** Janet Ann '76
(614) 461-5600 **Grubbs** Donell Roy '86
(614) 231-7090 **Gruber** M Ellen '80
(614) 249-9001 **Grubler** Gary L '85
(614) 244-0874 **Gruenbaum** Judith C '89
(614) 224-4411 **Gruhin** Lois A '73
(614) 462-3949 **Gubola** Michelle M '96
(614) 428-8555 **Gueli** Christopher G '95
(614) 267-2871 **Guerrieri** David D '02
(614) 220-9100 **Gugle** Kathryn R '92
Guiher Virgil L '56
(614) 466-7014 **Guldin** John R '67
(614) 469-3939 **Gunasekera** Eva U '04
(614) 466-7046 **Gunn** Jeannette E '94
(614) 228-1541 **Gunsett** Daniel J '74
(614) 445-2646 **Gurian** Jonathan G '85
(614) 228-6885 **Gurile** Melissa A '04
(614) 224-5161 **Gurvis** Anthony N '81
(614) 444-3900 **Gussler** Stephanie G '92
(614) 221-2300 **Gutentag** Mark S '93
(614) 466-2980 **Guthrie** James M '71
(614) 466-0722 **Guthrie** John A '80
(614) 431-1500 **Guthrie** Maria C '97
(614) 236-6500 **Guttenberg** Jack A '82
(614) 228-1541 **Guttman** Daniel J '97
(614) 292-0611 **Guttman** Todd G '96
(614) 752-1603 **Guy** James R '93
(614) 462-3194 **Guzman** Becky '01
(614) 221-9400 **Habash Reasoner & Frazier,LLP**
(614) 221-9400 **Habash** Stephen J '78
(614) 644-7250 **Hacker** Cheryl R '88
(614) 538-4256 **Hackett** Andrew M '95
(614) 221-3155 **Hackett** Daniel R '88
(614) 469-7447 **Hackett** Lawrence J '85
(614) 621-9000 **Hackett** Patricia A '93
(614) 431-2000 **Hadden** E Bruce '60
(614) 227-2000 **Hadden** James B '92
(614) 228-2945 **Haddow** Howard J '61
(614) 227-2320 **Haddox** Craig A '82
(614) 466-6696 **Haddox** Kelley R '97
(614) 464-2025 **Hafenstein** Kenneth S '94
(614) 228-6888 **Hager** Jackie L '00
(614) 341-6233 **Hagerott** Jacqueline C '99
(614) 324-5959 **Hahn** Halle B '94
(614) 236-6425 **Hahn** John V '91
(614) 221-0240 **Hahn Loeser & Parks LLP**
(614) 221-8448 **Hahn** Peter W '98
(614) 221-2223 **Hahn** Susie Lin '98
(614) 469-5715 **Hahnert** Robyn J '77
(614) 249-7191 **Haid** Amy E '01
(614) 644-2100 **Haight** Karen M '87
(614) 227-4079 **Haines** Kimberley K '90
(614) 466-5394 **Haire** Theresa G '82
(614) 228-1541 **Hairston** George W '68
(614) 221-4255 **Hale** Benjamin W Jr. '70
(614) 228-1541 **Hale** Mary A '96
(614) 462-5400 **Hall** Adam J '00
(614) 463-4212 **Hall** Alison Day '97
(614) 228-6345 **Hall** Andrew C '96
(614) 227-2000 **Hall** Brian D '85
(614) 249-7261 **Hall** Carrie Ann '01
(614) 225-9000 **Hall** Daniel M '93
(614) 267-2871 **Hall** Julie A '05
(614) 462-6641 **Hall** Kimberly L '98
(614) 365-4100 **Hall** Monique A '02
(614) 236-6719 **Hall** Nicole K '01
(614) 292-0748 **Hall** Patrick J '92
(614) 247-7898 **Hall** Peggy K '97
(614) 480-3663 **Hall** Sarah L '85
(614) 458-0025 **Hall** Stephen K '98
(614) 418-8019 **Hall** Timothy C Jr. '92
(800) 621-3216 **Hall** Timothy J '97
(614) 463-9441 **Haller** John E '86
(614) 292-5062 **Haller** Kathryn '75
(614) 445-8416 **Halley** Matthew S '99
(614) 292-7480 **Halpern** Sheldon W '97
(614) 466-7264 **Hamalian** Derek S '88
(614) 486-6967 **Hamelberg** William R '76
(614) 464-4532 **Hamilton** Andrew P '79
(614) 885-0038 **Hamilton** Elizabeth A '94
(614) 443-7920 **Hamilton** Karen E '95
(614) 464-6400 **Hamilton** Nathan C '89
(614) 469-3939 **Hamilton** Robert W '87
(614) 469-3939 **Hamilton McGranor** AshLee M '00
(614) 466-4395 **Hammerstein** Anne L '82
(614) 228-6061 **Hammond** Gary W '80
(614) 227-2000 **Hammond** Karen K '94
(614) 228-6061 **Hammond & Sewards**
Hampl Lisa S '96
(614) 365-2700 **Han** Kyu Chang '04
(614) 462-2288 **Han** Lisa Ge Shang '93
(614) 241-5111 **Handa** Charles Brent '85
(614) 461-9212 **Handelman & Kilroy**
(614) 252-2300 **Handelman** Robert B '76
(614) 461-9212 **Handelman** Robert K '72
(614) 462-5471 **Handlan** Allen L '72
(614) 677-4456 **Handley** Bobby J '98
(614) 444-4529 **Haney** Andrew R '99
(614) 227-2000 **Hanke** Paul A '61
(614) 463-4201 **Hankerson** Cheryl R '97
(614) 451-9999 **Hanks** John C '00
(614) 885-4009 **Hanley** Kathleen A '81
(614) 466-6939 **Hanna** Delbert P '93
(614) 621-1500 **Hannan** Lori L '98
(614) 792-5170 **Hanneman** James A '98
Hanselman Lisa N '01
(614) 466-5394 **Hanson** David F '92
(614) 462-3555 **Hanson** Denise L '94
(614) 431-7200 **Hanson** Robert E '79
Hanysh Jennifer M '03
(614) 469-7455 **Hanzel** Dennis J '81
(614) 231-0381 **Hapner** Priscilla L '96
Haque Masarath N '99
(614) 462-5523 **Harbage** Amy E '03
(614) 255-1140 **Harbold** Robert C '75
(614) 543-0369 **Hardesty** Christian P '04
(614) 466-7090 **Hardin** Jennifer A '89
(614) 466-5394 **Hardwick** Stephen P '94
(614) 464-6400 **Hardymon** David W '76
(614) 464-2770 **Harildstad** Timothy N '91
(614) 644-7257 **Harmon** Jessica M '01
(614) 249-7455 **Harmon** John T '94
(614) 387-9090 **Harold** David T '00
(614) 485-2010 **Harper** Michael Scott Jr. '99
(614) 228-5331 **Harper** Stephen L '81
(614) 469-6638 **Harraway** Andria M '04
(614) 644-6342 **Harrell** Eric C '99
(614) 464-2572 **Harris** James B '76
(614) 249-2300 **Harris** Jeffry D '03
(614) 224-7711 **Harris** John A IV '00
(614) 457-9731 **Harris** Kenneth E '75
(614) 469-5715 **Harris** Marcia J '79
(614) 457-9731 **Harris & Mazza**
(614) 464-2572 **Harris McClellan Binau & Cox,PLL**
(614) 645-8936 **Harris** Natalia S '00
(614) 227-2000 **Harris** Polly J '85
(614) 464-6400 **Harris** Robert A '92
(614) 451-5300 **Harris** Steven M '85
(614) 462-5466 **Harris** Stuart W '96
(614) 644-3374 **Harrison** James M '93
(614) 466-7264 **Harrison** John R '95
(614) 224-2428 **Harrison** Kimberly E '03
(614) 752-6291 **Harrison** Lemuel E Jr. '90
(614) 469-3939 **Harrison** Rebecca J '97
(614) 451-7066 **Harrison** Wade E '93
(614) 238-6738 **Hart** Elizabeth R '04
(614) 466-1305 **Hart** Robert M '82
(614) 462-3580 **Hartel** Jeffry A '00
(614) 276-8959 **Harter** Brian W '91
(614) 464-1211 **Harter** William M '00
(614) 227-2000 **Hartman** Elizabeth A '04
(614) 677-6367 **Hartman** Mark E '93
(614) 462-4941 **Hartmann** Philip K '92
(614) 463-8532 **Hartmann** Robert G '88
(614) 443-7920 **Hartnell** Molly Geyen '03
(614) 228-6885 **Hartranft** Jeffrey B '97
(614) 227-2000 **Hartranft** John C '67
(614) 227-2000 **Hartranft** John C Jr. '00
(614) 221-0922 **Hartshorn** Michael W '72
(614) 464-6400 **Harty** Susan Barrett '91
(614) 466-3615 **Hartzell** Julie C Kidwell '02
(614) 221-1216 **Hass** Cheri B '95
(614) 224-1222 **Hassay** Wayne E '91
(614) 229-4822 **Hatch** Colin K '80
(614) 628-0650 **Hatcher** Steven J '73
(614) 719-3300 **Hathaway** Amy D '02
(614) 677-8754 **Hatler** Patricia R '02
(614) 464-2392 **Hatten** Steven A '78
(614) 228-6888 **Hatzifotinos** Dimitrios G '04
(614) 278-6767 **Haubiel** Charles W II '92
(614) 239-1801 **Haught** Jack G '83
(614) 463-9770 **Haupt** Erika L '94
(614) 460-4649 **Hauschild** Neal T '03
(614) 644-9278 **Hauswirth** George M '68
(614) 466-6589 **Havener** John L '83
(614) 228-6888 **Havens** James R '81
(614) 464-6400 **Havens** Jolie N '00
(614) 228-6888 **Havens Willis LLC**
(614) 292-7970 **Haverkamp** Robert J '71
(614) 644-9272 **Hawk** Kristina P '96
(614) 462-3555 **Hawkins** Daniel R '01
Hawkins Mark E '00
(614) 341-6057 **Hawkins** Monica E '00
(614) 466-2980 **Hawkinson** Cheryl Rae '91
(614) 464-1877 **Hawley** Robert B II '96
(614) 248-5700 **Hay** David S '74
(614) 228-2612 **Hayden** William M '81
(614) 227-2000 **Hayes** Jeffrey T '79
(614) 280-9300 **Hayes** Michael J '98
(614) 462-3194 **Hayes** Thomas F '93
(614) 221-9500 **Haynes** Douglas J '82
(614) 221-9500 **Haynes** Eleanor E '84
(614) 466-4656 **Hays** Mark E '76
(614) 677-3463 **Hays** Michelle L '93
(614) 229-4955 **Hays** Robert D '91
(614) 466-4320 **Hazan** Naomi B '04
(614) 249-5169 **Hazelbaker** Elizabeth A '96
(614) 459-8900 **Head** Robert D '78
(614) 462-2272 **Headen** Raymond C '87
Heagerty Patrick J '04
(614) 466-1818 **Heaphy** William J III '75
(614) 481-6000 **Hebenstreit** Stephen L '67
(614) 292-0190 **Hébert** L Camille '90
(614) 224-1500 **Heck** Jeremiah E '03
(614) 224-7700 **Heckert** Christopher E '00
(614) 224-7700 **Heckert & Hockensmith Co,LPA**
(614) 228-0326 **Heckman** Clarence L '69
(614) 790-4265 **Hedden** David L '74
(614) 464-6400 **Hedden** Herbert A '90
(614) 538-5382 **Hedien** Mark J '95
(614) 466-0000 **Hedman** Sarah E '03
(614) 645-7483 **Hedrick** Billy Ray '96
(614) 365-2700 **Heer** Holly H '93
(614) 224-9207 **Heer** William C III '90
(614) 428-2102 **Heeter** Joseph L '88
(614) 258-6000 **Heffernan** Michael E '98
(614) 857-4390 **Heffernan** Terrence R '82
(614) 229-4431 **Heid** Brigid E '90
(614) 793-8470 **Heier** David S '79
(614) 229-7596 **Heier** Patricia W '79
(614) 228-8833 **Heinlein** David J '88
(614) 227-2000 **Heintz** Michael E '03
(614) 337-8366 **Heinzerling** Mark E '96
(614) 229-4722 **Heinzerling-Elkins** Mary '94
(614) 469-3289 **Helfrich** Kurt P '97
(614) 227-2000 **Helmreich** Richard J '89
(614) 547-0350 **Hemmer** Paul K '83
(614) 255-1140 **Hemminger** Chad K '04
(614) 461-5955 **Hemphill** John C '73
(614) 228-1541 **Hendershot** Elizabeth L '95
(614) 255-2040 **Henderson** Maurice M III '00
(614) 457-5600 **Henegar** Charles S III '94
(614) 464-6400 **Henke** Bruce R '79
(614) 466-8600 **Henkener** Ann E '74
(614) 340-3444 **Henley** Barron K '93
(614) 462-7450 **Hennebert** Shaunna L '96
(614) 224-8374 **Hennessey** Molly A '88
(614) 248-6691 **Hennessey** Thomas M '95
(614) 227-2000 **Henning** Harry L '71
(614) 224-9207 **Henry** George L '72
(614) 716-1612 **Henry** Janet Jay '84
(614) 486-4584 **Henry** William D '53
(614) 221-8448 **Hensel** Jan E '88
(614) 249-6584 **Hensley** Kimberly S '94
(614) 217-1111 **Henson** James J '79
(614) 249-4420 **Herath** Kirk Matthew '94
(614) 645-7657 **Herbert** Paul M II '87
(614) 464-6400 **Herbert** Sarah L '04
(614) 443-4866 **Herd** David A '92
(614) 444-5290 **Herder** Mark A '93
(614) 464-6400 **Herlihy** Kimberly Weber '97
(614) 292-2163 **Herman** Lawrence '53
(614) 221-1191 **Herman** Richard A '90
(614) 222-1889 **Herman** Steven E '98
(614) 221-8448 **Hernandez** Richard A '86
(614) 232-7072 **Herron** Katherine R '04
(614) 469-3939 **Hersch** Thomas J '01
(614) 466-3998 **Hersh** Jeffrey M '75
(614) 461-1156 **Hershberger** Eric B '91
(614) 466-8240 **Hertel** Kari B '96
(614) 463-9770 **Hertenstein** Edward C '76
(614) 644-2658 **Hertlein** Douglas L '88
(614) 827-7300 **Hess** Kevin E '04
(614) 445-8287 **Hess** Michael D '01
(614) 225-9000 **Hess** Paul J Jr. '81
(614) 462-5441 **Hess** Paul R '86
(614) 857-9590 **Hess** Rebecca J '84
(614) 462-5889 **Hess** Stephanie E '01
(614) 221-8448 **Hess** Thomas W '76
(614) 464-4100 **Hetterscheidt** Robert C '76
(614) 987-1500 **Heuer** Joseph Y '04
(614) 644-9529 **Heuerman** Mark R '89
(614) 253-5411 **Heyman** Ian A '98
(614) 225-9000 **Hickey** Michael J '68
(614) 644-7772 **Hicks** Britton M '03
(614) 644-1373 **Hicks** Cassandra L '83
(614) 487-5900 **Hicks** Sharon A '03
(614) 462-3555 **Hiers** Amy Lu '95
(614) 480-4282 **Higbee** Michael A '85
(614) 460-4653 **Higgins** Jenny L '91
(614) 248-9727 **Higgins** Thomas P '87
(614) 224-1222 **Hiland** Tammy L '97
(614) 221-8889 **Hilbert** Rebecca J '85
Hilbrands Kirk A '93
(614) 280-0570 **Hilburn** Regina L '91
(614) 466-7264 **Hildebrant** Kristin E '89
(614) 848-6500 **Hill Allison & DeWeese**
(614) 848-6500 **Hill** John W '52
(614) 848-6500 **Hill** John W Jr. '82
(614) 227-2000 **Hill** Kathleen B '98
(614) 462-5403 **Hill** Thomas W '70
(614) 221-2234 **Hiller** David P '69
(614) 466-8544 **Hillmer** Felicity M '89
(614) 466-4086 **Hills** William L '89
(614) 462-5451 **Hilson** Daniel G '86
(614) 462-4921 **Hilvert** Kevin '02
(614) 466-4882 **Himes** Lance D '98
(614) 224-7700 **Himes-Riley** Jennifer M '02
(614) 444-4455 **Himmelrick** Amy D '00
(614) 292-2694 **Hindes** Thomas J '84
(614) 234-1287 **Hines** Linda E '04
(614) 228-1541 **Hire** Charles H '66
(614) 464-2392 **Hirsch** Bruce L '79
(614) 236-6685 **Hirsch** Dennis D '03
(614) 644-5281 **Hissom** Heather L '97
(614) 445-2582 **Histed** Bradley J '81
(614) 677-3700 **Hjelle** Jennifer H '96
Hobday John D '66
(614) 469-2999 **Hobson** Gordon G Jr. '80
(614) 325-9144 **Hockenberry** Rebecca K '02
(614) 224-7700 **Hockensmith** Mark L '97
(614) 481-3127 **Hockstad** Karen S '93
(614) 221-4255 **Hodge** David L '02
(614) 462-5454 **Hoeffel** Melissa Rager '03
(614) 466-7447 **Hofacker-Carr** Velda K '88
(614) 752-1200 **Hoff** Walter A '76
(614) 421-2626 **Hoffman** Bradley E '83
(614) 645-8591 **Hoffman** Deborah F '81
(614) 222-0526 **Hoffman** Eric J '84
(614) 478-1975 **Hoffman** George M '79
(614) 466-2585 **Hoffman** Judith A '83
(614) 719-3393 **Hoffman** Kimberly E '95
(614) 459-4140 **Hogan** Christopher E '98
(614) 462-3555 **Hogan** Dennis A '75
(614) 387-9831 **Hogan** Lee '85
Hogan Mark E '03
(614) 221-4670 **Hohl** Ruth A '86
(614) 466-8600 **Hoke** Anne L '87
(614) 464-6400 **Holaday** Rodney A '97
(614) 462-3194 **Holben** Marla R '89
(614) 221-0422 **Holbrook** Michael J '83

(614) 292-7755 **Holder** Robert L '71
(614) 469-0180 **Holfinger** Alissa R '02
(614) 464-4100 **Holfinger** Jonathan L '02
(614) 466-8330 **Holko** Mark E '80
(614) 457-4837 **Holland** Robert J '63
(614) 466-6700 **Hollanshead** Susan M '85
(614) 228-6135 **Hollenbaugh** H Ritchey '73
(614) 228-4141 **Holley** Elisabeth M '01
(614) 221-2121 **Hollis** Matthew T '01
(614) 466-2653 **Hollon** Steven C '81
(614) 221-2121 **Holloway** James E '94
(614) 227-2348 **Holman** Michael S '72
(614) 848-4151 **Holmes** Christy M '98
(614) 644-9178 **Holmes** Douglas J '79
(614) 225-8516 **Holmquist** Paul R '97
(614) 227-2300 **Holodnak** Robert B '89
(614) 461-1311 **Holthus** Douglas P '86
(614) 462-2296 **Holz** Richard W '85
(614) 228-6885 **Holzhall** Vincent I '02
(614) 644-2657 **Hombach** Stephen C '88
(614) 462-3194 **Hood** James E '03
(614) 228-6345 **Hoppers** John W '68
(614) 462-2305 **Hopple** E James '63
Hopple Roy E Jr. '53
(614) 846-2000 **Hornbeck** David B '70
(614) 221-4000 **Horton** Timothy S '96
(614) 449-8282 **Horvath** Dennis E '01
(614) 253-2525 **Horvath** Thomas L '73
(614) 462-5310 **Hosafros** Rexann M '85
(614) 466-8600 **Hoskins** Patria V '86
(614) 488-2765 **Hotchkiss** Lawrence J '79
(614) 466-9563 **Hotz** Ann M '91
(614) 466-3947 **Houchen** Betsy J '95
(614) 480-5218 **Houck** Annette M '98
(614) 457-9731 **Houck** Rachael A '04
(614) 716-1630 **House** David C '92
(614) 461-1311 **House** Lisa R '03
(614) 223-9300 **House** Ronald L Jr. '86
(614) 462-4010 **House** Susan L '87
Householder David K '92
(614) 464-6400 **Howard** Stephen M '76
(614) 236-0011 **Howard** Ted R '64
(614) 469-0100 **Howarth** Robert F Jr. '70
(614) 222-8686 **Howenstein** C Bradley '91
(614) 462-3714 **Hoy** Suzanne H '88
(614) 644-0854 **Hoylman** Barbara N '90
(614) 228-1541 **Hoyt** Matthew W '00
(614) 461-1551 **Hrach** James A '91
(614) 466-5967 **Hubbard** Barton A '81
(614) 228-6885 **Hubbard** Edward G '97
(614) 469-1301 **Hubble** Adam J '94
(614) 228-3125 **Hubler** Julie P '86
(614) 228-3125 **Hubler** Lloyd E III '85
(614) 445-4455 **Huckaby** Kristen J '95
(614) 221-8800 **Hudak** Clara J '74
(614) 728-3053 **Hudak** Kimberly Z '96
(614) 488-7878 **Huddleston** Charles L III '77
(614) 464-6215 **Hudok** Timothy D '02
(614) 221-3155 **Hudson** Mary Jo '89
(614) 464-1211 **Hudson** Nicolette R '99
(614) 462-4461 **Hudson** Woodrow W '92
(614) 227-8791 **Huelsman** Douglas L '04
(614) 487-8667 **Huey** Donald Timothy '84
(614) 446-4470 **Huey** Karen J '93
(614) 387-0304 **Huff** H Delmar '03
(614) 227-2000 **Huff** Michael T '04
(614) 469-3939 **Huffman** Fordham E '84
(614) 466-6696 **Hufstader** Dennis L '75
(614) 227-2000 **Hughes** Anne M '01
(614) 410-6032 **Hughes** Darrell A '99
(614) 224-1222 **Hughes** Donald Timothy '84
(614) 365-2700 **Hughes** Donald W '97
(614) 451-4824 **Hughes** James E '72
(614) 227-2365 **Hughes** James J III '86
(614) 221-5216 **Hughes** James M '94
(614) 227-2000 **Hughes** Lawrence Bradfield '99
(614) 462-3555 **Hughes** Michael T '01
(614) 462-3194 **Hughes** Paula S '96
(614) 451-7060 **Hughes** Stephanie M '89
(614) 224-1222 **Hughes** Steven R '83
(614) 475-9511 **Huhn** Richard M '69
(614) 644-2640 **Hull** Melissa L '98
(614) 222-4139 **Hulthen** Amy M '88
(614) 462-4555 **Human** Randy E '94
(614) 645-6945 **Hummel** Gordon B '60
(614) 469-8000 **Hummel** Gretchen J '79
(614) 252-2300 **Hummel** Terry Van '82
(614) 220-9200 **Hummer** Brendan B '03
(614) 645-6822 **Hummer** Mark A '86
(614) 221-4000 **Humphrey** Guy R '84
Humphrey Ian C '02
(614) 241-5550 **Humphreys** Kevin E '98
(614) 488-7924 **Hunker** Frederick '81
(614) 451-1437 **Hunkins** Blaine B '52
(614) 228-1541 **Hunt** Ashanti T '02
(614) 466-2872 **Hunt** Holly J '02
(614) 466-6434 **Hunt** James F Jr. '76
(614) 466-8911 **Hunt** Jason M '98
(614) 415-7468 **Hunt** Jonathan J '00
(614) 444-3900 **Hunt** Mark M '97
(614) 442-5626 **Hunter Carnahan Shoub & Byard**
(614) 644-2658 **Hunter** Daniel J '81
(614) 221-2525 **Hunter** James K III '73
(614) 464-1969 **Hunter** Kyle L '98
(614) 442-5626 **Hunter** Michael J '85
(614) 461-1311 **Hunter** Thomas Day '72
(614) 326-3399 **Huntley** Jeffrey L '83
(614) 944-5220 **Huntley** Wendi R '92
(614) 876-0480 **Hurd** Dwight I '59
(614) 644-3037 **Hurdley** Jeffery H '89
(614) 621-8888 **Hurlbert** Jay J '96
(614) 221-1216 **Hurst** Rufus B '87
(614) 719-3200 **Hurst** Sarah E '02
(614) 462-3194 **Hurt** Emily '00
(614) 265-6565 **Hustead** Sherrie L '03
(614) 644-2658 **Huston** Daniel H '89
(614) 340-5000 **Hutchins** Antony Robert '85
(614) 228-5331 **Hutchins** William J III '71
(614) 466-3828 **Huth** Sandra D '91
(614) 228-6885 **Hutson** Jeffrey W '66
(614) 221-1000 **Huyghe** Ryan K '99
(614) 227-4093 **Hvizdos** Cynthia E '78
(614) 464-2572 **Hvizdos** John D '75
(614) 329-0732 **Hykes** John E '75
(614) 207-2441 **Hyre** John M III '96
(614) 228-6345 **Iannotta** Mark W '88
(614) 466-9511 **Iannotta** Melissa J '87
(614) 443-4866 **Ice** Matthew E '96
(614) 466-2766 **Idzkowski** Michael E '94
(614) 677-8223 **Ifeduba** Stephen E '97
(614) 261-9742 **Igo** Richard B '70
(614) 464-3332 **Igoe** Daniel J '68
(614) 228-6135 **Igoe** Michael H '75
(614) 224-0100 **Ihlendorf** Richard M '76
(614) 466-3615 **Imbrogno** Andre R '99
(614) 365-4100 **Imhoff** Caroline D '04
(614) 248-5656 **Imwalle** Randall J '88
(614) 464-6400 **Ingram** Bruce L '78
(614) 469-3939 **Ingram** Kasey T '02
(614) 466-8905 **Ingram** Meribethe Richards '04
(614) 888-9611 **Innis** Richard L '70
(614) 818-4098 **Innocenti** Trevor J '93
(614) 462-3555 **Insley** David W '81
(614) 224-0600 **Insley** Susan J '77
(614) 227-2376 **Intihar** Stephen '93
(614) 227-2000 **Ireton** C Andrew Jr. '73
(614) 292-0611 **Irvine** Joseph R '86
(614) 221-2121 **Isaac Brant Ledman & Teetor,LLP**
(614) 221-2121 **Isaac** Frederick M '66
(614) 275-2692 **Isern** Kathleen L '83
(614) 464-6400 **Ison** Richard G '53
(614) 365-2700 **Ita** Amy R '02
(614) 464-6400 **Iten** Jonathan D '81
(614) 461-1311 **Ivan** Paulette M '94
(614) 688-5683 **Iveson** Mary A '91
(614) 728-8400 **Izzo** John A '93
(614) 462-2472 **Jabarin** Nadia M '01
(614) 469-3939 **Jabe** Daniel N '03
(614) 228-6107 **Jack** Arnold L '64
(614) 221-2702 **Jackson** Douglas R '85
(614) 227-2700 **Jackson** Janet E '78
(614) 227-2000 **Jackson** Patrick I '02
(614) 464-6400 **Jackson** Reginald W '80
(614) 677-8212 **Jackson** Stephen M-L '04
(614) 466-4397 **Jackson-Forbes** Johnlander C '93
(614) 466-4605 **Jacobs** Bobbi-Lynn '92
(614) 463-9790 **Jacobs** Louis A '73
(614) 228-8400 **Jacobs** Rebecca B '97
(614) 466-0632 **Jacobsen** Lynda J '98
(614) 367-1493 **Jacobson** Michael T '01
(614) 227-2000 **Jacques** Laurie N '90
(614) 223-1634 **Jadwin** Jay E '87
(614) 443-7654 **Jaffe** Brett H '78
(614) 464-6400 **Jaffe** Dan L '90
(614) 228-6148 **Jaffy** Lynn S '97
(614) 228-6148 **Jaffy** Marc J '90
(614) 228-6148 **Jaffy** Rachel B '94
(614) 228-6148 **Jaffy** Stewart R '55
(614) 728-2845 **Jaite** Maura O'Neill '92
(614) 462-3555 **Jakubow** Michael R '90
(614) 252-0434 **James** Peter K '84
(614) 466-7900 **Jamieson** Duffy W '89
(614) 464-6400 **Jamieson** J Scott '79
(614) 719-8792 **Jamison** Terri B '04
(614) 228-8400 **Janes** Charles R '77
(614) 236-6779 **Janes** Kathryn B '00
(614) 224-7291 **Janes** Ronald B '69
(614) 466-5394 **Jaquith** Craig M '91
(614) 466-5394 **Jasiunas** J Banning '01
(614) 228-9550 **Javitch Block & Rathbone**
(614) 466-8911 **Jean** Martine '03
(614) 221-7711 **Jedinak** Thomas J '74
(800) 444-9950 **Jeffers** James B '95
(614) 464-6400 **Jeffries** Gretchen D '03
(614) 462-3194 **Jelen** Scott Z '86
(614) 464-6400 **Jenkins** George L '66
(614) 644-7342 **Jenkins** Vicki L '85
(614) 628-6880 **Jenkins** Wayne A '78
(614) 645-8205 **Jenkins** William B '52
(614) 221-2121 **Jennings** David G '88
(614) 466-0461 **Jennings** Lynn D '85
(614) 466-2872 **Jennings** Sharon A '91
(614) 995-1968 **Jensen** Mitchell A '04
(614) 469-3939 **Jernejcic** Junxia Tang '02
(614) 583-0088 **Jewel** Anne F '86
(614) 268-8661 **Jewett** James M '74
(614) 221-7663 **Jinkens** Jeffrey R '78
(614) 444-1190 **Jochim** Timothy C '76
(614) 224-5700 **Johan** Andrea H '85
Johns Alan L '78
(614) 752-6891 **Johns** Brian E '91
(614) 442-8885 **Johnson** Annrita S '76
(614) 466-3379 **Johnson** Bruce E '85
(614) 464-1904 **Johnson** Bryan B '83
(614) 464-3563 **Johnson** Calvin T Jr. '95
(614) 249-3951 **Johnson** Chris A '88
(614) 299-8235 **Johnson** Cleve M '79
(614) 221-2838 **Johnson** David L '71
(614) 466-6691 **Johnson** Denise M '87
(614) 436-6812 **Johnson** Doreen C '79
(614) 222-0535 **Johnson** Eric A '95
(614) 464-1877 **Johnson** Eric W '95
(614) 249-7187 **Johnson** Freddie L '93
(614) 716-2827 **Johnson** Gary L '98
(614) 365-5673 **Johnson** Giselle S '86
(614) 644-8878 **Johnson** Gregory K '80
(614) 457-4026 **Johnson** Jack L '61
(614) 224-1373 **Johnson** Jeremy W '02
(614) 241-2332 **Johnson** Jessica L '04
(614) 464-2025 **Johnson** John P II '93
(614) 444-4600 **Johnson** Katherine A '04
(614) 227-2322 **Johnson** Kenneth C '79
Johnson Kiehner '52
(614) 233-4710 **Johnson** Leslie S '97
(614) 462-3194 **Johnson** Lori A '04
Johnson Margaret L '02
(614) 221-0984 **Johnson** Margaret N '74
(614) 228-1541 **Johnson** Mark A '85
(614) 722-3940 **Johnson** Martha D '88
(614) 462-3555 **Johnson** Mary E '86
(614) 249-7918 **Johnson** Olivia B '86
(614) 466-5967 **Johnson** Russel J '04
(614) 466-4656 **Johnson** Stephen H '84
(614) 545-5555 **Johnson** Terri Len '95
(614) 462-3203 **Johnson** William C Jr. '91
(614) 716-1624 **Johnson** William E '95
(614) 227-2381 **Johnston** Gordon W '76
(614) 466-5032 **Johnston** Holly J '04
(614) 249-8613 **Johnston** LeRoy III '90
(614) 464-6400 **Johnston** Philip C '68
(614) 466-0924 **Johnston** William J '69
(614) 880-9085 **Johnston** William W '70
(614) 464-0082 **Johrendt Cook & Eberhart**
(614) 464-0082 **Johrendt** Michael J '77
(614) 628-6880 **Jolley** John D '97
(614) 251-4000 **Jolley** Lisa M '97
(614) 224-3855 **Jones** Belinda M '94
(614) 227-2000 **Jones** Bernard M '04
(614) 462-4427 **Jones** Charles P Jr. '81
(614) 621-1500 **Jones** Christopher '90
(614) 466-2980 **Jones** Daniel P '89
(614) 480-4258 **Jones** David A '78
(614) 469-3939 **Jones Day**
(614) 229-4606 **Jones** Donald L '82
(614) 221-2300 **Jones** Gary L '66
(614) 228-1398 **Jones** Grey W '80
(614) 223-9300 **Jones** James Allen III '00
(614) 462-2668 **Jones** Janine H '01
(614) 469-3939 **Jones** Jeffrey J '85
(614) 466-0463 **Jones** Jeffrey R '89
(614) 644-7233 **Jones** John H '91
(614) 466-2980 **Jones** Richard M '92
(614) 221-2300 **Jones** Robyn R '89
(614) 464-6400 **Jones** Stacia Marie '00
(614) 463-9770 **Jones** Stephen D '81
(614) 562-6458 **Jones** Terry T '90
(614) 227-2000 **Jordan** Donald W '76
(614) 939-9822 **Jordan** Jeffrey H '90
(614) 885-4828 **Jordan** Jerry D '63
(614) 462-2283 **Jordan** Michael S '97
(614) 466-8109 **Jordan** Suzanne S '97
(614) 462-3001 **Jorgensen** Hanne M '85
(614) 459-4014 **Josenhans** Paul J '72
(614) 449-8282 **Joseph** Jennifer J '91
(614) 449-8282 **Joseph** John J '81
(614) 644-7435 **Joyce** Deborah L '85
(614) 365-2700 **Judge** Corie Marty '98
(614) 719-3300 **Judge** Shawn K '98
(614) 461-5600 **Judy** Philip L '97
(614) 462-3555 **Julian** Christine S '92
(614) 462-3555 **Julian** Terry J '87
(614) 645-7031 **Jump** David S '81
(614) 481-4480 **Jump** W Mark '94
(614) 227-2000 **Jung** Jennifer L '00
(614) 462-3194 **Junga** Christopher T '00
(614) 228-6885 **Jurca** Jeffrey J '79
(614) 224-8374 **Jurcevich** Laura M '03
(614) 221-5824 **Jurkovac** Mark E '88
(614) 486-0297 **Jurus** Stanley R Jr. '54
(614) 258-1133 **Justice** Stewart III '01
(614) 228-1346 **Kacic** Glenn D '84
(614) 466-6511 **Kaczmarek** William F '89
(614) 463-4211 **Kadela** David A '86
(614) 466-2934 **Kading** Daniel J '87
(614) 464-6400 **Kahn** Benita A '82
(614) 221-7548 **Kaikis** Darla E '92
(614) 469-3939 **Kairis** Matthew A '91
Kaiser Jo E '00
(614) 213-7084 **Kalgreen** Andrew J '79
(614) 415-7078 **Kallner** Matthew G '90
(614) 224-1222 **Kaltenbach** Jerry L II '02
(614) 221-3151 **Kamb** William T '03
(614) 224-5205 **Kamer** Marc T '98
(614) 645-8896 **Kanai** Matthew A '00
(614) 221-3155 **Kandawalla** Darius N '96
Kane Ira O '73
(614) 227-2371 **Kane** Richard F '71
(614) 645-7385 **Kane** Wendy A '95
(614) 559-9000 **Kang** Catherine C '95
(614) 224-1118 **Kanter** Bernard E '57
(614) 466-6750 **Kantzer** Joseph C '87
(614) 645-4500 **Kanz** Gayle E Jr. '99
(614) 526-4795 **Kapitan** Robert J '64
(614) 228-4422 **Kaplan** Aimee L '03
(614) 228-5151 **Kaplan** Philip A '00
(614) 252-5233 **Kaplin** Thomas L Jr. '59
(614) 469-3939 **Kapp** Jeffrey L '93
(614) 764-4617 **Kaps** Charles G '77
(614) 677-6335 **Kapustin** Vladimir '89
(614) 294-0631 **Karam** Joseph D '57
(614) 228-8400 **Karl** Robert J '89
(614) 252-2300 **Karlock** Kenneth P '93
(614) 436-5466 **Karr** Douglas B '80
(614) 848-3100 **Karr** Glennon J '74
(614) 466-3998 **Karr** Heather E '99
(614) 478-6000 **Karr** Keith M '83
(614) 478-6000 **Karr & Sherman Co,LPA**
(614) 466-6290 **Kasai** Jerry K '84
(614) 444-7841 **Kass** Frederic R '72
(614) 461-1311 **Kasson** Donald P '91
(614) 462-4927 **Kastner** Beth '01
(614) 728-3676 **Katko** David P '90
(614) 227-4841 **Katz** Deborah A '89
(614) 466-5967 **Katz** Janyce C '89
(614) 227-2397 **Katz** Robert H '75
(614) 778-4414 **Kauffman** Andrew M '79
(614) 864-1200 **Kauffman** David E '95
(614) 719-1568 **Kauffman** Kelly L '99
(614) 464-8359 **Kaufman** David Jacob '04
Kaufman Jeffrey R '97
(614) 469-9650 **Kaufman** Philip B '78
(614) 221-3536 **Kavinsky** Keith A '92
(740) 450-5167 **Kawalec** Thomas C '68
(614) 462-3555 **Kaylor** Jamie Z '90
(614) 236-9900 **Kayne** Daniel J '76
(614) 462-3194 **Kazar** Michelle L '99
(614) 365-9900 **Keane** Aimee P '04
(614) 365-2700 **Kearns** Greta M '97
(614) 272-6560 **Keating** Bradley D '03
(614) 540-4000 **Keating** Van D '86
(614) 481-4466 **Keating** William H '72
(614) 645-7483 **Keck** Heather L '99
(614) 462-3194 **Keeling** John W '75
(614) 460-4682 **Keenan** David C '94
(614) 280-1100 **Keener Doucher Curley & Patterson,LPA**
(614) 280-1100 **Keener** Thomas J '75
(614) 462-5400 **Kegler Brown Hill & Ritter**
(614) 462-5446 **Kegler** Charles J '68
(614) 462-5409 **Kegler** Todd M '97
(614) 462-2279 **Keglewitsch** Josef Jr. '96
(614) 418-3100 **Keglewitsch** Rebecca A '97
(614) 442-9200 **Keister** David L '80
(614) 466-7264 **Keith** Harry B II '68
(614) 466-3014 **Keith** James R '79
(614) 213-8510 **Kelbick** Matt '02
(614) 445-2650 **Kelbley** Jeffrey P '77
(614) 442-1948 **Kelch** Donald F Jr. '68
(614) 444-5700 **Keller** Amy E '01
(614) 223-9300 **Keller** Donald M '04
(614) 227-2341 **Keller** Donald R '74
(614) 464-6400 **Keller** John K '75
(614) 459-5200 **Keller** Mark D '68
Keller Sandra L '99
(614) 469-2999 **Keller** Steven R '84
(614) 538-8155 **Kelley** Brendan W '88
(614) 469-5715 **Kelley** Kevin W '89
(614) 280-1100 **Kelley** Michael J '81
(614) 228-5775 **Kelley** Timothy M '83
(614) 469-1882 **Kelly** Elizabeth M '94
(614) 227-2308 **Kelly** Emmett M '99
(614) 280-1100 **Kelly** John T '87
(614) 223-7928 **Kelly** Jon F '76
(614) 241-2174 **Kelly** Joseph A '91
(614) 466-5638 **Kelly** Lori M '94
(614) 478-6000 **Kelly** Suzanne E '88
(614) 227-2000 **Kelly** William J Jr. '76
(614) 246-1000 **Kelm** Russell A '71
Kelsey Andrea M '85
(614) 228-8662 **Kelsey** Charles E '75
(614) 644-8390 **Kelsey** Mark G '82
(614) 228-1593 **Kelso** Daniel J '76
(614) 846-5069 **Kemp** Daniel W '70
(614) 224-2678 **Kemp** Harold R '74
(614) 224-2678 **Kemp** Jacqueline L '96
(614) 224-2678 **Kemp Schaeffer Rowe & Lardiere Co,LPA**
(614) 224-9221 **Kempf** Christopher J '84
(614) 469-1301 **Kendall** Darin G '82
(614) 469-3939 **Kennard** J Todd '97
(614) 221-8401 **Kennedy & Colasurd,LPA**
(614) 463-9770 **Kennedy** Douglas M '80
(614) 464-6400 **Kennedy** James P '60
(614) 221-8401 **Kennedy** Janice M '81
(614) 451-9660 **Kennedy** John W '89
(614) 488-1161 **Kennedy & Knoll**
(614) 488-1161 **Kennedy** Nicholas E '98
(614) 326-1222 **Kennedy** Robert G '92
(614) 644-7381 **Kennedy** Robert S '90
(614) 461-0256 **Kent** Joel S '87
(614) 248-7688 **Kent** Megan V '94
(614) 469-1882 **Kephart & Fisher LLP**
(614) 221-5121 **Kerber** Jacques C '75
(614) 227-2356 **Kerber** Steven R '76
(614) 223-9300 **Kern** Benjamen E '03
(614) 466-5610 **Kern** Charles D '00
(614) 466-2766 **Kern** Timothy J '86
(614) 486-2700 **Kerns** Keith R '00
(614) 462-5406 **Kerns** R Kevin '83
(614) 268-7250 **Kerns-Bidwell** Amy T '80
(614) 242-1000 **Kerpsack** Robert W Jr. '89
(614) 475-6440 **Kerscher** Martin J '77
(614) 462-2229 **Kerschner** Karl '01
(614) 459-4287 **Kersell** Nancy S '85
(614) 469-3939 **Kessler** Elizabeth P '93
(614) 221-0240 **Kessler** Marc J '92
(614) 888-3185 **Kessler** Russell W '80
(614) 444-3900 **Ketcham** Richard S '74
(614) 338-0163 **Keyser** Donald G '79
(614) 365-2700 **Keyser** Raymond C '02
(614) 462-5400 **Khan** Rasheeda Z '02
(614) 459-6331 **Khasawneh** Rateb M '00
(614) 857-9590 **Khorrami** Mina N '92
(614) 645-7483 **Khoury** Paul T '99
(614) 365-2700 **Kibbey** Thomas F '02
(614) 469-3200 **Kidd** Melissa L '99
(614) 278-7043 **Kidder** Charles L '90
(614) 228-5151 **Kielkopf** Andrew J '93
(614) 227-2000 **Kiger** Robert C '60
(614) 221-4221 **Kilbride** Randall J '96
(614) 794-6992 **Kilgore** Terry L '73
(614) 330-6844 **Killion** Christopher L '01
(614) 227-2334 **Killworth** Allen R '97
(614) 249-1698 **Killworth** Linda Klimas '97
(614) 542-9000 **Killworth** Melinda B '94
(614) 461-9212 **Kilroy** Mary J '81
(614) 221-1216 **Kim** Edward S '94
(614) 645-7547 **Kimball** Dennis R '82
(614) 227-2000 **Kimm** Lori-Lou '90
(614) 644-0258 **Kimmet** Kathryn A '91
(614) 224-7193 **Kincaid Randall & Craine**
(614) 228-1541 **Kincaid** Robert M Jr. '77
(614) 263-1810 **King** Carl R '81
(614) 222-0068 **King** Eric B '01
(614) 221-7201 **King** Eugene R '83
(614) 469-3939 **King** G Roger '71
(614) 784-8882 **King** Gerald L '78
(614) 889-2531 **King** Hamlin C Jr. '67
(614) 227-2000 **King** James A '88
(614) 469-3939 **King** James R '74
(614) 628-6880 **King** Michael J '00
(614) 462-3194 **King** Nancy B '80
(614) 644-7233 **King** Philip A '00
(614) 469-7404 **King** Robert C '75
(614) 716-1643 **King** Timothy A '84
(614) 621-0777 **King** Tunney L '74
(614) 466-8054 **Kingery** Jeanne W '81
(614) 644-8765 **Kingsley** Kay A '80
(614) 221-4000 **Kington** John A '80
(614) 225-4447 **Kinnan** Brent E '76
(614) 222-5853 **Kinnan** Jimmie L '79
(614) 227-2300 **Kinross** Kevin M '00
(800) 480-2265 **Kinross** Shannon C '01
(614) 466-6511 **Kinworthy** Christine M '89
(614) 464-6400 **Kinzer** Allen S '88
(614) 462-3979 **Kirby** Edwin Lee Jr. '74
(614) 462-4477 **Kirby** William J '80
(614) 236-6779 **Kirchner** Lina Nizar '02
(614) 221-3318 **Kirchner** Steven M '02
(614) 365-2700 **Kirila** Jill S '97
(614) 752-9039 **Kirk** Margaret '89
(614) 466-3180 **Kirk** Samuel J III '04
(614) 466-3998 **Kirkhope** Anne M '97
(614) 466-7264 **Kirkman** George M '80
(614) 462-3555 **Kirschman** Scott C '88
(614) 365-2700 **Kirsner** John M '92
(614) 246-4052 **Kirstein** Gregory W '82
(614) 461-1311 **Kish** Robert V III '03
(614) 280-4000 **Kissos** Dean G '85
(614) 462-5400 **Kitch** Thomas D '97

(614) 224-7711 **Kitrick & Lewis Co,LPA**
(614) 224-7711 **Kitrick** Mark M '81
(614) 224-7291 **Kizer** Tanya J '01
(614) 221-8889 **Klaben** Amy D '86
(614) 464-6400 **Kladder** Ronald A '79
(614) 466-6416 **Klatt** Andrew J '93
(614) 221-7548 **Klatt** Courtney Larrimer '96
(614) 221-5216 **Klausman** Charles W IV '94
(614) 462-3194 **Klecker** Theodore L '00
(614) 299-6139 **Klein** Andrew I '80
(614) 323-5225 **Klein** Jack A '76
(614) 645-7385 **Klein** John C III '79
Klein Mattie M '02
(614) 225-8703 **Klein** Michael A '80
(614) 224-0933 **Kleinman** Seth K '02
(614) 462-2700 **Kleinman** Stephen R '95
(614) 586-1310 **Kleiser** Christina M '98
(614) 466-3998 **Klemann** Michael A '72
(614) 232-8134 **Klenk** William C '90
Kline Carrie L '02
(614) 221-0090 **Kline** Kenneth R '01
(614) 466-4320 **Kline** Tiffany A '02
(614) 488-9233 **Klitch** Jennifer L '94
(614) 466-4656 **Klodell** Alan H '86
(614) 267-9581 **Klos** Daniel H '84
(614) 464-6400 **Kloss** William D Sr. '58
(614) 464-6400 **Kloss** William D Jr. '88
(614) 480-4579 **Klosz** Raymond T '88
(614) 547-0220 **Knapp** Curtis H '89
(614) 752-2045 **Knapp** Derrick L '04
(614) 461-1551 **Knapp** Ernestine M '91
(614) 462-3555 **Knapp** Irene L '00
(614) 466-2766 **Knapp** Jill L '03
(614) 227-2000 **Knapp** Kyle A '98
(614) 461-1311 **Kneafsey** Brian M Jr. '93
(614) 249-6618 **Knecht** Richard S '77
(614) 248-7689 **Knight** Barbara M '77
(614) 486-9503 **Knisley** Daniel S '86
(614) 486-9503 **Knisley** David L '89
(614) 486-9503 **Knisley** Dean A '86
(614) 486-9503 **Knisley** Douglas C '82
(614) 486-9503 **Knisley** Scott M '53
(614) 488-1161 **Knoll** Laren E '99
(614) 466-4199 **Knopp** Melissa Ann '95
(614) 464-6400 **Knueve** Mark A '96
(614) 464-6400 **Knueve** Meredith K '99
(614) 466-7447 **Knutti** Randall W '84
(614) 466-4961 **Kobalka** Walter S '76
(614) 236-6675 **Kobil** Daniel T '83
(614) 461-6666 **Koblentz** Robert A '70
(614) 288-4740 **Koch** Ronald J '03
(614) 220-5611 **Kochalski** Edward M '75
(614) 486-8905 **Kocher** Walter W '75
(614) 466-0605 **Kocsis** Alexander S '77
(614) 443-7455 **Koeck** Roger M '92
(614) 241-5902 **Koenig** Charles A '78
(614) 466-6750 **Koenig** Robert G Jr. '91
(614) 451-0713 **Koerner** Nancy L '84
(614) 481-4480 **Koffel** Bradley P '93
(614) 481-4480 **Koffel & Jump**
(614) 438-4080 **Kohler** Charles W '75
(614) 888-4911 **Kohler** Joseph E '75
(614) 466-2413 **Kohrt** Douglas H '74
(614) 232-0424 **Kokensparger** Steven J '94
(614) 466-2766 **Koladin Plantz** Summer '00
(614) 466-6750 **Kolb** Loretta R '74
(614) 466-4605 **Kolbash** Ronn L '97
(614) 462-5872 **Kolman** Marya C '78
(614) 241-5550 **Kolman** Michael S '81
(614) 221-1000 **Kolnicki** Shari A '00
(614) 462-3555 **Koltak** Joseph A '04
(614) 221-7381 **Koltak** Ronald J '77
(614) 365-2700 **Komasara** Tiffany L '01
(614) 644-2782 **Koncelik** Joseph P '93
(614) 227-2000 **Koogler** Mark B '80
(614) 461-1234 **Kooperman** Brian T '04
(614) 280-1100 **Koorn** Amy B '01
(614) 242-5931 **Kopech** David A '82
(614) 469-3200 **Kopf** John B III '02
(614) 278-2305 **Koprucki** Patricia J '81
(614) 224-4114 **Kormanik** Paul S '79
(614) 224-1222 **Korn** David G '76
(614) 221-2226 **Kort** Louis F '79
(614) 466-7090 **Korte** Julie M '93
(614) 462-3262 **Kosinski** Jeannie J '04
(614) 464-6400 **Kossoudji** Scott A '00
(614) 275-2460 **Kostelac** Gregory M '81
(614) 430-8885 **Kostreva** David R II '03
(614) 644-3037 **Kovac** Frances M '85
(614) 466-7751 **Kowalczyk** Elizabeth A '93
(614) 461-4014 **Kozelek** Edward F '96
(614) 801-2768 **Kozelek** James G '01
(614) 464-2572 **Kozich** John H '75
(614) 228-1541 **Kozlowski** Richard E '98
(614) 461-4455 **Kozlowski** Susan H '80
(614) 692-3284 **Kraft** Michael J '73
(614) 227-2300 **Kram** Elbert J '66
(614) 224-7771 **Kranstuber** Charles W '79
(614) 415-8397 **Kranyak** John T '97
(614) 462-3555 **Krapenc** Robert F '88
(614) 340-3444 **Krauss** M Samuel '03
(614) 466-2766 **Kravitz** Brett A '98
(614) 464-2000 **Kravitz** Janet E '87
(614) 464-2000 **Kravitz & Kravitz**
(614) 464-2000 **Kravitz** Max '73
(614) 529-5701 **Kreber** John F '91
(614) 246-2515 **Krebs** Kenneth J '84
(614) 249-6235 **Kreighbaum** John S '01
(614) 466-7788 **Kreiter** Robert D '87
(614) 228-8400 **Krejci** Matthew C '02
(614) 644-7257 **Kreps** Cavett R '02
(614) 415-7320 **Krier** Peter C '95
(614) 462-2209 **Krimm** John J '87
(614) 462-5316 **Krippel** Darrolyn C '80
(614) 228-8995 **Krivda** Pamela S '88
(614) 688-3062 **Krivoshey** Robert M '78
(614) 644-3037 **Kroeger** Susan C '92
(614) 451-7159 **Krone** Gilbert L '68
(614) 466-9378 **Krum** Jean Amy '90
(614) 466-1285 **Krumenacker** James R '76
(614) 249-3586 **Krumm** Nancy M '80
(614) 227-2000 **Krummen** Robert J '03
(614) 258-9300 **Krupman** Victor S '59
(614) 466-3998 **Kubli** David F '75
(614) 221-8500 **Kuehnle** Kenton L '70
(614) 262-2539 **Kuhlmann** Will '72
(614) 466-0182 **Kuhn** Amy K '94
(614) 224-8339 **Kuhn** Kristie Campbell '03
(614) 466-6750 **Kuhns** Keven J '89
(614) 464-6400 **Kulewicz** John J '81
(614) 462-3580 **Kullman** Jack R Jr. '77
(614) 469-3939 **Kulwicki** Laura A '87
(614) 888-4160 **Kundtz** Alan J '81
(614) 221-2121 **Kurek** Randy S '79
(614) 464-1610 **Kurgis** Kevin F '82
(614) 462-3194 **Kurila** Mary C '85
(614) 227-2000 **Kurtz** Charles J III '65
(614) 462-2252 **Kutell** Russell J '97
(614) 464-6400 **Kuykendall** Laura G '78
(614) 645-8210 **Kyle-Reno** Shelia Ann '83
(614) 221-1111 **LaBue** Anne M '91
(614) 716-0500 **LaBuhn** Matthew A '96
(614) 242-4242 **Lackey** David L '91
(614) 228-2154 **LaFayette** Eric L '04
(614) 466-5707 **LaFayette** Jennifer L '97
(614) 461-1311 **La Fayette** Paul-Michael '96
(614) 221-2121 **LaForge** Steven G '86
(614) 692-3284 **Lagana** Beth B '80
(614) 752-1767 **Lagana** Vincent E '89
(614) 222-0963 **Lahm** Gunther K '87
Lahmers Nancy K '80
(614) 716-2435 **Laing** David A '81
(614) 443-6721 **Laird** Eric M '98
(614) 464-6400 **Laliberte** Brian J '99
(614) 464-6400 **Laliberte** Elizabeth A '02
(614) 263-7809 **Lally** Mark S '75
(614) 469-1400 **Lambert** Marnie C '00
(614) 229-7631 **Lambert** Martha M '04
(614) 236-6779 **Lambert** Michelle R '01
(614) 224-8187 **Lamkin Van Emin Trimble Beals & Dougherty**
(614) 224-8187 **Lamkin** William W '66
(614) 267-6308 **Lamm** Russell E Jr. '63
(614) 469-3939 **Lampe** Matthew W '89
(614) 466-7447 **Lampke** Matthew J '97
(614) 227-2000 **Lampke** Monique B '97
(614) 462-5295 **Lampkin-Crafter** Odella '89
(614) 790-3019 **Lampkin-Isabel** Robin E '90
(614) 221-2400 **Lancaster** Leonard T '76
(614) 299-2100 **Lancione** David '77
(614) 228-6627 **Lancione** Robert M '76
(614) 221-2121 **Landes** Mark '82
(614) 464-6400 **Landolfi** John L '89
(614) 221-1662 **Landon** Laurence B '86
(614) 227-2000 **Landrum** Jaime T '03
(614) 449-0449 **Landusky** Joseph R II '86
(614) 228-6885 **Lane Alton & Horst LLC**
(614) 462-7450 **Lane** Jessica L '03
(614) 466-5394 **Lane** Robert L '81
(614) 221-3155 **Lane** Robert S '89
(614) 228-6885 **Lane** William M '60
(614) 462-3194 **Lang** Heather D '02
(614) 466-3636 **Lang** Robert K '89
(614) 466-3998 **Lange** Richard M '75
(614) 628-1602 **Langer** Jeffrey Ira '90
(614) 221-6969 **Langfelder** John O '02
(614) 213-2316 **Langley** Beverly J '91
(614) 451-2210 **Langlois** Jennifer L '97
(614) 486-0052 **Lanier** Lorelei M '81
(614) 231-4440 **Lanker** Lois L '57
(614) 228-2044 **Lantz** Susan M '83
(614) 728-5599 **Lapczynski** James '94
(614) 228-1541 **Lape** Marcella L '04
(614) 469-3939 **Lape** Rodd B '96
(614) 644-3037 **Lapp** Alan L '72
(614) 224-2678 **Lardiere** Christopher L '83
(614) 221-3318 **Laret** Joffre S '84
(614) 221-4400 **Larkin** Janet L '01
(614) 221-7548 **Larrimer** Craig E '97
(614) 221-7548 **Larrimer** Gavin R '61
(614) 221-7548 **Larrimer** John H '97
(614) 221-7548 **Larrimer** Kevin J '98
(614) 221-7548 **Larrimer** Terrence W '72
(614) 464-9112 **Larson** Steven A '80
(614) 466-6700 **LaSalle** Lawrence J '82
(614) 464-6400 **Lash** Lester S '61
(614) 227-2000 **Lashbrook** April D '01
(614) 233-4766 **Lashuk** Beth Anne S '94
(614) 677-4064 **Lashutka** Gregory S '74
(614) 365-2700 **Lasley** Aneca E '00
(614) 461-4455 **Latanick** David G '74
(614) 466-1283 **Latas** Michael D '85
(614) 644-6338 **Lathwell** Kyle E '99
(614) 464-6400 **LaTour** Randall D '87
(614) 462-2329 **Latsko** John M '81
(614) 255-4326 **Latta** Jennifer E '03
(614) 466-8104 **Latta** Robert E '81
(614) 466-7983 **Lau** Edward Ho '88
(614) 752-9677 **Laubert** Robert M '90
(614) 292-2448 **Laughlin** Stanley K Jr. '61
(614) 462-3194 **Laughlin-Schopis** Susan K '82
(614) 228-6885 **Lavelle** William S '80
(614) 628-6880 **Lavinsky** Rick A '69
(614) 228-6717 **Law** Sam S '99
(614) 228-3664 **Lawrence** Linda J '90
(614) 228-3664 **Lawrence** Rodd S '88
(614) 677-2069 **Lawrence** Stephanie D '00
(614) 227-2000 **Lawrence** Wayman C III '59
(614) 249-5706 **Lawroski** John P '82
(614) 292-0611 **Layish** Michael D '02
(614) 469-3939 **Laymon** Ronald E '97
(614) 236-6535 **Lazaroff** Risa D '88
(614) 221-1616 **Lazear** Bruce C '84
(614) 228-1541 **Lazear** Sherri B '85
(614) 466-4605 **Lazorishak** Karen L '85
(614) 221-8448 **Leach** Donald B Jr. '82
(614) 995-4198 **Leach** Ellen C '92
(614) 995-5287 **Leach** George W Jr. '01
(614) 249-4784 **Leahy** Walter R '71
(614) 466-1305 **Leahy-Connolly** Erin B '98
(614) 358-8056 **Lease** Charles H '85
(614) 628-8361 **Lease** Diane M '86
(614) 621-1500 **Lech** Robert R '00
(614) 422-5046 **Lechnowsky** Orest J '01
(614) 644-7257 **Lecklider** Timothy A '83
(614) 221-2121 **Ledman** James H '65
(614) 462-3555 **Lee** Catherine M '04
(614) 466-3636 **Lee** Denise C '94
(614) 236-4600 **Lee** James C '84
(614) 248-5590 **Lee** Matthew David '93
(614) 444-4999 **Lee** Paul W '78
(614) 249-2229 **Lee** Philip W '93
(614) 227-2300 **Lee** Phillip H '03
(614) 466-5394 **Lee** Thomas K '95
(614) 221-2223 **Leeseberg** Gerald S '79
(614) 221-2223 **Leeseberg & Valentine**
(614) 221-4221 **Leffel** Elizabeth C '89
(614) 466-8600 **Lefton** David E '85
(614) 466-4605 **Lehmann** Dale E III '95
(614) 258-1955 **Lehv** Michael S '94
(614) 464-2020 **Leidner** Ellen B '83
(614) 220-5611 **Leier** Rachel A '99
(614) 236-1075 **Leighton** Charles T '71
(614) 228-7771 **Leist** Darrin C '99
(614) 485-2010 **Leister** Craig D '74
(614) 228-6345 **Leithart** Paul W II '81
(614) 464-2819 **Lelli** Craig T '81
Lentz John C '98
(614) 452-8963 **Leo** James J '91
(614) 481-4480 **Leon** Robert J '04
(614) 462-6707 **Leonard** Edward J '91
(614) 436-3211 **Leonard** Tracey A '94
(614) 424-6760 **Leonatti** Adam H '97
(614) 227-2346 **Lerner** Marshall L '73
(614) 222-0526 **Lerner** Michael J '03
(614) 224-0401 **Leshner** Jay Harris '85
(614) 461-1178 **Leshy** George V '73
(614) 462-3194 **Lesley** Jane E '78
(614) 921-9487 **Leslie** Mark A '78
(614) 228-2226 **Lesser** Frances S '79
(614) 466-3191 **Lesser** Steven D '78
(614) 466-5204 **Lestini** Gregory J '03
(614) 228-6885 **Letcher** Barbara K '90
(614) 424-6424 **Letizia** Donald L '87
(614) 469-7404 **Letts** Richard D '74
(614) 273-1000 **Leuby** William A III '83
(614) 224-1222 **Leuchtag** Emery J '83
(614) 221-5627 **Leutz** John R '79
(614) 227-2328 **LeVere** T Earl '94
(614) 449-8282 **Leveridge** Julia L '00
(614) 645-7483 **Levering** Robert B '80
(614) 629-3002 **Levey** Jack S '83
(614) 224-5291 **Levine** Amy M '01
(614) 235-4340 **Levine** Cathy J '91
(614) 228-1541 **Levine** David C '89
(614) 463-9770 **Levine** Judith D '79
(614) 227-0300 **Levine** Richard L '84
(614) 228-4141 **Levinson** Lawrence L '94
(614) 252-1818 **Levy** Barbara '90
(614) 224-9550 **Levy** Stefan C '60
(614) 466-0570 **Lewis** Beth A '98
(614) 221-4000 **Lewis** Eugene B '82
(614) 221-3938 **Lewis** Gregg R '89
(614) 231-7513 **Lewis** Jacqueline '80
(614) 228-6885 **Lewis** James W '75
(614) 461-1100 **Lewis** Jeffrey M '81
(614) 231-5531 **Lewis** John F Jr. '87
(614) 224-7711 **Lewis** Mark D '94
(614) 253-9737 **Lewis** Milton E '95
(614) 466-4605 **Lewis** Randi G '78
(614) 469-3317 **Lewis** William Blair '98
(614) 227-2000 **Li** Christine D '04
(614) 462-4082 **Lieberman** Brett H '97
(614) 480-4434 **Liebersbach** John W '76
(614) 469-3939 **Liebman** Helen L '74
(614) 227-2399 **Liggett** Luther L '81
(614) 469-4778 **Lilly** Phillip G '87
(614) 644-2824 **Lim** Edwin Y '77
(614) 462-6004 **Lim** Lawrence S '92
(614) 488-2053 **Liming** Roxi A '98
(614) 719-3355 **Lin** Albert G '03
Lind Michael W '96
(614) 466-0195 **Lindamood** Suzanne '91
(614) 464-1211 **Lindemann** Jeffrey N '91
(614) 466-4395 **Lindgren** Thomas G '87
(614) 222-3924 **Lindholm** Jason P '04
(614) 466-3998 **Lindsay** George B '75
(614) 466-3998 **Lindsey** Kirk A '96
(614) 442-5858 **Lindsey** Scott T '96
(614) 442-5858 **Lindsey** Thomas H '65
(614) 583-5020 **Lindsey** Thomas K '86
(614) 365-9900 **Lindsmith** Quintin F '84
(614) 882-9803 **Lindwall** Robert R '73
(614) 228-6888 **Linhart** Brian E '99
(614) 451-0206 **Linville** James B '01
(614) 228-1541 **Linville** Ronald G '80
(614) 464-4644 **Lipchak** Melissa R '91
(614) 248-6508 **Lipovsek** Kimberly J '93
(614) 462-3555 **Lippe** Christine B '86
(614) 224-1979 **Lippe** Jerry L '67
(614) 937-1300 **Lippman** Allison J '02
(614) 365-4100 **Lipps** Jeffrey A '81
(614) 227-2000 **Lisle** Shawn G '01
(614) 221-1771 **Liss** Robert B '83
(614) 469-1400 **List** David Andrew '91
(614) 224-1222 **Lister** Kelli E '95
(614) 228-6131 **Liston** Dennis D '74
(614) 221-1341 **Liston** Jefferson E '78
(614) 645-8255 **Liston** Teresa Lea '82
(614) 469-3939 **Litle** Jeffrey D '99
(614) 365-2700 **Litle** T Bennett '04
(614) 227-2305 **Litt** Gordon F '85
(614) 424-5071 **Litteral** Malesa A '98
(614) 462-3555 **Little** Elza M '91
(614) 365-9900 **Little** Marion H Jr. '89
(614) 466-2980 **Little** Tamara S '83
(614) 540-3940 **Littlejohn** Glen E '95
(614) 463-4201 **Littler Mendelson,PC**
(614) 228-5151 **Littrell** Barry W '83
(614) 228-8400 **Littrell** Rex A '89
(614) 224-7771 **Livorno & Arnett Co,LPA**
(614) 224-7771 **Livorno** John F '72
(614) 292-9176 **Lloyd** Angela M '04
(614) 224-1222 **Lloyd** John A '00
(614) 365-4100 **Lloyd** Katheryn M '02
(614) 462-5034 **Lloyd** Melissa C '99
(614) 645-7385 **Lloyd** Paula J '85
(614) 752-2450 **Lobb** Christopher M '91
(614) 644-3372 **Lodge** Connie M '87
(614) 469-3246 **Lodge** Thomas E '81
(614) 365-2700 **Loewengart** Steven M '87
(614) 457-1010 **Logan** John A '78
(614) 221-7663 **Logan** William B Jr. '74
(614) 221-8500 **Lomax** Lisa A '93
Lombardo Margaret M '97
(614) 466-2166 **Long** Clare N '83
(614) 488-0681 **Long** James M '76
(614) 224-9207 **Long** Kelly A '01
(614) 466-4371 **Long** Kristin Jo '01
(614) 464-6400 **Long** Michael G '69
(614) 451-5300 **Long** Richard S '76
(614) 228-1541 **Long** Thomas L '76
(614) 644-0731 **Longo** Scott A '89
(614) 644-7073 **Lopez** A Ruben '92
(614) 227-3098 **Lopez** Christopher A '88
(614) 462-3555 **Lopez** Robert C '99
(614) 621-1500 **Losey** Mark A '94
(614) 463-8251 **Lossing** Roger A '83
(614) 462-5996 **Loucks** Nicole M '03
(614) 466-4961 **Loudenslagel** Mark T '78
(614) 228-5931 **Loughry** Michael S '01
(614) 466-2980 **Loughry** Timothy C '04
(614) 221-3155 **Louis** Harlan S '94
(614) 466-8181 **Loutzenhiser** Charles F Jr. '77
(614) 236-1075 **Love** Donald P '70
(614) 464-3563 **Loveland & Brosius**
(614) 227-2000 **Loveland** Curtis A '73
(614) 464-3563 **Loveland** Richard L '57
(614) 464-3563 **Loveland** William L '82
(614) 227-2307 **Lovering** Richard S III '80
(614) 462-3555 **Lowe** Amanda J '02
(614) 340-3895 **Lowe** David K '84
(614) 228-5331 **Lowe** Gregory A '93
(614) 784-0912 **Lowe** Howard P '55
(614) 462-3555 **Lowe** James L '94
(614) 462-5485 **Lowe** John IV '98
(614) 466-5394 **Lowe** Robert K '00
(614) 224-8446 **Lowenstein** Roy '76
(614) 229-4690 **Lowry** Bruce R '77
(614) 464-5052 **Lowther** John R '76
(614) 888-0040 **Lubow** Barry L '83
(614) 466-3934 **Lubow** Lauren '83
(614) 228-1541 **Lubow** Susan N '95
(614) 621-1500 **Lucas** Albert J '94
(614) 752-9740 **Lucas** Cynthia G '81
(614) 221-1364 **Lucas** George Robert II '68
(614) 326-0818 **Lucas** Jeffrey K '01
(614) 228-5711 **Lucas** John C '76
(614) 248-6115 **Lucas** Jonathan R '04
(614) 228-5711 **Lucas Prendergast Albright Gibson & Newman**
(614) 462-6041 **Luchsinger** Ann L '85
(614) 466-6700 **Luck** Rebecca R '79
(614) 464-4414 **Luckage** Eric J '97
(614) 221-9665 **Luckett** Ermel R Jr. '89
(614) 466-4395 **Luckey** Duane W '79
(614) 221-5265 **Luczkowski** Jean M '78
(614) 224-1500 **Luftman** Benjamin L '03
(614) 223-1646 **Luis** Michael R '69
(614) 228-5331 **Lukeman** Paul G '77
(614) 221-5212 **Lumpe** Joseph Richard '63
(614) 221-7663 **Luper** Frederick M '65
(614) 221-7663 **Luper Neidenthal & Logan,LPA**
(614) 464-6400 **Lusenhop** Peter A '98
(614) 462-3194 **Lutz** Carroll W '74
Lutz Matthew D '99
(614) 292-2681 **Lyke-Catalano** Heather R '97
(614) 462-6418 **Lyle** James K '00
(614) 466-3876 **Lyles** Andrew E '87
(614) 469-3939 **Lyles** Kevin D '86
(614) 252-0688 **Lyman** Chester T Jr. '82
(614) 365-2700 **Lynch** Chanda L '00
(614) 466-0451 **Lynn** James M '98
(614) 221-3155 **Lynn** Sarah E '92
(614) 466-1305 **Lynskey** Sandra L '97
(614) 464-6271 **Lyons** Christina M '04
(614) 228-1313 **Lyons** Gary W '64
(614) 286-9690 **Lyons** George A '84
(614) 228-5822 **Maas** Brandy M '03
(614) 249-8438 **Mabe** William E '76
(614) 443-1512 **Macali** Virginia L '85
(614) 278-6769 **Macbeth** William H III '95
MacDowell Benjamin J '02
(614) 719-3240 **Macias** Lisa A '96
(614) 716-1642 **Mack** Kevin D '86
(614) 462-5428 **Mackanos** Jennifer L '02
(614) 464-0011 **Macke** Francis J '75
(614) 464-0011 **Macke** Jason A '98
(614) 462-3580 **Macke** Kenneth W '77
(614) 221-2121 **MacKenzie** Paul A '92
(614) 221-8448 **Mackin** Kerry McConaghy '02
(614) 480-5120 **Mackin** William J '94
(614) 224-1008 **MacKinnon** John J '83
(614) 249-8720 **Macklin** George K '84
(614) 864-5200 **Mackura** Denise '82
MacLaughlin Lewis H III '73
(614) 462-5462 **MacMurray** Helen M '87
(614) 466-5610 **Macon-Bruce** Marcia J '90
(614) 221-1216 **Madden** Kathleen J '01
(614) 466-8911 **Madden** Thomas E '03
(614) 224-0933 **Maddox** Mark S '84
(614) 461-1100 **Madison** Timothy G '94
(614) 466-1604 **Madriguera** Christina M '00
(614) 272-6560 **Magelaner** Thomas L '90
(614) 464-2236 **Maggied** Pamela N '79
(614) 255-7552 **MaGinn** Tara M '04
(614) 371-1101 **Magnuson** James A '76
(614) 224-1222 **Maguire** Patrick D '76
(614) 224-1222 **Maguire & Schneider, LLP**
(614) 464-6400 **Mahaffey** Carol '83
(614) 462-3194 **Mahaffey** John P '80
(614) 279-5360 **Mahaffey** Morgan E '99
(614) 365-2700 **Maher** Daniel M '72
(614) 728-7055 **Maher** Stephen E '82
(614) 478-2302 **Mahler** Eric A '95
(614) 221-3155 **Mahoney** Michael P '72
(614) 469-7404 **Mahood** Margaret W '89
(614) 233-7910 **Mahota** John M '73
(614) 645-8980 **Maia** Elizabeth L '04
(614) 466-5967 **Maier** Robert C '90
(614) 221-1662 **Mains** Donald Leo Jr. '69

(614) 693-6837 **Majeski** Michael B '93
(614) 469-5715 **Malek** Andrew M '93
(614) 444-7440 **Malek** Edwin L '69
(614) 444-7440 **Malek** James E '95
(614) 444-7440 **Malek & Malek**
(614) 292-5062 **Malkoff** Daniel A '85
(614) 466-4882 **Malkoff** Tamara L '85
(614) 299-8321 **Mallett** Jeanne M '82
(614) 644-7233 **Mallory** Diane D '80
(614) 228-9707 **Mallory** Thomas H Jr. '95
(614) 228-9707 **Mallory & Tsibouris Co,LPA**
(614) 462-5011 **Malloy** Marie A '91
(614) 469-7130 **Malone** Andrew R '03
(614) 466-2766 **Malone** Margaret A '75
(614) 228-5271 **Maloney** Kevin M '85
(614) 221-4400 **Maloon** Jeffrey L '83
(614) 462-3555 **Maloon** Jerry L II '92
(614) 466-4961 **Manchak** John F III '74
(614) 644-7233 **Mancini** Joseph M '66
(614) 848-4300 **Maney** Thomas P Jr. '83
(614) 899-7477 **Mangan** Patrick F '79
(614) 645-7385 **Mangan** Timothy J '82
(614) 444-3036 **Mango** Dominic L '99
(614) 221-4000 **Maniace** James V '81
(614) 466-5414 **Manken** James T '94
(614) 220-5611 **Manley Deas & Kochalski, LLC**
(614) 220-5611 **Manley** Theodore K '92
(614) 224-2366 **Mann** Daniel L '55
(614) 462-3555 **Mann** Frederick M '68
(614) 464-6400 **Mann** Joseph B '04
(614) 224-5427 **Mann** Richard L '72
(614) 253-4090 **Mann** Robert J '88
(614) 224-4114 **Mann** William C '79
(614) 462-3555 **Manning** Jason P '01
(614) 677-8655 **Mannion** Brian L '97
(614) 262-2300 **Mannion** Laurel E '94
(614) 221-3155 **Manougian** Nancy J '85
(614) 221-1827 **Manring** Daniel Lee '76
(614) 221-1827 **Manring & Farrell**
(614) 469-3939 **Mansfield** Douglas M '94
(614) 424-6198 **Manuel** James C Jr. '83
(614) 387-9390 **Marbley** Janet Green '79
(614) 224-2062 **Marchese** Thomas J '85
(614) 466-4395 **Margard** Werner L III '82
(614) 466-8626 **Margulies** Pamela L '76
(614) 644-7250 **Marhevka** Donna M '84
(614) 299-9466 **Marinakis** Angela D '93
(614) 387-9030 **Marks** Caroline L '99
(614) 258-9300 **Marks** Irving B '71
(614) 462-2800 **Marks** Janine M '88
(614) 236-6545 **Markus** Kent R '84
(614) 241-2078 **Markworth** Thomas '68
(614) 227-2000 **Marlier** Haimavathi V '04
(614) 442-0002 **Marlin** James J Jr. '68
(614) 864-4352 **Marlin** Michael S '73
(614) 340-2699 **Marotta** Joseph M '01
(614) 466-4514 **Marotta** Melissa L '01
(614) 462-5435 **Marotta** Robert D '75
(614) 469-5715 **Marous** James M '79
(614) 336-8575 **Marsalka** Joseph P '58
(614) 227-2000 **Marsh** John F '95
(614) 464-6400 **Marsh** Judith L '00
(614) 228-6885 **Marsh** Rick E '60
(614) 227-2000 **Marshall** Colleen L '04
(614) 888-6533 **Marshall** Dwight A '69
(614) 463-9790 **Marshall** John S '83
(614) 387-9370 **Marshall** Jonathan W '70
(614) 469-0331 **Marshall** Joy L '02
(614) 459-8106 **Marshall** Michelle A '91
(614) 538-1840 **Marshall** Michelle L '03
(614) 463-9790 **Marshall & Morrow LLC**
(614) 466-3934 **Marshall** Rebecca J '99
(614) 279-8059 **Martello** Suzanne E '90
(614) 279-8059 **Martello** Thomas F Jr. '92
(614) 261-0143 **Martens** Franklin A '67
(614) 644-7233 **Marti** Todd R '83
(614) 224-1222 **Martin** Andrea E '82
(614) 466-2766 **Martin** Daniel J '95
(614) 424-5018 **Martin** David A '89
(614) 462-3396 **Martin** Don W '77
(614) 249-4217 **Martin** James D '96
(614) 221-0944 **Martin** John S '83
(614) 222-8686 **Martin** Julie C '91
(614) 466-4656 **Martin** Jutta E '87
(614) 719-3200 **Martin** Karen L '78
(614) 464-1626 **Martin** Kyle D '89
(614) 249-2490 **Martin** Lauren B '96
(614) 462-3555 **Martin** Mary J '96
(614) 224-1222 **Martin** Matthew F '91
(614) 577-0488 **Martin** Paige A '78
(614) 293-7149 **Martin** Suzanne C '83
(614) 227-2000 **Martin-Jones** Melanie '99
(614) 298-6488 **Martineau** Eric D '95
(614) 464-6400 **Martz** Michael D '91
(614) 466-3016 **Marvin** Robert E Jr. '80
(614) 466-2872 **Marziale** Arthur J Jr. '85
(614) 224-7291 **Mas** Joseph L '79
(614) 249-5736 **Mascarin** Paul E '95
(614) 466-0278 **Mase** Elizabeth K '85
(614) 466-5709 **Masek** Richard E '80
(614) 462-3194 **Masello** Dean J '03
(614) 457-6549 **Maskas** George P '72

(614) 224-8374 **Maskovyak** Joseph V '85
(614) 466-3905 **Mason** Donald L '89
(614) 621-1214 **Mason** Doris D '86
(614) 418-8044 **Mason** James Thomas '84
(614) 462-2275 **Mason** Jennifer '96
(614) 222-3060 **Mass** Amy '95
(614) 227-2000 **Massey** Daniel J '70
(614) 365-4100 **Massey** Daniel M '03
(614) 466-2766 **Massey** Lori A '90
(614) 221-0944 **Massucci** LeeAnn M '03
(614) 466-6696 **Mastrangelo** Joseph C '79
(614) 228-2678 **Matan** Eugene L '58
(614) 228-2678 **Matan Geer & Wright**
(614) 692-3284 **Matheke** Carol N '86
(614) 228-6885 **Mathews** Alvin E Jr. '87
(614) 415-7457 **Mathews** Colin A '96
(614) 645-8724 **Mathews** Denise R '93
(614) 387-9010 **Mathews** Gregory P '04
(614) 252-1333 **Mathless** Steven A '83
(614) 227-2000 **Matisziw** Kristin E '04
Matsa Aristotle R '84
(614) 628-6880 **Mattes** William M '88
(614) 466-5057 **Matthews** Christina '87
(614) 752-1200 **Matthews** Dale E Jr. '78
(614) 464-6400 **Matthews** Douglas R '87
(614) 462-5321 **Matthews** Jill A '02
(614) 227-2000 **Mattimoe** James M '89
(614) 486-5392 **Mattis Daniell Voltolini & Voltolini**
(614) 464-6400 **Mattis** Theodore P '91
(614) 227-2300 **Matto** Edward A '66
(614) 241-2156 **Mauger** Jud R '94
(614) 224-9223 **Maurer** James '64
(614) 262-9002 **Maurer** John W '79
(614) 771-0597 **Mauro** James C '83
(614) 269-4900 **Maxfield** Michael L '84
(614) 445-8287 **Maxfield** Sean H '76
(614) 466-8600 **Maxfield** Sheryl C '84
(614) 326-3960 **Maxwell** Amanda P '80
(614) 231-8529 **Maxwell** James Jr. '51
(614) 249-7822 **Maxwell** Mark D '96
(614) 527-7610 **May** Gregory D '88
(614) 249-7899 **May** Randall W '90
(614) 224-8374 **Mayer** Donna C '80
(614) 462-3555 **Mayer** James J III '00
(614) 985-3670 **Maynard** Jay W '88
(614) 258-6000 **Maynard** Jeffery S '01
(614) 645-8286 **Maynard** William D '86
(614) 236-6560 **Mays** Shirley L '88
(614) 466-5415 **Mayton** Craig R '80
(614) 228-5931 **Mazanec Raskin & Ryder Co,LPA**
(614) 228-8833 **Mazur** Alan E '96
(614) 457-9731 **Mazza** John P '77
(614) 229-4602 **Mazzoli** Joseph A '97
(614) 221-2838 **McAdams** Robert W Jr. '87
(614) 464-6400 **McAfee** Melinda R '95
(614) 469-8000 **McAlister** Lisa G '02
(614) 466-5394 **McAnespie** Molly Jo '99
(614) 227-2303 **McBeath** Gretchen A '82
(614) 621-1500 **McBride** Shelley A '82
(614) 258-6000 **McCaffrey** Patrick Jr. '96
(614) 466-7014 **McCallister** Michael D '95
(614) 801-2714 **McCandlish** Joseph M '01
(614) 422-7866 **McCane** Lisa A '99
(614) 424-6585 **McCann** Dennis J '81
(614) 228-2300 **McCann** George R '73
(614) 358-0880 **McCarter** Sean A '94
(614) 222-6466 **McCarthy** Deborah Beckerich '93
(614) 462-3555 **McCarthy** Sean V '00
(614) 462-4692 **McCarthy** Timothy P '73
(614) 462-5469 **McCarty** David M '92
(614) 236-6245 **McCaughan** Lorie L '96
(614) 275-2587 **McClaren** Robert J '90
(614) 462-5463 **McClatchey** Larry J '75
(614) 224-1222 **McClatchey** Ted P '94
(614) 464-2572 **McClellan** Edward T '75
(614) 340-0440 **McClelland** Jeffrey L '70
(614) 252-0688 **McCleskey** Harvey N Jr. '03
(614) 221-8448 **McCloskey** Christopher L '00
(614) 228-1398 **McCloskey** Kerri L '01
(614) 466-8081 **McCloud** Bradley L '88
(614) 466-4656 **McCloud** Stephanie B '96
(614) 227-2000 **McClure** Anthony R '03
(614) 421-7500 **McClure** David L '64
(614) 485-2010 **McClure** Lisa M '01
McCollister Sharon F '94
(614) 464-1266 **McCollum** James E '87
(614) 443-4063 **McCord** Lumumba T '96
(614) 221-2718 **McCormick** Jack E '69
(614) 444-9414 **McCormick** Kerry L '01
(614) 464-6433 **McCormick** Thomas N '02
(614) 464-1904 **McCormick** Tristan A '95
McCoy Karen C '99
(614) 481-8106 **McCoy** Steven J '74

(614) 227-2387 **McCreary** Charles H III '78
(614) 469-5614 **McCreary** Marcee C '81
(614) 466-3998 **McCue** Dana C '74
(614) 461-7596 **McCuen** Michael D '00
(614) 249-7636 **McCutchan** R. Lindsey '97
(614) 462-5009 **McDaniel** Jennifer M '02
(614) 462-5001 **McDermott** Kevin R '77
(614) 458-0025 **McDonald Hopkins Co, LPA**
(614) 462-2201 **McDonald** John C '61
(614) 228-4201 **McDonald** Susan J '02
(614) 466-6696 **McDonald** William J '75
(614) 716-1696 **McDonough** Kenneth E '84
(614) 462-5839 **McDougall** Ian '70
(614) 267-1306 **McElligott** Michael W '88
(614) 466-3998 **McElwee** Donald L '75
McEnaney Erin J '03
(614) 221-8868 **McFadden** Mary J '74
(614) 221-8868 **McFadden Winner & Savage**
(614) 885-4078 **McGaffick** Timothy D '88
(614) 466-8600 **McGann** Steven C '02
(614) 224-8374 **McGarvey** Kathleen C '03
(614) 466-3559 **McGee** Jonathon L '89
(614) 276-6555 **McGinley** John Michael '71
(614) 263-7000 **McGinnis** Mark A '03
(614) 227-8879 **McGlone** Sean M '02
(614) 221-5771 **McGough** John T '81
(614) 228-6061 **McGovern** James M '93
(614) 464-1969 **McGowan** Charles W '96
(614) 221-3155 **McGranor** Timothy B '00
(614) 645-7531 **McGrath** Barbara A '79
(614) 464-4201 **McGrath & Breitfeller LLP**
(614) 462-3555 **McGrath** Keith '92
(614) 464-4201 **McGrath** Thomas R '74
(614) 228-6345 **McGrath** Timothy J '69
(614) 217-4436 **McGraw** Christopher E '93
(614) 899-7477 **McGraw** Michael Scott '01
(614) 225-8700 **McGraw** Richard S '96
McGuigan Leigh A '92
(614) 431-1133 **McGuire** James W '60
(614) 466-5610 **McGuire** Robin L '96
(614) 462-5408 **McGuire** Traci A '99
(614) 466-5394 **McHenry** Jerry L '76
(614) 827-7300 **McIntosh** Sandra R '04
(614) 645-8081 **McIntosh** Stephen L '84
(614) 464-2235 **McInturff** Judith M '80
(614) 752-6417 **McIver** Kevin M '80
(614) 692-3284 **McKee** Susan E '84
(614) 227-2000 **McKenna** Alvin J '67
(614) 227-2000 **McKenzie** Myra L '02
(614) 621-2605 **McKenzie** William Locke Jr. '75
(614) 466-2980 **McKew** Barry D '80
(614) 255-1140 **McKinlay** Amy M '96
(614) 228-8833 **McLane** Michael J '87
(614) 583-7610 **McLaughlin** Patricia A '99
(614) 462-3194 **McLaughlin** Tara L '00
(614) 583-6731 **McLaughlin** Tracy A '97
(614) 462-3555 **McLean** Michael J '99
(614) 277-6598 **McLean** Patricia A '00
(614) 466-6700 **McLennan** Bruce A '87
(614) 228-1717 **McLeod** Mark A '87
(614) 232-9132 **McLeskey** Waymon B II '81
McMahon Maureen B '99
(614) 466-2766 **McManus** John K '86
(614) 224-2678 **McNair** Darren A '02
(614) 464-2770 **McNamara** Dennis W '76
(614) 461-5788 **McNamara** James D '74
(614) 228-6131 **McNamara** Keith '53
(614) 466-2980 **McNamara** Walter J IV '02
(614) 466-4395 **McNamee** Thomas W '79
(614) 224-7291 **McNeal** Earl D '92
(614) 451-2151 **McNeal** Kathleen K '82
(614) 227-2000 **McNealey** J Jeffrey '69
(614) 469-8000 **McNees Wallace & Nurick,LLC**
(614) 228-1541 **McNellie** Elizabeth A '90
(614) 444-8777 **McNichols** David J '83
(614) 449-8282 **McNinch** Deborah L '91
(614) 224-1244 **McNitt** Robert M '82
(614) 228-1128 **McPherson** Joel S '93
(614) 462-3118 **McPhillips** Michael C '95
(614) 461-1516 **McQuain** Larry G '96
(614) 227-2000 **McQuown** Richard C '86
(614) 221-1919 **McShane** Eugene F '71
(614) 263-7000 **McTigue** Donald J '79
(614) 444-3900 **McVay** Kirk A '95
(614) 995-5618 **Mead** Nancy L '87
(614) 921-2070 **Meagher** Stephen W '82
(614) 752-1200 **Mealey** Diane L '01
(614) 485-2010 **Means Bichimer Burkholder & Baker Co,LPA**
(614) 466-3998 **Meas** Loi L '00
(614) 464-5754 **Mechling** William C '83

(614) 236-1950 **Meckler** Marcia L '75
(614) 292-0943 **Meeks** James E '63
(614) 228-4141 **Meeks** Ralph W '75
(614) 267-2799 **Meena** James W '81
Meftah Diane M '89
(614) 644-7651 **Mehan** Patrick J '04
(614) 424-6760 **Meier** Harold C '56
(614) 424-6760 **Meier** William A '78
(614) 221-1644 **Meister** Frederick '80
(614) 258-1983 **Meizlish** Jodie K '87
(614) 221-4221 **Meizlish** Sanford A '79
(614) 466-8911 **Mekhjian** Ara G '97
(614) 566-5151 **Meldrum** Terri W '94
(614) 221-5216 **Melko** Mark C '98
(614) 461-5600 **Melle** James E '71
(614) 224-5205 **Melliere** Michael J '97
(614) 459-8912 **Mellon** Howard J '77
(614) 299-5522 **Meloun** Grant J '00
(614) 644-2548 **Melton** Katherine Jo '86
(614) 464-5275 **Melvin** John B '75
(614) 224-9223 **Melvin** William J '58
(614) 221-6500 **Menashe** Diane M '98
(614) 464-1626 **Mencer** Jetta L '83
(614) 466-6750 **Mendel** Janet J '87
(614) 464-6400 **Mendel** Linda R '81
(614) 644-9316 **Mengel** Marcia J '82
(614) 227-2300 **Mentel** Sean A '04
(614) 221-3329 **Mentser** Barry A '84
(614) 466-1797 **Merkel** Richard L '73
(614) 228-0068 **Merkle** Howard T '79
(614) 227-2000 **Merkle** Mark K Jr. '70
(614) 227-8871 **Merrill** Frank L '87
(614) 227-2000 **Merrill** Tracy L '01
(614) 221-4400 **Merry** Tony C '89
(614) 293-4296 **Mertz** Daniel T '92
(614) 365-2700 **Mertz** Mary C '02
(614) 443-7455 **Merullo Reister & Swinford Co,LPA**
(614) 443-7455 **Merullo** Victor D '73
(614) 222-4327 **Merz** Vincent P Jr. '98
(614) 227-2000 **Mescher** Richard M '93
(614) 645-7385 **Mesirow** Keith S '78
(614) 846-4318 **Mess** Michael A '79
(614) 444-7440 **Messenger** Walter W Jr. '01
(614) 469-2999 **Messmer** Jane S '98
(614) 469-1301 **Mets** Anthony D '98
(614) 225-8664 **Metz** Douglas O '84
(614) 463-4201 **Metzger** Thomas M '92
(614) 466-0722 **Metzler** Jonathan L '94
(614) 444-2144 **Meyer** Carl J '78
(614) 224-6000 **Meyer** David P '95
(614) 469-3939 **Meyer** H Theodore '62
(614) 237-3525 **Meyer** Jeffrey D '91
(614) 471-0085 **Meyer** Richard F '80
(614) 466-5394 **Meyers** Gregory W '83
(614) 221-9160 **Micciulla** James '90
(614) 466-8911 **Miceli** Julie '04
(614) 459-4840 **Michael** Barbara J '91
(614) 443-6262 **Michael** Jay E '85
(614) 644-7250 **Michael** Mark A '94
(614) 459-4840 **Michael** Susan J '92
(614) 621-1500 **Michael** William J '99
(614) 466-0356 **Midlam-Mohler** Tiffany J '04
(614) 462-1053 **Miele** Philip R '84
(614) 224-9985 **Mifsud** Charles A II '99
(614) 466-8574 **Migden** Janine Lee '81
(614) 644-7295 **Miglets** Michael P '81
(614) 466-3186 **Mihaly** Peter H '92
(614) 719-3371 **Mihocik** Eryn K '04
(614) 462-5414 **Mikes** Randall W '90
(614) 466-9261 **Miko** Matthew D '97
(614) 644-9279 **Miles** James R '61
(614) 476-0554 **Millard** William L '58
(614) 224-1222 **Miller** Adam C '94
(614) 644-6347 **Miller** Alan C '87
(614) 221-7711 **Miller** Alyson B '04
(614) 365-2700 **Miller** Andrew D M '02
Miller Angela W '95
(614) 221-0240 **Miller** Anthony J '00
(614) 221-8448 **Miller** Brett L '81
(614) 221-7791 **Miller** Brian G '94
(614) 462-5400 **Miller** Camille A '04
(614) 466-1251 **Miller** Charles M '01
(614) 462-5033 **Miller** Christopher L '94
(614) 224-9223 **Miller** Clifford W II '93
(614) 621-1500 **Miller** Courtney J '99
(614) 464-6400 **Miller** Darrell A '03
(614) 878-9262 **Miller** David L '80
(614) 227-2241 **Miller** Dixon F '76
(614) 462-3555 **Miller** Donald L '88
(614) 716-1645 **Miller** Donald Michael '75
(614) 644-3037 **Miller** Elissa B '00
(614) 485-2010 **Miller** Elizabeth L '01
(614) 466-5394 **Miller** Elizabeth R '04
(614) 228-1541 **Miller** Frank C V '99
(614) 466-4705 **Miller** Holly A '94
(614) 466-6114 **Miller** James W Jr. '78
(614) 466-2479 **Miller** Jane L '76
(614) 464-6400 **Miller** Jeffrey Allen '00
Miller Jeffrey D '96
(614) 228-6131 **Miller** John L '63
(614) 464-6400 **Miller** Joseph R '97

(614) 827-1465 **Miller** Kristian M '01
(614) 882-2500 **Miller** Larry B '86
(614) 267-1617 **Miller** Linda J '86
(614) 221-5627 **Miller** Maria G '81
(614) 227-0007 **Miller** Mark J '03
(614) 253-5297 **Miller** Mark S '81
(614) 248-5936 **Miller** Martha G '81
(614) 365-2700 **Miller** Matthew J '03
(614) 225-0980 **Miller** Melissa A '98
(614) 462-3896 **Miller** Michael L '79
(614) 221-4400 **Miller** Michael S '84
(614) 228-6885 **Miller** Monica L '99
(614) 292-7755 **Miller** Nancy J '79
(614) 466-3687 **Miller** Regina B '86
(614) 464-6400 **Miller** Richard T '91
(614) 469-3939 **Miller** Robert H '03
(614) 220-9200 **Miller** Robert P '00
(614) 462-5400 **Miller** S Michael '63
(614) 242-4242 **Miller** Steven V '95
(614) 227-2000 **Miller** Terrance M '72
(614) 464-6400 **Miller** Terry M '75
(614) 221-3155 **Miller** Tiffany C '00
(614) 221-2121 **Miller** Timothy E '86
(614) 443-4891 **Miller** Timothy T '93
Miller Wayne D '92
(614) 466-7264 **Miller-Coterel** Vanessa K '03
(614) 464-0011 **Milless** Charles K '75
Milligan William W '51
(614) 462-5310 **Milliken** Olga Bosques '86
(614) 221-2234 **Millisor & Nobil Co,LPA**
(614) 464-6400 **Mills** Frederick E '73
(614) 227-2000 **Mills** Jennifer T '83
(614) 299-6357 **Mills** Melanie '93
Milne Maurice N III '90
(614) 466-9566 **Milne** Susan E '94
(614) 227-2000 **Minck** Linda R '90
(614) 221-1125 **Mindzak** Stephen E '92
Mingo Clarence E II '99
(614) 785-1122 **Minister** Mark V '91
(614) 228-1541 **Minister** Michael E '74
(614) 481-7990 **Minnillo** Christopher J '79
(614) 464-6400 **Minor** Daniel J '81
(614) 464-6400 **Minor** Robert A '75
(614) 221-0090 **Mirman** Denise M '82
(614) 221-0922 **Mirman** Joel H '66
(614) 848-6611 **Mirras** Thomas J '71
(614) 249-1948 **Miskell** Jennifer L '98
(614) 463-7043 **Mitchell** Albert A '75
(614) 224-4114 **Mitchell Allen Catalano & Boda Co,LPA**
(614) 221-3318 **Mitchell** Gregory R '93
(614) 466-0722 **Mitchell** Keesha R '91
(614) 464-6400 **Mitchell** Melissa J '83
(614) 292-0611 **Mitchell** Michael A '91
(614) 464-6400 **Mitchell** Robert C '90
(614) 236-6500 **Mitchell** Roberta S '72
Mitchell Stephen D '78
(614) 221-2838 **Mitchell** Timothy B '82
(614) 462-3555 **Mitchell** Timothy K '80
(614) 221-5379 **Mittman** Lee C '58
(614) 443-8388 **Mix** Carol P '90
(614) 462-6033 **Mizelle** Brian D '01
(614) 801-2767 **Moats** Raymond F III '00
(614) 462-4556 **Mobley** Laura J '93
(614) 469-3206 **Moehring** Boyd K '89
(614) 501-1810 **Moesle** Eric J '94
(614) 461-1311 **Mokhtari** Alvand A '00
(614) 466-3180 **Moloney** Monica A '78
(614) 885-1901 **Moloney** Thomas E '74
(614) 224-2062 **Monast** James P '85
Mondon Dana S '96
(614) 752-9595 **Mone** Maria L '88
(614) 469-3203 **Mone** Robert P '59
(614) 692-3284 **Monta** Vasso K '77
(614) 466-4483 **Montgomery** Betty D '76
(614) 228-1541 **Montgomery** Henry P IV '79
(614) 291-3119 **Montgomery** John J '76
(614) 469-7404 **Montgomery** John R '81
(614) 462-3194 **Montgomery** Melissa A '00
(614) 462-3378 **Montgomery** Robert G '97
(614) 466-1291 **Mooney** Colleen L '84
(614) 466-5394 **Mooney** William J '75
(614) 645-8576 **Moore** Amy M '04
(614) 331-9556 **Moore** Candada J '81
(614) 221-2505 **Moore** Donald H Jr. '87
(614) 480-4435 **Moore** Elizabeth B '86
(614) 462-3555 **Moore** Jason A '96
(614) 462-5443 **Moore** Jayme P '03
(614) 227-2363 **Moore** Karen M '75
(614) 728-4792 **Moore** Karhlton F '98
(614) 279-6626 **Moore** Lillie B '83
(614) 462-4511 **Moore** Marchelle E '00
(614) 481-0550 **Moore** Michael G '79
(614) 462-3555 **Moore** Nancy D '89
(614) 224-1222 **Moore** Patricia L '91
(614) 227-2380 **Moore** Randall E '78
(614) 462-4551 **Moore** Thomas A '90
(614) 228-5711 **Moore** Tonda L '95
(614) 241-2156 **Moore** William J '82

(614) 241-2156 **Moore Yaklevich & Mauger**
(614) 459-4140 **Moots Carter & Hogan**
(614) 459-4140 **Moots** Philip R '65
(614) 365-4100 **Mordarski** Daniel R '94
(614) 621-1500 **Morgan** Douglas S '82
(614) 462-3555 **Morgan** Edward W '72
(614) 224-6488 **Morgan** Kara A '92
(614) 221-6837 **Morgan** Kelly M '77
(614) 462-3194 **Morgan** Michael W '92
(614) 227-2000 **Morgan** Robert J '01
(614) 258-1133 **Morgan** Thomas E '75
(614) 242-4242 **Morje** Robert J '75
(614) 227-2000 **Morris** Frank R Jr. '58
(614) 462-7585 **Morris** James E '86
(614) 227-2057 **Morris** Linda L '83
(614) 431-1500 **Morris** Troy B '89
(614) 485-2010 **Morrison** Dennis J '83
(614) 221-3600 **Morrison** Michael P '88
(614) 487-0007 **Morrison** Nancy E '83
(614) 469-6860 **Morrison** Philip D '96
(614) 221-4000 **Morrison** Sarah D '97
(614) 443-0352 **Morrissey** Michael J '72
(614) 485-2010 **Morrow** Robert M '83
(614) 213-5355 **Morse** Kerry L '90
(614) 466-3934 **Mortland** Karen H '79
(614) 480-5760 **Morton** Daniel W '89
(614) 464-2200 **Moser** Jack L Jr. '99
(614) 249-8226 **Moser** Michael R '94
(614) 418-1729 **Moses** Ambrose III '91
(614) 224-7291 **Moses** Michael A '77
(614) 644-7257 **Moss** Nicole S '94
(614) 466-6700 **Moss-Edwards** Linda A '80
(614) 488-7924 **Mote** Gretchen J '78
(614) 464-2572 **Mote** Scott R '77
(614) 227-4810 **Motter** Miranda C '01
(614) 469-0400 **Moul** Geoffrey J '99
(614) 469-3220 **Moul** William C '64
(614) 365-2700 **Mount** Steven F '86
(614) 292-0160 **Mowoe** Isaac J '82
(614) 228-8400 **Mowry** Sherry L '01
(614) 228-2552 **Moyer** Stephen A '81
(614) 436-0600 **Mueller** Jerry K Jr. '73
(614) 221-8448 **Mueller** Kevin M '02
(614) 436-0600 **Mueller & Smith,LPA**
(614) 885-2550 **Muenz** Donald P '74
(614) 299-7700 **Muetzel** Andrew T '99
(614) 464-6400 **Muklewicz** Jacob T '01
(614) 229-4429 **Mulchaey** Rachel A '01
(614) 233-4422 **Muldoon** Damon P '98
(614) 486-0297 **Muldoon** Michael J '76
(614) 221-3155 **Muller** David A '00
(614) 463-9770 **Mulligan** Richard S '79
(614) 466-4280 **Mullin** Philip A Jr. '74
(614) 466-4605 **Mullinax** Robert L '74
(614) 462-3194 **Mulrane** Kevin P '75
(614) 644-6803 **Mulrane-Meyers** Toni E '81
(614) 430-8885 **Mulvey** Thomas J '85
(614) 462-3555 **Muncy** Rebecca L '04
(614) 228-6885 **Munsell** Theodore M '79
(614) 462-3194 **Munson** Sheryl K '94
(614) 752-1795 **Murch** Elizabeth Z '97
(614) 462-2217 **Murch** Kevin L '96
(614) 272-7845 **Murdock** Elizabeth A '02
(614) 442-8040 **Murphey** David P '78
(614) 365-2700 **Murphey** Richard R Jr. '50
(614) 445-2583 **Murphy** Beth Williams '02
(614) 469-0400 **Murphy** Brian K '99
(614) 280-1100 **Murphy** Jenifer J '99
(614) 221-1266 **Murphy** John E '72
(614) 463-9770 **Murphy** Katherine L '98
(614) 752-8211 **Murphy** Sharon W '92
(614) 645-7483 **Murray** Anne M '94
(614) 462-3194 **Murray** Deborah A '99
(614) 469-0400 **Murray** Joseph F '94
(614) 469-0400 **Murray Murphy Moul & Basil LLP**
(614) 224-2678 **Murray** Richard G II '00
(614) 466-7788 **Murray** Susan J '88
(614) 278-5902 **Murrell** Julie L '02
(614) 466-3998 **Musheno** Allen R '75
(614) 221-3155 **Music** Amanda M '03
(614) 464-6400 **Musilli** Stephen C '00
(614) 583-7608 **Musselman** David T '86
(614) 451-5300 **Musser Long & Harris**
(614) 451-5300 **Musser** Philip S '75
(614) 462-7450 **Must** Jamie M '03
(614) 645-7483 **Myers** Amy M '89
(614) 292-1556 **Myers** Bradley A '80
(614) 638-3993 **Myers** Craig S '89
(614) 227-2000 **Myers** Eric C '02
(614) 469-3275 **Myers** Robert W '88
(614) 228-1432 **Myers** Stanley L '67
(614) 466-8600 **Myers** William S '88
(614) 221-9100 **Nacht** Beth J '03
(614) 466-2022 **Nagel** Susan K '90
(614) 224-8339 **Nagel** Tom H '71
(614) 221-2838 **Nagy** Timothy P '74
(614) 469-3939 **Nakasian** William E '90
(614) 728-2845 **Napier** Shawn P '01
(614) 458-0025 **Nardone** Vincent J '96
(614) 291-9590 **Narens** Mark E '98
(614) 227-2358 **Nathan** Jerry E '73
(614) 365-2700 **Nauman** Robert D '02
(614) 464-6400 **Naumoff** Jennifer A '01
(614) 227-2000 **Naumoff** Mitchell A Jr. '04
(614) 222-3142 **Naumoff** Paul A '95
(614) 644-3037 **Navarre** Mark J '80
(614) 221-7548 **Navin** Joseph F '88
(614) 221-8757 **Neal** John G '77
(614) 462-3998 **Neal** Marianne '88
(614) 466-8600 **Nealon** Dennis G '83
(614) 365-9900 **Nealy** Darren L '01
(614) 466-0722 **Nearhood** Constance A '82
(614) 239-5033 **Nederveld** Allen G '97
(614) 469-3939 **Needler-Turner** Shawn M '04
(614) 728-2849 **Neeley-See** Greta M '94
(614) 854-5934 **Neely** Demetries J '84
(614) 249-7606 **Neely** Sandra L '83
(614) 221-4221 **Neff** Frank J '60
(614) 228-2345 **Neff** Joseph H '90
(614) 221-7663 **Neidenthal** Kenneth W '71
(614) 248-6037 **Neidenthal** Randall C '79
(614) 469-8000 **Neilsen** Daniel J '03
(614) 276-8959 **Nein** James R '71
(614) 224-7141 **Nelson** Hugh W '59
(614) 864-5780 **Nelson** James A '53
(614) 227-2000 **Nelson** Janice A '92
(614) 228-1398 **Nelson Levine deLuca & Horst LLC**
(614) 628-8000 **Nelson** Vanessa A '00
(614) 227-4870 **Nelson Carney** Jennifer M '04
(614) 221-9790 **Nemann** Adam Lee '03
(614) 884-4800 **Nemecek** Julia Carrie '04
(614) 443-4866 **Nemeth** John C '71
(614) 586-1310 **Nesbit** Mark M '95
(614) 221-1934 **Nesser** J Michael '83
(614) 442-2502 **Nester** Elbert R '68
(614) 299-4975 **Neubauer** David M '75
(614) 889-4777 **Neuman** Todd H '92
(614) 644-4133 **Neville** William J Jr. '92
(614) 466-6928 **Newbold** Garold L '83
(614) 462-2257 **Newcomb** Angelique Paul '97
(614) 464-6400 **Newcomb** William S Jr. '69
(614) 272-1112 **Newcome** Ronald E '82
(614) 752-6864 **Newcomer** James D '64
(614) 228-6885 **Newhouse** D Wesley II '83
(614) 725-7055 **Newkirk** Todd W '03
(614) 221-2121 **Newman** Dennis R '68
(614) 228-5711 **Newman** William F '55
(614) 464-5000 **Newman-Coleman** Rosemarie '87
(614) 228-5551 **Newsom** Kimberly C '92
(614) 462-3194 **Neyerlin** Amy L '88
(614) 466-6750 **Nicely** Fredrick J '92
(614) 222-0050 **Nichelson** Lauren R '00
(614) 221-1111 **Nichols** Philip R '96
(614) 462-2234 **Nichols** Robert H '92
(614) 644-7784 **Nichols** Robin M '02
(614) 466-0722 **Nicholson** Claude V '91
(614) 466-7090 **Nick** Paul M '90
(614) 677-4251 **Nickell-Thomas** Jennifer A '91
(614) 220-8900 **Nickerson** George R '76
(614) 469-9500 **Niehoff** David O '66
(614) 222-4834 **Niermeyer** Kurt L '89
(614) 227-2700 **Ninos** Helen M '80
(614) 225-4791 **Nissl** Colleen K '75
(614) 222-4220 **Nobile Needleman & Thompson, LLC**
(614) 575-1188 **Nobile Needleman & Thompson, LLC**
(614) 469-3254 **Noble** Michele L '00
(614) 228-2678 **Noble** Robert D '88
(614) 466-0194 **Noel** Gerald T Jr. '94
(614) 469-3285 **Noel** Mark A '03
(614) 857-4383 **Noga** Ronald B '74
(614) 365-2700 **Nolan** William A '89
(614) 469-2999 **Nolder** Steven S '87
(614) 227-2000 **Nordstrom** Robert J '56
(614) 224-0933 **Norman** Arthur S '89
(614) 237-8050 **Norman** Craig A '83
(614) 464-6400 **Norman** Jonathan M '76
(614) 246-2508 **Norman** Nicole F '89
(614) 464-6400 **North** Chris J '80
North Pricilla Kress '02
(614) 227-2000 **North** Scott E '84
(614) 227-2000 **Northrop** David E '73
(614) 291-7306 **Northrup** Judith A '84
(614) 228-5151 **Nose** Kevin R '79
(614) 644-9292 **Noteman** Jennifer L '99
(614) 466-4395 **Nourse** Steven T '90
(614) 462-3418 **Novack** Nancy A '88
(614) 249-4669 **Nowak** Joseph P '92
(614) 422-5674 **Nowicki** Ronald C '76
(614) 462-3194 **Nowland** Matthew D '78
(614) 464-6400 **Nuber** Anna K '04
(614) 464-6400 **Nunnally** Phillip L '71
(614) 228-8622 **Nusken** Ralph E '70
(614) 572-0048 **Nussle** Patricia A '92
(614) 246-6173 **Nyce** Kinsley F '82
(614) 249-0617 **Oberholtzer** Todd L '95
(614) 462-2227 **Oberle** John H '01
(614) 249-7111 **Oberlin** Janet S '04
(614) 464-6400 **Obetz** Robin R '64
(614) 644-7233 **O'Brien** Carol A '83
(614) 538-0070 **O'Brien** Dennis L '94
(614) 415-1676 **O'Brien** Kathleen M '75
(614) 224-3080 **O'Brien** Kevin J '83
(614) 464-6400 **O'Brien** Michael F '93
(614) 326-7987 **O'Brien** Robert T '59
(614) 462-3555 **O'Brien** Ronald J '74
(614) 227-2335 **O'Brien** Thomas J '96
(614) 424-5400 **O'Bryan** Daniel W '80
(614) 463-9441 **O'Callaghan** Michael J '90
(614) 466-7900 **O'Carroll** Leah V Basobas '02
(614) 249-1941 **Ocheltree** Alan J '01
(614) 387-6118 **O'Connell** Thomas C '02
(614) 461-6066 **O'Connell** Thomas J '85
(614) 227-2000 **O'Conner** Adele E '76
(614) 621-1500 **O'Connor** Thomas E Jr. '67
(614) 457-3453 **Odita** Florence U '85
(614) 221-0888 **O'Donnell** Laura S '93
(614) 227-2345 **O'Donnell** Terrence N '01
(614) 469-3939 **Oellermann** Charles M '91
(614) 752-2438 **Oelslager** W Scott '02
(614) 716-0500 **Ogg** Benjamin W '03
(614) 488-7373 **Oglesbee** Carla E '99
O'Grady Michael P '79
(614) 752-6417 **Okano** Mary Lynne '78
(614) 236-1011 **O'Keefe** Bobbie C '92
(614) 469-6638 **O'Korn** Keith L '98
(614) 436-0600 **Okuley** John J '03
(614) 275-2620 **O'Leary** Anne C '89
(614) 227-2000 **Oliphant** James S '71
(614) 220-9100 **Oliver** Jami S '93
(614) 559-1100 **Olix** Thomas J '86
(614) 424-6580 **Olson** Kathy A '77
(614) 488-7373 **O'Malley** William J '91
(614) 464-6400 **Oman** Richard Heer '51
(614) 716-0500 **Onda LaBuhn & Rankin Co,LPA**
(614) 716-0500 **Onda** Robert J '83
(614) 249-8343 **O'Neil** Bonnie Irvin '87
(614) 792-2250 **O'Neil** Dennis M '92
(614) 235-1166 **O'Neil** Thomas G '95
(614) 464-6400 **O'Neill** C William '71
(614) 466-9858 **O'Neill** Michael J '89
(614) 462-3580 **O'Neill** Shari W '89
(614) 221-9055 **Onesto** John L '72
(614) 227-8822 **Oppenheimer** Susan L '94
(614) 469-3939 **Ording** Michael K '80
(614) 461-9335 **O'Reilly** Kelly C '96
(614) 457-6450 **Orenchuk** Robert P '96
(614) 227-2000 **Orensten** David K '02
(614) 469-3939 **Organ** Shawn J '93
(614) 416-5120 **Orlandini** David W '95
(614) 236-6448 **Orlando** Jacqueline M '88
(614) 857-2339 **Ormond** Regina R '97
(614) 466-8911 **Orosz** Nathaniel S '04
(614) 464-1999 **Osborn** Larissa D '01
(614) 224-7747 **Osborne Delaurentis & Sontich Co LPA**
(614) 644-7342 **Oser** Joseph M '76
(614) 224-3741 **Oser** Michael N '78
(614) 228-6885 **O'Shaughnessy** Christopher T '98
(614) 464-6400 **O'Shaughnessy** Margaret E '97
(614) 469-3200 **Oshima** June M '98
(614) 480-4540 **Oster** Jody M '89
(614) 463-9770 **Osterkamp** Kevin J '74
(614) 262-7880 **Osterman** Lewis N III '80
(614) 262-1269 **Osterman** Linda W '80
(614) 849-3000 **Ostrowski** Bernard A '83
(614) 222-8686 **Ostrowski** Edward L Jr. '95
(614) 462-2242 **Ouellette** Robert R '91
(614) 793-8000 **Overly** Niles C '88
(614) 221-8448 **Owen** Andrew W '92
(614) 436-3211 **Owen** James D '79
(614) 469-2004 **Owens** David L '78
(614) 438-4964 **Owens** Matthew A '03
(614) 228-8995 **Owens** Timothy J '84
(614) 459-0561 **Ozier** James M '84
(614) 645-6296 **Paat** Antonio B Jr. '88
(614) 252-4649 **Pacchino** Carmine E '94
(614) 221-2400 **Pace** Richard W '82
(614) 466-0601 **Packer** David R '77
(614) 839-0400 **Paddock** Harold D III '73
(614) 481-9792 **Padro** Ruben E '00
(614) 464-6359 **Paige** Bruce P '02
(614) 262-2724 **Painter** Dorothy S '96
(614) 224-3838 **Painter** Lori B '92
(614) 462-3555 **Painter** Nathan D '03
(614) 644-6526 **Palazij** Martha S '01
(614) 577-1330 **Paley** Eileen Y '88
(614) 224-7747 **Pallante** Jeffrey A '02
(614) 462-7145 **Palmer** Gina W '94
(614) 252-1780 **Palmer** Mark J '82
(614) 823-8577 **Palmer** Richard D '73
(614) 484-1200 **Palmer** Robert G '76
(614) 224-6142 **Palmer** Stephen E '95
(614) 469-4781 **Palmer** Thomas W '00
(614) 224-8374 **Palof** Marcia E '80
(614) 462-5041 **Pampush** Thomas A '93
(614) 566-5151 **Pandora** Frank T II '72
(614) 469-1301 **Pandora** Gary J '78
(614) 224-4004 **Panico** Paul R '90
(614) 221-3178 **Panitch** Harry F '92
(614) 466-2739 **Pannett** Thomas P '99
(614) 624-7093 **Pantelakis** Katherine J '93
(614) 466-2980 **Paoletti** Paula L '94
(614) 466-3615 **Papp** Dennis M '76
(614) 621-1500 **Pappas** Leah '93
(614) 621-2000 **Pappas** Thomas P '87
(614) 223-9300 **Paragas** Conrado David '90
(614) 221-2525 **Pardi** James J II '92
(614) 459-8620 **Parello** Raymond S '96
(614) 466-0400 **Parise** Rita R '85
(614) 253-1010 **Pariser** David B '74
(614) 217-2881 **Parisi** Donna J '01
(614) 459-3272 **Park** Chan W '00
(614) 445-3960 **Parker** Darryl O '99
(614) 466-1156 **Parker** Jennifer A '87
(614) 778-1695 **Parker** Shinerr J '04
(614) 462-3555 **Parker** Stacy '04
(614) 469-3939 **Parkhill-Krein** Gayle E '83
(614) 255-2006 **Parks** Edward Y '80
(614) 227-2386 **Parks** Gregory T '95
(614) 229-5142 **Parmer** Brandon J '03
(614) 464-4661 **Parrill** Kenneth W Jr. '83
(614) 462-3555 **Parris** Selena D '95
(614) 280-1804 **Parry** Richard B '95
(614) 365-9900 **Parsell** Stuart G '94
(614) 462-5412 **Parsons** Angela G '97
(614) 221-2838 **Parsons** Benjamin J '03
(614) 221-2121 **Passella** Michael V '00
(614) 645-6906 **Passmore** Sherrie Jo '80
(614) 459-0118 **Pasternack** Jacqueline B '94
(614) 466-7567 **Patchen** Robert W '84
(614) 227-2000 **Pate** Christina A '04
(614) 469-3200 **Patel** Akhil M '00
(614) 469-3939 **Patmon** William W III '93
(614) 248-6515 **Patrell** Gregory S '99
(614) 224-8374 **Patrick** Gail D '79
(614) 846-2000 **Patter** Jeffrey J '81
(614) 221-4799 **Patterson** David C '75
(614) 280-1100 **Patterson** David T '77
(614) 228-2722 **Patterson** Gregory L '79
(614) 466-2980 **Patterson** James R '83
(614) 228-7191 **Patterson** Jay M '88
(614) 466-2980 **Patterson** John E '82
(614) 462-7407 **Patton** Kelly C '00
(614) 365-4100 **Paul** Angela M '97
(614) 340-5000 **Paul** Jephtha J '00
(614) 848-8411 **Paulino** Harry R '59
Paulucci Thomas S '03
(614) 462-7250 **Pausch** Carma R '94
(614) 462-5016 **Pavarini** Peter A '81
(614) 222-3137 **Pavkov** Terracina '01
(614) 224-7883 **Pavlic** Paul V '70
(614) 221-3006 **Paxton** Robert C II '72
(614) 466-6696 **Payer** Charissa D '95
(614) 466-8911 **Payne** Lori A '01
(614) 466-5394 **Payne** Timothy R '00
(614) 221-4000 **Paynter** Craig B '82
(614) 229-3221 **Paynter** Donald G '71
(614) 466-7637 **Payton** G Michael '84
(614) 461-4455 **Pearsol-Christie** Erika L '98
(614) 462-4678 **Peck** Richard A '96
(614) 224-5205 **Peck Shaffer & Williams,LLP**
(614) 645-7385 **Peeples** Andrea C '94
(614) 228-6345 **Peer** Jerry E Jr. '02
(614) 759-1693 **Pehowic** Shoshana R '02
(614) 466-2765 **Pellitt** Robert M '82
(614) 224-3737 **Pelteson** Edward F '60
(614) 624-6300 **Pence-Lavy** Mary M '98
(614) 337-8366 **Pencheff & Fraley**
(614) 337-8366 **Pencheff** Peter M '52
(614) 445-3969 **Pennington** Crysta R '04
(614) 462-3896 **Peppers** Samuel A III '93
(614) 469-1400 **Perdue** Dale K '80
(614) 221-9222 **Perez** Jay G '97
(614) 431-1500 **Perez** Juan J '85
(614) 431-1500 **Perez & Morris LLC**
(614) 221-3155 **Perez** Rita A '04
(614) 249-1447 **Perin** Charles H Jr. '80
(614) 466-3664 **Perkins** Catherine C '84
(614) 462-2253 **Perlmuter** Jeffrey A '75
(614) 466-8600 **Perry** Gregory A '95
(614) 466-7264 **Perry** Jane Pat '85
(614) 629-3000 **Perry** Paul E '76
(614) 466-7447 **Pestello-Sharf** Stephanie D '79
(614) 732-0746 **Peter** Jennifer M '04
(614) 280-0203 **Peterman** Laura M '86
(614) 469-5715 **Peters** Dana M '86
(614) 857-4324 **Peters** Geoffrey J '94
(614) 228-1541 **Peters** Georgeann G '83
(614) 221-2121 **Peters** Joanne S '94
(614) 249-9001 **Peters** William L '80
(614) 466-2766 **Petersen** Shaun K '00
(614) 462-5200 **Peterson** Carolyn D '91
(614) 645-7385 **Peterson** David E '97
(614) 462-3555 **Peterson** Gregory S '93
(614) 325-0379 **Peterson** Kathleen S '80
(614) 228-4546 **Peterson** Mark A '89
(614) 466-3664 **Peterson** Michaela J '01
(614) 466-6511 **Peterson** Sonni G '93
(614) 228-4422 **Petitjean** David L '88
(614) 225-8853 **Petrecca** Michael A '85
(614) 436-1992 **Petrel** David B '84
(614) 466-4605 **Petrella** Barbara Jo '89
(614) 464-6400 **Petricoff** M Howard '74
(614) 227-2373 **Petrie** James G '92
(614) 466-8911 **Petro** James M '73
(614) 224-0531 **Petro** John J '62
(614) 224-0531 **Petro** John P '92
(614) 224-0531 **Petro** Susan S '90
(614) 466-0106 **Petrucci** Gretchen L '90
(614) 221-6837 **Petrucci** Mark C '90
(614) 224-4357 **Pettigrew** Grady L Jr. '71
(614) 466-7788 **Pettigrew** Lewis F '90
(614) 221-1111 **Pettit** Christopher R '98
(614) 228-3550 **Pettit** Susan '97
Petty Robert C '98
(614) 418-1810 **Pettys** Jeffrey C '93
(614) 466-2166 **Petzinger** John S '03
(614) 744-5070 **Peura** David A '02
(614) 583-5020 **Pfancuff** Sharon L '83
(614) 228-8191 **Pfau** Edward L '91
(614) 228-1541 **Pfefferle** Ben L III '79
(614) 466-8600 **Pfeiffer** Barbara J '85
(614) 645-7385 **Pfeiffer** Richard C Jr. '72
(614) 760-3502 **Pfeiffer** William W '83
(614) 469-2999 **Pfeuffer** Alan J '00
(614) 462-4242 **Phelps-White** Angela G '85
(614) 466-5092 **Philabaun** Michael A '83
(614) 224-7883 **Philbrick** Jon R '77
(614) 221-5216 **Phillips** Christopher G '01
(614) 464-6400 **Phillips** James E '75
(614) 228-5822 **Phillips** Mark E '84
(614) 462-7246 **Phillips** Patricia M '93
Phillips R L Kelly III '02
(614) 466-3180 **Phillips** Sherry M '91
(614) 645-7385 **Phillips** Westley M '04
(614) 469-1400 **Phipps** Karen Held '03
(614) 444-3036 **Piatt** Richard A '93
(614) 659-9616 **Piccin** Joseph L '00
(614) 462-3555 **Piccininni** Patrick J '91
(614) 406-8548 **Pickens** Jamie C '02
(614) 221-2121 **Pickett** Patrick M '89
(614) 228-1541 **Pickrel** Deborah A '04
(614) 645-7385 **Pieplow** Richard A '82
(614) 221-7791 **Pierce** Janica A '02
(614) 462-3194 **Pierce** Timothy E '89
(614) 249-3492 **Pierre** Darrell M Jr. '96
(614) 224-6525 **Pierre-Louis** Lloyd '97
(614) 462-2401 **Pierson** Anthony D '03
(614) 227-2000 **Pigman** Jack R '69
(614) 466-5146 **Pikosz** Michael J '99
(614) 752-8683 **Pilcher** Emily J '04
(614) 222-3062 **Pinkerton** Sandra E '93
(614) 460-6383 **Pino** Jovette S '84
(614) 248-6041 **Pioli** Robert J '85
(614) 221-5216 **Pipino** Samuel M '93
(800) 621-3216 **Pippin** Laura B '98
(614) 644-8955 **Pirik** Christine M '85
(614) 538-5375 **Pirtle** Timothy A '88
(614) 227-8815 **Pittner** Nicholas A '70
(614) 228-3372 **Placzkiewicz** James M '03
(614) 228-4546 **Plank** Donald T '79
(614) 293-8446 **Plant** John F III '03
(614) 644-7233 **Plate** Norman E '00
(614) 227-2000 **Plinke** Eric J '92
(614) 818-3222 **Pliskin** Lawrence E '94
(614) 235-5747 **Plummer** Angela K '92
(614) 629-3000 **Plunkett & Cooney,PC**
(614) 221-1166 **Plymale** Ronald E '68
(614) 244-6505 **Pocorus** Barbara '98
(614) 463-9770 **Poe** Michael A '78
(614) 466-4510 **Pohler** Susan J '85
(614) 227-2000 **Pohlman** James E '57
(614) 464-6400 **Pohlman** William J '88
(614) 466-2980 **Pokorny** Cheryl D '85
(614) 462-3194 **Pokorski** Rebecca R '87
(614) 221-2848 **Polhamus** William R '73
(614) 222-0052 **Pollak** Lawrence S '82
(614) 645-7745 **Pollitt** Harry W Jr. '74
(614) 444-7822 **Pomerants** Alex '98
(614) 944-5712 **Pomeroy** Lisa K '01
(614) 248-5654 **Pomeroy** Mark C '87
(614) 885-2101 **Pomeroy** Rosemary E '88
(614) 752-8855 **Pon** Christopher E '84
(614) 224-2291 **Pontius** Donald H '58
(614) 466-5610 **Poole** Mark R '01

(614) 225-8896 **Popelsky** Steven P '81
(614) 485-1800 **Popham** Kevin W '96
(614) 566-5151 **Porembski** Chester P '84
(614) 645-7717 **Porte** Stephen A '97
(614) 466-2872 **Porter** Elise W '91
(614) 462-5418 **Porter** Jeffrey D '96
(614) 466-5394 **Porter** Randall L '77
(614) 752-8211 **Porter** Richard G '86
(614) 227-2000 **Porter** Samuel H '53
(614) 462-2314 **Porter** Susan '86
(614) 464-6400 **Porter** William G II '84
(614) 227-2000 **Porter Wright Morris & Arthur LLP**
(614) 461-1234 **Portman Foley & Flint LLP**
(614) 461-1234 **Portman** Frederic A '73
(614) 227-2000 **Post** Andrew R '03
(614) 279-1700 **Post** Caris D '01
(614) 559-2502 **Post** Gerald R '71
(614) 457-2622 **Post** Roger C '66
(614) 228-1541 **Post** William R '00
(614) 486-2111 **Postlewaite** Charles C '82
(614) 738-2636 **Potash** Arlene N '00
(614) 227-2395 **Poth** Christine M '95
(614) 228-6885 **Poth** Jeffery M '96
(614) 228-2154 **Potts** Byron L '88
(614) 462-5427 **Pouget** Anne D '03
(614) 644-3345 **Pouliot** John A '00
(614) 466-2766 **Poulos** Gregory J '99
(614) 466-5394 **Powell** Amanda J '03
(614) 444-4445 **Powell** Bruce W '70
(614) 464-6400 **Powell** D Scott '92
(614) 228-9550 **Powell** David T '03
(614) 228-6107 **Powell** Shane M '03
(614) 462-5010 **Powers** Victoria E '91
(614) 224-5205 **Pratt** Glendon B '82
(614) 466-4328 **Pratt** Jennifer L '87
(614) 466-8600 **Pratt** Lawrence D '73
(614) 466-5394 **Pratt** Shelley M '98
(614) 224-7883 **Precario** Peter A '70
(614) 258-6000 **Prendergast** Melissa M '02
(614) 462-3555 **Press** Katherine J '82
(614) 272-6951 **Pressler** Timothy A '76
(614) 227-2000 **Pressley** Fred G Jr. '78
(614) 480-5297 **Preston** Carmen Kathryn '90
(614) 297-1000 **Preston** Charles A '97
(614) 719-3240 **Preston** Elizabeth A '94
(614) 221-8448 **Preston** Robert C '58
(614) 275-5927 **Pribich** Dan T '82
(614) 217-0448 **Price** Deborah E '93
(614) 224-2319 **Price** Gary P '73
(614) 466-3191 **Price** Gregory A '90
(614) 462-5411 **Price** Rebecca R '01
(614) 644-7233 **Price** Thelma T '76
(614) 221-3155 **Price** William E II '91
(614) 462-3555 **Prichard** Sheryl L '95
(614) 728-7055 **Prichard** Timothy D '92
(614) 462-6281 **Prillo** Jennifer A '01
(614) 227-2302 **Princehorn** Rebecca C '81
(614) 227-2000 **Prior** James H '85
(614) 645-7483 **Prisley** Michael A '91
(614) 469-1400 **Pritchard** Glen R '88
(614) 466-2980 **Pritchard** John J '01
(614) 227-2000 **Pritchard** W John '92
(614) 459-5200 **Pritchett** Clark P Jr. '68
(614) 224-2678 **Probst** Erica A '01
(614) 464-2025 **Probst** Michael S '99
(614) 566-5151 **Proctor** Penelope A '80
(614) 464-6400 **Proels** Sebastian E '99
(614) 228-6885 **Prophater** William H Jr. '93
(614) 462-2333 **Prosek** Bryan K '91
(614) 461-1311 **Proxmire** Mickey L '01
(614) 466-5394 **Prucha** Linda E '88
(614) 466-5394 **Prude-Smithers** Pamela J '93
(614) 387-9420 **Pruett** Catherine Eileen '81
(614) 444-7711 **Pruitt** Jacob E Jr. '76
(614) 677-3452 **Prunte** Thomas J '82
(614) 469-5614 **Pryce** Deborah D '76
(614) 228-5151 **Pryor** David W '84
(614) 224-2795 **Puckett** Milton A '70
(614) 224-3207 **Pullins** Scott A '03
(614) 443-3860 **Pursglove** Joseph II '75
(614) 447-0100 **Pusateri** Paul D '77
(614) 221-5627 **Putnam** Douglas T '83
(614) 436-3701 **Pyles** Clement W '75
(614) 463-4201 **Pyles** Tracy Stott '01
(614) 221-5121 **Quayle** Jeffrey D '78
(614) 464-3563 **Quenemoen** Helen M '85
(614) 292-1764 **Quigley** John B Jr. '73
(614) 644-7293 **Quinn** David M '78
(614) 466-2585 **Quinn** Gretchen A '87
(614) 445-5858 **Rabaa** Shareef S '03
(614) 221-5212 **Raber** David A '92
(614) 464-6400 **Radnor** Alan T '72
(614) 227-2306 **Rafferty** Robert C '84
Raish Todd A '94
(614) 457-7700 **Rakestraw** W Vincent '68

(614) 224-8178 **Ralston** Jay C '72
(614) 466-4605 **Ramos** Domingo '95
(614) 466-0306 **Ramos-Reardon** Diana L '97
(614) 227-2300 **Ramseyer** Becky L '03
(614) 459-5200 **Rance Pritchett Brantner Keller & Ely Co,LPA**
(614) 459-5200 **Rance** William E '51
(614) 225-8325 **Ranck** Stephen P '83
(614) 227-2000 **Randall** Nicole S '00
(614) 224-7193 **Randall** Samuel B '51
(614) 224-7193 **Randall** Samuel B II '93
(614) 469-8000 **Randazzo** Samuel C '75
(614) 228-6885 **Rankin** Gregory D '77
(614) 221-3600 **Rankin** Lisa V '91
(614) 241-5550 **Rankin** Michael R '79
(614) 628-8395 **Rankin** Timothy J '01
(614) 716-0500 **Rankin** Timothy S '92
(614) 464-6400 **Ransier** Frederick L '74
(614) 464-6400 **Ransier** Kathleen H '74
(614) 466-6363 **Ransom** Lenora S '99
(614) 227-2000 **Ransom** Tracie N '04
(614) 221-7777 **Ranum** Darrell B '86
Rastetter Richard C Jr. '93
(614) 459-6331 **Rasul** Ronnie A '95
(614) 459-0364 **Ratchford** Robert L Jr. '75
(614) 497-9918 **Rathburn** Dennis A '91
(614) 719-3240 **Rattan** James E '62
(614) 466-2112 **Rau** John E '97
(614) 462-3555 **Rausch** Jennifer M Gregg '02
(614) 466-2980 **Rausch** Monica L '03
(614) 628-0818 **Rawlings** Stephanie M '02
(614) 466-7090 **Rawski** John '88
(614) 466-4882 **Ray** Carol L '87
(614) 221-7791 **Ray** Frank A '73
(614) 227-2000 **Ray** Nicholas M J '97
(614) 248-6038 **Raybuck** David W '85
(614) 221-3377 **Readey** James A '70
(614) 466-7012 **Readey** Mary Lynn '87
(614) 469-3939 **Readler** Chad A '97
(614) 462-5027 **Readler** Jennifer Dutey '97
(614) 228-6400 **Real** Mark J '77
(614) 470-8527 **Reall** Christopher S '96
(614) 221-4859 **Reasoner** Willis Irl III '78
(614) 248-2517 **Reber** Aaron J '97
(614) 253-9737 **Recchie** Joseph J Jr. '82
(614) 221-1800 **Rechner** Carl J Jr. '83
(614) 224-1222 **Recker** Brice O '90
(614) 463-9441 **Reckless** Walter W '69
(614) 224-6210 **Rector** Neil K '83
(614) 462-2219 **Rector** Susan D '84
(614) 462-3593 **Reddington** William A '77
(614) 645-7385 **Redick** Glenn B '70
(614) 461-9300 **Redmon** Ronald L '74
(614) 223-9300 **Reed** Frank J Jr. '91
(614) 466-7014 **Reed** Heather S '98
(614) 221-5839 **Reed** Joseph D '83
(614) 365-2700 **Reed** Michael R '94
(614) 443-9401 **Reed** Robert R '52
(614) 469-2455 **Reed** Steven G '75
(614) 785-1301 **Reedus** Benita D '86
(614) 540-4000 **Reedy** Hollie F '95
(614) 488-8441 **Rees** William J '81
(614) 716-2956 **Reeves** James L '78
(614) 462-3555 **Reichel** Jeffrey L '89
(614) 486-4311 **Reichelderfer** Thomas S '99
(614) 228-1240 **Reichenbach** Seth T '93
(614) 466-7447 **Reichley** John P '90
(614) 227-2000 **Reichwein** Diane C '83
(614) 227-8812 **Reid** Nelson M '97
(614) 462-2207 **Reidy** Joseph M '85
(614) 466-4395 **Reilly** Stephen A '75
(614) 225-9000 **Reim** Sandee E '98
(614) 621-1500 **Reinhard** Daniel A '02
(614) 228-7771 **Reinhart** Harry R '78
(614) 728-7171 **Reinoehl** Erika M '00
(614) 801-2771 **Reis** Allen J '76
(614) 466-6696 **Reis** Kevin J '77
(614) 228-6888 **Reisinger** Lori L '00
(614) 293-8446 **Reissland** Gaibrelle M '89
(614) 443-7455 **Reister** Frederick T '72
(614) 464-6400 **Reisz** Lisa Pierce '92
(614) 464-6400 **Reitler** Angela K '03
(614) 466-2580 **Reitz** Lili C '90
(614) 462-5425 **Reitz** Mark R '96
(614) 221-7548 **Reitz** Thomas L '97
(614) 461-1311 **Reminger & Reminger**
(614) 469-7404 **Rendar** Gail M '92
(614) 466-7788 **Renick** Anderson M III '97
(614) 469-3939 **Renker** Kerry M '02
(614) 469-3284 **Renne** Michael A '87
(614) 644-1114 **Renner** Michael J '73
(614) 466-8288 **Rennick** Kyme W '82
(614) 716-1606 **Resnik** Marvin I '73
(614) 237-9308 **Retter** Erica E '87
(614) 462-3555 **Reulbach** Sue A '85
(614) 228-6885 **Reuss** James K '79
(614) 268-0534 **Reves** Randal M '94
(614) 221-8080 **Reynard** Jeffrey D '99

(614) 278-6800 **Reynolds** Chadwick P '99
(614) 221-2838 **Reynolds** Diane D '85
(614) 221-4255 **Reynolds** Jackson B III '93
(614) 677-6368 **Reynolds** Tyla L '96
(614) 462-2278 **Rhee** Hansel H '03
(614) 221-4670 **Rhiel** Susan L '86
(614) 242-4242 **Rhoad** Brant K '03
(614) 644-3037 **Rhoads** Kimberly A '93
(614) 466-9392 **Rhodebeck** Larry D '80
(614) 228-6321 **Rhodehamel** David R '90
(614) 365-2700 **Rhodes** Keely J '03
(614) 298-8600 **Ribar** Mark D '96
(614) 466-0722 **Rice** Chelsea S '03
(614) 559-2101 **Rice** Frederick W '78
Rice Scott E '99
(614) 228-5822 **Rich Crites & Dittmer,LLC**
(614) 228-5822 **Rich** Jeffrey A '70
(614) 227-8869 **Rich** Matthew A '04
(614) 457-9784 **Rich** Sandra L '86
(614) 249-6201 **Rich-Barge** Mario M '02
(614) 461-1156 **Richards** John R '93
(614) 221-7663 **Richards** Kenneth M '88
(614) 228-1128 **Richards** Robin S '01
(614) 464-6400 **Richards** Suzanne K '74
(614) 424-5612 **Richards** William B '99
Richardson Kristopher L '97
(614) 464-6400 **Richardson** Matthew J '03
(614) 878-9262 **Richardson** Randy '86
(614) 228-5151 **Richie** Crystal R '95
(614) 365-2700 **Richner** Kristin E '04
(614) 298-8150 **Richter** Jody R '99
(614) 728-9758 **Richter** Michael P '90
(614) 466-3205 **Richter** Philip C '95
(614) 365-2700 **Rickard** Erik J '97
(614) 464-6400 **Rickert** Benjamin J '03
(614) 358-8056 **Ricketts** Richard T '86
(614) 464-6400 **Ridgley** Thomas B '68
(614) 365-2700 **Rieck** Kim A '77
(614) 221-3155 **Riedel** Timothy A '87
(614) 462-3555 **Riedl** Daniel J '03
(614) 224-8160 **Riehl** Lawrence A '79
(614) 221-1216 **Riepenhoff** David A '02
(614) 466-7351 **Riesenberger** William A '76
(614) 444-6556 **Rieser** David P '80
(614) 466-5394 **Rigby** Kimberly S '04
(614) 248-6045 **Rigelman** Bruce D '96
(614) 444-3900 **Rigg** Brian J '87
(614) 228-6625 **Riggins** Melissa K '88
(614) 224-3208 **Riggs** Warren G '53
(614) 268-1493 **Rigney** Joseph K '74
(614) 221-0240 **Riley** Thomas J '69
(614) 365-6034 **Rilley** Karin W '90
(614) 466-2872 **Rimelspach** Rene L '01
(614) 444-4455 **Rinehart** Adam R '89
(614) 221-0717 **Rinehart** Dana G '73
(614) 221-0717 **Rinehart & Rishel,Ltd**
(614) 292-3694 **Rinehart-Thompson** Laurie '94
(614) 221-7548 **Riseling** Jerry L '62
(614) 221-0717 **Rishel** James R '72
(614) 221-0717 **Rishel** James R '02
(614) 224-8374 **Risley** Rebecca L '02
(614) 227-4857 **Ristau** Justin W '02
(614) 228-6675 **Ritenour** Margaret J '80
(614) 462-5442 **Ritter** Paul D Jr. '56
(614) 224-9207 **Ritterspach** Angela M '99
(614) 462-3555 **Ritterspach** Benjamin E '99
(614) 221-8800 **Roach** John R '74
(614) 445-2481 **Roark** David T '80
(614) 487-0700 **Roark** Sue D '80
(614) 221-1314 **Robbins** Pamela S '97
(614) 445-5858 **Robbins-Penniman** Gus E '78
(614) 464-1211 **Robek** Christine L '04
(614) 462-2294 **Robenalt** Robert M '89
(614) 645-6947 **Roberto** Cheryl L '87
(614) 885-8272 **Roberts** Cynthia B '91
(614) 466-4100 **Roberts** Daniel J '88
(614) 224-8374 **Roberts** Donald W '02
(614) 451-2210 **Roberts** Douglas S '76
(614) 466-4328 **Roberts** James C '04
(614) 462-4010 **Roberts** Janie D '85
(614) 464-6400 **Roberts** Jeffrey D '01
(614) 451-2210 **Roberts** Scott R '79
(614) 719-3410 **Roberts** Stacy E '02
(614) 901-8178 **Roberts** Stewart E '75
(614) 466-4605 **Robertson** David W '89
(614) 462-3664 **Robertson** Jan E '91
(614) 462-2218 **Robinett** John D '82
(614) 228-1541 **Robins** Harlan W '92
(614) 464-6400 **Robins** Ronald A Jr. '90
(614) 228-1541 **Robinson** Barry R '72
(614) 462-5052 **Robinson** David J '92
(614) 462-3555 **Robinson** Heather B '96
(614) 884-4800 **Robinson** Kenneth J '98
(614) 621-9000 **Robinson** Michelle K '96
(614) 221-9800 **Robinson** Rachel K '97
(614) 221-8900 **Robinson** Randal D '75

(614) 221-3318 **Robinson** Robert M '96
(614) 365-2700 **Robinson** Tim J '90
(614) 466-5610 **Robinson-Bond** Alice L '84
Robison Gary T '60
(614) 559-3839 **Robol** Richard T '96
(614) 430-8885 **Roby** Robert S '96
(614) 898-7100 **Rocco** Gerald A '86
(614) 221-1111 **Rocco** Thomas J '92
(614) 466-5394 **Roche** Susan M '00
(614) 457-9731 **Rocray** John N '96
(614) 221-8651 **Roderick** Gerald L '84
(614) 221-4000 **Rodgers** Todd M '93
(614) 224-7754 **Rodier** Ian H '89
Rodocker Peter B '97
(614) 464-6400 **Rodriguez** Joseph C '00
(614) 365-2700 **Roehm** Victor J III '01
(614) 469-3200 **Roehrenbeck** Gabriel J '04
(614) 559-1188 **Roesch** Robert C II '92
(614) 463-9770 **Roetzel & Andress,LPA**
(614) 466-3101 **Rogers** Clarence D Jr. '64
(614) 227-2367 **Rogers** David A '76
(614) 464-6400 **Rogers** Douglas L '71
(614) 462-3555 **Rogers** Jeffrey C '98
(614) 462-7450 **Rogers** Marilyn C '98
(614) 292-0574 **Rogers** Nancy Hardin '72
(614) 464-1211 **Rogovin** Richard D '68
(614) 387-9762 **Rohrs** Kenneth A '73
(614) 227-2000 **Rohyans** John B '69
(614) 466-1305 **Roller** Valerie A '87
(614) 466-5091 **Rolletta** Sandra M '83
(614) 469-5715 **Rolwing** Richard M '93
(614) 461-1311 **Romanello** George M '74
(614) 645-8287 **Romanoff** Marvin S '67
(614) 248-8039 **Romohr** Amy L '91
(614) 628-0650 **Rook** James E '93
(614) 221-5500 **Rooney** Kevin G '85
(614) 486-7884 **Rooney** Lisa A '85
(614) 365-2700 **Root** Emily E '03
(614) 221-2121 **Roper** James M '87
(614) 445-2744 **Rorapaugh** Michael B '82
(614) 461-1100 **Rosan** Kristin E '99
(614) 227-2321 **Rosati** Jack R Jr. '89
(614) 621-1500 **Rosato** Peter A '97
(614) 221-6969 **Roscoe** David A '01
Roscoe Roberta J '02
(614) 225-9700 **Rose** Bert L '92
(614) 415-7461 **Rose** Daniel A '88
(614) 444-8777 **Rose** James V '58
(614) 292-8626 **Rose** Michael D '63
(614) 268-8928 **Rose** Waldo B '69
(614) 645-7712 **Roseboro** Anthony M '86
(614) 797-9700 **Roseman** D Richard '95
(614) 466-8911 **Rosen** Erin G '99
(614) 249-7982 **Rosenbaum** Melissa G '92
(614) 461-1100 **Rosenberg** Eric J '98
(614) 228-6885 **Rosenberg** Karen Krisher '84
(614) 464-2213 **Rosenberg** Neil W '84
(614) 224-1690 **Rosenberger** John C '73
(614) 464-6400 **Rosenfeld** Aaron P '76
(614) 221-8448 **Rosenthal** Brent D '84
(614) 469-3245 **Rosenthal** Janis B '81
(614) 644-7257 **Rosenthal** Joseph N '84
(614) 864-4359 **Rosenthal** Lee S '82
(614) 716-1646 **Rosenthal** Martin S '85
(614) 464-6400 **Rosler** Russell R '87
(614) 519-2488 **Ross** Marcus A '97
(614) 485-2010 **Ross** Richard W '78
(614) 475-4845 **Ross** Ruth F '77
(614) 457-4104 **Ross** Stanley D '65
(614) 224-8374 **Ross** William H '80
(614) 888-1338 **Rossie** Linda M '90
(614) 469-3939 **Rossman** E Michael '98
(614) 523-4159 **Rossman** Jerry '87
(614) 523-4145 **Rossman** Kevin D '90
(614) 252-7824 **Roth** Bruce I '74
(614) 291-0826 **Rotondo** Eric P '75
(614) 221-7791 **Roubanes** Barbara A '97
(614) 273-6004 **Rouda** Harley E Jr. '87
(614) 220-9200 **Rourke & Blumenthal,LLP**
(614) 220-9200 **Rourke** Michael J '81
(614) 265-6883 **Rowan** Charles G '89
(614) 224-9004 **Rowan** Phyllis J '93
(614) 224-2678 **Rowe** Steven D '74
(614) 644-8912 **Rowland** David L '85
(614) 466-1826 **Rowland** Jill M '93
(614) 464-6400 **Rowland** Ronald L '72
(614) 466-0641 **Rowland** William G '93
(614) 221-2400 **Roy** Cynthia M '82
(614) 228-0704 **Royer** Barth E '72
(614) 227-2000 **Rozelle** Paul G '03
(614) 460-4639 **Rubadue** David W '84
(614) 228-5060 **Ruben** Donald B '64
(614) 365-2700 **Rubenstein** Richard W '80
(614) 719-3372 **Rubey** Rachel A '03
(614) 457-7700 **Rubin** Daniel R '84
(614) 752-8068 **Rubino** Joseph D '88
(614) 464-6400 **Ruby** Thomas O '82
(614) 445-3971 **Rucker** Retanio A '88

(614) 253-1010 **Rudolph** Timothy J '99
(614) 848-4999 **Rupert** David E '99
(614) 464-1211 **Rupert** Jeffrey G '95
(614) 466-1305 **Rupert** Rosemary E '89
(614) 249-7641 **Rupp** Daniel R '69
(614) 228-1541 **Rupp** Robert K '82
(614) 227-2000 **Ruscitti** Donna M '86
(614) 466-1560 **Rush** Deanna D '83
(614) 464-6400 **Rusie** Jennifer A '03
(614) 464-6400 **Rusie** Michael J '03
(614) 946-1966 **Russ** Andrew E '02
(614) 863-8880 **Russ** Jason H '94
(614) 227-2000 **Russell** Christopher C '88
(614) 464-6400 **Russell** Gregory D '92
(614) 466-4656 **Russell** Paul A '93
(614) 222-5809 **Russell** Susan L '88
(614) 228-6135 **Russell-Washington** Necol D '01
(614) 464-6400 **Russo** Gina R '02
(614) 227-8830 **Rutledge** James A '78
(614) 466-8911 **Ruttan** Mary Beth '93
(614) 464-6400 **Rutz** Allen L '98
(614) 447-2365 **Ruzicho** Andrew J '67
(614) 447-2365 **Ruzicho** Andrew J '94
(614) 228-1398 **Ryan** Cheryl L '97
(614) 228-6885 **Ryan** Corinne N '96
(614) 846-2000 **Ryan** Daniel F '80
(614) 221-3155 **Ryan** James G '85
(614) 488-4880 **Ryan** Joseph E Jr. '64
(614) 227-2000 **Ryan** Joseph W Jr. '78
(614) 228-4546 **Ryan** Michael F '88
(614) 249-0293 **Ryan** Paige L '97
(614) 228-5151 **Ryan** Timothy J '91
Ryerson John T Jr. '91
(614) 228-8833 **Rymers** Beau K '99
(614) 466-3180 **Rzymek** Michael A '88
(614) 457-5330 **Saad** James A '77
(614) 365-2700 **Saad** Michael D '66
(614) 464-6400 **Saalman** Gary J '89
(614) 222-0535 **Sabath** Mark K '92
(614) 229-3888 **Sabatino** Alessandro Jr. '93
(614) 462-5030 **Sabo** Roger L '71
(614) 871-8970 **Sabol** Garry A '82
(614) 445-0793 **Sabol** Suzanne K '83
(614) 462-3555 **Saeger** John S '89
(614) 466-3636 **Safko** Sheldon R '84
(614) 716-2430 **Sagan** Fredric L '81
(614) 365-2700 **Sagone** Matthew L '94
(614) 460-4652 **Sagun** Stanley J Jr. '92
(614) 853-2518 **Sahli** Richard C '80
(614) 444-3036 **Saia** Jon J '87
(614) 444-3036 **Saia & Piatt,PLL**
(614) 469-3939 **Saigo** Holly H '01
(614) 224-4114 **St Clair & Bainter,LLP**
(614) 224-4114 **St Clair** Robert B '77
(614) 716-1658 **St Pierre** Thomas G '89
(614) 488-9900 **Saker** Theodore R Jr. '84
(614) 239-5034 **Saleme** David W '97
(614) 292-2019 **Samansky** Allan J '95
(614) 221-3155 **Samples** Todd J '01
(614) 688-0052 **Sampson** Sara A '97
(614) 466-5744 **Samsel** Edward C '83
(614) 221-2580 **Samuels** Harvey M '74
(614) 231-9134 **Samuels** Margaret Ann '74
(614) 462-5021 **Samuels** Stephen P '75
(614) 889-2531 **Sanborn Brandon Duvall & Bobbitt Co,LPA**
(614) 462-5295 **Sanchez** Lorenzo '92
(614) 466-0284 **Sandberg** Elisabet K '98
(614) 221-5216 **Sander** Neil C '04
(614) 469-5715 **Sanders** Deborah F '89
(614) 728-0849 **Sanders** Howard M '75
(614) 228-0704 **Sanders** Judith B '77
(614) 466-5394 **Sandford** Kathryn L '94
(614) 225-8818 **Sandor** Louis J Jr. '78
(614) 462-5319 **Sanford** Jay H '72
(614) 443-4866 **Sant** Sanjeev J '01
(614) 227-2331 **Sant** Thomas R '73
(614) 222-2172 **Santangelo** Stephen A '78
(614) 469-9500 **Santellani** Lianne L '79
(614) 424-4164 **Santilli** Paul T '60
(614) 995-4399 **Sarko** Thomas L '91
(614) 275-2650 **Saros** John '74
(614) 469-3939 **Sarver** Todd L '93
(614) 995-2096 **Satterwhite** Matthew J '00
(614) 466-1312 **Sauer** Larry S '87
(614) 462-2260 **Saunders** Charles Jr. '72
(614) 644-6342 **Saunders** O'Neal '93
(614) 719-8766 **Saunders** Tyanika L '00
(614) 461-4455 **Sauter** Robert W '77
(614) 221-8868 **Savage** James S III '81
(614) 249-8537 **Savini** Steven R '91
(614) 431-1500 **Savino** Angela M '88
(614) 221-4000 **Saxbe** Charles R '75
(614) 249-3572 **Saxon** Anne D '89
(614) 445-2623 **Saylor** Lyle R '74
(614) 488-8930 **Schadek** Michael A '93
(614) 644-2640 **Schaefer** Carol L '75
(614) 644-2520 **Schaefer** Carol S '87
(614) 229-4766 **Schaefer** Robert B '87

(614) 249-1748 **Schaefer** Theresa R '85
(614) 221-3155 **Schaeffer** Matthew T '96
(614) 224-2678 **Schaeffer** Michael N '75
(614) 475-9511 **Schafer** Dale C '49
(614) 221-1000 **Schafer** Jennifer L '02
(614) 488-4484 **Schafer** Stephen E '73
(614) 464-2392 **Schaffer** Grier D '88
(614) 466-3998 **Schaffner** Jeffery O '84
(614) 223-9300 **Schantz** Roger L '91
(614) 469-3397 **Scheaf** Oral Judson III '88
(614) 224-8374 **Schear** Kathi L '78
(614) 466-7447 **Schedler** Karl W '76
(614) 628-8000 **Scheiderer** Judith M '91
(614) 462-4513 **Schelb** Jon E '99
(614) 228-6885 **Schellhaas** Kim M '93
(614) 431-7200 **Scherner** Hans '79
(614) 431-7200 **Scherner Hanson & Cornwell,LLC**
(614) 466-2801 **Schierholt** Steven W '03
(614) 224-1484 **Schiff** Lynda Z '88
(614) 449-4313 **Schiff** Michael S '86
(614) 621-8888 **Schiff** Scott W '82
(614) 464-6400 **Schimmer** Alexandra T '02
(614) 239-9980 **Schindler** Jerome R '68
(614) 464-6400 **Schira** David M '90
(614) 466-4656 **Schlatter** Robert L '83
(614) 297-1211 **Schlaufman** Darice L '01
(614) 249-4169 **Schleppi** William J '79
(614) 278-6807 **Schlonsky** Michael A '91
(614) 878-7251 **Schlosser** Jacob A '62
(614) 249-3606 **Schlosser** Nicole A '00
(614) 268-4993 **Schmalz** Kurt J '89
(614) 229-5260 **Schmarr** John M '76
(614) 621-9000 **Schmidt** George A '72
(614) 227-2000 **Schmidt** Robert J Jr. '93
(614) 466-7900 **Schmidt** Stefan J '90
(614) 466-3934 **Schmidt** William J '81
(614) 744-2217 **Schmitt** Grace E '96
(614) 540-4000 **Schmitz** Patrick J '91
(614) 462-3194 **Schneider** Carole B '79
(614) 645-8206 **Schneider** Charles A '76
(614) 224-1222 **Schneider** Karl H '82
(614) 224-1222 **Schneider** Keith W '89
(614) 292-0611 **Schneider** Mary F '89
(614) 466-4656 **Schoch** Frederick C '80
(614) 233-4742 **Schockman** Douglas J '94
(614) 464-6400 **Schoedinger** Daniel H '69
(614) 224-0531 **Schoenberger** Josh Logan '04
(614) 430-8885 **Schoenling** Lynne K '91
(614) 249-9005 **Scholl** Joseph M '79
(614) 466-7046 **Scholl** Marcie M '80
(614) 466-2765 **Scholl** Michael R '93
(614) 462-7245 **Scholl** Thomas W III '96
(614) 462-3194 **Schopis** Robert O '85
(614) 462-2266 **Schottenstein** Edwin E '82
(614) 464-1880 **Schottenstein** James M '72
(614) 462-2700 **Schottenstein Zox & Dunn**
(614) 461-1311 **Schrader** Matthew L '01
(614) 227-2000 **Schraff** Christopher R '72
(614) 464-6400 **Schrag** Edward A Jr. '61
(614) 228-9707 **Schreibeis** George Dennis '98
(614) 466-3578 **Schroeder** Anthony D '91
(614) 224-6220 **Schroeder** Sarah W '84
(614) 227-8839 **Schuck** James P '00
Schuck William B '82
(614) 221-8448 **Schuckmann** Frank '97
(614) 462-5440 **Schuermann** Richard W Jr. '83
(614) 224-1222 **Schuler** Robert C '91
(614) 462-5410 **Schuler** Robert G '87
(614) 222-4735 **Schulte** Kathaleen B '82
(614) 224-1500 **Schultz** David B '04
(614) 444-3900 **Schumacher** Donald C '74
(614) 827-7300 **Schumacher** Mark L '81
(614) 481-6900 **Schuman** John D '93
(614) 462-3194 **Schumann** George M '94
(614) 644-0876 **Schuster** Elizabeth L '97
(614) 436-2022 **Schuster** Richard C '81
(614) 464-6400 **Schuster** Richard D '81
(614) 644-7250 **Schuster** Saundra D '97
(614) 466-4489 **Schwab** Gregory B '92
(614) 466-4510 **Schwade** Joseph A '98
(614) 228-3727 **Schwager** Richard A '88
(614) 224-5205 **Schwallie** Dennis G '78
(614) 488-6005 **Schwart** Charles J '82
(614) 451-2191 **Schwartz** Heidi S '99
Schwartz Joel L '83
(614) 645-8828 **Schwarzwalder** Alan M '70
(614) 488-5008 **Schwenker** Charles V '40
(614) 466-8600 **Schwepe** Alan P '81
(614) 221-7161 **Scoliere** Michael E '86
(614) 224-7844 **Scopetti** Nina P '80
(614) 221-4400 **Scott** Craig P '89
(614) 229-4455 **Scott** David M '97
(614) 466-4034 **Scott** Elizabeth A '91
(614) 222-8686 **Scott** Gregory B '76
Scott James T '02
(614) 221-9790 **Scott** Joseph E '93
(614) 995-2170 **Scott** Keith A '97
(614) 464-0011 **Scott** Paul A '57
(614) 221-1578 **Scott** Paul A Jr. '92
(614) 469-1400 **Scott** Paul O '74
(614) 644-1773 **Scott** Richard M '88
(614) 463-1299 **Scott** Ryan M '97
(614) 222-8686 **Scott Scriven & Wahoff LLP**
(614) 471-7197 **Scott** Theodore Jr. '84
(614) 462-3555 **Scozzie** Nicole M '01
(614) 222-8686 **Scriven** Donald C '74
(614) 464-6400 **Scrutton** Suzanne J '90
(614) 466-3998 **Scull** John M '75
(614) 480-4393 **Scurti-Swain** Tiffany '01
(614) 365-2700 **Seamon** Aaron A '99
(614) 365-4100 **Sechler** Joel E '03
(614) 645-7483 **Seckerson** Cynthia L '95
(614) 224-1222 **Secrest** Jonathan R '02
(614) 728-2759 **See** Charles W '91
(614) 365-2700 **See** P Brian '00
(614) 365-4100 **See** Shana Y '04
(614) 365-2700 **Sefcovic** Paul F '71
(614) 224-7141 **Segal** David M '76
(614) 785-6461 **Segel** Benjamin B '79
(614) 227-2000 **Segelken** Edward M '84
(614) 221-8868 **Segerman** Douglas J '95
(614) 242-4242 **Seguin** James P '84
(614) 451-0694 **Seidel** Edward F Jr. '74
(614) 716-1638 **Seidensticker** John W '90
(614) 469-3939 **Seidt** Andrea L '98
(614) 461-4455 **Seifert** Kristin L '04
(614) 258-4401 **Seigerst** Edward G '93
(614) 460-4648 **Seiple** Stephen B '81
(614) 469-3939 **Selden** Brian G '95
(614) 224-2428 **Seliavski** Lioubov I '03
(614) 463-1986 **Sellman** Jerry B '75
(614) 227-2000 **Seltzer** Martin S '77
(614) 228-1930 **Semons** Tad A '98
(614) 228-1930 **Semons** William A '66
(614) 228-1541 **Senff** Mark D '71
(614) 221-1444 **Sentz** Barbara A '83
(614) 466-9565 **Serio** Joseph P '86
(614) 462-3580 **Serio** Kimberly K '86
(614) 221-3311 **Serrott** Mark A '79
(614) 469-1400 **Seskes** Brandi R '04
(614) 227-2000 **Sestile** Lindsay M '02
(614) 224-1222 **Seth** Nivita '03
(614) 436-3564 **Sethi** Neil K '99
(614) 445-0240 **Settina** William A '97
(614) 464-6400 **Settineri** Michael J '01
(614) 466-4656 **Severance** Gregory S '81
(614) 644-2186 **Severns** William C '75
(614) 224-0370 **Sevis** Chris S '97
(614) 336-3322 **Sewalk** Karen M '94
(614) 228-6061 **Sewards** Frederick A '90
(614) 221-4788 **Sexton** Robert E '61
(614) 221-4788 **Sexton** Thomas P '91
(614) 478-1540 **Seyfang** Matthew G '04
(614) 469-7404 **Sferrella** Nino A '64
(614) 462-5995 **Sgalla-McClure** Cynthia J '01
(614) 462-5630 **Shad** Matthew E '01
(614) 436-5424 **Shady** John M D '73
(614) 462-2270 **Shaffer** Anthony D '95
(614) 464-6400 **Shaffer** Jody G '04
(614) 462-2331 **Shah** Parag H '00
(614) 274-0033 **Shaid** Brett A '99
(614) 466-8054 **Shailer** John L '81
(614) 466-2766 **Shaklee** William V '02
(614) 223-9300 **Shamansky** Robert N '50
(614) 224-9078 **Shamansky** Ronda S '88
(614) 228-4141 **Shamansky** Samuel H '85
(614) 469-3939 **Shambaugh** Phyllis J '93
(614) 462-3555 **Shaner** Nellie J '81
(614) 227-2000 **Shank** Aaron M '98
(614) 326-1217 **Shank** Shirley A '80
(614) 466-6600 **Shannon** Ann M '92
(614) 752-5374 **Shannon** Desiree T '89
(614) 466-4585 **Shantz** Arthur W Jr. '71
(614) 644-3037 **Shapiro** Michael A '74
(614) 716-2927 **Shapiro** Rick J '94
(614) 221-9400 **Sharett** Anthony M '03
(614) 227-2300 **Sharett** Hope M '03
(614) 436-1240 **Sharma** Constance L '78
(614) 469-3939 **Sharp** Autumn L '03
(614) 424-4971 **Sharpe** Thomas E '89
(614) 462-3194 **Shartzer** Donald R '82
(614) 466-7788 **Shaver** Holly T '96
(614) 227-0007 **Shaw** Douglas W '76
(614) 221-6327 **Shaw** Elwin S '76
(614) 223-3070 **Shaw** James C '80
(614) 227-2000 **Shaw** Kyle T '04
(614) 228-6611 **Shaw** Mark A '92
(614) 462-3981 **Shaw** Richard T '81
(614) 457-2029 **Shay** William M '75
(614) 221-1111 **Shayne & Greenwald**
(614) 221-1111 **Shayne** Stanley H '69
(614) 462-3194 **Shea** Robert E '03
(614) 228-1541 **Shearer** William B '94
(614) 466-3998 **Sheehan** George M II '75
(614) 228-1541 **Sheely** Sommer L '03
(614) 728-0742 **Sheeran** Ellen J '81
(614) 462-3555 **Sheeran** Patrick E '76
(614) 466-2995 **Sheets** Kerry K '84
(614) 462-3555 **Sheets** Scott O '03
(614) 944-5134 **Sheffer** Brent A '90
(614) 228-1541 **Sheffer** Karen E '79
Sheffield Douglas M '76
(614) 221-1800 **Sheidlower** David T '86
(614) 237-5414 **Shelko** Susan L '91
(614) 227-2000 **Shepard** Darrell R '81
(614) 237-5414 **Shepard** Laura J '98
(614) 464-1211 **Shepard** Noel C '96
(614) 448-1035 **Shepardson** Cathleen B '96
(614) 621-8888 **Shepardson** Keith J '95
(614) 228-1541 **Shepherd** Amy M '89
(614) 692-9503 **Shepler** Marc A '77
(614) 273-3300 **Sheppard** Alan W '70
(614) 233-6950 **Sheraw** Brett R '01
(614) 644-9267 **Sheridan** James W '89
(614) 221-2001 **Sheridan** Philip H Jr. '73
(614) 221-8448 **Sheridan** Susan G '89
(614) 221-5216 **Sheriff** Mark J '70
(614) 716-0979 **Sherman** Bradley E '97
(614) 466-2166 **Sherman** Jeffrey P '77
(614) 365-2700 **Sherman** Kendra S '97
(614) 946-2259 **Sherman** Michael C '03
(614) 478-6000 **Sherman** Robert P '76
(614) 227-2000 **Sherman** Ryan P '02
(614) 444-8800 **Sherman** Terry K '71
(614) 995-3717 **Sherman** Thomas L '79
(614) 459-5582 **Sherowski** Elizabeth M '96
(614) 462-3194 **Sherwin** Dietra K '04
(614) 227-4803 **Shevelow** Douglas L '04
(614) 224-2428 **Shihab** Gus M '93
(614) 224-2428 **Shihab** Sam M '94
(614) 466-8950 **Shilling** Melissa M '94
(614) 644-8763 **Shillington** Beth C '90
(614) 466-2872 **Shimeall** Kent M '82
(614) 461-0256 **Shinn** Brian E '96
(614) 469-1301 **Shirey** Van R '76
(614) 365-4100 **Shoaff** Shannon M '01
(614) 229-5072 **Shockley** John L '95
(614) 469-5715 **Shoemaker** Brenda S '89
(614) 462-4485 **Shoemaker** Douglas Lyn '85
(614) 469-0100 **Shoemaker Howarth & Taylor LLP**
(614) 469-0100 **Shoemaker** Kevin L '79
(614) 464-1211 **Shook** Kevin T '01
(614) 469-3209 **Short** Jennifer E '98
(614) 464-4100 **Short** Jennifer E '04
(614) 462-5037 **Short** Michael T '98
(614) 442-5626 **Shoub** Grant D '77
(614) 227-2000 **Shouvlin** David P '96
(614) 461-1311 **Shrader** Rebecca R '03
(614) 228-6453 **Shroyer** David I '80
(614) 464-1610 **Shroyer** Gary S '84
Shroyer Melisa S '85
(614) 251-1700 **Shuler** Gordon P '73
(614) 228-4546 **Shuler Plank & Brahm,LPA**
(614) 228-4546 **Shuler** Samantha A '96
(614) 463-9441 **Shumaker Loop & Kendrick,LLP**
(614) 261-6331 **Shuman** Dennis L '77
(614) 365-2700 **Shumate** Alex '75
(614) 365-2700 **Shumate** Keith '91
(614) 292-0611 **Shumate** Kimberly A '92
(614) 469-3939 **Shurte** Matthew R '98
(614) 462-5400 **Shuster** Michele Ann '93
(614) 469-0180 **Shwartz** Myron '67
(614) 451-1580 **Sibbring** Donald A '55
(614) 466-2980 **Siciliano** Anthony D '01
(614) 466-6968 **Sico** Thomas '78
(614) 464-6400 **Sidman** Robert J '68
(614) 464-6400 **Sieck** William A '00
(614) 644-8329 **Sieg** Gary L '94
(614) 227-2000 **Siegel** Bradd N '78
(614) 442-8885 **Siegel Siegel Johnson & Jennings Co, LPA**
(614) 227-2000 **Siegfried** Erin Freund '96
(614) 752-1765 **Siegfried** Gregory M '03
(614) 227-2000 **Siegfried** Jeremy David '99
(614) 228-1541 **Siehl** Richard W '77
(614) 224-6488 **Siewert** Michael H '84
(614) 466-4656 **Sigal** Marc A '84
(614) 781-7686 **Sigall** Herschel M '65
(614) 221-8448 **Sigmund** Thomas J '78
(614) 716-1556 **Signet** Bradford R '81
(614) 227-2333 **Signoracci** Diane M '81
(614) 462-3555 **Sika** Warren J '75
(614) 236-6889 **Sikora** Alison D '99
(614) 827-7300 **Sikora** Charity Seabrook '02
(614) 466-8911 **Sikora** Damian W '02
(614) 461-1311 **Silk** Richard J Jr. '01
(614) 781-7686 **Silveira** Elaine N '00
(614) 221-2718 **Silver** Howard D '76
(614) 466-4605 **Silver** Joseph J '84
(614) 227-4812 **Silverberg** Karl J '04
(614) 249-7015 **Silverman** Karen L '03
(614) 464-2233 **Silverstein** Jerry '85
(614) 466-3417 **Silverstein** Michael L '84
(614) 237-8050 **Silvestri** Ralph S Jr. '92
(614) 249-7618 **Simaitis** David E '89
(614) 224-7291 **Simmons** Gerald G '71
(614) 249-8480 **Simmons** Kent N '85
(614) 258-4267 **Simmons** Pamela A '83
(614) 292-2829 **Simmons** Ric Lee '04
(614) 462-3555 **Simms** Brian E '94
(614) 227-0091 **Simon** William S '91
(614) 324-5959 **Simpson** Carol '04
(614) 227-2354 **Simpson** Richard C '72
(614) 628-8232 **Simpson** William F '82
(614) 224-8374 **Simunic** Nancy H '76
(614) 457-9655 **Singer** Lawrence A '70
(614) 221-4000 **Singh** Bobby '00
(614) 885-0038 **Sinno** Sheila M '87
(614) 464-6400 **Sinnott** Bradley K '86
(614) 387-5600 **Sirkle** Rebecca Haggar '04
(614) 365-2700 **Sisto** James E P '84
(614) 221-7614 **Sites** Richard L '75
(614) 469-3939 **Sjoberg-Witt** Kerstin E '03
(614) 221-9800 **Skaggs** Kimberly M '93
(614) 274-4700 **Skeeles** Rebecca L '99
(614) 462-4281 **Skeens** Edwin L Jr. '87
(614) 462-3194 **Skendelas** Paul '81
(614) 466-4605 **Skidmore** James R '84
(614) 469-3939 **Skingle** Denise L '96
(614) 227-2000 **Skinner** Karen R '99
(614) 466-3998 **Skovron** Richard C '74
(614) 233-6950 **Skrobot** David A '77
(614) 227-8826 **Slagle** Christopher N '04
(614) 228-1144 **Slagle** Ehren W '02
(614) 885-8272 **Slavin** Richard C '79
(614) 462-5047 **Slazyk** Denise R '01
(614) 487-2050 **Slee** Richard A '84
(614) 444-1500 **Slemmer** Greggory D '95
(614) 466-2765 **Slocum** Cynthia D '93
(614) 461-1516 **Slotnick** Lisa M '99
(614) 466-4605 **Slotnick** Marcia T '82
(614) 884-4800 **Slowik** Donald C '80
(614) 466-1292 **Small** Jeffrey L '93
(614) 464-6400 **Smallwood** Carl D '80
Smallwood Connie H '81
(614) 224-5209 **Smallwood** Howard '73
(614) 221-7201 **Smalz** Michael R '89
(614) 466-9581 **Smart** John R '89
(614) 486-3909 **Smiles** Terri-Lynne B '86
(614) 466-6700 **Smiseck** Steven L '93
(614) 462-2247 **Smith** Adam L '99
(614) 249-4323 **Smith** Alan B '69
(614) 464-6400 **Smith** Andrew C '84
(614) 228-8943 **Smith** Aria D '89
(614) 644-6429 **Smith** Brian L '85
(614) 463-9770 **Smith** Charles D '83
(614) 276-8959 **Smith** Charles J '84
(614) 221-0922 **Smith** Craig A '84
(614) 621-8888 **Smith** Craig T '00
(614) 487-1510 **Smith** Daniel S '85
(614) 692-3284 **Smith** Donald L Jr. '86
(614) 464-6400 **Smith** Elizabeth Hanning '03
(614) 728-6069 **Smith** Elizabeth T '84
(614) 466-2980 **Smith** Emily A '03
(614) 365-2700 **Smith** Fredric L '63
(614) 228-1233 **Smith** G Rand '74
(614) 436-0600 **Smith** Gerald L '76
(614) 559-1185 **Smith** Gregory D '96
(614) 221-4255 **Smith & Hale**
(614) 221-4255 **Smith** Harrison W Jr. '50
(614) 228-8400 **Smith** J Gregory '93
(614) 464-6400 **Smith** J Theodore '98
(614) 469-3204 **Smith** Jeffery E '79
(614) 228-6647 **Smith** Jeffrey S '02
(614) 221-4221 **Smith** Julie A '91
(614) 365-2700 **Smith** Julie Rinehart '04
(614) 227-2313 **Smith** Karen D '91
(614) 850-9472 **Smith** Karen Fuller '99
(614) 466-8600 **Smith** Kristin S '94
(614) 464-1626 **Smith** Lee M '78
(614) 466-5394 **Smith** M Kathryn '99
(614) 486-7182 **Smith** Mara C '96
(614) 888-4911 **Smith** Marc D '98
(614) 424-7554 **Smith** Mary K '91
(614) 221-9200 **Smith** Melita L '02
(614) 462-3555 **Smith** Nathan T '99
(614) 466-1814 **Smith** Patricia A '79
(614) 457-5600 **Smith** Patrick F '79
(614) 227-2000 **Smith** Patrick J '65
(614) 466-5394 **Smith** Raymond H Jr. '90
(614) 221-0446 **Smith** Rebecca Ann '96
(614) 644-2658 **Smith** Robert F III '78
(614) 728-5448 **Smith** Robin C '97
(614) 469-7130 **Smith Rolfes & Skavdahl Co,LPA**
(614) 466-7264 **Smith** Ronald L '83
(614) 462-3555 **Smith** Scott A '88
(614) 224-4424 **Smith** Scott E '82
(614) 462-2249 **Smith** Stephen J '71
(614) 462-2308 **Smith** Stephen J Jr. '99
(614) 228-6040 **Smith** Steven L '73
(614) 466-6750 **Smith** Susan L '93
(614) 228-6148 **Smith** Warren J '59
(614) 210-9259 **Smolik** Mark A '87
(614) 253-9000 **Smoot** Dana Dior '03
(614) 799-8899 **Snedaker** Robert H III '81
(614) 464-6400 **Snider** Blake A '99
(614) 227-2150 **Snider** Mark A '04
(614) 221-2121 **Sniderman** Jeffery J '95
(614) 340-2035 **Snitcher McQuain** Jill '99
(614) 463-9770 **Snyder** Bradley L '81
(614) 466-3947 **Snyder** Cynthia R '84
(614) 466-8600 **Snyder** Melinda Ryans '04
(614) 228-6107 **Snyder** Meredith A '95
(614) 463-9441 **Snyder** Michael A '98
(614) 466-3013 **Snyder** Patricia E '78
(614) 461-4455 **Snyder** Ronald H '80
Snyder Timothy J '95
(614) 222-8686 **Soards** Karla S '98
(614) 249-7610 **Soden** Glenn W '77
(614) 292-5354 **Solomon** Robert Lee Jr. '89
(614) 469-5715 **Solove** Deborah A '81
(614) 444-9414 **Solove** Ronald L '70
(614) 221-2121 **Soltis** Steve M '68
(614) 752-9038 **Sommer** Joseph C '83
(614) 258-6100 **Somos** Tom '99
(614) 460-4640 **Sonderman** Andrew J '79
(614) 466-3998 **Sonnen** Craig A '75
(614) 728-7189 **Sorem** Peter R '78
(614) 901-3376 **Sornabala** Jasmine '93
(614) 462-3555 **Soulas** Nick A Jr. '93
(614) 228-5822 **Sova** Rosemary L '84
(614) 464-1877 **Sowald** Beatrice K '66
(614) 464-1877 **Sowald** Heather Gay '79
(614) 464-1877 **Sowald Sowald & Clouse**
(614) 466-6696 **Sowell** Lasheyl N '03
(614) 466-3615 **Sowers** Amber D '04
(614) 466-4510 **Spahia-Carducci** Mary L '86
(614) 331-9104 **Spainhoward** Rebecca A '89
(614) 624-7359 **Spalding** Jennifer M '97
(614) 644-7257 **Spalding** Sloan T '97
(614) 248-0463 **Spangler** Melissa D '97
(614) 645-8739 **Sparks** Danielle R '91
(614) 469-5715 **Spartis** Gary L '79
(614) 222-4734 **Spater** Alexander M '73
(614) 644-6338 **Speakman** Claudia J '76
(614) 462-5530 **Speaks** George E '92
(614) 466-3627 **Speelman** Eleanor L '78
(614) 249-3671 **Spencer** Gilda L '93
(614) 227-2300 **Spencer** Maria E '94
(614) 228-9707 **Sperl** Kenneth J '02
(614) 227-2342 **Spialter** David C '82
(614) 221-7272 **Spiert** Kenneth R '87
(614) 719-1565 **Spina** Anthony '98
(614) 485-1800 **Spirito** Maryellen C '83
(614) 224-2104 **Spiroff** Christopher J '89
(614) 227-2315 **Sprader** Bobbie S '94
(614) 466-7046 **Sprague** James R '89
(614) 224-1222 **Sprankle** Tricia A '99
(614) 847-1007 **Spratley** William A '73
(614) 327-4636 **Sprayberry** Brad A '95
(614) 224-8374 **Springer** Jennifer L '01
(614) 224-8339 **Sproat** John W Jr. '87
(614) 228-8575 **Spurlock** Michael '74
(614) 227-2396 **Squeglia** Elisabeth A '79
(614) 628-6880 **Squillace** Michael L '80
(614) 723-2022 **Squillace** Vincent J III '02
(614) 228-6528 **Squire** Percy '81
(614) 365-2700 **Squire Sanders & Dempsey LLP**
(614) 469-5715 **Squires** Douglas W '01
(614) 463-4212 **Srsic** Daniel W '94
(614) 485-2010 **Stafford** Robert G '68
(614) 469-3939 **Stalnaker** R Alan '04
(614) 252-7601 **Stamatakos** John C '74
(614) 387-9030 **Stamp** Jennifer L '03
(614) 229-4753 **Stamp** Matthew E '98
(614) 221-2121 **Stankunas** Jeffrey A '00
(614) 466-3998 **Stanley** Dina R '92
(614) 221-4000 **Stanton** Elizabeth M '82
(614) 469-5715 **Stark** John J '03
(614) 228-1541 **Stark** Lisa R '02
(614) 462-4938 **Starkoff** Alan G '75
(614) 575-8440 **Stasiewicz** Suzanne M '88
(614) 466-2166 **Stauffer** Timothy D '82
(614) 644-8340 **Stavridis** John D '85
(614) 462-3555 **Stead** Douglas P '84
(614) 644-2438 **Stead** Susan T '84
(614) 228-9058 **Stebbins** David C '78
(614) 221-1000 **Stebbins** Steven C '00
Stedman Richard R '64
(614) 445-8870 **Steele** Athornia '77
(614) 462-3194 **Steele** Rebecca S '89
(614) 224-9223 **Steele** Thomas L '78
(614) 461-4455 **Steele** William J '83
(614) 279-9348 **Stefanelli** Luisa V '79
(614) 225-8757 **Steffes** James B '01
(614) 462-5495 **Steger** S Martijn '83

(614) 228-7888 **Stehura** Paul A '82
(614) 221-9100 **Stein Chapin & Associates LLC**
(614) 221-9100 **Stein** David K '89
(614) 469-5737 **Stein** Lesley E '03
(614) 224-7707 **Stein** Stanley R '71
(614) 221-1166 **Stein** Sydney DeWitt '03
(614) 466-3930 **Steiner** Paul J '81
(614) 224-8374 **Steinhoff** Rainer E '92
(614) 719-8770 **Steinkamp** Amy D '01
(614) 292-2631 **Steinke** Matthew R '00
(614) 221-7833 **Stelzer** Lawrence J Jr. '91
(614) 227-2000 **Stemm** Mark S '84
(614) 466-3379 **Stempfer** Robert P '87
(614) 577-9005 **Stempien** James H Jr. '87
(614) 444-5606 **Stephan** Randall L '88
(614) 227-2000 **Stephen** John M '79
(614) 466-9537 **Stephens** Eric B '94
(614) 227-2594 **Stephens** Lawrence G Jr. '81
(614) 227-2000 **Stephenson** H Grant '79
(614) 463-9790 **Stepter** Rayl L '90
(614) 462-5457 **Stern** Geoffrey '68
(614) 466-8600 **Steuk** Sally A '74
(614) 466-8911 **Stevens** Lori M '02
(614) 466-7046 **Stevenson** Elaine K '99
(614) 451-6313 **Stevenson** James S '95
(614) 469-6860 **Stevenson** Louis '75
(614) 644-1422 **Stevenson** Mary D '75
(614) 221-3938 **Steward** Anne C '04
(614) 221-7663 **Stewart** Jackie L '80
(614) 220-8625 **Stewart** Joseph R '73
(614) 278-5815 **Stewart** Lynne L '84
(614) 424-4692 **Stewart** Todd A '02
(614) 341-2393 **Stichter** Philip W '66
(614) 466-4320 **Stickan** Lisa M '01
(614) 462-3555 **Stickel** Paul M '79
(614) 469-3939 **Stiles** Kelli Jones '03
(614) 246-8257 **Still** Nan M '87
(614) 221-0240 **Stiltner** Jeffrey W '95
(614) 462-2332 **Stine** Joshua N '03
(614) 221-3155 **Stinson** Dane '81
(614) 445-6700 **Stith** Robin S '80
(614) 221-1111 **Stitt** Scott J '01
(614) 275-5871 **Stitt** Willie C '79
(614) 387-9033 **Stock** Christopher D '02
(614) 227-2323 **Stock** Elizabeth C '02
(614) 223-9300 **Stock** John F '81
(614) 469-3939 **Stock** Jonathan Kent '95
(614) 228-5931 **Stoffers** Robert H '82
(614) 628-8000 **Stolar** Margaret M '93
(614) 464-6400 **Stoll** Sheryl Clark '98
(614) 225-2024 **Stoll** William F Jr. '73
(614) 462-2255 **Stoller** Eric M '99
(614) 461-0256 **Stone** Amy C '92
(614) 466-5394 **Stone** Jill E '79
(614) 462-3896 **Stone** Thomas A '85
(614) 280-8769 **Stonecipher Price** Sheryl '75
(614) 466-6849 **Stoneking** Janet K '96
(614) 888-3560 **Stonerock** Bobbie J '93
(614) 480-5181 **Stopa** John R '94
(614) 249-9001 **Storck** Gail L '99
(614) 249-9086 **Storts** Mark E '04
(614) 227-8861 **Stout** Matthew L '99
(614) 752-1769 **Stout** Thomas A '77
(614) 221-8500 **Stovall** Richard K '85
(614) 487-4464 **Stover** Stephan W '75
(614) 466-7447 **Strait** Anne B '83
(614) 462-3194 **Strait** David L '01
(614) 242-4242 **Stranges** Jodelle N '01
(614) 847-9843 **Strasser** Thomas F '84
(614) 464-6400 **Strause** Edgar A III '54
(614) 462-5048 **Strauss** Catherine L '00
(614) 221-8401 **Strautz** Elizabeth M '97
(614) 438-4962 **Strayer** Brian S '90
(614) 228-4480 **Strayer** Herbert N Jr. '03
(614) 880-1907 **Strayer** Susan L '96
(614) 224-0200 **Streb** Joseph S '84
(614) 466-6750 **Strelou** Karen L '84
Stremski Janet R '93
(614) 466-2872 **Strigari** Frank M '04
(614) 228-6345 **Strip** Asriel C '60
(614) 228-6345 **Strip Hoppers Leithart McGrath & Terlecky Co LPA**
(614) 228-0207 **Strohm** Robin L '04
(614) 644-3037 **Stroup** Catherine A '89
(614) 324-5929 **Stuckey** Kent D '82
(614) 222-8686 **Stucko** James K Jr. '93
(614) 466-2766 **Studer** Raymond J '76
(614) 228-6131 **Sturges** Scott F '82
(614) 365-2700 **Sturtz** Craig A '92
(614) 365-2706 **Stutz** Heather L '04
(614) 464-6400 **Styduhar** Robert J '79
(614) 365-2700 **Stype** Gregory W '82
(614) 464-1880 **Subramaniam** Radha '01
(614) 462-3830 **Suffron** Benjamin F III '78
(614) 221-3155 **Sugar** Anthony J '91
(614) 462-5422 **Sugarman** Roger P '75
(614) 462-5476 **Suh** Jean Hinte '96
(614) 449-1200 **Suhr** Robert W '70
(614) 462-3194 **Sukienik** Harvey '91
(614) 462-4680 **Sullivan** Angela M '02
(614) 466-6541 **Sullivan** Christine A '79
(614) 460-4689 **Sullivan** Cynthia L '97
(614) 365-2700 **Sullivan** Johnathan E '00
(614) 224-8374 **Sullivan** Megan L '03
(614) 227-2337 **Sullivan** Michael F '67
(614) 466-7447 **Sullivan** Susan M '77
(614) 443-3930 **Sully** Ira B '74
(614) 464-6400 **Sumi** Christopher E '02
(614) 365-2700 **Summer** Fred A '74
(614) 645-7385 **Sumner** John H '80
(614) 227-2300 **Sun** Chuan '04
(614) 228-1200 **Sunbury** Gerald T '74
(614) 228-3822 **Sundberg & Fesenmyer,LLC**
(614) 228-3822 **Sundberg** Steven D '99
(614) 469-3207 **Sunderland** John T '83
(614) 462-5448 **Susalla** Malinda L '01
(614) 466-2872 **Susec** Martin D '96
(614) 221-2121 **Suter** Douglas J '88
(614) 461-1551 **Sutker** Dory A '78
(614) 248-6478 **Sutter** Andrew I '83
(614) 227-2000 **Sutter** Karl J '82
(614) 466-4510 **Sutter** Michelle T '81
(614) 248-6080 **Sutton** Gregory E '92
(614) 486-0297 **Sutton** Joseph R '95
(614) 462-3194 **Sutton** Maximillian C '98
(614) 469-1963 **Swaim** Stephen '79
Swain Paul A '02
(614) 716-1691 **Swaneck** Anthony J III '96
(614) 227-4895 **Swank** Christopher N '02
(614) 459-1355 **Swanson** Daniel T '86
(614) 246-2511 **Swanson** Kim L '72
(614) 644-7342 **Swart** Gregory W '80
(614) 469-3939 **Swatsler** Todd S '81
(614) 469-7130 **Sway** M Andrew '96
(614) 461-1100 **Swedlow Butler Levine Lewis & Dye Co,LPA**
(614) 461-1100 **Swedlow** Gerald H '61
(614) 466-3033 **Sweet** Sherry L '95
(614) 223-9300 **Sweterlitsch** Martha J '83
(614) 462-2225 **Swetnam** Daniel R '82
(614) 463-9770 **Swick** Jeffrey D '85
(614) 227-8850 **Swift** Betsy A '88
(614) 464-6400 **Swift** David A '78
(614) 227-2000 **Swinerton** Jenny T '04
(614) 443-7455 **Swinford** Leslie B Jr. '75
(614) 462-3555 **Swisher** Laura Rayce '99
(614) 221-3536 **Swisher** Sarah J '99
(614) 462-3555 **Swisher** Zachary M '03
(614) 233-4765 **Switzer** Thomas E '97
(614) 854-6680 **Sydney** Kristen J '87
(614) 462-5483 **Sykes** Kevin L '79
(614) 228-6131 **Szolosi** Michael R Sr. '69
(614) 644-1614 **Szudy** Katherine A '03
(614) 464-6400 **Szykowny** Thomas E '82
(614) 249-7840 **Tabb** Kimberly B '00
(614) 221-2838 **Taft Stettinius & Hollister LLP**
(614) 464-6400 **Taggart** Brent C '88
(614) 464-6400 **Taggart** Thomas M '65
(614) 466-0570 **Tait** Amy C '98
(614) 469-3939 **Tait** Mary E '99
(614) 464-6400 **Tait** Robert E '73
(614) 488-7590 **Talbott** Harold B '52
(614) 444-4455 **Talbott** Harold B '85
(614) 444-4455 **Talbott & Rinehart**
(614) 719-3719 **Talebi** Denise J '93
(614) 228-5151 **Tallan** Mitchell M '84
(614) 469-3200 **Tammaro** Bradford L '85
(614) 241-2181 **Taneff** Thomas N '88
(614) 239-4017 **Tanner** Robert E Jr. '89
(614) 644-9402 **Tannous** Marlo B '88
(614) 227-2000 **Tannous** Robert '87
(614) 447-1698 **Tanoury** John L '77
(614) 677-0281 **Tantra** Dina A '94
(614) 443-8000 **Taps** Richard T '78
(614) 463-9770 **Tarian** Brian A '82
(614) 464-6400 **Tarpy** Thomas M '69
(614) 462-2304 **Tarullo** Michael D '89
(614) 644-0876 **Tassie** James G '95
Tate Davie Jr. '83
(614) 469-3939 **Tate** Tracy C '03
(614) 466-3180 **Tate** Vivian P '92
(614) 224-2426 **Taylor** Amy S '83
(614) 462-3555 **Taylor** Cynthia L '88
(614) 228-8833 **Taylor** Daniel G '89
(614) 227-2000 **Taylor** Heather N '03
(614) 891-8422 **Taylor** James R '00
(614) 222-8686 **Taylor** Jodie M '95
(614) 228-9707 **Taylor** Josefina B '00
(614) 227-2000 **Taylor** K Michael '69
(614) 227-2000 **Taylor** M Todd '00
(614) 221-5216 **Taylor** Mary TenCyck '85
(614) 227-2317 **Taylor** Maureen P '97
(614) 469-0100 **Taylor** Robert H '74
(614) 462-3555 **Taylor** Steven L '90
(614) 443-3848 **Teaford** Hamilton J '66
(614) 263-4205 **Teaford** Murray R '89
(614) 462-5200 **Teague** Rodney B '74
(614) 358-8056 **Teeples** M Brandon '03
(614) 221-2121 **Teetor** John S '77
(614) 827-7676 **Teeven** William G '85
(614) 258-1969 **Tenenbaum** Lee J '78
(614) 621-1500 **Terakedis** J Troy '96
(614) 462-5002 **Terakedis** John Jr. '70
(614) 227-2000 **Terapak** Richard G '72
(614) 273-0448 **Terbeek** Jeffrey L '73
(614) 228-6345 **Terlecky** Myron N '84
(614) 644-9280 **Termuhlen** Maureen A '83
(614) 462-3555 **Termuhlen** Richard A II '83
(614) 677-9352 **Terveer** Thomas B '83
(614) 222-4735 **Terzian** Barbara A '75
(614) 227-2000 **Teteris** Jean Y '75
(614) 466-4605 **Thambuswamy** Ramesh '93
(614) 224-9221 **Thaxton** Larry R '97
(614) 249-9847 **Theiss** Douglas J '81
(614) 462-3643 **Theller** Robert T '98
(614) 466-9939 **Thernes** Linda J '89
(614) 227-2000 **Thien** John Kenneth '99
(614) 462-3555 **Thies** Arnold P '02
(614) 213-5832 **Tholt** Rita E '89
(614) 461-1311 **Thomas** Amy S '01
(614) 464-6400 **Thomas** Bethany R '02
(614) 280-1860 **Thomas** Collin N '95
(614) 228-4141 **Thomas** David H '99
(614) 464-6400 **Thomas** Duke W '64
(614) 252-2141 **Thomas** Fred Jr. '77
(614) 252-8788 **Thomas** Isabella D '88
(614) 221-2331 **Thomas** J Patrick '77
(614) 227-0366 **Thomas** James D '88
(614) 719-8813 **Thomas** Jodi L '02
(614) 462-5453 **Thomas** John R '68
(614) 252-8788 **Thomas** Larry W '87
(614) 464-6400 **Thomas** Michael R '85
(614) 462-5430 **Thomas** Patsy A '94
(614) 466-2980 **Thomas** Peter M '88
(614) 466-8600 **Thomas** Rebecca L '96
(614) 221-4400 **Thomas** Warner M Jr. '79
(614) 249-6768 **Thompson** Bruce R '85
(614) 728-7443 **Thompson** Christine E '91
Thompson David P '00
(614) 466-3934 **Thompson** Diann K '84
(614) 461-9000 **Thompson** Harold Lee '75
(614) 469-3200 **Thompson Hine LLP**
(614) 221-7777 **Thompson** Janice C '86
(614) 280-1500 **Thompson** Jeffrey G '94
(614) 236-6245 **Thompson** Jenifer S '02
(614) 462-3555 **Thompson** Lisa F '97
(614) 424-6760 **Thompson Meier & Dersom**
(614) 462-3118 **Thompson** Myron A '96
(614) 224-9207 **Thompson** Paul C '02
(614) 645-8226 **Thompson** Susan E '01
(614) 424-6760 **Thompson** Thomas D '71
(614) 825-4835 **Thompson** Toby G '82
(614) 644-3490 **Thomson** Anne E '92
(614) 227-2000 **Thomson** Terry L '03
(614) 224-3838 **Thorman** William A III '88
(614) 227-2000 **Thornton** Brett P '01
(614) 644-9110 **Thornton** Gregg B '91
(614) 365-2700 **Thurston** Pamela H '87
(614) 469-3225 **Ticknor** Charles E III '89
(614) 365-9900 **Tigges** Steven W '81
(614) 728-4639 **Tilton** Richard J '85
(614) 466-5394 **Timken** Kyle E '99
(614) 728-0449 **Timms** Lisa H '99
(614) 224-3303 **Tinianow** Jerome C '80
(614) 501-8012 **Tippins** Adria M '02
Tipton John G '93
(614) 644-5441 **Titchell** Alan L '71
(614) 221-2838 **Titus** Frank A '79
(614) 466-5394 **Tkacz** Ruth L '93
(614) 645-7483 **Tobias** Melanie R '99
(614) 645-8940 **Tobias** Robert S '95
(614) 466-7264 **Tobin** Susan G '81
(614) 242-4333 **Todaro** Frank E '87
(614) 485-1800 **Todaro** Gerald J '74
(614) 224-0933 **Todd** Adam R '04
(614) 365-2700 **Todd** William M '76
(614) 228-4141 **Tome** Lisa M '01
(614) 628-8000 **Tomkies** Michael C '86
(614) 262-9940 **Tomko** Carole W '81
(614) 258-1476 **Tongren** Robert S '72
(614) 431-1500 **Tonks** Paul H '96
(614) 224-4331 **Tonti** Alfred P '54
(614) 487-1630 **Toomey** Michael J '98
(614) 336-4401 **Tootle** Heather W '96
(614) 228-7747 **Tootle** Thomas C '93
(614) 486-4805 **Topper** Richard D Jr. '79
(614) 644-3037 **Tormey** Edmund J '90
(614) 261-7400 **Tornstrom** Megan M '00
(614) 221-1216 **Torriero** Dolores F '95
Totten Mark S '82
(614) 464-6400 **Tour** Jeffrey H '93
(614) 466-6859 **Touris** Jaimee L '91
(614) 463-9441 **Tournoux** Katie L '02
(614) 249-6184 **Towarnicky** John M '92
(614) 475-3493 **Tower** Jessie M '95
(614) 825-4029 **Townsend** Maureen M '00
(614) 466-7046 **Tracy** Roger W '64
(614) 227-2000 **Trafford** Kathleen McManus '79
(614) 227-2000 **Trafford** Robert W '77
(614) 213-7643 **Trail** Christopher D '81
(614) 248-7597 **Trail** Judith D '82
(614) 466-3947 **Tran** Terry D '04
(614) 292-2689 **Travalio** Gregory M '85
(614) 644-8969 **Travis** Michael '93
(614) 326-3200 **Travis** Paul D '73
Trefethern Randall J '95
(614) 228-3715 **Treneff** Craig P '81
(614) 292-0582 **Trethewey** Virginia M '77
(614) 781-8896 **Tribble** Judith E '01
(614) 224-8187 **Trimble** Thomas W '83
(614) 227-8918 **Trishman** Natalie C '02
(614) 752-1773 **Trout** Gregory C '78
(614) 466-8600 **Troutman** Mark H '03
(614) 466-5394 **Troutman** Rachel G '03
(614) 445-9293 **Troxell** Richard H '96
(614) 221-1511 **Truax** William H Jr. '76
(614) 469-3939 **True** Mary R '90
(614) 443-7000 **Truitt** Kevin J '04
(614) 228-9707 **Tsibouris** Dino '94
(614) 462-3570 **Tsitouris** Anne K '75
(614) 464-2211 **Tsitouris** Chris C '72
(614) 464-2211 **Tsitouris** Chris C '03
(614) 466-4882 **Tuch** Socrates H '95
(614) 464-6400 **Tucker** Jennifer L '04
(614) 466-5038 **Tucker** Jo-Ellyn H '02
(614) 223-9300 **Tucker** Mark D '86
(614) 336-4020 **Tugend** Stephen E '91
(614) 227-2000 **Tulencik** Aaron T '00
(614) 462-5464 **Tullis** Timothy T '89
Tulman Elizabeth E '82
(614) 227-2000 **Tumen** David A '81
(614) 227-8837 **Tunnell** Kurtis A '87
(614) 469-0100 **Turano** David A '71
(614) 223-9300 **Turk** Jennifer M '01
(614) 221-3155 **Turner** Jameel S '04
(614) 752-4260 **Turner** James N '78
(614) 225-8700 **Turner** Pete S '01
(614) 221-9400 **Turner** Tracy L '98
(614) 469-3939 **Turoff** S James '04
(614) 292-0611 **Tuttle** Amanda L '02
(614) 644-9274 **Tuttle** Cheryl L '86
(614) 224-8166 **Twyford & Donahey**
(614) 224-8166 **Twyford** Thomas L '65
(614) 221-1341 **Tyack Blackmore & Liston Co,PA**
(614) 445-0793 **Tyack** David B '82
(614) 221-1341 **Tyack** James P '00
(614) 221-1341 **Tyack** Jonathan T '96
(614) 466-6858 **Tyack** Matthew J '98
(614) 221-1341 **Tyack** Thomas M '65
(614) 253-7800 **Tyson** Renny J '81
(614) 547-0350 **Ucker** Timothy J '67
(614) 527-8979 **Uhlmann** Beth A '97
(614) 253-2532 **Ullmann** Victoria E '77
(614) 228-8400 **Ulmer & Berne LLP**
(614) 462-7450 **Ulrich** Matthew E '03
(614) 475-4493 **Umpleby** John I '74
(614) 466-4425 **Underhill** Aaron L '00
(614) 214-0459 **Underwood** Charles D Jr. '80
(614) 227-2000 **Underwood** Michael Joseph '80
(614) 340-3444 **Unger** Paul J '95
(614) 462-5487 **Union** Stephanie P '99
(614) 469-8000 **Urvan** Sean J '03
(614) 464-2704 **Utz** Richard A '77
(614) 281-3985 **Vaas** Jonathan M '04
(614) 221-2223 **Valentine** Anne M '82
(614) 461-1311 **Valentine** Michael J '87
(614) 644-2640 **Vamos** Stephen J III '81
(614) 336-3861 **Vance** Catherine E '97
(614) 221-8317 **Van De Mark** Julie A '82
(614) 645-8288 **VanDerKarr** Scott D '82
(614) 451-4224 **Van Dervoort** John W '54
(614) 451-0480 **van Deusen** Edwin H II '70
(614) 469-3286 **VandeWerken** Jerry '74
(614) 462-5372 **Van Dyke** Omia N '83
(614) 221-8668 **Van Dyne** Jean E Jr. '72
(614) 224-8187 **Van Eman** Timothy L '81
(614) 466-3180 **VanHeyde** George J '76
(614) 228-1541 **Van Heyde** J Stephen '68
(614) 463-9444 **VanHorn** Terry D '70
(614) 469-3200 **Van Hoy** Martha S '04
(614) 469-3939 **Van Kley** Jack A '79
(614) 485-1800 **Van Ligten** Peter F '96
(614) 292-0611 **Vannatta** Julie D '87
(614) 464-6400 **Vannatta** Mark E '87
(614) 644-0089 **VanNorman** John S '00
(614) 644-3037 **Vanterpool** Donald L '87
(614) 227-2000 **Van Vlerah** Darin L '03
(614) 220-9440 **Varanese** John R '90
(614) 469-3243 **Varchetti** Glen A '99
(614) 224-1222 **Vargo** James G '97
(614) 221-8004 **Vargo** Thomas W '72
(614) 645-7385 **Varhus** Alan P '74
(614) 224-8374 **Varnado** Leslie Jr. '74
(614) 644-7739 **Varveris** Nicholas M '91
(614) 258-6000 **Varwig** Audrey E '01
(614) 464-6400 **Vascura** Chelsey M '03
(614) 464-6400 **Vaughn** Jonathan R '82
(614) 387-9530 **Vaughn** Robert '98
(614) 466-2034 **Vawter** Jana R '90
(614) 846-2000 **Veatch** Alan K '82
(614) 552-0200 **Veigel** Thomas L '69
Velayudhan Krishna K '02
(614) 677-2366 **Venard** Catherine L '00
(614) 466-3615 **Vendel** Eric P '96
(614) 365-2700 **Venesy** Bryan J '88
(614) 752-0960 **Venters** Ellen W '00
(614) 462-3194 **Venters** Yeura R '78
(614) 292-1575 **Verdun** Vincene '90
(614) 466-3206 **Verich** Michael G '84
(614) 466-5610 **Verlaney** Georgia L '99
(614) 227-2000 **Verrett** Kendall S '03
(614) 523-4094 **Verwohlt** Jeffrey H '93
(614) 752-8683 **Vest** Pamela J '93
(614) 466-5394 **Vickers** Richard J '86
(614) 224-8160 **Vickery** Byron L '65
(614) 224-8160 **Vickery Riehl & Alter**
(614) 543-1305 **Vidmar** John M '03
(614) 242-4242 **Viets** James D '83
(614) 221-2121 **Vincent** John E Jr. '99
(614) 644-7250 **Vincent** Rachelle Peloquin '00
(614) 262-8283 **Virgil** Albert E '88
(614) 466-2766 **Vitale** Dale T '78
(614) 486-0297 **Vitale** Frank A '97
(614) 481-6000 **Vitale** Sheila P '97
(614) 436-0539 **Vivyan** Thomas F '71
(614) 481-6500 **Voelker** Dirken T '56
(614) 481-6500 **Voelker** Dow T '87
(614) 744-0132 **Vogel** John W '99
(614) 221-4400 **Volkema** Daniel R '79
(614) 221-4400 **Volkema Thomas Miller Burkett Scott & Merry, LPA**
(614) 466-4314 **Vollmer** Sara R '88
(614) 486-5392 **Voltolini** Bruno E '57
(614) 486-5392 **Voltolini** John P '86
(614) 486-5392 **Voltolini** Mathew J '88
(614) 242-4242 **Vonau** James M '81
(614) 825-4029 **Vornbrock** Kelley L '03
(614) 227-2394 **Vorys** Anne Sferra '85
(614) 464-6400 **Vorys** John C '80
(614) 464-6400 **Vorys Sater Seymour & Pease LLP**
(614) 464-6400 **Vorys** Webb I '85
(614) 466-6092 **Vorys** Yolanda V '81
(614) 487-5900 **Vourlis** Simina '90
(614) 462-3194 **Wachsman** Elizabeth E '03
(614) 431-1500 **Wachtman** Andrew D '93
(614) 415-7495 **Wachtman** Kristen A '93
(614) 466-3998 **Wachunas** Robert J '68
(614) 463-9518 **Waddy** John W Jr. '79
(614) 445-9300 **Wade** E Roberta '91
(614) 462-2276 **Wade** Felix C '77
(614) 466-3998 **Wade** Jared W '98
(614) 236-6549 **Wade** Robert J Jr. '72
(614) 228-1541 **Wadman** Gary A '85
(614) 228-5225 **Wafer** Lisa A '01
(614) 424-7927 **Wagenbach** Adam J '73
(614) 466-3016 **Wagenbrenner** Diane L '00
(614) 466-0281 **Wagner** Steven A '96
(614) 481-4480 **Wagoner** Jacob D '01
(614) 242-4333 **Wagoner** Robert J '98
(614) 442-1953 **Wahl** Eric M '01
(614) 224-8374 **Wahl** Janice K '04
(614) 365-2700 **Wahl** Jeffrey R '02
(614) 464-6400 **Wahl** Kyong W Nahm '00
(614) 464-6400 **Wahl** Travis J '00
(614) 621-1500 **Wahlers** Kristopher L '91
(614) 222-8686 **Wahoff** William J '82
(614) 227-3087 **Waid** Elizabeth O '85
(614) 221-3155 **Walden** Jon C '94
(614) 227-2339 **Walker** Charles H '76
(614) 466-7447 **Walker** Eric A '88
Walker Kris H '90
(614) 221-2838 **Walker** Lawrence D '73
(614) 466-6901 **Walker** Paul D '76
(614) 263-8750 **Walker** Richard L '66
(614) 469-3939 **Walker** Scott C '94
(614) 466-2872 **Walker** Susan C '90
(614) 340-8820 **Wall** Andrew J '93
(614) 628-6880 **Wall** Kirk M '93
(614) 365-4100 **Wallace** David A '85
(614) 221-3821 **Wallace** Paul L '80
(614) 228-2300 **Waller** Barry A '74
(614) 221-2121 **Walls** Jessica K '03
(614) 464-2392 **Walsh** Christopher R '95
(614) 719-8512 **Walsh** Lyndsay M '03
(614) 461-5600 **Walter** Robert J '72
(614) 464-3034 **Walter** Todd A '04
(614) 565-1050 **Walters** Ben R '88
(614) 628-6880 **Walters** Marilena R '84
(614) 469-3939 **Walters** Randall M '78
(614) 469-3939 **Walters** Ryan D '03
(614) 466-7447 **Walters** Sally A '80
(614) 246-4054 **Walton** Kelley K '01
(614) 462-3555 **Walton** William R II '01
(614) 462-3580 **Wambaugh** Carrie L '00
(614) 644-7250 **Wampler** Elizabeth Cole '02

(614) 227-4889 **Wampler** G Samuel '02
(614) 645-8815 **Wander** Michael H '96
(614) 466-6700 **Wang** Thomas L '77
(614) 466-0892 **Wanless** Brock A '03
(614) 464-2392 **Warburton** Dick M Jr. '61
(614) 621-1500 **Ward** Christopher M '03
(614) 224-9223 **Ward Kaps Bainbridge Maurer & Melvin**
(614) 466-1540 **Ward** Leora A '83
(614) 466-4320 **Ward** Lucas C '03
(614) 224-9223 **Ward** Paul F '39
(614) 466-2752 **Ware** John P '93
(614) 752-6417 **Warheit** Melissa A '79
(614) 227-2000 **Warner** Charles C '70
(614) 229-3888 **Warner** Matthew D '02
(614) 224-6000 **Warner** Patrick G '95
(614) 237-1221 **Warner** Robert S '80
(614) 221-3821 **Warner** Roger '81
(614) 221-5375 **Warner** Sheryl D '96
(614) 466-5610 **Warner** Stephanie L '00
(614) 436-5880 **Warrick** Glenn S '96
(614) 461-4455 **Washburn** Robert L Jr. '77
(614) 223-9300 **Washbush** Thomas C '91
(614) 221-2400 **Washington** Gloria B '91
(614) 789-5921 **Wasson** Christopher E '97
(614) 228-8400 **Watchorn** Christine E '03
(614) 462-5200 **Waterfield** Melissa A '00
(614) 227-2378 **Waterman** Charles H III '77
(614) 224-5205 **Waterman** Charles H IV '01
(614) 466-6696 **Waterman** Gerald H '74
(614) 898-2696 **Waterman** Joseph '59
(614) 228-4546 **Watkins** David '92
(614) 444-3036 **Watson** David C Jr. '85
(614) 443-1221 **Watson** James E '88
(614) 486-8827 **Watson** Robert T '87
(614) 644-7233 **Watson** Stephanie L '94
(614) 461-4455 **Watson** Sue A '97
(614) 464-6400 **Watt** Kristin L '89
(614) 221-4000 **Watters** Elizabeth J '91
(614) 464-6400 **Watts** Tamara J '02
(614) 464-6400 **Wautier** Nathan J '03
(614) 462-3580 **Weakley** Kyle D '03
Weaston Daniel Q '80
(614) 236-6531 **Weatherspoon** Floyd D '85
(614) 466-4605 **Weaver** Diane M '77
(614) 221-2121 **Weaver** Mark R '95
(614) 224-5811 **Weaver** Ruthellen Q '85
(614) 464-6400 **Webb-Lawton** Nina I '96
(614) 224-4149 **Webber** Marci L '97
(614) 462-5415 **Weber** Christopher J '92
(614) 227-2300 **Weber** Maggie F '03
(614) 466-2091 **Weber** Randall S '91
(614) 221-4000 **Weber** Todd A '96
(614) 464-6400 **Webner** Robert N '85
(614) 461-1156 **Webster** Geoffrey E '75
(614) 464-6400 **Webster** Norton R '52
(614) 466-6750 **Webster** Victoria G '77
(614) 224-9207 **Wecker** Andrew P '96
(614) 464-1626 **Weeden** Elizabeth S '89
(614) 241-5550 **Weeden** Eric L '87
(614) 221-7201 **Weeks** Thomas W '75
(614) 466-7264 **Weeks** Winnifred N '87
(614) 939-9822 **Wegener** Oliver H '03
(614) 365-2700 **Wehrer** Greg R '97
(614) 466-4605 **Weibl** Mona L '85
(614) 462-1057 **Weidenhamer** Evan R '99
(614) 645-7385 **Weidman** Nancy L '88
(614) 895-2000 **Weiland** Kurt H '76
(614) 221-4286 **Weiler** Robert J '83
(614) 464-6400 **Weimer** John B '89
(614) 645-7483 **Weinberg** Denice '92
(614) 866-1640 **Weiner** Jerry '52
(614) 443-6581 **Weiner** Samuel B '73
(614) 466-0507 **Weinfeld** Jennifer L '00
(614) 462-5450 **Weinstein** Melvin D '73
(614) 228-4200 **Weis** Amy Jo '96
(614) 464-6400 **Weis** Anthony D '99
(614) 228-1717 **Weis** Karen D '01
(614) 487-4414 **Weisenberg** William K '71
(614) 265-7062 **Weiser** Joan C '79
(614) 459-5600 **Weislogel** George S '80
(614) 462-3194 **Weisman** J S '90
(614) 466-4425 **Weisman** Lori J '84
(614) 462-5139 **Weisman** Robert D '75
(614) 431-0781 **Weiss** Daniel K '85
(614) 464-0381 **Weiss** Eugene P '72
(614) 228-6674 **Weiss** Stephen M '68
(614) 224-4155 **Weisz** Michael J '82
(614) 462-2800 **Welch** Christopher S '92
(614) 236-9066 **Welch** Derek W '01
(614) 223-2431 **Welch** Mark A '77
(614) 462-3555 **Welch** Ronald L '98
(614) 236-8000 **Welcome** Kristen J '99
Weldele Eric D '04
(614) 469-3269 **Welin** Peter D '88
(614) 228-4200 **Wellbaum** Gary S '85
(614) 224-9223 **Weller** Matthew A '93
(614) 464-6400 **Wellner** John P '79
(614) 229-4746 **Wells** Cheryl A '83
(614) 279-9929 **Wells** Joquetta S '81
(614) 466-5610 **Wells** Kimberley S '99
(614) 542-9358 **Welt** Richard J '79
(614) 228-7272 **Weltman Weinberg & Reis Co,LPA**
(614) 365-2700 **Wendel** Lee A '87
(614) 752-1765 **Wendell** Christina M '99
(614) 444-3003 **Wendt** Tracy Q '98
(614) 461-9212 **Wentz** Jonathan C '97
(614) 466-0501 **Wentzel** Jane E '96
(614) 464-6400 **Werth** Robert W '65
(614) 445-8218 **Wesner** Arthur G '58
(614) 228-5822 **Wesp** Edward Joel '70
(614) 445-2643 **West** Charles E '74
(614) 466-7014 **West** Sarah J '97
(614) 280-4141 **West** Scott B '82
(614) 268-0534 **Westbrook** Gayle R '80
(614) 466-6511 **Westerman** Matthew L '97
(614) 365-2700 **Westerman** Philip R '98
(614) 457-9731 **Westfall** Lee W '96
(614) 421-9200 **Weston** Bruce J '80
Wetterer Thomas R Jr. '83
(614) 249-4727 **Wetzel** Jonathan H '74
(614) 249-6910 **Wetzel** Sandra M '77
Weyls Donald R '01
(614) 292-3814 **Whaley** Douglas J '85
(614) 224-3208 **Wheatley** John C Jr. '52
(614) 221-5216 **Wheeler** James W '68
(614) 451-6803 **Wheeler** Pelton W '88
(614) 221-0944 **Wheeler** Terrence T '85
(614) 487-2050 **Whetzel** Eugene P '74
(614) 461-6006 **Whipps** Edward F '61
(614) 221-7663 **Whitaker** Roger T '76
(614) 228-1541 **Whitcomb** David A '92
(614) 469-3235 **White** Anthony C '93
(614) 485-9300 **White** Arnold S '69
(614) 249-7699 **White** David Lin '81
(614) 466-5967 **White** Duane M '76
White Janice G '78
(614) 464-6400 **White** Julia Falenski '96
(614) 438-2648 **Whitehead** Daniel P '98
(614) 644-9110 **Whitehouse** Richard A '87
(614) 236-2300 **Whiteside** Alba L Jr. '54
(614) 688-4225 **Whitney** Denton S '04
(614) 221-7663 **Whittaker** David M '79
(614) 644-7409 **Whitworth** Jill A '94
(614) 469-3297 **Wible** Michael V '04
(614) 228-1128 **Wichman** Jane C '89
(614) 221-7663 **Wickham** Henry P Jr. '79
(614) 299-2859 **Wickliffe** Marsha R '84
(614) 462-2204 **Wickline** Amanda L '03
(614) 224-8848 **Wideman** Clark W '75
(614) 221-9790 **Wideman** Matthew B '02
(614) 228-5711 **Wideman** Stacey Lane '03
(614) 466-4605 **Widener** China L '92
(614) 445-8801 **Widmaier** James L '65
(614) 224-3344 **Widman** Thomas G '92
(614) 559-1102 **Wiese** John A '87
(614) 424-6589 **Wiesmann** Klaus H '79
(614) 466-3801 **Wiest** Christopher D '04
(614) 203-4670 **Wiggin** James W '85
(614) 241-5550 **Wiggins** Jennifer A '01
(614) 228-1541 **Wightman** Alec '75
(614) 463-7241 **Wigton** Charles E III '76
(614) 466-8600 **Wilburn** Melissa L '89
(614) 365-9900 **Wilcox** Jonathan A '04
(614) 466-8600 **Wilcox** Kyle C '94
(614) 274-1107 **Wilcox** Ronald L '61
(614) 221-5216 **Wiles Boyle Burkholder & Bringardner Co,LPA**
(614) 221-5216 **Wiles** Daniel G '66
(614) 221-5216 **Wiles** James M '70
(614) 621-1500 **Wiley** Stephen C '97
(614) 447-0100 **Wilford** Barry W '77
(614) 488-2515 **Wilhelm** James E Jr. '64
(614) 466-5394 **Wilhelm** Joseph E '91
(614) 628-0790 **Wilkerson** John P Jr. '81
(614) 462-5417 **Wilkes** Nicholas E '95
(614) 447-7050 **Wilkins** Linda A '96
(614) 221-9800 **Wilkins** Paul G '02
(614) 469-3266 **Wilkinson** William C '76
(614) 621-1500 **Will** Anne E '03
(614) 466-3615 **Willard** Kirsten J '98
(614) 457-9731 **Willard** Robert H '80
(614) 221-4000 **Willcox** Roderick H '58
(614) 728-7055 **Wille** Charles L '79
(614) 888-7090 **Willi** Kaye P '83
(614) 466-3947 **Williams** Ayn Phalyn '93
(614) 228-0207 **Williams** Charles T '74
(614) 469-5715 **Williams** Dale E Jr. '79
(614) 415-1652 **Williams** Douglas L '80
(614) 221-0240 **Williams** Erica K '96
(614) 227-2374 **Williams** Faith M '96
(614) 228-1541 **Williams** Jeffrey T '88
(614) 466-2980 **Williams** John T '78
(614) 466-4801 **Williams** Julia K '95
(614) 220-5611 **Williams** Kevin L '93
(614) 224-7291 **Williams** Lewis E Jr. '74
(614) 221-8640 **Williams** McCullough A III '78
(614) 462-3988 **Williams** Megan J '92
(614) 221-8448 **Williams** Michael L '92
(614) 462-3194 **Williams** Mitchell A '97
(614) 224-0531 **Williams & Petro Co,LLC**
(614) 224-0531 **Williams** Richard A '82
(614) 716-0500 **Williams** Robert E '93
(614) 716-2037 **Williams** Sandra K '83
(614) 228-6061 **Williams** Scott E '92
(614) 464-1211 **Williams** Thomas V '77
(614) 228-6888 **Willis** William L Jr. '87
(614) 221-3938 **Willison** Eric E '96
(614) 469-7446 **Wilsbacher** MaryAnne B '91
(614) 292-3079 **Wilson** Charles E '86
(614) 462-4554 **Wilson** Courtney '97
(614) 464-6400 **Wilson** James A Jr. '85
(614) 469-5715 **Wilson** James C '03
(614) 228-1541 **Wilson** Leigh Ann '99
(614) 224-6969 **Wilson** Mark R '82
(614) 469-3939 **Wilson** Matthew R '00
Wilson Nicholas B '74
(614) 224-5205 **Wilson** Thomas A '90
(614) 644-3037 **Wilson** William S '82
(614) 469-3939 **Winchester** Jeffrey D '97
(614) 222-5853 **Winfree** James R '75
(614) 222-0535 **Winkle** Dawn M '04
(614) 466-9567 **Winkler** Dirken D '97
(614) 559-3839 **Winkler** John F '83
(614) 221-8868 **Winner** Joseph C '76
(614) 728-8400 **Winslow** Timothy C '99
(614) 592-1911 **Winston** Michael D '02
(614) 624-5686 **Winter** William J '91
(614) 888-8611 **Wintering** Michael R '78
(614) 221-3388 **Winters** Charles W '53
(614) 228-0068 **Winters** David C '75
(614) 365-2700 **Winters** Karen A '81
(614) 491-1401 **Winters** Leslie A '80
(614) 267-6401 **Winters** Susan J '82
(614) 464-6400 **Winters** Thomas R '84
Wirt Laurie B '95
(614) 443-4866 **Wirth** David S '01
(614) 221-1166 **Wise** C Michael '88
(614) 237-5414 **Wise** Janice W '81
(614) 247-5853 **Wise** Katherine J '97
(614) 466-8600 **Wise** Michael A '02
(614) 227-2310 **Wiseman** Randolph C '74
(614) 891-3512 **Wisner** Edwin A '66
(614) 461-6006 **Wistner** Robert N '62
(614) 469-3939 **Witalec** Joseph M '94
(614) 462-2202 **Withee** Stephen P '98
(614) 487-5100 **Witney** William P '90
(614) 466-4328 **Witten** Alan C '69
(614) 246-2500 **Witten** John P '77
(614) 258-1983 **Wittenberg** Eric J '87
(614) 227-2000 **Wobst** Franck G '83
(614) 462-3555 **Wodarcyk** Mark J '90
(614) 279-8188 **Woelfel** Bradford B '83
(614) 469-3939 **Wofford** Isaac S '02
(614) 228-4201 **Woggon** Linda S '92
(614) 262-3336 **Wolery** Don E '79
(614) 220-5611 **Wolf** Holly N '97
(614) 224-3080 **Wolfe** Carrie D '02
(614) 263-5297 **Wolfe** George M '94
(614) 221-2330 **Wolfe** Grant A '81
(614) 445-2644 **Wolfram** Jill A '96
(614) 228-1541 **Wolinetz** Barry H '71
(614) 466-4863 **Wollam** Shawn M '04
(614) 229-4755 **Wollett** Ronald S '94
(614) 280-1000 **Wolman** Benson A '88
(614) 885-7577 **Wolock** Margaret M '90
(614) 221-4000 **Wolper** Beatrice E '78
(614) 221-6969 **Wolske & Barclay,LPA**
(614) 221-6969 **Wolske** Walter J Jr. '56
(614) 221-6969 **Wolske-Donaldson** Sarah J '01
(614) 224-7291 **Wonnell** Nancy K '87
(614) 644-3037 **Wood** Ann M '95
(614) 857-4332 **Wood** Brian D '02
(614) 505-0808 **Wood** David W '86
(614) 228-4422 **Wood** Lee M '86
(614) 645-4530 **Wood** Melanie '98
(614) 337-2427 **Wood** Thomas C Jr. '74
(614) 466-4341 **Woodbeck** Charles A '91
(614) 461-1551 **Woodrow** Paul F '93
(614) 728-6487 **Woodruff** P Thomas '98
(614) 365-2700 **Woods** C Craig '81
(614) 431-1500 **Woods** Michelle Gehring '98
(614) 228-6131 **Woods** William H '73
(614) 719-3312 **Woodward** Lisa M '99
(614) 221-1662 **Wooldridge** Gregory D '88
(614) 462-4771 **Woolley** Julie M '03
(614) 460-6954 **Woosley** Stephen E '98
(614) 486-0297 **Workman** John R '74
(614) 644-8716 **Worley** Glenn T '83
(614) 644-7250 **Worly** Mindy A '86
(614) 299-6000 **Wrachford** Jason S '97
(614) 348-3847 **Wright** Beth A '95
(614) 224-2999 **Wright** Carol A '85
(614) 227-8874 **Wright** Harry IV '90
(614) 221-6969 **Wright** Jason K '01
(614) 692-3284 **Wright** Marsha M '84
(614) 644-9618 **Wright** Melissa G '04
(614) 224-1222 **Wright** Phillip L Jr. '00
(614) 228-2678 **Wright** Scott E '89
(614) 466-4395 **Wright** William L '84
(614) 255-3388 **Wrightsel** Bradley B '93
(614) 255-3388 **Wrightsel** Richard D '65
(614) 228-6885 **Wuerth** Richard O '73
(614) 744-3418 **Wurgler** Barry A '93
(614) 292-1056 **Wurster** Lee E '71
(614) 785-6600 **Wyatt** Thomas D '03
(614) 464-8354 **Wyckoff** Robin Grant '04
(614) 466-4961 **Wynsen** Pamela G '83
(614) 229-5052 **Xavier** Ronald E '98
(614) 228-6453 **Yacobozzi** Dennis V II '03
(614) 224-8187 **Yaeger** Keri N '01
(614) 221-1578 **Yaeger** Nicholas W '04
(614) 443-1333 **Yagoda** Andrea R '77
(614) 241-2156 **Yaklevich** John A '79
(614) 487-2050 **Yalamanchili** Kalpana '84
(614) 248-6207 **Yang** Carrie A '01
(614) 228-1541 **Yang** Rosanne T '99
(614) 464-6400 **Yano** James A '77
(614) 249-7150 **Yarbrough** Heather Ann '96
(614) 464-1211 **Yarbrough** Michael K '76
(614) 227-2180 **Yaross** Todd D '04
(614) 223-9300 **Yashko** Gary G '97
(614) 469-5715 **Yates** Christopher R '95
(614) 224-1979 **Yavitch** Bernard Z '71
(614) 224-6142 **Yavitch** Eric J '95
(614) 221-0240 **Yeager** Jeffrey A '97
(614) 457-6991 **Yearling** Joseph H '56
(614) 228-7005 **Yeazel** Keith A '89
(614) 228-2699 **Yemc** Michael J Jr. '95
(614) 464-6400 **Yeoman** Kelly J '04
(614) 469-7404 **Yerian** Paul E '82
(614) 351-8010 **Yiangou** Andrew '91
(614) 728-3053 **Yoakum** Kerry R '99
(440) 205-8525 **Yohman** Kathy A '94
(614) 462-3555 **Yosowitz** Andrew N '02
(614) 466-7264 **Yost** Cynthia A '89
(614) 466-7266 **Yost** Melissa R '99
(614) 341-6367 **Young** Betty K '00
(614) 466-6700 **Young** Carrie C '86
(614) 466-7046 **Young** Christopher R '89
(614) 228-1200 **Young** David C '86
(614) 365-2700 **Young** David J '55
(614) 442-1375 **Young** John Timothy '77
(614) 469-3939 **Young** Mary Beth Brookshire '01
(614) 227-2000 **Young** Nancy B '77
(614) 466-2590 **Young** Robert J '94
(614) 336-7072 **Young** Ronald G '96
(614) 752-1784 **Young** Stephen A '84
(614) 227-2000 **Young** Thomas A '73
(614) 462-3194 **Younger** Mary A '84
(614) 464-4100 **Younkin** Tracy A '94
(614) 227-2336 **Yount** Sue W '86
(614) 463-9770 **Youssef** Leslie Howard '04
(614) 228-6885 **Yurik** Stephen B '96
(614) 464-6400 **Yurkiw** Heidi L '99
(614) 227-2000 **Yurkiw** Jay A '97
(614) 224-8326 **Yurovich** Dale R '84
(614) 236-8000 **Zacks** Benjamin S '88
(614) 488-7847 **Zadnik** Rudolph S '51
(614) 719-3330 **Zafris** James L '89
(614) 458-0025 **Zaino** Thomas M '89
(614) 466-2765 **Zalenski** Scott T '90
(614) 221-3151 **Zalimeni** Gail M '90
(614) 221-1300 **Zamora** Charles '91
(614) 365-2700 **Zancourides** Lori Maiorca '03
(614) 466-8444 **Zapp** William A '72
(614) 229-4445 **Zaremski** Laura M '00
(614) 224-4411 **Zashin & Rich Co, LPA**
(614) 462-5497 **Zatezalo** Michael E '75
(614) 229-3888 **Zeehandelar** Steven J '82
(614) 224-9221 **Zeidan** Georges S '02
(614) 783-6479 **Zeidan** Tariq H '04
(614) 365-9900 **Zeiger** John W '72
(614) 365-9900 **Zeiger** Matthew S '02
(614) 365-9900 **Zeiger Tigges Little & Lindsmith, LLP**
(614) 464-6400 **Zelasko** Gregory J '81
(614) 462-3555 **Zeller** Jeanne M '03
(614) 723-2017 **Zervas** John A '89
(614) 462-2244 **Zets** Brian M '96
(614) 276-5263 **Zettler** Lois A '85
(614) 462-3555 **Zeyen** David F '97
(614) 464-6400 **Ziance** Scott J '97
(614) 221-9100 **Zibners** Amanda K '01
(614) 221-9100 **Zibners** Harry '03
(614) 481-9325 **Ziegler** Edward J '02
(614) 228-9550 **Ziegler** Elaine K '01
(614) 466-1305 **Ziegler** Michael S '89
(614) 241-5550 **Zikas** J Michael II '83
(614) 224-1979 **Zilka** Heather R '99
(614) 644-3037 **Zima** Bryan F '80
(614) 466-0750 **Zimmer** Dale A '78
(614) 462-3194 **Zimmer** Osias D '88
(614) 241-2227 **Zimmers** Neal F Jr. '67
(614) 249-9344 **Zisser** Steven L '83
(614) 227-2000 **Zola** George E '85
(614) 466-0212 **Zollinger** Sue A '04
Zonak Irene S '83
(614) 462-3221 **Zorn** James E Sr. '88
(614) 462-2216 **Zox** Benjamin L '62
(614) 462-2241 **Zox** Melissa L '90
(614) 255-3333 **Zox** William P '92
(614) 263-4299 **Zuber** Joan E '57
(614) 486-8052 **Zuber** Thomas J '58
(614) 228-5781 **Zuk** Nicholas W '78
(614) 224-8511 **Zunshine** Zach '91
(614) 229-3888 **Zury** James C '95
(614) 466-5205 **Zwyer** David A '77

COLUMBUS GROVE
Putnam County
(419) 659-2141 **Lehman** Scott C '93

CONCORD
Lake County
(440) 357-4601 **Andrews** Richard C '69
Brigham Anne T '99
(440) 942-7750 **Cantor** Abraham '73
(440) 639-9000 **Coffey** Michael D '60
(440) 354-4445 **Corbett** James J '78
(440) 357-6372 **Dalheim** Theodore J Jr. '90
(440) 350-0233 **Demeter** Richard V '84
(440) 639-9000 **DiPalma** William J '77
Eippert Tonya L '98
(440) 392-9580 **Gornik** David J '90
(440) 350-9270 **Higgins** Charles N Jr. '68
Hrenko Kimberly A '01
(440) 354-3917 **Nowak** Michael E '87
(440) 358-0534 **Pleska** Kenneth W '81
(440) 350-9273 **Sweeney** Maureen A '86
(440) 352-4004 **Vilsack** Robert D '87
Whitaker William S '85

CONNEAUT
Ashtabula County
(440) 593-6211 **Coxon** Gary L '71
(440) 593-2309 **Gallagher** Luke P '90
(440) 593-7410 **Harris** Thomas E '82
(440) 593-6457 **Iarocci** Nicholas A '89
(440) 593-2309 **Lafferty** Charles N Jr. '77
(440) 593-7413 **Lamer** Lori B '83
(440) 599-6708 **Naylor** Robert E '72
(440) 593-4900 **Richards** Sally E '82
(440) 593-6120 **Storm** Laverne Frederick '93
(440) 593-6120 **Storm** Mary E '91
(440) 593-6255 **Thayer** Walter E '50

COPLEY
Summit County
(330) 665-7200 **Garlock** Paul R '75
(330) 665-7200 **Gillis** Eugene G '78
Green Frederick J '90
(330) 666-7250 **Hewitt** William B '63
(330) 666-7250 **Hewitt** William W '84
(330) 665-7200 **Johanson** David M '00
Kozik Mary Ann J '96
McGown Daniel J '77
(330) 666-1650 **Robinson** David J '76
Schwartz Brenda S '94

CORTLAND
Trumbull County
(330) 638-1529 **Bishop** Jami L '03
(330) 638-7347 **Brooker** William H '81
(330) 638-1200 **Catuogno** J V '95
(330) 637-4600 **Franks** James D '84
(330) 637-3906 **Gessner** George E '69
(330) 637-3906 **Gessner & Platt Co, LPA**
(330) 637-9030 **Grundy** John C '87
(330) 638-1529 **Nosich** Marty D '03
(330) 637-3906 **Platt** Robert M Jr. '74
(330) 637-3906 **Platt** Robert M Sr. '54
(330) 637-3906 **Polak** Jenna Gessner '98
(330) 637-9030 **Rouzzo** David T '01
Zimmer Frederick C '59

COSHOCTON
Coshocton County
(740) 622-3566 **Batchelor** Robert J '92
(740) 622-3171 **Baxter** Terrence J '91
(740) 622-0130 **Blanchard** Van II '86
(740) 622-2011 **Burns** David W '68
(740) 623-0800 **Davitt** Norman S '77
(740) 622-6464 **Deadman** William G '77
(740) 622-1595 **Foster** Susan M '84
(740) 622-6872 **France** Timothy L '81
(740) 622-6464 **Frase Weir Baker & McCullough Co,LPA**
(740) 622-0166 **Given** Jason W '02
(740) 622-2871 **Hostetler** David L '76
(740) 622-8969 **Johnson** Antonia K '84
(740) 622-9801 **Kiracofe** Bruce H '81
(740) 622-0166 **Leech Scherbel & Peddicord**
(740) 622-0166 **Leech** Thomas B '46
(740) 622-3911 **Manning** Michael D '75
(740) 622-1051 **Mathay** Charles E '72

(740) 622-6464 **McCullough** Michael P '74
(740) 622-2011 **Nelson** Christie M '99
(740) 622-3911 **Owens** William M '72
(740) 622-0166 **Peddicord** Randall H '82
(740) 622-2011 **Pomerene Burns & Skelton**
(740) 622-0166 **Scherbel** Paul R '73
(740) 622-2011 **Skelton** James R '92
(740) 622-2011 **Skelton** Joseph R '74
(740) 622-2011 **Skelton** Robert A '90
(740) 622-6464 **Weir** Robert E '83

COVINGTON
Miami County
(937) 473-3161 **O'Donnell** James R '66

CRESTLINE
Crawford County
(419) 683-2214 **Berger** J Sebastian '03
(419) 683-2214 **Berger** John W '66
(419) 683-2214 **Garner & Berger**
(419) 683-3800 **Skropits** Amy E '96

CURTICE
Ottawa County
(419) 836-8246 **Carstensen** William J '94
(419) 836-9955 **Heyman** Richard A '98

CUSTAR
Wood County
(419) 669-8500 **Ferrell** Dennis L '79

CUYAHOGA FALLS
Summit County
(330) 928-7976 **Aldridge** James D '73
(330) 971-8190 **Arrington** Virgil E Jr. '82
Bailey Barbara E '92
(330) 762-2323 **Barrett** Gerald Van '85
(330) 762-0755 **Berkowitz** Richard E '96
(330) 945-6931 **Bowen** Kathleen K '98
(330) 928-7878 **Brouse** Karen H '02
(330) 971-7067 **Caldwell** Deborah A '98
(330) 922-4830 **Cazin** Tyler K '98
Chapman John E '02
(330) 971-8273 **Clark** John W '90
(330) 971-8256 **Coates** Lisa L '94
(330) 920-1210 **Colavecchio** Diana M '89
(330) 923-5315 **Cole** Leza A '02
(330) 971-8191 **Connolly** Lisa A '89
(330) 945-8070 **Cusimano** Christopher D '93
(330) 928-1576 **Dandrea** Victor A '71
Dean Melissa C '99
(330) 929-9222 **DeMarco** John C '92
(330) 929-4495 **Dietz** David R '82
(330) 929-4002 **Durr** Susan L '83
(330) 376-3572 **Eshelman** C Richard '68
(330) 926-9845 **Evans** Diane K '97
(330) 928-1040 **Falcone** Vincent J '80
(330) 535-2220 **Farine** Cheryl L '88
(330) 929-3777 **Farris** Vincent G '93
(330) 762-8773 **Folk** Alexander R '96
(330) 929-1195 **Frisby** John D Jr. '80
(330) 929-0507 **Gibson** Kenneth L '79
(330) 929-0507 **Ginther** Sharyl W '91
(330) 929-3168 **Godward** Eugene G '84
(330) 929-6212 **Gruber** Michael J Jr. '79
(330) 929-3324 **Hanlon** Herbert J '85
(330) 929-2676 **Haring** Brian J '99
(330) 929-2676 **Herrnstein** John M '83
(330) 929-2676 **Heydorn** Robert W '75
(330) 929-2676 **Hoover Heydorn & Herrnstein Co,LPA**
(330) 971-8209 **Hoover** Kim R '79
(330) 929-2676 **Hoover** Orval Ray '59
(330) 535-2220 **Hudak** Daniel J '69
(330) 535-2220 **Hudak** Daniel J Jr. '99
(330) 535-2220 **Hudak Shunk & Farine**
(330) 971-8190 **Jones** Dwayne K '87
(330) 971-8190 **Jones** Hope L '90
(330) 928-3373 **Kassinger** John R '84
(330) 929-4293 **Keith** George G '83
(330) 923-8758 **Kille** Angela M '04
(330) 923-5315 **Kreiner** Margaret H '85
(330) 945-7238 **Laing** Matthew A '92
(330) 945-7111 **LaPorte** Mary C '85
(330) 929-0507 **Larko** John '73
(330) 929-3160 **Learner** Edward C '84
(330) 923-2122 **Leipply** Gerald R '59
(330) 923-5315 **Little** Sarah L '04
(330) 971-8190 **Lohan** Angela F '03
(330) 929-0507 **Lowry** Randal A '76
(330) 971-8190 **Lynn** Stacy L '97
(330) 923-2316 **Maher** Edward C '49
(330) 929-9700 **Malyuk** Michael A '75
(330) 376-3572 **McCue** Kevin L '03
(330) 929-4291 **McDowall** Robert H '62
Mergl Marija '01
(330) 929-3337 **Moore** Robert S '61
(330) 929-0507 **Moran** Michael J '78
(330) 928-3373 **Nehrer** John A '66
(330) 928-3373 **Nehrer & Kassinger**
(330) 928-3373 **Nehrer** Lori S '85
(330) 376-3572 **Nestico** Alberto '99
(330) 247-1057 **Oettinger** Jennifer E '02
(330) 923-2211 **Ogden** James R '79
(330) 928-9791 **Oldham** Robert L '71
(330) 923-0401 **Pagel** Thomas R '79
(330) 926-2483 **Pannell** Linda L '86
(330) 922-0934 **Perdue** Stephen R '94
(330) 971-8280 **Pike** William B '58
(330) 376-3572 **Redick** Robert W '99
(330) 929-0507 **Reidy** Jerome G '74
(330) 929-6000 **Rice** Wayne M '76
(330) 294-1032 **Rogachefsky** Barbara J '97
(330) 535-2220 **Schmitz** Thomas M '67
(330) 971-8260 **Schwartz** Steven J '73
(330) 535-2220 **Shunk** Laura F '83
(330) 945-4800 **Snoderly** John A '59
(330) 922-0342 **Snyder** Gayle L '94
(330) 971-8256 **Teodosio** Linda T '82
(330) 929-0507 **Terilla** John A '73
(330) 618-0478 **Varga** Michael J '95
(330) 376-3572 **Vasvari** Thomas M '90
(330) 971-8190 **Ward** Gregory M '00
(330) 929-0507 **Weick** David C '84
(330) 929-0507 **Weick** Paul A '54
(330) 929-0507 **Weinberger** Mark S '84
(330) 929-0507 **Weinberger** Michael A '72
(330) 923-5315 **Weinschenk** Barbara J '04
(330) 923-0040 **Williams** Glen A '61

CUYAHOGA HEIGHTS
Cuyahoga County
(216) 271-8049 **Colgrove** John K '69
(216) 883-8888 **Friedman** Matthew S '93
(216) 271-8987 **King** Russell R '90
(216) 271-8254 **Pinzone** Charles R Jr. '92
(216) 271-8047 **Tetlak** Thomas E '76

DALTON
Wayne County
(330) 828-2288 **Kauffman** Roland B '82

DAMASCUS
Mahoning County
(330) 537-3739 **Bandy** Kenneth L '74
Grant Holly J '98

DAYTON
Montgomery County
(937) 252-2592 **Abbott** John M '72
(937) 226-1212 **Abboud** Antony A '04
(937) 643-3770 **Abdallah** Bahjat M '04
(937) 225-5779 **Abshire** Steven M '01
(937) 445-2966 **Ackermann** John R Jr. '91
(937) 224-5300 **Adams** Audrey S '01
(937) 294-2778 **Adams** Jay A '00
(937) 449-2800 **Adams** Karen R '91
(937) 223-1201 **Adkins** Dennis J '86
(937) 431-9660 **Adkinson** Patrick K '80
(937) 223-1201 **Adler** Deborah J '82
(937) 865-6800 **Agarwal** Neil P '96
(937) 276-6580 **Ahearn** Todd M '98
(937) 865-6800 **Akerson** Valerie L '95
(937) 275-7170 **Albert** Jeffrey P '71
(937) 443-6600 **Aldrich** Jeff Jr. '02
(937) 228-5912 **Allbery** Charles F III '78
(937) 228-5912 **Allbery Cross & Fogarty**
(937) 225-4464 **Allen** Pamela K '96
(937) 223-1201 **Altick & Corwin Co,LPA**
(937) 276-6560 **Amarante** John J '87
(937) 229-9999 **Ambrose** James T '75
(937) 461-4646 **Ames** Arthur A '69
(937) 224-8806 **Amos** John C '00
(937) 227-3700 **Anderson** Bradley D '93
(937) 865-6800 **Anderson** Christopher J '95
(937) 865-6800 **Anderson** Maureen H '96
(937) 225-7687 **Anderson** Thomas W Jr. '00
(937) 226-9354 **Andrade** David '00
(937) 225-4652 **Andrews** Charles G '80
(937) 223-5200 **Angelo** Thomas III '83
(937) 223-8177 **Anspach** Douglas C Jr. '01
(937) 278-4214 **Arkenberg** Kenneth J '53
(937) 225-5751 **Armanini** Debra B '82
(937) 296-4902 **Armanini** Joseph S '82
(937) 225-4892 **Armstead** Thaddeus J '82
(937) 461-4648 **Armstrong** James S '78
(937) 222-2424 **Arnold** Gordon D '75
(937) 222-3322 **Arnold Todaro & Welch**
(937) 224-0036 **Arntz** Matthew R '82
(937) 208-2525 **Arquilla** Thomas J '84
(937) 254-3738 **Arthur** Richard P '86
(937) 496-7428 **Ashbery** Lynda K '97
(937) 775-5857 **Ashelman** Scott A '01
(937) 865-6800 **Audi** Joseph F '97
(937) 865-6800 **August** James E '97
(937) 223-6003 **Auman** Gary W '76
(937) 449-5767 **Austin** Matthew D '03
(937) 443-6877 **Axtell** Stephen J '88
(937) 224-5300 **Azallion** Melissa G '95
(937) 223-8177 **Bach** Michelle D '95
(937) 865-6800 **Bacon** Leanna E '92
(937) 224-0963 **Bacon** Steven E '92
(937) 512-2376 **Badonsky** Deborah K '73
(937) 223-1201 **Baggott** Thomas M '71
(937) 227-6473 **Bailes** Michael S '93
(937) 223-4701 **Bailey Cavalieri LLC**
(937) 225-4652 **Bailey** Dennis L '82
(937) 228-8080 **Bailey** Kenneth L '60
(937) 227-3700 **Bair** Erin A '04
(937) 226-1990 **Baker** Theresa A '92
(937) 225-5887 **Baldwin** Bradley S '98
(937) 485-1708 **Ball** David E '92
(937) 225-4168 **Ballard** Nadine L '80
(937) 225-6104 **Ballard** Tracey L '98
(937) 534-0500 **Ballato** Lynnette P '95
(937) 228-2306 **Ballato** Thomas A '94
(937) 293-2141 **Balmer** Joseph E III '89
(937) 435-7500 **Baran** Heidi L '98
(937) 223-9133 **Barbato** Matthew J '03
(937) 865-6800 **Barber** Darin S '94
(937) 496-7740 **Barnes** Kevin R '94
(937) 223-6003 **Barney** William H III '77
(937) 225-5757 **Barrentine** Ward C '01
(937) 438-1001 **Bart** David R '71
(937) 227-3700 **Bartlett** Robert P '64
Barton Rebecca S '93
(937) 225-2516 **Baxley** Jessica Y '00
(937) 222-2424 **Bazelak** Leonard J '94
(937) 328-2653 **Bazeley** Christopher C '04
(937) 454-0039 **Beasley** Jesse B Jr. '88
(937) 495-3092 **Beasley** John H '93
(937) 449-6400 **Beckmann** Richard J '74
(937) 435-7500 **Behnke** Stephen D '00
(937) 291-2209 **Beitel** Stephanie A '82
(937) 225-7687 **Bennett** Cheryll A '94
(937) 449-6810 **Bennett** John Francis '02
(937) 224-9291 **Bennington** C Christopher '04
(937) 229-4211 **Bernal-Olson** Patricia '98
(937) 223-4701 **Berner** Robert B '84
(937) 277-0505 **Bernsen** Kenneth J '99
(937) 496-3686 **Bernstein** Elaine S '89
(937) 775-3488 **Bernstein** J Michael '71
(937) 278-0022 **Berry** Thomas D '81
(937) 449-6400 **Beyer** James E '95
(937) 222-2500 **Beyer** Martin A '92
(937) 224-1427 **Beyoglides** Harry G Jr. '78
(937) 223-8177 **Bhat** Aniruddha D '01
(937) 223-3277 **Bierman** Mary-Karen '02
(937) 223-3277 **Bieser Greer & Landis LLP**
(937) 223-3277 **Bieser** Irvin G Jr. '66
(937) 333-4413 **Bilott** Raymond L '83
(937) 222-1148 **Birt** James E '63
(937) 228-2666 **Bissonnette** Brett R '03
(937) 223-8177 **Blackburn** R Scott '79
(937) 223-8171 **Blair** Amy R '01
(937) 296-2384 **Blake** Jonathan I '01
(937) 252-1414 **Blaschak** Thomas R '92
(937) 222-2424 **Blasik-Miller** Susan '84
(937) 222-2424 **Blatt** Shawn M '91
(937) 485-4388 **Blattner** Elizabeth H '89
(937) 443-6539 **Blattner** James Wray '80
(937) 443-6964 **Block** Barry M '75
(937) 438-5310 **Bloomfield** Roger E '74
(937) 224-7200 **Blumenthal** Gary M '74
(937) 223-1130 **Bly** Loren M '89
(937) 271-2727 **Boddie** Kelvin L '85
(937) 223-3277 **Bodin** John D '03
(937) 898-1465 **Bodoh** Emily D '00
(937) 226-1200 **Bogin Patterson & Bohman**
(937) 226-1200 **Bohman** Jerome B '59
(937) 333-4100 **Bonfield** Patrick J '73
(937) 775-5857 **Booher** Michael R '81
(937) 222-2500 **Booth** Michael A '95
(937) 299-7482 **Bothmann** Randall N '70
(937) 435-7500 **Botros Behnke & Schulte,LLC**
(937) 435-7500 **Botros** Michael R '96
(937) 223-0122 **Boucher** Richard A '86
(937) 223-8177 **Bower** Glenn L '77
(937) 461-9297 **Bowers** Gwendolyn R '78
(937) 222-2500 **Bowman** Kevin A '97
(937) 333-4100 **Bradford** Tracy L '92
(937) 226-1212 **Bradley** Karen D '96
(937) 224-3741 **Brandt** Daniel J '97
(937) 225-5543 **Brandt** Kirsten A '98
(937) 222-9687 **Brandt** Stephen D '76
(937) 228-2306 **Brannon** Douglas D '03
(937) 228-2306 **Brannon** Dwight D '74
(937) 226-9354 **Branson** Paul M '01
(937) 222-3000 **Brasier** Susan M '88
(937) 396-0089 **Braum** Scott L '99
(937) 224-0963 **Breidenbach** Heidi S '95
(937) 224-0963 **Breidenbach** John E '68
(937) 224-9291 **Brennan** James M '57
(937) 586-3100 **Brenner** Joan B '81
(937) 222-2424 **Brewer** Steven L '98
(937) 512-2950 **Brigner** Victor M '77
(937) 226-1996 **Brinkman** Daniel E '82
(937) 223-8177 **Brinkman** Justin D '03
(937) 223-6003 **Brinsfield** Gary T '68
(937) 222-3000 **Brissie** William J '02
(937) 449-2800 **Broock** Richard A '72
(937) 228-9790 **Brooks** Adrienne D '04
(937) 225-4609 **Brooks** Richard C '68
(937) 222-2424 **Brooks** Richard C Jr. '02
(937) 643-9329 **Brown** Alan I '79
(937) 228-8088 **Brown** Branford D '89
(937) 449-2800 **Brown** Christopher M '03
(937) 461-5310 **Brown** Diana S '96
(937) 227-3700 **Brown** Jacqueline V '04
(937) 443-6557 **Brown** Robert J '68
(937) 225-4652 **Bruce** Kimberly L '04
(937) 223-8888 **Bruder** Matthew D '98
(937) 225-5757 **Brumby** Jennifer D '03
(937) 228-5600 **Brunner** Lowell K '73
(937) 512-1680 **Bruns** Julie A '96
(937) 449-2800 **Bruzzese** Anthony E '03
(937) 449-2800 **Bryant** Todd E '00
(937) 223-6211 **Buchanan** Joseph P '56
(937) 865-6800 **Buckley** Brian P '01
(937) 224-1981 **Burdge** Michael J '78
(937) 432-9500 **Burdge** Ronald L '78
(937) 443-6625 **Burick** Lawrence T '68
(937) 225-5798 **Burke** Nicole C '97
(937) 223-8888 **Burke** Robert A '79
(937) 865-6800 **Burneka** Joseph W III '96
(937) 443-5426 **Burns** Belinda A '79
(937) 865-6800 **Burns** Jonathan P '01
(937) 333-4400 **Burns-Smith** Andrea J '99
(937) 223-8000 **Bursey** Charles E II '01
(937) 227-3700 **Burton** Chad E '04
(937) 227-3700 **Burton** Donald E '88
(937) 227-3700 **Burton** Melinda K '95
(937) 297-1150 **Butler** Mariah D '03
(937) 445-7438 **Butler** Timothy R '83
(937) 865-6800 **Byrd** James E '84
(937) 445-6327 **Byrnes** John J '82
(937) 865-6800 **CaJacob** Jennifer G '00
(937) 225-4652 **Calaway** Scott M '97
(937) 225-4652 **Calaway** Todd E '99
(937) 913-2539 **Calvert** Christopher J '97
(937) 445-6662 **Campbell** Noelle D '94
(937) 865-6800 **Campbell** Samuel A '02
(937) 443-4367 **Cannon** James F '78
(937) 461-8800 **Capizzi** Anthony '79
(937) 223-2200 **Caras** Sam G '80
(937) 443-6520 **Carlile** Richard F '69
(937) 865-1711 **Carlisle** Lynn A '85
(937) 276-6577 **Carlson** John P '03
(937) 225-5782 **Carper** Margaret M '91
(937) 223-6003 **Carr** Richard L Jr. '84
(937) 222-2424 **Carrigg** Christopher W '85
(937) 890-8883 **Carson** Douglas T '86
(937) 898-7070 **Carson** Lloyd T '49
(937) 222-1366 **Carter** Jay B '89
(937) 445-2088 **Carver** Todd B '91
(937) 223-8177 **Cary** Dina M '97
(937) 449-2800 **Caspar** Frederick J '85
(937) 222-1232 **Cass** William O Jr. '86
(937) 461-0306 **Caudill** Mary B '83
(937) 223-1201 **Certo** Peter R Jr. '79
(937) 228-2666 **Cervay** John A '68
(937) 436-1893 **Chalker** Brad A '81
(937) 223-8177 **Chambers** John C '85
(937) 445-4956 **Chan** Michael '88
(937) 865-6800 **Chase** Barry E '01
(937) 225-2910 **Chema** J Richard '81
(937) 445-9787 **Chema** Susan R '82
(937) 365-6800 **Chen** Huiling K '93
(937) 449-2800 **Chernesky Heyman & Kress PLL**
(937) 449-2800 **Chernesky** Richard J '66
(937) 449-2800 **Cherney** Andrew K '73
(937) 865-1419 **Chillinsky** Michael J '88
(937) 224-9291 **Chilson** Mark R '81
(937) 226-9354 **Chinault** Elizabeth M '03
(937) 223-8888 **Chinault** Jeffrey G '03
(937) 461-0796 **Christon** Jimmie '87
(937) 443-6568 **Ciambrone** Richard A '80
(937) 424-5390 **Cicero** Anthony R '95
Claire Grace '02
(937) 225-9947 **Clark** Jan A '75
(937) 294-6573 **Clark** Robert L '01
(937) 222-2500 **Clawson** Carissa E '03
(937) 224-1427 **Claypool** Charles A '73
(937) 224-3740 **Claypoole** Erin L '97
(937) 443-6829 **Clifford** Joanne E '01
(937) 222-5552 **Cline** James T Jr. '70
(937) 223-8171 **Cloud** John M '76
(937) 223-1130 **Clough** John E '94
(937) 586-4654 **Coates** Joseph A '88
(937) 865-6800 **Coats** Wanda P '80
(937) 229-2332 **Cochran** Rebecca A '92
(937) 865-6800 **Cohen** Jonathan D '99
(937) 225-3991 **Colbert** Valerie L '01
(937) 225-4255 **Cole** James D '80
(937) 222-2500 **Coleman** Danyelle S '00
(937) 228-8104 **Coles** Gwendolyn D '93
(937) 865-6800 **Collins** David A '89
(937) 445-3690 **Collins** Lori J '87
(937) 227-3310 **Comunale** Anthony F '93
(937) 225-4652 **Comunale** Kristine E '93
(937) 223-8177 **Conard** Christopher R '88
(937) 237-9485 **Conboy** Patrick J '98
(937) 228-1111 **Conley** Andrew P '03
(937) 225-5762 **Connell** James M '69
(937) 222-2424 **Connell** Kevin C '94
(937) 229-3211 **Conte** Francis J '88
(937) 443-6840 **Conway** Mark A '91
(937) 294-8807 **Conway** William M '77
(937) 865-6800 **Cooley** Brian H '00
(937) 223-8177 **Coolidge Wall Womsley & Lombard**
(937) 443-6909 **Cooper** Charles D II '01
(937) 224-5300 **Cooper & Gentile Co,LPA**
(937) 224-5300 **Cooper** Janet K '78
(937) 223-8177 **Costello** Shannon L '98
(937) 224-1981 **Coughlin** Robert B '80
(937) 224-1611 **Cousineau** Richard L '59
(937) 222-2030 **Cowan** Christopher F '81
(937) 222-1090 **Cowdrey** Robert F '75
(937) 228-1975 **Cox** Bobby Joe '73
(937) 227-3700 **Cox** Jeffrey T '91
(937) 434-7114 **Cox** Ray A '68
(937) 225-4652 **Cox** Steven M '75
(937) 496-3210 **Cox** William C '89
(937) 865-6800 **Craig** Christopher J '99
(937) 223-1201 **Crane** Brent A '95
(937) 225-4250 **Cranmer** David J '87
(937) 208-2205 **Creech** Dale E Jr. '78
(937) 434-6227 **Creech** Herbert Jr. '73
(937) 223-6211 **Crew & Buchanan**
(937) 223-6211 **Crew** Robert B '36
(937) 434-6040 **Crews** Virginia L '04
(937) 276-5770 **Crim** Gary W '73
Croghan Harold H '67
(937) 225-2516 **Cross** Colleen R '96
(937) 294-6000 **Crossman** Frances A '89
(937) 225-6258 **Crowl** Thomas L Jr. '78
(937) 223-8177 **Crump** Edith E '91
(937) 264-5116 **Crump** James R '89
(937) 436-0033 **Cumbo** Jennifer S '01
(937) 496-7797 **Cumming** John A '73
(937) 865-6800 **Cummings** Brian K '95
(937) 865-7925 **Cummings** Carrie W '93
(937) 281-6273 **Cummiskey** John P '87
(937) 865-6800 **Cunningham** Melissa A '95
(937) 443-6511 **Curry** Robert M '78
(937) 865-6800 **Curtis-Austin** Kelli C '00
(937) 227-3700 **Czanik** Kara A '02
(937) 449-2800 **Czechowski** Thomas L '74
(937) 224-1514 **Dahms** Kenneth C '73
(937) 225-5766 **Daidone** Leon J '81
(937) 291-7025 **Daly** Denis G '69
(937) 222-0500 **Daly** William T '98
(937) 434-3197 **D'Amico** Rudolph A '51
(937) 461-8656 **Dancing** Tara C '04
(937) 225-4652 **Daniels** Ramona E '98
(937) 333-4100 **Danish** John J '90
(937) 643-9999 **Dankof** Steven K '76
(937) 228-8104 **Dannemann** Stephanie L '04
(937) 228-1525 **Dauber** Eric L '94
(937) 223-6211 **Davidek** Robert J '81
(937) 222-2500 **Davies** Scott S '03
(937) 223-8177 **Davis** Nicholas E Jr. '90
(937) 445-2914 **Davis** Peter W '91
(937) 443-6533 **Davis** Steven J '87
(937) 865-6800 **Dawe** Timothy J '90
(937) 449-6400 **Dawson** Wayne H '67
(937) 224-9291 **Dean** Steven O '83
(937) 449-6810 **Deas** William G III '72
(937) 443-6664 **DeBrosse** Thomas E '80
(937) 228-8088 **Decker-Hall** Sarah J '00
(937) 293-3058 **Deddens** Robert L '67
(937) 865-4324 **DeFazio** Judith D '80
(937) 225-4652 **Deffet** Michael E '91
(937) 865-6800 **DeFrench** Melissa K '95
(937) 898-7673 **Deitering** Joyce M '84
(937) 225-5765 **Delnicki** Christopher R '93
(937) 445-2701 **Demko** Thomas A '00
(937) 910-7550 **Denardo** Thomas R '81
(937) 223-6003 **Dendwick-Gordon** Laurie N '02
(937) 229-9999 **Dennis** James D '76
(937) 224-0039 **Denny** Larry J '74
(937) 445-5821 **Denny** Simone M '99
(937) 225-4253 **Denslow** Jeremiah J '02
(937) 434-6040 **Depoorter** Kent J '92
(937) 223-8177 **Derrien** Sylvie '00
(937) 225-6103 **Deschler** Robert C '92
(937) 865-6800 **DeSerna** Alexander C '89
(937) 223-8171 **DeSio** Laura C '04
(937) 449-8880 **Deuser** Charles W II '81
(937) 223-7170 **Deutsch** David M '69
(937) 252-2030 **DeVeny** Dain N '74
(937) 225-7233 **DeVenzio** William A '85

(937) 225-4652 **Dewar** Glen H '89
(937) 495-3143 **DeWolfe** Gregory S '73
(937) 225-5795 **Dezarn** Marcell N '83
(937) 222-8091 **DiCicco** Matthew D '00
(937) 333-4100 **Dickens** Norma M '93
(937) 228-1525 **Dickhaut** William A '92
(937) 433-8611 **Dineen** Thomas M '87
(937) 449-6400 **Dinsmore & Shohl LLP**
(937) 224-7200 **Dobson** Stephanie D '02
(937) 461-5310 **Doll Jansen & Ford**
(937) 461-5310 **Doll** John R '78
(937) 299-0893 **Donahue** John W '66
(937) 228-8183 **Donahue** Peter J '55
(937) 333-4100 **Donaldson** Lynn R '89
(937) 226-7501 **Donenfeld** Richard D '93
(937) 223-4400 **Donoff** Marilyn R '81
(937) 224-1427 **Douple** Daryl R '79
(937) 222-2333 **Dowd** Edward J '83
(937) 333-4100 **Downs** Timothy S '03
(937) 434-3556 **Dressel** Frederick W '81
(937) 254-2600 **Driscoll** Brian C '01
(937) 254-2600 **Driscoll** Daniel P '02
(937) 225-3499 **Droessler** Julie A '97
(937) 224-1006 **Ducker** John T '67
(937) 294-2778 **Duff** Trisha M '91
(937) 434-6040 **Duncan** Richard L '73
(937) 222-2500 **Duncombe** Barbara A '00
(937) 223-3277 **Dunlevey** Karen T '96
(937) 223-6003 **Dunlevey Mahan & Furry**
(937) 223-6003 **Dunlevey** Robert T '73
(937) 512-2935 **Dunn** Darlene Efinger '03
(937) 222-3000 **Dunphy** Patrick K '82
(937) 225-2910 **Dunsky** Gregory P '77
Duong Vy T '02
(937) 461-9400 **Durden** Aaron G '88
(937) 910-7530 **Durden** Paula V '86
(937) 445-5522 **Duren** Mark W '92
(937) 854-6686 **Durham** Joan D '82
(937) 297-1154 **Duwel** David M '73
(937) 297-1154 **Duwel** Kyle C '02
(937) 297-1154 **Duwel** Todd T '98
(937) 461-1142 **Dybvig** Roger S '60
(937) 223-8888 **Dyer Garofalo Mann & Schultz**
(937) 222-2500 **Dyer** James A '80
(937) 223-8888 **Dyer** Michael E '80
(937) 222-2500 **Early** Katherine L '02
(937) 865-6800 **Easter** Suzanne M '95
(937) 586-3100 **Ebenger** Joseph R '77
(937) 293-2392 **Eckhart** Michael R '73
(937) 294-5800 **Edelstein** Kimberly A '02
(937) 224-3724 **Ehrstine** William H '79
(937) 258-3668 **Eichelman** Nate '03
(937) 449-6810 **Eichner** Roland F '58
(937) 228-8183 **Eilerman** Robert J '57
(937) 439-4400 **Elinger** Abbey P '03
(937) 865-8868 **Elleman** Jennifer N '98
(937) 443-6838 **Elleman** Steven J '96
(937) 275-0944 **Ellerbrock** Michael J '79
(937) 228-1987 **Elliott** Steven E '89
(937) 264-8710 **Elliott** William B '75
(937) 865-6800 **Ellis** Charles M '92
(937) 226-1200 **Ellis** James C '81
(937) 222-1560 **Ellison** Kathy L '79
(937) 439-5642 **Emrick** Nicky R '82
(937) 299-1914 **Engler** Gregory T '88
(937) 223-3001 **Engling** Mark C '99
(937) 228-7511 **Epley** Christopher B '99
(937) 443-6814 **Erickson** Douglas E '89
(937) 233-5555 **Ernst** Daniel D '94
(937) 223-2002 **Ernst** Herbert Jr. '61
(937) 294-8420 **Ervin** Joanne J '91
(937) 298-0008 **Esler** Charles M Jr. '87
(937) 865-6800 **Esparza** Lorena '02
(937) 854-3788 **Evans** Meg M '86
(937) 276-6565 **Everett** John D '98
(937) 449-2800 **Evers** Bradley W '85
(937) 223-8177 **Ewers** Gregory M '97
(937) 222-7777 **Fadia** Jill D '04
(937) 223-8177 **Fague** Terence L '78
(937) 226-0070 **Falconer** Diane M '95
(937) 222-3000 **Falke & Dunphy LLC**
(937) 222-3000 **Falke** Lee C '55
(937) 225-4652 **Fallang** Dennis J '77
(937) 865-6800 **Fals** Mary M '91
(937) 643-1920 **Fannon** Patrick J '76
(937) 223-9133 **Farley** Keri E '03
(937) 225-4640 **Farmer** David M '81
(937) 643-1758 **Farquhar** Harold R '75
(937) 223-1201 **Farquhar** Robert N '61
(937) 227-3700 **Faruki** Charles J '74
(937) 227-3700 **Faruki Ireland & Cox PLL**
(937) 264-8710 **Faulkner** Jonathan E '04
(937) 225-2910 **Fehrman** Anne H '94
(937) 225-5637 **Feller** Gina A '98
(937) 223-3277 **Feller** Joseph L '98
(937) 225-4600 **Felsburg** Timothy A '98
(937) 865-6800 **Fening** Matthew B '94
(937) 865-6800 **Ferguson** Candice H '02
(937) 443-6740 **Ferrante** Francesco A '81
(937) 449-2800 **Feuer** Mark S '78
(937) 225-4600 **Fields** Sarah E '01
(937) 254-3767 **Fierst** David J '90
(937) 223-8177 **Finch** Kristin A '95
(937) 438-2819 **Finefrock** James L '75
(937) 228-7104 **Finke** R Peter '68
(937) 222-2500 **Finley** Gale S '81
(937) 225-5789 **Finn-DeLuca** Valerie M '94
(937) 227-3700 **Fischer** John A '97
(937) 225-2516 **Fischer** Susan K '82
(937) 433-2411 **Flaherty** Mimi K '91
(937) 223-5200 **Flanagan Lieberman Hoffman & Swaim**
(937) 223-5200 **Flanagan** Patrick A '67
(937) 223-3277 **Fleisher** James P '92
(937) 228-5912 **Fogarty** Canice J Jr. '83
(937) 836-4433 **Foley** Patrick J '56
(937) 225-5769 **Folfas** Paul A '72
(937) 461-8656 **Folkerth** John R Jr. '83
(937) 461-8656 **Folkerth** Karen S '86
(937) 438-6848 **Folkerts** Michael D '89
(937) 227-3700 **Foos** Martin A '95
(937) 445-3265 **Foote** Douglas S '85
(937) 461-5310 **Ford** Julie C '88
(937) 278-0651 **Foster** Mark S '80
(937) 258-3668 **Fox** Charles B '54
(937) 791-8161 **Fox** Randy E '87
(937) 485-4088 **Frame** Carla M '84
(937) 225-5783 **Franceschelli** David M '79
(937) 225-4987 **Francis** Jessica L '02
(937) 865-6800 **Frantz** Deborah A '00
(937) 223-8378 **Frapwell** William H '78
(937) 224-0076 **Frayne** Anne M '79
(937) 433-8985 **Frazee** Willis H Jr. '53
(937) 223-1201 **Freeman** Jonathan B '97
(937) 222-2424 **Freeze** Stephen V '74
(937) 454-1468 **Freiberger** Mary M '95
(937) 222-2424 **Freudiger** Ramon C '91
(937) 222-2424 **Freund Freeze & Arnold**
(937) 222-2424 **Freund** Neil F '70
(937) 449-6400 **Frey** Michael G '98
(937) 223-8177 **Frick** Dawn M '98
(937) 236-6444 **Fricker** Keith A '86
Friedlander Betsy A '02
(937) 224-4128 **Friesinger** Patricia J '00
(937) 226-1776 **Froelich** Gary L '68
(937) 226-1776 **Froelich & Weprin**
(937) 222-5992 **Frydman** Joel M '79
(937) 226-1996 **Fuchsman** David H '83
(937) 298-7677 **Fulero** Solomon M '80
(937) 228-5151 **Fullenkamp** James J '84
(937) 223-6003 **Furry** Richard L '64
(937) 222-5335 **Gabel** Alan D '84
(937) 865-6800 **Gaffin** Dana L '99
(937) 236-3020 **Gagnon** Kathleen D '94
(937) 225-4652 **Gaines** Kandis C '00
(937) 223-1113 **Galen** Barry S '89
(937) 225-4601 **Gallagher** Joseph S '77
(937) 445-4051 **Gallagher** Julie D '93
(937) 586-3100 **ES Gallon & Associates**
(937) 865-6800 **Galvin** Gregory M '02
(937) 223-8177 **Gambill** R Brent '97
(937) 449-6400 **Gambrel** Kimberly '88
(937) 433-4090 **Gammell Hoshor Kendo & Ross LLP**
(937) 433-4090 **Gammell** Jeffrey W '91
(937) 865-6800 **Ganote** David P '96
(937) 228-5912 **Gantt** Gregory M '95
(937) 449-6400 **Gardner** Ames Jr. '65
(937) 865-6800 **Gardner** Ann M '94
(937) 435-8780 **Garman** Richard K '57
(937) 223-8888 **Garofalo** Carmine M '74
(937) 433-2744 **Garrett** Dawn S '91
(937) 512-2349 **Garrison** Connie Lee '92
(937) 496-3226 **Gasper** Margaret Lee '75
(937) 333-4460 **Gehres** Daniel G '78
(937) 225-4892 **Gehres** Virginia P '78
(937) 223-5200 **Geidner** Charles F '73
(937) 224-5300 **Gentile** Diane L '86
(937) 222-2333 **Gentry** Boyd W '99
(937) 449-6810 **Gentry** Caroline H '96
(937) 224-7200 **Gerhardt** Cassandra S '99
(937) 229-3442 **Gerla** Harry S '76
(937) 299-3576 **German** Regina D '85
(937) 436-0033 **Getty** Daniel F '01
(937) 643-0600 **Gibson** Gregory C '77
(937) 224-7311 **Gilbert** Paul D '62
(937) 223-8177 **Gildner** Lance A '91
(937) 223-1130 **Gilene** Salvatore A '02
(937) 434-7114 **Ginger** David S '70
(937) 222-2500 **Glankler** John R '88
(937) 225-4892 **Glasper** Thomas '81
(937) 223-5200 **Goelz** Robert D '78
(937) 225-2910 **Goldberg** Dale A '82
(937) 254-4455 **Goldman Rubin & Shapiro**
(937) 226-3525 **Goodall** L S '93
(937) 431-9700 **Goodwin** Charles S '75
(937) 225-4652 **Goraleski** Carl G '83
(937) 865-6800 **Gordon** Erica J '04
(330) 562-2681 **Gorman** Lisa M '94
(937) 449-6810 **Gottman** Andrew J '99
(937) 449-6400 **Gottman** James F '74
(937) 496-7609 **Gottman** Virginia M '00
(937) 913-0200 **Gottschlich** Gary W '71
(937) 913-0200 **Gottschlich & Portune LLP**
(937) 226-1212 **Gounaris** Nicholas G '95
(937) 223-1201 **Grandjean** Dalma C '77
(937) 865-2012 **Grass** Joseph J '72
(937) 333-4457 **Greaney** Dennis J '79
(937) 865-6800 **Greathouse** M Gregory '92
(937) 223-8177 **Green** John L '82
(937) 224-3333 **Green** Thomas M '76
(937) 225-3991 **Greene** James F III '86
(937) 445-4276 **Greene** Nelson F '88
(937) 223-3277 **Greer** David C '62
(937) 223-3277 **Greer** James H '90
(937) 223-3153 **Greger** Lawrence J '80
(937) 223-4332 **Gregg** Douglas B '72
(937) 865-6800 **Gressly** Brian K '90
(937) 223-5200 **Grieshop** David B '71
(937) 225-6379 **Grilliot-Murty** Moira L '04
(937) 208-2237 **Grimes** Timothy M '89
(937) 341-9422 **Grodecki** Paul A '90
(937) 229-2919 **Groeber** Claudette M '84
(937) 225-4652 **Grove** Charles L III '81
(937) 223-8177 **Gruenberg** Jonas J '70
(937) 223-5200 **Gudorf** Theodore G '86
(937) 225-2910 **Guerrier** Mona '96
(937) 854-4900 **Gump** Dennis E '69
(937) 443-6822 **Haaker** Christine M '94
(937) 443-6931 **Hackert** Timothy J '88
(937) 222-2424 **Hadi** Vaseem S Y '02
(937) 429-8595 **Haffey** David A '73
(937) 449-6400 **Hagan** Timothy W '78
(937) 229-2423 **Hagel** Thomas L '83
(937) 449-6810 **Haggerty** Patrick H '02
(937) 222-1800 **Hahn** Douglas C '76
(937) 223-2200 **Hale** Tarin S '92
(937) 223-1201 **Hall** David L '68
(937) 228-1111 **Hall** Dennis L '69
(937) 461-8800 **Hall** Keith R '73
(937) 228-1111 **Hall & Mueller, LPA**
(937) 229-3031 **Hallinan** Charles G '78
(937) 449-6810 **Hallinan** Paul G '80
(937) 223-1100 **Hamilton** Adelina E '04
Hamilton Bethany J '02
(937) 223-1201 **Hammond** Julie G '00
(937) 223-4332 **Hamrick** Winn C '50
(937) 233-8194 **Hanaghan** Dennis M '66
(937) 223-6211 **Hann** Jennifer K '96
(937) 222-2500 **Hanseman** Robert G '00
(937) 223-8177 **Hansen** Chad D '02
(937) 224-1427 **Hansen** Thomas A '65
(937) 223-8888 **Hanson** Diane E '93
(937) 443-6600 **Haper** Cori R '04
(937) 461-8800 **Harker Capizzi & Hall**
(937) 461-8800 **Harker** Donald F III '75
(937) 298-1133 **Harlamert** Irvin H Jr. '55
(937) 643-0600 **Harlan** Camille L '94
(937) 485-4380 **Harman** Daniel T '77
(937) 865-6800 **Harmon** Joseph P '86
(937) 461-5980 **Harmon** Sean H '97
(937) 449-6400 **Harrelson** Laura G '83
(937) 223-1130 **Harrington** Thomas J '60
(937) 222-2424 **Harris** Justin D '04
(937) 461-4060 **Harrison** John C '66
(937) 496-3158 **Harshbarger** Kimberly K '92
(937) 443-6842 **Harson** Linn S '96
(937) 229-4333 **Hart** John E '86
(937) 449-6810 **Hart** Tami L '04
(937) 224-1718 **Hart** Terry R '97
(937) 439-5708 **Harvey** Anne '91
(937) 224-0076 **Hatton** Frederick B '00
(937) 225-5840 **Hatton** Nicole K '00
(937) 299-5530 **Havemann** William L '70
(937) 223-3277 **Haviland** John F '85
(937) 433-2880 **Hawkins** Homer D Jr. '53
(937) 434-8951 **Hayslip** Michael W '94
(937) 461-6200 **Hazlett** Jeffrey A '81
(937) 225-5757 **Heapy** Jennifer N '03
(937) 435-7500 **Hébert** Shireen J '04
(937) 228-6802 **Heck** Cynthia M '79
(937) 225-5757 **Heck** Mathias H Jr. '72
(937) 228-3889 **Hedrick** James E '78
(937) 228-3889 **Hedrick & Jordan Co,LPA**
(937) 227-3700 **Hedrick** R Holtzman '04
(937) 225-6308 **Hein** Sara L '95
(937) 461-5980 **Helms** Jeffrey R '02
(937) 224-9291 **Hemenway** James K '88
(937) 223-5200 **Hempfling** Richard '85
(937) 333-4450 **Henderson** Carl S '85
(937) 222-2500 **Henderson** Toby K '99
(937) 222-1090 **Hendrixson** Patricia L '00
(937) 461-9330 **Henke** Lawrence W III '70
(937) 222-5244 **Henley** Elizabeth J '79
(937) 228-5800 **Henrici** Kelly A '94
(937) 226-1212 **Henry** R Mark '93
(937) 223-8177 **Herbert** J Stephen '78
(937) 228-0894 **Herdman** Douglas '83
(937) 449-2800 **Herman** Carrie E '03
(937) 449-6810 **Heron** John J '65
(937) 443-6615 **Herr** James Michael '68
(937) 223-1201 **Herron** Philip B '66
(937) 222-2424 **Hesse** Lisa A '89
(937) 865-6800 **Hewitt** Robin R '96
(937) 449-2800 **Heyman** Ralph E '56
(937) 298-7584 **Hickey** James P '68
(937) 775-3326 **Hickey** Robert E Jr. '74
(937) 225-5770 **Hiett** Teresa M '92
(937) 222-2030 **Hilgeman** John P '83
(937) 223-3277 **Hill** Jennifer L '99
(937) 439-5708 **Hines** Dean E '94
(937) 228-8104 **Hirtle** Stanley A '73
(937) 225-5787 **Hobson** Sandra K '78
(937) 228-2666 **Hochman** James B '66
(937) 228-2666 **Hochman Roach & Plunkett Co,LPA**
(937) 297-1150 **Hochwalt** Michael A '84
(937) 297-1150 **Hochwalt & Schiff,LLP**
(937) 298-8191 **Hodapp** Ruey F Jr. '58
(937) 461-0009 **Hodge** Victor A '81
(937) 449-6810 **Hoffman** Craig A '02
(937) 223-5200 **Hoffman** Louis I '61
(937) 223-8177 **Hoffman** Timothy D '81
(937) 208-2266 **Hoffmann** John J '90
(937) 228-9179 **Hollencamp** Arthur R '80
(937) 449-6400 **Hollenkamp** Nicholas C '64
(937) 424-8556 **Hollingsworth** Jonathan '83
(937) 226-1973 **Holm** Carol J '82
(937) 443-6820 **Holmes** Nathan E '01
(937) 865-6800 **Holt** Jon D '96
(937) 449-6810 **Holton** Thomas A '67
(937) 299-8653 **Holz** Michael H '68
(937) 320-1047 **Holzer** Richard J '75
(937) 293-2141 **Holzfaster Cecil McKnight & Mues**
(937) 367-4784 **Hong** Thomas S '01
(937) 224-7200 **Horenstein Nicholson & Blumenthal**
(937) 224-7200 **Horenstein** Steven B '72
(937) 865-6800 **Horner** Kurt F '91
(937) 227-3700 **Horstman** Paul L '67
(937) 278-5100 **Horwitz** Jonathan A '75
(937) 225-4979 **Horwitz** Jonathan A '97
(937) 433-4090 **Hoshor** Peter B '92
(937) 222-2424 **Houston** M Cinamon '97
(937) 224-7847 **Hovey** Susan J '82
(937) 225-4652 **Howard** Kelli R '01
(937) 222-3000 **Howard** Robert J '02
(937) 225-5761 **Howland** Linda L '80
(937) 225-4053 **Howley** Michael J '96
(937) 223-5200 **Hruska** Gary M '80
(937) 225-4892 **Huber** Janna L '02
(937) 445-6546 **Huber** Matthew B '96
(937) 225-4652 **Huelsman** Brian D '91
(937) 228-2292 **Huffer** Brian R '82
(937) 865-6800 **Hughes** Kathleen M '93
(937) 222-1285 **Hungerford** Eric S '67
(937) 222-2500 **Hunt** Deborah D '88
(937) 222-1800 **Hunt** Kevin M '01
(937) 443-6908 **Hunt** Nathan C '01
(937) 865-6800 **Hunt** Paul D '88
(937) 222-1800 **Hunt** Richard M '66
(937) 228-8080 **Hunter** Stephen C '74
(937) 223-8888 **Hyde** Henry III '94
(937) 223-8888 **Ignozzi** Kenneth J '91
(937) 225-3444 **Ingram** Carley J '80
(937) 229-3028 **Ingram** Jefferson L '78
(937) 222-3000 **Intili** Thomas J '86
(937) 227-3700 **Ireland** D Jeffrey '80
(937) 865-6800 **Irizarry** Francisco A '88
(937) 226-1996 **Izenson** Fred M '59
(937) 461-5980 **Jablinski** David S '85
(937) 461-5980 **Jablinski Folino Roberts & Martin**
Jacklitch Thomas R Jr. '67
(937) 424-5390 **Jackson** Christopher L '03
(937) 222-4059 **Jacobs** Craig B '00
(937) 228-8104 **Jacobs** Ellis '81
(937) 439-1189 **Jacobs** Gary J '82
(937) 865-7206 **Jacobs** Richard E '80
(937) 223-1130 **Jacobson** James L '78
(937) 461-1776 **Jacobson** Jeffrey M '91
(937) 298-2811 **Jacox Meckstroth & Jenkins**
(937) 228-9179 **Jacques** Robert F '02
(937) 689-7360 **Jaeger** Charles E '71
(937) 438-5588 **James** Stacey D '99
(937) 439-1177 **James** William K '83
(937) 496-7428 **James-Cox** Mary E '91
(937) 461-6200 **Janes** Robert J '85
(937) 222-2424 **Janis** Patrick J '82
(937) 461-5310 **Jansen** Susan D '87
(937) 228-3889 **Jansing** John G '88
(937) 865-6800 **Jarvis** Ryan C '99
(937) 222-6090 **Jasinski** James E '81
(937) 223-8177 **Jefferson** My'chael D '03
(937) 298-2811 **Jenkins** Matthew R '82
(937) 223-8177 **Jenkins** Peter L '03
(937) 223-3001 **Jenks Pyper & Oxley Co, LPA**
(937) 223-3001 **Jenks** Thomas E '53
(937) 224-1981 **Jerardi** Peter J Jr. '65
(937) 276-6577 **Jermany** Sharon A '02
(937) 223-1130 **Jewson** Matthew T '94
(937) 449-6400 **Jividen** William A '99
(937) 445-2968 **Johnsen** Kirk D '87
(937) 449-6810 **Johnson** C Terry '64
(937) 224-1427 **Johnson** Charles A '72
(937) 222-2424 **Johnson** Christopher F '80
(937) 445-2928 **Johnson** Debbie Watts '91
(937) 865-6800 **Jones** Heather R '03
(937) 225-5437 **Jones** Melissa L '98
(937) 223-2175 **Jones** Robert W '84
(937) 449-6810 **Jones** Scott K '98
(937) 222-2841 **Jones** Taylor Jr. '76
(937) 443-6824 **Jones** Teresa D '88
(937) 276-1737 **Jones-Kelley** Helen E '86
(937) 461-6988 **Jonson** Michele R '99
(937) 228-3889 **Jordan** April A '87
(937) 208-6395 **Judge** Dianne D '93
(937) 228-2838 **Justice** J Steven '94
(937) 534-0500 **Justice** Tabitha '02
(937) 276-1900 **Kaiser** Robert T '79
(937) 443-6816 **Kane** John F '98
(937) 225-4892 **Kantosky** Dorothy A '77
(937) 223-8378 **Kantosky** William H '77
(937) 434-2249 **Kaplan** Richard L '81
(937) 225-4652 **Karns** Cynthia A '93
(937) 449-6400 **Kaskey** Gregory M '01
(937) 222-4301 **Katchman** Steven C '89
(937) 224-0036 **Katchmer** George A Jr. '81
(937) 223-8171 **Kearney** Keith R '84
(937) 256-1449 **Kearney** Philip F Jr. '75
(937) 223-5200 **Keck** Emerson R '75
(937) 223-1201 **Keeton** Anne Pennington '03
(937) 396-1269 **Kegelmeyer** Jack M '03
(937) 278-1543 **Keish** Rodney D '72
(937) 223-1130 **Kelleher** James W '79
(937) 225-2910 **Keller** Dwight K '02
(937) 222-7600 **Kellner** Jeffrey M '85
(937) 433-4090 **Kendo** Thomas W Jr. '92
(937) 239-2711 **Kennett** David H '82
(937) 225-7233 **Kenyon** Gregory G '93
(937) 449-6810 **Kessler** Philip E '99
(937) 449-6810 **Kidwell** Charles Y '85
(937) 227-9382 **Kiefaber** Robert W '02
(937) 223-6035 **Kilby** Kimberly A '98
(937) 226-2121 **Kilgo** David M '78
(937) 449-6400 **Killworth** Richard A '73
(937) 333-4400 **King** Addie J '01
(937) 222-2424 **King** Michele L '99
(937) 443-6560 **King** Scott A '86
(937) 223-8177 **Kingseed** C Mark '86
(937) 443-6922 **Kinlin** Donald J '84
(937) 226-1990 **Kinney** Winfield E III '61
(937) 223-0697 **Kirkland** James R '69
(937) 435-8780 **Kirkwood** Lori E '91
(937) 226-9354 **Kirtley** John F II '04
(937) 222-2424 **Kislig** Kimberly S '03
(937) 222-2500 **Klasing** Heather E '99
(937) 865-7947 **Klein** Daniel P '92
Klopsch Diane K '96
(937) 298-1988 **Knight** Randal S '92
(937) 278-0651 **Knostman** Richard G '72
(937) 443-6777 **Knoth** Thomas A '86
Koenig Joseph A '75
(937) 223-3001 **Kohler** Chad M '01
(937) 296-4153 **Kolberg** John F '83
(937) 424-5390 **Kollin** Thomas M '96
(937) 461-5297 **Kolotkin** Beth A '80
(937) 512-1532 **Konya** Janice R '97
(937) 865-6800 **Koorndyk** Jill A '95
(937) 223-8171 **Kordik** James G '83
(937) 223-8177 **Korte** David C '80
(937) 291-9339 **Kosanovich** Daniel N '77
(937) 222-2500 **Kost** Susan S '92
(937) 222-6926 **Koverman** John R Jr. '59
(937) 224-1427 **Kovich** Don E '78
(937) 222-6764 **Kozar** Ronald J '89
(937) 259-7215 **Koziar** Stephen F Jr. '71
(937) 227-3700 **Kraemer** Thomas R '92
(937) 512-1681 **Kraft** Julie A '95
(937) 264-5110 **Krall** Michael F '81
(937) 222-1700 **Kramer** Scott A '00
(937) 223-3277 **Krebs** Leo F '66
(937) 512-2724 **Krebs** William A '77
(937) 586-7242 **Kremer** Debra S '99
(937) 449-2800 **Kress** Edward M '74
(937) 223-3277 **Krisher** Howard P II '75
(937) 275-7170 **Krochmal** Kenneth J '81
(937) 225-5781 **Krumholtz** John F '76
(937) 223-3277 **Krumholtz** Michael W '79
(937) 333-4100 **Krygowski** Walter J '96
(937) 228-8367 **Kuczak** Konrad '69
(937) 278-9399 **Kuns** David E '91
(937) 865-6800 **Kurtz** Christy L '89
(937) 223-5200 **Lachey** Robert E '73
(937) 225-2910 **Lafferty** Sheila G '89
(937) 443-6600 **LaForte** Rene '93
(937) 293-2392 **Lair** Anthony R '54
(937) 293-2392 **Lair Owen & Meadows**
(937) 222-2500 **Lambert** William W '81
(937) 221-1540 **Lamme** Kathryn A '80

(937) 223-5533 **Lang** Wilbur S '58
(937) 496-3048 **Langemo** Bree D '03
(937) 837-3302 **Langhals** Joyce A '85
(937) 222-2333 **Lantz** Kevin A '94
(937) 865-6800 **La Porte** Justina M '95
(937) 223-1201 **Larson** David E '79
(937) 222-6699 **Lasky** Laurence A '77
(937) 222-6699 **Lasky & Scharrer**
(937) 225-8871 **Latham** Samuel S '95
(937) 226-1900 **Latimore** Caroll A '02
(937) 228-2666 **Lauer** Carla J '92
(937) 228-8088 **Lavey** Debra A '01
(937) 296-0365 **Layman** David L '83
(937) 496-7959 **LeBoeuf** Mary Carmichael '03
(937) 228-2696 **Ledbetter** Michael A '97
(937) 433-5753 **Lee** Roger A '76
(937) 438-6848 **Lees** Thomas E '98
(937) 312-3614 **Leesman** Michael G '03
(937) 259-7115 **Leffak** Ellen S '85
(937) 449-2800 **Leibold** William J '82
(937) 438-9985 **Leland** Robert G '64
(937) 227-3700 **LeMar** Andrew D '03
(937) 542-3007 **Lenehan** John F '67
(937) 223-9133 **Lennen** Kevin L '87
(937) 496-7487 **Lenski** Kathleen S '98
(937) 913-0200 **Lentz** Mary E '90
(937) 294-2778 **Leonard** Paul R '69
(937) 294-5959 **Leppla** Gary J '78
(937) 224-1427 **Leve** Stephen '66
(937) 222-7884 **Levine** Jeffrey L '76
(937) 225-5602 **Levinson** James R '73
(937) 443-6949 **Levy** Mark P '81
(937) 225-7687 **Lewis** Beth G '93
(937) 252-6683 **Lewis** David M '85
(937) 225-4652 **Lewis** Michael V '81
(937) 222-1234 **Lewis** Terry L '79
(937) 461-1900 **Lewis** Vincent A '99
(937) 223-1201 **Liberman** Scott A '92
(937) 223-5200 **Lieberman** Dennis A '78
(937) 443-6958 **Lienesch** Theodore D '80
(937) 225-4444 **Lindsay** Karen R '98
(937) 865-6800 **Lipchik** Marie-Lise '93
(937) 222-2424 **Lipcius** Jesse R '04
(937) 436-0033 **Lipowicz** Richard A '80
(937) 435-2322 **Lipp** Robert W III '00
(937) 434-6040 **Little** Don A '66
(937) 434-6040 **Little Duncan & Pinchot**
(937) 333-4369 **Littlejohn** Billy C '73
(937) 449-2800 **Littlejohn** Gail H '83
(937) 890-4787 **Litvin** Joseph '73
(937) 222-0500 **Livingston** Jeffrey D '93
(937) 225-2910 **Lockhart** Gregory G '76
(937) 333-4400 **Logan** Deirdre E '91
(937) 254-0054 **Logan** Ronald G '58
(937) 433-0624 **Logothetis** Sorrell '68
(937) 898-9440 **Loikoc** Edmund G '70
(937) 223-8177 **Lombard** John C '64
(937) 298-7794 **Lopez** Alvin J '86
(937) 222-2424 **Loridas** Heather M '01
(937) 223-8177 **Lounsbury** Joshua R '04
(937) 222-8091 **Lowe** Charles D '64
(937) 865-6800 **Lowe** Christopher P '95
(937) 865-1812 **Lowery** Kermit F '84
(937) 865-7634 **Ludlow** Vicki L '89
(937) 223-8171 **Lush** L Anthony '90
(937) 865-6800 **Lutsch** Eric C '95
(937) 443-6600 **Lux** Carl A '04
(937) 224-3333 **Lynch** Jane M '82
(937) 226-9354 **Macey & Chern**
(937) 496-3158 **Maciorowski** Michelle M '97
(937) 898-1465 **Mackin** Melanie R '84
(937) 461-6200 **Mackinnon** Douglas A '01
(937) 443-6730 **Macklin** Crofford J Jr. '77
(937) 443-6804 **Maffett** Jennifer L '02
(937) 225-4063 **Magee** Christine L '70
(937) 223-6003 **Mahan** Charles W '71
(937) 222-2424 **Mahoney** Bryan J '99
(937) 227-6531 **Mahoney** Joan A '95
(937) 208-3195 **Mahoney** Mark E '03
(937) 223-8888 **Maier** Frank M '81
(937) 502-4160 **Main** Chad W '04
(937) 223-8177 **Makley** Roger J '60
(937) 496-3220 **Malhotra** Rajshree R '93
(937) 586-3100 **Malloy** Martin L '77
(937) 461-0000 **Malocu** Frank A '91
(937) 586-3100 **Malone** Richard M '77
(937) 223-8171 **Mancz** Barry W '77
(937) 223-8888 **Mann** Douglas A '84
(937) 534-0500 **Mann** Nikolas P '97
(937) 225-3322 **Manovich** Mark E '83
(937) 865-6800 **Mantel** Kaila A '94
(937) 913-0200 **Maresca** Richard A '95
(937) 225-5780 **Mariani** Laura G '94
(937) 461-9330 **Markowski** Kristen A '99
(937) 223-8888 **Marquis** David W '91
(937) 333-4400 **Marsh-Cook** Stephanie L '96
(937) 222-2424 **Marsico** Lindsay N '04
(937) 225-4652 **Martin** Barbara J '92
(937) 865-6800 **Martin** Denise D '00
(937) 865-6800 **Martin** Kathleen A '91
(937) 278-2612 **Martin** Kenneth D '04
(937) 223-8177 **Martin** M Shannon '93
(937) 445-2990 **Martin** Paul W Jr. '91
(937) 461-5980 **Martin** Thomas P '75
(937) 865-1653 **Martino** Bruce F '82
(937) 443-6810 **Marx** Dianne F '82
(937) 865-6800 **Maschino** Lisa L '91
(937) 865-6800 **Massa** Susan '93
(937) 225-4348 **Matis** Michael M '97
(937) 461-9234 **Matlock** Michael D '85
(937) 427-2271 **Mattera** Joseph P '03
(937) 285-6500 **Matthews** Jason P '01
(937) 775-2475 **Mattison** Gwen M '84
(937) 293-3890 **Matusoff** Robert B '55
(937) 223-8177 **May** Jill A '00
(937) 226-2118 **Mayhew** Kimberly H '91
(937) 220-4904 **McCann** Gregory L Jr. '82
(937) 865-6800 **McCarty** Kimberly A '97
(937) 890-0826 **McCloskey** James B '94
(937) 225-4400 **McCollum** Alice O '72
(937) 913-0200 **McComas** Benjamin K '04
(937) 277-3984 **McCray** Risa C '74
(937) 865-6800 **McDermond** Lori A '00
(937) 428-9800 **McDonald** Christine M '93
(937) 223-1130 **McDonald** Gerald L '04
(937) 428-9800 **McDonald** Joseph P '91
(937) 439-1083 **McDonnell** Ronald H Jr. '52
(937) 224-7200 **McDougall** Kevin T '97
(937) 225-5773 **McGee-Cromartie** Frances E '83
(937) 224-1981 **McGinnis** Carlo C '79
(937) 267-7625 **McGuire** Dennis M '94
(937) 461-6200 **McHenry** Brian R '96
(937) 223-1201 **McHugh** Stephen M '79
(937) 333-4121 **McKenzie** Brent L '97
(937) 461-9000 **McKinney** Charles A '87
(937) 222-1242 **McLeran** William T Jr. '49
(937) 225-4892 **McMillin** Judson G '02
(937) 865-1464 **McMurry** Donna M '88
(937) 461-5310 **McNew** Michael A '99
(937) 865-6800 **McPeek** Anna L '85
(937) 865-6800 **McQuillan** Suzanne T '95
(937) 226-1212 **McQuiston** Jeffrey R '76
(937) 223-8177 **McQuown** Terence P '00
(937) 512-1572 **McShea** Michael B '89
(937) 225-4464 **McSherry** Shauna K '79
(937) 223-5200 **McTigue** Terrence P Jr. '93
(937) 293-2392 **Meadows** Jerry A '75
(937) 298-2811 **Meckstroth** Alan F '60
(937) 865-6800 **Meder** Frank C '99
(937) 432-9300 **Meehling** John C '04
(937) 461-7000 **Meily** William D '78
(937) 223-1201 **Mesaros** David P '83
(937) 443-6841 **Metzcar** Jeffrey C '00
(937) 259-7209 **Meyer** Arthur G '82
(937) 461-5310 **Meyer** Beverly A '94
(937) 495-3660 **Meyer** Donald E II '95
(937) 223-8177 **Michael** Allison D '99
(937) 461-1900 **Miles** Stephen D '77
(937) 223-8888 **Miley** Douglas R '93
(937) 222-2333 **Miller** Amy '04
(937) 229-1000 **Miller** Arvin S III '84
(937) 228-5415 **Miller** Joseph P '87
(937) 865-6800 **Miller** Karen S '00
(937) 228-2666 **Miller** Todd T '94
(937) 435-7500 **Miller** William R '97
(937) 438-3977 **Millonig** Michael J '81
(937) 223-8888 **Minella** Shirley L '92
(937) 223-6003 **Mitchell** Amy C '98
(937) 449-2800 **Mitchell** James R '72
(937) 222-2424 **Mitchell** Nicole A '97
(937) 865-6800 **Mitchell** Robert G II '91
(937) 913-0200 **Mohr** John R '72
(937) 449-6400 **Molloy** Matthew A '04
(937) 361-6497 **Moloney** Maureen A '82
(937) 222-2500 **Moloney** Michael P '80
(937) 222-2500 **Monday** Michael W '00
(937) 228-9000 **Mondock** Joseph J III '02
(937) 225-4652 **Monroe** William J '75
(937) 890-6921 **Monta** Michael L '73
(937) 223-1130 **Montgomery** David H Jr. '98
(937) 225-5774 **Montgomery** Mary E '98
(937) 224-3333 **Moore** Erin B '93
(937) 865-7536 **Moore** Michael E '88
(937) 643-1240 **Moore** Thomas E '78
(937) 333-4400 **Moorman** Colette E '92
(937) 223-3277 **Morman** Carla J '96
(937) 449-6810 **Morris** Jeffrey W '93
(937) 865-6800 **Mort** Charles D '78
(937) 865-6800 **Mosley** Lynne R '93
(937) 225-7233 **Motta** Elizabeth A '93
(937) 865-6800 **Mount** Barbara A '80
(937) 225-4464 **Mount** Ronald E '80
(937) 228-1111 **Mueller** Carolyn L '95
(937) 225-5757 **Muennich** Joshua M '01
(937) 293-2141 **Mues** Robert L '78
(937) 449-6400 **Muhic** Theresa M '88
(937) 298-2226 **Mulligan** James J '54
(937) 228-9790 **Mulligan** Leo Patrick '84
(937) 298-2226 **Mulligan** Patrick J '89
(937) 223-8177 **Mullins** Jeffrey A '90
(937) 227-3700 **Murphy** Michele A '85
(937) 865-6800 **Murphy** Rosemary A '87
(937) 228-7277 **Murraine** Fitzgerald T '01
(937) 865-1133 **Murray** Erin '87
(937) 461-0009 **Murry** Michael K '83
(937) 333-4400 **Musto** Amy B '99
(937) 333-4116 **Musto** John C '99
(937) 225-4892 **Myers** Beth L '99
(937) 224-0076 **Myers & Frayne Co,LPA**
(937) 224-0075 **Myers** Jacob A '59
(937) 913-0200 **Myers** Jeffrey R '99
Myers Karen G '83
(937) 225-4652 **Nailing** Joyce E '94
(937) 865-6800 **Nash** Nancy A '82
(937) 643-0980 **Nauman** Joseph G '53
(937) 865-7417 **Naumoff** Cynthia S '00
(937) 898-1465 **Neary** James G '82
(937) 277-0175 **Neef** James T '60
(937) 225-7233 **Neidhold** Terri W '94
(937) 224-3333 **Neltner** Michael M '94
(937) 208-2379 **Nestor** Amy Bertke '99
(937) 227-3700 **Neudorfer** Karl E '00
(937) 443-6775 **Neuhardt** David A '79
(937) 443-6705 **Neuhardt** Sharen S '76
Neuman Edward B '66
(937) 222-2333 **Nevherz** Rebekah Sinnott '00
(937) 434-2425 **Newlin** John R '49
(937) 224-7200 **Nicholson** Bruce I '77
(937) 865-7664 **Nicholson** Mark W '85
(937) 443-6808 **Nilles** Victoria L '03
(937) 228-7104 **Nolan Sprowl Smith & Finke**
(937) 222-1090 **Noland** Thomas R '70
(937) 223-3001 **Nordstrom** P Christian '95
(937) 443-6815 **Norris** Allen R '83
(937) 495-4341 **Norris** Patricia C '87
(937) 293-2141 **Nortman** Tammy C '01
(937) 225-7676 **Nothstine** Roberta L '93
(937) 222-1862 **Nowicki** Griff M '00
(937) 229-8366 **Nugent** Robert L '73
(937) 223-1011 **Nystrom** Richard A '88
(937) 228-6001 **O'Brien** Daniel J '61
(937) 225-7233 **O'Brien** Mychael P '95
(937) 225-4168 **O'Connell** Timothy N '80
O'Day Tracey K '88
(937) 427-2271 **O'Diam** Thomas M '85
(937) 223-3277 **Oehlers** Joseph C '95
(937) 449-2800 **O'Hara** Lloyd H '42
(937) 865-6800 **O'Keefe** Kelly E '93
(937) 643-0600 **O'Keefe** Stephen P '95
(937) 461-7000 **Olsvig** Josie '88
(937) 222-7773 **O'Neal** Raymond W Sr. '81
(937) 224-0963 **O'Neal** Robert M '84
(937) 225-5757 **Orlando** Elizabeth J '03
(937) 225-5757 **Osborn** Susan E '01
Ostgaard Andrea M '03
(937) 225-5910 **Otis** Erin D Matre '03
(937) 433-7755 **Otto** Craig W '78
(937) 228-0880 **Overholser** James N '72
(937) 276-6568 **Overholt** Matthew T '00
(937) 293-2392 **Owen** William J '73
(937) 275-6842 **Owens** Alvarene N '77
(937) 333-4300 **Owens** Mark E '81
(937) 223-3001 **Oxley** Scott G '87
(937) 865-6800 **Paczelt** Anna E '86
(937) 223-1130 **Page** Gregory S '95
(937) 254-7312 **Pappayliou** George S '90
(937) 225-4987 **Parson** Angela L '03
(937) 225-5601 **Patricoff** George B '79
(937) 226-1200 **Patterson** Dennis L '64
(937) 228-2838 **Patterson** Lisa L '96
(937) 225-5757 **Patzer** Jeffrey M '96
(937) 223-8177 **Paulus** Janice M '85
(937) 222-4529 **Payson** Frank M '91
(937) 223-0122 **Penick** Bryan K '99
(937) 223-8378 **Pensyl** Michelle L '88
(937) 225-4652 **Pentecost** Michael R '86
(937) 227-3700 **Pepper** Timothy G '99
(937) 229-4507 **Perna** Richard P '83
(937) 224-1518 **Pero** Maureen '83
(937) 496-3147 **Petrella** Jennifer A '04
(937) 228-0894 **Pfarrer** Stephen M '67
(937) 438-5588 **Phillips** Thomas M '87
(937) 225-5778 **Phipps** Michele D '98
(937) 333-4364 **Pickrel** John S '70
(937) 223-1130 **Pickrel Schaeffer & Ebeling**
(937) 223-8177 **Pierce** David P '93
(937) 449-2800 **Pierce** Lisa S '95
(937) 586-3100 **Piercy** James R '73
(937) 223-9133 **Pierson** Steven T '84
(937) 434-6040 **Pinchot** Pamela L '99
(937) 225-4652 **Piper** Angela F '96
(937) 228-2666 **Plunkett** Gary D '90
(937) 225-4228 **Pohlman** Kenneth R '74
(937) 223-9790 **Poley** John D '78
(937) 775-2056 **Polk** Simone G '96
(937) 222-8500 **Popp** Vincent P '77
(937) 449-6810 **Porter Wright Morris & Arthur LLP**
(937) 913-0200 **Portune** Robert E '73
(937) 293-0900 **Poulton** Thomas M '79
(937) 865-6800 **Powderly** Melanie C '96
(937) 208-2263 **Powers** Cara W '98
(937) 222-2424 **Pregon** Jamey T '02
(937) 227-3700 **Preston** K Lynn '04
(937) 223-8177 **Pretekin** Ronald S '66
(937) 294-5959 **Price-Testerman** Connie S '90
(937) 449-6400 **Prior** Patricia L '86
(937) 449-6810 **Proud** H John '04
(937) 223-3001 **Pyper** Thomas H '81
(937) 225-2910 **Quinn** Margaret M '80
(937) 225-2910 **Quinn** Patrick D '81
(937) 223-4101 **Radabaugh** Tom B '63
(937) 227-3700 **Raether** Ronald I Jr. '97
(937) 775-4894 **Raines** David A '90
(937) 228-2696 **Rakay** Peter J '68
(937) 276-6580 **Ramsey** Sarah V '04
(937) 496-7291 **Rauch** Thomas G '75
(937) 225-6370 **Rea** Darlene S '95
(937) 225-6070 **Reardon** Melinda Barnett '04
(937) 443-6833 **Redder** Edward C '98
(937) 865-6800 **Reece** Barbara W '96
(937) 223-8177 **Reed** David N '91
(937) 449-6400 **Reed** John D '97
(937) 445-2109 **Reed** Shelley A '80
(937) 225-5706 **Reid** Lorine M '73
(937) 461-9400 **Reid** Phillip A '79
(937) 331-9227 **Reid** Worrell A '92
(937) 227-3700 **Reitz** Andrew J '03
(937) 222-9687 **Reno** Barbara E '86
(937) 223-2100 **Replogle** Thomas J '89
(937) 898-7673 **Requarth** Ann '79
(937) 865-7591 **Reynolds** Lynn M '95
(937) 449-6810 **Reynolds** Walter '79
(937) 222-1366 **Rezabek** Jeffery S '98
(937) 222-2424 **Rhinehart** Michael N '03
(937) 865-6800 **Rice** Martha E '01
(937) 225-4652 **Rice** Ted W '67
(937) 259-7103 **Rice** Timothy G '79
(937) 865-6800 **Richardson** Lisa A '01
(937) 643-9999 **Rickert** David M '78
(937) 224-4128 **Rieser & Associates LLC**
(937) 224-4128 **Rieser** John P '81
(937) 293-1000 **Rife** Harry P '62
(937) 443-6586 **Rigot** Joseph M '73
(937) 223-1201 **Riley** Adele M '82
(937) 223-6003 **Rineer** Donald B '99
(937) 443-0121 **Rion** James P '69
(937) 223-9133 **Rion** John H '70
(937) 223-9133 **Rion** Jon P '96
(937) 259-7118 **Rizer** Edward N '83
(937) 228-2666 **Roach** David G '83
(937) 461-5980 **Roberts** Brian M '82
(937) 223-1100 **Roberts** Christopher D '00
(937) 222-2424 **Roberts** Shaun A '88
(937) 222-1440 **Robinson** Eugene '71
(937) 224-7625 **Rock** William Randall '84
(937) 443-6825 **Roddy** Joan H '81
(937) 293-9189 **Roderer** Paul B '67
(937) 293-9189 **Roderer** Paul B Jr. '94
(937) 449-2800 **Rodman** Rachael L '01
(937) 252-2030 **Roedersheimer** Charles J '68
(937) 223-8171 **Rogers & Greenberg**
(937) 438-0555 **Rogers** Richard H '74
(937) 223-8171 **Rogers** William A Jr. '60
(937) 228-9790 **Rohrer** David A '89
(937) 225-5964 **Rondy** Anny Kraynanski '03
(937) 433-2567 **Root** Frank M Jr. '51
(937) 225-5434 **Rosario** Kay M '84
(937) 223-1130 **Rosemeyer** Jon M '84
(937) 228-2465 **Ross** Anne E '95
(937) 225-4464 **Ross** Cheryl A '96
(937) 224-0039 **Ross** Marc T '99
(937) 433-4090 **Ross** Robert D '94
(937) 496-7646 **Rousseau** Patricia E '90
(937) 296-0650 **Routh** Paul J '86
(937) 254-4455 **Rubin** Ira '75
(937) 223-1201 **Ruchman** Marshall D '64
(937) 225-4892 **Rudd** Richard D '02
(937) 396-0089 **Rudd** Timothy R '02
(937) 438-4601 **Rudwall** David F '82
Rueth Joseph E '80
(937) 225-5609 **Ruf** Walter F '82
(937) 449-2800 **Ruffner** James David II '94
(937) 434-3556 **Ruffolo** John M '82
(937) 434-3556 **Ruffolo Stone Dressel & Lipowicz**
(937) 225-5799 **Russell** Michael '71
(937) 294-6000 **Rutledge** Marybeth W '82
(937) 433-9926 **Ryan** Edwin L Jr. '71
(937) 449-6810 **Ryan** Robin D '01
(937) 223-8888 **Saldanha** Jason J '03
(937) 586-3100 **Salyer** David R '91
(937) 225-6495 **Salyers** Lance S '00
(937) 223-8821 **Salzler** Mark J '76
(937) 865-7875 **Samonas** Michael '86
(937) 445-2908 **Samson** Paul M '01
(937) 445-4937 **Samuels** Ellen J '86
(937) 229-4333 **Sandner** Lisa A '94
(937) 223-1130 **Sandner** Michael W '94
(937) 227-3700 **Sanom** Laura A '87
(937) 643-3770 **Santiago** Miguel A '04
(937) 586-3100 **Saphire** David A '70
(937) 229-2820 **Saphire** Richard B '71
(937) 278-4858 **Saul** Irving I '52
(937) 424-0041 **Scaccia** John J '83
(937) 225-4464 **Scanlon** Erin E '94
(937) 449-6400 **Schaeff** B Joseph '75
(937) 223-1130 **Schaeffer** Alan B '74
(937) 222-0410 **Schaeffer** Beth W '75
(937) 228-8183 **Schaengold** Gary C '82
(937) 225-4652 **Schafer** Mary L '02
(937) 228-0880 **Schaffer** Thomas A '72
(937) 898-1465 **Scheuer Mackin & Breslin LLC**
(937) 225-5757 **Schierloh** Joshua R '04
(937) 297-1150 **Schiff** Thomas R '88
(937) 689-3529 **Schindler** Melissa K '00
(937) 299-1895 **Schmidt** David R '84
(937) 461-6200 **Schmidt** Matthew M '00
(937) 865-6800 **Schmidt** Michele H '91
(937) 223-3001 **Schmitt** J Jason '01
(937) 222-1232 **Schneble** Alfred William III '81
(937) 228-2735 **Schram** Deborah C '78
(937) 228-8158 **Schriber** Kenneth L '70
(937) 435-7500 **Schulte** Richard W '96
(937) 223-8177 **Schwartz** Richard A '78
(937) 223-1130 **Schweller** Donald G '57
(937) 223-1201 **Scott** Donald K '86
(937) 225-5757 **Scott** Elizabeth Chapin '03
(937) 225-4829 **Scott** Gregory T '84
(937) 496-7265 **Scott** John M Jr. '95
(937) 225-4892 **Scott** Thomas B '02
(937) 298-0008 **Scudder & Esler Co,LPA**
(937) 298-0008 **Scudder** Steven C '90
(937) 434-7218 **Seall** William H '68
(937) 222-2500 **Sebaly** Jon M '65
(937) 222-2500 **Sebaly Shillito & Dyer**
(937) 224-0076 **Seeberger** Sheryl S '92
(937) 222-2500 **Sefton** Warren J '02
(937) 439-0386 **Segreti** A Mark Jr. '70
(937) 229-3801 **Seielstad** Andrea M '98
(937) 454-1038 **Seligman** William S '93
(937) 865-7605 **Sempeles** Leigh A '83
(937) 223-1130 **Senney** Jeffrey S '86
(937) 436-6886 **Serr** Willis O II '75
(937) 333-4400 **Sexton** Andrew D '99
(937) 294-6000 **Shale** Rebecca A '88
(937) 512-2935 **Shane** Bonnie S '82
(937) 223-3277 **Shane** Charles F '93
(937) 222-1090 **Shaneyfelt** Paul H '95
(937) 865-6800 **Shank** Anne L '88
(937) 223-3277 **Shank** Edward L '56
(937) 254-4455 **Shapiro** Joel S '67
(937) 866-6719 **Shapiro** Kenneth H '78
(937) 227-3700 **Sharkey** Gerald S Jr. '97
(937) 298-0067 **Sharma** Meenu '97
(937) 229-2218 **Shaw** Lori E '87
(937) 237-0112 **Shearer** Robert B '68
(937) 256-5252 **Sheets** Michael A '91
(937) 443-6757 **Sherk** Arik A '84
(937) 225-4652 **Sherlock** Karen M '82
(937) 227-3700 **Sherman** Adam C '03
(937) 225-5600 **Shia** Johnna M '97
(937) 222-2500 **Shillito** Beverly F '78
(937) 223-3277 **Shook** Charles D '52
(937) 438-6848 **Showalter** Robert L '89
(937) 222-2500 **Shulman** Jeffrey B '63
Shumaker Dennis K '03
(937) 865-6800 **Silver** Harry R '88
(937) 228-3731 **Silverstein** Jeffrey M '80
(937) 865-6800 **Simmons** Stacy M '96
(937) 449-2800 **Simon** Kevin V '96
(937) 890-2889 **Simpson** Charles J '60
(937) 454-1468 **Simpson** Jay M '81
(937) 264-5116 **Singleton** Vicki C '87
(937) 225-4987 **Sink** Jill R '03
(937) 227-3700 **Sinkovits** Angela M '03
(937) 226-1212 **Skelton McQuiston Gounaris & Henry**
(937) 226-1212 **Skelton** Richard S '88
(937) 223-2214 **Skilken** Ralph A Jr. '68
(937) 223-6677 **Skilken** Thomas E '78
(937) 748-9771 **Skinn** Bryce W '87
(937) 286-2360 **Slagle** John W '76
(937) 226-1200 **Slaton** Curtis F '86
(937) 228-9179 **Slavens** John M '70
(937) 223-1100 **Slicer** Charles W III '92
(937) 223-1100 **Slicer** Charles W Jr. '66
(937) 775-2796 **Slonaker** William M Sr. '72
(937) 222-9687 **Slone** Lee A '02
(937) 222-9687 **Slone-Stiver** Ruth A '85
(937) 223-8888 **Smalley** John A '85
(937) 223-5200 **Smith** Bradley C '78
(937) 228-7104 **Smith** Edward M '74
(937) 865-6800 **Smith** Georgeana G '94
(937) 224-1981 **Smith** Larry A '67
(937) 227-3700 **Smith** Nicholas M '03
(937) 222-6926 **Smith** Patrick K '78
(937) 910-7500 **Smith** Randall J '82

(937) 274-2313 **Smith** Rebecca B '80
(937) 865-6800 **Smith** Rosemary E '94
(937) 223-5200 **Smith** Roy Todd '87
(937) 228-9000 **Snead** Jeffrey W '94
(937) 224-5297 **Snell** Richard G '56
(937) 228-2696 **Snyder** Gary A '60
(937) 439-3811 **Snyder** Jeffrey D '94
(937) 865-6800 **Snyder** Mark E '98
(937) 222-7777 **Snyder** Monte K '85
(937) 449-6810 **Snyder** R Bruce '73
(937) 228-2696 **Snyder Rakay & Spicer**
(937) 222-2424 **Snyder** Robert N '85
(937) 428-0540 **Soifer** Stacey M '93
(937) 496-3013 **Sollars** Karen L '94
(937) 449-2800 **Solle** Susan D '99
(937) 224-7200 **Sommer** Louis F III '99
(937) 435-7500 **Sommers** Brian A '00
(937) 225-5565 **Sorrell** Janet R '81
(937) 278-8275 **Soter** Mary K '75
(937) 226-9354 **Sottile** Derrick A '02
(937) 865-7786 **Southam** Sharon L '00
(937) 225-4652 **Souther** Susan F '92
(937) 222-1366 **Southern** Patrick A '04
(937) 228-8104 **Souvé** Todd W '86
(937) 221-1940 **Sowar** Gerard D '87
(937) 223-1655 **Spaeth** Paul H '83
(937) 222-3000 **Spears** Gregory P '82
(937) 224-4600 **Spells** Yashmin W '87
(937) 228-2696 **Spicer** Jerry A '78
(937) 461-5980 **Stachler** John H '94
(937) 865-6800 **Stafford** Mary J '81
(937) 898-9440 **Stamps** Dana A '77
(937) 898-9440 **Stamps** Eric A '99
(937) 225-2910 **Stanek** Pamela M '85
(937) 223-5200 **Stanley** Lu Ann '85
(937) 496-3033 **Starline** Tyler D '04
(937) 222-1090 **Statman Harris Siegel & Eyrich LLC**
(937) 227-3700 **Stefanec** Erin E '04
(937) 299-2899 **Steigerwald** Jean M '86
(937) 225-3981 **Stenson** David E '89
(937) 223-5200 **Stephan** Wayne P '74
(937) 438-6848 **Stevens** Richard C '82
(937) 438-6848 **Stevens & Showalter LLP**
(937) 443-0416 **Stewart** Beverly J '87
(937) 443-6859 **Stewart** Jeffry C '02
(937) 443-6806 **Stirling** Scott T '93
(937) 443-1000 **Stock** Otto F Jr. '66
(937) 454-1468 **Stocklin & Simpson Co LPA**
(937) 454-1468 **Stocklin** Valerie '81
(937) 225-4063 **Stoermer** Elaine M '81
(937) 223-1201 **Stokely** Matthew D '93
(937) 865-6800 **Stoll** Sandra J '99
(937) 436-0033 **Stone** Scot A '82
(937) 223-1130 **Storar** Andrew C '81
(937) 222-7600 **Stout** Scott G '82
(937) 276-3990 **Strahorn** Derrick A '86
(937) 223-3277 **Stueve** Jennifer L '02
(937) 438-6848 **Stukenborg** Charlene L '95
(937) 222-7777 **Stukey** Linda S '78
(937) 226-1200 **Stump** Randall L '84
(937) 298-7794 **Suarez** Isabel '84
(937) 228-1525 **Subashi** Deborah J '87
(937) 534-0500 **Subashi** Nicholas E '86
(937) 534-0500 **Subashi Wildermuth & Ballato**
(937) 640-5030 **Sullivan** Anthony W '93
(937) 222-2424 **Sullivan** Thomas P '04
(937) 222-2333 **Surdyk Dowd & Turner Co,LPA**
(937) 222-2333 **Surdyk** Robert J '72
(937) 228-0880 **Sutton Overholser & Schaffer**
(937) 228-0880 **Sutton** Richard S '72
(937) 223-5200 **Swaim** James E '71
(937) 449-6400 **Swanson** Kristina E '04
(937) 222-7477 **Swift** Ben M '95
(937) 223-6211 **Swillinger** Jeffrey A '79
(937) 228-9000 **Switala** Gilbert B '91
(937) 225-4063 **Sylvain** Nicholas P '93
(937) 228-2838 **Taft Stettinius & Hollister LLP**
(937) 224-1006 **Talbot** Thomas B Jr. '74
(937) 223-8177 **Talda** Richard A '82
(937) 227-3700 **Taronji** Ian A '03
(937) 226-5642 **Taylor** Countess R '88
(937) 278-2723 **Taylor** Edward M Jr. '51
(937) 865-6800 **Taylor** Kevin M '01
(937) 278-2723 **Taylor** Mary J '51
(937) 865-6800 **Taylor** Steven D '02
(937) 461-5980 **Theibert** Jennifer D '03
(937) 220-9139 **Thinnes** Mary A '82
(937) 865-6800 **Thomas** Angela M '94
(937) 225-5757 **Thomas** Nolan C '04
(937) 227-3310 **Thompson** Christopher W '91
(937) 294-5959 **Thompson** Eric S '99
(937) 443-6600 **Thompson Hine LLP**
(937) 865-7606 **Thompson** Kenneth R II '85
(937) 252-2030 **Thompson** Lester R II '74
(937) 224-4600 **Thompson** Michael C '89
(937) 228-9000 **Thorson** James M Jr. '90
(937) 228-9000 **Thorson Switala Wilkins & Snead, LLP**
(937) 225-7306 **Thurman** Brett L '85
(937) 229-8257 **Thurston** Heather L '95
(937) 225-3449 **Titus** Gary L '84
(937) 228-7511 **Tolliver** George W II '01
(937) 443-6600 **Trahan** Jeremy L '96
(937) 223-3277 **Treherne** Gretchen M '01
(937) 222-2424 **Treherne** Jason E '01
(937) 898-5870 **Trissell** Stanley L Jr. '92
(937) 449-6400 **Trott** Merideth A '75
(937) 226-9354 **Trout** Douglas M '00
(937) 229-2529 **Turner** Dennis J '70
(937) 228-2838 **Turner** Gregory '01
(937) 299-9900 **Turner** James D '84
(937) 222-2333 **Turner** Jeffrey C '94
(937) 461-6200 **Turner** Jonathan C '95
(937) 222-2424 **Turner** Julia A '03
(937) 222-8500 **Tuss** Mark A '81
(937) 449-2800 **Tweel** Donna S '90
(937) 222-2500 **Ulrich** Karl R '91
(937) 449-6400 **Ulrich** Paul M '99
(937) 223-8177 **Ungerman** Fred A Jr. '80
(937) 333-4400 **Utacht** Edward C II '74
(937) 225-5608 **Valley** Theodore D '99
(937) 278-0022 **Vallone** Sean J '94
(937) 333-4349 **Vanden Bosch** Virginia C '85
(937) 298-0008 **VanderSchaaff** Bertis J IV '96
(937) 222-7477 **VanNoy** Anthony S '96
(937) 225-5607 **Van Schaik** Chris R '70
(937) 225-4652 **Vaughn** Navay M '89
(937) 222-6635 **Vaughn** Noel W '79
(937) 264-5116 **Velten** Judy L '89
(937) 485-4241 **Ventura** Douglas M '85
(937) 259-7348 **Vinolus** Athan A '88
(937) 227-3700 **Voigt** Eric P '03
(937) 223-8171 **Vollmar** Michelle S '95
(937) 222-2424 **Vollmar** Thomas Andrew '94
(937) 222-6926 **Vonderwell-Hull** Marcy A '04
(937) 224-3333 **Von Meister** Peter F '72
(937) 223-8177 **Wachstein** Steven M '01
(937) 225-5885 **Wagenfeld** Steven L '90
(937) 294-2778 **Wagner** Henry C '74
(937) 227-3700 **Wahl** Katrina L '03
(937) 222-2424 **Waite** Wayne E '82
(937) 223-8177 **Wakefield** Brian M '04
(937) 434-9938 **Wald** Kathryn S '80
(937) 226-9000 **Walker** Christopher A '88
(937) 208-2183 **Walker** Geoffrey P '86
(937) 434-2885 **Walker** Joseph W '78
(937) 225-4600 **Walker** Steven H '76
(937) 228-2838 **Wall** Hugh E III '72
(937) 225-4887 **Wallace** Helen C '00
(937) 222-1148 **Walsh** James Joseph '63
(937) 224-8100 **Wampler** Earl J '65
(937) 252-0002 **Wampler** Harold W III '83
(937) 224-8100 **Wampler** Sherry L '77
(937) 264-5116 **Ward** Steven H '79
(937) 254-2600 **Warden & Driscoll LLP**
(937) 254-2600 **Warden** Joseph K '89
(937) 294-4100 **Ware** Mark F '50
(937) 865-6800 **Warling** Robin L '96
(937) 223-8177 **Warwar** Sam '81
(937) 222-2841 **Washington** Cheryl R '87
(937) 496-1450 **Washington** Dwight A '77
(937) 224-8763 **Waskowiak** Amy M '99
(937) 443-6812 **Wasylyna** Victor J '03
(937) 223-6003 **Watring** Stephen A '81
(937) 449-2800 **Watts** Steven R '81
(937) 229-2326 **Wawrose** Susan C '95
(937) 496-6616 **Waymire** William D II '95
(937) 225-4652 **Weaver** Brian D '69
(937) 225-4863 **Weber** Jennifer M '02
(937) 222-1800 **Wehner** David K '76
(937) 274-3026 **Wehrle-Einhorn** Robert J '85
(937) 461-6600 **Weiner** Daniel D '63
(937) 643-9999 **Weisbrod** Alfred J '69
(937) 643-9999 **Weisbrod & Dankof**
(937) 222-2500 **Welbaum** Heather N '99
(937) 225-4652 **Welch** Carla E '97
(937) 222-3322 **Welch** John B '91
(937) 432-9500 **Wells** Amy L '04
(937) 432-9500 **Wells** Elizabeth A '04
(937) 333-4400 **Welsh** Mary E '97
(937) 445-7679 **Weltner** Robert B '81
(937) 224-7200 **Wendling** Marcus N '02
(937) 865-6800 **Wenz** George L III '93
(937) 225-4652 **Wenzke** James F '69
Wenzke Margaret M '77
(937) 222-8885 **Weprin** Ellen C '89
(937) 226-1776 **Weprin** James I '67
(937) 865-6800 **Wertz** Jeanne D '94
(937) 223-1130 **Wessendarp** Richard J '80
(937) 445-5755 **Wheatley** Bryan C '97
(937) 449-2800 **Whelley** Thomas P II '77
(937) 225-5760 **Whisman** Victor T '82
(937) 224-3926 **White** David A '88
(937) 222-2424 **White** Jennifer M '04
(937) 294-5800 **White** Lawrence J '93
(937) 435-8780 **White** Thomas A III '61
(937) 219-7726 **Whiting** Kimberly M '03
(937) 255-5270 **Whitt** Gregory D '84
(937) 449-2800 **Wickham** David R '83
(937) 225-5705 **Wienekoski** Victoria E '93
(937) 224-9291 **Wiggins** Misty M '02
(937) 223-8177 **Wilberding** Merle F '73
(937) 496-7740 **Wilcoxson** Clinton R II '93
(937) 222-4529 **Wilder** Lucas W '01
(937) 534-0500 **Wildermuth** Brian L '96
(937) 865-7495 **Wildfeuer** Steven R '96
(937) 228-2838 **Wiles** Matthew J '02
(937) 496-3161 **Wilhelm** Jenifer L '90
(937) 298-0008 **Wilhite** Stacy E '98
(937) 228-9000 **Wilkins** Lawrence A '96
(937) 226-2069 **Williams** Frank B III '77
(937) 866-0352 **Williams** Karen S '78
(937) 277-2950 **Williams** Lawrence R Jr. '89
(937) 223-3277 **Williamson** David P '78
(937) 278-0652 **Wilmes** John A '76
(937) 496-6917 **Wilson** Laura L '97
(937) 432-9300 **Wilson** Melinda M '01
(937) 512-1531 **Winquist** Stephanie L '02
(937) 223-1130 **Winterhalter** Paul J '66
(937) 294-6000 **Winwood Crossman & Associates**
(937) 294-6000 **Winwood** Jeffrey A '72
(937) 223-8177 **Wiseman** Lisa K '01
(937) 227-3700 **Wiseman** Mary L '91
(937) 222-2424 **Witherspoon** John G Jr. '83
(937) 496-3212 **Wolf** Rebecca J '83
(937) 253-7171 **Wolff** David G '94
Wolk Reuben '57
(937) 225-4063 **Wood** Timothy D '84
(937) 223-8177 **Woods** Lowell T Jr. '97
(937) 222-1090 **Woods** Tina F '97
(937) 254-7325 **Woryk** Mildred P '84
(937) 225-4063 **Wright** Annette M '87
(937) 227-3700 **Wright** Brian D '02
(937) 222-7477 **Wright** Michael L '97
(937) 222-7477 **Wright & VanNoy,LPA**
(937) 223-5200 **Wuebben** Kristi A '00
(937) 222-2500 **Yates** Nita S '83
(937) 258-3668 **Yiambilis** Paulette '97
(937) 223-8888 **Yim** Edward C '96
(937) 865-6800 **Yonak** Christopher R '00
(937) 224-9291 **Young & Alexander Co,LPA**
(937) 461-4646 **Young** Margaret R '87
(937) 224-1981 **Young Pryor Lynn & Jerardi**
(937) 222-2424 **Young** Robert W '95
(937) 496-7478 **Young** Timothy '92
(937) 223-5200 **Yuhas** Steven E '86
(937) 438-2000 **Zavakos** Christ L '62
(937) 512-1550 **Zimmer** Patricia A '84
(937) 223-1130 **Zimmer** Paul E '73
(937) 227-3700 **Zink** Julie E '99
(937) 228-2666 **Zipperstein** Irvin J '49
(937) 890-1739 **Zugelder** Mark A '82
(937) 449-2800 **Zukowsky** Philip A '85

DEFIANCE
Defiance County

(419) 782-3010 **Aplin** Robert D '00
(419) 784-5622 **Archer** Stephen R '78
(419) 782-9881 **Arthur O'Neil Mertz & Michel Co,LPA**
(419) 782-9881 **Arthur** Rodney M '69
(419) 782-9500 **Bates** E C '86
(419) 782-9492 **Beckman** Tiffany R '99
(419) 782-9492 **Borland** James S '69
(419) 782-9881 **Brown** Jennifer N '01
(419) 782-6055 **Clemens Korhn Liming & Warncke, Ltd**
(419) 782-2253 **Dulebohn** Diana G '80
(419) 782-6055 **Essex** Troy A '00
(419) 784-4699 **Goldenetz** John P '69
(419) 782-7757 **Haver** Mark L '90
(800) 544-7369 **Hayman-Weaner** Pamela A '92
(419) 784-3700 **Herman** Russell R '97
(419) 782-5134 **Hitchcock** James E '68
(419) 782-2253 **Horvath** Jeffrey J '01
(419) 782-3010 **Hubbard** Stephen F '84
(419) 782-9881 **Hutchinson** Matthew O '03
(419) 782-7757 **Kight** Katrina Y '96
(419) 782-6055 **Korhn** Stephen F '72
(419) 784-1072 **Land** David A '89
(419) 782-6055 **Liming** John M '81
(800) 544-7369 **Mantel** Lisa L '01
(419) 782-9881 **Mertz** Eric A '79
(419) 782-9881 **Michel** Daniel R '96
(419) 784-3700 **Murray** Morris J '85
(419) 782-9881 **O'Neil** Joseph W '77
(419) 784-9982 **Penner** Ted W '91
(419) 782-7284 **Rath** Barbara A '83
(419) 784-1414 **Reeves** John D '75
(419) 784-2123 **Renollet** Tamara S '90
(419) 784-9982 **Richards** Jilene E '98
(419) 782-2253 **Schuller** Elizabeth J '96
(419) 784-0002 **Seibel** Peter R '71
(419) 784-3700 **Slade** Carson L '94
(419) 782-8846 **Snavely** Stephen K '73
(419) 784-9982 **Sondergaard** Steven J '91
(800) 544-7369 **Steinhauser** Rebecca J '96
(419) 784-3700 **Strausbaugh** Erin S '02
(419) 784-3700 **Strausbaugh** Jeffrey A '86
(419) 782-2253 **Trimboli** Dennis B '79
(419) 782-2253 **VanSickle** Mary J '87
(419) 782-6055 **Warncke** Marc F '89
(419) 782-3010 **Weaner** James K '96
(419) 782-3010 **Weaner** John W '64
(419) 782-3010 **Weaner Zimmerman Bacon Yoder & Hubbard,Ltd**
(419) 784-1072 **Williams** David H '76
(419) 784-3700 **Yoder** Jayne Z '79
(419) 782-3010 **Yoder** Stanley J '80

DE GRAFF
Logan County

(937) 585-5165 **Minnich** Michael G '87

DELAWARE
Delaware County

(740) 369-2423 **Abrams** Robert A '93
(740) 362-8341 **Anderson** John R '87
(740) 369-8229 **Ash** Charles W '93
(740) 368-1673 **Bennington** Daniel B '73
(740) 833-2690 **Betts** Christopher D '97
(740) 363-2223 **Birch** David H '85
(740) 363-9412 **Boger** Keith A '81
(740) 363-1213 **Brehm** David J '93
(740) 593-5046 **Brown** Susan A '93
(740) 363-2600 **Burkam Fuller & Herzog**
(740) 363-2600 **Burkam** Jeffrey A '79
(740) 369-7567 **Carney-DeBord** Jack W '91
(740) 369-2423 **Chambers** Lester A '90
(740) 363-9412 **Clark** Thomas C '60
(740) 363-9412 **Clark** Thomas C II '91
(740) 363-1925 **Clinger** Terrie L '86
(740) 363-1324 **Coldren** Robert H '59
(740) 363-1443 **Cole** April B '98
(740) 368-1545 **Corroto** Mark T '87
(740) 833-2690 **Darr** Frank P '82
(740) 363-1213 **Davis** Joanna R '03
(740) 363-1313 **Diersing** Charles M '94
(740) 363-1313 **Dietz** James M '85
(740) 833-2720 **Dobrovich** Christine E '96
Fenker Steven M '95
(740) 363-1324 **Fergus** William D Jr. '95
(740) 363-1213 **Firestone Brehm Hanson Nelson Wolf & Young,LLP**
(740) 369-4388 **Flahive** Edward F '77
(740) 363-1443 **Flahive** Terrence P '86
(740) 363-1443 **Flahive** Timothy I '83
(740) 363-2600 **Fuller** Randall D '95
(740) 363-7182 **Fulmer** Amy M '97
(740) 363-1324 **Gabel** Edna M '80
Ganim Sandra M '95
(740) 833-2690 **Garrett** Candace C '01
(740) 368-1865 **Givens** Erin K '87
(740) 363-1369 **Gordin** Robert H '80
(740) 363-8988 **Gordon** David J '69
(740) 363-8988 **Gordon** Linda M '86
(740) 833-2690 **Gray** Thayne D '92
(740) 369-1125 **Haines** Quentin R '77
(740) 363-1213 **Hanson** Lewis K III '95
(740) 363-1369 **Heald** Anthony M '74
(740) 363-1369 **Heald** Chad A '02
(740) 363-1369 **Heald & Long**
(740) 362-1988 **Heimlich** Michael M '84
(740) 833-2593 **Hejmanowski** David A '99
(740) 833-2690 **Hemmeter** Marianne T '97
(740) 363-2600 **Herzog** Louis H '98
(614) 369-5297 **Hoague** Michael C '83
(740) 369-0330 **Hutchins** Shelby V '61
(740) 369-6812 **Jones** Nicholas W '75
(740) 363-1931 **Kaiser** R Lamont '69
(740) 363-3211 **Klein** James H '83
(740) 362-2881 **Lewis** Jonathan C '74
(740) 363-1369 **Long** Oscar R '73
(740) 363-1313 **Manos Martin Pergram & Dietz Co,LPA**
(740) 368-0111 **Marrocco** Michael A '94
(740) 363-1313 **Martin** Stephen D '74
(740) 549-6188 **Martz** Gary R '82
(740) 363-1324 **Miller** G Scott '84
(740) 369-8900 **Monnaville** Robert H Jr. '73
(740) 363-1213 **Nelson** April D '90
(740) 363-9232 **Osborne** Wesley W '00
(740) 833-2690 **Owen** William J II '86
(740) 368-0008 **Owens** Robert M '98
(740) 363-1313 **Pergram** Dennis L '77
(740) 362-7729 **Petkovic** Wayne E '71
(740) 548-4802 **Preston** Ralph W '76
(740) 833-2690 **Reinhart** James G '03
(740) 368-1545 **Rohrer** Kyle E '96
(740) 368-1545 **Ruffing** Peter B '82
(740) 833-2534 **Schmansky** Joseph E '00
(740) 833-2690 **Sellers** Leah J '00
(740) 363-9232 **Shade** David C '73
(740) 363-9232 **Shade** Michael R '80
(740) 833-2690 **Skinner** Alison M '02
(740) 363-7182 **Stults** Loran K '01
(740) 368-1575 **Sunderman** David P '77
(740) 363-7182 **Thomas** William R '91
(740) 881-4689 **Urban** Raymond T '86
(740) 363-1259 **Vatsures** Peter T '54
(740) 363-1259 **Vatsures** Stephen J '96
(740) 363-1259 **Vatsures** Thomas P '89
(740) 833-2690 **Vick** Robert F '00
(740) 363-3100 **Warnock** Douglas W '78
(740) 833-2554 **Wolf** Alicia F '99
(740) 363-1213 **Wolf** Scott A '97
(740) 363-9192 **Worly** Donald G '89
(740) 833-2690 **Yost** David A '91
(740) 363-1213 **Young** Don J III '00
(740) 549-6073 **Young** Robert A '90

DELPHOS
Allen County

(419) 695-7050 **Antalis** Gregory M '78
(419) 692-9055 **Clark** Nicholas J '89
(419) 692-0931 **Lause** Glen D '73
(419) 695-0097 **Mansfield** Stephen J '77
(419) 692-0060 **Metzner** John A Jr. '57
(419) 692-0060 **Minzing** Paula A '50
(419) 695-9925 **Moening** Ronald S '73
(419) 695-8480 **Osting** Clayton P '84
(419) 695-9080 **Steffan** Christina L '02
(419) 695-9080 **Waldick** Juergen A '85

DELTA
Fulton County

(419) 822-3211 **Barber Kaper Stamm & Robinson**
(419) 822-3211 **Buehrer** Stephen P '97
(419) 822-3211 **Kaper** Terry J '68
(419) 822-4197 **Meister** Joan B '61
(419) 822-4197 **Meister** Sheldon C '52
(419) 822-3324 **Van Gunten** Amber L '99
(419) 822-3324 **Van Gunten** Gregory L '76

DESHLER
Henry County

(419) 278-7015 **Collier** John S '79
(419) 278-7015 **Gribbell Sunderman & Collier**
(419) 278-7015 **Rode** James D '99
(419) 278-2896 **Sunderman** John D '80

DIAMOND
Portage County

Henry Cynthia L '85

DILLONVALE
Jefferson County

(740) 769-7219 **Boothe** Lawrence I '79

DOVER
Tuscarawas County

(330) 364-6553 **Bauer** Erick L '91
(330) 364-6553 **Black McCuskey Hanhart Deeds & Bauer**
(330) 343-8848 **Bohse** Frederick H '68
(330) 878-5501 **Boynton** John R '69
(330) 343-6080 **Buckley-Mirhaidari** Sharon '84
(330) 343-5542 **Comella** Michael J '82
(330) 364-4414 **Corsi** Mario D '51
(330) 364-6553 **Deeds** Charles J '89
(330) 602-2833 **Engle** Susan C '93
(330) 364-6000 **Farone** Eric V '00
(330) 364-6621 **Fox** Thomas W '73
(330) 364-1477 **Gartrell** John A '03
(330) 364-1477 **Gartrell** John M '88
(330) 364-6553 **Hanhart** David M '80
(330) 343-8834 **Hisrich** Thomas H '66
Marazsky Stanley P '99
(330) 364-7421 **Markworth** Lawrence '72
(330) 364-2803 **Miller** Thomas E '55
(330) 364-3353 **Ostapuck** John A '72
(330) 364-6591 **Pietro** Frank W II '78
(330) 364-9900 **Renner** Richard R '81
(330) 364-5505 **Space** Socrates J '59
(330) 364-5505 **Space** Zachary T '86
(330) 364-9900 **Touschner** Anthony J '73
(330) 364-6621 **Traver** Dennis D '73
(330) 364-5505 **Weimer** Christine M '98
(330) 343-8848 **Woodard** John L '40
(330) 364-6553 **Zemis** Kristin R '93

DOYLESTOWN
Wayne County
(330) 352-1439 **Baldwin** David C '95
(330) 658-2960 **Hollis** Cheryl A '96

DUBLIN
Franklin County
(614) 764-6895 **Aebker** Jill E '97
(614) 799-2800 **Alex** Spero M '82
(614) 799-2800 **Arenstein** Gilbert G '94
(614) 791-4121 **Ayers** Elizabeth A '95
Babner David W '93
(614) 791-3245 **Baker** Matthew B '02
(614) 866-0666 **Banks** James H '80
(614) 757-4514 **Barnett** James E '99
(614) 210-1840 **Barrett** David C Jr. '81
(614) 210-1840 **Barrett Easterday Cunningham & Eselgroth LLP**
(614) 791-1600 **Bauer** Christy L '89
(513) 367-5401 **Beck** Gregory G '82
(614) 761-0402 **Bellinger** Scott P '92
(614) 761-8323 **Bennett** George H Jr. '78
(614) 757-5132 **Bennett** Jeffrey R '98
(614) 791-9413 **Berky** Robert R '88
(614) 923-6534 **Bernard** Bruce D '85
(614) 764-1444 **Birch** Elizabeth J '89
Blake Joseph G II '02
(614) 764-0681 **Blaugrund** David S '77
(614) 764-0681 **Blaugrund Herbert & Martin,Inc**
(614) 734-1270 **Boland** James A Jr. '02
(614) 659-1644 **Bosserman** Eric L '97
(614) 757-5913 **Brasel** Christine E '99
(614) 734-3337 **Brown** James R '94
(614) 798-1600 **Buckley** Michael E '98
(614) 286-9670 **Budde** Joseph E '83
(614) 761-9775 **Budde** Oscar A '99
(614) 789-9600 **Burda** Robert T '81
(614) 798-0971 **Burton** Robert E Jr. '67
(614) 764-6057 **Buzash** George E '90
(614) 761-1000 **Byrne** Laura D '84
(614) 761-1000 **Byrne** Thomas J '88
(888) 224-3993 **Cadwallader** John R '83
(614) 210-1840 **Callicoat** Troy A '03
(614) 846-2946 **Cameron** Phillip D '69
(614) 873-2219 **Capehart** Curtis R A '03
(614) 718-4416 **Carper** Tina L '91
(614) 921-8976 **Carrier** Frank L Jr. '00
Carton Thomas W Jr. '73
(614) 761-9273 **Castrodale** Gloria P '88
(614) 761-3200 **Catri** Jeffrey A '84
(614) 854-8673 **Caughey** Stacey L '95
(614) 793-7600 **Centolella** Paul A '81
(614) 799-0602 **Chapin** Don H '89
(614) 789-0240 **Choi** Monica H '98
(614) 526-1013 **Clancey** Michael T '96
(614) 757-5000 **Clark** Marla D '96
(614) 764-0681 **Cline** Christopher T '75
(614) 766-7910 **Coles** Carl E '91
(614) 757-5957 **Cook** John K '96
(614) 854-4840 **Coridan** Mary F '81
(614) 764-0681 **Corna** Maryellen '92
Cummings Lisa M '95
(614) 210-1840 **Cunningham** Russell N '89
(614) 791-9112 **Cutler** Kimberly M '02
(614) 798-1800 **Danison** Nancy L '77
(614) 210-0222 **Daugherty** Scott P '89
(614) 757-7775 **Davis** Carolyn L '04
(614) 793-1799 **Davis** Claudia L '02
(614) 410-4643 **Davis** Natasha N '01
(614) 734-1270 **Day** Barbara A '00
(614) 895-3095 **Demaree** Karin E '99
(614) 793-5964 **DeMatteo** Lucia Villari '00
(614) 761-0042 **DeVore** Cheryl H '91
(614) 761-2003 **DiRosario** Lewis J '57
(614) 761-0402 **Donahue** Kerry M '93
(800) 799-1770 **Dougherty** Patricia A '83
(614) 789-1086 **Dougherty** Timothy R '95
(614) 764-8459 **Dreitler** Beth L '93
(614) 764-8486 **Dunsizer** Jennifer B '93
(614) 761-1733 **Duren** David L '80
(614) 210-1840 **Easterday** Jeffrey A '83
(614) 798-1600 **Eichenberger** Jerry A '75
(614) 764-1444 **Einstein** Dianne D '97
(614) 798-0511 **Ellis** George M '74
(614) 757-5000 **Erickson** John C '03
(614) 210-1840 **Eselgroth** Carolyn D '92
(614) 757-5000 **Falk** Stephen T '94
(614) 761-2003 **Faoro** Therese M '88
(614) 734-1270 **Farlow** Beverly J '85
(800) 237-4148 **Farren** Kristy E '97
(614) 764-4840 **Fireman** Steven H '92
(614) 734-9450 **Flynn** Nicole A '01
(614) 210-1840 **Foltz** Terri H '91
(614) 757-7713 **Ford** Brendan A '86
(614) 889-1493 **Forman** Monica S '86
(614) 764-0681 **Gabel** Jonathan M '85
(614) 764-1444 **Galeano** Judith E '90
(614) 761-7701 **Gall** Heather R '99
(614) 526-2581 **Gaskill** Regina M '02
(614) 792-5555 **Gayan** Eric M '98
(614) 799-1040 **Gentry** Steven G '82
(614) 757-7721 **Giacalone** Robert P '02
(614) 889-0500 **Gilbert** James D '81
(614) 718-6249 **Giller** Victoria H '97
(614) 792-9358 **Gluck** Myriam W '91
(614) 718-2517 **Goble** Paula A '84
(614) 764-7800 **Goldberg** Scott D '90
(614) 757-5000 **Goodman** Heather E '93
(614) 792-5555 **Grant** Stephen L '88
Green James S '02
(614) 764-3005 **Hadley** Gregory A '88
(614) 356-5000 **Hart** Thomas L '94
(614) 791-3243 **Hegedus** Joseph M '91
(614) 771-7070 **Heine** Bruce V '71
(614) 757-7221 **Henchel** Gregory J '95
(614) 791-2622 **Hendrix** Robert S '86
(614) 764-0681 **Herbert** John W '75
(614) 442-5800 **Hess** Charles W '81
(614) 764-3174 **Hessler** Robert J '79
(614) 764-3596 **Hickman** Gregory A '88
(614) 766-6346 **Hillman** Steven E '73
(614) 932-7000 **Himmelrick** Matthew T '99
(614) 737-1358 **Hinze** Keith W '03
(614) 889-6600 **Hitsman** Michael R '88
(614) 766-7000 **Hoag** Wesley F '84
(614) 764-3214 **Hoffman** Cynthia Jo '91
(614) 757-5187 **Hoke** Robin S '88
(614) 792-1790 **Holderman** Mark V '80
(614) 210-1848 **Hoover** Larry E '96
(614) 889-1143 **Hopfinger** John M '97
Horner Robert W III '91
(614) 764-4346 **Houfek** James T '69
(614) 766-9100 **Howard** Charles C '94
Howard Steven W '85
(614) 799-2800 **Humphrey** David L '86
(614) 793-1770 **Hunter** Jason C '01
(614) 620-5754 **Inman** Karl R '80
(614) 764-6746 **Inzetta** Mark S '80
(614) 757-5811 **Jackson** John M '01
(614) 718-9205 **Jacobs** Francine I '80
(614) 718-4434 **Jagers** Susan M '93
(614) 764-2007 **Jankowski** Daniel R '01
(614) 764-9944 **Jennings** Charles F '94
(614) 932-9884 **Jensen** Judith K '94
Johnson Ray E '00
(614) 793-5163 **Johnston** Craig E '83
(614) 734-1270 **Johnston** Vicki '04
(614) 798-2110 **Jordan** Joan B '99
(614) 792-9133 **Kalson** Lisa S '95
(614) 457-0635 **Kaps** Dennis O '74
(614) 764-3242 **Karasarides** Shawn H '93
(614) 764-8404 **Karpowicz** Joseph R Jr. '81
(614) 757-5000 **Kennedy** Michael P '93
(614) 757-7992 **Kepner** Kristina S '96
(614) 764-0681 **Kessler** David S '89
(614) 764-3228 **Klein** Dana W '79
(614) 764-0681 **Kovacs** Francis A Jr. '80
(614) 336-2984 **Kozlowski** John F '81
(614) 766-7243 **Kramer** Ronald A '71
(614) 793-1770 **Kreiner & Peters Co,LPA**
(513) 367-5401 **Kreiner & Peters Co,LPA**
(614) 792-5555 **Kwak** James L '96
(614) 792-5703 **Lacksonen** Todd A '92
Larrison Anne M '86
LaTour Kathleen A '87
(614) 799-2800 **Lawrence** James J '78
(614) 791-9112 **Leonard** James K '87
(614) 923-7700 **Leslie** Richard L Jr. '93
(614) 734-6270 **Lewis** Emily J '86
(614) 764-1444 **Lillard** Samuel N '88
(614) 734-3320 **Lipari** Gretchen M '93
Lokai Jeffery M '00
Long Timothy C '88
Loveland Daniel R '86
(614) 793-7000 **Lowe** Justin D '00
(614) 923-7706 **Lucas** Mark J '81
(614) 793-1246 **Lyden** Terrence W '86
(614) 798-1616 **Maloon** Jerry L '75
(614) 734-1270 **Marquardt** Richard F '00
(614) 764-0681 **Martin** Steven A '88
(614) 734-9450 **Mason** Ronald L '78
(614) 766-8108 **Mazer** Bernard D '87
(614) 791-7648 **McCarthy** Mark M '89
(614) 761-9321 **McCash** Thomas M '92
(614) 764-3210 **McCorkle** Leon M Jr. '72
(614) 717-0768 **McCormick** Nicole D '98
(614) 790-3787 **McCune** Diana R '88
(614) 889-5718 **McCurdy** Gay L '88
(614) 764-1801 **McHenry** Linda F '82
(614) 764-7440 **McKirahan** Jay F '72
(614) 791-5181 **Mears** Rhonda L '01
(614) 793-7600 **Mentel** Michael C '88
(614) 792-1966 **Mesirow** Christine T '78
(614) 761-1733 **Metcalf Duren Morris Starkey & Waid,LLC**
(614) 761-1733 **Metcalf** Richard B '51
(614) 761-6196 **Meyer** Robert A Jr. '78
(614) 596-1719 **Michael** Thomas P '68
(614) 760-8119 **Miller** Paul A '83
(614) 764-0681 **Miller** Sharon Lou '79
(614) 761-1733 **Morris** Robert V II '79
(614) 761-5001 **Morrison** Melinda L '97
(614) 764-1444 **Mowery** James S Jr. '73
(614) 764-1444 **Mowery & Youell**
(614) 790-8737 **Mozakis** Lee W '98
(614) 761-9775 **Muchnicki** Edward D '74
(614) 356-5564 **Murry** Christine A '98
(614) 764-0681 **Myers** Marc E '76
(614) 873-0364 **Myers** Susan M '89
(614) 866-0666 **Najjar** Nina M '82
(614) 757-5000 **Nelson** Michael R '86
(614) 798-0150 **Nesdore** Bruce G '89
(614) 923-7700 **Nevada** Eugene P Jr. '76
(614) 757-5542 **Nickey** Donald O '76
(614) 792-5555 **Norris** Jeffrey C '96
(614) 757-7426 **Norris** Jennifer R '96
(614) 798-1012 **Obert** Carl R '95
(614) 764-8407 **O'Kane** Michael G '81
(614) 764-8455 **Opelt** Vivian Lee '85
(614) 791-8215 **Pahwa** Susan K '81
(614) 923-1000 **Parisi** Vincent A '01
(614) 790-3396 **Patterson** Matthew T '82
(614) 791-9112 **Pennington** David S '83
(614) 889-7567 **Permar** David B II '85
(614) 757-5427 **Pero** Brian V '88
(614) 793-1770 **Peters** James M '76
(614) 791-4121 **Peterson** Lauren M '82
(614) 889-1425 **Phillips** Thomas M '72
(614) 764-1444 **Poling** Karen L '98
(614) 764-0681 **Postalakis** Stephen P '94
(614) 764-6056 **Presas** Julie L '95
(614) 761-9990 **Purcell** Cary W '85
(614) 761-9990 **Purcell & Scott Co,LPA**
(614) 766-5800 **Rabe** Randall S '83
(614) 717-4444 **Radcliffe** Michael T '73
(614) 793-7600 **Ralph** Amanda S '83
(614) 764-0681 **Rasmussen** Teri G '84
(614) 336-3945 **Redman** Timothy D '89
(614) 734-2717 **Reed** Frederick R '73
(614) 766-9100 **Reich-Bruce** Sara A '97
(614) 760-1801 **Resch** Frederick D '78
(614) 764-3387 **Reynolds** Mark A '89
(614) 761-1010 **Rhoades** Joel D '93
(614) 792-5212 **Rhoads** Jennifer B '98
Rhodes Christopher R '00
(614) 764-8966 **Richards** R L '75
(614) 799-2800 **Rieger** Thaddeus T '89
(614) 764-8486 **Roberts** James E '92
(614) 893-2514 **Robinson** Evelyn R '82
(614) 854-3090 **Robinson** Kerry L '98
(614) 790-1556 **Roe** Michael S '93
(614) 789-5568 **Rogers** Brent A '97
(614) 210-7616 **Ronnebaum** Sherri L '94
(614) 760-1801 **Root** William K '78
(614) 792-1188 **Rose** David E '78
(614) 889-8160 **Rose** Donald G '66
Rowland Robert R '99
(614) 923-3300 **Ryan** Robert S '96
(614) 764-2007 **Ryser** Philip P '78
(614) 734-1270 **Sayers** Michelle R '04
(614) 793-1770 **Scherger** Scott C '02
(614) 764-3339 **Schuerman** Robert E '76
(614) 792-5555 **Scotney** Cheryl S '98
(614) 764-0681 **Scott** Geoffrey P '97
(614) 761-9930 **Scott** Peggy A '91
(614) 889-0234 **Sechler** Kenneth R '74
(614) 854-3437 **Senecal** Theodore F '72
(614) 757-5000 **Sherman** J Daniel '89
(614) 734-1270 **Sieloff** William L '01
(614) 854-5226 **Sigman** Timothy E '95
(614) 717-0768 **Sims** Leigh-Ann M '98
(614) 764-2007 **Smith** Eric M '96
(614) 792-0777 **Smith** Ruth A '77
(614) 792-5555 **Speed** Fred M Jr. '97
(614) 764-0423 **Sponseller** Nancy L '77
(614) 792-5555 **Standley** Jeffrey S '90
(614) 339-0171 **Stark** Andrew W '98
(614) 761-1733 **Starkey** David H '77
(614) 757-7861 **Steffensmeier** Michael D '93
(614) 932-6010 **Stelzer** Lorraine M '87
(614) 764-7440 **Stockamp** Deanna L '96
(614) 792-5555 **Stonebrook** Michael R '02
(614) 792-5555 **Stovsky** Carol G '94
(614) 761-6078 **Sugar** Joseph A III '94
(614) 923-7989 **Sweat** Katherine D '03
(614) 792-5555 **Szolosi** Michael Roy Jr. '95
(614) 757-5680 **Taylor** Ellisa A '93
(614) 761-1991 **Tenuta** Luigia '81
(614) 761-7701 **Thomas** Terry L '85
(614) 932-6369 **Tilton** Jerry E '75
(614) 734-9450 **Timms** David S '99
(614) 214-6720 **Toth** Timothy J '96
Troxell Elizabeth O M '90
Turner Amy J '01
(614) 792-7916 **Vaughn** Carol P '79
(614) 327-8500 **Vinson** Gary II '99
(614) 761-1733 **Waid** Phillip A '73
(614) 435-6675 **Walkup** Christine M '03
(614) 356-5000 **Ward** Thomas A II '96
(614) 766-1960 **Warren** Jeffrey S '99
(614) 766-1960 **Warren** Kenneth J '77
(614) 798-1321 **Waterman** Ronald L '01
(614) 764-1444 **Wayman** Merl H '83
(614) 764-0681 **Weiss** Carole D '86
(614) 932-7000 **Welch** Porter R '99
(614) 764-1900 **Welsh** Gerald D '72
(614) 764-7440 **Whann** Keith E '84
(614) 757-3428 **Willet** Debra A '89
(614) 757-7768 **Williams** Paul S '87
(614) 854-4841 **Williams** Thomas A '92
(614) 791-5730 **Wires** Eileen M '86
(614) 757-5000 **Withrow** Brent M '03
(800) 457-7703 **Wolery** Alan K '99
(614) 764-3323 **Wright** Herman L II '86
(614) 791-9112 **Wright** Paul Leo '78
(614) 757-7765 **Wulf** James V '91
(614) 764-1444 **Youell** Spencer M '74
(614) 799-2800 **Zaino & Humphrey LPA**
(614) 799-2800 **Zaino** Michael J '83
(614) 889-9282 **Zawaly** Peter P II '73
(614) 799-9494 **Zitesman** James A '93

EAST CLEVELAND
Cuyahoga County
(216) 321-7150 **Basie** Ramon '62
(216) 681-2393 **Curtis** Ronda G '92
Fakhir Ayana R '03
(216) 681-5020 **Jackson** Warner Lee '71
(216) 681-2214 **Keenon** Una H '75
(216) 451-4796 **McGowan** Harvey J '83
(216) 541-7000 **Nikiforovs** Andris G '91
(216) 371-0534 **Shelley** Howard A Jr. '66
(216) 851-0799 **Smith** Walterio S '60

EASTLAKE
Lake County
(440) 942-8544 **Brallier** Thomas B Jr. '95
(440) 942-6262 **Dame** Stacy E '02
(440) 953-9180 **George** Mark W '82
(440) 942-6262 **Germano** Michael P '88
(440) 951-6460 **Hawkins** John W '85
(440) 951-6460 **Hawkins** Judson J '77
(440) 289-6213 **Kasunick** Jason G '03
(440) 942-6262 **Lucas** Michael C '80
(440) 602-5120 **Myers** Neil '65
(440) 942-6262 **Richards** Daniel F '65
(440) 975-1003 **Rosenthal** Gary H '74
(440) 946-3946 **Shah** Indrawadan K '74
(440) 942-6262 **Simpson** Robert A '97
(440) 942-6262 **Spangler** Mathew E '02
(440) 918-6363 **Tekavec** James W '72
(440) 954-3744 **Vadnal** Richard A '88
(440) 942-6262 **Weaver** Geoffrey W '91
(440) 602-5135 **Wilcox** Richard K '85
(440) 942-6262 **Wiles** John W '59
(440) 942-6262 **Wiles & Richards**
(440) 602-5120 **Zele** Ronald J '71
(440) 602-5120 **Zele** Scott J '98
(440) 602-5120 **Zele** Zachary F '03

EAST LIVERPOOL
Columbiana County
(330) 385-3900 **Aronson Fineman & Davis Co, LPA**
(330) 385-3900 **Barnett** Troy D '00
(330) 386-5964 **Brookes** Timothy R '79
(330) 385-8590 **Buzzard** John D '69
(330) 385-5151 **Byers-Emmerling** Melissa '82
(330) 382-7455 **Ciccarelli** Mark A '99
(330) 382-0371 **Davidson** Marian D '96
(330) 385-3900 **Davis** William J '73
(330) 385-0419 **Emmerling** Frederick C '78
(330) 385-0850 **Fannin** Thomas N '68
(330) 385-3900 **Fineman** Bernard '58
(330) 385-5595 **Frank** Dominic A '92
(330) 385-7702 **Gbur** George A '94
(330) 386-3640 **Hoppel** Richard V '94
(330) 386-3640 **Hoppel & Yajko Co, LPA**
(330) 385-5595 **Kelly** Kyde L '02
(330) 385-0576 **King** Carl J '76
(330) 385-3900 **Kontnier** Kellie S '91
(330) 385-3137 **Lang** Mary S '74
(330) 385-3900 **Ludovici** Joseph L '86
(330) 385-8144 **Luther** Richard A '83
(330) 385-3900 **Osman** Daniel P '01
(330) 385-0351 **Payne** Charles L '83
(330) 385-3990 **Taylor** Hayes '82
(330) 385-3400 **Vodrey** Jackman S '63
(330) 386-3640 **Yajko** Mark A '83

EAST PALESTINE
Columbiana County
(330) 426-9076 **Allison** David M '02
(330) 426-9491 **Allison** James B '90
(330) 426-9491 **Blasdell** Daniel A '73
(330) 426-4121 **Dickey** Larry M '70
(330) 426-9296 **Ferris** Thomas A '82
(330) 426-3774 **Frost** Mark A '74
(330) 426-4121 **Hartford Dickey & Young Co, LPA**
(330) 426-4121 **Hartford** James T '79
(330) 426-3092 **Hill** Stephen A '79
(330) 426-4121 **King** Douglas A '91
(330) 426-2241 **Turner** Leevesta J '28

EAST ROCHESTER
Columbiana County
La Vallee Rebecca H '00

EATON
Preble County
(937) 456-8420 **Amiott** Laura M '95
(937) 456-4100 **Bennett** Gray W '91
(937) 456-1776 **Bruns** Stephen R '83
(937) 456-9999 **Clark** Karen M '90
(937) 456-4104 **Earley** Dirk E '00
(937) 456-4104 **Earley** George J '64
(937) 456-8156 **Ferguson** Rebecca J '75
(937) 456-4125 **Fisher** Donnette A '97
(937) 456-4941 **Henry** Paul D '81
(937) 456-2819 **Holtzmuller** Paul E '82
(937) 456-5581 **Hubler** Charles D '69
(937) 472-3648 **Kalil** Edmund H '89
(937) 456-5300 **Lindstrom** Carol P '80
(937) 456-8156 **Manning** Gracia S '98
(937) 456-8136 **Overmyer** Jenifer K '98
(937) 456-5544 **Peltier** Paul E '77
Petry John L '69
(937) 472-0193 **Ross** Augustus L III '75
Schilling Nancy A '89
(937) 456-8156 **Shaw** Byron K '00
(937) 456-6818 **Siehl** Andrew F '95
(937) 456-4103 **Thomas** James W '74
(937) 456-4103 **Thomas** James W Jr. '01
(937) 456-8156 **Votel** Martin P '97
(937) 456-8156 **Worthington** Kathryn M '01

EDON
Williams County
(419) 272-2521 **O'Donnell** Bruce V '86
(419) 272-2521 **Toner** John G '62

ELIDA
Allen County
(419) 229-2931 **Bender** Michael J Jr. '66

ELMORE
Ottawa County
McTague Jerome A '01
(419) 862-2415 **Weis** Kenton P '75

ELYRIA
Lorain County
(440) 326-1464 **Adams** Cynthia M '92
(440) 934-3700 **Anderson** Kurt D '90
(440) 328-2206 **Anderson-White** Charlita '88
(440) 284-5100 **Anglewicz** Gregory A '04
(440) 328-2205 **Arredondo** Michele S '81
(440) 326-4011 **Baggett** Jessica Ann '94
(440) 324-7577 **Baker** Edward J '89
(440) 365-2000 **Balena** William J '78
(440) 934-0044 **Balser** Brian K '87
(440) 329-5357 **Barilla** James V '92
(440) 326-4835 **Barilla** Jody L '92
(440) 323-8240 **Bartels** Victoria T '88
(440) 323-7070 **Becker** Michael F '76
(440) 323-7070 **Becker & Mishkind Co,LPA**
(440) 329-5389 **Belcher** Billie J '00
(440) 323-1808 **Bennett** Gary C '77
(440) 323-0687 **Berki** Jenifer C '04
(440) 323-1650 **Bilancini** Darrel A '78
(440) 366-5440 **Blaszak** James L '70
(440) 366-9930 **Blevins** Anne-Marie N '98
(440) 366-9930 **Blevins** Paul E '93
(440) 366-4792 **Bonham** Brian W '03
(440) 323-5813 **Boyson** Frank A Jr. '74
(440) 323-5700 **Breunig** Erik A '04
(440) 323-5700 **Breunig** Kurt A '79
(440) 324-5353 **Brill** Douglas M '78
(440) 323-7070 **Burnett** John W '87
(440) 323-5443 **Butler** Harry F '52
(440) 329-5416 **Butler** Linda M '88
(440) 329-5408 **Butler** Terrence R '84
(440) 323-6098 **Cabrera** Robert '94
(440) 934-3700 **Chavez** Stephen P '95
(440) 329-5456 **Cillo** Anthony D '93
Cirigliano Joseph E '52
(440) 365-1310 **Clemens** Timothy J '98
(440) 322-4548 **Clevenger** Sherman G '70
(440) 365-8388 **Cooke** Amanda M '03
(440) 324-5353 **Couch** James R '75
Craig Kristen L '02
(440) 323-8174 **Crobaugh** Christopher J '99
(440) 329-5193 **Csokmay** Jeffrey R '93
(440) 323-7066 **Dawson** Corinne K '78
(440) 329-5389 **Deery** Amanda R '04
(440) 323-9500 **Deery** James A '77
(440) 284-0800 **Dickson** Joyce M '97
(440) 329-3264 **Dlugosz** Robert W '85
(440) 934-3700 **Donovan** Kevin W '80
(440) 322-1329 **Dorsey** Jennifer M '03
(440) 323-6100 **Doyle** Michael D '91
(440) 329-5389 **Eckstein** Ann C '97

(440) 323-8004 **Edleman** Jeffrey G '94
(440) 323-3456 **Eschrich & Stoll Co,LPA**
(440) 322-5824 **Evanich** Jeanette M '92
(440) 329-5389 **Evard** Mary R '96
(440) 329-3255 **Farren** John E '99
(440) 934-3700 **Fauver Keyse-Walker & Donovan**
(440) 934-3700 **Fauver** Worth A Jr. '63
(440) 322-8236 **Ferguson** George H '56
(440) 329-5398 **Flanagan** Martin R '84
(440) 323-1203 **Fritz** Joel D '91
(440) 329-5389 **Gauthier** Peter J '91
(440) 328-2207 **Gemelas** James S '97
(440) 322-4548 **George** David C '56
(440) 365-8800 **Giamboi** Frank C II '86
Gibbons Daniel J '96
(440) 329-5390 **Gillette** Kimberly D '88
(440) 329-5455 **Glass** Sherry L '98
(440) 323-0866 **Godles** Michael J '89
(440) 329-5389 **Gronsky** Richard A '86
(440) 326-1464 **Grunda** Jay B '86
(440) 365-8800 **Hamamey** David A II '97
(440) 323-1145 **Hampole** Gowri V '97
(440) 329-5183 **Harkacz** Myron '79
(440) 322-4510 **Harkenrider** Lawrence E '99
(440) 323-6100 **Haynes** John S '68
(440) 323-1808 **Hendershot** Margaret A '98
(440) 323-7451 **Hubbard** Neal E '69
(440) 323-1019 **Hume** Ernest E '71
(440) 328-2250 **Ignatz-Hoover** Gail M '81
(440) 324-5353 **Illner** Michael D '85
(440) 329-5389 **Innes** Gerald A '75
(440) 329-5396 **Ioannidis** Amy '03
(440) 324-2409 **Janco** David J '89
(440) 965-7520 **Keressi** John S Jr. '79
(440) 329-5725 **Keys** John R '86
(440) 323-7946 **Keys** Michael B '78
(440) 934-3700 **Keyse-Walker** John L '81
(440) 323-8240 **Kile** Carol A '91
(440) 322-3800 **Kilfoyle** William E '56
(440) 934-3700 **King** Kristina M '01
(440) 329-5389 **Kinlin** Michael J '98
(440) 322-4657 **Knezevic** Samuel R Jr. '80
(440) 323-3456 **Kocsis** Paul M '99
(440) 329-5389 **Koury** George I Jr. '75
(440) 322-5985 **Kovacs** John J '77
(440) 322-5441 **Kryszak** Andrea C '03
(440) 366-9930 **Kuhn** Paula A '99
(440) 934-3700 **Lane** Howard T '93
(440) 329-9179 **LaPlaca** Anthony C '84
(440) 329-5389 **Lathwell** Lindsey C '04
(440) 322-5505 **Laubenthal** Marilu '82
(440) 323-4460 **Laux** Richard T '52
(440) 322-5441 **Lessing** Robert E Jr. '69
(440) 322-5441 **Lessing White & Roig Ltd**
(440) 323-6180 **Lieux** Kenneth M '84
(440) 329-5389 **List** Faye S '82
(440) 329-5389 **List** Stephen A '79
(440) 323-6545 **Locke Graves** Lisa A '91
(440) 323-1203 **Long** David C '75
(440) 329-5565 **Lubbe** Timothy P '98
(440) 323-2456 **Maiorca** Philip R '97
(440) 329-5389 **Malanowski** Stephanie '03
(440) 329-5389 **Mangan** Thomas M '81
(440) 322-0596 **McClain** James M '75
(440) 329-5389 **McConnell** Lucinda C '00
(440) 366-9930 **McCray Muzilla Smith & Meyers Co,LPA**
(440) 322-5770 **McGuire** James J '74
(440) 366-9930 **McGuire** Lisa J '01
(440) 324-5353 **Meckler** Stephen G '65
(440) 324-2409 **Mellion** Paul J '72
(440) 323-1203 **Merrill** Douglas W '00
(440) 366-9930 **Meyers** Kim R '84
(440) 329-6111 **Miklich** Thomas R '74
(440) 329-6660 **Miller** Bridget A '83
(440) 324-7607 **Morgan** Brian D '86
(440) 329-5389 **Morrisson** John G '77
(440) 323-3335 **Morrisson** John G '77
(440) 329-5389 **Muhek** David P '82
(440) 323-4903 **Musson** John R '75
(440) 366-9930 **Muzilla** Raymond A '58
(440) 366-9930 **Muzilla** Thomas A '86
(440) 323-1111 **Myers** David A '73
(440) 323-5646 **Nedwick** Michelle D '93
(440) 323-0687 **Nehr** David W '04
(440) 326-4399 **Nelson** Jill E '00
(440) 329-5389 **Nolan** Michael S '72
(440) 365-5000 **Pelka** Karen M '94
(440) 323-7070 **Peskin** Lawrence F '92
(440) 365-8800 **Petroff** Mark G '79
(440) 365-8388 **Piazza** Robert A '69
(440) 329-5389 **Pierre** Christopher J '02
(440) 324-5353 **Pocci** Marisa A '04
(440) 326-1464 **Powers** Linda M '93
(440) 322-1329 **Pulito** Gino '87
(440) 323-8240 **Ramage** Barbara K '80
(440) 329-5397 **Riedthaler** Jennifer M '01
(440) 326-4856 **Rising** June K '89
(440) 329-5286 **Robinson** Donald G '89
(440) 323-5700 **Robinson** James T '97
(440) 324-2409 **Robison** Deanne L '93
(440) 322-5441 **Roig** Delbert L '92
(440) 365-2880 **Rose** Carl J '04
(440) 322-7972 **Rosenbaum** Jonathan E '79
(440) 323-1203 **Rothgery** Eric J '99
(440) 323-1203 **Rothgery** Kenneth P '69
(440) 323-5646 **Rothschild** Honey '82
(440) 329-5521 **Russ** Catherine A '96
(440) 323-1808 **St Marie** Paul R '81
(440) 323-1808 **St Marie** Thomas A '75
(440) 323-3570 **Saunders** Kenneth G '96
(440) 323-1650 **Savoy** Jerome J '73
(440) 284-2883 **Sayre** James G '95
(440) 323-1774 **Schwartz** Richard K '85
(440) 329-5389 **Sheehan** Erin M '03
(440) 322-1329 **Shilling** Terry S '68
(440) 324-2409 **Silver** Michael D '88
(440) 458-4381 **Smith** Catherine K '96
(440) 323-2201 **Smith** Geoffrey R '83
(440) 366-9930 **Smith** Thomas J '66
(440) 326-4835 **Spenzer** Sherry N '78
(440) 324-5353 **Spike** Allen S '64
(440) 324-5353 **Spike & Meckler, LLP**
(440) 324-5353 **Spike** Neil H '97
(440) 329-5389 **Springfield** Freddie M '81
(440) 329-5246 **Strait** Gerald E '78
(440) 322-5441 **Stucke** Agnes C '02
(440) 329-5389 **Swansinger** Laura Ann '92
(440) 323-7433 **Szekely** Michael E '74
Tackett Joe L Jr. '03
(440) 323-5700 **Taylor Breunig & Robinson Co,LPA**
(440) 323-5700 **Taylor** James N '81
(440) 323-8240 **Taylor** William D '79
(440) 323-3335 **Tonry** Eugene A '57
(440) 233-8463 **Tweed** Guy E II '74
(440) 329-5297 **Waltz** Lisa L '94
(440) 329-5239 **Ward** Susan L '92
Weizel Hollace B '83
(440) 323-7510 **West** Harold A '54
(440) 322-5441 **White** Robert C '91
(440) 934-3700 **Wieber** Brett D '01
(440) 329-5389 **Will** Dennis P '87
(440) 329-9380 **Wolf** Scott A '00
(440) 329-5359 **Zafarana** Renee '86
(440) 934-7000 **Zagrans** Eric H '77
(440) 323-3334 **Zerbini** Elio P '65

ENGLEWOOD
Montgomery County
(937) 836-1013 **Crowell** Larry G '75
(937) 836-3648 **Cyester** Tod A '89
(937) 836-8639 **Geisenfeld** James R '64
(937) 832-1973 **Ledford** George W '74
(937) 836-3296 **Treherne** James E '73

ENON
Clark County
(937) 863-7593 **Cook** William R '98
(937) 864-2924 **Hollingsworth** David M '77

EUCLID
Cuyahoga County
Andreas Frederick W '91
(216) 692-6369 **Artuso** John D '86
(216) 481-0020 **Beni** Franklin '79
(216) 271-5665 **Brdar** Robert A '84
(216) 261-8839 **Cook** Gary '76
Cook Schuyler M '88
(216) 289-7600 **Davies** William B '83
(216) 261-0200 **Deyo** Kenneth D '63
(216) 589-9926 **Doyle** Barry T '77
Ekelman Beth A '91
(216) 486-2163 **Eyman** Culver F III '80
(216) 261-0200 **Fisher** Patricia A '88
(216) 481-2020 **Foti** Anthony L '88
(216) 289-2746 **Frey** Louis Christopher '87
(216) 732-9250 **Frye** Thomas E '72
(216) 261-0200 **Gargiulo** William C '69
(216) 289-4332 **Gilman** Aimee E '84
(216) 289-4500 **Giunta** Anthony J Jr. '88
(216) 481-0020 **Glitzenstein** Jonell R '93
(216) 481-0020 **Gonakis** Spiros E '75
(216) 481-0020 **Gonakis** Spiros E Jr. '03
(216) 261-0200 **Hribar** Joyce A '89
(216) 261-0200 **Hribar** Paul J '41
Janezic Christopher B '96
(216) 851-0800 **Johnson** Almeta A '71
(216) 692-7200 **Kold** Linda '01
(216) 261-1529 **Kowalski** Judith M '93
(216) 261-0200 **Lavigna** Michael P Jr. '74
(216) 289-2888 **LeBarron** Deborah A '84
(216) 481-0020 **Lombardo** David J '63
(216) 261-4004 **Lynch** David M '82
(216) 261-0200 **Mamrack** Edward D '79
(216) 533-3301 **McCafferty** Thomas M '02
(216) 481-6258 **McPhillips** Michael D '90
Meaney Thomas P Jr. '53
(216) 289-8322 **Meister** Brian H '96
(216) 261-7792 **Miller** Gregory J '78
(216) 481-2350 **Mock** Theron C '54
(216) 289-4500 **Molnar** Bruce F '74
(216) 289-2746 **Murphy** Patrick J '80
(216) 289-2746 **Oyaski** Paul F '77
(216) 481-0020 **Parker** Patrick R '93
(216) 731-3300 **Pearl** Robert M '77
(216) 261-0200 **Perme** Michael R '74
(216) 797-4489 **Peterson** Grace M '94
(216) 531-1766 **Picciano** Mary B '89
(216) 731-0050 **Pigman** Edwin P '82
(216) 692-7076 **Poeppelman** Robert L '89
(216) 261-0200 **Powall** Constance A '91
Pryatel Mark R '83
(216) 289-7600 **Quinn** Patrick D '76
(216) 289-4500 **Rich** Linda M '77
(216) 289-4500 **Rocco** Patrick R '69
(888) 901-4647 **Rupp-Autero** Margaret '98
(216) 732-9250 **Spechalske** Richard A '80
(216) 486-4868 **Speece** Janet L '87
(216) 481-4753 **Sweeney** Patrick J '70
(216) 289-5100 **Sweet** Barry L '82
(216) 731-2266 **Syracuse** Vetus '04
(216) 731-2266 **Syracuse** Vetus J '70
(216) 486-6888 **Testa** Paul A '88
(216) 289-8322 **Vento** Phyllis L '93
(216) 383-8413 **Vrabec** Craig S '85
(216) 692-3877 **White** James J '56
(216) 289-2700 **Wiegand** Richard A '78
(216) 289-5297 **Winfield** Patricia L '84

FAIRBORN
Greene County
(937) 754-3040 **Barber** Catherine Mae '79
(937) 879-2261 **Brezine & Bowers**
(937) 879-2261 **Brezine** Donald F '84
(937) 879-9542 **Brown** Richard T '82
(937) 912-9810 **Conley** Andrew P '03
(937) 878-8030 **Cusack** David J '94
(937) 878-8649 **Griggs** Peter N '01
(937) 912-9810 **Hall** Dennis L '69
(937) 912-9810 **Hall & Mueller, LPA**
(937) 879-9460 **Houston** Douglas G '95
(937) 878-3956 **Kramer** Thomas G '83
Limoli John K Jr. '92
(937) 878-8649 **Martin McCarty Wright & Roach**
(937) 878-8030 **Mayer & Cusack LLC**
(937) 878-8030 **Mayer** Michael A '94
(937) 878-5266 **Miles** David R '81
(937) 879-2261 **Morse** David R '00
(937) 912-9810 **Mueller** Carolyn L '95
(937) 878-8649 **Roach** Buddy R '95
(937) 754-3040 **Root** Beth W '92
(937) 879-2261 **Swigert** Daniel L '79
Vaughn Robert A '59
(937) 878-8649 **Wilson** Yvonne N '03

FAIRFIELD
Butler County
(513) 870-5000 **Atwell** Kevin H '85
(513) 603-5346 **Balzano** David J '93
(513) 939-3300 **Beeber** Kerry A '95
(513) 858-2400 **Billig** Gary A '75
(513) 892-8329 **Bruewer** Henry J '49
(513) 829-4579 **Carter** Bruce '92
(513) 829-6700 **Clemmons** John H '76
(513) 603-5032 **Collett** Keith W '98
(513) 860-5355 **Conliff** Charles M '92
(513) 870-2399 **Cracas** Teresa C '98
(513) 603-2213 **Crane** Debra K '96
(513) 829-7519 **DeCresce** Michele A '91
(513) 886-3829 **Felerski** Heather A '91
Gartner Leonard S '77
(513) 939-2439 **Goodman** Farrell J '92
(513) 829-6700 **Gressel** Michele M '78
(513) 829-2900 **Grove** Jack F '79
(513) 603-7176 **Hanna** David B '00
(513) 863-7771 **Irwin** James S '61
(513) 603-7991 **Kelly** Richard B '80
(513) 942-7900 **Kovach** Karen Sue '92
(513) 870-2989 **Kyrios** Helen '98
(513) 939-3300 **Leshner** Gerald R '77
(513) 942-7900 **Lewis** Stacy A '94
(513) 939-3300 **Lierman** Dale O '77
Losekamp Geoffrey M '96
(513) 867-5001 **Markstein** Peggy A '87
(513) 870-2000 **McGee** Joseph A '88
(513) 829-6700 **Millikin & Fitton**
(513) 674-6000 **Moore** Howard S '84
(513) 844-1960 **Moser** Donald K '87
(513) 645-1400 **Packer** Dennis M '92
(513) 603-5082 **Phillips** John P '04
(513) 603-2209 **Pustinger** David A '97
(513) 858-1258 **Rauh** Leslie H '94
(513) 603-2221 **Santez** David L '79
(513) 829-1590 **Schnell** James M '73
Semple Kathleen M '83
(513) 603-5097 **Skinner** Matthew R '91
(513) 868-1500 **Snyder** Richard D '88
(513) 870-2480 **Stofel** Steven F '01
(513) 867-5962 **Swaine** David A '85
(513) 829-7400 **Thompson** Grace H '86
(513) 939-3300 **Trokhan** Cynamon T '96
(513) 603-2316 **van Nuis** Rosalie P '85
(513) 603-5255 **Wainscott** Jason P '04
(513) 829-0300 **Wear** Maxwell N '67
(513) 829-6700 **Wolterman** Stephen J '94

FAIRLAWN
Summit County
(330) 253-1555 **Alejars** Stacey L '03
(330) 264-6464 **Behlke** William M '97
(330) 864-0500 **Boecker** Gary J '83
(330) 253-1555 **Booher** Debra E '97
(330) 666-5545 **Carlyon** Candice J '94
(330) 867-8422 **Cochran** Charles J Jr. '90
(330) 670-5213 **DelBene** Louis J '91
(330) 329-3792 **Fowler** Robert M '72
(330) 869-4262 **Gorenc** William Jr. '81
(330) 836-7040 **Graves** James R '57
(330) 668-3073 **Humphrey** Michael B '85
(330) 253-1555 **Joseph** John E '01
(330) 867-8422 **Kostoff** Thomas W '80
(330) 670-9777 **Kroeger** Tia M '94
(330) 869-4250 **LeMay** James C '82
(330) 253-1555 **Lichtman** Corey S '02
(330) 865-9250 **Mack** Michael R '73
(330) 253-1555 **Marinelli** Deborah M '01
(330) 666-6787 **Mullen** Thomas T '87
(330) 869-4257 **Nagucki** Robert E '93
(330) 869-0224 **Neiman** Robert E '81
(330) 864-3377 **Neman** Patrick J '67
(330) 864-0500 **Pappas** Angela M '99
(330) 376-6222 **Rackoff** Maryanne R '83
(330) 869-0263 **Robbins** Howard S '77
(330) 607-7298 **Rosen** Gerald M '99
(330) 869-4471 **Rywalski** Robert F '68
(330) 253-1555 **Scherf** Holly L '99
(330) 253-1555 **Schinker-Kuharich** Dynele L '98
Shaw Ronald R Jr. '91
(330) 865-4904 **Simonton** Stacey R '89
(330) 283-6950 **Sipplen** Eddie M '03
(330) 864-1923 **Stewart** Richard M '50
(330) 869-4200 **Syrvalin** Kristine C '93
(330) 867-1500 **Yashnik** Steven L '85

FAIRPORT HARBOR
Lake County
(440) 392-2737 **Warmeling** Jonathan R '94

FAIRVIEW PARK
Cuyahoga County
(440) 356-1100 **Allington** Frances Fitzgerald '97
Baumbick John J '98
(440) 333-4848 **Bennett** Robert T '67
(440) 356-2600 **Bliss** Thomas P '76
(440) 686-9000 **Bryan** Bradric T '90
(440) 777-6500 **Burke** James W Jr. '70
(440) 777-6500 **Burke Vannucci & Gallagher**
(440) 686-9000 **Carlin** Hugh A '83
(440) 356-0062 **Cullen** James P '85
Dever Veronica M '70
(440) 333-8088 **Ertle** John B Jr. '87
(440) 686-9000 **Esber** Kevin J '04
(440) 333-3100 **Farrell** Patrick M '83
(440) 895-1234 **Fox** Thomas C Jr. '92
(440) 779-1400 **Friedrich** Gordon R '73
(440) 777-6500 **Gallagher** James R '77
(440) 333-9001 **Gedeon** Carol R '84
(440) 686-9000 **Goodwin & Bryan LLP**
(440) 686-9000 **Goodwin** Elizabeth A '95
(440) 895-1510 **Gresko** Gary E '97
(440) 356-0062 **Hagan** Brian F '81
(440) 333-3100 **Hildebrand** John P Sr. '70
(440) 333-3100 **Hildebrand** John P Jr. '97
Holland Patrick J '91
(440) 979-1030 **Hom** Harold L '88
(440) 356-2600 **Hoty-Bliss** Diane '82
(440) 333-1296 **Jarrett** Rita M '92
(440) 331-2731 **Kowalski** Kathiann '79
(440) 356-4400 **Kowalski** Theodore R '67
(440) 331-0422 **Kreps** Robert C '75
(440) 331-8747 **Larimer** Leanne S '93
(440) 779-6383 **Larson** Patricia A '97
(440) 356-9575 **Lehman** Jeffrey K '84
(440) 356-2728 **Markus** Richard M '56
Mayer Michael P '94
(440) 333-4431 **Miclau** Daniel C '71
(440) 742-0241 **Miles** Stephen L '88
(440) 777-8497 **Mills** Barbara A '94
(440) 331-0266 **Murphy** Eugene D '51
(440) 331-8867 **Nanowsky** Gail A '91
(440) 777-6500 **O'Donnell** Deanna '93
(440) 356-0021 **Parasiliti** Mary F '01
(440) 895-1234 **Paulozzi** Joseph G '92
(440) 333-2500 **Penfield** George R '70
(440) 333-2503 **Perla** Randall M '74
(440) 895-1234 **Polito** Michael G '91
(440) 895-1234 **Polito Paulozzi & Rodstrom**
(440) 356-0062 **Rego Cullen & Hagan Co,LPA**
(440) 356-0062 **Rego** Lucian C '71
(440) 331-6671 **Rini** Charles A Jr. '92
(440) 895-1234 **Rodstrom** Derek N '96
(440) 777-6500 **Sage** Victoria M '88
(440) 686-9000 **Smith** Victoria N '95
(440) 777-6500 **Tittle** Donald S '75
(440) 777-6500 **Vannucci** Dominic J '74
(440) 333-3916 **Walsh** Mary K '94
(440) 333-6202 **White** Scott D '93
(440) 333-3100 **Williams** Robert H '80
(440) 331-7206 **Wukovich** George N '85
(440) 686-9000 **Yoder** Kimberly K '95

FAYETTE
Fulton County
(419) 237-2661 **Molitierno** Thomas S '82

FAYETTEVILLE
Brown County
(513) 875-3511 **Tissandier** Stephen J '90

FELICITY
Clermont County
(513) 876-4160 **Motta** Alan C '86

FINDLAY
Hancock County
(419) 421-2815 **Abke** Hope B '99
(419) 422-8906 **Alge** William S Jr. '73
(419) 422-2121 **Andes** Ronald L '88
(419) 420-3055 **Balega** Joseph R '86
(419) 421-4023 **Barto** Vincent A '85
(419) 423-2673 **Bauer** Bernard K '72
(419) 427-2406 **Baumgartner-Novak** Patti '91
(419) 424-1365 **Behrendt** Elizabeth A '94
(419) 427-3679 **Benson** Jeffrey L '76
(419) 422-2121 **Benson** Molly R '98
(419) 422-5565 **Betts Miller & Russo**
(419) 422-5565 **Betts** Stephen C '73
(419) 422-4014 **Beutler** Robert A Jr. '71
(419) 423-2200 **Blackwell** Robert B '89
(419) 422-2121 **Breidenbach** David C '77
(419) 422-8000 **Brimley** J Bruce '78
(419) 423-0242 **Brown** Garth W '93
(419) 422-2919 **Busey** Nicole M '02
(419) 421-3343 **Callahan-Brown** Linda J '93
(419) 424-7066 **Candler** Elizabeth P '80
Carrigan Martin D '85
(419) 424-7818 **Carson** Loretta A '82
(419) 422-7176 **Christopher** Steven D '84
(419) 422-2121 **Clark** Kristi L '96
(419) 423-0242 **Clark** William E '68
(419) 424-7286 **Collette** Daniel M '71
(419) 425-2769 **Crow** Robroy L '86
(419) 422-8713 **Davenport** Julie A '79
(419) 421-4476 **De La Cruz** Jaime J '00
(419) 423-2035 **Dibble** Barbara A '94
(419) 423-0242 **Drake Phillips Kuenzli & Clark**
(419) 423-0242 **Drake** Robert W '48
(419) 423-0242 **Drake** Thomas D '77
(419) 422-7178 **Elliott** Howard A II '86
(419) 424-3067 **Elliott** Karen E '83
(419) 421-3436 **Evans** Thomas D '80
(419) 421-3344 **Farmer** Clarence Eugene Jr. '86
(419) 422-4014 **Feighner** Robert E Jr. '99
(419) 427-9000 **Filkins** John C III '90
(419) 423-4321 **Firmin** John C '41
(419) 423-4321 **Firmin Sprague & Huffman Co,LPA**
(419) 420-9312 **Fitzgerald** Dennis M '76
(419) 423-1644 **Flowers** Richard W '96
(419) 424-7403 **Fry** Robert A '78
(419) 422-7700 **Fuller & Henry,Ltd**
(419) 423-8944 **Gaberman** Robert N '79
(419) 421-3112 **Gagle** Suzanne '92
(419) 424-7276 **Galose** Michael C '90
(419) 421-2386 **Gearheart** James W '03
(419) 424-1085 **Gilb** Michael E '85
(419) 422-2121 **Griffin** Daniel A '96
(419) 422-4014 **Hackenberg** Alan D '94
(419) 422-4014 **Hackenberg Beutler & Rasmussen**
(419) 429-7338 **Hackenberg** David A '68
(419) 421-3355 **Haffenden** Philip E '84
(419) 429-3500 **Hainley** Sharon H '88
(419) 421-3687 **Hancock** Paul D '78
(419) 421-3173 **Harwick** Cheryl L '91
(419) 424-9889 **Hauter** Gary M '88
(419) 422-4089 **Hawkins** Jeffrey Van '87
(419) 423-8746 **Higgins** Patterson W '72
(419) 422-8713 **Hollister** Robert B '77
(419) 424-1776 **Holmes** Linda S '84
(419) 448-4100 **Hool** Mary L '98
(419) 423-4321 **Huffman** Douglas W '76

(419) 421-2948 **Hunziker** Robin Morris '92
(419) 424-7089 **Johnson** Kristen K '93
(419) 423-4321 **Kemp** Thomas P '78
(419) 423-4676 **Kentris** George L '76
(419) 421-3370 **King** Virginia M '03
(419) 424-1365 **Kissh** John A Jr. '76
(419) 423-4321 **Klein** Matthew L '01
(419) 424-5847 **Koehler** John H '79
(419) 422-7700 **Kostyo** John F '81
(419) 423-0242 **Kuenzli** David P '64
(419) 424-7286 **Land** Lucinda M '89
(419) 424-5847 **Lather** Kenneth L '78
(419) 421-4476 **Lay** Lisa A '94
(419) 424-7276 **Maekask** Paul V '97
(419) 422-7393 **Magee** Timothy A '96
(419) 421-3277 **Maguire** John K '83
(419) 422-8716 **Malone** Michael J '73
(419) 424-4333 **McCracken** Jack J '90
(419) 421-3265 **Melin** Douglas R '78
(419) 424-4324 **Meyers** Gregory E '77
(419) 420-9312 **Mihalik** Drew Joseph '04
(419) 424-7089 **Miller** Mark C '91
(419) 422-5565 **Miller** Roger L '76
(419) 424-0202 **Needles** John Stanley '69
(419) 423-8055 **Niese** Andrew J '03
(419) 427-1355 **Noble** John D '61
(419) 422-1887 **Noggle** Michael C '86
(419) 423-0242 **Oman** John D '82
(419) 422-6486 **Opperman** Raymond J '54
(419) 422-8713 **Oxley Malone Hollister O'Malley & Warren, PLL**
(419) 424-4322 **Pinzone** Scott R '95
(419) 423-8668 **Powell** Steven M '93
(419) 424-7144 **Preston** Vernon L '80
(419) 423-4481 **Pry** C N '68
(419) 422-5387 **Rader** Roger L '79
(419) 422-9455 **Rakestraw** Adam E '01
(419) 422-9455 **Rakestraw** Gregory A '74
(419) 423-0242 **Ranzau** Christie L '02
(419) 422-4014 **Rasmussen** Donald J '84
Ricketts Anne E '93
(419) 424-7276 **Ried** Aaron J '00
(419) 424-7832 **Rinebolt** Richard J '48
(419) 421-2196 **Ritter** Robert H '88
(419) 423-4321 **Roepke** Stephen A '81
(419) 424-4323 **Roman** Bridgette C '88
(419) 423-0242 **Rooney** Philip L '92
Roszman Valerie Myers '89
(419) 423-0242 **Ruse** William E '72
(419) 422-5565 **Russo** Ralph D '78
(419) 424-7276 **Sass** Kenneth J '94
(419) 422-9693 **Sausser** John C '61
(419) 422-8111 **Schroeder** Jerome B '78
(419) 421-2598 **Schroeder** Kimberly B '92
(419) 422-2864 **Schuck** Robert E '83
(419) 423-5172 **Shaw** Patricia W '93
(419) 421-3261 **Simmons** Joe A '80
(419) 425-1110 **Smith** Kelton K '86
(419) 424-7144 **Smith** Kevin C '83
(419) 422-8906 **Snyder Alge & Welch,LPA**
(419) 422-8906 **Snyder** Daniel M '59
(419) 420-9312 **Spaeth** Bret A '97
(419) 423-4321 **Sprague** Robert F '68
(419) 427-4182 **Standley** Thomas R '81
(419) 424-7818 **Starn** Jonathan P '93
(419) 422-0288 **Swope** William L '85
(419) 424-4318 **Teeple** Richard D '67
(419) 423-8668 **Van Horn** Andrew J '97
(419) 423-8055 **Walter** Douglas M '84
(419) 422-8713 **Warren** Bradley S '95
(419) 423-5700 **Weasel** Charles W '76
(419) 422-8906 **Welch** Allen L '81
(419) 423-5090 **Wenner** Cheryl G '89
(419) 421-4121 **West** Elizabeth Ramsey '04
(419) 422-2121 **Whiteleather** Larry W '79
(419) 423-8055 **Whitman** Jeffrey J '77
(419) 423-8055 **Whitman Law Office, LLC**
(419) 421-2470 **Wilder** J. Michael '01
(419) 422-9875 **Winkeljohn** John T '72
(419) 424-7090 **Wortman** Drew A '00
(419) 425-2769 **Wykes** Stephanie M '03

FLAT ROCK
Seneca County
(419) 483-7330 **Talbott** Jacquie F '83

FLUSHING
Belmont County
(740) 968-1800 **Kelly** Claire R '03

FORT LORAMIE
Shelby County
(937) 295-2983 **Faulkner Garmhausen Keister & Shenk, LPA**
(937) 295-2983 **Shuffelton** David B '69

FOSTORIA
Seneca County
Alt Damon D '04
(419) 435-5566 **Bennett** Donald S '89
(419) 435-4809 **Burger** Robert M '54
(419) 435-9273 **Dauterman** Kurt A '03
(419) 435-9273 **Dauterman** William D '59
(419) 435-1886 **Guernsey** Donald J '77
(419) 435-8139 **Hadacek** John D '75
(419) 436-5613 **James** Richard P '92
(419) 435-7786 **Marley** Barbara L '73
(419) 435-7786 **Marley** Francis M Jr. '71
(419) 435-2359 **Mennel** Donald M '86
(419) 435-2284 **Murray** Gene P '76
(419) 435-5566 **Patel** Upendra K '96
(419) 435-1886 **Reffner** Carol L '87
(419) 435-0606 **Stotzer** Jonathan G '83
(419) 435-1039 **Wolph** Alexandra K '87

FRANKLIN
Warren County
(937) 746-2832 **Bronson** Barbara J '73
(937) 704-0220 **Bunce** Jack P '73
(937) 746-2832 **Burns** Joshua G '01
(937) 743-1500 **Chicarelli** David A '75
(513) 424-4863 **Foley** Darlene F '83
(513) 422-7665 **Green** Bryan L '01
(937) 743-1500 **Lahmann** Barbara A '87
(937) 746-9921 **Lukas** James M '96
(937) 746-6425 **Runge** Steven M '75
(937) 746-2832 **Ruppert Bronson & Ruppert Co, LPA**
(937) 746-2832 **Ruppert** James D '66
(937) 746-2832 **Ruppert** Jeffrey A '99
(937) 746-2832 **Ruppert** Ronald W '88
(937) 746-2832 **Ruppert** Rupert E '76

FREDERICKTOWN
Knox County
(740) 694-3015 **Bringman** William P '70
(740) 694-6315 **Connett** Kimberly M '96

FREMONT
Sandusky County
(419) 355-1372 **Adams** Herbert E '72
(419) 332-9999 **Albrechta** Joseph F '84
(419) 334-7436 **Ansted** Barbara J '78
(419) 355-5349 **Bilby** Cynthia A '95
(419) 332-8260 **Bowlus** Thomas M '94
(419) 332-8260 **Bowlus** William R '62
(419) 332-7161 **Bristley** C Wesley '51
(419) 334-8884 **Brudzinski** Daniel L '91
(419) 232-8810 **Chudzinski** Anthony A '76
(419) 332-5587 **Culbert** Roger A '73
(419) 332-1101 **Dorobek** David A '85
(419) 334-6222 **Elder** Benjamin R '98
(419) 332-4722 **Ellis** James H III '00
(419) 333-4345 **Fiegl** Christopher P '92
(419) 334-6211 **Geiger** Michael R '72
(419) 332-1670 **Hafford** Roger W '77
(419) 355-5374 **Haley** Nancy E '89
(419) 332-3800 **Hall** John F '70
(419) 332-5553 **Hart** Robert G '84
(419) 332-8111 **Heid** Robert C '64
(419) 332-8111 **Heid** Sally R '54
(419) 332-4463 **Ickes** Jon M '92
(419) 334-6446 **Ickes** Leslie S '75
(419) 334-2232 **Kane** Jeffrey A '87
(419) 334-6222 **Kolesar** John P '95
(419) 333-3552 **Lockshin** Andrew C '02
(419) 332-7301 **Luse** Barry F '85
(419) 334-8377 **Mayle** Ronald J '74
(419) 332-8828 **Melle** James F '94
(419) 334-2909 **Moreland** Ruth A '97
(800) 837-8908 **Nava-Wade** Nancy '93
(419) 334-2909 **Newell** Beverly S '96
(419) 334-8444 **Quigley** Richard W Jr. '73
(419) 334-9723 **Scranton** Nancy M '73
(419) 332-2221 **Semer** Jerry W '74
(419) 332-8293 **Sherick** Sara J '91
(419) 332-0550 **Smith** Bradley J '96
(419) 333-9918 **Snyder** Lisa M '98
(419) 334-9725 **Solze** Norman P '70
(419) 334-8937 **Stierwalt** Thomas L '75
Watkins Linda K '90
(419) 334-9501 **Wingard** William A '73
(800) 837-8908 **Wu** Karen P '04
(419) 332-5579 **Zinkand** John L '69

FRESNO
Coshocton County
(740) 622-3240 **Weber** Linda H '95

GAHANNA
Franklin County
(614) 478-9472 **Adjoua** Hakim B '99
Adler Allen P '71
(614) 476-5540 **Agin** Frank J '88
(614) 471-5881 **Angell** Robert C '93
(614) 883-7680 **Barnitz** David W '90
(614) 418-4740 **Benson** Michael E '97
(614) 939-9409 **Bicking** Carol D '94
(614) 478-8020 **Bonham** William T '88
Bring Dale V '74
(614) 428-6969 **Burnside-Kelly** Susan B '91
(614) 428-8540 **Cohen** Robert D '76
(614) 751-0444 **Connor** Kevin H '86
(614) 471-5150 **Creed** Lawrence C '97
(614) 337-0960 **Daneman** Sara J '79
Evans Scott L '95
(614) 471-7424 **Ewald** Shane W '00
(614) 475-6677 **Faist** Julia A '78
Friedman Kimberly J '89
(614) 414-0052 **Fulkerson** Kimberly Loughry '01
(614) 478-5555 **Hennis** Trina D '85
(614) 475-6677 **Johnson** Kathleen A '93
(614) 478-8616 **Jurca** Melanie C '84
(614) 471-8181 **King** Ray J '74
(614) 475-5174 **Leickly** James R '86
(614) 475-7040 **Mancuso** Anthony O '86
(614) 471-8194 **Mantel** James K '91
(614) 729-4900 **Melvin** Carolyn S '80
(614) 883-7698 **Miller** Regina A '96
(614) 476-6453 **Moran** Michael R '94
(614) 476-5252 **Morris** Richard L '90
(614) 939-1948 **Mosbacher** Linda F '89
(614) 471-8194 **Mularski** Raymond J '84
(614) 471-3113 **Murray** Bernard M '69
(614) 751-2650 **O'Connor** Robert F '79
(614) 428-7867 **Peden** John J '83
(614) 476-2222 **Richards** David J '77
(614) 478-3676 **Riddell** Peter H '74
Saken Elizabeta P '03
(614) 476-1596 **Schmidt** Thomas F '83
Snyder Larry H '52
(614) 729-4921 **Spencer** Robert W Jr. '98
(614) 337-0354 **Stehle** William L '64
(800) 686-0025 **Swisher** John R '95
(614) 475-2233 **Tripp** Thomas N '67
(614) 313-2389 **Vorys** George N '79
(614) 476-0350 **Weber** Thomas L '69
(614) 552-1696 **Yockey** Albert M III '94
(614) 729-4909 **Zablocki-Gage** Kathy L '99

GALENA
Delaware County
(740) 657-1661 **Faulkner** Steven L '93
(740) 965-0746 **Hartman** Ronald F '67
(740) 965-1855 **Head** Suzanne '89
(740) 965-3900 **Molnar** Kenneth J '74
O'Reilly Patrick F '04

GALION
Crawford County
(419) 468-6300 **Erlsten** Steven J '68
(419) 468-4933 **Garverick** Debra A '83
(419) 468-5044 **Garverick** Grant B '88
(419) 468-5044 **Garverick** Lowell B '59
(419) 468-1766 **Hesby** Philip S '50
(419) 468-5044 **Hottenroth** Earl R '62
(419) 468-5044 **Hottenroth Garverick Tilson & Garverick Co,LPA**
(419) 468-7766 **Keller** David W '82
(419) 468-7766 **Keller Zeisler & Murphy**
(419) 468-7766 **Murphy** Clifford J '94
(419) 462-7060 **Palmer** Thomas N '92
(419) 468-5044 **Tilson** Stephen F '74
(419) 468-1131 **Wagner** Jay D '84
(419) 468-1131 **Wagner** John L '55
(419) 468-7766 **Zeisler** Jeffrey D '93

GALLIPOLIS
Gallia County
(740) 446-0644 **Adkins** Charles Jeffrey '86
(740) 446-7890 **Calhoun** Ronald R '58
(740) 446-2922 **Cherrington Moulton & Evans**
(740) 446-0603 **Conley** William D '72
(740) 446-0644 **Cowles** Douglas M '76
(740) 446-8575 **Eachus** Michael N '03
(740) 446-8575 **Eachus** William N '74
(740) 446-1737 **Evans** David C '01
(740) 446-8575 **Finley** Jeffery L '98
(740) 446-7889 **Henry** James R '03
(740) 446-2968 **Jenkins** Robert W '61
(740) 446-1356 **Lentes** John R '85
(740) 446-2922 **Moulton** Thomas S Jr. '97
(740) 446-0603 **Mulford** Eric R '04
(740) 446-8880 **Roderick** Richard C Jr. '72
(740) 446-1652 **Saunders** Brent A '83
(740) 446-1652 **Sheets** Mark E '87
(740) 446-1652 **Sheets** Warren F '50
(740) 446-6921 **Wallen** Barbara A '81

GALLOWAY
Franklin County
Ayers April C '89
(614) 878-4281 **Birnbrich** Gilbert J '99
(614) 878-0287 **Clinkscale** Debra L '87
(614) 853-0294 **Erwin** Van III '95
(614) 877-3333 **Fink** Joan K '79
(614) 870-9669 **Gander** Van A '87
Grasham Matthew J '03
Greene Dara L '99
McCann Tricia A '00
(614) 851-0200 **Sanborn** Jeffrey W '91
(614) 879-5754 **Smith** Mary E '53
(614) 851-2631 **Worthington** Dianne '84

GAMBIER
Knox County
(740) 427-5164 **Fowler** Wendi M '01
Leech Charles R Jr. '55

GARFIELD HEIGHTS
Cuyahoga County
(216) 332-0400 **Adler** Steven M '97
Briggs Beverly M '72
(216) 581-7400 **Cifelli** Leo L '59
(216) 475-3655 **Demer** Margaret E '59
(216) 587-2120 **Grau** Paul A '76
(216) 581-0500 **Kenney** Carol A '85
(216) 587-2120 **Klonowski** Stephen M '74
(216) 475-5484 **Kuban** Noreen M '96
(216) 587-2120 **Leggett** Linda A '91
(216) 518-2200 **McGinnis** John P '78
McGinty John P '58
(216) 587-2120 **Meek** David E '72
(216) 475-5045 **Nicastro** Deborah J '79
(216) 587-8150 **Pietras** John S '95
(216) 587-2120 **Reddy** Francis X Jr. '65
(216) 587-2120 **Reddy Grau & Meek Co,LPA**
(216) 663-9852 **Rowinski** Gregory B '77
(216) 587-2120 **Schuman** Kenneth A '97
(216) 475-5045 **Spiegelberg** Wilhelm G II '82
(216) 475-0725 **Sturik** Mark M '83
(216) 518-2200 **Tater** Steve W '96
(216) 475-4927 **Weiler** Jennifer P '79
(216) 581-1644 **Winger** Lora A '96
(216) 475-8100 **Winton** Jeffrey D '79

GARRETTSVILLE
Portage County
(330) 527-7007 **Kohli** Susan Kim '94
(330) 527-4351 **Manlove** Mark L '74
(330) 527-2335 **Mishler** Robert E '60
(330) 527-4882 **Timmons** Dann S '87

GATES MILLS
Cuyahoga County
(440) 423-0606 **Bissell** Robert K '52
Campanella Phillip J '66
(440) 442-5224 **Fedor** Steven L '81
Frutig Thomas R '69
(440) 585-4448 **Jochum** F Eric '87
(440) 423-3420 **Kalberer** Jean C '81
Lamb Geoffrey R '95
(440) 461-0866 **Lawley** Patricia M '85
(440) 423-0909 **Mitchell** Thoral David '89
(440) 423-1288 **Puette** Thomas J '69
(440) 423-0792 **Reitman** Robert S '58
(440) 442-5550 **Schiemann** Jeffrey J '88

GENEVA
Ashtabula County
(440) 466-4624 **DiFabio** Louis A '68
(440) 466-7670 **Epstein** Sherry Stein '86
Mayle Timothy L '99
(440) 466-6455 **Michelson** Armand M '60
(440) 466-4818 **Pasqualone** Gary L '74
(440) 466-5200 **Piper** Kenneth L '75
(440) 466-6026 **Stevens** Richard Lee '77

GENOA
Ottawa County
(419) 855-7718 **Bowland** Denise M '85
(419) 855-9955 **Cottrell** Ernest E Jr. '85
(419) 855-7731 **Cottrell** Stephen E '73

GEORGETOWN
Brown County
(937) 378-6165 **Cutrell** Jay D '76
(937) 378-4151 **Grennan** Thomas F '75
(937) 378-1072 **Gusweiler** Scott T '90
(937) 446-1734 **Homan** Ruth E '92
(937) 378-4769 **Hornschemeier** Patrick M '77
(937) 378-4151 **Hunter** David Michael '03
(937) 378-6165 **McConn-Pirman** Julie A '79
(937) 378-4151 **McMullen** Mary G '96
Miller Kenneth M '90
(937) 378-4119 **Purdy** Stanley K '65
(937) 378-4151 **Reder** Joseph M '02
(937) 378-4119 **Ring** Charles N '93
(937) 378-3188 **Thompson** Nathan A '80
(937) 378-4121 **Worley** Joseph M '83

GERMANTOWN
Montgomery County
(937) 455-3352 **Hasbrook** Jay T '94
(937) 855-7111 **Izor** David E '74
(937) 855-6013 **Kelley** Lynn M '63
(937) 855-4166 **Rettich** Robert W III '78
(937) 855-2376 **Steel** Jennifer M '96

GETTYSBURG
Darke County
(937) 447-8111 **Wagner** Paul E '97

GIBSONBURG
Sandusky County
(419) 637-2168 **Beck** Ladd W '80

GIRARD
Trumbull County
(330) 545-6912 **Angelo** Barbara J '85
(330) 759-3758 **Bernard** Anthony M '46
(330) 545-3424 **Carson** Edward L '81
(330) 545-5506 **Cervello** Mark C '91
(330) 545-1550 **Daliman** John P '86
(330) 545-4250 **Denney** James A '77
(330) 545-4326 **DePietro** Harry J '89
(330) 545-9707 **Flevares** William M '92
(330) 545-2800 **Masternick** John '55
(330) 545-1550 **Masternick** John J '91
(330) 545-4326 **Snyder** Emmor F '70
(330) 545-6252 **Standohar** Mark M '92
Tauro Frank C '58
(330) 539-4490 **Tauro** Lori A '93
(330) 545-9707 **Thomas** James W '60
(330) 539-1052 **Zauderer** Philip Q '64

GLENDALE
Hamilton County
(513) 771-7800 **Slap** Albert J '02

GNADENHUTTEN
Tuscarawas County
(740) 254-9429 **Cochran** Michael A '75

GOSHEN
Clermont County
(513) 625-1111 **Corcoran** T J '94
(513) 722-2441 **Herzner** Richard S '01

GRAFTON
Lorain County
(440) 669-0876 **Longwell** Donald E Jr. '93

GRAND RAPIDS
Wood County
(419) 832-0626 **Battin** Robert C '88
(419) 875-5474 **Salmon** Joseph Michael '94

GRANDVIEW
Franklin County
(614) 487-8210 **Stumler** Rebecca J '90

GRANVILLE
Licking County
(740) 587-2889 **Adams** Russell J '76
(740) 587-4150 **Akin** Dain C '78
(740) 321-7162 **Barns** Stephen W '95
(740) 973-4326 **Bellman** Daniel A '80
(740) 587-4150 **Bocciardi** John G '96
Bolon Gordon K '53
(740) 587-4066 **Contini** Stephen A '83
(740) 587-4150 **Diewald** Jodi S '99
(740) 321-7173 **Eckert** Inger H '96
(740) 587-4682 **Ellis** Gary E '81
(740) 587-4480 **Helser** Gregory C '90
(740) 321-1650 **Hinton** Linda S '03
Jump James R '73
(740) 321-3080 **Laskiewicz** Larry K '82
(740) 321-6013 **Little** Anne C '95
(740) 587-2139 **Lowry** Carla E '95
(740) 587-4782 **Masterson** Hugh A '89
(740) 587-3633 **McFarland** Jonathan Drew '87
(740) 587-4150 **McMillan** Lori A '01
(740) 321-1212 **Mershon** Steven W '81
(740) 587-1900 **Minklei** Lisa A '87
(740) 334-1011 **Predieri** Stephen Craig '01
(740) 587-6293 **Sharkey** Gregory J '95
(740) 321-1741 **Todd** Sara L '81
Weeks Amy S '01
(740) 587-0157 **Wernet** William R '81
(740) 587-2209 **Wince** Philip D '76

GRAYTOWN
Ottawa County
Kline Dale A '64

GREEN
Summit County
(330) 896-5209 **DiCato** Edward M '91
(330) 896-0450 **Mucklow** David '00
(330) 896-3023 **Romig** Connie J '96
(330) 896-6250 **Storey** Harlan G '79

GREENFIELD
Highland County
(937) 981-7318 **Curren** Conrad A '59
(937) 981-3326 **Davis** Carol A '86
(937) 981-4403 **Hayes** Larry D '76
(937) 981-4403 **Judkins** Robert J '75
(937) 981-7318 **Lubbers** Carol A '02
(937) 981-4142 **Quance** Peter D '84

GREENFORD
Mahoning County
(330) 702-1869 **Hough** Thomas E '73

GREENVILLE
Darke County
(937) 548-1920 **Amick & Breaden**
(937) 548-1920 **Amick** Jeffrey L '77
(937) 548-1920 **Aslinger** Jason R '96
(937) 548-2211 **Brand** Eric H '78
(937) 548-1920 **Breaden** Randall E '79
(937) 548-1125 **Brown** Gary L '72
(937) 547-7360 **Brumbaugh** Anne J '78
(937) 547-0218 **Brumbaugh** Michael L '91
(937) 548-1157 **Cooper** William H '77
(937) 547-7350 **Deneke** Albert J Jr. '64
(937) 548-1157 **Detling** James S '89
(937) 548-6888 **Donadio** Raymond M Jr. '80
(937) 548-1157 **Dues** Gail M '03
(937) 548-2122 **Durham** Darrell T '96
Felton Mary K '99
(937) 548-3240 **Finnarn** Theodore O '76
(937) 548-0324 **Flinn** Gary L '78
(937) 548-4132 **Foley** Kandy H '89
(937) 548-2211 **Goubeaux** James J '61
(937) 548-1157 **Graber** Thomas H II '79
(937) 547-7380 **Green** Jesse J '88
(937) 548-1157 **Guillozet** Thomas L '85
(937) 548-1157 **Hanes Schipfer Cooper Graber Guillozet & Detling,**
(937) 548-8995 **Hayes** Margaret B '89
(937) 548-2211 **Heggie** Mark E '74
(937) 547-7380 **Hoover** Phillip D '86
(937) 547-7380 **Howell** Richard M '78
(937) 548-1125 **Marchal & Brown**
(937) 548-1125 **Marchal** John F '58
(937) 548-1125 **Marchal** John F '96
(937) 548-8098 **Monnin** Julie L '96
(937) 548-0324 **Muntean** Susan M '78
(937) 547-7380 **Ormsby** Rowland K III '80
(937) 547-0218 **Ross** Dean E '01
(937) 547-0218 **Rudnick** Scott D '79
(937) 548-1157 **Schipfer** Daniel C Jr. '70
(937) 547-0218 **Stollings** Jerry C '01

GROVE CITY
Franklin County
(614) 539-2533 **Anderson** Harold J III '92
(614) 875-4895 **Anderson** Jeffrey S '89
Bechtol Lew A II '89
(614) 871-9555 **Beck** Mary J '82
Boling Ellis D '82
(614) 895-1070 **Bootes** Wendi S '98
(614) 875-1777 **Bowshier** Stephen J '81
(614) 875-3227 **Breckenridge** Donald O '85
(614) 875-7220 **Buskirk** Jeffrey E '84
(614) 882-6334 **Cellura** Frank A '78
(614) 875-4895 **Clark** Thomas R '75
(614) 875-7233 **Compton** Jeffrey P '89
(614) 539-1661 **Cordray** Richard A '87
(614) 277-9001 **Daily** Ruth A '99
(614) 875-6661 **Edwards** Steve J '79
(614) 875-0490 **Elliott** Bryan K '95
(614) 871-5100 **Englert** Christopher L '94
(614) 871-5100 **Flory** Paul D '04
(614) 235-4436 **Galasso** John G '96
(614) 875-9619 **Hall** Connie L '86
(614) 875-4115 **Hamilton** Raymond K '96
(614) 875-4115 **Hawkins** Laney J '97
(614) 875-0490 **Hilt** John F Jr. '75
(614) 875-0490 **Hull** Joseph W '76
(614) 539-9994 **James** Stephen A '93
(614) 277-4577 **Johnston** James E '97
Kuehn Kevin '03
(614) 875-2301 **Lett** Ellsworth jack '51
(614) 539-1480 **McCarty** Robert L '50
Monta Niki K '02
(614) 875-2371 **Rieser** Richard E '89
(614) 875-9640 **Smith** Stanley S '64
(614) 539-6550 **Stratman** Michelle D '03
(614) 277-1000 **Tarbox** Eric J '89
(614) 853-1047 **Timmins** Patrick F Jr. '67
(614) 277-1000 **Vaughn** Corinna M '98
(614) 878-6553 **Walsh** Eugene J '59
(614) 575-3530 **Welch** Erin E '99
(614) 875-1408 **Wilcox** James L '64

GROVEPORT
Franklin County
(614) 836-9981 **Galeano** Michael J '89
(614) 836-7593 **Lucas** Barbara D '89
(614) 836-3124 **Mashburn** John B '74
(614) 836-1866 **McCarty** Kevin R '92
(614) 477-9844 **McClellan** Sharon A '80
(614) 836-3242 **Schockling** Scott D '94

GUYSVILLE
Athens County
(740) 662-5503 **McGuire** Thomas R '75
(740) 662-5297 **Wirtshafter** Don E '85

HAMILTON
Butler County
(513) 868-7100 **Adams** Dennis L '97
(513) 785-5880 **Adelmann** Laura A '99
(513) 737-5100 **Albrecht** David S '98
(513) 887-3474 **Aldridge** Averil A '98
(513) 844-1300 **Allen** James M '68
(513) 785-7030 **Ash** Kenya D '03
(513) 737-8000 **Barrett** Amanda R '02
(513) 867-8000 **Beane** Gregory S '80
(513) 892-8251 **Blauvelt** Scott N '97
(513) 785-7327 **Borst** Samuel D '89
(513) 892-3400 **Bowling** Jeffrey W '98
Boyer Todd F '99
(513) 892-3400 **Brandabur** Michael J '96
(513) 785-7006 **Brandenburger** Mark '74
(513) 863-6600 **Braun** Michael P '81
(513) 868-3663 **Brewer** David B '98
(513) 887-3313 **Bruewer** John T '88
(513) 887-3474 **Burress** Brad A '00
(513) 887-3364 **Cade** Daniel S '82
(513) 887-3586 **Cady** Heather L '03
(513) 868-3200 **Carlson** Timothy W '86
(513) 868-7474 **Carmella** Bradley R '86
(513) 785-5805 **Carter** Barbara S '91
(513) 896-4547 **Cohen** Jack E '75
(513) 844-1300 **Combs-Valerio** Traci M '04
(513) 737-7044 **Conese** Mark A '83
(513) 868-7500 **Connaughton** John B '64
(513) 868-3663 **Cooney** James E '75
(513) 227-9398 **Cooper** James T '94
(513) 887-7300 **Copeland** K Brent '90
(513) 863-5333 **Cornett** Jackie L '78
(513) 887-3474 **Cox** Brenda S '94
(513) 868-7100 **Creach** Larry H Jr. '99
(513) 868-9985 **Cummins** Bill W '96
(513) 863-6600 **Cunningham** Lyn A '89
(513) 868-3911 **Daiker** Victoria A '77
(513) 241-9400 **Daly** Gerald R '72
(513) 887-3474 **Dattilo** Christina R '02
(513) 868-7100 **Davidson Adams & Creach Co,LPA**
(513) 893-6122 **Davidson** Brian J '00
(513) 868-7100 **Davidson** David T '86
(513) 887-3474 **Davidson** Elizabeth A '87
(513) 737-6164 **Devney** Denise L '91
(513) 863-6700 **Dierling** Thomas A '01
(513) 856-8601 **Doellman** Norbert M Jr. '76
Dolan James H '50
Downing Patricia J '89
(513) 887-3257 **Duckett** Douglas E '82
(513) 844-8515 **Dudley** Mary K '83
(513) 785-7184 **Edmunds** Albert V '73
(513) 785-5880 **Effler** Julie K '98
(513) 887-3474 **Eichel** Daniel G '76
(513) 241-9400 **Elliott** Lori K '85
(513) 863-6700 **Evans** Catherine L '96
(513) 868-7600 **Evans** Timothy R '74
(513) 887-3474 **Ferguson** Danny L '86
(513) 896-7722 **Ferris** Carl D '80
(513) 896-7722 **Ferris** Donald L '52
(513) 785-4561 **Fette** Glenn P '92
(513) 887-7300 **Fiehrer Lane & Copeland**
(513) 887-7300 **Fiehrer** Lawrence P '74
(513) 896-6623 **Fischer** Daniel B '64
(513) 889-0007 **Forg** John H III '89
(513) 844-8888 **Fox** Jonathan N '88
(513) 863-6700 **Franke** John P '89
(513) 737-5100 **Frederick** Christopher P '03
(513) 737-5100 **Frederick** Scott J '94
(513) 863-6700 **Freisthler** Marlaina S '04
(513) 887-3474 **French** Rebecca S '01
(513) 863-7600 **Froelke** Frank J '66
(513) 863-0083 **Froelke** Gerald G '63
(513) 785-5880 **Froug** Randi E '00
(513) 863-8270 **Fryman** Robert E '53
(513) 863-6700 **Fulton** Michael A '70
(513) 863-6600 **Garretson** John A '77
(513) 737-9900 **Garretson** Patrick W '84
(513) 887-3478 **Gates** Roger S '79
(513) 737-8000 **Gattermeyer** Daniel J '83
(513) 737-8000 **Gattermeyer & McCracken LLC**
(513) 868-7600 **Gedling** James L '80
(513) 737-4347 **Gehr** Daniel W '98
(513) 892-8251 **Gmoser** Michael T '73
(513) 785-7327 **Goodyear** Brian E '98
(513) 863-4015 **Groth** William A '73
(513) 887-3474 **Gugino** R Paul '01
(513) 737-1369 **Haddad** Hanna B '03
(513) 785-6548 **Haferkamp** Shannon L '02
(513) 887-7300 **Halcomb** Margot B '93
(513) 867-1411 **Halverson** Damon L '01
(513) 785-5880 **Hamilton** Rodrick J '87
(513) 737-4000 **Hardig** Mark N '81
(513) 887-3474 **Harris** Karl R '91
(513) 867-1856 **Hatcher** Gregory E '83
(513) 887-3474 **Hawkins** Lawrence C III '03
(513) 887-3474 **Hedric** Craig D '86
(513) 887-4118 **Heffner** Jann K '75
(513) 785-5729 **Hider** Patricia A '95
(513) 863-8270 **Hirka** Sara C '97
(513) 868-7600 **Holbrock & Jonson Co,LPA**
(513) 892-8251 **Holcomb & Hyde LLP**
(513) 863-6600 **Holcomb** Jeffrey G '98
(513) 892-8251 **Holcomb** John M '91
(513) 894-2337 **Holden** Kathryn L '86
(513) 863-0660 **Hon** Michael D '00
(513) 863-0664 **Horwitz** Barbara L '94
(513) 868-3663 **Howard** John G '87
(513) 863-6700 **Hull** Gregory E '83
(513) 868-8721 **Humbach** Thomas E '77
(513) 867-1717 **Hurchanik** Richard L '82
(513) 863-0660 **Hurr** Daniel J '86
(513) 892-8251 **Hyde** Richard A '89
(513) 894-9916 **Imfeld** Bert C '55
(513) 867-4502 **Immelt** Mark W '76
(513) 887-3313 **Infantino** Barbara M '89
(513) 844-2000 **Jacobs** Michael E '97
(513) 887-4221 **Jewett** Bruce E '78
(513) 868-7600 **Jonson** George N '58
(513) 887-3474 **Kash** David L '79
(513) 887-3690 **Keating** Lori L '98
(513) 868-7100 **Keck** Jill A '99
(513) 863-6700 **Keck** William C '70
(513) 785-5805 **Kessler** Eva D '73
(513) 887-3474 **Kiesey** Cassandra E '90
(513) 887-5643 **Kindley** Zane E '88
(513) 868-0008 **Koehler** Richard N II '78
(513) 785-6531 **Krebs** Robert T '99
(513) 844-2288 **Kusel** Mary L '80
(513) 889-0400 **Lampe** Misty L '92
Landis David H '79
(513) 887-7300 **Lane** Stephen C '86
(513) 867-8200 **LeRoy** Donald C '77
(513) 863-6700 **Lewis** Heather Sanderson '98
(513) 863-8270 **Marcum** Stephen S '83
(513) 863-0660 **Masana** Michael P '74
(513) 867-4729 **McCauley-Myers** Janie P '94
(513) 737-8000 **McCracken** John J '89
(513) 844-6100 **McGee** Gary A '81
(513) 844-2000 **McGowan** Jack C '74
(513) 737-5180 **McKenzie** Kyle B '94
(513) 887-3821 **Milbauer** Jeffrey K '81
(513) 868-2909 **Miller** Fred S '79
(513) 785-7180 **Miller** Hillary G '84
(513) 863-6700 **Millikin & Fitton**
(513) 844-8515 **Moeller** Patrick G '84
(513) 887-3474 **Monk** James A '02
(513) 887-3352 **Moreland** Vickie G '77
(513) 867-1731 **Morgan** Ronald C '66
(513) 893-6122 **Morgenstern** Barbara L '86
(513) 893-6122 **Morgenstern** Carl '49
(513) 887-3474 **Muench-McElfresh** Jennifer R '97
(513) 868-8229 **Napier** Clayton G '83
(513) 887-3474 **Nardiello** Mary A '89
(513) 868-2731 **Nerenberg** Jonathon O '77
(513) 887-9595 **Newland** Michael A '89
(513) 887-5682 **O'Keefe** Kelly A '03
(513) 887-3474 **Oldendick** Lee A '80
(513) 867-8000 **Olivas** Adolf '81
(513) 887-3474 **Oster** Michael A Jr. '03
(513) 887-3778 **Parker** Deborah L '90
(513) 895-0044 **Parks** Brenda B '91
(513) 863-8270 **Parrish Fryman & Marcum Co,LPA**
(513) 863-8270 **Parrish** Lee H '68
(513) 887-3277 **Pater** Charles L '93
(513) 867-1411 **Pater** Clement A III '69
(513) 867-1411 **Pater** Gerald L '68
(513) 785-5880 **Pater** Raymond C III '91
(513) 868-1113 **Peck** Gregory L '88
(513) 887-3305 **Phillabaum** Jason R '00
(513) 887-3474 **Piper** Robert N III '82
(513) 868-2731 **Pollard** Nellie R '76
(513) 887-3592 **Reed** Harold M '01
(513) 863-6700 **Reister** John J '78
(513) 868-2731 **Reyes** Roger O '96
(513) 887-3265 **Rice** Kelli M '90
(513) 867-4822 **Roberts** Jeffrey C '98
(513) 887-3474 **Rodkey** Jessica M '01
Rohrkaste William D '85
(513) 362-2846 **Roosa** Kathryn L '02
(513) 887-3474 **Rossi** Glenn J '01
(513) 241-9400 **Rothstein** Debra D '86
(513) 863-6700 **Rullman** Stanley D '67
(513) 863-6700 **Rulon** Jeffrey L '83
(513) 785-5880 **Sauer** Gregory J '86
(513) 863-4200 **Schiavone** Frank J III '78
(513) 887-6400 **Schraffenberger** Mark D '90
(513) 867-4838 **Schul** David D '79
(513) 241-9400 **Seel** Thomas R '89
(513) 868-7600 **Shanks** Michael D '76
(513) 737-1540 **Sheets** Gary L '80
(513) 422-4488 **Sherron** James E '86
Smith-Johnston Glenda A '99
(513) 785-6549 **Smithson** Nicole M '02
(513) 737-5180 **Snyder** Christopher J '88
(513) 868-8229 **Songer** Diana L '93
(513) 887-3795 **Sorey** Roger L '86
(513) 737-5100 **Sphar** Kristen L '98
(513) 785-5880 **Startzman** Jeffrey P '79
(513) 887-3305 **Stephens** Gregory S '95
(513) 887-9595 **Stephenson** Nicole M '98
(513) 863-7600 **Stitsinger** Steven M '97
(513) 863-5888 **Straus** Stephen M '78
(513) 874-4422 **Tamborski** Peter E '82
(513) 785-7183 **Taylor** Colleen H '99
(513) 868-2838 **Temin** Andrew M '82
(513) 895-4200 **Thomas** Lawrence R III '00
(513) 863-6700 **Tooman** Steven A '96
(513) 868-3663 **Truesdell** Gwendolyn A '93
(513) 896-4411 **Tumblison** Joan M '99
(513) 868-8900 **Uhl** John W '70
(513) 887-3474 **Ulreich** Jacqueline M '01
(513) 867-4823 **Walsh** Dennis G '75
(513) 868-1113 **Walsh** Herbert V '72
(513) 867-3514 **Ware** Beth-Anne '93
(513) 737-5100 **Weisbrod** Michael P '85
(513) 863-0083 **Wessel & Froelke**
(513) 863-0083 **Wessel** Richard J '52
(513) 863-0083 **Wessel** Robert F '51
(513) 863-6700 **Whalen** Jon P '97
(513) 887-3318 **Wilkerson** Patricia A '93
(513) 844-8181 **Willard** John T '66
(513) 887-3844 **Winton** Joel F '04
(513) 896-7767 **Wittman** Dennis L '71
(513) 863-0664 **Wolf** Myron A '75
(513) 863-0664 **Wolf** Myron D III '80
(513) 868-2731 **Wolfgang** Rex A '88
(513) 868-3740 **Zettler** Jack A '77
(513) 737-9770 **Zornow** Harry B '84

HARRISON
Hamilton County
(513) 367-1332 **Charls** Jerome J '82
(513) 367-4861 **Haft** James E '72
(513) 367-1999 **Kluener** Thomas J '84
(513) 367-2141 **Loechel** Angela G '97
(513) 367-6133 **McKenery** Deborah L '85
(513) 367-2141 **Meyer** Donald J Jr. '76
Peters Craig M '90

HARTVILLE
Stark County
(330) 877-9479 **Buetel** Veronica K '00
(330) 877-2613 **Hite** Christopher E '69
(330) 877-0700 **Martin** Thomas H '04
(330) 877-0700 **Martin** Todd M '04
Ramsburg Cheryl L '96

HEATH
Licking County
(740) 323-4888 **Bindley** Richard S '78
(740) 522-8567 **Boeckman** Ronald P '87

HEBRON
Licking County
(740) 927-8790 **Peck** Jimmy R '04
(740) 928-3696 **Tosi** James G '71

HIGHLAND HEIGHTS
Cuyahoga County
(440) 256-3323 **Carlin** Joan L '86
(440) 461-0928 **Casper** Michael J '75
(440) 442-8800 **Catalano** Cynthia A '73
(440) 483-3000 **DeRamus** Monica D '01
(440) 395-9599 **Duvin** Deborah C '90
(440) 446-1327 **Feran** Amy R '83
(440) 461-1054 **Feuer** Charles E '89
(440) 473-3000 **Fry** John J '91
(440) 473-0200 **Ibold** Charles J '82
(440) 684-1090 **Jaffe** Michael A '93
(440) 483-3798 **Jelenic** Barbara A '96
(440) 684-9393 **Kotoch** Norman A '90
(440) 684-1090 **Kusner** Mark '80
(440) 684-1090 **McClure** Thomas D Jr. '03
(440) 684-1080 **Mesi** Douglas P '88
Murphy Cathlyn S '93
(440) 603-6335 **Riegel** Sharon A '93
Rogan Michael J '83
Rozario Charmaine C '99
(440) 449-1320 **Siegfried** John P '73
(440) 995-2027 **Syby** Craig W '93
Tripi Phillip G '57
(440) 449-3555 **Watson** David S '89

HIGHLAND HILLS
Cuyahoga County
(216) 987-2310 **Cieslak** James L '78

HILLIARD
Franklin County
(614) 777-1750 **Barth** David A '88
(614) 876-2689 **Behringer** Douglas J '96
(614) 777-9917 **Bell** Irene D '89
(614) 777-4600 **Bodycombe** Paul A '80
(614) 529-8600 **Bostic** Amy L '88
(614) 771-6933 **Broschak** Thomas J '80
(614) 527-6740 **Byers** William L IV '03
(614) 527-6199 **Callender** Carma L '03
(614) 527-0779 **Chanfrau** Graciela M '98
(614) 777-7610 **Chasser** Timothy G '76
(614) 876-2689 **Craig** Steve A '76
(614) 876-7511 **Crowley** James W '85
(614) 723-4197 **Davis** Jon T '96
(614) 876-7361 **DeDent** Pamela A '91
(614) 851-8810 **DeLaughter** Sharon D '93
(614) 921-1080 **Doucher** Kimberley A '96
(614) 527-6762 **Gillette** Nancy P '92
(614) 777-1203 **Gunner** Michael T '73
(614) 876-8888 **Haney** John L Jr. '76
Hansen Curtis A '90
(614) 777-4411 **Hyslop** Bruce A '66
(614) 777-4411 **Hyslop** Jean F '91
(614) 529-1742 **Jursek** Stephanie J '86
(614) 876-1700 **Keith** Charles L '80
(614) 527-6762 **Maglione** Timothy I '93
(614) 529-8988 **Meloun** Stacy A '00
(614) 486-2401 **Mulgrew** Donald B '75
(614) 777-4024 **Mullins** Lawrence G '75
(614) 529-8600 **Needleman** Scott R '91
(614) 777-3420 **Nisbet** Rebecca J '82
(614) 529-8600 **Nobile** James E '92
(614) 529-8600 **Nobile** Martin C '94
(614) 529-8600 **Nobile Needleman & Thompson, LLC**
(614) 334-3362 **Paparodis** Chris O '82
Petras David J '96
(614) 876-2689 **Prince** Stephanie N '04
(614) 529-8988 **Rager** Nicole E '04
(614) 771-2785 **Reid** David W '94
Rice Timothy S '01
Rothbaum Jennifer A '03
(614) 462-5408 **Russi** Steven R '84
(614) 575-1188 **Sarver** Eden R '02
(614) 777-9908 **Schumacher** Stacy M '02
Shaynak-Diaz Christina L '02
(614) 529-8988 **Shufeldt** Matthew D '01
(614) 527-7563 **Simmons** Robert M '99
(614) 777-8170 **Sullivan** James T '78
Swartwout Daniel A '00
(614) 529-8600 **Thompson** Matthew J '88
Turner Anne D '87
(614) 876-8240 **White** Daniel J '80
(614) 529-8988 **Willis** C Stanley II '91
(614) 529-8988 **Willis** Kelly A '92
(614) 529-8988 **Willis Shufeldt & Willis Co LPA**
(614) 847-1688 **Yannon** Albert A '57

HILLSBORO
Highland County
(937) 393-3397 **Armintrout** George W '84
(937) 393-1906 **Beery** Forrest F '50
(937) 393-1907 **Beery** Fred J '82
(937) 393-1850 **Coss** Rocky A '76
(937) 393-9285 **Daniels** Susan M '99
(937) 393-4000 **Davis** Susan L '80
(937) 393-1851 **Grandey** James B '77
(937) 393-3487 **Hapner** James D '51
(937) 393-3487 **Hapner** Jon C '58
(937) 393-3487 **Hapner** Mary K '96
(937) 393-1851 **Harrell** Shari Lee '97
(937) 393-4600 **Koogler** Lee D '01
(937) 393-4731 **Lyle** Jeffrey J '83
(937) 365-2080 **McGuire-Haines** Kimberly J '96
(937) 393-1814 **McKenna** David H '92
(937) 393-1102 **McKinney** Carroll V '60
(937) 393-4267 **Pence** David W '73
(937) 927-0154 **Stroop** Richele M '96
(937) 393-3185 **Swonger** Ronald L '60
(937) 393-1207 **Van Zant** Gregory F '88
(937) 393-2422 **Williams** Cynthia Ann '91

HINCKLEY
Medina County
Lutz Timothy R '89
(330) 278-2343 **Mason** Chris '01
(330) 556-3750 **Wochna** Donald A '83
(330) 278-2001 **Wolgamuth** Keith R '82
Zore Ernest F '78

HIRAM
Portage County
Macek Stephen G '82

HOLLAND
Lucas County
(419) 866-8900 **Atkinson** James R '80
(419) 861-7800 **Ayers** Andrew J '79
(419) 861-7800 **Bahret** Robert J '80
(419) 865-1251 **Bair** C William '83
(419) 243-4788 **Bender** Anthony J '83
(419) 865-1251 **Bialecki** Korleen M '89
(419) 865-1251 **Bish Wagoner** Helen '80
(419) 861-7800 **Charles** Jeffrey B '95
(419) 866-8900 **Craig** Brian D '80
(419) 861-2300 **Dennis** David A '85
(419) 861-7800 **Doerner** David W '76
(419) 868-1100 **Fadell** Frederick J '59
(419) 865-1251 **Friedmar** Richard S '76
(419) 861-7800 **Gerken** Mandy M '04
(419) 865-5586 **Greenfield** Donna J '74
(419) 865-6586 **Johnson** Willard A '54
Keller Dennis F '75
(419) 865-1251 **Kestner** Tara J '96
Kline James E '66
(419) 868-1162 **Kohli** Leslie A '00
(419) 861-0755 **Kowalski** Lawrence W '75
(419) 865-1251 **Kuhnle** Carl A '71
(419) 867-5294 **Lindower** Kurt J '90
(419) 861-7800 **Malkoski** Kathleen M '99
(419) 865-9622 **Meister** Marc J '79
(419) 868-8150 **Morgan** James E '76
(419) 865-1251 **Overley** Thomas G '84
(419) 865-4200 **Pizza** Anthony G '50
(419) 865-1251 **Post** Frederick R '74
(419) 868-5704 **Sanders** Richard L '81
(419) 865-6586 **Sharkey** Susan K '93
(419) 865-0852 **Snavely** David A '74
(419) 867-8090 **Snyder** Edward L '83
(419) 865-1251 **Steinberg** Harold M '66
(419) 865-1251 **Wagoner** John E '65
(419) 865-1251 **Wagoner** Mark D '68
(419) 865-1251 **Wagoner & Steinberg,Ltd**
(419) 865-1837 **Wilkerson** Carolyn S '74
(419) 865-5515 **Yoder** Thomas A '77
(419) 865-1251 **Zhang** Fan '99

HOWARD
Knox County
(740) 393-0405 **Lee** William J '48

HUBBARD
Trumbull County
(330) 534-1901 **Aurilio** Beth A '01
(330) 759-2044 **Chan** Grace Y '93
(330) 534-1901 **Daugherty** Teresa R '78
(330) 270-1700 **Duda** Donald A Jr. '94
(330) 534-6275 **Gilmartin** Gary M '76
(917) 902-2768 **Katz** Susan S '79
(330) 534-1481 **Knuth** Richard L '84
(330) 534-3139 **LaCivita** Richard J '75
Marks Ronald A '75
(330) 534-1901 **Rice** Ronald J '85
(330) 759-9838 **Roland** David K '86

HUBER HEIGHTS
Montgomery County
(937) 233-8492 **Bennington** Christopher '76
(937) 236-6444 **Caspar** Robert L Jr. '88
(937) 237-9485 **Fisher** Mark A '96
(937) 496-7231 **Hensley** James A Jr. '87
(937) 236-6444 **Herndon** John A '96
(937) 233-8492 **Piergies** James D '80
(937) 236-6444 **Posey** Terry W '88
(937) 237-9485 **Staton** James C '97
(937) 233-8605 **Tomlinson** Jon S '99

HUDSON
Summit County
(330) 650-0328 **Baker** Michael D '61
(330) 656-1272 **Bean** Thomas F '72
(330) 342-8203 **Billick** Timothy R '77
(330) 656-0495 **Birmingham** Fletcher A '88
(330) 342-9778 **Bockanic** William N '73
(330) 656-2702 **Breslin** Jordan K '84
Cesarik Joseph M '81
(330) 656-3633 **Cline** Carl L '94
(330) 342-8203 **Clunk** John D '82
(330) 650-7697 **Comery** Franklin B Jr. '75
Costello Fred P III '03
(330) 656-1266 **Cox** Anthony A Jr. '65
(330) 655-5800 **Crane** Robert L Jr. '73
(330) 554-1888 **Demyan** John W '02
(330) 656-3799 **Dye** Edward R '73
(330) 650-0419 **Ealy** Stephen T '90
(330) 650-4761 **Elliott** Frances C '83
(330) 655-7000 **Essner** Howard S '82
(330) 656-2600 **Ewald** Michael J '96
(330) 650-0551 **Fischer** Thomas J '91
(330) 621-9255 **Frangos** Gus '82
(330) 655-5722 **Gardner** Deborah F '83
(330) 655-5722 **Garrison** James E '84
(330) 387-2954 **Gasper** Carol L '88
Goodman Amy O '01
(330) 655-4980 **Green** Cynthia L '87
Haring Kimberly Koontz '02
Hauenstein Joan E '02
(330) 342-8203 **Hoose** Robert R '02
(330) 342-4910 **Hoover** Dean S '78
(330) 650-0525 **Hoover** John E '94
(330) 342-8203 **Humbert** Ted A '81
(330) 656-1572 **Jacobstein** Pamela G '82
(330) 656-2600 **Kaminski** Karen D '00
Klingshirn Nancy P '86
Korff Christopher J '03
Kuri Camille D '93
(330) 425-4501 **LeFaiver** William A '69
(330) 463-5738 **Lehman** David W '96
(330) 650-2200 **Maher** Robert V '49
Manak Charles R '92
(330) 342-1080 **Mastrangelo** Ellen L '89
McCaughey Maura A '98
(330) 653-9372 **McConnel** Stewart P Jr. '74
(330) 342-8203 **Michaels** Lisa M '96
Mosteller Brenda L '93
(330) 342-8203 **Paisley** Andrew A '89
(330) 342-3013 **Peterson** Kenneth B '81
(330) 650-4656 **Phillips** Robert D '75
(330) 650-0452 **Renner** Jack L '60
(330) 656-2702 **Rich** Eric A '94
(330) 650-0580 **Rischitelli** Robert J Jr. '95
Rosenberg-Webster Terri A '93
(330) 656-2600 **Rothenberg** Marc D '83
(330) 656-2600 **Sachs** Valerie G '81
(330) 656-2702 **Scheuer Mackin & Breslin LLC**
(330) 650-5444 **Sesny** Thomas A Jr. '92
(330) 650-4436 **Sharp** John M '81
(330) 528-3616 **Sley** Benjamin H '99
(330) 650-4436 **Umbaugh** David G '74
(330) 656-1530 **Walling** Richard R '55
(330) 650-4273 **Warburton** Phillip L '70
(330) 342-5515 **Weaver** Benjamin Wayne '04
(330) 342-8203 **Wiery** Michael L '97
(330) 253-9118 **Young** Peter F '62

HUNTSVILLE
Logan County
(937) 686-4625 **Bennett** Charles A '81
(937) 842-4258 **Graham** Joseph V '90
(937) 842-2479 **Heffner** Cynthia L '93
(937) 842-6159 **Taylor** Mary L '97

HURON
Erie County
(419) 433-3130 **DeLamatre** Richard D '58
(419) 625-8373 **Donnelly** Timothy J '77
Folger Will R '85
(419) 433-5798 **Hardy** Richard B III '97
(419) 433-3379 **Johnson** Lawrence P '80
(419) 433-4485 **Pfefferle** John A '66
(419) 433-3225 **Pisano** Ralph C Sr. '51
(419) 433-3225 **Pisano** Ralph C Jr. '90
(419) 433-5246 **Pokorny** Donald '65
(419) 433-2525 **Roshong** Alicia W '92

HYDE PARK
Hamilton County
(513) 561-6277 **Slutz** Leonard D '37

INDEPENDENCE
Cuyahoga County
(216) 674-0550 **Alkire** Richard C '80
(216) 573-6000 **Amato** Thomas S '92
(216) 447-3061 **Asseff** Carl F '84
(216) 524-5717 **Bajorek** Christine C '89
(216) 447-9500 **Bakula** Charles A '92
(216) 447-0070 **Balog** Joseph A '76
(216) 520-1464 **Belinger** Robert J '75
(216) 524-9438 **Bentkowski** David A '97
(440) 546-7500 **Bernard** Dale A '84
(216) 328-8080 **Bernstein** Stephen C '01
(216) 524-2212 **Brokaw** Glenn J '82
(216) 522-2763 **Brommer** Carolyn T '85
(216) 522-4820 **Buckingham** George W Jr. '92
(216) 328-2590 **Burke** John T '69
(216) 615-7600 **Burney** Stephanie B '00
(216) 520-5980 **Cassidy** Michael P '83
(216) 520-5980 **Cassidy** Paul W '47
(216) 328-0002 **Ciaravino** Michael G '91
(216) 642-3777 **Cichocki** Charles F '79
(216) 573-1776 **Cleary** Timothy R '75
(216) 241-5900 **Cook** Francis X '79
(216) 520-7060 **Courtney** Mary L '78
(216) 524-7979 **Cowan** Dale H '81
(216) 525-4283 **Daprile** Joseph R '86
(216) 328-2590 **Deegan** Jon F '86
(216) 524-4673 **DiGeronimo** Kellie L '00
(216) 447-9850 **Duffy** Matthew M '99
(216) 447-8800 **Eder** James R '89
(216) 573-6000 **Elliott** Zena B '91
(216) 520-7172 **Ellis** Brian R '73
(216) 642-0797 **Flask** John A '85
(216) 522-7121 **Franczak** Michael S '95
(216) 328-1677 **Fritz** Raymond N '78
(216) 328-2037 **Giffels** Thomas E II '87
(216) 674-7095 **Gordon** Eric S '98
(216) 447-4496 **Grabow** Raymond J '58
(216) 447-1161 **Grendel** David S '80
(216) 642-8961 **Gruber** Lynn F '82
(216) 447-9105 **Hehr** Albert G III '99
(216) 525-2626 **Hice** Brooke M '00
(216) 986-6656 **Homolak** Diane I '89
(216) 642-0030 **Hopkins** Kathleen C '89
(216) 986-0860 **Horvath** David J '91
Hritz Judith J '83
(216) 328-1100 **Incorvaia** Santo T '88
(216) 369-2600 **Incze** Norman E '95
(216) 525-7392 **Kelley** Steven K '84
(216) 643-2915 **King** Michael L '84
(216) 635-3980 **Klemenok** Kimberly A '98
(216) 328-2895 **Kline** Paul J '02
(216) 525-4300 **Klinge** Stephen D '01
(216) 328-2009 **Kola** Arthur A '64
(216) 520-8400 **Kordel** Douglas A '97
(216) 524-4260 **Kozelka** Frank J '71
(216) 337-3331 **Kulick** Martina '91
(216) 361-4169 **Leslie** Timothy C '94
(216) 573-6000 **Licata** Louis J '83
(216) 643-6952 **Maser** Douglas J '76
(216) 447-9850 **Matas** Richard S '95
(216) 642-3133 **Maybaum** Scott D '78
(216) 901-4824 **Mayer** John E '89
(216) 447-0070 **Mazur** Lloyd D '67
(216) 520-7177 **McAndrew** John A '69
(216) 520-7170 **McCarroll** Elaine A '77
(216) 642-9494 **McGrath** James J '67
(216) 573-6666 **Morell** Dan A Jr. '86
(216) 573-1223 **Moroz** Nicholas M '75
(216) 447-0070 **Moss** Debbie L '78
(216) 520-4700 **Murphy** Sandi R '91
(216) 520-5556 **Music-Biro** Kristina E '83
(216) 447-9105 **Myers** Richard A Jr. '88
(216) 674-0550 **Nieding** Dean C '83
(216) 986-6144 **Novak** Geoffrey '98
(216) 447-9500 **O'Rourke** R Russell '84
(216) 674-7094 **Oster** Alexis S '94
(216) 525-7392 **O'Sullivan** Cornelius J Jr. '90
(216) 901-1072 **Palmer** Matthew W '99
(216) 241-5900 **Payne** Kevin F '81
(216) 241-5900 **Payne Payne & Cook**
(216) 241-5900 **Payne** William A '84
(216) 642-9007 **Peterson** Robin J '92
(216) 573-6666 **Petropouleas** Jim '02
(216) 642-5353 **Pignatiello** Richard A '82
(216) 573-1776 **Pitcock** Danielle K '98
(216) 642-5812 **Plona** Alexander '92
(216) 642-1425 **Ramos** Fred P '78
(216) 643-6991 **Ricchetti** Eugene T '66
(216) 573-6666 **Roberto** Robert J '03
(216) 447-9850 **Rodman** John D '87
(216) 642-8722 **Roth** Randolph R '94
(216) 573-6000 **Ryan** Jody Le '91
(216) 520-7176 **Sabo** Aberdeen H '67
(216) 573-1800 **Schmid** Gordon E '76
(216) 573-9700 **Schwallie** Daniel P '91
(216) 746-0776 **Severyn** Myra S '90
(216) 526-2067 **Simmons** Milton L '59
(216) 573-1776 **Stiefvater** Robert G III '03
(216) 447-4496 **Tiktin** Roger D '74
(216) 520-5566 **Tomazic** Mary E '84
(216) 643-6659 **Visconsi** Thomas A Jr. '75
(216) 526-2144 **Wachs** William P '00
(216) 901-0219 **Wallace** Jodi M '98
(216) 520-7177 **Walsh** Terrence R '98
(216) 524-5700 **Wasserman** Robert '76
(216) 524-1891 **Weinreich** Thomas Wm '98
(216) 642-1105 **Weiss** Linda A '79
(216) 524-4855 **Williams** Monica B '84
(216) 525-7939 **Winans** Jill M '90
(216) 573-6000 **Wood** Jeremiah J '02
(216) 485-8400 **Woods** Jennifer A '03
(216) 520-1464 **Zaffiro** James A '97

INDIAN HILL
Hamilton County
(513) 561-1470 **Wilson** Harold G '89

INDIAN SPRINGS
Butler County
(513) 870-4980 **Cook-Reich** Melynda W '96
(513) 870-4980 **Schad** Kevin M '93

IRONTON
Lawrence County
(740) 533-1700 **Allen** Craig A '66
(740) 532-7779 **Anderson** Brigham M '04
(740) 532-4554 **Anderson** Curtis B '97
(740) 532-7779 **Anderson** Robert C '78
(740) 532-7779 **Anderson** William M '77
(740) 532-7000 **Bentley** Richard F '78
(740) 532-4333 **Bowling** Daniel S '97
(740) 532-8034 **Collier** James B Jr. '70
(740) 532-9772 **Collins** Mark A '82
(740) 532-4366 **Cooper** William C '73
(740) 532-8744 **Davis** J B '99
(740) 532-9422 **Destocki** Paul E '74
(740) 533-2720 **Dillon** David R '80
(740) 532-4554 **Edwards Klein Anderson & Shope Co LPA**
(740) 532-8744 **Fisher** Frederick C Jr. '03
(740) 532-9422 **Hampton** Carol J '69
(740) 532-4169 **Heald** Philip J '96
Kehoe John E '71
(740) 532-0814 **Kennedy** Richard D '88
(740) 532-0814 **Kennedy** William D '57
(740) 532-4554 **Klein** Charles C '49
(740) 532-4554 **Klein** Sara B '83
(740) 532-4554 **Klein** Thomas L '81
(740) 532-4333 **Lambert McWhorter & Bowling**
(740) 532-4333 **Lambert** Randall L '79
(740) 532-8744 **McCown** David H '60
(740) 532-8744 **McCown & Davis,LPA**
(740) 532-8744 **McCown** Mark K '97
(740) 532-4333 **McWhorter** Donald L II '87
(740) 532-4333 **Morris** Jeremy R '03
(740) 532-4333 **Sanders** Patricia S '96
(740) 532-4554 **Shope** Dru A '93
(740) 532-4911 **Smith** Jason P '99
(740) 532-9000 **Smith** Jeffrey M '84
(740) 532-6913 **Spears** David R '78
(740) 532-5815 **Spears** Harold D '48
(740) 532-4911 **Waldo** James M '78
(740) 532-4911 **Waldo** Kevin J '80
(740) 532-7000 **Wolfe & Bentley**
(740) 532-7000 **Wolfe** John H '69

JACKSON
Jackson County
(740) 286-5006 **Blanton** Jonathan D '98
(740) 286-5460 **Cole** William S '77
(740) 286-6408 **Cox** Donald A '79
(740) 286-1112 **Detty** John L '81
(740) 286-2223 **Forshey** Timothy E '87
(740) 286-2718 **Johnston** Lorene G '82
(740) 286-3735 **Kirby** Joseph D '91
(740) 286-5008 **Kunze** Mary B '50
(740) 286-0071 **Lewis** Richard M '82
(740) 286-8054 **Martin** William C '74
(740) 395-8303 **Matlack** Ross A III '01
(740) 286-4649 **Michael** Aaron C '02
(740) 286-0030 **Moore** Christopher Michael '99
(740) 286-4100 **Musick** Mark T '86
(740) 286-3601 **Regan** Christopher J '87
(740) 286-0071 **Shriver** Jill H '03
(740) 286-4649 **Smith** Barry L '81
(740) 286-0071 **White** Andrew T '01

JACKSON CENTER
Shelby County
Gudgel James R '02

JAMESTOWN
Greene County
(937) 223-4800 **Combs** Gardner J '90

JEFFERSON
Ashtabula County
(440) 576-3662 **Blankenship** Jodi Misinec '01
(440) 576-3662 **Burnside** Teri L '96
(440) 576-3662 **Colgan** Catherine R '01
(440) 576-3662 **Divoky** Rebecca K '99
Dodson Davida J '90
(440) 576-3489 **Foster** David F '84
(440) 576-3831 **Geary** Michael P '89
(440) 994-6012 **Gerken** Philip D '79
(440) 576-3662 **Herman** Robert L '92
(440) 576-4166 **Hiener** Michael A '86
(440) 576-3662 **Leikala** Brenda S '00
(440) 576-9104 **Lemieux** James M '82
(440) 576-9177 **Lemire** Jerome A '76
(440) 576-3831 **McNair** Robert M '70
(440) 576-9155 **Miller** Virginia K '89
(440) 576-3667 **Niemi** Ariana E '87
(440) 576-8120 **Reese** Anne M '85
(440) 576-3694 **Sartini** Thomas L '75
(440) 576-3662 **Scott** Angela M '99
(440) 576-3003 **Sezon** Marianne '98
(440) 576-6015 **Sims** Donald C '84
(440) 576-9155 **Smith** Kyle B '80
(440) 576-3662 **Smith** Patricia J '92
(440) 576-3662 **Specht** Harold E Jr. '00
(440) 576-3665 **Thomas** Susan R '96
(440) 576-8406 **Timonere** Jane '01
(440) 576-3009 **Toth** Jason M '01
(440) 576-3662 **Tylman** Stephen J '04
(440) 576-3699 **Walsh** Patricia M '80
(440) 576-3662 **Wetherholt** Tamara A '98
(440) 576-3027 **Williams** Susan J '93
(440) 576-9003 **Wynn** Robert S '73

JOHNSTOWN
Licking County
(740) 967-2261 **Furr** Jeffrey M '93
(740) 967-5555 **Nicks** John M '01
(740) 967-5555 **Shafer** Larry F '80
(740) 966-5866 **Utz** Dorothy A '95
(740) 967-3644 **Utz** Nancy A '89

JUNCTION CITY
Perry County
(740) 987-2521 **Vigue** Ronald R '84

KENT
Portage County
(330) 673-3444 **Antognoli** Benito C '79
(330) 673-1535 **Arthur** Francis L '74
(330) 673-9118 **Averill** Sue N '95
(330) 673-3444 **Can** Errol A '92
(330) 673-8600 **Clegg** C Bailey '76
(330) 673-9511 **Conner** Marjorie L '94
(330) 678-4677 **Coogan** Alan H '77
(330) 673-0114 **DeRhodes** Jon M '88
(330) 678-3088 **Dressler** Roy D '69
(330) 677-5298 **Dubetz** Shirley A '54
(330) 673-8336 **Dyer** James D '76
Farwell Theresa M '88
(330) 673-0114 **Flynn** John J '74
(330) 678-6595 **Grim** Nancy E '84
(330) 677-0785 **Grimm** Brian T '91
(330) 673-4181 **Hart** Timothy J '80
(330) 858-1375 **Hartman** Dawn E '96
(330) 672-2982 **Hawke** Constance N '78
(330) 677-0506 **Hirt** Lisa J '93
(330) 673-3444 **Ickes** James E '00
(330) 673-5512 **Jackman** Titus '54
(330) 673-3444 **Kratcoski** Peter C '88
(330) 673-6515 **Krutz** Deborah A '88
(330) 673-0142 **Lander** Byron G '74
(330) 673-2440 **Lorenz** Peter P '00
Lyle Roxana R '81
(330) 677-9000 **Marks** Richard S '94
(330) 673-4414 **Martyniuk** Andrew O '95
(330) 677-0645 **Megargel** Ralph C '92
(330) 673-1535 **Nome** William A '76
(330) 678-5525 **Oates** Ralph L '70
(330) 672-2982 **Ochmann** David L '92
(330) 678-0242 **Paoloni** Robert J '74
(330) 297-3628 **Pittman** Laurie J '86
Pryor Richard E II '84
(330) 673-4515 **Reeves** Troy A '98
(330) 673-5015 **Smith** Stephen J '91
(330) 672-2572 **Smith** Timothy D '77
(330) 672-2775 **van Dulmen-Krantz** Jennifer J '04
(330) 677-4549 **Vitone** Patrick M '83
(330) 672-2982 **Walker** Willis '81
(330) 672-2982 **Watson** James R '83
(330) 673-8047 **Weill** Leo '72
(330) 673-3444 **Welser** Howard T Jr. '69
(330) 673-3444 **Williams** David E '76
(330) 673-3444 **Williams Welser & Kratcowski**
(330) 678-2850 **Wilson** Richard A '74
(330) 678-5508 **Wolfson** Michael D '77

KENTON
Hardin County
(419) 673-8188 **Bailey** Bradford W '79
(419) 674-4031 **Barrett** Scott N '76
(419) 673-1292 **Cesner** Robert E Jr. '68
(419) 673-1128 **Crates** James L '65
(419) 673-5212 **Crates** Randy L '86
(419) 673-1444 **Fischmann** Garron R '97
(419) 673-1534 **Glover** Teresa S '91
(419) 674-2284 **Hursh** Tammie K '95
(419) 674-4502 **Lange** Keith A '81
(419) 674-2245 **Lay** Mark A '96
(419) 674-2284 **Limerick** Colleen P '93
(419) 674-2256 **Malkin** Leslie N '86
(419) 673-4176 **Markley** Frederick E '61
(419) 673-1128 **McKinley** Paul N Jr. '75
(419) 673-4176 **Miller** Jason M '01
(419) 673-1292 **Napier** Jane A '93
(419) 675-1297 **O'Connell** Colleen M '90
(419) 674-4031 **Roof** Thomas A '79
(419) 673-1534 **Santoro** Todd F '04
(419) 673-4176 **Schwemer** David J '70
(419) 673-4176 **Schwemer** John A '01

(419) 673-4176 **Schwemer** Mark B '02
(419) 673-3167 **Sherman** Dorothy J '83
(419) 673-8188 **Sinn-Bailey** Holly A '79
Smith Burke E '54
(419) 673-1292 **Tudor** John M '62
(419) 673-9424 **Watkins** Elizabeth M '87
(419) 673-4176 **Wetherill Schwemer Markley & Schwemer**
(419) 673-8188 **Zerby** Ryan A '97

KETTERING
Montgomery County
(937) 291-8646 **Biegel** Alan A '67
(937) 298-1054 **Blue** Charles M '01
(937) 293-2200 **Coen** William R '53
(937) 298-1054 **Compton** Brooks A '79
(937) 293-2016 **Cramer** Carl A '73
(937) 223-1788 **Daganhardt** Robert Casey '82
Eckert Valerie L '00
(937) 296-2456 **Eubank** David L '89
Gonsior David S '85
(937) 299-9607 **Greenberg** Marc N '04
(937) 296-2456 **Hamer** Theodore A III '89
(937) 296-2543 **Hanna** Thomas M '81
Havener Charles R '83
(937) 435-2118 **Hemmert** William F '73
(937) 223-1788 **Hess** Douglas A '84
(937) 294-7400 **Hohl** Lee E '84
(937) 293-6964 **Horn** Charles F '54
(937) 238-9211 **Kalafatas** Mark '02
(937) 294-1715 **Light** Ronald A '82
(937) 296-2456 **Long** James F '84
(937) 298-1054 **Macbeth** William H '63
(937) 293-1000 **Mischler** Frederick F '94
(937) 296-2466 **Moore** Robert L '72
(937) 298-1054 **Murr Compton Claypoole & Macbeth**
(937) 298-8908 **Nagle** Daniel A '59
(937) 296-2456 **Newberry** Forde J '73
Ostrowski Andrea G '02
(937) 298-1961 **Parisi** Georgianna I '82
(937) 485-9420 **Pica** Mary R '79
(937) 298-6105 **Puncer** William O '80
(937) 293-0110 **Reuther** Albert H '53
(937) 643-2000 **Roberson** Nancy A '82
(937) 299-5098 **Robinson** Constance M '90
(937) 298-0399 **Schmidt** Steven P '74
(937) 299-9607 **Sherrets** Carl D '88
(937) 291-8646 **Tye** Timothy N '78
(937) 299-1506 **Yung** Gerald E '75
(937) 294-9684 **Zimmerman** George E '55

KIMBOLTON
Guernsey County
(740) 498-6254 **Schreiner** Bernard J '76

KINGSTON
Ross County
(740) 655-2002 **Delong** Richard W '74

KINGSVILLE
Ashtabula County
(440) 998-6950 **Madden** Daniel L '75

KINSMAN
Trumbull County
(330) 876-1583 **Panak** Stephen D '86

KIRTLAND
Lake County
(440) 525-7352 **Barnard** Laura '83
(440) 256-8806 **Griffith** Pamela B '81
(440) 953-7348 **Lombardo** Catherine M '79
(440) 256-9210 **Lustri** Ralph R '87
(440) 256-4150 **Mitchell** Kenneth L '82
(440) 256-2990 **Podgurski** John A '84
(440) 256-1361 **Skeggs** David C '89
(440) 256-9213 **Smith** Arthur L '72
(440) 953-7077 **Tawil** Linda E '86
Theis Stuart H '70
(440) 256-6828 **Wilson** Jane P '84
(440) 256-4150 **Woodling Krost & Rust**

LAGRANGE
Lorain County
(440) 355-5297 **Fox** Kathleen N '95

LAKE MILTON
Mahoning County
(330) 654-5565 **Kelley** L. P Jr. '73

LAKESIDE MARBLEHEAD
Ottawa County
Gonda Douglas A '72

LAKEVIEW
Logan County
(937) 843-3152 **Schrader** Chris A '76
(937) 843-3152 **Shirk** William E '57
(937) 204-1724 **Wagner** Jared A '03

LAKEWOOD
Cuyahoga County
(216) 228-1166 **Bartos** David S '99
Bates George Del '51
Baxter Howard H '56
(216) 226-9463 **Becker** Thea G '84
(216) 221-2984 **Bennett** Paul E '73
(216) 579-9100 **Bodnar** Carol G '92
(216) 579-9100 **Bodnar** Mark S '91
(216) 221-2930 **Boutall** Thomas B '91
(216) 228-8850 **Bouvier** Jaime M '99
(216) 221-8825 **Burda** Joan M '82
(216) 529-6700 **Carroll** Patrick J '77
(216) 221-7044 **Chandra** Ashvin '93
(216) 228-7250 **Clevenger** Daniel E II '98
(216) 210-0470 **Conway** Thomas E '84
(216) 221-0560 **Cook** David R '76
(216) 226-8241 **Costanzo** Raymond J '78
(216) 228-0415 **Cox** Diane E '98
(216) 268-6511 **Cullen** Craig E '76
(216) 521-7151 **Curran** John J '57
(216) 521-6363 **De Gross** Louis G '83
(216) 221-1260 **Dowling** John L '77
(216) 228-6715 **D'Souza** Gerard I '96
(216) 228-9400 **Elliott** Daniel R III '89
(216) 221-1830 **Ellison** Wildon V '93
(216) 228-7550 **Endress** Jeffrey C '80
(216) 521-6552 **Essi** Brian J '84
(216) 521-8882 **Fagnilli** Sara J '85
(216) 221-8020 **Fegen** David A '73
(216) 221-1616 **Filak** John J '56
Fowerbaugh Andrew M '98
(216) 227-3340 **Friedman** Robert E '80
Froude Jeffrey R '02
(216) 496-3427 **Gallick** Donald M '01
(216) 221-8474 **Gauntner** Timothy J '70
(216) 228-8850 **Gelfand** Martin D '97
(216) 228-7250 **Glassman** Alan B '78
(216) 226-8800 **Gordon** Chester E '55
(216) 521-7525 **Gorie** Leo F Jr. '76
(216) 228-1166 **Graham** Edward M '71
Grossi Kelly '03
(216) 228-6996 **Gruss** Raymond S '91
Harley Rachel M '91
(216) 228-7835 **Harris** Russell W '75
(216) 226-5000 **Hiller** Deborah L '75
(216) 221-3100 **Horn** Dale W '73
(216) 227-3000 **Huffman** Donald J '77
(216) 529-6090 **Ittu** Yvette M '95
(216) 227-0900 **Jacobs** Joseph J Jr. '96
(216) 521-2595 **Jankite** Susan K '99
(216) 226-4200 **Jones** David W '87
(216) 221-3100 **Kerber** Anthony W '73
(216) 221-3142 **Kilcoyne** James F '62
(216) 623-6554 **Kindt** Mark D '79
(216) 227-0715 **Kirk** Christopher S '98
(216) 529-2870 **Kohler** John E '69
(216) 221-1215 **Konchan** James E '73
Kowalczyk Crystina M '93
(216) 226-8241 **Lazzaro** Robert E '78
(216) 221-3079 **Liguore** Maryann T '80
Malloy John R '56
(216) 521-7400 **Malloy** Mary A '92
(216) 226-1170 **Martinez** Richard D '62
(216) 221-8023 **McHugh** Terrence P '85
(216) 221-2323 **McLaughlin** Ronald L '86
(216) 529-6030 **Mladek** Jennifer L '98
(216) 228-6996 **Murman** Michael E '75
(216) 228-4545 **Nageotte** Edward C '99
(216) 529-6700 **Neff** Terease Z '92
(216) 521-1418 **Neumann** Arthur W '53
(216) 316-3161 **Ostrowski** Joseph T '97
(216) 226-0166 **O'Toole** Sean C '98
(216) 529-0030 **Pahys** Thomas R '74
(216) 228-7478 **Patta** John D '88
(216) 529-2870 **Paynter Kohler & Wagner**
Pinter Jessica A '03
(216) 496-3238 **Powers** Brian E '88
(216) 521-0771 **Presswala** Rashi R '98
(216) 228-7250 **Randall** Kerry L '84
(216) 228-7250 **Rasmussen** John V '85
(216) 521-8080 **Ray** Jared S '98
(216) 227-9000 **Reulbach** John L Jr. '86
(216) 469-3152 **Richards** Terri M '94
Roberts Neil E '73
(216) 529-6030 **Robinson** Andrew S Jr. '01
(216) 221-3993 **Rus** Vladimir M '81
Safos Kristine A '02
(216) 228-7250 **Saurman** Jan A '78
(216) 226-9530 **Schillawski** Philip C '87
Sharkin Brian W '02
(216) 221-2889 **Shields** Daniel E '85
(216) 228-4791 **Shinn** Maria L '97
(216) 221-3100 **Shively** Jeffrey A '77
(216) 221-2323 **Sinagra** Anthony C '67
(216) 331-1110 **Smith** Anna M '91
(216) 228-9191 **Smolka** Monica '79
(216) 228-7250 **Stanford** Teresa G '85
(216) 521-0200 **Stearns** Roger S '67
(216) 696-8440 **Strachan** Shannon C '89
(216) 529-0300 **Stroh** Thomas M '79
(216) 521-8080 **Sumpter** Chester L '85
(216) 226-4700 **Tibbetts** Roger D '69
(216) 227-3913 **Tomallo** Ronald P Jr. '96
(216) 227-8623 **Toth** Kathryn Ellen '91
(216) 228-1523 **Utrata** Carl I '72
(216) 226-7706 **Varga-Sinka** Michael '82
(216) 221-3100 **Waag** Christian F Jr. '57
(216) 529-2870 **Wagner** Steven B '94
(216) 221-8023 **Wehr** Karen R '90
(216) 271-5482 **Wilson** Marianne E '86

LANCASTER
Fairfield County
(740) 654-2325 **Aiman** Scott A '69
(740) 654-4141 **Aranda** James C '73
(740) 653-3281 **Barnes** Kenneth M '57
(740) 687-6513 **Beery** Edward T '70
(740) 687-7155 **Bender** Jeffrey F '86
(740) 687-5555 **Berens** Randall S '78
(740) 687-5555 **Berens** Richard E '85
(740) 653-6464 **Bibler** Robert M '81
(740) 653-4259 **Blaisdell** Julie S '92
(740) 653-1902 **Boltz** G Brian '59
(740) 654-5704 **Boone** Mary A '92
(740) 654-1892 **Booth** Victoria M '79
(740) 687-5645 **Bornstein** Meredith L '00
(740) 681-9290 **Brown** Tyler E '04
(740) 653-4400 **Calig & Handelman,LPA**
(740) 653-3281 **Christian** Thomas M '72
(740) 653-6464 **Clark** Jonathan C '02
(740) 687-7044 **Clark** Joseph T '66
(740) 653-7825 **Coen Wexler & Wentz**
(740) 653-6464 **Conrad** Aaron R '02
(740) 687-1450 **Corbin** Thomas J '78
(740) 653-4000 **Cornell** Raina D '94
(740) 653-6464 **Dagger Johnston Miller Ogilvie & Hampson**
Dailey Bruce R '03
(740) 654-4141 **Davis** Sandra W '91
(740) 689-3000 **Edgar** Michelle L '00
(740) 687-5803 **Edwards** James A '76
(740) 687-5803 **Edwards** Judith L '78
(614) 920-4302 **Ehrenborg** Carie A '93
(740) 689-1372 **Fields** James A '88
Finnen George R '65
(740) 654-4141 **Fruth** Daniel J '02
(740) 653-7705 **Gordon** Charles E '83
(740) 654-5603 **Green** Frank W '69
(740) 653-6464 **Griffith** D Joe '91
(740) 687-6616 **Griggs** Jason M '99
Grove Lance R '01
(740) 653-6464 **Happeney** Randy L '85
(740) 689-9007 **Harker** John D '74
(740) 653-4259 **Hart** Roy E '77
(740) 687-7155 **Haselberger** Christina E '03
(740) 654-4141 **Hensley** Paul R '97
(740) 653-4259 **Hilty** Julia C '98
(740) 687-0175 **Holt** William J '77
(740) 654-4141 **Johnson** Matthew E '99
(740) 653-6464 **Johnston** Robert E '54
(740) 653-3863 **Keaton** Ronald L '69
(740) 654-6161 **Kellner** George K Jr. '69
(740) 653-2616 **Krooner** Theresa M '01
(740) 653-4259 **Landefeld** David L '76
(740) 654-7777 **Lantz** James A '47
(740) 687-5025 **Lewis** Douglas A '01
(740) 687-6082 **Libert** Donald J '56
(740) 681-9290 **Linehan** James M '88
(740) 654-7777 **Lipp** Thomas C '78
(740) 653-4259 **MacFadden** Denise D '82
(740) 653-0100 **Maley** Lawrence M '91
(740) 687-9355 **Mann** Jayne H '88
(740) 687-9355 **Mann** Toby D '81
(740) 653-4259 **Markwood** Maureen L '03
(740) 653-2423 **Marx** Carol S '79
(740) 653-4259 **Marx** Gregg '79
(740) 653-6464 **Michalski** Raymond R '76
(740) 653-6464 **Miller** James W '55
(740) 687-7087 **Miller** Sandra Kay '93
(740) 653-8050 **Millisor** Kenneth C '94
(740) 687-1450 **Mongold** Jessica L '04
(740) 653-4259 **Morehart** Paul D '88
(740) 687-7155 **Mowry** Kathy S '81
(740) 687-6616 **Nelson** Stephanie A '01
(740) 654-9098 **Norman** Roger H '70
(740) 653-4259 **Northness** Robert C '87
(740) 681-1770 **Novak** Lawrence J '88
(740) 653-6464 **Ogilvie** Norman J Jr. '68
(740) 687-6725 **Orlando** Michael E '88
(740) 654-4141 **Pechar** Todd D '98
(740) 689-3000 **Price** Jason A '94
(740) 687-1405 **Reed** Charles E '51
(740) 653-6464 **Riegel** Mark R '85
(740) 687-1990 **Rose** Martha A '79
(740) 687-6152 **Russell** Theodore V '79
(740) 221-6211 **Ryan** Sherman '91
(740) 687-3339 **Seeley** Robert H '47
(740) 687-3339 **Seeley** Robert L '53
Selhorst Angela J '96
(740) 653-6464 **Shonk** Brian D '88
(740) 653-0461 **Sitterley & Vandervoort Ltd**
(740) 653-0461 **Sitterley** William J '73
(740) 687-7087 **Smith** Laura B '94
(740) 681-9499 **Smith** Margaret A '98
(740) 654-4141 **Snider** John M '82
(740) 654-4141 **Snider** Rick L '79
(740) 653-6464 **Snoke** Carrie S '02
(740) 653-6464 **Spangler** Jeffrey J '04
(740) 687-5535 **Spires** Jeremiah J '89
(740) 654-4141 **Stebelton Aranda & Snider,LPA**
(740) 654-4141 **Stebelton** Gerald L '70
(740) 653-0961 **Stevenson** Andrew H '92
(740) 653-0961 **Stevenson** H James '66
(740) 687-5962 **Stoughton** Ronald C Sr. '79
(740) 681-9290 **Tawney** David A '92
(740) 653-7678 **Thomas** Scott S '93
(740) 653-4400 **Thompson** Lee A '83
(740) 687-6616 **Trimmer** David A '93
(740) 687-7176 **Trotter** Kevin Jay '82
(740) 681-4759 **Vail** Madge E '83
(740) 653-0461 **Vandervoort** Craig M '92
(740) 653-0461 **Vandervoort** Jeffrey K '95
(740) 653-0461 **Vandervoort** Peter M '63
(740) 681-5023 **Vandervoort** Terre L '90
(740) 837-7146 **Wehrmann** Kristin A '01
(740) 653-7825 **Wentz** Gregory C '81
(740) 653-6464 **Wood** Scott P '94
(740) 653-8866 **Zimpfer** George F '41

LANDON
Warren County
(513) 218-5621 **Hoyt** Bradley R '82

LEBANON
Warren County
(513) 933-9011 **Allen** Mitchell W '91
(513) 695-1325 **Anderson** Keith W '83
Atkins William M '94
(513) 695-1325 **Beaton** James D Jr. '73
(513) 932-3263 **Bednarczuk** Robert '62
(513) 932-7699 **Bennett** Charles K '73
(513) 932-4284 **Bogen** Mark R '73
(513) 695-1569 **Bonham** Mitchell W '76
(513) 932-8000 **Busse** Robert L '84
(513) 933-5527 **Courtney** Darren L '96
(513) 932-2115 **Crist** Renee L '01
(513) 933-9011 **Crossley** Paige A '92
(513) 933-0032 **Darling** Suzanne J '02
(513) 932-2115 **Dearie** James A '00
(513) 932-2121 **Demos** Gregory J '94
(513) 932-2121 **Diehl & Demos**
(513) 932-2121 **Diehl** Thomas J '88
(513) 932-3145 **Dundes** Raymond J '89
(513) 932-2871 **Duning** James W '68
(513) 695-1732 **Duvelius** Carolyn A '88
(937) 743-2545 **Eagle** Thomas G '86
(513) 932-1836 **Elter** Nathan J '95
(513) 695-1325 **Engel** Joshua A '03
(513) 932-2214 **Ernst** David E '85
(513) 695-1325 **Faulkner** Derek B '99
(513) 932-1515 **Florence** Mark T '80
(513) 932-7444 **Fowler** William G '73
(513) 932-3221 **George** Andrew P '99
(513) 932-2871 **Gray & Duning**
Gray Jon F '86
(513) 695-1325 **Hand** Mary Kathleen '03
(513) 695-1459 **Hasselbach** William A '91
(513) 932-1836 **Hedges** Jackson C '63
(513) 932-3221 **Herdman** Paul N '51
(513) 934-0893 **Howard** Anne K '01
(513) 695-1548 **Howard** Thomas E A '04
(513) 932-2121 **Hubbell** Martin E '01
(513) 695-1325 **Hutzel** Rachel A '91
(513) 695-1344 **Iversen** Yvonne A '92
(513) 932-5792 **Jarnicki** Brent H '04
(513) 932-5792 **Jarnicki** Harold '74
(513) 932-1515 **Kaufman & Florence**
(513) 932-1515 **Kaufman** William H '71
(513) 932-1515 **Kaufman** William R '01
(513) 932-3931 **Kearin** Kathy H '76
(513) 934-3200 **Krehbiel** Anne E '80
(513) 695-1231 **Larez** Michael P '03
(513) 695-1325 **Loxley** Gary A '87
(513) 934-0038 **McCormick** Jeffrey A '02
(513) 932-1414 **McKay** Leroy F '83
(513) 932-2047 **Mengle** John S '78
(513) 695-1325 **Meyer** Leslie M '92
(513) 695-1781 **Nixon** Corwin K Jr. '99
(513) 932-3452 **Oliver** Lois A '76
(513) 695-1168 **Peters** Erik A '74
(513) 695-1325 **Planas** Melvin '01
(513) 425-1370 **Powers** Dallas P '68
(513) 932-5792 **Renneker** Erin C '03
(513) 932-2300 **Revelson** Jay D '76
(513) 695-1167 **Richards** Jeffery E '83
(513) 932-2115 **Rittgers** Charles H '78
(513) 932-2115 **Rittgers** Ellen B '79
(513) 933-1278 **Secrest** Elizabeth A '94
(513) 695-1325 **Shapiro** Peggy A '04
(513) 695-1759 **Sharkey** Bartholomew B '01
(513) 932-2047 **Short** Jane A '00
(513) 932-2115 **Showen** Jason A '00
(513) 695-1325 **Sievers** Andrew L '94
(513) 934-0522 **Staton** Roger D '75
(513) 932-7444 **Stueve** Jeffrey W '00
(513) 932-3221 **Summers** Jillora H '83
(513) 695-1325 **Tamashasky** Anne L '95
(513) 934-5512 **Tepe** Timothy N '84
(513) 932-4931 **Thornton** Kevin W '95
(513) 932-2871 **Watkins** Christopher A '83
(513) 932-1414 **Wright** Bernard H Jr. '75
Young Marvin E '40
(513) 932-3060 **Yurick** Mark S '87

LEETONIA
Columbiana County
(330) 427-2720 **Newton** Walter L Jr. '85
(330) 427-2303 **Shelar** Richard C '69
(330) 427-1823 **Zarnick** Jacklynn M '89

LEWISBURG
Preble County
Ditmer Mary A '96
(937) 962-4341 **Faber** Richard V Jr. '78
(937) 962-2712 **Hobbs** H Steven '83
(937) 962-9320 **Spencer** Maria L '00

LEWIS CENTER
Delaware County
(614) 203-2729 **Atway** Saed W '01
(740) 459-0116 **Ballou** Marie E '90
(740) 549-2202 **Blue** Allan M '67
(740) 549-1320 **Callahan** Thomas C '79
Graves Christine C '02
(740) 549-2444 **Master** John E '83
(740) 548-5654 **Pemberton** David L '66
Penn Ralph W '74
(740) 272-1723 **Schmitz** Elizabeth S '91
(614) 783-2279 **Welch** Rosemarie A '99
(740) 657-7810 **Whitney** Thomas R '73

LEWISTOWN
Logan County
(937) 843-9297 **Snyder** Cheryl Wright '81

LEXINGTON
Richland County
(419) 884-0655 **Brown** Russell J '84
(419) 884-9874 **Grey** Lawrence A '69

LIBERTY CENTER
Henry County
(419) 533-6472 **Busick** David M '93

LIBERTY TOWNSHIP
Butler County
Anderson Mary K '96
(513) 737-5473 **Maloney** James P II '93

LIMA
Allen County
(419) 228-6365 **Anderson** Michael P '87
(419) 227-9595 **Balyeat** Clay W '85
(419) 227-9595 **Balyeat** William B '57
(419) 222-9933 **Banks** Farley K '95
(419) 227-5858 **Baran Piper Tarkowsky Fitzgerald & Theis Co,LPA**
(419) 222-5045 **Bartels** N Shannon '94
(866) 794-7282 **Bashore** Sandra K '84
(419) 999-1256 **Baumeister** Michelle L '96
(419) 227-3423 **Becker** Stephen L '75
(419) 223-1861 **Bell** Tamara M '96
(419) 228-0189 **Benavidez** Joseph A '89
(419) 228-7640 **Berry** Melvin D '72
(419) 224-1353 **Blair** James F '74
(419) 222-1040 **Bollinger** Christine M '02
(419) 228-3700 **Bowers** David '70
(419) 227-3423 **Brock** Terry B II '93
(419) 225-8987 **Brown** Christi L '94
(419) 224-7133 **Chamberlain** Frank S '88
(419) 228-6365 **Cheney** David A '74
(419) 222-1155 **Cornwell** Ted E '76
(419) 228-6365 **Cory** Frank B '55
(419) 228-6365 **Cory Meredith Witter Rumer & Cheney,LPA**
(419) 229-0224 **Crawford** Leslie L '00
(419) 222-1155 **Cunningham** Mariah M '03
(419) 227-9595 **Daley Balyeat & Leahy LLC**
(419) 227-9595 **Daley** Charles W '49
(419) 227-9595 **Daley** Douglas A '80
Davis Mark E '99
(419) 224-0400 **DeLong** David C '83
(419) 227-5531 **Derryberry** Glenn H '77

(419) 227-5862 **DeStephens** Clifford R '75
(419) 225-4055 **Dickason** Miner O '67
(419) 225-4055 **Dickason** Oren E '38
(419) 221-5230 **DiPierro** Rocco W '02
(419) 223-1861 **Dobay** Nikki E '03
(419) 999-9999 **Dodson** James M Jr. '98
(419) 229-4529 **Donohue** Gregory W '80
(419) 228-2091 **Doute** Jerome R '88
(419) 223-8511 **Drexler** Deborah L '83
(419) 228-0189 **Dugan** Michael E '74
(419) 227-0061 **Easterday** Jennifer S '00
Eddy E R II '01
(419) 229-1161 **Emerick** Steven M '01
(419) 224-1353 **Emerick** William C '00
(419) 228-5111 **Evans** David R '93
(419) 999-4272 **Everett** Bonnie E '86
(419) 228-8403 **Fisher** James P '63
(419) 228-8403 **Fisher** John H '85
(419) 228-8403 **Fisher Vandemark & Fisher Co,LPA**
(419) 227-5858 **Fitzgerald** Robert B '82
(419) 999-3300 **Fox** Rebecca S '83
(419) 223-1861 **Franceschelli** Anna M '03
(419) 222-6266 **French** Diane W '88
(866) 794-7282 **Gabriele** Linda C '94
(419) 221-5183 **Geiger** Anthony L '83
(419) 227-4945 **Good** Danielle A '97
(419) 227-3423 **Gottschalk** Craig A '97
(419) 227-7193 **Graff** Melinda J '87
(419) 227-5531 **Grzybowski** Robert A '90
(419) 228-3700 **Gutman** Jana E '92
(419) 223-8501 **Hamman** Timothy C '73
(419) 225-5706 **Hawkins** Brandie L '04
(419) 221-5183 **Hawley** Kevin M '02
(419) 228-9002 **Hermon** Gary R '66
(419) 228-3300 **Honigford** Robert J '91
(419) 228-3700 **Hopkins** John J III '98
(419) 227-3423 **Huffman** John C '89
(419) 227-3423 **Huffman Kelley Becker & Brock LLC**
(419) 227-3423 **Huffman** Lawrence A '81
(419) 227-3423 **Huffman** Lawrence S '58
(419) 227-3423 **Huffman** Matthew C '85
(419) 222-1040 **Hunt** James Ira '48
(419) 222-1040 **Hunt & Johnson**
(419) 227-7775 **Huston-Kinworthy** Carlene '92
(419) 229-9800 **Jacobs** Ann E '77
(419) 229-9800 **Jacobs & Von der Embse**
(419) 995-8404 **Jenson-Schuck** Margaret I '84
(419) 222-1040 **Johnson** Jerry M '75
(419) 227-5858 **Jones** Michael L '94
(419) 222-1395 **Kaufman** Kurt A '92
(866) 794-7282 **Keenehan** John C '78
(419) 227-3423 **Kelley** Charles B '79
(419) 229-4077 **Kendall** William G '73
(419) 223-8511 **Kerber** Dennis S '91
(419) 224-1353 **King** Andrew B '95
(419) 224-1353 **King & Blair**
(419) 223-1861 **Klein** Zachary M '04
(419) 225-5706 **Kluge** William F '76
(419) 227-2631 **Koester** Mark A '93
(419) 223-1861 **Kohlrieser** Terri L '01
(419) 228-2122 **Kohlrieser** Todd E '02
(419) 228-2122 **Kuhn** Thomas R '70
(419) 227-6506 **Lawson** Walter M III '69
(419) 227-6506 **Lawson** Walter M Jr. '48
(419) 227-9595 **Leahy** John M '66
(419) 227-9595 **Leahy** John M '98
(419) 228-1020 **Leonard** Robert K '69
(419) 227-7193 **Lortie** Daniel J '95
(419) 223-1861 **Mahoney** Luke D '02
(419) 228-6365 **Maisch** Victoria U '94
(419) 224-1011 **Martin** Danny N '85
(419) 222-5045 **McCluskey** Holly Lee '93
(419) 224-0066 **McLeod** Katy J '89
(419) 228-6365 **Meredith** Robert J '88
(419) 229-5886 **Mihlbaugh** Michael P '93
(419) 229-5886 **Mihlbaugh** Robert H '57
(419) 223-1861 **Miller** Gregory B '91
(419) 227-9595 **Miller** Richard W III '96
(419) 229-5106 **Minnard** Lawrence R '68
(419) 224-2125 **Novak** Gregory M '72
(419) 222-4100 **Nyers** Athena J '92
(419) 227-3050 **Patrick** James P '72
(419) 228-8989 **Pedlow** Edward B IV '85
(419) 224-3828 **Perry** Jennifer J '03
(419) 221-5234 **Phipps** Heather L '02
(419) 225-5706 **Pitts** Jerry O '87
(419) 223-1861 **Prueter** Susan M '92
(419) 227-0506 **Quatman** George B III '72
(419) 229-0023 **Quatman** Janice A '91
(419) 227-0506 **Quatman** Joseph E '79
(419) 227-5858 **Reese** Richard T '81
(419) 228-2122 **Reeves** Randy L '80
Reinicke Daniel E '75
(419) 229-5106 **Rizor Minnard & Rizor Co,LPA**
(419) 229-5106 **Rizor** Paul D '76
(419) 229-0054 **Robenalt** John A '48
(419) 228-3300 **Rodabaugh** David A '77
(419) 225-2015 **Romey** Steven A '79
(419) 225-2015 **Romey & Vandemark**
(419) 221-6712 **Roush** Bradley C '79
(419) 229-0023 **Roush** William T '73
(419) 228-3700 **Routson** Jeffrey L '97
(419) 228-6365 **Rumer** Michael A '70
(419) 224-2125 **Sabol** John A '72
(419) 225-5707 **Santo** Maria '88
(419) 223-1861 **Scheeser** Amanda L '01
(419) 222-1155 **Scherner Hanson & Cornwell,LLC**
(419) 222-4100 **Schramski** Nancy S '87
(419) 229-3044 **Shenk** Robert E '80
(419) 221-5230 **Short** Michael J '94
(419) 222-5045 **Siferd & McCluskey LPA**
(419) 222-5045 **Siferd** Richard E '73
(419) 228-6365 **Smith** James A '89
(419) 228-3700 **Sterling** Alissa M '98
(419) 228-8989 **Stotts** Kevin J '98
(419) 225-2015 **Vandemark** Dale M '84
(419) 228-8403 **Vandemark** William C '62
(419) 227-5858 **Van Dyne** Mark A '90
(419) 223-1861 **Villarreal** Teresa A '89
(419) 229-9800 **Von der Embse** Marie A '83
(419) 228-6365 **Walters** Sumner E '74
(419) 221-5227 **Weir** Joseph H II '78
(419) 995-8386 **White** Terry L '82
(419) 227-6601 **White** Walter L '48
(419) 227-6601 **White** William H '70
(419) 227-5531 **Whitlatch** Robert E '82
(419) 228-8335 **Willamowski** John R '85
(419) 228-8335 **Willamowski** Mona L '87
(419) 993-2930 **Williams** Jeffrey G '83
(419) 228-6365 **Witter** Donald J '62
(419) 222-7861 **Workman** Rickard A '84
(419) 224-1353 **Younkman** Derek A '93

LISBON
Columbiana County

(330) 424-3211 **Barborak** Nicholas M '00
(330) 424-3211 **Barborak** Virginia M '97
(330) 424-7781 **Bush** Florence '84
(330) 424-7937 **Calhoun** Melody M '84
(330) 424-7777 **Dailey** Coleen H '81
(330) 424-4071 **Fitzpatrick** Charles E Jr. '81
(330) 424-0550 **Hanley** Cynthia A '85
(330) 420-0140 **Herron** Robert L '77
(330) 420-0019 **Horvath** Peter G '81
(330) 420-0140 **Jones** Tammie M '85
(330) 424-9383 **Kibler** Richard E '86
(330) 420-0140 **McNicol** Timothy J '91
(330) 424-7800 **Ward** Jerry J '74
(330) 424-7800 **Ward** John P '00
(330) 420-0140 **Weikart** Ryan P '03

LOGAN
Hocking County

(740) 385-5343 **Beal** Larry E '78
(740) 380-2941 **Brandon** Sandra L '88
(740) 385-2191 **Dillon** Cornelius W '52
(740) 380-0332 **Eaton** Jeffrey W '87
(740) 380-1704 **Frechette** Monica A '95
(740) 385-2153 **Gerken** Charles A '77
(740) 385-5909 **Henderson** William W '79
(740) 385-1078 **Henniger** Louis Jackson II '73
(740) 385-9611 **Jackson** Steven F '89
(740) 385-8551 **Johnston** Edwin C '56
(740) 385-2181 **Jordan** Laina Fetherolf '04
(740) 385-2121 **Kernen** Willard J '77
(740) 380-2561 **Lewis** James C III '79
(740) 385-2181 **Lilley** Robert L '72
(740) 380-1555 **Mackey** Carol A '80
(740) 385-7611 **Nangle** Patricia J '73
(740) 385-5604 **Proctor** Stephen E '82
(740) 385-5604 **Rolston** George Drew '72
(740) 385-1078 **Silcott** Lori L '94
(740) 385-9611 **Veidt** Christopher E '68
(740) 385-2614 **Wagner** Deborah A '87
(740) 385-3880 **Wallace** John T '86
(740) 385-2250 **Wallar** Richard M '81

LONDON
Madison County

(740) 845-0300 **Ailes** Aleita J '72
(740) 852-3065 **Alderman** Elizabeth C '02
(740) 852-9706 **Beathard** Maurice E '50
(740) 852-9706 **Beathard** Steven P '78
(740) 852-2445 **Brown** Christopher J '97
(740) 852-2259 **Costello** Eamon P '93
(740) 852-7130 **Creamer** Michael E Jr. '99
(740) 852-2746 **Dunkle** Richard A '90
(740) 852-3000 **Flax** Richard E '74
(740) 852-8383 **Freeman** Robin R '59
(740) 852-1576 **Hansgen** Shirley C '79
(740) 852-4085 **Hume** Stephen L '87
(740) 852-0424 **Jackman** David H '64
(740) 852-9777 **Lazaroff** Alan J '86
(740) 852-1126 **Londergan** Gary W '76
(740) 852-2259 **Merritt** Gregory T '71
(740) 852-3000 **Nichols Stonecipher & Flax**
(740) 852-1669 **Picken** Robert D '74
(740) 852-0112 **Pitstick** Mark J '92
(740) 852-2259 **Price** Rachel M '95
(740) 852-2259 **Pronai** Stephen J '84
(740) 852-2221 **Richmond** Charles D '50
(740) 852-3094 **Rolfes** James W Sr. '75
(740) 852-8383 **Schooley** Eric M '97
(740) 852-4133 **Scurry** Fred L '72
(740) 852-1576 **Siddiqi** Zahid Haq '97
(740) 852-2114 **Starr** Wendy J '96
(740) 852-3000 **Stonecipher** Timothy R '75
(740) 852-1576 **Tanner Mathewson & Hansgen**
(740) 852-5420 **Theodotou** Pamela I '89
(740) 852-0112 **Treynor** Shannon M '00
(740) 852-3164 **White** Monte C '70
(740) 852-8383 **Wildman** Austin P '71
(740) 852-8383 **Wildman Schooley LLC**
(740) 852-1073 **Woods** Corey R '00
(740) 852-1073 **Woods** Robert D '69
(740) 852-1576 **Zabloudil** Renae E '01

LONDONDERRY
Ross County

(740) 887-4987 **Childers** Pamela C '98

LORAIN
Lorain County

(440) 244-4839 **Angel** Stephen B '72
(440) 960-2520 **Arroyo** Angel L '77
(440) 277-1259 **Barkus** Michael M '79
(440) 233-1100 **Barrett** Benjamin F '66
(440) 233-1100 **Barrett** Benjamin F Jr. '87
(440) 233-1100 **Barrett** Matthew H '96
(440) 244-3177 **Berta** David J '94
(440) 245-3111 **Blake** Stephen K '00
(440) 244-1811 **Bradley** Jack W '77
(440) 282-9109 **Brosky** Michael E '92
(440) 282-6188 **Brosky** Robert E '69
(440) 244-1808 **Burge** James M '75
(440) 244-1808 **Burge** Susan C '97
(440) 245-4000 **Camera** Michael J '80
(440) 988-9000 **Colella** Richard '60
(440) 988-9000 **Colella** Richard J '93
(440) 988-9000 **Colella & Weir, PLL**
(440) 244-7350 **Conger** Neal A '69
(440) 246-2665 **Cook** D Christopher '93
(440) 282-7539 **Curci** Nicholas R '65
(440) 277-8265 **Cwalina** Daniel R '94
(440) 988-9500 **Dattilo** Brian G '01
(440) 277-4444 **Donohue** Paul C '84
(440) 244-4809 **Downie** Thomas A '78
(440) 244-2434 **Duff** Michael J '80
(440) 282-2121 **Elwell** Thomas J Jr. '78
(440) 246-2317 **Ewers** Raymond J '88
(440) 244-2166 **Ewers** Robert A '54
(440) 960-1670 **Gargasz** Robert J '83
(440) 244-4809 **Gary Naegele & Theado, LLC**
(440) 244-4809 **Gary** Robert D '66
(440) 277-8146 **Gehlmann** Donald E '60
(440) 244-1811 **Giardini** Anthony B '76
(440) 244-1640 **Goldberg** Hyman S '54
(440) 282-1200 **Gordon** Ronald H '63
(440) 244-1811 **Griffin** Paul A '01
(440) 244-1389 **Grunda** Joseph C '79
(440) 244-1389 **Grunda** Joseph R '58
(440) 282-5455 **Halasa** Ghada K '87
(440) 246-0045 **Heiland** Eric K '91
(440) 282-8101 **Hritsko** John J '54
(440) 245-1160 **Jesensky** Alex Jr. '71
(440) 960-5970 **Jones** Fred C '46
Kessler Robert S '61
(440) 244-2590 **Kilroy** John P '78
(440) 233-7626 **Kuzela** Dennis M '72
(440) 988-9000 **Lamb** Joshua E '03
(440) 277-2538 **Mahon** Richard J Jr. '92
(440) 246-2202 **Mase** Lawrence L II '81
(440) 282-6431 **McNamee** Brian F '88
(440) 988-9500 **Mellott** Richard R Jr. '84
(440) 204-2159 **Mihok** Mark J '82
(440) 233-1100 **Miraldi & Barrett Co,LPA**
(440) 233-1100 **Miraldi** David P '78
(440) 233-1100 **Miraldi** James L '77
(440) 989-8080 **Miraldi** John R '87
(440) 245-1558 **Miraldi** Karen K '88
Motsch Barry B '76
(440) 288-8192 **Mumford** David M '77
(440) 244-4809 **Naegele** Jori Bloom '80
(440) 244-7374 **Nocjar** David E '73
(440) 282-1616 **Nolan** Quentin J '74
(440) 204-2150 **Nunez** Gustalo '67
(440) 245-7000 **Ortner** Kenneth N '98
(440) 244-0826 **Otero** John B Jr. '74
(440) 244-1681 **Parobek** James S '52
(440) 246-2665 **Pena** Michelle Fernandez '04
(440) 240-1224 **Porter** Mary R '89
(440) 244-6133 **Provenza** Kenneth J '67
(440) 204-2250 **Provenza** Mark R '85
(440) 244-6133 **Provenza** Michael K '92
(440) 244-6133 **Provenza** Russell D '64
(440) 244-2434 **Prusak** John M '00
(440) 244-2120 **Quinn** Alexander J '72
(440) 989-8080 **Rabold** Charles S '80
(440) 989-5821 **Ramsey** Richard S '03
(440) 244-5214 **Resar** Kenneth R '79
(440) 244-5214 **Riley** Patrick D '79
(440) 244-1827 **Ruskan** Ronald J '77
(440) 244-0122 **Scherach** Michael J '71
(440) 989-2755 **Simonoff** Zachary B '98
(440) 244-2776 **Smith** Nancy A '83
(440) 988-9500 **Stephenson** Mark E '80
(440) 246-2800 **Stone** Russell B '83
(440) 989-2755 **Swenski** Lisa I '99
(440) 282-2079 **Szabo** Jeffrey S '78
(440) 244-2727 **Taylor** Phillip P '62
(440) 244-4809 **Theado** Thomas R '79
(440) 244-1811 **Tony** Michael J '89
(440) 988-9500 **Trigilio & Stephenson**
(440) 988-9500 **Trigilio** Timothy S '80
(440) 233-7232 **Tucholski** Karen L '96
(440) 244-3955 **Tully** Michael D '80
(440) 960-2525 **Walther** James T '87
(440) 246-1823 **Webber** Barbara A '89
(440) 246-1823 **Webber** Henry T '62
(440) 246-1823 **Webber** Linda A '93
Yanick Michael E '82
(440) 282-9109 **Zaleski** Donald M '84

LOUDONVILLE
Ashland County

(419) 994-4892 **Gilman** Thomas R '03
(419) 994-3141 **Hunter** David M '96
(419) 994-3269 **Hyde** Andrew G '94
(419) 994-4892 **Kick** Erin R '98

LOUISVILLE
Stark County

(330) 875-8555 **McCue** Thomas P '76
(330) 875-7300 **Mickley** Laurie A '02
Pugh Jason R '98
(330) 875-5487 **Regas** Steve G '64
(330) 875-3288 **Shockling** Robert J '49
(330) 875-3255 **Thorley** David A '84

LOVELAND
Clermont County

(513) 984-8313 **Arnold** James S '93
(513) 965-2962 **Barnett** Richard S '92
(513) 683-3221 **Bauer** Robert C '78
(513) 984-1160 **Benadum** Frederick L '58
(513) 677-1645 **Bodley** James C '78
Bright Robert P '04
(513) 268-8887 **Brueggeman** Edward P '72
(513) 697-6999 **Ewald** Brian A '98
(513) 722-3617 **Frank** Armin H '74
(513) 722-3617 **Frank** Rainer A '94
(513) 583-9221 **Geary** Brett A '96
(513) 697-6999 **Ipsaro** John R '93
(513) 631-1300 **Kathman** Edward T '91
(513) 677-2667 **Kime** Todd G '91
(513) 683-1427 **Kothman** David M '83
(513) 985-0390 **Minamyer** William E '79
(513) 683-5666 **Pedicone** Alfred J '97
(513) 677-9865 **Schickel** Joseph '91
(513) 984-8313 **Smith** Gregory E '04
(513) 583-9565 **Snyder** David B '92
(513) 965-2900 **Stall** Mark G '88
(513) 248-6000 **Stelter** Daniel C '97
(513) 683-3221 **Stiver** Shawn A '91
(513) 683-7539 **Street** Gary D '83
(513) 677-2782 **Voyles** David R '85
(513) 583-9221 **Werdmann** Timothy G '96
(859) 240-0653 **Wilson** John D '83

LYNDHURST
Cuyahoga County

(440) 449-4560 **Bell** Irving '59
(440) 720-3283 **Castell** Rebecca J '03
Ciocia James A '71
(440) 442-0022 **Goldstein** Bruce S '83
(440) 544-1122 **Groedel** Caryn M '92
(216) 374-7472 **Heller** Michael A '01
(216) 291-0143 **Holeski** Walter L '77
(216) 381-2900 **Hoy** Kelly M '89
(440) 461-4150 **Kehn** James M '71
(216) 382-5454 **Kingsbury** Dorothea J '81
(216) 382-9150 **Mancini** James M '69
(440) 461-9975 **Marek** Edward F '65
(440) 461-4980 **Moravick** Robert J '70
(440) 461-6500 **Morhard** Albert J '56
Pasiadis Christopher F '86
(440) 473-8944 **Rubenstein** Kenneth D '91
(440) 684-1164 **Schick** Brian S '91
(440) 544-1122 **Steiner** David J '02
(440) 446-0300 **Stuplinski** Linda A '94
(440) 442-4681 **Wojnar** Christopher F '92
(440) 461-1810 **Zaffiro** Carl J '66
(440) 449-8811 **Zaffiro** William T '73
(440) 449-8811 **Zaffiro** William T Jr. '04
(440) 646-9218 **Zuckerman** Richard '71

MACEDONIA
Summit County

(330) 650-2090 **Beres** Steven A '79
(330) 467-5030 **Colavecchio** Paul V '81
(330) 467-1065 **Day** John R '89
(330) 467-5030 **Hersch** John F '77
(440) 349-3432 **Klausman** Charles W III '67
(330) 467-5030 **Maddock** Darrell D '82
(330) 467-3300 **Martin** Kenneth C '87
(440) 349-3432 **Norwillo** Vincent T '90
(330) 468-4096 **Sciortino** Steven D '90
(330) 467-5030 **Wood** Kenneth '74
(330) 468-0700 **Zielinski** Richard J '95
(330) 425-1477 **Zupon** Janice E '92

MADISON
Lake County

Archinal David D '92
(440) 428-1136 **Lalka** Colman R '81
Laughlin David J '81
(440) 428-6226 **Schafer** Scott P '95
(440) 428-6044 **Vince** George A Jr. '84
(440) 298-3760 **Wagner** James L '75

MAGNOLIA
Stark County

(330) 866-4477 **Myers** Kent J '95

MAINEVILLE
Warren County

(513) 583-8888 **Brehm** John E Jr. '82
(513) 583-8888 **Heath** James J '88
(513) 583-8888 **Heath** James V '66
(513) 336-9940 **Heil** Michael F '87
(513) 583-8888 **Stolle** Linda K '87
(513) 398-6891 **Woodward** Richard H Jr. '77

MALVERN
Carroll County

(330) 863-9455 **Slabaugh** Vincent L '98

MANSFIELD
Richland County

(419) 755-9455 **Alesch-Scholl** Carol M '85
(419) 524-7788 **Allen** John W '74
(419) 524-8200 **Anderson Will O'Donnell & Kitzler LLP**
(419) 756-7711 **Ardis** Frank Jr. '74
(419) 755-9622 **Ault** Jerry E '78
(419) 525-0800 **Badnell** David C '94
(419) 524-6682 **Badnell** Kelly L '94
(419) 774-5676 **Baker** John W '81
(419) 524-6682 **Baran** Edward C Jr. '67
(419) 524-6682 **Baran** Gregory G '70
(419) 524-6682 **Baran Piper Tarkowsky Fitzgerald & Theis Co,LPA**
(419) 756-7711 **Bayer Jerger & Ardis**
(419) 522-6242 **Beddow** Kenneth R '81
(419) 522-2706 **Beilstein** Kathryn A '84
(419) 525-1611 **Bemiller** F Loyal '58
(419) 529-8764 **Blazef** Jaceda '00
(419) 522-6168 **Blunt** James L II '94
(419) 524-6011 **Bourdeau** Julia M '99
(419) 526-1176 **Bove** Ralph R '78
(419) 525-1611 **Brown Bemiller Murray & McIntyre**
(419) 524-4711 **Brown** Charles M '72
(419) 525-1611 **Brown** John T '58
(419) 522-2889 **Burton** Jon K '74
(419) 522-7776 **Busler** David E '77
(419) 524-6011 **Calhoun Kademenos Heichel & Childress Co,LPA**
(419) 755-9659 **Cannon** Karen L '92
(419) 524-9811 **Carto** David D '81
(419) 774-5676 **Castor** Robert D '76
(419) 524-6011 **Childress** James L '85
(419) 529-4560 **Chisnell** Brian J '80
(419) 524-6011 **Clark** Christopher S '91
(419) 522-8844 **Cockley** Mark W '92
(419) 522-2001 **Cockley** Stephen '76
(419) 524-4711 **Cole Brown & Fesmier**
(419) 524-4711 **Cole** Thomas L '61
(419) 755-9659 **Copp** Dianna B '85
(419) 524-1361 **Corley** Byron O '04
(419) 774-5676 **Couch** Bambi S '82
(419) 774-4100 **Cowell** Sheryl M '94
(419) 774-5569 **Dalbey** Garry D '79
(419) 529-1367 **Davidson** Lisa L '95
(419) 524-1213 **Davis** Bernard R '72
(419) 756-3687 **Davis** Harold H '68
(419) 524-3337 **Dees** Jodie D '87
(419) 525-0777 **Dilts** John S '88
(419) 525-1984 **Donaldson** John D '86
(419) 524-8011 **Dorner** Thomas M '74
(419) 755-1477 **Emmens** David P '74
(419) 522-2733 **Enderle** John R '74
(419) 524-4711 **Fesmier** Raymond G '85

(419) 522-7000 **Fithian** William C III '81
(419) 524-3603 **Flippin** Wilbur H Jr. '57
(419) 524-9811 **Fowler** Richard R Jr. '53
(419) 529-4560 **Freda** Michael M '72
(419) 526-1131 **Fry** Randall E '78
(419) 774-5727 **Fultz** Lisa R '92
(419) 526-1622 **Gandert** William F '50
(419) 524-5568 **Gerhardt** Dan E '87
Gilbert Louis H '03
(419) 526-3177 **Goldberger** Robert '76
(419) 524-9811 **Goldman** Catherine D '81
(419) 529-7657 **Guarnera** Anthony P '88
(419) 524-9811 **Hall** George '52
(419) 524-6682 **Hanke** Chad P '03
(419) 525-1611 **Haring** David N '94
(419) 524-1986 **Harper** Roeliff E '91
(419) 525-1611 **Heck** James J '88
(419) 524-6011 **Heichel** William D '72
(419) 526-2188 **Hendricks** Richard E '69
(419) 884-3522 **Hire** John S '82
(419) 524-7400 **Hitchman** Terry D '88
(419) 522-7999 **Hoard** JoAnn P '00
(419) 522-6242 **Hoerig** Joseph P '95
(419) 522-6242 **Hohenberger** Wayne P '73
(419) 524-9811 **Holmes** John A '94
(419) 524-9811 **Hoover** Donald E '80
(419) 755-9659 **Hoovler** Ryan M '01
(419) 522-2733 **Inscore** Larry Lee '59
(419) 522-2733 **Inscore** Michael Lee '84
(419) 522-3398 **Inscore Rinehardt Whitney & Enderle,LPA**
(419) 524-5568 **Jacobs** Thomas L '86
(419) 756-7711 **Jerger** Joseph L '90
(419) 525-1468 **Jones** Kenneth D Jr. '96
(419) 524-6011 **Kademenos** Victor P '71
(419) 524-6011 **Kamarados** John S '01
(419) 529-1367 **Karl** Melissa K '84
(877) 223-4633 **Keller** Jennifer D '01
(419) 526-2301 **Keyser** George R '73
(419) 524-8200 **Kitzler** Benjamin D '00
(419) 524-8200 **Kitzler** David L '76
(419) 524-8200 **Kitzler** Patricia O '88
(419) 524-5568 **Knell Dorner & Gerhardt Co,LPA**
(419) 524-0471 **Kopcial** Douglas J '87
(419) 522-7474 **Kramer** Jeffrey N '93
(419) 774-5573 **Linsker** Jeffrey A '76
(419) 522-3113 **Lowenkamp Cockley** Heather M '91
(419) 774-5700 **Lucas** Kelly L '91
(419) 525-1000 **Lynch** Charles D '75
(419) 524-1403 **Mabee & Mills**
(419) 524-1403 **Mabee** Robert E '50
(419) 524-4683 **Mack** Deborah L '96
(419) 529-1367 **Mahlay** Oleh '95
(419) 526-2223 **Marshall** Mark A '02
(419) 774-5676 **Massie** Nancy H '88
(419) 524-2444 **Mayer** Cassandra J '99
(419) 774-5676 **Mayer** James J Jr. '77
(419) 524-2444 **Mayer** Philip A '77
(419) 525-1611 **McIntyre** William T '75
(419) 774-5573 **McKinley** William S '98
(419) 529-4949 **Meyers** Robert J '73
(419) 522-6262 **Miller** Eric S '76
(419) 524-1403 **Mills** Reese F '75
(419) 521-6222 **Morrison** Jeffrey S '94
(419) 526-0050 **Morton** Norman R '73
(419) 525-1611 **Murray** David K '73
(419) 525-1611 **Murray** Jason B '95
(419) 774-5676 **Murray** Michael J '76
(419) 524-6522 **Musilli** Dale M '87
(419) 524-3700 **Naumoff** Annette R '95
(419) 524-3700 **Naumoff** Phillip S '94
(419) 524-3700 **Naumoff** William K '94
(419) 524-6011 **Naylor** Robert S '93
(419) 522-5900 **Neumann** James M '76
(419) 524-8200 **O'Donnell** James J '54
(419) 524-5555 **O'Donnell** John C III '80
(419) 524-9811 **Olecki** Joseph T '94
(419) 524-9811 **Otto** Richard H '81
(419) 524-7788 **Owens** Beth Allen '04
(419) 755-9616 **Payton** Jeff '75
(419) 529-4560 **Perry** Kathleen E '83
(419) 774-5751 **Persinger** Kathleen M '90
(419) 524-6682 **Piper** Gary A '75
(419) 774-5676 **Pitzer** Norma J '97
(419) 747-9100 **Price** Daniel E '02
(419) 774-5676 **Pscholka-Gartner** Kirsten L '04
(419) 529-8300 **Reichenbach** Gregory S '04
(419) 755-9659 **Remy** David L '75
(419) 522-3398 **Rinehardt** John J '56
(419) 529-2020 **Rinehardt** John K '86
(419) 774-5676 **Robinson** Brent N '94
(419) 524-6000 **Robinson** Charles T '66
(419) 522-6242 **Sauter Hohenberger & Beddow**
(419) 755-5725 **Schemine** Bryan A '95
(419) 774-5676 **Schoren** James A '84
(419) 774-1430 **Schulz** Alicia A '86
(419) 524-9811 **Siegenthaler** John H '64
Smith Craig E '02
(419) 525-1811 **Spaulding** Jonathon W '00
(419) 524-6011 **Spon** John R Jr. '73
(419) 525-8705 **Stewart** John P '91
(419) 774-5676 **Studenmund** John D '93
(419) 755-4778 **Sturgill** Judith L '85
(419) 755-4869 **Sukys** Paul A '80
(419) 755-5376 **Sullivan** Daniel W '87
(419) 524-6682 **Tarkowsky** John '78
(419) 524-6211 **Teffner** Donald R '77
(877) 223-4633 **Tenison** Dennis C '79
(419) 524-9811 **Them** Jerod M '04
(419) 529-8672 **Thomas** Rebecca M '92
(419) 522-5297 **Thompson** Charles R '76
Thompson Dale A '75
(419) 755-9659 **Thompson** Jerry W '01
(419) 522-0004 **Thrush** Douglas L '75
(419) 525-1611 **Turlo** Emily M '04
(419) 524-4402 **Tyree** James A '83
(419) 756-7711 **Underwood** Jeffrey A '96
(419) 525-1611 **Vetter** Adam Jr. '85
(419) 526-3300 **Wagner** James K '76
(419) 524-3334 **Wagner** Leslie K Jr. '67
(419) 522-3398 **Weiler** Samuel P '04
(419) 524-9811 **Weldon Huston & Keyser,LLP**
(419) 522-2889 **Welsh** Harry M '66
Wendling Anne C '89
(419) 522-2111 **Werstiuk** Allen D '82
(419) 522-3398 **Whitney** M Loré '92
(419) 522-3398 **Whitney** R Rolf '82
(419) 522-3398 **Whitney** Robert H '62
(419) 774-5676 **Wildermuth** Stephen M '89
(419) 524-5297 **Wolf** Marcus A '80
(419) 774-5575 **Woodward** Deborah E '89

MANTUA
Portage County

Ohlrich Holly A '04
Tighe James M '77

MAPLE HEIGHTS
Cuyahoga County

(216) 662-8631 **Augustine** Susan M '89
(216) 587-1245 **Bocci** Lawrence M '98
(216) 526-2068 **Broski** Gerald F '68
(216) 663-4552 **Canestraro** Donald C '66
(216) 475-8585 **Gorman** Joseph T Jr. '87
(216) 591-0909 **Heller** Renee P '94
(216) 475-3656 **Matlin** Judith L '91
(216) 663-4552 **Naffah** Eli Thomas '62
(216) 663-4552 **Naffah** Elias T Jr. '93
(216) 663-7991 **Siekierski** Diane M '83

MARBLEHEAD
Ottawa County

Ibos Robert J '66
(419) 798-5203 **Klaehn** John C '98
(419) 734-1969 **Mazur** James A '68

MARENGO
Morrow County

(419) 253-6091 **Bennett** Earl W '75
(740) 747-0336 **Minadeo** Joseph M '04
Vaile George Q '68

MARIETTA
Washington County

(740) 373-1335 **Adams** William J '85
(740) 373-6688 **Addison** James R Jr. '53
(740) 376-2400 **Archer** Michael D '00
(740) 373-4633 **Atkinson & Burton**
(740) 373-4633 **Atkinson** Thomas R '69
(740) 373-2420 **Baumgartel** Rolf E '89
(740) 373-1155 **Bertram & Halliday,LLC**
(740) 373-1155 **Bertram** Paul G III '89
(740) 373-1155 **Bertram** Paul G Jr. '62
(740) 374-2629 **Bozian** Robin A '77
(740) 373-5455 **Brock** Jerry A '63
(740) 374-2629 **Brockwell** Joseph H '81
(740) 373-4633 **Brum** Nancy E '02
(740) 373-3219 **Buell** Michael D '78
(740) 374-2241 **Burnworth** Randall G '76
(740) 373-4633 **Burton** William L '76
(740) 373-5455 **Carlisle** Matthew C '98
(740) 373-7624 **Cauthorn-Kreiss** Alison L '89
(740) 373-5455 **Cook** Colleen E '83
(740) 373-9324 **Danford** Barbara N '91
(740) 373-7572 **Davidson Heckler Riggs & Fouss**
(740) 374-5346 **Dehmlow** Jonathan C '00
(740) 373-4474 **Dotsenko** Juliana C '88
(740) 373-5513 **Dugger** Raymond E '99
(740) 373-8624 **Ellis** Robert '77
(740) 373-5455 **Erb** John E '69
(740) 373-3155 **Evans** Robert E '67
(740) 374-5346 **Fields** William A '64
(740) 373-6604 **Folwell** Norman L '91
(740) 373-7572 **Fouss** Daniel A '80
(740) 373-5455 **Frye** Gary F '68
(740) 373-6688 **Funk** Rustin J '77
(740) 373-2414 **Garrison** Jennifer D '87
(740) 373-1155 **Halliday** John M '93
(740) 374-2629 **Harrington** Dennis M '86
(740) 376-9669 **Hirschi** Helen '95
(740) 376-4804 **Hodson** Thomas S '73
(740) 373-5261 **Hollister** Jeffrey L '74
(740) 373-5455 **Huggins** James S '81
(740) 374-6109 **Hunsaker** Charles R '72
(740) 373-7618 **Jones** Donald L '63
Keegan Anne E '80
(740) 373-7624 **Kerenyi** Mark '96
(740) 373-5455 **Leeper** Myron D Jr. '74
(740) 373-4171 **Marsh** John H Jr. '00
(740) 373-1441 **McKim** Janet F '77
(740) 373-9447 **Miller** James M '82
(740) 373-7674 **Montera** Susan A '93
(740) 373-7674 **Newhart** Anita L '83
(740) 374-9000 **Nichols** Curtis B '80
(740) 373-4474 **Nuzum** William M III '81
(740) 373-4171 **Reynolds** Catherine I '92
(740) 373-8624 **Richardson** Lynn M '77
(740) 373-7572 **Riggs** Roland W III '72
(740) 373-7624 **Rings** Kevin A '87
(740) 373-5455 **Ritter** Khadine L '00
(740) 373-7624 **Schneider** James E '75
(740) 373-5455 **Sellers** Abraham '97
(740) 373-3219 **Sipe** Dennis L '73
(740) 373-7624 **Spahr** Michael G '74
(740) 373-5455 **Theisen Brock,LPA**
(740) 373-5455 **Theisen** Paul T '57
(740) 373-4171 **Thompson** Amy L '99
(740) 373-5455 **Triplett** John E Jr. '84
(740) 373-5455 **Vessels** Ethan T '03
(740) 374-6222 **Welch** Janet D '80
(740) 373-8151 **Wesel** Marilyn S '93
(740) 374-1581 **Westbrock** Paul G '93
(740) 373-4500 **Willard** Michele H '84
(740) 374-0664 **Wyant** Daniel M '95

MARION
Marion County

(740) 382-3221 **Anderson** Todd A '96
(740) 387-1613 **Armengau** Javier H '98
(740) 223-4290 **Babich** Lawrence H '75
(740) 387-5900 **Babich** Ted B '80
(740) 383-3377 **Ballinger** Teresa L '94
(740) 387-6000 **Bartram** John C '73
(740) 387-9704 **Bebout** Bradley C '80
Buck Christian L '01
(740) 223-4290 **Burggraf** Rhonda G '92
(740) 382-1121 **Burt** Jasper N '66
(740) 387-5297 **Chaffin** Steven E '81
(740) 233-1470 **Collins** Kevin P '85
(740) 233-1470 **Collins & Lowther**
(740) 382-2611 **Cordrick** Robert C '01
(740) 223-3322 **Coulter** Ted I '81
(740) 387-9093 **Cramer** Ronald D '75
(740) 223-4290 **Croskey** Jennifer S '00
(740) 387-0800 **Crowder** Mary K '92
(740) 233-1470 **Diequez** Douglas B '02
(740) 382-4445 **Dowler** Harry L Jr. '61
(740) 383-1151 **Ebert** Douglas E '76
(740) 387-9991 **Farrington** Barbara J '87
(740) 387-2020 **Finnegan** William R '79
(740) 387-5854 **Firstenberger** John P '59
(740) 387-7438 **Fragale** Robert D '82
(740) 387-7384 **Frericks & Howard,LPA**
(740) 387-7384 **Frericks** Theodore P '45
(740) 387-7384 **Frericks** Theodore P IV '70
(740) 387-7384 **Frericks** Thomas A '71
(740) 387-7384 **Frericks** Timothy M '74
(740) 382-4445 **Goodman** Malcolm L '74
(740) 383-6109 **Hall** Kevin R '87
(740) 382-5781 **Hardy** Charles T '84
(740) 387-1717 **Harraman** Brent M '77
(740) 383-1151 **Harris** James A '68
(740) 383-2446 **Heiser** Larry N '02
(740) 387-7799 **Hypes** Maria L '91
(740) 389-6283 **Jacob** Dean L '86
(740) 387-1120 **Kegler Brown Hill & Ritter**
(740) 387-0970 **Kochheiser** Keith A '78
(740) 383-2161 **Libster** Mitchell A '76
(740) 387-6688 **Logsdon-Babich** Sara E '84
(740) 233-1470 **Lowther** David H '96
(740) 382-6588 **Luton** James P '76
(740) 387-1613 **Martin** Denise '99
(740) 387-5854 **Mathews** Thomas A '77
(740) 387-1120 **McKinniss** Ted M '76
(740) 233-1470 **Minter** John A '04
(740) 382-1104 **Murphy** Matthew P '92
(740) 387-7438 **Nemo** Robert C '79
(740) 387-4998 **Panzer** John W '70
(740) 387-6727 **Piacentino** Charles M '73
(740) 223-4290 **Potts** Renee' L '90
(740) 383-6023 **Ratliff** J C '78
(740) 387-5308 **Reber** Frank K '73
(740) 382-1121 **Redmond** Dustin J Jr. '77
(740) 223-4060 **Reed** David T '94
(740) 223-4290 **Rich** J Anthony '96
(740) 387-0800 **Rogers** James W '62
(740) 382-2611 **Roston** Timothy A '02
(740) 387-8916 **Rowland** Brent A '80
(740) 387-3777 **Russell** Mark D '90
(740) 382-2277 **Scharer** Ronald J '73
(740) 223-4290 **Slagle** Jim '80
(740) 383-2161 **Smith** Donald B Jr. '97
(740) 387-0900 **Spohn** Clifford C '68
(740) 387-0900 **Spohn Spohn & Zeigler**
(740) 382-2153 **Taube** Donald H '73
(740) 383-2161 **Thomas** Staci K '00
(740) 382-1121 **Warner** Jason D '96
(740) 382-1027 **Williamson** David E '72
(740) 382-8892 **Williamson** Jonathan '76
(740) 387-0970 **Wilson** Robert E '68
(740) 387-1120 **Worobiec** Michele S '96
(740) 387-0900 **Zeigler** Fredrick S '69
(740) 383-4795 **Ziercher** Mark C '96

MARTINS FERRY
Belmont County

(740) 633-5551 **Berhalter** Christopher M '96
(740) 633-5551 **Liberati** David K '82
(740) 633-2954 **Sommer** Karl W Jr. '63
(740) 633-5551 **Sommer** Keith A '66
(740) 633-5551 **Sommer Liberati & Berhalter Co,LPA**

MARYSVILLE
Union County

(937) 642-4070 **Allen** David F '61
(937) 642-4070 **Allen Yurasek & Merklin**
(937) 644-8151 **Aslaner** Tim M '98
(937) 644-9111 **Behrens** Daniel E '68
(937) 645-3082 **Blackburn** Marcia V '85
(937) 644-9125 **Bridges** Robert L '79
(937) 578-4202 **Calloway** Sue Dill '83
(937) 644-9125 **Cannizzaro Fraser Bridges & Jillisky**
(937) 644-9125 **Cannizzaro** John F '80
(937) 645-4190 **Chase** Melissa A '89
(937) 644-8151 **Coleman Eufinger & Aslaner**
(937) 645-2787 **Coogle** Andrew B '96
(937) 644-3849 **Cox** Faye D '01
(937) 644-1010 **Dawson** Kerry B '89
(937) 642-6297 **Dennison** Judith L '96
(937) 644-6639 **DuBoise** Nancy F '00
(937) 642-9718 **Duke** John E '03
(937) 644-8151 **Dunbar** Stephen C '03
(937) 644-8151 **Eufinger** John M '72
(937) 644-6642 **Francis** Stephen S '84
(937) 644-9125 **Fraser** Don W '79
(937) 644-6634 **Goldfarb** Lewis H '88
(937) 644-6545 **Grady** Stephen L '97
(937) 645-8478 **Greeno** Pamela E '00
(937) 642-0515 **Grigsby** Joseph B '48
(937) 642-0686 **Grigsby** Michael J '80
(937) 642-5877 **Hamilton** Robert O '53
(937) 645-4190 **Hord** Terry Lee '82
(937) 644-3849 **Howard** Frank '75
(937) 644-6629 **Howard** Lowell B Jr. '87
(937) 644-6626 **Hust** Robert L '86
(937) 644-9125 **Jillisky** Donald R '93
(937) 644-9125 **Jillisky** Nancy L '95
(937) 645-2316 **Jimenez** Joseph V '02
(937) 644-3691 **Johnson** Frederick B '77
(937) 644-6640 **Kahle** John B '93
(937) 645-8425 **Konstantacos** Taso W '86
(937) 644-6630 **Korleski** Christopher '88
(937) 644-6631 **LaFleur** Joseph F '86
(937) 644-6645 **Long** Mark A '87
(937) 642-6297 **McDonald** Alan T '00
(937) 642-4070 **Merklin** Jeffrey A '85
(937) 642-4618 **Mickley** Richard S '71
(937) 642-3142 **Music** Lisa W '98
(937) 642-4070 **Owens-Ruff** Tina L '99
(937) 642-2950 **Parrott** Robert W '85
(937) 644-3144 **Parsons** Perry R '95
(937) 642-5627 **Pelanda** Dorothy K '82
(937) 642-8232 **Pelanda** Kevin L '81
(937) 645-4190 **Phillips** David W III '84
(937) 578-5509 **Proels** Allayne W '96
(937) 644-2626 **Ramsini** Hope J '94
(937) 645-3029 **Robinson-Walls** Sharon Kay '99
(937) 645-4190 **Rodger** Lester R Jr. '89
(937) 644-7606 **Schmenk** Christiane W '84
(937) 644-9488 **Schneider** Russell Larry '69
(937) 644-7888 **Schostek** Richard M '86
(937) 644-3849 **Schulze** Dennis A '68
(937) 644-3849 **Schulze Howard & Cox**
(937) 578-5237 **Smith** Ivan C '94
(937) 644-9125 **Streng** Michael J '00
(614) 563-2343 **Watson** Yvonne M '01
(937) 642-4070 **Yurasek** Stephen J '79

MASON
Warren County

(513) 622-1268 **Alexander** Richard L '02
(513) 229-7996 **Babcock** Kelly E '94
(513) 765-6331 **Barone** James J '95
(513) 398-8901 **Batsche** David A '96
(513) 398-8901 **Batsche** David K '66
(513) 336-2503 **Beck** Patrick E '92
(513) 336-2701 **Benintendi** Laurie H '91
(513) 765-6902 **Benton** James S '80
(513) 754-0564 **Coil** Nicole T '96
(513) 229-1000 **Corrado** Barry V '81
Cozine John C '98
(513) 701-5529 **Croskery** Robert F '95
(513) 765-6000 **Curtis** Mildred A '81
(513) 398-8885 **Davis** Betty J '87
(513) 398-9500 **Davis** Michael J '90
(513) 398-4891 **Donnelly** Karen S '90
(513) 229-0230 **Eichner** Claire S '99
(513) 573-4880 **Estenfelder** Regina L '95
(513) 336-4685 **Evans** Marlene M '91
(513) 398-4646 **Fischer** Robert S '99
Fliehman Travis L '00
(513) 765-6000 **Freytag** David M '89
(513) 459-1745 **Garner-Stark** Carol A '96
(513) 336-2546 **Gephardt** Stephanie M '88
(513) 701-3000 **Glass** Robert P '83
Goldman Elmer M '50
(513) 398-4891 **Graber** Matthew J '02
(513) 765-6000 **Griffiths** William D '80
(513) 229-0383 **Hasse** Donald E '78
(513) 229-0383 **Hasse & Nesbitt LLC**
(513) 622-1822 **Haughey** Angela K '03
(513) 765-4448 **Hayne** April M '01
(513) 459-0492 **Hicks** Andrea N '94
(513) 765-6351 **Holley** Cathy E '88
(513) 622-2184 **Howell** John M '88
(513) 229-6536 **Kammer** Richard E '90
(513) 829-0313 **Kauffman** Giles F III '95
(513) 774-8500 **Kincaid** Daniel E '95
(513) 229-7996 **Kircher** Konrad '92
(513) 701-5529 **Kinsley** Melinda E '84
(513) 622-1962 **Livingston** Jennifer Lyon '03
(513) 229-6537 **Longwell** Christopher D '00
(513) 770-3801 **Lopez** David B '63
(513) 765-6340 **Lovejoy** Wallace W '88
(513) 336-2702 **McDermott** Maureen A '96
(513) 398-4891 **McGary** Bruce A '91
(513) 622-5502 **McMahon** Mary P '92
(513) 229-7996 **Mongenas-Handorf** Jacqueline '92
Moser Devon L '02
(513) 229-0383 **Nesbitt** Daniel F '86
(513) 258-1991 **Parker** George M '90
(513) 398-4891 **Peeler McGary & Zopff**
(513) 398-4891 **Peeler** Robert W '83
(513) 336-2544 **Pershern** Judy L '84
(513) 258-1991 **Qucsai** Robert James III '04
(513) 398-0820 **Rice** Paul D '75
(513) 229-0383 **Richter** Ronald J '01
(513) 573-6606 **Rosen** Arthur M '81
(513) 459-1574 **Ross** Clara S '88
(513) 398-4646 **Sams Fischer & Schuessler**
(513) 398-4646 **Sams** Jonathan D '96
(513) 336-2704 **Sansbury** Amy Z '81
(513) 229-6777 **Schaller** Stephen J '95
(513) 398-4646 **Schuessler** Dolores C '89
(513) 398-8911 **Shackleford** Thomas D '68
(513) 229-0479 **Simon** Steven E '75
Slone Thomas J Sr. '79
(513) 765-6000 **Spitz** Mark A '89
Stegman David W II '01
(513) 336-2541 **Stubbers** Edward L '95
(513) 398-7300 **Tefend** Mark B '93
(513) 336-4628 **Thomas** Brian J '98
(513) 459-3622 **Ucros** Nancy '99
(513) 622-1825 **Upite** David V '00
(513) 622-4433 **Vago** James C '95
Valento James J '89
(513) 398-4891 **Wade** Teresa R '94
(513) 336-2545 **Weber** Jody E '95
(513) 398-1910 **Whitaker** James A Jr. '72
(513) 765-6000 **Wilson** Robin R '93
(513) 398-8900 **Wireman** Daniel R '95
(513) 765-6906 **Wood** Elizabeth H '89
(513) 622-3952 **Zea** Betty J '91

MASSILLON
Stark County

(330) 830-1718 **Andrews** Amy Sue '98
(330) 452-6567 **Beane** Frank L '73
(330) 837-9735 **Breyfogle** Edwin H '76
(330) 478-4333 **Burns** Susan H '94
(330) 830-0083 **Buttacavoli** Glen F '84
(330) 830-2682 **Centrone** Cataldo R '80
(330) 833-6315 **Chapis** Richard M '75
(330) 832-5999 **Christoff** William Z '76
(330) 830-2688 **Conley** James M '77
(330) 832-5211 **Connelly** Alan M '57
Dean Melissa K '99
(330) 832-1853 **DeLong** James C Sr. '57

(330) 833-9736 **Demsky** William E '76
(330) 832-1597 **Dummermuth** Karen S '93
(330) 834-3602 **Dunn** Karen A '90
(330) 833-8700 **Eisenbrei** Barbara Waltz '88
(330) 837-4678 **Fellmeth** Scott E '80
(330) 837-4678 **Ferrero** John Dee Jr. '81
(330) 837-4678 **Ferrero** Thomas V '72
(330) 832-9878 **Fichter** Joel C '84
Fichter Matthew R '03
(330) 832-2918 **Fitzgerald** Neal L '79
(330) 833-1734 **Frieg** John H '82
(330) 854-4619 **Fulmer** Claudia F '82
(330) 834-2709 **Geis** Raymond M '04
(330) 833-3183 **Harris** Henry G '70
(330) 832-8124 **Hutsell** Randall A '84
(330) 837-4678 **Jarvis** Keith L '69
(330) 833-2884 **Jollay** Robert D Jr. '74
(330) 830-1725 **Kettler** Richard T '74
(330) 837-4251 **Kimmins** Thomas W '63
(330) 832-1597 **Kincaid** Dale B '67
(330) 832-9878 **Kurtzman** John L '66
(330) 830-1718 **LaPenna** Anthony '83
Lewandowski Thomas P '70
(330) 832-9833 **Maier** Erich J '96
(330) 837-4678 **Matecheck** Vincent G '71
(330) 830-1555 **Milliken** Paul E '63
(330) 832-9744 **Netzly** Dwight H '52
Paxson Debra D '93
(330) 833-8521 **Percival** Mark R '78
(330) 832-4904 **Rea** Brenda J '94
(330) 830-1718 **Reed** Malynda M '97
(330) 830-1718 **Schurer** Laura A '98
(330) 837-4678 **Simpson** John H '85
(330) 832-9833 **Slagle** Larry V '77
(330) 837-4251 **Snively** James D '66
(330) 832-9878 **Stergios** John F '69
(330) 832-9878 **Stergios & Kurtzman Co,LPA**
(330) 832-9878 **Stergios** Paul J '61
(330) 832-9878 **Stergios** Pericles G '86
Tavaglione Barbara A '94
(330) 830-1718 **Warstler** Keith A Jr. '00

MAUMEE
Lucas County

(419) 897-7085 **Arnsby** John B '90
(419) 891-1510 **Asbury** Karen E '88
(419) 893-3360 **Baker** Chad R '99
Barciz Rosemarie A '83
(419) 897-6500 **Barkan & Robon Ltd**
(419) 897-6500 **Barkan** William Ira '55
(419) 891-8884 **Bayer Papay & Steiner Co,LPA**
(419) 893-7300 **Behrendt** Harry M Jr. '67
Bentley Michael L '02
Bergsmark Jean M '00
(419) 893-5555 **Boss** Charles M '81
(419) 893-5555 **Boss & Vitou Co,LPA**
(419) 724-7000 **Bostleman** William Lee '91
(419) 893-4880 **Brogan** Allan J '58
(419) 891-2024 **Bueter** Christopher R '02
(419) 897-7140 **Byers** Gary L '81
(419) 891-8884 **Chamberlain** Richard M '99
(419) 893-4836 **Coe** Helen M '73
(419) 891-7775 **Conrad** Mark A '83
(419) 897-6500 **Damicone** Jason S '03
(419) 897-6500 **Davis** Robert E '01
(419) 897-6500 **Elder** Gregory R '86
(419) 891-6474 **Fallat** Dale W '70
(419) 893-1444 **Farrar Naayers & Wilkinson,Ltd**
(419) 893-1444 **Farrar** Richard G '66
(419) 893-2195 **Fulop** Louis J '61
(419) 891-6473 **Hall** Elizabeth J '80
Hart Lori B '93
(419) 897-8200 **Isaac** Lynn A '80
(419) 897-8456 **Jensen** Julie A '98
(419) 891-9999 **Katz** Ian M '03
(419) 893-3360 **Keller** Stephen S '99
(419) 861-1100 **Klein** Daniel M '90
(419) 893-7600 **Kuns** Gary F '68
(419) 248-4611 **Lindsay** James M '86
(419) 893-4880 **Marsh** Benjamin F '55
(419) 893-4880 **Marsh McAdams Ltd**
(419) 893-4880 **McAdams** Sheilah H '78
(419) 893-5050 **McBride** Beverly J '66
(419) 893-9999 **Mikesell** Alan D '84
(419) 893-4836 **Millon** James W '76
(419) 897-5295 **Mlcek** Paula B '90
(419) 893-0011 **Moore** Everett D '77
(419) 893-1444 **Naayers** John A '86
(419) 893-4880 **Norton** Suzanne Belot '84
(419) 244-7563 **Orra** Said M '03
(419) 893-3374 **Oswald** Julie S '95
(419) 891-8884 **Papay** Debbie J '85
(419) 897-7439 **Patton** Diana R '97
(419) 536-9708 **Pesin** Donna K '92
(419) 891-8662 **Pettiford** Nadine S '95
(419) 897-6500 **Radon** Paul A '81
(419) 891-8884 **Raitz** Glenn N '63
(419) 865-0251 **Rasmusson** Deborah E '99
(419) 878-8760 **Restivo** Francis C '49
(419) 897-6500 **Robon** Marvin A '66
(419) 893-3798 **Runner** George F '75
(419) 893-3798 **Runner** Raymond A '76
(419) 891-5200 **Sandusky** Barbara J '92
Savage Barry E '65
(419) 893-4880 **Schaefer** Stephen A '73
(419) 897-5295 **Spidel** Douglas A '97
(419) 891-7909 **Stancati** Joseph A '72
(419) 891-8884 **Steiner** Chris E '78
(419) 893-3360 **Sterling** Robert V '71
(419) 893-4880 **Szozda** Veronica L '88
(419) 654-0199 **Taylor** Jayson A '04
(419) 897-6500 **Tesznar** Cynthia G '84
(419) 897-6500 **Torda** Joseph R '90
(419) 897-6500 **Tuschman** James M '66
(419) 893-6000 **Van Horn** Darrell V Jr. '72
(419) 893-5555 **Vitou** Mark F '79
(419) 893-3360 **Weber & Sterling,LLC**
(419) 893-1444 **Wilkinson** Grant W '87
(419) 893-3360 **Williams** Dennis P '90
(419) 893-5908 **Zouhary** Kathleen M '76

MAYFIELD
Cuyahoga County

(440) 473-1025 **Carbone** Rocco J '72
(440) 473-1025 **Murphy** Paul T '76

MAYFIELD HEIGHTS
Cuyahoga County

(440) 460-1415 **Agin** Bernard I '75
(440) 460-1415 **Agin** Sandra K '78
(440) 720-8500 **Arcara** Kristina A '01
(440) 442-6677 **Baran** Mark R '01
(440) 442-6677 **Baran** Mindy E '98
(440) 423-6532 **Becker** Gordon P '78
(440) 449-9690 **Bittenbender** Charles A '80
(440) 646-1881 **Bossin** Kenneth A '71
(440) 461-6000 **Brainard** Patrick J '93
(440) 646-3375 **Brezovec** Brian P '97
(440) 603-2376 **Burba** Christopher M '78
(440) 442-6800 **Calta** Diane A '99
(440) 473-2277 **Carr** Leonard B '96
(440) 473-2277 **Carr** Leonard F '74
(440) 442-6800 **Cartwright-Jones** Rhys B '04
(440) 442-6677 **Carty** Matthew J '02
(440) 442-6677 **Casey** James S '93
(440) 995-5100 **Clark** Daniel J '85
(440) 442-6677 **Cowan** Gary '88
(440) 603-2277 **Craig** Andre A '84
(440) 442-6677 **Crandall** Stephen S '94
(440) 442-6677 **Delahunty** Martin S III '87
(440) 442-6800 **Diemert** Joseph W Jr. '72
(216) 896-3000 **Doyle** Raymond E '80
(440) 461-9000 **Dyson Schmidlin & Foulds Co,LPA**
(440) 442-6677 **Elk** Arthur M '73
(440) 442-6677 **Elk** David J '65
(440) 442-6677 **Elk & Elk Co,LPA**
(440) 461-5000 **Elkins** Otto E Jr. '01
(440) 395-1315 **Evans** Joy M '92
(440) 460-0333 **Fierman** Scott A '94
(440) 461-9000 **Foulds** Robert J '81
(440) 603-7558 **Gamin** Mark A '83
(440) 473-2273 **Giaimo** Frank P '79
Greene Christopher L '89
(440) 446-0700 **Grossman** Jack N '82
(440) 442-6800 **Hanculak** Thomas M '75
(440) 461-9000 **Henderson** David B '92
(440) 646-3359 **Hill** Edwin V Jr. '67
(440) 446-1100 **Hoffman** Eric R '77
(440) 995-5300 **Horvitz** Richard A '78
(440) 603-7630 **Intili** Ann M '90
(440) 603-7531 **Jackson** Jennifer S '93
(440) 442-6677 **Kelley** James M III '93
(440) 442-6677 **Kelly** Thomas R '88
(440) 603-2301 **Kerwin** Timothy L '91
(440) 995-5100 **King** Charles H '92
(440) 995-5110 **Koval** William J Jr. '90
(440) 442-6677 **Kral** Donald J '89
(440) 684-8753 **Krantz** Michele L '93
(440) 461-5000 **Kuhlman** Kathleen L '95
(440) 603-2378 **LaCava** Robin K '90
(440) 720-1100 **Lang** Ronald J '68
(440) 646-9721 **Lilko** Robert J '87
Mann Robert K '84
(440) 461-9000 **Manway** Celeste M '87
(440) 603-2064 **Matoh** James E '85
(440) 603-7079 **McGrath** Kevin P '96
(440) 461-3461 **Misseldine** Russell W '96
(440) 720-8169 **Moses** Karen L '84
(440) 461-4433 **Nagle** Jamie M '02
(440) 646-0222 **Peterman** Michael J '73
(440) 603-2201 **Pisanelli** Ernest C '90
(440) 646-1677 **Rassin** Julius '59
(440) 646-3098 **Rivera-Sanchez** Kim M '94
(440) 461-9000 **Roberts** Kevin P '94
(440) 442-8383 **Rolla** Dudley B '57
(440) 442-6677 **Rosenberg** Todd O '86
Rosenberg Victor R '02
(440) 446-9366 **Rosenfeld** Robert T '58
(440) 442-6677 **Rost** Grant M '01
(440) 603-2367 **Salsbury** Sue E '89
(440) 603-2738 **Schenk** Jeffrey A '91
(440) 442-9500 **Schepis** Nicholas '84
(440) 449-9636 **Schilling** Kenneth C '85
(440) 461-9000 **Schmidlin** Raymond J '65
(440) 461-9000 **Schmidlin** Raymond J Jr. '89
Shenker Dina '04
(440) 544-1107 **Siegel** Edward F '74
(440) 603-7530 **Simmons** Laura M '92
(440) 684-6940 **Slezak** David G '85
(440) 603-2007 **Snow** Gina D '96
(440) 684-8740 **Sogg** Nancy W '75
(440) 442-6800 **Sokolowski** Jeffrey J '00
(440) 646-3009 **Speroff** Scott R '92
(440) 461-5000 **Sukel** Timothy M '85
(440) 461-6000 **Sweeney** David M '75
(440) 423-6805 **Tillman** John C '89
(440) 449-9692 **Tsipis** Constantine E '91
(440) 449-6482 **Tucker** Howard J '89
(440) 498-5170 **Vanderwist** Kathryn K '84
(440) 461-4433 **Van Ness** Charles J '90
(440) 473-5263 **Wagner** Mark R '80
Wells John N '94
(440) 603-7616 **Yokaitis-Skutnik** Judith A '86

MAYFIELD VILLAGE
Cuyahoga County

(440) 395-0251 **Albert** Peter J '88
(440) 449-3333 **Argie D'Amico & Vitantonio**
(440) 449-3333 **Argie** George J '82
(440) 473-1634 **Brown** Ronald B '68
(440) 473-1634 **Burr** Andrew M '93
(440) 395-0274 **Choi** Catherine K '98
(440) 473-1634 **Christensen** Romie M '03
(440) 395-0234 **Coffey** David M '86
(440) 395-0281 **Corwin** Patricia M '87
(440) 449-3333 **D'Amico** Louis A '88
(440) 720-3301 **Degnan** Martin J '74
(440) 603-3791 **Dobscha** Stephen F '87
(440) 395-3679 **Domeck** John W '88
(440) 449-6800 **Dunn** Paul L '91
(440) 395-0246 **Fitts** John T '77
(440) 395-0257 **Garfunkel** Steven B '72
(440) 395-3685 **Gerlack** Robert J '94
(440) 461-4019 **Hudacko** Andrew R '76
(440) 461-8880 **Hull** Jonathan '78
(440) 395-0237 **Hurst** John P '79
(440) 395-3692 **Jablonski** Richard W '94
(440) 473-9232 **Jarem** Helen S '97
Jarrett Charles E '86
(440) 395-3693 **Kerner** William J Jr. '91
(440) 395-3698 **Lamb** David C '90
(440) 395-0252 **Ling** Raymond S '90
(440) 395-0249 **Major** Lynn N '90
(440) 395-0400 **Mascaro** Daniel P '88
(440) 395-0303 **Melvin** Eva Y '99
(440) 395-3751 **Miller** Peter D '79
(440) 395-3742 **Mullen** Kristy M '03
(440) 395-0259 **Nash** Jeffrey P '85
Novak Scott J '98
(440) 395-9353 **Perry** William F '03
(440) 395-3760 **Rubesne** Kellie M '97
(440) 395-0256 **Ruppelt** Ronna F '85
(440) 395-3762 **Sablack** Michael A '96
(440) 395-3764 **Schwartz** Gregory E '94
Shaw Karen C '97
(440) 395-3765 **Shrallow** Dane A '71
(440) 449-6800 **Silver** Terry L '77
(440) 395-2269 **Steiner** Eric J '00
(440) 395-9729 **Sukel** Christine H '87
(440) 395-3769 **Sullivan** Mary B '01
(440) 395-3771 **Uth** Michael R '87
(440) 461-5000 **Vierkorn** Katherine A '92
(440) 449-3333 **Vitantonio** Dominic J '91
(440) 395-0246 **Wells** R Mark '90
(440) 395-0246 **Zielaskiewicz** Joshua M '03

MCARTHUR
Vinton County

(740) 596-5583 **Gleeson** Timothy P '90
(740) 596-5291 **Griffith** Jeffrey R '01
(740) 590-3969 **Kieckhefer** Frederick B Jr. '87
(740) 596-9371 **Kimes-Brown** Trecia M '98
(740) 596-5291 **Salyer** James P '94

MCCOMB
Hancock County

(419) 293-2911 **Johnson** Jack L '69

MCCONNELSVILLE
Morgan County

(740) 962-2262 **Christie** Robert J '74
(740) 962-4776 **Dye** Ralph D Jr. '58
(740) 962-2174 **Graham** Amy S '02
(740) 962-3862 **Lowe** Michael D '83
(740) 962-6478 **Welch** Richard D '84
(740) 962-2262 **Wells** John A '94

MC DERMOTT
Scioto County

(740) 259-6222 **Sesser** Stephen K '01

MC DONALD
Trumbull County

Chuparkoff Stephen J '87
(330) 530-1620 **Robinson** Lisa K '89
(330) 707-4000 **Tadla** James A '90

MECHANICSBURG
Champaign County

(937) 834-5000 **Bratka** Dan W '87
(937) 834-2170 **Dever** Jonathan T '02

MEDINA
Medina County

(330) 668-1324 **Abramson** Susan H '84
(330) 723-9797 **Afarin** Lisa M '87
(330) 725-8816 **Amodio** James A '78
(330) 764-9823 **Arnold** Alanna S '01
(330) 725-4209 **Bachtell** David J '92
(330) 725-0030 **Bailey** Steve C '89
(330) 334-2468 **Barber** Mark H '87
Barbera Richard '94
(330) 764-8752 **Barrington** Teresa '96
(330) 725-6666 **Batchelder** William G '39
(330) 723-9536 **Bennett** James R II '99
(330) 723-6404 **Berry** Robert C '91
(330) 723-4599 **Bougher** Frederick C '82
Bowers Edmond F '86
(330) 725-6666 **Bramley** Jeffrey L '81
(330) 722-6611 **Brandel** Lawrence S '75
(330) 722-1152 **Brobst** Lorie K '94
(330) 725-8816 **Brown & Amodio, LPA**
(330) 725-8816 **Brown** David N '72
(330) 722-4686 **Brown** Robert W '82
(330) 725-7045 **Brown** Stephen J '70
(330) 723-2200 **Butts** Michael T '90
(330) 725-6666 **Bux** Robert J '78
(330) 725-9709 **Buzzelli** Russell A '87
Cahill Ronald R '99
(330) 722-8989 **Cameron** John B '91
(330) 721-7819 **Campbell** Kevin R '82
(330) 725-0030 **Campbell** Robert B '92
(330) 725-0531 **Carey** Chris D '94
(330) 723-9536 **Chandler** Maryann C '04
(330) 723-3287 **Chase** Dale H '75
(330) 725-4935 **Cheek** Todd E '03
(330) 722-5000 **Ciccolini** James F '92
Ciupak Scott P '03
(330) 725-3456 **Corrigan** Mary B '89
(330) 725-8474 **Courtney** Lawrence J '73
(330) 723-6404 **Critchfield Critchfield & Johnston Ltd**
(330) 721-0131 **D'Amico** Tanya '01
(330) 723-6404 **Demlow** Amy D '94
(330) 723-9540 **Devanney** Katharina E '98
Dick Bernard E '76
(330) 723-8828 **Dolatowski** John J '87
Dressler Ronald L Jr. '97
(330) 723-6102 **Dunn** Kevin W '91
(330) 725-5297 **Edmonds** Marie M '79
(330) 764-8399 **Eisenhower** Anne E '96
(330) 239-5041 **Flickinger** Dare S '50
(330) 764-8731 **Francis** J Bruce '77
(330) 725-2348 **Frantz** William G '80
(330) 722-9099 **Funk** Susan L '88
(330) 725-9709 **Gallagher** Laura J '86
(330) 721-0000 **Gashel Dillon** Amanda M '98
(330) 722-9070 **Gates** Susan P '98
(330) 722-7171 **Gechter** Maureen F '89
(330) 723-4947 **Gedrock** David V '80
(330) 723-4656 **Gervinski** Nancy L '78
(330) 722-0330 **Haberman** Ian S '82
(330) 723-2200 **Hall** Eric D '97
Haller Sonja M '83
(330) 722-2144 **Hanwell** Robert M '85
(330) 723-7000 **Happ** Gregory W '76
Hartmann Lora A '02
(330) 725-4929 **Hathcock** Alicia M '04
(330) 722-9313 **Hendricks** Connie G '88
(330) 725-4929 **Henry** Phillip J '99
(330) 725-4929 **Hensal** Jennifer L '93
(330) 722-1957 **Herron** Sunny N '91
(330) 725-0531 **Hertrick** Paul W '75
(614) 860-2000 **Hirn** William E Jr. '88
(330) 722-9219 **Hirsch** Susan L '91
(330) 723-2000 **Hiteman** Carl G '83
(330) 723-9546 **Hitsman** David V '00
(330) 723-9536 **Holman** Dean '80
(330) 723-9536 **Hopkins** Russell A '94
(330) 725-1962 **Horvath** George '85
(330) 725-6666 **Huber** Gregory A '84
(330) 725-5233 **Huth** Jeffrey A '89
Jackson Alice M '02
(330) 725-4114 **Jeandrevin** John T '59
(330) 725-8816 **Jeppe** Gerald L '69
(330) 721-0000 **Jocke** Ralph E '81
(330) 725-6666 **Johnson** Carroll N Jr. '63
(330) 722-9099 **Jones Davies & Funk Co, LPA**
(330) 722-9099 **Jones** Glenn R '74
(330) 225-1234 **Jones** Lyle R '74
(330) 722-8138 **Jurewicz** Jessica Lynn '04
Kaminsky Michael P '79
(330) 723-6301 **Kasmer** Richard J '94
(330) 764-7253 **Kerr** Lisa M '93
(330) 725-4365 **Kinney** Jack M '58
(330) 472-5796 **Kipp** Jerald B '81
(330) 725-3636 **Korduba** Andrew M '98
(330) 721-0000 **Kramer** Patricia S '97
(330) 725-4935 **Lanier** J Matthew '98
Lapp Deborah A '85
(330) 723-8828 **Largent Berry Preston & Jamison Co,LPA**
(330) 725-0531 **Laribee** Gillian A '01
(330) 725-0531 **Laribee Hertrick & Kray**
(330) 725-0531 **Laribee** Michael L '96
(330) 725-0531 **Laribee** Ray E '68
(330) 723-4656 **Latchney** John D '90
(330) 723-3287 **Lawrie** Charles T '86
(330) 725-9729 **Leaver** James R '90
(330) 725-4929 **Lesiak** Theodore J '89
Lick Fred Jr. '61
(330) 721-0000 **Louke** Marcella R '03
(330) 722-0113 **Loving** Deborah G '79
(330) 723-2400 **Loyer** Richard A '78
(330) 721-0000 **Maag** Robert E Jr. '83
(330) 723-9536 **Magensky** Jill A '04
(330) 722-0836 **Mahon** Brian P '93
(330) 725-0030 **Marco** Kenneth J '91
(330) 725-0030 **Marco Marco & Bailey**
(330) 725-0030 **Marco** Richard J '57
(330) 725-0030 **Marco** Richard J Jr. '81
(330) 725-7045 **Matyac** Jennifer D '03
(330) 725-2116 **Maynard** Patricia F '89
(330) 723-1919 **McArtor** David L '95
(330) 239-6095 **Messer** Betty J '94
(330) 725-5005 **Michelson** Allan M '77
(330) 723-5082 **Moran** John D '84
Morgan Kelly A '00
(330) 725-4929 **Oberholtzer Filous & Lesiak**
(330) 725-4929 **Oberholtzer** John C '67
(330) 725-5936 **Oehlhof** Shayne M '01
(330) 722-8989 **Olson** Conrad G '95
(330) 764-8437 **O'Toole** Linda A '99
(330) 725-9132 **Owen** Jackie L '88
(330) 725-4935 **Palmquist** James B III '76
(330) 764-3101 **Parker** Andrew M '03
(330) 721-0000 **Parmelee** Christopher L '98
(330) 725-5439 **Patsouras-Vukovich** Rhonda '89
(330) 723-5082 **Patterson** Denise K '88
(330) 725-6082 **Paul** Dennis E '75
(330) 722-1234 **Pedro** Cameron B '01
(330) 723-2200 **Piszczek** Gerald D '77
(330) 764-8736 **Porzio** Barbara '79
Razavi Matthew K '96
(330) 721-0000 **Reeves** Nancy L '98
(330) 336-6405 **Reiter** Carol C '80
(330) 723-6120 **Renswick** Julien C '48
Russo Dorcas A '81
(330) 723-9536 **Salisbury** Scott G '88
(330) 725-1199 **Salzgeber** Joseph F Jr. '94
(330) 723-6024 **Schaffrath** Kurt A '73
(330) 722-2636 **Scheetz** Stanley D '74
(330) 721-0900 **Schultz** Beau A '01
(330) 725-7555 **Sharratt** Thomas W '52
(330) 722-8989 **Sheldon** David C '88
(330) 764-3582 **Shields** Jim A '91
Shirer Albert D '94
(330) 723-9536 **Shockley** Carol '87
(330) 725-8685 **Shulman** Gary A '90
(330) 598-1062 **Sisson** Edwin A '04
(330) 725-5936 **Skidmore** Claudia M '96
(330) 725-5936 **Skidmore & Hall**
(330) 725-5936 **Skidmore** Lee T '85
(330) 725-5936 **Skidmore** Robert C '01
(330) 725-4929 **Slimak** Michelle L '99
(330) 725-0030 **Spears** Ronald S '98
(330) 723-5450 **Spink** Prudence C '81
(330) 723-3830 **Stanley** Ronald R '74
(330) 723-1889 **Steigerwald** Dean R '73
(330) 725-6666 **Steingass** Jonathan M '87
(330) 722-3246 **Steinmetz** Robert F '76
(330) 723-9536 **Thorne** William L '73
(330) 725-4929 **Timer** Kimberly J '03
(330) 723-4656 **Tomino** Nick '78
(330) 273-8883 **Tompkins** Paul K '81
(330) 722-8290 **Truman** Kathryn M '96
(330) 722-8877 **Truman** Vance P '93
(330) 721-0000 **Walker & Jocke,LPA**
(330) 721-0000 **Walker** Patricia A '81
(330) 723-9546 **Weingart** Denise H '91

(330) 725-6666 **Williams & Batchelder, LLP**
(330) 714-0105 **Wright** Barbara E '87
(330) 725-0612 **Yoder** Lois J '80
(330) 764-6026 **Young** Brian R '04
(330) 725-6666 **Young** William B '78
(330) 764-7252 **Zachman** Janis H '95
(330) 721-5092 **Zanath** Debra A '91
(330) 725-8861 **Zee** Sharlene A '88

MENTOR
Lake County

(440) 255-4600 **Amery** Eric J '83
(440) 942-9980 **Arthur** Douglas W '93
(440) 257-5000 **Balin** Paulette F '78
(440) 225-1747 **Beach** Michael T '00
(440) 946-7739 **Bencin** Patricia D '81
(440) 255-5550 **Bernstein** Harry S '88
(440) 266-1700 **Biales** Robert C '93
(216) 781-1609 **Bielinis** Arunas P '76
(440) 205-3600 **Boles** Edgar H II '73
(440) 951-8889 **Brennan** Jane L '96
(440) 205-3600 **Brubaker** Carl Richard '60
(440) 954-4170 **Bush** Mary E '90
(440) 205-9303 **Callahan** Dennis M '70
(440) 255-9100 **Callender** James S Jr. '92
(440) 974-1273 **Canala** John S '89
(440) 255-1080 **Carr** Douglas L '94
(440) 392-7643 **Centanni** Michael A '84
(440) 257-1658 **Chopra** Mira B '92
(440) 974-0505 **Cipollo** Todd D '98
(440) 354-2600 **Clancy** Timothy G '88
(440) 639-4494 **Cohen** Gretchen Y '93
(440) 255-4244 **Collins** Leo R '62
Couhig Thomas N '02
(440) 205-0188 **D'Amico** Mitchell '96
(440) 205-3600 **Daugherty** Patrick J '93
(440) 951-6666 **Denman** Alfred '70
(440) 951-6666 **Denman & Lerner Co, LPA**
(440) 209-1600 **DePledge** Laura A '97
(440) 953-8888 **DiCello** Mark Andrew '94
(440) 953-8888 **DiCello** Robert F '00
(440) 953-8888 **DiCello** Robert J '71
(440) 354-2600 **Donnelly** Nancy H '91
(440) 205-3600 **Driggs** Charles M '51
(440) 205-3600 **Driggs Lucas Brubaker & Hogg Co,LPA**
(440) 255-1522 **Everett** P David II '85
(440) 974-0099 **Field** Harry E '71
(440) 942-2924 **Flaherty** James T '71
(440) 255-9100 **Freeman** Amy M '97
(440) 974-1173 **Gallovic** John G '75
(440) 225-0500 **Gibson Brelo Ziccarelli & Martello**
(440) 255-5998 **Goff** Robert E Sr. '68
(440) 974-5752 **Graham** Rondie M '87
Groves Kevanne M '95
Hadzinski Kenneth W '96
(440) 255-9100 **Hanrahan** Patrick R '74
(440) 951-6599 **Hartory** Timothy P '72
(440) 350-4600 **Hoffart** Michele R '87
(440) 205-3600 **Hogg** William N '59
(440) 350-5060 **Hutchinson** Trudy '83
(440) 350-5020 **Jerse** Joseph J '81
Kalski Steven F '85
(440) 639-4494 **Khan** Gulam A '93
(440) 974-8484 **Klammer** Darya J '97
(440) 974-8484 **Klammer** Joseph R '97
(440) 974-8484 **Klammer** Lisa M '99
(440) 974-9400 **Kleiman** Michael M '79
(440) 257-3060 **Kline** William S III '99
(440) 354-5923 **Klingenberg** Donald H '73
(440) 946-5155 **Knavel** Randolph L '94
(440) 392-7126 **Kuhel** Anthony E Jr. '00
(440) 951-6666 **Lerner** Michael J '92
(440) 951-6666 **Lerner** Susan D '92
(440) 255-9100 **Loxterman** Kirk F '85
(440) 205-3600 **Lucas** James A '64
(440) 269-8823 **Manning** Francis P '90
(440) 942-6405 **Manning** Joseph J Jr. '77
(440) 269-8823 **Manning** Karen T '95
(440) 225-0500 **Mayernik** Thomas J '89
(440) 354-6242 **McCarter** William K '67
(440) 392-7105 **McClaning** Kathy M '89
(440) 392-7056 **McGinley** Mark D '82
(440) 255-9100 **McNamara Hanrahan Callender & Loxterman**
(440) 255-9100 **McNamara** Walter J III '69
(440) 257-4372 **Mocilnikar** Frank C '76
(440) 942-1144 **Negin** Morton S '54
Niccum Robert F '57
(440) 257-8329 **Nierenberg** Alice S '87
(440) 946-1743 **O'Flaherty** Terence P '79
(440) 974-8081 **O'Leary** James R '96
(440) 392-7169 **Patton** Dennis P '77
(440) 974-4014 **Picardini** Joseph B '71
(440) 255-4838 **Richlak** Susan P '94
(440) 255-4444 **Rose** Ronald '91
(440) 241-1872 **Ryder** Blanche S '98
(440) 974-8081 **Sacerich** Thomas J '80
(440) 951-6666 **Salem** John S '96
(440) 974-8194 **Sassé** Cynthia A '89
(440) 350-5020 **Schaltenbrand** Eric J '95
(440) 974-1433 **Schroeder** David A '81
(440) 255-8000 **Seifert** Patricia L '89
(440) 205-0539 **Seman** Richard T Jr. '94
Sheridan Michael P '01
(440) 266-7777 **Sikora** Michael J III '98
(440) 392-7410 **Snyder** Ronald E '73
(440) 269-8823 **Spano** Lisa M '93
(440) 350-1327 **Stark** Paul S '92
Stefl Scott R '82
(440) 942-6267 **Sternberg** David J '73
(440) 269-1900 **Stewart** Michael J '86
(440) 974-5750 **Swain** Richard A '63
(440) 701-1253 **Taylor** Suzanne S '89
(440) 974-5750 **Trebets** John '82
(440) 974-8091 **Vaci** Elizabeth D '83
West Kathleen L '79
(440) 392-7108 **Zangerle** John A III '91
(440) 942-6267 **Zeid** Gary D '75
(440) 225-0500 **Ziccarelli** Mark A '79
(440) 255-2421 **Zuch** Frederic L '72

MIAMISBURG
Montgomery County

(937) 866-9933 **Attkisson** Kevin W '97
(937) 866-2485 **Bookwalter** Thomas E '70
(937) 910-4173 **Bragg** Holly J '83
(937) 847-6477 **Burk** Christine L '90
(937) 866-9933 **Callahan** Karl P '90
(937) 866-9933 **Casteel** Douglas '75
(937) 866-2922 **Croskey** Thomas P '80
(937) 910-2851 **Crumbley** Aimee L '02
(937) 603-5326 **Davenport** Andrew T '01
(800) 227-9597 **Deininger** Patrick J '04
(937) 866-8454 **Denny** Richard G '73
(937) 865-4637 **Ebersole** John M '00
(937) 910-4174 **Ellis** Robert C '79
(937) 865-6800 **Gordon** Rachel E '03
(937) 865-4772 **Holland** Renee S '81
(937) 865-6800 **Jeng** Kathryn L '02
(937) 865-6800 **Johnson** Mark A '93
(937) 866-1629 **Lehman** Joseph A '77
(937) 865-6800 **Lewis** Forrest R '98
(937) 866-8454 **Marsh** Michael T '92
(937) 865-6800 **Mathews** Maureen Ly '02
(937) 866-2203 **Messham** Robert E Jr. '72
(937) 865-1445 **Miller** Robin F '93
(937) 384-6286 **Mitchell** Richard J Jr. '90
Moreland Garnetta P '03
(937) 384-0079 **Petzold** John P '62
(937) 866-1629 **Ruschau & Lehman**
(937) 866-1629 **Ruschau** Steve J '77
(937) 865-8820 **Spaeth** Edward J '89
(937) 439-0281 **Sprowl** John O '93
(937) 226-5725 **Tassone** Joseph V '62
(937) 865-2810 **Teeters** Bruce A '91
(937) 866-2103 **Wilson** Vernon '52
(937) 866-8454 **Wirth** Gerald R '73
(937) 865-2057 **Woo-Haltresht** Roseanne M '96
(937) 866-1629 **Woodruff** Edward L '01

MIAMIVILLE
Clermont County

(513) 509-9961 **Chang** Nancy Schadler '96

MIDDLEBURG HEIGHTS
Cuyahoga County

(440) 826-4100 **Allen Ramsey Maynard & Associates**
(440) 243-5010 **Armstrong** Erin A '97
(440) 234-1100 **Brasfield** Lynne S '97
(440) 243-5010 **Briller** David D '77
(440) 846-2434 **Cain** Julia A '89
(440) 260-6612 **Camp** Margaret A '95
(440) 842-3500 **Carlisle-Kesling** Kathryn J '99
(440) 243-1198 **Cartwright** Mark J '98
(440) 886-7460 **Caster** Cynthia M '90
(216) 676-8131 **Caterini** Joseph W '62
(440) 243-2800 **Costabile** Gregory S '93
(440) 239-8881 **Doslak** William R '81
(440) 843-5193 **Franks** Steven L '94
(440) 243-5000 **Gaynor** Norman J III '74
(440) 816-1035 **Geiger** Warren P '60
(440) 243-5010 **Griffin** Rae E '84
(440) 243-1058 **Harpst** Ronald J '63
(440) 239-8881 **Haynes** Cheryl A '87
(440) 243-2458 **Herbers** Keith M '76
(440) 826-1250 **Hilliard** Carol R '84
(440) 843-1340 **Hopp** Fred G '86
(440) 243-5010 **Horvath** Carol D '81
(440) 234-8811 **Hull** Peter H '71
(440) 826-3333 **Jansen** Edward R '00
(440) 234-5795 **Jordan** Jill L '96
(440) 234-6699 **Kalapos** Michele A '90
(440) 274-2450 **Karris** Tom J '82
(440) 843-5320 **Kerns** Brian D '86
(440) 843-5320 **Kerns Hurt & Proe**
(440) 239-2090 **Kleiner** Stuart J '79
(440) 243-2800 **Madachik** Joseph M '96
(440) 826-4100 **Maynard** Jerry L '78
(440) 243-2800 **Mille** Dennis G '72
(440) 243-2800 **Newell** Monica M '01
Panek Jason M '04
(440) 243-2800 **Phillips Mille & Costabile Co,LPA**
(440) 243-2800 **Phillips** Nicholas E '73
(440) 843-5320 **Proe** Stephen J '96
(440) 843-5320 **Puin** Timothy J '95
(440) 826-4100 **Ramsey** Lloyd J '74
(440) 239-1109 **Reardon** Michael E '93
(440) 842-3500 **Russell** Monica E '02
(440) 362-0775 **Salmon** John G '65
(440) 816-6704 **Scheutzow** Susan O '82
(440) 234-7000 **Steiger** Daniel N '87
(440) 243-1458 **Tomsik** Donald M '59
(440) 843-5320 **Tyler** Charles Sr. '01
(440) 243-2800 **Wilson** Stewart S '79
(440) 239-8881 **Worthing** Donald E '77
(440) 826-3333 **Zalic** John D '91
(440) 816-1877 **Zito** Maureen F '86
(440) 888-9933 **Zomparelli** Gino '89

MIDDLEFIELD
Geauga County

Kmiec Thomas D '71
(440) 632-9090 **Ohly** Robert S '85

MIDDLEPORT
Meigs County

(740) 992-2117 **Custer** John S '87

MIDDLETOWN
Butler County

(513) 425-2602 **Allen** Jonathan P '92
(513) 424-2401 **Allen** Patrick W '65
(513) 422-2001 **Allen** Thomas B '94
(513) 424-2401 **Allen** William P '94
(513) 425-5000 **Appenzeller** Rebecca H '89
(513) 422-3658 **Atkins** Christopher G '84
Banks Gerald T '79
(513) 422-1997 **Barr** Eric J '81
(513) 423-1100 **Batliner** Jennifer J '82
(513) 424-2429 **Becker** Paul A '78
(513) 422-4861 **Bolinger** Bradley D '88
(513) 424-2050 **Bowen** William L '78
(513) 422-2001 **Brown** Daniel A '88
(513) 423-9291 **Bryant** Jerry M '72
(513) 425-2617 **Caneris** Thomas A '87
(513) 424-2401 **Casper** Arthur B '67
(513) 424-2401 **Casper & Casper**
(513) 424-2401 **Casper** Douglas W '75
(513) 424-2401 **Casper** E Jeffrey '72
(513) 424-2401 **Casper** Sanford I '81
(513) 425-6609 **Clark** Gregory M '86
(513) 424-1660 **Combs** Charles E Jr. '73
(513) 424-1660 **Combs & Schaefer**
(513) 425-6609 **Cooper** Matthew S '01
(513) 422-2001 **Crain** Donald L '73
(513) 422-1136 **Derivan** Hubert T '67
(513) 705-9000 **Dillon** Martina M '96
(513) 425-7012 **Dumes** Robert M '77
(513) 423-3654 **Elliott** George H '50
(513) 423-0194 **Ellis** Paris K '80
(513) 425-6609 **Engel** Scott H '92
(513) 425-6609 **Fantetti** James P '04
(513) 425-7990 **Fassler** Bruce E '79
(513) 424-2401 **Fogle** Stephen R '93
(513) 422-2001 **Frost Brown Todd LLC**
(513) 422-2001 **Fuller** Jennifer R '04
(513) 425-6609 **Furnish** William B '04
(513) 422-2001 **Gleason** Andrew D '00
(513) 425-6609 **Groom** Kathy J '93
(513) 425-6609 **Guinigundo** Billy W '04
(513) 424-2401 **Hallee** Michael J '02
(513) 422-4699 **Haugen** Halver H '68
(513) 425-6609 **Hein** Jonathan A '98
(513) 423-1680 **Herr** John W '66
(513) 424-2401 **Hollifield** Lisa S '03
(513) 425-2690 **Horn** David C '77
(513) 425-2805 **Hoyt** Lawrence K '87
(513) 425-5081 **Hritz** John G '85
(513) 422-4015 **Hudson** Eugene M Jr. '63
(513) 423-3462 **Imhoff** Don Jr. '72
(513) 423-8124 **Ingram** Robert A '79
(513) 705-9000 **Johnson** Eugene H '04
(513) 424-2401 **Kabakoff** Ronald M '77
(513) 423-2609 **Kash** Kevin '82
(513) 422-6378 **Kaup** Gerhard H '67
King Terri S '87
(513) 425-6609 **Kowalski** Susan M '98
(513) 425-5224 **Kuzman** John J Jr. '86
(513) 425-7714 **Landen** Leslie S '79
(513) 705-4104 **Langendorf** James P '97
(513) 422-5407 **Lazarow** Jeffrey W '77
(513) 423-9276 **Lord** Mary C '51
(513) 425-6609 **Manning** Bennett A '82
(513) 420-5653 **Martinez** Lisa A '91
(513) 705-6000 **Matejkovic** Joseph R '91
(513) 705-9000 **McCausland** Patrick E '98
(513) 424-2401 **McCollum** Margaret H '92
(513) 425-7899 **McKnight** Patrick E '97
(513) 425-7830 **Mills** Sara E '01
(513) 422-8443 **Newlin** Joseph E '68
(513) 425-2669 **O'Connor** John P Jr. '90
(513) 424-1823 **Pagan** Christopher J '94
(513) 705-9000 **Papakirk** James '94
(513) 424-2401 **Partin** Robin R '97
(513) 424-5000 **Peace** Candice R '83
(513) 705-7582 **Pickrel** Patricia A '99
(513) 425-5151 **Plye** Joseph W '83
(513) 777-6009 **Powell** Walter E '84
(513) 424-1823 **Powers** Noah E II '80
(513) 705-9000 **Pratt** Gregory K '77
(513) 705-9000 **Pratt Singer Papakirk Co,LPA**
(513) 424-1823 **Repper Powers & Pagan,LTD**
(513) 424-1823 **Repper** Theodore Jr. '55
(513) 424-2401 **Richards** Megan '83
(513) 705-9000 **Richmond** Vicki L '00
(513) 425-6609 **Ritter** Scot M '82
(513) 422-7184 **Robertson** Charles S '95
(513) 422-0158 **Romans** Kathleen A '83
(513) 420-5755 **Ross** JoAnn '93
(513) 423-5467 **Ryan** James D '62
(513) 423-9291 **Sanzone** Vincent A Jr. '75
(513) 424-1660 **Schaefer** Edward B '01
(513) 424-1660 **Schaefer** Gene E '64
(513) 422-2001 **Scholler** Warren J III '00
(513) 420-8774 **Schwartz** Peter J '77
(513) 422-4861 **Shew** James C '69
(513) 705-9000 **Singer** Andrew N '74
(513) 424-2600 **Smith** James C '84
(513) 424-2401 **Strady** Barbara L '91
(513) 424-1660 **Strand** Sheldon A '75
(513) 424-2401 **Summers** Mark A '85
(513) 422-2001 **Swope** Thomas A '78
(513) 239-4244 **Terhune** Charles P Jr. '78
(513) 425-0180 **Tucker** Curtis C '98
(513) 424-5000 **Venturella** John J '82
(513) 425-6609 **Wean** Sophie S '93
(513) 423-8951 **Weinrich** Lancer R Jr. '72
(513) 422-2001 **Wells** James R '00
(513) 423-1300 **Whittington** John A '77
(513) 424-2401 **Wilkinson** Rebecca L '83

MILAN
Erie County

(419) 499-4285 **Huber** Richard R '55
(419) 499-4605 **Ruffing** Vickie B '81
(419) 499-4605 **Strickler** Randal L '86
(419) 499-4605 **Vitaz** Heather M '97

MILFORD
Clermont County

(513) 576-0111 **Albenze-Smith** Nadine A '94
(513) 965-8302 **Anderson** Isaac L III '88
Anderson Robert N '94
(513) 248-0088 **Antell** Barbara B '77
(513) 831-2942 **Baird** Sharon C '82
(513) 965-9002 **Buschbacher** Michael S '73
(513) 576-1060 **Calderhead** David C '87
(513) 576-2801 **Campbell** Douglas W '88
(513) 248-9332 **Cassidy** Michael W '84
(513) 831-8700 **Cloud** Robert L '76
(513) 965-9260 **Condit** Thomas W '89
(513) 831-8511 **Crowe** Stephen C '76
(513) 831-8511 **Cushman** Christopher S '97
Dooley Lloyd D '66
(513) 831-6697 **Douglas** Flach '57
(513) 576-5952 **Eberle** Thomas F '80
(513) 831-1564 **Eckerson** Mark D '77
(513) 576-1060 **Franckewitz** Stephanie P '01
(513) 831-5604 **Hemminger** David G '65
Herriott Scott H '75
(800) 554-9406 **Holston** Timothy L '77
(513) 248-0317 **Hoseus** Edwin L Jr. '74
(513) 910-8391 **Jones** Erin Hogan '00
(513) 831-3223 **Kemper** Richard J '57
(513) 965-8012 **Marcin** Edward W '97
(513) 965-8012 **Marcin** Melissa A '98
(513) 563-3525 **Marler** Karen F '82
(513) 831-6697 **Martin** Charles R II '96
(513) 248-2820 **Mason** Ronald A '85
(513) 831-6444 **Masterson** Michael E '93
(513) 248-4497 **McCune** David S '79
(513) 248-0760 **Minniear** Michael T '73
(513) 248-9300 **Mitchell** Edward B Jr. '69
(513) 831-6660 **Nelson** Barry E '84
(513) 248-1526 **Parrish** Dawne M '96
(513) 576-1060 **Peschke** Joel L '00
(513) 248-0317 **Plank** Kevin D '79
(513) 248-1216 **Potter** Carolyn A '91
Reifin Melvin H '62
(513) 248-2527 **Reynolds** William J '93
(513) 831-2227 **Riley** Michael J '83
(513) 248-2580 **Schilling** William H '75
(513) 831-1200 **Schmieg** Michael M '78
(513) 831-5700 **Sieber** Steven J '82
(513) 831-2255 **Staley** James A '76
(513) 831-3373 **Thomson** Douglas W '78
(513) 722-3800 **Van Pelt** Jeanne A '97
(513) 248-0317 **Ward** Marcia A '78
(513) 831-8511 **Welch** Robert H III '04
(513) 831-8511 **Welch** Robert H Jr. '76
(513) 831-3373 **Zimmerman** Elizabeth W '92

MILLERSBURG
Holmes County

(330) 674-4300 **Baserman** Mark W Sr. '78
(330) 674-0499 **Bower** Blair A '89
(330) 674-3055 **Critchfield Critchfield & Johnston Ltd**
(330) 674-0457 **Dailey** Stephen P '80
(330) 676-5909 **Douglas** Thomas C '74
(330) 674-1555 **Gindlesberger** Thomas D '55
(330) 674-5086 **Ginsburg** Jeffrey M '90
(330) 674-1888 **Hines** Robert B II '76
(330) 674-1111 **Holtzmann** Cassandra A '99
(330) 674-0442 **Kellogg** Jeffrey G '97
(330) 674-9776 **Knowling** Stephen D '75
(330) 674-7070 **Lang** Kimberly A '98
(330) 674-3055 **Leininger** Mark E '95
(330) 674-7070 **Mason** Grant A III '94
(330) 674-7070 **Mast** Diane S '81
(330) 674-3055 **Mathie** Daniel L '83
(330) 674-7070 **Miller & Mast Ltd**
(330) 674-7070 **Miller** Max A '81
(330) 674-1080 **Miller** Paul A '72
(330) 674-1900 **Mullen** Jeffrey A '93
(330) 674-9776 **Rinfret** Robert D '72
(330) 674-3055 **Roach** Garrett M '92
(330) 674-6264 **Schmid** Laurel J '76
(330) 674-3055 **Shrock** Steven J '92
(330) 674-0001 **Steimel** Samuel M '83
(330) 674-3055 **Waltman** John R '70
(330) 674-3055 **Warner** Sean M '02

MILLERSPORT
Fairfield County

(740) 467-1308 **Louthen** Constance S '98

MINERVA
Stark County

(330) 868-4248 **Battista** Clark E '83
(330) 868-4210 **Chaddock** Susan C '97
(330) 868-6400 **Chapman** Martin A '85
(330) 868-4210 **Clark Clark & Chaddock**
(330) 868-4210 **Clark** Luther J Jr. '56
(330) 868-4210 **Clark** Robert A '91
(330) 868-1138 **Martin** Jack E '80
(330) 868-6161 **Martin** Robert D '69
Mount Dick W Jr. '75
(330) 868-7747 **Willen** Gary L '78

MINFORD
Scioto County

(740) 820-4131 **Wrage** Eric A '99

MINGO JUNCTION
Jefferson County

(740) 535-1643 **Wilson** William E '75

MINSTER
Auglaize County

(419) 628-3232 **Bernhold** James A '72

MOGADORE
Portage County

(330) 628-1446 **Brooks** Richard R '87
McDowall Robert T Jr. '84
(330) 699-1129 **Millard** William L '80
(330) 699-4094 **Steinle** Richard J '81
(330) 733-6291 **Ziga** Timothy P '83

MONCLOVA
Lucas County

(419) 865-3923 **Colburn** Anthony J '95
Ochu Ann M '83
(419) 872-6070 **Zoltanski** Edward F '58

MONROE
Butler County

Bevens Tonya R '95
(513) 539-3131 **Herbe** Diana J '82

MONROEVILLE
Huron County

Wensink Katherine E '02

MONTGOMERY
Hamilton County

(513) 793-3737 **Hamilton** Louis G '82
(513) 651-9440 **McCarthy** Dennis K '73
(513) 891-8261 **Payne** Thomas F '94

MONTPELIER
Williams County
(419) 485-3284 **Bechtol** Denver G '77
(419) 485-0255 **Sostoi** Martin W '82

MORELAND HILLS
Cuyahoga County
(440) 292-6445 **Bell** Helen M '89
(440) 247-2477 **Cameron** David K '78
(440) 893-9588 **Climaco** Michael L '73
Compton Lori '82
Groetzinger Jon Jr. '91
(440) 464-8388 **Klein** Roger D '98
(440) 247-9660 **Lang** Charles V '88
(440) 789-3848 **Rutigliano** Joseph E '82
(440) 519-0113 **Sokell** James C '87
(440) 247-1428 **Trimble** David L '90

MOSCOW
Clermont County
Daugherty David D Jr. '73

MOUNT CARMEL
Hamilton County
Benintendi Robert F '92

MOUNT GILEAD
Morrow County
(419) 947-4515 **Aebi** Ana Luz '00
(419) 947-9111 **Arnold** Michael F '03
(419) 946-2100 **Desmond** Earl K '78
(419) 946-7876 **Elkin** Tom C '83
(419) 946-2001 **Griffith** Matthew T '04
(419) 946-6055 **Hickson** Robert C Jr. '83
(419) 946-3868 **Hildebrand** Dale G '52
(419) 947-4426 **Howland** Charles S '83
(419) 947-4426 **Howland** Hollis L '85
(419) 947-5515 **Jensen** Jon L Jr. '00
(419) 947-9111 **Leppo** Erin L '03
(419) 947-9505 **Long** Frank G '87
(419) 947-5045 **McClelland** Lee W '74
(419) 946-2001 **McClelland** Shawn R '01
(419) 947-5575 **Phillips** Steven M '91
(419) 947-5545 **Ryan** Kathleen J '89
(419) 947-5515 **Stamolis** David J '02
(419) 947-8075 **Steiger** Amy '00
(419) 946-6367 **Wick** Donald K '83

MOUNT HOPE
Holmes County
(330) 674-7015 **Wolf** Donald D '77

MOUNT ORAB
Brown County
(937) 444-0403 **Bitzer** Frank J '88
(937) 444-2626 **Cassity** Michael E '72
(937) 444-2576 **Houser** John B '71
(937) 444-2563 **Kelly** Katherine M '02
(937) 444-2563 **Kelly** Michael P '73
(937) 444-2563 **Kelly** Timothy J '91
(937) 444-2563 **Kelly & Wallace Co,LPA**
(937) 444-2626 **Levine** Robin J '90
(937) 444-2563 **Lewis** Val E '99
(937) 444-2576 **Potts** Cecelia J '86
(937) 444-2563 **Wallace** Bruce S '83

MOUNT STERLING
Madison County
(740) 869-2393 **Baynes** Gerald T '64
(740) 869-4400 **Brooks** L Steven '87

MOUNT VERNON
Knox County
(740) 393-0771 **Aebi** John W '79
(740) 397-5262 **Alden** Noel B '96
(740) 393-6720 **Broeren** P Robert Jr. '98
(740) 393-6780 **Cohen** Linda M '90
(740) 397-4040 **Critchfield Critchfield & Johnston Ltd**
(740) 397-5262 **Cullers** James J '59
(740) 393-1122 **Demaree** Duff D '79
(740) 393-2718 **Dice** Daniel S '98
(740) 393-2718 **Drown** William T '98
(740) 397-5321 **Giles** James A '81
(740) 397-5262 **Grindle** Larry J '86
Hendrickson Sharon M '99
(740) 397-2443 **Kahrl** Clyde C '80
(740) 392-2900 **Kepko** William J '86
(740) 397-4040 **Landon** Adam B '01
(740) 393-0110 **Lane** Kenneth E '78
(740) 392-8838 **Lee** Robert D '79
(740) 393-2788 **Lehmkuhl** Phillip D '78
(740) 397-7420 **Malek** Bruce J '77
(740) 393-9562 **Mallory** Heidi A '00
(740) 397-7420 **Mayhew** Frederick E II '70
(740) 397-7420 **McDevitt Mayhew & Malek,LPA**
(740) 397-7474 **Murray** Richard B '77
(740) 397-4040 **Norris** James R '76
(740) 397-5262 **Railsback** David E '70
(740) 397-7474 **Rauzi** Robert L '72
(740) 397-0711 **Ressing** T Garrett '66
(740) 397-4040 **Ritter** Richard F '69
(740) 397-4040 **Rose** Kim M '81
(740) 397-7177 **Schlemmer** Michael D '74
(740) 393-9562 **Smith** William D '75
(740) 397-7177 **Stacker** Jean Lou '84
(740) 393-3339 **Stebbins** Carol G '90
(740) 397-4040 **Swihart** Kathy L '96
(740) 393-6720 **Thatcher** John C '89
(740) 397-4040 **Wakefield** Laura A '97
(740) 392-4151 **Walker** Harlow H '94
(740) 397-5262 **Weston** Robert B '71
(740) 393-6796 **Williams** Jeffrey C '87
(740) 397-7420 **Zanghi** Mark A '04
(740) 397-5262 **Zelkowitz Barry & Cullers**

MOUNT WASHINGTON
Hamilton County
Matthews David W '59

MUNROE FALLS
Summit County
(330) 688-8820 **Alexander** Ronald E '71
(330) 688-3355 **Damicone** Mary T '92
(330) 250-2746 **Figler** Susan M '92
(330) 283-6480 **Julius** Thomas N '73
(330) 688-7908 **McLeland** Joseph C '64
(330) 688-8821 **Seeling** Paul H '83
(330) 633-7373 **Strzala-Peters** Sheri A '91
Sweeney Mark L '03
(330) 633-7373 **Williger** Marta J '85

NAPOLEON
Henry County
(419) 592-5105 **Altman** Richard L '83
(419) 599-5590 **DelFavero** Christopher D '95
(419) 599-1936 **Donovan** John '83
(419) 592-3816 **Firestone** Melissa P '93
(419) 599-1010 **Fisher** Richard A '74
(419) 592-3503 **Grahn** David M '90
(419) 599-1010 **Hanna & Fisher**
(419) 599-1010 **Hanna** John H '72
(419) 591-1414 **Holcomb** Victor H '99
(419) 592-0010 **Lankenau** Jeffrey R '86
Laver Gerald D '83
(419) 592-3283 **Manahan** David A '87
(419) 592-8300 **Manahan** Thomas R '85
(419) 592-5926 **McColley** Denise A '81
(419) 592-6801 **Meekison** David F '72
(419) 592-6801 **Meekison** David P '36
(419) 533-7701 **Meister** Teckla H '87
(419) 592-3816 **Peper** Edmund G Jr. '57
(419) 748-8041 **Rogers** George C '74
(419) 599-1010 **Rosebrook** Amy C '98
(419) 599-0212 **Schnitkey** Mark D '84
(419) 592-0010 **Wesche** Michael J '73

NAVARRE
Stark County
(330) 879-2105 **Bentzel** Todd H '83
(330) 830-2689 **Chapanar** Lawrence E '84
(330) 879-9900 **Roth** Michael J '97
(330) 879-5017 **Shedlarz** Robert J '73

NELSONVILLE
Athens County
(740) 753-1111 **Baker** David S '93
(740) 753-1961 **Nolan** T Michael '69

NEW ALBANY
Franklin County
(614) 855-0383 **Belan** Laurie A '87
(614) 939-0985 **Bluestone** Charles L '93
(614) 222-0800 **Casey** Sean M '99
(614) 939-1235 **Cason-Adams** Sharon '97
(614) 939-1235 **Cohen** Lawrence H '97
(614) 289-5410 **Cohen** Richard '80
(614) 939-1235 **Demers & Cohen**
(614) 939-1235 **Demers** David J '91
Dengler Mary M '86
Dunn Sean P '94
(614) 775-3827 **Duprey** Mary E '85
Erlichman Sheryl D '85
(614) 939-0590 **Ferguson** Nancy H '80
(614) 855-5300 **Jeffers** Michael K '88
(614) 855-1867 **Klayman** Elliot I '69
(614) 855-5079 **Lanahan** Patrick M '96
Linhart Larry R '71
(614) 775-5278 **Major** Robert H '02
(614) 289-5430 **Mazzitti** Madeleine Linda '82
Michalsky Melissa F '01
(614) 855-7488 **Mozenter** Michael J '84
Newmark Lisa M '85
(614) 656-0000 **Phillips** Kimberly S '98
(614) 855-5223 **Prescott** Gary M '76
(614) 575-8965 **Reusser** Carl A '92
(614) 855-2292 **Roelle** Robert H '57
Schleeter Andrea R '97
(614) 283-6393 **Shubitowski** John K '80
(614) 855-2292 **Soska** Christine V '97
(614) 939-1235 **Speidel** Jamison S '01
(614) 775-5000 **Swartz** Dean E '74
(614) 933-1200 **VanSlyck** Steven B '86
(614) 855-2292 **Venard** Carl E '64
(614) 619-9256 **Waldo** David W '98
White Catherine M '01
Zeldin Laura Sue '94

NEWARK
Licking County
(740) 345-3431 **Albright** Mary M '97
(740) 345-9611 **Altmaier** Martin D '67
(740) 349-8581 **Anderson** Eric L '97
(740) 349-6575 **Baldwin** Craig R '92
(740) 349-2299 **Barrett** Thomas H II '86
(740) 345-2400 **Beck** Roland S '63
(740) 349-6195 **Becker** Robert L '74
(740) 349-6227 **Berryhill** John C '70
(740) 345-5535 **Branstool** William D '94
(740) 323-1545 **Bunning** Karen J '77
(740) 345-4429 **Burdick** Nancy N '88
(740) 345-0417 **Burkett** Julia Kristin '90
(740) 345-6454 **Calesaric** Robert E '94
(740) 349-8581 **Calig & Handelman,LPA**
(740) 349-8505 **Campbell** Thomas K '74
(740) 345-9611 **Carnes** Carolyn J '96
(740) 345-9722 **Carter** Gregory E '87
(740) 345-5171 **Castner** Joseph F '80
(740) 349-6640 **Chesrown** Jennifer L '95
(740) 349-7414 **Christiansen** Vicky M '79
(740) 349-6181 **Clark** Stephanie A '96
(740) 345-3431 **Clovis** Siobhan R '98
(740) 345-9611 **Cooper** James R '72
(740) 345-9611 **Cooper** Timothy M '98
(740) 345-3431 **Crawford** John A '81
(740) 345-3411 **Diernbach** Jonathan C '99
(740) 349-6051 **Dove** Dennis E '91
(740) 345-3431 **Drake** Robert N '72
(740) 349-7839 **Earl** Kathleen A '81
(740) 349-6898 **Ellsworth** Mary E '01
(740) 522-7106 **Ennen** Bruce A '79
(740) 349-7262 **Erhard** Robert T '77
(740) 349-6575 **Fleming** Mary E '88
(740) 349-3772 **Gard** John S '81
(740) 345-7955 **Gardner** Mark D '82
(740) 349-6195 **Gonzalez** Jenny R '98
(740) 345-9611 **Gordon** Leland J '53
(740) 349-8505 **Gramza** Michelle L '91
(740) 349-7075 **Green** Robin L '73
(740) 345-9611 **Greene** Steven T '73
(740) 349-6195 **Grenauer** Regina M '92
(614) 519-5817 **Hampton** Kevin M '04
(740) 349-8371 **Hand** James R '72
(740) 366-7446 **Harmon** Paul D '79
(740) 349-6652 **Higgins** Michael F '77
(740) 366-1525 **Hite** David L '46
(740) 345-0850 **Horne** Benjamin D '00
(740) 349-6663 **Hostetter** James W '76
(740) 349-6575 **Hottensmith** Mark H '89
(740) 348-4533 **Hubbuch** Carol A '99
(740) 345-9801 **Jones Norpell Miller & Howarth**
(740) 345-3431 **Kennedy** Ann M '81
(740) 345-5171 **Kenney** Deborah L '83
(740) 345-9801 **King** Joseph Michael '79
(740) 322-5770 **Kirsh** Andrea M '85
(740) 345-3431 **Klema** Connie J '96
(740) 349-5916 **Klockner** Tricia M '04
(740) 345-9801 **Koehler** Charles H '63
(740) 349-6575 **Lampl** Robert C '71
(740) 344-2518 **List** A David '58
(740) 345-3431 **Lowe** William Douglas '85
(740) 348-4000 **Mallett** Renee M '99
(740) 345-0850 **Mann** Laura S '98
(740) 349-8371 **Mantonya** John B '49
(740) 345-0850 **Marks** Anna L '02
Martin David L '73
(740) 828-4016 **Mason** Danielle M '89
(740) 345-4545 **McCoy** Carl E Jr. '82
(740) 322-5498 **McIntyre** Teresa O '87
(740) 345-3431 **Meyer** Christopher R '77
(740) 345-1040 **Monty** Michelle L '02
(740) 345-3488 **Morris** Robert L '85
(740) 349-7262 **Morrow** Clark A '71
(740) 345-9611 **Morrow** Elmer C '33
(740) 349-7262 **Morrow & Erhard Co,LPA**
(740) 345-9611 **Morrow Gordon & Byrd,Ltd**
(740) 345-3431 **Nelson** Rodney A '92
(740) 345-6961 **Obora** John H '85
(740) 349-6195 **Oswalt** Kenneth W '86
(740) 349-3629 **Plunkett** Jeffrey A '83
(740) 349-4716 **Proctor** Philip L '89
(740) 345-3431 **Reed** Brian C '00
(740) 345-3431 **Reese** John G '52
(740) 345-3431 **Reese Pyle Drake & Meyer,PLL**
(740) 322-5137 **Reidy** Thomas A '78
(740) 349-6215 **Rickrich** C William II '79
(740) 349-6663 **Rieser** Jack D '85
(740) 349-8714 **Ripko** Cindy L '82
(740) 345-5280 **Robertson** Robert C '77
(740) 345-9801 **Robison** Joseph A '75
(740) 345-9183 **Roland** Christian D '90
(740) 345-0850 **Romaker** Robert R '90
(740) 345-0417 **Sanderson** Andrew T '96
(740) 349-6131 **Sassen** Douglas E '86
(740) 349-8505 **Schaller Campbell & Untied**
(740) 349-8505 **Schaller** Stephen E '73
Schumaker Kenneth B '68
(740) 349-6169 **Seeds** Melinda G '94
(740) 345-6015 **Sewards** William B Jr. '86
(740) 345-3411 **Shapiro** Harvey H '71
(740) 349-6195 **Shenk** Brent W '76
(740) 349-6195 **Shipley** Rachel C '02
(740) 349-7262 **Snow** William P '81
(740) 349-6216 **Snyder** Ann E '92
(740) 345-0417 **Spangler** Melanie A '01
(740) 345-0417 **Stansbury** David N '99
(740) 349-7266 **Stokes** David B '79
(740) 349-6169 **Strefelt** Christopher A '94
(740) 364-3537 **Strefelt** Kari A '94
(740) 349-6575 **Stubbs** SaKeya M '99
(740) 345-3431 **Suskind** Ira R '71
(740) 345-1040 **Swank** James G '74
(740) 345-9611 **Treneff** Alexander T '72
(740) 344-6885 **Trifelos** James N '83
(740) 349-6663 **Tuhy** Elena V '95
(740) 349-8505 **Untied** Wesley K '85
(740) 345-3488 **Van Winkle** Richard M '75
(740) 345-9611 **Vernau** Adam K '89
(740) 349-6195 **Waltz** Brian T '00
(740) 345-0417 **Webb** Larry G Jr. '03
(740) 345-6611 **Weidaw** William W '73
(740) 345-3431 **Wenger** David W '79
(740) 349-7414 **Wentworth** Karen H '94
(740) 345-9611 **White** Glenn A '69
(740) 349-6580 **Whittington** John A '89
(740) 349-8505 **Wigginton** David Q '85
(740) 501-1332 **Wilson** Christina Ritchey '93
(740) 345-4550 **Wilson** Stephen B '88
(740) 345-6667 **Wright** Richard P '87
(740) 322-5341 **Zaleski** Aimee A '98

NEW BREMEN
Auglaize County
(419) 629-2311 **Hinders** Rodney J '85
(419) 629-2311 **Maxa** John G '75
(419) 629-2311 **Montgomery** Ogden K '78
(419) 629-3681 **Smith** Stephen L '72
(419) 629-2311 **Tate** John E '80
(419) 629-8108 **This** Jason E '92

NEWBURY
Geauga County
(440) 564-1480 **Davis** James B '59
(440) 564-9350 **Frimel** Michael P '96
Murphy Charles T Jr. '71
(440) 564-5525 **Paschke** Carolyn J '95
(440) 564-9111 **Peterson** Paul N '02
(440) 564-7528 **Schwartz** Lynn B '91
(440) 564-9111 **Slusarz** George V '81
(440) 564-9111 **Yaksic** Michael '81

NEW CARLISLE
Clark County
(937) 882-9305 **Baker** Wilburn L '03
(937) 845-8989 **Bartlett** Kelli A '04
(937) 845-3878 **Brichacek** John I '75
(937) 845-9485 **Daniel** Theodore D '73
(937) 777-1903 **Davenport** Michael S '97
(937) 845-3878 **Glew** James P '98
(937) 845-9759 **Janning** Charles W '67
(937) 882-9305 **Nelson** Gordon R '03
(937) 845-8776 **Wingert** Howard E '85

NEWCOMERSTOWN
Tuscarawas County
(740) 498-7860 **De Boer** Dirk P '00
(740) 498-7860 **Tarr** Patricia L '75

NEW KNOXVILLE
Auglaize County
(419) 753-2967 **Katterheinrich** Thomas H '78
Murphy Paul J '02

NEW LEBANON
Montgomery County
(937) 687-9099 **Hensley** James A Sr. '78
(937) 687-1388 **Keener** Ronald D '69
(937) 687-9099 **Manning** James L '74
(937) 687-1388 **Turrell** Claudia J '84

NEW LEXINGTON
Perry County
(740) 342-1534 **Allen** Joseph M '62
(740) 342-5520 **Boyer** Tina M '94
(740) 342-7324 **Dodd** Daniel F '03
(740) 342-7324 **Dodd** Maureen E '96
(740) 342-7324 **Dodd** Robert J Jr. '65
(740) 342-3576 **Flautt** Joseph A '80
(740) 342-5511 **Herendeen** Stephen R '85
(740) 342-3582 **Howdyshell** Mark J '91
(740) 342-3582 **Howdyshell & O'Neil Ltd**
(740) 342-4184 **Lewis** Thomas A '77
(740) 342-1611 **Miller** Robert A '89
(740) 342-3582 **O'Neil** Cindy M '99
(740) 342-1109 **Ridenour** Nancy N '96
(740) 342-2033 **Schnittke** Steven P '75
(740) 342-2033 **Smith** Linda Loy '76
Tackett Brian '02
(740) 342-3156 **Wilson** Dean L '83

NEW LONDON
Huron County
(419) 929-8352 **Bennett** Stephen K '75

NEW MIDDLETOWN
Mahoning County
(330) 542-0114 **Taylor** Douglas B '90

NEW PHILADELPHIA
Tuscarawas County
(330) 364-1614 **Anderson** Steven A '96
(330) 364-5538 **Barnhouse** James R '51
(330) 364-2881 **Barrow** James J '87
(330) 364-6441 **Bates** John R '93
(330) 365-3502 **Berry** Traci A '94
(330) 339-2806 **Blackwell** David L '94
(330) 365-3214 **Bornhorst** Amanda S '89
(330) 343-1614 **Bowers** Henry T '49
(330) 364-1112 **Brechbill** John M '96
(330) 365-3289 **Brown-Tolloti** Lisa M '96
(330) 339-6444 **Carrothers** James M '73
(330) 602-7767 **Collins** Ronald L '73
(330) 364-9070 **Cunningham** Arthur B '63
(330) 364-6888 **Deedrick** Robert S '92
(330) 364-1112 **De La Cruz** Christopher P '79
(330) 343-5585 **Durmann** Glenn G '72
(330) 343-6797 **Dzigiel** Judith E '99
(330) 343-0099 **Erdman** Deborah L '95
(330) 364-5593 **Ernest** Michael J '96
(330) 364-9599 **Fete** Marvin T '01
Fidel Ann A '01
(330) 339-3998 **Finzel** Kristen A '01
(330) 365-3269 **Fischer-Immke** Andrea L '99
(330) 364-0088 **Fisher** Michael R '96
(330) 364-1614 **Fitzpatrick Zimmerman & Rose Co LPA**
(330) 339-6322 **Goforth** Richard E '47
(330) 364-4491 **Gordon** Paul N '77
(330) 364-6825 **Greene** William C '92
(330) 339-9963 **Greenham** Deborah E '95
(330) 364-3523 **Greig** Gary L '89
(330) 364-9070 **Hardin & Schaffner, LPA**
(330) 364-9070 **Hardin** Thomas W '81
(330) 339-3998 **Harrington** Michael F '97
(330) 339-7791 **Haverfield** David W '95
(330) 364-3523 **Herman** Christopher T '03
(330) 364-6665 **Hinig** Richard W '79
(330) 343-2168 **Hipp** David C '76
(330) 343-6647 **Hoopingarner** John M '79
(330) 364-9070 **Iborra** Jose A '94
(330) 364-5593 **Johnson** Michael C '73
(330) 364-5593 **Johnson Urban & Range Co LPA**
(330) 343-9578 **Krugliak Wilkins Griffiths & Dougherty Co,LPA**
(330) 343-5585 **Kyler** William A '64
(330) 343-4540 **Latanich** Gerald A '81
(330) 364-4421 **Lehigh** Daniel T '57
(330) 364-2467 **Lorenz** Charles E II '84
(330) 343-5585 **Lundholm** John K '85
(330) 343-1614 **Mastin** Joseph S '77
(330) 364-9070 **Maxwell** John P '94
(330) 364-1811 **McLane** William G '69
(330) 343-8891 **Meyer** Hank F III '99
(330) 364-1614 **Miller** J G '90
(330) 343-5585 **Miller & Kyler, LPA**
(330) 343-5585 **Moore** Brent L '99
(330) 364-1614 **Nemitz** Eugene H Jr. '73
(330) 364-5531 **O'Meara** Douglas J '77
(330) 339-6444 **Ong** James J '97
(330) 343-5585 **Pringle** James J '79
(330) 339-3998 **Query** Callie S '04
(330) 364-5593 **Range** James A '80
(330) 364-8811 **Reed** Joy E '77
(330) 364-1614 **Rose** Frank J Jr. '74
(330) 364-9070 **Schaffner** David K '88
Shepperd Frederick M '79
(330) 364-4491 **Space** Mary E '81
(330) 364-4450 **Stephan** Nicole R '02
(330) 365-3299 **Stephenson** Elizabeth W '89
(330) 339-6444 **Stephenson** Richard L '58

(330) 339-6444 **Stephenson** Robert R II '86
(330) 339-6444 **Stephenson Stephenson & Carrothers**
(330) 343-0449 **Styer** Daniel M '94
(330) 343-0449 **Styer** Ryan D '98
(330) 343-8864 **Thomakos** Steven G '87
(330) 343-5585 **Tolhurst** Harry C III '00
(330) 343-0212 **Tripodi** Joseph I '67
(330) 364-5593 **Urban** Robert C Jr. '85
(330) 364-1112 **Von Allman** Nanette D '84
(330) 364-5066 **Wallick** Tina Galigher '86
(330) 339-2288 **Weygandt** Thomas J '95
(330) 602-9666 **Williams** Patrick J '92
(330) 365-3266 **Worth** David W '77
(330) 339-7272 **Wright** Edd K '68
(330) 365-3272 **Zajkowski** Karen B '93
(330) 364-1614 **Zimmerman** Donald B '78
(330) 364-1614 **Zimmerman** Donald W '51

NEW RICHMOND
Clermont County
(513) 553-3421 **Davis** Robert H '67
(513) 553-6286 **Griffiths** Nancy K '84
(513) 553-7740 **Hirschauer** Gregory A '93
(513) 553-2433 **Hollister** Lisa H '87
(513) 553-4713 **Lamb** Robert M '89
(513) 553-1323 **McCachran** Marshall T '79
McMillin Larry H '76

NEW STRAITSVILLE
Perry County
(740) 380-6346 **Weed** Charles B '71

NEWTON FALLS
Trumbull County
(330) 872-0918 **Buente** Victor O Jr. '80
(330) 872-0302 **Old** Thomas L '73
(330) 872-1617 **Palmer** Thomas H '69
(330) 872-0918 **Walrath** Terry J '70
(330) 872-7776 **Ziegler** Charles A '80

NEW VIENNA
Clinton County
(937) 987-2612 **Uible** Harold H '50

NEW WATERFORD
Columbiana County
(330) 457-2820 **Robb** Carol A '83

NILES
Trumbull County
(330) 505-1811 **Armstrong** Charles R '73
(330) 544-4002 **Blair** Matthew J Jr. '84
(330) 652-4529 **Bogen** Curt P '89
(330) 544-4002 **Boker** David E '75
(330) 652-8000 **Buckley & George Co, LPA**
(330) 652-8000 **Buckley** Robert J '80
(330) 652-8000 **Chapman** Dawn L '04
(330) 652-0190 **Coates** Michael J Jr. '86
(330) 544-0424 **DeMatteis** Martin D '80
(330) 652-5006 **Dull** Joseph T '76
(330) 652-8000 **George** Timothy F '86
(330) 652-8989 **Goodman** Richard L '74
(330) 544-7818 **Hickton** Dawne S '98
Jensen William A Jr. '96
(330) 652-0630 **Joseph** Michael D '73
(330) 544-4002 **Latell** Kurt D '93
(330) 652-1111 **Lorenzetti** Jack C Jr. '82
(330) 652-1749 **Neuman** Douglas J '77
(330) 652-1749 **Parry** Patrick E '94
(330) 652-8000 **Pluma** Richard S '92
(330) 652-8387 **Ryan** Allen L '97
(330) 652-2762 **Shaker** Christopher J '83
(330) 652-2762 **Shaker** Robert I '87
(330) 652-5863 **Townley** Thomas W '75
(330) 544-0424 **Witten** Debora Kay '80
(330) 652-1609 **Zuzolo** Christopher P '93
(330) 652-1609 **Zuzolo** Ralph A '68
(330) 652-1609 **Zuzolo** Ralph A Jr. '95

NORTH BALTIMORE
Wood County
(419) 257-3121 **Bechtel** Allen H '51
Bushey Jason D '03
(419) 257-2879 **Parsons** Glenn C '52
(419) 257-3121 **Thompson** George G '76

NORTH BEND
Hamilton County
(513) 721-1995 **James** Daniel J '77
(513) 721-1995 **James** Diane M '80
(513) 941-2668 **Salem** David A '95

NORTH CANTON
Stark County
(330) 966-9990 **Ashbrook** Julie D '88
Bendetta Gina M '00
(330) 305-6400 **Campbell** Kristen E '96
(330) 497-9700 **Carbenia** Brian P '03
(330) 244-8000 **Cox** Kevin C '01
(330) 497-5131 **Critchfield** Maureen C '98
(330) 490-5037 **Dettinger** Warren W '80
(330) 244-8000 **Dodson** Kara M '02
(330) 305-6400 **Evans** Cari F '93
(330) 305-6400 **Fischer** Mark F '91
(330) 490-5005 **Francis-Vogelsang** Charee '88
(330) 484-3302 **Gatien** John M '84
(330) 305-6400 **Geiser** Julie A '94
(330) 497-0979 **Gibbs** Richard P '79
(330) 305-6565 **Goff** Christopher V '00
(330) 494-1381 **Gonyias** Drew '93
(330) 497-3000 **Halkias** John W '88
(330) 494-7023 **Harbert** Robert P II '95
(330) 490-4522 **Hesse** Chad F '00
(330) 499-7453 **Howes** Hubert A '53
(330) 499-7453 **Howes** Shirley E '96
(330) 497-8274 **Konovsky** John T Jr. '98
(330) 499-4059 **Krum** Frederick J '80
(330) 497-8274 **Lensman** Todd A '92
(330) 490-4726 **Lindroos** Michael E '83
(330) 499-9200 **Lowe** Arnold B '75
(330) 497-9455 **Lyke** Trevor A '96
(330) 497-9700 **Machan** Sandra J '91
(330) 452-6180 **Milhoan** Douglas A '01
(330) 499-8223 **Miller** Michael Lee '84
Milligan John R Jr. '52
(330) 494-1815 **Morrison** John W '96
(330) 305-6400 **Pelini** Craig G '84
(330) 305-6400 **Pelini & Fischer,Ltd**
(330) 499-4121 **Pousoulides** Dimitrios S '90
(330) 499-8648 **Repella** Michael V II '04
(330) 305-6400 **Robbins** Donald L Jr. '02
(330) 490-5038 **Sekula** John W '73
(330) 497-7247 **Serra** Rosemary C '84
(330) 499-7946 **Shuttleworth** William L Jr. '51
Smith Heather A '02
(330) 244-8000 **Soles** Robert E Jr. '90
(330) 494-2970 **Stelea** Barbara J '89
(330) 497-5303 **Swope** Raymond A Jr. '71
(330) 494-8700 **Thomas** Christopher J '91
(330) 305-6400 **Traub** Randall M '99
(330) 494-1022 **Van Gaasbeek** David A '77
Vitale Joseph M '67
(330) 490-4746 **Warder** Gregory S '01
(330) 305-6400 **Williams** Eric J '00
(330) 966-0095 **Zackaroff** Peter T '80

NORTHFIELD
Summit County
(330) 650-0088 **Ania** Anthony L '91
(330) 650-0088 **Bates** David S '92
(330) 650-0088 **Bevan** Keith D '72
(330) 650-0088 **Bevan** Thomas W '91
(330) 468-3990 **Economus** Dale S '77
(330) 468-6300 **Fletcher** Peter F '82
(330) 468-1056 **Halberg** William S '70
(330) 468-1000 **Lepri** Attilio J '65
(330) 467-7131 **Marsh** Linda S '89
(330) 650-0088 **Mismas** John D '04
(330) 468-6333 **Moore** Eric J '95
(330) 468-3969 **Motsco** Dwight P '87
(330) 467-9776 **Neubert** Eleanore S '54
(330) 467-5002 **Pearl** James R Jr. '96
(330) 650-0088 **Powell** Raymond M '91
(330) 468-3990 **Rudder** Verner R Jr. '83
(330) 650-0088 **Stefancik** Christopher J '96
(330) 650-0088 **Walsh** Patrick M '03
(330) 468-3990 **Watson** James C '83
(330) 468-1056 **Weiss** Leslie A '91

NORTH JACKSON
Mahoning County
(330) 538-3863 **Kisan** Peter J '87
(330) 538-0066 **Kravitz** Cynthia A '83
(330) 538-0066 **Kravitz** Solomon J '82
(330) 547-3327 **Martin** Frances '99

NORTH KINGSVILLE
Ashtabula County
(440) 224-1606 **Irons** David R '80

NORTH LIMA
Mahoning County
(330) 549-2609 **Smith** Eugene R '56

NORTH OLMSTED
Cuyahoga County
Alston Richard N '79
(440) 779-6636 **Basladynsky** Myroslava A '94
(440) 734-6162 **Bates** Mickey C '89
(440) 734-7600 **Bayer** Paul A '88
(440) 734-8087 **Boehm** Keith D '81
Brown Jeffery S '01
(440) 777-5354 **Burnham** Francis N '68
(440) 734-7600 **Caron** Brian L '95
(440) 734-7600 **Dorchak** Thomas J '66
(440) 779-6722 **Drossis** Deborah A '86
(440) 734-7858 **Dubelko** James M '79
(440) 779-6636 **Duffy** John J '78
(440) 734-3194 **Fehribach** Michael R '92
(440) 777-1500 **Gareau** David M '96
(440) 777-1500 **Gareau** Michael R '67
(440) 777-1500 **Gareau** Michael R Jr. '96
(440) 301-5206 **Griswold** Desmond R '93
(440) 779-8300 **Haas** John M '67
(440) 669-8855 **Hargitai** Zoltan '04
(440) 777-6506 **Hayes** Catherine K '94
(440) 687-1111 **Hussey** Robert R '71
(440) 734-1276 **James** Teresa '81
(440) 734-8092 **Kasler** Carolyn J '89
Kovacik Gerard J '79
(440) 979-0775 **Kozel** Thomas '90
Kunz MK '03
(440) 777-0478 **Liedtke** William P '72
(440) 734-7600 **Marcoguiseppe** Joseph J '74
(216) 272-7750 **Martindale** John E '62
(440) 779-5815 **McCormick** Keith L '91
(440) 779-1430 **Menassa** Alexander '87
Oliver Randall C '79
(440) 734-1500 **O'Malley** Bryan P '88
(440) 734-7600 **Peterson** Eric S '02
(440) 779-6330 **Rudy** Donald M '68
(440) 734-3281 **Russell** William H '74
(440) 777-0639 **Shook** Ann J '56
(440) 777-0639 **Shook** Gene E Sr. '56
Sidloski Robert A '96
Sourek Michael J '02
(216) 536-9619 **Spreng** Michael R '87
(440) 777-1500 **Stehlik** Elizabeth A '04
(440) 899-9161 **Tararin** Alexander A '99
(440) 777-6332 **Thomay** John S '70
(440) 362-4820 **Ursu** Daniel J '86
(440) 716-2226 **Vernon** Eileen B '92
(440) 779-6632 **Wagoner** Byron R '70
(440) 734-6158 **Witt** Mark S '83

NORTH RANDALL
Cuyahoga County
(216) 662-0430 **O'Bannon** Pamela C '90

NORTH RIDGEVILLE
Lorain County
(440) 327-1925 **Andolsen** Robert R '94
(440) 327-5487 **Bryer** Terry A '85
(440) 327-9495 **Corcoran** Kevin '98
Eckstein Scott M '98
Ellis Jay B '59
Fredenburg Gary C '85
(440) 327-9811 **Gray** Robert W '65
(440) 327-5420 **Guerini** David W '89
(440) 327-6966 **Kikol** John C '70
(440) 327-5721 **Lissner** Joan E '90
(440) 327-1542 **McDonough** William F '74
McGuire Michelle K '03
Miller Stanley R '66
(440) 353-0848 **Morgan** Toni L '96
(440) 327-2700 **Ryan** Kevin M '98
(440) 327-1542 **Sfiscko** Johanna M '74
(440) 748-2115 **Terry** Robert M '95
(440) 353-3101 **Tobin** Mary L '84
(440) 272-6640 **Weissinger** Lee E '93

NORTH ROYALTON
Cuyahoga County
(440) 230-1700 **Anthony** David S '01
(440) 884-4300 **Boldt** David R '86
(440) 237-1100 **Broz** Glenn A '74
(440) 230-0978 **Dionisopoulos** Justine M '04
Drescher Cathy S '83
(440) 237-1681 **Evenchik** Aaron S '01
Gall Christine C '02
(440) 237-1100 **Hurley** Kenneth R '80
Julian Christopher T '03
(440) 884-4300 **Kirner & Boldt Co, LPA**
(440) 884-4300 **Kirner** Paul T '73
(440) 582-8180 **Kolozvary** Stephen P '79
(440) 582-2374 **Lord** John A '00
(440) 237-1679 **Lotenero** Dale J '75
(440) 237-3554 **Lukuch** Kollene '04
(440) 582-8080 **McGowan** Stephen '77
(440) 237-1100 **Osterland** Charles E '69
(440) 237-7900 **Powers** Kevin P '93
(440) 230-0388 **Rakic** Aleksandar '94
(440) 230-9230 **Riddle** James C '96
Romano Joseph M '02
(440) 888-5333 **Sands** John F '56
(440) 230-1700 **Sindyla Anthony & Sindyla**
(440) 230-1700 **Sindyla** John R '02
(440) 230-1700 **Sindyla** Robert J '71
Slain Roger S '93
(440) 237-2800 **Thomas** Mary A '84
(440) 237-2800 **Thomas** Phillip E '81
(440) 237-7900 **Volcheck** Mark J '94
(440) 582-6706 **Vozar** Donna M '92
(440) 237-7900 **Weltman** Stephen Randall '85
(440) 230-0800 **Wishnosky** David M '89

NORTHWOOD
Lucas County
(419) 698-1040 **Ballenger** Brian J '85
(419) 691-3542 **Krueger** Mary M '79
(419) 698-1040 **Moore** Troy L '85

NORTON
Summit County
(330) 706-1831 **Banas** James E '83
(330) 730-4317 **Crislip** Kenneth M '04
(330) 825-2477 **Gutbrod** James J '86
(330) 825-2450 **Headley** David L '58
(330) 706-1831 **Hoffer** Paul R '85
(330) 825-2477 **Kennedy** David R '86
Kondik Marie A '02
(330) 535-6957 **Millhoff** Patricia Ann '79
(330) 825-6089 **Sedmack** Jane P '78
(330) 825-2477 **Walkley Kennedy & Gutbrod Co,LPA**
(330) 825-2477 **Walkley** Thomas L '86

NORWALK
Huron County
(419) 668-8211 **Allton** John D '72
(419) 668-2311 **Baird** John D '75
(419) 660-8167 **Clifford** Timothy D '01
(419) 668-1616 **Conway** Danita G '91
(419) 663-6785 **Conway** James W '88
(419) 663-6634 **Derby** Charles P '91
(419) 668-4879 **Eschrich & Stoll Co,LPA**
(419) 668-4879 **Eschrich** T Craig '75
(419) 668-4896 **Eyster** Kathryn M '02
(419) 668-7828 **Ford** George C III '77
(419) 668-4484 **Freeman** Harold J '73
(419) 668-4896 **Freeman Laycock & McDaniel**
(419) 668-4896 **Freeman** Ronald H '66
(419) 668-4484 **Freeman** Thomas H '75
(419) 663-5554 **Gentzel** Robert W '78
(419) 668-8101 **Harwood** Sharon L '85
(419) 668-6524 **Hendrikson** Nancy E '83
(419) 668-8211 **Hiltz Wiedemann Allton & Koch Co,LPA**
(419) 668-8403 **Jackson** Michael B '91
(419) 668-2081 **Kalfs** William D '83
(419) 663-2320 **Kasper** Daivia S '95
(419) 668-8211 **Koch** Curtis J '85
(419) 668-4896 **Laycock** Jeffrey P '69
(419) 668-8215 **Leffler** Russell V '77
(419) 663-6400 **Lux** Paul G '81
(419) 668-8403 **Lynch** Richard S '74
(419) 668-8403 **Lynch & White Co,LPA**
(419) 668-4896 **McDaniel** Herman F Jr. '72
(419) 668-4879 **McGuire** Thomas J '01
(419) 663-6785 **O'Hara** George S Jr. '79
(419) 663-2871 **Owens** William W '69
(419) 663-6785 **Palmer** Steve Jr. '92
(419) 663-6771 **Ridge** John S '79
(419) 668-8540 **Ruggles** Warren W '65
(419) 660-8540 **Ruggles** West M '02
(419) 668-6162 **Sales** Bradley E '87
(419) 668-2552 **Schaechterle** Gordon E Jr. '80
(419) 663-1605 **Shell** Gregory A '91
(419) 668-4879 **Stoll** Thomas J '94
(419) 706-1645 **Swanson** Laura P '00
(419) 668-2067 **Waugh** Frederick F '63
(419) 668-1886 **White** Beverly M '60
(419) 668-8211 **Wiedemann** Robert A '52
(419) 668-6840 **Wineman** Reese M '76
(419) 668-8215 **Woodruff** Richard R '80
(419) 668-9830 **Young** Henry E '49
(419) 663-0934 **Zannieri** Joseph A '86

NORWOOD
Hamilton County
(513) 218-7370 **Fenton** John H '95
(513) 621-8267 **FitzGerald** Timothy J '91
(513) 531-3636 **Kelly** Robert G '77
(513) 458-4588 **Kiser** Theodore E '99
(513) 731-3800 **Wolf** James G '86

NOVELTY
Geauga County
(440) 785-8319 **Chambers** Gregory J '76
(440) 338-3264 **Evans** Clyde P Jr. '81
(440) 338-6117 **Lee** Dennis J '73
(440) 729-9621 **Meyers** Edward F Jr. '65
(440) 247-8178 **Miller** John F '58
Pitorak Larry J '74
(440) 338-1718 **Studen** Greg E '77
(440) 338-5051 **Williams** Donald '53
(440) 338-3392 **Wiseley** Paul J '50

OAK HARBOR
Ottawa County
(419) 898-0000 **Brikmanis** John A '89
(419) 898-6210 **Burns** Charles R '91
(419) 898-2671 **Christie** Michelle L '93
(419) 898-2671 **Graves Kohli & Christie**
(419) 898-0100 **Haar** Dawn M '93
(419) 898-2671 **Kohli** Gary A '71
(419) 898-3095 **McKean** Alan R '85
(419) 898-3095 **McKean** Pamela A '85
(419) 898-3688 **Patterson** Michael P '90
(419) 898-2921 **Robertson** Jerry D '74
(419) 898-0400 **Stanfa** Lori A '88

OAKWOOD VILLAGE
Cuyahoga County
(440) 232-6399 **Austin** Pamela J '01
(440) 232-9911 **Frank** Louis S '69
(440) 232-9911 **Hitzeman** Janice L '98
(440) 232-9911 **Holman** Robert B '00
(440) 232-9911 **McDonald Frank Hitzeman & Holman**
(440) 232-9911 **McDonald** Michael J '82
Scott Curtis Jr. '79

OBERLIN
Lorain County
(440) 775-1411 **Baxter** Norman T Jr. '69
(440) 775-1903 **Dougan** Thomas J '73
(440) 774-4382 **Eckstein** Barry S '71
(440) 774-7722 **Gottschling** Carol M '03
(440) 775-1751 **Heberling** Martin M '65
Mason Emma J '79
(440) 774-5114 **Miller** Mark N '84
(440) 774-3665 **Palmer** Robert A '76
(440) 774-7700 **Roose** Kirk B '81
(440) 774-7700 **Roose & Ressler PA**
(440) 775-1471 **Sarringhaus** Kurt G '76
(440) 774-1278 **Severs** Eric R '75
Shirokawer Leo '03
(440) 775-1751 **Walsh** James L '81

OKEANA
Butler County
Wesselman Christy Lee '98

OLMSTED FALLS
Cuyahoga County
(440) 427-9760 **Lowenkamp** Cynthia D '96
(440) 239-9376 **Rumes** Kevin W '97

OLMSTED TOWNSHIP
Cuyahoga County
(440) 234-2662 **Gandola** Paul D '69
(440) 891-9790 **Kasputis** Edward F '88
(440) 554-8588 **Kuzmickas** Paul S '03

OREGON
Lucas County
(419) 691-6844 **Bihn** Jane F '83
(419) 690-7100 **Bollinger** Ernest E '92
(419) 690-7100 **Bollinger** Mary M '84
(419) 690-8022 **Breier** Gary A '78
(419) 691-2435 **Bryce** Robert W '81
(419) 698-6626 **Davies** James L '97
(419) 242-5399 **DeSmith** Amber R '00
(419) 691-3051 **Dugan** Thomas A '74
(419) 698-4307 **Garand** John D '71
(419) 691-0182 **Garand** Richard C '64
(419) 725-0078 **Hohenberger** Christopher E '88
(419) 691-2435 **Kazee** Timothy S '02
(419) 691-8889 **Koehn** Richard W '79
(419) 698-9595 **Lorton** Michael D '79
(419) 691-2435 **Schlageter & Bryce Co,LPA**
(419) 691-2435 **Schlageter** Thomas G '75
(419) 691-6356 **Testa** Charles R '42
(419) 697-9672 **Todd** Virginia L '97
(419) 693-0610 **Vild** Jeffrey T '85
(419) 690-8022 **Winckowski** Scott A '89

ORRVILLE
Wayne County
(330) 684-3598 **Ekonomon** Adam M '89
(330) 683-4981 **Forrer** Carl E '72
(330) 684-3315 **Harlan** M Ann '85
(330) 683-0015 **Helmuth** Ricky J '79
(330) 683-5010 **Hohenberger** Raymond W '74
(330) 683-0015 **Johnson & Helmuth**
(330) 683-0015 **Johnson** John E '75
(330) 683-0015 **Johnson** John E Jr. '87
(330) 683-5010 **Kirkbride** Cheryl M '01
(330) 684-3000 **Knudsen** Jeannette L '98
(330) 683-5010 **Kropf** John W '68
(330) 683-5010 **Kropf Wagner Hohenberger & Lutz, LLP**
(330) 683-5010 **Lutz** Daniel R '87

(330) 682-3000 **Mackus** Eloise L '79
(330) 683-9474 **Moore** Marie L '98
(888) 550-9555 **Shinaberry** Shannon L '96
(330) 683-5010 **VanSickle** Timothy R '98
(330) 683-5010 **Wagner** Richard S '58
(330) 683-1025 **Waltman** Paul D '65

OTTAWA

Putnam County

(419) 523-5658 **Blankemeyer** Anna M '81
(419) 876-3600 **Bohrer** Bruce B '83
(419) 523-3322 **Borer** Michael A '86
(419) 523-3396 **Cunningham** Margaret A '68
(419) 523-3396 **Cunningham** Matthew A '99
(419) 523-5777 **Hermiller** Gregory J '99
(419) 523-6200 **Klausing** Jennifer L '04
(419) 523-5400 **Lammers** Gary L '89
(419) 523-5015 **Leopold** Lawrence E '74
(419) 523-5015 **Leopold Wildenhaus & Sahloff**
(419) 523-5777 **Niese** Chad C '97
(419) 523-5777 **Niese Hermiller & Schierloh, LLC**
(419) 523-6104 **O'Malley** Michael E '68
(419) 523-6104 **Oxley Malone Hollister O'Malley & Warren, PLL**
(419) 523-5015 **Sahloff** Kurt W '94
(419) 523-5777 **Schierloh** Keith H '99
(419) 523-5658 **Schroeder Blankemeyer & Schroeder**
(419) 523-5658 **Schroeder** Clyde A '70
(419) 523-5658 **Schroeder** Joseph C '91
(419) 523-5688 **Schroeder** Lee R '02
(419) 523-5658 **Schroeder** Todd C '02
(419) 523-9600 **Shartzer** D Jean '86
(419) 523-5015 **Welch** Jill S '99
(419) 523-5015 **Welch** Scott E '99
(419) 523-5015 **Wildenhaus** William J '75

OTWAY

Scioto County

(740) 372-0902 **Moore** Steven A '99

OXFORD

Butler County

(513) 523-4104 **Bennett** Jay C '74
(513) 523-6369 **Bolin** Larry R '97
(513) 529-4848 **Cramer** Philip W '71
(513) 524-5000 **Deters** Dennis P '00
(513) 523-6369 **Engel** Drew G '87
(513) 524-5000 **Haughey** Daniel E '00
(513) 529-2945 **Herron** Daniel J '78
(513) 523-6369 **Huss** Dan E '65
(513) 523-4111 **Lipnickey** Susan C '91
(513) 523-7722 **Meyer** Martha P '79
(513) 523-3700 **Michael** James E Jr. '73
(513) 523-3700 **Millikin & Fitton**
(513) 529-6734 **Parker** Robin L '82
(513) 529-8759 **Rice** Mackenzie L '02
(513) 523-4111 **Robinson** James G '74
(513) 524-1177 **Schoonover** Paul E '88
(513) 524-2453 **Spohn** Monica L '96
(513) 523-7722 **Staton** Wayne C '76
(513) 529-4151 **Thomas** Randi M '93

PAINESVILLE

Lake County

(440) 354-8859 **Alban** Robert J '73
(440) 639-0300 **Anderson** George F '81
(440) 357-5537 **Aveni** Anthony J '66
(440) 357-5537 **Aveni** Benjamin L '03
(440) 350-2299 **Baeppler** Michelle M '95
(440) 639-4890 **Baetzel** Robert C '96
(440) 354-4364 **Baker & Hackenberg Co,LPA**
(440) 350-2683 **Barner** Donald R '86
(440) 350-2684 **Bartolotta** Mark J '92
(440) 352-3391 **Berezin** Alec '74
(440) 357-5537 **Bevack** Gina M '03
(440) 350-3200 **Biddell** Nancy L '02
(440) 350-1616 **Black** Jeffrey H '92
(440) 350-2781 **Brown** Lora L '97
(440) 946-2322 **Buss** Ralph C '66
(440) 352-8977 **Cahill** Kenneth J '91
(440) 350-3200 **Campbell** Margaret S '95
(440) 357-5537 **Cannon Stern Aveni & Loiancono Co,LPA**
(440) 357-5537 **Cannon** Timothy P '80
Cave Gilbert T '60
(440) 350-2146 **Cheatham** Amy E '97
(440) 639-3000 **Chemnitz** Gregory R '84
(440) 350-3200 **Clapp** Vanessa R '92
(440) 350-2683 **Condon** Eric A '88
(440) 350-2683 **Condon** Patrick J '99
(440) 942-6957 **Conway** Neil J III '83
(440) 357-6211 **Cooper** Linda D '78
(440) 350-2683 **Cornachio** Marisa L '04
(440) 350-2663 **Corrigan** Victoria M '99
(440) 350-2684 **Coulson** Charles E '74
(440) 352-3391 **Coven** Steven H '03
(440) 352-4484 **Cruikshank** David E '73
(440) 357-5654 **Dalheim** Theodore J '70
(440) 352-8500 **Dana** Richard L Jr. '95
(440) 942-5232 **D'Angelo** Nicholas A '87
(440) 354-5636 **Dean** John T '59
(440) 350-2683 **De Leone** Michael L '01
(440) 352-5318 **Denman** Patrice F '89
(440) 357-6111 **DiFranco** Carl L II '98
(440) 352-4400 **Dray** Sandra A '81
(440) 350-2683 **Dugan** James R Jr. '80
(440) 352-3391 **Dworken & Bernstein Co,LPA**
(440) 352-3391 **Dworken** Marvin P '59
(440) 488-0287 **Dynes** Brandon D '97
(440) 350-2100 **Echols** Kelly A '03
(440) 352-6200 **Eiger** Marley F '74
(440) 350-2708 **Evans** Janice S '78
(440) 357-0939 **Farrell** James K Jr. '77
(440) 350-3200 **Farren** David E '83
(440) 350-3000 **Ferkol** Jeffrey C '86
(440) 350-2378 **Fiederer** Pamela A '85
(440) 357-6211 **Forbes** Glenn E '79
(440) 350-2708 **Fram** Jeffrey W '77
(440) 350-2683 **Gambol** Robert A '73
(440) 357-6129 **Gilson** Gregory M '72
(440) 350-2135 **Gorman** Thomas R '92
(440) 350-3200 **Grieshammer** Charles R '81
(440) 350-3200 **Grieshammer** Susan C '88
(440) 354-3800 **Gurley** Joanne G '81
(440) 354-3800 **Gurley** Joseph M '75
(440) 354-4364 **Hackenberg** Isaac J '64
(440) 350-2683 **Hackman** David J Jr. '90
(440) 354-3800 **Hanahan** Geoffrey C '79
(440) 352-4484 **Haskell** George B '75
(440) 354-4364 **Hennig** Richard A '83
(440) 350-3200 **Hess** Terry E '02
(440) 357-5558 **Hurley** John J Jr. '68
(440) 357-5558 **Hurley** Michael P '74
(440) 352-8500 **Ischie** Wilbur N '75
(440) 352-3360 **Jambor** Z Richard '67
(440) 357-5577 **Kaiser** Mark A '85
(440) 350-2683 **Kaplan** Paul E '91
(440) 392-0147 **Kidd** Patricia A '99
(440) 352-3003 **Kilpeck** Lori R '02
Koepper Engeline H '76
(440) 357-5577 **Koerner** David E '85
(440) 354-3800 **Koerner** James P '75
(440) 254-8818 **Kolkowski** Brian M '91
(440) 350-2683 **Kondas** Dale R '79
(440) 357-2683 **Kowall** Karen L '85
Kowalski Gregory J '83
(440) 352-3391 **Kraus** Keith R '84
(440) 350-1900 **Kubyn** R R '84
(440) 350-1900 **Kubyn** Stacey L '91
(440) 350-3200 **Kucharski** Carolyn M '93
(440) 352-0761 **LaForce** Robert W '81
(440) 350-3200 **LaPlante** Roland P '72
(440) 352-8700 **Lawson** Karen D '82
(440) 350-2683 **LeHoty-Ostry** Randi '89
(440) 350-2683 **Linden** Taylir K '94
(440) 350-2098 **Lister** Kevin S '86
(440) 350-1616 **Lobur** John S '01
(440) 357-5537 **Loiacono** James V III '78
(440) 352-3391 **Lowell** Staci D '04
(440) 357-5000 **Lyons** James M '78
(440) 357-5537 **Malchesky** Paul R '97
(440) 350-1174 **Marinucci** Daniel F '80
(440) 350-3200 **Mathews** James C '00
(440) 352-6200 **McGuinness** Clare I '85
(440) 350-2683 **Mijic-Barisic** Katarina V '95
(440) 350-2708 **Miller** Eileen N '86
(440) 357-6211 **Miller** Paul E '97
(440) 354-3585 **Moran** Mary A '83
(440) 357-6211 **Moseman** Heather L '03
(440) 352-3391 **Murphy** Patrick T '86
(440) 357-6111 **Murray** Michael D '88
(440) 357-5134 **Myers** Robert H Jr. '91
(440) 357-5558 **Nelson Sweet & Hurley**
(440) 350-2683 **Neroda** Lisa A '91
(440) 350-2683 **Neylon** Benjamin J '99
(440) 350-2683 **Nocero** Patricia A '80
(440) 350-3200 **O'Brien** Maryellen '01
(440) 357-5000 **O'Donnell** John P '87
(440) 352-3391 **Okin** Gary S '77
(440) 350-3200 **O'Neill** Melissa A '04
(440) 352-3324 **Orosz** Richard T '71
(440) 350-2684 **Patton** Robert J '96
(440) 352-3391 **Perotti** Patrick J '82
(440) 350-2318 **Peters** Jennifer L '99
(440) 639-0146 **Plassard** Brett J '85
(440) 352-3391 **Rabb** Howard S '86
(440) 352-3391 **Raj** Manav H '96
(440) 354-3800 **Rand Gurley Hanahan & Koerner**
(440) 357-6111 **Redmond** Edward C '57
(440) 357-6111 **Redmond Walker & Murray**
(440) 352-3391 **Resnick** Melvyn E '66
(440) 350-2742 **Rezaee** Alana A '04
(440) 352-3391 **Richards** David J Jr. '71
(440) 352-0716 **Richer** Donald A '75
(440) 350-3200 **Roessner** Pamela L '01
(440) 350-2683 **Rogers** John M '02
(440) 918-2720 **Roll** Kenneth R '80
(440) 352-3391 **Rosner** Irving '79
(440) 350-3200 **Schwartz** Aaron A '02
(440) 352-3391 **Selby** Richard N '92
(440) 350-2683 **Sheppert** Karen A '89
(440) 352-3391 **Sherlock** Kristen M '01
(440) 350-2683 **Sheroke** William L '71
(440) 354-2212 **Silakoski** Linda G '97
Simonelli Mark M '96
(440) 350-2394 **Smither** Wendy J '91
(440) 350-2707 **Sommers** JoAnne V '73
(440) 350-2683 **Stano** Brian W '03
(440) 352-3391 **Stender** Jonathan T '99
(440) 350-2683 **Stevenson** Leah J '99
(440) 352-6200 **Sweeney** Anne K '04
(440) 354-4364 **Szeman** Joseph P '95
(440) 358-4948 **Szmagala** Taras G Jr. '91
(440) 352-8500 **Talikka** Leo J '68
(440) 357-3428 **Tinkler** Timothy E '73
(440) 352-3391 **Tomaszewski** Jodi L '99
(440) 350-2683 **Tucci** Christopher P '03
(440) 352-3391 **Turoff** Geoffrey H '88
(440) 352-8977 **Ulrich** Joseph R '69
(440) 350-2708 **Umholtz** Marie L '89
(440) 354-1969 **Unterweiser** Carl H '84
(440) 357-7199 **Vazzana** James L '87
(440) 357-6111 **Walker** Gerald R '73
(440) 350-2624 **Waltonen** Andrea L '87
(440) 350-7035 **Weiss** Francis P '82
(440) 350-1909 **White** Mark C '83
(440) 358-1100 **Wilson** Neil R '73
(440) 350-2167 **Yohe** Lynne A '85
(440) 352-3003 **Ziegler Metzger & Miller LLP**

PANDORA

Putnam County

(419) 384-3238 **Diller** Jon N '75

PARMA

Cuyahoga County

(440) 843-9944 **Ade** Mark A '98
(216) 351-0100 **Bader** Thomas J '56
(440) 884-5015 **Bazarko** Volodymyr O '70
(440) 884-8018 **Belovich** Barbara A '86
(440) 884-8018 **Belovich** Robert F '52
(440) 884-8018 **Belovich** Robert S '77
(440) 886-3800 **Boyko** Timothy A '89
(216) 485-7970 **Britt** Stephen T '89
(440) 845-9050 **Bubna** Walter P '80
(216) 362-1880 **Chimples** Constantine G '73
(216) 749-2203 **Cichocki** Bruce M '75
Connors Maureen '01
(216) 485-7970 **Conrad** Michelle L '03
(440) 884-2675 **Corea** Charles '87
(216) 485-7970 **Courey** Bruce M '89
(440) 884-1309 **Csiszar-Highman** Debbie A '97
(216) 676-9840 **Davidson** Lauren E '03
(216) 485-7970 **DeGeeter** Timothy J '98
(216) 485-7970 **DePiero** Dean E '94
(440) 886-3800 **Dobeck** Timothy G '86
Dolan Michael K '02
(440) 884-5538 **Donahue** James R '57
(216) 351-2613 **Dorocak** John R '77
Dugan Thomas A '58
(440) 888-0843 **Durica** Terrence D '74
(440) 743-4043 **English** Monica L '89
(440) 842-0455 **Falconi** Ronald E '95
(440) 887-7400 **Fink** Edward J '76
(216) 674-1400 **Finnerty** David J '92
(440) 887-7458 **Gilligan** Timothy P '87
(216) 485-0600 **Gilmartin** Matthew T '82
(440) 885-8073 **Golubovic** Carla L '93
(440) 886-1900 **Graves** Harold D '61
(440) 842-9328 **Gvozdenovic** Milos '04
(440) 888-7000 **Hrisko** Paul A '69
(440) 843-5300 **Kelleher** Sean F '92
(440) 845-0500 **Koscianski** James P '88
(440) 845-0500 **Koscianski** John P '90
(440) 845-0500 **Koscianski** Raymond A '58
(440) 886-1332 **Kotulic** Irene M '55
(440) 885-2854 **Krafcik** Jamie R '95
(216) 676-2528 **Krogh** Timothy R '92
(440) 886-3000 **Lang** Daniel P '86
(440) 886-3000 **Leary** Lynn W '63
(440) 886-3000 **Leary Schifko Nobili & Lang**
(440) 888-4220 **Liscynesky** Marta L '93
(440) 888-4220 **Liscynesky** Orest W '83
(216) 485-7970 **McCauley** Christopher J '86
(216) 741-4486 **McGee** Kathleen H '79
(216) 749-7090 **Mottl** Ronald M '57
(440) 886-6394 **Naughton** John D '57
(440) 886-6112 **Nebesh** Eugene '71
(440) 886-3000 **Nobili** David L '71
(440) 845-4785 **Novak** Richard P '93
(440) 888-4888 **Ocampo** Benjamin T '87
(216) 485-7970 **O'Malley** Michael C '92
(440) 884-5015 **Oryshkewych** George R '92
Oryshkewych George V '71
(440) 843-3004 **Ott** Arthur E '88
Paul Ross R '90
(216) 351-2643 **Pilwallis** Clarence J '57
(440) 887-7400 **Purge** Sherry M '00
(440) 886-1900 **Riley** Victoria J '98
(440) 886-3000 **Schifko** Robert F '64
(440) 842-3848 **Schleicher** Albert G '56
(440) 891-8389 **Serrano** Mariela F '80
(216) 898-8399 **Sharvit** Eliav '04
(440) 885-8173 **Siegfried** Elayne M '94
(440) 843-8800 **Stanovic** James M '79
(440) 845-4140 **Stoken** Henry A '81
(440) 886-9999 **Thesling** William H '76
(440) 843-5300 **Toetz** David W '83
(440) 888-2889 **Wagner** Edwin J '67
(440) 886-2510 **Walick** Joseph A '63
(440) 398-7522 **Willmann** Wendel E '69
(440) 885-8132 **Zampedro** Anthony J '91
Zubricky Douglas J '03

PARMA HEIGHTS

Cuyahoga County

(440) 843-6670 **Bianchi** Robert C '84
(440) 842-6800 **Chizmar** Gregory A '77
(440) 888-8090 **Feola** Dennis L '74
(440) 884-6800 **Gartman** Thomas N '76
(440) 886-4556 **Glorioso** Russell J '67
(440) 884-6500 **Goldhamer** Stanley J '53
(440) 845-9040 **Higgins** John H '56
(440) 885-5559 **Homolak** Gloria R '81
(440) 886-7700 **Kulig** John J '60
(440) 845-1666 **McGhee** Shorain L '03
(440) 842-2770 **Milenkovich** Milosh D '75
(440) 845-9110 **Murphy** John F '80
(440) 743-7000 **Papcke** Mary E '84
(440) 845-3030 **Pelagalli** Rodger A '86
(440) 845-1900 **Senn** Richard A '66
(440) 382-5054 **Sobieski** Ernest F '75
Spanagel George W '50
(440) 888-2770 **Varga** Jane M '81
(440) 884-4844 **West** John H '82
(440) 845-1900 **Wilbur** Thomas B '68
(440) 886-5667 **Young** Robert H '86

PATASKALA

Licking County

(740) 927-8386 **Bennett** Richard T '75
(740) 927-2219 **Brush** C Bernard '75
(740) 927-7933 **Floyd** Dixie K '88
(740) 927-2927 **Hayes** Chester D '01
(740) 927-2927 **Hayes** William C '78
(740) 927-2927 **Hayes** William S '93
(740) 927-3859 **Peters** John I '75
(740) 927-9195 **Scott** Elaine R '84
(740) 927-8000 **Shackelford** Margaret O'Connor '87
(740) 927-9225 **Shaheen** Arnold E Jr. '74
(740) 927-7145 **Sims** August C '84
(740) 964-9271 **Veley** Jonathan A '92
Weber Joshua D '03
Woods Lisa A '02
Zochowski Myra M '02

PAULDING

Paulding County

(419) 399-2351 **Bandy** Erwin J '77
(419) 399-2181 **Burkard** Joseph R '92
(419) 399-2181 **Cook** Norman E '68
(419) 399-2181 **Cook Troth & Burkard,Ltd**
(419) 399-8270 **Crosley** Casey R '02
(419) 399-3801 **DeMuth** John A '79
(419) 399-2181 **Gorrell** Brian S '02
(419) 399-4916 **Hyman** David A '78
(419) 399-4911 **Jones** Michael C '79
(419) 399-3456 **Pieper** Timothy R '86
(419) 399-2217 **Sponseller** James M '74
(419) 399-4911 **Spriggs** James P '73
(419) 399-2181 **Troth** Glenn H '82

PEEBLES

Adams County

(937) 587-3119 **Kelley** Christopher D '93

PEMBERVILLE

Wood County

(419) 287-3233 **Davies** Richard N '76
(419) 287-4618 **Kuhlman** Robert A '79
(419) 287-9307 **Moffett** John J '72
(419) 287-3233 **Ruck** John D '98

PENINSULA

Summit County

(330) 322-8194 **Griffith** Anne Marie '04
(330) 459-6587 **Payne** Rex E III '97
Royer Christina M '01

PEPPER PIKE

Cuyahoga County

(216) 765-8520 **Aggers** David F '83
(216) 765-8520 **Aggers Joseph & Cheverine Co, LPA**
(216) 360-2124 **Arthur** Harry L '82
(216) 378-4136 **Bertea** Craig J '85
(216) 464-2153 **Bray** Christopher P '01
(216) 765-8004 **Brouman** Alvin '55
(216) 464-7988 **Brover** David R '85
(216) 831-3175 **Brown** Harvey A '65
(216) 378-0804 **Brown** Kristin M '91
(216) 514-5997 **Caplan** Leah M '86
(216) 831-4935 **Carlin** William A '78
(216) 765-8520 **Cheverine** Vincent L '95
(216) 831-5904 **Chilcote** Nancy A '83
Conte Richard M '83
(216) 206-1238 **Delventhal** Thomas M '91
(216) 464-6901 **Etowski** Earl J Jr. '74
(216) 464-6901 **Froelich** Georgia A '84
(440) 339-7607 **Ginsburg** Janice R '99
Gisser Sheldon M '63
(216) 831-2400 **Harding** Frank I III '69
(216) 360-9000 **Hendershott** Howard E Jr. '53
(216) 360-2124 **Higerd** Jeffrey Jay '75
(216) 464-2289 **Jacobson** Murray R '69
(216) 360-2124 **Jaros** Stanley T '73
(216) 765-8520 **Joseph** Kathryn Theresa '86
(216) 514-5997 **Khoury** Alisa K '99
(216) 514-5997 **Levinson** Jeffrey M '90
(216) 621-7337 **Lightbody** William S '77
(216) 514-8694 **Lissauer** Charles W '64
(440) 449-4200 **Lukas** Anne L '86
(216) 514-5997 **Margulies** James W '94
(216) 514-5997 **Margulies** Susan C '95
(216) 473-2530 **Matas** Vytas R '71
(216) 765-1240 **McKown** Michael O '77
(216) 360-2124 **Moriarty & Jaros,PLL**
(216) 360-2124 **Moriarty** Richard J Jr. '49
(216) 831-4935 **Ockington** William J '74
(216) 831-7338 **Palmeri** Charles J '77
(216) 831-4935 **Papa** Nicholas A '92
(216) 360-9969 **Parisi** Stephen T '66
(216) 360-2124 **Riley** David R '80
Rubenstein Ronald M '57
(216) 765-8520 **Scharon** John V '78
(216) 206-1239 **Sheppard** James F '82
(216) 831-4935 **Spremulli** Leonard A '75
(216) 378-0140 **Staph** Jack A '73
(216) 464-7986 **String** Cynthia M '91
(216) 831-0698 **Thompson** William H '84
(216) 378-2810 **Tognetti** Edward J '96
(216) 292-4932 **Tura** James V '77
Wallace-Curry Virginia M '88
(216) 241-8376 **Womer** George S '51
(216) 464-0001 **Wortzman** William A '74
(216) 831-1551 **Wymor** Larry L '61
(216) 360-9000 **Ziegler Metzger & Miller LLP**

PERRY

Lake County

(440) 259-5200 **Goldstein** Noreen K '90
(440) 259-3578 **Pikus** James X '85
(440) 259-0074 **Ponce de Leon** Agustin '97
(440) 259-0074 **Wadding** Edward A '01

PERRYSBURG

Wood County

Ahern William R '72
(419) 874-7188 **Allotta Farley & Widman Co, LPA**
(419) 874-3569 **Aubry** P M '82
(260) 668-8778 **Beech** Beth E '88
(419) 666-3417 **Beier** Gayle K '00
(419) 873-8401 **Blakley** Kim G '88
(419) 873-0009 **Brown** Matthew S '04
(419) 874-1633 **Callender** Calvin D '67
(419) 872-1688 **Caughey** William C '75
(419) 872-5695 **Celley & Sanderson,LLP**
(419) 872-5695 **Celley** Walter J '87
(419) 872-1290 **Clark** Mary C '93
(419) 874-5610 **Croy & Hendel,LLP**
(419) 874-5610 **Croy** Paul E '89
(419) 872-6600 **Csomos** Laura A '00
(419) 873-1814 **Dane** Stephen M '81
(419) 874-2535 **Davis** Paul A '81
(419) 874-3536 **Dombey** Philip L '73
(419) 874-4604 **Donahue** John P '83
(419) 874-9675 **Eckel** Paul C '91
(419) 874-2261 **Field** Peter F '96
(419) 874-1100 **Fraser** Donald R '63
(419) 874-1100 **Fraser Martin Buchanan Miller LLC**
(419) 874-7188 **Grachek** Ellen M '03
(419) 874-3569 **Gwyn** Peter D '68
(419) 872-1272 **Hafner** Mark A '87
(419) 872-6600 **Handwork** B Thomas Jr. '68

(419) 872-6600 **Handwork & Kerscher**
(419) 874-3536 **Hart** James H '74
(419) 874-5610 **Hendel** Sharon S '94
(419) 874-3536 **Howard** Kay L '92
(419) 872-2600 **Howard** Susan E '92
Hudson Marcia M '01
(419) 872-1998 **Huffstutler** Rahn M '79
(419) 874-3203 **Johnson** Robert W '78
(419) 873-8660 **Keller** Marvin E '75
(419) 872-6600 **Kerscher** Jeffrey M '93
Keune Grant M '91
(419) 874-6048 **Kienzle** David W '80
(419) 247-3758 **Kienzle** Susan S '77
(419) 872-6808 **Klapp** Austin F '00
(419) 874-3322 **Kobil** Gerald M '75
(419) 874-3536 **Leatherman** Wayne M '50
(419) 874-3536 **Leatherman Witzler Dombey & Hart**
(419) 874-5610 **Mackin** Thomas G '90
(419) 874-1100 **Martin** Richard G '90
(419) 874-5610 **Mattimoe** John I '89
(419) 874-3177 **McDermott** James A '96
McGrail Thomas E '77
Meyers Terri A '94
(419) 874-1100 **Miller** J Douglas '00
(419) 874-9500 **Montz** Lane A '93
(419) 872-2800 **Newcomer** Ned S '68
(419) 874-3536 **Noll** Todd H '82
(419) 872-7915 **Osterud** S D '74
(419) 874-3177 **Pheils** David R Jr. '74
(419) 874-3177 **Pheils & Wisniewski**
(419) 874-2261 **Prephan** Michael Jr. '87
(419) 874-6173 **Pummill** Brian S '89
(419) 666-2984 **Reams** Frazier Jr. '55
(419) 872-5695 **Sanderson** Dawn E '00
(419) 874-9300 **Sheppard** Kenneth L Jr. '03
(419) 874-9145 **Simmons** Donald D '58
(419) 874-3536 **Skaff** Paul A '98
(419) 666-3417 **Skiver** Stephen A '89
(419) 874-3569 **Smith** Cynthia B '88
(419) 666-1088 **Snyder** Bruce T '76
(419) 872-6808 **Spore** John S '86
(419) 874-5850 **Spore** Judson P Jr. '62
(419) 626-2709 **Sturgill** Russell I '53
(419) 872-6808 **Troendle** Janelle M '03
(419) 698-2968 **Varner** Philip W '92
(419) 874-2261 **Weiss** Dan M '96
(419) 661-9500 **Wetmore** Kenneth H '75
(419) 874-7188 **Widman** Marilyn L '97
(419) 874-3177 **Wisniewski** Marshall D '81

PERRYSVILLE
Ashland County

(419) 938-1740 **Kochensparger** Andrea S '01

PICKERINGTON
Fairfield County

Brown William F Jr. '73
(614) 837-6504 **Carlisle** Robert P '85
(614) 837-5992 **Daniel** F Toby T '75
(614) 927-9059 **Dye** James L Jr. '93
(614) 861-1916 **Edwards** John B '00
(614) 833-2531 **Elwing** Thomas R '98
(614) 548-0024 **England** Dale R Jr. '72
(614) 837-1870 **Feyko** Jeffrey '85
(614) 837-3980 **Fields** Orval E II '75
(614) 837-8210 **Flaugher** Robert A '96
(614) 759-9590 **Golowin** Serge A '79
Haywood Lisa M '99
(614) 751-9910 **Hoskinson** Marla D '99
Husted Gerald E '75
(614) 861-5362 **Kouns** Mark E '76
(614) 837-1889 **Mapes** Robert E '74
(614) 837-5077 **Mazel** Joel M '90
(614) 260-3797 **Moore** Michael M '85
(614) 834-1515 **Noethlich** Keith A '77
(614) 833-3777 **O'Reilly** Michael J '84
(614) 863-6220 **Ort** Mark P '82
(614) 837-5992 **Poston** David W '82
(614) 837-3980 **Regoli** Holly P '93
(614) 834-1200 **Rose** Sara L '95
(614) 322-7923 **Sams** Jeffrey B '88
(614) 833-6033 **Schwarz** Jerrold W '90
(614) 837-8433 **Shaver** David B '86
(614) 834-9879 **Snyder** Luann K '89
(614) 575-2500 **Szluzer** Cheryl E '01
(614) 866-9811 **Vanderhoff** Anna M '99
(614) 863-9372 **Willette** Philip B '76
(614) 866-3411 **Zuravsky** Marvin A '91

PIKETON
Pike County

(740) 289-2371 **James** Darin C '96

PIQUA
Miami County

(937) 778-8000 **Buecker** Thomas J '69
Cromley Charles T Jr. '97
(937) 773-3212 **Davis** Dale G '76
(937) 773-7621 **DePriest** Roy H '59
(937) 773-8054 **Dungan & LeFevre Co,LPA**
(937) 773-3212 **Gutmann** Michael E '84
(937) 778-0579 **Hardin** Paulette D '00
(937) 773-8054 **Hemm** John E '82
(937) 773-3212 **Hornish-Schlosser** Laura '00
(937) 773-8047 **Kindell** Louie R '83
(937) 773-3212 **McCulloch Felger Fite & Gutmann Co,LPA**
(937) 773-3212 **McNeil** William B '64
(937) 773-3212 **Neuenschwander** Jack L '67
(937) 773-3212 **Patrizio** Frank J '91
(937) 778-1770 **Pratt** Robert A '61
(937) 773-3212 **Ramer** Daniel E '79
(937) 778-8000 **Roberts** Roberta S '02
(937) 773-9290 **Tinkler** Cornelia E '96
(937) 778-0092 **Virzi** Frank S '72
(937) 773-8054 **Wannemacher** John A Jr. '93

PLAIN CITY
Madison County

(614) 873-3421 **Blevins** Melissa D '04
(614) 873-8566 **Chuha** Edward F '68
(614) 873-7171 **Endres** Louis P III '78
(614) 873-3421 **Houchard** John E '64
(614) 873-8227 **Janetzke** Ronald H '67
(614) 873-9668 **Johnson** Daniel E '84
(614) 733-0720 **Kincaid** Timothy J '96
(614) 873-4511 **Smith** Frank S '76
Suchta Arthur M '73
(614) 873-3421 **Valentine** Clifton G Jr. '82
(614) 873-8740 **White** Lisa A '03

PLEASANT PLAIN
Warren County

(513) 877-2900 **Cox** Michael G '81

POLAND
Mahoning County

(330) 758-3878 **Adler** Jeffrey D '90
(330) 757-2454 **Andrews** James H '82
(330) 707-0377 **Carlin** Clair M '73
(330) 757-7171 **Fortunato** Mark R '88
(330) 726-3736 **Gemma** Anthony N '76
(330) 707-0377 **Higgins** Amy L '02
(330) 757-9293 **Hoza** Michael L Jr. '94
(330) 757-7700 **Jones** James S '94
(330) 757-0333 **Katz** Louis E '75
(330) 757-1898 **Meloy** William S '62
(330) 757-1700 **Powers** John W '49

POMEROY
Meigs County

(740) 992-5730 **Bunce** Denise L '89
(740) 992-5132 **Crow** Irving C '75
(740) 992-7101 **Fultz** Bernard V '56
(740) 992-2090 **Knight** Charles H '74
(740) 992-6689 **Little** Douglas W '79
(740) 992-2186 **Little Sheets & Warner, LLP**
(740) 992-2381 **O'Brien** Patrick H '77
(740) 992-2151 **Sheets** Jennifer L '82
(740) 992-6371 **Story** Patrick R '91
(740) 992-6624 **Story** Steven L '79
(740) 992-6368 **Tenoglia** Christopher '91
(740) 992-2186 **Warner** Linda Rae '88

PORT CLINTON
Ottawa County

(419) 732-3135 **Barney** James C '94
Bierce James M '65
(419) 734-6845 **Boldt** David R '85
(419) 734-6790 **Boyd** Jason E '02
(419) 732-3145 **Brown** Bree Noblitt '01
(419) 734-6699 **Cabral** Allen M '75
(419) 734-3174 **Coppeler** John A '75
(419) 797-2377 **Corogin** Thomas L '53
(419) 734-6845 **Croy** Lorrain R '95
(419) 734-1528 **DeBacco** Thomas J '79
(419) 734-9009 **Dunn** Terry J '88
(419) 734-3174 **Flynn Py & Kruse,LPA**
(419) 732-1607 **Frederick** Mark A '87
(419) 732-3135 **Gillum** Richard R III '98
(419) 734-4142 **Gulas** Ruth M '87
(419) 734-4143 **Hany** Frederick C II '84
(419) 732-3135 **Heigel** Catherine Edwards '03
(419) 734-4928 **Johannsen** Kyle J '90
(419) 734-0235 **Kennedy** Shelly L '89
(419) 732-3135 **Kocher** John A '74
(419) 734-4142 **Kroeger-Baum** Linda Lee '93
(419) 732-1041 **Loeffler** Donald B '85
(419) 734-1528 **Marcinko** Christopher M '04
(419) 734-5700 **Melena** Donald R '57
(906) 458-2096 **Menucci** William R '78
(419) 734-6845 **Mulligan** Mark E '77
(419) 734-6997 **Nation** Sarah A '00
(419) 732-3145 **Noblitt** Larry L '68
(419) 734-6840 **Petersen** Barbara B '73
(419) 732-2521 **Petersen** Lowell S '52
(419) 734-1723 **Reinheimer** Frank W '65
(419) 734-1723 **Reinheimer** James L '92
(419) 732-3000 **Rudes** Terrence R '77
(419) 734-6511 **Sandwisch** Michael W '82
(419) 797-4783 **Wagner** Glen W '49
(419) 732-1041 **Wargo** Louis P III '81
(419) 734-4060 **Wilber** George C '77
(419) 734-6755 **Winters** Bruce A '88
Wood Wendy A '81
(419) 797-7311 **Woodson** Riley D '84

PORTSMOUTH
Scioto County

(740) 353-7548 **Aalyson** Mark E '80
(740) 353-2146 **Apel** John P '97
(740) 353-2146 **Apel-Miller** Margaret B '89
(740) 354-2334 **Ashburn** Randy D '89
(740) 353-1157 **Bannon Howland & Dever**
(740) 354-3214 **Beck** David B '97
(740) 353-4191 **Bender** Stanley C '76
(740) 355-8215 **Bennett** Rebecca L '92
(740) 353-4191 **Berry** John F '76
(740) 355-0073 **Book** Thomas T '94
(740) 355-9000 **Brown** J Rick '76
(740) 353-6604 **Buckler** Barry A '02
(740) 353-6604 **Buckler** Jerry L '96
(740) 353-6604 **Buckler** Ruth A '02
(740) 353-1540 **Burris** Diane '87
(740) 354-5659 **Campbell** Richard W '83
(740) 354-7563 **Cardosi** Mark J '88
(740) 354-3214 **Clark** Roger L '68
(800) 837-2508 **Crowder** Marjorie B '75
Danner John H Jr. '97
(740) 353-9805 **Davis** Anna Eva '00
(740) 353-4661 **Davis** George L III '80
(740) 353-1157 **Davis** Sherry D '97
(740) 353-1157 **Dever** Robert E '56
(740) 353-1157 **Dever** Robert R '80
(740) 355-3283 **Donohue** Stephen P '79
(740) 353-1509 **Edwards** Wallace E '82
(740) 354-2300 **Enriquez** Rick '87
(740) 354-3600 **Fitch** James C '55
(740) 354-3600 **Fitch** Lee O '50
(740) 354-3643 **Frost** Daphne J '04
(740) 354-2375 **Garaczkowski** Joan M '93
(740) 353-2187 **Gentner** Susan Smith '01
(740) 351-0499 **Gerard** Christopher C '00
(740) 354-7755 **Gerlach** Cynthia K '85
(740) 354-7755 **Gerlach** Franklin T '61
(740) 354-7755 **Gerlach & Gerlach**
(740) 354-7755 **Gerlach** Valarie K '87
(740) 354-7563 **Greenwald** Tammy L '00
(740) 353-9805 **Haas** John R '90
(740) 353-1629 **Hale** Joseph L '83
(740) 354-2300 **Hamm** George R '02
(740) 353-3113 **Harcha** Howard H Jr. '52
(740) 354-1000 **Hoover** Marie Moraleja '94
(740) 354-1000 **Hoover** Robert T '88
(740) 354-2375 **Hoover** Roxanne '96
(740) 354-4200 **Howard** Joshua D '04
(740) 353-8895 **Huddleston** David M '77
(740) 353-2155 **Hunter** Richard S '50
(740) 354-4200 **Johnson** C Clayton '70
(740) 354-2300 **Kleha** Jeffrey A '03
(740) 354-1454 **Kuhn** David W '69
(740) 355-8215 **Kuhn** Mark E '94
(740) 354-7563 **Leitzell** Karyn J '00
(740) 354-3600 **Lemons** Richard A '85
(740) 353-1800 **Marshall** John B Jr. '79
(740) 355-8301 **Marshall** William T '83
(740) 355-8306 **McFarland** Matthew W '92
(740) 354-8602 **McKenzie** Ronald E '75
(740) 354-3643 **Mearan** Michael H '71
(740) 354-3600 **Miller Searl & Fitch**
(740) 354-4200 **Oliver** Stephen L '81
(740) 354-1000 **Parker** Danielle M '03
(740) 355-8944 **Pekar** Patricia R '92
(740) 354-1300 **Rodeheffer** Stephen C '76
(740) 353-9805 **Ruggiero** Daniel P '73
(740) 353-9805 **Ruggiero & Haas**
(740) 354-3283 **Schisler** Richard T '68
(740) 351-0981 **Scott** Christine M '00
(740) 353-5191 **Shaw** William K Jr. '76
(740) 351-1243 **Skeens** Marcia S '87
(740) 353-1509 **Smith** James S '79
(740) 354-3761 **Stephenson** Marilee '91
(740) 354-5800 **Thatcher** John W '64
(740) 355-8306 **Tieman** Shane A '98
(740) 354-5098 **Tracy** Larry A '82
(740) 353-8111 **Triplett** Aaron R '83
(740) 353-5044 **Wheeler** Wayne B '82
(740) 353-1157 **Willard** Steven M '87
(740) 352-1646 **Willis** Jay S '95
(740) 354-3643 **Young** Jack D '61

POWELL
Delaware County

(614) 846-5005 **Brengartner** Beth A '99
Christensen Susan M '00
(614) 766-8475 **Clark** William J '77
(614) 873-8542 **Herb** Wendy M '91
(614) 888-7363 **Hodovanich** Dina L '01
(614) 792-2565 **Hoffman** Richard F '99
(614) 799-9996 **Irwin** Cynthia C '81
(614) 336-3083 **Ison** David A '83
(614) 888-8500 **Jones Troyan Pappas & Perkins,LPA**
(614) 846-1252 **Kauffman** Ronald P '61
(614) 985-0527 **Klein** John W '97
Lorenzo Paul S '94
(614) 846-1908 **McCarthy** Michael J '80
Messmer Gail E '83
(614) 847-3997 **Murphy** Timothy E '73
Nims Ronald K '82
(614) 888-8500 **Pappas** Robert T '84
(614) 888-8500 **Perkins** John R Jr. '84
(614) 888-2178 **Reeder** Donald R '81
(614) 889-6008 **Richardson** Herbert M III '86
(740) 881-0888 **Roberts** Mary A '81
(614) 361-6783 **Roeger** Deborah L '89
(614) 785-1700 **Scherner** Benjamin '97
(614) 799-2144 **Shoemaker** Larry B '90
(740) 881-3131 **Simile** Belinda H '87
(614) 436-8879 **Sobnosky** Edward N '56
Sturtz Laurence E '67
(614) 785-1700 **Sybert** Curtis J '87
(614) 888-8500 **Troyan** Gary M '78
(740) 549-2089 **Unver** Douglas R '91
Unver Karen A '91
(614) 760-0500 **Whitaker** Lowell D '86

PROCTORVILLE
Lawrence County

(740) 886-1616 **Hall** John E '76
Klein Mitchell L '84
(740) 886-2889 **Pierce** James A '92
(740) 886-5402 **Stillpass** Marty J '83

RAVENNA
Portage County

(330) 297-0881 **Aylward** James J '81
(330) 297-5531 **Badger** Richard J '73
(330) 297-3850 **Barone** Christina M '00
(330) 298-0065 **Bergener** Karin C '91
(330) 296-3884 **Berger** Robert W '78
(330) 296-2811 **Bertrand** Louis R '68
(330) 297-3850 **Bird** Tiffany D '97
(330) 297-3850 **Blakemore** Allison B '89
(330) 281-3936 **Bostick** Robin G '97
(330) 297-3850 **Brode** David M '90
(330) 296-7152 **Buchanan** Thomas R '87
(330) 297-5788 **Cimino** Frank J '72
(330) 297-2310 **Colecchi** Stephen '79
(330) 296-7447 **Cox** Thomas A '75
(330) 296-8186 **Earle** Paul M '84
(330) 297-7030 **Fankhauser** Mark K '98
(330) 296-3621 **Fenwick** Timothy S '91
(330) 297-3850 **Fink** Eric R '99
(330) 297-3850 **Finnegan** Eric P '03
(330) 297-3850 **Gallagher** Paul J '86
(330) 296-3884 **Giulitto & Berger**
(330) 296-3884 **Giulitto** Michael A '88
(330) 296-3884 **Giulitto** Paula C '92
(330) 296-4451 **Goodwin** Jerry A '81
(330) 296-3888 **Graham** Gerald B '70
(330) 297-3879 **Graham** Kent M '82
Gregel Robyn L '99
(330) 296-3868 **Grueschow** Michael E '77
(330) 297-3665 **Haupt** Natalie Rogal '02
(330) 297-6460 **Heisa** Mark H '78
(330) 296-9966 **Hogle** James E Jr. '65
(330) 297-3850 **Holder** Pamela J '00
(330) 296-5100 **Hostler** Michael J '04
(330) 972-7712 **Jalbert** Michael J '84
(330) 297-1569 **Jennings** Jonathan P '99
(330) 297-3631 **Jones** Erik E '02
(330) 296-3868 **Kane** Terrence G '77
(330) 296-6742 **Kehres** Douglas M '84
(330) 297-3665 **Lager** Dennis D '76
(330) 296-4451 **Lawson** Stephen C '90
(330) 297-5718 **Lentz** William D '76
(330) 296-2851 **Lichtenberger** Lisa K '95
(330) 296-5252 **Lombardi** Richard C '71
(330) 296-9654 **Ludick** Timothy D '78
(330) 296-9642 **Masi** James '89
(330) 297-3850 **Meduri** Christopher J '95
(330) 297-3850 **Michniak** Stephen A '00
(330) 296-5461 **Mostardi** Sharon R '00
(330) 296-4451 **Muldowney** Eugene L '89
(330) 296-5920 **Myers** Jeffery D '96
(330) 296-9199 **Myers** Louis R '72
Nolfi Edward A '83
(330) 297-2241 **Norman** Kelli Kay '97
(330) 297-3622 **O'Neill** John P '71
(330) 296-9199 **Plough** John J '73
(330) 296-8552 **Poland** Kevin T '86
(330) 297-3850 **Redman** Jennifer E '98
(330) 297-3850 **Ricciardi** Francis M '77
(330) 296-3434 **Rosenberg** Robert E '89
(330) 296-4336 **Roubic** Melissa R V '96
(330) 297-5718 **Sansom** Norman W '68
(330) 297-3850 **Scahill** Sean P '00
(330) 297-3850 **Scahill** Theresa M '04
(330) 297-5778 **Scavdis** Antonios C '74
(330) 297-5778 **Scavdis** Antonios C Jr. '01
(330) 296-9654 **Schneider** Oliver J '51
(330) 296-3599 **Sed** David A '77
(330) 297-3880 **Sendry** Douglas J '74
(330) 297-3665 **Shinn** Charles R Jr. '01
(330) 296-9999 **Sicuro** Thomas J '68
(330) 296-9999 **Simon** William G Jr. '72
(330) 297-3850 **Smith** Denise L '84
(330) 296-3434 **Stephens** Craig M '74
(330) 297-3850 **Stuck** Michele A '94
(330) 297-0881 **Szymanski** Joseph '90
(330) 296-3804 **Thomas** Timothy R '77
(330) 297-3850 **Vigluicci** Victor V '77
(330) 296-8000 **Weisenburger** Dan J '81
(330) 296-9642 **Wilson** Stephen M '79
(330) 298-4444 **Young** David A '95
(330) 296-8133 **Zavinski** Dennis M '74
(330) 297-2307 **Zawadski** Thaddeus F '75

RAYMOND
Union County

(937) 309-9297 **Duell** Mark E '94
(937) 645-8693 **Luang** Hsin-Wei '04
(937) 645-1973 **Millard** Christen M '97
(937) 645-6001 **Perin** Douglas E '89

READING
Hamilton County

(513) 769-9396 **Bernard** Christopher J '91
(513) 554-1868 **Gertz** Anthony J '72
(513) 554-1868 **Gertz** Anthony J II '02
(513) 554-1868 **Gertz** Susan M '95

REMINDERVILLE
Portage County

Thal Michael L '65

REYNOLDSBURG
Franklin County

(614) 868-0009 **Allen** Anthony J '89
(614) 866-9999 **Arbuckle** Charles H '90
(614) 866-6593 **Baer** Christopher J '82
(614) 644-2489 **Bally** James P '61
(614) 751-8611 **Berlin** Lawrence A '70
(614) 644-2613 **Brant** John W '77
(614) 863-0018 **Brusk** Norman '92
(614) 863-0018 **Brusk** Susan P '92
(614) 501-1460 **Carmany** Margaret R '89
Chasteen Kathleen C '02
(614) 863-4775 **Cochran** Shirley A '79
(614) 759-7100 **Corban** William V '71
Cox John M Jr. '78
(614) 864-8210 **D'Amico** Jodelle M '83
(614) 866-9999 **Derksen** Tina M '02
Dobbs Melvin Keith '71
(614) 868-0009 **Ebbeskotte** Mark J '89
Eckels Christopher R '95
(614) 866-9327 **Eichenberger** Raymond L III '80
(614) 728-6430 **Esselburne** Peter C '75
(614) 864-8210 **Friedman** Alan P '76
(614) 575-1145 **Gallutia** Christopher A '85
(614) 868-0009 **Hallowes Allen & Haynes**
(614) 868-0009 **Hallowes** Donald B '89
(614) 864-5600 **Hardgrove** James A '78
(614) 868-0009 **Haynes** Samuel S '92
Himes Steven C '98
(614) 466-0211 **Hix** John H Jr. '70
(614) 728-6430 **Hopper** William A Jr. '75
(614) 866-9154 **Koehler** Mark W '93
(614) 782-8727 **Leber** William E '75
(614) 866-5051 **Lepp** Michael '74
(614) 864-1117 **Lord** Richard E '79
Milliken Christopher M '86
(614) 644-2489 **Mull** Sharon A '91
(614) 644-2489 **Panzera** Dominic A Jr. '91
(614) 644-2489 **Patitsas** Peter D '86
(614) 577-9898 **Pinder** Dora P '89
(614) 864-5600 **Plank** Rhett A '82
(614) 728-3300 **Pursley** Gerald L '78
(614) 863-9470 **Reynolds** Cristyn G '92
(614) 863-6333 **Rogers** James T '68
(614) 866-1195 **Roth** Kelleen A '95
(614) 866-1195 **Roth** Matthew R '90
(614) 475-0911 **Rovito** Joel R '94
(614) 863-1369 **Sain** George R '98
(614) 864-8210 **Sanders** Robert M '68
(614) 644-2489 **Sarris** Michael J '84
(614) 866-1195 **Shannon** Kevin C '92
(614) 866-4025 **Sigall** Leonard S '59
(614) 577-1050 **Southern** James E '93
(614) 868-0009 **Spears** Jessica L '04
(614) 864-1054 **Stewart** John Douglas '79

(614) 864-5292 **Stobbs** Brent C '89
(614) 866-4025 **Stone** Deborah J '96
(614) 866-4025 **Stone** Steven D '96
(614) 332-1632 **Strawser** Eric J '00
(614) 866-1492 **Swope** Kristy J '86
(614) 866-1492 **Swope** Richard F '56
(614) 866-1436 **Thompson** James C '61
(614) 752-8200 **Thompson** Timothy C '93
(614) 728-6335 **Tiell** Jennifer R '77
(614) 866-1195 **Underwood** William F Jr. '74
Willer Glenn P '98

RICHFIELD
Summit County

(330) 659-3142 **Buser** Daniel C '88
(330) 659-5842 **Carpinelli** Ralph R '66
(330) 908-4429 **Elsmore** Venetia M '95
(330) 659-8900 **Inama** Tanya M '01
(330) 659-0416 **Lucas** Robert A '76
(330) 659-3296 **Lyons** Michael K '85
(330) 908-4512 **Mayland** Gail B '92
(330) 908-4149 **Morgan** Richard A '01
(330) 659-8900 **Moroney** Michael J '85
(330) 659-1690 **Musacchia** Jacqueline A '88
(330) 908-4276 **Rudolph** Jennifer L '98
(330) 659-8900 **Sandel** Kevin S '95
(330) 463-5024 **Siwik** Lori L '87
(330) 463-5000 **Siwik** Mark R '88
(330) 463-5000 **Talley** Douglas L '84
(330) 659-2578 **Thomas-Boehnlein** Karen M '91
(330) 659-2519 **Todaro** David M '03
(330) 659-8900 **Varcho** Raymond A '85

RICHMOND
Jefferson County

(740) 282-3019 **Reed** William E II '76

RICHMOND HEIGHTS
Cuyahoga County

(440) 446-5769 **Cherosky** Michael R '00
(440) 446-3078 **Crane** Roderick J '83
(216) 382-9109 **Dawson** James G '79
(216) 797-8780 **Fishman** Martin A '68
(216) 382-9950 **Granito** Michael B '84
(440) 603-5339 **Kienzl** William P '83
(216) 692-3312 **Kronenberg** Janet L '79
(216) 692-0577 **Lipold** Albin '55
(216) 261-2800 **Macauda** Vincent '91
(440) 461-8500 **Parker** Jason P '99
(440) 603-0066 **Richlak** James D '73
(440) 461-8500 **Rosalina** Gabriella M '98
(440) 461-8500 **Rosalina** Joseph K '01
(440) 461-8500 **Russo** Basil M '72
(216) 692-2227 **Spiccia** John C '84
(440) 461-8500 **Svec** Matthew J '00
(216) 381-2441 **Van Dyke** Anthony P '72
(216) 473-8783 **Weiss** Lita L '78
Wertheim Walter R '63

RICHWOOD
Union County

(740) 943-2325 **Evans Evans & Hoffman,LLP**
(740) 943-2325 **Evans** Jeffrey L '81
(740) 943-2325 **Evans** Robert E Jr. '55
(740) 943-2325 **Hoffman** Scott L '96
(740) 943-3739 **Holtschulte** Jeffery M '85

RIPLEY
Brown County

(937) 392-4371 **Grimes** David E '96
(937) 392-4371 **Pfeffer** Michael S '73

RITTMAN
Wayne County

(330) 925-9080 **Beaumont** Lynn A '72
(330) 927-5100 **Bower** George K '76
(330) 925-9010 **Clark** Mark C '74
(330) 925-9010 **Flynn** Thomas T '69
(330) 925-1010 **Landers** William D '91
(330) 927-3120 **Winchell** V Lee '77

ROCKBRIDGE
Hocking County

(740) 969-1101 **Moses** Frederick T '02
(740) 969-3171 **Moses** Robert P '70

ROCKY RIVER
Cuyahoga County

(440) 356-0373 **Adrain-Piccorelli** Suzanne H '86
(440) 356-1345 **Allen** Thomas E '54
(440) 331-0599 **Annandale** Melinda J '91
(440) 356-0838 **Aragones** Neil F '95
(440) 356-4604 **Barrett** Mary C '90
(440) 331-8850 **Batal** Susan E '82
(440) 895-9700 **Battle** Colleen P '86
(440) 895-9700 **Battle & Miller PLL**
(440) 331-0200 **Beebe** Linda G '82
Bennett Michael J '88
(440) 333-9270 **Biggins** Brian P '96
(440) 333-3386 **Blaha** Keith E '86
(440) 333-8960 **Bostwick** John M Jr. '86
(440) 333-5991 **Brumbaugh** Marian C '83
(440) 331-2478 **Caputo** Diane J '80
(440) 333-5700 **Ciocco** Mary B '94
(440) 331-8844 **Cleary** Edward F '88
(440) 333-0031 **Cook** David J '58
(440) 356-7255 **Cooper** Julianne B '98
(440) 356-6380 **Corso** Joseph J '61
(440) 895-1811 **Cowan** Elmer G Jr. '52
(440) 331-9599 **Cummings** David A '94
(440) 356-7456 **Davis** Robert S '83
(440) 356-5056 **Deese** James L '80
(440) 333-3708 **Delay** Brendan E '86
(440) 333-2508 **Distin** John H '90
Doan Amy Ingham '03
(440) 331-1010 **Dowling** Jerome E '82
(440) 356-7255 **Drain** Joseph A '82
Dreher Joseph M '80
(440) 331-3191 **Dunson** James A Jr. '79
(440) 331-3191 **Dunson** Richard W '88
(440) 895-9700 **Ellis** James W III '00
(440) 331-0801 **Farah** Benjamin F '81
Farley Nicole Hatem '03
(440) 333-8118 **Ferenczy-Furry** Deborah S '95
(440) 333-2755 **Flanagan** Patrick M '73
(440) 333-8119 **Foliano** Carrie A '89
(440) 333-1617 **Gallagher** Mary C '85
(440) 356-2828 **Ganor** Stacey M '99
(440) 333-9800 **Gorski** Pamela L '92
(440) 356-7255 **Grady** Francis X '84
(440) 895-0062 **Gravens** Maureen A '79
(440) 331-3949 **Gray** Susan M '93
Hahn Lesley W '77
(440) 228-3010 **Hart** Robert D '63
(440) 356-9108 **Harvey** Michael P '87
(440) 356-9991 **Havemann** Justin W '99
(440) 331-0108 **Hejra** Mary L '77
(440) 331-4660 **Herthneck** Richard E '73
Hoffman Linda G '89
(440) 403-0628 **Honohan** Michael T '61
(440) 356-2376 **Johnson** Christopher A '78
Joliet Amy Hathaway '03
(440) 333-9150 **Jones** Vickie L '99
(440) 331-8683 **Kadlec** Georgia M '89
(440) 333-1956 **Kanally** John E Jr. '72
(440) 895-9543 **Kelley** John J III '93
(440) 333-0637 **Kelly** Karen M '85
(440) 333-8960 **Kenneally** Sean M '98
(440) 333-8960 **Kenneally** Terrence J '78
(440) 333-3949 **Kennedy** Edwin A '56
(440) 356-5775 **Keshock** John P '89
(440) 333-0099 **Klima** Gregory K '86
(440) 356-9984 **Klima** Ronald E '76
Kranz Claire E '78
(440) 333-9270 **Kutsko** Douglas A '97
(440) 333-9000 **Lampus** Robert W '73
(440) 895-0041 **Larrick-Serrat** Kelly Ann '81
(440) 333-1445 **Lazzaro** Lynn A '75
(440) 356-1219 **Lehnowsky** Judith A '84
(440) 333-0011 **Lindon** Elizabeth A '99
(440) 333-0011 **Lindon** James Lee '97
(440) 331-2245 **Louth** Richard P '73
(440) 356-5775 **Manning** Anthony L '89
(440) 333-8603 **Markstrom** Paul F Jr. '72
Matyjasik Robert E '81
(440) 356-1650 **McDermott** John M '71
(216) 509-0140 **McDonough** Brian M '00
(440) 356-8050 **McDougal** Larry E '85
(440) 221-7238 **McDowell** James M '58
(440) 333-1277 **McNally** Thomas G '78
(440) 331-2328 **McQuillan** Jean M '80
(440) 356-2828 **Milano** Jerome A '81
(440) 895-9700 **Miller** Sharon L '91
(440) 333-5700 **Mills** Charles E '80
(440) 333-5700 **Mills** Ronald H '72
(440) 356-1650 **Monjot** James A '72
Moroney John K '80
Murphy Lynn G '95
(440) 895-9970 **Murphy** Michael H '94
(440) 331-9998 **Nagy** James E '91
(440) 781-8440 **Nixon** Patrick R '81
Papajcik Daniel A '04
Parrish Justin P '94
(440) 333-1445 **Pavlik** Lisa A '02
(440) 331-2127 **Pempus** Eric O '86
(440) 331-1850 **Percio** Joseph M '75
Pietrangelo Wendy D '95
(440) 333-7704 **Portmann** Richard W '50
(440) 356-7255 **Puglise** Scott M '00
(440) 331-5883 **Purcell** Kevin '81
(440) 331-5532 **Putka** Andrew C '52
(440) 356-0775 **Ramos** Edgar A '77
Rhein Clyde K '49
Romell William C '61
Ryan John D '66
(440) 895-5000 **Schill** William T '95
Schnalcer Theresa '02
(440) 333-1000 **Seelie** John F '68
(440) 331-8850 **Shalala** Edna C '52
(440) 331-2505 **Shepherd** John E '61
(440) 333-5370 **Simon** Charles T '77
(440) 333-0106 **Skillen** Richard Jr. '61
(440) 333-0653 **Skoch** Gerald '84
(440) 356-1910 **Skonce** Ralph T Jr. '79
(440) 895-4000 **Snyder** William F '50
Staub Stacey S '90
(440) 895-5000 **Streeter** David A Jr. '01
(440) 356-4165 **Sulin** Alton G '82
(440) 333-1333 **Taft** Homer S Jr. '70
(440) 331-1053 **Talbert** Richard C '65
(440) 356-9400 **Talty** Patrick E '87
(440) 331-4441 **Taylor** Timothy A '70
(440) 331-3410 **Teater** Christopher C '84
(440) 895-3511 **Telzrow** William J III '84
(440) 333-8153 **Tenwick** Thomas J '72
(440) 331-8026 **Thompson** Gregory L '00
(440) 331-8026 **Thompson** Rebecca A '99
(440) 333-0066 **Valponi** Barbara D '79
(440) 333-2572 **VanRooy** Mark J '91
(440) 333-2211 **Wagner** Paul C Jr. '54
(440) 331-1010 **Wall** Philip J '56
(440) 356-2828 **Weiser** Rachel E '98
(440) 331-1142 **Weston** William G Jr. '84
Wilcox Darlene A '98
(440) 610-4443 **Wills** Wendy I '83
(440) 356-2631 **Wojton-Grisanti** Francine J '94
(440) 356-4980 **Zapis** Donna M '88

ROME
Ashtabula County

(440) 563-4444 **Winer** Jonathan W '87

ROOTSTOWN
Portage County

(330) 325-1624 **Coffman** Brian L '98
(330) 325-1145 **Murdock** Chad E '91
(330) 325-1790 **Sabarese** Sharon A '89
(330) 325-2511 **Schimer** Maria R '84

ROSSFORD
Wood County

(419) 661-0800 **Burns** Brian P '94
(419) 666-6188 **Crosser** Joan M '93
(419) 662-9200 **Doss** Cynthia A '02
(419) 662-3100 **Galernik** Gerald E '89
(419) 662-3100 **Galernik** Melissa M '03
Gluckin Susan E '96
(419) 662-3100 **Heban** Kevin A '85
(419) 662-3113 **Meyer** Stephen A '91
(419) 666-3116 **Paterson** David G '82
(419) 666-5215 **Portnoy** Michael D '88
Schlageter Derek C '01

RUSHSYLVANIA
Logan County

(937) 468-9921 **Core** Anthony E '90

RUSSELL
Geauga County

(440) 336-0720 **Dangelo** Kathleen B '90

RUSSELL TOWNSHIP
Cuyahoga County

(440) 338-3097 **Langer** Warren D '53

SAGAMORE HILLS
Summit County

Arceci Richard M '81
(330) 908-0229 **Forrestal** Timothy J '93
(330) 468-4984 **Furber** Philip C '75
(330) 468-5303 **Goldberg** Mitchell B '68
(330) 468-0483 **Peters** Saundra L '85
(330) 467-9600 **Snell** Jeffrey J '88
(330) 468-0599 **Tuzi** Louis A '56
(330) 467-3575 **Utley** Sue E '70

SAINT CLAIRSVILLE
Belmont County

(740) 695-2929 **Barnes** David L '58
(740) 695-9202 **Barr** Jason '04
(740) 695-0532 **Bean** Charles H '72
(740) 695-1444 **Bench** Rebecca L '02
(740) 695-4821 **Burech** Stanley G '69
(740) 695-1327 **Busic** Amy L '99
(740) 695-0371 **Costine** Eric N '85
(740) 695-0371 **Costine** John O '51
(740) 695-4821 **Crow** Donna L '90
(740) 695-0114 **Dolan** Richard E '80
(740) 695-1444 **Duff** Gerald P '71
(740) 695-1444 **Estadt** John R '83
(740) 695-4412 **Fry** Daniel P '79
(740) 695-0532 **Glick** Elizabeth L '88
(740) 695-1444 **Hanlon Duff Estadt & McCormick Co,LPA**
(740) 695-1444 **Hanlon** Lodge L '58
(740) 695-9202 **Harper & Hazlett**
(740) 695-9202 **Harper** Marlin J '75
(740) 695-9202 **Hazlett** Thomas M '77
(740) 695-4817 **Hinzey** Gregory W '78
(740) 695-5866 **Kigerl** Jack J '74
(740) 695-1444 **McCormick** Michael P '89
(740) 695-1350 **Myers** Thomas M '80
(740) 695-5263 **Nicholson** James L '74
(740) 695-4331 **Nicholoff** Sandra L '95
(740) 695-5034 **Paleudis** John G '73
(740) 695-4412 **Pierce** George F '76
(740) 695-4412 **Quirk** Robert W '75
(740) 695-1444 **Schramm** Erik A '99
(740) 695-4448 **Shaheen** Michael J '89
(740) 695-4448 **Skorich** Elaine L '98
(740) 695-9335 **Thomas** Mark A '87
(740) 695-5263 **Thompson** Kirk M '81
(740) 695-0532 **Thornburg Bean & Glick**
(740) 695-8347 **Tomlan** John R '83
(740) 695-9202 **Trouten** David S Jr. '93
(740) 695-4331 **Vavra** John A '83
(740) 695-8987 **Verba** Steven J '92
(740) 695-4412 **Yonak** Helen '95

SAINT LOUISVILLE
Licking County

Adkins Stuart A '92

SAINT MARYS
Auglaize County

(419) 394-7432 **Hitchen** Kenneth E '71
(419) 394-7270 **Huber** William E '68
(419) 394-3341 **Kemp** Barrett G '59
(419) 394-2516 **Kuffner** John F '55
(419) 394-7441 **Montague** Eldon E '49
(419) 394-7441 **Moul** John F '69
(419) 394-7441 **Noble** Edward S '47
(419) 394-7441 **Noble** Kraig E '74
(419) 394-7441 **Noble Montague & Moul**
(419) 394-2516 **Pierce** Edwin A '80
(419) 394-7441 **Squire** Jeffrey P '93
(419) 394-2323 **Wilson** Eric J '93
(419) 394-2323 **Wilson** Gregory D '69

SAINT PARIS
Champaign County

Anderson Gerald L '77

SALEM
Columbiana County

(330) 337-6624 **Apple** Kenneth B '87
(330) 337-8761 **Barry** Timothy A '87
(330) 337-9173 **Bowman** Scott M '92
(330) 337-8761 **Cecil** Larry G '72
(330) 337-6586 **Conn** Harry R '73
Duff David W '74
(330) 337-8761 **Fitch Kendall Cecil Robinson & Barry**
(330) 222-4315 **Gamble** John E '89
(330) 337-9529 **Goll** Geoffrey S '73
(330) 337-9515 **Gorby** Jennifer A '01
(330) 337-8235 **Guehl** Robert L '73
(330) 337-6586 **Harrington Hoppe & Mitchell, Ltd**
(330) 337-7622 **Humphrey** Don W Jr. '77
(330) 337-9515 **Kirkland** Samuel Lee '85
(330) 337-7934 **Macala** Brian J '92
(330) 337-9587 **Miller** Earl R '52
(330) 337-9578 **Naragon** Frederic E '71
(330) 332-0852 **Plummer** Barbara J '85
(330) 337-9515 **Rice-Bartlett** Kathleen J '94
(330) 337-8761 **Robinson** Ian '79
(330) 337-8761 **Robinson** Whitman '03
(330) 337-3105 **Schiller** Royal A '73
(330) 337-3769 **Schory** Earl A II '75
(330) 332-8101 **Slack** Mark R '83
(330) 332-4147 **Tolson** Theresa T '97
(330) 337-3253 **Williams** Charles B '83
(330) 337-9515 **Yeagley Kirkland & Bartlett**
(330) 337-4820 **Zellers** Christopher B '93

SALINEVILLE
Columbiana County

(330) 679-2328 **Hull** Rick L '81

SANDUSKY
Erie County

(800) 224-7914 **Anderson** Carl W '90
(419) 626-3712 **Bacon** John O '75
(419) 625-6740 **Bailey** Kenneth R '83
(419) 627-0414 **Ball** John R '88
(419) 624-3000 **Bartle** William H '75
(419) 627-7697 **Barylski** Mary A '87
(419) 627-7697 **Baxter** Kevin J '82
(419) 624-3000 **Bechtel** Steven C '83
(419) 626-3800 **Boehk** Robert P '85
(419) 626-3800 **Bogden** Kenneth E '78
(419) 627-7774 **Bower** Mary M '86
(419) 626-3241 **Boyd** Melanie S '87
(419) 621-9214 **Brady** Daniel J '74
(419) 627-0414 **Buckingham Lucal McGookey & Zeiher Co, LPA**
(419) 625-7770 **Calhoun Kademenos Heichel & Childress Co,LPA**
(419) 609-0143 **Carman** Heather L '00
(419) 627-8075 **Chapman** Benjamin M '79
(419) 627-0414 **Claus** David J '99
(419) 627-7782 **Croteau** Bruce R '87
(419) 609-1311 **Cuneo** Richard P '98
(419) 433-5006 **Demmitt** Denise M '00
(419) 627-6207 **Dempsey** Timothy H '81
(419) 627-1371 **Deville** Patrick L '80
Duncan Lane S '02
(419) 626-3800 **Dusza** Thomas M '90
(419) 624-3000 **Earle** Vicki L '01
(419) 625-3957 **Eaton** Melissa L '93
(419) 626-3871 **Egger** Robert C '70
(419) 624-3000 **Evans** Donna Jean A '00
(419) 625-5901 **Evans** George M '94
(419) 626-3800 **Fantozzi** Joseph M '04
Feiszli William J '87
(419) 626-3800 **Ferber** Gary S '77
(419) 625-8324 **Flynn Py & Kruse,LPA**
(419) 627-0414 **Frankel** John D '75
(419) 624-8133 **Fritz-Gasteier** Linda M '93
(419) 626-8630 **Galloway** Duane L '77
(419) 627-5851 **Gast-King** Lynne A '90
(419) 626-6781 **Ghezzi** Karen B '89
(419) 624-1501 **Giesler** E Ann S '77
(419) 624-3000 **Goldsmith** Sylvia M '95
(419) 627-7697 **Goodrum** Cheryl Y '95
(419) 627-7697 **Griffith** Terry R '88
(419) 609-5000 **Gross** Gerhard R '00
(419) 609-5000 **Gross** Mark R '95
Gross Pamela A '97
(419) 626-0055 **Grubbe** Richard E '65
(419) 625-8324 **Hart** James W '81
(419) 627-7697 **Hayberger** Trevor M '02
(419) 609-1311 **Heebsh** Philip S '02
(419) 625-8324 **Hill** Mary J '84
(419) 625-7770 **Hines** Adrienne M '96
(419) 627-5851 **Icsman** Donald C '81
(419) 624-6882 **Jennings** Nancy L '04
(419) 626-6669 **Kaufman** Michael D '98
(419) 626-6669 **Kaufman** Ronald G '66
(419) 625-8735 **Kellam** James R '68
(419) 625-7377 **Kelsey** Robert T '82
(419) 626-1917 **Kirwan** John F '71
(419) 626-1681 **Koch** Richard D '80
(419) 626-3241 **Lawson** Michael J '87
(419) 625-3672 **Lehrer** John W '40
(419) 627-7696 **Lickfelt** Gary A '73
(419) 627-7697 **Lippert** Jeanne '92
(419) 499-8308 **Longo** David J '86
(800) 224-7914 **Longton** Erik W '01
(419) 627-0414 **Lucal** Dean S '62
(419) 627-0400 **Lucas** Thomas R '00
(419) 609-7000 **Lynch** Kula H '98
(419) 625-8324 **Marinko** Christopher M '88
(419) 627-0414 **McDermond** Maurice L Jr. '71
(419) 627-0414 **McGookey** Daniel L '79
(419) 625-4121 **McGookey** James E '75
(419) 627-7782 **McGory** Gregory S '96
(419) 626-0055 **McGory** Peter J '73
(419) 626-4700 **Miles** Gaye H '86
(419) 627-0414 **Milkie** Duffield E '91
(419) 626-0055 **Moir** Linda Tucker '87
(419) 626-3323 **Moore** Robert M '84
(419) 609-1311 **Moracz** Donald J '91
(419) 624-3000 **Moriarty** Mary M '00
(419) 627-6620 **Morris** Michael P '97
(419) 626-3323 **Muehlhauser** Eric M '93
(419) 626-3323 **Muehlhauser** George M III '55
(419) 626-3323 **Muehlhauser & Moore**
(419) 609-1311 **Mullin** Jeanne M '99
(419) 609-1311 **Murphy** Michael P '96
(419) 624-3000 **Murray** Charles M '91
(419) 624-3000 **Murray** Dennis E Jr. '87
(419) 624-3000 **Murray** Dennis E Sr. '64
(419) 624-3000 **Murray** James L '97
(419) 624-3000 **Murray** James T '65
(419) 624-3000 **Murray** John T '79
(419) 624-3000 **Murray** Margaret M '96
(419) 624-3000 **Murray** Michael T '70
(419) 624-3000 **Murray** Thomas J Jr. '65
(419) 624-3000 **Murray** William P '65
(419) 609-9207 **Nath** Michael J '76
(419) 627-5920 **O'Brien** Erich J '79
(419) 627-6674 **Ogden-Dellisanti** Nancy L '89
(419) 625-5901 **Oglesby** Lurlia A '84
(419) 624-3000 **O'Neill** Mary S '97
(419) 627-7697 **Palmer** Vicki R '79
(800) 224-7914 **Parish** Elinor G '90
(419) 625-8324 **Py** John D '73
(419) 626-3323 **Quinn** Patrick J '83
Ramsey Donald L '75

(419) 609-1311 **Reminger & Reminger**
(419) 627-0400 **Rengel** D Jeffery '82
(419) 626-3800 **Reno Bogden & Ferber Co,LPA**
(419) 626-3800 **Reno** Robert M '76
(419) 626-1915 **Rhode** Edward W III '80
(419) 625-0536 **Rice** Pamela D '97
(419) 625-8324 **Rosino** John E '77
(419) 625-3672 **Saferstein** Melvin A '86
(419) 609-1311 **Sammon** James P '94
(419) 625-0536 **See** Daniel E '81
(419) 627-8075 **Sipe** David Lee '73
(419) 624-3000 **Smith** Barbara Q '91
(419) 625-0536 **Smith** C Ross III '78
(419) 625-3672 **Smith & Lehrer,LPA**
(419) 626-0055 **Smith** Michele A '97
(419) 625-3672 **Smith** William H Jr. '69
(419) 621-7999 **Sprunk** Thomas R '97
(419) 626-0728 **Stacey** James A '52
(419) 624-6369 **Stallkamp** Christopher A '97
(419) 625-0536 **Stark** Roger S '01
(419) 625-8324 **Stauffer** Melvyn J '51
(419) 625-8324 **Steuk** William C '66
(419) 625-8324 **Steuk** William R '96
(419) 627-7723 **Stuckey** Mark A '85
(419) 627-6620 **Tandon** Harsh '99
(419) 624-3000 **Timmerberg** James S '97
(419) 626-0055 **Tone Grubbe McGory & Vermeeren**
(419) 626-0055 **Tone** Tygh M '89
(419) 625-4010 **Van Tine** Linda R '92
(419) 626-0055 **Vermeeren** Barry W '75
(419) 627-0414 **Waldock** Frederick D '54
(419) 627-7697 **Walsh** Katherine H '76
(419) 627-2087 **Webb** Rush P '59
(419) 627-6620 **Whitacre** Jeffrey J '88
(419) 625-6778 **Wilber** Elizabeth F '02
(419) 627-0414 **Wisehart** Troy D '91
(419) 626-2939 **Wood** Deborah L '88
(419) 627-0414 **Zeiher** Kevin J '77
(419) 625-6955 **Zelvy** Robert '69

SARDINIA
Brown County
(937) 446-2523 **Taylor** David J '96

SEBRING
Mahoning County
(330) 938-2161 **Cardinal** Kenneth J '74

SEVEN HILLS
Cuyahoga County
(216) 642-2273 **Bleisch** N D '98
(216) 524-9007 **Boulas** James E '98
(216) 520-1345 **Burkhart** Robert C '98
Carolin Thomas M '77
(216) 642-9969 **Curtis** Scott D '93
(216) 447-8500 **Dell'Aquilla** Richard P '78
(216) 642-5353 **DiChiro** Patrick '89
(216) 524-6207 **Koloda** Richard J '98
(216) 642-0931 **Miller** Stephen C '93
Naticchia Alfred D '86
(216) 520-0077 **Sacha** Laura J '97
(216) 447-0500 **Stachewicz** Gerald R '79
(216) 369-0100 **Tobin** Christine M '82

SEVILLE
Medina County
(330) 769-4544 **Doty** Joseph E '98
(330) 769-4470 **Noderer** Eric W '94

SHADYSIDE
Belmont County
(740) 676-6503 **Melanko** Richard E '74
(740) 671-9300 **Ryncarz** Thomas M '95

SHAKER HEIGHTS
Cuyahoga County
(216) 991-0731 **Adams** Craig A '85
(216) 932-9302 **Arrington** Curtis R '76
(216) 371-1154 **Bain** Jeffrey M '77
(216) 471-6900 **Banker** Amanda M '04
(216) 561-8999 **Baylog** Richard L '54
(216) 491-8446 **Bean** Marva J '87
Berman Paul B '80
(216) 751-6214 **Branagan** James J '68
(216) 991-4236 **Breidenbach** Paul C '49
(216) 991-5391 **Brenneman** Kathryn R '84
(216) 752-9930 **Brindza** Robert A II '89
(216) 932-1930 **Bulloff** Frances W '78
(216) 491-1381 **Byrne** Cornelia A '75
(216) 751-1490 **Caterino** Bartholomew M '61
(216) 426-0890 **Character** Dea L '89
(216) 426-0890 **Character-Johnson** Darla M '95
Childs Ishmael C '56
Clark Jill G '79
(216) 751-5546 **Cochran** Edward W '76
(216) 991-6200 **Coghlan** Owen Scott '92
(216) 752-4286 **Cone** Sanford A '61
(216) 299-2451 **Cord** Daniel A '04
(216) 752-9341 **Cox** Marion N '89
(216) 595-9225 **Cydulka** Michele L '85
(216) 991-0800 **Derrick** William A Jr. '69
(216) 650-2038 **Dori** Aryeh I '03
Durham Mary L '78
(216) 991-2295 **Edison** Glenn '83
(216) 921-0964 **Farmer** Constance G '84
(216) 991-6200 **Firstenberg** Barbara A '81
(216) 991-6200 **Foote** Richard C '76
(216) 991-8325 **Foster** Ivan V '76
(216) 295-2428 **Friedman** Sydney S '50
(216) 283-2323 **Gardner** Michael B '93
(216) 295-9394 **Gerhart** Ann T '72
(216) 496-3312 **Gleisser** Brian S '88
(216) 921-7589 **Gobel** John H '76
Goldstein Dana Ann '83
(216) 292-6592 **Greenslade** Victor F Jr. '53
Griswold Jane W '75
(216) 991-6200 **Gross** Robert E '79
(216) 491-1646 **Groves** Gregory '80
(216) 371-3570 **Gruber** William M Ondrey '82
(216) 595-0740 **Habat** John L '83
(216) 991-6200 **Hahn** Joseph A '95
(216) 991-3940 **Harkins** James L Jr. '54
(216) 292-8201 **Havighurst** Alan W '77
(216) 991-5560 **Hecht** Emanuel H '41
(216) 464-5383 **Heffernan** Thomas A '64
(216) 991-6200 **Hoffman** Mark L '76
(216) 751-7879 **Horvath** Theodore J '52
(216) 751-1490 **Hulett** W Michael '03
(216) 932-2800 **Jackson** Gary B '96
(216) 752-8000 **Jackson** Gerald M '72
(216) 991-1100 **Jacob** Richard K '71
(216) 921-9314 **Joseph** Jane E '02
Kaplan William '67
(216) 360-0479 **Katz** Richard B '77
(216) 752-1022 **Kelly** Michael F '78
(216) 752-1022 **Kenneweg** William W '70
(216) 896-9091 **Kidder** Stephen J '91
(216) 752-3590 **Killian** Karen L '97
(216) 561-6111 **Klein** Jonathan I '80
Koenemann Lynda '02
Lanzy Patricia A '01
(216) 752-1488 **Lester** Esther O '89
(216) 464-5778 **Levin** Paul F '74
(216) 561-4437 **Lewis** Robert J '50
(216) 443-4947 **Loeb** Lawrence R '72
(216) 921-7878 **Lurie** Elana Turoff '92
Lyren Philip S '93
(216) 283-5575 **Manuszak** Michael J '77
(216) 751-6000 **McCary** Renee D '83
(216) 283-4385 **McCord** Michael B '84
(216) 921-8718 **McDonald** Craig D '80
(216) 831-4884 **Melamed** Alan L '76
Merritt Diana B '97
(216) 752-3330 **Misra** Anand N '97
(216) 491-1442 **Montgomery** K J '77
(216) 421-8400 **Montlack** Kirt A '92
Moses Barry W '81
(216) 752-6965 **Nelson** Delos T '48
(216) 767-1361 **Neubert** William T '79
(216) 389-0079 **O'Connell** Martin James '03
(216) 751-9529 **Paley** Rochelle L '89
(216) 292-2711 **Polster** Dorothea M '88
(216) 991-3646 **Relic** Marianne D '78
(216) 491-1323 **Resnick** Lois S '82
(216) 291-9215 **Roe** Carol A '91
(216) 991-8880 **Rosch** Winn L '83
Rose Dora '04
(216) 491-1317 **Rosett** Wendy Sue '91
Roth Carole A '78
(216) 561-7419 **Roth** Laddie J '50
(216) 577-0166 **Saunders** James D '97
(216) 561-3278 **Schloss** John P '89
(216) 491-0161 **Seballos** Sandra K '86
(216) 283-2309 **Sgro** Valentina '80
(216) 991-6200 **Shibley** Cathy M '82
(216) 752-7400 **Sin** Nancy P '96
(216) 752-4200 **Sprague** Madelon '78
(216) 577-5021 **Stratman** John W '84
(216) 283-9289 **Thompson** Siobhan R '87
(216) 491-8398 **Toth** Barbara B '86
(216) 561-0566 **Tuffin** Paul J '57
(216) 921-7878 **Turoff** Carole R '70
(216) 292-6757 **Udisky** Warren L '65
(216) 751-0181 **Welsh** Martin J '60
(216) 921-6900 **White** Andrew D '96
(216) 283-8617 **Widder** John M '64
(216) 283-8617 **Widder** Margaret M '86
(216) 831-8139 **Woodling** George V Jr. '66
Yen Dominic F '81
(216) 752-4200 **Zamore** Joseph D '71
(216) 752-4200 **Zamore & Sprague**
Zavelson Andrew P '02
Zavelson Nancy F '91
(216) 991-6914 **Zohn** Patrick M '78
(216) 921-8627 **Zolich** Joseph '70

SHARON CENTER
Medina County
(330) 239-1230 **Brannon** Ellis B '51
Elias Eugene N '94
(330) 239-4480 **Holland** John J '88
(330) 239-4480 **Holland & Muirden**
(330) 239-1230 **Mantkowski** Gary T '82
(330) 239-4480 **Muirden** Marjorie A '89
(330) 334-4053 **Woodall** Forrest W '58

SHARONVILLE
Hamilton County
(513) 956-4620 **Hanket** Mark J '68
(513) 779-0237 **Rubenstein** Jeffrey B '83

SHEFFIELD LAKE
Lorain County
Jancura Diana D '98
(440) 949-5425 **Levin** Arnold S '34
(440) 949-1500 **Papandreas** George J '86

SHEFFIELD VILLAGE
Lorain County
(440) 930-4001 **Alderman** Larry D '75
(440) 930-4001 **Baumgartner** Charles E '73
(440) 930-4001 **Baumgartner & O'Toole**
(440) 930-4001 **Baumgartner** Todd C '02
(440) 930-4001 **Bond** Stephen P '76
(440) 930-4001 **Carlson** Frank S '74
(440) 930-4001 **Clark** Jonathan D '93
(440) 930-4001 **Coey** Laurent E '73
(440) 930-4001 **Hartung** Susan R '03
(440) 930-4001 **Keating** Susan E '02
(440) 934-3590 **Kolczun** Lee S '74
(440) 930-4001 **Lieberman** Abraham '76
(440) 930-4001 **Loughman** Michael J '73
(440) 930-4001 **Mason** Daniel D '91
(440) 930-4001 **McGlamery** Heidi K '98
(440) 930-4001 **McLaughlin** Russell T '74
(440) 930-4001 **O'Bryon** Margaret A '93
(440) 930-4001 **O'Toole** Dennis M '74
(440) 930-4001 **Pecora** Anthony R '98
(440) 930-4001 **Serazin** Scott F '77
(440) 930-4001 **Stumphauzer** Kenneth S '76
(440) 930-4001 **Warhola** Andrew J Sr. '51

SHELBY
Richland County
(419) 347-4900 **Benham** Frank L III '79
(419) 347-7421 **Depler** Thomas A '75
(419) 342-4261 **Eyster** Gordon M '01
(419) 347-2573 **Howard** David A '85
(419) 342-4261 **McKown** Neil A '78
(419) 347-7421 **Poland Depler & Shepherd,Co,LPA**
(419) 342-4261 **Ream** Jeffrey S '90
(419) 347-7421 **Shepherd** Richard L '77

SHERRODSVILLE
Carroll County
(772) 341-5038 **Burkhart** Sandra Edwards '01
(330) 735-2269 **Richards** Allan R '70

SIDNEY
Shelby County
(937) 497-7222 **Bauer** Ralph A '88
(937) 492-6125 **Beigel** Jeffrey J '86
(937) 492-1271 **Bensman** Daniel A '94
(937) 497-1000 **Blake** Kara M '04
(937) 497-1000 **Blake** Rodney R Jr. '66
(937) 492-6125 **Boller** Michael F '64
(937) 498-7230 **Carter** Gary J '83
(937) 492-4250 **Chrisman** James J '79
(937) 498-4981 **Clinard** Nathan '94
(937) 492-1271 **Deeds** John M '03
(937) 492-6191 **Elsass** Eugene P '57
(937) 492-6191 **Elsass Wallace Evans Schnelle & Co**
(937) 492-6191 **Evans** Stanley R '82
(937) 492-1271 **Faulkner Garmhausen Keister & Shenk, LPA**
(937) 492-1271 **Faulkner** Harry N '66
(937) 492-1271 **Garmhausen** John M '73
(937) 492-6191 **Geise** Steven J '94
(937) 492-6125 **Goettemoeller** Duane A '82
(937) 498-7265 **Guillozet** Melanie E '93
(937) 498-1311 **Hax** Priscilla L '77
(937) 492-6125 **Hegemann** Heath H '93
(937) 492-1271 **Keister** Ralph F '67
(937) 492-6125 **Kerrigan Boller Stevenson Goettemoeler & Biegel**
(937) 492-6125 **Kerrigan** Thomas W II '84
(937) 492-1271 **Koltak** Joshua A '04
(937) 492-1271 **Lang** William E Jr. '59
(937) 492-6125 **Leistner** Ann K '00
(937) 498-8119 **Luce** Donald G '76
(937) 498-2108 **May** Kelli E '00
(937) 497-0880 **Mazurowski** Suellen P '83
(937) 492-1271 **Niemeyer** Bryan A '97
(937) 498-4981 **Pertee** Lisa M '02
(937) 492-6191 **Posey** Terry W Jr. '04
(937) 492-1271 **Potts** Thomas J '88
(937) 492-6191 **Pulfer** Anthony R '88
(937) 498-4810 **Richard** Jonathan M '97
(937) 492-6191 **Schnelle** Keith M '81
(937) 492-9191 **Sell** Timothy S '83
(937) 498-3777 **Shannon** Michael K '01
(937) 492-1271 **Shenk** James R '75
(937) 492-4191 **Smith** Michael L '73
(937) 492-5592 **Snavley** James T '91
(937) 492-1271 **Staudt** Michael A '84
(937) 492-6125 **Stevenson** James F '75
(937) 492-6148 **Swinger** Welza L '60
(937) 492-1271 **Thieman** James L '80
(937) 498-8118 **Thieman** Tonya K '81
(937) 492-6101 **Thompson** Daniel K '79
(937) 492-6191 **Turner** Allison Scherger '04
(937) 492-6191 **Wallace** Richard H '75
(937) 492-1969 **Zimmerman** William R '79

SILVER LAKE
Summit County
Mulrooney Aaron L '90

SILVERTON
Hamilton County
(513) 793-7776 **Wang** Charleston C '82

SOLON
Cuyahoga County
(440) 498-4353 **Arnson** Gerald I '65
(440) 349-9000 **Asher** Anthony J '63
(440) 349-0044 **Barrat** Elliott S '86
(440) 542-1324 **Barsham** Kelly J '00
(440) 349-9000 **Basil** Deborah B '80
Bencivengo Mary L '80
(440) 248-7005 **Berman** David L '88
(440) 349-4889 **Bernstein** David J '83
(440) 349-5757 **Besman** Douglas B '90
(440) 577-1738 **Bieganski** Walter R '85
(440) 248-8787 **Bleiweiss** Gary L '81
(440) 349-9000 **Burns** Robert S '85
(440) 349-2712 **Chiarucci** Regina L '90
(440) 349-9966 **Chisling** Stephanie A '97
(440) 248-5010 **Church** Joseph Jeffrey '79
(440) 248-6728 **Condon** Amanda A '00
(440) 248-6728 **Condon** Frederick J '70
(440) 248-5151 **Crawford** James D '74
(440) 349-3813 **Creech** Nancy N '92
(440) 248-8811 **DeMarco** Robert P '69
(440) 498-4000 **DeRoche** James A '91
(440) 505-0040 **Dorer** William R Jr. '78
(440) 498-0070 **Emery** Marlene P '79
(440) 349-5757 **Erdelack** Wayne F '73
(440) 248-6700 **Fouts** Douglas R '75
(440) 914-0287 **Friedman** Susan L '96
(440) 349-3300 **Friedman** Ted S '82
(440) 248-0240 **Ganger** Milton E Jr. '62
(440) 542-1900 **Gerstenslager** William E '77
(440) 498-1911 **Glanz** David S '01
(440) 248-5151 **Glazer** Jeffrey S '71
(440) 498-9010 **Glazer** Neil T '85
(440) 519-9900 **Goldberg** J Michael '90
(440) 519-9900 **Goldberg** Steven M '89
(440) 349-1120 **Gordon** William J Jr. '73
(440) 248-8223 **Grugle** Scott D '95
(440) 349-4938 **Haber** Harry L '70
(440) 914-0400 **Habinski** Amy K '99
(440) 248-8448 **Hallberg** Charles E '77
(216) 521-6556 **Harriston** Michael A '96
(440) 424-0058 **Hicks** Robert C '99
(440) 498-7500 **Hoffmann** Andrew W '75
(440) 349-3301 **Jacob** Harry J III '81
(440) 542-2901 **Kalk** Daniel L '83
(440) 349-3200 **Kaufman** Craig I '81
(440) 349-0388 **Kolt** Jeffrey A '70
(440) 498-8237 **Konkol-Myers** Kim R '85
(440) 542-1307 **Korte** Peter B '93
(440) 248-2027 **Kundtz** John A '58
(440) 498-9510 **Maly** Michael P '92
(440) 248-0135 **Manning** Charles H '91
(440) 248-8873 **Marek** Robert J '69
(440) 248-8844 **Mazanec** David T '76
(440) 349-3300 **Mendelsohn** Richard A '81
(440) 542-1900 **Obert** Lisa M '87
(440) 248-8622 **Pelsozy** Dale F '78
Pelunis Robert N '99
(440) 655-3543 **Petrinovic** Peter A '79
(440) 264-5181 **Pilla** Mary Lee '81
(440) 914-5297 **Podor** Kenneth C '78
(440) 528-0200 **Pollock** Harold '76
(440) 914-5297 **Pyle** Thomas B '00
(440) 248-3363 **Ralls** Nancy E '86
(440) 914-5297 **Reuven** David W '92
(440) 556-4926 **Rosati** Flaviano P '79
(440) 248-8437 **Salada** Bernadette F '86
(440) 914-0400 **Schmidt** Courtney C '99
(440) 498-4120 **Shellito** Christopher J '97
(440) 349-3700 **Snider** Harvey A '61
(440) 519-3500 **Steinbock** Mark A '84
(440) 498-5363 **Thomas** Rita A '91
Townsend Danielle D '03
(440) 349-2110 **Trombetta** I Bernard '63
(440) 542-1330 **Vettel** Louis M '86
(440) 498-2126 **Wainblat** Julia L '92
(440) 914-2000 **Wimbiscus** Denise M '96
(440) 349-5955 **Winik** Jane L '96
(440) 498-9655 **Wolk** Alan M '55
(440) 349-5757 **Wyatt** Jack D '74
(440) 248-4200 **Zilich** George J '04

SOMERSET
Perry County
(740) 743-1669 **Derr** Vicki B '79

SOUTH BLOOMINGVILLE
Hocking County
(740) 332-1352 **Stohs** Daniel J '77

SOUTH CHARLESTON
Clark County
(937) 462-8361 **McAdow** Samuel J '64

SOUTH EUCLID
Cuyahoga County
(216) 691-8472 **Allen** Bruce C '80
(216) 691-8472 **Allen & Hodgman**
(216) 382-8422 **Christie** Edward C '70
(888) 397-9499 **Cweiber** Bruce E '94
(216) 291-9200 **Ginsberg** Melvin R '75
(216) 381-2162 **Gross** Judd H '67
(216) 691-8472 **Hodgman** Blair '78
(216) 691-8888 **Keller** Paul V '92
(216) 382-2394 **Kirn** John J Jr. '71
(216) 691-8472 **Kirshner** Adrienne B '02
(216) 381-2880 **Kleri** Patricia A '76
(216) 926-6305 **Link** David M Jr. '04
(216) 291-1159 **Lograsso** Michael P '92
Martin Rachael J '03
(216) 382-1370 **McKenna** Todd J '84
(216) 297-1040 **Niermann** Dennis J '81
(216) 381-0011 **Nittskoff** David '70
(216) 442-1700 **Patsch** Glenn F '75
(216) 765-0038 **Potash** Loree E '80
(216) 765-0038 **Potash** M. Steven '79
(216) 381-4050 **Robison** Nancy B '79
(216) 397-0111 **Schwartz** Fred P '78
Shaughnessy Michael P '02
Weiner Paul L '82
(216) 382-3666 **Wieder** Michael D '69
Zwick Coleman D '64

SOUTHINGTON
Trumbull County
(330) 898-5680 **Torres** Cindy J '01

SOUTH POINT
Lawrence County
(740) 377-2120 **Payne** James S '94
Zolman Courtney L '99

SOUTH RUSSELL
Cuyahoga County
(440) 338-4150 **Berger** Christopher J '86
(440) 338-8981 **Denney** Jon E '64

SOUTH VIENNA
Clark County
Tackett Natalie J '88

SOUTH WEBSTER
Scioto County
(740) 778-2982 **McHenry** John K '87

SOUTH ZANESVILLE
Muskingum County
(740) 450-9301 **Allen** John R '68
(740) 450-9301 **Baughman** Janice M '97

SPENCERVILLE
Allen County
(419) 647-6671 **Pohlman** James D '79

SPRINGBORO
Warren County
(937) 748-1004 **Brandenburg** Cynthia L '86
(937) 748-9447 **Cornyn** Christopher J '79
(937) 748-2522 **Czechowski** Donna K '89
(937) 748-1004 **D'Amico** Michael J '92
(937) 748-5162 **Eckert & Eckert, Co LPA**
(937) 748-5162 **Eckert** Roger C '91
(937) 748-3838 **Glaser-Atkins** Carol J '84
(937) 748-5162 **Henry** Deborah J '03
Hopper David M '98
(937) 748-9447 **Hughes** Kevin D '95
(937) 748-1749 **Jansing** Debra L '88

(937) 748-5162 **Kane** Sherry L '98
(937) 748-1004 **Kirby** Jeffrey T '88
(937) 748-1004 **Kirby** Joseph W '95
(937) 748-1004 **Kirby** Thomas B Jr. '68
(937) 748-1004 **Kirby & Thomas. LPA**
(937) 748-6700 **Kolb** Stanley E '59
(937) 369-6288 **Lachman** Marshall G '03
(937) 743-4878 **Laurito** Erin M '02
(937) 743-4878 **Laurito** Jeffrey V '73
(937) 748-9155 **Lawson** Eddie Jr. '66
(937) 746-1010 **Mattis** Scott W '81
(937) 746-1010 **May** Kenneth F '78
Mengel Kathryn T '86
(937) 746-1010 **Messer** Steven L '80
(937) 866-6251 **Michaud** Nancy A '80
(937) 746-4997 **Morrow** Edwin P III '98
(937) 746-1010 **Office** James R '82
(937) 746-1010 **Pinales** Ian M '94
(937) 886-1151 **Reiling** Richard B '96
(937) 748-0066 **Sauer** Rena G '95
(937) 748-2409 **Seaman** Edward G '67
(937) 748-2761 **Sharts** John E '74
(937) 748-2522 **Smith** John D '80
Susco Michael E '82
(937) 748-1004 **Thomas** Michael R '81
(937) 885-9860 **Thompson** Thomas L '93
(937) 748-5001 **Thomsen** Ira H '79
(937) 748-4080 **Tschanz** Bryan M '03
(937) 748-1749 **West** Richard E '86

SPRINGDALE

Hamilton County

(513) 246-0034 **Tormey** Randolph T '79

SPRINGFIELD

Clark County

(937) 328-2574 **Anderson** Susan H '82
(937) 323-9783 **Andreoff** Alexander '62
(937) 322-0891 **Angle** Tammi J '94
(937) 327-1700 **Armstrong** Melinda M '04
(937) 324-4566 **Baader** William F '75
(937) 323-6475 **Bailey** Edward G '70
(937) 322-0891 **Barnett** Cynthia S '94
(937) 324-5541 **Barnett** Hugh D '62
(937) 325-8822 **Beals** Scott B '91
Bennett Chad M '03
(937) 322-6611 **Berry** James A '53
(937) 323-8777 **Boblitt** Ronald R '86
(866) 837-8847 **Bonar** Byron K '79
(937) 323-0966 **Borley** Robert L '75
(937) 323-1171 **Brucker** Joseph C '52
Buchanan Leslie S '80
(937) 324-7353 **Burkholder** Andrew J '77
(937) 324-8482 **Busam** Thomas C '98
(937) 322-0891 **Butz** John R '69
Caplinger James L '62
(937) 325-4077 **Carey** Daniel D '91
(937) 328-2435 **Carey** Richard P '83
(937) 328-2575 **Carter** Darnell E '79
(866) 837-8847 **Catanzariti** Frank P '85
(937) 325-2459 **Catanzaro** Michael A '77
(937) 328-2640 **Chavez** Bjorn J '98
(937) 342-1896 **Chu** Jeannette A '04
(937) 322-0891 **Cole Acton Harmon & Dunn**
(937) 324-5541 **Collier** Glenn W '68
Collins Alan E '94
(937) 328-2574 **Collins** Stephen C '90
(937) 324-5541 **Comer** Randall M '00
(937) 328-2640 **Cox** Gregory D '91
(937) 325-3022 **Cushman** Linda J '89
(937) 525-5549 **D'Ambrosi** Bernard Jr. '93
(937) 324-7350 **DeBell** Robin B '78
(937) 864-3000 **Dimitry** Edward S '84
(866) 837-8847 **Dougherty** Kathryn C '92
(937) 323-3705 **Doughty** Jon A '78
(937) 325-7365 **Dressel** Quinton R '83
(937) 322-0891 **Dunn** Edward W '55
(937) 322-0891 **Dunn** Elizabeth J '92
(937) 322-0891 **Dunn** Joseph A '92
(937) 399-9709 **Elder** Andrew H '85
(937) 399-9709 **Elder** John M '68
(937) 399-9709 **Elder** Kenneth M '78
(937) 399-9709 **Elder Roberts & Elder**
(937) 325-7365 **Emerich** John D '64
(937) 325-7365 **Emerich Winks & Peifer**
(937) 323-0093 **Filhart** Eddie L '66
(937) 390-9701 **Fisher** Terry L '85
(937) 323-4004 **Flack** Sanford H '70
(937) 324-6905 **Foley** Margaret L '91
(937) 325-2000 **Geyer** Douglas W '68
(937) 325-7058 **Gorman Veskauf Henson & Wineberg**
(937) 323-7531 **Gould** John E '60
(937) 322-5242 **Griffin** James N '76
(937) 325-1333 **Grinvalds** Edwin A '83
(937) 324-5541 **Groves** William R '79
(937) 327-9370 **Hammond** John R '80
(937) 324-8482 **Harkins** Daniel C '85
(937) 324-5541 **Harley** Robert E '57
(937) 323-9739 **Hasselbach** Kurt S '75
(937) 325-2492 **Heath** James E '75
(937) 324-5541 **Heil** Richard F Jr. '86
(937) 325-2000 **Herier** David D '98
(937) 328-3741 **Hickey** Christopher J '99
(937) 322-0891 **Hicks** William C '74
(937) 324-2224 **Hofbauer** Lawrence J '96
(937) 328-2574 **Hoffman** William D '90
(937) 399-1429 **Husted** Stanley N II '72
(937) 324-8481 **Jewett** Reed P '60
(937) 399-8180 **Juergens** Carl E '54
(937) 399-8180 **Juergens** John C '86
(937) 325-8214 **Juergens** Joseph M '72
(937) 325-1588 **Juergens Wilt & Strileckyi**
(937) 328-2640 **Kaech** Noel E '71
(937) 322-0891 **Kavanagh** Paul J '95
(937) 327-3646 **Keener** Kyle B '00
(937) 325-1531 **Kellogg** Scott K '92
(937) 328-9079 **King** Courtney D '99
(937) 323-9739 **Kinsler** Christopher L '01
(937) 390-0695 **Knowlton** Peter M '59
(937) 324-3000 **Kohler** Anthony E '84
(937) 323-5555 **Lagos** James H '73
(937) 323-5555 **Lagos & Lagos**
(937) 323-5555 **Lagos** Thomas H '72
(937) 328-4645 **Lancaster** Katrine M '91
(937) 325-5500 **Lancaster** Robert N Jr. '87
(937) 325-7058 **Latham** William D '88
(937) 864-3000 **LeFevre** Deana L '83
(937) 322-2161 **Lehmkuhl** Allen M '74
(937) 525-0025 **Lind** Gregory K '91
(937) 399-8415 **Littleton** Charles D Jr. '51
(937) 327-1767 **Luthe** Suzanne M '93
(937) 323-3768 **Malina** Paul D '62
(937) 325-7058 **Marlow** Brandin D '03
(937) 324-2224 **Marshall** James D '83
(937) 324-5541 **Martin Browne Hull & Harper**
(937) 324-5000 **Martin** David M '75
(937) 323-4004 **Mayhall** Richard E '82
(937) 324-5541 **McCready** Steven J '83
(937) 323-3441 **McDonough** John P '54
(937) 328-2640 **Merrell** William N '77
(937) 328-2653 **Millspaugh** Theodore E '79
(937) 323-3768 **Mlicki** Teresa C '80
(937) 328-3741 **Moody** Denise L '90
(937) 328-2574 **Morris** Gregory M '89
(937) 328-2640 **Morris** Ronald E '83
(937) 328-2640 **Murphy** Shawn P '93
(937) 322-0891 **Nedelman** Phyllis S '82
(937) 328-3763 **Nevius** Eugene S '72
(937) 525-9460 **Niles** Lisa J '93
(937) 324-6807 **O'Keefe** Daniel M '69
(937) 324-5541 **Osborn** Robert M '95
(937) 322-6655 **Pappas** Panayotis F '67
(937) 328-9055 **Parks** Kimberly S '96
(937) 323-3768 **Parmley** Terri L '88
(937) 325-2459 **Pavlatos Catanzaro & Lancaster Co,LPA**
(937) 325-2459 **Pavlatos** Robert B '49
(937) 325-2459 **Pavlatos** Stacey R '77
(937) 323-1010 **Pedraza** Miguel A Jr. '85
(937) 325-7365 **Peifer** James F '72
(937) 325-4446 **Pennington** Anthony B '77
(937) 323-5555 **Petroff** Samuel J '80
(937) 328-4557 **Phillips** Patrick B '99
(937) 328-2574 **Pickering** Andrew P '97
(937) 325-9950 **Potter** Wilfred L '78
(937) 323-6120 **Powers** Paula M '77
(937) 328-2574 **Pryor** Johnny D '03
(937) 328-2574 **Rastatter** Douglas M '94
(937) 328-3741 **Reckley** Kathryn A '86
(937) 322-0891 **Reich** Barry P '70
(937) 323-8643 **Reynard** Jack P Jr. '64
(937) 325-6221 **Ricketts** Charles N '68
(937) 399-9709 **Roberts** Mark F '79
(937) 325-2492 **Ronemus** Thor G '55
(937) 324-5541 **Ross** Lauren M '84
(937) 390-7940 **Royer** Etta S '95
(937) 323-1007 **Rush** Kenneth G '57
(937) 328-4557 **Salway** Joel D '89
(937) 323-9739 **Schmenk** Gerald E '66
(937) 323-9739 **Schmenk Spencer & Hasselbach**
(937) 328-2574 **Schumaker** Stephen A '78
(937) 324-4442 **Schutte** Stephen E '73
(937) 324-5736 **Seall** Elizabeth A '00
(937) 328-3741 **Sheils** Michael F '84
(937) 328-6970 **Shipley** Alma H '86
(937) 322-6611 **Skogstrom** James W '80
(937) 328-2626 **Skogstrom** Janie O '80
(937) 328-2574 **Smith** David E '75
(937) 323-4641 **Smith** Elbert G '58
(937) 327-3687 **Smith** Nichol R '01
(937) 324-5260 **Snead** Cozette '95
(937) 325-1588 **Sommer** Eric M '96
(937) 324-5541 **Southward** Wayne E '83
(937) 325-8822 **Spencer** John M '83
(937) 323-9739 **Spencer** Richard A '72
(937) 322-2161 **Stegner** Dennis E '72
(937) 328-3758 **Stewart** Albert Jr. '73
(937) 324-5553 **Stoll** William J '50
(937) 325-1588 **Strileckyj** Wolodymyr '79
(937) 323-1010 **Strozdas** Jerome M '80
(937) 323-1010 **Strozdas & Pedraza LLP**
(937) 323-0488 **Swaney** Charles D '76
(937) 322-8600 **Taylor** Shawn M '96
(937) 964-8974 **Tenwick** David A '63
(937) 328-2640 **Thomas** Shawn A '88
(937) 322-3330 **Thoresen** Alice D '93
(937) 328-2574 **Trempe** Thomas E '80
(937) 325-2459 **Tyree** Sherry L '04
(937) 325-9000 **Valente** Paul R '67
(888) 695-1100 **Vandiford** Douglas A II '02
(937) 328-2574 **Ward** Roger A '95
(937) 323-1131 **Warren** James R '59
(937) 324-5541 **Weaver** David A '72
(937) 324-4171 **West** William D '65
(937) 324-5541 **Wildman** Walter A '68
(937) 864-3000 **Williams** Ralph B '77
(937) 328-2574 **Wilson** David A '01
(937) 324-5870 **Wilson** Thomas W '79
(937) 325-1588 **Wilt** Valerie J '88
(937) 325-7058 **Wineberg** Robert A '80
(937) 325-7365 **Winks** Paul W '71
(937) 322-1921 **Zimmerman** Charles B Jr. '58

STEUBENVILLE

Jefferson County

(740) 283-3330 **Abrams** Amanda Jo '02
(740) 283-3330 **Abrams** James T '73
(740) 282-6233 **Adulewicz** Casimir T '63
(740) 282-5323 **Agresta** Emanuela '90
(740) 282-2676 **Angel-Shaffer** Arlene B '81
(740) 283-1966 **Baes** Maresa R '03
(740) 264-1651 **Bednar** Michael C '84
(740) 282-6271 **Bianco** Dominic J '42
(740) 264-1651 **Blake Hershey & Bednar**
(740) 264-1651 **Blake** Shawn M '99
(740) 264-1651 **Blake** William F Jr. '74
(740) 283-2535 **Boswell** Jerry L '75
(740) 282-1911 **Brown** Jeffrey Orr '79
(740) 282-5323 **Bruzzese & Calabria**
(740) 282-5323 **Bruzzese** Frank J '74
(740) 282-5323 **Bruzzese** Jeffrey J '04
(740) 282-5323 **Calabria** Michael J '77
(740) 284-8008 **Carinci** Francesca T '94
(740) 859-5209 **Carpino** Joseph S '64
(740) 282-9784 **Chalfant** Robert P '65
(740) 283-3388 **Corabi** Joseph M '77
(740) 283-3388 **Corabi-Flenniken** Mary F '88
(740) 283-1966 **Cottrell** Cerryn R '01
(740) 284-1682 **Cozza** Piero P '00
(740) 282-6705 **D'Anniballe** Robert J Jr. '81
(740) 283-3300 **Dylewski** Mary C '92
(740) 264-6960 **Edwards** Charles W '51
(740) 283-1966 **Felmet** Bryan H '76
(740) 283-1966 **Ferro** Richard H '99
(740) 282-1911 **Fisher Brown & Peterson**
(740) 283-4781 **Gorman** David D '99
(740) 282-6705 **Gorman** Michelle L '96
(740) 266-2995 **Hallock** Gary M '77
(740) 282-1900 **Hargrave** Robert C '70
(740) 283-3693 **Hayman** Milton A '60
(740) 264-1651 **Hershey** Adrian V '75
(740) 264-3700 **Isla** Roger A '94
(740) 282-1900 **Jack** Otto A Jr. '74
(740) 283-4781 **Johns** Robert C '95
(740) 282-5323 **Keenan** Jane M '01
(740) 282-1900 **King Hargrave Scurti & Jack**
(740) 282-5122 **Lamatrice** Stephen B '82
(740) 284-1000 **LaRue** David A '88
(740) 284-8111 **Lyons** Meeta Bass '87
(740) 282-7400 **Marshall** Michael J '95
(740) 282-1544 **Mascio** John J '92
(740) 283-3330 **Mastros** Costa D '95
(740) 283-4529 **McDonald** Robert E '00
(740) 283-1966 **McKeegan** Terrence L '04
(740) 282-5323 **Moreland** Carl C '62
(740) 283-4529 **Noble** Frank W Jr. '95
(740) 282-4593 **Olivito** Dominick E Jr. '78
(740) 283-3341 **Olivito** Peter S '62
Olivito Richard A '89
(740) 282-2000 **Pate** Samuel A '80
(740) 282-1911 **Peterson** Howard W III '91
(740) 282-6705 **Pietragallo Bosick & Gordon**
(740) 283-6028 **Powell** Richard L '53
(740) 283-3711 **Prest** Joseph G '64
(740) 283-4781 **Raffaele** Christine L '94
(740) 282-7929 **Repella** Stephen G '79
(740) 283-1313 **Reszke** Eric M '93
(740) 283-4529 **Scarpone** David J '87
(740) 282-1900 **Scurti** Adam E '66
(740) 282-2676 **Shaffer** John R '81
(740) 282-6028 **Spahn** G Daniel '82
(740) 284-1211 **Stern** Gary M '78
(740) 282-5336 **Stern** James A '77
(740) 264-6060 **Stewart** Susan P '77
(740) 283-1966 **Straus** Thomas R '78
Taylor William W '95
(740) 282-1131 **Turrentine** Samuel M '96
(740) 282-9746 **Vukelic** David A '77
(740) 264-4024 **Wilson** Thomas S '76
(740) 283-4781 **Zani** Thomas E '99

STOW

Summit County

(330) 928-7840 **Buie** Mark J '86
(330) 678-6030 **Clem** Christopher '87
(330) 689-2700 **Deutsch** Gary B '97
(330) 678-3857 **Fanelly** Richard M '67
(330) 688-9900 **Greif** Carl '97
(330) 346-0674 **Guanciale** Christopher M '85
(330) 922-1771 **Haas** Richard H '67
(330) 689-2869 **Haefner** Joseph P '96
(330) 945-4234 **Hyland** Scott A '99
(330) 688-8484 **Kaminski** Edward C '59
(330) 688-8962 **Landi** Albert J '54
(330) 688-1806 **Loepp** Thomas C '90
(330) 688-1806 **Maistros** Georgia '90
(330) 688-1806 **Maistros & Loepp**
(330) 686-1708 **Martin** Richard P '77
(330) 297-7788 **Mitchell** Donald P Jr. '73
(330) 945-4234 **Nemer** Robert J '95
(330) 686-1708 **Perduk** David C '96
(330) 929-0161 **Pickut** Sandra J '76
(330) 689-2860 **Reali** Brian A '98
(330) 285-1563 **Schaffer** Lee A '90
(330) 689-2869 **Stanford** Tamara J '01
Watkins Richard D '94
(330) 686-8844 **Watkins** Thomas W '92
(330) 945-8322 **Wolfson** Daniel E '87
(330) 650-6000 **Worhatch** S David '81

STRASBURG

Tuscarawas County

(330) 878-5535 **Fox** Richard L '76

STREETSBORO

Portage County

(330) 626-2926 **Carothers** Deborah A '00
(330) 626-5600 **Cochran** George W Jr. '79
(330) 626-1118 **Markowski** Lucille '89
(330) 626-1990 **Rissland** Karl R '90
(330) 626-2525 **Ruppelt** Arthur G '89
(330) 422-1978 **Wood** Jodi L '85
(330) 626-1212 **Wood** Rick B '83

STRONGSVILLE

Cuyahoga County

(440) 268-4355 **Agnello Russo** Christine L '89
(440) 572-1450 **Alikhan** Cheryl A '89
(440) 238-7887 **Blech** Kenneth A '79
(440) 876-6338 **Buss** Dennis A '74
(440) 238-3331 **Cohen** Martin '85
(440) 572-5083 **Csank** James F '66
(440) 268-9212 **Esper** Thomas L '71
Ferreri Robert A '80
(440) 846-3666 **Fink** Joseph J '79
(440) 846-0000 **Foth** Arthur E '03
(440) 846-0000 **Foth** Arthur F Jr. '74
(440) 238-1070 **Gambino** Joseph A '72
(440) 533-7585 **Gawell** Lawrence E '75
(440) 878-9503 **Gibbons** Timothy J '89
Grieselhuber Pierre A '69
(440) 826-9497 **Hemingway** Christine A '94
(440) 572-2919 **Hopkins** William J '75
(440) 503-1795 **Jackel** Katherine E '04
(440) 238-7373 **Janowski** John T '94
(440) 878-2992 **Keenan** Alexis G '03
(440) 846-0000 **Kelly** Thomas A III '74
(440) 846-0000 **Kelly** Thomas J '02
(440) 572-2100 **Klatka** Edward J Jr. '81
(440) 238-5720 **Kraus** Kenneth A '72
Larissey Michele L '01
(440) 878-8200 **Li** Peter B '96
Lombardy Kelly L M '03
(440) 238-1070 **Lukcso** Andrew J '69
(440) 572-2100 **Lutz** Jeffrey J '91
(440) 846-1556 **Malone** Laurie A '97
(440) 572-3420 **McNamee** Michael M '97
(440) 238-0365 **Minni** Dennis E '73
(440) 572-3420 **Novak** Karen J '83
(440) 846-1661 **Papandreas** Joyce M '91
(440) 572-3300 **Pasz** David J '82
(440) 238-3373 **Ramsey** Bryan K '88
(440) 238-3373 **Ramsey Caputo & Ramsey**
(440) 238-3373 **Ramsey** Kenneth E '63
(440) 238-3373 **Ramsey-Caputo** Donna J '84
Russell Peter A '93
(440) 897-3180 **Sabrey** James F '00
Schneider Gregory A '97
(440) 238-3209 **Sedory** Allen R '61
(440) 846-0900 **Sheehe** Lawrence G Jr. '83
Shimko John A '69
(440) 238-1070 **Smith** Gary D '79
(440) 238-5468 **Stehman** Thomas E '77
(440) 572-1540 **Sullivan** Timothy M '93
(440) 846-3686 **Tomson** William L Jr. '71
Tymcio Deborah '00
(440) 846-0000 **Urban** John J '75
(440) 238-1011 **Westerhaus** Michael F '74

STRUTHERS

Mahoning County

(330) 755-1437 **Clemente** Michael C '53
(330) 750-9636 **Creighton** William S '91
(330) 755-1414 **Lewis** Lora L '89
(330) 755-1437 **Melone** James A '97
(330) 755-1437 **Wagner** Carol C '88

STRYKER

Williams County

(419) 682-6661 **Brenner** William J '77

SUGARCREEK

Tuscarawas County

(330) 852-2513 **Frautschy** Douglas D '99

SUNBURY

Delaware County

(740) 965-5119 **Adams** William Mark '87
(740) 965-8452 **Brammer** Celeste E '90
(740) 965-9697 **Heath** John F '69
(740) 965-3991 **Miller** Marvin C '64
(740) 548-4231 **Morris** David R '76
(740) 965-3991 **Schilder** Joseph W '64
(740) 965-9317 **Thompson** Jerry L '92

SWANTON

Fulton County

(419) 826-4866 **Gerbitz** Clayton M '92
(419) 826-4866 **Hallett** Christopher J '88
(419) 825-1330 **Keiser** Jed A '78
(419) 826-4866 **Kimmelman** William C '87
(419) 826-0055 **Lehenbauer** Alan J '84
(419) 826-5636 **McQuade** Colin J '80
(419) 826-0055 **McQuade** Daniel P '67
McQuade Richard B Jr. '65
(419) 825-5285 **Sheperak** Thomas J '66
(419) 825-2318 **Smith** Gary Lee '89

SYCAMORE

Hamilton County

(513) 489-2656 **Worth** Robert W '60

SYLVANIA

Lucas County

(419) 724-2600 **Abramson** Mark C '81
(419) 885-7442 **Antonini** Jennifer J '90
(419) 867-1800 **Beightol** Sharon S '80
(419) 344-7355 **Best** Steven K '99
(419) 882-4570 **Bocik** Edward J '74
(419) 882-7100 **Brinning** Leslie B '02
(419) 882-7100 **Burke** Steven M '82
(419) 885-3597 **Callahan** John J '52
(419) 842-0313 **Clair** Mark D '97
(419) 841-4400 **Contrada** Carol A '79
(419) 841-4400 **Contrada** Charles V '79
(419) 882-6285 **Cook** Linda S '93
(419) 517-7000 **Culver** Jeffery A '02
(419) 882-4707 **DeNune** Ralph III '75
Dorcas Carl F '51
(419) 882-2400 **Douglas** Thomas S '75
(419) 724-2600 **Downey** Patrick J '93
(419) 885-7515 **Drescher** Erich W '00
(419) 885-7515 **Drescher** Wolfgang '69
(419) 882-7100 **Dymarkowski** Douglas A '94
(419) 882-1144 **Gersz** Theodore '73
(419) 885-3597 **Gonzalez** Alfonso J '00
Grega Richard J '92
(419) 829-5297 **Gregory** Michele L '99
(419) 885-3683 **Gutchess** Allen D Jr. '60
(419) 517-7000 **Hensien** Christopher J '03
(419) 882-5755 **Hetzer** Nicholas W '78
(419) 829-2255 **Hizer** Brian A '02
(419) 882-0518 **Hunt** Charles N '58
(419) 882-0518 **Hunt Milliken DeVictor & O'Brien**
(419) 885-0234 **Jakubowski** James D '97
Jermann Edmond L Jr. '56
(419) 882-1718 **Jones** Brian D '77
(419) 882-7100 **Jones** Michael S '91
(419) 841-4400 **Jones** Russell W '94
(419) 824-0636 **Joyce** Kevin E '82
(419) 882-4686 **Justen** Frank A '70
(419) 517-7000 **Kalas** Brian C '99
(419) 882-4707 **Kalmbach** Frederick E '02
(419) 517-7000 **Kenney** Kevin J '81

(419) 517-7000 **Kenney & Niehaus,Ltd**
(419) 534-6833 **Kitchen** Margaret A '53
(419) 534-6833 **Kitchen** Margaret A '83
(419) 882-6528 **Kujawa** Kenneth T '71
(419) 882-0081 **LaValley** Daniel J '85
(419) 882-0081 **LaValley LaValley Todak & Schaefer Co,LPA**
(419) 882-0081 **LaValley** Richard G '53
(419) 882-0081 **LaValley** Richard G Jr. '83
(419) 885-3597 **Lemon** David B '94
(419) 885-4461 **Levine** Arleen R '82
(419) 882-0081 **Liedel** Deidre A '98
(419) 829-5297 **Lublin** Jeffery M '80
(419) 882-7100 **Lydy & Moan,Ltd**
(419) 882-7100 **Lydy** Robert J '72
(419) 829-2255 **Mahaffey** Ty S '02
(419) 885-2153 **Manning** Pamela M '99
(419) 885-3597 **McHugh DeNune & McCarthy,Ltd**
(419) 885-3597 **McHugh** John J III '76
(419) 885-7152 **Merritt** Daniel L '82
(419) 882-0518 **Millican** Patrick R '87
(419) 882-7100 **Moan** James E '72
(419) 885-3597 **Mosier** Stephen B '77
(419) 885-3229 **Nagle** Robert T '86
Nasatir Philippa H '84
Neff Theresa M '04
(419) 517-7000 **Niehaus** Charles D '86
(419) 882-0518 **O'Brien** Isobel T '89
(419) 882-7100 **O'Donnell** Michael W '84
(419) 885-7515 **Petitjean** David L '88
(419) 885-1819 **Pfeiffer** James J '57
(419) 885-8920 **Pyzik** Robert A '78
(419) 885-8975 **Ramey** Malcolm S '73
(419) 882-0790 **Richmond** Charles K Jr. '94
(419) 885-2153 **Rimelspach** Ron L '73
(419) 885-4200 **Rosenthal** James A '99
(419) 517-7000 **Sadowski** Stephen M '96
(419) 841-9800 **Saggese** Robert P '92
(419) 843-2777 **Schaefer** Debra G '80
(419) 882-0081 **Schaefer** James E '82
(419) 517-7000 **Schoonmaker** Laurie A '99
(419) 882-0081 **Semro** Timothy J '99
(419) 882-7100 **Spinazze** Anthony P '00
(419) 882-7100 **Spinazze** Dominic J '92
(419) 885-8877 **Strong** Dennis P '80
(419) 882-0081 **Todak** Michael J '82
(419) 724-2600 **Udell & Abramson Ltd**
(419) 724-2600 **Udell** Louis '83
(419) 885-8300 **Vinciguerra** Ralph D '76
(419) 885-8920 **Wagner** Michelle A '95
(419) 824-0241 **Warrick** Bert J '64
(419) 882-5755 **Webb** Linde Hurst '73
(419) 885-3597 **Wensink** Karen J '02
(419) 882-7100 **Wilson** Cecil G '77
(419) 824-8389 **Yarbrough** Stephen A '74
(419) 882-4546 **Zraik** Thomas G '64
(419) 882-2559 **Zraik** Thomas J '77

TALLMADGE
Summit County

(330) 818-0131 **Goodson-Beal** Amy E '03
(330) 634-8090 **Kamlowsky** Lisa M '93
(330) 633-0666 **Kimble** Matthew '04
(330) 630-9502 **Lawrence** Walter R '85
(330) 633-0666 **Maguire** Robert D '75
(330) 634-0220 **Miller** George M '68
(330) 761-9960 **Raber** Megan E '02
(330) 673-7000 **Salerno** Mark A '83
(330) 633-0859 **Schunk** Richard A '74
(330) 580-5229 **Siciliano** Patrick S '84
(330) 630-5077 **Simon** Shirley A '95
(330) 633-4865 **Smolk** Edward C '58
(330) 633-0859 **Taylor** Penelope K '87
(330) 633-2300 **Thomas** Esther L '98
(330) 630-2618 **Walters** Thomas E '85

TERRACE PARK
Hamilton County

(513) 248-0560 **Brown** Jack G '72
(513) 831-5250 **Olinger** Philip S '55
(513) 576-1590 **Thoman** Henry N '82
(513) 248-0121 **Willis** Nancy A '74

THE PLAINS
Athens County

(740) 593-5046 **Culp** Barbara V '84
(740) 593-5046 **Galbraith** Randall L '98
(740) 593-5046 **Huff** Debra K '83
(740) 593-5046 **Oakley** Gregg V '81

THORNVILLE
Perry County

(740) 246-5624 **Crandell** Riley C '01
(740) 246-4602 **Walser** Thomas E '83

TIFFIN
Seneca County

(419) 447-0507 **Anderson** Eleanor J '01
(419) 447-0507 **Barga** John T '76
(419) 448-4575 **Behm & Henry**
(419) 448-4575 **Behm** Karen S '89
(419) 448-8755 **Bendure** Randall S '73
(419) 447-6181 **Burtis** Paul F '90
(419) 448-4444 **Cable** Jonathan H '02
(419) 425-8594 **Campbell** Dow L '97
(419) 447-5255 **Claydon** Julianne '00
(419) 449-7800 **Crall** Matthew E '02
(419) 443-0689 **Curtin** John V '88
(419) 448-8000 **Davis** B Mark '80
(419) 447-6181 **Dell Burtis & Anspach,LLP**
(419) 447-6181 **Dell** Jane C '90
(419) 448-9250 **DeVine** Derek W '93
(419) 448-0204 **Eberly** Dennis J '85
(419) 448-0204 **Eberly** Thomas J '65
(419) 448-4444 **Egbert** Kenneth H Jr. '89
(419) 447-9121 **Forrest** Clair M Jr. '85
(419) 447-6181 **Fruth** James W '95
(419) 447-3023 **Gordon** Thomas J '68
(419) 447-7966 **Graham** Arthur F '60
(419) 447-5132 **Gucker** James R '88
(419) 443-9711 **Hall** Charles R Jr. '03
(419) 447-4912 **Hanson** Kathryn E '97
(419) 448-4575 **Henry** Dean C '90
(419) 447-2982 **Hoffman** Randy F '80
(419) 448-4444 **Hoover** Timothy J '04
(419) 447-2521 **Howard** Brent T '87
Howard Susan H '88
Huth Lester C '51
(419) 447-4999 **Jones** Susan M '90
(419) 443-1121 **Kahler** Jennifer L '97
(419) 443-1121 **Kahler** John M II '96
(419) 447-2285 **Kahler** Richard A '66
(419) 448-4620 **Klepatz** Mark A '84
(419) 447-2521 **Koop** Martin D '98
(419) 448-9250 **Lange** Anne M '00
(419) 448-9250 **Lange** Michael B '61
(419) 447-1632 **McKinney** Samuel R Jr. '75
(419) 447-5132 **Meyer** Gerald D '68
(419) 447-5132 **Meyer** Jay A '96
(419) 447-5132 **Meyer Meyer & Gucker,Ltd**
(419) 448-4444 **Molnar** Rhonda K '98
(419) 447-5011 **Moreland** Shannon A '03
(419) 443-9500 **Nord** Kent D '93
(419) 447-2521 **Nordholt** James S Jr. '74
Palau Lois V '88
(419) 448-5422 **Palau** Richard H '88
(419) 455-9508 **Patino** Leticia G '82
(419) 447-5011 **Perez** Victor H '02
(419) 447-4952 **Phillips** Susan J '90
(419) 447-8332 **Root** Dawn D '87
(419) 447-5011 **Sammet** Jenny L '02
(419) 448-3321 **Stockner** Jeffry J '85
(419) 447-2521 **Supance & Howard**
(419) 447-2521 **Supance** James D '72
(419) 448-4444 **Townsend** Matthew J '00
(419) 448-4575 **Van der Klooster** Susan C '89
(419) 448-4444 **Willman** Angela M '01

TILTONSVILLE
Jefferson County

(740) 859-2178 **Piergallini** Lawrence T '80

TIPP CITY
Miami County

(937) 667-4481 **Andersen** Nicholas I '04
(937) 667-6684 **Cochran** Thomas R '88
(937) 667-2466 **Davis** Richard S '74
(937) 667-4481 **Downing** Joseph A '98
(937) 667-4481 **Dysinger Stewart & Downing**
(937) 667-4481 **Dysinger** Thomas E '77
(937) 667-4481 **French** Andrew T '98
(937) 335-7783 **Hunt** Carroll E '51
(937) 667-8805 **Lovett** George H '88
(937) 667-8805 **Lovett** Roselyn G '89
(937) 667-8309 **Pearson** John D '70
(937) 667-4481 **Stewart** Andrew B '99
(937) 667-4481 **Stewart** Bryan K '89
(937) 667-8458 **Wist** Edmund J '68

TOLEDO
Lucas County

(419) 241-6000 **Abercrombie** Gene R '96
Abood Charles D '70
(419) 474-1218 **Abou-Arraj** Rochelle A '96
(419) 213-4700 **Accettola** Judith K '81
(419) 241-1150 **Accettola** Paul E '75
Adams Mark W '90
(419) 241-2000 **Adray** James S '76
(419) 252-8152 **Adusei-Poku** Marilyn S '97
(419) 243-6148 **Ahern** Stephen F '76
(419) 841-8584 **Albrechta & Coble**
(419) 471-1489 **Albright** Alfred Jr. '79
(419) 241-9000 **Alexander** Gregory G '54
(419) 213-4590 **Alexander** John P '85
(419) 259-2791 **Allen** James B '98
(419) 381-9368 **Alley** Timothy R '02
(419) 535-0075 **Allotta Farley & Widman Co, LPA**
(419) 535-0075 **Allotta** Joseph J '72
(419) 269-2156 **Altiere** James N III '90
(419) 242-7985 **Anagnos** Joyce '04
(419) 245-2740 **Anderson** Charles R II '78
(419) 252-6268 **Anderson** James C '79
(419) 213-4700 **Anderson** James Christopher '80
(419) 241-3213 **Andres** Van P '89
(419) 246-5757 **Anspach Meeks & Nunn,LLP**
(419) 246-5757 **Anspach** Robert M '73
(419) 242-2131 **Antonini** Michael J '83
(419) 249-7900 **Antonini** Thomas J '88
(419) 249-7100 **Arce** Roman '92
(419) 213-3000 **Armacost** James S '76
(419) 327-4303 **Armbruster** Clare C '86
(419) 259-7488 **Armstrong** Kristopher J '04
(419) 241-2200 **Arnold & Caruso,Ltd**
(419) 241-4441 **Arnold** Gregory L '80
(419) 241-2200 **Arnold** William D '87
(419) 843-3955 **Arnsby** Jeanette F '89
(419) 729-3752 **Arquette** James A '90
(419) 242-8900 **Ashley** William L '98
(419) 244-8384 **Aslinger** Julie A '03
(419) 213-4749 **Atkin** Jean E '79
(419) 213-4700 **Atkins** Maureen O '94
(419) 242-1400 **Aubry** Jude T '66
(419) 241-9000 **Aubry** M Scott '95
(419) 843-1333 **Ault** Tim A '86
(419) 531-9559 **Austin** Douglas V '78
(419) 254-1311 **Avery** Laura J '98
(419) 243-2100 **Avila** Janine T '91
(419) 474-1190 **Bacho** Teresa M '94
(419) 245-1503 **Bader** Carol J '01
(419) 242-1555 **Bader** David A '91
(419) 247-1032 **Baehren** James W '78
(419) 254-4300 **Baer** Elizabeth E '95
(419) 247-2523 **Bainbridge** David R '83
(419) 213-4700 **Bainbridge** Jennifer T '83
(419) 249-7900 **Baither** C Philip III '80
(419) 241-6000 **Baker** Kenneth C '77
(419) 241-6000 **Baker** Kimberly Sue '00
(419) 536-3260 **Baker** Richard S '57
(419) 213-3000 **Baker-Johnson** Elaine '89
(419) 865-8021 **Balk Hess & Miller**
(419) 321-6444 **Balyeat** Thomas M '76
(419) 255-7044 **Banks** Gerald W '73
(419) 241-2900 **Baran Piper Tarkowsky Fitzgerald & Theis Co,LPA**
(419) 241-6612 **Barber** Matthew J '04
(419) 885-3000 **Barger** Brian P '84
(419) 244-6788 **Barnes** Mark S '95
(419) 241-6000 **Barnett** Michael R '02
(419) 243-0020 **Baron** Joanna E '02
(419) 242-0280 **Baronas** Ann M '93
(419) 248-1432 **Barone** Gaetano '73
(419) 241-9000 **Barron** John C '78
(419) 241-6285 **Barry** Gordon R '76
(419) 213-4700 **Bates** Julia R '77
(419) 241-2100 **Bates** William F '69
(419) 885-0805 **Battani** Joseph A Jr. '87
(419) 213-3639 **Battles** Cynthia L '87
(419) 241-6000 **Bauer** Albin II '93
(419) 259-6376 **Bauer** David O '76
(419) 213-4700 **Baum** Eric A Jr. '91
(419) 472-0077 **Bayford** Anthony '74
(419) 249-7900 **Beach** William V '88
(419) 247-2500 **Beck** Margaret G '92
(419) 244-8500 **Beebe** Raymond L '81
(419) 241-2200 **Belazis** Paul T '79
(419) 842-8200 **Bell** Michael D '99
(419) 241-9000 **Bell** Neema M '87
(419) 244-9500 **Bella** Johna M '86
(419) 241-9000 **Belt** Jenifer A '95
(419) 252-5997 **Benavides** John J '87
(419) 249-7100 **Bennett** Marshall A Jr. '80
(419) 254-3106 **Bennett** Yvonne D '92
(419) 843-2689 **Benore** Charles J '85
(419) 245-4907 **Bensen** Eileen W '94
(419) 249-7900 **Benziger** Julia E '02
(419) 255-6500 **Berebitsky** Michael J '73
(419) 244-8138 **Bergman** Charles S '97
(419) 244-8138 **Bergman** Melissa R '97
(419) 245-1941 **Berling** Amy J '87
(419) 255-5058 **Berling** Mark D '83
(419) 248-7769 **Berry** Richard L Jr. '83
(419) 321-1326 **Best** Eileen M '93
(419) 241-1200 **Best** Libbey W '97
(419) 241-5522 **Best** Louis M '87
(419) 724-0030 **Bhatti** Kaser S '93
(419) 243-6678 **Biesiada** Shawn T '00
(419) 843-2001 **Biggert** Wayne W '04
(419) 243-9876 **Bingle** William J '71
(419) 531-9559 **Bires** Steven A '99
(419) 255-6810 **Birmingham** John D '90
(419) 242-1400 **Bishop** Daniel A '78
(419) 536-2066 **Bishop** Jerry J II '79
(419) 255-5058 **Bittner** Diana L '98
(419) 252-5770 **Bixler** Robert J '72
Blachman Marci L '95
(419) 255-5900 **Blake** Scott A '95
(419) 249-7900 **Blandin** Bradley L '04
(419) 241-9000 **Blank** Thomas C '81
(419) 255-7250 **Blaufuss** John A '91
(419) 241-1150 **Bloom** Charles E '72
(419) 241-6000 **Bluhm** Graham A '95
(419) 241-6000 **Bobowick** Morton '66
(419) 254-4300 **Bodie** John F Jr. '91
(419) 325-2458 **Boggioni** Nicholas A '95
(419) 241-6000 **Boggs** John H '72
(419) 476-7525 **Bohl** Steven C '80
(419) 213-4755 **Bohmer** Julie E '96
(419) 241-2100 **Bohmer** Robert W '94
Bohner Michael D '04
(419) 843-2001 **Boissoneault** Kevin J '88
(419) 726-3450 **Boldt** Daniel J '86
(419) 472-1900 **Bolotin** Samuel G '75
(419) 866-6060 **Bolotin** Sandra C '79
(419) 241-1200 **Boney** Jacqueline M '76
(419) 243-2100 **Bonfiglio** Michael A '85
(419) 241-9770 **Bonfiglio** Paul R '89
(419) 241-9000 **Bonini** Aleta M '79
(419) 213-2001 **Borell** John A '81
(419) 249-7100 **Borell** John A Jr. '97
(419) 841-9623 **Borgess** Pamela A '00
(419) 842-1166 **Borgstahl** Gene T '84
(419) 842-1166 **Borgstahl & Zychowicz**
(419) 247-1716 **Borman** Amy J '90
(419) 291-5826 **Borrillo** Donato J '97
(419) 727-5442 **Borysiak** David E '83
(419) 241-6000 **Boss** Mark H '97
(419) 247-2500 **Bostelman** Lisa L '01
(419) 243-1770 **Bovee** Megan E '88
(419) 475-7422 **Bower** Karen L '83
(419) 843-2001 **Bowman** Theodore A '79
(419) 243-6281 **Boxell** Charles K '74
(419) 241-8171 **Boyd** Kenneth E '80
(419) 246-5757 **Boyd** Nathan R '04
(419) 241-2300 **Boyer** Peter G '92
(419) 241-1395 **Boyk** Charles E '83
(419) 327-6160 **Boyk** Fredric M '94
(419) 213-4061 **Boyle** Joseph P III '89
(419) 885-3000 **Brady Coyle & Schmidt LLP**
(419) 885-3000 **Brady** Jack J '84
(419) 535-0075 **Brady** William D II '04
(419) 252-6271 **Bragg** Michael W '85
(419) 252-6216 **Bragg** Ralph E '59
Brant Travis W '90
(419) 213-4700 **Braun** Timothy F '87
(419) 249-7900 **Brazeau** James E '78
(419) 255-5111 **Brebberman** James A '82
(419) 536-8600 **Breese** Charles E '55
(419) 885-4149 **Breier** Gregory J '81
(419) 241-3601 **Brennan** William J '80
(419) 241-1200 **Bretzloff** Margaret E '85
(419) 255-0814 **Bridges** Angelita C '00
(419) 241-9000 **Briley** Michael M '69
(419) 321-1348 **Britton** Eric D '92
(419) 242-7415 **Britz** Harland M '56
(419) 243-4006 **Brossia** Anne M '01
(419) 534-2200 **Browarsky** Phillip D '78
(419) 243-6281 **Brown** Charles E '49
(419) 213-4755 **Browning** Melvin L '88
(419) 241-6000 **Brubaker** Marcus J '81
(419) 245-1829 **Bruce** Kerry D '77
(419) 213-4061 **Bruggeman** Carol L '84
(419) 246-5700 **Bruno** Dominic M '64
(419) 241-1395 **Bruno** Michael A '83
(419) 247-2500 **Bruss** Howard G Jr. '67
(419) 243-1239 **Bryan** David A '76
(419) 213-4772 **Buckley** Kevin P '82
(419) 244-6788 **Bugbee & Conkle**
(419) 241-9000 **Bula** Megan A '00
(419) 241-2777 **Bunda** Robert A '79
(419) 241-2777 **Bunda Stutz & DeWitt,PLL**
(419) 243-2283 **Burke** Hal D '98
(419) 243-9650 **Burke** Megan E '97
(419) 243-2283 **Burke** Michael J '73
(419) 245-1020 **Burkhardt** James G '76
(419) 536-6038 **Burkholder** Fred J '83
(419) 535-0075 **Burnard** Justin D '02
(419) 249-7100 **Burns** Craig P '90
(419) 248-3585 **Burns** Mary A '83
(419) 241-9000 **Burson** John H '68
(419) 213-4751 **Butler** Amy L '02
(419) 241-8013 **Byers** Frederick '84
(419) 213-6850 **Byrne** William A '81
(419) 247-2611 **Cabanski** Robert W '79
(419) 244-8989 **Cain** Dwight L '81
(419) 213-6744 **Cairl** Susan M '87
(419) 242-7985 **Calamunci** Anthony J '94
(419) 885-4149 **Calcamuggio** Larry G '77
(419) 255-0571 **Cameron** Donald H '80
(419) 843-4499 **Camick** Daniel G '87
(419) 841-0792 **Candiello** Vedo R '73
(419) 321-6444 **Canestraro** Eugene F '85
(419) 245-1020 **Cannon** Marci L '97
(419) 213-6951 **Carder** Kevin J '86
(419) 241-2100 **Carey** John M '78
(419) 535-1301 **Carlisle** James E '98
(419) 246-5757 **Carnes** James R '98
(419) 865-8021 **Carr** Richard H '83
(419) 246-5757 **Carr** Steven E '99
(419) 351-4005 **Carr** Tonya L '04
(419) 259-7778 **Carter** David W '98
(419) 241-2200 **Caruso** James D '78
(419) 255-3153 **Casey** Julia K '74
(419) 241-6000 **Casey** Peter R III '74
(419) 329-6500 **Catignani** Dean A '89
(419) 241-6000 **Cecil** Daniel O '04
(419) 841-3311 **Chabler** Allan J '61
(419) 537-2926 **Chapman** Douglas K '74
(419) 867-8900 **Chappell** Erik Grant '96
(419) 536-2066 **Chase Goff & Bishop**
(419) 536-2066 **Chase** Richard A '67
(419) 242-4969 **Cherry** Jonathan B '75
(419) 252-6208 **Choka** Byron S '80
(419) 843-2001 **Christen** Dawn T '01
(419) 249-7100 **Christensen** Allen T '77
(419) 248-7957 **Christy** John W '97
(419) 243-6148 **Chuparkoff** David F '88
(419) 242-8214 **Cimerman** Adrian P '79
(419) 241-1200 **Clark** E Sharon '01
(419) 691-5745 **Clark** Edward V '67
(419) 242-3900 **Clark** Michael Leo '89
(419) 213-3328 **Clark** Patricia J '82
(419) 213-4700 **Clark** Robert L Jr. '80
(419) 841-4672 **Clark** Roger N '67
(419) 213-4755 **Clarkson** Karin L '04
(419) 726-2645 **Clement** John K Jr. '87
(419) 321-6444 **Cline Cook & Weisenburger Co,LPA**
(419) 841-8584 **Coble** John A '84
(419) 841-8584 **Coble** Richard A '69
(419) 241-5506 **Cocoves** Spiros P '85
(419) 255-8260 **Cohen** Richard A '70
(419) 327-4303 **Cole** Christy L '01
(419) 244-8336 **Cole** David A '86
(419) 244-1742 **Cole** Eddie M '51
(419) 241-1200 **Coleman** Pariss M II '96
(419) 243-2100 **Collier** Steven P '81
(419) 255-3544 **Collins** Francis C '87
(419) 241-6000 **Collins** Myron C '95
(419) 245-1020 **Colturi** Jeffrey S '80
(419) 724-0030 **Comes** Robert J '82
(419) 535-4500 **Commons** Donald W '82
(419) 244-6788 **Conkle** Allan J '48
(419) 244-8336 **Conklin** George J '78
(419) 255-7600 **Conn** Charles L '75
(419) 243-2100 **Connelly Jackson & Collier LLP**
(419) 213-4700 **Connelly** Kathleen M '88
(419) 254-4300 **Connelly** Kristen A '98
(419) 243-2100 **Connelly** William M '64
(419) 255-5990 **Connelly** William M Jr. '00
(419) 478-2889 **Connolly** Thomas M '77
(419) 243-1818 **Cook** Stacy H '94
(419) 213-4700 **Cooper** Candace C '74
(419) 241-1200 **Cooper** Cary R '69
(419) 241-6000 **Cooper** David F '74
(419) 241-1200 **Cooper** David R '95
(419) 535-4569 **Cooper** Emily K '96
(419) 242-1555 **Cooper** Kevin J '01
(419) 241-1200 **Cooper & Walinski,LPA**
(419) 247-1500 **Cooperman** Ronald M '73
(419) 244-3053 **Corpening** Sarah A '00
(419) 244-8989 **Cosme** Keila D '94
(419) 241-9000 **Cotter** Thomas A '88
(419) 242-8214 **Cottier** Geoffrey A '76
(419) 243-1770 **Cottle** Christopher C '00
(419) 535-1840 **Covrett** Clinton C '75
(419) 536-8600 **Cox-Doty** Beverly J '91
(419) 249-7900 **Coy** Edwin A '74
(419) 243-8251 **Coy** Mary F '85
(419) 241-9000 **Coyle** David J '87
(419) 248-2600 **Coyle** Lori A '98
(419) 535-0111 **Cramer** Bruce A '68
(419) 241-9000 **Creamer** Jeffrey S '79
(419) 882-0877 **Crocker** Douglas J '04
(419) 248-2600 **Cron** Nicholas J '74
(419) 259-6376 **Croniser** Gretchen E '96
(419) 868-8788 **Crosgrove** Darrell M '93
(419) 297-3771 **Crossmock** Steven L '89
(419) 244-4605 **Crouch** Victor R '78
(419) 243-7243 **Cubbon** Frank W Jr. '53
(419) 243-7243 **Cubbon** Kyle A '84
(419) 243-7243 **Cubbon** Stuart F '81
(419) 242-1555 **Culbert** William M '64
(419) 241-1200 **Czarnecki** John '72
(419) 382-6888 **Czerniakowski** Joseph L '54
(419) 407-4355 **Damrauer** Carol L '82
(419) 244-8989 **D'Angelo** Joseph M '94
(419) 843-2001 **Dansack** Michael P Jr. '85
(419) 473-1346 **D'Arcangelo** Bradley M '97
(419) 473-1346 **D'Arcangelo** Joseph M '84
(419) 473-1346 **D'Arcangelo** Michael J '63
(419) 242-8214 **Davis** Carla B '84
(419) 472-2123 **Davis** Christopher W '93
(419) 241-9000 **Davis** Diane V '83

(419) 530-4236 **Davis** Gabrielle '91
(419) 245-1020 **Davis** Geoffrey H '73
(419) 297-5088 **Davis** Mark A '99
(419) 242-7447 **Davis** Philip C '77
(419) 241-9000 **Davis** Terrance K '89
(419) 249-7100 **Dawson** Jennifer J '84
(419) 241-9770 **Dawson** Joseph P '81
(419) 476-8000 **Day** Willis F IV '80
(419) 478-0474 **Dear** Harry J '77
(419) 530-5508 **Decatur** William R '83
(419) 241-5506 **Dech** Merle R Jr. '91
(419) 249-7100 **Decker** Lori W '78
(419) 255-5465 **Decker** Michael E '82
(419) 241-2122 **DeClark** Peter O '95
(419) 382-9590 **DeGidio** Anthony J Jr. '98
(419) 244-8351 **DeLand** Jennifer L '02
(419) 243-6148 **DeLaney** Cormac B '75
(419) 321-1378 **Deller** Scott G '90
(419) 241-9000 **Deller** Stefanie E '99
DeLong James C '83
(419) 255-8331 **Del Vecchio** Susan P '91
(419) 244-6788 **Denny** Gregory B '73
(419) 470-1487 **Desmond** Patrick J '97
(419) 243-6281 **Dettinger** James F '74
(419) 241-6000 **Devaney** Kevin D '91
(419) 254-4858 **Dever** Timothy J '88
(419) 530-7230 **Dewberry** Charlon K '79
(419) 243-6281 **Dewhirst** Peter A '94
(419) 254-3114 **DeWitt** Theresa R '83
(419) 259-8372 **Diener** Erwin '74
(419) 241-9000 **Diesing** Gary R '75
(419) 252-5851 **Diethelm** Joan P '84
(419) 843-9883 **DiLabbio** Larry V '84
(419) 241-9000 **Dillon** Thomas P '92
(419) 241-9770 **Dills** Alan B '73
(419) 255-0675 **DiSalle** Anthony B '66
(419) 930-5600 **DiSalle** John D '91
(419) 255-4543 **Dixon** Blondell '74
(419) 536-8600 **Dixon & Hayes,Ltd**
(419) 536-8600 **Dixon** Randall C '80
(419) 536-8600 **Dixon** Robert B '53
(419) 241-6000 **Dixon** Thomas A '82
(419) 249-7100 **Dolgorukov** D Edward '93
(419) 535-4739 **Doner** Gary W '90
(419) 213-6819 **Dong** Mui-Ling Y '92
(419) 241-1200 **Doniere** Brandi L '04
(419) 213-4700 **Donovan** Jennifer L '97
(419) 255-5990 **Donovan** Kimberly A '02
(419) 936-5120 **Dooley** Colleen M '84
(419) 244-4000 **Dorf & Kalniz**
(419) 244-4000 **Dorf** Michael D '66
(419) 327-4303 **Dorner** Renisa A '88
(419) 530-7230 **Doty** Robert L '90
(419) 242-7985 **Douglas** Julie A '01
(419) 255-5111 **Dow** Martin P '73
(419) 248-1500 **Doyle Lewis & Warner**
(419) 530-1486 **Drabik** Sandra A '80
(419) 248-1432 **Driscoll** Perry F '72
(419) 867-3946 **Ducey** Ernest D '83
(419) 867-3946 **Ducey & Reiwaldt**
(419) 536-1708 **Dudda-Sworden** Barbara '93
(419) 242-1400 **Duffin** John P '77
(419) 244-3393 **Duhart** Myron C II '97
(419) 536-2399 **Dunn** Darlene J '77
Dunn Owen B Jr. '02
(419) 241-0767 **Dustin** Ava M '92
(419) 243-6122 **Dustin** David C '92
(419) 471-1489 **Dworkin** David M '92
(419) 255-7300 **Dzienny** Michael A '86
(419) 259-6717 **Easterwood** Cynthia A '89
(419) 241-6000 **Eastman & Smith Ltd**
(419) 244-7655 **Effler** Fanny P II '79
(419) 321-6444 **Eickholt** William C '68
(419) 241-6000 **Eischen** Heidi N '01
(419) 246-5757 **Ellenberger** Richard F '65
(419) 244-8336 **Elliott** Brooke E '04
(419) 843-2720 **Elliott** Donna L '89
(419) 247-2500 **Ellis** Daniel T '87
(419) 241-1228 **Elrod** Bradley C '82
(419) 255-5900 **Emch** Gregg W '85
(419) 243-1294 **Emch** Richard D '63
(419) 243-1294 **Emch Schaffer Schaub & Porcello Co,LPA**
(419) 241-9000 **Emerson** Edwin G '66
(419) 243-6281 **Emery** Richard L '91
(419) 530-8411 **Engel** Lauri A '95
(419) 213-4700 **English** Ian B '01
(419) 246-5757 **Engwert** J Randall '99
(419) 242-1400 **Engwert-Loyd** Donna M '79
(419) 252-6225 **Entenmann** Richard A '54
(419) 537-1954 **Epstein** Robert '91
(419) 382-6888 **Errington** Michael D '70
(419) 247-2508 **Esch** Raymond G Jr. '65
(419) 255-3948 **Evans** Denise F '85
(419) 249-7100 **Evans** Stephen P '98
(419) 252-5572 **Ewing** Dana R '00
(419) 474-9514 **Farah** Asad S '96
(419) 843-1333 **Farell** Gregory C '84
(419) 535-0075 **Farley** Larry D '77
(419) 247-2500 **Farris** Ray A '75
(419) 249-4944 **Farthing** Dana M '99
(419) 242-0461 **Fech & Fech, LLC**
(419) 242-0461 **Fech** Matthew N '01
(419) 242-0461 **Fech** Nicole Y '01
(419) 241-6285 **Feit** Elliot H '76
(419) 243-5261 **Feldstein** Eden S '67
(419) 537-1954 **Feldstein** Jay E '79
(419) 537-6610 **Fell** George N '66
(419) 537-6610 **Fell & Marcus,LPA**
(419) 841-4294 **Ferguson** Kevin M '86
(419) 213-3000 **Ferguson** Twila R '94
(419) 213-4775 **Fernandes** Trevor N '95
(419) 259-6440 **Fickel** David J '78
(419) 244-4304 **Fiedler** Robert W Jr. '96
(419) 241-4400 **Findish** Marie E '95
(419) 530-4260 **Fink** Maara A '96
(419) 244-1680 **Fischer** Edward J '84
(419) 531-2514 **Fischer** Karen M '91
(419) 249-7100 **Fischer** Matthew J '91
(419) 241-9000 **Fischer** William G '73
(419) 535-3247 **Fisher** Allan S '72
(419) 843-2001 **Fisher** John B '91
(419) 245-1020 **Fiske** Rex D '89
(419) 241-6000 **Fissel** Barry W '81
(419) 385-5704 **FitzGerald** Sharon A '84
(419) 535-4652 **Fletcher** Pamela W '76
(419) 474-9623 **Flood** Judy A '00
(419) 255-0814 **Flowers** Phyllis D '01
(419) 244-7596 **Flynn** Abbey M '04
(419) 252-5653 **Foley** Elizabeth M '97
(419) 241-1200 **Foley** Janis E '86
(419) 321-1226 **Folk** Vivian C '76
(419) 244-4277 **Forcht** Melan M '01
(419) 243-1010 **Ford** Claudia A '00
Forejt Christopher A '03
(419) 213-6680 **Fornof** Judith A '73
(419) 241-9000 **Fort** Jeffrey E '82
(419) 243-6281 **Fournier** Heather J '02
(419) 241-2200 **Frank** Raymond M '71
(419) 255-5111 **Frankel** Paul D '77
(419) 243-9005 **Franklin** John D '91
(419) 473-3916 **Franklin** Pauline '00
(419) 242-5100 **Frederickson** Craig F '75
(419) 242-5100 **Frederickson Heintschel & King Co,LPA**
(419) 242-1400 **Frey** Francis C '75
(419) 327-3324 **Frey** Lou Ann '84
(419) 842-9902 **Friedes** David E '84
(419) 530-4131 **Friedman** Howard M '65
(419) 241-3101 **Friedman** Lawrence M '84
(419) 531-4431 **Fruth** Lynn L '76
(419) 242-7985 **Fugee** Patricia Brown '99
(419) 247-2500 **Fuller & Henry,Ltd**
(419) 241-9000 **Fulop** Sharon M '97
(419) 473-1346 **Furey** Thomas R '75
(419) 321-1290 **Fynes** Jack G '77
(419) 245-1975 **Gaich** Sharon D '96
(419) 474-5678 **Gall** Joanne F '79
(419) 241-4860 **Gallagher Sharp Fulton & Norman**
(419) 241-2122 **Gallagher** Thomas W '75
(419) 843-2001 **Gallon** Jack E '56
(419) 843-2001 **Gallon & Takacs Co,LPA**
(419) 867-8900 **Gant** Jim R '00
(419) 535-0075 **Garner** Mitchell E '04
(419) 259-9459 **Garrett** Laura A '88
(419) 471-1488 **Garrett** Stanley J '92
(419) 841-1440 **Garwood** John A '69
(419) 885-3000 **Gaynor** Christine M '96
(419) 531-0507 **Gehring** Edwin F '78
(419) 255-5917 **Geller** Paul L '71
(419) 241-3213 **George** Shannon J '97
(419) 247-2500 **George** Thomas M '75
(419) 241-4900 **Gerace** Ryan J '03
(419) 243-5552 **Gerken** George E '97
(419) 537-1954 **German** Bethany L '04
(419) 244-5831 **Gernot** George III '74
(419) 241-2100 **Gess** Thomas C '82
(419) 724-6294 **Gessel** Barbara F '87
(419) 241-5506 **Geudtner** Mark C '79
(419) 248-8148 **Gibb** James A '88
(419) 245-1060 **Gibbons** Julie A '96
(419) 241-6000 **Gibney** Thomas J '85
(419) 249-7900 **Gibson** Thomas A '86
(419) 841-7416 **Gibson** Willard L '73
(419) 242-1400 **Giha** Paul D '04
(419) 255-5900 **Gillespie** Ted C '75
(419) 241-6000 **Gilmer** Robert J Jr. '75
(419) 536-2066 **Goff** Martin E '85
(419) 882-2889 **Goldberg** Marvin E '84
(419) 843-5355 **Goldberg** Paul S '77
(419) 247-1623 **Goldberg** Stuart J '85
(419) 255-0030 **Goldstein** Jeffrey I '68
(419) 249-7100 **Gonzalez** Michael A '98
(419) 255-0814 **Goode** Victor L '98
(419) 249-6682 **Goodell** Brian C '84
(419) 936-5120 **Goodwin** Thomas P '90
(419) 244-9500 **Goranson** James E '78
(419) 244-9500 **Goranson Parker & Bella**
(419) 244-9500 **Goranson** Roger W '76
(419) 245-1944 **Gorman** Francis X '67
(419) 241-9000 **Gosline** William H '70
(419) 255-3344 **Gottlieb** Arnold N '78
(419) 385-8002 **Gottlieb** Judith B '81
(419) 248-7448 **Gould** Kenneth D '75
(419) 243-6281 **Goulding** Michael R '96
(419) 242-9900 **Gouttiere** John P '74
(419) 535-1840 **Graeff** Scott M '02
(419) 213-3030 **Graff** Walter J '82
(419) 252-2700 **Granata** Eileen M '85
(419) 245-2747 **Grant** Lloyd S '93
(419) 242-1400 **Graven** James P '90
(419) 241-2777 **Gray** David L '98
(419) 243-4006 **Greeley** Nancy P '86
(419) 241-2200 **Green** Merritt W III '76
(419) 536-6168 **Greenberg** Nathan '42
(419) 243-9005 **Greenfield** Richard Kevin '81
(419) 252-6211 **Greenwood** Truman A '79
(419) 241-6000 **Gregg** Joseph A '81
(419) 537-6610 **Grego** Lisa A '94
(419) 244-8336 **Gressley Kaplin & Parker**
(419) 255-8111 **Griffin** Sharon L '83
(419) 841-4294 **Griffith** Carl D '85
(419) 252-6261 **Grigsby** Teresa L '85
(419) 244-6700 **Grill** Donna M '93
(419) 213-4791 **Grine** Kathy J '89
(419) 241-2000 **Grna** Daniel H '76
(419) 930-3030 **Groth** Stevin J '94
(419) 472-9774 **Grude** David G '79
(419) 213-3115 **Gruenhagen** Alan M '88
(419) 242-7488 **Guerin** Marshall W '92
(419) 259-0252 **Gurecky** Marcia S '87
(419) 248-2419 **Gusses** George '73
(419) 255-3030 **Gustafson** John P '85
(419) 841-1571 **Guynes** Marlene F '90
(419) 259-6217 **Gwinn** Yolanda D '84
(419) 248-5701 **Haak** William H II '94
(419) 245-2740 **Habekost** Carl E '90
Hafner Barbara A '87
(419) 843-2001 **Haims** Bonnie E '00
(419) 241-1200 **Hales** Janet E '92
(419) 517-0090 **Hales** Steven C '99
(419) 241-9000 **Hall** Nathan A '03
(419) 382-0111 **Hall** Rhonda G '00
(419) 241-9000 **Halverson** Micah J '01
(419) 252-5935 **Hamel** Gregory J '94
(419) 531-1734 **Hamilton** Richard A '57
(419) 259-2891 **Hamilton** Sandra A '88
(419) 241-2100 **Hamner** Jessica R '03
(419) 255-1360 **Hamner** Scott E '78
(419) 213-4700 **Hanible** Khary L '03
(419) 213-6850 **Hanneman** Donna P '90
(419) 241-2201 **Hanson** Anastasia K '00
(419) 241-6000 **Harden** Gary M '80
(419) 213-6850 **Hargreaves** Carol J '78
(419) 247-1822 **Harper** Matthew D '92
(419) 472-1900 **Harrington** Dee A '00
(419) 243-1105 **Harris** John A III '69
(419) 255-5990 **Hartman** Stephen D '02
(419) 248-6330 **Harves** Donald Scott '96
(419) 242-7985 **Hasbrook** Denise M '84
(419) 242-1400 **Hasbrook** Richard C '77
(419) 249-7900 **Haselman** Scott A '95
(419) 252-5602 **Hathaway** Lisa A '89
(419) 252-6229 **Hattner** Louis J '68
(419) 472-9774 **Haughn** James E II '96
(419) 241-9000 **Hauptman** W Reed '98
(419) 536-8600 **Hayes-Deckebach** Jill L '90
(419) 241-9000 **Haynam** Douglas G '80
(419) 213-4700 **Hays** Patricia C '92
(419) 843-5355 **Hays** Thomas R '94
(419) 241-9000 **Hayward** John F '66
(419) 241-2201 **Hayward** John P '95
(419) 249-7900 **Hazard** Daniel G '01
(419) 242-1400 **Hazard** Elizabeth S '96
(419) 724-0030 **Heben** Mary Ellen '78
(419) 259-8530 **Heck** Richard W '91
(419) 242-5100 **Heintschel** Thomas W '79
(419) 882-0096 **Helberg** Tom R '84
(419) 255-0814 **Heller** Mark R '82
(419) 243-3800 **Helmick** Jeffrey J '88
(419) 213-4755 **Helmick** Karen H '89
(419) 241-2222 **Hendershott** Patrick D '93
(419) 243-7243 **Henderson** David T '96
(419) 213-2001 **Henderson** Karlene D '03
(419) 243-9876 **Henderson** Ronald Roy '73
(419) 242-1400 **Henning** Frederick E '66
(419) 241-6000 **Henry** Michael P '94
(419) 241-9000 **Herbert** Edwin L III '75
(419) 255-0814 **Hernandez** Patricia Y '94
(419) 213-4700 **Herr** Mark T '89
(419) 245-1020 **Herring** Barbara E '84
(419) 241-1150 **Herschel Accettola Bloom Mills & Manore**
(419) 241-1150 **Herschel** Henry B '67
(419) 244-8336 **Hershman** Howard B '78
(419) 245-1200 **Herwat** Stephen J '03
(419) 865-8021 **Hess** Harry R Jr. '70
(419) 241-6000 **Heuerman** Henry N '70
(419) 241-1200 **Heywood** Susan M '02
(419) 321-1262 **Heywood** William H III '69
(419) 382-0292 **Hickey** Charles J '88
(419) 383-5533 **Hickey** Daniel P '03
(419) 843-9883 **Hickman** Gregg D '78
(419) 381-1148 **Hicks** Cathy S '88
(419) 245-1060 **Hicks-Hudson** Paula S '82
(419) 246-5760 **Higley** William E II '76
(419) 321-1390 **Hilbert** John W II '71
(419) 243-2100 **Hill** Jason A '00
(419) 241-9000 **Hiller** Charles W '86
(419) 245-2740 **Hines** Richard S '83
(419) 531-1021 **Hirsch** Gordon H '72
(419) 255-5900 **Hitaffer** Thedford I '00
(419) 243-4006 **Hitaffer** Tiffany J '00
(419) 249-7100 **Hixon** Mark A '92
(419) 249-7100 **Hoblet** Vaughn A '74
(419) 865-8021 **Hoch** Brian J '82
(419) 213-3000 **Hoenig-Navarette** Kimberly S '97
(419) 242-1001 **Hoffer** Jeremiah A II '83
(419) 242-9281 **Hoffman** Edward L '73
(419) 693-0770 **Hoffman** Glen R '81
(419) 242-7985 **Hohman** Teresa E '00
(419) 254-5107 **Hollins** Sharon E '92
(419) 478-1700 **Holmberg** Claes S '67
(419) 243-6281 **Holmes** Martin J '71
(419) 243-6281 **Holmes** Martin J Jr. '95
(419) 471-1489 **Holmes** Terry S '96
(419) 727-7294 **Holt** William D '80
(419) 243-1239 **Honold** David L '79
(419) 243-3800 **Hoolahan** Catherine G '87
(419) 241-9000 **Hoover** Lynn M '90
(419) 213-4789 **Horen** Joanne E '96
(419) 478-6550 **Horn** Gary E '82
(419) 474-8377 **Horne** Timothy J '85
(419) 244-7753 **Horner** Patricia '88
(419) 382-3270 **Horrigan** Dean A '92
(419) 243-6148 **House** Stephen E '98
(419) 252-5523 **Hovland** Valerie B '93
(419) 241-1200 **Hubbell** Bradley F '02
(419) 251-0700 **Hudgin** Barry F '84
(419) 535-4825 **Huelsman** Lisa A '94
(419) 242-8461 **Huffman** John L '88
(419) 486-9999 **Hummer** Donal Jr. '83
(419) 255-4300 **Hunter** John J Jr. '86
(419) 255-4300 **Hunter & Schank Co,LPA**
Hurst Linda L '84
(419) 213-6685 **Hutcheson** William G '83
(419) 255-0126 **Hylant** Sandra M '81
(419) 248-1500 **Hyrne** Michael E '80
(419) 478-7078 **Iacoangeli** James T '92
(419) 475-9040 **Ibarra** David H '88
(419) 704-4191 **Ilstrup** Thomas G '89
(419) 244-7500 **Ingram** Arthur C '83
(419) 255-5900 **Inks** Allen W '92
(419) 472-9774 **Intagliata** John C '80
(419) 242-9363 **Intagliata** Patricia S '79
(419) 537-1954 **Iorio** Donato S '98
(419) 249-7100 **Irmen** James H '86
(419) 241-2201 **Jackson** Louise A '77
(419) 244-6788 **Jackson** Michael W '03
(419) 213-6951 **Jackson** Natalie J '03
(419) 243-2100 **Jackson** Reginald S Jr. '71
(419) 241-6000 **Jacobs** Frank D '59
(419) 248-3501 **Jacobs** Mark I '84
(419) 248-3501 **Jacobs** Marvin K '53
(419) 837-9016 **Jacobson** John L '75
(419) 243-6200 **James** Mary M '99
(419) 241-3213 **James** Timothy C '80
(419) 213-3000 **Jan** Christopher M '87
(419) 247-2500 **Janson** Scott T '91
(419) 724-5330 **Jaros** James J '93
(419) 249-7900 **Jarrett** Evy M '93
(419) 473-1350 **Jasin** Christopher A '85
(419) 473-1350 **Jasin Sallah & McHugh Co,LPA**
(419) 252-6226 **Jeffery** James R '65
(419) 843-9921 **Jennings** Debra M '92
(419) 244-2070 **Jennings** Linda J '89
(419) 244-2070 **Jennings** William G '86
(419) 241-2122 **Jilek** Michael F '70
(419) 478-1776 **Joelson** Philip R '61
(419) 255-0814 **Johns** Jeanne D '82
(419) 843-2424 **Johnson** Donald L Jr. '90
(419) 249-7900 **Johnson** Jennifer C '03
(419) 249-7100 **Johnson** Justice G Jr. '64
(419) 241-6000 **Johnson** Patrick J '67
(419) 241-6000 **Johnson** Richard L '78
(419) 241-6000 **Johnson** Richard Lee '94
(419) 536-6038 **Johnson** Robert G '81
(419) 241-3213 **Johnson** Wendy C '96
(419) 213-4700 **Johnston** Jeffery B '81
(419) 241-1200 **Johnston** Thomas S '70
(419) 213-4775 **Jomantas** Paul E '83
(419) 241-6450 **Jones** Christopher F '87
(419) 345-2970 **Jones** Ellen E G '80
(419) 244-3888 **Jones** Linda A '85
(419) 213-3000 **Jones** Robert J Jr. '97
(419) 241-6450 **Jones & Scheich**
(419) 248-3501 **Jones** Stewart W '89
(419) 936-5120 **Jordan** Douglas K '67
(419) 473-1300 **Jordan** Joseph P '62
(419) 531-9926 **Joseph** G Christopher '79
(419) 321-1435 **Joseph** Regina M '79
(419) 259-6197 **Juby** Alyce R '87
Kaczala Larry A '83
(419) 243-7500 **Kadri** Cherrefe A '93
(419) 254-5181 **Kale** Connie E '92
(419) 537-1954 **Kalniz** Burton A '67
(419) 537-1954 **Kalniz Iorio & Feldstein,LPA**
(419) 244-4000 **Kalniz** M '03
(419) 213-8803 **Kanios** Peter N '82
(419) 241-6168 **Kaplan** Robert Z '55
(419) 241-6168 **Kaplan** Samuel Z '93
(419) 255-1222 **Karcher** Richard A '80
(419) 259-6376 **Karol** Thomas A '78
(419) 241-4500 **Katz** Michael S '84
(419) 243-7281 **Katz** Randolph S '79
(419) 841-4300 **Kaufman** Steven R '82
(419) 843-9101 **Kean** John V '73
(419) 213-3362 **Keeler** Dianne L '80
(419) 213-4700 **Keiffer** Lance M '89
(419) 843-4499 **Keil** Dennis M '85
(419) 841-1148 **Keisser** Keith A '93
(419) 242-8900 **Keller** Jeffery B '88
(419) 321-6444 **Kelley** Thomas J '82
(419) 213-4001 **Kelly** Jill B '82
(419) 245-4742 **Kemnitz** Walter R Jr. '90
Kennedy Elizabeth N '03
(419) 537-2944 **Kennedy** Robin M '70
(419) 255-6252 **Kennedy** William R '51
(419) 255-5990 **Kerger** Richard M '74
Khoury Nicole I '02
(419) 241-2900 **Kidd** Tracy L '99
(419) 249-7100 **Killam** Thomas P '76
Kincade Donald H '80
(419) 242-5100 **King** Douglas W '91
(419) 213-4755 **King** Frances V '88
(419) 248-8000 **King** Ricardo A '95
(419) 244-6788 **King** Robert P '83
(419) 241-2000 **King** Thomas R '55
(419) 213-4755 **Kirby** JoAnne J '91
(419) 213-6850 **Kirby** Michael D '84
(419) 291-2192 **Kirkhope** Thomas G '91
Kirkpatrick Joel J '00
(419) 213-4755 **Kiroff** Donna L '80
(419) 259-6376 **Kiroff** Lawrence J '83
(419) 841-3311 **Kirshner** Alan R '75
(419) 243-4006 **Kitch Drutchas Wagner DeNardis & Valitutti,PC**
(419) 241-6000 **Klee** Roger P '74
(419) 885-3000 **Kleeberger** Patricia J '98
(419) 530-2948 **Klein** James M '69
(419) 213-4202 **Klosterman** Julie A '98
(419) 255-1102 **Klucas** David L '88
(419) 867-8900 **Klumb** Marci L '89
(419) 249-7900 **Knepp** James R II '92
(419) 213-3191 **Knepp** Linda M '92
(419) 842-1333 **Knoblauch** Diane J '94
(419) 472-9041 **Koder** Stephen D '78
(419) 241-9000 **Koenig** Robert A '83
(419) 255-0814 **Koeninger** Walter D '96
(419) 882-2142 **Kolb** Henry G '81
(419) 244-3006 **Kolb** Richard L '67
(419) 244-3006 **Kolb & Zigray**
(419) 241-5175 **Kolodgy** Kathleen W '85
(419) 241-2100 **Kondalski** Kimberly Sue '87
(419) 249-7900 **Konieczny** Timothy A '82
(419) 255-0571 **Konop** Alan S '63
(419) 691-2491 **Kontak** James R '76
(419) 244-5865 **Kosydar** Walter J '73
(419) 213-4700 **Kountouris** Louis E '82
(419) 245-1893 **Kovacik** Leslie A '98
(419) 843-2001 **Kovacs** Louis S '88
(419) 241-4050 **Kovacs** Patricia A '93
(419) 241-1200 **Kowalski** Gerald R '80
(419) 841-9623 **Kranz** Michelle L '93
(419) 249-7100 **Kraus** Paul M '57
(419) 321-1292 **Kress** Kathleen A '85
(419) 247-1679 **Krock** David C '82
(419) 473-1346 **Kroncke D'Arcangelo Sutter & Furey**
(419) 473-1346 **Kroncke** William G '64
(419) 249-7900 **Krugh** Timothy D '78
(419) 241-6000 **Kuhl** David L '75
(419) 473-1431 **Kuhl** John R '77
(419) 471-2034 **Kuhn** Jeffrey C '82
(419) 244-8336 **Kuhn** Todd J '02
(419) 242-8461 **Kurek-Maloney** Kimberly C '98
(419) 241-4288 **Kurt** Patricia H '82
(419) 248-2600 **Kurt** Ted '79
(419) 241-2777 **Kwapich** Christie M '99
Lackey Jane L '79
(419) 243-1105 **Lackey Nusbaum Harris Reny & Torzewski,LPA**
(419) 241-2122 **Lafferty** Jon A '73
(419) 248-2600 **Lah** Jack J '04
(419) 213-4687 **Lambdin** Jennifer M '98
(419) 243-1239 **Landry** Francis J '76
(419) 243-1239 **Landry** John A '77
(419) 241-6000 **Landwehr** John T '74
(419) 245-2550 **Lanzinger** Joshua W '98
(419) 843-5028 **LaRue** Lawrence B '75

(419) 213-4700 **Lastra** Andrew J '98
(419) 213-3000 **Lauback** Mary D '79
(419) 213-5131 **Lauer** Steven K '77
(419) 472-1900 **Lautar** Brian F '87
(419) 249-7900 **Lavalette** Peter N '94
(419) 243-2100 **Lavalette** Tammy G '99
(419) 244-3888 **Lavender** Barbara A '94
(419) 255-5202 **Lawrence** John H '81
(419) 255-5117 **Lawrence** Morgan A '83
(419) 241-6000 **Lazar** Bruce D '95
(419) 213-3000 **Lazar** Mary E '95
(419) 936-2290 **Lehman** Mary J '03
(419) 213-3000 **Lehman-Sentle** Susan K '00
(419) 243-1010 **Leizerman** Erwin J '76
(419) 842-8200 **Leizerman** Joseph-Jacques S '93
(419) 243-1010 **Leizerman** Michael J '94
(419) 885-0805 **Lenavitt** David J '95
(419) 885-0805 **Lenavitt** Jack M '65
(419) 535-4791 **Leonardi** Robert M '74
(419) 243-1010 **Leonhardt** Ronald F '92
(419) 213-6986 **Levin** Anita '98
(419) 535-4640 **Levin** Marc S '80
(419) 252-6274 **Levine** Joel A '63
(419) 843-2001 **Levine** Marilyn J Brenner '01
(419) 255-3360 **Levy** Jeffrey D '77
(419) 255-5111 **Lewis** Gina M '02
(419) 867-8900 **Liebenthal** Jon B '86
(419) 248-2600 **Light** C Randolph '66
(419) 242-1400 **Light** Neil H '79
(419) 242-4055 **Ligibel** Rebecca K '92
(419) 724-0030 **Lindberg** Mark S '88
(419) 255-1222 **Lindsley** William R Jr. '76
(419) 213-4700 **Lingo** Jeffrey D '90
(419) 530-3364 **Linker** Carol W '80
(419) 243-9005 **Lipinski** Tracy A '03
(419) 243-1088 **Lipton** Andrew S '80
(419) 241-1200 **Lockhart** Margaret J '88
(419) 241-9000 **Lodge** Gregory T '82
(419) 255-7552 **Lodge** Terry J '79
(419) 244-8351 **Loeffler** Joseph H '88
(419) 241-4900 **Logan** Amy M '04
(419) 213-4700 **Loisel** Michael J '98
(419) 242-1555 **Lombardo** Carla A '92
(419) 865-5743 **Loney** Brett A '00
(419) 241-2900 **Long** Stephen D '94
(419) 283-9888 **Longacre** Timothy W '92
(419) 245-1198 **Lopez** Anita L '99
(419) 245-1020 **Loukx** Adam W '93
(419) 321-6444 **Lowenstein** Jacob M '98
(419) 321-6444 **Lowenstein** Jay J '75
(419) 471-2281 **Luckner** Kleia R '91
(419) 321-1251 **Ludd** Oksana M '80
(419) 539-7449 **Ludd** Steven O '82
(419) 724-5240 **Luettke** Thomas E '99
(419) 252-6298 **Lupica** Thomas A '90
(419) 691-2150 **Luther** Lynn A '02
(419) 842-0600 **Lutton** Robert S '93
(419) 578-9211 **Lutz** Lonnie R '80
(419) 867-8900 **Lyden Liebenthal & Chappell,Ltd**
(419) 867-8900 **Lyden** Patricia G '80
(419) 247-2500 **Lyle** Dennis A '84
(419) 248-8000 **Lynch** Patricia Ann '75
Lyonette Desiree '01
(419) 936-5120 **MacHarg** James C '75
(419) 241-2777 **Machin** Barbara E '78
(419) 241-9000 **Mack** David J '00
(419) 729-3944 **Mack** James R '67
(419) 241-9000 **MacKay** John N '75
(419) 255-5900 **MacMillan** Richard S '80
(419) 255-5900 **MacMillan Sobanski & Todd,LLC**
(419) 245-1020 **Madigan** John T '73
(419) 243-6148 **Madrzykowski** Jeffrey Jon '92
(419) 249-7900 **Maguire** Edmund T '63
(419) 213-2001 **Majdalani** Brenda J '89
(419) 843-1333 **Malone Ault & Farell**
(419) 241-9000 **Malone** Nicholas D '04
(419) 843-1333 **Malone** Richard R '77
(419) 241-5175 **Maloney** Daniel J '98
(419) 241-5175 **Maloney McHugh & Kolodgy**
(419) 241-5175 **Maloney** William T '78
(419) 259-6803 **Manahan** Marsha A '81
(419) 243-6148 **Manahan** Michael J '79
(419) 243-6148 **Manahan Pietrykowski Bamman & DeLaney**
(419) 578-6300 **Mandell** Steven L '83
(419) 213-4700 **Mandross** Dean P '80
(419) 213-4061 **Mandross** Suzanne C '80
(419) 245-1975 **Manon** Lora L '86
(419) 241-1150 **Manore** John J III '94
(419) 535-7100 **Mansour-Ismail** Linda N '81
(419) 243-0922 **Mantel** Dianne Sue '93
(419) 242-1959 **March** Andrew G '96
(419) 213-3000 **Marciniak** Douglas G '87
(419) 537-6610 **Marcus** Steven E '78
(419) 244-4200 **Margelefsky** Michael P '77
(419) 241-6000 **Markakis** Maria Limbert '00
(419) 724-0030 **Marks** R Edward '94
(419) 321-7188 **Marley** James W '96
(419) 254-4300 **Marshall & Melhorn,LLC**
(419) 249-7100 **Marshall & Melhorn,LLC**
(419) 248-3318 **Martin** David L '88
(419) 248-4611 **Martin** John W '76
(419) 255-5900 **Martineau** Catherine B '82
(419) 241-2122 **Masse** Andrew R '84
(419) 843-2001 **Massey** Laura A '01
(419) 255-4864 **Mather** John G '83
(419) 213-4719 **Mathew** Anita '96
(419) 213-4700 **Matuszak** Thomas A II '97
Matuszynski Charles A '69
(419) 249-7100 **Mauer** Kenneth J '85
Maugeri Beatrice '92
(419) 247-2500 **Mauntler** John E '88
(419) 241-8195 **Mays** Richard D '78
(419) 472-8213 **Mazziotti** Mary L '67
(419) 243-7243 **McArdle** Thomas J '87
(419) 321-6444 **McBee** Clint M '79
(419) 252-6231 **McBride** Benjamin G '67
(419) 242-1400 **McBride** Mark R '81
(419) 255-9100 **McCarter** Charles T '71
(419) 241-9000 **McCarthy** Timothy C '79
(419) 241-2100 **McCauley** Ann M '99
(419) 476-7210 **McClanahan** Dawn M '95
(419) 241-9000 **McClay** Susan D '76
(419) 241-6282 **McConnell** Karyn R '98
(419) 829-2463 **McCormick** Daniel J '83
(419) 252-5958 **McCormick** Patricia A '95
(419) 213-6850 **McCourt** Ronald V '76
(419) 241-2122 **McCready** Jennifer C '99
(419) 241-3213 **McCready** William S '69
McCrory Dorothy B '65
(419) 473-3916 **McCrory** Paul A Jr. '65
(419) 471-1489 **McCrury** Lowell D '76
(419) 865-8021 **McCulley** David C '83
(419) 539-6000 **Mc Elfresh** Randall J '90
(419) 248-2600 **McElroy** Neil S '03
(419) 245-2740 **McGill** David C '84
(419) 213-6824 **McGowan** Lisa D '93
(419) 241-9000 **McGowan** Michael S '82
(419) 243-1105 **McGowan** Paul C '89
(419) 249-3325 **McGrail** Michael T '87
(419) 473-1350 **McHugh** Peter J '88
(419) 241-5175 **McHugh** Sarah A '83
(419) 241-1200 **McKee** William M '90
(419) 327-3314 **McLaughlin** Bruce D '73
(419) 241-9000 **McMahon** Brian N '78
(419) 254-9000 **McMahon** John W '94
(419) 242-1255 **McManus** Kevin P '88
(419) 242-1255 **McManus** Martin J '87
(419) 241-1200 **McNamara** Joseph V '03
(419) 244-6864 **McNulty** Michael S '94
(419) 247-1009 **McWeeny** Philip '65
McWilliam John L '86
(419) 249-7100 **Meacham** Ruth A '81
(419) 213-4700 **Meader** Jevne C '00
(419) 243-1294 **Meehan** Thomas A '62
(419) 246-5757 **Meeks** Mark D '88
(419) 249-7100 **Melhorn** Donald F Jr. '60
(419) 242-1555 **Menacher** William R '84
(419) 321-1436 **Mercer** Mark E '02
(419) 241-1200 **Mercurio** Meredith L '99
(419) 530-2949 **Merritt** Frank S '68
(419) 249-7900 **Messenger** Michael S '83
(419) 242-2488 **Metusalem** Mark J '87
(419) 249-7900 **Metz** Douglas E '65
(419) 255-0126 **Mewhort** Donald M III '91
(419) 241-9000 **Mewhort** Donald M Jr. '65
(419) 213-4700 **Meyer** Brenda G '86
(419) 244-4605 **Meyer** Frederick C '81
(419) 243-6148 **Meyer** Larry P '85
(419) 241-2201 **Meyer** Randy L '99
(419) 246-5722 **Meyer** William G '77
(419) 244-4200 **Mezinko** Vincent S '85
(419) 255-6171 **Michalak** Alan J '91
(419) 255-6171 **Michalak** Richard F '52
(419) 242-8461 **Mickel** Kenneth L '65
(419) 327-4336 **Mickel** Marilyn D Miller '82
(419) 724-3499 **Miesle** Gary E '81
(419) 213-3000 **Mikkonen** Michael P '88
(419) 473-9276 **Miller** Bennet M '79
(419) 247-1849 **Miller** Gary L '99
(419) 244-6788 **Miller** Harvey C Jr. '99
(419) 247-2729 **Miller** Jeffrey H '88
(419) 865-8021 **Miller** Jim '76
(419) 213-4755 **Miller** Joann Kay '88
(419) 327-4303 **Miller** Lisa A '02
(419) 213-4775 **Miller** Nancy A '88
(419) 242-7985 **Miller** Russell R Sr. '78
(419) 241-1150 **Mills** Gerald L '68
(419) 474-5020 **Mira** Charles J '83
(419) 241-1200 **Mistry** Jennifer S '01
(419) 213-6762 **Mitchell** Donna P '89
(419) 255-4480 **Mitchell** Keith L '87
(419) 213-4743 **Mitchell** Kristina L '96
(419) 842-1166 **Mitchell** Mary J '01
(419) 248-4256 **Mittelstaedt** David J '83
(419) 724-3499 **Mockensturm** Mark M '93
(419) 241-6000 **Modd** Anthony R '02
(419) 255-0814 **Mogavero** Mark N '97
(419) 242-7488 **Mohler** Edward T '89
(419) 243-6281 **Mohler** Martin E '73
(419) 242-1400 **Mohr** David M '66
(419) 249-7900 **Mohr** Kathryn M '87
(419) 213-4461 **Molaro** Catherine M '93
(419) 249-2707 **Molaro** Salvatore C Jr. '87
(419) 244-7500 **Mollenkamp** Alan L '74
(419) 255-5900 **Molnar** John B '83
(419) 243-5080 **Mondville** Jeffrey J '95
(419) 241-1200 **Monro** Susan E '93
(419) 254-4300 **Moody** Nancy D '82
(419) 385-0765 **Moran** James P '75
(419) 241-8171 **Moran** Mary B '89
(419) 241-8171 **Moran** Peter L '53
(419) 291-2419 **Morelli** Deborah A '02
(419) 248-4611 **Morgan** Frieda G '75
Morgan Harry W Jr. '71
(419) 213-4775 **Morgan** Maria Q '76
(419) 536-2663 **Morris** Robert G '51
(419) 244-4605 **Morrison** Jennifer L '86
(419) 251-2801 **Morrissey** Martin B '92
(419) 247-2509 **Morton** James M Jr. '67
(419) 255-9585 **Mosiniak** Gary J '90
(419) 213-4755 **Mowry** Paula C '88
(419) 539-6000 **Moyer** Kevin J '84
(419) 241-6000 **Mueller** Denise A '00
(419) 243-6126 **Mufleh** Ida B '95
(419) 724-0030 **Mulder** Kevin C '92
(419) 473-1431 **Mulkey** Chad T '00
(419) 213-3168 **Mull** Lawrence O '90
(419) 241-4400 **Munger** Peter C '89
(419) 241-4400 **Munger Watkins Co,LPA**
(419) 213-3000 **Murd** Pamela K '01
(419) 251-5263 **Murphree** R K '95
(419) 535-5650 **Musachio** Rosalie N '77
(419) 243-7720 **Muska** Susan Hartman '77
(419) 213-6850 **Mutchler** Alan D '76
(419) 243-2100 **Nackowicz** Timothy P '03
(419) 843-3168 **Nagy** Ronald L '99
(419) 241-6000 **Nahhas** Fadi V '00
(419) 213-4700 **Narges** Michael E '94
(419) 241-6168 **Nathan** Daniel M '04
(419) 249-7100 **Natyshak** Amy M '90
(419) 242-5485 **Nedom** Francis P '89
(419) 243-6281 **Neff** Carter P '68
(419) 241-1200 **Nelson** John K '79
(419) 252-6217 **Nelson** Susan B '81
(419) 345-7122 **Neumeyer** James D '04
(419) 242-3900 **Newberg** Brian A '92
(419) 254-1311 **Newman** Emily Weaver '04
(419) 213-3169 **Newnham** Gary C '79
(419) 241-6000 **Newsom** Scott D '96
(419) 248-2600 **Nicholson** Brent B '79
(419) 245-1975 **Niedzielski** Michael J '93
(419) 247-1500 **Nitschke** Drew A '00
(419) 243-6281 **Noble** Catherine H '78
(419) 679-6050 **Noble-Haggy** Laura L '01
(419) 327-4303 **Noe** Bernadette R '00
(419) 245-2740 **Nolte** Lynne R '83
(419) 241-6000 **Nooney** James F '66
(419) 241-3580 **Novak** Karen A '84
(419) 726-2605 **Nowak** James S '76
(419) 245-1020 **Nugent** Samuel J '78
(419) 241-6000 **Nunn** David W '91
(419) 578-9246 **Nunnari** Jeffrey P '92
(419) 255-6070 **Nusbaum** James B '95
(419) 243-1105 **Nusbaum** Melvin G '57
(419) 249-7100 **Oberlin** Phillip S '59
(419) 249-7900 **OBrien** Jean M '89
(419) 841-0881 **O'Brien** Shari L '87
(419) 249-7100 **O'Connell** David L '84
(419) 247-1500 **O'Connell** Katherine R '84
(419) 249-7900 **O'Connell** Maurice D '56
(419) 252-5523 **O'Connor** Kevin M '01
(419) 241-9000 **O'Doherty** James H '99
(419) 213-4700 **Olender** Lori L '97
(419) 247-2500 **Oostmeyer** Melissa M '99
(419) 213-6510 **Orlow** Gary M '78
(419) 842-8200 **Osborne** Gary W '75
(419) 213-4700 **Osgood** Marla R '78
(419) 531-1021 **Osnowitz** Samuel '75
(419) 245-1954 **Osowik** Thomas J '82
(419) 249-7900 **Ozimek** Mark A '04
(419) 243-1294 **Pacella** Patrick P '71
(419) 242-7985 **Palm-Kuebler** Lisa '01
(419) 476-1411 **Palmer** Robert C '78
(419) 249-7100 **Palmer** Thomas W '72
(419) 244-2201 **Pangle** Laurie J '83
(419) 537-8524 **Papadimos** Peter J '82
(419) 213-4700 **Papadimos** Steven J '83
(419) 475-7700 **Papurt** Richard A '90
(419) 475-6043 **Pardee** John K III '74
(419) 247-8707 **Parikh** Niravkumar D '91
(419) 244-9500 **Parker** Christopher F '84
(419) 255-4300 **Parker** Ericka S '97
(419) 244-8336 **Parker** Jerome R '73
(419) 213-3270 **Parker** Marilyn L '82
(419) 321-1347 **Patberg** William L '78
(419) 255-5900 **Pavelko** Douglas V '90
(419) 247-2500 **Pawlicki** Sarah E '03
(419) 251-3568 **Pazzo** Michael P '00
(419) 213-4700 **Pearson** Craig T '85
(419) 241-6000 **Peckinpaugh** Rudolph A Jr. '80
(419) 534-2304 **Penamon** Alan W '95
(419) 727-1040 **Pennington** Stephen T '84
(419) 249-7900 **Peppel** Gregg A '99
(419) 243-6281 **Perkins** Jeffrey J '82
(419) 478-1776 **Perlman** James M '80
(419) 241-4181 **Perlmutter** Steven J '87
(419) 243-4006 **Perne'** Lori L '01
(419) 843-1010 **Pertz** Frank E '83
(419) 213-4202 **Peters** Lora D '97
(419) 242-5429 **Peters** William J '73
(419) 244-8396 **Petlow** James J '67
Pheasant Merle E Jr. '72
(419) 530-4017 **Phelps** Amy B '02
(419) 724-0030 **Phifer** B Janelle Butler '75
(419) 255-6070 **Phillips** Jerome '69
Phillips Kenneth W '89
(419) 213-3000 **Phillips** Shannon L '93
(419) 243-6148 **Pietrykowski** William F '83
(419) 776-4567 **Pigott** Thomas D '94
(419) 247-1600 **Pilkington** Joseph H '59
(419) 245-1975 **Pilrose** Daniel R Jr. '86
(419) 385-8002 **Pinkus** Fredric '83
(419) 474-3380 **Pioch** Susan M '81
(419) 241-9000 **Pisanelli** Mary Ellen '82
(419) 241-3031 **Pitkin** Peter J '74
(419) 255-0126 **Pitman** Christopher '99
(419) 535-0311 **Pittman** Raymond H III '91
(419) 248-1500 **Pituch** Kevin A '88
(419) 252-6227 **Pizza** Lisa E '81
Platz Sarah L '94
(419) 241-6000 **Plessner** Dirk P '87
(419) 241-9000 **Pletz** Thomas G '71
(419) 241-9000 **Podolsky** Michael J '02
(419) 471-1489 **Poirier** Jennifer L '96
(419) 291-3706 **Polizzi** Arturo '97
(419) 245-2550 **Pollex** Yvonne T '84
(419) 535-4653 **Pollock** Robert E '71
(419) 241-7900 **Polofka** John R '80
(419) 843-1333 **Pommeranz** Milton E '02
(419) 242-3900 **Popil** James J '86
(419) 243-1294 **Porcello** James F Jr. '77
(419) 841-7211 **Porritt** Russell W II '93
(419) 255-2366 **Porz** Bonnie M '81
(419) 255-2366 **Porz** Susan G '80
(419) 213-4389 **Posner** Curtis E '67
(419) 255-2802 **Potts** John F '78
(419) 247-1500 **Poturalski** Steven J '97
(419) 244-4697 **Prephan** Michael Sr. '69
(419) 242-3540 **Price** Douglas R '75
(419) 255-0814 **Pridgeon** Merritt J '02
(419) 243-2042 **Priestap** Stephen T '92
Proctor James W '56
(419) 380-1330 **Puligandla** Bertrand R '93
(419) 213-1330 **Puligandla** Vijay K '88
(419) 473-2322 **Purcel** Jerry P '80
(419) 531-0599 **Purdue** David C '83
(419) 531-0599 **Purdue** John C '49
(419) 245-1278 **Quintero** Arturo M '79
(419) 885-4149 **Racine** Charles E '67
(419) 213-4458 **Raduege** Tammy J '89
(419) 247-1225 **Ragan** William A Jr. '94
(419) 474-8377 **Rahal** Ronald Lee '92
(419) 247-2524 **Rambo** Glenn L '80
(419) 843-6420 **Ramsey** Brian M '91
(419) 213-4700 **Ranazzi** Andrew K '88
(419) 243-5581 **Randall** Benjamin A '00
(419) 242-9405 **Randall** Jane S '83
(419) 242-4011 **Rankin** Bonnie Rae '93
(419) 861-1141 **Ray** Brenda A '98
(419) 537-1954 **Reardon** Christine A '86
(419) 241-9000 **Rectenwald** David J '86
(419) 530-3332 **Reed** Kathleen M '93
(419) 241-6000 **Regnier** Michael W '93
(419) 843-2001 **Reight** Rachel M '04
(419) 241-6000 **Reinbolt** Steven D '85
(419) 246-5757 **Reinker** Lisa M '03
(419) 242-9501 **Reiser** George K '87
(419) 244-8336 **Reiser** Rosalind A '86
(419) 248-6546 **Relation** Alfred J '83
(419) 254-1311 **Reminger & Reminger**
(419) 243-1105 **Reny** Dennis M '77
(419) 242-5485 **Repass** Michael D '84
(419) 241-9000 **Rerucha** Cynthia L '84
(419) 885-3000 **Restivo** James B '96
(419) 249-6743 **Restivo** Laura A '95
(419) 882-0533 **Retske** Robert A '70
(419) 243-6610 **Reynolds** Frank E '83
(419) 245-2550 **Reynolds** Susan J '84
(419) 255-6810 **Reynolds** Timothy R '79
(419) 255-0814 **Ricaurte** Eve K '93
(419) 531-5758 **Rice** Darrel L '77
(419) 480-1900 **Rice** Kollin L '96
(419) 243-1294 **Rice** Philip M '62
(419) 241-6168 **Richardson** Jon D '73
(419) 241-9000 **Rideout** Joseph A '76
(419) 535-4128 **Rider** John A III '94
(419) 247-4267 **Ries** Deborah K '01
(419) 246-5757 **Riesen** Kent D '89
(419) 251-3679 **Riethmiller** Michael K '84
(419) 867-3946 **Riewaldt** Martha L '80
(419) 244-4000 **Rife** Joan H '82
(419) 243-6148 **Riley** Ted B '88
(419) 242-2251 **Riley** Tyrone '85
(419) 241-3565 **Risner** Rick L '83
(419) 473-3450 **Ritson** Douglas J '92
(419) 241-3213 **Ritter Robinson McCready & James**
(419) 242-3900 **Roach** Stephen C '84
(419) 241-9000 **Roberts** H Buswell Jr. '75
(419) 244-4777 **Roberts** Richard L Sr. '89
(419) 255-5900 **Robinette** Gregory W '00
Robinson Mark A '79
(419) 724-0030 **Robinson** Tonya M '99
(419) 249-7900 **Robison Curphey & O'Connell**
(419) 843-2001 **Roca** John M '86
(419) 241-9000 **Rodgers** Damian M P '94
(419) 475-5151 **Roemer** Wellington F III '89
(419) 242-7985 **Roetzel & Andress,LPA**
(419) 241-6000 **Rogers** James L '88
(419) 245-4913 **Rogers** Jon A '83
(419) 248-2600 **Rohrbacher** David J '75
(419) 248-2600 **Rohrbacher** Matthew J '80
(419) 248-2600 **Rohrbachers Light Cron & Trimble Co,LPA**
(419) 249-7100 **Rollison** Gerardo R '80
(419) 241-6168 **Roman** Jane E '02
(419) 842-1252 **Romanoff** Rollind W '61
(419) 241-1200 **Romp** Janelle M '03
(419) 259-7633 **Romstadt** Lori A '99
(419) 242-1515 **Roose & Ressler PA**
(419) 249-7100 **Root** Bridgett J '98
(419) 249-7100 **Rose** Mark H '87
(419) 241-6168 **Rost** Peter G '77
(419) 389-6413 **Roth** Thomas J '85
(419) 241-9000 **Rothschild** James I '93
(419) 241-9000 **Rothschild** Stephen A '88
(419) 243-7281 **Rothstein** Scott D '91
(419) 535-4655 **Rotman** Phillip A II '93
(419) 241-8555 **Rowell** Charles S Jr. '74
(419) 252-6239 **Rowen** Theodore M '70
(419) 241-6612 **Royer** George R '66
(419) 252-5876 **Royer** Jeffrey T '88
(419) 243-6281 **Rozic** John W '78
(419) 244-7482 **Rubin** Daryl K '82
(419) 241-7211 **Rubin** Joanne '84
(419) 259-6470 **Rubin** Kenneth J '04
(419) 244-7482 **Rubin** Sheldon '53
(419) 241-2201 **Rubinoff** Norman J '66
(419) 213-3366 **Rudebock** David T '91
(419) 385-5721 **Rump** Deborah K '84
(419) 476-0347 **Rust** John G '48
(419) 213-6907 **Rutledge** Brenda I '88
(419) 259-6806 **Ruyle** James P '79
(419) 243-6450 **Saglioccolo** Gaetano '92
(419) 471-1489 **St Clair** Beverly J '93
St Clair Donald D '92
(419) 255-0814 **Salas** Jesus R '95
(419) 475-8665 **Salem** Nadeem S '96
(419) 537-4236 **Salem** Robert S '90
(419) 473-1350 **Sallah** Charles H '81
(419) 244-4605 **Salsberry** Tam E '91
(419) 241-9000 **Sanderson** Michael G '81
(419) 245-1975 **Santiago** Lourdes '79
(419) 213-4700 **Santoro** Jeremy J '01
(419) 243-8251 **Sapara** Matthew A '99
(419) 241-6000 **Sargeant** Richard T '75
(419) 843-3545 **Sass** James C '73
(419) 243-1144 **Saum** Scott J '75
(419) 242-8900 **Sawan** Dennis P '88
(419) 243-5581 **Sawers** Mary Lou '01
(419) 255-5917 **Scalzo** Joseph R Jr. '77
(419) 249-7100 **Scalzo** Michael S '79
(419) 243-1294 **Schaffer** Mark C '69
(419) 843-2001 **Schaffer** Thomas J '90
(419) 243-6281 **Schaller** James F II '03
(419) 245-2740 **Schank** Laura J '93
(419) 255-4300 **Schank** Thomas J '77
(419) 243-1294 **Schaub** Charles R '73
(419) 243-2283 **Scheer Green & Burke Co,LPA**
(419) 241-6450 **Scheich** Richard A '84
(419) 241-9000 **Scheidel** Rolf H '65
(419) 841-9113 **Schlachter** Thomas L '70
(419) 243-6281 **Schlageter** John J III '97
(419) 243-6281 **Schlageter** John J Jr. '73
(419) 241-1261 **Schlatter** Donald A '56
(419) 241-7371 **Schlaudecker** David G '76
(419) 885-3000 **Schmidt** Philip L '74
(419) 841-4294 **Schnorf** Brandon G Jr. '58
(419) 248-2646 **Schnorf** David M '64

(419) 841-4294 **Schnorf Ferguson & Griffith**
(419) 244-8336 **Schoenberger** Bruce S '83
(419) 213-3000 **Schreibman** Sydney A '94
(419) 244-3344 **Schroeder** Charles F '57
(419) 478-1776 **Schroeder** Jeffery A '94
(419) 244-3808 **Schuchmann** John J '54
(419) 535-0311 **Schuller** James L '77
(419) 249-7100 **Schurr** Donald A '89
(419) 241-9999 **Schwab** Stuart S '78
(419) 255-5900 **Schweikert** James D '03
(419) 255-5900 **Schweikert** Staci E '02
(419) 241-1200 **Schwieterman** Nicole K '99
(419) 530-1472 **Sciarini** James M '81
(419) 283-5444 **Scott** John N '84
(419) 241-5454 **Scott** Robert B '01
(419) 241-2122 **Scott** Robert M '84
(419) 213-4700 **Scott** Rose M '00
(419) 473-1300 **Scouten** John D '71
(419) 254-3121 **Sechrist** Rebecca C '86
(419) 259-6376 **Secor** Thomas O '77
(419) 241-3213 **Seitzinger** Mark P '89
(419) 248-2600 **Selis** Tracy B '01
(419) 262-9898 **Serraino** Stephen R '81
(419) 242-1400 **Shaffer** Russel E '72
(419) 255-5900 **Shah** Shital A '97
(419) 255-8260 **Sharfman** Mervin S '67
(419) 865-8021 **Shemas** James F '47
(419) 243-6281 **Shindler** James V Jr. '66
(419) 243-6281 **Shindler Neff Holmes & Schlageter,LLP**
(419) 242-7985 **Shinn** Jason M '01
(419) 254-3104 **Shook** David C '90
(419) 241-9000 **Shope** Gregory J '01
(419) 213-4775 **Shousher** Eileen S '90
(419) 241-8885 **Shousher** Mohamed Y '80
(419) 245-4944 **Shuba** John H '90
(419) 241-9000 **Shumaker** Gregory S '73
(419) 241-9000 **Shumaker Loop & Kendrick,LLP**
(419) 321-1377 **Siciliano** John J '78
(419) 383-3898 **Siegel** Gregory B '84
(419) 249-7900 **Sieler** Jean A '87
(419) 252-6214 **Sikkema** Gary D '75
(419) 241-2777 **Sikkema** Sue A '82
(419) 252-6282 **Silk** James P '62
(419) 252-6210 **Silk** James P Jr. '93
(419) 243-3261 **Silverman** Nathan Leo '61
(419) 241-9000 **Silverman** Peter R '84
(419) 474-9514 **Silvers** Kyle A '97
(419) 243-6281 **Simko** David J '75
(419) 213-6951 **Simko** Megan E '04
(419) 321-1389 **Simpson** Joseph S '88
(419) 245-1942 **Singer** Arlene '76
(419) 241-8811 **Skotynsky** Walter J '76
(419) 213-2001 **Skrzyniecki** Duane J '77
(419) 255-3153 **Slaybod** Sheldon M '75
Slayton Thomas F '75
(419) 841-0221 **Sloan** Aaron P '98
(419) 729-5448 **Sloma** Anthony P '97
(419) 325-2111 **Smith** Arthur H '60
(419) 241-6000 **Smith** Bruce L '66
(419) 244-8384 **Smith** Craig J '04
(419) 472-1720 **Smith** David E '90
(419) 249-7100 **Smith Gorski** Clare K '94
(419) 251-0714 **Smith** Harold T '93
(419) 244-0991 **Smith** J P '97
(419) 882-4131 **Smith** Jeffrey T '93
(419) 243-6281 **Smith** Mary E '85
(419) 243-2100 **Smith** Steven R '80
(419) 247-8699 **Smith** Susan L '00
(419) 245-1978 **Smith** Victoria L '87
(419) 247-1662 **Snavely** Jeffrey D '96
(419) 530-2418 **Snider** Stephen J '02
(419) 213-4700 **Sniderhan** James T '76
(419) 243-3800 **Snyder** Constance A '83
(419) 241-1200 **Snyder** Lucy M '96
(419) 255-5900 **Sobanski** Mark J '82
(419) 242-9908 **Sobecki** Thomas A '81
Sodeman William A Jr. '97
(419) 213-4754 **Sofia-Cerilli** Tamara L '97
(419) 248-3501 **Solomon** Joseph J Jr. '84
(419) 244-6788 **Solt** Robert L III '84
(419) 241-2100 **Sommer** Gary O '84
(419) 693-4433 **Sorah** Linda A '96
(419) 213-4700 **Sorg** Bruce J '92
(419) 841-2073 **Souders** Kenneth M '78
(419) 242-1400 **Sparrow** Keithley B '79
(419) 241-1200 **Spencer** Jodi D '01
(419) 242-8214 **Spencer** Scott E '79
(419) 241-2201 **Spengler Nathanson PLL**
(419) 249-4956 **Speyer** Sharon S '85
(419) 245-3016 **Spidel** Mara L '99
(419) 242-7985 **Spiker** Douglas E '86
(419) 242-1555 **Spitler** Steven M '81
(419) 242-1555 **Spitler & Williams-Young Co,LPA**
(419) 241-9000 **Spitzer** Lyman F '76
(419) 472-0535 **Spohler** Norman G '81
(419) 247-1731 **Sponseller** Carrie L '01
(419) 842-1035 **Sprenger** George F '74
(419) 243-9424 **Spychalski** Deborah K '93
(419) 243-8003 **Squillante** David G '82
(419) 255-0814 **Stafford** Ellen M '81
(419) 242-9393 **Stahlbush** Kristin A '94
(419) 244-8000 **Staler** John J Jr. '99
(419) 241-2777 **Stallings** Douglas E '94
(419) 247-2500 **Stanford** Stephen J '75
(419) 243-2042 **Stanton** Kristen A '01
(419) 724-3499 **Starbird** Debra L '93
(419) 251-3568 **Starcher** John M '01
(419) 241-6000 **Starr** Kimberly A '99
(419) 936-5120 **Stebbins** Thomas R '80
(419) 241-9000 **Steele** Cynthia L K '98
(419) 241-9000 **Steele** Jared B S '02
(419) 245-1975 **Steinberg** Stephen J '97
(419) 243-6200 **Steltenpohl** Darrell D '99
(419) 243-6200 **Steltenpohl James & Menacher Co,LPA**
(419) 241-1200 **Steves** Jennifer W '02
(419) 478-1776 **Stewart** John C '89
(419) 241-9000 **Stewart** Mark C '76
(419) 247-1500 **Stockwell & Cooperman,LPA**
(419) 247-1500 **Stockwell** John P '73
(419) 245-2550 **Stokes** Michael L '95
(419) 242-8214 **Stoner** Amy E '00
(419) 241-6000 **Stopar** Jeffrey M '96
(419) 472-1900 **Stough** Andrew J '01
(419) 246-5757 **Straub** Jessica Wilson '03
(419) 241-9000 **Straub** John L '70
(419) 472-9041 **Strauss** Robert D '92
(419) 241-1200 **Strup** David P '86
(419) 213-4745 **Strzesynski** Michelle A '96
(419) 255-7300 **Strzyinski** Kathy J '96
(419) 249-7900 **Stuckey** David W '75
(419) 241-6000 **Stump** Alexandra M '03
(419) 248-3563 **Stupsker** Charles A '65
(419) 241-6000 **Sturgeon** Margaret M '90
(419) 241-2777 **Stutz** Barbara J '83
(419) 241-4211 **Stutz** Paul F '56
(419) 242-3989 **Styblo** Jennifer F '99
(419) 243-6281 **Sulewski** James A '87
(419) 215-3194 **Sullivan** Daniel J '02
(419) 213-4758 **Sullivan** Mary A '89
(419) 535-0075 **Sullivan** Michelle T '99
(419) 259-6524 **Suplica** Marie E '98
(419) 255-5900 **Sutter** Gary M '84
(419) 473-1346 **Sutter** Jude F '59
(419) 936-5120 **Swanson** Mary S '82
(419) 248-4677 **Sweeney** Frederick J '78
(419) 247-1789 **Swemba** Connie S '03
(419) 259-6376 **Sydlow** Holly T '75
(419) 245-1020 **Syring** Paul F '90
(419) 242-1001 **Szczepaniak** Richard J Jr. '77
(419) 244-8989 **Szollosi** Matthew A '98
(419) 535-0075 **Szollosi** Wednesday M '02
(419) 252-6270 **Szuberla** Joan C '83
(419) 245-2465 **Szuch** David P '82
(419) 248-2419 **Szyperski** Joseph T '04
(419) 248-2419 **Szyperski** Thomas J '70
(419) 324-2407 **Tackett** Kevin A '95
(419) 255-0814 **Tafelski** Joseph R '71
(419) 843-2001 **Takacs** William E '76
(419) 249-7900 **Talbott** D Casey '90
(419) 321-6444 **Tantari** Mark R '86
(419) 248-2009 **Taoka** Leslie M '79
(419) 241-6000 **Tarini** Mary Jo '91
(419) 471-0211 **Tassie** Deborah S '79
(419) 535-0311 **Taylor** Allison M '02
(419) 244-1000 **Taylor** David R III '76
(419) 248-3503 **Taylor** Douglas A '01
(419) 245-1020 **Taylor** Gary R '88
(419) 241-8195 **Taylor** Richard P '75
(419) 241-1200 **Terpinski** Kimberly '98
(419) 241-1200 **Thacker** Joseph P '78
(419) 242-8900 **Thakur** Nirakar C Jr. '95
(419) 255-3035 **Thebes** John B '89
(419) 241-2900 **Theis** Donald E '79
(419) 321-6325 **Thie** Christopher J '00
(419) 249-7900 **Thomas** Kimberly M '03
Thomson Constance S '80
(419) 865-8021 **Thomson** Joseph M '80
(419) 241-6000 **Tice** Ronald J '73
(419) 248-1500 **Timonere** Steven '55
(419) 241-1200 **Tinsley** Dusty R '00
(419) 255-5900 **Todd** Oliver E Jr. '67
(419) 249-2703 **Tolliver** Lafayette E '77
(419) 213-4305 **Tomczak** Thomas N '68
(419) 243-1105 **Torzewski** Joan M '77
(419) 241-9000 **Tosi** Louis E '74
(419) 255-5900 **Toska** Anita S '03
(419) 245-1975 **Toska** David L '83
(419) 242-1400 **Traband** Charles M Jr. '78
(419) 241-6000 **Tracey** Shawn M '01
(419) 291-5959 **Trachsel** Kenneth R '89
(419) 248-2600 **Trimble** J Mark '90
(419) 245-1940 **Trimboli** Mary G '78
(419) 243-4006 **Trudel** Valerie A '97
(419) 255-0814 **Tucker** Robert P '70
(419) 248-3503 **Tucker** Theodore B III '76
(419) 536-5110 **Turin** John C '70
(419) 243-2100 **Turley** Anthony E '98
(419) 213-4700 **Turner** James D '72
(419) 241-2300 **Turvey-Albert** Michelle S '92
(419) 241-2122 **Tuschman** Chad M '02
(419) 213-6753 **Udell** Judith L '84
Ujvagi Matthew K '00
(419) 841-8584 **Urenovitch** Joseph J '96
(419) 472-2179 **Vail** James E Jr. '76
(419) 865-8021 **Valtin** James D '03
(419) 244-5000 **VanBerkom** Trevor P '99
(419) 255-6810 **Van Deilen** James W '79
(419) 866-0928 **Vaneck** Alexandria R '80
(419) 843-6581 **Van Gunten** Edward A '62
(419) 213-4746 **van het Kaar** Sally H '99
(419) 247-2500 **Van Horsten** Craig J '76
(419) 243-3800 **Van Huysen** Ian Scott '01
(419) 724-0030 **Varner** Julita '00
(419) 242-8214 **Varnes-Richardson** Jill M '96
(419) 241-9770 **Vassar Dills Dawson & Bonfiglio,LLC**
(419) 241-9770 **Vassar** James M '68
(419) 248-7848 **Vaughan** Deon '90
(419) 241-1969 **Vaughan** Elizabeth A '83
(419) 241-6168 **Vicente** Brian D '94
(419) 843-2001 **Vindas** Eva C '02
(419) 241-8811 **Viren** Jack P Jr. '78
(419) 693-4433 **Voller** Cindy M '92
(419) 936-3023 **Wachowiak** Joseph W '83
(419) 241-9000 **Wagenman** Barton L '67
(419) 213-6749 **Waggoner** Geoffrey M '80
(419) 213-6951 **Wagner** Melissa M '98
(419) 242-1400 **Wagner** Peter Jan '72
(419) 246-5757 **Wagoner** Gregory H '03
(419) 241-9000 **Wagoner** Mark D Jr. '97
(419) 241-2300 **Walerius** Timothy J '94
(419) 241-1200 **Walinski** Richard S '69
(419) 537-6700 **Wall** Virginia M '89
(419) 321-6444 **Walsh** Joseph M '82
(419) 213-4700 **Walter** James C '87
(419) 537-8679 **Walter** James E '67
(419) 213-4700 **Walz** Kenneth C '04
(419) 246-5757 **Wanick** John R '70
(419) 241-1200 **Ward** George C '76
(419) 243-6148 **Wasielewski** Glenn E '82
(419) 243-1239 **Wasserman Bryan Landry & Honold,LLP**
(419) 243-1239 **Wasserman** John C '64
(419) 243-4006 **Wasung** John S '91
(419) 241-9000 **Waterman** David F '79
(419) 241-2100 **Watkins Bates & Carey**
(419) 241-4400 **Watkins** Keith J '81
(419) 247-1687 **Watson** Laurie A '02
(419) 843-1333 **Waugh** Bradley R '99
(419) 535-4200 **Wawrzyniak** Jeffery J '93
(419) 535-7221 **Weaver** Donna M '82
(419) 241-9000 **Webb** Thomas I Jr. '73
(419) 245-1895 **Weber** Ford P '87
(419) 535-0075 **Webster** William H '81
(419) 537-2268 **Wedding** Donald K Sr. '67
(419) 213-4700 **Weglian** John J '72
(419) 245-1946 **Weiher** Roger R '56
(419) 882-0533 **Weinberg** Mark D '75
(419) 213-4755 **Weinstein** Andrea C '92
(419) 255-5111 **Weisberg** Joseph D '67
(419) 691-5745 **Weisenburger** Margaret M '78
(419) 321-6444 **Weisenburger** Thomas E '62
(419) 241-0767 **Weldon** Thomas P '94
(419) 244-7596 **Weller** Lucinda J '99
(419) 243-8251 **Wenk** Dawn M '97
(419) 241-7175 **Wenner** William E '83
(419) 473-1350 **Wenninger** Kenneth W '99
(419) 531-3887 **Werner** Kim W '71
(419) 241-9000 **Werner** Martin D '81
(419) 539-4092 **West-Estell** Rebecca L '00
(419) 241-2300 **Westfall** Sandra A '98
(419) 244-7041 **Westmeyer** Joseph W III '99
(419) 244-7041 **Westmeyer** Joseph W Jr. '66
(419) 244-9500 **Weston** Gretchen F Goranson '03
(419) 244-6788 **Wetli** John F '69
(419) 245-1080 **Wheelock** Donald S '96
(419) 241-4141 **Whitcomb** Howard C III '91
(419) 246-5757 **White** Garrick O '98
(419) 241-9000 **White** James F Jr. '65
(419) 479-3959 **White** James W Jr. '80
(419) 241-5522 **White** Kenneth I Sr. '61
(419) 254-4300 **White** Kenneth J '74
(419) 213-4755 **Wichowski** Judith E '87
(419) 241-9000 **Wicklund** David W '74
(419) 691-4232 **Wiley** David F '63
(419) 249-7900 **Wiley** Julia S '84
(419) 244-6788 **Wilhelms** Andrew Jon '96
(419) 244-6788 **Wilhelms** Tybo A '76
(419) 259-6420 **Wilhelmy** Kristi Kress '04
(419) 246-3777 **Wilkins** Douglas A '82
(419) 241-9770 **Wilkowski** Keith A '82
(419) 241-3310 **Willey** David S '02
(419) 241-6000 **Willey** John D Jr. '79
(419) 242-1515 **Willey** Loretta J '99
(419) 291-2034 **Williams** Anne K '94
(419) 243-6610 **Williams** Brian Ray '78
(419) 241-3213 **Williams** Gregory A '87
(419) 241-2122 **Williams Jilek Lafferty Gallagher & Scott Co,LPA**
(419) 241-2122 **Williams** Martin W '69
(419) 213-4061 **Williams** Robert B '67
(419) 843-2001 **Williams** Vernos J '76
(419) 882-0601 **Williams** Vesper C II '73
(419) 242-1555 **Williams-Young** Marc G '82
(419) 213-3203 **Williamson** Julie T '89
(419) 247-1808 **Williamson** Lane D '89
(419) 241-1200 **Wilson** Beth Ann '97
Wilson Jeffrey J '01
(419) 693-7717 **Wilson** John M '82
(419) 259-6376 **Wilson** Joseph R '81
(419) 843-2001 **Wilson** Martha J '97
(419) 486-9999 **Wineland** Erik J '00
(419) 243-3800 **Wingate** Ronnie L '79
(419) 241-9770 **Winterhalter** Keith J '87
(419) 321-6444 **Winters** Steven B '96
(419) 252-6228 **Wise** David G '67
(419) 327-4303 **Wise & Dorner,Ltd**
(419) 327-4300 **Wise** Patricia A '85
(419) 291-2034 **Wisniewski** Jeffrey T '00
(419) 241-5175 **Wisniewski** Samara L '04
(419) 243-9873 **Witcher** Jenelda E '95
(419) 241-9000 **Witherell** Dennis P '77
(419) 213-3000 **Witko** Michael G '83
(419) 241-3251 **Witt** Robert E '66
(419) 535-7444 **Wittenberg** Joseph L '72
(419) 255-6070 **Wittenberg Phillips Levy & Nusbaum**
(419) 255-6070 **Wittenberg** Sheldon S '69
(419) 242-6505 **Wohl** Doris K '73
(419) 930-3030 **Wojtas** Yvonne A '04
(419) 259-8158 **Wolf** Philip H '78
(419) 252-6238 **Wolff** Cheryl F '79
(419) 936-5120 **Wolff** Jill E '95
(419) 252-6253 **Wolff** Richard E '80
(419) 245-1862 **Wood** Karen E '89
(419) 255-3948 **Woodley** Robert A '77
(419) 249-6685 **Woods** Joyce Ann '80
(419) 241-9000 **Woodward** Kathryn J '87
(419) 243-6281 **Worline** Daniel A '74
(419) 248-2419 **Worline** Robin A '01
(419) 843-9960 **Wroblewski** Dennis E '79
(419) 535-4675 **Wurster** Lisa A '85
(419) 843-5355 **Wurster** Phillip D '84
(419) 247-2500 **Yates** James B '90
(419) 243-7243 **Yavorcik** James E '79
(419) 249-6745 **Yerman** John W Jr. '77
(419) 243-6281 **Yoppolo** Louis J '80
(419) 243-3261 **Young** Jeremy G '01
(419) 244-7885 **Young** Kurt M '93
(419) 259-6376 **Young** Robert G '71
(419) 247-1114 **Young** Thomas Lee '72
(419) 878-9988 **Youngston** Diane L '90
(419) 885-3000 **Youssef-Coyle** Lami H '84
(419) 252-5859 **Zalewski** Cynthia M '94
(419) 843-2001 **Zan** Kelley A '02
(419) 242-8214 **Zaner & Cimerman**
(419) 242-8214 **Zaner** Lorin Jay '76
(419) 254-5246 **Zaremba** Thomas S '77
(419) 321-1460 **Zarou** Mechelle '00
(419) 241-1200 **Zazycki** Suzanne '03
(419) 242-7415 **Zemmelman** Connie F '82
(419) 244-3006 **Zigray** Daniel F '91
(419) 255-1515 **Zilba** Jeffrey C '87
(419) 841-1411 **Zima** John P '87
(419) 531-4544 **Zimmerman** Roger K '79
(419) 248-2600 **Zimmerman** Todd M '97
(419) 241-1200 **Zinz** Marguerite A '01
(419) 841-9623 **Zoll** David W '77
(419) 841-9623 **Zoll & Kranz**
(419) 247-2500 **Zouhary** Jack '76
(419) 841-6786 **Zugay** Anthony A Jr. '70
(419) 842-1166 **Zychowicz** Michael J '85
(419) 213-4700 **Zychowicz** Ralph C '79
(419) 243-1144 **Zyndorf** Sol '74

TORONTO

Jefferson County

(740) 537-4687 **Allen** Craig J '90
(740) 537-3827 **Haynes** William Jr. '80

TRENTON

Butler County

(513) 988-9357 **Binns** Patrick A '76
(513) 988-6193 **Harrison** Brian K '96
(513) 988-6169 **Yauch** Elizabeth A '88

TROTWOOD

Montgomery County

(937) 854-3047 **Flora** Bruce J '81
(937) 854-1137 **Petroziello** Brian C '77

TROY

Miami County

(937) 332-7016 **Altenburger** Scott R '85
(937) 332-6848 **Altier** Mark W '73
(937) 339-0511 **Baer** Michael A '74
(937) 335-6495 **Bazler** Frank E '53
(937) 332-6993 **Beers** Gretchen K '84
(937) 440-9220 **Beitzel** David E '76
(937) 440-5960 **Bennett** James D '85
(937) 339-0511 **Brookshire** James D '91
(937) 332-0138 **Brumbaugh** Jeffrey S '01
(937) 332-9300 **Bucio** Christopher R '03
(937) 332-9300 **Bucio & Ehinger,LLP**
(937) 332-6936 **Caldwell** David J '93
(937) 339-0511 **Cargill** Michael L '79
(937) 335-7366 **Carter** Jack L '83
(937) 335-5658 **Clark** Christopher D '95
(937) 335-0570 **Cotner** John M '70
(937) 440-5960 **Dicks** James R Jr. '96
(937) 339-1500 **Dixon** William M Jr. '75
(937) 339-7181 **Donnelly** Dennis M '76
(937) 339-0511 **Dungan & LeFevre Co,LPA**
(937) 335-2928 **Earhart** Scott W '95
(937) 332-9300 **Ehinger** Mark A '03
(937) 339-2627 **Evans** Nika R '00
(937) 339-2627 **Farley** Jason R '02
(937) 335-8324 **Faust Harrelson Fulker McCarthy & Schlemmer**
(937) 335-8324 **Fraas** Richard J '59
(937) 335-8324 **Fulker** John E '53
(937) 335-8324 **Fulker** William J '82
(937) 339-0511 **Gearhardt** Michelle J '80
(937) 332-6836 **Gee** Christopher M '78
(937) 335-7963 **Geisinger** Bruce '66
(937) 339-0511 **Goodenough** Wendy J '98
(937) 335-2121 **Greenwald** Carol E '77
(937) 332-6971 **Gutmann** Elizabeth S '84
(937) 335-8324 **Harrelson** Robert M '82
(937) 335-3666 **Harvey** Randal A '85
(937) 332-6965 **Hemm** Michael W '74
(937) 335-0550 **Huffman Landis & Weaks Co,LPA**
(937) 335-0550 **Huffman** Robert J Jr. '88
(937) 335-0550 **Huffman** Samuel L '95
(937) 332-9300 **Ikramuddin** Asmina '03
(937) 339-2919 **Johnson** Kay F '91
(937) 339-1500 **Johnston** Robert C '78
(937) 335-8760 **Jones** Phillip M '74
(937) 339-0511 **Kappers** Alan M '77
(937) 332-6920 **Kemmer** Aubrey M '78
(937) 440-5960 **Kendell** Anthony E '96
(937) 339-1500 **Kerber** Grant D '97
(937) 332-9300 **Kim** Jonghoon James '03
(937) 339-2651 **King** Stephen W '72
(937) 332-2112 **Kremmel** Donn A '88
(937) 335-0550 **Landis** Raymond L '67
(937) 339-7161 **Lang** Michael L '79
(937) 322-6811 **Layman** Steven R '85
(937) 339-1500 **Livingston** James R '69
(937) 440-5960 **Long** Robert E III '96
(937) 335-5658 **Lopez** Jose M '79
(937) 335-5658 **Lopez Severt & Pratt Co,LPA**
(937) 335-5658 **Lucia** Andrew D '96
(937) 339-2627 **Luring** Roger E '75
(937) 332-9300 **Martin** Laura J '03
(937) 335-8324 **McCarthy** Robert A '55
(937) 339-0511 **McGraw** William J '73
(937) 339-1500 **Merritt** Tom O '96
(937) 339-0511 **Mikel** David L '89
(937) 339-2627 **Miller & Luring Co,LPA**
(937) 335-7142 **Morgan** Carol A '82
(937) 440-5960 **Nasal** Gary A '88
(937) 335-5658 **Pratt** Andrew R '94
(937) 440-5960 **Pratt** Jeannine N '95
(937) 339-2651 **Princi** Paul R '72
(937) 335-7142 **Ratcliff** Ann L '83
(937) 332-2114 **Rodgers** Thomas H '70
(937) 778-3800 **Rowley** Jamie P '01
(937) 335-8324 **Schlemmer** Robert N '69
(937) 339-1500 **Sell** Charles H II '73
(937) 332-6993 **Severt** Katherine K '91
(937) 335-5658 **Severt** Todd D '92
(937) 339-1500 **Shipman Dixon & Livingston**
(937) 339-4257 **Smith** De Wayne '72
(937) 339-0511 **Sorg** Matthew C '94
(937) 335-2622 **Utrecht** James D '77
(937) 339-7161 **Vest** Margaret E '89

(937) 332-7000 **Votava** Andrew R '94
(937) 335-0550 **Walters** Jennifer J '96
(937) 335-8760 **Wannemacher** John A '66
(937) 335-0550 **Weaks** Gary L '70
(937) 339-1180 **Weigl** William '58
(937) 335-2622 **Young** Fredric L '92
(937) 332-7084 **Zuhl** Gary E '76
(937) 335-5658 **Zweizig** Jonathan S '98

TWINSBURG
Summit County

(330) 425-4201 **Arnovitz** Michael S '86
(330) 425-4201 **Bailey** Edward A '97
(330) 425-4696 **Bartlebaugh** Thomas E '85
(330) 425-4201 **Bohnert** Edward G '80
(330) 486-4007 **Brady** Brooke M '00
(330) 425-9282 **Brown** Kevin E '80
(330) 405-5061 **Carr** Adam E '93
(330) 425-8520 **Casterline** Christopher S '01
(330) 405-3391 **Chapman** George B III '83
(216) 901-9111 **Chase** Michael G '98
(330) 425-4201 **Chernek** Ronald J '89
(330) 487-5151 **Doyle** Duane L '71
(330) 486-3100 **Dunn** Leslie D '75
(330) 963-7253 **Eyhusen** Edward A '85
(330) 425-8520 **Fox** Rosmarie T '86
(330) 425-4201 **Franks** Stephen R '02
(330) 405-5061 **Grigsby** Kelly N '96
(330) 405-5440 **Grist** Thomas '93
(330) 425-4201 **Gross** Adam L '91
(330) 963-3939 **Hults** Richard E '93
(330) 405-5061 **Hura** Mark S '85
(330) 486-3000 **Icsman** Robert D '94
(330) 425-4201 **Kalniz** Jeffrey T '96
(330) 425-4201 **Kanellis** Dean W '94
(800) 800-3106 **Katz** Richard S '84
(330) 405-5061 **Kosla** Phillip C '98
(330) 487-6965 **Kramer** Timothy E '69
(330) 486-0950 **Lah-O'Brien** Kristina I '94
(330) 963-5883 **Lentz** Karen C '95
(330) 425-8520 **Lerner Sampson & Rothfuss**
(330) 425-4201 **Locke** Faye D '02
(330) 425-4201 **Lorber** Michael F '73
(330) 425-8520 **Mandryk** Susan E '97
(330) 425-3500 **Martin** Donald L '64
(330) 425-4201 **Mehler** Peter L '02
(330) 405-5061 **Moliterno** Louis R '95
(330) 405-4736 **Mueller** Caroline A '92
(330) 425-2354 **Nelson** Sidney G Jr. '90
(330) 963-6600 **Pecchio** Robert A '84
(330) 963-0022 **Petsche** John A III '89
(330) 405-9005 **Rader** Clarence B III '89
(330) 425-9199 **Randazzo** Joseph C '99
(330) 272-2488 **Randazzo** Mary E '98
(330) 425-4201 **Reimer** Dennis '68
(330) 425-4201 **Reimer Lorber & Arnovitz Co, LPA**
(330) 425-2291 **Richner** Robert A '76
(330) 405-5061 **Sah** Perrin I '95
(330) 963-1015 **Seibert** Darrel L II '91
(330) 405-5061 **Sennett** James A '80
(330) 486-4058 **Shannon** Colleen M '89
(330) 486-3403 **Sherriff** David J '70
(330) 487-6520 **Swift** Dean A '78
(330) 405-5061 **Wantz** Joseph H '82
(330) 405-5061 **Williams** Roger H '79
(330) 405-5061 **Williams Sennett & Scully Co, LPA**
(330) 425-4201 **Wrentmore** James C '90

UHRICHSVILLE
Tuscarawas County

(740) 922-4161 **Connolly Hillyer & Welch**
(740) 922-4795 **Fragasse** Maria L '81
Gossett Jay M '87
(740) 922-4161 **Hillyer** Bradley L '81
(740) 922-4161 **Hillyer** William H '53
(740) 922-4161 **Jackson** Jason L '01
(740) 922-4161 **Welch** Kenneth R '79
(740) 922-1497 **Wheeler** Joseph A '84

UNIONTOWN
Summit County

(330) 877-8850 **Barnoff** Michelle S '88
(330) 699-6102 **Bates Bostian** Geneva R '80
(330) 896-7821 **Bucklew** Roger D '91
(330) 699-6703 **DeHaven** Darren W '95
(330) 699-6703 **Demczyk** Michael V '82
(330) 896-0300 **Donohew** Monty Lee '92
(330) 699-6703 **Fortado** Matthew '77
(330) 699-6703 **Freeman** Sidney N '77
(330) 896-9172 **Gibson** Joseph W '72
Lang Paul A '77
(330) 896-6162 **Lowrie** Scott R '84
Manning Jeffrey J '01
(330) 699-6703 **McNamara & Freeman Co, LPA**
(330) 699-6703 **McNamara** Robert F '77
(330) 899-0475 **Moore** Christopher J '95
(330) 699-5002 **Olson** Martin L '73
(330) 896-4500 **Weimer** David P '85
(330) 896-4500 **Weimer** Paul E '50

UNIONVILLE
Ashtabula County

(440) 428-1258 **Per Due** David W '86

UNIVERSITY HEIGHTS
Cuyahoga County

(216) 932-5556 **Adelman** Eugene M '56
Arons Murray H '95
Bendycki Richard T '81
(216) 932-1069 **Brooks** Ellen M '87
Delsander Dominic C '64
(216) 291-9905 **DeRocco** Gary D '74
(216) 321-8284 **Freedman** Leland S '56
(216) 397-4563 **Gross** Joanne '86
(216) 371-0568 **Katz** Roger J '82
(216) 765-1414 **Kenny** Robert E III '82
(216) 932-4961 **Kimball** Maynerd A '59
(216) 381-0315 **Kraus** William M '50
(216) 932-2902 **LoPresti** Carl L '76
Luxenburg Mitchel E '99
Mandel Stewart I '69
Marino Lucien R '72
(216) 691-0369 **Rubadue** Laura S '97
(216) 321-8033 **Sills** Alan J '82
(216) 371-4306 **Sugerman** Martin A '58
(216) 397-4434 **Swenson** Elizabeth v '86

UPPER ARLINGTON
Franklin County

(614) 538-2901 **Buck** Elaine S '81
(614) 583-5044 **Ford** Regina M '93
Gazivoda Jelena '90
(614) 799-1788 **Hagen** Theresa L '92
(614) 481-8608 **Halliburton-Cohen** Kim M '82
(614) 481-8608 **Kenney-Pfalzer** Susan M '03
(614) 451-3771 **Schaefer** Philip S '72
Schooley Ruth K '86
Truitt Susan '84

UPPER SANDUSKY
Wyandot County

(419) 294-2232 **Bacon** David F '77
(419) 294-2232 **Bacon** Forrest H '51
(419) 294-2924 **Bartholomew** Charles L '72
(419) 294-5781 **Beck** Bruce J '81
(419) 294-1333 **Brown** Richard R '68
(419) 294-5781 **Browne** David J '88
(419) 294-3132 **Collins** Kathryn M '98
(419) 294-3132 **Ellis** Mark J '77
(419) 273-2730 **Fox** Daniel E '86
(419) 294-2336 **Fox** Mary E '81
(419) 294-3533 **Funk** James C '83
(419) 294-1981 **Grafmiller** Richard A '73
(419) 294-4991 **Gray** Martha M '92
(419) 294-3132 **Mason** David C '61
(419) 294-3132 **Mason Mason & Ellis**
(419) 294-2232 **Miller** Jonathan K '95
(419) 294-2336 **Osborn & Fox,LPA**
(419) 294-2336 **Osborn** Thomas E '75
(419) 294-1200 **Pfeifer** Agnes A '86
(419) 294-1200 **Pfeifer** Dennis E '79
(419) 294-2532 **Pfeifer** E Michael '73
(419) 294-2232 **Roth Bacon Young**
(419) 294-1971 **Roth** Jeffrey P '72
(419) 294-1200 **Rowland** Douglas D '02
(419) 294-2336 **Ruhlen** James M '98
(419) 294-5701 **Scheck** Frederick L III '73
(419) 294-5701 **Scheck** Laurie A '97
(419) 294-5701 **Schoenberger** Loren C '49
(419) 294-9744 **Snyder** Mary F '97
(419) 294-5701 **Stansbery Schoenberger & Scheck**
(419) 294-4977 **Weaver** Stephanie A '92
(419) 294-2232 **Young** Kenneth L '93

URBANA
Champaign County

(937) 652-1606 **Berry** B Bradley '03
(937) 484-7303 **Brecount** Steven T '95
(937) 652-2224 **Bucci** Christopher M '01
(937) 653-7174 **Davidson** Harley A '77
(937) 653-7186 **Denkewalter** William F '95
(937) 484-2455 **Duggan** Scott T '99
(937) 652-2224 **Ellis** Kirk D '91
(937) 652-2224 **Feinstein** Mark M '95
(937) 653-7376 **Fornof-Lippencott** Susan J '89
(937) 653-7174 **Gilbert** Brett A '92
Hahn Joshua J '02
(937) 653-7186 **Harris** Richard O '58
(937) 653-4478 **Heckman** Darrell L '75
(937) 653-7186 **Houston Harris & Denkewalter**
(937) 653-7174 **Maurice** Allen R '70
(937) 652-2744 **Meyer** Richard A '74
(937) 653-8338 **Nau** Richard E '85
(937) 653-3501 **Navarre** Mark A '96
(937) 652-2700 **Pappas** George Z '86
(937) 653-5257 **Paulig** Karl E '53
(937) 653-5257 **Paulig Singer & Talebi**
(937) 653-5259 **Schneider** Philip S '68
(937) 652-1555 **Selvaggio** Nicola A '91
(937) 653-5257 **Singer** Bradley C '89
(937) 653-7186 **Smack** LeAnna D '02
(937) 653-8200 **Strapp** Robert M '76
(937) 653-5257 **Talebi** Kevin S '98
(937) 653-3467 **Tompkins** Ronald C '85
(937) 653-1729 **Valore** Joseph P '62
(937) 653-7174 **Wagner Maurice Davidson & Gilbert**
(937) 653-3170 **Weithman** Cathy J '78
(937) 653-3170 **Weithman** Gil S '83
(937) 652-1555 **Whitesell** Jack W Jr. '89

UTICA
Licking County

(740) 892-4444 **Gustafson** Alan P '73
(740) 892-3443 **Heath** F Richard '69
(740) 892-3443 **Hite & Heath**
(740) 892-3443 **Light** Sara G '87

VALLEY CITY
Medina County

Carroll Heidi R '02
(330) 483-3121 **Morton** Christopher R '04
(330) 225-6546 **Wootton** Arthur W '68

VALLEY VIEW
Cuyahoga County

(216) 328-0436 **Boncella** Gary A '78
(216) 447-0814 **Evangelista** James P '89
(216) 750-4511 **Gemperline** Richard B '80
(216) 778-6535 **Prokop** Josephine V '85
(216) 750-4529 **Stone** Alesia M '89

VANDALIA
Montgomery County

(937) 415-3300 **Babel** Thomas S '98
(937) 898-3996 **Bannister** Richard J '61
(937) 898-3990 **Courtney** Paul M '82
(937) 898-3911 **DeMarco** Alex U '61
(937) 898-4941 **Duffy** Edward J Jr. '51
(937) 264-8139 **Fischer** William E '77
(937) 264-1122 **Gibson** Joseph E '90
(937) 898-3975 **Gramza** Jeffrey T '91
Kiefer James C '58
(937) 890-5515 **Klein** Stephen E '75
(937) 454-9458 **Longo** James M '88
(937) 898-3975 **Moore** Joseph P '74
(937) 898-3996 **Rice** Bonnie B '79
(937) 890-2110 **Rollert** Joyce A '88
Scharff Martin '59
(937) 454-5544 **Slyman** Jeffrey D '79
(937) 415-3211 **Stipancich** John K '93

VAN WERT
Van Wert County

(419) 238-1010 **Bradford** Kent M '73
(419) 238-6553 **Burchfield** Martin D '86
(419) 238-5767 **Campbell** Phil W '76
(419) 238-6621 **Diller** Steven L '80
(419) 238-2057 **Gehres** Stephen P '76
(419) 238-0114 **Gordon** Scott R '88
(419) 238-6621 **Hatcher** John E '00
(419) 238-6621 **Hatcher** W Edward '74
(419) 238-4469 **Johnson** Donald J '74
(419) 238-2488 **Keister** Stephen E '74
(419) 238-0180 **Kennedy** Charles F III '79
(419) 238-0014 **Koch** Charles F '80
(419) 232-2700 **Leatherman** Jill T '02
(419) 238-2200 **Putman** Shaun A '02
(419) 238-6621 **Rauch** Kelly J '98
(419) 238-6621 **Rice** Earl J '80
(419) 238-2200 **Runser** C Allan '67
(419) 238-1010 **Summers** Jeffrey A '82
(419) 238-1166 **Taylor** Kevin H '77
(419) 238-5252 **Unterbrink** Gregory W '81
(419) 238-5307 **Wise** Perry G '50
Wolfrum Todd D '02
(419) 238-1166 **Yarger** Eva J '89
(419) 238-1166 **Young** Robert C '64
(419) 238-1166 **Young Taylor & Yarger**

VERMILION
Erie County

(440) 967-5195 **Adams** Charles F '70
(440) 967-2680 **Ashar** Michael K '85
Aukerman Russell R '89
Brown Susan R '87
(440) 967-6136 **Buckingham Lucal McGookey & Zeiher Co, LPA**
(440) 967-1513 **Chesky** Stuart B '03
(440) 967-0759 **Clark** Jonathan F '84
(440) 967-6136 **Dolyk** Walter Z '78
(440) 967-2060 **Downie** John F '59
(440) 967-0521 **Elden** John A '57
Fehr Jill D '90
(440) 984-2084 **Gammons** Patrick E '71
(440) 967-9065 **Kish** Robert A '90
(440) 967-8717 **Kishman** Henry W '76
(440) 967-6565 **Reeves** Gayle A '84
(440) 967-5695 **Schaffer** Gail M '77
(440) 967-5695 **Schaffer** Michael V '65

VERSAILLES
Darke County

(937) 526-3111 **Phelan** Brent J '95

VIENNA
Trumbull County

(330) 856-3898 **Lutseck** John P '84

WADSWORTH
Medina County

(330) 335-2304 **Bowers** Harold F Jr. '78
(330) 335-2748 **Brague** Norman E '71
(330) 336-7377 **Brewer** Scott E '88
(330) 334-6446 **Callow** Michael J '95
(330) 336-6666 **Crilly** John R '97
(330) 336-6666 **Dickey** Richard D '63
(330) 352-6090 **Dickinson** Joseph A '93
(330) 334-5255 **Foreman** Joseph E '65
(330) 336-3231 **Gerstenschlager** Neal J '76
(330) 336-3330 **Gigiano** Daniel F '99
Hall Jeffrey L '91
(330) 335-5961 **Hayne** James R '94
(330) 334-1536 **Hoffmann** Linda '84
(330) 334-1544 **Hogan** Roy F '88
(330) 336-3234 **Hood** Terry W '85
(330) 336-4455 **Jack** David C '83
(330) 334-2520 **Johnston** Charles F Jr. '54
(330) 334-9050 **Johnston** Wesley A '93
(330) 336-9561 **Krebs** Brian E '93
(330) 334-2877 **Manning** Elizabeth B '81
(330) 334-1536 **McIlvaine** Andrew S '96
(330) 334-1536 **McIlvaine** James R '69
(330) 335-1596 **McIlvaine** Stephen B '78
(330) 668-1163 **Michaels** Andrew '53
(330) 334-1536 **Morris** Thomas J '98
(330) 334-1536 **Morse** Mary J '83
(330) 334-4494 **Moss** John P '88
Mulhollan John S '94
(330) 334-6345 **Ondrey** Kevin P '99
(330) 334-1536 **Palecek McIlvaine Hoffmann & Morse Co LLP**
(330) 334-1536 **Palecek** Thomas E '69
(330) 336-4111 **Roberts** Nancy S '92
(330) 335-2749 **Schrock** Page C III '78
(330) 334-5258 **Thompson** Steven Forrest '94
Willis John M '89

WAKEMAN
Huron County

Hawley Matthew J '03

WALBRIDGE
Wood County

(419) 666-4974 **Perras** Douglas L '78

WALTON HILLS
Cuyahoga County

(440) 439-7700 **Churchmack** Allan G '89
(440) 439-1040 **Polster** Scott H '82
(440) 232-0505 **Sapir** George R '75
(440) 233-1283 **Turner** Deborah M '99

WAPAKONETA
Auglaize County

(419) 738-7180 **Allen** Eric J '01
(419) 738-9688 **Augsburger** Robert A '95
(419) 739-6510 **Brunner** John D '93
(419) 738-8165 **Burton** Courtney W '95
(419) 738-8165 **Burton** Michael A '95
(419) 738-7180 **Crisp** Jamie L '02
(419) 738-9678 **Derryberry** Quentin M II '70
(419) 738-4578 **Faller** Dennis P '79
(419) 738-9688 **Fox** Amy O '92
(419) 738-8171 **Hearn** James F '87
(419) 738-6768 **Holthaus** James H '81
(419) 738-9274 **Jauert** Douglas S '72
(419) 738-5215 **Kehoe** Robert W '89
(419) 738-1222 **Kentner** Matthew J '92
(419) 738-9688 **Meade** Darren L '94
(419) 738-8171 **Miller** Ronald H '68
(419) 738-7180 **Poppe** John A '72
(419) 738-7180 **Poppe** Kris R '93
(419) 738-7427 **Siesel** Gerald F '76
(419) 738-4417 **Stroebel** George E '42
(419) 738-7025 **Weller** Stanley M '79
(419) 738-8165 **Wiesenmayer** Robert C '65
(419) 738-8165 **Wiesenmayer** Robert C II '93

WARREN
Trumbull County

(330) 841-0985 **Allen** Thomas W '70
(330) 394-1501 **Alpern** Jack N '71
(330) 393-6400 **Ambrosy** Curtis J '77
(330) 675-2426 **Annos** LuWayne '91
(330) 399-6450 **Antonucci** Anthony L '80
(330) 399-5518 **Arbie** Phillip S '73
(330) 675-2426 **Bailey** Kenneth N '71
(330) 675-2426 **Barber** Diane L '98
(330) 395-9555 **Basile** Andrew R '86
(330) 393-3818 **Bauer** Roger R '73
(330) 675-2426 **Becker** Christopher D '90
(330) 399-3601 **Beil** Patricia S '93
(330) 394-1539 **Bennett** Bruce W '86
(330) 395-6444 **Berzonski** Laura Odenweller '04
(330) 395-3419 **Birrell** Bruce '53
(330) 392-5000 **Biviano** William R '74
(330) 399-4554 **Bluedorn** Samuel F '92
(330) 393-4060 **Bodor** Csaba A '72
(330) 399-2233 **Bodor** Frank R '56
(330) 373-7298 **Bombeck** Scott C '84
(330) 609-5515 **Bourne** Nicholas A '95
(330) 847-8383 **Brainard** Todd L '91
(330) 716-0855 **Braun** Gary L '83
(330) 392-1541 **Bricker** Gina DeGenova '00
(330) 609-5045 **Brutz** James M '84
(330) 373-1035 **Bumstead** Mark E '80
(330) 394-1501 **Burke** Charlene E '89
(330) 393-3200 **Burkey Burkey & Scher Co, LPA**
(330) 393-3200 **Burkey** Elise M '88
(330) 393-3200 **Burkey** Robert F '66
(330) 675-2426 **Burnett** Michael A '01
(330) 392-8551 **Buzulencia** Michael D '84
(330) 373-1717 **Cantalamessa** Enzo C '03
(330) 392-1541 **Carey** Thomas G Jr. '78
(330) 392-6171 **Carpenter** Dennis L '77
(330) 373-1221 **Carr** James C '73
Catipay Christina T '03
(330) 392-2505 **Cauffield** William G '70
(330) 395-9500 **Chaney** John H III '91
(330) 394-1539 **Christine** Anthony P '84
(330) 372-2010 **Collins** Susan P '88
(330) 393-7727 **Consoldane** Anthony V '72
(330) 675-2542 **Cornicelli** Anthony M '79
(330) 392-9329 **Costanzo** Maridee L '92
(330) 394-9692 **Crisan** James J '95
(330) 394-6711 **Culver** Fred A '60
(330) 609-9999 **Daniluk** Daniel P '79
(330) 392-6171 **Daugherty** David D '80
(330) 373-1717 **Davis & Young**
(330) 392-4176 **Del Bene LaPolla & Thomas**
(330) 369-1533 **Dixon** Rodger L '89
(330) 399-2632 **Donlin** Patrick J Sr. '71
(330) 399-3544 **Dull** David A Jr. '86
(330) 399-3544 **Dull** David A Sr. '56
(330) 373-1448 **Duricy** Patrick B '89
(330) 393-1584 **Durniok** Deborah S '95
(330) 675-2426 **Earnhart** Jason C '99
(330) 675-2426 **Elkins** Stanley A '85
(330) 824-7725 **Evans** Robert H '80
(330) 394-6148 **Finamore** Mark S '82
(330) 393-2519 **Fodor** Jeffrey W '73
(330) 856-6888 **Ford** Donald R Jr. '83
(330) 392-3991 **Fowler** John E II '94
(330) 393-6400 **Fredericka** James A '78
(330) 399-8500 **Fritz** Andrew J '91
(330) 393-3344 **Gargano** John R '83
(330) 392-2533 **Garris** Joshua M '01
(330) 373-3316 **Geisler** Brian T '03
(330) 399-8801 **Gensler** Robert L Jr. '02
(330) 373-1312 **Georgiadis** Michael '82
(330) 399-3555 **Gerin** Daniel N '78
(330) 394-8333 **Glaros-King** Koula E '83
(330) 392-1541 **Gold** Ned C Jr. '66
(330) 393-3400 **Goodman** Jeffrey V '91
(330) 841-2538 **Graham** Nicholas J '98
(330) 394-1539 **Graora** David J '86
(330) 856-7575 **Gray** James E '74
(330) 373-1035 **Griffith** Lynn B III '82
(330) 856-8800 **Grinstein** Jeffrey M '85
(330) 399-4556 **Grove** Michael E '78
(330) 393-7642 **Guarnieri** Donald L '60
(330) 393-1584 **Guarnieri & Secrest**
(330) 841-2515 **Gysegem** Thomas P '84
(330) 609-5057 **Hanshaw** William '78
(330) 392-1541 **Harrington Hoppe & Mitchell, Ltd**
(330) 841-0990 **Hatchner** Jeffrey A '79
(330) 392-1541 **Hawley** William L '79

(330) 392-4176 **Heltzel** Paul E '82
(330) 392-8397 **Hicks** Gregory V '85
(330) 373-1020 **Hill** Donald W '74
(330) 675-2600 **Hirschl** Rhonda S '01
(330) 856-7575 **Hlaudy** Richard S '01
(330) 675-2389 **Horton** Monte Jay '92
(330) 841-2566 **Iannucci** Anthony A Jr. '73
(330) 841-2518 **Ivanchak** Terry F '78
(330) 856-4115 **Johnson** Lisa L '03
(330) 373-6298 **Johnson** Robert L '89
(330) 394-5455 **Kafantaris** George N '81
(330) 392-7780 **Kearney** Patricia A '91
(330) 399-6847 **Keating** Brendan J '98
(330) 393-4611 **Keating** Daniel G '82
(330) 393-4611 **Keating Keating & Kuzman**
(330) 393-4611 **Keating** W Leo '50
(330) 609-5045 **Kelligher** William Chad '83
(330) 675-6682 **Kerr** Dax W A '02
(330) 394-3126 **King** John E '56
(330) 399-2649 **Knepp** Patricia A '93
(330) 394-5500 **Kovoor** Sarah T '98
(330) 373-1035 **Kragalott** Samuel R '82
(330) 399-1891 **Kurtz** John W '50
(330) 394-7580 **Lake** David G '84
(330) 675-2650 **Lamb** Matthew O '87
(330) 856-6868 **Lambert** Marc D '98
(330) 392-4176 **LaPolla** Thomas A '62
(330) 395-1490 **Large** John H '97
(330) 399-2216 **Larmi** Allan R '51
Laslo Tracey A '99
(330) 373-1035 **Lavelle** Edward L '73
(330) 399-2649 **Leopardi** John A '57
(330) 373-1035 **Letson** Daniel B '86
(330) 373-1035 **Letson Griffith Woodall Lavelle & Rosenberg**
(330) 373-1035 **Letson** Thomas B '88
(330) 373-1035 **Letson** William N '55
(330) 393-7727 **Lewis** James F '72
(330) 675-2521 **Lightbody** Susan M '87
(330) 373-1000 **Maas** Paula D '87
(330) 394-1587 **Makridis** Irene K '81
(330) 392-1541 **Marando** Michael G '74
(330) 675-2521 **Marik** Deborah E '91
(330) 395-5297 **Masek** Raymond J '77
(330) 675-2650 **Massacci** Shibani S '97
(330) 399-8801 **May** Joyce A '78
(330) 373-1000 **Maynard** Robert C '63
(330) 675-6687 **McBride** Michele L '02
(330) 675-2840 **McCarthy** Patrick F '90
(330) 392-1541 **McGee** Michael J '02
(330) 392-8800 **McGuire** William P '80
(330) 393-8200 **McLain** David H '92
(330) 372-3483 **McLain** William P '58
(330) 373-1717 **Meola** William Jack '84
(330) 395-7405 **Mickens** Charles G '91
(330) 675-2426 **Misocky** James J '78
Misocky Michael A '99
(330) 395-6444 **Morgan** Jonathan P '01
(330) 675-2426 **Morrow** Charles L '88
(330) 392-1541 **Murphy** Kevin P '85
(330) 395-7555 **Nader** Paul G '53
(330) 373-1448 **Nader** Rachel E '90
(330) 395-7555 **Nader** Thomas C '87
(330) 675-2601 **Natale** Anthony M '75
(330) 372-2010 **Neuman** Craig H '74
(330) 373-1221 **Nielsen** Dean E '89
(330) 675-2521 **Norton** Thomas F '69
(330) 675-2426 **O'Brien** Sean J '98
(330) 675-2650 **O'Day** Michael P '86
(330) 342-0222 **Ognibene** Michael A '81
(330) 399-4554 **Ohlin** Charles E '88
(330) 399-2070 **Ohlin** Joseph D '85
(330) 675-6684 **Oldfield** Charles W '99
(330) 393-3000 **Pentz** Matthew A '84
(330) 373-1639 **Phillips** Clifford L '72
(330) 675-7037 **Pico** John J '88
(330) 675-2650 **Pinzone** John D '02
Platenak Frank '03
(330) 392-1541 **Pogue** John L '69
(330) 392-5300 **Pond** George S '82
(330) 609-9999 **Poteet** Cherry L '85
(330) 675-6676 **Raphtis** Harry T '01
(330) 373-1448 **Reale-Gottfried** Elsa '92
(330) 841-9121 **Rexroad** Jeffrey D '81
(330) 394-6352 **Rich** Gary R '81
(330) 373-1000 **Richards** Charles L '69
(330) 392-6171 **Rieger** Gilbert L '70
(330) 392-6171 **Rieger Spencer Carpenter & Daugherty**
(330) 393-0851 **Ries** James R '75
(330) 395-7405 **Robinson** Learthon S Jr. '91
(330) 841-2605 **Rose** Traci T '98
(330) 373-1035 **Rosenberg** Michael W '66
(330) 395-9500 **Ross** Douglas W '97
(330) 393-1584 **Rossi** Anthony G '61
(330) 393-1584 **Rossi** Anthony G III '91
(330) 393-1584 **Rossi** Michael D '75
(330) 373-2587 **Rotar** Daniel R '90
(330) 395-9500 **Roux** William M '83
(330) 392-8392 **Rucker** Gilbert R III '86
(330) 393-1584 **Rudloff** Randil J '73
(330) 392-6171 **Rudnicki** Susan E '83
(330) 395-1800 **Safos** Robert P '77
(330) 675-2426 **Saker** James T '83
(330) 399-8801 **Sanders** James E '81
(330) 675-2317 **Savakis** Alexander J '78
(330) 393-0851 **Scala** Michael A '76
(330) 393-3200 **Scher** James R '91
(330) 399-5469 **Schubert** Thomas E '70
(330) 394-7445 **Schwartz** Richard F '83
(330) 399-2070 **Shackelford** William M '96
(330) 856-2922 **Shaw** Kenneth N '80
(330) 399-8801 **Shepherd** David A '81
(330) 675-2521 **Shorts** John T '00
(330) 675-2659 **Simmons** Cameron F '01
(330) 394-9692 **Sopkovich** Carol A '83
(330) 392-6171 **Spencer** Patricia L '79
(330) 373-1035 **Stack** Dene M '00
(330) 841-0234 **Stanitz** Christopher '74
(330) 373-1035 **Swader** David S '02
(330) 394-1586 **Swartz** Albert F '54
(330) 399-2306 **Swartz** Charles I '68
(330) 395-9500 **Swauger** Terry A '95
(330) 394-4488 **Tackett** Dennis W '91
(330) 856-7575 **Theisler** Charles W '93
(330) 392-4176 **Thomas** Daniel A '93
(330) 392-4176 **Thomas** Daniel P '66
(330) 369-1200 **Tisone** Raymond J '72
(330) 675-2426 **Toepfer** David M '97
(330) 399-8801 **Turner** Lawrence S '66
(330) 399-8801 **Turner May & Shepherd**
(330) 399-8801 **Turner** Stephen A '04
(330) 399-3229 **Ujczo** Dennis E '76
(330) 394-1539 **Urban** William J Jr. '69
(330) 675-5646 **Vazmina-Koltnow** Shelley C '89
(330) 393-3426 **Vennitti** Louis J '62
(330) 394-5880 **Vigorito** Philip M '89
(330) 393-3058 **Vingle** Joseph M '98
(330) 399-6434 **Walker** Keith M '76
(330) 856-8879 **Wallace** Lisa R '94
(330) 675-2426 **Watkins** Dennis '73
(330) 395-9500 **Weddell-Harwood** Sandra S '91
(330) 392-2533 **Wern** Charles E III '99
(330) 392-2533 **Wern** Charles E Jr. '59
(330) 394-9692 **White** Martin F '77
(330) 392-1541 **Wilson** Patrick K '88
(330) 373-1035 **Woodall** William D '67
(330) 399-1381 **Woodward** Calvin J Jr. '68
(330) 675-2426 **Wrenn** Thomas C '91
(330) 392-8200 **Yakubek** Nancy E '83
(330) 399-1481 **York** Robert L '67

WARRENSVILLE HEIGHTS
Cuyahoga County
(216) 766-6000 **Graines** Stuart J '72
(216) 360-9720 **Sampsel** Susan M '84
(216) 927-2030 **Shapiro** Alan J '62
(216) 927-2030 **Shapiro** Daniel L '92
(216) 927-2030 **Shapiro** Geoffrey J '93
(216) 491-7158 **Sullivan** Kerry H '88
(216) 587-6500 **Terry** Steven J '89
(216) 831-8678 **Zavarella** Gino P '95

WASHINGTON COURT HOUSE
Fayette County
(740) 335-2037 **Barr** Michael L '75
(740) 335-3826 **Bender** David B '86
(740) 335-4381 **Butler** James L '74
(740) 335-0888 **Eckstein** Steven H '86
(740) 335-8150 **Hammond** Robert L '67
(740) 335-3231 **Junk** William T '79
(740) 335-5271 **Kiger** David V '92
(740) 335-5271 **Kiger** James A '62
(740) 335-8060 **Lander** Michael J '75
(740) 335-4381 **Marshall** Dallas B '97
(740) 335-4750 **Mattingly** Dennis W '83
(740) 636-4164 **Miller** Mark S '99
(740) 335-0888 **Rooker** Kristina M '01
(740) 335-8765 **Roszmann** John H '73
(740) 335-0640 **Simmons** Melissa J '96
(740) 636-4164 **Smith** Matthew T '85
(740) 636-1830 **Terhune-Olaker** Landis L '01
(740) 335-8221 **Wead** John H '76

WAUSEON
Fulton County
(419) 337-9240 **Ahroni** Orly '94
(419) 337-5065 **Barber Kaper Stamm & Robinson**
(419) 335-5011 **Hallett Hallett & Nagel**
(419) 335-5011 **Hallett** Timothy W '72
(419) 337-9240 **Kennedy** Paul H '95
(419) 337-6116 **Nagel** Dale J '80
(419) 335-5011 **Nagel** Eric K '01
(419) 335-5011 **Nagel** Roger D '73
(419) 337-5065 **Nixon** Carrie J '00
(419) 337-4300 **Poorman** Gary L '84
(419) 335-3971 **Powers** Mark L '80
(419) 337-5065 **Robinson** Jeffrey L '77
(419) 337-5065 **Stamm** Jan H '78
(419) 335-2015 **Stuckey** Kurt A '87
(419) 337-9240 **Swigart** William R '76

WAVERLY
Pike County
(740) 226-4191 **Bevins** Walter A '91
(740) 947-2176 **Catanzaro** Jerome D '77
(740) 947-2176 **Catanzaro & Rosenberger**
(740) 947-1026 **Fosson** John L '75
(740) 947-2171 **Harrell** Kevin I '91
(740) 947-4323 **Junk** Charles R Jr. '91
McCleese Gary D '98
(740) 947-4323 **McDonald** Jessica S '02
(740) 947-2099 **Moraleja** Anthony A '92
(740) 947-7605 **Rhoads** Joseph E '82
(740) 947-2176 **Rosenberger** Robert N '81
(740) 947-7277 **Seif** D Dale Jr. '03
(740) 947-7232 **Seif** David D '74
(740) 947-7277 **Shugart** Jason V '02
(740) 947-7605 **Waterman** Deborah A '81
(740) 941-3287 **Weckbacher** Joseph H '83

WAYNE
Wood County
(800) 440-4284 **Hall** Michael D '93
(419) 288-3025 **Mitchell** L Snowden '60
(419) 288-2989 **Stewart** Beryl W '64

WAYNESFIELD
Auglaize County
(419) 568-5751 **Miltner** Ryan K '02
(419) 568-5751 **Reed** Kristine H '96
(419) 568-5751 **Yale** Benjamin F '80

WAYNESVILLE
Warren County
Beavers Timothy C '99
(513) 897-9738 **Dotson** Douglas C '74
Duchak Kathleen E '89
(513) 897-5901 **Krebs** Robert J Jr. '73
(513) 897-9222 **Mayer** Donald G '80
(513) 897-1310 **Opsahl** Yvonne G '93
(513) 897-0525 **Reynolds** Kimberly A '03
(513) 897-3055 **Thiemann** Charles L Jr. '01

WELLINGTON
Lorain County
(440) 647-4219 **Baumgartner & O'Toole**
(440) 647-4219 **Brownsberger** Alecia J '93

WELLSTON
Jackson County
(740) 384-5641 **Clark** John K Jr. '91
Dupree Randy H '02
(740) 384-5440 **Gilliland** Dana E '96
(740) 384-5440 **Gilliland Gilliland & Gilliland**
(740) 384-5440 **Gilliland** Kyle R '83
(740) 384-5440 **Gilliland** Roy J '52
(740) 384-2111 **Heiser** Lawrence A '73
(740) 384-2111 **Miller** Robert R '90
(740) 384-2111 **Ochsenbein** Mark A '77
(740) 384-2111 **Oths Heiser & Miller**
(740) 384-2111 **Oths** Joseph A '61
(740) 384-2111 **Weber** Shannon S '01

WELLSVILLE
Columbiana County
(330) 532-4658 **Amato** Charles C '90
(330) 532-4658 **Amato** Nicholas T '89
(330) 532-5955 **Beech** Andrew A '85

WEST CARROLLTON
Montgomery County
(937) 859-1323 **Carney** Patrick G '66
(937) 859-3628 **Galvas** Walter W '89
(937) 859-8026 **Haddick** Reid J '84
(937) 859-3628 **Tracy** Bridget A '84
(937) 859-3628 **Tracy** John P '84
(937) 859-3628 **Tracy** Louis E '52

WEST CHESTER
Butler County
(513) 779-4961 **Breissinger** Kirc J '96
(513) 777-2222 **Caparella** Courtney N '03
(513) 942-8855 **Casper** Sheldon Robert '72
(513) 723-8400 **Cliffel** Susan K '90
(513) 723-8400 **Coley** William P II '86
(513) 860-2560 **Colloton** Margaret C '82
(513) 777-2222 **Dehner** Jeffrey A '90
(513) 860-2560 **Doerflein** Angela L '04
(513) 779-5516 **Fernandez** Eric J '96
(513) 860-2560 **Fries** Winifred G '91
Gaffield Diane K '85
(513) 867-5070 **Hendrickson** Robert A '84
(513) 779-9850 **Hicks** Bryan S '95
(513) 634-9358 **Huston** Larry L '87
(513) 860-2560 **Jennings** Ann D '01
(513) 779-4601 **Kates** Rick D '95
(513) 349-1678 **Keys** James G Jr. '76
(513) 777-1545 **Kile** Paul R '85
(513) 759-6346 **Kirschner** Steven R '87
(513) 723-8400 **Kirtley** Emily A '03
(513) 777-2222 **Kraemer** Bradley M '98
(513) 942-6196 **Kravetz** Andrea F '83
(513) 777-7460 **Lamm** Dennis J '84
(513) 860-2560 **Lesick** John R II '71
(513) 634-5649 **Lewis** Leonard W '84
(513) 777-2222 **Lyons & Lyons Co,LPA**
(513) 777-2222 **Lyons** Robert H '80
(513) 634-9076 **McConihay** Julie A '04
(513) 777-2222 **Meadows** Jeffrey C '97
(513) 942-0224 **Mehrle** Joseph P '95
(513) 634-9359 **Meyer** Peter D '01
(513) 755-2600 **Nesbitt** Patrick T '81
(513) 779-0111 **Packard** Dwight A '77
(513) 870-9070 **Perrino** Nicholas D '91
(513) 860-1555 **Quraishi** Nadeem Z '00
(513) 723-8400 **Richards** Jeremy D '01
(513) 863-9100 **Rink** Martin D '03
(513) 723-8400 **Roberts** Robert C '04
Sager Barbara L '95
(513) 777-9800 **Schumacher** Lynn M '85
(513) 634-9397 **Stone** Angela M '99
(513) 759-4403 **Strobl** Lori A '01
Sweeney Mary F '01
(513) 708-3106 **Szydlowski** Christine H '91
(513) 723-8400 **Uhl** Leslee M '98
(513) 863-9100 **Yonas** John J '00

WESTERVILLE
Franklin County
(614) 898-9900 **Akin Guthrie LLC**
(614) 898-9900 **Akin** Sherrille D '92
(614) 823-6243 **Alexander** Nicholas Z '64
(614) 882-2327 **Bailey** Bruce E '78
(614) 794-0386 **Baldwin** Richard T '70
(614) 895-5600 **Bale** David G '78
(614) 523-1798 **Ball** Theodore C '54
(614) 901-5700 **Barone** Joseph J '75
(614) 776-1000 **Barren & Merry Co,LPA**
(614) 776-1000 **Barren** Michael J '83
(614) 891-2410 **Bates** Anna L '84
(614) 895-5600 **Begin** James S '73
(614) 899-1447 **Bell** Albert L '59
(614) 865-4700 **Bell** Sandra F '86
(614) 891-5378 **Blaine** Craig J '82
(614) 891-6920 **Bohan** Gerald F '77
(614) 891-6530 **Bolton** James G '82
(614) 865-8515 **Bondy** Michael S '01
(614) 890-2111 **Boston** Shannon C '97
Boyd Robert C II '94
(614) 890-5632 **Brewer** Lee M '89
(614) 899-6611 **Callander** Robert D '67
(614) 410-6740 **Carelli** Gail E '02
(614) 898-8903 **Clayton** Kelly L '91
Conrad Earl W Jr. '83
(614) 899-1119 **DiAlbert** John E '85
(614) 899-9014 **Dunkerley** Debra L '86
Easley Sue A '88
(614) 882-1425 **Feister** Ronald E '76
(614) 865-4700 **Fiely** Linda K '79
(614) 891-0336 **Fifner** William F '73
(614) 325-8525 **Flagler** Harold G '78
(614) 794-9595 **Flaherty** James G '84
(614) 834-4340 **Fleischer** David A '95
Floyd Marc L '00
(614) 882-5980 **Foley** J Edward '99
(614) 898-5200 **Foley** Megan D '97
Freed Irene K '93
(614) 523-7575 **Fusco Mackey Mathews Smith & Watkins,LLP**
(614) 523-7575 **Fusco** Michael J '79
(614) 895-9619 **Gannon** Patrick J '78
(614) 895-2000 **Gatherum** Kristin L '93
(614) 846-2001 **George** Michael F '74
(614) 823-6246 **Gervers** David '76
(614) 948-0817 **Gluntz** Paula S '98
(614) 882-3443 **Gonzales** John M '87
(614) 226-5991 **Graeff** David J '72
(614) 890-4543 **Griffith** Charles R '78
(614) 890-4543 **Griffith & Worth**
(614) 568-0030 **Guthrie** Graham D '93
(614) 794-9770 **Hane** Wilbur H III '01
(614) 818-1100 **Harley** Sean P '84
(614) 901-5700 **Harper** John D '89
(614) 895-0575 **Hartlaub** Joseph V '77
(614) 891-3589 **Hasselback** David G '85
(614) 865-6680 **Hatcher** Judi K '83
(614) 901-2203 **Hazelton** Peter M '92
(614) 776-1000 **Helkowski** Lawrence Scott '97
(614) 890-6696 **Helmer** Elena V '02
(614) 875-1041 **Helvey** Edward D '82
(614) 890-4801 **Herrington** Claudia S '97
(614) 410-6740 **Heydinger** Mark C '83
(614) 839-5700 **Hollern** Edwin J '88
(614) 882-2327 **Hollins** Eugene L '88
(614) 436-0346 **Holmes** Leanne M '03
(614) 508-7204 **Hondros** John G '72
(614) 794-9770 **Hulthen** Martin R '88
(614) 818-9014 **Huston** Catherine E '83
(614) 891-7112 **Irwin** Michael T '80
(614) 818-3800 **James** Edmund G Jr. '75
(614) 891-5923 **Jarosi** Michael J '03
(614) 891-0336 **Jeffers** Michael D '91
(614) 901-8380 **Jeffries** Bryan L '87
(614) 901-3676 **John** Sidney C '65
(614) 436-0346 **Johnson** Katryna L '99
Jones Michael F '89
(614) 890-2233 **Jordan** James W '66
(614) 406-4399 **Keefer** Stanislava '00
Kinkela John F '83
(614) 891-5133 **Kosmo** Megan E '00
Lancione Bernard G '65
Lanier Janice Kay '94
(614) 823-6290 **Leibrock** Robin D '93
(614) 438-7000 **Levine** Richard J '75
(614) 898-5200 **Levy** Yale R '95
(614) 901-7100 **Linch** Heather L '84
(614) 891-6363 **Linch** M Jebb '77
(614) 865-4700 **Linder** Mark E '89
(614) 895-1234 **Lonn** Thomas C '92
(614) 898-9522 **Lord** Shannon R '04
(614) 523-7575 **Mackey** Jeffrey D '81
(614) 436-0346 **Maguire** Peggy L '00
(614) 818-1100 **Makela** Charity R '01
(614) 436-8338 **Malech** Arnold M '80
(614) 895-9473 **Mallett** Jacqueline S '92
(614) 523-3575 **Marlatt** Jonathan Scott '03
(614) 523-7575 **Mathews** Gregory B '88
Mathews Larry D '83
(614) 431-9912 **Matthews** James S '88
(614) 818-1118 **McCormick** Marshall S '93
(614) 899-9194 **McCreary** David M '58
(614) 899-1700 **McDonald** Deborah A '84
(614) 410-6740 **McKinley** Kristen E '94
(614) 882-2327 **McLoughlin** William J '86
(614) 901-8380 **McQuown** Cara M '00
(614) 776-1000 **Merry** Thomas R '89
(614) 882-2327 **Metz & Bailey**
(614) 776-1000 **Miller** Beth M '00
(614) 895-8727 **Miller** James D '87
Miller Patrick S '82
(614) 891-6363 **Milligan** David T '68
(614) 891-6363 **Milligan** Frederick J Jr. '67
(614) 794-9595 **Mills** Julie S '98
(614) 523-3575 **Mills** Kathleen B '91
(614) 523-3575 **Mills** Luther J '89
(614) 899-0636 **Minor** Anne E '97
(614) 895-2302 **Moss** Judith D '78
(614) 865-2220 **Naumoff** George '88
(614) 839-5700 **Newsome** Romina P '03
(614) 523-7506 **Nordman** Eric R '80
(614) 898-9918 **Osif** Thomas J '75
(614) 891-2109 **Palmer** John W '63
(614) 898-8795 **Paragas** Leonore T '89
Pate Mary Ann '91
(614) 898-8078 **Payne** Walter R Jr. '78
(614) 682-2049 **Philabaum** Laura B '89
(614) 895-5500 **Piper** Brian S '76
(614) 898-5200 **Pope** Elaine A '01
(614) 898-5200 **Pope** Gregory S '95
(614) 898-5200 **Pope & Levy Co,LPA**
(614) 898-5200 **Poplaski** Leighann K '04
(614) 865-2611 **Porter** John T '86
(614) 891-9061 **Posani** John P '78
(614) 221-5143 **Press** Lawrence S '82
(614) 865-1560 **Price** Alise M '96
Prior Kelly K '91
(614) 794-0120 **Ritter** Stacy J '00
(614) 890-4543 **Roda** Matthew J '93
(614) 207-0070 **Salters** Gerald W '02
(614) 891-9522 **Sammons** Jeffery D '82
Samuel Marcy B '83
(740) 965-3570 **Sauter** John L '68
(614) 891-6920 **Schumann** William M '67
(614) 891-4158 **Shaw** Melissa J '97
Sherman Susan E '94
(614) 890-0834 **Shoemaker** Fred J '51
(614) 865-8263 **Sidor** David S '72
(614) 890-7004 **Sinkhorn** Mark W '74
(614) 898-9900 **Smith** Todd W '03
(614) 794-0221 **Snyder** Douglas A '81
(614) 436-0346 **Snyder** Tamie I '99
(614) 891-2560 **Soto** Michael '88
(614) 891-1041 **Steele** Lucinda G '00
(614) 885-2066 **Storey** Robert '80
(614) 882-2327 **Stroh** Kyle J '99
(614) 890-2900 **Struble** Carla I '84
(614) 508-7240 **Thompson** William A '81
(888) 371-6763 **Trout** Paula J '87
(614) 891-5555 **Tsiliacos** Narcus J '64
(614) 890-0093 **Turk** Thomas E '66
(614) 899-6868 **Uhrich** Jeffrey P '90
(614) 895-7962 **Ullom-Morse** Norman J '79

(614) 436-4154 **Van Runkle** Peter E '82
(614) 865-4724 **Varner** Carrie M '97
(614) 865-4700 **Vaughn** Allison J '97
(614) 217-8849 **Villwock** David S '97
(614) 523-3575 **Waldeck** Tom R '90
(614) 523-7575 **Watkins** Alison A '93
(614) 882-2339 **Westervelt** Charles E Jr. '48
(614) 891-2222 **Wetterauer** Damon E Jr. '74
(614) 865-8415 **Whipple** Robert C '02
(614) 865-4709 **Whitter** Herman S '90
(614) 890-3724 **Wilhelm** Anne M '84
Wood Robert C '00
(614) 890-4543 **Worth** Randall E '78
(614) 818-1100 **Zabkar** William J '76
(614) 839-5700 **Zimmerman** Kevin J '99

WEST FARMINGTON
Trumbull County

(330) 889-2515 **Granitto** Rhonda L '89

WESTFIELD CENTER
Medina County

(330) 887-0101 **Batchelder** John T '82
(800) 243-0210 **Brej** Christopher J '04
(800) 243-0210 **Brockman** Phoebe M '83
(800) 243-0210 **Carrino** Frank A '87
(330) 887-1036 **Carson** Kandie L '93
(330) 887-6930 **Cluse** Mark E '95
(330) 887-8365 **Cronin** Michael C '04
(800) 243-0210 **Croyle** Sherry A '87
(800) 243-0210 **Estvanic** Sally A '04
(330) 887-6422 **Hutson** William F '91
(330) 887-0143 **Kahelin** William J '74
Linnen Stephen P '99
(800) 243-0210 **Perry** Alfred C Jr. '99
(330) 887-0560 **Popelmayer** Richard A '86
(800) 243-0210 **Sandor** Frank J III '91
(330) 887-0162 **Sterling** William Fisher '83
(330) 887-0669 **Walker** James M '81
(800) 243-0210 **Winkler** Daniel A '94
(330) 887-0542 **Yogmour** Gus Jr. '85

WEST JEFFERSON
Madison County

(614) 879-4143 **Brockman** Blaine P '01
(614) 879-9413 **Flowers** Debra J '96
(614) 879-4062 **Green** Robin W '89
(614) 879-7606 **Murray** Joseph M '83
(614) 879-7606 **Parsons** Ronald C '67
(614) 879-8026 **Sams** David A '91

WESTLAKE
Cuyahoga County

(216) 299-7508 **Andrews** William H III '02
(440) 892-3000 **Baden** Steven L '84
(440) 871-4022 **Beranek** Steven B '96
(440) 414-6050 **Bercik** Joseph E '02
(440) 892-8846 **Bidari** Jayashree Y '92
(440) 871-0516 **Bittel** Patricia T '83
(440) 617-1900 **Blackburn** Douglas C '75
(440) 892-6800 **Bradford** Dale A '83
(440) 808-9743 **Brandt** Natasha E '90
(440) 892-8456 **Bullard** Marcia J '84
Burgett Clifford W '94
(440) 835-8200 **Burke** Joseph T '91
(440) 779-5920 **Cables** Thomas A '61
(440) 871-8900 **Cada** Dennis C '96
(440) 925-2802 **Carey** John T '83
(440) 899-1551 **Carney** Joseph D '77
(440) 835-6603 **Ciszczon** William J '83
Clarke Arthur F '74
Clarke Timothy P '93
(440) 871-1122 **Claypool** Oliver H Jr. '74
(440) 892-1580 **Coen** Beverly J '77
(440) 333-7330 **Coltman** Thomas J '64
(440) 979-0233 **Columbro** James R '78
(440) 892-0400 **Cook** Brian A '92
(440) 871-4022 **Corsaro** Joseph G '82
(440) 871-5020 **Costa** Gregory J '93
(440) 835-6304 **Costanza** James F '67
(440) 835-0600 **Coury** Elias J '87
(440) 835-0600 **Coyne** Michael P '79
(440) 333-7330 **Cruse** Brian C '89
(440) 808-0011 **Curatolo** Joseph G '77
(440) 835-8200 **Daray** Stephen E '97
(440) 871-2985 **Darling** Brian J '04
(440) 414-6001 **DeGrandis** Fred M '78
(440) 331-3232 **Donahue** Charles B II '67
(216) 410-1467 **Dowling** Dawn M '91
(440) 556-0719 **Duffy** Sheila A '86
(440) 892-6896 **DuVall** Michael A '75
(440) 250-4400 **Egert Mayer & Hack**
(440) 835-0600 **Egleston** James D '94
(440) 835-0600 **Ehrnfelt** Walter F III '88
(440) 250-9709 **Fedor** Robert J Jr. '89
(440) 871-5020 **Fifner** Douglas K '79
(440) 871-5020 **Fifner** Elaine S '79
(440) 808-8461 **Finnan** Gabrielle A '95
(440) 892-3460 **Fitz** Robert E '72
(440) 835-5497 **Froelich** Raymond R Jr. '73
(440) 871-8111 **Frost** Robert S '94
Furio Catherine A '91
(440) 899-8000 **Giesser** Rosemary A '81
(440) 835-0600 **Giganti** Mary J '91
(440) 892-3344 **Gogul** Ronald J '70
(440) 808-0163 **Good** John D '92
(440) 871-4022 **Gordon** Jeanne V '98
(440) 871-8288 **Gornik** James T '73
(440) 899-7377 **Grace** Charles H '71
(440) 250-4400 **Hack** Edward G '79
(440) 871-0026 **Hamilton** James L '73
(440) 250-9140 **Helfrich** Karl S '86
(440) 871-5151 **Hodous** David F '76
(440) 808-9100 **Hood** David R '93
(440) 835-0600 **Hoppe** Herbert J Jr. '53
(440) 892-1990 **Hotz** Gary A '77
(440) 892-8430 **House** Linda L '93
(440) 871-8111 **Huffman** Charles S Jr. '52
(440) 871-8111 **Huffman Isaac & Frost LLC**
(440) 871-8111 **Huffman** William C '80
(440) 892-0400 **Hunt** William H '75
(440) 871-8111 **Isaac** Frank K '52
(440) 899-1551 **Jancura** Scott E '95
(440) 892-1990 **Janis** Edward M '76
(440) 250-9709 **Jefson** Thomas A '02
(440) 835-2052 **Johanek** Mary A '80
(440) 871-4022 **Kikta** Mark A '92
(440) 892-3005 **King** James R '80
King John F '83
(440) 871-6300 **Kirchner** Lisa M '93
(440) 871-4858 **Kocian** Jeffrey L '66
(440) 835-1200 **Kolick** Daniel J '75
(440) 835-1200 **Kolick & Kondzer**
(440) 835-1200 **Kondzer** Thomas A '75
(440) 250-7015 **Koury** Elias G '53
(440) 250-7025 **Koury** Lee M '97
(440) 835-6212 **Krause** Marcella A '91
(440) 871-5020 **Kwarciany** Dale L '76
(440) 788-5097 **Lally** Sarah T '02
(440) 808-9138 **Landy** Pamela S '81
(440) 617-1200 **Lastovka** Terri A '96
(440) 835-3889 **Lauber** Richard E '81
(440) 871-4022 **Lauricia** Samuel J III '04
(440) 808-4472 **Lee** Steven C '89
(440) 808-3390 **Leroux** Clayton G Jr. '71
(440) 899-5130 **Levenberg** Jessica A '04
(440) 835-9535 **Liwosz** John C Jr. '64
(440) 899-6776 **Ljubi** Sharon J '81
(440) 871-4022 **Long** Clare S '84
(440) 356-9789 **Malloy** Anthony T '91
(440) 716-8562 **Maloney** Michael P '87
Maloof-Wolf Faye J '89
Marquard Robert J '54
(440) 835-5238 **Maruster** Robert F '75
(440) 835-1800 **Marx** James A '87
(440) 250-4400 **Mayer** Wallace J Jr. '70
(440) 835-0600 **McConville** Luke F '96
McCullough George V '52
(440) 871-6300 **McIntyre** Daniel M '90
(440) 871-0413 **Meslat** Lanene M '01
(440) 871-5151 **Miller** John J '66
(440) 333-6239 **Miller** Mark J '83
(440) 835-3511 **Minnich** William A '57
(440) 871-3131 **Mishler** Howard V '73
(440) 892-8380 **Mittendorf** William J '72
(440) 779-6613 **Mobberly** Patricia H '88
Moldaver Simon A '90
(440) 899-1551 **Mollohan** Bryan S '98
(440) 892-2040 **Musial** Lisa A '04
(440) 892-2040 **Musial** Mark N '85
(440) 892-2040 **Musial** Norman T '61
(440) 899-1551 **Nye** John R '89
(440) 808-0011 **Oehlenschlager** James E '01
(440) 899-1900 **Patton** Joseph M '90
(440) 898-3098 **Pembridge** Donald Timothy '82
(440) 835-8158 **Pophal** Michael C '92
(440) 899-6317 **Poulos** John D '88
(440) 892-1940 **Prendergast** Kevin P '87
(440) 892-4900 **Rains** Robert N '70
(440) 871-5072 **Rehor** Daniel J '64
(440) 899-6776 **Reichard** William E '68
(440) 808-0011 **Renner Kenner Greive Bobak Taylor & Weber, LPA**
(440) 414-5499 **Riddle** Susan L '90
(440) 808-8040 **Riley** David J '97
(440) 617-4233 **Rocco** Andrea F '93
(440) 871-1565 **Ruhe** Linda J '83
Russo Angelo '02
(440) 808-9494 **Ryser** Elizabeth H '91
(440) 835-2232 **Saggio** Joseph A '67
Sandalakis Athanasia C '90
(440) 356-6108 **Sava** Michael F '82
(440) 892-3000 **Scanlon** Patricia M '85
(440) 835-8200 **Sciangula** Francis A '63
(440) 899-9990 **Shepherd** John B Jr. '78
(440) 871-2122 **Sherman** David C '72
(440) 899-9990 **Short** Dale W '77
(440) 899-9990 **Short Shepherd & Stanton**
(440) 808-0011 **Sidoti** Salvatore A '99
(440) 871-0234 **Simiele** Thomas C '71
(440) 899-1911 **Skulina** Thomas R '59
(440) 892-1580 **Slattery** Raymond J III '83
(440) 835-4831 **Smith** Michael K '87
(440) 835-0600 **Smith** Susan F '88
(440) 871-3300 **Soeder** Robin L '93
(440) 835-8200 **Spalding** Walter T Jr. '56
Squeri Therese V '82
(440) 899-9990 **Stanton** Mark A '77
(440) 835-0600 **Swartz** Scott E '92
Tasse James L '80
(440) 250-9709 **Taylor** Susan Parker '04
(440) 899-1285 **Tellerd** Craig M '87
(440) 835-1200 **Thomas** Daniel J '89
(440) 871-4040 **Thomas** Joan Jacobs '84
(440) 779-6613 **Thompson** Brian '75
(440) 835-1800 **Traci** Robert V '75
(440) 835-8200 **Ujczo** Joseph E '81
(440) 333-7330 **Valore & Cruse Co,LPA**
(440) 333-7330 **Valore** Joseph A '70
(440) 250-4126 **Vaughn** Aaron M '02
(440) 414-5184 **Veillette** Robert E '78
(440) 835-0600 **Waldheger Coyne, LPA**
(440) 835-0600 **Waldheger** Ronald J '76
(440) 871-0394 **Weishar** Fred A '55
(440) 899-9425 **Wick** Bruce T '75
(440) 835-1200 **Yanok** Michelle A '01

WEST LIBERTY
Logan County

(937) 465-2002 **Brandt** Philip A '82
(937) 465-5056 **Fansler** Steven R '80
(937) 465-2002 **Moell** Christopher J '96

WEST MILTON
Miami County

(937) 698-4112 **Wagner** Allyn S '69

WEST PORTSMOUTH
Scioto County

(740) 858-6991 **Heid** Catherine S '83
(740) 858-6654 **Stevenson** John R '81

WEST SALEM
Wayne County

Millhoan Carol W '84
(419) 853-4603 **Williams** Barbara L '79

WEST UNION
Adams County

(937) 544-3331 **Armstrong** Kenneth L Jr. '77
(937) 544-5095 **Blanton** Kristofer D '01
(937) 544-2581 **Bubp** Danny R '84
(937) 544-5095 **Caldwell** John B '73
(937) 544-8655 **Carroll** Gregory A '88
(937) 544-5251 **Foster** Alan W '76
(937) 544-2831 **Gabbert** Roy E Jr. '89
(937) 544-3600 **Haslam** Aaron E '04
Lawler John H '89
(937) 544-2581 **Little** Jessica A '03
(937) 544-2371 **McFarland** Michelle Elrick '02
(937) 544-7900 **McIlwain** Douglas E '79
(937) 544-2500 **Moore-Eiterman** Barbara A '97
(937) 544-2581 **Purtell** Steven W '93
(937) 544-2101 **Schlueter** James W '74
(937) 544-3900 **Spencer** Brett M '89
(937) 544-6465 **Whalen** Dana N '00
(937) 544-2301 **Wilson** Charles H Jr. '59
(937) 544-5095 **Young & Caldwell**

WHEELERSBURG
Scioto County

(740) 574-2521 **Blume** Thurl K '81
(740) 574-4311 **Faulkner** Rickey L '79
(740) 574-4311 **Grimshaw** Lynn A '75
(740) 574-2521 **Mowery** Steven L '79
(740) 574-4311 **Porter** Kenneth W '81

WHITEHALL
Franklin County

(614) 444-2020 **Beagle** Peter F '78
(614) 442-1331 **Blair** Roger S '68
(614) 692-9704 **Castillo** Maria B '84
(614) 863-3150 **Fennessey** Dennis J '76
(614) 237-9802 **Gould** Craigg E '93
(614) 755-2424 **Strobl** Derrick B '93
(614) 235-6406 **Wood** Donald E '98

WHITEHOUSE
Lucas County

Bartman Christi S '94
(419) 872-5337 **Brown** Timothy J '84
Staffe Jeffrey C '82
(419) 877-5529 **Wells** Michael H '87

WICKLIFFE
Lake County

(440) 347-5668 **Bauer** Joseph W '81
(440) 943-7600 **Bednar** Gerald J '74
(440) 943-1200 **Day** Suzanne F '93
(440) 585-5111 **DiCicco** Richard D '66
(440) 516-6000 **Drake** Eric M '93
(440) 585-7968 **Forrester** Traci L '02
(440) 347-5094 **Gardiner** Archibald T III '75
(440) 347-5072 **Gilbert** Teresan W '83
(440) 585-0595 **Gregor** Robert J '67
(440) 943-4200 **Hansell** Herbert J '49
(440) 943-4200 **Harris** Tracy B '80
(440) 943-4200 **Kidder** Fred D '50
(440) 944-4470 **Kuhar** Fred '71
(440) 347-1541 **Laferty** Samuel B '83
(440) 943-6800 **Leach** Robert S '78
(440) 943-4200 **Lewis** Gregory R '93
Manley James R '69
(440) 943-4200 **Manson** William D '85
(440) 347-5487 **Marlowe** Cecil '88
(440) 944-7020 **Morrison** Richard P '80
(440) 347-5645 **Reynolds** Leslie M '88
(440) 347-5099 **Rosko** Christopher J '95
(440) 944-7020 **Shryock** John W '79
(440) 347-5781 **Silbiger** Mark C '88
(440) 347-5793 **Sussman** Jason R '99
(440) 347-5792 **Thiele** Terry V '96
(440) 943-5222 **Turi** Louis A Jr. '50
(440) 943-1200 **Webb** William J '75

WILBERFORCE
Greene County

(937) 376-6333 **Garland** John W '74
(937) 376-6629 **Hughey** Andrew C '99

WILLARD
Huron County

(419) 935-0171 **Harwood** David B '73
(419) 935-1681 **Hauser** Richard B '73
(419) 964-0423 **Martin** James J '74
(419) 935-0171 **Thornton** Kenneth Alec '85
(419) 935-0171 **Thornton** Robert F '58
(419) 935-0171 **Thornton Thornton & Harwood**
(419) 935-0171 **Weisenburger** Eric R '90

WILLIAMSBURG
Clermont County

(513) 724-2252 **Burgess** Terry David '71
(513) 724-2969 **Littman** Donald F '65

WILLOUGHBY
Lake County

(440) 953-4183 **Allen** Bruce L '72
(440) 942-7757 **Andrews** Charles M '78
(440) 942-7757 **Andrews** Junior Melvin '50
(440) 946-9646 **Baker** Benjamin B '99
(440) 942-7935 **Behnke** Mark L '81
(440) 954-3111 **Bergen** Ann S '92
Botek Frederick G '96
(440) 946-6958 **Brancatelli** Frank R '73
(440) 951-2303 **Byron** Barry M '56
(440) 951-2303 **Byron** Stephen L '91
(440) 953-9355 **Cantrell** Doreen M '88
(440) 946-9469 **Chapman** James E '03
(440) 942-6675 **Christman** Katie E '03
(440) 942-6675 **Clair** Mary J '77
(440) 209-0609 **Crotser** Michele L '85
(440) 953-2000 **Davies** David H '73
(440) 953-9064 **Deeb** Charles G '76
(440) 953-9064 **Deeb** Timothy S '98
(440) 953-1771 **Doganiero** John A III '78
(440) 951-1525 **Dudley** Celine M '87
(440) 942-8650 **Eager** David T '01
(440) 953-1310 **Ezzone** Donald J '75
(440) 954-3111 **Feczko** Christopher E '96
(440) 946-9469 **Freeburg** Antoinette E '99
(440) 943-4700 **Frost** Merrie M '92
(440) 951-5400 **Fudale** William F '67
(440) 946-1380 **Futterer** Stephen J '75
(440) 953-1771 **Glinski** Mark A '79
(440) 954-9455 **Gockel** Laura C '91
(440) 951-9000 **Gordon** Lesley A '99
(440) 256-2394 **Haines** Jeffrey D '92
(440) 951-1181 **Hegyes** Bryan F '02
(440) 951-1181 **Hegyes** Dean K '92
(440) 942-5900 **Hentemann** Paul H '62
(440) 951-1848 **Hutton** Bruce A '76
(440) 951-6665 **Jurjans** Peteris '72
(440) 946-9469 **Kasunic** Carl P Jr. '86
(440) 954-9455 **King** David M '84
(440) 954-9455 **King** Philip G '02
(440) 944-4580 **Krebs** Scott T '89
(440) 256-1395 **Misny** Timothy P '81
Nelson Lisa V '99
(440) 943-4700 **Patterson** David N '64
(440) 953-1310 **Perez** Richard J '74
(440) 255-8888 **Plasco** Marvin R '69
(440) 951-2323 **Purola** Albert L '70
(440) 953-1310 **Rosplock** Robert S '73
(440) 942-2454 **Rubin** Irl D '76
(440) 951-9246 **Sandrey** Holly J '93
(440) 954-9455 **Schraff & King Co,LPA**
(440) 954-9455 **Schraff** Patricia J '80
(440) 946-8990 **Simms** Michael A '73
(440) 953-2870 **Slattery** Lisa J '86
Taber Timothy J '75
(440) 942-8886 **Wilt** Daniel D '70
(440) 951-6245 **Zatyko** Donald R '75

WILLOUGHBY HILLS
Lake County

(440) 951-4879 **Gainar** Ronald A '96
(440) 942-6276 **Heyl** Bonnie M '87
(440) 918-1850 **Ledman** David E '87
(440) 585-0919 **McDevitt** John F '57
(440) 951-4679 **McGregor** John T '76
(440) 951-3565 **Patronite** Gerald J '73
(440) 951-4660 **Poklar** Michael A '73
(440) 943-6489 **Ristity** Donald W '66
(440) 946-7450 **Tassi** M Elaine '79
(440) 944-3660 **Watling** Justin J '80

WILLOWICK
Lake County

(440) 944-4443 **Bosco** John W '72
(440) 943-7080 **Foxx** John E '65
(440) 944-2736 **Hutchison** Edward L '95
(440) 585-1441 **Komarjanski** Stephen '71
(440) 943-6888 **Rozanc** Frank J '90

WILMINGTON
Clinton County

(800) 736-3973 **Albl** Suzanne Scheiner '01
(937) 382-1494 **Armour** Scott A '85
Besser Jason A '03
(937) 382-4030 **Blake** John F '70
(937) 383-1422 **Bowling** Larry R '88
(937) 382-1494 **Brake** Daniel J '93
(937) 382-7777 **Bryant** Jerry D '74
(937) 382-4454 **Buckley** Frederick J '50
(937) 382-0946 **Buckley** Karen '86
(937) 382-0946 **Buckley Miller & Wright**
(937) 382-2838 **Campbell** Michael T '98
(937) 382-0955 **Carey** Ronald C '64
(937) 382-1497 **Caudill** David R Jr. '91
(937) 382-1497 **Cook** Charles T '00
(937) 382-0045 **Daugherty** Michael T '94
(800) 543-5589 **DeLuca** Donald R '94
(937) 382-1497 **Denier** Charles P '03
(937) 382-3831 **Dennis** Joseph H '86
(937) 382-2838 **Dobyns** John M '80
(937) 382-8747 **Elder** Steven E '81
(937) 382-2838 **Federle** Richard L Jr. '93
(937) 382-5509 **Fife** David M '75
(937) 382-5509 **Fife** Elaine H '75
(937) 382-1000 **Foster** Brett L '94
(937) 241-9400 **Gamble** Kathy L '73
(937) 382-3320 **Gano** Judy A '86
(937) 382-4559 **Henry** David M '91
(937) 382-1000 **Hoskins** Joseph C '93
(937) 382-2838 **Jeffries** Jacob M '04
(937) 382-1200 **Johnson-Hebb** Inza E '88
(937) 383-0050 **Kornman** Sharon A '94
Lacy David L '77
(937) 382-0581 **McCracken** William B '72
(937) 382-3640 **McElwee** Mary H '77
(937) 382-7777 **Miars** Mark J '78
(937) 382-0946 **Miller** James P '63
(937) 382-6661 **Moke** Paul F '82
(937) 382-4559 **Moyer** Richard W '88
(937) 382-1316 **Newburger** Craig A '01
(937) 382-0201 **Nowel** Lynne M '95
(937) 241-9400 **Ondre** Schaunette Marie '98
(937) 382-5591 **Payne** William J '92
(937) 382-1497 **Peelle** Carol S '86
(937) 382-1497 **Peelle** Chaley E '04
(937) 382-1497 **Peelle** Robert C '76
(937) 382-1497 **Peelle** William E '75
(937) 382-0045 **Peterson** Shaun D '91
(937) 382-8747 **Polly-Murphy** Michelle L '00
(937) 382-2838 **Porter** John S '96
(937) 382-4559 **Quigley** Deborah S '91
(937) 382-0946 **Raizk** Lauren E '04
(937) 382-4559 **Randolph** William C '95
(937) 382-2838 **Rose & Dobyns Co,LPA**
(937) 382-2838 **Rose** Gordon L '80
(937) 383-2067 **Rowlands** Helen L '97
(937) 382-1316 **Szelagiewicz** Steven N '01
(937) 383-2067 **Turner** Lynn W '92
(937) 382-1494 **Wade** Jeffrey C '94
(937) 382-3831 **Williams** James H '79
(937) 382-0946 **Wright** Jeffrey L '74

WINTERSVILLE
Jefferson County

(740) 264-6441 **Evans** Augustus H Jr. '51
(740) 264-0661 **Ferguson** Lisa K '02

WOODLAWN
Hamilton County

Willingham Layla K '02

WOODMERE
Cuyahoga County

(216) 831-6580 **Bergrin** Irving S '76
(216) 464-6744 **Davis** William T '86
(216) 464-2860 **Greenfield** Mark R '81
(216) 831-6580 **Hartman** Alan S '65
(216) 831-6580 **Hartman & Kahn Co,LPA**
(216) 831-6580 **Kahn** Ronald S '74
(216) 831-9110 **Kertesz** Ronnie M '81
(216) 763-2200 **Leska** Abbie B '92
(216) 378-9730 **Lodwick** Sheila A '82
(216) 292-2913 **Marshek** Ronald S '73
(216) 464-2860 **Rubin** Steven K '04
(216) 464-6744 **Seders** Julianne M '97
(216) 378-9730 **Shapiro** Fred D '54

WOODSFIELD
Monroe County

(740) 472-1647 **Coury** Robert G '67
(740) 472-0708 **Frank** William E Jr. '90
(740) 472-0703 **Morrison** C Mark '75
(740) 472-1681 **Peters** James W '81
(740) 472-1158 **Riethmiller** Lynn K '77
(740) 472-1647 **Selmon** Julie R '99
(740) 472-1647 **Smith & Coury**
(740) 472-1647 **Smith** Gary W '82
(740) 472-0707 **Yoss** Richard A '68

WOOSTER
Wayne County

(330) 262-8871 **Anfang** William F III '83
(330) 287-5575 **Bailey** Kenneth W '78
(330) 264-4444 **Baker** Susan E '92
(330) 262-3030 **Ball** Brian A '04
(330) 264-9456 **Barnard** Bryan K '03
(330) 264-9456 **Barnard** George K '71
(330) 264-8679 **Barrington** John C '68
(330) 287-5545 **Bauders** Jerry A '74
Beckler Mark M '02
(330) 263-5248 **Benson** Richard R Jr. '82
(330) 264-9897 **Broehl** Margo E '77
(330) 287-5490 **Brown** Lisa A '95
(330) 262-7555 **Buytendyk** Michael G '86
(330) 262-7555 **Cicconetti** Francis E '69
(330) 264-9454 **Connelly** James J '79
(330) 264-4444 **Critchfield Critchfield & Johnston Ltd**
Cullis David H '80
(330) 345-8100 **Dark** Edward A '89
(330) 262-3030 **Desiderio** Jason B '02
(330) 264-4444 **Drushal** Bonnie C '82
(330) 264-4444 **Drushal** Jeff D '77
(330) 287-5663 **Evans** Dafydd W Jr. '73
(330) 264-1222 **Evans** Matthew C '00
(330) 262-3030 **Fink** Michelle Ann '89
(330) 262-3030 **Frantz** Martin H '78
(330) 264-6911 **Gluck** Robert N '69
(330) 264-4444 **Gorman** Robert C '95
(330) 264-8161 **Graven** Marion F III '69
(330) 262-3030 **Harp** Bradley R '99
(330) 287-5561 **Hemphill** Joi E '87
(330) 264-6115 **Holtman** Ronald E '67
(330) 264-6115 **Hostetler** Daniel J '73
(330) 264-2216 **Jackwood** Renee J '95
(330) 262-9060 **Jarrett** David L '93
(330) 264-4444 **Johnston** John C III '75
(330) 264-7355 **Kaufman** Daniel W '02
(330) 262-2916 **Keating** John T '83
(330) 262-2916 **Keating** Louise W '80
(330) 262-2916 **Keating** Richard M '52
(330) 262-7555 **Kennedy** Charles A '69
(330) 262-7555 **Kennedy Cicconetti Knowlton & Buytendyk**
(330) 287-5560 **Kienzle** Roger W Jr. '74
(330) 262-7555 **Knowlton** David C '92
(330) 264-5141 **Lanham** James J '85
(330) 264-6115 **Lehman** Ralph E '79
(330) 287-5490 **Leonard** John J '96
(330) 264-6115 **Logee Hostetler Stutzman & Lehman**
(330) 264-4444 **Lycans** Andrew P '04
(330) 262-2350 **Mast** Thomas K '80
(330) 264-4444 **McAllister** Kevin J '04
(330) 264-6911 **Miller** Norman R Jr. '91
(330) 287-5663 **Miller** Stuart K '74
(330) 263-2984 **Miyashita** Monica L '00
(330) 262-9060 **Murphy** John P Jr. '80
(330) 264-5141 **Musselman** Jeffrey D '97
(330) 262-5246 **Oehl** Frank C '86
(330) 264-4444 **Oviatt** Lincoln P '56
(330) 262-2667 **Owens** Clarke W '99
(330) 264-6115 **Packard** Jerry S '77
(330) 264-4444 **Pettorini** Timothy B '98
(330) 264-4444 **Plant** Tricia L '02
(330) 264-4444 **Plumly** Daniel H '78
(330) 264-4444 **Proper** Roger D Jr. '97
(330) 262-7555 **Rauckhorst** Robert J Jr. '99
(330) 345-7055 **Rehm** Ronald L '79
(330) 263-5333 **Ressler** Jon H '97
(330) 264-1150 **Reynolds** Craig R '86
(330) 264-1150 **Reynolds** Don L '57
(330) 264-1150 **Reynolds & Richard**
(330) 264-1150 **Reynolds** Robert J '82
(330) 264-1150 **Richard** James M '74
(330) 263-5333 **Roose & Ressler PA**
(330) 262-2350 **Rosebrough-Schneider** Christina A '94
(330) 264-1213 **Ross** Ford G '35
(330) 264-1213 **Ross** James H '81
(330) 264-1213 **Ross** William F '75
(330) 345-4639 **Rudawsky** Larry W '82
(330) 287-5490 **Rudy** Michael S '95
(330) 264-4444 **Schaeffer** John H '89
(330) 264-4500 **Schmitt** Christopher A '94
(330) 264-4444 **Schmitz** Peggy Jo '78
(330) 262-3030 **Schumacher** Jodie M '04
(330) 264-9454 **Sherrin** Michele P '92
(330) 287-5542 **Shriner** Rosanne K '02
(330) 345-5340 **Simmons** Lisa M '95
(330) 264-8956 **Spector** David N '83
(330) 287-5663 **Spitler** Corey E '88
(330) 262-3030 **Stefancin** Jocelyn '90
(330) 262-5246 **Stone** Meredith Blake '73
(330) 263-9011 **Storck** Jason '03
(330) 264-6115 **Stutzman** Morris '75
(330) 345-7949 **Thomas** James A '76
(330) 263-2984 **Thompson** Heather Walters '03
(330) 345-8100 **Tschantz** David E '89
(330) 262-2510 **Vinion** Lon R '79
(330) 264-1164 **Waldron** Suzanne M '89
(330) 262-3030 **Watkins** Deborah C '02
(330) 264-9454 **Whitney** Richard K '87
(330) 287-5574 **Wiest** Karin C '85
(330) 264-4444 **Wigham** David J '92
(330) 262-4781 **Wigham** John T '54
(330) 262-3030 **Wiles** Latecia E '04
(330) 683-5285 **Williams** Christine C '96
(330) 262-3030 **Williams** John M '85
(330) 287-5490 **Wire** Beverly J '85
(330) 264-4444 **Wright** Elizabeth L '01
(330) 264-5141 **Zacour** Wayne A '79

WORTHINGTON
Franklin County

(614) 433-9612 **Acklin** Kristina L '96
(614) 340-4044 **Alban** David R '55
(614) 340-4044 **Alban** Glenn F '92
(614) 433-9612 **Albert** Robert H '60
(614) 433-7941 **Anderson** Hugh Russell III '72
(614) 848-9600 **Appel** Jeffrey L '99
(614) 436-0093 **Arnold** William H '77
(614) 436-3555 **Atzberger** Thomas W '76
(614) 436-2750 **Aultman** Mark H '68
(614) 841-1994 **Avery** Barbara '75
(614) 431-8110 **Baxter** Thomas E '74
(614) 802-0150 **Bean** Mark W '79
(614) 470-2063 **Beckley** John G '91
(614) 841-2635 **Blazek** James N '93
(614) 430-9258 **Bolen** Alan L '83
(614) 785-0054 **Boord** Lawrence F '75
(614) 431-8110 **Borowicz** Louis M '04
(614) 885-4980 **Boyd** Jeffrey D '82
(614) 854-9968 **Butts** Diana F '89
(614) 340-4044 **Carlson** Valerie H '90
Caruso Daniel R '95
(614) 848-7882 **Coffman** Joseph G '75
(614) 888-3177 **Compton** John S '77
(614) 848-7883 **Crowley** Timothy G '75
(614) 880-0888 **Cusack** Mary Jo '59
(614) 847-1660 **DeBoard** James C '77
(614) 433-9612 **Diehl** William D '66
(614) 985-0556 **Dominy** Shawn R '97
Drumm Cynthia J '91
(614) 841-1620 **Evans** Craig E '73
(614) 436-3681 **Eyerman** Philip L '81
(614) 637-9994 **Fein** Henry L '81
Foster Kimberley S '93
(614) 985-1493 **Gilbert** Stacey A '01
(614) 847-8255 **Gloeckner** George N '72
(614) 841-0559 **Goelz** Marilyn M '82
(614) 885-0554 **Good** William A '80
(614) 436-8010 **Goodrich** Kyle S '04
(614) 436-3437 **Graham** Richard E '78
(614) 841-1918 **Grayson** R S '85
(614) 410-1700 **Green** Rebecca M '88
(614) 433-9612 **Groeber** John A '90
(614) 885-3500 **Hall** James A '79
(614) 880-0883 **Hardesty** Michael J '66
(614) 433-9502 **Harmon** Phillip L '80
(614) 847-1660 **Hayes** Susan N '92
(614) 802-2900 **Heiser** Steven L '79
Hellstedt Jonathan E '99
(614) 885-5112 **Holmes** Robert D '49
(614) 885-5112 **Holmes** Scott D '80
Holschuh Nathan W '02
(614) 436-1001 **Hoover** Douglas E '73
(614) 781-1400 **Hrabcak** Michael '91
(614) 545-4118 **Huddle** William G '81
(614) 410-1700 **Hughes** Martin J '83
(614) 844-5208 **Johnson** Keisha D '02
(614) 885-8118 **Jones** John S '76
(614) 436-7599 **Juhola** Michael D '80
(614) 433-9612 **Kagay Albert Diehl & Groeber**
(614) 841-1500 **Kelleher** W Sean '74
(614) 785-9420 **Kerns** Ralph A '81
(614) 436-2750 **Kettlewell** Charles J '00
(614) 846-2626 **King** Gale R III '72
(614) 841-1620 **Kirk** Edward R '73
(614) 888-2600 **Kobee** Robert F '62
(614) 847-0309 **Landers** Mary M '86
(614) 888-2033 **Lehman** David B '74
(614) 885-4980 **Little** Shawn A '91
(614) 431-2600 **Lorimer** James J '69
(614) 888-4017 **Machle** Kathi J '87
(614) 431-1763 **Malley** Kingston E '72
(614) 841-1918 **Massengill** Kimberly A '92
McCormac John W '61
(614) 431-0851 **McElwee** Larry A '91
(614) 841-1918 **McLinden** Peter M '97
McNeil Christopher B '89
Michael Bonnie B '84
(614) 848-4442 **Mills** Steven R '85
(614) 848-9600 **Minton** Harvey S '62
(614) 848-7812 **Mong** James F '84
(614) 844-5208 **Mortimer** Pamela A '98
(614) 841-1918 **Moss** Patricia A '81
(614) 802-0150 **Novack** Thomas J '87
(614) 846-1700 **Phillips** Janet L '97
Piero Jeffrey D '00
(614) 547-0370 **Reeve** Gary A '95
(614) 547-0370 **Reeve & Watts**
(614) 221-0002 **Reibel** Linda L '96
(614) 781-1400 **Richards** Jason W '98
(614) 841-9282 **Rouch** Kevin C '85
(614) 433-0467 **Sarap** George M '77
(614) 846-4100 **Simon** Frederick J '59
(614) 781-1400 **Smith** Heidi A '03
Sowash Allan D '02
(614) 431-6436 **Stanger** Philip C '77
Szymanski Duane R '94
(614) 846-5080 **Thomas** Arthur H Jr. '64
(614) 781-6500 **Uldricks** David M '99
(614) 846-6783 **Van Sickle** John A '83
(614) 888-0666 **Vierow** Frederick A '60
(614) 848-5888 **Walker** Brian A '89
(614) 436-1197 **Welsh** Jeannette M '89
(614) 888-7686 **Whitaker** Philip W '69
(614) 888-7126 **Whitlock** Scott N '67

WRIGHT PATTERSON AFB
Greene County

(937) 255-6111 **Babbitt** Edwin R III '81
(937) 255-6111 **Beckett** Janice C '85
(937) 255-6111 **Bird** Karl C '88
(937) 257-6142 **Brown** Darryl D '93
(937) 904-2156 **Brubaker** James D '77
(937) 257-5958 **Campbell** Douglas L '76
(937) 255-6111 **Case** John A '83
(937) 257-4124 **Cavanaugh** William D Jr. '86
(937) 904-2176 **Clayton** Robert B '71
(937) 255-6111 **Curp** Sharon A '89
Dattilo Anthony P '81
(937) 257-7143 **Diaz** Norbert J '82
(937) 255-6111 **Dickinson** Diana S '89
(937) 255-5270 **Ditalia** Peter M '81
(937) 255-5270 **Edsall** Richard L '82
(937) 257-5868 **Hilker** Samuel R '76
(937) 255-2838 **Hollins** Gerald B '70
(937) 255-5270 **Klein** Charles M '86
(937) 257-8189 **Kramer** Gary M '91
(937) 255-2838 **Kundert** Thomas L '87
(937) 904-5041 **Kurtz** Marcia L '81
(937) 255-5270 **Lyons** Bridget E '98
(937) 255-6111 **Marcey** Thomas S '75
(937) 255-5270 **Mullin** Michael J '75
(937) 255-5270 **Nihiser** Nike '86
(937) 255-4600 **Owens** Jeffrey R '99
(937) 255-6113 **Perfilio** Anthony J '80
(937) 255-6111 **Peterson** Sigurd R Jr. '87
(937) 255-5270 **Reist** Robert M '86
(937) 257-5728 **Robb** Jeffrey L '84
(937) 257-9996 **Rudolph** Thomas E '83
(937) 257-3851 **Satterfield** Carol A '79
(937) 255-2838 **Scearce** Bobby D '72
(937) 255-5270 **Schumann** Ronald G '92
(937) 255-2872 **Sinder** Fredric L '75
(937) 255-2838 **Tollefson** Gina S '94
(937) 255-6111 **Underwood** Denise A '85
(937) 255-7777 **Whalen** Paul L '93
(937) 255-5270 **Zimmerle** Sandra G '84

WYOMING
Hamilton County

Gentry Vanessa L '82
(513) 632-9555 **Stonehill** David N '80

XENIA
Greene County

(937) 372-4436 **Anderson** Alan G '73
(937) 372-8055 **Baker** R J '92
(937) 372-4404 **Barrett** Paul W '80
(937) 372-4411 **Beard** Phillip L '73
(937) 372-4411 **Brandabur Finlay Johnson Weckstein & Beard**
(937) 372-4411 **Brandabur** James F '59
(937) 372-6000 **Buckwalter** Michael A '84
(937) 372-4431 **Carrera** Nicholas A '62
(937) 374-0077 **Chappars** Timothy S '78
(937) 372-6921 **Cox** David W '76
(937) 372-6921 **Cox Keller & Rowland**
(937) 372-3584 **Donatelli** Mark J '79
(937) 562-5250 **Ellis** Elizabeth A '01
(937) 372-9963 **Ferguson** Lester L '69
(937) 372-4411 **Finlay** John A '66
(937) 372-8055 **Finney** Charles R '49
(937) 562-5250 **Foley** Michael E '77
(937) 562-5250 **Gall** Garrett T '77
(937) 372-4404 **Gibney Stephan Barrett & Root**
(937) 376-7299 **Goldie** Susan L '78
(937) 562-5041 **Graf** Joseph C '75
(937) 562-5250 **Haller** Stephen K '75
(937) 562-5250 **Hayes** David D '04
(937) 562-5250 **Hendrix** Robert K '86
(937) 562-5250 **Hunt** Andrew J '01
(937) 562-5250 **Hunter** Jeffrey D '93
(937) 372-4411 **Johnson** Gary R '72
(937) 372-6921 **Keller** Ronald P '83
(937) 562-6249 **Kelly** Kristen '95
Lennon Cynthia A '81
(937) 562-4000 **Lewis** Amy H '92
(937) 376-7303 **Lewis** Ronald C '93
(937) 372-9981 **Massie** Marshall J '51
(937) 376-5429 **Mathewson** Thomas G '96
(937) 372-8055 **McKeown** Noel K '72
(937) 372-8055 **Miller Finney McKeown & Baker**
(937) 562-5250 **Miller** Thomas C '03
(937) 431-0509 **Moran** Timothy J '94
(937) 562-5250 **Murray** Christopher A '92
(937) 372-4411 **Neal** Scott E '98
(937) 372-9236 **Orlins** David A '75
(937) 372-4919 **Pendry** David L '80
(937) 372-3584 **Peterson** David S '84
(937) 372-3584 **Peterson** Marshall E '55
(937) 372-4436 **Phipps** David L '75
(937) 372-3101 **Pitts** Teddy L '78
(937) 372-4404 **Root** John A '92
(937) 372-6921 **Rowland** Charles M II '95
(937) 372-4919 **Saunders** Craig W '00
(937) 562-5250 **Schenck** William F Jr. '70
(937) 372-5591 **Schmidt** James W '73
(937) 562-5250 **Schmidt** Suzanne M '79
(937) 372-7243 **Schornak** Donald G '56
(937) 562-5134 **Shaver** Mark A '98
(937) 376-3548 **Sheets** Kenneth R '84
(937) 376-9454 **Sidell** Arthur L III '73
(937) 372-9236 **Silverberg** Eric '69
(937) 372-9236 **Silverberg Zaharieff & Orlins Co,LPA**
(937) 426-6633 **Stafford** Thomas R '77
(937) 372-4404 **Stephan** Peter D '74
(937) 372-4404 **Stephan** Stephanie B '03
(937) 562-5250 **Stout** Cheri L '01
(937) 562-5249 **Stump** Kimberly Metzler '96
(937) 376-1937 **Theodor** Christ '77
(937) 562-4000 **Thompson** Cynthia L '87
(937) 562-5250 **Tornichio** Adolfo A '99
(937) 372-4436 **Wead Anderson Phipps & Aultman**
(937) 372-4436 **Wead** Richard A '67
(937) 372-4411 **Weckstein** Donald '62
(937) 562-5250 **Womack** Tamela A '98
(937) 372-7605 **Zachritz** James D '65
(937) 372-9236 **Zaharieff** Anthony J '70

YELLOW SPRINGS
Greene County

(937) 767-2741 **Boettcher** Barbara E '03
Stoner Carol M '79

YOUNGSTOWN
Mahoning County

(330) 742-4255 **Abrams** Karen H '81
(330) 743-5101 **Abrams** Richard A '80
(330) 740-2073 **Akins** Kim F '90
Ally Bassil S '99
(330) 742-8791 **Almasy** Dionne M '92
(330) 629-9030 **Amendolara** Samuel G '79
(330) 792-6611 **Ames** Clarence D '92
(330) 702-9700 **Ams** John A '02
(330) 744-4137 **Amstutz** Clarence John Jr. '60
(330) 740-2330 **Andrews** Robert J '89
(330) 792-6033 **Anzellotti Sperling Pazol & Small Co, LPA**
(330) 743-6300 **Atway & Cochran,LLC**
(330) 743-6300 **Atway** Neal G '92
(330) 726-1654 **Ausnehmer** John E '80
(330) 747-4404 **Baker** Brent E '00
Bannon Charles J '58
(330) 758-6731 **Bannon** Robert W '84
(330) 744-5211 **Barbee** David S '86
(330) 744-1111 **Baronzzi** Christopher J '04
(330) 746-8491 **Bartels** Charles B '96
(330) 740-2180 **Bateman** Melissa F '01
(330) 744-1111 **Beard** Ralph A '75
(330) 743-1171 **Beatrice** Mark A '81
(330) 747-2661 **Beck** Mark J '91
(330) 744-3523 **Belinky** Mark A '77
(330) 744-4351 **Bennett** Franklin S Jr. '80
(330) 744-5284 **Bernard** Elizabeth A '88
(330) 799-7711 **Bernard** Roberta M '00
(330) 740-0200 **Billak** Damian A '95
(330) 744-0291 **Bins-Castronovo** Matthew N '99
(330) 744-5211 **Bishara** Joseph C '96
(330) 744-0440 **Blackstone** Jay C '83
(330) 744-5211 **Blair** Richard B '70
(330) 742-8941 **Blanchard** William J '96
(330) 744-1111 **Blomstrom** James L '74
(330) 792-3313 **Bobovnyik** David A '86
(330) 792-1063 **Bodzenta** Dwayne J '88
(330) 744-1111 **Boetcher** Martin J '87
(330) 743-1171 **Bolton** Stephen T '72
(330) 726-5518 **Bouffard** Robert S '79
(330) 744-0291 **Boyd** John C '66
(330) 744-0291 **Boyd Rummell Carach & Curry Co LPA**
(330) 743-4116 **Brennan Frederick Vouros & Yarwood,Ltd**
(330) 758-0080 **Briach** George G '82
(330) 965-5195 **Bricker** Dale E '61
(330) 259-0612 **Bricker** Thomas R '00
(330) 965-2323 **Bruno** Lynn S '83
(330) 744-1148 **Bryan** Jerome M '91
(330) 746-5643 **Buck** Marshall D '81
(330) 740-2180 **Budinsky** Robert '78
(330) 743-9383 **Burgess** Richard L '84
(330) 743-2987 **Burns** Susan A '97
(330) 799-5940 **Bush** Joseph J III '87
(330) 743-5101 **Bush** Richard T '83
(330) 742-8921 **Bush** Robert E Jr. '92
(330) 743-1171 **Bushey** Martha L '89
(330) 759-9350 **Caccarozzo** Joey L '03
(330) 744-3198 **Callen** James B '76
(330) 744-0291 **Carach** Herman J Jr. '77
(330) 788-2480 **Carfolo** Mark A '91
Carnie William T '79
(330) 740-2073 **Caroline** John C '95
(330) 793-4419 **Casale** Carl L '84
(330) 744-2125 **Christian** Robert J '77
(330) 744-1111 **Christian** Shirley J '86
(330) 742-7031 **Cloonan** Terrence F '81
(330) 788-3971 **Close** Arthur L Jr. '58
(330) 743-6300 **Cochran** Scott R '95
(330) 740-2158 **Coles-Jones** Jacquelyn '01
(330) 788-3666 **Collins** William M '58
(330) 746-5643 **Comstock** David C '59
(330) 746-5643 **Comstock** David C Jr. '88
(330) 746-5643 **Comstock Springer & Wilson Co,LPA**
(330) 746-6301 **Conn** Paul C '92
(330) 744-1111 **Coombs** Frederick S III '75
(330) 743-4116 **Corroto** Thomas L Jr. '48
(330) 747-2661 **Corsell** Joseph D '96
(330) 743-4116 **Crawford** Anne F '91
(330) 743-5101 **Cunning** Patrick P '84
(330) 744-0291 **Curry** Robert J '95
(330) 746-7027 **Cusick** Kelly R '03
(330) 740-2180 **Czopur-Gaffney** Melanie A '01
(330) 759-4155 **Dann** Marc E '87
(330) 783-9222 **D'Apolito** Anthony M '94
(330) 783-9222 **D'Apolito** David A '89
(330) 783-9222 **D'Apolito** Loumano A '73
(330) 744-4137 **Dascenzo** Daniel P '98
(330) 747-2661 **Davis** Richard T '76
(330) 743-1717 **Davis & Young**
(330) 740-2055 **Dawson** Thomas D '88
(330) 726-0484 **DeAngelo** Edward S '85
(330) 744-5211 **DeBonis** Scott R '95
(330) 782-3000 **DeFabio** Louis M '92
(330) 743-4116 **DeGenova** Damian P '94
(330) 744-1111 **Dellick** John T '85
(330) 965-2323 **Delost** Raymond M '80
(330) 742-2340 **Denman** Sandra L '88
(330) 747-2661 **DeSalvo** Donald J '69
(330) 758-3878 **DeSanto** Donald J '81
(330) 758-3878 **DeSanto** Jeanne Bitonte '87
(330) 758-3878 **DeSanto** Joseph D '68
(330) 740-2330 **Desmond** Martin P '04
(330) 743-1171 **Detec** David A '80
(330) 744-4137 **Dietz** James B '91
Dinsio Melissa D '97
(330) 726-0484 **DiSalvo-LaCivita** Renee M '97
(330) 744-0202 **Dixon** John J '76
(330) 747-2661 **Dobran** James M '82
(330) 792-0827 **Dockry** Michael B '82

(330) 726-0484 **Donofrio** Anthony '91
(330) 744-3196 **Dougan** Patricia '94
(330) 742-8857 **Douglas** Robert A Jr. '80
(330) 629-9030 **Douglass** Anthony R '01
(330) 758-1781 **Draa** Charles M '81
(330) 740-2330 **Duffrin** Robert E '93
(330) 629-8877 **Dunn** James C '86
(330) 740-2330 **Durkin** Dawn M '98
(330) 744-1111 **Dutton** Paul M '72
(330) 744-5029 **Economus** Basil G '99
(330) 744-5029 **Economus** George C '64
(330) 744-1111 **Erb** Shawna L '96
(330) 744-1148 **Essad** Scott C '96
(330) 726-0484 **Fabrizi** Mary A '85
(330) 759-4155 **Falgiani** John D Jr. '85
(330) 747-2661 **Fantauzzi** David A '81
(330) 743-6004 **Farris** Anthony J '91
(330) 740-2161 **Fehr** Eugene J '78
(330) 744-0202 **Ferris** Ted A '79
(330) 726-5518 **Fire** Patrick C '88
(330) 759-3232 **Flanagan** Edward J '79
(330) 726-8700 **Fleck** Jeffrey B '67
(330) 743-3232 **Fleming** Alfred J '75
(330) 747-4404 **Floyd** James G '71
(330) 746-5643 **Flynt** Bobbie L '96
(330) 792-6611 **Foley** Robert J Jr. '98
(330) 746-5643 **Fowler** William S '84
(330) 744-5284 **Fox** Eugene B '52
(330) 549-2497 **Franken** Timothy E '79
(330) 743-4116 **Frederick** Harry '51
(330) 744-4137 **Friedman & Rummell Co, LPA**
(330) 747-4404 **Fulton** Robert S '72
(330) 740-2330 **Gaglione** Karen M '92
(330) 740-2330 **Gains** Paul J '82
(330) 726-5518 **Galip** Ronald G '57
(330) 726-8700 **Gallitto** Robyn R '01
(330) 744-0247 **Gallo** Michael A Jr. '67
(330) 629-7510 **Garea** Stephen R '77
(330) 792-3423 **Gattozzi** Lisa B '94
(330) 884-6264 **Gaughan** Patrick H '89
(330) 746-5000 **Gentile** James S '76
(330) 746-1712 **Gerson** Rebecca M '94
(330) 726-0484 **Giannini** Matthew C '78
(330) 792-1063 **Gibbons** John D '83
(330) 744-3010 **Gilmartin** Vincent E '54
(330) 746-5643 **Golden** Kenneth L '04
(330) 782-6470 **Gollings** Michael L '96
(330) 744-5139 **Greaves** Elaine B '91
(330) 743-5101 **Green Haines & Sgambati, Co LPA**
(330) 746-3251 **Grinstein** Deborah L '85
(330) 744-0247 **Grinstein** Peter B '61
(330) 742-8874 **Guarnieri** Dana C '98
(330) 742-8874 **Guglucello** Iris T '82
(330) 744-1111 **Gurbach** Matthew D '03
(330) 740-2330 **Hackett** Sharon K '84
(330) 792-2336 **Hackett** Timothy R '84
(330) 740-2073 **Hafiz** Ishraq A '83
(330) 743-5101 **Haines** Dennis '62
(330) 747-2661 **Hall** Leonard D '85
(330) 746-6301 **Hanni** Don L '53
(330) 744-5284 **Harlan** Michael D '98
(330) 744-1111 **Harrington Hoppe & Mitchell, Ltd**
(330) 744-5284 **Harshman Bernard & Ramage**
(330) 744-5284 **Harshman** Michael S '66
(330) 744-0247 **Hartford** Robert S Jr. '74
(330) 792-2336 **Hartwig** Edward J '98
(330) 740-2330 **Hawn** Kerry L '03
(330) 744-1148 **Heino** John T '96
(330) 747-2661 **Heinrich** Julian '02
(330) 743-1171 **Heintz** Jeffrey D '84
(330) 261-2486 **Helbley** William C Jr. '89
(330) 792-6611 **Heller Maas Moro & Magill Co LPA**
(330) 792-6611 **Heller** Robert L '81
(330) 744-1148 **Henderson Covington Messenger Newman & Thomas Co,**
(330) 740-2180 **Hendrickson** Jeffrey E '00
(330) 746-8491 **Henkin** Robert A '73
(330) 797-1717 **Hepfner** Donald C '89
(330) 744-4481 **Herberger** Robert J Jr. '90
(330) 747-4404 **Herriott** Donald P '74
(330) 740-2180 **Hively** Aaron A '99
(330) 744-1148 **Holmquist** David K '61
(330) 726-8939 **Horlick** Chester W '58
(330) 726-8939 **Horlick** Todd M '92
(330) 743-1171 **Houser** Joseph M '81
(330) 747-4404 **Houser** Mary Beth M '82
(330) 799-7711 **Housley** Brett A '99
(330) 744-3198 **Howard** Cherie H '82
(330) 740-2208 **Huberman** Mark A '76
(330) 792-6612 **Hudak** Ann C '71
(330) 792-1063 **Hudzik** John C '83
(330) 759-0102 **Hull** Victor C '96
(330) 746-8491 **Hume** Martin S '81
(330) 726-0484 **Infante** Thomas E '72
(330) 965-2000 **Inglis** Patricia M '83

(330) 743-1171 **Jacob** Timothy J '77
(330) 941-2340 **Jacobs** Holly A '91
(330) 884-1046 **Jacobson** Patricia F '80
(330) 782-8301 **James** Carl G III '77
(330) 792-2336 **Jeren** John A Jr. '73
(330) 744-1311 **Johns** Kelly A '00
(330) 740-2330 **Johnson** Greta L '04
(330) 759-4155 **Joltin** Benjamin '00
(330) 782-5674 **Jones** Anissa M '97
Kalafut George E '72
(330) 743-5181 **Kannensohn** Fredric A '64
(330) 740-2208 **Kaufmann** Deborah A '97
(330) 744-0291 **Kaufmann** Walter '73
(330) 744-4137 **Kelley** Michael J '89
(330) 792-1063 **Khavari** Bijan A '93
(330) 629-8877 **Kissinger** William J Jr. '92
(330) 746-6301 **Kivlighan** Michael O '03
(330) 744-5284 **Kmetz** Kimberlee Jo '94
(330) 758-0377 **Knickerbocker** Ronald E '82
(330) 746-6591 **Kolmacic** Mark J '82
(330) 743-5101 **Kondela** Joseph D '99
(330) 729-9000 **Koval** Margaret '84
(330) 740-2330 **Kralj** Kevin M '92
(330) 742-8791 **Krause** Michael J '97
(330) 746-5643 **Kress** Douglas J '94
(330) 746-0171 **Kretzer** Alan R '68
(330) 740-2330 **Krueger** Dawn P '02
(330) 743-1171 **Krzys** Jerry R II '04
(330) 746-6301 **Kurz** Jeffrey A '02
(330) 758-9525 **Kutlick** Paula '94
(330) 744-5211 **Lacich** Christopher P '93
(330) 788-2480 **Laczko** John P '91
(330) 743-5101 **Laine** Barry Robert '73
(330) 743-1171 **Lanz** Charles Scott '80
(330) 782-8283 **Lanzo** James E '98
(330) 743-3988 **Latas** Mark A '81
(330) 743-3998 **Latas** Milan '58
(330) 743-5101 **Lavelle** Gregory J '75
(330) 758-6900 **Lavelle** Mark J '93
(330) 744-3196 **Legow** Christine Blair '79
(330) 759-7988 **Legow** Elliot P '78
(330) 744-3198 **Lehere** Allyson L '95
(330) 746-5652 **Leone** Donald P '76
(330) 799-7711 **Lilly** Jeffrey A '99
(330) 726-6999 **Limbian** John J '90
(330) 743-1171 **Lipka** Thomas J '96
(330) 744-5211 **Lodge** Thomas J '77
(330) 744-1311 **Longbrake** W Bradford '95
(330) 744-0247 **Lucci** Joseph C '78
(330) 792-6611 **Maas** Steven D '82
(330) 792-0439 **MacDonald** Stewart D '72
(330) 740-2330 **Macejko** Joseph R '98
(330) 744-9007 **Macejko** Melissa M '99
(330) 746-1054 **Macejko** Theodore T Jr. '63
(330) 747-2661 **Mackall** Robert L III '00
(330) 746-6301 **Mager** Kevin D '91
(330) 792-6611 **Magill** Richard L '87
(330) 747-6548 **Maillis** Michael J '95
(330) 740-2970 **Malkin** Michael L '81
(330) 744-0291 **Malkoff** Solomon '42
(330) 740-2073 **Malmisur** Joanna M '92
(330) 740-2311 **Maloney** Timothy P '85
(330) 743-1171 **Manchester Bennett Powers & Ullman**
(330) 726-1444 **Mangie** Mark G '75
(330) 740-2600 **Manigault** Kimberly A '93
(330) 702-9700 **Marando** Michael P '77
(330) 629-9030 **Maro** Lynn A '91
(330) 746-6301 **Marshall** William M Jr. '74
(330) 726-5888 **Matavich** Alan J '76
(330) 744-0247 **Matune** Frank J '98
(330) 747-2661 **Matune** Timothy J '84
(330) 629-8977 **Maxin** Joseph J '87
(330) 629-8977 **Maxin** Joseph W '61
(330) 744-1111 **Maxwell** Neil H '84
(330) 743-6300 **McBride** Michael J '02
(330) 740-2278 **McCollum** Donna J '85
(330) 792-1063 **McKinney** Debra J '92
(330) 744-4481 **McLaughlin** Richard P '62
(330) 744-4481 **McLaughlin & McNally**
(330) 744-4481 **McNally** John A III '71
(330) 742-8874 **McNally** John A IV '96
(330) 744-8973 **Melnick** Robert R '83
(330) 746-5643 **Meola** Margo Stoffel '95
(330) 782-3000 **Meranto** Anthony P '96
(330) 744-1148 **Messenger** James L '67
(330) 743-1171 **Meub** Janet K '01
(330) 747-2661 **Miklandric** William J Jr. '01
(330) 792-6033 **Mikulka** Angela J '84
(330) 792-6033 **Mikulka** Thomas L '98
(330) 742-4309 **Millich** George P Jr. '00
(330) 743-5101 **Mirkin** Ira J '79
(330) 793-2698 **Modarelli** Nicholas E '83
(330) 759-8664 **Mogul** Michael L '77
(330) 744-5211 **Moore** David M '93
(330) 742-8874 **Morgione** Gregory G '98
(330) 726-5518 **Morley** Michael J '81
(330) 792-6611 **Moro** Joseph A '85
(330) 744-1111 **Morrison** Kelly J '85

(330) 744-1111 **Morrison** Lance A '92
(330) 744-3196 **Mostov** Jan R '84
(330) 799-5940 **Muldowney** Shawn R '92
(330) 747-2661 **Mulligan** Joseph P '91
(330) 629-8860 **Mumaw** Daniel J '86
(330) 788-2804 **Myers** William A '93
(330) 744-0247 **Nadler Nadler & Burdman Co, LPA**
(330) 744-1148 **Newman** Christopher J '73
(330) 747-4404 **Newman** John M '42
(330) 747-4404 **Newman Olson & Kerr,LPA**
(330) 742-0572 **Nohra** Jude J '97
(330) 629-9030 **Ocasio** Miriam M '00
(330) 792-6220 **O'Halloran** Janice T '82
(330) 792-6220 **Ohanian** Eric J '94
(330) 740-2180 **O'Horo** Kristen L '98
(330) 743-5101 **Okusewsky** Stanley J III '03
(330) 747-4404 **Olson** Leonard A '53
(330) 747-2661 **Orlando** Jacqueline A '98
(330) 747-2579 **Palagano** Michael Jr. '79
(330) 744-4137 **Palma** Robert M '75
(330) 629-9030 **Palombaro** Albert A '84
Palusak Julie D '04
(330) 884-4913 **Parker** Gerald M '71
(330) 744-4137 **Patrick** Walter Terry '77
(330) 792-6033 **Pazol** James L '62
(330) 740-2073 **Petraglia** Catherine T '80
(330) 744-0247 **Petrony** John F '93
(330) 740-2208 **Petruska** Heidi M '98
(330) 702-9700 **Pfau** John C '80
(330) 702-9700 **Pfau Pfau & Marando**
(330) 702-9700 **Pfau** William E III '79
(330) 758-9525 **Philibin** Gary J '87
(330) 740-2330 **Phillips** Elizabeth M '96
(330) 743-5101 **Piatt** Timothy R '88
(330) 740-2330 **Pierce** Constance E '95
(330) 743-7000 **Pilcher** Gary L '76
(330) 726-8177 **Pipino** James D '85
(330) 747-2661 **Placanica** Maria '97
(330) 793-3171 **Pochiro** Patrick R '67
(330) 759-2115 **Politi** Jonathan D '93
(330) 740-2330 **Popio** Kerry '03
(330) 744-3198 **Powell** Barbara E '83
(330) 744-5211 **Pridham** Herbert H '55
(330) 799-4311 **Pritchard** Warren G '82
(330) 747-4404 **Puhalla** Leo J '96
(330) 788-5555 **Rafidi** Joseph F '00
(330) 744-4137 **Rafoth** Carl D '68
(330) 758-0575 **Rafoth** James '89
(330) 744-5284 **Ramage** William C III '69
(330) 744-0247 **Reardon** Timothy M '92
(330) 758-2146 **Reich** Jerry '55
(330) 744-5211 **Reid** Wayne P '96
(330) 744-1311 **Reminger & Reminger**
(330) 743-1171 **Ricchiuti** Doralice Tavolario '04
(330) 743-3232 **Richards** Lawrence H '76
(330) 743-1171 **Richardson** Gina Agresta '99
(330) 746-0171 **Ridder** Bryan M '83
(330) 744-5147 **Rinehart** James P '80
(330) 629-8371 **Ritchie** Walter D '91
(330) 744-5211 **Roberts** James E '74
(330) 744-5201 **Rohde** R Keller '75
(330) 783-9222 **Rohrbaugh** Robert J II '99
(330) 743-1171 **Romero** Edwin '78
(330) 740-2180 **Rorick** Christina M '99
(330) 744-0247 **Rosenblum** Donn D '79
(330) 744-2667 **Rosenthal** Patty B '81
(330) 747-2661 **Ross** Ronald J '65
(330) 788-4922 **Rossi** Armond V '56
(330) 744-8695 **Rossi** Dan L '52
(330) 743-1191 **Rossi** Eugene J '78
(330) 744-8695 **Rossi** Gregg A '90
(330) 744-8695 **Rossi & Rossi**
(330) 744-5211 **Roth Blair Roberts Strasfeld & Lodge,LPA**
(330) 744-5211 **Roth** Daniel B '56
(330) 744-0291 **Rummell** Randall W '83
(330) 747-1954 **Saadi** Edward T '03
(330) 742-7021 **Sabine** John D '67
(330) 565-5160 **Sammarone** Christopher '99
(330) 744-3196 **Sarna** Wayne W '83
(330) 746-5000 **Saunders** Linda Sue '82
(330) 743-1171 **Savage** John T '01
(330) 758-2308 **Scarsella** Paul L '97
(330) 743-5101 **Scharf** Shawn D '98
(330) 744-4137 **Schiavone** Christopher J '01
(330) 744-4137 **Schiavone** Leonard D '77
(330) 799-5940 **Schiavoni** Louis J '83
(330) 799-5940 **Schiavoni Schiavoni & Bush Co, LPA**
(330) 743-1040 **Schiraldi** Richard J '81
(330) 965-9910 **Schoenike** Jonathan K '91
(330) 744-1111 **Schor** Neil D '89
(330) 744-5211 **Schwartz** Glenn J '74
(330) 799-7711 **Schwartz** Richard N '82

(330) 747-4404 **Sebastiano** Patrick A '82
(330) 758-8369 **Seely** Donald R '65
(330) 799-7711 **Sekerak** Diane M '95
(330) 742-8823 **Sertick** Anthony Jr. '91
(330) 759-6711 **Shagrin** Steven S '81
(330) 799-7717 **Sheftel** Lynn A '66
(330) 740-2330 **Shells-Conne** Lori Lei '91
(330) 726-8700 **Siciliano** Anthony '89
(330) 743-7000 **Sisek** James H '74
(330) 744-0247 **Skolnick** Jay M '67
(330) 792-2336 **Skoufatos** Nikitas '88
(330) 742-8800 **Slavens** Kathleen M '92
(330) 744-0247 **Smith** Edward F '88
(330) 758-3075 **Smith** Wade W Jr. '82
(330) 743-9509 **Sofranko** George B Jr. '83
(330) 792-6033 **Sperling** Adam L '94
(330) 792-6033 **Sperling** Victor '60
(330) 746-5643 **Springer** Lawrence R '61
(330) 783-9222 **Stanos** Steve P '58
(330) 757-4347 **Stavick** Margaret A '74
(330) 746-3291 **Stebelton** Richard A '59
(330) 792-6220 **Stefanski** Dale Kim '80
(330) 744-0247 **Stein** Marc S '75
(330) 799-9977 **Steiskal** Arthur R '70
(330) 792-1063 **Stone** Marc D '79
(330) 744-5211 **Strasfeld** Stuart A '77
(330) 740-2330 **Stratford** Linette M '90
(330) 782-3000 **Sturgeon** Edward F '79
(330) 744-9007 **Suhar** Andrew W '92
(330) 744-2161 **Suhar** Kandis W '94
(330) 744-5145 **Szabados** Lester M '86
(330) 746-6612 **Theofilos** Gus K '77
(330) 744-1148 **Thomas** Richard J '87
(330) 743-1171 **Thompson** Jon M '04
(330) 747-4404 **Thornton** Edward C Jr. '71
(330) 792-2336 **Tiberio** Michael A '93
(330) 742-7032 **Tomlinson** Kimberly A '94
(330) 480-3203 **Tonies** Theresa M '95
(330) 743-5101 **Torba** Carla Jo '92
(330) 687-5324 **Trefethern** Thomas N '01
(330) 759-7499 **Tribby** Alfred G Jr. '81
(330) 726-8669 **Turner** Roklyn M '01
(330) 744-4495 **Tzagournis** George A '60
(330) 746-7830 **Ujczo** Daniel D '02
(330) 746-5000 **Van Brocklin** Gary L '75
(330) 744-4495 **Vaporis** John M '60
(330) 726-1654 **Vaughn** Jack R '77
(330) 746-1064 **Vereb** Melodie E '02
(330) 742-1574 **Vergon** Charles B '72
(330) 740-2330 **Villani** Michael T '96
(330) 720-6012 **Virostek** Janet E '82
(330) 726-5518 **Vivo** James S Jr. '00
(330) 743-4116 **Vouros** Joseph E '50
(330) 742-0500 **Wagner** Michael J '81
(330) 744-3196 **Walling** Michael I '65
(330) 793-5488 **Weber** Kirk D '82
(330) 746-1064 **Weimer** William A '75
(330) 792-2336 **Wellman Jeren Hackett & Skoufatos Co,LPA**
(330) 740-2104 **Welsh** Kathi M '85
(330) 480-5225 **Welsh** Timothy G '86
(330) 744-1111 **Wenger** Alan D '77
(330) 792-6033 **Wexler** Ilan '80
(330) 744-1148 **White** George L IV '96
(330) 758-0080 **White** Richard N '76
(330) 743-1717 **Wilkes** Larry D '84
(330) 746-5643 **Wilson** Thomas J '76
(330) 747-1471 **Wiseman** Robert L Jr. '78
(330) 744-5321 **Wittman** Donald B '00
(330) 729-9000 **Wloch** Vincent J '74
(330) 729-9835 **Wolfcale** Arthur D Jr. '54
(330) 746-6301 **Wolff** Heidi A '02
(330) 740-2330 **Workman** James E Jr. '78
(330) 744-8695 **Wright** Thomas R '91
(330) 744-3196 **Wrona** Michelle A '99
(330) 743-4116 **Yarwood** Ronald D '97
Yavorcik Martin E '99
(330) 743-1171 **Young** Joseph R Jr. '82
(330) 747-2661 **Yourstowsky** Ronald J '91
(330) 729-9823 **Zahar** Deborah A '92
(330) 726-1654 **Zamary** Gary M '83
(330) 629-9030 **Zena** Thomas E '72
(330) 744-5211 **Zomoida** John N Jr. '00

ZANESVILLE

Muskingum County

(740) 452-8426 **Baker** Herbert W Jr. '76
(740) 454-2545 **Baldwin** Steven R '83
(740) 452-8439 **Barclay** Adam T '03
(740) 454-8585 **Barclay** Katherine M '04
(740) 452-7555 **Beam** James R '60
(740) 452-7555 **Beam** Jeff R '82
(740) 453-6475 **Benbow** Brian W '99
(740) 454-2545 **Bopeley** Thomas R '58
(740) 455-7123 **Borowitz** Paul J '65
(740) 453-0888 **Brown** James P '84
(740) 452-8484 **Bryan** Michael T '01
(740) 453-0351 **Buck** Steven E '75
(740) 455-7123 **Chess** Walter K Jr. '75
(740) 454-1010 **Coffman** Ward D III '78
(740) 453-1130 **Couch** Ronald C '83

(740) 455-7123 **Crawmer** Shawn E '95
(740) 453-0888 **Cultice & Brown**
(740) 453-0888 **Cultice** Peter N '83
(740) 453-0888 **Cultice Brown** Susan C '83
(740) 452-7555 **Dal Ponte** Don A '73
Davis Wesley R '03
(740) 453-2566 **Deitrick** Robert L '90
Dick Trafford '83
(740) 452-2757 **Dickman** James L '65
(740) 454-8585 **Dye** Scott A '02
(740) 454-2591 **Eickelberger** Scott D '91
(740) 452-8485 **Erhard** Gerald A Jr. '79
(740) 452-8431 **Fitz** Todd B '96
(740) 452-9311 **Fox** Rose M '98
(740) 452-7555 **Fries** Miles D '78
(740) 452-7555 **Gerstner** Cole J '82
(740) 454-2591 **Geyer** Robert W '05
(740) 452-7555 **Gottlieb Johnston Beam & Dal Ponte,PLL**
(740) 454-8585 **Graham** Clay P '80
(740) 454-8585 **Graham** David A '83
(740) 454-8585 **Graham** James F '52
(740) 454-8585 **Graham McClelland & Ransbottom Co,LPA**
(740) 454-8585 **Graham** Robert P '79
(740) 452-9311 **Greenberger** Bruce L '74
(740) 454-1223 **Gullifer** Amy E '01
(740) 452-4192 **Haas** Susan J '85
(740) 455-7123 **Haddox** Dennis M '82
(740) 455-3350 **Hillis** Scott T '89
(740) 454-1223 **Itani** Stuart Y '02
(740) 452-5403 **Jones Funk & Payne**
(740) 452-7555 **Kaido** Mark E '91
(740) 455-7123 **Kalis** Maria N '01
Kalis Perry M II '99
(740) 454-2591 **Kincaid Taylor & Geyer**
(740) 452-7555 **Krischak** James R '77
(740) 455-7123 **LaAsmar** Ronald G '69
(740) 452-4574 **Levion** Leon L '52
(740) 454-1223 **Little** David A '67
(740) 452-8431 **Magaziner** Blair L '84
(740) 452-8431 **Magaziner McGlade & Fitz**
(740) 453-8900 **Marczewski** Mitchell C '01
(740) 455-7123 **Martin** Eric D '95
(740) 453-5544 **Massey** Jefferson H '75
(740) 454-8585 **McCann** Stephen R '76
(740) 454-8585 **McClelland** Jack J '73
(740) 452-8431 **McGlade** Roger D '89
(740) 454-2545 **McLendon** Jeremy M '02
(740) 454-8585 **Mellor** Adam K '99
(740) 454-8585 **Merry** Joseph W '80
(740) 454-2545 **Micheli Baldwin Northrup Co,LPA**
(740) 454-2545 **Micheli** Frank J '53
(740) 454-2545 **Micheli** Michael J '80
(740) 453-1317 **Mills** Thomas M '82
(740) 452-9960 **Moorehead** Douglas A '78
(740) 454-2545 **Mortimer** David E '02
(740) 454-2545 **Northrup** Michael A '79
(740) 455-3448 **Patterson** Ronald S '86
(740) 452-5403 **Pattison** Jeff A '98
(740) 452-5403 **Payne** Thomas '52
(740) 452-7555 **Phillips** Aaron B '00
(740) 452-7555 **Phillips** Philip S '75
(740) 452-7555 **Phillips** Wayne W II '72
(740) 588-6745 **Randles** Steven G '89
(740) 452-2045 **Rankin** D Scott '99
(740) 454-8585 **Ransbottom** James W '77
(740) 453-8737 **Ryan** Sherry L '74
(740) 455-3350 **Small** Susan E '96
(740) 454-8585 **Smith** Gary M '77
(740) 455-7123 **Smith** Robert L '83
(740) 455-7146 **Starcher** Gregory A '91
(740) 452-8484 **Stubbins** Brent A '78
(740) 452-8484 **Stubbins** James B '43
(740) 452-8484 **Stubbins** Mark W '83
(740) 452-8484 **Stubbins Watson & Erhard Co LPA**
(740) 455-7190 **Sugar** Susan N '92
(740) 454-2591 **Tarbert** David J '93
(740) 452-5403 **Tarbert** Molly L '93
(740) 454-2591 **Taylor** William J '73
(740) 454-2591 **Tiberio** Gerald J '04
(740) 455-7190 **Tompkins** Thomas Jay '85
(740) 452-8430 **Van Horn** Kevin R '85
(740) 455-9377 **Vinsel** Jay F '83
(740) 452-8484 **Watson** Mark A '83
(740) 452-7555 **Wietmarschen** Donald A '81
Wilson Amy J '04
(740) 450-1559 **Winnefeld** Sheila M A '03
(740) 453-9600 **Wolfe** James B '96
(740) 455-7142 **Wolfe** William Allen '71
(740) 452-8439 **Zellar** Crystal I '87

LOAN AMORTIZATION TABLE

TERM RATE %	5 YEARS	10 YEARS	15 YEARS	20 YEARS	25 YEARS	30 YEARS	35 YEARS
3.00	17.96869	9.65607	6.90582	5.54598	4.74211	4.21604	3.84850
3.25	18.08000	9.77190	7.02669	5.67196	4.87316	4.35206	3.98937
3.50	18.19174	9.88859	7.14883	5.79960	5.00624	4.49045	4.13291
3.75	18.30392	10.00612	7.27222	5.92888	5.14131	4.63116	4.27905
4.00	18.41652	10.12451	7.39688	6.05980	5.27837	4.77415	4.42775
4.25	18.52956	10.24375	7.52278	6.19234	5.41738	4.91940	4.57894
4.50	18.64302	10.36384	7.64993	6.32649	5.55832	5.06685	4.73257
4.75	18.75691	10.48477	7.77832	6.46224	5.70117	5.21647	4.88857
5.00	18.87123	10.60655	7.90794	6.59956	5.84590	5.36822	5.04688
5.25	18.98598	10.72917	8.03878	6.73844	5.99248	5.52204	5.20743
5.50	19.10116	10.85263	8.17083	6.87887	6.14087	5.67789	5.37016
5.75	19.21677	10.97692	8.30410	7.02084	6.29106	5.83573	5.53501
6.00	19.33280	11.10205	8.43857	7.16431	6.44301	5.99551	5.70190
6.25	19.44926	11.22801	8.57423	7.30928	6.59669	6.15717	5.87076
6.50	19.56615	11.35480	8.71107	7.45573	6.75207	6.32068	6.04154
6.75	19.68346	11.48241	8.84909	7.60364	6.90912	6.48598	6.21417
7.00	19.80120	11.61085	8.98828	7.75299	7.06779	6.65302	6.38856
7.25	19.91936	11.74010	9.12863	7.90376	7.22807	6.82176	6.56467
7.50	20.03795	11.87018	9.27012	8.05593	7.38991	6.99215	6.74243
7.75	20.15696	12.00106	9.41276	8.20949	7.55329	7.16412	6.92176
8.00	20.27639	12.13276	9.55652	8.36440	7.71816	7.33765	7.10261
8.25	20.39625	12.26526	9.70140	8.52066	7.88450	7.51267	7.28491
8.50	20.51653	12.39857	9.84740	8.67823	8.05227	7.68913	7.46861
8.75	20.63723	12.53268	9.99449	8.83711	8.22144	7.86700	7.65363
9.00	20.75836	12.66758	10.14267	8.99726	8.39196	8.04623	7.83993
9.25	20.87990	12.80327	10.29192	9.15867	8.56382	8.22675	8.02744
9.50	21.00186	12.93976	10.44225	9.32131	8.73697	8.40854	8.21612
9.75	21.12424	13.07702	10.59363	9.48517	8.91137	8.59154	8.40589
10.00	21.24704	13.21507	10.74605	9.65022	9.08701	8.77572	8.59672
10.25	21.37026	13.35390	10.89951	9.81643	9.26383	8.96101	8.78856
10.50	21.49390	13.49350	11.05399	9.98380	9.44182	9.14739	8.98134
10.75	21.61795	13.63387	11.20948	10.15229	9.62093	9.33481	9.17503
11.00	21.74242	13.77500	11.36597	10.32188	9.80113	9.52323	9.36958
11.25	21.86731	13.91689	11.52345	10.49256	9.98240	9.71261	9.56494
11.50	21.99261	14.05954	11.68190	10.66430	10.16469	9.90291	9.76107
11.75	22.11832	14.20295	11.84131	10.83707	10.34798	10.09410	9.95794
12.00	22.24445	14.34709	12.00168	11.01086	10.53224	10.28613	10.15550
12.25	22.37099	14.49199	12.16299	11.18565	10.71744	10.47896	10.35371
12.50	22.49794	14.63762	12.32522	11.36141	10.90354	10.67258	10.55254
12.75	22.62530	14.78398	12.48837	11.53812	11.09052	10.86693	10.75196
13.00	22.75307	14.93107	12.65242	11.71576	11.27835	11.06200	10.95193
13.25	22.88126	15.07889	12.81736	11.89431	11.46700	11.25774	11.15242
13.50	23.00985	15.22743	12.98319	12.07375	11.65645	11.45412	11.35341
13.75	23.13884	15.37668	13.14987	12.25405	11.84666	11.65113	11.55485
14.00	23.26825	15.52664	13.31741	12.43521	12.03761	11.84872	11.75673
14.25	23.39806	15.67731	13.48580	12.61719	12.22928	12.04687	11.95903
14.50	23.52828	15.82868	13.65501	12.79998	12.42163	12.24556	12.16171
14.75	23.65890	15.98074	13.82504	12.98355	12.61465	12.44476	12.36475
15.00	23.78993	16.13350	13.99587	13.16790	12.80831	12.64444	12.56813
15.25	23.92136	16.28693	14.16750	13.35299	13.00258	12.84459	12.77184
15.50	24.05319	16.44105	14.33990	13.53881	13.19745	13.04517	12.97585
15.75	24.18542	16.59585	14.51308	13.72534	13.39290	13.24617	13.18014
16.00	24.31806	16.75131	14.68701	13.91256	13.58889	13.44757	13.38469
16.25	24.45109	16.90744	14.86168	14.10046	13.78541	13.64935	13.58950
16.50	24.58452	17.06423	15.03709	14.28901	13.98245	13.85148	13.79454
16.75	24.71835	17.22167	15.21321	14.47820	14.17997	14.05396	13.99980
17.00	24.85258	17.37977	15.39004	14.66801	14.37797	14.25675	14.20526
17.25	24.98720	17.53850	15.56757	14.85842	14.57641	14.45986	14.41092
17.50	25.12221	17.69788	15.74578	15.04942	14.77530	14.66325	14.61675
17.75	25.25762	17.85788	15.92467	15.24099	14.97460	14.86692	14.82276
18.00	25.39343	18.01852	16.10421	15.43312	15.17430	15.07085	15.02892
18.25	25.52962	18.17978	16.28440	15.62578	15.37439	15.27503	15.23523
18.50	25.66621	18.34165	16.46523	15.81897	15.57484	15.47945	15.44168
18.75	25.80319	18.50414	16.64669	16.01266	15.77565	15.68408	15.64825
19.00	25.94055	18.66724	16.82876	16.20685	15.97680	15.88892	15.85495
19.25	26.07830	18.83093	17.01143	16.40152	16.17827	16.09397	16.06176
19.50	26.21645	18.99522	17.19470	16.59665	16.38006	16.29920	16.26867
19.75	26.35497	19.16010	17.37855	16.79223	16.58215	16.50461	16.47568
20.00	26.49388	19.32557	17.56297	16.98825	16.78452	16.71019	16.68278

Use this table to find the monthly payment for any loan amount for the term of years and rates shown above. The dollar amount represents the monthly payment for a $1,000 loan. To compute for a different amount, divide that amount by 1,000 and multiply by the monthly payment.

Example:
The monthly payment for a loan of $172,500 for 30 years at 7% would be 172.5 x 6.65302 = $1,147.65

ATTORNEYS GROUPED BY AREAS OF PRACTICE

The following attorneys have listed themselves under various fields of law. These listings do not imply special abilities or competency, merely that they are available to consult or associate with other attorneys under the particular field of law. Attorneys who limit their practice to a particular field of law, or who are admitted in other jurisdictions, or who are certified, may have these facts indicated in italics.

BANKRUPTCY LAW

(419) 241-4050
FAX 241-8726
PATRICIA A. KOVACS, ESQ.
500 Madison Avenue, Suite 525, Toledo, OH 43604

(440) 323-7433
FAX 322-6474
MICHAEL E. SZEKELY, ESQ.
230 Third Street, Suite 200, Elyria, OH 44035

DOMESTIC RELATIONS LAW

(937) 393-3487
FAX 393-5388
HAPNER & HAPNER
127 North High Street, Hillsboro, OH 45133

ESTATE PLANNING & PROBATE LAW

(440) 323-7433
FAX 322-6474
MICHAEL E. SZEKELY, ESQ.
230 Third Street, Suite 200, Elyria, OH 44035

LEGAL MALPRACTICE

(330) 373-1000
FAX 394-5291
LAW OFFICE OF CHARLES L. RICHARDS
159 East Market Street, Suite 300, Warren, OH 44481
Defense only, including disciplinary actions.

LEMON LAW

(937) 432-9500
FAX 432-9503
BURDGE LAW OFFICE CO., LPA
2299 Miamisburg-Centerville Road, Dayton, OH 45459

PATENT, COPYRIGHT & TRADEMARK LAW

(513) 241-2324
FAX 241-6234
WOOD, HERRON & EVANS, L.L.P.
2700 Carew Tower, 441 Vine Street, Cincinnati, OH 45202
Website: www.whepatent.com

REAL ESTATE LAW

(937) 393-3487
FAX 393-5388
HAPNER & HAPNER
127 North High Street, Hillsboro, OH 45133

ATTORNEYS ACCORDING TO AREAS OF PRACTICE

the legal pages®
Category Index

PROFESSIONAL PRODUCTS AND SERVICES

the legal pages® reaches over 10,000 lawyers, judges, government officials and other members of the legal community. If you want to do business with these people, your business should be represented in *the legal pages*®. Call us to learn how. (800) 444-4041, ext. 4.

ABATEMENT SERVICES
(See ENVIRONMENTAL—CONSULTANTS)

ABSTRACTERS
(See Also TITLE INSURANCE COMPANIES & AGENTS; and SEARCH SERVICES)

ABSTRACT TITLE CO
318 DORNEY PLZ #310, FINDLAY 45840 . . . . (419) 420-1544
ACCUSEARCH
815 SUPERIOR AVE E #1218, CLEVELAND 44114 . . . . . (216) 771-7667
ALPHA LAND TITLE AGENCY INC
PO BOX 35003, CANTON 44735 . . . . (330) 490-2910
AREA TITLE AGENCY INC
709 MADISON AVE #101, TOLEDO 43624 . . . . (419) 242-5485
ASSURED TITLE AGENCY
102 S WASHINGTON ST, TIFFIN 44883 . . . . (419) 447-7126
BEACON TITLE AGENCY INC
4715 FULTON DR NW, CANTON 44718 . . . . (330) 492-3090
BENNETT TITLE AGENCY INC
126 N 9TH ST, CAMBRIDGE 43725 . . . . (740) 432-2561
BROOKLYN TITLE AGENCY INC
4355 RIDGE RD, CLEVELAND 44144 . . . . (216) 739-9988
C M PENTELLO & ASSOC
373 S HIGH ST, COLUMBUS 43215 . . . . (614) 621-0531
CHICAGO TITLE AGENCY OF S OHIO
PO BOX 1384, PORTSMOUTH 45662 . . . . (740) 353-1157
COMMONWEALTH LAND TITLE CO
PO BOX 219, YOUNGSTOWN 44501 . . . . (330) 746-3291
COSHOCTON COUNTY LAND TITLE
305 MAIN ST #302, COSHOCTON 43812 . . . . (740) 622-5653
GENERAL TITLE AGENCY INC
629 EUCLID AVE #1020, CLEVELAND 44114 . . . . (216) 696-3252
GEORGE D REZENDES EXAMINING
PO BOX 21, NEW PHILADELPHIA 44663 . . . . (330) 364-8898
GOLDEN KEY TITLE AGENCY INC
239 S MAIN ST, FINDLAY 45840 . . . . (419) 420-3055
HANCOCK TITLE AGENCY INC
101 W SANDUSKY ST, FINDLAY 45840 . . . . (419) 422-5400
HOME TITLE AGENCY INC
PO BOX 963, FINDLAY 45839 . . . . (419) 424-8889
HOMESTEAD LAND TITLES
5080 CLARK STATION RD, GREENVILLE 45331 . . . . . . (937) 547-6085
INDEPENDENT ABSTRACT INC
PO BOX 114, BATAVIA 45103 . . . . (513) 831-5002
ITS TITLE EXAMINING
220 MARKET AVE S #608, CANTON 44702 . . . . (330) 456-4668
KANE & KANE
PO BOX 167, RAVENNA 44266 . . . . (330) 296-3868
LAWYERS TITLE AGENCY
PO BOX 1505, PORTSMOUTH 45662 . . . . (740) 354-4200
LAWYERS TITLE INSURANCE CORP
201 MAIN ST, CHARDON 44024 . . . . (440) 285-2129
LOUISVILLE TITLE AGENCY
626 MADISON AVE #100, TOLEDO 43604 . . . . (419) 248-4611
MECKSTROTH ABSTRACT SERV INC
7539 BERMUDA TER, W CHESTER 45069 . . . . (513) 777-9200
METROPOLITAN TITLE AGENCY
300 W MONUMENT AVE #100, DAYTON 45402 . . . . . . (937) 228-2465
MID AMERICA LAND TITLE AGENCY
7925 PARAGON RD, DAYTON 45459 . . . . (937) 434-7366
155 TRI COUNTY PKWY #280, CINCINNATI 45246 . . . . . . (513) 771-0990
MID-AMERICAN TITLE AGENCY
100 E MAIN CROSS ST, FINDLAY 45840 . . . . (419) 423-8500
NORTHWEST TITLE AGENCY-OH & MI
328 N ERIE ST, TOLEDO 43624 . . . . (419) 241-8195
PAYSOURCE PLUS INC
1640 FRANKLIN AVE #7, KENT 44240 . . . . (330) 673-4497
PORT CLINTON LAND TITLE INC
208 MADISON ST, PORT CLINTON 43452 . . . . (419) 734-4068
PORT LAWRENCE TITLE & TRUST CO
616 MADISON AVE, TOLEDO 43604 . . . . (419) 244-4605
PRESTIGE TITLE
914 MAIN ST #500, CINCINNATI 45202 . . . . (513) 421-6555
ROSEBERRY ROBIN L
451 W 3RD ST, DAYTON 45422 . . . . (937) 226-7487
SAMPSON JUDY A
451 W 3RD ST, DAYTON 45422 . . . . (937) 228-7215
SURETY TITLE AGENCY INC
526 SUPERIOR AVE E #1010, CLEVELAND 44114 . . . . . . (216) 589-8399
THOMAS JULIA
209 S MAIN ST #505, AKRON 44308 . . . . (330) 762-6388

TITLE CO OF SO OH
9050 OHIO RIVER RD, WHEELERSBURG 45694 . . . . . . (740) 574-2521
TITLE POINTE AGENCY INC
7700 PARAGON RD, DAYTON 45459 . . . . (937) 223-2263
TLT TITLES
451 W 3RD ST, DAYTON 45422 . . . . (937) 586-0895
TOWNE & COUNTRY LAND TITLE INC
1113 E MAIN ST, GREENVILLE 45331 . . . . (937) 547-0412
TRIAD TITLE AGENCY
PO BOX 251, BELLBROOK 45305 . . . . (937) 848-6450
TRUMBULL COUNTY ABSTRACT CO
174 N PARK AVE #10, WARREN 44481 . . . . (330) 399-1891
TUCKER ABSTRACT & TITLE CO
26 E MAIN ST, NORWALK 44857 . . . . (419) 668-2081
WILLIAM A ZECK INC
229 3RD ST NW #200, CANTON 44702 . . . . (330) 452-2567
YOUNGSTOWN TITLE ABSTRACT INC
5069 LAMME RD, DAYTON 45439 . . . . (330) 758-2206
ZANE TITLE
59 N 4TH ST, ZANESVILLE 43701 . . . . (740) 452-8484

ACCIDENT EXPERTS
(See EXPERTS—ACCIDENTS)

ACCIDENT RECONSTRUCTION SERVICES
(See Also EXPERTS—RECREATION & SAFETY; EXPERTS—FORENSICS; and EXPERTS—ACCIDENTS)

CLEVELAND BRIDGE BUILDERS
1331 EUCLID AVE #3, CLEVELAND 44115 . . . . (216) 685-0874
COLLISION RESEARCH & GRAPHICS
25 WALNUT ST #7, LEXINGTON 44904 . . . . (419) 884-2005
FRED LICKERT INC
16 DUNNINGTON CT, SPRINGBORO 45066 . . . . (937) 748-1102
INTROTECH INC
1006 VIVIAN DR W, GRAFTON 44044 . . . . (440) 926-2627
LEADING TECH FORENSIC
WWW.LTFEXPERTS.COM . . . . (419) 452-6992
MEREDITH ENTERPRISES
16040 WAKE ROBIN DR, NEWBURY 44065 . . . . (440) 564-7173
MIDWEST TRAFFIC ACCIDENT CO
9790 PLEASANT PLAIN RD, BROOKVILLE 45309 . . . . (937) 833-5399
PATRIDGE PROFESSIONAL SRVYRS
9464 DUBLIN RD, POWELL 43065 . . . . (614) 799-0031
RESTAURANT SPECIALTIES
1881 POLARIS PKWY, COLUMBUS 43240 . . . . (614) 848-3591
STANDARDS TESTING LABS INC
1845 HARSH AVE SE, MASSILLON 44648 . . . . (330) 833-8548
STAR INVESTIGATIONS
1545 EDGE ST, PIQUA 45356 . . . . (937) 778-8529
VALLEY TECHNICAL SVC
14143 STATION RD, COLUMBIA STA 44028 . . . . (440) 236-3702

ACCOUNTANTS
(See EXPERTS—ACCOUNTING; and ACCOUNTANTS—CERTIFIED PUBLIC)

ACCOUNTANTS-CERTIFIED PUBLIC
(See Also EXPERTS—ACCOUNTING)

MARK P MURPHY & ASSOCS
1051 OLD HENDERSON RD #A, COLUMBUS 43220 . . . . . . (614) 888-1512
A S FRICANO & CO
123 W 5TH ST, E LIVERPOOL 43920 . . . . (330) 385-2160
ABC ACCOUNTING SVC
3681 GREEN RD #203, CLEVELAND 44122 . . . . (216) 292-9800
ABC SOLUTIONS
3964 BROWN PARK DR #A, HILLIARD 43026 . . . . (614) 850-9440
ABRAR CPA INC
15736 LORAIN AVE, CLEVELAND 44111 . . . . (216) 941-3144
ASCHLIMAN & CO
201 DITTO ST, ARCHBOLD 43502 . . . . (419) 446-2250
ASHWORTH BARRETT & CO CPA
6862 ENGLE RD #202, CLEVELAND 44130 . . . . (440) 260-2000
ASSOCIATED BUSINESS SVC
4213 HARWOOD RD, CLEVELAND 44121 . . . . (216) 382-4209
AUER CHARLES J
191 W NATIONWIDE BLVD, COLUMBUS 43215 . . . . . . (614) 249-2320
AUGUR HALE & CO
579 HIGH ST, WORTHINGTON 43085 . . . . (614) 436-8193

ACCOUNTANTS-CERTIFIED PUBLIC (Cont'd)

AUSTIN ASSOCIATES INC
12560 CHILLICOTHE RD #1, CHESTERLAND 44026 . . . . (440) 729-8299
BUELOW FRED C CPA
2172 BROWN RD, CLEVELAND 44107 . . . . (216) 521-6666
BUILDERS SQUARE CONSTRUCTION
27801 EUCLID AVE #203, CLEVELAND 44132 . . . . (216) 261-0624
BURDEN & CO
623 PARK MEADOW RD #M, WESTERVILLE 43081 . . . . (614) 818-9910
BURNS OHARE & BELLA INC
565 N BROAD ST, CANFIELD 44406 . . . . (330) 533-9909
BURROUGHS ASSOC INC
PO BOX 2376, COLUMBUS 43216 . . . . (614) 833-2475
BUSINESS MANAGEMENT SVCS
2855 MADISON RD, CINCINNATI 45209 . . . . (513) 531-1166
C B BUSINESS CONSLNTS & ASSOC
1416 W PLEASANT VALLEY RD, CLEVELAND 44134 . . . . (440) 866-1040
CHARLILLO CLAUDE M CPA
10280 MATAIRE LN, STRONGSVILLE 44136 . . . . (440) 238-2044
CULKAR STACHOWICZ & CO
17601 W 130TH ST #3, CLEVELAND 44133 . . . . (440) 230-5260
CUMMINS KRASIK & HOHL CO
2 MIRANOVA PL, COLUMBUS 43215 . . . . (614) 224-7800
CUMMINS REUSSER & ASSOC INC
515 VALLEYVIEW DR, KENT 44240 . . . . (330) 923-9400
CURTIN JAMES S CPA
1629 W 1ST AVE, COLUMBUS 43212 . . . . (614) 486-1421
CUTTER LEWIS R CPA
815 WARREN RD #3, NILES 44446 . . . . (330) 544-2214
CUYAHOGA ACCOUNTING & MGMT SVC
15707 DETROIT AVE #213, LAKEWOOD 44107 . . . . (216) 221-1220

DAVID R SNYDER CPA INC
4097 YOUNGSTOWN RD SE, WARREN 44484. . . **(330) 369-3961**

DUANE C ARCARO INC
5223 N RIDGE RD W #2, ASHTABULA 44004 . . . . (440) 969-1220
DUCATO & KOESEL
3681 GREEN RD #300, CLEVELAND 44122 . . . . (216) 464-2100
DUDLEY & ASSOC
11823 BROWNING AVE, CLEVELAND 44120 . . . . (216) 707-0441
DUFFY & CO
15400 PEARL RD #255, CLEVELAND 44136 . . . . (440) 846-0500
DUNCAN & ASSOC BUSINESS & TAX
33 MONUMENT SQ, URBANA 43078 . . . . (937) 653-4144
DUNN JAMES
6703 THOREAU DR, CLEVELAND 44129 . . . . (440) 842-4586
DUNPHY FINANCIAL SVCS INC
100 TECHNE CENTER DR #200, MILFORD 45150 . . . . (513) 528-2721
DUVALL & ASSOCS INC CPA
301 W 1ST ST #200, DAYTON 45402 . . . . (937) 228-4272
EBERWEIN RUSSELL R CPA
67 E WILSON BRIDGE RD, WORTHINGTON 43085 . . . . (614) 847-0073
GUDAITIS ACCOUNTING & TAX SVC
278 E 208TH ST, CLEVELAND 44123 . . . . (216) 486-1040
GUNDIN FINANCIAL SVC CO
2101 S HAMILTON RD #201, COLUMBUS 43232 . . . . (614) 863-2667
GUZZO ANTHONY T
1249 HOLGATE AVE, MAUMEE 43537 . . . . (419) 893-2348
HUDAK & VRANA
1422 EUCLID AVE # 662, CLEVELAND 44115 . . . . (216) 621-3440
HUGH G STIFFLER & ASSOC
1172 W GALBRAITH RD #112, CINCINNATI 45231 . . . . (513) 729-2234
HUNTER JENNIFER S CPA
25 W 5TH ST #A-B, LONDON 43140 . . . . (740) 852-6960
IBEW
626 N 4TH ST # 106, STEUBENVILLE 43952 . . . . (740) 282-1251
ICKERT & CO L L C
280 N HIGH ST #800, COLUMBUS 43215 . . . . (614) 464-3343
KIRSCH LUDWIN CPA GROUP LLC
925 DEIS DR #A, FAIRFIELD 45014 . . . . (513) 858-6040
KUBINEC BURG & CO
1370 ONTARIO ST #400, CLEVELAND 44113 . . . . (216) 696-5650
KUHN ACCOUNTING & FINANCIAL
6460 W BROAD ST, GALLOWAY 43119 . . . . (614) 879-6243
KUHNS & ASSOC
9700 ROCKSIDE RD #350, CLEVELAND 44125 . . . . (216) 573-7395
KUPER HILTON & KAMINSKI
23790 LORAIN RD, N OLMSTED 44070 . . . . (440) 779-0303
LBK HEALTH CARE INC
7445 LIBERTY WOODS LN, DAYTON 45459 . . . . (937) 296-1550

LISHAWA ACCOUNTING & TAX LTD
335 S BLANCHARD ST, FINDLAY 45840 . . . . **(419) 422-2851**

LUBLIN SUSSMAN ROSENBERG
3166 N REPUBLIC BLVD, TOLEDO 43615 . . . . (419) 841-2848
LUKANC JOHN CPA
20325 CENTER RIDGE RD #513, CLEVELAND 44116 . . . . . (440) 356-9095
MULLIGAN & ASSOC
20545 CENTER RIDGE RD #409, ROCKY RIVER 44116 . . . . (440) 356-6095
MULLIGAN TOPY & CO
196 W JOHNSTOWN RD, GAHANNA 43230 . . . . (614) 471-1040
MUNSHOWER WILLIAM J CPA
6060 ROYALTON RD, CLEVELAND 44133 . . . . (440) 237-8284
MURRAY MIKA INC
509 S OTTERBEIN AVE #5, WESTERVILLE 43081 . . . . (614) 794-1818

MURRAY WELLS WENDELN ROBINSON
PO BOX 613, PIQUA 45356 . . . . (937) 773-6373
MUSULIN WILLIAM B
1001 LAKESIDE AVE E, CLEVELAND 44114 . . . . (216) 522-1017
OBRIEN KIERAN D CPA
145 CANTON RD, WINTERSVILLE 43953 . . . . (740) 264-4753
OSSIO & MASON
25 BENNETT BLVD, WINTERSVILLE 43953 . . . . (740) 264-4185
PHILLIPS ORGANIZATION THE
3924 CLEVELAND AVE NW, CANTON 44709 . . . . (330) 493-3928
PLAVECSKI & ASSOCIATES
3 SUMMIT PARK DR #610, INDEPENDENCE 44131 . . . . . . (216) 524-3814
PUSATERI NICHOLS & CO
115 COMMERCE PARK DR, WESTERVILLE 43082 . . . . (614) 891-5423
R S ACCOUNTING SVC
393 W FRONT ST, LOGAN 43138 . . . . (740) 385-0019
RUSCHEL BRIAN G CPA
925 EUCLID AVE #660, CLEVELAND 44115 . . . . (216) 621-3370
SCHMITZ CORRIGAN KRAUSE & CO
19111 DETROIT RD #201, ROCKY RIVER 44116 . . . . (440) 356-9009
SCHNEIDER DOWNS & CO INC
WWW.SCHNEIDERDOWNS.COM . . . . (614) 621-4060
SS&G FINANCIAL SERVICES
WWW.SSANDG.COM . . . . **(800) 869-1834**
SUCCESS BUILDERS
3725 WENZLER DR, KETTERING 45429 . . . . (937) 297-0900
SULLENS ROBERT T CPA
1414 S GREEN RD #205, CLEVELAND 44121 . . . . (216) 381-6607
SUSNIK & CORSELLO CPAS
5005 ROCKSIDE RD, CLEVELAND 44131 . . . . (216) 573-3777
SUSSMAN & ASSOC INC
125 W BOYER ST, WADSWORTH 44281 . . . . (330) 334-3641
SUSTIN BARTELL & WALDMAN LTD
1801 E 9TH ST #920, CLEVELAND 44114 . . . . (216) 621-1180
TUCKER STEIN KISSLING BUELTEL INC
608 4TH ST, TOLEDO 43605 . . . . (419) 693-2693
ZUCCARO & ASSOC
16600 W SPRAGUE RD, CLEVELAND 44130 . . . . (440) 243-8585
ZUZAK JEAN CPA
16029 MESSENGER RD, BURTON 44021 . . . . (440) 543-4618

ACCOUNTING EXPERTS
(See EXPERTS—ACCOUNTING)

ADDICTION TREATMENT
(See ALCOHOL & DRUG TREATMENT CENTERS)

ADJUSTERS

A-WARD ADJUSTING SVC
1353 RD 216, BELLEFONTAINE 43311 . . . . (937) 592-9273
ADJUSTING SERVICES UNLIMITED
5755 GRANGER RD #830, CLEVELAND 44131 . . . . (216) 459-8600
PO BOX 230, WATERVILLE 43566 . . . . (419) 535-1691
ALEX N SILL ADJUSTMENT CO
6000 LOMBARDO CTR #600, CLEVELAND 44131 . . . . (216) 524-9999
ALPS CLAIMS SVC
10653 CHESTER RD, CINCINNATI 45215 . . . . (513) 671-6300
APAC1 INC
6176 LOOKOVER CT, TOLEDO 43612 . . . . (419) 478-7757
ASSOCIATED PUBLIC ADJUSTERS
2000 AUBURN DR, CLEVELAND 44122 . . . . (216) 292-8292
ASU
129 COSMOS LN SW, PATASKALA 43062 . . . . (614) 888-5916
BLAHA FINANCIAL SVC
18500 LAKE RD #220, CLEVELAND 44116 . . . . (440) 356-8889
BREWER MCGRAW & ASSOC
1001 EASTWIND DR #203, WESTERVILLE 43081 . . . . (614) 890-5632
CINCINNATI INSURANCE CO
PO BOX 2576, ZANESVILLE 43702 . . . . (740) 453-4924
CINCINNATI INSURANCE CO
PO BOX 122, CLAY CENTER 43408 . . . . (419) 855-4345
CINTI CREDIT COUNSELING SVC
4424 AICHOLTZ RD #H, CINCINNATI 45245 . . . . (513) 621-1737
CLEVELAND ADJUSTING & MARINE
15515 DETROIT AVE, CLEVELAND 44107 . . . . (216) 221-1187
CRAWFORD & CO
7271 ENGLE RD, CLEVELAND 44130 . . . . (440) 891-9156
2780 S ARLINGTON RD, AKRON 44312 . . . . (330) 644-9926
4464 CARVER WOODS DR #100, CINCINNATI 45242 . . . . . (513) 984-9950
6401 HAMILTON DR, HOLLAND 43528 . . . . (419) 866-6611
400 W OLD WILSON BRIDGE RD #150, WORTHINGTON 43085 (614) 846-0161
CUNNINGHAM LINDSEY INC
PO BOX 292545, COLUMBUS 43229 . . . . (614) 848-4444
20525 CENTER RIDGE RD #614, CLEVELAND 44116 . . . . . (440) 331-4040
644 LINN ST #1220, CINCINNATI 45203 . . . . (513) 621-2266
CUSTARD INSURANCE ADJUSTERS
6161 BUSCH BLVD #312, COLUMBUS 43229 . . . . (614) 431-1328
5151 MONROE ST #205, TOLEDO 43623 . . . . (419) 841-1126
5339 RIDGE RD #202, CLEVELAND 44129 . . . . (440) 888-6007
110 BOGGS LN #155, CINCINNATI 45246 . . . . (513) 326-5900
1149 LYONS RD #D, DAYTON 45458 . . . . (937) 291-3710
DEIST & ASSOC
PO BOX 53487, CINCINNATI 45253 . . . . (513) 522-8080

ADJUSTERS (Cont'd)

FARMERS INSURANCE
969 CRYSTAL CAY CT, COLUMBUS 43230 . . . . (614) 418-5055
FRONTIER ADJUSTERS
21 JUANITA CT, SPRINGBORO 45066 . . . . (937) 438-9411
3956 BROWN PARK DR #A, HILLIARD 43026 . . . . (614) 486-0073
977 FREDERICK BLVD, AKRON 44320 . . . . (330) 867-3353
PO BOX 140534, TOLEDO 43614 . . . . (419) 893-8939
17200 W TEN MILE #205, S FIELD, MI 48075 . . . . (419) 255-4995
G K WYMER INC
14155 US HWY 24, GRAND RAPIDS 43522 . . . . (419) 832-3100
GAB
PO BOX 589, GREEN 44232 . . . . (330) 896-7220
5533 SOUTHWYCK BLVD #201, TOLEDO 43614 . . . . (419) 866-4405
612 S MAIN ST #205, FINDLAY 45840 . . . . (419) 423-0734
8595 OHIO RIVER RD, WHEELERSBURG 45694 . . . . (740) 574-5700
2935 KENNY RD #225, COLUMBUS 43221 . . . . (614) 451-8012
6155 ROCKSIDE RD #110, CLEVELAND 44131 . . . . (216) 696-3700
HAND GROUP INC
104 N 5TH ST, MARTINS FERRY 43935 . . . . (740) 635-1127
HARTFORD
PO BOX 3008, CENTER LINE, MI 48015 . . . . (330) 346-0537
7100 E PLEASANT VALLEY RD #200, INDEPENDENCE 44131 . (216) 447-1000
HILLIARD BUILDING
1419 W 9TH ST #3, CLEVELAND 44113 . . . . (216) 241-3993
HOLLOWAY & ASSOC INC
1550 OLD HENDERSON RD, COLUMBUS 43220 . . . . (614) 442-1504
HURSEYS ADJUSTING SVCS
240 E MAIN ST, GRATIOT 43740 . . . . (740) 787-1420
INTERSTATE CASUALTY CLAIMS SVC
1425 E DUBLIN GRANVLL RD #104, COLUMBUS 43229 . . . . . . (614) 436-2991
ITEN INSURANCE SVC
13716 OTUSSO DR, PERRYSBURG 43551 . . . . (419) 874-4333
ITS INC
54 WINTHROP RD, COLUMBUS 43214 . . . . (614) 262-9440
J H MOORHEAD & ASSOC INC
1414 S GREEN RD #112, CLEVELAND 44121 . . . . (216) 382-0277
JAMES FLAUTO ADJUSTER SVC
7087 WEST BLVD #8, YOUNGSTOWN 44512 . . . . (330) 726-0106
L CHARLES AUCK & ASSOC
3645 WARRENSVILLE CENTER RD #129, CLEVELAND 44122 . (216) 751-7720
LARRY ENGLAND & ASSOC INC
2541 HARRISBURG PIKE, GROVE CITY 43123 . . . . (614) 871-4400
LELUX CO
3230 N HIGH ST, COLUMBUS 43202 . . . . (614) 267-6992
NATIONWIDE INSURANCE CO
8300 TYLER BLVD #200, MENTOR 44060 . . . . (440) 205-8955

NORTH AMERICA CLAIMS SVC CO
4608 ST CLAIR AVE, CLEVELAND 44103 . . . . (216) 621-5040
PROPERTY DAMAGE APPRAISERS
4292 OLD SCIOTO TRL, PORTSMOUTH 45662 . . . . (740) 353-0100
PO BOX 122, CALDWELL 43724 . . . . (740) 732-2677
R S LANDEN ADJ CO
4920 REED RD #E, COLUMBUS 43220 . . . . (614) 459-3400
RIDAR ADJUSTING CO
210 E KIRACOFE AVE, ELIDA 45807 . . . . (419) 339-0156
RITTEL HILL & ZIMMERMAN INS
4920 REED RD #E, COLUMBUS 43220 . . . . (614) 457-7765
SKIPCO FINANCIAL ADJUSTERS
332 MORTON AVE, DAYTON 45410 . . . . (937) 222-7901
SMOCK LUTZ & ASSOC LTD
3820 MICHAEL LN, ZANESVILLE 43701 . . . . (740) 453-5379
STATE AUTO INSURANCE CO
PO BOX 756, ST CLAIRSVILLE 43950 . . . . (740) 699-1245
STERLING EXPRESS
77 N DUTOIT ST, DAYTON 45402 . . . . (937) 461-4008
T F GEBHARDT ASSOC
254 6TH ST, ELYRIA 44035 . . . . (440) 323-2200
TOLEDO CLAIM SVC
4230 SHADE TREE DR, TOLEDO 43615 . . . . (419) 385-3418
TURNER CLAIMS SVC DBA HOLLOWAY & ASSOC
1675 E MAIN ST #248, KENT 44240 . . . . (330) 673-2726
VERICLAIM INC
25651 DETROIT RD #305, CLEVELAND 44145 . . . . (440) 871-3847
WARD NORTH AMERICA
650 SALISBURY RD, COLUMBUS 43204 . . . . (614) 274-8916
WARNER ADJUSTMENT CO
5461 SOUTHWYCK BLVD, TOLEDO 43614 . . . . (419) 865-1332
WESTERN RESERVE GROUP
PO BOX 18334, CINCINNATI 45218 . . . . (513) 742-2142
WESTFALL ADJUSTMENTS
6736 HATHAWAY RD, CLEVELAND 44125 . . . . (216) 524-4202
YORK CLAIMS SVC
16560 COMMERCE CT, CLEVELAND 44130 . . . . (440) 243-8409

ADR SERVICES

BEECH ACRES MEDIATION CENTER
6881 BEECHMONT AVE, CINCINNATI 45230 . . . . (513) 231-6630
CENTER FOR RESOLUTION OF DISPUTES INC
8 W NINTH ST, CINCINNATI 45202 . . . . (513) 721-4466
JUDICIAL ALTERNATIVES OF OHIO INC
See Our Display Ad Under This Heading
7419 JACKSON PIKE, LOCKBOURNE 43137 . . . . **(888) 629-3793**

ADVERTISING AGENCIES
(See MARKETING FIRMS & CONSULTANTS)

ALCOHOL & DRUG TREATMENT CENTERS
OHIO LAWYERS ASSISTANCE PROGRAM INC
  37 W BROAD ST, COLUMBUS 43215. . . . . (800) 348-4343
RECOVERY RESOURCES
  3950 CHESTER AVE, CLEVELAND 44114 . . . . (216) 431-4131
SOUTHEAST INC
  1455 S 4TH ST, COLUMBUS 43207 . . . . (614) 444-0800
SUBSTANCE ABUSE SVC
  1832 ADAMS ST, TOLEDO 43624 . . . . (419) 243-7274
UNIVERSITY HOSPITALS HEALTH SYSTEM
  WWW.LAURELWOODHOSPITAL.COM . . . . (440) 953-3000

APPELLATE PRINTERS
(See PRINTERS—LEGAL & FINANCIAL)

APPRAISAL SERVICES
(See Also ESTATE LIQUIDATORS; and VALUATION SERVICES)

A E ASEBROOK JR APPRAISER
  201 E WASHINGTON ST, SPRINGFIELD 45502 . . . . (937) 322-4927
ANTIQUES APPRAISER THE
  2811 28TH CT, JUPITER, FL 33477. . . . . (800) 486-0134
ANTIQUES AT OCONNORS
  2700 COLCHESTER RD, STRONGSVILLE 44136 . . . . (216) 238-3632
CENTURY ANTIQUES & APPRAISALS INC
  3255 GLENCARIN RD, SHAKER HTS 44122 . . . . (216) 991-2356
CHURCH ON THE LANE ANTIQUES
  2170 W LANE AVE, COLUMBUS 43221 . . . . (614) 488-3606
DESIGNERS LOFT
  555 COMPTON RD, CINCINNATI 45231 . . . . (513) 521-5434
ENTERPRISE DEVELOPMENT RESOURCES INC
  3659 GREEN RD #100, CLEVELAND 44122 . . . . (216) 765-0845
IMAGES GALLERY
  4343 W BANCROFT ST #4F, TOLEDO 43615 . . . . (419) 537-1400
JUNE GREENWALD ANTIQUES
  3096 MAYFIELD RD, CLEVELAND HTS 44188. . . . . (216) 932-5535
MAHONING AUTO
  11110 MAHONING AVE BX 244, N JACKSON 44451 . . . . (330) 538-3246
MCILWAIN LIONEL R
  PO BOX 8723, TOLEDO 43623 . . . . (419) 843-1759
MEDICAL EQUIPMENT APPRAISAL SPECIALISTS
  3891-2 LANDER RD, CLEVELAND 44022 . . . . (216) 464-0999
RUDIG CHARLES
  6420 MIAMI RD, CINCINNATI 45243 . . . . (513) 561-8093
WAYNE SIDDENS INC
  5270 W ALEXIS RD, SYLVANIA 43560 . . . . (419) 882-1557

APPRAISAL SERVICES-COINS
LINDHEIM LEON T
  23511 CHAGRIN BLVD #501, BEACHWOOD 44122 . . . . (216) 464-3517

APPRAISAL SERVICES-JEWELRY
(See APPRAISAL SERVICES)

APPRAISAL SERVICES-PERSONAL PROPERTY
BROWN AUCTION SVC
  5316 GENNY DR, MEDINA 44256 . . . . (330) 725-2395
COPLEY ANTIQUE MALL
  1451 S CLEVELAND MASSILLON RD, COPLEY 44321 . . . . . (330) 665-5581
CORCORAN FINE ARTS LIMITED
  WWW.CORCORANFINEARTS.COM . . . . (216) 767-0770
GARTHS AUCTIONS INC
  2690 STRAFFORD RD, DELAWARE 43015. . . . . . **(740) 363-2158**
GENE SIMPKINS & SON ALL AMERICAN AUCTIONS
  2633 SHERIDAN DR, CINCINNATI 45212 . . . . (513) 731-1792
LAST MOVING PICTURE CO THE
  10535 CHILLICOTHE RD, KIRTLAND 44094 . . . . (440) 256-3660
OLD WEST END COLLECTORS CORNER
  2502 COLLINGWOOD BLVD, TOLEDO 43610 . . . . (419) 244-0004
WIESCHAUS & COMPANY
  PO BOX 9660, CANTON 44711 . . . . (330) 456-6600

APPRAISAL SERVICES-REAL ESTATE
(See Also REAL ESTATE CONSULTANTS)

A BETTER APPRAISAL INC
  7145 FOX LEDGES LN, CHAGRIN FALLS 44022 . . . . (440) 918-7990
A THOMAS ASSOC APPRAISAL
  427 S BROAD ST, CANFIELD 44406 . . . . (330) 533-2428
ACCURATE APPRAISAL SERVICES INC
  114 SEYFFER DR, LOVELAND 45140 . . . . (513) 697-6666

ASHLEY JAMES APPRAISALS REAL ESTATE
  323 GREENHILL RD, MARIETTA 45750 . . . . (740) 374-6209
ASSURED APPRAISALS
  3645 WARRENSVILLE RD #311, SHAKER HTS 44122 . . . . . . (216) 561-7135
AUSTIN APPRAISALS
  1988 E STATE ROUTE 73, WAYNESVILLE 45068 . . . . (937) 436-1765
BARNHORN APPRAISAL SVCS
  31 E GALBRAITH RD, CINCINNATI 45216 . . . . (888) 948-0948
BECKER & COLE INC
  69 HIGH HAVE DR, TORONTO 43964 . . . . (740) 264-7701
BERMAN SANFORD W
  401 MARKET ST #527, STEUBENVILLE 43952 . . . . (740) 282-9736
BETHEL AGENCY
  209 CUNNINGHAM LN, WINTERSVILLE 43953 . . . . (740) 264-5581
C E STUMP & ASSOC INC
  543 STEPHENS RD, AKRON 44312 . . . . (330) 733-8260
CAROL STRAUME - HEARTH REALTY INC
  1368 LUDLOW RD, XENIA 45385 . . . . (937) 427-8837
CERTIFIED REAL ESTATE APPRAISL
  PO BOX 55, ENGLEWOOD 45322. . . . . (937) 836-7546
COE LELAND M MAI CCIM CRE
  120 LINWOOD ST, DAYTON 45405 . . . . **(937) 226-1504**
CONTINENTAL APPRAISAL CO
  1111 SCHROCK RD, COLUMBUS 43229 . . . . (614) 221-5173
DENNIS B PELL CO
  36345 DETROIT RD, AVON 44011 . . . . (440) 899-1405
DEVCO INC
  1649 DEIST RD, MIDDLE BASS 43446 . . . . (419) 285-5871
DEVITT & ASSOCIATES INC
  WWW.DEVITTASSOCIATES.COM . . . . (513) 241-7688
EARHART APPRAISALS
  5940 CLEVER RD, BELLVILLE 44813 . . . . (419) 886-4342
F F APPRAISAL SVC
  PO BOX 864, LANCASTER 43130 . . . . (740) 743-3918
FEATHERINGHAM REALTY & AUCTION
  1060 CANTON RD, WINTERSVILLE 43953 . . . . (740) 264-7131
GEAUGA COUNTY ASSN-REALTORS
  17711 RAVENNA RD, BURTON 44021 . . . . (440) 834-8000
GEER REALTY
  730 DRESDEN AVE, E LIVERPOOL 43920 . . . . (330) 386-9066
GEORGE BUCHANAN REAL ESTATE
  490 DEERFIELD RD, ZANESVILLE 43701 . . . . (740) 872-6117
GRISWOLD REALTY
  343 NEW TOWNE SQUARE DR, TOLEDO 43612 . . . . (419) 476-9540
HABITAT APPRAISAL LTD
  1397 WARREN RD, LAKEWOOD 44107 . . . . (216) 227-4700
HENDERSON LAND INVESTMENT CO
  PO BOX 820, ST PARIS 43072 . . . . (937) 663-4184
HER PARRY REAL ESTATE
  1620 E WHEELING AVE, CAMBRIDGE 43725 . . . . (740) 439-1111
HERB FARROW & ASSOC INC
  PO BOX 524, BURTON 44021 . . . . (440) 834-8301
J E HUNTZINGER REAL ESTATE APPRAISALS
  688 LINDSEY RD, PIQUA 45356 . . . . (937) 492-3600
JAN ROSEBERRY APPRAISALS
  214 W 21ST ST, DOVER 44622. . . . . (330) 364-4367
KENDALL APPRAISAL GROUP INC
  2056 PORTAGE RD #5, WOOSTER 44691. . . . . (330) 345-7217
  1260 LEXINGTON AVE #4, MANSFIELD 44907 . . . . (419) 522-8405
KEYES GATEWAY INC REALTORS
  65 S PROGRESS DR, XENIA 45385 . . . . (937) 376-8477
L T DAVIS & ASSOC INC
  3596 LYTLE RD, CLEVELAND 44122 . . . . (216) 561-2900
LIMING & ASSOC INC
  670 N DETROIT ST, XENIA 45385. . . . . (937) 372-2553
MASSENGALE APPRAISALS INC
  6241 KINGOAK DR, CINCINNATI 45248 . . . . (513) 451-9268
MEDINA APPRAISAL GROUP LTD
  229 HARDING ST, MEDINA 44256 . . . . (330) 725-7223
MERIDIAN APPRAISAL
  324 E 3RD ST, PERRYSBURG 43551. . . . . (419) 354-0270
METROPOLITAN REALTY RESEARCH
  2220 SHOREHAM RD, COLUMBUS 43220. . . . . (614) 457-7500

MICHAEL S FOLKMAN & ASSOC INC

  EXPERT/STATE CERT/RESIDENTIAL & COMRCL
  DIVORCE/EMINENT DOMAIN OTHR LITIGATION
  DISPOSITION/ACQUISITION/MORTGAGE LOAN

  WWW.FOLKMANAPPRAISALS.COM . . . . **(216) 831-8210**

OHIO REAL ESTATE CONSULTANTS INC
  201 BRADENTON AVE, DUBLIN 43017 . . . . (614) 791-0038
REAL ESTATE APPRAISAL SVC INC
  4209 PEARL RD, CLEVELAND 44109 . . . . (216) 398-2900
  337 N HURON ST, TOLEDO 43602 . . . . (419) 259-5092
REAL PROPERTY ANALYSTS INC
  6929 W 130TH ST #102, CLEVELAND 44130 . . . . (216) 591-9211
REALTY MARKET PLACE
  5900 RIDGE RD #1, CLEVELAND 44129 . . . . (216) 475-4310
REALTY ONE
  8251 MAYFIELD RD #100, CHESTERLAND 44026 . . . . (440) 729-3300
REALTY WORLD - STOTZ REALTY
  16281 COUNTY RD G, BRYAN 43506 . . . . (419) 636-7355

APPRAISAL SERVICES-REAL ESTATE
(Cont'd)

REBERA APPRAISAL SVC
  1614 WARRICK DR, ASHTABULA 44004 . . . . (440) 964-2503
RENFREW OLDE TOWN AUCTION
  224 N 4TH ST, COSHOCTON 43812. . . . . (740) 622-3669
RESIDENTIAL REAL ESTATE APPRAISAL INC
  402 BOWLING GREEN PL, COLUMBUS 43230 . . . . (614) 337-0748
SAI GROUP INC
  1130 CHANNINGWAY DR, FAIRBORN 45324 . . . . (937) 436-3924
SEASONS REAL ESTATE COUNSELORS
  1288 W PERRY ST, SALEM 44460 . . . . (330) 332-1598
SEPTEMBER & ASSOC LTD
  2353 ROXBURY RD, AVON 44011 . . . . (440) 937-4488
SKIFFEY APPRAISERS
  5978 YOUNGSTOWN RD, NILES 44446 . . . . (330) 652-1781
SOINSKI INSURANCE AGCY
  8050 CORPORATE CIR, N ROYALTON 44133 . . . . (440) 843-8988
STATE WIDE APRAISING
  PO BOX 377, WORTHINGTON 43085 . . . . (614) 841-9967
STEFANO & ASSOC INC
  PO BOX 595, HUDSON 44236 . . . . (330) 425-3733
STEFFL APPRAISAL SVC
  PO BOX 352, MT PLEASANT 43939 . . . . (740) 769-7639
STEVEN GENTRY & ASSOC
  PO BOX 210, MILFORD 45150. . . . . (513) 248-4004
STEVEN M HENLEY APPRAISAL SVC
  6302 FAR HILLS AVE, DAYTON 45459 . . . . (937) 436-3555
STH HILL REAL ESTATE INC
  PO BOX 543, SOMERSET 43783 . . . . (740) 743-2435
STICKELMAN SCHNEIDER & ASSOCS
  2520 HARRIS AVE, CINCINNATI 45212 . . . . (513) 475-6000
STONE VALLEY APPRAISAL
  346 E HUNTER ST, LOGAN 43138 . . . . (740) 380-0450
STUBBS BRADLEY M
  920 CENTER CT, ZANESVILLE 43701 . . . . (740) 454-2184
TELZROW J APPRAISALS
  517 BROADWAY ST #403, E LIVERPOOL 43920. . . . . . . (330) 382-0285
VIOLET APPRAISAL SVC INC
  PO BOX 394, BRUNSWICK 44212 . . . . (330) 225-6947
WEBER & ASSOC REAL ESTATE
  1171 S CREEKWAY CT, COLUMBUS 43230 . . . . (614) 428-8620
WELLES BOWEN REALTORS
  1224 W WOOSTER ST #B, BOWLING GREEN 43402. . . . . . . (419) 352-6565
WESLEY BAKER & ASSOCIATES
  14 1/2 N MAIN ST, CHAGRIN FALLS 44022 . . . . (440) 247-3161
WESTERN RESERVE APPRAISAL CO
  PO BOX 416, CHARDON 44024 . . . . (440) 639-1144
WETZEL-VALLEY AGENCIES INC
  PO BOX 129, HANNIBAL 43931 . . . . (740) 483-1707
WILLIAM J GAYDOS & ASSOC
  14714 DETROIT AVE, LAKEWOOD 44107 . . . . (216) 529-1966
ZEIGLER REALTY SVC
  2200 VICTORY PKWY #709, CINCINNATI 45206 . . . . (513) 242-7740
ZENDERS APPRAISAL SVC
  934 ALLENDALE AVE, AKRON 44306 . . . . (330) 785-9275

ARBITRATION SERVICES
(See ADR SERVICES)

ARCHITECTS
(See EXPERTS—ARCHITECTURAL)

ARCHIVAL SERVICES
(See OFFICE RECORDS—STORAGE)

ASBESTOS SERVICES
(See Also ENVIRONMENTAL—CONSULTANTS)

EA GROUP
  7118 INDUSTRIAL PARK BLVD, MENTOR 44060 . . . . (440) 951-3514

ASSOCIATIONS-LEGAL & PROFESSIONAL
OH STATE BAR ASSN
  1700 LAKE SHORE DR, COLUMBUS 43204 . . . . (614) 487-2050

ATHLETIC & RECREATION EXPERTS
*(See EXPERTS—SAFETY & SECURITY; and
EXPERTS—RECREATION & SAFETY)*

ATTORNEY TRUST ACCOUNT SERVICES
(See BANKS)

AUCTIONEERS
*(See Also ESTATE LIQUIDATORS; and APPRAISAL
SERVICES)*

ASPIRE AUCTIONS INC
  12730 LARCHMERE BLVD, CLEVELAND 44120 . . . . (216) 231-5515
AUCTIONS BY MAGGIE INC
  3350 HARRISON AVE, CINCINNATI 45211 . . . . . . **(800) 745-3557**
BALDWIN AUCTIONEERING
  PO BOX 342, N HAMPTON 45349 . . . . (937) 964-5040
BARGAIN TELEVISION
  64 ENTERPRISE PL, CHILLICOTHE 45601 . . . . (740) 779-1776
BARNHART AUCTION
  47222 UNIONVALE RD, CADIZ 43907 . . . . (740) 942-9999
BARRY ALLEN AUCTIONEER
  PO BOX 314, MARIETTA 45750 . . . . (740) 373-1763
BASINGER AUCTION SVC
  11120 MARKET ST, N LIMA 44452 . . . . (330) 549-3555
BRIAN HENNING AUCTION CO
  445 E OHIO ST #2810, CHICAGO, IL 60611 . . . . (440) 327-5111
BROUGH CHAD W
  3303 S STATE RT 19, OAK HARBOR 43449 . . . . (419) 898-0290
BRUCE GUILFORD REAL ESTATE
  103 E HIGH ST, HICKSVILLE 43526 . . . . (419) 542-6637
CAPRAS AUCTION CO
  PO BOX 10262, CLEVELAND 44110 . . . . (216) 541-1225
CARLIN CO
  5653 STATE RT 15, BRYAN 43506 . . . . (419) 636-5622
CASSEL & ASSOC AUCTIONEERS
  6827 N HIGH ST #109, WORTHINGTON 43085 . . . . (614) 433-7355
COLLECTORS AUCTIONEER THE
  302 GRANGER RD, MEDINA 44256 . . . . (330) 239-1944
CREMEANS ERNESTINE AUCTION
  8557 STATE RT 56 E, CIRCLEVILLE 43113 . . . . (740) 420-7734
DALE GRESS REAL ESTATE
  316 W MAIN ST, W LAFAYETTE 43845 . . . . (740) 545-7186
DANNY WESTLAKE AUCTIONEER
  17183 MACKAN RD, MARYSVILLE 43040 . . . . (937) 642-2546
DARREL D YODER AUCTIONEER
  PO BOX 391, LYONS 43533. . . . . (419) 923-7705
DAVE KAUFMAN REALTY & AUCTIONS INC
  WWW.KAUFMANREALTY.COM . . . . (330) 852-4111
DAVID A FLOOD AUCTIONEER
  4540 VISTA DR, CANAL WINCHESTER 43110 . . . . (614) 834-3300
DAVID J DOUGLAS & ASSOC INC
  5766 FISHERMANS WHARF RD, HILLSBORO 45133 . . . . (937) 393-9999
DAVID JONES AUCTIONS
  PO BOX 467, FLUSHING 43977. . . . . (740) 968-3710
DAVY AUCTION SVC
  8945 JASPER DR, ZANESVILLE 43701 . . . . (740) 454-1495
DIMMERLING REALTY & AUCTIONEERS INC
  1736 CLEVELAND AVE NW, CANTON 44703 . . . . (330) 492-1112
DON GLEIM AUCTION SVCS
  1091 POPLAR FORK RD, FRANKLIN FURNACE 45629 . . . . . (740) 574-2657
FARMERS REALTY & AUCTION CO
  1001 S MAIN ST, BALTIMORE 43105 . . . . (740) 862-4146
FREEDOM REALTY & AUCTION SVC
  706 N MAIN ST, WELLINGTON 44090 . . . . (440) 647-6777
FUSCO AUCTIONS
  4134 ERIE ST, WILLOUGHBY 44094 . . . . (440) 975-8938
GALLOWAY AUCTION CO
  2840 W BROAD ST, COLUMBUS 43204 . . . . (614) 851-1496
GARTHS AUCTIONS INC
  2690 STRAFFORD RD, DELAWARE 43015 . . . . . . **(740) 363-2158**
GARY W CAIN REALTORS & AUCTNRS
  2724 SUNSET BLVD, STEUBENVILLE 43952 . . . . (740) 266-2246
GIBBS AUCTION SVC
  206 N LONDON ST, MT STERLING 43143 . . . . (740) 869-4525
GREEN & GREEN AUCTIONEERS
  14610 E STATE ROUTE 37, SUNBURY 43074 . . . . (740) 965-9140
HALLOCK REALTY INC & AUCTION
  114 W HIGH ST, BRYAN 43506. . . . . (419) 636-3116
HAMILTONS AUCTION HOUSE
  3519 N RIDGE W, ASHTABULA 44004 . . . . (440) 992-1405
HOFFMAN MICHAEL AUCTIONEER
  WWW.SPIFFYAUCTIONS.COM . . . . (614) 866-6512
HOMESTEAD AUCTIONS
  1384 VANDERHOOF RD, BARBERTON 44203 . . . . (330) 644-4563
JACK WINBORNE AUCTIONEER
  1213 SANDLIN AVE, COLUMBUS 43224 . . . . (614) 291-9400
JACKSON LIVESTOCK AUCTION
  PO BOX 58, DE GRAFF 43318. (937) 585-5635
JAMES J AURAND AUCTIONEER
  916 BEXLEY DR, PERRYSBURG 43551 . . . . (419) 874-8550
JOSEPH DISHER AUCTION CO
  1928 W SYLVANIA AVE, TOLEDO 43613 . . . . (419) 292-1781
KIKO AUCTIONEERS
  2805 FULTON DR NW, CANTON 44718 . . . . (800) 533-5456
KREINER CHUCK
  14244 ATWATER AVE NE, ALLIANCE 44601 . . . . (330) 821-3232
LAHMERS AUCTION SVC
  2121 MONTGOMERY RD, NEWARK 43055 . . . . (740) 763-2952
LARRY HALL AUCTION SVC
  337 MARTHA AVE, COLUMBUS 43223 . . . . (614) 274-1499

AUCTIONEERS (Cont'd)

LARRY K BOGGS AUCTIONEER
  325 BOGGS RD, STOCKPORT 43787 . . . . (740) 551-2455
MABRY AUCTION SVC
  212 E CHURCH ST, URBANA 43078. . . . . (937) 653-3068
MARK HAGANS AUCTIONEER
  731 HARRISBURG PIKE, COLUMBUS 43223. . . . . (614) 278-9291
MARK N HARRIS AUCTIONEER
  5855 GLENN HWY, CAMBRIDGE 43725. . . . . (740) 432-7400
MARK WELLS AUCTIONEER
  1049 COOPERS RUN, AMHERST 44001 . . . . (440) 984-4477
MARLBORO COUNTRY AUCTION
  644 S ROCKHILL AVE, ALLIANCE 44601 . . . . (330) 821-5670
MARY STOLLER REALTY & AUCTION
  116 N MAIN ST, BRYAN 43506 . . . . (419) 636-5656
OSBORNE & ASSOC AUCTION
  1012 RALSTON AVE, DEFIANCE 43512. . . . . (419) 782-7916
PACHELIEFF TOM JR
  550 E FLORENCE AVE #302, TOLEDO 43605 . . . . (419) 691-7313
PATRICK E GAMMONS ATTY AT LAW
  1610 COOPER FOSTER PARK RD, VERMILION 44089 . . . . . . (440) 984-2084
PATTISON CO
  5778 GLENN HWY, CAMBRIDGE 43725. . . . . (740) 439-5388
PRESIDENTIAL HOMES REALTY CO
  215 HARDING WAY W, GALION 44833 . . . . (740) 382-9158
PRYOR & SON AUCTIONEERS
  59960 PIGEON POINT RD, BARNESVILLE 43713 . . . . (740) 425-3397
R & R AUCTION
  10272 TRI COUNTY RD, WINCHESTER 45697 . . . . (513) 509-3803
RANDY POLLOCK AUCTIONEER
  68045 READ RD, CAMBRIDGE 43725. . . . . (740) 432-4974
SALSBERRY THOMAS E
  6150 N CHANTICLEER DR, MAUMEE 43537 . . . . (419) 861-7433
SALVAGE POOL AUCTION
  286 E TWINSBURG RD, NORTHFIELD 44067 . . . . (330) 468-1500
SAM SWITZER REALTY
  322 N CLINTON ST, DEFIANCE 43512 . . . . (419) 782-4116
STANLEY & SON INC
  86 N PAINT ST, CHILLICOTHE 45601 . . . . (740) 775-3330
TRI STATE AUCTIONS
  681 WASHINGTON ST, VAN WERT 45891. . . . . (419) 238-9732
TRI STATE VEHICLE MARKETING
  14125 COUNTY RD M50, MONTPELIER 43543 . . . . (419) 485-5414
TRI-GREEN INTERSTATE EQUIPMENT
  1499 US HWY 42 NE, LONDON 43140 . . . . (614) 879-7731
TRUSKOWSKI GEORGE
  128 JACKSON ST, AMHERST 44001 . . . . (440) 985-1764
USA-1 REAL ESTATE
  1676 BRICE RD, REYNOLDSBURG 43068 . . . . (614) 866-1800
WADE E FLORY & ASSOC
  1386 DAYTON GERMANTOWN PIKE, GERMANTOWN 45327. . . (937) 855-6052
WALTER BROS INC
  901 N MAIN ST, FINDLAY 45840 . . . . (419) 424-0944
WALTER REAL ESTATE & AUCTION
  16394 TOWNSHIP HWY 20, CAREY 43316 . . . . (419) 396-6064
WARREN W CAMPBELL AUCTION SVC
  10995 HEIGLE RD SW, STOUTSVILLE 43154 . . . . (740) 477-6302
WATSON AUCTION & REAL
  4156 S TOWNSHIP RD #17, TIFFIN 44883 . . . . (419) 443-7653
WAYNE LUOMA AUCTION CO
  PO BOX 308, GENEVA 44041 . . . . (440) 466-8383

BAIL BONDS

(See Also BONDS-SURETY & FIDELITY)

A BAIL BONDS
  2030 SILVER GLOBE RD, MARIETTA 45750 . . . . (740) 695-0423
  PO BOX 216, MIDDLEBRANCH 44652 . . . . (330) 830-1430
  144 S FAYETTE ST, WASHINGTON CT HS 43160 . . . . (740) 335-0212
ABC BAIL BONDS
  1370 W 6TH ST #213, CLEVELAND 44113 . . . . (216) 696-4866
CHUCK BROWN BAIL BOND AGENCY
  342 S HIGH ST, COLUMBUS 43215 . . . . (614) 224-0788
SIMPSONS EZ BAIL BOND
  14218 EUCLID AVE, CLEVELAND 44112 . . . . (216) 541-2245
THOMAS E SHORT & CO
  130 W 2ND ST #1636, DAYTON 45402 . . . . (800) 801-6010

BANKS

ANDOVER BANK
  PO BOX 405, JEFFERSON 44047 . . . . (440) 576-2265
  PO BOX 88, GENEVA 44041 . . . . (440) 466-3040
  PO BOX 500, CONNEAUT 44030 . . . . (440) 593-6595
  PO BOX 273, AUSTINBURG 44010 . . . . (440) 275-3333
  PO BOX 3138, ASHTABULA 44005 . . . . (440) 964-8999
  PO BOX 1300, ANDOVER 44003 . . . . (440) 293-7605
  PO BOX 136, PIERPONT 44082 . . . . (440) 577-1124

ANDREW YANOK INSURANCE
  PO BOX 38, ST CLAIRSVILLE 43950 . . . . (740) 695-0954
ANTWERP EXCHANGE BANK
  PO BOX 727, ANTWERP 45813 . . . . (419) 258-5351
BANK SKY
  1103 W SYLVANIA AVE, TOLEDO 43612 . . . . (419) 254-7020
EXCHANGE BANK THE
  610 E SOUTH BOUNDRY ST, PERRYSBURG 43551 . . . . . . (419) 874-2090
HUNTINGTON NATIONAL BANK
  41 S HIGH ST, COLUMBUS 43215 . . . . (614) 480-4433
INDEPENDENCE BANK
  PO BOX 318048, CLEVELAND 44131 . . . . (216) 447-1444
INDIAN VILLAGE COMMUNITY BANK
  PO BOX 830, GNADENHUTTEN 44629 . . . . (740) 254-4313
  635 W HIGH AVE, NEW PHILADELPHIA 44663 . . . . (330) 308-4867
INTEGRA BANK
  130 STIVERS RD, ABERDEEN 45101 . . . . (937) 795-2248
KEYCENTERS
  120 N DETROIT ST, XENIA 45385. . . . . (937) 372-8035
LNB BANCORP INC
  457 BROADWAY, LORAIN 44052 . . . . (440) 244-6000
MT VICTORY STATE BANK
  PO BOX 67, MT VICTORY 43340. . . . . (937) 354-3171
OLD FORT BANK
  300 W STATE ST, FREMONT 43420. . . . . (419) 254-7020
PNC BANK
  1375 E 9TH ST #1250, CLEVELAND 44114 . . . . (216) 781-9050
STANDARD FEDERAL BANK
  3131 EXECUTIVE PKWY #101, TOLEDO 43606 . . . . (419) 535-6045
STANDING STONE NATIONAL BANK
  PO BOX 2610, LANCASTER 43130 . . . . (740) 689-5001
STARK FEDERAL CREDIT UNION
  3426 CLEVELAND AVE NW, CANTON 44709 . . . . (330) 493-8325
STATE BANK & TRUST CO
  515 PARKVIEW ST, WAUSEON 43567 . . . . (419) 335-0070
  312 MAIN ST, DELTA 43515 . . . . (419) 822-3311
  1991 CROCKER RD #204, CLEVELAND 44145 . . . . (440) 871-9394
STATE BANK THE
  PO BOX 467, DEFIANCE 43512. . . . . (419) 587-3500
STEBBINS NATIONAL BANK
  PO BOX 1112, CRESTON 44217 . . . . (330) 435-6371
STEEL VALLEY BANK
  68400 STEWART DR, ST CLAIRSVILLE 43950 . . . . (740) 695-9910
  PO BOX 128, TILTONSVILLE 43963 . . . . (740) 769-2313
STRASBURG SAVINGS BANK
  224 N BODMER AVE BX 107, STRASBURG 44680 . . . . . . (330) 878-5555
UNION SAVINGS BANK
  1654 E MAIN ST, LANCASTER 43130 . . . . (740) 653-3730
  3550 W DUBLIN GRANVILLE RD, COLUMBUS 43235. . . . . (614) 761-9700
  1320 BRICE RD, REYNOLDSBURG 43068 . . . . (614) 861-9003
  1330 MORSE RD, COLUMBUS 43229 . . . . (614) 781-8896
UNITED BANK
  685 DELAWARE AVE #115, MARION 43302 . . . . (740) 383-3355
  3198 BELMONT ST, BELLAIRE 43906 . . . . (740) 676-2361
UNITED MIDWEST SAVINGS BANK
  4848 REED RD, COLUMBUS 43220 . . . . (614) 538-9400
  PO BOX 159, DE GRAFF 43318. . . . . (937) 585-5861
UNITED NATIONAL BANK & TRUST
  4086 MASSILLON RD, UNIONTOWN 44685. . . . . (330) 438-1200
UNITY NATIONAL BANK
  PO BOX 913, PIQUA 45356 . . . . (937) 778-4617
UNIZAN BANK
  5665 N HAMILTON RD, COLUMBUS 43230 . . . . (614) 478-9183
  3005 NORTHWEST BLVD, COLUMBUS 43221 . . . . (614) 486-7703
  66 S 3RD ST, COLUMBUS 43215 . . . . (614) 462-2800
  2585 E MAIN ST, COLUMBUS 43209 . . . . (614) 237-3777
  PO BOX 24190, CANTON 44701 . . . . (330) 438-1200
  5414 FULTON DR NW, CANTON 44718 . . . . (330) 966-5227
  PO BOX 616, UTICA 43080 . . . . (740) 892-3301
  36 W BROAD ST, PATASKALA 43062 . . . . (740) 927-1347
  580 HEBRON RD, HEATH 43056. . . . . (740) 522-2144
  973 N 21ST ST, NEWARK 43055. . . . . (740) 366-3364
  42 N 3RD ST, NEWARK 43055. . . . . (740) 345-9751
  222 BROADWAY E, GRANVILLE 43023 . . . . (740) 587-3133
  4311 N HIGH ST, COLUMBUS 43214 . . . . (614) 263-5053
  PO BOX 42, DRESDEN 43821. (740) 754-2881
  965 E CHERRY ST, CANAL FULTON 44614 . . . . (330) 882-3263
  2 W STATE ST, ALLIANCE 44601 . . . . (330) 829-3200
  965 CHERRY ST E, CANAL FULTON 44614 . . . . (330) 854-3666
  650 W MAPLE ST, HARTVILLE 44632 . . . . (330) 877-2215
  153 LINCOLN WAY E, MASSILLON 44646 . . . . (330) 830-7231
  450 LAKE AVE NE, MASSILLON 44646 . . . . (330) 830-7290
  2021 MAHONING RD NE, CANTON 44705 . . . . (330) 438-1070
  PO BOX 52, FRAZEYSBURG 43822 . . . . (740) 828-3401
  220 MARKET AVE S, CANTON 44702. . . . . (330) 438-1230
  PO BOX 239, NEW CONCORD 43762 . . . . (740) 826-4455
  PO BOX 217, DUNCAN FALLS 43734 . . . . (740) 674-4373
  PO BOX 4658, ZANESVILLE 43702. . . . . (740) 452-8444
  3573 MAPLE AVE, ZANESVILLE 43701 . . . . (740) 455-7059
  225 N MAYSVILLE AVE, ZANESVILLE 43701 . . . . (740) 455-7055
  2801 MAPLE AVE, ZANESVILLE 43701 . . . . (740) 455-7048
  3562 COMMERCE PKWY, WOOSTER 44691 . . . . (330) 345-2031
  6140 W CREEK RD, CLEVELAND 44131 . . . . (216) 901-4728
  2625 LINCOLN WAY E, MASSILLON 44646 . . . . (330) 830-7295
UNIZAN BANK MORTGAGE
  4086 MASSILLON RD, UNIONTOWN 44685. . . . . (330) 305-6685

BANKS-TRUST SERVICES
(See BANKS)

BILLING SYSTEMS
(See COMPUTERS—LEGAL SOFTWARE)

BONDS
(See BAIL BONDS; and BONDS—SURETY & FIDELITY)

BONDS-SURETY & FIDELITY
(See Also BAIL BONDS)

A-1 BAIL BONDING
2205 BROADWAY, LORAIN 44052 . . . . (440) 960-2066
A-1 BOND SVC
1220 W 3RD ST, CLEVELAND 44113 . . . . (216) 781-2221
A-ONE LIBERTY BELL BONDING INC
PO BOX 1345, YOUNGSTOWN 44501 . . . . (330) 545-4900
ALAN R DYNES INSURANCE INC
2603 RIVERSIDE DR #200, PAINESVILLE 44077 . . . . (440) 357-8200
ALL BOND INSURANCE
5706 TURNEY RD, CLEVELAND 44125 . . . . (216) 662-9121
AMERICAN CONTRACTING SVC INC
12333 RIDGE RD #1B, CLEVELAND 44133 . . . . (440) 237-5700
AMERICAN CONTRACTORS CO
4030 MT CARMEL TOBASCO #221, CINCINNATI 45255 . . . . . (513) 688-0800
ANAST-YATES INSURANCE
314 W MAIN CROSS ST, FINDLAY 45840 . . . . (419) 422-3453
ARCADE INSURANCE INC
1168 E TALLMADGE AVE, CUYAHOGA FALLS 44221 . . . . (330) 630-2801
ARCHER MEEK WEILER INC
150 E MOUND ST #308, COLUMBUS 43215 . . . . (614) 221-3225
ATLAS BONDING
1324 W 54TH ST, CLEVELAND 44102 . . . . (216) 961-1967
BAIL BONDS
PO BOX 307, LEHIGH ACRES, FL 33970 . . . . (419) 332-8012
BENEDICT INSURANCE INC
PO BOX 87, PAINESVILLE 44077 . . . . (440) 354-4308
BERWANGER OVERMYER ASSOC
PO BOX 20945, COLUMBUS 43220 . . . . (614) 457-7000
BILL RYAN BAIL BOND
134 W MAIN ST, HILLSBORO 45133 . . . . (937) 393-0559
BROCKMEYER & WEAN
9350 READING RD #1, CINCINNATI 45215 . . . . (513) 733-4200
BROOKS INSURANCE
1120 MADISON AVE, TOLEDO 43624 . . . . (419) 243-1191
BROWER INSURANCE
110 N MAIN ST #1400, DAYTON 45402 . . . . (937) 228-4135
BURTCH CONSOLIDATED
500 E CENTER ST, MARION 43302 . . . . (740) 387-3374
CARABOOLAD INSURANCE
614 W SUPERIOR AVE #1106, CLEVELAND 44113 . . . . (216) 522-1222
CASTLE BAIL BONDS
39 GREENE ST, XENIA 45385 . . . . (937) 372-5878
CHANEY & THOMAS INSURANCE
PO BOX 228, LONDON 43140 . . . . (740) 852-2323
CLEVELAND BONDING & INSURANCE
1370 ONTARIO ST #1014, CLEVELAND 44113 . . . . (216) 696-4733
COOPER INSURANCE INC
166 MAIN ST, PAINESVILLE 44077 . . . . (440) 953-0355
D-N-M ENTERPRISES
4542 STATE RT 314, CHESTERVILLE 43317 . . . . (419) 768-2500
DANIEL KELLY BAIL BONDS
851 BRILL MILL RD, CLEVELAND 44145 . . . . (216) 781-2322
DENNISON & ASSOC
900 FRONT ST, MARIETTA 45750 . . . . (740) 373-2604
ENDSLEY AGENCY REAL ESTATE
433 WALNUT ST, COSHOCTON 43812 . . . . (740) 622-5881
EOFF INSURANCE INC
PO BOX 187, FINDLAY 45839 . . . . (419) 422-1323
FISH & SON INSURANCE
116 N MARKET ST, WAVERLY 45690 . . . . (740) 947-7777
FLANDERS BROTHERS INSURANCE
220 PUTNAM ST, MARIETTA 45750 . . . . (740) 373-1345
FRANCIS C BERG BAIL BOND
PO BOX 302, LORAIN 44052 . . . . (440) 365-3505
FREEDOM BAIL BOND
601 N 4TH ST, STEUBENVILLE 43952 . . . . (740) 283-1696
GLADSTONE INSURANCE
PO BOX 1328, CAMBRIDGE 43725 . . . . (740) 439-4045
GOODWINS INSURANCE
PO BOX 7, COLUMBUS GROVE 45830 . . . . (419) 659-2523
GRUBERS COLUMBUS AGENCY
3040 RIVERSIDE DR #104, UPPER ARLINGTON 43221 . . . . . (614) 486-0611
HAYES INSURANCE
PO BOX 636, MARIETTA 45750 . . . . (740) 373-2347
HEMPHILL INSURANCE
9930 JOHNNYCAKE RIDGE RD, MENTOR 44060 . . . . (440) 357-1800
HOUSTON INSURANCE
PO BOX 1832, ZANESVILLE 43702 . . . . (740) 453-3609
HUBER HARGER WELT & SMITH
209 W POE RD, BOWLING GREEN 43402 . . . . (419) 353-8611

J C BAIL BONDING
322 BROAD ST, ELYRIA 44035 . . . . (440) 323-7200
JORDAN
PO BOX 42133, MIDDLETOWN 45042 . . . . (513) 423-1821
KAMINSKI MENS BELL & ASSOC INC
1789 INDIAN WOOD CIR #100, MAUMEE 43537 . . . . (419) 891-4666
KELLER-ALGE INSURANCE
341 E LINCOLN ST, FINDLAY 45840 . . . . (419) 422-2272
KELLY INSURANCE INC
PO BOX 381, CUYAHOGA FALLS 44222 . . . . (330) 929-3056
KNERR INSURANCE INC
3481 OFFICE PARK DR #100, DAYTON 45439 . . . . (937) 299-4200
KUNDTZ NICHOLS INSURANCE
14414 DETROIT AVE #104, CLEVELAND 44107 . . . . (216) 521-6821
LANDMAN INSURANCE
7946 US HWY 22 E, NEW HOLLAND 43145 . . . . (740) 495-5234
LENT INSURANCE INC
6651 CENTERVLE BUSINESS PKWY 2, DAYTON 45459 . . . . (937) 435-4788
LEUSCH INSURANCE SVC
16903 FISCHER RD #2, CLEVELAND 44107 . . . . (216) 228-3333
LINSCO PRIVATE LEDGER
1360 E 9TH ST #610, CLEVELAND 44114 . . . . (216) 367-8787
MEGA INSURANCE GROUP
15858 SAINT CLAIR AVE, E LIVERPOOL 43920 . . . . (330) 385-0688
MORGAN HOFFMAN INSURANCE
9424 MAIN ST, CINCINNATI 45242 . . . . (513) 891-8338
NORTHERN OHIO INSURANCE
8039 MAYFIELD RD, CHESTERLAND 44026 . . . . (440) 946-7600
ODELL INSURANCE
136 S STYGLER RD, GAHANNA 43230 . . . . (614) 475-4786
OHIO CASUALTY CORP
9450 SEWARD RD, FAIRFIELD 45014 . . . . (513) 603-2400
PEACH BONDING & INSURANCE
301 OFFNERE ST, PORTSMOUTH 45662 . . . . (740) 353-2009
PUTNAM WHITE & LEWIS
4161 N HIGH ST, COLUMBUS 43214 . . . . (614) 267-1269
REED-MOTE-STALEY INSURANCE INC
PO BOX 505, PIQUA 45356 . . . . (937) 773-1734
RENO INSURANCE
320 LINWOOD ST #1C, DAYTON 45405 . . . . (937) 223-5235
ROBERT A RYAN INSURANCE INC
2212 VICTORY PKWY, CINCINNATI 45206 . . . . (513) 221-1454
SCHWABLE KAREN
PO BOX 472, FREMONT 43420 . . . . (419) 626-4459
SECURANCE SERVICE INC
416 CROGHAN ST, FREMONT 43420 . . . . (419) 332-5081
PO BOX 67, GIBSONBURG 43431 . . . . (419) 637-2196
SHAFER INSURANCE INC
PO BOX 667, CAMBRIDGE 43725 . . . . (740) 439-2737
SPEAR LEEDS & KELLOGG
1375 E 9TH ST #2425, CLEVELAND 44114 . . . . (216) 623-4800
STEELE INSURANCE ASSOC INC
109 E CHURCH ST, BARNESVILLE 43713 . . . . (740) 926-1100
607 HANOVER ST, MARTINS FERRY 43935 . . . . (740) 633-0010
48259 NATIONAL RD W, ST CLAIRSVILLE 43950 . . . . (740) 695-8200
TRANS-OHIO BONDING AGENCY
306 MARKET AVE N #700, CANTON 44702 . . . . (330) 456-7380
UNITED INSURANCE SVC
PO BOX 690, SANDUSKY 44870 . . . . (419) 625-5464
W B GREEN & CO
626 WHEELING AVE, CAMBRIDGE 43725 . . . . (740) 439-1329
WALTER P DOLLE INSURANCE INC
201 E 5TH ST #1000, CINCINNATI 45202 . . . . (513) 421-6515
WEICKERT INSURANCE
2274 W STATE ST #A, FREMONT 43420 . . . . (419) 332-6423
WITTENBERG ASSOC AGENCY INC
1700 CANTON AVE #4, TOLEDO 43624 . . . . (419) 241-9711

BOOKKEEPING SERVICES
FACTS INC
311 WALNUT ST, CINCINNATI 45216 . . . . (513) 242-3613

BUILDING INSPECTION SERVICES
A ABLE HOME INSPECTION SVC
24419 DUFFIELD RD, CLEVELAND 44122 . . . . (216) 292-6047
A-1 PEST CONTROL
3378 SULLIVANT AVE, COLUMBUS 43204 . . . . (614) 276-2350
ABCO & ASSOC CONSULTING
5174 SCHUYLKILL ST, COLUMBUS 43220 . . . . (614) 459-5363
ABLE BUILDERS & INSPECTING
6690 CANAAN CIR, DUBLIN 43017 . . . . (614) 889-8880
ACKERMAN ENGINEERS
7050 ENGLE RD #100, CLEVELAND 44130 . . . . (440) 234-5233
ACTION PEST CONTROL INC
750 CROSS POINTE RD #A, COLUMBUS 43230 . . . . (614) 367-9500
AFFORDABLE INSPECTION SVC
PO BOX 44249, CLEVELAND 44144 . . . . (216) 341-0601
AHC INC
1251 S FRONT ST, COLUMBUS 43206 . . . . (614) 228-7892
ALL-AMERICAN HOME INSPECTION
2017 DORITY RD, TOLEDO 43615 . . . . (419) 537-0333
ALLIED HOME INSPECTIONS
17877 HUNT RD, CLEVELAND 44136 . . . . (440) 846-2599

BUILDING INSPECTION SERVICES (Cont'd)

AMBASSADOR CONSTRUCTION INC
1501 SPRING GARDEN AVE, CLEVELAND 44107 . . . . (216) 431-8378
AMERICAN BUILDING INSPECTIONS
6928 WEATHERBY DR, MENTOR 44060 . . . . (440) 951-1655
AMERICAN ELECTRICAL SYSTEMS
3529 ALBANY AVE, LORAIN 44055. . . . . (440) 233-5910
AMERICAN PRIDE HOME INSPECTION
5032 EAST BLVD NW, CANTON 44718 . . . . (330) 497-1213
AMERISPEC HOME INSPECTION SVC
PO BOX 670, COLUMBIA STA 44028 . . . . (440) 427-1252
ARCHER HOME INSPECTIONS
26250 EUCLID AVE #531L, CLEVELAND 44132 . . . . (216) 731-2001
BEST BUILDING INSPECTIONS
68290 ELDER AVE, ST CLAIRSVILLE 43950 . . . . (740) 695-4375
BRADY & HENDERSON INSPECTIONS
7079 NAVAJO TRL, CLEVELAND 44139. . . . . (440) 349-3919
BRICK KICKER
9928 COUNTY RD 7-2, DELTA 43515 . . . . (419) 389-9163
BTI HOME INSPECTION
1 WOODCREST CT, HIGHLAND HTS, KY 41076 . . . . (513) 651-1841
BUCCILLI HOME INSPECTION
5362 HARLESTON DR, CLEVELAND 44124. . . . . (216) 381-8935
BUCKEYE INSPECTIONS
17204 DORCHESTER DR, CLEVELAND 44119 . . . . (216) 486-4663
BUCKEYE PEST MANAGEMENT INC
PO BOX 327, ST CLAIRSVILLE 43950 . . . . (740) 283-9700
BUILDING INSPECTOR-MOIR INC
25732 CENTER RIDGE RD, CLEVELAND 44145 . . . . (440) 892-8997
BUYERS INSPECTION SVC
7686 RAGALL PKWY, CLEVELAND 44130. . . . . (440) 243-7166
CARROLL GROUP INC
405 MEADOWCREST RD, CINCINNATI 45231 . . . . (513) 522-7400
CASTLE ENTERPRISES INC
5519 PEARL RD, CLEVELAND 44129. . . . . (440) 888-8815
CONSTRUCTION INSPECTING SVC
7609 EUCLID AVE, CLEVELAND 44103 . . . . (216) 391-1980
CRAINE ENGINEERING CONSULTANTS
PO BOX 14733, COLUMBUS 43214 . . . . (614) 847-1141
CRITERIUM VAN SICKLE ENGINEERS
4421 HAMILTON CLEVES RD #6, HAMILTON 45013. . . . . . . (513) 738-4323
CRITERIUM WITHEM & LISZKAY
110 N HIGH ST #207, GAHANNA 43230 . . . . (614) 418-7200
CUSTOM HOME INSPECTION
5003 ROBINHOOD DR, WILLOUGHBY 44094 . . . . (440) 953-4663
DETECTIVE HOMES INSPECTION LTD
2511 STATE ST NW, UNIONTOWN 44685. . . . . (330) 494-4663
EGAL AMERICAS BEST HOME INSPC
PO BOX 391083, SOLON 44139 . . . . (440) 248-4438
FAMILY HOME INSPECTION SVC
7174 HODGSON RD, MENTOR 44060 . . . . (440) 953-9290
FRED LAUFFER INSPECTION SVC
4418 EAGLEHURST RD, SYLVANIA 43560 . . . . (419) 885-3033
GREATER CLEVELAND HOME INSPCTN
3169 BERKSHIRE RD, CLEVELAND 44118 . . . . (216) 371-3394
HOME & BUILDING INSPECTION SVC
RR 1 BX 637, SUGAR GROVE 43155 . . . . (740) 929-1180
HOME BUYER CONSULTANTS
4088 SIERRA PARK TER, DAYTON 45440 . . . . (937) 426-4138
HOME PRIDE INSPECTION CO
19101 BREWSTER RD, AURORA 44202 . . . . (216) 956-7736
HOMEPRO SYSTEMS OF COLUMBUS
2394 SHERWOOD RD, COLUMBUS 43209 . . . . (614) 236-2525
HOMETEAM INSPECTION SVC
6128 NEW LONDON RD, ASHTABULA 44004 . . . . (440) 969-7480
HOUSE DETECTIVE
PO BOX 727, HOLLAND 43528 . . . . (419) 865-8282
KING HOME INSPECTIONS INC
11514 LOWER GREEN VALLEY RD, MT VERNON 43050. . . . . (740) 397-3517
KOZUSKOS HOME INSPECTION SVC
430 THOMAS ALVA DR, VERMILION 44089. . . . . (440) 967-4300
LAKESIDE HOMEPRO SVC
1606 ELMWOOD AVE, CLEVELAND 44107 . . . . (216) 228-7866
LANE & SON PEST MANAGEMENT LTD
2055 S MAIN ST, AKRON 44301 . . . . (330) 724-0007
MARRELLI JOHN R
9988 CONCORD POINT CT, MENTOR 44060 . . . . (440) 639-0850
MARTIN ASSOCIATES ARCHITECTS
1617 AKRON PENINSULA RD #201, AKRON 44313 . . . . (330) 928-5585
MONTGOMERY HOME INSPECTION CO
7908 CINCINNATI DAYTON RD #K, W CHESTER 45069 . . . . . (513) 777-0010
NATIONAL HOME INSPECTION SVC
960 N MORRISON RD, REYNOLDSBURG 43068 . . . . (614) 755-9922
NATIONAL PROPERTY INSPECTIONS
1212 LYONS RD, MINFORD 45653 . . . . (740) 534-9533
NATIONAL RISK MANAGEMENT
3179 LIVINGSTON RD, CLEVELAND 44120. . . . . (216) 752-3200
NEMASTIL HOME INSPECTIONS
2140 LEE RD #202, CLEVELAND 44118. . . . . (216) 371-4096
NEWCOMERS INSPECTION SVC
24050 BRIAR PATCH DR, OLMSTED FALLS 44138 . . . . (440) 427-9666
NMD CONSULTANTS INC
34861 GLEN DR, WILLOWICK 44095 . . . . (440) 951-4822
OHIO CHAPTER OF AMERICAN
2996 DEVAN VALE DR, CUYAHOGA FALLS 44223 . . . . (330) 929-5239

PILLAR TO POST
1079 BARTLETT RD, AURORA 44202 . . . . (330) 274-5450
PREFERRED HOME INSPECTIONS
2340 PINKERTON LN, ZANESVILLE 43701 . . . . (740) 452-3155
PRO CHECK ENGINEERING INC
700 MORSE RD #210, COLUMBUS 43214 . . . . (614) 841-0217
PROFESSIONAL PROPERTY INSPCTN
4857 WINTERSET DR, COLUMBUS 43220 . . . . (614) 459-5941
PROFESSIONAL REAL ESTATE SVC
6012 SAINT REGIS DR, CINCINNATI 45236. . . . . (513) 831-3455
PROTECTION HOME INSPECTION
750 FOX CREEK LN, CINCINNATI 45245 . . . . (513) 752-1110
SAFE & SOUND LTD
4635 SULGRACE DR, TOLEDO 43623 . . . . (419) 843-5660
SEAGATE INSPECTIONS INC
PO BOX 351976, TOLEDO 43635 . . . . (419) 865-6238
SEARCHMASTER PROPERTY INSPCTN
6703 DUNHAM AVE, CLEVELAND 44103. . . . . (216) 881-2898
SEBRING HOME INSPECTION CO
775 WESTWOOD DR, PAINESVILLE 44077. . . . . (440) 354-8768
SGS AUTOMOTIVE
5050 GROVEPORT RD, OBETZ 43207 . . . . (614) 497-1710
SOWRIGHT SEED CO
21488 SCHENCK CREEK RD, HOWARD 43028 . . . . (740) 427-2300
TEAM ENVIRONMENTAL SVC INC
1275 W 74TH ST, CLEVELAND 44102 . . . . (216) 687-8200
TOTAL HOME INSPECTION INC
4373 GLENDALE AVE, TOLEDO 43614 . . . . (419) 382-8811
TRI-STATE INSPECTION SVC
4981 WAYNE TRACE RD, MIDDLETOWN 45042 . . . . (513) 726-6817
UNITED HOME PRO SYSTEMS INC
4667 DOVER CENTER RD, N OLMSTED 44070. . . . . (440) 734-1502
W P HICKMAN SYSTEMS
41 S GRANT AVE, COLUMBUS 43215 . . . . (614) 291-8528
WING INSPECTION GROUP INC
3009 COLUMBUS ST #104, GROVE CITY 43123 . . . . (614) 871-8787

BUSINESS BROKERS

BUSINESS LATITUDES
5570 HURON ST, VERMILION 44089 . . . . (440) 967-8500
BUSINESS RESOURCE GROUP LLC
527 N MARKET ST #100, WOOSTER 44691 . . . . (330) 202-9054
TRANSACTION BUSINESS SVCS
1338 WREN LN, POWELL 43065 . . . . (614) 888-7616

BUSINESS VALUATION SERVICES
(See VALUATION SERVICES)

CHEMICAL ENGINEERS
*(See ENGINEERS—CHEMICAL; EXPERTS—CHEMISTRY; and
LABORATORIES—TESTING)*

CHEMISTRY EXPERTS
*(See ENGINEERS—CHEMICAL; EXPERTS—CHEMISTRY; and
LABORATORIES—TESTING)*

CHIROPRACTIC EXPERTS
(See EXPERTS—CHIROPRACTIC)

CIVIL ENGINEERS
(See ENGINEERS—CIVIL; and ENGINEERS—CONSULTING)

CLAIMS ADJUSTERS
(See ADJUSTERS; and APPRAISAL SERVICES)

COMPUTER CONSULTANTS
(See COMPUTERS—PROGRAMMING AND CONSULTING)

COMPUTERS-HARDWARE & SOFTWARE
(See COMPUTERS—LEGAL SOFTWARE)

COMPUTERS-LEGAL SOFTWARE

ABSI LEGAL TECHNOLOGY LTD
28111 KNICKERBOCKER RD, CLEVELAND 44140 . . . . (440) 250-0608
ABSTRACT PRO SOFTWARE
6706 RAVEN CT, HAMILTON 45011 . . . . (513) 755-7404
BEC LEGAL SYSTEMS
175 TRI COUNTY PKWY #120, CINCINNATI 25246 . . . . (513) 948-1500
HENSCHEN AND ASSOCIATES INC
See Our Display Ad On First Page of Book
432 W GYPSY LANE RD, BWLING GREEN 43402. . **(419) 352-5454**
NEEDLES CASE MANAGEMENT
8 E MUSIC FAIR RD, OWINGS MILLS, MD 21117 . . . . (410) 363-1976

COMPUTERS-PROGRAMMING & CONSULTING

HORIZON COMPUTER SEMINARS
  3136 BIRD DR, RAVENNA 44266 . . . . (330) 296-3439
INTERACTIVE BUSINESS SYSTEMS INC
  144 MERCHANT ST #160, CINCINNATI 45246 . . . . (513) 984-2205
NET ENTERPRISES INC
  18 W STIMSON AVE, ATHENS 45701 . . . . (740) 594-3400
REGNILLOH & ASSOC INC
  1564 VICGROSS AVE, AKRON 44310 . . . . (330) 633-3016
RESOURCE TEAM
  WWW.RESOURCETEAM.COM . . . . (216) 292-9355
SS&G FINANCIAL SERVICES
  WWW.SSANDG.COM . . . . **(800) 869-1834**
WALKINGSTICK PRODUCTIONS INC
  232 PORTAGE TRAIL #F, CUYAHOGA FALLS 44221 . . . . (330) 923-7708

CONSTRUCTION CONSULTANTS
(See BUILDING INSPECTION SERVICES; REAL ESTATE CONSULTANTS; and EXPERTS—CONSTRUCTION)

CONSULTING ENGINEERS
(See EXPERTS—ENGINEERING; and ENGINEERS—CONSULTING)

COPIERS
(See OFFICE EQUIPMENT)

COPYING SERVICES

ADKINS & CO
  14541 MADISON AVE, CLEVELAND 44107 . . . . (216) 521-0237
ARCHIVE REPROGRAPHIC CTR INC
  175 S 3RD ST #170, COLUMBUS 43215 . . . . (614) 224-9100
BOARDMAN PRINTING
  PO BOX 5122, YOUNGSTOWN 44514 . . . . (330) 788-9608
BOBELS OFFICE PLUS
  1953 COOPER FOSTER PARK RD, AMHERST 44001 . . . . (440) 960-7070
COLOR BAR CORP
  26310 EMERY RD, CLEVELAND 44128 . . . . (216) 595-3939
COMMERCIAL INDUSTRIAL
  212 WARDEN AVE, ELYRIA 44035 . . . . (440) 323-9665
COMMERCIAL PRINTING
  PO BOX 2550, LANCASTER 43130 . . . . (740) 687-6000
COMP COS BUSINESS PRINTING & COPYING SVC
  PO BOX 58541, CINCINNATI 45258 . . . . (513) 347-7055
CONRADS PRINTING SVC
  135 N COLUMBUS ST, LANCASTER 43130 . . . . (740) 654-6248
COP-EZ
  1664 NEIL AVE, COLUMBUS 43201 . . . . (614) 292-4576
COPIER GUY
  3800 W 152ND ST, CLEVELAND 44111 . . . . (216) 252-8775
COPY CENTER WEST PRINTING CO
  9 N ROCKY RIVER DR, BEREA 44017 . . . . (440) 243-6410
COPY KING
  2905 CHESTER AVE, CLEVELAND 44114 . . . . (216) 861-3377
COPY MAX
  7850 MENTOR AVE #4, MENTOR 44060 . . . . (440) 974-4773
  87 HUBER VILLAGE BLVD, WESTERVILLE 43081 . . . . (614) 823-6846
  26035 LORAIN RD, N OLMSTED 44070 . . . . (440) 734-5020
  5221 MONROE ST, TOLEDO 43623 . . . . (419) 843-5374
COPY PRINT
  9799 RAVENNA RD, TWINSBURG 44087 . . . . (330) 425-9599
COPY QUEST
  180 MAIN ST, PAINESVILLE 44077 . . . . (440) 354-6606
COPY SYSTEMS INC
  4549 STERLINGRIDGE CT, CINCINNATI 45247 . . . . (513) 245-0879
COPY THIS INC
  5764 WESTBOURNE AVE, COLUMBUS 43213 . . . . (614) 337-2679
COPYPLUS
  32730 WALKER RD #E2, AVON LAKE 44012 . . . . (440) 933-2881
CORD CAMERA & VIDEO INC
  1364 RIVER VALLEY BLVD, LANCASTER 43130 . . . . (740) 654-4000
  2631 E MAIN ST, COLUMBUS 43209 . . . . (614) 236-9040
  PO BOX 44406, COLUMBUS 43204 . . . . (614) 457-5554
  2250 STRINGTOWN RD, GROVE CITY 43123 . . . . (614) 539-0255
  17 W SCHROCK RD, WESTERVILLE 43081 . . . . (614) 891-1500
  6950 E MAIN ST, REYNOLDSBURG 43068 . . . . (614) 864-0200
  1158 POLARIS PK WAY, COLUMBUS 43240 . . . . (614) 846-2673
  4760 SAWMILL RD, COLUMBUS 43235 . . . . (614) 889-8444
  23789 LORAIN RD, N OLMSTED 44070 . . . . (440) 801-1000

CORD CAMERA 55 MINUTE PHOTO
  3544 SOLDARO BLVD, COLUMBUS 43228 . . . . (614) 278-2673
  9552 MENTOR AVE, MENTOR 44060 . . . . (440) 352-6656
CREATIVE GRAPHICS OF OHIO
  17 S 4TH ST, ZANESVILLE 43701 . . . . (740) 453-6665
DOCUMENT SOLUTIONS
  131 W MAIN ST, LANCASTER 43130 . . . . (740) 653-1100
  100 E CAMPUS VIEW BLVD #105, COLUMBUS 43235 . . . . . . (614) 846-2400
DOCUMENT SYSTEMS INC
  PO BOX 461, MONROE, MI 48161 . . . . (419) 720-0800
DOPCO-DIGITAL OFFICE PRODS
  812 S MAIN ST, N CANTON 44720 . . . . (216) 459-2790
  8351 N HIGH ST #149, COLUMBUS 43235 . . . . (614) 885-9832
DOWNTOWN PRINT SHOP
  520 MADISON AVE #11, TOLEDO 43604 . . . . (419) 242-9164
ERIEVIEW REPRODUCTION CTR
  2254 E ENTERPRISE PKWY, TWINSBURG 44087 . . . . (330) 487-0900
FREISMUTH PRINTING
  2193 NATIONAL RD, WHEELING, WV 26003 . . . . (740) 676-6264
GOODMAN CRAIG
  2647 BROADMORE LN, WESTLAKE 44145 . . . . (440) 871-1963
GORMANS PHOTO CTR
  53 E BRIDGE ST, BEREA 44017 . . . . (440) 234-2284
GREENWOOD PRINTING & GRAPHICS
  3615 STICKNEY AVE, TOLEDO 43608 . . . . (419) 476-1325
HOT GRAPHIC SVC
  PO BOX 307, TOLEDO 43697 . . . . (419) 242-7000
KOPY KAT
  PO BOX 593, NEWBURY 44065 . . . . (440) 564-9006
KOPY KWIK
  35756 VINE ST, WILLOWICK 44095 . . . . (440) 951-7300
LEGAL IMAGES
  2000 E 9TH ST #320, CLEVELAND 44115 . . . . (216) 861-4600
LOOK A LIKE COPIES
  14544 ELLETT RD, BELOIT 44609 . . . . (330) 537-3300
LORAIN QUICKPRINT & COPY
  1219 COOPER FOSTER PARK RD #C, LORAIN 44053 . . . . . (440) 960-2280
LOVE PHOTOGRAPHY
  44 W BAGLEY RD, BEREA 44017 . . . . (440) 243-5683
MONKS COPY SHOPS INC
  645 DEARBORN PARK LN, WORTHINGTON 43085 . . . . (614) 885-7228
NORTH END PRESS INC
  235 S COLUMBUS ST, LANCASTER 43130 . . . . (740) 653-6514
NORTHCOAST CREATIVE BUSINESS
  PO BOX 417, ELYRIA 44036 . . . . (440) 322-2115
OFFICE GRAPHICS
  223 COURT ST, HAMILTON 45011 . . . . (513) 863-3393
ORIGINAL DOCUMENTS SVC INC
  1717 E 36TH ST, CLEVELAND 44114 . . . . (216) 923-0046
PAK MAIL
  825 N HOUK RD, DELAWARE 43015 . . . . (740) 363-5530
POSTNET POSTAL & BUSINESS SVC
  8535 TANGLEWOOD SQ #5, CHAGRIN FALLS 44023 . . . . . (440) 543-2599
  8210 MACEDONIA COMMONS BLVD, MACEDONIA 44056 . . . (330) 468-0029
PRESSMARK INC
  PO BOX 1203, MARIETTA 45750 . . . . (740) 373-6005
PRIME DIGITAL PRINTING
  24 RANDOLPH ST, WILMINGTON 45177 . . . . (937) 382-2582
PRINT N COPY
  104 N MARIETTA ST, ST CLAIRSVILLE 43950 . . . . (740) 695-3616
PRINT SHOP
  6536 PROMLER ST NW, N CANTON 44720 . . . . (330) 452-3232
PRINTING & SUCH INC
  3550 EXECUTIVE PKWY, TOLEDO 43606 . . . . (419) 537-6631
PRINTING PARTNERS
  13437 DETROIT AVE, CLEVELAND 44107 . . . . (216) 221-7117
  5063 TURNEY RD, CLEVELAND 44125 . . . . (216) 663-6400
PRINTMARK INC
  400 S BROAD ST, LANCASTER 43130 . . . . (740) 653-7319
QUICK COPY-PRINT CTR
  253 W MAIN ST, RAVENNA 44266 . . . . (330) 296-0123
ROCKSIDE 21 PRINTING
  6901 ROCKSIDE RD, CLEVELAND 44131 . . . . (216) 328-9930
ROUTE 60 U-STOR-ALL
  1612 STATE RD, VERMILION 44089 . . . . (440) 967-7867
TOMAHAWK PRINTING INC
  4017 COUNTY ROAD 11, WAUSEON 43567 . . . . (419) 335-3161
TOMS PRINT SHOP
  PO BOX 146, ZANESVILLE 43702 . . . . (740) 452-7100
WRAP N POST
  3901 LAYBOURNE RD, SPRINGFIELD 45505 . . . . (937) 323-0003
WRAYS ENTERPRISES INC
  197-B MARYBILL DR, TROY 45373 . . . . (937) 335-7401

COPYRIGHT AGENTS
(See PATENT COPYRIGHT & TRADEMARK AGENTS & SERVICES)

COURIER SERVICES
(See MESSENGER SERVICES)

Tackla & Associates

Court Reporting & Videotaping

- Court Reporting
- Videotaping
- Two-Camera Videotaping
- A-Day-in-the-Life Videotaping
- Process Serving
- Real-Time Reporting
- Big Screen Playback
- Still Pictures From Videotapes
- Video Editing
- Video Teleconferencing
- Interpreting Services
- Private Investigator
- MINI Transcripts
- ASCII, Discovery ZX, WP Disks
- Digital Still Photos on Disk

• Power Point Presentations for Court

1020 Ohio Savings Plaza
1801 E. 9th Street
Cleveland, OH 44114

216-241-3918
Fax 216-241-3935
Lautst@aol.com

COURT REPORTERS

(See Also TRANSCRIPTION SERVICES)

ACBA SVCS INC
400 KOPPERS BLDG 436 7TH AVE, PITTSBURGH, PA 15219 . (412) 261-5588
ACCUSCRIBES REPORTING LTD
206 S BROAD ST BX 2466, LANCASTER 43130. . **(740) 689-1680**
ACE REPORTING SERVICES
30 GARFIELD #620, CINCINNATI 45202. . . . . (800) 277-7165

ANDERSON REPORTING SVCS

CERTIFIED LIVE NOTE SERVICE PROVIDER
CONFERENCE ROOMS * VIDEOCONFERENCING
REAL TIME REPORTING * SUBPOENA SERVICES

3242 W HENDERSON RD #A, COLUMBUS 43220 . . **(614) 326-0177**

ARIZONA COURT REPORTING
177 N CHURCH AVE #1006, TUCSON, AZ 85701 . . . . (520) 623-3375
ARMSTRONG & OKEY INC
185 S FIFTH ST #101, COLUMBUS 43215 . . . . (800) 223-9481
ASSOCIATED COURT REPORTING INC
1 CASCADE PLZ #1025, AKRON 44308. . . . . (330) 434-8800

BISH & ASSOCIATES INC

VIDEO CONFERENCING * CONFERENCE ROOMS
ONLINE DOCUMENT REPOSITORY
SUBPOENA SERVICE AVAILABLE

159 S MAIN ST #812, AKRON 44308. . . . . **(330) 762-0031**

CADY REPORTING SERVICES INC
55 PUBLIC SQ #1225, CLEVELAND 44113 . . . . . **(216) 861-9270**
CAMILLO & CLARK COURT REPORTERS
589 W BROAD ST, ELYRIA 44035 . . . . **(440) 323-3381**
CEFARATTI GROUP
4608 ST CLAIR AVE, CLEVELAND 44103. . . . . (216) 696-1161
CHARLENE E NICHOLAS & ASSOCS LLC
5136 PHILLIPSBURG-UNION RD, ENGLEWOOD 45322. . . . . . (937) 836-7878
CIN-TEL CORP
813 BROADWAY ST, CINCINNATI 45202. . . . . (513) 621-7723
COLLINS REPORTING SVC INC
405 W HURON ST 1ST FL, TOLEDO 43604 . . . . (419) 255-1010
CORSILLO & GRANDILLO COURT REPORTERS
850 EUCLID AVE CITY CLUB BLDG #700, CLEVELAND 44114 . (216) 523-1700
COURT REPORTERS OF AKRON CANTON & CLEVELAND
40 E BUCHTEL AVE, AKRON 44308 . . . . **(330) 376-8100**
COURT REPORTING PLUS INC
PO BOX 418, WORTHINGTON 43085. . . . . (614) 840-0129
DEPO SVC
1464 TUCKER HILL RD, WAITSFIELD, VT 05673 . . . . (802) 244-8440
DRAPER & OESTREICHER
3609 W EIGHTH ST, CINCINNATI 45205 . . . . (513) 244-2223
DROGELL & ASSOCS
301 LANDMARK BLDG 7 W BOWERY ST, AKRON 44308 . . . . . (330) 253-8307
DUNN & GOUDREAU COURT RPTG SVC
1 STATE ST #115, BOSTON, MA 02109 . . . . (617) 742-6900

FINCUN-MANCINI INC

FULL SERVICE COURT/DIGITAL REPORTING
PROCESS AND VIDEOTAPING SERVICES
VIDEO/TEXT SYNC - CONFERENCE SUITES

1801 E 9TH ST #1720, CLEVELAND 44114. . . . . **(877) 696-3376**

HUNTLEY REPORTING SVC
912 PERRY ST, SANDUSKY 44870. . . . . (419) 626-4039
JUDY JETTKE & ASSOCS
309 SOUTHBOUND GRATIOT AV #2, MT CLEMENTS, MI 48043 (586) 783-0060

KNAPP DEBORAH
36 ISLAND PK, IPSWICH, MA 01938. . . . . (978) 356-0234
KRYSCHTAL KLEAR COURT REPORTING SVC
1017 W RIVER RD N, ELYRIA 44035. . . . . (440) 277-8440
M & M REPORTING INC
ONE PIERCE PL #295-E, ITASCA, IL 60143 . . . . (312) 266-4900
MCGINNIS & ASSOCS
175 S THIRD ST #540, COLUMBUS 43215. . . . . (800) 498-2451
MEHLER & HAGESTROM
1015 KEY BLDG, AKRON 44308 . . . . (800) 562-7100
MERIT REPORTING SVC
8193 AVERY RD #201, BROADVIEW HTS 44147 . . . . (800) 528-9475
MIZANIN REPORTING SERVICE INC
50 PUBLIC SQ 1511 TRMNL TWR, CLVLND 44113 **(216) 241-0331**
MOLER REPORTING SERVICE
2115 HARKER WAITS RD, WILLIAMSBURG 45176. . . . . (937) 444-4565
MONNA MCCORMICK & ASSOC
PO BOX 752283, DAYTON 45475 . . . . (937) 291-3334
NAGY-BAKER COURT REPORTING INC
26 MARKET ST #810, YOUNGSTOWN 44503 . . . . (800) 964-3376
ODONNELL BOYER & MCGHEE
44 PARK AVE W #203, MANSFIELD 44902 . . . . (419) 522-9700
ON-TIME REPORTING
8739 LANDEN DR, MAINEVILLE 45039 . . . . (513) 677-6188
PAM LATHER & ASSOC
220 W HARDIN ST, FINDLAY 45840 . . . . (419) 422-6749
PATTERSON-GORDON REPORTING INC
11221 PEARL RD, STRONGSVILLE 44136. . . . . (216) 771-0717
POWERS GARRISON & HUGHES
600 WARNER CTR 332 FIFTH AVE, PITTSBURGH, PA 15222 . . (412) 263-2088
PROFESSIONAL REPORTERS INC
398 S WASHINGTON AVE, COLUMBUS 43215 . . . . (800) 229-0675

RUA REPORTING SVC

MEDICAL-TECHNICAL EXPERTISE
PROFESSIONAL VIDEOTAPE SERVICES
DEPOSITION SUITE

55 PUBLIC SQ #1160, CLEVELAND 44113. . . . . **(216) 241-5500**

SEAGATE REPORTING SERVICE INC
WWW.SEAGATEREPORTINGSERVICE.COM . . . . (888) 419-2070
SHELL COURT REPORTING
9201 EBY RD, GERMANTOWN 45327 . . . . (937) 855-3406
SNYDER REPORTING SVCS
2233 WILLIAM PENN HWY, PITTSBURGH, PA 15235. . . . . . . (412) 243-3644
SPECTRUM REPORTING LLC
333 E STEWART AVE, COLUMBUS 43206 . . . . (800) 635-9071
STRESKI REPORTING & VIDEO SVC
7000 HAMPTON CTR #E, MORGANTOWN, WV 26505. . . . . . (304) 598-9292
625 LIBERTY AVE 28TH FL, PITTSBURGH, PA 15222 . . . . . . (412) 566-2249
SUMMIT CITY REPORTING INC
3492-B STELLHORN RD, FT WAYNE, IN 46815. . . . . (800) 977-3376
TACKLA & ASSOCIATES
See Our Display Ad Under This Heading
1801 E 9TH ST, CLEVELAND 44114 . . . . **(216) 241-3918**
TRI-COUNTY COURT REPORTING
95 S FOURTH ST, BATAVIA 45103 . . . . (513) 732-1477

COURTROOM EXHIBITS
(See Also VIDEO PRODUCTION SERVICES—LEGAL; and PHOTOGRAPHERS—LEGAL)

ALPINE VIEW IMAGES LTD
　7971 E DUBLIN GRANVILLE RD, NEW ALBANY 43054 . . . . (614) 789-9277
GAYLE HOLTON DESIGN
　6089 FRANZ RD #101, DUBLIN 43017 . . . . (614) 764-9181
VIDEO DISCOVERY INC
　See Our Display Ad Under This Heading
　14245 CEDAR RD, CLEVELAND 44121 . . . . **(216) 382-1043**
VISUAL ANATOMY
　See Our Display Ad Under This Heading
　WWW.VISUALANATOMY.COM . . . . **(937) 390-8984**
VISUAL EVIDENCE CO
　1140 EUCLID AVE, CLEVELAND 44115 . . . . (216) 241-3443
VISUAL MEDICINE
　4661 CODDINGVILLE RD, MEDINA 44256 . . . . (330) 239-2007

CPAS
(See ACCOUNTANTS—CERTIFIED PUBLIC)

DELIVERY SERVICES
(See MESSENGER SERVICES)

DESTRUCTION-OFFICE RECORDS
(See OFFICE RECORDS—DESTRUCTION)

DETECTIVE AGENCIES
(See INVESTIGATORS & DETECTIVE AGENCIES)

DOCUMENT EXPERTS
(See EXPERTS—DOCUMENTS)

DOCUMENT FILING & RETRIEVAL
KEYSTROKES BY KELLY
　KEYSTROKES@COLUMBUS.RR.COM . . . . **(614) 875-9590**
LEGAL EASE OF OHIO LLC
　WWW.LEGALEASEOFOHIO.COM . . . . (800) 519-6331
NATIONAL SERVICE INFORMATION INC
　WWW.NSII.NET . . . . **(800) 235-0337**

DOCUMENT MANAGEMENT
IBEAM SOLUTIONS
　10 S HIGH ST, CANAL WINCHESTER 43110 . . . . (614) 833-9713

EMPLOYABILITY EXPERTS
(See EXPERTS—EMPLOYABILITY)

EMPLOYMENT AGENCIES
(See Also EXECUTIVE SEARCH FIRMS; and LEGAL PLACEMENT SERVICES)

CARPENTER LEGAL SEARCH INC
　301 GRANT ST #3030, PITTSBURGH, PA 15219 . . . . (412) 255-3770
CONTRACT COUNSEL
　470 OLDE WORTHINGTON RD, COLUMBUS 43282 . . . . (614) 410-6749
L STEVENS & CO EMPLOYMENT SPECIALISTS
　WWW.LSTEVENSEMPLOYMENT.COM . . . . **(216) 523-1800**
LEGAL EMPLOYMENT SOLUTIONS
　571 HIGH ST, WORTHINGTON 43085 . . . . (614) 825-6188
MAJOR LEGAL SVCS LLC
　WWW.MAJORLEGALSERVICES.COM . . . . **(216) 579-9782**
SPHERION
　5151 PFEIFFER RD #120, CINCINNATI 45242 . . . . (937) 853-0140

ENGINEERS-CHEMICAL
(See Also EXPERTS—CHEMISTRY)

TECHNICAL SOLUTION SPECIALISTS
　4203 MALSBARY RD, CINCINNATI 45242 . . . . (513) 793-7919
TRIAD RESOURCES
　5038 BEECH ST, NORWOOD 45212. . . . . (513) 631-5400

ENGINEERS-CIVIL
AZTECH ENGINEERING & SURVEYING
　38879 MENTOR AVE #A, WILLOUGHBY 44094 . . . . (440) 602-9071
JUDGE ENGINEERING CO
　1201 E DAVID RD #105, KETTERING 45429 . . . . (937) 294-1441
WELLERT CORP
　5136 BEACH RD, MEDINA 44256 . . . . (888) 935-5378

ENGINEERS-CONSULTING
(See Also EXPERTS—ENGINEERING)

AES GROUP LLC
　230 NORTHLAND BLVD, CINCINNATI 45246 . . . . (513) 771-2374
AS 1 TECHNOLOGIES
　34452 HEATHERWOOD, AVON 44011 . . . . (440) 937-7752
BAKER & ASSOC
　2000 E 9TH ST #1220, CLEVELAND 44115 . . . . (216) 664-6493
BARR ENGINEERING INC
　4410 KING GRAVES RD, VIENNA 44473 . . . . (330) 856-5355
BATTELLE
　20455 EMERALD PKWY #200, CLEVELAND 44135. . . . . (440) 734-0094
BAUER DAVIDSON & MERCHANT INC
　255 GREEN MEADOWS DR S, WESTERVILLE 43081 . . . . (614) 846-3393
BELARDO TECHNOLOGIES INC
　1260 ARLINGTON RD, CLEVELAND 44107 . . . . (216) 521-4077
BELCAN CORP
　28999 AURORA RD, CLEVELAND 44139 . . . . (440) 349-5200
BENATEC ASSOCIATES
　119 DILLMONT DR #200, COLUMBUS 43235. . . . . (614) 431-1116
BENZ TECHNOLOGY INTL INC
　2305 CLARKSVILLE RD, CLARKSVILLE 45113 . . . . (937) 289-4504
BHE ENVIRONMENTAL
　11733 CHESTERDALE RD, CINCINNATI 45246 . . . . (513) 326-1500
CAD ZONE INC
　4480 LAKE FOREST DR #410, CINCINNATI 45242 . . . . (513) 769-9901
CAR SOURCE
　1200 STRINGTOWN RD, GROVE CITY 43123 . . . . (614) 801-9400
CARDINAL CONSULTING LTD
　2580 WYNDBEND BLVD, POWELL 43065 . . . . (614) 436-5122
CATES & ASSOC INC
　200 TECHNE CENTER DR #215, MILFORD 45150 . . . . (513) 831-0551
CHARLES W JENKINS CONSULTING
　4074 HEDGEWOOD DR, MEDINA 44256 . . . . (330) 764-3326
DENNMARK CONSULTANTS INC
　6000 CORNELL RD, CINCINNATI 45242. . . . . (513) 530-9984
DESIGNEERS MIDWEST
　7817 COOPER RD #B, CINCINNATI 45242. . . . . (513) 793-6670
EER ENGINEERS
　PO BOX 153, ORRVILLE 44667. (330) 682-4007
FACILITY SERVICES & CONSULTING
　744 CAMDEN LN, BRUNSWICK 44212. . . . . (330) 273-1260
GANNETT FLEMING ENGINEERS
　4151 EXECUTIVE PKWY #350, WESTERVILLE 43081 . . . . (614) 794-9424
GAS TECH PRODUCTS INC
　7547 KELLOGG RD, PAINESVILLE 44077 . . . . (440) 392-0500
GEODETIC CONSULTING SVC
　235 S MAIN ST, COLUMBIANA 44408. . . . . (330) 482-3117
GEORGE A FIEDLER & ASSOC
　PO BOX 146, DOVER 44622 . . . . (330) 364-2122
GEORGE A MARA ENGINEERING INC
　55 E 2ND ST, LOGAN 43138 . . . . (740) 385-8138
HANSEN LEGAL NURSE CONSULTING
　5401 W BANCROFT ST, TOLEDO 43615 . . . . (419) 698-0406

ENGINEERS-CONSULTING (Cont'd)

HUGHES RICHARD T PE
506 KREBS AVE, CLEARFIELD, PA 16830 . . . . (800) 819-1004
J A WOLF ENTERPRISES LTD
133 LAKE BLUFF DR, COLUMBUS 43235 . . . . (614) 846-3039
JABLONSKI & AUSTRIAN INC
1422 EUCLID AVE #840, CLEVELAND 44115. . . . . (216) 621-6631
JEDSON ENGINEERING
5300 DUPONT CIR #B, MILFORD 45150 . . . . (513) 271-9999
KADUNC DONALD A PHD
681 FAIRLAWN DR, CIRCLEVILLE 43113 . . . . (740) 420-7306
KEANEY & CO
1314 OAKVIEW DR, COLUMBUS 43235 . . . . (614) 846-9923
KEOGH CONSULTING
10217 BRECKSVILLE RD, CLEVELAND 44141 . . . . (440) 526-2002
KORDA NEMETH ENGINEERING INC
1650 WATERMARK DR #200, COLUMBUS 43215 . . . . (614) 487-1650
LAKE ERIE MEP
1310 W 4TH ST, MANSFIELD 44862. . . . . (419) 529-8334
LEE ROBINSON CONSULTING
PO BOX 319, MOGADORE 44260 . . . . (330) 628-0834
LEE S GOOD PE INC
10483 CLEVELAND AVE NW, UNIONTOWN 44685. . . . . (330) 494-1574
MANUFACTURING RESOURCES INC
7813 FIRST PL, CLEVELAND 44146. . . . . (440) 786-3390
MARNELL GROUP
704 BENNETT CIR, SIDNEY 45365 . . . . (513) 232-3225
MARTI TECHNOLOGY US INC
3057 NATIONWIDE PKWY, BRUNSWICK 44212 . . . . (330) 220-0833
MAUMEE RESEARCH & ENGINEERING
27439 HOLIDAY LN, PERRYSBURG 43551 . . . . (419) 666-4188
METCALF & EDDY INC
1300 E 9TH ST, CLEVELAND 44114 . . . . (216) 910-2000
2800 CORPORATE EXCHANGE #250, COLUMBUS 43231. . (614) 890-5501
NEFF & ASSOC
6405 YORK RD, CLEVELAND 44130 . . . . (440) 884-3100
NEW PRODUCT ENT
16938 LEFFINGWELL RD, BERLIN CENTER 44401 . . . . (330) 547-2533
PARALLEL DESIGN INC
1588 N GEYERS CHAPEL RD, WOOSTER 44691 . . . . (330) 345-1660
PAUL F TREMBLY & ASSOC
2114 W RESERVE CIR, AVON 44011 . . . . (440) 934-5283
PERMA PIPE INSPECTION SVC
151 PORTAGE TRL #149, CUYAHOGA FALLS 44221 . . . . . . (330) 945-9970
PETERS GROUP
PO BOX 111, CHESTERHILL 43728 . . . . (614) 577-9960
PGM DIVERSIFIED INDUSTRIES
6514 ALEXANDRIA DR, PARMA HTS 44130 . . . . . (440) 885-3500
R E KNIGHT ASSOC INC
3933 CENTER RD, BRUNSWICK 44212 . . . . (330) 225-4515
RADLINSKI & ASSOC INC
3143 COUNTY RD 154, E LIBERTY 43319 . . . . (937) 666-5006
RALPH TYLER CO
1120 CHESTER AVE #200, CLEVELAND 44114 . . . . (216) 623-0808
RAVEN SYSTEMS DESIGN
6931 GRANDVIEW DR, CLEVELAND 44131 . . . . (216) 524-7030
RESOURCE FUELS
17 S HIGH ST #1220, COLUMBUS 43215 . . . . (614) 233-6350
S A E C
10300 ALLIANCE RD #550, CINCINNATI 45242 . . . . (513) 793-4959
SADIA
1737 GEORGETOWN RD, HUDSON 44236 . . . . (330) 342-5503
SAFETY BY DESIGN BY LJB INC
WWW.LJBINC.COM . . . . (877) 886-5301
SALEM CONSULTING
14622 CAMDEN CIR, CLEVELAND 44136 . . . . (440) 238-5325
SAVAGE WALKER & ASSOC INC
756 CINCINNATI BATAVIA PIKE #C, CINCINNATI 45245 . . . . . (513) 793-7410
SAYER & ASSOC INC
3730 CLAY MOUNTAIN DR, MEDINA 44256. . . . . (330) 725-4621
SEDLAK MANAGEMENT CONSULTANTS
4020 KINROSS LAKES PKWY, RICHFIELD 44286. . . . . (330) 908-2100
SEG DESIGN LTD
1369 DEPOT ST, CLEVELAND 44116. . . . . (440) 356-7045
TECHNICAL ASSURANCE CONSULTING
38112 2ND ST, WILLOUGHBY 44094 . . . . (440) 953-3147
TECHSOLVE
6705 STEGER DR, CINCINNATI 45237. . . . . (513) 948-2000
THOMAS C GREEN & ASSOC
21 E STATE ST #1100, COLUMBUS 43215 . . . . (614) 224-3321
THORSON BAKER & ASSOC
3030 W STREETSBORO RD, RICHFIELD 44286 . . . . (330) 659-6688
VARO ENGINEERS LTD
2790 COLUMBUS RD #70, GRANVILLE 43023 . . . . (740) 927-3277
2233 N BANK DR, COLUMBUS 43220 . . . . (614) 459-0424
VEROSTKO CONSULTING ENGINEER
1216 AMERITECH BLVD, YOUNGSTOWN 44509 . . . . (330) 799-1339
W E QUICKSALL & ASSOC INC
554 W HIGH AVE, NEW PHILADELPHIA 44663 . . . . (330) 339-6676
WARMUS & ASSOC INC
PO BOX 807, BATH 44213 . . . . (330) 659-4440
WEAVER & ASSOC
51 N 3RD ST, NEWARK 43055 . . . . (740) 345-4260
WELDED TUBE PROS
16574 OLD CHIPPEWA TRL, DOYLESTOWN 44230 . . . . (330) 658-7070

YAGER CONSULTANTS INC
2650 N REYNOLDS RD #1, TOLEDO 43615 . . . . (419) 537-9479

ENGINEERS-ELECTRICAL

ADVANCED AUTOMATION INC
406 E 4TH ST, GENOA 43430 . . . . (419) 855-1353
BOWSHOT COOPER & ODONNELL
19571 ROSELAND AVE, CLEVELAND 44117. . . . . (216) 692-0460
CINCINNATI TECHNOLOGIES LTD
4700 DUKE DR #200, MASON 45040 . . . . (513) 754-8935
D C ENGINEERING INC
1071 BANDANNA DR, CINCINNATI 45238 . . . . (513) 922-3551
DESIGN ENGINEERS & CONSULTING
415 CONANT ST, MAUMEE 43537 . . . . (419) 891-0022
ELECTRIC GROUP INC
14923 STATE ROUTE 104, ASHVILLE 43103. . . . . (740) 983-6626
ELECTROL SYSTEMS INC
10025 PRINCETON GLENDALE RD, CINCINNATI 45246 . . . . . (513) 942-7777
GEDEON FREDERICK & CO
26031 CENTER RIDGE RD #D, CLEVELAND 44145 . . . . (440) 892-0490
GOLIVER & ASSOC INC
2040 BRICE RD #120, REYNOLDSBURG 43068 . . . . (614) 759-2275
H T BERNSDORFF INC
2735 N HOLLAND SYLVANIA RD #A3, TOLEDO 43615. . . . . . (419) 535-1616
HAWA INC
980 OLD HENDERSON RD, COLUMBUS 43220 . . . . (614) 451-1711
HORN ELECTRIC CO
PO BOX 493, DOVER 44622 . . . . (330) 364-7784
JDRM ENGINEERING INC
5604 MAIN ST #200, SYLVANIA 43560 . . . . (419) 824-2400
JESS HOWARD ELECTRIC CO
6630 TAYLOR RD, BLACKLICK 43004 . . . . (614) 861-1300
JMP & ASSOC
666 REDNA TER #100, CINCINNATI 45215 . . . . (513) 771-3002
KOESTER CORP
136 FOX RUN DR, DEFIANCE 43512 . . . . (419) 782-0291
LENZ ENGINEERING & COMM SVC
1880 MILDEN RD, COLUMBUS 43221 . . . . (614) 459-3920
LUMAY DESIGN SVC
5400 W MONROE CONCORD RD, W MILTON 45383 . . . . . . (937) 698-1004
MICROCONTROLS
223 FAIRGROUND RD, XENIA 45385 . . . . (937) 374-1192
MKC ASSOC INC
3021 BETHEL RD, COLUMBUS 43220 . . . . (614) 326-0248
MORRIS JAMES H PE
864 E BROWN AVE, BELLEFONTAINE 43311 . . . . (419) 478-5110
PAHL ENGINEERING
1493 S HOME RD, MANSFIELD 44904 . . . . (419) 756-8430
PCE-PRIORITY-BASED CONTROL
6063 FRANTZ RD #205, DUBLIN 43017 . . . . (614) 799-0300
PETERS TSCHANTZ & BANDWEN INC
275 SPRINGSIDE DR #300, AKRON 44333 . . . . (330) 666-3702
POWER SYSTEM SOLUTIONS
6914 ASBURY CIRCLE NE, CANTON 44721 . . . . . (330) 497-8250
PYRAMID TECHOLOGIES
1718 N QUAIL, MESA, AZ 85205 . . . . (480) 507-0088
RALPH & CURL LIGHTING ENGINEER
3720 E 5TH AVE, COLUMBUS 43219 . . . . (614) 237-8416
REESE ENGINEERING
2651 BELL RD, MANSFIELD 44904. . . . . (419) 884-9660
ROEHRENBECK ELECTRIC INC
2525 ENGLISH RD, COLUMBUS 43207 . . . . (614) 443-9709
SCHOOLEY CALDWELL ASSOC
300 MARCONI BLVD #100, COLUMBUS 43215 . . . . (614) 628-0300
SCITECH NATIONAL
9506 CENTERBROOK CT, DAYTON 45458 . . . . (937) 885-1723
SEMCOR INC
5100 SPRINGFIELD ST #109, BEAVERCREEK 45431 . . . . . . (937) 258-0217
SINGLE SOURCE AUTOMATION
116 GRAND AVE, DEFIANCE 43512. . . . . (419) 784-1558
STELLAR SYSTEMS INC
1944 HARRISON AVE, CINCINNATI 45214. . . . . (513) 921-8748
SUPERIOR AUTOMOTIVE ELECTRIC
44 25TH ST NW, BARBERTON 44203 . . . . (330) 706-9136
TECHNICAL SVC
321 TOWNSHIP RD 16, CENTERBURG 43011 . . . . (740) 625-9000
W M ENGINEERING
7100 HUNTLEY RD #204N, COLUMBUS 43229 . . . . (614) 431-1181
W M LEWIS & ASSOC INC
500 CHILLICOTHE ST #300, PORTSMOUTH 45662 . . . . (740) 354-3238

ENGINEERS-ENVIRONMENTAL

*(See Also ENVIRONMENTAL—CONSULTANTS; and
EXPERTS—ENVIRONMENTAL)*

2 E INC
PO BOX 41008, CLEVELAND 44141 . . . . (440) 717-0750
A & A ENGINEERING
4209 MONROE ST, TOLEDO 43606 . . . . (419) 292-1983
A & S ENTERPRISE
7949 STONEHURST DR, DUBLIN 43016 . . . . (614) 792-5214
ALT & WITZIG ENGINEERING INC
10178 INTERNATIONAL BLVD, CINCINNATI 45246 . . . . (513) 874-9494

ENGINEERS-ENVIRONMENTAL (Cont'd)

ARCADIS
284 CRAMER CREEK CT, DUBLIN 43017 . . . . (614) 764-2310
ATC ASSOCIATES
2027 SPRINGBORO RD W, DAYTON 45439 . . . . (937) 297-6600
11121 CANAL RD, CINCINNATI 45241 . . . . (513) 771-2112
950 TAYLOR STATION RD #V, GAHANNA 43230 . . . . (614) 416-8028
BARGE WAGGONER SUMNER & CANNON
8280 YANKEE ST, DAYTON 45458 . . . . (937) 438-0378
BBC & M ENGINEERING
8555 SWEET VALLEY DR #S, CLEVELAND 44125 . . . . (440) 585-9995
BENNETT & WILLIAMS INC
2700 E DUBLIN GRANVILLE #400, COLUMBUS 43231 . . . . . (614) 882-9122
BHE ENVIRONMENTAL
1335 DUBLIN RD #126D, COLUMBUS 43215 . . . . (614) 487-7831
BROWN & CALDWELL
2674 FEDERATED BLVD, COLUMBUS 43235 . . . . (614) 410-6144
BRUMBAUGH & HERRICK
3026 STRATHMOOR AVE, TOLEDO 43614 . . . . (419) 475-1253
BURGESS & NIPLE LTD
5085 REED RD, COLUMBUS 43220 . . . . (614) 459-2050
CAMP DRESSER & MCKEE INC
1100 SUPERIOR AVE E #620, CLEVELAND 44114 . . . . (216) 579-0404
8805 GOVERNORS HILL DR #260, CINCINNATI 45249 . . . . (513) 583-9800
CHEM-TECH CONSULTANTS INC
559 STATE RT 97 E, BELLVILLE 44813 . . . . (419) 886-4375
CLEAN CEMP-CONSTRUCTION ENGRNG
3619 WALTON AVE #5, CLEVELAND 44113 . . . . (216) 651-3000
CONESTOGA ROVER & ASSOC
7704 MILAN RD, SANDUSKY 44870 . . . . (419) 609-1339
CRA INC
9033 MERIDIAN WAY, W CHESTER 45069 . . . . (513) 942-4750
DLZ OHIO INC
6121 HUNTLEY RD, COLUMBUS 43229 . . . . (614) 848-4141
EASTON ENVIRONMENTAL ENGINEER
337 SLATE RUN DR, POWELL 43065 . . . . (740) 549-9938
EDP CONSULTANTS INC
9375 CHILLICOTHE RD, WILLOUGHBY 44094 . . . . (440) 256-6500
EHS TECHNOLOGY GROUP
PO BOX 3040, MIAMISBURG 45343 . . . . (937) 865-3553
EMH & T INC
170 MILL ST, GAHANNA 43230 . . . . (614) 471-5150
ENVIROMATRIX
PO BOX 488, BATH 44210 . . . . (216) 524-0888
ENVIROMENTAL CONTROL LABS
38818 TAYLOR PKWY, ELYRIA 44035 . . . . (440) 353-3700
ENVIRONMENTAL ENGINEERING SVC
3575 COLUMBIA RD, LEBANON 45036 . . . . (513) 934-1512
ENVIRONMENTAL TECH & COMMS INC
31 TRIANGLE PARK DR #3103, CINCINNATI 45246 . . . . . . (513) 772-7903
ERM-MIDWEST INC
8101 N HIGH ST #30, COLUMBUS 43235 . . . . (614) 433-7900
FINKBEINER PETTIS & STROUT INC
310 W LAKESIDE AVE #100, CLEVELAND 44113 . . . . (216) 781-6177
FOPPE TECHNICAL GROUP INC
11415 CENTURY CIR W, CINCINNATI 45246 . . . . (513) 671-8144
FRANKLIN-CT CONSULTANTS INC
2700 E DUBLIN GRANVILLE RD, COLUMBUS 43231 . . . . . (614) 891-6000
FRX INC
11582 KEMPER WOODS DR, CINCINNATI 45249 . . . . (513) 469-6040
FULLER MOSSBARGER SCOTT & MAY
10018 INTERNATIONAL BLVD, CINCINNATI 45246 . . . . . . (513) 860-1070
6600 BUSCH BLVD # 100, COLUMBUS 43229 . . . . (614) 846-1400
GANDEE & ASSOC INC
4488 MOBILE DR, COLUMBUS 43220 . . . . (614) 459-8338
GARRETT & CLEMMER INC
2398 E ENTERPRISE PKWY, TWINSBURG 44087 . . . . (330) 425-7901
GEOTECHNICAL CONSULTANTS INC
720 GREEN CREST DR, WESTERVILLE 43081 . . . . (614) 895-1400
HAMILTON ENGINEERING & CNSLTNG
3999 PARKWAY LN, HILLIARD 43026 . . . . (614) 684-0077
HARDING ESE
521 BYERS RD #101, MIAMISBURG 45342 . . . . (937) 859-3600
HAZCORP ENVIRONMENTAL SVC
404 S REYNOLDS RD, TOLEDO 43615 . . . . (419) 537-6000
HULL & ASSOC INC
3401 GLENDALE AVE #300, TOLEDO 43614 . . . . (419) 385-2018
6161 COCHRAN RD #A, CLEVELAND 44139 . . . . (440) 519-2555
6397 EMERALD PKWY #200, DUBLIN 43016 . . . . (614) 793-8777
4900 PARKWAY DR #100, MASON 45040 . . . . (513) 459-9677
I T CORP
5050 SECTION AVE, CINCINNATI 45212 . . . . (513) 782-4700
JERRY HAMMOND & ASSOC
137 E STATE ST, COLUMBUS 43215 . . . . (614) 621-3222
JONES & HENRY ENGINEERS INC
2000 W CENTRAL AVE, TOLEDO 43606 . . . . (419) 473-9611
KIRK & BLUM MFG CO
3120 FORRER ST, CINCINNATI 45209 . . . . (513) 458-2600
LAWHON & ASSOC INC
975 E WIND DR #190, WESTERVILLE 43081 . . . . (513) 936-9233
LEWANDOWSKI ENGINEERS
234 N ERIE ST, TOLEDO 43624 . . . . (419) 255-4111
M S CONSULTANTS INC
2221 SCHROCK RD, COLUMBUS 43229 . . . . (614) 898-7100
MALCOLM PIRNIE INC
5800 CLEVELAND MEMORIAL SH, CLEVELAND 44102 . . . . (216) 631-8172

MCCARTHY ENVIRONMENTAL
100 FENWAY RD, COLUMBUS 43214 . . . . (614) 436-5879
MCNAMEE INDUSTRIAL SVC
420 MADISON AVE, TOLEDO 43604 . . . . (419) 255-4497
MIAMI GROUP INC
1048 BAXTER RD, LOVELAND 45140 . . . . (513) 683-3326
MIDDOUGH ENVIRONMENTAL SVC INC
1901 E 13TH ST #400, CLEVELAND 44114 . . . . (216) 367-6000
OXBOW RIVER & STREAM RSTRTN
2905 KLONDIKE RD, DELAWARE 43015 . . . . (740) 362-4134
PARSONS ENGINEERING SCIENCE
2443 CROWNE POINT DR, CINCINNATI 45241 . . . . (513) 326-3040
PARSONS TRANSPORTATION GROUP
902 N CAPITOL AVE #301, INDIANAPOLIS, IN 46204 . . . . . (614) 543-7030
PEGASUS TECHNICAL SVC
10901 REED HARTMAN HWY #203, CINCINNATI 45242 . . . . (513) 793-0094
PROFESSIONAL SERVICE IND
4960 VULCAN AVE #C, COLUMBUS 43228 . . . . (614) 876-8000
PSARA TECHNOLOGIES INC
10925 REED HARTMAN HWY #220, CINCINNATI 45242 . . . . (513) 791-4418
R D ZANDE & ASSOC INC
11500 NORTHLAKE DR #150, CINCINNATI 45249 . . . . . . (513) 769-5009
R E WARNER & ASSOC
25777 DETROIT RD #200, WESTLAKE 44145 . . . . (440) 835-9400
RAYMOND PROFESSIONAL GROUP INC
550 W VAN BUREN ST #500, CHICAGO, IL 60607 . . . . . . (630) 771-1827
RCE - NORTHWEST OHIO
28 LANSDOWNE RD, TOLEDO 43623 . . . . (888) 940-9800
RED WING ENGINEERING
3791 BAKER RD, ALBANY 45710 . . . . (740) 698-6056
REED & ASSOC INC
11500 ROCKFIELD CT, CINCINNATI 45241 . . . . (513) 772-8686
ROY F WESTON INC
6777 ENGLE RD, CLEVELAND 44130 . . . . (440) 888-6317
2566 KOHNLE DR, MIAMISBURG 45342 . . . . (937) 384-4200
SAFE X
140 N OTTERBINE AVE, WESTERVILLE 43081 . . . . (614) 890-0800
SCS ENGINEERS
2060 READING RD #200, CINCINNATI 45202 . . . . (513) 421-5353
SOLAR TESTING LABORATORIES
5399 LANCASTER DR #1, CLEVELAND 44131 . . . . (216) 741-7007
SPENCE ENVIRONMENTAL CONSULTNG
12671 OAKMERE DR, PICKERINGTON 43147 . . . . (614) 755-4750
STEPHEN J SEBESTA & ASSOC
6777 ENGLE RD #O, CLEVELAND 44130 . . . . (440) 781-0060
STONE ENVIRONMENTAL
14 W 1ST ST, DAYTON 45402 . . . . (937) 223-5807
6460 BUSCH BLVD #105, COLUMBUS 43229 . . . . (614) 888-8041
SYRACUSE RESEARCH CORP
2300 MONTANA AVE #217, CINCINNATI 45211 . . . . (513) 542-2296
T M GATES INC
787 ROUND BOTTOM RD, MILFORD 45150 . . . . (513) 248-1025
TETRA TECH
250 W COURT ST #200W, CINCINNATI 45202 . . . . (513) 241-0149
TRINITY ENGINEERING ASSOC
8832 FALMOUTH DR, CINCINNATI 45231 . . . . (513) 521-3515
URS CORP
800 W ST CLAIR AVE, CLEVELAND 44113 . . . . (216) 622-2400
277 W NATIONWIDE BLVD, COLUMBUS 43215 . . . . (614) 464-4500
WATSON MONTGOMERY
1300 E 9TH ST #1100, CLEVELAND 44114 . . . . (513) 241-9522
WEBCO ENVIRONMENTL MGMT INC
6645 MIAMI TRAILS DR, LOVELAND 45140 . . . . (513) 605-8999

ENGINEERS-INDUSTRIAL

ARISE INC
6940 S EDGERTON RD, CLEVELAND 44141 . . . . (440) 746-8860
BREAKTHROUGH PERFORMANCE INC
308 EASTMOOR BLVD, COLUMBUS 43209 . . . . (614) 231-1777
FUTURE SYSTEMS INTL
4811 OLD HICKORY PL, DAYTON 45426 . . . . (937) 274-9414
INDUSTRIAL ENGINEERING TECH
3539 GLENDALE AVE, TOLEDO 43614 . . . . (419) 385-1233
MR TECH INC
PO BOX 1746, W CHESTER 45071 . . . . (513) 755-6675
VENTURA ENGINEERING
7610 OLENTANGY RIVER RD #100, COLUMBUS 43235 . . . . (614) 847-1110

ENGINEERS-MECHANICAL

ADI MACHINING
4686 FRENCH CREEK RD, SHEFFIELD VLG 44054 . . . . . . (440) 277-4141
ANDON JERAR
98 LOMA MEDIA RD, SANTA BARBARA, CA 93103 . . . . . . (805) 965-7707
APPLIED ENGINEERING GROUP
7402 E BROAD ST, BLACKLICK 43004 . . . . (614) 322-7050
APPLIED THERMAL ENGINEERING
7400 BROWN RD #200, OSTRANDER 43061 . . . . (740) 666-4872
BOILER & BURNER SYSTEMS
1130 CONGRESS AVE #C, CINCINNATI 45246 . . . . (513) 772-3963
C G TECH
PO BOX 157, FINDLAY 45839 . . . . (419) 420-0096
CTL ENGINEERING INC
P O BOX 44548, COLUMBUS 43204 . . . . (614) 276-8123

ENGINEERS-MECHANICAL (Cont'd)

DYNAMECH DESIGN LTD
751 CHERITON DR, CLEVELAND 44143 .... (440) 442-6774
E QUEST
1983 W 28TH ST, CLEVELAND 44113 .... (216) 621-9490
ENGINEERING ELEMENTS INC
4950 E 345TH ST, WILLOUGHBY 44094 .... (440) 951-6700
FACILICORP
11400 GROOMS RD, CINCINNATI 45242 .... (513) 469-7000
FORCE DESIGN INC
20 HIGH ST, COVINGTON 45318 .... (937) 473-3737
FUTURE ENGINEERED PRODUCTS
2742 W SPRAGUE RD, CLEVELAND 44134 .... (440) 888-1616
IMPRESSION TECHNOLOGY
1730 E ALEX BELL RD, DAYTON 45459 .... (937) 428-5641
INTERTECH DESIGN SVC INC
9900 CARVER RD #200, CINCINNATI 45242 .... (513) 791-5588
ITE INTEGRATED TECHNOLOGIES
424 WARDS CORNER RD, LOVELAND 45140 .... (513) 576-6200
K B ENGINEERING
6939B WATKINS RD, DELAWARE 43015 .... (614) 299-0803
NAV-TECH INDUSTRIES INC
505 HIGHLAND RD E, MACEDONIA 44056 .... (330) 467-7301
OXFORD RESOURCE GROUP
PO BOX 621223, CINCINNATI 45262 .... (513) 777-2111
PATRIOT ENGINEERING CO
16937 MUNN RD, CHAGRIN FALLS 44023 .... (440) 543-3100
PINNACLE INC
8035 DARBYS RUN, CHAGRIN FALLS 44023 .... (440) 543-4333
POWER ENGINEERING
7840 COLTON LN, CINCINNATI 45236 .... (513) 793-5800
PRATER ENGINEERING ASSOC
6130 WILCOX RD, DUBLIN 43016 .... (614) 766-4896
PREFERRED ENGINEERING ASSOC
7778 COLERAIN AVE, CINCINNATI 45239 .... (513) 931-7973
PROGRESSIVE CONSULTING ENGNR
4700 REED RD #H, COLUMBUS 43220 .... (614) 451-4410
PROTHERM INC
18151 JEFFERSON PARK RD #101, CLEVELAND 44130 ..... (440) 234-2666
QUALITY MACHINE DESIGN CORP
4771 GERALDINE RD, CLEVELAND 44143 .... (216) 382-0177
REESE MACHINE CO
PO BOX 1396, ASHTABULA 44005 .... (440) 992-3942
SCHMIDT ASSOC
7333 FAIROAKS RD, CLEVELAND 44146 .... (440) 439-7300
STORK HERRON TESTING LABORATORIES INC
5405 E SCHAAF RD, CLEVELAND 44131 .... **(216) 524-1450**
STRUCTURE MECHANICS CORP
PO BOX 58177, CINCINNATI 45258 .... (513) 598-1600
TK ENGINEERING ASSOC INC
55 MERCHANT ST #220, CINCINNATI 45246 .... (513) 552-5013
WAFIOS MACHINERY CORP
7051 KRICK RD, CLEVELAND 44146 .... (440) 786-1518
WIKOFF CONCEPTS
11260 CORNELL PARK DR #702, CINCINNATI 45242 .... (513) 791-8558
ZDS DESIGN-CONSULTING SVC
11258 CORNELL PARK DR #600, CINCINNATI 45242 ...... (513) 247-0270

ENGINEERS-STRUCTURAL

BARBER & HOFFMAN INC
1100 W 9TH ST, CLEVELAND 44113 .... (216) 875-0100
BUDAI ENGINEERING INC
365 DUMBARTON BLVD, CLEVELAND 44143 .... (216) 531-5922
CDS ASSOC INC
11120 KENWOOD RD, CINCINNATI 45242 .... (513) 791-1700
CHRISTIAN & KLOPPER INC
3570 WARRENSVILLE CTR #106, CLEVELAND 44122 .... (216) 283-1300
CON AD SVC INC
502 SOTER PL, VANDALIA 45377 .... (937) 890-7603
DAVID L GERINGER PE
201 DITTO ST, ARCHBOLD 43502 .... (419) 446-2118
DYNATEK DEVELOPMENTAL SVC
PO BOX 175, TRANSFER, PA 16154 .... (330) 759-8404
DYNOTEC INC
1925 E DUBLIN GRANVILLE RD #106, COLUMBUS 43229 ..... (614) 880-7320
E A SATLER CONSULTING ENGINEER
4148 WHITE CEDAR PL, PERRY 44081 .... (440) 259-2848
EEMAN & BLINN INC
4351 DALE DR #250, DUBLIN 43017 .... (614) 791-1575
ERG STRUCTURAL ENGINEERS
7972 BLAIRHOUSE DR, CINCINNATI 45244 .... (513) 281-0209
FAST LARRY L
4615 MITCHAW RD, SYLVANIA 43560 .... (419) 885-4258
GENSERT BRETNALL ASSOC
29065 CLEMENS RD #400, CLEVELAND 44145 .... (440) 663-0208
HASBROUCK ENGINEERING
1080 KINGSMILL PKWY #110, COLUMBUS 43229 .... (614) 888-3918
HUFFMAN LEVIGNE ASSOC INC
26031 CENTER RIDGE RD #C, CLEVELAND 44145 .... (440) 899-2970
INFRASTRUCTURE SERVICES INC
55 E CUYAHOGA FALLS AVE, AKRON 44310 .... (330) 253-4888
J & Y ENGINEERING SVC
6777 ENGLE RD #B, CLEVELAND 44130 .... (440) 891-1130

J MULLER INTL
9771 BURTON DR, TWINSBURG 44087 .... (330) 405-5780
JACK D WALTERS & ASSOC
PO BOX 855, DUBLIN 43017 .... (614) 889-2516
JEZERINAC GEERS & ASSOC INC
5640 FRANTZ RD, DUBLIN 43017 .... (614) 766-0066
KABIL ASSOC INC
5900 SHARON WOODS BLVD #B, COLUMBUS 43229 .... (614) 899-6707
KAV CONSULTING ENGINEERS
1158 YELLOWSTONE RD, CLEVELAND 44121 .... (216) 381-7333
KLENKE THOMAS PE
4409 ANDREA DR, KETTERING 45429 .... (937) 294-8897
LANTZ JONES & NEBRASKA INC
1166 DUBLIN RD, COLUMBUS 43215 .... (614) 481-9800
LKL ENGINEERS
2735 N HOLLAND SYLVANIA RD #A2, TOLEDO 43615 .... (419) 578-0195
MODERN COMPUTATIONAL TECHS INC
8723 TIBURON DR, CINCINNATI 45249 .... (513) 745-0457
PAUL J FORD & CO
250 E BROAD ST #1500, COLUMBUS 43215 .... (614) 221-6679
PELLER & ASSOCIATES INC
821 WESTPOINT PARKWAY #910, CLEVELAND 44145 ..... (440) 899-1661
PINNACLE ENGINEERING INC
4520 COOPER RD #300, CINCINNATI 45242 .... (513) 984-1663
PRETZINGER ROBERT PE
2519 S DIXIE DR #2, DAYTON 45409 .... (937) 298-5411
RICHLAND ENGINEERING LTD
29 PARK ST N, MANSFIELD 44902 .... (419) 524-0074
ROBERT P MADISON INTL
2930 EUCLID AVE, CLEVELAND 44115 .... (216) 861-8195
ROSSI ASSOCIATES INC
PO BOX 140818, TOLEDO 43614 .... (419) 385-6633
S M HAW ASSOC INC
2234 E ENTERPRISE PKWY, TWINSBURG 44087 .... (330) 405-4480
SCOTT ENGINEERING INC
733 MOUNT PARNASSUS DR, GRANVILLE 43023 .... (614) 579-2482
SHELL & MEYER ASSOC INC
2202 S PATTERSON BLVD, DAYTON 45409 .... (937) 298-4631
SHEPHERD ENGINEERING
705 LAKEVIEW PLAZA BLVD, WORTHINGTON 43085 .... (614) 846-6889
SHIRK WILLIAM F
370 E WILSON BRIDGE RD, WORTHINGTON 43085 .... (614) 436-6465
SIGMART & ASSOC
PO BOX 351856, TOLEDO 43635 .... (419) 885-2049
SKJ ENGINEERING ASSOC INC
4895 MONROE ST #202, TOLEDO 43623 .... (419) 480-1394
SMITH ROBERTS & ASSOC INC
4010 EXECUTIVE PARK DR #400, CINCINNATI 45241 .... (513) 769-5111
STEVEN SCHAEFER ASSOC
10411 MEDALLION DR, CINCINNATI 45241 .... (513) 542-3300
STRUCTURAL DESIGN SYSTEMS
12875 ECKEL JUNCTION RD #A, PERRYSBURG 43551 ..... (419) 872-7103
THOMAS FOK & ASSOC LTD
278 MONROE ST NW, WARREN 44483 .... (330) 394-7624
THP LTD INC
100 E 8TH ST #9, CINCINNATI 45202 .... (513) 241-3222
TRUMAN P YOUNG & ASSOC
1216 E MCMILLAN ST #302, CINCINNATI 45206 .... (513) 861-5655
W R BIRD & CO
4525 INDIANOLA AVE, COLUMBUS 43214 .... (614) 261-0921
WORLINE & ASSOC INC
210 S MAIN ST, SWANTON 43558 .... (419) 825-1103
PO BOX 671, NAPOLEON 43545 .... (419) 592-9661

ENVIRONMENTAL-CONSULTANTS
*(See Also ENGINEERS—ENVIRONMENTAL; and
EXPERTS—ENVIRONMENTAL)*

CIERRA ENVIRONMENTAL
3015 QUEEN RD, RAVENNA 44266 .... (330) 325-0675
ENSAFE INC
4545 FULLER DR #326, IRVING, TX 75038 .... (901) 372-7962
ERATECH ENVIRONMENTAL
4505 INFIRMARY RD, W CARROLLTON 45449 .... (937) 859-8998
H C NUTTING COMPANY
611 LUNKEN PARK DR, CINCINNATI 45226 .... (513) 321-5816
HALEY & ALDRICH
465 MEDFORD ST, BOSTON, MA 02129 .... (617) 886-7400
MANNIK & SMITH GROUP INC
1800 INDIAN WOOD CIR, MAUMEE 43537 .... (419) 891-2222
MIAMI GEOLOGICAL SERVICES INC
P O BOX 462, W UNION 45693 .... (937) 587-2995
PAYNE FIRM INC
11231 CORNELL PARK DR, CINCINNATI 45242 .... (513) 489-2255
RD ZANDE & ASSOC INC
1500 LAKE SHORE DR, COLUMBUS 43204 .... (614) 486-4383
WAGNER ENVIRONMENTAL CONSULTANTS INC
PO BOX 465, TALLMADGE 44278 .... (330) 633-0660

ESCROW SERVICES
(See BANKS)

ESTATE LIQUIDATORS
(See Also APPRAISAL SERVICES; and AUCTIONEERS)

HOUSE OF WILHELM
17960 PEARL RD, STRONGSVILLE 44149 . . . . (440) 572-1932
N GOGOLICK & SON CORP
850 EUCLID AVE #901, CLEVELAND 44114 . . . . (216) 241-5422

EXECUTIVE SEARCH FIRMS
(See Also EMPLOYMENT AGENCIES; and LEGAL PLACEMENT SERVICES)

BASON ASSOC INC
250 E 5TH ST #1500, CINCINNATI 45202 . . . . (513) 762-7633
BELL ASSOCIATES
34 S MAIN ST, CHAGRIN FALLS 44022 . . . . (440) 247-9322
BRYAN & LOUIS RESEARCH
14055 CEDAR RD #302, CLEVELAND 44124 . . . . (440) 442-8744
CALLOS PERSONNEL SVC
3340 W MARKET ST, FAIRLAWN 44333 . . . . (330) 864-1220
CAPPAMORE INC
7247 S KIPLING PL, PAINESVILLE 44077 . . . . (440) 357-7631
CAPSTONE SEARCH GROUP
2460 NORTHWEST BLVD, COLUMBUS 43221 . . . . (614) 486-1388
CAREER PLANNING
24600 CENTER RIDGE RD #460, CLEVELAND 44145 . . . . (440) 899-0161
CONNECTING CLEVELAND
8039 BROADMOOR RD #12, MENTOR 44060 . . . . (440) 942-1775
CONSULT FORBES
1149 REGENCY DR, COLUMBUS 43220 . . . . (614) 538-1109
CONTINENTAL SEARCH ASSOC
PO BOX 14, PICKERINGTON 43147 . . . . (513) 921-3946
CORNERSTONE HEALTH SVC
PO BOX 282, WICKLIFFE 44092 . . . . (440) 944-3365
CORNERSTONE PARTNERS
1240 MARLYN DR, COLUMBUS 43220 . . . . (614) 481-9080
COURTNEY TEMPORARY SVCS
PO BOX 340013, COLUMBUS 43234 . . . . (614) 761-3337
DANKOWSKI & ASSOC
6479 STONEY RIDGE RD, N RIDGEVILLE 44039 . . . . (440) 327-8717
DEFFET GROUP INC
7801 MARYSVILLE RD, OSTRANDER 43061 . . . . (740) 666-7600
DELTA MEDICAL SEARCH ASSOC
844 BROOKPARK RD #101, MARION 43302 . . . . (614) 878-0550
DEVLIN GROUP
56 MILFORD DR #403, HUDSON 44236 . . . . (330) 342-5636
DISE & CO
20600 CHAGRIN BLVD #925, CLEVELAND 44122 . . . . (216) 752-1700
FAST SWITCH LTD
37 W BRIDGE ST #200, DUBLIN 43017 . . . . (614) 336-3690
GAMMILL GROUP
9200 WORTHINGTON RD #101, WESTERVILLE 43082 . . . . . . (614) 848-7726
GARDNER MALIN & ASSOC
20600 CHAGRIN BLVD, BEACHWOOD 44122 . . . . (216) 283-3311
GAYHART & ASSOC
1250 OLD RIVER RD #2, CLEVELAND 44113 . . . . (216) 861-7010
GRISCHAM & PROUT
1111 SUPERIOR AVE E, CLEVELAND 44114 . . . . (216) 771-5530
GROM JOHN C
868 THELMA DR, WADSWORTH 44281 . . . . (330) 336-2213
HALF ROBERT
277 W NATIONWIDE BLVD #200, COLUMBUS 43215 . . . . (614) 365-7442
HARCOURT GROUP LTD
2178 HARCOURT DR, CLEVELAND 44106 . . . . (216) 791-6000
HARRIS & ASSOC
4236 TULLER RD, DUBLIN 43017 . . . . (614) 798-8500
HEIDRICK & STRUGGLES
600 SUPERIOR AVE E, CLEVELAND 44114 . . . . (216) 241-0020
HITE EXECUTIVE SEARCH
1300 LAKE RD, CONNEAUT 44030 . . . . (440) 599-1600
KESIC & CO
23400 MERCANTILE RD #5, BEACHWOOD 44122 . . . . (216) 378-2020
LAUGHLIN & ASSOCS
129 TWIN LAKES DR, FAIRFIELD 45014 . . . . (513) 772-1082
MAIOLA & CO
12900 LAKE AVE #29, CLEVELAND 44107 . . . . (216) 521-0011
MANAGEMENT RECRUITERS
8039 BROADMOOR RD #20, MENTOR 44060 . . . . (440) 946-2355
10104 BREWSTER LN #150, POWELL 43065 . . . . (614) 336-3637
38036 2ND ST, WILLOUGHBY 44094 . . . . (440) 953-9559
8 E 4TH ST, CINCINNATI 45202 . . . . (513) 742-9424
1900 W MARKET ST, AKRON 44313 . . . . (330) 867-2900
20600 CHAGRIN BLVD #703, BEACHWOOD 44122 . . . . (216) 561-6776
200 PUBLIC SQ #31, CLEVELAND 44114 . . . . (216) 696-1122
MANNING GROUP
700 W ST CLAIR AVE #218, CLEVELAND 44113 . . . . (216) 664-1857
MAS RESOURCES CORP
4042 INDIAN RIPPLE RD #B, DAYTON 45440 . . . . (937) 431-1000
MIDWEST EXECUTIVES INC
4825 BRANTFORD CT, W CHESTER 45069 . . . . (513) 942-7286
MRI-CLEVE
9930 JOHNNYCAKE RIDGE RD #3F, MENTOR 44060 . . . . . . (440) 352-7599
NORTHPOINT PROFESSIONAL SEARCH
4570 FISHCREEK RD, STOW 44224 . . . . (330) 655-3655
POOLE PROFESSIONAL RESOURCES
3011 BETHEL RD, COLUMBUS 43220 . . . . (614) 538-0321

PRECISION SEARCH INC
10357 BELLEAU DR, TWINSBURG 44087 . . . . (330) 963-4943
PREMIER SEARCH ASSOC
8114 DANBURY CT, MENTOR 44060 . . . . (440) 209-7736
PROFESSIONAL SEARCH
PO BOX 20245, COLUMBUS 43220 . . . . (614) 457-7789
PROVIDENCE PERSONNEL CONSLNTS
2404 4TH ST #1, CUYAHOGA FALLS 44221 . . . . (330) 929-6431
RATLIFF & TAYLOR
31105 BAINBRIDGE RD #4, SOLON 44139 . . . . (216) 328-9494
READ SOURCE LTD
8417 KIRKALDY CT, DUBLIN 43017 . . . . (614) 764-8666
REQUEST PEOPLE
1930 N OLD STATE RD, DELAWARE 43015 . . . . (614) 267-7200
REVERE ASSOCIATES
PO BOX 498, BATH 44210 . . . . (330) 666-6442
RICHARD L BENCIN & ASSOC
8553 TIMBER TR, BRECKSVILLE 44141 . . . . (440) 526-6726
RICHARDS TERRY
36 PUBLIC SQ, WILLOUGHBY 44094 . . . . (440) 918-1800
ROGISH ASSOC
615 COPELAND MILL RD, WESTERVILLE 43081 . . . . (614) 899-2525
ROSE SANFORD ASSOC
2280 HENDERSON RD #214, COLUMBUS 43220 . . . . (614) 273-0874
428 BEECHER RD, COLUMBUS 43230 . . . . (614) 939-1309
SALES CONSULTANTS OF TOLEDO
5600 MONROE ST #206B, SYLVANIA 43560 . . . . (419) 882-5088
SEARCH MASTERS
1148 EUCLID AVE #509, CLEVELAND 44115 . . . . (216) 781-5311
SEARCH PRO 1
14701 DETROIT AVE, CLEVELAND 44107 . . . . (216) 226-1796
SEARCHMARK MEDICAL
10466 TORRINGTON DR, POWELL 43065 . . . . (614) 760-5447
SELECTIVE SEARCH ASSOCS
4565 DRESSLER RD NW #106, CANTON 44718 . . . . (330) 494-5584
SELL & ASSOC
511 N PARK ST, COLUMBUS 43215 . . . . (614) 221-8199
SIDICK-MEYER GROUP
9 LIBERTY ST, COLUMBUS 43215 . . . . (614) 885-7210
TABB & ASSOC
PO BOX 340888, COLUMBUS 43234 . . . . (614) 880-0000
TECH PERSONNEL STAFFING
11590 CENTURY BLVD #119, CINCINNATI 45246 . . . . (513) 779-7753
TECHSOURCE SOLUTIONS
35249 SPINNAKER DR, AVON LAKE 44012 . . . . (440) 725-8101
TIM SPRINGER & ASSOC
230 INDIAN RUN RD, DUBLIN 43017 . . . . (614) 792-5701
URBANA RECRUITING OFFICE
1412 N MAIN ST, URBANA 43078 . . . . (937) 484-3016
VORTECHS GROUP
8227 CHATEAU LN, WESTERVILLE 43082 . . . . (614) 755-2222
WARNER & ASSOC INC
101 E COLLEGE AVE, WESTERVILLE 43081 . . . . (614) 891-9003
WELLS INC
PO BOX 21010, COLUMBUS 43221 . . . . (614) 876-0651
YAEKLE & CO
65 DENISON DR, GRANVILLE 43023 . . . . (740) 587-7366
YORK & ASSOC
51 N 3RD ST #409, NEWARK 43055 . . . . (740) 345-0400

EXHIBITS
(See COURTROOM EXHIBITS)

EXPERT REFERRAL SERVICES

PRIDE CONSULTING
787 ONEIDA TRAIL, FRANKLIN LKS, NJ 07417 . . . . (212) 650-5203
TASA GROUP THE
See Our Display Ad Under This Heading
WWW.TASANET.COM . . . . **(800) 523-2319**
WOLF TECHNICAL SVCS
6836 HAWTHORN PARK DR, INDIANAPOLIS, IN 46220 . . . . . . (317) 842-6075

EXPERTS

The individuals and businesses listed in the following fields of specialty have designated themselves as available to the legal community for a wide range of services, including review, consultation, investigation, research and testimony:

-ACCIDENTS	-CRIME SCENES	-FIREARMS	-PHOTOGRAPHY
-ACCOUNTING	-DENTAL	-FORENSICS	-PODIATRY
-ACOUSTICS	-DOCUMENTS	-FRAUD	-PSYCHIATRIC
-ACTUARIAL	-DRINKING & DRIVING	-GEOLOGY	-PSYCHOLOGICAL
-AGRICULTURAL	-ECONOMICS	-HORTICULTURE	-REAL ESTATE
-APPRAISING	-EDUCATIONAL	-INSURANCE	-RECREATION & SAFETY
-ARCHITECTURAL	-ELEVATORS	-MARITIME	-SAFETY & SECURITY
-AUDIO & VIDEO	-EMPLOYABILITY	-MEDICAL	-SURVEYING
-AVIATION	-ENGINEERING	-METALLURGICAL	-TELECOMMUNICATIONS
-CHEMISTRY	-ENTOMOLOGY	-METEOROLOGY &	-TOXICOLOGY
-CHIROPRACTIC	-ENVIRONMENTAL	WEATHER	-TRAFFIC
-COMPUTERS	-ERGONOMICS	-NEUROPSYCHOLOGY	-TRANSPORTATION
-CONSTRUCTION	-FINANCIAL	-NURSING	-WOOD SCIENCES
-CONSUMER PRODUCTS	-FIRE & ARSON	-PATHOLOGY	

*Help a business associate. Do you know of any expert witnesses who should be listed in **the legal pages**®? Contact (800) 444-4041, ext. 4.*

EXPERTS-ACCIDENTS

(See Also ACCIDENT RECONSTRUCTION SERVICES)

ACCIDENT RECONSTRUCTION SVCS
202 GERRYMANDER AVE, SONORA, CA 95370 . . . . (209) 532-6459
ARCCA INC
2288 2ND ST PIKE, PENNSPARK, PA 18943 . . . . (215) 598-9750
AUTOMOBILE COLLISION CAUSE ANALYSIS
2768 GRANDVIEW ST, SAN DIEGO, CA 92110 . . . . (619) 275-1455
BARNES RESEARCH GROUP
2625 SPALDING DR, LAS VEGAS, NV 89134 . . . . (702) 360-6660
BARNES W MCCORMICK PHD PE
611 GLENN RD, STATE COLLEGE, PA 16803 . . . . (814) 863-0602
CARS INC
5258 N BEACON DR, YOUNGSTOWN 44515 . . . . (330) 503-1070
ENGLISH WILLIAM
PO BOX 985, ALVA, FL 33920 . . . . (239) 728-3254
KOBAYASHI TED
59 RICKENBACKER CIR, LIVERMORE, CA 94550 . . . . (415) 447-6495
LEADING TECH FORENSIC
WWW.LTFEXPERTS.COM . . . . (419) 452-6992
LITIGATION CONSULTANT UNITED PERSONNEL SVCS
1735 CRISLER WAY, LOS ANGELES, CA 90069 . . . . (415) 327-2300
LS HARRIS CORPORATION
30285 BRUCE INDSTRL PKWY #C2, CLVLND 44139 **(440) 331-1443**
MORRIS & WARD CONSULTING ENGINEERS
4938 HAMPDEN LN #114, BETHESDA, MD 20814 . . . . (301) 320-4900
NUGENT OWEN J JR
208 WYNCOTE RD, JENKINTOWN, PA 19046 . . . . (215) 887-0626
RICHMAN DENNIS A
8240 ROUTE 83, HARTLAND, WI 53029 . . . . (414) 966-7355
TAYLOR JAMES A
3510 KIRKWOOD DR, FAIRFAX, VA 22031 . . . . (703) 591-5593
TIRE CONSULTANTS INC
3330 LAKEWIND WAY, ALPHARETTA, GA 30202 . . . . (800) 882-7006
TONER ASSOCIATES
5446 OTTAWATTAMIE DR, PENTWATER, MI 49449 . . . . (810) 683-8390

EXPERTS-ACCOUNTING

AMERICAN EXPRESS TAX & BUSINESS SVCS
1185 AVE OF THE AMERICAS 5TH FL, NEW YORK, NY 10036 . (212) 372-1242
COHEN MORRIS A
1601 MARKET ST, PHIL . . . . (215) 567-8000
DAVID R SNYDER CPA INC
See Our Display Ad Under This Heading
4097 YOUNGSTOWN RD SE, WARREN 44484 . . . **(330) 369-3961**
HALL KISTLER & COMPANY LLP
220 MARKET AVENUE S #700, CANTON 44702 . . . . (330) 453-7633
INVESTIGATIVE & FORENSIC ACCOUNTING SERVICES LLC
6100 OAK TREE BLVD, INDEPENDENCE 44131 . . . . (216) 643-6784
JOHN & DOTY CPA INC
563 W SPRING ST, LIMA 45801 . . . . (419) 222-6826
MARKS PANETH & SHRON LLP
622 THIRD AVE, NEW YORK, NY 10017 . . . . (212) 503-8853
PLANTE & MORAN L L P
65 E STATE ST #600, COLUMBUS 43215 . . . . (614) 791-9200
SCHNEIDER DOWNS & CO INC
WWW.SCHNEIDERDOWNS.COM . . . . (614) 621-4060
SS&G FINANCIAL SERVICES
See Our Display Ad Under This Heading
WWW.SSANDG.COM . . . . **(800) 869-1834**
TUCKER ALAN INC
100 W BIG BEAVER RD #200, TROY, MI 48084 . . . . (248) 526-0500
WISEHART & WISEHART INC
WWW.WISEHART-WISEHART.COM . . . . (614) 791-2100

EXPERTS-ACOUSTICS

MILLER HENNING ASSOCS INC
  23 WHITTIER AVE #101, MCLEAN, VA 22101 . . . . (703) 506-0005

EXPERTS-ACTUARIAL

BURROWS RICHARD A FSA MAAA
  110 E STATE ST #3, KENNETT SQ, PA 19348 . . . . (610) 444-1820
J L PENSION ACTUARIAL
  400 E MAIN ST, LANSDALE, PA 19446 . . . . (215) 362-2248

EXPERTS-AGRICULTURAL

BANCROFT ROBERT PHD
  HC #64 BX 582A, WESTFORD, VT 05494 . . . . (802) 879-7386
BOMMER ROBERT H JR
  2701 WHITNEY DR, YORK, PA 17402 . . . . (717) 741-3010
DELLAVALLE LABORATORY INC
  1910 W MCKINLEY, FRESNO, CA 93728 . . . . (559) 233-6129
GEOPHYTA INC
  2685 COUNTY RD 254, VICKERY 43464 . . . . (419) 547-8538
RICKS H PLUENNEKE & ASSOC
  6155 DICK PRICE RD, FT WORTH, TX 76140 . . . . (817) 478-0761

EXPERTS-APPRAISING

(See Also APPRAISAL SERVICES)

EQUINE APPRAISING
  3031 COVENTRYVILLE RD, POTTSTOWN, PA 19465 . . . . (610) 469-0433

EXPERTS-ARCHITECTURAL

DELLINGER ARCHITECTS
  6920 PLAINFIELD RD, CINCINNATI 45236 . . . . (513) 793-9055
NBBJ
  1555 LAKE SHORE DR, COLUMBUS 43204 . . . . (614) 224-7145
RICHARD FLEISCHMAN & PARTNERS-ARCHITECTS & PLANNERS
  1025 HURON RD, CLEVELAND 44115 . . . . (216) 771-0090

EXPERTS-AUDIO & VIDEO

TEAM AUDIO
  See Our Display Ad Under This Heading
  WWW.AUDIORESTORATION.COM . . . . **(419) 243-3000**

EXPERTS-AVIATION

AIROSCOPE INC
  11750 AIRPORT WY #B12B, BROOMFIELD, CO 80021 . . . . (303) 465-4414
COASTAL AVIATION INDUSTRIES INC
  14 MIRY BROOK RD, DANBURY, CT 06810 . . . . (203) 748-7303
HICKSONS DOWNEY & TRAVELSTED
  PO BOX 3250, BOWLING GREEN, KY 42101 . . . . (502) 782-3580
MARKOWSKI MICHAEL A
  1 OAKGLADE CIR, HUMMELSTOWN, PA 17036 . . . . (717) 566-0468
ROBERT SHAW CONSULTING
  190 OAKHILL DR, LOMPOC, CA 93436 . . . . (805) 733-1414
WACHS MILLER A
  852 WILCOXSON AVE, STRATFORD, CT 06497 . . . . (203) 380-2499

EXPERTS-CHEMISTRY

*(See Also LABORATORIES—TESTING; and
ENGINEERS—CHEMICAL)*

ADHESIVE CONSULTANTS INC
  383 STANTON AVE, AKRON 44301 . . . . (330) 773-9161
AL-SAIGH ZEKI PHD
  4225 UNIVERSITY AVE, COLUMBUS, GA 31907 . . . . (706) 568-2075

CARLITZ IRWIN H
  6529 N 13TH ST, PHIL 19126 . . . . (215) 924-1144
CHEMSULTANTS INC
  9349 HAMILTON DRIVE, MENTOR 44060 . . . . (440) 352-0218
GEORGETOWN UNIVERSITY
  37TH & O STREETS NW, WASHINGTON, DC 20057 . . . . (202) 625-4065
GIRARD JAMES
  6328 KARMICH ST, FAIRFAX STA, VA 22039 . . . . (703) 425-4280
GREENWOOD LABORATORIES
  437 GREENWOOD RD, KENNETT SQ, PA 19348 . . . . (610) 388-7295
J PRANE INDUSTRIAL CONSULTANT
  213 CHUCH RD, ELKINS PK, PA 19027 . . . . (215) 635-2008
KHB CONSULTING SVCS
  1212 ELMWOOD AVE, EVANSTON, IL 60202 . . . . (866) 243-6397
LEMKE ROBERT H
  PO BOX 1632, TULLYTOWN, PA 19007 . . . . (215) 946-3998
MICHELSON LABORATORIES INC
  6280 CHALET DR, COMMERCE, CA 90040 . . . . (213) 928-0553
POLYMER DIAGNOSTICS INC
  33587 WALKER RD, AVON LAKE 44012 . . . . (800) 438-2335
PURICONS INC
  101 QUAKER AVE, MALVERN, PA 19355 . . . . (610) 644-5488
SCIENTIFIC INVESTIGATIONS CO
  6719 MAINSGATE RD, WICHITA, KS 67226 . . . . (316) 651-0485
STORK HERRON TESTING LABORATORIES INC
  5405 E SCHAAF RD, CLEVELAND 44131 . . . . **(216) 524-1450**

EXPERTS-CHIROPRACTIC

(See Also EXPERTS-MEDICAL)

EDWARDS LONNEY D
  1570 N WISHON, FRESNO, CA 93728 . . . . (209) 266-7356
MCFARLAND DEBORAH DC
  221 FRONT ST SW, NEW PHILADELPHIA 44663 . . . . (330) 339-6730

EXPERTS-COMPUTERS

ASSIST.COM
  2790 FISHER RD STE A, COLUMBUS 43204 . . . . (614) 846-9000
INFOSCI INC
  BOX 7117, MENLO PK, CA 94026 . . . . (415) 854-1567
INTERHACK
  5 EAST LONG ST #1101, COLUMBUS 43215 . . . . (614) 545-4225
PETTEYS CONSULTING INC
  9270 KENT AVE NE, CANTON 41002 . . . . (877) 738-8397
RLRA INC
  3813 EASY ST, ALVARADO, TX 76009 . . . . (817) 790-6556
SS&G FINANCIAL SERVICES
  WWW.SSANDG.COM . . . . **(800) 869-1834**

EXPERTS-CONSTRUCTION

(See Also BUILDING INSPECTION SERVICES)

ARNOLD ENGINEERING CO INC
  20 MURON AVE, BELLINGHAM, MA 02109 . . . . (508) 883-3400
BARNES FRANKLIN C
  6423 HESPERIA AVE, RESEDA, CA 91311 . . . . (818) 708-9669
BKB ENTERPRISES INC
  17709 WHITEHEAD RD, LAGRANGE 44050 . . . . (440) 355-4307
BORNSTEIN BARRY A CONSTRUCTION CNSLTNTS
  400 GREENWOOD AVE, WYNCOTE, PA 19095 . . . . (215) 572-0666
CADY PHILIP D
  200 SHADY DR BX 158, LEMONT, PA 16851 . . . . (814) 238-5234
FERRARO & ASSOCIATES
  32800 PETTIBONE RD, CLEVELAND 44139 . . . . (330) 656-4697
INSTITUTE FOR PRODUCTS ENGINEERING & CONSTRUCTION
  34522 N SCOTTSDALE RD #D-8-160, SCOTTSDALE, AZ 85262 (888) 212-1155
JC CHEW CONSULTING INC
  8691 WESTFIELD RD BX 215, WESTFIELD CTR 44251 . . . . . . (330) 887-1400
JENNINGS & ASSOC
  333 DODD ST, E ORANGE, NJ 07017 . . . . (973) 672-1562
JHD ENTERPRISES
  7250 LEDGEWOOD DR, KIRTLAND 44094 . . . . (440) 256-9274
KOEHLER CONSTRUCTION INC
  3169 HERON CV, GOSHEN 45122 . . . . (513) 827-6800
MCHUGH BROS
  152 MONROE AVE, PENNDEL, PA 19047 . . . . (800) 624-8447
QEI ENGINEERS
  561 CONGRESS PARK DR, DAYTON 45459 . . . . (937) 438-8635
RL SEILER & ASSOC LLC
  PO BOX 215, DOYLESTOWN 44230 . . . . (330) 697-8555
SAM THOMPSON CONSTRUCTION
  827 2ND ST PK, SOUTHAMPTON, PA 18966 . . . . (215) 355-6989
WGK & ASSOCIATES INC
  6600 W 95TH ST #209, OVERLAND PK, KS 66212 . . . . (913) 648-0096

EXPERTS-CONSUMER PRODUCTS

*(See Also EXPERTS—SAFETY & SECURITY; and
EXPERTS—RECREATION & SAFETY)*

BTI CONSULTANTS
  1937 E BROADWAY RD, TEMPE, AZ 85282 . . . . (602) 967-1000

EXPERTS-CRIME SCENES
GARY A RINI MFS DABFE
    PO BOX 81098, CLEVELAND 44181 . . . . (440) 979-5271

EXPERTS-DENTAL
CAPTLINE ANTHONY M DR
    890 BEAVER GRADE RD, CORAOPOLIS, PA 15108 . . . . (412) 262-3370
GOLDBERG HERBERT DDS
    528 DELANCEY ST, PHIL 19106 . . . . (215) 925-9551
HIGDON SAMUEL J DDS
    2250 NW FLANDERS ST #111, PORTLAND, OR 97210 . . . . . . (503) 227-4844
KIRSCHNER HOWARD J
    338 BEACH 54TH ST, ROCKAWAY BCH, NY 11692 . . . . (800) 258-2113
MANNA RALPH JR DMD
    4701 DUKE ST, HARRISBURG, PA 17109 . . . . (717) 657-3441
MARKS JAY M DMD FAGD
    25 PADANARAM RD #93, DANBURY, CT 06811 . . . . (203) 792-3131
MEDILEX INC
    175 E 96TH ST #8H, NEW YORK, NY 10128 . . . . . **(888) 633-4539**
NEER RONALD L DDS
    22199 OSBORN RD, HIGGINSVILLE, MO 64037 . . . . (660) 584-5804
O'SHAUGHNESSY TERRENCE
    9245 PITCHING WEDGE, LAS VEGAS, NV 89134 . . . . (702) 240-4957

EXPERTS-DOCUMENTS
CHARLES BEHLOW ASSOCIATES
    1310 PENDLETON ST #807 UNIT 41, CINCINNATI 45202 . . . . (513) 651-5122
DAVENPORT VIRGINIA WINN
    11855 BURNING BEND ST, SAN ANTONIO, TX 78249 . . . . . . (512) 699-1922
DOCUMENT CONSULTANTS
    340 WINDSOR AVE, SOUTHAMPTON, PA 18966 . . . . (215) 357-3083
FORENSIC CONSULTANTS
    PO BOX 1177, PENNSAUKEN, NJ 08109 . . . . (800) 231-7891
FORENSIC EXAMINER OF QUESTIONED DOCUMENTS
    218 MERRYMONT DR, AUGUSTA, GA 30907 . . . . (706) 860-4267
GRIMES DAVID P
    8502 HITCHING POST LN, ALEXANDRIA, VA 22308 . . . . (703) 360-2715
HANDWRITING CONSULTANTS OF PA
    780 SOUTH 60TH, HARRISBURG, PA 17111 . . . . (717) 564-5769
KILLELEA THOMAS J
    42 CHESTNUT DR, CHELSEA, MI 48118 . . . . (313) 475-9977
MILLER JAMES T
    12716 BERMUDA LN, BOWIE, MD 20715 . . . . (301) 262-5213
ORTRUD KUNZMANN BOWMAN
    409 VALLEYBROOK DR, LANCASTER, PA 17601 . . . . (717) 569-6200
PATCHIS & WAYNE
    67 S FAIR ST, WARWICK, RI 02888 . . . . (401) 467-5641
PHILASCRIPT CO INC
    2131 WELSH RD #116, PHIL 19115 . . . . (215) 698-8411
RUSSO JOSEPH F
    27 SPRING VALLEY LN, STREAMWOOD, IL 60107 . . . . (708) 837-9348
SEIFER HANDWRITING CONSULTANTS
    PO BOX 32, KINGSTON, RI 02881 . . . . (401) 294-2414
SHANEYFELT LYNDAL
    6125 VERNON TERR, ALEXANDRIA, VA 22307 . . . . (703) 329-1331
SHIPP RICHARD L
    P O BOX 30172, CINCINNATI 45230 . . . . (513) 232-0844
SPECKIN FORENSIC
    1903 YMA TRAIL, OKEMOS, MI 48864 . . . . (517) 349-4014
WILKINSON R D
    244 S DILLWYN RD, NEWARK, DE 19711 . . . . (302) 366-0571
WILL EMILY
    PO BOX 58552, RALEIGH, NC 27658 . . . . (877) 699-7414
WILLARD VICKIE L
    526 SUPERIOR AVE #935, CLEVELAND 44114 . . . . (216) 520-1520

EXPERTS-DRINKING & DRIVING
DITZE DAVID
    500 PAXINOSA AVE, EASTON, PA 18042 . . . . (215) 258-5169

EXPERTS-ECONOMICS
ANALYSIS GROUP
    111 HUNTINGTON AVE, BOSTON, MA 02199 . . . . (617) 425-8000
ECONALYSIS
    PO BOX 35970, HOUSTON, TX 77235 . . . . (713) 728-3317
ECONOMIC EVALUATION GRP
    272 CHELTENHAM LN, MUNROE FALLS 44262 . . . . (330) 630-3363
ECONOMISTS INC
    1200 NEW HAMPSHIRE AV NW #400, WSHNGTN, DC 20036 . . (202) 223-4700
EDWARD ROSENBAUM INC
    29485 BERMUDA LN, SOUTHFIELD, MI 48076 . . . . (248) 357-0575
FARRELL BLOCH ASSOCIATES
    4813 41ST ST NW, WASHINGTON, DC 20016 . . . . (202) 362-5795
GUSTAFSON COLE R PHD
    3698 FAIRWAY, FARGO, ND 58102 . . . . (701) 280-9413
HUVER & ASSOC INC
    125 JOHN ROBERT THOMAS DR BX 1539, EXTON, PA 19341 . (610) 594-1999
LEGAL ECONOMETRICS INC
    1527 BASSWOOD CIR, GLENVIEW, IL 60025 . . . . (847) 729-6154
LEGAL ECONOMIC EVALUATIONS INC
    1000 ELWELL CT, PALO ALTO, CA 94303 . . . . (800) 221-6826

LITIGATION ECONOMICS LLC
    34 JEROME AVENUE, BLOOMFIELD, CT 06002 . . . . (860) 243-5862
MAHER CRAKES & ASSOC
    860 WARD LN, CHESHIRE, CT 06410 . . . . (203) 272-1205
MEDVOPRO
    3620 N HIGH ST, #B-4, COLUMBUS 43214 . . . . . . **(614) 539-1150**
NATHAN ASSOCIATES INC
    2101 WILSON BLVD, ARLINGTON, VA 22201 . . . . (703) 516-7700
RODGERS JAMES D
    347 KOEBNER CIRCLE, STATE COLLEGE, PA 16801 . . . . . . (814) 237-9322
WISEHART & WISEHART INC
    WWW.WISEHART-WISEHART.COM . . . . (614) 791-2100
WISNIEWSKI STANLEY C
    PO BOX 33367, WASHINGTON, DC 20033 . . . . (202) 223-9191

EXPERTS-EDUCATIONAL
FAR HORIZONS EDUCATIONAL CONSULTANTS
    955 PRINCESS DR, YARDLEY, PA 19067 . . . . (215) 493-1225
SCHOOL MATCH BY PUBLIC PRIORITY SYSTEMS INC
    5027 PINE CREEK DR, WESTERVILLE 43081 . . . . (614) 890-1573

EXPERTS-ELEVATORS
CUNNINGHAM JOE
    9709 S BLACKWELDER, OKLAHOMA CITY, OK 73159 . . . . . (405) 691-1272
DONNELLY & ASSOCIATES INC
    1807 GLENVIEW RD #207, GLENVIEW, IL 60025 . . . . (800) 248-7911

EXPERTS-EMPLOYABILITY

BARRETT & ASSOCIATES
    1772 STATE RD, CUYAHOGA FALLS 44223 . . . . (330) 928-2323
CASTON & ASSOCIATES INC
    10999 REED HARTMAN HWY #214, CINCINNATI 45242 . . . . . (513) 985-9151
CESTAR RAYMOND MD
    PO BOX 4478, WALLINGFORD, CT 06492 . . . . (203) 265-6676
CHAPMAN & ASSOCIATES
    PO BOX 831, MAUMEE 43537 . . . . (419) 867-7879
GROWICK BRUCE S PHD
    1945 N HIGH ST #356, COLUMBUS 43210 . . . . (614) 292-8463
HARTUNG & ASSOCS INC
    3911 BROADWAY, GROVE CITY 43123 . . . . (614) 871-6164
HR RESOURCES
    1716 N RD, WARREN 44484 . . . . (330) 399-1700
INDEPENDENT ASSESSMENT SERVICES
    33 DONALD DR #7, FAIRFIELD 45014 . . . . (513) 858-2300
JOHNSTON VOCATIONAL CONSULTING
    2915 85TH ST, LUBBOCK, TX 79432 . . . . (614) 314-3413
KENNETH J MANGES PHD AND ASSOCIATES INC
    105 W FOURTH ST, CINCINNATI 45202 . . . . (888) 590-9623

LEE DEBORAH MRC CRC LPC

VOCATIONAL SERVICES & CONSULTING
EMPLOYABILITY OPINION ASSESSMENT
LOSS OF EARNING CAPACITY

CLEVELAND 44129 . . . . **(440) 843-7147**

LM KAUFMAN & ASSOCS
    1979 HAVERTON DR, REYNOLDSBURG 43068 . . . . (614) 864-5806
LUSTBADER EDWARD DR
    1018 BELL LN, MAPLE GLEN, PA 19002 . . . . (215) 542-9380
MEDVOPRO
    See Our Display Ad Under This Heading
    3620 N HIGH ST, #B-4, COLUMBUS 43214 . . . . . . **(614) 539-1150**
PARMAN & ASSOCS INC
    4501 HILTON CORPORATE DR, COLUMBUS 43232 . . . . (614) 575-9400
REHABILITATION SUPPORT SVCS INC
    16 ELMDALE AVE, AKRON 44313 . . . . (330) 867-0170
RETURN TO WORK REHAB SVCS
    9553 CARROLL CT, LOVELAND 45140 . . . . (513) 683-6036

EXPERTS-EMPLOYABILITY (Cont'd)

VECTOR INC
13822 BEACH BLVD, WESTMINSTER, CA 92683 . . . . (714) 898-5533
VOCARE SERVICES INC
4670 RICHMOND RD #150, CLEVELAND 44128 . . . . (216) 514-1221
VOCATIONAL CONSULTATION SVCS INC
1350 W 5TH AVE #10A, COLUMBUS 43212 . . . . (614) 486-1378
VOCATIONAL REHAB CONSULTANTS
23250 CHAGRIN BLVD #425, BEACHWOOD 44122 . . . . (216) 397-0207
VOCATIONAL SVCS TEAM
5626 BROADVIEW RD, CLEVELAND 44134 . . . . (216) 635-7777

EXPERTS-ENGINEERING

(See Also ENGINEERS)

ACRE LAND SURVEYORS
PO BOX 600, FEASTERVILLE, PA 19053 . . . . (215) 752-2000
ANDERSON HILBERT J
2422 S QUEEN ST, YORK, PA 17402 . . . . (717) 741-0884
ARTHUR T FINE CO
9 NUTMEG LN, BLOOMFIELD, CT 06002 . . . . (203) 242-2942
BUSKE ENGINEERING
302 MARINA VILLAGE WY, BENICIA, CA 94510 . . . . (707) 745-6400
CHOU TSU-WEI
304 BARTRAN LN, HOCKESSIN, DE 19707 . . . . (302) 239-3175
CHRISTENSON CONSULTANTS INC
1123 GLENCOE AVE, PITTSBURGH, PA 15220 . . . . (412) 921-0115
CRITERIUM VAN SICKLE ENGINEERS
4421 HAMILTON CLEVES RD #6, HAMILTON 45013 . . . . (513) 738-4323
DILLING SCOTT A PE
6391 HARBORVIEW AVE NW, CANTON 44718 . . . . (330) 966-7251
ENGINEERING ANALYSIS ASSOC
28635 MOUND RD, WARREN, MI 48092 . . . . (586) 574-2332
FONDA ENGINEERING ASSOC
649 S HENDERSON RD C-307, KING OF PRUSSIA, PA 19406 . . (215) 337-3311

FORENSIC ANALYST

ROGER L BOYELL - ELECTRONICS
ELECTRICAL & COMMUNICATION SYSTEMS
E-MAIL: BOYELL@IEEE.ORG

WWW.BOYELL.COM . . . . (856) 234-5800

FRANK JOHN C
804 WHT OAKS CIR, PITTSBURGH, PA 15228 . . . . (412) 531-0514
FRUMERMAN ASSOC INC
5423 DARLINGTON RD, PITTSBURGH, PA 15217 . . . . (412) 371-7800
JOLTES RICHARD
4 QUAIL CT, EXPORT, PA 15632 . . . . (781) 246-5695

JORDAN CONSULTING SVCS
435 LA JOYA ST, SANT FE, NM 87501 . . . . (602) 893-2595
KMS ENGINEERING CONSULTANTS INC
See Our Display Ad Under This Heading
287 CHURCH HILL RD, VENETIA, PA 15367 . . . . . **(724) 348-7606**
900 E 8TH AV #300, KNG OF PRSSIA, PA 19406 . **(610) 768-8011**
67 PUBLIC SQ #500, WILKES-BARRE, PA 18701 . **(570) 825-9490**
LAMAR OLIVER D III
9641 OLD KUMMER RD, ALLISON PK, PA 15101 . . . . (412) 366-0824
LAWRENCE ARATA ASSOC
628 LAWSON AVE, HAVERTOWN, PA 19083 . . . . (215) 446-7079
LAWRENCE G SPIELVOGEL INC
203 HUGHES RD, KING OF PRUSSIA, PA 19406 . . . . (610) 783-6350
LEADING TECH FORENSIC
WWW.LTFEXPERTS.COM . . . . (419) 452-6992
LS HARRIS CORPORATION
See Our Display Ad Under This Heading
30285 BRUCE INDSTRL PKWY #C2, CLVLND 44139 **(440) 331-1443**
MAZER WILLIAM M
1421 34TH ST NW, WASHINGTON, DC 20007 . . . . (202) 338-0669
MCCABE ENGINEERING
529 N FRIESLAND DR, RICHBORO, PA 18954 . . . . (215) 355-3524
NORTHBROOK ENGINEERING
690 SANDERS RD, NORTHBROOK, IL 60062 . . . . (847) 272-8236
ORTH-RODGERS & ASSOC INC
230 S BROAD ST, PHIL 19102 . . . . (908) 218-1932
PBS ENGINEERING INC
7355 WILMINGTON PK, CENTERVILLE 45459 . . . . (937) 369-8227

PGM DIVERSIFIED INDUSTRIES

FORENSIC ENGINEERING - WE CAN PROVIDE:
UNIVERSITY AFFILIATED PHD EXPERTS
PRODUCT FAILURE ANALYSIS
SOFTWARE FAILURE ANALYSIS
COMPUTER ANIMATION / MODEL FABRICATION
ATTORNEY / JURY EDUCATION

6514 ALEXANDRIA DR, PARMA HTS 44130 . . . . **(440) 885-3500**
POWER SYSTEM SOLUTIONS
See Our Display Ad Under This Heading
6914 ASBURY CIRCLE NE, CANTON 44721 . . . . . **(330) 497-8250**
RALPH C DUMACK PE & ASSOC
102 BLUE SPRUCE LN, LEVITTOWN, PA 19054 . . . . (215) 945-4700
RIDGE & ASSOCIATES INC
PO BOX 1091, FINDLAY 45839 . . . . (419) 423-3641
ROBSON LAPINA
503 S FRONT ST #205, COLUMBUS 43215 . . . . (800) 654-4344

EXPERTS-ENGINEERING (Cont'd)

SCHACHT CONSULTING SERVICES
12 HOLLAND RD, PITTSBURGH, PA 15235 . . . . (412) 242-9906
STERLING MURRAY A
539 NEWPORT CIR E, LANGHORNE, PA 19047 . . . . (215) 357-7783
STORK HERRON TESTING LABORATORIES INC
5405 E SCHAAF RD, CLEVELAND 44131 . . . . **(216) 524-1450**
THOMPSON JOSEPH A PE
604 HAMPTON AVE, SOUTHAMPTON, PA 18966 . . . . (215) 322-0781
TVE CORP
3609 CHAPEL RD, NEWTOWN SQ, PA 19073 . . . . (610) 356-6100
UNIV OF PITTSBURGH
OHARA & N BOUQUET STS, PITTSBURGH, PA 15261 . . . . (412) 624-9727

EXPERTS-ENTOMOLOGY

ENTSULT ASSOCIATES INC
14 BOBBIE LN, RYE BROOK, NY 10573 . . . . (914) 939-0917
GARY NORMAN E PHD
U CAL-ENTOMOLOGY DEPT, DAVIS, CA 95616 . . . . (916) 752-0480

EXPERTS-ENVIRONMENTAL

*(See Also ENVIRONMENTAL—CONSULTANTS; and
ENGINEERS—ENVIRONMENTAL)*

AB ENVIRONMENTAL SERVICES
23 E MERCER AVE, HAVERTOWN, PA 19083 . . . . (610) 853-9370
ENGINEERS COLLABORATIVE INC
5 GARRISON PL, NEWTOWN, PA 18940 . . . . (215) 968-0762
ENVIRO TEAM
1280 SW 36TH AVE #104, POMPANO BEACH, FL 33069 . . . . . . (877) 440-9528
ENVIRONMENTAL RESEARCH ASSOC INC
414 MILL RD, HAVERTOWN, PA 19083 . . . . (610) 449-7400
H C NUTTING COMPANY
611 LUNKEN PARK DR, CINCINNATI 45226 . . . . (513) 321-5816
KERRI KENNETH D
5839 SHEPARD AVE, SACRAMENTO, CA 95819 . . . . (916) 456-3584
LINCOLN ENVIRONMENTAL INC
333 WASHINGTON HWY, SMITHFIELD, RI 02917 . . . . (978) 392-7971
MARCHESANI VINCENT J DR
980 WINDSONG RD, W CHESTER, PA 19380 . . . . (215) 696-4744
PAYNE FIRM INC
11231 CORNELL PARK DR, CINCINNATI 45242 . . . . (513) 489-2255
PRINCETON-SOMERSET GROUP INC
4 CARROLL DR, HILLSBOROUGH, NJ 08844 . . . . **(800) 597-8836**
R A WEST ASSOCIATES INC
2865 S EAGLE RD #359, NEWTOWN, PA 18940 . . . . (215) 860-5026

RESOURCE RECOVERY RESEARCH
5313 38TH ST NW, WASHINGTON, DC 20015 . . . . (202) 362-6034
WARD JOHN B
256 HILLDALE RD, VILLANOVA, PA 19085 . . . . (215) 525-3307
WEBSTERS NURSERY
619 3RD ST SE, MASON CITY, IA 50401 . . . . (319) 266-4516

EXPERTS-ERGONOMICS

JOSHUA TECHNOLOGY GROUP
WWW.JOSHUATECHNOLOGY.COM . . . . (937) 271-6765

EXPERTS-FINANCIAL

KUSHELL ASSOC INC
235 FEARRINGTON POST, PITTSBORO, NC 27312 . . . . (919) 542-3500
SIERRA TRADING CO
2045 PALISADES AVE, FULLERTON, CA 92631 . . . . (714) 992-2150
WILLAMETTE MANAGEMENT ASSOC
111 SW 5TH AVE #2150, PORTLAND, OR 97204 . . . . (503) 222-0577

EXPERTS-FIRE & ARSON

CASALINOVA INVESTIGATIONS
PO BOX 1260, NORTON 44203 . . . . (330) 335-0192
FIRE PROTECTION CONSULTANTS INC
2251 COLONIAL CT, WALNUT CREEK, CA 94598 . . . . (415) 932-4490
KMS ENGINEERING CONSULTANTS INC
287 CHURCH HILL RD, VENETIA, PA 15367 . . . . . . **(724) 348-7606**
900 E 8TH AV #300, KNG OF PRSSIA, PA 19406 . **(610) 768-8011**
67 PUBLIC SQ #500, WILKES-BARRE, PA 18701 . **(570) 825-9490**
LAWRENCE J DOVE ASSOC
6860 STATE RD, PHIL 19135 . . . . (800) 441-3683
LEADING TECH FORENSIC
WWW.LTFEXPERTS.COM . . . . (419) 452-6992
UNIFIED INVESTIGATIONS & SCNCS
6520A HUNTLEY RD, COLUMBUS 43229 . . . . (614) 430-0813
WILLIAM D GROW & ASSOC INC
5986 WASHINGTON LN, BENSALEM, PA 19020 . . . . (215) 245-5622

EXPERTS-FIREARMS

BALLISTIC ARMOR RESEARCH GRP LLC
PO BOX 432, BOYNE CITY, MI 49712 . . . . (888) 844-5721
PEREGRINE CORP THE
PO BOX 170, BOWERS, PA 19511 . . . . (610) 682-7147

EXPERTS-FORENSICS

AIR BRAKE CONSULTANTS INC
PO BOX 905, JACKSONVILLE, AL 36265 . . . . (205) 435-5925
ANAMET LABORATORIES INC
3400 INVESTMENT BLVD, HAYWARD, CA 94545 . . . . (510) 887-8811
AUGSPURGER KOMM ENGINEERING INC
15455 N GREENWAY-HAYDEN LP #C-14, SCTTSDL, AZ 85260 (480) 483-5966
FORENSIC INK ANLYSTS
4632 PENDELTON COURT, MILTON, WI 53563 . . . . (608) 752-8220
FORENSIC SCIENCES INC
606 BRUMAR DR, HATBORO, PA 19040 . . . . (215) 773-0332
GLATER IRVING W PE
277 N QUAKER LN, W HARTFORD, CT 06119 . . . . (860) 236-5141
LEADING TECH FORENSIC
WWW.LTFEXPERTS.COM . . . . (419) 452-6992
MATERIALS ANALYTICAL SVCS
3945 LAKEFIELD DR, SUWANEE, GA 30024 . . . . (800) 421-8451
MCCRONE ASSOCIATES INC
850 PASQUINELLI DR, WESTMONT, IL 60559 . . . . (708) 887-7100
PHOENIX LABORATORIES
9704 W 10TH ST, WICHITA, KS 67212 . . . . (316) 722-8285

EXPERTS-FRAUD

FORENSIC FRAUD RESEARCH INC
PO BOX 36058, CANTON 44735 . . . . (330) 936-9998

EXPERTS-GEOLOGY

ALEXANDER SHELTON S
537 DEIKE PENN STATE UNIV, UNIVERSITY PK, PA 16802 . . . (814) 863-7246
ERLIN CO THE
1693 CLEARVIEW DR, LATROBE, PA 15650 . . . . (412) 539-1800
GEOCHEMISTRY UNLIMITED
2207 BLACKHORSE DR, WARRINGTON, PA 18976 . . . . (215) 343-3689
MILLER GLENN
6236 W GRAND RIVER, BRIGHTON, MI 48116 . . . . (800) 872-3981
VIBRA-TECH ENGINEERS INC
109 E 1ST ST, HAZELTON, PA 18201 . . . . (717) 455-5861

EXPERTS-HORTICULTURE

FEATHER FRANK B
   737 ALONDRA LN NW, ALBUQUERQUE, NM 87114 . . . . (505) 898-4268
INT DEVELOPMENT ASSOC
   2512 Q ST NW, WASHINGTON, DC 20007 . . . . (202) 338-5034
TREE DOCTOR INC THE
   PO BOX 1340, HENDERSONVILLE, NC 28793 . . . . (828) 693-8733

EXPERTS-INSURANCE

CUMMINS J DAVID DR
   3641 LOCUST WALK, PHIL 19174 . . . . (215) 898-5644
GAISER RONALD O JR
   1906 CAHABA RD, BIRMINGHAM, AL 35223 . . . . (205) 251-2380
HATFIELD GROUP
   1735 POST RD, FAIRFIELD, CT 06430 . . . . (203) 256-5660
KAUFMAN FINANCIAL SVCS
   1702 LOVERING AVE #2, WILMINGTON, DE 19806 . . . . (302) 658-1111

RECTOR & ASSOCS
   172 E STATE ST, COLUMBUS 43215 . . . . (614) 224-6200
RISK ASSESSMENTS GROUP INC
   1024 ASHLAND DR, BATON ROUGE, LA 70806 . . . . (504) 927-5149
WINDT ALAN D
   1760 MARKET ST, PHIL 19102 . . . . (215) 563-4335

EXPERTS-MARITIME

ARTHUR H SULZER ASSOCIATES INC
   688 BEATTY RD, SPRINGFIELD, PA 19064 . . . . (610) 543-5884
CAPT HENRY HELGESEN & ASSOC
   2002 WYCLIFFE CT, WILMINGTON, NC 28405 . . . . (910) 509-9763
DWORKIN GERALD M
   10 MAIN ST BX 905, HARRISVILLE, NH 03450 . . . . (603) 827-4139

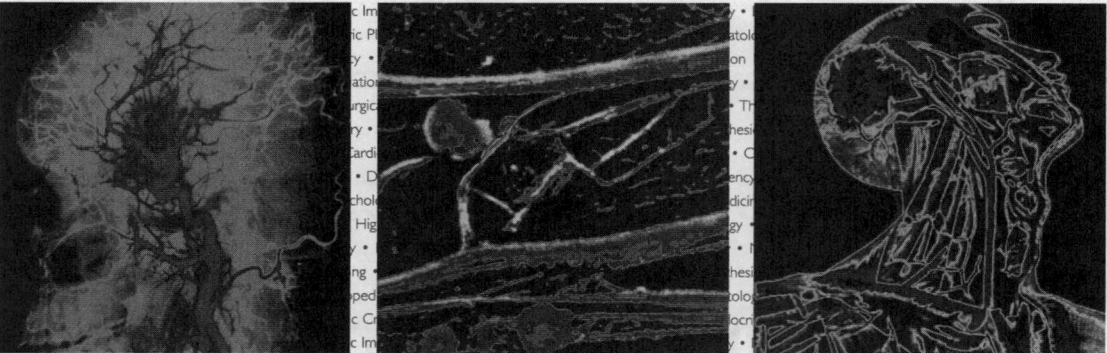

EXPERTS-MEDICAL
(See Also EXPERTS—CHIROPRACTIC)

ACADEMIC MEDICAL CONSULTANTS
PO BOX 670528, CINCINNATI 45267 . . . . (513) 558-5392
AMERICAN AMPUTEE FOUNDATION INC
PO BOX 250218, LITTLE ROCK, AR 72225 . . . . (501) 666-2523
AMERICAN COUNCIL OF THE BLIND
1155 15TH ST NW, WASHINGTON, DC 20005. . . . . (202) 467-5081
BRONSTON DR PAUL
1 JIB ST #202, MARINA DEL REY, CA 90292 . . . . (310) 301-9426

BURDGE JEREMY J MD
PLASTIC AND RECONSTRUCTIVE SURGEON
SPECIALIZING IN BURNS, WOUND HEALING
& MAXILLOFACIAL TRAUMA

3732C OLENTANGY RVR RD, COLUMBIA 43214. . . **(614) 451-0411**

CENTRAL OHIO PULMONARY DISEASE INC
745 W STATE ST #510, COLUMBUS 43222 . . . . . **(614) 464-0788**
CITRON DR RONALD
4189 SILVERADO TRL, CALISTOGA, CA 94515 . . . . (707) 948-5818
DEMIRJIAN NEUROLOGY & PAIN MANAGEMENT INC
See Our Display Ad Under This Heading
3732 BLOSSOM HEATH RD, DAYTON 45419. . . . **(937) 298-3800**
DESALVO ANTHONY R MD
1842 E MARKET ST, WARREN 44483 . . . . (330) 856-7212
ECRI
5200 BUTLER PK, PLYMOUTH MEETING, PA 19462 . . . . (215) 825-6000
ED QUALITY SOLUTIONS INC
PO BOX 39158, CLEVELAND 44139 . . . . (440) 349-3310
EXPERT MEDICAL WITNESSES INC
85 LOGAN BLVD, ALTOONA, PA 16602 . . . . (888) 944-8456
GENESIS MEDICAL INC
6520 HARBOR VIEW CIRCLE, PRIOR LAKE, MN 55372 . . . . . . (612) 445-7280
GRIGG JOHN W MD
1003 MULHOLLAND ST, BAY CITY, MI 48708 . . . . (989) 894-2823
HALL THOMAS C
1348 SUDDEN VALLEY, BELLINGHAM, WA 98226 . . . . (206) 734-8170
HARRIS STEVEN MD
400 PARNASSUS AVE, SAN FRANCISCO, CA 94143 . . . . (415) 476-1053
HUFFMAN GROUP THE
402 TOD LN, YOUNGSTOWN 44504 . . . . (330) 743-9596
IMEX ASSOCIATES INC
3601 S GREEN RD #314, BEACHWOOD 44122. . . . . (216) 504-0400
JD MD INC
PO BOX 11733, ATLANTA, GA 30355 . . . . (800) 225-5363
KIBLER GORDON E
9303 TIMBERSIDE, HOUSTON, TX 77025 . . . . (713) 668-5510
KLEIN IRA DR
10565 KATY FREEWAY #305, HOUSTON, TX 77024 . . . . (713) 932-8651
LEGAL INDEPENDENT NURSE CONSULTANTS LLC
WWW.LINCME.COM . . . . (513) 652-3392
LITIGATION MANAGEMENT INC
300 ALLEN-BRADLEY DR, MAYFIELD HTS 44124. . . . . (440) 484-2000
MARGULIES SHELDON MD JD
705 KERSEY RD, SILVER SPRING, MD 20902. . . . . (301) 649-6400
MEDI-LEGAL SVCS
PO BOX 1464, EL CAJON, CA 92022 . . . . (800) 343-2135
MEDICAL ADVISERS PC
14-14 BONNIE LN, BAYSIDE, NY 11360 . . . . (718) 423-9167
MEDICAL FACT FINDING SVCS
5630 LK MENDOTA DR, MADISON, WI 53705 . . . . (608) 238-4043
MEDICALLY SPEAKING-MEDICAL LEGAL CONSULTANTS
186 ATTORNEYS COM CT, LAKE HELEN, FL 32744 . . . . (909) 446-8866
MEDILEX INC
See Our Display Ad Under This Heading
175 E 96TH ST #8H, NEW YORK, NY 10128 . . . . . **(888) 633-4539**
MEDMAL CONSULTING
See Our Display Ad Under This Heading
WWW.MEDMALCONSULTING.COM . . . . **(440) 248-8242**
MEDVOPRO
See Our Display Ad Under This Heading
3620 N HIGH ST, #B-4, COLUMBUS 43214 . . . . . . **(614) 539-1150**
NEUROPSYCHIATRY CONSULTANTS INC
1005 BELLEFONTAINE AVE #360, LIMA 45804 . . **(419) 229-0415**

NEWMAN ANDREW MD
1331 E WYOMING AVE, PHIL 19124. . . . . (215) 537-8880
PHYSICIANS FOR QUALITY
PO BOX 730, BOORNE, TX 78006. . . . . (800) 284-3627
RECORD REVIEW MEDPSYCH OF OHIO VALLEY INC
2000 POLARIS PKWY #100, COLUMBUS 43240. . **(800) 251-0799**
SATALOFF ROBERT T MD
1721 PINE ST, PHIL 19103. . . . . (215) 545-3322
STASCHAK M C
308 HALLSBOROUGH DR, PITTSBURGH, PA 15238 . . . . (412) 963-6139
TASAMED
WWW.TASANET.COM . . . . **(800) 659-8464**
WASH OCCUPATIONAL HEALTH ASSOC INC
1120 19TH ST NW #410, WASHINGTON, DC 20036 . . . . (202) 463-6698

EXPERTS-METALLURGICAL

CORROSION TESTING LABS INC
60 BLUE HEN DR, NEWARK, DE 19713 . . . . (302) 454-8200
ENGINEERING MATERIALS & PROCESSES
121 EDGEWOOD AVE, PITTSBURGH, PA 15218 . . . . (412) 242-9333
EVANS JAMES W
530 BLVD WY, PIEDMONT, CA 94610 . . . . (415) 642-3807
FAAS METALLURGICAL SVC INC
22907 FELBAR AVE, TORRANCE, CA 90505 . . . . (310) 530-5664
FORENSIC METALLURGY ASSOC INC
7503 MARITIME LN, SPRINGFIELD, VA 22153 . . . . (703) 455-4446
JONAS E A CONSULTANT
620 BIERYS BRIDGE RD, BETHLEHEM, PA 18017 . . . . (610) 865-3300
MATERIALS ANALYSIS INC
10338 MILLER RD, DALLAS, TX 75238 . . . . (214) 343-3811
MATERIALS SCIENCE ASSOCIATES
1 RICHMOND SQUARE, PROVIDENCE, RI 02906 . . . . (800) 672-6721
RAYMOND K HART LTD
145 GROGAN LAKES DR, ATLANTA, GA 30350 . . . . (404) 396-3579
SEAL LABORATORIES
250 N NASH ST, EL SEGUNDO, CA 90245 . . . . (310) 322-2011
STRUCTURE PROBE INC
PO BOX 656, W CHESTER, PA 19381 . . . . (610) 436-5400

EXPERTS-METEOROLOGY & WEATHER

ATMOSPHERIC INFORMATION SVCS
255 FULLER RD, ALBANY, NY 12203 . . . . (518) 437-8712
CLIMATOLOGICAL CONSULTING CORP
7338 155TH PL N, PALM BEACH GARDENS, FL 33418 . . . . . . (561) 744-4889
DBS ASSOCIATES
881 WELLMAN AVE, N CHELMSFORD, MA 01863 . . . . (888) 422-8844
RAHN JAMES J PHD
202 N 25TH ST, CAMP HILL, PA 17011 . . . . (717) 737-4772
WRIGHT WEATHER
PO BOX 117, NEW YORK, NY 10108 . . . . (212) 582-7434

EXPERTS-NEUROPSYCHOLOGY

DELLA MORA CATHY PH D
7870 OLENTANGY RVR RD, COLUMBUS 43235 . . . . (614) 433-2558

RECORD REVIEW MEDPSYCH OF OHIO VALLEY INC

NEUROPSYCHOLOGY INDEPENDENT MEDICAL EXAMS
CASE REVIEW * DEFENSE/SETTLEMENT STRATEGIES
PREPARATION OF ATTYS FOR DEPOSITIONS & LITIGATION

2000 POLARIS PKWY #100, COLUMBUS 43240 . . . **(800) 251-0799**

WALLACE-KETTERING NEUROSCIENCE INSTITUTE THE
See Our Display Ad Under This Heading
3533 STHRN BLVD #5200, KETTERING 45429. . . **(937) 395-8043**

EXPERTS-NURSING
(See Also NURSING CONSULTANTS)

MED-LAW NURSE CONSULTANTS INC
277 TRIPLE CROWN CIR, SPRINGBORO 45066 . . . . (937) 432-6894
MEDICAL DIRECTIONS
39 ELGIN AVE, N KINGSTOWN, RI 02852 . . . . (401) 884-1999
RESH CAROL A
3607 DREXEL ST, HOUSTON, TX 77027 . . . . (713) 621-9578

EXPERTS-PATHOLOGY
(See Also EXPERTS-MEDICAL)

WEBPATHOLOGY2NDOPINION.COM
197 GREAT OAKS TRL, WADSWORTH 44281 . . . . (330) 618-2576

EXPERTS-PHOTOGRAPHY
(See Also PHOTOGRAPHERS-LEGAL)

THE FOTO-TECHNIKS GROUP
1845 W GALBRAITH RD, CINCINNATI 45239 . . . . (513) 522-4861

EXPERTS-PODIATRY
(See Also EXPERTS—MEDICAL)

MEDILEX INC
175 E 96TH ST #8H, NEW YORK, NY 10128 . . . . . **(888) 633-4539**

EXPERTS-PSYCHIATRIC

ACCREDITED PSYCHIATRY & MEDICINE
96 LARCHWOOD DR, CAMBRIDGE, MA 02138 . . . . (617) 492-8366
ALLIED COUNSELING CTRS
8631 W 3RD ST, LOS ANGELES, CA 90048 . . . . (310) 657-8558
CODISPOTI V MD
#2 SALEM BUSINESS CTR S, SALEM, FL 62881 . . . . (618) 548-0400
DENSEN-GERBER JUDIANNE JD MD
5 HEDLEY FARMS RD, WESTFORD, CT 06880 . . . . (203) 255-4198
DISABILITY & IMPAIRMENT EVALUATIONS INC
5370 SOM CENTER RD, WILLOUGHBY 44094 . . . . (440) 946-4007
LIMOGES RICHARD F DR
822 PINE ST ST REGIS CT #1B, PHIL 19107 . . . . (215) 627-5650
MEDILEX INC
175 E 96TH ST #8H, NEW YORK, NY 10128 . . . . . **(888) 633-4539**

NEUROPSYCHIATRY CONSULTANTS INC

RICHARD NOCKOWITZ, MD
MASSACHUSETTS GENERAL HOSP/HARVARD UNIV
TRAINED/MEDICOLEGAL CASE REVIEW, OPINIONS
& EXPERT TESTIMONY/EXPERT IN ALL AREAS OF
PSYCHIATRY, NEUROPSYCHIATRY, PSYCHIATRIC
MEDICINE & CLINICAL PSYCHOPHARMACOLOGY

1005 BELLEFONTAINE AVE #360, LIMA 45804 . . . . **(419) 229-0415**

SADOFF ROBERT L DR
326 BENJAMIN FOX PVLN, JENKINTOWN, PA 19046 . . . . (215) 887-6144
UNIVERSITY PSYCHIATRY
231 ALBERT SABIN WAY, CINCINNATI 45267 . . . . (513) 584-3194

EXPERTS-PSYCHOLOGICAL

BLOOM RICHARD F PHD
292 POST RD EAST, W PORT, CT 06880 . . . . (203) 226-6456
CAILLER CLINIC LTD
505 S DEWEY ST, EAU CLAIRE, WI 54701 . . . . (715) 836-0064
CAROL L PATRICK PHD & ASSOC
1037 W MARKET ST, LIMA 45805 . . . . (419) 222-5077
CENTERS LOUISE C PHD
25052 SHERWOOD CIR, SOUTHFIELD, MI 48075 . . . . (248) 559-6914
CHILDRENS PSYCHOLOGICAL TRAUMA TEAM THE
2024 DIVISADERO ST, SAN FRANCISCO, CA 94115 . . . . (415) 474-0955
COLUMBUS TRAUMATIC STRESS CTR
7750 PINGUE DR, WORTHINGTON 43085 . . . . (614) 436-9985
DENT CONSTANCE P DR
11 SALLY ANN RD, MERTZTOWN, PA 19539 . . . . (610) 682-2246
DIAMOND PSYCH SERVICES CORP
445 ROSEWOOD AVE #M, CAMARILLO, CA 93010 . . . . (805) 482-5166
FARRAR WILLIAM E PHD
572 S FOREST DR, BIRMINGHAM, AL 35209 . . . . (205) 871-0679
FORENSIC PSYCHOLOGY ASSOC
330 NORWOOD AVE, PROVIDENCE, RI 02905 . . . . (401) 941-1717
FOX DAVID D PHD
1560 E CHEVY CHASE DR #130, GLENDALE, CA 91206 . . . . . (818) 246-3937
HATZENBUEHLER LINDA C PHD
452 S 6TH AVE, POCATELLO, ID 83201 . . . . (208) 232-6998
INTERPSYCH ASSOC
700 S HENDERSON RD, KING OF PRUSSIA, PA 19406 . . . . . . (215) 265-6464
LEE HOWARD INC
822 S HIGH ST, COLUMBUS 43206 . . . . (614) 444-0961
M*A*T*C*H
8905 PATTON RD, WYNDMOOR, GLENSIDE, PA 19038 . . . . . (215) 204-6109
MALINKY JOHN M PHD
647A PARK MEADOW RD, WESTERVILLE 43081 . . . . (614) 898-0443
PALUMBO STANLEY J PHD
314 CHURCHILL-HUBBARD RD #A, YOUNGSTOWN 44505 . . . (330) 759-0943
RELINGER HELMUT PHD
2999 REGENT ST, BERKELEY, CA 94705 . . . . (415) 540-8389
RIDENOUR MARCELLA V DR
143 FRNBROOK AVE, WYNCOTE, PA 19095 . . . . (215) 576-0928
WALLACE-KETTERING NEUROSCIENCE INSTITUTE THE
3533 STHRN BLVD #5200, KETTERING 45429 . . . **(937) 395-8043**

EXPERTS-REAL ESTATE
(See Also REAL ESTATE CONSULTANTS)

CENTURY 21
  600 COLUMBUS AVE, LEBANON 45036 . . . . (513) 932-2335
  19220 LORAIN RD, CLEVELAND 44126 . . . . (800) 377-5354
  6370 YORK RD, CLEVELAND 44130. (440) 842-7200
  1108 MAPLE AVE, ZANESVILLE 43701 . . . . (740) 454-6777
  51 PRICE RD, NEWARK 43055 . . . . (740) 366-3940
HENKALINE & ASSOCIATES INC
  5791 FAR HILLS AVENUE, DAYTON 45429 . . . . (937) 436-7804

EXPERTS-RECREATION & SAFETY

GREENLAW MARTIN
  25 EL PLAZUELA ST, SAN FRANCISCO, CA 94127 . . . . (415) 333-5832
LAKESIDE CONSULTING DESIGN & EDUCATION INC
  PO BOX 543, N OLMSTED 44070 . . . . (440) 235-8210
PLAYGROUND CLEARING HOUSE INC
  238 SYCAMORE LN, PHOENIXVILLE, PA 19460 . . . . (610) 935-1549

EXPERTS-SAFETY & SECURITY
(See Also SAFETY & SECURITY CONSULTANTS)

ADT SECURITY SERVICES INC
  5590 LAUBY RD N W, N CANTON 44720 . . . . (330) 497-5325
ALDERSON CLARK & MAY LTD
  PO BOX 40035, BAY VILLAGE 44140 . . . . (440) 930-5066
BLACK THOMAS L
  PO BOX 729, RANCHO SANTE FE, CA 92067 . . . . (619) 756-1235
BUNK KENNETH H
  3702 HICKORY HILL RD, BETHLEHEM, PA 18015 . . . . (215) 866-0622
CONSTRUCTION SAFETY ENGINEERS
  3250 FAIRCHILD AVE S, MINNEAPOLIS, MN 55391 . . . . (612) 935-0235
ERROR ANALYSIS INC
  5811 AMAYA DR #205, LA MESA, CA 91942 . . . . (619) 464-4427
EXECUTIVE SECURITY CONSULTANTS
  PO BOX 350, GLADWYNE, PA 19035 . . . . (610) 687-2999

FORENSIC ANALYST

ROGER L BOYELL - ELECTRONICS
TELECOMMUNICATION & SECURITY SYSTEMS
E-MAIL: BOYELL@IEEE.ORG

WWW.BOYELL.COM . . . . **(856) 234-5800**

HARPER WALTER R
  2612 SAMARKAND DR, SANTA BARBARA, CA 93105 . . . . (805) 687-5717
INTL MANAGEMENT ASSISTANCE CORP
  15830 FOLTZ INDUSTRIAL PKWY, CLEVELAND 44149 . . . . . . (440) 878-7621
JD SECURITY CONSULTANTS
  630 LANCASTER CT, DOWNINGTOWN, PA 19335 . . . . (610) 269-8086
KEVIN PARSONS & ASSOC INC
  PO BOX 356, APPLETON, WI 54912 . . . . (414) 731-8893
LABORATORY TESTING INC
  2331 TOPAZ DR, HATFIELD, PA 19440 . . . . (215) 355-5420
LARRY TALLEY & ASSOC
  5375 CHAMBLEE DUNWOODY RD, DUNWOODY, GA 30338 . . (770) 394-0127
LOSS MANAGEMENT CONSULTANTS
  PO BOX 775, PLYMOUTH MEETING, PA 19462 . . . . (610) 279-5450
MBE ASSOC
  4047 BALCONY DR, WOODLAND HILLS, CA 91364 . . . . (818) 347-2666
MCCAULEY R PAUL PHD
  4620 LUCERNE RD, INDIANA, PA 15701 . . . . (412) 349-9676
MIDDLECAMP WALTER J JR
  2168 SW MAIN, PORTLAND, OR 97205 . . . . (503) 222-2968
OMNI TECH INTERNATIONAL LTD
  2715 ASHMAN ST, MIDLAND, MI 48640 . . . . (989) 631-3377
PANKAU CONSULTING
  PO BOX 9797, THE WOODLAND, TX 77219 . . . . (713) 224-3777
RYAN JOSEPH P PHD
  1925 OVERVIEW DR, CASTLE ROCK, CO 80104 . . . . (303) 660-8243
SCHAIBLE ASSOCIATES
  1008 COUNTRY PLACE DR, LANCASTER, PA 17601 . . . . (800) 832-5564
SECURITY LITIGATION GROUP INC
  6099 RIVERSIDE DR #102, DUBLIN 43017 . . . . (614) 793-1614
SENNEWALD CHARLES A
  28004 LAKE MEADOW ST, ESCONDIDO, CA 92026 . . . . (619) 749-7527
THOMAS INVESTIGATIVE SVCS
  810 PENDLETON DR, COMSTOCK PK, MI 49321 . . . . (616) 784-0490
WITHERSPOON SECURITY CONSULTING
  22021 BROOKPARK RD, CLEVELAND 44126 . . . . (440) 779-3803

EXPERTS-SURVEYING

THOMAS ENGINEERING AND SURVEYING CO THE
  PO BOX 28098, COLUMBUS 43228 . . . . (614) 276-2619

EXPERTS-TELECOMMUNICATIONS

DITTENBERNER ASSOCIATES
  4641 MONTGOMERY AVE, BETHESDA, MD 20814 . . . . (301) 652-8350

EXPERTS-TOXICOLOGY

A & L SHATTO INC
  336 S MAIN ST, BEL AIR, MD 21014 . . . . (410) 836-0922
CLINICAL CONSULTANTS
  986 HARBOR OAKS DR, CHARLESTON, SC 29412 . . . . (843) 795-9595
CONSELTECH ENGINEERING
  3003 VAN NESS NW, WASHINGTON, DC 20008. . . . . (202) 364-6152
COWAN JONATHAN PHD
  1103 HOLLENDALE WAY, GOSHEN, KY 40026. . . . . (502) 228-1552
D J OBRIEN & ASSOCIATES INC
  1953 E FRONTIER LN, OLATHE, KS 66062 . . . . (913) 764-8957
DRUG SCAN INC
  PO BOX 2969, WARMINSTER, PA 18974. . . . . (215) 674-9310
KELLER JOHN G
  4504 TOURNAY RD, BETHESDA, MD 20814 . . . . (301) 229-0843
LEVINE BARRY
  111 PENN ST, BALTIMORE, MD 21201 . . . . (301) 333-3242
MEDILEX INC
  175 E 96TH ST #8H, NEW YORK, NY 10128 . . . . . **(888) 633-4539**
MMK CONSULTING
  9458 MACOMBER LN, COLUMBIA, MD 21045 . . . . (410) 992-4048
NATIONAL MEDICAL SERVICES INC
  3701 WELSH RD, WILLOW GROVE, PA 19090 . . . . (215) 657-4900
NATIONAL SCIENTIFIC SVCS
  3411 PHILIPS DR, BALTIMORE, MD 21208 . . . . (410) 486-7486
PRINCETON-SOMERSET GROUP INC
  See Our Display Ad Under This Heading
  4 CARROLL DR, HILLSBOROUGH, NJ 08844. . . . **(800) 597-8836**
SCIENTIFIC RESEARCH ASSOC
  1920 L ST NW #420, WASHINGTON, DC 20036. . . . . (202) 728-1400

EXPERTS-TRAFFIC

RICHARD N BEST ASSOC INC
  15 TRAIL RD, LEVITTOWN, PA 19056 . . . . (215) 945-9240

EXPERTS-TRANSPORTATION

TBB GLOBAL LOGISTICS
  9 NEWMAN AVE #5, RUMFORD, RI 02916. . . . . (401) 431-0296
UHER RICHARD A DR
  2013 COUNTRY CLUB DR, MCKEESPORT, PA 15135 . . . . (412) 751-8470

EXPERTS-WOOD SCIENCES

BLANKENHORN PAUL R
  310 FOREST RESOURCES LAB, UNIVERSITY PK, PA 16802 . . (814) 865-6972

FIDELITY BONDS
(See BAIL BONDS; BONDS—SURETY & FIDELITY; and INSURANCE AGENCIES)

FINANCIAL INSTITUTIONS
(See BANKS)

FINANCIAL PLANNING CONSULTANTS
(See INVESTMENT SERVICES)

FINANCIAL SERVICES

JONES EDWARD
  6052 WILMINGTON PIKE, DAYTON 45459 . . . . (937) 848-8740
ROBERT W BAIRD & CO INC
  4030 SMITH RD #100, CINCINNATI 45209 . . . . (513) 421-4530
WALLER FINANCIAL PLANNING GROUP
  941 CHATHAM LN #212, COLUMBUS 43221. . . . . (614) 457-7026
WEALTH PRESERVATION PLANNERS INC
  9639 LEEBROOK DR, CINCINNATI 45231 . . . . (513) 521-8000

FINGERPRINTS
(See POLYGRAPH & LIE DETECTION SERVICES; EXPERTS—FORENSICS; and INVESTIGATORS & DETECTIVE AGENCIES)

FIRE & ARSON EXPERTS
(See EXPERTS—FIRE & ARSON)

FLOOD HAZARD SEARCHES
(See TITLE INSURANCE COMPANIES & AGENTS; and SEARCH SERVICES)

FORENSICS
(See EXPERTS; POLYGRAPH & LIE DETECTION SERVICES; and INVESTIGATORS & DETECTIVE AGENCIES)

FORMS-BUSINESS & LEGAL
(See OFFICE SUPPLIES; and PRINTERS—LEGAL & FINANCIAL)

GENEALOGICAL & TITLE RESEARCH
(See Also SEARCH SERVICES; and HEIR TRACERS)

AFRICAN AMERICAN GENEALOGY GRP
   175 MIAMI DR, YELLOW SPRINGS 45387 . . . . (937) 767-1949
FRANKLIN COUNTY GENEALOGICAL
   570 W BROAD ST, COLUMBUS 43215 . . . . (614) 469-1300
GENEALOGICAL RESEARCH SVC
   628 HARTFORD ST, WORTHINGTON 43085 . . . . (614) 885-8151
HOLMES COUNTY GENEALOGY SOC
   100 W MILLERSBURG ST, NASHVILLE 44661 . . . . (330) 378-2314
LOGAN COUNTY GENEALOGICAL SOC
   521 E COLUMBUS AVE, BELLEFONTAINE 43311 . . . . (937) 593-7811
MINDWARE TECHNOLOGIES
   135 JUNIPER AVE, WESTERVILLE 43081 . . . . (614) 895-2837
OHIO HISTORICAL SOCIETY
   1982 VELMA AVE, COLUMBUS 43211 . . . . (614) 297-2510
PALATINES TO AMERICA
   611 E WEBER RD, COLUMBUS 43211 . . . . (614) 267-4700
RALPH C REED LAND SURVEYOR
   127 VENTURA AVE, DAYTON 45417 . . . . (937) 263-4151
WELLS CONSULTING SVC
   PO BOX 281, VANLUE 45890 . . . . (419) 387-7393

HANDWRITING EXPERTS
(See EXPERTS—DOCUMENTS)

HEIR TRACERS
(See Also GENEALOGICAL & TITLE RESEARCH)

AMERICAN RESEARCH BUREAU INC
   2386 E HERITAGE WAY, SALT LAKE CITY, UT 84109 . . . . (800) 628-7221
INTERNATIONAL GENEALOGICAL SEARCH INC
   PO BOX 34000, SEATTLE, WA 98124 . . . . (800) 663-2255
JOSH BUTLER & CO INC
   201 E COMMERCE ST, YOUNGSTOWN 44503 . . . . (800) 567-8434
LANDEX RESEARCH
   2 N LASALLE ST, CHICAGO, IL 60602 . . . . (800) 844-6778

HOME HEALTH CARE SERVICES
COMMUNITY HEALTH PROFESSIONALS
   1159 WESTWOOD DR, VAN WERT 45891 . . . . (419) 238-9223
HEARTLAND HOME HEALTH CARE AND HOSPICE
   3450 W CENTRAL AVE #230, TOLEDO 43606 . . . . (419) 531-0440
INTERIM HEALTH CARE OF NORTHWESTERN OHIO INC
   3745 SHAWNEE RD #108, LIMA 45806 . . . . (419) 228-2535
MAXIM HEALTHCARE SVC
   1880 E DUBLIN GRANVILLE RD #200, COLUMBUS 43229 . . . . . (614) 882-6400
WILLCARE HOME HEALTHCARE
   25000 EUCLID AVE #300, EUCLID 44117 . . . . (216) 289-5300

HOME INSPECTION SERVICES
(See BUILDING INSPECTION SERVICES)

HOUSE ARREST SERVICES

Complete Home Incarceration Service
• Alternative to Jail
• Alcohol & Curfew Monitoring
• We can monitor anywhere in the U.S.

800-253-2447   FAX: 513/931-9300
email: cdachip@fuse.net

CDA ELECTRONIC MONITORING
See Our Display Ad Under This Heading
CDACHIP@FUSE.NET . . . . **(800) 253-2447**

INCORPORATION SERVICES
(See SEARCH SERVICES)

INDEPENDENT FEE APPRAISERS
(See Also APPRAISAL SERVICES—REAL ESTATE)

ABRECHT JULIE P IFA
   PO BOX 39455, SOLON 44139 . . . . (440) 349-2554
ADAMS ZEDDIE E
   PO BOX 22394, BEACHWOOD 44122 . . . . (216) 514-8006
AIRHART MICHAEL S IFA
   50 N ERIE ST #200, MASSILLON 44646 . . . . (330) 830-2121
ASCHENBACK WANDA E IFA
   155 N LEAVITT RD #102, AMHERST 44001 . . . . (440) 988-2335
BLACKMAN TRAVIS L
   9925 S BLVD, CLEVELAND 44108 . . . . (216) 721-9750
BODENHOFF ROBINA S IFA
   26404 CENTER RIDGE RD, WESTLAKE 44145 . . . . (440) 871-3315
BRYLL ERIC R IFA
   6048 BLAKLEY DR, HIGHLAND HTS 44143 . . . . (440) 449-2063
CASTO CYNTHIA C IFA
   17930 OWEN RD, MIDDLEFIELD 44062 . . . . (440) 548-5718
CATHER CHARLES L IFA
   2451 RAVENNA AVE SE, E CANTON 44730 . . . . (216) 398-2900
CERNY ROBERT J IFA
   PO BOX 704, WOOSTER 44691 . . . . (800) 577-6480
CHANCE JOHN K IFAS
   PO BOX 105, URBANA 43078 . . . . (937) 653-3441
CHAPMAN SHERYL IFAS
   125 BUCKEYE BLVD, PORT CLINTON 43452 . . . . (419) 734-0411
CLARK FRANK IFA
   2907 LANDON DR, COLUMBUS 43209 . . . . (614) 236-5452
COOK WILLIAM R IFA
   421 VIOLA AVE, HUBBARD 44425 . . . . (330) 534-0861
COOKSON CLAYTON G JR
   17312 AKITA CT, STRONGSVILLE 44136 . . . . (440) 846-0872

INDEPENDENT MEDICAL EXAMINERS
INPHYNET MEDICAL MGMT INC
   2620 RIDGEWOOD RD, AKRON 44313 . . . . (330) 867-9470

INFORMATION BUREAUS
(See LITIGATION SUPPORT SERVICES)

INSPECTION SERVICES
(See BUILDING INSPECTION SERVICES)

INSURANCE ADJUSTERS
(See ADJUSTERS)

INSURANCE AGENCIES

A BETTER AUTO INSURANCE
3645 WARRENSVILLE CENTER RD, CLEVELAND 44122 . . . . . (216) 752-6365
A-1 AFFORDABLE HEALTH INSURANCE
713 FOX CREEK LN #4, CINCINNATI 45245 . . . . (513) 753-7318
ABBINGTON FINANCIAL
210 BELL ST, CHAGRIN FALLS 44022 . . . . (440) 247-3500
866 E 185TH ST, CHAGRIN FALLS 44022 . . . . (216) 692-8700
ABC AUTO INSURANCE
105 FRONT ST, BEREA 44017 . . . . (440) 243-6650
PO BOX 6118, CLEVELAND 44101 . . . . (216) 881-2600
ABE AMERICAN AUTO INSURANCE
25550 CHAGRIN BLVD, CLEVELAND 44122 . . . . (216) 464-4872
ABSOLUTE AUTO INSURANCE
107 W JOHNSTOWN RD, GAHANNA 43230 . . . . (614) 476-6960
ACACIA LIFE INSURANCE CO
135 N HAMILTON RD, GAHANNA 43230 . . . . (614) 475-0667
ACCELERATION NATIONAL INS CO
1366 DUBLIN RD, COLUMBUS 43215. . . . . (614) 764-0616
ACCEPTANCE INSURANCE CO
139 S 3RD ST, COSHOCTON 43812 . . . . (740) 622-8000
7866 BROADVIEW RD, CLEVELAND 44134 . . . . (216) 328-5990
ACCURATE INSURANCE
2000 WARRENSVILLE CENTER RD, CLEVELAND 44121 . . . . (216) 691-0000
ACME BONDING AGENCY
22 W BOARDMAN ST, YOUNGSTOWN 44503 . . . . (330) 746-2130
ACORDIA
580 N 4TH ST #400, COLUMBUS 43215 . . . . (614) 228-5565
BBB HEALTHCARE SVC CTR
1100 SUPERIOR AVE E #1700, CLEVELAND 44114 . . . . . . (330) 425-1870
CBIZ BENEFITS & INSURANCE SVC
34920 RIDGE RD, WILLOUGHBY 44094. . . . . (440) 602-6493
6050 OAK TREE BLVD #500, CLEVELAND 44131 . . . . (216) 328-1300
D B INDEPENDENT INSURANCE
1 VICTORIA SQ, PAINESVILLE 44077 . . . . (440) 354-1566
ECS RISK CONTROL INC
364 COLONY RD, ROSSFORD 43460. . . . . (419) 662-9274
G E FINANCIAL ASSURANCE LONG TERM CARE DIVISION
6610 W BROAD ST, RICHMOND, VA 23230 . . . . (804) 281-6000
GOLDEN HORIZONS INS INC
5874 FULTON DR NW, CANTON 44718. . . . . (330) 499-2444
GROVE CITY INSURANCE
1600 GATEWAY CTR, GROVE CITY 43123 . . . . (614) 846-1173
HERCHELL MCCOY
15904 HENLEY RD, CLEVELAND 44112 . . . . (216) 932-7515
INGRAM & ASSOCIATES INC
6768 LOOP RD, CENTERVILLE 45459 . . . . (937) 434-8989
INSURANCE AGENCIES OF THE MAUMEE VLY
6729 PROVIDENCE ST, WHITEHOUSE 43571 . . . . (419) 829-4414
JAMES B OSWALD CO THE
1360 E NINTH ST, CLEVELAND 44114 . . . . (216) 622-7400
M & C INSURANCE INC
PO BOX 446, RICHFIELD 44286 . . . . (330) 659-4866
M C ROBINSON & ASSOC INC
2381 LOCUST ST S, CANAL FULTON 44614 . . . . (330) 854-9300
M C THOMAS INSURANCE INC
892 NATIONAL RD, BRIDGEPORT 43912 . . . . (740) 635-0873
MANAGED CARE CONSULTANTS INC
6150 PARKLAND BLVD #105, CLEVELAND 44124 . . . . (440) 442-0002
MASS MUTUAL FINANCIAL GROUP CHRIS COLLIER CLU
300 E BUSINESS WAY #390, CINCINNATI 45241 . . . . (513) 579-8555
MBA MONTGOMERY BLUE ASH INS
9501 UNION CEMETERY RD, LOVELAND 45140 . . . . (513) 605-3500
MCBANE INSURANCE INC
100 N 4TH ST #325, STEUBENVILLE 43952. . . . . (740) 282-9708
PO BOX 340, BERGHOLZ 43908. (740) 768-2121
591 6TH ST NW, CARROLLTON 44615 . . . . (330) 627-7717
MCCARTHY STEVENOT AGENCY
10921 REED HARTMAN HWY #310, CINCINNATI 45242 . . . (513) 891-9888
MCCLELLAND & ASSOC
PO BOX 43, WESTERVILLE 43086 . . . . (740) 965-6466
MCCLENAGHAN & ASSOC
403 1/2 E MAIN ST, LANCASTER 43130 . . . . (740) 653-6744
MCCLOY FINANCIAL SVC
921 CHATHAM LN #300, COLUMBUS 43221 . . . . (614) 457-6233
MCFARLAND INSURANCE
PO BOX 323, W UNION 45693 . . . . (937) 544-2397
MCGOHAN BRABENDER FINANCIAL
3931 S DIXIE DR, DAYTON 45439. . . . . (937) 293-1600
MCGRAW AGENCY
821 ELLIOTT DR, MIDDLETOWN 45044 . . . . (513) 423-0772
MCKEE INSURANCE INC
601 MARKET ST, ZANESVILLE 43701 . . . . (740) 452-2735
MCKISSON SWEENEY GROUP
4159 N HOLLAND SYLVANIA RD #101, TOLEDO 43623 . . . (419) 885-8485
MCLAUGHLIN FINANCIAL
747 W ELM ST, WASHINGTON CT HS 43160 . . . . (740) 335-4215
MCNELLY-PATRICK INSURANCE
135 E HURON ST #100, JACKSON 45640 . . . . (740) 286-4175
MCNUTT INSURANCE INC
PO BOX 84, E LIVERPOOL 43920 . . . . (330) 385-9293
MCPHERSON JOHN F
912 S MAIN ST, FINDLAY 45840 . . . . (419) 422-4727
MCQUISTON INSURANCE
PO BOX 18309, FAIRFIELD 45018 . . . . (513) 868-9625

MCVICKER INSURANCE
5825 WECKERLY RD, WHITEHOUSE 43571 . . . . (419) 877-5326
N CAROL INSURANCE INC
1989 W 5TH AVE #6, COLUMBUS 43212 . . . . (614) 486-1666
OCONNELL INSURANCE
31715 VINE ST, WILLOWICK 44095 . . . . (440) 943-5484
SCHAFFER INSURANCE AGCY
1451 N MAIN AVE, SIDNEY 45365 . . . . (937) 492-0600
SCHANZ INSURANCE
15732 LORAIN AVE, CLEVELAND 44111 . . . . (216) 941-7555
SCHEETZ AGENCY INC
114 ORCHARD DR, BALTIC 43804 . . . . (330) 897-3811
SCHEIB-SNOW & CO
3700 N HOLLAND SYLVANIA #101, TOLEDO 43615 . . . . (419) 841-3300
SCHIEFER INSURANCE
225 CLEVELAND AVE, AMHERST 44001 . . . . (440) 984-2414
SCHLEMMER INSURANCE INC
26777 LORAIN RD #708, N OLMSTED 44070 . . . . (440) 779-6210
SCHMIDT THERESA
8412 WAINSTEAD DR, CLEVELAND 44129 . . . . (440) 845-1447
SCHRAFF-SHARPE INSURANCE
20325 CENTER RIDGE RD #704, CLEVELAND 44116 . . . . . . (440) 356-0300
SCHRIVER INSURANCE
22 S MAIN ST, JEFFERSONVILLE 43128 . . . . (740) 426-8418
SCHROEDER INSURANCE
8150 CORPORATE PARK DR #100, CINCINNATI 45242 . . . . (513) 489-9909
SCHUBERT SCHEHR INSURANCE INC
4141 N BEND, CINCINNATI 45211 . . . . (513) 923-4500
SCHULTHEIS INSURANCE INC
30 W HUNTER ST, LOGAN 43138. . . . . (740) 385-2532
SCHUSTER-TRINTER INSURANCE
157 CLEVELAND AVE, AMHERST 44001 . . . . (440) 988-4461
SCHWALL-BECHTEL INSURANCE
138 N FULTON ST, WAUSEON 43567 . . . . (419) 335-6962
SCHWENDEMAN AGENCY INC
109 PUTNAM ST, MARIETTA 45750 . . . . (740) 373-6793
SCOTT GOOD INSURANCE
1631 NW PROFESSIONAL PLZ, COLUMBUS 43220. . . . . . . (614) 326-6401
SCOTT INSURANCE
PO BOX 323, ALBANY 45710. . . . . (740) 698-4011
SCOTT TAYLOR INSURANCE
21 CROZIER CT, GRANVILLE 43023 . . . . (740) 587-7447
SCOTT-MARSHALL INSURANCE INC
PO BOX 190, NEWCOMERSTOWN 43832 . . . . (740) 498-5114
SCUREMAN & ASSOC
2000 E 9TH ST #500, CLEVELAND 44115 . . . . (216) 621-3033
SZARKA FINANCIAL MANAGEMENT
29691 LORAIN RD, N OLMSTED 44070 . . . . (440) 777-4330
SZUCS INSURANCE
5679 LIBERTY AVE, VERMILION 44089 . . . . (440) 967-1555

INSURANCE-PROFESSIONAL LIABILITY

FERNEDING INSURANCE
533 E STROOP RD, DAYTON 45429. . . . . (937) 294-1755

PROFESSIONAL LIABILITY SERVICES INC

SPECIALIZING IN LIABILTY COVERAGE FOR
LAWYERS * LAW FIRMS * TITLE AGENCIES
WWW.ATTORNEYSLIABILITY.COM

6701 ROCKSIDE RD, CLEVELAND 44131 . . . . **(888) 475-5001**

PRONATIONAL INSURANCE CO

LAWYERCARE-PROFESSIONAL LIABILITY
INSURANCE FOR LAWYERS AND LAW FIRMS

WWW.PRONATIONAL.COM . . . . **(800) 292-1036**

INTERNET SERVICES

GOOD PENNYS
10758 CHILDRESS CT, CINCINNATI 45240 . . . . (513) 851-5514

INTERPRETERS & TRANSLATORS

A SPANISH INTERPRETER
2950 E MAIN ST, COLUMBUS 43209 . . . . (614) 231-4744
A TECHNICAL TRANSLATION SVC
37841 EUCLID AVE, WILLOUGHBY 44094. . . . . (440) 942-3130
A-1 CONVERSA LANGUAGE CTR
817 MAIN ST #6, CINCINNATI 45202 . . . . (513) 651-5679
ABC TRANSLATIONS
3419 S CLUB CREST AVE, CINCINNATI 45209 . . . . (513) 321-5054
ADVANCED TRANSLATION SVC
3751 WILLOW RUN, CLEVELAND 44145 . . . . (440) 716-0820
AJI TRANSLATION & WEB SVC
7652 SAWMILL RD, DUBLIN 43016 . . . . (614) 791-0134
ALLIANCE FRANCAISE DE TOLEDO
1700 N REYNOLDS RD, TOLEDO 43615 . . . . (419) 537-9024
ALTCO TRANSLATIONS
1426 RIDGEVIEW RD, COLUMBUS 43221 . . . . (614) 486-2014

INTERPRETERS & TRANSLATORS (Cont'd)

AMERICAN INSTITUTE OF LANGUAGE
1990 N CLEVELAND MASSILLON RD, AKRON 44333 . . . . (330) 666-8133
AMERILINGUA TRANSLATION SVC
2545 FISHINGER RD, COLUMBUS 43221 . . . . (614) 451-0714
ARAB AMERICAN SVC
14235 DETROIT AVE, CLEVELAND 44107 . . . . (216) 226-6330
AROUND THE WORLD TRANSLATIONS
See Our Display Ad Under This Heading
WWW.ATWTRANSLATION.COM . . . . **(614) 575-2424**
AROUND WORLD INC
12281 BUTTERFIELD DR, PICKERINGTON 43147 . . . . (614) 575-2424
ASIST TRANSLATION SVC
4891 SAWMILL RD #200, COLUMBUS 43235 . . . . (614) 451-6744
BERLITZ LANGUAGE CTR
6133 ROCKSIDE RD #101, INDEPENDENCE 44131 . . . . (216) 861-0907
CHINESE TRANSLATION SVC
3225 BRAINARD RD, PEPPER PK 44124 . . . . (216) 378-0503
CINCILINGUA TRANSLATION SVC
322 E 4TH ST, CINCINNATI 45202 . . . . (513) 721-8782
COMMUNITY SERVICES-THE DEAF
212 E EXCHANGE ST, AKRON 44304 . . . . (330) 376-9494
CONVERSA LANGUAGE CTR
817 MAIN ST #6, CINCINNATI 45202 . . . . (513) 651-5679
CORVUS TRANSLATIONS
1018 24TH ST NE, CANTON 44714 . . . . (330) 456-0978

DEAF INITELY IT
4235 MONROE ST, TOLEDO 43606 . . . . (419) 472-8377
DEAF RESOURCE CTR
1801 ADAMS ST, TOLEDO 43624 . . . . (419) 243-1111
DEAF SERVICES CTR INC COMM
5830 N HIGH ST, WORTHINGTON 43085 . . . . (614) 841-9991
E TU ASSOC
5027 MADISON RD, CINCINNATI 45227 . . . . (513) 561-1010
FRENCH INTERFACE TRANSLATIONS
5607 N GREENWAY CT B, CLEVELAND 44143 . . . . (440) 684-0944
GEMO
6952 PONTEBERRY ST NW, CANTON 44718 . . . . (330) 499-2023
5037 SOUTHWAY ST SW, CANTON 44706 . . . . (330) 479-2720
GRACOR LANGUAGE SVC
159 BARANOF W, WESTERVILLE 43081 . . . . (614) 818-3220
H I TRANSLATION SVC
31500 SHAKER BLVD, PEPPER PK 44124 . . . . (216) 514-0210
INTER NET SVC
8202 MARKET PLACE LN, CINCINNATI 45242 . . . . (513) 891-2923
INTERNATIONAL INSTITUTE
2040 SCOTTWOOD AVE, TOLEDO 43620 . . . . (419) 241-9178
207 E TALLMADGE AVE, AKRON 44310 . . . . (330) 376-5106
INTERNATIONAL LANGUAGE PLUS
9403 KENWOOD RD #A203, CINCINNATI 45242 . . . . (513) 791-9293
INTERNATIONAL LANGUAGE SOURCE
PO BOX 338, HOLLAND 43528 . . . . (419) 865-4374
INTERNATIONAL SERVICES CTR
1836 EUCLID AVE #200, CLEVELAND 44115 . . . . (216) 781-4560
INTERPRETERS & TRANSLATORS
1680 NORTON CT, COLUMBUS 43228 . . . . (614) 346-3414
JAPAN SERVICES LTD
630 S PEARL ST, COLUMBUS 43206 . . . . (614) 464-9570
JAPANESE BUSINESS SVC
23220 SHAKER BLVD, CLEVELAND 44122 . . . . (216) 295-8283
JAPANESE TRANSLATION SVC
17215 ERNADALE AVE, CLEVELAND 44111 . . . . (216) 252-0777
JEWISH RESETTLEMENT
24075 COMMERCEE PARK ST $105, CLEVELAND 44122 . . . . . (216) 932-9200
KELEMEN & CO
6101 STOW RD, HUDSON 44236 . . . . (330) 463-5451
LANGUAGE BANK
200 MCFARLAND, CINCINNATI 45202 . . . . (513) 721-7660
LANGUAGE COMMUNICATIONS
6060 RAFTON DR, NEW ALBANY 43054 . . . . (614) 764-9210
LANGUAGE SOURCE
1043 PIERMONT RD, CLEVELAND 44121 . . . . (216) 381-2313
LEGAL LANGUAGE SERVICES
See Our Display Ad Under This Heading
WWW.LEGALLANGUAGE.COM . . . . **(800) 322-0284**
LINGUA INTERNATIONAL
3055 BETHEL RD, COLUMBUS 43220 . . . . (614) 457-8911
LINGUA TECH
368 WINTERSET DR, ENGLEWOOD 45322 . . . . (937) 832-3186
MCB TRANSLATIONS
965 GARDEN RD, COLUMBUS 43224 . . . . (614) 262-4111
MIAMI VALLEY INTERPRETERS LLC
1 ELIZABETH PL #SW10, DAYTON 45408 . . . . (937) 222-8200
MULTILINGUAL SVC INC
15139 72ND N, W PALM BEACH, FL 33418 . . . . (513) 934-2160
NATIVE TRANSLATIONS.COM
PO BOX 123, BATH 44210 . . . . (330) 659-4219
PROFESSIONAL TRANSLATION
10413 LORAIN AVE, CLEVELAND 44111 . . . . (216) 252-7088
RUSSIAN TRANSLATION SVC
8077 BARBERRY HILL DR, MENTOR 44060 . . . . (216) 573-7321
SPANISH AMERICAN COMMITTEE
4407 LORAIN AVE, CLEVELAND 44113 . . . . (216) 961-2100
SPANISH ONLY TRANSLATION SVC
184 OAKDALE AVE, AKRON 44302 . . . . (330) 535-4370
STROMAN & ASSOC
10022 WREN RD, MECHANICSBURG 43044 . . . . (937) 834-2021
SUMMIT TECHNICAL COMMUNICATION
3085 BRUSH RD, RICHFIELD 44286 . . . . (330) 659-3794
SYSTEMS INTERNATIONAL LANGUAGE
209 CAMBRIDGE AVE, TERRACE PK 45174 . . . . (513) 831-7474
TOBAR-THE WORLD OF LANGUAGES
1170 MEADOWIND CT, CINCINNATI 45231 . . . . (513) 784-1119
TONGUE TIED INC
835 MARILYN DR, WOOSTER 44691 . . . . (330) 262-7906
TRANSLATIONS UNLTD
1951 FALLBROOK LN, CINCINNATI 45240 . . . . (513) 674-0716
TRI-STATE INTERPRETING
455 BEECHTREE DR, CINCINNATI 45224 . . . . (513) 761-7761
VICE VERSA TRANSLATION SVC
1190 HATTERAS LN, HOLLYWOOD, FL 33019 . . . . (513) 677-5338
VOCALINK
40 S PERRY ST #135, DAYTON 45402 . . . . (937) 223-1415
WESTERN RESERVE TRANSLATORS
10160 DALE DR, WADSWORTH 44281 . . . . (330) 334-0457
WRIGHT & ASSOC
PO BOX 994, KENT 44240 . . . . (330) 673-0043

INVENTORY CONSULTANTS
(See VALUATION SERVICES)

INVESTIGATORS & DETECTIVE AGENCIES

A1 INVESTIGATIONS
  114 N WEST ST #205, LIMA 45801 . . . . (419) 229-1955
ABACUS INVESTIGATIONS
  611 W FRONT ST, FINDLAY 45840 . . . . (419) 722-7730
ACKERMAN KING & ASSOC
  4991 ALMONT DR, COLUMBUS 43229 . . . . (614) 436-4969
ALTECH DATA SVCS
  1144 TULSA DR, COLUMBUS 43229 . . . . (877) 541-3503
ANGELOTTA INVESTIGATIONS
  11510 BUCKEYE RD, CLEVELAND 44104 . . . . (216) 721-7700
ARGUS INVESTIGATIONS AGENCY
  9391 MENTOR AVE #313, MENTOR 44060 . . . . (440) 942-2389
B B ENTERPRISES
  2034 ANDERSON FERRY RD, CINCINNATI 45238 . . . . (513) 471-5777
B C & M INVESTIGATIONS & SCRTS
  179 DOGWOOD DR, DELAWARE 43015 . . . . (740) 369-8133
BALDUCCI ENTERPRISES
  31469 LORAIN RD #104, N OLMSTED 44070 . . . . (440) 979-0078
BOERGER INVESTIGATIVE SVCS
  PO BOX 1794, COLUMBUS 43216 . . . . (877) 754-8295
BUREAU OF RESEARCH INC
  75 PUBLIC SQ #1210, CLEVELAND 44113 . . . . (216) 589-0540
CLEVELAND SERVICE AGY
  PO BOX 93447, CLEVELAND 44101 . . . . (888) 212-5614
CORPORATE INVESTIGATIVE SERVICES INC
  31400 BRADLEY RD, N OLMSTED 44070 . . . . (800) 899-1173
DATA RESEARCH INC
  5650 W CENTRAL AVE #D, TOLEDO 43615 . . . . (419) 534-5422
DESMITH CONSULTING GRP INC
  9862 FREMONT DR, COLUMBIA STA 44028 . . . . (440) 236-9609
DLB & ASSOC INVESTIGATIONS
  148 BARBERRY DR, BEREA 44017 . . . . (440) 260-7567
DRISCOLL & ASSOC
  PO BOX 273, SUNBURY 43074 . . . . (740) 965-3023
GENERAL CORPORATE INVESTIGATION INC
  PO BOX 2657, CINCINNATI 45201 . . . . (859) 491-5341
GENERAL DETECTIVE AGENCY
  3699 WILLOW RUN, CLEVELAND 44145 . . . . (440) 734-4780
GLOBAL ONE SECURITY
  171 E LIVINGSTON AVE, COLUMBUS 43215 . . . . (614) 501-8490
GRAY SECURITY INC
  5136 RICHMOND RD, CLEVELAND 44146 . . . . (216) 595-9800
GSA PRIVATE INVESTIGATORS
  10383 LORETO RIDGE DR, KIRTLAND 44094 . . . . (440) 256-2505
HALL & ASSOC INC
  894 VILLAGE BROOK WAY, COLUMBUS 43235 . . . . (614) 785-1777
HENSLEY & MCCRACKEN INVSTGTNS
  4745 WOLF CREEK PIKE, DAYTON 45427 . . . . (937) 275-3000
HOLMES DETECTIVE GROUP
  36 E 7TH ST #2121, CINCINNATI 45202 . . . . (513) 651-5150
INFO-TRAK INVESTIGATIONS
  1604 WALKER LAKE RD, MANSFIELD 44906 . . . . (419) 747-9296

INFOCORP INVESTIGATIVE SVCS LLC
  See Our Display Ad Under This Heading
  PO BOX 120, LEWIS CTR 43035 . . . . **(888) 989-9894**
INFORMATION SEARCH GROUP LTD
  PO BOX 6557, COLUMBUS 43026 . . . . (614) 449-2828
INNOVATIVE INVESTIGATIONS
  3476 IRWIN SIMPSON RD #110A, MASON 45040 . . . . (513) 229-0015
INSIGHT CONSULTANTS INC
  PO BOX 29280, COLUMBUS 43229 . . . . (614) 460-7409
INTEGRITY SECURITY SVCS INC
  6511 EASTLAND RD, BROOKPARK 44142 . . . . (440) 816-2070
INTELL NORTH INVESTIGATIONS
  7955 SETHWICK RD, DUBLIN 43016 . . . . (614) 789-9277
ISIS INVESTIGATIONS
  5642 WALES AVE NW, MASSILLON 44646 . . . . (330) 498-4747
J & G INVESTIGATIONS
  6924 SPRING VALLEY DR #180, HOLLAND 43528 . . . . (419) 244-0221

LEGAL INVESTIGATION SERVICES
  See Our Display Ad Under This Heading
  PO BOX 10633, DAYTON 45402 . . . . **(937) 547-1710**

MATRIX INVESTIGATIONS & CONSULTING INC
  See Our Display Ad Under This Heading
  1776 MENTOR AVE, CINCINNATI 45212 . . . . **(877) 550-7573**
METRO CLEVELAND SECURITY INC
  5627 MEMPHIS AVE, CLEVELAND 44144 . . . . (216) 398-0924
N I S INC
  597 PARK AVE E #228, MANSFIELD 44905 . . . . (419) 756-3711

Civil, Criminal, Corporate & Insurance Investigations

- **Worker's Compensation Fraud**
- **Insurance Fraud**
- **Disability Fraud**
- **Undercover Operations**
- **Background Checks**
- **Witness Locates, Interviews & Statements**

VIDEO SURVEILLANCE SPECIALISTS

If a picture is worth 1000 words, what is a video worth?

Matrix Investigations & Consulting, Inc.
1776 Mentor Avenue, Cincinnati, OH 45212

877-550-7573
www.mtrxinc.com

Toll Free
888-989-9894

- **Private Investigations**
  - * Corporate Fraud   * Financial Fraud
  - * Worker's Compensation Fraud
  - * Domestic   * Construction Fraud
- **Skip-Tracing**
  - * Locates * Adoption Cases - Nationwide
- **Process Service - Available Nationwide**
- **Attorney Support**   *Licensed in the state of Ohio - Fully Insured*

P.O. Box 120   **Local: 614-785-1669**
Lewis Center, Ohio 43035   **Fax: 614-340-7179**

NATIONAL SECURITY INVESTIGATIVE AGCY INC
  72 REESE RD, PORTSMOUTH 45662 . . . . (740) 776-2400
NIAM ENTERPRISES
  118 W STREETSBORO ST, HUDSON 44236 . . . . (330) 342-0838
NORTH AMERICAN SECURITY SLTNS
  2844 E RIVER RD, DAYTON 45439 . . . . (937) 890-4300
NORTH COAST INVESTIGATIONS
  PO BOX 99311, CLEVELAND 44199 . . . . (800) 231-6132
OFFICIAL INVESTIGATIONS INC
  PO BOX 317725, CINCINNATI 45231 . . . . (513) 931-7448
PICA CORP
  551 S 3RD ST, COLUMBUS 43215 . . . . (614) 228-7422
PINKERTON INVESTIGATION SVC
  1 SUMMIT PARK DR #630, INDEPENDENCE 44131 . . . . (216) 520-5400
PINKERTON SECURITY SVC
  12000 SNOW RD #5, CLEVELAND 44130 . . . . (216) 351-5652
PROFESSIONAL INVESTIGATION SVC
  5451 BROADVIEW RD, CLEVELAND 44134 . . . . (216) 661-1366

INVESTIGATORS & DETECTIVE AGENCIES
(Cont'd)

QUEST ASSOCIATES OF OHIO LLC
See Our Display Ad Under This Heading
4771 GLENDALE MILFORD RD, CNCNNT 45242 . **(800) 354-9907**
R C BECKETT INVESTIGATIONS
PO BOX 750503, CENTERVILLE 45475 . . . . (937) 433-6385
REA INVESTIGATIONS
PO BOX 30143, MIDDLEBURG HTS 44130 . . . . . . **(216) 433-7685**
REGIONAL INVESTIGATIONS INC
5440 FULTON DR NW #205, CANTON 44718 . . . . (330) 497-4977
RESEARCH ASSOC INC
27999 CLEMENS RD, COLUMBUS 44145 . . . . (440) 892-1000
RICK SHEASBY & ASSOC
7901 BEVELHEIMER RD, NEW ALBANY 43054 . . . . (614) 855-2500
RISC GROUP THE
PO BOX 11023, CHARLESTON, WV 25339 . . . . (888) 568-6500
S T & D INVESTIGATIVE SVC GRP
110 N HIGH ST #201, GAHANNA 43230 . . . . (614) 552-0196
SADLER & ASSOCIATES INC
PO BOX 249 227 MAIN ST, LUCKEY 43443 . . . . (419) 833-8222
SAFE PLACE
3573 WOODSTONE DR, LEWIS CTR 43035 . . . . (614) 798-4200
SATIRA DATA NETWORK
PO BOX 294, BURTON 44021 . . . . (440) 834-4037
SCREENPOINTE
500 S FRONT ST #102, COLUMBUS 43215 . . . . (614) 224-8622
SECURE SYSTEMS GROUP LTD
958 INDEPENDENCE DR, DAYTON 45429 . . . . (937) 673-4546
SECURITY ENGINEERING
249 S PAINT ST #102, CHILLICOTHE 45601 . . . . (740) 773-5700
SEMAPHORE INVESTIGATIONS & SECURITY
PO BOX 304, BOWERSVILLE 45307. . . . . (937) 681-4758
SENTINEL PROTECTION SVCS INC
400 ORANGE ST, ASHLAND 44805 . . . . (419) 289-8595
SPARTAN ENTERPRISES
1854 ELDON DR, WICKLIFFE 44092 . . . . (440) 944-4898
STARDUST INVESTIGATIONS
PO BOX 325, BATH 44210 . . . . (330) 244-9581
SUR-TECH SPY STORE
580 MIAMISBURG CENTERVILLE RD, DAYTON 45459 . . . . . . (937) 293-8414
SYDNEY R MICHAEL INVESTIGATIONS
7360 W BLVD #102, YOUNGSTOWN 44512. . . . . (330) 726-6475
TECH EVIDENCE INC
WWW.TECHEVIDENCE.COM . . . . (937) 238-8064
TENABLE PROTECTIVE SVCS
2423 PAYNE AVE, CLEVELAND 44114 . . . . (216) 361-0002
TRI VALLEY PROTECTIVE SVC
735 E MAIN ST, SMITHVILLE 44677 . . . . (330) 669-2539
TRIAL PREP INVESTIGATIONS
2701 CLEVELAND AVE NW #G, CANTON 44709 . . . . (330) 456-2207
UNIQUE INVESTIGATIVE SVC
2374 N BILLMAN RD, GENOA 43430 . . . . (419) 855-3679
UNITED NATIONAL SECURITY INC
7900 WHIPPLE AVE NW, N CANTON 44720 . . . . (330) 966-0019
WHITESTONE GROUP INC
PO BOX 499, PICKERINGTON 43147 . . . . (614) 501-7007
WILLIAM ANDERSON INVESTIGATIONS
PO BOX 1408, CUMMING, GA 30028 . . . . (801) 282-2132

INVESTMENT SERVICES
PINNACLE INVESTORS ADVISORY CORP
6 W 3RD ST #100, MANSFIELD 44902 . . . . (419) 526-5226

JUDGEMENT SEARCHES
(See SEARCH SERVICES; TITLE INSURANCE COMPANIES & AGENTS; and ABSTRACTERS)

JURY CONSULTANTS
(See LITIGATION SUPPORT SERVICES)

LABORATORIES-TESTING

ACCURATE BIOMEDICAL LABORATORY
PO BOX 248137, CLEVELAND 44124 . . . . (216) 691-1182
ADENA HEALTH CTR
PO BOX 830, JACKSON 45640 . . . . (740) 286-9040
ADVANCED ANALYTICS
1025 CONCORD AVE, COLUMBUS 43212 . . . . (614) 299-9922
ADVANCED QUALITY GROUP INC-NDT
1090 ERIE RD #F, WILLOUGHBY 44095. . . . . (440) 954-9404
AERODYN ENGINEERING INC
4954 PROVIDENT DR, CINCINNATI 45246. . . . . (513) 674-9520
AGGREGATE & CONCRETE TESTING
POB 873, GNADENHUTTEN 44629. . . . . (740) 254-1018
AKRON RUBBER DEVELOPMENT LAB
2887 GILCHRIST RD, AKRON 44305 . . . . (330) 794-6600
AMERICAN POLYMER STANDARDS
8680 TYLER BLVD, MENTOR 44060. . . . . (440) 255-2211
AMKO SERVICE CO
2296 LARSON RD SE, GNADENHUTTEN 44629 . . . . (740) 254-4020
AUTOMOTIVE SAFETY TESTING INC
1723 COUNTY ROAD 130, BELLEFONTAINE 43311 . . . . . (937) 593-0340
BASEDOW FAMILY CLINIC
2111 S 7TH ST, IRONTON 45638 . . . . (740) 533-2156
C C TECHNOLOGIES
5777 FRANZ RD, DUBLIN 43017 . . . . (614) 761-1214
CAL MAR SOIL TESTING LAB
130 S STATE ST, WESTERVILLE 43081 . . . . (614) 523-1005
CARDINAL ANALYTICAL LAB
650 MCCREADY AVE, CADIZ 43907. . . . . (740) 942-2117
CENTRAL TESTING LABORATORIES
5265 TRANSPORTATION BLVD, CLEVELAND 44125. . . . . . (216) 475-9000
CLC LABS
325 VENTURE DR, WESTERVILLE 43081 . . . . (614) 888-1663
COLUMBUS WATER & CHEMICAL TEST
4628 INDIANOLA AVE, COLUMBUS 43214 . . . . (614) 262-4372
COMMERCIAL TESTING & ENGRNG
2979 E CENTER ST, CONNEAUT 44030 . . . . (440) 224-2261
CONCRETE RESEARCH & TESTING
400 FRANK RD, COLUMBUS 43207 . . . . (614) 443-0085
COSHOCTON ENVIRONMENTAL INC
709 MAIN ST, COSHOCTON 43812 . . . . (740) 622-3328
CSA INTL
8501 E PLEASANT VALLEY RD, CLEVELAND 44131 . . . . . . (216) 524-4990
CTC ANALYTICAL SVC INC
18419 EUCLID AVE, CLEVELAND 44112 . . . . (216) 383-8200
CTX ACCRA LABORATORIES
1393 HIGHLAND RD, TWINSBURG 44087. . . . . (330) 405-6830
DANIEL T CLANCY & ASSOC
5827 ALBERTA DR, CLEVELAND 44124 . . . . (440) 461-0720
DATA ANALYSIS TECHNOLOGIES INC
7715 CORPORATE BLVD, PLAIN CITY 43064 . . . . (614) 873-0710
DAYTON TESTING LAB
125 WESTPARK RD, DAYTON 45459. . . . . (937) 890-6350
DHI COOPERATIVE INC
7849 E LINCOLN WAY, APPLE CREEK 44606 . . . . (330) 264-0411
EDISON WELDING INSTITUTE INC
1250 ARTHUR E ADAMS DR, COLUMBUS 43221 . . . . . . (614) 688-5000
ETC TESTING LABORATORIES
29633 LAKELAND BLVD, WICKLIFFE 44092 . . . . (440) 944-3665
EXPERIOR TESTING NETWORK
6000 LOMBARDO CTR #220, CLEVELAND 44131 . . . . . . (216) 642-7369
F SQUARED LABORATORIES
14333 KINSMAN RD, BURTON 44021. . . . . (440) 834-8926
FIRSTECH INC
19701 S MILES RD #52, CLEVELAND 44128 . . . . (216) 663-0808
FISCHER ENGINEERING
8220 EXPANSION WAY, DAYTON 45424 . . . . (937) 754-1750

LABORATORIES-TESTING (Cont'd)

FTI-SEA INC
  7349 WORTHINGTON GALENA RD, WORTHINGTON 43085 . . (614) 888-4160
HAYDEN ENVIRONMENTAL GROUP I
  PO BOX 751401, DAYTON 45475 . . . . (937) 439-3764
INDEPENDENT HEALTH SVC
  4400 N HIGH ST #207, COLUMBUS 43214 . . . . (614) 267-4222
INSIGHT SERVICE
  12703 TRISKETT RD, CLEVELAND 44111 . . . . (216) 251-2510
ITS CALEB BRETT USA INC
  4760 RIVER RD, CINCINNATI 43616 . . . . (419) 693-4007
JFP TECHNICAL SVC
  7552 ST CLAIR AVE #G, MENTOR 44060 . . . . (440) 946-6577
KAVON TESTING LABS
  12275 BEAN RD, CHARDON 44024 . . . . (440) 918-9128
LABORATORY CONSULTANTS
  7454 S TIPP COWLESVILLE RD, TIPP CITY 45371 . . . . . . (937) 438-2984
LANKARD MATERIALS LAB INC
  400 FRANK RD, COLUMBUS 43207 . . . . (614) 443-3303
MACTEC ENGINEERING
  413 APPLE GROVE NW #100, N CANTON 44720 . . . . (330) 244-1541
MARLIN MANUFACTURING CORP
  PO BOX 118000, CLEVELAND 44111 . . . . (216) 941-6200
MARSHFIELD LABORATORIES
  15473 NEO PKWY, CLEVELAND 44128 . . . . (216) 475-6601
MATERIALS EVALUATION BUREAU
  7809 HARVARD AVE, CLEVELAND 44105 . . . . (216) 341-8096
MATERIALS JOINING CONSULTANTS
  790 MORRISON RD, COLUMBUS 43230 . . . . (614) 863-9626
MCGAW TECHNOLOGY INC
  17439 LAKE AVE, CLEVELAND 44107 . . . . (216) 521-3490
NCS CORP
  1385 W GOODALE BLVD, COLUMBUS 43212 . . . . (614) 340-3700
NSL ANALYTICAL SVC
  7650 HUB PKWY, CLEVELAND 44125 . . . . (216) 447-1550
ONCODIAGNOSTICS LABORATORY INC
  2351 E 22ND ST, CLEVELAND 44115 . . . . (216) 861-5845
ORBIT INDUSTRIES
  6840 LAKE ABRAMS DR, CLEVELAND 44130 . . . . (440) 243-3311
PORTER LABORATORIES INC
  1829 E LONG ST, COLUMBUS 43203 . . . . (614) 252-3560
PREDICT
  9555 ROCKSIDE RD, CLEVELAND 44125 . . . . (216) 642-3223
PSI
  5555 CANAL RD, CLEVELAND 44125 . . . . (216) 447-1335
RICERCA INC
  7528 AUBURN RD, PAINESVILLE 44077 . . . . (440) 357-3261
RMI TESTING
  9933 CHILLICOTHE RD, WILLOUGHBY 44094 . . . . (440) 256-1463
SGS COMMERCIAL TESTING
  2979 E CENTER ST, CONNEAUT 44030 . . . . (440) 224-2261
SPECTRUM ANALYTIC INC
  1087 JAMISON RD NW, WASHINGTON CT HS 43160 . . . . (740) 335-1562
STORK HERRON TESTING LABORATORIES INC
  See Our Display Ad Under This Heading
  5405 E SCHAAF RD, CLEVELAND 44131 . . . . . . **(216) 524-1450**
SUPERIOR LABORATORIES
  168 DORCHESTER SQ S, WESTERVILLE 43081 . . . . (614) 793-8778
TALCO SYSTEMS LLC
  4690 INTERSTATE DR #P, CINCINNATI 45246 . . . . (513) 874-8445
TENSILE TESTING METALLURGICAL
  7815 HARVARD AVE, CLEVELAND 44105 . . . . (216) 641-3290
TIMMERMAN GEOTECHNICAL GROUP
  2685 GILCHRIST RD, AKRON 44305 . . . . (330) 434-3494
TOLEDO FOREST PRODUCTS LAB INC
  6540 W CENTRAL AVE #J, TOLEDO 43617 . . . . (419) 841-7663
TOTALMED LABS
  1328 DUBLIN RD #21, COLUMBUS 43215 . . . . (614) 481-4425
TOXICOLOGY ASSOC INC
  999 BETHEL RD #3000, COLUMBUS 43214 . . . . (614) 459-2307
U S INSPECTION SVC
  1864 ENTERPRISE PKWY #D, TWINSBURG 44087 . . . . . . (330) 405-8991
ULTRA LABS INC
  19600 ST CLAIR AVE, CLEVELAND 44117 . . . . (216) 531-8107
UNDERWRITERS LABORATORIES INC
  1445 WORTHINGTON WDS, WORTHINGTON 43085 . . . . (614) 841-0333
WELDING CONSULTANTS INC
  889 N 22ND ST, COLUMBUS 43219 . . . . (614) 258-7018
WILSON ENVIRONMENTAL LABS INC
  4834 CRAZY HORSE LN, WESTERVILLE 43081 . . . . (614) 431-0010
WORLD INTERNATIONAL TESTING CO
  2229 SUNSET BLVD, STEUBENVILLE 43952 . . . . (740) 264-1111
XRI TESTING
  5403 E SCHAAF RD, CLEVELAND 44131 . . . . (216) 642-0100

LAND SURVEYORS
  (See ENGINEERS—CIVIL; and SURVEYORS—LAND)

LANGUAGE SERVICES
  (See INTERPRETERS & TRANSLATORS)

LEGAL PLACEMENT SERVICES
  (See Also EMPLOYMENT AGENCIES; EXECUTIVE SEARCH FIRMS; and PARALEGAL SERVICES)

CARPENTER LEGAL SEARCH INC
  301 GRANT ST #3030, PITTSBURGH, PA 15219 . **(412) 255-3770**
J MONAGHAN & ASSOCIATES LLC
  1550 OLD HENDERSON RD, COLUMBUS 43220 . . . . (614) 273-0545

L STEVENS & CO EMPLOYMENT SPECIALISTS

THE LEGAL STAFFING PROFESSIONALS
ATTORNEYS * PARALEGALS * LEGAL SECRETARIES
DIRECT HIRE * CONTRACT * TEMPORARY

WWW.LSTEVENSEMPLOYMENT.COM . . . . **(216) 523-1800**
MAJOR LEGAL SVCS LLC
  WWW.MAJORLEGALSERVICES.COM . . . . **(216) 579-9782**
MARVEL CONSULTANTS INC
  See Our Display Ad Under This Heading
  28601 CHAGRIN BLVD #670, CLEVELAND 44122 **(216) 292-2855**

LEGAL RESEARCH SERVICES
  (See Also LITIGATION SUPPORT SERVICES; and PARALEGAL SERVICES)

WESTGROUP
  600 SUPERIOR AVE E #2550, CLEVELAND 44114 . . . . (216) 623-0880

LEGAL SOFTWARE
  (See COMPUTERS—LEGAL SOFTWARE)

LIABILITY INSURANCE
  (See INSURANCE—PROFESSIONAL LIABILITY; and INSURANCE AGENCIES)

LIBRARY SERVICES
  (See LEGAL RESEARCH SERVICES)

LIE DETECTION SERVICES
  (See POLYGRAPH & LIE DETECTION SERVICES)

LIEN SEARCHES
  (See SEARCH SERVICES; ABSTRACTERS; and TITLE INSURANCE COMPANIES & AGENTS)

MEDVOPRO
MEDICAL VOCATIONAL PROFESSIONALS

LIFE CARE PLANNING • FUTURE NEEDS ASSESSMENT
MEDICARE SET-ASIDE ALLOCATIONS
MEDICAL RECORD REVIEW • VOCATIONAL COUNSELING

PERSONAL INJURY • CATASTROPHIC ILLNESS
WORKERS COMPENSATION • DISABILITY

Contact: Karen Conrad
(614) 539-1150
3620 North High Street, Suite B-4 • Columbus, Ohio 43214
W W W . M E D V O P R O . C O M

LIFE CARE PLANNING

BENOIT ROXANNE N
  BENOITCLCP@CS.COM . . . . (614) 799-2859

COLBERT BETTYE J RN CDMS CCM CLCP

CATASTROPHIC CASE MANAGEMENT * LEGAL
NURSE CONSULTING * LIFE CARE PLANNING
MEDICARE SET-ASIDE

PO BOX 340641, COLUMBUS 43234 . . . . **(614) 284-9716**

GRAESSLE & ASSOCIATES INC
  GRAESSLEASSOC@AOL.COM . . . . (937) 312-1511
LIFE CARE PLAN CONSULTING
  BALESCLCP@AOL.COM . . . . (614) 231-1720
LIFE CARE PLANNING INC
  PO BOX 06423, COLUMBUS 43206 . . . . (614) 228-7513

LIFE CARE SOLUTIONS INC

PROVIDING CASE MANAGEMENT &
LIFE CARE PLANNING FOR CHILDREN
& ADULTS WITH CATASTROPHIC INJURIES

LCSCMS@INSIGHTBB.COM . . . . **(502) 243-9745**

MEDVOPRO
See Our Display Ad Under This Heading
  3620 N HIGH ST, #B-4, COLUMBUS 43214 . . . . . . **(614) 539-1150**
MOSLEY ROBERT A PHD CLCP
  13938A CEDAR RD #240, UNIVERSITY HTS 44118 . . . . (216) 321-5674
QUALITY REHABILITATION & CONSULTING SVCS LLC
  391 SADDLE PATH LN, PATASKALA 43062 . . . . . . **(740) 964-9366**
RICKARD-WATSON MIKKI L RN BSN CLCP CRRN LNC
  NURSINGCO@MSN.COM . . . . **(304) 638-1791**
RINEHART JENNIFER A RN CLCP
  12313 N HOGAN RD, AURORA, IN 47001 . . . . **(513) 564-8163**
SHEILA J COTTLE & ASSOCIATES
  SCOTTLE@CINCI.RR.COM . . . . (513) 742-1111
VILLAGE AT ST EDWARD THE
  3125 SMITH RD, FAIRLAWN 44333 . . . . (330) 668-2828
VITACARE CONSULTING LLC
  CHAPMAN43112@AOL.COM . . . . (614) 833-9470
VOCWORKS
  5555 GLENDON CT, DUBLIN 43016 . . . . (614) 760-3889
ZALAC JONI RN MSN CRRN CLCP
  OSSIJZ@ZOOMINTERNET.NET . . . . (330) 758-6527

LITIGATION SUPPORT SERVICES
(See Also LEGAL RESEARCH SERVICES; and PARALEGAL SERVICES)

COMPUSERVE INC
  5000 ARLINGTON CTR BLVD, COLUMBUS 43220 . . . . (800) 848-8199
COMPUTERS 4 US
  181 ELM RD, WARREN 44483. . . . . (330) 373-0990
MARK W BOSLETT INC CPA
  PREFERREDTAX@ALLTEL.NET. . . . . **(330) 650-4033**
NORMAN JONES ENLOW & CO
  530 W SPRING ST, COLUMBUS 43215 . . . . (740) 453-0515
R L STEVENS & ASSOC INC
  5005 ROCKSIDE RD #900, INDEPENDENCE 44131 . . . . (216) 642-1933
SCHNEIDER DOWNS & CO INC
  WWW.SCHNEIDERDOWNS.COM . . . . (614) 621-4060
SEATON DELTA CONSULTING
  7251 DOVER-ZOAR RD NE, DOVER 44622. . . . . (330) 343-5621

LOSS ADJUSTERS
(See ADJUSTERS)

MANAGEMENT CONSULTANTS
DMA GRP INC
  239 DRAKESIDE RD, HAMPTON, NH 03842 . . . . (800) 370-3362

MARKETING FIRMS & CONSULTANTS
BUSINESS & PROFESSIONAL IMAGES
  506 W MAIN ST, NEWARK 43055 . . . . (740) 787-2947

MARRIAGE & FAMILY COUNSELORS
(See Also ADR SERVICES)

A CENTER FOR PSYCHOLOGICAL SVC
  5060 BRADENTON AVE #A, DUBLIN 43017 . . . . (614) 766-6688
A MEDIATION GRP
  11125 SW 177 ST, MIAMI, FL 33157 . . . . (305) 255-5190
ACCESS BEHAVIORAL CARE INC
  PO BOX 603918, CLEVELAND 44103 . . . . (440) 777-7574
ACKERLEY DIANA G PHD
  305 E STROOP RD, DAYTON 45429. . . . . (937) 294-1689
ADDICTION & PSYCHOTHERAPY SVCS INC
  7086 CORPORATE WAY, CENTERVILLE 45459 . . . . (937) 435-5200
ADKINS RICHARDSON & STOKES
  PO BOX 864, BELLEFONTAINE 43311 . . . . (937) 599-2662
ALEXANDER LEON PHD
  101 LONGVUE AVE, MINGO JUNCTION 43938 . . . . (740) 282-5335
BELMONT PSYCHIATRIC SVC
  300 HOWARD ST #4, BRIDGEPORT 43912 . . . . (740) 635-7792
BENDER NATHAN J PHD
  386 TRUSSEL RD, PETAL, MS 39465. . . . . (601) 582-5294
BETHESDA COUNSELING MINISTRIES
  PO BOX 193, WESTFIELD CTR 44251 . . . . (330) 769-1930
CENTER FOR CHILD PSYCHOLOGY
  9853 JOHNNYCAKE RIDGE RD, MENTOR 44060 . . . . (440) 352-6848
CENTER FOR COGNITIVE THERAPY
  2121 BETHEL RD #D, COLUMBUS 43220 . . . . (614) 459-4490
CENTER FOR FAMILIES & CHILDREN
  4500 EUCLID AVE, CLEVELAND 44103 . . . . (216) 431-5800
  3929 ROCKY RIVER DR, CLEVELAND 44111 . . . . (216) 252-5800
CENTER FOR FAMILY DEVELOPMENT
  8 MAIN ST, ZANESVILLE 43701 . . . . (740) 453-9089
CENTER-RELATIONSHIP SUCCESS
  979 HIGH ST, WORTHINGTON 43085 . . . . (614) 846-6743
CENTRAL BEHAVIORAL HEALTHCARE
  5965 RENAISSANCE PL, TOLEDO 43623 . . . . (419) 841-5934
CENTRAL OHIO MENTAL HEALTH CTR
  950 MEADOW DR #A, MT GILEAD 43338. . . . . (419) 947-4560
D & E COUNSELING
  108 E OHIO AVE, SEBRING 44672 . . . . (330) 938-2364
DEEPERLIFE MINISTRIES
  5123 CONVERSE HUFF RD, PLAIN CITY 43064 . . . . (614) 873-8811
DELAWARE CHRISTIAN CHURCH
  2280 MARYSVILLE RD, DELAWARE 43015 . . . . (740) 369-2929
DELAWARE INTERNAL MEDICNE
  454 W CENTRAL AVE, DELAWARE 43015 . . . . (740) 369-2058
DELTA PSYCHOLOGICAL SVC
  3865 ROCKY RIVER DR #3, CLEVELAND 44111 . . . . (216) 671-4508
DELTA PSYCHOLOGY CTR
  848 SCIOTO ST #B, URBANA 43078. . . . . (937) 652-1474
DENNISON & ASSOC INC
  97 S LIBERTY ST, POWELL 43065 . . . . (614) 888-8440
DESIGN FOR INDIVIDUAL FAMILY
  461 W LORAIN ST, OBERLIN 44074. . . . . (440) 775-2905
EMOTIONAL HEALTH COUNSELING CTR
  28906 LORAIN RD #104, N OLMSTED 44070. . . . . (440) 777-5151
FAMILY VISITATION & MEDIATION SVC INC
  143 NORTHWEST AVE #102, TALLMADGE 44278. . . . . (330) 630-1868
GEBHART JAMES E PHD
  3400 KENNY RD, COLUMBUS 43221 . . . . (614) 451-8132
GENESIS COUNSELING CTR INC
  17747 CHILLICOTHE RD #202, CHAGRIN FALLS 44023 . . . . (440) 543-8880
GENTLE SHEPHERD COUNSELING CTR
  1469 S MAIN ST, N CANTON 44720 . . . . (330) 499-3065
GERLACH LEAR & ASSOC
  45 W 2ND ST #C, CHILLICOTHE 45601 . . . . (740) 773-4521
JEFFERSON BEHAVIORAL HEALTH
  740 N 6TH AVE, STEUBENVILLE 43952. . . . . (740) 282-5338
  3200 JOHNSON RD, STEUBENVILLE 43952 . . . . (740) 264-7751
  100 N 4TH ST #200, STEUBENVILLE 43952. . . . . (740) 284-7165
  524 MADISON AVE, STEUBENVILLE 43952 . . . . (740) 284-1400
KENNEDY CONSULTING
  PO BOX 944, WILMINGTON 45177 . . . . (937) 383-3565
KENT A YOUNG & ASSOC
  9500 MENTOR AVE #320, MENTOR 44060 . . . . (440) 639-1221
KEROSKY MICHAEL
  6635 W CENTRAL AVE, TOLEDO 43617 . . . . (419) 841-5042
L-C CONSOLIDATED CARE INC
  PO BOX 817, W LIBERTY 43357 . . . . (937) 465-8065
LENGERICH THERESA C
  10915 READING RD, CINCINNATI 45241 . . . . (513) 891-6040
MCELROY CYNTHIA
  130 N PROSPECT ST, GRANVILLE 43023 . . . . (740) 587-2902
MCGLOSHEN THOMAS H PHD
  5178 BLAZER PKWY #A, DUBLIN 43017 . . . . (614) 889-2223

MARRIAGE & FAMILY COUNSELORS
(Cont'd)

MCVEY PHYLISS MSW LISW
2691 E MAIN ST #203, COLUMBUS 43209 . . . . (614) 237-0309

MEEKS PHIL
621 FRANKLIN AVE, COLUMBUS 43215 . . . . (614) 469-4720

MEERS INC
3246 HENDERSON RD, COLUMBUS 43220. . . . . (614) 451-0176

MELANIE THOMBRE MD & ASSOC
2639 UPTON AVE, TOLEDO 43606. . . . . (419) 471-1848

MELVIN PAINTER INC
14701 DETROIT AVE, CLEVELAND 44107. . . . . (216) 226-4610

MELYMBROSIA ASSOC
315 TUSCARAWAS ST W #500, CANTON 44702 . . . . (330) 455-2145

MENTAL WELLNESS CTR
230 STONE BRIDGE RD, NORTHFIELD 44067 . . . . . . (330) 665-8055

NEW CREATION COUNSELING CTR
7695 S COUNTY ROAD 25A, TIPP CITY 45371 . . . . . . (937) 667-4678

NEW DIRECTIONS COUNSELING CTR
1575 MARION AVE, MANSFIELD 44906 . . . . (419) 529-9941

NEW LIFE COMMUNITY CHURCH
PO BOX 293, W CHESTER 45071 . . . . (513) 759-6040

NEW LIFE COUNSELING SVC
125 E 2ND ST, DOVER 44622 . . . . (330) 343-6600

NEW LIFE MINISTRIES
8000 PLAZA BLVD #140, MENTOR 44060 . . . . (440) 946-5686

NEWARK-GRANVILLE PSYCHOLOGICAL
1943 NEWARK GRANVILLE RD, GRANVILLE 43023. . . . . (740) 587-5252

OZER MINISTRIES
407 N MARKET ST, E PALESTINE 44413 . . . . (330) 426-2147

PAMELA VENUS
1397 WARREN RD, CLEVELAND 44107 . . . . (216) 221-3137

PENGILLY MORRIS R
3865 ROCKY RIVER DR #2, CLEVELAND 44111 . . . . . (216) 941-0230

PERSONAL GROWTH COUNSELING
1128 W MARKET ST, LIMA 45805 . . . . (419) 222-2255

PERSONAL MARRIAGE-FAMILY
2044 SCENIC DR NW, LANCASTER 43130 . . . . (740) 687-6429

PERSONALIZED ART LTD
4015 FENWICK RD, COLUMBUS 43220 . . . . (614) 457-5112

PERSPECTIVES COUNSELING SVC
1114 BOURGOGNE AVE, BOWLING GREEN 43402 . . . . (419) 353-8430

REGINALD C BLUE PHD & ASSOCS
20310 CHAGRIN BLVD #5, SHAKER HTS 44122 . . . . . (216) 991-3500

ROBINWOOD PSYCHOSOCIAL SVC
2400 ROBINWOOD AVE, TOLEDO 43620 . . . . (419) 241-2433

SCHULZ GEORGE O PHD
361 UPPER VALLEY PIKE, SPRINGFIELD 45504 . . . . . (937) 322-3523

SCIOTO PAINT VALLEY MENTAL CTR
1300 E PAINT ST, WASHINGTON CT HS 43160 . . . . . (740) 333-1675
145 MORRIS RD, CIRCLEVILLE 43113. . . . . (740) 474-8874

SEASONS OF LIFE COUNSELING INC
4444 GALLOWAY RD, SANDUSKY 44870 . . . . (419) 621-8773

WEAVER JEAN MS LPCC
42 E RAHN RD #209, DAYTON 45429. . . . . (937) 667-9597

WELLNESS INSTITUTE
1000 HIGH ST, WORTHINGTON 43085 . . . . (614) 888-5885

WESTARK FAMILY SVC
42 1ST ST NE, MASSILLON 44646 . . . . (330) 832-5043

WESTERN RESERVE COUNSELING
1 VICTORIA SQ #105, PAINESVILLE 44077 . . . . . . (440) 352-8954

WESTERVILLE FAMILY CNSLTN CTR
1001 EASTWIND DR #201, WESTERVILLE 43081 . . . . (614) 882-3684

ZECK THOMAS F PHD
1740 COOPER FOSTER PARK RD #E, LORAIN 44053 . . . (440) 282-1383

MEDIATION SERVICES
(See ADR SERVICES)

MEDICAL EXPERTS
(See EXPERTS—MEDICAL)

MEDICARE SET-ASIDES

MEDVOPRO
3620 N HIGH ST, #B-4, COLUMBUS 43214 . . . . . . **(614) 539-1150**

QUALITY REHABILITATION & CONSULTING SVCS LLC
391 SADDLE PATH LN, PATASKALA 43062. . . . . (740) 964-9366

MENTAL HEALTH SERVICES

WOODLAND CENTERS INC
3086 STATE RT 160, GALLIPOLIS 45631 . . . . (740) 446-3022

MESSENGER SERVICES
(See Also PROCESS & SUBPOENA SERVICES)

ADVANCED DELIVERY SVC INC
PO BOX 751892, DAYTON 45475 . . . . (937) 433-6898

ALL-AMERICAN COURIER CORPS
245 ASHLEY CT, GAHANNA 43230. . . . . (614) 863-2617

BEST COURIER INC
1200 TECHNOLOGY DR, COLUMBUS 43230 . . . . (614) 475-8900

BLACK & WHITE CAB CO
44 HILLWYCK DR, TOLEDO 43615. . . . . (419) 381-5900

BOLT EXPRESS
5515 SOUTHWYCK BLVD, TOLEDO 43614 . . . . (419) 865-2500

C & R EXPRESS INC
PO BOX 2957, YOUNGSTOWN 44511 . . . . (330) 799-4488

CENTRAL CONTROL DELIVERY INC
1424 E 25TH ST, CLEVELAND 44114. . . . . (216) 781-0707

CINCINNATI EXPRESS DELIVERY
1150 W 8TH ST #252, CINCINNATI 45203 . . . . (513) 721-1900

CLOCKWORK COURIER INC
4765 E 131ST ST, CLEVELAND 44105 . . . . (216) 581-0707

COAST TO COAST COURIER DLVRY
PO BOX 490, DAYTON 45404 . . . . (937) 222-8700

COLUMBUS CORPORATE COURIER
5905 GREEN POINTE DR S #H, GROVEPORT 43125. . . . . (614) 492-8221

COMMAND COURIER SVCS INC
668 ROANOKE AVE, CUYAHOGA FALLS 44221 . . . . . . (330) 650-2841

CORPORATE COURIER
PO BOX 32341, CLEVELAND 44132. . . . . (440) 951-3556

DIRECT EXPRESS DELIVERY
PO BOX 403, LEWIS CTR 43035 . . . . (614) 846-8970

DYNAMEX
2475 SCIOTO HARPER DR, COLUMBUS 43204 . . . . . . (614) 276-6000

EXECUTIVE CHOICE DELIVERY
PO BOX 40938, CINCINNATI 45240 . . . . (513) 489-8883

EXPRESS MESSENGER SVC INC
PO BOX 27154, COLUMBUS 43227 . . . . (614) 237-7707

GOPHERS OHIO X-PRESS INC
2475 STATE RD, CUYAHOGA FALLS 44223 . . . . (330) 923-1343

LOCAL MAIL & FREIGHT
PO BOX 23118, COLUMBUS 43223 . . . . (614) 875-2044

MERCURY MESSENGER INC
16172 IMPERIAL PKWY, STRONGSVILLE 44149 . . . . . (440) 808-8700

METRO PACKAGE SYSTEMS
1374 KING AVE, COLUMBUS 43212 . . . . (614) 488-0666

MIDWAY DELIVERY SVC
4420 SUPERIOR AVE, CLEVELAND 44103 . . . . (216) 391-0700

NOVA EXPRESS SVC
2160 BRITAINS LN, COLUMBUS 43224 . . . . (614) 447-8840

PRIORITY DISPATCH INC
25671 FT MEIGS RD #A, PERRYSBURG 43551 . . . . . (419) 480-1500
4204 E RIVER RD, DAYTON 45439 . . . . (937) 294-8200
4665 MALSBARY RD, CINCINNATI 45242 . . . . (513) 791-1300
1110 CLAYCRAFT RD, COLUMBUS 43230 . . . . (614) 258-8558
6180 HALLE DR, CLEVELAND 44125 . . . . (216) 328-0030

PROEX
5195 ENGLE RD, CLEVELAND 44142. . . . . (216) 898-1930

QUICKSILVER MESSENGER SVC
10100 BRECKSVILLE RD, BRECKSVILLE 44141. . . . . (330) 908-0707

QUIKPRO EXPRESS
700 MORSE RD #200, COLUMBUS 43214 . . . . (614) 888-6164

RAPID DELIVERY SVC CO
529 N WAYNE AVE, CINCINNATI 45215. . . . . (513) 733-0500

ROADRUNNERS DELIVERY INC
PO BOX 669088, CLEVELAND 44109 . . . . (216) 579-0700

RUSH TRANSPORTATION/LOGISTICS
2388 ARBOR BLVD, DAYTON 45439 . . . . (937) 297-6182

S & L DELIVERY & COURIER SVC
8604 EDGEWATER AVE, GALLOWAY 43119 . . . . (614) 851-1301

SPECIAL D RAPID INC
1145 HIGHBROOK ST #401, AKRON 44301. . . . . . . (330) 374-0550

STAT COURIER INC
7423 ROYALTON RD, CLEVELAND 44133. . . . . (440) 237-6226

STERLING DELIVERY SVC INC
1425 E DUBLIN GRANVILLE RD #99, COLUMBUS 43229. . . (614) 880-1494

TRI COUNTY EXPRESS DELIVERY
8099 GLEN PARK RD, WILLOUGHBY 44094 . . . . (440) 256-3994

U S CARGO
2074 INTEGRITY DR N, COLUMBUS 43209. . . . . . . (614) 449-2854
6969 COMMODORE DR, WALBRIDGE 43465 . . . . . . (419) 666-3500
9350 MIDWEST AVE, CLEVELAND 44125 . . . . (216) 332-0500

UPS STORE THE
15741 US HWY 36, MARYSVILLE 43040 . . . . (937) 642-9528
6724 PERIMETER LOOP RD, DUBLIN 43017 . . . . . . (614) 791-0289
365 DOWNTOWNER PLZ, COSHOCTON 43812 . . . . . (740) 622-8606

YELLOW TAXI-MARIETTA
111 STRECKER HL, MARIETTA 45750 . . . . (740) 374-9999

MICROFILM SERVICES, EQUIPMENT & SUPPLIES
(See OFFICE EQUIPMENT)

MOCK TRIALS

JUDICIAL ALTERNATIVES OF OHIO INC
7419 JACKSON PIKE, LOCKBOURNE 43137 . . . . **(888) 629-3793**

NATIONAL LEGAL PROFESSIONAL ASSOC
11331 GROOMS RD #1000, CINCINNATI 45242 . . . . . . (513) 247-0082

MORTGAGE CONSULTANTS
ALPINE MORTGAGE
1643 S BREIEL BLVD, MIDDLETOWN 45044 . . . . (513) 420-9469
ARROWHEAD FINANCIAL GROUP
WWW.HOTMORTGAGERATE.COM . . . . (888) 825-1177
GOOD FAITH MORTGAGE INC
4720 WARNER RD, GARFIELD HTS 44125 . . . . (216) 271-9800
UNM FINANCIAL CO
8241 DOW CIR W, STRONGSVILLE 44136 . . . . (440) 816-1800
WATERFIELD FINANCIAL CORP
150 E WILSON BRIDGE RD #100, WORTHINGTON 43085 . . . . . (614) 846-2266

NURSING CONSULTANTS
(See Also EXPERTS-NURSING)

BEVERLY HEALTH AND REHAB CTR
1425 YORKLAND RD, COLUMBUS 43232 . . . . (614) 861-6666
COLBERT CLEVENGER & ASSOCIATES
PO BOX 340641, COLUMBUS 43234. . . . . **(614) 284-9716**
KMR LEGAL NURSE CONSULTANTS
4514 BROOKLYN AVE, CLEVELAND 44109 . . . . (216) 398-7995
LEGAL INDEPENDENT NURSE CONSULTANTS LLC
WWW.LINCME.COM . . . . **(513) 652-3392**
MEDVOPRO
3620 N HIGH ST, #B-4, COLUMBUS 43214 . . . . . . **(614) 539-1150**
MIDWEST LEGAL NURSE CONSULTANTS
10999 REID HARTMAN HWY, CINCINNATI 45242 . . . . (513) 891-5088

NURSING EXPERTS
(See EXPERTS—NURSING)

OFFICE EQUIPMENT
(See Also OFFICE SUPPLIES)

BAKER OFFICE EQUIPMENT CO
PO BOX 187, ELYRIA 44036 . . . . (440) 322-4617
FERRARELLI INC
3646 GLENMORE AVE, CINCINNATI 45211 . . . . (513) 481-6116
OFFICE SUITES PLUS
2333 ALEXANDRIA DR, LEXINGTON, KY 40504 . . . . (859) 514-2160

OFFICE FURNITURE
AFFORDABLE OFFICE FURNITURE
11965 CAVES RD, CHESTERLAND 44026 . . . . (216) 431-2020
BASIC OFFICE SUPPLIES
4425 GLENBROOK RD, WILLOUGHBY 44094 . . . . (440) 951-7316
CADDO DESIGN & OFFICE PRODUCTS
5443 DUFF DR, CINCINNATI 45246 . . . . (513) 771-3808
CAPITOL OFFICE SUPPLY
777 DEARBORN PARK LN #L, COLUMBUS 43085 . . . . (614) 846-7303
CFIS-EXPRESS BID
9089 JOHNNYCAKE RIDGE RD, MENTOR 44060 . . . . (440) 255-9511
COCONIS FURNITURE INC
4 S MAYSVILLE AVE, ZANESVILLE 43701 . . . . (740) 452-1231
COMMERCIAL OFFICE FURNITURE
7228 WALTON RD, CLEVELAND 44146 . . . . (440) 439-1960
CONNELLS HOME FURNISHINGS
11359 UPPER GILCHRIST RD, MT VERNON 43050 . . . . (740) 392-9116
CONSOLIDATED BUSINESS PRODUCTS
6141 MARKET AVE, MIDDLETOWN 45042 . . . . (513) 423-6591
CONTINENTAL EDUCATIONAL ENVIRONMENTS
2561 SILVER DR, COLUMBUS 43211 . . . . (614) 262-7600
CONTINENTAL OFFICE MOVES
5063 FREEWAY DR E, COLUMBUS 43229 . . . . (614) 781-0080
CONTRACT FURNITURE GROUP
1407 ARGONNE RD, CLEVELAND 44121 . . . . (216) 381-3113
CONTRACT INTERIORS
580 N 4TH ST #190, COLUMBUS 43215 . . . . (614) 228-1582
CONTRACT SOURCE INC
1440 SNOW RD #216, CLEVELAND 44134 . . . . (216) 351-7575
COPENHAGEN SCANDINAVIAN FURN
1077 BETHEL RD, COLUMBUS 43220 . . . . (614) 459-7773
COPLEYS OFFICE FURNITURE
6658 DAYTON BRANDT RD, TIPP CITY 45371 . . . . (937) 692-5237
CORPORATE EXPRESS
4170 HIGHLANDER PKWY, RICHFIELD 44286 . . . . (216) 416-7700
CORPORATE EXPRESS IMAGING
2228 CITYGATE DR, COLUMBUS 43219 . . . . (614) 472-3505
D & AA AFFORDABLE OFFICE FRNT
3140 LYNN RD, FRANKLIN 45005 . . . . (513) 727-0658
DELAMOTTE CO
111 N ST CLAIR ST, PAINESVILLE 44077 . . . . (440) 352-3931
DELUXE OFFICE FURNITURE
8340 KINSMAN RD, NOVELTY 44072 . . . . (216) 382-8895
FALLON INDUSTRIAL RESOURCES
20950 CENTER RIDGE RD, CLEVELAND 44116 . . . . (440) 356-1300
19706 CENTER RIDGE RD #DN, CLEVELAND 44116 . . . . (440) 356-1170
FELBER INDUSTRIAL
4100 PAYNE AVE 2ND FL, CLEVELAND 44103 . . . . (216) 831-6262
GALLERY POSTER SHOPPE
4725 REED RD, COLUMBUS 43220 . . . . (614) 538-9040

GEIGER BRICKEL
27596 DETROIT RD, CLEVELAND 44145 . . . . (440) 871-9130
HERMAN MILLER WORKPLACE
1240 HURON RD E, CLEVELAND 44115 . . . . (216) 781-9911
HON OFFICE FURNITURE SALES
3545 CHRISFIELD DR, CLEVELAND 44116 . . . . (440) 356-6565
JAMES & WEAVER FURNITURE
22 W WOOD ST, YOUNGSTOWN 44503 . . . . (330) 744-4427
JEFFERYS FURNITURE NOW
762 READING RD, MASON 45040 . . . . (513) 398-9869
KENT OFFICE SUPPLY & BUS MACHS
948 CHERRY ST, KENT 44240 . . . . (330) 673-6115
MACK BAILEY ENTERPRISES
14475 STATE RT 93 S, LOGAN 43138 . . . . (740) 380-3409
MARYSVILLE OFFICE CTR
116 S MAIN ST, MARYSVILLE 43040 . . . . (937) 642-8893
MODULAR SYSTEMS TECHNICIANS
5504 VALLEY BELT RD #F, BROOKLYN HTS 44131 . . . . (216) 459-2630
MONARCH SALES & MARKETING
7555 AIRPORT HWY #A, HOLLAND 43528 . . . . (419) 861-0336
MORRIS INTERIOR CONTRACTING
319 KATIEBUD DR, CINCINNATI 45238 . . . . (513) 751-5065
MOURNINGS INC OFFICE EQUIP
427 E MAIN ST, JACKSON 45640 . . . . (740) 286-5011
NATIONAL OFFICE SVC INC
15655 BROOKPARK RD, CLEVELAND 44142 . . . . (216) 898-0080
NATIONAL OFFICE WAREHOUSE
500 W BROAD ST, COLUMBUS 43215 . . . . (614) 228-2233
NORTH COAST ELECTRO-COATERS
3083 ENDICOTT WAY, SILVER LK 44224 . . . . (330) 688-2260
NORTH COAST OFFICE FURNITURE
13000 ATHENS AVE #2, CLEVELAND 44107 . . . . (216) 228-9900
NORTHEAST FURNITURE RENTAL
34601 RIDGE RD, WILLOUGHBY 44094. . . . . (440) 449-1400
2350 GILCHRIST RD, AKRON 44305 . . . . (330) 726-6666
OFFICE CITY EXPRESS
PO BOX 942, LOGAN 43138 . . . . (740) 385-2621
25 E 2ND ST, CHILLICOTHE 45601. . . . . (740) 774-2181
27 W WILLIAM ST, DELAWARE 43015 . . . . (740) 363-1765
OFFICE DEPOT
1680 MARION MOUNT GILEAD RD, MARION 43302 . . . . (740) 386-2552
OFFICE EMPORIUM FURNITURE
761 BETA DR, CLEVELAND 44143 . . . . (440) 753-0021
OFFICE ENVIRONMENTS
PO BOX 41067, CLEVELAND 44141 . . . . (440) 526-9400
OFFICE EQUIPMENT SPECIALIST
4365 PARKTON DR, CLEVELAND 44128 . . . . (216) 475-8877
OFFICE FACTORY
181 SCHOFIELD DR, COLUMBUS 43213 . . . . (614) 367-1072
OFFICE FURNITURE OUTLET
4521 MARKET ST, YOUNGSTOWN 44512 . . . . (330) 746-6105
OFFICE FURNITURE SOURCE
2920 E KEMPER RD, CINCINNATI 45241 . . . . (513) 531-0900
OFFICE FURNITURE USA
1213 PROSPECT AVE E, CLEVELAND 44115 . . . . (330) 926-8200
OFFICE FURNITURE WAREHOUSE
4100 PAYNE AVE #2, CLEVELAND 44103 . . . . (216) 431-2700
OFFICE INVENTIONS & DESIGN INC
1195 ESSEX AVE, COLUMBUS 43085 . . . . (614) 475-7134
OFFICE MART
1151 E MAIN ST, LANCASTER 43130 . . . . (740) 687-1707
OFFICE MAX
PO BOX 228070, CLEVELAND 44122 . . . . (216) 471-6900
OFFICE SUPPLY CTR
122 WINCKLES ST, ELYRIA 44035 . . . . (440) 365-2221
OHIO PAPER & SUPPLY CO INC
PO BOX 227, CANTON 44720 . . . . (330) 499-8001
PAN L TEK INC
4220 PERIMETER DR, COLUMBUS 43228. . . . . (614) 274-9421
RELIABLE OFFICE SUPPLY INC
112 S ERIE ST, MASSILLON 44646. . . . . (800) 750-1716
REMANUFACTURED BUSINESS FURN
1225 WESTERN AVE, CINCINNATI 45944 . . . . (513) 232-3363
SEAGATE OFFICE PRODUCTS
1044 HAMILTON DR, HOLLAND 43528. . . . . (419) 861-6161
TAB PRODUCTS CO
23400 AURORA RD #C, CLEVELAND 44146 . . . . (440) 439-8270
TAYLOR RESOURCES
200 PUBLIC SQ #224, CLEVELAND 44114. . . . . (216) 694-4444
TODAYS BUSINESS PRODUCTS INC
12985 SNOW RD, CLEVELAND 44130 . . . . (216) 267-5000
TODDS OFFICE SUPPLIES INC
171 N HAMILTON RD, COLUMBUS 43213 . . . . (614) 864-6117
WARREN CHANEY OFFICE FURNITURE
3200 EUCLID AVE, CLEVELAND 44115 . . . . (216) 391-3337
WATSON OFFICE SUPPLY & EQUIP
224 W COURT ST, WASHINGTON CT HS 43160 . . . . (740) 335-5544
WEILAND OFFICE MACHINES
706 S EWING ST, LANCASTER 43130 . . . . (740) 653-7787
WESTERN RESERVE OFFICE SUPPLY
11993 RAVENNA RD #2, CHARDON 44024 . . . . (440) 285-2303
WOOSTER OFFICE EQUIPMENT INC
160 S COLUMBUS AVE, WOOSTER 44691 . . . . (330) 264-1200
WORK STYLES
1240 HURON RD E, CLEVELAND 44115 . . . . (216) 621-4590

OFFICE RECORDS-DESTRUCTION

ABC MOBILE SHREDDING INC
  PO BOX 5519, WILLOWICK 44095 . . . . (440) 943-1995
ACCUSHRED LLC
  1114 W CENTRAL AVE, TOLEDO 43610 . . . . (800) 747-3341
ALL SHRED
  PO BOX 177, LAURA 45337 . . . . (937) 845-2300
ALLSHRED SERVICES INC
  715 SPENCER ST, TOLEDO 43609 . . . . (419) 381-7762
CDD INC
  300 W CHESTNUT ST, WAUSEON 43567 . . . . (419) 337-4085
CHAR-MAC DOCUMENT DESTRUCTION
  1441 SPRING LAWN AVE, CINCINNATI 45223 . . . . (513) 681-2172
COMPASS SHREDDING SVC
  4431 OLD SPRINGFIELD RD, VANDALIA 45377 . . . . (937) 890-6739
CONFIDENTIAL MATERIAL DESTRUCT
  2609 NORDIC RD, DAYTON 45414 . . . . (937) 233-2800
DATA SECURITY INC
  26800 FARGO AVE #F, CLEVELAND 44146 . . . . (216) 831-2260
DOCU-SHRED
  707 S ELLSWORTH AVE, SALEM 44460 . . . . (330) 332-0024
ERTH SYSTEMS
  5574 GLEN OAK, MASON 45040 . . . . (513) 459-8810
FIREPROOF RECORDS CTR
  1024 N HIGH ST, COLUMBUS 43201 . . . . (614) 299-2122
INFORMATION DESTRUCTION SVC
  9030 HOCKING HILLS DR, THE PLAINS 45780 . . . . (740) 593-5316
INFOSHRED.NET
  7255 FREE AVE, CLEVELAND 44146 . . . . (440) 439-0200
LA GORE OFFICE EQUIPMENT
  1741 CRESTWOOD RD, CLEVELAND 44124 . . . . (440) 449-3650
LOTT INDUSTRIES INC
  5500 TELEGRAPH RD, TOLEDO 43612 . . . . (419) 476-2516
  3350 HILL AVE, TOLEDO 43607 . . . . (419) 534-4980
MAXWELL RECYCLING
  480 5TH ST NE, BARBERTON 44203 . . . . (330) 848-1815
NEO SHRED
  621 E TALLMADGE AVE, AKRON 44310 . . . . (330) 633-6799
NICHAL COMPANIES
  4041 BATTON ST NW #110, N CANTON 44720 . . . . (330) 498-9750
NORTHCOAST INC RECYCLING SPEC
  1305 LLYOD RD, WICKLIFFE 44092 . . . . (440) 943-6968
OHIO MOBILE SHREDDING
  PO BOX 307206, COLUMBUS 43230 . . . . (614) 236-1979
PELTZ GROUP OF OHIO
  965 WAYSIDE RD, CLEVELAND 44110 . . . . (216) 481-3200
ROYAL DOCUMENT DESTRUCTION
  1300 NORTON RD, COLUMBUS 43228 . . . . (614) 751-9731
S SLESNICK CO
  700 3RD ST SE, CANTON 44707 . . . . (330) 454-5101
SECURE SHRED
  3711 STARRS CENTRE DR, CANFIELD 44406 . . . . (330) 629-7158
SECURITY SHREDDERS INC
  4718 GUERLEY RD, CINCINNATI 45238 . . . . (513) 681-4003
SHRED-IT
  6777 ENGLE RD #I, CLEVELAND 44130 . . . . (440) 243-8500
  9860 WINDISCH RD, W CHESTER 45069 . . . . (513) 777-3327
  596 CLAYCRAFT RD, COLUMBUS 43230 . . . . (614) 231-7470
SHREDDED BEDDING CORP
  6589 BENNINGTON CHAPEL RD, CENTERBURG 43011 . . . . . (740) 893-3567
SHREDDING SOLUTIONS
  9011 FREEWAY DR, MACEDONIA 44056 . . . . (330) 468-2700
SMARTSHRED
  11340 DONWIDDLE DR, LOVELAND 45140 . . . . (513) 677-2443

OFFICE RECORDS-STORAGE

ARCHIVE AMERICA
  3455 NW 54TH ST, MIAMI, FL 33142 . . . . (800) 273-8587
BRENDAMOUR WAREHOUSING & SVC
  11400 GROOMS RD, CINCINNATI 45242 . . . . (513) 247-0077
BUSINESS INFORMATION STORAGE
  2201 SPRING GROVE AVE, CINCINNATI 45214 . . . . (513) 721-3453
CROWN STORAGE
  1292 ELMRIDGE DR, AMELIA 45102 . . . . (513) 752-9266
DATA STORAGE CTR
  690 E CRESCENTVILLE RD, CINCINNATI 45246 . . . . (513) 671-7717
GENERAL ELECTRONICS SECURITY
  6114 MADISON RD, CINCINNATI 45227 . . . . (513) 271-4466
INFOMANAGEMENT
  903 DANCE CT, CINCINNATI 45203 . . . . (513) 621-5706
IRON MOUNTAIN
  5845 HIGHLAND RIDGE DR, CINCINNATI 45232 . . . . (513) 242-0707
  324 CHESTNUT ST, TOLEDO 43604 . . . . (513) 874-3535
  5057 FREEWAY DR E, COLUMBUS 43229 . . . . (614) 840-9321
QUEEN CITY SELF STORAGE
  4775 RED BANK RD, CINCINNATI 45227 . . . . (513) 271-5599
WALKERLY MOVING & STORAGE
  2730 AKRON RD, WOOSTER 44691 . . . . (330) 263-0515

OFFICE SUPPLIES
(See Also OFFICE EQUIPMENT)

AFFORDABLE BUSINESS SUPPLIES
  568 SHELDON AVE, COLUMBUS 43207 . . . . (614) 542-0877
ARVEY PAPER & OFFICE PRODUCTS
  See Our Display Ad Under This Heading
  914 DALTON ST, CINCINNATI 45203 . . . . **(513) 421-5300**
  431 E LIVINGSTON, COLUMBUS 43215 . . . . **(614) 221-0153**
BOISE CASCADE OFFICE PRODUCTS
  13301 STEVENS RD, WARREN, MI 48089 . . . . (419) 891-1070
BOLINDS SOLUTIONS SVC INC
  PO BOX 670482, NORTHFIELD 44067 . . . . (330) 468-1554
BUCKEYE OFFICE PRODUCTS
  2700 E 6TH AVE, COLUMBUS 43219 . . . . (614) 737-0050
BUELL INC
  PO BOX 340, ASHVILLE 43103 . . . . (614) 486-4359
BULLDOG OFFICE PRODUCTS INC
  6950 AMERICANA PKWY #E, REYNOLDSBURG 43068 . . . (614) 501-8380
CENTRAL OHIO COPIER SUPPLY
  6838 NEW ALBANY CONDIT RD, NEW ALBANY 43054 . . . (614) 855-9315
CENTURION OFFICE SUPPLY
  480 SCHROCK RD #H, COLUMBUS 43229 . . . . (614) 436-5162
CONCORD OFFICE PRODUCTS
  PO BOX 21176, COLUMBUS 43221 . . . . (614) 488-9717
CORPORATE EXPRESS
  5443 DUFF DR, CINCINNATI 45246 . . . . (513) 631-3752
CROWN RUBBER STAMP & OFC SUPL
  17019 LORAIN AVE, CLEVELAND 44111 . . . . (216) 251-3272
D R MILLER OFFICE SUPPLIES
  4290 N HIGH ST, COLUMBUS 43214 . . . . (614) 447-0096
DAVID W MALLOY CO
  2210 AGLER RD, COLUMBUS 43224 . . . . (614) 475-7905
DISCOUNT TAPE N ROLL
  246 E 131ST ST, CLEVELAND 44108 . . . . (216) 761-7000
DITEC CORP
  4185 E MAIN ST, COLUMBUS 43213 . . . . (614) 231-2751
ECOMART
  2606 JAY AVE, CLEVELAND 44113 . . . . (216) 781-7701
ERGOSOURCE
  8779 HILLTOP DR, MENTOR 44060 . . . . (440) 257-9235
F & E CHECK PROTECTOR & CHECK
  PO BOX 670289, NORTHFIELD 44067 . . . . (440) 845-6606
FRANKLIN COVEY STORE
  RT 82, STRONGSVILLE 44136 . . . . (440) 238-0590
GARRIGANS OFFICE PLUS
  234 W COLUMBIA, SPRINGFIELD 45504 . . . . (937) 298-9866
GATEWAY OFFICE PRODUCTS
  2020 EUCLID AVE, CLEVELAND 44115 . . . . (216) 623-0700
HEIMBERGER OFFICE MACHINES
  664 E MAIN ST, LANCASTER 43130 . . . . (740) 653-1458

OFFICE SUPPLIES (Cont'd)

HOLCOMBS KNOWPLACE
PO BOX 94636, CLEVELAND 44101 . . . . (216) 341-3000
HOME OFFICE SUPPLY
120 S SANDUSKY AVE, BUCYRUS 44820 . . . . (419) 562-6831
120 SOUTH SANDUSKY AVE, BUCYRUS 44820 . . . . (419) 462-5422
HORIZON USA DATA SPLS INC
2297 SOUTHWEST BLVD #H, GROVE CITY 43123 . . . . (614) 539-8150
JUST THINGS
108 S MAIN ST, CADIZ 43907 . . . . (740) 942-2390
KE-WA-PA SALES
78 N COLUMBUS ST, SUNBURY 43074 . . . . (740) 965-5404
KIMCO BUSINESS SUPPLIES
9337 RAVENNA RD #L, TWINSBURG 44087 . . . . (330) 405-2883
LAKE OFFICE SUPPLY
1430 LLOYD RD, WICKLIFFE 44092 . . . . (440) 944-5324
LASER CONNECTION
418 MAIN ST, TOLEDO 43605 . . . . (419) 691-3333
LASER LINE INC
6953 MCNERNEY DR, NORTHWOOD 43619 . . . . (419) 666-8288
LAUGHLINS INC
21 FOREST COVE DR, AKRON 44319 . . . . (330) 745-2925
M 2 FORMS & SYSTEMS INC
5445 BEAVERCREST DR, LORAIN 44053 . . . . (440) 960-1832
MARIOTTI PRINTING CO
513 E 28TH ST, LORAIN 44055 . . . . (440) 245-4120
MARTINS FERRY OFFICE SUPPLY
305 S 4TH ST, MARTINS FERRY 43935 . . . . (740) 633-2301
MCCLINTOCK BUSINESS MACHINES
69505 BIRMINGHAM RD N, LORE CITY 43755 . . . . (740) 489-5411
MEEK STATIONERY CO
124 N PLEASANT DR, E PALESTINE 44413 . . . . (330) 426-9593
MODERN OFFICE METHODS INC
816 GREEN CREST DR, WESTERVILLE 43081 . . . . (614) 891-3693
MOODYS PRINTING & OFFICE
559 HIGH ST, WORTHINGTON 43085 . . . . (614) 885-9964
MORNINGSTAR BUSINESS PRODUCTS
35620 STEVENS BLVD, WILLOUGHBY 44095 . . . . (440) 946-9074
NORLSON INC
3681 GREEN RD #212, CLEVELAND 44122 . . . . (216) 566-0809
NORTH COAST OFFICE PRODUCTS
30043 FORESTGROVE RD, WILLOWICK 44095 . . . . (440) 951-8432
NORTH COAST REFILL
4503 STATE RD, CLEVELAND 44109 . . . . (216) 661-2973
OFFICE DEPOT
11711 PRINCETON PIKE, CINCINNATI 45246 . . . . (513) 671-4421
OFFICE DEPOT BUSINESS SVC DIV
9880 SWEET VALLEY DR, CLEVELAND 44125 . . . . (216) 986-0856
OFFICE LINK
10054 BISSELL DR, TWINSBURG 44087 . . . . (330) 425-8007
OFFICE MAX
23355 MERCANTILE RD, CLEVELAND 44122 . . . . (216) 896-9330
370 HOWE AVE, AKRON 44320 . . . . (330) 929-2204
9151 FIELDS ERTEL RD, CINCINNATI 45249 . . . . (513) 794-9523
1541 RIVER VALLEY CIR N, LANCASTER 43130 . . . . (740) 653-8941
8443 DAY DR, CLEVELAND 44129 . . . . (440) 842-1662
21950 CENTER RIDGE RD, CLEVELAND 44116 . . . . (440) 356-2550
3462 MAYFIELD RD, CLEVELAND 44118 . . . . (216) 297-9789
300 S HOLLYWOOD BLVD, STEUBENVILLE 43952 . . . . . . (740) 264-7884
3315 N RIDGE RD E, ASHTABULA 44004 . . . . (440) 992-5188
285 MIDWAY BLVD, ELYRIA 44035 . . . . (440) 324-5571
23550 COMMERCE PARK, CLEVELAND 44122 . . . . (216) 292-2163
36415 EUCLID AVE, WILLOUGHBY 44094 . . . . (440) 946-1241
27845 CHARDON RD, WICKLIFFE 44092 . . . . (440) 943-7680
QUALITY RIBBONS & SUPPLIES
2769 COMMERCIAL RD, CLEVELAND 44113 . . . . (216) 579-6200
RECIO OFFICE SUPPLY
PO BOX 28166, COLUMBUS 43228 . . . . (614) 279-6636
STAPLES THE OFFICE SUPERSTORE
50585 VALLEY PLAZA DR, ST CLAIRSVILLE 43950 . . . . . (740) 695-9647
1558 COSHOCTON AVE, MT VERNON 43050 . . . . (740) 392-2155
STAPLETON OFFICE SUPPLY INC
PO BOX 550, DUNBAR, WV 25064 . . . . (740) 353-1187
STERLING OFFICE SUPPLIES & SVC
125 CHESTNUT ST, MT STERLING 43143 . . . . (740) 869-2222
SUPPLY SIDE
23750 ST CLAIR AVE, CLEVELAND 44117 . . . . (216) 738-1200
SUPPLYROOM INC
7127 TIFFANY BLVD, YOUNGSTOWN 44514 . . . . (330) 759-7057
TEAM OFFICE PRODUCTS & SVC
110 FEDERAL PLZ W, YOUNGSTOWN 44503 . . . . (330) 744-1984
TOPS BUSINESS FORMS
962 WHISPERING PINE WAY, LEBANON 45036 . . . . (513) 934-1867
VIKING OFFICE PRODUCTS INC
PO BOX 780692, WICHITA, KS 67278 . . . . (513) 874-5720
WOOLUMS BUSINESS PRODUCTS
203 BROADWAY ST, JACKSON 45640 . . . . (740) 286-4560
XEROX-ARWEBB OFFICE EQUIPMENT
PO BOX 5090, NEWARK 43058 . . . . (740) 349-8348

ONE-WRITE SYSTEMS
(See OFFICE SUPPLIES)

OPTICAL IMAGING
IMAGING TECHNOLOGIES INC
PO BOX 33517, N ROYALTON 44133 . . . . (216) 573-6763

PACKAGE DELIVERY
(See MESSENGER SERVICES)

PAPER SHREDDING MACHINES
(See OFFICE EQUIPMENT)

PAPER SHREDDING SERVICES
(See OFFICE RECORDS—DESTRUCTION)

PARALEGAL SERVICES
(See Also LEGAL RESEARCH SERVICES; LEGAL PLACEMENT SERVICES; and LITIGATION SUPPORT SERVICES)

ADAMS PARALEGAL SVC
35671 STEVENS BLVD, WILLOUGHBY 44095 . . . . (440) 975-8500
BARRETT JOE
3214 MIDDLE CT, MILLERSPORT 43046 . . . . (740) 467-7042
CHELSEY PARALEGAL SVC
4254 DUBLIN RD, COLUMBUS 43221 . . . . (614) 777-1175
CIMS COLLEGE
5340 E MAIN ST #209, COLUMBUS 43213 . . . . (614) 367-2467
CYNTHIA H MILLER PARALEGAL SVC
931 WATCH CREEK DR, CINCINNATI 45230 . . . . (513) 624-0858
EXECUTIVE LEGAL SVC
7140 KLEBER CT, CLEVELAND 44131 . . . . (216) 447-7979
HAMANN & ASSOC INC
520 MADISON AVE, TOLEDO 43604 . . . . (419) 255-5205
J & A SOTERIADES INC
4181 E MAIN ST, COLUMBUS 43213 . . . . (614) 237-8050
KERNS PAULA A
865 EASTWIND DR, WESTERVILLE 43081 . . . . (614) 891-8777

KEYSTROKES BY KELLY

*SECRETARIAL SVCS*ACCESS TO PUBLIC RECORDS
*DIRECT MAILING/ADVERTISING
FAX # (614) 871-4836

KEYSTROKES@COLUMBUS.RR.COM . . . . **(614) 875-9590**

LEGAL ADVANTAGE
432 WALNUT ST #200, CINCINNATI 45202 . . . . (513) 651-2252
LEGAL TIME
344 PROMONTORY PLZ, WILLOWICK 44095 . . . . (440) 946-8463
MEDICAL RECORDS CONSULTING
2710 EUCLID AVE, CINCINNATI 45219 . . . . (513) 284-2683
MOYER PARALEGAL SVC
50 W BOWERY ST, AKRON 44308 . . . . (330) 849-0148
NJL PARALEGAL SVC INC
1458 YANKEE PARK PL, DAYTON 45458 . . . . (937) 434-4442
PARALEGAL ASSN OF CENTRAL OHIO
89 E NATIONWIDE BLVD, COLUMBUS 43215 . . . . (614) 224-9700
PENROD CHARLES ECCP
PO BOX 184, MOGADORE 44260 . . . . (330) 699-5577
PFENNING JULIE M
4568 MAYFIELD RD #112, CLEVELAND 44121 . . . . (216) 896-9530
SECURE CHECK
190 N UNION ST #101, AKRON 44303 . . . . (330) 253-7410
SLIVE & SLIVE CO
526 SUPERIOR AVE E #935, CLEVELAND 44114 . . . . . . (216) 566-1111
SUSAN L KATHERMAN PROBATE
325 ACTON RD, COLUMBUS 43214 . . . . (614) 268-0325

PATENT ILLUSTRATION
DAKATEC
2360 FORDYCE RD, CLARKSVILLE 45113 . . . . (937) 289-3505

PATENT, COPYRIGHT & TRADEMARK AGENTS & SERVICES
EPE INCORPORATED
PO BOX 361551, STRONGSVILLE 44136 . . . . (440) 238-7000
HARPMAN & HARPMAN
819 SOUTHWESTERN RN, YOUNGSTOWN 44514 . . . . . . (330) 758-7505

PERSONAL PROPERTY APPRAISERS
(See APPRAISAL SERVICES—PERSONAL PROPERTY)

PHOTOGRAPHERS-LEGAL
(See Also VIDEO PRODUCTION SERVICES—LEGAL; and COURTROOM EXHIBITS)

AGI PHOTOGRAPHIC IMAGING
2495 TECHNICAL DR, MIAMISBURG 45342 . . . . (937) 866-9314
CHARLES BEHLOW PHOTOGRAPHY
1310 PENDLETON ST #807 UNIT 41, CINCINNATI 45202 . . . . . . (513) 651-5122
EFFECTS PRODUCTIONS INC
6167 GRAND VISTA AVE, CINCINNATI 45213 . . . . (513) 351-6224
INCAMERA STUDIOS
620 HASKINS RD, BOWLING GREEN 43402 . . . . (800) 832-4882

PHYSICAL THERAPISTS
(See REHABILITATION SERVICES)

PLACEMENT SERVICES
(See LEGAL PLACEMENT SERVICES; EXECUTIVE SEARCH FIRMS; and EMPLOYMENT AGENCIES)

POLYGRAPH & LIE DETECTION SERVICES
(See Also INVESTIGATORS & DETECTIVE AGENCIES)

A J BUREAU OF INVESTIGATION
PO BOX 796, TOLEDO 43697 . . . . (419) 691-1199
A PROFESSIONAL INFORMATION & TESTING SVCS INC
3609 W ALEXIS RD #202, TOLEDO 43625 . . . . . . **(419) 473-2973**
ALPHA OMEGA POLYGRAPH SVC
PO BOX 245, GALLOWAY 43119 . . . . (614) 851-1817

ASSOCIATED LIE DETECTION SERVICE INC

30 YEARS OF LAW ENFORCEMENT EXPERIENCE
MEMBER OF AMERICAN POLYGRAPH ASSOCIATION
STATEWIDE SERVICE AVAILABLE

1100 W BAGLEY RD #203, BEREA 44017 . . . . **(216) 375-7307**

BRENTLEY INSTITUTE INC
PO BOX 20724, CLEVELAND 44120 . . . . (216) 231-2333
CLARK-DYE & ASSOC INC
10921 REED HARTMAN HWY #224, CINCINNATI 45242 . . . . . . (513) 891-8869
GLOBAL POLYGRAPH NETWORK
553 MAIN ST, STROUDSBURG, PA 18360 . . . . (877) 765-9837
INTEGRITY VERIFICATIONS INC
7515 PEARL RD, CLEVELAND 44130 . . . . (440) 234-9000
735 N COURT ST #D, MEDINA 44256 . . . . (330) 725-3866
JAMES W BASSETT CO
151 W 4TH ST #1L, CINCINNATI 45202 . . . . (513) 421-9604
MID-OHIO TRUTH VERIFICATION
876 OLD ELM RD, CHILLICOTHE 45601 . . . . (740) 775-8271
MONAHAN MICHAEL P
630 VINE ST, CINCINNATI 45202 . . . . (513) 579-8488
PINPOINT
PO BOX 9023, CANTON 44711 . . . . (330) 471-8800
POLY-TECH ASSOC INC
209 S MAIN ST #403, AKRON 44308 . . . . (330) 434-2344
4403 ST CLAIR AVE, CLEVELAND 44103 . . . . (216) 241-4661
POLYGRAPH BUREAU LTD
6161 BUSCH BLVD #336, COLUMBUS 43229 . . . . (614) 781-0255
PROFESSIONAL INFORMATION
3609 W ALEXIS RD, TOLEDO 43623 . . . . (419) 473-2973
QUEST POLYGRAPH CONSULTANTS
DONNE_2000@YAHOO.COM . . . . (740) 363-8122
REEDER FORENSIC SVC INC
4130 LINDEN AVE, DAYTON 45432 . . . . (937) 256-3660
SCIENTIFIC TRUTH VERIFICATION
125 E 9TH ST #400A, CINCINNATI 45202 . . . . (513) 621-6229
SECURITY & POLYGRAPH CONSLNTS
25200 MILES RD, CLEVELAND 44146 . . . . (216) 831-3447
TRI-STATE POLYGRAPH ASSOC
4030 MOUNT CARMEL TOBASCO RD, CINCINNATI 45255 . . . . (513) 528-6717
TRUTHGRAPH LTD
248 W MAIN ST #C, NORWALK 44857 . . . . (419) 668-0961

PRINTERS-LEGAL & FINANCIAL

BLACKIE & ASSOC
20220 CENTER RIDGE RD #304, CLEVELAND 44116 . . . . (440) 895-2560
DAVID VALINSKY ASSOC
1269 GRANDVIEW AVE, COLUMBUS 43212 . . . . (614) 485-1246
VAN DYNE CROTTY INC
7830 DIVISION DR, MENTOR 44060 . . . . (440) 205-2561

PRIVATE DETECTIVES & INVESTIGATORS
(See INVESTIGATORS & DETECTIVE AGENCIES; and SKIP TRACERS)

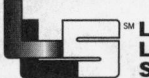

PROCESS & SUBPOENA SERVICES

A J PAINE & ASSOC
PO BOX 363, DAYTON 45404 . . . . (937) 228-6169
ADB INC
4239 HAMILTON AVE, CINCINNATI 45223 . . . . (800) 405-4006
AMERICAN EXPEDITING CO
325 KEN MAR INDUSTRIAL PKWY, BROADVIEW HTS 44147 . . (800) 220-1624
ASAP ATTORNEY SVC
131 N LUDLOW ST #275, DAYTON 45402 . . . . (937) 222-7821
ATTORNEY SVCS OF NE OHIO
40 E BUCHTEL AVE, AKRON 44308 . . . . (330) 376-8100
ATTORNEYS SERVICES INC
3214 PROSPECT AVE E, CLEVELAND 44115 . . . . (216) 431-7400
CAL CRIM INC
11177 READING RD, CINCINNATI 45241 . . . . (800) 899-1225
CERTIFIED LEGAL SVC
PO BOX 891, MIAMISBURG 45343 . . . . (937) 859-4775
CLEVELAND PROCESS SVC LLC
521 LITERARY RD, CLEVELAND 44113 . . . . (216) 357-4098
COMMERCIAL RECOVERY INC - CRI
167 WASHINGTON ST, NORWELL, MA 02061 . . . . (888) 522-2235
COMPLETE OHIO PROCESS SERVERS
1695 FRANKLIN AVE, COLUMBUS 43205 . . . . (614) 231-5595
CONFIDENTIAL SVCS INC
1156 ALUM CREEK DR, COLUMBUS 43209 . . . . (800) 752-4581
ELECTRONIC MERCHANT SYSTEMS
5005 ROCKSIDE RD #100, CLEVELAND 44131 . . . . (216) 524-0900
GREAT LAKES INVESTIGATIVE SVCS
PO BOX 6874, TOLEDO 43612 . . . . (419) 254-9553
HOLZBERGER & ASSOCS INC
217 COURT ST, HAMILTON 45011 . . . . (513) 737-7700
HUNTERS NORTH ASSOCS LLC
1757 RT 9, SPOFFORD, NH 03462 . . . . (888) 363-8200
HUTTER LEGAL SVCS
6195 SHERWOOD DR, N OLMSTED 44070 . . . . (440) 779-6429
INFOCORP INVESTIGATIVE SVCS LLC
PO BOX 120, LEWIS CTR 43035 . . . . **(866) 989-9894**
JOHN R BAHS & ASSOCS
115 W OAK ST, OAK HARBOR 43449 . . . . (866) 879-2247

LEGAL INVESTIGATION SERVICES

SERVING MONTGOMERY & SURROUNDING COUNTIES
LICENSED & BONDED INVESTIGATION AGENCY
CIVIL * CRIMINAL * INSURANCE & DOMESTIC CASES

PO BOX 10633, DAYTON 45402 . . . . **(937) 608-1920**

LEGAL LANGUAGE SERVICES
See Our Display Ad Under This Heading
WWW.LEGALLANGUAGE.COM . . . . **(800) 755-5775**
MARSHALL & ASSOCS INC
PO BOX 498789, CINCINNATI 45249 . . . . (800) 541-0634
MATRIX INVESTIGATIONS & CONSULTING INC
1776 MENTOR AVE, CINCINNATI 45212 . . . . **(877) 550-7973**
MIAMI VALLEY INVESTIGATIONS
3503 ALFRED CT, COLUMBUS 43221 . . . . (614) 595-7401
MIDWEST INVESTIGATIVE SVCS INC
6077 FAR HILLS AVE #215, DAYTON 45459 . . . . (937) 433-9903
MIKE MOBLEY REPORTING
334 S MAIN ST, DAYTON 45402 . . . . (937) 222-2259
MOLING & ASSOC INC
425 BRICE RD N, BLACKLICK 43004 . . . . (614) 759-7433
OHIORECORDS.NET
PO BOX 1794, COLUMBUS 43126 . . . . (614) 298-0026
PEERLESS PROCESS SVC
840 UNION BLVD #203, ENGLEWOOD 45406 . . . . (937) 279-9395
PRECISION INVESTIGATIONS & CNSLTNG
8216 PRINCETON GLENDALE RD, W CHESTER 45069 . . . . . . (513) 895-5400
PRO SURV INVESTIGATIONS INC
PO BOX 292680, DAYTON 45429 . . . . (937) 299-9004

PROCESS & SUBPOENA SERVICES (Cont'd)

PRO-SERVE INC
4456 WINCHESTER SOUTHERN RD, CANAL WNCHSTR 43110. (800) 664-1408
PROCESS SERVERS OF NW OHIO
715 GOULD ST, NORTHWOOD 43619 . . . . (419) 698-9605
PROCESS SERVICE CO
14671 PEARL RD #272, CLEVELAND 44136 . . . . (440) 382-3638
QUEST ASSOCIATES OF OHIO LLC
4771 GLENDALE MILFORD RD, CNCNNT 45242 . **(800) 354-9907**
R STUART & ASSOCS
6959 TAYLOR RD, CINCINNATI 45248 . . . . (513) 598-9852
RAINBOW EXPRESS
2000 S HIGH ST 2ND FL, COLUMBUS 43207 . . . . (614) 444-5600
621 E MEHRING WY #418, CINCINNATI 45202 . . . . (513) 579-1947
RENNILLO RPTG SVCS
1301 E 9TH ST #2500, CLEVELAND 44114 . . . . (888) 391-3376
SOUTHERN OHIO LEGAL SVC
952 WOODBRIAR LN, CINCINNATI 45238 . . . . (888) 802-6601
STERLING LEGAL SVC
1220 N BECHTLE AVE, SPRINGFIELD 45504 . . . . (937) 322-9131
WITTENBERG PROCESS SVC INC
5767 W MAPLE, W BLOOMFIELD, MI 48322 . . . . (248) 855-6531

PROFESSIONAL LIABILITY INSURANCE
(See INSURANCE—PROFESSIONAL LIABILITY)

PROMOTABILITY EXPERTS
(See EXPERTS—EMPLOYABILITY)

PSYCHIATRIC EXPERTS
(See EXPERTS—PSYCHIATRIC)

PSYCHOLOGICAL EXPERTS
(See EXPERTS—PSYCHOLOGICAL)

PUBLIC RELATIONS FIRMS
(See MARKETING FIRMS & CONSULTANTS)

PUBLISHING COMPANIES
LEGAL PAGES THE
See Our Display Ad Under This Heading
WWW.LAWDIARY.COM . . . . **(800) 444-4041**

RADON TESTING SERVICES
(See BUILDING INSPECTION SERVICES)

REAL ESTATE APPRAISERS
(See APPRAISAL SERVICES—REAL ESTATE)

REAL ESTATE CONSULTANTS
(See Also APPRAISAL SERVICES—REAL ESTATE)

AKRON APPRAISAL GRP INC
3560 W MARKET ST #120, FAIRLAWN 44333 . . . . (330) 867-4585
ANDERSON LAYMAN CO
9 N THIRD ST, NEWARK 43055 . . . . (740) 349-7844
ASSOCIATED ESTATES RLTY
5025 SWETLAND CT, RICHMOND HTS 44143 . . . . (216) 261-5000
CARNEGIE GRP THE
75 E MARKET ST #230, AKRON 44308. . . . . (330) 253-1702
CB RICHARD ELLIS COMMERICAL REAL ESTATE
27500 DETROIT RD, WESTLAKE 44145 . . . . (440) 250-3260

CENTURY 21 RUMBAUGH INC REALTY

RESIDENTIAL, FARMS, COMMERCIAL, LAND DEVELOPMENT
WHERE INTEGRITY, QUALITY AND SERVICE PREVAIL
CALL AND ASK FOR JOHN, WANDA OR RANDAL
WE STRIVE FOR EXCELLENCE
E-MAIL: C21RUMBA@ZOOMINTERNET.NET
FAX# 419-281-8348

1250 CLAREMONT AVE, ASHLAND 44805 . . . . **(419) 289-2828**

CHELM PROPERTIES INC
31000 AURORA, SOLON 44139 . . . . (440) 349-4300
CONWAY LAND TITLE CO
162 MAIN ST, PAINESVILLE 44077 . . . . (440) 357-7225
RE-MAX KEYSTONE REALTY-SHIRLEY COONS
55 SHIAWASSEE, AKRON 44333 . . . . (330) 867-1045
STEVE BROWNLEE REALTY INC
802 N LIMESTONE ST, SPRINGFIELD 45503 . . . . (937) 324-5756
USA MANAGEMENT & DEVL INC
35110 EUCLID AVE 2ND FL, WILLOUGHBY 44094 . . . . (440) 942-8770

RECREATION SAFETY EXPERTS
(See EXPERTS—RECREATION & SAFETY)

RECRUITERS
(See LEGAL PLACEMENT SERVICES; EMPLOYMENT AGENCIES; and EXECUTIVE SEARCH FIRMS)

REHABILITATION SERVICES
(See Also ALCOHOL & DRUG TREATMENT CENTERS)

MORAKIS MASSOTHERAPY INC
  7291 WEST BLVD, YOUNGSTOWN 44512 . . . . (330) 758-1111

REPORTERS
(See COURT REPORTERS; and TRANSCRIPTION SERVICES)

RESEARCH SERVICES
(See LEGAL RESEARCH SERVICES; PARALEGAL SERVICES; GENEALOGICAL & TITLE RESEARCH; and LITIGATION SUPPORT SERVICES)

SAFETY & SECURITY CONSULTANTS
(See Also EXPERTS—SAFETY & SECURITY)

STEPHEN B OGLE & ASSOC INC
  823 NORTH ST, CALDWELL 43724 . . . . (740) 732-2399
TODAYS RESOURCES INC
  5690 CLYDE MOORE DR, GROVEPORT 43125 . . . . (800) 233-8725

SAFETY EXPERTS
(See EXPERTS—SAFETY & SECURITY)

SEARCH FIRMS
(See EXECUTIVE SEARCH FIRMS; EMPLOYMENT AGENCIES; and LEGAL PLACEMENT SERVICES)

SEARCH SERVICES
(See Also ABSTRACTERS; GENEALOGICAL & TITLE RESEARCH; and TITLE INSURANCE COMPANIES & AGENTS)

NSI

National Service Information Inc

Servicing law firms, financial institutions & corporations for more than 15 years

www.nsii.net

800-235-0337

NATIONWIDE SERVICES:
(FIRST SEARCH NO SERVICE FEE)

SECURED TRANSACTIONS
SEARCH, FILE & RETRIEVE UCC'S, SUITS, JUDGMENTS, MORTGAGES, BANKRUPTCY, TAXES, ETC.

CORPORATE SERVICES
DOCUMENT PREPARATION & FILING
GOOD STANDINGS
ARTICLES OF INCORPORATION
NAME AVAILABILITY

REGISTERED AGENT SERVICES
NATIONWIDE NETWORK
DOCUMENT LIBRARY, 8,000 CORPORATE FORMS
ON-LINE TAX CALENDAR
FREE OF CHARGE CHANGE-OVER
20-40% SAVINGS

CENTRAL CITY TITLE AGENCY INC
  PO BOX 1008, COLUMBUS 43216 . . . . (614) 341-7950
DETECTALL INC
  25 WALNUT ST, LEXINGTON 44904 . . . . (419) 884-9131
EAGLE COMMUNICATIONS
  4568 MAYFIELD RD #213, CLEVELAND 44121 . . . . (216) 297-3200
HERES WHERE
  6605 MASEFIELD ST, WORTHINGTON 43085 . . . . (614) 221-4636
INTER-COUNTY INC-MIDLAND TITLE
  8166 MARKET ST #N, YOUNGSTOWN 44512 . . . . (330) 758-8369
MCS GROUP INC THE
  1301 E 9TH ST #2500TO, CLEVELAND 44114 . . . . (216) 621-9660
MIDWEST SEARCH & ASSOC
  22576 BEECHNUT LN, CLEVELAND 44116 . . . . (440) 331-5551
MYERS RESEARCH & CONSULTING
  PO BOX 833, CANFIELD 44406 . . . . (330) 533-1880
  PO BOX 1395, STOW 44224 . . . . (330) 688-3004
NATIONAL SERVICE INFORMATION INC
  See Our Display Ad Under This Heading
  WWW.NSII.NET . . . . **(800) 235-0337**
PAN TRAVELS.COM
  8855 EAST PIKE, NORWICH 43767 . . . . (740) 872-3040
PRITCHARD ROGER M
  145 BUCKEYE CIR, COLUMBUS 43217 . . . . (614) 497-8686
RELIABLE TITLE AGENCY INC
  7301 WEST BLVD #C2, YOUNGSTOWN 44512 . . . . (330) 965-0110
VIN-MAR INC
  209 S MAIN ST, AKRON 44308 . . . . (330) 253-9353

SECRETARIAL SERVICES
ADECCO
  905 EUCLID AVE, CLEVELAND 44115 . . . . (216) 861-1900
  1366 CHERRY BOTTOM RD, GAHANNA 43230 . . . . (614) 476-4850
ADMINISTRATIVE RESOURCES
  1999 EDMUNDS CT, POWELL 43065 . . . . (614) 923-0170
ANDRAKO SECRETARIAL SVC
  20575 CENTER RIDGE RD #318, CLEVELAND 44116 . . . . (440) 356-2117
APS3 INC
  35100 CENTER RIDGE RD, N RIDGEVILLE 44039 . . . . (440) 327-2122
AREA EAST SECRETARIAL SVC
  7668 SLATE RIDGE BLVD, REYNOLDSBURG 43068 . . . . (614) 864-2840
AS NEEDED OFFICE HELP
  PO BOX 292612, DAYTON 45429 . . . . (937) 296-0321
ASSISTANTS
  20545 CENTER RIDGE RD #422, CLEVELAND 44116 . . . . (440) 331-2711
BEREA BUSINESS SVC
  117 DELAWARE CIRCLE, ELYRIA 44035 . . . . (440) 234-4379
BRIDGET VAUGHN OFFICE SVC
  2603 CANTERBURY RD, CLEVELAND 44118 . . . . (216) 371-3044
BUSINESS OFFICE CTR
  6745 ENGLE RD #110, CLEVELAND 44130 . . . . (440) 826-5050
BUSINESS RESOURCES UNLIMITED
  3055 TEMPLETON RD, COLUMBUS 43209 . . . . (614) 235-7532
C OFFICE-WORKS
  2 N MAIN ST, LONDON 43140 . . . . (740) 852-7877
CG SECRETARIAL SERVICES
  870 ROBINWOOD AVE, SHEFFIELD LK 44054 . . . . (440) 949-1807
CINCINNATI STENOGRAPHIC
  7908 CINCINNATI DAYTON RD, W CHESTER 45069 . . . . (513) 737-0880
COLONEL GLENN EXECUTIVE SUITES
  2661 COMMON BLVD, DAYTON 45431 . . . . (937) 427-9700
COMPLETE SECRETARY
  2686 MCVEY BLVD W, COLUMBUS 43235 . . . . (614) 262-8000
COMPUTE-A-WORD SECRETARIAL SVC
  9853 JOHNNYCAKE RIDGE RD #207, MENTOR 44060 . . . . (440) 357-7259
CONCISE CLERICAL SVCS INC
  7162 READING RD #405, CINCINNATI 45237 . . . . (513) 761-8832
CROWN SERVICES TEMPORARY PRSNL
  77 N WILSON RD, COLUMBUS 43204 . . . . (614) 276-9696
CURTIS SECRETARIAL
  19615 LAKE RD, CLEVELAND 44116 . . . . (440) 331-6262
CUSTOM STAFFING
  232 N MAIN ST #G, MARYSVILLE 43040 . . . . (614) 351-4473
DELAWARE OFFICE SYSTEM
  98 W CENTRAL AVE, DELAWARE 43015 . . . . (740) 369-5636
DIVERSIFIED SERVICES GROUP INC
  35 S PARK PL # 202, NEWARK 43055 . . . . (740) 349-2238
DIVINE INTERVENTION
  14807 ELM AVE, CLEVELAND 44112 . . . . (216) 851-1760
DOCUMENT EXPRESS
  520 MADISON AVE #9, TOLEDO 43604 . . . . (419) 242-9919
EXECENTER
  7784 REYNOLDS RD, MENTOR 44060 . . . . (440) 946-9919
EXECUTIVE CONCEPTS
  3530 WARRENSVILLE CTR RD, BEACHWOOD 44122 . . . . (216) 472-0250
EXECUTIVE OFFICE PLACE
  100 E BROAD ST, COLUMBUS 43215 . . . . (614) 464-1025
  2720 AIRPORT DR #100, COLUMBUS 43219 . . . . (614) 418-1700
  200 E CAMPUS VIEW BLVD #200, COLUMBUS 43235 . . . . (614) 985-3600
GOLDEN TOUCH SECRETARIAL
  209 S MAIN ST #203, AKRON 44308 . . . . (330) 376-7672
GOLDIE BROWN & ASSOC
  4601 N HIGH ST #204, COLUMBUS 43214 . . . . (614) 263-8533
HAYDEN & HAYDEN
  7050 ENGLE RD #105, CLEVELAND 44130 . . . . (440) 234-3515
JUST YOUR TYPE BUSINESS SVC
  4360 FERGUSON DR, CINCINNATI 45245 . . . . (513) 943-7780
KELLY SERVICES
  120 E 4TH ST, CINCINNATI 45202 . . . . (513) 241-3161
L A BUSINESS SVC
  1775 E 45TH ST, CLEVELAND 44103 . . . . (216) 431-4597
LIBERTY SQUARE SECRETARIAL SVC
  110 W STREETSBORO ST #15, HUDSON 44236 . . . . (330) 650-6939
MARIE FLYNN SECRETARIAL SVC
  1395 GRANDVIEW AVE #4, COLUMBUS 43212 . . . . (614) 487-0501
MED QUIST INC
  7010 ENGLE RD #100, MIDDLEBURG HTS 44130 . . . . (330) 598-2000
  700 ACKERMAN RD #375, COLUMBUS 43202 . . . . (513) 612-6800
MOLLIES LETTER PERFECT
  1204 GORDON RD, CLEVELAND 44124 . . . . (440) 442-1157
MR PROCESSSERVER
  3108 W 146TH ST, CLEVELAND 44111 . . . . (216) 476-9760
NEWHOUSE & ASSOC
  3280 SUMMIT RD SW, PATASKALA 43062 . . . . (740) 362-5072
OFFICE ANGEL
  PO BOX 854, AMHERST, NH 03031 . . . . (603) 672-5249
OFFICE ANGELS
  115 W AURORA RD, NORTHFIELD 44067 . . . . (330) 467-3143
OFFICE MANAGEMENT BY KAREN
  1036 16TH ST, PORTSMOUTH 45662 . . . . (740) 355-1546
OFFICE PRO INC
  3001 AEROSPACE PKWY, BROOK PARK 44142 . . . . (216) 925-0017
OFFICE SERVICE CTR OF OHIO
  2532 LAFAYETTE DR, CLEVELAND 44118 . . . . (216) 291-3660

SECRETARIAL SERVICES (Cont'd)

P S EXECUTIVE CTR INC
4807 ROCKSIDE RD #400, CLEVELAND 44131 . . . . (216) 642-8269
5005 ROCKSIDE RD #600, CLEVELAND 44131 . . . . (216) 573-3791
3401 ENTERPRISE PKWY #340, BEACHWOOD 44122 . . . . (216) 766-5769
PARKER TYPING SVC
295 ARCHWOOD AVE, MUNROE FALLS 44262 . . . . (330) 688-5757
PERFECT WORD CO
3309 E FAIRFAX RD, CLEVELAND 44118 . . . . (216) 321-2600
PRECISION TYPING SVC-PTS
318 N HARMONY ST, MEDINA 44256 . . . . (330) 723-0552
PREMIER SUITES BUSINESS CTR
55 SOUTHWEST AVE, TALLMADGE 44278 . . . . (330) 434-4200
RESUME SOLUTIONS
675 W MARKET ST #208, LIMA 45801 . . . . (419) 227-7000
RIDGE SECRETARIAL SVC
3540 RIDGE RD, CLEVELAND 44102 . . . . (216) 961-9100
RIGHT IMAGE
7891 MANNING RD, MIAMISBURG 45342 . . . . (937) 866-4441
SECRETAIRE EXTRAORDINAIRE
3610 SILSBY RD, CLEVELAND 44118 . . . . (216) 932-2292
SECRETARIAL OFFICE SVC
PO BOX 531089, CINCINNATI 45253 . . . . (513) 381-2277
SECRETARIAL PLUS
PO BOX 521, SIDNEY 45365 . . . . (937) 492-0545
SECRETARIAT INC
165 STANFORD DR, BEREA 44017 . . . . (440) 234-4913
SPACE
65 E GAY ST #200, COLUMBUS 43215 . . . . (614) 652-5968
STONEMAN N
21000 ST CLAIR AVE, CLEVELAND 44117 . . . . (216) 738-1384
TEMPO HELP INC
777 COLUMBUS AVE #8L, LEBANON 45036 . . . . (740) 773-7519
TER SECRETARIAL SVC
608 MADISON AVE, TOLEDO 43604 . . . . (419) 242-1400
TOWER SECRETARIAL SVC
20600 CHAGRIN BLVD, CLEVELAND 44122 . . . . (216) 295-9600
TRI-CITY SECRETARIAL SVC
5990 HERITAGE KNOLL TERR, FAIRFIELD 45014 . . . . (513) 825-2623
TRIPLE J WORD PROCESSING CO
PO BOX 10635, CLEVELAND 44110 . . . . (216) 761-1911
WERE AT YOUR SVC
232 DANHURST RD, COLUMBUS 43228 . . . . (614) 851-8120
WORD PROCESSABILITIES
8881 STONEHENGE CIR, PICKERINGTON 43147 . . . . (740) 927-9977
YOUR PERSONAL SECRETARY INC
35401 EUCLID AVE #100, WILLOUGHBY 44094 . . . . (440) 942-0076
YOUR PRIVATE SECRETARY
3033 KETTERING BLVD #210, DAYTON 45439 . . . . (937) 298-4654
YOUR SECRETARY INC
1631 NW PROFESSIONAL PLZ #101, COLUMBUS 43220 . . . . . (614) 451-5657

SECURITY EXPERTS
(See EXPERTS—SAFETY & SECURITY)

SERVICE OF PROCESS
(See PROCESS & SUBPOENA SERVICES)

SHORTHAND REPORTERS
(See COURT REPORTERS; and TRANSCRIPTION SERVICES)

SHREDDING MACHINES
(See OFFICE EQUIPMENT)

SKIP TRACERS
(See Also INVESTIGATORS & DETECTIVE AGENCIES)

ALL ABOUT RECOVERY
5 E LONG ST, COLUMBUS 43215 . . . . (614) 228-9096
DBS COLLECTION AGENCY
2936 MAPLE AVE, ZANESVILLE 43701 . . . . (740) 454-3224
GRACE RECOVERY SVC
8346 TYLER BLVD, MENTOR 44060 . . . . (440) 255-1300
HELTON & ASSOCS
31 CRAWFORD ST, MIDDLETOWN 45044 . . . . (513) 423-5011
RICH & ASSOCS
PO BOX 421362, MIDDLETOWN 45042 . . . . (513) 422-0725

STENOGRAPHERS
(See TRANSCRIPTION SERVICES; and COURT REPORTERS)

STORAGE SERVICES
(See OFFICE RECORDS—STORAGE)

STRUCTURED SETTLEMENTS
ASSURED STRUCTURED SETTLEMENTS
8 MYSTIC LN, MALVERN, PA 19355 . . . . (610) 647-2611

SUBPOENA SERVICES
(See PROCESS & SUBPOENA SERVICES)

SURETY BONDS
(See INSURANCE AGENCIES; and BONDS—SURETY & FIDELITY)

SURVEYORS-LAND

(See Also ENGINEERS—CONSULTING; ENGINEERS—CIVIL; and EXPERTS—SURVEYING)

AAA LAND SURVEYING
7147 N QUEENSFERRY PL, PAINESVILLE 44077 . . . . (440) 352-9097
AAA LAND SURVEYING
100 CENTER ST, CHARDON 44024 . . . . (440) 286-2393
AMERICAN LAND SURVEYS INC
2008 GLENN PKWY, BATAVIA 45103 . . . . (513) 735-4200
AZTEC LIMITED
7739 VIEWMOUNT DR, PAINESVILLE 44077 . . . . (440) 352-1446
BABCOCK-JONES & ASSOC
1924 MENTOR AVE, PAINESVILLE 44077 . . . . (440) 357-1811
BALL SURVEYING
PO BOX 5241, NEWARK 43055 . . . . (740) 345-5791
BASE LINE SURVEYING INC
4183 CHERRYSHIRE DR, BRUNSWICK 44212 . . . . (330) 225-6321
BAUER SURVEYS CO
4705 STATE RD, CLEVELAND 44109 . . . . (440) 461-4140
BOCK & CLARK
WWW.1800SURVEYS.COM . . . . (800) 787-8397
BONAR SURVEYING
2041 TOWNSHIP RD 267, AMSTERDAM 43903 . . . . (740) 768-2591
BOUTWELL LAND SURVEYING
4058 COLONEL GLENN HWY, DAYTON 45431 . . . . (937) 237-3036
BYRNSIDE SURVEYING INC
1971 8 MILE RD, CINCINNATI 45255 . . . . (513) 474-6020
CAMPBELL & ASSOC INC
5415 E SCHAAF RD #206, CLEVELAND 44131 . . . . (216) 642-8555
PO BOX 460, CANFIELD 44406 . . . . (330) 702-0512
CAPITOL SURVEY CO
6545 STRATHMORE DR, CLEVELAND 44125 . . . . (216) 447-9227
CARDINAL SURVEYS
7449 DAVIS DR, N RIDGEVILLE 44039 . . . . (440) 327-1833
CARLSON SURVEYS
15878 COWLEY RD, GRAFTON 44044 . . . . (440) 926-0200
CHEGRIN VALLEY ENGINEERING
22999 FORBES RD #B, OAKWOOD VLG 44146 . . . . (440) 585-2700
COLLINS-SADDLER & ASSOC
1599 N CENTRAL DR, DAYTON 45432 . . . . (937) 426-8145
COLUMBUS ENGINEERING CONSLNTS
840 MICHIGAN AVE, COLUMBUS 43215 . . . . (614) 228-3500
COMPTON SURVEYING CO
2844 JOHNSTOWN RD, COLUMBUS 43219 . . . . (614) 475-6550
CONKLE JIRIMIAH P S
4814 SMOKETALK LN, WESTERVILLE 43081 . . . . (614) 882-1672
CONSERVATION TECHNOLOGIES
212 W HIGH ST, LONDON 43140 . . . . (740) 852-1300
CONTRACT SURVEYING SVC
2003 W FAIR AVE, LANCASTER 43130 . . . . (740) 653-6381
COR CONSULTANTS
23 S FOREST ST, GENEVA 44041 . . . . (440) 466-8085
CORNER STONE PROFESSIONAL
4123 WEYMOUTH RD, MEDINA 44256 . . . . (330) 723-2612
COTTRILL SURVEYING
8256 STATE RT 207, MT STERLING 43143 . . . . (740) 869-3811
DADECO ENGINEERING INC
715 RICHEY RD, ZANESVILLE 43701 . . . . (740) 452-7262
DALLIS DAWSON & ASSOC
PO BOX 2568, E LIVERPOOL 43920 . . . . (330) 385-7836
DANIEL D TURNER & ASSOC INC
19 S PLUM ST, TROY 45373 . . . . (937) 335-8444
DOUGLAS MC LAUGHLIN & ASSOC
1720 RIDGEWOOD RD, WADSWORTH 44281 . . . . (330) 239-0135
FAIRVIEW LAND SURVEYING
21055 LORAIN RD, CLEVELAND 44126 . . . . (440) 331-8414
FORESIGHT ENGINEERING GROUP
320 CENTER ST # F, CHARDON 44024 . . . . (440) 286-1010
GARDNER SURVEYING
60707 STEWART RD, CAMBRIDGE 43725 . . . . (740) 432-5369
GARRETT & ASSOC INC
2030 W 19TH ST, CLEVELAND 44113 . . . . (216) 696-6080
HAINES SURVEYORS
354 KESSLER ST, GROVEPORT 43125 . . . . (614) 837-2181
HAMMONTREE & ASSOC LTD
5233 STONEHAM RD, N CANTON 44720 . . . . (330) 499-8817
HAPONEK & ASSOC INC
5444 STONEY RIDGE RD, N RIDGEVILLE 44039 . . . . (440) 327-4776
HOFMANN-METZKER INC
24 BEECH ST, BEREA 44017 . . . . (440) 234-7350
HOY SURVEYING SVC INC
5750 CHANDLER CT, WESTERVILLE 43082 . . . . (614) 895-1922

J & J SURVEYING SVC INC
6515 E LIVINGSTON AVE #12, REYNOLDSBURG 43230 . . . . . . (614) 866-9158
JAMES B ROOT & ASSOC
200 ELLEN DR, BEREA 44017 . . . . (440) 243-9843
JAMES J PERK & ASSOC
3319 NORRIS AVE, CLEVELAND 44134 . . . . (440) 842-6000
JOBES HENDERSON & ASSOC INC
59 GRANT ST, NEWARK 43055 . . . . (740) 344-5451
JOHN DAVID JONES CO
7110 WHIPPLE AVE NW, N CANTON 44720 . . . . (330) 494-0804
JOHN R HOY & ASSOC
4562 W 130TH ST, CLEVELAND 44135 . . . . (216) 476-3600
K MCGERVEY ENGINEERING
2643 JOSEPH ST, AVON 44011 . . . . (440) 937-4188
KOEHLER SURVEYING
PO BOX 28, UPPER SANDUSKY 43351 . . . . (419) 294-5388
KOHN & ASSOC
1400 CHAPEL WAY #B21, HEATH 43056 . . . . (740) 587-1792
LAKEWOOD SURVEYS
14567 MADISON AVE #601, CLEVELAND 44107 . . . . (216) 521-6960
LANDMARK SURVEY GROUP INC
1015 ORCHARD ST, COSHOCTON 43812 . . . . (740) 623-0993
2099 W 5TH AVE, COLUMBUS 43212 . . . . (614) 445-6001
LAUNDON SIMON KELSER ASSOC INC
110 MIDDLE AVE, ELYRIA 44035 . . . . (440) 322-7625
LAUX & ASSOC
8200 GARFIELD RD, MENTOR 44060 . . . . (440) 974-0037
LOCKWOOD LANIER MATHIAS &
2475 SUGAR GROVE RD SE, LANCASTER 43130 . . . . (740) 687-5542
MACKAY ENGINEERING & SURVEY
7017 PEARL RD, CLEVELAND 44130 . . . . (440) 886-4500
MAF SURVEYING
PO BOX 163, MADISON 44057 . . . . (440) 428-9563
MARKER ENGINEERING & SURVEYING
529 E MAIN ST, GNADENHUTTEN 44629 . . . . (330) 343-3444
MATMAR CO
4225 DONLYN CT, COLUMBUS 43232 . . . . (614) 863-2633
MAXSON & ASSOC
PO BOX 8, WAUSEON 43567 . . . . (419) 337-7806
MONTGOMERY SURVEYING
1712 PENNINGTON RD, WAVERLY 45690 . . . . (740) 947-8203
MORRIS & ASSOC INC
40 W LOCUST ST #22A, NEWARK 43055 . . . . (740) 349-7144
P A ROSEBECK & ASSOC
705 WILLOW CREEK DR, AMHERST 44001 . . . . (440) 988-4657
PAUL R COUCH LAND SURVEYOR
PO BOX 2192, HUDSON 44236 . . . . (330) 342-5596
POMEROY & ASSOC
599 SCHERERS CT, WORTHINGTON 43085 . . . . (614) 885-2498
R M KOLE ASSOC
5316 RIDGE RD, CLEVELAND 44129 . . . . (440) 885-7136
RAAB SURVEYING
852 MARION RD, COLUMBUS 43207 . . . . (614) 445-7103
ROBINSON & ASSOC SURVEYING INC
5490 ELECTION HOUSE RD, CARROLL 43112 . . . . (740) 756-4007
ROY E YEAGER SURVEYING CO
401 N OHIO AVE, FREMONT 43420 . . . . (419) 334-8348
SMART ENGINEERING & SURVEYING
1705 1/2 BLUE JAY RD, HEATH 43056 . . . . (740) 345-4700
TOBIN-MCFARLAND SURVEYING INC
111 W WHEELING ST #202, LANCASTER 43130 . . . . (740) 687-1710
TRI-STATE LOCATION SERVICES INC
See Our Display Ad Under This Heading
722 NILLES RD, FAIRFIELD 45014 . . . . **(513) 829-7722**
VANCE SURVEYING
28 CLINTON RD, MT VERNON 43050 . . . . (740) 397-6296
YODER SURVEYING
944 JONES AVE NW, CARROLLTON 44615 . . . . (330) 627-2614
ZARANEC SURVEYING CO
16722 W PARK CIRCLE DR, CHAGRIN FALLS 44023 . . . . (440) 543-1403

TAX CONSULTANTS
(See ACCOUNTANTS—CERTIFIED PUBLIC)

TITLE INSURANCE COMPANIES & AGENTS
(See Also ABSTRACTERS)

AGGRESSIVE TITLE AGENCY INC
222 DEPOT ST #N, WAUSEON 43567 . . . . (419) 335-4410
ASHTABULA LAND TITLE AGENCY
3503 CARPENTER RD, ASHTABULA 44004 . . . . (440) 964-2700
ASPEN TITLE AGENCY INC
8401 CLAUDE THOMAS RD #16, FRANKLIN 45005 . . . . (937) 704-0526
ASSOCIATED LAND TITLE AGENCY
973 W LIBERTY ST, HUBBARD 44425 . . . . (330) 534-3139
ATI TITLE AGENCY OF OHIO INC
4365 HARRISON AVE, CINCINNATI 45211 . . . . (513) 598-8844
BOULEVARD TITLE AGENCY INC
29525 CHAGRIN BLVD #314, CLEVELAND 44122 . . . . (216) 464-9618
BUCKEYE TITLE AGENCY INC
6788 LOOP RD, DAYTON 45459 . . . . (937) 435-1888
CHICAGO TITLE INSURANCE CO
5150 REED RD, COLUMBUS 43220 . . . . (614) 459-0721
CITIZENS LAND TITLE CO
233 S SCIOTO ST, CIRCLEVILLE 43113 . . . . (740) 477-2566
CITY TITLE CO
709 BROOKPARK RD, CLEVELAND 44109 . . . . (216) 741-2250
CIVIC TITLE CO
143 W FRANKLIN ST, CIRCLEVILLE 43113 . . . . (740) 474-1020
CRIMS TITLE RESEARCH
4235 STATE RT 213, STEUBENVILLE 43952 . . . . (740) 346-0116
FIDELITY NATIONAL TITLE
4416 PLYMOUTH ROCK CT, COLUMBUS 43230 . . . . (614) 498-1280
6011 COLUMBUS PIKE, LEWIS CTR 43035 . . . . (740) 657-3800
FIDELITY TITLE & CLOSING SVCS INC
112 N MAIN ST, MT VERNON 43050 . . . . (740) 393-2718
FIRELANDS ABSTRACT & TITLE
1243 NAPOLEON ST, FREMONT 43420 . . . . (419) 332-0500
8 E SEMINARY ST, NORWALK 44857 . . . . (419) 663-6300
FIRST AMERICAN EQUITY LOAN SVC
1228 EUCLID AVE #400, CLEVELAND 44115 . . . . (216) 241-1278
616 MADISON AVE, TOLEDO 43604 . . . . (419) 243-3483
495 S HIGH ST, COLUMBUS 43215 . . . . (614) 461-7701
1219 ONTARIO ST, CLEVELAND 44113 . . . . (216) 241-7898
FIRST AMERICAN TITLE INS CO
12360 MANCHESTER #100, DES PERES 63131 . . . . (314) 821-5515
1392 HIGH ST, WADSWORTH 44281 . . . . (330) 334-5115
FIRST CAPITAL TITLE SVCS INC
405 MADISON AVE #1350, TOLEDO 43604 . . . . (419) 255-5800
FIRST CLASS TITLE AGENCY INC
6611 ROCKSIDE RD #110, INDEPENDENCE 44131 . . . . (614) 337-2766
FIRST FINANCIAL TITLE AGENCY
1500 W 3RD ST #400, CLEVELAND 44113 . . . . (216) 664-1920
FIRST HOLMES TITLE
5797 TOWNSHIP RD 353, MILLERSBURG 44654 . . . . (330) 674-1080
FIRST SERVICE TITLE AGENCY INC
5810 SOUTHWYCK BLVD #102, TOLEDO 43614 . . . . (419) 861-0931
FIRST TITLE OF MIAMI COUNTY
1900 W STANFIELD RD, TROY 45373 . . . . (937) 332-0335
HIGHLAND TITLE SVC
1530 METZGER RD, VALLEY CITY 44280 . . . . (330) 225-1907
INSIGNIA TITLE AGENCY
6000 ROCKSIDE WOODS BLVD #220, INDEPENDENCE 44131 (216) 642-5680
LIBERTY TAX SVC
5700 BRIDGE AVE, CLEVELAND 44102 . . . . (216) 651-8200
LIBERTY TITLE INSURANCE INC
4204 DETROIT AVE, CLEVELAND 44113 . . . . (216) 961-2310
MAUMEE VLY TITLE AGENCY INC
514 W THIRD ST, DEFIANCE 43512 . . . . (419) 782-3334
MID OHIO TITLE AGENCY INC
601 MAIN ST, ZANESVILLE 43701 . . . . (740) 454-2988
MIDLAND CELTIC TITLE GROUP
341 S 3RD ST #200, COLUMBUS 43026 . . . . (614) 771-2705
6877 N HIGH ST #100, WORTHINGTON 43085 . . . . (614) 786-1885
MIDLAND COMMERCE GROUP
121 S MAIN ST #400, AKRON 44308 . . . . (330) 896-0800
MIDLAND TITLE SECURITY INC
10 W ERIE ST #100, PAINESVILLE 44077 . . . . (440) 354-3400
961 LINDEN AVE, ZANESVILLE 43701 . . . . (740) 450-0006
149 N PROSPECT ST, RAVENNA 44266 . . . . (440) 232-7720
111 N HAMBDEN ST, CHARDON 44024 . . . . (440) 285-2266
30 W WALNUT ST, JEFFERSON 44047 . . . . (440) 576-5858
1270 N ABBE RD, ELYRIA 44035 . . . . (440) 365-9000
420 MADISON AVE #1200, TOLEDO 43604 . . . . (419) 255-0126
3103 EXECUTIVE PKWY #101, TOLEDO 43606 . . . . (419) 843-2273
KEY BANK BLDG, CLEVELAND 44102 . . . . (216) 861-6707
4665 CORNELL RD #245, CINCINNATI 45241 . . . . (513) 489-0404
MIDWEST ABSTRACT CO
40 S MAIN ST #600, DAYTON 45402 . . . . (937) 898-5785
MINGLEWOOD TITLE RESEARCH
1500 W 3RD ST #1, CLEVELAND 44113 . . . . (216) 621-0416
OXFORD TITLE AGENCY INC
3814 WEST ST, CINCINNATI 45227 . . . . (513) 561-3313
PILLAR TITLE AGENCY
33 E NORTH ST #100, WORTHINGTON 43085 . . . . (614) 841-2553
PIPER TITLE AGENCY
185 WATER ST, GENEVA 44041 . . . . (440) 466-5200
SOUTHERN TITLE OF OHIO LTD
58 W THIRD ST, MANSFIELD 44902 . . . . (419) 525-4600

STEWART TITLE GUARANTY
501 W SCHROCK RD, WESTERVILLE 43081 . . . . (888) 307-2193
TITLE ACCESS
20006 DETROIT RD #200, ROCKY RIVER 44116 . . . . (440) 333-0099
TITLE FIRM
2347 MAPLE AVE, ZANESVILLE 43701 . . . . (740) 452-3062
TITLE FIRST AGENCY INC
6641 N HIGH ST #202, WORTHINGTON 43085 . . . . (614) 431-0400
555 S FRONT ST #400, COLUMBUS 43215 . . . . (614) 224-9207
541 BUTTERMILK PK, CRESCENT SPRINGS 41017 . . . . . . (513) 577-7700
2070 STRINGTOWN RD, GROVE CITY 43123 . . . . (614) 871-4222
495 EXECUTIVE CAMPUS DR #110, WESTERVILLE 43082. . (614) 895-3165
250 E 5TH ST #1500, CINCINNATI 45202 . . . . (513) 381-7444
TITLE LINK
500 W WILSON BRIDGE RD #125, WORTHINGTON 43085 . . (614) 438-5900
TITLE PRO
2020 BRICE RD, REYNOLDSBURG 43068 . . . . (614) 759-4716
TITLE PROFESSIONALS INC
295 HARMON AVE NW, WARREN 44483 . . . . (330) 392-7780
TITLE WORKS AGENCY
8228 E MARKET ST #A, WARREN 44484 . . . . (330) 609-5515
TITLE XPERTS AGENCY INC
1500 W 3RD ST, CLEVELAND 44113 . . . . (216) 696-5160
614 W SUPERIOR AVE #1111, CLEVELAND 44113 . . . . (216) 861-5226
205 MAIN ST, CHARDON 44024 . . . . (440) 286-6750
TITLECO TITLE AGENCY LTD
7281 PEARL RD, CLEVELAND 44130 . . . . (440) 842-7787
TITLES ETC INC
9821 OLDE 8 RD, NORTHFIELD 44067 . . . . (330) 468-0609
U S TITLE AGENCY INC
1111 CHESTER AVE #400, CLEVELAND 44114 . . . . (216) 621-1424
VIRTUAL TITLE AGENCY INC
801 W CHERRY ST, SUNBURY 43074 . . . . (740) 965-5688
WILLARD & ASSOC TITLE SEARCH SVCS LLC
12954-A STONECREEK DR NW, PICKERINGTON 43147 . . . . (614) 751-1810

TRADEMARK AGENTS
(See PATENT, COPYRIGHT & TRADEMARK AGENTS & SERVICES)

TRANSCRIPTION SERVICES
(See Also COURT REPORTERS; and SECRETARIAL SERVICES)

2 M SOFTWARE ASSOC
30285 BRUCE INDUSTRIAL PKWY #C, CLEVELAND 44139 . . . (440) 498-7484
A SECRETARIAL SVC-LONGWORTH
700 W PETE ROSE WAY, CINCINNATI 45203 . . . . (513) 381-6277
A-1 ACTION AGENCY
1080 WITTSHIRE LN #A, CINCINNATI 45255. . . . . (513) 232-3338
AT YOUR SVC
352 MORNINGSIDE DR, WINTERSVILLE 43953 . . . . (740) 266-7500
BROWNING MEDICAL TRANSCRIPTION
2954 PERTHWOOD DR, CINCINNATI 45244 . . . . (513) 232-2007
CLERICAL PLUS
9093 ARROWHEAD CT, CINCINNATI 45231 . . . . (513) 729-3009
COMMUNITY SECRETARIAL SVC
4100 EXECUTIVE PARK DR #16, CINCINNATI 45241 . . . . . . (513) 563-2525
ELECTRONIC DOCUMENT SVC
5933 COACHMONT DR, FAIRFIELD 45014 . . . . (513) 829-7101
ELECTRONIC TRANSCRIPTION INC
3609 W 8TH ST, CINCINNATI 45205 . . . . (513) 244-2223
INTERNATIONAL TRANSCRIPTION
3308 JEFFERSON AVE, CINCINNATI 45220 . . . . (513) 569-9100
JMS MEDICAL SVC
1392 LINDEN CREEK DR, MILFORD 45150 . . . . (513) 575-5335
K T CODING & TRANSCIPTION
920 S MAIN ST #202, N CANTON 44720 . . . . (330) 498-8499
LANTECH
7504 GRACELY DR, CINCINNATI 45233 . . . . (513) 941-3836
LEGAL LANGUAGE SERVICES
WWW.LEGALLANGUAGE.COM . . . . **(800) 322-0284**
LEGAL TRANSCRIPTION GROUP
6381 EUCLID RD, CINCINNATI 45236. . . . . (513) 984-5567
M T EXPRESS
8500 YALE RD, ROOTHPOWN 44272. . . . . (330) 654-2962
MEDWORDS INC
512 AUXIER DR, CINCINNATI 45244 . . . . (513) 474-6263
MEM MEDICAL TRANSCRIPTION
3863 MONROE AVE, DAYTON 45416. . . . . (937) 277-9920
OFFICE EXCHANGE INC
665 COOPER RD, COLUMBUS 43081 . . . . (614) 882-3267
OFFICE LINK
4704 DUNEDEN AVE, CINCINNATI 45236 . . . . (513) 984-1604
PHILLIPS TRANSCRIPTION
4325 PHOENIX DR, SPRINGFIELD 45503 . . . . (937) 342-9375
PREMIER TRANSCRIPTION SVC
9620 COLERAIN AVE #20, CINCINNATI 45251 . . . . (513) 741-9666
SHAMAN TRANSCRIPTION SVC
2904 RIDGE AVE, DAYTON 45414 . . . . (937) 275-9798
SUMMIT MEDICAL TRANSCRIPTION
376 SUMATRA AVE, AKRON 45305 . . . . (330) 784-2533
TURNAROUND
1091 PENNINGTON CT #4, CINCINNATI 45240 . . . . (513) 851-0355

TRANSLATORS
(See INTERPRETERS & TRANSLATORS)

TREATMENT CENTERS
(See ALCOHOL & DRUG TREATMENT CENTERS; MARRIAGE & FAMILY COUNSELORS; and REHABILITATION SERVICES)

TRIAL CONSULTANTS
DIRECTED DECISIONS
1220 W 6TH ST #400, CLEVELAND 44113 . . . . (866) 344-9404

VALUATION SERVICES
(See Also APPRAISAL SERVICES)

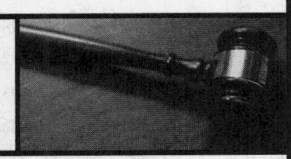

Litigation Consulting Services

As one of Ohio's largest financial services firms, our credentialed professionals are experienced in:

- Financial Analyses
- Business Valuations
- Expert Witness Testimony
- Economic Damages
- Forensic Analyses and Investigations
- Preferential and Fraudulent Transfers
- Accounting, Auditing & Tax Issues
- Dispute Resolution
- Settlement Structure
- Computer Forensics
- Electronic Recovery

For more information about how SS&G can help your firm, please contact one of our experts:

800.869.1834
Lewis Baum, CPA, CVA
Ed Blaugrund, CPA/ABV, CFE
Jeff Firestone, CPA, CFE
Robert Greenwald, CPA/ABV, JD, CFE
Mark Kutylowski, MBA, CIRA
Elaine Rockwell, CPA, CVA

800.869.1835
Steve Goykhberg, MBA, CBA
Christopher Szuch, CPA, CFE
Mark Stepka, CPA, CVA
Tami Bolder, CPA/ABV, MBA

SS&G *Financial Services*
Beyond Expectations
www.SSandG.com

Cleveland   Akron   Columbus   Cincinnati

ANTHONY F MOLLICA AND ASSOCIATES
1601 BETHEL RD #220, COLUMBUS 43220 . . . . (614) 459-1140
BEULE DAVID T CPA CVA
220 MARKET AVE S #700, CANTON 44702 . . . . (330) 453-7633
BUSINESS LATITUDES
5570 HURON ST, VERMILION 44089 . . . . (440) 967-8500
CHAPIN ASSOCS LTD
2441 FOX MEADOW CT, NORTHFIELD, IL 60093 . . . . (847) 441-2400
CIUNI & PANICHI INC
25201 CHAGRIN BLVD, CLEVELAND 44122 . . . . (216) 831-7171
DAVID R SNYDER CPA INC
4097 YOUNGSTOWN RD SE, WARREN 44484 . . . (330) 369-3961
EBERHART MICHAEL G CPA CVA
220 MARKET AVE S #700, CANTON 44702 . . . . (330) 453-7633
FAMENT INC
505 ACTON RD, COLUMBUS 43214 . . . . (614) 261-0552
GBQ PARTNERS
PO BOX 182108, COLUMBUS 43218 . . . . (614) 221-1120
HOLBROOK & MANTER CPAS
100 N MAIN ST, MARYSVILLE 43040 . . . . (937) 644-8175
HUDSON VALUATION ADVISORS INC
PO BOX 1474, HUDSON 44236 . . . . (330) 655-9730
LEVIN SWEDLER & COMPANY INC
3501 EMBASSY PKWY #200, AKRON 44333 . . . . (330) 666-4199
LEMKE VALUATION GROUP THE
PO BOX 584, MANSFIELD 44901 . . . . (419) 566-8904

LISHAWA ACCOUNTING & TAX LTD

C RANDAL LISHAWA CPA CVA
BUSINESS VALUATION & LITIGATION SUPPORT
335 S BLANCHARD ST, FINDLAY, OH 45840

LACCTAX@BRIGHT.NET . . . . **(419) 422-2851**

LYNCH ANSELMO OTT BRYAN & CO
2550 SOM CENTER RD, WILLOUGHBY HILLS 44094 . . . . (440) 585-1120
MARK W BOSLETT INC CPA

MARK W BOSLETT CPA CVA
CERTIFIED VALUATION ANALYST
1737 GEORGETOWN RD STE J HUDSON OH

PREFERREDTAX@ALLTEL.NET . . . . **(330) 650-4033**
MARTIN-MOLLICA SANDRA K CPA ASA
1601 BETHEL RD #220, COLUMBUS 43220 . . . . (614) 459-1140
MARTINET MARTINET & RECCHIA INC
35000 KAISER CT #201, WILLOUGHBY 44094 . . . . (440) 942-3900
PHILLIPS RUSSELL JR CPA CVA
3924 CLEVELAND AVE NW, CANTON 44709 . . . . **(330) 493-3928**
PLAVECSKI & ASSOCIATES
3 SUMMIT PARK DR #610, INDPNDNCE 44131 . . **(216) 524-3814**
SAETTEL & ASSOCS
7969 WASHINGTON WOODS DR, DAYTON 45459 . . . . (937) 433-7711
SCHMITZ ROBERT A CPA ABV CVA
19111 DETROIT RD #201, ROCKY RIVER 44116 . **(440) 356-9009**
SCHNEIDER DOWNS & CO INC
WWW.SCHNEIDERDOWNS.COM . . . . (614) 621-4060
SS&G FINANCIAL SERVICES
See Our Display Ad Under This Heading
WWW.SSANDG.COM . . . . **(800) 869-1834**
WHALEN & CO CPAS
250 W OLD WILSON BRIDGE RD, WORTHINGTON 43085 . . . . (614) 396-4200
WISEHART & WISEHART INC
WWW.WISEHART-WISEHART.COM . . . . (614) 791-2100

VIDEO PRODUCTION SERVICES-LEGAL

VIDEO DISCOVERY, INC.
Legal Video Specialists

Enter the digital age of courtroom visual presentations.

Litigation Support Services
- Trial/Discovery Videotape Depositions
  - 1 or 2 Camera • - Document Camera
- Large Screen High Resolution Playbacks
- Day-in-the-Life Documentaries
- Settlement Videos
- Site Inspections
- Property Damage and Personal Injury Photography

- 2-D and 3-D Animation
- Accident Reconstruction/Re-enactment
- CD-Rom Technology
- Text-to-Video Sync
- Document/Image Integration
- Courtroom Trial Support
- Document/Image Scanning and Enhancement
- Mock Trial Presentations
- Linear/Non-Linear Editing Suites

14245 Cedar Road • Cleveland, Ohio 44121 - Contact: Barry Hersch
Phone: (216) 382-1043 • Fax: (216) 382-9696
Toll Free: 1 (888) 720-7206 Pin# 2757 • www.videodiscoveryinc.com

A WORLD OF VIDEO-PRODUCTIONS
46 N MERIDIAN RD, YOUNGSTOWN 44509 . . . . (330) 797-0009
ACCURATE LEGAL VIDEOS LLC
11021 BROKEN WOODS DR, DAYTON 45342 . . . . (888) 875-1011
ANDERSON REPORTING SVCS
3242 W HENDERSON RD #A, CLMBS 43220 . . . . **(614) 326-0177**
AUGUST PRODUCTIONS COMPLETE
1858 KENNY RD, COLUMBUS 43212 . . . . (614) 487-7211
AUMAN RECORDING STUDIO
4316 MURRAY RD NW, DOVER 44622 . . . . (330) 343-2297
BERGDORF CO
3558 PORTAGE POINT BLVD, AKRON 44319 . . . . (330) 644-4444
BEST IMAGE VIDEO & PHOTOGRAPHY
1375 RICHMOND RD, CLEVELAND 44124 . . . . (216) 381-6395
BILL LEVY PRODUCTIONS
1267 W 9TH ST #200, CLEVELAND 44113 . . . . (216) 861-6778
BUZZ CUTS
2 1/2 N STATE ST, WESTERVILLE 43081 . . . . (614) 891-6700
CENTURY VIDEO PRODUCTIONS
10545 KLEY RD, VANDALIA 45377 . . . . (937) 898-3512
CINCINNATI VIDEO
PO BOX 30168, CINCINNATI 45230 . . . . (513) 231-5666
CINECRAFT PRODUCTIONS INC
2515 FRANKLIN BLVD, CLEVELAND 44113 . . . . (216) 781-2300
CURTIS INC
2025 READING RD, CINCINNATI 45202 . . . . (937) 293-2191
DEAL VIDEO & EDITING
16 FESCUE CT, CINCINNATI 41042 . . . . (859) 657-6000
DIAMOND VIDEO
30510 LAKE SHORE BLVD, WILLOWICK 44095 . . . . (440) 943-2109
DIGITAL ART VIDEO PRODUCTIONS
PO BOX 489, GREEN 44232 . . . . (330) 896-9318
DIGITAL DREAMS DJ & VIDEOGRPH
140 WOODLAND PL, CLYDE 43410 . . . . (419) 547-6724
DIGITAL EDGE
2182 COVENTRY RD, CLEVELAND 44118 . . . . (216) 321-1955

VIDEO PRODUCTION SERVICES-LEGAL
(Cont'd)

DIVITAS PHOTOGRAPHY
35595 CURTIS BLVD, EASTLAKE 44095 . . . . (440) 946-4020
DOWNTOWN MEDIA
140 GLENWOOD CIR, WILMINGTON 45177 . . . . (937) 382-5987
FALLEN 8 PRODUCTIONS
1700 MADISON RD, CINCINNATI 45206. . . . . (513) 553-6913

FINCUN-MANCINI INC
1801 E 9TH ST #1720, CLEVELAND 44114 . . . . . **(216) 696-2272**

FINE ARTS PHOTOGRAPHY & VIDEO
1191 HOLMDEN AVE, CLEVELAND 44109. . . . . (216) 771-4268
GEMINI PRODUCTIONS
12801 BEREA RD, CLEVELAND 44111 . . . . (216) 252-4640
GILLMAN PHOTOGRAPHY & VIDEO
5273 SPRINGFIELD DR, WESTERVILLE 43081. . . . . (614) 891-5886
GURA VIDEO MEMORIES
20030 PARKVIEW AVE, ROCKY RIVER 44116 . . . . (330) 757-4664
HEIRLOOM VIDEO PRODUCTIONS
24603 MAIDSTONE LN, CLEVELAND 44122 . . . . (216) 464-1696
JEFF PHELPS VIDEO PRODUCTIONS
3293 RUMSON RD, CLEVELAND 44118. . . . . (216) 321-8090
KELLNER STUDIOS INC
10237 BEREA RD #K, CLEVELAND 44102. . . . . (216) 651-2700
KERN VIDEO PRODUCTIONS
417 GRANTS TRL, CENTERVILLE 45459. . . . . (937) 428-0962
KIBBY-RAYNOR PRODUCTIONS
24 WHITNEY DR #G, MILFORD 45150 . . . . (513) 248-1611
LE CRONE COMMUNICATIONS
3700 LACON RD #1, HILLIARD 43026. . . . . (614) 777-2920
LEGAL ELECTRONIC RECORDING INC
5230 ST CLAIR AVE, CLEVELAND 44103. . . . . (216) 881-6272
LIGHTBORNE
212 E 14TH ST, CINCINNATI 45202. . . . . (513) 721-2272
LITIGATION SUPPORT SVC
817 MAIN ST #400, CINCINNATI 45202 . . . . (513) 241-5605
LP VIDEO PRODUCTION
4489 EVA LN, BATAVIA 45103 . . . . (513) 753-4604
MEDIA MAGIC PRODUCTIONS
4504 STATE ROUTE 46 S, JEFFERSON 44047 . . . . (440) 294-2492
MEHLER & HAGESTROM
1750 MIDLAND BLDG, CLEVELAND 44115 . . . . (216) 621-4984
MEMORY LANE PRODUCTIONS
878 HAMPTON CT, NORTHFIELD 44067 . . . . (330) 468-5241
METATEC INTERNATIONAL INC
7001 METATEC BLVD, DUBLIN 43017 . . . . (614) 761-2000
METRO VIDEO PRODUCTIONS INC
463 S CENTRAL AVE, LIMA 45804 . . . . (419) 991-8433
MILLS-JAMES PRODUCTIONS
3545 FISHINGER BLVD, HILLIARD 43026 . . . . (614) 777-9933
MIZANIN REPORTING SERVICE INC
50 PUBLIC SQ 1511 TERMINAL TOWER, CLEVELAND 44113. . (216) 241-0331
MULTI VIDEO SERVICE INC
7303 STATE RT 43, KENT 44240 . . . . (888) 908-4336
MULTIMEDIA FARMS
PO BOX 633, CANFIELD 44406. . . . . (330) 533-6988
OMEGA INTELLIGENCE INC
PO BOX 11023, CHARLESTON, WV 25339 . . . . (304) 344-0406
PEAKS VILLE POST
3723 PEARL RD, CLEVELAND 44109 . . . . (216) 635-0971
PICTURE YOURSELF STUDIO
3434 MEMPHIS AVE, CLEVELAND 44109 . . . . (216) 661-3384
QUEEN CITY PHOTOGRAPHY & VIDEO
284 SEBASTIAN CT, CINCINNATI 45238 . . . . (513) 922-3370
REMEMBER WHEN VIDEO PRODUCTION
25919 HENDON RD, CLEVELAND 44122 . . . . (216) 514-1567
REMINGTON PRODUCTIONS INC
1455 W 29TH ST, CLEVELAND 44113 . . . . (216) 241-1440
RISE
3849 WASHINGTON AVE, CINCINNATI 45229 . . . . (513) 721-0221
SEBO VIDEO GRAPHICS
23366 COMMERCE PARK #101A, CLEVELAND 44122. . . . . (216) 464-6840
SOLID VIDEO PRODUCTIONS
PO BOX NINE, WILBERFORCE 45384 . . . . (937) 374-1207

TACKLA & ASSOCIATES
1801 E 9TH ST, CLEVELAND 44114 . . . . **(216) 241-3918**

TED BACHO PRODUCTIONS
5900 DONCASTER DR, CHARLOTTE, NC 28211 . . . . (704) 366-6640
TELSTAR PRODUCTION
1 GOJO PLZ #75, AKRON 44311 . . . . (330) 467-5578
TM VIDEO PRODUCTIONS & SON
335 HARMONY DR, WINTERSVILLE 43953 . . . . (740) 264-1591

VICO SOLUTIONS
10124 DESMOND PL, PERRYSBURG 43551 . . . . (419) 867-8426
VIDEO DATA SVC
94 W CHURCH ST, PICKERINGTON 43147 . . . . (614) 837-8273

VIDEO DISCOVERY INC
See Our Display Ad Under This Heading
14245 CEDAR RD, CLEVELAND 44121. . . . . **(216) 382-1043**

VIDEO DUPLICATION SVC INC
3827 BROOKHAM DR, GROVE CITY 43123 . . . . (614) 871-3827
VIDEO EVIDENCE INC
1511 TERMINAL TOWER, CLEVELAND 44113 . . . . (216) 241-0506
VIDEO FEATURES INC
680 NORTHLAND BLVD, CINCINNATI 45240. . . . . (513) 742-6262
VIDEO GRAYPHICS
5787 RAPID RUN RD, CINCINNATI 45233 . . . . (513) 451-4869
VIDEO GT
8553 LANCASTER RD, HEBRON 43025 . . . . (740) 928-6297
VIDEO IMPRESSIONS
2096 MIRAMAR BLVD, CLEVELAND 44121 . . . . (216) 291-0622
VIDEO ONE PRODUCTIONS
6099 FREEMAN RD, WESTERVILLE 43082. . . . . (614) 898-9721
VIDEO POST PRODUCTIONS INC
6011 RENNAISSANCE PL #3, TOLEDO 43623. . . . . (419) 885-8433
VIDEO TREASURES
1474 CAMBRIA MILL RD, GRANVILLE 43023. . . . . (740) 587-2360
VIDEOGENIC
103 S COURT ST #114, CLEVELAND 38732 . . . . (662) 843-1943
VIDEOGRAPHICS-LEGAL VIDEO
419 DOVER CENTER RD, CLEVELAND 44140 . . . . (440) 899-2999
VIDEOWORKS
5301 SOUTHWYCK BLVD #205, TOLEDO 43614 . . . . (419) 865-6800
WILLIAMS CORPORATE COMMS
4553 WELDWOOD LN, SYLVANIA 43560. . . . . (419) 885-8385
WILSON TERRY CCV
141 S COLUMBUS ST, LANCASTER 43130 . . . . (740) 689-9125

VIDEO TAPE DEPOSITIONS

ACCUSCRIBES REPORTING LTD
206 S BROAD ST BX 2466, LANCASTER 43130 . . . . (740) 689-1680
LEGAL VIDEO SVC
9242 STATE RT 7S, GALLIPOLIS 45631 . . . . (740) 446-4500
MIRROR IMAGE VIDEO & PHOTOGRAPHY
4274 CHEVAL CIR, STOW 44224 . . . . (330) 945-4477
MULTI VIDEO SERVICE INC
7303 STATE RT 43, KENT 44240 . . . . (888) 908-4336
VIDEO DISCOVERY INC
14245 CEDAR RD, CLEVELAND 44121. . . . . **(216) 382-1043**

VIDEO TAPE DUPLICATION SERVICES
(See Also COPYING SERVICES)

HAVE INC
309 POWER AVE, HUDSON, NY 12534 . . . . (888) 999-4283
TAPE CO THE
11240 CORNELL PARK DR #100, BLUE ASH 45242 . . . . (800) 851-3113
USA DUBS & REPLICATION
29 W 38TH ST 4TH FL, NEW YORK, NY 10018 . . . . (800) 872-3821
VIDEO DUPLICATION SVC INC
2882 S DIXIE DR, DAYTON 45409. . . . . (888) 837-3827
4485 W 160TH ST, CLEVELAND 44135 . . . . (216) 676-3827
WESTERN MEDIA ONLINE
30941 W AGOURA RD, WESTLAKE VLG, CA 91361 . . . . (800) 648-8006

VIDEOCONFERENCING SERVICES

FINCUN-MANCINI INC

DOWNTOWN CLEVELAND LOCATION
VIDEOTAPING SERVICES
FAX AND INTERNET AVAILABLE

1801 E 9TH ST #1720, CLEVELAND 44114. . . . . **(216) 696-2272**

WORD PROCESSING SERVICES
(See SECRETARIAL SERVICES)

WRONGFUL DISCHARGE EXPERTS
(See EXPERTS—EMPLOYABILITY)

the legal pages®
Advertiser Index

INDEX

Index

Index

Index

Index